SUPE

RACES AND RACE HORSES

FLAT 1987

COMPLETE RESULTS OF 1986 FLAT SEASON

Foreword

For over twelve years John Haig Scotch Whisky have sponsored this annual, but following the sale of the company we no longer enjoy this sponsorship.

However the name change to Superform brings a better - and larger annual! We have now broken the thousand page barrier with the addition of the expanded index which shows each horse's full race ferences, form figures and total of win and place prize money.

The 1980's have produced some outstanding performances. In 1982 Shergar rated 97 after his amazing 10 length Derby win. In 1984 El Gran Senor shot to 106 in a tremendously fast run Two Thousand Guineas. In 1986 Dancing Brave thrilled us with high class performances over a mile, and then ten furlongs. Finally over one and a half miles, this remarkably versatile star produced a rating of 101 defeating one of the strongest fields ever to contest the Prix de L'Arc de Triomphe. What does 1987 hold? Read on! All at Superform wish you every success in the new season.

Photographs by Alec Russell, Huttons Ambo, York

Front cover (paperback only)
Sharastani (Walter Swinburn) holds off **Dancing Brave** in the 1986 Ever Ready Derby

CONTENTS

Publisher Kevin Gilroy, thanks the following for their tremendous help in the compilation of this Annual.

A O Bentley

A Dadswell

K Ducie

D Nemeth

M Simmons

P Towning

V Towning

D Wenham

Printed by Billings Ltd , Worcester.

Published by Furlong Press
High Street, Shoreham, West Sussex.

INTRODUCTION

The race results in this book cover every horse in each race in Britain.

The results and commentaries are published in weekly parts
throughout the season
The commentaries cover the first six horses past the post - plus all
horses, up to and including 10/1 in the betting.

WHY IS SUPERFORM DIFFERENT?
Our principal task in Superform, is not to report the results, but to
interpret them. Race results/form have little meaning unless the reader can
grasp the value or worth of the form. Why is the form of one handicap,
maiden race, or 2 y o race, likely to prove better than any other? Ratings
of ability/merit, calculated for the first six in every race, immediately
reveal the likely worth of the form, but to calculate and tabulate ratings
for over 7000 horses each season is beyond the resources of most people.
Superform does this thoroughly. You may not agree with our ratings but at
least they provide a consistent yardstick for informed discussion.
There are other vital aspects of form study which the bare results do not
reveal. If a horse runs badly, we search for the likely cause: when it runs
well we pinpoint the conditions which favour success. Race results give no
indication of where (or whether) a horse has won in the past. Superform
lists all wins in the past two years for every horse! Form figures printed
beside the first six horses in each race reveal whether the winner beat
consistent performers or disappointing types. The optimum going, distance
and track preferences for each horse are written up in full and we make
particular note of long absences from the track. The bare results never
indicate whether a horse is likely to be suited by a longer distance or
whether a newcomer is closely related to high class performers. Only a
study of breeding can reveal such potential. Such research is time
consuming and the tools of reference are costly. Superform does it all for
you.

There is considerable interest in race timings but a race time by itself
reveals nothing. It is meaningful only when compared with some standard or
average. Consistent methods must then be used to evaluate the condition of
the track. Superform produce pace and going figures which both pinpoint
fast run races and reflect the condition of the track. Often our 'going'
figures differ from the official going report supplied by the racecourse.!
More information on time & pace figures appear on page 1035.

STARTING PRICES
Starting prices are included, not for the purpose of settling bets, but as a
guide to the relative chance of each horse expressed by the bookmakers at
the track, on the day. There are times, possibly because of industrial
action, when we must formulate our own prices about unplaced horses but such
differences of opinion should only amount to half a point or so.

CHARACTER SUMMARIES
To obtain a character summary simply refer to the horse's last race. This
race will either provide the summary or point out where the latest summary
is printed with the reference "see --". With this method of reference you
will gain an expertise and feel for the form book which is impossible to
achieve where horses and summaries are listed individually in A - Z fashion.

USING SUPERFORM (cont.)

RATINGS

The ratings published here are expressions of opinion, based wherever possible on collateral form. Our ratings are presented on the 0 - 100 scale as used by the official Jockey Club Handicappers.

In the index at the back of this annual, following the horse's name, there appears in bold type, the end of season **Superform rating** for each horse. This rating is usually the best attained in the last three races and this figure should be used in all calculations.

We usually downrate a horse after 3 poor runs but if the horse shows itself to be less than enthusiastic the downrating often takes place more quickly. Dont be too surprised if you come across a higher rating when searching back in a horse'e form. Unfortunately more horses go back or deteriorate than improve.

For full information on how to use the private handicap ratings, see page 1033

FAST TIMERS

Horses which win in a time of 10 Fast or more are marked with a + sign instead of the usual asterisk. Horses which finish second, beaten 3 lengths or less in a similarly fast time, are marked - These symbols are placed after the latest race reference. A fuller explanation of the time and pace figures can be found on page 1035

COURSE REQUIREMENTS

In the race results we describe the type of race and note the prize money for the winner. The distance of each race, the prevailing going and the pace of the race are also noted. At the beginning of each race meeting there is a brief comment on the course characteristics. Generally it is more important to note whether the course was sharp. Horses which win on sharp tracks usually need a similar course before they produce their best form. However, horses that win on galloping tracks are usually able to win anywhere. It takes an honest sort to win at Newmarket or Newbury but tracks like Chester and Epsom throw up true course specialists.

WEIGHTS

Regarding the weights shown in the results, these are the weights (plus overweights) alloted to the horse by the handicapper. We do not subtract rider's allowances. The rider's allowance is noted in brackets. Penalties are marked with an x: ow signifies overweight and oh notes that the horse was carrying more than the long handicap weight set originally by the handicapper.

LONG HANDICAP WEIGHTS

Handicaps are made from the highest rated horse downwards. The topweight is usually set to carry at least 9-7. As the minimum weight in a Flat handicap is fixed at no lower than 7-7, any horse rated more than 28 pounds below the topweight will have to carry the minimum weight, not that alloted by the Handicapper. It is the original alloted weight which is known as the LONG HANDICAP WEIGHT. When a horse originally set to carry 7-1 runs in a handicap he will have to carry the minimum weight of 7-7 and is therefore said to be 6 lbs out of the (long) handicap.

OFFICIAL RATINGS

At the start of each handicap race, in the right hand margin, the figure in brackets represents the Official Rating of a horse set to carry 10-0 in that race. If the figure is 50, horse B carrying 10-0 is officially rated 50. Horse C, set to carry 8-8 is rated 30 since it carries 20lb less than 10-0 - and so on. In this way it is possible to work out the official mark of each horse in any handicap right through the season.

ABBREVIATIONS

Abs	= Absent or Absence		Impr	= Improved or Improving
Al	= Always		Juv	= Juvenile (i.e. a 2YO)
Bkd	= Backed		Ld	= Lead
bl	= Blinkers		Mdn	= Maiden
BL	= Blinkers for the first time		Mid-Div	= Mid-Division
Btn	= Beaten		Mkt	= (Betting) Market
Btr	= Better		Mod	= Moderate
C/D	= Course and Distance		Poss	= Possibly
Ch	= Chance		Press	= Pressure
Chall	= Challenge(d)		Prog	= Progress
Clr	= Clear		Prom	= Prominent
Cmftbly	= Comfortably		P.U.	= Pulled Up
Disapp	= Disappointing		Qcknd	= Quickened
Dist	= Distance (i.e. a point 240yd		Rem	= Remainder
from the winning post)			Sev	= Several
Dsptd	= Dispute(d)		Sft	= Soft going
Eff	=(i) Effort (eg. good effort)		Sh	= Short
	(ii)Effective(eg.eff at 6f)		Shrp	= Sharp
Ev	= Every		Sn	= Soon
Fav	=(i) after S.P.= Favourite		T.O.	= Tailed Off
	(ii) in text = favoured		Trk	= Track
Fdd	= Faded		Unbtn	= Unbeaten
Fin	= Finished		vis	= Visor
Fm	= Firm going		VIS	= Visor for the first time
Gall	= Galloping		Wknd	= Weakened
Gd	= Good going		Wl	= Well
Gr	= Group (i.e. Pattern Race)		Yld	= Yielding going
Hd	= Head			
Hdd	= Headed			
Hdwy	= Headway			
Hmpd	= Hampered			
Hvy	= Heavy going			

SUPERFORM TOP RATED IN 1986

11f Upwards		8 - 10f		5 - 7f	
101 DANCING BRAVE	3	98 DANCING BRAVE	3	90 LAST TYCOON	3
97 BERING	3	92 SKYWALKER	4	90 SMILE	4
95 SHAHRASTANI	3	91 CELESTIAL STORM	3	88 GREEN DESERT	3
94 SOUTHJET	3	TRIPTYCH	4	87 DOUBLE SCHWARTZ	5
SHARDARI	4	90 ESTRAPADE	6	86 HALLGATE	3
93 MANILA	3	FAST TOPAZE	3	85 LEAD ON TIME	3
91 TRIPTYCH	4	SONIC LADY	3	84 PARIOLI	6
90 THEATRICAL	4	89 TELEPROMPTER	6	83 HADEER	4
89 ACATENANGO	4	LAST TYCOON	3	LUCKY RING	4
MOON MADNESS	3	88 SCOTTISH REEL	4	PINE TREE LANE	4
TURKOMAN	4	THRILL SHOW	3	82 POLYKRATIS	4
88 ALTAYAN	3	PARK EXPRESS	3	BEDSIDE PROMISE	4
COLORSPIN	3	PRECISIONIST	5	81 BAISER VOLE	3
DARARA	3	87 PENNINE WALK	4	COMRADE IN ARMS	6
MIDWAY LADY	3	PALACE MUSIC	5	FIRM LANDING	3
SLIP ANCHOR	4	SURE BLADE	3	POWDER KEG	4
87 PETOSKI	4	86 DOUBLE BED	3	SARAB	5
86 BONHOMIE	3	85 FERDINAND	3	80 CYRANO DE BERGERAC	3
DAMISTER	4	DIVULGE	4	GREY DESIRE	6
LACOVIA	3	LIRUNG	4	GWYDION	3
SAINT ESTEPHE	4	84 BAILLAMONT	4	MISTER WONDERFUL	3
UNTOLD	3	EFISIO	4	NORTHERN PREMIER	3
85 ANAZID	3	MAYSOON	3	OR VISION	3
DANGERS HOUR	4	THEN AGAIN	3	SPERRY	3
EL CUITE	3	UN DESPARADO	3	FAUSTUS	3
IVORS IMAGE	3	UPTOWN SWELL	4		
84 ALESSO	3	83 BOLD ARRANGEMENT	3		
AUTHAAL	3	HUNTINGDALE	3		
ATHEUS	4	MAGICAL WONDER	3		
MERSEY	4	WASSL TOUCH	3		
NOBLE FIGHTER	4	82 BONNE ILE	5		
83 BABYTURK	4	ELLE SEULE	3		
FARAWAY DANCER	3	FLASH OF STEEL	3		
GALLA PLACIDA	4	FIELD HAND	4		
JUPITER ISLAND	7	FLYING PIDGEON	5		
LONGBOAT	5	HIGHEST HONOR	3		
MASHKOUR	3	SHAROOD	3		
NISNAS	3	REGAL STATE	3		
ROYAL TREASURER	6	BEDTIME	6		
VALUABLE WITNESS	6	81 ART FRANCAIS	3		
VERD ANTIQUE	3	AROKAR	3		
82 AIR DE COUR	4	CAROTENE	3		
ALLEZ MILORD	3	CONQUERING HERO	3		
BALITOU	7	DALLAS	3		
BAKHAROFF	3	DIRECTING	3		
DIHISTAN	4	OVER THE OCEAN	4		
IADES	4	PRADIER .	3		
KAZAROUN	4	SECRET FORM	3		
SWINK	3	TOP CORSAGE	3		
TOMMY WAY	3	80 BARJER	3		
ZAHDAM	3	ENGLISH SPRING	3		
81 CELESTIAL STORM	3	FITNAH	4		
EASTERN MYSTIC	4	FLEUR ROYALE	3		
GULL NOOK	3	GALUNPE	3		
NEMAIN	4	IMPERIAL FALCON	3		
SIRK	3	KADROU	3		
80 EAGLING	4	TOCA MADERA	3		
SEISMIC WAVE	4				
SIRIUS SYMBOLI	4				

8

SUPERFORM TOP RATED IN 1986
2 Year Olds

86 REFERENCE POINT	72 PERCYS LASS
85 FOREST FLOWER	MR EATS
AJDAL	MELBURY LAD
83 MINSTRELLA	LOVE THE GROOM
MIESQUE	LALUCHE
81 SHADY HEIGHTS	GULF KING
80 RISK ME	CUTTING BALDE
MILLIGRAM	CHIME TIME
FOTITIENG	AT RISK
BELLOTTO	71 WILLESDON
79 SAKURA REIKO	TARTUFFE
INVITED GUEST	TAHILLA
78 SUHAILIE	ROUNDLET
SIZZLING MELODY	NAHEEZ
POLONIA	KALGOORLIE
NOBLE MINSTREL	IMPERIAL FRONTIER
LOCKTON	GOLD FEE
DONT FORGET ME	GLORY FOREVER
DANISHKADA	BEESHI
BENGAL FIRE	ARABIAN SHEIK
77 SANAM	AMIGO SUCIO
MOST WELCOME	70 ZAJAL
MANSOOJ	TWYLA
GENGHIZ	THREE TAILS
GAYANE	SINGING STEVEN
DEPUTY GOVERNOR	SEA DARA
76 WIGANTHORPE	NEW ATTITUDE
LEGAL BID	LINDAS MAGIC
HIAAM	HYDRAULIC POWER
BALBONELLA	GRAND CHELEM
75 SHY PRINCESS	GOLDEN BRAID
SHINING WATER	EXPORT PRICE
RICH CHARLIE	DON MARIO
PRINCESSE DU BOURG	BESTPLAN
MIDYAN	BALI MAGIC
GROOM DANCER	BABA KARAM
CLASSIC TALE	
ANGARA ABYSS	
74 WHO KNOWS	
THREE GENERATIONS	
MISTER MAJESTIC	
INTERVAL	
DOMINION ROYALE	
73 ZAIBAQ	
WHAKILYRIC	
MOUNTAIN MEMORY	
IOSIFA	
GRECIAN URN	
DARCYS THATCHER	
CAROLS TREASURE	
CANADIAN MILL	
BALAKIREV	

Index To Race Meetings By Page Number

1   ARTESIUM R Johnson Houghton -00
BEAU MIRAGE C Booth -010 (10f Heavy, £4,140)
CARRIBEAN TYME C Booth -000
EMERALD EAGLE C Booth -01 (1m Good, £3,228)
REPEALED W Hastings Bass -032
SOCKS UP R Johnson Houghton -0
SOVEREIGN LOVE W Hastings Bass -0031 (1m Heavy £4,140)
VAGUE LASS W Hastings Bass -31 (6.5f Heavy £4,600)
VILLAGE HERO W Hastings Bass -0000
WAGONER P Walwyn -22

SAINT CLOUD   Thursday March 13

Official Going Given as Good

2   PRIX EDMOND BLANC GROUP III 4YO+   £15640   1m   Good

--   EPHIALTES (C Milbank) 4-9-0 A Junk .: -43-001: Smart colt: impressive 4L winner of
Group 3 Prix Edmond Blanc at Saint Cloud March 13: fit from 2 recent runs at Cagnes: eff.
around 1m, stays 11f: acts on good ground.   **80**
--   STELLA GRANDE (J Chevigny) 4-8-11 F Head : 10002-2: Ran on well final 1f: formerly
trained by R Sheather , winning a Gr. 3 event first time out last season at Epsom: later a
fine 5th in the 1,000 Guineas: eff. around 1m on firm and yielding.   **70**
--   HERALDISTE (P Biancone) 4-9-0 E Legrix : 23100-3: The favourite: ev.ch.: in 84/85
won a Gr. 3 race at Deauville: smart 2yo when trained by H Cecil: eff at 1m on firm and soft. **72**
3 ran   4,hd.   C Milbank France.

DONCASTER   Thursday March 20th   Lefthand Galloping Track

Official Going Given as Gd/Firm Round Course: Good Straight Course: However all times slow due to very strong winds.

3   PHILIP CORNES BROCKLESBY STAKES 2YO   £3002   5f   Good Slow

--   BLUEMEDE (M Brittain) 2-8-11 K Darley 4/1: 1: 2 ch c Blue Cashmere - Knavesmire
(Runnymede): Prom colt: nicely bckd: led over 3f and again inside the final 1f, gamely in the
Brocklesby Stakes at Doncaster Mar.20: cost only 1,500 gns: eff at 5f: speedily bred and
does well with forcing tactics: acts on good ground.   **52**
--   AUTHENTIC (N Tinkler) 2-8-11 T Ives 2/1 FAV: 2: Well bckd: dsptd lead ½way: led
over 1f out till inside final 1f: 4L clear 3rd: should find a similar event at this stage
of the season: brother to winning juvenile Johnny Nobody: cost 13,000 gns and should be
suited by further than 5f.   **50**
--   PANBOY (T Fairhurst) 2-8-11 C Coates(5) 10/1: 3: Never nearer: speedily bred and
should impr: acts on good.   **38**
--   LAURIES WARRIOR (R Boss) 2-8-11 M Miller 9/2: 4: Friendless in mkt: no real threat:
cost 10,000 gns. should do better next time on sounder surface.   **38**
--   MUNTAG 2-8-11 D Nicholls 12/1: 0: Sn prom: should stay further.   **36**
--   TEAM EFFORT 2-8-11 R P Elliott 7/1: 0: Lightly bckd: cost I.R. 2,300.   **34**
--   DEINOPUS 2-8-11 P Robinson 6/1: 0: No threat: cost 7,400 gns: will stay further.   **00**
--   BOY SINGER 2-8-11 C Dwyer 6/1: 0: Slow start: 5,000 gns purchase.   **00**
--   LUCEDEO 2-8-11 S Perks 7/1: 0: Missed the
break: always rear.   **00**
9 ran   ½,4,hd,½,½,nk,1½   (P J Armstrong)   M Brittain Warthill, Yorks

4   BERTIE BASSETT STAKES HANDICAP 0-60   £3324   1m 4f   Good Slow   [52]

--   TIVIAN (I Matthews) 6-8-3(vis) N Day 7/1: 13010-1: 6 b g Busted - Jovian
(Hardicanute):
First time out, al prom and led over 2f out, ridden out in the Bertie Bassett h'cap at
Doncaster Mar.20: in 84/85 won h'caps at Newmarket and Folkestone and also a maiden at
Doncaster on the opening day of the season: well suited by 12f: acts on firm and yld and
on any trk: goes well when fresh.   **39**
--   PAGAN SUN (A Bailey) 5-8-9 B Thomson 6/1: 40040-2: Prom, ran on well final 1f: fit
from hurdling: in 84/85 won an app. h'cap at Haydock: previous season won at this opening
meeting: eff at 10f, stays 12f: acts on gd/firm and soft and may win soon.   **42**
--   REGAL STEEL (R Hollinshead) 8-7-11 A Culhane(7) 11/1: 00000-3: Led till over 2f out:
kept on: failed to win last season: in 83/84 won twice here: eff over 12/14f: acts on gd/
firm and yld.   **29**
--   ROSTHERNE (K Stone) 4-8-6 A Murray 10/1: 00023-4: Kept on, no threat: in 84/85 won
the valuable XYZ h'cap at Newcastle: eff at 10f, stays 12f: acts on gd & yld & a gall trk.   **35**

DONCASTER   Thursday March 20th   - Cont'd

--	VINTAGE TOLL 6-9-8 J Lowe 11/1: 20000-0: Gd hdway over 1f out: no extra.	47
--	DICK KNIGHT 5-7-9(2ow)(2oh) R Fox 20/1: 01000-0: Prom, ev ch.	16
--	HONEYDEW WONDER 5-9-1 Pat Eddery 10/3 FAV: 11103-0: Disap fav, never nearer.	00
--	GAY CAPTAIN 4-9-13 W Carson 10/1: 1-00-0: Never in the hunt.	00

-- Golden Fancy 9-8-5   -- Bamdoro 7-7-7(1oh)   -- Kentucky Quest 4-9-4
-- Bold Connection 6-10-0   -- Four Star Thrust 4-8-4
-- Holy Spark 6-8-13
14 ran   1½,shhd,1½,2,2,1,½,1½   (Lady Matthews)   ·   I Matthews Newmarket

5   RACING POST MILE LISTED RACE   £10516   1m   Good Slow

-- **MACS REEF** [3] (M Ryan) 4-9-3 G Starkey 9/1: 03202-1: 4 b c Main Reef - Avereen (Averof): Smart colt: outsider of 4, but ran on well final 1f to win valuable Racing Post Mile (Listed race) at Doncaster Mar.20: unlucky not to win last season: fin a fine 4th in Irish 2,000 Guineas: in 83/84 won at Goodwood and York: eff over 1m, stays 12f well: acts on firm and yld: has been difficult to place. **77**

-- **TREMBLANT** [1] (R Smyth) 5-9-0 Pat Eddery 6/4 FAV: 30111-2: Heavily bckd on seasonal debut: set moderate pace: hdd inside final 1f: smart and much impr colt in 84/85, winning valuable h'caps at Doncaster, Newmarket and Ascot, culminating in an easy win in the Cambridgeshire, again at Newmarket: in '84 won at Kempton, Salisbury and Newmarket: very eff over 7-9f and may stay even further: acts on gd and firm ground and is well suited by a stiff, gall trk: thoroughly game and genuine and a credit to his trainer: capable of winning a Group race. **70**

-- **BOLD ARRANGEMENT** [4] (C Brittain) 3-8-0 P Robinson 9/4: 1322D-3: Chall over 1f out: very smart 2yo, winning at Sandown, Leicester, Nottingham and Goodwood: on last start fin an excellent 2nd to Bakharoff in the Futurity at Doncaster, but subs. disq. and placed 4th: very eff over 7f/1m: acts on firm and yld: genuine and consistent: possibly going for the Kentucky Derby. **74**

-- **SULAAFAH** [2] (H T Jones) 4-9-7 A Murray 5/2: 01010-4: Fdd over 1f out: very smart colt, who last season won a valuable h'cap at Newmarket and a Gr.3 event at Baden Baden: in '84 won at Redcar and again at Baden Baden: very eff at 7f/1m: acts on gd/frm and soft. **57**
4 ran   1½,shhd,15.   (T P Ramsden)   M Ryan Newmarket

6   BATHYANY HANDICAP STAKES 3YO 0-50   £2519   5f   Good Slow   [57]

-- **ROVE** [2] (S Norton) 3-7-11 J Lowe 4/1: 0301-1: 3 gr c Mummy's Pet - Glenburnie (Green God): First time out, sn prom and led well over 1f out, holding on by ½L in a 3yo h'cap at Doncaster Mar.20: in 84/85 won a 2yo maiden at Edinburgh: speedily bred and is well suited by 5f: acts on gd and firm and on any trk, though likes a sharp one. **38**

-- **AMBER CLOWN** [8] (W Wharton) 3-7-7(3oh) N Carlisle 14/1: 03000-2: Ran on well final 1f: eff over 5f, suited by 6f: acts on gd and firm. will find a race on this form. **31**

-- **MAYOR** [13] (M Leach) 3-8-13 D Nicholls 10/1: 43110-3: Under the whip over 1f out: finished really well: in 84/85 won a Nursery h'cap at Warwick and a valuable seller at York: eff over 5/6f: acts on gd/firm and yld and on any trk: should find a similar event soon **49**

-- **THE HILCOTE CLUB** [7] (M Mccormack) 3-8-10 R Cochrane 7/2 FAV: 00044-4: Well bckd: ev ch: in fine form early last season, winning at Pontefract and Ayr: speedily bred: eff over 5f on gd and heavy. should find a race soon. **40**

-- **SEW HIGH** [6] 3-7-13 A Roper(7) 10/1: 01041-0: Ev ch over 1f out. **27**
-- **BRADBURY HALL** [10] 3-7-7 G Carter(0) 25/1: 000-0: Al there. **16**
-- **KEN SIDDALL** [5] 3-7-10(bl) L Charnock 10/1: 00032-0: Early speed, fdd. **00**
-- **RUNAWAY** [9] 3-9-7(VIS) S Perks 11/2: 20004-0: Led over 3f: btr for race. **00**
-- **OLE FLO** [1] 3-7-12 S Whitworth 6/1: 24233-0: Easy to back: prom early. **00**
-- **MY DERYA** [3] 3-7-7(15oh) R Morse(3) 10/1: 10000-0: Springer in mkt: no show. **00**
-- **Running Rainbow** [11] 3-7-7(7oh)   -- **Planter** [12] 3-7-7(bl)(13oh)
-- **Percipio** [4] 3-7-7
13 ran   ½,1,1½,½,1½,2½,1,shhd   (Peter Wetzel)   S Norton High Hoyland, Yorks

7   SPRING APPRENTICE HANDICAP 0-45   £1970   1m 2f   Good Slow   [40]

-- **BALGOWNIE** [2] (J Mulhall) 6-7-7(1oh) S P Griffiths(5) 20/1: 00042-1: 6 br m Prince Tenderfoot - Grandee Ann (Cyane): Led approaching final 1f, driven out for a 20/1 success in an app. h'cap at Doncaster Mar.20: first success: eff over 10f, stays 12f: acts on any ground **15**

-- **PATCHBURG** [12] (W Haigh) 4-8-5 J H Brown(5) 14/1: 20002-2: Led 2f out: 2yo winner at Hamilton: eff at 7f, stays 10f: acts on gd/firm and yld. **24**

-- **LOVELY BUTTERFLY** [17] (M Brittain) 5-7-9 A Munro(5) 33/1: 00000-3: Nearest fin: has been running over hurdles: no form last season: stays 10f and acts on good. **13**

-- **DUELLING** [10] (P Mitchell) 5-8-8(vis) G Carter(5) 11/4 FAV: 01330-4: Well bckd: ev ch straight: last season won a h'cap at Lingfield, also successful at Cagnes: very eff over 10f on firm and yld: likes a sharpish trk, though acts on any. **21**

-- **TAKE A CARD** [4] 7-7-10 D Williams(7) 14/1: 00404-0: Active in mkt: ev ch over 1f out. **08**
-- **SKYBOOT** [13] 7-8-2 Wendy Carter(3) 14/1: 00440-0: Fit from hurdling, never nearer. **04**
-- **PARIS TRADER** [5] 4-9-2(bl) M Hindley(3) 6/1: 40102-0: Late headway: dual winner over hurdles in '85. **00**

--   JOLIS GIRL [18] 4-9-10 P Barnard(7) 10/1: 40420-0: Never beyond mid-div.   00
--   RIDGEFIELD [1] 8-9-5 Gay Kelleway(5) 10/1: 00000-0: No progress straight.   00
--   BACHAGHA [6] 5-8-3 K Radcliffe(5) 6/1: 34040/0: Well bckd: prom ½way: has been hurdling.00
--   DICKS FOLLY [9] 7-8-8 L Riggio 9/1: 1224-0: Never in it.   00
--   North Star Sam [7] 5-8-0   --   Screes [14] 5-8-10   --   Miss Morley [16] 4-7-13
--   Noble Mount [11] 5-8-2(BL)   --   Absonant [3] 4-8-1
--   Letby [8] 4-7-8   --   Coded Love [15] 4-7-10
18 ran   1½,nk,2½,½,6,shhd,2   (Ray Vardy)   J Mulhall York, Yorkshire

8 HALL GATE MAIDEN STAKES   £959   1m 2f   Good Slow

--   JACKS LUCK [3] (M Tompkins) 5-9-0 M Rimmer 25/1: -1: 5 b g Lucky Wednesday - Miss Deed
(David Jack): Made a winning Flat race debut, stayed on well to get up in the last strides
in a maiden at Doncaster Mar.20: fit from hurdling: eff at 10f, should stay further: acts
on gd and yld.   31
--   CAREEN [17] (M Pipe) 5-9-0 S Whitworth 12/1: 40030-2: Led 2f out, just caught:
has been hurdling: has ability but is still a maiden: stays 12f and acts on gd and firm.   29
--   CORAL HARBOUR [2] (G Pritchard Gordon) 4-9-0 G Duffield 9/1: 40300-3: Led over 3f out:
7L clear rest: eff around 10f: acts on gd and firm.   27
--   APPEALING [18] (G Blum) 4-8-11 Pat Eddery 10/1: -000-4: Fdd 2f out: lightly raced
filly: acts on gd and soft.   12
--   LADY FIREPOWER [8] 4-8-11 R Fox 14/1: -0002-0: Never nearer: stays 10f.   12
--   STONEBROKER [14] 4-8-11 J Reid 33/1: 00-00-0: Has been hurdling.   07
--   MEXICAN MILL [27] 4-9-0 S Perks 10/1: 03000-0: Mkt drifter: never beyond mid-div.   00
--   PRINCE RELKO [30] 4-9-0 R Cochrane 6/1: -0: Very active in mkt: no show.   00
--   ALPHABETICAL ORDER [11] 4-9-0 B Crossley 9/2 FAV: -02-0: Uneasy fav and no show.   00
--   RUSTLING [20] 4-8-11 W R Swinburn 15/2: 00320-0: Mkt drifter: wknd 3f out.   00
--   RESPONDER [25] 4-8-11 D Nicholls 8/1: -230-0: Prom early, fdd.   00
--   Delicate Design [29] 4-8-11   --   Ardoon Prince [4] 4-9-0
--   Nikoola Eve [15] 4-8-11   --   Al Alam [7] 4-9-0   --   Al Misk [23] 4-9-0
--   Ocean Life [21] 4-9-0   --   Vesuve [10] 4-9-0   --   Dimension [12] 4-9-0
--   African Magic [13] 5-9-0   --   Celtic Quest [28] 5-9-0 --   Cluga Gurm [19] 5-9-0
--   Cut A Caper [9] 4-9-0   --   Golden Boy [26] 4-9-0 --   Harbour Bazaar [22] 6-9-0(bl)
--   Johnny Frenchman [6] 5-9-0   --   Two Counties [5] 4-9-0
--   Keredem [24] 4-8-11   --   Great Relative [16] 4-9-0 --   Welsh Guard [1] 4-9-0
30 ran   ½,1,7,hd,3.   (J Jiggens)   M Tompkins Newmarket

Official Going Given as Good

9 HAYWARDS PICKLE STAKES (AMA.RIDERS)   £2743   1m 2f   Yielding 92 -20 Slow

--   BRUNICO [4] (R Simpson) 4-11-2 Mr T Thomson Jones 9/4 FAV: -1: 4 br g Bruni -
Cartridge (Jim French) Smart hurdler who made a winning Flat debut in this country: easily
led 1f out in amateur riders event at Doncaster Mar 21: last week fin. unlucky 2nd in the
Triumph Hurdle: last year 1m winner in France: eff. over 10f: should stay further: acts on
good/firm and soft: looks sure to win more races and rate more highly.   54
--   ARGES [30] (R Hollinshead) 5-10-3 Maxine Juster 10/1: 22422-2: Led well over 1f out:
placed many times last year but yet to get his head in front: eff over 8/12f: acts on good
and yielding and galloping track: certainly due a change of luck.   33
--   BOOM PATROL [6] (G Pritchard Gordon) 4-10-12 Mr S Bullard(5) 7/1: 31000-3: Prom, ran on
well: winner over hurdles in '85: last year won maiden at Leicester: eff at 10f and acts
on good but suited by yldg/soft: quite nicely h'capped at present: suited by stiff track.   41
--   HOLYPORT VICTORY [14] (M Usher) 4-10-8 Ann Newnes(5) 20/1: 32230-4: Never closer:
placed sev. times in h'caps last year: runs well at Folkestone and won there at 2 years:
eff over 1m-12f: acts on good and yld.   31
--   COUNT COLOURS [28] Mr T Walford 10/1: 20204-0: 2nd straight, faded: first
time out winner in 85 at Ayr: stays 12f: acts on gd/firm and heavy.   29
--   WISE CRACKER [2] 5-10-8 Mr P Doyle(5) 25/1: -0: Made most, faded.   24
--   ORYX MINOR [29] 6-10-12 Dana Mellor(5) 15/2: 20401-0: Ev ch.   00
--   Crown Estate [18] 4-10-3   --   Mister Point [10] 4-11-2
--   Arrow Beak [15] 5-11-2   --   Little Sloop [19] 4-10-5
--   Lo Broadway [3] 8-10-5   --   Cradle Of Jazz [1] 6-10-12
--   Favourite Nephew [20] 5-10-3   --   High Reef [17] 5-10-12
--   Love Walked In [9] 5-10-3   --   Magic Mink [22] 6-11-2(vis)
--   Swiftspender [7] 5-10-3   --   Tit Willow [16] 4-10-3
--   Winning Star [25] 5-10-8   --   Master Blow [11] 7-11-2
--   Rheinford [26] 10-11-2   --   Some Jet [27] 8-11-2
--   Jubilant Lady [13] 5-10-13   --   Heldigvis [23] 6-10-9
--   Arancia Doro [21] 11-10-3   --   Cri De Grace [5] 11-10-3
--   Whoknowsthebowler [12] 4-10-3   --   Pinwiddie [8] 4-10-0
29 ran   3,½,3,1,2½.   (T Ramsden)   R Simpson Upper Lambourn,Berks

10   LEGER WAY HANDICAP STAKES (0-35)   £3040   1m   Yielding 92 -22 Slow   [34]

-- **FORMATUNE** [14] (D Arbuthnot) 4-9-4(bl) W R Swinburn 14/1: 00003-1: 4 b c Double Form - Native Melody (Tudor Music): First time out, held on well final 1f in a h'cap at Doncaster Mar.21: in '85 won a maiden at Beverley: eff over 5/6f, stays 1m well: acts on firm and yld.   32

-- **VERBARIUM** [21] (J Ramsden) 6-8-11 R Hills 14/1: 41031-2: Ran on well final 1f and just failed: gd effort: most consistent last season, winning at Haydock, Newcastle, Ayr and the Isle Of Man: very eff at 8/10f: acts on firm and soft and a stiff gall trk: goes well when fresh.   24

1 **REPEALED** [8] (W Hastings Bass) 4-9-0 W Carson 7/1 FAV: 00-0323: Fit from Cagnes and well bckd: ev ch final 1f and just btn in close fin: ran only twice on the Flat last season: eff over 1m on yld. due a change of luck.   26

-- **HINCKLEY LANE** [19] (M W Easterby) 4-8-9 M Hindley(3) 16/1: -000-4: Ev ch straight: fit from hurdling: lightly raced on the Flat last season: eff over 1m on yld ground.   18

-- **LEMELASOR** [16] 6-9-6 D Williams(7) 14/1: 30420-0: No real threat.   21

-- **MRS CHRIS** [1] 4-8-12 M Miller 14/1: 34400-0: Prom, ev ch.   09

-- **SWIFT PALM** [17] 9-9-4 G Duffield 15/2: 24330-0: Mkt drifter and never showed.   00

-- **FOOT PATROL** [13] 5-9-4 Pat Eddery 8/1: 00310-0: Mkt drifter, never dangerous   00

-- **PALMION** [5] 4-9-5 S Perks 10/1: 02240-0: Been running over hurdles.   00

-- **FOOLISH TOUCH** [10] 4-9-5(vis) C Dwyer 10/1: 00001-0: Never in the hunt.   00

--	Easy Day [25] 4-8-13	--	Miss Aggro [9] 4-9-0	--	Moondawn [22] 5-9-4	
--	Pliant [20] 6-8-10	--	Sway [4] 4-8-10	--	Aqaba Prince [18] 6-9-0	
--	Night Warrior [12] 4-9-7(vis)			--	Kings Badge [15] 4-9-10	
--	My Handsome Boy [6] 4-8-11			--	Kamaress [23] 4-9-1	
--	Timewaster [7] 4-8-12	--	Kelly Bay [24] 5-8-11	--	Mrs Sauga [11] 4-8-8	
--	Henrys Place [3] 4-8-8			--	Lilting Lad [2] 4-8-3	

25 ran   nk,hd,1½,4,2   (G Ward)   D Arbuthnot Newbury

11   RACING POST MARATHON (H'CAP)   £10410   2m 2f Yielding 92 +16 Fast   [52]

-- **WITHY BANK** [7] (M H Easterby) 4-8-0 W Carson 10/1: 40220-1: 4 b g Blakeney - Chiltern Lass (High Hat): Winner over hurdles last Sat. and made full use of his fitness, led over 1f out, forged clear in a fast run h'cap at Doncaster Mar.21: stays 2m2f really well: acts on yld and soft and likes a gall trk.   36

-- **MEADOWBROOK** [3] (I Balding) 5-8-8 P Eddery 11/2 FAV: 31423-2: Led briefly over 1f out: gd effort: in '85 won valuable h'cap at Royal Ascot: also successful at Pontefract & Haydock: in '84 won at Doncaster: stays 2½m well: acts on any going: genuine and consistent.   36

-- **ACCURACY** [10] (G Balding) 5-8-2 R Fox 7/1: 20200-3: Fit from hurdling, ev ch: failed to win last season: in '84 won at Catterick, Nottingham and Doncaster: needs an extreme test of stamina nowadays: acts on gd and soft.   28

-- **AULD LANG SYNE** [2] (J Jefferson) 7-7-7(bl)(7oh) L Charnock 16/1: 33-30-4: Led 2f out, fdd: fit from hurdling: ran only twice on the Flat in '85: stays really well and acts on gd & soft   18

-- **TOM SHARP** [6] 6-8-4 G Duffield 8/1: 04000-0: Led over 2f out, wknd.   27

-- **TRESIDDER** [4] 4-9-1 K Hodgson 10/1: 13410-0: No real threat.   37

-- **TRAPEZE ARTIST** [14] 5-8-12(vis) S Cauthen 9/1: 00300-0: Never beyond mid-div.   00

-- **TUGBOAT** [18] 7-7-7(2oh) G Carter(5) 10/1: 34104-0: Never held a hope.   00

--	Canio [5] 9-7-7(2oh)	--	Ibn Majed [12] 4-7-12	--	All Is Revealed [8] 4-8-8(vis)	
--	Petrizzo [15] 5-9-10	--	Cool Decision [16] 9-7-11			
--	Flying Officer [21] 9-8-13(vis)			--	Morgans Choice [1] 9-8-13	
--	Jackdaw [20] 6-8-1	--	Milton Burn [9] 5-7-10			
--	Symbolic [13] 6-8-10	--	Knights Heir [17] 5-7-7(7oh)			
--	My Challenge [19] 8-7-7(bl)(17oh)					

20 ran   7,2,½,2,nk   (H Cooper)   M H Easterby Malton, Yorks

12   WILL SCOTT HANDICAP (0-50)   £2616   5f   Yielding 92 -07 Slow   [50]

-- **WILL GEORGE** [13] (C Horgan) 7-8-9 Pat Eddery 6/1 FAV: 22003-1: 7 gr g Abwah - Grey Miss (Grey Sovereign): Fin really well to lead inside final 1f, comfortably in a h'cap at Doncaster Mar.21: in '85 won a h'cap at Newbury: previous season won at Lingfield and Windsor: eff over 5f: acts on gd and soft and on any trk: genuine sort who may win again.   43

-- **SPACEMAKER BOY** [11] (R Nicholls) 6-8-9 N Howe 10/1: 00020-2: Led inside final 1f: in '85 won h'caps at Pontefract, Hamilton and Haydock: very eff over 5f: acts on firm and yld and on any trk: suited by forcing tactics.   37

-- **HILTON BROWN** [10] (P Cundell) 5-10-0 P Cook 13/2: 20000-3: Gd effort under 10-0: failed to win last season, but in '84 was in excellent form, winning 2 valuable h'caps at Ascot and a h'cap at Newmarket: very eff at 5f: acts on firm and soft: genuine and consistent.   55

-- **COOL ENOUGH** [12] (A Bailey) 5-7-12 R Hills 20/1: 00000-4: Ev ch final 1f: first time out last season won a seller at Thirsk: formerly a winner in Ireland: eff at 5-7f: acts on gd and yld.   21

-- **BINCLEAVES** [2] 8-8-0 R Street 8/1: -1010-0: Dsptd lead ½way: fdd final 1f.   20

-- **BROADWATER MUSIC** [3] 5-9-5 R Cochrane 10/1: 41210-0: Btr for race.   37

-- **CHAPLINS CLUB** [1] 6-10-0 D Nicholls 8/1: 04021-0: Should do btr next time.   00

14

--	Schula [7] 6-7-7	--	Bay Bazaar [6] 4-8-3	--	Farmer Jock [15] 4-8-1(vis)
--	Parade Girl [18] 4-7-7(4oh)			--	Philip [17] 4-9-3
--	Brampton Grace [4] 4-9-2			--	Top That [9] 5-8-2
--	Bubs Boy [5] 4-7-9	--	Monswart [16] 5-7-7(2oh)		
--	Warthill Lady [8] 4-7-7(3oh)			--	Krislin [14] 4-7-7(5oh)
18 ran	2,½,1½,1,¾	(R Scott)		C Horgan Billingbear	

13 SOUTH YORKS. MAIDEN SELLER (2-Y-O)   £684   5f   Yielding 92 -69 Slow

-- HELENS CONTACT [4] (M Brittain) 2-8-11 K Darley 9/2: 1: 2 ch f Crofter - First
Contact (Simbir): Made all readily first time out in a maiden seller at Doncaster Mar.21:
half sister to a 7f winner in '85: should stay 6f: acts on yld: sold 5,800 gns.   25

-- DEAR GLENDA [3] (J Berry) 2-8-11 W Carson 3/1 FAV: 2: Gd late prog: should win a
similar race soon: acts on yld.   20

-- MI OH MY [9] (K Stone) 2-8-11 G Brown(5) 4/1: 3: Al there: very active in the mkt:
will benefit from the experience and should pick up a seller.   16

-- BUMI HILLS [5] (P Haslam) 2-8-11 T Williams 5/1: 4: Wknd 1½ out.   06

-- VICHY VAL [2] 2-8-11 M L Thomas 9/1: 0: Late prog: wk in mkt.   00

-- HARRYS COMING [10] 2-9-0 C Coates(5) 9/1: 0: No threat.   00

-- TANGDONTPAY [11] 2-8-11 J H Brown(5) 9/2: 0: Very wk in mkt.   00

-- HEXTHORPE DELL [1] 2-8-11 K Hodgson 7/1: 0: Prom early, fdd.   00

-- Middlelane Lad [8] 2-9-0   -- Kamstar [6] 2-8-11

-- My Mabel [7] 2-8-11

11 ran   1½,1½,4,4,1.   (Mrs H Mills)   M Brittain Warthill

14 FRENCH GATE MAIDEN STAKES (3-Y-O)   £959   1m   Yielding 92 -10 Slow

-- JAZETAS [2] (N Callaghan) 3-9-0 Pat Eddery 6/4 FAV: 4-1: 3 ch c Jaazeiro - Mil Pesetas
(Hot Foot): Well bckd, led 1½ out easily in a 22 runner maiden race at Doncaster Mar.21:
in '85 fin a promising 4th to Dancing Brave at Newmarket: acts on firm and yld and on a gall.
trk: looks certain to be suited by further than 1m and should win btr races.   50

-- BENISA RYDER [10] (C Horgan) 3-9-0 P Cook 2/1: 03-2: Kept on well: acts on yld and
stays 1m: should find a similar maiden race.   38

-- HONEST TOIL [6] (R Whitaker) 3-9-0 D Mckeown 33/1: 00000-3: Al prom: an impr effort:
acts on yld and will probably be suited by further than 1m: half brother to several winners
incl Wealthy, Honest Record and All Fair.   34

-- BILLS AHEAD [11] (G Moore) 3-8-11 W Carson 20/1: 12000-4: Al there: in '85 won a
maiden auction race at Catterick over 7f: stays 1m, acts on firm and yld and does well on
a sharp trk like Catterick.   31

-- ELEGANT BILL [15] 3-9-0 M Beecroft 33/1: 00000-0: Ev ch: stays 1m and acts on yld.   26

-- NORTHERN MELODY [8] 3-9-0 P Bloomfield 25/1: -0: Gd late prog, might have been closer
with more luck in running.   25

--	Knoydart [3] 3-9-0	--	Mistress Charley [22] 3-8-11		
--	Qualitair King [17] 3-9-0			--	The Lidgate Star [21] 3-9-0
--	Tower Fame [20] 3-9-0	--	Grey Dragon [7] 3-9-0	--	Jimmys Secret [14] 3-9-0
--	Take The Biscuit [16] 3-9-0			--	Capistrano Climax [18] 3-9-0
--	Dearham Bridge [13] 3-9-0			--	Izzy Gunner [9] 3-9-0
--	Swynford Prince [19] 3-9-0			--	Frandie Miss [12] 3-8-11
--	Gunner Go [1] 3-8-11	--	Standon Mill [5] 3-8-11		
--	Auction Man [4] 3-9-0				
22 ran	4,1½,shhd,4,½.	(G Cooke)		N Callaghan Newmarket	

Official Going Given as Good

15 MAIL ON SUNDAY 3YO SERIES HCAP 0-60   £3739   7f   Soft 127 -03 Slow   [67]

-- MISNAAD [2] (B Hanbury) 3-7-13 W Carson 5/1: 4220-1: 3 ch c Sauce Boat - Dawn Sky
(Imbros): First time out, led inside final 1f, ridden out in a 3yo h'cap at Doncaster Mar.22:
speedily bred sort, last season fin a close 2nd to Cyrano De Bergerac at Lingfield: stays 7f:
acts on gd and yld and on any trk.   50

-- PLANET ASH [9] (A Bailey) 3-7-13 G Carter(5) 9/2: 320-2: Well bckd: led over 1f
out: kept on: gd effort: showed promise as a 2yo: eff at 7f on firm and yld.   46

1 SOVEREIGN LOVE [7] (W Hastings Bass) 3-7-8 R Lines(0) 10/30 FAV: 2-00313: Fit from a
recent win at Cagnes and well bckd: ev ch 2f out: in 84/85 fin 2nd at Wolverhampton: eff at
7f and stays 1m: acts on firm and heavy.   31

-- BERESQUE [3] (G Lewis) 3-8-5 P Waldron 8/1: 030-4: Al up there: in '85 was a most
promising 3rd in a 7f maiden at Newmarket: cost 180,000 gns and is a half brother to several
winners: eff over 7f on firm and soft.   41

-- CRETE CARGO [8] 3-8-13 Paul Eddery 14/1: 00100-0: Led well over 1f out: fdd on
seasonal debut: btr for race: useful 2yo, winning at Bath, Folkestone and Chepstow: eff
around 5/6f: acts on firm and soft and on any trk.   43

-- ANDARTIS [12] 3-9-7 R Hills 8/1: 01002-0: AI mid-div: very useful 2yo, winning twice
at Newmarket: eff at 7f and stays 1m: likes fast ground and a stiff trk.   41
-- Touch Of Grey [4] 7-12   -- Supreme Kingdom [10] 8-4
-- Tanias Dad [5] 7-7(6oh)   -- Bernigra Girl [4] 7-8
-- Meadow Moor [1] 8-1
11 ran   1½,4,hd,2½,4,1½   (Maktoum Al Maktoum)   B Hanbury Newmarket

16   RACING POST MAIDEN STAKES UNRACED 3YO   £3743   7f   Soft 127 -44 Slow

-- MY KIND OF TOWN [2] (R Williams) 3-9-0 T Ives 8/1: -1: 3 b c Camden Town - Bonny Rand
(Hillary): Ran on well final 1f, gamely getting up close home in a slow run 3yo maiden at
Doncaster Mar.22: eff at 7f and should be suited by 1m plus: acts on soft ground and a
stiff track.   40
-- IYAMSKI [10] (W Hastings Bass) 3-8-11 R Lines 6/1: -2: Led over 1f out: ran green in
front and caught near fin: sure to impr for this initial outing and win a similar event:
eff over 7f on soft ground.   36
-- FALINE [4] (M Francis) 3-8-11 Paul Eddery 5/1: -3: Ev ch 2f out: should do btr: eff
over 7f on soft ground.   33
-- SOXOPH [1] (M H Easterby) 3-8-11 W Carson 13/2: -4: Led 2f out: half sister to the
speedy 2yo Domynsky: should impr.   30
-- BOLD SEA ROVER [6] 3-9-0 M Birch 7/1: -0: Very active in mkt: ev ch 2f out: acts soft. 31
-- PELLS CLOSE [9] 3-9-0 K Hodgson 14/1: -0: Mkt drifter, never nearer.   29
-- ROWIE [5] 3-9-0 T Quinn 5/2 FAV: -0: Very wk fav: wknd after ½way: big strong sort
who should do much btr: half brother to the smart Tremblant.   00
-- Big League [3] 9-0   -- Oscar De Sousa [7] 9-0
-- Petencore [8] 9-0
10 ran   hd,1½,1½,½,½   (Arno Rudolf)   R Williams Newmarket

17   WILLIAM HILL LINCOLN HANDICAP 0-75   £22402   1m   Soft 127 +43 Fast   [68]

-- K BATTERY [12] (W Elsey) 5-8-4 J Lowe 25/1: 00000-1: 5 ch h Gunner B - Kajetna
(Caro): Useful horse: ran on well under press to lead inside final 1f in the valuable and
fast run William Hill Lincoln h'cap at Doncaster Mar.22: in '85 won the valuable Zetland Gold
Cup at Redcar: in '84 won at Newmarket, York, Carlisle and Newcastle (2): very eff over
1m/10f: acts on firm and soft and a stiff track.   57
-- WELL RIGGED [1] (M H Easterby) 5-7-10 G Carter(5) 4/1 FAV: 31321-2: A major gamble:
led till inside final 1f: most gallant effort to make all: in excellent form in '85, winning
at Doncaster, Thirsk and Beverley (2): very eff at 8/9f: acts on firm and soft ground and
on any trk: tough and genuine.   46
-- FUSILIER [9] (C Brittain) 4-7-10(bl)(3ow)(2oh) A Mackay 35/1: 03003-3: Kept on well
final 1f: gd effort: eff over 1m/10f: acts on firm and soft and a gall trk: goes well
when fresh, but yet to win a race.   43
-- XHAI [15] (M Tompkins) 4-7-8 R Morse(4) 25/1: 22110-4: Ev ch from 2 out: ran well:
in '85 won h'caps at Haydock and Ayr: half brother to several winners: equally eff at
1m/10f: acts on firm, suited by soft or heavy and a gall trk.   40
-- KAMPGLOW [8] 4-7-7(5oh) R Fox 50/1: 00004-0: Sn prom, ran well.   38
-- MOORES METAL [10] 6-8-1 W Ryan 25/1: 03000-0: AI there.   44
1   EMERALD EAGLE [19] 5-7-7(7ex) A Shoults(0) 25/1: 1000-01: Fit from Cagnes: fin 7th. 00
-- RANA PRATAP [7] 6-8-0 M L Thomas 13/1: 00144-0: Prom, ev ch.   00
-- RUNNING FLUSH [13] 4-7-9 B Crossley 18/1: 34040-0: Prom over 6f.   00
-- STAR OF A GUNNER [4] 6-7-13 S Dawson(3) 14/1: 00100-0: Fit from hurdling, ev ch.   00
-- VIRGIN ISLE [16] 5-7-11 T Williams 16/1: 13034-0: Prom 5f.   00
-- EMPAPAHERO [14] 4-8-11 G Baxter 16/1: 22001-0: No show, fin lame.   00
-- SHARP NOBLE [24] 4-8-8 W Carson 22/1: 12001-0: Badly drawn.   00
-- CHRISTIAN SCHAD [26] 4-8-10 S Cauthen 14/1: 30040-0: Been hurdling, but badly drawn. 00
-- Inishpour [11] 8-2   -- Bollin Knight [18] 9-10
-- Conmayjo [23] 7-9   -- Qualitair Flyer [3] 8-13
-- Shellman [2] 8-1   -- Gundreda [6] 8-6   -- Dorset Cottage [5] 8-9
-- Well Covered [22] 7-7   -- Senor Ramos [21] 7-11 -- Hay Street [17] 8-3
-- Merry Measure [25] 7-7(4oh)
25 ran   1½,1½,½,¾,shhd,1,2,1½   (Mrs M C Butler)   W Elsey Malton, Yorks

18   CAMMIDGE TROPHY LISTED 3YO+   £8834   6f   Soft 127 +22 Fast

-- GREY DESIRE [5] (M Brittain) 6-9-10 K Darley 7/4 FAV: 00301-1: 6 gr h Habat - Noddy
Time (Gratitude): Smart horse: first time out, ran on under press to lead well inside final
1f in valuable Cammridge Trophy (Listed race) at Doncaster Mar.22: in excellent form early
last season, winning Listed races at Haydock and Newmarket, also won the Quail Stakes at
Kempton: in '84 won at Newmarket and Thirsk (2): eff at 6f, stays 7f really well: acts on
any going and has retained his form well: a credit to his trainer.   84
-- SHARP ROMANCE [4] (B Hanbury) 4-9-7 Pat Eddery 13/2: 00000-2: Led over 1f out till
inside final 1f: gd effort: in '85 was an easy winner of a 4 runner Listed race at Haydock:
in '84 won at Newmarket: very eff over 5/6f, stays 7f: acts on firm and yld ground: likes a
stiff trk and goes well when fresh.   77

--   QUE SYMPATICA [10] (R Boss) 4-9-4 M Miller 11/2: 00404-3: Ev ch over 1f out: first time
out in '85 won at Kempton, later tried over longer distances. but seems best at 6f/1m: in
'84 won sole start at Yarmouth: acts on gd/firm and soft. and does well when fresh.   71
--   VORVADOS [6] (M Haynes) 9-9-10 T Ives 16/1: 00004-4: Ev ch, never nearer: failed to
win last season: in '83 and '84 won this race: also in '83 won at Doncaster and Gr.3 event
at York: eff at 6/7f: acts on firm and heavy and a stiff trk.   69
--   AMIGO LOCO [1] 5-9-4(bl) S Whitworth 10/1: 04240-0: Sn prom and ev ch.   60
1   VAGUE LASS [13] 3-8-1 W Carson 7/1: 320-310: Fit from Cagnes, led ½way.   55
--   ATALL ATALL [2] 3-8-10 S Cauthen 11/2: 12030-0: Sn prom, fdd.   00

--	Jarrovian [8] 7-10	--	Dawns Delight [3] 9-10		
--	John Patrick [7] 9-7	--	Corncharm [12] 9-0	--	Gentileschi [11] 9-0
--	Tanfen [9] 9-0				

13 ran   1½,1,3,1,1,2,1,½   (Mel Brittain)   M Brittain Warthill, Yorks

19   MARCH MAIDEN STAKES 4YO+   £959   1m 6f   Soft 127 +10 Fast

--   MR QUICK [5] (W Wharton) 7-9-0 M Hindley(3) 13/2: -1: 7 b g Saucy Kit - Tesco Maid
(Miss Audrey): Fit from a recent win over hurdles and made a winning Flat race debut, led
over 1f out, ridden out in a maiden at Doncaster Mar.22: stays 14f well: acts on yld and
soft and on any trk.   34
1   ARTESIUM [10] (R Houghton) 4-9-0 J Reid 8/1: 434-002: Led 3f out: stayed: fit from
2 runs at Cagnes: tried in bl last season: stays 2m and acts on gd/firm and soft.   32
--   CHRISTO [4] (R Simpson) 4-9-0 S Whitworth 5/1: -3: Fit from hurdling: stayed on
under press: acts on gd/firm and soft.   28
--   PRIVATE AUDITION [13] (M Usher) 4-9-0 M Wigham 14/1: -4: Been hurdling: led 5f out:
acts on yld.   25
--   R NANCY [9] 5-8-11 D Nicholls 16/1: 0--00-0: Winner over hurdles in '85: ev ch straight   18
--   SANDYLA [12] 5-9-0(bl) M Miller 20/1: 20--0-0: Ev ch over 3f out.   20
--   LADY WOODPECKER [17] 4-8-11 G Starkey 10/30 FAV: 00003-0: Well bckd fav, fin 9th.   00
--   NORTHERN HOPE [16] 4-8-11 P Cook 6/1: 03000-0: Recent hurdles winner, fdd straight.   00
--   RECHARGE [11] 4-9-0 S Perks 6/1: 204-0: Led ½way, wknd.   00

--	Scholar [6] 9-0	--	Dew [15] 8-11	--	Dawn Spirit [3] 9-0
--	Rapidan [8] 9-0	--	Lush Path [1] 8-11	--	Norwhistle [2] 9-0
--	New Times [14] 9-0	--	Precipice Will [7] 9-0		

17 ran   1,3,2,3,nk   (Charles B Sanderson)   W Wharton Melton Mowbray, Leics

20   GREY FRIARS MAIDEN STAKES 2YO   £1162   5f   Soft 127 -25 Slow

--   QUEL ESPRIT [8] (M Mccormack) 2-9-0 R Cochrane 11/8 FAV: 1: 2 b c What A Guest -
Les Sylphides (Kashmir II): Well regarded colt: heavily bckd and led after ½way, readily in a
2yo maiden at Doncaster Mar.22: cost 10,000 gns: eff at 5f and should stay 6f plus: acts
on soft ground and a gall trk: should win more races.   55
--   HAZELS GIRL [10] (A Madwar) 2-8-11 M Miller 14/1: 2: Mkt drifter: nearest fin: showing
promise: should be suited by 1m plus: acts on soft ground.   42
--   TAKE EFFECT [6] (M Brittain) 2-9-0 K Darley 4/1: 3: Al there: cost only I.R. 2,000:
should stay further: acts on soft.   43
--   MADDYBENNY [9] (K Stone) 2-8-11 C Dwyer 10/1: 4: Mkt drifter: gd late hdway: 37
--   TOUCH OF SPEED [4] 2-9-0 S Perks 6/1: 0: Pleasing debut: half brother to several
winners, incl smart 5f filly Storm Warning: sure to impr.   38
--   ARTFUL MAID [2] 2-8-11 D Nicholls 14/1: 0: Led over 2f: cost I.R. 7,400: bred to
stay further.   32
--   GAME FEATHERS [7] 2-8-11 N Carlisle 9/2: 0: Wk in mkt, fin 7th.   00
--   BOOTHAM LAD [5] 2-9-0 M Irving(7) 10/1: 0: Wknd 2f out.   00
--   CAMMAC LAD [3] 2-9-0 M Birch 10/1: 0: Early speed.   00
--   Caringmore [1] 8-11

10 ran   4,½,1,½,nk,1   (International Vacationers)   M Mccormack Sparsholt, Oxon

Official Going Given as Soft

21   KNIGHTON MAIDEN AUCTION STAKES 2YO   £1159   5f   Soft 140 +08 Fast

-- PEATSWOOD SHOOTER [2] (M Brittain) 2-8-2 K Darley 7/2: 1: 2 gr c Windjammer - Raffinata (Raffingora): Made ev yd, comfortably in quite a fast run 2yo maiden auction at Leicester Mar.24: eff at 5f, should stay 6f: acts on good ground and a stiff trk: seems suited by forcing tactics.   **40**

-- MELBURY LAD [6] (C Hill) 2-8-8(1ow) T Ives 7/2: 2: Springer in mkt: ev ch final 2f: good debut and should find a similar event: eff at 5f, should stay further: acts on soft and a gall trk.   **40**

-- SPARSHOLT [4] (P Cole) 2-8-0 T Quinn 11/10 FAV: 3: Sn prom, stays well: heavily bckd today: eff at 5f on soft ground.   **29**

-- PREMIUM GOLD [1] (K Cunningham Brown) 2-7-11 J Lowe 20/1: 4: Al prom, 10L clear rem: eff at 5f on soft ground.   **25**

-- RING BACK [7] 2-8-0 A Proud 16/1: 0: No show: may improve.   **04**

-- SUTTERS MILL [17] 2-8-1(1ow) M Miller 12/1: 0: Friendless in mkt: fdd.   **03**

-- KILVARNET [13] 2-8-10(3ow) S Perks 8/1: 0: Active in mkt: half brother to useful sprinter Young Inca.   **00**

-- Tawny Pipit [10] 7-11	-- Sarasota [8] 8-0	-- Cutler Ridge [5] 8-0
-- Cold Laser [9] 8-6	-- Bold Difference [14] 7-11	
-- Quick Sticks [16] 7-11		-- Petrus Seventy [11] 8-13
-- Roweking [12] 8-7	-- Valdosta [15] 8-0(3ow)	

16 ran   1½,1,nk,10,¾,hd,2½   (G G Ashton)   M Brittain Warthill, Yorks

22   BILLESDON SELLING HCAP STKS 0-25   £708   1m   Soft 140 -30 Slow   [20]

-- CAVALIERAVANTGARDE [4] (P Wigham) 4-9-5 J Reid 10/1: -0000-1: 4 b g Rarity - Erica (Ballyciptic): Mkt drifter, but led 1½f out, comfortably in a 3 & 4yo selling h'cap at Leicester Mar.24 (no bid): little form previously: eff at 8/9f: acts on gd/firm and soft and a gall trk.   **21**

-- DANEDANCER [5] (K Cunningham Brown) 4-8-9(BL) T Ives 12/1: 30040-2: Fit from hurdling: always there: placed in sellers last season: eff around 1m on gd/firm and soft.   **03**

-- PEN TAW [10] (C Hill) 4-9-1(BL) G Starkey 9/1: -0200-3: Has been hurdling: mkt drifter, made most: in '85 fin 2nd in a seller at Bath: eff at 1m on firm.   **06**

-- SNAKE RIVER [11] (D Nicholson) 4-9-11 Pat Eddery 5/1: 24001-4: Mkt drifter: fdd 2 out: in '85 won a 3yo seller at Wolverhampton: eff at 6-11f: acts on gd and firm and a gall trk.   **06**

-- FRISCO [1] 4-9-10 G Baxter 11/8 FAV: 30041-0: Well bckd: prom, ev ch: in '85 won a seller at Hamilton: eff over 6f, stays 1m: acts on gd/firm and heavy: likes a sharpish trk: formerly trained by C Thornton, now with R Akehurst.   **03**

-- SWEET GEMMA [9] 4-8-13 Kim Tinkler(7) 7/1: 00-40-0: Mkt drifter, never showed.   **00**

-- Raceform Rhapsody [2] 7-9(2ow)		-- Meganot [8] 8-8
-- The Dabber [3] 8-0	-- Vaigly Tyresome [12] 8-7	
-- Turffontein [6] 8-13	-- Mattsaward [7] 9-1	

12 ran   4,1½,6,¾,6.   (Cavalier Carpets Ltd)   P Wigham Scagglethorpe, Yorks

23   KINGFISHER HANDICAP STAKES 0-35 4YO+   £2470   1m 4f   Soft 140 -07 Slow   [35]

-- BOLD ILLUSION [11] (M Eckley) 8-8-2 L Riggio(7) 3/1 FAV: 20104-1: 8 ch g Grey Mirage - Savette (Frigid Aire)   Fit from hurdling, led entering straight, forged clear and kept on well in a h'cap at Leicester Mar.24: in '85 won h'caps at Chester and Nottingham: useful performer over hurdles: very eff over 10/12f: acts on any going, but is favoured by some give.   **22**

-- RECORD WING [3] (D Haydn Jones) 8-9-2 R Hills 5/1: 14000-2: Easy recent winner over hurdles: 2nd from 2 out: 7L clear 3rd: in '85 won a h'cap at Chester after several placings: in '84 won again at Chester and likes that very sharp trk: stays 12f well: acts on gd and firm, but likes soft ground.   **29**

-- CHRISTMAS HOLLY [5] (G Reveley) 5-7-8 M Fry 25/1: -000-3: Fit from hurdling: ev ch: lightly raced and no form on the Flat.   **00**

-- SKI RUN [9] (P Wigham) 11-7-10(2ow) J Lowe 20/1: 03-00-4: Sn prom: ran only twice last season.   **00**

-- DON RUNI [2] 4-9-5 G Duffield 20/1: 13000-0: Ev ch straight: in '85 won a 2m maiden at Beverley: stays really well, acts on gd and heavy.   **17**

-- APPLE WINE [12] 9-8-8 D Nicholls 14/1: 00000-0: Mkt drifter, been hurdling.   **04**

-- GWYN HOWARD [13] 4-8-10 R Mcghin 13/2: 30000-0: Sn prom, fdd.   **00**

-- HUNTERS FEN [17] 4-9-0(VIS) S Perks 13/2: 02340-0: Never beyond mid-div.   **00**

-- JACKS ISLAND [14] 4-9-8 Pat Eddery 7/1: 11031-0: Friendless in mkt, wknd straight.   **00**

7   RIDGEFIELD [18] 8-9-10 G Starkey 7/1: 0000-00: Wknd: won this race in '85.   **00**

9 Love Walked In [19] 7-11		-- My Charade [10] 8-11(bl)
4 Bamdoro [7] 8-9	-- Jackies Lass [6] 7-7	-- Trikkala Star [15] 8-2
-- Jonix [20] 8-7	-- Welsh Spy [16] 8-4	-- Butts Bay [1] 8-4
-- Master Carl [8] 8-8		

19 ran   5,7,3,¾,1½,hd   (H M Thursfield)   M Eckley Brimfield, Salop

24   BURTON OVERY EBF STAKES 3YO   £4269   7f   Soft 140 -23 Slow

-- FLEET FORM [2] (C Nelson) 3-8-11 J Reid 9/2: 01300-1: 3 ch c Double Form - Fleetsin (Jim French): Useful colt: first time out, led after 3f out, comfortably in valuable 4 runner minor event at Leicester Mar.24: in '85 won a maiden at Bath: eff at 6/7f on firm and soft: likes a gall trk.   66

-- LANCE [4] (P Cole) 3-8-13 T Quinn 4/1: 02200-2: No extra final 1f: ran well: in '85 won first time out at Kempton: eff at 6/7f on firm and soft.   63

-- BRIGHT AS NIGHT [3] (M Ryan) 3-8-8 G Starkey 4/9 FAV: 22240-3: Eased when btn: ran well in smart company last season, fin 2nd 3 times: eff at 7f, stays 1m well: acts well on good/firm.   48

-- ROBIS [1] (N Macauley) 3-8-5 R Hills 33/1: 33000-4: Led over 4f: impossible task: eff at 7f on gd ground: suited by a sharp track.   00

4 ran   2½,6,dist   (James L Mamakos)   C Nelson Upper Lambourn, Berks

25   SIMON DE MONTFORT MAIDEN STAKES 3YO   £1109   1m 2f   Soft 140 -36 Slow

-- PRINCE MERANDI [8] (M Francis) 3-9-0 Paul Eddery 20/1: 0-1: 3 b c Blakeney - Copt Hall Princess (Crowned Prince)   Wk in mkt, but ran on under press to lead closing stages in a 3yo maiden at Leicester Mar.24: ran only once last season: eff at 10f, may stay further: acts on soft ground and a gall trk.   44

-- MR WHATS HIS NAME [12] (I Matthews) 3-9-0 A Weiss(5) 14/1: 4400-2: Ran on really well: eff at 10f, may stay further: acts on gd/firm and soft: should find a maiden.   42

-- HUBBARDS LODGE [3] (P Kelleway) 3-9-0 P Cook 5/6 FAV: 0032-3: Heavily bckd: led straight till close home: eff at 10f on firm and soft: suited by a gall trk and should strip fitter next time.   41

-- OSRIC [7] (M Ryan) 3-9-0 P Robinson 20/1: -4: Unfancied on racecourse debut: kept on and 7L clear rem: half brother to 9f winner Joli's Girl: acts on soft.   38

-- TARGET SIGHTED [4] 3-9-0 J Reid 9/2: 2-0: Mkt drifter: wknd: 2nd on sole start in '85, a maiden at Warwick: eff at 1m on gd/firm.   26

-- QUICK REACTION [11] 3-9-0 G Starkey 7/1: 0-0: Wknd straight.   14

-- ROYAL EFFIGY [9] 3-9-0 G Baxter 8/1: 000-0: Led till straight.   00

-- Appealiana [2] 9-0   -- Larches [6] 8-11   -- Lineout Lady [1] 8-11
-- Master Music [10] 9-0
11 ran   1,hd,1½,7,7,5   (Merandi Bloodstock Ltd)   M Francis Lambourn, Berks

26   LODDINGTON EBF STAKES 3YO   £2380   6f   Soft 140 -01 Slow

-- KING OF SPADES [2] (N Vigors) 3-8-10 P Cook 5/1: 3013-1: 3 b c King Of Spain - Blueit (Bold Lad) (Ireland): Useful colt: first time out, led well over 1f out, ridden out in a 3yo stakes at Leicester Mar.24: in '85 won a maiden at Wolverhampton: does well when fresh: eff at 5/6f: acts on gd/firm and soft.   59

-- GLIKIAA MOU [3] (R Boss) 3-8-5 M Miller 7/2: 2F00-2: Not qckn close home: good seasonal debut: first time out in '85 fin. a nk 2nd to Queen Mary winner Gwydion, but fell at Brighton on her next start and was off the trk for a long time: eff at 5/6f on firm and soft: should have no trouble finding a race.   51

-- NICCOLO POLO [6] (B Hanbury) 3-9-3 A Geran(7) 5/2 FAV: 10300-3: Chall approaching final 1f: not btn far: first time out in '85 won a maiden at Haydock: eff at 5/6f on firm and soft.   62

-- VOLIDA [4] (C Brittain) 3-9-1 P Robinson 7/2: 10400-4: Made most: a maiden winner at York last season: half sister to the smart Supreme Leader: acts on soft, likes good/firm.   52

-- YOUNG PUGGY [8] 3-8-12 S Perks 10/1: 304C0-0: Mkt drifter, no show.   43

-- MIAMI BLUES [7] 3-8-5 Paul Eddery 10/1: 000-0: Prom, fdd.   16

-- OUR TILLY [5] 3-8-10 W R Swinburn 9/2: 2120-0: Early speed.   00

-- Arranmore Girl [1] 8-5
8 ran   1,hd,3,2½,10,5,3   (Avon Industries Ltd)   N Vigors Upper Lambourn, Berks

---

FOLKESTONE   Monday March 24th   Righthand Undulating Track

Official Going Given as Soft

27   HEADCORN STAKES 2YO   £684   5f   Yield/Soft 113 -15 Slow

-- MISTER COLIN [6] (R Hannon) 2-8-11 L Jones[5] 11/8 jt fav: 1: 2 b c Lord Gayle - Silk Lady (Tribal Chief): First time out, well bckd and led dist. for a comfortable 8L success in a 2yo minor race at Folkestone Mar.24: cost 14,000 gns: brother to '83 juvenile winner Rix Woodcock (subsq. successful over hurdles) and half brother to winning miler Silk Imp: eff at 5f and soft ground: likely to stay further: typical smallish, sharp, early type who could win again.   40

-- LADY PAT [2] (M Mccormack) 2-8-8 R Cochrane 11/8 jt fav: 2: Led over 3f: half sister to 4 winners, though none of them successful as 2yos: acts on soft going: eff at 5f and will stay further.   25

--	**MIDDAY SANITO** [1] (P Mitchell) 2-8-11 A Mcglone 12/1: 3: Outpcd: half brother to winning '85 2yo Track The Black: sprint bred and likely to prove best around 5/6f.	23
--	**CHERRYWOOD SAM** [3] (H O'neill) 2-8-11 I Johnson 10/1: 4: Sprint bred colt who may improve on this first effort.	14
--	**CAWSTONS COMEDIAN** [7] 2-8-8 R P Elliott 12/1: 0: Early speed.	01
--	**PRINCE MAC** [5] 2-8-11 C Rutter[5] 25/1: 0: Al outpcd.	00
--	**FLAKY LADY** [4] 2-8-8 S Whitworth 12/1: 0: Al outpcd.	00

7 ran   8,4,6,7,6.   (Major Es'ad Tarik)   R Hannon East Everleigh, Wilts

28   ALKHAM SELLING H'CAP 3Y+ 0-25   £739   1m 2f   Yield/Soft 113 -72 Slow   [24]

--	**ICEN** [8] (W Musson) 8-8-11 M Wigham 11/8 fav: 04400/1: 8 b g Tycoon II - Pepstep (Polic): Fit from hurdling and proved an easy 6L winner of a slowly run selling h'cap at Folkestone Mar.24 (bought in 1,550 gns): recent easy winner of a selling hurdle at Lingfield having been off the trk previously since May '84: in '82 won at Kempton and Ascot: stays 10f well: likely to stay 12f: acts on gd/firm but well suited by soft going and an undulating trk: likely to win again in similar company.	17
--	**VAIGLY REL** [4] (B Forsey) 6-9-7 R Cochrane 7/2: 04/0-2 Ev ch, outpcd final 2f: fit from hurdling and was a recent winner at Worcester: acts well on soft and heavy going: winner at Warwick on the Flat in '83: eff 1m, stays 10f.	18
--	**HOT BETTY** [11] (P Butler) 6-8-13 R Guest 12/1: 31000-3: Mkt drifter, late prog: won a selling h'cap at Brighton in Sept.'85, has since changed stables: in '84 won at Redcar: eff at 10 and 12f and on gd and firm going.	03
--	**BLAIRS WINNIE** [10] (Pat Mitchell) 4-8-4 W Woods[3] 6/1: 10000-4: Sn prom: won a poor selling h'cap at Folkestone in Aug.'85, sole success to date: acts on gd and yld and on an undulating trk: stays 10f.	00
--	**GREATEST HITS** [3] 9-8-12 C Rutter[5] 14/1: 04041/0: Fit from hurdling but unraced on the Flat since successful at Bath in '83: stays 10f and acts on gd and heavy.	00
--	**TAXINETTE** [6] 4-8-4 D Gibson 25/1: 04000-0: No threat from this maiden.	00
--	**OG BOY** [12] 4-8-5(BL) S Whitworth 8/1: 4-000-0: Soon weakened.	00

--	Tame Duchess [14] 8-11	--	Alcazaba [2] 8-9
--	Charisma Music [7] 8-10	--	Court Jewel [13] 8-4
--	Modern Man [1] 8-4(BL)	--	Bulandshar [9] 8-4
--	Fleur De Thistle [5] 7-7		

14 ran   6,7,4,7,1½   (N Donald)   W Musson Newmarket

29   KINGSNORTH HANDICAP 3YO 0-35   £1082   1m 4f   Yield/Soft 113 -157 Slow   [38]

--	**THE WOODEN HUT** [1] (R Voorspuy) 3-7-9 D Brown 8/1: 00430-1: 7 ch c Windjammer - Bunduq (Scottish Rifle): First time out, led under press final 1f in a very slowly run 3yo h'cap at Folkestone Mar.24: lightly raced in '85: evidently well suited by soft going and an undulating trk: stays 12f.	13
--	**FOUL SHOT** [3] (W Musson) 3-7-12 A Mackay 7/1: 000-2: Well bckd, kept on: showed nothing in 3 outings in '85 but evidently suited by middle distances and soft going: half brother to a couple of winners: could win while fitness is at a premium.	13
--	**HELENS PLEASURE** [6] (I Matthews) 3-9-5 W Woods[3] 15/2: 04404-3: Made most: rated 45 when 4th in a minor race at Ayr (6f, heavy) in Sept.'85: may not stay 12f.	34
--	**RED BILLY** [4] (C Brittain) 3-8-2 C Rutter[5] 11/4: 04000-4: Dsptd lead thro'out, not btn far: close 4th to smart Water Cay at Doncaster in May '85 on 2nd outing but has been disapp since: stays 12f and acts on soft.	16
--	**NORTHINCH** [5] 3-9-1 J Williams 20/1: 000-0: Btr for race: no form in 3 outings in '85 but bred to be a btr 3yo.	19
--	**ICARO** [7] 3-9-7 G Carter[5] 13/8 fav: 02301-0: Prom 10f: well bckd disapp: needed race?	22
--	**HOLIDAY MILL** [2] 3-9-6 Gay Kelleway[5] 5/1: 30300-0: Should benefit from the race.	00

7 ran   2½,hd,½,8,3.   (F J Bull)   R Voorspuy Folkington, Sussex

30   ALDINGTON HANDICAP 3YO+ 0-35   £1223   5f   Yield/Soft 113 +33 Fast   [25]

--	**PERION** [10] (G Lewis) 4-9-13 P Waldron 9/2: 04000-1: 4 ch g Northfields - Relanca (Relic): First time out, led dist readily in a fast run h'cap at Folkestone Mar.24: quite lightly raced in '85 and showed little form: in '84 won at Newmarket (5f, good): suited by the minimum trip and acts on gd and soft going: likely to win again.	35
--	**ROYAL BEAR** [14] (J Bradley) 4-8-3 C Rutter[5] 25/1: 00000-2: Made much: ddhtd in a 3yo seller at Chepstow in May '85, sole success to date: eff at 5f, probably stays 1m: acts on firm and soft.	04
--	**MANGO MAN** [13] (Pat Mitchell) 5-8-10(bl) R Cochrane 16/1: 00000-3: Al there: unsuccessful in '85, previous season won at Brighton: stays 7f and is well suited by soft going.	11
--	**PRINCESS WENDY** [16] (N Callaghan) 4-10-0 G Carter[5] 12/1: 44141/4: Gd late prog and will strip much fitter next time: off the trk in '85, the previous season winner twice at Edinburgh (rated 51): very eff at 5f on firm or good ground, also seems to acts on soft: not badly h'capped and is sure to take a deal of beating next time.	24

-- JACKIE BLAIR [2] 4-9-13 N Howe 7/2 fav: 40040-0: Well bckd, ev ch.   23
12 SCHULA [6] 6-9-4 I Johnson 11/2: 0400-00: No danger.   13
-- HOKUSAN [3] 4-9-2 A Shoults[5] 7/1: 00001-0: Nicely bckd, started slowly, do
better next time.   00
-- ALICE HILL [17] 3-9-0 R Curant 10/1: 10040-0: Early speed: btr for race.   00
-- Thatchville [5] 9-12   -- Lottie [18] 8-4(BL)(1ow)
-- Edwins Princess [7] 8-8(bl)   -- Russell Flyer [11] 9-10(bl)
-- Belle Tower [8] 9-10   -- Lean Streak [4] 8-11(bl)
-- St Terramar [1] 8-3(bl)   -- Hampton Walk [9] 8-3
-- Mr Rose [12] 9-1
17 ran   4,hd,4,shhd,½,1½,1½   (J W Wheatland)   G Lewis Epsom, Surrey

---

31 ROCHESTER STAKES 3YO UPWARDS   £684   6f   Yield/Soft 113 -18 Slow

-- GOLD PROSPECT [11] (G Balding) 4-9-0 J Williams 5/2 fav: 20-1: 4 b g Wolverlife -
Golden Darling (Darling Boy): Uneasy fav first time out but comfortably won a minor event
at Folkestone Mar.24: gd 2nd on debut in '84, disapp on sole subsequent start: half brother
to winning sprinters Pitboy, Portal Lad and About Turn: likely to prove best around 5/6f:
acts well on soft: rated 62 first time out in '85.   32
-- SHIRLY ANN [17] (N Macauley) 4-8-11 S P Griffiths[5] 33/1: 00000/2: Rank outsider, ran
well: off the trk last season and has yet to win: half sister to 4 winners, notably useful
miler Majestic Nurse: could win a h'cap while fitness is at a premium.   22
-- BLACK SPOUT [8] (H O'neill) 5-9-0 I Johnson 33/1: 00000-3: Rank outsider, led 5f:
officially rated 00: no worthwhile form in '85 and remains a maiden.   19
-- LINGFIELD LADY [18] (W Kemp) 4-8-11 B Thomson 13/2: 00400-4: Fit from hurdling and
a gamble, wknd final 1f: placed on the Flat last season and has yet to win.   10
-- DALSAAN BAY [4] 3-7-11 S Dawson[5] 33/1: 00-0: Speed 4f.   00
-- MR MCGREGOR [7] 4-9-0 S Whitworth 12/1: 03440-0: Wknd final 2f: btr for race.   05
-- VISUAL IDENTITY [3] 4-9-0 A Mcglone 7/2: 30020-0: No threat.   00
-- NORTHERN GUNNER [13] 3-7-11 M L Thomas 15/2: 02000-0: Fin 9th.   00
-- PULSINGH [1] 4-9-0 B Rouse 7/1: -0: Early speed.   00
-- REST AND WELCOME [15] 4-8-11 J Matthias 11/2: 40030-0: Mkt drifter, btr for race.   00
-- Passooner [12] 7-11   -- Matelot Royale [16] 7-11
-- Miletrians Lass [5] 8-11   -- Young Boris [10] 9-0
-- Jeldora [9] 8-11
15 ran   3,2½,3,¾,3,1,1,1,½   (Harvey Spack)   G Balding Fyfield, Hants

---

32 SHORNCLIFFE STAKES 3YO   £684   1m 4f   Yield/Soft 113 -72 Slow

-- TRUELY BILLY [4] (I Matthews) 3-9-0 N Day 5/4 fav: 32-1: 2 ch c Hello Gorgeous -
Vraiment (Relko): First time out, led dist readily in a minor 3yo race at Folkestone Mar.24:
placed in both outings in '85 when trained by J Hindley: appears to act on firm and soft
going: well suited by 12f: half brother to smart '79 2yo Varingo.   43
-- COUNTLESS COUNTESS [2] (R Williams) 3-8-11 R Cochrane 11/2: -2: Racecourse debut, late
hdway and will benefit from the experience: suited by 12f and acts on soft.   28
-- OWL CASTLE [6] (M Usher) 3-9-0 A Mcglone 14/1: 00000-3: Made much, wknd: showed some
ability last season: may prove best at 10f with forcing tactics: acts on soft.   30
-- STRONGARM [5] (I Matthews) 3-9-0(BL) G Dickie 14/1: -4: Stable companion of winner
and bl first time on a racecourse: may impr.   27
-- MIGHT MOVE [8] 3-9-0 C Rutter[5] 11/4: 003-0: Much btr final outing of '85 over 7f
on firm ground.   00
-- NEVER BEE [9] 3-9-0 N Dawe 16/1: 00-0: Dsptd lead much: lightly raced.   00
-- Wing Bee [1] 9-0   -- Highland Daisy [3] 8-11
8 ran   6,½,1½,20,hd.   (Lord Matthews)   I Matthews Newmarket

---

LEICESTER   Tuesday March 25th   Righthand Galloping Track

Official Going Given as Soft

33 KEYTHORPE MAIDEN STAKES 3YO   £1021   7f   Soft 120 -01 Slow

-- EMRYS [7] (N Vigors) 3-9-0 P Cook 2/1 FAV: 002-1: 3 ch c Welsh Pageant - Sun Approach
(Sun Prince): Despite hanging inside the final 1f, led on the line in a 3yo maiden at
Leicester Mar.25: in '85 fin 2nd in a maiden at Newbury: eff at 7f: acts on gd and soft
and a gall trk.   45
-- PRINCELY ESTATE [4] (J Winter) 3-9-0 W R Swinburn 16/1: 000-2: Led/dsptd lead: caught
post: no form in 3 outings last season, but seems to have impr: eff over 7f on soft ground. 45
-- PRETTY GREAT [6] (I Matthews) 3-8-11 N Day 20/1: -3: Led to ½way: promising racecourse debut: half brother to 3 winners, incl the speedy Crews Hill: eff at 7f on soft. 38
-- MISS BRADY [1] (M Ryan) 3-8-11 S Perks 20/1: 0-4: Under press, hmpd dist: ran only
once in '85: half sister to useful 10f winner Brady.   35

-- PENTLAND HAWK [11] 3-9-0 S Perks 5/1: 04-0: Mkt drifter: never nearer: 4th in a maiden at Doncaster in '85: acts on gd and soft. **36**
-- ALPHA HELIX [2] 3-9-0 S Whitworth 14/1: -0: Friendless in mkt on racecourse debut: half brother to Emir Sultan and should do btr over further. **32**
-- NO RESTRAINT [9] 3-8-11 Pat Eddery 11/4: -0: Well fancied: there halfway. **00**
-- TRIXIE BELLE [8] 3-8-11 G Starkey 13/2: 0-0: Early speed. **00**
-- Marina Plata [10] 8-11   -- Harmony Bowl [12] 9-0
-- Country Craft [5] 8-11   -- Geoffs Folly [3] 9-0
12 ran   shhd,2,2,½,1½,1½   (Lady d'Avigdor Goldsmid)   N Vigors Upper Lambourn, Berks

34 BESCABY MAIDEN STAKES 2YO   £1101   5f   Soft 120 +06 Fast

-- SIZZLING MELODY [9] (Lord John Fitzgerald) 2-9-0 R Hills 9/2: 1: 2 br c Song - Mrs Bacon (Balliol): Promising colt: ready 4L winner of a 2yo maiden at Leicester Mar.25: cost 14,000 gns and is held in some regard: eff at 5f, will be suited by 6f: acts well on soft ground and should win more races. **57**
-- WINDMEDE [8] (M Brittain) 2-9-0 K Darley 7/2: 2: Led 4f: 5L clear 3rd: gd effort: cost 1,500 gns: half brother to winning 2yo Descartes: acts on soft ground. **45**
-- UNOS PET [6] (K Stone) 2-9-0 G Brown(5) 16/1: 3: Never nearer: should impr: acts on soft ground. **33**
-- LAWNSWOOD LAD [10] (R Hollinshead) 2-9-0 S Perks 10/1: 4: Kept on well, showing promise **23**
-- LATE PROGRESS [3] 3-8-11 W Carson 3/1 FAV: -0: Well bckd: early speed. **18**
-- HERR FLICK [11] 2-9-0 N Day 13/2: 0: Chall 2f out: fdd: half brother to several winners and bred to stay further. **18**
-- QUITE SO [4] 3-8-11 W R Swinburn 5/1: -0: Active in mkt: fdd 2 out. **00**
-- MISS PISA [1] 3-8-11 J Ward(7) 10/1: -0: Prom early: cost I.R. 1,000. **00**
-- Four Laffs [5] 8-11   -- Swynford Princess [2] 8-11
-- Mark Seagull [7] 9-0
11 ran   4,5,4,1,1½,6.   (Mrs Mary Watt)   Lord John Fitzgerald Newmarket

35 KIBWORTH CLAIMING STAKES 3YO   £1917   1m 4f   Soft 120 -55 Slow

-- CHUMMYS OWN [1] (N Callaghan) 3-8-8 Pat Eddery 11/8 FAV: 0-1: 3 ch c Sagaro - Monagram (Mon Fetiche): Heavily bckd and led over 2f out, pushed out in a 3yo claimer at Leicester Mar.25: ran only once last season: half brother to several winners incl winning stayer Appeal To Me: eff at 12f, should stay further: acts on soft and a gall trk. **32**
-- S S SANTO [3] (M Tompkins) 3-8-5 M Rimmer 9/2: 0-2: Very active in mkt: not pace of winner, but 6L clear 3rd: eff at 12f on soft ground. **22**
-- HOT RULER [5] (M Brittain) 3-9-0 K Darley 5/1: 0202-3: Friendless in mkt: ev ch: in '85 fin 2nd in sellers at Hamilton and Leicester: eff at 8/10f, stays 12f: acts on any ground. **21**
-- ANDREAS PRIDE [2] (P Haslam) 3-8-3 T Williams 12/1: 004-4: Made most: fdd: stays 10f. **05**
-- FAST AND FRIENDLY [4] 3-8-4 A Whitehall(7) 8/1: 0000-0: Never dangerous. **04**
-- TARA DANCER [7] 3-8-6(bl) C Dwyer 6/1: 00010-0: Led early. **05**
-- ARCH PRINCESS [8] 3-8-11(BL) R Cochrane 11/2: 000-0: Fdd straight. **00**
-- Star Command [6] 9-0
8 ran   2,6,3,1½,nk,10   (C Gaventa)   N Callaghan Newmarket

36 GREYHOUND HANDICAP STAKES 0-35   £2418   1m 2f   Soft 120 -35 Slow   [33]

*7 BALGOWNIE [16] (J Mulhall) 6-7-13 S P Griffiths(5) 5/1 FAV: 0042-11: 6 br m Prince Tenderfoot - Grandee Ann (Cyane): In gd form, ran on well to lead inside the final 1f, comfortably in a h'cap at Leicester Mar.25: last week won an app. h'cap at Doncaster: eff over 10f, stays 12f: acts on any ground. **16**
7 LOVELY BUTTERFLY [5] (M Brittain) 5-8-2 K Darley 7/1: 0000-32: Running well: acts on gd and soft: see 7. **13**
-- WELL MEET AGAIN [4] (C Benstead) 9-9-4 B Rouse 7/1: 34-20-3: Mkt drifter: led 2 out, wknd on seasonal debut: ran only twice in '85, first time out fin 2nd in a h'cap at Lingfield: in '83 won at Goodwood and Leicester: best around 10f: likes soft ground and normally comes late. **29**
-- BWANA KALI [11] (M Tompkins) 4-9-7 R Cochrane 9/1: 04010-4: Active in mkt: ev ch from 2 out: in '85 won a minor event at Edinburgh: very eff at 1m on gd and soft ground. **30**
-- GODS HOPE [13] 4-8-10 G Baxter 25/1: 0--00-0: Al there: ran only twice last season: yet to win. **15**
-- RECORD RED [2] 5-7-9 P Hill(7) 25/1: -0: Dddhtd 5th: maiden. **00**
8 LADY FIREPOWER [9] 4-7-10 R Fox 13/2: 0002-00: Wknd over 2f out: btr in 8 (good). **00**
-- TIMURS GIFT [7] 4-8-11 A Murray 7/1: -0000-0: Never showed. **00**
-- COUNT BERTRAND [14] 5-8-13 R Morse(7) 10/1: 30302-0: Mkt drifter, ev ch. **00**
-- TRUMPS [17] 6-8-4 W Carson 8/1: 23104-0: Dist last. **00**
-- Monclare Trophy [1] 8-13   -- Floreat Floreat [6] 8-5
-- Mr Music Man [8] 8-9   -- Shad Rabugk [12] 8-8 -- Toda Forca Avanti [10] 8-10
-- Pokey [3] 8-11(bl)   -- Superfrost [18] 8-10 -- Nordic Hawk [19] 7-11
-- Sherpaman [15] 7-9
19 ran   2½,¼,¼,2½,ddht,2.   (Ray Vardy)   J Mulhall York

37 HARBOROUGH FILLIES EBF STAKES 3YO   £2275   1m   Soft 120 -02 Slow

-- HIDDEN BRIEF [2] (R Boss) 3-8-10 M Miller 11/4: 41400-1: 3 ch f Pyjama Hunt -
Himalia (High Line): Useful filly: easy to back, but made ev yd, comfortably in a 3yo fillies
stakes at Leicester Mar.25: in '85 won a maiden auction event at Redcar: later a fine 4th in
Gr.3 Hoover Fillies Mile at Ascot: very eff at 1m on firm and soft: best with forcing tactics.   56
-- SHINING POPPY [4] (P Cole) 3-8-11 T Quinn 8/11 FAV: 23244-2: Heavily bckd: ev ch:
8L clear 3rd: consistent sort in '85, winning at Brighton first time out: eff at 7f/1m: acts
on soft: likes gd/firm: acts on any trk.   47
-- HIGHEST NOTE [3] (G Blum) 3-8-8 G Duffield 20/1: 00400-3: Stiff task: eff at 7/8f
on good and soft.   26
-- UPTOWN RANDBS [6] (G Moore) 3-9-1 J Lowe 8/1: 21040-4: There ½way: in '85 won a
nursery h'cap at Catterick: acts on firm and soft and on any trk.   13
-- CHALFONT MO [1] 3-8-8 P Cook 10/1: 03000-0: Mkt drifter: prom 5f.   01
-- NANOR [5] 3-8-11 C Rutter(5) 14/1: 20314-0: There ½way, wknd.   00
6 ran   4,8,10,2½,2½   (K Bethel)   R Boss Newmarket

38 BUTLER HANDICAP STAKES 3YO 0-35   £1721   5f   Soft 120 -04 Slow   [40]

-- COPPERMILL LAD [2] (L Holt) 3-8-2 N Adams 20/1: 03000-1: 3 ch c Ardoon - Felin Geri
(Silly Season): Unfancied, but ran on well to get up near the line in a 3yo h'cap at
Leicester Mar.25: eff at 6f on soft ground: acts on any track.   23
-- TAYLOR OF SOHAM [15] (D Leslie) 3-8-8(bl) M Rimmer 12/1: 40000-2: Led final 1f: caught
post: placed several times in '85, but failed to win: eff at 5f on firm and soft: deserves
a change of luck.   28
-- MERCIA GOLD [6] (B Morgan) 3-8-5 B Crossley 20/1: 03000-3: Al prom and not btn far in
close finish: in '85 fin 3rd in a 5 runner maiden at Warwick: eff at 5f on firm and soft.   24
6 AMBER CLOWN [13] (W Wharton) 3-8-7 N Carlisle 7/4 FAV: 3000-24: Much btr in 6 (good).16
-- GOLDEN GUILDER [3] 3-8-4(3ow) K Hodgson 14/1: 40000-0: Prom, ev ch: eff over 5f on
yld and soft.   12
-- LEFT RIGHT [11] 3-8-8(bl) Gay Kelleway(5) 20/1: 04400-0: Led till 1f out.   15
6 MY DERYA [8] 3-7-9 R Morse(5) 6/1: 0000-00: Never in it after slow start.   00
-- YOUNG JASON [10] 3-9-7 P Waldron 7/1: 40011-0: No show: btr for race.   00
-- EL ALAMEIN [4] 3-8-7 N Day 10/1: 01004-0: Mkt drifter: early speed.   00
6 BRADBURY HALL [1] 3-8-10(VIS) C Dwyer 7/1: 000-00: Prom early: btr in 6 (good).   00
-- Hobournes Katie [5] 8-6   -- Lady La Paz [7] 8-8
-- Feather Girl [14] 7-7(5oh)   -- Stromberg [9] 7-7(2oh)
-- Kiki Green [12] 7-9(2ow)(5oh)
15 ran   shhd,nk,4,½,½   (Mrs J K Sargood)   L Holt Tunworth, Hants

39 KEYTHORPE MAIDEN STAKES 3YO   £1021   7f   Soft 120 -37 Slow

-- RHAPSODY IN BLACK [8] (M Ryan) 3-9-0 M Giles 7/1: -1: 3 b c Sexton Blake - Goldwyn
Princess (Native Prince): First time out, ran on well under press to get up near line in a
3yo maiden at Leicester Mar.25: half brother to useful 2yo Cornwall: eff at 7f and should
stay further: acts on soft ground.   31
-- TEED BORE [2] (W Musson) 3-8-11 M Wigham 25/1: 0-2: Just btn.: ran only once in '85:
half sister to the very smart stayer Ore and should be suited by further: acts on soft.   27
-- COOPER RACING NAIL [9] (J Berry) 3-8-11 W Carson 5/2 FAV: 00322-3: Led ½way till close
close home: placed several times last season in sellers and should win in plating company:
eff at 6/7f and likes soft ground.   27
-- NATCHAKAM [11] (G Lewis) 3-9-0 P Waldron 5/1: -4: Fdd final 1f on racecourse debut.   19
-- BAXTERGATE [3] 3-9-0 R P Elliott 16/1: 0000-0: Never beyond mid-div.   14
-- COOL OPERATOR [10] 3-9-0 R Cochrane 8/1: 000-0: Fdd after 1f out.   12
-- DELTA LIMA [6] 3-9-0 J Reid 7/1: 4200-0: Mkt drifter, fin 7th.   00
-- GLORIANT [5] 3-9-0 K Darley 4/1: 00040-0: Wknd 2f out.   00
-- THE LITTLE JOKER [1] 3-8-11 J Lowe 10/1: 0000-0: Led to ½way.   00
-- BOLD LOREN [7] 3-8-11 T Quinn 10/1: -0: Prom, fdd.   00
-- Bryanthus [4] 8-11
11 ran   nk,hd,5,2½,1,1½   (T P Ramsden)   M Ryan Newmarket

Official Going Given as Good/Soft

40   EBF ORAN MAIDEN STAKES 2YO   £1031   5f   Good/Soft 110 -06 Slow

20   ARTFUL MAID [5] (R Stubbs) 2-8-11 D Nicholls 7/2: 01: 2 gr f Artaius - Snow Maid (High Top): Impr filly: made ev yd, stayed on well in a 2yo maiden at Catterick Mar.26: cost I.R. 7,400: eff at 5f and should stay further: acts on soft ground and on any trk, though is suited by forcing tactics on a sharpish one.   **42**

-- **WHISTLING WONDER** [10] (M Brittain) 2-9-0 K Darley 3/1: 2: Cheaply acquired colt: al up there: kept on well: should find a small maiden: eff at 5f on soft ground.   **40**

-- **BANTEL BLAZER** [9] (I Bell) 2-9-0 N Carlisle 16/1: 3: Sn prom: speedily bred: acts on yld and a sharp trk.   **34**

-- **SEATON GIRL** [1] (D Barron) 2-8-11 S Webster 11/4 FAV: 4: Stayed on under press. wl bkd. **26**

-- **MR GRUMPY** [7] 2-9-0 M Fry 12/1: 0: Nearest fin and should do btr next time.   **22**

-- **BENFIELD MORPETH** [2] 2-9-0 C Dwyer 9/1: 0: No real threat.   **16**

-- **MARK OF GOLD** [4] 2-8-11 J Reid 6/1: 0: Never in it: half sister to useful sprinter Pip'em and should do btr than this.   **00**

-- Scarning Sparkler [8] 9-0   -- Creole Bay [6] 8-11

9 ran   1½,2,1½,3,2   (Glenwright Bloodstock Co ltd)   R Stubbs Middleham, Yorks

41   FORCETT PARK SELLING STAKES 3 & 4YO   £1130   7f   Good/Soft 110 -11 Slow

-- **BRAMPTON IMPERIAL** [2] (D Chapman) 4-9-7 D Nicholls 12/1: 00000-1: 4 b g Imperial Fling - Cereum (Tudor Grey): First time out, led over 1f out, comfortably in a 3 & 4yo seller at Catterick Mar.26 (no bid): in '85 won selling h'caps at Ripon and Redcar: eff at 6f, stays 9f: acts on firm and soft and on any track, though likes a sharpish one.   **18**

9   **TIT WILLOW** [4] (S Wiles) 4-9-7 S Keightley 10/1: 0300-02: Lightly bckd: kept on under press: maiden: eff at 7f/1m on gd and yld: likes a sharpish trk.   **13**

14   **GUNNER GO** [10] (Ron Thompson) 3-8-3 R P Elliott 33/1: 000-03: Made most: lightly raced: eff at 7f on yld and a tight trk.   **06**

-- **SISTER NANCY** [17] (M Lambert) 3-8-3 P Burke(7) 16/1: 40000-4: Ran on : not well drawn   **05**

-- **MUSIC TEACHER** [15] 3-8-4(1ow) J Bleasdale 10/1: 03300-0: Ev ch: eff at 5/6f last season on gd and heavy.   **02**

-- **LADY GRIM** [8] 4-9-4 G Carter(5) 6/1 FAV: 10000-0: Al there: has been hurdling: first time out last season won this same race: eff at 7f on yld and a sharp trk.   **00**

-- **CALL ME CLAIRE** [20] A Murray 13/2: 04000-0: Fit from hurdling: prom. fdd.   **00**

-- **BUCKS BOLT** [16] 4-9-7 M Fry 7/1: 00000-0: Bckd from 12/1: no show. not well drawn.   **00**

-- **GRAND CELEBRATION** [14] 4-9-7 S Whitworth 7/1: -0-0: Mkt drifter: never beyond mid-div. **00**

-- **SAREMA** [6] 4-9-4 J Reid 10/1: -0424-0: Never in it.   **00**

-- Blue Piazza [1] 9-4   -- Poco Loco [12] 9-7   8   Ardoon Prince [18] 9-7

-- Martella [9] 9-7   -- Fields Diamond [5] 8-6

-- Run For Fred [3] 9-7   -- Louisalex [13] 8-6(BL)

22   The Dabber [19] 8-3

18 ran   2,2½,½,1½,½.   (W G Swiers)   D Chapman Stillington, Yorks

42   RACE AROUND YORKSHIRE HANDICAP 0-35   £1276   6f   Good/Soft 110 +30 Fast [29]

-- **GODS SOLUTION** [10] (D Barron) 5-9-7 B Mcgiff(7) 4/1 Jt.FAV: 00300-1: 5 gr h Godswalk - Campitello (Hornbeam): First time out, made most for a ready 7L win in a fast run h'cap at Catterick Mar.26: in '85 was in gd form, winning 3 times at Beverley & Catterick (2): eff over a stiff 5f, stays 6f well: acts on firm & soft & on any trk, though likes Catterick.   **36**

12   **BAY BAZAAR** [5] (M W Easterby) 4-9-10 M Hindley(3) 5/1: 0022-02: No chance with winner: in '85 fin 2nd 3 times but failed to win: in '84 won at Ayr: eff at 5f, stays 6f: acts on good/firm and yld.   **24**

-- **CAERNARVON BOY** [6] (J Kettlewell) 4-7-13 A Proud 20/1: 00000-3: Sn prom: first time out in '85 fin 2nd at Carlisle but subs. failed to make the frame: in '84 won a selling h'cap at Ripon: eff at 6f on firm & yld.   **00**

-- **SINGLE HAND** [8] (D Chapman) 6-9-1 N Leach(7) 9/1: 00020-4: Ran on final 1f: failed to win in '85: previous season won h'caps at Newcastle & Nottingham: eff over 6/7f: stays 1m: acts on any going and usually comes late.   **13**

-- **SPOILT FOR CHOICE** [2] 8-9-5 D Nicholls 10/1: 40000-0: Every chance.   **09**

-- **HENRYS VENTURE** [13] 4-8-1 S P Griffiths(5) 20/1: 00000-0: Sn prom, wknd.   **00**

-- **MR JAY ZEE** [1] 4-9-10 G Carter(5) 4/1 Jt.FAV: 00000-0: Very active in mkt: has regressed 00

-- **ILLINEY GIRL** [7] 4-9-8 G Duffield 15/2: -0410-0: Made no show.   **00**

-- Low Flyer [11] 8-8   -- Go Spectrum [4] 7-13(bl)

-- Crowfoots Couture [9] 8-2(vis)   -- Off Your Mark [12] 8-7

-- Gold Duchess [3] 8-9

13 ran   7,nk,½,3,hd   (Peter Jones)   D Barron Maunby, Yorks

43   TOYTOP STAKES 2YO   £1136   5f   Good/Soft 110 +01 Fast

*3   **BLUEMEDE** [5] (M Brittain) 2-9-4 K Darley 4/11 FAV: 11: 2 ch c Blue Cashmere - Knavesmire (Runnymede): Useful colt: led from the stalls for a facile win in the Toytop Stakes at Catterick Mar.26: last week won the Brocklebsy at Doncaster: cost only 15,000 gns and looks a bargain: eff at 5f: speedily bred and does well with forcing tactics: acts on good and yielding.   **59**

-- **LATERAL** [1] (J Berry) 2-8-11 M Fry 10/1: 2: Bolted before start: kept on well though no chance with easy winner: half brother to 12f winner Pine Ridge and should be suited by further: acts on yld. 42

3   **TEAM EFFORT** [4] (Ron Thompson) 2-8-11 R P Elliott 5/1: 03: Al prom: cost I.R. 2,300 and acts on good and yielding. 34

-- **ATHENS LADY** [6] (A Smith) 2-8-8 S Webster 16/1: 4: Never going pace. 11

-- **ROYAL ILLUSION** [3] 2-8-11 J Lowe 12/1: 0: Never in it. 10

-- **GILLOT BAR** [2] 2-8-8 K Hodgson 9/1: 0: Friendless in mkt and al there. 00

6 ran   1½,3,8,2,4   (P J Armstrong)   M Brittain Warthill, Yorks

---

44   YARM HANDICAP 0-35   £1394   2m   Good/Soft 110 -05 Slow   [35]

-- **CARNEADES** [6] (M H Easterby) 6-8-0(vis) G Carter(5) 2/1 FAV: 1000-1: 6 b g Homing - Connarca (Connaught): Fit from hurdling, led over 2f out, very easily in a h'cap at Catterick Mar.26: lightly raced on the Flat: first time out in '85 won this same race: stays 2m really well: acts on yld and heavy: likes Catterick. should win again. 20

-- **BUSTOFF** [15] (S Hall) 6-7-12 N Carlisle 16/1: 00--0-2: Led over 3f out: fit from hurdling: lightly raced on the Flat: stays 2m. 09

-- **TIMMINION** [10] (K Stone) 4-8-9 C Dwyer 12/1: 03330-3: Nearest fin on seasonal debut: btr for race: in '85 won at Catterick and Pontefract: eff at 12f, stays 2m: acts on firm and yld: likes a sharpish trk. 17

-- **RED DUSTER** [11] (T Fairhurst) 6-9-1 M Beecroft 7/1: 41100-4: Fit from hurdles: in '85 won h'caps at Catterick and Redcar: in '84 won again at Catterick: stays 2m really well: acts on firm and soft: likes Catterick. 11

-- **NO FLUKE** [5] 6-7-7 Kim Tinkler(3) 33/1: -0: Been hurdling: stays 2m. 00

-- **OCEANUS** [2] 5-7-10(1ow) L Charnock 9/1: 23000-0: Nearest fin: hurdles winner in '85. 00

-- **DUKE OF DOLLIS** [3] 7-8-4 S Whitworth 9/1: -0102-0: Mkt drifter: never showed. 00

-- **RIBBONS OF BLUE** [1] 6-7-13 K Darley 10/1: -1320-0: Fdd 4f out. 00

-- **MEIKLEOUR** [9] 7-10-0 A Murray 13/2: 12100-0: Made most, weakened. 00

-- Mount Rule [8] 7-9   -- Gainville Lad [4] 8-5   11   Symbolic [14] 9-13
-- Baval [12] 8-0(5ow)   -- Prime Stone [7] 8-5   9   Jubilant Lady [13] 7-12
-- Thunder Rock [16] 7-7

16 ran   5,3,12,½,½.   (Timeform Social Club Owners Group)   M H Easterby Great Hapton

---

45   WHORLTON MAIDEN FILLIES STAKES 3YO   £684   1m 4f   Good/Soft 110 -84 Slow

-- **NIMBLE NATIVE** [3] (S Norton) 3-8-11 J Lowe 4/1: 000-1: 8 ch f Our Native - Fleeting Vision (Pronto): Led over 3f out, comfortably in a very slowly run 3yo maiden fillies stakes at Catterick Mar.26: no form in 3 outings in '85: eff at 12f on yld ground and a sharp trk. 31

-- **SAY SOMETHING** [1] (J Winter) 3-8-11 G Duffield 9/4: 000-2: Well bckd: came to chall over 1f out: half sister to several winners and this was impr form: eff at 12f on yld ground and a tight track. should find a similar maiden. 27

-- **WHITTINGHAM VALE** [2] (W Elsey) 3-8-11 C Dwyer 14/1: -3: Hung left approaching dist on racecourse debut: stays 12f and acts on yld. 20

-- **MADAM GERARD** [6] (W Wharton) 3-8-11 N Carlisle 12/1: 02000-4: Made most: fdd: best effort in '85 when 2nd in a seller at Thirsk: acts on firm and yld. 08

-- **GILSAN GREY** [5] 3-8-11 C Coates(5) 50/1: 0-0: Led early: lightly raced. 00

-- **MOHICAN** [4] 3-8-11 J Bleasdale 7/4 FAV: 3220-0: Very uneasy in the mkt and btn a long way out: in '85 was placed in maidens: stays 1m and acts on gd and yld. 00

-- Solent Breeze [8] 8-11   -- Parkes Special [7] 8-11

8 ran   2,4,8,6,nk   (Bahman Abtahl)   S Norton High Hoyland, Yorks

---

46   SPRINGTIME APPRENTICES HANDICAP 0-35   £931   7f   Good/Soft 110 -10 Slow   [25]

-- **JANES BRAVE BOY** [5] (D Chapman) 4-9-1 N Leach(7) 9/1: 10003-1: 4 b g Brave Shot - Jane Merryn (Above Suspicion): First time out, led over 2f out, readily in an app. h'cap at Catterick Mar.26: in '85 won a seller at Beverley: eff at 6-8f: acts on gd and yld and on any trk. 21

-- **JOHN GILPIN** [6] (W Haigh) 4-8-11(bl) J Quinn 9/1: 04100-2: Prom and kept on well: last season won an app. selling h'cap at Windsor: also won a seller at Ayr: eff at 6f, stays 7f: acts on gd and heavy and on any trk. 10

-- **RAPID ACTION** [8] (G Moore) 5-9-5 S Wood(7) 7/1: 03420-3: Ev ch in straight: fit from hurdling: placed on several occasions in '85 but failed to win: eff at 7f/1m on gd and yld. 14

10   **MRS CHRIS** [14] (M Naughton) 4-9-7 G King(7) 15/2: 4400-04: Ev ch: failed to win last season: in '84 won at Pontefract: eff at 7f on a sharpish trk. 16

-- **BLOW MY TOP** [6] 7-8-10 A Dicks 15/2: 10002/0: Sn prom: been hurdling. 00

-- **BLACK RIVER** [4] 5-8-4 Wendy Carter 5/1 FAV: 00040-0: A big gamble: hmpd 2f out when starting a run: has been running over hurdles: lightly raced on the Flat: half brother to four winners. one to keep an eye on. 00

-- **MURILLO** [15] 10-9-5 J Carr 10/1: 04032-0: Never showed. 00

-- **YELLOW BEAR** [10] 4-9-0 T Parkes(7) 15/2: 00001-0: Fit from hurdling. 00

--	AMPLIFY [2] 3-7-7 A Munro(5) 10/1: 03020-0: Mkt drifter and never in it.				00
10	Lilting Lad [16] 8-12			-- Miami Dolphin [1] 8-3	
--	Malmo [17] 9-2	--	Willie Gan [6] 9-1	-- Remainder Tip [11] 8-6	
--	Red Vanity [7] 8-5	--	Scoop The Kitty [13] 8-3		
--	Bold Rowley [3] 8-3				
17 ran	2½,1½,shhd,2½,nk	(J Eddell)		D Chapman Stillington, Yorks	

Official Going Given as Heavy: All Times Slow

47   PHILIP CORNES MAIDEN AUCTION STKS 2YO   £2070   5f   Heavy Slow

-- NAIVE CHARM [11] (R Boss) 2-8-9 E Guest(3) 2/1 FAV: 1: 2 b f Milford - Proper Madam (Mummy's Pet): Heavily bckd on racecourse debut and made most for a ready win in a 2yo maiden auction stakes at Haydock Mar.29: clearly well suited by the minimum trip though should stay further: acts on heavy ground and on a stiff trk: well regarded and should win again.   53

-- CLOWN STREAKER [4] (M H Easterby) 2-8-7 K Hodgson 7/2: 2: Well bckd debutant: showed good pace and should find a similar race soon: acts on heavy ground and on a gall trk.   46

20 TAKE EFFECT [5] (M Brittain) 2-8-6 M Wigham 5/1: 33: Easy to back: smartly away, behind ¼way and ran on well: acts on soft and heavy ground: see 20.   42

-- EMMER GREEN [10] (J Berry) 2-8-7 M Fry 10/1: 4: Mkt drifter on debut: close up over ½way and seems sure to impr for this experience: acts on heavy ground and on a gall trk.   35

-- WOLF J FLYWHEEL [3] 2-8-6 M Wood 20/1: 0: Al mid-div, kept on same pace.   33

3 LUCEDEO [8] 2-8-12 S Perks 10/1: 00: Dsptd lead till ½way: btr effort.   31

20 MADDYBENNY [2] 2-8-3 L Charnock 9/2: 40: Lost place ½way: btr in 20 (soft).   00

-- Prior Well [13] 8-3   -- Real Rustle [6] 8-6   -- Sinclair Lady [12] 8-11
-- Miss Drummond [9] 8-8   -- Royal Treaty [7] 8-7   -- Miss Bolero [1] 8-3
13 ran   1,1½,4,nk,4,1½   (K Bethel)   R Boss Newmarket

48   HOLSTEN DIAT PILS MAIDEN STKS 3YO   £2679   1m 2f   Heavy Slow

-- SIRK [2] (C Brittain) 3-9-0 A Murray 5/6 FAV: 423-1: 3 ch c Kris - Belle Viking (Riverman): Useful colt: well bckd on reappearance and was al going well, led 3f out for a cosy win in a 3yo stakes at Haydock Mar.29: showed plenty of promise to be placed in all his starts last season, notably when running up to Mashkour at Goodwood: half brother to Beowulf: acts on firm and heavy ground: eff over 8/10f and is sure to stay further: acts on any trk: should win more races.   46

-- DENBERDAR [1] (R Hollinshead) 3-9-0 S Perks 16/1: 0-2: Ran on well, just btn: good effort: unplaced in a maiden at Redcar on sole start last season: clearly well suited by 10f on heavy ground: acts on a gall trk. should win again.   40

-- TAYLORMADE BOY [3] (Denys Smith) 3-9-0 W Carson 5/1: 0330-3: Led early, ran on same pace: placed a couple of times in minor events last season: stays 10f: acts on yld and heavy ground.   36

14 HONEST TOIL [4] (R Whitaker) 3-9-0 D Mckeown 7/4: 0000-34: Held up, no extra below distance: btr in 14 (1m yld).   24

4 ran   nk,2½,8.   (Capt M Lemos)   C Brittain Newmarket

49   MNCHESTER SINGAPORE STKS 3YO HCP 0-70   £5962   1m   Heavy Slow   [50]

-- AMONGST THE STARS [1] (S Norton) 3-8-10 J Quinn(7) 9/1: 41200-1: 3 br f Proctor - Out Of This World (High Top): First time out, led below dist and forged clear in a 3yo h'cap at Haydock Mar.29: last season was visored when winning a nursery h'cap at Wolverhampton on much faster ground: also won a fillies maiden at Catterick last term: well suited by 1m: acts on gd/firm and heavy ground and on any trk.   44

15 SOVEREIGN LOVE [4] (W Hastings Bass) 3-8-11 R Lines(3) 10/3: -003132: Led before ½way: clear of rem: see 15.   39

15 SUPREME KINGDOM [2] (R Hollinshead) 3-9-7 S Perks 14/1: 2210-03: Al prom: a fair effort on this testing ground: showed useful form last season, placed several times before making all in a nursery at Haydock (good): very eff over 7/8f: acts on firm and heavy ground: suited by forcing tactics and acts well on a gall trk.   41

15 PLANET ASH [5] (A Bailey) 3-9-2 W Carson 13/8 FAV: 320-24: Well bckd: never got in a blow, much btr over 7f on soft ground in 15.   28

-- FLEET FOOTED [6] 3-8-12 W Ryan 8/1: 31004-0: No threat on seasonal debut: quite a useful colt, won a maiden at Catterick last term and was later placed in a nursery at Doncaster: half brother to Pipyn Bach: eff over 6/7f on firm and soft ground: acts on any trk: shoul do btr next time on a sounder surface.   16

-- LADY ST CLAIR [8] 3-8-8 L Charnock 16/1: 1404-0: Al behind on reappearance.   12

-- RETHYMNO [7] 3-9-7 A Murray 5/1: 04000-0: Sn led, hdd after ½way and sn btn.   00

1 Carribean Tyme [3] 9-7
8 ran   6,8,8,8,shhd,4   (Mrs Malcolm Keogh)   S Norton Barnsley, Yorks

50   DANNY MAHER HANDICAP 0-50   £2968   2m   **Heavy Slow**   [44]

+11   WITHY BANK [5] (M H Easterby) 4-9-0 W Carson 5/6 FAV: 0220-11: 4 b g Blakeney - Chiltern Lass (High Hat): In fine form, was well bckd and cruised into lead 3f out for an easy win in a h'cap at Haydock Mar.29: earlier won a fast run h'cap at Doncaster and also successful recently over hurdles: stays 2m2f really well: acts on yld and heavy ground and on a gall trk: should complete the hat trick.   45

11   AULD LANG SYNE [9] (J Jefferson) 7-7-8(VIS) L Charnock 9/2: 3/30-42: Stayed on though no impression on winner: acts on gd and heavy ground and on a gall trk: see 11.   12

44   RED DUSTER [8] (T Fairhurst) 6-8-6 M Beecroft 6/1: 1100-43: Al close up: good effort.   22

--   WESSEX [2] (N Tinkler) 4-8-0(bl) Kim Tinkler(7) 14/1: 20333-4: Stayed on well, never nearer: fit from hurdling: eff though seems btr suited by 2m: acts on gd and heavy ground and on a gall trk: usually bl nowadays.   15

23   DON RUNI [1] 4-8-10 A Murray 14/1: 3000-00: Made most, one-pace run in.   21

--   ARIBIAN [7] 5-7-8 T Williams 20/1: 04400-0: Close up most of the way: fit from hurdling   00

--   ARTAIUS MEAD [6] 4-9-9 S Perks 10/1: 11314-0: Fit from hurdling: tough task under top weight on this testing ground.   00

23   Bamdoro [3] 8-0   **--   Scottish Rose** [4] 8-1
9 ran   6,1½,1,2½,10   (H J B Cooper)   M H Easterby Great Habton, Yorks

51   TOD SLOAN MAIDEN SELLING STKS 3YO   £1115   6f   **Heavy Slow**

6   PLANTER [9] (T Fairhurst) 3-9-0(bl) M Beecroft 5/2 FAV: 4033-01: 3 b g Manor Farm Boy - Pangkor (Tribal Chief): Dropped to selling company and comfortably justified fav. led below dist in a 3yo maiden seller at Haydock Mar.29: placed several times in non-selling company last season: eff over 5/6f on gd and heavy ground: acts on any trk: seems best in blinkers.   22

--   LITTLE ARMIER [4] (K Stone) 3-8-11 A Murray 9/1: 00000-2: Mkt drifter on re-appearance: ran on well, never nearer: no worthwhile form in similar company last season: acts on heavy ground and on a gall trk: may improve enough to win a similar race.   10

--   RAPID STAR [5] (G Harman) 3-8-11 W Carson 16/1: 00000-3: Mkt drifter: al there: showed a little ability last term: eff over 5/6f on firm and heavy ground.   08

--   CHAUTAUQUA [7] (P Haslam) 3-9-0 T Williams 7/1: 0-4: Easy to back: broke well, hdd well over 1f out: unplaced in a maiden at Yarmouth on sole start last season: should be btr on a sounder surface.   03

--   RICH BITCH [3] 3-8-11 N Leach(7) 25/1: 0-0: Never dangerous on reappearance.   00

--   FOURNO TRUMPS [10] 3-9-0 L Charnock 25/1: 000-0: Some late prog on seasonal debut.   00

--   THE STRAY BULLETT [6] 3-9-0(bl) J Hillis(5) 3/1: 30030-0: No extra below dist: can do much better.   00

--   COMICAL LAD [2] 3-9-0 P Bloomfield 10/1: 0-0: Mkt drifter: no threat.   00

--   MY CUP OF TEA [1] 3-9-0 D Mckeown 10/1: 0-0: Never going well on reappearance.   00

--   Duke Of Milltimber [8] 9-0
10 ran   5,1,4,2,1   (C D Barber-Lomax)   T Fairhurst Middleham, Yorks

52   HERBERT JONES HANDICAP 0-50   £2890   1m 4f   **Heavy Slow**   [49]

--   CAROS GIFT [2] (N Tinkler) 5-9-6 Kim Tinkler(7) 9/1: 30003-1: 5 gr h Caro - Christmas Belle (Santa Claus): Useful horse: fit from hurdling, led 3f out and ran on gamely to win a h'cap at Haydock Mar.29: last season won a fast run h'cap at Brighton: in '84 won 3 times: well suited by 12/14f: acts on firm and heavy ground and on any trk: genuine sort who carries weight well.   52

4   ROSTHERNE [6] (K Stone) 4-8-9 A Murray 3/1: 0023-42: Full of running dist, not quicken and just btn: acts on heavy ground: see 4.   40

4   VINTAGE TOLL [3] (S Norton) 6-9-11 J G Murray(7) 8/1: 0000-03: Mkt drifter: ev ch: good effort under top weight: useful h'capper who won a fast run race at Pontefract last term: eff over 7/10f and stays 12f well: acts on firm and heavy ground and on any trk: carries weight well.   46

11   TRESIDDER [1] (M W Easterby) 4-9-4 K Hodgson 11/4 FAV: 3410-04: Switched to stands side straight, ran on same pace: last season was an easy winner of a 3yo h'cap at Newcastle, after 2 earlier wins at Catterick: very eff over 14f/2m: well suited by some give in the ground: acts on any trk.   39

--   WARWICK SUITE [4] 4-8-0 W Carson 11/2: 03000-0: Wknd early in straight: fit from hurdling: a winner in Cagnes early last season, though yet to win in this country: eff over 10/12f: well suited by heavy ground.   07

4   REGAL STEEL [5] 8-8-0 A Culhane 3/1: 0000-30: Made most, sn btn when hdd: much btr on gd ground in 4.   07

6 ran   nk,6,hd,10,hd   (Full Circle Thoroughbreds Ltd)   N Tinkler Malton, Yorks

NEWCASTLE   Saturday March 29th   Lefthand, Stiff Galloping Track

Official Going Given as Soft

53 CAMBOIS 3YO FILLIES MAIDEN STKS   £1553   1m   Heavy Slow

16 SOXOPH [5] (M H Easterby) 3-8-11 M Birch 2/1: -41: 3 br f Hotfoot - My Therape
(Jimmy Reppin): Impr filly: fit from her run last week, led dist, comfortably in a 5 runner
3yo fillies maiden at Newcastle Mar.29: half sister to the speedy 2yo Domynsky: stays 1m well
and seems suited by heavy ground and a gall trk.   41
-- HOIST THE AXE [2] (B Hanbury) 3-8-11 G Baxter 5/2: -2: Led over 2f out: 5L clear 3rd:
wk in mkt today and should impr: acts on heavy ground.   37
-- KEEP COOL [4] (P Kelleway) 3-8-11 Gay Kelleway(5) 7/4 FAV: 003-3: Well bckd on seasonal
debut: ev ch: rated 44 in '85 when 3rd in a maiden at Leicester: acts well on firm ground:
stays 1m.   27
-- ZEELANDIA [3] (T Fairhurst) 3-8-11 C Coates(5) 14/1: 0000-4: Prom, fdd: no form in
'85, though is a half sister to several winners.   20
-- BLUE BELLS STAR [1] 3-8-11 J Lowe 14/1: 0000-0: Made most.   17
5 ran   1,5,3,1½   (Mrs Anthony Vandervell)   M H Easterby Great Habton, Yorks

54 BLAGDON HANDICAP 3YO 0-35   £1824   1m 2f   Heavy Slow   [42]

-- CHEVET LADY [5] (R Whitaker) 3-7-12 S P Griffiths(5) 15/2: 00100-1: 3 gr f John De -
Coombe - Beamless (Hornbeam): First time out, led over 2f out, driven out in a 3yo h'cap at
Newcastle Mar.29: in '85 won a nursery selling h'cap at Beverley: eff at 1m, stays 10f well:
half sister to several winners: acts on firm and heavy and a stiff trk.   24
1 , BEAU MIRAGE [4] (C Booth) 3-9-7 J H Brown(5) 7/1: 03-0102: Ev ch over 1f out: fit
from a recent Cagnes win: stays 10f and acts well on heavy.   42
-- LAUGH A LOT [8] (W Wharton) 3-8-6 N Carlisle 10/1: 42223-3: Sn prom: kept on: btr for
race: placed on numerous occasions in '85 in selling company, though failed to win: stays
10f: acts on any ground.   24
29 RED BILLY [6] (C Brittain) 3-7-12 G Carter(5) 7/4 FAV: 4000-44: Dsptd lead 2f out.   15
-- PULHAM MILLS [1] 3-9-1 A Mackay 6/1: 04400-0: Prom 7f: placed several times last
season, but did not win: stays 7f and acts on firm and soft.   12
14 SWYNFORD PRINCE [7] 3-8-3(1ow) M Birch 14/1: 0003-00: Never in it.   00
35 TARA DANCER [9] 3-8-6(bl)(2ow) C Dwyer 8/1: 0010-00: Made most till 2 out.   00
-- PAULS SECRET [3] 3-8-12 T Ives 17/2: 03000-0: Never threatened.   00
14 Take The Biscuit [10] 8-7   **-- Octiga** [2] 8-3
10 ran   3,1½,hd,15,shhd   (D m Gibbons)   R Whitaker Wetherby, Yorks

55 BRUNSWICK HANDICAP 3YO+ 0-70   £5414   7f   Heavy Slow   [69]

17 BOLLIN KNIGHT [1] (M H Easterby) 4-9-9 M Birch 1/1 FAV: -01: 4 b g Immortal Knight -
Lush Secret (Most Secret): Very useful gelding: well bckd and led all the way for a ready
win in a h'cap at Newcastle Mar.29: off the trk last season: smart 2yo, winning at Doncaster,
Catterick and Ayr: very eff over 6/7f: acts on yld and heavy: genuine sort.   75
-- BATON BOY [3] (M Brittain) 5-7-8(1ow) J Lowe 4/1: 44000-2: Not pace of winner: did
not win in '85 but in '84 won over this C/D: acts on gd and heavy: has been tried in bl.   40
17 SHELLMAN [4] (K Stone) 4-8-0 G Carter(5) 9/2: 0010-03: No real threat: useful colt
on his day: in '85 won a valuable h'cap at Newmarket, earlier won a h'cap at Haydock: in
'84 won at Hamilton and Haydock: well suited by 8/9f: acts on any going: likes a gall trk.   40
-- TRANSFLASH [2] (E Eldin) 7-8-5(bl) A Mackay 5/1: 01000-4: Fdd over 1f out: btr for
race: in '85 won h'caps at Newcastle and Nottingham: in '84 won at York, Thirsk and
Nottingham: very eff at 5/6f: acts on firm and yld.   42
4 ran   1½,3,1½   (N G Westbrook)   M H Easterby Great Habton, Yorks

56 MONKSEATON HANDICAP 4Y+ 0-35   £2043   5f   Heavy +20 Fast   [27]

12 PARADE GIRL [3] (J Kettlewell) 4-8-12 N Connorton 6/1 Co.FAV: 0003-01: 4 br f Swing Easy
Dauphiness (Supreme Sovereign): Made ev yd, driven out in a fast run h'cap at Newcastle
Mar.29: in '85 won a h'cap at Redcar: very eff at 5f with forcing tactics: acts on firm
and heavy and a gall trk: may win again.   27
-- MENDICK ADVENTURE [1] (D Smith) 5-10-0 T Ives 6/1 Co.FAV: 00240-2: Sn prom: 10L clear
rest: fine effort under 10-0: in '85 "won" a h'cap at Ripon, subs. disq: previous season
won at Thirsk: very eff at 5/6f, stays 7f: acts on any ground: carries weight well.   39
-- VELOCIDAD [7] (J Glover) 6-9-6 G Carter(5) 8/1: 0010-3: Raced centre of rthe trk
and never near the first 2 on the favoured far side: in '85 won a minor event at Redcar:
in '84 won at Doncaster: best over 5f: acts on firm and soft.   11
12 WARTHILL LADY [2] (M Brittain) 4-8-13 K Darley 13/2: 0000-04: Never in it: won a h'cap
at Ayr last season: eff over 5f on firm and yld.   03
-- PERGODA [6] 8-9-12(bl) R Vickers(7) 16/1: 00000-0: Prom centre of track.   14
-- FAIRGREEN [5] 8-8-11 D Nicholls 7/1: 00403-0: Prom, fdd.   00
12 TOP THAT [4] 5-9-11 B Mcgiff(7) 6/1 Co.FAV: 0000-00: Sn struggling.   00
-- TRADESMAN [9] 6-8-1(bl) A Shoults(7) 15/2: 23433-0: Prom halfway.   00
12 FARMER JOCK [10] 4-9-10 S Keightley 6/1 Co.FAV: 0340-00: Al rear. badly drawn.   00
-- Jo Andrew [8] 8-1(bl)
10 ran   1½,10,nk,½,1½   (Mrs R Olivier)   J Kettlewell Catterick, Yorks

28

57   NEWCASTLE SELLING STAKES 2YO   £1303   5f   Heavy Slow

-- PASHMINA [3] (T Fairhurst) 2-8-8 C Coates(5) 16/1: 1: 2 b f Blue Cashmere - Petploy (Faberge II): Unfancied, but led over 2f out, driven out in a 2yo seller at Newcastle Mar.29 (no bid): half sister to 2 winners: eff at 5f on heavy. 23
-- MOONEE POND [9] (M H Easterby) 2-8-8 M Birch 10/1: 2: Ran on well final 1f: should be suited by further than 5f: acts on heavy. 19
-- GALLIC TIMES [6] (I Bell) 2-8-11 N Carlisle 6/1: 3: Prom, ev ch: half brother to 4 winners incl the speedy Ferriby Hall: acts on heavy. 21
-- ATHALEA CYNTRA [2] (N Tinkler) 2-8-8 J H Brown(5) 20/1: 4: Never nearer on racecourse debut: should be suited by further. 17
13 MI OH MY [7] 2-8-8 G Brown(5) 4/1: 30: Ran on final 1f: see 13. 16
-- MINIZEN LADY [5] 2-8-8 K Darley 5/1: 0: Mkt drifter: stayed on well: should impr: will be suited by further. 16
-- GAELIC CROSS [8] 2-8-11 D Nicholls 7/1: 0: Led over 2f: active in mkt. 00
-- FANTINE [11] 2-8-8 T Ives 6/1: 0: Mkt drifter: prom, fdd. 00
13 VICHY VAL [1] 2-8-8 G Carter(5) 7/2 FAV: 00: Never in it. should do better than this. 00
-- Millie Duffer [4] 8-8   13 My Mabel [12] 8-8   -- Above The Salt [10] 8-11
12 ran   1½,nk,½,½,shhd   (Mrs M I Morley)   T Fairhurst Middleham, Yorks

58   HOLYSTONE MAIDEN STAKES   £1151   1m 2f   Heavy Slow

8 APPEALING [7] (G Blum) 4-9-4 M Birch 5/2 FAV: -000-41: 4 b f Star Appeal - Mayfell (Rockefella): Led on bit over 2f out and kept on well to win a maiden at Newcastle Mar.29: lightly raced previously: stays 10f well: acts on gd, well suited by heavy. 30
-- TRY SCORER [9] (D Smith) 4-9-7 T Ives 9/2: 00004-2: Ev ch final 2f: first time out last season fin 2nd in a maiden at Pontefract: eff at 1m, stays 10f: acts on gd and heavy. 30
8 NIKOOLA EVE [5] (J Glover) 4-9-4 M Rimmer 7/1: -03: Led 3f out: very lightly raced: stays 10f and acts on heavy. 22
-- TREYARNON [12] (S Norton) 4-9-7 J Lowe 4/1: 24400-4: Ev ch 2f out: 2nd in this same race last season: eff at 10f on heavy ground. 17
-- BANTEL BUCCANEER [10] 4-9-7 N Carlisle 14/1: 03--0-0: There 1m: lightly raced sort. 05
8 WELSH GUARD [2] 4-9-7 K Darley 14/1: -00: Mkt drifter and no show. 04
-- SING OUT LOUD [8] 4-9-4 M Hindley(3) 10/1: -0: Tailed off on racecourse debut. 00
-- SINFEROPOLI [4] 4-9-4 N Carson(7) 7/1: 33-00-0: Made most: soon fdd. 00
-- Nordic Secret [1] 9-7   -- Jalome [3] 9-4   -- Little Newington [11] 9-4
8 Great Relative [6] 9-7
12 ran   1½,3,5,8,½   (D J Simpson)   G Blum Newmarket

58A   QUEENS PRIZE HANDICAP 0-60   £4705   2m   Soft/Heavy 157 –09 Slow   [52]

11 MILTON BURN [3] (H O'neill) 5-7-10 S Dawson[3] 33/1: 2240-01: 5 b h Sexton Blake - Neasden Belle (Sovereign Path): Held up, came with a strong late chall when narrowly winning a valuable h'cap at Kempton Mar.29: in '85 won a 2m h'cap at Nottingham and in '84 won at Warwick and again at Nottingham: well suited by 2m and seems to act on any going: goes well for S Dawson and needs to be held up. 30
11 ACCURACY [14] (G Balding) 5-8-2 R Fox 15/2: 0200-32: Strong chall final 2f, just caught: in grand form: due a change of luck and should find a race soon: see 11. 36
11 MEADOWBROOK [1] (I Balding) 5-8-8 Pat Eddery 6/4 fav: 1423-23: Nearly made all: see 11. 40
11 TRAPEZE ARTIST [13] (N Vigors) 5-8-12(vis) S Cauthen 12/1: 0300-04: Al there: carries weight well and in '85 won a 14f h'cap at Newmarket under 9-10: in '84 won at Chester: eff at 14f and stays extreme distances: acts on gd/firm and soft: usually bl. 43
-- REVISIT [7] 4-9-2 W R Swinburn 14/1: 12101-0: Btr for race: useful filly last year winning at Redcar, Ayr and Yarmouth: eff at 13f and stays 2m 1f: acts on firm and soft and on any track. 43

-- POPSIS JOY [9] 11-8-6 J Reid 16/1: 00001-0: Wknd 2 out: not getting any younger but
still able to win a race and in '85 picked up a h'cap at Warwick: in '84 won at Newmarket
and does well there, having run well several times in the Cesarewitch: needs a good test
of stamina and is well fav by a stiff trk: probably acts on any: acts on firm and soft.   23
-- WESTERN DANCER [15] 5-9-11 P Cook 12/1: 12124-0: Looks quite nicely h'capped, btr
for race.   00
-- NAFTILOS [10] 4-9-2 P Robinson 14/1: 11120-0: Active in mkt, no threat.   00
-- Peggy Carolyn [11] 9-2   -- Shiny Copper [2] 7-7
-- Sylvan Joker [4] 7-7(vis)(1oh)   11 Petrizzo [12] 9-10
-- Majestic Ring [8] 8-8   -- Derby Day [6] 7-7(7oh) 11 Morgans Choice [5] 8-13
15 ran   nk,1½,½,4,10   (A J Richards)   H O'neill Coldharbour, Surrey

59 BONUSPRINT MASAKA STAKES 3YO FILLIES   £6933   7f   Soft/Heavy 157 +11 Fast

-- STATELY LASS [3] (J Winter) 3-8-4(1ow) R Cochrane 9/2: 23-1: 3 br f Free State -
Jackyda (Royal Palm): Ran on gamely and sprinted clear in final furlong in a valuable fillies
event at Kempton Mar.29: half sister to several winners incl the useful sprinter Overtrick:
seems to act on firm and soft ground: possibly fav by a stiff trk: stays 7f and will
probably stay 1m.   64
•37 HIDDEN BRIEF [5] (R Boss) 3-8-9 M Miller 15/8 fav: 1400-12: Made most, gd effort: see 37 57
-- MEASURING [4] (I Balding) 3-8-13 S Cauthen 6/1: 11320-3: Mkt drifter, no threat, btr
for race: ran most consistently in '85 winning her first 3 races on the trot at Windsor,
Sandown and Newbury and was placed in good company: half sister to several winners including.
the smart Devon Ditty: cost 46,000 gns: very eff at 6f, probably stays 7f and so far best
on gd/firm and yld.   59
-- APPRILA [1] (C Brittain) 3-8-3 P Robinson 16/1: -4: Mkt drifter, never in it: half
sister to minor 5f winner Blessit: will probably need further and btr for this race.   39
-- FLYAWAY BRIDE [2] 3-8-9 Pat Eddery 2/1: 0131-0: 2nd 2 out: can do btr: very useful
filly winning twice at Bath in '85 and fin a close 3rd in a Gr.1 race at the Curragh:
so far best at 5f with forcing tactics: acts on yld and soft ground and on a stiff trk:
might not stay 7f.   43
5 ran   8,2,5,2½.   (D O McIntyre)   J Winter Newmarket

60 BONUSPRINT EASTER STAKES 3YO C & G   £7362   1m   Soft/Heavy 157 -08 Slow

-- TISNT [3] (P Cole) 3-8-4 P Waldron 5/1: -1: 8 gr c Shergar - Zabarella (Clouet II):
Very promising colt: first time out led 1 out and kept on well under press in a Listed race
at Kempton Mar.29: acts on soft ground and stays 1m: half brother to 17f winner Zeratino:
looks sure to suited by at least 1½m: can only impr for this race and is one to keep on
the right side.   75
-- HELLO ERNANI [9] (I Balding) 3-8-4 Pat Eddery 2/1 fav: 203-2: Kept on well, narrowly
beaten: acts on firm and soft ground and looks sure to be suited by 10f: 3rd in the Horace
Hills stakes at Newbury last year: fin clear of the rest and should soon find compensation.   71
-- FOUZ [7] (P Cole) 3-8-10 T Quinn 8/1: 13020-3: Led on the far side 2 out, ran well:
in good form early in '85 winning 3 of his first 4 races at Catterick, Thirsk and Kempton:
eff at 6f and probably stays 1m: acts on firm and soft and does well on a sharp trk.   70
-- LANDSKI [1] (M Ryan) 3-8-4 B Thomson 25/1: -4: Late prog: very promising first effort
from this half brother to the useful 5/7f winner Amerone: stays 1m, acts on soft ground and
should soon find a maiden race.   62
-- CELTIC HEIR [8] 3-9-3 G Duffield 15/2: 02010-0: Btr for race: in '85 won Gr.3 Horace
Hill Stakes at Newbury after an abs: earlier won at Redcar and fin a good 6th in the
Coventry Stakes at Royal Ascot: very eff at 6 and 7f on gd and firm ground: probably stays 1m.   69
-- MIRAGE DANCER [4] 3-8-4 S Whitworth 10/1: 0204-0: Every chance.   54
-- LIAM [5] 3-8-4 P Robinson 4/1: 222-0: Well bckd, fin 7th: can do better.   00
-- Poderoso [2] 8-4   -- Marshal Macdonald [6] 8-4
9 ran   ¾,4,½,6,2   (F N Sahadi)   P Cole Whatcombe, Oxon

61 EBF REDFERN MAIDEN STAKES 2YO C & G   £1650   5f   Soft/Heavy 157 -28 Slow

-- PENSURCHIN [3] (D Elsworth) 2-9-0 A Mcglone 8/1: 1: 2 ch c Creetown - Coriace
(Prince Consort): Came with a strong run and readily led final 1f in a maiden race at
Kempton Mar.29: eff at 5f on soft ground but looks sure to be suited by a stiffer trk and 6f.   53
-- MARK ANGELO [4] (R Boss) 2-9-0 M Miller 7/2: 2: Well bckd, led 2 out: acts on soft
ground, should soon find a maiden race.   48
34 WINDMEDE [2] (M Brittain) 2-9-0 Pat Eddery 5/6 fav: 23: Dsptd lead 3f: see 34.   42
-- SAMLEON [6] (R Hannon) 2-9-0 L Jones[5] 5/1: 4: Drifted badly in mkt, btr for race.   39
-- CHOCO [1] 2-9-0 N Day 16/1: 0: Ev ch: half brother to an 11f winner: might need further.   39
27 CHERRYWOOD SAM [5] 2-9-0 I Johnson 25/1: 40: Early ldr: see 27.   14
6 ran   1½,2½,1½,hd,15   (Mrs H P Ralton)   D Elsworth Whitsbury, Hants

62   QUEEN ELIZABETH STAKES HCAP 3YO 0-50   £2464   6f   Soft/Heavy 157 +13 Fast   [56]

--   LOFT BOY [2] (N Vigors) 3-8-4 S Dawson[3] 14/1: 030-1: 3 b g Cawston's Clown -
Burglar Tip (Burglar): First time out picked up a h'cap at Kempton Mar.29, comfortably
leading 1 out: had been abs since very early in '85: eff at 5 and 6f and seems to act on
firm and soft ground: put up a good time and could win again.   43
--   SITZCARRALDO [3] (R Hannon) 3-7-12 A Mcglone 16/1: 03300-2: Not much luck in running,
good effort: placed in several maiden races last year and has been tried in bl: eff at
5 and 6f and acts on any going and on any trk.   31
--   WEST CARRACK [4] (A Ingham) 3-9-7 S Cauthen 10/1: 12120-3: Gd effort under top weight:
has been abs since very early in '85 when won 2 of his first 3 races at Beverley and Lingfield: very eff at 5/6f, acts on firm but seems to do well on soft ground: could find a
h'cap in the near future: acts on any trk: genuine sort.   52
--   MUDRIK [1] (C Benstead) 3-9-0 B Rouse 5/1: 00041-4: Looks well h'capped following a
win in a h'cap at Newbury in Oct.'85: half brother to the smart Cragside: very eff at 6f
acts on soft but so far best on gd and firm ground: probably best on a stiff trk.   44
--   STEEL CYGNET [9] 3-8-12 J Reid 10/1: 11002-0: Prom.: genuine sort who won 3 times
last year at Goodwood, Lingfield and Kempton: eff at 5/6f, acts on gd/firm and yld: fav by
a sharpish or an undulating trk. not well drawn.   41
15   MEADOW MOOR [6] 3-8-12(vis) I Johnson 8/1: 1020-00: Led 3f: winner at Salisbury and
Bath in '85: wears a visor: eff at 5/6f, acts on any going and is well suited by a gall trk.   36
--   HYMN OF HARLECH [7] 3-9-3 G Duffield 10/1: 21300-0: Finished 8th.   00
15   TOUCH OF GREY [13] 3-8-9 M L Thomas 10/1: 0210-00: Speed over 4f.   00
6   THE HILCOTE CLUB [10] 3-8-11 Pat Eddery 11/4: 0044-40: Missed the break: btr 6.   00
--   Home Rule [5] 9-3   --   Major Jacko [11] 8-2   --   Stanbo [8] 8-1(2ow)
--   Northern Lad [12] 8-1(2ow)
13 ran   3,¾,nk,½,3   (Mrs Bernie Allwright)   N Vigors Upper Lambourn, Berks

63   CHATSWORTH HANDICAP STAKES 3YO 0-50   £2401   1m 2f Soft/Heavy 157 -09 Slow [51]

--   SWIFT TROOPER [3] (R Williams) 3-8-13(bl) R Cochrane 4/1: 30410-1: 3 br c Air Trooper -
Kemoening (Falcon): First time out, well bckd and readily led 1 out in a h'cap at Kempton
Mar.29: in '85 won at Edinburgh (8f good): half brother to a couple of winners incl the
useful hurdler Saxon Farm: eff over 8/10f and seems to act on firm and soft ground: goes
well on a sharpish trk and wears bl.   48
--   STRAIGHT THROUGH [7] (J Winter) 3-7-12 R Fox 9/2: 00024-2: Led 2 out: placed in 2m
h'caps in '85 and has been tried in a visor: eff at 8/10f and acts on gd and soft: goes
well on a sharpish trk: should find a maiden race: well clear of the rest.   30
--   ARE YOU GUILTY [4] (M Ryan) 3-8-5 Paul Eddery 8/1: 20003-3: Tried in bl last year
and ran well in h'cap company over 6 & 7f: acts on any trk though seems best on a sharp one.   27
--   POUNELTA [6] (R Hannon) 3-9-6 S Cauthen 7/2 fav: 34133-4: Led 7f: stiff task at the
weights: was very consistently last year winning a h'cap at Epsom: acts on firm and yld: very
eff at 7/8f and may not stay 10f.   30
--   UP TO UNCLE [5] 3-8-3 R Wernham 12/1: 22444-0: No threat.   12
--   SILENT RUNNING [9] 3-7-13 A Mcglone 14/1: F000-0: No show.   00
--   COMMON FARM [8] 3-8-13 Pat Eddery 5/1: 00304-0: Active in mkt, no threat.   00
--   ATIG [2] 3-9-7 J Reid 7/1: 41404-0: Active in mkt, no show.   00
8 ran   1½,10,12,1½,8   (Swift Racing Services Ltd)   R Williams Newmarket

Official Going Given as Soft

64   ROBIN HOOD MAIDEN STAKES 3YO   £959   6f   Soft

--   EASY LINE [5] (P Haslam) 3-9-0 J Scally(7) 16/1: -1: 3 ch g Swing Easy - Impromptu
(My Swanee): Made a successful racecourse debut, led after ½way and ran on well for a narrow
win in a 3yo maiden at Nottingham Mar.31: half brother to a couple of winners: eff over
6f and should stay further: acts on soft ground and on a gall trk: should win more races.   40
--   ABSOLUTE MASTER [9] (M Jarvis) 3-9-0 T Ives 8/1: 000-2: Stayed on well, just btn:
speedily bred colt: acts on gd and soft ground: best effort to date.   38
--   TOUCH ME NOT [6] (R Hollinshead) 3-9-0 S Perks 10/1: 40000-3: Led over ½way, not
btn far: showed some promise last season over 5/6f: acts on firm and soft ground and on
any trk: seems suited by forcing tactics.   36
--   VAIGLIAN [7] (J Bethell) 3-9-0 W R Swinburn 10/11 FAV: 42303-4: Well bckd on seasonal
debut: stayed on same pace: showed some useful form last term in good class nurseries:
eff over 5/6f and is sure to be suited by further: acts on firm and soft ground and on
any trk: should come on for this outing and win a good race.   30
--   LOCH FORM [8] 3-8-11 M Wood 33/1: 00-0: Stayed on late on seasonal debut.   26
--   CHABLISSE [10] 3-8-11 D Mckeown 8/1: 000-0: Good speed over ½way: btr for race.   24
6   KEN SIDDALL [4] 3-9-0 C Dwyer 6/1: 0032-00: No extra below dist over this longer trip.   00

-- **LUIGIS STAR** [2] 3-9-0 S Whitworth 7/1: 0-0: Loss place after ½way: lightly raced.   00
-- **Belvel** [3] 9-0 ·   -- **The Mechanic** [1] 9-0
10 ran   nk,¾,2½,¾,1,6   (B Lasala)   P Haslam Newmarket

65   BROXTOWE HANDICAP 0-35   £1744   6f   Soft   [33]

-- **SUDDEN IMPACT** [1] (K Brassey) 4-9-10 S Whitworth 10/1: 00040-1: 4 b c Be Friendly -
False Evidence (Counsel): Gamely defied top weight on seasonal debut, led dist. and ran on
well to win a h'cap at Nottingham Mar.31: proved disapp last season when trained by G Lewis
but in '84 was a useful juvenile, winning nurseries at Newmarket and Nottingham: very eff
over 6/7f and should stay 1m: acts on gd & soft ground & on a gall trk: runs well when fresh.   40
-- **REVEILLE** [5] (M Jarvis) 4-9-8 T Ives 8/1: 00000-2: Nicely bckd first time out: led
briefly below dist. kept on well: unplaced in all his starts last season but looks well
h'capped on his juvenile form, when successful at Carlisle and Wolverhampton: eff over 6/7f:
acts on firm and soft ground and is well suited by a gall trk: could win soon.   35
-- **STEVEJAN** [8] (B Morgan) 4-7-8 G Carter(2) 14/1: 00000-3: Good effort, not btn far:
showed his best form early last season, when placed in gd h'caps at Leicester and Haydock:
in '84 won a nursery at Wolverhampton: eff over 5/6f and is well suited by plenty of give
in the ground.   06
-- **HOPEFUL KATIE** [4] (D Leslie) 4-8-9(hd) J Williams 12/1: 10000-4: No extra close home:
btr for race: had a good season in '85, winning h'caps at Yarmouth, Folkestone and Ripon:
well suited by 6f: acts on firm and soft ground: genuine filly.   17
42   **SINGLE HAND** [1] 6-8-10 S P Griffiths(5) 5/1: 0020-40: Stayed on well: see 42.   14
+42   **GODS SOLUTION** [10] 5-9-2(5ex) B Mcghiff(7) 3/1 FAV: 0300-10: Close up most of way:
much btr in 42 (tight track).   19
6   **SEW HIGH** [11] 3-8-7 J Hills 7/2: 1041-00: Nicely bckd: made most: not btn that far.   00
12   **COOL ENOUGH** [2] 5-9-0 R Carter(5) 10/3: 0000-40: Raced alone and al last: see 12.   00
-- **Wesbree Bay** [7] 7-11(3ow)   10   **Foolish Touch** [3] 9-5(vis)
-- **Holt Row** [9] 8-11
11 ran   1,½,2,2,½   (R Chiarella)   K Brassey Newmarket

66   CLUMBER STAKES 3YO   £959   1m 2f   Soft

-- **DUSTY DIPLOMACY** [5] (M Jarvis) 3-8-11 T Ives 9/2: 0-1: 3 b c Run Dusty Run - Faithful
Diplomacy (Diplomat Way): First time out, al close up and was switched to chall inside dist
and although just held was placed 1st in a 3yo stakes at Nottingham Mar.31: raced only once
last season: clearly stays 10f well on soft ground: acts on a gall trk: impr likely.   40
25   **ROYAL EFFIGY** [4] (D Leslie) 3-8-11 J Williams 9/1:000-01D:Nicely bckd: led below
dist: held on well though adjudged to have interfered with the runner up and subsequently
relegated to 2nd: however this was an impr effort and should find consolation soon: well
suited by 10f: acts on firm and soft ground and on a gall trk.   40
-- **CAGLIOSTRO** [7] (L Piggott) 3-8-11 W R Swinburn 4/5 FAV: -3: Heavily bckd on racecourse
debut: made most and was not given a hard race when hdd: promising effort by this nicely
bred colt who cost 60,000 gns as a yearling: should stay 10f: will do btr on a sounder surface   36
-- **SAGAREME** [3] (M Haynes) 3-8-8 S Whitworth 9/1: 00400-4: No threat final 2f: although
quite highly tried showed promise last season and should do btr than this: eff over 7/10f:
acts on gd and soft ground and on a gall trk.   27
25   **QUICK REACTION** [6] 3-8-11 M Giles 9/2: 0-00: Sn recovered from a slow start, no
extra 3 out.   22
-- **COMMON ACCORD** [1] 3-8-11 G Duffield 5/1: 000-0: Never dngr on reappearance.   18
-- **Histon Bronze** [2] 8-11
7 ran   ½,4,6,8,2½   (Jacques Lamote)   M Jarvis Newmarket

67   COUNTY CLAIMING STAKES 3YO   £1312   1m   Soft

-- **COSMIC FLIGHT** [14] (M Usher) 3-8-9 G Duffield 14/1: 00000-1: 3 b f Cosmo - Sweet
Flight (Falcon): First time out was a surprise winner, led early and again over 2f out for
a game win in a 3yo claiming stakes at Nottingham Mar.31: showed a modicum of ability over
sprint distances last term: half sister to a couple of winners: stays 1m well: acts on
firm and soft grnd and on any trk.   24
-- **FLYING FLYNN** [11] (N Callaghan) 3-8-11 G Carter(5) 4/1: 321-2: Ev ch on seasonal
debut: ended last season with a win in a seller at Hamilton: stays 1m well: acts on firm and
heavy ground and on a gall trk: should win a small race.   22
-- **MISS TONILEE** [2] (D Haydn Jones) 3-8-4 J Williams 9/2: 03-3: No extra close home:
lightly raced last season, being placed in a seller at Haydock on latter start: eff over
6/8f: acts on gd/firm and soft ground and on a gall trk: has enough ability to win a seller.   13
-- **PATS JESTER** [12] (H Rohan) 3-8-11 M Wood 14/1: 00040-4: Al there: placed in selling
company last season at Haydock: seems suited by 1m on soft ground: best effort to date.   15
-- **DORS GEM** [5] 3-8-7 S Morris 20/1: 000-0: Unfancied on seasonal debut: al there.   08
-- **SANDRON** [9] 3-9-0(BL) S Whitworth 7/1: 00020-0: Close up till dist: btr for race.   08
14   **NORTHERN MELODY** [8] 3-9-0(bl) P Bloomfield 6/4 FAV: -00: Dropped to selling company
and heavily bckd: close up over ½way, sn no extra: ex Irish colt who performed much btr
in a maiden at Doncaster recently: sure to win a seller on that form: see 14.   00

32

--	FIREPROOF [6] 3-9-0 W R Swinburn 7/1: 00-0: Never got in a blow.		00
25	LARCHES [13] 3-8-4 M Giles 8/1: 00-00: Led briefly after ¼way: wknd into 9th.		00
--	MERRY RIDGE [3] 3-9-0 P Hutton(7) 8/1: -0: Never beyond mid-div.		00
16	OSCAR DE SOUSA [10] 3-9-0 T Ives 9/2: -00: Never dangerous.		00
--	MISS HARLEQUIN [5] 3-8-9 L Jones(5) 8/1: 0200-0: Fin last: should be btr next time.		00

--   Way Above [7] 9-0   --   Colonel Hall [4] 9-0
14 ran   1½,1,2½,1½,4   (E Peate)   M Usher Lambourn, Berks

---

68   LITTLE JOHN EBF STAKES 3YO   £2271   1m   Soft

--   CRESTA AUCTION [5] (G Pritchard Gordon) 3-9-3 G Duffield 3/1: 0413-1: 3 b c Auction Ring-Baby Clair (Gulf Pearl): Useful colt: first time out was al close up, led well over 2f out for a comfortable win in a 3yo stakes at Nottingham Mar.31: last season made most to win a maiden at Brighton: subsequently was placed in a valuable stakes at Newmarket: eff over 6/7f and clearly stays 1m well: acts on firm and soft grnd and on any trk: genuine sort.   **56**

--   GEORDIES DELIGHT [2] (L Piggott) 3-9-0 W R Swinburn 9/2: 0-2: Ran on same pace: unplaced on sole start last season when trained by J Ciechanowski: eff over 1m on soft ground: acts on a gall trk: likely to impr further and should find a race.   **46**

--   PASTICCIO [1] (M Jarvis) 3-9-6 T Ives 1/1 FAV: 1-3: Well bckd on reappearance: ev ch below dist: narrow winner of a maiden at Leicester on sole outing last season: eff over 7f and should stay at least 1m: acts on firm and soft ground and on a gall trk: likely to do better next time.   **46**

--   JOHN TULLY [4] (M Haynes) 3-9-0 S Whitworth 14/1: 0-4: Mkt drifter: short lived effort after halfway: raced only once last season: acts on soft ground and on a gall trk.   **28**

*39   RHAPSODY IN BLACK [3] 3-9-3 M Giles 4/1: -10: Made most, sn btn when hdd: much better in 39 (7f).   **19**
5 ran   3,3,7,7   (Miss H F Gevers)   G Pritchard Gordon Newmarket

---

69   NOTTINGHAM HANDICAP STAKES 0-35   £1446   1m 6f   Soft   [29]

--   INTUITION [3] (M Usher) 4-9-7 J Carter(7) 20/1: 00000-1: 4 b g Busted - She's The One (Sword Dancer): First time out, comfortably defied top weight in a h'cap at Nottingham Mar.31, led over 3f out and was soon clear: first success: well suited by middle distances: acts on gd and soft ground and turns well on a gall trk: can win again.   **40**

--   LEPRECHAUN LADY [1] (S Norton) 4-9-4 J Murray(7) 12/1: 20040-2: Stayed on though no threat to easy winner: last season won a h'cap at Hamilton: in '84 won a seller at Haydock: stays 14f well: acts on gd and soft ground and on a gall trk.   **24**

*44   CARNEADES [9] (M H Easterby) 6-8-11(vis) G Carter(5) 4/6 FAV: 1000-13: Heavily bckd: some late prog though never threatened leaders: btr over a longer trip in 44.   **14**

23   HUNTERS FEN [7] (R Hollinshead) 4-9-6(vis) S Perks 11/2: 2340-04: Active in mkt: nearest fin: ran several good races last term, notably when twice successful at Leicester: eff over 8/10f and stays 14f well: acts on any going and is well suited by a gall. track.   **13**

--   BOREHAM DOWN [4] 7-7-13 M Richardson(4) 33/1: 00400-0: Unfancied: stayed on same pace.   00

44   TIMMINION [5] 4-9-1 C Dwyer 10/1: 3330-30: Mkt drifter: al there: see 44.   **04**

--   BLUEBIRDINO [2] 7-8-2 M Wood 10/1: 1D000-0: Never dangerous on reappearance.   00

--   MISS BLACKTHORN [6] 4-9-2 W R Swinburn 10/1: 00001-0: Easy to back: fin last.   00

35   Hot Ruler [8] 7-7   --   Paternoster Row [11] 9-1(bl)
7   North Star Sam [10] 8-11
11 ran   8,2½,10,1½,½,nk,nk   (J Cohen)   M Usher Lambourn, Berks

---

KEMPTON   Monday March 31st   Righthand Sharpish Track

Official Going Given as Soft: Based on Time Soft 135 Straight Course, **Heavy** 175 Round Course

70   QUAIL STAKES 3YO UPWARDS   £4604   6f   Soft 135 +09 Fast

+18   GREY DESIRE [7] (M Brittain) 6-9-10 K Darley 8/11 FAV: 0301-11: 6 gr h Habat - Noddy Time (Gratitude): Very smart sprinter: led approaching final 1f and soon clear in the valuable Quail Stakes at Kempton Mar.31: first time out won a Listed race at Doncaster: in excellent form early last season, winning Listed races at Haydock & Newmarket, also this same race: in '84 won at Newmarket & Thirsk (2): eff at 6f, stays 7f really well: acts on any going and has retained his form well: a credit to his trainer.   **85**

18   AMIGO LOCO [5] (K Brassey) 5-9-5(bl) N Adams 16/1: 4240-02: Made most and ran well: consistent performer, who in '85 won h'caps at Lingfield and Doncaster: in '84 won at York, Wolverhampton, Bath & Doncaster: very eff at 5/6f: acts on any ground: wears bl but is thoroughly genuine: carries weight well.   **71**

-18   SHARP ROMANCE [4] (B Hanbury) 4-9-10 W Carson 15/2: 0000-23: Kept on well: see 18.   **75**

--   MELODY PARK [12] (M Ryan) 4-8-11 G Starkey 10/1: 33404-4: Fdd final 1f on seasonal debut: good effort: in '85 failed to win but previous season was a very useful 2yo, winning at Ayr, Lingfield & Yarmouth: very eff at 5/6f with forcing tactics: acts on firm and yld.   **61**

-- FARNCOMBE [8] 3-8-1(1ow) G Baxter 25/1: 00-0: Ran on well on seasonal debut: ran only
twice last season: should be suited by further than 6f as he is a half brother to the useful
10f winner Miramar Reef: acts on gd/firm and soft: one to keep an eye on.   60
18 VORVADOS [14] 9-9-10 S Cauthen 16/1: 0004-40: Never nearer: see 18.   67
-- OUR JOCK [10] 4-9-0 P Cook 9/1: 12200-0: Early speed, fdd.   00
15 Crete Cargo [9] 8-2(2ow)   -- Ocean Trader [6] 8-0(bl)
-- Really Honest [2] 9-5   18 Gentileschi [11] 9-0   -- Miracles Take Time [15] 9-0
-- Mount Argus [13] 9-0   31 Pulsingh [3] 9-0   -- Cockalorum [1] 9-0
15 ran   3,nk,½,2½,nk   (Mel Brittain)   M Brittain Warthill, Yorks

71 CAPITALCARD H'CAP 4YO+ 0-50   £2548   1m   Heavy 175 +17 Fast   [47]

-- KAZAROW [3] (H Collingridge) 5-8-8 G Starkey 8/1: 02022-1: 5 ch h Blue Cashmere -
Sardara (Alcide): First time out, al prom and led over 2f out, readily in a fast run h'cap
at Kempton Mar.31: 2nd on 3 occasions in '85, but failed to win: in '84 won at Folkestone:
acts on gd, likes soft ground: stays 1m well: acts on any trk and may win again.   42
-- READY WIT [10] (R Hannon) 5-8-10 S Cauthen 20/1: 01000-2: Kept on well but no chance
with winner: good seasonal debut: in '85 won a 25 runner selling h'cap at Doncaster: won as
a 2yo at Chepstow: stays 1m: acts on gd & soft.   38
17 KAMPGLOW [13] (D Thom) 4-8-9 R Fox 6/1: 0004-03: Ev ch final 2f: showed promise in
'84 & '85, but has yet to get his head in front: stays 1m well and likes soft ground.   33
17 RANA PRATAP [8] (G Lewis) 6-9-7 P Waldron 13/2: 0144-04: Ev ch after 2f out: in
'85 won a h'cap at York: in '82 won twice as a 2yo: eff at 7f, stays 1m: acts on gd & soft.   44
-- THE HOWARD [5] 4-9-3 N Day 20/1: -0101-0: Al there on seasonal debut: in '85 won 2
of 4 starts, a h'cap at Carlisle and a maiden at Edinburgh: stays 1m well: acts on firm
and soft and on any trk: has run well in bl and should strip fitter next time.   39
-- ALQIRM [6] 4-9-0 B Rouse 9/1: 02400-0: Sn prom.   34
*10 FORMATUNE [11] 4-8-12(7ex) J Reid 8/1: 0003-10: Never nearer: much btr in 10 (yld).   00
-- CORN STREET [14] 8-9-6 Pat Eddery 5/1 FAV: 102D4-0: Prom over 6f.   00
17 FUSILIER [9] 4-8-12(bl) G Baxter 13/2: 3003-30: Pounds below form 17 (stiffer trk).   00
-- Classic Capistrano [2] 9-1   -- Jimjams [12] 8-8
-- Quiet Riot [4] 9-10   17 Merry Measure [7] 8-10
-- Kalkour [15] 9-7   31 Mr Mcgregor [1] 9-1
15 ran   2,2,¾,½,½   (Mrs V M McKinney)   H Collingridge Newmarket

72 ROSEBERRY H'CAP 4YO+ 0-70   £7726   1m 2f   Heavy 175 -18 Slow   [62]

-- NEBRIS [5] (R Akehurst) 5-8-10 Pat Eddery 14/1: 10110-1: 5 b h Nebbiolo - Magic Quiz
(Quisling): Made a winning seasonal debut, led approaching final 1f, readily in the valuable
Roseberry Stakes (h'cap) at Kempton Mar.31: smart hurdler: in fine form on the Flat in '85,
winning h'caps at Epsom and Newmarket: earlier an amateur riders race at Lingfield: very
eff at 10/11f: acts on gd/firm and soft and on any trk: genuine sort.   58
-- ABU KADRA [15] (W Musson) 5-9-1(BL) M Wigham 12/1: 00000-2: Fit from hurdling: chance
final 1f: good effort: below his best last season: in '84 was in fine form winning 4 times,
incl valuable November H'cap when trained by M Stoute: eff over 8/10, stays 12f really well:
acts on firm and soft.   57
7   JOLIS GIRL [6] (M Ryan) 4-8-2 Paul Eddery 14/1: 0420-03: Ran on well final 1f:
should go close next time: in '85 won a h'cap at Ripon: eff at 9f, stays 12f: acts on gd/
firm and soft: has worn blinkers.   44
23 RIDGEFIELD [3] (D Thom) 8-7-11 M L Thomas 14/1: 000-004: Never nearer: first time out
last season won a h'cap at Leicester: in '84 won again at Leicester: in '83 won 3 times:
eff over 12f and acts on any ground.   32
9   BOOM PATROL [13] 4-8-2 W Ryan 8/1: 1000-30: Ev ch straight, btr in 9.   33
7   DUELLING [2] 5-7-7(vis)(7oh) N Adams 9/1: 1330-40: Led over 2f out: see 7.   20
17 XHAI [1] 4-8-0 R Morse(7) 4/1 FAV: 2110-40: Disapp fav: btr in 17 (1m).   00
38 WELL MEET AGAIN [10] 9-7-7(4oh) S Dawson(1) 9/1: 4-20-30: Never sighted: much btr 36.   00
17 GUNDREDA [9] 4-8-12 P Robinson 10/1: 1000-00: Made most: fdd.   00
-- Shostakovitch [8] 8-1   -- Thats Your Lot [12] 10-0
4   Kentucky Quest [14] 8-8   -- All Fair [7] 9-2
7   Gay Captain [11] 9-3   -- Marley Roofus [4] 8-6
15 ran   2,nk,4,2½,2   (D S Collinge)   R Akehurst Epsom, Surrey

73 REDSHANK 2YO MAIDEN FILLIES STAKES   £1832   5f   Soft 135 -60 Slow

-- MY IMAGINATION [5] (P Kelleway) 2-8-11 P Cook 5/1: 1: 2 b f What A Guest - Tutti
Frutti (Tarboosh): Promising filly: led approaching final 1f and was sn clear in a slow run
2yo maiden fillies stakes at Kempton Mar.31: cost I.R. 10,000: eff at 5f and should stay
further: acts on soft and should win more races.   59
-- SHADES OF NIGHT [10] (J Winter) 2-8-11 Pat Eddery 6/1: 2: made most, showing promise:
cost 15,000 gns and a half sister to useful 2yo Running Princess: sire, Red Sunset, won
the Coventry Stakes at Royal Ascot: eff at 5f, should stay further: acts on soft.   46
-- ALWAYS A LADY [3] (M Usher) 2-8-11 B Thomson 14/1: 3: Sn prom: half sister to 2 winners,
incl useful Netsuke, a 2yo winner in '83: should stay further than 5f: acts on soft.   42

-- JOHNKEINA [2] (W Jarvis) 2-8-11 B Rouse 8/1: 4: Lightly bckd: nearest fin: French bred
filly who should impr: acts on soft.   41
-- OUR PET [11] 2-8-11 S Cauthen 7/2 FAV: 0: Late hdway and should do btr next time:
cost 21,000 gns and is a half sister to 3 winners.   38
-- PINTAFORY [4] 2-8-11 G Starkey 10/1: 0: Wknd final 1f: should do btr next time:
should stay further.   32
-- ROYAL RABBLE [14] 2-8-11 A Mcglone 5/1: 0: Mkt drifter and never threatened: cost
3,400 gns and is a half sister to 3 winners.   00
-- TILTING YARD [6] 2-8-11 R Cochrane 10/1: 0: Fin 9th on racecourse debut: stoutly bred
and should do better in time.   00
-- FOWL PLAY [8] 2-8-11 N Day 8/1: 0: Mkt drifter: fdd app. final 1f: cost 13,000 gns.   00
-- Double Talk [7] 8-11   -- Bastilla [13] 8-11   -- Saucier [1] 8-11
-- Revelina [12] 8-11   -- Betta Win [14] 8-11
14 ran   5,2,½,1½,3   (Roldvale Ltd)   P Kelleway Newmarket

74 MIDDLESEX HANDICAP 3YO 0-50   £2502   1m   Heavy 175 -32 Slow   [52]

-- BELOW ZERO [2] (A Bailey) 3-8-6 R Cochrane 4/1: 20402-1: 3 ch c Northfields - Indigine
(Raise A Native): First time out, led over 1f out, comfortably in a 3yo h'cap at Kempton
Mar.31: placed several times last season, but failed to win: eff at 7f, stays 1m well: acts
on gd/firm and soft.   43
-- FARAG [7] (P Walwyn) 3-8-5 Paul Eddery 5/2 FAV: 44031-2: Led 2f out, 12L clear 3rd:
on final outing last season won a nursery h'cap at Nottingham: eff at 1m: acts on firm and
soft and on any trk.   36
-- GIVING IT ALL AWAY [6] (H Beasley) 3-8-3 D Mckay 16/1: 00000-3: Showed some promise
in '85: eff at 7f and should stay 1m: acts on gd.   14
-- CEROC [1] (J Bethell) 3-7-12 W Carson 10/1: 000-4: Sn prom, ev ch: unplaced in 3
outings last season: eff at 7f on good.   06
-- GORGEOUS ALGERNON [3] 3-9-7 S Cauthen 5/1: 24030-0: Wknd over 2f out.   24
-- QUICKEN THE BID [5] 3-7-9(2oh) R Fox 10/1: 00400-0: Made most, fdd.   00
-- BAKERS DOUGH [4] 3-8-2 P Waldron 5/1: 0011-0: No real threat: fin 8th.   00
-- Brent Riverside [9] 8-1   -- Hooray Hamilton [8] 7-10(1oh)
9 ran   2¼,12,1½,3,10   (T P Ramsden)   A Bailey Newmarket

75 RUTH WOOD MAIDEN STAKES 3YO   £1643   1m 4f   Heavy 175 -33 Slow

-- LONGGHURST [5] (C Horgan) 3-9-0 Pat Eddery 4/1: 00-1: 3 b c Camden Town - Olanrose
(Kythnos): Mkt drifter, but made ev yd, responding well to press for a narrow win in a
3yo maiden at Kempton Mar.31: half brother to several winners: acts well on heavy ground:
genuine and can continue to improve.   45
25 TARGET SIGHTED [1] (C Nelson) 3-9-0 J Reid 7/1: 2-02: Chall final 1f and 10L clear
3rd: on sole start last season, fin 2nd in a maiden at Warwick: stays 12f well: acts on
gd/firm and soft and should find a maiden.   44
25 HUBBARDS LODGE [7] (P Kelleway) 3-9-0 P Cook 7/4 FAV: 0032-33: Again well bckd:
ev ch: see 25.   29
-- GROVE TOWER [8] (R Nicholls) 3-9-0 N Howe 12/1: 003-4: Fdd 3f out on seasonal debut:
rated 36 last season when 3rd in a 10f maiden at Doncaster on soft ground.   27
-- DISCIPLE [3] 3-9-0 P Waldron 8/1: -0: Never in it on racecourse debut.   25
-- PARTS IS PARTS [2] 3-8-11 R Cochrane 4/1: -0: Friendless in mkt and well btn.   00
-- Markelius 0 9-0   -- Quarterflash [6] 9-0
8 ran   hd,10,1½,1½,dist   (John D Terry)   C Horgan Billingbear, Berks

76 PADDOCK HANDICAP 3YO+ 0-50   £2427   5f   Soft 135 -08 Slow   [50]

12 HILTON BROWN [4] (P Cundell) 5-10-0 P Cook 7/1: 0000-31: 5 br h Daring March -
Holiday Season (Silly Season): Defied 10-0, led dist. comfortably in a h'cap at Kempton
Mar.31: failed to win last season, but in '84 was in excellent form, winning 2 valuable
h'caps at Ascot and a h'cap at Newmarket: very eff at 5f: acts on firm & soft: genuine
and consistent and carries weight well.   62
-- BRIDGE STREET LADY [3] (J Bosley) 5-9-5 G Baxter 8/1: 04200-2: Led till inside
final 1f on seasonal debut: good effort: in '85 was a fine 2nd in the Wokingham at Royal
Ascot: earlier won a h'cap at Nottingham: in '84 won a h'cap at Chepstow: very eff at
5/6f, stays 7f: acts on gd and heavy: best with forcing tactics: genuine mare.   47
*12 WILL GEORGE [6] (C Horgan) 7-9-2(7ex) Pat Eddery 4/1 Jt.FAV: 2003-13: Fin well: in
good form: see 12.   43
12 SPACEMACER BOY [5] (R Nicholls) 6-8-9 N Howe 13/2: 0020-24: Al there: see 12.   35
-- DAVILL [1] 4-8-11 B Rouse 4/1 Jt.FAV: 10212-0: Well bckd, but never showed on
seasonal debut: in '85 was in good form, winning h'caps at Wolverhampton and Sandown and
a fillies maiden at Lingfield: very eff over 5f, stays 6f: acts on firm & soft and on
any track.   30
12 BRAMPTON GRACE [8] 4-9-2 W Carson 16/1: 0000-00: Never showed.   20
12 CHAPLINS CLUB [9] 6-10-0 D Nicholls 10/1: 4021-00: Wknd 2f out.   00
31 Miletrians Lass [10] 7-7(14oh)   -- Cronks Quality [11] 8-12
9 ran   2,¾,nk,3,8   (Lord McAlpine)   P Cundell Compton, Berks

Official Going Given as Soft

77   JESMOND STAKES 2YO   £1789   5f   Heavy 168 +12 Fast

57   **GALLIC TIMES** [1] (I Bell) 2-8-11 N Carlisle 14/1: 31: 2 ch c Good Times - Gallic
Law (Galivanter): Impr colt: having 2nd race in 48 hours, responded well to press to lead
final 1f in a fast run 2yo minor race at Newcastle Mar.31: btn in a seller first time out!
half brother to 4 winning sprinters, notably the very useful Ferriby Hall: likely to prove
best around 5/6f: acts well on soft ground, on a stiff trk.   46
+43   **BLUEMEDE** [2] (M Brittain) 2-9-7 A Bacon[7] 4/5 fav: 112: Having 3rd race in 11 days,
clear ldr till wknd final 1f and was below his best: btr 43.   53
--   **TOOTSIE JAY** [3] (P Feilden) 2-8-8 R Hills 14/1: 3: Never in it: cost only 3,000 gns:
should improve.   30
3   **BOY SINGER** [5] (K Stone) 2-8-11 G Brown[5] 3/1: 04: Wknd ½way: cost 5,000 gns and
is sprint bred.   33
--   **REVOLVER VIDEO** [6] 2-8-8 M Fry 9/1: 0: No threat: bargain basement buy who is sprint bred.18
--   **JJ JIMMY** [4] 2-8-11 M Birch 10/1: 0: No danger: sprint bred.   18
6 ran   2½,4,hd,6,2½   (Mrs E Taylor)   I Bell Hawick, Roxburghshire

78   MELDON MAIDEN STAKES 3YO   £1177   1m   Heavy 168 -55 Slow

--   **SPROWSTON BOY** [3] (P Kelleway) 3-9-0 Gay Kelleway[5] 7/2: 04322-1: 3 ch g Dominion -
·Cavalier's Blush (King's Troop): First time out, made most, keeping up gamely for a narrow
win in a 3yo maiden at Newcastle Mar.31: placed several times in '85, showing particular
liking for heavy going which he once again emphasised here: stays 1m and acts on a stiff trk.   45
--   **WESHAAM** [5] (B Hanbury) 3-9-0 R Hills 8/15 fav: 30-2: Led 2f out, no extra near fin.
but a dist clear of rest: showed promise both outings in '85 on firm & good going, possibly
not at home on this testing surface: stays at least 7f, probably 1m.   43
14   **QUALITAIR KING** [2] (K Stone) 3-9-0 S Keightley 9/1: 04-03: Fdd final 4f: rated 33
when 4th in a maiden at Yarmouth in '85, only ran twice: possibly btr suited by good
than heavy going.   00
--   **NOBLE SAXON** [1] (S Norton) 3-9-0 J Lowe 14/1: 000-4: Never landed a blow: only ran
three times in '85.   00
--   **CLAWSON THORNS** [4] 3-9-0 M Birch 14/1: 0000-0: Fdd quickly str: rated 32 on final
outing of '85 when 5th of 12 in a maiden at Redcar on firm ground: unsuited by heavy?   00
5 ran   1,dist,15,dist   (Geoff Whiting)   P Kelleway Newmarket

79   NEWCASTLE CENTENARY HCAP STAKES 0-60   £4401   1m   Heavy 168 -18 Slow   [49]

-17   **WELL RIGGED** [4] (M H Easterby) 5-9-1 M Birch 5/4 fav: 1321-21: 5 ch g Windjammer -
Topless Dancer (Northfields): Useful gelding: never hdd when readily winning quite a valuable
h'cap at Newcastle Mar.31 fav. when 2nd in the Lincoln first time out: in '85 won at Doncaster, Thirsk and Beverley (2): very eff over 1m/9f: acts on firm & heavy and on any trk:
tough and genuine front runner.   46
17   **VIRGIN ISLE** [6] (P Haslam) 5-9-2 R Hills 9/1: 3034-02: Al in vain pursuit: had a
busy season in '85 winning at Newmarket and Doncaster: also won twice in '84: eff over 7f/1m:
acts on any going: likes a gall trk.   40
10   **VERBARIUM** [2] (J Ramsden) 6-7-10 J Quinn[7] 3/1: 1031-23: Strong fin: too much to do?   19
--   **TUTBURY** [1] (W Wharton) 4-8-3 N Carlisle 9/1: 42102-4: Should benefit from this first
race since June '85: consistent last season winning at Redcar & Nottingham: very eff over
7f/1m on a gall trk: acts on any going: will do btr next time.   26
17   **EMERALD EAGLE** [5] 5-8-0 A Shoults[5] 6/1: 000-0100: Wknd 2f out: fit from recent
success at Cagnes: last season won at Ayr: best form around 1m on yld but also acts on firm.   18
--   **TRY TO STOP ME** [3] 5-9-7 M Fry 14/1: 13000-0: The first beaten.   34
6 ran   4,1,shhd,3,4   (Mrs J B Mountfield)   M H Easterby Malton, Yorks

80   FOREST HALL HANDICAP STAKES 0-35   £2131   1m 4f   Heavy 168 -125 Slow   [31]

23   **SKI RUN** [9] (P Wigham)⁻11-7-12 J Lowe 7/1: 3-00-41: 11 b g Workboy - Snow Run
(Quorum): Led on bit inside final 3f comfortably in a very slowly run h'cap at Newcastle
Mar.31: ran only twice in '85 and last successful in '82 at Haydock (2): acts on firm &
heavy going: eff at 10f: stays 12f: has been a good stable servant.   10
--   **LEON** [6] (N Tinkler) 4-9-10 Kim Tinkler[7] 8/1: 41104-2: Fin well on seasonal debut:
trained by L Cumani in '85 winning at Leicester, Salisbury, Lingfield and Doncaster: eff over
10/12f: best form on firm or good going but seems also to act on heavy: sure to go close
next time.   34
--   **DESCARTES** [5] (M W Easterby) 4-8-11(bl) K Hodgson 10/1: 20001/3: Led 10f: fit from
a recent success over hurdles: acts well on heavy going: off the trk in '85 but the previous
season won a seller at Redcar over 7f on good going.   18
7   **TAKE A CARD** [1] (J Ramsden) 7-8-5 A Shoults[5] 5/1 fav: 0404-04: Seemed to run in
snatches: quite lightly raced in '85 without success: in '83 won at Newmarket: stays at
least 10f: acts on firm and heavy.   12

36   POKEY   [10] 4-8-13 M Hindley[3] 14/1: 3000-00: Ran 8 times without success in '85:
in '84 won over 5f at Haydock on firm going.   16
7   MISS MORLEY   [12] 4-8-8 J Bleasdale 11/1: 0100-00: Well there 10f.   08
44   RIBBONS OF BLUE   [11] 6-8-3 N Connorton 6/1: 1320-00: Pressed ldrs till 2f out, fin 7th   00
--   HOLLY BUOY   [4] 6-9-0 E Guest[3] 6/1: 13211-0: Should benefit from seasonal debut.   00
--   IVOROSKI   [7] 4-9-2 M Birch 8/1: 44400-0: Seemed totally unsuited by the going.   00
--   Tharaleos   [2] 7-12   --   Higham Grey   [8] 9-1
11 ran   1½,1½,hd,4,2½   (P Wigham)   P Wigham Malton, Yorks

81   NORTHERN HANDICAP STAKES 3YO   £2861   7f   Heavy 168 -40 Slow   [43]

--   GOOSE HILL   [3] (M W Easterby) 3-9-4 K Hodgson 5/1: 10-1: 3 b f Don-Magic Lady (Gala
Performance): First time out, comfortably led dist. in a slowly run 3yo h'cap at Newcastle
Mar.31: also won first time out in '85, a seller at Newcastle and likes this stiff track:
very eff over 6/7f and should stay 1m: acts on yld and heavy going.   43
--   IMPROVISE   [4] (Ron Thompson) 3-8-13 R P Elliott 8/1: 30010-2: Ev ch final 1f: good
seasonal debut: winner of a seller and a nursery at Carlisle & Catterick in '85: very eff
over 7f/1m: acts on firm and heavy: cheaply bought.   33
37   UPTOWN RANDBS   [1] (G Moore) 3-8-6 S Wood[7] 8/1: 1040-43: Led over 5f: see 37.   22
--   DANCING TOM   [2] (T Fairhurst) 3-9-7 C Coates[5] 7/2: 3101-4: Pressed ldr over 5f,
should benefit from seasonal debut: won 2 out of his 4 races in '85 at Ripon and Redcar:
eff over 5/6f and is suited by yld or soft going.   27
38   BRADBURY HALL   [5] 3-8-7 L Charnock 12/1: 000-000: No threat, remains a maiden.   13
--   KO ISLAND   [7] 3-8-2 M Fry 11/2: 32000-0: Never posed a threat on seasonal debut.   00
--   CUMBRIAN DANCER   [6] 3-8-10 M Birch 6/4 fav: 00212-0: Ran badly on seasonal debut.   00
7 ran   2½,2½,8,shhd,20.   (Hippodromo Racing)   M W Easterby Sheriff Hutton, Yorks

82   KILLINGWORTH MAIDEN STAKES 3YO   £1103   7f   Heavy 168 -38 Slow

53   HOIST THE AXE   [5] (B Hanbury) 3-8-11 A Geran[7] 13/8: -21: 3 gr f Al Hattab -
Naval Orange (Hoist The Flag): Having 2nd race in 24 hours, making most readily in a 3yo
maiden at Newcastle Mar.31: evidently well at home in testing going on a stiff trk: likes
to stay at least 1m.   45
--   JENIFER BROWNING   [3] (T Barron) 3-8-11 E Guest[3] 12/1: 00-2: No chance with winner:
no form in 2 outings last season: half sister to a couple of minor winners: likely to
prove best around 7f.   25
16   BOLD SEA ROVER   [4] (M H Easterby) 3-9-0 M Birch 11/8 fav: -03: Slightly hmpd but
would not have btn this easy winner in any event: see 16.   28
--   MR COFFEY   [2] (S Norton) 3-9-0 J Lowe 8/1: 0000-4: Held up, no chance from ½way:
no form in 4 outings last season.   16
--   RAVELSTON   [6] 3-9-0 R Hills 14/1: 00-0: Early ldr, fdd quickly: lightly raced maiden.   00
--   COLWAY RADIAL   [1] 3-9-0 M Fry 10/1: 00-0: Wknd after 3f: lightly raced.   00
6 ran   20,nk,12,25,12   (T P Whitney)   B Hanbury Newmarket

WARWICK   Monday March 31st   Lefthanded Sharp Track

83   MARTON STAKES (3-Y-O)   £684   6f   Soft 159 +22 Fast

--   HEART OF GLASS   [1] (P Fielden) 3-8-11 M Hills 10/1: 4-1: 3 b c Music Boy - Handle With
Care (Jutland): First time out, made all gamely in a fast run minor event at Warwick Mar.31:
stays 6f: evidently suited by a sharp trk, front running tactics and soft ground: could
win better races.   43
--   BOOFY   [7] (C Nelson) 3-8-11 A Clark 5/4 FAV: 0340-2: Just failed under strong press:
should stay further than 6f: half brother to several winners incl Get The Message and
Royal Home: seems to go well on soft ground and on a sharpish trk: should soon find a
maiden race.   42
--   REIGNBEAU   [4] (G Lewis) 3-8-11 G Sexton 7/4: 03-3: Al close up and not btn far: acts
on soft ground, should stay further than 6f and might do btr on a more gall trk.   40
--   TOLLYS ALE   [3] (I Matthews) 3-8-8 W Woods(3) 25/1: 40304-4: Ev ch: abs since last
July: eff at 5 & 6f.   25
38   MERCIA GOLD   [8] 3-8-11 B Crossley 10/1: 3000-30: Much btr in 38.   16
--   GALAXY PATH   [5] 3-8-11 T Johnson 25/1: 0-0: Every chance.   15
--   LOW KEY   [6] 3-8-11 T Lucas 10/1: 2-0: Fin well behind: half brother to 12f winner
Sir Crusty: just btn in a seller at Ripon in '85 over 5f on good ground.   00
--   Saxon Bazaar   [2] 8-11   --   Royal Berks   [10] 8-11   --   Ivory Fire   [9] 8-8
10 ran   nk,¾,4,4,shhd   (P J Feilden)   P Fielden Exning, Suffolk

84   WARWICKSHIRE SPRINT H'CAP 3YO+ (0-35)   £1257   5f   Soft 159 +07 Fast   [26]

--   RIVERSIDE WRITER   [2] (K Bridgwater) 4-9-4 P D'arcy 13/2: 924-4: 4 b g African Sky -
Fair Darling (Darling Boy): Well bckd, first time out winner of a h'cap at Warwick Mar.31,
getting up on the post: first ever success: suited by 5/6f and goes well on soft ground:
possibly well h'capped, early in '85 was rated 36.   37   24

30   ROYAL BEAR [5] (J Bradley) 4-8-2 M Miller 7/1: 0000-22: Led 1 out, just caught:
deserves to find a similar race soon: acts on soft: see 30.   07
38   TAYLOR OF SOHAM [6] (D Leslie) 3-8-9(bl) M Rimmer 11/2: 0000-23: Al prom: see 38.   24
--   PINE HAWK [3] (D Haydn Jones) 5-8-7 D Williams(7) 8/1: 43004-4: Still a maiden, best
effort was when 2nd over 5f at Warwick last year on soft ground.   06
+30   PERION [7] 4-10-5(7ex) J Adams(7) 5/4 FAV: 4000-10: Made most, stiff task: see 30.   25
12   KRISLIN [1] 4-8-12 S Webster 25/1: -00: Early speed.   00
--   ROBROB [8] 4-9-8 I Johnson 9/1: 14000-0: Wk in mkt: no threat: 5f winner at Chepstow
in '85 on soft ground: stays 6f and also acts on gd/firm.   00
--   FAIRDALE [4] 8-8-7 R Guest 33/1: -0: Early ldr, fdd.   00
8 ran   nk,1,1,2½,10   (G K Kattou)   K Bridgwater Lapworth, Warwickshire

85   HEART OF ENGLAND H'CAP 4YO+ (0-50)   £2494   1m 6f   Soft 159 44 Slow   [42]

--   PEARL RUN [9] (G Price) 5-8-4 G King(7) 2/1 FAV: -1320-1: 5 ch g Gulf Pearl - Deep
Down (Deep Run): First time out, well bckd, led 2 out readily in a h'cap at Warwick Mar.31:
also won this race last year: eff at 14f and stays 2m2f: seems to act on firm & heavy ground:
runs particularly well at Warwick and looks nicely h'capped.   28
11   KNIGHTS HEIR [1] (L Lightbrown) 5-7-10 W Woods(1) 12/1: 2030-02: Made most: very fit
following his recent win   in a selling hurdle: stays extreme distances and probably acts
on any going.   16
--   AVEBURY [4] (F Jordan) 4-9-1 A Clark 9/2: 01433-3: Led 4 out: fit from hurdling:
winner at Newcastle in '85 over 14f: suited by a stiff track and acts on gd and soft.   28
--   DOWN FLIGHT [2] (C Holmes) 6-9-5(BL) M Hills 7/1: 30000-4: Well bckd: ran well early
in '85 but has not won since '83 when successful at York & Wolverhampton: stays at least
2m2f and best on yld and heavy.   18
9   HOLYPORT VICTORY [8] 4-8-6 R Curant 9/2: 2230-40: Not stay 14f? see 9.   04
--   BALKASH [6] 5-7-7(BL)(5oh) D Williams(7) 25/1: -0000-0: Never in it.   00
--   AGRA KNIGHT [7] 4-9-10(bl) A Murray 9/2: 12131-0: Wknd 4 out: fit from hurdling:
proved most consistent on the Flat last year winning at Edinburgh (2) & Newcastle when
trained by J Hindley: stays 2m and acts on gd & yld: best in bl.   00
--   Librate [5] 7-10   --   Faidros [10] 8-4(1ow)
9 ran   2,5,10,nk,12   (R Squires)   G Price Leominster, Herefordshire

86   BIDFORD SELLING STAKES (2-Y-O)   £578   5f   Soft 159 35 Slow

--   GOLDORINA [5] (W Turner) 2-8-11 R Curant 10/1: 1: 2 ch c Gold Song - Dobrina
(Our Mirage): Active in mkt: first time out got up close home in a seller at Warwick Mar.31:
bought in 3,450 gns: suited by 5f, sharpish trk and soft ground.   24
21   ROWEKING [9] (P Haslam) 2-8-11(VIS) M Hills 4/1: 02: Tried in a visor, just failed
to make all: acts on soft ground: should find a seller on a similar sharp trk.   23
--   SAMS REFRAIN [10] (D Haydn Jones) 2-8-8 D Williams(7) 16/1: 3: Not recover from
a slow start, could do btr next time: acts on soft.   08
57   ATHALEA CYNTRA [8] (N Tinkler) 2-8-8(BL) J H Brown(5) 7/4 FAV: 44: Bl for the first
time, proved a disapp fav: btr in 57.   04
--   MONS FUTURE [4] 2-8-8 I Johnson 10/1: 0: Every chance.   00
--   ANONA BELLE [1] 2-8-8 B Crossley 14/1: 0: Fdd 2 out.   00
--   MARTHAS PRIDE [6] 2-8-8 S Webster 5/1: 0: Ran disapp: half sister to several winners
over 5-10f: worth another chance.   00
21   CUTLER RIDGE [2] 2-8-11 J Matthias 10/1: 00: Early speed: mkt drifter.   00
21   Valdosta [3] 8-8   --   High Town [7] 8-8
10 ran   hd,4,1½,2½,1½   (E Goody)   W Turner Corton Denham

87   SNITTERFIELD MAIDEN FILLIES STAKES 3YO   £684   5f   Soft 159 +09 Fast

--   WESSEX KINGDOM [4] (M Mccormack) 3-8-11 M Hills 3/1: 0-1: 3 ch f Vaigly Great -
Kingdom Come (Klondyke Bill): First time out made all easily in a maiden fillies race at
Warwick Mar.31: well bckd: does well when fresh, suited by 5f, sharp trk and front running
tactics: acts on soft ground: a half sister to 5 winners from 5-16f: should win btr races.   48
--   MADAM MUFFIN [3] (J Bethell) 3-8-11 J Mattias 2/1 FAV: 2-2: 2nd in a Newmarket seller
last year over 6f on firm ground: possibly acts on firm & soft & should pick up a small race.   28
--   KNIGHTLY DIA [5] (L Piggott) 3-8-11 B Crossley 4/1: -3: Late prog: will probably
need more time.   26
--   PROMISING TIMES [2] (M Jarvis) 3-8-11 W Woods(3) 6/1: -4: Ch. 2 out: might do
better on a sounder surface.   20
--   CATECHISM [6] 3-8-11 A Mackay 7/2: -0: Disapp debut: half sister to an 8f winner:
might do better over 6f plus.   14
--   SOMEWAY [1] 3-8-11 Amanda Clayford(7) 14/1: 03-0: Early speed.   11
6 ran   8,½,2,2,1   (P W Bennett)   M Mccormack Sparsholt, Oxon

88   WEST MIDLANDS HANDICAP 4YO+ (0-35)   £1249   1m 2f   Soft 159 11 Slow   [28]

--   STAR OF IRELAND   [2] (G Price) 6-9-0 G King(7) 3/1 JTFAV: 3--00-1: 6 b g Star Appeal - Belligerent (Roan Rocket): First time out, easily led 2 out in a h'cap at Warwick Mar.31: fit from a recent win over hurdles: in '84 won at Lingfield and in '83 at Kempton: acts on firm & heavy and eff at 8/10f: also seems to do well on a sharpish trk and should win again.   29

7   SCREES   [1] (J H Wilson) 5-9-7 Julie Bowker(7) 16/1: -02: Made most: in '83 won a minor race at Catterick: well suited by forcing tactics, a sharp trk: should stay well: acts on soft & yld.   20

7   SKYBOOT   [3] (E Carter) 7-9-0 Wendy Carter(7) 5/1: 0440-03: Fit from hurdling: failed to win last year but in '84 at the end of the season won h'caps at Wolverhampton and Redcar (app.): very eff around 8/9f and acts on any going though fav. by soft.   11

9   ARROW BEAK   [7] (I Matthews) 5-9-10 W Woods(3) 3/1 JTFAV: 2011-04: Difficult task at the weights: in '85 at the end of the season won at Edinburgh and Hamilton: in '84 won at Goodwood (seller): eff at 10/12f and acts on good and heavy ground.   09

--   FLAME FLOWER   [9] 4-8-5 R Street 14/1: 30030-0: 2nd till 1½ out: best effort in '85 when just failed to make all in an 11f h'cap at Bath but remains a maiden: stays 12f and acts on soft ground.   00

--   COFFEE HOUSE   [4] 11-8-0 S O Gorman(7) 14/1: 00000-0: Never closer.   00

9   CRADLE OF JAZZ   [8] 6-9-0 A Murray 5/1: 2000-00: Ran well early in '85, placed on heavy ground at Leicester & Haydock: in '83 won at Yarmouth: stays 12f and also acts on a sound surface.   00

36   Superfrost   [5] 9-1   --   Karamoun   [10] 8-9   --   Minibank   [6] 8-0
10 ran   10,1,8,¾,4.   (H K Strickland)   G Price Leominster, Hereford

89   LEEK WOOTON FILLIES STAKES 3-Y-O   £684   1m   Soft 159 23 Slow

--   HIGH HALO   [2] (I Balding) 3-8-11 J Matthias 7/2: 0-1: 3 b f High Top - Halomata (Hallez): Made all and held on well in a minor race at Warwick Mar.31, first time out: certain to impr for the experience and looks sure to be suited by longer distances than 1m: goes well with forcing tactics on soft ground: acts on a sharp trk.   37

--   HOT MOMMA   [4] (R Boss) 3-8-11 M Miller 1/1 FAV: 02022-2: Held up, ev ch, clear of the rest but has proved frustrating since her 4th in the Cherry Hinton at Newmarket last year: probably stays 1m and acts on any going.   35

--   BOXERS SHUKEE   [6] (J Bradley) 3-8-11 B Crossley 33/1: 0000-3: Never a threat: probably stays 1m: btn in a seller last year.   19

--   NATIVE HABITAT   [1] (M Jarvis) 3-8-11 W Woods(3) 3/1: -4: Well bckd, a half sister to the useful Eastform, winning at 5-8f: ran disapp: might do btr on a sounder surface.   07

--   MOLLY PARTRIDGE   [3] 3-8-11 R Guest 14/1: 04203-0: 2nd in a 6f seller at Newcastle last year on soft ground: also acts on yld.   00

--   AUSSIE GIRL   [7] 3-8-11 M Hills 14/1: 00-0: Never in it.   00

6 ran   ½,8,7,7,1   (Mrs Michael Wates)   I Balding Kingsclere, Hants

Official Going Given as Soft: Races 90, 91 & 93 were started by flag

90   CHANDLER SUITE 3YO MAIDEN STAKES   £684   1m   Soft 148 -03 Slow

--   PROHIBITED   [5] (P Cole) 3-9-0 T Quinn 3/1 FAV: 00-1: 3 br c Formidable - Deed (Derring-Do): First time out, led final 1f, driven out in a 3yo maiden at Warwick Apr.1: 100,000 gns purchase who is a half brother to several winners, incl the smart Busaco: stays 1m well: acts on soft and a sharpish trk: should continue to impr.   40

39   NATCHAKAM   [12] (G Lewis) 3-9-0 P Waldron 4/1: -42: Led over 1f out: on the up grade: eff over 1m on soft ground and a sharp trk.   36

33   ALPHA HELIX   [7] (K Brassey) 3-9-0 S Whitworth 10/1: -03: Al prom: 7L clear rem: stays 1m: acts on soft ground: see 33.   32

--   KINGS CRUSADE   [11] (G Lewis) 3-9-0 G Sexton 25/1: -4: Fdd on racecourse debut: should do better: brother to 10f winner in '85 Historical Fact .   19

--   ENFOLD   [3] 3-9-0 Pat Eddery 5/1: -0: Led 6f: impr likely.   13

--   ROUGH PASSAGE   [9] 3-9-0 M Wigham 20/1: -0: Prom 5f.   01

14   TOWER FAME   [2] 3-9-0 M L Thomas 8/1: 04-00: Active in mkt: no show: rated 36 when 4th in a 2yo stakes at Yarmouth in '85 (6f firm): half brother to a winning stayer.   00

--   HUNTING IRISH   [6] 3-9-0 W R Swinburn 9/1: -0: Friendless in mkt: no threat.   00

--   Fire Rocket   [8] 9-0   --   Summerhill Rock   [10] 9-0
--   Sir Brett   [1] 9-0   --   Cornish Prince   [4] 9-0

12 ran   2,1½,7,3,6   (F Salman)   P Cole Lambourn, Berks

91   ARC WEEKEND HANDICAP STAKES (0-35)   £1442   1m   Soft 148 +13 Fast   [33]

-- DE RIGUEUR [19] (J Bethell) 4-9-9 W Carson 15/2: 34324-1: 4 b g Derrylin - Northern
Lady (The Brianstan): Led approaching final 1f, comfortably in quite a fast run h'cap at
Warwick Apr.1: consistent performer in '85 winning a h'cap at Wolverhampton: eff at 1m:
acts on gd and soft and on any trk: genuine sort who does well when fresh.   40
-- VAGUE MELODY [15] (L Piggott) 4-9-8 W R Swinburn 13/2: 04214-2: Gd effort on seasonal
debut: trained by G Balding in '85 to win a h'cap at Leicester: now with L Piggott: eff
at 1m, stays 10f well: acts on gd and soft and on any trk.   34
10 LEMELASOR [3] (D Haydn Jones) 6-9-7 D J Williams(7) 5/1 FAV: 0420-03: Ran on well
final 1f: in '85 won app. h'caps at Wolverhampton and Chester: eff over 7/9f: acts on gd
and soft ground and on any trk: may be winning soon.   33
-- CHAISE LONGUE [2] (H O'neill) 4-8-10 S Whitworth 33/1: 00000-4: Led/dsptd lead:
little form in '85: a shhd 2nd at Goodwood as a 2yo: eff at 6/7f: acts well on a sharpish
track: should find a seller.   16
-- MARSOOM [8] 4-8-5 D Mckay 25/1: 32010-0: Mkt drifter but al prom.   06
-- MISS APEX [12] 4-8-7 I Johnson 14/1: 04032-0: Led briefly 2f out, fdd.   03
10 MISS AGGRO [17] 4-9-1 G Starkey 6/1: 0000-00: Made most.   00
-- FEI LOONG [14] 5-9-5 G King(7) 8/1: 11400-0: Btr for race.   00
-- KAVAKA [6] 4-9-2 A Mcglone 8/1: 40-00-0: Fin mid-div.   00
39 BAXTERGATE [10] 3-7-7 N Carlisle 10/1: 0000-00: Active in mkt but well btn.   00
-- Bit Of A State [4] 9-3   -- Avraeas [9] 8-2
-- Dallas Smith [16] 7-13   10 Kamaress [5] 9-2
-- Craven Boy [1] 7-10   -- Venture To Reform [18] 8-0
-- Throw Me Over [11] 8-5(BL) P
17 ran   2,nk,3,2½,2½,½,nk   (Mrs Christopher Heath)   J Bethell Chilton, Oxon

92   PARIS HANDICAP STAKES (0-50) 4YO+   £2388   1m 4f   Soft 148 -35 Slow   [46]

23 RECORD WING [12] (D Haydn Jones) 8-8-5 D J Williams(7) 2/1 FAV: 4000-21: 8 b g Record
Run - O'Flynn (Prince Regent): Heavily bckd, led after 2f out, easily in a h'cap at Warwick
Apr.1: recently an emphatic winner over hurdles: in '85 won a h'cap at Chester after several
placings: in.'84 won again at Chester and likes that very sharp trk: stays 12f well: acts
on good but hates soft.   34
-- MR GARDINER [10] (W Brooks) 4-8-10 J Bray(7) 16/1: 20401-2: Led briefly 2 out: 8L
clear 3rd: trained by P Cole in '85 to win an app. stakes at Doncaster: half brother to
several winners incl the very smart Royal Heroine: eff over 8/10f, stays 12f well: acts
on any going and on any trk.   24
-- FOGAR [4] (D Murray Smith) 4-8-11 S Cauthen 12/1: -10-3: Made most: has been hurdling:
very lightly raced gelding who first time out in '85 won a stakes event at Lingfield:
stays 12f well: likes to force the pace on a sharpish trk: acts on firm and soft.   15
-- KADESH [7] (F Yardley) 5-7-11 A Proud 25/1: 00024-4: Ev ch in straight: lightly
raced maiden who has been placed on several occasions: eff at 10f, stays 12f: acts on gd/
firm and soft: has been tried in a visor.   01
-- DERRYRING [3] 4-9-4 C Rutter(5) 16/1: 10210-0: Prom, fdd final 1f.   22
-- JANUS [5] 8-8-5 B Rouse 11/1: /0-40-0: Has been hurdling.   03
-- MOON JESTER [8] 6-8-4 D Mckay 6/1: 00040-0: Never nearer.   00
-- BUCKMINSTER BOY [9] 5-7-12 N Carlisle 10/1: -0010-0: Never showed: fit from hurdling.   00
-- NESTOR [1] 6-9-10 J Adams(7) 10/1: 12000-0: Never in it.   00
*4 TIVIAN [11] 6-9-3(vis)(8ex) N Day 5/1: 3010-10: Unsuited by soft? much btr in 4.   00
-- Royal Craftsman [6] 7-8(BL)(1ow)   -- Signorina Odone [2] 8-9
-- Shipwright [13] 8-0
13 ran   10,8,nk,hd,4   (Mrs P A Long)   D Haydn Jones Efailisaf, Glam.

93   KINGSWOOD SELLING H'CAP (0-25) 3YO   £599   7f   Soft 148 -74 Slow   [17]

-- CHEPSTOWED [1] (D Haydn Jones) 3-8-13 John Williams 6/1: 00000-1: 3 b c Welsh Captain -
Kelly Green (Kelly): Nicely bckd when an easy 7L winner of a very slowly run selling h'cap
for 3yos at Warwick Apr.1: no form in '85 but is a half brother to several winners: eff
at 7f on soft ground and a sharp trk.   14
-- JULTOWN LAD [2] (H Beasley) 3-8-13 R Morse(7) 16/1: 40000-2: Al up there, no chance
with winner: eff at 6/7f on gd and soft and a sharp trk.   01
46 AMPLIFY [8] (M Brittain) 3-9-3 K Darley 15/8 FAV: 3020-03: Uneasy fav: never nearer:
eff at 6f on soft and heavy.   00
-- MR JESTER [4] (N Macauley) 3-9-7 Gay Kelleway(5) 12/1: 000-4: Made most 5f: no
form in 3 outings in '85.   00
-- ASHRAF [7] 3-9-3 M Lynch(7) 16/1: 000-0: Early leader.   00
-- THE TENDER MATADOR [6] 3-9-2 P Waldron 9/4: 34010-0: Active in mkt, there halfway.   00
-- ANDERBY [5] 3-9-0 J Ward(7) 8/1: 00400-0: Never showed.   00
7 ran   7,4,4,10,½   (W H Jones)   D Haydn Jones Efailisaf, Glam.

94   E.B.F.COMPTON VERNEY MAIDEN 2YO STAKES   £975   5f   Soft 148 -38 Slow

40   WHISTLING WONDER [3] (M Brittain) 2-9-0 K Darley 2/1 FAV: 21: 2 ch c Whistling Deer -
Divided Loyalties (Balidar): Driven out to lead dist. in a 2yo maiden at Warwick Apr.1:
cheaply acquired colt: eff at 5f on soft ground and a sharp trk.   40
34   HERR FLICK [1] (I Matthews) 2-9-0 N Day 7/1: 02: Led approaching final 1f: impr:
acts on soft and a sharp trk: see 34.   37
34   UNOS PET [5] (K Stone) 2-9-0 Pat Eddery 2/1 Jt.FAV: 33: Hmpd approaching final 1f
and would have fin. much closer: see 34.   32
--   THATCH AVON [7] (A Smith) 2-9-0 S Webster 25/1: 4: Al there on racecourse debut:
half brother to 9f winner Bold Lady.   24
--   ORIOLE DANCER [4] 2-9-0 M L Thomas 14/1: 0: Made most: should do btr: cost 3,300 gns:
bred to stay further.   24
--   GEORGE HARRY [9] 2-9-0 J Reid 5/1: 0: Early speed, fdd.   18
21   Sarasota [6] 9-0   --   Pertain [2] 9-0
8 ran   1,2½,2,hd,2   (Mel Brittain)   M Brittain Warthill, Yorks

95   CASTLE SUITE MAIDEN STAKES 3YO   £684   1m 2f Soft 148 -56 Slow

--   WISHLON [7] (R Smyth) 3-9-0 Pat Eddery 11/2: -1: 3 b c Lyphard's Wish - Swiss Swish
(Wajima): Promising colt: led on bit over 1f out, easily in a 3yo maiden at Warwick Apr.1:
eff at 10f, should stay 12f: acts on soft ground and a sharp trk: should rate more highly.   45
32   OWL CASTLE [8] (M Usher) 3-9-0 A Mcglone 9/2: 0000-32: Led ½way till hdd approaching
final 1f: 20L clear rest: should find a small maiden: seems to like a sharpish track: see 32.   32
--   WELSH CROWN [2] (A Ingham) 3-9-0 J Reid 4/1: -3: Active in mkt: ev ch on racecourse
debut: half brother to smart 7/8f winner Protection and should do btr than this.   07
25   MR WHATS HIS NAME [1] (I Matthews) 3-9-0 N Day 15/8 FAV: 4400-24: Heavily bckd:
lbs below form 25 (gall trk).   07
--   EASTERN PLAYER [3] 3-9-0 C Rutter(5) 33/1: 0000-0: No threat: little form in '85.   00
32   MIGHT MOVE [6] 3-9-0 S Whitworth 10/1: 003-00: Prom 1m: seems unsuited by soft:
rated 46 on final outing last season when 3rd in a 2yo stakes at Lingfield (7.5f firm).   00
--   Cheetak [5] 9-0   --   Swallow Time [4] 9-0
8 ran   4,20,hd,8,5.   (K Abdulla)   R Smyth Epsom, Surrey

ST CLOUD   Friday March 21st

96   GROUP III PRIX EXBURY 4YO+   £18211   1m 2f Soft -

--   NEW TARGET (E Lellouche) 5-9-0 J Breux 1: -20-1: Very useful French colt: unfncd,
but led into straight and held on by a sh nk in Gr.3 Prix Exbury at St Cloud Mar.21: stays
10f and acts on soft ground.   77
--   VERTIGE (P Biancone) 4-8-12 E Legrix 1: 13420-2: First time out, fin well and just
denied: early last season trained by H Cecil to win at Ascot: very eff over 9/10f: acts
on firm and soft.   74
2   STELLA GRANDE (J Chevigny) 4-8-13 F Head 1: 0002-23: Ran on well and just beaten.   75
3 ran   shnk, hd   E Lellouche France

ST CLOUD   Saturday March 29th

97   GROUP III PRIX PENELOPE 3YO FILLIES   £17851   1m 2f Heavy -

--   TERMIENNE (J Gallorini) 3-8-12 D Boeuf   : -41-1: Very promising 3yo filly: 1L
winner of Gr.3 Prix Penelope at St Cloud Mar.29: stays 10f really well and acts on heavy.   76
--   TOP AND LADY (P Biancone) 3-8-12 G Mosse   : ----1-2: Ran well: won sole start
in '85: stays 10f and acts on testing ground.   74
--   RIVER TOWER (D Smaga) 3-8-12 A Lequeux   : -1-43:   71
3 ran   1,1½   (P Faucampre)   J Gallorini

Official Going Given as Heavy

98 GROUP III PRIX DES ORANGIS   £17792   1m   Heavy –

-- VERTIGE (P Biancone) 4-8-12 E Legrix   : 13420-1: 4 b c Lyphards Wish - Valhalla
(New Chapter): Smart colt: responded gamely in the final 1f to get up close home by a nk in
Gr.3 Prix De Ris Orangis at Evry Mar.30: see race 96.   75
-- ETAT MAJOR (B Morettie) 4-8-12 C Asmussen   : -0-02: Led inside final 1f: just
caught: eff at 1m on heavy.   74
-- BLUE TIP (P Biancone) 4-8-11 G Mosse   : -1103-3: Going on fin and btr for this
race: last season won the Gr.3 Prix Penelope: eff at 1m, stays 10½m well: acts well on
heavy ground.   69
3 ran   nk,1½   (D Wildenstein)   P Biancone France

Official Going Given as Soft: No Times Available

99 BANANA RUM MAIDEN STKS 3YO   £968   1m   Soft –

33 MARINA PLATA [7] (D Chapman) 3-8-11 D Nicholls 7/1: 0-01: 3 b f Julio Mariner -
Mar Del Plata (Crowned Prince)): Fit from recent run, chall 2 out, driven out final
1f for a hard earned 1½L win in a 3yo maiden at Hamilton Apr.2: dam won over 1m at 3 years:
acts on soft ground and should get further than 1m.   31
-- LOST OPPORTUNITY [8] (B Hanbury) 3-9-0 G Baxter 13/8 FAV: 4-2: Uneasy fav: led 2
out, ev ch: trained by C Horgan in '85 when 4th at Brighton: cost 24,000 gns as a yearling:
eff at 7f, stays 1m: acts on soft and should find a small maiden.   31
-- MR KEWMILL [4] (M Tompkins) 3-9-0 R Cochrane 9/4: 000-3: Stayed on, never nearer:
well clear of rem: showed some promise as a 2yo when trained by M Pipe: acts on soft,
possibly btr suited by a sounder surface: stays 1m.   30
-- VAN DER PUP [5] (Z Green) 3-9-0 S Keightley 25/1: 000-4: Wknd 3f out: no form in '85.   00
-- BANTEL BEAU [6] 3-9-0 N Carlisle 20/1: 0-0: Made most, fdd: unplcd on sole start in '85   00
-- NORTHERN FLING [3] 3-8-11 G Duffield 12/1: -0: Prom halfway.   00
25 Master Music [2] 9-0   -- Moving Performance [1] 9-0
8 ran   1½,¾,30,15,1   (David W Chapman)   D Chapman Stillington, Yorks

100 BROMISTA RUM HANDICAP 3YO 0-35   £1163   1m 1f Soft –   [37]

14 ELEGANT BILL [3] (T Fairhurst) 3-8-3 M Beecroft 5/2: 0000-01: 3 ch c Nicholas Bill-
Elegant Star (Star Moss): Benefitted from recent run, making ev yd, driven out in a 3yo
h'cap at Hamilton Apr.2: eff at 1m, stays 9f: acts on yld and soft.   21
-- BRAVE AND BOLD [4] (N Callaghan) 3-8-8(bl) R Cochrane 10/11 FAV: 42001-2: Ev ch final
1f: clear 3rd: on final outing in '85 won a nursery h'cap at Edinburgh: eff at 7f, stays
9f: acts on firm and soft and on any trk: best in bl.   25
-- CAROUSEL ROCKET [1] (J Wilson) 3-9-7 G Duffield 10/3: 23033-3: Prom, fdd on seasonal
debut: btr for race: failed to win in '85, though placed on several occasions: eff at 7f
on firm and yld.   26
-- BELHILL [2] (D Chapman) 3-8-0 S P Griffiths(5) 16/1: 00000-4: Fdd quickly 2f out:
best effort in '85 when 4th in a maiden at Nottingham: subs. disapp: half sister to 2
winning platers.   02
4 ran   ½,8,1½   (T E Herring)   T Fairhurst Middleham, Yorks

101 LANGS SUPREME WHISKY H'CAP 3YO+ 0-35   £2194   1m   Soft –   [24]

46 JOHN GILPIN [11] (W Haigh) 4-8-12(bl) R Cochrane 5/1: 4100-21: 4 b c Comedy Star (USA)
Double Grand (Coronation Year): Led inside the final 1f, ridden out in a h'cap at Hamilton
Apr.2: in '85 won an app. selling h'cap at Windsor and a seller at Ayr: eff at 6f, stays
1m: acts on gd and heavy and on any trk.   16
-- PRINCE OBERON [1] (R Allan) 5-8-8(bl) S Webster 14/1: 00000-2: Led over 2f out:
5L clear 3rd: little form in '85: in '84 won at Beverley: eff over 8/10f: acts on firm
and soft.   06
-- QUALITAIRESS [7] (K Stone) 4-8-6(2ow) A Murray 12/1: 43000-3: Chall 2f out: fdd
final 1f: best effort in '85 when 2nd in a h'cap at Carlisle: eff at 6/7f on gd/firm & soft.   00
58 LITTLE NEWINGTON [9] (N Bycroft) 5-8-4 A Shoults 33/1: 0000-04: Little form to date.   00
50 BAMDORO [2] 7-9-6(bl) M Richardson 15/2: 20-0000: Prom 2f out: in '85 won at Catterick
and this same race: eff at 1m, stays 12f well: acts on gd and soft, likes a sharp trk.   04
10 HINCKLEY LANE [5] 4-9-5 M Hindley(3) 2/1 FAV: -000-40: Heavily bckd: btr in 10 (yld).   00
10 SWAY [10] 4-9-6 G Baxter 8/1: 1030-00: Never threatened.   00
*46 JANES BRAVE BOY [6] 4-9-2 D Nicholls 11/2: 0003-10: Mkt drifter: beat winner in 46.   00
-- Barnes Star [3] 9-7   10 My Handsome Boy [8] 9-7
-- High Port [4] 9-0
11 ran   3,5,nk,3,12   (A Barker)   W Haigh Malton, Yorks

102   ZAREVICH VODKA SELLING STAKES 2YO   £736   5f   Soft -

13   TANGDONTPAY [8] (N Tinkler) 2-8-8 J H Brown(5) 15/2: 01: 2 b f Magnolia Lad -
Rocket Star (Roan Rocket): Impr filly: fin well to lead final 1f in a 2yo seller at
Hamilton Apr.2 (sold 2,200 gns): eff at 5f, should stay 6f: acts on soft ground.   21
13   HARRYS COMING [2] (T Fairhurst) 2-8-11 C Coates(5) 11/1: 02: Led over 2f out, just
caught: btr effort from this cheap purchase: eff at 5f on soft: could find a similar event
on a sharper trk.   21
57   MINIZEN LADY [6] (M Brittain) 2-8-8 K Darley 4/1 Jt.FAV: 03: Al there: btr 57.   10
--   BROONS ADDITION [10] (K Stone) 2-8-8 G Brown 33/1: 4: Rank outsider: sn prom.   08
57   MILLIE DUFFER [4] 2-8-8 M Beecroft 11/2: 00: Ev ch: acts on soft.   06
57   VICHY VAL [7] 2-8-8(BL) R Cochrane 5/1: 000: Bl first time: never nearer.   01
57   GAELIC CROSS [9] 2-8-11 S Webster 4/1 Jt.FAV: 00: Fdd: half brother to winning
2yo Eloisey.   00
--   WINNER ALRIGHT [1] 2-8-11 M Fry 10/1: 0: Never in it.   00
13   Middlelane Lad [5] 8-11(BL)   --   Broons Answer [3] 8-8
10 ran   1,3,$\frac{3}{4}$,$\frac{3}{4}$,2   (W Tang)   N Tinkler Malton, Yorks

103   GLENGOYNE MALT WHISKY H'CAP 3YO 0-35   £1660   5f   Soft -   [26]

--   SONNENELLE [1] (J S Wilson) 3-9-0(vis) G Duffield 11/4: 43422-1: 3 b f Sonnen Gold -
Touch Of Dutch (Goldhill): First time out, made ev yd, comfortably in a 3yo h'cap at
Hamilton Apr.2: consistent performer in '85: eff at 5/6f on any ground.   23
--   OUR MUMSIE [2] (N Bycroft) 3-8-9 M Richardson 8/1: 00040-2: Ev ch final 1f: eff
over 5f on soft/heavy: may do btr in selling company.   10
38   MY DERYA [3] (M Tompkins) 3-8-9 R Cochrane 7/4 FAV: 000-003: Again well bckd: never
nearer: early in '85 won a 5f seller at Warwick: eff at 5f on soft/heavy.   08
--   PUNCLE CREAK [4] (G Moore) 3-8-11 S Wood(5) 10/1: 00S00-4: Sn prom, ev ch: eff at
5/6f: likes gd/firm and a sharp track.   03
38   EL ALAMEIN [5] 3-9-7(bl) W Woods(3) 10/3: 1004-00: Prom halfway: in '85 won at
Epsom but little form afterwards: eff at 5f with forcing tactics on a sharpish trk: acts
on gd/firm and soft.   08
5 ran   3,$\frac{3}{4}$,2$\frac{1}{2}$,1$\frac{1}{2}$ (J S Wilson)   J S Wilson Ayr, Scotland

104   TOTTER HOME MAIDEN STAKES 4YO UPWARDS   £1109   1m 3f   Soft -

--   IMPECUNIOSITY [8] (J S Wilson) 4-9-0 D Nicholls 5/1: 30300-1: 4 gr g Free State -
Lydiate (Tower Walk): In good form after a recent hurdles win, led close home under press
in a maiden at Hamilton Apr.2: eff at 11/12f: acts well on soft & heavy.   32
--   REGAL CAPISTRANO [10] (M Prescott) 4-9-0 G Duffield 11/2: 32040-2: Led straight till
close home: 5L clear 3rd: showed some form in '85: stays 12f and acts on firm & soft:
has been tried in bl: officially rated only 14.   31
--   RACING DEMON [3] (F Carr) 4-9-0 S Morris 25/1: 03404-3: Ev ch 2 out: stays 12f
and acts on firm & soft.   23
--   WHAT A LINE [9] (G Reveley) 4-9-0 E Guest(3) 5/1: -2430-4: Dsptd lead over 2f out:
no extra: lightly raced in '85, but showed fair form when 2nd in a h'cap at Kempton when
trained by B Hills: stays 10f and acts on gd/firm and heavy.   21
9   FAVOURITE NEPHEW [4] 5-9-0 R Vickers(7) 25/1: -00: Never nearer: saddle slipped.   18
--   SONNY ONE SHINE [2] 5-9-0 A Shoults(5) 10/3 FAV: -0-0: Fit from hurdling: no threat.   08
8   AL MISK [1] 4-9-0 A Murray 7/2: -00: Led till straight.   00
58   Welsh Guard [6] 9-0   --   Kept On Ice [5] 9-0   --   Jimmy Tarps [7] 9-0
10 ran $\frac{1}{2}$,5,1$\frac{1}{2}$,2$\frac{1}{2}$,8   (David Landa)   J S Wilson Ayr, Scotland

---

Official Going Given as Soft: No Times Available

105   AUCHINRAITH APPR. HANDICAP   0-35   £895   1m 3f   Soft

23   CHRISTMAS HOLLY [2] (G Reveley) 5-8-7 G Craggs(3) 7/1: /000-31: 5 b g Blind Harbour -
Holly Doon (Doon): Finally lost his maiden tag, ran on well to lead inside final 1f,
comfortably in an app h'cap at Hamilton Apr.3: placed on several occasions previously over
hurdles: eff at 11/12f: acts on soft ground.   10
--   STARS DELIGHT [5] (F Carr) 4-8-7 J Quinn 9/2: 00030-2: Led approaching final 1f:
fit from a recent hurdles win: fair form as a 2yo: stays 11f: likes soft/heavy and a
sharpish track.   06
--   MR LION [7] (F Carr) 4-8-6 J Carr 14/1: 00000-3: Ev ch final 1f: no form in '85:
winning juvenile on this track: stays 11f and acts on yld.   05
--   SULTAN ZAMAN [10] (J Wilson) 5-9-0 E Turner 14/1: /0004-4: Made most: clr rest: fit
from hurdling: lightly raced on Flat: acts on soft.   11
*36   BALGOWNIE [8] 6-9-1(5ex) M Richardson 11/4 FAV: 042-110: Disapp run: btr 36 (10f).   02

43

4   DICK KNIGHT [6] 5-9-7 L Ford(3) 7/2: 1000-00: Never nearer: in '85 won h'caps at
Warwick and Hamilton (app.): eff over 11/12f: acts on firm & soft and on any trk.   02
--   MUSICAL WILL [3] 4-9-3 M Taylor(3) 8/1: /0210-0: There 1m.   00
--   Rural Scene [1] 8-12   28   Taxinette [4] 8-6   36   Sherpaman [9] 8-7
10 ran   2½,hd,1½,10,6.   (R S Wood)   G Reveley Lingdale, Cleveland

106   HOLYTOWN MAIDEN STAKES 3YO+   £836   1m 1f   Soft .

--   FORCELLO [8] (S Norton) 3-8-3 J Lowe 4/6 FAV: 40342-1: 3 b c Forli - Heavenly Bow
(Gun Bow): Had a simple task and made ev yd in a canter to win a 3yo maiden at Hamilton Apr.3
placed several times in '85: eff at 7-9f on gd and soft ground.   26
--   BANTEL BUSHY [9] (I Bell) 3-8-3 N Carlisle 14/1: 000-2: Al prom: no chance with
winner: lightly raced and no form in '85: eff at 9f on soft.   10
41   POCO LOCO [5] (A Davison) 4-9-7 G Baxter 8/1: 0-03: Ev ch: has been hurdling: very
lightly raced on the Flat.   02
41   GRAND CELEBRATION [4] (W Storey) 4-9-7 S Whitworth 13/2: -0-04: There 1m: little form.00
--   PHILLY ATHLETIC [2] 4-9-4 N Connorton 8/1: 00-0: Fit from hurdling, fdd straight.   00
--   ACKAS BOY [3] 4-9-7 S Keightley 10/1: -0: Wknd in straight.   00
--   Pretty Amazing [7] 9-7   --   Golden Boy [6] 9-7
8 ran   10,8,3,4,5   (BTRBplc)   S Norton High Hoyland, Sth Yorks

107   QUARRY SELLING H'CAP (0-25) 3 & 4YO   £681   1m   Soft .   [9]

--   BANTEL BOWLER [1] (I Bell) 3-8-11 J Quinn(7) 6/1: 44400-1: 3 ch g Beverley Boy -
Cutler Heights (Galivanter): Mkt drifter, but led well over 1f out for a simple 12L win in
a 3 & 4yo selling h'cap at Hamilton Apr.3 (sold 2,900 gns): placed in similar events in
'85: eff at 7f/1m on gd/firm & soft.   20
22   SWEET GEMMA [5] (N Tinkler) 4-9-10 J Brown(5) 7/2: 0-40-02: Sn prom: fdd final 1f:
lightly raced and little form on the Flat.   00
41   MARTELLA [6] (M Brittain) 4-9-5 K Darley 7/1: 0000-03: Clear ldr till well over
1f out: no form in '85: may prefer a sharper track.   00
--   CONERSER [3] (J Berry) 3-9-0 M Fry 3/1 FAV: 00000-4: Wknd well over 2f out: best
effort in '85 when 6th in a maiden at Edinburgh (1m good).   00
58   JALOME [4] 4-9-8 D Nicholls 4/1: 0000-00: Al behind.   00
--   GILLANBONE [2] 4-9-9 J Hills(5) 6/1: 30004-0: Btn a distance.   00
6 ran   12,8,5,7,dist   (Bantel Ltd)   I Bell Hawick, Scotland

108   E.B.F. CAMPSIE MAIDEN STAKES 2YO   £880   5f   Soft .

3   PANBOY [5] (T Fairhurst) 2-9-0 C Coates(5) 7/2: 31: 2 br c Sparkling Boy - Pakpao
(Mansingh): Impr colt: led final 1f, ridden out in a 2yo maiden at Hamilton Apr.3: speedily
bred sort who should stay 6f: acts on good and soft: half brother to winning 2yo Pandan.   42
40   SEATON GIRL [4] (D Barron) 2-8-11 S Webster 13/2: 42: Prom all the way: impr:
should stay further: acts on yld and soft.   34
--   SCOTTISH FLING [10] (J Wilson) 2-9-0 E Turner(7) 14/1: 3: Mkt drifter on debut:
led after 2f till over 1f out: half brother to 3 winners and should impr: acts on soft.   34
--   AREA CODE [2] (G Reveley) 2-9-0 E Guest(3) 16/1: 4: Lightly bckd: kept on well,
showing promise: will do btr over longer distances: acts on soft.   33
40   BANTEL BLAZER [1] 2-9-0 N Carlisle 8/1: 30: Led over 2f: btr in 40 (sharp, yld).   28
-43   LATERAL [7] 2-9-0 M Fry 5/2 FAV: 20: Never in it: much btr 43 (yld).   26
--   U BIX COPY [8] 2-9-0 C Dwyer 10/1: 0: Never nearer 7th: half brother to 2 winners
and should improve.   00
--   GEOBRITONY [9] 2-9-0 G Duffield 6/1: 0: Never showed: half brother to a winning 2yo:
bred to stay much further.   00
21   Quick Sticks [12] 8-11   --   Minizen Lad [6] 9-0
--   Megs Money [11] 8-11
11 ran   2,1½,½,2½,¾   (C D Barber-Lomax)   T Fairhurst Middleham, Yorks

109   DECHMONT MAIDEN STAKES 3YO   £778   6f   Soft .

--   TARANGA [6] (M Tompkins) 3-9-0 R Cochrane 5/4 FAV: 43002-1: 3 b g Music Boy -
Emblazon (Wolver Holow): Useful gelding: gained a deserved success, led 3f for an easy 6L
win in a 3yo maiden at Hamilton Apr.3: most unlucky not to win last season, running well on
all his starts: eff at 6f on firm and soft: no track preferences and should win more races. 48
--   RAAS [1] (S Norton) 3-9-0 J Lowe 3/1: 0-2: Not pace of winner, but 15L clear 3rd:
good seasonal debut: unplaced on sole start in '85: cost 100,000 gns and is closely related
to the smart Petorius: looks sure to find a small maiden: eff at 6f on soft.   32
39   GLORIANT [4] (M Brittain) 3-9-0 K Darley 16/1: 0040-03: Never nearer: little form
in '85: eff at 6f on soft.   00
14   DEARHAM BRIDGE [7] (D Moffatt) 3-9-0 C Dwyer 20/1: 000-04: Never in it: no form in '8500
16   FALINE [8] 3-8-11 Paul Eddery 7/2: -30: Mkt drifter and no show: much btr 16 (7f). 00
--   BANTEL BANZAI [5] 3-9-0(bl) N Carlisle 33/1: 00-0: Outsider, there ½way: no form
in 2 outings in '85.   00

44

-- **ADHARI** [2] 3-8-11(BL) G Baxter 10/1: -0: Bl debutant: mkt drifter, fin 7th: half
brother to very useful sprinter Time Machine and should do btr than this.   00
16 **Petencore** [3] 9-0
8 ran   6,15,3,3,2   (Stanley Squires)   M Tompkins Newmarket

110 MIDDLEWARD HANDICAP (0-35) 3YO+   £1623   6f   Soft .   [33]

-- **IDLE TIMES** [7] (C Elsey) 4-8-4 J Lowe 10/1: 04200-1: 4 b f Faraway Times - Ibolya
Princess (Crowned Prince): First time out, led over 1f out, soon clear in a h'cap at Hamilton
Apr.3: winning 2yo at Yarmouth: eff at 5/6f on gd/firm and soft.   20
-- **SHANOUSKA** [2] (J Harris) 6-7-9 A Mackay 10/1: 0/400-2: First time out, made most:
last won in '83 at Salisbury and has been lightly raced: eff at 6f on soft and heavy.   01
-- **VIA SATELLITE** [1] (R Simpson) 4-8-5 S Whitworth 5/1: 23440-3: Al there: early in
'85 showed fair form when 2nd at Bath and Haydock, but has been disapp since and has
tumbled down the h'cap: eff at 5/6f: seems best on good/firm.   10
42 **BAY BAZAAR** [5] (M W Easterby) 4-9-6 M Hindley(3) 5/1: 022-024: Below form of 42 (yld). 20
46 **YELLOW BEAR** [4] 4-8-6 T Parkes(7) 8/1: 0001-00: No show after slow start: has been
hurdling: on final start in '85 won a seller at h'cap on this trk: earlier won a seller at
Leicester: eff at 6f, stays further: acts on good and heavy.   00
12 **BUBS BOY** [3] 4-8-12 E Guest(3) 4/1 : 0011-00: Early speed.   00
-- **MARY MAGUIRE** [6] 9-10-0 D Nicholls 8/1: 20100-0: Never dngr: btr for race.   00
-- **FLOMEGAS DAY** [9] 4-9-4(bl) J Hills(5) 6/1: 10000-0: Last to finish.   00
-- **Trade High** [8] 8-13   -- **Pentoff** [8] 4-8-10
10 ran   5,nk,3,8,10,2   (C W C Elsey)   C Elsey Malton, Yorks

---

Official Going Given as Good/Soft (Straight): Heavy (Round Course).

111 OXTED STAKES (3-Y-O)   £959   6f   Soft 124 +07 Fast

-- **PLATINE** [4] (R Simpson) 3-8-11 K Radcliffe(7) 20/1: 00-1: 3 gr f Rarity - El Diana
(Tarboosh)   : Active in mkt on seasonal debut and made most on the far side in a fast
run 3yo stakes at Lingfield Apr.5: unplaced in both his starts last season: clearly well
suited by 6f on soft ground: acts on an undulating track: should win more races.   42
*38 **COPPERMILL LAD** [8] (L Holt) 3-9-5(5ex) Angela Frampton(7) 12/1: 3000-12: Veered badly dist:
ran on well again and just held: in fine form at present: eff over 5/6f: officially rated
only 14 and should win again in h'cap company: see 38.   46
+62 **LOFT BOY** [2] (N Vigors) 3-9-5(5ex) S Dawson(3) 11/10 FAV: 030-13: Well bckd, al close
up and fin. clear of rem: in good form: see 62.   44
31 **DALSAAN BAY** [10] (Pat Mitchell) 3-9-0 J Reid 14/1: 00-04: Lost touch dist: however
this was an impr effort: eff over 6f on soft ground: acts on an undulating trk.   25
+83 **HEART OF GLASS** [3] 3-9-5(5ex) M Hills 5/1: 4-10: Rather disapp after fast time win in 83 26
-- **RAYHAAN** [15] 3-8-11 B Rouse 6/1: -0: Mkt drifter on racecourse debut: close up over
½way and is expected to impr on this effort next time: well bred filly who cost I.R.
250,000 gns as a yearling: should be well suited by sprint distances: acts on soft ground.   17
-- **HACHIMITSU** [5] 3-8-11 M Wigham 33/1: 00-0: Unfncd on reappearance: made eye catching
late progress and should do btr next time: lightly raced last season: eff over 6f on soft
ground: acts on a sharpish track.   00
-- **Count Almaviva** [11] 9-0   74 **Hooray Hamilton** [12] 9-0
-- **Rebello Imp** [16] 9-0   33 **Harmony Bowl** [6] 9-0   -- **Tuneful Lass** [14] 8-11
-- **Valvinora** [7] 9-0   -- **Bellepheron** [1] 9-0   -- **Sunset Dancer** [9] 8-11
-- **First Orbit** [13] 9-0
16 ran   1,½,6,1½,½,hd   (Gordian Troeller Bloodstock Ltd)   R Simpson Upper Lambourn

112 APRIL STAKES (H'CAP) (0-35) 4YO+   £2348   7f   Soft 124 +01 Fast   [35]

-- **KING OF SPEED** [9] (B Wise) 7-8-8 B Rouse 10/1: 20300-1: 7 b h Blue Cashmere -
Celeste (Sing Sing): First time out, fin strongly to lead close home in quite a fast run
h'cap at Lingfield Apr.5: consistent performer last season, won a h'cap at Brighton and was
also placed on many occasions: ran well on reappearance last term and does well when fresh:
seems best over 7f though does stay 10f: acts on firm and soft ground and is well suited by
a sharp, undulating trk.   26
-71 **READY WIT** [5] (R Hannon) 5-9-8 S Cauthen 10/3 FAV: 1000-22: Nicely bckd: ran on
strongly, just btn: in good form and should go one btr soon: see 71.   39
10 **REPEALED** [6] (W Hastings Bass) 4-8-13 R Lines(3) 7/1: 0-03232: Led below dist, just
caught and ddhtd for 2nd: in fine form at present and he should lose his maiden tag sn: see 10   30
-- **EVERY EFFORT** [14] (R Holder) 4-9-4 J Reid 20/1: 01000-4: Stayed on well on reappearance:
last season made most when successful in a maiden at Edinburgh: eff at 7/8f: acts on firm
and soft ground and is well suited by a sharpish trk.   33
-- **SINGLE** [12] 4-8-11 D Eddery(7) 20/1: 00020-0: Bckd at long odds on reappearance:
led ½way, not btn far: quite consistent last season when winning at Bath and Newbury: well
suited by 1m: acts on firm though possibly btr on good or heavy ground: acts on any trk
though favours a gall one.   21

17   RUNNING FLUSH [15] 4-10-0 P Cook 11/2: 4040-00: Ran well: useful colt who was in
good form early last season, when successful twice in h'caps at Lingfield: eff over 7/8f and
stays 10f really well: acts on fast & heavy ground: well suited by this sharp undulating trk.   38
10   SWIFT PALM [2] 9-9-3 G Duffield 9/1: 4330-00: First time out winner of an app. h'cap
at Doncaster last season and is a useful h'capper on his day: in '84 won twice: eff over
7/8f and stays 10f well: acts on firm & soft ground.   00
--   PANDI CLUB [17] 4-8-7 P Waldron 10/1: 00000-0: Easy to back: led briefly after ½way.   00
--   High Pitched [10] 9-5   --   Peanday [7] 8-13   --   Irish Cookie [4] 9-2
--   Dolly [11] 9-2   --   Mels Choice [16] 9-3 --   Abloom [3] 9-8
--   Crown Counsel [8] 8-4   --   Golden Slade [13] 9-4 -- Westerham [1] 9-3
17 ran   hd,ddht,1,3,hd   (John Wilberforce)   B Wise Polegate, Sussex

113 NUTLEY SELLING STAKES (3-Y-O)   £841   7f   Soft 124 -40 Slow

31   MATELOT ROYALE [1] (A Davison) 3-9-0 J Reid 10/1: 0-01: 3 b g Le Dauphin - Starboard Belle (Right Tack): Dropped to selling company and was nicely bckd when leading inside
dist, comfortably in a 3yo seller at Lingfield Apr.5 (no bid): lightly raced colt who is
clearly suited by 7/8f on soft ground: acts on an undulating trk: half sister to the useful
staying hurdler Micks Star.   22
--   BANDYANN [2] (P Mitchell) 3-8-11 A Clark 6/1: 00-2: Active in mkt on reappearance:
went on ½way and was soon clear, though caught close home: lightly raced last season: suited
by 7/8f on soft grund: should win a similar race.   15
51   MY CUP OF TEA [8] (P Haslam) 3-8-11 J Scally(7) 20/1: 0-03: Mkt drifter: late prog:
should be suited by a longer trip or a more gall trk: acts on soft ground.   08
67   OSCAR DE SOUSA [6] (P Haslam) 3-9-0(BL) T Williams 11/2: -004: Dropped in class and
bl first time: wandered under press and no threat: half sister to several winners and should
do better than this.   00
--   THAI SKY [5] 3-8-11 R Cochrane 11/2: 03440-0: Should do btr next time.   00
--   ODERVY [7] 3-9-0 P Waldron 20/1: 00000-0: Easy to back on reappearance: no threat.   00
--   JADE ESSENCE [4] 3-8-11 G Sexton 7/1: 000-0: Lost place ½way on reappearance.   00
51   COMICAL LAD [9] 3-9-0(BL) P Bloomfield 10/1: 0-00: Bl first time: mkt drifter and
btn halfway.   00
--   DYNAMIC BABY [10] 3-8-11 R Curant 7/2 FAV: 00000-0: Well bckd on seasonal debut:
led till ½way: previously had shown enough in btr company to suggest a seller should not
be beyond her: eff over 5f on firm and soft grund: has been tried in bl.   00
31   PASSOONER [3] 3-9-0 B Rouse 7/1: 0P-00: Dropped in class: lost place ½way.   00
10 ran   2½,7,5,2½,shhd.   (Miss Lynne Ennis)   A Davison Caterham, Surrey

114 NEW FLAT HANDICAP STAKES (0-35) 3YO+   £1604   6f   Soft 124 -06 Slow   [35]

76   WILL GEORGE [8] (C Horgan) 7-10-3(7ex) P Cook 2/1 FAV: 003-131: 7 gr g Abwah -
Grey Miss (Grey Sovereign): Useful sprint h'capper: comfortably defied top weight when making
most in a h'cap at Lingfield Apr.5: began the season with a ready win in a similar event at
Doncaster: last season won a h'cap at Newbury and the previous season won at Lingfield and
Windsor: very eff over 5/6f: acts on gd and soft ground and on any trk: genuine and
consistent sort who carries weight well.   48
31   BLACK SPOUT [3] (H O'neill) 5-7-7 S Dawson(1) 11/2: 0000-32: Ev ch: flattered in 31.   00
--   EXERT [6] (R Akehurst) 4-8-10 N Adams 7/1: 04400-3: Stayed on again late on reappearance and should do better next time: gained his first win in a h'cap at Brighton last
season: eff over 6/7f: acts on firm & soft ground & is well suited by a sharp undulating trk.   12
30   THATCHVILLE [8] (I Matthews) 4-9-2(19oh) W Woods(3) 7/1: 4040-04: Ev ch after a tardy
start: a comfortable winner of a h'cap at Catterick last season: eff over 6f, stays 1m:
acts on good/firm ground though best form on easier surface: acts on any trk though
probably best on a sharp one.   16
30   MANGO MAN [2] 5-8-4(bl)(4ow) R Cochrane 3/1: 0000-30: Denied a clear run: btr in 30(5f).02
--   JAMES DE COOMBE [4] 4-8-5 P Waldron 9/1: 00230-0: Mkt drifter on reappearance: btr
for race: remains a maiden though only just denied in a selling h'cap at Windsor last season
and should find a small race this year: eff over 6f on firm & soft ground : suited by a
sharp track.   00
10   Henrys Place [7] 8-7(bl)   76   Miletrians Lass [5] 7-8(BL)
8 ran   4,2,1,1,2   (Robert Scott)   C Horgan Billingbear, Berks

115 WESTERHAM STAKES (2-Y-O)   £959   5f   Soft 124 -01 Slow

+34   SIZZLING MELODY [3] (Lord J Fitzgerald) 2-9-3 R Hills 10/11 FAV: 11: 2 br c Song -
Mrs Bacon (Balliol): Very promising juvenile: heavily bckd and again showed a smart turn
of foot to win a 2yo stakes at Lingfield Apr.5: on racecourse debut was a ready winner of a
maiden at Leicester: cost 14,000 gns: very eff over the minimum trip and looks sure to
stay further: acts on soft ground and seems to act on any trk: well regarded and should
complete the hat trick.   64
*27   MISTER COLIN [1] (R Hannon) 2-9-3 L Jones(5) 9/2: 12: Led briefly below dist: no
chance with easy winner though beat the rem decisively and looks a promising sort: acts on
a sharpish trk: should win again soon: see 27.   53
*61   PENSURCHIN [6] (D Elsworth) 2-9-3 A Mcglone 10/3: 13: Outpcd inside dist: possibly
flattered in 61.   43

-- HONEY PLUM [7] (M Usher) 2-8-8 M Wigham 16/1: 4: Made most on racecourse debut: promising effort: cost 8,400 gns as a yearling: evidently possesses plenty of pace: probably will do better on less testing ground: acts on a sharp trk.   30
-- CABALLINE [5] 2-8-11 P Cook 33/1: 0: Unfancied on racecourse debut: no threat: cheaply acquired colt.   23
-- MUKHABBR [2] 2-8-11 B Rouse 12/1: 0: No real threat after a slow start: should impr.   11
-- Jans Decision [4] 8-11
7 ran   6,4,2,5,6   (Mrs Mary Watt)   Lord J Fitzgerald Newmarket

116 EAST GRINSTEAD STAKES (3-Y-O)   £1722   1m 2f Soft 124 -74 Slow

-- ONISKY [3] (P Cole) 3-9-7 T Quinn 2/1: 410-1: 3 b c Niniski (USA) - Orma (Double Jump): Useful colt: first time out, led early and again ½way for a comfortable win in a slowly run 3yo stakes at Lingfield Apr.5: lightly raced last season when winning a maiden at Brighton (1m, firm): clearly stays 12f well: acts on firm and soft ground and is well suited by a sharp, undulating trk.   54
-- SOLVENT [4] (M Jarvis) 3-9-0 T Ives 8/11 FAV: 4-2: Heavily bckd on reappearance: soon led though hdd ½way and although clear of rem could not reach winner: was a promising 4th to Mashkour in a valuable race at Goodwood on sole start last year: half brother to several winners: eff over 8/12f: acts on good/firm and soft ground and on a sharp, undulating track: sure to find a race in time.   44
*25 PRINCE MERANDI [1] (M Francis) 3-9-7 Paul Eddery 5/1: 0-13: No chance with principals: see 25 (10f).   28
-- SONG AN DANCE MAN [2] (M Mccourt) 3-9-7 R Wernham 16/1: 10000-4: Outsider: al last and btn a long way: won a small race in Ireland last season (1m, good/firm).   00
4 ran   1½,15,dist.   (Fahd Salman)   P Cole Whatcombe, Oxon

117 WEARE HANDICAP STAKES (0-35) 3YO   £1668   1m 2f Soft 124 -88 Slow   [37]

-- FEDRA [2] (Lord J Fitzgerald) 3-9-0 R Hills 25/1: 0000-1: 3 b f Grundy - Zebra Grass (Rum The Gantlet): Active in mkt on reappearance, denied a clear run though quickened well to lead close home in a slowly run 3yo h'cap at Lingfield Apr.5: unplaced in all her starts last season though did show some promise in fair company: stoutly bred filly who cost 41,000 gns: stays 10f well and should be suited by further: acts on firm and soft ground and on any trk.   32
67 FLYING FLYNN [4] (N Callaghan) 3-8-9 G Carter(5) 7/4 FAV: 321-22: Gambled on: fin strongly, though just too late: stays 10f well: in good form and should get her head in front soon: see 67.   25
-- STILLOU [9] (P Mitchell) 3-8-8 T Williams 7/2: 04104-3: Ran well on reappearance: showed some fair form last season, though her win came in selling company at Redcar: eff over 7/8f and stays 10f: acts on firm and soft ground and on any trk: btr for race.   21
95 OWL CASTLE [3] (M Usher) 3-9-7 A Mcglone 5/1: 000-324: Easy to back: led early and again ½way: consistent: see 32.   32
-- ITTIHAAD [1] 3-9-7 B Rouse 14/1: 000-0: Led briefly below dist. though lack of fitness soon told: lightly raced last season: should be well suited by middle distances: acts on soft ground and on an undulating trk.   31
63 UP TO UNCLE [6] 3-9-3 R Wernham 9/2: 2444-00: Btr effort: showed some fair form in nurseries last season, after winning a seller at Brighton: eff over 8/10f and should stay further: acts on gd/firm & soft grund and is well suited by a sharpish trk: consistent.   26
-- Priok [8] 8-4   -- Trelawney [5] 8-13   -- Walcisin [7] 8-13
9 ran   ¾,1½,1½,nk,¾   (Mrs H GCambanis)   Lord J Fitzgerald Newmarket

---

Official Going Given as Heavy. All races started by flag

118 HOTHFIELD 2YO STAKES   £684   5f   Heavy 189 -01 Slow

-- MISS SUNDAY SPORT [10] (P Kelleway) 2-8-8 P Cook 5/1: 1: 2 b f Sharpo - High Move (High Top): Promising filly: nicely bckd on debut and made virtually ev yd on the favoured far side for a decisive win in a 2yo stakes at Folkestone Apr.7: speedily bred juvenile who clearly handles heavy ground well: likely to stay further than this minimum trip: acts on a sharp trk: should win again.   52
73 ROYAL RABBLE [11] (D Elsworth) 2-8-8 A Mcglone 10/1: 02: Easy to back: stayed on though no threat to winner: half sister to several winners, incl 10f winner Tinoco: eff over 5f on heavy ground and should stay further: acts on a sharpish trk: improving.   33
20 HAZELS GIRL [4] (A Madwar) 2-8-8 M Miller 7/4 FAV: 23: Gambled on: led stands side though no chance with first 2 inside dist: cost only 660 gns as a yearling: acts on a testing surface & on any trk: best in 20.   31
115 MISTER COLIN [5] (R Hannon) 2-9-2 L Jones(5) 9/4: 124: Quick reappearance: ev ch though btr on less testing ground in 115: see 27.   38

FOLKESTONE   Monday April 7th   - Cont'd

•94   WHISTLING WONDER [2] 2-9-2 B Thomson 7/1: 210: Al front rank stands side: acts on
heavy: see 94.   38
--   **PARKLANDS BELLE** [3] 2-8-8 J Reid 33/1: 0: Unfncd on racecourse debut: close up till
below dist and should impr for this experience: acts on heavy ground and on a sharpish trk.   29
--   **MASTER DRUMMER** [7] 2-8-11 R P Elliott 12/1: 0: Bckd at long odds on debut though al last
                                                                                                      00
--   Pilgrim Prince [1] 8-11   27   Midday Sanito [8] 8-11
--   Minobee [9] 8-8   --   Telegraph Folly [6] 8-11
11 ran   8,1,hd,shhd,nk   (Roldvale Ltd)   P Kelleway Newmarket

119 FAVERSHAM SELLING HCAP STAKES 0-25   £704   1m 1f Heavy 189 +11 Fast   [21]

--   **TOPORI** [6] (S Woodman) 7-8-7 P Cook 16/1: 40000/1: 7 br g High Top - Lady Oriana
(Tudor Melody): Fit from hurdling, led 4f out and stayed on well to win a fast run selling
h'cap at Folkestone Apr.7 (no bid): no worthwhile form on the Flat for sometime and last
won in '82 at Epsom: eff over 8/10f, stays 12f: seems to act on any going and is well suited
by a sharp trk.   08
--   **MEZIARA** [5] (A Ingham) 5-9-7(bl) J Reid 11/4 FAV: 00420-2: Well bckd on reappearance:
stayed on under press: failed to win last season though in '84 won at Brighton and Yarmouth:
also a winner over hurdles: eff over 10/12f: acts on good & heavy ground and is suited by
forcing tactics: wears bl.   17
--   **GAMBART** [1] (B Stevens) 4-9-10(VIS) R Carter(5) 10/1: 40000-3: Easy to back on
seasonal debut: remains a maiden: quite lightly raced last season and showed his best form
over 10f on good/firm ground: also acts on heavy: half brother to several winners.   12
28   **TAME DUCHESS** [13] (A Moore) 4-9-0 D Brown 16/1: 0040-04: Has shown only modest form
to date: eff over 6/7f and probably stays 10f: suited by some give in the ground.   01
--   **SHALLAAL** [3] 7-8-13(bl) R Guest 12/1: 03300/0: Mkt drifter: has been hurdling.   00
--   **PAMELA HEANEY** [15] 4-9-4 D Mckay 5/1: 00030-0: No real threat on reappearance.   03
28   **BLAIRS WINNIE** [8] 4-8-7 M Miller 6/1: 0000-40: Mkt drifter: unsuited by ground: see 28.   00
36   **MR MUSIC MAN** [14] 12-9-7 S Whitworth 5/1: 2400-00: Easy to back: never dangerous.   00
--   **UNIT TENT** [11] 8-8-11 G Sexton 7/1: 00314-0: Has changed stables: needed this race.   00
28   Greatest Hits [4] 9-1(bl)   --   Maiden Bidder [2] 8-12
--   CalisoJon [9] 8-7   --   Liberty Walk [7] 8-11
13 ran   3,6,½,2,shhd   (John Pegley)   S Woodman East Lavant, Sussex

120 WESTENHANGER HOUSE HCAP STKS 3YO 0-35   £1220   1m 2f Heavy 189 -05 Slow   [37]

63   **STRAIGHT THROUGH** [12] (J Winter) 3-8-12 B Rouse 13/8 FAV: 0024-21: 3 br g Pitskelly -
Queen Of Time (Charlottown): Nicely bckd when a comfortable winner of a 3yo h'cap at
Folkestone Apr.7: led early and again over 3f out: placed a couple of times last season
though this was his first win: eff over 8/10f: acts on gd and heavy ground & runs well on
a sharpish trk: half brother to several winners: was tried in a visor last season.   32
•29 **THE WOODEN HUT** [9] (R Voorspuy) 3-8-0 D Brown 13/2: 0430-12: In good form: acts on
heavy: see 29.   09
--   **VANTASTIC** [10] (B Stevens) 3-7-8 G Carter(1) 20/1: 000-3: Stayed on well on seasonal
debut: behind in his 3 starts last season: evidently stays 10f and acts on heavy ground:
acts on a sharpish trk.   00
53   **KEEP COOL** [2] (P Kelleway) 3-9-7 P Cook 10/1: 003-34: Ev ch: stays 10f on heavy ground.   20
29   **HELENS PLEASURE** [7] 3-9-6 W Woods(3) 13/2: 4404-30: Mkt drifter: much btr over 12f
here in 29 (soft).   00
--   **REFORM PRINCESS** [4] 3-9-2 M Giles 14/1: 32000-0: Easy to back on reappearance:no threat. 00
--   **PARKIES BAR** [11] 3-8-13 J Matthias 8/1: 00100-0: Active in mkt on seasonal debut:
better for race: last season won twice at Lingfield, after a maiden success at Leicester:
half brother to several winners: eff over 5/7f and should stay further: best form on soft/
heavy ground though does act on good.   00
--   **ALL A DREAM** [3] 3-8-11 M Wigham 13/2: 04000-0: Well bckd: no extra straight.   00
--   **PASSION PLAY** [8] 3-8-6 T Williams 7/1: 003-0: Fin last on seasonal debut.   00
--   Fic Vic [6] 7-(1oh)   --   Angel Drummer [5] 8-4
11 ran   7,5,3,25,nk   (J A Prenn)   J Winter Newmarket

121 WHITSTABLE HANDICAP 4YO UPWARDS 0-35   £1335   1m 7f Heavy 189 -15 Slow   [35]

--   **BRIGADIER JACQUES** [3] (C Austin) 5-8-2(2ow) A Clark 12/1: 02210-1: 5 b g Brigadier Gerard -
Statuesque (Djakao): First time out, led after ½way and stayed on well to win a h'cap at
Folkestone Apr.7: won a seller at Edinburgh at the back end of last season: eff over 12f and
stays 2m: acts on gd/firm and heavy ground and on any trk: sometimes bl.   18
-19 **ARTESIUM** [9] (R Johnson Houghton) 4-9-3 J Reid 7/1: 34-0022: Stayed on well: in gd
form: acts on heavy ground and on any trk: see 19.   29
--   **CHARTFIELD** [6] (B Sanders) 6-7-8 L Riggio(7) 20/1: 00000/3: Led briefly before ½way:
fit from hurdling though last ran on the Flat in '84, though showed no worthwhile form: stays
15f well: acts on heavy ground and a sharpish trk.   05
23   **GWYN HOWARD** [5] (A Pitt) 4-8-10 R Mcghin 4/1 Jt FAV: 0000-04: Well bckd: fin clear
of rem: half brother to useful 8/10f winner Silver Season: probably stays 15f: seems to
act on any going.   20

48

58a SHINY COPPER [14] 8-8-10 D Brown 4/1 Jt FAV: 0000-00: Well behind ½way, fin well:
began last season with h'cap wins at Lingfield and Folkestone though subsq. was disapp:
stays well: best with plenty of give in the ground.   08
28   HOT BETTY [4] 5-8-10(4ow) R Guest 12/1: 1000-30: Easy to back: see 28.   00
--   PATRALAN [1] 4-8-9 M Wigham 8/1: 10000-0: Likely to do btr next time.   00
--   COLLISTO [2] 5-9-2 S Whitworth 5/1: 03010-0: Well bckd on reappearance: lost place ½way. 00
85   DOWN FLIGHT [8] 6-9-12(BL) W Woods(3) 13/2: 0000-40: Bl first time: btr on soft in 85. 00
--   Keeley Louise [13] 7-8   -- The Betsy [11] 7-8
23 Jonix [15] 8-7   -- Rika Mia [7] 7-8   -- Divine Truth [10] 7-9
-- Lord Butch [12] 8-9
15 ran   2½,nk,¾,12,7   (A J Richards)   C Austin Wokingham, Berks

122 LYMINGE APP.H'CAP 3YO+ 0-35   £751   6f   Heavy 189 -64 Slow   [28]

--   ANOTHER BING [3] (A Moore) 4-8-0 L Riggio 20/1: 00400-1: 4 b g Crooner - Swing Gently
(Swing Easy): Rank outsider though led below dist and ran on well to win a slowly run app.
h'cap at Folkestone Apr.7: first success: little form last season and was btn in selling
company: well suited by 5/6f: acts on firm & heavy ground and is well suited by a sharpish trk 10
30   BELLE TOWER [7] (R Smyth) 4-9-7 A Cole 7/2: 0000-02: Stayed on well: clear of rem:
last season made all in a h'cap at Folkestone: eff over 6/7f: acts on any going and is well
suited by this sharpish trk.   26
30   HOKUSAN [1] (K Ivory) 4-8-13 G Mash 4/1: 0001-03: Btr effort: modest h'capper who
is eff over 5/6f on good and heavy ground: suited by a sharpish course.   10
--   SPARKFORD LAD [2] (D Elsworth) 4-9-10(bl) Debra Wheatley(5) 11/2: 40003-4: Remains a
maiden: eff over 5/6f though possibly btr suited by 7f: seems to act on any going btr for race 18
30   RUSSELL FLYER [9] 4-9-7(bl) L Johnsey 6/1: 0420-00: Never dngr on seasonal debut. 07
--   MUSIC MACHINE [5] 5-9-13 J Scally 5/2 FAV: 04010-0: Quickly away, clear ldr over
½way: had a tough task under top weight on this testing ground and should do btr next time
on a sounder surface   08
--   LEAP YEAR [8] 4-9-3 Sharon Greenway(5) 8/1: /0000-0: Active in mkt though sn behind. 00
7 ran   2½,5,1½,4,3   (Miss Beryl M Patching)   A Moore Woodingdean, Sussex

123 CHILHAM FILLIES STAKES 3YO   £684   1m 4f Heavy 189 -39 Slow

--   BRIDE [2] (R Boss) 3-8-11 M Miller 7/1: 00-1: 3 ch f Remainder Man - Rebid (Jimmy
Reppin): First time out, led over 2f out for a comfortable win in a 3yo fillies stakes at
Folkestone Apr.7: lightly raced last season though did show some promise and is likely to
impr further: half sister to middle dist. winner Call Again: stays 12f well: acts on firm
and heavy ground and on any trk.   37
45   SAY SOMETHING [7] (J Winter) 3-8-11 J Reid 6/4 FAV: 000-22: Weighted most: acts on
heavy: see 45.   30
--   WRANGBROOK [1] (W Jarvis) 3-8-11 B Thomson 10/1: 0-3: Al front rank on reappearance:
slowly away when unplaced on her only start last season: stays 12f on heavy grund: acts on
a sharpish trk: should impr on this start.   20
--   SANET [5] (P Kelleway) 3-8-11 P Cook 9/4: -4: Active in mkt on racecourse debut:
should be well suited by middle distances: acts on heavy ground.   12
66   SAGAREME [4] 3-8-11 S Whitworth 10/1: 0400-40: Not quicken str: btr over 10f in 66(sft) 00
39   TEED BORE [3] 3-8-11 M Wigham 4/1: 0-20: Much btr over 7f in 39 (gall trk, soft). 00
--   Miss Brahms [6] 8-11
7 ran   4,7,6,10,1½   (K Bethel)   R Boss Newmarket

NOTTINGHAM   Monday April 7th   Lefthand Fair Track

Official Going Given as Good/Soft First 3: Remainder Soft

124 FELSTEAD HANDICAP 0-35   £1345   6f   Yielding +10 Fast   [29]

--   ROSIE DICKINS [2] (R Hollinshead) 4-8-8 R Lappin(7) 11/1: 00300-1: 4 b f Blue Cashmere -
Deva Rose (Chestergate): First time out, led then, ridden out in quite a fast run h'cap at
Nottingham Apr.7: failed to win in '85 and was rather frustrating: in '84 won a nursery h'cap
at Haydock: eff at 5/6f on gd and soft ground.   20
56   TOP THAT [4] (D Barron) 5-9-9 G Baxter 10/1: 000-002: Mkt drifter: made most: good
effort: lightly raced in '85: in '84 won 3 times: very eff at 5f with forcing tactics, stays
6f: acts on firm & yld ground: likes Catterick.   33
65   STEVEJAN [7] (B Morgan) 4-8-0(1ow) P Robinson 10/3 FAV: 0000-33: Al prom: not btn
far: see 65.   09
42   GOLD DUCHESS [5] (M W Easterby) 4-8-9(BL) K Hodgson 14/1: 0000-04: Friendless in mkt:
sn prom: best effort in '85 when 5th at Thirsk: eff at 5/6f on gd and yld.   14
65   SINGLE HAND [8] 6-9-1 A Proud 8/1: 020-400: Ev ch 2f out: see 42.   19
84   ROYAL BEAR [3] 4-7-13 C Rutter(5) 5/1: 000-220: Early speed: see 84 (5f).   00
•84 RIVERSIDE WRITER [14] 4-9-8(7ex) P Darcy 9/2: 2000-10: Poorly drawn: btr 84 (5f shrp) 00

--	NAME THE GAME [13] 4-7-13 A Mackay 10/1: 00000-0: Fdd final 2f.	00
--	MAFTIR [11] 4-9-8(bl) Pat Eddery 8/1: 12000-0: Never dangerous.	00

65   Single Hand [8] 9-1   --   Sullys Choice [12] 9-10
--   Norcool [1] 7-11(1ow)   --   My Annadetsky [9] 7-8 46   Remainder Tip [10] 8-2
14 ran   ½,hd,1½,nk,1   (Dickins Ltd)   R Hollinshead Upper Longdon, Staffs

125   ABOYEUR SELLING STAKES 2YO   £821   5f   Yielding Slow

--   SKYDREAM [7] (M Brittain) 2-8-11 K Darley 11/4 : 1: 2 b c Skyliner - Archers Dream
(Guillaume): Easy to back, but driven out to get up close home in a 2yo seller at Nottingham
Apr.7: eff at 5f, should stay further: acts on yld ground sold today 4, 200 gns.   20
86   ANONA BELLE [4] (C Wildman) 2-8-8 J Williams 7/1: 02: Nearly made all: impr: should
stay further: acts on soft.   16
--   DORCET PLAN [2] (M H Easterby) 2-8-8 M Birch 15/8 FAV: 3: Well bckd debutant: nearest
fin: should impr and be placed to win a similar event: acts on yld.   10
102   MILLIE DUFFER [6] (J Kettlewell) 2-8-8 M Beecroft 16/1: 004: Ev ch: acts on soft & yld.   04
--   IRISH LINK [5] 2-8-8 Pat Eddery 8/1: 0: Mkt drifter: prom 4f: cheaply acquired.   00
57   ABOVE THE SALT [1] 2-8-11 P Robinson 11/4: 00: Speed ½way: half brother to winning
3yo Hafeaf: should stay further.   00
--   Keiths Wish [8] 8-8
7 ran   ½,2½,2,1½,4   (Mel Brittain)   M Brittain Warthill, Yorks

126   CALL BOY HANDICAP 0-35   £1534   1m 3f   Soft Slow   [35]

23   LOVE WALKED IN [14] (W Holden) 5-7-11 R Morse(7) 6/1: 000-001: 5 ch g Hotfoot -
Love Resolved (Dan Cupid): Nicely bckd and fin well to lead inside final 1f in a h'cap at
Nottingham Apr.7: first success: stays 14f well and acts on soft ground.   14
80   LEON [16] (N Tinkler) 4-9-6 W R Swinburn 9/4 FAV: 1104-22: Led 2f out: just caught:
good effort under 9-6 in this soft ground: should win soon: see 80.   35
--   ALACAZAM [1] (J Spearing) 4-7-12(2ow) W Carson 20/1: 00000-3: Al up there on seasonal
debut: made: stays 14f and acts on soft.   10
9   PINWIDDIE [11] (P Rohan) 4-7-9 J Quinn(3) 20/1: 0003-04: Led over 3f out: in '85 fin
3rd in a 12f seller at Thirsk: acts on soft.   00
88   COFFEE HOUSE [4] 11-7-7 M Marshall(7) 20/1: 0000-00: Some late hdway: in '84 won over
12f at Leicester: acts on good/firm and soft.   00
--   CAWARRA BELLE [6] 5-7-9 R Fox 10/1: 4--00-0: Never nearer: lightly raced on the Flat.   00
105   BALGOWNIE [15] 6-7-11 P Burke(1) 10/1: 42-1100: Again below form 36 (10f).   00
--   SEASONS DELIGHT [9] 7-8-3 S Dawson(3) 10/1: 00/40-0: There 1m: been hurdling.   00
69   BLUEBIRDINO [5] 7-7-10 A Mackay 8/1: D000-00: Led till over 3f out: in '85 "won"
h'caps at Haydock and Ayr, but had the misfortune to be demoted on each occasion: maiden
on the Flat but a winner over hurdles: well suited by 14f/2m: acts on gd & yld.   00
--   WESTRAY [2] 4-9-11 S Perks 10/1: 00130-0: Fdd 4f out on seasonal debut.   00
85   Librate [8] 8-3   --   Sailors Reward [13] 9-9
44   Gainville Lad [3] 8-5   --   Mossberry Fair [10] 7-9
--   Action Time [17] 9-5   --   Wandering Walter [7] 9-3
69   North Star Sam [12] 8-5
17 ran   1,3,6,4,1   (Whitting Commodities Ltd)   W Holden Newmarket

127   SLIP ANCHOR STAKES 3YO   £1856   1m   Very Soft Slow

*14   JAZETAS [8] (N Callaghan) 3-9-3 Pat Eddery 5/4 FAV: 4-11: 3 ch c Jaazeiro - Mil
Pesetas (Hotfoot): Useful colt: led 2f out, for a cosy nk success in a 3yo stakes at
Nottingham Apr.7: first time out an easy winner of a maiden at Doncaster: in '85 was a
promising 4th to Dancing Brave at Newmarket: acts son firm & soft and a gall trk: eff at
1m and should stay further: acts on soft.   53
--   MOONSTRUCK [1] (M Ryan) 3-9-0 P Robinson 6/1: 0-2: Led 6f: kept on well and 10L clear
3rd: good seasonal debut: on sole start in '85 finished 5th in a 2yo stakes at Doncaster:
half brother to several American winners: stays 1m and acts on good and soft: should
find a maiden.   45
--   PORO BOY [10] (C Williams) 3-9-0 P Waldron 33/1: 00-3: Sn prom: fdd final 1f: little form
in 2 outings in '85: half brother to 2m winner in Ireland Mad About Ya: eff at 1m on soft.   25
--   PELLINKO [3] (E Eldin) 3-9-0 A Mackay 33/1: 00-4: Never nearer on seasonal debut:
highly tried in 2 outings in '85: half brother to winning 2yo Sandy Cap: eff at 1m and should
get further: acts on soft.   19
*53   SOXOPH [5] 3-9-2 M Birch 7/2: -410: Much btr in 53.   17
16   IYAMSKI [2] 3-8-11 W Carson 9/4: -20: Well bckd: much btr 16 (7f).   09
--   Geraghty Again [6] 9-0   --   Simons Fantasy [4] 9-0
39   Bryanthus [9] 8-11
9 ran   nk,10,3,2,1½   (G S B Cooke)   N Callaghan Newmarket

128   OH SO SHARP EBF STAKES 3YO FILLIES   £1900   1m 2f   Very Soft Slow

-- SUE GRUNDY [3] (G Wragg) 3-9-6 S Cauthen 11/8 FAV: 013-1: 3 b f Grundy - Susanna (Nijinsky): Very useful filly: had a simple task on seasonal debut and led 1½f out, easily in a 4 runner 3yo fillies stakes at Nottingham Apr.7: in '85 fin a fine 3rd in Gr.3 Hoover Fillies Mile at Ascot: earlier won a maiden at Salisbury: eff at 1m/10f and may stay further: acts on firm and soft and should win more races.   59

-- MARIE GALANTE [4] (C Brittain) 3-8-11 P Robinson 7/1: 300-2: No chance with winner but ran well: in '85 fin 3rd in a 2yo fillies maiden at Sandown: stays 10f and acts on firm and soft.   40

-- MYSTERIOUS DANCER [2] (I Balding) 3-9-0 Pat Eddery 2/1: 010-3: Led over 1m: btr for race: in '85 won a fillies maiden at Wolverhampton: well bred filly who is a half sister to 2 winners: eff at 9f, should stay further: acts on good ground and should do btr than this.   31

-- DAVEMMA [1] (P Kelleway) 3-8-11 G Starkey 7/2: 0-4: Dist. last: on sole start in '85 fin 7th in a 29 runner maiden at Newmarket: sister to Bonus Print Masaka Stakes winner Sul-El-Ah: should do btr than this.   08

4 ran   2,8,15   (E B Moller)   G Wragg Newmarket

129   BBC RADIO NOTTINGHAM HCAP 0-35   £1547   1m 2f   Very Soft Slow   [34]

-- GULFLAND [3] (G Pritchard Gordon) 5-8-10 S Childs(7) 25/1: 00-00-1: 5 ch g Gulf Pearl - Sunland Park (Baragoi): First time out, unfncd, but led 2f out, comfortably in a h'cap at Nottingham Apr.7: in '84 won at Kempton: has been lightly raced: stays 10f well: acts on firm and soft.   28

8 CAREEN [2] (M Pipe) 5-8-6 S Cauthen 4/1: 0030-22: Ev ch str: see 8.   16

-91 VAGUE MELODY [11] (L Piggott) 4-9-7 W R Swinburn 7/4 FAV: 4214-23: Heavily bckd but much better 91 (1m sharp).   19

36 RECORD RED [16] (J Spearing) 5-7-9 P Hill(7) 14/1: 0000/04: Sn prom: fdd.   00

36 GODS HOPE [1] 4-8-9 G Baxter 10/1: --00-00: Led over 4f out: see 36.   00

-- BOSSANOVA BOY [14] 7-9-5 T Quinn 10/1: 33230-0: Btr for race: consistent in '85, but failed to win: in '84 won twice at Ayr: eff over 10/12f: acts on any ground.   03

10 PLIANT [12] 6-8-10 Pat Eddery 10/3: 0000-00: Active in mkt, but last to fin: failed to win in '85: in '84 won at Sandown: eff at 1m on firm & heavy.   00

36 Shad Rabugk [7] 8-7   -- Deerfield Beach [6] 8-4

-- Manabel [8] 9-1   -- Absurd [15] 8-7   -- Gorgeous Princess [10] 8-8

80 Miss Morley [13] 8-5   -- Super Trip [4] 9-11   -- Cuddly [9] 9-1

15 ran   4,8,4,1½,3,hd   (G Pritchard-Gordon)   G Pritchard Gordon Newmarket

---

AYR   Monday April 7th   Lefthand Galloping Track

Official Going Given as Good to Soft

130   GREENAN MAIDEN STAKES 3YO   £959   1m 3f   Heavy 170 -49 Slow

100 CAROUSEL ROCKET [7] (J S Wilson) 3-9-0 G Duffield 7/2: 3033-31: 3 ch c Whistling Deer - Fairy Tree (Varano): Prom and driven out to gain the day in the final 100 yds in a 3yo maiden at Ayr Apr.7: placed several times last season: well suited by 11f and soft/heavy going though probably acts also on firm.   26

106 BANTEL BUSHY [2] (I M Bell) 3-9-0 N Carlisle 20/1: 000-22: Led after 1m, caught close home clear of rest: seems suited by 11f and soft/heavy going: may find a small maiden race soon.   23

-- BENAROSA [6] (P Kelleway) 3-8-11 Gay Kelleway[5] 13/8 fav: -3: Led ½way, wknd on racecourse debut: dam a winner over middle distances: acts on heavy: should impr next time. 12

53 BLUE BELLS STAR [8] (S Norton) 3-8-11 J Lowe 12/1: 0000-04: No extra final 2f: dam won the Lincoln: may prove btr around 1m.   00

-- NITIDA [10] 3-8-11 E Guest[5] 7/1: 03-0: Should benefit from seasonal debut: ran only twice in '85, rated 57 when 3rd in a minor race at Hamilton over 1m on soft: dam a useful middle dist. performer who has already thrown 3 winners: should do btr.   00

99 VAN DER PUP [1] 3-9-0 D Nicholls 50/1: 000-40: Outsider, seems moderate.   00

-- MADISON GIRL [3] 3-8-11 D Mckeown 6/1: 02300-0: Fin 7th: btr for race?   00

45 Gilsan Grey [4] 8-11   -- Spinning Turn [9] 9-0   -- Justthewayyouare [5] 9-0

10 ran   1½,5,10,4,3   (A Saccomando)   J S Wilson Ayr

131   RAVENSPARK SELL.H'CAP 3YO+ 0-25   £909   1m   Heavy 170 -49 Slow   [18]

101 LITTLE NEWINGTON [3] (N Bycroft) 5-8-10 A Shoults[5] 8/1: 000-041: 5 b m Most Secret- Kathy King (Space King): Gained her first success, leading on bit 2f out in a selling h'cap at Ayr Apr.7 (no bid): only moderate form in the past: evidently well suited by 1m on heavy going.   07

-- SWIFT RIVER [5] (I M Bell) 4-8-10 N Carlisle 12/1: -00/0-2: Fin well, clear of rest: very lightly raced in last 2 seasons but in '84 won at Edinburgh: stays 1m well: eff at shorter distances: appears to act on good and heavy.   05

-- RUSTIC TRACK [1] (Denys Smith) 6-9-0 T Ives 5/1: 00031-3: Ev ch on seasonal debut: winner twice in '85 at Redcar and Beverley: eff over 1m/10f: well suited by firm or good going and a stiff trk.   00

42   CROWFOOTS COUTURE [11] (J Parkes) 5-8-13 T Parkes[7] 14/1: 0000-04: Made much: winner
at Bath in '85: eff around 1m on firm going.   00
--   CLUEDO [2] 5-9-3(bl) Sharron James 10/1: 10000-0: Fit from hurdling, no dngr.   01
46   MURILLO [10] 10-9-12(bl) J Carr[7] 6/1: 4032-00: Ev ch: has regressed?   09
*41   BRAMPTON IMPERIAL [4] 4-9-8(5ex) D Nicholls 2/1 fav: 0000-10: Uneasy fav: wknd into
8th: better 41 (yielding, sharp track).   00
51   RAPID STAR [8] 3-7-11 J Lowe 8/1: 0000-30: Fin 9th: btr 51 (6f).   00
42   Go Spectrum [6] 8-10(bl)   -- Ailsa Pearl [7] 8-10
10   Kelly Bay [9] 9-13
11 ran   ¾,7,hd,½,¾,1½   (M J Pound)   N Bycroft Brandsby, Yorks

132 GARNOCK HANDICAP 3YO 0-35   £1994   1m 2f Heavy 170 –90 Slow   [39]

*78   SPROWSTON BOY [7] (P Kelleway) 3-9-9(5ex) Gay Kelleway[5] 5/2 jt fav: 4322-11: 3 ch g
Dominion - Cavalier's Blush (King's Troop): Unbtn in 2 races this season, the latest a h'cap
at Ayr Apr.7 when making all: won a maiden at Newcastle Mar.31: placed several times in '85:
eff at 1m, stays 10f: likes a gall trk: suited by forcing tactics & heavy going.   45
*54   CHEVET LADY [1] (R Whitaker) 3-8-6(5ex) K Bradshaw[5] 5/2 jt fav: 0100-12: Came from off
the pace and is in fine form.   24
100   BELHILL [5] (D Chapman) 3-7-12 S P Griffiths[5] 16/1: 0000-43: Ev ch: stays 10f? acts
on soft/heavy: see 100.   12
--   SPACE TROOPER [2] (T Fairhurst) 3-8-1 M Hills 10/1: 0400-4: Sn prom on seasonal debut:
lightly raced in '85, showing best form over 6f on firm going: should stay 1m.   13
49   LADY ST CLAIR [4] 3-9-5 L Charnock 9/1: 1404-00: Ev ch: first time out winner of a
fillies event at Ayr in May '85: half sister to several winners mainly over jumps incl the
smart but ill fated The Grey Bomber: runs well on good going: probably stays 10f.   29
14   STANDON MILL [6] 3-8-4 D Nicholls 33/1: 000-00: Fair effort from this lightly
raced maiden.   13
--   LADY BRIT [3] 3-9-7 E Guest[3] 15/2: 00020-0: Fin 7th: btr for race?   00
--   ROCKALL [8] 3-9-1 J Lowe 7/1: 34030-0: Close up 1m on seasonal debut.   00
8 ran   1½,2,1½,1½,1,shhd,2   (Geoff Whiting)   P Kelleway Newmarket

133 EBF KIDSNEUK MAIDEN STAKES 2YO   £1411   5f   Heavy 170 –27 Slow

--   THE GRANITTON [1] (R Whitaker) 2-9-0 D Mckeown 5/1: 1: 2 br c Free State - Petrinella
(Mummy's Pet): First time out, never hdd when readily winning a 4 horse 2yo maiden at Ayr
Apr.7: cheaply acquired son of a winning juvenile and is speedily bred: acts on heavy:
should stay 6f.   45
40   MR GRUMPY [3] (Denys Smith) 2-9-0 T Ives 2/1 fav: 02: Well bckd, ev ch: acts on
heavy: speedily bred.   38
108   BANTEL BLAZER [4] (I M Bell) 2-9-0 N Carlisle 11/4: 303: Speed over 3f: see 40 (yld).   26
--   MUSEVENI [2] (P Calver) 2-9-0 M Fry 9/4: 4: Close up 3f, btr for race: cost 17,000 gns:
should benefit from this experience.   18
4 ran   2,7,4   (D Gill)   R Whitaker Scarcroft, Yorks

134 LADYKIRK STAKES 3YO   £959   6f   Heavy 170 +12 Fast

*109 TARANGA [5] (M H Tompkins) 3-9-3 R Cochrane 6/5 fav: 3002-11: 3 b g Music Boy -
Embluzon (Wolver Hollow): Unbtn in 2 minor races this season, the latest at Ayr Apr.5 when
hacking up in a true run race: first time out winner at Hamilton Apr.3: unlucky not to win
in '85, running well on all starts: very eff over 6f on soft/heavy: also acts on fast going:
looks sure to pick up a h'cap in the near future.   47
--   SANA SONG [6] (C Parker) 3-8-10 D Nicholls 25/1: 040-2: Creditable effort though always
outpcd on seasonal debut: lightly raced but showed promise in '85: running best over 6f on
firm ground at Newcastle on penultimate outing: seems to also act on heavy: appears
reasonably h'capped at present and could win soon.   28
--   NOT A PROBLEM [2] (Denys Smith) 3-8-10 T Ives 25/1: 30000-3: Never closer on seasonal
debut: lightly raced and little worthwhile form in '85: may do btr this season.   23
18   JARROVIAN [1] (T Fairhurst) 3-8-10 J Lowe 11/4: 3000-04: Speed 4f: showed btr form
last season and was rated 41 when bl for the first time in a maiden at Doncaster in Nov.   13
--   TURN EM BACK JACK [4] 3-8-10 P Bloomfield 25/1: -0: Should benefit from this racecourse
debut: related to a couple of winners abroad.   05
*87   WESSEX KINGDOM [3] 3-9-0 M Hills 5/2: 0-10: Fdd quickly ½way, disapp after 87 (5f).   05
6 ran   2½,2½,7,5,2½   (Stanley Squires)   M H Tompkins Newmarket

135 SEAFIELD HANDICAP 3YO+ 0-35   £1807   6f   Heavy 170 +29 Fast   [34]

110   SHANOUSKA [2] (J S Wilson) 6-7-8 S P Griffiths[5] 5/2 fav: /400-21: 6 b g He Loves Me-
Khadija (Habat): Rewarded strong support when making all very easily in a fast run h'cap at
Ayr Apr.5: lightly raced since winning in '83 at Salisbury: well suited by 6f, soft/heavy
going and front running tactics: should win again.   13
18   CORNCHARM [3] (M Mccormack) 5-9-7 R Cochrane 11/4: 0100-02: In vain pursuit final
2f: winner twice at Folkestone in '85: eff between 5 & 7f and on any going: suited by
forcing tactics: likes a sharpish trk, especially Folkestone.   30

-56 **MENDICK ADVENTURE** [7] (Denys Smith) 5-9-7 T Ives 3/1: 0240-23: Outpcd, much btr 56(5f27
--   **EMERGENCY PLUMBER** [1] (T Barron) 5-9-2 B Mcgiff[7] 5/1: 00400-4: Prom, wknd: btr for
race? rated 41 when a creditable 4th in a valuable h'cap at Nottingham in July, below that
form 2 subsequent outings: last won in '83 at Nottingham and runs well on that trk: best
at 6f on fast going.   17
--   **TIDDLYEYETYE** [4] 5-8-3(bl) S Webster 14/1: 21440-0: No dngr: btr for race.   00
--   **TOLLYMORE** [6] 7-7-13 M Fry 20/1: 03004-0: Abs since June '85: btr for race.   00
12   Monswart [5] 8-7
7 ran   10,2,4,3,¾,3   (Allan Fowler)   J S Wilson Ayr

NOTTINGHAM   Tuesday April 8th   Lefthand Fair Track

Official Going Given as Soft: Based on times soft and deteriorating

136 OLD TRAFFORD MAIDEN STAKES 2-Y-O   £921   5f   Soft +10 fast

34   **LAWNSWOOD LAD** [10] (R Hollinshead) 2-9-0 S Perks 3/1 Co.FAV: 41: 2 b c Runnymede -
Combe Grove Lady (Simbir): Impr colt: led after ½way, comfortably in quite a fast run 2yo
maiden at Nottingham Apr.8: cost 1,450 gns: eff at 5f and should stay 6/7f: acts well on
soft ground.   45
34   **FOUR LAFFS** [5] (D Leslie) 2-8-11 J Williams 14/1: -02: Kept on well final 1f, showing
impr: should be suited by 6/7f: acts on soft ground.   32
47   **TAKE EFFECT** [6] (M Brittain) 2-9-0(BL) K Darley 3/1 Co.FAV: 333: Made most to ½way:
better 47: see 20: bl first time today.   33
94   **PERTAIN** [11] (W Wharton) 2-9-0 W Ryan 14/1: 04: Sn prom: btr effort: cost 2,600 gns:
acts on soft.   28
21   **BOLD DIFFERENCE** [1] 2-8-11 I Johnson 20/1: 00: Never showed: cost only 800 gns. 17
--   **NOALIMBA** [9] 2-9-0 Mark Wood(7) 14/1: 0: Soon prominent on racecourse debut:
cost 1,850 gns: should impr.   20
--   **MASTER POKEY** [2] 2-9-0 W Carson 11/2: 0: Mkt drifter on racecourse debut: there ½way:
cost 1,000 gns.   00
--   **HOMING IN** [4] 2-8-11 G Carter(5) 3/1 Co.FAV: 0: Early ldr: sn fdd: cost 8,800 gns. 00
20   Cammac Lad [7] 9-0
9 ran   4,1,2½,3,shhd,¾   (A S Hill)   R Hollinshead Upper Longdon, Staffs

137 TRENT BRIDGE HANDICAP (0-35) 4YO+   £1509   2m 2f   Soft Slow   [30]

+85 **PEARL RUN** [14] (G Price) 5-9-7(5ex) G King(7) 5/1: 1320-11: 5 ch h Gulf Pearl -
Deep Down (Deep Run): In good form, led approaching final 1f, ridden out in a h'cap at
Nottingham Apr.8: last time out won a h'cap at Warwick: in '85 won again at Warwick: eff
at 14f, stays 2m2f: acts on any ground and on any trk though likes Warwick: may complete
the hat trick.   32
--   **CHEKA** [2] (I Balding) 10-8-5 Pat Eddery 14/1: 00000-2: Led home turn till over 1f
out: fair seasonal debut: in '85 won a h'cap at Bath: in '84 won at Epsom: needs an extreme
test of stamina nowadays: acts on firm and soft and on any trk.   15
--   **PELHAM LINE** [5] (W Musson) 6-8-3 M Wigham 20/1: -3: Ev ch over 1f out: 15L clear rest:
lightly raced sort: stays 2m2f and acts on soft.   13
--   **BEAKER** [7] (M Naughton) 6-8-2(2ow) M Miller 16/1: 40000-4: Fit from hurdling: made most
till str: in '84 won at Lingfield: acts on soft.   00
--   **LADY TUT** [3] 6-8-5 P Robinson 6/1: 0-010-0: Nicely bckd: ev ch: has been hurdling:
in '85 won a h'cap at Carlisle: stays 12f and acts on any grund.   00
--   **MICHELE MY BELLE** [16] 4-7-12 N Howe 33/1: 00000-0: Sn prom: has been hurdling. 00
-85 **KNIGHTS HEIR** [6] 5-8-8 W Woods(3) 10/1: 030-020: Much btr in 85 (1m6f).   00
--   **DANCING ADMIRAL** [17] 6-9-7(vis) S Cauthen 10/1: 04000-0: Fdd: recent winner over hurdles.00
69   **CARNEADES** [15] 6-8-10(vis)(5ex) G Carter(5) 3/1 FAV: 000-130: Twice below 44 (sharp). 00
50   Don Runi [9] 9-10   50   Aribian [18] 8-8   69   Boreham Down [12] 7-12
44   No Fluke [4] 7-12   --   Corston Springs [10] 9-3
11   Jackdaw [11] 9-9   --   Hayashi [8] 7-12   --   Americk [13] 9-6
9   Rheinford [1] 7-13
18 ran   ¾,hd,15,3,20   (R Squires)   G Price Leominster, Herefordshire

138 HEADINGLEY E.B.F. STAKES 3-Y-O   £2460   6f   Soft +10 Fast

--   **KEDRON** [1] (R Laing) 3-9-1 W Carson 7/4 Jt.FAV: 012-1: 3 gr c Absalom - Top Stream
(Highland Melody): First time out, led nearing final 1f, comfortably in quite a fast run
3yo stakes at Nottingham Apr.8: in '85 won a 2yo maiden at Folkestone: cheaply acquired:
eff at 6f & soft: seems to like a sharp/easy trk.   52
26   **YOUNG PUGGY** [2] (R Hollinshead) 3-9-1 S Perks 7/4 Jt.FAV: 0400-02: Sn prom: in '85 won
at Thirsk and was placed on several occasions: half brother to several winners: eff at 5/6f
on good/firm and yld.   40

67   NORTHERN MELODY [4] (A Bailey) 3-8-10(bl) P Bloomfield 14/1: -003: Made much: see 67, **34**
--   LJAAM [3] (H T Jones) 3-9-6 A Murray 9/2: 1040-4: Mkt drifter and no show: first time
out in '85 won at Chepstow: eff at 6f on good ground.   **40**
--   ANGELS ARE BLUE [5] 3-8-7 P Robinson 5/1: -0: Mkt drifter on racecourse debut: should
impr: half sister to useful sprinter Polykratis.   **23**
5 ran   5,½,1½,1½   (G J Burgess)   R Laing Lambourn, Berks

139   TAVERN SELLING STAKES 3-Y-O   £687   1m 2f Very Soft Slow

67   DORS GEM [7] (P Rohan) 3-9-0 Pat Eddery 6/4 FAV: 000-01: 3 b g Brigadier Gerard -
Siraf (Alcide): Dropped to selling company and heavily bckd for an easy win in a 3yo seller
at Nottingham Apr.8 (bought in 1,100 gns): eff at 10f: acts well on soft ground.   **16**
--   SOLENT LAD [4] (B Stevens) 3-9-0 R Carter(5) 7/2: 00000-2: Al there on seasonal debut:
placed in sellers in '85: may stay 10f: acts on good and heavy.   **00**
41   THE DABBER [8] (G Harman) 3-8-11(BL) G Duffield 25/1: 000-003: Prom 3f out: little form. **00**
--   GRAND FLING [3] (R Laing) 3-9-0 C Rutter(5) 4/1: 00000-4: Wknd str: no form in '85.   **00**
--   HANNAH REED [6] 3-8-11 S Whitworth 14/1: 44000-0: Never in it.   **00**
22   RACEFORM RHAPSODY [1] 3-8-11 R P Elliott 25/1: 0000-00: Made much: wknd.   **00**
35   ANDREAS PRIDE [5] 3-9-0 T Williams 4/1: 004-40: Much b'tr in 35 (12f).   **00**
--   Platinum Star [2] 8-11
8 ran   7,5,¾,7,1,1   (Mrs Frank Reihill)   P Rohan Norton, Yorks

140   OVAL MAIDEN STAKES 3-Y-O   £1272   1m 2f Very Soft Slow

--   PEARL FISHER [2] (J Francome) 3-9-0 S Cauthen 6/1: -1: 3 b g Ile De Bourbon -
Perliere (Rheingold): Made a winning racecourse debut, led nearing final 1f, easily in a
3yo maiden at Nottingham Apr.8: trained by H Cecil in '85 but never ran: cost $35,000
as a yearling and seems a well bred sort: eff at 10f, should stay 12f: acts on soft.   **45**
--   HIGHEST PEAK [1] (G Pritchard Gordon) 3-9-0 G Duffield 11/4 FAV: 000-2: Well bckd:
led over 3f out: swamped for foot by the winner: ran only 3 times in '85: half brother to
several winners incl smart Explorer King: stays 10f and acts on soft ground: should find
a maiden.   **35**
--   BETTER BEWARE [8] (I Balding) 3-9-0 Pat Eddery 15/2: 00-3: Led approaching str: unplaced
in 2 outings in '85: half brother to 6f winner Inspire: stays 10f: acts on soft.   **33**
66   ROYAL EFFIGY [14] (D Leslie) 3-9-0 J Williams 8/1: 00-01D4: B'tr in 66 (C/D).   **31**
--   PRINCE SATIRE [6] 3-9-0 T Ives 10/1: -0: Al prom on racecourse debut: acts on soft.   **20**
--   IDLE SONG [4] 3-9-0 S Perks 12/1: -0: Chance 2 out: should do btr.   **18**
--   OUT OF STOCK [3] 3-9-0 W R Swinburn 3/1: 00000-0: Fdd str: showed some promise in
'85 but failed to make the frame: eff at 7f/1m: acts on good and soft.   **00**
--   IRISH DILEMMA [9] 3-9-0 P Bloomfield 7/1: -0: Mkt drifter: wknd in straight.   **00**
--   Crown Mine [12] 9-0   --   Blushing Spy [13] 9-0   --   Sharp Times [11] 9-0
--   Supreme Command [7] 9-0   66   Histon Bronze [5] 9-0
14   Grey Dragon [10] 9-0(BL)
14 ran   4,1½,1½,7,1,6   (Sheikh Mohammed)   J Francome Lambourn, Berks

141   LORDS HANDICAP (0-35) 3YO   £1394   1m   Very Soft Slow   [39]

--   BARLEY BILL [12] (L Cumani) 3-9-7 R Guest 4/1 Jt.FAV: 022-1: 3 ch c Nicholas Bill -
Oatfield (Great Nephew): Easy to back, but led final 1f, easily in a 3yo h'cap at Nottingham
Apr.8: in '85 finished 2nd at Brighton and .Newcastle: stoutly bred and is a half brother to
2m winner High Plains: eff at 1m, will stay much further: acts on firm and soft.   **46**
--   FAIR ATLANTA [4] (M Usher) 3-8-8 A Mcglone 4/1 Jt.FAV: 4003-2: Kept on under press:
eff at 6/7f: stays 1m: acts on soft and heavy: half sister to several winners.   **23**
14   AUCTION MAN [2] (R Hollinshead) 3-9-6 S Perks 13/2: 0003-03: Led well over 1f out:
in '85 fin. 3rd in a maiden at Redcar (6f, good/firm): half brother to several winners.   **34**
--   UNEXPLAINED [8] (R Armstrong) 3-9-0 V Smith(7) 16/1: 000-4: Led 3f out: fdd final
1f: good seasonal debut: unplaced in 3 outings in '85: half brother to several winners and
should find a small h'cap.   **28**
--   ARCTIC KEN [13] 3-8-6 J Reid 20/1: 0040-0: Ev ch 2f out.   **14**
--   ARROW EXPRESS [1] 3-9-0 G Sexton 20/1: 000-0: Early ldr.   **16**
--   PHILOSOPHICAL [5] 3-8-13 M Wigham 11/2: 02041-0: Mkt drifter: fin 7th.   **00**
74   CEROC [11] 3-8-11 W Carson 13/2: 000-40: Made most: see 74.   **00**
--   Hare Hill [7] 8-1   --   Sporting Sovereign [3] 9-0
39   Delta Lima [10] 8-4(BL)   --   Mabel Alice [6] 9-0
--   Folkswood [14] 8-3
13 ran   2,¾,shhd,3,3,¾   (G Keller)   L Cumani Newmarket

Official Going Given as Good/Soft

142 CASTLEHILL APPR HCAP 0-35   £1297   1m 2f   Soft 150 -60 Slow   [31]

7   PATCHBURG [9] (W Haigh) 4-9-0 B Mcghiff 3/1 FAV: 0002-21: 4 b g Remainder Man -
Voleur Vert (Burglar): In good form, led below dist. for a comfortable win in an app. h'cap
at Ayr Apr.8: failed to win last season though won at Hamilton as a juvenile: eff over 7f,
stays 10f well: acts on good/firm and soft ground: acts on a gall trk.   28
88   SKYBOOT [8] (E Carter) 7-8-11 Wendy Carter 6/1: 440-032: Stayed on well: see 88.   18
58   TREYARNON [5] (S Norton) 4-8-6(VIS) J G Murray(5) 10/1: 4400-43: Easy to back: did
not get into the race until late on: well suited by a gall trk: will stay further: see 58.   10
--   QUALITY CHORISTER [1] (G Moore) 5-8-9 M Richardson 9/1: 00002-4: Made most till lack
of fitness told inside dist: last season was never hdd in a similar event at Newcastle and
in '84 won at Ayr: eff over 8/10f: acts on good and soft ground and is well suited by a
galloping track.   12
8   RESPONDER [12] 4-9-2 N Leach 16/1: /230-00: Ran to her best: lightly raced last
season though showed promise in maiden company and will find a race in time: should be
suited by further than todays trip: acts on gd and soft ground and on a gall trk.   17
4   GOLDEN FANCY [11] 9-9-12 R Vickers(5) 9/2: 2201-00: Very slowly into his stride and
this effort is best ignored: very versatile gelding who has won over both hurdles and
fences, and won on the Flat at Doncaster last season: eff over middle distances, stays 2m:
acts on any going.   22
46   MRS CHRIS [2] 4-9-1 David Eddery 8/1: 400-040: Btr over 7f in 46 (tight track).   00
105 MR LION [3] 4-7-11 J Carr 6/1: 0000-30: Ran better in 105 (11f).   00
--   Mark Edelson [7] 7-12   131 Kelly Bay [6] 9-0
10 ran   4,2,hd,1,3,1½   (W W Haigh)   W Haigh Malton, Yorks

143 AUCHANS MAIDEN STAKES 3 & 4YO   £959   1m   Soft 150 -32 Slow

58   TRY SCORER [3] (Denys Smith) 4-9-9 D Nicholls 6/1: 0004-21 4 b g Gulf Pearl -
Just Frolicking (Pals Passage): His fitness advantage proved decisive, went on 2 out to
score readily in a maiden at Ayr Apr.8: placed several times in similar company previously
though seemed to lack a turn of foot: eff over 8/10f: acts on good and heavy ground and
on any track.   46
--   MERHI [5] (S Norton) 3-8-5 J Lowe 3/1: 200-2: Kept on under press on reappearance and
beat the rem. decisively: half brother to several winners and he showed plenty of promise
last season, notably when 5th to Nomrood at Newmarket: eff over 8f and should stay further:
acts on firm and soft ground: sure to find a race this season.   40
--   SOPHYS FOLLY [4] (J Wilson) 4-9-9 Gay Kelleway(5) 33/1: -00-3: The outsider: led
early, kept on late: well btn in both starts last season and should do btr when tackling
longer distances: acts on soft/heavy ground & on a gall trk.   22
--   POP THE CORK [2] (M Francis) 3-8-5 Paul Eddery 6/1: 220-4: Well bckd on reappearance:
found little when below dist: showed plenty of ability last season, when placed at
Doncaster and Ascot over 6f: possibly unsuited by todays going and should do much btr on
a sounder surface: has plenty of scope and should certainly find a race in due course.   22
--   BOYNTON [1] 3-8-5 A Shoults(5) 11/1: 0004-0: Easy to back: fin last on reappearance:
ran his best race on final outing last season at Edinburgh (1m gd) & should do btr next time.   14
5 ran   3,12,shhd,4   (D Knights)   Denys Smith Bishop Auckland, Co Durham

144 COODHAM HANDICAP 0-35   £2169   1m 5f   Soft 150 -44 Slow   [34]

50   WESSEX [6] (N Tinkler) 4-8-10(bl) Kim Tinkler(7) 6/1: 0333-41: 4 b c Free State -
Bonandra (Andrea Mantegna): Came with a smooth chall to lead dist, comfortably in a h'cap at
Ayr Apr.8: first success: placed several times in similar company last season and subsq. made
the frame over hurdles: eff over 12f though is better suited by a test of stamina: acts on
any going: suited by a gall trk.   26
--   RULE OF THE SEA [3] (A Scott) 5-9-11 R Cochrane 10/1: 13000/2: Ran on late: fit from
a successful spell of hurdling though this was a fine effort under top weight: last won on
the Flat in '83 at Sandown: stays 2m: eff over 8/14f & soft ground & on a gall trk.   35
80   DESCARTES [1] (M W Easterby) 4-8-8 A Shoults(5) 7/1: 0001/33: Went on 3 out: in gd
form: see 80.   14
50   AULD LANG SYNE [9] (J Jefferson) 7-8-4(vis) L Charnock 9/2 Jt FAV: /30-424: Stayed on   07
80   HIGHAM GREY [5] 10-8-12 D Nicholls 12/1: 0010-00: Led briefly 2f out: last season won
at Warwick & Ayr: eff over 10f plus, stays 2m well: probably acts on any going: often bl.   14
44   OCEANUS [7] 5-7-10 M Fry 8/1: 3000-00: Remains a maiden: stays well: acts on soft grnd.   00
69   LEPRECHAUN LADY [10] 4-8-13 J Lowe 9/2 Jt FAV: 0040-20: Much btr over 14f in 69.   00
--   MARLION [4] 5-9-8 E Guest(3) 15/2: 10120-0: Needed the race:will be straighter next time   00
105 SULTAN ZAMAN [8] 5-8-3(1ow) Paul Eddery 13/2: 0004-40: led over ½way: fin last.   00
58   Bantel Buccaneer [2] 7-13
10 ran   3,3,2,nk,1½,2½   (Full Circle Thoroughbreds Ltd)   N Tinkler Malton, Yorks

145   LAMLASH SELLING STAKES 3 & 4YO   £888   6f   Soft 150 -04 Slow

41   MUSIC TEACHER [10] (A Robson) 3-7-10(1ow) A Shoults(0) 5/1: 3300-01: 3 ch f Record Token-
Tarte Aux Pommes (Song): Despite carrying 6lbs overweight, led close home in a 3 and 4yo
seller at Ayr Apr.8 (bought in 1,250 gns), though hung left dist and had to survive a
stewards enquiry: placed several times last season though this was her first win: eff over
5/6f on good and heavy ground: tried in bl last season.   17
42   CAERNARVON BOY [5] (J Kettlewell) 4-9-4 M Richardson(7) 10/1: 0000-32: Ev ch: running
well: see 42.   20
101   BARNES STAR [3] (P Monteith) 4-8-13 S Keightley 6/1: 2000-03: Strong late chall, not
btn far: placed a couple of times last season over longer trips: eff over sprint distances
though does stay 12f: acts on firm & soft ground.   14
--   THE CHALICEWELL [13] (M James) 4-8-13 Sharron James 14/1: 00200-4: Led/dsptd lead
most of way: good effort on seasonal debut and he could find a similar race soon on a
sharper trk: eff over 5/6f: acts on gd and soft ground.   13
65   WESBREE BAY [4] 4-8-13 L Charnock 10/1: 0004-00: Just needed this race: eff over
5/6f and should stay further: best form last season on fast ground though would appear to
act on soft.   08
51   LITTLE ARMIER [1] 3-7-9 J Lowe: 0000-20: Ran better in 51(heavy)   00
*51   PLANTER [8] 3-8-3(bl) M Beecroft 4/1 Jt FAV: 033-010: Much btr on heavy ground in 51. 00
46   MALMO [7] 4-8-10 R Cochrane 5/1: -000-00: Lost touch with ldrs from ½way.   00
51   RICH BITCH [11] 3-7-9 S P Griffiths(5) 10/1: 0-00: Has been well btn in all her starts 00
99   Bantel Beau [2] 7-12(BL)   --   Valdarno [12] 7-12
--   Grand Queen [6] 8-10
12 ran   1½,½,½,2½,3,nk   (David S Blake)   A Robson Stockton On Tees, Co Cleveland

146   HILLHOUSE STAKES 2YO   £959   5f   Soft 150 +13 Fast

+77   GALLIC TIMES [4] (I Bell) 2-9-4 N Carlisle 3/1: 311: 2 ch c Good Times - Gallic Law
(Gallivanter): Much impr colt: ridden out to lead close home in a fast run 2yo stakes at
Ayr Apr.8: recently beat dual winner Bluemede in a similar race at Newcastle: incredibly was
beaten in a seller on his debut: half brother to several winning sprinters, notably the
very useful Ferriby Hall: very eff over this minimum trip: acts well on soft ground and on
a galloping track.   54
*20   QUEL ESPRIT [3] (M Mccormack) 2-9-4 R Cochrane 1/2 FAV: 12: Well bckd, made most: see 20.51
108   SCOTTISH FLING [2] (J Wilson) 2-8-11 E Turner(7) 5/1: 33: Ev ch, not btn far:
stable is in good form and he should find a small race soon: see 108.   40
--   SWIFT CHALLENGER [1] (R Stubbs) 2-8-11 D Nicholls 33/1: 4: Friendless in mkt and
soon behind on racecourse debut.   00
4 ran   ½,1½,25   (Miss Elva M Taylor)   I Bell Hawick, Borders

147   SMITHSTONE HANDICAP 0-35 3YO   £1666   5f   Soft 150 +17 Fast   [36]

--   CAPEABILITY POUND [4] (N Bycroft) 3-9-7 M Richardson(7) 8/1: 20000-1: 3 ro g Balboa -
Olibanum (Frankincense): First time out, made virtually ev yd under top weight to win a
fast run 3yo h'cap at Ayr Apr.8: began last season with an all the way success in a maiden at
Thirsk: subsq. placed at Beverley though then suffered from a virus and lost his form: half
brother to winning sprinter Blockhairn Skolar: eff over 5f on gd/firm and soft ground: likes
to be out in front and should win more races this term.   38
*103   SONNENELLE [1] (J Wilson) 3-8-11(vis)(7ex) Gay Kelleway(5) 5/4 FAV: 3422-12: Pressed winner
throughout: ran well under his penalty: see 103.   25
--   WOW WOW WOW [5] (N Tinkler) 3-9-0 Kim Tinkler(7) 5/1: 10110-3: Ran on again close
home and this was a fair effort: last season won at Ayr, Edinburgh and Thirsk: well suited
by 5f on firm & soft ground: half sister to several minor winners: should go close next time. 25
103   MY DERYA [6] (M Tompkins) 3-8-3(BL)(4ow) R Cochrane 7/2: 00-0034: Bl first time: btr in 103.00
--   BEECHWOOD COTTAGE [2] 3-8-4(bl) J Carr(7) 15/2: 00010-0: Needed the race and should
dp btr next time: was a comfortable winner of a nursery at Hamilton last season: needs
further than this minimum trip: stays 7f and will stay further: acts on gd/firm & soft ground. 00
103   PUNCLE CREAK [3] 3-8-1 J Lowe 12/1: 0S00-40: Easy to back: see 103.   00
6 ran   ½,1½,6,1½,10   (M J Pound)   N Bycroft Brandsby, Yorks

---

PHOENIX PARK   Saturday April 5   Left & Right Handed Sharpish Track

Official Going Given as Soft/Heavy

148   TULLAMAINE CASTLE STUD 3YO FILLIES   £3450   1m   Very Soft

--   PARK EXPRESS (J Bolger) 3-8-7 D Gillespie 8/15 FAV: 02-1: 3 br f Ahoonora - Matcher
First time out, an easy winner of a 3yo fillies event at Phoenix Park April 5: very smart
juvenile, first time out winner at Leopardstown: subs. fin. a fine 5th in Gr.1 Cheveley Park
at Newmarket behind Embla: eff. at 6f, stays 1m well: acts on firm and soft/heavy: should win
some good races this season.   73
--   SHERKRAINE (C Collins) 3-8-11 P Shanahan 4/1: 32-2: No chance with winner, though ran
well: first time out in '85 won over 6f here: later a good 3rd to Roaring Riva in Gr.1
Phoenix Stakes on this course: stays 1m: likes soft ground.   67

```
--   CATHERINE MARY  (L Browne) 3-8-4 S Craine 7/1: -3: Not disgraced on stiff debut.        52
--   ST CROINS CASTLE  (M Connolly) 3-8-7 C Roche 12/1: 00020-4: Ex-English filly.
     HEADIN WEST 3-8-7 M J Kinane 8/1: -0::: J Bolger , Ireland
5 Ran     4,4,6,2½      (P Burns)           J Bolger, Ireland
```

149 HORSE FRANCE IRELAND RACE 2YO   £3450   Very Soft

```
--   WITH GODS HELP  (A Geraghty) 2-8-12 Pat Eddery 7/1: 1: 2 br c Godswalk - Social
Partner: Made a winning racecourse debut, led after ½-way, gamely by a sh.hd. in Horse France
Ireland Stakes at Phoenix Park April 5: eff. at 5f on soft/heavy ground.                      56
--   HARRY QUINN  (K Prendergast) 2-8-12 G Curran 4/6 FAV: 22: Chall. final 1f: just denied
also fin. 2nd on his debut at Leopardstown: eff. over 5f on soft/heavy.                        55
--   SNAPPY DRESSER  (P Doyle) 2-8-9 S Craine 7/2: 23: Eff. at 5f on soft/heavy.               48
--   LYREEN RIVER  (N Mcgrath) 2-8-12 J T Hyde(5) 12/1: 4:
--   COLLEGE BOY  2-8-12 D Duggan 14/1: 0:                                                     42
--   HURRICANE DODO  2-8-9 C Roche 10/1: 0:                                                    33
--   Hedera Helix  8-12
7 ran     sh.hd.,2,nk,2,2½        (Mrs I Foley)           A Geraghty , Ireland
```

150 PEGAGUS STUD MAIDEN 3YO C & G   £5175   1m 2f   Very Soft

```
--   IMPERIAL FALCON  (M V O'brien) 3-9-0 Pat Eddery 4/6 FAV: -0-1: 3 b c Northern Dancer -
Ballade: Highly prom. colt: led inside final 2f for a facile win in a 3yo maiden at Phoenix
Park April 5: cost a huge $8.2m as a yearling: ½-brother to useful though frustrating Ma
Petite Jolie: eff. at 10f and should stay further: being aimed for the Derby.                 75
--   ALONE SUCCESS  (V Bowens) 3-9-0 D Parnell 14/1: -034-2: Not pace of winner: stays 10f:
acts on soft/heavy ground.                                                                    58
--   RIVER BLUES  (L Browne) 3-9-0 S Craine 6/1: -04-3: Ran to his best: 4th in a maiden at
Leopardstown in '85.                                                                          57
--   REHEARSING  (D Weld) 3-9-0 M J Kinane 12/1: -4: Mkt. drifter on debut: should improve.   53
--   MY GREAT MONTI  3-9-0 D Gillespie 20/1: -0: Mkt. drifter: ½-brother to very useful
10f winner in '85, Kings Head.                                                                50
--   CARORIVER  3-9-0 P Shanahan 10/1: -0-0:                                                   48
13 ran     3,nk,2        (Sheikh Mohammed)           M V O'brien , Ireland
```

151 WINDFIELDS MINSTREL STAKES 3YO LISTED   £12975   1m   Very Soft

```
--   GOLD CARAT  (M V O'brien) 3-8-11 Pat Eddery 5/4 FAV: -1: 3 br c Mr Prospector - Gaite
Prom. colt: well bckd. on racecourse debut and proved an easy winner of val. Listed Race at
Phoenix Park April 5: eff. at 1m, should stay further: acts on soft ground.                   74
--   AIR DISPLAY  (M O'toole) 3-9-4 D Gillespie 6/1: 31220-2: Ex-English colt: not pace of
winner : recently successful at Leopardstown: eff. at 1m on good and soft ground.             68
--   DEVILS RUN  (L Browne) 3-8-11 S Craine 4/1: 10010-3: Mkt. drifter: in '85 won a Listed
Race at The Curragh: eff. at 7/8f: acts on soft ground.                                       57
--   FORT PROSPECT  (D Weld) 3-9-0 M J Kinane 4/1: -1-4: Not disgraced: on sole start in
'85 won a maiden at Navan: acts on yielding.                                                  60
--   MUFARRIH  3-9-0 G Curran 20/1: 00120-0:                                                   52
--   DAWN COYOTE  3-8-11 D Parnell 14/1: -0:                                                   48
6 ran     2½,1½,sh.hd.,3½        (R Sangster)           M V O'brien , Ireland
```

LONGCHAMP   Sunday April 6   Right handed Track

Official Going Given as Soft

152 GROUP 3 PRIX DE FONTAINBLEU (3YO COLTS) £15639   1m   Soft

```
--   FAST TOPAZE  (G Mikhalides) 3-9-2 C Asmussen 1: -1: 3 b c Far North - Pink Topaze:
Very useful French colt: comfortable winner of Gr.3 event at Longchamp April 6: smart 2yo,
winning Gr.2 Grand Criterium De Saint-Cloud: eff. at 1m, should stay further: acts on soft.   75
--   KALISTAN  (France) 3-9-2 G Mosse 1: -2: Eff. at 1m on soft.                               67
--   EXOTIC RIVER  (France) 3-9-2 Y Saint Martin 1: -3: Nearest finish: acts oon soft.        62
10 ran     2,1½        (M Fustok)           G Mikhalides, France
```

153 GROUP 3 PRIX DE PARBEVILLE   £15639   2m   Soft

```
--   DENEL  (P Bary) 7-8-12 C Asmussen 1: 40/43-1: 7 ch h Devon Vernel: Group 3 winner at
Longchamp April 6: 3rd in this same race last year: stays 2m well: acts on soft/heavy.        75
--   AIR DE COUR  (P Biancone) 4-9-2 E Legrix 1: 11241-2: Stays 2m: smart performer in '85,
winning Gr.2 Grand Prix de Deauville and also minor events at Longchamp(2): loves soft/hvy.   76
--   GRANDCOURT  (France) 4-8-12 F Head 1: -3: -                                               68
9 ran     1,3,2½        (Mme. S Nathan)           P Bary , France
```

154 GROUP TWO PRIX HARCOURT   £18399   1m 2f   Soft

-- SAINT ESTEPHE (A Fabre) 4-9-2 A Gibert 1: 32123-1: 4 b c Top Ville - Une Tornade:
Smart French colt: impressive winner of Gr.2 Prix Harcourt at Longchamp April 6: consistent
in '85, winning at Saint-Cloud(2): eff. at 10/12f: acts on firm and soft.   86
-- OVER THE OCEAN (G Mikhalides) 4-9-0 C Asmussen 1: /1003-2: No chance with winner:
trained by O Douieb last year to win European Free H'cap at Newmarket: eff. over 7/8f:
seems to stay 10f: acts on soft, likes good and firm ground.   74
-- BAILLAMONT (France) 4-9-4 F Head 1: 10030-3: Very smart French colt in '85, winning
Gr.1 Prix Jean Prat at Chantilly: eff. at 9/10f: acts on soft ground.   75
11 ran   6,1½   (Y Houyvet)   A Fabre , France

Official Going Given as Very Heavy

155 PRIX IMPRUDENCE (LISTED) 3YO FILLIES   £10120   7f   Very Heavy

-- OR VISION (F Boutin) 3-9-2 F Head 1: 1300-1: 3 ch f Irish River - Luv Luv'in: Smart
filly: found the best ground, and ran on well to win val. Prix Imprudence at M-Laffitte April
8: very eff. over 6/7f with some give in the ground.   80
-- MARIE DE BEAUJEU (France) 3-9-2 E Legrix 1: -2: Kept on well on this testing ground.   78
-- GLIFHADA (France) 3-9-2 A Lequeux 1: -3: Clearly a very useful filly: fin. 3rd to
Lead On Time in the Criterium on this track last season: stays 7f.   72
-- RIVER DANCER (J Cunnington Jr) - 1: 124-4: Certainly not disgraced on this
unsuitably heavy ground: last year won a maiden at Deauville: eff. over 6/7f on fm. and hvy. 70
-- BAISER VOLE 3-9-2 - 1: 11131-0: Needed this race: never going particularly well and
was not given a hard race: proved herself a very smart filly last term when gaining Gr.1 wins
at Longchamp and M-Laffitte: also won two small races on latter track: stays 7f: acts on
acts on firm and soft: genuine sort.   69
-- ROSE OF THE SEA 3-9-2 - 1: 43-0: Front rank early on: winner of a minor race on
this track last year, subs. placed in good company (notably when 3rd to Embla in Cheveley
Park Stakes at Newmrkt.): stays 6f: acts on good/firm and soft ground.   61
8 ran   ¾,4,1½,½,6   (S Niarchos)   F Boutin , France

156 PRIX DJEBEL (LISTED) 3YO COLTS   £10120   7f   Very Heavy

-- HIGHEST HONOR (P Bary) 3-9-2 C Asmussen 1: -1: 3 gr c Kenmare - High River: Very prom
colt: always going well, led 2 out comfortably in val. Prix Djebel at M-Laffitte April 8:
clearly well suited by 7f and handles testing ground well: looks sure to win some nice prizes. 75
-- TAKFA YAHMED (France) 3-9-2 A Lequeux 1: 11140-2: Kept on well to take the minor
honours: trained by S.Norton in this country last year, showing smart form to win at Beverley
Newcastle and Leicester: later ran creditably in top-class juvenile company: very eff. over
7f and stay at least 1m: acts on any going: well suited by forcing tactics.   68
-- CRICKET BALL (France) 3-9-2 G W Moore 1: -3: Ran well on this heavy ground.   63
-- WASTBELL (France) 3-9-2 - 1: -4: -   57
8 ran   4,3,4,nose,2½   (E Manneville)   P Bary , France

Official Going Given as Good/Soft

157 DAMERHAM HANDICAP STAKES (0-50) 3YO   £2544   1m   Good/Soft 88 -29 Slow   [50]

-- BOWL OVER [6] (P Makin) 3-8-12 G Baxter 5/1: 04302-1: 3 ch g Hard Green - Light Jumper
(Red God): Mkt. drifter on seasonal debut but led inside dist., gamely in a 3yo h'cap at
Salisbury April 9: 2nd in a nursery at Nottingham in '85: stays 1m well: acts on firm and
yielding: half-brother to sev. winners.   46
-- ELWADHNA [3] (H T Jones) 3-9-7 A Murray 7/4 FAV: 21-2: Well backed first time out, led
appr. final 1f: just denied: in '85 was a game winner of a 29-runner fillies maiden at
Newmarket: cost $750,000 as a yearling: eff. over 7f, stays 1m well: acts on fast and
yielding ground and on a galloping track: should be winning soon.   55
-- MODENA REEF [5] (I Balding) 3-8-10 Pat Eddery 7/1: 300-3: Stayed on well: not btn far:
first time out last year fin. 3rd in a Newbury maiden: suited by 1m and may stay further:
acts on good and yielding.   43
-- ATROMITOS [2] (C Brittain) 3-9-4 P Robinson 11/4: 041-4: Made much: better for race:
on final outing in '85 won at Haydock: stays 1m well: acts on gd/fm and soft and any track. 47
-- STRIVE [1] 3-9-6 R Cochrane 12/1: 23100-0: Mkt. drifter: better for race.   44
83 SAXON BAZAAR [4] 3-8-5 M Wigham 33/1: 004-00: Always trailing.   21
6 ran   sh.hd,½,2,2½,,4   (A R Hobbs)   P Makin , Ogbourne Maisey, Wilts.

SALISBURY   Wednesday April 9 - Cont'd

158 B.B.A. SALISBURY 1000 GUINEAS TRIAL   £5712   7f   Good/Soft 88 -33 Slow

--   MIGIYAS [4] (P Cole) 3-8-9 T Quinn 7/2: 1240-1: 3 b f Kings Lake - Rajastar (Raja Baba)
Very useful filly: first time out, led below dist., ridden out in val., but slow run,
4-runner 1,000 Gns.Trial at Salisbury April 9: began last season with a win in a fillies race
at Newbury: cost 94,000 gns. as a yearling: eff. over 7f, should stay 1m, on good and yld.   60
--   SWEET ADELAIDE [3] (B Hills) 3-8-13 B Thomson 4/7 FAV: 130-2: Heavily bckd.: front rank,
led 3f out: first time out in '85 won a fillies event at York: eff. at 6/7f: acts on yld.   61
--   SHEREEKA [1] (H T Jones) 3-8-6 A Murray 7/2: 2-3: No extra final 1f: good effort: on sole
start in '85 fin. a promising 2nd in a fillies mdn. at Leicester: ½-sister to sev. winners:
stays 7f and acts on firm and yielding.   49
--   LADY WINDMILL [2] (M Usher) 3-8-6 M Wigham 20/1: 000-4: Led/dsptd. lead: unplaced last
year, though showed some promise: eff. at 6f, should stay further: acts on yielding.   38
4 ran   ¾,2,5   (F Salman)   P Cole , Whatcombe, Oxon

159 GROUP 3 SALISBURY 2000 GUINEAS TRIAL   £14104   7f   Good/Soft 88 +05 Fast

--   ZAHDAM [5] (G Harwood) 3-8-10 G Starkey 8/11 FAV: 11-1: 3 b c Elocutionist - Delray
Dancer (Chageaugay): Smart colt: justified strong support with an emphatic win in Gr.3 2,000
Gns.Trial at Salisbury April 9: easy winner of both races in '85, at Ascot and Salisbury:
½-brother to sev. winners: eff. at 7f, will stay further: acts on fm. & yld. & on a stiff trk.   77
--   HARD ROUND [1] (R Hannon) 3-8-10 S Cauthen 8/1: 041-2: Not pace of winner, though ran a
good race: on final outing in '85 won a maiden at Epsom: eff. at 6/7f, should stay further:
acts on gd/fm and yielding and on any track.   67
--   SIT THIS ONE OUT [3] (R Laing) 3-8-10 W Carson 2/1: 32110-3: Made most: better for race:
in '85 won twice at York, including val. Champion Racehorse Futurity: eff. over 6/7f, should
get 1m: acts on firm and yld. and a stiff track.   57
--   AL DIWAN [2] (D Arbuthnot) 3-8-10 R Street 16/1: 20-4: Stiff task: better for race: ran
only twice in '85, first time out fin. 2nd to Bold Arrangement in a Goodwood maiden(5f,good).   27
70   FARNCOMBE [4] 3-8-10 G Baxter 7/1: 00-00: Mkt. drifter: flattered in 70 ? (6f,soft).   21
5 ran   2,5,15,2½   (Sheikh Mohammed)   G Harwood , Pulborough, Sussex

160 CRANBORNE SPRINT H'CAP (0-35) 4YO+   £1612   6f   Good/Soft 88 -05 Slow   [32]

*114 WILL GEORGE [3] (C Horgan) 7-10-6(7ex) P Cook 5/4 FAV: 03-1311: 7 gr g Abwah - Grey Miss
(Grey Sovereign): In excellent form, led after 3f, hdd. briefly inside dist though rallied
gamely under top-weight to win a h'cap at Salisbury April 9: recent winner of similar events
at Lingfield and Doncaster: in '85 won at Newbury: prev. season won at Lingfield and Windsor:
very eff. over 5/6f: acts on good and soft and on any trk: genuine and carries weight well.   47
--   SHADES OF BLUE [6] (M Blanshard) 5-9-2 R Cochrane 8/1: 03000-2: Led briefly inside dist.:
4l clear 3rd: last season won at Leicester and runs well on that track: in '84 won at Warwick
eff. over 6f on any ground: best when up with the pace.   28
--   LADY NATIVELY [5] (P Makin) 4-8-9 T Quinn 12/1: 00000-3: Ev.ch. over 2f out: eff. at 6f
on firm and yielding.   12
122 HOKUSAN [4] (K Ivory) 4-8-9 A Shoults(5) 9/2: 001-034: Never nearer: see 122.   11
30   LOTTIE [8] 4-7-10(bl) T Williams 25/1: -400-00: Early leader: lightlyraced performer
who has been beaten in a seller.   00
--   IDEOLIGIA [7] 4-8-0 C Rutter(5) 16/1: 00020-0: Prom. ½-way.   00
30   Mr Rose [1] 8-8   10   Timewaster [2] 9-0
8 ran   Sh.hd,4,½,15,nk   (Robert Scott)   C Horgan , Billingbear, Berks.

161 WALLOP HANDICAP STAKES (0-35) 3YO   £1648   5f   Good/Soft 88 +04 Fast   [35]

--   STEPHENS SONG [5] (N Vigors) 3-9-2 S Dawson(3) 11/2: 24000-1: 3 b g Song - Train Of
Thought (Bay Express): Made a winning seasonal debut, led below dist., ridden out in a 3yo
h'cap at Salisbury April 9: placed sev. times in '85 but failed to win: eff. over 5f on firm
and soft: acts on any track.   34
--   FOUNTAIN BELLS [2] (R Hannon) 3-9-7 L Jones(5) 25/1: 04000-2: Al. up there: 6l clear 3rd:
eff. at 5f on gd/firm and yielding: goes well on a stiff track.   36
6   OLE FLO [4] (K Brassey) 3-9-6 G Duffield 4/1: 4233-03: No real threat: in '85 won at
Brighton and was placed sev. times: acts on any ground: likes a sharpish track.   23
--   LIBERTON BRAE [7] (J Bethell) 3-8-13 W Carson 11/2: 40020-4: Better for race: failed to
win in '85 though placed sev. times: eff. over 5/6f: likes good/firm ground: acts on any track   11
--   NO JAZZ [3] 3-8-11 B Rouse 16/1: 0000-0: Never dangerous: no form in '85.   08
6   PERCIPIO [8] 3-9-1(vis) A Shoults(5) 12/1: 0300-00: Made much, faded.   09
62   SITZCARRALDO [1] 3-9-5 S Cauthen 2/1 FAV: 3300-20: Dwelt start: much better in 62(6f). 00
--   Mister March [6] 8-5
8 ran   ¾,6,2½,½,1½   (tom Nicholson)   N Vigors , Upper Lambourn, Berks.

59

162 ANDOVER MAIDEN FILLIES STAKES (3YO)   £1302   1m 2f   Good/Soft 88 -04 Slow

--   GESEDEH [3] (M Jarvis) 3-8-11 W Carson 2/1 FAV: -1: 3 ch f Ela Mana Mou - Le Melody
(Levmoss): Highly prom. filly: well bckd. on racecourse debut and made hacks of her rivals,
going clear in straight to win a 3yo fillies maiden at Salisbury April 9: very well-bred,
being a half-sister to sev. winners, notably top-class middle-dist. winner Ardross: cost
200,000 gns. as a yearling: eff. at 10f and sure to stay further: acts on yielding ground and
on a galloping track: can only improve and looks a top-class prospect.   70
--   FAREWELL TO LOVE [8] (I Balding) 3-8-11 Pat Eddery 4/1: 20-2: Made most: swamped for foot
by winner: first time out last year fin. 2nd in a fillies mdn. at Goodwood: stays 10f: acts
on good and yielding and should find a small maiden.   45
--   BAG LADY [5] (P Walwyn) 3-8-11 Paul Eddery 9/4: 04034-3: Mkt. drifter: al. there: in '85
was placed on 3 occasions: eff. over 1m, seems to stay 10f: acts on firm and yld.   40
--   ANNABELLINA [2] (G Wragg) 3-8-11 S Cauthen 5/1: 0000-4: No extra final 2f: clear of rest:
best effort in '85 when 5th in a fillies maiden at Newbury(6f,yld).   35
--   LISAKATY [4] 3-8-11 R Wernham 33/1: 00200-0: Very stiff task: in '85 fin. 2nd in a
seller at Nottingham: eff. at 6f, should stay further: acts on firm and yld.   15
--   MIRANOL VENTURE [1] 3-8-11 B Rouse 25/1: 000-0: There half-way.   07
--   Tharita [7] 8-11   --   Battle Fleet [6] 8-11
8 ran   12,3,2½,12,4   (Sheikh Mohammed)   M Jarvis , Newmarket

---

HAYDOCK   Wednesday, April 9   Left Handed Galloping Track

Official Going Given as Good/Soft Based on time: straight - gd/soft, remainder - soft.
                                              Times slow except 165.
163   FRAANK WOOTOON SELLING HCAP 0-25   £1471   1m   Soft Slow   [25]

--   HIGHDALE [9] (J Cosgrave) 4-8-3 W Hayes(4) 33/1: 00404-1: 4 b f Hillandale - Fast Buck
(Clear River): First time out, led straight for an easy win in a selling h'cap at Haydock
April 9(no bid): first success: eff. at 1m on good/firm and soft.   12
41   TIT WILLOW [11] (S Wiles) 4-9-1 S Keightley 9/1: 300-022: No impression from 2f out:
acts on any track: see 41.   15
--   QUICK FLING [16] (D Haydn Jones) 5-8-9 J Williams 5/1 FAV: 00000/3: Stayed on well: didn't
race on the Flat in '85: eff. at 1m, should stay further: acts on soft and a gall. track.   07
80   POKEY [8] (M W Easterby) 4-9-5(bl) M Hindley(3) 9/1: 000-004: Al. prom.: stays 1m and
acts on firm and soft ground: see 80.   16
--   ROYAL EXPORT [2] 6-8-3 M Wood 20/1: -0000-0: Sn. prom.: lightly raced in recent years:
in '83 won at Catterick: acts on firm.   00
56   FAIRGREEN [14] 8-8-13 S P Griffiths(5) 12/1: 0403-00: Mkt. drifter: fdd. over 2f out:
best form previously over 5f: in '84 won at Edinburgh and Ayr: acts on good and heavy.   00
--   BRANKSOME TOWERS [3] 6-8-4 A Mackay 7/1: 01000-0: Better for race: early in '85 won a
h'cap at Chepstow: eff. at 5/7f: acts on good and yielding.   00
41   LADY GRIM [5] 4-8-11 G Carter(5) 8/1: 0000-00: Prom. ½-way: see 41.   00
91   Avraeas [15] 8-10   36   Monclare Trophy [4] 7-9-7
42   Spoilt For Choice [2] 8-9-9   --   Dreamcoat [13] 8-5
--   Cadenette [12] 8-12   46   Scoop The Kitty [17] 8-3(bl)
--   Teejay [1] 8-10   --   Composer [18] 8-10   9   Arancia Doro [6] 8-3
17 ran   5,1½,sh.hd.,1½,6   (Mrs P Cosgrave)   J Cosgrave , Cheltenham, Glos.

164   ECONOMIST MAIDEN STAKES   £1654   1m 4f   Soft Slow

--   MURFAX [16] (J Glover) 3-8-5 D Mckeown 10/1: -04-1: 3 gr c Jellaby - Coral Flower
(Quorum) First time out, led 3f out, driven out, in a maiden at Haydock April 9:
ran only twice in '85, on last start fin. 4th to Faraway Dancer on this track: stays 12f
well: acts on soft ground and a galloping track.   36
--   TAP EM TWICE [20] (M Jarvis) 3-8-5 T Ives 10/3 FAV: 04-2: Chall. final 2f: just btn
and 10L clear 3rd: promising 4th in a maiden at Leicester in '85: stays 12f: acts on
good/firm and soft.   35
--   FREE TO GO [9] (M Naughton) 4-9-8 M Miller 8/1: 0-3: Recent winner over hurdles: led on
far side: acts on soft ground and on any track.   18
45   MADAM GERARD [15] (W Wharton) 3-8-2 N Carlisle 20/1: 2000-44: Acts on firm & soft.   12
--   RAGABURY [18] 6-9-11 D Nicholls 25/1: 0-000-0: Never nearer: lightly raced , little form. 05
19   RECHARGE [4] 4-9-11 W R Swinburn 6/1: 204-00: Front rank 1m: best eff. in '85 when 2nd
at Windsor: seems best over 10f on good ground and a sharp track.   04
75   DISCIPLE [2] 3-8-5 P Waldron 9/1: -00: Lightly backed, but no show.   00
--   TOUCH OF LUCK [13] 4-9-8 S Perks 7/1: 00333-0: There 1m, faded.   00
--   VISTULE [5] 4-9-11 G Landau(7) 6/1: 00-00: No show : better for race.   00
--   Ryans Dove [11] 9-8   --   Haddak [19] 9-11   --   Raisabillion [12] 9-11 •
--   Marcellina [17] 9-8   19   Scholar [1] 9-11   --   One For The Ditch [7] 9-8
--   Easy Kin [10] 9-11   --   Shake The King [14] 8-5
19   Lush Path [6] 9-8   --   Lady Abinger [8] 9-8
19 ran   ¾,10,4,10,½.   H E Waller   J Glover Carburton, Notts.

165 FIELD MARSHAL STAKES LISTED   £7134   5f   Good/Soft +25 Fast

12   BROADWATER MUSIC [8] (M Tompkins) 5-8-13 M Rimmer 12/1: 1210-01: 5 b g Music Boy -
La Presidente(Primera) Very useful sprinter: led from the stalls, staying on well in valuable
Field Marshal Stks(Listed) at Haydock April 9: in good form in '85, winning valuable h'cap at
Newbury and a stks event at Haydock: in '83 won 3 times: very eff. at 5f: acts on good/firm
and soft and on any track: genuine sort.   70
70   AMIGO LOCO [10] (K Brassey) 5-8-13(bl) S Whitworth 2/1 FAV: 240-022: Al. prom: see 70.68
70   SHARP ROMANCE [6] (B Hanbury) 4-9-6 W R Swinburn 4/1: 000-233: Sn. prom: best 18. 70
--   ROARING RIVA [7] (D Laing) 3-8-10 T Ives 9/1: 21000-4: Mkt drifter on seasonal debut:
never nearer: better for race: very useful 2yo, winning twice at Windsor and later very
valuable Group 1 Phoenix Stakes at Phoenix Park: very eff at 6f: acts on firm and soft and on
any track: should win races this season.   69
--   CLANTIME [1] 5-8-13 D Mckeown 20/1: 22100-0: Early speed: should strip fitter next time
in '85 won a valuable h'cap at Epsom: in '84 won at Chester: 4 times a winner as a 2yo: very
eff. over 5f and is well suited by forcing tactics: acts on any going and on any track:
sometimes blinkered, but is a genuine sort.   49
--   CRAGSIDE [5] 4-8-13(bl) P Waldron 11/2: -0302-0: Speed 3f on seasonal debut: lightly
raced in '85, being placed in Group races in France: winning 2yo at Newmarket: equally eff.
at 5/6f: acts on firm and soft and likes a stiff track.   46
--   ARDROX LAD [4] 6-8-13 N Adams 10/1: 00000-0: No real threat.   00
76   CHAPLINS CLUB [9] 6-8-13 D Nicholls 15/2: 021-000: No form this season.   00
18   Dawns Delight [3] 8-13   6   Runaway [2] 8-0
10 ran   ½,2,2½,4,1½.   (P H Betts Holdings)   M Tompkins Newmarket.

166 FREDDY FOX HANDICAP 0-50   £2919   1m 2f   Good/Soft Slow   [50]

--   MASKED BALL [6] (P Calver) 6-7-12 M Fry 10/1: 11230-1: 6 b h Thatch(USA) - Miss Mahal
(Taj Dewan): Mkt. drifter but led into straight, driven out in a h'cap at Haydock April 9:
in '85 won two h'caps at Newcastle: in '84 won at Thirsk: very eff. over 10f, stays 12f: acts
on good and yielding and on any track.   30
17   SHARP NOBLE [10] (B Hanbury) 4-9-12 M Hills 5/1: 2001-02: Fin. well but the post came
just too soon: grand eff. under 9-12 and should go one better soon: in '85 won minor races at
Warwick and Nott.: eff. at 10/11f: acts on gd/fm and yielding and on any track: genuine sort.   57
17   CONMAYJO [2] (D Haydn Jones) 5-8-13 J Reid 13/2: 1020-03: Kept on well: in '85 won
h'caps at Salisbury and Haydock: in '83 won at Chepstow & Bath: eff. at 7/8f, seems to stay
10f: acts on good and soft ground.   40
9   LO BROADWAY [3] (D Moffatt) 8-7-9 J Lowe 5/1: 1000-04: Sn. prom.: in '85 won a moderate
maiden at Hamilton: useful hurdler: eff. at 10/11f: acts on soft ground.   18
--   BALLYDURROW [1] 9-8-9 D Nicholls 3/1 FAV: 01113-0: Never nearer on seasonal debut:
in excellent form last term, winning at Newbury, Haydock, Ayr and Edinburgh(2): in '84 won at
Hamilton: eff. over 10/11f and stays further: equally eff. on any going or trk.:
needs to be come with a late challenge.   31
--   GRUNDY LANE [8] 4-10-0(VIS) T Ives 10/1: /0234-0: Fit from hurdling, but no show.   46
8   MEXICAN MILL [7] 4-8-0(1ow) W Ryan 5/1: 3000-00: There 1m, faded.   00
--   EVROS [5] 4-9-8 R Hills 11/2: 10004-0: Last to finish, better for race.   00
9   Mister Point [9] 8-5   --   Dipyn Bach [4] 8-9
10 ran   Hd.,1½,2½,nk,2½   (P Calver)   P Calver , Ripon , Yorks.

167 EBF MORNINGTON CANNON 2YO FILLIES MDN   £1634   5f   Good/Soft Slow

21   KILVARNET [3] (R Hollinshead) 2-8-11 S Perks 10/1: 01: 2 b f Furry Glen - Sunny Eyes
(Reliance): Evidently benefitted considerably fromhis recent debut, made every yard for a
runaway win in a 2yo fillies maiden at Haydock April 9: half-sister to useful sprinter
Young Inca: eff. at 5f and should stay at least 6f: acts on yielding ground & a gall. track.   50
--   MISS SHEGAS [5] (J Berry) 2-8-11 M Fry 14/1: 2: Sn. Prom.: no chance with easy winner:
cost 3,200 gns.: eff. over 5f on yielding ground.   35
34   MISS PISA [4] (W Wharton) 2-8-11 G Carter(5) 14/1: -03: Al. up there: better eff.:
cheaply acquired.   34
--   PHILEARN [2] (M Brittain) 2-8-11 K Darley 6/1: 4: Prom., ev.ch. on debut: cost IR 2,600:
should improve for this experience.   29
--   MEATH PRINCESS [9] 2-8-11 J Lowe 8/1: 0: Bred to stay 1m: acts on yielding.   26
--   SHEER ROYALTY [8] 2-8-11 T Ives 8/11 FAV: 0: Faded 2f out on debut: well bckd. today:
cost 62,000 gns and should improve on this effort next time.   20
73   JOHNKEINA [1] 2-8-11 M Hills 5/1: 40: Well below form shown in 73(sharpish track).   00
43   Gillot Bar [7] 8-11   40   Mark Of Gold [6] 8-11
9 ran   8,hd,2,1½,3   (Noel Sweeney)   R Hollinshead , Upper Longdon, Staffs.

168 JOHNNY OSBORNE HANDICAP 0-50 3YO   £2920   6f   Good/Soft Slow   [49]

-- **EXAMINATION** [2] (A Bailey) 3-8-3(bl)(1ow) S Whitworth 10/1: 00030-1: 3 b g Cawston's Clown -
Ixia (I Say): Outsider of the party but led below dist.,comfortably in a 3yo h'cap at
Haydock April 9: early in '85 won at Catterick: ½-brother to two winners: eff. at 5/6f, may
stay 7f: acts on good and soft ground and on any track.
                                                                                              40
38 **GOLDEN GUILDER** [4] (M W Easterby) 3-7-7(BL)(1oh) G Carter(1) 4/1: 0000-02: Made much:
eff. over 5/6f on yielding/soft ground: seems suited by forcing tactics.   21
-- **CARELESS WHISPER** [7] (I Matthews) 3-9-1 N Day 7/1: 010-3: Mkt. drifter: no extra final 1f
better for race: in '85 won a fillies maiden at Lingfield: ½-sister to useful 1m winner
Pictograph: eff. at 5/6f and should get further: acts on firm and yielding.   36
6 **MAYOR** [1] (M Leach) 3-9-7 D Nicholls 9/2: 3110-34: Much better in 6(good).   40
-- **NEW EDITION** [5] 3-8-6(bl) M Hills 6/1: 10000-0: Faded below dist.: in '85 won a fillies
maiden at York but subsequently disappointed: eff. at 5f on yielding.   17
81 **DANCING TOM** [6] 3-9-1(bl) C Coates(5) 9/4 FAV: 3101-40: Disappointing fav.: see 81. 23
64 **TOUCH ME NOT** [3] 3-7-10 A Culhane(7) 5/1: 0000-30: No show: faltered in 64 ?   00
7 ran   3,2½,1,4,1½   (T P Ramsden)   A Bailey , Newmarket

Official Going Given as Soft

169 ST ARVANS MDN FILLIES STKS 3YO DIV I   £888   1m 2f   Yielding 102 -44 Slow

89 **NATIVE HABITAT** [2] (M Jarvis) 3-8-11 T Ives 9/2: -41: 3 ch f Habitat - Nip In The
Air (Northern Dancer): Clearly benefitted considerably from her recent debut, and
lead early in str for a comfortable win in quite a slowly run 3yo fillies stakes at Chepstow
Apr.10: cost 66,000 gns as a yearling and is a half sister to several winners, incl the
useful Eastform: seems well suited by 10f and likely to stay further: acts on yld ground
and on a gall trk.   36
35 **S S SANTO** [5] (M Tompkins) 3-8-11 M Rimmer 7/2: 0-22: Fin clear of rem: in good
form and should find a small race soon: cost 7,000 gns as a yearling: eff over 10/12f: see 35. 18
-- **MRS SCATTERCASH** [1] (C Brittain) 3-8-11 G Baxter 11/2: -3: Never dngr on her racecourse debut though should be btr for this experience: bred to be suited by todays trip.   02
-- **CELTIC DOVE** [4] (G Price) 3-8-11 J Williams 12/1: -4: Slowly into her stride and
never got into the race.   02
-- **TONDELA** [3] 3-8-11 Pat Eddery 5/4 FAV: 4-0: Led over ½way though wknd quickly str
and trailed in last: showed promise in sole start at Lingfield last season on fast grnd:
half sister to a couple of minor winners in France and should be well suited by middle dists. 00
5 ran   8,10,shhd,8   (Ralph C Wilson Jnr)   M Jarvis Newmarket

170 EBF ST BRIAVELS MAIDEN STAKES 2YO   £1019   5f   Yielding 102 +02 Fast

-21 **MELBURY LAD** [1] (C Hill) 2-9-0 W Carson 9/4: 21: 2 ch c Free State - Lucky Kim
(Whistling Wind): Impr colt: nicely bckd and made most for a ready win in quite a fast run
2yo maiden at Chepstow Apr.10: cost 3,200 gns as a yearling: well suited by this minimum trip
though should stay further: acts on yld and soft ground & on a gall trk.   44
-- **ARAPITI** [6] (K Brassey) 2-9-0 S Whitworth 6/4 FAV: 2: Well bckd on racecourse debut:
led briefly dist and fin 4L clear of rem: speedily bred colt whom cost 8,600 gns as a
yearling: acts on yld ground and on a gall trk: should find a race.   36
-- **SHARPHAVEN** [3] (M Brittain) 2-8-11 K Darley 6/1: 3: Sprint bred debutant by Sharpo
stayed on from ½way and should do btr next time: cheaply acquired: acts on yld ground and
on a gall trk.   25
73 **DOUBLE TALK** [5] (H Oneill) 2-8-11 G Baxter 14/1: 04: Close up over ½way: sprint bred
filly who acts on yld ground and on a gall trk.   17
-- **DIAMOND FLIGHT** [11] 2-9-0 Pat Eddery 5/1: 0: Active in mkt on debut though never
threatened: cheaply acquired colt who should do btr next time.   08
-- **TEZ SHIKARI** [4] 2-9-0 N Carlisle 16/1: 0: Bckd at long odds on racecourse debut:
front rank early though soon ran out of steam: cost 4,400 gns and is a half sister to
winning Legalize: should impr.   06
-- Setter Country [8] 8-11   -- Swallow Bay [9] 8-11
-- Clearway [10] 9-0   -- Brushford [2] 9-0
10 ran   3,4,2½,5,1   (C John Hill)   C Hill Barnstaple, Devon

171 HOLLYWOOD STAKES HANDICAP 3YO 0-35   £1156   1m 4f   Yielding 102 -62 Slow   [41]

117 **OWL CASTLE** [3] (M Usher) 3-9-3 P Eddery 11/4: 00-3241: 3 b c Bold Owl - My Duty
(Sea Hawk II): Gained a deserved win, led well over 1f out, ridden out in a 3yo h'cap at
Chepstow Apr.10: showed some promise last season and has been placed in all his starts this
term: eff over 10/12f on yld and soft ground: half brother to 10f winner Boom Patrol: genuine
and consistent best when held up now.   42
29 **FOUL SHOT** [8] (W Musson) 3-7-9 A Mackay 5/2 FAV: 000-22: Made most: in gd form.   14
-- **MOUNT SCHIEHALLION** [2] (K Brassey) 3-9-7 S Whitworth 8/1: 02030-3: Btr for race: showed
some promise in nurseries last season: eff over 1m and should be suited by 10/12f: acts
on gd/firm and yld ground: half brother to several winners, incl fair stayer Trapeze Artist. 35

-- NOBLE HILL [5] (D Arbuthnot) 3-8-13 J Williams 10/3: 31-4: Never beyond mid-div and
sure to come on for this race: was an easy winner of a seller at Leicester last season:
half brother to several winners: eff over 8/10f and should stay further: acts on firm &
yld ground & on any trk.   27
35 FAST AND FRIENDLY [4] 3-8-13 S Perks 12/1: 0000-00: Mkt drifter: btr effort and
seems suited by 12f on yld ground.   21
-- GROVECOTE [1] 3-8-4 G Baxter 14/1: 003-0: Led early: wknd quickly str.   00
-- ROCKHOLD PRINCESS [7] 3-8-2 W Carson 9/1: 000-0: Al behind on seasonal debut.   00
7 ran   2,3,shhd,2,25   (Brian over)   M Usher Lambourn, Berks

172 MERCURY STAKES HANDICAP 0-60   £4674   6f   Yielding 102 +22 Fast   [53]

71 CORN STREET [12] (J Bosley) 8-9-0 Pat Eddery 5/1: 02D4-01: 8 ch g Decoy Boy -
Diamond Talk (Counsel): Useful h'capper: was nicely bckd when an easy winner of a fast run
h'cap at Chepstow Apr.10: led below dist, pushed out: last season also scored comfortably
over 7f on this course: very eff over 6/8f: has won on fast ground though is fav. by some
give: acts on any trk: could win again.   52
65 REVEILLE [14] (M Jarvis) 4-8-3 T Ives 13/2: 0000-22: Not btn far: in good form: see 65. 36
-- BAY PRESTO [10] (K Brassey) 4-8-6(bl) S Whitworth 20/1: 00200-3: Fin strongly, not
btn far on seasonal debut: just btn by Coincidental in a valuable h'cap at Newmarket last
season and again won in '84 at Catterick: eff over 5/6f: acts on firm & yld ground and
on any trk: looks well h'capped on his best form and could win soon.   35
-- PRINCE SKY [1] (P Cole) 4-8-13 T Quinn 10/3 FAV: 40114-4: Made most, lack of fitness
told close home and he should take some catching next time: won successive races at Brighton
and Windsor last season: very eff over this trip: acts on gd & yld ground and is well suited
by a sharpish trk.   34
-- QUARRYVILLE [6] 3-9-3 N Adams 14/1: 24413-0: Ev ch on reappearance though possibly
btr on a faster surface: consistent last season, won at Bangor early on and later a nursery
at Folkestone: very eff over 5/6f: closely related to several winners: should come on
for this race.   51
-- FAWLEYS GIRL [9] 4-8-1(1ow) W Ryan 12/1: 31000-0: Bckd at long odds on reapp.   12
70 VORVADOS [8] 9-9-4 W Carson 4/1: 0Q4-400: Never threatened: much btr in 18.   00
70 Crete Cargo [2] 8-12   -- Manimstar [4] 9-12   -- Elmdon [3] 7-7(2oh)
-- Derry River [7] 8-5   -- Postorage [13] 9-13   84 Robrob [5] 7-9
76 Brampton Grace [11] 8-13
14 ran   ¾,1½,3,¾,3,nk   (M A Wilkins)   J Bosley Bampton, Oxon

173 ST ARVANS MDN FILLIES STKS 3YO DIV II   £893   1m 2f Yielding 102 -48 Slow

-- MYCENAE CHERRY [4] (G Wragg) 3-8-11 Paul Eddery 5/2: 0-1: 3 ch f Troy - Cherry Hinton
(Nijinsky): Prom filly: first time out made steady prog to lead inside dist in quite a
slowly run 3yo fillies maiden at Chepstow Apr.10: unplaced in a good race at Newmarket last
season: half sister to the very smart Cherry Ridge: clearly suited by 10f on yld ground:
acts on a gall trk: sure to impr further and win more races.   49
-- FLAMING DANCER [6] (J Winter) 3-8-11 W Carson 5/1: 0-2: Made most to ½way, just btn
and this was a good effort: cost 15,000 gns and is a half sister to smart 10f winner Goody
Blake: likely to be suited by further: acts on yld ground and on a gall trk: should find
a race soon.   47
-- DONNAS DREAM [1] (J Tree) 3-8-11 Pat Eddery 11/10 FAV: 40-3: Well bckd on reappearance:
led below dist, caught close home and just btn: cost 82,500 gns and is closely related to
several winners, incl smart middle dist. winner Town And Country: stays 10f: acts on firm
and yld ground and on a gall trk: sure to find a race this season.   46
-- TUDOR DOR [3] (A James) 3-8-11 M Hills 33/1: -4: Outsider: went on before ½way, no
extra dist: fair effort on her debut: acts on yld ground and on a gall trk: should impr. 31
32 COUNTLESS COUNTESS [5] 3-8-11 T Ives 5/1: -20: Led briefly str: see 32.   38
-- LONGRIVER LADY [2] 3-8-11 D Kemp(7) 33/1: -0: Dwelt, never going well and fin well btn.00
6 ran   ¾,nk,10,2,30   (E B Moller)   G Wragg Newmarket

174 ST LEONARDS STKS HANDICAP 0-35   £1383   7f   Yielding 102 +15 Fast   [34]

112 SINGLE [6] (W Wightman) 4-8-12 Pat Eddery 4/1: 0020-01: 4 b c Jellaby - Miss Solo
(Runnymede): In good form; led below dist for an easy win in a fast run h'cap at Chepstow
Apr.10: ran consistently last season when winning at Bath and Newbury: eff over 7/8f: acts
on fast ground though is fav. by some give: acts on any trk though does particularly well
on a gall one.   34
91 LEMELASOR [7] (D Haydn Jones) 6-9-6 D Williams(7) 11/4 FAV: 420-032: Led after ½way,
no chance with winner though another good effort: see 91.   30
-- ARTISTIC CHAMPION [13] (M Pipe) 3-8-2(2ow) Paul Eddery 6/1: 000-3: Stayed on from ½way:
good effort and should do btr next time: lightly raced last season in fair company: cost
11,000 gns: stays 7f: acts on gd & yld ground and on a gall trk.   24
-- GAUHAR [1] (M Blanshard) 5-8-8 N Adams 16/1: 00300-4: Just needed this race: failed
to win last season though in '84 won at Salisbury & Lingfield: eff over 7/8f: acts on any going. 10

63

--   MISTA SPOOF [12] 4-7-11 R Street 20/1: 24004-0: Ran on well after a slow start: and should impr on this effort next time: half brother to a couple of winners, incl winning sprinter Welsh Folly: placed several times last season though yet to win: stays 10f: seems best with some give. 00
112   MELS CHOICE [8] 8-9-4 K Darley 13/2: 0040-00: Smartly away though soon mid-div: useful sprinter on his day: landed a gamble at York last season: in '84 won at Ascot & Ayr: eff over 7f on gd/firm and soft ground: sometimes bl. 03
--   TALK OF GLORY [5] 5-8-13 N Carlisle 10/1: 03000-0: Easy to back and no threat on reapp. 00
91   CHAISE LONGUE [15] 4-8-9 S Whitworth 15/2: 0000-40: Never reached leaders: btr in 91. 00
31   REST AND WELCOME [9] 4-8-2 T Quinn 10/1: 0030-00: Mkt drifter: no threat. 00
--   Santella Pal [11] 7-11   71 Mr Mcgregor [2] 10-0
84   Fairdale [10] 7-13   -- Sharasar [4] 7-11   -- Mister Prelude [14] 8-12
14 ran   5,2,2,1½,8   (A G Lansley)   W Wightman Upham, Hants

---

Official Going Given as Good/Soft

175 SEVEN DIALS STAKES 3YO   £1660   6f   Good 54 +16 Fast

83   REIGNBEAU [2] (G Lewis) 3-9-0 P Waldron 2/1: 03-31: 3 b c Runnett - Queensworthy (Capistrano): Led str, stayed on well under press in a fast run stakes event at Brighton Apr.10: eff at 6f, should stay further: acts on gd & soft & on any trk. 45
-83   BOOFY [12] (C Nelson) 3-9-0(BL) J Reid 7/4 FAV: 0340-22: Bl first time: kept on final 1f: beat winner 83 (soft): also acts on good. 40
83   TOLLYS ALE [7] (I Matthews) 3-8-11 A Weiss(5) 12/1: 0304-43: Led to ½way: kept on: eff at 5/6f on gd and soft. 29
--   PORTHMEOR [9] (M Bolton) 3-9-0 S Cauthen 7/1: 22044-4: Mkt drifter: nearest fin and btr for race: rated 39 in '85 when 4th to Resourceful Falcon at Lingfield: eff at 6f and acts on gd/firm and yld. 27
--   TIPPLE TIME [8] 3-8-11 C Rutter(5) 12/1: 03300-0: Mkt drifter: late hdway and should strip fitter next time: best effort in '85 when 3rd at Warwick: eff at 5/6f on gd & firm: has been tried in bl. 23
64   LUIGIS LASS [3] 3-9-0 R Cochrane 20/1: 0-00: Prom, ev ch: lightly raced: acts on gd. 19
111   DALSAAN BAY [10] 3-9-0 G Carter(5) 15/2: 00-040: Sn prom: much btr in 111 (soft). 00
--   Bold Archer [11] 9-0   -- Sir Speedy [6] 9-0   -- Hello Blue [5] 9-0
--   Baliview [1] 8-11   -- Lightning Byte [4] 9-0
--   Lochanier [13] 8-11
13 ran   1½,3,1½,nk,2½,¾   (Mrs B M Clarke)   G Lewis Epsom, Surrey

176 PYECOMBE APP.STAKES 4YO UPWARDS   £1434   1m 2f Good 54 -20 Slow

--   THATCHINGLY [3] (M Bolton) 5-8-3 R Carter 25/1: 23300-1: 5 gr g Thatching - Lady Rushen (Dancers Image): First time out, kept on up the hill to lead near fin in an app. stakes at Brighton Apr.10: placed on many occasions in '85 but failed to win: eff at 1m/11f: acts on good & soft & on any trk. 33
--   ROYAL HALO [1] (G Harwood) 5-9-3 P Mose 3/1 FAV: 30234-2: Made most: just caught: failed to win in '85: in '84 won at Kempton: eff at 1m, stays 10f: acts on gd/firm & soft and on any trk. 46
19   PRIVATE AUDITION [4] (M Usher) 4-8-3 J Carter 10/1: -43: Never nearer: acts on gd & soft 26
--   BANK PARADE [21] (J Davies) 5-9-3 L Ashworth(5) 4/1: 00424-4: Active in mkt on seasonal debut: ev ch 2f out: last won in '84 at Ripon & Newmarket (Wood Ditton): eff at 1m, stays 10f: acts on good & firm. 39
4   BOLD CONNECTION [10] 6-9-3 P Barnard(5) 9/1: 0200-00: Mkt drifter: well below the form of last season when 2nd to Royal Coach in a stakes event at Lingfield: first time out in '85 2nd to King Of Clubs in a Listed race at Doncaster: in '84 won at Leopardstown: eff at 1m, stays 2m: acts on firm & yld. 33
--   MAGNIFICA [18] 5-8-0 R Morse 20/1: -00-0: Mkt drifter: never nearer. 13
--   BLAZE OF TARA [7] 5-8-10 P Miller(5) 7/1: 00-42-0: Op.3/1: never in it. 00
--   THE HEIGHTS [2] 4-8-3 M Lynch 8/1: -0: Friendless in mkt on racecourse debut: well bred sort who cost I.R.200,000 gns as a yearling: may do btr. 00
112   Pandi Club [16] 8-3(bl)   -- Kilimanjaro Bob [13] 8-3
7   Bachagha [5] 8-3   -- Kala Nashan [9] 8-0   -- Old Malton [8] 8-3
8   Cluga Gurm [14] 8-3   -- Courageous Charger [20] 8-3
--   Hollow Oak [6] 8-3   -- Pett Velero [15] 8-3   -- Praos [19] 8-3
70   Pulsingh [11] 8-3   -- Rosanna Of Tedfold [12] 8-0
--   Stardyn [22] 8-0   -- Elephant Boy [17] 8-3
22 ran   nk,3,¼,3,1½,1   (D J Adamson)   M Bolton Felcourt, Sussex

177 HURSTPIERPOINT SELL. H'CAP 3YO+ 0-25   £890   7f   Good 54 +14 Fast   [34]

-- GOLD LOFT [8] (P Mitchell) 4-8-0 G Carter(5) 4/1: 0--02-1: 4 b g Stanford - Wendela
(Manacle): Well bckd and led 2f out, easily in a selling h'cap at Brighton Apr.10 (no bid):
in '85 fin 2nd in a 29 runner selling h'cap at Newmarket and has been lightly raced: eff at
6/7f, should stay 1m: acts on gd & firm and on any trk: may win again in similar company.   18

-- HIT THE HEIGHTS [6] (M Pipe) 5-8-6 S Cauthen 9/2: 00000-2: Nicely bckd on seasonal
debut: no form in '85: in '84 won at Epsom, but has regressed: eff at 7-10f: acts on gd & soft   13

71 CLASSIC CAPISTRANO [12] (G Gracey) 4-10-0 M Wigham 7/2 FAV: 13D4/03: Well bckd: ev ch
2f out: trained by M Prescott in '85 to win at Nottingham: eff at 6/7f on gd & firm.   30

-- NICANIC [10] (D Tucker) 5-7-8 Dale Gibson(6) 33/1: 00000-4: Never nearer: 7L clear rest:
no form in '85: eff at 7f on good.   00

31 LINGFIELD LADY [3] 4-8-7 B Thomson 6/1: 0400-40: Mkt drifter: btr in 31 (yld/soft).   00

-- CANDAULES [13] 8-7-8 R Fox 16/1: -0: Nearest fin: has been off the trk for a long time.   00

28 CHARISMA MUSIC [16] 4-8-0 C Rutter(5) 10/1: 3002-00: Fdd over 2f out.   00

-- FORT DUCHESNE [1] 4-8-7(1ow) R Guest 10/1: 33140-0: Mkt drifter: no show.   00

-- MAJORS REVIEW [2] 4-9-4 P Cook 13/2: 10300-0: Active in mkt: never threatened.   00

-- ELMCOTE LAD [14] 4-7-8 M L Thomas 10/1: 40000-0: Last to fin.   00

-- Roberts Girl [7] 7-12(1ow)   30   Lean Streak [15] 8-2(bl)

28 Fleur De Thistle [9] 7-8(1ow)(7oh)   113 Thai Sky [11] 7-7(14oh)

28 Og Boy [4] 7-9   -- Letoile Du Palais [5] 7-12(5ow)(9oh)

-- Clever Angle [17] 7-8(bl)

17 ran   4,2½,½,7,1,nk   (E Benfield)   P Mitchell Epsom, Surrey

178 BRIGHTON FESTIVAL H'CAP 3YO 0-60   £2684   1m   Good 54 -11 Slow   [60]

74 GORGEOUS ALGERNON [3] (C Brittain) 3-8-13 C Rutter(5) 10/1: 4030-01: 3 b c Hello
Gorgeous - Hail to Vail (Hail To Reason): Outsider of the party, but led 2f out, holding on
by ¼L in a 3yo h'cap at Brighton Apr.10: useful 2yo, winning at Newbury: eff at 6f, stays
1m well: acts on gd & yld and on any trk.   57

*74 BELOW ZERO [4] (A Bailey) 3-8-3 R Cochrane 5/4 FAV: 0402-12: Chall final 1f and
just btn: 6L clear 3rd and is in good form: see 74.   46

49 SOVEREIGN LOVE [2] (W Hastings Bass) 3-8-1 R Lines(3) 11/2: 0031323: Btr in 49, heavy.   32

-- DOGMATIC [5] (R Johnson Houghton) 3-9-7 S Cauthen 4/1: 2301-4: Made most on seasonal
debut: on final outing in '85 won a nursery h'cap at Doncaster: eff at 7f, should stay 1m:
acts on firm & yld and runs well on a stiff trk: likes to force the pace.   52

15 BERESQUE [1] 3-8-12 P Waldron 3/1: 030-40: Fdd 1f out: see 15 (7f).   40

5 ran   ½,6,hd,1½   (W J Gredley)   C Brittain Newmarket

179 OVINGDEAN HANDICAP 3YO+ 0-35   £2565   1m 2f   Good 54 -32 slow   [30]

-- DHOFAR [4] (G Pritchard Gordon) 6-9-8 S Childs(7) 9/2: -1000-1: 6 ch g Octavo (USA) -
Cress (Crepello): Fighting fit and led/dsptd lead after ½way, drawing clear in the final 1f
for an easy win in a h'cap at Brighton Apr.10: has been running well over hdles: first time
out in '85 won at this same meeting: eff at 10/12f: acts on any grnd & on any trk: genuine
sort who does well on a sharp track like Brighton.   35

-- DETROIT SAM [1] (R Akehurst) 5-9-9 J Reid 14/1: 00000-2: Mkt drifter: al up there:
last won in '83 at Lingfield: eff at 7f, stays 12f: acts on gd/firm & heavy & likes a
sharpish track.   29

-- LONGSTOP [3] (P Makin) 4-9-7 T Williams 7/1: 11134-3: Led ½m out: should strip
fitter next time: course specialist here, in '85 won twice at Brighton and loves the sea air:
also won at Goodwood & Wolverhampton: winning 2yo: stays 12f well: acts
on good & firm & on any trk, though likes a sharpish one: genuine and consistent.   21

-- PELLINCOURT [5] (A Pitt) 4-9-5 B Rouse 5/1: 00320-4: Active in mkt: showed some
promise in '85 when trained by G Wragg: eff at 10f, should stay 12f: acts on any ground.   19

*28 ICEN [6] 8-8-8 M Wigham 11/4Jt.FAV: 4400/10: Much btr in 28 (yld/soft, seller).   08

-- BIDDABLE [7] 7-8-1 C Rutter(5) 12/1: -0200-0: Has been hurdling.   00

92 MR GARDINER [9] 4-9-12 S Cauthen 11/4 Jt.FAV: 0401-20: Much btr 92 (soft): ran
poorly at Brighton last year. best on flat track?   00

23 Trikkala Star [2] 8-7   121 Divine Truth [8] 8-0

9 ran   3,3,shhd,shhd,3   (Lt Col E K Phillips)   G Pritchard Gordon Newmarket

180 SOUTHWICK MAIDEN STAKES 2YO   £959   5f   Good 54 -22 Slow

-- STRIKE RATE [5] (R Hannon) 2-9-0 A Mcglone 7/4: 1: 2 b c Wolver Hollow - Rixensart
(Credo): First time out, led final 1f, comfortably in a 2yo maiden at Brighton Apr.10: cost
14,000 gns and is a half brother to 3 winners: eff at 5f, will stay further: acts on gd
ground & a sharpish trk: should rate more highly.   47

-- CLARENTIA [1] (M Usher) 2-8-11 M Wigham 4/1: 2: Led briefly final 1f: Not btn far:
should stay further: acts on gd ground and a sharpish trk.   41

-- SANDHURST [3] (P Cundell) 2-9-0 P Cook 11/8 FAV: 3: Well bckd: made most: btn when
hmpd final 1f: speedily bred colt who cost 8,200 gns: impr likely.   40

-- TAKE A HINT [4] (M Fetherston Godley) 2-9-0 R Hills 9/2: 4: Fdd final 1f: cost I.R. 6,000
and should do btr over longer distances.   20

-- RIBO BE GOOD [2] 2-8-11 N Dawe 20/1: 0: Friendless in mkt: wknd: should do btr in time.   00

5 ran   ¾,1½,10,6   (John Horgan)   R Hannon East Everley, Wilts

Official Going Given as Good/Soft. All times slow except race 182.

181   SCARBOROUGH SPA SELLING STAKES 2YO   £901   5f   Good/Soft Slow

102 HARRYS COMING [9] (T Fairhurst) 2-8-11 C Coates(5) 7/4 FAV: 021: 8 b c Marching On –
Elegant Star (Star Moss): Comfortably justified fav. in making virtually ev yd in a 2yo
seller at Beverley Apr.11 (bought in 1,150 gns): cheaply acquired colt who is well suited by
this minimum trip: acts on yld & soft ground & is suited by forcing tactics: acts on a stiff track.   28
57   MI OH MY [8] (K Stone) 2-8-8 C Dwyer 5/2: 302: Kept on well under press and she
should find a similar race soon, possibly over a longer trip: acts on yld & heavy grnd: see 13   20
--   GIFT OF PEARL [7] (J Berry) 2-8-8 M Fry 6/1: 3: Showed plenty of pace in this modest
company on her racecourse debut and she should find a similar race in the near future: acts
on yld grnd and cn a stiff trk.   15
125 ABOVE THE SALT [10] (N Tinkler) 2-8-11(BL) Kim Tinkler(7) 7/1: 004: Kept on nicely
and this was an impr effort: seems well suited by yld ground: should stay further than this
minimum trip.   14
102 BROONS ANSWER [6] 2-8-8 G Brown(5) 10/1: 00: No extra dist though not btn that far.   10
40   SCARNING SPARKLER [3] 2-8-11 S Morris 12/1: 00: No threat from ½way.   01
--   Rose Duet [4] 8-8   86   High Town [11] 8-8   13   Kamstar [1] 8-8
9 ran   1,2,1½,hd,5 .   (T Fairhurst)   T Fairhurst Middleham, Yorks

182   WITHERNSEA HANDICAP STAKES (0-35) 3YO+   £1423   5f   Good/Soft +30 Fast   [35]

12   BINCLEAVES [9] (M Mccormack) 8-9-1 G Baxter 9/4 FAV: 1010-01: 8 ch h Tumblewind –
Pink Doll (Palestine): Was a game winner of a fast run h'cap at Beverley Apr.11, just got up
under strong press: lightly raced though was quite consistent early last season, winning
h'caps at Doncaster & Haydock: eff over 5/6f: seems to act on any going though fav. by some
give in the ground: genuine sort.   30
124 GOLD DUCHESS [8] (M W Easterby) 4-8-0 L Charnock 10/1: 000-042: Just failed to make all
and this was a good effort: likes to be up with the pace: see 124.   14
124 RIVERSIDE WRITER [5] (K Bridgwater) 4-9-0(5ex) P D'arcy 11/1: 000-103: Not btn far: in
good form: see 84.   26
--   ALNASHME [8] (D Thom) 4-8-3 A Murray 14/1: 0/004-4: Easy to back on reappearance: al
front rank: lightly raced over sprint distances last season: acts on firm & yld ground and
is suited by forcing tactics.   10
42   HENRYS VENTURE [4] 4-7-7 S P Griffiths(5) 20/1: 0000-00: Stayed on well: maiden who
seems best over sprint dist: acts on gd/firm & yld ground.   00
+56 PARADE GIRL [3] 4-8-12(8ex) N Connorton 7/1: 003-010: Market drifter: better 56(hvy)   1½
56   WARTHILL LADY [10] 4-8-5 K Darley 13/2: 000-040: Close up most of the way: see 56.   00
--   THRONE OF GLORY [11] 5-10-0 D Nicholls 10/1: 00000-0: No threat:.   00
56   VELOCIDAD [3] 6-8-12 G Carter(5) 15/2: 0010-30: Btr on hvy ground in 56.   00
--   Grey Starlight [6] 8-2(2ow)   --   Workaday [1] 10-0
56   Pergoda [12] 9-4
12 ran   shhd,¾,2,2,hd,1   (M McCormack)   M Mccormack Sparsholt, Oxon

183   LECONFIELD MAIDEN STAKES 3YO   £822   1m   Good/Soft Slow

49   PLANET ASH [5] (A Bailey) 3-9-0 G Carter(5) 5/4 FAV: 320-241: 3 b c Star Appeal –
Cinderwench (Crooner): Heavily bckd when a comfortable winner of a 3yo maiden at Beverley
Apr.11: ran up to Misnaad in a h'cap at Doncaster first time out and was unsuited by the
bottomless ground when a disapp fav last time: showed promise last season: eff over 7/8f on
firm & soft ground: quite consistent.   45
--   OPTIMISM FLAMED [14] (C Brittain) 3-9-0 G Baxter 5/1: 033-2: Nicely bckd on his
seasonal debut: led after ½way till dist: good effort: placed twice in similar company last
season, once over this C/D and is clearly well suited by this stiff course: acts on firm &
soft grund: should impr for this outing and win a race soon.   38
--   MAKE PEACE [15] (I Balding) 3-9-0 J Matthias 10/3: 3-3: Nicely bckd on reappearance: al
close up and this was a fair effort: placed behind Picatrix over 7f at Chepstow on sole
start last year: cost 36,000 gns and is a half brother to several winners, incl the smart
Doobie Do: stays 1m: acts on gd & yld ground and on a stiff trk.   36
39   COOL OPERATOR [2] (R Williams) 3-9-0 R Hills 14/1: 000-04: Made eye catching late prog
after a tardy start: on the up grade and will be suited by a longer trip: acts on yld ground.   34
--   SNAPDRAGON [9] 3-9-0 J Bleasdale 10/1: 0-0: Just needed this race and should do btr
next time: showed promise in a Newcastle maiden on sole start last year (7f, good): brother
to several winners: should stay further than todays trip: acts on yld ground.   32
--   COUNTRY CARNIVAL [7] 3-8-11 N Day 16/1: 00200-0: No extra close home and btr for race   28
--   FINAL CURTAIN [1] 3-9-0 M Hills 8/1: 00-0: Never reached ldrs on reappearance.   00
--   MR PASTRY [16] 3-9-0 G Duffield 15/2: -0: Prom for a long way and should do btr next time.   00
--   Saiyyaaf [10] 9-0   --   Dress In Spring [8] 8-11
--   Rapid Flight [12] 9-0   --   Katie Rhodes [6] 8-11 --   Motor Master [4] 9-0
--   Our Annie [3] 8-11   78   Noble Saxon [11] 9-0(VIS)
--   Lottie Limejuice [13] 8-11
16 ran   4,1,1,¾,½,6.   (T P Ramsden)   A Bailey Newmarket

184   HORNSEA MERE HANDICAP (0-35) 3YO+   £1569   1m 2f   Good/Soft Slow   [32]

--   SEVEN SWALLOWS [10] (H Collingridge) 5-9-4 M Rimmer 10/1: 01230-1: 5 br h Radetzky -
Polysee (Polyfoto): First time out, led into str and ran on well to win a h'cap at Beverley
Apr.11: was a surprise winner of an amateur riders h'cap at Haydock last season: in '84 won
at Edinburgh: eff over 8/10f on gd & soft ground: seems to act on any trk: clearly does well
when fresh. carries weight well.   30
*58   APPEALING [3] (G Blum) 4-8-7(5ex) M Birch 4/1 FAV: 000-412: Easy to back: in gd form
and had ev ch: looks well h'capped on his recent success at Newcastle and should be winning
again soon: see 58.   17
*80   SKI RUN [13] (P Wigham) 11-8-5(8ex) J Lowe 5/1: /00-413: Ran well under penalty: see 80. 10
8   DELICATE DESIGN [1] (J Leigh) 4-9-0 G Carter(5) 7/1: -034-04: Nicely bckd and had
ev ch: lightly raced last season though showed some promise and is likely to impr further:
eff over 10f on firm & yld ground.   16
*105 CHRISTMAS HOLLY [7] 5-7-12 M Fry 6/1: 000-310: Never nearer after a slow start: btr
judged on his win in 105.   00
10   NIGHT WARRIOR [2] 4-9-7 J Bleasdale 16/1: 0000-00: Kept on late though may need further 18
104   REGAL CAPISTRANO [11] 4-8-10 G Duffield 13/2: 2040-20: Led over ½way, sn btn when hdd
and much btr when ridden with more restraint in 104 (11f, soft).   00
36   LOVELY BUTTERFLY [8] 5-8-4 K Darley 11/2: 000-320: Below par effort: much btr in 7.   00
--   Rashah [9] 8-10   *131 Little Newington [6] 7-10(5ex)
*22   Cavalieravantgarde [5] 8-11   --   Loch Laddie [12] 8-3
--   Sound Work [4] 8-7
13 ran ¾,3,1½,¾   (Mrs G E Davidson)   H Collingridge Newmarket

185   BRIDLINGTON BAY MAIDEN STAKES   £1412   2m   Good/Soft Slow

--   WIDE BOY [11] (I Balding) 4-9-9 J Matthias 15/8: 03230-1: 4 b g Decoy Boy - Wide Of The
Mark (Gulf Pearl): Landed some nice bets on his reappearance, led before str for a game win
in a maiden at Beverley Apr.11: placed several times in maiden & h'cap company last term
though this was his first win: has been hurdling this winter: stays well: acts on firm &
soft ground and on a gall trk. good weight carrier.   32
19   CHRISTO [14] (R Simpson) 4-9-9 S Whitworth 11/8 FAV: -32: Was heavily bckd and only
just went down after a sustained chall: well suited by this test of stamina & given similar
conditions he could win soon: see 19.   30
--   MENINGI [15] (N Tinkler) 5-9-9 J H Brown 11/1: 00-00-3: Fit from hurdling and ran
well: lightly raced on the Flat last season, over shorter trips though clearly stays 2m well:
acts on gd & yld ground.   25
--   BLUFF COVE [17] (R Hollinshead) 4-9-9 S Perks 10/1: 04000-4: Easy to back despite
being fit from hurdling: al there: placed a couple of times last season and ran to his
best here: stays well: suited by some give.   24
104   FAVOURITE NEPHEW [12] 4-9-9 D Nicholls 10/1: -000: Bckd from 20/1: stayed on late
though no reach ldrs: clearly suited by a test of stamina: acts on yld ground.   09
69   HOT RULER [7] 3-8-4 K Darley 16/1: 202-300: Led briefly before str: btr over 12f in 35. 05
--   Smack [10] 9-9   45   Whittingham Vale [3] 8-1
--   War Palace [1] 8-4   --   Baton Match [4] 9-9   --   Perfect Double [2] 9-6
50   Scottish Rose [13] 9-6   --   Deekays [9] 9-9(BL)
--   Eyton Milady [16] 9-6   --   Velindre [6] 9-6   --   Cashed In [5] 9-9
16 ran ½,3,1,15,7,1½   (Lord Porchester)   I Balding Kingsclere, Hants

186   FILEY MAIDEN AUCTION STAKES 2YO   £824   5f   Good/Soft Slow

--   GOOD BUY BAILEYS [18] (G Blum) 2-7-10 A Mackay 12/1: 1: 2 b f Good Times - Justine
(Luciano): Easy to back and showed a nice turn of foot to lead inside dist in a 2yo maiden
auction stakes at Beverley Apr.11: clearly well suited by this minimum trip: acts on yld
ground & on a stiff track.   38
47   WOLF J FLYWHEEL [19] (C Tinkler) 2-7-13 M Wood 7/1: 02: Easy to back: al front rank
though did show signs of greenness and should continue to impr: acts on yld & heavy ground
and on a stiff track.   35
102   BROONS ADDITION [5] (K Stone) 2-7-10 P Burke(7) 16/1: 43: Stayed on well from ½way:
btr effort: eff over 5f on yld/soft ground: cheaply acquired filly.   30
--   TAP THAT BATON [7] (M Tompkins) 2-8-11 M Rimmer 4/1 FAV: 4: Well bckd on racecourse
debut and showed plenty of promise under top weight: cost 6,200 gns as a yearling: acts on
yld ground: looks sure to find a race.   44
47   MADDYBENNY [1] 2-7-10 L Charnock 16/1: 400: With ldrs most of way: flattered in 20?   24
94   ORIOLE DANCER [13] 2-8-2 G Duffield 6/1: 00: Tried to make all and may win a small
race over a less exerting course: acts on yld/soft: suited by forcing tactics: see 94.   28
61   CHOCO [6] 2-8-2 N Day 15/2: 00: Never reached ldrs: btr in 61 (soft/hvy).   00
47   ROYAL TREATY [3] 2-8-2(3ow) J H Brown(0) 20/1: 00: Never beyond mid-div.   00
--   PRINCESS SINGH [15] 2-7-10 M Fry 5/1: 0: Nicely bckd on racecourse debut though beat
only 2 home: should do btr than this.   00
20   Bootham Lad [10] 7-13   --   Stage [14] 8-5
47   Prior Well [2] 7-10   94   Thatch Avon [4] 7-13 --   Five Sixes [20] 8-0(1ow)
--   Call For Taylor [16] 7-13   --   Victoria Star [11] 7-13 -- Medallion Man [8] 8-2
--   Pay Dirt [9] 8-2   108 Minizen Lad [12] 7-13 21 Tawny Pipit [17] 7-10(BL)
20 ran 2½,¾,¾,nk,2,¾.   (Baileys Horse Feeds)   G Blum, Newmarket.

Official Going Given as Good/Soft

187 POLYANTHUS MAIDEN STAKES 2YO   £1944   5f   Good/Soft 105 -36 Slow

-- **ENCHANTED TIMES** [7] (C Horgan) 2-9-0 Pat Eddery 9/2: 1: 2 b c Enchantment - Miss Times
(Major Portion): Sn prom and led inside the final 1f in a 2yo maiden at Kempton Apr.11:
cost 7,400 gns: speedily bred: acts on gd/soft and a sharpish trk: should impr on this.   50
-- **FRENCH TUITION** [9] (R Hannon) 2-9-0 A Mcglone 3/1 FAV: 2: Well bckd debutant: made
most: 6L clear 3rd: half brother to speedy 2yo Cronk's Image: eff at 5f and should stay
further: acts on yld ground and should have no trouble finding a similar event.   47
-- **MICRO LOVE** [4] (H O'neill) 2-9-0 J Williams 25/1: 3: Rank outsider: al there, showing
promise: should stay further than 5f: acts on yld.   32
-- **QUICK SNAP** [5] (A Ingham) 2-9-0 J Reid 4/1: 4: Very active in mkt: sn prom: should be
suited by further than 5f and will come on for this run.   29
-- **CASTLE CORNET** [8] 2-9-0 B Rouse 10/1: 0: Slowly away on seasonal debut: impr likely
from this 10,500 gns purchase: sire the smart stayer Castle Keep and should do btr over
longer distances.   28
-- **MOON INDIGO** [3] 2-9-0 M Roberts 8/1: 0: Cost 24,000 gns and is a half brother to
10f winner Lakh: should do btr.   27
-- **MAKIN MISCHIEF** [6] 2-9-0 C Rutter(5) 6/1: 0: Ev ch ½way: cost 9,600 gns.   00
-- **FATHER TIME** [2] 2-9-0 G Starkey 5/1: 0: No show: half brother to several winners,
incl the smart sprinter Grey Desire.   00
-- Shenley Romp [1] 9-0
9 ran   ¾,6,1,½,½   (Mrs H Corbett)   C Horgan Billingbear, Berks

188 FLORENCE NAGLE GIRL APPR MDN STKS 3YO   £1867   1m 1f   Good/Soft 105 -18 Slow

-- **TOP WING** [3] (J Hindley) 3-9-0 Alison Harper(5) 7/4: 2-1: 3 b c High Top - Be Faithful
(Val De Loir): Useful colt: led 2½f out, comfortably in a girls app. maiden at Kempton
Apr.11: showed a deal of promise on sole start in '85, fin 2nd to high class prospect Winds
Of Light in a Newmarket maiden: half brother to a couple of winners abroad: eff at 9f, should
stay further: acts on gd/firm and yld and should win more races.   50
14 **BENISA RYDER** [5] (C Horgan) 3-9-0 Gay Kelleway 10/11 FAV: 03-22: Heavily bckd: ev ch
final 1f: 10L clear 3rd: stays 9f and acts on yld ground: should find a small maiden.   44
-- **SAFFAN** [4] (M Prescott) 3-9-0 Wendy Carter 7/1: 03-3: Friendless in mkt: btr for race:
in '85 fin 3rd to Swift Trooper in an Edinburgh maiden: eff at 1m on firm & soft.   26
-- **MR ADVISER** [2] (F Durr) 3-9-0 Debbie Price(5) 14/1: -00-4: Wknd: no form in 2 outings
in '85: should do btr.   21
32 **NEVER BEE** [1] 3-9-0 Sharon Greenway(5) 50/1: 00-00: Made most.   00
5 ran   2,10,2,30   (K Al-Said)   J Hindley Newmarket

189 JONNIE MULLINGS MEM HCAP STKS 0-60   £3189   1m 4f   Good/Soft 105 -17 Slow   [56]

4 **HOLY SPARK** [8] (D Elsworth) 6-8-2 D Brown 33/1 : -01: 6 b g Sparkler - Saintly Miss
(St Paddy): Ran on well inside final 1f to get up close home in a h'cap at Kempton Apr.11:
off the trk in '85: useful 2yo winning at Newmarket and Nottingham, but has had training
problems: stays 12f well: acts on gd and soft.   42
72 **KENTUCKY QUEST** [5] (M Pipe) 4-8-11 J Reid 25/1: 000-002: Ran on well final 1f: much
btr effort: lightly raced and off form in '85: fair 2yo, winning at Epsom: half brother to
2,000 gns winner Mon Fils: stays 12f well: acts on gd/firm and yld.   48
-- **POCHARD** [7] (P Cole) 4-9-0 T Quinn 11/2: 12323-3: Made most at good pace until
final 1f: btr for race and should be winning soon: consistent performer in '85, winning at
Carlisle, Wolverhampton & Kempton: stays 12f well, acts on firm & yld.   48
-- **FOLK DANCE** [9] (I Balding) 4-9-0 S Cauthen 8/1: 32441-4: Ev ch over 2f out: should
strip fitter next time: in '85 won at Leicester & Lingfield: stays 12f well: acts on gd &
yld & on any trk.   48
92 **MOON JESTER** [3] 6-7-10(2ow) D Mckay 6/1: 0040-00: Ev ch 2f out: kept on.   29
72 **ABU KADRA** [6] 5-9-7(bl) M Wigham 9/2 Jt.FAV: 0000-20: Never nearer: btr 72 (hvy).   51
-- **STATELY FORM** [10] 4-9-10 Pat Eddery 10/1: 41140-0: Friendless in mkt: btr for race.   00
92 **NESTOR** [1] 6-9-0 P Waldron 9/1: 2000-00: Wknd straight.   00
72 **JOLIS GIRL** [2] 4-8-8 P Robinson 9/2 Jt.FAV: 420-030: Fin last! much btr 72 (10f, hvy).   00
72 Shostakovitch [12] 8-7   -- Alsiba [11] 7-10
-- Free On Board [4] 7-10
12 ran   1½,1½,shhd,1,2.   (J A Leek)   D Elsworth Whitsbury, Hants

190 LABURNHAM STAKES 3YO   £3908   1m   Good/Soft 105 +11 Fast

-- **NISNAS** [5] (P Cole) 3-8-9 T Quinn 7/1: 143-1: 3 ch c Tap On Wood - Suemette (Danseur):
Very useful colt: mkt drifter, but led over 1½f out, ridden out in a stakes event at Kempton
Apr.11: first time out in '85 won a maiden at Salisbury and does well when fresh: eff at 1m,
should stay further: acts on gd/firm and yld and on any trk.   68

-- ESDALE [1] (J Tree) 3-8-9 Pat Eddery 7/4 FAV: 2-2: Heavily bckd: chall over 1f out:
12L clear 3rd: good effort and should be winning soon: well regarded sort, 2nd to Zahdam at
Ascot on sole start in '85: half brother to a couple of winners: eff at 1m, should stay
further: acts on firm & yld.   66

-- BADARBAK [3] (R Johnson Houghton) 3-8-9 S Cauthen 4/1: 103-3: Mkt drifter: fdd: first
time out in '85 was an easy winner at Windsor: half brother to 12f winner Vadalushka and
should be suited by further than 1m: acts on yld, well suited by fast ground.   46

-- CROMWELL PARK [4] (M Ryan) 3-9-0 P Robinson 9/4: 1-4: Wknd 2f out: won sole start
in '85, a 26 runner Newmarket maiden: eff at 7f, should stay 1m: acts well on firm ground
and a gall trk: should do btr than this.   41

-- GOVERNOR GENERAL [2] 3-8-9 R Cochrane 20/1: 001-0: Led 6f: on final outing in '85 won
a fast run maiden at Goodwood: half brother to 2 winners: eff at 6f: acts on gd/firm and
a sharpish trk: likes to force the pace.   30

5 ran   ¾,12,5,3   (Fahd Salman)   P Cole Whatcombe, Oxon

191 MAGNOLIA STAKES 3YO   £2372   1m 3f   Good/Soft 105 -27 Slow

-- TORWADA [8] (P Cole) 3-8-11 T Quinn 7/2 Jt.FAV: 204-1: 3 b c Troy - Miss By Miles
(Milesian): Promising colt: led after 1m, and went clear in the final 1f for an easy win in
a 3yo stakes at Kempton Apr.11: first time out in '85 fin 2nd at Sandown: well regarded sort
who is a half brother to 2 winners, incl the smart Missed Blessing: eff at 11f, sure to
stay 12f plus: acts on firm & yld & should win more races.   58

-- RUSSIAN LOGIC [6] (G Harwood) 3-8-11 G Starkey 7/2 Jt.FAV: -2: Easy to back on racecourse debut: chall 2f out: eased when btn: promising debut from this $500,000 buy: should
stay 12f: acts on yld and should have no trouble finding a maiden.   48

-- NORFOLK SONATA [5] (R Boss) 3-9-4 M Miller 9/2: 0431-3: Sn prom: rated 52 last year: on
final outing in '85 won at Goodwood: eff at 7f, should stay 11f plus: acts on firm & yld.   43

90 KINGS CRUSADE [9] (G Lewis) 3-8-11 P Waldron 15/2: -44: On the up grade: stays 11f.   35

*75 LONGGHURST [1] 3-9-4 Pat Eddery 5/1: 00-10: Made most: acts on yld & heavy: see 75.   42

-- GORGEOUS STRIKE [10] 3-9-4 J Reid 7/1: 123-0: Wknd str: btr for race: first time out
in '85 beat Torwada in a maiden at Sandown: eff at 7f, but should be suited by middle dists:
acts on firm & yld and a gall trk.   34

-- Great Topic [2] 8-11   95 Eastern Player [7] 8-11
116 Song An Dance Man [4] 9-4   66 Common Accord [3] 8-11
10 ran   6,7,nk,shhd,4   (Fahd Salman)   P Cole Whatcombe, Oxon

192 SYRINGA HANDICAP STAKES 0-50   £2712   6f   Good/Soft 105 +28 Fast   [50]

-- TYROLLIE [8] (N Vigors) 4-9-3 P Cook 11/1: 00402-1: 4 br f Balidar - Segos (Runnymede):
Useful filly: first time out, sn prom and led well over 1f out, ridden out in a fast run
h'cap at Kempton Apr.11: in '85 was in good form, winning at Sandown & Newbury: also a
"winner" at Epsom (subs. disq): in '84 won at Folkestone: eff at 5f, stays 6f: acts on
firm & soft: thoroughly genuine.   53

*31 GOLD PROSPECT [5] (G Balding) 4-8-8 J Williams 11/1: 20-12: Kept on well: in fine form.   40

55 TRANSFLASH [12] (E Eldin) 7-9-10 G King(7) 12/1: 1000-43: Btr effort: see 55.   49

-- MATOU [11] (G Pritchard Gordon) 6-9-10 W Ryan 10/1: 20011-4: Kept on well: stiff task:
btr for race: in good form at the back end of '85, winning h'caps at Doncaster, Haydock &
Pontefract: in '83 won twice at Newmarket: very eff at 6f: does stay 10f: acts on any grnd.   47

-- AMEGHINO [14] 6-9-6 R Wernham 12/1: 43000-0: Sn prom: fair seasonal debut: in gd form
early last season, winning a h'cap at Kempton: in '83 won at Goodwood: best over 5/6f: acts
on gd/firm & yld: should do btr next time.   41

18 JOHN PATRICK [6] 5-9-2 T Ives 10/1: 0003-00: No show: puzzling sort: early in '85
won Listed race at Doncaster and also won at Cagnes: eff at 6/7f: acts well on soft & heavy.   31

-- DUCK FLIGHT [17] 4-9-4 S Cauthen 13/2: 00030-0: Fdd over 1f out.   00

76 BRIDGE STREET LADY [3] 5-9-5 Pat Eddery 4/1 FAV: 4200-20: Much btr in 76 (5f, soft).   00

-- CANIF [13] 5-8-10 G Starkey 6/1: 04000-0: Very active in mkt.   00

-- Eecee Tree [7] 7-12   -- Deputy Head [15] 9-0   -- Al Amead [9] 9-7
-- Lyric Way [1] 8-10   -- Hello Sunshine [2] 9-0
70 Miracles Take Time [4] 8-4   -- Kellys Royale [10] 9-12
16 ran   1,2½,½,½,2½   (Lady D'Avigdor Goldsmid)   N Vigors Upper Lambourn, Berks

193 PAMIANTHE HANDICAP STAKES 3YO 0-50   £2670   1m 2f   Good/Soft 105 -06 Slow   [43]

-- SAMANPOUR [4] (R Johnson Houghton) 3-9-1 S Cauthen 6/1: 0001-1: First time out, led
1½f out, comfortably, a 3yo h'cap at Kempton Apr.11: on final outing in '85 won a maiden at
Nottingham: very eff at 10f: acts on fast & yld & on any trk.   42

*63 SWIFT TROOPER [3] (R Williams) 3-10-0(bl)(7ex) R Cochrane 3/1 FAV: 0410-12: Heavily bckd:
in fine form: see 63.   49

*132 SPROWSTON BOY [7] (P Kelleway) 3-9-7(7ex) Gay Kelleway(5) 11/2: 322-113: Led 3f out:
better 132 (soft).   45

117 FLYING FLYNN [1] (N Callaghan) 3-8-3 M L Thomas 11/2: 321-224: Better 117.   26

-- GOLDEN CROFT [9] 3-8-5 S Dawson(3) 12/1: 000-0: Sn prom on seasonal debut: no form
in '85: eff at 10f on yld.   13

KEMPTON   Friday April 11th   - Cont'd

KEMPTON   Friday April 11th   - Cont'd

-- **TOM RUM** [8] 3-8-5 L Riggio(7) 12/1: 000-0: No threat: showed promise in '85 when 6th to Ininsky in a maiden at Sandown: half brother to 3 winners: acts on gd/firm.   **03**

-- **Adeem** [5] 9-1   54 **Beau Mirage** [6] 9-6   *67 **Cosmic Flight** [11] 8-4(7ex)
-- **Palewells Comet** [12] 9-1   -- **Black Comedy** [2] 8-13
-- **Roaming Weir** [10] 9-6
12 ran   3,4,1½,1½,5   (H H Aga Khan)   R Johnson Houghton Blewbury, Oxon

---

BEVERLEY   Saturday April 12th   Righthanded Track, Stiff Uphill Finish

Official Going Given as Soft

194 JUDI MERDEN MAIDEN STAKES 3YO   £1408   1m 2f   Yielding 107 +09 Fast

-- **TOP GUEST** [2] (G Wragg) 3-9-0 A Murray 11/8 FAV: 0222-1: 3 ch c Be My Guest - Topsy (Habitat): Very useful colt: first time out was nicely bckd, led early in str for a comfortable win in quite a fast run 3yo maiden at Beverley Apr.12: found one too good in 3 of his 4 starts last season, incl twice at Newmarket: half brother to Rye Tops and Troytops: clearly stays 10f well: acts on firm & yld ground & on a stiff trk: genuine & consistent & should win more races.   **56**

-- **BANANAS** [16] (O Douieb) 3-9-0 R Hills 15/8: -2: Well touted newcomer: slowly away though sn had ev ch: cost 20,000 gns as a yearling and is a half brother to Ananas who won her only start last term: evidently suited by 10f on yld ground: acts on a stiff trk: should go one btr soon.   **48**

-- **SARONICOS** [9] (C Brittain) 3-9-0 P Robinson 20/1: 00-3: Easy to back on reappearance though showed much impr form and fin clear of rem: trailed in last in both his races last season: half brother to several winners, incl fair middle dist performer Snow Mallard: stays 10f well: acts on yld ground and on a stiff track.   **46**

-- **AGATHIST** [8] (G Pritchard Gordon) 3-9-0 G Duffield 13/2: 00-4: Active in mkt on reappearance: no extra below dist though should impr for this run: showed some promise last season: eff over 10f on yld ground: should impr and win a race this season.   **35**

-- **RANELAGH** [1] 3-9-0 J Reid 33/1: 00-0: Outsider: led ½way till early in str: down the field in his 2 starts last season though should do btr this term: acts on yld ground.   **27**

14 **IZZY GUNNER** [5] 3-9-0 J Bleasdale 25/1: 0030-00: Wknd str: fair effort: showed his best form with forcing tactics when placed at Hamilton last season: eff over 8/10f on gd/firm & soft ground.   **19**

-- **RUN BY JOVE** [11] 3-9-0 J Lowe 14/1: 0300-0: Bckd at long odds on reappearance: stayed on late and never nearer: should impr considerably next time.   **00**

-- **Fancy Pan** [6] 8-11   -- **Come Pour The Wine** [4] 8-11
-- **Helsanon** [15] 8-11   -- **Johnstan Boy** [12] 9-0 -- **Glory Time** [7] 9-0
25 **Lineout Lady** [13] 8-11   -- **Fissure** [10] 8-11
99 **Master Music** [3] 9-0   -- **Redally** [14] 9-0
16 ran   3,1,7,5,5   (E B Moller)   G Wragg, Newmarket

195 STEVE MASSAM SELLING STAKES 3YO   £897   7f   Yielding 107 -25 Slow

138 **NORTHERN MELODY** [2] (A Bailey) 3-8-10(bl) P Bloomfield 11/10 FAV: -0031: 3 b c Northfields - Melodramatic (Tudor Melody): Back to selling company, and proved an easy winner, led below dist and was sn clear in a 3yo seller at Beverley Apr.12 (bought in 7,400 gns): cost 17,500 gns as a yearling and earlier had shown promise in btr company: ex Irish colt who is well suited by 7/8f: suited by some give: acts on a gall trk.   **32**

145 **PLANTER** [6] (T Fairhurst) 3-9-1(bl) M Beecroft 11/2: 33-0102: Stayed on well from ½way and beat the rem decisively: should win again in similar company soon: sure to stay 1m: see 51   **22**

41 **SISTER NANCY** [1] (M Lambert) 3-8-7 P Burke(7) 12/1: 0000-43: Kept on: appears to be impr: eff around 7f on yld ground and seems to acts on any trk.   **06**

-- **FOREVER YOUNG** [5] (M Lambert) 3-8-10 L Charnock 33/1: 000-4: Late prog & should do btr next time: showed no worthwhile form last season: acts on yld ground & should be suited by further.   **07**

-- **BONNY BRIGHT EYES** [14] 3-8-7 S Perks 12/1: 04000-0: Front rank most of the way.   **01**

41 **GUNNER GO** [10] 3-8-7 R P Elliott 14/1: 000-030: Failed to stay this extended trip: better in 41 (tight track).   **00**

145 **LITTLE ARMIER** [3] 3-8-7(VIS) A Murray 8/1: 000-200: Fitted with a visor: ran on late though best in 51 (6f, heavy).   **00**

-- **Creetown Sally** [9] 8-7   145 **Valdarno** [4] 8-10
145 **Rich Bitch** [13] 8-7   45 **Parkes Special** [8] 8-7
-- **Balidareen** [12] 8-7   131 **Rapid Star** [7] 8-7   33 **Geoffs Folly** [11] 8-10
14 ran   8,4,1½,1,1,nk   (T P Ramsden)   A Bailey Newmarket

196 RADIO HUMBERSIDE H'CAP (0-50) 3YO+   £3277   1m   Yielding 107 +06 Fast   [44]

17 **STAR OF A GUNNER** [5] (R Holder) 6-9-8 J Reid 15/2: 0100-01: 6 ch g Gunner B - Starkist (So Blessed): Made steady prog to lead inside dist, ridden out in quite a fast run h'cap at Beverley Apr.12: has been hurdling this winter: won on the Flat in Goodwood (2) and Warwick last season: very eff around 1m: acts on any going & on any trk though is particularly suited by a sharpish one.   **48**

70

10   PALMION [14] (R Hollinshead) 4-8-9 S Perks 14/1: 2240-02: Led briefly dist: good
effort: consistent h'capper last season, won at Thirsk and was placed on many occasions:
eff around 1m on firm & soft ground: well suited by a sharpish trk.   32
36   BWANA KALI [9] (M Tompkins) 4-8-10 R Cochrane 6/1: 4010-43: Ev ch, not btn far:
in good form: see 36.   30
79   TUTBURY [7] (W Wharton) 4-8-8 G Carter(5) 13/2: 2102-44: Nicely bckd: ev ch: see 79.   26
--   BURAAG [17] 5-9-4 K Hodgson 20/1: 40000-0: Gd late prog on seasonal debut & sure
to be straighter next time: last season won over 10f at Newmarket (gd/firm) and probably
needs further than todays trip: also acts on yld ground.   35
46   RAPID ACTION [1] 5-8-0 J Lowe 12/1: 3420-30: Fair effort over this slightly longer trip   18
+91 DE RIGUEUR [12] 4-9-3 W Carson 4/1 FAV: 4324-10: Led into str. hdd dist: btr in 91.   00
129 Menabel [13] 8-5   --   Rocabay Blue [15] 9-6 91   Bit Of A State [7] 8-6(bl)
--   Assaglawl [11] 8-13   71   Merry Measure [18] 8-13(BL)
--   Romantic Uncle [10] 8-9   --   Nicoridge [2] 10-0
--   Keats [4] 8-13   63   Common Farm [6] 8-2 --   Fleet Special [8] 9-8
--   Bundaburg [16] 9-9
18 ran   1,1½,1,1,hd,hd   (James Neville)   R Holder Portbury, Avon

197 CHARLIE PARTRIDGE GRIMSBY STAKES 2YO   £2225   5f   Yielding 107 +01 Fast

+21 PEATSWOOD SHOOTER [10] (M Brittain) 2-9-2 K Darley 6/5 FAV: 11: 2 gr c Windjammer -
Raffinata (Raffingora): Fast impr juvenile: heavily bckd and was al going like the winner,
led ½way for an easy win in quite a fast run 2yo stakes at Beverley Apr.12: also clocked a
fast time when making all in a maiden auction race at Leicester: very eff over 5f and sure to
stay further: acts on yld/soft grnd and on a stiff trk: suited by forcing tactics: in fine
form and should complete his hat trick.   55
*108 PANBOY [8] (T Fairhurst) 2-9-2 C Coates(5) 7/2: 312: Set off in front, comfortably held
by winner though is in good form and should win again soon: see 108.   42
--   OYSTER GRAY [13] (C Gray) 2-8-8 I Johnson 14/1: 3: Ev ch after a slow start: cheaply
acquired filly who seems sure to impr for this experience: acts on yld ground & on a stiff trk   30
--   JAYS SPECIAL [1] (M W Easterby) 2-8-11 M Hindley(3) 14/1: 4: Stayed on well from ½way:
mkt drifter today and is bound to impr on this effort next time: half sister to a couple of
sprint winners: acts on yld ground and on a stiff trk.   31
43   TEAM EFFORT [7] 2-8-11 R P Elliott 14/1: 030: Easy to back: btr on a tight trk in 43.   23
47   SINCLAIR LADY [6] 2-8-8 G Duffield 12/1: 00: Lost touch from halfway.   06
--   DEBACH DEITY [12] 2-8-8 R Cochrane 8/1: 0: Active in mkt on racecourse debut: sn behind
and beat only one home: cost 11,000 gns: bred to stay further than todays trip.   00
--   FAIRBURN [4] 2-8-11 A Murray 13/2: 0: Last to fin on racecourse debut: however showed
plenty of pace in the early stages and he should do btr than this.   00
--   Hunters Leap [11] 8-11   3   Muntag [2] 8-11
--   Rosies Image [9] 8-8   --   La Verte Gleam [5] 8-8
12 ran   4,2,1,2,6,1   (G Ashton)   M Brittain Warthill, Yorks

198 ROBIN PULFORD HANDICAP (0-35) 3YO   £1704   5f   Yielding 107 -09 Slow   [32]

168 GOLDEN GUILDER [7] (M W Easterby) 3-8-12 K Hodgson 2/1 FAV: 000-021: 3 b f Sonnen Gold-
Dutch Gold (Goldhill): In gd form, fin strongly to lead on the line in a 3yo h'cap at
Beverley Apr.12 and landed some nice bets: earlier this week ran up to Examination in a
similar event at Haydock: half sister to winning sprinter Dutch Gold: well suited by 5/6f:
acts on yld/soft ground and on a stiff trk.   25
--   PETILLER [8] (W Watts) 3-7-11 S P Griffiths(5) 20/1: 0000-2: Easy to back on reappearance though only just failed to make ev yd: lightly raced though showed little form
last season: clearly suited by forcing tactics over this minimum trip: acts on yld ground:
could win a small race on a sharper trk.   09
42   LOW FLYER [2] (G Oldroyd) 3-9-4 M Birch 4/1: 0004-03: Nicely bckd: just failed to
get up: won a small race at Beverley last season on heavy ground: eff over 5/6f on gd &
soft ground: seems to act on any trk.   30
64   KEN SIDDALL [13] (K Stone) 3-9-7 G Brown(7) 8/1: 032-004: Not btn far and this was
an impr effort: narrowly btn by Mayor in a nursery at Warwick last season (5f, gd/firm)
though remains a maiden: also acts on soft.   29
147 BEECHWOOD COTTAGE [5] 3-8-8(bl) G Carter(5) 6/1: 0010-00: Close up thro'out: see 147. 12
*145 MUSIC TEACHER [1] 3-8-6(7ex) A Shoults(5) 9/1: 300-010: Fair effort under her penalty.   05
103 OUR MUMSIE [12] 3-8-3 L Charnock 9/2: 0040-20: Nicely bckd though btr on soft in 103.   00
--   Haddon Lad [14] 9-0   --   Virajendra [11] 9-1   38   Kiki Green [9] 7-13(BL)(3ow)
--   The Bight [10] 9-6   --   Red Zulu [6] 8-10
12 ran   hd,hd,1½,1½,2,3   (C Buckton)   M W Easterby Sherriff Hutton, Yorks

199 ERIC SMITH BREAKFAST STAKES 3YO+   £1555   1m 4f Yielding 107 -09 Slow

--   COLONEL JAMES [10] (S Oliver) 4-9-6 R Cochrane 5/2 : 02200-1: 4 br c Captain James -
Faraday Girl (Frigid Aire): Nicely bckd, led inside dist, ridden out in a stakes event at
Beverley Apr.12: ex Irish trained colt who has been showing good form over timber this
Winter: last season won a minor event at Navan on the Flat: eff over 1m, stays 12f well:
suited by some give in the ground.   32

*8   JACKS LUCK [11] (M Tompkins) 5-9-6 M Rimmer 9/4 FAV: -12: Well bckd: stayed on well
though could not quite reach the winner: in good form: stays 12f well: see 8.   30
185   CHRISTO [7] (R Simpson) 4-9-2 S Whitworth 6/1: -323: Led into str: consistent
performer over hurdles and on the Flat though has yet to get in head in front: stays well.   25
8   HARBOUR BAZAAR [5] (M Chapman) 6-9-2(vis) J Williams 50/1: /000-04: Made most: had been
busy chasing this Winter: suited by middle dists and some give in the ground: remains a mdn.   19
41   ARDOON PRINCE [9] 4-9-2 C Dwyer 33/1: 000-000: Outsider: some late prog.   07
9   WISE CRACKER [15] 5-9-5 J Carroll(7) 9/1: 0021/00: Gambled on: chance early in
str though sn btn: ex Irish trained gelding who won a small race at Ballinrobe though failed
to appear last season: stays 12f well: acts on firm & yld ground.   02
--   CASTIGLIONE [14] 4-9-2 S Keightley 9/1: -32-0: Stayed on late: made the frame in
both his starts last season and has since been placed over timber: eff around 9f and is
sure to be suited by middle dists: seems to act on any going.   00

-- What Will I Wear [4] 9-6(bl)		-- Electrified [12] 8-13
-- Porter [2] 9-7	70 Mount Argus [16] 9-2	9 Winning Star [3] 9-6
23 Welsh Spy [8] 9-8(bl)	-- Far To Go [6] 9-2	-- Go Lissava [1] 9-2(bl)
-- Fill Abumper [13] 8-13		

16 ran   ½,½,4,8,5,5   (D O'Callaghan)   S Oliver Suckley, Worcs

---

Official Going Given as Soft (first 2 races): Heavy (remainder). All races except 2.15 started by flag

200 CHATHAM STAKES 2-Y-O   £684   5f   Soft 137 -01 Slow

61   SAMLEON [5] (R Hannon) 2-8-11 L Jones(5) 4/1: 41: 2 gr c King Of Hush - Perlease
(Bold Lad): Useful colt: easy to back, led below dist for an easy win in a 2yo stakes at
Folkestone Apr.14: said to have been unsuited by the testing surface on his debut though took
this similar ground in his stride: sprint bred: cost 3,000 gns as a yearling: looks sure to
win more races, especially on btr ground.   50
--   SCALLYKATH [2] (R Holder) 2-8-8 M Wigham 20/1: 2: Bckd at long odds on racecourse debut:
led over ½way: fair effort on this testing ground: evidently has plenty of pace and should
do btr on faster ground: acts on a sharpish trk.   30
115   CABALLINE [6] (M Haynes) 2-8-11 P Cook 7/1: 03: Ran on late: seems sure to be suited
by a longer trip: acts on soft/heavy ground: on the up grade: see 115.   29
--   ZOLA ZOOM [3] (P Kelleway) 2-8-8 Gay Kelleway(5) 4/6 FAV: 4: Odds on flop on racecourse
debut: showed good speed till below dist and should do btr than this: speedily bred filly who
cost 6,800 gns: probably needs faster ground.   25
--   MISS MARJORIE [4] 2-8-8 P Waldron 8/1: 0: Active in mkt on debut: outpcd after ½way
though should impr for this racing: daughter of useful miler Swing Easy.   19
--   PIPERS ENTERPRISE [1] 2-8-11 R Morse(7) 20/1: 0: Outsider though did attract some
support on racecourse debut: brought wide after ½way and trailed in last: should be well
suited by this minimum trip.   00
6 ran   6,2,½,2½,15   (G Howard-Spink)   R Hannon Marlborough, Wilts

201 GILLINGHAM SELLING H'CAP (0-25) 3YO+   £774   1m 2f Soft 137 -46 Slow   [23]

--   FLAMING PEARL [14] (B Stevens) 5-9-9(vis) R Carter(5) 3/1 FAV: 33/20-1: 5 b m Junius -
Carol Barnett (Frigid Aire): Fit from hurdling and was nicely bckd when winning a slowly run
selling h'cap at Folkestone Apr.14 (no bid): stayed on well to lead close home: placed in
similar company in a light season last year, and won at Haydock, Salisbury & Redcar in '84:
well suited by 10f: acts on any going and on any trk.and carries weight well.   28
119   MEZIARA [9] (A Ingham) 5-9-5(bl) L Riggio(7) 10/3: 0420-22: Led into str: in fine
form: see 119. should win a seller soon.   20
+119 TOPORI [6] (S Woodman) 7-8-10(5ex) P Cook 7/2: 0000/13: Had ev ch and ran well under
his penalty: see 119.   04
119   UNIT TENT [8] (B Sanders) 8-8-9(bl) G Sexton 14/1: 0314-04: Stayed on: trained by
G Lewis when winning a small race at Warwick last season: well suited by this trip: acts on
any going and does well on a turning course.   00
119   BLAIRS WINNIE [10] 4-8-4 Paul Eddery 11/1: 000-400: Active in mkt: led early though
no extra dist: has twice run below par on soft/heavy recently and need btr ground: see 28.   00
--   METELSKI [13] 5-9-10 G Duffield 8/1: 40100-0: Stayed on after a slow start: btr for
race: gained his first win in a similar event at Yarmouth last season: well suited by 10f on
gd and fast ground.   02
--   TRACK THE BEAR [4] 3-8-0 N Adams 9/1: 20000-0: Nicely bckd on seasonal debut: slowly
away and no threat: showed his best form early last season, when twice a runner up in sellers
over sprint dist: should stay 10f on breeding: acts on gd & soft grnd: should do btr next time   00

-- Najam [7] 8-5	-- Casbar Kid [3] 8-5(vis)	
-- Californian Link [12] 8-12		-- Tomorrows World [1] 8-5(BL)
121 Lord Butch [2] 9-7	-- Gold Floor [5] 8-5(bl)	

13 ran   1½,4,7,3,1,1½   (Nathan Lee Jnr)   B Stevens Lewes, Sussex

202 SALTWOOD HANDICAP STAKES (0-35) 3YO+   £1248   1m 4f   Soft 137 -72 Slow   [35]

85   HOLYPORT VICTORY   (M Usher) 4-8-13 M Wigham 3/1: 230-401: 4 br c Free State - Snow
Goose (Santa Claus): Led early in str for a comfortable win in a h'cap at Folkestone Apr.14:
placed several times in similar company last season, running well on this course several
times and gained his only win previous here as a juvenile: well suited by 10/12f: acts on
gd & soft/heavy grnd and is well suited by a sharpish trk. should win again.   32
92   JANUS   (N Smith) 8-9-2 B Rouse 7/2: 0/40-02: Led briefly approaching str, just held
on to 2nd place: ran well over hurdles last week and clearly is in good form: last won on
the Flat in '83, at Epsom, Folkestone, Brighton & Goodwood: eff over 12f and is suited by
a test of stamina: acts on gd & heavy grnd.   22
--   LADY LIZA   (B Stevens) 5-8-4 R Carter(5) 8/1: 10400-3: Fit from a recent run over
hurdles: ran to her best: won a seller at Windsor last season (1m, good): stays 12f well:
acts on any going.   10
184   APPEALING   (G Blum) 4-8-6(7ex) G Duffield 7/4 FAV: 00-4124: Quick reappearance: held up:
much better 184,58.   12
--   MASTER FRANCIS   4-9-6 P Cook 14/1: 20300-0: Lost place approaching str and should
do btr next time: maiden who fin 2nd on 3 occasions last season, once when just btn by
Wallah Wassl over this C/D: acts on firm & soft ground: well suited by a sharpish trk:
should find a small race this term.   00
129   DEERFIELD BEACH   4-8-3 J Williams 14/1: 0021-00: Made most till str: successful in
selling company at Leicester on her final start last term: stays 12f: acts on firm & soft grnd
                                                                                               00
--   ASSAIL   5-10-2 A Cole(7) 12/1: -310/0: Mkt drifter after a lengthy abs: led early
though clearly needed this race: trained by G Harwood when a runaway winner of a Kempton
maiden as a 3yo: now with   Ron Smyth: eff over 8/10f on gd/firm ground.   00
--   Ricco Star 0 8-9
8 ran   8,hd,shhd,20,6,10   (Holyport Bloodstock Ltd)   M Usher Lambourn, Berks

203 PRIVY COUNCILLOR E.B.F STAKES 3YO   £2460   6f   Soft 137 -06 Slow

--   TUSSAC (H Cecil) 3-9-3 S Cauthen 4/7 FAV: 112-1: 3 b c Miswaki - Cast The Die (Olden
Times): Smart colt: heavily bckd on reappearance, led below dist for an easy win in quite a
valuable 3yo stakes at Folkestone Apr.14: most impressive when gaining all the way wins at
Warwick & Newmarket last season, only just denied his hat trick by shock winner Hotbee in
Gr.3 Molecomb Stakes at Goodwood: very eff over 5/6f: acts on fast & soft grnd: evidently has
wintered well and should win some nice prizes this term.   77
--   TARIB (H Thomson Jones) 3-9-0 A Murray 4/1: 21112-2: Tried to make all on seasonal
debut, lacked foot of easy winner: very useful filly who won successive races at Beverley,
Catterick & Redcar last season: very eff over sprint distances with forcing tactics: acts on
firm & soft ground & has no track preferences: straighter for this race and sure to be
winning soon.   54
62   WEST CARRACK   (A Ingham) 3-9-3 L Riggio(7) 6/1: 2120-33: Stayed on late: tough task.   49
--   SEQUESTRATION   (C Austin) 3-8-8 A Clark 50/1: 00-4: No chance from ½way on reappearance: well btn in both his starts last season though is a half brother to several
winners and he could win a small race this season: suited by sprint distances.   20
--   BOLIVIA 3-9-0 C Mcnamee 10/1: 11040-0: Never a factor on her debut in this country:
dual winner in Germany last season: eff over 5/6f and is sure to do btr on faster ground.   12
5 ran   10,4,10,8   (Peter Burrell)   H Cecil Newmarket

204 GRAVESEND HANDICAP (0-35) 3YO+   £1317   1m 7f   Soft 137 -39 Slow   [29]

--   GOING BROKE (D Murray Smith) 6-8-2 Paul Eddery 8/1: 4/342-1: 6 b h Bustino - Spring
Maiden (Silly Season): First time out, led dist, ridden out to win a h'cap at Folkestone
Apr.14: had been hurdling during the Winter though has not run over timber for sometime after
suffering from a virus: made the frame in his 3 starts on the Flat early last season and in
'84 won at Yarmouth: well suited by 12/16f: acts on any going and is suited by a turning trk:
does well when fresh and runs very well h'capped: should win again.   12
121   SHINY COPPER   (N Smith) 8-9-2 B Rouse 4/1: 000-002: Led into str: good effort and he
usually runs well on this sharpish trk: see 121.   24
*126   LOVE WALKED IN   (W Holden) 5-8-10(7ex) R Morse(7) 9/4 FAV: 00-0013: Not btn far: 15L
clear of rem: in good form at present and clearly is well suited by a test of stamina: see 126   18
*121   BRIGADIER JACQUES   (C Austin) 5-8-10(4ex) A Clark 11/2: 2210+14: Much btr over this
C/D in 121 on similar ground.   03
23   MY CHARADE 5-9-0 J Williams 20/1: 0040-00: Some late prog: lightly raced last
season and last successful in '84 at Haydock: stays well: acts on any going.   06
--   JENNY WYLLIE 5-8-13 S Cauthen 9/1: 32300-0: Made most till str: easy to back today
and should come on for this race: maiden whose best effort last year was her ½L 2nd to
Nastilos on fast ground at Beverley: suited by a test of stamina: equally eff on an easy trk.   00
--   SAN CARLOS 4-9-7 P Waldron 10/1: 04340-0: Fit from hurdling: lost place appr. str.   00
121   CHARTFIELD 6-8-0 L Riggio(7) 9/1: 0000/30: Fin last and much btr over this C/D in 121.   00
--   Relkisha 8-13   121   Keeley Louise 8-0   --   Spring Philtre 8-10
11 ran   1,hd,15,½,12,2   (J G O'Neill)   D Murray Smith Newbury, Berks

FOLKESTONE   Monday April 14th   - Cont'd

205 DARTFORD FILLIES MAIDEN 3YO   £684   5f   Soft 137 +07 Fast

-- **CORRALS JOY** (J Winter) 3-8-11 B Rouse 2/1 FAV: 03200-1: 3 b f Absalom - Pahaska
(Wolver Hollow): Landed some nice bets on her reappearance, made all and was ridden out to
win a fast run 3yo fillies maiden at Folkestone Apr.14: showed some promise last season: eff
over 5f on gd & soft grnd: likes a sharp trk & is clearly well suited by forcing tactics. 43
-- **NAWADDER** (B Hanbury) 3-8-11 M Hills 7/2: 0-2: Sustained chall inside dist, not quite
reach winner: highly tried on her sole start last season though is a half sister to useful
10f winner Trojan Prince and she should find a small race: eff over 5f on soft ground:
seems suited by a sharpish trk. 39
-- **CRESTA LEAP** (R Hannon) 3-8-11 S Cauthen 6/1: 24340-3: Ran well on her reappearance:
placed several times last season though had been off the trk since last July: eff over 5f
on firm & soft ground. 34
-- **ASTARTE** (G Pritchard Gordon) 3-8-11 Abigail Richards(3) 8/1: 23330-4: Easy to back on
seasonal debut: chased winner most of way: ran consistently in similar company last season:
eff over 5f on firm & soft ground: should win a small race in due course. 32
-- **TURNAWAY** 3-8-11 E Guest(3) 7/2: 0220-0: Appeared unsuited by this testing ground on
her reappearance: showed promise when running up to Kharrana over this C/D last season on
fast ground: speedily bred filly who should do btr than this. 22
-- **MEGADYNE** 3-8-11 R Morse(7) 20/1: -0: Easy to back: stayed on late. 16
-- Sweet Fool 8-11   89 Boxers Shukee 8-11   -- Winters Beta 8-11
-- Divine Fling 8-11   -- Kelly Lindo 8-11   175 Lochanier 8-11
87 Someway 8-11
13 ran   1,2,1,5,3   (A Th Van der Lecq)   J Winter Newmarket

---

WOLVERHAMPTON   Monday April 14th   Lefthand Easy track

Official Going Given as Soft

206 TRILLIUM MAIDEN STAKES 2YO   £822   5f   Heavy 161 -25 Slow

-- **ASTON LASS** [1] (L Barratt) 2-8-11 A Proud 20/1: 1: 2 b f Headin' Up - Ritzy Dreamer
(High Line): Led well inside final 1f, under press in a 2yo maiden at Wolverhampton Apr.14:
home bred filly: eff at 5f, should stay further: acts on heavy ground and an easy track. 38
-- **AKII BUA** [7] (R Sheather) 2-9-0 R Cochrane 11/10 FAV: 2: Heavily bckd: led 1f out:
half brother to 1m winner Essam and should find a small maiden: eff at 5f on heavy ground. 37
-- **LAST RECOVERY** [9] (M Ryan) 2-8-11 P Robinson 5/1: 3: Mkt drifter: made most: cost
2,500 gns: dam a winning sprinter: acts on heavy. 28
-- **STARCH BROOK** [4] (R Hollinshead) 2-8-11 S Perks 8/1: 4: Nearest fin: speedily bred
and should impr: acts on heavy. 25
-- **DECCAN PRINCE** [3] 2-9-0 G Baxter 5/1: 0: Mkt drifter, no show: cost 2,600 gns and is
a brother to winning 2yo in '83 Deccan Queen: should impr. 14
-- **SKRAGGS PLUS TWO** [2] 2-9-0 M Rimmer 20/1: 0: Mkt drifter and no show. 00
-- **RECORD FLIGHT** [8] 2-8-11 W Carson 11/2: 0: Al rear: should be suited by longer dists. 00
-- **KNOWLES BANK** [6] 2-9-0 M Fry 10/1: 0: Prom early. 00
8 ran   1½,2,1,6,6,2,½   (L Barratt)   L Barratt Oswestry, Salop

207 WALLFLOWER SELLING HANDICAP 0-25   £757   1m   Heavy 161 -11 Slow   [17]

120 **FIC VIC** [2] (B Stevens) 3-7-8 C Rutter(0) 8/1: 0000-01: 3 br g Take A Reef -
Westerlands Finis (Owen Anthony): Active in mkt, led under strong press final 1f in a 3 &
4yo selling h'cap at Wolverhampton Apr.14 (bought in 2,600 gns): lightly raced previously:
eff at 7f/1m: acts on gd/firm & heavy and runs well at Wolverhampton. 09
8 **CUT A CAPER** [8] (B Preece) 4-9-7 S Keightley 10/1: 0002-02: Springer in mkt: ran on
under press: winning plater over hurdles: eff at 1m on gd/firm & heavy. should win a seller. 16
22 **SNAKE RIVER** [5] (D Nicholson) 4-9-13 W Hayes(7) 10/1: 4001-43: Mkt drifter: led 3f
out: acts on any grnd: see 22. carries weight well. 20
8 **STONEBROKER** [9] (D Haydn Jones) 4-8-13 J Reid 2/1 FAV: 0-00-04: Well bckd: ev ch:
eff at 1m/10f on gd & heavy. 05
22 **PEN TAW** [3] 4-9-4(bl) G Starke 5/2: 0200-30: Btr on gd & firm: see 22. 06
-- **DECEMBRE** [7] 4-9-7 A Proud 20/1: 0-000-0: Ran on final 2f: fit from hurdling: should
stay further than 1m: acts on heavy. 05
139 Hannah Reed [11] 7-13   22 Meganot [1] 8-9   -- Another Glamgram [6] 8-1(2ow)
-- Lochfast [10] 9-9   -- Holme Code [12] 8-11   -- Sweet Explanation [4] 9-6(BL)
12 ran   1,1,½,2,2½,shhd   (Vic Searle)   B Stevens Bramley, Surrey

208 HYACINTH HANDICAP STAKES 4YO+ 0-50   £2524 1m 4f Heavy 161 -10 Slow   [43]

88 **SCREES** [13] (J H Wilson) 5-8-7 D Nicholls 12/1: -021: 5 gr g Precipice Wood -
Chieftain's Lady (Border Chief): Made virtually ev yd, comfortably in a h'cap at Wolverhampton Apr.14: last won in '83 at Catterick & Chester: stays 12f well: best with forcing
tactics on a sharp/easy trk: acts on gd & heavy. 32

74

--   **MILLERS TALE** [10] (I Balding) 4-9-1 S Payne 8/1: 00002-2: Led nearing final 1f, sn wknd: btr for race: first time out in '85 was an easy winner of a maiden at Bath: eff at 12f and may stay further: acts on gd/firm & heavy.   **33**

*92   **RECORD WING** [1] (D Haydn Jones) 8-9-2(5ex) D Williams(7) 11/4 FAV: 000-213: In gd form. **30**

--   **THE MISSISSIPPIAN** [7] (M Eckley) 5-7-7(6oh) M Fry 8/1: 00000-4: Active in mkt: sn prom: in '84 won at Leicester: btn in sellers in '85: eff at 10/12f: acts on gd/firm & heavy.   **07**

126   **BALGOWNIE** [3] 6-7-8 P Burke(5) 16/1: 2-11000: Disapp since 36 (10f).   **03**

--   **STANS PRIDE** [16] 9-9-7 P Robinson 5/1: -1124-0: Fit from hurdling: late hdway: in '85 won a h'cap on this trk and a maiden at Haydock: eff at 12f, suited by further on the Flat: acts on firm & heavy: genuine & consistent and should do btr next time.   **28**

--   **LOBKOWIEZ** [4] 7-9-6 W Carson 9/1: 00210-0: Sn prom, fdd on seasonal debut: in '85 won h'caps at Ripon & Kempton (first time out): in '84 won at Haydock: very eff at 12f: acts on any ground and on any trk.   **00**

--   **BALMACARA** [9] 5-7-13 A Shoults(3) 9/1: 32230-0: Btr for race: in '85 won an amateur h'cap at Carlisle and was placed on numerous occasions: in '84 won at Wolverhampton: eff at 8/9f, stays 12f well: acts on firm & soft & on any trk.   **00**

129   **BOSSANOVA BOY** [8] 7-8-10 G Baxter 8/1: 2230-00: Well btn: see 129.   **00**

--	Baluchi [11] 7-8	--	Crook N Honest [2] 7-7(1oh)		
--	Kates Pride [5] 9-3	--	Changanoor [6] 9-0	--	Fleurcone [12] 8-0
160	Timewaster [14] 8-2				

15 ran   4,2,hd,3,¾   (Mrs G S Rees)   J H Wilson Tarleton, Lancs

---

209   BLUEBELL FILLIES STAKES 3YO   £1145   1m 1f   Heavy 161 -06 Slow

--   **BELICE** [9] (S Mellor) 3-8-11 N Howe 25/1: -1: 3 b f Super Concorde - Hopeful Road (Hasty Road): Ex French trained filly: made a winning seasonal debut, led nearing final 1f comfortably in a 3yo fillies stakes at Wolverhampton Apr.14: eff at 9f and should stay further: acts on heavy grnd and an easy trk.   **46**

--   **SECRET WEDDING** [16] (W Hern) 3-8-11 W Carson 6/1: 30310-2: Al prom: in '85 won the Newmarket Challenge Cup: half sister to several winners, incl useful Falstaff: stays 9f: acts on gd/firm & soft.   **36**

--   **FLYING FAIRY** [8] (H Cecil) 3-8-11 W Ryan 9/4 FAV: 00-3: Well bckd: dsptd lead 3f out: very well bred filly who showed promise on both outings in '85: acts on heavy, possibly btr on good & firm and should find a maiden.   **34**

141   **FAIR ATLANTA** [5] (M Usher) 3-8-11 A Mcglone 10/1: 4003-24: Stays 9f: gd effort: see 141   **30**

--   **ARMOUR OF LIGHT** [10] 3-8-11 S Whitworth 20/1: -0: Made most on racecourse debut, showing promise: half sister to 7f winner Thats Magic: acts on heavy ground.   **29**

--   **TAKE A BREAK** [19] 3-8-11 C Rutter(5) 25/1: 20020-0: Late hdway on seasonal debut: 2nd in sellers at Wolverhampton & Warwick in '85: stays 9f and acts on firm & heavy.   **20**

--   **TRANSCENDENCE** [1] 3-8-11 G Baxter 7/1: -0: Prom ½way: stoutly bred filly who should do btr in time.   **00**

--   **STRAW BOATER** [7] 3-8-11 R Guest 4/1: -0: Easy to back: al trailing: half sister to Coming Generation and should impr.   **00**

--	Yamma [12] 8-11	37	Highest Note [15] 8-11		
--	Janie O [14] 8-11	169	Celtic Dove [11] 8-11	--	Miss Aron [6] 8-11
--	Damascus Dew [13] 8-11			--	Miss Betel [3] 8-11
75	Parts Is Parts [11] 8-11			--	Crimson Robes [18] 8-11
--	Sallow Kitten [2] 8-11				

18 ran   5,¾,2,nk,5,¾   (Mrs Paulette Meynet)   S Mellor Lambourn, Berks

---

210   CROCUS EBF STAKES 3YO   £2675   1m   Heavy 161 +11 Fast

*68   **CRESTA AUCTION** [2] (G Pritchard Gordon) 3-9-6 G Carter(5) 9/2: 0413-11: 3 b c Auction Ring - Baby Clair (Gulf Pearl): Very useful colt: led from the stalls, comfortably in quite a fast run 3yo stakes at Wolverhampton Apr.14: first time out won at Nottingham: in '85 won a maiden at Brighton: eff over 6/7f, stays 1m really well: acts on firm & soft & on any trk: consistent sort who should win more races.   **65**

*24   **FLEET FORM** [3] (C Nelson) 3-9-6 J Reid 3/1: 1300-12: Al prom: stays 1m: see 24 (7f).   **55**

--   **PICATRIX** [1] (G Harwood) 3-9-6 G Starkey 4/7 FAV: 00111-3: Odds on flop on seasonal debut: unsuited by heavy? in fine form late last season winning at Chepstow & Brighton (2): very eff at 7f, stays 1m: acts on firm & yld and likes an undulating trk: should do much btr than this.   **49**

127   **GERAGHTY AGAIN** [6] (A Bailey) 3-8-11 K Hodgson 33/1: 00-04: Prom over 5f: best effort yet: stays 1m and acts on good & heavy: half brother to winning 2yo Standing Order.   **36**

191   **SONG AN DANCE MAN** [5] 3-9-2 R Wernham 33/1: 000-400: Impossible task: see 116.   **00**

5 ran   6,4,¾,25   (Mrs H F Gevers)   G Pritchard Gordon Newmarket

---

211   DAFFODIL HANDICAP STAKES 0-35   £1760   5f   Heavy 161 +15 Fast   **[38]**

76   **SPACEMAKER BOY** [5] (R Nicholls) 6-9-7 N Howe 3/1 Co.FAV: 020-241: 6 b h Realm - Glounanarrig (Dike): Made all on the far side (top weight) in a fast run h'cap at Wolverhampton Apr.14: in '85 won h'caps at Pontefract, Hamilton & Haydock: very eff over 5f: acts on any ground & on any trk, though likes a sharp/easy one: suited by forcing tactics.   **40**

+124 ROSIE DICKINS [14] (R Hollinshead) 4-8-6(7ex) R Lappin(7) 3/1 Co.FAV: 0300-12: Nearly got up:
in fine form: see 124. seems to love the mud.   24
30   JACKIE BLAIR [10] (M Mccormack) 4-8-12(BL) W Carson 3/1 Co.FAV: 0040-03: Led stands side:
in '85 made ev yd in a h'cap at Warwick: winning 2yo at Salisbury: eff at 5f: worth another chance.19
124 ROYAL BEAR [15] (J Bradley) 4-7-8(1ow)(3oh) C Rutter(0) 10/1: 00-2204: Mkt drifter:
better 84 (sharp): see 30.   00
--   HILMAY [6] 4-8-2 P Robinson 33/1: 02000-0: Prom far side: maiden: eff over 5f on
gd & yld: runs well on a sharp/easy trk.   06
--   LUCKY STARKIST [12] 4-8-0 R Fox 20/1: 00410-0: Btr for race: in '85 won a seller at
Edinburgh: eff over 5/6f on firm & yld: best with forcing tactics on a sharp trk.   00
--   High Eagle [9] 8-10   --   Pinetum [8] 8-12   --   Even Banker [3] 7-12(1ow)
--   Native Ruler [2] 7-7(3oh)   --   The Manor [11] 7-7(3oh)
--   Aphrodisiac [13] 8-1   --   Tollys Best [1] 7-7(3oh)
--   Taw Crossing [7] 7-8(BL)(1ow)(3oh)
14 ran   nk,5,$\frac{1}{2}$,$\frac{3}{4}$,5   (T Drake)   R Nicholls Somerby, Leics

---

NEWMARKET   Tuesday April 15th   Righthand, Stiff Galloping Track

Official Going Given as Good/Soft

212 EBF STUNTNEY MAIDEN STAKES 2YO C & G   £2385   5f   Good/Soft 113 -15 Slow
--   MISTER MAJESTIC [4] (R Williams) 2-9-0 R Cochrane 4/1: 1: 2 b c Tumble Wind - Our
Village (Ballymore): First time out, led 1$\frac{1}{2}$f out, ridden out in a 4 runner 2yo maiden at
Newmarket Apr.15: cost I.R. 26,000 and is a half brother to 2yo winner Clotilda: eff at
5f, should stay further: acts on yld & a gall trk.   56
--   ONE LINER [1] (N Callaghan) 2-9-0 Pat Eddery 15/8 : 2: Led/dsptd lead: kept on well:
cost 14,000 gns: should stay further than 5f: acts on yld and a gall trk: should find a maiden race. 52
187 FRENCH TUITION [3] (R Hannon) 2-9-0 A Mcglone 7/4 FAV: 23: Led/disputed lead:
better 187 (sharper track).   44
--   JONLEAT [2] (L Piggott) 2-9-0 W R Swinburn 10/3: 4: Friendless in mkt: al rear:
cost 14,000 gns and should impr.   33
4 ran   1$\frac{1}{2}$,3,3   (D A Johnson)   R Williams Newmarket

213 GEOFFREY BARLING MAIDEN 3YO FILLIES   £3814   7f   Good/Soft 113 -03 Slow
--   ZALATIA [2] (W Jarvis) 3-8-11 B Rouse 14/1: 22-1: 3 b f Music Boy - Zepha (Great
Nephew): Useful filly: first time out, led nearing final 1f, comfortably in a valuable 3yo
fillies maiden at Newmarket Apr.15: 2nd on both her starts at Doncaster and on this trk in
'85: eff at 7f, should stay further: acts on firm & yld ground & likes a gall trk: should
win more races.   58
--   ABSENCE OF MALICE [4] (B Hanbury) 3-8-11 R Cochrane 33/1: -2: Ran on well final 1f,
showing much promise: eff at 7f, should stay 1m: acts on yld ground & a gall trk: should
have no trouble finding a similar event.   53
--   GREEN FOR DANGER [16] (J Hindley) 3-8-11 M Hills 33/1: -3: Ex Irish filly: made most
and ran well: unplaced in 2 outings in '85: half sister to winning 2yo Red Roman: eff at
7f on yld ground.   48
--   NIHAD [3] (B Hanbury) 3-8-11 G Baxter 33/1: 0-4: Al there and ran well: unplaced
behind Twice Bold in a Lingfield maiden in '85: eff at 7f, should stay further: acts on yld
ground & a galal trk: should find a maiden.   44
--   MISS TIMED [7] 3-8-11 M Roberts 33/1: -0: Nearest finish on racecourse debut: impr
likely: half sister to numerous winners: eff at 7f, should stay 1m: acts on yld.   40
--   VIANORA [6] 3-8-11 G Starkey 8/1: 3-0: Mkt drifter: sn prom: on sole start in '85
fin 3rd to Elwadhna in a maiden on this trk: bred to stay 1m: acts on firm & yld.   39
--   GREAT LEIGHS [9] 3-8-11 B Thomson 12/1: 02-0: in '85 fin 2nd to
Niccolo Polo in a Haydock maiden: eff at 5f, stays 7f: acts on gd & yld.   00
--   ROYAL NUGGET [5] 3-8-11 W R Swinburn 15/8 FAV: 322-0: Heavily bckd: wknd well over
1f out: eased: ran really well in top company in her 3 outings in '85, fin 2nd to Kingscote
and Ala Mahlik: very eff at 6f, possibly btr on gd or firm & should do much btr than this. 00
--   LIKENESS [1] 3-8-11 W Carson 8/1: 033-0: Wknd well over 1f out.   00
--   SOEMBA [14] 3-8-11 Paul Eddery 13/2: 4-0: No threat.   00
--   ZUMURRUDAH [19] 3-8-11 A Murray 5/1: -0: Prom $\frac{1}{2}$way on racecourse debut.   00
--   Aphrosina [8] 8-11   --   Eastern House [17] 8-11
--   Hardy Chance [11] 8-11   --   Highland Ball [12] 8-11
--   Miss Hicks [15] 8-11   --   Queen Of Battle [18] 8-11
--   Gavea [13] 8-11
18 ran   2$\frac{1}{2}$,2$\frac{1}{2}$,1$\frac{1}{2}$,2$\frac{1}{2}$,$\frac{1}{2}$,nk   (R E Waugh)   W Jarvis Newmarket

214 GROUP 3 NELL GWYN STAKES 3YO FILLIES   £14440   7f   Good/Soft 113 +22 Fast

-- SONIC LADY [4] (M Stoute) 3-8-7 W R Swinburn 13/8 FAV: 1-1: 3 b f Nureyev - Stumped
(Owen Anthony): Potentially top class filly: first time out, justified strong support, making
almost all for an impressive 3L win in fast run Gr.3 Nell Gwyn Stakes at Newmarket Apr.15:
on sole outing in '85 was a runaway winner of valuable Blue Seal Stakes (Listed race) at
Ascot: cost $500,000 as a yearling: very eff at 6/7f, looks sure to stay 1m: acts on firm &
yld & a gall trk: held in very high regard and looks certain to play a major role in
the 1,000 Guineas.   86
-- LADY SOPHIE [8] (H Cecil) 3-8-7 S Cauthen 10/1: 01-2: Stayed on well final 1f:
excellent effort: on final outing in '85 won a 2yo fillies maiden at Yarmouth: half sister to
'82 Lincoln winner King's Glory: eff at 7f, certain to stay 1m: acts on gd/firm & yld &
should win more good races.   77
-- ALA MAHLIK [9] (F Durr) 3-8-7 G Starkey 11/4 : 11-3: Dsptd lead over 5f: smart filly
who won both her starts in '85 at Salisbury & Newmarket: very eff at 6/7f on gd/firm & yld:
runs well on a gall trk.   76
-- EMBLA [3] (L Cumani) 3-8-12 Pat Eddery 9/2: 2111-4: Mkt drifter: disliked this yielding
ground: very smart filly in '85, winning at Ripon & Kempton: on final outing won the Gr.1
Cheveley Park Stakes on this trk: half sister to very useful 3yo Tantino: eff over 6f, should
stay 1m: acts on gd/firm & on any trk: will do much btr than this. rated 85 last year.   68
-- BUSTARA [6] 3-8-7 P Robinson 33/1: 010-0: Sn prom: good effort: in '85 won a maiden
at Goodwood: eff at 7f, should be suited by 1m: acts on gd/firm & yld.   61
-- BAMBOLONA [5] 3-8-7 R Cochrane 16/1: 210-0: No real threat: smart filly in '85, winning
a Listed race at Kempton: cost only 8,200 gns: eff at 6/7f, may stay 1m: acts on yld, well
suited by firm ground.   58
-- Mrs Waddilove [1] 8-7   -- Meteoric [2] 8-7   -- Moonlight Lady [7] 8-7
9 ran   3,hd,7,¾,1½   (Sheikh Mohammed)   M Stoute Newmarket

215 JERRY SPENCER SMITH MEMORIAL HCAP 0-70   £5390   1m 6f Good/Soft 113 -10 Slow   [62]

52 ROSTHERNE [10] (K Stone) 4-7-10 L Charnock 8/1: 023-421: 4 ch.g Crimson Beau -
Correct Approach (Right Tack): Ran on well final 1f to get up close home in a close fin to
a h'cap at Newmarket Apr.15: in '85 won the valuable XYZ h'cap at Newcastle: eff at 10f,
stays 14f and may get 2m: acts on gd & yld and runs well on a gall trk: genuine.   43
58a NAFTILOS [5] (C Brittain) 4-8-6 P Robinson 12/1: 1120-02: led briefly final 1f:
btn a whisker: good effort: in '85 won h'caps at Wolverhampton & Beverley, also won a
maiden again at Beverley: eff at 14f, stays 2m well: acts on firm & yld and likes a stiff
trk: should be winning soon.   52
-- CADMIUM [4] (P Cole) 4-8-9 Pat Eddery 11/2 Co.FAV: 13331-3: Just failed: disptd lead 6f
out: good seasonal debut: in '85 won at Catterick & Sandown: eff over 12f, stays 14f well:
acts on firm & yld & on any trk.   54
-- BACKCHAT [8] (G Harwood) 4-9-2 G Starkey 8/1: 0-411-4: Friendless in mkt: led 2f out:
in '85 won at Newmarket and Bath: very eff over 13/14f: acts on gd/firm & yld & a stiff trk.   59
-- PATHS SISTER [7] 5-7-12 W Carson 11/2 Co.FAV: 13111-0: Never nearer, but not btn far:
in fine form in '85, winning h'caps at Doncaster, Haydock (2), Newcastle & Ayr (awarded
race): in '84 won at Edinburgh & Doncaster: closely related to useful stayer/hurdler
Path Of Peace: eff over 14f, stays 2m2f: acts on any going & on any trk: genuine.   38
-- INDE PULSE [3] 4-9-10 M Hills 10/1: 11100-0: Gd effort under 9-10.   62
58a TRAPEZE ARTIST [2] 5-8-1(vis) S Dawson(3) 11/2 Co.FAV: 300-040: Al trailing: much
better 58a (soft/heavy).   00
58a Popsis Joy [12] 7-10   -- Dominate [1] 7-7(1oh)   92   Tivian [6] 7-12
-- Stan The Man [11] 8-10   -- Rikki Tavi [9] 7-11
12 ran   shhd,nk,1½,2½,2   (Mrs N Nuttall)   K Stone Malton, Yorks

216 LADBROKE HANDICAP 3YO 0-60   £5064   7f   Good/Soft 113 +05 Fast   [65]

-- DIGGERS REST [16] (G Wragg) 3-9-2 Pat Eddery 11/1: 303-1: 3 b c Mr Prospector -
Loralane (Habitat): Very useful colt: first time out, led 1½f out, comfortably in a valuable
h'cap at Newmarket Apr.15: dam is a half sister to 1,000 Guineas winner On The House: eff
at 7f, should be suited by 1m plus: acts on gd/firm & yld & runs well at Newmarket.   68
178 BELOW ZERO [8] (A Bailey) 3-7-12(5ex) C Rutter(5) 5/1: 402-122: Heavily bckd: ev ch
over 1f out: in excellent form: see 74.   44
-- MISTER WONDERFUL [15] (J Dunlop) 3-9-7 W Carson 16/1: 210-3: Kept on well final 1f:
fine effort under top weighht: in '85 won a valuable maiden at Ascot: eff at 6/7f, should
stay 1m: acts on firm & yld & a gall trk: should be winning soon.   67
-- DUNLORING [12] (G Pritchard Gordon) 3-8-5 W Ryan 25/1: 20000-4: Sn prom: gd effort:
first time out in '85 won at Haydock and does well when fresh: stays 7f: acts on gd & yld
and on any trk.   48
*81 GOOSE HILL [9] 3-8-1(5ex) G Carter(3) 9/2: 10-10: Made much: in gd form: see 81.   43
-- CHINOISERIE [13] 3-8-9 R Guest 10/1: 022-0: Gd late hdway and should do btr next
time: showed a deal of promise in '85 finishing 2nd to Andartis on this trk and Queens
Soldier at Yarmouth: eff at 7f, will be suited by 1m plus: acts on gd/firm & yld.   49
-- LASTCOMER [11] 3-8-11 W R Swinburn 4/1 FAV: 1-0: Uneasy fav: wknd: on sole start in
'85 won a fast run maiden at Doncaster: half sister to several winners: eff at 6f, bred
to stay 1m: acts on yld & should do btr than this.   00

*33   EMRYS [14] 3-7-10 S Dawson(3) 9/1: 002-10: Slow start: btr 33 (soft).   **00**

62	Hymn Of Harlech [4] 8-8			**99**	Mr Kewmill [17] 7-7(11oh)
--	Swifts Pal [2] 8-12	--	Thalassino Asteri [3] 8-12		
168	Mayor [5] 8-5	--	Town Jester [7] 8-13	--	Kings Touch [6] 8-5
--	Edgewise [1] 8-12	--	Hot Gem [10] 8-9		

17 ran   2½,hd,1½,nk,¾   (Sir Philip Oppenheimer)   G Wragg Newmarket

217 STETCHWORTH MAIDEN STAKES 3YO   £3613   6f   Good/Soft 113 -02 Slow

--   NO BEATING HARTS [3] (M Mccormack) 3-9-0 S Cauthen 9/1: 00320-1: 3 b g London Bells - Movement (Daring Display): Made most, staying on well in a 3yo maiden at Newmarket Apr.15: eff at 6/7f on any trk: acts on firm & yld ground.   **52**

--   RESPECT [2] (R Laing) 3-9-0 W Carson 13/2: 243-2: Duelled with winner final 1f: just btn: gd effort: speedily bred sort, who is a half brother to several winners: eff at 6f: acts on gd/firm & yld & a gall trk: yet to fin out of the frame and should win soon.   **50**

--   BONNY LIGHT [1] (R Sheather) 3-9-0 R Cochrane 13/2: 204-3: Chance 1f out: gd effort: lightly raced 2yo: eff at 5/6f on firm & yld.   **42**

33   PRETTY GREAT [10] (I Matthews) 3-8-11 G Carter(3) 10/1: -34: Sn prom: in gd form: eff at 6/7f on yld & soft: may win soon at one of the lesser trks: see 33.   **39**

--   BERTIE WOOSTER [11] 3-9-0 W R Swinburn 13/2: 320-0: Ev ch 1½f out: btr for race: mkt drifter today: trained by P Makin last season now with L Piggott: eff at 5/6f on gd & yld.   **41**

--   CHUMMYS PET [6] 3-9-0 M L Thomas 20/1: -0: Mkt drifter on racecourse debut: sn prom.   **38**

--   CODICES [20] 3-9-0 G Starkey 4/1 FAV: 42340-0: Fin 9th on seasonal debut: showed a deal of promise in '85 but failed to win: stays 1m: acts on yld, likes gd/firm.   **00**

--   SHAYI [7] 3-9-0 M Roberts 9/1: -0: Al mid-div.   **00**

--	Homme Daffaire [8] 9-0			--	Needlewoman [4] 8-11
--	Gregorian Chant [15] 9-0			--	Hansom Lad [22] 9-0
--	Khamsin Red [21] 9-0	--	Khlestakov [5] 9-0	**83**	Low Key [17] 9-0
--	Muhtaris [13] 9-0	--	Winning Format [9] 9-0		
--	Angel Target [14] 8-11			--	Georgian Rose [12] 8-11
--	Pleasure Island [19] 8-11			--	Pointed Lady [18] 8-11
--	Pact [16] 9-0				

22 ran   ¾,3,hd,½,1,hd   (Tony Hart)   M Mccormack Sparsholt, Berks

---

Official Going Given as Good/Soft

218 WOOD DITTON STAKES (3-Y-O)   £5400   1m   Good/Yld 78 +17 Fast

--   ARMADA [5] (G Harwood) 3-9-0 G Starkey 4/5 FAV: -1: 3 b c Shirley Heights - If (Kashmir II): Top class prospect: heavily bckd on racecourse debut, led 2 out in fast time and drew right away for a highly impressive win in the Wood Ditton Stakes at Newmarket Apr.16: cost 1 million guineas as a yearling: eff at 1m: looks sure to be suited by 10/12f: acts on yld ground and a stiff trk: entered in the English, Irish & French Derbys and can only improve.   **82**

--   DARE SAY [6] (J Tree) 3-9-0 Pat Eddery 10/1: -2: Kept on well final 1f: no chance with winner, though ran well: half brother to several winners, incl the smart sprinter Kafu: eff at 1m, may stay further: acts on gd/yld & a gall trk and should find a maiden soon.   **60**

--   TOP DEBUTANTE [15] (M Jarvis) 3-8-11 T Ives 33/1: -3: Led/dsptd lead: good effort: half sister to a minor 10f winner: eff at 1m on gd/yld and a stiff trk: should have no trouble finding a maiden.   **55**

--   HAWARDEN [3] (B Hills) 3-9-0 B Thomson 10/1: -4: Sn prom: promising debut: should stay further than 1m: acts on gd/yld and a stiff trk.   **57**

--   PRASINA MATIA [9] 3-9-0 Paul Eddery 20/1: -0: Mkt drifter: made much: U.S. bred colt: acts on good/yielding.   **54**

--   MONA LISA [1] 3-8-11 P Cook 33/1: -0: Nearest fin, showing promise: should be suited by further: acts on gd/yld.   **49**

--   BEAU SHER [21] 3-9-0 G Baxter 25/1: -0: Ran on final 2f: impr likely.   **00**

--   DALLAS [12] 3-9-0 R Guest 8/1: -0: No real threat: seems well regarded & should do better than this.   **00**

--	Bien Dorado [10] 9-0	--	Martessana Dancer [16] 8-11		
--	Ebolito [13] 9-0	--	Fast Realm [20] 9-0	--	Fly My Star [17] 9-0
--	Jaryan [7] 9-0	--	Nawob [14] 9-0	--	Paris Turf [22] 9-0
--	Pegmarine [19] 9-0	--	Sharpetto [8] 9-0	--	Sutimark [18] 9-0
--	Bitofagirl [2] 8-11				

20 ran   8,¾,nk,1½,1½,2   (K Abdulla)   G Harwood Pulborough, Sussex

219 APRIL MAIDEN STAKES (3-Y-O)   £3060   1m 4f   Good/Yld 78 -64 Slow

--   MUBAARIS [3] (P Walwyn) 3-9-0 Paul Eddery 10/1: 3-1: 3 ch c Hello Gorgeous - Aloft (High Top): Led over 2f out, staying on under press in a slowly run 3yo maiden at Newmarket Apr.16: on sole start in '85 fin 3rd to Secret Wedding on this trk: stays 12f well: acts on gd/firm & yld and a stiff trk.   **45**

-- JUMBO HIRT [4] (B Hills) 3-9-0 B Thomson 11/2: 30-2: Switched inside final 1f: not btn far: good effort: cost $500,000 as a yearling and is closely related to several useful winners: stays 12f: acts on gd/firm & yld and should find a maiden soon.. **44**

-- WELSH BARON [1] (M Albina) 3-9-0(VIS) S Cauthen 14/1: 00-3: Led over 3f out: visored first time: showed some promise in '85: half brother to several winners: stays 12f and acts on firm & yld. **40**

-- PEARLY KING [2] (G Harwood) 3-9-0 G Starkey 11/2: -4: Wknd 3f out on racecourse debut: easy to back today and should impr: half brother to 2 winners. **28**

116 SOLVENT [6] 3-9-0 T Ives 15/8 FAV: 4-20: Much btr in 116 (10f, sharp). **08**

-- POKEYS PRIDE [5] 3-9-0 R Cochrane 7/2: 0020-0: Prom, ev ch. **02**

95 CHEETAK [7] 3-9-0 J Reid 20/1: -00: Early ldr, fdd. **00**

7 ran   ¾,2,7,12,4   (Hamdan Al-Maktoum)   P Walwyn Lambourn, Berks

---

220 LADBROKE EUROPEAN FREE HANDICAP 3YO   £22292   7f   Good/Yld 78 -22 Slow [82]

-- GREEN DESERT [6] (M Stoute) 3-9-7 W R Swinburn 11/2: 21214-1: 3 b c Danzig - Foreign Courier (Sir Ivor): Very smart colt: defied top weight, led inside the final 1f, ridden out in rather slowly run, but valuable European Free H'cap (Listed) at Newmarket Apr.16: in '85 was a clever winner of Gr.2 Flying Childers Stakes at Doncaster: earlier won Gr.3 July Stakes at Newmarket: eff at 5/6f, stays 7f and should get 1m on gd ground: acts on yld, likes fast going & a gall trk: has a fine turn of foot and should run well in the Guineas. **88**

-- SPERRY [3] (P Walwyn) 3-8-11 Paul Eddery 9/1: 03210-2: Made most, kept on gamely: fine effort: in '85 won at Newmarket and Salisbury (first time out): eff over 6f, stays 7f: acts on yld, likes fast ground: acts on any trk and is best when forcing the pace: genuine. **75**

-- PILOT JET [9] (R Williams) 3-8-10 R Cochrane 5/1: 41-3: Ch over 1f out: good effort: on final outing in '85 was a ready winner of a maiden at Newmarket: cost only 12,500 gns: half brother to several winners: eff at 6/7f on gd & yld. **69**

60 FOUZ [8] (P Cole) 3-8-10 T Quinn 9/2 FAV: 3020-34: Much btr in 60 (1m, sharper trk). **55**

-- TOP RULER [1] 3-8-13 W Carson 8/1: 134-0: Never nearer: btr for race: first time out in '85 won a valuable event at York: eff over 6/7f, should stay further: acts on gd/firm & yld and a stiff trk. **57**

-- NATIVE WIZARD [5] 3-8-10 A Murray 7/1: 3012-0: Never in it. **47**

-- BRIDESMAID [4] 3-8-10(VIS) B Thomson 12/1: 21430-0: Early speed, wknd. **00**

-- LUNA BID [2] 3-8-10 Pat Eddery 5/1: 11130-0: Fdd quickly over 2f out. **00**

8 ran   1,2½,7,½,4,shhd   (Maktoum Al-Maktoum)   M Stoute Newmarket

---

221 GROUP 3 EARL OF SEFTON E.B.F. STAKES   £22794   1m 1f Good/Yld 78 +01 Fast

-- SUPREME LEADER [2] (C Brittain) 4-8-10 P Robinson 7/2: 40030-1: 4 b c Bustino - Princess Zena (Habitat): Very smart colt: not the best of runs, but led final 1f, comfortably in valuable Earl Of Sefton Stakes at Newmarket Apr.16: early in '85 won at Sandown, later ran fine races when 3rd in the 1,000 Guineas and 4th in the Epsom Derby: very eff over 8/10f, though does stay 12f: acts on yld, likes gd & firm: suited by a gall trk & should win more good races. **88**

-- FIELD HAND [5] (B Hills) 4-8-10 B Thomson 14/1: 03121-2: Led 2f out: 6L clear 3rd: fine effort on seasonal debut: much impr in '85, winning at Haydock, Ascot (Ladies race) and Chester: half brother to the smart Prego: very eff over 8/9f: acts on firm & yld & on any trk: should be winning very soon. **80**

-- DAMISTER [7] (J Tree) 4-9-1 Pat Eddery 6/4 FAV: 13313-3: Heavily bckd: ch 2f out: btr for race: in '85 was a model of consistency, winning Gr.2 Mecca Dante at York and Gr.3 Guardian Classic Trial at Sandown: also controversially awarded Gr.2 Great Voltigeur at York after fin a nk behind Shardari: also placed in both English & Irish Derbys: winning 2yo at Newmarket: eff over 8/10f, stays 12f well: acts on gd/firm & yld & on any trk: genuine **73**

-- ENGLISH SPRING [1] (I Balding) 4-8-10 S Cauthen 8/1: 00112-4: Held up: never nearer: should strip fitter next time: in fine form at the backend of '85 winning Gr.3 event in Italy and a valuable fillies race at Ascot: also successful at Wolverhampton & Epsom (h'cap): very eff over 1m/9f: acts on any going & on any trk: genuine filly. **66**

+17 K BATTERY [4] 5-8-10 T Ives 16/1: 0000-10: Al there: fine effort in this high class company: see 17. **65**

-- BIG REEF [10] 4-8-10 G Duffield 20/1: 2211-0: Hmpd in run in: btr for race: in '85 won at Newcastle & York: eff 8/9f, should stay further: acts on firm & soft & a gall trk. **64**

-- Phardante [9] 8-10   -- Line Of Fire [3] 8-10   -- Celebrity [11] 8-7

-- Lightning Dealer [8] 8-13

10 ran   3,6,½,hd,nk   (Capt M Lemos)   C Brittain Newmarket

---

222 ABERNANT STAKES (LISTED RACE)   £7609   6f   Good/Yld 78 +05 Fast

-- HOMO SAPIEN [3] (H Cecil) 4-9-2 S Cauthen 7/1: 11--2-1: 4 b c Lord Gayle - Bold Caress (Bold Lad)(Ire): First time out, edged left final 1f, but ran on to lead close home in valuable Abernant Stakes (Listed) at Newmarket Apr.16: smart colt, but has had training problems: on sole start in '85 was a fine 2nd to Efisio at Goodwood: won both his starts as a 2yo at Nottingham & Leicester: eff at 6/7f, should stay 1m: acts on fast & yld. **78**

*70   GREY DESIRE [1] (M Brittain) 6-9-12 K Darley 6/4 FAV: 301-112: Led over 1f out, just
btn: remains in excellent form: see 70. carries weight well.   87
18   QUE SYMPATICA [2] (R Boss) 4-9-6 M Miller 12/1: 0404-33: Al there: good effort: see 18.   76
--   PRINCE REYMO [6] (R Armstrong) 6-9-12 W Carson 12/1: 302D2-4: Made most: wkning· when
hmpd final 1f: most consistent in '85, winning at Thirsk and placed on numerous occasions:
in '84 won valuable events at Doncaster & Ostend: very eff at 5/6f: acts on firm & soft.   74
--   POLYKRATIS [4] 4-9-2 Paul Eddery 25/1: 42030-0: Never nearer: btr for race: in '85
won at h'cap at Nottingham: also a fine 2nd to Storm Warning in a Listed race at Doncaster:
in '84 won at Salisburyy: very eff at 5/6f, stays 7f: acts on gd & firm & a gall trk.   52
--   OROJOYA [9] 4-9-12 M Hills 4/1: 31313-0: Prom over 3f: should strip fitter next time:
very smart colt: much impr in '85, winning Gr.2 Vernons Sprint Cup at Haydock: also won
valuable h'cap at Newcastle and minor events at Kempton & Warwick: eff at 5-7f: acts on
firm, suited by gd or yld: acts on any trk: genuine & consistent.   52
--   BLUE EYED BOY [7] 3-8-2 B Rouse 5/1: 221-0: Active in mkt: fdd.   00
--   Atoka [8] 8-13   165 Cragside [5] 9-12(bl)
9 ran   ½,1½,3,6,4   (Mrs Maria Niarchos)   H Cecil Newmarket

223 E.B.F. BARTLOW FILLIES MAIDEN 2YO   £2518   5f   Good/Yld 78 -55 Slow

--   REGENCY FILLE [8] (R Williams) 2-8-11 R Cochrane 7/2: 1: 2 gr f Tanfirion - Regency
Girl (Right Boy): Led inside the final 1f, under press in a maiden at Newmarket Apr.16: cost
6,200 gns & is a half sister to several winners: eff at 5f on yld grnd & a gall trk.   52
--   STAY LOW [6] (G Blum) 2-8-11 G Duffield 33/1: 2: Fin well and nearly got up: cheaply
acquired: speedily bred filly who should win a maiden soon: eff at 5f on yld ground & a
stiff trk.   51
--   BECHEMAL [1] (B Hills) 2-8-11 B Thomson 5/1: 3: Slow start: led briefly final 1f:
impr likely from this $85,000 purchase: eff at 5f on yld.   45
--   NATURALLY FRESH [4] (J Winter) 2-8-11 Pat Eddery 6/4 FAV: 4: Much touted debutant:
never nearer: should impr: cost 6,000 gns: should be suited by further than 5f: better for race. 44
77   TOOTSIE JAY [9] 2-8-11 Paul Eddery 14/1: 30: Led/dsptd lead: acts on yld & heavy
and a gall track.   34
--   TOP AND TAIL [10] 2-8-11 P Robinson 14/1: 0: Sn prom, fdd: cost $24,000.   27
73   OUR PET [7] 2-8-11 A Mcglone 11/2: 00: Ev ch, bumped 2f out: see 73.   00
--   FLAPPER GIRL [2] 2-8-11 W R Swinburn 8/1: 0: Slow start, no show.   00
73   Revelina [3] 8-11   -- Game Light [5] 8-11
10 ran   hd,2½,nk,4,3   (C F Linney)   R Williams Newmarket

Official Going Given as Soft

224 GERRY FEILDEN STAKES (LISTED RACE) 3YO   £9786   1m 1f   Soft 140 +27 Fast

--   FLYING TRIO [3] (L Cumani) 3-9-4 Pat Eddery 3/1: 21102-1: 3 b c Trio - Griffade
(Ribocarre): Very smart ex French colt: led approaching final 1f, comfortably in fast run
and valuable Gerry Feilden (Listed race) at Newmarket Apr.17: one of the top French 2yos in
'85, winning at Every, Deauville & St Cloud: eff at 8/9f, should be suited by 10/12f: acts
on firm, suited by soft ground: sure to win more good races.   80
*60   TISNT [9] (P Cole) 3-9-4 T Quinn 5/1: -12: Chall from 2f out: in excellent form:
stays 9f: acts on any trk: see 60.   75
--   PLAID [2] (P Walwyn) 3-9-1 Paul Eddery 33/1: 132-3: Led over 2f out: fine seasonal debut:
first time out in '85 won valuable maiden at Ascot and does well when fresh: half brother
to winners abroad: stays 9f: acts on firm & soft.   67
--   SHIBIL [8] (M Stoute) 3-8-11 W R Swinburn 12/1: 33-4: Mkt drifter: al there: good
effort: showed promise on both starts in '85: eff at 9f and should be suited by 12f: acts
on gd/firm & soft.   51
--   WINDS OF LIGHT [4] 3-9-1 S Cauthen 2/1 FAV: 1-0: Heavily bckd: never nearer: unsuited
by soft? highly impressive winner of a 24 runner Newmarket maiden on sole start in '85:
should be suited by middle distances: acts on gd/firm & a gall trk: will do much btr than this 47
--   FESTIVAL CITY USA [6] 3a-4 B Thomson 14/1:   3-0: No threat: btr for race: on
sole start in '85 fin a promising 3rd to Soughaan in a valuable event at Ascot: well bred
sort who should be suited by middle distances: acts on gd/firm & soft.   29
--   MY TON TON [5] 3-9-1 P Robinson 16/1: 00410-0: Mkt drifter: made much.   00
--   CLIVEDEN [7] 3-9-1 G Starkey 7/1: 213-0: Mkt drifter: wknd 2f out.   00
--   Three Times A Lady [1] 8-8   -- Shahaab [11] 9-1
--   Happy Breed [10] 9-1
11 ran   1½,2,6,4,7,nk   (C A B St George)   L Cumani Newmarket

225 REMY MARTIN COGNAC H'CAP (0-50) 4YO+   £3002   1m 4f   Soft 140 -35 Slow   [49]

--   PUBBY [8] (J Toller) 5-8-2 G Duffield 7/1: 13310-1: 5 b m Doctor Wall - Snotch
(Current Coin): First time out, led approaching final 1f, comfortably, in a slow run h'cap
at Newmarket Apr.17: in '85 was in good form, winning at Haydock & Yarmouth: eff at 10f,
stays 12f well: acts on firm, suited by soft ground: genuine.   35

--   WITCHCRAFT [6] (G Wragg) 4-8-13 Pat Eddery 5/1: 00020-2: Led 2f out: kept on well: early
in '85 won a maiden at Haydock: eff at 10f, stays 12f really well: acts on gd & heavy &
likes a gall trk.   42
189 JOLIS GIRL [10] (M Ryan) 4-9-1 P Robinson 7/1: 20-0303: Good hdway over 1f out:
no extra inside final 1f: good effort: see 72.   43
--   SAFE RIVER [9] (L Cumani) 4-9-10 R Guest 7/1: 01221-4: No real threat: btr for race:
most consistent in '85, winning twice at Redcar: half brother to the smart stayer Protection
Racket and is well suited by 14f: acts on soft, likes gd/firm: likes a gall trk.   32
--   THE CLOWN [4] 5-7-8 J Lowe 3/1 FAV: 22200-0: Led 10f: fit from hurdling: in '85 won
a h'cap at Beverley and was quite consistent: eff at 12f on firm & yld.   01
--   ABSENT LOVER [5] 5-9-4 I Johnson 15/2: 31240-0: Never in it: btr for race.   15
126 WESTRAY [2] 4-8-11 S Perks 15/2: 0130-00: Dsptd lead, going well over 3f out: wknd:
in '85 won a maiden at Chester: eff at 12f, stays 14f: acts on gd & firm & on any trk.   00
166 Evros [3] 9-9   --   Touchez Le Bois [7] 8-12
--   Aylesfield [1] 9-3
10 ran   1½,nk,15,½,8   (A J Morrison)   J Toller Newmarket

226 GROUP 3 CRAVEN STAKES 3YO   £15400   1m   Soft 140 -09 Slow

--   DANCING BRAVE [6] (G Harwood) 3-8-7 G Starkey 11/8 FAV: 11-1: 3 b c Lyphard - Navajo
Princess (Drone): Potential top class colt: first time out, heavily bckd and led over 1f
out, comfortably in Gr.3 Craven Stakes at Newmarket Apr.17: easy winner of both starts in
'85, at Newmarket and Sandown: cost $200,000 as a yearling: very eff over 1m and should be
suited by 10/12f: acts on soft, well suited by fast ground: very highly regarded and there
is more impr to come: has a fine turn of foot & will be hard to beat this season.   88
--   FARAWAY DANCER [11] (H Cecil) 3-8-7 S Cauthen 9/2: 111-2: Led over 2f out: kept on
well and ran a fine race: unbtn in 3 starts in '85, at Sandown, Haydock & Goodwood: half
brother to a smart American sprinter: very eff at 1m & should stay further: acts on firm &
soft & on any trk: should win more good races.   82
--   MASHKOUR [9] (H Cecil) 3-8-7 W Ryan 14/1: 2211-3: Ch final 1f: very gd effort: in '85
won at Goodwood and Yarmouth: eff at 1m and looks sure to stay further: acts on firm & soft
and on any trk.   80
*127 JAZETAS [3] (N Callaghan) 3-8-7 Pat Eddery 25/1: 4-114: In excellent form: see 127.   65
--   EVES ERROR [7] 3-8-7 W R Swinburn 10/1: 112-0: Never nearer:'btr for race: smart 2yo,
winning at Epsom & Nottingham: on final outing fin 2nd to Flash Of Steel in Gr.2 event at
the Curragh: half brother to several winners, incl Apples Of Gold: eff at 1m, may stay
further: acts on gd/firm & soft & on any trk.   61
--   RESOURCEFUL FALCON [8] 3-8-7 T Quinn 16/1: 0111-0: Never beyond mid-div.   51
--   SHARROOD [10] 3-8-7 W Carson 11/2: 01111-0: Hdway when badly hmpd 2f out: best ignored:
smart 2yo in '85, winning at Newbury, Doncaster, Chester & Goodwood: cost $1.1 million:
eff at 7f, should be suited by 1m & further: acts on gd/firm & yld: highly regarded and is
much better than this.   00
--   SILVINO [4] 3-8-7 B Thomson 10/1: 31032-0: Led over 5f: btr for race.   00
60 Liam [2] 8-7   --   Illumineux [1] 8-7   60 Poderoso [5] 8-7
11 ran   1,½,6,2,6   (K Abdulla)   G Harwood Pulborough, Sussex

227 KRUG CHAMPAGNE STAKES 3YO   £2944   6f   Soft 140 -12 slow

62 HOME RULE [3] (M Mccormack) 3-8-13 Pat Eddery 10/3: 1200-01: 3 b c Home Guard -
Sierra (March Past): Fit from recent run, well bckd and led from the stalls, easily in a
4 runner event at Newmarket Apr.17: in '85 was quite consistent, winning at Carlisle: half
brother to several winners in France: very eff at 6f on gd/firm & soft & on a stiff trk.   59
--   MANTON DAN [2] (N Vigors) 3-9-1 P Cook 6/4 FAV: 012-2: Heavily bckd on seasonal debut:
al 2nd: useful 2yo, winning at Goodwood: half brother to several winners incl useful sprinter
Street Market: eff at 6f, may stay further: acts on soft, likes fast grund: seems to handle
any trk and is suited by forcing tactics.   49
--   MUMMYS SECRET [1] (G Pritchard Gordon) 3-8-13 G Duffield 7/1: 20400-3: Btr for race: in
'85 won at Windsor and Lingfield (subs. disq): half brother to 3 winners: eff over 5/6f:
acts on soft, likes fast ground.   40
--   ALKAASEH [4] (H T Jones) 3-9-6 A Murray 2/1: 210-4: Friendless in mkt: no threat:
unsuited by soft? highly promising 2yo, winning at Yarmouth: half brother to a useful Irish
sprinter: very eff at 6f, should stay further: acts on fast ground.   43
4 ran   5,3,1½   (J Wenman)   M Mccormack Sparsholt, Berks

228 LADBROKES BOLDBOY SPRINT H'CAP 0-60 3YO   £4760   6f   Soft 140 -07 Slow   [64]

62 MAJOR JACKO [1] (R Hannon) 3-7-10(2ow) D Mckay 50/1: 000-01: 3 b c Mandrake Major -
Toreadora (Matador): Rank outsider, but ran on strongly final 1f to lead close home in a
h'cap at Newmarket Apr.17: no form previously but had been working well at home: eff at 6f,
should stay 7f: acts on soft ground & a stiff trk: may win again.   44
*168 EXAMINATION [2] (A Bailey) 3-7-8(bl)(7ex) G Carter(1) 7/1: 0030-12: Made almost all:
in fine form: see 168.   40

--   OH BOYAR [3] (J Sutcliffe) 3-9-4 Pat Eddery 16/1: 1300-3: Ev ch over 1f out: good
seasonal debut: first time out in '85 won at Sandown: eff at 5/6f, may stay further: acts
on good and soft.   57

26   GLIKIAA MOU [7] (R Boss) 3-7-7(1oh) S Dawson(0) 3/1 FAV: 2F00-24: A handicap "good
thing": much btr 26: erroneously given 14lbs less to carry and she will now find it
very difficult to win off her proper mark.   27

--   COLWAY COMET [4] 3-9-3 T Ives 14/1: 21203-0: Sn prom on seasonal debut: very useful
2yo, winning at Ayr & Newcastle and was most consistent: eff at 6f, stays 7f well: acts on
firm & yld & seems best on a gall trk.   47

18   VAGUE LASS [10] 3-9-0 R Lines(3) 25/1: 20-3100: Al prom: winner at Cagnes in Mar:
eff at 6f on any ground: acts on any trk.   44

+134 TARANGA [15] 3-8-6(7ex) R Cochrane · 6/1: 002-110: Adverse draw: btr 134.   00

--   SKEEB [12] 3-9-3 W R Swinburn 11/2: 3114-0: No real threat: btr for race.   00

38	Young Jason [14] 7-9	--	Tufuh [13] 9-6	--	Topeka Express [8] 7-8
--	Helawe [6] 7-10	168	Careless Whisper [11] 8-0		
172	Quarryville [5] 9-7	*26	King Of Spades [9] 9-3		

15 ran   ¾,3,2,1½,shhd   (John Horgan)   R Hannon East Everleigh, Wilts

---

229   ROWLEY MAIDEN STAKES 3YO   £3652   7f   Soft 140 -28 Slow

--   NIGHT OUT PERHAPS [8] (G Wragg) 3-9-0 P Robinson 4/1 Jt.FAV: 0-1: 3 b c Cure The
Blues - Pipina (Sir Gaylord): Made a winning seasonal debut, very wl bkd: led over 1f
comfortably in a 3yo maiden at Newmarket Apr.17: ran only once in '85, fin 5th at Newmarket:
eff at 7f, should stay 1m: acts on gd & soft & a gall trk: should continue to impr.   50

--   HABER [14] (B Hills) 3-9-0 M Hills 14/1: -2: Active in mkt: ran on well final 1f:
eff at 7f, should stay 1m: acts on soft ground & a gall trk: should find a maiden shortly.   45

--   FIRST DIBS [10] (M Stoute) 3-9-0 W R Swinburn 4/1 Jt.FAV: 2-3: Well bckd: ch final 1f:
on sole start in '85 fin 2nd to Faustus at Nottingham: half brother to several winners and
should have no trouble finding a maiden: eff at 7f and acts on gd & soft.   41

--   GEORGES QUAY [2] (R Hannon) 3-9-0 A Mcglone 20/1: 000-4: Made much: half brother to
several winners: stays 7f and acts on firm & soft.   40

--   PENWARD [3] 3-9-0 Pat Eddery 9/2: 0-0: Easy to back: fdd final 1f: btr for race:
promising 6th to Soughaan at Ascot on sole start in '85: half brother to 1m winner Destina
and will impr on this: possibly btr on faster ground.   30

--   STAR SHINER [16] 3-9-0 P Waldron 33/1: -00-0: Nearest fin: will be suited by 1m plus:
acts on gd/firm & soft and should be placed to find a small maiden.   29

--   ROYAL TROUBADOR [11] 3-9-0 B Thomson 9/1: 0-0: Led/dsptd lead, fdd.   00

--   EXCLUSIVE NORTH [15] 3-9-0 W Carson 8/1: 2330-0: Never threatened.   00

--	Auction Time [5] 9-0	--	Al Bashaama [13] 9-0	--	Sahraan [17] 9-0
--	Persian Ballet [7] 9-0			--	On Water [1] 9-0
99	Lost Opportunity [4] 9-0			14	The Lidgate Star [12] 9-0
--	Willwood [6] 9-0				

16 ran   1½,1½,nk,5,½   (E B Moller)   G Wragg Newmarket

Official Going Given as Soft

230   BECKHAMPTON MAIDEN STAKES 2YO   £3268   5f   Heavy 170 -14 Slow

170 ARAPITI [8] (K Brassey) 2-9-0 S Whitworth 9/4: 21: 2 b c Runnett - Amiga Mia
(Be Friendly): Impr colt: well bckd: led over 2f out and drew right away for an impressive
win in a 2yo maiden at Newbury Apr.18: first time out fin 2nd at Chepstow: speedily bred sort
who cost 8,600 gns: eff at 5f, should stay 6f: acts on yld & heavy & a gall trk: should win
more races.   55

--   SEGOVIAN [7] (W Wightman) 2-9-0 Pat Eddery 7/4 FAV: 2: Well bckd debutant: no chance
with winner, though showed promise: eff at 5f on heavy ground & a gall trk: speedily bred
sort who should not be long in winning.   40

--   ACQUISITIVE [9] (M Usher) 2-9-0 M Wigham 12/1: 3: Never nearer on debut: impr likely
and should stay further than 5f: acts on heavy ground & a gall trk.   39

--   RIMBEAU [1] (C Nelson) 2-9-0 J Reid 7/1: 4: Led 3f on debut: cost 12,000 gns and
should impr: acts on heavy: should win soon on a sharper trk.   35

--   SOMEONE ELSE [2] 2-9-0 S Cauthen 8/1: 0: Late hdway: cost 8,600 gns and is a half
brother to several winners: acts on heavy: impr likely over longer distances.   29

--   PARIS GUEST [10] 2-9-0 R Cochrane 10/1: 0: Mkt drifter: sn prom, wknd: half brother to
smart '84 2yo Northern Chimes and will do btr than this, possibly on btr ground.   23

| -- | Leading Role [5] 9-0 | -- | Divine Charger [4] 9-0 |
| -- | Panache [3] 9-0 | | |

9 ran   7,½,1½,2½,2½   (P C Bourke)   K Brassey Upper Lambourn, Berks

231 SPRING MAIDEN STAKES 3YO   £3323   1m 3f Heavy 170 –05 Slow

-- **PAEAN** [2] (H Cecil) 3-9-0 S Cauthen 5/6 FAV: 2-1: 3 b c Bustino - Mixed Applause (Nijinsky): Very promising colt: heavily bckd and led over 2f out, easily in a maiden at Newbury Apr.18: on sole start in '85 was just btn by Kolgong Heights in a maiden on this trk: very well bred sort who should be suited by 12f: acts on yld & heavy & a gall trk: well regarded and should rate more highly.   **61**

-- **ROSEDALE USA** [14] (J Dunlop) 3-9-0 W Carson 10/1: ----2-2: Led str till over 2f out: stayed on well & should have no trouble finding a maiden: on sole start in '85 fin 2nd to Tommy Way in a Haydock maiden: eff at 11f, should be suited by 12f: acts on soft & heavy & a gall trk.   **54**

-- **LAABAS** [12] (P Cole) 3-9-0 T Quinn 12/1: 04-3: Good seasonal debut: lightly raced in '85: half brother to 12f winner Librate and should be suited by 12f himself: acts on gd/firm and heavy and will have no trouble finding a maiden.   **48**

-- **LOCAL HERBERT** [4] (I Balding) 3-9-0 G Starkey 15/2: 02-4: Ev ch str: 10L clear rem: on final outing in '85 fin 2nd to Comme Letoile in a maiden at Haydock: eff at 1m, stays 11f: acts on soft & heavy & a gall trk.   **40**

-- **FOXY PRINCE** [6] 3-9-0 J Matthias 16/1: -0: Late hdway on racecourse debut: friendless in mkt today and will impr.   **20**

-- **DUNCAN IDAHO** [1] 3-9-0 J Reid 7/1: -0: Not clear run into str: will do much btr than this: full brother to the 12f winner Jasper: one to keep an eye on.   **18**

-- **Euphemism** [10] 9-0   -- **Shirzad** [7] 8-11   -- **Billilla** [3] 9-0
164 Disciple [8] 9-0   -- **Chauve Souris** [11] 9-0
-- **Eaton Square** [9] 9-0   -- **Music Minstrel** [5] 9-0
-- **Keepcalm** [13] 9-0
14 ran   1½,2½,4,10,½,shhd   (Lord Howard de Walden)   H Cecil Newmarket

232 GROUP 3 FRED DARLING STAKES 3YO FILLIES   £17780   7f   Heavy 170 +09 Fast

-- **MAYSOON** [1] (M Stoute) 3-9-0 W R Swinburn 11/2: 130-1: 3 b f Shergar - Triple First (High Top): Very smart filly: first time out, well bckd and led well over 2f out, comfortably in quite fast run Gr.3 Fred Darling Stakes at Newbury Apr.18: first time out in '85 was an easy winner of a valuable maiden at Ascot: half sister to the smart Triagonal: eff over 6/7f: will be suited by 1m & further: acts on fast ground, well suited by heavy: should run well in the 1,000 Guineas, especially if the ground is riding soft.   **84**

-- **ASTEROID FIELD** [7] (B Hills) 3-9-0 B Thomson 7/1: 2114-2: Kept on well final 1f: fine seasonal debut: smart 2yo, winning Gr.3 event at Goodwood & a fillies maiden at Sandown: also an excellent 4th in Gr.1 Cheveley Park Stakes at Newmarket: eff at 6/7f, should be suited bt 1m: acts on gfirm & heavy & on any trk: should win more good races.   **80**

-- **TANOUMA** [10] (J Dunlop) 3-9-0 W Carson 7/1: 1-3: Fine effort after being off the trk since successful in a Goodwood maiden in May '85: eff over 6/7f: may stay 1m: acts on gd/firm & heavy and on any trk: should be winning soon.   **73**

-- **GWYDION** [4] (H Cecil) 3-9-0 S Cauthen 9/4 FAV: 11-4: Ev ch 2f out on seasonal debut: possibly unsuited by this heavy ground: smart, unbtn filly in '85, winning Gr.3 Queen Mary Stakes at Royal Ascot and first time out a fillies maiden at Newmarket: half sister to the Irish St Leger winner Opale and should stay 1m: acts well on firm ground & will do much btr on a sounder surface.   **65**

-- **KINGSCOTE** [3] 3-9-0 Pat Eddery 3/1: 13112-0: Easy to back: not quicken in this heavy ground: very smart 2yo, easy winner of Gr.2 Lowther Stakes (bt winner at York): also won Princess Margaret Stakes at Ascot & a fillies maiden at Salisbury: on final outing an excellent 2nd to Embla in Gr.1 Cheveley Park Stakes at Newmarket: eff at 6f, should be suited by 7f/1m: acts on heavy, but much btr on gd & firm.   **64**

-- **FASHADA** [2] 3-9-0 J Reid 8/1: 01-0: Stiff task on seasonal debut.   **56**
-- **NORTHERN ETERNITY** [5] 3-9-0 G Starkey 10/1: 112-0: Prom over 4f, btr for race.   **00**
-- **Smooch** [9] 9-0   *82 **Hoist The Axe** [8] 9-0 O
158 Lady Windmill [6] 9-0
10 ran   1½,3,4,½,4,shhd   (Maktoum Al-Maktoum)   M Stoute newmarket

233 CHEVELEY HANDICAP STAKES 3YO 0-50   £3726   5f   Heavy 170 –05 slow   [52]

*161 **STEPHENS SONG** [8] (N Vigors) 3-8-6(7ex) S Dawson(3) 9/2: 4000-11: 3 b g Song - Train Of Thought (Bay Express): In fine form, led over 2f out, gamely in a 3yo h'cap at Newbury Apr.18: first time out won a similar event at Salisbury: very eff over 5f on any ground and on any trk: genuine.   **41**

*6 **ROVE** [9] (S Norton) 3-8-7 G Baxter 10/3 FAV: 0301-12: Slightly hmpd 1f out but just btn: : acts on any ground & on any trk: see 6.   **39**

-- **NORTHERN TRUST** [7] (C Nelson) 3-9-5 I Johnson 16/1: -1020-3: Ran on well final 1f: and just btn: good effort: first time out in '85 won at Bath and does well when fresh: eff over 5f, should stay 6f: acts on gd/firm & heavy & likes a stiff, gall trk: should go close next time.   **51**

-- **AU DESSUS** [3] (J Winter) 3-9-2 W R Swinburn 10/1: 33110-4: Ev ch inside final 1f: good seasonal debut: in '85 won at Catterick and Nottingham: very eff at 5f: acts on gd/firm & heavy: well suited by front running tactics & likes a sharpish trk, though acts on any.   **44**

161 FOUNTAIN BELLS [4] 3-8-4 L Jones(5) 5/1: 4000-20: Much closer to winner 161 (yld).   27
62   STEEL CYGNET [1] 3-9-2 J Reid 9/2: 1002-00: Prom, fdd: see 62 (sharper trk).   31
62   STANBO [5] 3-8-1 W Carson 15/2: 2300-00: Active in mkt: no show.   00
--   HAIL AND HEARTY [2] 3-7-13 T Williams 10/1: 400-0: Btr for race.   00
76   CRONKS QUALITY [6] 3-9-7(BL) P Waldron 9/1: 4000-00: Led over 2f, fdd.   00
9 ran   ¼,nk,1½,1½,3   (Tom Nicholson)   N Vigors Upper Lambourn, Berks

234   STROUD GREEN STAKES 3YO HCAP 0-60   £4409   1m   Heavy 170 -09 Slow   [63]

62   MUDRIK [11] (C Benstead) 3-8-7 B Rouse 11/2: 0041-41: 3 b c Sparkler - Amerella
(Welsh Pageant): Useful colt: ran on well to lead inside final 1f, comfortably in a 3yo
h'cap at Newbury Apr.18: won again at Newbury: half brother to the very useful
sprinter Cragside : very eff at 6f, stays 1m well: acts on any grnd, but likes a stiff trk.   55
*15 MISNAAD [2] (B Hanbury) 3-8-8 W Carson 9/2 FAV: 4220-12: Hmpd inside final 1f: fin
3rd, placed 2nd: in fine form: stays 1m: acts on good & heavy: see 15.   51
--   FRAMLINGTON COURT [3] (P Walwyn) 3-8-1(1ow) Paul Eddery 16/1: 0200-2D: Led well over
1f out: drifted left inside the final 1f: fin 2nd, placed 3rd on seasonal debut: showed
promise in '85, but was not too consistent: however, is well h'capped on his best form:
half brother to 2 winners: eff at 6f, stays 1m: acts on gd & heavy and should find a h'cap.   45
--   LUCKY SO SO [5] (S Norton) 3-8-7 G Baxter 10/1: 134-4: Al up there on seasonal debut:
first time out winner in '85 at Ayr: half sister to the useful High Cannon: should be suited
by 1m plus: acts on any ground: likes a gall trk.   41
157 ATROMITOS [13] 3-8-5 P Robinson 6/1: 041-40: Led briefly 2f out: btr 157 (yld).   37
--   TOBAGO DANCER [14] 3-8-3 A Mcglone 12/1: 02404-0: Prom over 6f, btr for race.   32
--   STAGE HAND [9] 3-9-7 S Cauthen 7/1: 010-0: Fin 7th: btr for race.   00
--   HAWAIIAN PALM [7] 3-9-6 Pat Eddery 10/1: 13-0: Never sighted on seasonal debut.   00
--   FARM CLUB [15] 3-8-10 B Thomson 8/1: 10-0: Prom over 5f, fdd.   00
178 BERESQUE [12] 3-8-7(BL) P Waldron 8/1: 030-400: Bl first time, led 6f: best 15 (7f)   00
--   Bold Borderer [4] 8-8   62   Meadow Moor [10] 8-2(vis)
--   Tap Duet [6] 7-9   --   Halo Hatch [1] 8-11   74   Brent Riverside [8] 7-8(1ow)(5oh)
15 ran   ½,¾,5,½,1½,1   (Hamdan Al-Maktoun)   C Benstead Epsom, Surrey

235   THATCHAM STAKES HANDICAP 0-50   £4630   2m   Heavy 170 +09 Fast   [45]

58a ACCURACY [6] (G Balding) 5-8-11 R Fox 5/1: 200-321: 5 ch m Gunner B - Veracious
(Astec): Gained a deserved success, led 3f out, held on gamely in quite a fast run h'cap at
Newbury Apr.18: failed to win last season: in '84 won at Catterick, Nottingham & Doncaster:
eff at 2m, stays 2½m well: acts on yld, likes soft/heavy needs a fast run race.   39
--   ACE OF SPIES [8] (L Kennard) 5-8-10 W R Swinburn 14/1: 22/00-2: Fit from hurdling: kept
on well final 1f: good effort: lightly raced on the Flat in '85: in '84 won at Kempton,
Thirsk & Leicester: eff over 10/12f: stays 2m really well: acts on any going: likes a
gall trk: genuine sort.   36
--   CIMA [14] (J Old) 8-9-2 R Cochrane 16/1: 10020/3: Fit from hurdling/chasing: al up
there: most versatile sort: last successful on the Flat in '82: recent winner over fences:
stays 2m: acts on gd & heavy.   40
204 SHINY COPPER [15] (N Smith) 8-7-11 G Carter(3) 12/1: 00-0024: Running well: see 204.   19
--   HIGH PLAINS [1] 4-9-5 S Cauthen 4/1 FAV: 21010-0: Well bckd on seasonal debut: ch 2f
out: will come on for this run: in '85 was an easy winner of a h'cap at Chester and a
maiden at Lingfield: well suited by 2m: acts on heavy, well suited by good/firm: acts on
any trk, but likes a sharp one: well h'capped & should be winning soon.   41
--   BLOODLESS COUP [18] 4-9-8 D Mckay 20/1: 41000-0: Al up there: good effort.   41
*69 INTUITION [3] 4-8-12 J Carter(7) 8/1: 0000-10: Fdd: much btr 69 (14f).   00
--   ORANGE HILL [2] 4-8-13 Pat Eddery 10/1: 0001-0: Mkt drifter: no show.   00
--   CUMREW [11] 6-7-7(bl)(1oh) S Dawson(1) 10/1: 0--00-0: Made much, wknd.   00
*137 PEARL RUN [4] 5-8-12(6ex) G King(7) 6/1: 320-110: Well below form 137 (easier trk).   00
--   Sugar Palm [13] 8-5(bl)   --   Storm Cloud [5] 9-6
--   Vickstown [9] 9-2   121 Down Flight [16] 8-13   121 Collisto [7] 8-6
--   Commonty [17] 7-13   --   Romana [12] 9-0
17 ran   1½,1½,1½,shhd,3   (Miss B Swire)   G Balding Fyfield, Hants

---

THIRSK   Friday April 18th   Lefthand Fair Track

236   E.B.F. BRITON MAIDEN STAKES 2-Y-O   £3078   5f   Soft 135 -13 Slow

--   MARCHING MOTH [11] (M Camacho) 2-8-11 N Connorton 14/1: 1: 2 br f Radetzky - Crescent
Dart (Sing Sing): First time out, made most and kept on strongly in a 2yo maiden at Thirsk
Apr.18: speedily bred but should stay at least 6f: acts well on soft ground and is suited
by forcing tactics.   46
--   DOMINO ROSE [1] (N Tinkler) 2-8-11 T Ives 6/1: 2: Sn prom: good racecourse debut:
should be well suited by further than 5f: act on soft.   40
186 PAY DIRT [3] (T Fairhurst) 2-9-0 C Coates(5) 12/1: 03: Al prom: cheaply bought May
foal: on the up grade: acts on soft.   36

-- FISHERGATE [8] (M W Easterby) 2-9-0 K Hodgson 8/1: 4: No extra final 1f but is sure
to benefit from the outing: very speedily bred: should go close next time.   35
-- MAESTROMAN [9] 2-9-0 K Darley 13/2: 0: Al prom: cheaply bought Apr. foal who should
be suited by 6f.   29
197 HUNTERS LEAP [14] 2-9-0 J Lowe 7/1: 00: Early speed: speedily bred.   26
-- RAINTREE COUNTY [13] 2-9-0 D Mckeown 11/2 Jt.FAV: 0:Wl bkd:nt recover from slowstart.   00
34 LATE PROGRESS [5] 2-8-11 M Fry 6/1: -00: Early speed from a poor draw: see 34.   00
-- MISS DISPLAY [12] 2-8-11 D Nicholls 10/1: 0: No threat but should benefit from the race   00
-- RABENHAM [4] 2-9-0 M Roberts 11/2 Jt.FAV: 0: Well bckd, no show from a poor draw:
half brother to useful '79 2yo Schweppeshire Spy   00
-- PRINCEGATE [7] 2-9-0 M Beecroft 7/1: 0: Speedily bred: never got into the race on debut   00
-- Miss Lamb   8-11   -- Dream Ticket [10] 9-0
13 ran   2½,3,nk,2½,1   (Lady Durham)   M Camacho Malton, Yorks

237 KNAYTON SELLING STAKES 3-Y-O   £1059   6f   Soft 135 -35 Slow

147 WOW WOW WOW [4] (N Tinkler) 3-9-3 Kim Tinkler(7) 10/3 FAV: 0110-31: 3 b f Comedy Star-
True Dresden (Vilmoray): Uneasy fav. but driven into lead close home in a 3yo seller at
Thirsk Apr.18 (no bid): in '85 won at Ayr, Edinburgh & Thirsk: very eff over 5/6f & acts
on firm & soft: half sister to several minor winners.   30
39 COOPER RACING NAIL [14] (J Berry) 3-8-11 M Fry 7/2: 0322-32: Just failed to make
all, clear of rest and deserves one final chance to lose her maiden tag: see 39.   22
67 SANDRON [3] (K Brassey) 3-9-0(bl) N Adams 5/1: 0020-03: Outpcd final 1f: rated 25 when
close 2nd in a selling nursery at Lingfield last Oct, best effort in '85: eff around 6f
on gd/firm going, also seems to handle soft.   13
195 PLANTER [6] (T Fairhurst) 3-9-6(bl) M Beecroft 8/1: 3-01024: Ev ch: see 51, 195.   17
-- LULLABY BLUES [9] 3-9-0 M Birch 7/2: -0: Ran well 4f on racecourse debut: speedily bred
half brother to winning '83 juvenile Sing To Me: will trip fitter next time and can win
a similar race.   11
67 COLONEL HALL [5] 3-9-0 M Roberts 20/1: 000-00: Shaped well final 1f: lightly raced
in '85: worth noting in selling company next time.   06
93 AMPLIFY [12] 3-9-0 K Darley 10/1: 020-030: Early speed: see 93.   00
195 GUNNER GO [2] 3-8-11 R P Elliott 6/1: 00-0300: Poorly drawn: see 41.   00
-- Samba Lass [1] 8-11   -- Galaxy Gala [5] 9-0   -- Waterford Way [7] 9-0
14 Frandie Miss [10] 8-11   -- First Alarm [11] 9-0
198 Kiki Green [8] 9-0   195 Geoffs Folly [13] 9-0
15 ran   ½,5,1,shhd,3   (Full Circle Thoroughbreds Ltd)   N Tinkler Malton, Yorks

238 BIRDFORTH HANDICAP STAKES (0-50)   £2666   1m   Soft 135 -10 Slow   [44]

196 TUTBURY [6] (W Wharton) 4-8-8 N Carlisle 6/1: 102-441: 4 b g Camden Town - Bravour II
(Birkhahn): Prom, led inside final 3f readily in a h'cap at Thirsk Apr.18: winner at Redcar
and Nottingham in '85 (did not race after June): very eff over 7f/1m on a fair gall trk:
probably acts on any going: could win again.   37
79 VERBARIUM [2] (J Ramsden) 6-8-11 M Roberts 9/2 Jt.FAV: 031-232: Stayed on: see 10.   22
196 BWANA KALI [7] (M Tompkins) 4-8-10 M Rimmer 9/2 Jt.FAV: 010-433: Sn prom: consistent but
seems to lack foot: see 36.   30
184 NIGHT WARRIOR [10] (A Robson) 4-8-8 J Bleasdale 14/1: 000-004: Outpcd final 1f: winner
at Hamilton & Edinburgh in '85: acts on gd & heavy: eff around 7f/1m, probably stays 10f.   27
71 KAMPGLOW [11] 4-8-13 Gay Kelleway(5) 5/1: 004-030: Chall dist: see 71.   20
105 DICK KNIGHT [1] 5-7-13 A Mackay 14/1: 000-000: Made most: see 105.   03
71 THE HOWARD [12] 4-9-7 N Day 8/1: 0101-00: Ev ch: btr 71 (heavy).   00
-- MAGIC BID [8] 4-9-7 M Hills 9/1: 03212-0: Should benefit from seasonal debut:
consistent in '85 winning at Thirsk (7f, gd/firm): acts on firm & yld & is very eff at 7f.   00
79 Emerald Eagle [5] 8-5   -- Pacific Princess [9] 9-4
163 Cadenette [13] 7-8(BL)(1ow)   -- Russell Creek [4] 9-5
12 ran   2,nk,½,7,1½   (G Adshead)   W Wharton Melton Mowbray, Leics

239 SOWERBY E.B.F. STAKES 3-Y-O   £3165   1m 4f   Soft 135 -38 Slow

-- BLOCKADE [5] (P Cole) 3-8-10 T Ives 85/40: 02-1: 3 br c Mill Reef - Edwinarowe
(Blakeney): Led 4 out and hung on gamely, first time out in a minor race at Thirsk Apr.18:
seems to act on firm & soft ground: stays 12f, certain to be suited by further and looks a
useful young stayer in the making.   54
-- KUDZ [1] (H Cecil) 3-8-10 W Ryan 11/10 FAV: 22-2: Chall over final 2f: stays 12f, seems
to act on firm & soft ground: half brother to several winners incl Lucky North: sure to find
a maiden race soon, might benefit from bl.   50
128 MARIE GALANTE [3] (C Brittain) 3-8-7 M Roberts 7/2: 300-23: Stiff task, possibly stays
12f: btr 128 over 10f.   33
*164 MURFAX [2] (J Glover) 3-9-4 D Mckeown 14/1: -04-14: Not disgraced: see 164.   40
130 JUSTTHEWAYYOUARE [4] 3-8-10(BL) P Bloomfield 50/1: 0000-00: Led till 4 out.   00
-- GUNNER MAC [6] 3-8-10 M Richardson 50/1: 0-0: Fin well behind.   00
6 ran   1½,8,2½,dist,nk   (Fahd Salman)   P Cole Whatcombe, Oxon

240   OAKSTRIPE HANDICAP STAKES (0-35)   £2407   7f   Soft 135 +17 Fast   [35]

*110 IDLE TIMES [8] (W Elsey) 4-8-8(6ex) C Dwyer 11/4 FAV: 4200-11: 4 b f Faraway Times -
Ibolya Princess (Crowned Prince): Easily made practically all impressively in a fast run
h'cap at Thirsk Apr.18: won first time out at Hamilton: in '85 won at Yarmouth: eff at 5/7f
and seems to act on firm & soft: impr filly who looks sure to win again next time.   28
194 IZZY GUNNER [7] (A Robson) 3-7-7(1oh) S P Griffiths(5) 9/1: 030-002: Al 2nd, active in
mkt: seems suited by 7f but ran last time over 10f: well clear of the rest.   14
65   HOPEFUL KATIE [2] (D Leslie) 4-8-8(hd) J Williams 8/1: 0000-43: Ev ch: stays 7f? see 65   00
-182 GOLD DUCHESS [3] (M W Easterby) 4-8-0(bl) K Darley 7/2: 00-0424: Btr 182 (5f).   00
--   CREEAGER [4] 4-9-8 N Carlisle 9/1: 20040-0: Winner at Thirsk in '85 over 1m and also
ran well later at Newmarket over 7f: probably acts on any trk, best form on a sound surface.   08
110 PENTOFF [9] 4-8-8 D Nicholls 12/1: 1000-00: Winner at Hamilton in '85 over 6f &
heavy ground: probably acts on any going and on any trk: best when held up.   00
101 QUALITAIRESS [5] 4-7-8(1ow)(2oh) L Charnock 8/1: 3000-30: Btr 101.   00
81   UPTOWN RANDBS [1] 3-7-11 J Lowe 8/1: 040-430: Needs stiff trk? see 81, 37.   00
--   Princess Pamela [6] 7-10   -- Darnit [11] 9-11
124 Name The Game [10] 7-10(3ow)
11 ran   6,10,shhd,hd,hd   (C W Elsey)   W Elsey Malton, Yorks

241   HAMBLETON STAKES 3-Y-O   £1614   5f   Soft 135 +05 Fast

--   ALKAAYED [9] (H T Jones) 3-9-0 A Murray 7/1: 40-1: 3 ch c hard Fought - Red Jade (Red
God): Just got up in a close fin to a minor race at Thirsk Apr.18 (first time out): very eff
at 5f on a soft surface but should stay further: half brother to the top class filly Mahogany.   41
134 JARROVIAN [6] (T Fairhurst) 3-9-0 C Coates(5) 4/1: 000-042: Led inside final 1f, just
failed: evidently suited by 5f & acts on soft: see 134: should find a maiden race in the North   40
109 RAAS [2] (S Norton) 3-9-0 J Lowe 7/4 FAV: 0-23: Heavily bckd, just failed to make all
in a tight fin: seems equally eff over 5 & 6f and compensation awaits: see 109.   39
84   TAYLOR OF SOHAM [4] (D Leslie) 3-8-11(bl) M Rimmer 7/1: 000-234: Consistent: see 38.   27
--   SILENT MAJORITY [8] 3-9-0 T Ives 6/1: 44-0: Seems best at 5f & acts on firm & yld.   15
198 OUR MUMSIE [10] 3-8-11 M Richardson(7) 14/1: 040-200: Disapp since 103.   00
168 TOUCH ME NOT [1] 3-9-0 S Perks 10/1: 000-300: Disapp since 64.   00
134 WESSEX KINGDOM [5] 3-9-4(bl) M Hills 6/1: 0-100: Tried in bl: possibly needs to
make all but has been disapp since 134.   00
6   Running Rainbow [3] 8-11   109 Petencore [7] 9-0
10 ran   nk,nk,4,7,5   (Hamdan Al-Maktoum)   H T Jones Newmarket

242   CLIFTON STAKES 2-Y-O   £2469   5f   Yielding 115 -13 Slow

--   DEMDERISE [2] (N Tinkler) 2-8-8 T Ives 11/2: 1: 2 ch f Vaigly Great - Kanvita (Home
Guard): Promising filly: nicely bckd on racecourse debut, led inside dist and ran on well in
a 2yo stakes at Thirsk Apr.19: half sister to winning sprinters Alpine Strings and Carolyn
Christensen: clearly well suited by 5f on a sharpish trk: acts on yld ground, likely to impr
and win more races.   48
77   BLUEMEDE [3] (M Brittain) 2-9-4 K Darley 11/10 FAV: 1122: Led ½way: consistent: see 77.   52
146 SCOTTISH FLING [5] (J Wilson) 2-8-11 E Turner(7) 6/1: 333: Ran on well & beat rem
decisively: continues to impr: acts on any going: see 146 and 108.   44
197 PANBOY [6] (T Fairhurst) 2-9-4 C Coates(5) 11/2: 3124: Rem. in gd form: see 197 & 108.   37
--   FIRMLY ATTACHED [1] 2-8-11 S Webster 6/1: 0: Sn behind though sure to impr for this
experience: speedily bred colt who cost 6,600 gns as a yearling: seems to act on yld grnd.   28
--   WIGANTHORPE [4] 2-8-11 M Hindley(3) 12/1: 0: No threat after a slow start on racecourse
debut: cost 18,500 gns: should be suited by a longer trip.   27
-86 Roweking [7] 8-11(vis)
7 ran   1,hd,6,½,½,½   (Mrs D Wright)   N Tinkler Malton, Yorks

243   TELEPROMPTER HANDICAP STAKES (0-50)   £2582   1m 4f Yielding 115 -15 Slow   [48]

--   WILDRUSH [13] (W Watts) 7-7-10(2ow) A Shoults(0) 14/1: 10002-1: 7 b g Free State -
Ribble Reed (Bullrush): First time out, led dist for a narrow win in a h'cap at Thirsk Apr.19
last season made when successful in a h'cap at Ripon: in '84 won at Hamilton & Beverley:
eff over 10/12: acts on gd & yld ground & is well suited by a sharpish course.   26
52   REGAL STEEL [10] (R Hollinshead) 8-7-12 A Culhane(5) 7/1: 000-302: Tried to make all:
fin clear of rem and ran to his best: acts on any trk: see 4.   27
*52 CAROS GIFT [8] (N Tinkler) 5-9-11 Kim Tinkler(7) 4/1: 0003-13: Ran in snatches: btr
on heavy in 52 (gall trk).   40
166 LO BROADWAY [9] (D Moffatt) 8-7-11 J Quinn(5) 10/1: 000-044: Btr on a gall trk in 166.   09
196 BURAAG [7] 5-9-0 T Lucas 7/2 FAV: 0000-00: Never reached ldrs: btr in 196 (1m).   26

--   DOUBLE BENZ [1] 4-9-2 M Birch 12/1: 12200-0: No extra str & should do btr next time:
quite consistent gelding who won at Haydock last season, and at Redcar in '84: eff over
1m, stays 12f: acts on gd & yld ground and is well suited by a gall trk.   23
52   VINTAGE TOLL [5] 6-9-9(vis) J Lowe 9/2: 000-030: Much btr on hvy grnd in 52 (gall trk)   00
208 Balgownie [12] 7-7(4oh)   126 North Star Sam [3] 7-7(5oh)
--   Campus Boy [11] 7-9   --   Strathearn [4] 8-5
11 ran   nk,10,2,shhd,3   (W C Watts)   W Watts Bridlington, Nth Humberside

244 CIMTAX CLASSIC TRIAL STAKES 3-Y-O   £4838   1m   Yielding 115 -21 Slow

--   SURE BLADE [5] (B Hills) 3-9-3 B Thomson 2/7 FAV: 1113-1: 3 b c Kris - Double Lock
(Home Guard): Very smart colt: easily landed the odds on his reappearance, leading 2f out in
quite a valuable 3yo stakes at Thirsk Apr.19: began last season by winning a maiden at
Newmarket, later successful in Gr.3 Coventry Stakes at Royal Ascot and Gr.2 Laurent Perrier
Champagne Stakes at Doncaster: then narrowly btn behind Huntingdale in Gr.1 Dewhurst Stakes
at Newmarket: cost 270,000 gns as a yearling: very effective over 7/8f and seems sure to stay at
least 10f: acts on good/firm and yielding ground and on any trk: looks sure to run well in the
2,000 Guineas.   66
49   SUPREME KINGDOM [4] (R Hollinshead) 3-8-11 S Perks 33/1: 210-032: Led briefly in str:
outclass by winner: however a most creditable effort and she should be winning soon: see 49.   42
143 MERHI [2] (S Norton) 3-8-7 J Lowe 33/1: 200-23: Led over ½way: fair effort: see 143.   32
--   CENTREPOINT [1] (J Etherington) 3-9-0 T Ives 12/1: 001-4: Short lived effort early
in str: btr for race: lightly raced last season, when winning a maiden at Newcastle on
his last start: eff over 7/8f: acts on yld ground and is suited by a gall trk.   34
--   JELLYGOLD [3] 3-9-0(bl) M L Thomas 4/1: 01100-0: Nicely bckd on reappearance though
btn early in str: did not wear bl when winning successive fillies races at Haydock & Newmarket last season: very eff over 6/7f on gd & yld ground: probably btr suited bu a gall trk.   18
5 ran   5,3,2½,10   (Sheikh Mohammed)   B Hills Lambourn, Berks

245 THIRSK HALL E.B.F. STAKES 3YO+   £8255   6f   Yielding 115 +18 Fast

--   POWDER KEG [5] (J Hindley) 4-10-0 M Hills 85/40 FAV: 11113-1: 4 ch c Tap On Wood -
Live Ammo (Home Guard): Very smart colt: first time out put up a typically game performance
when leading close home in a fast run & valuable stakes at Thirsk Apr.19: made tremendous
impr last season, when winning at Folkestone, Ayr, Pontefract, Newcastle, Newmarket & York:
also won a valuable sprint in Stockholm: on final start was just btn by Efisio in Group
company at Newmarket: very eff over 6/7f: acts on gd/firm & soft grnd & on any trk: very game
& genuine sort who carries weight well: should win a Group race this term.   80
-165 AMIGO LOCO [2] (K Brassey) 5-9-10(bl) S Whitworth 4/1: 40-0222: Just failed to make all:
in fine form at present and is certainly due a change of luck: see 70.   74
70   MELODY PARK [3] (M Ryan) 4-8-11(vis) P Robinson 5/2: 3404-43: Ev ch: in gd form: see 70.56
--   SI SIGNOR [7] (P Cole) 4-10-0 J Reid 6/1: 11040-4: Ran to his best on reappearance:
smart colt who scored successive h'cap wins at Chepstow, Goodwood & York last season: lightly
raced in '84 when winning at Haydock: very eff over 6/8f: acts on any going & on any trk:
has a fine turn of foot and should win some good races this season.   72
--   LOCHONICA [6] 3-8-8 D Nicholls 11/2: 42140-0: Close up most of way & should do
btr next time: very useful, consistent colt last season who won early on at Epsom & Ayr,
and later quite a valuable race at the latter trk: very eff over 5/6f: acts on fast ground
though btr suited by good or yld: genuine sort who has no trk preferences.   56
--   PARIS MATCH [1] 4-9-10 B Thomson 33/1: 21040-0: Front rank till ½way: had a stiff
task: last season made all in a h'cap at Beverley & is well suited by forcing tactics: half
brother to several winners, incl Miss Saint Cloud: btr suited by 1m on faster ground.   42
--   Simla Ridge [4] 8-9
7 ran   hd,2,½,4,7   (J E Nash)   J Hindley Newmarket

246 RACE AROUND YORKSHIRE H'CAP 0-50 3YO   £2443   5f   Yielding 115 +12 Fast   [41]

65   SEW HIGH [2] (B Mcmahon) 3-8-12 J Hills(7) 5/1: 041-001: 3 b g Nicholas Bill - Sew
Nice (Tower Walk): Nicely bckd, led dist for a comfortable win in a fast run 3yo h'cap at
Thirsk Apr.19: last season won sellers at Ripon & Haydock: well suited by sprint dists: acts
on fast & soft ground and likes to be up with the pace.   38
--   RESTLESS RHAPSODY [4] (K Brassey) 3-8-13(bl) S Whitworth 4/1 FAV: 23134-2: Made most on
reappearance: most consistent last season when he was rarely out of the frame, and made all
in a maiden at Catterick: very eff over 5f on a sharp trk: acts on firm & yld ground: wears
bl: should go close next time.   31
38   HOBOURNES KATIE [7] (R Hollinshead) 3-8-3 A Culhane(7) 14/1: 0000-03: Ran on well:
showed some promise in fillies maidens last season over this minimum trip: suited by some
give under foot: acts on any trk.   20
198 KEN SIDDALL [3] (K Stone) 3-8-8 G Brown(5) 11/2: 32-0044: Running well at present.   24
--   GODS ISLE [5] 3-9-7 M Birch 5/1: 41010-0: Dsptd lead over ½way: fair effort under
top weight and she should impr next time: won a maiden auction at Haydock & a fast run
nursery at Thirsk last season: very eff over 5f on gd & yld ground: acts on any trk.   36
38   AMBER CLOWN [9] 3-8-4 N Carlisle 9/2: 000-240: Needs btr ground: see 6.   00
83   MERCIA GOLD [8] 3-8-0 P Robinson 9/2: 000-300: Twice disapp since 38 (gall trk, soft).   00
39   The Little Joker [6] 7-12   --   Spring Garden [1] 7-7(1oh)
9 ran   3,½,nk,nk,10,hd   (R Thornhill)   B Mcmahon Hopwas Hill, Staffs

247   BYLAND MAIDEN STAKES 3-Y-O   £2655   1m   Yielding 115 -25 Slow

--   HEAVY BRIGADE [13] (W O'gorman) 3-9-0 T Ives 7/4 FAV: -1: 3 ch c Hard Fought - Victorian
Pageant (Welsh Pageant): Heavily bckd on racecourse debut and stayed on well to lead in the
final stride in a 3yo maiden at Thirsk Apr.19: clearly well suited by 1m & is certain to
be suited by further: acts on yld ground & on a sharpish trk: should rate more highly.   44
141 AUCTION MAN [16] (R Hollinshead) 3-9-0 S Perks 6/1: 003-032: Led early in str, just
caught: is impr steadily & should make amends soon: acts on any trk: see 141.   42
90   ALPHA HELIX [8] (K Brassey) 3-9-0 S Whitworth 8/1: -033: Stayed on: in gd form: see 90.   32
--   CHANCE REMARK [14] (B Hills) 3-9-0 B Thomson 5/1: 0-4: Nicely bckd on racecourse debut:
al there and should impr : stays 1m: acts on yld grnd and on a sharpish trk.   31
--   PRIME NUMBER [17] 3-9-0 J Reid 7/1: 0-0: Late prog after a slow start: unplaced behind
Shtaifeh in a stakes at Nottingham (1m, firm) on sole start last year: cost I.R. 9,000:
also acts on yld ground.   29
54   PULHAM MILLS [4] 3-9-0 P Robinson 10/1: 4400-00: Led over ½way, sn btn: see 54.   13
--   Rose Window [7] 8-11   --   Couture Color [10] 9-0
--   Mawdlyn Gate [12] 9-0   --   Scarborough [2] 9-0   183 Rapid Flight [11] 9-0
16   Pells Close [6] 9-0   134 Turn Em Back Jack [5] 9-0
--   Hill Ryde [1] 9-0   --   Oriental Express [3] 9-0
--   Strawberry Split [9] 8-11   99 Moving Performance [18] 9-0
17 ran   shhd,5,¾,1½,8   (Mrs P L Yong)   W O'gorman Newmarket

---

Official Going Given as Soft

248   MELLOWES PPG SPRING CUP H'CAP 4Y+ 0-70   £6888   1m   Soft 143 +17 Fast   [70]

*196 STAR OF A GUNNER [11] (R Holder) 6-8-3(7ex) S Dawson(3) 12/1: 100-011: 6 ch h Gunner B -
Starkist (So Blessed): Useful horse who is in fine form: led approaching final 1f, staying
on under press in fast run & valuable Newbury Spring Cup (h'cap) at Newbury Apr.19: last season
      won at Goodwood (2) & Warwick: very eff around 1m: acts on gd/firm, likes yld/soft: acts
on any trk, though runs well on a sharpish one.   57
--   PATRIACH [12] (J Dunlop) 4-8-0 T Quinn 16/1: 03411-2: Ev ch over 1f out: fine seasonal
debut: in '85 won a h'cap at Leicester & a maiden at Lingfield: very eff over 7f/1m: acts
on gd/firm & soft & on any trk: should be winning soon.   53
71   RANA PRATAP [21] (G Lewis) 6-7-11 R Fox 11/1: 144-043: Ev ch final 1f: in gd form: see 7147
112 RUNNING FLUSH [19] (D Oughton) 4-7-8(1ow) B Crossley 20/1: 040-004: Led early, al prom
and ran well: finding his form and may win a h'cap soon: see 112.   44
79   VIRGIN ISLE [18] 5-7-10 T Williams 14/1: 034-020: Led 2f out: good effort: see 79.   45
--   TRULY RARE [8] 4-8-8 W R Swinburn 13/2 FAV: -4141-0: Well bckd on seasonal debut:
promising run 3f out: btr for race: in '85 won h'caps at York & Leicester: in '84 won again at
Leicester: very eff around 1m/9f: acts on firm 7 soft and a gall trk.   55
--   INDIAN HAL [15] 4-8-3 Paul Eddery 20/1: 24231-0: Not btn far in 7th on seasonal debut:
in good form in '85, winning h'caps at Newmarket, Salisbury & Pontefract: eff at 1m, stays
10f: acts on firm & soft & on any trk: consistent sort.   49
+172 CORN STREET [4] 8-8-4(7ex) G Baxter 11/1: 2D4-010: Close up 8th: in gd form: see 172.   50
--   ROCKMARTIN [16] 4-8-3 S Payne 11/1: 10020-0: Never nearer in 9th: btr for race.   00
55   SHELLMAN [3] 4-7-11 G Carter(3) 12/1: 010-030: Btr in 55 (7f heavy).   00
--   ADVANCE [13] 5-9-4 S Cauthen 20/1: 22101-0: Btr for race, prefers faster ground.   00
--   GO BANANAS [2] 5-9-0 R Cochrane 7/1: 31000-0: No real threat: well bckd.   00
--   Boldden [17] 8-7   --   Portogon [5] 8-2   --   Korypheos [10] 7-13
--   Bold Indian [14] 9-13   72   Thats Your Lot [20] 8-13
70   Really Honest [9] 8-12   --   Barry Sheene [6] 8-6
196 Bundaburg [7] 7-11   72   All Fair [1] 8-6
21 ran   ½,1½,hd,nk,¾,nk,shhd   (James Neville)   R Holder Portbury, Avon

---

249   GRP 3 CLERICAL MEDICAL GREENHAM STKS 3Y   £27201   7f   Soft 143 -13 Slow

--   FAUSTUS [5] (H Cecil) 3-9-0 S Cauthen 5/1: 11112-1: 3 b c Robellino - B F's Salingal
(Sail On Sail): Smart colt: made a winning seasonal debut in Gr.3 Greenham Stakes at Newbury
Apr.19: ran on well final 1f under press to get up near the line: in excellent form thro'out
'85, winning his first 5 starts, at Newbury, Goodwood (Lanson Champagne Stakes), Newmarket,
Nottingham & Yarmouth: has met defeat only once when 2nd to Sure Blade in Gr.2 event at
Doncaster: eff at 7f, looks sure to be suited by 1m plus: acts on firm & soft & on a gall trk:
most genuine colt who should win more good races.   80
--   LEAD ON TIME [3] (A Badel) 3-9-0 O Douieb 7/4 FAV: 121-2: Heavily bckd: led from the
stalls: caught post: fine effort: smart performer in '85, first time out winner at Newmarket
& on final outing won Gr.2 Criterium De Maisons Laffitte: half brother to a very useful
French miler and should stay 1m: acts on gd/firm & soft & should win more races.   80
--   HALLGATE [7] (S Hall) 3-9-0 K Hodgson 8/1: 11111-3: Waited with: ev ch 1f out:
not quicken close home: excellent effort: one of the most impr performers in '85, on final
outing won Gr.3 Cornwallis Stakes at Ascot, earlier winning at Ripon, Redcar, Pontefract,
Edinburgh & Hamilton (2): very eff over 5/6f, stays 7f & should get 1m: acts on firm & soft
& on any trk: genuine & consistent and has a useful turn of foot.   79

165   ROARING RIVA [6] (R Laing) 3-9-0 R Cochrane 33/1: 1000-44: Fine effort: stays 7f: see 165 73
--   NOMINATION [2] 3-9-0 T Quinn 4/1: 01104-0: Seems btr over 6f: very smart colt in
'85, winning Gr.2 Richmond Stakes at Goodwood, also successful twice at York & first time out
at Newbury: very eff over 5/6f: acts on gd & firm, though likes soft ground: has a smart
turn of foot & should do well in the top sprint events this season.   67
--   VAINGLORIOUS [4] 3-9-0 G Starkey 33/1: 31102-0: Stiff task, ran well.   66
--   WASSL TOUCH [1] 3-9-0 W Carson 6/1: 1-0: Prom 4f: sn wknd.   00
60   Celtic Heir [8] 9-0   --   Barclay Street [9] 9-0
9 ran   shhd,hd,3,3,½   (S S Niarchos)   H Cecil Newmarket

250   BRIDGET 3YO MAIDEN FILLIES STAKES   £4194   7f   Soft 143 -18 Slow

--   ARGON LASER [1] (J Dunlop) 3-8-11 W Carson 9/2: -1: 3 b f Kris - Lighted Lamp
(Sir Gaylord): Very prom filly: showed a good turn of foot to lead inside final 1f for a
comfortable win in a valuable 3yo fillies maiden at Newbury Apr.19: well bred sort who is a
half sister to numerous winners: eff at 7f, should be suited by 1m plus: acts on soft grnd
& a gall trk and should rate more highly/win more races.   66
--   SOMEONE SPECIAL [12] (P Cole) 3-8-11 P Waldron 15/2: -2: Made much: fine racecourse
debut: dam won the 1,000 Guineas: eff at 7f and should stay 1m: acts on soft ground & a
gall trk and should have no trouble finding a maiden.   58
--   FLUTTERY [13] (G Wragg) 3-8-11 S Cauthen 4/1 FAV: -3: Well bckd: ev ch over 1f out:
promising debut from this half sister to the smart 6f winner Al Sylah: eff at 7f & acts on
soft ground: should be winning soon.   52
--   QUEENS VISIT [14] (P Walwyn) 3-8-11 Paul Eddery 6/1: -4: Active in mkt: chance 2f out:
U.S. bred filly who should come on for this run: eff at 7f & should stay 1m: acts on soft grnd   46
--   ANDIKA [9] 3-8-11 S Raymont 20/1: -0: Never nearer: impr likely from this half sister
to 2 winners, notably smart 12f performer John French: should be suited by 1m plus: acts
on soft ground.   45
--   BUTTERFLY KISS [6] 3-8-11 G Duffield 25/1: -0: Never nearer 6th: will impr : half
sister to several winners, incl the very useful 1m winner Kufuma: should be suited by 1m
plus: acts on soft ground.   44
--   CRYSTAL MOSS [4] 3-8-11 T Quinn 5/1: -0: Wknd over 1f out: will impr.   40
--   GLITTER [7] 3-8-11 G Starkey 10/1: -0: Fin 9th: half sister to numerous winners &
should do btr next time.   00
--   LAKE ONEGA [3] 3-8-11 W R Swinburn 8/1: -0: Never in it.   00
--   Solo Singer [11] 8-11   --   Bet Oliver [10] 8-11   --   High Image [5] 8-11
--   Calvinette [2] 8-11   --   Fidaytik [8] 8-11
14 ran   3,2½,3,½,½   (Dr J A E Hobby)   J Dunlop Arundel, Sussex

251   LANES END JOHN PORTER STKS GROUP 3   £25540   1m 4f Soft 143 +16 Fast

--   LEMHILL [5] (M Blanshard) 4-8-8 R Cochrane 15/2: 1D232-1: 4 b c He Loves Me -
Moonscape (Ribero): Smart colt: first time out, landed some good bets in Gr.3 John Porter
Stakes at Newbury Apr.19: al going well & led over 1f out, comfortably in a fast run race:
admirably consistent in '85 winning at Newbury and was most unlucky to be disq. when winning
valuable Morland Brewery h'cap on this trk: very eff at 12/13f: acts on any grnd, though
likes yld/soft: most genuine & his gameness should win him more good races.   82
--   EAGLING [8] (H Cecil) 4-8-8 S Cauthen 9/2: 11310-2: Led over 2f out: fine seasonal
debut: smart colt, who in '85 won the Scottish Derby at Ayr: also successful at Haydock &
Leicester: half brother to several winners: very eff over 10/12f: acts on firm & soft & likes
a gall trk: game & genuine and likes to be up with the pace.   80
--   GOLD AND IVORY [4] (I Balding) 5-9-0 B Rouse 13/8 FAV: 99670-3: Led over 4f out: ev ch:
heavily bckd today: much travelled in '85 winning Gr.1 event at Baden Baden: first time out
won on this trk: in '84 won Gr.1 events at San Siro and Cologne: very eff at 12/13f: acts on
good & heavy ground: genuine sort who should again be placed to advantage on the Continent
this season.   77
--   LEADING STAR [3] (I Balding) 4-8-8 G Starkey 7/1: 1-010-4: Ev ch in str: very useful
colt, who in '85 won a valuable h'cap on this trk: very lightly raced performer who won sole
start as a 2yo at Newmarket: half brother to useful duo Church Parade and Castle Rising: very
eff at 10f, stays 12f and may get further: acts on firm & soft & a gall trk: should win
races this season.   69
--   CHAUMIERE [1] 5-8-8(vis) W Carson 10/1: 34023-0: Never in it.   49
--   SOLAR CLOUD [6] 4-8-8(vis) A Murray 33/1: -0: Triumph Hurdle winner: there 1m.   25
--   KUBLAI [7] 4-8-8 P Waldron 16/1: 12200-0: Made much, fdd.   00
--   SEISMIC WAVE [2] 5-8-11 R Hills 9/2: 00122-0: Last to fin: btr for race.   00
8 ran   ½,5,½,10,12,½   (Stanley Hinton)   M Blanshard Lambourn, Berks

252   EBF ST ANNES MAIDEN FILLIES STKS 2YO   £3255   5f   Soft 143 -60 Slow

--   ABUZZ [5] (C Brittain) 2-8-11 M Roberts 5/4 FAV: 1: 2 ch f Absalom - Sorebella
(Prince Tenderfoot): Heavily bckd on racecourse debut and led final 1f, comfortably in a
slow run 2yo fillies maiden at Newbury Apr.19: speedily bred filly: eff at 5f, should stay
6f: acts on soft ground & a gall trk: well regarded & should rate more highly.   52

73   SHADES OF NIGHT [6] (J Winter) 2-8-11 W R Swinburn 2/1: 22: Led over 1f out: in good
form: should open her account soon: see 73.   45
136   FOUR LAFFS [10] (D Leslie) 2-8-11 J Williams 14/1: -023: Ran on final 1f: on the up
grade: should find a small maiden: see 136.   43
--   SONOCO [3] (W Brooks) 2-8-11 T Quinn 20/1: 4: Led 2f out: speedily bred filly who
should impr: acts on soft ground.   37
--   WISE TIMES [2] 2-8-11 M Wigham 20/1: 0: Mkt drifter: ch over 1f out: cost 4,800 gns
and should impr: half sister to 1m winning h'capper Lafrowda   : acts on soft.   29
--   INDIAN SET [4] 2-8-11 P Waldron 12/1: 0: Led 3f.   09
--   Folly Gale [11] 8-11   --   Perigris [8] 8-11   --   War Child [1] 8-11
--   Semis [9] 8-11   --   Santo Princess [7] 8-11
11 ran   1½,nk,2,3,8,½   (Mrs C E Brittain)   C Brittain Newmarket

253   COMPTON MAIDEN STAKES 3YO   £3442   1m   Soft 143 -50 Slow

--   SIR PERCY [1] (G Wragg) 3-9-0 S Cauthen 4/1: -1: 3 b c Blakeney - Nicolletta (Busted):
Made a winning racecourse debut, led over 1f out, comfortably in a slow run 3yo maiden at
Newbury Apr.19: stoutly bred colt who should be suited by further than todays 1m trip: acts
on soft ground & a gall trk: should rate more highly.   55
--   AMIR ALBADEIA [5] (C Benstead) 3-9-0 Paul Eddery 11/4 FAV: 04-2: Led 3f out: fin 3rd,
placed 2nd: well bckd today: showed promise in '85 when 4th to Ininsky in a Sandown maiden:
half brother to 2 winners: stays 1m: acts on gd/firm & soft & a gall trk.   46
--   DUSTY DOLLAR [9] (W Hern) 3-8-11 W Carson 4/1: 44-3: Well bckd: made much: fin 4th,
placed 3rd: showed promise on both her starts in '85 in very good company: 4th to Lady
Brideshead in a fillies maiden at Newmarket and 4th to Kingscote in a valuable event at
Ascot: half sister to the smart Kind Of Hush: acts on soft, suited by firm ground: stays
1m and should have no trouble finding a maiden.   41
--   BARRACUDA BAY [6] (P Makin) 3-9-0 T Quinn 20/1: 00-4: Under press, badly bumped dist:
good effort: stays 1m & acts on gd/firm & soft.   42
--   LLANARMON [2] 3-9-0 R Street 16/1: 0-0: Nearest fin: btr for race: unplaced on sole
start in '85: half sister to several winners: stays 1m & acts son soft.   40
--   ZAUBARR [8] 3-9-0 R Fox 16/1: 00-0: Not the best of runs: fin well & should do much
btr next time: half brother to several winners: should be suited by further than 1m:
acts on soft ground and will find a maiden soon.   38
--   WASMI [12] 3-9-0 G Duffield 9/2: 00-2D: Switched and bumped over 1f out: ran on to
fin 2nd, but disq. and placed last: showed promise on both starts in '85: half brother to
useful sprinter Al Amead: stays 1m: acts on gd/firm & soft.   00
--   Triple Bluff [10] 9-0   --   The Quietstan [3] 9-0   --   Almutanabbi [13] 9-0
--   Top Range [11] 9-0   --   Our Craig [4] 9-0
12 ran   2,3,1,1,1½,1½   (E B Moller)   G Wragg Newmarket

WOLVERHAMPTON	Tuesday April 15th	Waterlogged

RIPON	Wednesday April 16th	Waterlogged

WOLVERHAMPTON	Monday April 21st	Waterlogged

EDINBURGH	Monday April 21st	Righthand, Sharp Track

Official Going Given as Good

254 CARBERRY MAIDEN AUCTION STKS 2YO   £547   5f   Good/Soft 106 +06 Fast

197 **TEAM EFFORT** [7] (Ron Thompson) 2-7-13 R P Elliott 11/2: 0301: 2 b c Stanford - Bap's Miracle (Track Spare): Led from the stalls comfortably in a maiden auction stakes at Edinburgh Apr.21: cost I.R. 2,300: acts on gd & yld: suited by an easy 5f with forcing tactics — 38
-- **SCOTCH IMP** [6] (D Chapman) 2-8-1 S P Griffiths(5) 16/1: 2: Unfancied: kept on closing stages on racecourse debut: cost 2,400 gns: eff at 5f, should stay further: acts on yld. — 31
-- **AFRABELA** [2] (M Brittain) 2-8-1 K Darley 7/1: 3: Nearest fin: impr likely from this 2,500 gns purchase: half sister to 7f winner Baton Boy. — 30
186 **BROONS ADDITION** [1] (K Stone) 2-8-1 L Charnock 9/2: 434: Al there: needs 6f? see 186. — 28
167 **MISS PISA** [5] 2-7-10 N Carlisle 9/2: -030: Sn prom, ev ch: btr 167 (stiffer trk). — 23
-- **MR BERKELEY** [4] 2-9-0 M Birch 5/1: 0: Active in mkt but no show on debut: cost 4,600 gns: should do btr: acts on yldhad a very stiff task at the weights — 26
118 **HAZELS GIRL** [3] 2-7-10 G Carter(3) 2/1 FAV: 230: Disapp fav: twice below form 20: see 118: possibly needs a stiffer trk. — 00
7 ran   4,$\frac{1}{2}$,$\frac{1}{2}$,hd,6   (George Mansell)   Ron Thompson Stainforth, Yorks

255 NORTH BERWICK STAKES 3YO   £547   5f   Good/Soft 106 +19 Fast

64 **LOCH FORM** [7] (C Tinkler) 3-8-8 M Birch 12/1: 00-01: 3 b f Lochnager - Good Form (Deep Diver): Impr filly: led well over 1f out, comfortably in a fast run 3yo stakes at Edinburgh Apr.21: speedily bred sort: eff at 6f on yld & soft: acts on any trk, though seems to like a sharpish one. — 38
217 **CHUMMYS PET** [2] (N Callaghan) 3-8-11 R Cochrane 3/1: -02: Ev ch over 1f out: 4L clear 3rd: eff at 5/6f: acts on yld ground and should find a maiden in the North. — 33
38 **LEFT RIGHT** [3] (N Macauley) 3-8-8(bl) Gay Kelleway(5) 12/1: 4400-03: Sn prom, btr effort: placed several times in '85: eff over 5f on gd & heavy & on any trk. — 21
241 **RAAS** [5] (S Norton) 3-8-11(BL) J Lowe 6/4 FAV: 0-234: Again heavily bckd: led over 3f: found little: bl first time today: see 241, 109 (soft ground). — 19
109 **BANTEL BANZAI** [1] 3-8-11 J Quinn(7) 33/1: 00-00: Nearest fin: impr effort: eff at 5/6f on yld & soft. — 15
-147 **SONNENELLE** [8] 3-9-4(vis) G Duffield 5/1: 422-120: Much btr 147, 103 (soft). — 16
111 **HEART OF GLASS** [4] 3-9-4 A Shoults(5) 11/2: 4-100: Twice well below form 83 (6f, turning track, soft). — 00
195 **Balidareen** [6] 8-8
8 ran   3,4,2,1,2.   (Walter Bulmer)   C Tinkler Malton, Yorks

256 MUSSELBURGH SPRING HCAP 0-35   £1662   1m 4f Good/Soft 106 -13 Slow   [33]

-- **SILENT JOURNEY** [10] (J Watts) 4-9-3 N Connorton 11/2: -3030-1: 4 br g Gregorian - Slow March (Queens Hussar): First time out, led final 1f, under press in a h'cap at Edinburgh Apr.21: first success: eff at 12/13f on yld & heavy: seems best when fresh. — 31
23 **APPLE WINE** [3] (D Chapman) 9-8-10 D Nicholls 13/2: 0000-02: Very fit: made almost all: good effort: in fine form last June/July, winning twice at Hamilton in '84 won at Ripon (2), Edinburgh & Hamilton: well suited by forcing tactics: suited by 11f-13f: acts on any ground, though likes soft: course specialist at Hamilton, likes a sharpish trk. — 23
*208 **SCREES** [9] (J H Wilson) 5-9-10(7ex) R Cochrane 5/1: -0213: Just btn under top weight — 36
80 **HOLLY BUOY** [7] (G Reveley) 6-8-9 D Leadbetter(5) 4/1 FAV: 3211-04: Ev ch str: in good form on the Flat early in '85, winning h'caps at Beverley, Hamilton & Edinburgh (this race): eff at 12f, stays 2m well: acts on fast & yld & on any trk. — 13
142 **GOLDEN FANCY** [8] 9-9-10 R Vickers(7) 11/2: 201-000: Al there, saddled slipped see 142 — 24
137 **BOREHAM DOWN** [4] 7-7-9 L Charnock 25/1: 400-000: Prom, wknd over 2f out. — 00
-- **BULLOM** [5] 6-8-1(bl) M Fry 9/1: -0: Been hurdling. — 00
184 **LOVELY BUTTERFLY** [11] 5-8-3 K Darley 9/1: 00-3200: Btr 36, 7 (10f, stiff trk). — 00
-- **Verbading** [6] 8-2   -- **Allez** [2] 7-9   -- **Lochabbey** [1] 8-5
11 ran $\frac{1}{2}$,nk,5,3,3   (R E Sangster)   J Watts Richmond, Yorks

257   ABERLADY SELLING HANDICAP 0-25   £762   1m 3f   Good/Soft 106 -36 Slow   [18]

--   FRASASS [7] (D Chapman) 9-9-1 D Nicholls 11/2: 00000-1: 9 b g Sassafrass - Desert
Flame (Baldric II): Made ev yd, comfortably in a slow run selling h'cap at Edinburgh Apr.21:
(bought in 920 gns)): in '84 won at Warwick & Ayr: eff over 12/13f, stays 2m: acts on any
going, but needs to be out in front.   13
131 CROWFOOTS COUTURE [5] (J Parkes) 5-8-10 T Parkes(7) 9/2: 000-042: Ev ch final 1f:
stays 1m3f and acts on firm and soft.   04
131 MURILLO [8] (F Carr) 10-9-10(bl) J Carr(7) 6/1: 032-003: Hdway over 1f out: not
keen: not getting any younger: placed on numerous occasions in '85: last won in '81: acts
on good, likes soft/heavy: eff at 7f, stays 11f.   13
--   PENRYN BOY [6] (Ron Thompson) 3-7-12(2ow) R P Elliott 9/1: 00000-4: Prom over 1m: no
form previously: probably stays 11f: acts on yld & a sharp trk.   00
--   HONEST TOKEN [3] 7-8-11 C Dwyer 10/1: 40000-0: Prom 1m: in '84 won at Beverley:
eff over 1m, stays 10f: acts on gd & firm.   00
184 LITTLE NEWINGTON [1] 5-8-13(5ex) Amanda Bycroft(7) 3/1 FAV: 0-04100: Twice below form
131 (1m, heavy).   00
--   Quivering [4] 7-8(1ow)(2oh)   131   Go Spectrum [9] 8-10
22   Turffontein [2] 8-12
9 ran   2,2,6,7,shhd,shhd   (David W Chapman)   D Chapman Stillington, Yorks

258   INVERESK MAIDEN STAKES 3 & 4YO   £547   1m   Good/Soft 106 -15 Slow

48   TAYLORMADE BOY [12] (D Smith) 3-8-6 L Charnock 7/2: 0330-31: 3 b c Dominion -
Ash Gayle (Lord Gayle): Led over 2f out, comfortably in a 3 & 4yo maiden at Edinburgh Apr.21:
eff at 1m, stays 10f: acts on yld & heavy & on any trk.   39
--   TABLE TURNING [1] (J Watts) 3-8-3 N Connorton 10/1: 00-2: Al up there: kept on: best
effort yet from this half sister to the very smart Teleprompter: highly tried in 2 outings
in '85: eff at 1m, may stay further: acts on yld & should impr.   26
229 AUCTION TIME [10] (M Prescott) 3-8-6 G Duffield 6/4 FAV: -03: Well bckd, ev ch:
very lightly raced colt: eff at 1m, may stay further: acts on yld ground: may do btr on
a more gall trk.   25
194 MASTER MUSIC [8] (M Brittain) 3-8-6 K Darley 25/1: 00-0004: Never nearer: no form
previously: stays 1m & acts on yld ground.   20
143 SOPHYS FOLLY [2] 4-9-9 Gay Kelleway(5) 10/1: -00-30: Made much: effective over
1m on yld and soft.   18
--   GENERATION GAP [7] 4-9-6 Dale Gibson(7) 25/1: -00-0: Fdd 2f out on seasonal debut:
half brother to several winners, though has shown little in his 3 races to date.   00
183 SAIYYAAF [6] 3-8-6 A Murray 7/1: -00: Lightly bckd, fin 9th.   00
134 SANA SONG [3] 3-8-6 D Nicholls 9/1: 040-20: Well below form 134 (6f, heavy).   00
--   Fencalina [1] 9-6   99   Northern Fling [5] 8-3
8   Two Counties [4] 9-9   145   Bantel Beau [9] 8-6
12 ran   5,2,2,¾,10   (Bryan Robson)   D Smith Bishop Auckland, Co Durham

259   INVERESK MAIDEN STAKES 3 & 4YO   £547   1m   Good/Soft 106 -01 Slow

--   LONDON BUS [11] (J Watts) 3-8-6 N Connorton 2/1: 00-1: 3 b c London Bells - Miss
Robust (Busted): Made a winning seasonal debut, led from the stalls, comfortably in a 3
& 4yo maiden at Edinburgh Apr.21: lightly raced in '85, but showed promise on both starts:
half brother to 3 winners: eff at 1m on gd & yld: eff with forcing tactics on a sharpish
trk, though seems to act on any: should rate more highly and win better races   47
33   PRINCELY ESTATE [3] (J Winter) 3-8-6 A Mackay 13/8 FAV : 000-22: Heavily bckd,
al prom: eff over 7f/1m on yld & soft & on any trk: should find a small maiden.   40
142 RESPONDER [7] (R Stubbs) 4-9-6 D Nicholls 14/1: 230-003: Sn prom: no chance with
first 2: see 142.   19
--   THIRTEENTH FRIDAY [12] (W Pearce) 4-9-9 M Hindley(3) 33/1: -0000-4: No real threat
on seasonal debut: lightly raced colt who showed promise as a 2yo: eff at 1m on yld ground.   17
81   KO ISLAND [8] 3-8-6(BL) M Fry 25/1: 2000-00: Never nearer: best effort in '85 when
2nd to Chartino at Ayr and would find a small event on that form: eff at 7f on gd/firm & yld.   15
--   BAYVIEW GAL [10] 3-8-3 R P Elliott 33/1: 0-0: Never threatened.   06
104 WHAT A LINE [6] 4-9-9 D Leadbetter(5) 9/1: 2430-40: Well btn: has regressed: see 104.   00
--   Ultressa [4] 8-3   --   Nicky Dawn [5] 9-6   106 Ackas Boy [1] 9-9
58   Sinferopoli [9] 9-6
11 ran   2,10,2½,½,1   (Sheikh Mohammed)   J Watts Richmond, Yorks

260   DALMENY HANDICAP 3YO+ 0-35   £954   7f   Good/Soft 106 -34 Slow   [35]

--   VENDREDI TREIZE [14] (W Pearce) 3-8-11 N Connorton 12/1: 42100-1: 3 b c Lucky Wednesday-
Angel Row (Prince Regent): First time out, made almost all, ridden out in a h'cap at
Edinburgh Apr.21: in '85 won a maiden at Newcastle and was placed on several occasions:
acts on fast ground, suited by yld: eff at 6/7f with forcing tactics on any trk should stay 1m.   44

-- **MONINSKY** [1] (N Bycroft) 5-8-7 M Richardson(6) 8/1: 02332-2: Kept on well: good seasonal debut: failed to win in '85, though placed on several occasions: in '84 won at Ayr & Pontefract: eff at 6/7f on any grnd: likes a sharpish trk, though acts on any.   20

145 **BARNES STAR** [12] (P Monteith) 4-8-8 B Mcgiff(7) 16/1: 000-033: Nearest fin: needs further? see 145.   18

163 **FAIRGREEN** [15] (D Chapman) 8-8-3 A Proud 20/1: 403-004: Btr effort: see 163 (seller).   11

124 **MAFTIR** [11] 4-9-2(bl) R Cochrane 11/1: 2000-00: Kept on final 1f: in '85 won a h'cap at Nottingham: eff at 6f, stays 1m: acts on gd/firm & yld and on any trk: best in bl.   21

*143 **TRY SCORER** [7] 4-9-2(5ex) L Charnock 5/1: 004-210: Much btr 143 (1m, soft).   20

110 **TRADE HIGH** [5] 7-8-11 R Vickers(7) 20/1: 0000-00: Late hdway: should do btr next time: early last season won a selling h'cap at Pontefract: in '83 won at Carlisle: eff at 5f, stays 7f: acts well on gd & firm & should be noted if dropped to selling company.   00

-- **ZIO PEPPINO** [16] 5-8-6(1ow) E Guest(0) 10/1: 00000-0: Never nearer 9th.   00

182 **ALNASHME** [9] 4-8-5(2ow) A Murray 4/1 FAV: /004-40: Dissapp Fav: 00
expected to do better: see 182.   00

--	Illicit [13] 8-7	182	Throne Of Glory [10] 10-0		
--	O I Oyston [2] 9-3	124	Single Hand [4] 8-8(BL)		
174	Mels Choice [3] 9-3	10	Kings Badge [6] 9-9	58	Great Relative [8] 7-12

16 ran   1¼,1½,½,1½,nk   (P B Raymond)   W Pearce Thirsk, Yorks

---

EPSOM   Tuesday April 22nd   Lefthand, Sharp Undulating Track

Official Going Given as Soft (Heavy in patches)

261 CUDDINGTON MAIDEN AUCTION STKS 2YO   £2110   5f   Soft 143 -05 Slow

170 **DIAMOND FLIGHT** [6] (R Hannon) 2-8-12 Pat Eddery 9/4 FAV: 01: 2 b c Skyliner - Blajina (Bold Lad) (Ire): Impr colt: well bckd and led inside the final 1f, under press in a maiden auction stakes at Epsom Apr.22: cost 3,200 gns: eff at 5f, should stay 6f: acts on yld & soft & seems suited by a sharpish trk.   43

167 **MISS SHEGAS** [4] (J Berry) 2-8-9 W Carson 5/2: 22: Well bckd: made almost all: good effort: acts on any trk and should find a small event: acts on soft & yld: see 167.   35

223 **REVELINA** [9] (D Thom) 2-8-3 M L Thomas 11/1: 003: Never nearer: impr effort from this cheaply acquired filly: acts on soft and a sharpish trk.   22

115 **HONEY PLUM** [8] (M Usher) 2-8-3 M Wigham 5/1: 44: Bumped early on: btr 115.   16

118 **ROYAL RABBLE** [7] 2-8-9 A Mcglone 8/1: 020: Outpcd early: nearest fin: needs further and possibly a stiffer trk: see 118.   22

-- **GLORY GOLD** [3] 2-8-3 K Darley 6/1: 0: Sn prom on debut: cheaply acquired.   11

186 **ORIOLE DANCER** [1] 2-8-12 G Duffield 10/1: 000: Much btr in 186 (yld).   00

180 **Ribo Be Good** [2] 8-3
8 ran   1½,3,2½,shhd,1½   (P W Talbot-Ponsonby)   R Hannon East Everleigh, Wilts

262 EVELYN APP.HANDICAP 3Y+ 0-35   £2428   1m   Soft 143 -30 Slow   [34]

+174 **SINGLE** [6] (W Wightman) 4-9-1(5ex) David Eddery(3) 11/2 Jt.FAV: 020-011: 4 b c Yellaby - Miss Solo (Runnymede): In fine form, despite hanging badly left, led inside the final 1f, comfortably in an app h'cap at Epsom Apr.22: last time out won a h'cap at Chepstow: in '85 won at Bath & Newbury: eff over 7/8f: acts on firm grnd, though likes soft/yld: acts on well on undulating track.   35

-- **TAMERTOWN LAD** [3] (J Jenkins) 5-8-13 L Riggio(5) 12/1: 40000-2: Made much: hmpd nearing final 1f, fin 3rd, placed 2nd: fair effort: in '85 won this same race: in '84 won at Brighton: eff at 7f, stays 1m well: acts on soft, likes good/firm: definitely best on a sharpish trk and does well when fresh.   18

36 **TODA FORCA AVANTI** [7] (A Davison) 4-8-7 I Jupp(7) 16/1: 000-02D: Led over 1f out: not much room final 1f: fin. 2nd, placed 3rd: in '85 won a selling h'cap at Lingfield: eff at 1m/10f: acts on yld & soft & a sharp trk.   16

91 **FEI LOONG** [18] (E Eldin) 5-9-4 G King(3) 9/1: 1400-04: Ran on final 1f: in '85 was in good form, winning twice at Windsor, and likes a sharp trk: eff at 6f-1m: acts on gd/firm & soft.   22

41 **BUCKS BOLT** [5] 4-8-5 S P Griffiths 33/1: 0000-00: Sn prom: in '85 won sellers at Catterick & Haydock: eff at 6/7f, stays 1m: acts on gd & soft: likes a sharpish trk.   08

-- **TOP FEATHER** [2] 4-8-13 M Lynch 20/1: 4004-0: Al there.   13

+177 **GOLD LOFT** [14] 4-8-5(5ex) G Carter 11/2 Jt.FAV: --02-10: No show: much btr 177 (7f gd) 00

*112 **KING OF SPEED** [4] 7-9-0(5ex) R Teague(5) 8/1: 0300-10: Much btr in 112 (7f).   00

112 **HIGH PITCHED** [10] 7-9-6(VIS) P Sargent(7) 10/1: 0404-00: Visored first time: fdd.   00

--	Follow The Band [16] 9-8	--	Rear Action [11] 9-6	--	Any Business [1] 9-12
46	Blow My Top [15] 7-13	--	Young Angel [17] 9-10(vis)	176	Pandi Club [12] 8-8(bl)
160	Mr Rose [20] 8-3	--	Hunts Katie [8] 8-10		
--	Denboy [19] 8-11	--	Pitkaithly [13] 8-12	--	Vitigeson [9] 8-10

20 ran   7,2,½,nk,1½   (A G Lansley)   W Wightman Upham, Hants

263   GREAT METROPOLITAN H'CAP 4Y+ 0-50   £4305   1m 4f   Soft 143 -03 Slow   [50]

--   OWENS PRIDE [10] (R Akehurst) 4-8-0 P Robinson 14/1: 03000-1: 4 b c Owen Dudley - Beech Tree (Fighting Ship): Fit from recent win over hurdles; led over 1f out, ridden out in a h'cap at Epsom Apr.22: in '85 was trained by M Brittain to win a maiden at Hamilton: eff at 10f, stays 15f: best on soft/heavy ground.   37

166 SHARP NOBLE [4] (B Hanbury) 4-9-12 G Baxter 14/1: 001-022: Led over 2f out: 10L clear 3rd: anchored by his big weight: in fine form: stays 12f: see 166.   56

208 RECORD WING [9] (D Haydn Jones) 8-8-8 D Williams(7) 12/1: 00-2133: Ch 2f out: best 92.   26

--   BOLD REX [2] (J Dunlop) 4-9-10 W Carson 8/1: 12031-4: Sn prom on seasonal debut: better for race: in gd form in '85, winning at Chester and Thirsk and on final outing valuable Nov. H'cap at Doncaster: winner in France in '84: stays 12f well: acts on any grnd, though likes some give: genuine & consistent: should be dtr next time.   38

176 BACHAGHA [17] 5-7-7 A Mackay 16/1: 000: Led/dsptd lead: wknd: winner over hurdles, but little form on the Flat.   02

*184 SEVEN SWALLOWS [15] 5-8-3(5ex) M Rimmer 10/1: 1230-10: Led 4f out: btr 184 (10f yld)   07

189 KENTUCKY QUEST [16] 4-8-13(vis) J Reid 8/1: 00-0020: Well below form 189 (yld).   00

*23 BOLD ILLUSION [13] 8-7-8 L Riggio(7) 4/1 FAV: 0104-1U: Heavily bckd: u.r. eff 4f: see 23.   00

121 Hot Betty [3] 7-7(6oh)   121 Gwyn Howard [11] 7-7   -- Electropet [14] 7-10
*176 Thatchingly [6] 7-7(4oh)   -- Otabari [1] 9-8
--   Inherit [8] 7-7(8oh)   -- The Footman [12] 9-6   72 Marley Roofus [5] 9-1
--   Koffi [7] 9-11
17 ran   5,10,3,4,4   (Venture Chemical Products Ltd)   R Akehurst Epsom, Surrey

264   PRINCESS ELIZABETH STKS 3YO FILLIES   £8389   1m   Soft 143 -22 Slow

218 MONA LISA [5] (P Kelleway) 3-8-5 P Cook 10/1: -01: 3 b f Henbit - House Maid (Habitat): Prom filly: ev ch when not much room final 1f: btn a nk by Land Of Ivory, but subsq. awarded Princess Elizabeth Stakes (Listed race) at Epsom Apr.22: did not race as a 2yo: cost I.R. 50,000 gns as a yearling: eff at 1m, should stay further: acts on yld & soft & on any trk: should win more races.   62

--   CHERNICHERVA [2] (H Cecil) 3-8-9 S Cauthen 7/2: 113-2: Easy to back: led over 1f out till inside final 1f: fin 3rd, placed 2nd: won first 2 starts in '85, at Haydock & Goodwood: half sister to 2 winners: eff at 7f, stays 1m: acts on gd/firm & soft grnd & on any trk.   65

--   REJUVENATE [9] (B Hills) 3-8-5 B Thomson 10/1: -3: Ev ch when stopped in her tracks final 1f: unlucky?: promising racecourse debut from this half sister to several winners: eff at 1m, should stay further: acts on soft ground & should be winning soon.   60

--   LAND OF IVORY [1] (I Balding) 3-8-9 Pat Eddery 12/1: 1404-1D: Led, but hung badly left final 1f to get home by a nk: disq. & placed 4th, giving P Eddery 7 days suspension: in '85 won a fillies maiden at Sandown: half sister to the smart Gold And Ivory and should be suited by further than 1m: acts on good & soft grnd and on any trk: should gain compensation soon.   67

-89 HOT MOMMA [8] 3-8-5 M Miller 25/1: 2022-20: Frustrating filly but a fair effort: 89.   46

--   ENTRANCING [4] 3-8-9 W Carson 5/2 FAV: 12-0: Well bckd on seasonal debut, made much sn wknd: should do much btr than this: first time out in '85 won at Goodwood: eff at 7f, should be suited by 1m: acts on soft, possibly best on a sounder surface.   40

*213 ZALATIA [6] 3-8-9 B Rouse 3/1: 22-10: Much btr in 213 (7f, yld, gall trk).   00

--   KICK THE HABIT [3] 3-8-5 P Robinson 6/1: 0-0: Active in mkt: no show.   00

--   LIGHT BEE [7] 3-8-9 A Murray 16/1: 12103-0: Fdd: btr for race.   00
9 ran   nk,nk,½,7,6   (Roldvale Ltd)   P Kelleway Newmarket

265   CITY AND SUBURBAN H'CAP 3YO+ 0-60   £11449   1m 2f   Soft 143 +01 Fast   [55]

*72 NEBRIS [8] (R Akehurst) 5-9-8 Pat Eddery 11/2 FAV: 0110-11: 5 b h Nebbiolo - Magic Quiz (Quisling): Very useful horse: well bckd and led 2f out, easily in a valuable h'cap at Epsom Apr.22: in fine form, first time out was a ready winner of valuable Rosebery Stakes (h'cap) at Kempton: smart hurdler: in fine form on the Flat in '85, winning h'caps at Epsom and Newmarket: earlier won an amateur riders race at Lingfield: very eff at 10/11f: acts on good/firm and soft and on any trk: genuine and consistent: will win again: carries weight well.   65

--   ESQUIRE [3] (B Hills) 4-9-3 B Thomson 14/1: 44010-2: Led 2f out: 8L clear 3rd: in '85 won a 3yo maiden at Newbury: eff at 9/10f: acts on gd & soft & on any trk: goes well when fresh.   51

--   TABARDAR [11] (R Johnson Houghton) 4-9-4 S Cauthen 16/1: 03400-3: Made much: lightly raced maiden who showed promise in '85: eff at 10/11f on gd/firm & soft ground.   40

--   THE GAMES UP [7] (P Haslam) 5-7-10 T Williams 25/1: 30300-4: No real threat on seasonal debut: failed to win in '85: in '84 won at Windsor and Hamilton: eff at 1m, stays 10f: acts on gd/firm & soft.   16

72   DUELLING [12] 5-7-7(vis) G Carter(0) 8/1: 330-400: Best in 7 (good).   08

--   HOUSE HUNTER [4] 5-9-2 I Salmon 25/1: 34000-0: Nearest fin: btr for race.   27

*9   BRUNICO [9] 4-9-9 S Whitworth 15/2: -10: No show: much btr in 9 (yld, gall trk).   00

+71 KAZAROW [21] 5-8-6 M Rimmer 8/1: 2022-10: Wknd: much btr in 71 (1m).   00

176 ROYAL HALO [13] 5-9-5 G Starkey 9/1: 0234-20: Much btr 176 (good).   00

--	Master Line [19] 8-9	--	Pictograph [5] 9-3	72	Gay Captain [15] 9-6	
17	Christian Schad [6] 9-8			189	Abu Kadra [20] 9-9(bl)	
--	Chiclet [2] 9-6	--	The Nub [16] 9-0	71	Alqirm [14] 8-6	
189	Shostakovitch [10] 8-6(BL)			179	Pellincourt [18] 7-8	

19 ran   3,8,¾,2½,2   (D S Collinge)   R Akehurst, Epsom Surrey

---

266 KINGSWOOD HANDICAP 4YO+ 0-35   £2502   6f   Soft 143 +28 Fast   [31]

122 BELLE TOWER [13] (R Smyth) 4-9-2 C Rutter(5) 8/1: 000-021: 4 Tower Walk - Sarum Lady (Floribunda): In good form, ran on well to lead inside final 1f, under press in a fast run h'cap at Epsom Apr.22: in '85 won a h'cap at Folkestone: eff over 6/7f: acts on any going, but is definitely best on a sharp trk.   29

-- FREMONT BOY [10] (C James) 4-8-11 W Carson 25/1: 03000-2: Strong run final 1f and nearly got up: good seasonal debut: failed to win in '85: in '84 won at Redcar & Windsor: eff at 5f on gd/firm & soft: acts on any trk, though likes a sharp trk.   23

211 ROYAL BEAR [7] (J Bradley) 4-8-0 T Williams 14/1: 0-22043: Led ½way: caught inside final 1f: loves a sharp trk: see 84.   08

114 EXERT [5] (R Akehurst) 4-9-0 N Adams 8/1: 4400-34: Nearest fin: in good form: see 114.   21

135 CORNCHARM [6] 5-9-10 S Cauthen 9/1: 100-020: Sn prom: see 135.   31

114 BLACK SPOUT [1] 5-7-11 S Dawson(3) 12/1: 000-320: Mkt drifter: wknd final 1f: flattered in 31.   00

110 VIA SATELLITE [14] 4-8-7 S Whitworth 4/1 FAV: 3440-30: Well bckd: btr 110 needs a stiff track. 00

182 PARADE GIRL [12] 4-8-13 Pat Eddery 7/1: 03-0100: Early ldr: best 56 (5f hvy stiff trk)   00

160 SHADES OF BLUE [2] 5-9-3 R Cochrane 5/1: 3000-20: Well below form 160 (yld stiff trk)   00

182 HENRYS VENTURE [11] 4-7-11 J Lowe 9/1: 000-000: Al rear: see 182.   00

--	Port Mist [3] 7-11	122	Sparkford Lad [15] 9-7(bl)		
160	Lottie [4] 7-11(bl)	--	Hildalarious [9] 7-12	--	Linton Starchy [8] 8-0(3ow)

15 ran   nk,1½,1,¾,shhd,2½   (Mrs G R Smith)   R Smyth Epsom, Surrey

---

CURRAGH   Saturday April 12th   Righthand Galloping Track

Official Going Given as Yielding

267 MICHAEL SMURFITT GLADNESS STKS LISTED   £12739   7f   Yielding -   [2]

-- LIDHAME (K Prendergast) 4-9-11 G Curran 10/1: 3-100-1: 4 br c Nureyev - Red Berry: Smart colt: led over 2f out, ridden out in Gladness Stakes (Listed Race) at the Curragh Apr.12: trained by J Dunlop in '85 to win Gr.3 event at Salisbury: very eff at 7f: acts on gd/firm & heavy grnd and a gall trk.   78

151 MR DISPLAY [3] (M O'toole) 3-8-6 D Gillespie 8/1: 220-122: Not much room over 1f out: in fine form: see 151.   72

-- TATE GALLERY [1] (M V O'brien) 3-8-12 Pat Eddery 2/7 FAV: --011-3: Long odds on: ev ch over 2f out: failed to quicken up: has now been taken out of the 2,000 Guineas betting: in '85 won twice, incl Gr.1 National Stakes on this trk: full brother to the top class Sadlers Wells: eff at 7f, should stay much further: acts on yld grnd: should do much btr than this.   74

-- MIAMI COUNT [5] (D Weld) 4-9-8 M J Kinane 6/1: 24200-4: Now trained by D Weld: failed to win in '85: 3 times a winner as a 2yo: very eff over 7f: acts on firm & heavy.   66

-- SUNSTART [7] 4-9-11 G Mcgrath 20/1: 11-21-0: Btr for race: lightly raced in '85, winning Gr.3 event on this trk: eff at 1m, stays 10f: acts on firm & soft: has run well in blinkers.   65

-- SPEAR DANCE [6] 4-9-5(bl) S Craine 50/1: 1400-00: Led over 4f.   55

6 ran   ¾,2,¾,2,1½   (Hamdan Al-Maktoum)   K Prendergast Ireland

---

268 BANDON EBF 2YO MAIDEN   £2415   5f   Yielding -

-- HIGH WIND [5] (J Murphy) 2-9-0 D J Murphy 3/1 Jt.FAV: 1: 2 b c Wind And Wuthering Easter Joy: Made a winning racecourse debut: comfortable 2L winner of a maiden at the Curragh Apr.12: eff at 5f, should stay further: acts on yld & a gall trk.   52

-- CORRIENDO LIBRE [3] (C Collins) 2-9-0 P Shanahan 5/1: 2: Promising debut: eff at 5f, should stay further: acts on yld.   46

-- CAJUN MELODY [9] (A Leahy) 2-8-11 J Nolan(5) 12/1: 3: Impr likely.   42

-- ON THE STEEL [2] (E Lynam) 2-9-0 J Coogan 9/2: 4:   43

-- GAELGOIR [7] 2-9-0 G Curran 3/1 Jt.FAV: 0:   38

-- SOLE JUSTICE [4] 2-9-0 C Roche 5/1: 0:   34

-- SECONDS OUT [6] 2-9-0 D Parnell 8/1: 0:   00

--	Blundell Wood [8] 9-0	--	She Is A Beauty [1] 8-11

9 ran   2,nk,¾,2m1½   (S Hayden)   J Murphy Ireland

269   WASSL MARBAYEH 3YO FILLIES LISTED   £8889   7f   Yielding -

--   **WEIGHT IN GOLD** [8] (J Bolger) 3-8-8 D Gillespie 5/4 FAV: -121-11: 3 b f Dalsaan -
Albigold: Very useful Irish filly: made ev yd, comfortably in a valuable fillies Listed race
at the Curragh Apr.12: first time out won at Leopardstown, again making all: very eff at
7f with forcing tactics: acts on yld & heavy.   70
--   **CARHUE LADY** [4] (P O'leary) 3-8-8 Pat Eddery 4/1: 22142-2: Good seasonal debut:
in '85 won a fillies maiden at the Curragh: on final outing was a fine 2nd to Gayle Gal in
Gr.1 event again at the Curragh and runs well here: eff at 6/7f on gd & soft.   65
--   **CALAMETTA** [5] (D Hughes) 3-8-8 S Craine 20/1: -022-3: Outsider: gd effort: eff at
7f on soft & yld.   63
--   **SANTOLINE** [3] (N Meade) 3-8-8 P V Gilson 5/1: -0101-4: Not disgraced: in '85 won at
the Curragh and Down Royal: eff at 7f, stays 9f: acts on yld & soft.   62
--   **WELSH FANTASY** [2] 3-8-12 P Shanahan 10/1: -210-0: In '85 won over 6f at Phoenix Park:
acts on gd/yld & soft.   65
--   **BUSHY BELLE** [7] 3-8-8 C Roche 14/1: 3140-20: Recent 2nd, albeit at 10L to Weight In
Gold at Leopardstown: acts on yld & heavy.   60
--   **CAROLS LUCK** [6] 3-8-9(1ow) D Murphy 4/1: -1-0: On final outing in '85 won a fillies
maiden at Naas: acts on yld.   00
--   **Pickety Place** [1] 8-8
8 ran   2,¼,½,hd,½   (Mrs O White)   J Bolger Ireland

EPSOM   Wednesday April 23rd   Lefthand, Sharp, Undulating Track

Official Going Given as Heavy: Time Slow except race 272

270   113TH EBF HYDE PARK MAIDEN 2YO STAKES   £1668   5f   Heavy Slow

--   **OLORE MALLE** [3] (R Hannon) 2-9-0 R Wernham 10/1: 1: 2 ch c Camden Town - Grace Poole
(Sallust): First time out, led inside the final 1f, ridden out in a 2yo maiden at Epsom
Apr.23: cost I.R. 5,000: eff at 5f, should be suited by 6f plus: acts on heavy ground and
a sharpish trk: should rate more highly.   45
118 **PARKLANDS BELLE** [2] (M Haynes) 2-8-11 P Cook 20/1: 02: Led over 1f out: 8L clear
3rd and is on the up grade: should find a small maiden: see 118.   37
115 **MUKHABBR** [6] (C Benstead) 2-9-0 B Rouse 7/2: 03: Made much: btr effort: cost
I.R.18,000: half brother to very useful sprinter Pampas and like her may prefer faster
ground: should continue to impr.   24
--   **OUR FREDDIE** [7] (A Ingham) 2-9-0 J Reid 6/1: 4: Outpcd early: nearest fin: half brother
to several winners and should impr.   04
--   **SYLVAN ORIENT** [9] 2-9-0 A Mcglone 7/1: 0: No threat: cost ₹1,000 gns.   00
--   **NIPPED OFF** [8] 2-9-0 Pat Eddery 13/8 FAV: 0: Well bckd fav: no show after slow start:
cost 5,400 gns and should do btr than this.   00
--   **Hit Lucky** [4] 8-11   --   **Pink Pumpkin** [5] 8-11
8 ran   1½,8,10,3,2   (Mrs J Reglar)   R Hannon East Everleigh, Wiltshire

271   RACAL ELECTRONICS HANDICAP 3YO   £3811   8.5f   Heavy Slow   [62]

--   **BRAZZAKA** [4] (M Jarvis) 3-8-11 T Ives 13/2: 22221-1: 3 ch f Barrera - Irish Reel
(Irish Lancer): Useful filly : led after 3f, comfortably in a 3yo fillies h'cap at Epsom
Apr.23: in '85 was most consistent, winning at Hamilton after 4 2nds in a row: eff at 7f,
stays 1m well: acts on firm, seems well suited by heavy ground: acts on any trk.   59
63   **POUNELTA** [7] (R Hannon) 3-8-8(BL) S Cauthen 7/2: 4133-42: Well bckd: ev ch final
1f: good effort: runs well here: acts on any grnd and may win soon: see 63.   53
--   **MIRATAINE VENTURE** [1] (R Akehurst) 3-8-6 G Baxter 12/1: 00022-3: Early ldr: al prom
on seasonal debut: showed promise in '85, though yet to win: eff at 7f, stays 1m: acts on
firm and heavy and on any trk.   46
+89 **HIGH HALO** [3] (I Balding) 3-8-3 B Rouse 4/1: 0-14: Much btr in 89 (made all).   27
--   **GREY WALLS** [6] 3-9-1 Pat Eddery 2/1 FAV: 013-0: Heavily bckd: wknd 2f out: in '85
won a fillies maiden at Yarmouth: half sister to 3 winners, notably very smart Pelerin: eff
at 6f, should be suited by 1m: possibly btr on good ground and is worth keeping an eye on.   31
--   **NORMANBY LASS** [2] 3-9-7 Paul Eddery 16/1: 00320-0: Mkt drifter: fdd on seasonal debut:
in '85 won at Warwick: eff at 7f and should be suited by 1m plus: acts on firm & yld and
on any trk.   33
--   **LA SERENATA** [5] 3-7-10 M L Thomas 10/1: 0340-0: Sn struggling.   00
7 ran   ¼,2½,8,4,2   (Tjo Tek Tan)   M Jarvis Newmarket

272   MINORU STKS HANDICAP   £3791   5f   Heavy +25 Fast   [60]

84   **PERION** [3] (G Lewis) 4-7-13 M L Thomas 5/1: 000-101: 4 ch g Northfields - Relanca
(Relic): Well bckd and led inside final 1f, under press in a 5f h'cap at Epsom Apr.23:
first time out won a h'cap at Folkestone: lightly raced in '85: in '84 won at Newmarket:
very eff at 5f, acts on gd, well suited by soft/heavy and seems best when held up for
a late chall.   45

165 CLANTIME [6] (R Whitaker) 5-8-11 D Mckeown 7/1: 2100-02: Led over 1f out: likes
Epsom: in '85 won a valuable h'cap on this trk: in '84 won at Chester: 4 times a winner as
a 2yo: very eff over 5f with forcing tactics: acts on any going & on any trk though likes
a sharpish one: sometimes bl but is a genuine sort.   51
*76   HILTON BROWN [9] (P Cundell) 5-9-8 P Cook 5/2 FAV: 000-313: Heavily bckd: nearest
fin: in good form: see 76.   58
122 MUSIC MACHINE [4] (P Haslam) 5-7-9 T Williams 13/2: 4010-04: Made much: in '85 won
at Pontefract, Warwick & Ripon: in '84 won at Ayr: very eff at 5f, stays 6f: acts on any
grnd and on any trk though seems best forcing the pace on a sharpish one.   30
+211 SPACEMAKER BOY [8] 6-8-6(7ex) N Howe 10/1: 20-2410: Btr 211 (made all).   29
172 DERRY RIVER [2] 5-7-12(bl) W Carson 14/1: 0322-00: Active in mkt: prom 4f: last won
in '83 at Wolverhampton, but ran well when 2nd to Broadwater Music in a valuable h'cap at
Newbury in '85: eff at 5f on gd/firm & yld.   19
+165 BROADWATER MUSIC [ı] 5-9-5(10ex) R Cochrane 9/2: 210-010: No show: btr 165 (stiffer trk)00
211 Jackie Blair [1] 7-7(BL)(3oh)   165 Ardrox Lad [5] 10-0
9 ran   2½,2,nk,6,½   (John W Wheatland)   G Lewis Epsom, Surrey

273 RACAL VODAPHONE BLUE RIBAND TRIAL 3YO   £11550   1m4f   Heavy Slow

--   BELDALE STAR [7] (G Harwood) 3-8-12 G Starkey 9/2: 21120-1: 3 b c Beldale Flutter-
Little White Star (Mill Reef): Smart colt: easy to back on seasonal debut, but made hacks of
his rivals with an easy 4L win in valuable Blue Riband Trial Stakes (Listed race) at
Epsom Apr.23: in good form in '85, winning at Kempton & Salisbury: also a fine neck 2nd
to Faustus in Listed race at Goodwood: stays 1½m well: acts on gd/firm, seems well suited
by heavy grnd: acts on any trk: should win more races.   76
--   DANCING ZETA [3] (P Kelleway) 3-8-12 P Cook 9/2: 13013-2: Made much till inside
final 1f: no chance with winner, but ran well: in '85 won at York & Ayr: eff at 1m, stays
12f: acts on any grnd and on any trk: suited by forcing tactics.   64
--   COMME LETOILE [1] (J Hindley) 3-8-12 M Hills 3/1 FAV: 121-3: Heavily bckd on seasonal
debut: ev ch str: in '85 won at Doncaster & Haydock: eff at 10f, stays 12f: acts on firm,
suited by soft/heavy: acts on any trk.   59
123 SANET [6] (P Kelleway) 3-8-5 T Quinn 25/1: -44: No real threat thogh is fast impr:
stays 12f well: suited by heavy grnd & a sharpish trk & should find a small maiden.   50
--   WAR HERO [8] 3-8-12 W Carson 8/1: 013-0: Early ldr: wknd on seasonal debut: last
season won at Goodwood: eff at 1m, probably stays 12f: acts on gd/firm & heavy.   51
60   LANDSKI [4] 3-8-8 S Whitworth 8/1: -40: Much btr in 60 (1m).   47
75   GROVE TOWER [5] 3-8-8 N Howe 33/1: 003-40: Rank outsider: led 3f: see 75.   00
--   EMERALD POINT [2] 3-8-8 Pat Eddery 15/2: 3-0: Fdd str: unsuited by heavy?   00
--   KOLGONG HEIGHTS [9] 3-9-1 R Cochrane 8/1: 1300-0: Never in it.   00
9 ran   4,2½,1,3,hd   (N A Solomons)   G Harwood Pulborough, Sussex

274 PRINCES STAND HANDICAP 3YO   £2978   7f   Heavy Slow   [45]

+175 REIGNBEAU [4] (G Lewis) 3-9-13(6ex) P Waldron 4/1: 03-311: 3 b c Runnett - Queens
worthy (Capistrano): Useful, impr colt: made ev yd, driven out in a 3yo h'cap at Epsom
Apr.23: last time out won a fast run stakes event at Brighton: eff at 6/7f: acts on gd &
heavy and on any trk, though likes a sharpish one: seems suited by front running tactics. 54
95   MIGHT MOVE [3] (R Smyth) 3-8-13 W Carson 10/1: 003-002: Ch final 1f, good effort:
has been running over 10/12f: seems btr suited by this shorter trip: acts on firm & heavy
and a sharpish trk.   39
--   PROBLEM CHILD [9] (R Smyth) 3-8-7 S Whitworth 16/1: 00003-3: Ran on final 1f and
narrowly btn: good seasonal debut: on final outing in '85 fin 3rd in a maiden at Lingfield:
eff at 7f/1m: acts on any grnd: seems to like a sharpish trk.   32
*228 MAJOR JACKO [2] (R Hannon) 3-9-3(6ex) S Cauthen 11/8 FAV: 000-014: Much better
228 (6f, stiff track).   36
--   SUMMERHILL SPRUCE [1] 3-8-1 G Carter(3) 16/1: 00000-0: Ch over 1f out: btr for
race: showed some form in '85, notably when 2nd in a Kempton maiden: eff at 5f, stays 6f:
acts on gd & firm & a sharpish trk.   08
--   BLUE STEEL [8] 3-8-3 N Adams 25/1: 00000-0: Bumped 3f out on seasonal debut.   05
--   BLUE HORIZON [5] 3-8-4 M L Thomas 15/2: 41303-0: There ½way.   00
--   LABRAG [7] 3-8-10 Paul Eddery 3/1: 0300-0: Unsuited by heavy.   00
37   Nanor [6] 7-13
9 ran   nk,nk,3,7,3   (Mrs B M Clarke)   G Lewis Epsom, Surrey

275 WESTMINSTER STAKES HANDICAP 3YO   £2358   10f   Heavy Slow   [42]

*193 SAMANPOUR [2] (R Johnson Houghton) 3-9-7(5ex) S Cauthen 5/2 FAV: 0001-11: 3 gr c Nishapour -
Sellasia (Dankaro): In fine form, heavily bckd and led near line in a 3yo h'cap at Epsom
Apr.23: last time out won a similar event at Kempton: on final outing in '85 won a maiden
at Nottingham: very eff at 10f: acts on any grnd & on any trk.   44
*120 STRAIGHT THROUGH [18] (J Winter) 3-8-13(5ex) B Rouse 10/3: 024-212: Well bckd: led over
3f out: caught near line: in fine form: 5L clear rem: see 120.   35

117 PRIOK [15] (W Wightman) 3-7-13 M L Thomas 20/1: 0000-03: Dsptd lead 3f out: btr
effort from this maiden: eff over 10f on heavy grnd and a sharpish trk.   12
117 STILLOU [6] (P Mitchell) 3-8-3 G Carter(3) 6/1: 4104-34: Mkt drifter: al there: see 117.   13
*171 OWL CASTLE [11] 3-9-12(5ex) Pat Eddery 14/1: 0-32410: Much btr in 171 (12f, yld).   24
120 REFORM PRINCESS [9] 3-8-11 P Robinson 20/1: 2000-00: Never nearer: showed some form
in '85, notably when 2nd at 10L to Rethymno in a Kempton maiden: eff over 7f, may stay
10f: acts on yld & soft.   05

--	Be Positive [8] 7-11	--	Sales Promoter [5] 8-11		
117	Walcisin [7] 8-8	191	Common Accord [10] 8-10		
193	Roaming Weir [16] 9-7	--	Puppywalker [17] 7-7(vis)(7oh)		
--	On To Glory [12] 9-5	--	Raffia Run [14] 8-10	--	Fastway Flyer [3] 8-1
120	Angel Drummer [13] 8-1(2ow)				

16 ran   shhd,5,1½,7,2,nk   (Aga Khan)   R Johnson Houghton Blewbury, Oxon

276 BANSTEAD MAIDEN STAKES 3YO   £1716   7f   Heavy Slow

-- MIRANDA JULIA [3] (D Elsworth) 3-8-11 A Mcglone 10/3: 0440-1: 3 b f Julio Mariner -
La Miranda (Miralgo): First time out, led inside final 1f, under press in a 3yo maiden at
Epsom Apr.23: half sister to several winners, incl the useful sprinter Ferryman: eff at 6f,
stays 7f: acts on gd/firm & heavy & seems to like a sharpish trk.   33
237 COOPER RACING NAIL [6] (J Berry) 3-8-11 J Reid 9/2: 322-322: Led over 6f: see 237 (seller)28
-- MIGHTILY [1] (D Wilson) 3-9-0 B Rouse 16/1: 0-3: Fair seasonal debut: unplaced on
sole start in '85: eff at 7f, though on breeding should be well suited by 1m plus: acts
on heavy.   23
111 BELLEPHERON [2] (G Lewis) 3-9-0 P Waldron 10/1: 0-04: Al there: best effort yet:
eff at 7f on heavy.   17
-- BLUE BRILLIANT [9] 3-9-0 B Thomson 11/4 FAV: 00-0: Ev ch when hmpd 2f out, ending
his chances: highly tried in 2 outings in '85: acts on heavy: should stay 1m & will do
btr next time.   13
-- COMEDY PRINCE [11] 3-9-0 S Whitworth 20/1: 000-0: Never beyond mid-div: acts on heavy. 10
111 VALVINORA [4] 3-9-0 P O'leary 9/1: 00-00: Very active in mkt: prom over 4f: wknd.   00

32	Wing Bee 0 9-0	83	Galaxy Path 0 9-0	113	Dynamic Baby 0 8-11

10 ran   2,4,3,3,1½   (D L C Hodges)   D Elsworth Whitsbury, Hants

277 BANSTEAD MAIDEN STAKES 3YO   £1704   7f   Heavy Slow

68 GEORDIES DELIGHT [10] (L Piggott) 3-9-0 T Ives 7/4 FAV: 0-21: 3 b c Northern Baby -
Shout For Joy (Court Martial): Heavily bckd and led 2f out, comfortably in a maiden at
Epsom Apr.23: first success for L Piggott as a trainer: unplaced on sole start in '85 when
trained by J Ciechanowski: eff over 7f/1m on soft & heavy: acts on any trk.   46
175 PORTHMEOR [1] (M Bolton) 3-9-0 S Cauthen 4/1: 2044-42: Made much: 5L clear 3rd:
good effort: stays 7f & seems to act on any grnd: likes a sharpish trk: should find a small race . 36
175 LIGHTNING BYTE [2] (G Gracey) 3-9-0 G Carter(3) 33/1: -03: Ch over 2f out: impr
effort: stays 7f: acts on heavy & a sharpish trk.   25
-- OMANIA [8] (R Hannon) 3-8-11 A Mcglone 8/1: 400-4: Btr for race: lightly raced in '85:
half sister to 2 winning sprinters: acts on firm & heavy & on any trk.   19
-- LINAVOS [4] 3-9-0 T Quinn 25/1: 000-0: Speed 4f on seasonal debut: unplaced in 3
outings in '85.   14
-- SWEET DOMAIN [9] 3-8-11 W Carson 2/1: 0320-0: Well bckd: unsuited by heavy? showed
fair form in '85, notably when 2nd to Resourceful Falcon at Nottingham: eff at 6f: acts
on gd/firm & yld.   05

117	Trelawney 0 9-0	91	Baxtergate 0 9-0	162	Lisakaty 0 8-11

9 ran   4,5,1½,4,3   (Sheikh Mohammed)   L Piggott Newmarket

Official Going Given as Soft with Heavy Patches: On Time Heavy and deteriorating.

278 BEAST FAIR MAIDEN STKS 2YO   £1935   5f   Heavy +05 Fast

+197 PEATSWOOD SHOOTER [5] (M Brittain) 2-9-6 K Darley 5/4 FAV: 111: 2 gr c Windjammer -
Raffinata (Raffingora): Useful colt: unbtn in 3 races, the latest at Pontefract Apr.23 when
making all keeping on well: winner at Beverley & Leicester (first time out) previously:
very eff over 5f, shld stay at least 6f: acts on yld & heavy going and runs well on a
stiff trk though probably acts on any: suited by front running tactics: all 3 of his wins
have been in fast times & he must still be followed until btn.   58
*200 SAMLEON [2] (R Hannon) 2-9-3 G Duffield 4/1: 412: Kept on well: fine effort and
will not often meet one as good as this winner at this stage of the season: see 200.   52
*167 KILVARNET [6] (R Hollinshead) 2-9-3 S Perks 9/4: 013: Al well there: possibly btr
suited by gd/soft in 167.   44

-- DANADN [1] (Ron Thompson) 2-8-11 R P Elliott 33/1: 4: Slow start, kept on well
showing promise: should be well suited by 6f: a May foal who should impr.   33
94 UNOS PET [4] 2-8-11 C Dwyer 20/1: 330: Never closer: would be hard to beat in a
seller: see 94, 34.   33
223 TOOTSIE JAY [3] 2-8-8 R Hills 9/1: 300: Ran poorly, btr 223 (gd/yld).   00
6 ran   1,3,2,shhd,15   (G Ashton)   M Brittain Warthill, Yorks

279 BENTLEY MEMORIAL SELL HCAP 3YO   £842   8f   Heavy Slow   [20]

-- BILLYS DANCER [7] (D Dale) 3-9-7 G King(7) 11/4: 040-1: 3 ch c Piaffer - Hay-Hay
(Hook Money): Made a winning seasonal reappearance, leading final 100 yds in a 3yo selling
h'cap at Pontefract Apr.23: lightly raced but showed some promise in sellers in '85; notably
when bl on one occasion: appears to act on firm & heavy: stays 1m and runs as if further
will suit.   22
*93 CHEPSTOWED [3] (D Haydn Jones) 3-9-3 D J Williams(7) 7/4 FAV: 0000-12: Led 3f out
under strong driving, outpcd by winner: well clear of rest and is in gd form: see 93.   10
139 THE DABBER [4] (G Harman) 3-8-13(bl) G Duffield 10/1: 00-0033: Ev ch: appears moderate. 00
51 DUKE OF MILLTIMBER [10] (P Rohan) 3-8-9 S Morris 14/1: 000-04: Ev ch: lightly raced
and no worthwhile form.   00
-- FIRE LORD [8] 3-8-10 D Casey(7) 25/1: 00000-0: No threat on seasonal debut: only poor fσm.00
183 OUR ANNIE [1] 3-9-6 Wendy Carter(7) 25/1: 000-00: No threat: no form.   00
107 CONERSER [9] 3-9-7(bl) Gay Kelleway(5) 9/1: 0000-40: Led around ½way, wknd: rated
18 last season: see 107-   00
-- MAX CLOWN [6] 3-8-13 N Carlisle 9/1: 000-0: No threat from this lightly raced maiden.   00
-- LA MANGA PRINCE [2] 3-9-5 G Brown(5) 11/2: 30000-0: Fin last: creditable 3rd in a
valuable seller at York in July '85, has run badly since.   00
-- Gemma Louise [5] 9-2
10 ran   5,12,2½,hd,3   (F Phoenix)   D Dale Newmarket

280 HEY SOFT DRINKS EBF STAKES   £3720   17f   Heavy Slow

215 INDE PULSE [3] (J Hindley) 4-9-3 R Hills 1/4 FAV: 1100-01: 4 b c Troy - Divine
Thought (Javelot): Very useful stayer: al there and led finally 4f out for a clever 2L
success in a 4 runner minor race at Pontefract Apr.23: in '85 was trained by F Durr and
completed a hat trick at York (2) & Chepstow: eff 2m, stays really well: acts on firm & heavy
and on any trk.   50
-- NORTHERN RULER [1] (L Lightbrown) 4-8-9 G Duffield 8/1: 20000-2: Flattered by proximity
to tenderly ridden winner: winner at Redcar & Hamilton in '85: eff around 12f, evidently
stays very well: winning form on fast going but ran creditably here in heavy.   34
-- AYRES ROCK [4] (M Haynes) 5-9-1 R Fox 10/1: 03000-3: Made much on seasonal debut:
Irish import who won at Thurles in '85: best form on firm & good going: now stays 2m.   25
58a MAJESTIC RING [2] (P Kelleway) 4-8-9 Gay Kelleway 10/1: 0012-04: No threat: trained by
G Harwood in '85 & won a claiming stakes at Sandown: eff around 11f & fast going on a stiff trk. 07
4 ran   2,12,10   (R J McAlpine)   J Hindley Newmarket

281 HARDWICK HANDICAP STKS   £2253   8f   Heavy Slow   [32]

-- SILVER CANNON [18] (R Woodhouse) 4-9-7 K Darley 25/1: 21000-1: 4 gr g Lot O'Gold -
So High (Sea-Bird II): Turned up at 25/1 on seasonal debut, making most comfortably in a
h'cap at Pontefract Apr.23: fairly consistent last season winning a h'cap at Edinburgh:
half brother to several winners, notably the useful High Cannon: best form over 1m with front
running tactics & likes a sharp or turning trk, particularly Edinburgh: wore visor when
successful last season but not today: has changed stables since last season.   34
131 RUSTIC TRACK [11] (D Smith) 6-8-0 M Fry 25/1: 0031-32: Fin very strongly from an
impossible position: in good form: seems to act on firm & heavy: see 131.   10
*142 PATCHBURG [3] (W Haigh) 4-9-0 J H Brown(5) 5/1: 002-213: Stayed on under press:
better 142 (10f).   21
10 EASY DAY [10] (E Eldin) 4-9-1 A Mackay 14/1: 0000-04: Ev ch: placed on a few occasions
last season but yet to break his maiden tag: has been tried in a visor: probably stays 1m.   17
-- GOLDEN BEAU [14] 4-9-2 M Birch 12/1: 40040-0: Ev ch, should benefit from the race:
failed to win in '85 but the previous season successful at Yarmouth, Brighton & Epsom:
best form around 7f/1m: acts on gd & soft & on any trk though runs well on an undulating one. 11
238 VERBARIUM [2] 6-8-13 D J Williams(7) 3/1 FAV: 31-2320: Once again kept on late and
seems a difficult ride: see 10.   00
142 MRS CHRIS [7] 4-9-0(vis) M Miller 10/1: 00-0400: Led around ½way: twice below 46.   00
112 REPEALED [15] 4-9-2(BL) R Lines(3) 5/1: -032320: Ran poorly: bl for the first time
and seems btr without: see 71, 112.   00
36 COUNT BERTRAND [9] 5-9-0 R Morse(5) 10/1: 0302-00: Fin last: remains a maiden.   00
-- Glenderry [13] 8-10   -- Minus Man [1] 8-4   142 Quality Chorister [4] 8-8
-- Fair Trader [6] 7-10   -- Welsh Medley [12] 9-3   163 Spoilt For Choice [5] 9-0
15 ran   1,1½,2½,4,5   (Couture Marketing Ltd)   R Woodhouse Whitewell On The Hill

PONTEFRACT   Wednesday April 23rd   – Cont'd

282 FRYSTON EBF STAKES   £2863   12f   Heavy Slow

58   NIKOOLA EVE [9] (J Glover) 4-8-4 M Birch 11/1: -031: Al there and readily came clear
final 2f in a minor race at Pontefract Apr.23: did not race last season: suited by 12f on
heavy going: impr type who should win again.   30
--   GENTLE STREAM [1] (J Toller) 4-9-1 R Hills 10/1: 00000-2: Prom, ev ch: Irish import who
was successful twice at Killarney in '85: very eff around 12f on firm or gd going, probably
also acts on heavy.   26
176 PRIVATE AUDITION [3] (M Usher) 4-8-7 M Wigham 5/1 Jt.FAV: -433: Much btr 176 (10f gd).08
--   HYOKIN [13] (M Morley) 4-8-7 G Duffield 8/1: 00242-4: Placed in his last 3 in '85 but
remains a maiden: wore a visor several times last season: stays 12f: runs well on fast gng:
should do better next time.   07
--   GREENACRES GIRL [5] 5-8-4 A Roper(5) 25/1: -0-0: Fit from hurdling but is a very
lightly raced maiden on the Flat.   01
--   CANE MILL [2] 4-9-4 M Tebbutt(7) 7/1: 2142-0: Made most: easily won a maiden at
Nottingham early in '85 when trained by H Cecil, has since changed stables: acts on yld
going: stays 10f well.   09
208 CHANGANOOR [8] 4-8-7 S Perks 7/1: 0432-00: Fin. in pleasing style: placed several
times last season though has yet to win a race.   00
--   IVOR ANTHONY [18] 5-8-7 J Matthias 5/1 Jt.FAV: -0: Well btn on Flat debut: showed a
little promise over hurdles in the Winter.   00
--   AL MURTAJAZ [10] 5-9-4 D Nicholls 10/1: 30210-0: Irish import who won at Naas in
'85 on good going over 2m.   00
199 What Will I Wear [14] 9-4(bl)   199 Wise Cracker [4] 9-4
--   Dubavarna [15] 8-4   --   Glenmore Captain [16] 8-7
--   Penthouse C [17] 8-7   199 Winning Star 11 5-9-4
15 ran   15,8,1,2½,5   (Mrs S Glover)   J Glover Worksop, Notts

283 WAKEFIELD MAIDEN STAKES 3YO   £684   6f   Heavy Slow

--   JOVEWORTH [6] (J Glover) 3-9-0 M Birch 10/1: 00440-1: 3 gr c Monsanto - Flitterdale
(Abwah): Well bckd and readily led dist. in a 3yo maiden at Pontefract Apr.23: showed ability
last season: acts on gd, well at home on soft or heavy going: very eff at 6f.   39
--   SAALIB [5] (H T Jones) 3-9-0 A Murray 13/2: 40-2: Dsptd lead most, outpcd final 1f:
ran only twice in '85, showing promise on debut at Nottingham: sure to be suited by further
than 6f.   29
--   TAMALPAIS [7] (H Collingridge) 3-8-11 G Sexton 16/1: 000-3: Dsptd lead most: had only
3 late season runs in '85: may impr.   19
217 GEORGIAN ROSE [3] (K Ivory) 3-8-11 G Morgan 20/1: 0-04: Ev ch: half sister to 4
winners incl fair sprinter Minstrel: should stay further than 6f.   12
87   MADAM MUFFIN [1] 3-8-11 J Matthias 4/1: 2-20: Dsptd lead around ½way: btr 87 (5f).   03
198 VIRAJENDRA [4] 3-9-0 D Nicholls 33/1: 0200-00: Early speed: best effort in '85 was
6L 2nd of 6 in a maiden at Hamilton on heavy going.   00
--   JOHN SAXON [11] 3-9-0 W R Swinburn 11/10 FAV: 033-0: Well bckd and had a clear chance
on last seasons form,   may have been unsuited by this desperate going: worth another chance
on better ground.   00
--   Tachometer [9] 9-0   --   Findon Manor [10] 9-0   217 Pact [8] 9-0
10 ran   5,3,4,5,20   (D Cooper)   J Glover Worksop, Notts

284 WAKEFIELD MAIDEN STAKES 3YO   £684   6f   Heavy Slow

--   GOLDEN ANCONA [3] (E Eldin) 3-9-0 E Guest(3) 2/1: 0000-1: 3 ch c London Bells -
Golden Darling (Darling Boy): First time out, came from behind to lead inside final 1f
narrowly in a 3yo maiden at Pontefract Apr.23: lightly raced in '85 but showed ability:
sprint bred: eff at 6f on heavy.   38
217 HANSOM LAD [5] (W Haigh) 3-9-0 D Nicholls 11/2: 0303-02: Led 2f out, kept on under
press, just btn and well clear of rest: should find a similar race soon: showed some promise
towards the end of last season on fast going but also acts on heavy.   37
217 BERTIE WOOSTER [7] (L Piggott) 3-9-0 W R Swinburn 15/8 FAV: 320-03: Al there: uneasy
fav: see 217: unsuited by heavy?   19
109 GLORIANT [4] (M Brittain) 3-9-0 K Darley 14/1: 040-034: Ev ch: see 109.   09
183 KATIE RHODES [2] 3-8-11 S Perks 25/1: 000-00: No dngr: no form last season.   02
14   MISTRESS CHARLEY [1] 3-8-11 J Lowe 20/1: 00-00: Made much: lightly raced.   00
78   QUALITAIR KING [6] 3-9-0 S Keightley 8/1: 04-030: Again seemed unsuited by hvy: see 78. 00
--   Pendor Dancer [8] 9-0   --   Dorade [9] 9-0   --   Selorcele [10] 9-0 U
10 ran   nk,12,6,2½,2   (D Gorton)   E Eldin Newmarket

100

285   ---

286   GROUP 1 PREMIO PARIOLI (3YO COLTS)   £28956   1m   Good/Soft .

-- SVELT (A Botti) 3-9-2 J Heloury:-11D1:3 b c African Sky - Christine: Smart Italian
colt: narrow head winner of Gr.1 Premio Parioli at Capannelle Apr.12: in fine form, winning
both his previous races this season, but subs. disq. in one of them: eff at 1m on gd/soft.   75
60   HELLO ERNANI (I Balding) 3-9-2 W R Swinburn   : 203-22: Led 1f out: just caught:
fine effort and is in good form: see 60.   74
-- MISCROWN (Italy) 3-9-2 C Asmussen   : 11320-3: Ex English colt: chance 1f out: not
much room final 1f: fine effort: in '85 won at Thirsk & Yarmouth: stays 1m well: acts on
fast & yld.   73
-- SOUTH THATCH (Italy) 3-9-2 S Dettori   : -4: Btn less than 1L: ran well.   73
-- LUQMAN 3-9-2 Paul Eddery   : 14114-0: Ch. 1f out: not btn far: good effort as he
seemed just in need of this race: tremendously impr in '85, winning at Kempton, Chester (2),
Chepstow & Gr.2 Mill Reef Stakes at Newbury: very eff over 6f, seems to stay 1m: acts on
firm & yld & on any trk.   72
24   BRIGHT AS NIGHT 3-9-2 G Starkey   : 2240-30: Creditable 8th: see 24.   64

-- Alex Nureyev 9-2	-- Max Dor 9-2	-- Bestebreuje 9-2
-- Karmo 9-2	-- For Dear Life 9-2	-- Tanque Verde 9-2
-- Rusty Salt 9-2	-- Creese 9-2	

14 ran   hd,¾,shhd,nk,hd   (Scuderia Rencate)   A Botti Italy

---

Official Going given as Good

287   GROUP 3 PREMIO NATALE DI ROMA 4YO+   £10324   1m   Heavy .

-- MALEVIC (L Brogi) 5-8-13 S Dettori   : -1: 5 br c Hawaiian Sound - My Room: Very
useful Italian colt: fin really well to lead well inside the final 1f in Gr.3 Premio Natale
Di Roma at Capannelle Apr.13: stays 1m well and acts on heavy ground.   71
-- CAPO NORD (Italy) 4-9-2 M Depalmas   : 1343-2: Caught close home: gd effort: in '85
won a Gr.3 event on this trk: very eff at 1m: acts on gd & heavy.   73
-- CHAPEL COTTAGE (M Ryan) 5-8-6 G Starkey   : 00020-3: Unstd by this heavy ground:
smart filly who in '85 won Gr.3 event at York & also a valuable stakes at Thirsk: smart
2yo when trained by M W Easterby, winning Gr.3 Cherry Hinton Stakes at Newmarket: very eff
over 6/7f, stays 1m: best on good & firm ground & should win races this season.   60
3 ran   nk,2,1.   (Scuderia Cleffedi)   L Brogi Italy

Official Going Given as Heavy

288   GROUP 3 PRIX DE LA GROTTE 3YO FILLIES   £15639   1m   Heavy .

-- NORTHERN PREMIER (G Mikhalides) 3-9-2 C Asmussen   : /031-01: 3 b f Northern Baby -
Madame Premier: Smart French filly: led inside the final 2f, holding on by a hd in Gr.3
Prix De La Grotte at Longchamp Apr.13: eff at 1m, may stay further: acts on heavy & a gall trk   74
-- BEAUJOLAISE (D Sepulchre) 3-9-2 M Philipperon   : 20142-2: led over 2f out: kept on
well: fine effort: smart 2yo, ready winner of a Gr.3 event at St Cloud: eff at 6f, stays 1m:
acts on gd & heavy.   73
-- CARNATION (M Zilber) 3-9-2 A Lequeux   : /0414-3: Just btn in close fin: good effort:
eff at 1m on gd & heavy.   72
-- REGAL STATE (J Fellows) 3-9-2 G Guignard   : 31120-4: Btn ¼L on seasonal debut: very
smart 2yo in '85, winning Gr.1 Prix Morny at Deauville and later a shnk 2nd to Baiser Vole
in Gr.1 event at Longchamp: eff at 7f, should be suited by 1m plus: acts on any ground:
likes a gall trk & should do btr next time.   71
-- MERCADAH 3-9-2 G Mosse   : 31340-0: Ran to her best.   70
-- PALLANZA 3-9-2 G Moore   : -21-0: Fair seasonal
debut: ready 6L winner of her final outing in '85: should come on for this race.   68

-- Kariya 9-2	-- Fieldy 9-2	-- Yoko 9-2
-- Suprematie 9-2	-- Prospect Tora 9-2	-- Carnet Solaire 9-2
-- Kanmary 9-2		

13 ran   hd,hd,nk,½,1   (M Fustok)   G Mikhalides France

---

289   GROUP 2 PRIX GREFFULHE 3YO   £22978   1m 2f Heavy .

-- AROKAR (J De Chevigny) 3-9-2 C Asmussen   : --101-1: 3 br c Akarad - Arosa: Very smart
French colt: made a winning seasonal debut, led 2f out and drew right away for an impressive
4L win in Gr.2 Prix Greffulhe at Longchamp Apr.13: in '85 won Gr.3 events at Longchamp
first time out won at Maisons Laffitte: very eff at 9/10f and should stay 12f: acts on any
grnd: likes a gall trk and should win more good races.   84

LONGCHAMP		Sunday April 13th	- Cont'd

-- **CLOVIO** (P L Biancone) 3-9-2 E Legrix : -1-2: No ch with winner, though kept on well:
won sole start in '85: stays 10f & acts on heavy.   75
-- **BAROOD** (A Fabre) 3-9-2 A Gibert : -32-3: Caught for 2nd close home: ran well.   73
-- **MINATZIN** (G Bonnaventure) 3-9-2 Pat Eddery : -1431-4: In '85 won Gr.3 event at
Longchamp: eff at 1m, stays 10f well: acts on firm & heavy.   70
-- **NORTHERN DATE** 3-9-2 D Gillespie : -41-0: Irish colt: made much.   68
-- **GAMBERO** 3-9-2 F Head : -1-0: Sn prom.   67
-- **Prince De La Tour** 9-2   -- **Manndesh** 9-2
8 ran   4,1,2,1,1   (Prince K Al Said)   J De Chevigny France

---

GELSENKIRCHEN HORST   Sunday April 13th

Official Going Given as

290 GROUP 3 GROSSER PREIS DER GELSENKIRCHEN £9887   1m 4f . .

-- **LOVE LETTER** (S Von Mitzlaff) 5-8-12 P Schade : 32-1: 5 b h Luciano - Lhasa: Very
useful German horse: kept on well under press for a narrow ¾L win in Gr.3 event at Gelsenkirchen Horse Apr.13: stays 12f really well.   70
-- **HYDROS** (Germany) 4-8-8 L Mader : -2: Ran on well final 1f.   65
-- **MANTELANO** (Germany) 6-8-12 P Gilson : 23-3: Led/dsptd lead: fdd final 1f.   67
3 ran   ½,½.   (Gestut Ittlingen)   S Von Mitzlaff Germany

MAISONS LAFFITTE   Friday April 18th

Official Going Given as Soft

291 PRIX MONTENICA 3YO   **£11040   7f   . .**

156 **TAKFA YAHMED** (M Saliba) 3-8-11 Y Saint Martin : 140-221: 3 ch c Main Reef - Gelder
Shiel (Grundy): Smart colt: ran out an easy 4L winner of valuable Prix Montenica at
Maisons-Lafitte Apr.18: formerly trained by S Norton, winning at Beverley, Newcastle &
Leicester: later ran creditably in top class juvenile company: very eff over 7f, looks sure
to stay 1m: acts on any going and likes to be up with the pace: has run well in bl.   72
-- **EASTBELL** (P L Biancone) 3-8-11 E Legrix : --13-42: No ch with winner: trained by
D O'Brien in '85 winning at Phoenix Park: eff at 7f, should stay 1m: acts on firm & heavy.   62
156 **CRICKET BALL** (J Fellows) 3-9-2 G W Moore : --21-33: Consistent: eff at 7f on heavy.   65
3 ran   4,1,2.   (Yazid Saud)   M Saliba France

PHOENIX PARK	Saturday April 19th	Left & Righthand Sharpish Track

Official Going Given as Heavy

292 HERON BLOODSTOCK 2YO MAIDEN   **£4140   5f   Heavy 166 -32 Slow**

-- **SAY PRINCESS** [9] (L Browne) 2-8-11 M T Browne 10/1: 1: 2 b f Saher - Galtee Princess:
Promising filly: first time out was a ¾L winner of valuable 2yo maiden at Phoenix Park
Apr.19: half sister to a 9f winner: eff at 5f, should stay further: acts on heavy ground.   58
-- **ESTATE CARLTON** [5] (D Weld) 2-8-11 M J Kinane 4/1: 2: Good racecourse debut: should
be suited by further than 5f: acts on heavy.   56
-- **SAY YES** [8] (L Browne) 2-8-11 Pat Eddery 4/1: 3: Impr likely.   53
-- **TOWN ABLAZE** [4] (C Ryan) 2-8-11 R Hogan 20/1: 4: Outsider: fair effort.   48
-- **FAIRWAY LADY** [6] 2-8-11 S Craine 3/1 FAV: 0: Well bckd debutant: should rate more highly 41
-- **BONVIN** [2] 2-8-11 G Curran 5/1: 0: --   00
268 **ON THE STEEL** [1] 2-9-0 J Coogan 8/1: 40: Fin. 8th: btr 268 (yld).   00
-- **CIVIC DANCER** [7] 2-9-0 P Shanahan 5/1: 0: Last to finish.   00
268 **Seconds Out** 0 9-0
9 ran   ½,1½,2½,hd,3½   (A Scott)   L Browne Ireland

293 GROUP 3 GALLAGHER'S 2 £15805   Heavy 166 -10 Slow

-- **TOCA MADERA** [3] (L Browne) 3-8-10 S Craine 6/4 Jt FAV: ---11-1: 3 b c Taufan -
Genisis: Very smart colt: first time out, qcknd really well 2f out for an impressive win in
Gr.3 2,000 Guineas trial at Phoenix Park Apr.19: unbtn in 2 starts as a 2yo, a Gr.3 event
at Leopardstown & first time out a maiden at Phoenix Park: eff at 7f/1m: should be suited
by 10f: acts on any going: should run well in the 2,000 Guineas, especially if the going is
on the soft side: should win more good races.   83
-- **LONDON TOWER** [5] (D Weld) 3-8-7 M J Kinane 4/1: -12: Chall final 1f, not pace of
winner, though ran really well: 6L clear 3rd: first time out won a maiden at Naas and
is rapidly impr: full brother to the very smart filly Marwell: eff at 6/7f: acts well on
heavy ground and further successes look assured.   77

PHOENIX PARK   Saturday April 19th   - Cont'd

-- GRANNYS MONEY [6] (M O'toole) 3-8-7 D Gillespie 16/1: -030-33: Ran to his best.   66
-- CURRENT WAVE [1] (T Curtin) 3-8-7 K Moses 33/1: -2140-4: Fair seasonal debut: in '85
won a maiden on this trk: eff over 6/7f: acts on any ground.   65
-- ROCK ALLEY [4] 3-8-7 D Parnell 50/1: --03-00: Impossible task: not disgraced.   53
*151 GOLD CARAT [2] 3-8-10 Pat Eddery 6/4 Jt FAV: -10: Most disapp after 151 (1m, soft).   45
6 ran   1½,6,nk,6,4   (Miss D Threadwell)   L Browne Ireland

294 GROUP 3 1000GNS TRIAL 3YO FILLIES   HEAVY 166

-- THE BEAN SIDHE [5] (J Hayden) 3-8-7 F Swan 25/1: 03110-1: 3 b f Corvaro - Whisky
Mountain: Smart Irish filly: first time out, caused a 25/1 surprise, holding on by a hd in
Gr.3 1,000 Guineas trial at Phoenix Park Apr.19: in '85 won h'caps at Naas and Phoenix Park:
eff at 6/7f, may stay 1m: acts on good & heavy.   71
269 CAROLS LUCK [4] (J Murphy) 3-8-7(bl) J T Hyde 16/1: ---1-02: Ran on well and just
failed to get up: fine effort and should be winning soon: see 269.   70
*148 PARK EXPRESS [11] (J Bolger) 3-8-7 D Gillespie 1/1 FAV: 1102-13: Unstd by this very
heavy ground: see 148.   64
-- EPICURES GARDEN [9] (D Weld) 3-8-7 M J Kinane 8/1: ---13-4: Good seasonal debut: in
'85 won over this C/D: acts on gd/firm & heavy.   63
148 SHERKRAINE [7] 3-8-7 P Shanahan 8/1: -132-20: Ran to her best: see 148.   61
-- LADY RIDER [8] 3-8-7 D Manning 25/1: -000: Rank outsider: acts on heavy.   49
-- GONE FOR GOOD [1] 3-8-7 G Curran 8/1: --0-410: Fin 7th: recent winner over this C/D.   00
59 FLYAWAY BRIDE [3] 3-8-7 Pat Eddery 6/1: 0131-00: Again well below 2yo form: see 59.   00
-- Future Shock 0 8-7   -- Sunbed 0 8-7
10 ran   hd,3,hd,1,7   (Mrs B Hayden)   J Hayden Ireland

295 MILL RIDGE STAKES (LISTED) 3YO   £14313   6f   Heavy 166 +09 Fast

-- YOUNG BLADE [7] (M O'toole) 3-8-9 C Roche 6/1: 01103-1: 3 gr g Silent Dignity -
Grey Axe: Smart young sprinter: made ev yd on the stands side and came home on his own
in quite fast run & valuable Listed race at Phoenix Park Apr.19: first time out fin 2nd to
Air Display at Leopardstown: twice a winner in '85: very eff at 6f on heavy grnd and looks
sure to win more races.   74
-- DOBEY THATCHER [3] (M Kauntze) 3-8-9 P Shanahan 10/1: ---1-42: No chance with winner:
recent 4th to Gone For Good on this trk: in '85 won at Naas: acts on yld & heavy.   62
-- WOODMAN [2] (M V O'brien) 3-9-2 Pat Eddery 4/7 FAV: -1110-3: Al struggling on seasonal
debut: much btr than this: in '85 was a smart 2yo, winning Gr.3 event at the Curragh after
2 earlier wins again at the Curragh: very eff over 6f, stays 1m well: acts on gd & yld,
possibly unsuited by todays heavy ground: worth another chance.   61
-- SO DIRECTED [5] (M Kauntze) 3-8-13 K Moses 8/1: 2220-04: No real threat.   50
-- MYSTICAL MAN [6] 3-8-9 S Craine 10/1: 423-030: --   40
5 ran   8,4,3,2½   (Mr M O'Toole)   M O'toole Ireland

SAN SIRO   Sunday April 20th

Official Going Given as Heavy

296 GROUP 3 PREMIO D'APRILE 4YO+   £10700   1m 2f   Heavy .

-- DON ORAZIO (F Jovine) 4-8-11 M Jerome   : -1120-1: Smart Italian colt: had a simple
task and was an easy 5L winner of slow run Gr.3 Premio D'Aprile at San Siro Apr.20: in fine
form in '85, winning the Derby Italiano at Capannelle and a Gr.2 event on this trk: also
a good 7th in the Arc de Triomphe: eff over 10f, stays 12f well: acts on gd/firm & soft.   72
-- PIQUE PAN (Italy) 4-8-11 G Dettori   : -2: No ch with winner.   62
-- MICRO UMBRO (Italy) 5-8-11 V Panici   : -3: --   60
-- GOLDEN BOY(ITA) (Italy) 5-8-11 U Suter   : -4: --   59
4 ran   5,1,3   (Lady M Scuderia)   F Jovine Italy

297 GROUP 2 PREMIO EMANUELE FILBERTO 3YO   £15434   1m 2f   Heavy .

-- CAPTAIN HAWAI (U Pandolfi) 3-9-2 J Heloury   -1: 3 br c Hawaii - Bags In Orbit: Very
useful colt: got up close home for a narrow win in Gr.3 event at San Siro Apr.20: eff at
10f, should stay further: acts on heavy.   69
-- ASSISI DEL SANTO (Italy) 3-9-2 A Dinardo   : 12-2: Caught close home: good effort:
Gr.3 winner on this trk in '85: stays 10f and acts on yld & heavy.   68
-- BE MY MASTER (Italy) 3-9-2 G Dettori   : -3: Not btn far: good effort: stoutly bred.   65
3 ran   shthd,nk,2   (Scuderia La Tesa)   U Pandolfi

SAINT CLOUD   Saturday April 19th   Lefthand, Galloping Track

Official Going Given as Very Heavy
298 GROUP 3 PRIX CORRIDA 4YO+   £16776   1m 2f Very Heavy .

-- GALLA PLACIDIA (A Fabre) 4-9-4 A Gibert : 11030-1: 4 b f Crystal Palace - Golden
Gleam (Lyphard): Smart French filly: first time out, easy winner of Gr.3 Prix Corrida at
St Cloud Apr.19: in fine form in '85, winning on 5 occasions, incl Gr.2 event at Deauville
& Gr.3 event at Chantilly: very well suited by soft & heavy grnd: eff at 10f, stays 13f well. 80
98 BLUE TIP (France) 4-9-2 E Legrix : 1103-32: Not pace of winner: good effort: see 98. 72
-- STAR ROSE (J Audon) 4-9-0(.) G Guignard : --221-3: Ran a good race. 67
-- REINE KA (M Boulard) 4-9-2 M Boulard : --1-004: -- 65
-- LADY DAY 4-9-0 G W Moore : 011D4-0: -- 61
-- ROBERTOS FIGHTER 4-8-12 F Head : 00403-0: -- 56
-- Topeka 8-12   -- Vivre En Paix 8-12   -- Belly Dancer 8-12
-- Luth Celtique 9-0   -- Green Light 8-12
11 ran   2,1½,2½,1½,2   (W Kazan)   A Fabre France

LONGCHAMP   Sunday April 20th

Official Going Given as Very Heavy
299 GROUP 3 PRIX D'HEDOUVILLE 4YO+   £17852   1m 4f Very Heavy .

-- BABY TURK [3] (A Royer Dupre) 4-8-9   Y Saint Martin : --21-01: 4 b c Northern Baby -
Vieílle Villa (Kashmir II): Smart French colt: got the btr of King Luthier by 1L in Gr.3
event at Longchamp Apr.20: a fine 2nd to Jupiter Island in Gr.2 event at Longchamp: very
eff at 12f: acts on firm & heavy. 77
-- KING LUTHIER [4] (A Fabre) 4-8-9 A Gibert : 0244-12: Btn 1L and 5L clear 3rd: trained
by G Lewis in '85 to win at Epsom & Warwick (subs. disq.): eff at 12f, stays 14f well:
acts on gd/firm & heavy and on any trk. 74
-- NOBLE FIGHTER [1] (M Saliba) 4-9-2 C Asmussen : 12310-3: Ev ch: showed much impr
form in '85 to win Gr.1 Turf Classic at Belmont Park (rated 85): acts on heavy, but very
well suited by 12f on firm grnd. 74
-- PREMIER ROLE [5] (J Cunnington) 4-8-9 M Philipperon : 23443-4: Btr for race: stays
12f & acts on any ground. 64
-- SIRIUS SYMBOLI [6] 4-9-2 G Mosse : 003-0: Best effort in '85 when a fine 3rd to
Mersey in Gr.1 Prix Royal Oak on this trk: stays 15f: acts on heavy, but seems best on firm. 68
*96 NEW TARGET [2] 5-8-11 J M Breux : -20-100: Dist. last: twice below form 96 (10f). 51
6 ran   1,5,2,2,12   (Mme A M d'Estainville)   A Royer Dupre France

300 GROUP 3 PRIX VANTEAUX 3YO FILLIES   £19287   1m 2f Very Heavy .

-- BARJER [13] (P L Biancone) 3-9-2 G Mosse : --23-11: 3 b f Riverman - Trillion
(How To Reason): Smart, very promising French filly: led 1f out, comfortably in Gr.3 Prix
Vanteaux at Longchamp Apr.20: sister to top class filly Triptych: eff at 9f, should stay
12f and is entered in both the English and French Oaks: acts on heavy grnd: further
successes look assured. 80
-- LACOVIA [2] (F Boutin) 3-9-2 F Head : ---01-2: Hdd over 1f out: kept on well: fine
effort: eff at 9f: acts on heavy. 72
*97 TERMIENNE [4] (J Gallorini) 3-9-2 D Boeuf : -41-13: See 97. 65
-- EL FABULOUS [8] (C Head) 3-9-2 G W Moore : -4: Btr for race. 58
-- GALUNPE [10] 3-9-2 J L Kessas : 114-0: Btr for race: smart 2yo, winning Gr.3 event
at Longchamp: acts well on gd/firm. 53
-- TICAROCK [5] 3-9-2 J C Desaint : --02-00: -- 46
-- Rivine 0 9-2   -- Secret Life 0 9-2   -- Dahsala 0 9-2
-- Rivers Of Mist 0 9-2   -- Al Joharah 0 9-2   -- Rivertower 0 9-2
-- Femme Elite 0 9-2
13 ran   1½,4,4,3,4   (N B Hunt)   P L Biancone France

301 GROUP 2 PRIX NOAILLES 3YO   £27603   1m 3f Very Heavy .

-- BERING [9] (C Head) 3-9-2 G Moore : -31-1: 3 ch c Arctic Tern - Beaune (Lyphard): Smart,
very promising colt: first time out, drew right away for an easy 8L win in Gr.2 Prix Noailles
at Longchamp Apr.20: eff at 11f, should be suited by 12f: acts well on heavy ground and
should win more good races. 80
-- POINT DARTOIS [6] (B Secly) 3-9-2 J L Kessas : -31-2: No ch with winner: good effort. 66
-- PORT ETIENNE [7] (J Cunnington Jr) 3-9-2 M Philipperon : -01-13: Made much, fdd. 65
-- LOUP DOR [1] (F Palmer) 3-9-2 M Gentile : -1134: -- 65
-- TAMBOUR BATTANT [3] 3-9-2 C Asmussen : -0-310: -- 62
-- SYNDROM [5] 3-9-2 Y Saint Martin : -10: -- 00
-- Kadrou [8] 9-2   -- Milouin 0 9-2   -- Grand Palace 0 9-2
9 ran   8,nk,shhd,2,20   (Madam A Head)   C Head France

302   GROUP 3 PRIX DE GUICHE 3YO COLTS   £19108   1m 2f   Very Heavy .

--   **BAD CONDUCT** [8] (P L Biancone) 3-9-2 E Legrix 1: -2211: 3 b c Stalwart - White Lie
(Bald Eagle): Smart French colt: led dist. comfortably in Gr.3 Prix De Guiche at Longchamp
Apr.20: eff at 9f, should stay further: acts well on heavy ground.   75
--   **HAIL TO ROBERTO** [7] (G Mikhalides) 3-9-2 C Asmussen 1: -12: The fav: led 2f out: acts
on heavy, but btr suited by faster ground.   71
--   **DOUBLE BED** [3] (F Doumen) 3-9-2 J L Kessas 1: -223: Eff at 9f on heavy.   70
--   **MALAKIM** [4] (A Royer Dupre) 3-9-2 Y Saint Martin 1: -2-14: --   66
--   **UN DESPERADO** [1] 3-9-2 A Gibert 1: 12-0: --   62
--   **ARCTIC BLAST** [2] 3-9-2 G W Moore 1: -1-20: --   62
--   **Persian Mews** 0 9-2   --   **Crystal De Roche** 0 9-2
8 ran   1½,hd,2½,2½,shhd   (J T Lundy)   P L Biancone France

SAINT CLOUD   Tuesday April 22nd

Official Going Given As Very Heavy

303   PRIX LA SORELLINA 3YO   £8280   1m 2f   Very Heavy .

--   **PRADIER** (P L Biancone) 3-9-2 E Legrix 1: -11: 3 b c Lightning - Plencia (La Haar):
Very promising French colt: unbtn in 2 outings to date, on latest start was a comfortable 4L
winner in valuable Prix la Sorellina at St Cloud Apr.22: first time out won again at
Longchamp: half brother to the top class Pawneese: eff at 10f, should be suited by 12f:
acts well on heavy ground and is being aimed for the Epsom Derby.   80+
--   **SUN** (B Secly) 3-9-2 A Badel 1: 001-222: No ch with winner, though is in good form:
stays 10f well & acts on heavy ground.   70
--   **SALYF** (A Royer Dupre) 3-8-12 Y Saint Martin 1: -3134-3: --   64
--   **CHERCHEUR DOR** (C Head) 3-9-2 G W Moore 1: -310-4: --   64
--   **SILVER BAND** 3-8-12 C Asmussen 1: -1-0: --   56
--   **MAZMAN** 3-8-12 A Lequeux 1: 4421-30: --   46
--   **Juba Dollar** 9-2
7 ran   4,1,2½,4,5   (D Wildenstein)   P L Biancone France

THIRSK   Friday April 25th   Lefthanded Sharpish Track

Official Going Given as Soft

304   BARTON COTTAGE STAKES 2YO   £2374   5f   Soft/Heavy 156 +20 Fast

*242   **DEMDERISE** [2] (N Tinkler) 2-9-1 T Ives 6/5 FAV: 11: 2 ch f Vaigly Great - Kanvita
(Home Guard): Very promising juvenile: comfortably led fav. quickened nicely to lead
below dist and clocked a very good time when winning a 2yo stakes at Thirsk Apr.25: won a
similar event over this C/D on her racecourse debut recently: half sister to winning
sprinters Alpine Strings & Carolyn Christensen: very eff over this minimum trip: acts on
yld & soft/heavy grnd & on a sharpish trk: should complete her hat trick next time.   56
242   **FIRMLY ATTACHED** [6] (T Barron) 2-8-11 S Webster 1: 02: Friendless in mkt: no
ch with winner though ran well to take the minor honours: on the up grade & should win a
race soon: acts on soft/heavy: see 242.   43
+146   **GALLIC TIMES** [8] (I Bell) 2-9-4 N Carlisle 5/2: 3113: Remains in fine form: see 146.   50
118   **WHISTLING WONDER** [4] (M Brittain) 2-9-1 K Darley 12/1: 2104: Made most: consistent: see 9. 39
--   **WENSLEYDALEWARRIOR** [3] 2-8-11 N Crowther 33/1: 0: Unfncd on racecourse debut: stayed
on from ½way and should benefit from this experience: half brother to 10f winner The Villain:
acts on soft/heavy grnd and on a sharpish trk.   29
--   **INGLISTON** [7] 2-8-11 M Birch 33/1: 0: Easy to back on racecourse debut: never really
on terms: cost 6,800 gns and may do btr on a more gall trk.   28
*133   **THE GRANITTON** [9] 2-9-1 D Mckeown 11/2: 10: Lost touch ½way: much btr in 133 (gall trk) 00
--   **Dockin Hill** [1] 8-11   --   **Ra Raver** [5] 8-11
9 ran   3,shhd,4,2½,hd   (Mrs D Wright)   N Tinkler Langton, Yorks

305   NESS SELLING STAKES 3YO   £1098   1m   Soft/Heavy 156 -45 Slow

--   **DIX ETOILES** [2] (J Fitzgerald) 3-8-11 A Murray 5/1: 4-1: 3 br f Monsanto - Wharton
Manor (Gallivanter): First time out, led from the stalls and ran on strongly to win a
3yo seller at Thirsk Apr.25 (no bid): last to fin behind New Edition in a fillies maiden at
York on her only start last term: eff over 1m: clearly well suited by forcing tactics on
a sharp trk: acts on gd & soft/heavy ground.   18
140   **SHARP TIMES** [10] (W Musson) 3-9-0 M Wigham 11/10 FAV: 0-02: Dropped to selling company
& well bckd: stayed on well: seems well suited by 1m on soft/heavy grnd: acts on any trk.   15
237   **AMPLIFY** [6] (M Brittain) 3-9-0 K Darley 10/1: 20-0303: Chased winner most of way:
stays 1m: see 93.   10
237   **WATERFORD WAY** [3] (R Hollinshead) 3-9-0 S Perks 16/1: 00-04: No real threat after a
slow start: however an impr effort: eff over 1m with plenty of give.   09

237 FIRST ALARM [8] 3-9-0 S Morris 20/1: -00: Never beyond mid-div.   07
237 PLANTER [5] 3-9-0(bl) M Beecroft 11/4: -010240: Front rank till below dist: much
btr in 195 (7f).   06
195 SISTER NANCY [7] 3-8-11 P Burke(7) 10/1: 000-430: Ev ch when hung left early in str.   00
195 Rapid Star [9] 8-11   93 Mr Jester [1] 9-0(bl)   -- Classy Scouse [4] 9-0
10 ran   3,2½,1,¾,¾.   (Mrs E C York)   J Fitzgerald Norton, Yorks

306 HICKLETON HANDICAP STAKES 0-50   £2897   6f   Soft/Hvy 156 +09 Fast   [49]

--   BOOT POLISH [19] (J Watts) 4-8-13 N Connorton 12/1: 10104-1: 4 gr g Godswalk -
Flirting Countess (Ridan): First time out, led below dist, ridden out to win quite a fast
run h'cap at Thirsk Apr.25: twice successful in h'caps over this trip at Redcar last season:
in '84 won a maiden at Newcastle: very eff over 5/6f: previously had shown his best form
on fast ground though clearly also acts on soft/heavy: no trk preferences.   46
135 EMERGENCY PLUMBER [9] (T Barron) 5-8-0 S Webster 8/1: 0400-42: Led early in str, kept
on well: acts on soft/heavy grnd & on a sharpish trk: see 135.   30
65   FOOLISH TOUCH [8] (K Stone) 4-8-3 P Burke(7) 16/1: 001-003: Al front rank: much
btr effort: landed a gamble on his final start last season in a selling h'cap at Newmarket:
earlier had won first time out at Ayr: in '84 also well bckd when winning a seller at
Yarmouth and a market move is worth heeding when he is dropped in class: eff over 5/7f:
acts on any going & on any trk.   26
182 RIVERSIDE WRITER [11] (K Bridgwater) 4-8-0 P D'arcy 10/1: 00-1034: Not clear run,
fin strongly: see 84.   22
*65   SUDDEN IMPACT [16] 4-8-12 S Whitworth 4/1 FAV: 0040-10: Al close up though btr in
65 (galloping trk).   33
110 MARY MAGUIRE [10] 9-8-12 D Nicholls 16/1: 0100-00: led over ½way: last season won
h'caps at Hamilton & York and in '84 scored a hat trick of wins at Ayr: eff over 6/7f: acts
on any going though seems fav. by some give: well suited by a gall trk.   33
65   COOL ENOUGH [15] 5-7-11 T Williams 12/1: 000-400: Stayed on late: see 12.   00
--   VALLEY MILLS [4] 6-10-0 B Mcghiff(7) 10/1: 31000-0: Not well drawn: late prog and
should impr.   00
192 JOHN PATRICK [3] 5-9-3(BL) T Ives 11/2: 003-000: Ldr on far side till ½way: fin last.   00
12   Philip [13] 9-3   -- Bollin Emily [5] 9-7   -- Oxhey Bay [12] 8-12
--   Karens Star [1] 8-6   172 Fawleys Girl [18] 8-4   -- Taskforce Victory [17] 8-0
110 Bay Bazaar [2] 8-3   -- Ra Ra Girl [14] 8-12   182 Warthill Lady [6] 7-7(3oh)
245 Paris Match [7] 9-3
19 ran   1,3,½,½,hd,½   (G B Parkinson)   J Watts Richmond, Yorks

307 BYWELL MAIDEN STAKES 3YO   £1232   2m   Soft/Hvy 156 -89 Slow

173 COUNTLESS COUNTESS [9] (R Williams) 3-8-11 T Ives 7/2: -201: 3 gr f Morston -
Noble Company (Young Emperor): Made steady progress to lead below dist in a slowly run 3yo
maiden at Thirsk Apr.25: eff over 10/12f and clearly stays 2m well: acts on yld & soft/heavy
ground and does well on a sharpish trk.   36
130 BANTEL BUSHY [8] (I Bell) 3-9-0 N Carlisle 13/2: 000-222: Continues to impr: led
before ½way and kept on well when hdd: stays 2m: acts on any trk: see 130.   33
171 MOUNT SCHIEHALLION [4] (K Brassey) 3-9-0 S Whitworth 9/4 FAV: 2030-33: Uneasy fav:
btr over 12f in 171 (yld).   25
--   PHEASANT HEIGHTS [6] (H Candy) 3-8-11 R Curant 11/2: 00000-4: Fair effort on re-
appearance: one paced run in though clear of rem: half sister to a couple of winners incl
consistent plater Topsoil: clearly stays well & is suited by some give in the ground.   20
--   THE LEGGETT [3] 3-9-0 S Keightley 8/1: R0024-0: Btn turning for home: run up to
Hardly Fair in a seller at Redcar late last season (1m, firm) and subsq. ran well in btr
company: does act on soft though should do btr on faster grnd: suited by a gall trk.   00
--   SANDMOOR PRINCE [5] 3-9-0(bl) M Birch 10/1: 000-0: Lost touch before ½way: well btn.   00
--   QUARANTINO [7] 3-9-0 K Darley 10/1: 0000-0: Made most till ½way, sn btn.   00
164 Shake The King [2] 9-0   -- Daneagle Glory [1] 9-0
9 ran   4,8,1½,dist,hd   (A J Lavell)   R Williams Newmarket

308 BROMPTON HANDICAP STAKES 0-35   £2351   1m 4f   Soft/Hvy 156 -43 Slow   [35]

185 MENINGI [9] (N Tinkler) 5-8-10 J Brown(5) 11/2 Jt FAV: 0-00-31: 5 ch g Bustino -
Miss Filbert (Compensation): Was nicely bckd and led 2f out, gamely in a h'cap at Thirsk
Apr.25: first success on the Flat though proved himself a very useful novice hurdler last
winter when gaining 3 wins: eff over 12f, stays 2m well: acts on gd & soft/hvy ground and
on any trk.   26
*256 SILENT JOURNEY [16] (J Watts) 4-9-1(4ex) T Ives 11/2 Jt FAV: 3030-12: Well bckd to
defy his penalty: sustained chall inside dist and just held: remains in fine form: acts
on soft/heavy ground: see 256.   30
--   BOLLIN PALACE [17] (M H Easterby) 4-9-4 M Birch 10/1: 02000-3: Active in mkt on
reappearance: led 3f out, not btn far: in gd form early last season when twice successful in
h'caps at Catterick: eff over 12/14f: acts on any going & on any trk, though is suited by
a sharp one: genuine & consistent.   32
142 SKYBOOT [13] (E Carter) 7-8-7 Wendy Carter(6) 10/1: 40-0324: In gd form: stays 12f: see 88 17

144 RULE OF THE SEA [1] 5-10-1 G Carter(3) 10/1: 3000/20: Another good effort under
top weight: see 144.   38
243 REGAL STEEL [18] 8-8-11 A Culhane(7) 10/1: 00-3020: Al front rank: best in 243 (C/D yld) 16
184 SKI RUN [5] 11-8-1 J Lowe 10/1: 00-4130: Btr over this trip in 80 (gall trk).   00

--	String Of Beads [19] 8-2(bl)			101	Bamdoro [12] 8-3(2ow)
137	Don Runi [4] 8-11	8	Ocean Life [7] 8-8	69	Timminion [14] 8-6(1ow)
256	Apple Wine [3] 8-8	199	Electrified [8] 8-10	17	Senor Ramos [11] 10-0
121	Patralan [2] 8-7	--	Billidor [20] 8-8	105	Rural Scene [6] 7-13
--	Boldera [10] 8-11	4	Four Star Thrust [15] 9-4		

20 ran   nk,¼,3,nk,3   (Full Circle Thoroughbreds Ltd)   N Tinkler Langton, Yorks

---

309 ABBEY LANE STAKES 3YO   £1803   6f   Soft/Hvy 156 -21 Slow

241 JARROVIAN [11] (T Fairhurst) 3-8-11 C Coates(5) 11/2: 00-0421: 3 ch c Moorestyle -
Shady desire (Meldrum): Went on ½way and ran on well to win a 3yo stakes at Thirsk Apr.25:
earlier had been comfortably btn by todays winner up in similar conditions at Ayr & this is
clearly on the up grade: eff over 5/6f with plenty of give in the grnd: acts on any trk:
well suited by this sharp course though acts on any.   46
228 TARANGA [10] (M Tompkins) 3-9-3 R Cochrane 7/4 FAV: 02-1102: Made early running,
kept on under press: remains in gd form though btr in 134.   45
--   ELSOCKO [15] (B Mcmahon) 3-8-8 J Hills(5) 10/1: 0300-3: Ev ch on reappearance: quite
highly tried last season, showing some promise: half sister to a couple of winners, incl
fair stayer San Carlos Bay: eff over 5/6f on gd/firm & soft grnd: acts on any trk.   35
--   IMPERIAL SUNRISE [4] (M W Easterby) 3-8-8 S Hustler(4) 33/1: 42044-4: Mkt drifter on
seasonal debut: al there and kept on well: placed several times in selling company last
season: eff over 6/7f on firm & soft grnd: acts on any trk.   34
--   HARRY HULL [14] 3-8-11 M Hindley 16/1: 000-0: Ran on late: lightly raced last
season: half brother to useful sprinter Able Albert: acts on gd/firm & soft grnd & on a
sharpish track.   31
--   HAITI MILL [1] 3-8-8 N Carlisle 12/1: 303-0: Al there & should do btr next time:
placed in 2 of her 3 starts last term, showing plenty of promise: eff over 5/6f on gd &
soft grnd: acts on any trk.   19
*241 ALKAAYED [2] 3-9-3 A Murray 7/2: 40-10: Never going well: much btr over 5f here in 241. 00

247	Pells Close [5] 8-11(BL)			134	Not A Problem [13] 8-11
198	Red Zulu [18] 8-11	237	Galaxy Gala [8] 8-11	--	Watendlath [3] 8-8
--	Crisp Metcalfe [7] 8-11			246	The Little Joker [12] 8-8
--	Shy Mistress [17] 8-8	--	Polly Worth [6] 8-8	--	Tip Top Boy [16] 8-11

17 ran   3,nk,nk,3,4,1½   (A J Le Blond)   T Fairhurst Middleham, Yorks

---

310 LEVY BOARD APPRENTICE STAKES 0-35   £1091   1m   Soft/Hvy 156 -27 Slow   [33]

*141 BARLEY BILL [4] (L Cumani) 3-9-6 S Quane 6/5 FAV: 022-11: 3 ch c Nicholas Bill -
Oatfield (Great Nephew): Useful colt: easily justified fav. in an app. h'cap at Thirsk
Apr.25: led below dist and was sn clear: recently won a h'cap at Nottingham and in '85
fin. runner up at Brighton & Newcastle on his final 2 starts: half brother to 2m winner
High Plains: very eff over 1m and is sure to stay further: acts on firm & soft/hvy grnd
& on any trk: in fine form & should win again and carries weight well.   60+
--   SAMHAAN [17] (B Hanbury) 4-8-10(bl) A Geran 20/1: 0040-2: Unfncd on reappearance:
stayed on well: showed plenty of promise early on last season, was rated 43 when btn less
than 7f by Ramadi Dawn at redcar (10f, firm) and should certainly win a race off his present
mark on that form: probably found todays trip inadequate: acts on any track and on any going. 18
196 RAPID ACTION [14] (G Moore) 5-8-11 D Casey 10/1: 420-303: Remains in gd form: acts
on soft: see 46.   16
--   DOMINION PRINCESS [7] (H Rohan) 5-8-4 J Quinn 12/1: 32000-4: Some late prog and will
strip fitter next time: placed several times in selling company last season, though failed
to get her head in front: eff over 1m on firm & soft grnd: acts on any trk.   09
240 DARNIT [11] 4-9-13 M Tebbutt 20/1: 3000-00: Late hdway: btr effort: placed several
times last season & was a ready winner of a maiden over 7f at Thirsk: stays 1m well: acts on
firm & soft grnd & on any trk.   31
238 BWANA KALI [8] 4-9-7 B Cook(7) 7/1: 10-4330: Stayed on too late: see 238.   23
260 TRY SCORER [13] 4-9-5 A Nixon(7) 9/1: 04-2100: Led briefly ½way: twice disapp
since 143 (gall trk).   00
238 NIGHT WARRIOR [1] 4-9-6 R Vickers(7) 10/1: 00-0040: Much btr over this C/D in 238. 00

46	Lilting Lad [15] 8-1	91	Miss Aggro [5] 8-12	--	Pershing [9] 8-11
101	Janes Brave Boy [16] 8-11			91	Kamaress [10] 8-12
9	Crown Estate [12] 9-4			--	Charming View [2] 8-0
--	Sweet Eire [3] 8-2	--	Elarim [18] 9-9	--	Short Sleeves [6] 10-0

18 ran   4,1½,shhd,½,1½   (G Keller)   L Cumani Newmarket

Official Going Given as Soft (Heavy patches)

311 JUVENILE MAIDEN FILLIES' STAKES 2YO   £2569   5f   Soft 153 -33 Slow

--   **SAXON STAR** [5] (J Winter) 2-8-11 Pat Eddery 11/2: 1: 2 b f Comedy Star - True Dresden
(Vilmoray): Prom filly: mkt drifter, but led inside final 1f and drew clear in a 2yo fillies
maiden at Sandown Apr.25: half sister to several winners: eff at 5f, should stay 6f: acts
on soft/heavy and a gall trk.   58

--   **BLUE TANGO** [4] (R Laing) 2-8-11 W Carson 4/1: 2: Led 2f: kept on inside final 1f to
snatch 2nd: good debut: eff at 5f, should stay 6f: acts on soft/heavy & should find a small
maiden, possibly on a sharper trk.   44

223 **BECHEMAL** [4] (B Hills) 2-8-11 B Thomson 8/13 FAV: 33: Heavily bckd: led after ½way:
tired badly final 1f: see 223 (gd/yld).   44

--   **SHUTTLECOCK GIRL** [3] (W Jarvis) 2-8-11 W R Swinburn 12/1: 4: Early speed: mkt drifter:
half sister to numerous winners, should stay 6f.   34

252 **WISE TIMES** [2] 2-8-11 A Mcglone 12/1: 00: Dwelt start: best 252.   22

73   **BETTA WIN** [1] 2-8-12(1ow) N Dawe 33/1: 00: Prom early: very cheaply acquired.   00

6 ran   6,hd,4,6,20   (John Ratcliffe)   J Winter Newmarket

---

312 AUDI SPORT HANDICAP STAKES (0-60)   £4900   1m 6f   Soft/Heavy 153 +10 Fast   [44]

•58a **MILTON BURN** [7] (H O'neill) 5-8-8 S Dawson(3) 13/2: 240-011: 5 b h Sexton Blake -
Neasden Belle (Sovereign Path): In fine form, led well over 1f out, comfortably in quite a
fast run h'cap at Sandown Apr.25: last time out won a similar event at Kempton: in '85
won a 2m h'cap at Nottingham: in '84 won at Warwick & again at Nottingham: eff at 14f,
stays 2m really well: acts on any going, but relishes soft/heavy: goes well for S Dawson and
is best when held up.   36

•189 **HOLY SPARK** [5] (D Elsworth) 6-9-4(4ex) Pat Eddery 7/1: 000/012: Led over 2f out, came
again final 1f: another good effort and is running well: stays 14f: see 189.   44

235 **BLOODLESS COUP** [10] (M Usher) 4-9-9 D Mckay 4/1 Jt.FAV: 1000-03: Well bckd: prom,
dropped back 2f out: stayed on final 1f under   his   big weight: in '85 won at Kempton
(first time out) and Newbury: also awarded valuable Morland Brewery H'cap again at Newbury:
in '84 won at Salisbury: eff at 41f, stays 2m: acts on gd/firm & heavy & on any trk, though
runs well at Newbury.could soon go one better.   44

--   **ALDO KING** [3] (D Oughton) 5-8-10 B Crossley 6/1: -1000-4: Recent winner over hurdles:
no real threat: first time out in '85 won a h'cap at Newbury: in '84 won at redcar &
Catterick: stays 2m really well: acts on gd & heavy & on any trk.   30

58a **REVISIT** [6] 4-9-10 W R Swinburn 4/1 Jt.FAV: 2101-00: Wknd over 1f out: see 58a.   43

--   **FOR A LARK** [1] 4-8-13 S Cauthen 10/1: 01300-0: Fit from hurdling: led over 2f out:
in '85 won at Hamilton & Edinburgh: eff at 12f, stays 14f: acts on gd & soft & on any trk,
though is probably best forcing the pace on a sharpish one.   29

235 **CIMA** [9] 8-9-3 J Reid 8/1: 0020/30: Much btr 235 (2m).   00

--   **Full Of Dreams** [11] 7-7(bl)(9oh)   --   **Shuttlecock Star** [8] 7-7(5oh)

--   **Bellanoora** [4] 8-3   189 **Alsiba** [2] 8-8

11 ran   ¼,4,hd,hd,2¼.   (Mrs E W Richards)   H O'neill Coldharbour, Surrey

---

313 GROUP 2 TRUSTHOUSE FORTE MILE   £28480   1m   Soft/Heavy 153 +20 Fast

221 **FIELD HAND** [3] (B Hills) 4-9-0 B Thomson 11/2: 3121-21: 4 ch c Crofter - Audrey Joan
(Doutelle): Very smart colt: led well over 1f out, driven out close home to win fast run
Gr.2 Trusthouse Forte Mile at Sandown Apr.25: first time out was a fine 2nd to Supreme Leader
in Gr.3 Earl of Sefton Stakes at Newmarket: in '85 won at Haydock, Ascot (Ladies race) &
Chester: half brother to the very smart Prego: very eff over 8/9f: acts on any ground &
on any trk: has not stopped impr & further successes look assured.   82

--   **SCOTTISH REEL** [5] (M Stoute) 4-9-3 W R Swinburn 11/10 FAV: 11240-2: Made much: rallied
gamely final 1f & just held: fine seasonal debut from this very smart colt: in excellent
form in '85, winning his first 4 starts, Gr.3 Diamond Stakes at minor events at
Warwick, Ripon & York: also a grand 2nd to Bairn in Gr.2 St James Palace Stakes at Royal
Ascot: very eff over 7f/1m: acts on gd, suited by soft/heavy: no trk preferences & should
be winning soon.   83

--   **PROTECTION** [4] (H Cecil) 4-9-0 S Cauthen 10/1: 12110-3: Al prom: gd seasonal debut
and 12L clear rest: last season won a valuable event at Lingfield, Britannia H'cap at
Royal Ascot & minor events at Beverley & Leicester: very eff at 7f/1m, should sta further:
acts on yld & soft, likes fast grnd: suited by a gall trk: should win races this season.   75

--   **YOUNG RUNAWAY** [1] (G Harwood) 4-9-5 G Starkey 10/1: 41010-4: Mkt drifter: btr for
race: smart colt who in '85 won a Gr.2 event at Dusseldorf and a stakes event at Goodwood:
very useful 2yo, winning at Goodwood & Gr.2 Laurent Perrier Champagne Stakes at Doncaster:
very eff over 7/8f: acts on firm & soft & on any trk.   62

--   **VIN DE FRANCE** [2] 4-9-7 E Legrix 5/1: 23140-0: Mkt drifter: no threat: btr for race:
in fine form in '85, winning Gr.1 Prix Jacques Le Marois at Deauville and also a maiden at
Kempton when trained by H Cecil: half brother to the smart Vacarme: eff at 1m, stays 10f:
acts on gd/firm & soft.   63

--   **EFISIO** [6] 4-9-3 W Carson 12/1: 02110-0: Prom 6f, wknd.   58

221 **LIGHTNING DEALER** [7] 4-9-3 P Cook 33/1: 21-1-00: Never in it.   00

7 ran   nk,3,12,nk,nk   (R E Sangster)   B Hills Lambourn, Berks

314   MARCUS BERESFORD HANDICAP 0-50 (3YO)   £3074   5f   Soft/Heavy 153 -23 Slow   [57]

--   TREASURE KAY [9] (P Makin) 3-9-7 B Thomson 14/1: 010-1: 3 b c Mummy's Pet - Welsh
Blossom (Welsh Saint): Useful colt: first time out led approaching final 1f and despite
stumbling was an easy winner of a 3yo h'cap at Sandown Apr.25: in '85 won a maiden at
Newbury: speedily bred colt whose dam was a very successful sprinter: very eff at 5f
on firm & heavy: acts on a gall trk & should win more races.   64
111   LOFT BOY [7] (N Vigors) 3-8-10 S Dawson(3) 4/1: 030-132: Led 2f out: in fine form: see 62 43
233   NORTHERN TRUST [10] (C Nelson) 3-9-0 J Reid 9/4 FAV: 1020-33: Al prom good run see 233 45
--   LA MALMAISON [8] (R Hannon) 3-7-8(1ow)(1oh) R Fox 14/1: 000-4: Made much on seasonal
debut: unplaced in 3 outings in '85: eff at 5f and acts on yld & heavy.   23
203   WEST CARRACK [6] 3-9-6 S Cauthen 5/1: 120-330: Al there: best 62 (6f).   45
172   CRETE CARGO [5] 3-9-7 Paul Eddery 20/1: 00-0000: Early speed: best 15.   36
--   COMPLEAT [4] 3-9-6 P Waldron 8/1: 02331-0: Prom 3f: btr for race: on final outing in
'85 won a 2yo maiden at Wolverhampton: consistent sort who is a half brother to the good
sprinter Boezinge: very eff over 5f, should stay 6f: best form so far on gd & firm grnd.   00
*111 PLATINE [1] 3-8-5 K Radcliffe(7) 13/2: 00-10: Much btr 111 (sharp, undulating trk).   00
--   Little Pipers [3] 9-6   62 Northern Lad [2] 8-7 7-12
10 ran   5,1,1,2,5,shhd   (G W Yates)   P Makin Ogbourne Maisey, Wilts

315   CHILDWICK BURY FILLIES MAIDEN 3YO   £2813   1m 2f   Soft/Heavy 153 -53 Slow

162   FAREWELL TO LOVE [1] (I Balding) 3-8-11 Pat Eddery 13/2: 20-21: 3 b f Key To Content -
Farewell Letter (Arts And Letters): Useful, impr filly: led well over 2f out, ridden out
in a slow run 3yo fillies maiden at Sandown Apr.25: eff at 10f, should stay further: acts
on gd & heavy & on any trk: on the up grade paid a fine complement to Gesedeh.   58
--   MAGIC SLIPPER [7] (H Cecil) 3-8-7 S Cauthen 5/4 FAV: -2: Heavily bckd debutant: kept
on well and should be winning shortly: very well bred filly who is a half sister to several
winners incl Light Cavalry, Fairy Footsteps & Royal
Coach: eff at 10f, may stay further: acts on soft/heavy, should impr on btr grnd.   50
--   ROSI NOA [2] (P Kelleway) 3-8-11 Gay Kelleway(5) 33/1: 0-3: Rank outsider: good
seasonal debut: highly tried on sole outing in '85: eff at 10f on soft/heavy & a gall trk:
should find a small maiden.   46
--   CHALICE OF SILVER [4] (M Jarvis) 3-8-11 W Woods(3) 9/1: 30-4: Sn prom on seasonal debut:
first time out in '85 fin 3rd in a 24 runner maiden at Newmarket: half sister to a couple
of winners abroad: should be suited by 10f: acts on gd/firm & soft: should do btr next time.   38
213   NIHAD [3] 3-8-11 G Baxter 4/1: 0-40: Never nearer: btr 213 (7f).   36
--   ANOTHER PAGEANT [6] 3-8-7 W Carson 12/1: -0: Should impr on this, her racecourse debut:
should be suited by 10f plus: will do btr than this.   27
--   Veronica Ann [8] 8-7   162 Annabellina [5] 8-11
8 ran   2,4,4,1,2½   (Paul Mellon)   I Balding Kingsclere, Hants

316   THE 81ST RENEWAL OF THE TUDOR STAKES   £2821   1m   Soft/Heavy 153 -13 Slow

*90   PROHIBITED [6] (P Cole) 3-9-2 T Quinn 9/1: 00-11: 3 br c Formidable - Deed
(Derring-Do): Useful, impr colt who is in fine form: led under press inside final 1f in
a stakes event at Sandown Apr.25: first time out won a Warwick maiden: 100,000 gns purchase
who is a half brother to several winners, incl the smart Busaco: eff at 1m, should stay
further: acts well on soft grnd & on any trk: fast impr colt who should win more races.   52
253   AMIR ALBADEIA [8] (P Walwyn) 3-8-11 Paul Eddery 7/2: 04-22: led over 2f out: just
btn and is in gd form: should be winning soon: see 253.   46
--   DALGADIYR [7] (M Stoute) 3-8-11 W R Swinburn 11/2: -3: Friendless in mkt on debut:
nearest fin & should do much btr next time: half brother to a smart French colt: should be
suited by 10f plus: acts on soft/heavy.   42
--   THORCASTLE [2] (C Brittain) 3-8-11 S Cauthen 13/8 FAV: -4: Much touted debutant and
heavily bckd: led briefly 3f out: obviously well regarded & should do much btr than this.   40
--   PLAXTOL [5] 3-8-11 Pat Eddery 13/2: -0: Ch 3f out: impr likely froms U.S. bred colt:
one to keep an eye on.   32
--   COUNTERMINE [4] 3-8-11 B Thomson 20/1: 03-0: Wknd over 2f out: on final outing in
'85 fin 3rd in a Chester maiden: half brother to several winners, incl the smart Seismic Wave
possibly btr on gd/firm.   18
--   Cardave [9] 8-11   140 Out Of Stock [1] 8-11   -- Coleman Hawkins [3] 8-11
9 ran   ½,2,1,4,8   (F Salmon)   P Cole Whatcombe, Oxon

Official Going Given as Soft with Heavy Patches

317   NORTHERN TRAINERS 2YO FILLIES MAIDEN   £2630   5f   Soft 125 -01 Slow

-- **NUTWOOD LIL** [6] (E Eldin) 2-8-11 A Mackay 7/2: 1: 2 b f Vaigly Great - Sterlonia (Sterling Bay): First time out, landed a gamble, making most, ridden out in a 2yo fillies maiden at Ripon Apr.26: half sister to '85 2yo winner Atromitos: eff at 5f, should be suited by 6f: acts on soft ground and a sharpish trk: seems suited by forcing tactics.   **40**

-- **LINN ODEE** [4] (M W Easterby) 2-8-11 M Hindley(3) 25/1: 2: Ran on well, btn ¼L, showing future promise: cost 8,200 gns and is speedily bred: eff at 5f, should stay further: acts on soft & a sharpish trk: should go one better soon.   **38**

-- **BUNDUKEYA** [3] (H T Jones) 2-8-11 A Murray 10/3: 3: Wk in mkt: nt btn far: cost 74,000 gns and should come on for this race: eff at 5f, should stay 6f: acts on soft.   **37**

170 **SHARPHAVEN** [11] (M Brittain) 2-8-11 K Darley 5/2 FAV: 34: Well bckd: not beaten far: impr: see 170.   **35**

-- **LYN RAE** [1] 2-8-11 J Bleasdale 10/1: 0: Mkt drifter on debut: nearest fin: impr likely: half sister to 5/6f winner Brampton Grace: acts on soft.   **31**

57 **MOONEE POND** [5] 2-8-11 K Hodgson 8/1: 20: Good effort in this btr company: will definitely find a seller on this form: acts on soft/heavy on any trk: see 57.   **30**

-- **MISS LAMB** [10] 2-8-11 M Beecroft 10/1: 0: Sn prom: fdd: half sister to a couple of winners, incl useful hurdler Vurns: should be suited by much further.   **00**

-- Dancing Belle [7] 8-11   -- **Miss Sherbrooke** [2] 8-11
197 Sinclair Lady [12] 8-11   -- Deftly [9] 8-11
-- Sue Forever [8] 8-11
12 ran   ¾,½,¾,2,shhd   (A E Hutley)   E Eldin, Newmarket

318   ASBAH SELLING STAKES 3YO   £1380   1m 1f   Soft 125 -43 Slow

-- **CRAMMING** [9] (W Musson) 3-8-9(2ow) P Gunn 7/1: 000-1: 3 b g Viking - Damaring (Saidam): First time out, made ev yd, easily in a slow run 3yo seller at Ripon Apr.26 (sold 6,000 gns): unplaced in 3 outings in '85: eff at 9f on soft ground and a sharpish trk.   **32**

54 **LAUGH A LOT** [7] (W Wharton) 3-8-7 N Carlisle 7/4 FAV: 2223-32: Ev ch str: see 54.   **21**

-- **STEP ON** [8] (C Thornton) 3-8-7 J Bleasdale 20/1: 00-3: Al prom on seasonal debut: stays 9f and acts on soft: suited by a sharpish trk.   **16**

234 **TAP DUET** [2] (B Hills) 3-8-7 M Hills 11/2: 000-04: Mkt drifter: no threat: unplaced in 3 non sellers in '85: may do better.   **06**

120 **ALL A DREAM** [5] 3-8-7 A Mackay 7/1: 4000-00: Never nearer: showed some form in '85, though yet to win: stays 9f: acts on soft, suited by gd/firm ground.   **03**

-- **TROPICO** [10] 3-8-7 J Scally(7) 15/2: 02-0: Nearest fin on seasonal debut and impr likely next time: on final outing in '85 fin 2nd in a Newmarket seller: stays 9f: acts on soft, suited by gd/firm ground and should find a seller in the near future.   **02**

-- **NIPPY CHIPPY** [6] 3-9-0 K Hodgson 10/1: 0041-0: Wknd: btr for race.   **00**

82 **JENIFER BROWNING** [1] 3-8-4 S Webster 13/2: 00-20: Never in it: much btr 82 (7f stiff).   **00**

-- **SKELTON** [4] 3-8-11 M Hindley(3) 10/1: 20100-0: Al trailing.   **00**

255 Balidareen [3] 8-4   54 Tara Dancer [12] 9-7(bl)
11 ran   4,2½,5,1½,½   (Mrs Catherine Perkins)   W Musson Newmarket

319   C B HUTCHINSON MEM.CUP H'CAP 4Y+ 0-50   £3137   2m   Soft 125 -29 Slow   [40]

243 **DOUBLE BENZ** [9] (M H Easterby) 4-9-10 K Hodgson 4/1: 2200-01: 4 chc Busted - Estructura (Gulf Pearl): Cruised into lead over 1f out, under 9-10 in a h'cap at Ripon Apr.26: in '85 won at Haydock and in '84 won at Redcar: eff over 1m, nowadays suited by 12f/2m: acts on gd & soft ground and on any trk: consistent: carries weight well and should win again.   **46**

*144 **WESSEX** [3] (N Tinkler) 4-8-12(bl) Kim Tinkler(7) 11/4 FAV: 333-412: In fine form: stays 2m: see 144.   **31**

-- **STANWOOD BOY** [7] (W Musson) 4-8-5 A Mackay 7/1: 30100-3: Nearest fin on seasonal debut: should do btr next time: has been hurdling: in '85 won a h'cap at Ayr: eff at 10f, stays 2m: acts on any grnd: likes a gall trk.   **23**

-- **RUSHMOOR** [5] (R Peacock) 8-9-4 L Charnock 10/1: -0330-4: Led ½m out: lightly raced on the Flat in '85: very useful hurdler: last won on the Flat in '81: stays 2m plus: acts on any ground.   **34**

144 **LEPRECHAUN LADY** [2] 4-8-6 J Lowe 9/1: 040-200: Never nearer: stays 2m: see 69.   **20**

-- **SANDCRACKER** [6] 7-7-7(bl)(1oh) J Quinn(3) 50/1: -0: Rank outsider: sn prom: been chasing.   **00**

-- **STONE JUG** [4] 6-8-0 S Webster 10/1: 03401-0: Led 6f out: btr for race.   **00**

50 **RED DUSTER** [8] 6-8-10 M Beecroft 7/2: 100-430: Better 50: likes Catterick: see 44.   **00**

-- **LHASA** [1] 4-9-6 E Guest(3) 6/1: 43200-0: Made mu   **00**

9 ran   1½,½,⁻,1½,1½,7   (T Bennett)   M H Easterby, Great Habton, Yorks

320   SOUTHERN TRAINERS 2YO STAKES   £1720   5f   Soft 125 +05 Fast

*73 MY IMAGINATION [6] (P Kelleway) 2-8-13 Gay Kelleway(7) 1/1 FAV: 11: 2 b f What A Guest-
Tutti Frutti (Tarboosh): Useful filly: led 1½f out, easily in quite a fast run 2yo event
at Ripon Apr.26: first time out was a similarly easy winner of a fillies maiden at Kempton:
cost I.R. 10,000: eff at 5f, should stay further: acts on soft & should win more races.   55
242 WIGANTHORPE [4] (M W Easterby) 2-8-11 M Hindley(3) 4/1: 02: Led after 2f, no chance
with winner, though is on the up grade: should find a Northern maiden soon: acts on soft
ground: see 242.   45
--   HARRY HUNT [2] (J Berry) 2-8-11 M Fry 7/1: 3: Sn prom: promising debut: sire was a
speedy sort, but his dam seems an influence for stamina: acts on soft grnd & should impr.   35
--   REGENT LAD [5] (L Siddall) 2-8-11 G Gosney 16/1: 4: Never nearer on debut: cost
5,000 gns: half brother to several winners, incl the fair sprint h'capper Gamblers Dream.   30
236 RAINTREE COUNTY [3] 2-8-11 D Mckeown 5/1: 00: Led over 2f: impr effort from this
8,000 gns purchase: acts on soft.   24
--   GLENCROFT [7] 2-8-11 D Nicholls 12/1: 0: Wknd over 1f out on debut: cost 6,200 gns.   18
--   DAMART [1] 2-8-11 E Guest(3) 10/1: 0: Al rear: half brother to '85 winning 2yo Floating
Asset: should do btr.   00
7 ran   2½,4,2½,2½,6   (Roldvale Ltd)   P Kelleway Newmarket

321   TURN TO YORKSHIRE H'CAP 3YO+ 0-50   £2070   6f   Soft 125 +15 Fast   [43]

124 SULLYS CHOICE [6] (D Chapman) 5-8-10 D Nicholls 16/1: 0000-01: 5 b g King Pellinore-
Salute The Coates (Solar Salute): Ran on under press to get up on the line in a fast run
h'cap at Ripon Apr.26: little form in '85, but in good form in '84 winning at Ripon and was
placed on many occasions: eff over 5/6f, stays 1m: acts on soft, likes gd/firm: has run
well in blinkers.   36
--   EASTBROOK [5] (S Hall) 6-7-8(1ow) L Charnock 8/1: 00000-2: Nearly made all: caught
post: fine seasonal debut: early in '85 won a h'cap at Hamilton: eff at 5/6f on gd & soft
ground: best out in front and likes a sharpish trk.   20
+240 IDLE TIMES [7] (W Elsey) 4-8-5(5ex) J Lowe 1/1 FAV: 200-113: Heavily bckd: sn prom:
good effort but btr 240 (7f).   25
240 PENTOFF [3] (D Chapman) 4-8-0 S P Griffiths(5) 16/1: 000-004: Hung right over 1f
out: seems a difficult ride: see 240.   12
--   JAMES PAL [1] 4-9-7 M Hindley(3) 7/2: 00211-0: Should strip fitter next time: in
fine form at the back end of '85, winning a stakes event at Thirsk and a h'cap at Hamilton:
very eff at 6f: acts on any grnd & on any trk, though seems to like a sharpish one.   17
46   WILLIE GAN [2] 8-7-9 M Fry 16/1: 0000-00: No show.   00
192 LYRIC WAY [9] 4-9-3 S Derham(7) 7/1: 2200-00: Prom 4f.   00
172 BRAMPTON GRACE [8] 4-9-7 E Guest(3) 14/1: 00-0000: Slow start, no show.   00
--   THE MAZALL [4] 6-8-3 G Gosney 10/1: 22010-0: Btr for race.   00
9 ran   shhd,2½,3,8,4   (William Chapman)   D Chapman Stillington, Yorks

322   OWNERS STAKES 3YO   £1720   1m   Soft 125 -16 Slow

*99 MARINA PLATA [4] (D Chapman) 3-9-2 D Nicholls 17/2: 0-011: 3 b f Julio Mariner -
Mar Del Plata (Crowned Prince): Fast impr filly: sn prom, led over 2f out and held on
gamely under press in a 3yo stakes at Ripon Apr.26: last time out won a 3yo maiden at
Hamilton: dam won over 1m at 3 years: well suited by soft grnd: acts on any trk: should
stay further than 1m: seems a genuine sort and should win more races.   44
--   ALBERT HALL [1] (B Hills) 3-9-0 M Hills 5/4 FAV: 0002-2: Chall final 1f: btn a
whisker on seasonal debut: good effort: on final outing in '85 fin. 2nd to Mighty Memory
at Bath: eff at 1m, should stay further: acts on gd/firm & soft & on any trk: should find
a maiden.   42
--   KNYF [5] (E Weymes) 3-9-0 E Guest(3) 4/1: 332-3: Ch final 1f: fair seasonal debut:
placed on all 3 starts in '85: should be suited by 1m plus: acts on gd/firm & soft.   39
--   HELLO BENZ [6] (M H Easterby) 3-9-0 J Lowe 12/1: -4: Al up there on racecourse debut,
showing promise: half brother to 12f winner Wild Ginger: should stay 10f: acts on soft.   32
127 SOXOPH [7] 3-9-5 K Hodgson 7/1: -4100: Ev ch: best 53.   36
*100 ELEGANT BILL [9] 3-9-5 C Coates(5) 6/1: 000-010: Made much: gd effort: see 100.   24
--   Lucky West [11] 8-11   --   Manvil [3] 9-0   54 Pauls Secret [8] 9-0
--   Spansyke [2] 9-0
10 ran   shhd,1½,3,nk,5.   (Miss Sarah Hills)   D Chapman Stillington, Yorks

---

SANDOWN   Saturday April 26th   Righthand Stiff Galloping Track

Official Going Given as Soft with Heavy Patches

323   SANDOWN PARK 2YO MAIDEN STAKES   £3043   5f   Soft 129 -13 Slow

--   RISK ME [5] (P Kelleway) 2-9-0 P Cook 1/1 fav: 1: 2 ch c Sharpo - Run The Risk
(Run The Gantlet): Very useful colt in the making: first time out, heavily bckd and led
before ¼way when hacking up by 8L in a 2yo maiden at Sandown Apr.26: half brother to 3
winners, all of whom stayed extremely well: acts on soft grnd & a stiff trk: certain to
stay beyond 5f: has been burning up the gallops at home & is not one to oppose in his
next few engagements.   85
111

230 ACQUISITIVE [1] (M Usher) 2-9-0 M Wigham 4/1: 32: No ch with winner: see 230.   39

187 QUICK SNAP [6] (A Ingham) 2-9-0(BL) S Cauthen 13/2: 43: Bl first time, showed
some impr: seems suited by this stiff 5f: see 187.   39

--   HAILEYS RUN [2] (G P Gordon) 2-9-0 W Carson 13/2: 4: May benefit from the outing:
sprint bred: cost I.R. 10,000.   31

--   CAPITAL FLOW [3] 2-9-0 A Mcglone 12/1: 0: Mkt drifter on debut: sprint bred.   28

5 ran   8,hd,4,1½   (L H Norris)   P Kelleway Newmarket

324 GROUP 3 GUARDIAN CLASSIC TRIAL 3YO   £19845   1m 2f   Soft 129 -08 Slow

--   SHAHRASTANI [1] (M Stoute) 3-8-7 W R Swinburn 2/1: 2-1: 3 ch c Nijinsky - Shademah
(Thatch): Smart colt: trked Bonhomie till sprinting clear over 2f out for a ready and
impressive win in Gr.3 Guardian Classic Trial at Sandown Apr.26: unlucky in running on sole
start in '85 but is known to be held in high regard by his powerful stable: stays 10f well
and will have no difficulty staying 12f: acts on gd/firm & soft going & is suited by a
gall trk: not one to oppose lightly, whatever the class of the opposition.   83

--   BONHOMIE [3] (H Cecil) 3-8-12 S Cauthen 7/4 fav: 111-2: Led almost 1m, swamped for
foot by the winner: unbtn in 3 outings in '85 at Yarmouth, Lingfield & Royal Lodge Stakes
at Ascot: half brother to several winners: eff over 1m, stays 10f & should stay 12f: acts
on soft, probably btr suited by firm or good going: likes to force the pace and is a
genuine sort.   78

*48 SIRK [2] (C Brittain) 3-8-7 P Robinson 20/1: 423-13: No ch with first 2 but had an
impossible task here and should win more races back in his proper grade: see 48.   63

--   PRIMARY [4] (G Harwood) 3-8-7 G Starkey 2/1: 01-4: Well bckd on seasonal debut,
unable to give his true running as jockey Greville Starkey injured his arm exiting the
stalls: ran only twice in '85, winning a backend maiden at Lingfield on final outing: eff
7f, bred to stay middle dists: acts on firm going: certain to impr this season.   00

4 ran   4,5,dist   (H H Aga Khan)   M Stoute Newmarket

325 GROUP 3 WESTBURY E.B.F STAKES 4YO+   £21600   1m 2f   Soft 129 -20 Slow

*221 SUPREME LEADER [3] (C Brittain) 4-8-12 P Robinson 1/2 fav: 0030-11: 4 b c Bustino -
Princess Zena (Habitat): Very smart colt: patiently ridden and had to be really stoked up to
get the btr of a close fin to rather slowly run Gr.3 Westbury Stakes at Sandown Apr.26:
comfortable winner of valuable Earl of Sefton Stakes at Newmarket first time out: early in
'85 won at Sandown and also placed 3rd in the 1,000 Guineas & 4th in the Derby: stays 10/12f
but said by his trainer to be an outstanding miler and will revert to the shorter dists now:
acts on yld or soft going, also on good or firm and has a smart turn of foot.   85

--   IROKO [5] (M Stoute) 4-8-8 W R Swinburn 6/1: 20111-2: Prom, led str and battled on
gamely, just btn: fine seasonal debut from this much impr colt: ended last season by
recording a hat trick at Sandown & Goodwood (2) (incl Valdoe Stakes): earlier won at Windsor:
half brother to top class French horse Manado: equally eff at 10 & 12f & acts on firm &
soft going & on any trk: game & genuine sort who is sure to win more races.   79

--   RAMICH JOHN [1] (L Browne) 4-8-5 A Mcglone 10/1: 2D-0113: Battled it out thro'out final
2f, just btn & clear of rest: Irish chall. who has gained 2 recent wins in her native
country: well at home in soft or heavy going: eff at 10 & 12f.   76

221 ENGLISH SPRING [6] (I Balding) 4-8-9 S Cauthen 7/1: 0112-44: Ev ch: see 221.   70

221 K BATTERY [8] 5-8-8 P Cook 33/1: 000-100: Far from disgraced in this company and
has much impr this season: see 17.   69

--   SEVERN BORE [4] 4-8-8 G Starkey 20/1: 32203-0: No dngr on seasonal debut: gained
only success so far in a Listed race at Kempton first time out in '85 though subsequently
ran several good races, notably when a close 3rd in a valuable h'cap at York (rated 77): best
form around 1m on good or soft going though also acts on firm: will strip fitter next time.   64

251 Chaumiere [2] 8-8(vis)   221 Big Reef [7] 8-8

--   Thalestria [9] 8-5

9 ran   nk,shhd,6,shhd,4   (Capt M Lemos)   C Brittain Newmarket

326 ESHER CUP (HANDICAP) 0-70 3YO   £12271   1m   Soft 129 +08 Fast   [68]

193 SWIFT TROOPER [3] (R Williams) 3-8-5(bl) R Cochrane 7/2 fav: 410-121: 3 br c Air
Trooper - Kemoening (Falcon): Useful colt: made ev yd, staying on strongly for a 2L success
in quite fast run & valuable Esher Cup H'cap (3yo) at Sandown Apr.26: ready first time out
winner at Kempton: in '85 won at Edinburgh: half brother to a couple of winners incl the
useful hurdler Saxon Farm: eff over 1m/10f and acts on gd & soft going: acts on any trk:
best form in bl: could win again.   59

--   SIMSIM [9] (J Dunlop) 3-9-5 W Carson 8/1: 41-2: Fin in good style, showing bags of
promise on seasonal debut: ran only twice in '85 winning a maiden at York: acts on gd/firm
and soft going: stays 1m & should stay at least 10f: one to be on next time.   69

--   TERMINATOR [5] (H Candy) 3-7-12 L Riggio[7] 11/2: 341-3: Close up final 3f and will
strip fitter for this seasonal debut: ran only 3 times in '85 winning final outing, a maiden
at Lingfield: acts on firm & soft going: suited by 1m & should stay further: well h'capped
and should not be missed next time.   48

*183 **PLANET ASH** [6] (A Bailey) 3-8-3(5ex) S Dawson[3] 13/2: 20-2414: Kept on well: another
good effort & continues to impr: likely to win again soon: see 183.   52
--   **NERVOUS RIDE** [2] 3-9-7 S Cauthen 7/1: 1-0: Prom str: probably just needed race:
winner of sole outing in '85, prevailing in a blanket fin to a Newmarket maiden: acts on
soft but possibly more at home on a sounder surface: will stay at least 1m: does not seem
well h'capped.   68
--   **SYLVAN EXPRESS** [4] 3-8-2 G Carter[3] 9/2: 00211-0: A gamble, wknd str: easy winner
of valuable nurseries at Newmarket & Ascot at the end of '85: very eff over 7f on gd or
firm going and may not be suited by soft, though sire (Baptism) acted well in such going.   39
*178 **GORGEOUS ALGERNON** [1] 3-8-10(5ex) C Rutter[5] 7/1: 030-010: Much btr 178 (gd, sharp track).00
216   Hot Gem [7] 8-6   216 Swifts Pal [8] 8-9   26   Our Tilly [10] 8-0
10 ran   2,nk,½,1,8   (Swift Racing Services Ltd)   R Williams Newmarket

327 ATHLONE HANDICAP STAKES 4YO+ 0-60   £3695   5f   Soft 129 +32 Fast   [52]

192   **BRIDGE STREET LADY** [10] (J Bosley) 5-9-3 G Baxter 11/4 fav: 200-201: 5 b m Decoy Boy -
Diamond Talk (Counsel): Useful sprinter: made most readily in a fast run h'cap at Sandown
Aor.26: in '85 won at Nottingham and was a fine 2nd in the Wokingham at Royal Ascot: in
'84 won at Chepstow: very eff over 5/6f, stays 7f: best on gd or heavy grnd with forcing
tactics: could win again.   55
192   **EECEE TREE** [9] (J Sutcliffe) 4-7-11(1ow) A Mcglone 6/1: 1000-02: Al chasing winner:
in '85 successful at Newmarket (seller) & Chepstow (h'cap): eff over 6/7f with front running
tactics and a gall trk: acts on soft, well suited by firm or gd going.   23
--   **CREE BAY** [6] (J Spearing) 7-9-3 W Carson 11/1: 40040-3: Late hdway and will strip
fitter next time: failed to win in '85 though placed several times: in '84 won at Pontefract
(2) & Warwick: eff at 5 & 6f and probably best on gd or firm grnd though ran well on soft here   42
192   **DUCK FLIGHT** [5] (J Douglas Home) 4-9-2 S Cauthen 9/2: 0030-04: Ev ch: first time out
winner at Leicester and subsq. at Chester in '85: eff at 5 & 6f on gd & heavy going.   39
--   **LOCHTILLUM** [1] 7-9-4 R Cochrane 12/1: 10100-0: Fin in pleasing style: ran valuable
h'caps at Newcastle & Doncaster (Portland H'cap) in '85: very eff over 5/6f though seems to
act on any going: best form on a stiff trk: should run well next time.   39
192   **DEPUTY HEAD** [4] 6-8-12 J Matthias 12/1: 4000-00: No dngr: failed to win in '85,
previous season won at Newbury & Ascot: eff over 5/6f but acts on any going.   28
*122 **ANOTHER BING** [8] 4-7-7(12oh) L Riggio[7] 9/1: 0400-10: Very stiff task: see 122.   00
--   **ALL AGREED** [3] 5-9-5 W R Swinburn 4/1: 10204-0: Should benefit from race.   00
192   Kellys Royale [7] 9-10   122 Russell Flyer [2] 7-9
10 ran   6,½,1,¾,3,2,10,nk   (M Wilkins)   J Bosley Lower Haddon, Oxon

---

328 HOLSTEN DIAT PILS MAIDEN STAKES 3YO   £2674   1m   Soft 125 +03 Fast

--   **STARTINO** [12] (H Cecil) 3-8-11 W Ryan 5/6 FAV: 2-1: 3 b f Bustino - Western Star
(Alcide): Promising filly: justified fav. on her reappearance, led after ½way and was soon
clear for an easy win in quite a fast run 3yo maiden at Leicester Apr.26: just btn by
Entrancing in a fillies race at Goodwood on her only start last term: half sister to a
winning sprinter and is also closely related to the smart Mr Fluorocarbon: very eff over 1m
on a stiff trk & looks sure to be suited by further: acts on firm & soft grnd: takes a strong
hold and does well with forcing tactics: should win again.   56
--   **ASHINGTON GROVE** [7] (D Murray Smith) 3-9-0 T Quinn 25/1: 00-2: Ran on well from ½way
though no chance with winner: unplaced in both starts last season though has clearly wintered
well: eff over 1m on soft grnd: acts on a stiff trk: should find a similar race.   42
253   **TOP RANGE** [16] (M Jarvis) 3-9-0 T Ives 16/1: -03: Al prom: btr effort: eff over
1m on a gall trk: suited by some give in the ground.   41
--   **FRANGNITO** [5] (R Johnson Houghton) 3-9-0 J Reid 15/2: 0-4: Active in mkt on seasonal
debut: ran on too late: showed promise on his only start last season: is closely related to
several winners, incl Assert and Bikala: acts on soft grnd & on a gall trk: sure to impr
on this effort, especially over a longer trip.   40
157   **SAXON BAZAAR** [18] 3-9-0 F Roberts(7) 50/1: 004-000: Outsider: led briefly ½way: sn
btn though this was an impr effort: full brother to useful sprinter Crofthall: acts on
firm & soft ground: should do btr on a less exacting course.   26
--   **COUNTRY GENTLEMAN** [2] 3-9-0 R Fox 9/1: 040-0: Mkt drifter on reappearnce: btr for race.23
90   **NATCHAKAM** [15] 3-9-0 P Waldron 11/2: -420: Close up over ½way: see 90.   00
218   **PARIS TURF** [1] 3-9-0 G Duffield 7/1: -00: Nicely bckd though no threat from ½way.   00
218   Sutimark [9] 9-0   247 Rose Window [17] 8-11   --   Cheal [19] 9-0
247   Mawdlyn Gate [14] 9-0   --   Grendel [20] 9-0   247 Couture Color [21] 9-0
--   Guymyson [6] 9-0   194 Johnstan Boy [3] 9-0   --   Man In The Moon [11] 9-0(BL)
140   Supreme Command [10] 9-0   --   Starboard [4] 8-11
--   Tamana Dancer [13] 8-11   247 Strawberry Split [8] 8-11
21 ran   7,½,¾,7,1½   (Mrs James McAllister)   H Cecil Newmarket

329 GADSBY SELLING STAKES 2YO   £685   5f   Soft 125 -29 Slow

170 SETTER COUNTRY [5] (C Hill) 2-8-8 A Clark 5/4 FAV: 01: 2 b f Town And Country -
Top Soprano (High Top): Dropped to selling company and landed a gamble when a comfortable
winner of a 2yo seller at Leicester Apr.26: led 2f out and was sn clear (bought in 3,700 gns)
half brother to winning hurdler Jack Ramsey: eff over 5f & sure to stay further: acts on
soft grnd & on a stiff trk.   26
--   BINGO QUEEN [7] (J Berry) 2-8-8 G Duffield 7/2: 2: Nicely bckd on racecourse debut:
kept on under press and would not have to impr much to win a small race: eff over 5f on soft
grnd: acts on a gall trk.   18
181 MI OH MY [2] (K Stone) 2-8-8 C Dwyer 3/1: 3023: No extra inside dist: best in 181 (yld)   16
118 TELEGRAPH FOLLY [1] (R Hoad) 2-8-11 B Crossley 12/1: 04: Mkt drifter: ran on from
½way: acts on soft grnd & on a gall trk.   15
86   CUTLER RIDGE [3] 2-8-11(bl) J Reid 7/1: 000: Led over ½way: cheaply acquired colt.   13
181 SCARNING SPARKLER [6] 2-8-11 J Carr(7) 12/1: 00P: Sn behind and p.u. before ½way.   00
6 ran   4,1½,1,1   (A G Newcombe)   C Hill Barnstaple, Devon

330 HOLSTEN PILS TROPHY EBF STKS   £7105   7f   Soft 125 +19 Fast

•55 BOLLIN KNIGHT [2] (M H Easterby) 4-8-13 M Birch 11/2: 211/011: 4 b g Immortal Knight-
Lush Secret (Most Secret): Smart gelding: led below dist and ran on well to win a fast run
& valuable stakes at Leicester Apr.26: last month made all readily in a h'cap at Newcastle:
off the trk last season though a smart juvenile in '84, winning at Doncaster, Catterick &
Ayr: very eff over 6/7f: acts on yld & heavy grnd & on any trk: genuine & consistent.   78
--   SHMAIREEKH [7] (P Walwyn) 5-8-13 N Howe 11/1: 22000-2: Mkt drifter on seasonal debut
though led after ½way and ran a fine race: early last season won a valuable h'cap at Epsom
and later ran creditably abroad: in '84 won at Newmarket, Sandown & Newbury: very eff
over 7/8f: acts on any going, though best on a faster surface: well suited by a gall trk:
genuine colt who will be winning soon.   74
•222 HOMO SAPIEN [5] (H Cecil) 4-8-13 W Ryan 10/11 FAV: 11/2-13: Al close up, ran on well
close home: 10L clear of rem: good effort on unsuitably soft grnd: see 222.   73
--   SIYAH KALEM [6] (J Dunlop) 4-8-13 T Ives 10/1: 00211-4: Ran on late on reappearance:
useful colt who ended last season with wins at Newmarket & Leicester: half brother to several
winners, incl Bel Bolide: very eff over 1m on fast grnd, though does act on soft: well
suited by a gall trk: btr for race.   55
17   QUALITAIR FLYER [11] 4-8-13 G Brown 25/1: 0200-00: Easy to back: not disgraced in
this hot company: early last season won a 3yo h'cap at Haydock and was later placed several
times in good company: in '84 won at York & Leicester: well suited by 7/8f: acts on any
going and is suited by a gall trk.   54
--   NORTHERN ASPEN [10] 4-8-13 R Hills 10/3: 1001-0: Close up over ½way on her reappearance:
smart filly was lightly raced last season, when winning at Sandown: later a Gr.2 race at
Deauville: eff over 1m, stays 10f well: acts on gd/firm & soft grnd & on a gall trk: will
be straighter next time.   50
222 Atoka [8] 8-4   -- Cabral [4] 8-7   -- Muswell Hill [9] 8-7
245 Simla Ridge [1] 8-7
10 ran   1½,nk,10,hd,2½,2   (N G Westbrook)   M H Easterby Great Habton, Yorks

331 SPRING HANDICAP STAKES 3YO 0-35   £2351   1m 4f Soft 125 -14 Slow   [37]

54   SWYNFORD PRINCE [14] (K Stone) 3-8-5(vis) G Brown(3) 20/1: 003-001: 3 br c Kampala -
Derry Willow (Sunny Way): Gained a surprise first success, led 2f out for a comfortable win
in a 3yo h'cap at Leicester Apr.26: half brother to several winners: eff around 1m & stays
12f well: acts on firm & heavy grnd and is well suited by this stiff trk.   25
•117 FEDRA [8] (Lord J Fitzgerald) 3-9-3 R Hills 4/1 Jt FAV: 0000-12: Remains in gd form:
stays 12f: see 117.   29
117 ITTIHAAD [13] (C Benstead) 3-9-7 B Rouse 14/1: 000-03: Nicely bckd: stayed on: see 117.   32
132 CHEVET LADY [15] (R Whitaker) 3-8-10 K Bradshaw(5) 6/1: 100-124: Led after 1m, appeared
not to stay this longer trip: btr over 10f in 54.   13
193 GOLDEN CROFT [10] 3-8-11 J Reid 13/2: 000-00: Some late prog: see 193.   12
171 FOUL SHOT [11] 3-8-0 R Fox 10/1: 000-220: Btr when making most in 171 (yld).   00
•66 DUSTY DIPLOMACY [4] 3-9-5 T Ives 4/1 Jt FAV: 0-10: Much btr over 10f in 66.   00
•45 NIMBLE NATIVE [5] 3-9-2 J Murray(7) 9/1: 000-10: No threat: much btr in 45 (tight trk).   00
193 BLACK COMEDY [12] 3-9-5 P Waldron 10/1: 001-00: Easy to back: last to fin.   00
--   G G Magic [1] 9-1   29 Northinch [6] 8-13   120 Vantastic [3] 7-8
120 The Wooden Hut [7] 8-1   193 Tom Rum [2] 8-11
--   Dads Gunner [9] 7-10(3ow)(2oh)
15 ran   5,nk,7,2,2,½   (Qualitair Engineering Ltd)   K Stone Malton, Yorks

332 WOOLSTHORPE MAIDEN STAKES 2YO   £688   5f   Soft 125 -07 Slow

212 JONLEAT [10] (L Piggott) 2-9-0 T Lucas 11/8 FAV: 41: 2 b c Longleat - Swing Gently
(Swing Easy): Impr young colt: landed a gamble in a 2yo maiden at Leicester Apr.26, led
after ½way and again inside dist for a narrow win: cost 14,000 gns: eff over 5f & should
stay further: acts on yld & soft grnd & on a stiff trk: should continue to impr.   45

-- SINGING STEVEN [11] (R Hannon) 2-9-0 B Rouse 6/1: 2: Quite well fancied on racecourse debut: led below dist though winner's experience told close home: cost 3,000 gns: half brother to fair h'capper Minus Man: acts on soft grnd & on a gall trk: should go one btr soon.   42
-- SILVER ANCONA [4] (E Eldin) 2-9-0 T Ives 6/1: 3: Bumped start, not btn that far & fin clear of rest: gd effort by this half brother to a couple of winning sprinters: acts on soft grnd & on a stiff trk: will win a small race on this evidence.   39
-- MCCALLUN [3] (M Brittain) 2-9-0 A Bacon(7) 16/1: 4: Mkt drifter: kept on under press: cost 2,500 gns: acts on soft grnd: should impr.   23
-- LITTLE SACY [7] 2-9-0 J Williams 25/1: 0: Outsider on debut: al mid-div.   15
136 TAKE EFFECT [1] 2-9-0 G Duffield 11/2: 3330: Led over ½way: much btr in 47.   13
186 WOLF J FLYWHEEL [6] 2-9-0 M Birch 9/2: 020: Well there till ½way: much btr in 186.   00
230 Panache [9] 9-0   -- Master Knowall [2] 9-0(BL)
-- Penny Lover [5] 9-0
10 ran   ¾,1,8,4,¾   (Mrs C Dickson)   L Piggott Newmarket

333 WEIGHING ROOM HANDICAP 0-35   £2778   1m   2f Soft 125 -01 Slow   [35]

-- STATE BUDGET [14] (W Musson) 5-9-5 M Wigham 6/1: 31230-1: 5 b g Free State - Novelista (El Gallo): Fit from hurdling and proved an easy winner, led below dist and was sn clear in a h'cap at Leicester Apr.26: quite consistent on the Flat last season, when winning another h'cap over this C/D: in '84 won at Redcar: eff over 10/12f: acts on firm though relishes soft grnd: well suited by this stiff trk.   36
243 BALGOWNIE [12] (J Mulhall) 6-8-2 P Burke(7) 12/1: 1100002: Btr effort after a string of disapp. runs: well suited by soft grnd & loves this stiff course: see 36.   12
*129 GULFLAND [13] (G Pritchard Gordon) 5-9-7 J Cahill(7) 7/1: 0-00-13: Stayed on: in gd form: see 129.   28
243 NORTH STAR SAM [9] (J Ramsden) 5-7-12 R Morse(7) 33/1: -00004: Tried to make all: maiden who is eff over middle dists on gd & soft grnd: front runner.   03
72 WELL MEET AGAIN [15] 9-9-3 B Rouse 9/2: -20-300: Much btr over this C/D in 36.   19
129 SHAD RABUGK [3] 4-8-3 R Street 33/1: 0-0-000: Mkt drifter: maiden with little worthwhile form to his name: acts on firm & soft grnd.   00
+88 STAR OF IRELAND [2] 6-9-3 Catherine Strickland(7) 2/1 FAV: --00-10: Disapp fav: much btr in 88 (sharp trk).   00
164 RECHARGE [11] 4-8-7 S Perks 8/1: 204-000: Never beyond mid-div: see 164.   00
238 Dick Knight [8] 8-5   -- Lucksin [1] 8-0   -- Deramin [7] 9-6
-- Singing Boy [19] 9-4   174 Mister Prelude [16] 8-11
208 Fleurcone [5] 8-8   129 Absurd [17] 8-6   119 Mr Music Man [10] 8-4
129 Miss Morley [18] 8-0   -- Turcy Boy [4] 7-13(1ow)
-- Armorad [6] 9-4
19 ran   3,2,1½,2½,4,7   (A P Field)   W Musson Newmarket

---

334 LOVELY ROSA 3YO STAKES   £913   7f   Yielding 108 +01 Fast

127 PELLINKO [5] (E Eldin) 3-9-0 A Mackay 14/1: 00-41: Impr colt: easy to back though ran on strongly to lead inside dist. in quite a fast run 3yo stakes at Warwick Apr.28: half brother to winning sprinter Sandy Cap: very eff over 7/8f and should stay further: acts on yld & soft grnd and on any trk.   54
-- THRESH IT OUT [17] (M Stoute) 3-9-0 W R Swinburn 11/10 FAV: 0223-2: Heavily bckd on reappearance: ran on well, though too late: placed in gd class company in 3 of his 4 starts last season, notably when 3rd to Resourceful Falcon in a nursery at Doncaster: full brother to smart milers Final Straw and Achieve: very eff over 6/7f: sure to stay at least 1m: acts on firm & soft grnd & on any trk: sure to go one btr soon.   46+
-- AUTUMN FLUTTER [4] (R Hannon) 3-9-0 L Jones(5) 50/1: 00-3: Friendless in mkt on seasonal debut: kept on well and this was a promising run: lightly raced last season: eff over 7f on gd/firm & yld grnd: seems to act on any trk.   42
-175 BOOFY [10] (C Nelson) 3-9-0(bl) J Reid 8/1: 340-224: Again ran well: stays 7f: see 175   38
-- RETRIEVE [18] 3-9-0 B Thomson 4/1: -0: Well bckd on racecourse debut: led early & again briefly below dist, sn btn: half brother to several winners incl useful miler Long Row: acts on yld grnd & on a sharpish trk: clearly quite well regarded and should impr next time.   38
-- FAATIK [6] 3-9-0 N Howe 33/1: 03400-0: Mkt drifter on reappearance: led/dsptd lead most of way: showed promise over sprint distances last season: acts on gd/firm & yld grnd and on any track.   30
66 CAGLIOSTRO [1] 3-9-0 T Lucas 12/1: -30: Again set the pace, btn dist: see 66.   00
-- DESERT OF WIND [8] 3-9-0 R Guest 12/1: -0: Mkt drifter on racecourse debut: should impr.   00
-- Golden Straw [3] 9-0   247 Prime Number [2] 9-0   -- Beau Dire [16] 9-0
-- Charcoal [9] 9-0   -- Eagle Destiny [13] 9-0
-- King Tefkros [19] 9-0   229 On Water [15] 9-0   258 Saiyyaaf [7] 9-0
-- The Moon And Back [14] 9-0   64 Absolute Master [12] 9-0
18 ran   4,¾,2½,hd,4   (L Westbury)   E Eldin Newmarket

335 SOUTH BANK APP.H'CAP 3YO 0-35   £1184   1m   Yielding 108 +04 Fast   [42]

*16   MY KIND OF TOWN [4] (R Williams) 3-9-12 C Barnfather(7) 12/1: -11: 3 b c Camden Town-
Bonny Rand (Hillary): Useful colt: gamely defied top weight in an app. h'cap at Warwick
Apr.28, leading close home: earlier just got up to win a maiden at Doncaster on his debut:
eff over 7/8f & should stay further: acts on yld & soft grnd & on any trk: suited by waiting
tactics: genuine sort.   50
141   UNEXPLAINED [3] (R Armstrong) 3-8-11 V Smith(7) 9/1: 0000-42: Sn led, caught near
fin: seems much impr this season and should find a small race: seems to act on any trk: see 141   32
*279 BILLYS DANCER [5] (D Dale) 3-8-9 G King 5/1: 040-13: Not btn far: in gd form: see 279.   29
123   TEED BORE [8] (W Musson) 3-8-2 B Uniacke(4) 11/1: 0-204: Never nearer: needs further.   19
100   BRAVE AND BOLD [6] 3-8-3(bl) G Bardwell(3) 5/1: 2001-20: Stayed on late: btr in 100 (9f).17
174   ARTISTIC CHAMPION [13] 3-8-8 D Eddery 9/2 FAV: 000-30: Ran btr over 7f in 174 (gall trk) 15
209   FAIR ATLANTA [16] 3-8-6 F Roberts(7) 6/1: 003-240: Never dngr 8th: btr in 209 (9f).   00
117   UP TO UNCLE [12] 3-8-8 L Jones 6/1: 444-000: Nicely bckd though btr over 10f in 117.   00
--   Rupert Brooke [1] 8-0   --   Monstrosa [2] 8-1   --   Time Bird [10] 8-13
--   Winding Path [7] 8-7   141   Ceroc [17] 8-8   --   Whirling Words [15] 8-6
--   The Sportsman [11] 8-1   147   My Derya [9] 7-7(2oh)
279   Chepstowed [14] 7-9
17 ran   1½,shhd,2,½,3   (A Rudolf)   R Williams Newmarket

336 GODIVA H'CAP 4YO UPWARDS 0-50   £2639   2m 2f   Yielding 108 -07 Slow   [39]

235   PEARL RUN [11] (G Price) 5-9-2 J Williams 7/1: 20-1101: 5 ch h Gulf Pearl - Deep Down
(Deep Run): Returned to winning form, led below dist and was sn clear in a h'cap at Warwick
Apr.28: earlier won similar events at Nottingham & Warwick (first time out): last season
again won at Warwick and he clearly loves this turning trk: eff over 14f, stays 2m2f really
well: acts on any grnd & on any trk: should win again on this evidence.   40
137   BEAKER [8] (M Naughton) 6-7-7(2oh) J Lowe 14/1: 0000-42: Led 4f out, no ch with
winner: placed over hurdles since running in 137.   02
235   CUMREW [4] (N Vigors) 6-7-12(bl) S Dawson(3) 10/1: 0/00-03: Recent winner over hdles
though has been lightly raced on the Flat in recent seasons, and last won in '83 at Newmarket: suited by a test of stamina: seems to act on any going & on any trk.   04
11   FLYING OFFICER [1] (M Pipe) 9-8-9(vis) S Cauthen 7/1: 0040-04: Made most: has been
hurdling this Winter, winning at Devon: last won on the Flat in '83, at Warwick, Lingfield,
Wolverhampton & Bath: stays well: acts on any going & on any trk.   11
137   CHEKA [14] 10-7-12 S O'gorman(7) 7/1: 0000-20: Never nearer: btr over this trip in 137.   00
263   HOT BETTY [3] 6-7-12 A Proud 25/1: 00-3000: No threat: see 28 (10f).   00
204   RELKISHA [10] 5-8-3 N Adams 16/1: 1000-00: Stayed on too late.   00
--   TERN [13] 5-8-10 M Birch 3/1 FAV: 21000-0: Fit from hurdling: disapp fav: last season
won a h'cap at Pontefract: stays forever: acts on gd & heavy grnd and is well suited by a
sharp track.   00
--   Zircons Sun [12] 7-7(4oh)   58a Morgans Choice [2] 9-7
126   Alacazam [5] 7-9   137   Jackdaw [6] 8-8   235   Storm Cloud [9] 9-12
--   Mitilini [7] 7-10   --   Wordsworth [15] 7-7(4oh)
15 ran   12,2½,4,nk,2   (R Squires)   G Price Llangorse, Brecon.

337 ROCKFEL 2YO MAIDEN SELLING STKS   £544   5f   Yielding 108 -54 Slow

200   MISS MARJORIE [4] (L Holt) 2-8-11 P Waldron 6/4 FAV: 01: 2 ch f Swing Easy - Flying
Molly (Shiny Tenth): Dropped to selling company and was well bckd, just btn by Five Sixes
though had been impeded by that winner and she was awarded the race in the stewards room, in
a 2yo seller at Warwick Apr.28 (bought in 1,100 gns): eff over 5f on yld/soft grnd: seems
suited by a sharpish trk.   23
186   FIVE SIXES [2] (W Pearce) 2-9-0 N Connorton 7/4: -01D: Made ev yd though hung
right from ½way & although he just held on he was demoted to 2nd: well bckd today & should
make amends in a similar race soon: cost 2,600 gns & is a half brother to winning miler
Mitilini: eff over 5f on yld grnd: suited by forcing tactics.   26
86   VALDOSTA [7] (C Wildman) 2-8-11 R Hills 33/1: 003: Friendless in mkt though al close
up: cheaply acquired filly who acts on yld grnd.   15
--   SANDIS GOLD [5] (D Wintle) 2-8-11 R Byrne(7) 7/1: 4: Mkt drifter on debut: stayed on
after a slow start & should do btr next time: speedily bred filly who acts on yld grnd.   12
--   SPARKLING JUDY [6] 2-8-11 A Mackay 20/1: 0: Mkt drifter: there till ½way.   04
--   FLYING SILENTLY [1] 2-8-11 J Reid 5/1: 0: Never dngr after a tardy start.   04
--   DEEP TAW [8] 2-8-11 N Day 12/1: 0: Friendless in mkt: never a factor.   00
7 ran   nk,2½,1½,3,shhd   (A V Dittrich)   L Holt Long Sutton, Hants

338 LIGHT BROCADE STAKES 3YO FILLIES   £1322   1m   Yielding 108 -02 Slow

173   DONNAS DREAM [19] (J Tree) 3-8-11 Pat Eddery 5/2 FAV: 40-31: 3 br f Young Generation-
First Huntress (Primera): Useful filly: well bckd when an easy all the way winner of a 3yo
fillies stakes at Warwick Apr.28: showed promise on both starts last season & was a
narrowly btn fav at Chepstow first time out: cost 82,000 gns and is closely related to
several winners, incl smart middle dist. winner Town And Country: very eff over 8/10f: acts
on firm & yld grnd & on any trk: sure to win more races.   62

--   FIREAL [12] (H Cecil) 3-8-11 S Cauthen 11/4: 4-2: Easy to back on her reappearance: stayed on well though no chance with winner: placed behind Holbrooke Sutton in a similar race at Newmarket on sole start last season: eff over 1m: acts on firm & yld grnd & on any trk: should find a race soon.   **48**

--   WHILE IT LASTS [3] (L Cumani) 3-8-11 R Guest 4/1: -3: Gambled on from 16/1 on racecourse debut: kept on promisingly from ¼way: American bred filly who is out of a half sister to high class Stage Door Johnny: eff over 1m on yld grnd: clearly held in some regard and should find a race.   **38**

209 CELTIC DOVE [6] (G Price) 3-8-11 J Williams 50/1: -404: Ran on well after a slow start: much impr effort: eff over 8/10f on yld grnd: seems to act on any trk though clearly suited by a sharpish one.   **34**

--   SIRDAR FLYER [20] 3-8-11 I Johnson 33/1: 4300-0: Fair effort on reappearance: speedily bred filly who showed some promise last term: acts on gd & yld grnd & on any trk.   **30**

--   AUNT ETTY [1] 3-8-11 S Keightley 50/1: -0: Kept on late on reappearance.   **29**

--   SWEDISH PRINCESS [11] 3-8-11 R Hills 8/1: -0: Easy to back and lost place ½way.   **00**

--	Lady Bishop [2] 8-11	111	Hachimitsu [10] 8-11	--	Sybil Fawlty [7] 8-11(HD)
--	Dasa Queen [14] 8-11	--	Velvet Pearl [13] 8-11.		
--	Aircraftie [15] 8-11	213	Hardy Chance [8] 8-11	--	La Chula [4] 8-11
123	Miss Brahms [17] 8-11	--	Naughty Nighty [18] 8-11		
--	Sokolova [9] 8-11	--	Young Heroine [5] 8-11		
--	Eastern Lass [16] 8-11				

20 ran   6,4,1½,1½,½,¼   (Donald T Johnson)   J Tree Beckhampton Wilts

339 AVON HANDICAP 3YO 0-35   £1238   5f   Yielding 108 +06 Fast   [41]

--   IMPALA LASS [4] (B Mcmahon) 3-8-7 J Hills(5) 7/1: 40301-1: 3 b f Kampala or Malinowski - Shell-Na-Gig (Ridan): Nicely bckd on reappearance and gamely made all in quite a fast run 3yo h'cap at Warwick Apr.28: ended last season with an all the way win in a seller at Catterick, after earlier being placed in similar company: well suited by this minimum trip: acts on gd/firm & yld grnd: best with forcing tactics on a sharpish trk: could win again.   **32**

+255 LOCH FORM [3] (C Tinkler) 3-8-11(7ex) M Birch 11/4 FAV: 00-012: Came late, just failed: good effort under her penalty: see 255.   **33**

161 OLE FLO [12] (K Brassey) 3-8-12(BL) T Ives 4/1: 233-033: Bl first time: ran on well and not btn far: a good effort: see 161.   **33**

161 LIBERTON BRAE [14] (J Bethell) 3-8-6 J Reid 10/1: 0020-44: Stayed on late: see 161.   **23**

205 CRESTA LEAP [1] 3-9-7 S Cauthen 11/2: 4340-30: Remains in gd form: see 205.   **34**

--   GLEADHILL PARK [7] 3-8-11 N Adams 20/1: 004-0: Some late prog & should do btr next time: showed impr form on his final start last season when 4th to Merlin's Magic at Folkestone: eff over 5/6f on firm & yld grnd: suited by a sharpish trk.   **15**

246	Hobournes Katie [10] 8-5			--	Commander Meaden [8] 8-5(7ow)
38	Stromberg [11] 7-7(3oh)			--	Taylors Taylormade [9] 8-2
205	Kelly Lindo [6] 7-13	--	Choristers Dream [5] 8-8(bl)		
--	Metal Woods Rule [2] 7-13			--	Skylin [13] 8-7

14 ran   ¾,hd,1½,1½,3   (P Willett)   B Mcmahon Tamworth, Staffs

---

BRIGHTON   Monday April 28th   Lefthand, Sharpish Undulating Track

Official Going Given as Good/Soft

340 CONFLANS HANDICAP 0-35 3YO   £2278   6f   Good 57 +02 Fast   [39]

228 EXAMINATION [4] (A Bailey) 3-9-7(bl) G Carter(3) 9/4 FAV: 030-121: 3 b g Cawston's Clown - Ixia (I Say): In fine form, well bckd and led inside the final 1f, driven out in a 3yo h'cap at Brighton Apr.28: first time out won similar event at Haydock: also just btn in a 3yo h'cap at Newmarket: in '85 won at Catterick: half brother to 2 winners: eff at 5/6f, may stay 7f: acts on gd & soft grnd & on any trk: seemed a genuine sort though wears bl.   **43**

233 HAIL AND HEARTY [3] (R Smyth) 3-8-12 P Robinson 12/1: 400-02: Led ½way: gd effort: lightly raced in '85, half brother to 7/8f winner Imperial Salute: stays 6f: acts on gd & firm & on any trk.   **30**

274 NANOR [7] (W Kemp) 3-8-5 C Rutter(5) 12/1: 314-003: Ev ch over 1f out: impr effort: in '85 won a nursery selling h'cap at Lingfield: eff over 6f, stays 1m: acts on firm & yld and on any trk.   **18**

--   DEPUTY TIM [8] (J Bethell) 3-9-5(bl) W Carson 9/1: 0002-4: Good late hdway on seasonal debut and should do much btr next time: on final outing in '85 fin 2nd to Young Jason at Leicester: eff at 6f, may stay further: acts on gd & firm grnd & on any trk.   **32**

--   WILLBE WILLBE [6] 3-8-5 G Baxter 20/1: 30000-0: Ev ch over 2f out: btr for race: first time out in '85 fin 3rd in a fillies maiden at Newcastle: eff at 5/6f: acts on gd ground and on any trk.   **13**

111 COUNT ALMAVIVA [9] ⁻3-8-13 R Cochrane 20/1: 000-00: Never nearer: lightly raced in '85, but showed some promise: half brother to winning sprinter Boot Polish.   **20**

-- **WAVEGUIDE** [10] 3-9-5 P Cook 11/2: 424-0: Never nearer 7th on seasonal debut: placed on all 3 outings in '85: speedily bred and is a half sister to several winners: acts on gd & firm & on any trk: should be btr next time. **00**

-- **TUMBLE FAIR** [16] 3-9-3 R Wernham 9/1: 4014-0: There ½way on seasonal debut: btr for race: in '85 won a maiden at Bath: half sister to several winners: eff at 5f on gd/firm & yld & a gall trk. **00**

30	ALICE HILL [12] 3-8-11 T Williams 10/1: 0040-00: Mkt drifter: early ldr.					**00**
--	Witham Girl [15] 8-3	228	Topeka Express [14] 9-5			
--	Hopefull Dancer [13] 8-13			111	Rebello Imp [17] 8-7(BL)	
--	Delta Rose [1] 8-9	--	Noras Boy [2] 8-7	111	Hooray Hamilton [11] 8-6	
--	Pegasus Lady [18] 8-4	--	Fancy Pages [5] 8-8			
18 ran	2,2,nk,1½,½	(T P Ramsden)		A Bailey Newmarket		

341   TOWN PURSE HANDICAP 0-35   £1934   1m 2f   Good 57 +09 Fast   [34]

*202 **HOLYPORT VICTORY** [13] (M Usher) 4-9-4(4ex) M Wigham 9/2: 30-4011: 4 br c Free State - Snow Goose (Santa Claus): In fine form, led inside the final 1f, ridden out in quite a fast run h'cap at Brighton Apr.28: last time out won a similar event at Folkestone: winning 2yo again at Folkestone: eff at 10/12f: acts on gd & soft/heavy grnd and likes a sharpish, undulating trk, especially Folkestone. **35**

179 **DETROIT SAM** [16] (R Akehurst) 5-9-5 G Baxter 7/2 FAV: 0000-22: Led 3f out: just btn and 8L clear 3rd: in good form and should win soon: see 179. **34**

235 **SUGAR PALM** [11] (R Hannon) 5-9-2(bl) A Mcglone 8/1: 0010-03: Al up there: in '85 won a Lingfield & Leicester: eff over 10/12f, stays 2m plus: acts on any going and seems suited by forcing tactics. **19**

-- **THE YOMPER** [1] (D Elsworth) 4-9-3 P Mcentee(7) 11/1: -0200-4: Fit from hurdling: made most: maiden over both hurdles & on the Flat: best effort in '85 when 2nd in a h'cap at Kempton: suited by forcing tactics over 12f on a sharpish trk: acts on gd & yld. **15**

-- **PRIMROSE WAY** [4] 4-8-4 R Cochrane 16/1: 30000-0: Al there on seasonal debut: maiden: best effort in '85 when 3rd in a stakes event at Windsor: eff at 10/12f: acts on good & soft & likes a sharpish trk. **00**

92 **ROYAL CRAFTSMAN** [3] 5-8-3 P Robinson 14/1: 0-10-00: Nearest fin: lightly raced on the Flat in '85, winning over this C/D: eff at 12f, stays further: acts on gd & heavy. **00**

36	FLOREAT FLOREAT [14] 4-8-3 W Carson 10/1: 3300-00: Very active in mkt, but no show.				**00**
--	Fort Nayef [8] 8-11	208	Crook N Honest [20] 8-1		
--	Wild Ginger [18] 8-11	--	Kiki Star [6] 8-11	--	Inchgower [2] 8-6
--	Mishrif [9] 9-7	201	Topori [17] 7-11	--	Pooella [12] 8-1
--	True Weight [19] 9-1	129	Gorgeous Princess [15] 8-6		
88	Flame Flower [10] 7-13(BL)			--	Janaab [5] 9-0
--	Mijas Golf [7] 8-3 P				
20 ran	¾,8,3,1,1	(Holyport Bloodstock Ltd)		M Usher Lambourn, Berks	

342   PRINCE OF WALES STAKES 3YO   £3350   1m 2f   Good 57 -11 Slow

+218 **ARMADA** [3] (G Harwood) 3-9-9 G Starkey 1/5 FAV: -11: 3 b c Shirley Heights - If (Kashmir II): Smart colt: had a simple task and gained a cheeky neck success in a 4 runner stakes event at Brighton Apr.28: first time out was a highly impressive 8L winner of the Wood Ditton at Newmarket: cost 1 million gns as a yearling: eff at 1m, stays 10f & should get 12f: acts on gd & yld & on any trk: now going for the Mecca-Dante at York & will probably by-pass the Epsom Derby & possibly go for the French equivalent. **75**

-- **WASSL REEF** [1] (J Dunlop) 3-9-0 W Carson 5/1: 22-2: Ran on well final 1f to get within a neck of Armada but the winner was only toying with him: nevertheless a good seasonal debut: fin 2nd both starts in '85, at Doncaster & York: cost 480,000 gns: eff at 10f, should be suited by 12f: acts on gd & yld & on any trk: should be winning soon. **59**

193 **SPROWSTON BOY** [4] (P Kelleway) 3-9-9 Gay Kelleway(5) 25/1: 22-1133: Stiff task: led ½way: see 132: acts on good & heavy. **38**

275 **SALES PROMOTER** [2] (K Cunningham Brown) 3-9-0 S Whitworth 100/1: 000-04: Impossible task: led 5f. **00**

4 ran   nk,20,dist   (K Abdulla)   G Harwood Pulborough, Sussex

343   PETWORTH SELLING HANDICAP 3YO+ 0-25   £1033   1m 2f   Good 57 -18 Slow   [24]

177 **CANDAULES** [8] (C James) 8-8-4 B Rouse 25/1: -01: 8 b g Supreme Sovereign - Sweet And Naughty (Connaught): Caused a 25/1 surprise, led approaching final 1f, ridden out in a selling h'cap at Brighton Apr.28 (bought in 1,700 gns): eff at 10f on gd ground: seems best on a sharpish trk. **09**

10 **MOONDAWN** [9] (M Usher) 5-10-0 R Cochrane 9/1: 0040-02: Ran on well under top weight: good effort: in '85 won a h'cap at Hamilton and a selling h'cap (awarded race) at Salisbury: in '84 won at Newbury & Haydock: eff at 6f, stays 10f: acts on firm & soft grnd & on any trk: carries weight well. **28**

-- TRACK MARSHALL [17] (J Davies) 4-9-1 M Wigham 8/1: 00300-3: Kept on well on seasonal debut: best effort in '85 when 3rd in an app. stakes at Leicester: eff at 10f on gd & firm ground: trained by H Candy last season.   14

201 MEZIARA [15] (A Ingham) 5-9-4(bl) L Riggio(7) 7/1: 420-224: Made much: btr 201 (soft).   13

-- NOBLE PHILIP [13] 9-8-4 A Clark 20/1: -0: Early ldr, rem. prom: off the trk for a long time: in '81 won at Lingfield: probably stays 10f: acts on firm & yld.   00

-- RESISTER [12] 6-8-5 C Rutter(5) 10/1: -0: Active in mkt: prom, ev ch: last won in '83 at Edinburgh: acts on gd ground.   00

-- UNDER THE STARS [4] 4-9-4 G Baxter 9/2 FAV: 00300-0: Well bckd: ev ch 1m: best effort in '85 when 3rd in a 6 runner maiden at Epsom: eff over 1m on fast grnd & a sharpish trk: should win a seller.   00

36 TRUMPS [2] 6-8-13 W Carson 5/1: 3104-00: No threat.   00

119 GAMBART [20] 4-9-6(vis) R Carter(5) 11/2: 0000-30: Btr in 119 (9f, heavy).   00

--	Chalet Waldegg [3] 8-6			201	Blairs Winnie [22] 8-2(1ow)
22	Danedancer [7] 8-5(bl)			201	Unit Tent [5] 8-6(bl)
177	Roberts Girl [6] 8-7	119	Tame Duchess [14] 8-9	201	Lord Butch [10] 9-2
--	Gold Hunter [1] 8-8	--	Fire Chieftain [11] 8-4		
201	Casbar Kid [16] 8-4(vis)			177	Nicanic [18] 8-4
--	Havers Road [19] 8-6				

21 ran   3,shhd,2,7,¾   (C James)   C James East Garston, Berks

---

344   SIDNEY THOMPSON MEM EBF STAKES 3YO+   £3915   1m   Good 57 -01 Slow

-- PRESIDIUM [15] (H Cecil) 4-9-0 W Ryan 5/1: 12-03-1: 4 b c General Assembly - Doubly Sure (Reliance II): Very useful colt: led fully 3f out and stayed on gamely by a shhd in a stakes event at Brighton Apr.28: lightly raced in '85, as he suffered a back problem: very smart 2yo, winning a minor event at Yarmouth and then fin 2nd to Local Suitor in Mill Reef Stakes at Newbury: eff over 6f, stays 1m well: acts on firm & yld grnd: genuine sort who is a full brother to the top class miler Kris.   65

+210 CRESTA AUCTION [3] (G Pritchard Gordon) 3-8-1 G Carter(3) 15/8 FAV: 413-112: Chall final 1f: btn a whisker and 5L clear 3rd: in excellent form this season: should win more races.   68

17 DORSET COTTAGE [8] (W Jarvis) 4-9-0 B Rouse 20/1: -021-03: No ch with first 2 but a good effort: lightly raced gelding who in '85 broke the course record in a maiden at Beverley: very eff at 1m on gd & firm grnd: acts on any trk.   53

-- FREEDOMS CHOICE [2] (J Dunlop) 4-9-7 W Carson 12/1: 21213-4: Mkt drifter, nearest fin on seasonal debut: should do btr next time: in grand form in the second half of '85, winning at Newbury & Haydock and was placed on several occasions: very eff over 1m, stays 10f: acts on gd/firm & soft and on any trk: genuine & should be winning soon.   53

220 FOUZ [11] 3-8-1 T Quinn 5/2: 020-340: Well bckd: never nearer: best in 60 (soft/heavy).   50

112 DOLLY [17] 4-8-11 M Wigham 33/1: 0000-00: Ran remarkably well: officially rated 23: in '85 won a moderate fillies maiden at Lingfield: eff at 6f, stays 1m: acts on gd/firm & soft: best on a sharpish trk.   36

*277 GEORDIES DELIGHT [10] 3-7-11 B Crossley 6/1: 0-210: Btr in 277 (7f, heavy).   00

203	Gibbous Moon [16] 9-0	--	Marsh Harrier [13] 9-4		
203	Bolivia [7] 8-4	49	Rethymno [6] 8-1	--	Clarances Hope [1] 9-0
--	Mind The Time [4] 9-0	199	Mount Argus [5] 9-0	174	Mr Mcgregor [14] 9-0
--	Angies Video [12] 8-11			--	Zeldas Fancy [9] 9-0

17 ran   shhd,5,3,shhd,1½   (Lord Howard de Walden)   H Cecil Newmarket

---

345   ORLEANS MAIDEN STAKES 2YO   £959   5f   Good 57 -43 Slow

-- EASA [3] (M Tompkins) 2-9-0 R Cochrane 12/1: 1: 2 b c Scorpio - Gavina (Val De Loir): Made a winning racecourse debut, led inside the final 1f, ridden out in a maiden at Brighton Apr.28: cost 3,200 gns and is a half brother to 10-14f winner Purns Mill: eff at 5f, looks sure to stay much further: acts on gd grnd and a sharpish trk.   43

230 RIMBEAU [6] (C Nelson) 2-9-0 A Clark 3/1 FAV: 42: Led 2f till inside final 1f: good effort: acts on gd & heavy: see 230.   39

-- LOMA BREEZE [8] (P Kelleway) 2-8-11 P Cook 7/2: -3: Mkt drifter: kept on well final 1f, showing some promise: eff at 5f, should stay further: acts on gd grnd & a sharpish trk.   32

-- LITTLE KEY [10] (N Callaghan) 2-9-0 M L Thomas 12/1: 4: Never nearer: should impr: bred to stay further than 5f.   25

206 LAST RECOVERY [9] 2-8-11 P Robinson 5/1: 30: Btr in 206 (heavy).   20

-- CHERRYWOOD STAR [1] 2-9-0 G Baxter 16/1: 0: Mkt drifter: no show: speedily bred.   22

-- GLAMIS GIRL [4] 2-8-11 S Whitworth 4/1: -0: Mkt drifter: early ldr: speedily bred.   00

252 PERIGRIS [2] 2-8-11 A Mcglone 7/2: 00: Well bckd: fdd: cost I.R. 7,000: half sister to winning 2yo General Breyfax.   00

--	Downsview Lady [5] 8-11		27	Prince Mac [7] 9-0

10 ran   1½,1½,4,½,hd   (Stanley Squires)   M Tompkins Newmarket

BATH   Tuesday April 29th   Lefthanded Galloping Track

Official Going Given as Good

346 SPA SELLING STAKES 3YO   £834   1m   Yielding 98 -20 Slow

209 TAKE A BREAK [14] (D Laing) 3-8-4 S Dawson(3) 5/4 FAV: 0020-01: 3 br f Take A Reef -
Vacation (Remainder): Comfortably justified fav. in a 3yo seller at Bath Apr.29, led below
dist and ridden out: ran up in similar company at Wolverhampton & Warwick last season: eff
over 8/9f on firm & heavy grnd: well suited by a gall trk.   20
111 FIRST ORBIT [10] (M Mccormack) 3-8-7 R Wernham 9/1: 0000-02: Dropped to selling
company and trying a longer trip: ev ch, kept on well: eff over 5/6f & stays 1m: suited by
some give in the ground.   16
141 DELTA LIMA [7] (G Kindersley) 3-8-7(bl) J Reid 11/2: 200-003: Dropped in class: made
most: ran up to Moorgate Man in a stakes at Windsor early last season, subsq. lightly raced:
stays 1m: acts on gd/firm & soft ground & on any trk: should find a seller.   15
-- BAO [4] (J Cosgrave) 3-8-4 W Hayes(7) 8/1: -4: Bckd from 33/1 on racecourse debut:
ran on too late: eff over 1m on yld grnd: acts on a gall trk: worth noting next time.   07
*207 FIC VIC [9] 3-8-12 C Rutter(5) 17/2: 000-010: Btr on an easier trk in 207.   00
-- TINSEL ROSE [11] 3-8-4 P Cook 33/1: 40-0: Nearest fin on reappearance: only ran twice
last season and was well btn in modest company on both occasions: half sister to a couple of
winners: acts on yld grnd & on a gall trk.   00
207 Hannah Reed [8] 8-4   205 Winters Beta [5] 8-4   93 Jultown Lad [3] 8-7
205 Sweet Fool [13] 8-4   -- Chagunola [6] 8-4   -- Nenuco [12] 8-4
93 The Tender Matador [2] 8-12   -- Jeanne Jugan [1] 8-4
14 ran   3,hd,3,8,1,½   (Ian M McGready)   D Laing Lambourn, Berks

347 BLATHWYATT MAIDEN STAKES 3YO   £1176   1m 4f Yielding 98 +01 Fast

231 ROSEDALE USA [14] (J Dunlop) 3-9-0 B Thomson 10/11 FAV: -2-21: 3 b c Vaguely Noble -
Ivory (Riverman): Useful colt: heavily bckd when leading 2 out, staying on under press in
a 3yo maiden at Bath Apr.29: ran up to Tommy Way in a similar race at Haydock last term and
recently fin. 2nd to Paean at Newbury: eff around 11/12f: acts on yld & heavy grnd and
on a gall trk.   50
-- ACTINIUM [13] (P Cole) 3-9-0 T Quinn 10/1: 043-2: Stayed on well & should win a
similar race soon: placed in 2 of his 3 starts last season and is a half brother to several
winners: eff around 10/12f on firm & yld grnd: runs well on a gall trk.   46
231 DUNCAN IDAHO [11] (R Johnson Houghton) 3-9-0 J Reid 11/2: -03: Al up there and ran
well: eff around 11f on yld & heavy grnd: acts on a gall trk: on the up grade: see 231.   42
140 BETTER BEWARE [4] (I Balding) 3-9-0 Pat Eddery 9/1: 00-34: Had ev ch: stays 11f: see 140 35
-- BEYBARS [5] 3-9-0 W Carson 14/1: 230-0: Active in mkt on reapp: led ½way till 2f
out: btr for race: showed plenty of promise last season, when twice placed in fair company:
cost 530,000gns : is a half brother to several winners, incl smart sprinter Music Maestro: eff
over 8/11f: acts on gd & yld grnd and on any trk.   28
-- TURFAH [12] 3-9-0 N Howe 7/1: 3400-0: Short lived effort early in str: nicely bred
colt who showed promise last season, notably when 4th to Oriental Soldier at Salisbury:
eff over 7/8f and should stay this trip: acts on gd & yld grnd & on any trk.   23
-- IGHTHAM [7] 3-9-0 G Starkey 9/1: -0: Debutant who never threatened after a slow start.   00
-- Polecroft [15] 9-0(BL)   -- Abydos [16] 9-0
231 Billilla [6] 9-0   -- Hello Georgie [10] 9-0
139 Grand Fling [9] 9-0   162 Miranol Venture [3] 8-11
-- Nautical Step [2] 8-11
14 ran   2,2½,4,4,3,1½   (N B Hunt)   J Dunlop Arundel, Sussex

348 SOMERSET EBF STAKES 3YO   £4103   1m 2f Yielding 98 +06 Fast

224 PLAID [2] (P Walwyn) 3-8-13 N Howe 11/10 FAV: 132-31: 3 b c Martinmas - Lanata
(Charlottown): Very useful colt: easily justified fav. leading over 2f out in quite a fast
run 3yo stakes at Bath Apr.29: last season won a valuable maiden at Ascot and first time out
this term was a fine 3rd to Flying Trio at Newmarket: half brother to winners abroad: very
eff over 9/10f: acts on firm & soft grnd & is well suited by a gall trk: looks sure to
win more races.   68
191 GORGEOUS STRIKE [6] (C Nelson) 3-8-13 J Reid 12/1: 123-02: Not reach winner though
stayed on well: comfortably beat the rem: see 191.   55
116 PRINCE MERANDI [1] (M Francis) 3-8-8 A Clark 25/1: 0-133: Led before ½way: good effort
in this top company: well suited by a gall trk: see 25.   38
-- ROBBAMA [4] (J Dunlop) 3-8-13 R Fox 9/4: 110-4: Never a threat on reappearance and
needs faster ground: very promising juvenile last season when winning at Goodwood and
Sandown: cost $700,000: very eff over 1m and looks sure to stay further: acts on any trk:
sure to win more races when the ground dries out.   35
-- FAMILY FRIEND [5] 3-8-13 W Carson 15/2: 41240-4: Led early: btr for race: last season
made all, gamely at Sandown: later was just btn by Oriental Soldier at Salisbury: very eff
over 7/8f: acts on firm & yld grnd and is suited by a gall trk.   35
-- LANDMARK [3] 3-8-8 Pat Eddery 11/2: -0: Nicely bckd on racecourse debut, though slowly
away and never reached ldrs: half brother to several winners, incl very useful pair Castle
Rising and Leading Star: sure to be suited by middle dists: acts on yld grnd: will do
btr next time.   28
6 ran   5,7,5,ddht,1   (A D Oldrey)   P Walwyn, Lambourn, Berks

349   EMPIRE HANDICAP STAKES 0-50 4YO+   £2897   1m 4f   Yielding 98 +04 Fast   [50]

333 STAR OF IRELAND [13] (G Price) 6-8-2 G King(7) 15/2: -00-101: 6 b g Star Appeal -
Belligerent (Roan Rocket): Made a quick reapp. and proved an effortless winner, led 3f out
and cruised clear in quite a fast run h'cap at Bath Apr.29: recent winner over hurdles and
won a h'cap at Warwick last month with similar ease: last season won at Lingfield & in '83
at Kempton: eff over 8/12f on firm & heavy grnd: acts on any trk, though does well on a
sharpish one: should certainly win again in this form.   40
189 MOON JESTER [10] (M Usher) 6-7-12 D Mckay 8/1: 040-002: Stayed on well to take the
minor honours: nicely bckd today: last won in '83, at Newbury & Kempton: eff over 8/12f on
good/firm & soft ground: acts on any trk.   20
--   BALLET CHAMP [17] (R Holder) 8-7-13 A Proud 20/1: 10042-3: Easy to back on seasonal
debut: nearest fin and needs further: last season won at Ascot & Warwick: eff over 2/2m2f:
acts on firm & yld grnd & on any trk: has to be held up for a late chall.   20
263 BOLD ILLUSION [3] (M Eckley) 8-7-8 L Riggio(7) 4/1 FAV: 104-1U4: Bolted before
start, went on after ½way: fair effort though btr judged on his win in 23.   14
--   MOORLAND LADY [16] 4-8-7 G Carter(3) 25/1: 20130-0: Mkt drifter on reappearance:
quite consistent last season, when successful in a fillies maiden at Haydock: eff over
10/11f: acts on yld/soft grnd & on a gall trk.   25
--   GOING GOING [9] 7-9-2 P Johnson(7) 12/1: 42114-0: Nearest fin on reappearance: should
do btr next time: useful h'capper who won at Epsom, Windsor & Kempton last season: in '84
also won at Windsor: eff over 11/12f: genuine & consistent sort who acts on any going &
on any trk: carries weight well.   32
--   PARANG [12] 5-7-12 N Howe 9/1: 01230-0: Fit from hurdling: nicely bckd, no threat.   00
179 LONGSTOP [5] 4-8-1 G Baxter 6/1: 1134-30: Well bckd though ran below par: see 179.   00
--   BASSIM [1] 4-9-8(BL) Pat Eddery 9/1: --431-0: Bl first time: never beyond mid-div.   00
--   KUWAIT MUTAR [11] 4-8-1 A Shoults(5) 7/1: 00-0-0: Gambled on though was last to fin.   00
--   Traffitanzi [3] 7-7(3oh)   92   Derryring [20] 9-0
--   Dancing Barron [14] 8-6   4   Honeydew Wonder [6] 9-1
--   Anything Else [2] 8-4   --   Picadilly Prince [7] 8-7
265 Christian Schad [19] 9-13   92   Signorina Odone [4] 7-13
202 Ricco Star [8] 7-8(BL)
19 ran   4,1,hd,1,1,shhd   (H K Strickland)   G Price Leominster, Hereford

350   EBF HODCOTT MAIDEN STAKES 2YO   £1264   5f   Yielding 98 -26 Slow

--   JAISALMER [5] (D Elsworth) 2-8-11 A Mcglone 5/1: 1: 2 b f Castle Keep - Sabala
(Tribal Chief): Active in mkt on racecourse debut, was a ready winner, led inside dist. in
a 2yo maiden at Bath Apr.29: half sister to a couple of winners: ef, over 5f: sure to stay
further: acts on yld grnd & on a gall trk: promising filly who should win more races.   48
--   JAH BLESS [5] (P Haynes) 2-9-0 N Howe 20/1: 2: Led briefly inside dist: promising
effort from this 13,000 gns purchase: suited by this minimum trip: acts on yld grnd & on
a stiff trk.   40
--   THE DOMINICAN [1] (B Hills) 2-9-0 B Thomson 7/2: 3: Nicely bckd debutant: ran on
promisingly, never nearer: cost 19,000 gns as a yearling: speedily bred colt who acts on
yld ground & on a gall trk: seems sure to improve.   36
170 TEZ SHIKARI [7] (L Cottrell) 2-9-0 N Carlisle 20/1: 04: Friendless in mkt though
al front rank: impr effort & should win a small race on a sharp trk: acts on yld: see 170.   35
--   SPANISH SKY [2] 2-8-11 P Cook 15/8 FAV: 0: Heavily bckd debutant: broke well and
made most: cost 8,400 gns and is a half brother to middle dist. winner Glideaway: acts on
yld grnd and on a gall trk: should impr for this experience.   24
--   THE LIONHEART [11] 2-9-0 R Street 16/1: 0: Stayed on promisingly and will do btr
next time.   27
34   MARK SEAGULL [8] 2-9-0 W Carson 10/1: 00: Mkt drifter: showed some impr today.   00
--   IMAGINARY SKY [9] 2-9-0 R Cochrane 9/1: 0: Mkt drifter on debut: never dangerous.   00
187 CASTLE CORNET [14] 2-9-0 Pat Eddery 7/1: 00: Easy to back: showed plenty of pace till
½way: see 187.   00
--   Imperial Friend [6] 8-11   --   Sleepline For Pine [10] 9-0
206 Record Flight [3] 8-11   252 Folly Gale [4] 8-11
170 Brushford [13] 9-0
14 ran   3,1½,shhd,4,shhd   (Lady Scott)   D Elsworth Whitsbury, Hants

351   BLATHWYATT MAIDEN STAKES 3YO   £1171   1m 4f   Yielding 98 -03 Slow

--   GOLDEN HEIGHTS [7] (P Walwyn) 3-9-0 Pat Eddery 1/1 FAV: 43-1: 3 b c Shirley Heights -
Yelney (Blakeney): Heavily bckd on reappearance, led in str for a decisive win in a
3yo maiden at Bath Apr.29: nicely bred colt who cost 74,000 gns as a yearling: showed promise
on both starts last season: acts on gd & yld grnd and on a gall trk: should win more races
over middle dists this term.   58
--   ALLATUM [1] (B Hills) 3-8-11 B Thomson 20/1: -2: Friendless in the mkt on racecourse
debut though showed plenty of promise and should certainly find a small race soon: stays
11f well: acts on yld grnd & on a gall trk.   42

-- BASTINADO [16] (I Balding) 3-9-0 J Matthias 20/1: -3: Easy to back: kept on well and
is certain to impr for this experience: half brother to the fair River Spey: acts on yld
ground and on a stiff trk: should find a similar race in the near future.   45
-- ALARM CALL [2] (3/1) 3-9-0 G Starkey 3/1: -4: Had ev ch on his racecourse debut:
clearly acts on yld grnd and on a gall trk.   41
-- LAW COURT [3] 3-9-0 R Curant 8/1: 0-0: Nicely bckd, stayed on well in str and should
do btr next time.   31
-- SHIRLSTAR TAXSAVER [4] 3-9-0 W Carson 33/1: 00-0: Ran on well from the rear: friendless
in the mkt today and should impr on this effort next time.   29
-- MINISTRAILIS [13] 3-9-0 T Quinn 6/1: 00-0: Nicely bckd on reappearance: al mid-div.   00
276 Mightily [11] 9-0   173 Tudor Dor [9] 8-11   162 Battle Fleet [10] 8-11
140 Blushing Spy [6] 9-0   -- Gay Caruso [14] 9-0   191 Eastern Player [5] 9-0
-- Tremendous Jet [15] 9-0   -- Deruta [8] 8-11
90 Summerhill Rock [12] 9-0
16 ran   8,hd,1½,6,1½,2   (P Goulandris)   P Walwyn Lambourn, Berks

352 ILCHESTER HANDICAP STAKES 3YO 0-50   £2704   1m   Yielding 98 -08 Slow   [43]

234 FRAMLINGTON COURT [8] (P Walwyn) 3-9-6 N Howe 7/1: 200-2D1: 3 gr c High Top -
Princess Runnymede (Runnymede): Useful colt on his day: ran on strongly to lead close home
in a 3yo h'cap at Bath Apr.29: showed promise, without winning, last season though did show
signs of temperament: half brother to a couple of winners: eff over 6/8f: acts on gd &
heavy ground and is suited by a gall trk.   45
-- MEET THE GREEK [2] (D Laing) 3-9-2 J Reid 10/1: 20202-2: Led below dist, just caught
on reappearance: fine effort: showed plenty of promise last season, especially early on when
running up to Bakharoff and Cliveden at Sandown & Goodwood respectively: stays 1m well:
acts on firm & yld grnd & on any trk: looks fairly h'capped.   40
216 EMRYS [4] (N Vigors) 3-9-4 P Cook 10/1: 002-103: Ev ch, not btn far: stays 1m: see 33.   40
127 PORO BOY [7] (C Williams) 3-9-7 P Waldron 9/1: 00-34: Ran on too late: still a good
effort: see 127.   40
216 BELOW ZERO [6] 3-9-7 G Carter(3) 3/1: 02-1220: Well bckd: slightly below par: see 216.   35
-- ARABIAN BLUES [3] 3-8-6 D Mckay 11/1: 001-0: Never nearer on seasonal debut: ended
last term with a decisive win on heavy ground at Hamilton: stays 1m: suited by some give
in the ground.   16
*157 BOWL OVER [9] 3-9-7 G Baxter 11/2: 4302-10: Went on 2f out, soon lost his pitch
and this run can be ignored: much btr in 157.   00
-- SYNTHETIC [12] 3-9-2 W Carson 13/2: 4010-0: Nicely bckd though never threatened on
reappearance.   00
157 MODENA REEF [11] 3-9-3(BL) Pat Eddery 11/4 FAV: 300-30: Bl first time: trailed in
last after making most: btr in 157.   00
67 Miss Harlequin [10] 7-11   -- Stanford Vale [1] 8-5
-- Spinnaker Lady [5] 7-13
12 ran   ½,1,2,2,2½   (L A Smith)   P Walwyn Lambourn, Berks

NOTTINGHAM   Tuesday April 29th   Lefthand, Fair Track

Official Going Given as Good/Soft

353 CINDERHILL MAIDEN FILLIES STAKES 2YO   £1022   5f   Soft 139 -35 Slow

252 FOUR LAFFS [6] (D Leslie)   2-8-11 John Williams 10/3 FAV: -0231: 2 ch f Free State -
Spur Ride (Comedy Star): Gained a deserved success, led inside the final 1f, ridden out in
a fillies maiden at Nottingham Apr.29: eff at 5f, should be suited by 6/7f: acts on
soft ground.   42
170 DOUBLE TALK [10] (H O'neill) 2-8-11 S Whitworth 20/1: 042: Mkt drifter: tried to
make all: good effort and is on the up grade: speedily bred filly who acts on soft & yld
and should find a small maiden on an easy/sharpish trk.   37
-- CHEVSKA [8] (D Morley) 2-8-11 M Birch 16/1: 3: Sn prom on debut: good effort: cost
10,000 gns: half sister to winning 2yo Northern Trust: should be suited by further than
5f: acts on soft grnd: impr likely.   37
-- ROUMELI [2] (Lord J Fitzgerald) 2-8-11 R Hills 15/2: 4: Mkt drifter on debut: kept
on and should impr: half sister to winning 2yos Andrios and Fassa: should be suited by 6f
plus: acts on soft.   30
73 PINTAFORY [14] 2-8-11 A Mackay 5/1: 00: Mkt drifter: btr 73.   26
223 FLAPPER GIRL [9] 2-8-11 W R Swinburn 7/2: 00: Sn prom: impr: dam lightly raced: acts
on soft.   25
-- SPEEDBIRD [1] 2-8-11 P Robinson 8/1: 0: Early speed on debut: fin 7th: half sister
to middle. dist. winner Joli's Girl: should do btr.   00
-- Belle Of Stars [4] 8-11   -- Thats Motoring [7] 8-11
-- Greens Gallery [3] 8-11   -- Peggys Treasure [12] 8-11
-- Linpac North Moor [11] 8-11   -- Nofandancer [13] 8-11
-- Dungehill Star [15] 8-11
14 ran   1½,hd,3,1½,½   (A C Birkle)   D Leslie Goadby, Leics

354 BAGTHORPE SELLING STAKES 2YO   £760   5f   Soft 139 -43 Slow

86   MONS FUTURE [3] (H O'neill) 2-8-8 S Whitworth 9/1: 01: 2 b f Monsanto - Future
Chance (Hopeful Venture): Made almost all, ridden out in a slow run 2yo seller at Nottingham
Apr.29 (bought in 1,600 gns): eff at 5f, should stay further: acts on soft grnd and seems
suited by forcing tactics.   24
94   SARASOTA [6] (C Wildman) 2-8-11 P Robinson 11/2: 002: Dropped to selling company:
stayed on well: cheaply acquired, but should find a seller: acts on soft grnd.   21
329   MI OH MY [1] (K Stone) 2-8-8 C Dwyer 8/1: 30233: Al there: consistent: see 181.   15
--   BAD PAYER [8] (M W Easterby) 2-8-9(1ow) M Hindley(0) 16/1: 4:.Nearest fin on debut:
cost 4,400 gns: acts on soft.   13
86   SAMS REFRAIN [5] 2-8-8 D Williams(7) 4/1: 30: Never nearer: see 86.   12
186   PRINCESS SINGH [4] 2-8-8 S Webster 2/1 FAV: 00: Again well bckd: wknd final 1f:
half sister to winning plater Kiki Star.   12
--   GLORIAD [2] 2-8-8 K Darley 7/1: 0: No show on debut.   00
329   BINGO QUEEN [7] 2-8-8 M Fry 7/2: 20: Much btr in 329 (stiff trk).   00
8 ran   2,1,1,shhd,shhd   (H O'Neill)   H O'Neill Coldharbour, Surrey

355 EASTWOOD HANDICAP (0-35) 3YO+   £1976   6f   Soft 139 +01 Fast   [35]

84   PINE HAWK [18] (D Haydn Jones) 5-7-12 D Williams(7) 12/1: 3004-41: 5 b h Algora   -
Paridance (Doudance): Led dist, ridden out in a h'cap at Nottingham Apr.29: first success:
eff at 5/6f: suited by soft grnd: acts on any trk.   16
-211 ROSIE DICKINS [4] (R Hollinshead) 4-8-8 R Lappin(7) 7/2 FAV: 300-122: Just btn: in
fine form: see 124.   24
240   GOLD DUCHESS [3] (M W Easterby) 4-8-0(bl) L Charnock 10/1: 0-04243: Made much: running
well: see 182, 124.   10
*283 JOVEWORTH [9] (J Glover) 3-8-9(7ex) M Birch 6/1: 0440-14: Hmpd slightly nearing final
1f: in good form: see 283.   30
--   CAPTAINS BIDD [15] 6-7-7(bl) M Fry 33/1: 04300-0: Sn prom on seasonal debut: yet to
win, but has been placed on several occasions: eff at 5/6f: acts on soft, suited by good
and firm: likes to force the pace.   00
211   EVEN BANKER [17] 7-8-0 K Darley 33/1: 0-00-00: Al there: last won in '82 at Kempton
and Doncaster and has been lightly raced since: stays 10f: acts on firm & soft.   01
240   HOPEFUL KATIE [7] 4-8-8(bl) J Williams 10/1: 000-430: Mkt drifter: best 65 (6f).   00
306   MARY MAGUIRE [1] 9-9-12 D Nicholls 15/2: 100-000: Sn prom, fin 9th: btr 306 (6f).   00
124   STEVEJAN [2] 4-7-8(BL) T Williams 11/2: 000-330: Bl first time: btr 124, 65 (6f).   00
211   Hilmay [11] 8-5   266 Port Mist [8] 7-8(1ow)   114 James De Coombe [6] 8-3
260   Throne Of Glory [16] 10-0   306 Karens Star [12] 9-6
--   Paddystown [14] 9-4   --   Philstar [13] 9-2   182 Grey Starlight [5] 8-2(2ow)
260   Great Relative [10] 7-12(BL)
18 ran   ½,2,1½,1,¾,shhd   (Mrs Jacqueline Wilkinson)   D Haydn Jones Efall Isaf, Glam

356 LANGWITH CLAIMING STAKES 3YO   £1476   1m 2f   Soft 139 -11 Slow

67   PATS JESTER [18] (P Rohan) 3-8-11 M Wood 8/1: 0040-41: 3 ch c Orchestra - Owey
(Sovereign Gleam): Impr colt: suited by extra 2f and led inside the final 1f, drawing clear
in a 3yo claimer at Nottingham Apr.29: first success: eff at 1m, suited by 10f: acts on
soft grnd and runs well at Nottingham.   25
*113 MATELOT ROYALE [11] (A Davison) 3-9-0 N Adams 14/1: 0-012: Fin well: in good form:
suited by 10f and may get further: should win again in selling company: see 113.   20
193   COSMIC FLIGHT [14] (M Usher) 3-9-1 M Wigham 14/1: 000-103: Led 3 out: beat winner
in 67 (1m).   19
171   FAST AND FRIENDLY [19] (R Hollinshead) 3-8-9 S Perks 16/1: 000-004: Ran on well and
going on fin: btr 171 (12f).   07
193   FLYING FLYNN [21] 3-8-11 S Cauthen 3/1 FAV: 21-2240: Btr 117 (sharper trk): see 67 (1m) 08
169   S S SANTO [12] 3-8-8 M Rimmer 11/1: 0-220: Much btr 169, 35.   00
--   LADY OWEN [9] 3-8-11 R Morse(5) 8/1: 2004-0: Never nearer 7th: should strip fitter
next time: lightly raced in '85, showing promise: eff at 10f, may stay 12f: acts on firm
and soft and should find a small event.   00
--   FOXCROFT [8] 3-8-6(vis) T Williams 8/1: 10022-0: Led over 4f on seasonal debut:
in '85 won a seller at Beverley: eff at 7f, stays 1m: acts on gd & firm & likes a stiff trk.   00
--   STANGRAVE [5] 3-8-11 M Miller 7/1: 33330-0: Mkt drifter: no show.   00
35   Arch Princess [20] 8-8(bl)   139 Solent Lad [16] 9-0
--   Holme Rook [22] 8-11   --   Grandangus [13] 8-10
--   Wine Festival [1] 8-8   120 Parkies Bar [3] 9-4(bl)
--   Resha [23] 9-0   --   Spring Flight [4] 9-0   --   Super Smart [10] 9-0
67   Way Above [2] 9-0   64   Belvel [18] 8-11   --   Tyrannise [15] 8-11
237   Geoffs Folly [6] 8-7
23 ran   5,1,3,¼,4,hd   (Yorkshire Racing Club Ltd)   P Rohan Norton, Yorks

357   FLYING HORSE MAIDEN STAKES 3YO   £2176   1m 2f   Soft 139 +01 Fast

-- **MILTESCENS** [1] (A Jarvis) 3-9-0 D Nicholls 20/1: 40033-1: 3 ch c Milford - Lutescens
(Skymaster): Made a winning seasonal debut, getting up on the post in a 3yo maiden at
Nottingham Apr.29: placed several times in '85: eff at 1m/10f, may stay 12f: acts on firm
& soft & a gall trk.   46
-- **ENBARR** [8] (H Cecil) 3-9-0 S Cauthen 8/11 FAV: 0-2: Heavily bckd on reappearance:
led inside final 1f, caught death: on sole start in '85, showed much promise when 5th in
a valuable maiden behind Simsim   at York: half brother to Cheshire Oaks winner
Hunston: eff at 10f, may stay further: acts on yld & soft: should go one btr next time.   46
140 **HIGHEST PEAK** [13] (G Pritchard Gordon) 3-9-0 W Ryan 7/1: 000-23: Led 2f out: good
effort and is on the up grade: should win soon: see 140.   44
-- **CALL TO HONOR** [11] (O Douieb)(BL) R Machado 14/1: -4: Bl debutant: never nearer:
impr likely: dam a prolific winner: eff at 10f, should stay 12f: acts on soft ground.   41
-- **MOUNT OLYMPUS** [5] 3-9-0 T Ives 7/2: 04-0: Nicely bckd on seasonal debut: made much:
btr for race: showed promise on both starts in '85, notably when 4th to Nomrood in a
competitive maiden at Newmarket: brother to the useful 1m winner Crampon: eff at 1m, should
stay 10f: acts on firm & soft grnd.   32
-- **ALDINO** [12] 3-9-0 M Roberts 33/1: 00-0: Good seasonal debut: highly tried in 2
outings in '85: eff at 1m on soft grnd: should continue to impr.   29

--	Le Moulin [9] 9-0	194	Run By Jove [19] 9-0(BL)			
--	Noble Viking [16] 9-0	140	Royal Effigy [18] 9-0	--	Kookys Pet [10] 9-0	
--	Quezal [17] 9-0	--	Rye Hill Mariner [22] 9-0			
--	Tender Type [20] 9-0	--	Canadian Star [6] 9-0	--	Dunston [3] 9-0	
--	Hidden Move [14] 9-0	--	Majestician [7] 9-0	--	Sender [21] 9-0	
--	Ashford Lass [1] 8-11	--	Tanagon [2] 8-11	229	Willwood [4] 9-0	

22 ran   shhd,1,1½,5,1½,1½   (A H Mansfield)   A Jarvis Royston, Herts

358   FOREST HANDICAP (0-35) 4YO+   £1578   1m 6f   Soft 139 +07 Fast   [34]

204 **LOVE WALKED IN** [18] (W Holden) 5-8-4 R Morse(5) 3/1 FAV: 0-00131: 5 ch c Hotfoot -
Love Resolved (Dan Cupid): In fine form, ran on well to lead close home in quite a fast run
h'cap at Nottingham Apr.29: earlier won a similar event again at Nottingham: stays 14f well
and seems well suited by soft ground: likes Nottingham.   20
208 **THE MISSISSIPPIAN** [13] (M Eckley) 5-7-10 T Williams 8/1: 0000-42: Led 2 out: just
caught: in good form: stays 14f: eff on yld & soft.   11
-- **SUPER GRASS** [14] (S Mellor) 7-7-12 B Crossley 20/1: 00--0-3: Fit from hurdling: stayed
on well and not btn far: lightly raced on the Flat and last successful in '82 at Pontefract:
stays 14f well: acts on gd/firm & soft.   11
319 **WESSEX** [4] (N Tinkler) 4-9-4(bl) Kim Tinkler(7) 4/1: 33-4124: Fin well and not btn
far: remains in good form: very eff at 14f/2m: see 144.   30
280 **NORTHERN RULER** [10] 4-9-7 M Fry 8/1: 0000-20: Good effort: stays well: see 280.   31
121 **ARTESIUM** [7] 4-9-5 S Cauthen 7/1: 4-00220: Loves soft ground: see 121, 19.   26
-- **BLENDERS CHOICE** [17] 4-8-10 S Whitworth 9/1: 00300-0: Led ½m out on seasonal debut:
btr for race: maiden: stays 14f: acts on good/firm.   00
235 **INTUITION** [9] 4-9-9 M Wigham 7/1: 000-100: Wknd, best first time out in 69 (C/D).   00
164 **TOUCH OF LUCK** [2] 4-8-12 S Perks 10/1: 0333-00: Fdd str.   00

204	My Charade [20] 8-9 (bl)	243	Campus Boy [16] 8-9	208	Baluchi [3] 8-3	
104	Welsh Guard [6] 8-0	--	Amigo Estimado [11] 9-1			
126	Wandering Walter [15] 9-4			144	Higham Grey [12] 8-10	
199	Far To Go [19] 8-8	92	Shipwright [5] 8-6			

18 ran   ¾,1½,¾,1½,3,¾   (Whitting Commodities Ltd)   W Holden Newmarket

---

Official Going Given as Good/Soft

359   INSULPACK STAKES 3YO FILLIES   £8051   1m   Yld/Soft 116 -20 Slow

213 **GREAT LEIGHS** [1] (B Hills) 3-8-11 B Thomson 12/1: 02-01: 3 b f Vaigly Great - Goosie
Gantlet (Run The Gantlet): Useful, impr filly: led final 1f, ridden out in a valuable fillies
stakes at Ascot Apr.30: in '85 fin 2nd to Niccolo Polo in a maiden at Haydock: eff at 1m,
may stay 10f: half sister to 4 winners, incl the speedy Ulla Laing and the stayer Rikki Tavi:
acts on gd & yld/soft and a gall trk.   58
-- **FLOWER BOWL** [8] (J Dunlop) 3-8-11 W Carson 9/4 FAV: 22-2: Heavily bckd on seasonal
debut: led inside final 2f: stayed on well and 5L clear 3rd: 2nd on both outings in '85,
behind Possedyno at Newmarket and Royal Loft at Doncaster: eff at 1m, may stay 10f: acts
on firm & yld/soft and a gall trk: looks sure to find a maiden in the near future.   55
250 **GLITTER** [7] (I Balding) 3-8-11 S Cauthen 14/1: -03: Al there: on the up grade:
half sister to numerous winners: stays 1m & acts on yld/soft grnd.   45
-- **BALLAD ROSE** [6] (P Cole) 3-8-11 T Quinn 12/1: 323-4: Wknd final 1f: good seasonal debut:
placed on all 3 outings in '85: half sister to 12f winner Vouchsafe: stays 1m: acts on
gd & heavy.   43

218 TOP DEBUTANTE [4] 3-8-11 G Starkey 11/4: -30: Led/dsptd lead: much btr 218 (gd/yld).   38
250 QUEENS VISIT [3] 3-8-11 N Howe 9/1: -40: Never nearer: best 250 (7f).   36
250 ANDIKA [9] 3-8-11 Pat Eddery 7/2: -00: Led after 3f: much btr 250 (7f).   00
--   **Lumiere** [2] 8-11   --   **Private Sue** [5] 8-11
9 ran   1½,5,¼,3,1   (A W Boon)   B Hills Lambourn, Berks

360 GR 3 INSULPAK SAGARO EBF STAKES   £24388   2m   Yld/Soft 116 -21 Slow

--   VALUABLE WITNESS [1] (J Tree) 6-9-0 Pat Eddery 10/11 FAV: -1111-1: 6 b g Val De
L'Orne - Friendly Witness (Northern Dancer): Very smart stayer: first time out, ran on
strongly under press final 1f to collar Ramich John close home in valuable Gr.3 Sagaro Stakes
at Ascot Apr.30: in excellent form in '85, being unbtn in all 4 starts, Gr.2 Goodwood Cup
at Goodwood, Listed race at Royal Ascot & easy wins at Haydock & Sandown: in '84 won again at
Ascot & fin 2nd in Tote Cesarewitch: eff over 14f: stays extreme dists really well: acts on
firm and is definitely best on soft ground: very game and consistent performer who carries weight
extremely well: sure to win more good races.   85
325 RAMICH JOHN [10] (L Browne) 4-8-5 B Thomson 11/2: D-01132: Led well over 1f out:
caught dying strides: unlucky: in fine form: eff from 10f-2m: seems a very genuine filly.   75
--   SPICY STORY [5] (I Balding) 5-8-11 S Cauthen 5/1: 04214-3: Led into str: btr for
race: in '85 won Gr.3 Doncaster Cup and first time out was an unlucky 3rd in this same
event: in '84 won at Newbury & York: eff at 14f, stays 2m3f really well: acts on fast and
soft ground and a gall trk: very genuine.   74
--   EASTERN MYSTIC [9] (L Cumani) 4-8-8 R Guest 7/1: 21211-4: Ev ch str: btr for race:
one of the most impr performers of '85, winning valuable Coral Autumn Cup at Newbury,
breaking the course record in a valuable h'cap at Doncaster and also won an amateur riders
event at Newmarket: half brother to the smart Treizieme: eff over 12f, well suited by 14f
plus: acts on soft grnd but is much btr on gd & firm: suited by a gall trk: very consistent
and a credit to his trainer.   59
280 AYRES ROCK [6] 5-8-8 W R Swinburn 66/1: 3000-30: Never nearer, but an amazing effort
at the weights: seems very eff at 2m on soft grnd: should find a race on this form.   54
*280 INDE PULSE [2] 4-8-8 M Hills 8/1: 100-010: Fdd 2f out: see 280.   46
--   Contester [3] 8-8   58a Petrizzo [4] 8-8   235 Vickstown [7] 8-8
199 Christo [8] 8-8
10 ran   shhd,4,6,2½,8   (S S Niarchos)   J Tree Marlborough, Wilts

361 INSULPAK VICTORIA CUP H'CAP 0-75   £12902   7f   Yld/Soft 116 +16 Fast   [60]

112 READY WIT [4] (R Hannon) 5-7-13 D Mckay 7/1: 000-221: 5 br h Bay Express - Brevity
(Pindari): In fine form, led 2f out, comfortably in fast run and valuable Victoria Cup
(H'cap) at Ascot Apr.30: in '85 won a competitive selling h'cap at Doncaster: winning 2yo
at Chepstow: very eff at 7f/1m: acts on gd/firm & soft and on any trk.   45
72   XHAI [1] (M Tompkins) 7-8-2 M Rimmer 14/1: 110-402: Ran on final 1f, not get to
winner: good effort: eff at 7f, though well suited by 1m/10f: see 17.   42
166 CONMAYJO [12] (D Haydn Jones) 5-8-2 D Williams(7) 13/2 Jt.FAV: 020-033: Nearest fin:
in good form: see 166.   41
248 CORN STREET [13] (J Bosley) 8-8-13(6ex) Pat Eddery 7/1: D4-0104: Ch over 1f out:
running well: see 172.   50
248 VIRGIN ISLE [2] 5-8-6 T Williams 13/2 Jt.FAV: 34-0200: Ran well: should find a
h'cap soon: see 248, 79.   43
70   OUR JOCK [7] 4-9-7 W Carson 12/1: 2200-00: Al there: btr effort: in good form in
'85, winning 3yo h'cap at Windsor & Kempton (first time out): also btn shhds in the Stewards
Cup at Goodwood and Great St Winifred H'cap at Ripon: in '84 won first time out at Kempton:
eff at 5/6f, stays 7f: acts on firm & soft and on any trk: genuine sort.   52
245 MELODY PARK [3] 4-9-3(vis) P Robinson 9/1: 404-430: Btr 245, 70 (6f).   00
172 POSTORAGE [5] 4-9-5 S Cauthen 10/1: 0020-00: Early ldr: wknd: in good form in '85
winning 4 h'caps on the trot at Sandown, Wolverhampton, Salisbury & Warwick: in '84 won at
Nottingham: very eff at 6/7f: acts on yld, well suited by good & firm: acts on any trk:
carries weight well and is a genuine sort.   00
172 Manimstar [8] 9-4(vis)   192 Transflash [11] 8-12
248 Korypheos [9] 8-7   --   Maazi [14] 8-8   --   Red Russell [10] 9-7
71   Fusilier [6] 8-2
14 ran   3,nk,1,hd,3   (Mrs R Tennant)   R Hannon East Everleigh, Wilts.

362 WHITE ROSE STAKES 3YO   £8402   10f   Yld/Soft 116 -11 Slow

226 MASHKOUR [3] (H Cecil) 3-9-0 S Cauthen 15/8 : 2211-31: 3 ch c Irish River - Sancta
Rose (Karabas): Smart colt: ridden along ¼way, but was back on the bit in the str and led
2f out, readily drawing clear for an impressive win in valuable White Rose Stakes at Ascot
Apr.30: first time out fin an excellent 3rd to Dancing Brave in Gr.3 Craven Stakes at
Newmarket: in '85 won at Goodwood and Yarmouth: eff at 1m, stays 10f well: acts on firm &
soft ground and on any trk: sure to win more good races.   83
60   MIRAGE DANCER [5] (R Smyth) 3-8-9 P Robinson 50/1: 0204-02: No ch with winner, though
ran well: ran well on several occasions in '85 in good company, though yet to win: however
should find a maiden in the very near future: stays 10f well: acts on gd/firm & soft and a
gall trk: half brother to several winners incl the smart stayer General Ironside.   59

+190 NISNAS [6] (P Cole) 3-9-0 T Quinn 7/1: 143-13: Led 3f out: stays 10f: see 190.   63
  --   SHIP OF STATE [4] (I Balding) 3-8-9 Pat Eddery 10/1: 23-4: Led after 3f: good seasonal
debut: placed on both starts in '85 in very good company: eff at 7f, stays 10f: half brother
to 12f winner Sea Raider: acts on gd & yld/soft and should have no trouble finding a maiden.   52
  --   DANISHGAR [1] 3-8-9 W R Swinburn 1/1 FAV: 22-0: Heavily bckd: led ½way, going well:
sn in trouble when the pace quickened: continues to work very well at home, though has yet
to reproduce that form on the racecourse: in '85 fin. 2nd on both starts, behind Janiski
at Doncaster and Nomrood at Newmarket: should be suited by 10f plus: acts on firm & soft:
highly regarded.   51
159 SIT THIS ONE OUT [2] 3-9-7 W Carson 25/1: 2110-30: Stiff task: btr 159 (7f)   13
6 ran   8,¾,4,1,30   (Prince Ahmed Salman)   H Cecil Newmarket

363 CHOBHAM APPRENTICE H'CAP 0-60   £3178   12f   Yld/Soft 116 -05 Slow   [51]

*225 PUBBY [7] (J Toller) 5-8-4(4ex) Jackie Houston(10) 7/1: 3310-11: 5 b m Doctor Wall -
Snotch (Current Coin): In fine form, led 2f out for an easy win in an app. h'cap at Ascot
Apr.30: first time out was a comfortable winner of a h'cap at Newmarket: in '85 was in
good form, winning at Haydock & Yarmouth: eff at 10f, stays 12f really well: acts on firm,
likes soft ground: genuine & consistent and may complete the hat trick.   40
265 HOUSE HUNTER [8] (C Horgan) 5-9-6 P Skelton(10) 12/1: 4000-02: No ch with winner,
though is running into form: in good form last Aug, winning a h'cap at Brighton: in '84
won app. events at Chepstow, Bath & Leicester: also a dual winner at Folkestone: eff over
10f, stays 12f well: acts on firm & soft & on any trk: genuine sort who carries weight well
and goes well for an app.   46
*263 OWENS PRIDE [1] (R Akehurst) 4-8-3(4ex) G Carter 7/4 FAV: 3000-13: Heavily bckd: btr
263 (softer ground).   28
225 SAFE RIVER [4] (L Cumani) 4-9-8 S Quaine(6) 11/2: 1221-44: Well bckd: possibly needs
14f/better ground: see 225.   45
208 MILLERS TALE [6] 4-8-7 M Marshall(10) 8/1: 0002-20: Well below form 208 (heavy).   24
243 CAROS GIFT [3] 5-9-8 Kim Tinkler(6) 11/2: 003-130: Best first time out in 52.   38
  --   POSITIVE [2] 4-10-0 A Riding(10) 9/1: 21120-0: Btr for race: admirably consistent
in '85 winning at Salisbury & Newmarket (2): half brother to several winners: well suited
by 12f: acts on firm & soft grnd and likes a stiff trk, especially Newmarket.   00
225 JOLIS GIRL [9] 4-8-13 S Hibble(10) 8/1: 0-03030: Much btr 225: see 72.   00
  --   Watford Gap [5] 8-0   --   Key Royal [10] 7-12
10 ran   6,1,1½,5,1,shhd   (A J Morrison)   J Toller Newmarket

364 SEDBURY MAIDEN AUCTION STAKES 2YO   £684   5f   Yielding 97 +01 Fast

47 CLOWN STREAKER [4] (M H Easterby) 2-8-11 M Birch 4/6 FAV: 21: 2 ch c Cawston's Clown -
Velour Streak (Firestreak): Useful colt: made virtually ev yd for a ready win in quite a fast
run maiden auction race at Catterick Apr.30: earlier ran up to Naive Charm in a similar race
at Haydock: well suited by this minimum trip: acts on yld & heavy grnd and on any trk:
well suited by forcing tactics: should impr further.   46
254 AFRABELA [10] (M Brittain) 2-8-8 K Darley 8/1: 32: Dspt lead over ½way and kept on
well: handles a tight track well: acts on yld grnd: should win a small race soon: see 254.   35
  --   RHABDOMANCER [6] (J Watts) 2-8-11 T Ives 9/1: 3: Kept on promisingly on racecourse
debut: half sister to 2 winning juveniles: acts on yld grnd & on a tight trk: should impr.   32
108 GEOBRITONY [5] (D Moffatt) 2-8-11 J Lowe 14/1: 04: Ran on under press: should do
btr over a longer trip: acts on yld grnd: see 108.   31
  --   KALAS IMAGE [3] 2-8-5 N Crowther 33/1: 0: Ran on late & should impr for this
experience: cheaply acquired filly who acts on yld grnd & on a sharp trk.   24
  --   SAWDUST JACK [9] 2-9-0 M Hindley(3) 33/1: 0: Never reached ldrs on racecourse debut.   27
  --   GET SET LISA [7] 2-8-8 M Wood 10/1: 0: Never beyond mid-div on debut.   00
  --   Eurocon [12] 8-11   --   Gwynbrook [8] 8-8   --   Jean Jeanie [2] 8-8
  --   Miss Diamante [11] 8-5
11 ran   2½,3,nk,½,3,¾   (W Steels)   M H Easterby Norton, Yorks

365 JOCKEY CAP SELLING STAKES 3YO   £928   12f   Yielding 97 -20 Slow

*139 DORS GEM [7] (H Rohan) 3-8-10 T Ives 8/15 FAV: 000-011: 3 b g Brigadier Gerard -
Siraf (Alcide): Easily landed the odds, led below dist. and cruised clear in a 3yo seller
at Catterick Apr.30 (sold for 3,200 gns): recently again justified fav. in a similar event
at Nottingham: eff over 10/12f: acts on yld & soft grnd & on any trk: in good form and
may win a small h'cap.   25
  --   LUCKY HUMBUG [4] (W Pearce) 3-8-10 N Connorton 8/1: 00-2: Led into str, no ch with
winner though comfortably beat rem: twice well btn in btr company last term and is more at
home in this grade: stays 12f on a tight trk: acts on gd & yld grnd.   14

185 HOT RULER [2] (M Brittain) 3-8-10 K Darley 4/1: 02-3003: Back to 12f and made most
till run in: best on a gall trk in 35.   02
45 SOLENT BREEZE [6] (W Turner) 3-8-7 R Curant 25/1: 0000-04: Dropped to selling company
though fin well btn over this longer trip: no form to date.   00
257 PENRYN BOY [5] 3-8-10 R P Elliott 10/1: 0000-40: No extra run in: see 257.   00
257 QUIVERING [3] 3-8-7 J Lowe 20/1: 0000-00: With ldr ½way: no form to date.   00
6 ran   3,10,12,1¼,8   (Mrs Frank Reihill)   H Rohan Norton, Yorks

---

366 BRIDGE HANDICAP 0-35   £1861   15.9f Yielding 97 -08 Slow   [33]

-- MARINERS DREAM [14] (R Hollinshead) 5-7-11 A Culhane(7) 25/1: 00000-1: 5 br h Julio
Mainer - My Ginny (Palestine): Fit from hurdling and gained a surprise win in a h'cap at
Catterick Apr.30, leading inside final 1f for his first success on the Flat: last season won
4 times over hurdles though had been rather disapp this Winter: stays 2m well: acts on
firm & soft ground & on any trk.   11
126 PINWIDDIE [12] (H Rohan) 4-7-11 L Charnock 14/1: 003-042: Led run in, kept on well:
good effort over this longer trip: acts on gd & soft grnd: see 126.   07
*204 GOING BROKE [2] (D Murray Smith) 6-8-2(4ex) S Whitworth 5/2 FAV: /342-13: Al close up and
is in good form: see 204.   10
-- SUN STREET [6] (C Brittain) 4-9-3 T Ives 11/1: 12240-4: Stayed on: fair effort on
reapp. and should come on for this run: quite consistent last season, when gaining an early
win in a maiden on this course: eff over 14f, stays 2m: acts on firm & yld grnd and is well
suited by a sharp trk.   24
137 CARNEADES [10] 6-8-9(vis) M Birch 11/2: 00-1300: Btr effort & runs well here: see 44.   15
184 CHRISTMAS HOLLY [16] 5-8-1 G Craggs(5) 11/1: 00-3100: Late prog: stays 2m on a
sharp trk: see 105.   06
319 RED DUSTER [8] 6-9-3 M Beecroft 8/1: 00-4300: Usually runs well here: see 44.   00
144 MARLION [1] 5-9-7 E Guest(3) 13/2: 0120-00: Never beyond mid-div: last season won
h'caps at Redcar & Catterick: in '84 won & has also been successful over timber:
stays well: btr suited by faster ground.   00
144 Bantel Buccaneer [15] 7-11   104 Racing Demon [9] 8-4
44   Duke Of Dollis [5] 8-6   --   Grey Card [13] 7-11
256 Allez [3] 7-9   199 Porter [4] 8-1(6ow)   --   Abbee Valley [11] 8-11
85   Balkash [7] 7-11(bl)   *257 Frasass [17] 8-4(4ex)
17 ran   2¼,2,¾,1,¾   (Dennis Newton)   R Hollinshead Upper Longdon, Staffs

---

367 RICHMOND STAKES 2YO   £1202   5f   Yielding 97 -19 Slow

242 ROWEKING [5] (L Lightbrown) 2-8-11 J Bleasdale 10/1: 0201: 2 b c Mandrake Major -
Dalesview (Mummy's Pet): Was not visored today and duly produced an impr effort, led below
dist for a comfortable win in a 2yo stakes at Catterick Apr.30: cost 3,100 gns and is a half
brother to a winning juvenile: eff over 5f on yld/soft grnd: best when up with the pace on
a sharp trk.   40
133 MR GRUMPY [4] (Denys Smith) 2-8-11 M Fry 9/2: 022: Made most and is in good form:
acts on yld & heavy grnd & on any trk: see 133.   35
304 WHISTLING WONDER [2] (M Brittain) 2-9-2 K Darley 7/2: 21043: Again had ev ch: has
not run a bad race since winning in 94.   40
*236 MARCHING MOTH [7] (M Camacho) 2-9-2 N Connorton 1/1 FAV: 14: Well btn fav, though
her bit slipped ½way and she had no chance thereafter: btr judged on her promising win in 236.   20
-- BRIARQUEEN [6] 2-8-8 D Nicholls 20/1: 0: No ch after a slow start   00
40   CREOLE BAY [3] 2-8-8 C Coates(5) 14/1: 00: Trailed in last.   00
6 ran   1½,shhd,10,2,6   (Jeffrey Ross)   L Lightbrown Costock Grange, Leicestershire

---

368 HURGILL LODGE STAKES 3YO   £728   7f   Yielding 97 +10 Fast

229 AL BASHAAMA [5] (L Cumani) 3-9-0 P Hamblett 8/15 FAV: -01: 3 b c Vice Regent -
Noble Fancy (Vaguely Noble): Heavily bckd in this lesser company, led below dist for an easy
win in a fast run 3yo stakes at Catterick Apr.30: half brother to a couple of winners:
clearly very eff over 7f and seems certain to stay further: acts on yld grnd & on a tight
trk: should win btr races.   48
-- CARRIBEAN SOUND [9] (C Brittain) 3-8-11 J Lowe 13/2: 04000-2: No ch with winner though
kept on well: half sister to Carribean Song: showed some promise last term over 6/7f: acts
on gd & yld grnd & on any trk.   30
258 AUCTION TIME [3] (M Prescott) 3-9-0 C Nutter 13/2: -033: Had ev ch: needs further.   33
-- MISS LAURA LEE [10] (P Felgate) 3-8-11 Gay Kelleway(5) 33/1: 40-4: Hmpd early in str,
kept on: lightly raced last season, showing promise: closely related to a couple of winners:
acts on firm & yld grnd and seems suited by a sharp trk: should be btr over a longer trip.   25
24   ROBIS [2] 3-8-11 S P Griffiths(5) 50/1: 3000-40: Kept on same pace: see 24.   24
-- LARNEM [11] 3-8-11 C Coates(5) 50/1: 4000-0: Stayed on from rear on reapp: should impr.   18
284 Gloriant [4] 9-0   82 Bold Sea Rover [8] 9-0
258 Bantel Beau [7] 9-0(bl)   -- Cherry Lustre [6] 9-0
-- Bollin Uncle [1] 9-0
11 ran   6,shhd,2¼,¼,4   (Sheikh Mohammed)   L Cumani Newmarket

369   SPRING HANDICAP 0-35   £1316   6f   Yielding 97 -03 Slow   [29]

-321 EASTBROOK [10] (S Hall) 6-8-7 K Hodgson 7/2 Jt FAV: 0000-21: 6 b g Lochnager - Lush
Gold (Goldhill): Made a quick reapp. and comfortably made ev yd in a h'cap at Catterick
Apr.30: just failed with similar tactics at Ripon on Saturday: in '85 won a h'cap at
Hamilton: eff over 5/6f on gd & soft grnd: well suited by a sharp trk and does well with
forcing tactics.   18
281   SPOILT FOR CHOICE [9] (D Chapman) 8-9-1 D Nicholls 16/1: 00-0002: Btr effort: ran
on well: failed to win last season though in '84 won at Hamilton & Catterick (2): eff between
5 & 7f: stays 1m: acts on any going & on any trk.   21
18   TANFEN [13] (T Craig) 5-9-3 N Carlisle 12/1: 1200-03: Ran on well: last season won h'caps
at Newcastle, Hamilton & Catterick: eff over sprint dists: acts on any going and on any trk
and is suited by forcing tactics.   21
65   GODS SOLUTION [6] (T Barron) 5-10-0 B Mcghiff(7) 11/2: 300-104: Al up there: runs well
here: see 2.   32
110   FLOMEGAS DAY [4] 4-9-8(bl) J Hills(5) 12/1: 0000-00: Stayed on after a slow start:
last season won at Ripon, Catterick & Pontefract: eff over 5/6f on gd & soft grnd: well
suited by a sharpish trk.   25
260   FAIRGREEN [12] 8-8-9 N Leach(7) 14/1: 03-0040: In fair form: see 163.   11
+135 SHANOUSKA [5] 6-8-11 S P Griffths(5) 7/2 Jt FAV: 400-210: Never going well: much
btr in 135 (gall trk).   00
266   VIA SATELLITE [2] 4-8-9(bl) S Whitworth 11/2: 440-300: Only beat one home: btr in 110.   00
--   Dorame [7] 8-7   306 Bay Bazaar [1] 9-9   135 Monswart [11] 8-10
--   Godlord [8] 9-0   --   Tricenco [3] 9-1
13 ran   1½,1,shhd,nk,½   (Hippodromo Racing Ltd)   S Hall Middleham, Yorks

---

NEWMARKET   Thursday May 1st   Righthand, Stiff Galloping Track

Official Going Given as Good

370   MAY STAKES 3YO   £4467   1m 1f   Good 42 +11 Fast

--   ALLEZ MILORD [6] (G Harwood) 3-9-6 G Starkey 2/1 FAV: 1-1: 3 b c Tom Rolfe - Why Me
Lord (Bold Reasoning): Smart colt: heavily bckd and made a winning seasonal debut, led after
3f out, qcknd over 1f out, but had to be ridden out close home in a fast run May stakes
Newmarket May 1: on sole start in '85 romped home by 7L in a valuable 2yo maiden again at
Newmarket: half brother to several winners: eff over 9f, should stay 10f plus: acts on
good & firm grnd and a gall trk: has a smart turn of foot and should win more good races.   80
--   ALL HASTE [5] (H Cecil) 3-8-7 S Cauthen 13/2: -2: Ran on well final 1f: just btn:
fine racecourse debut from this well bred colt: eff at 9f, should be suited by 10f plus:
acts on gd grnd and a stiff trk: should be winning very soon.   66
--   VERARDI [10] (W Hastings Bass) 3-8-7 T Ives 33/1: -3: Ran on well final 1f on racecourse debut: most promising effort, eff at 9f, should stay 12f: acts on gd grnd & a gall
trk: a maiden is well within his grasp.   63
--   HIGH CROWN [4] (L Cumani) 3-8-7 P Hamblett 33/1: -4: Dsptd lead 3f out: promising colt:
eff at 9f, should stay further: acts on gd grnd & a gall trk: will find a race.   61
--   NADEED [7] 3-8-7 W R Swinburn 9/1: -0: Ch 2f out: encouraging effort: impr likely and
should have no trouble finding a race: eff at 9f, should stay further: acts on gd grnd &
a gall trk.   60
*95   WISHLON [1] 3-8-8 S Whitworth 33/1: -10: Never nearer 6th, but acquitted himself
well in this very good company: should win more races: acts on gd & soft grnd & on any trk.   60
-190 ESDALE [9] 3-8-7 C Asmussen 11/4: 2-20: Hmpd slightly dist: btr 190 (1m yld).   00
*188 TOP WING [11] 3-8-7 M Hills 14/1: 2-10: Not disgraced: see 188.   00
--   SILK THREAD [3] 3-8-7 W Carson 9/1: 2-0: Prom 7f: btr for race.   00
127   Moonstruck [8] 8-7   --   Is Bello [2] 8-7   234 Stage Hand [12] 9-2
12 ran   hd,1½,1,nk,shhd   (Jerome Brody)   G Harwood Pulborough, Sussex

371   HASTINGS MAIDEN STAKES 3YO   £4786   1m   Good 42 -15 Slow

--   NINO BIBBIA [18] (L Cumani) 3-9-0 R Guest 7/2 FAV: 2-1: 3 b c Cresta Rider - Native
Tan (Exclusive Native): Very useful colt: first time out, led well over 1f out, comfortably
in a valuable maiden at Newmarket May 1: on sole outing in '85 fin 2nd to Ghika in a stakes
event at Yarmouth: half brother to 2 winners: eff at 1m & will stay further: acts on gd &
firm grnd and a gall trk: further impr likely and should rate more highly.   69
--   KADIAL [6] (R Johnson Houghton) 3-9-0 Y Saint Martin 12/1: -2: Led/dsptd lead over
6f: kept on well: very promising racecourse debut from this half brother to the smart Kalim:
eff at 1m, should be suited by further: acts on gd grnd & a stiff trk: will be winning soon.   66
--   BROWN THATCH [17] (H Cecil) 3-9-0 S Cauthen 5/1: -3: Ran on well final 1f on debut:
impr likely: eff at 1m, should stay further: acts on gd grnd & a gall trk & should win soon.   61
--   PICEA [11] (M Jarvis) 3-9-0 T Ives 13/2: 42-4: Ch 2f out: btr for race: showed a deal
of promise in '85 notably when 2nd to Laughter in a Listed race at Newmarket: dam the
smart May Hill: stays 1m: acts on gd & firm & a gall trk.   57

-- AMJAAD [4] 3-9-0 W R Swinburn 4/1: -0: Well bckd debutant: kept on well, showing promise: U.S. bred colt who should impr for this run: eff at 1m, should stay further: acts on good ground. 55

-- SAKER [19] 3-9-0 P Hamblett 33/1: -0: Nearest fin: stable companion of winner and should do btr next time: will be suited by further than 1m: should have no trouble finding a race. 54

-- AITCH N BEE [3] 3-9-0 R Fox 33/1: -0: Never nearer 7th: promising run and impr likely. 53

-- MOEL FAMMAU [2] 3-9-0 R Hills 33/1: -0: Fin 8th on debut, showing future promise. 52

-- STEP IN TIME [5] 3-9-0 T Quinn 33/1: -0: Fin 9th: half brother to the fair stayer and smart hurdler Pike's Peak: acts on good ground. 51

-- MOORE STYLISH [16] 3-8-11 G Sexton 33/1: -0: Impr likely from this half sister to several winners. 50

--	Absheer [1] 9-0	218	Prasina Matia [12] 9-0		
218	Bien Dorado [7] 9-0	--	Asseer [10] 9-0	--	Shareef [13] 9-0
--	Burning Bright [15] 9-0			--	Crystal Glass [9] 9-0
--	Royal Dynasty [14] 9-0			--	Gundulina [8] 8-11

19 ran   ¾,3,2,½,½,½,nk,nk,hd   (Sheikh Mohammed)   L Cumani Newmarket

372 PRETTY POLLY STAKES 3YO FILLIES   £9864   1m 2f   Good 42 +01 Fast

*162 GESEDEH [10] (M Jarvis) 3-8-10 T Ives 15/8 FAV: -11: 3 ch f Ela-Mana-Mou - Le Melody (Levmoss): Smart filly: heavily bckd and qcknd well to lead 1f out, comfortably in valuable Pretty Polly Stakes (Listed race) at Newmarket May 1: first time out demolished a field of maidens at Salisbury: very well bred, being half sister to several winners, notably the cop class middle dist winner Ardross: cost 200,000 gns as a yearling: eff at 10f, sure to stay further: acts on gd & yld & a gall trk: more impr to come & looks a top class prospect. should run well in the Oaks. 79

-- SANTIKI [11] (M Stoute) 3-8-5 W R Swinburn 9/4: 3-2: Heavily bckd on seasonal debut: led 2f out: kept on well and this was a fine effort: on sole start in '85 was a promising 3rd to Lady Sophie in a fillies maiden at Yarmouth: half sister to the smart Shearwalk: eff at 10f should stay 12f: acts on gd & firm grnd & a gall trk: should go one btr next time and caught a tartar today. 68

-- MILL ON THE FLOSS [4] (H Cecil) 3-9-2 S Cauthen 9/1: 10-3: Mkt drifter: al prom: very good seasonal debut: first time out in '85 beat Queen Helen in valuable fillies event at Newbury: half sister to 6 winners: eff at 10f, should be suited by 12f: suited by a stiff trk and acts on gd/firm & a gall trk: should win some good races this season. 75

130 BENAROSA [1] (P Kelleway) 3-8-5 C Asmussen 33/1: -34: Stayed on well: 3rd at Ayr first time out! very eff at 10f on good grnd & a gall trk: dam a middle dist winner and Benarosa should find a maiden soon. 56

-- COCOTTE [9] 3-8-5 W Carson 6/1: 224-0: Led 3f out on seasonal debut: btf for race: ran well on all 3 starts in '85, 2nd to Maysoon in the Virginia Water at Ascot first time out: eff at 1m, should be suited by 10f plus: acts on gd & firm grnd. 36

*49 AMONGST THE STARS [6] 3-9-2 J Lowe 33/1: 1200-10: Not disgraced: in good form: see 49. 41

-- INTRINSIC [8] 3-8-7(2ow) G Starkey 9/1: -0: Mkt drifter: no show on debut: half sister to numerous winners and should do much btr than this. 00

224	Three Times A Lady [7] 8-5			--	Lost In France [12] 8-5
128	Davemma [2] 8-5	--	Shehana [3] 8-10	213	Queen Of Battle [5] 8-5

12 ran   1¼,2,3,12,3,hd   (Sheikh Ahmed Al Maktoum)   M Jarvis Newmarket

373 GROUP 1 GENERAL ACCIDENT 1000 GUINEAS   £101244   1m   Good 42 -02 Slow

-- MIDWAY LADY [1] (B Hanbury) 3-9-0 R Cochrane 10/1: 2111-1: 3 b f Alleged - Smooth Bore (His Highness): Very smart filly: made a winning seasonal debut in Gr.1 1,000 Guineas at Newmarket May 1: made good hdway 2f out and led inside the final 1f, under press in a close fin: in excellent form in '85, winning Gr.1 Prix Marcel Boussac at Longchamp, Gr.3 May Hill Stakes at Doncaster & a fillies maiden at Yarmouth: very eff over 1m, seems certain to stay 12f: acts on gd & firm ground and a gall trk: held in very high regard and is a worthy fav. for the Oaks. 86

*232 MAYSOON [12] (M Stoute) 3-9-0 Y Saint Martin 15/2: 130-12: Led briefly final 1f: ran on well: excellent effort from this genuine filly: acts on any grnd: will be suited by further than 1m: see 232. 84

+214 SONIC LADY [11] (M Stoute) 3-9-0 W R Swinburn 6/4 FAV: 1-13: Led well over 2f out: ran on well under press and btn less than 1L: excellent effort & stays 1m: certain to win more good races: see 214. 84

214 ALA MAHLIK [8] (F Durr) 3-9-0 G Starkey 14/1: 11-34: Al there: fine effort: stays 1m well: should be winning again soon: see 214. 82

214 EMBLA [14] 3-9-0 T Ives 6/1: 2111-40: Ev ch 2f out: btr effort, but below her 2yo form: stays 1m: see 214. 78

*269 WEIGHT IN GOLD [5] 3-9-0 D Gillespie 50/1: 21-1410: Sn prom: fine effort from this smart Irish filly: stays 1m: acts on gd & heavy: see 269. 74

26 VOLIDA [3] 3-9-0 P Robinson 200/1: 0400-40: Never nearer 7th: ran remarkably well: suited by 1m: rated only 51 officially: should win soon: see 26. 67

-- DEAR MARGIE [2] 3-9-0 E Legrix 25/1: -0-110: French chall: never nearer 8th: recent winner at St Cloud and Maison Laffitte: eff at 1m, stays 10f: acts on gd, suited by soft/hvy. 65

214 LADY SOPHIE [13] 3-9-0 S Cauthen 9/1: 01-20: Much btr 214 (yld).   59
--   Spun Gold [9] 9-0   220 Bridesmaid [10] 9-0(vis)
--   Tender Loving Care [7] 9-0   81   Improvise [15] 9-0
--   Grande Couture [4] 9-0   155 Rose Of The Sea [6] 9-0
15 ran   ¾,shhd,2½,¾,1½,1½,3   (H H Rainier)   B Hanbury Newmarket

374 BRETBY HANDICAP 4YO+ 0-60   £5708   6f   Good 42 +04 Fast   [55]

--   HO MI CHINH [15] (C Brittain) 4-9-2 S Cauthen 12/1: 44000-1: 4 ch c Homing - Fiordiligi
(Khalkis): Useful colt: first time cut for his new stable, led well over 1f out, holding on
under press in a valuable h'cap at Newmarket May 1: trained by M H Easterby in '85: first
time out won at Pontefract: in '84 won at Newcastle: very eff at 6f, stays 1m: acts on firm
& yld grnd and on any trk.   56
-192 GOLD PROSPECT [9] (G Balding) 4-8-3 T Quinn 5/1 FAV: 20-122: Just touched off: in
excellent form: acts on gd & soft grnd and should win again soon: see 31.   42
--   BRIG CHOP [5] (P Walwyn) 5-9-9 R Guest 10/1: 00004-3: Ch over 1f out: good seasonal
debut: first time out in '85 won this same race: in '84 won at Kempton: eff over 6f, stays
7f really well: acts on gd & firm grnd: likes Newmarket.   57
306 EMERGENCY PLUMBER [11] (D Barron) 5-7-8 T Williams 13/2: 400-424: Nicely bckd: al prom 25
--   BROWN BEAR BOY [18] 4-8-1 W Carson 12/1: 00400-0: Made much on seasonal debut: early
in '85 won at Cagnes: fair 2yo, winning at Ripon: eff at sprint dist: stays 1m: acts on
gd/firm & yld.   29
--   SAILORS SONG [14] 4-9-7 P Cook 10/1: 30224-0: Sn prom: most consistent in '85, winning
at Pontefract and placed on numerous occasions: equally eff at 5/6f: acts on gd ' firm grnd.   46
-172 REVEILLE [17] 4-8-1 W Woods(3) 7/1: 000-220: Much btr 172, 65 (yld/soft).   00
--   ROYSIA BOY [1] 6-8-13 W Ryan 9/1: 01101-0: No show: btr for race.   00
--   Our Dynasty [12] 9-12   --   Chicago Bid [8] 7-9   --   Dorking Lad [4] 9-9
172 Vorvados [2] 9-2   17   Inishpour [6] 9-1   306 John Patrick [3] 8-11
306 Paris Match [13] 8-11   238 Kampglow [7] 8-2   260 Maftir [16] 7-10(bl)
17 ran   hd,2,¾,¾,¾   (Phil Bull)   C Brittain Newmarket

375 MARCH HANDICAP 4YO+ 0-60   £5308   2m   Good 42 -27 Slow   [47]

--   SNEAK PREVIEW [10] (H Candy) 6-8-9 C Asmussen 11/2: 01043-1: 6 b g Quiet Fling -
Glimmer Of Hope (Never Say Die): First time out, nicely bckd and led inside the final 1f,
under press in a valuable h'cap at Newmarket May 1: in good form in '85, winning h'caps at
Wolverhampton & Salisbury (first time out): also an excellent 4th in Tote Cesarewitch on
this trk: stays 2m2f really well: acts on gd & firm grnd & a gall trk: genuine.   40
--   WATERLOW PARK [6] (I Balding) 4-8-10 S Cauthen 4/1 FAV: 42422-2: Heavily bckd: led 3f
out till inside final 1f: battled on gamely: good seasonal debut: was placed to win, but placed
on several occasions: stays 2m well: acts on gd/firm & yld & a gall trk: seems best up
with the pace.   40
215 RIKKI TAVI [9] (B Hills) 6-8-12 B Thomson 8/1: 1213-03: Ev ch final 1f: btn 1L and
10L clear rem: good effort: in '85 won h'caps at Ascot & Doncaster: in '84 won at Warwick:
well suited by 2m plus: acts on any trk, but likes a gall one: acts on gd & yld grnd.   41
11   ALL IS REVEALED [1] (D Thom) 4-8-11 G Starkey 10/1: 1310-04: Never nearer: unusual
tactics adopted for this well known trail blazer and should do btr next time: in '85 was
in fine form, making all in h'caps at Ascot, Sandown (course record) & Yarmouth: also won
a seller at Newmarket: eff at 14f, stays 2m well: acts on yld, likes good/firm: goes well
on a stiff, gall trk: best forcing the pace in a bl/visor though did not wear one today.   30
215 NAFTILOS [5] 4-9-7 P Robinson 5/1: 120-020: Never nearer: much btr 215 (yld, 14f).   38
--   SECURITY CLEARANCE [8] 5-9-0 M Rimmer 50/1: 00000-0: Outsider, no real threat.   29
215 CADMIUM [7] 4-9-10 M Lynch(5) 11/2: 3331-30: Led/dsptd lead much: btr 215 (yld 14f).   00
11   TOM SHARP [3] 6-8-8 S Dawson(3) 15/2: 4000-00: Led 1m: wknd ½m out.   00
215 Trapeze Artist [2] 9-2(vis)   215 Popsis Joy [11] 8-10
235 Romana [4] 8-12   137 Corston Springs [12] 7-10
12 ran   nk,¾,10,1½,1½   (Mrs C E Gross)   H Candy Kingstone Warren, Oxon

CARLISLE   Friday May 2nd   Righthanded Undulating track, Stiff Uphill Finish

Official Going Given as Good/Soft with final 2f described as Heavy

376 E.B.F. HIGH STILE FILLIES MAIDEN 2YO   £830   5f   Yielding 101 -51 Slow

252 SHADES OF NIGHT [1] (J Winter) 2-8-11 A Mackay 5/4 FAV: 221: 2 b f Red Sunset -
Purple Princess (Right Tack): Gained a deserved win in justifying fav. in a slowly run 2yo
fillies maiden at Carlisle May 2, led below dist and driven out: r.u. in both her previous
starts: cost 15,000 gns and is a half sister to useful juvenile Running Princess: well
suited by this minimum trip, though should stay further: acts on yld/soft grnd and on any
trk: consistent filly.   42
167 MEATH PRINCESS [3] (S Norton) 2-8-11 J Lowe 9/1: 02: Stayed on well under press:
impr effort & should do even btr over a longer trip: acts on yld/soft grnd & seems suited by
a stiff trk: see 167.   40

254 BROONS ADDITION [6] (K Stone) 2-8-11 G Brown(5) 14/1: 4343: Broke well & made most.   36
167 PHILEARN [8] (M Brittain) 2-8-11 K Darley 9/1: 44: No extra dist: acts on yld: see 167.   24
317 DANCING BELLE [9] 2-8-11 C Coates(5) 5/1: 00: Nicely bckd though would prefer
faster ground.   23
108 SEATON GIRL [4] 2-8-11 S Webster 13/2: 420: Showed speed till ½way: btr in 108.   23
--   ROSIES GLORY [2] 2-8-11 M Birch 10/1: 0: Showed signs of greeness & will do btr
next time: mare was a juvenile winner: acts on yld grnd.   00
--   Benfield Newcastle [5] 8-11   -- Dear Dolly [10] 8-11
--   Bantel Bouquet [7] 8-11
10 ran   ¾,1½,6,nk,shhd,1   (P K Nurse)   J Winter Newmarket

377 BRANDRETH CLAIMING STAKES 3YO   £697   5f   Yielding 101 -03 Slow

255 CHUMMYS PET [5] (N Callaghan) 3-9-0 J Matthias 11/8 FAV: -021: 3 b g Song - Hodstock
Venture (Major Portion): Had to be switched though just got up in a 3yo claiming stakes at
Carlisle May 2: eff over 5/6f with some give in the grnd: seems to act on any trk.   35
51   CHAUTAUQUA [10] (P Haslam) 3-8-8 T Williams 7/1: 0-42: Just failed to make all,
though comfortably beat rem and should find a similar race soon: eff over 5/6f: suited by
a stiff trk: see 51.   28
237 SAMBA LASS [2] (T Barron) 3-8-5 G Carter(3) 9/1: 000-03: Ran on late: best effort
to date: eff over 5f on yld grnd.   17
--   MAYBE JAYNE [1] (A Jones) 3-8-11 C Dwyer 33/1: 0-4: Friendless in mkt: late prog and
should impr: only ran once last season but unplaced in a Haydock seller: acts on yld grnd &
on a stiff trk.   11
255 BANTEL BANZAI [7] 3-8-6 J Quinn(5) 20/1: 00-000: Late prog after a slow start:
btr in 255.   05
241 TOUCH ME NOT [8] 3-9-0 S Perks 9/1: 00-3000: Speed over ½way: easily best in 64 (6f soft).09
237 LULLABY BLUES [3] 3-9-0 M Birch 9/1: -00: Never beyond mid-div: see 237.   00
237 SANDRON [6] 3-8-10(bl) S Whitworth 8/1: 020-030: Only beat 1 home: much btr in 237   00
51   The Stray Bullett [4] 9-0(bl)   -- Heavenly Hoofer [11] 8-6
--   Bavarian Princess [13] 8-11   147 Puncle Creak [12] 8-11(vis)
284 Mistress Charley [9] 8-11(BL)
13 ran   hd,3,5,½,1½,½,1½   (C Gaventa)   N Callaghan Newmarket

378 GRASMERE HANDICAP (0-35) 3YO+   £1962   6f   Yielding 101 -04 Slow   [25]

257 LITTLE NEWINGTON [13] (N Bycroft) 5-8-5(BL) M Richardson(7) 14/1: -041001: 5 b m Most
Secret - Kathy King (Space King): Returned to winning form, scrubbed along early though led
inside dist in a h'cap at Carlisle May 2: earlier was a comfortable winner of a selling
h'cap at Ayr: eff over a stiff 6f, stays 1m well: acts on yld & heavy grnd and does well
on a gall trk.   12
114 HENRYS PLACE [7] (D Chapman) 4-9-1 D Nicholls 12/1: 300-002: Led briefly inside dist:
rem a maiden: eff over 6f, stays 1m: acts on firm & yld grnd: tried in bl last season.   17
260 TRADE HIGH [5] (G Richards) 7-9-7 R Vickers(7) 10/1: 000-003: Ran on well from the
rear, not btn far: btr effort: see 260.   22
355 STEVEJAN [9] (B Morgan) 4-8-4 G Carter(3) 6/1: 00-3304: Ran on well, not btn far: see 65 05
46   MIAMI DOLPHIN [2] 6-8-3 M Fry 14/1: 0000-00: Led briefly below dist: maiden who
has shown little worthwhile form in sprint h'caps: acts on gd/firm & yld grnd & seems to
have no trk preferences.   03
106 GOLDEN BOY [1] 4-8-4 J Quinn(5) 16/1: 0--0-00: Lightly raced gelding who was bckd
at long odds today: raced wide thro'out and never reached ldrs: acts on yld.   01
260 BARNES STAR [14] 4-9-2 B Mcghiff(7) 15/2: 00-0330: Fin 9th: much btr on soft in 145.   00
46   BLACK RIVER [4] 5-8-4 J Lowe 5/1 FAV: 0040-00: Never beyond mid-div: see 46.   00
145 CAERNARVON BOY [17] 4-8-3 M Beecroft 6/1: 000-320: Speed over ½way: btr in 145 (soft). 00
131 Swift River [12] 8-4   240 Qualitairess [3] 8-1   163 Composer [11] 8-7
--   Hoptons Chance [8] 8-10(bl)   -- Remembrance [10] 9-6
260 Illicit [6] 9-3   -- Culminate [18] 8-3   131 Ailsa Pearl [16] 8-1
17 ran   1½,nk,shhd,½,1½,¾   (M J Pount)   N Bycroft Brandsby, Yorks

379 BOW FELL FILLIES MAIDEN 3YO   £1034   1m 1f   Yielding 101 -05 Slow

--   NORTHERN MEETING [3] (I BalJing) 3-8-11 J Matthias 8/1: 000-1: 3 b f Young Generation -
Tartan Pimpernel (Blakeney): Unruly at the start though settled nicely and went on 2f out
for a ready win in a 3yo fillies maiden at Carlisle May 2: half sister to several winners
and showed some promise last season, when she again showed signs of temperament: eff over
9f and should stay further: acts on gd/firm & yld/soft grnd and on any trk.   45
--   NICE LADY [12] (J Winter) 3-8-11 A Mackay 6/1: -2: Ex Irish trained filly: stayed on
again and beat rem decisively: should stay further than this trip: acts on yld grnd & on
a stiff trk.   36
209 JANIE O [2] (M Ryan) 3-8-11 G Carter(3) 12/1: -03: Stayed on too late: btr effort:
eff over 9f on yld grnd: acts on a stiff trk.   24
209 CRIMSON ROBES [10] (R Hollinshead) 3-8-11 S Perks 16/1: -04: Late prog: seems likely
to appreciate a longer trip: acts on yld grnd & on a stiff trk.   23

194 COME POUR THE WINE [13] 3-8-11 D Nicholls 25/1: 00-00: First signs of form: acts on yld. 21
--   BILLS DAUGHTER [9] 3-8-11 J Carroll(7) 25/1: -0: Should impr for this initial outing:
acts on yielding.   17
209 ARMOUR OF LIGHT [14] 3-8-11 S Whitworth 6/1: -00: Active in mkt: btr on heavy in 209.   00
132 LADY BRIT [11] 3-8-11 E Guest(3) 6/1: 0020-00: Led into str, wknd into 8th.   00
--   MRS MAINWARING [6] 3-8-11 J Lowe 11/2 FAV: 03-0: Short lived effort early in str:
fin 9th & btr for race: lightly raced last season, placed in a maiden at Hamilton on final
start: acts on yld & heavy grnd and on a stiff trk.   00
--   GLACIER LASS [5] 3-8-11(BL) R Fox 6/1: 00-0: Bl first time, never going well on reapp.   00
--   Pinturicchia [4] 8-11   --   Tieatre [16] 8-11   --   Star Of Tara [7] 8-11
53   Zeelandia [8] 8-11   --   Town Of Ennis [15] 8-11
--   Hiya Bud [1] 8-11
16 ran   3,8,nk,shhd,1½   (The Queen)   I Balding Kingsclere, Hants

380 SCAFELL HANDICAP (0-35) 3YO   £1791   1m 1f   Yielding 101 -14 Slow   [31]

322 ELEGANT BILL [7] (T Fairhurst) 3-8-10 M Beecroft 7/2 Jt FAV: 00-0101: 3 ch g Nicholas
Bill - Elegant Star (Star Moss): Led below dist, ridden out in a 3yo h'cap at Carlisle May 2:
earlier made all in a similar event at Hamilton: eff over 8/9f: acts on yld & soft grnd
and does well on an undulating trk.   24
29   ICARO [1] (N Callaghan) 3-9-7 J Matthias 7/2 Jt FAV: 2301-02: Sustained chall final
1f, just held: ended last season with a decisive win in an Edinburgh maiden: half brother to
several winners: well suited by 8/9f and will stay further: acts on gd & heavy grnd
and on any trk: looks fairly h'capped and may win soon.   34
331 G G MAGIC [3] (M Morley) 3-9-7 M Birch 7/1: 2200-03: Stayed on from the rear: good
effort: half brother to several minor winners and won a seller at Catterick last season:
eff over 7/9f: acts on gd/firm & yld grnd & on any trk: genuine sort.   27
132 ROCKALL [8] (S Norton) 3-9-7(BL) J Lowe 8/1: 4030-04: Made most: began last season
with a narrow win in an Ayr maiden: later placed several times: cost $280,000: eff over
8/9f: acts on gd/firm & heavy grnd & on a gall trk.   20
130 VAN DER PUP [10] 3-8-7 S Keightley 33/1: 000-400: Kept on same pace: see 99.   03
--   GREENHILLS GIRL [5] 3-8-12 G Carter(3) 4/1: 001-0: Never beyond mid-div on reapp: ended
last season with a win in a fillies maiden at Hamilton (5f, heavy): seems sure to prove eff
beyond sprint dists and should be btr for this run.   03
*107 BANTEL BOWLER [6] 3-9-2 J Quinn(5) 8/1: 4400-10: Fin 8th: much btr over 1m in 107.   00
--   Bold Answer [2] 8-7   --   Allisterdransfield [4] 8-8
109 Dearham Bridge [9] 8-9
10 ran   hd,4,3,1½,3   (T Herring)   T Fairhurst Middleham, Yorks

381 GREAT GAMBLE STAKES 3YO+   £1179   1m 4f   Yielding 101 +12 Fast

*219 MUBAARIS [20] (P Walwyn) 3-8-6 N Howe 4/5 FAV: 3-11: 3 ch c Hello Gorgeous -
Aloft (High Top): Had to be strongly ridden when a narrow winner of a fast run 3yo stakes
at Carlisle May 2: first time out again kept on well under press to win a maiden at Newmarket: well suited by 12f: acts on gd/firm & yld grnd & on a stiff trk.   46
307 BANTEL BUSHY [13] (I Bell) 3-7-10 N Carlisle 8/1: 00-2222: Led into str, ran on
gamely when hdd: again clear of rem and is certainly due a change of luck: see 307 & 130.   34
--   TARTAN TAILOR [15] (G Richards) 5-9-0 J Carroll 20/1: -3: Stayed on well run in:
fair debut: evidently suited bt 12f on a stiff trk: acts on yld grnd.   22
--   COUNTRY JIMMY [14] (C Tinkler) 4-9-0 M Wood 20/1: 00-4: Stayed on from rear: lightly
raced last season: eff over 12f and should stay further: acts on yld grnd.   15
130 NITIDA [9] 3-7-7 L Charnock 8/1: 03-00: Yet to fulfil her juvenile promise: see 130.   08
--   SHANDON BELLS [2] 4-9-0 J Lowe 20/1: -0: Slowly away on racecourse debut: some late
prog and should do btr next time.   08
123 SAY SOMETHING [5] 3-7-7 A Mackay 5/1: 000-220: Made most till home turn: better in 123. 00
185 Favourite Nephew [18] 9-0   --   Paravane [8] 8-11
--   Brigadier Troy [16] 9-0   58   Nordic Secret [7] 9-0
164 Easy Kin [19] 9-0   8   Celtic Quest [11] 9-0
164 Marcellina [1] 8-11
239 Gunner Mac [6] 7-10   --   Hoad Hill [17] 7-10   --   Say Please [3] 8-11
307 Quarantino [10] 7-12(2ow)   247 Moving Performance [12] 7-10
--   Marinaville [4] 8-11
20 ran   ½,8,5,1½,2   (Hamdan Al-Maktoum)   P Walwyn Lambourn, Berks

Official Going Given as Good

382 ARLINGTON STAKES 2YO   £3074   5f   Good/Firm 38 -40 Slow

-146 QUEL ESPRIT [1] (M Mccormack) 2-9-0 S Cauthen 10/3: 121: 2 b c What A Guest -
Les Sylphides (Kashmir II): Useful colt: made almost all, comfortably in a 2yo stakes at
Newmarket May 2: first time out won a maiden at Doncaster: cost 10,000 gns: eff at 5f, should
stay 6f plus: acts on gd & soft grnd & a gall trk: held in high regard by his stable and
should win more races.   55

*212 MISTER MAJESTIC [6] (R Williams) 2-9-4 R Cochrane 11/10 FAV: 12: Heavily bckd: chall
final 1f: just btn and is in fine form: acts on gd/firm & yld: see 212.   56
--   ALKADI [3] (W O'gorman) 2-8-11 T Ives 5/1: 3: Active in mkt on debut: should impr:
eff at 5f, should stay further: acts on gd grnd and a gall trk: should find a maiden.   42
--   BUDDY RICH [8] (W O'gorman) 2-8-11 M L Thomas 16/1: 4: Mkt drifter: sn prom:
48,000 gns purchase: should be suited by further than 5f: half brother to useful winning
2yo Fleet Form.   32
--   RIOT BRIGADE [7] 2-8-11 G Baxter 8/1: 0: Mkt drifter on debut: impr likely from this
11,500 gns buy: half brother to several winners: should stay further than 5f.   26
--   MIGHTY BOLD [5] 2-8-11 W Carson 14/1: 0: Mkt drifter: prom early: cost I.R. 18,000
and will do better.   25
--   Sohams Taylor [4] 8-11
7 ran   ½,2½,4,2,nk   (Miss Laura Morgan)   M Mccormack Sparsholt, Oxon

383 EBF WILBRAHAM MAIDEN STAKES 2YO   £3197   5f   Good/Firm 38 -05 Slow

223 NATURALLY FRESH [12] (J Winter) 2-8-11 W R Swinburn 9/4 FAV: 41: Very promising filly:
landed many hefty bets when making ev yd for an impressive 7L win in a 2yo maiden at Newmarket May 2: also heavily bckd in running when 4th to Regency Fille
again at Newmarket: cost only 6,000 gns as a yearling and looks a bargain: eff at 5f,
should stay further: held in high regard & should continue to improve.   65
--   PLUM DROP [7] (R Armstrong) 2-8-11 W Carson 33/1: 2: Nearest fin on debut and impr
very likely: eff at 5f, should stay further: acts on gd/firm & a gall trk.   47
--   JAY GEE ELL [9] (E Eldin) 2-8-11 M L Thomas 20/1: 3: Sn prom: promising debut from
this cheaply acquired filly: half sister to a minor 5f winner: acts on gd/firm & a gall trk.   43
--   MINSTRELLA [6] (C Nelson) 2-8-11 J Reid 3/1: 4: Well bckd on debut: al prom and
will impr: should be suited by further than 5f: acts on gd/firm & should have no trouble
finding a maiden.   43
--   GO MY PET [11] 2-8-11 S Cauthen 10/3: 0: Active in mkt: sn prom and is a speedily
bred sort: half sister to a couple of sprint winners: possibly one to note on a sharper
trk: acts on gd/firm.   41
--   SILVERS ERA [2] 2-8-11 R Cochrane 20/1: 0: Early speed on debut: sprint bred who is
a half sister to several winners.   39
--   GARNET [3] 2-8-11 M Miller 14/1: 0: Mkt drifter: early speed: half sister to a minor
7f winner.   00
--   QUEEN MATILDA [10] 2-8-11 G Baxter 8/1: 0: Dwelt and no threat: should do btr over
longer distances.   00
--   Little Upstart [8] 8-11   186 Call For Taylor [5] 8-11
--   Ring Of Pearl [4] 8-11   --   Mariko Gold [1] 8-11
12 ran   7,1½,nk,½,½,   (G S Shropshire)   J Winter Newmarket

384 CORAL NEWMARKET STAKES 3YO LISTED   £12564   1m 2f Good/Firm 38 +07 Fast

--   VERD ANTIQUE [2] (H Cecil) 3-8-6(1ow) S Cauthen 11/10 FAV: -1: 3 b c Shirley Heights -
Vejana (Braccia Da Montone): Smart, highly promising colt: heavily bckd and came with a
strong run to lead inside the final 1f, comfortably in fast run Newmarket Stakes (Listed
race) at Newmarket May 2: has been working very well at home: eff at 10f, should stay 12f:
highly regarded & can only improve.   75
--   DANSKI [5] (P Cole) 3-8-5 T Quinn 16/1: 22322-2: Led 2f out: caught inside final
1f: luckless colt: excellent seasonal debut: showed very useful form as a 2yo, but met
some smart performers and is yet to get his head in front: eff at 10f, may stay 12f:
acts on firm & yld grnd and on any trk: must lose his maiden tag soon.   69
286 HELLO ERNANI [4] (I Balding) 3-8-5 T Ives 9/2: 203-223: Ran on well final 1f and
continues in fine form: see 60: stays 10f and will win soon.   67
224 SHIBIL [9] (M Stoute) 3-8-6(1ow) W R Swinburn 12/1: 33-44: Ch over 1f out: very
good effort: should be winning in the near future: see 224.   67
224 CLIVEDEN [10] 3-8-10 G Starkey 10/1: 213-00: Not btn far: ran well: very useful 2yo,
winning at Goodwood and also close up 3rd in Gr.3 Coventry Stakes at Royal Ascot: stays
10f: acts well on gd & firm grnd.   69
--   MILLERS DUST [1] 3-8-5 W Ryan 16/1: -0: Stable mate of winner: al there: prom debut:
eff at 10f, should stay 12f: half brother to 10f winner Dundy: acts on gd/firm & a gall trk:
should find a maiden.   58
--   JEWELLED REEF [8] 3-9-2 M Hills 16/1: 10-0: Made much, btr for race.   00
218 HAWARDEN [3] 3-8-5 B Thomson 11/1: -40: No threat: btr 218 (gd/yld).   00
--   FINAL TRY [7] 3-9-2 W Carson 33/1: 01230-0: Al there on seasonal debut.   00
--   SOUGHAAN [6] 3-9-2 A Murray 10/1: 1-0: Dsptd lead over 3f out: wknd.   00
10 ran   1½,½,½,1,3   (Sheikh Mohammed)   H Cecil Newmarket

385   GROUP 2 GEN. ACCIDENT JOCKEY CLUB STKS   £26008   1m 4f Good/Firm 38 +01 Fast

221   PHARDANTE [2] (G Harwood) 4-8-7 G Starkey 11/2: 0230-01: 4 b c Pharly - Pallante
(Taj Dewan): Smart colt: floored the odds on Slip Anchor in Gr.3 Jockey Club Stakes at
Newmarket May 2: given a fine ride by G Starkey, running on well to lead near fin: failed
to win in '85, though a fine 2nd to Oh So Sharp in the St Leger at Doncaster: smart 2yo,
winning at Ascot, Kempton, Salisbury & Lingfield: eff at 12f, stays 14f: best on gd & firm
grnd: genuine.   84
--   SLIP ANCHOR [3] (H Cecil) 4-8-12 S Cauthen 4/11 FAV: 11122-2: Led till close home:
pulled hard and this was probably his downfall: top class colt who in '85 was a runaway
winner of the Epsom Derby: earlier made all to win Gr.3 Derby Trial Stakes at Lingfield and
valuable Hethorn Stakes at Newmarket: on final outing was a gallant 2nd to Pebbles in Gr.1
Dubai Champion Stakes at Newmarket: winning 2yo at Nottingham: eff over 10f, nowadays suited
by 12f: acts on firm & soft grnd & on any trk: game & genuine: likes to be out in front and   88
will definitely come on for this race.   88
251   SEISMIC WAVE [1] (B Hills) 5-8-7 B Thomson 11/2: 0122-03: Dsptd lead going well 2f
out: wknd final 1f: good effort: running into form: smart colt who in '85 won Gr.3 Ormonde
Stakes at Chester and is again being aimed for that race next week: winning 2yo at Doncaster:
eff over 10f, stays 13f well: acts on gd & firm grnd & on any trk.   77
3 ran   nk,4.   (Simon Karmel)   G Harwood Pulborough, Sussex

386   CHARLES HEIDSIECK CHAMPAGNE HCP 3YO 0-6   £4978   1m   Good/Firm 38 -24 Slow [61]

--   KABIYLA [6] (M Stoute) 3-8-6(1ow) W R Swinburn 11/4 FAV: 1-1: 3 b f Busted - Karera
(Kalamoun): Useful filly: well bckd on seasonal debut and led over 2f out, easily in a slow
run, but valuable h'cap at Newmarket May 2: won sole start in '85 at Leicester: eff at
1m, may stay further: acts on gd & firm grnd & a gall trk and should continue to impr.   54
--   AUCTION FEVER [10] (B Hills) 3-8-10 B Thomson 12/1: 00333-2: Not the best of runs:
fin well: fine seasonal debut: showed promise in '85 but yet to win: eff at 1m, should be
suited by further: acts on gd/firm & yld & a gall trk: should find a h'cap soon.   50
--   DANCING EAGLE [4] (M Jarvis) 3-8-9 T Ives 25/1: 01-3: Ev ch over 1f out: good effort:
on final outing in '85 won at Lingfield: half brother to 2 winners, incl useful Italian
performer Will Dancer: eff at 7f, stays 1m: acts on gd & firm grnd & on any trk.   48
--   FLOATING ASSET [12] (P Walwyn) 3-8-6 G Baxter 16/1: 00124-4: Al up there on seasonal
debut: in '85 won a maiden at Leicester: eff at 7f, stays 1m: acts on gd & firm grnd and
a gall trk.   42
234   FARM CLUB [14] 3-8-12 G Duffield 14/1: 10-00: Ch over 1f out: good effort: first time
out in '85 won at Bath: eff at 1m, should be suited by further: acts on gd & yld.   47
--   SOMETHING CASUAL [5] 3-9-3 R Guest 33/1: 10-0: Stayed on well final 1f: pleasing
seasonal debut: first time out in '85 won at Doncaster: eff at 7f, should be suited by
1m plus: acts on gd grnd & a gall trk.   51
74   FARAG [7] 3-7-12 W Carson 3/1: 4031-20: Heavily bckd: btr 74 (heavy).   00
229   GEORGES QUAY [2] 3-7-8 D Mckay 7/1: 000-40: No show: btr 229 (7f, soft).   00
--   TWICE BOLD [8] 3-9-0 S Cauthen 7/1: 01-0: Wknd, btr for race.   00
141   Arrow Express [13] 7-7(BL)(1oh)   --   Palaestra [9] 9-7
216   Thalassino Asteri [3] 9-2   33   Pentland Hawk [1] 8-5
--   Pitprop [11] 8-5
14 ran   2½,hd,1½,¾,¾,½   (H H Aga Khan)   M Stoute Newmarket

387   ELY HANDICAP 3YO 0-70   £6659   6f   Good/Firm 38 -03 Slow   [69]

--   MERDON MELODY [8] (R Sheather) 3-7-9 M L Thomas 12/1: 01034-1: 3 b c Mummy's Pet -
Singing (Petingo): Useful colt: first time out, ran on well to lead post in a valuable 3yo
h'cap at Newmarket May 2: consistent performer in '85, being awarded a maiden at Sandown:
cost 44,000 gns: half brother to the useful Durham Place: eff at 4/6f: acts on firm &
soft grnd: seems a genuine sort.   49
220   LUNA BID [9] (M Blanshard) 3-9-5 R Cochrane 12/1: 1130-02: Led over 2f out: caught
near line: gallant effort from this very useful gelding: in fine form in '85, winning at
Newmarket, Salisbury & Kempton: half brother to the smart and much impr middle dist. winner
Lemhill and like him is a genuine sort. eff over 6f, should stay further: acts on firm &
soft grnd & likes to be up with the pace.   72
26   NICCOLO POLO [16] (B Hanbury) 3-8-9 W R Swinburn 8/1: 0300-33: Ch final 1f: ran
well: see 26.   58
228   QUARRYVILLE [7] (K Brassey) 3-9-2 R Hills 20/1: 413-004: Ran on well final 1f: good
effort and may win soon: consistent performer in '85, winning at Bath and Folkestone: eff
at 5f, stays 6f well: acts on firm & yld.   65
228   OH BOYAR [2] 3-8-13 B Thomson 6/1: 1300-30: Kept on well final 1f: in gd form: see 228. 62
138   YOUNG PUGGY [11] 3-8-1 W Ryan 14/1: 400-020: Nicely bckd: ran well: see 138.   49
241   TAYLOR OF SOHAM [12] 3-7-7(8oh) N Adams 33/1: 00-2340: Fin 7th: most consistent: see 38.00
274   MAJOR JACKO [14] 3-7-8 D Mckay 6/1: 00-0140: Twice below form: see 228 (soft). 00
70   OCEAN TRADER [10] 3-8-11(bl) P Waldron 16/1: 0122-00: Led 3f: fin 9th.   00

228	COLWAY COMET [1] 3-8-12(VIS) T Ives 10/1: 1203-00: Wknd over 1f out: btr 228 (soft).					00
227	MANTON DAN [6] 3-8-10 P Cook 5/1: 012-20: Well bckd: see 227.					00
314	Little Pipers [4] 8-8	--	Safeera [15] 8-3	*284	Golden Ancona [5] 8-3(7ex)	
245	Lochonica [18] 9-7	60	Marshal Macdonald [13] 9-0			
*309	Jarrovian [3] 8-1(7ex)			214	Mrs Waddilove [17] 7-7(5oh)	

18 ran　　shhd,1½,shhd,shhd,½,1,hd　　　　(J C Smith)　　　　　　　　　R Sheather Newmarket

---

388　NEWMARKET CHALLENGE WHIP 3YO MAIDEN　　　£0　　1m　　Good/Firm 38 -23 Slow

-- 　TIMBERWOOD [2] (H T Jones) 3-9-0 A Murray 5/2: 4040-1: 3 b c Tap On Wood - Enchanted
(Song): First time out, made most and gamely forced his head in front again on the post in
a rather slowly run 3yo maiden at Newmarket May 2: showed ability last season, notably when
a close 4th behind Tanaos in a maiden on this trk: well suited by fast going: stays 1m well.　　48
194　SARONICOS [4] (C Brittain) 3-9-0 P Robinson 11/10 FAV: 00-32: Led under press near
fin, hdd post: should find a maiden soon: see 194.　　47
130　SPINNING TURN [3] (P Calver) 3-9-0 S Cauthen 12/1: -03: Kept on under press and
this was a much impr effort: suited by a stiff 1m, likely to stay 10f: should find a maiden
in the North.　　45
-- 　STAVORDALE [1] (H T Jones) 3-9-0 R Hills 4/1: 0-4: Ev ch: stable companion of winner:
showed promise on only outing last season (rated 44): likely to impr.　　38
-- 　QUADRILLE [5] 3-8-11 G Duffield 8/1: 0-0: Btn a long way at the fin: unplaced only
outing in '85.　　10
5 ran　　hd,¾,4,20　　　　(Mrs H T Jones)　　　　　H T Jones Newmarket

389　DUBAI POULE DESSAI DES POULAINS GR 1　　£97241　　1m　　Very heavy -

*152　FAST TOPAZE [3] (G mikhalides) 3-9-2 C asmussen　: -11: 3 br c Far North - Pink Topaze
Hvly bkd fav, proved a decisive winner of Gr 1 Dubai Poule D'Essai des Poulains at Longchamp
Apr 27 and is now unbeaten in three races: earlier won Gr 3 race at Longchamp and in '85 won
Gr 2 race at St Cloud: very eff at 1m and looks sure to stay 12f: however all form so far
on soft or heavy ground: should rate more highly: likely to go for the French derby.　　85
*156　HIGHEST HONOR [6] (P bary) 3-9-2 F head　: -12: Continues to improve and fin well:
eff at 7f and looks sure to stay at least 10f: goes well in the mud: see 156.　　82
-- 　ART FRANCAIS [1] (P biancone) 3-9-2 E legrix　: -3: Much improved this season and a
winner last time at M-Laffitte on heavy ground: sure to be suited by 10f.　　81
-- 　SPLENDID MOMENT 0 (R collet) 3-9-2 Y st Martin　: 310-4: Ran well on unsuitable going:
winner of a Gr.3 race at Longchamp in '85 over 1m on firm grnd: will be suited by 10f.　　73
152　KALISTAN 0 3-9-2 J bernard　: -20: Led 5 out: fin well: see 152.　　69
-- 　ROCK ISLET 0 3-9-2 A badel　: -0: Earlier a winner at M'Laffitte: far from disgraced
and will be suited by 10f.　　66
-- 　MANETHO 0 3-9-2 A lequeux　: 32-0: Ran well last year on firm grnd, btn a whisker in
a Gr.3 race at Longchamp over 10f: sure to be suited by 12f this year.　　00
*159　ZAHDAM 0 3-9-2 G starkey　: 11-10: Most disapp on this heavy grnd: this was not
his running and is certainly worth another chance.　　00
8 ran　　1½,½,5,2½,1½,1½　　　　(M Fustok)　　　　　G mikhalides France

390　PRIX VICOMTESSE VIGIER GROUP 2　　　£21150　　2m　　Very Heavy -

153　AIR DE COUR (P biancone) 4-9-1 E legrix　: 1241-21: 4 b c Vigors - Amya: Developed
into a smart stayer and comfortably made all the running in a Gr.2 race at Longchamp Apr.27:
also won twice at Longchamp last year and also picked up a Gr.2 race at Deauville: stays
extremely well and loves soft/heavy.　　82
*153　DENEL (P bary) 7-8-13 C asmussen　: 0/43-12: Another good effort: see 153.　　75
153　GRANDCOURT (F boutin) 4-8-11 F head　: -33: --　　72
-- 　SOUTH GALE (C bartholemew) 6-8-11 A lequeux　: 33020-4: --　　64
-- 　ROYAL CHARTER 4-8-11 A gibert　: -0: --　　52
5 ran　　1½,nk,5,8　　　　(D Wildenstein)　　　　P biancone France

Official Going Given as Soft

391　GROUP 3 PRIX DU MUGUET 4YO　　　£17493　　1m　　Soft -

-- 　APELDOORN (P barbe) 4-8-7 M philliperon　: 023-1: 4 b c R B Chesne - Grey Magic:
Winning 2nd race on the trot, got up with a strong late run in a Gr.3 race at St Cloud May 1:
very eff at 1m on soft grnd.　　78
*2　EPHIALTES (C milbank) 4-8-11 A junk　: 43-0012: Just failed: remains in grand form.　　81
154　OVER THE OCEAN (G mikhalides) 4-8-11 A badel　: 1003-23: Fav, just went down in a
finish of heads: see 154.　　80

SAINT CLOUD   Thursday May 1ast - Cont'd

298	**BLUE TIP** (P biancone) 4-8-8 G mosse 1: 103-324: See 98, 298.	67
--	**THIRSTY** (R collet) 4-8-4 A gibert 1: -0: --	58
5 ran	hd,hd,6,2½ (P Barbe) P barbe France	

TURIN   Thursday May 1st

Official Going Given as Good to Soft

392 **GRAN PREMIO CITTA DI TORINO GR 3**   **£10862**   **1m**   **Yielding -**

-- **MANTERO** (G miliani) 5-9-2 A parravani : -1: 5 b h Derrylin - Sorato: Kept on
strongly when winning this Gr.3 race for the 2nd year running: well suited by 1m and acts
well on soft grnd.   **74**
-- **KATELL** (Italy) 7-9-2 M planard : -1112: Unbtn in 3 races this year, tried to make all **72**
5 **SULAAFAH** (H t jones) 4-9-2 A murray 1: 1010-43: Distant third, not yet back to
his best: see 5.   **63**
-- **SINSA** (Italy) 4-8-13 V panici : -4:   **57**
-- **MARY GUARD** 4-8-13 J heloury : 1-0:   **53**
-- **EXECUTIVE MAN** 5-9-2 F dessi : 040-0-0:   **52**
6 ran   1,5,1½,1½   (S Genzianella)   G miliani Italy

EVRY   Saturday April 26th

Official Going Given as Heavy

393 **PRIX DE LA BEAUCE 3YO MAIDEN C & G**   **£6440**   **1m**   **Heavy -**

-- **MAGICAL WONDER** (G mikhalides) 3-8-11 C asmussen : 4-1: 3 ch c Storm Bird - Fiona
Ardiente: Looked a high class prospect in the making when coming home in a canter in a
valuable maiden race at Evry Apr.26: very eff over 1m & acts on heavy grnd: should stay 10f.
certain to rate more highly.   **79+**
-- **FORBIDDING** (France) 3-8-11 Y st Martin : -2:   **65**
-- **STEINLEN** (France) 3-8-11 E legrix .: -3:   **57**
-- **SPACE HUNTER** (France) 3-8-11 - : -4:   **49**
-- **Northern Sham** 3-8-11   -- **Kirinyagga** 3-8-11
6 ran   5,4,4   (M Fustok)   G mikhalides France

CURRAGH   Saturday April 26th   Righthanded, Stiff Galloping Track

Official Going Given as Yielding/Soft

394 **GR 3 MT COOTE STUD ATHASI STKS 3YO F**   **£11550**   **7f**   **Yielding -**

-- **KEMAGO** [5] (J oxx) 3-8-7 Pat Eddery 11/2: -1-1: 3 b f Prince Tenderfoot - Pale Ivory:
Ran on well under press to win a fillies Gr.3 race at the Curragh Apr.26: also won over 7f at
the Curragh in '85: impr filly who acts on soft but does much btr on a sound surface.   **68**
-- **LADY LOIRE** [2] (C collins) 3-8-7 P shanahan 9/2: -011-2: Unbtn in her last 3 races,
kept on strongly and just btn.   **66**
*294 **THE BEAN SIDHE** [8] (J hayden) 3-9-0 C swan 12/1: 3110-13:   **70**
-- **CLASSIC STYLE** [16] (D weld) 3-8-11 M kinane 12/1: 0-4:   **66**
158 **SWEET ADELAIDE** [7] 3-8-11 B thomson 4/1 FAV: 130-20: Disapp fav: btr 158.   **65**
15ran   ½,1,nk,shhd,½   (B Cooke)   J oxx Ireland

395 **TETRARCH STAKES GROUP 3 3YO COLTS**   **£11550**   **7f**   **Yielding -**

-- **FLASH OF STEEL** (D weld) 3-9-2 M kinane 7/2: -0111-1: 3 b c Kris - Spark Of Fire:
Gamely led inside final 1f in a Gr.3 race at the Curragh Apr.26: has now won 4 races on the
trot and is very eff at 7/8f: possibly acts on any going.   **81**
-- **EQUATOR** (M v obrien) 3-8-7 Pat Eddery 5/1: -2: Ran most promisingly on debut, not
btn far but certain to be suited by 1m and impr likely next time.   **70**
267 **AIR DISPLAY** (M otoole) 3-8-7 D manning 5/4 FAV: 220-223: Well bckd, nearly made all
and not btn far: seems very genuine & consistent: see 267, 151.   **69**
-- **MR JOHN** (L browne) 3-8-11 M browne 20/1: 13100-4: Good seasonal debut and not btn far
on a close fin: a winner twice last year at Leopardstown and Naas: should be suited by 1m:
acts on soft but possibly btr on fast grnd.   **72**
8 ran   ½,shhd,shhd   (B Firestone)   D weld Ireland

396 BALLYSAX 3YO RACE   £5520   1m 2f Yielding

*150 IMPERIAL FALCON [1] (M v obrien) 3-9-2 Pat Eddery 4/7 FAV: -0-11: 3 b c Northern Dancer-
Ballade: Very promising colt: readily led 2 out in a valuable minor race at the Curragh
Apr.26: also easily won a maiden race at Phoenix Park Apr.5: cost a huge $8.2m as a yearling:
half brother to the useful though frustrating Ma Petite Jolie: eff at 10f & sure to stay
further:being aimed at the Derby: difficult to rate accurately.   80
269 WELSH FANTASY [8] (C collins) 3-8-11 P Shanahan 14/1: -210-02: Kept on well and looks
sure to be suited by 12f.   70
--   WORLD COURT [4] (T curtin) 3-8-11 K moses 16/1: -00-13:   64
--   EURIPUS [3] (M ryan) 3-8-11 D murphy 25/1: -00-204:   62
11 ran   1½,3,½,   .   (Sheikh Mohammed)   M v obrien Ireland

---

Official Going Given as Yielding

397 GROUP 2 PREMIO REGINA ELENA 3YO   £41552   1m   Yielding

--   DANZICA [1] (E Borromeo) 3-8-11(0) W carson : 4-4-31: 3 b f Rusticaro - Dupple:
Unlucky in running last time, gamely kept on to win a Gr.1 fillies race at Capannelle
Apr.27: eff at 1m & acts on soft grnd.   64
--   RUSSIAN LADY 0   3-8-11 G dettori   -12: Led over 3 out and ran very well.   61
--   VICTORIA FALLS 0   3-8-11 M paganini : 0432-13:   60
214 BUSTARA 0 (G wragg) 3-8-11 S cauthen : 010-04: Never closer but not disgraced.   58
--   ROMAN ELSIE 0 3-8-11 B jovine : 0-0:   56
--   SOL SYMPHON? 0 3-8-11 J Heloury : -0:   55
17 ran   1,½,½,1,hd   (M Borromeo)   E Borromeo Italy

Official Going Given as Very Heavy

398 GROUP 3 COPPA D'ORO DI MILANO 4YO+   £15176   1m 7f Very Heavy

--   ALAN FORD (V di Maggio) 6-8-11 V di Maggio : 440-111: 6 b h Run The Gantlet -
Chapeau Bleu: Came with a late chall and won easily and completed a hat trick of wins: seems
to love heavy grnd & stays very well.   75
1   WAGONER (France) 6-8-11 B thomson : 040-222:   71
--   TARVISIO   4-8-11 V Panici : -3:   59
6 ran   3,10,10   (S Emanuela)   V di Maggio Italy

Official Going Given as Good/Firm

399 AMBITION APP. HANDICAP 3YO+ (0-35)   £2068   1m   Good 55 -07 Slow   [34]

8   DIMENSION [13] (N Smith) 4-8-2(bl) J Carter(5) 33/1: 00-01: 4 b c Dominion - Airy
Queen (Sadair): Was a surprise winner, ran on strongly to lead close home in an app. h'cap
at Kempton May 3: lightly raced last season, showing some promise in maiden company: half
brother to several winners: seems best over 1m on fast grnd: well suited by a sharpish trk. 16
--   FLYHOME [1] (P Cundell) 5-9-13 C Carter(5) 11/1: 03200-2: Just failed in a blanket
fin on his reapp: quite a consistent h'capper who won a similar event at Sandown last season
and in '84 won at Bath & Wolverhampton: eff over 8/10f: well suited by gd/firm grnd: acts
on any trk: genuine sort who carries weight well.   40
--   HEATHGRIFF [17] (N Callaghan) 4-8-4 G Bardwell(5) 16/1: 20102-3: Narrowly btn on
seasonal debut: won a seller at Pontefract late last season: eff over 8f, stays 10f well:
well suited by fast grnd & a sharpish trk.   16
*262 SINGLE [5] (W Wightman) 4-9-13(5ex) David Eddery(5) 7/4 FAV: 20-0114: Led below dist till
close home: not btn far and remains in fine form: still looks fairly h'capped: see 262.   38
--   AUGUST [3] 5-9-10 J Dunne(5) 20/1: 04000-0: Made eye catching late prog. on reapp and
should go close next time: failed to win last season though in '84 won at Ayr: eff over
1m though seems btr suited by 10f: best on fast grnd and is well suited by forcing tactics. 32
262 GOLD LOFT [20] 4-8-10 P Simms(5) 12/1: -02-100: Good effort and clearly stays 1m
well: see 177.   17
112 SWIFT PALM [18] 9-9-3 D Price(3) 10/1: 330-000: Ran on too late though a fair effort. 00
340 NANOR [9] 3-7-8 P Hill(5) 8/1: 14-0030: Disapp run: much btr on yld in 340 (6f).   00

262	Any Business [7] 9-12	--	Long Bay [11] 8-11	--	Eucharis [23] 8-0	
--	The Ute [8] 7-7(bl)(1oh)			--	Running Bull [16] 9-0	
266	Sparkford Lad [4] 9-4	--	Spring Pursuit [22] 9-2			
10	Aqaba Prince [14] 9-0			174	Chaise Longue [21] 8-7	
--	Ostentatious [15] 8-3	333	Turcy Boy [19] 7-13	--	Dellwood Renown [6] 7-10	
343	Danedancer [10] 7-10(bl)(1ow)			--	Dukeswood [12] 7-8	
10	Foot Patrol [2] 9-4					
23 ran	nk,hd,nk,2,nk		(M A Ingram)		N Smith Lambourn, Berks.	

400   E.B.F. MENTMORE FILLIES MAIDEN 2YO   £2455   5f   Good 55 -07 Slow

180   CLARENTIA [3] (M Usher) 2-8-11 M Wigham 7/2: 21: 2 ch f Ballad Rock - Laharden (Mount Hagen): Impr filly: went on ½way and kept on well to win a 2yo fillies maiden at Kempton May 3: missed the break when narrowly btn by Strike Rate on her debut at Brighton last month: well suited by 5f on a sharpish trk: acts on gd/firm grnd.   **47**

--   MARIMBA [9] (J Winter) 2-8-11 B Rouse 11/10 FAV: 2: Heavily bckd debutant: ran on strongly though not reach winner: sprint bred filly who is a half sister to the very useful 6/8f winner Larionov: acts on gd grnd & on a sharpish trk: clearly has plenty of pace and should be winning soon.   **45**

--   RECREATION [10] (W Jarvis) 2-8-11 W Ryan 14/1: 3: Easy to back on debut: outpcd early though had ev ch inside dist and should impr for this experience: acts on gd grnd & on a sharpish trk: should stay further in time.   **38**

270   PARKLANDS BELLE [2] (M Haynes) 2-8-11 R Fox 11/2: 024: Ran on late: in good form: acts on good: see 270.   **37**

--   EBONY PRIDE [7] 2-8-11 G Duffield 20/1: 0: Front rank most of way on debut: speedily bred filly who cost I.R. 3,700 as a yearling: acts on gd grnd & on a sharpish trk: should do better.   **35**

270   HIT LUCKY [5] 2-8-11 S Whitworth 20/1: 00: Broke well, hdd ½way and sn no extra: half sister to a couple of winners and showed signs of impr here.   **25**

--   WATER OF LOVE [4] 2-8-11 P Cook 6/1: 0: Never in it on debut: fin 8th.   **00**

--	Surely Great [6] 8-11	--	French Plait [1] 8-11	--	Eileen A Lee [8] 8-11	
10 ran	¾,2½,nk,½,5		(Mrs Nicholas Kairis)		M Usher Lambourn, Berks	

401   HAWKINS HARROW HANDICAP 3YO+ (0-60)   £5103   6f   Good 55 +13 Fast   [54]

306   FOOLISH TOUCH [6] (K Stone) 4-7-12(vis) P Burke(7) 7/1: 01-0031: 4 b g Hot Spark - Nushka II (Tom Fool): Led before ½way and ran on well to win a fast run and valuable h'cap at Kempton May 3: last season was a well bckd winner of a selling h'cap at Newmarket, earlier won first time out at Ayr: in '84 won at Yarmouth: eff over 5/7f: acts on any going & on any trk: in good form.   **35**

+192   TYROLLIE [10] (N Vigors) 4-9-4 P Cook 5/1: 0402-12: Kept on well: in fine form: see 192.   **49**

--   MANCHESTERSKYTRAIN [1] (L Cottrell) 7-9-3 I Johnson 16/1: 14200-3: Stayed on well final 1f on seasonal debut: useful h'capper who won a valuable race at Ascot last season: in '84 won at Goodwood, Brighton & Bath: very eff over 5/7f: acts on any going & on any trk: should go close next time.   **48**

266   EXERT [14] (R Akehurst) 4-7-7(2oh) N Adams 12/1: 400-344: Al close up, not btn far: see 111. **23**

192   AMEGHINO [12] 6-9-2 R Wernham 9/2 FAV: 3000-00: Stayed on well: gd effort: see 192.   **45**

165   DAWNS DELIGHT [8] 8-9-7 W Woods(3) 10/1: 140-000: Fair effort under top weight: scored in valuable h'caps at Doncaster and Haydock last term and in '84 was successful at Doncaster, Salisbury & Lingfield: very eff over 5/6f: acts on firm & soft grnd & on any trk.   **46**

172   BAY PRESTO [7] 4-8-5(bl) S Whitworth 6/1: 0200-30: Al close up: fin 7th: see 172.   **00**

*160   WILL GEORGE [2] 7-9-2 W Ryan 5/1: 3-13110: Fin 8th: btr on yld in 160 (gall trk).   **00**

--   GREEN DOLLAR [4] 3-8-13 G Duffield 9/1: 10210-0: Close up over ½way on seasonal debut: useful colt who used front running tactics when twice successful at Windsor last season: eff over 5/6f: acts on gd & firm grnd & is well suited by a sharp trk: btr for race.   **00**

327	Deputy Head [13] 8-10	--	Ferryman [3] 8-11	--	Armitage [9] 8-9	
314	Crete Cargo [11] 8-11	112	Peanday [15] 7-10(2ow)	--	Cats Lullaby [16] 7-7(4oh)	
15 ran	2,shhd,nk,hd,2,nk		(M Chandler)		K Stone Malton, Yorks	

402   WINDSOR PARK MAIDEN STAKES 3YO   £4783   1m   Good 55 +01 Fast

213   VIANORA [13] (G Harwood) 3-8-11 A Clark 7/4 FAV: 3-01: 3 ch f Ahonoora - Miss Portal (St Paddy): Useful filly: showed a good turn of foot to lead close home in a 3yo maiden at Kempton May 3: placed behind Elwadhna in a Newmarket maiden on sole start last term: eff over 7/8f: acts on firm & yld grnd & on any trk.   **54**

218   BEAU SHER [8] (B Hanbury) 3-9-0 A J Geran(7) 20/1: -02: Easy to back: effort after ½way, kept on well & just btn: half brother to 7f winner Salala: eff over 1m on gd & yld grnd seems to act on any trk: should lose his maiden tag soon.   **56**

--   DUFF [5] (D Elsworth) 3-9-0 D Brown 11/2: 0423-3: Led/dsptd lead all the way, just btn: showed plenty of promise last season when placed in 3 of his 4 starts, notably when 3rd to Cromwell Park in a Newmarket maiden on final start: eff over 7/8f: acts on firm & yld grnd & on any trk: suited by forcing tactics: progressive type who is sure to win a race.   **55**

--   SHAFY [20] (M Stoute) 3-9-0 A Kimberley 11/4: 32-4: Well bckd on reapp. and put up a good effort: showed plenty of promise last season when placed in both starts, running up to Illumineux in a Newmarket maiden last backend: eff over 7/8f on gd & firm grnd: must find a race this season.   **54**

--   KENANGA [21] 3-8-11 W Ryan 7/2: -0: Kept on promisingly on racecourse debut: half sister to Ribblesdale winner Strigida: clearly eff over 1m on a sharpish trk, though will be suited by a longer trip: acts on gd ground: nicely bckd today & should go close when stepping up in distance.   **49**

217 NEEDLEWOMAN [26] 3-8-11 V Smith(6) 50/1: -00: Never nearer over this longer trip: impr effort.   **45**

--   LAJNATA [16] 3-8-11 D Price 50/1: -0: Unfancied on racecourse debut: al there and should improve.   **44**

234 BOLD BORDERER [10] 3-9-0 N Adams 50/1: 3300-00: Fin 8th though not btn that far.   **46**

218 Sharpetto [27] 9-0	-- Coccoluto [12] 9-0	-- Admirals All [23] 9-0	
328 Frangnito [17] 9-0	-- Forward Move [7] 9-0	198 Haddon Lad [24] 9-0	
277 Lightning Byte [1] 9-0		-- Orange Dale [18] 9-0	
-- Quick Dancer [22] 9-0	-- Royal Loch [19] 9-0	-- Saryan [4] 9-0	
-- Soho Sam [6] 9-0	-- Tebitto [2] 9-0	253 The Quietstan [28] 9-0	
-- Bibi Khatoun [3] 8-11	-- Great Dilemma [11] 8-11		
-- Princess Andromeda [15] 8-11		-- Ikraam [9] 9-0	
26 ran nk,½,nk,1,2½,hd	(J Richmond-Watson)	G Harwood Pulborough, Sussex	

---

403   PRINCESS HANDICAP STAKES 4YO+ (0-60)   £3163   1m 4f Good 55 +10 Fast   [55]

189 POCHARD [9] (P Cole) 4-9-1 T Quinn 5/2 FAV: 2323-31: 4 b c Affirmed - Telferner (Tell): Useful colt: again set off in front and held on well for a narrow win in a fast run h'cap at Kempton May 3: consistent performer last season, winning at Carlisle, Wolverhampton and Kempton: well suited by 12f: acts on firm & yld grnd & on any trk: suited by forcing tactics and may win again.   **55**

-312 HOLY SPARK [6] (D Elsworth) 6-8-8 A Mcglone 5/1: -0122: Ran on gamely, just denied.   **47**

--   CONVINCED [5] (G Harwood) 4-9-7 A Clark 10/1: 1100-3: Fine effort under top weight on seasonal debut: was a comfortable winner at Pontefract & Goodwood in June last year, though subsq. rather disapp in h'cap company: half brother to useful miler Teamwork: eff over 10/12f: acts on gd/firm grnd & on a sharpish trk.   **58**

263 BOLD REX [8] (J Dunlop) 4-9-5 B Rouse 7/2: 2031-44: Not btn far, clear of rem: see 263   **55**

--   SAINTLY LAD [7] 4-8-2 N Adams 20/1: 0004-0: Ran on well from rear: never nearer: best effort last season when placed behind Ladys Bridge in a Newbury maiden on final start in July: eff over 11/13f: acts on gd & yld grnd: looks fairly h'capped.   **28**

225 EVROS [1] 4-8-13 T Lucas 16/1: 004-000: Lost place early in str: should do btr when reverting to 10f: last season won at Sandown, Nottingham & Haydock: acts on gd/firm & yld grnd and is suited by a gall trk.   **36**

312 BLOODLESS COUP [4] 4-8-12 D Mckay 7/2: 000-030: Much btr over 14f in 312 (easier grnd). **00**

--   JAZAIR [2] 4-8-4 P Cook 9/1: 10000-0: Btn approaching str: fin 8th on reappearance.   **00**

--   Easter Rambler [3] 7-7(5oh)   312 Full Of Dreams [10] 7-7(20oh)

10 ran   nk,2,hd,10,1   (Fahd Salman)   P Cole Whatcombe, Oxon

---

404   WATERLOO MAIDEN AUCTION STAKES 2YO   £2210   5f   Good 55 -12 Slow

230 PARIS GUEST [11] (Pat Mitchell) 2-8-5 G Duffield 11/1: 01: 2 b c What A Guest - Gay Pariso (Sir Gaylord): Impr colt: smartly away and made virtually ev yd, comfortably in a 2yo maiden auction race at Kempton May 3: half brother to smart juvenile winner Northern Chimes: eff over 5f on gd grnd: well suited by forcing tactics on a sharpish trk.   **42**

261 ORIOLE DANCER [12] (D Thom) 2-8-3 T Quinn 25/1: 0002: Dsptd lead till ½way: good effort: see 186.   **34**

186 TAP THE BATON [10] (M Tompkins) 2-8-9 M Rimmer 13/2: 43: Kept on under press: in good form: see 186.   **40**

254 HAZELS GIRL [4] (A Madwar) 2-8-0 R Morse(5) 14/1:   -2304: Mkt drifter: 5L clear of rem: see 118 & 20.   **30**

--   GREY WOLF TIGER [6] 2-8-3 A Mcglone 12/1: 0: Ran on too late, though should do btr next time: acts on gd grnd: maybe btr suited by a gall trk.   **23**

--   DERRING DEE [4] 2-8-0 N Adams 25/1: 0: Nearest fin on racecourse debut: sprint bred filly who cost 3,000 gns as a yearling: acts on gd grnd & on a sharpish trk.   **20**

--   CALIBOGUE [3] 2-8-7 B Rouse 8/1: 0: Showed gd speed over ½way and should impr.   **00**

180 SANDHURST [2] 2-8-11 P Cook 13/8 FAV: 30: Well bckd: disapp effort after promising debut in 180.   **00**

323 ACQUISITIVE [14] 2-8-5 M Wigham 7/2: 320: Nicely bckd though never in it: btr in 230.   **00**

-- Briggs Builders [5] 8-3		3 Lauries Warrior [7] 9-0	
-- Pearlitic [1] 8-3	-- Branstown Sunset [9] 8-11		
-- Kieron Press [13] 8-7			
14 ran 2,shhd,½,5,hd,shhd	(A J Cousins)	Pat Mitchell Polegate, Sussex	

Official Going Given as Good

405   PHILIP CORNES MAIDEN STAKES 2YO   £3249   5f   Firm 15 -12 Slow

--   **ZAIBAQ** [3] (H T Jones) 2-9-0 A Murray 15/8 fav: 1: 2 b c Danzig - Sounds Of Secret
(Secretariat): Very prom colt: first time out, gained a pillar-to-post success comfortably in
a 2yo maiden at Newmarket May 3: cost $1.6m and is very highly regarded by his powerful
stable: sure to stay 6f & probably further: must be followed until btn.   62

--   **SAMEEK** [1] (R Armstrong) 2-9-0 W Carson 20/1: 2: Kept on well, good debut from this
24,000 gns purchase: speedily bred (sire won the Coventry Stakes): hard to beat next time.   57

--   **MANSOOJ** [9] (N Callaghan) 2-9-0 R Cochrane 7/2: 3: Al prom, not btn far: good effort
from this 42,000 gns Feb. colt: well bckd today and should gain compensation before long.   54

--   **DUTCH COURAGE** [7] (D Morley) 2-9-0 S Cauthen 16/1: 4: Ev ch: good debut: certain to
stay at least 6f: should have no difficulty winning a maiden in the Midlands/North.   48

--   **GULF KING** [6] 2-9-0 C Asmussen 11/1: 0: Mkt drifter and ran on only 3 shoes, performed
creditably in circumstances: half brother to 5 winners incl useful hurdlers Star Burst and
Copse And Robbers: sure to be suited by 6f & further: acts on firm: will impr on this next time.   39

--   **LACK A STYLE** [4] 2-9-0 S Craine 33/1: 0: Fell out of the stalls, outpcd till late
prog: quite cheaply acquired: may need further than 5f.   34

--   **BESTPLAN** [10] 2-9-0 T Ives 7/2: 0: Heavily bdkd debutant, early speed, fin 7th:
half brother to smart sprinter Sayf El Arab and useful sprinter Eagle's Landed: speedily bred
sort who should impr on this next time.   33

--   **Melody Maker** [2] 9-0   --   **On Your Princess** [5] 9-0

--   **Pacific Basin** [8] 9-0

10 ran   ¾,1,2,3,1½   (Hamdan Al-Maktoum)   H T Jones Newmarket

406   LADBROKES HANDICAP 3YO 0-70   £9614   7f   Firm 15 +13 Fast   [75]

326   **SYLVAN EXPRESS** [2] (P Mitchell) 3-7-9 G Carter[2] 6/1: 0211-01: 3 b c Baptism -
Folle Remont (Prince Tenderfoot): Useful colt: led dist. and held on to win a fast run &
valuable 3yo h'cap at Newmarket May 3: easy winner of valuable nurseries at Newmarket & Ascot
at the end of '85: seems best around 7f on gd or firm going (below his best in 326 over 1m
on soft): still impr.   56

210   **FLEET FORM** [3] (C Nelson) 3-8-8 J Reid 20/1: 300-122: Denied a clear run dist, fin
strongly: unlucky? continues to impr and should win again soon: see 24.   68

216   **MISTER WONDERFUL** [9] (J Dunlop) 3-8-11 W Carson 7/2 jt fav: 210-33: Running on only
3 shoes, took an age to find his stride but fin in good style: how far would he have won if
correctly shod? compensation awaits next time: see 216: will stay 1m.   70

--   **NATIVE OAK** [8] (H Cecil) 3-9-2 S Cauthen 7/2 jt fav: 313-4: Al there, not btn far in
a driving fin and ran a   fine seasonal debut: won 1 of his 3 races in '85 but has been
working very well on the home gallops recently: well suited by 7f, will stay at least 1m:
acts on firm & good grnd & on a gall trk: sure to run well next time.   75

78   **WESHAAM** [7] 3-7-7(1oh) N Carlisle 8/1: 30-20: Al prom, not btn far in a gd finish:
a certainty for a maiden race: see 78.   49

220   **SPERRY** [4] 3-9-7 C Asmussen 5/1: 3210-20: Made most, kept on gamely in usual
fashion: see 220.   74

59   **Firm Landing** [5] 9-0   --   **Prince Pecadillo** [1] 9-5

59   **Hidden Brief** [10] 8-9   --   **Basoof** [6] 8-1

10 ran   ½,¾,nk,½,¾   (Mrs R A Johnson)   P Mitchell Epsom, Surrey

407   GROUP 1 GEN. ACCIDENT 2000 GUINEAS 3YO   £107145   1m   Firm 15 -10 Slow

*226   **DANCING BRAVE** [3] (G Harwood) 3-9-0 G Starkey 15/8 fav: 11-11: 3 b c Lyphard -
Navajo Princess (Drone): Top class colt: al prom, chall 2f out and slaughtered his rivals
for foot when sprinting clear in the final 1f to win slowly run Gr.1 2,000 Guineas at
Newmarket May 3: first time out, comfortably won Craven Stakes, again at Newmarket: easy
winner of both starts in '85, at Newmarket & Sandown: very eff over 1m should be well suited
by further: acts on soft but his fine action is well suited by firm or good grnd: regarded by
his powerful stable as being the best miler they have trained: not one to oppose this season.   98

*220   **GREEN DESERT** [9] (M Stoute) 3-9-0 W R Swinburn 12/1: 1214-12: Top class colt: led inside
final 3f, kept on well and lost nothing in defeat against this exceptional winner: sure to
win more top class races: see 220.   88

--   **HUNTINGDALE** [12] (J Hindley) 3-9-0 M Hills 6/1: 221-3: Well bckd on seasonal debut,
kept on well against press: seemed to run up to his best: lightly raced in '85 winning the
Dewhurst on final outing at Newmarket: eff at 7f, stays 1m & may well stay further: acts on
firm & yld & is suited by a stiff gall trk: should win decent races over 1m so long as he
does not come up against Dancing Brave again.   83

226   **SHARROOD** [1] (W Hern) 3-9-0 W Carson 14/1: 1111-04: Kept on well to be a close 4th:
grand effort and continues to impr: see 226.   82

*244   **SURE BLADE** [6] 3-9-0 B Thompson 13/2: 1113-10: Al well there, just lacks top class foot   78

302   **HAIL TO ROBERTO** [7] 3-9-0 C Asmussen 66/1: 20: French chall: led almost 6f: good
effort & acts on firm & heavy: see 302.   76

249 VAINGLORIOUS [2] 3-9-0 R Curant 66/1: 1102-00: Highly creditable 7th and is evidently still on the up grade: winner at Lingfield & Newmarket in '85: seems to act on gd/firm & softish going: eff 6f and stays 1m: genuine sort.   76

*249 FAUSTUS [11] 3-9-0 S Cauthen 12/1: 1112-10: Ev ch, fin 8th: btr 249 (soft).   70

*293 TOCA MADERA [5] 3-9-0 S Craine 9/1: --11-10: Outpcd in 9th: said to be suited by firm but looks a mud-lark: see 293 (heavy).   70

267 TATE GALLERY [10] 3-9-0 T Ives 12/1: -011-30: Last to fin and has been totally disapp this season so far: see 267.

226	Jazetas [4] 9-0	152	Exotic River [13] 9-0	249	Hallgate [15] 9-0
--	Alshinfarah [14] 9-0	159	Farncombe [8] 9-0 R		

15 ran   3,1½,hd,1½,¾,shhd,2½,shhd   (K Abdulla)   G Harwood Pulborough, Sussex

---

408 GROUP 3 PALACE HOUSE STAKES 3YO+   £15118 5f Firm 15 +22 Fast

-- DOUBLE SCHWARTZ [13] (C Nelson) 5-8-10 B Thompson 12/1: 1D012-1: 5 b h Double Form - Cassy's Pet (Sing Sing): Smart sprinter: first time out, led dist, comfortably in very fast run Gr.3 Palace House Stakes at Newmarket May 3: in '85 won a valuable event at Newmarket and was also first past the post in a Gr.3 race at Phoenix Park but subsq. disq: stays 6f, possibly best at 5f: acts on gd/firm & on any trk.   78

272 CLANTIME [12] (R Whitaker) 5-8-10 D Mckeown 25/1: 100-022: Made most: remarkable effort for one rated only 43 by the h'capper: would trot up in the h'cap if reproducing this form: see 272.   73

-- IMPERIAL JADE [11] (A Jarvis) 4-8-7 J Lowe 33/1: 42030-3: Al there, not btn far: good seasonal debut: carried top weight to victory in a h'cap at Salisbury in '85: very eff over 5f on firm grnd on a stiff trk: probably acts on any going: genuine filly who carries weight well.   69

-- WELSH NOTE [1] (I Balding) 3-7-9 G Carter 11/2: 22214-4: Poorly drawn, creditable seasonal debut in the circumstances: most consistent filly in '85 winning first 2 outings at Lingfield & Windsor and subsq. a valuable Listed race in Ireland: also 2nd 4 times, notably in the Queen Mary Stakes at Royal Ascot: very eff at 5f though probably acts on firm & soft grnd.   63

222 QUE SYMPATICA [3] 4-8-7 M Miller 11/1: 404-330: Btr 222 (6f).   57

-- MAROUBLE [4] 3-8-2 J Reid 15/2: 14023-0: Al prom: very consistent in '85, winning Norfolk Stakes at Royal Ascot and placed in 3 of his 4 subsequent runs, notably when narrowly btn by Hallgate, again at Ascot: acts well on firm grnd: is very eff around 5f.   62

-245 AMIGO LOCO [7] 5-8-10(bl) M Hills 10/1: 0-02220: Ev ch, fin 7th: btr 245 (6f, yld).   58

-- STORM WARNING [2] 4-8-7 T Ives 5/1: -4310-0: Early speed, fin 8th & should benefit from seasonal debut.   00

-- PRINCE SABO [9] 4-9-4 W R Swinburn 4/1 fav: 41020-0: No dngr & should benefit from seasonal debut.   00

222 PRINCE REYMO [5] 6-9-0 S Cauthen 15/2: 02D2-40: Poorly drawn? btr 222 (6f).   00

-- DUBLIN LAD [10] 3-7-12 W Carson 7/1: 13200-0: Well bckd seasonal debutant, early speed and should impr for the outing.   00

--	Modest [8] 8-7	272	Broadwater Music [6] 8-10

13 ran   1,hd,1½,2½,hd,½   (R Sangster)   C Nelson Upper Lambourn, Berks

---

409 CULFORD STAKES 3YO   £4240 1m 4f Firm 15 -12 Slow

-- HEIGHLAD [2] (O Douieb) 3-9-0 W R Swinburn 10/1: -1: 3 b c Shirley Heights - Good Lass (Reform): Prom colt: first time out, led 3f out & despite showing signs of inexperience, held on well to win quite a valuable minor event at Newmarket May 3: unraced in '85: half brother to useful Bonne Ile: well suited by 12f on firm going: sure to impr further & win more races.   60

*231 PAEAN [8] (H Cecil) 3-9-7 S Cauthen 8/13 fav: 2-12: Fin strongly, just failing to land the odds: continues to impr and will win more races: will stay further than 12f: acts on firm & heavy: see 231.   66

-- STORMY PROSPECT [5] (M Jarvis) 3-9-0 T Ives 20/1: -3: Al well there, good racecourse debut: half brother to useful winners Felthorpe Mariner & Footshore: stays 12f but may possibly prove just as effective over 10f (if not more so): acts on firm: sure to win soon.   54

-- WHITE REEF [1] (W Hern) 3-9-0 W Carson 5/1:   -3-4: Dsptd lead 10f: good seasonal debut: rated 57 when close 3rd to smart Nomrood in a backend maiden at Newmarket: half brother to several useful winners incl Irish Oaks winner Swiftfoot: sure to be suited by 12f: acts on firm grnd: will strip much fitter next time.   42

-- FRENCH FLUTTER [3] 3-9-0 R Cochrane 25/1: 30020-0: Made much: needed race? good 2nd under 9-7 in a nursery at Pontefract last season (1m, good): should be suited by 12f.   35

-- VERITABLE [4] 3-9-0 T Williams 20/1: 43-0: Prom over 1m on seasonal debut: placed both outings '85: half brother to smart Ulterior Motive should have no problem picking up a middle dist maiden in the near future.   25

219 PEARLY KING [7] 3-9-0 G Starkey 12/1: -40: Ran as if something badly amiss: see 219.   00

--	Turmeric [6] 9-0	--	Hopeful Line [9] 8-11

9 ran   hd,2½,8,5,7   (Sheikh Mohammed)   O Douieb Newmarket

410   TURN OF THE LANDS HANDICAP 0-60 4YO+   £5572   1m 2f Firm 15 -01 Slow   [55]

--   BEN ADHEM [5] (H Candy) 4-8-1 T Williams 7/1: 03014-1: 4 b g Hotfoot - Heaven Chosen
(High Top): First time out, led dist. under press in a close fin to a h'cap at Newmarket
May 3: lightly raced prior to winning a h'cap at Lingfield in Oct.'85: well suited by 10f
and fast going: acts on any trk: continues to impr.   38
--   WYLFA [4] (J Shaw) 5-8-11 P Robinson 11/1: 11140/2: Fin strongly, fine effort in
first outing since Oct.'84: last season successful at Newmarket, Redcar & Sandown: best
form on firm or good going over 10f & likes a gall trk: rated 65 in '84 & looks very well
h'capped at present: should not be missed next time.   46
--   MIN BALADI [2] (S Norton) 4-7-13 J Lowe 3/1 fav: 3411-3: Chall. final 1f, not btn
far: good seasonal debut: lightly raced in '85 winning final 2 on the trot, both at Redcar:
equally eff at 10 & 12f, suited by firm grnd: runs well at Redcar: should go well next time. 32
176 BANK PARADE [6] (J Davies) 5-9-5 J Reid 12/1: 0424-44: Chall 2f out: see 176.   50
--   HANDLEBAR [7] 4-8-2 W Carson 5/1: -0031-0: Well bckd on seasonal debut, ev ch:
lightly raced in '85 winning a maiden at Beverley: stays 10f well & acts on firm & good:
will strip fitter next time.   27
--   ISLAND SET [10] 4-8-10 R Guest 8/1: 03411-0: Creditable seasonal debut: winner of
minor races at Goodwood & Yarmouth on final 2 outings in '85: suited by 10f & firm or good
going: fairly h'capped at present.   33
4   PAGAN SUN [8] 5-8-8 G Thomas[7] 7/1: 0040-20: Dsptd lead after ½way, fin 9th: btr 4(12f) 00

--   Asswan [1] 9-9   **333** Deramin [3] 8-0   --   Joli Wasfi [12] 8-4(1ow)
248 Shellman [9] 8-12   **17**   Well Covered [11] 8-5(1ow)
12 ran   ¾,½,½,3,½   (Gerald Kidd)   H Candy Wantage, Oxon

Official Going Given as Good

411   SIR RICHARD FAIREY MEM.STAKES 3YO   £2637   1m 2f Yielding 95 +01 Fast

190 BADARBAK [5] (R Johnson Houghton) 3-8-12 K Darley 2/1 FAV: 103-31: 3 b c Julio Mariner -
Bengala (Hard To Beat): Useful colt: led 2f out, staying on gamely in a 3yo stakes at Haydock
May 3: first time out in '85 won at Windsor: half brother to 12f winner Badalushka and is
stamina endowed: eff at 10f, should stay 12f: acts on firm & yld & on any trk: genuine sort
who should win more races.   59
231 LOCAL HERBERT [7] (I Balding) 3-8-11 J Matthias 4/1: 02-42: Chall final 1f: just
btn: fine effort: acts on yld & heavy & should have no trouble finding a maiden: see 231.   57
--   TOMMY WAY [3] (J Dunlop) 3-9-2 G Baxter 3/1: -021-3: Al prom: good seasonal debut:
8L clear rem: in '85 was an impressive 8L winner of a maiden at Haydock: eff at 1m, stays
10f: acts on gd/firm & soft grnd and on any trk: should be winning soon.   60
244 CENTREPOINT [4] (J Etherington) 3-9-4 M Wood 11/1: 001-44: Stays 10f: see 244.   48
48 DENBERDAR [1] 3-8-11 S Perks 10/1: 0-20: Stiff task: no show: eff at 10f on yld &
heavy grnd & a gall trk.   38
348 GORGEOUS STRIKE [6] 3-9-4 R Hills 13/2: 123-020: Led ½m out: too soon after 348?   44
--   CASHEW KING [2] 3-8-13 J Hillis(5) 33/1: 0010-0: Made much 1m.   00
7 ran   ½,1½,8,1½,hd   (H H Aga Khan)   R Johnson Houghton Didcot, Oxon

412   STOCKPORT HANDICAP 3YO UPWARDS 0-50   £2934   5f   Yielding 95 +09 Fast   [42]

355 GOLD DUCHESS [4] (M W Easterby) 4-7-7 L Charnock 11/2: -042431: 4 b f Sonnen Gold -
Dutch Gold (Goldhill): Impr filly: made almost all, comfortably in quite a fast run h'cap
at Haydock May 3 (first success): eff at 5/6f on gd & soft grnd: acts on any trk.   19
--   GEORGE WILLIAM [1] (P Bevan) 5-8-13 P Waldron 10/1: 30000-2: Ev ch over 1f out: good
seasonal debut: in good form in '85, winning h'caps at Wolverhampton (2), Doncaster & Ripon:
very eff over 5f, stays 6f well: acts on any trk.   33
+**321** SULLYS CHOICE [2] (D Chapman) 5-9-4(7ex) D Nicholls 7/1: 000-013: In good form: see 321 30
+**182** BINCLEAVES [10] (M Mccormack) 8-8-12 G Baxter 9/2: 010-014: Never nearer: btr 182.   20
306 RIVERSIDE WRITER [7] 4-8-7 P Darcy 6/1: 0-10340: Never nearer: best 84 (sharpish trk). 13
--   STONEYDALE [3] 4-9-1 N Connorton 16/1: 33000-0: No threat on seasonal debut: failed
to win in '85, though a useful 2yo, winning at Warwick, Beverley, Hamilton & Edinburgh: very
eff over 5f on fast grnd: goes well on a sharpish trk, though acts on any.   15
369 SHANOUSKA [8] 6-7-12(VIS) S P Griffiths(5) 8/1: 00-2100: Twice below form 135 (heavy). 00
--   UPTOWN GIRL [5] 6-8-0 R Hills 7/2 FAV: 00111-0: First time out: early speed: btr
for race: in fine form at the backend of '85, completing a hat trick at Warwick, Haydock &
Beverley: in '84 won at Edinburgh: very eff over 5f, stays 7f: acts on firm & soft grnd &
on any trk.   00
70 Gentileschi [9] 9-9   --   Russian Winter [6] 7-7(7oh)
10 ran   2,3,1½,¾,2½   (C F Buckton)   M W Easterby Sheriff Hutton, Yorks

413   FAIREY SPRING TROPHY 3YO UPWARDS   £9182   7f   Yielding 95 -06 Slow

+330 BOLLIN KNIGHT [3] (M H Easterby) 4-9-4 M Birch 3/1: -0111: 4 b g Immortal Knight -
Lush Secret (Most Secret): Smart, impr gelding: well ridden to get up close home, under press
in a valuable Listed race at Haydock May 3: in fine form, earlier winning a valuable stakes
at Leicester and a ready winner of a h'cap at Newcastle: off the trk in '85, though a smart
juvenile in '84, winning at Doncaster, Catterick & Ayr: very eff over 6/7f: acts on yld &
heavy grnd & on any trk: genuine & consistent & should win more races.   84
222   OROJOYA [5] (J Hindley) 4-9-7 R Hills 7/2: 1313-02: Led over 1f out, looking an
assured winner: caught near fin: fine effort and will be winning soon: see 222.   86
--   SARAB [4] (P Coole) 5-9-4 P Waldron 7/2: 10304-3: Ev ch over 1f out: not btn far:
good seasonal debut: most consistent in '85, winning Listed races at Newcastle & Haydock:
in '84 won at Goodwood, Doncaster, Newmarket, Haydock & Beverley: very eff at 7f, stays 1m:
acts on firm & soft: usually held up and possesses a fine turn of foot: should win races
this season.   79
222   GREY DESIRE [2] (M Brittain) 6-9-4 K Darley 7/4 FAV: 01-1124: Never nearer: not btn
far, though btr 222 (6f).   78
325   SEVERN BORE [6] 4-9-4 G Baxter 16/1: 2203-00: Led after ½way: not btn far in close
fin: good effort: see 325.   76
330   ATOKA [1] 4-8-8 P D'arcy 100/1: -000: No show: has been very highly tried this season:
ex German filly who would appreciate a drop in class.   36
238   PACIFIC PRINCESS [7] 4-8-12(BL) M Wood 100/1: 1B40-00: Led 4f: bl first time.   00
7 ran   nk,1½,½,1,12   (N G Westbrook)   M H Easterby Great Habton, Yorks

414   BOTANY BAY AMATEUR RIDERS STKS 3YO   £1755   1m   Yielding 95 -19 Slow

*310 BARLEY BILL [5] (L Cumani) 3-9-12 Sara Cumani 11/8 FAV: 022-111: 3 ch c Nicholas Bill -
Oatfield (Great Nephew): Very useful, impr colt: in excellent form and led 2f out for an
easy win in an amateur riders event at Haydock May 3: earlier was not troubled to win h'caps
at Thirsk and Nottingham: stamina endowed and is a half brother to 2m winner High Plains:
very eff over 1m: sure to stay further: acts on any grnd & on any trk: can maintain his
winning sequence.   67
24   LANCE [8] (P Cole) 3-10-1 Mr L Wyer 10/3: 2200-22: No ch with winner though ran
well: stays 1m: see 24.   60
--   VERDANT BOY [1] (M Stoute) 3-9-7 Maxine Juster 7/4 : 03-3: Well bckd: sn prom on
seasonal debut: showed promise on both starts in '85 in good company: stays 1m: acts on
firm & yld grnd & a gall trk: well regarded & should have no trouble finding a race.   47
328   MAWDLYN GATE [4] (M H Easterby) 3-9-7 Leila Easterby(0) 50/1: 0-004: Led ½way, showing
impr form: stays 1m and acts on yld grnd: half brother to 2 winners, Nonabella and
Ho Mi Chinh.   35
*322 MARINA PLATA [6] 3-9-9 Sarah Hills(4) 12/1: 0-0110: Stiff task: btr 322 (soft).   34
140   IDLE SONG [2] 3-9-7 Jennie Goulding 50/1: -00: Never in it, but a btr effort:
stays 1m and acts on yld.   31
--   Annual Event [3] 9-13(6ow)   259 Ko Island [9] 9-7
--   Shark Fighter [7] 9-12
9 ran   4,2½,5,1½,nk   (G Keller)   L Cumani Newmarket

415   SALFORD MAIDEN AUCTION STKS 2YO   £1901   5f   Yielding 95 -14 Slow

--   THEKKIAN [9] (R Hollinshead) 2-8-11 S Perks 7/1: 1: 2 ch c Thatching - Debian (Relko):
First time out led 2f out, comfortably in a maiden auction at Haydock May 3: cost only
3,800 gns: eff at 5f should stay 6f plus: acts on yld grnd & a gall trk: should rate more highly. 37
186   PRIOR WELL [13] (M W Easterby) 2-7-13(BL) L Charnock 13/8 FAV: 002: Gambled on: not
pace of winner, though an impr effort: bl first time today: eff at 5f, should stay further:
acts on yld grnd.   18
--   CREES FIGURINE [8] (M Fetherston Godley) 2-8-5 R Hills 12/1: 3: Dsptd lead ½way:
kept on well: 2,100 gns purchase: eff at 5f on yld grnd.   22
--   HUGO Z HACKENBUSH [5] (C Tinkler) 2-8-8 M Wood 16/1: 4: Mkt drifter: nearest fin
and should impr for this initial outing: cost 2,400 gns and is a half brother to a minor
winner: eff at 5f and will stay further: acts on yld grnd.   25
21   RING BACK [7] 2-8-5 N Howe 12/1: 00: Sn prom: btr effort: speedily bred: eff at
5f on yld grnd: should find a seller on a sharper trk.   14
261   GLORY GOLD [10] 2-7-13 K Darley 13/2: 00: Led over 2f: eff over 5f on soft & yld:
may prefer a sharper trk.   04
--   BOLT UP [4] 2-8-8 J Bleasdale 20/1: 0: Mkt drifter: never nearer 8th: should do btr
than this: cost 2,500 gns.   00
--   PUBLIC PRAISE [11] 2-8-8 M Birch 15/2: 0: Dwelt & no show on debut: speedily bred.   00
186   MADDYBENNY [6] 2-7-13 S Webster 7/1: 4000: Early speed: best first time out in 20 (soft 00
236   PAY DIRT [14] 2-8-11 C Coates(5) 6/1: 030: Prom early: btr 236 (sharpish trk).   00
108   Quick Sticks [15] 7-13   --   Hilliard [1] 8-2
--   The Brazilian [12] 8-8   --   Brookhead Girl [3] 8-0(1ow)
--   Cream And Green [2] 8-8
15 ran   2½,½,nk,3,1½   (F H Lee)   R Hollinshead Upper Longdon, Staffs

416   FAN MAKERS HANDICAP 3YO 0-50   £2963   1m 4f   Yielding 95 +04 Fast   [52]

-- **AL SALITE** [9] (J Dunlop) 3-9-7 G Baxter 4/1: 412-1: 3 ch c High Line - Delicia
(Sovereign Path): Useful colt: made a winning seasonal debut, led ½m out, staying on well
in quite a fast run h'cap at Haydock May 3: winning 2yo at Nottingham: cost I.R. 80,000 as
a yearling: eff at 10f, stays 12f well: acts on firm & soft grnd & a gall trk: should win
more races.   57
*331 **SWYNFORD PRINCE** [10] (K Stone) 3-7-8(vis)(4ex) L Charnock 4/1: 03-0012: 8L clear 3rd:
in fine form: see 331.   26
*140 **PEARL FISHER** [2] (J Francome) 3-9-1 M Birch 5/2 FAV: -13: Well bckd: took a strong
hold : btr 140 (very soft).   35
331 **NIMBLE NATIVE** [7] (S Norton) 3-8-1 J Quinn(5) 12/1: 000-104: No threat: best first
time out in 45 (sharp trk).   09
*35 **CHUMMYS OWN** [1] 3-7-8 S P Griffiths(5) 6/1: 0-10: Made much 1m: btr in 35 (Claimer). 00
-- **QUEEN OF SWORDS** [11] 3-8-7 S Perks 20/1: 40400-0: No threat on seasonal debut: failed
to win in '85: dam a genuine middle dist. h'capper: acts on yld grnd.   11
*130 **CAROUSEL ROCKET** [6] 3-8-5(1ow) D Nicholls 9/1: 033-310: Well below form 130 (11f, heavy)00

| 273 Grove Tower [5] 8-4 | 132 Standon Mill [8] 7-7(3oh) |
| 193 Beau Mirage [4] 8-10 | 239 Murfax [3] 9-1 |

11 ran   2,8,6,2½,hd   (Hamdan Al-Maktoum)   J Dunlop Arundel, Sussex

---

Official Going Given as Firm

417   EBF PRIMROSE MAIDEN FILLIES STKS 2YO   £1045   5f   Good 40 -22 Slow

-- **SUMMER SKY** [2] (P Cole) 2-8-11 T Quinn 4/6 FAV: 1: 2 br f Skyliner - Soft Pedal
(Hotfoot): Promising filly: easily justified fav. on debut, making all in a 2yo fillies
maiden at Warwick May 5: half sister to winning juvenile Lucky Scott: clearly very eff over
the minimum trip, though sure to stay further: acts on gd grnd & on a sharpish trk: sure to
win more races.   55
-- **DANCING DIANA** [1] (R Hannon) 2-8-11 J Matthias 12/1: 2: Ran on promisingly on debut:
caught a tartar here and should find a small race soon: eff over 5f on gd grnd: acts on a
sharpish trk.   36
-- **TANGALOOMA** [4] (L Piggott) 2-8-11 B Thomson 7/1: 3: Chased winner most of way: fair
effort and should impr: cost 22,000 gns and is bred to stay further than todays trip: acts
on good grnd & on a sharpish trk.   35
261 **ROYAL RABBLE** [3] (D Elsworth) 2-8-11(BL) A Mcglone 12/1: 0204: Bl first time: al
there: see 118.   31
317 **SHARPHAVEN** [8] 2-8-11 M Wigham 7/1: 340: Best on soft in 317: see 170.   19
-- **ARDNACROSS** [5] 2-8-11 R Cochrane 25/1: 0: Mkt drifter on debut: slow start, no threat. 18
-- **ROSE LOUBEL** [6] 2-8-11 P D'arcy 11/1: 0: Never troubled ldrs after a slow start.   00
353 **FLAPPER GIRL** [7] 2-8-11 B Crossley 9/1: 000: Close up over ½way: fin last.   00
8 ran   6,nk,1½,5,nk   (D Rowland)   P Cole Whatcombe, Berks

418   LEVY BOARD APPR. HANDICAP 0-35   £1127   5f   Good 40 +06 Fast   [35]

-- **ROTHERFIELD GREYS** [7] (C Bell) 4-9-7 J Leech(5) 20/1: 00000-1: 4 b g Mummy's Pet -
Relicia (Relko): First time out, made ev yd to score unchall in an app. h'cap at Warwick
May 5: disapp last season when suffering from a virus though had useful juvenile form in
'84 when twice successful at Redcar: very eff over 5/6f on gd & firm grnd: well suited by
a sharpish trk and does well with forcing tactics: looks well h'capped & can win again.   42
-- **LALESTON** [14] (G Huffer) 3-8-6 W Litwin(5) 8/1: 10400-2: Fin strongly on reapp:
good effort: won a fillies maiden over this C/D last season: eff over 5f and will stay
further: acts on gd & yld grnd & runs well on this sharpish trk.   30
355 **HILMAY** [4] (W Charles) 4-8-5(BL) R Lappin 14/1: 000-003: Al close up: impr effort.   15
-- **MISS METAL WOODS** [11] (S Mellor) 4-8-0 J Carter 8/1: 00423-4: Al front rank on reapp:
front running maiden was placed several times late last season and looks quite well h'capped:
eff over 5f & should stay 6f: acts on gd & yld grnd & on any trk.   03
-- **LADY OF LEISURE** [9] 5-8-10 R Vickers(5) 20/1: 00000-0: Ran a good race on her reapp.   12
211 **APHRODISIAC** [13] 5-8-4(bl) A Roper 20/1: 000-00: Ran on too late: needs a longer trip. 06
314 **LA MALMAISON** [19] 3-8-3 R Perham(5) 9/1: 000-40: Late prog into 7th: see 314.   00
*355 **PINE HAWK** [15] 5-8-5(7ex) D Williams 11/2: 004-410: Ruined his chance with a slow
start: see 355.   00
272 **SPACEMAKER BOY** [1] 6-10-1 S Gregory(5) 5/1 FAV: 0-24100: Had ev ch: best when making
all in 211 (heavy).   00
268 **ROYAL BEAR** [2] 4-7-9 G King 13/2: -220430: Much btr over 6f in 266 (soft).   00

-- Sing Galvo Sing [6] 7-10	327 Another Bing [20] 7-12
174 Fairdale [16] 7-10	211 High Eagle [18] 8-13	-- Sleepline Duchess [17] 8-2
-- Blochairn Skolar [8] 7-9	91 Craven Boy [10] 7-8
339 Kelly Lindo [5] 7-8	175 Baliview [12] 7-8	-- Manilow [3] 8-13

20 ran   2½,1,3,nk,hd,½   (Mrs D Gleeson)   C Bell Sparsholt, Oxon

419   RADIO W M HANDICAP STAKES 0-50   £2526   1m 6f   Good 40 +05 Fast   [40]

--   LADYS BRIDGE [2] (I Balding) 4-9-13 J Matthias 7/4 FAV: 214-1: 4 b f Sir Ivor - Colony
Club (Tom Rolfe): Useful filly: easily defied top weight on her reappearance, making all
in quite a fast run h'cap at Warwick May 5: lightly raced last season when a comfortable
winner of a Newbury maiden: eff over 11/12f and stays 14f really well: acts on gd & yld grnd
and on any trk: should go in again.   54
--   FISHPOND [4] (D Elsworth) 5-9-2 A Mcglone 5/1: 23240-2: Well bckd on reapp: chased
winner run in and comfortably beat rem: ran consistently, without winning, last season and
remains a maiden: eff over 12/14f and stays 2m: acts on fast & heavy grnd & on any trk:
should find a race this term.   34
69   MISS BLACKTHORN [1] (N Vigors) 4-8-2 R Curant 16/1: 0001-03: Stayed on late: won a
seller at Wolverhampton on her final start last season: eff over 12/14f: acts on gd &
firm grnd & on any trk.   10
308   FOUR STAR THRUST [9] (R Whitaker) 4-8-13 K Bradshaw(5) 14/1: 321-004: Btr effort:
ended last season with a win in a minor event at Edinburgh, after a succession of placings:
eff over 12/14f: acts on gd & firm grnd & on any trk: consistent filly.   20
208   STANS PRIDE [13] 9-9-10 J Williams 4/1: 1124-00: No extra below dist: see 208.   30
--   HARLESTONE LAKE [15] 4-8-10 J Reid 10/1: 40320-0: Close up most of way & btr for race. 15
204   JENNY WYLLIE [10] 5-7-13 M Hills 7/1: 2300-00: Never going well: fin 9th: see 204.   00
--   Thetford Chase [12] 8-1(6ow)   336   Relkisha [6] 7-13
--   Annie Ra [11] 7-9   319   Leprechaun Lady [5] 8-6(bl)
131   Cluedo [3] 7-7(bl)   44   Jubilant Lady [8] 7-7(2oh)
336   Hot Betty [7] 7-11
14 ran   2½,8,¾,½,¾   (Paul Mellon)   I Balding Kingsclere, Hants

420   WARWICK SPRING HANDICAP STKS 0-35   £2385   1m 2f   Good 40 -03 Slow   [34]

163   MONCLARE TROPHY [2] (P Bevan) 7-8-9 R Curant 20/1: 010-001: 7 ch h Sandford Lad -
Blue Warbler (Worden II): Produced a much impr effort when a comfortable winner of a h'cap
at Warwick May 5, led below dist and ridden out: well btn in a seller last time though in
'85 showed fair form to win h'caps at Hamilton & Brighton: in '84 won at Folkestone: eff
over 10/11f: acts on firm & soft grnd & is well suited by a sharpish trk: carries weight well   26
--   SPANISH REEL [1] (J Edwards) 4-9-4 B Thomson 12/1: 14040-2: Stayed on well on reapp:
quite consistent last season when making all in a h'cap at Pontefract: eff over 7/8f and
clearly stays 10f well: acts on firm & yld grnd & on any trk: should go close next time.   30
281   WELSH MEDLEY [9] (D Haydn Jones) 4-9-1 J Reid 14/1: 4000-03: Ran well on his seasonal
debut: last successful in '84 at Chester: eff around 1m, stays 10f well: acts on gd/firm
grnd & is suited by a sharp trk.   20
91   MISS APEX [15] (F Yardley) 4-8-6 I Johnson 14/1: 4032-04: Led briefly 2f out: quite
consistent filly last season when only twice out of the frame, and a first time out winner
of a Haydock seller: eff over 7/8f and stays 10f: acts on firm & soft grnd & on any trk.   10
176   KALA NASHAN [18] 4-8-13 A Mcglone 10/1: 0020-00: Some late prog: returning to form.   17
--   ELEGANT FASHION [11] 4-8-12 R Cochrane 12/1: 00200-0: Nearest fin on seasonal debut:
better for race.   15
202   LADY LIZA [20] 5-8-5 R Carter(5) 10/1: 04U0-30: No threat: much btr over 12f in 202.   00
*349   STAR OF IRELAND [8] 6-9-11(7ex) G King(7) 7/4 FAV: 00-1010: Most disapp fav: much
better in 349.   00
349   BOLD ILLUSION [19] 8-8-10 L Riggio(7) 7/2: 04-1U40: Never threatened leaders:
best in 23 (12f, soft).   00
208   Kates Pride [3] 9-6   --   Karnatak [13] 8-3   164   Scholar [16] 8-6
342   Sales Promoter [5] 8-3   --   My Son My Son [4] 9-8
--   Gourtionist [17] 8-13   349   Ricco Star [12] 8-6(bl)
281   Count Bertrand [14] 8-12
17 ran   3,4,½,shhd,1   (Monclare Products Ltd)   P Bevan Kingstone, Staffs

421   STONEBRIDGE 2YO MAIDEN SELLING STKS   £547   5f   Good 40 -60 Slow

--   SPITTIN MICK [4] (J Berry) 2-9-0 Sharron James 6/1: 1: 2 b g The Brianstan - La Fille
(Crooner): Led inside final 1f, ridden out in a slowly run 2yo seller at Warwick May 5
(no bid): clearly well suited by this minimum trip: acts on gd grnd & on a sharpish trk.   26
--   BARLEY TWIST [2] (H Rohan) 2-9-0 S Morris 7/4: 2: Had ev ch & kept on well: speedily
bred colt who acts on good grnd & on a sharpish trk.   23
337   FLYING SILENTLY [1] (H O'neill) 2-8-11 J Reid 4/1: 03: Went on ½way, fin clear of
rem and this was a btr effort: cheaply bought filly who is eff over 5f on a sharp trk.   16
329   CUTLER RIDGE [5] (C Wildman) 2-9-0(bl) M Hills 12/1: 0004: Again made the early
running: see 329.   05
--   DUBLIN DANCER [6] 2-8-11 A Mcglone 4/1: 0: Ran on late on racecourse debut: should impr.00
--   YOUNG FOOL [7] 2-9-0 J Williams 10/1: 0: Sn behind on racecourse debut.   00
115   JANS DECISION [3] 2-9-0 J Matthias 6/4 FAV: 00: Well bckd fav: gd speed over ½way
though soon btn: cost 2,500 gns as a yearling: fin last in both his starts to date.   00
7 ran   ¾,1½,6,2½,nk   (Mrs J Berry)   J Berry Cockerham, Lancs

422   ALVESTON MAIDEN FILLIES STKS 3YO   £728   1m   Good 40 +05 Fast

--   NICKLE A KISS [8] (L Cumani) 3-8-11 R Guest 4/1: 4-1: 4 b f Plugged Knickle - Kiss-
apotamus (Illustrious): Prom filly: first time out, easy to back though led dist and held on
well in quite a fast run 3yo fillies maiden at Warwick May 5: showed promise behind Tucson
Princess in a Yarmouth maiden on sole start last season: nicely bred filly who is by champion
sprinter Plugged Nickle: stays 1m well: acts on gd & yld grnd & on an easy/sharp trk: should
rate more highly.   49
218   MARTESSANA DANCER [10] (B Hills) 3-8-11 B Thomson 3/1: -02: Fin well, just failed:
well suited by 1m on gd grnd: seems to act on any trk: on the up grade & should go one
better soon.   48
--   KALANDARIYA [4] (R Johnson Houghton) 3-8-11 J Reid 9/2: 4-3: Al front rank on reapp:
good effort and should impr next time: half sister to a couple of winners & ran well behind
Blue Eyed Boy at Doncaster on her sole outing last term: stays 1m: acts on gd grnd & on
any track.   42
--   TAIS TOI [7] (M Fetherston Godley) 3-8-11 R Cochrane 33/1: 00-4: Outsider though kept
on well to show impr form: highly tried in both starts last season: eff over 1m on gd &
soft grnd: seems suited by forcing tactics.   36
--   MALEIHA [2] 3-8-11 R Curant 12/1: -0: Led/dsptd lead till dist: quite a promising
debut: acts on gd grnd & on a sharpish trk: seems suited by forcing tactics.   35
338   SOKOLOVA [3] 3-8-11 A Mcglone 25/1: 30-00: Never reached ldrs after a slow start.   34
158   SHEREEKA [1] 3-8-11 P D'arcy 2/1 FAV: 2-30: Dsptd lead 6f: much btr 158 (7f gall trk). 00
--   Rabab [6] 8-11   89 Aussie Girl [11] 8-11   --   Morgiana [9] 8-11
--   Pladda Princess [14] 8-11   --   Easy Romance [5] 8-11
--   Humble Beauty [13] 8-11   --   Glamgram [12] 8-11
14 ran   nk,3,3,1,½   (Warren Rosenthal)   L Cumani Newmarket

423   ALVESTON MAIDEN FILLIES STKS 3YO   £717   1m   Good 40 -11 Slow

--   RIYDA [4] (R Johnson Houghton) 3-8-11 J Reid 7/1: -1: 3 ch f Be My Guest - Relisa
(St Paddy): Friendless in mkt on racecourse debut though burst into the lead inside dist
to win a fillies maiden at Warwick may 5: clearly suited by 1m though should stay further:
acts on gd grnd & on a sharpish trk: has a good turn of foot and may win again.   45
127   IYAMSKI [1] (W Hastings Bass) 3-8-11 R Lines(3) 12/1: Had ev ch: btr effort
on this sounder surface: stays 1m & acts on a sharpish trk: see 16.   40
338   HARDY CHANCE [11] (B Hills) 3-8-11 B Thomson 16/1: 0-003: Led below dist: impr effort:
half sister to several winners: well suited by 1m on good ground.   32
--   NAOUSSA [6] (J Dunlop) 3-8-11 N Dawe 14/1: 03-4: Mkt drifter on reapp: kept on late
and should do btr next time: lightly raced, showing promise last season when a close 3rd
to Merlins Magic at Folkestone: acts on gd & firm grnd & does well on a sharpish trk.   29
315   ROSI NOA [10] 3-8-11 Gay Kelleway(5) 10/1: 0-30: Mkt drifter: led ½way: much btr 315. 27
--   MARY MILFORD [7] 3-8-11 T Quinn 12/1: 0-0: Al mid-div on reappearance.   23
--   SUNLEY SAINT [2] 3-8-11 N Howe 7/1: 20-0: Front rank over ¼ way: will do btr next time. 00
87   KNIGHTLY DIA [5] 3-8-11 B Crossley 7/1: -30: Fin 8th over this longer trip: see 87. 00
--   OUR NOORA [8] 3-8-11 R Cochrane 7/1: -0: Active in mkt: never reached ldrs.   00
213   MISS TIMED [14] 3-8-11(VIS) M Roberts 5/4 FAV: -00: Disapp fav: made most till
½way and dropped out tamely: much btr over 7f on a gall trk in 213: deserves another chance. 00
338   Miss Brahms [9] 8-11   --   Mahabad [12] 8-11   283 Georgian Rose [13] 8-11
111   Sunset Dancer [3] 8-11
14 ran   1½,4,2½,nk,2½   (H H Aga Khan)   R Johnson Houghton Blewbury, Oxon

424   WOODLAND HANDICAP STAKES 3YO 0-35   £1601   7f   Good 40 -08 Slow   [39]

141   ARCTIC KEN [17] (C Nelson) 3-8-6 J Reid 9/2 FAV: 0040-01: 3 ch c Stanford - Peggy
Dell (Sovereign Gleam): Nicely bckd when a comfortable winner of a 3yo h'cap at Warwick
May 5: led 2f out and ridden out: half brother to useful juvenule winner Prairie Dunes: eff
over 7f on gd grnd: seems suited by a sharpish trk.   26
--   STILL DREAMING [5] (N Vigors) 3-9-0 R Curant 6/1: 030-2: Fin strongly on reapp:
lightly raced last season, her best effort being a close 3rd to Cafe Noir in a fillies maiden
at Folkestone: eff over 6/8f & should stay much further: acts on gd & yld grnd & on a
sharpish trk.   30
--   LA JAMBALAYA [6] (P Makin) 3-8-6 T Quinn 20/1: 040-3: Not btn far on seasonal debut:
lightly raced last term & showing some promise over the minimum trip: stays 7f: acts on
gd grnd & on any trk.   21
31   NORTHERN GUNNER [3] (W Jarvis) 3-8-8 R Guest 8/1: 2000-04: Never nearer after a
slow start: looks fairly h'capped on his best form of '85 when placed a couple of times:
eff over 7f & should stay further: suited by fast grnd.   17
334   FAATIK [2] 3-8-9 N Howe 7/1: 3400-00: Had ev ch: see 334.   15
--   SEQUESTRATOR [12] 3-8-13 M Wigham 16/1: 03000-0: Easy to back & should do btr next time. 16
120   KEEP COOL [1] 3-9-5 Gay Kelleway(5) 6/1: 003-340: Front rank most of way: see 120. 00

33	COUNTRY CRAFT [16] 3-9-0 A Mcglone 9/1: 00-00: Never threatened leaders.					00
175	BOLD ARCHER [14] 3-8-2 M Hills 7/1: 400-00: Easy to back and never beyond mid-div.					00
175	LUIGIS STAR [7] 3-8-9 R Cochrane 10/1: 0-000: Speed over ½way: see 175.					00
33	COUNTRY CRAFT [16] 3-9-0 J Williams 7/1: 00-00: Well btn in both starts this season.					00
205	Boxers Shukee [9] 7-10			--	Athletes Week [11] 8-3	
340	Rebello Imp [8] 8-7(bl)			--	Buhaaz [20] 8-5	
205	Someway [10] 9-1	--	Pokeree [13] 8-7	64	Chablisse 0 8-4 P	
--	Highland Tale [18] 8-9					

19 ran   1½,shhd,4,¾,2   (R Mello)   C Nelson Upper Lambourn, Berks

---

DONCASTER   Monday May 5th   Lefthand Galloping Track

Official Going Given as Good on Str Course: Good/Firm on Round Course

425 WISETON MAIDEN AUCTION STKS 2YO   £959   5f   Good 64 +15 Fast

223 STAY LOW [14] (G Blum) 2-8-2 G Duffield 11/4: 21: 2 ch f Tina's Pet - Pickled (Pitcairn): Mkt drifter but led before ½way and stayed on much too well for her rivals in a fast run maiden auction race at Doncaster May 5: speedily bred filly who is likely to prove best around 5/6f: acts on gd & yld & runs well on a stiff trk: should be able to win in better grade.   51

197 OYSTER GRAY [6] (C Gray) 2-7-13 S Webster 10/1: 32: Prom, kept on well & caught a tartar here: should win a similar race soon.   40

317 LINN ODEE [13] (M W Easterby) 2-7-10 L Charnock 2/1 fav: 23: Heavily bckd: chall 2f out: seems to act on gd & soft: see 317.   33

-- SNO SURPRISE [1] (R Boss) 2-8-5 M Miller 8/1: 4: Kept on well and this was a fair debut from this cheaply bought Apr. foal: speedily bred sort who should know more about the game next time.   37

136 PERTAIN [16] 2-8-5 N Carlisle 12/1: 040: Early ldr: acts on gd & soft: see 136.   31

-- SQUIGGLE [7] 2-8-11 P Bloomfield 12/1: 0: Speed to ½way: may impr.   36

223 GAME LIGHT [15] 2-7-13 S P Griffiths[5] 25/1: 00: Fin 7th & could be worth noting in a seller.   20

-- BROOM STAR [5] 2-8-8 W Ryan 7/1: 0: A gamble, plenty of early pace, fin 8th: very speedily bred: should impr.   29

47 MISS BOLERO [8] 2-7-13 J Lowe 7/1: 00: Fin last.   00

--	Galway Express [14] 8-2			186	Royal Treaty [3] 8-5
--	The Mague [12] 8-5	186	Bootham Lad [10] 8-5	--	Mere Music [17] 8-11
47	Real Rustle [11] 7-13	--	Trafford Way [4] 8-11	--	Oconnell Street [2] 8-11

17 ran   2½,1½,2,2½,2½,½,hd,2   (G Blum)   G Blum Newmarket

426 BAWTRY 3YO SELLING STAKES   £1167   7f   Good 64 -39 Slow

-- SOHO SUE [17] (D Ancil) 3-8-11 A Mackay 10/1: 00040-1: 3 ch f Red Regent - Reluctant Maid (Relko): First time out, never hdd and held on well to win a slowly run 3yo seller at Doncaster May 5 (no bid): 4th in a 2yo seller at Warwick in Oct.'85, best effort last season: eff over 7f/1m on good going: suited by forcing tactics.   16

67 MISS TONILEE [14] (D H Jones) 3-8-11 A Clark 100/30: 03-32: only btn ¾L: ran well and should find a similar race soon: see 67.   14

346 BAO [12] (J Cosgrave) 3-8-11 A Shoults[5] 9/1: -43: Not clear run, fin well: should be borne in mind for a similar event: see 346.   12

309 GALAXY GALA [8] (J Redfern) 3-9-0(BL) S Keightley 12/1: 000-004: Ev ch: stays 7f: acts on good.   11

284 DORADE [20] 3-9-0 M Birch 10/1: 0000-00: No worthwhile form last season: showed little impr today: suited by 7f, should stay 1m: acts on good.   10

-- MEDDY [6] 3-9-0 J H Brown[5] 14/1: 0403-0: Ev ch: 3rd of 16 in a 2yo seller at Haydock in Oct.'85: best effort yet: acts well on soft: should stay 1m.   05

305 PLANTER [9] 3-9-0(bl) M Beecroft 10/1: 0102400: Fin 7th: twice below 237 (6f, soft).   03

*305 DIX ETOILES [12] 3-8-11 J Lowe 6/4 fav: 4-10: Well bckd, much btr 305 (soft/heavy).   00

237	Frandie Miss [13] 8-11(bl)			309	Red Zulu [19] 9-0
328	Supreme Command [3] 9-0			--	Miss Beswick [15] 8-11
279	La Manga Prince [2] 9-0			284	Selorcele [7] 9-0(BL)
93	Anderby [10] 9-0	140	Histon Bronze [21] 9-0		
82	Ravelston [11] 9-0	305	Amplify [4] 9-0	305	First Alarm [1] 9-0
305	Classy Scouse [5] 9-0				

20 ran   ¾,1,2,½,3,1½   (D Ancil)   D Ancil Banbury, Oxon

427 A F BUDGE HANDICAP 3YO 0-50   £4227   1m   Good 64 -11 Slow   [51]

234 LUCKY SO SO [4] (S Norton) 3-9-5 J Lowe 5/1: 134-41: 3 b g What Luck - So High (Sea Bird II): Came from behind and responded gamely under press, gaining the day on the post in a 3yo h'cap at Doncaster May 5: first time out winner at Ayr in '85: half sister to the useful High Cannon: eff 1m, runs as if 10f will suit well: probably acts on any going: suited by a gall trk.   53

68   PASTICCIO [1] (M Jarvis) 3-9-7 G Duffield 5/1: 1-32: Ran on steadily, overcame
difficulties in running to lead final 1f, caught death: compensation next time: stays 1m well.   55
--   BEAUCLERC [9] (P Kelleway) 3-8-2 P Robinson 20/1: 00000-3: Al prom: gd seasonal debut:
no form last season, has evidently impr over the Winter: stays 1m & acts on good going.   33
326   PLANET ASH [5] (A Bailey) 3-9-1 G Carter[3] 7/2: 0-24144: Never going well, kept
on: much btr 326 (soft).   45
335   UNEXPLAINED [10] 3-8-2(BL) R Still 13/2: 000-420: Bl. first time, ev ch: see 335.   32
247   PULHAM MILLS [3] 3-8-4(BL) A Mackay 8/1: 400-000: Set up a clear lead, fdd final
1f: good effort: seems suited by a sound surface: see 54.   31
81   Bradbury Hall [2] 7-9   **234** Beresque [6] 9-3   **216** Mayor [7] 9-1
9 ran   shhd,1½,¾,shhd,1½   (Peter Wetzel)   S Norton High Hoyland, Sth Yorks

428   COAL MINER HANDICAP 3YO UPWARDS 0-60   £3811   5f   Good 64 +11 Fast   [46]

+272   PERION [4] (G Lewis) 4-9-1(5ex) P Waldron 7/4 fav: 00-1011: 4 ch g Northfields -
Relanca (Relic): Useful sprinter who has now won 3 out of 4 races this season: on latest
success showed a good turn of foot to lead final 1f, comfortably in a fast run h'cap at
Doncaster May 5: successful in similar h'caps at Epsom & Folkestone (first time out):
lightly raced in '85, in '84 won at Newmarket: very eff at 5f: acts on gd & soft/heavy:
suited by waiting tactics.   45
306   BOLLIN EMILY [1] (M H Easterby) 5-9-10 M Birch 7/1: 2314-02: Tried to make all: fine
effort: quite lightly raced in '85, placed most outings & won a valuable h'cap at York:
in July: very eff over 5f, stays 6f: suited by forcing tactics & a gall trk: acts on firm
& yld: should run well next time.   49
327   CREE BAY [6] (J Spearing) 7-9-9 P Robinson 10/1: 0040-33: Kept on under press: see 327.   46
233   ROVE [3] (S Norton) 3-8-2(BL) J Lowe 11/2: 301-124: Bl first time: btr 6 (C/D).   29
65   HOLT ROW [10] 5-7-12 W Woods[3] 25/1: 0000-00: Never closer: failed to win in '85,
'84 successful at Pontefract: acts on hard & gd going: best form around 5f on a sharpish
turning track.   13
-124   TOP THAT [8] 5-8-5 G Carter[3] 11/2: 00-0020: Prom most: btr 124 (yld).   20
76   DAVILL [2] 4-9-1 G Duffield 5/1: 0212-00: Plenty of early pace: fin 7th: see 76.   00
306   Philip [11] 9-6(bl)   **355** Philstar [9] 8-5   **355** Karens Star [7] 8-9
--   Tobermory Boy [5] 9-8
11 ran   1½,¾,2½,½,shhd,1½   (J W Wheatland)   G Lewis Epsom, Surrey

429   MAY DAY SPRING HANDICAP 4YO+ 0-50   £4298   1m 2f   Good 64 -17 Slow   [49]

71   QUIET RIOT [6] (R Armstrong) 4-9-7 V Smith[7] 10/1: 4304-01: 4 b c Hotfoot - Tuyenu
(Welsh Pageant): Came from behind to lead dist. and also hanging under press, kept on well
to win a h'cap at Doncaster May 5: first time out winner of a maiden at Thirsk in Apr.'85,
placed most subsequent outings: stays 10f well: acts on gd going.   52
333   GULFLAND [12] (G P Gordon) 5-8-8 S Childs[7] 4/1 fav: -00-132: Ev ch final 4f: in
fine form: see 129.   35
--   FENCHURCH COLONY [8] (M H Easterby) 5-8-6 M Birch 14/1: -3: Prom, led ½m out: good
effort on first outing since Oct.'84 successful at Beverley (1m, good) that season: possibly
btr over 1m than longer dists: acts on gd going & on a stiff trk: should run well next time.   29
243   BURAAG [14] (M W Easterby) 5-8-13 K Hodgson 8/1: 000-004: Kept on well but too late.   35
256   GOLDEN FANCY [10] 9-8-6 D Nicholls 11/1: 01-0000: Never closer: see 142.   27
333   BALGOWNIE [1] 6-7-7(6oh) J O'reilly[7] 9/1: 1000020: Came from off the pace: see 36, 333   12
281   PATCHBURG [15] 4-8-0 J H Brown[1] 8/1: 02-2130: No threat in 8th: best 142 (soft).   00
--   SITTING BULL [4] 4-9-1 P Robinson 6/1: 10300-0: Fin 9th: btr for race? winner at
Newcastle & Pontefract in '85: suited by 10f & good or firm going.   00
•238   TUTBURY [9] 4-8-7(4ex) N Carlisle 9/2: 02-4410: Much btr 238 (1m soft).   00
112   ABLOOM [5] 4-8-8 S Keightley 9/1: 2000-00: A gamble, prom 6f.   00
308   Senor Ramos [7] 9-0   **--** Sillitoe [2] 8-5   **--** Luminate [3] 8-13
257   Crowfoots Couture [11] 7-7(14oh)   **•163** Highdale [13] 7-7(6oh)
15 ran   1¼,2,1½,¾,2½   (R J Arculli)   R Armstrong Newmarket

430   RACE AROUND YORKSHIRE 3YO MAIDEN STKS   £1132   1m 4f   Good 64 -35 Slow

--   FIRST DIVISION [8] (G P Gordon) 3-9-0 Dominic Gibson 25/1: 000-1: 3 b c Wolver Hollow -
Home And Away (Home Guard): First time out, caused a 25/1 surprise, coming from well behind
to lead close home in a slowly run 3yo maiden at Doncaster May 5: no form in 3 outings last
season: half brother to minor winner Top Of The League: stays 12f well: acts on gd going.   50
--   LOCH SEAFORTH [7] (H Cecil) 3-9-0 W Ryan 7/2: 44-2: Wk in mkt, sn in a clear lead, hdd
near fin: rated 60 when close 4th in a valuable 2yo race at Doncaster in Sept.'85: should
be suited by 12f: acts on firm & gd going & seems suited by forcing tactics: should easily
find a maiden soon.   49
164   TAP EM TWICE [1] (M Jarvis) 3-9-0 W Woods[3] 7/1: 04-23: Al there, ran on & clear
of rest: should win a maiden soon: see 164.   47

-- GOODTIME HAL [10] (J Hindley) 3-9-0 A Shoults[5] 12/1: 0-4: Ev ch on seasonal debut: lightly raced half brother to winning sprinter Chantaco but stays much btr than him: acts on good going: should improve.   37
-- SARFRAZ [11] 3-9-0 A Clark 13/8 fav: 42-0: Heavily bckd, ev ch: placed both outings in '85 showing form over 10f on firm & yld.   36
219 WELSH BARON [4] 3-9-0(vis) P Waldron 9/1: 00-30: Prom most: btr 219 (vis. first time).   33
-- SHIPBOURNE [13] 3-9-0 K Butler 9/1: -0: Steady late prog into 8th & should improve enormously for this first experience of the racecourse: probably stays 12f: well bred colt who can improve.   00
-- DAVALLIA [3] 3-8-11 M Birch 7/1: 3-0: Nicely bckd, wknd str: rated 41 when 3rd of 16 in a minor event at Doncaster in Nov.'85, only previous outing: bred to stay well: acts on soft.   00

-- L B Laughs [15] 9-0	90 Cornish Prince [2] 9-0	
-- Baytino [14] 8-11	-- Rivers Nephew [5] 9-0(BL)	
140 Irish Dilemma [6] 9-0	-- Lyon Coeur [9] 9-0	307 The Leggett [12] 9-0
15 ran ½,1,6,½,1½,1½,1	(William Du Pont III)	G P Gordon Newmarket

---

KEMPTON   Monday May 5th   Righthand, Sharpish Track

Official Going Given as Good/Firm

431 BLACKBUSN CAR AUCTION STAKES 3YO   £3823   6f   Good 43 -07 Slow

111 RAYHAAN [14] (C Benstead) 3-8-10 B Rouse 12/1: -01: 3 b f Kings Lake - Welshwyn (Welsh Saint): Impr filly: played up start, but led well over 2f out and held on in a blanket fin to a 3yo fillies stakes at Kempton May 5: dam a smart sprinter: cost I.R. 250,000 gns as a yearling: eff at 6f: acts on gd & soft & a sharpish trk.   40
339 CRESTA LEAP [24] (R Hannon) 3-8-10 L Jones(5) 14/1: 340-302: Al prom: just btn: good effort: in good form this season: eff at 5/6f on firm & soft grnd and a sharpish trk: should find a small event.   39
-- CHARDONNAY [25] (R Laing) 3-8-10 G Sexton 33/1: 0-3: Ran on, jut btn on seasonal debut: unplaced on sole outing in '85: eff at 6f, may stay 7f: acts on gd grnd on a sharpish trk.   38
250 SOLO SINGER [4] (P Cole) 3-8-10 G Baxter 12/1: -04: Kept on well final 1f: btn less than 1L: speedily bred: eff at 6f on gd grnd & a sharpish trk: should find a small event.   38
-- BUTSOVA [15] 3-8-10 W Carson 13/2: -0: Active in mkt on debut and was not btn far: half sister to winning 10f performer Young Nicholas: should stay further than 6f: acts on gd grnd & a sharpish trk.   38
39 BOLD LOREN [22] 3-8-10 S Whitworth 33/1: -00: Al up there: narrowly btn and is impr: half sister to a minor winner: eff at 6f, may stay further: acts on gd grnd & a sharpish trk.   38
-- FESTIVITY [8] 3-8-10 D Mckay 20/1: 000-0: Close up 7th: best effort yet: unplaced in 3 outings in '85: should stay further than 6f: acts on gd/firm grnd.   37
-- BUTHAYNA [3] 3-8-10 R Hills 7/1: 022-0: Never nearer 8th: btr for race: showed good form in '85, notably when splitting Lady Sophie and Santiki in a Yarmouth fillies maiden: half sister to the smart 2yo Reach: should stay further than 6f: acts on gd/firm grnd and a maiden should be well within her grasp.   36
213 APHROSINA [23] 3-8-10 S Cauthen 9/2 FAV: -00: Never nearer: btr effort from this half sister to several winners: should stay further than 6f: acts on gd/firm.   30
*205 CORRALS JOY [21] 3-9-3 W R Swinburn 8/1: 3200-10: Led 3f: btr 205 (5f).   00
-- SHARP STABLE [19] 3-8-10 G Starkey 8/1: 0-0: Friendless in mkt and no show.   00

205 Astarte [1] 8-10	-- Aclia [13] 8-10	-- Another Western [2] 8-10
-- Emancipated Lady [16] 8-10		-- Esfahan [10] 8-10
-- Far Too Busy [9] 8-10	-- Lone Galaxie [5] 8-10	26 Miami Blues [11] 8-10
-- Miss Moth [17] 8-10	-- Shades Of Autumn [18] 8-10	
-- Spanish Intent [12] 8-10		111 Tuneful Lass [7] 8-10
-- Maries Valentine [6] 8-10		-- Jianna [20] 8-10
25 ran nk,nk,shhd,hd,hd.	(Hamdan Al-Maktoum)	C Benstead Epsom, Surrey

432 B.C.A. UNION JACK CLUB H'CAP (0-50)   £2788   1m 2f   Good 43 +11 Fast   [50]

71 KALKOUR [6] (M Haynes) 4-9-2 W R Swinburn 33/1: 10-0-01: 4 ch c General Assembly - Crepellana (Crepello): Useful colt: fin well to get up well inside the final 1f in a fast run h'cap at Kempton May 5: useful 2yo when trained by M Stoute winning at Sandown, but suffered from sore shins and has been lightly raced: stays 10f well: acts on gd & firm grnd & on any trk.   51
265 CHICLET [1] (P Walwyn) 4-9-11 Paul Eddery 9/1: 2130-02: Ran on well: just btn: fine effort under top weight & should be winning soon: in '85 won a valuable h'cap at Newmarket and a stakes event at Windsor: eff over 1m, stays 10f well: acts on any trk, but is definitely best on gd & firm grnd: genuine & consistent.   58
-- PROMISED ISLE [5] (Lady Herries) 5-9-7 W Carson. 7/1: 32002-3: Led briefly final 1f: just btn good seasonal debut: trained by J Dunlop in '85 and was placed on several occasions: in '84 won at Salisbury: half brother to numerous winners: eff over 8/10f: acts on firm & yld and on any trk.   54

--   **DASHING LIGHT** [14] (D Morley) 5-7-10 S Dawson(3) 16/1: 03002-4: Led till inside final
1f: good seasonal debut: confirmed front runner who in '85 won at h'cap at Folkestone:
in '84 won again at Folkestone & likes that undulating trk: eff over 10/12f: acts on any
going but is definitely best out in front: may win soon.   26
265 **DUELLING** [9] 5-7-12(vis) T Williams 8/1: 30-4000: Ev ch str: see 7.   27
265 **PELLINCOURT** [7] 4-7-13 S Whitworth 12/1: 320-400: Late hdway: btr effort: see 179.   26
248 **ROCKMARTIN** [8] 4-9-9 S Cauthen 7/2 FAV: 0020-00: Well bckd: no show: lightly raced
in '85: first time out won a maiden at Newbury: eff at 1m, stays 10f: acts on gd & firm
grnd & on any trk: should be nearing peak fitness.   00
--   **HEART OF STONE** [13] 4-7-7 N Adams 13/2: 00000-0: Active in mkt after recent wins over
hurdles: fin 8th: little form on the Flat.   00
--   **PULSATE** [4] 5-8-2 B Rouse 9/1: 02002-0: Wknd str: btr for race.   00
189 **Free On Board** [2] 7-13   129 **Super Trip** [12] 8-9
349 **Derryring** [3] 9-0   225 **Aylesfield** [10] 9-2   176 **Rosanna Of Tedfold** [11] 7-7(9c
14 ran   ¾,shhd,1½,hd,1   (David Myers)   M Haynes Epsom, Surrey

---

433 BRITISH CAR AUCTIONS JUBILEE H'CAP 0-75 £17246   1m   Good 43 +06 Fast   [74]

--   **PENNINE WALK** [1] (J Tree) 4-9-11 S Cauthen 16/1: 13140-1: 4 b c Persian Bold - Tifrums
(Thatch): Smart colt: first time out, comfortably defied top weight in a valuable & quite
fast run Jubilee H'cap at Kempton May 5: in '85 was a ready winner of a valuable 3yo h'cap
at Newmarket: earlier a game winner of Gr.3 Jersey Stakes at Royal Ascot: in '84 won at York,
Epsom & Newbury: eff at 7f, stays 1m well: best on gd & firm grnd: acts on any trk: genuine &
consistent & should win more good races.   86
248 **BOLD INDIAN** [16] 5-9-9 R Hills 33/1: 0020/02: Fin fast: excellent effort
under 9-9 and is clearly back to his best: in '84 won at Chester & Newmarket: also a fine
2nd in the AndyCapp H'cap at Redcar: eff at 1m, stays 10f well: acts well on gd & firm grnd
and should win soon.   82
248 **TRULY RARE** [21] (M Stoute) 4-8-3 W R Swinburn 8/1: 4141-03: Led 2f out: not btn
far: good effort: should find a h'cap soon.   61
248 **INDIAN HAL** [9] (P Walwyn) 4-7-13 P Hamblett 16/1: 4231-04: Ran on well final 1f:
good effort: see 248.   56
330 **QUALITAIR FLYER** [13] 4-8-7 G Brown(7) 20/1: 200-000: Ev ch over 1f out: not btn far.   63
--   **GILDERDALE** [15] 4-7-9 S Dawson(3) 25/1: 04310-0: Unlucky in running and would have fin
a lot closer: fine seasonal debut: in excellent form in '85, winning at Ascot, Leicester,
Epsom (2) & Wolverhampton: very eff at 7f/1m: acts on gd & firm grnd & on any trk: genuine,
consistent sort who goes well for S Dawson.   51
-330 **SHMAIREEKH** [17] 5-9-7 Paul Eddery 12/1: 2000-20: Not btn far in 7th: see 330.   00
5   **TREMBLANT** [7] 5-9-4 S Whitworth 9/2: 0111-20: Ev ch str: will do btr than this: see 5.   00
-248 **PATRIACH** [11] 4-7-10 W Carson 7/2 FAV: 3411-20: Well bckd: much btr 248 (soft).   00
+361 **READY WIT** [4] 5-7-7(8ex) G French 11/1: 00-2210: No show under penalty: see 361.   00
--   **Roman Beach** [23] 7-8   265 **Tabardar** [10] 7-13   248 **Go Bananas** [3] 8-10
--   **Bold And Beautiful** [22] 8-10   248 **Really Honest** [20] 8-8
--   **Merle** [8] 8-5   -- **October** [18] 8-4(1ow)   +248 **Star Of A Gunner** [12] 8-3(8ex)
248 **Barry Sheene** [2] 8-2   248 **Portogon** [5] 7-12   -- **Aconitum** [6] 7-9
238 **Russell Creek** [11] 7-7(4oh)   -- **Purchasepaperchase** [14] 9-0
23 ran   ¾,½,½,½,hd,½   (Mrs Maria Niarchos)   J Tree Beckhampton, Wilts

---

434 ORCHARD HOUSE STAKES 2YO   £2866   5f   Good 43 -21 Slow

115 **PENSURCHIN** [1] (D Elsworth) 2-9-4 S Cauthen 9/4: 131: 2 ch c Creetown - Coriace
(Prince Consort): Led well over 1f out, staying on under press in a slow run 4 runner 2yo
stakes at Kempton May 5: first time out won a maiden over this C/D: eff at 5f, should stay
6f: acts on gd & soft grnd & seems to like Kempton.   52
*180 **STRIKE RATE** [3] (R Hannon) 2-9-4 L Jones(5) 5/4 FAV: 12: Made much: kept on well
and is in good form: see 180.   50
--   **SWIFT PURCHASE** [2] (R Hannon) 2-8-11 P Cook 10/1: 3: No threat to first 2 on seasonal
debut: cost 7,000 gns and should stay further: closely related to numerous winners.   28
--   **TASJIL** [4] (C Benstead) 2-8-11 B Rouse 7/2: 4: Lightly bckd on debut: should impr:
cost 60,000 gns & should be suited by further.   12
4 ran   ½,8,8   (Mrs H Penelope Ralton)   D Elsworth Whitsbury, Hants

---

435 PARTH STAKES 3YO   £2394   1m 4f Good 43 +01 Fast

224 **WINDS OF LIGHT** [5] (H Cecil) 3-9-5 S Cauthen 13/8: 1-01: 3 b c Majestic Light -
Dancing Detente (Nijinsky): Very useful colt: well bckd & made ev yd, comfortably in a 5
runner stakes event at Kempton May 5: on sole start in '85 was an impressive winner of a
24 runner Newmarket maiden: stays 12f well: acts on gd/firm & a gall trk: seemed unsuited
by soft in 224: should win more races.   67
*351 **GOLDEN HEIGHTS** [2] (P Walwyn) 3-9-5 Paul Eddery 4/1: 43-12: Ch over 1f out: in
fine form: see 351.   62
--   **OSTENSIBLE** [3] (G Harwood) 3-9-5 G Starkey 11/8 FAV: 1-3: Uneasy fav on seasonal
debut: prom, ev ch: on sole start in '85 won a maiden at Leicester: cost $200,000 and is a
brother to useful winning 2yo Ghaiya: eff at 1m, stays 12f: acts on gd/firm grnd & should
do btr next time.   55

--   MARICAMA [4] (C Horgan) 3-9-0 P Cook 20/1: -4: Stiff task on debut: half brother to
the high class colt Lanfranco and should do much btr than this: worth keeping an eye on
in lesser company.   00
344 BOLIVIA [1] 3-9-5 C Mcnamee 50/1: 040-000: Again well btn: see 203.   00
5 ran   ·2½,4,30,dist   (S S Niarchos)   H Cecil Newmarket

436   APPLECORE HANDICAP 0-50 3YO   £2792   7f   Good 43 -13 Slow   [53]

--   VAGUE SHOT [4] (C Horgan) 3-8-13 P Cook 9/2: 40300-1: 3 ch c Vaigly Great - Cease
Fire (Martial): First time out, landed a gamble in a 3yo h'cap at Kempton May 5: led inside
the final 1f, comfortably: this was his first success, but ran well on several occasions in
'85 notably when a close up 6th to Green Desert in Gr.3 July Stakes at Newmarket: eff at 7f,
stays 1m: acts on gd & firm grnd & on any trk: has been tried in bl.   50
157 STRIVE [8] (M Blanshard) 3-9-1 W R Swinburn 10/1: 3100-02: Led 2f out: good effort:
in '85 won a maiden at Pontefract & ran consistently: stays 7f well: acts on gd/firm & yld
grnd & on any trk: may find a h'cap in the near future.   46
--   SUPER PUNK [7] (G Hunter) 3-9-7 R Hills 12/1: 031-3: Ran on well final 1f: good effort
under top weight: on final outing in '85 won a maiden at Nottingham: eff at 6f, stays 7f
well: acts on gd & firm grnd and on any trk.   52
--   BATH [3] (J Toller) 3-8-8 Jackie Houston(7) 33/1: 0300-4: Led 2f out: good seasonal
debut: best effort in '85 when 3rd in a fillies maiden at Newbury: eff at 6f, stays 7f:
acts on gd & yld grnd & on any trk: should find a small race.   38
64   VAIGLIAN [1] 3-8-8 Paul Eddery 10/1: 2303-40: Never nearer: running into form:
stays 7f: see 64.   37
*64   EASY LINE [6] 3-8-5 T Williams 10/1: -10: No show: btr in 64 (6f, soft).   32
161 SITZCARRALDO [9] 3-8-1 R Fox 10/1: 300-200: Twice below 62 (6f, soft/heavy).   00
--   FRUITY OROONEY [10] 3-9-5 S Cauthen 11/2: 0062-0: Made much, fdd: btr for race.   00
274 MIGHT MOVE [2] 3-8-5 W Carson 11/4 FAV: 03-0020: Well below form: see 74 (heavy).   00
--   Carnival Rose [11] 7-12   74   Giving It All Away [12] 8-2
338 Lady Bishop [5] 7-9
12 ran   2,shhd,nk,½,¾,3   (A W Anthony)   C Horgan Billingbear, Berks

---

Official Going Given as Good: Pace Figures Inapplicable

437   E.B.F. DARWEN STAKES 2YO   £2448   5f   Good Inapplicable

--   KHADRUF [1] (H T Jones) 2-9-0 A Murray 4/5 fav: 1: 2 ch c Blushing Groom - Call Me
Goddess (Prince John): First time out, well bckd and led inside final 2f comfortably in a 2yo
maiden at Haydock May 5: cost $685,000: evidently a speedy sort but should stay 6f &
probably further: acts on gd going: further impr likely.   45
--   COLWAY RALLY [10] (J W Watts) 2-9-0 T Ives 9/2: 2: Fin well, encouraging debut: sure
to be suited by 6f: acts on gd grnd: should find a maiden in the North.   42
77   BOY SINGER [2] (K Stone) 2-9-0 C Dwyer 20/1: 043: Mkt drifter, ev ch: seems to act
on gd & heavy: see 77.   39
332 SILVER ANCONA [6] 2-9-0 J Bleasdale 7/2: 34: Al well there: see 332: acts
on good and soft.   36
236 FISHERGATE [9] 2-9-0 T Lucas 11/1: 40: Dsptd lead 2f out: acts on gd & soft: see 236.   35
108 LATERAL [8] 2-9-0 K Darley 14/1: 200: Early speed: best 43 (sharp trk).   34
20   Touch Of Speed [7] 9-0   320   Damart [4] 9-0
--   Emsleys Heights [3] 8-11   --   Candle Dancer [5] 9-0
10 ran   ¾,¾,1,nk,nk   (Hamdan Al-Maktoum)   H T Jones Newmarket

438   MANCHESTER MAIDEN STAKES 3YO   £2404   6f   Good Inapplicable

--   QUINTA REEF [4] (M Jarvis) 3-9-0 T Ives 20/1: 00-1: 3 b f Main Reef - La Quinta
(Thatch): First time out, caused a 33/1 surprise leading dist. comfortably in a 3yo maiden
at Haydock May 5: showed nothing in 2 outings last season, has evidently greatly impr over
the Winter: eff at 6f, bred to stay at least 1m: acts on gd going: should win more races.   51
--   SATIAPOUR [12] (R J Houghton) 3-9-0 K Darley 9/4: 043-2: Made most: rated 51 when 3rd
in a maiden at Sandown in Oct.'85: suited by forcing tactics over 6/7f on gd or firm going:
wore a visor last season, not today.   46
--   BREAKFAST IN BED [13] (W Haigh) 3-8-11 N Day 7/1: 0030-3: A gamble, kept on: showed
promise last season: may well be suited by 7f this term: acts on gd & firm.   37
205 NAWADDER [10] (B Hanbury) 3-8-11 T Lucas 2/1 fav: 0-24: Heavily bckd, dsptd lead much:
btr 205 (5f, good).   27
--   TRY SIR [6] 3-9-0 N Connorton 16/1: -0: Quite a prom. debut: sure to impr for the
experience: acts on gd going.   24

159 AL DIWAN [14] 3-9-0 R Street 7/1: 20-40: Prom most: rated 47 last season: see 159.   24
283 SAALIB [3] 3-9-0 A Murray 5/1: 40-20: Ev ch, fin 7th: btr 283 (heavy).   00
309 The Little Joker [11] 8-11(BL)   --   The Stamp Dealer [1] 9-0
283 Pact [5] 9-0   -- Mark Eden [2] 9-0   -- Super Fresco [7] 9-0
--   Twicknam Garden [8] 9-0   --   Royal Fan [9] 9-0
14 ran   1½,2½,4,2½,hd   (F H Lee)   M Jarvis Newmarket

439   CASTLE IRWELL HANDICAP (0-60)   £3132   1m 2f   Good Inapplicable   [50]

*166 MASKED BALL [8] (P Calver) 6-8-0 M Fry 2/1 fav: 1230-11: 6 b h Thatch - Miss Mahal
(Taj Dewan): Winner of both his races this season, the latest a h'cap at Haydock May 5 when
leading 2f out comfortably: first time out winner over same C/D Apr.9: in '85 won 2 h'caps
at Newcastle: very eff 10f, stays 12f: acts on gd & yld & on any trk but likes a gall one,
especially Haydock.   31
*101 JOHN GILPIN [4] (W Haigh) 4-7-7(3oh) J Quinn[3] 15/2: 100-212: Came from off the
pace: in fine form & stays 10f well: see 101 well clear remainder.   21
--   PONTYATES [7] (J S Wilson) 4-8-6(6ow) C Dwyer 13/2: 0--24-3: Al prom on seasonal debut:
only ran twice last season, rated 41 when 4th in a minor race at Haydock in Oct: stays 12f
and best run on soft/yld.   24
--   THE CRYING GAME [6] (B Morgan) 4-7-7(14oh) P Hill[7] 25/1: 00000-4: Stiff task for this
maiden: 2nd of 8 in a seller at Doncaster in May '85, best effort last term: stays at
least 1m & acts on good.   10
243   VINTAGE TOLL [9] 6-9-7 T Lucas 5/1: 00-0300: Disapp type: see 52.   28
263   SEVEN SWALLOWS [5] 5-8-3 M Rimmer 7/2: 230-100: Dsptd lead 3f out: best 184.   08
--   ARISTOCRAT VELVET [3] 4-9-3 T Ives 9/1: 00023-0: Fin 7th, btr for race: failed to
win in '85, previous season successful at Ayr & Pontefract: acts on firm & yld & winning
form over 1m but probably stays 10f.   00
--   MARTIAN BABY [1] 4-8-10(bl) S Perks 8/1: 00200-0: Dsptd lead 7f: winner of C/D last
season, sole success so far: has been hurdling: acts on good going, on a gall trk: wears bl.   00
333   Recharge [2] 7-7(1oh)
9 ran   1½,6,¾,7,1½   (P Calver)   P Calver Ripon, Yorks

Official Going Given as Good/Soft

440   LILY AGNES STAKES 2YO   £3004   5f   Good 68 -14 Slow

*252 ABUZZ [1] (C Brittain) 2-9-0 M Roberts 7/2: 11: 2 ch f Absalom - Sorebelle (Prince
Tenderfoot): Very useful, impr filly: made ev yd, easily in a 2yo stakes at Chester May 6:
first time out was a comfortable winner of a fillies maiden at Newbury: speedily bred sort:
eff at 5f, should stay 6f: acts on gd & soft grnd & on any trk: well regarded & should
win more races.   60
*230 ARAPITI [3] (K Brassey) 2-9-3 S Whitworth 2/1 Jt.FAV: 212: Al there: in gd form:
acts on gd & heavy & on any trk: see 230.   54
*367 ROWEKING [2] (L Lightbrown) 2-8-11 G Starkey 20/1: 02013: Dsptd lead 3f: well suited
by a sharp trk: acts on gd & soft grnd: see 367. beaten in seller in race 86.   45
*206 ASTON LASS [4] (L Barratt) 2-8-8 A Proud 12/1: 14: Nearest fin: ran well: acts on
good & heavy: see 206.   38
+320 MY IMAGINATION [5] 2-8-8 P Cook 2/1 Jt.FAV: 110: Never going well: unsuited by this
tight track? btr 320 (soft).   35
242   PANBOY [6] 2-8-11 C Coates(5) 14/1: 31240: Prom ½way: btr 242 (yld): see 197, 108.   18
6 ran   3,1,1½,1,8   (Mrs Brittain)   C Brittain Newmarket

441   HOLSTEN DIAT PILS HCAP STAKES 4YO+ 0-60 £4155   7.5f   Good 68 +08 Fast   [53]

240   CREEAGER [2] (W Wharton) 4-8-4 N Carlisle 15/2: 0040-01: 4 b g Creetown - Teenager
(Never Say Die): Ran on under press to lead inside the final 1f in quite a valuable h'cap at
Chester May 6: in good form in '85, winning at Thirsk and also just btn by Powder Keg at
Newmarket: eff at 7f/1m: acts on any trk, but is best on gd & firm grnd.   40
--   KNIGHTS SECRET [1] (M H Easterby) 5-7-8 J Lowe 10/1: 00000-2: Btn only ¾L: led final
1f: good seasonal debut: first time out in '85 won a h'cap at Pontefract and does welk
when fresh: in '83 won 3 times: eff at 6f, stays 1m: acts on any grnd & on any track, but
likes a sharpish one: seems best when up with the pace.   28
174   LEMELASR [4] (D Haydn Jones) 6-8-3 D Williams(7) 7/1: 20-0323: Ran on well final
1f and continues in fine form: see 174, 91.   34
--   GRACIOUS HOMES [3] (D Haydn Jones) 5-7-7(1oh) R Fox 16/1: 02004-4: Late hdway on
seasonal debut: impr likely: failed to win in '85, but ran well on several occasions: in
'84 won at Windsor: eff at 6/7f, stays 1m: acts on firm & soft grnd & on any trk, though
likes a sharp one.   19

17   MOORES METAL [13] 6-9-2 S Perks 10/1: 3000-00: Nearest fin: useful colt on his day,
but is difficult to win on: in '85 won a valuable h'cap at Newcastle: in '84 won again at
Newcastle and likes that trk: stays 10f, but best form around 1m: acts on any going: carries
weight well, but has to be held up for a late run.   37
--   BABY SIGH [5] 4-8-5 B Thomson 9/1: 3-200-0: Fit from hurdling: late hdway: lightly
race on the Flat in '85, first time out fin 2nd to Shellman in a h'cap at Haydock: in '84
won at Chepstow: eff over 6/7f, stays 1m: acts on gd & firm grnd & on any trk.   26
*281 SILVER CANNON [17] 4-8-8(7ex) S Cauthen 13/2 FAV: 1000-10: Well bckd: no show: much
better 281 (heavy).   00

260	O I Oyston [9] 7-13	--	Young Bruss [6] 7-7(1oh)		
196	Manabel [7] 7-8	306	Ra Ra Girl [14] 8-8	135	Mendick Adventure [11] 8-1
196	Nicoridge [18] 9-5	196	Keats [10] 8-4	--	Soon To Be [8] 8-11
259	Responder [15] 7-7(2oh)			374	Paris Match [16] 8-13(BL)
--	Come On The Blues [12] 9-10				

18 ran   ¾,1½,3,2½,shhd   (J M Berry)   W Wharton Melton Mowbray, Leicester

---

442 DALHAM CHESTER VASE LISTED RACE   £21120   1m 4f Good 68 -07 Slow

--   NOMROOD [6] (P Cole) 3-8-12 T Quinn 11/2: 12-1: 3 b c Alleged - Sweet Habit (Habat):
Smart colt: made a winning seasonal debut, led nearing final 1f, under press in slow run but
valuable Chester Vase at Chester May 6: first time out in '85 beat Danishgar in a valuable
maiden at Newmarket: on only other start was an excellent 2nd to Bakharoff in Gr.1 William
Hill Futurity at Doncaster: brother to the high class performer Alleging: eff at 1m, stays 1m
4f: acts on gd & firm grnd & on any trk, though likes a stiff one: should win more races.   67
324 SIRK [7] (C Brittain) 3-8-12 P Robinson 28/1: 423-132: Ran on strongly final 1f and
nearly got up: in fine form this season: stays 12f and continues to impr: acts on any trk:
see 324, 48.   66
219 JUMBO HIRT [3] (B Hills) 3-8-8 B Thomson 25/1: 30-23: Ran on well final 1f: not btn
far and this was much impr form: acts on any trk: certain to win races on this form: on
the up grade: see 219.   60
362 DANISHGAR [4] (M Stoute) 3-8-8 W R Swinburn 10/1: 22-04: Made much: btr effort:
seems to stay 12f: possibly suited by front running tactics: see 362.   59
+224 FLYING TRIO [5] 3-8-12 Paul Eddery 5/2: 1102-10: Well below form 224 (gall trk soft)
and is much btr than this.   53
*273 BELDALE STAR [2] 3-8-12 G Starkey 9/4 FAV: 1120-10: Unsuited by slow pace: much
btr 273 (heavy).   50
*253 SIR PERCY [1] 3-8-12 S Cauthen 7/2: -10: Well bckd: btr 253 (soft, gall trk).   0u
7 ran   nk,1,1½,5,1½   (Fahd Salman)   P Cole Whatcombe, Oxon

---

443 PRINCE OF WALES HANDICAP STKS 3YO 0-60   £3934   5f   Good 68 -15 Slow   [62]

*339 IMPALA LASS [3] (B Mcmahon) 3-7-7(7ex) J Lowe 7/1: 0301-11: 3 b f Kampala or
Malinowski - Sheil-Na-Gig (Ridan): In fine form and led from the stalls, staying on well
under press in a h'cap at Chester May 6: first time out won a h'cap at Warwick: on final
outing in '85 made ev yd in a seller at Catterick and seems best out in front on a sharpish
trk: very eff at 5f: acts on gd/firm & yld ground.   37
246 GODS ISLE [4] (M H Easterby) 3-8-2 W Carson 9/2: 1010-02: Kept on well final 1f and
just went under: good effort: may be winning soon: see 246.   45
233 STEEL CYGNET [5] (Pat Mitchell) 3-8-6 M Miller 14/1: 002-003: Ran on well final 1f
and just btn in a close fin: finding his form: loves a sharp trk: see 62.   48
--   DANCING SARAH [2] (D Haydn Jones) 3-7-12 D Williams(7) 10/1: 42210-4: Btn 1L: good
seasonal debut: in '85 won a nursery h'cap at Chepstow: eff at 5f, stays 6f: acts on
firm & yld on any trk.   39
*233 STEPHENS SONG [1] 3-8-0 S Dawson(3) 4/1 FAV: 000-110: Narrowly btn: in fine form.   41
--   TRUE NORA [8] 3-9-7 J Reid 9/1: 01110-0: Slow start: not btn far and ran well on
seasonal debut: in good form in '85, completing a hat trick at Folkestone, Warwick &
Wolverhampton: half sister to the smart Mac's Reef: very eff over 5f with forcing tactics:
should stay 6f: acts on gd/firm & yld & seems to like a sharp/easy trk.   60
233 AU DESSUS [9] 3-8-7(1ow) W R Swinburn 11/2: 3110-40: Mkt drifter: no show: btr 233 (hvy). 00
+147 CAPEABILITY POUND [7] 3-7-11 M Richardson(0) 9/1: 0000-10: Sn prom, fdd: btr 147
(soft, stiffer track).   00

314	Platine [11] 8-1(1ow)	165	Runaway [6] 9-0	233	Cronks Quality [10] 8-11

11 ran   nk,¼,nk,ddht,1   (P Willett)   B Mcmahon Tamworth, Staffs

---

444 GROSVENOR STAKES 3YO   £3147   1m 2f Good 68 +17 Fast

--   OLD DOMESDAY BOOK [5] (J Winter) 3-8-9 W Carson 5/2 FAV: 0-1: 3 b f High Top -
Broken Record (Busted): Promising filly: heavily bckd on seasonal debut and led over 1f out
for an impressive win in a fast run 3yo stakes at Chester May 6: unplaced on sole outing
in '85: eff at 10f, should be suited by 12f: acts on gd grnd & a sharpish trk: should
rate more highly/win more races one to follow.   57

CHESTER   Tuesday May 6th   - Cont'd

*106 FORCELLO [6] (S Norton) 3-9-5 J Lowe 5/1: 0342-12: Made much: no ch with winner,
though ran very well: stays 10f: seems suited by a sharpish trk, though acts on any:
officially rated only 28 and should win a h'cap on this form: see 106.   50
253 LLANARMON [1] (B Hills) 3-8-12 B Thomson 10/3: 0-03: Never nearer: stays 10f:
acts on gd & soft: should find a maiden: see 253.   40
231 KEEPCALM [3] (G Wragg) 3-8-12 S Cauthen 7/2: -04: Sn prom: on the up grade: stays
10f and acts on gd grnd.   37
--   HITCHENSTOWN [2] 3-8-12 W R Swinburn 20/1: 0000-0: No show on seasonal debut: best
effort in '85 when 5th to Edgewise in a Haydock maiden: acts on yld.   12
352 PORO BOY [4] 3-8-12 P Waldron 10/1: 00-340: Prom, wknd str: btr 352 (1m yld): see 127. 07
--   SHOWDANCE [7] 3-8-12 S Perks 20/1: 0-0: Al rear.   00
7 ran   6,1½,1½,12,2½   (Lord Derby)   J Winter Newmarket

445 LADBROKE RACING HANDICAP 4YO+ 0-60   £3843   1m 2f Good 68 +01 Fast   [55]

265 ESQUIRE [11] (B Hills) 4-9-3 B Thomson 3/1 FAV: 4010-21: 4 ch c High Line - Monroe
(Sir Ivor): Useful colt: al prom and led over 2f out, comfortably in a h'cap at Chester
May 6: first time out was a good 2nd to Nebris in a h'cap at Epsom: in '85 won a 2yo maiden
at Newbury: eff at 9/10f, may stay further: acts on gd & soft grnd and on any trk: may
win again.   57
263 SHARP NOBLE [9] (B Hanbury) 4-9-8 W R Swinburn 4/1: 01-0222: Kept on well final 1f
and is due a change of luck: see 263, 166.   57
248 RANA PRATAP [3] (G Lewis) 6-8-12 P Waldron 7/1: 44-0433: Kept on under press: good
effort: running well: see 248, 71: stays 10f.   45
265 THE GAMES UP [7] (P Haslam) 5-7-10 T Williams 10/1: 0300-44: Never nearer: btr
effort: see 265 well suited by sharp track: 27
--   MILL PLANTATION [1] 7-9-8 S Cauthen 7/1: -0110-0: Nearest fin: should strip fitter
next time: lightly raced in '85, winning at Chepstow & this same race: in 83/84 won at
York: very eff at 10f, though does stay 12f: acts on gd & yld & on any trk: carries
weight well: genuine sort.   53
361 CONMAYJO [6] 5-8-7 J Reid 6/1: 20-0330: Prom, not btn far: see 361, 166.   36
265 MASTER LINE [2] 5-8-9 C Rutter(5) 8/1: 0110-00: Never nearer next time: should do
better next time: in '85 won h'caps at York & Newmarket (awarded race): eff over 9/10f:
stays 12f: acts on any grnd: likes a gall trk: goes well for an app.   00
248 Thats Your Lot [10] 10-0   176 Blaze Of Tara [5] 9-2(vis)
--   Mairs Girl [8] 7-7(20oh)   --   Polemistis [4] 7-8(bl)(1ow)(20oh)
11 ran   2,1,1,hd,¾   (K Abdulla)   B Hills Lambourn, Berks

REDCAR   Tuesday May 6th   Lefthanded Galloping Track

446 KILTON SELLING STAKES 2YO   £986   5f   Good 42 -26 Slow

--   HORNBLOWER GIRL [5] (P Rohan) 2-8-8 S Morris 5/1: 1: 2 br f Faraway Times - Ibolya
Princess (Crowned Prince): Nicely bckd on racecourse debut & led below dist, driven out
in a 2yo seller at Redcar May 6 (no bid): cost 3,200 gns as a yearling & is a half sister
to a couple of winning sprinters: eff over 5f on a gall trk: acts on gd ground.   25
353 BELLE OF STARS [1] (M Usher) 2-8-8 M Wigham 7/1: 02: Dropped in class: mkt drifter
though al close up and only just btn: cost 10,000 gns as a yearling: eff over 5f on gd grnd:
suited by a gall trk.   25
108 U BIX COPY [1] (J Wilson) 2-8-11 D Nicholls 5/2 FAV: 03: Kept on well: promises to
be well suited by a longer trip: acts on gd & soft grnd & on a gall trk.   22
34   SWYNFORD PRINCESS [18] (K Stone) 2-8-8 L Charnock 5/1: -04: Dropped to selling
company: made most: acts on gd grnd & on a gall trk: will stay further in time.   18
181 ROSE DUET [9] 2-8-8 S Webster 14/1: 00: Denied a clear run dist: ran on late:
half sister to winning sprinter Royal Question: acts on gd grnd & on a gall trk.   17
--   PATELS GOLD [7] 2-8-8 N Connorton 20/1: 0: Unfancied on debut, though al close up. 11
317 MOONEE POND [8] 2-8-8 M Birch 5/1: 200: Well below form shown in 317 (soft, shrp trk). 00
40   Benfield Morpeth [3] 8-11   167 Mark Of Gold [20] 8-8
57   Fantine [2] 8-8   354 Gloriad [17] 8-8   57   My Mabel [14] 8-9(1ow)
--   Fultons Flyer [1] 8-8   --   Julios Lad [6] 8-11   --   Chunky Supreme [21] 8-11
--   Avinasesh [13] 8-11   --   Cawkell Trooper [19] 8-11
--   Millfield Blue [10] 8-11   181 High Town [16] 8-8
353 Nofandancer [4] 8-8   --   Bloopers [22] 8-11
21 ran   shhd,2,¼,nk,2½,1   (E McMahon)   P Rohan Norton, Yorks

154

447   MACKINLAY MEM. HANDICAP STAKES 3YO 0-35   £2400   6f   Good 42 +02 Fast   [36]

--   MADRACO [8] (P Calver) 3-8-2 M Fry 13/2: 0404-1: 3 b c Hot Spark - Aberdeen Lassie
(Aberdeen): Well bckd on reapp and made most, comfortably in a 3yo h'cap at Redcar May 6:
lightly raced last season, showing some promise in maiden company: sprint bred colt who
acts on gd & firm ground & appears to have no trk preferences: well suited by forcing
tactics: can go in again.   25
*198 GOLDEN GUILDER [11] (M W Easterby) 3-8-13 K Hodgson 7/1: 00-0212: Was never going
to peg back winner though ran another good race: see 198.   30
284   HANSOM LAD [7] (W Haigh) 3-9-2 D Nicholls 8/1: 303-023: Switched below dist, fin
well: in fine form at present: acts on any trk: see 284.   32
81   CUMBRIAN DANCER [10] (M H Easterby) 3-9-2(vis) M Birch 14/1: 0212-04: Al close up: btr
effort: in gd form last backend, gained a runaway win in a nursery at Hamilton on heavy
grnd: equally eff over 6 & 7f: acts on firm & heavy grnd & is suited by a stiff trk.   23
198   LOW FLYER [21] 3-9-1 M Hindley(3) 10/1: 004-030: Ran on again late: see 198 not well drawn. 20
--   NEW EVIDENCE [17] 3-9-0 A Mackay 14/1: 00400-0: Fair effort on reapp: btr for race.   18
--   LUNAR SHAMAL GAL [24] 3-9-5 W Ryan 5/1 FAV: 01-0: Some late prog on seasonal debut
and should do btr next time: lightly raced last season when winning a maiden auction race
at Warwick on final start: eff over 5/6f on good & firm grnd: seems to act on any trk.   00
+246 SEW HIGH [12] 3-9-12(7ex) J Hills(5) 11/2: 41-0010: Dsptd lead to ½way: btr on
a sharp trk in 246 (5f, yld).   00
--   DOUBLE CHAI [23] 3-9-2(bl) T Ives 7/1: 04300-0: Never beyond mid-div on seasonal debut.   00
309   IMPERIAL SUNRISE [9] 3-8-6 T Lucas 8/1: 2044-40: Btr on soft grnd in 309 (sharp trk).   00

368	Larnem [16] 7-11	--	Jeldaire [5] 8-7	284	Qualitair King [22] 9-0
*237	Wow Wow Wow [15] 9-7(7ex)			--	Alexanjo [1] 9-4
--	Psalm [20] 9-6	--	Neds Expressa [3] 9-2	--	Tricky [6] 8-10
--	Henry Padwick [4] 8-4	--	Crown Colony [2] 8-2	--	Murryl Cannon [25] 8-2
--	La Belle Of Santo [26] 7-13			--	Spanish Infanta [18] 7-12
38	Feather Girl [14] 7-7(1oh)			246	Spring Garden [13] 8-0(1ow)
--	Aitchandoubleyou [19] 9-7				

26 ran   1½,½,4,1,½,1   (B W Hampson)   P Calver Ripon, Yorks

448   DANBY MAIDEN STAKES   £762   1m 2f Good 42 -16 Slow

--   LIE IN WAIT [7] (G Pritchard Gordon) 3-8-5 G Duffield 6/1: 0-1: 3 ch c Mill Reef -
Pitiless Panther (No Mercy): First time out, led below dist for a comfortable win in a
3yo maiden at Redcar May 6: unplaced on his sole start last term: evidently suited by 10f
on a gall trk: acts on gd grnd: progressive sort who should rate more highly.   47
--   SPARTAN VALLEY [11] (B Hills) 3-8-5 M Hills 4/1: -0-2: Ran on well on seasonal debut:
showed promise behind Hawaiian Palm in a Salisbury maiden on only outing last season: cost
$150,000 as a yearling: eff over 10f on gd grnd: acts on a gall trk.   42
--   CRICCEITH [8] (Denys Smith) 4-9-4 L Charnock 20/1: 00-3: Hmpd below dist, ran on
again: sure to have been closer if a clear run: unplaced in both starts last season though
looks an impr sort: eff over 10f: acts on gd grnd and on a gall trk.   35
--   MUHAJJAL [12] (H Thomson Jones) 4-9-7 A Murray 4/1: -4: Mkt drifter on racecourse
debut: hdway on bit to lead well over 2f out, ran green when chall and sure to do btr
next time: well bred colt who acts on gd grnd and on a gall trk.   32
368   CHERRY LUSTRE [9] 3-8-5 N Connorton 10/1: -00: Btr effort over this longer trip.   31
--   SAGAX [15] 4-9-7 M Birch 20/1: -0: Stayed on most promisingly on racecourse debut
and seems certain to impr next time, especially if tackling a longer trip.   30
141   MABEL ALICE [4] 3-8-2 A Mackay 20/1: 0040-00: Stayed on from the rear.   00
262   FOLLOW THE BAND [2] 4-9-7 E Guest(3) 11/4 FAV: 3200-00: Close up for 1m: fin 9th
and is proving disapp: just btn by Khandjar in a stakes race at Wolverhampton last season,
after earlier being twice placed in maidens: eff around 8/9f on gd/firm grnd: acts on any trk.   00

58	Sing Out Loud 9-4			104	Al Misk [16] 9-7
259	Nicky Dawn [6] 9-4	--	Snowfire Chap [5] 8-5	--	Porto Green [13] 9-7
199	Fill Abumper [3] 9-4	--	Hi Diddle [1] 9-4	--	Taufast [17] 8-5

16 ran   2½,2,2½,1½,1,1½   (William Du Pont III)   G Pritchard Gordon Newmarket

449   HUNTCLIFFE HANDICAP 3YO+ 0-35 ꜱ·`   £1993   1m 4f Good 42 -04 Slow   [31]

366   PINWIDDIE [5] (P Rohan) 4-7-13 L Charnock 7/1: 03-0421: 4 b f Moulton - Bombay Duck
(Ballyciptic): Made steady prog to lead dist, ridden out in a h'cap at Redcar May 6 for
her first success: eff over 11/12f and stays 2m: acts on gd & soft grnd & on any trk.   12
--   SUNAPAS OWLET [10] (A Jarvis) 5-8-7 T Ives 16/1: 00000-2: Fin in gd style on seasonal
debut: string of ducks eggs last season though in '84 was in good form, winning at Redcar,
Yarmouth & Nottingham: eff over 10/12f: acts on gd & firm grnd & is suited by a gall trk.   15
*341 HOLYPORT VICTORY [6] (M Usher) 4-10-0(4ex) M Wigham 5/1 Jt FAV: 0-40113: Another good
effort: see 341.   35
142   TREYARNON [3] (S Norton) 4-8-5 J Quinn(5) 12/1: 400-434: Led after 1m, hdd dist: see 142 08

```
--    ISHKHARA [4] 4-8-11 G Craggs(7) 20/1: 400-0: Stayed on well on reapp: lightly raced,
showing signs of promise last season and is a half sister to very useful hurdler Prideaux
Boy: stays 12f well: acts on gd grnd & on a gall trk.                                        10
243   STRATHEARN [12] 5-9-8 A Murray 12/1: 4400/00: Held up, never reached leaders.         20
199   CASTIGLIONE [2] 4-8-11 S Keightley 8/1: -32-00: Never a factor: see 199.              00
308   TIMMINION [9] 4-8-9 C Dwyer 5/1 Jt FAV: 30-3000: Only beat one home: btr in 44 (shp trk 00
126   Mossberry Fair [16] 7-11                                  23   Master Carl [7] 8-7
363   Key Royal [11] 9-4                308  Boldera [18] 9-1   366  Grey Card [14] 7-13
308   String Of Beads [17] 8-6(bl)                             --   Dark Cygnet [20] 8-0
--    Spend It Lass [8] 9-1            184  Sound Work [15] 8-7  164  Raisabillion [13] 8-6
308   Bamdoro [19] 8-5
19 ran    3,nk,3,4,1½         (Mrs D Williams)        P Rohan Norton, Yorks
```

---

450   E.B.F. AYTON STAKES 2YO   £1707   5f   Good 42 +18 Fast

*317 NUTWOOD LIL [6] (E Eldin) 2-9-1 A Mackay 9/2: 11: 2 b f Vaigly Great - Sterlonia
(Sterling Bay): Prom juvenile: easy to back though went on before ½way and ran on strongly
to win a very fast run 2yo stakes at Redcar May 6: well bckd when making most in a fillies
maiden at Ripon on her debut: half sister to winning juvenile Atromitos: very eff over 5f
and should be suited by further: acts on gd & soft grnd & on any trk: suited by forcing
tactics: on the up grade & should win again.   54
*223 REGENCY FILLE [4] (R Williams) 2-9-1 R Cochrane 5/4 FAV: 12: Well bckd: ran on well,
just held: lost nothing in defeat & should be winning again soon: see 223.   52
--   BALIDUCK [3] (P Rohan) 2-8-8 M Wood 16/1: 3: Prom debut: not btn far and comfortably
beat rem: half brother to winning miler Bombil and should stay further than this minimum
trip: acts on gd grnd & on a gall trk: should impr.   41
--   SPANISH SLIPPER [11] (W Haigh) 2-8-8 N Day 20/1: 4: Kept on from ½way: fair debut
from this cheaply acquired filly: half sister to a couple of winners: acts on gd grnd &
on a gall trk.   31
367   MARCHING MOTH [7] 2-9-1 N Connorton 7/1: 140: Led early, btn dist: best on soft
in 236 (sharp trk).   38
--   AIR OF SPRING [2] 2-8-8 S Webster 4/1: 0: Tardy start: close up most of way.   30
--   MINIZEN LASS [12] 2-8-8 K Darley 12/1: 0: Easy to back: no threat on debut.   00
--   MY SERENADE [10] 2-8-8 T Ives 11/2: 0: Early speed, fin 8th on racecourse debut.   00
--   Leven Lass [5] 8-8   --   Rose Meadow [1] 8-8   --   Sunny Gibraltar [8] 8-8
317   Miss Sherbrooke [9] 8-8
12 ran   ½,1½,4,shhd,nk   (A E Hutley)   E Eldin Newmarket

---

451   ESTON HANDICAP STAKES 0-35 3YO   £2015   1m   Good 42 -08 Slow   [37]

216   MR KEWMILL [1] (M Tompkins) 3-8-10 M Rimmer 11/1: 000-301: 3 b c Homing - Muninga
(St Alphage): Led dist and ran on well to win a 3yo h'cap at Redcar May 6: showed some
promise last season when trained by M Pipe: eff over 1m on firm & soft grnd: suited by a
gall trk.   30
335   BRAVE AND BOLD [15] (N Callaghan) 3-8-8(bl) G Duffield 8/1: 001-202: Ev ch: good
effort: see 100.   24
--   HUDSONS MEWS [10] (M W Easterby) 3-8-11 K Hodgson 5/4 FAV: 000-3: A big gamble on
his reapp: kept on under strong press and not btn far: lightly raced last season: eff over
1m on gd grnd: acts on a gall trk.   27
--   GOLD CHIP [26] (J Watts) 3-9-3 A Gorman(7) 14/1: 00013-4: Dsptd lead most of way on
reapp: in gd form last backend, comfortably winning a nursery at Edinburgh: half brother to
several winners: eff over 7/8f on gd & yld grnd: acts on any trk.   29
48   HONEST TOIL [22] 3-8-11 D Mckeown 12/1: 000-340: Had ev ch: best on yld in 14.   20
183   COOL OPERATOR [11] 3-9-7 R Cochrane 10/1: 000-040: Ran on late: needs further: see 183. 28
*195 NORTHERN MELODY [8] 3-9-2(bl) P Bloomfield 8/1: -00310: Never nearer in 7th: see 195. 00
--   BLACK DIAMOND [14] 3-9-0 T Ives 10/1: 0000-0: Bckd from 20/1 on reapp: no show.   00
--   WATERDALE [12] 3-8-9 T Lucas 10/1: 000-0: No threat on seasonal debut.   00
132   Belhill [4] 7-13   247 Rapid Flight [2] 7-13   183 Country Carnival [5] 8-8
--   Jersey Maid [6] 9-3   318 Tara Dancer [3] 8-8(vis)
258   Master Music [23] 8-1   318 Nippy Chippy [28] 8-13
--   Affaitati [27] 8-11   --   Owls Way [18] 8-11   240 Princess Pamela [16] 8-9
--   Daisy Star [17] 8-7   --   Crownit [24] 8-6   --   Desarem [24] 8-7
141   Hare Hill [25] 8-3   309 Not A Problem [19] 8-3
132   Space Trooper [21] 8-3   284 Katie Rhodes [13] 8-1
237   Colonel Hall [20] 7-12   195 Valdarno [9] 8-0(1ow)
28 ran   1½,hd,2½,1½,1,1½   (Brian D Cantle)   M Tompkins Newmarket

---

452   DANBY MAIDEN STAKES   £721   1m 2f   Good 42 +05 Fast

--   GLOWING PROMISE [11] (B Hills) 3-8-2 M Hills 5/1: 02-1: 3 b f Tap On Wood - Manx
Retreat (Habitat): Prom filly: first time out, went on 2f out for a comfortable win in quite
a fast run 3yo maiden at Redcar May 6: showed plenty of promise in her 2 starts last
season, notably when running up to Chernicherva at Haydock: stays 10f well: acts on gd &
soft grnd & on a gall trk: should win more races.   56
```
```

-- TOSARA [16] (H Candy) 4-9-4 R Curant 9/2: 0-2: Well bckd on her reapp: slowly away
though had ev ch: only raced once last season though is a half sister to several winners,
incl useful Border Dawn and is clearly quite useful: eff over 10f on gd grnd: should stay
12f: acts on a gall trk.   50
-- COMELY DANCER [12] (J Watts) 3-8-5 T Ives 11/4 FAV: 4-3: Ran well on his reapp:
showed promise behind Gracious Fan in a Ayr maiden last season: eff over 10f on gd grnd,
and on a gall trk: seems quite well regarded.   50
-- POWER BENDER [8] (G Pritchard Gordon) 4-9-7 G Duffield 12/1: 00222-4: Easy to back:
led 3f out: btr for race: runner up in his last 3 starts in '85, notably when behind Capricorn Son in a Newcastle maiden: eff over 8/10f and should stay further: acts on gd grnd
and on a gall trk: consistent sort.   45
-- JACQUETTE [9] 3-8-2 R Machado 8/1: -0: Nicely bckd debutant: ran on well.   42
-- HURRICANE HENRY [10] 3-8-5 K Bradshaw(5) 5/1: 02-0: Some late prog and should do
btr next time.   40
-- IRISH HERO [13] 4-9-7 M Birch 10/1: 42-0: Never dngr in 7th.   00
-- GREEN STEPS [5] 4-9-7 B Crossley 7/1: -0: Never going well on racecourse debut.   00
8   PRINCE RELKO [3] 4-9-7 R Cochrane 10/1: -00: Shown little in his 2 starts to date.   00
357 Hidden Move [2] 8-5   196 Assaglawi [6] 9-7   -- Game Set Match [15] 8-5
--   Debach Revenge [4] 9-4   101 My Handsome Boy [1] 9-7
--   Stanelly [14] 9-7   -- Bels Angel [17] 9-4   -- Ernies Choice [7] 9-7
17 ran   2,2,2,½,3,2½   (Pioneer Bloodstock Farm Ltd)   B Hills Lambourn, Berks

---

Official Going Given as Soft

453 WILTSHIRE HANDICAP STKES 0-60   £2884   8f   Yielding 85 +01 Fast   [45]

196 DE RIGUEUR [11] (J Bethell) 4-9-1 Paul Eddery 8/1: 324-101: 4 b g Derrylin - Northern
Lady (The Brianstan): Useful h'capper: led dist for an easy win in a h'cap at Salisbury
May 7: first time out won a similar event at Warwick: consistent performer last season,
winning at Wolverhampton: very eff over 1m on gd & soft grnd: acts on any trk: genuine
sort who is in good form.   46
174 TALK OF GLORY [2] (L Cottrell) 5-8-2 G Baxter 20/1: 3000-02: Tried to make all:
beat the rem decisively and should go one btr soon: last successful in '83, in a maiden at
Lingfield: eff over 8/12f: acts on firm & soft grnd: btr 248.   27
248 RUNNING FLUSH [5] (D Oughton) 4-9-3 A Clark 6/1 FAV: 40-0043: Fair effort: btr 248.   30
*399 DIMENSION [16] (N Smith) 7-7-7(bl)(2oh) J Carter(1) 14/1: 00-014: Ev ch: best in 399.   02
-- LADY EUROLINK [10] 4-8-9 J Matthias 25/1: -1000-0: Ran on too late on reapp: does
well when fresh, won a fillies race at Leicester first time out last season: best form over
1m though does stay further: acts on gd & heavy grnd & is suited by a stiff trk.   18
265 KAZAROW [9] 5-9-2 M Rimmer 7/1: 022-100: Much btr on heavy in 71 (sharper trk).   25
-- TOM FORRESTER [13] 5-8-7 T Quinn 10/1: 20003-0: Speed over ½way on seasonal debut:
better for race: consistent h'capper who made all to win at Sandown last season, later
controversially demoted after again making all at Kempton: in '84 won at Lingfield: eff over
7/8f: acts on any going & on any trk: suied by forcing tactics.   00
-- GURTEEN BOY [12] 4-9-2 A Mcglone 10/1: 10001-0: Btr for race: scored successive h'cap
wins at Newbury, Brighton & Lingfield last season and ended his campaign by winning again
at Nottingham: eff over 7/8f on firm & soft grnd: acts on any trk.   00
-- BOLD PILLAGER [17] 4-8-11 B Rouse 8/1: 020-0: Lightly raced colt: will do btr next time. 00
--   New Central [7] 8-2   399 Foot Patrol [3] 8-7   399 Aqaba Prince [1] 8-3
--   Safe Custody [4] 8-12   265 Shostakovitch [14] 9-2
248 Bundaburg [8] 9-8   --   Taj Singh [15] 7-11(1ow)
91   Marsoom [18] 7-10(3ow)   --   Bel Oscar [3] 9-9
18 ran   2,8,2,hd,hd,½   (Mrs Christopher Heath)   J Bethell Chilton, Oxon

454 LEVY BOARD APP H'CAP 3YO 0-35   £1226   6f   Yielding 85 -15 Slow   [39]

-- AMBROSINI [7] (M Jarvis) 3-9-7 P Hutton(5) 8/1: 20231-1: 3 ro f Drone - Mother Nature
(David Jack): Useful filly: quickened well to lead inside dist in an app. h'cap at Salisbury
May 7: impr steadily last season, winning a backend maiden at Redcar: half sister to several
winners: very eff over 6f: acts on any going & is suited by a gall trk: genuine filly who
carries weight well.   46
-- CELESTIAL DRIVE [2] (R Hannon) 3-8-12 A Lappin(5) 9/1: 23000-2: Led briefly inside
final 1f: good effort on her reapp: showed enough ability to win a race last season, notably
when running up to Nashia in a fillies maiden here: half sister to several winners, incl
very useful stayer Another Sam: eff over 5/6f: acts on gd & soft grnd & is well suited by
this gall trk.   28
-- SOLO STYLE [1] (G Lewis) 3-9-1 G Kennedy(5) 12/1: 000-3: Kept on well: speedily bred
colt who was lightly raced last season: eff over 6f on yld grnd: acts on a gall trk.   25

38   LADY LA PAZ [13] (P Cundell) 3-8-9 J Kennedy(5) 20/1: 000-04: Half sister to several
winners, incl true middle dist performer Hazel Bush: eff over 6f and should stay further:
acts on yld grnd & on a gall trk.   15
83   ROYAL BERKS [4] 3-8-6 T Lang(5) 20/1: 3000-00: Made most: btr effort.   12
113   BANDYANN [8] 3-7-9 P Sims(3) 11/2: 00-20: Much btr over 7f in 113 (sharper trk).   00
339   GLEADHILL PARK [14] 3-8-12 D Williams 7/1: 004-00: Again never nearer: needs
further: see 339.   00
217   WINNING FORMAT [15] 3-9-0 A Ball(5) 15/2: 00-00: Speed to ½way, sn btn.   00
--   OUT OF HARMONY [6] 3-9-1 P Skelton(5) 5/1 FAV: 010-0: Well bckd & had ev ch.   00
175   TIPPLE TIME [10] 3-9-0 A Cole(5) 8/1: 3300-00: Btr on a sharper trk in 175.   00
--   Helvick Bay [5] 8-7   175 Hello Blue [9] 8-4   -- Prissy Miss [12] 9-3
340   Noras Boy [16] 8-7   --   Georges Choice [11] 7-13(3ow)
15 ran   3,2½,1½,shhd,2½,2½   (Ananda Krishnan)   M Jarvis Newmarket

455   OAKLEY H'CAP 3YO 0-50   £2686   7f   Yielding 85 -05 Slow   [56]

+138 KEDRON [18] (D Laing) 3-8-12 S Whitworth 10/3 FAV: 012-11: 3 gr c Absalom - Top
Stream (Highland Melody): Useful colt: led below dist, readily in a 3yo h'cap at Salisbury
May 7: earlier won a 3yo stakes at Nottingham: in '85 won a Folkestone maiden: very eff
over 6/7f on firm & soft grnd: acts on any trk: in fine form & may win again.   54
*234 MUDRIK [10] (C Benstead) 3-9-6(6ex) B Rouse 6/1: 041-412: Another gd effort: see 234.   55
*276 MIRANDA JULIA [17] (D Elsworth) 3-8-1(6ex) A Mcglone 10/1: 0440-13: Not clear run,
fin well: see 276.   30
216   KINGS TOUCH [2] (P Makin) 3-9-0 G Baxter 12/1: 01-04: Led 2f out: btr effort:
lightly raced last season, when making all in a Redcar maiden: eff over 6/7f on gd/firm &
yld grnd: suited by a gall trk.   41
--   HIGHEST PRAISE [8] 3-8-4 S Payne 6/1: 403-0: Kept on well & should do btr next time:
lightly raced last year when twice placed in maidens, incl once here: eff over 6/7f on gd
& yld grnd: acts on a gall trk.   31
--   SEE NO EVIL [5] 3-7-7(6oh) G French 25/1: 40000-0: Al prom on reapp: best effort
last year when 4th to Nagajaya in a Brighton nursery: sprint bred colt who stays 7f well:
acts on gd & heavy grnd & on any trk.   19
216   DUNLORING [1] 3-9-0 W Ryan 13/2: 0000-40: Hmpd dist, not recover: btr judged on 216.   00
--   Empire Blue [4] 9-0   --   Kimble Blue [12] 8-8   340 Witham Girl [11] 7-7(7oh)
--   Bronze Opal [6] 9-4   --   Burhaain [19] 8-3   216 Edgewise [14] 9-7
--   Zulu Knight [20] 9-0   --   Miss Venezuela [7] 8-1
--   Young Flame [3] 7-11   340 Hopefull Dancer [13] 7-10
--   Harleyford Lad [15] 7-8   -- Monatation [16] 7-7(10oh)
19 ran   2½,3,¾,shhd,¾   (G Burgess)   D Laing Lambourn, Berks

456   SALISBURY STAKES 2YO   £2765   5f   Yielding 85 -03 Slow

*382 QUEL ESPRIT [1] (M Mccormack) 2-9-4 R Wernham 1/1 FAV: 1211: 2 b c What A Guest -
les Sylphides (Kashmir II): Very useful juvenile: again made all for an easy win in a 2yo
stakes at Salisbury May 7: earlier a comfortable winner at Newmarket: won at maiden at
Doncaster on his debut: cost 10,000 gns: very eff over 5f & should stay 6f plus: acts on
gd & soft grnd & on a gall trk: well regarded colt: looks certain to enjoy further successes. 65
323   QUICK SNAP [3] (A Ingham) 2-8-11 R Curant 16/1: 432: Kept on well: continues to
impr and must find a race soon: should stay further: see 323.   45
*187 ENCHANTED TIMES [4] (C Horgan) 2-9-1 T Quinn 7/4: 13: No extra dist: comfortably beat
todays r.u. in 187 (sharper trk).   41
*261 DIAMOND FLIGHT [5] (R Hannon) 2-9-1 A Mcglone 9/2: 014: Btr on a sharper trk in 261.   37
4 ran   4,3,1½   (Miss Laura Morgan)   M Mccormack Sparsholt, Oxon

457   EBF WARMINSTER 2YO MAIDEN STAKES   £1204   5f   Yielding 85 -04 Slow

--   AMIGO SUCIO [8] (K Brassey) 2-9-0 S Whitworth 10/3: 1: 2 gr c Stanford - Haunting
(Lord Gayle): Made a successful racecourse debut in a 2yo maiden at Salisbury May 7, led
inside dist and won going away: cost 17,000 gns as a yearling and is a half brother to
several winners, incl useful Valley Mills: eff over a stiff 5f and sure to stay further:
acts on yld grnd & on a gall trk.   54
332   SINGING STEVEN [5] (R Hannon) 2-9-0 B Rouse 10/3: 22: Just failed to make all: on
the up grade & sure to win soon: acts on gd & soft grnd: see 332.   51
--   MUNAASIB [3] (P Walwyn) 2-9-0 Paul Eddery 11/4 FAV: 3: Very well bckd, ran on well
late and impr seems certain: cost I.R. 24,000 as a yearling: acts on yld grnd & on a gall trk. 44
270   OUR FREDDIE [2] (A Ingham) 2-9-0 R Curant 16/1: 44: Kept on under press: impr effort:
eff over 5f on yld grnd: seems suited by a gall trk: see 270.   34
367   MR GRUMPY [10] (D Nicholls) 2-9-0 D Nicholls 7/1: 0220: Dsptd lead ½way: see 367 & 133. 32
--   AUGUST HILL [4] 2-9-0 R Hills 25/1: 0: Ran on late & should impr next time.   20
--   SHARP REMINDER [7] 2-9-0 G Sexton 9/2: 0: Should benefit from this initial outing.   00
--   Hard Act [1] 9-0   --   Comedy Sail [9] 9-0   -- Court Command [6] 9-0
10 ran   ¾,2½,4,¾,5,nk   (John Li)   K Brassey Upper Lambourn, Berks

458   DRUIDS STAKES 3YO FILLIES   £1333   1m4f   Yielding 85 -22 Slow

--   NICOLA WYNN [13] (D Elsworth) 3-8-11 A Mcglone 20/1: -1: 3 ch f Nicholas Bill -
Clouded Lamp (Nimbus): Was a surprise winner on her racecourse debut, led inside final 1f
comfortably in a 3yo fillies stakes at Salisbury May 7: clearly well suited by 12f and
should stay further: acts on yld grnd & on a gall trk: should win more races & rate more highly.   50
239   MARIE GALANTE [11] (C Brittain) 3-8-11 T Ives 9/1: 300-232: Led after 4f: good
effort & stays 12f on a stiff trk: see 128.   44
--   RED SHOES [10] (W Hern) 3-8-11 B Procter 8/1: 0-3: Led home turn, no extra close
home but still a prom effort: only ran once last season: acts on yld grnd & on a gall trk:
stays 12f & should find a race.   40
*173 MYCENAE CHERRY [12] (G Wragg) 3-9-2 Paul Eddery 7/4 FAV: 0-14: Well bckd: led early,
btr over 10f in 173.   39
--   TEMPLE HEIGHTS [7] 3-8-11 B Rouse 10/1: -0: Outsider: never nearer after a slow
start: stays 12f well: acts on yld grnd & on a gall trk.   28
338   AUNT ETTY [8] 3-8-11 S Keightley 33/1: -00: Fair effort over this longer trip.   24
--   TORREYA [1] 3-8-11 A Shoults(5) 7/1: -0: Backed from 33/1 on debut: prom over 1m:
fin 8th: half sister to fair Torrey: acts on yld grnd & on a gall trk: should impr.   00
231   SHIRZAD [5] 3-8-11 S Raymont 7/2: 0-00: Well bckd: last to fin.   00
351   Tudor Dor [3] 8-11   --   Molucella [4] 8-11   --   Cherry Glory [6] 8-11
347   Nautical Step [2] 8-11   --   Plum Bossy [14] 8-11
--   Tymbal [9] 8-11
14 ran   2½,2½,4,5,3   (C J harper)   D Elsworth Whitsbury, Hants

459   DEVIZES HANDICAP STAKES 3YO 0-50   £2406   10f   Yielding 85 +09 Fast   [53]

217   HOMME DAFFAIRE [1] (G Lewis) 3-8-1 P Waldron 9/4 Jt FAV: 000-01: 3 br c Lord Gayle -
French Cracker (Klairon): Landed a gamble when leading below dist, comfortably in quite a
fast run 3yo h'cap at Salisbury May 7: lightly raced last season and this was his first win:
half brother to 12f winner Royal Cracker: eff over 10f and should stay further: acts on
good and soft grnd & is suited by a stiff trk.   38
--   MUSICAL YOUTH [2] (C Horgan) 3-8-1 R Hills 10/1: 004-2: Slow start: fin full of
running though not reach winner: brother to very useful sprinter Prince Sabo: clearly stays
10f well: acts on firm & yld grnd & on any trk: see 169.   33
*169 NATIVE HABITAT [9] (M Jarvis) 3-7-12 W Woods(3) 9/4 Jt FAV: -413: Led home turn:
in good form: see 169.   23
--   ELAAFUUR [11] (P Walwyn) 3-9-1 Paul Eddery 13/2: 100-4: Led briefly 4f out: btr for
race: lightly raced last season winning at Chepstow maiden first time out: cost $625,000:
should be suited by middle dists: acts on gd & soft grnd & on a gall trk: well clear of remainder.   35
275   WALCISIN [10] 3-7-9(1ow) D Mckay 25/1: 000-000: Stayed on too late.   03
331   BLACK COMEDY [7] 3-8-3 M L Thomas 25/1: 001-000: Late prog: yet to recapture his
form shown last backend, when winning a maiden at Warwick: half brother to a couple of
winners: eff around 1m, stays 12f: acts on gd/firm & soft grnd & on any trk.   07
--   DUNOOF [6] 3-9-1 G Baxter 7/1: 012-0: Prom. over ½way: strip fitter next time.   00
271   POUNELTA [5] 3-9-3(vis) A Mcglone 15/2: 133-420: Led to ½way: much btr over 1m in 271.   00
331   Ittihaad [13] 8-5   348   Prince Merandi [3] 8-9
275   Roaming Weir [8] 8-7   90   Fire Rocket [4] 7-7
12 ran   3,4,3,12,1½,1½   (Mrs L R Baerlein)   G Lewis Epsom, Surrey

---

Official Going Given as Good/Soft

460   RED DRAGON MAIDEN STAKES 2YO   £2252   5f   Good/Yld 79 -22 Slow

--   FLAXLEY [6] (R Hollinshead) 2-9-0 S Perks 20/1: 1: 2 b c Godswalk - Touch My Heart
(Steel Heart): Prom colt: made a winning racecourse debut, ran on well to lead inside final
1f in a 2yo stakes at Chester May 7: cost 9,500 gns: first foal: speedily bred: eff at 5f:
acts on a sharp trk & gd/yld grnd.   53
212   ONE LINER [3] (N Callaghan) 2-9-0 S Cauthen 6/5 FAV: 22: Heavily bckd: nearly made
all: in gd form: acts on any trk: see 212.   48
--   SUPREME OPTIMIST [4] (R Peacock) 2-9-0 W Carson 16/1: 3: Al up there on debut:
prom effort: should stay 6f: acts on gd/yld & a sharp trk: should find a small maiden.   46
345   RIMBEAU [5] (C Nelson) 2-9-0 J Reid 5/1: 424: Dsptd lead: fdd: consistent but
seems to only just get 5f at present: see 345, 230.   38
--   MY BUDDY [7] 2-9-0 R Cochrane 5/1: 0: Slow start: no show on debut: cost 6,000 gns:
should do better next time.   33
--   RUN BY [2] 2-9-0 J Lowe 5/1: 0: Al rear on debut: cost 41,000 gns & should impr.   27
--   EL BE DOUBLEYOU [1] 2-9-0 P Cook 10/1: 0: No show.   00
7 ran   1½,½,3,2,2   (S C Reakes)   R Hollinshead Upper Longdon, Staffs

159

461   CHESHIRE REGIMENT H'CAP 0-60   £3596   12f   Good/Yld 79 -07 Slow   [59]

273 COMME LETOILE [7] (J Hindley) 3-9-7 M Hills 2/1 FAV: 121-31: 2 b c Star Appeal-
The Yellow Girl (Yellow God): Very useful colt: well bckd and led ½m out, easily in a h'cap
at Chester May 7: winning 2yo at Doncaster & Haydock: eff at 10f, stays 12f well and will
be suited by further: acts on firm, suited by soft & heavy: no trk preferences: should
win more races: carries weight well.   65
331 CHEVET LADY [3] (R Whitaker) 3-7-7(6oh) S P Griffiths(5) 10/1: 00-1242: Hmpd 3 out:
kept on final 1f, though no ch with winner: gd effort at the weights: stays 12f on a
sharp trk: see 54.   26
380 ROCKALL [4] (S Norton) 3-7-7(bl)(1oh) J Lowe 8/1: 030-043: Ev ch str: stays 12f: clear rest:
acts on any trk: see 380.   22
416 BEAU MIRAGE [1] (C Booth) 3-8-2(vis) R Lines(5) 12/1: 0102004: Wknd str: best 54
(10f, heavy).   00
244 SUPREME KINGDOM [2] (J Hindley) 3-8-9 S Perks 5/1: 10-0320: Fdd: much btr 244 (1m): see 49. 00
49   FLEET FOOTED [5] 3-8-2 G Duffield 6/1: 1004-00: Not stay 12f? see 49.   00
--   MILEOMETER [6] 3-8-3(1ow) B Thomson 5/1: 0020-0: Led 1m on seasonal debut: btr
for race: in '85 fin 2nd to Navarzato in a maiden on this trk: half brother to several
winners incl useful sprinter Numismatist: may not stay 12f: acts on gd/firm grnd.   00
7 ran   5,2,20,15,3   (K Al-Said)   J Hindley Newmarket

462   LADBROKE CHESTER CUP H'CAP 0-75   £17846   2m2f   Good/Yld 79 +21 Fast   [62]

58a WESTERN DANCER [8] (C Horgan) 5-9-0 P Cook 14/1: 2124-01: 5 b g Free State -
Polyandrist (Polic): Very useful, genuine gelding: led over 1f out, gamely by a shhd in
valuable & fast run Chester Cup (h'cap) at Chester May 7: in fine form in '85, winning
valuable Tote Ebor H'cap at York, also won h'caps at Salisbury & Kempton: in '84 won at
Redcar: very eff over 12/14f: stays 2m 2f on a sharp trk: acts on firm 7 yld grnd and carries
weight well: a credit to his trainer.   60
*336 PEARL RUN [2] (G Price) 5-7-12(5ow)(4oh) P Robinson 10/1: 0-11012: Ran on really well
and btn a whisker: carried 5lbs overweight and this may have made the difference: in
excellent form this season: loves a sharp trk.   44
*50 WITHY BANK [12] (M H Easterby) 4-8-7 M Birch 8/1: 220-113: Ch 1f out: continues in
fine form: acts on any trk: should win again soon.   50
360 INDE PULSE [1] (J Hindley) 4-9-13(3ex) M Hills 25/1: 00-0104: Tried to make all:
grand effort under 9-13: stays 2m2f: seems suited by front running tactics: see 280.   69
--   STERNE [21] 4-8-7 M Wigham 12/1: 2--11-0: Fit from a recent win over hurdles: hmpd
early on: late hdway: in '85 was trained by G Harwood, winning both starts at Folkestone
and Hamilton: eff at 12f, stays 18f: acts on any grnd & on any trk.   43
312 FOR A LARK [19] 4-7-9 C Rutter(1) 33/1: 1300-00: Never nearer: stays 2m2f: see 312. 31
312 REVISIT [11] 4-8-6 G Duffield 25/1: 101-000: Fin 7th: see 58A.   00
312 ALDO KING [13] 5-7-9(2ow)(1oh) B Crossley 22/1: 1000-40: Late hdway, never nearer. 00
235 HIGH PLAINS [9] 4-8-2 T Williams 6/1 FAV: 1010-00: Wknd in str: see 235.   00
*235 ACCURACY [10] 5-7-11(3ex) R Fox 8/1: 00-3210: Whipped round start: no show: see 235. 00
215 BACKCHAT [18] 4-9-2 G Starkey 8/1: -411-40: Wknd: btr 215 (gall trk).   00

215	Paths Sister [4] 7-12	336	Morgans Choice [16] 7-12		
--	Dan Marino [5] 9-3	85	Avebury [3] 7-8	336	Jackdaw [15] 7-7(5oh)
235	Orange Hill [22] 7-10	319	Rushmoor [22] 7-10	358	Northern Ruler [20] 7-7
366	Red Duster [7] 7-7(5oh)			366	Sun Street [14] 7-7(5oh)
360	Contester [17] 8-3				

22 ran   shhd,3,1,7,shhd,¾,1½,nk   (Mrs G R H Stone)   C Horgan Billingbear, Berks

463   CHESHIRE OAKS 3YO FILLIES   £15686   1m4f   Good/Yld 79 -05 Slow

--   SALCHOW [9] (W Hern) 3-9-0 W Carson 4/1: 1112-1: 3 b f Niniski - Spin (High Top):
Smart filly: first time out, stayed on well to lead inside the final 1f in Cheshire Oaks
(Listed race) at Chester May 7: very useful 2yo, winning her first 3 at Leicester, Doncaster
& Wolverhampton: on only other start was a fine 2nd to Colorstin in a valuable Listed race
at Newbury: stays 12f really well: acts on firm & yld & on any trk: should win more gd races. 75
--   ALTIYNA [2] (M Stoute) 3-9-0 G Starkey 8/1: 1-2: Ev ch final 1f: fine seasonal debut:
easy winner of sole start in '85, a fillies maiden at Leicester: half sister to several
winners: stays 12f: acts on firm & yld & on any trk: should be winning soon.   71
--   LUCAYAN PRINCESS [3] (H Cecil) 3-9-0 S Cauthen 4/1: 110-3: Made much: came again:
good effort: smart 2yo, winning Sweet Solera Stakes at Newmarket and first time out a maiden
at Yarmouth: stays 12f well: acts on firm & yld & on any trk: genuine sort who should win
races this season.   70
--   IVORS IMAGE [8] (M Stoute) 3-9-0 W R Swinburn 5/1: 21301-4: Led nearing final 1f:
good seasonal debut & 20L clear rest: in '85 won a Gr.2 event at San Siro & a fillies maiden
at Yarmouth: stays 12f: acts on firm & yld & on any trk.   68

351 ALLATUM [6] 3-8-10 B Thomson 14/1: -20: No show: btr 351 (gall trk).	35
*315 FAREWELL TO LOVE [5] 3-9-0 R Cochrane 12/1: 20-210: Wknd 3f out: much btr 315 (10f).	33
*128 SUE GRUNDY [7] 3-9-0 P Robinson 10/3 FAV: 013-10: Heavily bckd: much btr 128 (10f).	00
*123 BRIDE [4] 3-9-0 M Miller 25/1: 00-10: There 7f: stiff task: btr 123.	00
*264 MONA LISA [1] 3-9-0 P Cook 8/1: -010: Prom 7f: much btr 264: something amiss?	00

9 ran   2,nk,1½,20,4   (Mrs W R Hern)   W Hern West Ilsley, Berks

---

464   SEFTON MAIDEN 3YO FILLIES STAKES   £3392   7.5f   Good/Yld 79 -24 Slow

234 TOBAGO DANCER [1] (R Hannon) 3-8-11 G Starkey 7/1: 2404-01: 3 ch f Viking - Perbury
(Grisaille): Not the best of runs, but led close home in a 3yo fillies maiden at Chester
May 7: placed several times in '85 and this was a deserved success: eff at 7f, stays 1m:
acts on firm & yld & on any trk.   50
--   INDIAN LOVE SONG [10] (R Hollinshead) 3-8-11 S Perks 25/1: -0400-2: Ex Irish filly:
led over 1f out: just caught: good effort: half sister to a minor winner: eff at 7f on gd/
yld & a sharp trk: should find a maiden.   48
--   RAISINHELL [2] (W Jarvis) 3-8-11 S Cauthen 4/1: 0200-3: Lef briefly over 1f out: just btn.:
good seasonal debut: showed gd promise in '85: best effort when 2nd to Embla at Kempton:
half sister to 2 winners: eff at 6/7f: acts on firm & yld & should find a maiden.   48
264 HOT MOMMA [5] (R Boss) 3-8-11 M Miller 10/1: 022-204: Again ev ch: see 264, 89.   40
309 ELSOCKO [7] 3-8-11 W Carson 14/1: 0300-30: Made much: stays 7f: see 309.   38
213 ABSENCE OF MALICE [8] 3-8-11 R Cochrane 5/2 FAV: -20: Uneasy fav: no show: btr 213.   35
213 GREEN FOR DANGER [6] 3-8-11 M Hills 4/1: -300-30: Wknd: much btr 213 (gall trk).   00
217 Pleasure Island [3] 8-11   276 Cooper Racing Nail [11] 8-11
--   What A Party [9] 8-11(BL)   340 Pegasus Lady [4] 8-11
11 ran   ½,shhd,4,¾,2   (D A Lucie-Smith)   R Hannon East Everleigh, Wilts

---

465   ROODEYE EBF 3YO STAKES   £3941   7.5f   Good/Yld 79 -12 Slow

*229 NIGHT OUT PERHAPS [3] (G Wragg) 3-9-3 S Cauthen 3/1: 0-11: 3 b c Cure The Blues -
Pipina (Sir Gaylord): Useful, impr colt: ran on well under press to lead on the line in a
stakes event at Chester May 7: first time out was a comfortable winner of a maiden at
Newmarket: showed promise on sole start in '85: eff at 7f, should stay 1m: acts on gd &
soft grnd & on any trk: on the up grade & should win more races.   62
322 KNYF [5] (E Weymes) 3-8-9 W Carson 10/1: 332-32: Led over 1f out: caught post:
deserves a change of luck: runs well on a sharpish trk: see 322.   53
229 HABER [8] (B Hills) 3-8-9 B Thomson 15/8 FAV: -23: Heavily bckd: ch final 1f: acts
on any trk: should be suited by 1m: see 229: sure to find a race soon. .   45
159 HARD ROUND [1] (R Hannon) 3-8-12 G Starkey 7/2: 041-24: Made much: eased when btn.   40
--   DARK PROMISE [4] 3-8-12 S Perks 16/1: 21020-0: Early ldr: wknd str: btr for race:
most consistent in '85, winning at Wolverhampton: eff at 5f, stays 7f: acts on gd & soft grnd
and on any trk.   30
--   MASHHUR [6] 3-8-12 W R Swinburn 8/1: 02301-0: Fdd str on seasonal debut: on final
outing in '85 won a nursery at Nottingham: first time out won at Goodwood: stays 1m well:
acts on good & firm grnd & on any trk: has worn a visor: better for race.   16
--   SURE LANDING [7] 3-8-9 J Reid 10/1: -0: No show on racecourse debut: half brother to
a minor 5f winner.   00
414 SHARK FIGHTER [2] 3-8-12 L Charnock 33/1: 1310-00: Rank outsider: never in it.   00
8 ran   shhd,5,5,6,8   (E B Moller)   G Wragg Newmarket

Official Going Given as Soft

466   SWETTENHAM STUD RACE   £4140   1m   Soft .

--   FIORAVANTI (D O'brien) 3-9-0 C Roche 4/5 FAV: 11-1: 3 b c Northern Dancer-Pitasia:
Smart Irish colt: led approaching final 1f for a very clever nk success in Swettenham Stud
Race at Phoenix Park May 3: unbtn in 2 outings as a 2yo, at Phoenix Park & the Curragh: eff
at 1m & should stay further: acts on soft, well suited by good grnd: no trk preferences:
should come on for this first run of the season and the plan is the Irish 2,000 Guineas
followed by the Epsom Derby: highly regarded.   78
--   LIVING ROUGH (V Kennedy) 3-8-4 R Carroll 14/1:   2-2: Flattered by proximity to
winner, but a good effort: on sole start in '85 fin 2nd to Park Express in a maiden at
Leopardstown: stays 1m: acts on gd/firm & soft.   62
--   GOLDEN ORIOLE (M O'brien) 3-8-4 V Rossiter 14/1: -3: Promising racecourse debut
from this very well bred filly, being a full sister to the brilliant El Gran Senor: sure
to win races.   56
--   JAZZ MUSICIAN (M Kauntze) 3-8-10 P Shanahan 12/1: 24200-4: Not disgraced.   60
8 ran   nk,3,1   (Sheikh Mohammed)   D O'brien Ireland

467   DUBAI POULE DESSAI GR 1 3YO FILLIES   £64937   1m   Soft .

155   BAISER VOLE [4] (C Head) 3-9-2 G Guignard 1: 1131-01: 3 b f Foolish Pleasure -
River Rose: Very smart French filly: led 1f out, holding on by a nk in Gr.1 French 1,000
Guineas at Longchamp May 4: one of the top French 2yos in '85, gaining Gr.1 wins at Longchamp
and Maison Laffitte: also won 2 small races on the latter trk: eff at 7f, stays 1m: acts
on any grnd and is a most genuine filly.   81
--   SECRET FORM [5] (P Bary) 3-9-2 A Badel 1: -11-2: Fin really well and just denied:
smart filly: very eff at 1m on soft grnd.   80
155   RIVER DANCER [3] (J Cunnington) 3-9-2 M Philipperon 1: 124-43: Fine effort: stays 1m.   76
--   GLIFAHDA [9] (D Smaga) 3-9-2 A Lequeux 1: --03-34: Unfancied: not btn far: stays
1m well: acts on gd/firm & soft.   75
232   TANOUMA [2] 3-9-2 W Carson 1: 1-30: Acquitted herself well in this top class company:
stays 1m: see 232.   74
232   ASTEROID FIELD [13] 3-9-2 B Thomson 1: 2114-20: Below her best: see 232.   72
300   TICAROCK [1] 3-9-2 J C Desaint 1: 00: Not btn far in close fin & ran very well.   72
288   REGAL STATE [15] 3-9-2 Y Saint Martin 1: 1120-40: Close up 8th: see 288.   71
*288 NORTHERN PREMIER [7] 3-9-2 C Asmussen 1: 10: In good form: see 288.   70
288   KANMARY [6] 3-9-2 M Mosse 1: 4130-00: Fin 10th.   69
18 ran   nk,2,nk,nk,1,shhd,nk,hd,¼   (R Sangster)   C Head France

468   GROUP 1 PRIX GANAY 4YO +   £41398   1m 2f   Soft .

154   BAILLAMONT [7] (F Boutin) 4-9-2 F Head 1: 0030-31: 4 b c Blushing Groom - Lodeve:
Very smart French colt: fin well to get up in the final strides in Gr.1 Prix Ganay at
Longchamp May 4: in '85 won Gr.1 Prix Jean Prat at Chantilly: very eff at 9/10f: loves soft grnd. 86
--   MERSEY [3] (P L Biancone) 4-8-13 E Legrix 1: 23111-2: Caught close home: fine
seasonal debut from this very smart French filly: in excellent form at the end of last
season: on final outing won Gr.1 Prix Royal Oak at Longchamp: also won Gr.3 event at Longchamp and successful at Evry: eff at 10f, stays 15f: acts on firm & soft grnd & likes Longchamp. 83
*154 SAINT ESTEPHE [2] (A Fabre) 4-9-2 A Gibert 1: 2123-13: Not btn far in close fin:
continues in fine form: beat winner 154.   85
--   TRIPTYCH [5] (P L Biancone) 4-8-13 G Mosse 1: 20303-4: Good seasonal debut: trained
by D V O'Brien in '85 and was in excellent form, making history when the first filly to
win the Irish 2,000 Guineas: also successful in a Gr.3 event at Phoenix Park and a fine
2nd to the top class Oh So Sharp in the Oaks: eff at 1m, stays 12f: acts on gd, likes
yld/soft ground: thoroughly genuine and holds her form remarkably well.   80
*299 BABY TURK [10] 4-9-2 Y Saint Martin 1: 10: Fine 5th: see 299.   82
221   DAMISTER [9] 4-9-2 S Cauthen 1: 3313-30: Slightly disapp 6th: see 221.   80
+313 FIELD HAND [1] 4-9-2 B Thomson 1: 121-210: Fin 7th: much btr 313 (1m).   00
--   MORESPEED [6] 4-9-2 J L Kessas 1: 13043-0: Stiff task.   00
2   HERALDISTE [4] 4-9-2 D Boeuf 1: 3100-30: Fin 9th, see 2.   00
360   RAMICH JOHN [8] 4-8-13 W Carson 1: 320: Last to fin: has been very busy lately:
better 360, 325.   00
10 ran   shhd,½,1,1,1½   (S Niarchos)   F Boutin France

Official Going Given as Fast

469   GRADE ONE KENTUCKY DERBY 3YO   £244755   1m 2f   Fast .

--   FERDINAND [1] (C Whittingham) 3-9-0 W Shoemaker 1: 3-21321: 3 ch c Nijinsky -
Banja Luka: Very smart American colt: led inside the final 1f in Grade 1 Kentucky Derby at
Churchill Downs May 4: eff at 10f: acts well on fast grnd.   85
5   BOLD ARRANGEMENT [4] (C Brittain) 3-9-0 C Mccarron 1: 22D-332: Led 2f out: kept on
gamely and this was a fine performance: eff at 10f and may stay 12f: should win more gd races.   82
--   BROAD BRUSH [9] (R Small) 3-9-0 V Bracciale 1: 2111113: Very consistent.   80
--   RAMPAGE [5] (B Thomas) 3-9-0 P Day 1: 0-11414: --   79
16 ran   2¼,¾,nk,1½   (Howard B Keck)   C Whittingham U.S.A.

470   HERMITAGE FARM FILLIES STKS LISTED   £14472   1m 1f   Heavy Slow

294   EPICURES GARDEN (D Weld) 3-8-10 M J Kinane 4/1 Co FAV: --13-41: 3 ch f Affirmed -
Ralking Picture: Very useful Irish filly: led close home in a Listed race at Phoenix Park
May 7: in '85 won again at Phoenix Park: eff at 7f, stays 9f: acts on gd/firm & heavy grnd.   72
--   HALINA (J Oxx) 3-8-3 D Hogan 8/1: -3-2: Just touched off: fine seasonal debut:
on sole outing in '85 fin 3rd at the Curragh: stays 9f: acts well on soft grnd.   64
--   BEES NEST (M Kauntze) 3-8-10 D Manning 11/2: ---4-13: Gd effort: recent winner over
10f at Navan: acts on yld & heavy.   69

-- FAIR OF THE FURZE (L Browne) 4-10-1 M T Browne 10/1: /2201-4: Btr for race: on
final outing in '85 won a Listed race at Leopardstown: earlier a fine 5th to Helen Street
in the Irish Oaks: stays 12f: acts on gd/firm & soft grnd.   71
294 CAROLS LUCK 3-8-10 D J Murphy 4/1 Co FAV: -1-0200: Well bckd: beat winner in 264. 63
-- RIVER MYSTERY 3-8-10 K Moses 14/1: --30-10: Recent winner at Leopardstown(1m,hvy). 00
10 ran   nk,1½,nk,3   (Moyglare Stud Farm)   D Weld Ireland

471 LANES END FARM STKS LISTED RACE   £24459   1m   Heavy Slow

395 MR JOHN (L Browne) 3-8-10 M T Browne 7/1: 3100-41: 3 ch c Northfields - Ashton
Amber: Smart Irish colt: just got up in a 3 way photo to Lanes End Farm Stakes (Listed
race) at Phoenix Park May 7: in '85 won at Naas and Leopardstown: eff at 7f, stays 1m well:
acts on gd/firm & heavy grnd.   77
373 WEIGHT IN GOLD (J Bolger) 3-8-7 D Gillespie 11/4: 1-14102: Btn a whisker: in fine
form: see 373, 269.   74
-- FORLAWAY (D O'brien) 4-9-9 C Roche 6/1: 12202-3: Btn 2 shhds: fine seasonal debut:
in '85 won over 9f at Leopardstown and was most consistent: stays 10f: acts on gd/firm & soft. 74
150 RIVER BLUES (L Browne) 3-8-7 P V Gilson 20/1: -04-334: Gd effort: on the up grade. 71
293 LONDON TOWER 3-8-7 M J Kinane 2/1 FAV: -120: Well bckd, but not stay the trip.   67
-- HUNGRY GIANT 3-8-7 D Hogan 7/1: -220-0:   00
9 ran   shhd,shhd,1½,2½   (J Michael)   L Browne Ireland

472 BBA SPRING STAKES LISTED RACE   £8587   6f   Heavy Fast

*295 YOUNG BLADE (M O'toole) 3-8-12 C Roche 4/1: 1103-11: 3 gr c Silent Dignity - Grey
Axe: Smart Irish colt who is in fine form at present: comfortable 3L winner of fast run
Listed race at Phoenix Park May 7th: last time out was an easy winner of a Listed race
again at Phoenix Park: in '85 won at Punchestown & Gowran: very eff at 6f: acts on gd &
heavy: sure to win more races.   78
295 DOBEY THATCHER (M Kauntze) 3-8-7 P Shanahan 12/1: -1-422: Another good effort
and is impr: acts well on heavy: see 295.   65
-- RUSTIC AMBER (J Oxx) 3-8-12 D Hogan 4/1: 02210-3: Gd seasonal debut: in '85 won
over 5f at the Curragh: stays 6f: acts on gd & heavy.   69
-- STEEL COMMANDER (D Weld) 8-9-6 M J Kinane 5/2 FAV: 02032-4: Well bckd on seasonal
debut: btr for race: smart horse who in '85 won at Phoenix Park and is a winner 4 times
on this trk: very eff at 5/6f: acts on gd/firm & soft.   62
-- SNOWTOP 3-8-9 G Curran 10/1: 43D1-00:   54
394 THE BEAN SIDHE 3-8-11 C F Swan 9/2: 110-130: Best in 294 (7f).   55
10 ran   3,½,½,5,½   (Mrs M O'Toole)   M O'toole Ireland

CHESTER   Thursday May 8th   lefthand Very Sharp Track

Official Going Given as Soft

473 EBF SCEPTRE MAIDEN FILLIES STKS 2YO   £3059   5f   Soft/Heavy 157 -24 Slow

261 MISS SHEGAS [4] (J Berry) 2-8-11 W Carson 5/1: 221: 2 b f Rabdan - Rather Easy
(Swing Easy): Impr filly: made ev yd, just holding on in a 2yo fillies maiden at Chester
May 8: earlier fin 2nd at Epsom & Haydock: eff at 5f with forcing tactics: acts on soft &
yld grnd and on any trk, though likes a sharpish one.   42
383 SILVERS ERA [3] (N Callaghan) 2-8-11 Paat Eddery 9/2: 02: Ev ch final 1f: btn a
whisker: good effort: should find a small event: acts on gd/firm & soft & on any trk: see 383. 41
236 DOMINO ROSE [6] (N Tinkler) 2-8-11 T Ives 3/1: 23: Sn prom: will be suited by 6f. 39
-- CITY FINAL [2] (R Hollinshead) 2-8-11 S Perks 14/1: 4: Slow start, proved fatal:
should impr: cheaply acquired & should be suited by further than 5f.   23
-- VERYAN BAY [5] 2-8-11 S Cauthen 13/8 FAV: 0: Well bckd, but never in it: well bred
sort who should do much btr than this: possibly on btr grnd/stiffer trk.   09
73 SAUCIER [1] 2-8-11 B Thomson 25/1: 00: Prom early: cost 4,100 gns.   00
6 ran   shhd,½,8,7,15   (John Taylor (Shudehill) Ltd)   J Berry Cockerham, lancs

474 EATON HANDICAP 0-60   £3895   1m 4f   Soft/Heavy 157 +12 Fast   [54]

410 PAGAN SUN [4] (A Bailey) 5-8-9 Paul Eddery 9/1: 040-201: 5 ch c Mount Hagen -
Europeana (Dual): Fairly useful horse: ran on gamely to get up close home in quite a fast
run h'cap at Chester May 8: in '85 won an app h'cap at Haydock: previous season won at
Doncaster: eff at 10f, well suited by 12f: acts on gd/firm & soft & on any trk: genuine sort. 46
189 STATELY FORM [5] (J Tree) 4-9-10 Pat Eddery 11/4: 1140-02: Dsptd lead: just btn
and may be winning soon: in good form in '85, winning h'caps at Kempton, Goodwood & Sandown:
also won a minor event at Windsor: half brother to several winners: eff at 10f, stays 12f
well: acts on soft, likes firm grnd: no trk preferences.   60

308 REGAL STEEL [3] (R Hollinshead) 8-7-7(1oh) A Culhane(7) 14/1: 0-30203: Nearly made
all: likes this sharp trk: see 243, 4.   29
*199 COLONEL JAMES [8] (S Oliver) 4-8-6 R Cochranee 8/1: 2200-14: Lightly bckd: ch 1f
out: acts on any trk: in gd form: see 199.   38
308 BOLLIN PALACE [11] 4-7-13 N Carlisle 5/1 Jt.FAV: 2000-30: Ch 1f out: wknd: see 308.   27
360 PETRIZZO [2] 5-9-1 S Cauthen 16/1: 04-0000: Never nearer: failed to win in '85, but
in '84 won the Gr.3 Doncaster Cup at Doncaster, only to be controversially relegated to
2nd: eff over 13/14f: stays 2m plus: acts on firm & yld grnd.   34
263 RECORD WING [6] 8-8-4 D Williams(7) 6/1: 0-21330: No show: best in 92.   00
308 SILENT JOURNEY [10] 4-8-2(6ex) N Connorton 5/1 Jt.FAV: 030-120: Wknd: btr 308, 256.   00
--   STANDARD BREAKFAST [1] 4-8-12 B Thomson 10/1: -1400-0: No show on seasonal debut:
first time out in '85 won a maiden at Newbury: eff at 12f on yld grnd: acts on a gall trk.   00
308 Skyboot [9] 7-7(5oh)   --   Vouchsafe [12] 9-8
11 ran   nk,shhd,2½,2½,6.   (T P Ramsden)   A Bailey Newmarket

475 ORMONDE EBF STAKES GROUP 3   £24514   1m 5f Soft/Heavy 157 -25 Slow

265 BRUNICO [4] (R Simpson) 4-8-10 B Thomson 33/1: 000-101: 4 gr g Bruni - Cartridge
(Jim French): Smart colt: showed much impr form when led inside the final 1f, under press
to win Gr.3 Ormonde Stakes at Chester May 8: first time out was an easy winner of an amateur
riders event at Doncaster: also an unlucky 2nd in the Triumph Hurdle and is a smart performer
in that sphere: 1m winner in France in '85: eff over 10f, stays 13f: acts on gd/firm &
soft/heavy grnd: no trk preferences & should win more races.   77
--   SHARDARI [3] (M Stoute) 4-9-0 W R Swinburn 6/5 FAV: 21D11-2: Heavily bckd: led 4f out
till inside final 1f and was obviously in need of the race: top class colt who in '85 gave
Free Guest a 15L beating in Gr.3 St Simons Stakes at Newbury: also successful in Gr.3
Cumberland Lodge Stakes at Ascot and fast run events at Folkestone & Sandown: also "won"
Gr.2 Great Voltigeur at York, beating Damister a nk, but subsq. demoted: very eff over
10/12f: stays 13f: acts on firm & soft grnd & on any trk: genuine & consistent and will come
on for this race: sure to win some good races this season.   79
+251 LEMHILL [1] (M Blanshard) 4-9-0 R Cochrane 6/1: D232-13: Never nearer: btr 251.   70
--   RISING [2] (K Prendergast) 4-8-10 G Curran 6/1: 0030-14: Sn prom, fdd str: recent
winner of a Listed race at the Curragh: in '85 won at Down Royal: stays 2m: acts on firm
and soft ground.   66
325 CHAUMIERE [6] 5-8-10(vis) T Ives 33/1: 023-000: No show, but a btr effort: in
good form in '85, winning valuable John Smiths Magnet Cup at York and placed on several
occasions: in '84 won a valuable h'cap at Newmarket and a stakes event at York: eff at
8/10f, stays 12f: acts on any grnd: suited by a gall trk: genuine & consistent and
carries weight well.   56
251 GOLD AND IVORY [7] 5-9-4(VIS) Pat Eddery 6/1: 1200-30: Visored first time and led
over 1m: btr 251.   56
-251 EAGLING [5] 4-8-10 S Cauthen 6/1: 1310-20: Wknd: much btr 251 (gall trk).   00
+312 MILTON BURN [9] 5-8-10 S Dawson 50/1: 40-0110: Stiff task: see 312.   00
8 ran   1½,7,nk,8,6   (T P Ramsden)   R Simpson Upper Lambourn, Berks

476 DEE STAKES 3YO LISTED RACE   £16960   1m 2f Soft/Hvy 157 -04 Slow

226 FARAWAY DANCER [5] (H Cecil) 3-8-12 S Cauthen 4/5 FAV: 111-21: 3 br c Far North -
Prove Us Royal (Prove It): Smart colt: heavily bckd and led into str, easily in valuable
Dee Stakes (Listed race) at Chester May 8: first time out was an excellent 2nd to Dancing
Brave in Gr.3 Craven Stakes at Newmarket: unbtn in 3 outings in '85, at Sandown, Haydock
& Goodwood: half brother to a smart American sprinter: eff at 1m/10f, may stay further:
acts on any grnd & on any trk: has a gd turn of foot & should win more gd races.   82
*194 TOP GUEST [3] (G Wragg) 3-8-12 Pat Eddery 11/2: 0222-12: Sn prom: fine effort and
will be winning again soon: should stay 12f: acts on any trk and on any grnd.   68
*348 PLAID [6] (P Walwyn) 3-9-2 Paul Eddery 6/1: 132-313: Led 1m: acts on any trk:
continues in good form: see 348.   69
226 EVES ERROR [1] (M Stoute) 3-8-12 W R Swinburn 6/1: 112-04: Sn prom: stays 10f: see 226.   65
--   ORIENTAL SOLDIER [4] 3-8-12 B Thomson 10/1: 12210-0: Outsider: wknd on seasonal
debut: most consistent in '85, winning at Salisbury & Haydock and was placed on several
occasions: eff at 7f, should stay 1m plus: acts on yld, though likes firm grnd: runs well
on a stiff trk and should do btr than this.   35
5 ran   5,2,shhd,15   (Peter Burrell)   H Cecil Newmarket

477 OULTON HANDICAP STAKES 0-60   £3915   5f Soft/Heavy 157 +03 Fast   [47]

+428 PERION [6] (G Lewis) 4-9-2(7ex) P Waldron 2/1 FAV: 0-10111: 4 ch g Northfields -
Relanca (Relic): Useful gelding who is in excellent form: completed the hat trick, led 1f
out, comfortably in a h'cap at Chester May 8: earlier successful in similar event at
Doncaster, Epsom & Folkestone: lightly raced in '85: in '84 won at Newmarket: very eff
at 5f, acts on gd but is well suited by soft/heavy grnd & is best when held up for a
late chall: most consistent this season & acts on any trk.   46

+327 BRIDGE STREET LADY [7] (J Bosley) 5-10-0(7ex) Pat Eddery 9/2: 00-2012: Led briefly
over 1f out: in fine form: acts on any trk: see 327.   55
428 PHILIP [1] (N Tinkler) 4-9-5(bl) L Charnock 8/1: 00-0003: Nicely bckd: nearest fin:
btr effort: in '85 won 3yo h'caps at Doncaster, Haydock & Perth: in '84 won at Hamilton:
eff over 5/6f: acts on firm & soft grnd & on any trk: may find a h'cap shortly.   42
272 MUSIC MACHINE [3] (P Haslam) 5-8-8 T Williams 9/2: 010-044: Led/dsptd lead over 3f.   23
272 DERRY RIVER [8] 5-8-11(bl) N Carlisle 12/1: 322-000: Led ½way: fdd: see 272.   18
327 DUCK FLIGHT [5] 4-9-7 S Cauthen 5/1: 030-040: No show: much btr 327.   26
--   Little Starchy [4] 8-4(3ow)   --   Little Bori [2] 7-7(4oh)
8 ran   1,1½,4,4,¾   (John W Wheatland)   G Lewis Epsom, Surrey

478 LADBROKE HOTELS HANDICAP 3YO 0-60   £3980   7f   Soft/Heavy 157 -12 Slow [61]

178 DOGMATIC [2] (R Johnson Houghton) 3-9-6(bl) S Cauthen 9/2 Co.FAV: 2301-41: 3 b c Welsh
Pageant - Self Satisfied (Great Nephew): Very useful colt: led from the stalls, gamely in
a 3yo h'cap at Chester May 8: on final outing in '85 won a nursery h'cap at Doncaster:
eff at 7f: acts on any grnd & on any trk and seems best out in front.   65
196 ROMANTIC UNCLE [3] (H Wharton) 3-8-10 J H Brown(5) 15/2: 3021-02: Ran on well final
1f and just btn: gd effort and should be winning soon: in '85 won a nursery h'cap at
Haydock and was placed on several occasions: eff at 6f, stays 7f well: acts on firm, loves
soft/heavy grnd: acts on any trk.   54
216 HYMN OF HARLECH [1] (G Pritchard Gordon) 3-8-10 G Duffield 8/1: 300-003: Al prom: not
btn far: gd effort: useful 2yo, winning at Epsom and awarded a race at Pontefract: eff
over 7f, stays 7f: acts on gd/firm & soft and likes a sharpish trk.   52
247 AUCTION MAN [5] (R Hollinshead) 3-7-12 A Culhane(7) 9/2 Co.FAV: 03-0324: Btn 1L in
close fin: acts on any going: see 247, 141.   39
*335 MY KIND OF TOWN [4] 3-8-7 T Ives 11/2: -110: Sn prom: better 335 (1m).   43
168 DANCING TOM [8] 3-8-0 M Beecroft 14/1: 101-400: Wknd str: better 6f?: see 81.   24
*340 EXAMINATION [6] 3-8-6(bl)(7ex) G Carter(3) 9/2 Co.FAV: 30-1210: No show: btr 340.   00
--   TOPPESHAMME [9] 3-9-5 W Carson 8/1: 2311-0: Prom, faded: better for race: trained by
H Cecil in '85 winning fillies event at Haydock & Chepstow: now with E Weymes: eff at 7f
but should stay further: acts on firm and soft and on galloping track.   00
--   HARAABAH [7] 3-9-7 R Hills 14/1: 00200-0: Btr for race.   00
9 ran   hd,¾,hd,3,8.   (A G Samuel)   R Johnson Houghton Blewbury, Oxon.

Official Going Given as Soft

479 WINCANTON MAIDEN STAKES 3YO   £1249   1m 2f   Yielding 106 -03 Slow

--   FLEETING AFFAIR [10] (G Harwood) 3-8-11 G Starkey 8/1: -1: 3 b f Hotfoot - My Own II
(El Relicario): Prom filly: easy to back on debut though ran on strongly for a comfortable
win in a 3yo maiden at Salisbury May 8: half sister to several winners, incl the very useful
Haul Knight: clearly eff over 10f on a stiff trk, and should stay further: acts on yld
grnd: should win more races and rate highly.   52
--   MTOTO [1] (A Stewart) 3-9-0 M Roberts 4/5 FAV: 3-2: Heavily bckd on reapp: led below
dist: narrowly btn and this was a good effort: placed behind Queens Soldier in a Yarmouth
maiden on only outing last season: cost 110,000 gns and is closely related to several winners
incl smart French filly Button Up: stays 10f on a stiff trk: acts on gd & yld grnd: should
win soon.   51
--   SLANGI VAH [9] (H Candy) 3-9-0 R Curant 12/1: -3: Mkt drifter but just beaten:
led 3f out and kept on well when hdd: promising effort: clearly suited by 10f on a gall trk:
acts on yld grnd: should find a race soon.   50
--   TABACOS [3] (D Elsworth) 3-9-0 A Mcglone 15/2: 0-4: Never nearer on seasonal debut:
showed promise after a slow start behind Happy Breed on sole start at Lingfield last season:
eff over 10f and stays further: acts on firm & yld grnd & on a gall trk.   42
--   KRISWICK [11] 3-8-11 B Rouse 8/1: -0: Led briefly 3f out: well bred debutant who
cost 96,000 gns as a yearling and is a half sister to a very useful middle dist winner
Santella Man: should impr.   34
218 PEGMARINE [8] 3-9-0 W Woods(3) 16/1: -00: Never threatened though showed some impr.   31
--   Assembly [6] 9-0   --   Demon Fate [13] 9-0   231 Eaton Square [4] 9-0
--   Russki [2] 9-0   --   Alceba [5] 8-11   357 Ashford Lass [12] 8-11
12 ran   ¾,½,5,2,4,3   (Mrs S E Lakin)   G Harwood Pulborough, Sussex

480 DORSET HANDICAP (0-35) 3YO   £2536   1m   Yielding 106 -01 Slow [40]

386 GEORGES QUAY [5] (R Hannon) 3-9-1 A Mcglone 4/1: 000-401: 3 br g Prince Tenderfoot-
Princess Quay (Babur): Nicely bckd when making most in a 3yo h'cap at Salisbury May 8:
first success: half brother to several winners: eff over 7/8f on firm & soft grnd: well
suited by a stiff trk.   39

352 **STANFORD VALE** [7] (C Nelson) 3-8-8 J Reid 8/1: 400-02: Led over 2f out: impr effort:
lightly raced last season: half brother to several winners: stays 1m well: acts on gd &
yld grnd & on a gall trk.   26

356 **COSMIC FLIGHT** [9] (M Usher) 3-8-4 M Wigham 8/1: 00-1033: Gd effort: see 67.   20

67   **FIREPROOF** [15] (D Marks) 3-8-4 A Clark 16/1: 00-04: Stayed on late but should do
btr over a longer trip: acts on gd/firm & soft grnd & on any trk.   10

351 **EASTERN PLAYER** [1] 3-8-8 S Whitworth 33/1: 00-0000: Btr effort over this shorter trip.   11

274 **PROBLEM CHILD** [11] 3-8-12 C Rutter(5) 10/3 FAV: 0003-30: Had ev ch: much btr over
7f in 274 (sharp trk, heavy).   15

--   **AVENTINO** [8] 3-8-6 B Crossley 8/1: 0001-0: Mkt drifter and no threat on reapp: ended
last season a narrow win in a Newmarket seller: eff over 7f & should stay further:
acts on fast grnd & on a stiff trk: looks fairly h'capped & should do btr next time.   00

234	Brent Riverside [4] 8-12			335	Whirling Words [13] 8-8
275	On To Glory [6] 9-7	338	Hachimitsu [2] 8-12	--	Balnacraig [10] 8-9
--	Merrymoles [3] 8-12	--	No Stopping [12] 8-9	--	Cracon Girl [16] 8-6
161	No Jazz [17] 8-5	--	Csillag [14] 8-3		

17 ran   3,1,6,2,hd,2   (John Horgan)   R Hannon East Everleigh, Wilts

481 **STOCKBRIDGE HANDICAP (0-50)**   £2914   7f   Yielding 106 +05 Fast   [44]

399 **SINGLE** [11] (W Wightman) 4-8-12 D Mckay 3/1 FAV: 0-01141: 4 b c Jellaby – Miss Solo
(Runymede): Made a quick reapp and proved a comfortable winner of quite a fast run h'cap at
Salisbury May 8: led inside dist and won going away: last time narrowly btn in a blanket
fin at Kempton: earlier won successive h'caps at Chepstow & Epsom: in '85 won at Bath &
Newbury: eff over 7/8f: acts on firm & yld/soft grnd: seems equally eff on any trk: in
fine form.   38

71   **FORMATUNE** [12] (D Arbuthnot) 4-8-10(bl) J Reid 8/1: 003-102: Ran on well: gd effort.   32

401 **PEANDAY** [2] (H Beasley) 5-8-4 R Morse(5) 16/1: 000-003: Switched below dist, fin
well and not btn far: gd form early last season when twice a r.u. in h'caps: in '84 won at
Brighton, Windsor and Folkestone: eff over sprint distances & stays 10f: acts on any going
and on any trk, though all winning form has been on sharper courses.   25

355 **HOPEFUL KATIE** [15] (D Leslie) 4-7-13(hd) N Adams 16/1: 00-4304: Fin a close 5th,
promoted to 4th: see 65.   18

91   **KAVAKA** [18] 4-8-4 R Fox 16/1: 0-00-00: Stayed on well: btr effort.   22

--   **SANDBOURNE** [17] 4-8-6 J Williams 33/1: 30-00-0: Ev ch on reapp: maiden who only raced
twice early last season and seems sure to come on for this run: eff over 6/8f: acts on
gd & soft grnd and on any trk.   .   23

112 **EVERY EFFORT** [8] 4-8-9 G Starkey 7/2: 1000-40: Fin 7th: fair effort though btr in 112.   00

344 **DOLLY** (7) 4-8-7 M Wigham 11/1: 0000-004D: Led over 2f out, kept on to fin 4th though
slightly hmpd Every Effort inside dist and subs disq and placed last: see 344.   00

--	Habs Lad [3] 10-0	--	Fair Country [16] 9-3	192	Hello Sunshine [20] 9-4
374	Kampglow [14] 8-13	88	Superfrost [9] 7-12(2ow)		
--	Silent Gain [10] 7-8	--	April Fool [13] 8-13	262	High Pitched [4] 8-10
--	Nicky Nick [6] 8-5	--	Jabaraba [5] 8-2		
--	Crimbourne [1] 8-12				

19 ran   ¾,½,½,1,shhd,¾   (A G Lansley)   W Wightman Upham, Hants

482 **REDENHAM MAIDEN FILLIES STAKES 2YO**   £1199   5f   Yielding 106 -16 Slow

--   **MY ISABEL** [5] (R Hannon) 2-8-11 A Mcglone 14/1: 1: 2 b f Mummy's Game – Pied A Terre
(Ribocco): Prom filly: easy to back though ran on strongly to lead inside final 1f in a
2yo fillies maiden at Salisbury May 8: cost 8,800 gns as a yearling and is a half sister to
a couple of juvenile winners: eff over 5f and seems certain to stay further: acts on yld
grand & on a gall trk.   47

--   **JANS CONTESSA** [2] (R Boss) 2-8-11 M Miller 9/1: 2: Ev ch inside dist, just btn:
speedily bred filly who cost 16,500 gns and is a half sister to juvenile winner Doppio:
acts on yld grnd & on a gall trk: should win a race.   45

--   **WABARAH** [3] (H Thomson Jones) 2-8-11 A Murray 2/1: 3: Just failed to make all: not btn
far: promising effort: daughter of Shirley Heights who cost 160,000 gns as a yearling: sure
to be suited by a longer trip in time: acts on yld grnd & on a gall trk.   45

311 **BLUE TANGO** [10] (D Laing) 2-8-11 S Whitworth 1/1 FAV: 24: No extra dist though again
ran well: see 311.   35

--   **YAVARRO** [1] 2-8-11 M Malham 10/1: 0: Showed some promise on her debut: friendless
in the mkt today and should do btr next time: half sister to several winners: acts on yld
grnd and on a gall trk: bred to stay further.   30

--   **JOSIE SMITH** [9] 2-8-11 T Quinn 8/1: 0: Never really threatened after a slow start.   30

345	Downsview Lady [7] 8-11	--	Phoebe [8] 8-11
--	Ballantrae [4] 8-11		

9 ran   ½,hd,4,2½,shhd   (Derek Joseph)   R Hannon East Everleigh, Wilts

483 EDDIE REAVEY MAIDEN AUCTION STAKES 2YO   £1014   5f   Yielding 106 +09 Fast

21   SPARSHOLT [10] (P Cole) 2-8-4 K Powdrell 11/10 FAV: 31: 2 b c Miner's Lamp -
Hark Hark (Sing Sing): Easily justified heavy support in a fast run maiden auction race
at Salisbury May 8, making virtually all ev yd: was also well bckd when a close 3rd to Peatswood
Shooter at Leicester last month: half brother to several winners: well suited by forcing
tactics over this minimum trip & should stay further: acts on yld/soft grnd: could win again.   42
404 GREY WOLF TIGER [2] (R Hannon) 2-8-4 L Jones(5) 7/1: 02: Ran on late: on the up grade:
acts on gd & soft grnd: should stay further: see 404.   29
21   PREMIUM GOLD [5] (K Cunningham Brown) 2-8-1 A Mcglone 5/1: 43: Mkt drifter: chased
winner thro'out: see 21.   22
354 SARASOTA [7] (A Pitt) 2-8-4 B Rouse 16/1: 0024: Seems sure to stay further: see 354.   15
--   HIGHFALUTIN LYMEY [8] 2-8-4 R Wernham 12/1: 0: Short lived effort ½way, should impr
for this experience: cheaply acquired colt who should stay further than this minimum trip.   05
261 REVELINA [9] 2-8-1 M L Thomas 8/1: 0030: No threat: btr in 261 (sharp trk).   00
--   BIOTIN [11] 2-8-4 N Howe 5/1: 0: Good early speed on racecourse debut.   00
21   SUTTERS MILL [1] 2-8-4 M Miller 8/1: 00: Al behind and fin last.   00
252 Santo Princess [4] 8-1   -- Snapshot Baby [3] 8-1
10 ran   4,1½,4,4,¾,hd,1½   (W H Ponsonby)   P Cole Whatcombe, Oxon

484 WINCANTON MAIDEN STAKES 3YO   £1244   1m 2f Yielding 106 -19 Slow

--   MOON MADNESS [10] (J Dunlop) 3-9-0 B Rouse 6/1: 4-1: 3 b c Vitiges - Castle Moon
(Kalamoun): Useful colt: first time out impr well to lead inside dist, comfortably in a
3yo maiden at Salisbury May 8: showed plenty of promise on his sole start last term when a
never nearer 4th to Faraway Dancer in a Goodwood maiden: half brother to a couple of middle
distance winners: eff over 10f on a gall trk, and sure to stay further: acts on gd & yld
grnd: will impr for this race.   51
--   COINAGE [11] (R Johnson Houghton) 3-9-0 J Reid 9/2: 3-2: Nicely bckd on reapp: led
after ½way and again below dist: showed promise when placed behind Innishmore Island in
a maiden at Warwick on sole start last term: half brother to several winners: eff over
8/10f on gd/firm & yld grnd: seems to act on any trk: should find a race.   47
183 MAKE PEACE [14] (I Balding) 3-9-0 J Matthias 8/1: 3-33: Kept on well: stays 10f: see 183.   43
188 BENISA RYDER [7] (J Dunlop) 3-9-0 P Cook 11/4 FAV: 3-224: Proving expensive to
follow: led over 3f out, not qckn dist: eff over 8/10f on any trk: see 188.   40
334 AUTUMN FLUTTER [4] 3-9-0 L Jones(5) 10/1: 00-30: Kept on well: stays 10f: see 334.   37
191 KINGS CRUSADE [3] 3-9-0 G Sexton 8/1: -440: One paced though consistent: see 191.   32
--   FRITHIOF [9] 3-9-0 G Starkey 11/2: -0: Stayed on well after slow start: sure to do btr.   00
--   BILLET [5] 3-9-0 R Curant 10/1: 0-0: Fin 9th, btr for race.   00
--   Full Speed Ahead [8] 9-0   -- Gratify [13] 8-11
--   Home Or Away [12] 9-0   -- Mr Savvas [2] 9-0   -- Tonquin [1] 8-11
13 ran   ¾,2,1½,2,3,2½   (Lavinia, Duchess of Norfolk)   J Dunlop Arundel, Sussex

485 CITY BOWL HANDICAP STAKES (0-50)   £2750   1m 6f Yielding 106 -02 Slow   [46]

358 MY CHARADE [8] (B Waring) 5-7-7(vis) R Fox 20/1: 40-0001: 5 b m Cawston's Clown-
Schull (Yorick II): Showed impr form, led well over 2f out, comfortably in a h'cap at
Salisbury May 8: lightly raced in '85: in '84 won at Haydock: eff at 14f, stays 2m: seems
to act on any grnd well suited by galloping track and should win again.   25
341 WILD GINGER [5] (D Oughton) 4-7-13(bl) B Crossley 14/1: 0030-02: Led over 3f out: gd
effort: in '85 won a h'cap at Beverley: eff at 12f, stays 14f: acts on firm & yld & a
stiff trk, especially Beverley: best in bl.   21
341 INCHGOWER [2] (W Wightman) 9-7-8 M L Thomas 12/1: 0000-03: Nearest fin: in '85 won
a h'cap at Leicester: in '84 won at Brighton & Salisbury: eff at 12f, stays 14f: acts on
gd/firm & yld & on any trk, though likes Brighton.   08
189 FOLK DANCE [9] (I Balding) 4-9-10 J Matthias 7/4 FAV: 2441-44: Ch 2f out: btr 189.   34
235 COLLISTO [11] 5-8-3 S Whitworth 12/1: 010-000: Sn prom: fdd: lightly raced in '85,
winning a h'cap at Sandown: eff at 14f, probably stays 2m: acts on gd & heavy & a gall trk.   06
341 SUGAR PALM [3] 5-8-4(bl) B Rouse 6/1: 010-030: Wknd: btr 341 (10f sharp trk).   03
204 BRIGADIER JACQUES [6] 5-7-7 C Rutter(5) 8/1: 210-140: Twice well below form 121.   00
358 INTUITION [1] 4-8-11 J Kennedy(7) 7/1: 00-1000: Disapp since first time out in 69.   00
126 CAWARRA BELLE [10] 5-7-7(BL)(9oh) J Carter(2) 10/1: --00-00: Made no show.   00
--   Noster Puer [7] 8-0   202 Master Francis [4] 8-6
11 ran   5,6,3,7,4,nk   (T McCarthy)   Mrs B Waring Chedglow, Wilts

486 WINCANTON MAIDEN STAKES 3YO   £1238   1m 2f Yielding 106 -10 Slow

--   BROKEN WAVE [3] (H Candy) 3-8-11 R Curant 14/1: -1: 3 b f Bustino - Brittania's
Rule (Blakeney): Prom filly: ran on strongly to lead on the post in a 3yo maiden at Salisbury
May 8: well bred, being a half sister to smart middle dist winner Henry The Lion: eff over 10f
and sure to stay further: acts on yld grnd and on a stiff trk: genuine filly who should
enjoy further successes.   51

-- **BUSHIDO** [5] (G Harwood) 3-9-0 G Starkey 5/2: -2: Switched and led below dist, caught final stride: well clear of rem & sure to win a race soon: half brother to several winners, incl smart middle dist performer Yawa: eff over 10f on yld grnd: acts on a gall trk.   54

-- **ZAAJER** [11] (H Thomson Jones) 3-9-0 B Rouse 4/1: -3: Ran on too late on racecourse debut, though sure to do btr next time: half brother to a couple of winners, incl the useful miler Artiste: eff over 10f on yld grnd: acts on a stiff trk.   38

-- **HOTU** [1] (J Dunlop) 3-9-0 R Fox 20/1: -4: Quite a prom debut: acts on yld grnd & on a gall trk: backed at long odds today and may do btr.   37

316 **COLEMAN HAWKINS** [13] 3-9-0 T Quinn 33/1: -00: Showed some impr here: led ½way till below dist: acts on yld grnd & on a gall trk: on the up grade.   36

-- **FLORAL CHARGE** [9] 3-9-0 J Reid 11/8 FAV: 2-0: Heavily bckd: ev ch below dist: was a fast fin r.u. to Comme Letoile at Doncaster last backend: eff over 10f and should stay further: acts on yld/soft grnd and on a stiff trk: sure to do btr than this.   31

-- Diwaan [6] 9-0	-- Vitry [2] 8-11	-- Ma Feathers [14] 8-11
-- Bernigra Boy [7] 9-0	-- Danribo [10] 9-0	351 Gay Caruso [12] 9-0
-- Thereafter [8] 8-11		

13 ran   shhd,12,nk,½,3,2,1   (L B Holliday)   H Candy Wantage, Oxon

---

All races started by flag

487   WINCANTON MAIDEN STAKES 3YO   £1238   1m 2f   Yielding 106 –10 Slow

247 **ORIENTAL EXPRESS** [2] (F Carr) 3-8-7 J Carr 20/1: 000-01: 3 b g Whitstead – Miss Argyle (Mountain Call): Easy to back though led below dist for a decisive win in a 3yo maiden app stakes at Hamilton May 9: down the field in his 3 starts last season: half brother to several winners: well suited by 1m on a stiff trk: handles heavy grnd well.   36

-- **BREGUET** [3] (Don Enrico Incisa) 3-8-4 J Callaghan 20/1: 00-2: Almost made all on reapp: unplaced in both her starts last season and this was an impr showing: eff over 1m on heavy grnd: seems well suited by forcing tactics.   28

-- **SEATYRN** [9] (S Norton) 3-8-7 J Murray(2) 5/2: 42430-3: Had ev ch on reapp: btr for race: placed in most of his starts last season over 7/8f: acts on any going and on any trk.   30

451 **COOL OPERATOR** [6] (R Williams) 3-8-7 C Barnfather(5) 7/4 FAV: 00-0404: Clear of rem: acts on heavy: see 183.   27

-- **SEVEN HILLS** [10] 3-8-4 R Brown 8/1: 000-0: Wknd quickly below dist: btr for race.   16

377 **BAVARIAN PRINCESS** [1] 3-8-4 Wendy Carter 12/1: -00: No threat over this longer trip.   13

379 **BILLS DAUGHTER** [7] 3-8-4 J Carroll 10/1: -00: Close up over ½way, wknd into 8th.   00

195 Parkes Special [4] 8-4   424 Pokeree [8] 8-7

-- Cricket House [5] 8-7

10 ran   3,1,2½,8,3   (Danny Ho)   F Carr Malton, Nth Yorks

488   E.B.F. MANDORA MAIDEN STAKES 2YO   £1216   5f   Heavy 194 –10 Slow

320 **HARRY HUNT** [6] (J Berry) 2-9-0 M Fry 7/4 FAV: 31: 2 b c Longleat – Ardice (Hard Tack): Gamely justified fav. in a 2yo maiden at Hamilton May 9, led dist and stayed on well: eff over 5f in testing conditions and sure to stay further: acts on soft/heavy grnd & on any trk.   38

446 **U BIX COPY** [4] (J Wilson) 2-9-0 D Nicholls 9/2: 032: Led to ½way, kept on well and only just denied: acts on gd & heavy grnd: on the up grade & should win a race soon.   36

304 **INGLISTON** [9] (M H Easterby) 2-9-0 M Birch 8/1: 03: Dsptd lead till went on ½way: no extra close home: should certainly be capable of winning a seller: see 304.   28

-- **YOUNG WARRIOR** [7] (I Bell) 2-9-0 N Carlisle 16/1: 4: Showed good speed over ½way on his debut and should do btr next time: sprint bred: acts on heavy grnd.   22

-- **DORMESTONE LAD** [2] 2-9-0 J H Brown(5) 16/1: 0: Never reached ldrs after a slow start.   12

376 **MEATH PRINCESS** [1] 2-8-11 J Lowe 5/2: 020: Much btr on yld in 376.   07

-- Arishan [8] 9-0   -- Send It Down [5] 9-0   376 Bantel Bouquet [3] 8-11

9 ran   hd,4,3,5,1   (J K Brown)   J Berry Cockerham, Lancs

489   EARL OF ANGUS SELLING STAKES 3 & 4YO   £764   5f   Heavy 194 –02 Slow

377 **LULLABY BLUES** [4] (M H Easterby) 3-8-3 M Birch 4/1: -001: 3 br g Lochnager – Sunset Song (Song): Nicely bckd and led dist, running on strongly to win a seller at Hamilton May 9 (bought in 2,200 gns): speedily bred gelding who is a half brother to winning juvenile Sing To Me: eff over 5/6f on soft & heavy grnd: seems to act on any track.   20

198 **MUSIC TEACHER** [8] (A Robson) 3-8-7 A Shoults(5) 6/1: 00-0102: led below dist: gd effort.   18

339 **TAYLORS TAYLORMADE** [3] (M Tompkins) 3-8-3 M Rimmer 11/4 FAV: 0020-03: Well bckd: al close up & ran a fair race on unsuitable soft grnd: showed his best form on a sound surface last term, when running up to Impala Lass in a seller at Catterick: acts on any trk.   10

377 **MAYBE JAYNE** [1] 3-8-0 J Quinn(5) 6/1: 0-44: Nicely bckd: kept on: see 377.   05

145 **THE CHALICEWELL** [6] 4-9-0 Sharron James 8/1: 0200-40: led over ½way: btr on soft in 145   00

335 **WINDING PATH** [7] 3-8-7 A Whitehall(7) 5/1: 3120-00: Outpcd after ½way over this shorter trip: led close home in a seller at Ripon last season over 6f and probably finds this minimum trip inadequate: acts on gd/firm & soft grnd & on any trk.   00

145 Grand Queen [2] 8-11   -- Mrs Barrie [9] 8-11

8 ran   2,1½,1,4,3   (P D Savill)   M H Easterby Great Habton, Nth Yorks

490   BLENHEIM HANDICAP STAKES 0-35   £1440   6f   Heavy 194 +14 Fast   [33]

378 MIAMI DOLPHIN [14] (J Berry) 6-7-9 M Fry 15/2: 000-001: 6 b m Derrylin – Magibbillibyte
(Constable): Led below dist, forging clear on this testing grnd for a decisive win in a
fast run h'cap at Hamilton May 9: first success: eff over 6f on gd/firm & heavy grnd: seems
to act on any trk, though clearly well suited by a stiff one.   16
355 ROSIE DICKINS [9] (R Hollinshead) 4-9-1 R Lappin(7) 3/1 FAV: 00-1222: Clear of rem.   22
260 ZIO PEPPINO [5] (T Craig) 5-8-7 E Guest(2) 16/1: 0000-03: Al chasing ldrs: useful
h'capper on his day, made all at Ayr last season and later just btn by Scotch Rocket in
another h'cap on the same trk: stays 1m: acts on heavy though btr suited by
fast ground: fairly h'capped on his best form.   04
321 PENTOFF [4] (D Chapman) 4-8-9(VIS) J Lowe 15/2: 00-0044: Fitted with a visor: never
nearer: see 321 and 240.   04
--   NIPKNOWES [1] 5-8-5 N Carlisle 33/1: 40000-0: No threat on reapp, though btr for race:
eff over 6/8f: acts on any going & is suited by a gall trk.   00
355 MARY MAGUIRE [12] 9-10-0 D Nicholls 10/1: 00-0000: No threat under top weight: see 306 17
56   TRADESMAN [2] 6-8-0(bl)(5ow) K Darley 10/1: 3433-00: Clear ldr over ½way: quite
consistent sprint h'capper who made all to win at Hamilton last season, and was placed on
many occasions: eff over 5f and should stay 6f: acts on any going & on any trk: suited by
front running tactics.   00
378 TRADE HIGH [7] 7-8-12 R Vickers(7) 5/1: 00-0030: Short lived effort ½way: fin 9th.   00
378 GOLDEN BOY [11] 4-7-10 J Quinn(5) 10/1: --0-000: Never threatened: see 378.   00
441 Responder [6] 8-11   --   Peters Kiddie [8] 7-9   --   Its Heaven [13] 7-10(3ow)
--   Lauras Choice [3] 7-10(1ow)
13 ran   8,5,1,2½,nk,hd   (j Barrett)   J Berry Cockerham, Lancs.

491   SCOTTISH RIFLES HANDICAP STAKES 3YO   £836   1m   Heavy 194 -81 Slow   [35]

305 WATERFORD WAY [4] (R Hollinshead) 3-8-2 W Ryan 10/1: 00-041: 3 ch g Double Form –
Lovettsville (Le Levanstell): Stayed on gamely under press to lead close home in a 3yo h'cap
at Hamilton May 9: first success: half brother to a couple of winners: eff around 1m with
plenty of give in the grnd: seems to act on any trk.   16
240 IZZY GUNNER [1] (A Robson) 3-8-6 J Bleasdale 6/1: 30-0022: Went clear over 4f out,
caught near fin: good effort & stays 1m on heavy grnd: see 240.   19
283 VIRAJENDRA [9] (W Pearce) 3-8-11(BL) M Hindley(3) 20/1: 200-003: Bl first time: fin
well, not btn far: much impr effort over this longer trip: seems best with plenty of cut
in the grnd: see 283.   24
416 CAROUSEL ROCKET [6] (J Wilson) 3-9-7 David Eddery(7) 10/1: 33-3104: Ran on late: gd
effort: see 130.   32
414 KO ISLAND [12] 3-8-7 K Darley 14/1: 00-0000: Kept on under press: see 259.   16
414 MARINA PLATA [2] 3-9-3(5ex) D Nicholls 7/2 Jt FAV: 0-01100: Never nearer: much btr
over C/D in 99: see 322.   22
451 BRAVE AND BOLD [13] 3-8-10(bl) G Duffield 7/2 Jt FAV: 01-2020: Much btr on gd
ground in 451: see 100.   00
*380 ELEGANT BILL [7] 3-8-11(5ex) M Beecroft 9/2: 0-01010: Much btr on yld in 380 (9f).   00
451 Colonel Hall [11] 8-0   380 Van Der Pup [8] 8-3(BL)
124 Norcool [10] 8-5   54   Take The Biscuit [5] 8-10(bl)
183 Motor Master [3] 8-5
13 ran   nk,hd,1½,1½,3,½   (P Savill)   R Hollinshead Upper Longdon, Staffs

492   LORD LYNDOCH STAKES   £1139   1m 3f Heavy 194 -63 Slow

140 PRINCE SATIRE [6] (M Jarvis) 3-8-8 W Woods(3) 11/4 Jt FAV: 00-1: 3 b c Sensitive
Prince – No Comedy (Droll Role): Lear early in str and stayed on well to win a slowly run
maiden at Hamilton May 9: on the up going: stays 11f well and should be suited by further:
handles heavy grnd well: acts on a stiff trk.   32
-381 BANTEL BUSHY [8] (I Bell) 3-8-8 N Carlisle 11/4 Jt FAV: 0-22222: 2nd again! see 381. 34
45   MOHICAN [7] (C Thornton) 3-8-5(BL) J Bleasdale 6/1: 3220-03: Bl first time: remote 3rd. 14
247 SCARBOROUGH [2] (C Elsey) 3-8-8 G Duffield 12/1: 000-04: Led briefly home turn: no
extra: lightly raced colt who showed some impr here: best on heavy.   16
--   MAELSTROM [5] 3-8-8 M Birch 7/2: 30-0: Btr for race: lightly raced last term, showing
promise when placed behind Faraway Dancer and Plaid over 1m at Haydock on his debut: sure
to be suited by middle distances: acts on soft grnd & on a gall trk.   06
381 SHANDON BELLS [4] 4-9-7 J Lowe 14/1: -00: Led till home turn, sn btn: see 381.   00
--   Blencathra Boy [3] 8-8   --   Princess Bella [6] 9-4
8 ran   5,15,nk,8,8   (H A Grant Jr)   M Jarvis Newmarket

493   CAMERONIANS HANDICAP STAKES 0-35   £1755   1m 4f Heavy 194 -65 Slow   [30]

142 MR LION [4] (F Carr) 4-7-12(1ow) J Carr(0) 12/1: 000-301: 4 b g Windjammer - Polly
Darling (Darling Boy): Stayed on well to lead close home in a slowly run h'cap at Hamilton
May 9: all his best form is on this stiff trk, having won here as a juvenile: eff around
11/12f with some give in the grnd.   10

366 **CHRISTMAS HOLLY** [2] (G Reveley) 5-8-4 D Leadbitter(2) 7/1: 0-31002: Just btn: clear
of rem: gd effort & seems well suited by this stiff course, having won here in 105.   15
199 **JACKS LUCK** [8] (M Tompkins) 5-9-10 M Rimmer 7/2: -123: Kept on late: see 199 & 8.   28
*308 **MENINGI** [1] (N Tinkler) 5-9-8(7ex) J H Brown(3) 3/1 FAV: -00-314: Led over 2f out:
good effort: see 308.   16
308 **APPLE WINE** [6] 9-9-1 D Nicholls 5/1: 00-0200: Much btr on yld in 256 (sharp trk).   01
*243 **WILDRUSH** [5] 7-9-6 A Shoults(5) 4/1: 0002-10: Much btr on a sharper trk in 243 (yld).   00
185 **PERFECT DOUBLE** [7] 5-8-4 N Connorton 10/1: -32-00: Last to fin: needs btr grnd.   00
366 **Porter** [3] 8-0(bl)(2ow)
8 ran   nk,5,nk,10,8   (Mrs Jane V Kent)   F Carr Malton, Nth Yorks

---

Official Going Given as Good/Soft

494 HAWTHORN EBF 3YO STAKES   £2641   12f   Good 53 –07 Slow

362 **NISNAS** [6] (P Cole) 3-9-4 T Quinn 12/1: 143-131: 3 ch c Tap On Wood – Suemette
(Danseur): Smart colt: floored the odds on Verd Antique, led inside the final 1f under press
in a 3yo stakes at Lingfield May 9: first time out beat Esdale at Kempton: in '85 won a
maiden at Salisbury: eff at 1m, stays 12f well: acts on gd/firm & yld and on any trk: seems
a genuine sort.   74
*384 **VERD ANTIQUE** [3] (H Cecil) 3-9-4 S Cauthen 4/9 FAV: -12: Led till inside final 1f:
well clear 3rd and should win more gd races: stays 12f: possibly btr on a more gall trk.   73
362 **MIRAGE DANCER** [2] (R Smyth) 3-8-11 P Robinson 20/1: 204-023: In front of winner in
362 (yld/soft): stays 12f.   46
324 **PRIMARY** [4] (G Harwood) 3-9-4 A Clark 3/1: 01-44: Reared up start: ev ch: probably
stays 12f: should do btr: see 324.   52
435 **MARICAMA** [1] 3-8-11 P Cook 50/1: -40: Very stiff task: see 435.   39
-- **ELEGANT GUEST** [5] 3-8-11 T Ives 50/1: -0: Very tough debut: prom 1m: half brother to
the very useful 12/14f winner Polar Cub.   14
6 ran   ½,15,nk,3,15   (Fahd Salman)   P Cole Whatcombe, Oxon

495 SLEEPING PARTNER SELLING HANDICAP 0-25   £968   6f   Good 53 –01 Slow   [24]

260 **ALNASHME** [5] (D Thom) 4-9-0 W R Swinburn 4/1 FAV: 004-401: 4 ro g Godswalk – Fandetta
(Gay Fandango): Dropped to selling company and landed a gamble, led well over 1f out,
comfortably in a selling h'cap at Lingfield May 9 (bought in 5,800 gns): little form in '85
when trained by H T Jones: eff at 5/6f on firm & yld grnd: suited by forcing tactics on
a sharpish trk should win again.   20
119 **MAIDEN BIDDER** [16] (H Beasley) 4-8-8 R Morse(5) 25/1: 0000-02: No ch with winner, but
an impr effort from this maiden: eff at 6f on gd & firm grnd: acts on any trk.   08
418 **FAIRDALE** [9] (L Cottrell) 8-8-7 J Williams 33/1: -0003: Ch 2f out: 8yo maiden who
was unraced in '85: stays 6f: acts on gd grnd & a sharpish trk.   00
106 **POCO LOCO** [6] (A Davison) 4-8-9 J Reid 7/1: 0-034: Gambled on: al up there: eff at
6f, stays 9f: acts on gd & soft.   00
399 **SPARKFORD LAD** [8] 4-9-12 Debbie Wheatley(7) 16/1: 03-4000: Mkt drifter: nearest fin:
dropped to selling company today: should find a similar event, possibly over 7f.   09
343 **TAME DUCHESS** [7] 4-8-9 M Wigham 33/1: 40-0400: Never nearer: see 119.   00
160 **LADY NATIVELY** [19] 4-9-3 T Quinn 7/1: 0000-30: Mkt drifter: led 3f: btr 160 (yld).   00
418 **ANOTHER BING** [13] 4-8-9 P Cook 10/1: 00-1000: No show: best first time out in 122 (hvy). 00
217 **KHAMSIN RED** [12] 3-8-11 G Starkey 8/1: 0000-00: Al rear: maiden: should be suited
by 7f plus: acts on firm.   00
172 **Robrob** [3] 9-9(BL)   369 **Fairgreen** [10] 9-0(bl)
418 **Sing Galvo Sing** [11] 8-7   177 **Majors Review** [4] 10-0
327 **Russell Flyer** [15] 9-9(bl)   172 **Elmdon** [20] 9-6
177 **Fort Duchesne** [2] 9-2   -- **Bakers Double** [17] 8-11
114 **Mango Man** [1] 8-11(bl)   177 **Lean Streak** [14] 8-9(bl)
177 **Charisma Music** [18] 8-8
20 ran   2½,4,1½,1½,shhd   (Bob Honess)   D Thom Newmarket

496 CHARLES HEIDSIECK H'CAP 0-50 3YO   £2771   6f   Good 53 –01 Slow   [52]

284 **BERTIE WOOSTER** [3] (L Piggott) 3-8-9 W R Swinburn 7/1: 320-031: 3 ch c Homeboy –
Peace Of Mind (Midsummer Night II): Fairly useful
colt: led approaching final 1f, comfortably in a 3yo h'cap at Lingfield May 9: seemed
unsuited by heavy last time out: trained by P Makin in '85: very eff at 5/6f: acts on gd &
yld grnd and on any trk, though seems to like a sharpish trk.   46
*387 **MERDON MELODY** [10] (R Sheather) 3-9-3 R Cochrane 3/1 FAV: 1034-12: Kept on well:
in fine form: see 387: acts on any trk carried 5lb penalty.   47
314 **LOFT BOY** [12] (N Vigors) 3-9-2(5ex) S Dawson(3) 9/2: 30-1323: Led 2f out: most
consistent: see 62.   45
277 **PORTHMEOR** [13] (M Bolton) 3-8-10 S Cauthen 7/1: 044-424: Made much: gd effort: see 277. 36

15   BERNIGRA GIRL [5] 3-8-6 W Carson 13/2: 2331-00: Ch 2f out: on final outing in '85
won a nursery h'cap at Goodwood: eff at 6f, acts on firm & yld & likes an undulating trk.   21
––   DREAM CHASER [4] 3-9-7 L Johnsey(7) 12/1: 0024U-0: Never nearer: btr for race: will
impr next time: first time out in '85 won at Epsom: later a fine 2nd to Sperry in a valuable
nursery h'cap at Newmarket: very eff at 6f: acts on fast & yld & on any trk.   35
––   Mudisha [14] 9-6   ––   Sparky Lad [6] 9-7   234   Meadow Moor [7] 8-9(vis)
175   Dalsaan Bay [11] 8-1   ––   La Divina [9] 7-9   203   Sequestration [2] 7-8
––   Viceroy Major [1] 8-8
13 ran   2½,½,1,5,½   (Miss Amanda J Rawdin)   L Piggott Newmarket

497   ROBERTS MAIDEN 2YO STAKES   £2876   5f   Good 43 +09 Fast

405   BESTPLAN [13] (W O'gorman) 2-9-0 T Ives 4/1: 01: 2 b c Try My Best – Make Plans
(Go Marching): Useful, impr colt: made almost all, comfortably in a fast run 2yo maiden at
Lingfield May 9: half brother to smart sprinter Sayf El Arab & useful sprinter Eagles Landed:
speedily bred sort who seemed well suited by this sharpish trk: acts son grnd & firm grnd &
should win more races/rate more highly.   50
350   JAH BLESS [1] (P Haynes) 2-9-0 N Howe 14/1: 22: Mkt drifter: raced alone: another
good effort: acts on gd & yld & on any trk: should find a small event: see 350.   46
––   MUBKIR [4] (P Walwyn) 2-9-0 Paul Eddery 15/8 FAV: 3: Heavily bckd debutant: ch 2f
out: impr likely from this 100,000 gns purchase: very speedily bred sort: acts on gd grnd
and should find a race.   40
400   EBONY PRIDE [15] (Pat Mitchell) 2-8-11 M Miller 20/1: 04: Mkt drifter: ch 2f out.   35
––   MADAME FLORA [16] 2-8-11 J Williams 33/1: 0: Never nearer: should impr on this initial
effort: will be suited by further than 5f: acts on gd grnd.   28
––   LAST DANCE [6] 2-9-0 G Starkey 12/1: 0: Late hdway: easy to back today & will do btr.   25
––   FINAL DELIGHT [11] 2-9-0 S Whitworth 10/1: 0: Mkt drifter: no show: should be
suited by longer distances.   00
230   SEGOVIAN [17] 2-9-0 Pat Eddery 4/1: 20: Wk in mkt: much btr 230 (heavy).   00
––   Tauber [12] 9-0   ––   Its Varadan [7] 9-0   ––   Bold Mojacques [9] 9-0
––   Born Free Again [8] 9-0   ––   Flag Bearer [14] 9-0
––   Grey Rod [5] 9-0   ––   Young Moreton [10] 9-0
345   Loma Breeze [2] 8-11   ––   Timurtasch [3] 9-0
17 ran   1,2½,½,3,2½   (Mrs P L Yong)   W O'gorman Newmarket

498   GINEVRA SWEEPSTAKES 3YO   £959   7f   Good 53 –03 Slow

––   NIORO [10] (R Johnson Houghton) 3-9-0 Pat Eddery 5/1: 40-1: 3 gr c Blushing Groom –
Nasseem (Zeddaan): Useful filly: first time out, led well inside the final 1f in a 3yo stakes
at Lingfield May 9: first time out in '85 fin 4th at Bath: eff at 7f, should stay 1m: acts on
gd & firm grnd & on any trk.   50
––   SUNNY LIZ [2] (G Harwood) 3-8-11 G Starkey 4/6 FAV: 2-2: Led over 1f out: 5L clear
3rd: on sole start in '85 was a highly promising 2nd to Queen Helen in a Listed race at
Ascot: cost 80,000 gns and is a half sister to several winners: should be suited by further
than 7f: acts on gd & firm grnd & must find a maiden.   46
––   RUE ST JACQUES [6] (D Arbuthnot) 3-9-0 S Cauthen 12/1: 0-3: Nicely bckd: ch over
1f out: gd seasonal debut: unplaced on sole outing in '85: should stay 1m: acts on gd grnd
and a sharpish trk.   38
––   UPHORIA [11] (P Cole) 3-8-11 T Quinn 9/2: 3020-4: Led well over 2f out on seasonal
debut: showed promise in '85, notably when 2nd to Skeeb in a fillies maiden at Nottingham:
eff at 6f, stays 7f: acts on gd/firm & soft & on any trk.   35
––   HOLLY BROWN [5] 3-8-11 M Hills 50/1: -0: Never nearer on racecourse debut: should impr:
acts on gd grnd & a sharpish trk.   35
277   BAXTERGATE [9] 3-9-0 P Darcy 50/1: 00-0000: No threat but an impr effort: eff at
7f/1m: acts on gd & soft & seems suited by a sharpish trk.   25
––   Mostango [16] 9-0   334   The Moon And Back [14] 9-0
334   Charcoal [3] 9-0   276   Valvinora [7] 9-0   ––   Demisemiquaver [13] 9-0
175   Sir Speedy [12] 9-0   ––   Miss Maggie [1] 8-11   ––   Trent End [4] 9-0
14 ran   ½,5,shhd,shhd,5   (H H Aga Khan)   R Johnson Houghton Blewbury, Oxon

499   MAY STAKES HANDICAP 0-35   £2029   7.5f   Good 53 +02 Fast   [32]

281   EASY DAY [4] (E Eldin) 4-9-1 A Mackay 14/1: 000-041: 4 ch c Swing Easy – Break Of
Day (On Your Mark): Led well over 1f out, driven out in a h'cap at Lingfield May 9: first
success: eff at 7f/1m: acts on gd & heavy grnd & seems suited by a sharpish trk: has worn
a visor.   29
––   TORREY [5] (W Hern) 7-9-7(bl) T Sprake(7) 12/1: 00-10-2: Raced alone: al prom, jut btn:
ran on well: gd seasonal debut: ran only twice in '85: first time out won an app h'cap at
Lingfield & does well when fresh: eff at 7f on gd grnd: likes a sharpish/undulating trk.   34
281   GOLDEN BEAU [12] (D Morley) 4-9-2 B Rouse 11/2: 0040-03: Led over 2f out: btr effort.   21
262   KING OF SPEED [6] (B Wise) 7-9-2 L Riggio(7) 9/1: 300-104: Never nearer: best first
time out in 112 (C/D).   15
355   EVEN BANKER [13] 7-8-3 R Street 16/1: -00-000: No threat: see 355.   00
378   HENRYS PLACE [9] 4-8-8(bl) S Keightley 10/1: 00-0020: Wknd final 1f: btr 378 (6f).   04

171

262   TAMERTOWN LAD [10] 5-9-1 S Cauthen 5/1 FAV: 0000-20: Well bckd: made much: btr 262. 00
399   GOLD LOFT [16] 4-8-7 G Carter(3) 8/1: 02-1000: Btr 399: see 177.   00
369   VIA SATELLITE [11] 4-8-4(BL) S Whitworth 9/1: 40-3000: Bl first time: there 5f: see 110. 00
399   Turcy Boy [1] 8-1   --   Sharp Shot [18] 9-9   262 Rear Action [8] 9-8(bl)
112   Golden Slade [20] 9-7   Tars Hill [17] 9-4   262 Top Feather [15] 9-1
177   Lingfield Lady [7] 8-8   176 Pulsingh [14] 8-8
31   Young Boris [2] 8-8   --   Petit Bot [19] 8-2   174 Rest And Welcome [3] 8-2
20 ran   ½,4,3,1,½.   (D W Rolt)   E Eldin Newmarket

---

500   GINEVRA SWEEPSTAKES 3YO   £959   7f   Good 53 +05 Fast

•402   VIANORA [1] (G Harwood) 3-9-4 G Starkey 8/11 FAV: 3-011: 3 ch f Ahonoora - Miss
Portal (St Paddy): Useful, impr filly: led inside the final 1f, comfortably in quie a fast
run 3yo stakes at Lingfield May 9: last time out was a narrow winner of a maiden at Kempton:
eff over 7/8f: acts on firm & yld & on any trk, though seems to like a sharpish one.   56
387   MRS WADDILOVE [11] (P Kelleway) 3-8-11 Gay Kelleway(5) 14/1: 304-002: Ch final 1f:
good effort: showed some promise in '85: eff at 6/7f on gd & firm grnd & seems unsuited by hvy 40
--   GAELIC FLUTTER [9] (K Brassey) 3-9-0 S Whitworth 7/2: 4200-3: Well bckd on seasonal
debut: led well over 2f out: 6L clear 4th: best effort in '85 when 2nd to Beldale Star
at Kempton: stays 7f well: acts on gd & firm grnd & on any trk.   43
--   GIRDLE NESS [3] (J Dunlop) 3-8-11 W Carson 13/2: 0-4: Ch over 1f out: unplaced on
sole outing in '85: eff at 7f, should stay 1m: acts on gd grnd & a sharpish trk.   28
277   LISAKATY [10] 3-8-11 R Wernham 50/1: 200-000: Ch 2f out: gd effort: see 162.   16
--   PLAIN TALK [13] 3-9-0 R Guest 25/1: 04-0: Btr for race: on final outing in '85 fin 4th
in a maiden on this trk: eff at 7f on gd & firm grnd & a sharpish trk.   17
424   Highland Tale [6] 8-11   -- Mistral Magic [7] 8-11
--   Opal Flower [4] 8-11   --   Northern Impulse [5] 9-0
--   Kaasib [14] 9-0   334 Golden Straw [2] 9-0   -- Sea Trouper [12] 9-0
--   Porte Dauphine [15] 8-11   -- Recapture [8] 8-11
15 ran   3,hd,6,5,¾   (J H Richmond-Watson)   G Harwood Pulborough, Sussex

---

501   GINEVRA SWEEPSTAKES 3YO   £959   7f   Good 53 -12 Slow

--   HAUWMAL [3] (W Hern) 3-9-0 W Carson 3/1: 020-1: 3 ch c Troy - Sovereign Rose
(Sharpen Up): Useful colt: made a winning seasonal debut, led inside the final 1f, ridden
out in a 3yo stakes at Lingfield May 9: best effort in '85 when a gd 2nd to Rackstraw in a
valuable maiden at Ascot: eff at 7f: should be suited by 1m plus: acts on gd/yld & firm
grnd & on any trk: can continue to improve.   54
•274   REIGNBEAU [4] (G Lewis) 3-9-7 P Waldron 13/8 FAV: 03-3112: Made most: in fine form.   57
--   LOVE AT LAST [9] (W Hastings Bass) 3-8-11 R Lines 20/1: -3: Ch 1f out: promising racecourse debut from this half sister to a 7f winner: should stay 1m: acts on gd grnd & a
sharpish track.   41
--   BASICALLY BETTER [2] (P Walwyn) 3-8-11 Paul Eddery 5/1: 20-4: Al up there on seasonal
debut: best effort in '85 when 2nd to Sue Grundy in a fillies maiden at Salisbury: eff at
7f, should stay 1m: acts on gd & firm grnd & on any trk.   40
338   VELVET PEARL [10] 3-8-11 T Quinn 50/1: -00: Ran on well final 1f and is on the up
grade: half sister to Mohar: should stay 1m: acts on gd grnd.   39
--   SILVER DRAGON [6] 3-9-0 R Fox 16/1: -0: Mkt drifter: dsptd lead: should impr: half
brother to several winners.   40
--   BE SO BOLD [12] 3-8-11 P Robinson 15/2: -0: Active in mkt on debut, but no threat:
half sister to smart 1m/10f winner Princess Gate & will impr.   00
422   HUMBLE BEAUTY [1] 3-8-11 P Cook 33/1: -00: Quick reappear: well there 1 out.   00
--   Jaaziel [8] 9-0   --   Deputy Governor [14] 9-0
--   Baby Ravenna [7] 8-11   431 Spanish Intent [13] 8-11
--   Mr Matchmaker [15] 9-0(BL)
13 ran   1½,3,hd,nk,1   (Sheikh Mohammed)   W Hern West Ilsley, Berks

---

BATH   Saturday May 10th   Lefthand Galloping Track

Official Going Given as Good to Soft

502   FRANCASAL SELLING STAKES 2YO   £823   5f   Yielding 84 -80 Slow

170   CLEARWAY [5] (C Hill) 2-8-11 A Clark 7/4 FAV: 01: 2 b c Bold Owl - Subtle Answer
(Stephen Geroge): Landed a gamble, courtesy of the Stewards when awarded a 2yo seller at
Bath May 10 after fin a shhd 2nd (bought in 2,600 gns): cheaply acquired colt: eff over 5f
on a stiff trk, sure to be suited by 6f: acts on yld.   26
354   SAMS REFRAIN [7] (D Haydn Jones) 2-8-8 J Reid 5/1: 301D: Made most, held on gamely
but disq. for "bumping" inside final 50yds: deserves compensation in similar company: see 86. 23
329   TELEGRAPH FOLLY [8] (R Hoad) 2-8-11 T Ives 13/2: 043: Prom, ev ch: see 329.   14
337   DEEP TAW [2] (C Hill) 2-8-8 N Day 14/1: 04: Slow start: may impr: sprint bred.   07
337   VALDOSTA [1] 2-8-8 R Hills 8/1: 0030: Never closer: btr 337 (sharp trk).   06

-- JUST ENCHANTING [6] 2-8-8 G Baxter 9/2: 0: Ev ch: sprint bred filly: may impr.   02
-- ROMANY LAD [3] 2-8-11 R Curant 11/4: 0: Speed over 3f on debut: sprint bred.   00
-- Floret [4] 8-8
8 ran   shhd,4,1½,nk,1½   (C J Hill)   C Hill Fremington, Devon

503 EBF MONUMENT MAIDEN STAKES 2YO   £1611   5f   Yielding 84 –26 Slow

382 ALKADI [4] (W O'gorman) 2-9-0 T Ives 8/11 FAV: 31: 2 ch c Formidable - Sa-Vegas
(Star Appeal): Landed the odds, cleverly going ahead close home in a 2yo maiden at Bath
May 10: eff over a stiff 5f, sure to stay 6f & probably further: acts on gd/firm & yld &
likes a stiff trk: likely to impr further.   48
350 THE DOMINICAN [1] (B Hills) 2-9-0 B Thomson 9/4: 32: Just failed to make all:
clear of rest: impr & should find a similar race soon: likes a stiff trk: see 350.   45
-- ABSOLUTION [5] (K Brassey) 2-9-0 R Hills 15/2: 3: Should impr on this quite prom debut:
half brother to useful winning sprinter Peckitts Well: sure to strip fitter next time: may
prefer an easier trk where his speed can be exploited.   30
-- SAY YOU WILL [7] (P Makin) 2-9-0 J Reid 20/1: 4: Wk in mkt, never closer: bred to
need further than 5f.   28
-- CARJUJEN [2] 2-9-0 R Wernham 11/1: 0: No threat: speedily bred.   16
350 BRUSHFORD [3] 2-9-0(BL) I Johnson 25/1: 000: Appears moderate.   00
6 ran   nk,5,¾,5,12   (M Khalid)   W O'gorman Newmarket

504 BOOX HANDICAP STAKES 0-50   £2792   2m 1f   Yielding 84 –05 Slow   [39]

336 CHEKA [11] (I Balding) 10-7-10 G French 9/1: 000-201: 10 b g Russian Bank - Sweet
Seventeen (Country Delight): Stayed on well to get up close home in a h'cap at Bath May 10:
also successful in this race last year, and in '84 won at Epsom: suited by a test of stamina
nowadays: acts on firm & soft grnd & on any trk.   16
375 WATERLOW PARK [12] (I Balding) 4-9-4 J Matthias 2/1 FAV: 2422-22: Led over 2f out,
just caught and is certainly due a change of luck: see 375.   37
235 SHINY COPPER [7] (N Smith) 8-8-4(1ow) B Thomson 9/1: 0-00243: Not btn far: gd effort.   22
126 SAILORS REWARD [9] (J King) 4-9-3 J Williams 16/1: 3004-04: Gd effort over this
longer trip: stays 2m well: placed several times in gd class h'caps last season and looks
fairly treated on his best form: eff over middle dists on firm & soft grnd: suited by gall trk   32
349 BALLET CHAMP [2] 8-8-10 A Proud 5/2: 0042-30: Not btn that far & well clear of rem:
btr suited by this test of stamina: see 349.   23
312 SHUTTLECOCK STAR [3] 4-7-11(4ow) G King(0) 33/1: 3300-00: Outsider: lngr trip: not stay? 00
336 FLYING OFFICER [8] 9-8-9(vis) M Roberts 10/1: 040-040: Made most: fin 7th: see 336.   00
366 GOING BROKE [5] 6-7-9 S Dawson(3) 5/1: 342-130: Fin 9th: btr in 204 (15f, soft).   00
137 Americk [1] 8-6   58a Sylvan Joker [13] 8-5(vis)
462 Morgans Choice [6] 9-7   341 Kiki Star [4] 8-6
12 ran   ½,½,3,1½,15,3   (I Balding)   I Balding Kingsclere, Hants

505 MIDSOMER NORTON FILLIES HCAP 3YO 0-50   £2473   1m 2f   Yielding 84 –16 Slow   [55]

335 FAIR ATLANTA [7] (M Usher) 3-7-7 R Street 4/1: 33-2401: 3 ch f Tachypous - Enlighten
(Twilight Alley): Made all gamely in a fillies h'cap at Bath May 10: half sister to several
winners: seems well suited by forcing tactics and is eff at 8/10f: acts on soft & hvy grnd.   27
-- ZINDELINA [2] (R Hannon) 3-8-5 A Mcglone 11/2: 0440-2: Just failed with a strong
late chall: probably acts on firm & soft grnd, stays 10f & will stay further: could pick up
a maiden race soon.   37
209 SECRET WEDDING [4] (W Hern) 3-9-7 W Carson 1/1 FAV: 0310-23: Heavily bckd, al there:
probably stays 10f & goes well on a gall trk: see 209.   50
-- SLAP BANG [6] (N Vigors) 3-7-7(3oh) S Dawson(1) 20/1: 40000-4: May not stay 10f: possibly
acts on firm & soft: tried last year in a visor.   20
-- APPRECIATIVE [1] 3-8-0 N Howe 10/1: 000-0: Probably stays 10f: sister to Bloodless Coup.   19
275 STILLOU [3] 3-7-7(4oh) A Proud 13/2: 104-340: Best 117 (sharp trk).   10
338 Sirdar Flyer [5] 7-7(3oh)
7 ran   nk,1½,1½,8,1,12   (Mrs A M Riney)   M Usher Lambourn, Berks

506 WEST LITTLETON MAIDEN STAKES 3YO   £1899   1m 3f   Yielding 84 +01 Fast

-- JUST DAVID [8] (A Stewart) 3-9-0 M Roberts 16/1: -1: 3 b c Blakeney - Reltop (High Top):
Great big strong colt: looked in need of the race but trotted up by 8l in a maiden event at
Bath May 10, easily leading final 1f: stays 11f and looks the sort who will be suited by 2m:
acts on yld: looks certain to rate more highly and win again: promising young stayer.   55
-- EXCELBELLE [15] (J Dunlop) 3-8-11 W Carson 7/1: -2: Wk in mkt but led 2 out: prom
first effort: looks sure to be suited by 12f, acts on yld & should find a maiden race.   38
347 BETTER BEWARE [19] (I Balding) 3-9-0 J Matthias 8/1: 00-343: Led briefly 2½ out:
stays 11f & acts on yld: see 140: consistent: should find a maiden.   30
-- SAVAGE LOVE [17] (J Dunlop) 3-8-11 B Thomson 8/1: 30-4: Fin well: btr for race:
rated 45 last year when 3rd at Haydock on soft grnd: should be suited by 12f.   26
338 CELTIC DOVE [5] 3-8-11 J Williams 10/1: -4040: Al there: see 338.   24

357 ROYAL EFFIGY [14] 3-9-0 P Robinson 14/1: -01D400: Disapp since 66 (10f, soft).   26
--   SURE GROUND [2] 3-9-0 N Howe 5/1: -00-0: Active in mkt, made much: should stay 11f:
might do btr on a sound surface.   00
351 LAW COURT [10] 3-9-0 R Curant 9/4 FAV: 0-00: Well bckd disapp: see 351.   00
--   SNOW WIZARD [1] 3-9-0 R Hills 7/2: -0: Slow start, hmpd in running: expected to do btr.   00
--   CORNISH PIXIE [3] 3-9-0 G Baxter 9/1: -P: Drifter from 9/2 but got t.o. & was p.u.
1 out: should be suited at least 10f.   00
231 Music Minstrel [7] 9-0   --   Tears Of Laughter [18] 9-0
357 Dunston [12] 9-0   --   Mists Of Time [13] 9-0
331 Vantastic [4] 9-0   347 Hello Georgie [9] 9-0   188 Never Bee [11] 9-0(BL)
140 Crown Mine [16] 9-0   426 Bao [6] 9-0
19 ran   8,5,¾,2,nk   (A Leftwich)   A Stewart Newmarket

507 CHAPEL FARM HANDICAP STAKES 3YO 0-50   £2624   5f   Yielding 84 +20 Fast   [46]

233 FOUNTAIN BELLS [9] (R Hannon) 3-8-8 A Mcglone 7/1: 000-201: 3 b f London Bells -
Irish Summer (Sun Prince): Led below dist and qcknd well to win a fast run 3yo h'cap at Bath
May 10: first success: eff around 5f on a gall trk, a looks sure to be suited by 6f: acts
on gd/firm & yld grnd.   38
217 MUHTARIS [5] (C Benstead) 3-8-4 W Carson 4/1: 00-02: Switched after ½way, fin well:
lightly raced colt who is a half brother to useful 9f winner Tizzy: will be suited by 6f:
acts on yld grnd & on a stiff trk.   26
--   GYPSYS PROPHECY [8] (G Harwood) 3-8-8 A Clark 10/3 FAV: 0230-3: Nicely bckd on reappearance: kept on well: speedily bred colt who cost $67,000 as a yearling: showed promise
last season: eff over 5/6f and stays 7f: acts on firm & yld grnd & on a gall trk.   29
276 GALAXY PATH [10] (L Cottrell) 3-8-4 R Hills 20/1: 0-004: Fin well over this shorter
trip: btr effort: suited by some give in the grnd: seems to act on any trk.   22
--   USEFUL [11] 3-9-5 B Thomson 8/1: 31020-0: No extra close home in reapp: btr for
race: useful filly who was an easy winner of a Bath maiden last season and later ran up
in a Nottingham nursery (rated 50): eff over 5/6f: acts on gd/firm & soft grnd & on a gall trk   35
339 CHORISTERS DREAM [14] 3-8-3(bl) N Howe 20/1: 1440-00: Yet to reproduce his best form
of last season, when successful in an Edinburgh maiden and later placed behind Deadbolt
in a Haydock nursery: eff over 5/6f on gd/firm & soft grnd: acts on any trk.   19
340 HAIL AND HEARTY [13] 3-8-5 P Robinson 6/1: 400-020: Made most: fin 7th: btr in 340 (6f).00
339 OLE FLO [4] 3-8-8(bl)(1ow) T Ives 6/1: 33-0330: Never dngr 8th: btr 339.   00
--   TZU-WONG [1] 3-9-4 M Roberts 7/1: 424-0 Slowly away, no threat on reapp.   00
--   HERMINDA [12] 3-8-8 S Dawson(3) 8/1: 024-0: Ev ch below dist: btr for race.   00
--   Sunny Match [7] 8-2   174 Sharasar [6] 8-1   --   Websters Feast [3] 9-4
62   The Hilcote Club [2] 9-7
14 ran   2½,hd,1½,nk,hd,1½   (R I Khan)   R Hannon East Everleigh, Wilts

Official Going Given as Good to Soft for first 2 races: Soft for remainder

508 KAYNE HANDICAP 4YO UPWARDS 0-50   £2876   6f   Good 63 +10 Fast   [48]

112 IRISH COOKIE [1] (I Matthews) 4-8-3 W Woods[3] 16/1: 1320-01: 4 ch f Try My Best -
Irish Kick (Windjammer): Well drawn and led final 1f under press in quite a fast run h'cap
at Lingfield May 10: in '85 made all in a fillies maiden at Chepstow and placed on several
other occasions: eff over 6/7f: acts on soft, well suited by firm or gd ground.   33
374 BROWN BEAR BOY [2] (R Armstrong) 4-8-8 W Carson 13/2: 0400-02: Chall final 2f: gd
effort and may win soon: see 374.   35
266 CORNCHARM [9] (M Mccormack) 5-8-7 S Cauthen 9/1: 00-0203: Kept on under press to
ddht for 2nd: in gd form & should find a race soon: see 135.   34
401 EXERT [7] (R Akehurst) 4-7-10 B Crossley 10/1: 00-3444: Fin well: needs 7f? see 114.   21
+266 BELLE TOWER [6] 4-8-4 C Rutter[5] 8/1: 00-0210: Al well there, ddhtd for 5th: see 266.   24
--   LAURIE LORMAN [16] 4-9-2 R Wernham 25/1: 02300-0: Dsptd lead most from a bad draw:
good seasonal debut: in '85 won twice at Wolverhampton: best form so far at 5f on firm or
good going: worth noting next time if conditions are favourable.   36
374 VORVADOS [4] 9-9-9 P Sargent[7] 33/1: 4-40000: Never closer in 7th: see 18 (rated 69!).   00
327 EECEE TREE [15] 4-8-0 A Mcglone 10/1: 000-020: Badly drawn, disptd lead 4f, fin 8th.   00
192 AL AMEAD [20] 6-9-8 B Rouse 11/2 fav: 0004-00: Speed 4f from a poor draw: winner of
the race last season and a real Lingfield specialist with 6 course successes to his name:
(has never won anywhere else): equally eff at 6 & 7f & acts on gd/firm & soft.   00
361 CORN STREET [19] 8-9-10 W R Swinburn 9/1: 4-01040: No threat, poorly drawn: btr 172, 36100
401 WILL GEORGE [12] 7-9-8 P Cook 10/1: -131100: Early speed, best 160.   00
361 Transflash [11] 9-10   --   Native Skier [5] 9-8   --   Delaware River [3] 7-12
266 Shades Of Blue [17] 8-4   192 Miracles Take Time [13] 8-6
--   Dorney [14] 7-10   262 Young Angel [8] 8-10(bl)
401 Cats Lullaby [10] 7-7(40oh)   266 Hildalarious [18] 7-7(13oh)
20 ran   ¾,ddht,1,2,ddht   (Lord Matthews)   I Matthews Newmarket

509 MARLEY ROOF OAKS TRIAL STAKES 3YO F   £15608   1m 4f Good 63 –01 Slow

372 **MILL ON THE FLOSS** [8] (H Cecil) 3-8-9 S Cauthen 5/2: 10-31: 3 ch f Mill Reef - Milly Moss (Crepello): Smart filly: showed herself well suited by 12f when staying on dourly in the final.½m to win Oaks Trial at Lingfield May 10: first time out in '85 beat Queen Helen in a valuable fillies event at Newbury: half sister to 6 winners: eff at 10f, probably btr suited by 12f: acts on gd & firm going: should continue to impr.   78

-- **LAUGHTER** [4] (W Hern) 3-8-9 W Carson 5/1: 1-2: Gd seasonal debut: chall. 1f out: winner of only outing in '85, Horton Stakes at Newmarket: half brother to several winners and dam is sister to top class High Clere: acts on firm & gd grnd: well suited by 12f: sure to impr and is a definite Oaks prospect.   75

-- **SINGLETTA** [5] (M Stoute) 3-8-9 W R Swinburn 15/8 fav: 12-3: Chall going well 2f out, no extra: easy winner of a minor event at Ascot (first time out) from only 2 outings in '85: eff over 7f, should stay 12f: acts on firm & gd grnd.   72

373 **SPUN GOLD** [1] (P Cole) 3-8-9 T Quinn 9/1: 14-04: Fin well: gd effort: first time out winner of a minor event at York in oct. '85 & only ran once more: eff over 7f, clearly stays 12f well: acts on gd going: the type to impr further.   70

372 **DAVEMMA** [3] 3-8-6 Gay Kelleway 100/1: 0-400: No dngr but earned a high rating & could be improving: stays 12f: see 128.   55

372 **BENAROSA** [6] 3-8-6 P Cook 20/1: -340: Stiff task: see 372 (10f).   54

372 **INTRINSIC** [2] 3-8-6 G Starkey 7/1: -00: Fin last: highly tried: see 372.   00

173 Flaming Dancer [7] 8-6

8 ran   2,2,½,5,1½   (Louis Freedman)   H Cecil Newmarket

510 HIGHLAND SPRING DERBY TRIAL 3YO   £48573   1m 4f Good 63 –14 Slow

*362 **MASHKOUR** [3] (H Cecil) 3-9-0 S Cauthen 7/4: 211-311: 3 ch c Irish River - Sancta Rose (Karabas): Very smart colt: ridden to lead dist and pulled out extra when chall. to gain a narrow success in Gr.3 Derby Trial at Lingfield May 10: ready winner of valuable White Rose Stakes at Ascot Apr.30 & first time out 3rd to Dancing Brave in the Craven: in '85 won at Goodwood & Yarmouth: eff over 1m, nowadays well suited by 10/12f: acts on firm & soft & on any trk: genuine type who keeps finding extra under press & should win more races.   83

-- **BAKHAROFF** [6] (G Harwood) 3-9-0 G Starkey 11/10 fav: 11321-2: Dsptd lead 1f out, just no extra and this was a fine seasonal debut:the Officially top rated2yo last season following his success in the Futurity Stakes at Doncaster: earlier won at Royal Ascot & Sandown and was 2nd to Huntingdale in the Dewhurst: eff over 1m but is very well suited by 12f: now: acts on firm & gd grnd & on a gall trk: should impr for this race and will be a force in all the middle dist. events this season.   83

-224 **TISNT** [1] (P Cole) 3-9-0 T Quinn 13/2: -123: Al prom, kept on well & continues to impr: fairly well suited by 12f: acts òn gd & soft: see 60.   80

-- **NEW TROJAN** [2] (W Hern) 3-9-0 W Carson 12/1: 140-4: Stiff task, no dngr: first time out winner of a maiden at Goodwood in '85, only ran twice more: eff over 7f, should be suited by middle dists: acts on softish going.   60

191 **NORFOLK SONATA** [5] 3-9-0 M Miller 50/1: 0431-30: Led 3f out: stiff task & was far from disgraced: see 191.   58

224 **MY TON TON** [4] 3-9-0 P Robinson 25/1: 0410-00: Made much: narrowly beat Shahrastani in a valuable event at Newbury in '85: eff over 1m & gd/firm grnd: not certain to stay 12f.   48

6 ran   ½,1½,10,1,6   (Sheikh Mohammed)   H Cecil Newmarket

511 WILLIAMS DE BROE LIM.H'CAP 3YO+0-70   £6108   1m 2f Good 63 –01 Slow   [64]

*265 **NEBRIS** [7] (R Akehurst) 5-9-8 P Cook 10/11 fav: 110-111: 5 b h Nebbiolo - Magic Quiz (Quisling): Very useful horse who remains unbtn this season and completed a hat trick leading dist. in a valuable limited h'cap at Lingfield May 10: easy winner of similar valuable h'caps at Epsom & Kempton previously: smart hurdler: in fine form in '85 winning at Epsom (again), Newmarket & Lingfield: very eff around 10/11f but acts on any going & on any trk: genuine & consistent sort who will now step up to Pattern Race company next time.   71

265 **GAY CAPTAIN** [1] (J Bethell) 4-8-6 R Fox 7/1: 00-0002: Chall winner final 1f: much impr effort: only ran twice in '85 the previous season successful at Newbury: stays 10f well: acts on gd & heavy going: should find a race soon on this evidence.   53

-- **KAYTU** [3] (C Brittain) 5-9-4 S Cauthen 10/1: -0000-3: Made most: lightly raced & below his best in '85: winner of the Chester Vase in '84: eff over 12/14f: suited by a sound surface but probably acts on any trk: not badly h'capped.   64

-- **MAILMAN** [4] (I Balding) 7-8-8 T Quinn 8/1: 31000-4: Quite a gd seasonal debut from this tough h'capper: in '85 won at Doncaster & Lingfield: eff 1m, stays 11f well: acts on gd & firm: goes well for a boy.   50

-- **PATO** [5] 4-8-10 B Rouse 8/1: 03210-0: Dsptd lead 3f out on seasonal debut: winner of 2 h'caps at Lingfield & another at Yarmouth in '85: very eff over 10f but acts on firm & soft & on any trk though runs well at Lingfield.   52

221 **LINE OF FIRE** [6] 4-10-0 Paul Eddery 6/1: -021-00: Fin well btn: only ran 3 times early in '85, winning a minor event at York: half brother to 3 winners, notably One In A Million: suited by 10f & a gall trk: acts on firm & yld.   50

262 Toda Forca Avanti [2] 7-7(15oh)

7 ran   1,¼,2,shhd,15   (D Collinge)   R Akehurst Epsom, Surrey

512   TIOXIDE STAKES 3YO   £3132   1m 2f   Good 63 -16 Slow

357 QUEZAL [12] (H Cecil) 3-8-11 S Cauthen 6/1: 00-01: 3 b c Grundy - Quexine (Sir Gaylord):
Impr colt: gained a pillar-to-post success, holding on gamely in a 3yo minor race at Lingfield May 10: well bred colt who is suited by 10f and should stay 12f: acts on gd grnd: does
well with forcing tactics: likely to impr further.   44
357 HIGHEST PEAK [3] (G P Gordon) 3-8-11 W Ryan 5/2 fav: 000-232: Chall winner final 1f,
just btn & clear of rest: deserves a race: acts on gd & soft: see 140.   44
--   SWISS NEPHEW [1] (J Dunlop) 3-8-11 W R Swinburn 10/1: 00-3: Shaped promisingly final
2f on seasonal debut: no form on 2 outings last term but is a half sister to the smart stayer
Harly: sure to be suited by 12f & further: will be hard to beat next time in similar company. 37
90   SIR BRETT [10] (P Kelleway) 3-8-11 Gay Kelleway[5] 33/1: -04: Prom, ev ch: half
brother to winning middle dist filly Altana: impr jort who should be suited by 12f.   35
315 ANOTHER PAGEANT [4] 3-8-8 B Rouse 3/1: -00: Heavily bckd stable companion of Swiss
Nephew, ev ch: see 315.   22
--   GODS PATH [6] 3-8-11 D Brown 10/1: 000-0: Bckd from 25/1 but no dngr: no form in 3
outings last season but is a half brother to 6 winners over varying dists: obviously held
in some regard and can be expected to impr on this next time.   19
--   PILFER [7] 3-8-8 G Starkey 6/1: 3030-0: Ev ch, wknd into 9th: rated 48 when a close
3rd in a minor 2yo event at Sandown in '85: stays at least 7f and acts on gd/firm.   00
357 Kookys Pet [11] 8-11   351 Mightily [9] 8-11   402 Lightning Byte [5] 8-11
-- Last Polonaise [2] 8-8
11 ran   shhd,5,½,5,3   (Dr Carlo Vittadini)   H Cecil Newmarket

513   TULYAR AUCTION STAKES 2YO   £2805   5f   Good 63 +10 Fast

+425 STAY LOW [1] (G Blum) 2-8-6 M Rimmer 9/4 jt fav: 211: 2 ch f Tina's Pet - Pickled
(Pitcairn): Useful, impr filly: gained 2nd win in 5 days, drawing clear in the final 2f
in a fast run 2yo auction event at Lingfield May 10: picked up a fast run similar race at
Doncaster May 5: speedily bred filly who is very eff over 5f on gd or yld going: acts on
any trk: not one to oppose lightly.   57
311 WISE TIMES [3] (M Usher) 2-8-4 M Wigham 16/1: 002: Outpcd final 2f, caught a tartar
here and can win an auction event soon: see 252.   40
-278 SAMLEON [8] (R Hannon) 2-8-9 G Starkey 3/1: 4123: Led 3f: btr 278 (heavy).   44
--   LIGHTNING LEGEND [6] (P Kelleway) 2-8-10 P Cook 9/4 jt fav: 4: Well bckd debutant,
btr for race: half sister to 4 winners and is speedily bred: sure to impr & win a race soon. 40
--   BRADMORES SONG [9] 2-8-12 R Sidebottom 50/1: 0: Rank outsider, no dngr: may do btr
on a stiff trk over further.   36
--   GAMESHOW [4] 2-8-11 T Quinn 50/1: 0: Early speed: half brother to winning '85 2yo
Nagajaya: should improve.   30
270 SYLVAN ORIENT [5] 2-8-13 G Carter[3] 20/1: 00: No dngr in 7th: speedily bred colt.   27
*404 PARIS GUEST [2] 2-8-11 M Miller 5/1: 010: Fin 8th & much btr 404.   25
-- Marquee Cafe [10] 8-11   187 Shenley Romp [7] 8-4
10 ran   5,½,2,3,2   (G Blum)   G Blum Newmarket

514   PLOUGH HANDICAP 3YO 0-50   £2826   7f   Good 63 +07 Fast   [56]

352 MEET THE GREEK [12] (R Laing) 3-8-3 P Cook 7/2 fav: 0202-21: 3 b c Formidable -
Edelliette (Edellic): Fulfilled the promise shown last time, coming from behind to lead final
1f comfortably in quite a fast run 3yo h'cap at Lingfield May 10: showed plenty of promise
last season notably when 2nd to Bakahroff at Sandown: eff over 7f/1m: acts on firm & yld &
on any trk: could win again.   42
386 ARROW EXPRESS [3] (R Armstrong) 3-7-11(bl) M L Thomas 6/1: 000-002: Al well there,
not btn far: best effort yet though showed some promise last season: very eff over 7.5f on gd grnd. 33
352 BOWL OVER [10] (P Makin) 3-8-8(BL) T Quinn 6/1: 302-103: Fin well: good effort
and is in fine form: see 157.   42
--   LIGHTNING WIND [8] (M Usher) 3-8-4 M Wigham 16/1: 04300-4: Al prom on seasonal debut:
showed some promise last season (rated 43) but has yet to win: acts on gd.   36
--   IVORY GULL [7] 3-8-11 B Rouse 5/1: 041-0: Made most: won a maiden at Leicester on
final outing in '85: eff at 6f on firm grnd: should be well suited by longer distances.   38
352 BELOW ZERO [2] 3-8-9 Paul Eddery 8/1: 2-12200: Prom most: best 74.   34
--   DARTIGNY [6] 3-9-0 S Whitworth 9/2: 01-0: Speed 6f, fin 7th: well bckd: ran only
twice in '85 winning a maiden at Brighton: eff 6f on gd grnd & a sharpish undulating trk.   00
274 Summerhill Spruce [11] 7-7(3oh)   -- War Wagon [9] 8-8
356 Grandangus [5] 7-7(11oh)   314 West Carrack [4] 9-7
11 ran   ½,1,½,2,½   (P Goulandris)   R Laing Lambourn, Berks

Official Going Given as Good/Soft

515   MARKET PLACE 2YO AUCTIONS STAKES   £1363   5f   Good/Yld 77 +01 Fast

278   KILVARNET [7] (R Hollinshead) 2-8-9 S Perks 5/2 FAV: 0131: 2 b f Furry Glen - Sunny Eyes
(Reliance 11) Al prom, led final 1f, gamely in 2yo maiden auction at Thirsk May 10: earlier
easy winner of fillies maiden at Haydock: half sister to Young Inca: very eff at 5f and
should stay 6f: acts on heavy, suited by good/yld: acts on any track.   50
  --   CHAYOFA [12] (K Stone) 2-8-0 P Burke(7) 14/1: 2: Ran on well and just btn: good debut:
half sister to 2 winners: will be suited by further: acts on gd/yld: will find a race.   39
450   AIR OF SPRING [15] (D Barron) 2-8-2 S Webster 7/2: 03: Wl bkd, nearly made all:
just btn and on the upgrade: acts on gd/yldg: should find similar race: see 450.   41
*186   GOOD BUY BAILEYS [8] (G Blum) 2-8-6 A Mackay 7/1: 14: Mkt drfter: al prom: see 186.   38
+364   CLOWN STREAKER [4] 2-8-11 M Birch 4/1: 210: Wk in mkt: al prom: running well.   42
364   SAWDUST JACK [10] 2-8-5 T Lucas 14/1: 00: Fin well: impr: cost 3,300 gns: should be
suited by much further than 5f: acts on yld: will do btr on a stiffer trk.   34
236   RABENHAM [9] 2-8-8 R Cochrane 8/1: 00: Never nearer: see 236.   00
  --   THE DEVILS MUSIC [14] 2-8-6 L Charnock 15/2: 0: Very active in mkt: early speed from
this 4,400 gns purchase: stoutly bred on dam's side.   00
367   WHISTLING WONDER [6] 2-8-9 K Darley 10/1: 210430: Early speed: btr 367, 94 (sharp).   00
  --   SALLY FOXTROT [5] 2-8-2 J Bleasdale 10/1: 0: No show: cost 4,000 gns.   00
  --   Ben Ledi [18] 8-4   **364** Get Set Lisa [3] 8-1   --   Nations Song [17] 8-0
  --   James Owl [13] 8-8   **320** Glencroft [1] 8-8   --   Roker Roar [16] 8-8
364 Gwynbrook [11] 8-5(3ow)   --   Noble Kala [2] 8-8
18 ran   ¾,shhd,3,nk,1,½,½   (Noel Sweeney)   R Hollinshead Upper Longden, Staffs

516   SOBA MAIDEN 3YO STAKES   £2008   5f   Good/Yld 77 +03 Fast

  --   LATCH STRING [8] (L Piggott) 3-8-11 T Lucas 5/2 FAV: 40024-1: 3 b f Thatch (USA) -
Bentinck Hotel (Red God): Ex Irish filly who landed a gamble in a 3yo maiden at Thirsk
May 10: sn prom and got up close home under press: placed several times in Ireland in '85:
half sister to 3 winners: eff at·5f, should stay further: acts on gd & yld & a sharpish trk.   40
228   GLIKIAA MOU [1] (R Boss) 3-8-11 E Guest(3) 9/2: F00-242: Raced on her own on the far
side and nearly made all: should find a small event, but seems flattered in 26: see 228.   39
  --   SUPERCOOMBE [6] (P Cole) 3-9-0 M Lynch(5) 4/1: 4-3: Al prom on seasonal debut: good
effort: on sole outing in '85 fin 4th to Lastcomer in a maiden at Doncaster: half brother to
useful sprinter Ardrox Lad: eff at 5/6f: acts on gd & yld & on any trk: should find a race
and will impr for this run.   39
  --   WINSONG MELODY [13] (P Cundell) 3-8-11 J Kennedy(7) 25/1: -4: Led stands side: prom
racecourse debut & should stay further than 5f: half sister to a 1m winner: acts on gd/yld &
a sharpish trk.   31
438   SUPER FRESCO [10] 3-9-0 A Geran(7) 14/1: 0-00: Al there: best effort yet: eff at
5f on gd/yld & a sharpish trk: half brother to a sprint winner.   33
  --   SANDITTON PALACE [3] 3-9-0 M Fry 33/1: 00000-0: Sn prom: best effort yet and is
officially rated only 08: little form in '85: eff at 5f on gd/yld & a sharpish trk: should
find a seller.   32
  --   MURPHYS WHEELS [11] 3-9-0 J Lowe 8/1: 3-0: Nearest fin: btr for race: on sole start
in '85 was a fair 3rd to Bold Arrangement in a 5 runner stakes at Nottingham: half brother to
2 sprint winners: eff at 5/6f on gd & yld.   00
309   HARRY HULL [5] 3-9-0 S Perks 10/1: 000-00: Never nearer: btr 309: will do much btr
than this: mkt drifter today: see 309.   00
  --   FAUVE [2] 3-8-11 N Connorton 7/1: 42-0: Early speed on seasonal debut: showed fair
form on both starts in '85: on final outing fin 2nd to Tarib in a fillies event at Redcar:
eff at 5/6f on gd/firm grnd.   00
217   KHLESTAKOV [14] 3-9-0 M Birch 10/1: -00: No show.   00
  --   Roper Row [12] 9-0   --   Highland Glen [16] 9-0
  --   Marcredea [4] 8-11   **426** Selorcele [15] 9-0(bl)
309 Tip Top Boy [7] 9-0   **309** Crisp Metcalfe [17] 9-0
  --   Eastern Heights [9] 9-0
17 ran   nk,1,1½,nk,nk,2,hd   (Mrs Bertram R Firestone)   L Piggott Newmarket

517   MAY SELLING STAKES 3YO   £1031   12f   Good/Yld 77 -57 Slow

  --   MIAMI IN SPRING [10] (R Stubbs) 3-9-0 D Nicholls 12/1: 3000-1: 3 ch g Miami Springs -
Fado (Ribero): First time out, led well over 1f out, comfortably in a slow run 3yo seller
at Thirsk May 10 (bought in 4,600 gns): stays 12f well: acts on gd/yld & heavy, possibly
not firm: likes a sharpish trk.   21
365   LUCKY HUMBUG [7] (W Pearce) 3-9-0 N Connorton 5/1: 00-22: Al prom: in gd form: see 365   16
356   FAST AND FRIENDLY [12] (R Hollinshead) 3-9-0 S Perks 9/4 FAV: 00-0043: Came too late
(again): dropped to selling company today: eff at 12f on soft & yld.   15
164   MADAM GERARD [9] (W Wharton) 3-8-11(bl) N Carlisle 5/1: 000-444: Dropped in class: led
over 3f out: stays 12f: acts on firm & soft.   11
279   FIRE LORD [3] 3-9-0 D Casey(7) 20/1: 0000-00: Dsptd lead over 7f: fdd.   00
365   PENRYN BOY [5] 3-9-0(bl) R P Elliott 25/1: 000-400: Wknd str: see 257.   00

356 **WINE FESTIVAL** [8] 3-8-11 G Duffield 5/1: -00: Led into str, wknd.   00
51   **FOURNO TRUMPS** [2] 3-9-0 J Bleasdale 6/1: 000-00: Dsptd lead over 7f: fdd.   00
--   **ROBBIE GRANT** [11] 3-9-0 E Guest(3) 10/1: 000-0: There 1m.   00
451 **DESAREM** [6] 3-9-0 M Fry 9/1: 0000-00: Came in last: maiden.   00
279 **Our Annie** [1] 8-11
11 ran   1½,½,½,¾,12,5   (W J Blakey)   R Stubbs Middleham, Yorks

518   **MAIL ON SUNDAY 3YO HANDICAP 0-50**   £2855   7f   Good/Yld 77 -14 Slow   [55]

--   **TRICK OR TREAT** [2] (J Watts) 3-8-10 N Connorton 9/1: 1300-1: 3 ch f Wolverlife –
Sirmio (Shantung): First time out, kept on well to lead close home in a 3yo h'cap at
Thirsk May 10: first time out in '85 won at Doncaster and does well when fresh: eff at
7f, may stay 1m: acts on gd/firm & yld & on any trk.   48
*334 **PELLINKO** [5] (E Eldin) 3-8-12(6ex) A Mackay 9/4 FAV: 00-412: Waited with: stayed on
well: in gd form: suited by 1m: see 334.   46
447 **CUMBRIAN DANCER** [12] (M H Easterby) 3-7-11(vis) N Carlisle 6/1: 212-043: Made almost all:
kept on well: gd effort: stays 7f: see 518.   31
368 **CARRIBEAN SOUND** [6] (C Brittain) 3-8-2 J Lowe 8/1: 4000-24: Nearest fin: see 368.   33
--   **IRISH PASSAGE** [1] 3-8-3 S Webster 7/2: 1-0: Ev ch str on seasonal debut: btr for
race: won sole outing in '85, a stakes event at Ripon: eff at 6f, should be suited by
further: acts on firm grnd.   28
240 **UPTOWN RANDBS** [3] 3-7-7(4oh) S Wood(7) 20/1: 40-4300: Ev ch str: stays 7f: see 37.   17
*260 **VENDREDI TREIZE** [7] 3-8-10 M Hindley(3) 6/1: 2100-10: Fdd: much btr 260.   00
373 **IMPROVISE** [11] 3-8-1 R P Elliott 9/1: 010-200: Fdd str: best first time out in 81.   00
--   **Mandrake Madam** [4] 9-7   --   **Sidons Daughter** [9] 8-10
--   **Security Pacific** [10] 8-10   309 **Polly Worth** [8] 7-7(10oh)
12 ran   2,shhd,1½,3,½,1½   (Philip Newton)   J Watts Richmond, Yorks

519   **COFFEE TIME STKS AMATEUR RIDERS**   £1402   12f   Good/Yld 77 -40 Slow

*116 **ONISKY** [11] (P Cole) 3-10-1 Mr T Easterby 5/2 FAV: 410-11: 3 b c Niniski (U) – Orma
(Double Jump): Useful colt: led after ½way, readily drawing clear in an amateur riders stakes
at Thirsk May 10: first time out won a stakes event at Lingfield: lightly raced in '85
winning a maiden at Brighton: stays 12f really well: acts on firm & soft grnd & seems to
like a sharpish trk.   52
--   **DUAL VENTURE** [12] (J Fitzgerald) 4-11-5 Mr T Fitzgerald(1) 10/1: 00-42-2: Chall over 2f
out: ran only twice in '85: winning 2yo at Newcastle: stays 12f: acts on gd & soft grnd.   38
9   **ORYX MINOR** [15] (S Mellor) 6-11-5 Dana Mellor(3) 12/1: 0401-03: Al there: gd effort:
in '85 won a Ladies race at Chepstow: also a winning hurdler: eff at 10f, stays 12f: acts
on gd & soft.   36
439 **PONTYATES** [8] (J S Wilson) 4-11-0 Mr G Mclaren(3) 16/1: --24-34: Nearest fin: stays 12f.   25
416 **NIMBLE NATIVE** [17] 3-9-12 Sandy Brook(3) 20/1: 00-1040: Prom, ev ch: best first
time out in 45 (sharp trk).   25
363 **SAFE RIVER** [2] 4-11-5 Sara Cumani 11/4: 221-440: Hmpd home turn: best ignored: see 225.   28
--   **GENTLE FAVOR** [18] 5-11-2 Maxine Juster 7/1: 01210-0: Never nearer in 7th: ex Irish
colt who won twice in '85 : stays 14f: acts on firm & soft.   00
251 **SOLAR CLOUD** [16] 4-11-0(vis) Princess Anne(3) 10/1: -00: Wknd 3f out: maiden on
the Flat but the '86 Triumph Hurdle winner: stays 10f: acts on soft, likes firm grnd.   00
--   **Trojan Way** [19] 11-0   --   **Castle Pool** [7] 11-5   282 **Cane Mill** [1] 11-5
282 **Gentle Stream** [9] 11-2   --   **Pajanjo** [6] 11-5
--   **Excavator Lady** [3] 11-8(6ow)   381 **Easy Kin** [5] 11-0
--   **Pinctada** [4] 11-5   --   **Walter The Great** [10] 11-5
80   **Ivoroski** [20] 11-5   137 **Rheinford** [14] 11-5   282 **Al Murtajaz** [13] 11-5
20 ran   8,¾,4,1,½   (Fahd Salman)   P Cole Whatcombe, Oxon

520   **WM HILL FIRST FOR PRICES HCAP 0-50**   £2754   6f   Good/Yld 77 +11 Fast   [49]

412 **SULLYS CHOICE** [3] (D Chapman) 5-8-11(bl)(7ex) D Nicholls 9/2 FAV: 00-0131: 5 b g King
Pellinore – Salute The Coates (Solar Salute): In fine form, led well over 1f out, driven out
in quite a fast run h'cap at Thirsk May 10: earlier won a similar event at Ripon: little form
in '85 but in gd form in '84, winning at Ripon & was placed on many occasions: very eff
over 5/6f, though does stay 1m: acts on gd/firm & soft: eff with or without blinkers.   41
306 **FAWLEYS GIRL** [8] (R Hollinshead) 4-8-3 A Culhane(7) 12/1: 000-002: Sn prom: gd
effort: in '85 won a h'cap at Chester: eff at 6f on gd/firm & yld and a sharp trk.   32
306 **VALLEY MILLS** [7] (D Barron) 6-10-0 B Mcgiff(7) 13/2: 1000-03: Switched 2f out: stayed
on well: running into the form which enabled him to win valuable h'caps at York & Ayr in
'85: in '84 won at Doncaster, Leicester, Newcastle & Thirsk: equally eff over 6/7f: acts
on any going & likes a gall trk: genuine sort.   52
114 **THATCHVILLE** [2] (I Matthews) 4-8-0 G Dickie 8/1: 040-044: Al there: see 114.   22
306 **OXHEY BAY** [5] 4-8-12 V Smith(7) 6/1: 3112-00: Made much: in gd form at the backend
of '85, winning at Warwick & Folkestone: equally eff at 6/7f: acts on gd & yld grnd &
likes a sharp/undulating trk.   31

211 PINETUM [12] 4-7-12 K Darley 8/1: --01-00: Btr effort: very lightly raced in '85,
winning a moderate maiden at Kempton: speedily bred colt, but has been lightly raced due
to leg trouble: eff at 5/6f: likes firm grnd.   13
306 COOL ENOUGH [1] 5-7-11 T Williams 7/1: 00-4000: Fin 7th: see 12.   00
--   SHARLIES WIMPY [6] 7-9-5 M Hindley(3) 10/1: 00400-0: Fin 8th: btr for race: in gd form
in '85, winning h'caps at Chester and Hemilton (2): in '84 won first time out at Ripon: acts
on any trk: best over 6f on a sound surface: carries weight well.   00
--   PANNANICH WELLS [4] 3-7-8 L Charnock 8/1: 00430-0: Btr for race: failed to win in
'85 though showed some ability: eff at 6/7f on firm & yld: has been tried in bl.   00
369 GODS SOLUTION [9] 5-8-8 S Webster 11/2: 00-1040: Prom 4f: btr 369, 42 (Catterick).   00
46   Bold Rowley [11] 7-7(14oh)   321 Brampton Grace [10] 9-1(BL)
12 ran   ½,2½,¾,1,1½,2,2   (William Chapman)   D Chapman Stillington, Yorks

---

521   THIRSK HUNT CUP HANDICAP 0-70   £8350   1m   Good/Yld 77 -04 Slow   [57]

310 SHORT SLEEVES [8] (S Hall) 4-8-4 S P Griffiths 20/1: -310-01: 4 b f Move Off -
Red Jeans (Manacle): Waited with: ran on well to lead inside final 1f, comfortably in
valuable Thirsk Hunt Cup (h'cap) at Thirsk May 10: in '85 won a maiden at Ripon: eff at 1m,
stays 10f: acts on gd & yld & seems to like a sharpish trk.   45
•79   WELL RIGGED [1] (M H Easterby) 5-9-0 M Birch 9/4 FAV: 321-212: Led/dsptd lead: hdd
well inside final 1f: another game effort:4L clear 3rd: see 79.   52
310 RAPID ACTION [9] (G Moore) 5-7-7(6oh) J Lowe 12/1: 20-3033: Never nearer: in gd form:
eff at 1m on gd & soft grnd: see 46.   24
429 BURAAG [11] (M W Easterby) 5-8-5(1ow) T Lucas 10/1: 00-0044: Stayed on: consistent:
needs 10f? see 196.   35
429 TUTBURY [3] 4-8-0 N Carlisle 10/1: 2-44100: Twice below form 238 (C/D).   28
248 ALL FAIR [12] 5-9-1 T Williams 10/1: 002-000: No dngr: in '85 won h'caps at York &
Ripon: previous season won at Newbury & Haydock: eff over 8/10f: acts on firm & soft grnd
and likes a gall trk: does well when up with the pace.   39
--   CASCABEL [2] 5-8-4 R Cochrane 11/2: 00012-0: Fin 8th on seasonal debut: in fine form
in '85, winning h'caps at Edinburgh, Brighton & Salisbury: in '84 won at Catterick and
Edinburgh: equally eff over 7/8f: acts on firm & soft grnd & on any trk, though likes a
sharpish one: btr for race.   00
196 PALMION [10] 4-7-11 A Culhane(7) 3/1: 240-020: Well bckd: much btr 196 (C/D).   00
441 SILVER CANNON [4] 4-8-3(vis) G Duffield 8/1: 000-100: Twice below form 281 (heavy).   00
361 Red Russell [5] 9-10   182 Workaday [6] 8-4   441 Paris Match [7] 8-9(bl)
12 ran   1½,4,¾,¾,2,2½   (Miss S E Hall)   S Hall Middleham, Yorks

---

522 OSSETT SELLING STAKES 3 & 4-Y-O   £872   1m 2f   Soft 141 +01 Fast

--   MILL TERN [6] (A Potts) 4-9-1(BL) S Webster 8/1: 00200-1: 4 ch g Milford - Mitsuki
(Crowned Prince): First time out, dropped to selling company and ran on strongly to lead
close home in a modest race at Pontefract May 12: rated 40 when 2nd to Pochard in a non-
seller at Carlisle: (bought in 3,200 gns): eff over 10/12 on gd/firm & soft grnd: acts on
any trk.   16
378 SWIFT RIVER [11] (I Bell) 4-9-6 N Carlisle 11/1: 0/0-202: Slow start, led dist and
only just caught: impr effort over this longer trip: well suited by plenty of give: acts
on any trk: has been hurdling since 131.   20
--   NARCISSUS [2] (R Akehurst) 4-9-1 G Baxter 6/1: -0-3: Stayed on well on seasonal debut:
on sole outing last term was unplaced in France: half brother to very useful miler Petronici:
acts on soft ground &on a sharp trk: should impr.   13
238 CADENETTE [10] (M Camacho) 4-8-12 N Connorton 6/1: 030-004: Al there: placed in
similar company last season: eff over 8/10 on gd & heavy grnd: acts on any trk: half sister
to useful hurdler Lanhydrock.   07
381 MARCELLINA [5] 4-8-12 N Crowther 7/2: -00-000: Dropped to selling company and gambled
on: shorter trip and ran on too late: acts on soft grnd & on a sharp trk.   06
107 JALOME [7] 4-8-12 R Cochrane 33/1: 000-000: Late prog.   05
276 COMEDY PRINCE [1] 3-8-1 S Whitworth 7/4 FAV: 000-00: Heavily bckd: led below dist,
sn btn: dropped in class today and can do btr than this.   00
259 WHAAG [4] 4-9-1 D Leadbitter(7) 8/1: 430-400: Led ¼way: wknd into 8th: see 10400
517 Penryn Boy [3] 8-1(bl)   448 Porto Green [12] 9-1
--   Carlops [9] 8-12
11 ran   hd,1½,1½,½,¾   (S Stacey)   A Potts Horkstow, Sth Humberside

---

523 SNAITH 2YO STAKES   £2421   5f   Soft 141 -09 Slow

--   COUNT TREVISIO [3] (R Sheather) 2-8-11 R Cochrane 12/1: 1: 2 b c Lochnager - Spring
Clump (Mount Hagen): Made virtually ev yd to win a 2yo stakes at Pontefract May 12: speedily
bred colt who cost 17,000 gns as a yearling: sure to appreciate another furlong: acts on
soft grnd & on a sharp trk: should rate more highly & win more races.   45

*332 JONLEAT [7] (L Piggott) 2-9-3 T Lucas 5/4 FAV: 412: Again heavily bckd: ev ch and
is in fine form: acts on any trk: see 332.   48
304 WENSLEYDALEWARRIOR [8] (G Moore) 2-8-11 N Crowther 14/1: 03: Lost place after ½way,
fin strongly: looks sure to be suited by 6f plus: on the up grade: see 304.   37
440 ROWEKING [5] (L Lightbrown) 2-9-3 J Bleasdale 11/2: 020134: Consistent sort: see 367.   37
--   BENNETTHORPE [4] 2-8-11 K Hodgson 14/1: 0: Mkt drifter on debut: speed over ½way and
should impr for this experience: cost 11,500 gns: acts on soft grnd & on a sharp trk.   30
--   STAR PLAY [2] 2-8-11 C Dwyer 14/1: 0: Fair effort on racecourse debut: half sister
to several winning sprinters, incl the useful Not For Show: acts on soft grnd & on a sharp
trk: should improve.   29
382 BUDDY RICH [10] 2-8-11 T Ives 2/1: 40: Early speed from an adverse draw: fin 7th
and btr on fast grnd in 382 (stiff trk): worth another chance.   00
--   Commonsidr Gypsy [6] 8-11   197 Rosies Image [9] 8-8
--   Melgrove [1] 8-11
10 ran   ½,2,2,½,nk,3   (M S Hartley)   R Sheather Newmarket

524 OSSETT SELLING STAKES 3 & 4-Y-O   £872   1m 2f   Soft 141 -24 Slow

310 LILTING LAD [2] (W Wharton) 4-9-1 M Birch 4/1: 00-0001: 4 ch c Tower Walk – Lilting
Lady (Crooner): Dropped in class and stayed on well to lead near fin in a slowly run seller
at Pontefract May 12 (bought in 1,500 gns): eff over 8/10f with some cut in the grnd: seems
well suited by a sharp trk.   14
256 VERBADING [5] (S Norton) 4-8-12(VIS) J Lowe 11/2: 2000-02: Dropped to selling company
and visored first time: just failed to make all: rated 34 when 2nd to National Dress in a
fillies maiden at Catterick first time out last year (12f yld): well suited by an easy surface 10
--   GREEN ARCHER [1] (J Ramsden) 3-8-11 M Wood 16/1: -3: Ran on late on racecourse debut:
stays 10f on a sharp trk: acts on soft grnd.   14
--   EL HAR LE HAR [7] (W Musson) 4-9-1 P Waldron 7/2 FAV: 0-020-4: Ev ch on reapp: has
been hurdling this Winter though lightly raced on the Flat last year, when placed in a
similar race at Redcar: eff over 8/10f on firm & soft grnd: acts on any trk.   08
--   PROHIBITION BOY [10] 4-9-1 S Hustler(7) 20/1: 0-000-0: Fit from hurdling:
disputed lead to halfway.   07
305 RAPID STAR [4] 3-7-13(1ow) P Robinson 20/1: 0-30000: Nearest fin: stays 10f: see 51.   04
451 TARA DANCER [8] 3-8-7(1ow) C Dwyer 5/1: 0-00000: Dropped in class: no threat.   00
207 DECEMBRE [3] 4-9-1(VIS) A Proud 9/1: -000-00: Never dngr 8th: see 207.   00
426 FIRST ALARM [6] 3-8-1 J Quinn(5) 15/2: -0000: Close up to ½way: fin 9th.   00
356 Tyrannise [9] 7-12   279 Conerser [11] 8-1(bl)   426 Classy Scouse [12] 8-1
12 ran   ½,1½,1½,nk,2,nk   (L Chamberlain)   W Wharton Melton Mowbray, Leics

525 HEY GROUP SPRINT H'CAP 4YO+ 0-50   £2737   6f   Soft 141 +21 Fast   [44]

369 TANFEN [11] (T Craig) 5-8-2 N Carlisle 12/1: 200-031: 5 b g Tanfirion – Lady Mary
(Sallust): Went on 2f out for a comfortable win in a fast run h'cap at Pontefract May 12:
last season won similar races at Newcastle, Hamilton & Catterick: best form over 6f: acts
on any going & on any trk & does well with forcing tactics.   28
412 GEORGE WILLIAM [5] (P Bevan) 5-8-11 P Waldron 5/1: 0000-22: Finished strongly:
in good form: see 412.   32
--   CABANAX [10] (E Weymes) 4-9-9 E Guest(3) 33/1: 0-220-3: Unfancied on seasonal debut:
ran a good race under top weight: off the trk since early last season when running up to
Lyric Way and Powder Keg at Pontefract & Ayr respectively: eff over 5/6f on gd & soft grnd:
acts on any trk: looks fairly h'capped and should go close next time.   42
412 RIVERSIDE WRITER [7] (K Bridgwater) 4-8-5 P D'arcy 12/1: -103404: Kept on late:
good effort: see 84.   24
428 HOLT ROW [2] 5-8-0 W Woods(3) 11/1: 000-000: Made most: stays 6f: see 428.   19
369 FLOMEGAS DAY [3] 4-8-7(bl) J Hills(5) 13/2: 000-000: Slow start, fin well: see 369.   26
*412 GOLD DUCHESS [12] 4-7-13(bl)(9ex) L Charnock 9/1: 0424310: Ran on late: fin 7th:
best in 412 (5f).   00
361 XHAI [6] 4-9-4 R Cochrane 6/1: 10-4020: Shorter trip: much btr in 361 (7f stiff trk).   00
306 SUDDEN IMPACT [4] 4-9-3 S Whitworth 7/1: 040-100: Speed over ½way: best 65 (gall track).00
374 EMERGENCY PLUMBER [1] 5-8-5 S Webster 10/3 FAV: 00-4240: Disapp fav: fin 9th: see 306.00
369 Spoilt For Choice [8] 7-13   260 Single Hand [9] 7-11
12 ran   2,½,shhd,shhd,½,nk   (William Burns)   T Craig, West Barns, Lothian

526 TOTE MARATHON HANDICAP 4YO+ 0-35   £1780   2m 5f   Soft 141 -31 Slow   [33]

137 PELHAM LINE [4] (W Musson) 6-8-0 P Robinson 3/1 FAV: 0003/31: 6 ch m High Line –
Pelham Wood (Marmaduke): Went on home turn for an easy win in a h'cap at Pontefract May 12:
first success: lightly raced mare who is well suited by a test of stamina: acts on soft grnd
and does well on a sharp/easy course.   20
--   WRITE THE MUSIC [8] (P Felgate) 5-9-3(vis) M Hindley(3) 12/1: 12200-2: Stayed on, no ch
with winner though well clear of rem: last season won a similar race at Beverley: needs a
test of stamina: acts on gd/firm & soft grnd & on any trk: gd effort.   28

336 BEAKER [9] (M Naughton) 6-7-11 J Lowe 5/1: 000-423: Led briefly 3f out, hdd and
soon eased: see 336.   00
--   NEWMARKET SAUSAGE [1] (G Moore) 5-8-9 S Wood(7) 11/1: 0/000-4: Close up till home
turn: lightly raced over similar trips last season though has enjoyed a most successful spell
of hurdling recently, winning twice last month: stays well: suited by some give in the grnd:
best form on a sharp/easy trk.   00
358 HIGHAM GREY [10] 10-8-11 D Nicholls 14/1: 10-0000: Longer trip: no extra str: see 144.   00
--   IMPERIUM [5] 9-7-10 M Fry 12/1: 00000-0: Fit from hurdling: al behind.   00
336 TERN [3] 5-9-2(bl) M Birch 11/2: 1000-00: Most most: wknd quickly home turn: see 336.   00
360 CHRISTO [6] 4-9-2(BL) S Whitworth 5/1: -32300: Bl first time: remote 9th and this
running can be ignored: see 199.   00
137 Michele My Belle [11] 7-9   375 Romana [7] 9-7
--   Henry Geary Steels [2] 8-8(1ow)
11 ran   5,25,3,2,7,½   (C Weeks)   W Musson Newmarket

527 PONTEFRACT MAIDEN MILE CHAMP. 3YO   £2012   1m   Soft 141 +01 Fast

371 ABSHEER [8] (G Harwood) 3-9-0 G Starkey 4/1: -01: 3 b c Double Form - Milaire
(Tudor Melody): Prom colt: btr for recent run & ran on strongly to lead close home in quite
a fast run 3yo maiden at Pontefract May 12: earlier shaped promisingly behind Nino Bibbia in
a well contested Newmarket maiden: clearly very eff over 1m but will stay further: acts on
gd & soft grnd & on any trk: will win more races.   65
218 DALLAS [13] (L Cumani) 3-9-0 R Guest 2/1: -02: Well bckd and ran a fine race: led
after ½way, touched off close home though beat the rem decisively: well regarded colt who is
very eff over 1m on gd & soft grnd: acts on any trk: sure to go one btr soon.   64
371 MOEL FAMMAU [2] (J Toller) 3-9-0 P Robinson 10/1: -03: Ran on same pace: should find
a run of the mill maiden: eff over 1m on gd & soft grnd: acts on any trk.   52
253 WASMI [6] (J Dunlop) 3-9-0 G Baxter 7/4 FAV: 00-2D4: Well bckd: ev ch: see 253.   51
334 BEAU DIRE [5] 3-9-0 R Hills 50/1: -00: No extra str: however a fair effort in this
hot company: eff over 1m on soft grnd: acts on a sharp trk.   35
414 MAWDLYN GATE [3] 3-9-0 K Hodgson 14/1: 0.-0040: Op. 20/1: fair effort: see 414.   27
188 Mr Adviser [11] 9-0   -- Vikris [1] 8-11   380 Bold Answer [9] 9-0
259 Bayview Gal [4] 8-11   -- Dallona 0 8-11   --   Court Ruler [12] 9-0
12 ran   ½,7,½,10,5   (Prince Ahmed Salman)   G Harwood Pulborough, Sussex

528' PONTEFRACT MAIDEN MILE CHAMP. 3YO   £1998   1m   Soft 141 -15 Slow

--   ASIAN CUP [7] (G Harwood) 3-9-0 G Starkey 7/4 FAV: 02-1: 3 b c Irish Tower - Suzmatic
(Ace Of Aces): Useful colt: first time out easily justified fav. in a 3yo maiden at Pontefract May 12, led 3f out and sn quickened clear: cost $125,000 as a yearling & showed promise
in both his starts last season, running up to C Jam Blues at Salisbury: clearly well suited
by 1m & likely to stay further: acts on firm & soft grnd & on any trk: should win btr races. 54
229 SAHRAAN [1] (A Stewart) 3-9-0 M Banner 10/3: -02: Nicely bckd: led briefly ½way, no
ch with easy winner: seems suited by 1m on a sharp trk: acts on soft grnd: should impr further
                                                                                              34
--   ADAMSTOWN [9] (M Prescott) 3-9-0 C Nutter 20/1: -3: Active in mkt on racecourse debut:
ran in snatches, staying on late and seems certain to impr next time: eff over 1m on soft
grnd: acts on a sharp trk.   32
--   POUSSEZ [11] (O Douieb) 3-8-11 G Machado 5/1: -4: Showed some promise & btr for race:
speedily bred filly who is a half sister to a couple of winners: acts on soft grnd & on
a sharp trk.   28
368 BOLLIN UNCLE [4] 3-9-0 M Birch 16/1: 000-00: Clear of rem: impr effort.   25
--   SUNMAIDEN [2] 3-8-11 M Wood 33/1: 00-0: Unfancied & never threatened ldrs.   02
--   HAMLOUL [6] 3-9-0 R Hills 7/1: 00030-0: Speed over ½way: btr for race.   00
--   ENGLE DALE [12] 3-9-0 G French 9/1: -0: Lost place soon after ½way, only beat 1 home.   00
--   Sioux Sweet 0 8-11   -- Cover Inn 0 8-11   328 Couture Color 0 9-0
11 ran   5,1,hd,2,10   (Prince Ahmed Salman)   G Harwood Pulborough, Sussex

529 GARFORTH APP.H'CAP 3YO 0-35   £1040   5f   Soft 141 +03 Fast   [37]

--   BRIDGE OF GOLD [1] (D Barron) 3-9-0 B Mcghiff 7/1: 120-1: 3 b f Balidar - Nancy Brig
(Brigadier Gerard): First time out led inside dist and held on gamely in a 3yo h'cap at
Pontefract May 12: lightly raced last season, winning a seller at Catterick on her racecourse
debut: later ran up to Gods Isle in a nursery at Thirsk: very eff over 5f on a sharp trk
and should stay further: acts on firm & soft grnd: genuine filly who looks well h'capped
and may win again.   34
377 THE STRAY BULLETT [6] (B Mcmahon) 3-8-4(bl) A Roper 12/1: 030-002: Just failed to get
up: returning to form: half brother to sprinter Will George who acts on firm & soft grnd
and is well suited by a sharp trk: should again go close next time.   23
309 WATENDLATH [3] (E Weymes) 3-7-13 R Lappin 10/1: 0330-03: Ran on too late: lightly
raced when twice placed in modest company last term: eff over 5f though should do btr over a
longer trip: acts on gd & heavy grnd & on any trk.   11

246	RESTLESS RHAPSODY [5] (K Brassey) 3-9-7(bl) A Whitehall(4) 5/1: 3134-24: Al front rank.		30
339	LOCH FORM [4] 3-9-4 M Richardson 5/2 FAV: 00-0120: Made most: best in 255.		19
103	EL ALAMEIN [2] 3-8-8(bl) J Carr 8/1: 004-000: Nvr dngr: see 103.		01
198	PETILLER [9] 3-7-8 P Burke(3) 5/1: 0000-20: Early speed: fin 8th: btr in 198.		00
447	Murryl Cannon 0 8-1	-- Jessie Ellis 0 8-6	
9 ran	hd,3,$\frac{3}{4}$,4,2$\frac{1}{2}$,1	(T D Barron) D Barron Maunby, Yorks	

Official Going Given as Good/Firm

530   TORRISH SELLING HCAP STKS 0-25 4 & 5YO   £934   1m 2f   Firm 18 -12 Slow   [24]

262 PITKAITHLY [20] (J Jenkins) 4-9-4(BL) B Rouse 10/1: 4300-01: 5 b g Mansingh - Naughty
But Nice (Daring Display): Bl first time and active in mkt: led approaching final 1f, under
press in a selling h'cap at Windsor May 12 (bought in 2,700 gns): first success: stays 10f:
acts on fast grnd & on any trk.   23

177 HIT THE HEIGHTS [17] (M Pipe) 5-9-2(vis) S Cauthen 10/3*FAV: 0000-22: Ch final 1f:
good effort: likes a sharpish trk: acts on firm & soft grnd: see 177.   17

207 SNAKE RIVER [11] (D Nicholson) 4-9-5 Pat Eddery 15/2: 001-433: Ch over 1f out:
see 207, 22.   16

207 STONEBROKER [14] (D Haydn Jones) 4-8-5 R Curant 8/1: -00-044: Led over 2f out: see 207.   00

343 MEZIARA [19] 5-9-4(bl) C Rutter(5) 10/1: 20-2240: Mkt drifter: made much: best 201.   00

*201 FLAMING PEARL [3] 5-9-10(vis) R Carter(5) 8/1: 3/20-10: Mkt drifter: much btr 201 (soft) 01

-- VICEROY BOY [8] 4-8-13 N Byrne(7) 33/1: 00000-0: Never nearer on seasonal debut:
maiden: stays 10f: acts on fast grnd.   00

105 MUSICAL WILL [7] 4-9-1 C Coates(5) 15/2: 0210-00: Fin 8th: in '85 won a selling
h'cap at Newcastle: eff at 10f on gd/firm & yld & a gall trk.   00

129 RECORD RED [18] 5-8-5 W Carson 9/1: -040: Mkt drifter: no show.   00

343 UNDER THE STARS [2] 4-9-4(BL) B Crossley 7/1: 0300-00: Early ldr: btr 1m? see 343.   00

403 EASTER RAMBLER [5] 4-9-5 A Mackay 10/1: 1100-00: Wknd str.   00

--	Purple [16] 8-11	499	Lingfield Lady [21] 9-2		
418	Craven Boy [10] 8-5	202	Deerfield Beach [1] 8-10		
420	Scholar [4] 9-2(BL)	--	Asticot [9] 9-6(BL)	--	Manhattan Boy [15] 9-8
--	Maori Warrior [13] 8-13(bl)			--	Video Lad [12] 8-11
201	Tomorrows World [6] 8-2				
21 ran	2,2,5,5,1$\frac{1}{2}$hd,$\frac{1}{2}$,2	(Jeffrey Ross)	J Jenkins Epsom, Surrey		

531   EBF BLUE CHARM MAIDEN STKS 2YO   £931   5f   Firm 18 -06 Slow

417 DANCING DIANA [7] (R Hannon) 2-8-11 Pat Eddery 7/2: 21: 2 gr f Raga Navarro -
Lovely Diana (Supreme Sovereign): Useful, impr filly: led 2f out, cleverly holding the
heavily bckd Timeswitch by a nk in a 2yo maiden at Windsor May 12: eff at 5f, should be
suited by further: acts on gd & firm & seems to like a sharpish trk: should win more races.   49

-- TIMESWITCH [10] (W O'gorman) 2-9-0 T Ives 11/10 FAV: 2: Much touted debutant and
well bckd: just btn and will impr: half brother to the winning juvenile Indigo Jones:
should stay further than 5f: acts on firm grnd & should go one btr next time.   50

-- BATTLEAXE [6] (J Toller) 2-9-0 W Carson 12/1: 3: Sn prom: gd racecourse debut from
this 5,400 gns purchase: sure to be suited by further than 5f: acts on firm grnd & should
find a race.   43

-- KEEN EDGE [5] (P Mitchell) 2-9-0 A Mcglone 20/1: 4: Led 3f on debut: cost 8,800 gns:
acts on firm grnd.   35

-- GEMINI FIRE [1] 2-9-0 S Cauthen 10/1: 0: Sn prom: fdd final 1f: promising debut from
this 18,000 gns purchase: speedily bred, being a full brother to the useful sprinter Singing
Sailor: impr likely: acts on firm grnd.   28

404 BRANSTOWN SUNSET [8] 2-9-0 A Clark 33/1: 00: Rank outsider: no show, but a btr effort:
cost 8,200 gns and is a half brother to 3 minor winners: should be suited by further than 5f.   21

-- STARS IN MOTION [11] 2-9-0 W R Swinburn 12/1: 0: Early speed on debut: cost I.R. 9,000:
half brother to 2 winners and should stay further than 5f.   00

497 ITS VARADAN [4] 2-9-0 B Thomson 10/1: 00: Fin 8th: half brother to several winners,
notably the smart hurdler Ra Nova: may need further than 5f.   00

-- LAZIM [12] 2-9-0 B Rouse 15/2: 0: No show: cost I.R. 64,000: should impr.   00

--	Akrotiri Bay [3] 9-0	--	Lynda Broad [9] 8-11	--	Hennerton [2] 9-0
12 ran	nk,2$\frac{1}{2}$,3,2$\frac{1}{2}$,2$\frac{1}{2}$,shhd,1,2$\frac{1}{2}$	(G A Bosley)	R Hannon East Everleigh, Wilts		

532   DUSTY MILLER HCAP STAKES 0-50   £2893   1m 4f   Firm 18 -17 Slow   [45]

349 GOING GOING [18] (H Candy) 7-9-7 P Johnson(7) 5/1 FAV: 2114-01: 7 b g Auction Ring -
Whitethorn (Gulf Pearl): Remains a useful gelding: ran on under press to lead near line in
a h'cap at Windsor May 12: in '85 won h'caps at Epsom, Windsor & Kempton and was most
consistent: in '84 won again at Windsor and likes this trk: eff over 11/12f: genuine &
consistent sort who acts on any going & on any trk: carries weight well.   48

432 PELLINCOURT [9] (A Pitt) 4-8-0 C Rutter(5) 9/1: 20-4002: Led 2f out, caught near fin:
good effort: stays 12f: likes a sharpish trk: see 179.   26
449 HOLYPORT VICTORY [1] (M Usher) 4-9-1(5ex) W Carson 6/1: -401133: Continues in fine form38
349 MOON JESTER [10] (M Usher) 6-8-3(vis) D Mckay 6/1: 40-0024: Ran on well: nowadays suited
by 12f: see 349.   25
--   KUWAIT MOON [17] 4-9-3 Pat Eddery 10/1: 23202-0: Ev ch str on seasonal debut: consistent
performer in '85, but has yet to get his head in front: stays 12f: acts on firm & soft grnd
and likes a sharpish track.   38
432 DUELLING [6] 5-7-13(vis) A Mcglone 8/1: 0-40000: Led 3f out: see 7.   18
92   FOGAR [2] 4-8-12 S Cauthen 11/2: -10-30: Led 1m: see 92.   00

176	Old Malton [16] 7-11	349	Dancing Barron [5] 8-11		
263	Otabari [14] 9-10	--	Perisian Knight [12] 8-11		
--	New Zealand [11] 8-6	341	Janaab [7] 8-5(2ow)	403	Saintly Lad [4] 8-12
420	Lady Liza [8] 7-8	--	Hive Off [19] 8-0	--	Bay Pond [13] 7-13
333	Dick Knight [3] 7-9	262	Denboy [15] 8-3(5ow)		
19 ran	shhd,1½,nk,nk,1,5	(Henry Candy)	H Candy Kingstone Warren, Oxon		

---

533 LADY CAROLINE STAKES 2YO FILLIES   £1678   5f   Firm 18 +14 Fast

404 DERRING DEE [4] (P Cundell) 2-8-8 N Adams 33/1: 01: 2 b f Derrylin – Insurance
(Yellow God): Fast impr filly: stayed on well under press to lead close home in a fast run
2yo fillies stakes at Windsor May 12: cost only 3,000 gns as a yearling and seems a bargain:
sister to fair h'capper Killyglen: eff at 5f, should stay further: acts on gd & firm grnd
& a sharpish trk: should win more races.   55
--   SCIERPAN [6] (J Tree) 2-8-8 Pat Eddery 9/4: 2: Well bckd on debut: led 2f out: just
caught: good effort from this half sister to very useful 2yo winners Solo Native and In Toto:
eff at 5f, should stay further: acts on firm grnd & should have no trouble finding a race.   54
--   ULTRA NOVA [3] (P Cole) 2-8-8 T Quinn 13/8 FAV: 3: Heavily bckd debutant: led to ½way:
cost 6,600 gns and is obviously held in high regard: speedily bred & should not be hard
pressed to find a race: eff at 5f on firm grnd.   48
*400 CLARENTIA [2] (M Usher) 2-9-2 W Carson 7/1: 214: Giving 8lbs all round: another
good effort: see 400.   49
73   BASTILLIA [7] 2-8-8 W R Swinburn 33/1: 0: Impr effort: half sister to 3 sprint
winners: eff at 5f on firm grnd.   34
--   EDRAIANTHUS [9] 2-8-8 M Malham 33/1: 0: No threat on debut: cost 26,000 gns and is a
half sister to the useful Electrifying: should be suited by further than 5f: acts on firm grnd   32
383 GO MY PET [10] 2-8-8 S Cauthen 9/2: 00: Early speed: btr 383.   00
*57 PASHMINA [5] 2-8-8 C Coates(5) 16/1: 10: Sn prom, fdd: see 57 (seller heavy).   00

483	Premium Gold [11] 8-8	--	Good Time Girl [1] 8-8		
--	Princess Michico [12] 8-8			--	Spanish Melody [8] 8-8
12 ran	½,2½,3,2,¾,2,shhd	(Archie Hornall)	P Cundell Compton, Berks		

---

534 JOCK SCOTT HANDICAP STAKES 3YO 0-50   £2500   6f   Firm 18 +18 Fast   [48]

62   TOUCH OF GREY [3] (D Thom) 3-9-1 W R Swinburn 12/1: 210-001: 3 br c Blakeney –
Belle Den (Comedy Star): Useful colt: led approaching final 1f, readily in a fast run h'cap
at Windsor May 12: in '85 won a nursery h'cap at Ascot: very eff at 6f on fast grnd and
seems best when up with the pace: may win again.   49
--   FUDGE [1] (N Vigors) 3-8-0 S Dawson(3) 16/1: 000-2: No ch with winner, though a good
seasonal debut: no form in 3 outings in '85: half sister to several winners: eff at 6f: acts
well on firm grnd.   22
*217 NO BEATING HARTS [4] (M Mccormack) 3-9-5 S Cauthen 15/8 FAV: 0320-13: Well bckd: made
much: better 217 (yld).   39
436 STRIVE [2] (M Blanshard) 3-9-6 R Cochrane 6/1: 100-024: Sn prom: btr 436 (7f).   39
478 DANCING TOM [12] 3-8-13 C Coates(5) 11/1: 01-4000: Prom over 4f: see 81.   30
--   LIGHT HILLS [1] 3-8-12 K Radcliffe(7) 14/1: 10440-0: No show on seasonal debut: in
'85 won a h'cap at Sandown & a seller at Windsor: very eff at 5f: acts on yld, likes firm grnd   24
454 OUT OF HARMONY [9] 3-8-6 P Cook 3/1: 010-00: Well bckd but no show: in '85 won a
fillies maiden at Lingfield: speedily bred filly who is eff over 5f on firm grnd & a
sharpish track.   00
138 LJAAM [8] 3-9-7(BL) A Murray 10/1: 1040-40: Bl first time: btr 138: unsuited by firm?   00
--   FULL OF LIFE [5] 3-9-5 Paul Eddery 10/1: 4321-0: There 4f on seasonal debut.   00

--	Mitner [7] 8-5	480	No Stopping [10] 8-1	283	Tamalpais [6] 8-9
12 ran	5,1,¾,¾,2,1,shhd	(T M Jennings)	D Thom Newmarket		

---

535 MAR LODGE STAKES 3YO C & G   £1054   1m 2f   Firm 18 -14 Slow

357 ENBARR [12] (H Cecil) 3-9-0 S Cauthen 8/11 FAV: 0-21: 3 b c Kings Lake – Catherine
Wheel (Roan Rocket): Impr colt: heavily bckd & made almost all, comfortably in a 3yo stakes
at Windsor May 12: first time out just btn by Miltescens in a maiden at Nottingham: half
brother to Cheshire Oaks winner Hunston: eff at 10f, should stay 12f: acts on firm & soft
grnd & on any trk: can continue to impr/win more races.   50
328 ASHINGTON GROVE [5] (D Murray Smith) 3-9-0 Pat Eddery 8/1: 00-22: Ch over 1f out:
another good effort & is running well: stays 10f: acts on firm & soft & on any trk: see 328.   43

370 IS BELLO [13] (L Cumani) 3-9-0 R Guest 25/1: -03: Mkt drifter: ev ch over 1f out:
on the up grade: half brother to 2 winners: eff at 10f on firm grnd & a sharpish trk:
should find a maiden.   41
--   STARMAST [14] (W Hern) 3-9-0 W Carson 4/1: 0-4: Well bckd on seasonal debut: al up
there: kept on: btr for race: showed promise on sole start in '85: eff at 10f, should stay
12f: half brother to 3 winners incl useful types Baltic & Baffin: acts on firm grnd.   34
430 IRISH DILEMMA [7] 3-9-0(BL) P Bloomfield 33/1: -0: Bl first time: sn prom and
is on the up grade: acts on firm grnd and a sharp trk.   34
--   CHEERFUL TIMES [18] 3-9-0 W Woods(5) 50/1: 000-0: Never nearer on seasonal debut:
highly tried in 3 outings in '85: stays 10f and acts on firm ground.   32
63   SILENT RUNNING [23] 3-9-0 G Carter(3) 25/1: F000-0: Never nearer 7th: acts on firm.   00
--   KING JACK [3] 3-9-0 B Thomson 50/1: -0: Sn prom: fin 8th on racecourse debut: half
brother to 3 winners: should be suited by 10f plus.   00
--   ROI DE SOLEIL [8] 3-9-0 R Cochrane 50/1: 000-0: No form in 3 outings in '85: should
be suited by 10f plus: acts on firm.   00
--   Native Image [11] 9-0   --   Arrow Of Light [25] 9-0
--   Final Alma [16] 9-0   --   Gex [10] 9-0   --   Silca Chiavi [4] 9-0
--   Son Of Sparkler [22] 9-0   --   Bully Boy [20] 9-0
--   Celtic Sword [6] 9-0   402 Ikraam [17] 9-0   357 Noble Viking [19] 9-0
402 Soho Sam [15] 9-0   331 Tom Rum [2] 9-0   351 Tremendous Jet [21] 9-0
356 Super Smart [24] 9-0
23 ran   2½,½,4,hd,1,hd,½,½   (S S Niarchos)   H Cecil Newmarket

---

Official Going Given as Good to Soft

536 LICHFIELD MAIDEN AUCT. STAKES 2YO   £822   5f   Yielding 85 +03 Fast

457 SINGING STEVEN [10] (R Hannon) 2-8-5 B Rouse 11/8 fav: 221: 2 b c Balliol - Chebs
Honour (Cheb's Lad): Gained a deserved succes, holding on gamely to score a pillar-to-
post win in quite a fast run 2yo maiden auction stakes at Wolverhampton May 12: cheaply
bought half brother to winning h'capper Minus Man: acts on yld & soft going: front runner
who should be well suited by a sharp trk: likely to prove best at sprint distances.   47
350 TEZ SHIKARI [1] (L Cottrell) 2-8-7 W Carson 8/1: 042: Kept on well, almost getting up
in the last stride: impr sort who should win soon: see 350.   49
364 KALAS IMAGE [7] (G Moore) 2-7-13 A Mackay 20/1: 03: Prom thro'out: impr: sure to
be suited by 6f: see 364.   37
180 TAKE A HINT [3] (M Fetherston Godley) 2-8-5 M Hills 20/1: 44: Well outpcd final 1f.   13
118 PILGRIM PRINCE [6] 2-8-6(VIS)(1ow) M Wigham 33/1: 00: Visored first time: early speed.   09
415 HUGO Z HACKENBUSH [4] 2-8-4 G Carter[3] 12/1: 40: Early speed: btr 415.   02
--   MY ELANE [14] 2-8-5 Paul Eddery 8/1: 0: Fin 9th on debut: 5,000 gns Apr. foal:
speedily bred: half sister to 7f winner Amber Windsor.   00
353 CHEVSKA [13] 2-8-11 G Duffield 10/1: 30: Outpcd final 2f: much btr 353 (soft).   00
425 SNO SURPRISE [5] 2-8-5 M Miller 5/2: 40: Heavily bckd, much btr 425.   00
425 Oconnell Street [12] 8-8   --   Crofters Cline [9] 8-3
--   Chamber Master [11] 8-8   437 Lateral [8] 8-5(BL)
364 Afrabela [15] 8-1   415 Cream And Green [2] 8-4
15 ran   shhd,1,10,2,2   (Dr Steve Bennett)   R Hannon Marlborough, Wilts

537 TAMWORTH SELLING STAKES 2YO   £758   5f   Yielding 85 -37 Slow

181 BROONS ANSWER [3] (K Stone) 2-8-8(BL) G Brown[5] 12/1: 001: 2 br f Junius - Party
Dancer (Be My Guest): Impr by the fitting of bl for the first time when leading close home
under strong press in a 2yo seller at Wolverhampton May 12 (bought in 1,900 gns): acts on
yld going, eff at 5f, sure to be suited by 6f & probably further.   21
354 BINGO QUEEN [1] (J Berry) 2-8-8 Sharron James 9/2: 202: Made much, caught post: clear
of rest and a good effort: should find a seller soon: see 329: acts on yld & soft.   20
421 FLYING SILENTLY [6] (D H Jones) 2-8-8 J Reid 9/4 fav: 033: Well bckd, ev ch: btr 421.   10
415 GLORY GOLD [8] (M Brittain) 2-8-8 K Darley 7/2: 004: Mkt drifter: early ldr: see 415.   00
415 BROOKHEAD GIRL [2] 2-8-8 Paul Eddery 16/1: 00: Dsptd lead 3f: very cheaply bought
sprint bred filly.   00
446 MARK OF GOLD [7] 2-8-8 A Mackay 8/1: 0000: Prom much: appears moderate.   00
--   Great Stands By [4] 8-11   --   Pialuci [9] 8-11
8 ran   hd,5,10,nk,7   (W S Brown)   K Stone Malton, York

538 MIDLAND SPRING HANDICAP 3YO 0-50   £2747   1m   Yielding 85 +19 Fast   [49]

*414 BARLEY BILL [6] (L Cumani) 3-9-12(5ex) S Quane[7] 10/11 fav: 22-1111: 3 ch c Nicholas
Bill - Oatfield (Great Nephew): Very useful, fast impr colt who is unbtn in 4 races this
season: on latest success readily came 10L clear in the final 3f in a fast run 3yo h'cap
at Wolverhampton May 12: earlier won similar h'caps at Thirsk & Nottingham and an amateur
riders event at Haydock: very eff over 1m but bred to be suited by further (half brother to
2m winner High Plains): appears to act on any going & on any trk: must be followed until btn.   67

480 STANFORD VALE [5] (C Nelson) 3-7-13 S Dawson[3] 20/1: 400-022: Came from off the
pace, caught a real tartar here: see 480.   25
352 EMRYS [7] (N Vigors) 3-8-10 P Cook 15/2: 02-1033: Ev ch: best 33 (7f, soft).   34
275 RAFFIA RUN [11] (J Dunlop) 3-8-1 W Carson 10/1: 040-04: No real threat: showed some
ability in only 3 outings last season: sprint bred and may be suited by shorter distances.   22
335 MONSTROSA [3] 3-7-8 P Hill 33/1: 0300-00: No dngr: won a claimer at Leicester early
in '85: best form so far around sprint distances with give in the grnd.   15
352 SPINNAKER LADY [9] 3-7-1 J Carter[1] 33/1: 0020-00: Prom much: close 2nd in a seller
at York at the end of '85, best effort yet: best form over 6f on an easy surface.   09
*316 PROHIBITED [4] 3-9-4(5ex) T Quinn 100/30: 00-110: Well below best: see 316.   00
335 Rupert Brooke [8] 7-7   **231** Disciple [10] 8-4   **461** Supreme Kingdom [1] 9-6
--   Seclusive [12] 9-1   **315** Annabellina [2] 9-1
12 ran   10,1,2½,shhd,5   (G Keller)   L Cumani Newmarket

539 WATLING STREET EBF FILLIES STKS 3YO   £3069   1m 1f Yielding 85 –43 Slow

--   **PRINCESS NAWAAL** [7] (J Dunlop) 3-8-11 W Carson 11/10 fav: 44-1: 3 br f Seattle Slew
Ferly (Traffic Judge): First time out, well bckd & led inside final 3f for a narrow win in a
slowly run 3yo fillies race at Wolverhampton May 12: 4th in useful company on both outings
in '85: stays 9f well: acts on yld & firm.   48
338 DASA QUEEN [5] (W Casey) 3-8-11 J Reid 11/1: 3223-02: Ev ch final 1f: rated 58 on
best form in '85 and was placed on final 4 outings: seems to act on gd & yld: stays at
least 9f.   47
338 WHILE IT LASTS [3] (L Cumani) 3-8-11 Paul Eddery 5/4: -33: Made most: see 338.   42
--   **ALICE PARRY** [6] (J Douglas Home) 3-8-11 P Cook 66/1: -4: Not recover from a slow start
and should benefit from this experience: dam a winner over 10f.   30
250 BET OLIVER [2] 3-8-11 A Mcglone 16/1: -00: No dngr str: quite speedily bred.   10
--   **CULLENS PET** [4] 3-8-11 M Wigham 66/1: 0-0: Soon no dngr.   00
--   Leanders Pearl [1] 8-11
7 ran   ½,2½,5,10,15   (Sheikh Ahmed Al Maktoum)   J Dunlop Arundel, Sussex

540 ATHERSTONE HANDICAP STAKES 3YO+ 0-35   £2175   7f   Yielding 85 –19 Slow   [26]

*424 ARCTIC KEN [14] (C Nelson) 3-8-12(7ex) J Reid 7/2 fav: 040-011: 3 ch c Stanford –
Peggy Dell (Sovereign Gleam): Defied a 7lbs penalty when streaking clear in the final 1f to
win a h'cap at Wolverhampton May 12: comfortably won similar h'cap at Warwick May 5: half
brother to useful juvenile winner Prairie Dunes: very eff at 7f on gd/yld going: can win again   38
174 SANTELLA PAL [16] (L Cottrell) 5-8-5 P Cook 20/1: 0000-02: Made much: only success so
far came at Chepstow in '84: stays 10f.   02
262 BUCKS BOLT [4] (J Berry) 4-8-13 Gay Kelleway[5] 9/1: 000-003: Never closer: see 262.   05
378 REMEMBRANCE [8] (R Peacock) 5-9-5 J Matthias 20/1: 0000-04: Ev ch: ran 16 times in
'85, each placed once and than was successful at Ayr (7f, yld): inconsistent type.   06
--   **CENTRALSPIRES BEST** [9] 3-8-13 M Wigham 20/1: 00440-0: May impr for the outing: maiden
who showed some ability over 6/7f last season: acts on firm.   14
424 ATHLETES WEEK [13] 3-8-2 M Roberts 33/1: 0000-00: Ev ch maiden with only moderate form 00
163 BRANKSOME TOWERS [7] 6-8-2 L Riggio[7] 9/1: 1000-00: Slow start, fin 7th: see 163.   00
369 GODLORD [11] 6-9-3 G Duffield 7/1: 0000-00: Fin 8th: winner at Catterick (2) & Newcastle in the first half of '85, then rather lost his form: a specialist around 7f but
acts on any going: likes Catterick.   00
399 EUCHARIS [12] 4-8-8 A Shoults[5] 10/1: 0000-00: Ev ch, fin 9th: showed only moderate
form last season & remains a maiden.   00
402 HADDON LAD [1] 3-8-5 P Bloomfield 7/1: 000-000: Well bckd, never looked likely to
lose his maiden tag here.   00
--   **CINDYS GOLD** [17] 4-8-10 K Darley 7/1: 20000-0: Nicely bckd seasonal debutant, prom
much: won a selling h'cap at Redcar in '85, sole success to date: stays 6f: best on firm
or gd ground but seems to act on any trk: wore bl when successful.   00
129 Cuddly [2] 9-7   **91** Venture To Reform [6] 8-4
--   Billy Whiteshoes [3] 9-4   --   Little Dimple [15] 8-7
174 Mista Spoof [10] 8-5   --   Mr Panache [5] 9-3
17 ran   7,2,2,hd,3   (R H Mello)   C Nelson Lambourn, Berks

541 RUGELEY HANDICAP STAKES 4YO+ 0-35   £2133   1m 6f Yielding 85 –28 Slow   [34]

358 SUPER GRASS [6] (S Mellor) 7-7-12 R Fox 7/2 fav: 00/0-31: 7 br g Thatch – Pepi Image
(National): Well bckd, leading final furlong holding on gamely in a h'cap at Wolverhampton
May 12: lightly raced on the Flat and last successful at Pontefract in '82: has won several
times over hurdles in the intervening years: suited by 14f & yld or soft going.   11
419 MISS BLACKTHORN [3] (N Vigors) 4-8-8 P Cook 6/1: 001-032: Came from behind to chall
final 1f, just held: can win soon: see 419.   21
485 INTUITION [1] (M Usher) 4-9-6(VIS) J Carter[7] 14/1: 0-10003: Chall. 2f out:
best effort since 69.   29
--   **PERFECT APPROACH** [12] (I Balding) 4-9-5 J Matthias 6/1: 4030-4: Ev ch: placed in
maidens last season but has yet to win: stays at least 12f & acts on soft.   27

358 AMIGO ESTIMADO [2] 4-9-1 I Johnson 20/1: 0000-00: Led str, wknd: maiden who showed
little worthwhile form last season: bred to stay well.   20
319 STANWOOD BOY [14] 4-8-11 M Wigham 6/1: 0100-30: Much btr 319 (2m, soft).   06
462 AVEBURY [4] 4-9-8 N Howe 8/1: 433-300: Dsptd lead after 1m, wknd: twice below 85.   00
358 Touch Of Luck [10] 8-12   263 Gwyn Howard [9] 8-9
358 Wandering Walter [11] 9-4   --   Joist [8] 9-6
366 Frasass [7] 8-3   381 Celtic Quest [13] 7-11
--   Morocco Bound [5] 7-8
14 ran   shhd,3,½,2,8   (Mrs M Michael)   S Mellor Lambourn, Berks

---

542 MAPPERLEY HANDICAP 4YO+ (0-35)   £1562   2m   Yielding 84 +10 Fast   [33]

*185 WIDE BOY [7] (I Balding) 4-9-4 J Matthias 7/1: 3230-11: 4 b g Decoy Boy - Wide Of
The Mark (Gulf Pearl): In good form, led dist and although caught close home was awarded the
race in the Stewards Room, a fast run h'cap at Nottingham May 13: earlier a well bckd winner
of a Beverley maiden: showed good form over hurdles this Winter and was placed several times
on the Flat last term: stays 2m well: acts on firm & soft grnd & on a gall trk: genuine sort
who carries weight well.   32
358 THE MISSISSIPPIAN [4] (M Eckley) 5-8-3 L Riggio(7) 8/1: 00-421D: Led early & again
over 2f out, got up close home though demoted to 2nd: due a change of luck: clearly stays
2m well: see 358 and 208.   17
358 WESSEX [17] (N Tinkler) 4-9-5(bl) Kim Tinkler(7) 8/1: 3-41243: Switched dist, fin
well: hasn't run a bad race this season: see 144.   30
341 CROOK N HONEST [3] (R Holder) 4-8-0 A Proud 14/1: 040-004: Stayed on well over this
longer trip: nicely bckd: maiden who is eff over 10/12f & stays 2m well: suited by some give
in the ground.   07
--   SUPER EXPRESS [20] 5-8-12 R Byrnes(7) 33/1: -3P00-0: Slow start, fin well: has been
running over hurdles: last successful in '84, when winning h'caps at Kempton & Redcar: stays
2m really well: acts on gd & yld grnd.   18
504 GOING BROKE [10] 6-8-3(2ow) R Cochrane 9/1: 42-1300: Kept on late: see 204.   08
358 CAMPUS BOY [6] 5-8-7 S Webster 10/1: 032-000: Nearest fin and a btr effort: last
won in '84, a seller at Pontefract: eff over 10/12f & clearly stays 2m: acts on firm & soft
grnd & on any track.   00
+19 MR QUICK [13] 7-9-9 M Hindley(3) 8/1: -10: Longer trip: abs since 19 (14f, gall trk). 00
--   ISLAND EXILE [15] 4-9-6 T Ives 11/2 FAV: 10344-0: Close up till home turn: btr for race. 00
419 Harlestone Lake [18] 9-3   137 Aribian [1] 8-2(4ow)
375 Security Clearance [5] 10-0   485 Collisto [14] 8-13
--   American Girl [12] 8-10   358 Shipwright [19] 8-7
185 Smack [9] 8-6   --   Beau Navet [8] 7-13   105 Sherpaman [11] 7-7
--   Taxiads [2] 9-2
19 ran   hd,2½,4,½,½   (Lord Porchester)   I Balding Kingsclere, Hants

543 ST ANNS SELLING STAKES 2YO   £898   5f   Yielding 84 -68 Slow

446 SWYNFORD PRINCESS [5] (K Stone) 2-8-8 G Brown(5) 5/4 FAV: -041: 2 b f Raga Navarro -
Comtec Princess (Gulf Pearl): Comfortably justified fav. in a slowly run 2yo seller at
Nottingham May 13, led inside dist and ran on strongly: recently made most when placed behind
Hornblower Girl at Redcar: eff over 5f on gd & yld grnd: seems to act on any trk.   20
446 BENFIELD MORPETH [7] (J Berry) 2-8-11 M Fry 10/1: 002: Ran on well: btr effort from
this cheaply acquired gelding: well suited by this minimum trip: acts on yld grnd.   16
--   FALDWYN [2] (T Bill) 2-8-8(BL) N Carlisle 16/1: 3: Bl on racecourse debut: broke well
and almost made all: cheaply bought filly who will be suited by further in time: acts on
yld grnd: should find a seller.   12
446 FANTINE [1] (N Tinkler) 2-8-8 Kim Tinkler(7) 12/1: 004: Al well there: btr effort:
acts on gd & yld grrnd and on a fair trk.   12
446 GLORIAD [12] 2-8-8 K Darley 10/1: 000: Never nearer after slow start: acts on yld.   12
337 SANDIS GOLD [4] 2-8-8 S Whitworth 10/1: 40: Easy to back: early speed: see 337.   08
--   CARAS QUEST [6] 2-8-8 M Hindley(0) 15/2: 0: Al behind after slow start on debut.   00
367 BRIARQUEEN [8] 2-8-8 R Guest 5/2: 00: Dropped in class though soon outpcd.   00
421 Young Fool [9] 8-11   --   The White Lion [10] 8-8
337 Sparkling Judy [3] 8-8   86 Marthas Pride [11] 8-8
12 ran   2½,shhd,hd,1½,nk   (Qualitair Hotels Ltd)   K Stone Malton, Yorks

544 E.B.F. NETHERFIELD MAIDEN STAKES 2YO   £1409   6f   Yielding 84 -51 Slow

--   CONNAUGHT FLYER [13] (C Tinkler) 2-9-0 M Birch 16/1: 1: 3 gr c Connaught - Foothold
(Hotfoot): Ran on strongly on racecourse debut to lead close home in a slowly run 2yo maiden
at Nottingham May 13: cost 2,700 gns as a yearling: clearly eff over 6f though seems sure to
do btr over longer trips: acts on yld grnd & on a fair trk.   36

236 HUNTERS LEAP [15] (G Moore) 2-9-0 J Lowe 25/1: 002: Led dist, just caught: best effort
to date: cost 5,200 gns: eff over 5/6f on a sharp/easy trk: acts on gd & soft ground.   36
--   PALEFACE [7] (L Piggott) 2-9-0 T Ives 5/1: 3: Nicely bckd debutant: fin well, not
btn far & should find a race on this evidence: will be suited by another furlong: acts on
yielding ground.   35
353 ROUMELI [14] (J Fitzgerald) 2-8-11 M Hills 10/1: 44: Had ev ch: stays 6f: see 353.   28
200 CABALLINE [19] 2-9-0 S Cauthen 10/1: 030: Kept on under press: stays 6f: see 200.   27
--   ARIZONA SUN [22] 2-9-0 A Murray 14/1: 0: At front rank on racecourse debut: cost
8,200 gns and is a half brother to 6 winners: speedily bred colt who acts on yld grnd &
should impr for this experience.   26
450 BALIDUCK [21] 2-8-11 M Wood 9/4 FAV: 30: Disapp fav: prom over ½way though much
btr over 5f in 450 (good): deserves another chance.   00

-- Lightning Laser [12] 8-11	278 Danadn [20] 9-0	
94 George Harry [9] 9-0	-- Balquhidder Boy [3] 9-0	
-- Stelby [8] 9-0	-- Abidjan [5] 9-0	-- Fourwalk [10] 9-0
-- Gold State [4] 9-0	236 Maestroman [18] 9-0	133 Museveni [6] 9-0
332 Penny Lover [2] 9-0	-- Westgale [16] 9-0	376 Benfield Newcastle [11] 8-11
-- Corofin Lass [1] 8-11	-- Mission Bird [17] 8-11	

22 ran   shhd,½,1½,1½,½,hd   (J J Ryan)   C Tinkler Malton, Yorks

545 CLIFTON SPRINT H'CAP (0-35) 3YO   £2561   6f   Yielding 84 –08 Slow   [39]

*447 MADRACO [19] (P Calver) 3-8-6(7ex) M Fry 6/1 Jt FAV: 0404-11: 3 b c Hot Spark -
Aberdeen Lassie (Aberdeen): Uneasy fav though led before ½way and ran on well to win a 3yo
h'cap at Nottingham May 13: earlier made most in a similar race at Redcar: lightly raced
last season, showing promise in maiden races: very eff over 6f on firm & yld grnd: acts on
any trk: suited by forcing tactics: in fine form.   29
447 LOW FLYER [13] (G Oldroyd) 3-8-12 M Hindley(3) 16/1: 04-0302: Finished well:
fine effort: see 198.   32
387 TAYLOR OF SOHAM [25] (D Leslie) 3-8-11 M Rimmer 12/1: 0-23403: Ran on strongly: see 38 29
339 LIBERTON BRAE [22] (J Bethell) 3-8-8 J Reid 16/1: 020-444: Mkt drifter: led early,
not btn far: see 161.   24
454 WINNING FORMAT [26] 3-9-0 B Thomson 25/1: 00-000: Mkt drifter: close up thro'out:
impr effort: speedily bred colt who acts on gd & soft grnd.   22
368 ROBIS [24] 3-8-11 S P Griffiths(5) 25/1: 000-400: Never nearer over this shorter trip.   18
447 WOW WOW WOW [18] 3-8-11 Kim Tinkler(7) 10/1: 10-3100: Never nearer 8th: in good form.   00
447 GOLDEN GUILDER [14] 3-8-10 K Hodgson 6/1 Jt FAV: 0-02120: No show: much btr in 447.   00
175 TOLLYS ALE [21] 3-8-3 W Woods(3) 15/2: 304-430: Speed over ½way: btr in 175.   00
447 NEW EVIDENCE [5] 3-8-11(BL) A Mackay 15/2: 0400-00: Front rank to ½way: bl first time.   00

447 Neds Expressa [4] 8-13		480 Merrymoles [9] 8-13
-- Ardent Partner [6] 8-3		-- Blow The Whistle [16] 9-3
246 Amber Clown [12] 8-5(vis)		340 Willbe Willbe [10] 8-5
-- Miss Primula [23] 9-7	-- Azelly [8] 9-6	454 Gleadhill Park [3] 8-12(BL)
-- Princess Rymer [15] 8-10		339 Metal Woods Rule [20] 8-1
195 Bonny Bright Eyes [7] 7-13		-- Dicks Boy [2] 7-13
451 Valdarno [17] 7-11	195 Rich Bitch [11] 7-7(2oh)	

25 ran   ½,1,½,4,½,½,hd   (B W Hampson)   P Calver Ripon, Yorks

546 SNEINTON STAKES 3YO   £3027   1m   Yielding 84 +03 Fast

--   GEORGIA RIVER [4] (O Douieb) 3-9-0 R Hills 7/2: 3-1: 3 ch c Irish River - Prize Spot
(Little Current): Very useful colt: nicely bckd when quickening well to lead close home in
quite a fast run 3yo stakes at Nottingham May 13: shaped promisingly on sole outing last
term Tanaos in a Newmarket maiden: well bred colt who cost $330,000: very eff over 1m
and should stay further: acts on gd/firm & yld grnd & on any trk: the type to win more races.   62
371 PICEA [1] (M Jarvis) 3-9-0 T Ives 11/4 Jt FAV: 42-42: Ran on well: another gd effort:
sure to get off the mark soon: see 371.   58
+368 AL BASHAAMA [15] (L Cumani) 3-9-2 R Guest 11/4 Jt FAV: -013: Well bckd: led below
dist, hdd near fin and narrowly btn: fine effort in this btr company: stays 1m well: see 368.   60
--   MASTER THAMES [14] (M Stoute) 3-9-0 W R Swinburn 12/1: 2-4: Easy to back on reapp:
made most and kept on well: ran up to Roaring Riva on sole start last Summer: closely related
to several winners, being a full brother to useful performer Miss Thames: stays 1m well: acts
on gd/firm and yld grnd & on a sharp/easy course: sure to find a race.   56
--   SEVERS [3] 3-9-0 S Cauthen 5/1: -0: Showed plenty of promise on his debut and should
improve for this experience: half brother to several winners, incl useful sprinter Apollo
Nine: acts on yld grnd & on an easy course.   50
--   LYPHLAW [17] 3-9-0 B Rouse 25/1: 0-0: Friendless in mkt on reapp: gd late prog after
a slow start: cost 100,000 gns and is bred to stay further than todays trip: acts on gd/firm
& yielding ground.   49

402 Needlewoman [13] 8-11	-- Bon Accueil [11] 9-0	328 Grendel [5] 9-0
-- Choral Park [10] 8-11	438 Mark Eden [9] 9-0	-- Sell It Kilroy [7] 9-0
-- Windbound Lass [12] 8-11		-- Saxelbye Park [8] 9-0
-- Shesingh [2] 8-11		

15 ran   1,shhd,1½,2½,½   (Allen E Paulson)   O Douieb Newmarket

547   WOODTHORPE HANDICAP (0–35)   £1776   1m 2f   Yielding 84 –04 Slow   [34]

*275 SAMANPOUR [16] (R Johnson Houghton) 3-9-3 S Cauthen 7/4 FAV: 001-111: 3 gr c Nishapour –
Sellasia (Dankaro): Comfortably completed his hat trick, quickening well to lead close home
in a h'cap at Nottingham May 13: earlier won similar events at Epsom and Kempton: ended last
season with a maiden success over this C/D: very eff over 10f: acts on any grnd & on any trk:
has a good turn of foot and seems likely to win again.   52
420   WELSH MEDLEY [10] (D Haydn Jones) 4-8-13 J Reid 20/1: 000-032: Tried to make all:
good effort: acts on yld grnd: see 420.   27
*333 STATE BUDGET [3] (W Musson) 5-9-8(7ex) M Wigham 3/1: 1230-13: Ran well under his
penalty: see 333.   33
420   KATES PRIDE [20] (M Eckley) 4-9-6 L Riggio(7) 25/1: 244-004: Ev ch: btr effort:
half brother to several winners and showed promise last season, notably when shhd by Sharp
Noble over this C/D (rated 50): stays 12f: acts on gd & soft grnd: capable of winning
a small race.   27
--   RHEIN COURT [13] 6-8-1 D Williams(7) 33/1: 13000-0: Fin strongly on reapp: last season
won a h'cap at Wolverhampton: eff over 10/11f on gd/firm & soft grnd: suited by an easy trk. 08
--   LOTUS PRINCESS [15] 5-8-11 C Rutter(5) 33/1: 33203-0: Stayed on after a slow start:
btr for race: placed in 4 of her 6 outings last season and in '84 won a selling h'cap at
Newmarket: eff around 1m, stays 10f: acts on firm & soft grnd & on any trk.   17
--   RIMAH [19] 5-10-0(bl) A Murray 8/1: 20340-0: Well bckd: ev ch dist: fin 8th: early last
season was a good 2nd to Mailman in a valuable h'cap at Doncaster though last successful in
'84, at Goodwood: eff over 8/10f on firm & yld grnd: acts on any trk: should do btr next time. 00

--	New Barnet [21] 8-8	--	Forgiving [1] 8-9	*420	Monclare Trophy [23] 9-1(7ex)
333	Shad Rabugk [4] 8-4	--	Nugola [6] 8-6	--	Forever Tingo [7] 8-8
7	Paris Trader [14] 9-8			333	Well Meet Again [8] 9-4
449	Boldera [17] 8-12	--	Clipsall [22] 8-9	449	Sound Work [11] 8-4
207	Cut A Caper [9] 8-4	--	Top Gold [5] 8-2	88	Karamoun [2] 8-1
281	Minus Man [18] 8-1	420	My Son My Son [12] 9-8		

23 ran   ½,1½,2,1,nk,hd   (Aga Khan)   R Johnson Houghton Blewbury, Oxon

Official Going Given as Good

548   EBF ZETLAND STAKES 2YO FILLIES MAIDEN   £3837   5f   Good 42 –27 Slow

383   JAY GEE ELL [1] (E Eldin) 2-8-11 A Mackay 4/1: 31: 2 ch f Vaigly Great – Calarette
(Caliban): Useful, impr filly: led from the stalls, staying on well under press in a fillies
maiden at York May 13: cheaply acquired half sister to a minor 5f winner: eff at 5f, should
stay 6f: acts on gd grnd & a stiff trk: can continue to impr.   52
383   MINSTRELLA [6] (C Nelson) 2-8-11 J Reid 15/8 FAV: 42: Again well bckd: sn 2nd and ev ch:
4L clear 3rd: ran well: see 383 should find a small maiden soon.   45
--   GLOW AGAIN [4] (J Etherington) 2-8-11 M Wood 12/1: 3: Stayed on well final 1f on
racecourse debut and impr likely: half sister to the versatile The Small Miracle: should stay
further than 5f: acts on gd grnd.   36
450   MINIZEN LASS [5] (M Brittain) 2-8-11 K Darley 14/1: 04: Sn prom: on the up grade:
cost only 2,500 gns: should stay further than 5f: acts on gd ground.   35
--   CASHEL VIEW [7] 2-8-11 W R Swinburn 15/2: 0: No threat, but given a tender introduction
to racing and should impr: half sister to winning 2yos Oh Boyar and Rainbow Vision: should be
suited by further than 5f: acts on gd grnd & should do btr next time.   23
--   INDIRAJI [2] 2-8-11 S Cauthen 3/1: 0: Slow start and no show on debut: cost 52,000 gns
and should do much btr than this.   21
--   Mazurkanova [8] 8-11   -- Bold Event [3] 8-11
8 ran   3,4,hd,7,hd   (Barry Linford)   E Eldin Newmarket

549   BBA MIDDLETON STAKES 3YO FILLIES   £3603   1m 2f   Good 42 –48 Slow

--   GULL NOOK [4] (J Dunlop) 3-8-4 Pat Eddery 3/1 FAV: -1: 3 b f Mill Reef – Bempton
(Blakeney): Prom filly: made a winning racecourse debut, led well over 1f out and readily
drew clear in a slow run 3yo fillies stakes at York May 13: sister to fair 12f winner Primose
Valley: eff at 10f, will be well suited by 12f plus: acts on gd grnd & a gall trkk: should
win more races.   58
209   TRANSCENDENCE [9] (B Hanbury) 3-8-7 G Baxter 7/1: -02: Kept on well under press
and stayed this 10½f trip well: stoutly bred filly who should be suited by 12f: acts on
gd ground & a gall trk and should find a maiden.   47
--   HUSNAH [5] (L Cumani) 3-8-7 R Guest 10/3: 02-3: Easy to back on seasonal debut:
al there: on final outing in '85 was a gd 2nd to Chernicherva in a fillies maiden at Goodwood
half sister to 4 winners: stays 10f: acts on gd & firm grnd & on any trk: should do btr next time. 46

359 QUEENS VISIT [3] (P Walwyn) 3-8-7 Paul Eddery 8/1: -404: Set slow pace over 1m:
stays 10f: acts on gd & soft grnd & a gall trk: see 260.   46
315 VERONICA ANN [7] 3-8-7 J Reid 14/1: -00: With leader str: on the up grade and stays
10f: acts on gd grnd and a gall trk: see 46.   46
--   DUWANTO [2] 3-8-4 M Hills 10/1: -0: Never nearer, should impr: sister to winning 2yo
Dewanadance: acts on gd ground.   41
--   SHINY KAY [1] 3-8-4 J Lowe 33/1: -0: Stayed on: fair racecourse debut: half sister to
useful 1m/10f K-Battery & should impr: acts on gd grnd.   00
213 ZUMURRUDAH [8] 3-8-7 A Murray 5/1: -00: Mkt drifter: no threat: half sister to 3
winners, incl the smart Awaasif.   00
--   SUBLIME MIME [6] 3-8-4 A Geran(7) 25/1: -0: No show.   00
9 ran   5,nk,shhd,hd,1   (Lord Halifax)   J Dunlop Arundel, Sussex

550 DAVID DIXON SPRINT TROPHY HCAP 0-75   £9630   5f   Good 42 +18 Fast   [65]

477 PHILIP [6] (N Tinkler) 4-8-4(bl) Pat Eddery 10/1: 0-00031: 4 b g Kala Shikari -
Canteen Katie (King's Troop): Useful sprinter, led over 1f out and qcknd right away for an
impressive win in a fast run h'cap at York May 13: in '85 won 3yo h'caps at Doncaster,
Haydock & Thirsk: in '84 won at Hamilton: equally eff over 5/6f: acts on firm & soft grnd &
on any trk: should go in again.   56
428 CREE BAY [7] (J Spearing) 7-8-4(bl) W Carson 9/1: 040-332: Stayed on under press:
consistent: see 327.   46
-408 CLANTIME [10] (R Whitaker) 5-8-6 D Mckeown 9/2 Jt.FAV: 00-0223: Made much: kept on:
good effort, but btr 208 (firm): see 272.   48
-428 BOLLIN EMILY [12] (M H Easterby) 5-8-5 M Birch 9/2 Jt.FAV: 314-024: Sn prom: in
good form: see 428.   45
327 KELLYS ROYALE [8] 4-8-9 I Johnson 20/1: 000-000: Al there: btr effort: won this
race in '85: in '84 won at Sandown & Windsor: very eff at 5f on firm & gd/yld: acts on any
trk: best when up with the pace.   47
327 LOCHTILLUM [13] 7-8-5 R Cochrane 10/1: 0100-00: Switched 2f out: nearest fin:
should run well next time: see 327.   42
272 ARDROX LAD [11] 6-9-6 N Adams 20/1: 000-000: No threat in 7th: in gd form in the
first half of last season, winning h'caps at Sandown, Goodwood & Haydock (first time out):
in '84 won at York & Haydock: eff at 5/6f: acts on any going & on any grnd: genuine.   00
272 HILTON BROWN [15] 5-9-3 P Cook 11/2: 00-3130: Best 272, 76.   00
443 TRUE NORA [1] 3-8-7 J Reid 8/1: 1110-00: Early speed: much btr 443 (sharp).   00
327 ALL AGREED [5] 5-8-6 W R Swinburn 10/1: 0204-00: No show: in '85 won at Beverley &
Sandown: in '83 won twice: eff over 5/6f: likes a stiff trk: acts on any grnd, but seems
suited by good & firm.   00
412 Stoneydale [2] 7-7(1oh)   441 Mendick Adventure [9] 7-7(4oh)
--   China Gold [3] 8-0(4ow)   --   Yani [14] 7-7(30oh)
408 Dublin Lad [4] 9-8
15 ran   4,hd,¾,1,1   (D Marley)   N Tinkler Malton, Yorks

551 GR 3 TATTERSALLS MUSIDORA STKS 3YO F   £36105   1m 2f Good 42 -03 Slow

264 REJUVENATE [5] (B Hills) 3-8-11 B Thomson 9/2: -31: 3 b f Ile De Bourbon - Miss
Petard (Petingo): Smart, fast impr filly: led over 1f out, holding on well in Gr.3 Musidora
Stakes at York May 13: first time out was unlucky in running when 3rd to Mona Lisa in a
Listed race at Epsom: half sister to several winners: eff at 10f & should be suited by 12f:
acts on gd & soft grnd & on any trk: sure to win more races.   80
373 ALA MAHLIK [2] (F Durr) 3-8-11 G Starkey 11/4: 11-342: Held up to get the trip and
made up a tremendous amount of grnd in the str to be beaten only a nk: in fine form and
stays 10½f: may get 12f and is being aimed for the Oaks: see 373, 214.   79
--   COLORSPIN [4] (M Stoute) 3-8-11 S Cauthen 5/1: 11-3: Wk in mkt on seasonal debut:
could not quicken over 2f out but stayed on really well in the closing stages: btr for race
and should be winning soon: smart 2yo in '85 winning both starts, a maiden at Nottingham and
a fast run Listed race at Newbury: very well bred, being a half sister to Rappa Tap Tap and
Bella Colora: eff at 10f, should be suited by 12f: acts on gd grnd & a gall trk.   76
372 SANTIKI [7] (M Stoute) 3-8-11 W R Swinburn 5/2 FAV: 3-24: Heavily bckd: made much:
another good effort & must win soon: see 372.   74
*250 ARGON LASER [3] 3-8-11 Pat Eddery 11/2: -10: Stays 10f: acts on gd & soft: see 250.   62
372 THREE TIMES A LADY [6] 3-8-11 P Cook 33/1: -000: Ev ch str: not disgraced in this
very good company: on the up grade: half sister to 12f winner Saba Nejd.   51
264 KICK THE HABIT [1] 3-8-11 P Robinson 25/1: 0-00: Prom 1m.   00
7 ran   nk,2,¾,5,4   (K Abdulla)   B Hills Lambourn, Berks

552 LAMBSON STAKES 3YO   £3232   1m 6f Good 42 -12 Slow

+381 MUBAARIS [3] (P Walwyn) 3-8-13 Paul Eddery 10/1: 3-111: 3 ch c Hello Gorgeous -
Aloft (High Top): Very useful, impr colt: cleverly ridden to lead well inside the final 1f
and hold on by a shhd in a 3yo stakes at York May 13: last time out scraped home at Carlisle:
first time out won at Newmarket: eff at 12f, stays 14f well: acts on gd/firm & yld grnd and
a stiff trk: seems best when held up for a late chall.   63

•347 ROSEDALE USA [4] (J Dunlop) 3-8-10 Pat Eddery 13/8 : --2-212: Heavily bckd: led 2f
out and ran on gamely under press: still impr: stays 14f & should win more races: see 347.   59
•409 HEIGHLAD [5] (O Douieb) 3-8-13 W R Swinburn 5/4 FAV: -13: Made much: btr 409 (12f).   50
347 DUNCAN IDAHO [1] (R Johnson Houghton) 3-8-7 J Reid 15/2: -034: Led early: stiff task:
see 347, 231.   42
•357 MILTESCENS [2] 3-8-10 D Nicholls 25/1: 0033-10: Difficult task: see 357 (10f).   45
5 ran   shhd,8,1½,hd   (Hamdan Al-Maktoum)   P Walwyn Lambourn, Berks

553   SLEDMERE STAKES HCAP 3YO 0-60   £3246   1m 1f Good 42 -06 Slow   [65]

•259 LONDON BUS [7] (J Watts) 3-7-12 W Carson 7/2: 00-11: 3 b c London Bells - Miss Robust
(Busted): In fine form, made almost all, staying on gamely under press in a 3yo h'cap at
York May 13: first time out made all in a maiden at Edinburgh: lightly raced in '85: half
brother to 3 winners: eff at 1m/9f: acts on gd & yld & on any trk: does well with forcing
tactics and is an impr sort.   48
•258 TAYLORMADE BOY [8] (D Smith) 3-7-7(4oh) L Charnock 10/1: 330-312: Ev ch str: in
fine form: acts on gd & heavy grnd: should find a h'cap:see 258.   40
15 ANDARTIS [2] (Lord J Fitzgerald) 3-9-7 R Hills 14/1: 1002-03: Stayed on well and
nearest fin: should do btr next time: eff at 9f and should be suited by 10f: see 15.   65
444 FORCELLO [6] (S Norton) 3-7-7(2oh) J Lowe 3/1: 342-124: Well bckd, but btr 444 (sharp trk) 37
-- SURPRISE CALL [5] 3-7-12 G Carter(3) 12/1: 310-0: Wknd over 1f out on seasonal debut:
in '85 won a maiden auction at Doncaster: should be suited by 9f plus: acts on gd & firm
grnd & a gall trk.   32
386 AUCTION FEVER [4] 3-8-6 B Thomson 5/2 FAV: 0333-20: Well bckd: much btr 386 (1m).   39
183 OPTIMISM FLAMED [10] 3-7-11 M Roberts 17/2: 033-20: Mkt drifter: much btr 183 (1m yld). 00
-- Charlton Kings [1] 8-11   -- Linton Springtime [9] 7-9
451 Honest Toil [3] 7-7(10oh)
10 ran   1½,1½,hd,6,1   (Sheikh Mohammed)   J Watts Richmond, Yorks

LONGCHAMP   Thursday May 8th   Right Hand, Galloping track.

Official Going Given as Soft

554   PRIX DU SURESNES (LISTED RACE) 3YO   £9200   1m 2f Soft .

•303 PRADIER (P Biancone) 3-8-12 E Legrix 1: 11: 3 b c Lightning - Plencia (Le Haar)
Smart colt: unbeaten in 3 races: showed courage, leading 5 out but struggled to win listed
race at Longchamp May 8: earlier won at Longchamp and St Cloud: stays 10f and will be suited
by 12f: acts well on soft and heavy, yet to run on firm: half brother to top class Pawneese:
can continue to improve but is reported uncertain to come to Epsom.   81
-- ALTAYAN (France) 3-8-9 Y Saint Martin 1: -2: Led 1f out, just failed to hold on: fine
effort: stays 10f well and acts on soft.   77
302 UN DESPERADO (France) 3-8-9 A Gibert 1: 12-03: Dispd ld straight: ran well.   73
-- ELESKIRT (France) 3-8-6 G W Moore 1: -4: -   62
4 ran   hd,3,5.   (D Wildenstein)   P Biancone France.

CAPPANNELLE   Sunday May 11th   -

Official Going Given as Good

555   GROUP 1 DERBY ITALIANO 3YO   £62040   1m 4f Good .

411 TOMMY WAY (J Dunlop) 3-9-2 W Carson 1: -021-31: 3 b c Thatch - Tilia Very useful
improving colt: led 1f out, holding on by nk in Gr 1 Derby Italiano at Cappannelle May 11:
in '85 was easy 8L winner of maiden at Haydock: eff at 10f, stays 12f well: acts on gd/fm
and soft ground and on any track: should win more races: cleverly placed by trainer.   71
297 BE MY MASTER (Italy) 3-9-2 G Dettori 1: -32: Fin well: just beaten: good effort:
clearly well suited by 12f and acts on good and heavy: see 297.   70
384 SHIBIL (M Stoute) 3-9-2 W R Swinburn 1: 33-443: Nt btn far and ran well: stays 12f
well: see 384, 224: should soon pick up a race.   68
-- TONY BIN (Italy) 3-9-2 L Picuciello 1: 3-4: -   67
-- NORTH VERDICT 3-9-2 T Ives 1: 210-0: Gd seasonal debut: won at York in '85 and fin
good 6th to Bakharoff in Gr 1 Futurity Stks at Doncaster: half brother to sev winners: stays
12f: acts on good and yielding and should do well this season.   66
411 LOCAL HERBERT 3-9-2 Pat Eddery 1: 02-420: Fin 8th: beat winner in 411: see 231.   60
6 ran   nk,1¾,1,¾.   (Scuderia Erasec)   J Dunlop Arundel, Sussex.

556   GROUP 3 PREMIO SPRING 3YO C & G   £13349   1m   Good .

-- SARATOGA SPRING (L D'auria) 3-8-7 M Planard 1: -1: 3 b c Miami Spring - Twaddle 11
Very useful Italian colt: made all, gamely in Gr 3 race at Capannelle May 11: in fine form
lately: eff at 1m on good ground with forcing tactics.   70
386 DANCING EAGLE (M Jarvis) 3-8-7 T Ives 1: 01-32: Just btn: excellent effort: only
rated 42 officially: should be winning soon: see 386.   68

-- LORD HONING (Italy) 3-8-7 G Dettori 1: 4-3: Nt btn far.   66
286 LUQMAN (P Walwyn) 3-8-7 Paul Eddery 1: 4114-04: Chall 2 out: may benefit from a
shorter trip: see 286.   65
286 SOUTH THATCH 3-8-11 S Dettori 1: -40: Best 286 (yld).   00
5 ran   nose,1½,nk.   (Scuderia Scorpion)   L D'auria Italy.

557 ` GROUP 2 PREMIO MELTON 3YO+   £15388   6f   Good .

-- TINTEROSSE (G Benetti) 3-8-8 A Di Nardo 1: -1: 3 b c Kemare - Dressed in Red Smart
Italian colt: dispd lead all way and held on gamely in Gr 2 event at Capannelle May 11:
speedy sort who is very eff over 6f: acts on good.   80
-- NACACYTE (Italy) 4-9-3 T Ives 1: 42-2: Al prom: just btn: eff at 5/6f on gd & yld.   75
+245 POWDER KEG (J Hindley) 4-9-3 M Hills 1: 1113-13: Just denied in a close finish:
most consistent: see 245.   75
-- SESIN (Italy) 5-9-3 G Dettori 1: -1-4: -   69
4 ran   nk,shhd,2   (Scuderia Fert)   G Benetti Italy.

LEOPARDSTOWN   Monda May 12th   Left Hand Galloping Track.

Official Going Given as Good

558 SANDY COVE E.B.F. FILLIES MAIDEN 2YO   £2072   6f   Good .

-- POLONIA [13] (J Bolger) 2-9-0 D Gillespie 11/4 FAV: 1: 2 b f Danzig - Moss Very promising
Irish filly: first time out, led 2f out and sprinted clear for an impressive win in 2yo
fillies maiden at Leopardstown May 12: eff at 6f and should stay further: should win again.   65
-- INDEXS [5] (D Weld) 2-9-0 M J Kinane 4/1: 2: No chance with winner but this well
bred filly by Storm Bird ran a pleasing debut.   51
-- SABLE LAKE [3] (E O'grady) 2-9-0 S Craine 12/1: 3: Half sister to numerous winners.   48
-- EMPERORS FAN [6] (Ireland) 2-9-0 D Manning(3) 7/1: 4: -   41
4 ran   3,1,2½.   (H de Kwiatkowski)   J Bolger Ireland

LEOPARDSTOWN   Saturday May 10th   Left Hand Galloping Track.

Official Going Given as Good to Yielding

559 GROUP 2 DERRINSTOWN STUD DERBY TRIAL   £29200   1m 2f Good/Yld .

407 TOCA MADERA (L Browne) 3-9-0 C Roche 9/4: -11-101: 3 b c Taufan - Genesis Fin well
to get up close home by hd in Gr 2 Derby Trial at Leopardstown May 10: first time out was
impressive winner of Gr 3 race at Phoenix Park: below his best when 9th in the 2,000 Guineas:
unbtn 2yo winning Gr 3 race at Leopardstown and first time out at Phoenix Park: eff at 1m
and stays 10f well: acts on any going and should win more race.   78
-- WISE COUNCILLOR (M V O'brien) 3-8-11 Pat Eddery 4/5 FAV: -12: Hvly backed, dictated
a slow pace: qknd on home turn but unable to get clear and just caught: good effort: first
time out was easy winner of maiden at the Curragh: acts on good and soft: stays 10f.   74
-- INISHEER (D Weld) 3-8-11 M J Kinane 12/1: 1413-23: Ran on well: good effort: in '85
won over 7f at Limerick: well suited by 10f: acts on gd/fm and yldg.   70
-- SIMPLON (M Grassick) 3-8-6 D Parnell 20/1: -0-04: -   64
-- BANK STEP 3-8-11 S Craine 33/1: -4-10: First time out winner at Phoenix P(9f hvy).   65
395 AIR DISPLAY 3-8-11 G Curran 12/1: 0-12230: Stays 10f but better 395 (7f).   65
289 Northern Date 8-11   -- Full Flow 8-11   -- Sweet Move 8-3
9 ran   hd,2½,hd,2,shd.   (Mrs D Threadwell)   L Browne Ireland

560 WASSL RACE 3YO FILLIES   £6175   1m   Good/Yld .

-- LAKE CHAMPLAIN [8] (D Weld) 3-8-9 M J Kinane 5/4 FAV: -2-21: 3 b f Kings lake -
Sensibility Very useful Irish filly: wl bkd and led final 1f, cmftbly in valuable fillies
race at Leopardstown May 10: eff at 1m, may stay further: acts on firm and soft: improving.   68
-- LOUD APPLAUSE [7] (J Oxx) 3-8-9 D Hogan 8/1: -22: Fine effort: must win maiden soon.   62
269 CALAMETTA [5] (D Hughes) 3-8-9 S Craine 6/1: 22-30D3: Consistent: stays 1m: see 269.   60
394 LADY LOIRE [1] (C Collins) 3-9-3 P Shanahan 6/1: 11-1244: In gd form: 65
-- GAILY GAILY [4] 3-9-5 D Parnell 14/1: --141-0: Good seasonal debut: very useful 2yo
winning Gr 2 race at Phoenix Park and stks race at Navan: stays 1m: acts on gd/fm & yldg.   66
-- ARTHURS GIRL [6] 3-8-9 M T Browne 40/1: -00: -   54
-- River Lullaby 0 8-9   -- Christabelle 0 8-9
8 ran   3,¾,1½,nk,1.   (Mrs B Firestone)   D Weld Ireland.

SAINT CLOUD   Saturday May 10th   Left hand track

Official Going Given as Soft

561   GROUP 3 PRIX CLEOPATRE 3YO FILLIES   £17134   1m 2f   Soft .

300   EL FABULOUS [2] (C Head) 3-8-7 G W Moore 1: --01-41: 3 ch f Fabulous Dancer - El Mina
Led 1 out, gamely, in Gr 3 event at St Cloud May 10: wl suited by 10f, may stay 12f: acts
on soft ground: entered in the Oaks but not a certain runner.   73
97   TOP AND LADY [4] (P Biancone) 3-8-7 E Legrix 1: --1-122: Ran on well and just btn:
in fine form: see 97.   72
--   RESTIVER [8] (F Boutin) 3-8-11 F Head 1: --411-3: Tried to make all and nt btn far on
seasonal debut: in '85 won Gr 3 race at Longchamp: stays 10f: acts on firm and soft.   75
264   LAND OF IVORY [7] (I Balding) 3-8-7 C Asmussen 1: 404-1D4: Not disgraced: possibly
stays 10f but might prove best around 1m: see 264.   66
4 ran   shhd,½,3.   (Ecurie Aland)   C Head France

LONGCHAMP   Sunday May 11th   Right Hand Galloping Track

Official Going Given as Yielding

562   GROUP 2 PRIX HOCQUART 3YO   £30712   1m 4f   Good/Soft .

*301   BERING (C Head) 3-9-2 G W Moore 1: -31-11: 3 ch c Arctic tern - Beaune Smart French
colt: unbeaten last 3 races: led 2 out, very easily in Gr 2 Prix Hoquart at Longchamp
May 11: first time out, ready winner of gr 2 Prix Noailles again at Longchamp: very eff at 11
-12f: acts on yldg and heavy: likely to go for Prix du Jockey Club and will be hard to beat. 83
301   POINT DARTOIS (B Secly) 3-9-2 J L Kessas 1: -31-22: No chance with winner: but is
in good form: stays 12f and acts on yld and heavy.   70
303   SILVER BAND (J Chevigny) 3-9-2 C Asmussen 1: -1-03: -   64
289   CLOVIO (P Biancone) 3-9-2 E Legrix 1: -1-24: Better 289 (hvy).   61
4 ran   2,4,2.   (MMe A Head)   C Head France

563   GROUP 3 PRIX DE SAINT GEORGES 3YO   £17194   5f   Good/Soft .

--   LAST TYCOON [9] (R Collet) 3-8-13 A Lequeux 1: --10-01: 3 b c Try My Best - Mill
Princess   Smart French colt: fin very well to get up close home in Gr 3 race at Longchamp
May 11: in '85 won Gr 3 race at Longchamp and later was fine 5th in the Prix L'Abbaye: very
eff at 5f: acts on gd/fm and yldg.   72
--   BATAVE [3] (P Biancone) 4-9-3 E Legrix 1: --11-12: Ran on well: just btn: fine effort:
formerly trained by H Cecil, winning at Kempton in '85: smart 2yo: very eff over 5/6f:
acts on gd/fm and yielding: should benefit from a longer trip.   74
408   STORM WARNING [5] (W Hastings Bass) 4-9-1 B Thomson 1: 4310-03: Ran fine race, nearly
made all, just caught: back to her best: in 85 won listed race at Doncaster and also won at
Nottingham: very eff at 5f on firm and yldg: genuine filly who should win a Gr 3 race.   71
--   RISK FACTOR [1] (J Fellows) 3-8-8 G W Moore 1: -10-04: -   52
4 ran   hd,nk,5.   (R Strauss)   R Collet France.

BRIGHTON   Wednesday May 14th   Left Hand, Sharpish, Undualting track.

564   GORING SELLING STAKES   £820   8f   Good/Firm 35 -21 Slow

522   COMEDY PRINCE [4] (R Simpson) 3-8-7 S Whitworth 15/8 FAV: 000-001: 3 b g Comedy Prince
- Get Involved (Shiny Tenth) Made a quick reapp. over a shorter trip and comftbly led 2f out
in a seller at Brighton May 14, v wl bkd: (bght in 4,200gns): lightly raced last year:
effective over 7/8f and should stay further: seems suited by fast ground and sharpish track. 24
399   THE UTE [6] (L Bower) 3-8-7(bl) N Adams 5/1: 0200-02: Dropped to sell company: ev ch:
twice runner up in similar races last year, both on this sharp course: stays 9f: suited by
good or faster ground.   14
335   MY DERYA [5] (M Tompkins) 3-8-7 (bl) R Cochrane 4/1: -003403: Better effort: stays 1m
on a sharp track: acts on gd/fm and soft: see 103.   10
--   SOLSTICE BELL [2] (R Voorspuy) 4-9-6 (bl) M Roberts 14/1: 00440-4: Better for race: placed
sev times in similar company last year where usually up with the pace: eff at 9f on fast going
and suited by a sharpish track.   00
495   TAME DUCHESS [7] 4-9-6 M Wigham 5/1: 0-04000: No threat after slow start: see 119.   00
176   ELEPHANT BOY [3] 4-9-9 J Adams(7) 14/1: -00: Dropped to sell company: no show.   00
335   The Sportsman [1] 8-7   --   Persian Person [8] 9-6
346   Sweet Fool [10] 8-4   --   Care In The Air [11] 8-4(VIS)
10ran4,2,6,4,3   (F Rujas)   R Simpson Upper Lambourn, Berks.

565   EBF DITCHLING MAIDEN 2YO STAKES   £1781   5f   Good/Firm 35 -33 Slow

34   QUITE SO [6] (W Jarvis) 2-8-11 R Cochrane 12/1: -01: 2 br f Mansingh - Chiquitita
(Reliance 11) Got through to lead close home in a close finish in 2yo maiden at Brighton May
14: speedily bred filly: cost 2,200gns as yearling: acts on gd/fm and soft: improving type.   46
--   FLEET FACT [4] (B Hills) 2-8-11 G Starkey 11/2: 2: Mkt drifter on debut: just btn
despite a slow start: half sister to a couple of winners and should be suited by further than
5f: acts on gd/fm and on a sharpish track: should find a similar race.   44
212   FRENCH TUITION [2] (R Hannon) 2-9-0 A Mcglone 3/1: 233: Led over ½way: narrowly
btn: seems well suited by sharp track: acts on gd/fm and yldg: see 187: consistent.   46
405   DUTCH COURAGE [8] (D Morley) 2-9-0 B Rouse 11/8 FAV: 44: Hvly bkd, led after ½way, just
btn: acts on fast ground: will be suited by further: see 405.   46
--   INTHAR [7] 2-9-0 P Tulk 8/1: 0: Slow start on debut: better for experience: cost
60,000gns: may do better on more galloping track: acts on gd/fm.   41
497   SEGOVIAN [1] 2-9-0 D Mckay 8/1: 200: Led 3f: acts on gd/fm: see 230.   35
118   Minobee [3] 8-11
7 ran   ½,hd,shhd,2,4.   (Mrs Nigel Farmer)   W Jarvis Newmarket.

566   ALDRINGTON H'CAP 0-50   £2674   7f   Good/Firm 35 -05 Slow   [44]

499   KING OF SPEED [13] (B Wise) 7-8-4 L Riggio(7) 6/1: 00-1041: 7 b h Blue Cashmere -
Celeste (Sing Sing) Came strong and late to win h'cap at Brighton May 14: won first time out
at Lingfield: ran consistently last year again winning here: also placed many times: seems
best over 7f on a sharp track though does stay 10f: acts on firm and soft.   28
361   KORYPHEOS [11] (S Dow) 7-9-8 W Ryan 8/1: 000-002: Led 1 out, just caught: dropped in
class and ran well under top weight: last year won fast run h'cap at Newmarket and in '84 won
twice on that stiff track, and at Salisbury: suited by 7/8f on any ground or track.   46
499   GOLDEN BEAU [5] (D Morley) 4-8-4 B Rouse 5/1: 040-033: Another good effort: see 281   27
262   FEI LOONG [8] (E Eldin) 5-8-8 G King(7) 9/2 FAV: 400-044: Dispd ld all way: see 262   21
--   BOND DEALER [10] 9-8-5 M Wigham 16/1: 03200-0: Late prog: will do better next time: last
won in '84, an app. h'cap at Epsom: goes well on this sharp track: eff at 1m on any going.   17
453   GURTEEN BOY [7] 4-9-3 A Mcglone 7/1: 0001-00: Ev ch dist: see 453.   28
7   DICKS FOLLY [3] 7-8-4 N Howe 9/1: 1224-00: Nvr dangerous 8th after fair absence:
first time out winner over 10f at Brighton last year: best on a sound surface, but acts on sft   00
453   SAFE CUSTODY [4] 4-8-13 G Starkey 10/1: 0100-00: Made most: made all when won h'cap at
Haydock in '85: suited by 6/7f but shld stay 1m: acts on gd & fm and any track.   00
374   MAFTIR [9] 4-8-6 R Cochrane 9/1: 00-0000: Never a factor: see 260.   00
401   BAY PRESTO [6] 4-9-1(bl) S Whitworth 9/1: 200-300: No threat over longer trip: see172   00
176   Pett Velero [1] 7-7(9oh)   343   Nicanic [2] 7-7(10oh)
355   James De Coombe [12] 7-8
13 ran   shd,½,5,nk,½,¾   (John Wilberforce)   B Wise Polegate, Sussex.

567   DAVIES & TATE ANNIVERSARY STAKES 3YO   £2603   6f   Good/Firm 35 +03 Fast

*203 TUSSAC [1] (H Cecil) 3-9-8 W Ryan 1/2 FAV: 112-11: 3 b c Miswaki - Cast The Die
(Olden Times) Smart colt: has won 4 of his 5 races: missed the break but came smoothly
through final 1f to win going away in minor event at Brighton May 14: easy winner at Folkestone: won at Warwick and Newmarket in '85: later just pipped by Hotbee in Gr 3 Molecomb Stks
at Goodwood: eff at 5/6f and will stay further: acts on firm & soft grnd & on any trk:
sure to win better races this season-   70+
228   TUFUH [6] (A Stewart) 3-9-8 M Roberts 16/1: 1140-02: Sn held a clear lead, caught
near fin though still a fine effort: last season won a maiden at Folkestone and a fast run
nursery at Windsor: half brother to several winners: well suited by 6f & should stay further:
acts on firm & yld grnd and is well suited by a sharp trk: sure to win a race soon.   65
500   NORTHERN IMPULSE [4] (B Gubby) 3-9-0 M Wigham 50/1: -03: Kept on well: rank outsider today and showed considerable impr here: speedily bred colt who acts on gd/firm grnd
and on a sharpish course: will find a race.   53
387   QUARRYVILLE [3] (K Brassey) 3-9-8 G Duffield 4/1: 13-0044: Ran on too late: see 387.   55
--   FORLIS FAIR [2] 3-8-11 R Machado 12/1: -0: Easy to back on debut: stayed on after
a slow start: half sister to several winners, incl English & Irish Oaks heroine Fair Salinia:
will be suited by a more testing trip: acts on fast grnd: seems sure to impr.   42
--   ANN AESTHETIC [5] 3-9-2 A Mcglone 16/1: 0014-0: Btr for race: won a fillies maiden
at Lingfield last season and subsq. placed behind Northern Eternity in a valuable stakes race
at Newbury: very eff over 6f on gd ground: acts on any trk.   47
217   Pointed Lady [8] 8-11   74   Bakers Dough [7] 9-5
8 ran   ½,1½,2½,½,shhd   (Peter Burrell)   H Cecil Newmarket

568 GORING SELLING STAKES   £816   8f   Good/Firm 35 -24 Slow

481 SUPERFROST [4] (J Fox) 4-9-6 B Crossley 9/4 FAV: 30-0001: 4 ch f Tickled Pink –
Joshua's Daughter (Joshua): Dropped to selling company and was well bckd when leading below
dist, comfortably in a modest race at Brighton May 14 (bought in 1,650gns).
rated 37 last year: well suited by 1m: acts on gd/firm & yld grnd and on any trk.   22
177 ELMCOTE LAD [8] (C Holmes) 4-9-9 J Williams 20/1: 0000-02: Mkt drifter: led after
½way, no chance with winner though clear of rem: best effort for sometime: eff over 1m on
fast ground.   10
426 DORADE [6] (D Morley) 3-8-7 G Duffield 10/3: 000-003: Led over ½way: btr in 426 (7f).   00
177 LETOILE DU PALAIS [3] (B Stevens) 3-8-4(bl) R Carter(4) 12/1: 040-04: Nearest fin and
seems suited by this longer trip: lightly raced last season, showing no worthwhile form:
acts on gd & firm grnd.   00
140 GREY DRAGON [9] 3-8-7(bl) R Curant 8/1: 004-000: Dropped in class: fin well btn.   00
--   NIGHT WALLER [7] 4-9-9 N Dawe 20/1: 00000-0: Mkt drifter: some late prog.   00
276 DYNAMIC BABY [10] 3-8-5(1ow) J Reid 6/1: 000-000: Prom over ½way: fin 9th: see 113.   00
--   EQUIPPED FOR DUTY [2] 4-9-9(VIS) R Cochrane 15/2: 0-400-0: Never dngr 8th: visored today   00
399 Dukeswood [1] 9-6   -- Miracle Tool [5] 9-9(vis)
10 ran   6,8,hd,6,2½   (Bar Equipment & Refrigeration Co Ltd)   J Fox Winterbourne Stoke,

569 MADEIRA HANDICAP 0-60   £2924   12f   Good/Firm 35 +08 Fast   [48]

341 DETROIT SAM [2] (R Akehurst) 5-8-8 G Baxter 7/4 FAV: 000-221: 5 br h Green Dancer –
Tocqueville (Sir Gaylord): Gained a deserved success, regaining lead below dist for a
comfortable win in a fast run h'cap at Brighton May 14: 2nd twice in similar events over
10f here previously this season, and last won in '83 at Lingfield: clearly well suited by
a sharpish, undulating trk: eff over 10f, stays 12f well: acts on gd/firm & heavy ground:
in good form.   38
--   VORACITY [5] (J Winter) 7-9-10 G Starkey 8/1: 0/004-2: Kept on well: gd effort under
top weight on seasonal debut: useful h'capper who was lightly raced last season: in '84 was
most consistent, winning a valuable race at Haydock: in '83 won at Ascot & Newmarket: very
eff over 10/12f on firm & gd grnd: game & genuine sort: acts on any track.   48
176 STARDYN [7] (P Mitchell) 4-7-7(4oh) G Carter(0) 10/1: 00-03: Bckd from 33/1: stayed
on too late though still an impr effort: half sister to useful middle dist winner Southern
Dynasty: lightly raced filly who acts on gd/firm ground & on a sharp course.   16
263 THATCHINGLY [8] (M Bolton) 4-8-3 R Carter(2) 20/1: 300-104: Clear of rem: runs well
here: see 176.   25
349 LONGSTOP [4] 4-8-3 T Williams 6/1: 134-300: Mkt drifter: twice disapp since 179 (10f).   11
202 JANUS [1] 8-8-3 B Rouse 9/2: -40-020: Needs softer grnd: btr in 202.   07
282 HYOKIN [9] 4-7-13(1ow) G Duffield 8/1: 0242-40: Fin 7th: can do btr: see 282.   00
349 TRAFFITANZI [6] 5-7-7(1oh) D Brown 6/1: 30/2-00: Led to ½way: only ran once on the
Flat last season, fin 2nd to Topsoil in a Folkestone seller: stays 12f: acts on firm & yld   00
504 Kiki Star [3] 7-11
9 ran   3,½,½,10,3,shhd   (Mrs S Akehurst)   R Akehurst Epsom, Surrey

570 MARINA STAKES 3YO   £959   10f   Good/Firm 35 +03 Fast

*479 FLEETING AFFAIR [7] (G Harwood) 3-9-3 G Starkey 4/5 FAV: -11: 3 b f Hotfoot – My Own II
(El Relicario): Very useful filly: made steady prog to lead inside dist, pushed out in quite
a fast run 3yo stakes at Brighton May 14: earlier a similarly comfortable winner of a
maiden at Salisbury: half sister to several winners, incl the useful Haul Knight: very eff
over 10f & should stay further: acts on gd/frm & yld grnd & on any trk: should win more races.   56
259 PRINCELY ESTATE [4] (J Winter) 3-9-0 J Reid 6/1: 000-222: Led 2f out, comfortably held
though is impr steadily & should find a race soon: stays 10f on a sharp trk: see 259.   44
234 HALO HATCH [3] (K Brassey) 3-9-0 S Whitworth 9/2: 2203-03: Kept on same pace: showed
plenty of promise when placed in 4 of his 5 starts last term, notably when 3rd to Tyrian
Noble in a Bath nursery (rated 55): eff over 8/10f: well suited by fast grnd & acts on any trk   40
277 OMANIA [11] (R Hannon) 3-8-11 A Mcglone 33/1: 400-44: Made most: on the up grade
and seems to stay 10f on a sharp course: see 277.   31
--   LOBBINO [8] 3-8-11 B Rouse 10/1: 03-0: Mkt drifter on debut: stayed on promisingly and
should do btr next time: half sister to the very useful Lobbit: showed promise in both her
starts last season and should find a small ace: suited by fast grnd & a sharpish trk.   30
357 TENDER TYPE [2] 3-9-0 R Cochrane 50/1: -00: Never reached ldrs after a slow start:
stays 10f on a sharp trk: acts on fast grnd.   31
351 Ministrailis [1] 9-0   409 Turmeric [10] 9-0   316 Cardave [6] 9-0
--   Turn For Thebetter [9] 9-0   422 Rabab [5] 8-11
11 ran   1½,3,4,1,½   (Mrs F Lakin)   G Harwood Pulborough, Sussex

Official Going Given as Good first 4 races: Good to Soft last 2

571   RACE A ROUND YORKSHIRE 2YO STAKES   £3340   6f   Good/Firm 30 +01 Fast

*456   QUEL ESPRIT [8] (M Mccormack) 2-9-3 S Cauthen 11/4 FAV: 12111: 2 b c What A Guest - Les Sylphides (Kashmir II): Very useful, consistent colt: led/dsptd lead all the way, running on well in a valuable 2yo stakes at York May 14: earlier won at Salisbury, Newmarket & Doncaster: cost 10,000 gns: eff at 5f, suited by 6f and may get further: acts on gd/firm & soft grnd and a gall trk: genuine sort who should win more good races.   68

405   GULF KING [15] (P Kelleway) 2-8-11 P Cook 6/1: 02: Ran on well final 1f and was well suited by this 6f trip: should be winning soon: see 405.   60

+304   DEMDERISE [9] (N Tinkler) 2-9-0 T Ives 4/1: 113: Al up there: in fine form: stays 6f: acts on any grnd & on any trk: see 304.   56

--   CHECKPOINT [1] (C Brittain) 2-8-11 Pat Eddery 10/1: 4: Dsptd lead: promising racecourse debut from this full brother to the smart Mr Fluorocarbon: should be suited by further than 6f: acts on gd/firm & should have no trouble finding a maiden.   45

304   GALLIC TIMES [2] 2-9-3 N Carlisle 14/1: 31130: Sn prom: stays 6f: acts on any grnd, but beat winner 146 (soft).   49

61   MARK ANGELO [4] 2-8-11 M Miller 9/1: 20: Sn prom: abs since 61: stays 6f: acts on gd/frm & heavy.   36

--   MIAMI BAY [7] 2-8-11 A Bacon(7) 25/1: 0: Nearest fin on racecourse debut and impr likely: cost I.R. 3,900: half brother to a 2yo winner: acts on gd/firm grnd & should find a maiden in the North.   35

+278   PEATSWOOD SHOOTER [10] 2-9-3 K Darley 8/1: 1110: Prom, wknd: btr 278 (5f, heavy).   00

242 Scottish Fling [13] 8-11		320 Regent Lad [3] 8-11
437 Boy Singer [5] 8-11	-- Rodomont [6] 8-11	-- Stillman [12] 8-11
-- Danum Dancer [14] 8-11		-- Force Majeure [11] 8-11
15 ran ½,2½,3,¾,2½,shhd	(Miss Laura Morgan)	M Mccormack Sparsholt, Oxon

572   GLASGOW STAKES 3YO   £3438   10.5f   Good/Firm 30 -25 Slow

371   KADIAL [3] (R Johnson Houghton) 3-8-10 S Cauthen 4/1: -21: 3 b c Niniski - Khadaeen (Lyphard): Smart, fast impr colt: sn prom and led well over 2f out, readily drawing clear for an impressive win in a valuable 3yo stakes at York May 14: first time out was a fine 2nd to Nino Bibbia in a maiden at Newmarket: half brother to the smart Kalim: eff at 1m/10f, should be suited by 12f: acts on gd/firm grnd & a gall trk & can continue to impr/win more gd races.   74

231   CHAUVE SOURIS [4] (G Wragg) 3-8-10 P Robinson 20/1: 0-02: Stayed on well: very gd effort: eff at 10f & should be suited by 12f: half brother to smart performers Bold Indian and Assemblyman: acts on gd/firm grnd & a gall trk: should be winning soon.   60

342   WASSL REEF [2] (J Dunlop) 3-8-10 W Carson 13/2: 22-23: Ran on well under press: another gd effort: see 342.   59

371   SAKER [3] (L Cumani) 3-8-10 R Guest 7/2 Jt.FAV: -04: Well bckd: ev ch str: on the up grade: stays 10f: see 371.   59

316   PLAXTOL [9] 3-8-10 Pat Eddery 8/1: -00: Made much: gd effort and is impr fast: eff at 10f, should stay 12f: acts on soft: likes gd/firm grnd: should find a maiden.   55

370   VERARDI [7] 3-8-10 T Ives 7/2 Jt.FAV: -30: Much btr 370 (9f).   48

362   SHIP OF STATE [8] 3-8-10 W R Swinburn 15/2: 23-40: No threat: btr 362 (yld/soft).   00

-- Up To Me [1] 8-7	-- Past Glories [5] 8-10	194 Ranelagh [6] 8-10
10 ran 5,nk,shhd,2,4	(H H Aga Khan)	R Johnson Houghton Blewbury, Oxon

573   HOLSTEN PILS LTD H'CAP 0-75   £10035   8f   Good/Firm 30 -01 Slow   [67]

*445   ESQUIRE [2] (B Hills) 4-8-13(5ex) B Thomson 11/2: 010-211: 4 ch c High Line - Monroe (Sir Ivor): Very useful colt who is in fine form: made ev yd for a ready success in a valuable h'cap at York May 14: last time out won a h'cap at Chester: in '85 won a 3yo maiden at Newbury: eff at 1m, stays 10f well: acts on gd/firm & soft grnd & on any trk: seems to do well forcing the pace and should complete the hat trick.   67

344   DORSET COTTAGE [4] (W Jarvis) 4-8-10 T Ives 12/1: 021-032: Stayed on: no ch with winner: fin 3rd, placed 2nd: good effort: see 344.   56

433   ACONITUM [5] (J Bethell) 5-8-2 Paul Eddery 11/1: 0120-03: Nearest fin and is running into form: fin 4th, placed 3rd: in gd form in '85, winning a valuable h'cap at Ascot and placed on several occasions: in '84 won at Redcar & Yarmouth: eff at 7f, well suited by 1m nowadays: acts on firm & yld grnd & likes a gall trk.   41

*441   CREEAGER [1] (W Wharton) 4-8-0(5ex) N Carlisle 14/1: 040-014: Hmpd over 1f out: not recover: still a good effort: in fine form: see 441.   35

433   MERLE [9] 4-8-12 S Cauthen 10/1: 0000-00: Never nearer 6th, placed 5th: early last season was trained by R Sheather to win a Listed race at Newbury but subsq. failed to run up to that form: now with C Brittain: in '85 won at Leicester & Wolverhampton: eff at 1m, stays 10f really well: acts on gd/firm & yld grnd.   46

344   FREEDOMS CHOICE [13] 4-8-10 W Carson 11/2: 213-42D: 2nd when hung left over 1f out: fin 2nd: disq. and placed last: see 344.   56

433   QUALITAIR FLYER [6] 4-9-0 G Brown(5) 9/1: 00-0000: Much btr 433: see 330.   00

248 ADVANCE [8] 5-9-7 Pat Eddery 10/3 FAV: 2101-00: Well bckd: no show: very useful
gelding who in '85 won 2 valuable h'caps at Ascot: in '84 won at York: well suited by a
stiff 1m: acts on yld, best on firm grnd: should do btr than this.   00
441 Moores Metal [12] 8-2   --   Windpipe [7] 8-0   433 October [11] 8-10
433 Go Bananas [3] 9-1   433 Star Of A Gunner [10] 8-10
13 ran   3,shhd,3,2½,hd   (K Abdulla)   B Hills Lambourn, Berks

574 GR 2 MECCA DANTE STAKES 3YO   £80454   10.5f Good/Firm 30 +01 Fast

*324 SHAHRASTANI [4] (M Stoute) 3-9-0 W R Swinburn 10/11 FAV: 2-11: 3 ch c Nijinsky -
Shademah (Thatch): Smart colt: heavily bckd: led over 2f out, but had to be ridden out, for a
workmanlike rather than impressive win in Gr.2 Mecca-Dante Stakes at York May 14: first time
out was a ready winner of Gr.3 Guardian Classic Trial at Sandown: unlucky in running when 2nd
at Newbury to My Ton Ton on sole start in '85: eff at 10f, should be suited by 12f: acts
on gd/firm & soft grnd and is suited by a gall trk: should run well in the Derby, but failed
to show the acceleration of race 324 today.   82
*442 NOMROOD [2] (P Cole) 3-9-0 T Quinn 11/2: 12-12: Sn prom: not much room 3f out: kept
on well: in fine form: see 442.   78
442 SIRK [1] (C Brittain) 3-9-0 P Robinson 14/1: 23-1323: Ran on final 1f and is impr all
the time: see 442, 48.   76
442 FLYING TRIO [5] (L Cumani) 3-9-0 Pat Eddery 15/2: 102-104: Twice below form 224(9f,soft). 66
273 DANCING ZETA [6] 3-9-0(vis) P Cook 50/1: 3013-20: Made much: gd effort: see 273.   61
220 TOP RULER [3] 3-9-0 W Carson 50/1: 134-00: Wknd 2f out: not disgraced: probably
stays 10f: see 220.   60
-370 ALL HASTE [7] 3-9-0 S Cauthen 9/2 : -20: Wknd quickly in str and this was not his
running: something amiss? see 370.   00
7 ran   1½,1,5,2½,hd   (H H Aga Khan)   M Stoute Newmarket

575 MAIL ON SUNDAY 3YO FILLIES H'CAP 0-60   £4274   8f   Good 52 +03 Fast   [66]

*271 BRAZZAKA [6] (M Jarvis) 3-8-10 T Ives 11/4 FAV: 2221-11: 3 ch f Barrera - Irish Reel
(Irish Lancer): Very useful, consistent filly: well bckd and led 2f out, staying on well
in a valuable 3yo fillies h'cap at York May 14: first time out won a similar event at Epsom:
in '85 won at Hamilton after 4 2nds in a row and has yet to fin out of the first 2: stays 1m
well: acts on gd, suited by heavy grnd: no trk preferences: should win more races.   60
*359 GREAT LEIGHS [9] (B Hills) 3-8-10(8ex) B Thomson 4/1: 02-012: Kept on well: gd effort
under 8lbs penalty: see 359.   55
518 CARRIBEAN SOUND [5] (C Brittain) 3-7-7(2oh) J Lowe 14/1: 000-243: Made much: gd
run: stays 1m: see 368.   37
216 GOOSE HILL [1] (M W Easterby) 3-8-1 W Carson 5/1: 10-104: Ev ch str: consistent.   37
232 SMOOCH [2] 3-9-7 Pat Eddery 8/1: 103-00: Nearest fin: btr effort: very useful filly
in '85: first time out an easy winner at Salisbury: later a fine 3rd to Northern Eternity in
a Listed race at Newbury: stays 1m: acts on gd & firm grnd & runs well on a stiff trk.   56
271 NORMANBY LASS [7] 3-9-2 Paul Eddery 20/1: 0320-00: No show: see 271.   37
352 SYNTHETIC [4] 3-7-7 G French 20/1: 4010-00: No threat in 7th: in '85 won a fillies
maiden at Hamilton: eff at 6f, should stay further: acts on firm & heavy.   00
213 HIGHLAND BALL [8] 3-8-0 P Robinson 8/1: 00-00: Fin 8th: showed promise on both outings
in '85: half sister to 2 winners: should be suited by 1m plus: will impr.   00
386 SOMETHING CASUAL [3] 3-8-12 R Guest 13/2: 10-00: Wknd str: btr 386.   00
--   QUICKSAND [10] 3-7-7(1oh) M L Thomas 7/1: 2202-0: Active in mkt: btn early in str:
showed useful form as a 2yo, on final outing fin 2nd to Kabiyla in a fillies maiden at
Leicester: half sister to several winners: eff at 7f, should stay 1m: acts on gd & firm grnd. 00
10 ran   2,nk,4,½,8   (Tjo Tek Tan)   M Jarvis Newmarket

576 WILKINSON MEMORIAL 3YO MAIDEN STKS   £3525   7f   Good 52 -03 Slow

402 SHARPETTO [4] (M Albina) 3-9-0 T Ives 14/1: -001: 3 ch c Sharpen Up - Morelle
(Vitello): Impr colt: made ev yd, just holding on in a 3yo maiden at York May 14: stays 7f:
possesses a good deal of speed and may return to 6f next time: acts on gd grnd & a gall trk:
suited by forcing tactics.   47
431 ESFAHAN [5] (J Dunlop) 3-8-11 Pat Eddery 7/2 FAV: -02: Ran on well under press and
btn a whisker: impr filly: should be well suited by 1m: acts on gd grnd & a gall trk &
should find a maiden.   43
328 PARIS TURF [11] (G Wragg) 3-9-0 P Robinson 14/1: -003: Kept on under press: impr
colt: half brother to several winners, incl the useful sort Miss Longchamp, Miss St Cloud
and Paris Match: should stay 1m: acts on gd grnd & a gall trk.   44
371 BIEN DORADO [6] (B Hanbury) 3-9-0 S Cauthen 4/1: -004: Never nearer: btr effort:
should be suited by 1m: acts on gd grnd.   34
--   ABADJERO [3] 3-9-0 A Murray 14/1: -0: Nearest fin: should impr on this initial effort:
half brother to several winners.   29
371 SHAREEF [8] 3-9-0 W Carson 9/2: -00: Well bckd: wknd 2f out: well bred colt who
should do btr than this.   17

--	VITAL FORM [9] 3-9-0(BL) R Hills 13/2: -0: Bl on debut: no show.	00
--	GRIMESGILL [2] 3-8-11 M Hills 10/1: -0: Wknd over 2f out.	00
--	MOZART [7] 3-9-0 W R Swinburn 7/1: -0: Fin 9th.	00
--	DOWNTOWN BROWN [10] 3-9-0 T Quinn 9/1: -0: Never in it on debut.	00
217	GREGORIAN CHANT [1] 3-9-0 Paul Eddery 10/1: -00: Dsptd lead to ½way, fdd.	00

11 ran   shhd,¾,5,3,8   (Mahmoud Fustok)   M Albina Newmarket

---

SANDOWN   Thursday May 15th   Righthanded Stiff Galloping Track

577 MAY MAIDEN STAKES 2YO   £2611   5f   Good 48 -31 Slow

-- **WHIPPET** [8] (C Brittain) 2-9-0 P Robinson 7/1: 1: 2 b c Sparkler - St Louis Sue (Nonoalco): Prom colt: mkt drifter though al prom and led inside dist for a narrow win in a 2yo maiden at Sandown May 15: clearly well suited by a stiff 5f and sure to stay further in time: acts on gd grnd & on a gall trk: should impr for this race.   46
531 **KEEN EDGE** [4] (P Mitchell) 2-9-0 G Starkey 9/2: 42: Quick reapp. & just failed to make all: rallied gamely & clear of rem: acts on gd & firm grnd & on any trk: on the up grade and should win a race soon: see 531.   45
230 **SOMEONE ELSE** [3] (R Hannon) 2-9-0 A Mcglone 4/1: 03: Ran on well from ½way: sure to be suited by another furlong: acts on gd & heavy: see 230.   35
-- **BOLD AS BOLD** [6] (M Usher) 2-9-0 M Wigham 10/1: 4: Active in mkt on racecourse debut: stayed on promisingly from ½way and should impr next time: half brother to smart stayer Ore and sure to be suited by longer dists in time: acts on gd grnd & on a gall trk: should impr.   25
460 **MY BUDDY** [5] 2-9-0 R Cochrane 9/4 FAV: 00: Heavily bckd: speed over ½way: evidently well regarded & should do btr than this: acts on gd & yld: see 460.   23
187 **MAKIN MISCHIEF** [7] 2-9-0 C Rutter(5) 25/1: 00: No threat: should stay further in time.   19
252 **SEMIS** [2] 2-8-11 D Mckay 20/1: 00: Early speed: half sister to 1m winner Greek Banker.   00
457 **COMEDY SAIL** [1] 2-9-0 Paul Eddery 12/1: 00: Sn outpcd: cost 30,000 gns: should stay further. 00
8 ran   nk,4,4,½,1½,5   (A J Richards)   C Brittain Newmarket

578 BRIDGE APP. STAKES (H'CAP) (0-35)   £2446   1m   Good 48 +01 Fast   [35]

453 **DIMENSION** [17] (N Smith) 4-8-6(bl)(5ex) J Carter 12/1: 00-0141: 4 b c Dominion - Airy Queen (Sadair): Stayed on strongly to lead inside dist in an app h'cap at Sandown May 15: first time out was a surprise winner of a similar event at Kempton: lightly raced last season showing some promise in maiden company: half brother to several winners: best form over 1m on fast grnd: acts on any trk.   25
399 **FLYHOME** [9] (P Cundell) 5-9-12 C Carter(7) 11/2 FAV: 3200-22: Weighted to reverse form shown in 399 though had no answer to winners late burst: however another gd effort: see 399.   41
453 **TOM FORRESTER** [16] (A Pitt) 5-9-3 J Adams 11/1: 0003-03: Led below dist: gd effort.   31
310 **SAMHAAN** [20] (B Hanbury) 4-8-8 A Geran(7) 15/2: 0040-24: Not btn far: needs further.   20
*453 **DE RIGUEUR** [13] 4-10-2(5ex) B Lynch(7) 8/1: 24-1010: Another gd effort: see 453.   41
399 **HEATHGRIFF** [11] 4-8-3 G Bardwell(3) 10/1: 0102-30: Led briefly 2f out: see 399.   11
429 **HIGHDALE** [5] 4-8-1 W Hayes(3) 20/1: 404-100: Fin 7th: fair effort: see 163.   00
31 **VISUAL IDENTITY** [21] 4-8-13 P Sims(7) 33/1: 0020-00: Fin 8th after abs: maiden who was placed several times over sprint dists last season, though stays 1m: suited by fast grnd & a gall trk.   00

--	Fast Service [2] 9-7	499	Tamertown Lad [1] 8-12			
399	Any Business [8] 9-11	--	Big Pal [23] 9-11	399	August [7] 9-9	
333	Armorad [3] 9-4	333	Singing Boy [4] 9-4	481	High Pitched [6] 9-3	
196	Merry Measure [24] 9-3			499	Top Feather [12] 8-13(1ow)	
420	Elegant Fashion [14] 8-11(bl)			262	Pandi Club [18] 8-5(bl)	
119	Pamela Heaney [19] 8-3			--	Sweet Andy [22] 7-8	
--	Karamanad [10] 7-8					

23 ran   1½,hd,1½,¾,1½,3   (M A Ingram)   N Smith Lambourn, Berks

579 BLACKBIRD STAKES 3YO   £2582   1m   Good 48 -04 Slow

*371 **NINO BIBBIA** [3] (L Cumani) 3-9-4 R Guest 4/5 FAV: 2-11: 3 b c Cresta Rider - Native Tan (Exclusive Native): Smart colt: went on over 2f out and was sn clear for an impressive win in a 3yo stakes at Sandown May 15: earlier a comfortable winner of a valuable maiden at Newmarket: only ran once last season, fin 2nd to Ghika in a Stakes race at Yarmouth: half brother to 2 winners: very eff over 1m & will stay further: acts on gd & firm grnd & on a stiff trk: has a fine turn of foot & sure to win some good races this term.   76
*500 **VIANORA** [6] (G Harwood) 3-9-1 G Starkey 9/4: 3-0112: Well bckd: tried to make all though no chance with easy winner: still impr and will win more races: see 500.   62
-- **ALECS DREAM** [5] (A Stewart) 3-8-11 M Roberts 25/1: -3: Almost snatched 2nd place: prom racecourse debut: clearly well suited by a stiff 1m: acts on gd grnd: should certainly find a race on this evidence.   57
402 **DUFF** [10] (D Elsworth) 3-8-11 Pat Eddery 7/1: 0423-34: Al prom: clear of rem: see 402.   56
402 **QUICK DANCER** [7] 3-8-11 R Mcghin 50/1: 00-00: No extra below dist: half brother to a couple of winners, notably useful miler Cornish Gem: acts on gd grnd & on a gall trk.   40

-- **RESCUE PACKAGE** [2] 3-8-11 P Waldron 50/1: 4-0: Sn recovered from a slow start, no
extra 2f out though btr for race: half brother to several winners, incl smart middle dist
winner M'Lolshan: will stay further: acts on gd & firm grnd & on a gall trk.   39
-- **Shahs Choice** [9] 8-11   371 **Crystal Glass** [1] 8-11
-- **Bears Revenge** [4] 8-11   -- **Naskracker** [8] 8-11
10 ran   3,nk,¾,8,hd   (Sheikh Mohammed)   L Cumani Newmarket

580 BERRYLANDS STAKES (H'CAP) (0-50) 3YO   £3130   5f   Good 48 -17 Slow   [56]

217 **RESPECT** [8] (D Laing) 3-8-9 Pat Eddery 7/2 Jt FAV: 243-21: 3 b c Mummy's Pet -
Restive (Relic): Useful colt: cruised into lead ¼way to win unchall in a 3yo h'cap at
Sandown May 15: speedily bred sort who is a half brother to several winners: very eff over
5/6f on gd/firm & yld grnd: suited by a stiff trk: most consistent colt who should win again.   52
507 **MUHTARIS** [3] (C Benstead) 3-7-8 T Williams 7/2 Jt FAV: 00-022: Ran on well to take
2nd: heavily bckd today and should recoup losses when stepping up in dist: acts on gd &
yld: see 507.   30
228 **HELAWE** [10] (J Winter) 3-8-2(bl) R Hills 10/1: 2100-03: Stayed on well under press:
ran most consistently last season, when winning a nursery at Redcar: very eff over 5f on
fast grnd: suited by a gall trk.   34
443 **STEEL CYGNET** [6] (Pat Mitchell) 3-8-10 R Cochrane 11/2: 02-0034: Fin well: see 443 & 62. 40
496 **BERNIGRA GIRL** [1] 3-8-2 W Carson 10/1: 331-000: Never nearer: returning to form: see 496. 30
314 **NORTHERN LAD** [12] 3-7-13 N Adams 20/1: 200-000: Front rank till dist: half brother
to a couple of winners & produced his best effort last season when 2nd to easy winner
Welsh Note at Lingfield: eff over 5f on gd & firm grnd: acts on any trk.   17
418 **LA MALMAISON** [2] 3-7-8(1ow) R Fox 25/1: 000-400: Gd early speed: see 314.   00
496 **SPARKY LAD** [4] 3-9-3 D Nicholls 20/1: 10-00: Fin 8th though not btn that far: lightly
raced last season when a first time out winner of a Newcastle maiden: should stay 6f: acts
on gd & yld grnd and on a gall trk.   00
314 **NORTHERN TRUST** [9] 3-9-1 J Reid 10/1: 020-330: Fin 9th: btr on soft over this C/D in 314. 00
443 **DANCING SARAH** [11] 3-8-4 P Robinson 10/1: 2210-40: Btr last time in 443 (tight trk).   00
314 **COMPLEAT** [5] 3-9-7 P Waldron 10/1: 2331-00: Early speed: see 314.   00
418 **Baliview** [7] 7-7(9oh)
12 ran   1½,1½,¾,1,4,hd,1,½,2   (R Richmond Watson)   D Laing Lambourn, Berks

581 GOLF CLUB MAIDEN FILLIES STAKES 3YO   £2175   1m 2f   Good 48 -02 Slow

-- **SMASHING MILLIE** [6] (P Cole) 3-8-11 T Quinn 15/2: 0-1: 3 b f Mill Reef - Smash
(Busted): Very useful filly: first time out went on over 2f out and qcknd clear for a
comfortable win in a 3yo fillies maiden at Sandown May 15: shaped promisingly behind
Mysterious Dancer in a Wolverhampton maiden on sole start last term: clearly very eff over
10f & will stay further: acts on gd grnd & on a gall trk: sure to win more races over 12f plus. 64
-- **TASHTIYA** [15] (M Stoute) 3-8-11 A Kimberley 6/1: 0-2: Ran on well on seasonal debut
and caught a tartar here: only ran once last season, making gd late prog behind Elwadhna in a
Newmarket maiden: stays 10f well: acts on gd & firm grnd & on a stiff trk: should win soon.   56
-- **PRELUDE** [1] (W Hern) 3-8-11 W Carson 10/3 FAV: 3-3: Well bckd on reapp: kept on
under press: ran on well when placed behind El Cuite in a valuable race at Newbury last
season: half sister to Insular: eff over 10f on gd grnd: suited by a gall trk.   50
-- **ENZELIYA** [7] (R Johnson Houghton) 3-8-11 S Cauthen 7/1: 3-4: Made most: gd effort: also
showed plenty of promise on her only outing last season, in a staying on 3rd to Santella Mac
in a Lingfield maiden: should be well suied by middle dists: acts on gd & firm grnd.   50
-- **CURVACEOUS** [3] 3-8-11 W R Swinburn 12/1: -0: Al prom on racecourse debut: lesser
fancied stable mate of r.u: acts on gd grnd & on a gall trk: should impr.   47
-- **NORDICA** [16] 3-8-11 M Roberts 16/1: -0: Dwelt, stayed on promisingly and nearest fin:
should impr for this initial outing: acts on gd grnd & on a stiff trk.   47
250 **BUTTERFLY KISS** [13] 3-8-11 Pat Eddery 7/1: -00: No extra dist: fin 7th: see 250.   00
-- **PARSONS CHILD** [4] 3-8-11 R Guest 16/1: -0: Prog when hung right 2f out: sn btn though
certain to do btr next time: half sister to useful stayer Overtura: acts on gd grnd & on
a gall trk.   00
-- **Mighty Flash** [2] 8-11   -- **Mistakemenot** [11] 8-11
-- **Magic Vision** [10] 8-11   -- **La Grande Dame** [9] 8-11
-- **On The Agenda** [14] 8-11   250 **Lake Onega** [12] 8-11
-- **Miss Jade** [8] 8-11   -- **Barleybree** [5] 8-11
16 ran   3,3,hd,1½,hd   (Guiting Stud Ltd)   P Cole Whatcombe, Oxon

582 WOODLANDS STAKES (H'CAP) (0-50) 4YO+   £3185   1m 6f   Good 48 +24 Fast   [49]

375 **ALL IS REVEALED** [8] (D Thom) 4-8-9(vis) G Starkey 9/4 FAV: 310-041: 4 b g Welsh Pageant-
Senorita Rugby (Forward Pass): Very useful stayer on his day: set off in front and was sn
clear for a comfortable win in a very fast run h'cap at Sandown May 15: in fine form last
season, when making all in h'caps at Ascot , Sandown (course record) and Yarmouth: also won
a seller at Newmarket: eff over 14f, stays 2m well: acts on gd/frm & yld grnd & goes well
on a stiff trk: best forcing the pace: wore a visor today.   42
375 **TRAPEZE ARTIST** [6] (N Vigors) 5-8-11 S Dawson(3) 12/1: 0-04002: Stayed on well though
was never going to peg back winner: see 58a.   38

341 ROYAL CRAFTSMAN [2] (N Smith) 5-7-7(5oh) N Adams 25/1: -10-003: Good effort at the
weights: well suited by this longer trip: see 341.   18
*485 MY CHARADE [15] (B Waring) 5-7-9(vis)(5ex) R Fox 13/2: 0-00014: Never nearer: best 485. 16
126 LEON [9] 4-8-10 Kim Tinkler(7) 3/1: 104-220: Another gd effort: stays 14f: see 80.   29
449 CASTIGLIONE [3] 4-7-7(BL) C Rutter(5) 12/1: -32-000: Active in mkt: no extra below
dist: trying a longer trip today: see 199.   09
--   BOCODA LAD [12] 5-8-4 B Rouse 10/1: 44004-0: No threat: btr for race: tough &
consistent colt who won valuable h'caps at Sandown & Newmarket last season: in '84 won at
Lingfield: half brother to a couple of sprinters though needs a test of stamina himself: acts
on firm & hvy grnd & on any trk, though is well suited by a stiff one.   00
375 Naftilos [1] 9-7   -- Holliston [4] 9-3   403 Jazair [7] 8-10
204 Chartfield [13] 7-7(14oh)   312 Alsiba [5] 8-0
349 Moorland Lady [11] 8-8   -- Coastal Plain [10] 8-4
--   Paddycoup [14] 8-7
15 ran   3,1,4,1½,3   (Mrs I Norman)   D Thom Newmarket

Official Going Given as Good/Soft: High winds throughout the afternoon

583   YORKSHIRE MAIDEN STAKES 2YO   £3277   5f   Yld/Soft 115 -07 Slow

405 SAMEEK [2] (R Armstrong) 2-9-0 W Carson 6/5 FAV: 21: 2 b c Red Sunset -
Wilderness (Martinmas): Prom colt: heavily bckd & made ev yd, ridden out in a valuable
maiden at York May 15: first time out was a fine 2nd to the very promising Zaibaq in a
Newmarket maiden: eff at 5f, should stay 6f: acts on firm & yld grnd & a gall trk: should
win more good races.   60
--   GOVERNORSHIP [4] (C Nelson) 2-9-0 J Reid 15/2: 2: Fin really well and looks a certain
future winner: cost 110,000 gns and is a half brother to 3 winners, incl fair stayer Broad
Beam: should be well suited by 6f plus: acts on yld grnd & a gall trk & will open his
account soon.   56
--   SONG N JEST [3] (J Fitzgerald) 2-9-0 S Cauthen 7/1: 3: Sn prom: gd racecourse debut
from this very speedily bred colt: full brother to the smart Reesh and very useful Imperial
Jade: eff at 5f on yld grnd: looks sure to find a maiden.   51
--   SANDALL PARK [7] (M W Easterby) 2-9-0 K Hodgson 14/1: 4: Kept on well on racecourse
debut showing future promise: cost 11,000 gns: speedily bred colt who should have no
trouble finding a race: acts on yld grnd.   51
--   BALKAN LEADER [10] 2-9-0 A Murray 12/1: 0: Mkt drifter: al there: gd effort: cost
14,500 gns and is a half brother to several winners: speedily bred sort: acts on yld grnd.   44
437 COLWAY RALLY [9] 2-9-0 T Ives 9/2: 20: Dsptd lead: acts on gd & yld: see 437.   38
--   BEAU BENZ [6] 2-9-0 M Birch 10/1: 0: Never nearer 7th: should do btr: cost 11,500 gns:
half brother to several winners.   00
--   GOOD POINT [8] 2-9-0 M Hills 13/2: 0: No show: cost I.R. 50,000.   00
--   Northern Decree [5] 9-0   -- The Great Match [1] 9-0
10 ran   1½,1½,shhd,2½,2   (Hamdan Al-Maktoum)   R Armstrong Newmarket

584   TURN TO YORKSHIRE STKS HCAP 0-60   £3371   1m 4f   Yld/Soft 115 +09 Fast   [52]

403 BOLD REX [9] (J Dunlop) 4-9-6 W Carson 5/1: 031-441: 4 b c Rex Magna - Lady Bold
(Bold Lad) (Ire): Useful colt: ran on gamely to get up last stride in a fast run h'cap at
York May 15: in fine form in '85 winning at Chester & Thirsk and on final outing valuable
November H'cap at Doncaster: winner in France in '84: stays 12f really well: acts on any
grnd though likes some give: genuine & consistent: should win more races.   59
*363 PUBBY [8] (J Toller) 5-8-3 G Duffield 5/2 FAV: 310-112: Well bckd: led 2f out: tired
close home & caught last stride: remains in excellent form: 5L clear 3rd: see 363.   41
439 VINTAGE TOLL [4] (S Norton) 6-9-2 S Cauthen 16/1: 0-03003: Ev ch over 1f out: well
clear rem: see 52.   46
225 WITCHCRAFT [12] (G Wragg) 4-8-11 Pat Eddery 9/2: 0020-24: Never nearer: much btr 225.   25
410 HANDLEBAR [11] 4-8-5(BL) T Ives 8/1: 0031-00: Bl first time: no real threat: see 410.   16
410 SHELLMAN [13] 4-9-0 G Brown(5) 16/1: 0-03000: No show over this longer trip: see 55 (7f) 24
360 VICKSTOWN [3] 4-8-6 T Quinn 16/1: 010-000: Made much: fin 7th: in '85 won h'caps at
York & Wolverhampton: suited by 12f: acts on firm & yld & on a gall trk.   00
--   FIVE FARTHINGS [10] 4-8-6 W R Swinburn 10/1: 23100-0: Led 3f out on seasonal debut:
btr for race: in '85 was an easy winner of a maiden at Yarmouth: eff at 12f, stays 14f well:
acts on gd & firm & a gall trk.   00
--   Romiosini [2] 8-9   215 Tivian [5] 8-6(vis)   449 Strathearn [6] 7-10
--   Singers Tryst [14] 9-8   429 Senor Ramos [7] 8-11
439 Aristocrat Velvet [1] 9-1
14 ran   hd,5,12,2½,½,1   (Lord Granard)   J Dunlop Arundel, Sussex

585   YORKSHIRE CUP GROUP 2   £22086   1m 6f   Yld/Soft 115 -08 Slow

360 EASTERN MYSTIC [2] (L Cumani) 4-8-9 Pat Eddery 9/4 FAV: 1211-41: 4 b c Elocutionist -
Belle Pensee (Ribot): Very useful colt: ran on well under press to lead close home in Gr.2
Yorkshire Cup at York May 15: one of the most impr performers of '85, winning valuable Coral
Autumn Cup at Newbury, breaking course record in valuable h'cap at Doncaster and also won
amateur riders event at Newmarket: half brother to the smart Treizieme: eff over 12f, suited
by 14f plus: acts on soft grnd, is much btr on gd & firm: likes a gall trk: genuine &
consistent and a credit to his trainer.   76
385 SEISMIC WAVE [3] (B Hills) 5-8-9 B Thomson 7/2: 122-032: Led 4f out: just caught:
excellent effort & should win soon: acts on yld/soft, but much btr on a sounder surface:
stays 14f: see 385.   74
474 PETRIZZO [4] (C Brittain) 5-8-9 S Cauthen 20/1: 4-00003: Stayed on well & btn
only 2L in this very good company: would be a h'cap snip next time out if running up to
this form: likes a stiff trk: see 474.   72
--   BOURBON BOY [6] (M Stoute) 4-8-9 W R Swinburn 3/1: 10123-4: Ev ch over 3f out:
should strip fitter next time: in fine form in '85, winning valuable h'caps at York & Ayr:
also a h'cap winner at Nottingham & Ripon: on final outing fin 3rd in Tote Cesarewitch: eff
at 12f, well suited by 14f & stays 2m: acts on firm & yld: most genuine & consistent: should
win races this season.   67
--   TALE QUALE [10] 4-8-9 T Ives 4/1: 11301-0: Ev ch str: btr for race: much impr thro'out
'85, winning early in the season at Thirsk & Nottingham, but on final outing was an easy
winner of fast run Gr.3 Jockey Club Cup at Newmarket: full brother to several winners incl
Centroline and Nicholas Bill: stamina endowed: stays 2m well: well suited by gd & firm
grnd: acts on any trk.   57
*215 ROSTHERNE [1] 5-8-9 A Murray 33/1: 23-4210: Very stiff task: see 215.   39
--   COLD LINE [9] 4-8-6 J Lowe 33/1: 210-0: Made much on seasonal debut.   00
7 ran   1½,½,3,6,12   (Maarden)   L Cumani Newmarket

586   NORWEST HOLST TROPHY HCAP 3YO 0-75   £12700   7f   Yld/Soft 115 +05 Fast   [65]

-406 FLEET FORM [8] (C Nelson) 3-9-4 J Reid 6/1: 00-1221: 3 ch c Double Form - Fleetsin
(Jim French): Very useful colt who is in fine form at present: led final 1f, comfortably in
a valuable 3yo h'cap at York May 15: an unlucky 2nd last time out to Sylvan Express in a
similar event at Newmarket: first time out won a minor event at Leicester: in '85 won a
Bath maiden: very eff at 7f, should stay 1m: acts on firm & soft grnd & likes a gall trk:
should win more races.   70
226 RESOURCEFUL FALCON [13] (P Makin) 3-9-7 T Quinn 8/1: 0111-02: Led over 2f out: fine
effort under top weight: in '85 ran up a hat trick of successes, a fast run & valuable
nursery h'cap at Doncaster and earlier stake events at Lingfield & Nottingham: very eff at
7f, acts on firm & soft grnd & on any trk: genuine sort.   68
334 THRESH IT OUT [11] (M Stoute) 3-9-1 W R Swinburn 9/1: 0223-23: Ch over 1f out, gd
effort: see 334.   56
407 VAINGLORIOUS [6] (H Candy) 3-9-4 R Curant 11/4 FAV: 102-004: Nearest fin: h'cap snip
on running in the 2,000 Guineas: possibly needs 1m & btr grnd.   55
465 DARK PROMISE [7] 3-8-11 S Perks 25/1: 1020-00: Rank outsider: sn prom: gd effort.   46
226 ILLUMINEUX [4] 3-9-7 S Cauthen 14/1: 1-00: Ev ch: on final outing in '85 was a ready
winner of a maiden at Newmarket: very eff over 7f: acts on yld, likes firm grnd.   50
455 BRONZE OPAL [12] 3-8-9 J Lowe 16/1: 3320-00: Never nearer 7th: showed a good deal
of promise in '85 and should have no trouble finding a race: half brother to several winners:
eff at 6/7f on gd & yld grnd.   00
234 HAWAIIAN PALM [3] 3-9-4 Pat Eddery 8/1: 13-00: Prom over 5f: first time out in '85
won a maiden at Salisbury: half brother to several winners: eff at 7f, should stay 1m: acts
on gd/firm & a gall trk.   00
478 ROMANTIC UNCLE [1] 3-8-6 J H Brown(5) 7/1: 021-020: Fdd: much btr 478 (soft/hvy).   00
387 Golden Ancona [10] 8-0   387 Jarrovian [9] 7-12
232 Hoist The Axe [5] 8-3   111 Coppermill Lad [2] 8-3
13 ran   1½,3,2,¾,3   (James L Mamakos)   C Nelson Upper Lambourn, berks

587   GROUP 3 DUKE OF YORK STKS   £19350   6f   Yld/Soft 115 +01 Fast

413 GREY DESIRE [10] (M Brittain) 6-9-0 K Darley 4/1: 1-11241: Smart horse: led over 1f
out for a ready win in Gr.3 Duke Of York Stakes at York May 15: in excellent form this
season, earlier winning valuable events at Kempton & Doncaster (first time out): in '85 won
valuable events at Haydock, Newmarket & Kempton: previous season won 3 times: very eff at
6f stays 7f: acts on any going and on any trk & retains his form really well: genuine sort
who is a credit to his trainer.   85
245 SI SIGNOR [11] (P Cole) 4-9-0 T Quinn 12/1: 1040-42: Made much: fine effort & should
win soon: see 245.   75
374 OUR DYNASTY [9] (J Winter) 5-9-0 S Cauthen 100/1: 0000-03: 100-1 outsider: ran on
well and this was a remarkable effort: officially rated only 53: in '85 won a h'cap at Epsom
smart 2yo, winning at Doncaster, Thirsk, Newmarket & Kempton: eff over 6f, stays 7f: acts
on gd, likes yld/soft grnd: no trk preferences.   74

407 HALLGATE [7] (S Hall) 3-8-5(BL) K Hodgson 11/4 FAV: 111-304: Bl first time: held up
as usual: not qckn over 1f out: gd effort: see 249.   77
408 AMIGO LOCO [2] 5-9-0(bl) S Whitworth 25/1: -022200: Dsptd lead: difficult to place,
but deserves a win: see 245, 70.   69
408 QUE SYMPATICA [6] 4-8-11 Pat Eddery 14/1: 04-3300: Sn prom: see 18.   64
413 OROJOYA [4] 4-9-8 M Hills 3/1: 313-020: Stiff task at weights: btr 413 (7f): see 222. 00
--   PRIMO DOMINIE [1] 4-9-4 W R Swinburn 9/2: 41220-0: Fin 9th on seasonal debut: btr
for race: in fine form thro'out '85, winning Gr.3 King George Stakes at Goodwood: also fine
2nd to Never So Bold in Gr.1 Kings Stand Stakes at Royal Ascot & Gr.1 Spring Championship
at York: also 2nd to Orojoya in Gr.2 Vernon Sprint Cup at Haydock: top class 2yo, winning 4
times: very eff at 5/6f: acts on any going/trk: genuine sort.   00
--   Nashia [8] 7-12   401 Green Dollar [5] 8-1(VIS)
10 ran   3,shhd,nk,1½,¾   (M Brittain)   M Brittain Warthill, Yorks

588 SCARBOROUGH STKS 3YO HCAP 0-60   £3350   6f   Yld/Soft 115 -29 Slow   [58]

--   ELNAWAAGI [10] (H T Jones) 3-9-7 A Murray 10/1: 31123-1: 3 b c Roberto - Gurkhas Band
(Lurullah): Very useful colt: first time out, switched dead. and ran on well to get up close
home in a h'cap at York May 15: consistent 2yo, winning fast run events at Windsor & Thirsk:
very eff over 6f & should stay further: acts on firm & yld/soft and on any trk: very well
bred sort who should win more races this season.   65
520 PANNANICH WELLS [6] (M W Easterby) 3-7-12 L Charnock 16/1: 0430-02: Bumped 2f out:
led over 1f out, just btn: 3L clear 3rd: excellent effort: should win soon: see 520.   39
*455 KEDRON [1] (R Laing) 3-9-3(7ex) S Whitworth 10/3: 012-113: Sn prom: in gd form: see 455. 51
--   DEBBIE DO [9] (C Thornton) 3-9-1 J Bleasdale 12/1: 11322-4: Made much: not much room
final 1f: good seasonal debut: most consistent 2yo, winning at Hamilton & Carlisle and has
yet to fin out of the first 4: equally eff at 5 & 6f: acts on firm & soft & likes a gall trk. 44
443 GODS ISLE [3] 3-8-5(BL) M Birch 7/2: 010-020: Hmpd after 2f out: see 443, 246.   30
*454 AMBROSINI [2] 3-8-2 W Woods(5) 5/2 FAV: 0231-10: Heavily bckd: never nearer: btr 454. 24
228 KING OF SPADES [4] 3-9-6 P Cook 10/1: 013-100: Best first time out in 26.   00
387 Young Puggy [5] 8-12   --   Catherines Well [8] 8-12
9 ran   ½,3,2½,2,1½   (Handab Al-Maktoum)   H T Jones Newmarket

---

589 LUND SELLING STAKES 2YO   £982   5f   Good 50 -38 Slow

353 GREENS GALLERY [3] (G Blum) 2-8-8 M L Thomas 9/2: 01: 2 ch f Alias Smith - Celeste
(Sing Sing): Dropped to selling company, well bckd when winning at Beverley May 16, comfortably coming clear 1f out: bought in 3,000 gns: goes well on a stiff trk.   34
421 BARLEY TWIST [9] (P Rohan) 2-8-11 S Morris 11/10 FAV: 22: Heavily bckd, fin well:
looks sure to be suited by 6f & should win at least a seller: see 421.   29
278 TOOTSIE JAY [6] (P Feilden) 2-8-8 N Day 11/2: 3003: Fin well after slow start: see 223. 18
354 MI OH MY [7] (K Stone) 2-8-8 C Dwyer 7/1: 302334: Al there: consistent: see 181.   16
--   PETERS BLUE [1] 2-8-11 A Murray 8/1: 0: Led 2 out, prom debut: impr likely next time:
might do btr on a sharper trk.   18
446 MOONEE POND [2] 2-8-8(VIS) K Hodgson 11/2: 2000: Led 3f: see 317 (soft, sharp trk).   14
--   Tuesday Evening [4] 8-8   446 Cawkell Trooper [8] 8-11(VIS)
446 Millfield Blue [5] 8-11
9 ran   3,2½,nk,½,½   (Richard Green Fine Paintings)   G Blum Newmarket

590 ESK HANDICAP (0-35)   £1643   2m   Good 50 -22 Slow   [35]

419 LEPRECHAUN LADY [14] (S Norton) 4-8-8 M L Thomas 10/1: 0-20001: 4 b f Royal Blend -
Country Bee (Ribero): Al prom, led 2 out gamely in a 16 runner h'cap at Beverley May 16: in
'85 won at Hamilton and in '84 won at Haydock (seller): eff at 14f & stays 2m welel: seems
to act on gd & soft grnd & on a stiff trk: carries weight well.   22
--   SOUND DIFFUSION [4] (R Whitaker) 4-8-7 K Bradshaw(5) 14/1: 00030-2: Only btn ¼L, gd
seasonal debut: ran well twice at Redcar last year winning there over 2m in July: acts on
gd & firm.   20
542 SECURITY CLEARANCE [8] (G Blum) 5-9-12 M Rimmer 10/1: 000-003: Met trouble in running,
kept on and ran remarkably well under top weight: should be suited by 2m plus.   38
319 STONE JUG [16] (S Hall) 6-8-4 K Hodgson 6/1: 3401-04: Never closer: a winner at
Edinburgh (2) and Catterick in '85: eff at 12f & stays 2m2f well: acts on any grnd & goes
well on a sharp trk: coming into form.   15
449 MASTER CARL [10] 7-8-3 D Leadbitter(0) 10/1: 230-000: Not much luck in running: coming
back to form? last won in '82 at Hamilton: eff at 12f & stays 2m: acts on any going.   14
493 CHRISTMAS HOLLY [5] 5-7-13 S Webster 7/1: -310020: Btr 493, 105 (12f, soft).   09
--   ALFIE DICKINS [9] 8-7-12 P Hill(7) 5/1 FAV: 00130-0: Fit from hurdling: held up,
fin 7th: goes well at Beverley winning here twice last year and at Carlisle: eff at 12f
and stays 19f: acts on firm & soft & does well when fresh.   00
144 AULD LANG SYNE [3] 7-8-4(bl) A Shoults(5) 6/1: 30-4240: Much btr 50.   00
462 NORTHERN RULER [12] 4-9-6 G Duffield 8/1: 00-2000: Best 280.   00

358 ARTESIUM [11] 4-9-1 J Reid 13/2: -002200: Led 14f: best 121 (heavy). 00
308 ELECTRIFIED [6] 5-8-3 M Roberts 10/1: 040-000: There 2 out: best 12f? 00
358 **Welsh Guard** [15] 7-8 358 **Far To Go** [7] 8-2(2ow) -- **La Rose Grise** [1] 8-11
366 **Racing Demon** [13] 7-12 449 **Spend It Lass** [2] 8-11
16 ran ½,1,½,shhd,1,hd (G Corbett) S Norton Barnsley, Yorks

591 **RISBY HANDICAP (0-35)** **£1758 1m 4f Good 50 +02 Fast** **[31]**

493 **MENINGI** [10] (N Tinkler) 5-9-4 Kim Tinkler(7) 5/1: 00-3141: 5 ch g Bustino - Miss Filbert (Compensation): In grand form and winning for a 2nd time in last 3 races when picking up a h'cap at Beverley May 16: led 1 out & came clear, readily: earlier won at Thirsk: useful over hurdles, winning 3 times: eff over 12f & stays 2m well: acts on gd & soft/hvy grnd & on any track. 32
*493 **MR LION** [6] (F Carr) 4-8-2(6ex) J Carr(4) 8/1: 00-3012: Kept on, ran well under penalty: stays 12f & might be suited by 2m now. 12
493 **WILDRUSH** [15] (W Watts) 7-9-3 A Shoults(5) 8/1: 002-103: Al prom, gd effort: see 243. 24
-- **STERLING VIRTUE** [2] (B Mcmahon) 5-8-0 S Webster 14/1: 0-004-4: Maiden, acts on firm & soft & stays at least 12f. 06
429 **FENCHURCH COLONY** [8] 5-9-10 K Hodgson 8/1: 4000/30: Ran well over this 12f trip & is possibly btr at shorter distances: see 429. 29
-- **VERY SPECIAL** [4] 4-9-7 R Morse(5) 6/1: 10143-0: Well there 2 out: btr for race: front running winner of h'caps at Sandown & Thirsk in '85: well suited by 11/12f & seems best on fast grnd: goes well for an app. and should run well next time. 25
432 **DASHING LIGHT** [3] 5-9-1 G Duffield 3/1 FAV: 3002-40: Made most: see 432. 00
199 **ARDOON PRINCE** [7] 4-8-3 P Burke(7) 8/1: -0000: No threat: recent dual winner over hurdles: goes well in the mud. 00
493 **APPLE WINE** [12] 9-9-0 C Dwyer 10/1: 0-02000: Early ldr: btr 256 (sharp trk). 00
202 **APPEALING** [5] 4-8-11 M Rimmer 8/1: 0-41240: Best 184, 58 (10f heavy). 00
439 **The Crying Game** [16] 7-12 449 **Ishkhara** [11] 8-11
-- **Skerne Spark** [13] 8-9 -- **Cloud Dancer** [14] 7-13
14 ran 2½,2½,¾,nk,nk (Full Circle Thoroughbreds Ltd) N Tinkler Malton, Yorks

592 **EVERINGHAM MAIDEN STAKES 3YO+** **£684 1m 4f Good 50 +01 Fast**

239 **KUDZ** [3] (H Cecil) 3-8-3 N Day 2/7 FAV: 22-21: 3 br c Master Willie - Lucky Ole Me (Olden Times): Long odds on, led 2 out & came clear under press in a maiden race at Beverley May 16: stays 12f & acts on firm & soft grnd: half brother to several winners incl Lucky North: will probably be suited by 2m. 32
341 **THE YOMPER** [1] (D Elsworth) 4-9-6 A Mcglone 5/1: 0200-42: Made most: not an easy ride and is a hard puller: will probably stay further than 12f & goes well on soft grnd: should find a maiden. 25
430 **BAYTINO** [4] (H Collingridge) 3-8-0 M Rimmer 33/1: -03: Some late prog: will stay 2m. 12
-- **NADAS** [7] (S Norton) 3-8-3(BL) G Duffield 20/1: -4: Early ldr, tried in bl for the first time: probably stays 12f. 14
-- **MOULKINS** [8] 4-9-6 Julie Bowker(7) 33/1: 000-0: Never closer. 15
19 **RAPIDAN** [1] 5-9-6 K Hodgson 20/1: 30-00: No threat: needs 2m? 14
-- **Capitation** [5] 8-3 -- **Film Consultant** [10] 9-6
-- **Le Marsh** [9] 9-3 -- **Oeil De Tigre** [6] 9-6
10 ran 4,4,¾,¾,½ (Sheikh Mohammed) H Cecil Newmarket

593 **HOUGHTON MAIDEN STAKES 3YO** **£879 5f Good 50 +06 Fast**

-- **ORIENT** [12] (R Whitaker) 3-8-11 D Mckeown 8/1: 40-1: 3 b f Bay Express - Gundi (Mummy's Pet): Bckd from 20/1, led 3 out, came clear when readily winning a 19 runner maiden race at Beverley May 16, not very well drawn: a speedy & impr filly who is very eff at 5f and will probably stay 6f: goes well on a stiff trk & should win again. 44
-- **RESTORE** [19] (G Lewis) 3-9-0 P Waldron 15/8 FAV: 23-2: Heavily bckd, caught a tartar: acts on gd & firm grnd & very eff at 5f but might now be suited by 6f: seems sure to find a maiden race soon. 40
-- **MARGAM** [13] (P Walwyn) 3-9-0 A Mcglone 10/1: 0-3: Very wk in mkt but led ½way and ran well: should find a 5f maiden race. 40
-- **PAS DE REGRETS** [17] (D Arbuthnot) 3-9-0 J Williams 12/1: 04-4: Kept on: on the up grade: probably stays 6f & might be btr suited by 7f. 33
-- **MAWSUFF** [9] 3-9-0 A Murray 5/2: -0: Well bckd, not well drawn & fin strongly: probably btr than this and impr likely next time. 30
217 **PRETTY GREAT** [7] 3-8-11 A Shoults(5) 15/2: -340: Dsptd lead 3f: btr 217 (6f). 19
438 **SATIAPOUR** [4] 3-9-0(vis) J Reid 9/2: 043-20: Tried in a visor but badly drawn and never in it: worth another chance: see 438: needs at least 6f. 00
-- **Package Perfection** [8] 8-11 438 **Royal Fan** [2] 9-0
431 **Aclia** [6] 8-11 -- **Gary And Larry** [14] 9-0
283 **Findon Manor** [11] 9-0 328 **Tamana Dancer** [5] 8-11
-- **Dads Line** [15] 9-0 -- **Whoberley Wheels** [3] 9-0
529 **Watendlath** [1] 8-11 338 **Eastern Lass** [18] 8-11
328 **Strawberry Split** [10] 8-11 -- **Panova** [8] 8-11
19 ran 1½,shhd,2½,1½,2 (Mrs R T Watson) R Whitaker Wetherby, Yorks

594   BESWICK HANDICAP STAKES (0-35)   £1716   7f   Good 50 -06 Slow   [35]

--   ABLE MAYBOB [18] (H Collingridge) 4-8-0(3ow) M Rimmer 14/1: 20000-1: 4 ch c Goldhill's
Pride - Alarica (Cantab): Despite o.w. & difficulty in running, got up inside final 1f in a
h'cap at Beverley May 16, first time out: probably stays 1m but seems best at 6/7f on gd
grnd: probably acts on any trk: could win again.   15
*378 LITTLE NEWINGTON [10] (N Bycroft) 5-8-2(bl) M Richardson(5) 8/1: 0410012: Fin well
in gd form: see 378.   14
--   CBM GIRL [9] (R Woodhouse) 5-8-13 C Dwyer 8/1: 10000-3: Well bckd, gd seasonal debut
from an unfavourable draw: a winner 3 times last year at Ayr, Chepstow & Wolverhampton: in
'84 won at Ayr: acts on gd & yld & suited by 7/8f: best on a stiff trk: rated 34 last year
and should go well next time.   23
--   SIGNORE ODONE [17] (M H Easterby) 4-9-5 K Hodgson 13/2: 0-320-4: Al there: tried in bl
last year but ran btr without them & is possibly best around 1m on a sharpish trk: does
best when fresh but still a maiden.   28
321 THE MAZALL [19] 6-8-10 G Gosney 9/2: 2010-00: Despite slow start, led 1 out and
not btn far: coming back to form: best around 6/7f & in '85 won at Redcar & Carlisle: in
'84 won at Nottingham: acts on firm & soft & well suited by front running tactics.   19
310 DARNIT [8] 4-9-10 E Guest(3) 4/1 FAV: 000-000: Well bckd fav: chall 1 out: see 310.   31
310 JANES BRAVE BOY [13] 4-8-7 J Callaghan(7) 14/1: 03-1000: Fin 7th: best 46 (firm/yld).   00
--   Gods Law [2] 7-8   378 Hoptons Chance [16] 8-0
--   Grey Cree [14] 8-8   101 High Port [15] 8-0   -- Sky Mariner [11] 7-8
521 Workaday [1] 9-12   355 Paddystown [3] 9-3   -- Valrach [5] 9-3
--   Doppio [4] 8-8   110 Yellow Bear [6] 8-2   8   Johnny Frenchman [7] 7-13
18 ran   1,1,nk,shhd,1,½   (A Crawford)   H Collingridge Newmarket

595   EVERINGHAM MAIDEN STAKES 3YO+   £684   1m 4f Good 50 -26 Slow

357 SENDER [6] (A Stewart) 3-8-3 M Roberts 5/4 FAV: -01: Led 2 out under press in a slow
run maiden race at Beverley May 16: stays 12f & looks sure to be suited by further.   28
--   FOURTH TUDOR [4] (B Hanbury) 4-9-6 A Geran(7) 5/2: -2: Well bckd, kept on and will
be suited by farther than 12f.   26
185 BATON MATCH [5] (M Chapman) 6-9-6 N Day 12/1: 0000-03: Fit from hurdling, made most.   22
121 THE BETSY [9] (D Elsworth) 4-9-3 A Mcglone 7/1: 0000-04: Early ldr: stays 12?   15
333 FLEURCONE [7] 4-9-6 J Williams 7/1: 000-000: Probably stays 12f.   10
--   GARTHMAN [3] 3-8-3 M Miller 20/1: -0: Started slowly, never a threat.   05
430 RIVERS NEPHEW [8] 3-8-3(bl) R Machado 11/4: -00: Will be hard pushed to win a race
on this showing: tried in bl last time.   00
381 QUARANTINO [1] 3-8-3 M L Thomas 8/1: 000-000: Al behind.   00
8 ran   1½,2,2½,5,2½   (N B Hunt)   A Stewart Newmarket

NEWBURY   Friday May 16th   Lefthand, Galloping Track

Official Going Given as Good/Soft

596   TRENCHERWOOD SELLING STAKES 2YO   £2994   5f   Good 53 -25 Slow

*446 HORNBLOWER GIRL [2] (P Rohan) 2-8-8 Pat Eddery 5/2 FAV: 11: 2 br f Faraway Times-
Ibolya Princess (Crowned Prince): Impr filly: well bckd and made almost all, easily in a
2yo seller at Newbury May 16 (bought in 5,800 gns): first time out won a similar event at
Redcar): cost 3,200 gns as a yearling and is a half sister to a couple of winning sprinters:
eff over 5f, may stay further: acts on gd grnd & a gall trk & may win outside same company.   35
460 EL BE DOUBLEYOU [8] (N Callaghan) 2-8-11 P Cook 11/2: 02: Dropped in grade & well
bckd: no ch with winner, but can find a similar event: eff at 5f, should stay further: acts
on gd grnd & a gall trk.   28
--   BLOFFA [4] (P Cundell) 2-8-8 N Adams 25/1: 3: Mkt drifter on debut: kept on: cost only
2,000 gns & should be suited by much further than 5f: acts on gd grnd.   24
*329 SETTER COUNTRY [17] (R Hodges) 2-8-8 A Clark 5/1: 014: Nearest fin: acts on gd &
soft grnd: should be suited by 6f: see 329.   23
206 DECCAN PRINCE [7] 2-8-11 W R Swinburn 11/1: 00: No show: see 206.   15
*337 MISS MARJORIE [1] 2-8-8 J Matthias 8/1: 010: Prom over 3f: acts on gd & yld/soft:
possibly needs a sharper trk: see 337.   10
483 HIGHFALUTIN LYMEY [15] 2-8-11 R Wernham 10/1: 00: Mkt drrifter: fdd over 1f out:see 483 00
382 SOHAMS TAYLOR [12] 2-8-11 G Starkey 10/1: 00: Active in mkt, but no show: half
brother to a 9f winner and should be suited by further.   00
400 HIT LUCKY [5] 2-8-8 W Carson 8/1: 000: Btr in 400 (sharper trk).   00
170 Swallow Bay [1] 8-8   488 Dormestone Lad [18] 8-11
--   African Safari [9] 8-11   21   Petrus Seventy [13] 8-11
--   Sky Robber [14] 8-11   350 Sleepline For Pine [16] 8-11
--   Survival Kit [10] 8-8   311 Betta Win [3] 8-8(BL)
17 ran   3,hd,nk,5,1   (E McMahon)   P Rohan Malton, Yorks

203

597   ULTRAMAR STAKES 3YO HANDICAP 0-70   £6076   1m 4f   Good 53 -28 Slow   [71]

•416   AL SALITE [4] (J Dunlop) 3-8-8(6ex) Pat Eddery 7/4 FAV: 412-11: 3 ch c High Line -
Delicia (Sovereign Path): Very useful, impr colt: al going well and led over 1f out, soon
clear for an impressive win in valuable 3yo h'cap at Newbury May 16: first time out won a
h'cap at Haydock: winning 2yo at Nottingham: eff at 10f, well suited by 12f: acts on firm
& soft grnd & a gall trk: should win more races & is a progressive type.   67

273   KOLGONG HEIGHTS [3] (B Hanbury) 3-9-7 W R Swinburn 25/1: 1300-02: Kept on well final
1f: good effort under top weight: first time out in '85 won a maiden on this trk: well
suited by 12f: acts on firm & yld grnd trk.   70

357   MOUNT OLYMPUS [2] (J Watts) 3-7-8 R Fox 10/1: 04-03: Ev ch over 2f out: stays 12f
and should find a race soon.   43

348   FAMILY FRIEND [9] (W Hern) 3-9-6 W Carson 14/1: 1240-44: Led 2f out: good run: stays 12f.69

273   WAR HERO [8] 3-9-3 B Rouse 25/1: 013-00: Prom str: not btn far in close fin for
2nd: stays 12f: see 273.   66

442   JUMBO HIRT [1] 3-8-1(1ow) B Thomson 2/1: 30-230: Going well over 2f out but found
little when the pace qcknd: much btr 442 (sharp trk) and was a h'cap snip on that form: 45

435   OSTENSIBLE [7] 3-8-9 G Starkey 13/2: 1-30: There 10f: btr 435.   00

63   Atig [6] 8-1(2ow)   **191   Longghurst** [5] 7-10
9 ran   2¼,hd,nk,nk,2½   (Hamden Al-Maktoum)   J Dunlop Arundel, Sussex

598   JUDDMONTE LOCKINGE STAKES   GROUP 2   £29680   1m   Good 53 +26 Fast

-313   SCOTTISH REEL [1] (M Stoute) 4-9-1 W R Swinburn 4/1: 1240-21: 4 ch c Northfields -
Dance All Night (Double-U-Jay): Top class miler: sn prom and led inside the final 1f, ridden
out in very fast run Gr.2 Juddmonte Lockinge Stakes at Newbury May 16: first time out just
btn in Gr.2 Trust House Forte Mile at Sandown: in excellent form in '85 winning his first
4 starts, Gr.3 Diamond Stakes at Epsom & minor events at Warwick, Ripon & York: also a grand
2nd to Bairn in Gr.2 St James Palace Stakes at Royal Ascot: very eff over 7f/1m: acts on gd,
loves soft/heavy: no trk preferences: certain to win more good races & is a credit to his trainer.   88

--   TELEPROMPTER [5] (J Watts) 6-9-6(vis) T Ives 9/1: 12120-2: Led ½way till inside final
1f: fine seasonal debut from this top class gelding: in excellent form thro'out '85, his most
notable success when making all in Gr.1 Arlington Million at Arlington Park USA: also won
Gr.3 race at Pheonix Park & narrowly btn in this same race: later fin 2nd to Shadeed in Gr.2
Queen Elizabeth II Stakes at Ascot: in '84 won that same race & Gr.3 event at Deauville, the
Curragh & Phoenix Park: also won a h'cap at York: very eff over 8/9f: stays 10f on a fast
trk: acts on firm 7 yld grnd 7 is best out in front: wears a visor but is thoroughly genuine and
should win some good races in '86.   89

•325   SUPREME LEADER [3] (C Brittain) 4-9-1 P Robinson 6/4 FAV: 030-113: Al niggled along:
needs 10f? see 325.   80

313   EFISIO [8] (J Dunlop) 4-9-1 Pat Eddery 14/1: 2110-04: Gd hdway over 1f out: one pace
final 1f: fine run and is approaching peak form: very smart colt who in '85 won Gr.3 event at
Newmarket and a Listed race at Goodwood: unbtn 2yo, winning Gr.3 Horris Hill Stakes at
Newbury after wins at Salisbury, Goodwood & Ascot: very eff at 7f/1m: acts on firm & yld grnd
& on any trk: genuine & consistent.   77

•413   BOLLIN KNIGHT [7] 4-9-1 M Birch 10/1: -01110: Another good effort: stays 1m: see 413.   76

313   PROTECTION [6] 4-9-1 S Cauthen 9/2: 2110-30: Wknd over 1f out: see 313.   76

--   LUCKY RING [2] 4-9-1 W Carson 12/1: 21114-0: Btr for this seasonal debut.   00

--   Grand Harbour [4] 9-1
8 ran   1½,2,1½,¾,hd   (Cheveley Park Stud)   M Stoute Newmarket

599   SIR CHARLES CLORE. MEM. STKS 3YO FILLIES £8506   1m 2f   Good 53 -05 Slow

--   PILOT BIRD [3] (W Hern) 3-8-6 W Carson 14/1: 3-1: 3 b g Blakeney - The Dancer
(Green Dancer): Very useful filly: first time out, responded to press to lead over 1f out
and despite going left, was sn clear in Sir Charles Clore Memorial Stakes (Listed race) at
Newbury May 16: on sole start in '85 fin 3rd to Pilot Jet in a maiden on this trk: well bred
filly who looks certain to stay 12f: acts on gd grnd & a gall trk & should win more races.   60

•386   KABIYLA [7] (M Stoute) 3-9-0 W R Swinburn 13/8 FAV: 1-12: Well bckd: led 4f out:
stays 10f: see 386 (1m).   62

+444   OLD DOMESDAY BOOK [10] (J Winter) 3-8-9 G Starkey 10/3: 0-13: Slightly hmpd over
1f out: kept on and nearly got 2nd: gd effort: should be suited by 12f: acts on any trk.   57

--   EXCEPTIONAL BEAUTY [4] (M Jarvis) 3-8-6 T Ives 16/1: 02-4: Fin well and this was a
most encouraging seasonal debut: on final outing in '85 fin 2nd to Elwadhna in a Newmarket
fillies maiden: half sister to 3 winners: eff at 10f, should get 12f: acts on gd & firm grnd
and a gall trk: should be winning soon.   49

359   GLITTER [9] 3-8-6 Pat Eddery 14/1: -030: Ch over 2f out: another gd run and is
sure to find a maiden: stays 10f: acts on gd & yld/soft: see 359.   48

•209   BELICE [5] 3-8-9 M Wigham 25/1: -10: Never nearer: in gd form: stays 10f: acts on
gd & heavy: see 209.   51

264   CHERNICHERVA [2] 3-8-9 S Cauthen 7/2: 113-20: Mkt drifter: led 6f: sn wknd: much
better 264 (1m).   00

214   BAMBOLONA [1] 3-9-0 R Cochrane 10/1: 210-00: Wknd str: not stay 10f? see 214.   00

372   Lost In France [8] 8-6   **--   Fete Champetre** [6] 8-6
10 ran   2,hd,2½,¾,shhd   (Sir John Astor)   W Hern West Ilsley, Berks

600   HUE WILLIAMS STKS 3yo   £4971   6f   Good 53 15 Fast

190 GOVERNOR GENERAL [5] (L Cottrell) 3-8-9 G Starkey 20/1: 001-01: 3 b c Dominion -
Law And Impulse (Roan Rocket): Smart, much impr colt: caused a 20/1 surprise, led well over
1f out and sn clear for an easy win in fast run & valuable Hue-Williams Stakes at Newbury
May 16: in '85 won a fast run maiden at Goodwood: half brother to 2 winners: very eff at
6f: acts on gd & firm & on any trk: should win more good races.   74
406 NATIVE OAK [4] (H Cecil) 3-8-9 S Cauthen 9/4 FAV: 313-42: Al prom: no ch with winner
though again ran well: may need further than 6f: see 406.   64
232 FASHADA [10] (R Johnson Houghton) 3-8-6 W Carson 8/1: 01-03: Not clear run 2f out:
ran on well: good effort & should be winning soon: lightly raced in '85, winning final outing
at York: very eff over 6f though should be suited by further: acts on gd/firm & yld.   58
*314 TREASURE KAY [12] (P Makin) 3-8-9 B Rouse 11/2: 010-14: Ch over 2f out: in gd form:
stays 6f: see 314.   58
--   FAYRUZ [6] 3-8-9(BL) T Ives 7/1: 11022-0: Made much on seasonal debut: btr for race:
bl first time today: smart 2yo, winning 6 in a row at Newbury, Lingfield, Kempton, Ripon,
Thirsk and Windsor: subsq. was off the trk for sometime after chipping a bone: on final
outing was a find nk 2nd to Hallgate in Gr.3 Corn Wallis Stakes at Ascot: very eff at 5f:
acts on firm & yld & on any trk: game & consistent & should do btr next time.   54
--   GOSSIPER [8] 3-8-6 W Woods 33/1: 41400-0: Fair seasonal debut: in '85 won a nursery
at Warwick & a maiden at Wolverhampton (first time out): stays 6f: acts on firm & yld &
on any trk.   49
59   MEASURING [13] 3-8-6 Pat Eddery 8/1: 1320-30: Early speed: see 59.   00
*227 HOME RULE [11] 3-8-9 S Whitworth 9/1: 200-010: Mkt drifter: there 4f: stiff task.   00
387 LUNA BID [9] 3-9-0 R Cochrane 9/2: 130-020: Well bckd, but no show: much btr 387.   00
387 Niccolo Polo [7] 8-9   229 Royal Troubador [1] 8-9
143 Pop The Cork [2] 8-9   -- Avalon [3] 8-9
13 ran   5,2,1,1½,½   (Ray Richards)   L Cottrell Cullompton, devon

601   VOLVO GUARANTEED STAKES 2YO   £3200   5f   Good 53 -13 Slow

--   FOREST FLOWER [7] (I Balding) 2-8-8 S Cauthen 6/4 FAV: 1: 2 ch c Green Forest -
Leap Lively (Nijinsky): Very prom filly: first time out, well bckd and led inside the final
1f, easily in a 2yo stakes at Newbury May 16: well bred sort, being a first foal of
Lingfield Oaks Trial winner Leap Lively: eff at 6f, will be suited by further: acts on gd
grnd & a gall trk and can only improve and rate more highly.   66
--   BINT PASHA [6] (P Cole) 2-8-8 W Carson 12/1: 2: Friendless in mkt: no ch with winner
but this was a most promising run: cost $220,000 & should be suited by further than 6f:
acts on gd grnd & a gall trk: must find a maiden soon.   56
--   BASIC BLISS [1] (P Walwyn) 2-8-8 Paul Eddery 7/1: 3: Led over 1f out: gd racecourse
debut from this 13,000 gns purchase: eff at 6f, should stay further: acts on gd grnd & a
gall trk & should have no trouble finding a race.   53
*311 SAXON STAR [4] (J Winter) 2-9-1 Pat Eddery 13/8: 14: Stiff task at weights: led
½way: acts on gd & soft: see 311.   57
--   NAJABA [3] 2-8-8 B Rouse 16/1: 0: Mkt drifter: no show on debut: 140,000 gns purchase
who should do much btr than this: half sister to 2 winners: should be suited by further than 6 f. 34
--   ZILDA [2] 2-8-8 P Cook 14/1: 0: Mkt drifter: led 3f: French bred filly who should impr. 24
--   Lady Westgate [5] 8-8
7 ran   3,1,1,8,4   (Paul Mellon)   I Balding Kingsclere, Hants

NEWCASTLE   Friday May 16th   Lefthanded Galloping Track

Official Going Given as Good/Soft

602 EBF BLANCHLAND MAIDEN STAKES 2YO   £2714   5f   Good 63 +11 Fast

515 GLENCROFT [7] (D Chapman) 2-9-0 D Nicholls 12/1: 001: 2 b g Crofter - Native Fleet
(Fleet Nasrullah): Showed impr form when just getting up to win a fast run 2yo maiden at
Newcastle May 16: cost 6,200 gns as a yearling: acts on gd & yld grnd & on a gall trk.   57
320 WIGANTHORPE [3] (M W Easterby) 2-9-0 T Lucas 10/11 FAV: 022: Just failed to make all,
though beat rem decisively and should recoup losses soon: acts on any trk: see 320 & 242.   50
--   COME ON CHASE ME [13] (J Etherington) 2-9-0 M Wood 8/1: 3: Chased winner over ½way:
no extra dist though should impr for this race: speedily bred colt whose dam was twice
successful as a juvenile: acts on gd/yld grnd & on a gall trk.   35
--   KACERE [9] (P Calver) 2-9-0 M Fry 20/1: 4: Mkt drifter on racecourse debut: kept on
promisingly and should impr: cost I.R. 9,500gns and is a half brother to several winners:
sure to stay further: acts on gd grnd & on a gall trk.   27
345 LITTLE KEY [11] 2-9-0 D Manning(3) 4/1: 40: Early speed: btr on a sharp trk in 345.   13
353 LINPAC NORTH MOOR [4] 2-8-11 J Lowe 20/1: 00: Speed over ½way: half sister to winning
miler Linpac Leaf.   10
77   JJ JIMMY [2] 2-9-0(VIS) W Ryan 10/1: 00: Speed to ½way: fin 7th.   00
3   DEINOPUS [12] 2-9-0 G Baxter 7/1: 00: Mkt drifter: never going well after abs.   00
488 Bantel Bouquet [6] 8-11   425 Mere Music [5] 9-0
--   Causeway Foot [10] 9-0   -- Bejant Skite [1] 9-0
--   Queens Connection [8] 8-11
13 ran   hd,7,3,7,shhd   (W G Swiers)   D Chapman Stillington, Yorks

---

603 RIDSDALE SELLING STAKES 2YO   £1356   5f   Good 63 -13 Slow

376 BROONS ADDITION [6] (K Stone) 2-8-8 G Brown(5) 6/1: 43431: 3 b f Enchantment - Belinda Mede (Runnymede): Gaining a deserved success when leading inside dist, comfortably in a 2yo seller at Newcastle May 16 (bought in 1,600 gns): cheaply acquired filly who has been placed in all her races to date: eff over 5f on gd & soft grnd & should stay further: well suited by a gall trk. — **32**

533 PASHMINA [4] (T Fairhurst) 2-8-8 C Coates(5) 6/1: 102: Tried to make all: no extra close home: well suited by this gall trk: see 57. — **26**

354 BAD PAYER [5] (M W Easterby) 2-8-8 M Hindley(0) 12/1: 43: Denied a clear run dist, fin well: should win a similar event soon: see 354. — **26**

515 NATIONS SONG [9] (R Stubbs) 2-8-8 D Nicholls 10/1: 04: Al front rank: impr effort from this cheaply bought filly: acts on gd grnd & on a gall trk. — **23**

133 BANTEL BLAZER [2] 2-8-11 J Lowe 12/1: 3030: Al up there: acts on any trk: see 40. — **22**

515 SAWDUST JACK [10] 2-8-11 T Lucas 8/11 FAV: 000: Dropped in class: gambled on and showed good speed over ½way: however much btr in 515 (sharp trk). — **16**

136 BOLD DIFFERENCE [8] 2-8-8 N Carlisle 8/1: 000: Never threatened leaders. — **00**

236 LATE PROGRESS [7] 2-8-8 M Fry 10/1: -000: Never on terms. — **00**

543 Gloriad [3] 8-8   **450** Sunny Gibraltar [11] 8-8
10 ran   1½,hd,1,1½,3   (W S Brown)   K Stone Malton, Nth Yorks

---

604 XYZ HANDICAP STAKES 3YO 0-70   £6368   1m 2f Good 63 -09 Slow   [66]

372 AMONGST THE STARS [6] (S Norton) 3-7-13 J Lowe 6/1: 200-101: 3 br f Proctor - Out Of This World (High Top): Switched & qcknd well to lead inside dist in a valuable h'cap at Newcastle May 16: first time out winner of a similar event at Haydock, and last season won a Wolverhampton nursery and a fillies maiden at Catterick: very eff over 1m, stays 10f well: acts on gd/firm & heavy grnd & on a gall trk. — **51**

553 FORCELLO [1] (S Norton) 3-7-7(3oh) J Quinn(3) 11/2: 42-1242: Made most: has been busy lately though continues to run well: see 444. — **42**

326 SIMSIM [9] (J Dunlop) 3-9-7 G Baxter 9/4 FAV: 41-23: Ran on too late: stays 10f: see 326 — **68**

244 MERHI [5] (S Norton) 3-7-13(3ow) R Hills 14/1: 200-234: Never nearer: gd effort: stays 10f: see 143. — **44**

*352 FRAMLINGTON COURT [3] 3-8-0 N Howe 11/2: 00-2D10: Another gd effort: stays 10f: — **22**

342 SPROWSTON BOY [2] 3-8-1 Gay Kelleway(2) 12/1: 2-11330: Remains in gd form: see 342, 13238

427 PLANET ASH [7] 3-8-4 G Carter(3) 8/1: -241440: Al behind & is btr than this: see 326. — **00**

322 SOXOPH [4] 3-7-9(BL) M Fry 14/1: -41000: Held up, no threat: much btr here in 53 (1m). — **00**

553 OPTIMISM FLAMED [8] 3-7-10 A Mackay 10/1: 033-200: Trailed in last: much btr 183 (1m). — **00**
9 ran   1½,1½,1½,1½,3   (Mrs Malcolm Keogh)   S Norton Barnsley Sth Yorks

---

605 EARSDON EBF STAKES 3YO   £3880   1m   Good 63 -36 Slow

414 LANCE [5] (P Cole) 3-8-11 T Quinn 6/1: 200-221: 3 b c Main Reef - Kilcurley Lass (Huntercombe): Sn lead & only had to be pushed out to win a slowly run 3yo stakes at Newcastle May 16: deserved this win after running up to useful duo Barley Bill and Fleet Form in his previous outings this season: in '85 won a maiden at Bath: very eff over 7/8f: acts on firm & soft grnd & a gall trk. — **68**

326 NERVOUS RIDE [8] (H Cecil) 3-8-11 W Ryan 2/1 FAV: 1-02: Kept on though was never going to catch this easy winner: nevertheless ran a good race: see 326. — **60**

*216 DIGGERS REST [3] (G Wragg) 3-9-4 R Hills 5/2: 303-13: In good form: stays 1m: see 216. — **66**

407 JAZETAS [9] (N Callaghan) 3-9-1 D Manning(3) 7/2: 4-11404: Eased in class and ran to his best: well suited by a gall trk: see 127. — **62**

479 DEMON FATE [10] 3-8-11 K Darley 33/1: 04-00: Well btn though not disgraced in this hot company: lightly raced last season when showing promise behind Mazaad at Pontefract on final outing: half brother to a couple of winners: stays 1m: acts on gd grnd & on any trk. — **42**

-- LUCKY BLAKE [1] 3-8-11 M Wood 33/1: -0: Tough task on debut: ran on late, showing plenty of promise: half brother to winning sprinter Lucky Hunter though seems well suited by 1m himself: acts on gd grnd and on a gall trk. — **41**

-- Son Of Absalom [2] 8-11   **258** Sana Song [6] 8-11
-- Mahogany Run [11] 8-11   -- Jelly Jill [4] 8-8
10 ran   4,½,nk,8,¾,1   (Fahd Salman)   P Cole Lambourn, Berks

---

606 OTTERBURN HANDICAP 4YO UPWARDS 0-35   £2400   7f   Good 63 +10 Fast   [35]

441 KNIGHTS SECRET [4] (M H Easterby) 5-8-12 J Lowe 4/1 FAV: 0000-21: 5 ch h Immortal Knight - Lush Secret (Most Secret): Nicely bckd when qckning well to lead inside final 1f in a fast run h'cap at Newcastle May 16: first time out last season won a h'cap at Pontefract and does well when fresh: in '83 won at Catterick, Beverley & Redcar: eff over 6f though seems btr over 7/8f: acts on any grnd & on any trk: in gd form. — **30**

490 ZIO PEPPINO [9] (T Craig) 5-8-5 T Lucas 9/1: 000-032: Led after ½way till near fin: in gd form & could win a similar race soon: see 490. — **20**

441 O I OYSTON [3] (J Berry) 10-9-2 A Woods(7) 16/1: 000-003: Confirmed front runner who again tried to make all: best effort for sometime: early last season made all in an app. h'cap at Catterick: in '84 won at Edinburgh: acts on fast grnd though is fav by some give: eff over 7/8f: acts on any trk: grand stable servant. — **25**

310 DOMINION PRINCESS [8] (P Rohan) 5-8-2 J Quinn(5) 11/1: 2000-44: Ran on too late: see 310. 10
-- ITALIAN SECRET [2] 5-8-8 T Quinn 20/1: 30000-0: Al prom on her reapp: modest sprint
h'capper who last won in '83, at Wolverhampton & Beverley: well suited by fast grnd, though
does act on soft: should be btr for this outing. 08
-- BELLA BANUS [5] 4-9-5 M Hindley(3) 16/1: 10302-0: Gd late prog and btr for race:
in fine form last backend, winning at Newcastle & Redcar before finishing an unlucky 2nd to
Nuravia again at Redcar: eff over 7/8f: acts on gd & firm grnd & is suited by a stiff trk. 18
*499 EASY DAY [1] 4-9-2(4ex) A Mckay 9/2: 00-0410: Front rank till dist: see 499. 00
55 BATON BOY [14] 5-10-0 K Darley 10/1: 4000-20: No threat after fair abs: see 55. 00
260 MONINSKY [15] 5-8-7 L Charnock 8/1: 2332-20: Early speed though btr in 260 (sharp trk). 00

453	Taj Singh [16] 8-6		355	Throne Of Glory [6] 9-12			
490	Pentoff [10] 8-6(bl)		441	Young Bruss [12] 8-10	--	Show Of Hands [11] 8-8	
522	Swift River [7] 7-8		--	Marsiliana [13] 7-12	490	Nipknowes [17] 8-3	
17 ran	1,3,nk,5,½,1,1½		(N G Westbrook)		M H Easterby Great Habton, Nth Yorks		

---

607   HENSHAW STAKES 3YO UPWARDS   £1582   1m 4f Good 63 -29 Slow

409 PAEAN [4] (H Cecil) 3-8-13 W Ryan 8/15 FAV: 2-121: 3 b c Bustino - Mixed Applause
(Nijinsky): Very useful colt: landed the odds with the minimum of fuss, making most for an
easy win in a stakes race at Newcastle May 16: first time out won a Newbury maiden and
subsq. just failed to overhaul Heighlad in a valuable race at Newmarket: on sole start last
season was just btn by Kolgong Heights in a Newbury maiden: very well bred colt who is very
eff around 12f: acts on firm & heavy grnd & is well suited by a gall trk. 68
-- CUILLIN SOUND [5] (C Brittain) 3-8-5 G Baxtar 12/1: 0-2: No ch with winner though ran
well to take the minor honours on his reapp: last to fin behind Zahdan in a valuable race at
Ascot on sole start last season: clearly stays 12f well: acts on gd grnd & on a stiff trk:
should find a small race. 44
*239 BLOCKADE [6] (P Cole) 3-8-13 T Quinn 85/40: 02-13: In gd form: see 239. 48
388 SPINNING TURN [2] (P Calver) 3-8-5 M Fry 12/1: -034: Fin well btn & btr over 1m in 388. 24
381 SAY PLEASE [1] 7-9-4 S P Griffiths(5) 100/1: -00: Rank outsider and trailed in last. 00
5 ran   6,2½,10,dist   (Lord Howard de Walden)   H Cecil Newmarket

---

608   ROWLEY SELLING STAKES 3YO   £1033   7f   Good 55 No Standard Time

377 HEAVENLY HOOFER [5] (Denys Smith) 3-8-7 D Leadbitter(5) 12/1: 2000-01: 3 b g Dance
In Time - Heavenly Chord (Hittite Glory): Came with a late run when readily winning a seller
at Beverley May 17 (bought in 2,800 gns): eff at 7f should stay further: goes well on
a stiff track. 19
14 KNOYDART [2] (P Haslam) 3-8-7 G French 10/1: -02: Fin strongly after a slow start,
not btn far: looks sure to be suited by 1m & should find a seller. 18
-- HARSLEY SURPRISE [19] (N Tinkler) 3-8-4 J H Brown(5) 16/1: 4040-3: Not btn far in close
fin: good seasonal debut: stays 7f on a stiff trk. 15
377 TOUCH ME NOT [12] (R Hollinshead) 3-8-7(BL) S Perks 7/1: 0-30004: Bl first time,
nearly made all (6f). 16
426 MISS BESWICK [17] 3-8-4 I Johnson 25/1: 0000-00: Early leader. 10
426 MEDDY [8] 3-8-7 R Cochrane 8/1: 0403-00: Ev ch: see 426. 09
506 BAO [6] 3-8-4 J Scally(7) 13/2: -4300: Fin 7th after bad swerve: see 426. 00
489 MUSIC TEACHER [16] 3-8-11 A Shoults(5) 11/2: 0-01020: Not well drawn: see 489. 00
426 RED ZULU [14] 3-8-7 M Fry 9/1: 03-0000: Ev ch, fin 9th. 00
318 STEP ON [15] 3-8-7 J Bleasdale 3/1 FAV: 00-30: Well bckd fav: btr 218 (9f soft). 00
322 LUCKY WEST [4] 3-8-4 S Wood(7) 8/1: -00: Never dngr 10th. 00

305	Sister Nancy [1] 8-4(VIS)		--	Last Jewel [13] 8-4	
318	Balidareen [1] 8-9(5ow)		447	Crown Colony [3] 8-7	
--	Manasta [18] 8-4	380	Allisterdransfield [7] 9-0		
17 ran	½,shhd,1,1½,2	(T Gibson)	Denys Smith Bishop Auckland, Co Durham		

---

609   RAPID LAD HANDICAP (0-35) 3YO+   £2460   1m 2f Good 55 -02 Slow   [34]

-- FORWARD RALLY [16] (M Prescott) 4-9-6 G Duffield 9/1: 0021-1: 4 c f Formidable (USA) -
Rally (Relko): First time out led 2 out and came clear comfortably winning a h'cap at
Beverley May 17: in '85 won on heavy grnd at Hamilton: also acts on firm: goes well on a
stiff trk and seems to stay 10f well: impr filly. 35
380 ICARO [8] (N Callaghan) 3-8-3(1ow) R Cochrane 7/4 FAV: 301-022: Heavily bckd fav:
ran on well but too late: stays 10f well, good effort against older horses: should find
a race soon. 32
310 NIGHT WARRIOR [11] (A Robson) 4-9-3 J Bleasdale 16/1: 0-00403: Fin well: see 238. 28
429 BALGOWNIE [2] (J Mulhall) 6-8-4 P Burke(7) 12/1: 0000204: Chall wide & kept on
strongly at the finish: goes particularly well on a stiff trk: see 333, 36. 13
547 PARIS TRADER [4] 4-9-8(bl) T Lucas 16/1: 102-000: Returning to form? twice won
sellers in '85 at Haydock & Redcar: very eff at 8/9f & acts on gd & soft grnd: usually bl. 30

281 RUSTIC TRACK [6] 6-8-2 M Fry 8/1: 031-320: Again fin strongly after getting well
behind: puzzling sort who usually runs well at Beverley: see 281, 131.   10
439 SEVEN SWALLOWS [1] 5-9-5 M Rimmer 9/1: 30-1000: Fin 8th: best 184.   00
166 MISTER POINT [13] 4-9-3 M Birch 10/1: 200-000: Ran well out in front for most of the
way: returning to form? in '85 won h'caps at Hamilton & Beverley: suited by a stiff trk &
heavy grnd: also acts on gd: eff at 9/10f.   00
461 ROCKALL [3] 3-8-2(bl) J Lowe 8/1: 30-0430: Well bckd, slow start: btr 461 (12f).   00

333	North Star Sam [7] 7-11			410	Well Covered [10] 9-11
282	Dubavarna [14] 8-8	310	Elarim [12] 9-8(bl)	--	Bundling Bed [15] 7-11
184	Cavalieravantgarde [9] 8-7			429	Crowfoots Couture [5] 7-9
--	Arabian Sea [18] 9-11				

17 ran   1,1,1½,½,shhd   (Lady Macdonald Buchanan)   M Prescott Newmarket

610 HULL DAILY MAIL STAKES 2YO   £2725   5f   Good 55 -05 Slow

382 MISTER MAJESTIC [7] (R Williams) 2-9-3 R Cochrane 1/2 FAV: 121: 2 b c Tumble Wind -
Our Village (Ballymore): Led 3f and came again gamely close home in a minor race at Beverley
May 17, odds on: earlier won at Newmarket: half brother to Clotilda: should be suited by
further than 5f, acts on gd & yld & on a stiff trk: genuine.   56
*503 ALKADI [6] (W O'gorman) 2-9-1 M L Thomas 9/4 : 312: Prom, led 1 out and was just
caught: impr & genuine colt: see 503.   53
523 ROWEKING [3] (L Lightbrown) 2-9-0 J Bleasdale 20/1: 0201343: Dsptd lead most: see 367.   40
--   CHESWOLD [4] (M H Easterby) 2-8-11 M Birch 25/1: 4: Met trouble in running, sure to
fin closer next time: cost 22,000 gns: probably suited by 6f.   35
523 ROSIES IMAGE [1] 2-8-8 A Shoults(5) 100/1: 000: Never in it.   00
--   BECKINGHAM BEN [2] 2-8-11 S Morris 100/1: 0: Al behind.   00
6 ran   shhd,4,½,10,½   (D A Johnson)   R Williams Newmarket

611 TURN TO YORKSHIRE HANDICAP (0-35) 3YO+   £2302   1m   Good 55 +10 Fast   [33]

429 PATCHBURG [5] (W Haigh) 4-9-2 R Cochrane 11/2: 2-21301: 4 b g Remainder Man -
Voleur Vert (Burglar): Held up, got up close home in quite a fast run h'cap at Beverley
May 17: earlier won an app h'cap at Ayr: failed to win last year but won at Hamilton as a
2yo: eff between 7-10f: acts on gd/firm but seems to prefer softish grnd: goes well on
a stiff track.   28
310 PERSHING [1] (J Leigh) 5-8-11 M Miller 12/1: 3100-02: Slow start but fin strongly and
just btn: seems to run very well at Beverley and won there in '85 (selling h'cap): suited by
1m & should stay further: at his best on a sound surface & bl when winning.   23
105 STARS DELIGHT [7] (F Carr) 4-7-11 G Carter(3) 8/1: 0030-23: Dsptd lead & went clear,
just caught: in good form & is probably btr suited by a sharpish trk: see 105.   09
378 BLACK RIVER [13] (M H Easterby) 5-7-10 J Lowe 13/2: 040-004: Early ldr: see 46: stays 1m?07
196 BIT OF A STATE [11] 6-9-1(bl) D Nicholls 8/1: 300-000: Well bckd, never closer:
returning to form & bl when winning twice on the trot in '85 at Redcar & Beverley: in '84
won at Beverley & Pontefract & seems to do very well at Beverley: very eff at 1m on gd grnd
but probably acts on any: likes a stiff trk: rated 33 last year.   22
491 IZZY GUNNER [14] 3-7-7 M L Thomas 7/2 FAV: 0-00220: Well bckd fav but btr 491.   10
399 LONG BAY [10] 4-8-12 M Rimmer 8/1: 0001-00: Active in mkt, no show: landed a gamble
in a selling h'cap at Brighton in '85 over 7f on gd grnd: goes well on a sharp trk.   00
281 GLENDERRY [4] 4-8-9 W Ryan 8/1: 0100-00: Eff in mkt, no show: tried in bl when
winning a h'cap at Ripon in '85 & also won at Ripon first time out (seller) last year! in '84
won a selling h'cap at Beverley: suited by 8/9f & acts on firm & yld.   00
310 TRY SCORER [9] 4-9-3 D Leadbitter(5) 7/1: 4-21000: Disapp since 143 (soft).   00
521 PALMION [3] 4-9-7 S Perks 6/1: 40-0200: Made much: best 196 (C/D).   00

449	Grey Card [12] 7-8	--	Boy Sandford [8] 8-1	490	Peters Kiddie [2] 7-9
196	Common Farm [6] 8-11				

14 ran   shhd,nk,2,2½,2½   (T G kelso)   W Haigh Malton, Yorks

612 LECONFIELD MAIDEN AUCTION STAKES 2YO   £908   5f   Good 55 -03 Slow

536 CROFTERS CLINE [3] (J Wilson) 2-8-8 Julie Bowker(7) 33/1: 01: 2 br c Crofter -
Modena (Sassafras): Comfortably made all in a maiden auction event at Beverley May 17:
suited by front running tactics, goes well on a stiff trk & should be suited by 6f.   45
--   OUR HORIZON [18] (D Barron) 2-8-5 S Webster 20/1: 2: Fin best of all after running
green: good debut: will probably be suited by 6f: is a half brother to '85 winner Runaway
Lover: should find a similar race.   33
364 RHABDOMANCER [38] (J Watts) 2-8-7 N Connorton 4/1: 33: Kept on well: consistent: see 364.33
536 HUGO Z HACKENBUSH [20] (C Tinkler) 2-8-8 M Wood 16/1: 404: Al prom: see 415.   30
425 OYSTER GRAY [7] 2-8-5 I Johnson 2/1 FAV: 320: Al there: much btr 425.   26
--   MARKET MAN [14] 2-8-8 G Carter(3) 20/1: 0: Never closer: cost only I.R. 1,700.   25
425 PERTAIN [10] 2-8-8(VIS) N Carlisle 20/1: 0400: Tried in a visor, fin 7th: see 425, 136.   00
473 CITY FINAL [17] 2-8-9 S Perks 7/1: 40: Active in mkt: btr 473.   00
--   BLOW FOR HOME [9] 2-8-10 G Duffield 10/1: 0: Fin 9th, never closer.   00
--   GREAT MEMORY [2] 2-8-12 E Guest(3) 5/1: 0: Very well bckd but no show: cost 6,000 gns:
should do better next time.   00

425 SQUIGGLE [12] 2-8-12 R Cochrane 9/1: 00: Better 425.   00
--   Grecian Jos [23] 8-8   404 Pearlitic [22] 8-10   425 Broom Star [4] 8-10
425 The Mague [21] 8-8   -- Maybemusic [11] 8-8   -- Oxford Place [8] 8-12
--   Mayspark [13] 8-11   446 Chunky Supreme [19] 8-8
21   Cold Laser [15] 8-8   -- Cowlam Boy [24] 8-8   -- Sound As A Pound [25] 8-8
22 ran ⊢ 3,hd,1½,½,1½   (Mrs G S Rees)   J Wilson Tarleton, Lancs

613   RISBY MAIDEN STAKES 3YO+   £2013   1m 4f   Good 55 -16 Slow

430 LOCH SEAFORTH [15] (H Cecil) 3-8-5 W Ryan 1/1 FAV: 44-21: 3 b c Tyrnavos - Marypark
(Charlottown): Led 2½ out and held on under press in a maiden race at Beverley May 17:
probably suited by forcing tactics, acts on firm & gd grnd: stays 12f & should be suited
by further: rated 60 last year.   52
--   THE PRUDENT PRINCE [6] (W Jarvis) 4-9-7 R Cochrane 9/1: 32-2: Al prom, kept on strongly
and just btn: a lightly raced 4yo maiden, eff at 10/12f & will probably stay further:
takes a strong hold & suited by forcing tactics: acts on gd & yld & should certainly find
a maiden race.   48
357 CALL TO HONOR [12] (O Douieb) 3-8-5(bl) R Machado 5/1: -43: Al there: stays 12f: see 357,45
452 TOSARA [2] (H Candy) 4-9-4 R Curant 4/1: 0-24: A little disapp after 452: possibly
btr 10f but is bred to stay this trip: worth another chance.   40
--   SOMETHING SIMILAR [9] 3-8-5 M Wood 14/1: 0204-0: Bckd at long odds: probably stays 12f:
also eff at 7/8f & acts on gd/firm & yld: ran well at Redcar last year.   43
402 FRANGNITO [3] 3-8-5 K Darley 7/1: 0-400: Probably stays 12f: see 328.   37
--   Bernish Lady [5] 9-4   -- Relatively Easy [14] 8-2
430 Cornish Prince [4] 8-5   381 Brigadier Troy [8] 9-7
--   Sir Chester [11] 8-5   448 Sagax [16] 9-7   130 Blue Bells Star [13] 8-2
166 Mexican Mill [1] 9-7   452 Debach Revenge [10] 9-4
15 ran   ¾,2½,hd,½,4   (Sir David Wills)   H Cecil Newmarket

NEWBURY   Saturday May 17th   Lefthanded, Stiff Galloping Track

Official Going Given as Good to Soft First Two, Soft Remainder

614   PHILIP CORNES NICKEL ALLOYS STKS 2YO   £4123   5f   Good/Soft 82 -33 Slow

*497 BESTPLAN [4] (W O'gorman) 2-9-3 T Ives 15/8 FAV: 011: 2 b c Try My Best - Make Plans
(Go Marching): Made all but just held on in £4123 event at Newbury May 17: probably btr on
faster grnd when winning at Lingfield May 9: half brother to the smart Sayf El Arab and
the useful Eagles Landed: speedily bred sort who acts on yld: probably btr on a sounder
surface: fast time winner last time. speedy sort·   62
--   CAROLS TREASURE [2] (B Hills) 2-8-11 B Thomson 20/1: 2: Unlucky, met trouble in
running and just failed to get up: a promising sort who will soon find compensation.   55
--   MEBHIL [7] (P Kelleway) 2-8-11 S Cauthen 12/1: 3: Al there, prom debut: will probably
be suited by 6f: cost 15,000 gns: well clear of the rest: sure to find a maiden race.   50
--   MILEAGE BANK [8] (P Cole) 2-8-11 P Waldron 3/1: 4: Well bckd, expected to do btr:
cost $230,000 as a yearling and is a full brother to the smart '84 2yo Overtrump: should
do better next time.   39
440 ARAPITI [5] 2-9-3 S Whitworth 7/2: 2120: Much btr 442, 230.   44
434 SWIFT PURCHASE [9] 2-8-11 P Cook 16/1: 30: No threat: see 434.   24
--   MAHRAJAN [6] 2-8-11 B Rouse 20/1: 0: Cost 120,000 gns: half brother to Domynga and
a full brother to Fair Dominion, twice a winner over 5/6f in '83: should do btr.   00
404 SANDHURST [3] 2-8-11(BL) J Reid 33/1: 300: Disapp since 180.   00
--   KAMENSKY [1] 2-8-11 C Rutter 33/1: 0: Al behind after slow start: half brother to
several winners and cost 16,000 gns: will probably need further than 5f.   00
9 ran   hd,1,4,nk,6 ,shhd.   (Mrs P L Yong)   W O'gorman Newmarket

615   MAIL ON SUNDAY 3YO SERIES HCAP 3YO 0-50   £4493   1m   Good/Soft 82 +10 Fast   [54]

--   HILLS BID [8] (B Hills) 3-9-6 B Thomson 14/1: 00212-1: 3 b c Temperance Hill -
Davelle's Bid (Bold Bidder): First time out, led 1f out readily in a fast run 3yo h'cap at
Newbury May 17: in '85 won at Doncaster & Haydock: very eff at 1m & should stay 10f: acts
on gd/firm & yld & goes well on a stiff trk: genuine sort who also does well with forcing
tactics: impr sort who could win Gr 3 race.   60
326 GORGEOUS ALGERNON [9] (C Brittain) 3-9-7 G Baxter 20/1: 30-0102: Led 1½ out, gd
effort under top weight: possibly unsuited by soft but runs well at Newbury: clear of the rest.   57
*480 GEORGES QUAY [5] (R Hannon) 3-8-8 A Mcglone 8/1: 00-4013: Again ran well: see 480.   35
455 MUDRIK [12] (C Benstead) 3-9-7 B Rouse 7/1: 41-4124: Gd effort: btr 234 (heavy).   45
386 FLOATING ASSET [4] 3-8-13 S Cauthen 7/1: 0124-40: Can do btr: see 386.   34
444 PORO BOY [15] 3-8-9 L Jones(5) 33/1: 00-3400: Best 352 (1m yld): see 127.   28
518 PELLINKO [1] 3-9-1 A Mackay 7/1: 00-4120: Fin 7th, much btr 518, 334.   00
459 BLACK COMEDY [17] 3-7-11 R Fox 33/1: 01-0000: Fin 8th: returning to form? see 459.   00
326 TERMINATOR [16] 3-8-12 C Rutter(5) 9/2 FAV: 341-30: Disapp fav following 326.   00

514	Lightning Wind [10] 8-6			427	Beauclerc [3] 7-13
455	Miss Venezuela [18] 8-3			283	John Saxon [13] 9-0
334	Prime Number [19] 7-13(1ow)			209	Miss Aron [11] 9-3
--	Global [6] 8-3	436	Giving It All Away [14] 8-2(1ow)		
--	Gay Appeal [7] 8-13	436	Carnival Rose [2] 7-11		
19 ran	1½,5,1½,1½,¾		(Sheikh Mohammed)		B Hills Lambourn, Berks

616   TOWRY LAW INSURANCE HANDICAP 0-70   £10534   6f   Good/Soft 86 +16 Fast   [58]

401 DAWNS DELIGHT [5] (K Ivory) 8-9-3(vis) W Woods(3) 25/1: 40-0001: 8 b g Dawn Review - Bird Of Passage (Falcon): Led over 1 out and readily came clear in a valuable, fast run h'cap at Newbury May 17: in '85 won valuable h'caps at Doncaster & Haydock and in '84 won at Doncaster, Salisbury & Lingfield: very eff at 5/6f: acts on firm but possibly fav by softish grnd nowadays.   61

401 TYROLLIE [3] (N Vigors) 4-9-0 S Dawson(3) 12/1: 402-122: Led 2 out, in fine form: see 192 51

172 PRINCE SKY [10] (P Cole) 4-8-8 P Waldron 14/1: 0114-43: Kept on well: gd effort on this stiff trk but will do btr next time on a sharpish course: see 172.   44

401 AMEGHINO [8] (M Mccourt) 6-8-12 M Morse(5) 16/1: 000-004: Al there: running well: see 192 47

566 BAY PRESTO [4] 4-8-1(bl) S Whitworth 33/1: 00-3000: Ran well in the lead for a long way on the far side, quick reapp: might do btr on a sharper trk: see 172.   30

374 SAILORS SONG [17] 4-9-4(BL) P Cook 12/1: 0224-00: Tried in bl, running well: see 374.   46

387 MAJOR JACKO [13] 3-7-10 A Mcglone 20/1: 0-01400: Fin 7th: best on soft in 228.   00

361 OUR JOCK [1] 4-9-7 C Rutter(5) 20/1: 200-000: Fin 8th: not well drawn: see 361.   00

374 GOLD PROSPECT [11] 4-8-2 A Mackay 7/1: 20-1220: Mucn btr 374, 192.   00

520 VALLEY MILLS [19] 6-9-4 T Ives 8/1: 000-030: Fin 10th, btr 520.   00

401 MANCHESTERSKYTRAIN [22] 7-8-13 S Cauthen 5/1 FAV: 4200-30: Fin well down the field, disapp fav: much btr 401: worth another chance.   00

374 BRIG CHOP [14] 5-9-6 Paul Eddery 12/1: 0004-30: Refused to race: see 374.   00

361	Manimstar [6] 9-5(vis)			--	Stock Hill Lass [18] 8-10
481	Habs Lad [15] 9-0	401	Deputy Head [9] 8-5	--	Padre Pio [2] 8-12
--	Bold Realm [23] 8-0	441	Soon To Be [21] 8-6	--	Al Trui [12] 9-2
--	Young Inca [7] 9-6	374	Dorking Lad [20] 9-6		
22 ran	2½,nk,nk,2,nk,hd,nk		(K T Ivory)		K Ivory Radlett, herts

617   ASTON PARK STAKES   £8129   1m 5f   Good/Soft 90 -26 Slow

511 KAYTU [7] (C Brittain) 5-8-7 M Roberts 12/1: 0000-31: 5 b h High Top - Arawak (Seminole II): Surprise winner of Aston Park Stakes at Newbury May 17: led 3 out and held on gamely: lightly raced & below his best last year but won the Chester Vase in '84: eff over 12/14f and acts on firm & yld: acts on any trk & seems to do well when up with the pace.   74

-- MANGO EXPRESS [1] (C Horgan) 4-8-7 P Cook 9/2: -1124-2: Just failed with a strong chall, excellent seasonal debut: won his first 2 races in '85 at Lingfield & Newbury & fin. 4L 2nd to Lanfranco in a Gr.2 race at Royal Ascot: acts on firm & yld & well suited by 12f: goes well when fresh & should find a Gr.3 race this year.   73

251 LEADING STAR [13] (I Balding) 4-8-7 B Thomson 4/1: -010-43: Ran well & coming back to his best: was rated 75 last year: see 251.   69

360 AYRES ROCK [3] (M Haynes) 5-8-7 J Reid 50/1: 000-304: Fin well: another grand effort: see 360.   68

-- RANGE ROVER [11] 4-8-7 G Starkey 8/1: 13041-0: Well there 1 out, btr for race: in '85 won gamely at Goodwood & Chester: eff at 10-14f: acts on gd/firm & yld & on any trk: genuine sort who carries weight well.   68

-- LONGBOAT [2] 5-8-7 B Rouse 13/2: 3-142-0: Needs much further and in '85 was just btn by Gildoran in the Ascot Gold Cup over 2m4f: also won Gr.3 race at Ascot last year and in '84 won at Chester, Kempton, Bath & Goodwood: suited by 2m plus & best on firm grnd.   63

475 EAGLING [5] 4-8-7 S Cauthen 5/2 FAV: 310-200: Twice disapp since 251.   00

--	Ore [4] 8-7		--	Lundylux [14] 8-4	475	Chaumiere [8] 8-7(vis)
--	High Debate [9] 8-7		--	Vintage Port [12] 8-7	--	Broken Tackle [6] 8-2
519	Gentle Stream [10] 8-4					
14 ran	nk,2,½,hd,2½		(R N Khan)		C Brittain Newmarket	

618   LONDON GOLD CUP HCAP 0-60 4YO+   £4110   1m 3f   Good/Soft 90 -06 Slow   [54]

547 STATE BUDGET [8] (W Musson) 5-8-5 P Waldron 11/2: 230-131: 5 b g Free State - Novelista (El Gallo): In grand form and has won 2 of last 3 races: led 1½ out, comfortably in a valuable h'cap at Newbury May 17: earlier an easy winner at Leicester over 10f: also won at Leicester in '86 and in '84 at Redcar: eff at 10/12f & acts on firm but relishes soft: well suited by a stiff trk: could win again.   45

-- HIGH TENSION [3] (G Pritchard Gordon) 4-8-6 T Ives 5/1: 20044-2: Well bckd on seasonal debut, kept on well: in grand form early last year winning at Yarmouth & Redcar (course record): eff at 10/12f: evidently acts on yld, possibly btr on gd/firm grnd: nicely h'capped.   38

-- INSULAR [5] (I Balding) 6-9-8 S Cauthen 4/1: 00421-3: Led 5 out, gd seasonal debut: in '85 made all when winning an app. h'cap at Ascot and also won at Newmarket: in '84 won at York: eff over 12f & stays 2m very well: acts on any going and is suited by a gall trk: genuine sort.   53

NEWBURY   Saturday May 17th - Cont'd

445 SHARP NOBLE [11] (B Hanbury) 4-9-12 Paul Eddery 6/1: 1-02224: Another good effort:
see 263, 166.   56
453 RUNNING FLUSH [6] 4-8-10 B Crossley 10/1: 0-00430: Ran well on this stiff trk but is
possibly btr on a sharper trk: goes particularly well at Lingfield: see 112.   38
363 OWENS PRIDE [13] 4-8-3 P Robinson 3/1 FAV: 000-130: Disapp fav: btr 263.   17
532 Saintly Lad [9] 8-3   280 Majestic Ring [12] 8-3(BL)
58a Derby Day [7] 7-7(9oh)   --   Winter Palace [1] 8-5(3ow)
410 Joli Wasfi [10] 8-4(bl)   325 Thalestria [4] 8-13
--   Levigatus [2] 7-8
13 ran   4,½,½,1,8   (A Field)   W Musson Newmarket

619 SHAW MAIDEN STAKES 3YO   £3820   1m 3f Good/Soft 90 -29 Slow

--   SENOR TOMAS [19] (J Dunlop) 3-9-0 R Fox 16/1: -1: 3 b c Sparkler - Pearlemor (Gulf
Pearl): Surprise winner of a maiden race at Newbury May 17: comfortably led 1½f out after a
slow start: evidently well suited by soft grnd and looks certain to stay further than 11f:
should win btr races.   62
--   SATISFACTION [6] (W Hern) 3-9-0 B Proctor 16/1: 00-2: Led 2 out, evidently on the up
grade: will be suited by further than 11f: acts on soft and this half brother to the smart
Morcon will have no difficulty finding a maiden race: well clear of the rest.   58
--   DUNAN HILL [4] (I Balding) 3-9-0 J Matthias 20/1: -3: Kept on well at the fin & should
stay further than 11f: acts on soft: half brother to Almeda, a winner over 8f last year.   36
--   DHONI [9] (W Hern) 3-9-0 A Murray 14/1: 0-4: Led 3 out: should be suited by test of stamin 33
--   DARK HERITAGE [7] 3-9-0 J Reid 33/1: 00-0: Dsptd lead most of the way, probably stay 12f 30
348 LANDMARK [22] 3-9-0 T Ives 10/1: -00: Late prog: see 348.   29
--   BOON POINT [17] 3-9-0 B Thomson 2/1 FAV: 3-0: Evidently unsuited by the soft grnd:
rated 57 last year when 5L behind Queen Helen in a valuable 7f event at Ascot on firm grnd:
should be suited by 12f and will do much better than this on better ground.   00
430 SHIPBOURNE [11] 3-9-0 G Starkey 6/1: -00: Op.5/2: no show: see 430.   00
--   CIGAR [13] 3-9-0 P Robinson 11/2: 00-0: Well bckd, no show: ran in gd company last
year and seems highly regarded: should be suited by middle distances and is a half brother
to Abingdon, Kirtling & Crossways.   00
479 TABACOS [20] 3-9-0 A Mcglone 7/1: 0-40: No show: btr 479.   00
--   Deafening [1] 9-0   --   Northern Society [12] 9-0
484 Billet [14] 9-0   --   Burning Ambition [18] 8-11
--   Head Of School [10] 9-0   357 Le Moulin [8] 9-0
253 Almutanabbi [16] 9-0   --   Adbury [5] 9-0   347 Polecroft [3] 9-0(vis)
402 Forward Move [2] 9-0
20 ran   2,15,2,1½,1   (M Berger)   J Dunlop Arundel, Sussex

WINDSOR   Monday May 19th   Left & Righthand Sharpish Track

Official Going Given as Good/Firm

620 SERPENTINE SELLING H'CAP (0-25)   £966   1m   Firm 16 +04 Fast   [24]

530 SNAKE RIVER [7] (D Nicholson) 4-9-5 I Johnson 7/1: 01-4331: 4 ch g Miami Springs -
Gay Donna (Tudor Jinks): Led 3f out, ridden out in a 3 & 4yo selling h'cap at Windsor May 19
(sold 3,200 gns): in '85 won a 3yo seller at Wolverhampton: eff at 1m, stays 10f well: acts
on any grnd: likes a sharp/easy trk, though acts on any.   26
275 ANGEL DRUMMER [14] (A Ingham) 3-7-13 G Carter(3) 13/2: 010-002: Ev ch str: btr effort:
in '85 won a 2yo seller at Wolverhampton: stays 1m: acts on yld, likes gd/firm grnd.   13
399 OSTENTATIOUS [4] (C Wildman) 4-8-13 Pat Eddery 5/1 FAV: 0400-03: Gambled on: ch 2f out:
maiden: stays 1m well: acts on gd & soft grnd & goes well at Windsor.   10
--   HARD AS IRON [17] (P Haslam) 3-8-7 G French 14/1: 000-4: Nearest fin on seasonal debut:
should do btr next time: very lightly raced in '85: eff at 1m, should stay 10f: acts on gd/
firm grnd & a sharpish trk: should find a similar event.   17
262 HUNTS KATIE [16] 4-9-6 P Cook 25/1: 0030-00: Never nearer: mkt drifter: placed on
several occasions in '85 outside selling company: eff at 6/7f: seems to stay 1m: should do
better next time.   11
160 HOKUSAN [20] 4-9-1 A Shoults(5) 9/1: 01-0340: Never nearer: see 122: probably stays
1m: acts on any grnd: in '85 won a selling h'cap at Leicester.   04
274 BLUE STEEL [11] 3-8-9 S Whitworth 7/1: 0000-00: No show on first venture into
selling company: has shown enough ability to win a similar event: acts on gd/yld grnd.   00
356 FOXCROFT [3] 3-8-8 J Scally(7) 15/2: 0022-00: No dngr: see 356.   00
344 ANGIES VIDEO [2] 4-8-6 A Proud 10/1: -00: Springer in mkt: no threat.   00
564 THE UTE [8] 3-8-3(bl) M L Thomas 10/1: 200-00: Much btr 564.   00
346 FIRST ORBIT [11] 3-7-13(1ow) R Hills 15/2: 000-020: Wknd over 3f out: btr 346 (yld). 00
352 MISS HARLEQUIN [13] 3-7-11(BL)(1ow) A Mcglone 9/1: 200-000: Prom, wknd: 2nd in a
Newmarket seller in '85 over 7f on firm grnd: yet to reproduce that run.   00
530 Easter Rambler [18] 9-5   171 Grovecote [10] 8-1
--   Foxy Dyke [15] 9-13   495 Charisma Music [5] 8-8
--   On Impulse [19] 8-7   540 Venture To Reform [9] 8-6
568 Night Waller [21] 8-4   399 Nanor [6] 8-2   201 Track The Bear [1] 8-2
21 ran   4,½,1½,2,1   (R Bickley)   D Nicholson Condicote, Glos.

211

621 WHITEHALL STAKES 2YO   £959   5f   Firm 16 -08 Slow

383 PLUM DROP [9] (R Armstrong) 2-8-8 W Carson 2/1: 21: 2 gr f Take By Storm - Plum Blossom
(Gallant Romeo): Useful, impr filly: led from the stalls comfortably in a 2yo fillies stakes
at Windsor May 19: first time out was a promising 2nd to runaway winner Naturally Fresh in a
valuable maiden at Newmarket: eff at 5f, should stay further: acts on fast grnd & on any
trk: seems suited by forcing tactics: should win more races/rate more highly.   58
400 SURELY GREAT [8] (D Thom) 2-8-8 M L Thomas 25/1: 02: Kept on well and is fast impr:
cost only 1,800 gns: half sister to 6f winner Sandy Reef: should be suited by extra furlong:
acts on firm grnd & a sharpish trk & should find a maiden.   48
+**513 STAY LOW** [5] (G Blum) 2-9-4 G Duffield 4/1: 2113: Mkt drifter: another gd effort:
acts on firm & yld: see 513.   57
-- **BERTRADE** [6] (P Makin) 2-8-8 W R Swinburn 10/1: 4: Mkt drifter: promising debut:
should be suited by further than 5f: sister to smart '84 2yo Hi-Tech-Girl: sure to impr
on this run: acts on firm grnd.   40
-- **PINEAPPLES PRIDE** [4] 2-8-8 N Adams 33/1: 0: Never nearer on racecourse debut: should
do better: acts on firm grnd.   34
-- **RIPE CHRISTINA** [12] 2-8-8 Pat Eddery 7/4 FAV: 0: A big gamble on racecourse debut:
gd early speed: wknd over 1f out: dam a winning 3yo: obviously well regarded and should
impr on this.   28
-- **Infanta Maria** [2] 8-8   -- **Countess Bree** [3] 8-8   -- **Wind And Wave** [10] 8-8
-- **Nerrad** [7] 8-8   -- **Peroy** [11] 8-8   -- **Relampego** [1] 8-8
12 ran   3,hd,2½,2½,2.   (Charles H Wacker III)   R Armstrong Newmarket

622 CHARING CROSS STAKES 2YO   £1592   5f   Firm 16 -20 Slow

457 MUNAASIB [2] (P Walwyn) 2-8-11 Paul Eddery 10/11 FAV: 31: 2 ch g Dara Monarch -
Nagin (Pretense): Impr gelding: heavily bckd and led over 1f out, comfortably in a 2yo stakes
at Windsor May 19: first time out fin 3rd to Amego Sucio at Salisbury: cost I.R. 24,000 as a
yearling: acts on firm & yld grnd & on any trk: should be suited by 6f.   52
404 TAP THE BATON [4] (M Tompkins) 2-8-11 R Cochrane 6/1: 432: Made much: another gd
effort: acts on firm & yld grnd & on any trk: should be suited by further than 5f.   45
118 MISTER COLIN [6] (R Hannon) 2-9-4 Pat Eddery 4/1: 1243: Never nearer: acts on firm
& soft: see 27.   50
404 ORIOLE DANCER [3] (D Thom) 2-8-11 W R Swinburn 11/1: 00024: Ch 2f out: btr 404:see 186. 31
-- **HIGHLAND LODGE** [5] 2-8-11 T Quinn 9/2: 0: Never in it on racecourse debut: cost
9,400 gns and is a half brother to useful sprinter Kelly's Royale: should impr.   29
-- **TECHNOCRAT** [1] 2-8-11 P Cook 33/1: 0: Slow start: no show: half brother to 2 winners:
should be suited by further.   25
483 BIOTIN [7] 2-8-11 N Howe 33/1: 00: Reared up start & never in it: cheaply bought.   00
7 ran   2,½,5,1,2   (Hamdan Al-Maktoum)   P Walwyn Lambourn, Berks

623 WESTMINSTER HANDICAP STAKES 3YO 0-50 £2378 1m 4f Firm 16 -22 Slow   [52]

370 WISHLON [3] (R Smyth) 3-9-7 Pat Eddery 10/3 FAV: -101: 3 b c Lyphard's Wish -
Swiss Swish (Wajima): Useful colt: well bckd and led dist, driven out in a 3yo h'cap at
Windsor May 19: first time out won an easy winner of a maiden at Warwick and subs. was a
fine 6th to Allez Milord in a valuable event at Newmarket: eff at 10f, stays 12f: acts on
firm & soft grnd & on any trk.   54
480 FIREPROOF [10] (D Marks) 3-7-7(1oh) M L Thomas 12/1: 00-042: Stayed on well final 1f
and just btn: gd effort: clearly well suited by 12f: see 480.   24
416 PEARL FISHER [1] (J Francome) 3-9-1 S Cauthen 4/1: -133: Led 3f out: acts on firm
& soft: stays 12f: see 140.   41
331 GOLDEN CROFT [11] (N Vigors) 3-7-7(1oh) S Dawson(0) 12/1: 000-004: Ch 3f out: stays
12f: acts on firm & yld grnd.   17
506 BETTER BEWARE [5] 3-8-7 J Matthias 10/1: 00-3430: Ev ch str: acts on any grnd: stays
12f: see 506, 140.   28
505 ZINDELINA [9] 3-8-8 A Mcglone 7/1: 0440-20: Fdd: btr 505 (10f yld).   26
535 SILENT RUNNING [2] 3-7-10 G Carter(3) 3/1 FAV: 000-000: Gambled on, but never
nearer 7th: btr 535 (10f).   00
506 Royal Effigy [7] 8-0   **331 The Wooden Hut** [6] 7-7(10oh)
480 Balnacraig [8] 7-11   -- **Diva Encore** [4] 9-0
11 ran   ½,3,1,2,2½   (K Abdulla)   R Smyth Epsom, Surrey

624 JACK BARCLAY HANDICAP 3YO 0-50   £3157   6f   Firm 16 +14 Fast   [56]

+**534 TOUCH OF GREY** [20] (D Thom) 3-9-0(7ex) G Starkey 7/2 FAV: 10-0011: 3 br c Blakeney -
Belle (Comedy Star): Useful colt who is in fine form: well bckd and led well over 1f out,
comfortably in a fast run h'cap at Windsor May 19: last time out won a similar event again
at Windsor: in '85 won a nursery h'cap at Ascot: very eff at 6f on fast grnd & seems best
when up with the pace: likes a sharpish trk, though acts on any.   55
507 GYPSYS PROPHECY [14] (G Harwood) 3-7-12 W Woods(3) 10/1: 0230-32: Mkt drifter: ch
final 1f: 3L clear 3rd: should find a similar event: see 507.   35
241 SILENT MAJORITY [24] (W O'gorman) 3-7-8 M L Thomas 25/1: 44-03: Mkt drifter: made
much: gd effort: eff at 5/6f on a sharpish trk: acts on soft, likes fast grnd.   24

455 KIMBLE BLUE [19] (M Mccormack) 3-8-8 Pat Eddery 11/2: 1300-04: Ran on late: in '85
won twice at Pontefract & likes that trk: eff at 5f, stays 6f: acts on firm & soft grnd.   36
436 EASY LINE [11] 3-7-7(1oh) T Williams 12/1: -100: Ch over 1f out: acts on firm, but
best 64 (soft).   20
454 LADY LA PAZ [10] 3-7-7(1oh) G French 25/1: 000-040: Never nearer: see 454.   19
436 VAIGLIAN [12] 3-8-2 P Cook 16/1: 303-400: Ev ch: fin 7th: btr 436 (7f): see 64.   00
*496 BERTIE WOOSTER [2] 3-8-12(7ex) W R Swinburn 5/1: 20-0310: Heavily bckd: sn prom: btr 496   00
--   RIVIERA SCENE [6] 3-9-2 W Carson 9/1: 022-0: Mkt drifter: btr for race: on final outing
in '85 fin a close 2nd to the much impr Governor General in quite a fast run Goodwood maiden:
eff at 6f on fast grnd & a sharpish trk: impr likely.   00
--   MISS KNOW ALL [23] 3-8-8 B Thomson 10/1: 10-0: Sn prom: fdd: btr for race: first time
out in '85 was a ready winner of a fillies maiden at Wolverhampton: should be suited by 6f
plus: acts on fast grnd.   00

496	Loft Boy [9] 8-12	455	Edgewise [3] 9-7	401	Crete Cargo [22] 9-4
436	Fruity Orooney [15] 9-2			527	Tzu Wong [16] 8-8
436	Bath [17] 8-5	--	Harmony Heights [18] 8-4		
454	Prissy Miss [21] 8-0	424	Someway [25] 7-12	454	Solo Style [1] 7-12
283	Tachometer [4] 7-8	340	Delta Rose [5] 7-7(1oh)		
--	Stock Phrase [8] 7-7(1oh)			454	Bandyann [13] 7-7(15oh)
24 ran	1,3,1,nk,nk,½,1	(T M Jennings)		D Thom Newmarket	

625 MAYFAIR STAKES 3YO COLTS & GELDINGS   £1136   1m 2f Firm 16 -10 Slow

316 DALGADIYR [4] (M Stoute) 3-8-11 W R Swinburn 10/11 FAV: -31: 3 ch c Nishapour -
Djebellina (Charlottesville): Useful, fast impr colt: heavily bckd: led nearing final 1f,
driven out in a 3yo stakes at Windsor May 19: half brother to a smart French colt: eff at
10f, may stay further: acts on firm & soft grnd & on any trk: should win more races.   58
--   DAARKOM [12] (A Stewart) 3-8-11 M Roberts 14/1: -2: Kept on well under press: 5L clear
3rd: most promising racecourse debut: eff at 10f, should be suited by 12f: acts on firm grnd
and a sharpish trk & should have no trouble finding a maiden.   56
--   NORTHERN AMETHYST [16] (G Huffer) 3-8-11 G Carter(3) 13/2: 022-3: Mkt drifter on
seasonal debut: nearest fin & impr likely next time: in final outing in '85 was a fine 2nd
to Dancing Brave in a good event at Newmarket: eff at 10f, should stay 12f: acts well on
fast grnd & will find a maiden soon.   48
--   FREE HAND [15] (H Cecil) 3-8-11 S Cauthen 10/1: 3-4: Friendless in mkt: nearest fin:
ddhtd 4th on seasonal debut: on sole start in '85 fin 3rd to Barclay Street in a maiden at
Leicester: should be suited by 12f: acts on firm grnd & on any trk.   48
328 TOP RANGE [3] 3-8-11 M Jarvis 14/1: -030: Kept on well: ddhtd 4th: on the up grade
and should find a maiden: stays 10f: acts on firm & soft grnd.   48
--   NEXT DANCE [5] 3-8-11 C Rutter(5) 33/1: -0: Ch over 1f out: promising debut: eff
at 10f on firm grnd: should find a maiden.   47
535 STARMAST [17] 3-8-11 W Carson 13/2: 0-40: Made much: see 535.   00
484 MAKE PEACE [6] 3-8-11 Pat Eddery 10/1: 3-330: Wknd over 1f out: btr 484 (yld): see 183.   00

334	King Tefkros [2] 8-11	484	Mr Savvas [18] 8-11	535	Final Alma [13] 8-11
486	Floral Charge [1] 8-11			486	Gay Caruso [10] 8-11(BL)
--	Kheta King [11] 8-11	--	Lockwood Prince [9] 8-11		
535	Native Image [20] 8-11			--	Risk Another [7] 8-11
--	Run High [8] 8-11	535	Tremendous Jet [19] 8-11		
--	Willow Gorge [14] 8-11				
20 ran	1,5,hd,ddht,½	(H H Aga Khan)		M Stoute newmarket	

Official Going Given as Good/Firm

626 LEITH RACES APPR. HANDICAP 3YO+ 0-35   £1802   5f   Good/Firm 31 -01 Slow   [34]

*418 ROTHERFIELD GREYS [12] (C Bell) 4-10-0(6ex) J Leech 9/4 FAV: 0000-11: 4 b g Mummy's Pet -
Relicia (Relko): In fine form, led from the stalls, readily, in an app. h'cap at Edinburgh
May 19: first time out again made ev yd in a similar event at Warwick: lost his form in '85
when a virus sufferer, but was a useful 2yo, winning twice at Redcar: very eff over 5/6f:
acts well on gd & firm grnd: best out in front on a sharpish trk & may complete the hat trick.   46
412 UPTOWN GIRL [14] (D Barron) 6-8-8 B Mcgiff 4/1: 0111-02: Sn prom: 5L clear 3rd: gd
effort: may win soon: see 412.   18
+490 MIAMI DOLPHIN [10] (J Berry) 6-8-0(6ex) J Quinn 13/2: 00-0013: Sn prom: btr 490 (heavy).   00
82   COLWAY RADIAL [9] (D Smith) 3-7-8 P Hill 33/1: 00-04: Nearest fin: lightly raced
maiden: should be suited by 6f: acts on gd & firm grnd.   02
182 PERGODA [11] 8-9-4(bl) R Vickers(5) 12/1: 000-000: Never nearer: btr effort: reserves
his best for this trk: in '85 won twice at Edinburgh and is a course winner here on no
less than 7 occasions: very eff over 5f with forcing tactics, though does stay 6f: acts on
any going, but is fav. by fast grnd: usually bl: goes well for an app.   15
418 APHRODISIAC [5] 5-8-5(bl) A Roper 14/1: 010-000: Never nearer: in '85 won an app h'cap
at Catterick, winning 2yo at Haydock: eff at 5f, though does stay 7f: acts on any going
and on any trk.   02

-- RAMBLING RIVER [7] 9-10-0(vis) D Eddery 10/1: 40010-0: Early speed: btr for race: in '85 won h'caps at Edinburgh & Newmarket: in '83 won 4 times: equally eff at 5/6f: acts on any going and on any trk.   00
490 TRADESMAN [2] 6-7-8(bl) P Burke 8/1: 433-000: Early speed: see 490.   00
-- Last Secret [3] 7-13   211 Tollys Best [13] 7-8   426 Frandie Miss [1] 7-11(bl)
-- Marshall Drills [6] 7-8(1ow)(2oh)   418 Blochairn Skolar [8] 7-10
378 Culminate [4] 7-8
14 ran   2,5,shhd,nk,shhd,nk   (Mrs D Gleeson)   C Bell Sparsholt, Berks

627 EBF PEOPLES MAIDEN STAKES 2YO   £1260   5f   Good/Firm 31 -31 Slow

-- DUNLIN [14] (S Norton) 2-9-0 J Lowe 7/1: 1: 2 ch c Miswaki - Vita Mia (Ribot): Sn prom and led final 1f, under press in a 2yo maiden at Edinburgh May 19: cost $21,000 as a yearling: eff at 5f, should be suited by further: acts on gd/firm grnd & a sharpish trk.   40
523 WENSLEYDALEWARRIOR [11] (G Moore) 2-9-0 N Crowther 11/1: 032: Led/dsptd lead all the way: just went under and is an impr sort: deserves a small race: see 523, 304: acts on any grnd.   40
-- PREMIER VIDEO [12] (J Berry) 2-8-11 M Fry 14/1: 3: Al there on debut: eff at 5f on gd/firm grnd & a sharpish trk.   30
544 DANADN [8] (Ron Thompson) 2-9-0 R P Elliott 12/1: 404: Sn prom: see 278.   32
-- CARSE KELLY [13] 2-8-11 L Charnock 25/1: 0: Al there on debut: half sister to 3 winners: acts on gd/firm grnd & a sharpish trk.   28
473 SILVERS ERA [15] 2-8-11 A Murray 6/4 FAV: 020: Well below form 473, 383.   26
515 AIR OF SPRING [5] 2-8-11(BL) G Baxter 7/1: 030: Dsptd lead: fdd: btr 515 (gd/yld).   00
437 FISHERGATE [6] 2-9-0 K Hodgson 5/1: 400: No show: btr 437: see 236.   00
-- BRUTUS [7] 2-9-0 M Birch 9/1: 0: Racecourse debut: should impr: cost 11,500 gns.   00
236 Miss Display [2] 8-11   364 Geobritony [17] 9-0   -- Rivers Secret [1] 8-11
488 Young Warrior [16] 9-0   -- Choice Match [3] 8-11
-- Mr Tink [10] 9-0   488 Arishan [4] 9-0
16 ran   shhd,3,nk,nk,1,1½,hd   (Charles Buddeke)   S Norton Barnsley, Yorks

628 WAVERLEY MARKET EBF STAKES   £2194   5f   Good/Firm 31 -15 Slow

330 SIMLA RIDGE [8] (A Hide) 4-9-0 K Darley 5/1: -001: 4 br c Bay Express - Halliana (Bold Reason): Landed a big gamble: led final 1f under press for a narrow success in a stakes event at Edinburgh May 19: very lightly raced previously: seems a speedy sort: acts on gd/firm grnd & a sharpish trk.   45
-- IBERIAN START [4] (D Barron) 3-8-6 G Baxter 10/3: 00302-2: Led briefly final 1f: just btn: gd seasonal debut: first time out in '85 was an easy winner of a fillies event at Redcar and does well when fresh: very eff at 5f: acts on firm & soft grnd & on any trk.   46
545 MISS PRIMULA [7] (W Bentley) 3-8-10 K Hodgson 14/1: 4000-03: Kept on well: gd effort: in '85 won a maiden at Newmarket: eff at 5f, suited by 6f: acts on any trk, though is definitely best on fast grnd.   47
309 ALKAAYED [12] (H T Jones) 3-8-8 A Murray 9/2: 40-104: Nearest fin: possibly needs 6f on a sharpish trk: acts on firm & soft: see 241.   44
418 LADY OF LEISURE [2] 5-8-13 R Vickers(7) 14/1: 0000-00: Led centre of trk: gd effort at the weights: in '84 won at Haydock and in '83 won at Edinburgh: eff at 5f: seems best on fast ground.   38
588 DEBBIE DO [3] 3-8-6 J Bleasdale 3/1 FAV: 1322-40: Led/dsptd lead over 4f: see 588.   41
525 Gold Duchess [11] 9-6(bl)   266 Parade Girl [5] 9-6
-- Softly Spoken [1] 8-2   490 Its Heaven [6] 8-11   -- Waller Field [13] 9-0
259 Ackas Boy [10] 9-0   428 Philstar [9] 9-7(bl)
13 ran   nk,1,nk,nk,shhd   (John Medler)   A Hide Newmarket

629 EDINBURGH GOLD CUP HCAP 0-50   £3210   1m 4f   Good/Firm 31 +19 Fast   [43]

166 BALLYDURROW [8] (R Fisher) 9-9-1 D Nicholls 11/4: 1113-01: 9 ch g Doon - Even Tint (Even Money): Fair h'capper: well bckd and cruised into lead 1f out, easily in a fast run h'cap at Edinburgh May 19: in excellent form in '85, winning at Newbury, Haydock, Ayr & Edinburgh (2): in '84 won at Hamilton: eff over 10f, stays 12f well: acts on any going & on any trk: best when held up for a late chal & should win again.   45
410 MIN BALADI [2] 4-8-11 Lowe 5/2 FAV: 3411-32: No ch with winner, but is in gd form: see 410.   33
-- AUCHINLEA [11] (J Fitzgerald) 4-9-10 A Murray 6/1: 41000-3: Led briefly 2f out: gd seasonal debut: in '85 broke course record in a h'cap at Carlisle and was a fast run maiden winner at Beverley: very eff over 10/12f: acts on gd/firm & yld & likes a stiff trk, acts on any.   43
-- COMMANDER ROBERT [3] (J Hanson) 4-9-2 J H Brown(5) 8/1: 02000-4: Al there on seasonal debut: maiden: eff at 10f, stays 12f: acts on any trk.   33
419 FOUR STAR THRUST [4] 4-8-6 K Bradshaw(5) 14/1: 21-0040: Ch over 2f out: see 419.   23
519 EXCAVATOR LADY [6] 7-7-7(bl)(5oh) P Hill(7) 33/1: 0303-00: Dsptd lead over 2f out: in '84 won at Hamilton: eff at 12/13f: acts on yld: best on fast grnd.   09
584 Senor Ramos [10] 9-3(BL)   243 Lo Broadway [1] 8-0
-- Mend It [7] 7-8(bl)(1ow)(1oh)   144 Descartes [9] 8-1(VIS)
101 Prince Oberon [13] 7-7(bl)(4oh)   -- El Fayez [5] 9-8
519 Ivoroski [12] 7-13
13 ran   3,1½,1,shhd,½,2   (N Jaffer)   R Fisher Ulverston, Cumbria

630   COMMONWEALTH GAMES SELL HCAP 0-25   £1013   1m   Good/Firm 31 -05 Slow [18]

163 AVRAEAS [12] (R Morris) 7-9-0 L Charnock 13/2: 204-001: 7 b h Key To The Mint -
Rosewater (Sir Ivor): Led approaching final 1f, comfortably in a selling h'cap at Edinburgh
May 19 (bought in 1,500 gns): in '85 won a similar event at Haydock: subs. placed in non
selling company: very eff at 1m: acts on gd/firm & heavy grnd.   14
257· MURILLO [2] (F Carr) 10-9-5(bl) J Carr(7) 10/1: 32-0032: Chall final 2f: see 257.   13
--   REFORMED HABIT [5] (W Pearce) 4-8-10 N Connorton 20/1: 0-000-3: Al up there: very
lightly raced maiden: eff at 1m on gd/firm grnd & a sharpish trk.   00
541 FRASASS [9] (D Chapman) 9-9-4 D Nicholls 10/1: 00-1004: Led 4f out: best 257 (11f).   06
540 BUCKS BOLT [14] 4-9-7 Gay Kelleway(5) 9/2 FAV: 00-0030: Never nearer: see 262.   09
609 CROWFOOTS COUTURE [6] 5-8-11(vis) S Webster 14/1: -042000: Ran on too late: see 257.   00
378 CAERNARVON BOY [10] 4-8-10 M Beecroft 8/1: 00-3200: Not clear run into str: best 145.   00
257 HONEST TOKEN [11] 7-8-7(BL) N Carlisle 6/1: 0000-00: Bl first time: fdd: see 257.   00
258 SOPHYS FOLLY [7] 4-9-5 M Birch 5/1: -00-300: Led over 4f: btr 258 (yld).   00
--   Marton Boy [1] 8-10   139 Raceform Rhapsody [8] 7-9
377 Bantel Banzai [3] 8-10   377 Mistress Charley [15] 8-7
490 Lauras Choice [13] 8-10
14 ran   2¼,2,1,hd,½   (Mrs E A Davies)   R Morris Welshpool.

631   EDINBURGH INTERNATIONAL FEST. STKS   £963   1m 4f Good/Firm 31 -22 Slow

452 COMELY DANCER [12] (J Watts) 3-8-5 N Connorton 10/11 FAV: 4-31: 3 b c Northern Baby -
Abordage (Luthier): Led 2f out, staying on well in a minor event at Edinburgh May 19: first
time out was gd 3rd to Glowing Promise in a maiden at Redcar: eff over 10f, stays 12f well:
acts on gd & firm grnd & on any trk: should win btr races.   39
492 BANTEL BUSHY [10] (I Bell) 3-8-5 N Carlisle 11/2: -222222: Made much: kept on,
but the bridesmaid again: acts on any grnd & on any trk: see 381: rather frustrating, but
definitely has the ability to find a race.   34
449 TREYARNON [5] (S Norton) 4-9-9 J Lowe 14/1: 00-4343: Ev ch 2f out: gd effort:
4th when rated 08 in a h'cap last time out and treat this rating with caution: stays 12f:
acts on any grnd: maiden.   33
448 CRICCEITH [11] (D Smith) 4-9-6 L Charnock 9/2: 00-34: Ev ch str: btr 448: stays 12f.   27
--   NIGHT GUEST [7] 4-9-9 S Keightley 50/1: 04000-0: Ev ch: maiden: stays 12f: acts on
gd/firm & a sharpish trk.   12
452 HIDDEN MOVE [4] 3-8-5 M Birch 8/1: 000-000: Btr effort: acts on gd/firm.   10
*487 ORIENTAL EXPRESS [8] 3-8-5 J Carr(7) 9/1: 000-010: Fdd: much btr 487 and please note
dist of race was 1m and not 1m2f as printed.   00
379 Star Of Tara [3] 8-2   381 Gunner Mac [1] 8-5   --   Jessie Timmins [6] 8-2
381 Hoad Hill [9] 8-5   449 Dark Cygnet [2] 9-9
12 ran   2,shhd,¾,7,nk   (Joe L Allbritton)   J Watts Richmond, Yorks

632   E.B.F. PENKRIDGE MAIDEN STAKES 2YO   £1145   5f   Good 64 -12 Slow

457 HARD ACT [4] (R Hannon) 2-9-0 R Wernham 33/1: 01: 2 b c Hard Fought - Excruciating
(Bold Forbes): Was a surprise winner, led ½way and kept on gamely for a narrow success in a
2yo maiden at Wolverhampton May 19: well btn on soft grnd on his debut at Salisbury earlier
this month and clearly much btr suited by this faster grnd: cost 12,000 gns as a yearling:
eff over 5f on a gall trk.   46
544 STELBY [7] (O Brennan) 2-9-0 M Brennan(2) 33/1: 02: Ran on well under press, showing
much impr form: clearly suited by 5f on a gall trk: seems to prefer faster grnd.   44
323 HAILEYS RUN [3] (G Pritchard Gordon) 2-9-0 G Duffield 25/1: 43: Al close up: acts
on gd & soft grnd & on a gall trk: see 323.   36
--   DOMINION ROYALE [5] (R Williams) 2-9-0 R Cochrane 7/2: 4: Well bckd debutant: front rank
till dist: not given a hard race & seems certain to impr next time: should app another
furlong: acts on gd grnd & on a gall trk.   35
531 TIMESWITCH [1] 2-9-0 T Ives 13/8 FAV: 20: Again heavily bckd: speed to ½way though
sn under press: deserves another chance after prom debut in 531 (sharp trk, firm).   34
497 MUBKIR [10] 2-9-0 Paul Eddery 2/1: 30: Well bckd disapp: led to ½way though dropped
out tamely and can do much btr than this: see 497.   22
460 SUPREME OPTIMIST [11] 2-9-0 W Carson 8/1: 30: Gd early speed: btn into 7th and
much btr in 460 (tight trk).   00
186 Stage [9] 9-0   --   Taliesin [8] 9-0   --   Parkers Joy [6] 9-0
--   Gunship [2] 9-0
11 ran   ½,3,½,nk,5,1   (G Howard Spink)   R Hannon East Everleigh, Wilts

633 HIMLEY SELLING STAKES 2YO   £823   5f   Good 64 -28 Slow

536 CHAMBER MASTER [8] (R Howe) 2-8-11 P D'arcy 7/1: 01: 2 ch c Jasmine Star - Golden
Darling (Darling Boy): Led early & again below dist, comfortably led in a 2yo seller at Wolverhampton May 19 (bought in 3,400 gns): cheaply bought colt who is a half brother to several
winning sprinters: eff over 5f on a gall trk & looks certain to stay further: acts on gd
grnd: could win again on this grade.   28
537 BINGO QUEEN [3] (J Berry) 2-8-8 W Carson 7/4 FAV: 2022: Again found one too good:
due a change of luck: see 537 and 329.   15
*537 BROONS ANSWER [5] (K Stone) 2-8-12(bl) G Brown(5) 7/1: 0013: In gd form: see 537. 18
-- RUN TO WORK [1] (G Moore) 2-8-11 D Casey(7) 9/1: 4: Showed good early speed on racecourse debut, wknd dist though would not have to impr much to win a similar race: acts on
gd grnd & on a gall trk.   17
502 SAMS REFRAIN [2] 2-8-8 J Reid 5/1: 301D0: No extra dist: btr on yld in 502.   06
417 ARDNACROSS [6] 2-8-8 R Cochrane 7/2: 00: Speed over ½way: btr in 417 (sharp trk).   00
537 Pialuci [10] 8-11   -- Solent Gold [4] 8-8   -- Pullandese [7] 8-8
-- Star City [9] 8-8   -- Boxers Choice [11] 8-8
11 ran   3,nk,hd,3,3   (T B Rayner)   R Howe Epsom, Surrey

634 SHREWSBURY HANDICAP STAKES (0-50) 4YO+   £2763   2m 1f   Good 64 +06 Fast   [41]

504 SAILORS REWARD [1] (J King) 4-9-1 W Carson 12/1: 004-041: 4 b c Absalom - Barchessa
(Prince Chevalier): Went on 2f out and rallied gamely to regain lead near fin in quite a fast
run h'cap at Wolverhampton May 19: first success though last season was placed several times
in quite competitive hcps: eff over middle dist: stays 2m well: acts on firm & soft grnd
and is suited by a gall trk.   39
-462 PEARL RUN [4] (G Price) 5-9-10 P Robinson 4/1: -110122: Led dist, caught close home
though remains in excellent form despite rising sharply in the weights: see 462 & 336. 47
462 JACKDAW [10] (R Hollinshead) 6-8-2 W Ryan 16/1: 0-00003: Ran on too late, though a
btr effort: fair stayer on his day: rated 42 when winning a valuable h'cap at Newmarket last
season: in '84 again won at Newmarket, and also at Beverley & Haydock: very well suited by
2m: acts on firm & yld grnd & likes a gall trk.   22
312 CIMA [6] (J Old) 8-9-6 J Reid 14/1: 020/304: Made much: gd effort: see 235.   36
*526 PELHAM LINE [2] 6-7-10(4ex) R Fox 7/4 FAV: 003/310: Never reach ldrs and btr judged
on her recent win in 526, over a longer trip on soft ground.   12
235 ACE OF SPIES [5] 5-9-3 R Cochrane 9/2: 2/00-20: In gd form: see 235.   29
504 Flying Officer [11] 8-5(vis)   526 Write The Music [9] 8-9(vis)
541 Joist [8] 8-13   462 Rushmoor [3] 9-2
10 ran   ½,3,2½,nk,2½   (F J Carter)   J King Uffcote, Wilts

635 PENN FIELDS STAKES 3YO   £959   1m 4f   Good 64 -38 Slow

435 GOLDEN HEIGHTS [7] (P Walwyn) 3-9-2 Paul Eddery 8/13 FAV: 43-121: 3 b c Shirley Heights-
Yelney (Blakeney): Useful colt: easily landed the odds in a 3yo stakes at Wolverhampton
May 19, qknd clear after 1m and eased close home: first time out winner of a Bath maiden and
subs. ran up to Winds Of Light at Kempton: well bred colt who cost 74,000 gns as a yearling:
showed promise on both outings last season: very eff over 12f on gd & yld grnd: suited by
a gall trk: will win more races.   50
-- MYSTERY CLOCK [8] (P Bailey) 3-8-11(BL) J Williams 66/1: 0000-2: Rank outsider on reapp:
kept on well under press to take the minor honours: unplaced in all his starts last season
over shorter trips & clearly is btr suited by middle distances: acts on gd grnd & on a
gall track.   35
552 MILTESCENS [1] (A Jarvis) 3-9-2 J Matthias 9/2: 033-103: Ran on late: stays 12f: see 357.   38
351 SHIRLSTAR TAXSAVER [4] (J Bethell) 3-8-11 W Carson 7/1: 00-04: Early ldr: acts on
gd & yld: see 351.   32
414 IDLE SONG [6] 3-8-11 S Perks 12/1: -000: No threat over this longer trip: see 414. 18
191 GREAT TOPIC [9] 3-8-11 G Duffield 25/1: 0-00: Btn early in str: no form to date.   00
506 Crown Mine [3] 8-11   -- Tumba [2] 8-11   535 Irish Dilemma [5] 8-11(bl)
9 ran   2½,1,½,10,12   (P G Goulandris)   P Walwyn Lambourn, Berks

636 COMPTON HANDICAP STAKES (0-35) 4YO+   £2183   7f   Good 64 -37 Slow   [35]

566 BOND DEALER [7] (R Hodges) 9-9-0 A Dicks(7) 10/1: 3200-01: 9 ro g Habat - Sounion
(Vimy): Stayed on well to lead close home in a h'cap at Wolverhampton May 19, though fin
lame: failed to win last season though in '84 won an app h'cap at Epsom: best form over 7/8f
acts on any going & on any trk.   28
441 LEMELASOR [4] (D Haydn Jones) 6-9-7 D Williams(5) 5/1: 0-03232: Just btn: see 441.   34
525 FLOMEGAS DAY [5] (B Mcmahon) 4-9-1(bl) J Hills(5) 3/1 FAV: 00-0003: Gambled on: kept
on well under press and narrowly btn in a close fin: stays 7f: see 369.   28
262 MR ROSE [12] (R Hutchinson) 6-8-0 R Fox 10/1: 00-0004: Led below dist, hdd near fin
and not btn far: last season won at Beverley & Catterick & in '84 at Folkestone: best form
over 7f on gd or faster grnd: acts on any trk.   11
453 NEW CENTRAL [2] 4-8-12 R Cochrane 12/1: 1400-00: Led early, gd effort: last season won
a seller at Bath & later a h'cap at Kempton: in '84 won at Newmarket: eff over 7/8f: best
on fast grnd: acts on any trk.   23

441 GRACIOUS HOMES [1] 5-8-10 J Reid 5/1: 2004-40: Ran on too late: see 441.   20
481 SANDBOURNE [6] 4-9-1 J Williams 12/1: 0-00-00: Nearest fin: see 481.   00
490 GOLDEN BOY [13] 4-7-8 L Riggio(5) 25/1: -0-0000: Fin 8th though not btn that far.   00
418 HILMAY [9] 4-8-3(bl) P Robinson 8/1: 00-0030: Ran on late: fin 9th: see 418.   00
453 Marsoom [3] 8-3   508 Young Angel [10] 9-9   540 Remembrance [17] 8-10
--   Sue Clare [14] 7-10   495 Sing Galvo Sing [11] 7-12(2ow)
211 The Manor [16] 7-7   --   Toms Nap Hand [8] 7-7 --   Huytons Hope [15] 7-8(1ow)
17 ran   ½,shhd,¾,shhd,½,nk   (Ron Osborne)   R Hodges Charlton Adam, Somerset

637 CANNOCK HANDICAP STAKES (0-35) 3YO   £2404   1m   Good 64 +06 Fast   [38]

--   AL ZUMURRUD [16] (R Armstrong) 3-9-0 W Carson 9/1: 00400-1: 3 ch f Be My Guest -
Mey (Canisbay): First time out, stayed on well to lead near fin in quite a fast run 3yo h'cap
at Wolverhampton May 19: cost 52,000 gns and is a half sister to several winners: showed some
promise last season: eff over 1m though seems sure to be suited by further: acts on gd &
fast grnd & on any trk: should defy a penalty, especially over a longer trip.   35
*318 CRAMMING [14] (W Musson) 3-9-2 P Waldron 7/2: 000-12: Made most: in fine form: see 318. 34
436 LADY BISHOP [4] (R Hannon) 3-8-10(BL) R Wernham 25/1: 000-003: Ran on well and this
was an impr effort: half sister to a winning sprinter though is well suited by 1m herself
and should stay further: acts on gd grnd & a gall trk.   26
--   FRIVOLE [19] (P Cole) 3-8-10 M Lynch(5) 25/1: 000-4: Ran on strongly after slow start
and sure to do btr next time: lightly raced last season, showing gradual impr: cheaply
acquired filly who is eff over 7/8f & should stay further: acts on gd & firm grnd & on
any track.   26
538 SPINNAKER LADY [8] 3-8-2 D Mckay 20/1: 020-000: Never nearer: see 538.   17
335 CEROC [18] 3-8-7 J Reid 14/1: 00-4000: Not pace to chall: see 74.   16
540 CENTRALSPIRES BEST [20] 3-9-1 N Day 25/1: 0440-00: Ev ch dist: see 540.   00
318 TROPICO [15] 3-8-6 T Williams 16/1: 02-00: Raised in class: fin 8th: see 318.   00
478 AUCTION MAN [13] 3-9-7 S Perks 7/2 Jt FAV: 3-03240: Ch dist: fin 9th & much btr in 478. 00
451 PRINCESS PAMELA [7] 3-8-7 M Miller 8/1: 010-000: Won a maiden auction race at
Catterick last season (rated 38), though yet to recapture that form this term: appeared not
to stay todays trip but may impr when reverting to sprint dists: acts on gd grnd & on
a sharp track.   00
455 See No Evil [17] 8-5   --   London Contact [9] 9-7
500 Highland Tale [10] 8-10   424 Keep Cool [3] 9-6
--   Tempest Tossed [11] 9-5   14   Bills Ahead [1] 8-10
--   Saughtrees [6] 8-9   540 Athletes Week [12] 8-4
*346 Take A Break [2] 8-2
19 ran   1¼,1,hd,nk,3,shhd   (Hamdan Al-Maktoum)   R Armstrong Newmarket

CURRAGH   Saturday May 17th   Righthand, Stiff Galloping Track

Official Going Given as Heavy

638 ORAL B MARBLE HILL 2YO STAKES LISTED   £8236   5f   Very Heavy 198 -30 Slow

--   KEEN CUT [4] (D Weld) 2-8-8 M J Kinane 9/2: 11: 2 b c Sharpo - Diamond Land
(Sparkler): Prom Irish filly: winner of both outings to date, on latest start was a narrow
winner of a valuable Listed race at the Curragh May 17: first time out just got up to beat
Harry Quinn in a Leopardstown maiden: eff at 5f, may stay 6f: acts on yld & hvy grnd &
a gall trk.   60
--   LOVELY BAND [1] (E Lynam) 2-8-8 J Coogan 10/1: 1322: Just btn and is a most consistent
sort: first time out won at Leopardstown: acts on yld & heavy grnd.   59
--   KALORAMA [5] (K Prendergast) 2-8-9 G Curran 2/1 FAV: 13: Narrowly btn in tight finish:
first time out was an easy winner over 5f at Phoenix Park: acts on hvy grnd.   60
*268 HIGH WIND [2] (J Murphy) 2-8-12 D J Murphy 9/2: 14: Stiff task at weights, but just
btn: fine effort: acts on yld & hvy grnd.   63
292 FAIRWAY LADY [3] 2-8-9 S Craine 5/1: 010: Not disgraced: last time out won over this
C/D: acts on yld & heavy.   50
268 CORRIENDO LIBRE [7] 2-8-8 P Shanahan 10/1: 20: Stiff task: see 268.   49
*292 SAY PRINCESS [6] 2-8-12 M T Browne 7/1: 110: Last to fin: btr 292.   00
7 ran   hd,shhd,hd,4½,shhd   (B Firestone)   D Weld Ireland

639 GR 3 CURRAGH BLOODSTOCK GREENLANDS STKS £11550   6f   Very Heavy 198 +13 Fast

472 RUSTIC AMBER [10] (J Oxx) 3-8-11 Pat Eddery 6/1: 2210-31: 3 b c Thatching - Forever
Amber (Bold Lad (Ire)): Smart Irish colt: ready winner of fast run Gr.3 event at the Curragh
May 17: in '85 won over 5f at the Curragh: speedy sort who is equally eff at 5/6f: acts on
gd, likes heavy grnd.   80
249 NOMINATION [3] (P Cole) 3-9-3 T Quinn 9/4 FAV: 1104-02: Swerved at the start: gd
effort under the circumstances: should be winning soon: see 249.   81
471 LONDON TOWER [6] (D Weld) 3-8-6(bl) M J Kinane 11/2: ---1203: Tried in bl: gd effort.   68
267 MIAMI COUNT [2] (D Weld) 4-9-4 D Parnell 14/1: 4200-44: See 267.   64
--   WOLVERSTAR [9] 4-9-1 W Carson 8/1: 03-2010: Not btn far: last time out won a 5f h'cap
at Phoenix Park: well suited by soft/heavy.   61

*472 YOUNG BLADE [11] 3-9-0 C Roche 9/2: 103-110: Fin 7th: well below form 472 (beat winner).58
11ran   2,½,1½,hd   (R More O'Ferrall)   J Oxx Ireland

640 GR 1 AIRLIE COOLMORE IRISH 2000 GUINEAS £98600   1m   Very Heavy 198 -06 Slow

*395 FLASH OF STEEL [2] (D Weld) 3-9-0 M J Kinane 9/2: 0111-11: 3 b c Kris - Spark Of Fire
(Run the Gantlet): Very smart Irish colt: led 1f out, driven out in Gr.1 Irish 2,000 gns at
the Curragh May 17: first time out won a Gr.3 event at the Curragh: has not stopped impr and
is a winner of his last 5 races: stays 1m well: should get further: seems to act on any grnd.   82
*471 MR JOHN [5] (L Browne) 3-9-0 M T Browne 25/1: 100-412: Rank outsider, but al prom and
slightly hmpd inside final 1f: excellent effort and is still impr: should win more races:
seems to love heavy grnd: see 471.   80
407 SHARROOD [6] (W Hern) 3-9-0 W Carson 3/1 FAV: 111-043: Made much: wknd final 1f:
good effort on this rain sodden grnd: see 407, 226.   73
407 HUNTINGDALE [4] (J Hindley) 3-9-0 M Hills 7/2: 221-34: Ev ch over 1f out: probably
unsuited by the grnd: see 407.   71
*466 FIORAVANTI [1] 3-9-0 C Roche 9/2: 11-10: Lost his unbtn record today & is much
btr on a sounder surface: see 466.   67
407 GREEN DESERT [3] 3-9-0 W R Swinburn 4/1: 214-120: Said to be hating the grnd and
was never in it: much btr 407 (firm).   65
6 ran   ½,4,1½,2½,1   (B Firestone)   D Weld Ireland

641 GROUP 2 TATTERSALLS ROGERS GOLD CUP   £57500   1m 2f Very Heavy 198 -10 Slow

470 FAIR OF THE FURZE [2] (L Browne) 4-8-9 W Carson 9/2: 2201-41: 4 b f Ela-Mana-Mou
Autocratic (Tyrant): Smart Irish filly: led 2f out & readily drew clear in Gr.2 event at the
Curragh May 17: in fine form in '85, winning a Listed race at Leopardstown & earlier a fine
5th to Helen Street in the Irish Oaks: very eff at 10f, stays 12f: acts on gd/firm & hvy
grnd: should win more gd races.   85
-- NEMAIN [4] (D V O'brien) 4-9-1 C Roche 8/1: 03414-2: Made much on seasonal debut:
gd effort: consistent colt who in '85 won a Gr.2 event at the Curragh and also a fine 4th
to Oh So Sharp in St Leger: eff at 10f, stays 14f: acts on gd/firm & hvy grnd: genuine sort.   79
-- SUPER MOVE [3] (L Browne) 4-8-12 M T Browne 14/1: 1200-13: Ran well in this high class
company: first time out ran well at Leopardstown: eff at 10f, stays 2m: acts on gd & hvy grnd.   74
468 DAMISTER [5] (J Tree) 4-9-1(BL) Pat Eddery 5/4 FAV: 313-304: Tried in bl: never nearer:
below his best this season: unsuited by heavy? see 221.   73
-- DARK RAVEN [7] 4-8-12(bl) M J Kinane 14/1: -111200: Not disgraced: winner of first 3
outings this season: very eff at 10f, stays 12f: acts on yld & heavy.   69
*98 VERTIGE [8] 4-8-12 E Legrix 9/2: 420-210: Never in it: much btr 98.   49
*267 LIDHAME [6] 4-8-12 G Curran 8/1: -100-10: Last to fin: much btr 267 (7f).   00
7 ran   6,¾,2½,½,12   (Mrs s Rogers)   L Browne Ireland

Official Going Given as Good

642 GROUP 1 OAKS D'ITALIA 3YO FILLIES   £44741   1m 3f Good .

463 IVORS IMAGE (M Stoute) 3-8-11 W R Swinburn 1: 1301-41: 3 b f Sir Ivor - Embryo
(Busted): Smart filly: led over 1f out, comfortably in the Italian Oaks at San Siro May 18:
in '85 won a Gr.2 event again at San Siro and also a fillles maiden at Yarmouth: very eff
at 11f, stays 12f: acts on firm & yld grnd & on any trk: should win more races.   72
*397 DANZICA (E Borromeo) 3-8-11 M Planard 1: 12: Nearest fin in fine form: stays 11f:
acts on gd & soft grnd: see 397.   67
-- CRODAS (E Camici) 3-8-11 A Parravani 1: -3: Sn prom: gd effort.   66
-- MARIA ROBERTA (A Botti) 3-8-11 G Dettori 1: -4: Not btn far: ran well.   65
459 DUNOOF 3-8-11 A Murray 1: 012-00: No threat in 9th: stiff task: in '85 won a
fillies maiden at Leicester: closely related to several winners, incl the smart High Hawk:
should be suited by 11/12f: acts on gd & firm grnd.   49
11ran   2,½,nk   (Sir Gordon White)   M Stoute Newmarket

Official Going Given as Firm

643 GROUP 1 PRIX LUPIN 3YO COLTS & FILLIES   £60529   1m 2f Firm .

*389 FAST TOPAZE [3] (G Mikhalides) 3-9-2 C Asmussen 1: --1-111: 3 b c Far North - Pink
Topaze (Djakao): Very smart French colt: remains unbtn after a comfortable win in Gr.1 Prix
Lupin at Longchamp May 18: earlier won Gr.1 event & Gr.3 event again at Longchamp: on sole
start in '85 won a Gr.2 race at St Cloud: eff at 1m, stays 10f well: acts on any grnd and
should run well in the Prix du Jockey-Club.   86
*289 AROKAR [4] (J De Chevigny) 3-9-2 Y Saint Martin 1: -011-12: Kept on well and is
in fine form: should stay 12f: now bound for the Epsom Derby: see 289.   84

•302 BAD CONDUCT [6] (P Biancone) 3-9-2 E Legrix 1: --22113: Fine effort in this high class
company: eff at 10f: acts on any grnd: see 302.   79
289 MINATZIN [7] (G Bonnaventure) 3-9-2 Pat Eddery 1: 1431-44: Stiff task: ran well: see 289.   72
301 PORT ETIENNE [5] 3-9-2 M Philipperon 1: -01-130: Stiff task: not disgraced.   69
301 TAMBOUR BATTANT [1] 3-9-2 A Badel 1: -0-0100:   53
--   MISTER BIG LOUIE [2] 3-9-2 G Mosse 1: --0-400: --   00
7 ran   1,2,3,1½,10   (M Fustok)   G Mikhalides France

644 GROUP 3 PRIX DE LA JONCHERE 3YO   £18390   1m   Firm .

•393 MAGICAL WONDER [9] (G Mikhalides) 3-8-8 C Asmussen 1: 4-11: 3 ch c Storm Bird -
Flama Ardiente (Crimson Satan): Smart French colt: despite losing his action well inside the
final 1f, was a comfortable winner of Gr.3 event at Longchamp May 18: first time out won in
a canter at Evry: very eff at 1m, should be suited by further: seems to act on any grnd:
further impr likely & should win more gd races.   76
301 KADROU [6] (J Laumain) 3-9-0 A Lequeux 1: 130-102: Just btn: fine effort: first time
out won at St Cloud: smart 2yo: very eff at 1m: acts on firm & soft.   80
302 CRYSTAL DE ROCHE [1] 3-8-8 F Head 1: --1-003: Not btn far: gd run.   70
•291 TAKFA YAHMED [5] (M Saliba) 3-8-11 Y Saint Martin 1: 40-2214: In fine form: stays 1m.   71
--   MANIFIC [8] 3-8-11 G Guignard 1: 330-0P0: --   70
291 CRICKET BALL [4] 3-8-11 G W Moore 1: -330: Stays 1m: acts on firm & heavy.   66
9 ran   hd,1½,¾,nk,2   (M Fustok)   G Mikhalides France

645 GROUP 2 PRIX JEAN DE CHAUDENAY 3YO+   £27599   1m 4f   Good/Firm .

299 PREMIER ROLE [7] (J Cunnington) 4-9-2   M Philipperon 1: 3443-41: 4 ch c Golden
Act - Misty Princess: Smart French colt: led inside the final 1f, narrowly, in a Gr.2 event
at St Cloud May 19: stays 12f well: acts on any grnd & is a consistent sort.   78
--   BALITOU [8] (P Biancone) 7-9-8   E Legrix 1: 11410-2: Just btn: fine seasonal
debut: in fine form in '85, winning 3 times at Longchamp, incl a Gr.1 event and first time
out the Grand Prix at Cagnes: eff at 12f, well suited by 2½m: likes gd & firm grnd: genuine
and consistent: heading for the Ascot Gold Cup.   82
299 NOBLE FIGHTER [6] (M Saliba) 4-9-8 C Asmussen 1: 2310-33: Another gd effort: see 299.   80
--   IADES [3] (C Head) 4-9-2   F Head 1: 12200-4: Fair effort: equally eff at
10/12f: acts on firm & yld grnd.   73
468 BABY TURK [2] 4-9-4   Y Saint Martin 1: 100: Btr 468 (10f, soft): see 299.   00
•298 GALLA PLACIDIA [1] 3-8-5 A Gibert 1: 1030-10: Much btr 298 (heavy grnd).   00
8 ran   ½,1,¼.   (P De Moussac)   J Cunnington France

Official Going Given as Soft

646 EBF ST MARYGATE 2YO STAKES   £2026   5f   Yielding 96 -04 Slow

--   INSHIRAH [7] (H Thomson Jones) 2-8-8 A Murray 11/2: 1: 2 gr f Caro - Endurable Heights
(Graustark): Prom filly: went on below dist and ran on strongly to win a 2yo stakes at Ripon
May 21: American bred filly who cost $260,000 as a yearling: should be suited by another
furlong: acts on yld grnd & on a gall trk.   50
--   STEELOCK [5] (M H Easterby) 2-8-8 M Birch 14/1: 2: Ran on promisingly from ½way and
should impr for this experience: full sister to several winning sprinters, incl Benfen: acts
on yld grnd & on a gall trk.   46
--   GARDENIA LADY [4] (D Barron) 2-8-8 T Lucas 9/2: 3: Not btn far on racecourse debut,
and fin clear of rem: half sister to winning sprinter Meneghini Rose: acts on yld grnd
and on a gall trk: should impr and find a race.   45
•548 JAY GEE ELL [3] (E Eldin) 2-8-13 A Mackay 1/2 FAV: 314: Heavily bckd: led over ½way
though sn btn: much btr on faster grnd in 548 and deserves another chance.   34
--   BABY COME HOME [10] 2-8-8 J Quinn(5) 50/1: 0: Tardy start: ran on promisingly and
seems certain to impr: half sister to middle dist winner Timminion: acts on yld grnd and
on a gall trk.   27
--   BOLD AD [6] 2-8-8 J Bleasdale 50/1: 0: Showed good early speed on racecourse debut:
not given a hard race and should impr next time: full sister to 7f winner Bold Way: acts
on yld grnd.   21
47   Miss Drummond [1] 8-8   364 Jean Jeanie [2] 8-8
8 ran   1,nk,8,¾,4,hd   (Hamdan Al-Maktoum)   H Thomson Jones Newmarket

647 WESTGATE SELLING STAKES 2YO   £1305   5f   Yielding 96 +04 Fast

457 MR GRUMPY [4] (Denys Smith) 2-8-11 D Nicholls 5/4 FAV: 02201: 2 ch c The Brianstan -
Handy Dancer (Green Dancer): Dropped in class and proved a comfortable winner of quite a
fast run 2yo seller at Ripon May 21: led below dist and soon clear: bought in 3,900 gns:
speedily bred colt who earlier had been placed in btr company: well suited by some cut in
the ground: acts on any trk.   38
*421 SPITTIN MICK [1] (J Berry) 2-9-2 Gay Kelleway(5) 7/1: 12: Al front rank: kept on
well to take the minor honours and should win more races in this grade: acts on gd & yld
and on any trk: see 421.   35
254 MISS PISA [9] (W Wharton) 2-8-8 N Carlisle 7/1: -0303: Dropped in class: al up there
and looks good enough to win a similar race: acts on gd & yld grnd: see 167.   23
337 FIVE SIXES [5] (N Tinkler) 2-8-11 S Keightley 11/4: 01D4: Led over ½way: in good form.   20
*543 SWYNFORD PRINCESS [6] 2-9-2 G Brown(5) 4/1: -0410: Never going well: btr in 543.   13
603 SUNNY GIBRALTAR [8] 2-8-8 Kim Tinkler(7) 20/1: 000: Never a factor & seems modest.   00
543 Caras Quest [3] 8-8
7 ran   2½,1½,2½,5,7   (K Higson)   Denys Smith Bishop Auckland, Co. Durham

648 RACE A ROUND YORKSHIRE H'CAP 3YO   £1814   1m 4f Yielding 96 -33 Slow   [42]

*430 FIRST DIVISION [18] (G Pritchard Gordon) 3-9-7(5ex) G Duffield 9/2 Jt FAV: 000-11: 3 b c
Wolver Hollow - Home And Away (Home Guard): Useful colt: looked well h'capped and led on bit
below dist for an easy win in a 3yo h'cap at Ripon May 21: first time out was a surprise
winner of a maiden at Doncaster: lightly raced, showing no worthwhile form last season:
half brother to minor winner Top Of The League: very eff over 12f on gd & yld grnd: well
suited by a gall trk: should win again.   48
331 FEDRA [8] (Lord J Fitzgerald) 3-9-0 T Lucas 7/1: 000-122: Led after 1m: no ch with
this easy winner though ran another gd race: see 117.   32
*356 PATS JESTER [14] (P Rohan) 3-8-11 M Wood 8/1: 040-413: Ran on late: gd effort over
this longer trip: acts on a gall trk: see 356.   28
416 STANDON MILL [11] (J Wilson) 3-8-0 Julie Bowker(7) 33/1: 00-0004: Kept on late: stays
12f: see 132.   12
519 NIMBLE NATIVE [10] 3-8-9 J Lowe 16/1: 0-10400: Led briefly 4f out: best in 45 (tight trk). 17
487 SEVEN HILLS [15] 3-8-11 R Brown(7) 20/1: 000-00: Slow start, some late prog: lightly
raced filly who has shown little form herself though is a half sister to several winners:
acts on gd & soft grnd & on a gall trk.   11
25 APPEALIANA [12] 3-8-2 A Mackay 25/1: 00-00: Slowly away and no threat after fair abs.   00
*365 DORS GEM [17] 3-8-4 R Fox 10/1: 00-0110: Fin 8th in this btr company: see 3¦5.   00
357 ALDINO [1] 3-9-9 R Carter(5) 9/2 Jt FAV: 00-00: Well bckd: btr over 10f in 357.   00
416 SWYNFORD PRINCE [5] 3-8-11(vis) G Brown(5) 11/2: 3-00120: Mkt drifter: much btr in 331.   00
461 CHEVET LADY [2] 3-8-5 D Mckeown 8/1: 0-12420: No threat: much btr on a tight trk in 461   00
451 Belhill [16] 7-8   491 Elegant Bill [4] 8-6(5ex)
318 Laugh A Lot [9] 8-5   -- Storm Lord [7] 8-1   *491 Waterford Way [6] 8-0(5ex)
307 Sandmoor Prince [13] 8-1(bl)   380 G G Magic [3] 8-7
18 ran   4,½,3,3,6   (William Du Pont III)   G Pritchard Gordon Newmarket

649 SKELLGATE HANDICAP 0-50   £3306   6f   Yielding 96 +01 Fast   [49]

428 TOP THAT [10] (D Barron) 5-8-0 N Carlisle 11/2: 0-00201: 5 br g Legal Eagle -
Zellamaid (Runnymede): Gamely made ev yd in a h'cap at Ripon May 21: lightly raced last
season and last won in '84, at Catterick (2) and Hamilton: eff over 5/6f: acts on any grnd,
though seems fav by some give: well suited by forcing tactics.   30
525 XHAI [5] (M Tompkins) 4-8-13 M Rimmer 6/1: 0-40202: Outpcd ½way, stayed on well though
the post came too soon and todays trip seems inadequate: see 361 and 17.   38
520 OXHEY BAY [9] (K White) 4-8-11 A Murray 11/2: 112-003: Fin well: in gd form: see 520.   36
490 ROSIE DICKINS [3] (R Hollinshead) 4-7-13 A Culhane(7) 6/1: 0-12224: Model of consistency
this season: see 124.   24
520 COOL ENOUGH [11] 5-7-10 M Fry 14/1: 0-40000: Fin well and not btn far: see 12.   20
369 BAY BAZAAR [12] 4-8-2 K Darley 11/1: -024000: Al front rank, hung close home: see 42.   24
534 NO BEATING HARTS [10] 3-8-6 J Reid 4/1 FAV: 320-130: Dsptd lead most of way: gd
effort against older horses: see 217.   00
--   MELAURA BELLE [17] 5-9-1 T Lucas 10/1: 04004-0: Al behind on reapp: quite a useful
filly on her day, defied top weight in a Thirsk h'cap last season and first time out was
just pipped by Chaplins Club in this same race: eff over 5/6f on firm & soft grnd: acts
on any trk: should do btr next time.   00
428 Karens Star [6] 8-4   -- Air Command [8] 9-10   -- Hopeful Heights [14] 9-2
306 Taskforce Victory [13] 7-13
12 ran   1½,shhd,hd,½,½   (T D Barron)   D Barron Maunby, Yorks

650 KIRKGATE HANDICAP 3YO 0-35   £2192   8f   Yielding 96 -34 Slow   [35]

451 HUDSONS MEWS [6] (M W Easterby) 3-8-13 K Hodgson 5/2 FAV: 000-31: 3 b g Young Generation - Cuba Libre (Rum): Again nicely bckd and ran on well under press to lead close home
in a 3yo h'cap at Ripon May 21: failed to land a massive gamble when placed behind Mr Kewmill
at Redcar first time out: seems well suited by 1m on gd & yld grnd: acts on a gall trk.   30

451 AFFAITATI [18] (Don Enrico Incisa) 3-8-13 M Beecroft 25/1: 030-02: Ran on well, fin 3rd
and placed 2nd: lightly raced colt who stays 1m well: acts on yld grnd & on a gall trk.   24
335 TEED BORE [14] (W Musson) 3-8-9 A Mackay 6/1: 0-2043: Never nearer: fin 4th, placed 3rd. 19
-- MRS NAUGHTY [9] (W Wharton) 3-8-10 N Carlisle 8/1: 42000-4: Hmpd over 2f out, sn
no extra: fin 5th, placed 4th: won a seller at Haydock last season and was later placed in
a Catterick nursery: should be suited by this trip: acts on gd/firm and soft grnd & on
any trk: has run well in bl.   18
427 BRADBURY HALL [8] 3-8-11 C Dwyer 20/1: 0-00000: Made much: fin 6th, placed 5th: see 81. 18
318 SKELTON [3] 3-8-9 M Hindley(3) 14/1: 0100-00: Btr for race: landed a gamble in a
seller at Haydock last season, earlier having won at Thirsk: eff over 7/8f: acts on firm
& soft grnd & on any trk.   12
427 UNEXPLAINED [20] 3-9-6(bl) V Smith(5) 10/3: 0-4202D: Led early & again over 2f out:
held on to 2nd place though caused interference when coming to chall and subs. disq. and
placed last: see 335.   00

--	Balnerino [16] 8-10	**90**	Tower Fame [17] 8-13	--	Colonial King [10] 9-1
--	Cumbrian Nijo [2] 9-7	**379**	Hiya Bud [11] 8-8	**322**	Pauls Secret [1] 8-7
451	Crownit [12] 8-8	--	Capricorn Blue [5] 8-13		
328	Johnstan Boy [4] 8-11	**451**	Jersey Maid [7] 9-5		

17 ran   1½,2½,hd,¾,nk,2,1½,1½   (Hippodromo Racing Ltd)   M W Easterby Sherrif Hutto

651 STONEBRIDGEGATE EBF STAKES   £2895   9f   Yielding 96 -55 Slow

325 ENGLISH SPRING [8] (I Balding) 4-9-7 J Matthias 2/5 FAV: 112-441: 4 gr f Grey Dawn II -
Spring Is Here (In Reality): Very useful filly: took a big drop in class and only had to be
pushed out to land the odds in quite a valuable stakes at Ripon May 21: earlier had twice
fin 4th in Group company this season and was in fine form last backend, winning a Gr.3
event in Italy & a valuable fillies race at Ascot: also won at Wolverhampton & Epsom last
season: very eff over 8/9f: acts on any going & on any trk: genuine filly.who carries weight well.   64
-- INFANTRY OFFICER [13] (M Prescott) 4-9-7 G Duffield 7/1: -2: Led below dist and kept
on well on his debut in this country: first time out winner at Phoenix Park when trained by
J Oxx last season: very eff over 9f on gd/firm & soft grnd: acts on any trk: should find
a race soon.   59
452 POWER BENDER [4] (G Pritchard Gordon) 4-8-6 W Ryan 9/2: 0222-43: Ran on well: see 452. 40
-- PORT PLEASE [2] (M H Easterby) 3-7-7 J Lowe 50/1: -4: Led early in str: no extra
dist though still ran a gd race on her debut: acts on yld grnd & on a gall trk: should impr
enough to win a small race.   38
448 MABEL ALICE [7] 3-7-9(2ow) A Mackay 100/1: 040-000: No real threat: lightly raced
filly who is a half sister to several winners: eff around 1m on gd & soft grnd: acts on
a gall trk.   26
519 PAJANJO [11] 7-9-7 R Brown(7) 50/1: -00: Never dngr: half brother to a couple of
winners, incl useful sprinter Gunfighter.   31

379	Town Of Ennis [10] 8-0(7ow)		**448**	Sing Out Loud [9] 8-3
--	Aqualon [3] 9-4	**524** Green Archer [5] 7-10	**522**	Carlops [6] 8-3
--	Ammeed [12] 8-6	-- Rock Salt [1] 8-6		

13 ran   1,2,2,7,3.   (Paul Mellon)   I Balding Kingsclere, Hants

GOODWOOD   Wednesday May 21st   Righthand, Sharpish, Undulating Track

Official Going Given as First 3 races soft, heavy remainder: Visibility very poor first race.

652 CHICHESTER FESTIVAL THEATRE H'CAP 0-60   £3371   1m2f   Heavy 161 +04 Fast   [54]

433 TABARDAR [11] (R Johnson Houghton) 4-9-5 S Cauthen 7/1: 400-301: In lead 1f out, stayed
on under press in a h'cap at Goodwood may 21: first success, but showed promise in '85:
eff at 10f, stays 11f well: acts on gd/firm & heavy grnd & on any trk.   57
*573 ESQUIRE [13] (B Hills) 4-10-1(8ex) B Thomson 7/2: 10-2112: Grand effort under 10-1.   66
420 KALA NASHAN [12] (P Mitchell) 4-7-7 G Carter(0) 12/1: 020-003: Wknd final 1f: fair
effort: maiden: best effort in '85 when 2nd to Dance Machine in a 3yo fillies stakes at
Salisbury: stays 10f: acts on yld & heavy & on any trk.   23
403 EVROS [9] (Lord J Fitzgerald) 4-9-0 R Hills 16/1: 04-0004: Acts on any grnd: see 403.   34
238 THE HOWARD [7] 4-8-6 N Day 20/1: 101-000: Best in 71 (1m).   18
547 WELL MEET AGAIN [5] 9-7-11 A Mcglone 7/1: 0-30000: Best first time out in 36.   05
432 HEART OF STONE [6] 4-7-7(4oh) C Rutter(0) 10/1: 0000-00: Again active in mkt: see 432. 00
361 VIRGIN ISLE [2] 5-8-11 T Williams 10/1: 4-02000: New trip: btr 361 (7f): see 248, 79.   00
248 BOLDDEN [8] 4-9-9 W Carson 7/1: 1210-00: Yet to hit form: in '85 was most consistent,
winning at Wolverhampton & Newbury: also a fine 2nd to Fish 'N Chips in Extel H'cap on this
trk: very eff at 8/10f: acts on gd & soft grnd & seems suited by forcing tactics: genuine.   00
445 MILL PLANTATION [10] 7-9-9 Pat Eddery 10/3 FAV: 0110-00: Well bckd, but well btn.   00
569 Thatchingly [3] 7-11   -- Salloom [4] 8-10   **263** Bachagha [1] 7-7(BL)(8oh)
13 ran   ¼,4,5,4,2   (H H Aga Khan)   R Johnson Houghton Blewbury, Oxon

653 CLIVE GRAHAM STAKES LISTED RACE   £11218   1m2f   Heavy 161 +07 Fast

--   DIHISTAN [6] (M Stoute) 4-8-11 W R Swinburn 11/4 FAV: 01112-1: 4 b c Tyrnavos -
Damosa (Abdos): Smart colt: first time out, picked the best grnd and led stands side after 3f
out for a very easy win in valuable Clive Graham Stakes (Listed race) at Goodwood May 21:
in fine form in '85, winning h'caps at Leicester & Yarmouth (2): winning 2yo at Hamilton:
half brother to the smart Dazari: very eff over 10f, should stay further: acts on firm &
heavy grnd & on any trk: should win more gd races.   78
511 LINE OF FIRE [8] (P Walwyn) 4-8-11 G Baxter 7/1: 021-002: No ch with winner: btr
effort: acts on firm & heavy: see 511.   58
--● KHOZDAR [3] (W Hern) 4-8-11 W Carson 7/2: 10120-3: Made much on seasonal debut: btr
for race: smart colt who in '85 won twice at Newmarket: eff at 10f, well suited by 12f:
half brother to top class middle dist performer Ardross: well suited by fast grnd & a
stiff trk.   50
--   WINDSOR KNOT [1] (P Walwyn) 4-8-11 Paul Eddery 12/1: 31000-4: Never in it on seasonal
debut: ex French colt who was a winner in '85: difficult to assess.   34
617 VINTAGE PORT [2] 4-8-11 B Rouse 25/1: 3010-00: Impossible task: ex Irish colt who
was a winner at Down Royal in '85: stays 14f: acts on gd grnd.   16
*344 PRESIDIUM [5] 4-8-11 S Cauthen 10/3: 2-03-10: Mkt drifter: see 344 (1m, good).   16
--   ST HILARION [4] 4-9-6 G Starkey 5/1: 33111-0: Friendless in mkt and was well btn
in these atrocious conditions: very smart performer in '85 winning 2 Gr.1 events at San Siro
and an amateur riders event at Kempton: smart 2yo, winning at Goodwood & Newmarket: very eff
at 12f: acts on yld, best on gd & firm grnd: game & genuine & is much btr than this.   00
7 ran   12,5,10,12,hd   (H H Aga khan)   M Stoute Newmarket

654 SCHRODER PREDOMINATE STKS 3YO LSTD RACE £16934   1m 4f Heavy 161 -05 Slow

+370 ALLEZ MILORD [6] (G Harwood) 3-8-12 G Starkey 5/6 FAV: 1-11: 3 b c Tom Rolfe -
Why Me Lord (Bold Reasoning): Smart, unbtn colt: heavily bckd and led over 2f out, easily in
valuable Listed race at Goodwood May 21: first time out won a fast run event at Newmarket:
on sole outing in '85 was a runaway winner of valuable 2yo maiden again at Newmarket: half
brother to several winners: stays 12f: acts on heavy, suited by gd & firm grnd: has a smart
turn of foot and should win more good races.   81
*411 BADARBAK [1] (R Johnson Houghton) 3-8-12 B Thomson 10/1: 103-312: No ch with winner
but is in fine form: stays 12f: acts on any grnd: see 411.   64
231 LAABAS [4] (P Cole) 3-8-12 T Quinn 16/1: 04-33: 20L clear rest: stays 12f and is on
the up grade: see 231.   58
--   JANISKI [8] (W Hern) 3-8-12(BL) B Rouse 33/1: 100-4: Bl first time on seasonal debut:
no show: first time out in '85 won a valuable stakes at Doncaster: should be suited by 10f
plus: acts on fast grnd & a gall trk.   28
*435 WINDS OF LIGHT [2] 3-8-12 S Cauthen 6/1: 1-010: Made most: unsuited by heavy: see 435. 18
597 KOLGONG HEIGHTS [9] 3-8-12 W R Swinburn 11/1: 300-020: Dist. 6th: much btr 597 (gd).   00
510 NEW TROJAN [3] 3-8-12 W Carson 8/1: 140-40: Al trailing: btr than this: see 510.   00
442 Sir Percy [7] 8-12
8 ran   5,3,20,6.   (Jerome Brody)   G Harwood Pulborough, Sussex

655 EBF CUCUMBER STAKES 2YO FILLIES   £2315   6f   Heavy 161 -10 Slow

--   TENDER TIFF [6] (M Mccormack) 2-8-8 S Cauthen 5/2: 1: 2 b f Prince Tenderfoot -
Tsar's Bride (Song): Prom filly: first time out, well bckd & led inside the final 1f,
comfortably in a 2yo fillies stakes at Goodwood May 21: half sister to 10f winner Winter
Palace: eff at 6f, should stay further: acts on heavy grnd & a sharpish trk: should rate
more highly.   56
-450 REGENCY FILLE [7] (R Williams) 2-9-2 R Cochrane 11/2: 122: Led over 2f out: caught
inside final 1f: stays 6f & continues in fine form: acts on gd & heavy: see 450, 223.   56
400 RECREATION [9] (W Jarvis) 2-8-8 B Rouse 5/1: 33: Ev ch halfway: stays 6f: acts on
good & heavy: see 400.   38
513 LIGHTNING LEGEND [1] (P Kelleway) 2-8-8 P Cook 5/1: 44: Led over 3f: btr 513 (5f, gd). 28
*350 JAISALMER [8] 2-8-13 A Mcglone 6/4 FAV: 10: Disapp effort: much btr 350 (yld):
worth another chance.   27
400 PARKLANDS BELLE [2] 2-8-8 W R Swinburn 14/1: 0240: No show: btr 400, 270 (5f).   00
6 ran   2,5,5,3,20   (A C L Sturge)   M Mccormack Sparsholt, Oxon

656 BOXGROVE MAIDEN 3YO FILLIES STAKES   £959   7f   Heavy 161 -27 Slow

464 RAISINHELL [15] (W Jarvis) 3-8-11 S Cauthen 11/2: 0200-31: 3 b f Good Times - Saltana
(Darius): Useful filly: led close home in a fillies maiden at Goodwood May 21: showed promise
in '85, notably when 2nd to Embla at Kempton: half sister to 2 winners: eff at 7f, may
stay 1m: acts on any grnd: seems to like a sharpish trk.   50
422 MALEIHA [13] (N Vigors) 3-8-11 P Cook 25/1: -02: Led over 1f out: caught near fin:
on the up grade: acts on gd & heavy grnd & seems well suited by a sharpish trk: see 422. 48
359 BALLAD ROSE [10] (P Cole) 3-8-11 T Quinn 7/2 FAV: 323-43: Heavily bckd: made much.   43
338 SYBIL FAWLTY [14] (R Laing) 3-8-11 S Whitworth 20/1: 020-04: Sn prom: btr effort:
in '85 fin 2nd in a fillies maiden at Nottingham: acts on gd & heavy: should stay 1m.   39

431 BUTHAYNA [1] 3-8-11 R Hills 6/1: 022-00: Mkt drifter: never nearer: needs faster ground? see 431.   25
--   PAUSE FOR APPLAUSE [19] 3-8-11 W R Swinburn 33/1: 00-0½ No show on seasonal debut: showed some promise from 2 outings in '85: eff at 7f, should stay further: acts on gd & heavy.   20
-- ·CLEOFE [12] 3-8-11 R Guest 6/1: 044-0: Fin 7th: btr for race: showed promise in '85: on final outing was a good 4th to Elwadhna in a fillies maiden at Newmarket: eff at 7f: probably best on fast ground.   00
271 MIRATAINE VENTURE [7] 3-8-11 G Baxter 8/1: 0022-30: Prom, fdd: btr 271.   00
501 BE SO BOLD [18] 3-8-11 P Robinson 10/1: -00: Active in mkt but no threat: see 501.   00
--   MY DARLING [11] 3-8-11 Pat Eddery 9/1: -0: Never sighted on racecourse debut: bred to stay middle distances.   00

-- **Miss Kola** [6] 8-11		-- **Absolutely Bonkers** [20] 8-11	
-- **Collyweston** [5] 8-11		**402 Great Dilemma** [16] 8-11	
-- **Lucy Aura** [2] 8-11		**431 Shades Of Autumn** [4] 8-11	
-- **Straightaway Star** [17] 8-11			-- **Sunk Island** [8] 8-11
-- **Sweet Spice** [3] 8-11			

19 ran   1,2½,2,8,3   (G Hughes)   W Jarvis Newmarket

657 WESTERTON APP HCAP 3YO 0-50   £2611   6f   Heavy 161 -04 Slow   [57]

--   PRECIOUS METAL [2] (A Ingham) 3-9-7 A Shoults 5/2 FAV: 21200-1: 3 b c Mummy's Pet - Golden Treasure (Crepello): Useful colt: first time out, defied top weight, led 2f out in an app. h'cap at Goodwood May 21: useful 2yo, winning a maiden at Salisbury and subs. a fine 2nd to Hallgate in a valuable 2yo event at Ripon: very eff at 6f: acts on gd, suited by soft/heavy grnd: genuine colt who should win more races.   61
--   KENOOZ [6] (A Stewart) 3-8-0 W Hayes(3) 10/1: 0040-2: Ch final 1f: kept on well and just btn: gd seasonal debut: lightly raced 2yo: eff at 6f on gd & hvy grnd: should find a race   38
451 BLACK DIAMOND [4] (A Jarvis) 3-7-8 T Crowe(7) 20/1: 0000-03: Rank outsider: nearest fin: half brother to several winners incl useful sprinter Bold Bob: eff at 6f, stays 7f: acts on firm & heavy grnd.   28
431 CRESTA LEAP [3] (R Hannon) 3-8-3 L Jones 7/2: 40-3024: Mkt drifter: btr 431 (gd).   32
--   SILVER FORM [8] 3-7-7(3oh) J Carter(2) 16/1: 00400-0: No show on seasonal debut: in '85 fin 4th in a fillies maiden at Lingfield: half sister to 2 winners: eff at 6f on soft grnd & a sharpish trk.   17
443 PLATINE [7] 3-8-3 K Radcliffe 6/1: 00-1000: Disapp since first time out in 111.   15
283 MADAM MUFFIN [1] 3-7-7 P Mcgurk(3) 7/1: 2-200: Again below form 87 (5f).   00
496 PORTHMEOR [5] 3-8-5 G Carter 5/1: 44-4240: Prom, fdd: much btr 496 (gd): see 277.   00
8 ran   nk,2,2½,2½,6   (G Moore)   A Ingham Epsom, Surrey

658 BOXGROVE MAIDEN 3YO FILLIES STAKES   £2611   7f   Heavy 161 -18 Slow

250 SOMEONE SPECIAL [8] (P Cole) 3-8-11 T Quinn 9/4 FAV: -21: 3 b f Habitat - One In A Million (Rarity): Useful filly: well bckd and led 2f out, under press in a fillies maiden at Goodwood May 21: dam won the 1,000 Guineas: eff at 7f, should stay 1m: acts on soft & heavy grnd and on any trk: should win more races.   56
--   INDIAN SUMMER [18] (H Candy) 3-8-11 T Williams 14/1: 0-2: Dsptd lead 3f out: kept on well: gd seasonal debut: unplaced on sole outing in '85: eff at 7f, should stay 1m: acts on heavy grnd & can find a maiden.   49
--   STICKY GREENE [20] (B Hills) 3-8-11 B Thomson 15/2: 0-3: Nearest fin: gd seasonal debut: on sole start in '85 fin 6th to Bustara on this trk: well bred filly: acts on yld & hvy grnd & should do btr next time.   43
--   SUMMER GARDEN [13] (I Balding) 3-8-11 S Payne 20/1: -4: Never nearer on racecourse debut: impr likely from this half sister to useful stayer Crusader Castle & should do much btr over longer dists.   33
--   FREE CLARE [12] 3-8-11 C Nutter 12/1: 0-0: No threat: fin 5th in a Beverley maiden on sole start in '85: half sister to numerous winners.   33
431 FAR TOO BUSY [15] 3-8-11 N Howe 20/1: -00: Prom: ev ch: acts on heavy.   32
498 SUNNY LIZ [2] 3-8-11 G Starkey 5/2: 2-20: Easy to back and again below her 2yo form: unsuited by heavy grnd: see 498.   00

431 Chardonnay [7] 8-11	-- **Sweepy** [16] 8-11	**424 Country Craft** [10] 8-11	
205 Divine Fling [5] 8-11	**501 Humble Beauty** [11] 8-11		
-- **Mumtaz Mayfly** [19] 8-11		**171 Rockhold Princess** [9] 8-11	
-- **Zillebeke** [17] 8-11			

15 ran   3,3,6,½,½   (Helena Springfield Ltd)   P Cole Whatcombe, Oxon

Official Going Given as Soft

659   MAIL ON SUNDAY 3YO HANDICAP 0-60   £4227   1m   Yld/Soft 117 -35 Slow   [54]

*436   VAGUE SHOT [6] (C Horgan) 3-9-3(5ex) P Cook 9/4 FAV: 0300-11: 3 ch c Vaigly Great -
Cease Fire (Martial): Impr colt who is in fine form: well bckd and led nearing final 1f,
comfortably in a 3yo h'cap at Goodwood May 22: first time out landed a gamble in a similar
event at Kempton: ran well on several occasions in '85, notably when a close up 6th to
Green Desert in Gr.3 July Stakes at Newmarket: eff at 7f, stays 1m: acts on firm & yld/soft
grnd & on any trk.   55

*464   TOBAGO DANCER [3] (R Hannon) 3-9-3(5ex) G Starkey 5/2: 404-012: Led over 2f out:
in fine form: should win again soon.   49

••   ASK MAMA [5] (J Dunlop) 3-9-7 W Carson 12/1: 002-3: Mkt drifter: promising seasonal
debut: on final outing in '85 fin 2nd to Secret Wedding at Newmarket: half sister to several
winners: eff at 7f, stays 1m: acts on gd/firm & yld/soft. will find maiden race soon.   49

480   COSMIC FLIGHT [4] (M Usher) 3-7-11 A O'reilly(5) 10/1: 0-10334: Sn prom, ev ch:
in gd form: see 67.   22

75   MARKELIUS [1] 3-7-10 A Mackay 33/1: 000-00: Abs: never nearer: lightly raced colt:
probably stays 1m: acts on gd/firm & yld/soft.   17

455   MIRANDA JULIA [7] 3-8-5 A Mcglone 5/1: 440-130: Made much: btr 455, 276 (7f).   23

253   BARRACUDA BAY [2] 3-8-11 T Quinn 6/1: 00-40: No threat: btr 253 (stiffer trk).   00

7 ran   3,2½,1½,2,1½   (A W Anthony)   C Horgan Billingbear, Berks

660   RACELINE STAKES HANDICAP 3YO+ 0-70   £12096   5f   Yld/Soft 117 +38 Fast   [65]

508   LAURIE LORMAN [10] (M Mccourt) 4-7-13 T Williams 12/1: 2300-01: 4 b g Kampala -
Romanee Conti (Will Somers): Fair h'capper: ran on gamely under press to get up close home
in a fast run & valuable h'cap at Goodwood May 22: in '85 won twice at Wolverhampton: eff
at 5f, stays 6f on an easy trk: acts on firm & yld/soft grnd & seems a genuine sort.   49

550   BOLLIN EMILY [15] (M H Easterby) 5-8-4 M Birch 13/2: 14-0242: Led over 1f out: fine
effort: must win soon: see 428.   63

*580   RESPECT [13] (R Laing) 3-7-10(6ex) C Rutter(5) 4/1: 243-213: Kept on well: good
effort under penalty: in fine form: acts on gd/firm & yld/soft grnd & on any trk: see 580.   50

550   CLANTIME [2] (R Whitaker) 5-8-6 W R Swinburn 4/1: 0-02234: Ch over 1f out: gd effort:
best 408: see 272.   49

477   BRIDGE STREET LADY [11] 5-8-12 P Eddery 7/2 FAV: 0-20120: Sn prom: gd effort, but
btr 477, 327.   51

550   ARDROX LAD [6] 6-9-6 N Adams 14/1: 00-0000: Never nearer: see 550.   49

550   Dublin Lad [4] 9-9   **401   Ferryman** [8] 8-0   **477   Derry River** [5] 7-7(bl)
616   Young Inca [9] 8-13   **408   Broadwater Music** [7] 9-0
--   Perfect Timing [1] 8-5
12 ran   nk,2,nk,2,5   (A J Bingley)   M Mccourt Letcombe Regis, Oxon

661   LUPE STAKES LISTED 3YO FILLIES   £11959   1m 2f   Yld/Soft 117 -25 Slow

--   TRALTHEE [2] (L Cumani) 3-8-11 Pat Eddery 9/4: 31-1: 3 ch f Tromos - Swalthee
(Sword Dancer): Smart filly: heavily bckd on seasonal debut: led 2f out, easily in Lupe
Stakes (Listed) at Goodwood May 22: very useful 2yo, ready winner of valuable Rockfel Stakes
at Newmarket: eff at 10f, should stay 12f: acts on yld/soft, suited by fast grnd: acts on
any trk & does well when fresh: should run well in the Oaks.   81

463   ALTIYNA [6] (M Stoute) 3-8-11 W R Swinburn 13/8 FAV: 1-22: Made much: kept on well:
in good form, though no ch with this smart winner: see 463.   71

561   LAND OF IVORY [5] (I Balding) 3-8-11 S Cauthen 4/1: 04-1D43: Ch over 1f out: another
good run: stays 10f: see 264.   70

373   VOLIDA [7] (C Brittain) 3-8-11 P Robinson 8/1: 400-404: New trip: should win maiden:see 373 62

--   GEMMA KAYE [3] 3-8-11 C Asmussen 50/1: 00-0: Rank outsider: fdd final ½m: showed some
promise in 2 outings in '85: half sister to several winners & should be suited by 10/12f:
acts on gd/firm & soft grnd.   42

--   WARM WELCOME [4] 3-8-11 Paul Eddery 14/1: 42-0: Prom over 7f on seasonal debut:
btr for race: showed promise in both outings in '85: on final start was a good 2nd to runaway
winner Sonic Lady in Blue Seal Stakes at Ascot: well bred filly, being a half sister to the
useful Mill Plantation and the smart Hot Touch: should be suited by 10f plus & btr grnd.   17

6 ran   2½,hd,4,10,12   (Alan Clore)   L Cumani Newmarket

662   GOODWOOD AIRFIELD MAIDEN STKS 2YO COLTS £1677   5f   Yld/Soft 117 -04 Slow

--   MANDUB [5] (H T Jones) 2-9-0 A Murray 1/1 FAV: 1: 2 b c Topsider - Tzarina (Gallant
Romeo): Very prom colt: heavily bckd & made virtually all, easily in a 2yo maiden at Goodwood
May 22: eff at 5f, should be suited by further: acts on yld/soft & a sharpish trk: should
rate more highly and win more races.   51

--   BOIS DE BOULOGNE [6] (L Piggott) 2-9-0 W R Swinburn 7/1: 2: Ran on well final 1f:
showing future promise: should be well suited by 6f plus: acts on yld/soft & a sharpish trk
and should have no trouble finding a maiden.   41

--   TRIPLE ENTENTE [2] (H Candy) 2-9-0 C Asmussen 7/1: 3: Showed gd speed till wknd
final 1f: promising racecourse debut from this 50,000 gns purchase: well bred colt: eff
at 5f on yld/soft grnd & should be winning soon.   38

--   **VAIGLY BLAZED** [4] (C Horgan) 2-9-0 P Cook 8/1: 4: Mkt drifter and never in it: should improve: cost 7,600 gns and is a half brother to several winners: should be suited by further than 5f.   30

--   **PERSIAN STYLE** [3] 2-9-0 Pat Eddery 9/2: 0: No threat: impr likely from this half brother to several minor winners, incl out and out stayer Tern.   16

--   **COMBINED EXERCISE** [8] 2-9-0 W Carson 14/1: 0: No show: brother to 1m winner Double Quick Time.   09

--   **MOTOR BROKER** [7] 2-9-0 S Whitworth 14/1: 0: Never in it: ½ brother to 10f winner Marsoom 00
7 ran   3,1½,3,6,3   (Hamdan Al-Maktoum)   H T Jones newmarket

663   KINCSEM STAKES HANDICAP 4YO+ 0-60   £4025   2m 3f   Yld/Soft 117 -18 Slow   [45]

462   **ACCURACY** [4] (G Balding) 5-9-1 J Williams 5/1: 0-32101: 5 ch m Gunner B - Veracious (Astec): Made ev yd, coming home on her own in a h'cap at Goodwood May 22: in gd form this season, earlier winning a fast run h'cap at Newbury: failed to win in '85: in '84 won at Catterick, Nottingham & Doncaster: eff at 2m, well suited by 2½m: acts on yld, likes soft/heavy & seems well suited by forcing tactics.   43

11   **TUGBOAT** [2] (P Mitchell) 7-7-12 G Carter(3) 6/1: 04104-02: No ch with winner: in '85 won a h'cap at Ayr: previous season won again at Ayr: stays all day: acts on any going and on any track.   14

504   **SHINY COPPER** [6] (N Smith) 8-7-11 R Fox 7/1: -002433: Btr 504, see 204.   10

462   **ALDO KING** [12] (D Oughton) 5-8-9 B Crossley 8/1: 000-404: Ev ch str: see 312.   21

462   **STERNE** [9] 4-9-10 G Landau(7) 9/2 FAV: --11-00: Well bckd: wknd over 2f out: see 462.   35

419   **FISHPOND** [13] 5-8-11 A Mcglone 8/1: 3240-20: Never in it: btr 419 (14f, gd).   17

*634   **SAILORS REWARD** [7] 4-9-0(3ex) W Carson 5/1: 04-0410: Prom 2m: much btr 634 (2m1f gd). 00

504   Shuttlecock Star [10] 7-7(8oh)   --   Captain Webster [11] 7-8(bl)

541   Intuition [1] 8-9(vis)   582   Paddycoup [3] 8-11
11 ran   12,3,nk,1,5   (Miss B Swire)   G Balding Fyfield, Hants

664   EBF HALNAKER STAKES 2YO   £3297   6f   Yld/Soft 117 -13 Slow

-571   **GULF KING** [7] (P Kelleway) 2-8-11 C Asmussen 5/6 FAV: 021: 2 ch c Kings Lake - Pearl Star (Gulf Pearl: Led well over 1f out, readily drew clear in a 2yo stakes at Goodwood May 22: last time out was a find 2nd to Quel Esprit at York: half brother to 5 winners, incl useful hurdlers Star Burst and Copse & Robbers: well suited by 6f, will have no trouble getting 7f plus: acts on firm & soft grnd & on any trk: should win more races.   61

523   **JONLEAT** [2] (L Piggott) 2-9-2 Pat Eddery 4/1: 4122: Never nearer: again ran well but no ch with this easy winner: stays 6f & acts on any trk: see 332.   46

--   **TOUGH N GENTLE** [6] (L Piggott) 2-8-11 W R Swinburn 12/1: 3: Made much: prom racecourse debut from this half brother to a dual 5f winner: stays 6f: acts on yld/soft.   37

*270   **OLORE MALLE** [5] (R Hannon) 2-9-2 R Wernham 15/2: 14: Mkt drifter: btr 270.   36

--   **CAMBRIDGE REBEL** [9] 2-8-11 S Cauthen 12/1: 0: Mkt drifter: speed 4f: cost 8,200 gns and should be suited by further.   31

--   **LORD WESTGATE** [8] 2-8-11 B Thomson 20/1: 0: Mkt drifter: should do btr: cost I.R. 10,000 26

577   Makin Mischief [3] 8-11   --   Cee En Cee [1] 8-11

--   Baumaniere [4] 8-11
9 ran   8,2½,3,hd,2½   (Roldvale Ltd)   P Kelleway Newmarket

HAYDOCK   Friday May 23rd   Lefthand, Galloping Track

Official Going Given as Good/Soft

665   EBF ST HELENS MAIDEN FILLIES STKS 2YO   £1907   5f   Yld/Soft 117 -39 Slow

425   **LINN ODEE** [1] (M W Easterby) 2-8-11 K Hodgson 4/6 FAV: 231: 2 b g King Of Spain - Heavenly Chorus (Green God): Slow start, though led ½way for an easy win in a 3 runner fillies maiden at Haydock May 23: placed in her 2 previous outings: cost 8,200 gns and is a speedily bred sort: eff at 5f, should stay further: acts on gd & soft grnd & on any trk.   38

602   **LINPAC NORTH MOOR** [2] (W Elsey) 2-8-11 J Lowe 8/1: 002: Early ldr: see 602: impr: acts on gd & yld/soft.   25

548   **CASHEL VIEW** [3] (N Tinkler) 2-8-11 T Ives 13/8 : 03: Prom early: see 548 (good).   13
3 ran   4,4   (C F Spence)   M W Easterby Sheriff Hutton, Yorks

666   STRETFORD SELLING STKS 3YOO   £1444   7f   Yld/Soft 117 -28 Slow

447   **JELDAIRE** [2] (P Rohan) 3-8-11 Gay Kelleway(5) 6/1: 0000-01: 3 br f Radetzky - Jeldi (Tribal Chief): Dropped to selling company and led inside the final 1f in a 3yo seller at Haydock May 23 (no bid): useful early 2yo, winning first 2 starts at Beverley & Doncaster, but then lost her form: stays 7f: likes soft & hvy grnd & a stiff trk.   19

426   **MISS TONILEE** [13] (D H Jones) 3-8-11 A Clark 11/2: 03-322: Led over 1f out: in good form: see 426, 67.   15

358   **STANGRAVE** [8] (R Boss) 3-9-0 M Miller 11/2: 3330-03: Ch over 1f out: maiden, but placed on several occasions in '85: stays 7f: acts on gd & heavy & on any trk: has been tried in blinkers.   16

535 SOHO SAM [3] (W Musson) 3-9-0 P Waldron 15/2: -004: led ½way: best effort yet and fin 8L clear of rem: stays 7f & acts on soft grrnd: may find a seller.   15

464 COOPER RACING NAIL [9] 3-8-11 W Carson 4/1: 2-32200: Btr 276, 237.   00

141 PHILOSOPHICAL [11] 3-8-11 A Mackay 3/1 FAV: 2041-00: Mkt drifter: no show: should do btr than this: in '85 won sellers at Haydock (nursery) and Windsor: half sister to several winners: eff over 6/7f: should stay 1m: acts on any grnd & on any trk.   00

516 Crisp Metcalfe [10] 9-0		608 Bao [12] 8-11(BL)	
424 Rebello Imp [6] 9-0(bl)		-- Klammering [1] 9-0	
608 Sister Nancy [5] 8-11(bl)		-- Raj Kumari [7] 8-11	
12 ran 2,¾,nk,8,2½,nk,hd (Mrs Frank Reihill)		P Rohan Malton, Yorks	

667 SYDNEY SANDON STKS 3YO   £3574   1m   Yld/Soft 117 -30 Slow

465 HABER [1] (B Hills) 3-9-0 B Thomson 5/4: -231: 3 b c Habitat - Satu (Primera): Useful, impr colt: dictated the pace for an easy win in a 4-runner 3yo stakes at Haydock May 23: placed on both previous outings at Chester & Newmarket: stays 1m well: acts on gd & soft grnd & on any trk, but seems best on a gall one: should win more races.   58

*501 HAUWMAL [3] (W Hern) 3-9-2 W Carson 5/6 FAV: 020-12: Not clear run when the pace qcknd: stays 1m: acts on soft, but btr 501.   50

-- NORDIC PLEASURE [4] (B Hills) 3-9-0 R Street 9/1: -3: Stable mate of winner: should improve: well bred colt, being a half brother to 2 winners, notably At Talaq: stays 1m: acts on soft grnd.   42

-- ORTICA [2] (J Etherington) 3-8-11 M Wood 33/1: -4: Sn prom, fdd over 1f out: should impr: half sister to the useful 7/8f winner Zaide.   21

4 ran   5,3,7   (Alan Clore)   B Hills Newmarket

668 JOHN DAVIES HANDICAP STAKES 0-60   £4077   7f   Yld/Soft 117 -22 Slow   [43]

445 CONMAYJO [1] (D H Jones) 5-9-5 D Williams(7) 10/3: 0-03301: 5 b g Condorcet - Pricey Maid (Home Guard): Well bckd and led inside the final 1f, ridden out in a h'cap at Haydock May 23: in gd form this season: in '85 won at Salisbury & Haydock: previous season won at Chepstow & Bath: equally eff at 7/8f, just stays 10f: acts on gd & soft grnd & likes a gall trk: consistent sort.   43

566 FEI LOONG [7] (E Eldin) 5-8-9 A Mackay 13/2: 00-0442: Led ½way till inside final 1f: good effort and may win soon: see 262.   32

481 FORMATUNE [5] (D Arbuthnot) 4-8-11(bl) W R Swinburn 3/1 FAV: 03-1023: Ran on final 1f and not btn far: another gd run: possibly best over 1m: see 10.   33

573 WINDPIPE [9] (J Watts) 8-9-7 T Ives 12/1: 0040-04: Ch 1f out: not btn far: running into form: lightly raced in '85 & failed to win: in '84 won at Ayr (3) and Newcastle (2): in '83 won again at Ayr & likes that trk: eff at 7f & stays 1m really well: acts on firm & yld/soft and on any trk.   42

606 BATON BOY [8] 5-9-6 J H Brown(5) 10/1: 000-200: Never nearer: see 55.   38

566 GURTEEN BOY [6] 4-9-4 A Mcglone 4/1: 001-000: Ev ch nearing final 1f: see 453.   35

260 MELS CHOICE [3] 8-8-7 K Darley 10/1: 40-0000: Led 3f: see 174.   00

630 Bucks Bolt [2] 7-10(bl)   520 Thatchville [4] 8-6

9 ran   ½,¾,nk,1½,nk,7,6   (J Gibbs)   D H Jones Efail Isaf, Glam.

669 NEWTON MAIDEN STAKES 3YO   £2513   1m 4f   Yld/Soft 117 -20 Sow

351 ALARM CALL [6] (G Harwood) 3-9-0 G Starkey 3/1: 41: 3 b c Alleged - Sunelianne (Cyane): Impr colt: led well over 2f out, driven out in a maiden at Haydock May 23: stays 12f well: acts on yld & soft grnd & a gall trk & seems a genuine sort.   45

592 NADAS [1] (S Norton) 3-9-0(bl) J Lowe 16/1: -42: Ev ch over 1f out: out battled by winner but ran well: fast impr: stays 12f & acts on gd & soft grnd: half brother to 2 winners, incl useful sprinter Fly Baby.   42

347 BEYBARS [5] (W Hern) 3-9-0 W Carson 11/2: 230-03: Never nearer: stays 12f: acts on gd & soft grnd: see 347.   38

409 STORMY PROSPECT [3] (M Jarvis) 3-9-0 T Ives 11/8 FAV: -34: Heavily bckd, but well below form 409 (firm).   29

-- MILFORD QUAY [2] 3-9-0 D Nicholls 14/1: -0: Wknd over 1f out on racecourse debut: should do btr: acts on soft.   25

619 SHIPBOURNE [8] 3-9-0 A Clark 11/1: -000: Led after 1m: fdd: not stay 12f? see 430.   20

357 Majestician [7] 9-0   458 Nautical Step [4] 8-11

8 ran   1,2,5,2½,3,½,dist   (Sheikh Mohammed)   G Harwood Pulborough, Sussex

670 ALTCAR APPRENTICE HCAP 3YO 0-35   £1802   5f   Yld/Soft 117 +19 Fast   [38]

377 CHAUTAUQUA [5] (P Haslam) 3-8-7 K Radcliffe(7) 11/2: 0-421: 3 b c Standford - Pitmilly (Pitskelly): Made most, staying on well in a fast run app. h'cap at Haydock May 23: in gd form this season: very eff over 5f, stays 6f: acts on yld & hvy grnd & likes a stiff trk   28

545 WOW WOW WOW [9] (N Tinkler) 3-8-10 Kim Tinkler(7) 6/1: 0-31002: Ran on well final 1f: good run: needs 6f? see 237.   28

545 GOLDEN GUILDER [10] (M W Easterby) 3-8-12(bl) M Hindley 7/2 FAV: -021203: Ran on final 1f: gd effort: not btn far: see 447, 198.   30

141 SPORTING SOVEREIGN [2] (M Jarvis) 3-8-12 P Hutton(7) 14/1: 000-04: Nearest fin after slow start: should be suited by further than 5f: acts on gd/firm & soft grnd.   24

443 CAPEABILITY POUND [7] 3-9-7 M Richardson(7) 12/1: 000-100: Dsptd lead early: best
first time out 147.   27
489 WINDING PATH [6] 3-8-9 A Whitehall(7) 16/1: 120-000: No show: needs further than 5f.   05
246 KEN SIDDALL [4] 3-8-8 G Brown(3) 11/2: 2-00440: Early speed: btr 246, 198.   00
•443 IMPALA LASS [8] 3-9-6 J Hillis(3) 4/1: 301-110: Prom 3f: well below formm 443 (sharp track) 00
516 SANDITTON PALACE [1] 3-7-12 P Hills(7) 6/1: 0000-00: No show: btr 516 (none h'cap).   00
-- Miss Taufan [3] 7-7(1oh)
10 ran   ½,shhd,3,2,4,½,3   (T C Ellis)   P Haslam Newmarket

671   BE FRIENDLY HANDICAP 3YO 0-50   £3282   6f   Yld/Soft 117 +24 Fast   [51]

588 PANNANICH WELLS [8] (M W Easterby) 3-8-5 W Carson 6/4 FAV: 430-021: 3 b c Lochnager -
Gold Poulet (Goldhill): Well bckd, led over 1f out and came again gamely to get up close
home in a fast run 3yo h'cap at Haydock May 23: last time out a find 2nd to Elnawagi in a
similar event at Newmarket: equally eff at 6/7f: acts on firm & yld/soft grnd.   40
•438 QUINTA REEF [7] (M Jarvis) 3-9-6 T Ives 9/2: 00-12: led final 1f: just caught: in
fine form: acts on gd & yld/soft: see 438. carries weight well.   53
λ28 ROVE [11] (S Norton) 3-8-9 J Lowe 13/2: 01-1243: Ch over 1f out: gd effort: acts
on firm & yld/soft: see 6.   37
545 LOW FLYER [5] (G Oldroyd) 3-7-12 L Charnock 9/2: 4-03024: Led over 2f out: btr 545.   25
-- VILTASH [10] 3-9-7 M Hindley(3) 16/1: 32000-0: No show on seasonal debut: in gd form
in the first half of last season, winning at Ayr & Thirsk & was most consistent: equally eff
at 5/6f: acts on any grnd & on any trk.   43
454 HELVICK BAY [1] 3-7-9 R Fox 20/1: 0000-00: Slow start: little form in '85.   07
534 DANCING TOM [9] 3-8-10 C Coates(5) 9/1: 1-40000: Fdd final 1f: see 81.   00
580 Dancing Sarah [4] 8-8   **-- Tax Roy** [2] 9-1   **-- Dawn Love** [3] 8-2
10 ran   ½,1½,nk,1½,4,1,2   (Mrs Robert Sangster)   M W Easterby Sheriff Hutton, Yorks

---

672   TTHE SYCAMORE STAKES 2YO   £2400   5f   Good/Soft 93 -15 Slow

548 GLOW AGAIN [6] (J Etherington) 2-8-4 M Wood 2/1 FAV: 31: 2 br f The Brianstan -
Grey Aglow (Aglojo): Impr filly: led below dist and comfortably justified fav. in a 2yo
stakes at Pontefract May 23: half sister to the versatile The Small Miracle: eff over 5f
and should stay further: acts on gd & yld grnd & on any trk.   42
548 MINIZEN LASS [1] (M Brittain) 2-8-4 K Darley 7/2: 042: Tried to make all: has good
early speed and should find a small race on a tighter course: see 548.   30
-- FREV OFF [4] (M H Easterby) 2-8-4 M Birch 8/1: 3: Irish bred filly who should impr
for this initial outing: half sister to a couple of winning sprinters: acts on yld grnd.   22
•354 MONS FUTURE [7] (W Pearce) 2-8-8 N Connorton 12/1: 014: Ran to her best in this
btr company: see 354.   25
-- KATIE SAYS [5] 2-8-4 A Murray 10/1: 0: Ran on late after a slow start: speedily bred
filly who cost 12,500 gns as a yearling: acts on yld grnd: should do btr next time.   13
415 PRIOR WELL [9] 2-8-4 K Hodgson 10/3: 0020: Close up after ½way: best in 415.   09
-- Shady Blade [8] 8-7(3ow)   **543 Briarqueen** [10] 8-6(2ow)
8 ran   4,3,½,1,½,½   (Mrs G Liversidge)   J Etherington Malton, Yorks

673   BEECH SELLING HANDICAP (0-25)   £1051   1m   Good/Soft 93 -11 Slow   [17]

310 CHARMING VIEW [4] (H Jones) 4-9-4   W Ryan 10/1: 0400-01: Led 1f out, comfortably
in a selling h'cap at Pontefract May 23 (bought in 1,400 gns): made most to win at York as
a juvenile and was quite lightly raced last season: stays 1m: well suited by some cut in
the ground: acts on any trk.   16
609 BUNDLING BED [1] (R Woodhouse) 4-9-0 A Proud 15/2: 0000-02: Dropped in class &
nicely bckd: ran on late: in '84 won a small race at Nottingham though showed little form
in h'caps last season: eff over 8/10f: acts on firm & yld grnd.   06
420 MISS APEX [13] (F Yardley) 4-9-6 I Johnson 10/3: 032-043: Led into str: in fair
form: see 420.   08
-- RECORD HAULIER [2] (W Haigh) 4-8-12 S Lawes 20/1: 00400/4: No threat after a lengthy
abs: showed no worthwhile form in '84: stays 1m: acts on firm & yld.   00
-- VIDEO [8] 4-9-7 M Brennan(7) 16/1: 03000-0: Al mid-div on reapp: first time out in
'84 won a seller at Nottingham & was placed in similar company last season: eff over 7/8f:
best form on faster ground.   00
107 GILLANBONE [10] 4-8-12 T Ives 11/1: 0004-00: Never dangerous.   00
-- EMPIRE SANDS [7] 4-8-11(bl) Gay Kelleway(5) 8/1: 00440-0: Fin 7th: btr for race.   00
491 COLONEL HALL [5] 3-7-11 M Fry 5/2 FAV: 0-00000: Never nearer in 8th.   00
568 DORADE [14] 3-8-10 M Birch 7/1: 00-0030: Last to fin: see 426.   00
630 Sophys Folly [9] 9-6   **279 The Dabber** [3] 8-1(bl)(2ow)
-- Ebor Grey [11] 8-11   **139 Platinum Star** [6] 7-13
279 Gemma Louise [12] 7-11
14 ran   2,2,5,hd,2½   (Mrs A M Jones)   H Jones Malton, Yorks

674 **FARNDON RACING LTD. HANDICAP (0-50)**   £3052   1m   Good/Soft 93 -21 Slow   **[44]**

357 RUN BY JOVE [3] (S Norton) 3-8-8(VIS) J Lowe 13/2: 300-001: 3 gr c Northern Jove -
Running Eagle (Bald Eagle): Went on below dist and kept on gamely to win a 3yo h'cap at
Pontefract May 23: visored for the first time today: eff over 1m, stays 10f: acts on gd
& yld grnd & on any trk.   34
--   GIBBERISH [8] (M Prescott) 3-7-10 M Fry 10/1: 03000-2: Led/dsptd lead thro'out: gd
effort on reapp: lightly raced last season: clearly stays 1m: suited by some cut in the grnd.   20
253 TRIPLE BLUFF [7] (B Hills) 3-8-12 B Thomson 6/4 FAV: 00-03: Dropped in class & well
bckd: al close up: highly tried in both starts last season & again on reapp: stays 1m:
acts on gd & soft grnd & on any trk.   33
538 SECLUSIVE [6] (C Tinkler) 3-9-6 M Wood 6/1: 1400-04: Denied a clear run dist: ran
on well and this was a btr effort: last season won a nursery over 6f at Pontefract: stays
1m: acts on firm & yld grnd & on any trk.   35
379 LADY BRIT [2] 3-8-9 G Duffield 8/1: 020-000: No threat: best effort last season when
running up to Mal Y Pense in a fillies maiden at Catterick: eff over 7/8f on firm & yld grnd.   23
89   MOLLY PARTRIDGE [9] 3-7-10 N Carlisle 10/1: 4203-00: No threat after fair abs.   10
402 BOLD BORDERER [5] 3-9-7 J Reid 6/1: 300-000: Fin 7th: showed promise last season when
placed a Goodwood and Salisbury: stays 1m: acts on firm & yld grnd & on any trk.   00
--   KIRKELLA [1] 3-8-8 A Murray 14/1: 0000-0: No extra dist: fin 8th.   00
--   QURRAT AL AIN [4] 3-8-4 M Birch 10/1: 000-0: Led over ½way: fin last though btr
for race.   00
9 ran   ¾,1½,3,nk,shhd   (Peter Wetzel)   S Norton Barnsley, Yorks

675 **SAFEGUARD INVESTMENTS H'CAP (0-35)**   £1870   1m 4f   Good/Soft 93 -31 Slow   **[34]**

381 NORDIC SECRET [11] (Denys Smith) 4-7-12 L Charnock 25/1: 000-001: 4 b c Thatching -
Secret Isle (Voluntario III): Led into str and ran on well to win a h'cap at Pontefract
May 23: no worthwhile form previously: stays 12f: acts on yld grnd.   18
582 LEON [12] (N Tinkler) 4-9-11 Kim Tinkler(7) 11/4 FAV: 04-2202: Just held: under 9-11:see 30 35
591 ISHKHARA [2] (G Reveley) 4-8-6 D Leadbitter(3) 12/1: 400-003: Al close up: see 449.   13
526 HIGHAM GREY [7] (D Chapman) 10-8-6 D Nicholls 9/1: 0-00004: Made much: fair effort.   12
--   DONT RING ME [5] 4-9-3 R Lines(3) 5/1: 43100-0: Lost place home turn, stayed on again
and should do btr next time: comfortable winner of a Ripon maiden last season: stays 12f
well: acts on gd & hvy grnd: progressive filly.   22
--   LAKINO [1] 4-9-2 A Murray 12/1: 000-1-0: Never nearer on reapp: won his only start
last season, a selling h'cap at Beverley: eff over 10f, stays 12f: acts on firm & yld.   20
590 CHRISTMAS HOLLY [3] 5-8-0 M Fry 5/1: 3100200: Much btr in 105.   00
569 Hyokin [10] 8-12(vis)   --   Ramilie [8] 8-8   519 Trojan Way [13] 9-5
--   Hobournes [6] 8-8   381 Country Jimmy [9] 8-12
12 ran   ¾,2,hd,¾,¾,1½   (Denys Smith)   Denys Smith Bishop Auckland, Co Durham

676 **WALNUT E.B.F. STAKES 3YO+**   £3078   1m 2f   Good/Soft 93 +07 Fast

--   THEN AGAIN [2] (L Cumani) 3-8-8 Paul Eddery 4/6 FAV: -01-1: 3 b c Jazzeiro - New Light
(Reform): Very useful colt: first time out was heavily bckd when leading close home in
quite a fast run 3yo stakes at Pontefract May 23: big strong colt who won at the Curragh as
a juvenile: stays 10f well: acts on gd & yld grnd: well regarded & should win more races.   65
553 AUCTION FEVER [4] (B Hills) 3-7-13 M Hills 9/2: 333-202: Ran on well over this
longer trip: gd effort: see 386. must soon find a maiden   53
344 CRESTA AUCTION [7] (G Pritchard Gordon) 3-8-12 G Duffield 3/1: 13-1123: Qcknd clear
early in str: collared close home: stays 10f: remains in gd form: see 344.   63
535 ARROW OF LIGHT [3] (O Douieb) 3-7-13 R Hills 12/1: -04: Never dngr in this good
company: seems to stay 10f: acts on firm & yld grnd.   38
368 MISS LAURA LEE [5] 3-7-10 A Mackay 50/1: 40-40: Made much over this longer trip.   27
445 POLEMISTIS [6] 7-9-8(vis) Sharron James 100/1: 0000-00: Btn home turn trailed in last. 00
6 ran   ¾,2,7,5,25   (R J Shannon)   L Cumani Newmarket

677 **CEDAR MAIDEN STAKES 3YO**   £779   6f   Good/Soft 93 +18 Fast

455 HIGHEST PRAISE [4] (I Balding) 3-9-0 J Matthias 5/1: 403-01: 3 ch g Topsider -
Prides Promise (Crozier): Responded well to strong press to lead inside dist in a fast run
3yo maiden at Pontefract May 23: lightly raced last season when twice placed in similar
company: eff over 6/7f on gd & yld grnd: seems to act on any trk: clocked a good time
here and may win again. only rated 32 officially.   49
--   CHIEF PAL [11] (P Walwyn) 3-9-0 Paul Eddery 7/2: 4-2: Ran on well under press: gd
seasonal debut: placed behind Zahdam in a competitive race at Ascot on his only start last
season & should get off the mark soonn: brother to the useful h'capper Qualitair Flyer:
eff over 6/7f on firm & yld grnd.   44
464 ELSOCKO [1] (B Mcmahon) 3-8-11 J Hills(5) 14/1: 300-303: Tried to make all: not
btn far & comfortably beat rem: should find a race: see 309.   40
516 MURPHYS WHEELS [8] (A Jarvis) 3-9-0 D Nicholls 4/1: 3-04: No extra dist: see 516.   33
334 BOOFY [5] 3-9-0(bl) J Reid 7/1: 40-2240: Close up till dist: see 175.   31
255 RAAS [3] 3-9-0 J Lowe 12/1: 0-2340: Twice disapp since narrowly btn in 241 (5f).   28
516 SUPERCOOMBE [14] 3-9-0 T Quinn 11/4 FAV: 4-30: Front rank over ½way: much btr 516 (5f) 00

451 **Owls Way** [13] 8-11   **--** **Bickerman** [15] 9-0   **--** **Gardas Gold** [7] 9-0
447 **Qualitair King** [16] 9-0   **--** **Skybird** [9] 9-0
593 **Package Perfection** [17] 8-11   334 **Absolute Master** [10] 9-0(BL)
339 **Hobournes Katie** [12] 8-11
15 ran   1½,¼,½,5,1,1½   (Paul Mellon)   I Balding Kingsclere, Berks

---

LINGFIELD   Saturday May 24th   Lefthanded, Sharpish Undulating Track

Official Going Given as Good/Soft

678 E.B.F. SALFORDS MAIDEN STAKES 2YO   £2644   5f   Good 53 -05 Slow

565 **FRENCH TUITION** [4] (R Hannon) 2-9-0 S Cauthen 9/2: 2331: 2 b c Martinmas - French Pearl
(Gulf Pearl): Consistent colt: adopted different tactics, held up and led inside dist in a
2yo maiden at Lingfield May 24: in his earlier starts had tried to make all, most notably
when just btn by Enchanted Times at Kempton: half brother to speedy juvenile Cronk's Image:
very eff over 5f and should stay further: acts on gd/firm & yld grnd & is well suited by
a sharpish trk.   48
577 **KEEN EDGE** [8] (P Mitchell) 2-9-0 A Mcglone 7/4 FAV: 422: Well bckd: tried to make all:
another good effort and must get off the mark soon: see 577.   46
614 **KAMENSKY** [2] (R Smyth) 2-9-0 C Rutter(5) 50/1: 03: Friendless in mkt though had ev ch
and was not btn far: eff over 5f on a sharpish trk: acts on gd & yld grnd: see 614.   45
-- **JUST ONE MORE** [1] (E Eldin) 2-9-0 E Guest(3) 14/1: 4: Ev ch dist: gd racecourse debut:
speedily bred colt who fetched 5,200 gns as a yearling: acts on a sharpish trk.   37
-- **JABE MAC** [7] 2-9-0 R Curant 50/1: 0: Ran on quite promisingly after a slow start:
should do btr next time: half brother to a couple of winning sprinters: acts on gd grnd
and oon a sharpish trk.   29
457 **COURT COMMAND** [6] 2-9-0 N Adams 50/1: 00: Never dngr, though did show a little
improvement here.   23
-- **SANTELLA GREY** [3] 2-9-0 G Starkey 11/4: 0: Well bckd debutant: never reached ldrs
though will be btr for this experience: sprint bred colt who cost 9,200 gns as a yearling.   00
270 **MUKHABBR** [11] 2-9-0 B Rouse 12/1: 030: Mkt drifter: speed over ½way: see 270.   00
-- Mr Mumbles [9] 9-0   **--** Spy Tower [10] 9-0   **--** Kingswood Resopal [12] 9-0
565 Segovian [5] 9-0
12 ran   ¾,hd,3,4,1½,1,shhd   (R G Bedwell)   R Hannon East Everleigh, Wilts

679 REDHILL HANDICAP (0-35)   £2341   6f   Good 53 -05 Slow   [28]

418 **PINE HAWK** [16] (D Haydn Jones) 5-8-11 D Williams(7) 11/2: 04-4101: 5 b h Algora -
paridance (Doudance): Went on ½way and held on well in a h'cap at Lingfield May 24: last
month gained his first win in a similar event at Nottingham: eff over 5/6f: acts on any
grnd, though is suited by some give: no trk preferences: in gd form at present.   20
566 **JAMES DE COOMBE** [6] (M Bolton) 4-8-8 S Cauthen 10/1: 30-0002: Just failed: gd effort.   15
-266 **FREMONT BOY** [5] (C James) 4-9-1 B Rouse 5/1 FAV: 3000-23: Narrowly btn: in fine form. 22
*495 **ALNASHME** [11] (D Thom) 4-9-3(7ex) P Bloomfield 6/1: 04-4014: Ran on too late: see 495. 12
578 **SWEET ANDY** [13] 7-8-1 C Rutter(5) 25/1: 0200/00: Late prog: lightly raced on the
Flat and remains a maiden: best effort to date when placed in a Pontefract seller in 83/84:
stays 1m: acts son gd & soft grnd & on any trk.   00
495 **FAIRDALE** [7] 8-8-2(1ow) John Williams 14/1: -00030: Never reached ldrs: see 495.   00
355 **PORT MIST** [9] 4-7-13 S Meacock(5) 14/1: 000-000: Ddhtd for 6th: modest sprint h'capper
who has yet to win: acts on any going and on any trk.   00
355 **CAPTAINS BIDD** [1] 6-8-0(bl) M L Thomas 7/1: 4300-00: Speed over ½way: fin 8th: see 355. 00
508 **DORNEY** [4] 6-9-2 W Carson 6/1: 0240-00: Gd early speed: ran some gd races last
season though last won in '84 at Leicester: well suited by 6f on fast grnd: acts on any trk.   00
508 Cats Lullaby [15] 9-1(bl)   **--** Pommes Chateau [8] 9-10
495 Sparkford Lad [17] 9-6(bl)   **--** Gallant Hope [14] 8-7
-• Saravanta [19] 8-5   495 Another Bing [12] 8-3   **--** Italian Spring [10] 8-0
266 Linton Starchy [18] 8-2(4ow)
17 ran   hd,shhd,5,shhd,1,ddht   (Mrs Jacqueline Wilkinson)   D Haydn Jones Pontypridd

680 QUEEN ELIZABETH HANDICAP (0-60)   £4129   7f   Good 53 +10 Fast   [53]

578 **DE RIGUEUR** [3] (J Bethell) 4-9-0 S Cauthen 6/1: 4-10101: 4 b g Derrylin - Northern Lady
(The Brianstan): In tremendous form, held up and qcknd well to lead inside dist in a fast
run and valuable h'cap at Lingfield May 24: earlier successful in similar events at Salisbury
& Warwick: consistent performer last season winning at Wolverhampton: very eff over 7/8f on
gd & soft grnd: acts on any trk: genuine sort.   50
432 **SUPER TRIP** [6] (M Fetherston Godley) 5-8-1 C Rutter(5) 12/1: 400-002: Led below dist:
much btr effort: last season won a h'cap at Nottingham and in '84 won at Haydock & Pontefract: eff around 1m, stays 10f well: acts on gd & firm grnd & on any trk: carries weight well   33

566 GOLDEN BEAU [7] (D Morley) 4-7-9 T Williams 8/1: 40-0333: Al front rank: see 281.   22
573 GO BANANAS [10] (K Ivory) 5-10-0 G Mash(7) 12/1: 00-0004: Kept on well under top
weight: useful h'capper who won a h'cap at Newbury last season, after hacking up in Newbury
Spring Cup on that same course: very eff over 7/8f: acts on firm & soft grnd & on any trk:
carries weight well: seems to be returning to form.   50
508 AL AMEAD [2] 6-9-3 B Rouse 8/1: 004-000: Course specialist: made a lot of the running
and again ran well on this sharpish trk: see 508.   36
433 ROMAN BEACH [12] 6-8-13 N Day 8/1: 4400-00: Al up there: quite lightly raced in
recent seasons and last won in '84 at Doncaster: suited by 1m: acts on firm & yld grnd &
on any trk.   30
578 TOM FORRESTER [9] 5-7-12 W Carson 2/1 FAV: 003-030: Dsptd lead most of way: see 453.   00
636 LEMELASOR [13] 6-8-3 D Williams(7) 7/1: -032320: Fin 9th: see 441.   00
481 Hello Sunshine [8] 8-9   481 Kavaka [1] 7-9
578 Visual Identity [5] 7-11(2ow)   481 Jabaraba [4] 7-7
540 Billy Whiteshoes [11] 7-7(2oh)
13 ran   1½,2½,2½,1½,1,1,shhd   (Mrs Christopher Heath)   J Bethell Chilton, Oxon

681 EARLSWOOD SELLING STAKES 2YO   £891   5f   Good 53 -23 Slow

603 NATIONS SONG [2] (R Stubbs) 2-8-8 J H Brown(5) 6/1: 041: 2 b f Gold Song - Girl
Commander (Bold Commander): Left inside dist, driven out to win a 2yo seller at Lingfield
May 24 (bought in 3,400 gns): cheaply bought filly who has impr with every race: eff over
5f on gd & yld grnd: acts on any trk.   36
417 ROYAL RABBLE [5] (D Elsworth) 2-8-8 A Mcglone 11/8 FAV: 02042: Dropped in class &
gambled on: led after ½way, just held and well clear of rem: should certainly win a seller: 33
502 TELEGRAPH FOLLY [7] (R Hoad) 2-8-11 B Rouse 12/1: 0433: No extra dist: see 329.   16
-- KIND LADY [8] (J Winter) 2-8-8 S Cauthen 3/1: 4: Nicely bckd on racecourse debut
outpcd early though kept on Ite & should do btr next time: acts on gd grnd & on a sharpish trk   12
482 PHOEBE [9] 2-8-8 John Williams 14/1: 00: Bckd at long odds: speed over ½way.   04
421 JANS DECISION [6] 2-8-11 N Adams 12/1: 000: Led to ½way, sn wknd: see 421.   00
-- ALN WATER [10] 2-8-8 W Carson 6/1: 0: Never nearer after a slow start: half sister
to 8/10f winner Four For Uncle: btr for this experience.   00
483 Snapshot Baby [3] 8-8   -- Palace Fields [1] 8-8   502 Floret [4] 8-8
10 ran   1,7,½,3,6   (Nation Wide Racing Ltd)   R Stubbs Middleham, Yorks

682 REIGATE E.B.F. STAKES   £4971   1m 2f   Good 53 -04 Slow

-- BONSHAMILE [1] (A Hide) 3-8-5 R Guest 11/8: 1-1: 3 b f Ile De Bourbon - Narration
(Sham): Very useful filly: first time out was never hdd when an impressive winner of a
valuable stakes at Lingfield May 24: surprise winner of her only start last season, beat
Al Salite at Doncaster: very eff over 10f & sure to stay further: acts on gd & soft grnd
and on any trk: sure to come on for this race: well regarded and will now go for the Oaks.   64
-- ANCILLA [2] (P Kelleway) 4-9-2 S Cauthen 7/1: -2-2: Never reached winner though ran
a pleasing race on reapp: ran up to Vienna Belle in a fillies stakes at Ayr on sole outing
last season: nicely bred filly: stays 10f well: acts on gd & hvy grnd & on any trk: likely
to impr further & should win a race soon.   48
549 HUSNAH [3] (L Cumani) 3-8-0 W Carson 5/6 FAV: 02-33: Heavily bckd disapp: chased
winner most of way though btn early in str: btr in 549.   34
3 ran   6,10   (Edwin Turner)   A Hide Newmarket

683 BLETCHINGLEY HANDICAP (0-50)   £2599   1m 4f   Good 53 +02 Fast   [49]

-• RA NOVA [4] (I Matthews) 7-7-7 G Dickie 10/1: 00001/1: 7 b h Ragstone - Miss Casanova
(Galivanter): Fit from hurdling: led early in str & held on gamely in quite a fast run h'cap
at Lingfield May 24: successful on his last outing on the Flat in an amateur riders h'cap on
this course in '84: in '83 won at Chepstow & again at Lingfield: eff around 10/12f and will
stay further: acts on any going & on any trk, though does particularly well at Lingfield.   26
403 CONVINCED [5] (G Harwood) 4-10-0 G Starkey 10/3: 1100-32: Just failed to defy top
weight: but rem decisively and this was another fine effort: see 403.   60
•547 SAMANPOUR [1] (R Johnson Houghton) 3-8-6(4ex) S Cauthen 11/8 FAV: 01-1113: Heavily bckd:
ev ch over this longer trip & remains in tremendous form: see 547.   49
-- SITAR THEME [2] (R Akehurst) 4-7-12 C Rutter(5) 16/1: 003-4: Fit from hurdling: led
over 1m: fair effort: lightly raced on the Flat last season & remains a maiden: eff over
12/14f on gd & yld grnd.   22
485 WILD GINGER [6] 4-7-9(bl)(2ow) B Crossley 10/1: 030-020: Btr over 14f in 485 (stiff trk).   14
532 HOLYPORT VICTORY [9] 4-8-12 A O'reilly(7) 11/2: 4011330: Best over 10f in 341.   23
569 STARDYN [10] 4-7-7(5oh) T Williams 7/1: 00-030: Well placed till home turn: see 569.   00
532 Fogar [7] 8-8(bl)   -- Overule [8] 7-7(14oh)
9 ran   ½,4,1½,3,6   (Lady Matthews)   I Matthews Newmarket

230

684   FRICKLEY SELLING STAKES 3YO   £1041   1m   **Good 64 -26 Slow**

451   HARE HILL [1] (P Rohan) 3-8-11(BL) J Bleasdale 13/8 fav: 010-001: 3 b f Lochnager -
Chuchilla (Comedy Star): Led 3f out, hdd final 1f and was only 2nd best on merit when awarded
a 3yo seller at Doncaster May 24 (no bid): winner at Haydock in '85: acts on gd & soft:
eff over 1m on a gall trk. and improved by blinkers.   19
--   HAJ [9] (N Macauley) 3-9-0 W Wharton 14/1: 02-2: Came from off the pace, gd finish:
2nd in a seller at Yarmouth last season on second of only 2 outings: stays 1m well: acts
on gd: should find a seller.   22
620   ON IMPULSE [10] (K Brassey) 3-8-11 S Whitworth 11/4: 0000-03: Heavily bckd, ev ch:
lightly raced and no form last season: stays 1m & acts on gd.   09
--   LADY OF HAMPTON [5] (P Rohan) 3-8-11 S Morris 25/1: -4: Never closer on racecourse
debut: stable companion of Hare Hill: should impr.   08
426   SUPREME COMMAND [2] 3-9-0 D Nicholls 14/1: -0000: Prom most: best effort yet.   09
527   BEAU DIRE [4] 3-9-0 R Hills 100/30: -001D: Led 1f out & came home by 3L but was disq
and placed last for barging early in the str: unlucky loser and will gain compensation.   29
430   THE LEGGETT [4] 3-9-0 (C Drew) 7/1: 024-000: Ev ch: see 307.   00
                            608 Manasta [7] 8-11   **--   Rose Port** [3] 8-11
9 ran   3,shhd,5,½,1   (Mrs J P Bissill)   P Rohan Malton, Yorks

685   ZETLAND MAIDEN STAKES 2YO   £1342   6f   **Good 64 -11 SLow**

--   POLEMOS [15] (H T Jones) 2-9-0 R Hills 4/5 fav: 1: 2 ch c Formidable - Polemia
(Roi Dagobert): Prom colt: first time out, landed the odds making most comfortably in a
2yo maiden at Doncaster May 24: cost 105,000 gns: eff 6f, sure to stay further: acts on
gd going: likely to rate more highly & win more races.   56
523   COMMONSIDR GIPSY [19] (O Brennan) 2-9-0 M Brennan[4] 33/1: 02 Belied his SP, fin in
grand fashion: cheaply bought colt who looks sure to win a maiden on this form: will stay
further than 6f: acts on gd.   50
--   CUTTING BLADE [22] (L Piggott) 2-9-0 J Matthias 12/1: 3: Al prom, kept on well: gd
debut: sprint bred & should not be long impr on this.   50
--   LACK OF PEARLS [17] (R Woodhouse) 2-8-11 A Shoults[5] 33/1: 4: Prom thro'out: creditable
effort and impr likely.   37
571   DANUM DANCER [11] 2-9-0 K Hodgson 20/1: 00: Dsptd lead much and is on the up grade:
dam a smart sprinter and has already produced the smart sprinter Able Albert.   40
--   HAYTAL [10] 2-9-0 J Reid 10/1: 0: Prom much: will stay further than 6f.   39
--   NAVOS [6] 2-8-11 D Nicholls 33/1: 0: Gd late prog into 7th: will be suited by 7f:
sure to impr on this promising effort.   00
571   BOY SINGER [8] 2-9-0(HOOD) C Dwyer 14/1: 04300: Wearing a hood for the first time,
fin 8th: see 77.   00
571   MARK ANGELO [9] 2-9-0 P Cook 13/2: 200: Ev ch, fin 9th: best 61 (heavy). .   00
--   High Chateau [18] 9-0   **571 Regent Lad** [16] 9-0   **136 Cammac Lad** [21] 9-0
--   Brewin Time [13] 9-0   **544 Abidjan** [4] 9-0   **--   Banks And Braes** [14] 9-0
--   Born To Race [5] 9-0   **--   Combermere** [3] 9-0   **544 Maestroman** [12] 9-0(BL)
--   Sergeant Meryll [7] 9-0   **186 Thatch Avon** [1] 9-0
544 Westgale [2] 9-0
21 ran   1½,shhd,4,shhd,nk   (Hamdan Al-Maktoum)   H T Jones Newmarket

686   ROSEHILL HANDICAP 0-50   £3303   1m 4f   **Good 64 -06 Slow**   [46]

429   GULFLAND [5] (G P Gordon) 5-9-0 Abigail Richards[7] 8/1: 00-1321: 5 ch g Gulf Pearl -
Sunland Park (Baragoi): Came from behind and overcame difficulties in running when leading
near fin in a h'cap at Doncaster May 24: first time out won similar h'cap at Nottingham:
in '84 won at Kempton: suited by 10/12f: seems to act on firm & soft.   40
474   REGAL STEEL [2] (R Hollinshead) 8-7-11 A Culhane[7] 9/2: -302032: Just failed to
make all: gd effort but rated higher 474 (sharp trk).   21
591   VERY SPECIAL [4] (W Holden) 4-8-6 R Morse[5] 7/2 fav: 0143-03: Chall. final 1f: see 591. 29
585   ROSTHERNE [7] (K Stone) 4-9-0 G Brown[5] 7/2 jt fav: 3-42104: Ev ch: clear of rest. 35
584   STRATHEARN [8] 5-8-2 M Wood 9/1: 0000: Prom much: off the trk last season, in '83
won at Redcar: possibly stays 12f: best form over 1m/10f: acts on gd.   16
493   JACKS LUCK [6] 5-8-8 M Rimmer 11/2: -1230: Best 8 (10f).   20
532   KUWAIT MOON [3] 4-9-2 S Keightley 11/2: 3202-00: Ev ch: see 532 (firm).   00
--   Lysander [1] 9-7
8 ran   1,½,1,5,1½   (G P Gordon)   G P Gordon Newmarket

687   PRIORY PLACE HANDICAP 3YO+ 0-60   £4240   6f   **Good 64 +07 Fast** [56]

•374   HO MI CHINH [11] (C Brittain) 4-9-7 M Roberts 8/1: 4000-11: 4 ch c Homing - Fiordiligi
(Khalkis): Useful sprinter: led dist. and held on gamely in quite a fast run h'cap at
Doncaster May 24: first time out winner of valuable h'cap at Newmarket: also first time out
winner at Pontefract in '85 when trained by M H Easterby: stays 1m but very eff over 6f:
acts on firm & yld & likes a gall trk: does well when fresh.   60

520 SHARLIES WIMPY [3] (W Pearce) 7-8-12 M Hindley[3] 14/1: 0400-02: Well bckd at long
odds: came to chall final 1f: back to his best & should be kept on the right side next time.   48
-525 GEORGE WILLIAM [12] (P Bevan) 5-8-2 R Fox 11/2: 000-223: Well bckd, had anything but
a clear run and was possibly an unlucky loser: sure to find a race soon: see 412.   35
+508 IRISH COOKIE [4] (I Matthews) 4-8-0(5ex) M Woods[3] 12/1: 320-014: Gd effort under
her penalty: see 508.   31
*306 BOOT POLISH [5] 4-8-10 N Connorton 9/2 fav: 0104-10: Not clear run & should be
forgiven this effort: see 306.   40
508 CORN STREET [13] 8-9-2 W Hayes[7] 14/1: -010400: Dsptd lead much: best 172.   39
616 SAILORS SONG [9] 4-9-6(bl) P Cook 7/1: 224-000: Close up 7th: see 374.   00
587 OUR DYNASTY [7] 5-9-10 J Matthias 9/1: 000-030: Back to h'cap company, ev ch in 8th:
flattered 587.   00
+525 TANFEN [6] 5-7-8 N Carlisle 9/1: 00-0310: Dsptd lead most, fin 9th: btr 525 (soft).   00
+520 SULLYS CHOICE [10] 5-8-7(bl)(5ex) D Nicholls 10/1: 0-01310: Prom much: best 520.   00
-520 Fawleys Girl [14] 7-10   616 Stock Hill Lass [2] 8-12
616 Brig Chop [1] 9-9   +401 Foolish Touch [8] 8-3(vis)
14 ran   ½,1,½,hd,2½,1,½   (Phil Bull)   C Brittain Newmarket

688   RIFLE BUTTS STAKES 3YO   £1269   1m 2f Good 64 +12 Fast

--   HOLLOW HAND [7] (C Horgan) 3-8-11 P Cook 4/9 fav: 22-1: 3 b c Wolver Hollow -
Fingers (Lord Gayle): Comfortably landed the odds on seasonal debut in a fast run 3yo minor
event at Doncaster May 24: 2nd on both outings in '85, valuable events at Ascot & Newbury:
suited by 10f, may stay further: acts on gd going, on a gall trk: the sort to win more races.   62
463 FAREWELL TO LOVE [6] (I Balding) 3-9-2 J Matthias 13/2: 20-2102: Tried to make all:
gd effort and caught a tartar here: seems best at 10f: see 315.   59
--   AL KAAHIR [10] (H T Jones) 3-8-11 R Hills 5/1: 202-3: Kept on and this was a fair
seasonal debut: 2nd in 2 of his 3 outings in '85: acts on gd going: stays 10f: sure to
find a maiden.   51
*448 LIE IN WAIT [2] (G P Gordon) 3-9-2 J Reid 8/1: 0-14: Prom, ev ch and a gd effort: see 448 53
--   SHAKEEB [9] 3-8-11 G French 25/1: 00-0: Prom much: lightly raced in '85: should stay.   28
379 PINTURICCHIA [5] 3-8-8 M Beecroft 33/1: 00-00: No threat: lightly raced but showed
some ability last season.   20
--   Samosa [8] 8-8   --   Achillean [1] 8-11   --   Sonnendew [3] 8-11
--   The Godfather [4] 8-11
10 ran   2½,1½,½,10,3,nk   (Mrs Seamus Purcell)   C Horgan Wokingham.

689   GRESLEY HANDICAP 3YO+ 0-35   £2981   1m   Good 64 -03 Slow   [35]

578 SAMHAAN [2] (B Hanbury) 4-8-9(bl) R Hills 7/2: 040-241: 4 ch c Niniski - Mai Pussy
(Realm): Prom and led final 1f, narrowly, in a h'cap at Doncaster May 24: rated 43 at one
stage last season but this was first success: stays 10f but well suited by 1m: acts on gd &
heavy: wore bl today, though not for the first time.   27
*594 ABLE MAYBOB [7] (H Collingridge) 4-8-2 M Rimmer 7/1: 0000-12: Chall final 1f, just
btn and in fine form: see 594: stays 1m.   17
238 EMERALD EAGLE [5] (C Booth) 5-8-12 J Matthias 10/1: -010003: Led ½way, one paced
final 1f: see 79.   21
378 QUALITAIRESS [4] (K Stone) 4-7-7(3oh) P Burke[4] 25/1: 00-3004: Prom thro'out: see 101.   01
260 KINGS BADGE [6] 4-9-7 N Carlisle 20/1: 000-000: Prom most: in '85 winner at Edinburgh,
Redcar & Hamilton: eff 6f, stays 1m: acts on gd going: usually a front runner.   28
*422 NICKLE A KISS [12] 3-9-8 S Quane[7] 7/4 fav: 4-10: Ev ch, not disgraced though btr 422.   43
*530 PITKAITHLY [9] 4-8-12(bl)(5ex) J Bleasdale 8/1: 300-010: Btr 530 (seller).   00
343 MOONDAWN [8] 5-9-3 C Dwyer 10/1: 040-020: No threat: btr 343 (seller).   00
547 Nugola [3] 8-5   499 Henrys Place [10] 8-5   420 Count Bertrand [13] 8-4
540 Cuddly [14] 8-12   545 Willbe Willbe [15] 7-11(3ow)
547 Forever Tingo [11] 8-7   -- Musical Shadow [1] 9-1
15 ran   ½,3,½,hd,nk,shhd   (O Zawawi)   B Hanbury Newmarket

Official Going Given as Good/Soft

690   MAIL ON SUNDAY 3YO SERIES HCAP 0-50   £3042   1m 2f Good/Soft 104 -33 Slow   [48]

484 AUTUMN FLUTTER [1] (R Hannon) 3-8-10 R Cochrane 8/1: 00-301: 3 b g Beldale Flutter -
Crofting (Crepello): Al prom and led approaching final 1f, under press in a slow run 3yo
h'cap at Haydock May 24: stays 10f well: acts on gd/firm, suited by yld grnd: acts on any trk.   43
*452 GLOWING PROMISE [3] (B Hills) 3-9-7 M Hills 10/3: 02-12: Made most: in gd form: see 452. 50
553 TAYLORMADE BOY [2] (D Smith) 3-8-6 L Charnock 6/5 FAV: 30-3123: Well bckd: disapp
after 553: see 258.   27
--   MASTER LAMB [5] (S Hall) 4-7-9 J Lowe 25/1: 000-4: Fdd final 2f: lightly raced in
'85: may not stay 10f: acts on yld grnd.   14

219 SOLVENT [6] 3-8-12 M Jarvis 9/2: 4-200: Never in it: twice below form 116 (sharper trk)   **17**
335 BILLYS DANCER [4] 3-8-5 D Mckeown 7/1: 040-130: Ran wide str: btr 335, 279 (1m).   **08**
6 ran   2,4,¾,7,1   (Dr C Kenny)   R Hannon East Everleigh, Wilts

691 SANDY LANE STAKES 3YO LISTED   £9489   6f   Good/Soft 104 +29 Fast

373 BRIDESMAID [3] (B Hills) 3-8-13(vis) R Hills 16/1: 430-001: 3 ro f London Bells -
Zameen (Armistice): Smart filly on her day: led inside the final 1f, driven out in a fast
run and valuable listed race at Haydock May 24: in fine form in '85, winning at Epson,
Ripon & Newcastle: also fine 3rd to Storm Star in Gr.3 Cherry Hinton at Newmarket: very
eff at 6f: acts on firm & yld grnd: seems best in a visor.   **77**
406 SPERRY [7] (P Walwyn) 3-8-9 Paul Eddery 2/1: 210-202: Well bckd: made much and
kept on well for 2nd: gd effort: see 220.   **70**
*567 TUSSAC [5] (H Cecil) 3-9-2 W Ryan 13/8 FAV: 112-113: Well bckd: led briefly over 1f
out: another gd effort: see 567.   **76**
220 PILOT JET [1] (R Williams) 3-8-9 R Cochrane 5/1: 41-34: Nearest fin: maybe btr
suited by 7f: in gd form: see 220.   **68**
600 GOSSIPER [2] 3-8-6 T Ives 25/1: 1400-00: Stiff task: see 600.   **59**
249 ROARING RIVA [4] 3-9-5 M Wigham 7/1: 000-440: Has changed stables: ch 2f out: see 165.   **66**
295 SO DIRECTED [6] 3-8-6 G Duffield 11/1: 40: Irish filly: wknd over 1f out.   **00**
7 ran   1,nk,½,2½,2½   (R E Sangster)   B Hills Lambourn, Berks

692 TOTE DUAL FORECAST HANDICAP 3YO 0-75   £17220   1m   Good/Soft 104 +04 Fast [73]

546 AL BASHAAMA [8] (L Cumani) 3-7-10 P Hamblett 8/1: -0131: 3 b c Vice Regent - Noble
Fancy (Vaguely Noble): Very useful colt: nicely h'capped and led well inside the final 1f
in valuable and competitive Tote Dual Forecast H'cap at Haydock May 24: earlier won at
Catterick & last time out ran well when 3rd to Georgia River at Nottingham: stays 1m really
well: acts on yld grnd & on any trk: certain to win more races.   **56**
586 RESOURCEFUL FALCON [12] (P Makin) 3-8-13 T Quinn 8/1: 111-022: Led briefly finaal
1f: excellent effort and must win soon: stays 1m: see 586.   **70**
406 MISTER WONDERFUL [11] (J Dunlop) 3-9-0 T Ives 7/1: 210-333: Ch final 1f: another gd
run & stayed todays 1m trip: in fine form: see 406, 216.   **70**
*326 SWIFT TROOPER [1] (R Williams) 3-8-4(bl) R Cochrane 11/1: 10-1214: Led over 2f out:
in grand form: see 326.   **56**
386 FARM CLUB [4] 3-7-11 G Carter(3) 10/1: 10-000: Nearest fin: gd effort: see 386.   **44**
*427 LUCKY SO SO [3] 3-8-1 J Lowe 14/1: 134-410: Lightly bckd: btr 427.   **44**
-615 GORGEOUS ALGERNON [7] 3-8-2 G Baxter 9/1: 0-01020: Fdd: much btr 615: see 178.   **00**
599 KABIYLA [2] 3-8-5 A Kimberley 5/2 FAV: 1-120: Heavily bckd: much btr 599 (gd).   **00**
+615 HILLS BID [5] 3-8-8(7ex) M Hills 6/1: 0212-10: Wknd qckly over 2f out: well below 615.   **00**
386 Pentland Hawk [10] 7-7(6oh)   **455** Dunloring [9] 7-9
406 Prince Pecadillo [14] 9-7   **465** Knyf [6] 7-11
13 ran   1,1,2,3,2   (Sheikh Mohammed)   L Cumani Newmarket

693 LYMM STAKES   £3876   2m   Good/Soft 104 -05 Slow

617 ORE [2] (W Musson) 8-9-7 M Wigham 11/2: -01: 8 ch h Ballymore - Minatonka (Linacre):
Remains a useful stayer: led close home, cheekily in a stakes event at Haydock may 24:
off the trk last season: in '83 won a Gr .3 event at Sandown and Aston Park Stakes at Newbury: stays extreme dists well: probably acts on any grnd.   **67**
634 PEARL RUN [1] (G Price) 5-8-9 P Robinson 10/3: 1101222: Led final 1f: remains
in grand form: see 462, 336.   **54**
462 INDE PULSE [4] (J Hindley) 4-9-3 M Hills 4/5 FAV: 0-01043: Made much: btr 462 (sh. trk).   **60**
519 GENTLE FAVOR [3] (M Prescott) 5-8-6 G Duffield 14/1: 1210-04: Wknd str: see 519.   **19**
-- THE JOKER [6] 6-8-9 R Weaver 10/1: -0: Flat race debut in this country: wknd in str:
ex French horse who was a winner in '85: stays 2m1f: acts on gd grnd.   **16**
-- BRIGHT BIRD [5] 4-9-3 T Ives 12/1: -0: Prom over 12f: ex French colt who was a
winner at St Cloud in '85: acts on soft.   **19**
6 ran   ¾,1½,25,6,3   (O Zawawij)   W Musson Newmarket

694 EBF SKELMERSDALE MAIDEN STAKES 2YO   £2022   5f   Good/Soft 104 -07 Slow

-- IBNALMAGHITH [5] (H T Jones) 2-9-0 P D'arcy 4/1: 1: 2 ch c Kris - Lareyna (Welsh
Pageant): Prom colt: first time out, showed a gd turn of foot to lead inside the final 1f in
a maiden at Haydock May 24: cost 100,000 gns as a yearling and is a half brother to 12f
winner Larive: eff at 5f, should stay further: acts on gd/soft & a gall trk: should rate
more highly.   **50**
503 THE DOMINICAN [1] (B Hills) 2-9-0 M Hills 7/4 FAV: 322: Well bckd: made much,
caught close home: will win soon: see 503, 350.   **47**
-- SCHUYGULLA [9] (M Jarvis) 2-9-0 T Ives 13/2: 3: Early ldr, rem. prom: gd racecourse
debut from this I.R. 10,000 purchase: should be suited by further than 5f: acts on yld grnd
and should find a maiden.   **42**

-- **SKY CAT** [2] (J Wilson) 2-9-0 Julie Bowker(7) 33/1: 4: Slow start: fair racecourse debut:
bred to stay further: acts on yld grnd.   37
583 **BEAU BENZ** [7] 2-9-0 M Birch 8/1: 00: Never nearer: on the up grade: should be
suited by 6f: see 583.   29
-- **TAHARD** [11] 2-9-0 S Perks 20/1: 0: Nearest fin: should impr: cost 8,000 gns: should be
suited by 6f.   23
-- **AFRICAN OPERA** [10] 2-9-0 J Lowe 33/1: 0: No sh'● on racecourse debut: cost I.R. 16,000. 00
382 **RIOT BRIGADE** [4] 2-9-0 G Baxter 3/1: 00: Well bckd: fdd: btr 382 (gd/firm).   00
602 Causeway Foot [8] 9-0   -- Joe Sugden [6] 9-0   531 Stars In Motion [3] 9-0
11 ran   1,1½,1½,3,2½,1,hd   (Hamdan Al-Maktoum)   H T Jones Newmarket

695 **LOWTON HANDICAP STAKES 0-60**   £3908   1m 4f   Good/Soft 104 -16 Sloww   [52]

363 **POSITIVE** [5] (H T Jones) 4-9-10 P D'Arcy 13/2: 1120-01 Led 3f out, but lost weight cloth
2½L "winner" but disq. and placed last: see 363.   40
-- **MAIN REASON** [6] (F Lee) 4-9-0 S Perks 12/1: 41002-2: 4 b g Main Reef - Get Ahead
(Silly Season): Kept on well to fin 2nd: placed first in a h'cap at Haydock May 24: pulled
up twice over hurdles in 84/85: last season won a stakes event at Lingfield: in '84 won
again at Lingfield: eff at 10f, stays 12f well: acts on any grnd & on any trk. likes Lingfield. 45
*319 **DOUBLE BENZ** [2] (M H Easterby) 4-9-3 M Birch 5/2: 200-013: Ev ch 2f out: in gd form.   47
-- **ELPLOTINO** [3] (R Williams) 4-9-2 J Lowe 7/1: 21100-4: First time out: wknd over 1f out:
fin 4th, placed 3rd: btr for race: in '85 won at Sandown, Yarmouth (2) and Ayr: very eff
over 10/12f, stays 14f: acts on firm & yld & a gall trk.   42
584 **ROMIOSINI** [7] 4-8-9 Kim Tinkler 16/1: 2103-00: Never nearer: winner over hurdles
last Autumn: in '85 won a maiden at Ripon and was placed on several occasions: eff over
10f, stays 12f: best on gd & firm grnd, when up with the pace.   32
*584 **BOLD REX** [4] 4-9-12 T Ives 6/4 FAV: 31-4410: Well below form 584: deserves another ch. 47
225 **WESTRAY** [1] 4-8-4 W Ryan 14/1: 130-000: Made much: see 225.   00
7 ran   2½,¾,2½,2,1½   (F H Lee)   H T Jones Wilmslow

REDCAR   Monday May 26th   Lefthanded Galloping Track

Official Going Given as Good/Firm

696 **SANDHILL SELLING STAKES 2YO**   £958   5f   Firm 11 -25 Slow

603 **PASHMINA** [9] (T Fairhurst) 2-8-8 C Coates(5) 9/4: 1021: 2 b f Blue Cashmere -
Petploy (Faberge II): Smartly away & was never hdd when a comfortable winner of a 2yo seller
at Redcar May 26 (no bid): surprise winner of a similar event at Newcastle on racecourse
debut: half sister to a couple of winners: eff over 5f with forcing tactics: acts on any
going & is suited by a gall trk.   28
672 **MONS FUTURE** [4] (W Pearce) 2-8-8 D Nicholls 15/8 FAV: 0142: Al up there: see 354.   22
354 **PRINCESS SINGH** [8] (L Lightbrown) 2-8-8 J Bleasdale 8/1: 003: Al front rank: on the up
grade: eff over 5f on firm & soft grnd: acts on a gall trk: stro bay & see 354.   19
612 **THE MAGUE** [6] (L Siddall) 2-8-11 G Gosney 9/2: 004: Dropped in class: ran on well
after a slow start: eff over 5f on fast grnd: acts on a gall trk.   10
425 **BOOTHAM LAD** [3] 2-8-11(BL) J Lowe 10/1: 0000: Never reached ldrs: cheaply bought colt
who wore bl today and did show some impr here.   07
-- **NIFTY GRIFF** [7] 2-8-11 K Bradshaw(5) 10/1: 0: Kept on late after slow start: cheaply
bought colt who will be suited by another furlong: acts on fast grnd & on a gall trk.   03
589 **MI OH MY** [1] 2-8-8(BL) C Dwyer 8/1: 3023340: Bl first time: no threat after slow
start and can do btr than this: see 181.   00
446 **FULTONS FLYER** [5] 2-8-8 R Vickers(7) 20/1: 00: Early speed: fin 8th.   00
627 **CHOICE MATCH** [2] 2-8-8 R Guest 10/1: 00: Dropped in class: speed over ½way.   00
9 ran   2½,1,4,1,1½,1,shhd,1½   (Mrs M Morley)   T Fairhurst Middleham, Yorks

697 **RACE AROUND YORKSHIRE H'CAP 3YO 0-35**   £1674   1m 6f   Firm 11 -49 Slow   [39]

194 **AGATHIST** [7] (G Pritchard Gordon) 3-9-7 G Duffield 2/1 FAV: 00-41: 3 ch c Bon Mot III-
We Try Harder (Blue Prince II): Easily justified fav. led over 3f out and was sn clear in
a slowly run 3yo h'cap at Redcar May 26: earlier had shown promise over shorter trips though
clearly relished this test of stamina: acts on firm & yld grnd & on any trk: on the up grade
& could win again.   46
517 **LUCKY HUMBUG** [10] (W Pearce) 3-8-1 L Charnock 7/1: 00-222: Led before home turn:
no ch with easy winner though has been most consistent this term: stays 14f well: acts on
firm: see 365.   16
-- **REGENCY SQUARE** [6] (P Feilden) 3-7-10 G Dickie 25/1: 000-3: Ran on too late: should
do btr next time: half brother to 7f winner Travelguard: seems suited by a distance of grnd
himself: acts on firm grnd & on a gall trk.   10
356 **ARCH PRINCESS** [2] (R Sheather) 3-7-10(bl) M Fry 14/1: 000-004: Some late prog and
seems btr suited by this longer trip: acts on fast grnd & on a gall trk.   07
506 **TEARS OF LAUGHTER** [9] 3-8-5 R Hills 12/1: 000-00: First signs of form.   06

623   BETTER BEWARE [4] 3-9-6 S Payne 10/3: 0-34300: Best over 12f in 347 (yld): see 506.   21
492   MOHICAN [8] 3-8-5 J Bleasdale 15/2: 220-030: Disapp 9th: can do btr: see 45.   00
648   Belhill [1] 7-10   307   Shake The King [5] 8-6
648   Sandmoor Prince [3] 8-4(vis)
10 ran   5,nk,2½,8,shhd.   (William Du Pont III)   G Pritchard Gordon Newmarket

---

698   ZETLAND GOLD CUP H'CAP 0-60   £12042   1m 2f Firm 11 +20 Fast   [54]

*609 FORWARD RALLY [6] (M Prescott) 4-8-0 G Duffield 7/1: 0021-11: 4 b f Formidable -
Rally (Relko): In fine form, led early in str & held on gamely to win fast run & valuable
Zetland Gold Cup at Redcar May 26: recently a comfortable winner of a h'cap at Beverley:
last season won at Hamilton: very eff over 10f: acts on any going & is well suited by a
gall trk: genuine filly.   38
*439 MASKED BALL [3] (P Calver) 6-7-13 M Fry 12/1: 230-112: Post came just too soon:
still a fine effort & should win again soon off his present mark: acts on fast grnd: see 439.   36
604   MERHI [16] (S Norton) 3-7-7(1oh) J Lowe 16/1: 00-2343: Led home turn: consistent: see 143.   44
584   VINTAGE TOLL [9] (S Norton) 6-8-13 N Day 16/1: -030034: Not btn far: see 52.   46
--   SILLY BOY [10] 6-8-8 M Richardson(7) 25/1: 04000-0: Stayed on: gd effort on reapp:
early last season won an app h'cap at Thirsk after just failing to hold Hooligan on that
same trk first time out: in '84 won at Hamilton & Carlisle: eff over 8/10f: acts on any
grnd & on any trk: genuine sort who carries weight well and does well when fresh.   36
584   SHELLMAN [7] 4-8-10 C Dwyer 25/1: -030000: Ran on too late: see 55.   32
+629 BALLYDURROW [15] 9-8-10(6ex) D Nicholls 13/2: 113-010: Held up, no threat: much
btr in 629 (12f).   00
-432 CHICLET [2] 4-9-7 B Crossley 9/1: 130-020: Slowly away: fin 9th: btr in 432.   00
573   ACONITUM [17] 5-9-0 R Fox 10/1: 120-030: Longer trip: much btr over 1m in 573.   00
584   PUBBY [12] 5-8-9 R Hills 10/1: 10-1120: Much btr over 12f in 584 with some give: see 363   00
+538 BARLEY BILL [11] 3-9-3 R Guest 2/1 FAV: 2-11110: Struck into home turn, sn eased
and this run can be ignored: bred to be well suited by this trip: see 538.   00
79   Try To Stop Me [14] 9-0   594 Signore Odone [1] 8-0
433 Barry Sheene [4] 9-3   629 Commander Robert [5] 8-7
*429 Quiet Riot [8] 9-9   584 Tivian [13] 8-4(vis)
17 ran   nk,1,¾,3,4,1   (Lady Macdonald-Buchanan)   Sir M Prescott Newmarket

---

699   BILLINGHAM MAIDEN STAKES 3YO   £3022   1m 2f Firm 11 -12 Slow

--   AL SHAMIKH [1] (H Thomson Jones) 3-9-0 R Hills 11/2: 00-1: 3 ch c Czarevich -
Miss Nymph (Perugin): Useful colt: first time out, led over 2f out and although narrowly btn
had been bumped inside dist and was placed 1st in a 3yo maiden at Redcar May 26: cost
$220,000 as a yearling & showed some promise, when highly tried in both starts last season:
clearly well suited by 10f on fast grnd: acts on a gall trk.   52
322   ALBERT HALL [4] (B Hills) 3-9-0 R Fox 5/4 FAV: 002-21D: Ran on well to lead inside
dist though hung right, interfering with r.u. & was subs. placed 2nd: gd effort over this
longer trip & should make amends soon: see 322.   52
572   PAST GLORIES [6] (C Elsey) 3-9-0 C Dwyer 10/1: 200-03: Made most: gd effort: btn
the minimum dist by Sit This One Out in a York maiden last Summer: half brother to several
middle dist. winners: eff over 10f & likely to stay further: acts on gd & fast grnd & on
a gall track.   46
487   SEATYRN [13] (S Norton) 3-9-0 B Crossley 14/1: 2430-34: Gd effort: stays 10f: see 487.   45
--   DESERTED [5] 3-8-11 G Duffield 14/1: 00-0: Ran on same pace, showing impr on her
form of last season: stays 10f: acts on fast grnd & on a gall trk.   38
527   MOEL FAMMAU [10] 3-9-0 R Guest 7/1: -030: Ran on too late: stays 10f: acts on
fast grnd: best effort yet over 1m in 527 (soft).   40
322   HELLO BENZ [7] 3-9-0 J Lowe 9/2: -40: Fin 7th after being bumped over 2f out:
btr judged on his promising run in 322: acts on fast grrnd.   00
479 Pegmarine [2] 9-0   -- The Canny Man [8] 9-0   607 Spinning Turn [12] 9-0
--   Lauries Trojan [9] 9-0   528 Sunmaiden [11] 8-11
--   Goldena [3] 8-11
13 ran   nk,4,½,2,½,½   (Hamdan Al-Maktoum)   H Thomson Jones Newmarket

---

700   SPRING BANK HOLIDAY H'CAP 0-50   £2662   7f   Firm 11 +08 Fast   [41]

594   THE MAZALL [11] (L Siddall) 6-8-4(bl) G Gosney 11/2: 010-001: 6 br g Persian Bold -
Dance All Night (Double-U-Jay): Broke well & sn held a clear lead when comfortably winning a
fast run h'cap at Redcar May 26: last season won at Redcar & Carlisle & in '84 was successful
at Nottingham: best form around 6/7f: acts on firm & soft grnd & on any trk: well suited by
front running tactics.   28
374   CHICAGO BID [2] (R Armstrong) 5-8-8 V Smith(5) 4/1: 0023-02: No ch with easy winner
though ran a gd race: last successful in '83, at Newmarket: eff over 6/7f: acts on any
grnd & on any trk.   24
525   EMERGENCY PLUMBER [6] (D Barron) 5-8-9 R Hills 9/2: 0-42403: Al up there: stays 7f.   23
424   CHABLISSE [10] (R Whitaker) 3-7-7(4oh) J Lowe 20/1: 000-0P4: Never nearer: btr effort
from this half sister to winning sprinter Tuxford Hideway: stays 7f: well suited by fast
grnd & a gall trk.   16
611   BIT OF A STATE [5] 6-8-7(bl) D Nicholls 8/1: 00-0000: Not clear run ½way: btr 611 (1m)   13

611 TRY SCORER [4] 4-8-9 L Charnock 12/1: -210000: Front rank over ½way: best in 143 (1m).   14
238 MAGIC BID [12] 4-9-10 R Fox 7/2 FAV: 3212-00: Trailed in last: see 238.   00
490 Trade High [7] 8-4   521 Paris Match [9] 9-8   -- Always Native [8] 8-3
525 Single Hand [1] 8-2(2ow)   649 Hopeful Heights [3] 9-10
12 ran   4,1,2½,2,nk,nk   (David Wright)   L Siddall Tadcaster, Yorks

701 LANGBAUGH MAIDEN AUCTION 2YO STAKES   £920   5f   Firm 11 -13 Slow

--   BOTHY BALLAD [4] (P Calver) 2-7-13 M Fry 9/1: 1: 2 ch c Final Straw - Zanubia
(Nonoalco): Al close up on racecourse debut and led inside dist, readily in a 2yo maiden
auction stakes at Redcar May 26: cost 2,600 gns as a yearling: speedy colt who is clearly
well suited by fast grnd & a gall trk: can only improve.   40
515 JAMES OWL [7] (W Pearce) 2-8-8 M Hindley(0) 7/1: 02: Led after ½way: much btr effort:
cost 6,800 gns as a yearling: eff over 5f on fast grnd: acts on a gall trk: on the up grade
and should win a race.   45
612 RHABDOMANCER [6] (J Watts) 2-7-13 R Fox 10/3: 333: Led over ½way: see 364.   28
--   PETROC CONCERT [2] (R Whitaker) 2-7-10 A Cunningham(1) 16/1: 4: Ran on promisingly after
a slow start & sure to do btr next time: cost 3,000 gns as a yearling: acts on fast grnd
and on a gall trk.   17
612 OUR HORIZON [1] 2-7-10 L Charnock 10/11 FAV: 20: Early speed: much btr in 612 (gd).   01
602 BEJANT SKITE [5] 2-8-8 D Nicholls 20/1: 00: Speed to ½way: speedily bred colt who
cost 6,800 gns as a yearling: well btn in both starts to date: seems suited by fast grnd.   09
--   MISTY RUNNER [8] 2-7-10 J Lowe 6/1: 0: No threat after a slow start: half sister to
several winning sprinters and likely to impr next time.   00
--   Miss Emily [3] 7-10
8 ran   1,3,3,8,¾   (P Calver)   P Calver Ripon, Yorks

702 BILLINGHAM MAIDEN STAKES 3YO   £3008   1m 2f Firm 11 -27 Slow

444 LLANARMON [1] (B Hills) 3-9-0 R Fox 7/2: 0-031: 3 b c Lochnager - Quite Sweet (Super
Sam): Led after home turn and stayed on well to win a 3yo maiden at redcar May 26: half
sister to several winners: well suited by 10f: acts on firm & soft grnd & on any trk.   42
576 ABADJERO [8] (J Fitzgerald) 3-9-0 G Duffield 7/4 FAV: -02: Well bckd: ran on strongly:
not quite reach winner: stays 10f well: acts on gd & firm grnd & on a gall trk: should
win soon: see 576.   40
535 ASHINGTON GROVE [4] (D Murray Smith) 3-9-0 W Ryan 11/4: 00-223: Al front rank: see 535   35
451 NOT A PROBLEM [10] (Denys Smith) 3-9-0 D Nicholls 20/1: 00-3004: Bckd at long odds:
al close up though not qckn nr dist: stays 10f: acts on any going & is suited by a gall trk.   29
--   TAXI MAN [6] 3-9-0 R Hills 33/1: 00000-0: Slowly away, stayed on well & never nearer
on reapp: quite busy last season, when twice placed in maidens early on: stays 10f well:
best form on fast grnd.   29
549 SHINY KAY [5] 3-8-11 J Lowe 13/2: -00: Nearest fin: stays 10f well: acts on gd &
firm grnd & on a gall trk: see 549.   26
162 THARITA [11] 3-8-11 N Day 8/1: -00: Nicely bckd: close up over ½way: fair abs.   00
--   Jurisprudence [7] 9-0   16 Big League [12] 9-0   322 Manvil [3] 9-0
527 Vikris [2] 8-11   -- Sunlit [9] 8-11
12 ran   ½,2,2½,shhd,shhd   (R J McAlpine)   B Hills Lambourn, Berks

Official Going Given as Good

703 SAXONE HANDICAP STAKES (0-50) 3YO   £3617   7f   Good/Firm 39 -15 Slow   [53]

455 BURHAAIN [9] (P Walwyn) 3-8-4 Paul Eddery 20/1: 033-01: 3 b c Formidable - Blue Rag
(Ragusa): Ran on to lead inside final 1f, ridden out in a 3yo h'cap at Sandown May 26: first
success: eff at 7f: may stay 1m: acts on fast grnd & on any trk.   40
615 JOHN SAXON [16] (M Stoute) 3-9-1 W R Swinburn 12/1: 033-002: Not clear run 2f out:
ran on well & just failed to get up: unlucky? stays 7f & seems best on fast grnd: should
win soon: see 283.   50
*377 CHUMMYS PET [10] (N Callaghan) 3-7-10 D Browne 7/1: -0213: Mkt drifter: ch final
1f: in gd form: stays 7f: see 377.   29
328 NATCHAKAM [5] (G Lewis) 3-8-2(BL) P Waldron 13/2: -4204: Bl first time & well bckd:
nearest fin: needs 1m? acts on gd/firm & soft & on any trk: see 90.   31
514 WAR WAGON [14] 3-8-11 C Asmussen 14/1: 0000-00: Made much: lightly raced & little
form as a 2yo: eff at 7f on gd/firm & a gall trk.   37
496 VICEROY MAJOR [11] 3-8-7 W Carson 25/1: 4040-00: Never nearer: should do btr next time:
showed promise on several occasions in '85, notably when a gd 4th to Sperry in a nursery
h'cap at Newmarket: stays 7f well: acts on fast grnd.   26
276 BLUE BRILLIANT [17] 3-8-4 B Thomson 10/1: 00-00: Again not the best of runs: active
in mkt today: see 276.   00
424 STILL DREAMING [3] 3-8-0 S Dawson(3) 4/1 FAV: 030-20: Prom, ev ch: btr 424 (shpr trk). 00
*540 ARCTIC KEN [8] 3-8-3(5ex) M Hills 9/2: 40-0110: Slow start: no show: much btr 540, 424. 00
436 SUPER PUNK [13] 3-9-7 Pat Eddery 13/2: 031-30: Fdd 2f out: btr 436.   00

340   DEPUTY TIM [6] 3-8-5(bl) K Darley 10/1: 0002-40: Led briefly ½way: btr 340 (6f).   00
615   Miss Venezuela [4] 8-2   387   Little Pipers [15] 9-7
615   Global [1] 8-4   624   Stock Phrase [2] 7-9   455   Zulu Knight [7] 9-1
16 ran   nk,¼,1½,1,3   (Hamdan Al-Maktoum)   P Walwyn Lambourn, Berks

---

704   GROUP 3 HENRY II STAKES   £18675   2m   Good/Firm 39 +02 Fast

617   LONGBOAT [4] (W Hern) 5-8-11 W Carson 4/1: -142-01: 5 b h Welsh Pageant - Pirogue
(Reliance II): Very smart stayer: sn prom and led well over 2f out, ridden clear in Gr.3
Henry II Stakes at Sandown May 26: in '85 won a Gr.3 event at Ascot and was also just btn
by Gildoran in the Ascot Gold Cup and has a fine chance to gain compensation this season:
in '84 won at Chester, Kempton, Bath & Goodwood: eff at 2m, well suited by 2½m: best on
fast grnd.   83
585   SEISMIC WAVE [2] (B Hills) 5-8-11 B Thomson 5/1: 22-0322: Chall over 1f out: in
fine form: seems best when held up for a late run: see 585, 385: stays 2m.   79
•585   EASTERN MYSTIC [3] (L Cumani) 4-9-0 Pat Eddery 7/2 FAV: 211-413: Led over 13f: came
again final 1f: another fine effort: stays 2m well: see 585.   81
585   TALE QUALE [7] (H Candy) 4-8-11 T Ives 10/1: 1301-04: Kept on late: will be well suited
by further than 2m: see 585.   76
617   MANGO EXPRESS [1] 4-8-8 P Cook 4/1: 1124-20: Going well when chall after 2f out:
not quite stay 2m: gd effort: see 617.   73
251   KUBLAI [10] 4-8-8 P Waldron 50/1: 2200-00: No show: ddhtd 6th: in fine form in '85,
winning a valuable h'cap at Epsom: also fine 2nd to Wassl Merbayeh in Gr.3 Qleens Vase at
Royal Ascot & also 2nd to Valuable Witness in Gr.2 Goodwood Cup: winning 2yo at Newmarket:
eff at 12f, stays 2½m: acts on hvy: well suited by fast grnd.   72
•475   BRUNICO [9] 4-8-11 C Asmussen 14/1: -1010: No show: ddhtd 6th: fair effort: stays 2m.   75
585   BOURBON BOY [8] 4-8-8 W R Swinburn 11/2: 0123-40: Prom, fdd: see 585.   00
585   Petrizzo [6] 8-8   --   I Want To Be [5] 8-11
10 ran   2½,¾,1½,hd,1,ddht   (R D Hollingsworth)   W Hern West Ilsley, Berks

---

705   GROUP 3 SEARS TEMPLE STAKES   £19170   5f   Good/Firm 39 -01 Slow

+408   DOUBLE SCHWARTZ [9] (C Nelson) 5-9-3 Pat Eddery 10/3 FAV: D012-11: 5 b h Double Form -
Cassy's Pet (Sing Sing): Very smart sprinter: al going well and readily drew clear final 1f
for an impressive win in Gr.3 Temple Stakes at Sandown May 26: first time out won Gr.3 Palace
House Stakes at Newmarket: in '85 won again at Newmarket: also "won" a Gr.3 race at Phoenlx
Park, but subs. disq: very eff at 5f, though does stay 6f: acts on gd & firm grnd & on
any trk: should be hard to beat in the major sprint events this season.   85
•587   GREY DESIRE [6] (M Brittain) 6-9-3 K Darley 5/1: -112412: Hmpd 2f out: flying at
the finish: another grand effort over a trip short of his best: in excellent form: see 587.   80
--   PETROVICH [8] (R Hannon) 4-9-0 B Thomson 20/1: 11120-3: Got on well on seasonal debut
and this was a most encouraging run: in grand form in '85, winning h'caps at Haydock, Goodwood, Newmarket & Ascot: in '84 won at Sandown: very eff over 5f, stays 6f: acts on firm &
yld grnd on any trk: suited by a stiff one: much impr & should be winning soon.   75
557   POWDER KEG [3] (J Hindley) 4-9-7 M Hills 10/1: 113-134: Stayed on well final 1f:
model of consistency: see 245.   79
165   SHARP ROMANCE [7] 4-9-0 W Carson 10/1: 00-2330: Slowly away: gd effort: see 18.   70
600   FAYRUZ [10] 3-8-5(bl) T Ives 9/2: 1022-00: Led over 3f: see 600.   67
587   PRIMO DOMINIE [5] 4-9-5 W R Swinburn 7/2: 1220-00: Yet to hit form: see 587.   00
408   Prince Reymo [1] 9-3   408   Imperial Jade [4] 8-11
587   Nashia [2] 8-2
10 ran   2,nk,1,¾,1½   (R E Sangster)   C Nelson Lambourn, Berks

---

706   SELFRIDGES WHITSUN CUP (H'CAP) (0-70)   £13344   1m   Good/Firm 39 +16 Fast   [69]

330   SIYAH KALEM [13] (J Dunlop) 4-8-10 W Carson 10/1: 0211-41: 4 ch c Mr Prospector -
Lady Graustark (Graustark): Very useful colt: led dist, comfortably in fast run & valuable
h'cap at Sandown May 26: in '85 won at Newmarket & Leicester: half brother to several winners
incl the smart Bel Bolide: very eff over 1m on fast grnd though does act on soft: suited by
a galt trk: consistent sort.   65
432   PROMISED ISLE [9] (Lady Herries) 5-8-4 B Rouse 16/1: 2002-32: Ran on final 1f: in
excellent form: see 432.   55
578   FLYHOME [7] (P Cundell) 5-7-9 S Dawson(2) 9/1: 200-223: Ran on well final 1f: gd
run: should win soon: see 578, 399.   45
433   INDIAN HAL [6] (P Walwyn) 4-8-6 Paul Eddery 9/1: 231-044: Kept on final 1f: in gd
form: see 248.   56
511   GAY CAPTAIN [17] 4-8-3 P Robinson 12/1: 0-00020: Fin in gd style: eff at 1m, but well
suited by 10f: will win soon: see 511.   49
453   TALK OF GLORY [19] 5-7-7(8oh) D Browne 33/1: 000-020: Led 2f out: in gd form: see 453.   36
433   GILDERDALE [1] 4-8-2 P Cook 15/2: 4310-00: Never nearer: see 433.   00
--   LES ARCS [5] 4-9-7 W R Swinburn 5/1 FAV: 0-144-0: Going well 2f out, but got no sort
of a run: ignore this seasonal debut: lightly raced colt: first time out in '85 won Listed
race at Newmarket: very eff at 9f: acts on gd & firm grnd: should do much btr next time.   00
521   WELL RIGGED [4] 5-8-4 K Darley 7/1: 21-2120: Prom, wknd: btr 521: see 79.   00

605 Jazetas [14] 8-5	680 Roman Beach [3] 7-13	433 Ready Wit [10] 7-13
680 Go Bananas [18] 9-0	616 Habs Lad [20] 8-5	573 Merle [16] 8-10
573 Qualitair Flyer [11] 9-0		445 Thats Your Lot [12] 8-9(BL)
616 Manchesterskytrain [8] 8-4		441 Come On The Blues [21] 8-9
578 Fast Service [2] 7-7(4oh)		-- Chance Ina Million [15] 8-7
21 ran 1½,nk,shhd,2,1½	(Dana Stud Ltd)	J Dunlop Arundel, Sussex

707 MISS SELFRIDGE FILLIES MAIDEN 2YO   £3548   5f   Good/Firm 39 -35 Slow

-- INDIAN LILY [2] (C Brittain) 2-8-11 P Robinson 5/4 FAV: 1: 2 b f Indian King - Wave
Tree (Realm): Very prom filly: well bckd on racecourse debut and showed a gd turn of foot
to lead inside the final 1f in a slow run 2yo fillies maiden at Sandown May 26: cost I.R.
62,000 and is a half sister to 2 winners: eff at 5f, should be suited by 6f: acts on gd/
firm grnd & a gall trk: should rate more highly & win more races.   50

-- VEVILA [7] (L Cumani) 2-8-11 Pat Eddery 7/1: 2: Stayed on well final 1f: promising
racecourse debut: should be well suited by 6f plus: acts on gd/firm & can win soon.   45

400 MARIMBA [4] (J Winter) 2-8-11 W R Swinburn 11/2: 23: Made much: fine effort in this
gd company: acts on any trk: see 400.   44

-- PERSIAN TAPESTRY [10] (J Francome) 2-8-11 T Ives .14/1: 4: Ran on well final 1f,
showing future promise: will be well suited by 6f: acts on gd/firm & should have no trouble
finding a maiden.   43

-- FRESH THOUGHTS [1] 2-8-11 C Asmussen 16/1: 0: Sn prom: easy to back & should impr:
half sister to winning 3yo Session: should be suited by further than 5f: acts on gd/firm. 35

601 BASIC BLISS [6] 2-8-11 Paul Eddery 5/1: 30: Dsptd lead over 2f out: btr 601.   29

621 SURELY GREAT [8] 2-8-11 W Carson 10/1: 020: Stiff task: see 621.   00

621 BERTRADE [9] 2-8-11 P Cook 12/1: 40: Prom early: see 621.   00

-- LISIANTHUS [3] 2-8-11 B Rouse 33/1: 0: No show on racecourse debut: should impr.   00

9 ran   1,nk,nk,3,2   (Sheikh Mohammed)   C Brittain Newmarket

708 WALLIS FILLIES STAKES   £8129   1m   Good/Firm 39 +13 Fast

433 PURCHASEPAPERCHASE [8] (R Armstrong) 4-9-3 C Asmussen 16/1: 0000-01: 4 b f Young
Generation - Tin Goddess (Petingo): Led dist, ridden clear in fast run & valuable fillies
stakes at Sandown May 26: in gd form early in '85, first time out winning at Ascot &
subs. an excellent 2nd to Fitnah in Gr.1 event at Longchamp then lost her form: eff at
1m, stays 10f well: acts on gd & firm grnd & a gall trk: should win more races.   70

-- CHALK STREAM [7] (I Balding) 3-8-4(2ow) Pat Eddery 2/1 FAV: 21124-2: Ch final 1f:
gd seasonal debut: in '85 won a Listed race at Salisbury & a maiden at Lingfield: also fine
2nd to Storm Star in Gr.3 Cherry Hinton at Newmarket: eff at 6f, should be suited by 1m:
acts on gd & firm grnd & on any trk.   62

394 SWEET ADELAIDE [6] (B Hills) 3-8-2 B Thomson 8/1: 130-203: Nearest fin: gd effort:
seems suited by 1m: acts on gd/firm & yld grnd: see 158.   58

-- LADY FOR TWO [4] (M Stoute) 3-7-11 M Giles 33/1: -4: Rank outsider: ran on well final
1f on racecourse debut: promising effort: eff at 1m, may stay further: acts on gd/firm &
a gall trk & should have no trouble finding a race.   53

-- CHARGE ALONG [3] 4-9-3 W R Swinburn 8/1: 34400-0: Made much on seasonal debut:
first time out in '85 won at Leicester: eff at 7f on any grnd.   57

372 COCOTTE [2] 3-7-11 W Carson 9/4: 224-00: Prom, fdd: yet to find her 2yo form: see 372. 58

-- ARAB HERITAGE [5] 3-7-11 P Robinson 8/1: -0: Sn prom, fdd: from the same family as top
class filly Oh So Sharp: dam fin 2nd in the 1,000 Guineas: should do btr next time.   00

264 ENTRANCING [1] 3-8-2 B Rouse 8/1: 12-00: No show: see 264.   00

8 ran   5,¾,shhd,nk,1½   (John Bray)   R Armstrong Newmarket

709 OLYMPUS SPORT HANDICAP STAKES 0-35   £2926   1m 2f Good/Firm 39 -13 Slow   [35]

445 MASTER LINE [10] (H Candy) 5-9-10 C Asmussen 11/2: 110-001: 5 ch h High Line - Fair
Winter (Set Fair): Well bckd when romping home in a h'cap at Sandown May 26: in '85 won
h'caps at York & Newmarket (awarded race): equally eff over 9/10f: stays 12f: acts on any
grnd & likes a gall trk: should win again.   45

432 FREE ON BOARD [13] (C Horgan) 4-8-10 Paul Eddery 33/1: 000-002: Stayed on well: btr
effort from this maiden: first time out in '85 was trained by C Bell when 3rd to Que
Sympatica in a valuable fillies event at Kempton: eff at 1m, stays 10f: acts on gd/firm
& soft grnd.   19

399 DELLWOOD RENOWN [14] (W Holden) 4-7-7 S Dawson(0) 33/1: -000-03: Sn prom, ev ch:
maiden: eff at 10f on gd/firm.   00

591 DASHING LIGHT [12] (D Morley) 5-8-11 B Rouse 14/1: 002-404: Sn clear ldr: see 432.   17

344 GIBBOUS MOON [4] 4-8-11 W Carson 11/2: 20-00: Active in mkt: nearest fin: first time
out in '85 fin 2nd in a maiden at Warwick: stays 10f: acts on gd & firm grnd.   16

532 DUELLING [17] 5-8-10(vis) T Fahey 12/1: -400000: Never nearer: see 7.   13

*578 DIMENSION [19] 4-8-3(bl) B Thomson 7/2 FAV: 0-01410: Never nearer: btr 578 (1m).   00

-- TIP TAP [7] 4-9-0 M Hills 8/1: 02003-0: No show on seasonal debut: showed some form
in '85 over 1m/10f: acts well on firm grnd.   00

344 MARSH HARRIER [5] 5-9-0 P Cook 8/1: 4011-00: Nicely bckd: fdd over 2f out: in gd
form in '85, winning h'caps at Folkestone & Lingfield & a Ladies race at Brighton: eff at
10f, stays 12f: acts well on gd & firm grnd & a sharpish, undulating trk.   00

578 HEATHGRIFF [15] 4-8-4 Pat Eddery 9/1: 102-300: Wknd: see 399 (sharper trk).   00

499 Pulsingh [3] 8-5	499 Even Banker [16] 7-12	263 Electropet [20] 8-11
578 Any Business [1] 9-8	-- Tournament Leader [2] 7-13	
532 Janaab [13] 8-10	-- Trackers Jewel [8] 8-5	
432 Rosanna Of Tedfold [18] 7-13		564 Solstice Bell [11] 7-7(bl)

19 ran   5,1½,hd,½,1   (Mrs D Anderson)   H Candy Kingstone Warren, Oxon

---

DONCASTER   Monday May 26th   Lefthand Galloping Track

Official Going Given as Firm

710   BBC RADIO SHEFFIELD APP. H'CAP (0-35)   £1545   7f   Good/Firm 38 -16 Slow   [32]

594 GODS LAW [8] (G Reveley) 5-7-11 Julie Bowker[7] 20/1: 0000-01: 5 b g Godswalk -
Fiuently (Ragusa): Turned up at 20/1 qckning inside final 1f comfortably in an app. h'cap
at Doncaster May 26: unplaced in all 6 outings last season, but winner twice at Beverley in
'84: best form around 7f/1m on gd or firm grnd: can win again.   12

499 TORREY [3] (W Hern) 7-9-7(bl) T Sprake[7] 4/1 fav: 0-10-22: Uneasy fav: led 2f out
and ran well: see 499.   31

110 BUBS BOY [2] (G Reveley) 4-8-11 D Leadbitter[5] 12/1: 011-003: Prom, ev ch: gd effort:
ran only 4 times in '85 winning final 2 starts, sellers at Hamilton & Ayr in July : eff at
6f, stays 7f: acts on gd/firm, suited by yld or soft grnd.   20

-- GOLDEN DISC [11] (M Camacho) 4-7-10 W Woods[1] 25/1: 03333-4: Al there on seasonal
debut: fin 3rd on final 4 outings last season but has yet to lose to maiden tag.   01

547 MINUS MAN [4] 8-8-3 R Morse[5] 9/1: 200-000: Fin well & is returning to form: won a
h'cap at Kempton in '85 & also won the same race in '84: very eff over 1m: acts on firm &
yld & on any trk though runs well at Kempton.   07

606 O I OYSTON [6] 10-9-2 A Woods[7] 8/1: 00-0030: Made much: btr 606.   19

-606 ZIO PEPPINO [7] 5-8-8 G Carter[3] 9/2: 00-0320: Fin 7th: btr 606.   00

481 HOPEFUL KATIE [9] 4-8-9(hd) Gay Kelleway[7] 8/1: 0-43040: Poor effort: see 65, 481. 00

-- Highly Placed [14] 7-11		-- Monticelli [17] 7-10
499 Petit Bot [1] 8-2	-- Eyelight [18] 7-10	31 Shirly Ann [15] 8-1
-- Via Vitae [12] 7-13	594 Janes Brave Boy [16] 8-10	
-- Royaber [10] 8-0	620 Hokusan [13] 8-7	41 Sarema [5] 8-1

18 ran   1½,nk,1½,nk,½,nk   (Mrs V Robson)   G Reveley Saltburn, Cleveland

711   RANSKILL SELLING STAKES 2YO   £1035   5f   Good/Firm 38 -44 Slow

446 ROSE DUET [4] (D Barron) 2-8-4 N Connorton 15/8 fav: 001: 2 ro f Grey Ghost -
Royal Raintree (Royal Duet): Well bckd when making all under press in a 2yo seller at
Doncaster May 26 (no bid): half sister to winning sprinter Royal Question: suited by gd
or firm grnd, forcing tactics & 5f.   24

589 TOOTSIE JAY [7] (P Feilden) 2-8-4 G Carter[3] 2/1: 30032: Well bckd, fin well &
just btn: rated 34 in 223 (yld).   23

*181 HARRYS COMING [3] (T Fairhurst) 2-8-11 J Callaghan[7] 5/1: 0213: Abs: not btn far
and a gd effort: acts on firm & soft: see 181.   28

543 FANTINE [1] (N Tinkler) 2-8-4 K Hodgson 6/1: 0044: Mkt drifter, early speed: acts
on firm: see 543.   17

43 ATHENS LADY [5] 2-8-4 S Webster 12/1: 40: Early speed after abs since 43.   05

-- ROAN REEF [2] 2-8-7 Gay Kelleway[5] 12/1: 0: Unruly in stalls on debut.   04

-- Sweet Ribot [6] 8-4

7 ran   ½,½,1½,4,1½,   (J Greaves)   D Barron Maunby, Yorks

712   HAREWOOD HANDICAP (0-60)   £3147   2m 2f Good/Firm 38 +16 Fast   [44]

*375 SNEAK PREVIEW [14] (H Candy) 6-9-2 C Rutter[5] 7/2 fav: 1043-11: 6 b g Quiet Fling -
Glimmer Of Hope (Never Say Die): Useful stayer who is unbtn this season and on latest
success, came from well behind to readily sprint clear in the final 1f in a fast run h'cap
at Doncaster May 26: first time out winner of valuable h'cap at Newmarket May 1: in '85 won
at Wolverhampton & Salisbury (first time out): also 4th in the Cesarewitch: eff 2m, stays
forever: acts on firm & gd going & is suited by a galltrk: genuine sort who does well when
fresh and should win more races.   44

590 SOUND DIFFUSION [1] (R Whitaker) 4-7-13(1ow) D Mckeown 12/1: 0030-22: Chall 2f out:
gd effort & deserves a race: stays 2m2f: see 590.   22

375 RIKKI TAVI [7] (B Hills) 6-9-1 R Street 4/1: 213-033: Ev ch: see 375.   37

542 ISLAND EXILE [6] (J Watts) 4-8-9 N Connorton 11/1: 0344-04: Led str: wknd: won a
maiden in '85 & lightly raced: not certain to stay 2m2f & winning form over
middle dists: acts on gd grnd & is suited by forcing tactics.   27

634 JACKDAW [4] 6-7-13 A Culhane[7] 10/1: -000030: Ev ch: btr 634.   14

-- TURI [11] 7-7-7(8oh) G French 33/1: 00040/0: Fit from hurdling, ev ch: not disgraced at
the weights: did not race on the level last season and is a maiden in this sphere.   07

*358 LOVE WALKED IN [12] 5-7-13 R Morse[5] 8/1: -001310: Fin 7th: btr 358 (14f soft). 00

*504 CHEKA [5] 10-7-7(4ex)(2oh) M Marshall[3] 15/2: 00-2010: Much btr 504 (yld).   00

462 WITHY BANK [10] 4-9-13 M Brennan[7] 6/1: 20-1130: Much btr 50 (heavy).   00
462 Sun Street [9] 8-4   137 Knights Heir [3] 7-10   634 Pelham Line [13] 7-7(4ex)(4oh)
590 Security Clearance [8] 8-12
13 ran   2½,¾,2½,3,1,½   (Mrs C Gross)   H Candy Kingstone Warren, Oxon

713 DURHAM HANDICAP STAKES (0-60) 3YO   £4292 7f   Good/Firm 38 -03 Slow   [47]

575 CARRIBEAN SOUND [3] (C Brittain) 3-8-3 M Roberts 13/2: 00-2431: 3 ch f Good Times -
Aruba (Amber Rama): Came from behind to lead final 1f, comfortably in a 3yo h'cap at
Doncaster May 26: lightly raced but showed promise in '85: acts on firm & yld going: suited
by 7f & waiting tactics.   41
427 PASTICCIO [7] (M Jarvis) 3-9-7 W Woods[3] 4/1 co fav: 1-322: Dsptd lead from ½way
and deserves a race soon: see 68.   55
370 TOP WING [5] (J Hindley) 3-9-6 G Starkey 11/2: 2-103: Kept on well and is in fine
form: see 188.   50
*650 HUDSONS MEWS [8] (M W Easterby) 3-8-2(6ex) K Hodgson 4/1 co fav: 000-314: Made much: gd
effort & acts on firm & yld: see 650.   32
518 CUMBRIAN DANCER [6] 3-7-10(vis) R Street 6/1: 12-0430: Chall 2f out: much btr 518.   22
-- NAP MAJESTICA [1] 3-8-8 N Connorton 25/1: 42300-0: Prom most on seasonal debut: placed
in 4 of his 6 races last season but yet to win.   30
500 GAELIC FLUTTER [2] 3-9-5 S Whitworth 6/1: 4200-30: Chall 2f out: btr 500 (sharp trk).   00
514 IVORY GULL [4] 3-8-13 M Birch 4/1 co fav: 041-00: Btr 514 (sharpish trk).   00
8 ran   1½,1½,shhd,2,2½,shhd   (Mrs C Brittain)   C Brittain Newmarket

714 STAND MAIDEN STAKES 3YO   £1358 1m 4f   Good/Firm 38 +13 Fast

-- COX GREEN [12] (G Harwood) 3-9-0 G Starkey 4/6 fav: -1: 3 ch c Cox's Ridge - Love You
Dearly (Sadair): Landed the odds on his racecourse debut, readily leading dist. in a fast run
3yo maiden at Doncaster May 26: should be well suited by 12f & promises to stay further:
acts on fast going: further impr certain and will win more races.   46
572 UP TO ME [3] (P Kelleway) 3-9-0 Gay Kelleway[5] 25/1: -02: Led briefly 2f out, clear
of rest & is going the right way: suited by 12f, a gall trk & fast going: a maiden awaits.   43
506 DUNSTON [1] (F Durr) 3-9-0 G French 33/1: 0-003: Fin well to ddht for 3rd: improving:
stays 12f well & acts on fast going.   36
-- RHODE ISLAND RED [6] (J Watts) 3-9-0 N Connorton 33/1: -4: Never closer: showing
promise on racecourse debut: half brother to winning sprinter/hurdler Dont Annoy Me:
clearly stays 12f well & should not be long in impr on this.   36
-- HANKLEY DOWN [9] 3-9-0 M Birch 33/1: -0: Promising racecourse debut: may stay beyond 12f. 35
-- MR MOSS [7] 3-9-0 M Roberts 33/1: -0: Should benefit from this racecourse debut:
bred to stay very well.   23
572 SAKER [8] 3-9-0 P Hamblett 5/2: -040: Friendless in mkt, led 1m, fin 9th: much btr 572. 00
506 Snow Wizard [13] 9-0(BL)   613 Something Similar [4] 9-0
451 Waterdale [15] 9-0   -- Lakiste [11] 9-0   430 L B Laughs [2] 9-0
409 Pearly King [14] 9-0   479 Assembly [10] 9-0(BL)   347 Abydos [16] 9-0
351 Battle Fleet [5] 8-11(VIS)
16 ran   ¾,4,ddht,1,8   (K Abdulla)   G Harwood Pulborough, Sussex

715 E.B.F. VYNER MAIDEN STAKES 2YO   £2395 5f   Good/Firm 38 -01 Slow

614 CAROLS TREASURE [7] (B Hills) 2-9-0 R Street 1/1 fav: 21: 2 b c Balidar - Really
Sharp (Sharpen Up): Al prom & comfortably led inside final 1f in a 2yo maiden at Doncaster
May 26: sprint bred colt who is very eff at 5f & should stay at least 6f: acts on firm & yld
and on a gall trk.   57
583 SONG N JEST [9] (J Fitzgerald) 2-9-0 M Birch 4/1: 32: Pressed leaders thro'out and
will find a maiden soon: acts on firm & yld: see 583.   52
-- JOINT SERVICES [11] (P Rohan) 2-9-0 S Morris 12/1: 3: Made a fine racecourse debut &
should be all the btr for this experience: half brother to 4 winners, most of them sprinters:
should find a Northern maiden without too much trouble.   48
-- SHABIB [4] (L Cumani) 2-9-0 P Hamblett 9/2: 4: Al there: $225,000 purchase who should impr. 47
632 TIMESWITCH [8] 2-9-0(BL) M L Thomas 4/1: 200: Bl for the first time, made much:
twice below 531 (sharp trk).   40
583 THE GREAT MATCH [3] 2-9-0 D Mckeown 14/1: 00: Pressed ldrs much & showed impr: cheaply
bought half brother to winning '85 juvenile Sharp Reply: sure to stay at least 6f.   39
-- Gypsys Barn Rat [1] 8-11   -- Fenn Trap [6] 9-0
-- Coast Boy [2] 9-0
9 ran   1½,1½,nk,3,hd,2½   (Mrs C Lane)   B Hills Lambourn, Berks

716 ARKSEY HANDICAP STAKES (0-50) 3YO   £2746 1m 2f   Good/Firm 38 -14 Slow   [55]

406 WESHAAM [7] (B Hanbury) 3-8-13 G Starkey 7/4 fav: 30-201: 3 b c Fappiano - Priceless
Asset (What A Pleasure): Useful colt: led dist. comfortably in a slowly run 3yo h'cap at
Doncaster May 26: showed promise both outings in '85: acts on hvy but best form on firm
or gd ground: stays 10f well.   50
535 CHEERFUL TIMES [8] (K Ivory) 3-7-7 R Street 10/1: 000-02: Led 2f out: rated 32 in 535.   25

553 SURPRISE CALL [2] (M H Easterby) 3-8-8 M Birch 6/1: 310-03: Came from off the pace
and should stay beyond 10f: see 553.   34
553 CHARLTON KINGS [1] (R Hollinshead) 3-9-7 R Lappin[7] 12/1: 0030-04: Prom most:
winner at Ripon & Pontefract in '85 over sprint distances & did not seem to stay todays 10f
trip: suited by firm grnd.   32
575 GOOSE HILL [5] 3-8-12 K Hodgson 13/2: 10-1040: Rear, badly hmpd 2f out: best 81.   00
-- MANTIQUE [3] 3-7-7(1oh) G Carter[3] 8/1: 20000-F: Made much but on the retreat when
falling inside final 2f: placed first 2 outings last season but has yet to win.   00
331 DUSTY DIPLOMACY [6] 3-7-13 W Woods[3] 11/2: 0-10B: Btn 4th, b.d. inside final 2f: best 66. 00
480 ON TO GLORY [4] 3-8-5 M Roberts 7/1: 000-00B: Hdway, b.d. 2f out: showed some
promise last season and is the type to appreciate middle dists this term.   00
8 ran   3,4,10,25   (Maktoum Al-Maktoum)   B Hanbury Newmarket

---

Official Going Given as Good based on time Good/Firm

717 VICTORIA CLAIMING STAKES 2YO   £1920   5f   Good/Firm 28 -02 Slow

460 RIMBEAU [13] (C Nelson) 2-9-0 J Reid 3/1 FAV: 4241: 2 b c Runnett - Miss Morgan
(Native Prince): Prom, came clear 1 out comfortably in a claiming race at Leicester May 26:
a consistent sort who seems to act on any trk & is probably best on a sound surface at 5f.   48
544 BALIDUCK [12] (P Rohan) 2-8-5 M Wood 4/1: 302: Well bckd: kept on well: ran poorly
last time over 6f but does seem best on gd/firm grnd.   33
332 PANACHE [2] (P Haslam) 2-8-12 T Williams 25/1: 003: Making impr: might be suited by 6f
and could find a small race.   33
621 NERRAD [9] (P Cundell) 2-8-10 G Baxter 16/1: 04: Ran well in front 4f.   27
596 EL BE DOUBLEYOU [7] 2-9-0 S Cauthen 9/2: 020: Late prog: see 596.   26
206 STARCH BROOK [5] 2-8-7 S Perks 12/1: 40: Not disgraced: see 206.   15

633 Broons Answer [8] 8-2(bl)   544 Penny Lover [10] 8-7
353 Peggys Treasure [6] 8-5   73   Tilting Yard [11] 8-6
502 Just Enchanting [3] 8-2   612 Blow For Home [4] 9-0
--   Musical Chorus [1] 8-6
13 ran   2,2½,1½,2,1½   (Gordian Troeller Bloodstock Ltd)   C Nelson Upper Lambourn.

718 ANSTEY SELLING HCAP 3 & 4YO 0-25   £748   1m 2f Good/Firm 28 -17 Slow   [18]

530 STONEBROKER [7] (D H Jones) 4-8-11 J Reid 3/1 Jt.FAV: 00-0441: 4 ch f Morston -
Overspent (Busted): Held up, easily led 1 out in a selling h'cap at Leicester May 26: bought
in 1,600 gns: very eff at 1m/10f & acts on gd/firm grnd: could quickly pick up another seller.   10
343 TRACK MARSHALL [8] (J Davies) 4-9-7 J Adams(7) 3/1 Jt.FAV: 0300-32: Despite slow start,
led 1½ out: seems to do particularly well at Leicester & should win a seller: see 343.   12
540 LITTLE DIMPLE [6] (B Preece) 4-9-1 S Keightley 20/1: -03: Made most: stays 10f.   00
346 JULTOWN LAD [3] (H Beasley) 3-7-10 Kim Tinkler(6) 14/1: 000-204: Stays 10f? see 93.   00
279 MAX CLOWN [1] 3-7-10 A Mackay 10/1: 000-00: Some late prog.   00
426 AMPLIFY [4] 3-8-1 A Mcglone 10/1: -030300: Btr '305 (1m).   00
524 FIRST ALARM [2] 3-8-2(BL) M Wood 9/1: -00000: Tried in bl, fdd 2 out.   00
-- DONT TELL VANESSA [11] 3-8-1 T Williams 5/1: 0000-0: Active in mkt but fin last.   00
93 Ashraf [9] 7-12   426 Ravelston [10] 8-1   331 Dads Gunner [5] 7-8
11 ran   4,5,nk,shhd,4,2   (E Angel)   D H Jones Efail Isaf, Glamorgan.

719 FOXTON HANDICAP STAKES 3YO 0-60   £4963   1m   Good/Firm 28 +23 Fast   [59]

*514 MEET THE GREEK [1] (R Laing) 3-8-7(5ex) J Reid 5/1: 202-211: 3 b c Formidable -
Edelliette (Edellic): In grand form and won 2nd race on the trot when again coming with a
late run to lead on the post in a fast run h'cap at Leicester May 26: earlier won a fast run
h'cap at Lingfield May 10: very eff over 7/8f & acts on firm & yld.   48
604 FRAMLINGTON COURT [3] (P Walwyn) 3-8-7 N Howe 5/1: 0-2D102: Just failed with a
strong late chall: in great form & seems to act on gd/firm & heavy grnd: see 352.   47
538 STANFORD VALE [4] (C Nelson) 3-7-8(1ow)(5oh) A Mackay 12/1: 00-0223: Set a fast pace,
just failed: is due a change of luck soon and certain to pick up at least a maiden: see 480.   34
344 GEORDIES DELIGHT [6] (L Piggott) 3-8-12 R Cochrane 9/1: 0-2104: Continues on this
firmer grnd: continues in gd form: consistent sort who might need further than 1m: see 277.   50
386 PALAESTRA [2] 3-9-7 G Baxter 10/1: 0212-00: Fin behind: coming back to form: gd
effort at the weights: gamely made the running when winning a maiden at Redcar in '85: well
suited by 7/8f and is sure to stay further: suited by gd/firm grnd.   57
340 TOPEKA EXPRESS [5] 3-7-10(BL) R Still 33/1: 000-000: Tried in bl, no threat.   25
623 PEARL FISHER [10] 3-8-8 S Cauthen 7/2: -1330: Well bckd, helped to set a fast pace:
acts on firm but possibly btr on soft: see 140, 623.   00
586 THRESH IT OUT [7] 3-9-5 A Kimberley 11/4 FAV: 223-230: No luck in running: btr 586.   00
352 Arabian Blues [9] 7-7(4oh)   605 Mahogany Run [8] 9-7
10 ran   hd,shhd,1,¾,4   (P G Goulandris)   R Laing Lambourn, Berks.

720 GROSBY MAIDEN STAKES 3YO   £964   1m 2f   Good/Firm 28 +11 Fast

--   KATHY W [13] (H Cecil) 3-8-11 S Cauthen 7/2: -1: 3 gr f Grey Dawn II - Pretty Fresh
(Forli): Prom filly: first time out led well inside final 1f, readily in a fast run maiden
race at Leicester May 26: eff at 10f on fast grnd, will probably stay further & can only impr.   50
--   ENSIGNE [2] (H Candy) 3-9-0 T Williams 16/1: -2: Bckd at long odds, led 1½ out, very
prom debut: acts on gd/firm & sure to be suited by 12f: will pick up a maiden soon.   48
484   COINAGE [3] (R Johnson Houghton) 3-9-0 J Reid 5/2 FAV: 3-23: Consistent and is due
a change of luck: this half brother to several winners should find a maiden race.   48
388   STAVORDALE [9] (H T Jones) 3-9-0 A Murray 4/1: 0-44: Close up, ran well: stays 10f.   47
371   ROYAL DYNASTY [14] 3-9-0 D Surrey(7) 33/1: -00: Ran well in front for a long way &
was not btn far: stays 10f, acts on gd/firm & should find a maiden.   47
338   SWEDISH PRINCESS [1] 3-8-11 R Cochrane 12/1: -00: Some late prog: needs 12f?   35
535   KING JACK [17] 3-9-0 G Baxter 16/1: -00: Dsptd lead a long way, fin 7th: see 535.   00
--   CORNISH CASTLE [16] 3-9-0 A Kimberley 11/2: -0: Wk in mkt, fin last but one: cost
115,000 gns and is a half brother to Yabis: looks likely to be suited by a test of stamina
and btr things are expected.   00
416   Queen Of Swords [11] 8-11   --   Jubilee Jamboree [8] 8-11
--   Azusa [15] 9-0   --   Ricmar [6] 9-0   512   Kookys Pet [12] 9-0
--   Imperial Palace [4] 9-0   --   Pied Dor [7] 8-11
--   Marcee [10] 8-11
16 ran   1½,hd,½,hd,5   (Marvin Waldman)   H Cecil Newmarket

721 TIGERS APPRENTICES HANDICAP 4YO+ 0-35   £1889   1m 4f   Good/Firm 28 -13 Slow   [33]

*449 PINWIDDIE [12] (P Rohan) 4-8-5 J Quinn 4/1: 3-04211: 4 b f Moulton - Bombay Duck
(Ballyciptic): Despite a slow start, came with a late run to win an app h'cap at Leicester
May 26, 2nd success on the trot following a win in a h'cap at Redcar: very eff over 11/12 &
stays 2m: acts on gd/firm & soft & on any trk but seems fav by a gall one.   19
591   MR LION [10] (F Carr) 4-7-13(5ex) J Carr(3) 5/1: 0-30122: Led 2 out, just failed
to hold on: in great form at present: see 591, 493.   12
590   MASTER CARL [11] (G Reveley) 7-8-1 D Leadbitter 10/1: 30-0003: Led 2 out, ran well.   12
*591 MENINGI [2] (N Tinkler) 5-9-7(5ex) Kim Tinkler(3) 10/3 FAV: 0-31414: Al there, gd run.   30
519   ORYX MINOR [13] 6-8-12 G Landau(3) 5/1: 401-030: Made much: btr 519.   19
609   BALGOWNIE [5] 6-8-5 P Burke(3) 10/1: 0002040: Btr 609: see 333, 36.   06
*-   AIRLANKA [4] 4-7-10 P Johnson(3) 25/1: 00000-0: Fin well: btn in sellers last year:
probably stays 12f.   00
683   HOLYPORT VICTORY [6] 4-10-0 A O'reilly(7) 7/1: 0113300: Led 4½ out, fdd: see 341, 449.   00
343   Gambart [1] 8-6   590   Spend It Lass [7] 8-9   547   Karamoun [3] 8-2
11 ran   nk,1,1,1½,4   (Mrs D Williams)   P Rohan Norton, Yorks

722 LIONESS 2YO FILLIES MAIDEN   £964   6f   Good/Firm 28 -14 Slow

--   PEN BAL LADY [1] (G Pritchard Gordon) 2-8-11 Dominic Gibson 25/1: 1: 2 ch f Mummy's
Game - Northern Queen (Northfields): Surprise winner of a maiden race at Leicester May 26,
leading 1½ out under press: seems well suited by 6f & acts on gd/firm grnd: will probably
stay 7f: cost only 5,000 gns and looks a bargain.   40
544   ROUMELI [6] (Lord J Fitzgerald) 2-8-11 T Lucas 8/1: 442: Dsptd lead all the way:
gd effort from this impr filly who is well suited by this 6f trip: probably acts on soft
& gd/firm.   36
311   SHUTTLECOCK GIRL [11] (W Jarvis) 2-8-11 R Cochrane 7/1: 43: Led/dsptd lead till
½way: probably stays 6f: might be btr at 5f: see 311: acts on gd/firm.   35
317   BUNDUKEYA [15] (H Thomson Jones) 2-8-11 A Murray 11/10 FAV: 34: A little disapp
after 317 but not very well drawn: certainly worth another chance.   33
--   SYSTEMS GO [8] 2-8-11 J Reid 20/1: 0: Well there 4f.   23
--   BROADWAY STOMP [2] 2-8-11 G Sexton 10/1: 0: Bckd at long odds.   18
--   FRIVOLOUS FANCY [9] 2-8-11 A Mcglone 25/1: 0: Never nearer in 7th.   00
*-   OUR LUCKY NATIVE [12] 2-8-11 S Cauthen 11/2: 0: Well bckd filly: cost 7,200 gns:
showed speed but not too well drawn: half sister to Beldale Concorde: sure to stay 6f
and worth another chance.   00
353   Pintafory [14] 8-11   --   Our Lena [3] 8-11   376   Philearn [7] 8-11
544   Corofin Lass [13] 8-11   --   Timella [10] 8-11
531   Lynda Broad [4] 8-11
14 ran   1,shhd,½,4,2,1½   (G T Park)   G Pritchard Gordon Newmarket

723 GROSBY MAIDEN STAKES 3YO   £964   1m 2f   Good/Firm 28 +12 Fast

--   FIRST KISS [2] (J Dunlop) 3-8-11 G Baxter 20/1: -1: 3 b f Kris - Primatie (Vaguely
Noble): Despite a slow start, comfortably led final 1f in a fast run maiden race at Leicester
May 26: very wk in mkt: half sister to the smart Millers Mate: very eff at 10f on gd/firm
grnd and will probably stay further: should win btr races & rate more highly.   54
535   IS BELLO [10] (L Cumani) 3-9-0 C Rate(7) 10/1: -032: Led 1½ out & continues to impr:
will probably be suited by 12f & should find a maiden race soon.   50
--   EYE SIGHT [5] (R Johnson Houghton) 3-8-11 J Reid 20/1: -3: Eyecatching late prog:
sure to do btr next time: a half sister to many winners: will probably be suited by further
than 10f & should soon pick up a maiden.   43

242

422 MARTESSANA DANCER [9] (B Hills) 3-8-11 R Cochrane 6/1: -024: Al there: btr 422 (1m).   40
615 PORO BOY [11] 3-9-0 L Jones(5) 50/1: 0-34000: Made much: stays 10f: see 352, 127.   36
570 TURMERIC [8] 3-9-0 N Crowther 50/1: 442-000: Rated 42 last year when a dist 2nd
to Faraway Dancer: has twice run well at Sandown & stays at least 1m.   28
371 BROWN THATCH [3] 3-9-0 S Cauthen 4/11 FAV: -30: Odds on flop & fin last but one:
reported to have choked on his tongue and is btr judged on effort in 371: should stay 10f.   00
486 Vitry [4] 8-11   -- River Gambler [16] 9-0
480 Eastern Player [7] 9-0   486 Ma Feathers [15] 8-11
528 Engle Dale [14] 9-0   -- Stop The Clock [1] 8-11
458 Aunt Etty [13] 8-12(1ow)   539 Leanders Pearl [6] 8-11
15 ran   3,2½,1½,5,6   (Sheikh Mohammed)   J Dunlop Arundel, Sussex

---

CHEPSTOW   Monday May 26th   Lefthanded, Galloping Track

724 NEWICK STAKES HANDICAP 0-50   £2411   1m 2f   Good 62 +07 Fast   [46]

547 WELSH MEDLEY [10] (D H Jones) 4-8-1 D Williams[7] 9/2 fav: 00-0321: 4 b g Connaught -
Blessed Beauty (Rustam): Led 2 out and came clear in a h'cap at Chepstow May 26: last won
in '84 at Chester: very eff at 8/10f: acts on gd/firm grnd & on yld: possibly fav by a
sharpish trk & forcing tactics.   29
499 TARS HILL [12] (L Cottrell) 5-8-4 N Carlisle 6/1: 0012-02: Led over 3 out, back to
his best: seems to love Chepstow and won here twice last year: eff at 10/12f & acts on
gd & yld grnd: goes well on an undulating trk & has also run well at Lingfield: should find
a race soon.   27
547 KATES PRIDE [14] (M Eckley) 4-8-6(VIS) T Quinn 7/1: 44-0043: Running well: see 547.   27
420 STAR OF IRELAND [3] (G Price) 6-8-13 Catherine Strickland[7] 7/1: 0-10104: Wk in mkt,
late prog: best 349 (12f yld).   33
23   BUTTS BAY [6] 4-7-7(5oh) R Teague[7] 25/1: -000-00: Abs since 23, stays 10f.   13
--   DISPORT [2] 4-7-8 N Adams 25/1: 00000-0: Led early.   11
432 ROCKMARTIN [4] 4-9-12 J Matthias 11/2: 020-000: Stiff task, fin 7th: see 432.   00
420 SPANISH REEL [8] 4-8-6 I Johnson 6/1: 4040-20: Friendless in the mkt, never in it:
puzzling after 420: worth another chance.   00
481 PEANDAY [5] 5-8-1 J Carter[7] 5/1: 00-0030: Best on a sharp trk: see 481.   00
445 Mairs Girl [1] 7-7(11oh)   -- Quiet Country [11] 8-3(vis)(6ow)
578 Highdale [9] 7-7(3oh)   521 Silver Cannon [13] 9-0
420 Ricco Star [7] 7-7(bl)(4oh)
14 ran   3,1½,½,hd,2,2½   (North Cheshire Trading & Storage ltd)   D H Jones Pontypridd

725 BADMINTON STAKES 2YO FILLIES   £1461   5f   Good 62 -30 Slow

*417 SUMMER SKY [5] (P Cole) 2-9-0 T Quinn 2/5 fav: 11: 2 br f Skyliner - Soft Pedal
(Hotfoot): Made easily in a minor race at Chepstow May 26: also easy 6L winner of a
earlier race at Warwick: half sister to winning juvenile Lucky Scott: clearly well suited by
5f but is sure to stay further: acts on gd grnd & looks sure to rate more highly: speedy filly   57
*482 MY ISABEL [2] (R Hannon) 2-9-0 R Wernham 9/2: 12: Al there: caught a tartar: see 482.   45
--   BO BABBITY [3] (D H Jones) 2-8-8 D William[7] 15/2: 3: Pleasing debut by this half
sister to In Slips and Anitas Prince (smart sprinter): impr likely next time.   39
533 EDRAIANTHUS [1] (R Laing) 2-8-8 M Malham 12/1: 04: Al prom: needs 6f? see 533.   38
--   LUNDY ISLE [4] 2-8-8 N Adams 50/1: 0: Never in it.   26
--   SAUNDERS LASS [7] 2-8-8 A Proud 50/1: 0: Al behind.   00
6 ran   5,hd,nk,4,15   (D A R Rowland)   P Cole Whatcombe, Berks

726 ST JOHN SELLING STAKES 3YO   £804   5f   Good 62 -28 Slow

418 KELLY LINDO [2] (B Stevens) 3-8-8 R Wernham 12/1: 00-0001: 3 b f Kala Shikari -
Whitton lane (Narrator): Bckd at long odds when winning a seller at Chepstow May 26, readily
led 1½ out: should stay further but evidently suited by 5f: shrewdly placed by trainer.   20
424 BOXERS SHUKEE [7] (J Bradley) 3-8-8 John Williams 11/2: 00-3002: Al there: see 89.   15
339 COMMANDER MEADEN [3] (D O'donnell) 3-8-11 M Lynch 3/1: 000-03: Dropped in class, tried
to make all: might do btr on a sharper trk: could find a seller.   12
496 LA DIVINA [5] (G Lewis) 3-8-8 T Quinn 1/1 fav: 004-04: Dropped in class, held up but
proved a disapp fav: closely related to many sprint winners: might do btr in bl.   08
507 SHARASAR [4] 3-8-8(bl) A Dicks[7] 7/1: 400-000: Fdd 2 out.   00
346 NENUCO [8] 3-8-8 A Proud 25/1: 004-00: Never a threat.   00
593 Eastern Lass [6] 8-8
7 ran   1½,2,nk,7,2½   (R Cheetham)   B Stevens Bramley, Surrey

727 SEVERN STAKES HANDICAP 0-35 4YO+   £1482   7f   Good 62 -06 Slow   [32]

566 PETT VELERO [7] (S Dow) 7-7-10 P Simms[2] 33/1: 0/0-001: 7 b g Pitcairn - Naval
Artiste (Captain's Gig): Surprise winner of a h'cap at Chepstow May 26, readily led inside
final 1f: first success: suited by 7f and an undulating trk: will probably stay further.   07

594 CBM GIRL [20] (R Woodhouse) 5-9-2 A Bond 3/1 fav: 0000-32: Led 2½ out, gd effort and
again not well drawn: won this race last year: will find a race soon: see 594.   23
578 PAMELA HEANEY [9] (H Beasley) 4-8-6 J Carter[7] 11/1: 030-003: Ran on, coming back
to form: won a 7f seller at Beverley last year but does stay 10f: acts on firm & heavy.   10
174 GAUHAR [15] (M Blanshard) 5-8-10 N Adams 8/1: 0300-44: Abs since 174: wk in mkt.   13
679 FAIRDALE [4] 8-8-3(3ow) P Finn 16/1: -000300: Al prom, stays 7f: see 495.   04
495 POCO LOCO [16] 4-8-1 R Teague[7] 14/1: 0-0340: Led 4 out: see 495: wk in mkt.   02
540 BRANKSOME TOWERS [17] 6-7-10 G Bradwell[7] 9/1: 000-000: Bckd at long odds, fin 7th.   00
636 GRACIOUS HOMES [12] 5-8-13(bl) D Williams[7] 11/2: 004-400: Btr 636, 441.   00
540 SANTELLA PAL [21] 5-7-13 N Carlisle 15/2: 000-020: Led 3f, much btr 540.   00

547	Clipsall [22] 8-11	499	Turcy Boy [5] 8-3(3ow)	495	Elmdon [2] 8-12
--	Macmillion [10] 9-7	--	Formidable Lady [8] 8-11		
636	Sue Clare [7] 7-13	620	Angies Video [14] 7-12(BL)		
321	Lyric Way [11] 9-7	540	Mista Spoof 0 7-13	--	Maundy Gift [13] 7-10
636	Toms Nap Hand [18] 7-12(1ow)			122	Leap Year [3] 8-13
21 ran	1½,1½,hd,½,hd,2	(Mrs Hilly Beaufort)		S Dow Bramley, Surrey	

Official Going Given as Good/Firm

728 E.B.F. WOODHOUSE EAVES MAIDEN 2YO   £1784   5f   Firm 08 +02 Fast

-- FLOOSE [3] (P Cole) 2-9-0 T Quinn 5/1: 1: 2 b c Ballad Rock - Carnival Dance (Welsh
Pageant): Prom colt: led below dist, comfortably when making a winning debut in quite a fast
run 2yo maiden at Leicester May 27: half brother to the smart 7f winner Sarab and should stay
further than this minimum trip: acts on fast grnd & on a gall trk.   55
-536 TEZ SHIKARI [11] (L Cottrell) 2-9-0 W Carson 11/4 Jt FAV: 0422: Led briefly after
½way: no ch with easy winner though again ran well & should find a race soon: acts on
firm: see 350.   45
565 DUTCH COURAGE [6] (D Morley) 2-9-0 T Ives 11/2: 443: Ran on well & sure to appreciate
another furlong: acts on firm grnd & on any trk: consistent sort: see 405.   40
523 BUDDY RICH [9] (W O'gorman) 2-9-0(BL) T Ives 17/2: 404: Bl. first time: see 382.   38
437 TOUCH OF SPEED [8] 2-9-0 S Perks 16/1: 000: Led over ½way: clearly has plenty of
pace & should do btr on a sharper trk: acts on firm & soft grnd: see 20.   37
612 GREAT MEMORY [10] 2-9-0 B Crossley 8/1: 00: Al up there: acts on gd & firm: see 612.   36
-- SARIHAH [7] 2-9-0 A Murray 11/4 Jt FAV: 0: Nicely bckd debutant: showed gd early
speed and will impr for this experience: cost $140,000 as a yearling: acts on fast grnd.   30

--	Morning Flower [4] 9-0			--	Badoglio [4] 9-0
503	Say You Will [14] 9-0	--	Young Centurion [13] 9-0		
596	Sohams Taylor [2] 9-0	--	Sweet Piccolo [12] 9-0		
544	Gold State [1] 9-0				
14 ran	2½,2,½,hd,hd	(Fahd Salman)		P Cole Whatcombe, Oxon	

729 TOTE EACH WAY SELLING STAKES 3YO   £734   6f   Firm 08 -14 Slow

-- GERSHWIN [6] (D O'donnell) 3-8-6 A Clark 20/1: 000-1: 3 b g Gold Song - Firey Kim
(Cannonade): Was a surprise winner on seasonal debut, al close up and gamely led on the line
in a 3yo seller at Leicester May 27 (no bid): lightly raced last season in much btr company:
eff over 6f & sure to stay further: suited by fast grnd & a gall trk.   20
377 SAMBA LASS [2] 3-8-3 N Carlisle 7/2: 000-032: Btn a whisker: in gd form
and was well suited by this longer trip: acts on firm & yld grnd & a stiff trk.   16
195 CREETOWN SALLY [14] (A King) 3-8-4(1ow) I Johnson 33/1: 00-03: Just failed to make
all: impr effort from this lightly raced filly: eff over 6f on fast grnd: well suited by
forcing tactics.   15
309 SHY MISTRESS [9] 3-8-3 G Duffield 10/1: -04: Fin strongly, not btn far:
eff over 6f on fast grnd: acts on a gall trk.   12
608 TOUCH ME NOT [7] 3-8-6(bl) S Perks 11/2: -300040: Fair effort though best on soft in 64   11
593 GARY AND LARRY [10] 3-8-6 Pat Eddery 6/4 FAV: 00-00: Dropped in class & well bckd:
no extra dist: little form to date: eff over 5/6f: seems to act on any going.   09
422 EASY ROMANCE [4] 3-8-3 T Quinn 4/1: 00-00: Speed over ½way: fin 7th.   00
-- SALTCOTE HOPEFUL [13] 3-8-8 R Cochrane 8/1: 13100-0: Mkt drifter on reapp: btr for race:
last season won sellers at Yarmouth & Nottingham: well suited by 6f: acts on any going
and on any trk.   00

--	Trelales [1] 8-3	305	Mr Jester [5] 8-6	--	Nipper Smith [11] 8-6
620	Track The Bear [3] 8-6			--	Hillingdon Jim [12] 8-6
--	Dashaki Gold [8] 8-3(bl)				
14 ran	shhd,½,½,1,½	(Mrs E O'Donnell)		D O'donnell Upper Lambourn, Berks	

730 TOTE CREDIT HANDICAP (0-50) 3YO   £2687   1m 2f   Firm 08 -11 Slow   [38]

352 MODENA REEF [6] (I Balding) 3-9-7 Pat Eddery 11/2: 300-301: 3 gr c Mill Reef -
Mary Of Modena (Crowned Prince): Ran on well to lead close home in a 3yo h'cap at Leicester
May 27: nicely bred colt who had shown promise previously: eff over 1m, stays 10f well:
acts on firm & yld grnd & seems best on a gall trk: tried in bl last time though clearly
better without.   42

*637 AL ZUMURRUD [10] (R Armstrong) 3-9-5(5ex) W Carson 7/4 FAV: 0400-12: Led over 2f
out, just btn: gd effort under her penalty: stays 10f well: see 637.   40

637 CRAMMING [5] (W Musson) 3-9-2 M Wigham 7/1: 000-123: Denied a clear run dist, kept
on well & remains in gd form: stays 10f: acts on fast grnd: see 318.   33

*512 QUEZAL [1] (H Cecil) 3-9-11(5ex) S Cauthen 3/1: 00-014: Led 6f out, sn btn when
hdd & btr on a sharper trk in 512 (gd).   32

623 BALNACRAIG [7] 3-8-11 R Cochrane 33/1: 010-000: Mkt drifter though ran a fair
race: last season was a surprise winner of a small race at Yarmouth: stays 10f: suited
by fast ground.   15

506 CELTIC DOVE [3] 3-8-7 J Williams 14/1: -40400: Best over 1m in 338 (yld).   08

356 Lady Owen [8] 8-12	637 Spinnaker Lady [4] 8-2
486 Thereafter [2] 8-8	-- Baydon Queen [9] 9-1

10 ran   shhd,2,6,1½,2   (Sheikh Ali Abu Khamsin)   I Balding Kingsclere, hants

731 TOTE DUAL FORECAST HANDICAP (0-35)   £2390   1m 4f   Firm 08 -20 Slow   [28]

532 DENBOY [7] (B Stevens) 4-9-1 R Carter(5) 12/1: 400-001: 4 ch g On Your Mark -
Petal (Whistler): Led inside dist and just held on in a h'cap at Leicester May 27: best
effort last season when narrowly btn by London Leader in a Hamilton maiden first time out:
stays 12f: acts on firm & soft grnd & is suited by a stiff trk.   22

308 DON RUNI [13] (D Morley) 4-9-0 A Murray 16/1: 0-00002: Just btn: gd effort: see 23.   20

358 BLENDERS CHOICE [12] (K Brassey) 4-9-0 N Adams 12/1: 0300-03: Just failed to make
all: see 358.   19

--   PALACE YARD [6] (J Jenkins) 4-8-11 Pat Eddery 8/1: 0240-4: Al up on seasonal debut:
showed promise in maiden company last season: eff over 12/14f: acts on fast grnd and is
suited by a gall trk.   11

582 CASTIGLIONE [3] 4-8-10(bl) S Cauthen 6/1: 32-0000: Little form this season: see 199.   09

532 MOON JESTER [17] 6-9-7 D Mckay 4/1 FAV: 0-00240: Late prog: best in 349.   15

547 MONCLARE TROPHY [9] 7-9-7 R Curant 8/1: 0-00100: Best over 10f in 420 (sharp trk).   00

341 PRIMROSE WAY [4] 4-8-10 J Reid 8/1: 0000-00: Fin 9th: see 341.   00

485 INCHGOWER [11] 9-8-10 B Rouse 5/1: 000-030: Al rear: btr over 14f in 485 (yld).   00

547 Shad Rabugk [16] 8-7	92 Kadesh [1] 9-1(vis)	126 Action Time [15] 9-10 U
308 Patralan [10] 8-11	547 Cut A Caper [14] 8-10	-- Theresa [2] 8-4
591 The Crying Game [5] 8-2		526 Michele My Belle [8] 8-0

17 ran   nk,nk,3,¾,4   (Martin Coles)   B Stevens Bramley, Surrey

732 TOTE FILLIES E.B.F. STAKES 3YO   £4285   6f   Firm 08 +23 Fast

496 DREAM CHASER [8] (P Cole) 3-9-2 T Quinn 4/1: 024U-01: 3 b f Record Token - Hot
Sun (Hotfoot): Useful filly: led below dist, readily in a very fast run 3yo stakes at
Leicester May 27: first time out last season won at Epsom and later ran up to Sperry in a
valuable nursery at Newmarket: very eff over 6f & will stay further: acts on firm & yld
grnd & on any trk: should win again in this form.   65

294 FLYAWAY BRIDE [6] (I Balding) 3-9-2 Pat Eddery 6/4 FAV: 131-002: Tried to make all:
beat rem decisively: much btr effort on this faster grnd: see 59.   57

228 SKEEB [7] (M Stoute) 3-9-1 W R Swinburn 2/1: 3114-03: Stayed on though no threat
to leaders: useful filly last season, winning at Pontefract & Nottingham: stays 6f really
well: suited by fast grnd: acts on any trk.   32

--   RAFFLES VIRGINIA [1] (B Mcmahon) 3-8-7 R Cochrane 33/1: 02000-4: Late prog & btr
for race: best effort last season when 2nd to Chishtiya in a fillies maiden at Chester
(rated 32): eff over 5/6f: acts on firm & gd grnd & on any trk.   16

--   COOL GALES [5] 3-8-7 G Duffield 10/1: 33003-0: Placed behind Cyrano de Bergerac &
Tarib in a valuable Newmarket nursery on final start last season (rated 47) and will be
btr for this race: eff over 5/6f on gd & firm grnd: suited by a stiff trk.   10

--   FOUNDRY FLYER [10] 3-8-7 E Guest(3) 16/1: -0: Bckd at long odds: speed over ½way
on racecourse debut: acts on fast grnd   04

-- Springwell [3] 8-7	431 Miss Moth [2] 8-7	-- Chart Climber [9] 8-7
-- Rodistyle [4] 8-7		

10 ran   2,10,2½,2½,2½   (T A Johnsey)   P Cole Whatcombe, Oxon

733 TOTE PLACEPOT E.B.F. STAKES 3YO   £2460   7f   Firm 08 -01 Slow

600 NATIVE OAK [6] (H Cecil) 3-9-3 S Cauthen 4/7 FAV: 313-421: 3 b c Tower Walk -
Be Royal (Royal Palm): Useful colt: was heavily bckd when making all, comfortably in a
3yo stakes at Leicester May 27: lightly raced last season, winning a small race at Yarmouth:
very eff over 6/7f & sure to stay further: acts on firm & gd grnd & on a gall trk: does
well with front running tactics.   65

•423 RIYDA [12] (R Johnson Houghton) 3-8-10 J Reid 6/1: -12: Al close up, kept on well
and comfortably beat the rem: acts on gd & firm grnd & on a gall trk: on the up grade: see 423   55
--   BOLD ADMIRAL [4] (M Stoute) 3-8-11 W R Swinburn 10/1: -3: Friendless in the mkt on
racecourse debut: chased winner till dist: well bred colt who cost 160,000 gns as a yearling:
acts on firm grnd & on a gall trk: should impr.   48
--   ICHNUSA [10] (J Dunlop) 3-8-8 W Carson 9/2: -4: Prog ½way: not qknd dist though
should impr for this race: half sister to several winners, incl useful stayer Rollrights:
acts on fast grnd & on a gall trk.   39
498 HOLLY BROWN [16] 3-8-8 M Hills 50/1: -00: Al close up: acts on firm: see 498.   35
546 BON ACCUEIL [13] 3-8-11 P Hamblett 7/1: 42-00: Nicely bckd & al prom: placed in
both starts last season, being narrowly btn by Palaestra in a Redcar maiden on final start:
half brother to a couple of winners: eff over 7f on fast grnd: suited by a gall trk.   37
438 THE STAMP DEALER [7] 3-8-11 G Sexton 50/1: -00: Fin 7th: seems suited by fast grnd.   00
576 VITAL FORM [5] 3-8-11(bl) Pat Eddery 14/1: -00: Al in mid field: fin 8th: acts on
good and firm.   00

545	Robis [8] 8-8	227	Mummys Secret [1] 9-0	546	Saxelbye Park [18] 8-11
579	Bears Revenge [9] 8-11			486	Danribo [11] 8-11
498	Mostango [3] 8-11	501	Mr Matchmaker [20] 8-11(bl)		
183	Dress In Spring [15] 8-8			205	Megadyne [17] 8-8
545	Princess Rymer [2] 8-8			--	Waverley Rose [14] 8-8

19 ran   ¾,4,3,1½,½,hd,nk   (C d'Alessio)   H Cecil Newmarket

---

Official Going Given as Good

734 RAILWAY HANDICAP STAKES (0-35) 3YO+   £2595   5f   Good 46 -25 Slow   [35]

550 STONEYDALE [11] (N Callaghan) 4-9-8 G Starkey 8/1: 000-001: 4 b f Tickled Pink -
Toccatina (Bleep-Bleep): Fin well to get up close home in a slow run h'cap at Sandown May 27:
failed to win in '85 but a useful 2yo, winning at Warwick, Beverley, Hamilton & Edinburgh:
very eff over 5f on fast grnd: goes well on a sharpish trk, though acts on any.   38
580 MUHTARIS [8] (C Benstead) 3-8-5 B Rouse 5/2 FAV: 00-0222: Led over 2f out: in
fine form: see 580, 507.   30
-508 BROWN BEAR BOY [6] (R Armstrong) 4-9-7 W Carson 3/1: 400-023: Led inside final 1f:
just btn: well bckd here: in gd form: see 508, 374.   35
508 MIRACLES TAKE TIME [2] (D Elsworth) 4-9-5 Pat Eddery 15/2: 03-0004: Ran on final 1f
and just btn in a close fin: returning to form: in '85 won at Lingfield & likes a sharpish
trk: eff at 5f, suited by 6f: acts on gd & yld grnd.   33
--   SHALBEE [12] 4-8-8 R Guest 33/1: 00000-0: Never nearer on seasonal debut: winner
at Ascot as a 2yo: best over 5f on firm & gd/yld.   14
--   SITEX [5] 8-7-7 R Still 33/1: 22000-0: Ch over 1f out on seasonal debut: placed several
times in '85 but failed to get his head in front: eff at 6f, stays 7f: acts on any grnd:
likes a sharpish trk.   00
418 ROYAL BEAR [14] 4-7-8 T Williams 6/1: 2204300: Mkt drifter: early speed: btr 266.   00

550	Yani [9] 7-7	--	Silbando [4] 8-5	679	Dorney [13] 8-9
--	Paddington Belle [15] 8-2(2ow)			464	Pegasus Lady [7] 7-12(BL)
498	Valvinora [10] 7-12	--	Sharad [1] 7-7		

14 ran   hd,nk,hd,3,1,¾   (J Cresswell)   N Callaghan Newmarket

735 MILLER INSURANCE GRP. H'CAP (0-50)   £3501   1m 6f   Good 46 +29 Fast   [48]

582 TRAPEZE ARTIST [8] (N Vigors) 5-8-9 S Dawson(3) 8/1: -040021: 5 b h High Line -
Maternal (High Top): Led 1½f out, driven out in a fast run h'cap at Sandown May 27: in
'85 won a h'cap at Newmarket: in '84 won at Chester: eff at 14f, stays further: acts on
gd/firm & soft: has worn bl: carries weight well.   41
475 MILTON BURN [5] (H O'neill) 5-8-9 G Baxter 16/1: 0-01102: Another gd effort: see 312.   38
+582 ALL IS REVEALED [11] (D Thom) 4-8-11(vis)(4ex) G Starkey 6/4 FAV: 10-0413: Led 12f: good
effort but better 582(C/D).   37
582 BOCODA LAD [14] (C Benstead) 5-8-5 B Rouse 14/1: 4004-04: Nearest fin: running into form   27
618 OWENS PRIDE [10] 4-8-9 W Carson 12/1: 00-1300: Fair effort, but btr 263 (soft grnd).   29
215 DOMINATE [7] 5-8-6 T Ives 16/1: 3002-00: No threat: winner over hurdles recently:
failed to win in '85 though in '84 won at Chester & Goodwood: eff at 14f, stays 2m:
acts well on gd/firm: no track preferences.   24
504 WATERLOW PARK [1] 4-8-11 Pat Eddery 3/1: 422-22P: P.u: something amiss? see 504, 375.   00

582	My Charade [12] 8-4(vis)(9ow)(4ex)			336	Alacazam [4] 7-10(3ow)(10oh)
--	King Of Comedy [9] 9-12			462	For A Lark [13] 8-8
--	Tana Mist [2] 8-0	403	Bloodless Coup [3] 9-3		
542	Shipwright [6] 7-7(8oh)				

14 ran   2½,3,4,1½,1½   (Introgroup Holdings Ltd)   N Vigors Upper Lambourn, Berks

736 GROUP 3 BRIGADIER GERARD STAKES   £18405   1m 2f   Good 46 +02 Fast

--   BEDTIME [7] (W Hern) 6-8-10 W Carson 5/2: -1: 6 ch g Bustino - Sweet Hour (Primera): Very smart gelding: despite a very long abs, was brilliantly produced by his trainer to win Gr.3 Brigadier Gerard Stakes at Sandown May 27: led approaching final 1f and ridden clear: in excellent form in '84 winning Gr.3 events at Ascot & Deauville: also successful at Kempton (2) & Ayr: on final outing fin 2nd in the Japan Cup: a prolific scorer in '83, winning 4 times: acts on firm & soft grnd: very eff at 10f, stays 12f well: seems sure to come on for this race and is not one to oppose lightly.   **82**

410   WYLFA [2] (J Shaw) 5-8-10 B Rouse 50/1: 22: Ch final 1f: excellent effort at these weights: will definitely win soon: see 410.   **76**

598   SUPREME LEADER [6] (C Brittain) 4-9-1 P Robinson 7/4 FAV: 30-1133: Ev ch over 1f out: btr 325: see 221.   **80**

325   IROKO [1] (M Stoute) 4-8-13 W R Swinburn 7/2: 0111-24: Led 3f out: another gd run.   **77**

*511   NEBRIS [4] 5-8-13 Pat Eddery 11/2: 10-1110: Upped in class: in fine form: see 511.   **75**

598   PROTECTION [5] 4-8-13 S Cauthen 12/1: 110-300: Made much: fdd: see 313 (1m).   **70**

--   KUFUMA [3] 4-8-10 G Starkey 33/1: 23220-0: No show on seasonal debut.   **00**

7 ran   2,nk,½,1,2,1½   (Lord Halifax)   W Hern West Ilsley, Berks

737 NATIONAL STAKES 2YO   £6128   5f   Good 46 -09 Slow

*323   RISK ME [4] (P Kelleway) 2-9-0 Pat Eddery 1/1 FAV: 11: 2 ch c Sharpo - Run The Risk (Run The Gantlet): Smart, very promising colt: led well over 1f out and had only to be pushed out for a comfortable win in National 2yo Stakes (Listed) at Sandown May 27: first time out was a runaway winner over this C/D: half brother to 3 winners, all of whom stayed well: acts on gd & soft grnd & a stiff trk: looks certain to be suited by 6f: sure to win more races & can be followed with confidence.   **71**

*577   WHIPPET [2] (C Brittain) 2-9-0 P Robinson 14/1: 12: Al up there: excellent effort from this fast impr colt: certain to win more races: see 577.   **63**

*405   ZAIBAQ [1] (H T Jones) 2-9-0 A Murray 11/10 : 13: Heavily bckd: made much: gd effort and will win again soon: see 405.   **62**

601   SAXON STAR [3] (J Winter) 2-8-11 W R Swinburn 33/1: 144: Nearest fin & will appreciate 6f: another gd effort: acts on gd & soft grnd: see 311.   **57**

353   DOUBLE TALK [5] 2-8-8 G Baxter 100/1: 0420: Impossible task: see 353.   **19**

5 ran   2½,nk,½,12   (Lewis H Norris)   P Kelleway Newmarket

738 ESHER PLACE HANDICAP STAKES (0-50) 3YO   £3189   1m 3f   Good 46 -19 Slow   [47]

402   TEBITTO [7] (N Vigors) 3-8-8 P Cook 20/1: 000-01: 3 b g Derrylin - Over Beyond (Bold Lad)(Ire): Led from the stalls, staying on under press in a h'cap at Sandown May 27: highly tried in 3 outings in '85: eff at 11f with forcing tactics: acts well on a gall trk and good ground.   **36**

648   APPEALIANA [9] (W Musson) 3-7-11 A Mackay 8/1: 00-002: Nearest fin: best effort yet from this half brother to 4 winners: should be suited by 12f: acts on gd grnd & a gall trk.   **22**

648   SWYNFORD PRINCE [10] (K Stone) 3-8-6 G Brown(5) 9/2 Jt.FAV: -001203: Al up there: gd effort: see 331.   **31**

538   DISCIPLE [12] (G Lewis) 3-8-6 P Waldron 11/2: -00004: Gambled on: much impr effort: probably stays 12f: acts on gd grnd & a gall trk.   **29**

505   STILLOU [3] 3-7-11 T Williams 12/1: 04-3400: Ch 2f out: see 117 (10f).   **15**

452   HURRICANE HENRY [11] 3-9-7 W R Swinburn 9/2 Jt.FAV: 02-00: Mkt drifter: never nearer: will do btr than this: on final outing in '85 was rated 48 when 2nd to Innishmore Island in a Warwick maiden: half brother to 2 winners & should be well suited by 12f: acts on fast grnd.   **38**

275   OWL CASTLE [5] 3-9-2 Pat Eddery 6/1: -324100: Prom over 1m: abs: best 171 (12f yld).   **00**

356   Matelot Royale [8] 8-4   623   The Wooden Hut [1] 7-7(5oh)

512   Mightily [2] 8-1   623 Diva Encore [6] 9-5   461 Beau Mirage [4] 8-10(vis)

12 ran   1½,shhd,1,2½,½   (Lady d'Avigdor Goldsmid)   N Vigors Upper Lambourn, Berks

739 WHEATSHEAF MAIDEN STAKES 3YO   £4046   1m 2f   Good 46 -04 Slow

442   DANISHGAR [11] (M Stoute) 3-9-0 W R Swinburn 13/8 FAV: 22-041: 3 b c Shergar - Demia (Abdos): Heavily bckd & led inside the final 1f, under press in a 3yo maiden at Sandown May 27: highly regarded 2yo, fin 2nd on both starts in gd company: eff at 10f, seems to stay 12f: acts on firm & soft grnd.   **58**

388   SARONICOS [8] (C Brittain) 3-9-0 P Robinson 12/1: 00-322: Led 3f out: kept on well and is in fine form: may stay 12f: see 388, 194.   **55**

194   BANANAS [15] (O Douieb) 3-9-0 R Hills 9/4: -23: Well bckd: led 2f out: not btn far and 5L clear 3rd: acts on gd & yld grnd & will have no trouble finding a maiden: see 194.   **54**

546   NEEDLEWOMAN [21] (R Armstrong) 3-8-11 G Sexton 33/1: -0004: Nearest fin: should do btr next time: speedily bred, but seems to stay 10f well: acts on gd grnd & should find a race.   **42**

--   DOM STAR [15] 3-9-0 Paul Eddery 33/1: -0: Mkt drifter on racecourse debut: gd effort: stays 10f: acts on gd grnd & a gall trk.   **44**

371 STEP IN TIME [23] 3-9-0 T Quinn 20/1: -00: Stayed on well final 1f: another good
run: stays 10f: see 371.   43
370 SILK THREAD [7] 3-9-0 W Carson 6/1: 2-00: Mkt drifter: never nearer: a fine 2nd to
El Cuite in a 27 runner race at Newbury on sole start in '85 and will be a certainty for
a maiden on that form: half brother to several winners, incl very useful Silken Knot:
should be suited by middle dists: acts on gd grnd & a gall trk.   00
--   GUESSING [5] 3-9-0 G Starkey 10/1: -0: Never showed on racecourse debut: should
do better than this.   00

-- Strike Home [6] 8-11	-- Loreef [1] 8-11	-- Barsham [9] 8-11
-- Bustamente [2] 9-0	619 Cigar [22] 9-0	619 Forward Move [12] 9-0
484 Full Speed Ahead [13] 9-0		512 Gods Path [17] 9-0
-- Lucky Lad [14] 9-0	506 Never Bee [19] 9-0	625 Risk Another [20] 9-0
-- Woodlands Crown [18] 9-0		581 Barleybree [4] 8-11
444 Keepcalm [3] 9-0		

22 ran   1¼,¼,½,5,½,½   (H H Aga Khan)   M Stoute Newmarket

REDCAR   Tuesday May 27th   Lefthand, Galloping Track

Official Going Given as Good/Firm

740 PETER HIGGINS SELLING H'CAP 0-25 3YO   £892   1m   Firm 07 -06 Slow   [24]

356 SPRING FLIGHT [4] (A Jarvis) 3-8-11 J Lowe 9/2: 000-01: 3 b c Captain James -
Late Swallow (My Swallow): Landed a gamble, led final 1f, ridden out in a selling h'cap at
Redcar May 27 (no bid): eff at 1m on a stiff trk: acts well on firm grnd.   14
356 HILL RYDE [1] (J Harris) 3-9-2 M Birch 8/1: 000-002: Led ½way: gd effort: showed
some form in '85: stays 1m: acts on firm & yld grnd & should find a similar event: 8L clear rem. 15
608 HARSLEY SURPRISE [2] (N Tinkler) 3-9-0(bl) D Nicholls 2/1 fav: 4040-33: Sn prom: btr 608. 01
241 OUR MUMSIE [9] (N Bycroft) 3-8-9 M Richardson 12/1: 40-2004: Led 4f: best 103.   00
141 FOLKSWOOD [8] 3-8-12 N Connorton 20/1: 0000-00: Never nearer: little form.   00
491 KO ISLAND [5] 3-9-4 S Morris 5/1: 0-00000: Dropped in class: btr 491 (heavy).   00
620 GROVECOTE [10] 3-9-2 B Thomson 5/1: 003-000: Speed over 5f: on final outing in '85
fin 3rd in a seller over this C/D.   00
67   LARCHES [7] 3-9-3 P Robinson 7/1: 00-000: Abs: no show.   00

491 Take The Biscuit [3] 9-7		54 Octiga [6] 9-5

10 ran   1½,8,2,½,2½   (Mrs M A Jarvis)   A Jarvis Royston, Herts

741 E.B.F. JOHN CROSS MAIDEN STAKES 2YO   £1641   6f   Firm 07 -13 Slow

--   CHIME TIME [2] (C Tinkler) 2-9-0 T Lucas 12/1: 1: 2 b c Good Times - Balnespick
(Charlottown): Prom colt: made ev yd, comfortably in a 2yo maiden at Redcar May 27: well
bckd today: cost only 3,400 gns: half brother to fair 1m/10f winner Kaukas: eff at 6f,
should stay further: acts on firm grnd &a gall trk.   49
--   MUBDI [12] (H T Jones) 2-9-0 M Hills 2/1 fav: 2: Well bckd: ran on final 1f: impr
likely: should be suited by further than 6f: acts on fast grnd.   41
437 SILVER ANCONA [17] (E Eldin) 2-9-0 A Mackay 5/1: 343: Al prom: consistent: stays 6f.   36
515 RABENHAM [21] (D Barron) 2-9-0 W Ryan 20/1: 004: Gd effort: stays 6f: see 236:
acts on firm.   35
-602 WIGANTHORPE [8] 2-9-0 M Hindley[3] 6/1: 0220: Ev ch: btr 602 (5f).   31
544 MUSEVENI [15] 2-9-0 M Fry 20/1: 400: Sn prom: best effort yet: stays 6f.   27
497 FINAL DELIGHT [16] 2-9-0 S Whitworth 9/1: 00: No show: see 497.   00
--   WIND OF PEACE [18] 2-8-11 N Connorton 8/1: 0: Prom early on racecourse debut: half
sister to very useful stayer Prince Of Peace: may need further.   00

571 Stillman [17] 9-0	-- Be My Prospect [14] 9-0	
197 La Verte Gleam [13] 8-11		450 Leven Lass [20] 8-11
317 Deftly [7] 8-11	571 Force Majeure [10] 9-0	
206 Knowles Bank [4] 9-0	415 Public Praise [1] 9-0	523 Star Play [5] 9-0
-- Straight Edge [11] 9-0		-- Madame Laffitte [19] 8-11
-- Step By Step [3] 9-0		

20 ran   3,2,½,1½,2   (Red Lion Inn & Motel Ltd)   C Tinkler Malton, Yorks

742 SPRINT HANDICAP (0-50) 3YO+   £4103   5f   Firm 07 +29 Fast   [50]

+550 PHILIP [10] (N Tinkler) 4-9-10(bl)(10ex) Kim Tinkler[7] 13/8 fav: -000311: 4 b g Kala
Shikari - Canteen Katie (Kings Troop): Very useful gelding who is in excellent form: readily
defied a 10lbs penalty in a fast run h'cap at Redcar May 27: last time out won impressively
at York: in '85 won h'caps at Doncaster, Haydock & Thirsk: winning 2yo at Hamilton: equally
eff over 5/6f: acts on firm & soft grnd & on any trk.   59
626 RAMBLING RIVER [4] (W Stephenson) 9-8-12(vis) M Hindley[3] 7/1: 0010-02: Sn prom: gd
effort: see 626.   40
418 SPACEMAKER BOY [7] (R Nicholls) 6-9-0 N Howe 6/1: -241003: Led/dsptd lead: ran well.   38
606 THRONE OF GLORY [3] (D Chapman) 5-8-11 S Keightley 10/1: 0-00004: Nearest fin: best
effort this season: in '85 was trained by C Brittain, best effort when 3rd in a valuable
h'cap at Newbury: winner 3 times in '83: eff at 6f on a stiff trk: likes gd & firm grnd.   34

428 TOBERMORY BOY [1] 9-9-3 D Mckeown 5/1: 0002-00: Al there: btr effort: in '85 won a
h'cap at Nottingham: in '84 won at Doncaster and again at Nottingham: equally eff over
5/6f: probably acts on any grnd: likes a gall trk & carries weight well.   38
--   **CELTIC BIRD** [8] 6-7-11 A Mackay 10/1: 34000-0: Led/dsptd lead: btr for race: in
'85 won a fast run h'cap at Thirsk: in '84 won at Haydock: in '83 won 3 times: very eff at
5f: acts on gd/firm & soft & likes to force the pace.   17
--   **SHOW HOME** [11] 4-8-13 M Miller 5/1: 2-233-0: Fin 7th on seasonal debut: lightly raced
in '85, but showed fair form: winning 2yo at Leicester: eff over 5f, stays 6f: acts on
fast ground.   00
--   **Carpenters Boy** [5] 7-11   412 **Gentileschi** [2] 8-8
--   **Lady Cara** [12] 7-10   165 **Chaplins Club** [6] 9-12
11 ran   2½,1½,nk,¾,½,1½   (D Marley)   N Tinkler Malton, Yorks

---

743   REDCAR AMATEUR RIDERS STAKES   £1392   1m 4f Firm 07 -33 Slow

542 TAXIADS [10] (C Nelson) 4-11-7 Miss J Allison[7] 20/1: 0200-01: 4 b c Radetzky -
Florabette (Floribunda): Led 2f out and held on well in an amateur riders stakes at Redcar
May 27: first success on the Flat though did win over hurdles this Winter: half brother to
several winners: eff over 12f, stays 2m well: acts on any going & on any trk.   42
--   **HERRADURA** [6] (M Prescott) 5-11-7 Maxine Juster 7/1: 13042-2: Sustained chall final
1f: just held: most consistent in this type of race in recent seasons: in '85 won at
Pontefract & Thirsk & in '84 won 7 times: eff over 10/12f & stays 2m well: acts on gd &
firm grnd & on any trk, though does seem fav by a sharp one: genuine sort who carries
weight well.   42
375 CADMIUM [7] (P Cole) 4-11-7 Mr T T Jones 5/4 fav: 331-303: Led over 3f out: btr in 214.   35
519 CASTLE POOL [2] (D Gandolfo) 4-11-7 Elizabeth Gandolfo[5] 20/1: -04: Ran on same pace:
better effort: half brother to very useful miler Spanish Pool: last season trained in
Ireland and won at Naas: stays 12f well: seems suited by fast grnd & a stiff trk.   33
419 ANNIE RA [8] 4-11-4 Mr R Bevan[5] 33/1: 0-00-00: Some late prog: stays 12f: acts
on firm grnd & on a gall trk.   25
629 MIN BALADI [12] 4-11-7(BL) Mr T Easterby 7/2: 411-320: Bl first time: btn 2f out
and ran disapp: much btr over this trip in 629: see 410.   23
519 **Walter The Great** [9] 11-7   519 **Pinctada** [11] 11-7
--   **Noble Jack** [1] 11-7   519 **Pontyates** 0 11-7   432 **Aylesfield** [4] 11-7(BL)
282 **Greenacres Girl** (5) 11-4
12 ran   hd,7,2,5,5,2½   (Silux UK Ltd)   C Nelson Lambourn, Berks

---

744   MALCOLM WINTERS MAIDEN STAKES 3YO   £934   1m 3f Firm 07 -06 Slow

--   **BISHAH** [6] (H Cecil) 3-8-11 W Ryan 15/8 fav: 2-1: 3 gr f Balzac - Paaora (Sea Hawk II):
Useful filly: well bckd first time out and led over 2f out, readily in a 3yo maiden at
Redcar May 27: narrowly btn by Mount Martha in a fillies maiden at Goodwood on sole start
last season: stays 11f well: acts on fast grnd & on any trk: has a gd turn of foot and
should win more races.   55
597 MOUNT OLYMPUS [1] (J Watts) 3-9-0 N Connorton 11/4: 04-032: No ch with winner: see 597.   43
448 SPARTAN VALLEY [9] (B Hills) 3-9-0 B Thomson 9/2: -0-23: Ran well: stays 11f: see 448.   42
581 ENZELIYA [11] (R J Houghton) 3-8-11 K Darley 4/1: 3-44: Ran on same pace: stays 11f:
better when making the running in 581 (10f).   35
--   **DEPUTY MONARCH** [2] 3-9-0 M Fry 33/1: 040-0: Led over 3f out: btr for race: lightly
raced last season: should be suited by middle dists: acts on firm & yld grnd & on a gall trk.   36
--   **DENALTO** [5] 3-9-0 D Leadbitter 50/1: 00-0: Unfancied though was close up most
of way: showed little in his 2 starts last season: seems suited by fast grnd.   26
--   **State Jester** [3] 9-0   218 **Bitofagirl** [10] 8-11   -- **Red Breeze** [8] 9-0
322 **Spansyke** [7] 9-0   --   **Only Flower** [4] 8-11
11 ran   10,½,2½,1½,8   (Prince A Faisal)   H Cecil Newmarket

---

745   FRED ANDERSON HANDICAP (0-35) 3YO+   £1928   1m 1f Firm 07 -03 Slow   [34]

413 ATOKA [17] (Lord J Fitzgerald) 4-9-5 P Darcy 14/1: -0001: 4 b f Kaiseradler -
Ambivalenz (Orsini): Dropped in class & ran on well to lead close home in a h'cap at Redcar
May 27: ex German filly who stays 9f well: acts on fast grnd & on a gall trk.   34
--   **RABIRIUS** [2] (Denys Smith) 5-9-10 B Thomson 7/1: 0-010-2: Led below dist: gd seasonal
debut: lightly raced last season, when narrowly defying top weight in a Carlisle h'cap: also
a dual winner over hurdles: stays 9f well: acts on gd & firm grnd & is well suited by
a gall trk.   34
606 DOMINION PRINCESS [12] (P Rohan) 5-8-3 J Quinn[5] 11/2 Jt fav: 000-443: Fin well:
stays 9f: see 310.   10
611 STARS DELIGHT [14] (W Storey) 4-7-13(3ow) S Whitworth 7/1: 030-234: Al up there: see 611 05
*620 **SNAKE RIVER** [6] 4-9-2(7ex) W Hayes[7] 16/1: 1-43310: led over 2f out: in gd form: see 620 20
609 ELARIM [3] 7-9-8 C Coates[5] 6/1: 010-000: Front rank till dist: quite useful on his
day: won h'caps at Beverley & Redcar last season: eff over 1m & stays 11f well: best form
on fast grnd: carries weight well & goes well for an app.   19

REDCAR   Tuesday May 27th - Cont'd

-611 PERSHING [10] 5-8-10 M Miller 11/2 jt fav: 100-020: Much btr over 1m in 611 (gd).   00
609 NIGHT WARRIOR [13] 4-9-3 J Bleasdale 7/1: -004030: Btr on gd ground in 609 (10f):see 238 00
429 Sillitoe [5] 9-3   611 Glenderry [16] 8-8(bl)
310 Kamaress [11] 8-6   9   Swiftspender [15] 7-12
--   Sean Be Friendly [4] 7-8   689 Henrys Place [9] 8-6
547 New Barnet 0 8-8   --   Ravens Peak 0 8-6   259 Thirteenth Friday [7] 7-11
17 ran   2,1½,½,1,4,shhd,½   (Richard Kaselowsky)   Lord J Fitzgerald Newmarket

---

BRIGHTON   Wednesday May 28th   Lefthanded, Sharpish Undulating Track

746 SHOREHAM FILLIES 2YO STAKES   £1796   5f   Good/Firm 22 -50 Slow

533 BASTILLIA [3] (D Arbuthnot) 2-8-8 J Reid 14/1: 001: 2 b f Derrylin - Liberation
(Native Prince): Impr with ev race, smartly away & made virtually all to win a slowly run
2yo fillies stakes at Brighton May 28: half sister to several winning sprinters: eff over
5f: acts on fast grnd & is well suited by a sharpish trk: clearly suited by forcing tactics.   46
--   LADY BEHAVE [4] (R Hannon) 2-8-8 S Cauthen 9/4: 302: Ex Irish filly who led briefly
around ½way & kept on nicely: placed behind Keen Cut on her debut at Leopardstown in Mar:
acts on gd/firm & soft grnd & seems to have no trk preferences.   42
482 BLUE TANGO [5] (D Laing) 2-8-8 R Curant 13/2: 243: Mkt drifter: al up there &
acts on fast grnd: acts on any trk: best on soft in 311.   36
417 TANGALOOMA [6] (L Piggott) 2-8-8 W R Swinburn 11/8 FAV: 34: Heavily bckd: had ev ch
though failed to impr on her promising debut on similar grnd in 417.   30
497 LOMA BREEZE [1] 2-8-8 P Cook 9/1: -300: No threat: btr over this C/D in 345 (gd).   22
--   BAY WONDER [2] 2-8-8 D Gibson 9/1: 0: No threat after a slow start, though should
impr for this initial outing: speedily bred filly who fetched 3,000 gns as a yearling: acts
on gd/firm grnd.   16
197 Debach Deity [7] 8-8
7 ran   1½,2,2½,4,2,8   (M J Peters)   D Arbuthnot Compton, Berks

747 CLAYTON HANDICAP 3YO 0-60   £3056   7f   Good/Firm 22 -09 Slow   [60]

414 VERDANT BOY [10] (M Stoute) 3-9-7 W R Swinburn 7/2: 03-31: 3 br g Green Dancer -
Favourite Prospect (Mr Prospector): Dropped in class & comfortably defied top weight in a
h'cap at Brighton May 28, led dist and sn clear: earlier placed behind the smart Barley Bill
and also showed promise on both his starts last season: very eff over 7/8f: acts on firm
& yld grnd & on any trk: carries weight well.   68
478 HYMN OF HARLECH [2] (G Pritchard Gordon) 3-8-11 G Duffield 3/1 FAV: 00-0032: Kept on
well, though no ch with easy winner: gd form: see 478.   49
703 ARCTIC KEN [5] (C Nelson) 3-7-12(7ex) S Dawson(3) 5/1: 0-01103: Quick reapp: led
2f out: remains in gd form: see 540.   35
*451 MR KEWMILL [4] (M Tompkins) 3-7-7(1oh) R Morse(3) 13/2: 00-3014: Another gd effort.   28
427 PULHAM MILLS [7] 3-7-8(bl)(1ow)(1oh) A Mackay 14/1: 00-0000: Made most: see 427 & 54.   22
--   PINSTRIPE [3] 3-8-7 R Cochrane 20/1: 0330-0: Late prog & btr for race: rated 44
when placed behind Bonhomie & Kudz in a Yarmouth maiden last season: stays 7f well: acts
on gd & firm grnd & on any trk.   32
514 DARTIGNY [6] 3-8-10 S Whitworth 10/1: 01-00: Fin 7th: acts on gd/firm: see 514.   00
277 SWEET DOMAIN [9] 3-9-1 W Carson 9/1: 0320-00: No threat in 8th: see 277.   00
534 Light Hills [1] 8-0   496 Mudisha [8] 8-12
10 ran   4,½,1,4,2,1   (Sheikh Mohammed)   M Stoute Newmarket

748 FLANAGAND AND ALLEN H'CAP 0-50   £2939   6f   Good/Firm 22 +12 Fast   [48]

566 KORYPHEOS [2] (S Dow) 7-9-3 P Tulk 5/1: 00-0021: 7 b g He Loves Me - Silly Song
(Silly Season): In gd form, led dist for a ready win in a fast run h'cap at Brighton May 28:
just pipped by King Of Speed in a similar race over 7f here recently: last season won a
fast run h'cap at Newmarket and in '84 won twice on that stiff trk, & also at Salisbury:
eff over 7/8f: acts on any grnd & on any trk.   48
508 DELAWARE RIVER [6] (B Gubby) 4-7-12 A Mcglone 33/1: 4000-02: Outsider though fin
in gd style & seems to be returning to the form which won him a maiden at Folkestone last
season (rated 30): eff over 6f on fast & yld grnd: likes a sharpish, undulating trk.   23
499 REAR ACTION [1] (R Smyth) 6-8-6(bl) R Curant 8/1: 001-003: Never nearer after a
slow start: returning to form: last backend won a fast run h'cap at Lingfield, earlier
successful over 1m here: very eff over 6/8f: acts on gd & firm grnd & on any trk, though
is well suited by a sharpish one, especially Lingfield & Brighton.   30
508 SHADES OF BLUE [11] (M Blanshard) 5-8-4 N Adams 14/1: 00-2004: led after ½way: best
effort since 160.   25
616 AMEGHINO [5] 6-9-8 R Wernham 10/3 FAV: 00-0040: No extra dist: best in 616: see 192.   41
550 KELLYS ROYALE [4] 4-9-10 I Johnson 9/1: 00-0000: Btr over 5f in 550 (gd).   39
649 XHAI [8] 4-9-0 M Rimmer 7/1: -402020: Never dngr: see 649.   00
508 EXERT [7] 4-7-13 B Crossley 4/1: 0-34440: Fin 8th: better in 508: see 114.   00

250

--   DOWNSVIEW [10] 4-9-0 P Waldron 8/1: 00000-0: Well bckd on reapp: led over ½way:
sn dropped out: course specialist who won 3 times on this sharpish trk last season, incl
first time out, and has yet to win on any other course: equally eff over 5 & 6f: acts on
firm & gd grnd & is best with front runninng tactics, looks well h'capped on his best form.   **00**
495 Majors Review [3] 8-4   -- Catman [9] 7-7(bl)(1oh)
11 ran   2,nk,1,¾,1½,¾,2   (C Papaioannou)   S Dow Bramley, Surrey

749 SEAFORD SELLING STAKES 3YO   £853   1m   Good/Firm 22 -42 Slow

431 MIAMI BLUES [3] (M Francis) 3-8-11 Paul Eddery 5/1: 000-001: 6 b f Palm Track -
Blue Empress (Blue Cashmere): Dropped in class & proved an easy winner, led below dist &
sn clear in a 3yo seller at Brighton May 28 (bought in 2,600 gns): no worthwhile form last
season: stays 1m well: seems suited by fast grnd & a sharpish trk.   **24**
620 THE UTE [6] (L Bower) 3-9-0(bl) R Guest 5/1: 00-0202: Again ran well here: see 564.   **14**
177 FLEUR DE THISTLE [4] (A Davison) 3-9-0 J Reid 14/1: 000-003: First signs of form:
led 1m on fast grnd & seems suited by a sharpish trk.   **12**
620 FIRST ORBIT [5] (M Mccourt) 3-9-0 R Wernham 9/2: 00-0204: Led/dsptd lead over ½way.   **10**
620 BLUE STEEL   [9] 3-8-11 S Whitworth 5/2 FAV 000-000:Led over 3f out, eased when hdd:
acts on firm & yld grnd: see 620.   **00**
--   SPLENDID MAGNOLIA [10] 3-9-0 P Simms(7) 25/1: 00000-0: Ran on too late: no form in '85. **00**
346 THE TENDER MATADOR [8] 3-9-0 P Waldron 6/1: 010-000: Last season won a seller at
Yarmouth: stays 6f well: acts on gd & soft grnd.   **00**
--   BLUE FANTASY [9] 3-8-11 R Carter(5) 8/1: 300-0: Led/dsptd lead to ½way: lightly raced
last season: showed gd early speed on final start and may do btr over sprint distances.   **00**
346 Tinsel Rose [12] 8-11
9 ran   5,1,1,5,2,1½   (Mrs Merrick Francis)   M Francis Lambourn, Berks

750 CHANNEL HANDICAP   0-50   £2565   1m 2f   Good/Firm 22 +02 fast   [39]

--   REDDEN [11] (M Bolton) 8-9-0 S Cauthen 15/2: 14000-1: 8 ch g Red God - Portden
(Worden II): First time out, led below dist and ran on well to win a h'cap at Brighton May
28: lightly raced over hurdles this Winter: last season won h'caps at Lingfield & Epsom:
in '84 won over this C/D & todays success was his 5th here: very eff over 10f: acts on
gd & firm grnd & carries weight well: best form on
switchback tracks.   **32**
636 MARSOOM [9] (H Beasley) 4-7-11 R Morse(5) 33/1: 10-0002: Ran on well and just held:
last season won a seller at Salisbury over this trip: acts on gd & firm grnd & on any trk:
seems to be returning to form.   **14**
569 LONGSTOP [5] (P Makin) 4-8-9 T Williams 8/1: 34-3003: Fin strongly, not btn far:
loves this sharp trk: see 179.   **25**
618 DERBY DAY [2] (D Wilson) 5-7-13(bl) C Rutter(5) 6/1: 030-004: Just failed to make
all: employed similar front running tactics when winning this same race last year: suited
by 10f on a sound surface: best with front running tactics on a sharpish trk.   **15**
532 PELLINCOURT [7] 4-8-6 P Robinson 4/1 FAV: 0-40020: Not btn far: gd effort: see 532.   **20**
310 BWANA KALI [14] 4-9-0(BL) R Cochrane 14/1: 0-43300: Bl first time: ran on too late.   **28**
*566 KING OF SPEED [1] 7-8-9(5ex) S Dawson(3) 8/1: 0-10410: Best over 7f here in 566.   **00**
532 DANCING BARRON [3] 5-9-1 B Rouse 10/1: 004-000: Nicely bckd though no threat: won
a similar race at Kempton last season: won on this course in '83: eff over 10/12f: acts
on gd & firm grnd & is suited by a sharpish trk.   **00**
652 EVROS [13] 4-9-10 R Hills 10/1: 4-00040: Can do much btr: see 403.   **00**
652 KALA NASHAN [8] 4-8-6 A Mcglone 8/1: 20-0030: Btr with some give: see 652.   **00**
453 Bel Oscar [10] 9-10   419 Jenny Wyllie [6] 7-11   --   Young Daniel [12] 9-4
511 Toda Forca Avanti [4] 8-5(2ow)   343 Trumps [15] 7-7(1oh)
15 ran   ½,½,shhd,½,hd,1   (John Honeysett)   M Bolton Felcourt, Sussex

751 REGENCY MAIDEN STAKES   £959   1m 4f Good/Firm 22 -05 Slow

648 ALDINO [12] (A Stewart) 3-8-5(bl) M Roberts 7/1: 00-001: 3 ch c Artaius - Allotria
(Red God): Fitted with bl when making all, gamely in a maiden at Brighton May 28: eff over 1m,
suited by 12f: acts on gd/firm & soft grnd & seems well suited by forcing tactics
on a sharpish trk.   **46**
--   GANOON [7] (P Cole) 3-8-5 T Quinn 3/1: 2200-2: Hmpd dist, ran on well: gd effort
on his seasonal debut: fin 2nd on his first 2 starts last season, notably behind Beldale Star
in a Salisbury maiden first time out: half brother to a couple of winners: stays 12f:
acts on gd/firm & yld grnd & on any trk: should find a race.   **42**
--   MISS SHIRLEY [13] (J Dunlop) 3-8-5(3ow) J Reid 12/1: 0-3: Ran well on seasonal debut,
beating her btr fancied stablemate decisively: stays 12f: acts on fast grnd & on a
sharpish trk.   **38**
351 BLUSHING SPY [8] (M Fetherston Godley) 3-8-5(BL) R Hills 50/1: -004: Hung left below
dist, no extra: however showed impr form here: half brother to very useful middle dist
winner Abu Kadra: acts on gd/firm grnd & on a sharpish track: bl. first time here.   **33**
512 SWISS NEPHEW [15] 3-8-5 W Carson 13/8 FAV: 00-30: Bumped below dist, not recover: btr512 **29**

595 THE BETSY [2] 4-9-5 A Mcglone 20/1: 000-040: Nearest fin & stayed 12f well: acts
on gd & fast grnd & on any trk.   25
595 FOURTH TUDOR [11] 4-9-8 W R Swinburn 7/1: -20: Fin 7th: btr in 595.   00
--   MELENDEZ [5] 3-8-7(2ow) G Starkey 7/1: -0: Active in mkt on debut: never dngr &
should do btr though this.   00
617 Broken Tackle [4] 9-8   595 Rivers Nephew [10] 8-5
176 Cluga Gurm [9] 9-8   --   Fred The Thread [14] 9-8
709 Janaab [6] 9-8   --   Grosvenor Court [1] 8-5
570 Turn For Thbetter [3] 8-5
15 ran   2½,2½,3,2½,1,nk   (A Boyd-Rochfort)   A Stewart Newmarket

---

Official Going Given as Good/Yielding

752 MAGIN TV STAKES 2YO   £5624   6f   Good/Soft 106 -08 Slow

*558 POLONIA [4] (J Bolger) 2-8-6 D Gillespie 4/5 FAV: 11: 2 b f Danizig - Moss (Round
Table): Smart, highly promising Irish filly: made almost all, easily in valuable 2yo stakes
at the Curragh May 24: first time out won in similar fashion at Leopardstown: eff at 6f,
should be suited by further: acts on gd & yld grnd & is not one to oppose lightly: Royal
Ascot bound.   70
638 FAIRWAY LADY [12] (D Hughes) 2-8-6 S Craine 14/1:   -0102: No ch with winner: but
another gd effort: see 638: stays 6f.   51
149 HARRY QUINN [13] (K Prendergast) 2-8-13 G Curran 8/1: 2213: Consistent: stays 6f:
last time out was an easy winner at Phoenix Park: acts on yld & heavy.   55
--   EVER SO GENTLE [8] (N Meade) 2-8-6 P V Gilson 20/1: 4: Stiff task on racecourse
debut: not disgraced.   40
--   ROCKFAST [14] 2-8-9 M J Kinane 10/1: 0: Racecourse debut & should impr.   41
--   SOUTH MEADOW [9] 2-8-6 C Roche 20/1: 0: Half sister to several winners.   30
*149 WITH GODS HELP [3] 2-8-13 Pat Eddery 9/2: 10: Disapp after 149 (5f, heavy).   00
11 ran   5,1,3,½,3   (H De Kwiatkowski)   J Bolger Ireland

753 GROUP 2 WINDFIELDS FARM GALLINULE STKS   £23100   1m 2f Good/Soft 106 -16 Slow

396 WELSH FANTASY [7] (C Collins) 3-8-7 P Shanahan 6/1: 210-021: 3 ch f Welsh Pageant -
Santarelle (Jim French): Smart Irish filly: nicely bckd, led well over 1f out, staying on
well by a nk in Gr.2 event at the Curragh May 24: winning 2yo at Phoenix Park: eff at
10f, looks sure to be suited by 12f: acts on gd & soft grnd.   73
384 HELLO ERNANI [5] (I Balding) 3-8-6(1ow) W R Swinburn 4/1: 03-2232: Well bckd & just
btn: most consistent & must lose his maiden tag soon: see 384, 60.   71
--   PACIFIC DRIFT [2] (B Kelly) 3-8-10 Y Saint Martin 15/2: 0-01013: Not btn far:
fine effort: last time out won over 10f at Phoenix Park: acts on gd & soft grnd.   74
559 NORTHERN DATE [10] (J Bolger) 3-8-10 D Gillespie 20/1: -41-004: Btn just over 1L in
close fin: best effort yet: winner at Leopardstown in Mar: stays 10f & acts on gd & heavy.   73
150 ALONE SUCCESS [8] 3-8-5 D Parnell 20/1: 34-2320: Ran well: see 150.   64
559 BANK STEP [3] 3-8-10 S Craine 14/1: 00: See 559.   65
395 EQUATOR [11] 3-8-5 Pat Eddery 2/1 FAV: -20: Disapp fav: much btr 395 (7f, yld).   00
12 ran   nk,½,nk,1½,2   (Mrs J Mullion)   C Collins Ireland

754 GROUP 1 GOFFS IRISH 1000 GUINEAS 3YO F   £78900   1m   Good/Soft 106 +08 Fast

373 SONIC LADY [3] (M Stoute) 3-9-0 W R Swinburn 4/1 Jt.FAV: 1-131: 3 b f Nureyev -
Stumped (Owen Anthony): Top class filly: al going well and led well over 1f out for an easy
win in Gr.1 Irish 1,000 Guineas at the Curragh May 24: first time out was an impressive
winner of Gr.3 Nell Gwyn Stakes at Newmarket: in between was an excellent 3rd in the 1,000
Guineas at Newmarket: runaway winner of Blue Seal Stakes (Listed) at Ascot on sole outing in
'85: very eff at 7f, stays 1m well: acts on firm & yld & a gall trk: not one to oppose lightly   88
*560 LAKE CHAMPLAIN [5] (D Weld) 3-9-0 D Parnell 20/1: --2-212: Fin in gd style & is
fast impr: should win more gd races: see 560.   80
467 ASTEROID FIELD [19] (B Hills) 3-9-0 B Thomson 7/1: 114-203: Ran a fine race: stays 1m.   80
*467 BAISER VOLE [8] (C Head) 3-9-0 G Moore 4/1 Jt.FAV: 131-014: Hmpd but appeared held
final 1f: fin 5th, placed 4th: another gd effort: see 467.   76
466 LIVING ROUGH [7] 3-9-0 R Carroll 20/1: 2-24D: Ev ch over 1f out: drifted right final
1f: fin 4th, placed 5th: fast impr: see 466.   78
470 BEES NEST [6] 3-9-0 D Manning 25/1:   4-130: Consistent filly: see 470.   71
560 GAILY GAILY [11] 3-9-0(bl) M J Kinane 10/1: -141-010: Never nearer 7th: see 560.   00
294 PARK EXPRESS [16] 3-9-0 D Gillespie 8/1: 02-130: Wknd over 1f out: see 148.   00
*394 KEMAGO [18] 3-9-0 D Hogan 10/1: -1-10: No show: stiff task: see 394.   00
467 TANOUMA [19] 3-9-0 Y Saint Martin 7/1: 1-300: Btr 467: see 232.   00
269 Carhue Lady 0 9-0   --   Fleur Royale 0 9-0(bl)
560 Calametta 0 9-0(bl)   466 Golden Oriole 0 9-0   560 Loud Applause 0 9-0
294 Sherkraine 0 9-0   472 Snowtop 0 9-0   --   Atlantic Dream 0 9-0
--   Cova Kestrel 0 9-0
19 ran   2,shhd,½,1,2,shhd   (Sheikh Mohammed)   M Stoute Newmarket

Official Going Given as Firm

755 PRIX SAINT ALARY GROUP 1 3YO FILLIES   £57185   1m 2f   Firm -

300 LACOVIA [5] (F Boutin) 3-9-2 F Head   --01-21: 3 b f Majestic Light - Hope For All
(Secretariat): Very smart French filly: led into str and drew right away for   an impressive
win in Gr.1 Prix Saint-Alary at Longchamp May 25: acts on hvy, but seems much btr on
fast grnd: eff at 10f, should stay 12f: acts on a gall trk: should win more gd races.   84
467 SECRET FORM [2] (P Bary) 3-9-2 A Badel   11-22: No ch with winner, but another
gd effort: stays 10f: acts on firm & soft grnd.   74
--   BARGER [1] (P Biancone) 3-9-2 C Asmussen 23-113:Ran well, but beat winner here earlier
in the season on her favoured soft grnd.   73
--   FABULOUS QUEEN [4] (C Head) 3-9-2 G Moore 1-14: Comfortable winner at Evry in
Apr: gd effort here.   72
288 CARNATION [3] 3-9-2 A Lequeux   0414-30: Never nearer after slow start: stays 10f well   72
300 GALUNPE [8] 3-9-2 J L Kessas   114-00: See 300.   71
--   QUEEN HELEN [6] 3-9-2 W Carson   21-0: Made her seasonal debut here, but no show:
btr for race: on final outing in '85 was a ready winner of a Listed race at Ascot: eff at
7f, seems sure to be suited by middle dists: acts well on gd & firm grnd.   00
--   Welcome Valentine 0 9-2   --   Haute Autorite 0 9-2
9 ran   4,shnk,¼,nose,nk   (G Oldham)   F Boutin France

756 PRIX DU CADRAN GROUP I 4YO+   £30110   2m 4f   Firm -

*390 AIR DE COUR [7] (P Biancone) 4-9-2 E Legrix   241-211: 4 b c Vigors (USA) -
Amya (Sanctus): Very smart French stayer: led over 1f out, staying on well in Gr.1 Prix
du Cadran at Longchamp May 25: last time out made ev yd in a Gr.2 event again at Longchamp:
in '85 won at Longchamp (2) and a Gr.2 event at Deauville: stays really well: acts on firm,
loves heavy grnd.   80
--   FONDOUK [4] (H Van De Poule) 5-9-2 G Guignard   00-4012: Kept on well & ran a
fine race: stays extreme distances: acts well on firm.   77
--   GREEN [5] (J Beguigne) 5-9-2 Y Saint Martin   020-313: Recent winner at Evry:
gd effort: stays 2½m well: likes fast grnd.   76
390 SOUTH GALE [3] (C Bartholomew) 6-9-2 A Lequeux   3020-44: Not btn far.   74
398 WAGONER [5] 6-9-2 J L Kessas   40-2220: --   73
360 SPICY STORY [1] 5-9-2 Pat Eddery   4214-30: Not btn far, but may not have stayed
this 2½m: can do btr: see 360.   73
6 ran   1½,½,1½,½,nk   (D Wildenstein)   P Biancone France

757 PRIX LA FORCE GROUP 3 3YO   £20005   1m 2f   Firm -

--   LOYAL DOUBLE [7] (P Biancone) 3-8-12 G Mosse   0-13121: 3 b c Nodouble - Saygood
(Royal Ascot): The pacemaker for Savoldo, but made ev yd & just held on in Gr.3 event at
Longchamp May 25: stays 10f: seems well suited by fast grnd.   74
--   ISTIKAL [4] (A De Royer Dupre) 3-8-9 Y Saint Martin   -212: Just failed to get up:
winner at St Cloud early in the month: acts well on fast grnd.   71
644 TAKFA YAHMED [10] (M Saliba) 3-8-12 G Guignard   40-2143: Another gd effort:
stays 10f: see 291.   70
--   MAJESTIC VOICE [1] (G Mikhalides) 3-8-9 C Asmussen   -314: Not btn far in 4th.   67
--   SAVOLDO [3] 3-8-9 E Legrix   -10: Strongly fancied, but fin 9th: first time out won
at Longchamp over 12f: half brother to top class Sagace: should do much btr than this.   60
11 ran   shhd,2,nose   (J T Lundy)   P Biancone France

Official Going Given as Good

758 SCHERPING RENNEN LISTED 3YO   £8475   5f   Good -

203 TARIB (H T Jones) 3-8-11 A Murray   1112-21: 3 ch f Habitat - Red Coral: Very useful filly: won a Listed race at Baden Baden May 24: in '85 completed a hat trick of wins
at Beverley, Catterick & Redcar: very eff over 5f: acts on firm & soft grnd & on any trk:
should win more races.   69
--   WITH HOPE   3-9-4 M Dureuil   : 4-2: Gd effort at the weights.   73
--   ALIAS ROCKET   3-9-0 L Mader . -3:   64
--   AUENLIEBE   3-8-5 H Remmert : -4:   53
12 ran   1,1½,½.   (Hamdan Al Maktoum)   H T Jones Newmarket

759   BADENER MEILE GROUP 3   £12712   1m   Good -

413   SARAB (P Cole) 5-9-7 R Quinn   0304-31: 5 b h Prince Tenderfoot - Carnival Dance:
Smart horse: led dist, staying on well in a Gr.3 event at Baden Baden May 25: most consistent
in '85 winning Listed races at Newcastle & Haydock: in '84 won at Goodwood, Doncaster,
Newmarket, Haydock & Beverley: very eff at 7f, stays 1m: acts on firm & soft grnd: usually
held up as he possesses a fine turn of foot: genuine sort.   80
--   LIRUNG (Germany) 4-9-9 G Bocksai   1311-12: Top German miler: stuck on well and
just btn: first time out winner at Cologne: winner 5 times in '85, incl German 2,000 Guineas:
very eff at 1m/10f, acts on gd grnd.   80
433   BOLD AND BEAUTIFUL (G Pritchard Gordon) 4-8-10 G Duffield   1D10-03: Not disgraced:
returning to form: useful filly, who in '85 won at Kempton, Goodwood & Warwick: also "won"
at Newcastle, but subs. disq: eff at 1m, stays 9f: acts on gd & firm grnd & on any trk:
genuine & consistent.   60
--   GRAUER WICHT (Germany) 5-9-0 P Schiergen   -4: --   59
392   SULAAFAH 4-9-7 A Murray   010-430: Fin 5th: see 5.   64
7 ran   ½,3½,2½,¾   (F Salman)   P Cole Whatcombe, Oxon

---

760   WALLY COOMES HANDICAP (0-50) 3YO   £2628   5f   Good/Firm 28 +04 Fast   **[49]**

418   LALESTON [3] (G Huffer) 3-8-5 M Miller 11/2: 0400-21: Led below dist for a comfortable
win in quite a fast run 3yo h'cap at Brighton may 29: last season won a fillies maiden at
Warwick: well suited by this minimum trip though should stay further: acts on gd/firm & yld
grnd & does well on a sharpish trk: can defy a penalty.   40
657   PLATINE [14] (R Simpson) 3-8-11 S Cauthen 16/1: 0-10002: Returned to form, running on
well under press: well suited by a sharpish, undulating trk: eff over 5/6f on gd/firm &
soft: see 111.   38
--   EXCLUSIVE CAT [15] (I Balding) 3-9-5 Pat Eddery 9/1: 4312-3: Gd seasonal debut:
should go close next time: last season won a small maiden at Windsor & was placed in her
other 3 starts: speedily bred filly who should stay 6f: acts on firm & yld grnd & on
any trk: genuine sort who carries weight well.   46
+670   CHAUTAUQUA [12] (P Haslam) 3-7-10 T Williams 11/4 FAV: 0-4214: Front rank, no
extra dist: acts on fast grnd: best out in front in 670.   21
593   FINDON MANOR [8] 3-8-0(BL) M Rimmer 33/1: 340-000: Bl first time: fin well & this
was an impr effort: twice placed over 6f on this sharp trk last season in maiden company:
suited by gd or faster grnd: runs well at Brighton.   23
507   HAIL AND HEARTY [4] 3-8-2 P Robinson 10/1: 00-0200: Led over ½way: best over 6f
here in 340.   20
529   RESTLESS RHAPSODY [5] 3-8-9(bl) S Whitworth 9/1: 134-240: Early speed: much btr in 246.   00
340   ALICE HILL [10] 3-7-13 C Rutter(5) 5/1: 040-000: Btn dist: twice successful over
this trip last season, before winning a nursery h'cap at Folkestone: eff over 5f & should
stay 6f: suited by fast grnd & a sharpish trk: can do much btr than this.   00
496   Sequestration [11] 7-11   284   Pendor Dancer [9] 7-12
545   Ardent Partner [1] 7-7   580   Northern Trust [7] 9-7
431   Astarte [6] 8-5   580   La Malmaison [13] 8-1   431   Jianna [2] 7-12
340   Fancy Pages [16] 7-13(1ow)
16 ran   2,shhd,1,½,2   (K J Mercer)   G Huffer Newmarket

761   E.COOMES APPRENTICE H'CAP (0-35)   £2103   1m 4f Good/Firm 28 -29 Slow   **[35]**

363   MILLERS TALE [4] (I Balding) 4-9-9 P Francis(5) 5/1: 002-201: 4 b c Mill Reef -
Canterbury Tale (Exbury): Led early in str for a comfortable win in an app. h'cap at
Brighton May 29: last season was an easy winner of a Bath maiden: well suited by 12f:
acts on gd/firm & heavy grnd and on any trk: carries weight well.   38
459   WALCISIN [1] (R Hannon) 3-7-7(1oh) A Lappin 14/1: 00-0002: Stayed on strongly over
this longer trip: gd effort: stays 12f: best form on fast grnd: acts on any trk.   22
349   PARANG [9] (P Walwyn) 5-8-10 A Corney(5) 6/1: 1230-03: Kept on well & not btn
far: clear of rem: last term won a h'cap at Bath and has been hurdling this Winter: stays
13f: acts on gd/firm & soft grnd & on any trk.   20
683   STARDYN [8] (P Mitchell) 4-8-2 P Simms 3/1: 00-0304: Much btr over this C/D in 569.   03
419   HOT BETTY [5] 6-7-11 A Geran 16/1: -300000: Well placed till home turn: see 28.   00
403   FULL OF DREAMS [7] 5-7-7(bl) G Bardwell 33/1: -000: Well btn: showed glimpses of
ability in '84 when 2nd in a Newcastle seller though has since been disapp: stays 10f:
acts on gd/firm & soft grnd & on any trk.   00
582   JAZAIR [2] 4-9-7 P Skelton(5) 5/2 FAV: 000-000: Sn led, held a clear advantage till
run in: last season won over this trip at Beverley: well suited by fast grnd: acts on
any trk.   00
569   TRAFFITANZI [10] 5-8-5(BL) P Mcentee(5) 8/1: --2-000: Close up over ½way: fin 8th.   00
343   Chalet Waldegg [6] 7-7   652   Bachagha [3] 8-4
10 ran   1,½,6,8,5   (Paul Mellon)   I Balding Kingsclere, Hants

762   E.COOMES FILLIES HANDICAP (0-60)   £3830   1m   Good/Firm 28 -01 Slow   [38]

499 GOLDEN SLADE [5] (M Mccourt) 4-9-1 A Tucker(7) 9/1: 114-001: 4 ch f Octavo - Eastern
Isle (Gulf Pearl): Gaining her 3rd win on this course, leading inside dist, readily in a
fillies h'cap at Brighton May 29: dual winner on this sharpish trk last season, when she
also won at Wolverhampton: eff over 7/8f: best form on fast grnd: acts on any trk though
does particularly well at Brighton.   34
162 BAG LADY [3] (P Walwyn) 3-9-1 Paul Eddery 5/1: 4034-32: Ran on well: gd effort: see 162.   44
481 FAIR COUNTRY [2] (D Elsworth) 4-9-9 P Mcentee(7) 16/1: 0300-03: Nearest fin after a
slow start: returning to form: last season won an app. h'cap at Newbury: eff over 7/8f:
acts on firm & yld grnd & on any trk.   36
623 ZINDELINA [9] (R Hannon) 3-8-7 S Cauthen 7/2 FAV: 440-204: Led over 2f out: see 505.   34
659 COSMIC FLIGHT [4] 3-7-12 W Carson 9/1: -103340: Early ldr: hmpd below dist & not
recover: hasn't run a bad race since winning in 67.   23
481 DOLLY [7] 4-8-13 P Cook 4/1: 0-004D0: Stayed on much too late: see 481 & 344.   11
--   BLACK SOPHIE [8] 3-8-12 S Whitworth 8/1: 14303-0: Led 3f out: wknd into 7th: surprise
first time out winner of a Newbury maiden last season & subs. ran well to be placed in
gd class nurseries: stays 7f well: acts on gd & firm grnd & on any trk: btr for race.   00
--   ASTICOUR [6] 3-9-10 Pat Eddery 13/2: 2124-0: Led/dsptd lead for 6f: eased when btn
and will be btr for this run: useful filly who made all in a stakes race at Windsor last
season, and made the frame in her other 3 starts: very eff over 7f & sure to stay 1m:
acts on gd/firm & yld grnd & on any trk.   00
668 THATCHVILLE [1] 4-8-11(BL) G Starkey 8/1: 0-04400: Longer trip: made most over ½way.   00
9 ran   2½,nk,nk,1,8   (M McCourt)   M Mccourt Letcombe Regis, Oxon

763   E.COOMES SELLING STAKES 2YO   £808   5f   Good/Firm 28 -44 Slow

533 GOOD TIME GIRL [1] (R Hannon) 2-8-8 A Mcglone 3/1: 01: 2 b f Good Times - Inca Girl
(Tribal Chief): Dropped in class & nicely bckd when showing a gd turn of foot to lead close
home in a 2yo seller at Brighton May 29 (no bid): should stay another furlong: acts on fast
grnd & on a sharpish trk.   24
502 ROMANY LAD [6] (W Turner) 2-8-11 B Rouse 9/2: 02: Just failed to make all: btr
effort from this speedily bred colt: seems suited by fast grnd & a sharpish trk.   24
200 PIPERS ENTERPRISE [2] (W Holden) 2-8-11 R Morse(5) 8/1: 03: Eased in class: had
ev ch: seemed btr suited by todays faster grnd: acts on a sharp trk: see 200.   17
415 RING DANCE [5] (R Nicholls) 2-8-8 N Howe 6/4 FAV: 004: Heavily bckd: acts on gd/firm.   10
502 VALDOSTA [4] 2-8-8 R Hills 13/2: 00300: Led/dsptd lead till dist: best in 337.   04
497 GREY ROD [3] 2-8-11 R Mcghin 12/1: 00: Al behind and seems moderate.   03
6 ran   ¾,2½,1½,2½,1½   (D O'Brien)   R Hannon East Everleigh, Wilts

764   E.COOMES SENIOR CITIZENS STAKES 3YO   £2813   7f   Good/Firm 28 +02 Fast

527 DALLAS [7] (L Cumani) 3-9-0 Pat Eddery 10/11 FAV: -021: 3 gr c Blushing Groom -
Flordelisada (Drone): Useful colt: heavily bckd when leading inside dist, easily in a 3yo
stakes at Brighton May 29: earlier just failed to justify fav. when btn by Absheer in a
Pontefract maiden: very eff over 7/8f: acts on gd/firm & soft grnd & on any trk: well
regarded colt who should supplement this win.   55
593 MAWSUFF [2] (H Thomson Jones) 3-9-0 A Murray 11/2: -02: Tried to make all, comfortably
held by winner though did beat rem decisively: stays 7f well: acts on gd/firm grnd & on
any trk: on the up grade & should be winning soon.   48
498 RUE ST JACQUES [1] (D Arbuthnot) 3-9-0 S Cauthen 9/1: 0-33: Ran on in gd style &
sure to be suited by further: acts on fast grnd: can continue to impr: see 498.   42
465 SURE LANDING [6] (C Nelson) 3-9-0 J Reid 16/1: -04: Al up there & showed considerable
impr here: eff over 7f on fast grnd: acts on a sharpish trk.   37
501 JAAZIEL [3] 3-9-0 T Quinn 50/1: -00: On the up grade: acts on fast grnd & on
a sharpish trk.   29
--   UMBELATA [4] 3-9-0 R Weaver 50/1: -0: Outsider: stayed on well from ½way & should
do btr next time: acts on gd/firm grnd & on a sharp course.   26
402 ORANGE DALE [10] 3-9-0 P Waldron 50/1: 0-00: Late prog into 7th: btr effort
from this half brother to useful middle dist. winner Prime Assett: acts on gd/firm grnd.   00
*528 ASIAN CUP [15] 3-9-8 G Starkey 5/1: 02-10: Disapp 8th: much btr over 1m in 528 (soft).   00
501 BASICALLY BETTER [12] 3-8-11 Paul Eddery 10/1: 20-40: Fin 9th: can do btr: see 501.   00
--   Alburuj [14] 9-0   512 Lightning Byte [8] 9-0
658 Chardonnay [11] 8-11   500 Girdle Ness [9] 8-11   423 Mahabad [5] 8-11
500 Porte Dauphine [16] 8-11   --   Sheer Class [13] 8-11
501 Spanish Intent [17] 8-11
17 ran   1½,3,2½,4,½   (Richard I Duchossois)   L Cumani Newmarket

765   CATFORD MAIDEN STAKES 3YO   £959   1m 2f   Good/Firm 28 +01 Fast

273 LANDSKI [5] (R Simpson) 3-9-0 S Whitworth 7/2: -401: 3 b c Niniski - Misacre
(St Alphage): Useful colt: well bckd when leading below dist, ridden out in a 3yo maiden at
Brighton May 29: half brother to useful 6/8f winner Amarone: eff over 1m, stays 10f well:
acts on firm & soft grnd & does well on a sharpish trk.   50

BRIGHTON   Thursday May 29th   - Cont'd

613 FRANGNITO [12] (R Johnson Houghton) 3-9-0 S Cauthen 12/1: 0-4002: Game effort and made
most i: comfortably beat rem & should win a race soon if reproducing this form: suited
by forcing tactics: acts on fast grnd: goes well on sharp track: prob. stays 12f: see 328.   48
402 ADMIRALS ALL [14] (J Winter) 3-9-0 Pat Eddery 6/1: 00-03: Early ldr, kept on well
showing impr form: half brother to smart miler Larionov: stays 10f on fast grnd.   38
494 MIRAGE DANCER [1] (R Smyth) 3-9-0 P Robinson 10/3 FAV: 04-0234: Twice disapp since 36237
--   LORD IT OVER [3] 3-9-0 G Starkey 5/1: -0: Mkt drifter on debut: fair effort &
likely to impr: should stay further: acts on fast grnd & on a sharpish trk.   35
218 FAST REALM [4] 3-9-0 T Quinn 12/1: -00: Btr effort from this half brother to
several winners, incl very useful 8/12f winner Jalmood: seems suited by fast ground.   32
619 DEAFENING [6] 3-9-0 M Roberts 16/1: 0-00: Wknd into 7th: acts on gd/firm grnd.   00
422 SOKOLOVA [18] 3-8-11 J Reid 16/1: 30-000: Fin 8th: best effort last season when
3rd to Tucson Princess in a Yarmouth maiden (rated 50): on breeding should be well suited
by this trip: acts on gd/firm & yld grnd.   00
486 HOTU [7] 3-9-0 W Carson 10/1: -4P: Broke down inside dist, destroyed: see 486.   00
--   Kitty Clare [11] 8-11   484 Home Or Away [16] 9-0 498 Sir Speedy [10] 9-0
--   Soft Shoe Shuffle [2] 9-0   --   Ashshafak [9] 8-11
539 Bet Oliver [17] 8-11   250 Fidaytik [15] 8-11   --   Keep Hoping [13] 8-11
17 ran   ½,6,½,1,1½   (Broderick Munro-Wilson)   R Simpson Lambourn, Berks

CATTERICK   Thursday May 29th   Lefthand, Very Sharp Track

Official Going Given as Firm

766 EBF STAPLETON STAKES 2YO O   £1204   5f   Firm 15 -17 Slow

--   ECHOING [1] (J Watts) 2-8-8 N Connorton 6/1: 1: 2 b f Formidable - Siren Sound
(Manado): First time out, al prom and led inside final 1f, driven out in a 2yo stakes at
Catterick May 29: eff at 5f: should be suited by further: acts on firm grnd & a sharp trk.   39
627 AIR OF SPRING [2] (D Barron) 2-8-8 R Cochrane 3/1: 0302: Made much: kept on well
and just btn: gd effort: acts on firm & yld: tried in bl last time but seems btr without:
acts on a sharp trk.   38
*415 THEKKIAN [4] (R Hollinshead) 2-9-4 S Perks 5/2: 13: Ev ch: acts on firm & yld & will
be suited by 6f: see 415.   40
*665 LINN ODEE [3] (M W Easterby) 2-9-1 T Lucas 7/4 FAV: 2314: Slow start proved costly.   27
--   ABSALOUTE HEAVEN [6] 2-8-8 D Nicholls 12/1: 0: Early speed: cost 3,200 gns and is
a speedily bred filly: half sister to a 2yo winner.   14
602 MERE MUSIC [5] 2-8-11 K Darley 33/1: 000: Rank outsider: behind ½way.   05
6 ran   hd,3,5,2½,4   (C C Campbell Golding)   J Watts Richmond, Yorks

767 PEN HILL CLAIMING STAKES 3YO   £998   1m 4f Firm 15 -18 Slow

517 FAST AND FRIENDLY [2] (R Hollinshead) 3-9-0 S Perks 3/1 FAV: 0-00431: 3 ch c Lord Gayle-
Raubritter (Levmoss): Led well over 1f out comfortably in a 3yo claimer at Catterick May 29:
first success: stays 12f well: acts on firm & soft grnd & on any trk.   28
318 TAP DUET [9] (M Naughton) 3-9-0(VIS) M Hills 7/1: 000-042: Has changed stables:
led after 1m: stayed: eff at 12f on firm & a sharpish trk.   24
631 ORIENTAL EXPRESS [3] (F Carr) 3-9-0 J Carr(7) 6/1: 00-0103: Never nearer: stays
12f, but best 487 (1m, heavy).   18
209 MISS BETEL [5] (J Harris) 3-8-11 M Birch 20/1: 000-04: Led 1m: first signs of form:
probably stays 12f: acts on firm & a sharp trk.   03
684 LADY OF HAMPTON [8] 3-8-7 S Morris 9/2: -40: Some late hdway: btr 684.   00
524 TARA DANCER [1] 3-9-3 C Dwyer 10/1: -000000: Held up: no show: in '85 made most to
win a nursery h'cap at Hamilton: eff at 1m: should stay further: best form on soft & hvy grnd.   00
356 HOLME ROOK [7] 3-8-11 E Guest(3) 15/2: -00: No threat.   00
185 WHITTINGHAM VALE [4] 3-8-11(BL) J Lowe 11/2: -300: Took a strong hold: wknd: best
first time out in 45 (C/D, yld).   00
35   Star Command [6] 8-8
9 ran   nk,3,6,1,5   (J T Lawlor)   R Hollinshead Upper Longdon, Staffs

768 HAWES HANDICAP 3YO 0-35   £1853   6f   Firm 15 -02 Slow   [40]

274 BLUE HORIZON [6] (W Jarvis) 3-8-9 R Cochrane 5/1: 1303-01: 3 b c African Sky - Blue
Nose (Windjammer): Appeared well h'capped and led inside the final 1f, under press in a
3yo h'cap at Catterick May 29: in '85 won at Folkestone: very eff at 6f: best on fast grnd
and a sharpish trk.   32
--   FELIPE TORO [1] (M H Easterby) 3-8-8(BL) M Birch 16/1: 00000-2: Bl first time on
seasonal debut: nearly made all: gd effort: showed some form in '85: acts on firm & yld
grnd & on any trk.   29
447 IMPERIAL SUNRISE [4] (M W Easterby) 3-8-8 T Lucas 12/1: 044-403: Al prom: likes a
sharp trk: see 309.   27
309 HAITI MILL [5] (W Wharton) 3-8-13 N Carlisle 8/1: 303-04: Nearest fin: running into form.

256

529 THE STRAY BULLETT [8] 3-7-12(bl) J Lowe 11/2: 30-0020: Sn prom: btr 529 (soft).   13
-670 WOW WOW WOW [9] 3-8-8 Kim Tinkler(7) 4/1 FAV: -310020: Well bckd: btr 670: see 237.   22
*529 BRIDGE OF GOLD [11] 3-8-11 G Duffield 5/1: 120-10: Fin 9th: much btr 529 (5f, soft).   00
671 Dancing Tom [10] 9-7(BL)   --   Bargain Pack [2] 7-12
677 Skybird [12] 9-1   608 Music Teacher [13] 8-0
11 ran   ¾,¾,shhd,1½,½   (G E K Teo)   W Jarvis Newmarket

769   MUKON MAIDEN STAKES   £728   1m 6f Firm 15 +06 Fast

613 THE PRUDENT PRINCE [7] (W Jarvis) 4-9-9 R Cochrane 11/10 FAV: 32-21: 4 b c Grundy -
Ragirl (Ragusa): Heavily bckd & led ½way, easily in quite a fast run maiden at Catterick
May 29: first time out a gd 2nd to Loch Seaforth at Beverley: lightly raced previously:
eff at 12/14f, should stay even further: acts on firm & yld grnd & on any trk.   48
--   IN DREAMS [11] (M Prescott) 3-8-5 G Duffield 7/1: 40-2: Kept on well on seasonal debut,
but no threat to winner: stoutly bred colt who stays this trip very well: acts on firm grnd.   39
430 GOODTIME HAL [4] (J Hindley) 3-8-5 M Hills 5/2: 0-43: Led to ½way: stays 14f: see 430.   34
720 QUEEN OF SWORDS [10] (R Hollinshead) 3-8-2 A Culhane(7) 14/1: 400-004: Never nearer
over this longer trip: acts on firm & yld: see 416.   15
648 STORM LORD [5] 3-8-5 J Bleasdale 33/1: 000-00: Some late hdway: best effort yet:
acts on firm grnd.   14
308 BILLIDOR [1] 4-9-9 M Birch 20/1: 0040-00: Wknd in str: maiden: showed some form
in '85: stays 14f but possibly best at 12f: acts on gd & firm grnd.   13
381 SAY SOMETHING [2] 3-8-2 J Lowe 10/1: 00-2200: Fdd in str: twice below form 123 (12f, he 00
194 Lineout Lady [3] 8-2   --   Fanny Robin [9] 8-2   --   Sians Pet [13] 8-2
164 One For The Ditch [14] 9-6   --   Gyps Gift 0 9-6
12 ran   2,3,10,3,1½   (J M Greetham)   W Jarvis Newmarket

770   WIN WITH THE TOTE MAIDEN STAKES   £1076   1m 4f Firm 15 +02 Fast

--   PLYMOUTH HOE [8] (L Cumani) 3-8-7 R Guest 5/2 FAV: -1: 3 b c Busted - Pluvial
(Habat): First time out, easy to back, but led final 1f, comfortably in a maiden at Catterick
May 29: stays 12f: acts on firm grnd & a sharp trk: should rate more highly.   40
669 MAJESTICIAN [7] (G Pritchard Gordon) 3-8-7 G Duffield 11/2: -002: Led over 4f out:
impr effort: stays 12f: acts on a sharp trk & firm grnd.   32
130 MADISON GIRL [4] (R Whitaker) 3-8-4 K Bradshaw(5) 10/1: 2300-03: Sn prom: ev ch:
seems to stay 1½m: best form on gd & firm grnd: acts on any trk, runs well at Beverley.   24
493 PERFECT DOUBLE [1] (W Pearce) 5-9-7 N Connorton 20/1: -32-004: Sn prom: fdd str:
in final outing in '85 fin 2nd in a seller at Edinburgh: stays 12f & acts on gd grnd.   16
--   THE HOUGH [11] 5-9-10 D Leadbitter(5) 33/1: -0: Never nearer on racecourse debut
at the age of 5: seems to stay 12f well: acts on firm grnd.   18
449 MOSSBERRY FAIR [6] 5-9-7 N Day 16/1: 000-000: Some late hdway: eff at 12f on
firm & soft grnd.   05
123 WRANGBROOK [9] 3-8-4 M Hills 11/4: 0-30: Well bckd, much btr 123 (heavy).   00
--   LA CAZADORA [13] 3-8-4 R Cochrane 7/1: -0: Mkt drifter & no show on racecourse debut:
should do better.   00
492 Shandon Bells [2] 9-10   --   Bombard [3] 9-10
--   Jupiters Gem [12] 9-7   449 Raisabillion [14] 9-10
--   Wongalilli [5] 9-7   448 Nicky Dawn [10] 9-7
14 ran   4,2½,4,nk,5   (Lady Drake)   L Cumani Newmarket

771   GRINTON STAKES 2YO   £1256   5f   Firm 15 -47 Slow

583 SANDALL PARK [3] (M W Easterby) 2-8-11 K Hodgson 4/11 FAV: 41; 2 br c Frimley Park-
Imacarboncopy (Iamacornishprince): Confirmed the promise of his debut, led inside the final
1f, comfortably in a slow run 3 horse 2yo stakes at Catterick May 29: promising 4th to
Sameek at York first time out: cost 11,000 gns: speedily bred colt who acts on firm & yld
grnd: no trk preferences: should win more races.   52
242 BLUEMEDE [1] (M Brittain) 2-9-9 K Darley 4/1: 11222: Made much: no ch with winner:
stiff task at the weights: see 77.   55
--   SWING SINGER [2] (J Watts) 2-8-11(BL) N Connorton 7/1: 3: Bl on racecourse debut:
nearest fin: showing some promise: should be suited by 5f: acts on firm grnd.   38
3 ran   2½,1½,   (Hippodromo Racing)   M W Easterby Sheriff Hutton, Yorks

772   TAN HILL HANDICAP 0-35   £1337   1m 4f Firm 15 -03 Slow   [26]

*541 SUPER GRASS [8] (S Mellor) 7-8-12(4ex) M Wigham 9/4 FAV: --0-311: 7 br g Thatch -
Pepi Image (National): In fine form and led well over 1f out, driven out close home in a
h'cap at Catterick May 29: last time out won a h'cap at Wolverhampton: lightly raced on the
Flat: in '82 won at Pontefract: useful hurdler: eff at 12f, stays 14f: acts on firm, likes
yld & soft grnd.   19
*675 NORDIC SECRET [2] (D Smith) 4-8-10(4ex) L Charnock 4/1: 00-0012: Made much: kept on
well & just btn: gd effort under penalty: acts on firm & yld grnd.   16
44 BUSTOFF [4] (S Hall) 6-8-10 K Hodgson 5/1: 0--0-23: Ev ch over 1f out: abs since 44:
acts on firm & yld.   13

629 EXCAVATOR LADY [3] (R Whitaker) 7-8-5(bl) K Bradshaw(7) 8/1: 303-004: Sn prom, ev ch. 04
449 STRING OF BEADS [9] 4-8-6 G Duffield 6/1: 200-000: Maiden: stays 12f: acts on any grnd. 00
592 MOULKINS [6] 4-8-11 Julie Bowker(7) 20/1: 000-00: Prom 7f: btr 592. 00
731 KADESH [7] 5-9-3(vis) I Johnson 8/1: 024-400: Wknd in str: best first time out in 92. 00
592 **Rapidan** [1] 9-4   541 **Wandering Walter** [5] 9-7
9 ran   nk,1½,2½,4,2½   (Mrs M Michael)   S Mellor Lambourn, Berks

---

Official Going Given as Good to Firm

773 EXNING CHURCH 1350TH ANNIV. STAKES 2YO   £3210   5f   Firm 00 +03 Fast

*383 NATURALLY FRESH [6] (J Winter) 2-9-1 W R Swinburn 8/13 FAV: 411: 2 b f Thatching -
Lady Gaylord (Double Jump): Smart filly: readily landed the odds when scoring a pillar-to-
post success in quite a valuable 2yo fillies race at Newmarket May 30: also made all over
the same C/D last time: cost only 6,000 gns as a yearling and is a bargain: very eff with
forcing tactics over 5f, should stay 6f: acts well on fast going, on a gall trk: hard to
beat in any company. 68
655 JAISALMER [10] (D Elsworth) 2-8-11 A Mcglone 16/1: 102: Kept on and a much btr
effort: clearly unsuited by heavy in 655: acts on firm & yld: see 350. 56
--   LASHING [3] (L Cumani) 2-8-8 Pat Eddery 9/1: 3: Showed plenty of promise on racecourse debut: cost almost $⅓m and is from a top class family which includes smart middle
dist. performer Ack Ack: sure to find a race soon, probably over 6f plus. 46
*655 TENDER TIFF [2] (M Mccormack) 2-8-13 S Cauthen 15/2: 14: Speed 4f & seems to act on
firm & heavy: see 655. 49
--   UN BEL DI [8] 2-8-8 R Hills 5/1: 0: No threat but
should impr for this first experience of racing: American bred filly. 39
--   DREAM LAUNCH [1] 2-8-8 G Baxter 50/1: 0: Pressed leaders till after ½way: cost $57,000:
impr likely. 39
--   Russian Waltz [7] 8-8   -- Flair Park [5] 8-8   -- Last Stand [9] 8-8
9 ran   3,1½,¾,1½,shhd,1,shhd   (G Shropshire)   J Winter Newmarket

774 COWLINGE SELLING STAKES 3YO   £1830   1m   Firm 00 -33 Slow

637 KEEP COOL [14] (P Kelleway) 3-8-11 S Cauthen 7/2 FAV: 3-34001: 3 ch f Northern
Treat - Douce Grece (Timmy My Boy): Dropped in class and led inside final 2f in a 3yo
seller at Newmarket May 30: placed in btr company last season: well suited by firm grnd
though also seemed to handle heavy: stays 1m well & likes a stiff trk. 26
424 COUNT ALMAVIVA [9] (M Blanshard) 3-9-0 N Adams 12/1: 00-0002: Al there: gd effort. 25
120 PASSION PLAY [5] (P Haslam) 3-9-0 T Williams 5/1: 003-03: Abs: made much: 3rd in
a seller over C/D on final outing in '85: acts on gd & firm grnd & stays 1m. 25
608 RED ZULU [6] (L Lightbrown) 3-9-0 M Hills 33/1: 3-00004: Best effort this season
from this maiden: may stay beyond 1m: acts on firm. 23
729 GARY AND LARRY [7] 3-9-0 G Starkey 10/1: 00-000: Fin well: needs further? see 729. 21
658 ROCKHOLD PRINCESS [10] 3-8-11 R Guest 20/1: 000-000: Never closer: first signs of
form and looks likely to be suited by 10f: acts on firm. 13
356 S S SANTO [8] 3-8-11 M Rimmer 9/2: 0-2200: Ev ch, fin 7th: best 169 (10f yld). 00
402 PRINCESS ANDROMEDA [2] 3-8-11 Pat Eddery 13/2: 0-00: Fin 8th: lightly raced. 00
423 Georgian Rose [13] 8-11   -- Golden Bourne [1] 9-0
--   Alice Holt [11] 8-11   213 Gavea [15] 8-11   -- Nelsonsuperyankee [12] 9-0
546 Shesingh [3] 8-11
14 ran   1½,shhd,¾,1,2½   (N Mandell)   P Kelleway Newmarket

775 FAMOUS GROUSE SCOTCH WHISKEY H'CAP 0-50 £3402   7f   Firm 00 +03 Fast   [46]

*247 HEAVY BRIGADE [2] (W O'gorman) 3-8-5 T Ives 4/1 FAV: -11: 3 ch c Hard Fought -
Victoria Pageant (Welsh Pageant): Unbtn colt who was strongly supported when landing his
2nd successive win in a h'cap at Newmarket May 20: led close home in a tight fin: first time
out winner of a maiden at Thirsk and unraced last season: eff 7f, stays 1m well: acts on
firm & yld & on any trk: the type to impr further & win more races. 48
636 MR ROSE [17] (R Hutchinson) 6-7-7(4oh) G French 20/1: 0-00042: Ran well at the weights,
keeping on final 1f: should find a race if dropped in class next time: see 636. 19
453 BOLD PILLAGER [3] (J Dunlop) 4-8-8 B Rouse 13/2: 020-03: Nicely bckd, prom; thro'out
and not btn far: lightly raced in '85 fin 2nd to Vin De France in a Kempton maiden on
firm grnd over 1m: not badly h'capped on that performance: should be winning soon. 33
573 OCTOBER [9] (R Armstrong) 4-10-0 W Carson 10/1: 000-004: Made much: winner at Goodwood
& Lingfield in '85 then rather lost his form: verv eff over 7f on a sharpish, undulating
trk: acts on gd & heavy. grand effort at the weights today. 52
441 NICORIDGE [12] 4-9-10 S Bridle(7) 20/1: 330-000: Ev ch: placed most outings last
term but somewhat frustrating and has yet to win: stays at least 1m. 42
453 BUNDABURG [11] 6-9-2 R Wernham 10/1: 31-0000: Possibly coming back to form: winner
at Bath, Sandown & Goodwood in '85: eff over 7f/1m on firm or yld going. 32

636   NEW CENTRAL [6] 4-8-1 N Adams 10/1: 400-000: Fin. 9th: btr 636.   00
445   Blaze Of Tara [1] 9-9(bl)   521   All Fair [5] 9-9
668   Baton Boy [15] 9-3   512   Pilfer [10] 8-1(BL)   578   Merry Measure [7] 8-6
--   Reindeer Walk [16] 9-10   566   Safe Custody [13] 8-9
--   Dealt [14] 7-9   534   Mitner [8] 7-7(4oh)   --   Winter Words [4] 7-7(3oh)
17 ran   ½,nk,nk,2½,1,1   (Mrs P L Young)   W O'gorman Newmarket

776   BBA QUEENSBURY FILLIES STAKES 3YO   £4201   6f   Firm 00 +15 Fast

214   METEORIC [8] (W Hern) 3-8-13 W Carson 7/4 FAV: 0120-01: 3 ch f High Line - Metair
(Laster Light): Smart filly: well bckd and was driven into lead final 1f in a minor race
for 3yo fillies at Newmarket May 30: winner of a fillies maiden over this C/D last season
when lightly raced: dam a very useful sprinter: eff at 6f, should stay at least 7f: acts
well on fast grnd & on a gall trk, particularly Newmarket.   65
264   ZALATIA [1] (W Jarvis) 3-9-0 B Rouse 12/1: 22-102: Prom, kept on well and is suited
by this stiff trk: eff 6f, probably btr over 7f & further: see 213.   61
431   BUTSOVA [3] (R Armstrong) 3-8-5 M Roberts 14/1: -03: Led/dsptd lead most: impr & should
have little difficulty in finding a maiden: see 431.   50
213   ROYAL NUGGET [9] (M Stoute) 3-8-5 W R Swinburn 2/1 : 322-04: Chall. 2f out, found
little and has disapp. both starts this term: see 213.   44
567   ANN AESTHETIC [4] 3-8-8 Pat Eddery 12/1: 0014-00: Seemed to run to her best and will
find an easier opportunity: see 567.   46
431   SOLO SINGER [10] 3-8-5 T Quinn 16/1: -040: Difficult task, not disgraced: see 431.   40
658   INDIAN SUMMER [7] 3-8-5 H Candy 15/2: 0-20: Ran poorly, much btr 658 (heavy).   00
567   Forlis Fair [6] 8-5   --   Danesmoor [11] 8-5   315   Nihad [2] 8-5
576   Grimesgill [5] 8-5
11 ran   1½,½,½,2,hd,1,2½   (K Abdulla)   W Hern West Ilsley, Berks

777   E.B.F. ASHLEY MAIDEN STAKES 2YO   £3548   6f   Firm 00 -13 Slow

--   ALBASAR [2] (P Walwyn) 2-9-0 M Hills 12/1: 1: 2 b c Roberto - Kiva (Tom Rolfe)
Made a winning racecourse debut, forging clear in the final 2f in a 2yo maiden at Newmarket
May 30: cost $200,000 and is out of the winning juvenile Kiva: eff 6f, sure to stay further:
goes well on firm grnd & a stiff trk: will win more races.   60
583   GOOD POINT [1] (J Hindley) 2-9-0 M Hills 33/1: 02: Made most, gd effort: cost I.R.
50,000: sprint bred: sure to pick up a maiden soon, possibly on a sharper trk.   54
--   BRAVE DANCER [8] (G Harwood) 2-9-0 G Starkey 9/2: 3: Gd finish from this half brother
to a winning French colt: will impr & win a race.   50
--   OUR ZOUZOU [6] (M Jarvis) 2-9-0 T Ives 33/1: 4: Prom thro'out: cost 54,000 gns:
should impr for this experiennce.   47
--   MAINTAIN [5] 2-9-0 Pat Eddery 10/11 FAV: 0: Prom most & will impr for this race:
half brother to a couple of juvenile winners incl the fairly useful Test Of Time: will do
btr next time.   44
--   MUSICAL BELLS [11] 2-9-0 B Crossley 33/1: 0: Likely to benefit from the outing.   41
--   FORESIGHT [10] 2-9-0 W R Swinburn 15/2: 0: Not recover from a slow start: cost
47,000 gns: on breeding will be well suited by much longer distances.   00
--   King Balladeer [9] 9-0   --   Highland Laird [3] 9-0
187   Father Time [4] 9-0   --   Vivaldi [7] 9-0
11 ran   2,1½,1,1,1   (Hamdam Al-Maktoum)   P Walwyn Lambourn, Berks

778   THURLOW HANDICAP STAKES (0-50)   £3173   1m 6f   Firm 00 -08 Slow   [48]

618   INSULAR [6] (I Balding) 6-10-0 Pat Eddery 7/4 FAV: 0421-31: 6 b g Moulton - Pas De
Deux (Nijinsky): Useful stayer: well bckd & led inside final 2f, comfortably in a h'cap at
Newmarket May 30: fit from a successful spell of hurdling and last season won again at
Newmarket & also at Ascot on the Flat: eff 12f, stays 2m: acts on any going but is well
suited by a stiff gall trk: genuine sort. carries weight well.   60
--   NEWSELLS PARK [9] (J Winter) 5-9-2 W R Swinburn 25/1: 312-P-2: Fin in gd style:
p.u. only outing last season but in '84 won at Beverley & was rated 55: well suited by fast
going & is eff over 12/14f: likely to stay 2m: well h'capped & will be hard to beat next time.   45
532   OTABARI [5] (P Cole) 4-9-2 T Quinn 16/1: 414-003: Prom thro'out: winner at Leicester
in '85 & Lingfield in '84: acts on gd & hvy going: stays at least 12f.   42
675   LEON [4] (N Tinkler) 4-8-11 Kim Tinkler(7) 10/1: 4-22024: Ev ch, not btn far and is
running well: see 80.   36
--   SPECIAL VINTAGE [12] 6-9-8 R Brown(7) 20/1: 02114/0: Tried to make all and this was
a fine comeback effort after being off the trk last season: in '84 won at Sandown & Redcar:
well suited by 2m & fast going: sure to run well next time.   46
532   OLD MALTON [1] 4-7-7(2oh) Dale Gibson(7) 10/1: 0-4-000: Prom most: very lightly
raced maiden.   11
629   AUCHINLEA [8] 4-9-5 S Cauthen 10/3: 1000-30: Wknd final 2f: btr 12f? see 629.   00
585   Cold Line [10] 9-0   58a   Peggy Carolyn [2] 9-5   590   Northern Ruler [7] 8-2
215   Stan The Man [3] 9-8   *282   Nikoola Eve [11] 8-8
12 ran   1½,3,1,½,6   (H M The Queen)   I Balding Kingsclere, Berks

259

Official Going Given as Good

779 ELMIRE MAIDEN 3YO FILLIES STAKES   £2180   1m 4f   Firm 18 - 34 Slow

551 SANTIKI [10] (M Stoute) 3-8-11 A Kimberley 4/11 FAV: 3-241: 3 ch f Be My Guest - Sairshea (Simbir): Smart filly, had an easy task & led approaching final 1f, readily in a 3yo fillies maiden at Thirsk May 30: in fine form this season, first time out fin 2nd to Gesedeh in a Pretty Polly at Newmarket & last time out fin 4th to Rejuvenate in Gr.3 Musidora Stakes at York: half sister to the smart Sheerwalk: eff at 10f, stays 12f well: acts on gd 7 firm grnd 7 on any trk: certain to win more good races.   55
505 SECRET WEDDING [2] (W Hern) 3-8-11 G Duffield 6/1: 310-232: Al prom, no ch with easy winner: another good run: stays 12f: should win soon: see 209.   45
--   GREAT EXCEPTION [6] (H Candy) 3-8-11 C Rutter(5) 10/1: 0232-3: Nearest fin on seasonal debut: prom effort: showed useful form as a 2yo: stays 12f: acts on firm & soft grnd & should find a maiden.   44
458 TORREYA [1] (J Hindley) 3-8-11 R Cochrane 20/1: -04: Led over 2f out: impr: stays 12f: acts well on firm grnd: see 458.   42
--   RIBO MELODY [4] 3-8-11 J Reid 100/1: 00000-0: Rank outsider: ran remarkably well and was btn in a seller as a 2yo: stays 12f: acts on yld, seems well suited by firm grnd.   35
--   MEGANS MOVE [9] 3-8-11 L Charnock 50/1: 004-0: Never nearer on seasonal debut: btr for race: on final outing in '85 fin 4th in a fillies maiden at Beverley: seems suited by 12f: acts well on firm grnd.   32

--	Elvire [13] 8-11	--	Gone Overboard [11] 8-11		
379	Crimson Robes [5] 8-11			--	Lady Attiva [12] 8-11
--	Nicolini [8] 8-11	381	Nitida [15] 8-11	259	Ultressa [7] 8-11
676	Miss Laura Lee [3] 8-11			194	Helsanon [14] 8-11

15 ran   2½,nk,½,2,1   (R E Sangster)   M Stoute Newmarket

780 EBF STATION ROAD MAIDEN STAKES 2YO   £1458   5f   Firm 08 +10 Fast

602 COME ON CHASE ME [13] (J Etherington) 2-9-0 M Wood 6/1: 31: Fast impr colt: made almost all, running on gamely to win a fast run 2yo maiden at Thirsk May 30: speedily bred colt whose dam won twice as a 2yo: very eff at 5f on gd & firm grnd: acts on any trk, but seems well at home on a sharpish one: should win more races.   45
583 BALKAN LEADER [11] (J Fitzgerald) 2-9-0 S Perks 9/4 FAV: 02: Led briefly well inside final 1f: just caught: compensation awaits: acts on firm & yld grnd: see 583.   44
--   LAMB BECK [6] (J Jefferson) 2-9-0 J Reid 20/1: 3: Sn prom: stayed on well: promising racecourse debut from this brother to a winning 2yo: eff at 5f on firm grnd: should find a small event.   38
531 GEMINI FIRE [2] (P Felgate) 2-9-0 G Duffield 10/1: 04: Sn prom: on the up grade.   32
678 JUST ONE MORE [5] 2-9-0 A Mackay 9/2: 40: Al prom: btr 678 (good).   23
602 KACERE [4] 2-9-0 M Fry 14/1: 40: Never nearer: btr 602 (stiff trk).   23
523 BENNETTHORPE [10] 2-9-0 K Hodgson 7/1: 00: Made no show: btr 523 (soft grnd).   00
497 BORN FREE AGAIN [1] 2-9-0 T Lucas 10/1: 00: Never in it: half brother to smart sprinter Prince Reymo: should be able to do btr than this.   00

515	Roker Roar [9] 9-0	--	Buckswill [15] 9-0	612	Cowlam Boy [14] 9-0
544	Fourwalk [17] 9-0	--	Master Pippin [12] 9-0		
583	Northern Decree [7] 9-0			--	Premier Lad [8] 9-0
--	Seabury [16] 9-0	--	Sparkler Boy [3] 9-0		

17 ran   hd,2,2,3,shhd   (Duncan Norvelle)   J Etherington Norton, Yorks

781 DSRM SPORTING SALVER STAKES 2YO   £3329   6f   Firm 08 08 Slow

*457 AMIGO SUCIO [7] (K Brassey) 2-9-3 S Whitworth 13/8 FAV: 11: 2 gr c Stanford - Haunting (Lord Gayle): Very prom juvenile: well bckd when leading inside dist, ridden out in quite a valuable stakes at Thirsk May 30: quite impressive winner of a Salisbury maiden on his racecourse debut recently: cost 17,000 gns as a yearling and is a half brother to several winners, incl useful Valley Mills: very eff over 5/6f: acts on firm & yld grnd & on any trk: likely to take his chance in the Coventry Stakes.   63
--   SILVER HAZE [1] (S Hall) 2-8-11 M Birch 20/1: 2: Unfancied though ran a fine race on his racecourse debut & will be hard to beat next time: half brother to winning miler Absonant: clearly stays 6f well: acts on fast grnd & on a shrp trk: can only improve.   54
*460 FLAXLEY [4] (R Hollinshead) 2-9-3 S Perks 5/1: 13: Led till dist: gd effort over this longer trip: acts on firm grnd: see 460.   53
571 GALLIC TIMES [3] (I Bell) 2-9-3 J Reid 6/1: 311304: No extra dist: best over 5f in 146 (soft).   41
197 MUNTAG [5] 2-8-11 D Nicholls 33/1: 000: Pushed along thro'out & never reached ldrs: seems suited by gd or faster grnd: acts on any trk.   32
*523 COUNT TREVISIO [6] 2-9-3 R Cochrane 2/1: 10: Early speed: btr over 5f in 523 (soft).   37
627 Danadn [2] 8-11
7 ran   ½,2½,5,1,½,1½   (John Li)   K Brassey Upper Lambourn, Berks

782 JOHNS SMITHS HANDICAP STKS 0-50   £2544   1m 4f   Firm 08   02 Slow   [47]

*592 KUDZ [2] (H Cecil) 3-8-10(4ex) W Ryan 11/4 FAV: 22-211: 3 br c Master Willie -
Lucky Ole Me (Olden Times): In gd form, led 4f out and again inside dist to win a h'cap at
Thirsk May 30: recently had a confidence boosting win in a Beverley maiden: half brother to
several winners, incl Lucky North: stays 12f well & will be suited by further: acts on firm
& soft grnd & on any trk.   57

519 DUAL VENTURE [3] (J Fitzgerald) 4-9-9 G Duffield 8/1: 0-42-22: Led briefly dist:
beat rem decisively & should win soon: acts on fast grnd: see 519. carries weight well.   51

*532 GOING GOING [9] (H Candy) 7-9-9 P Johnson(7) 3/1: 114-013: Ran on same pace: best in 532.40

166 DIPYN BACH [1] (M Camacho) 4-8-10 R Cochrane 14/1: 1000-04: Looks to be returning
to form: in fine form early on last season, winning h'caps at Beverley, Ayr & redcar:
well suited by middle distances: acts on firm & soft grnd & on any trk: well h'capped on
his best form.   25

-- BUCKLOW HILL [8] 9-9-6 C Dwyer 14/1: 30010-0: Held up & no threat, though will come
on for this race: useful stayer who defied top weight in h'caps at Doncaster, Beverley &
Catterick last season: very eff around 12/15f & is well suited by fast grnd: acts on any
trk: best giving weight.   25

695 ELPLOTINO [6] 4-9-7 J Lowe 3/1: 1100-40: Much btr in 695 (yld) though has won
on fast ground.   23

-- TROJAN PRINCE [7] 4-9-10(bl) T Lucas 15/2: 00133-0: Led 1m: fin last: trained by
W Hern last season, when he made all in a Newmarket maiden: stays 10f well & will get
further: suited by fast grnd & forcing tactics: acts on any trk: looks fairly treated &
could go close next time.   00

553 Linton Springtime [5] 7-7(2oh)   333 Miss Morley [4] 7-7(9oh)
9 ran   1,7,1½,6,1½,nk   (Sheikh Mohammed)   H Cecil Newmarket

783 MOWBRAY SELLING STAKES   £1101   1m 4f   Firm 08   -57 Slow

184 REGAL CAPISTRANO [2] (M Prescott) 4-9-7 G Duffield 13/8 FAV: 040-201: 4 ch g Hotfoot -
Twill (Crocket): Stayed on well to lead inside dist in a slowly run seller at Thirsk May 30
(sold for 4,600 gns): first time out was narrowly btn by Impecuniosity in a Hamilton maiden,
and also showed some fair form last seasonl stays 12f well: acts on firm & soft grnd &
on any trk: has worn bl in the past.   22

718 TRACK MARSHALL [8] (J Davies) 4-9-7 M Wigham 7/2: 300-322: Stayed on gamely, just
btn: in gd form & appeared well suited by this longer trip: see 343.   20

524 VERBADING [1] (S Norton) 4-9-4(vis) J Murray(7) 13/2: 000-023: Made most: acts on firm.   14

530 MUSICAL WILL [7] (T Fairhurst) 4-9-7 C Coates(5) 8/1: 210-004: Ran in snatches though
had ev ch and was not btn far: stays 12f: acts on any trk: see 530.   16

379 COME POUR THE WINE [11] 3-8-1 M L Thomas 9/2: 00-000: Dropped in class: not btn
that far & has impr of late: stays 12f: acts on firm & yld grnd.   10

338 LA CHULA [6] 3-8-1(BL) J Reid 10/1: 0000-00: Eased in class: first signs of form:
acts on firm grnd & on a sharpish trk.   07

-- LOW MOOR [3] 4-9-7 M Hindley(3) 10/1: 03304-0: Lost place ½way: fin last: placed
several times in none selling company last season & should win a race if kept in this grade:
stays 2m: acts on gd/firm & soft grnd.   00

522 Marcellina [5] 9-4   524 Prohibition Boy [9] 9-7
195 Forever Young [10] 8-4   620 Venture To Reform [4] 9-7
11 ran   ½,1½,nk,1½,1½   (Graham Maynard)   Sir M Prescott, Newmarket

784 NORBY STKS HCAP 0-35   £2197   5f   Firm 08   +02 Fast   [35]

628 SOFTLY SPOKEN [1] (R Whitaker) 3-7-13 T Lucas 20/1: 0100-01: 3 b f Mummy's Pet -
Tender Answer (Prince Tenderfoot): Held up, fin well to lead close home in a h'cap at Thirsk
May 30: last season won a fillies event at Edinburgh: well suited by this minimum trip: acts
on firm & yld grnd & seems best on a sharpish trk.   26

628 GOLD DUCHESS [6] (M W Easterby) 4-8-7(bl) T Lucas 8/1: 2431002: Led inside dist,
just btn: see 412.   22

550 CHINA GOLD [2] (L Siddall) 7-9-12 G Gosney 10/1: 3000-03: Gd effort: useful sprint
h'capper on his day: won at Carlisle last season & in '84 won at Edinburgh (2) and Ripon:
very eff over 5f, stays 6f: best on fast grnd: acts on any trk & is well suited by forcing tac   45

626 COLWAY RADIAL [9] (D Smith) 3-7-7 L Charnock 12/1: 00-044: Fin well: see 626.   12

742 RAMBLING RIVER [10] 9-9-13(vis) M Hindley(3) 7/1: 010-020: Al up there: see 742.   36

-- RAPID MISS [7] 6-8-11 S P Griffiths(5) 14/1: 20000-0: Not btn that far & ran well
on her reapp: failed to win last season though ran some gd races: in '84 won at Leicester,
Yarmouth & Thirsk: best form over 5f on fast grnd.   19

624 SILENT MAJORITY [15] 3-8-5 M L Thomas 4/1: 44-030: Early speed: btr over 6f in 624.   00

742 CELTIC BIRD [13] 6-8-12 E Guest(3) 6/1: 4000-00: Made most: fin 7th: see 742.   00

272 Jackie Blair [4] 9-3(bl)   628 Lady Of Leisure [5] 8-10
-- Swinging Gold [3] 9-4   -- First Experience [14] 8-8
241 Running Rainbow [12] 7-7(2oh)   540 Mr Panache [8] 8-7
-- Miss Serlby [11] 8-0
15 ran   ½,2,hd,shhd,nk,hd ,½,½   (J David Abell)   R Whitaker Grimston, Leics.

HAMILTON Friday May 30th Righthanded Undulating Trac, Stiff Finish

Official Going Given as Soft (final furlong Heavy) based on times: run-in Heavy 170, rem Heavy 247.
All Times Slow except race 787.

785 EBF DRUMLOCH STAKES 2YO £1000 5f Heavy 170 Slow

+647 **MR GRUMPY** [8] (Denys Smith) 2-8-11 D Nicholls 4/1: 022011: 2 ch c The Brianstan - Handy Dancer (Green God): Impr colt: broke well and was never hdd when a comfortable winner of a 2yo stakes at Hamilton May 30: recently justified fav. in quite a fast run seller at Ripon: speedily bred colt who had earlier been placed in company similar to todays: will stay another furlong: well suited by some give in the grnd: acts on any trk. 40
•627 **DUNLIN** [2] (S Norton) 2-9-4 J Lowe 3/1 Jt FAV: 12: Ran on well though comfortably held by winner: not inconvenienced by this rather testing grnd: acts on any trk: half brother to several winners in the States: see 627. 40
488 **INGLISTON** [3] (M H Easterby) 2-8-11 M Birch 6/1: 033: Continues to impr: see 488. 32
612 **HUGO Z HACKENBUSH** [9] (C Tinkler) 2-8-11 M Wood 8/1: 4044: No extra dist: see 415. 22
•488 **HARRY HUNT** [7] 2-9-4 Gay Kelleway(5) 3/1 Jt FAV: 310: Speed over ½way: btr over this C/D in 488. 27
•681 **NATIONS SONG** [6] 2-8-8 J H Brown(5) 8/1: 0410: Much btr on gd grnd in 681. 00
488 **Send It Down** [5] 8-11 -- **Embarcadero** [4] 8-11
8 ran 2,½,5,1,15,10 (K Higson) Denys Smith Bishop Auckland, Co Durham

786 HIGHLAND PARK SINGLE MALT H'CAP 0-35 £2236 5f Heavy 170 Slow [30]

626 **MIAMI DOLPHIN** [8] (J Berry) 6-8-3 M Fry 2/1 FAV: 0-00131: 6 b m Derrylin - Magibbillibyte (Constable): Went on dist and held on gamely to win a h'cap at Hamilton May 30: earlier this month won on similar grnd on this trk & seems to revel in the mud: also acts on gd/firm: eff over 5/6f: seems to act on any trk, though clearly well suited by a stiff one. 14
•489 **LULLABY BLUES** [2] (M H Easterby) 3-8-10 M Birch 9/2: -0012: Just held: liked this trk: see 489. 28
649 **BAY BAZAAR** [4] (M W Easterby) 4-9-7 K Darley 6/1: 0240003: Not btn far: gd effort and is well suited by some cut in the grnd: acts on any trk: see 42. 27
628 **PARADE GIRL** [7] (J Kettlewell) 4-8-12 N Connorton 9/1: -010004: Made most: clear of rem: see 56. 16
679 **PORT MIST** [1] 4-7-11(bl) J Lowe 6/1: 00-0000: Ran on well after slow start: see 679. 00
626 **TRADESMAN** [3] 6-7-12 J Quinn(5) 10/1: 33-0000: Front rank to ½way: see 490. 00
-- **Musical Aid** [5] 8-5 106 **Grand Celebration** [6] 8-1
8 ran ¾,¾,1,4,2½,1½,6 (J W Barrett) J Berry Cockerham, Lancs

787 PTMARMIGAN MAIDEN STAKES 3YO £1010 6f Heavy 170 +16 Fast

593 **MARGAM** [2] (P Walwyn) 3-9-0 N Howe 6/4 FAV: 0-31: 3 b c African Sky - Valley Farm (Red God): Led dist and stayed on under press to win quite a fast run 3yo maiden at Hamilton May 30: earlier placed behind Orient over the minimum trip at Beverley: half brother to several winners, incl fair stayer Ragabash: stays 6f well: acts on gd & hvy grnd & stiff trk. 36
677 **RAAS** [3] (S Norton) 3-9-0 J Lowe 8/1: 0-23402: Tried to make all: clear of rem and certainly seems best when forcing the pace: acts on hvy grnd: see 241 & 109. 34
677 **GARDAS GOLD** [5] (M Brittain) 3-9-0 K Darley 14/1: 0033-03: Never nearer after a tardy start: maiden who showed impr form last backend when twice placed in fair company: eff over 5/6f: acts son gd/firm & hvy grnd & on any trk: running off a fair mark & could pick up a small h'cap. 24
438 **TRY SIR** [8] (J Watts) 3-9-0 N Connorton 4/1: -04: Btr on gd grnd in 438. 18
-- **BROOKS DILEMMA** [1] 3-8-11 A Bond 11/2: -0: No extra dist: half sister to a couple of winners & likely to impr for this experience, especially on btr grnd. 01
576 **MOZART** [7] 3-9-0 R Cochrane 4/1: -00: Speed to ½way: no form yet. 00
487 **Bavarian Princess** [6] 8-11 381 **Moving Performance** [4] 9-0
8 ran 1,5,2,7,12,3 (Hamdam-Al-Maktoum) P Walwyn Lambourn, Berks

788 TAMDHU SINGLE MALT SELLING H'CAP 0-25 £947 1m Heavy 247 Slow [14]

-- **ABJAD** [3] (R Woodhouse) 5-9-6 A Bond 12/1: 10000-1: 5 b g Mummy's Pet - Maxim's (Major Portion): First time out, broke well and proceeded to make all, readily in a selling h'cap at Hamilton May 30 (bought in 1,050 gns): wore bl when successful in a similar event at Leicester last season, subs. well btn in none selling company: eff over 7/8f: acts on any going: likes a stiff trk: can win again. 18
-- **TARLETON** [6] (P Rohan) 9-9-1 J Quinn(5) 11/2: 00300-2: Nicely bckd on reapp: ran on well to beat rem decisively: does well when fresh: began last season with an easy win in a similar race at Ayr: well suited by 1m on a stiff trk: acts on gd grnd though revels in the mud. 03
606 **SWIFT RIVER** [1] (I Bell) 4-9-12 J Lowe 11/2: 0-20203: Best over 10f in 522 (soft). 10
495 **FAIRGREEN** [10] (D Chapman) 8-9-7 D Nicholls 7/1: -004004: Btr over 6f in 369 (yld). 01
524 **RAPID STAR** [4] 3-7-13(BL) G Duffield 10/1: -300000: Bl first time: maiden: see 51. 00
630 **MURILLO** [7] 10-9-9(bl) J Carr(7) 7/2 FAV: 2-00320: Much btr on fast grnd in 630. 00
107 **Martella** [12] 8-12 369 **Tricenco** [2] 10-0 19 **Norwhistle** [5] 9-1
630 **Honest Token** [11] 8-11(bl) 240 **Name The Game** [13] 8-11
11 ran 4,2½,2½,8,1,4 (G A Farndon Eng. Co Ltd) R Woodhouse Welburn, Yorks

789 FAMOUS GROUSE H'CAP STAKES 0-50   £2662   1m 1f Heavy 247 Slow   [40]

547 LOTUS PRINCESS [2] (K Bridgwater) 5-8-5 P D'arcy 9/1: 3203-01: 5 ch m Camden Town -
Karlaine (Tutankhamen): Ran on strongly to lead inside dist in a h'cap at Hamilton May 30:
ran consistently without winning last season: in '84 won a selling h'cap at Newmarket:
eff over 8/10f: acts on firm & hvy grnd & on any trk.   25

*674 RUN BY JOVE [1] (S Norton) 3-8-5(vis)(8ex) J Lowe 11/2: 00-0012: Led over 2f out: gd
effort under his penalty: acts on hvy grnd: see 674.   36

611 BOY SANDFORD [3] (W Mackie) 7-7-8 N Carlisle 14/1: 0220-03: Not btn far & clear of
rem: gd effort on his fav. trk: in '84 won on fast grnd here & the previous year won twice
at Hamilton & also at Ayr: eff over 8/9f: acts on any grnd.   10

710 ZIO PEPPINO [5] (T Craig) 5-7-10 A Mackay 9/2: 0-03204: Much btr on gd in 606 (7f).   00

727 CBM GIRL [10] 5-8-8 A Bond 5/2 FAV: 000-320: Heavily bckd: no extra dist & much
btr on good grnd in 727 (7f): see 594.   04

611 COMMON FARM [6] 3-8-4 K Darley 14/1: 04-0000: Little form this season but rated
43 when winning a nursery h'cap at Beverley last season: eff over 7/8f: best form on faster
ground than todays.   05

689 MOONDAWN [9] 5-8-12 C Dwyer 9/1: 40-0200: Fin 9th: twice disapp since 343 (10f gd).   00

689 NUGOLA [8] 4-8-8(9ow) M Beecroft 7/1: 040-000: No form this term: surprise winner
first time out last season in a maiden over this C/D: stays 10f: acts on gd/firm & yld grnd
and on a stiff track.   00

413 Pacific Princess [11] 9-6   196 Rocabay Blue [4] 9-10
519 Al Murtajaz [7] 8-5(bl)(12ow)
11 ran   1½,hd,8,6,8,1½   (Mss S Evans)   K Bridgwater Lapworth, Warks

---

790 PINTAIL MAIDEN STAKES 3YO   £1339   1m 4f Heavy 247 Slow

512 SIR BRETT [3] (P Kelleway) 3-9-0 Gay Kelleway(5) 6/1: -041: 3 ch g Star Appeal -
Bessie Wallis (Prince de Galles): Impr gelding: ran on strongly to lead close home in a
3yo maiden at Hamilton May 30: half brother to winning middle dist filly Altana: stays 12f
well: acts on gd & hvy grnd & on any trk.   35

75 TARGET SIGHTED [8] (C Nelson) 3-9-0 J Reid 13/8 FAV: 2-022: Led dist, just caught
though ran a gd race after a fair abs: should recoup todays losses soon: see 75.   34

669 NADAS [2] (S Norton) 3-9-0(bl) J Lowe 3/1: -423: Went on ½way, rallied well when hdd
and not btn far: well clear of rem: acts on heavy: see 669.   33

95 MR WHATS HIS NAME [5] (I Matthews) 3-9-0 A Bond 7/1: 400-244: Well placed till 2f
out: see 25.   18

492 MAELSTROM [10] 3-9-0 M Birch 12/1: 30-00: Btn below dist: see 492.   16

635 IDLE SONG [6] 3-9-0 S Perks 12/1: -0000: No extra run in: best over 1m in 414.   14

631 Jessie Timmins [1] 8-11   452 Game Set Match [9] 9-0
699 The Canny Man [7] 9-0   625 Native Image [4] 9-0
10 ran   ¾,1,15,1,1½,8   (Roldvale Ltd)   P Kelleway Newmarket

---

Official Going Given as Good: Based on times Good/Firm

800 E.B.F. RIVERMEAD MAIDEN STAKES 2YO   £3043   5f   Good/Firm 39 +04 Fast

632 DOMINION ROYALE [6] (R Williams) 2-9-0 R Cochrane 3/1: 41: 2 ch c Dominion - Bahamas
Princess (Sharpen Up): Useful colt: led below dist, comfortably in quite a fast run 2yo
maiden at Kempton May 31: showed promise behind Hard Act at Wolverhampton on his debut: very
eff over 5f and will stay further: acts on gd & fast grnd & on any trk: well regarded and
will now go to Royal Ascot.   58

-- ROCKFELLA [3] (R Johnson Houghton) 2-9-0 S Cauthen 11/10 FAV: 2: Heavily bckd debutant:
ran on promisingly and looks a certain future winner: will be suited by 6f: acts on gd/firm
grnd & on a sharpish trk.   50

-- COPPER RED [5] (P Makin) 2-9-0 W Ryan 16/1: 3: Led briefly over 1f out: promising
effort: sprint colt who cost 9,400 gns as a yearling: acts on fast grnd & on a sharpish
trk: should be placed to win.   48

-- GAYS FLUTTER [4] (C Nelson) 2-8-11 J Reid 10/1: 4: Led over ¼ way: should impr for
this initial outing: nicely bred filly who cost 30,000 gns as a yearling: acts on fast grnd
and on a sharpish trk.   42

-- ONGOING SITUATION [2] 2-9-0 S Dawson(3) 25/1: 0: Ran on well: quite a promising debut:
speedily bred colt who acts on fast grnd & on a sharpish trk.   44

544 LIGHTNING LASER [10] 2-8-11 Pat Eddery 9/1: 00: Well placed till dist: should stay
further: acts on gd/firm & yld grnd & on a sharpish trk.   25

-- CHESTER TERRACE [13] 2-9-0 Paul Eddery 10/1: 0: Will impr for this race: half brother
to winning juvenile Realert.   00

-- Young Lochinvar [12] 9-0   -- Greens Herring [8] 9-0
-- Mughtanim [1] 9-0   -- Murajah [7] 9-0 383 Ring Of Pearl [9] 8-11
12 ran   2¼,1½,nk,nk,7   (David Robinson)   R Williams Newmarket

---

801 H.S. PEARCE MEM. STAKES (H'CAP)(0-50)   £2788   2m   Good/Firm 39 -03 Slow   [47]

519 SAFE RIVER [11] (L Cumani) 4-9-5 R Guest 11/2: 21-4401: 4 b c Riverman - Protectora
(Prologo): Well suited by this longer trip: ran on strongly to lead near fin in a h'cap at
Kempton May 31: most consistent last season, winning twice at Redcar: half brother to the
smart stayer Protection Racket: eff over 12/14f, stays 2m well: acts on yld grnd though best
form on a sound surface: acts on any trk.   48
735 MILTON BURN [3] (H O'neill) 5-8-10 Pat Eddery 5/1: -011022: Led inside dist, just
btn: in fine form and loves this sharp trk: see 312.   38
462 REVISIT [10] (J Winter) 4-9-5 W R Swinburn 13/2: 01-0003: Led dist, kept on well
and not btn far: gd effort: see 58A.   46
485 SUGAR PALM [7] (R Hannon) 5-7-13(bl) A Mcglone 20/1: 10-0304: Made most: ran well: see 341.25
462 HIGH PLAINS [12] 4-8-13 S Cauthen 4/1 FAV: 010-000: Led below dist, ran on same pace.   38
--   TESTIMONIAL [9] 4-7-12(1ow) W Carson 10/1: 2--00-0: Ran on too late: recent winner
over hurdles, though lightly raced on the Flat and yet to win: half brother to several
winners, incl Rhythmic Pastimes: stays 2m well: acts on fast & soft grnd & on any trk.   21
735 BOCODA LAD [14] 5-8-6 P Cook 10/1: 004-040: Fin 8th: see 582.   00
*663 ACCURACY [4] 5-9-3(4ex) J Williams 6/1: -321010: Went on ½way: fin 9th & btr with
some give in 663.   00

541 Miss Blackthorn [13] 7-12		263 Koffi [2] 9-10
363 House Hunter [15] 9-8	-- No U Turn [5] 9-5	-- Water Cannon [6] 9-2
582 Alsiba [1] 7-12	121 Jonix [8] 7-7(3oh)	-- Regent Leisure [16] 7-7(7oh)

16 ran   hd,¼,¾,nk,2   (S Fradkoff)   L Cumani Newmarket

---

802 HERON STAKES 3YO   £8090   1m   Good/Firm 39 +04 Fast

407 FAUSTUS [6] (H Cecil) 3-9-2 S Cauthen 7/4 FAV: 112-101: 3 b c Robellino - B F's Sall-
ingal (Sail On Sail On): Smart colt: qcknd impressively to lead inside dist in valuable &
quite fast run Heron Stakes at Kempton May 31: first time out won Gr.3 Greenham Stakes at
Newbury and subs. unplaced in the 2,000 Guineas in tremendous form last season, winning
successive races at Newbury, Goodwood (Lanson Champagne Stakes), Newmarket, Nottingham &
Yarmouth: sole defeat came when 2nd to Sure Blade in a Gr.2 race at Doncaster: very eff over
7/8f and will stay further: acts on firm & soft grnd and on any trk: most genuine & consistent.   76
--   BRAVE OWEN [4] (H Cecil) 3-8-11 W Ryan 11/2: 13-2: Led 2f out, narrowly btn by his
stable mate: fine effort after a lengthy abs: well regarded colt who made all, easily in a
maiden at Newmarket last season and then was a close 3rd to Luqman in Mill Reef Stakes at
Newbury though subs. suffered a setback: full brother to winning miler Welsh Warrior: stays
1m well: acts on fast grnd & on any trk: sure to be winning soon.   68
362 SIT THIS ONE OUT [8] (D Laing) 3-9-0 P Cook 33/1: 110-303: Ran on well under strong
press: not btn far: fine effort & clearly stays 1m: see 159.   70
465 HARD ROUND [7] (R Hannon) 3-8-11 Pat Eddery 20/1: 041-244: Led briefly 2f out: ran
to his best: stays 1m: see 159.   62
*605 LANCE [3] 3-8-11 T Quinn 11/2: 00-2210: Raised in class & tried to make all: btr in 605   54
574 TOP RULER [5] 3-8-11 W Carson 20/1: 134-000: Never dngr: see 220.   44
--   CHARTINO [1] 3-9-0 M Miller 9/1: 11112-0: No extra below dist: well btn though will
be btr for this race: useful colt who won successive races at Ayr, Catterick, Redcar &
Deauville last season: very eff over 7/8f: acts on any going & on any trk.   00
7 ran   ½,hd,2½,4,12   (S S Niarchos)   H Cecil Newmarket

---

803 VENUS FILLIES STAKES 3YO   £7856   1m   Good/Firm 39 -06 Slow

--   DOLKA [7] (M Stoute) 3-8-5 W R Swinburn 9/4: 1-1: 3 b f Shergar - Dumka (Kashmir II):
Smart filly: mkt drifter on her reapp though showed a fine turn of foot to lead inside dist
easily in a valuable 3yo fillies stakes at Kempton May 31: heavily bckd when comfortably
winning her only race at Newmarket last season: well bred, being a half sister to several
winners, incl the smart duo Dafayna and Dalsaan: very eff over 1m & sure to stay further:
acts on fast grnd & on any trk: scope for improvement & will win more races.   70
*575 BRAZZAKA [5] (M Jarvis) 3-8-5 T Ives 5/1: 221-112: Tried to make all, cleverly held
by winner though remains in tremendous form: acts on fast grnd: see 575.   60
*658 SOMEONE SPECIAL [2] (P Cole) 3-8-5 T Quinn 4/1: -213: Had ev ch and stayed this
longer trip well: acts on fast grnd: in fine form: see 658.   58
--   SALLY SAYS SO [6] (S Norton) 3-8-7(2ow) S Cauthen 16/1: 10-4: Outsider: gd seasonal
debut: first time out winner of a fillies maiden at Ayr last season: half sister to several
winners, incl Mr Meeka and Meeka Gold: stays 1m: well suited by fast grnd: acts on any trk.   55
551 ARGON LASER [3] 3-8-5 W Carson 6/5 FAV: -100: Heavily bckd disapp: btn 2f out: much
btr over 10f in 551 (good): see 250.   43
551 KICK THE HABIT [4] 3-8-5 P Robinson 16/1: 0-000: Bckd at long odds: highly tried
this season: half sister to several winners, notably smart miler Capricorn Belle: stays 1m:
seems suited by fast grnd.   39
6 ran   2,1,2½,6,1½   (H H Aga Khan)   M Stoute Newmarket

---

804 MANOR TWO YEAR OLD STAKES   £2763   6f   Good/Firm 39 +01 Fast

*610 MISTER MAJESTIC [6] (R Williams) 2-9-2 R Cochrane 4/1: 1211: 2 b c Tumble Wind -
Our Village (Ballymore): Very useful juvenile: led soon after ½way for a comfortable win in
quite a fast run 2yo stakes at Kempton May 31: earlier successful at Newmarket & Beverley,
in between narrowly btn by Quel Esprit: half brother to Clotilda: very eff over 5/6f: acts
on gd/firm & yld grnd & on any trk: genuine & consistent.   60
*434 PENSURCHIN [3] (D Elsworth) 2-9-2 A Mcglone 11/2: 1312: Ran on well: stays 6f: see 434.   52
614 MEBHIL [7] (P Kelleway) 2-8-11 S Cauthen 6/5 FAV: 33: Heavily bckd: ev ch: stays 6f:
acts on gd/firm & yld grnd & on any trk: see 614.   46
456 DIAMOND FLIGHT [9] (R Hannon) 2-9-2 Pat Eddery 12/1: 0144: Never nearer: stays 6f:
acts on fast grnd: best effort to date: see 261.   50
662 VAIGLY BLAZED [8] 2-8-11 P Cook 9/1: 40: Ran on too late: stays 6f: see 662.   27
187 MICRO LOVE [4] 2-8-11 J Williams 20/1: 30: Early speed: acts on gd/firm: abs since 187.   25
457 SHARP REMINDER [5] 2-8-11 W Carson 9/1: 00: Led over ½way: not given a hard race
when hdd: acts on fast grnd: see 457.   00
--   Bold Intention [2] 8-11   664 Cee En Cee [1] 8-11
9 ran   2½,hd,nk,7,1,shhd   (D A Johnson)   R Williams Newmarket

805 KINGFISHER HANDICAP STAKES (0-50)   £2616   1m 3f Good/Firm 39 -03 Slow   [49]

+403 POCHARD [7] (P Cole) 4-9-10 T Quinn 9/2: 323-311: 4 b c Affirmed - Telferner (Tell):
In fine form, again made all to score unchall in a h'cap at Kempton May 31: loves this sharp
course, recently won a similar race here and last season won at Carlisle, Wolverhampton &
again at Kempton: very eff around 12f: acts on firm & yld grnd & on any trk: well suited by
forcing tactics.   60
--   JOUVENCELLE [1] (H Candy) 4-7-12 T Williams 16/1: -0244-2: Ran on well on her reapp:
good effort and will be btr for this race: maiden who was rated 36 when 2nd to High Tern in
a Warwick maiden last season: eff over 11/12f & stays 14f well: runs well on fast grnd:
should find a h'cap off her present mark.   29
683 CONVINCED [2] (G Harwood) 4-10-0 G Starkey 2/1 Jt FAV: 100-323: Again ran well under
top weight: see 683.   55
618 HIGH TENSION [4] (G Pritchard Gordon) 4-8-11 W Carson 2/1 Jt FAV: 0044-24: Heavily bckd:
ran on: see 618.   32
459 PRINCE MERANDI [5] 3-7-10 B Crossley 20/1: 0-13300: Close up thro'out: see 348.   28
+432 KALKOUR [6] 4-9-5 Pat Eddery 9/2: 0-0-010: Nearest fin: much btr here in 432 (10f gd).   28
--   Iktiyar [3] 8-4   --   Beau Vista [8] 8-0
8 ran   3,2½,4,4,6.   (Fahd Salman)   P Cole Whatcombe, Oxon

NEWMARKET   Saturday May 31st   Righthand Stiff Galloping Track

Official Going Given as Good/Firm

806 HOLSTEN DIAT PILS MAIDEN STAKES 3YO   £4464   1m   Firm 19 +15 FAst

--   FARAJULLAH [4] (G Huffer) 3-9-0 M Miller 11/4 fav: -1: 3 b c Jaazeiro - Coup De Veine
(Gift Card): Very promising colt: landed a gamble on racecourse debut, leading inside final
3f readily to win a fast run 3yo maiden at Newmarket May 31: stays 1m well: acts on firm grnd
& on a stiff gall trk: very highly regarded by his stable & will now tackle Pattern company
in the Jersey Stakes at Royal Ascot: sure to win more races.   70
--   WALK ON AIR [11] (O Douieb) 3-8-11 R Cochrane 20/1: -2: Kept on well, highly prom debut
and caught a real tartar on this occasion: half brother to winning '80 juvenile Will Of
Victory: eff 1m, should stay further: acts on firm grnd: a maiden is a formality.   57
--   FLASHDANCE [21] (G Harwood) 3-8-11 G Starkey 16/1: -3: Never closer on racecourse
debut: prom first effort by this half sister to winning juveniles New Dimension and Prince
Hab: stays 1m well: acts on firm grnd: sure to win a maiden.   52
--   SHERZAD [25] (M Stoute) 3-9-0 W R Swinburn 6/1: -4: Steady late hdway from this half
brother to the top class duo Shergar and Shernazar: suited by 1m: will stay at least 10f:
acts well on firm grnd: hard to beat next time.   55
371 ASSEER [10] 3-9-0 W Ryan 25/1: -00: Al prom: impr colt who stays 1m & acts on firm:
will not be hard to place.   54
--   NILAMBAR [9] 3-9-0 S Cauthen 7/1: 02-0: Sure to benefit from seasonal debut: only ran
twice, late in '85, splitting North Verdict & Miltescens in a minor event at York on yielding
going: half brother to 3 winners, notable Nasseem: bred to stay beyond 1m.   53
--   RIVART [30] 3-9-0 P Eddery 12/1: -0: Never closer in 7th: promising first effort
and looks certain to impr on it next time.   00
--   BALTHUS [28] 3-9-0 David Eddery[7] 11/1: -0: Fin 8th & should benefit from this first
experience of racing: acts on firm grnd: stays 1m.   00
402 BEAU SHER [13] 3-9-0 Paul Eddery 6/1: -020: Fin mid-div: disapp after 402 (sharp trk).   00
--   SEA POWER [6] 3-8-11 W Carson 11/1: 03-0: Mkt drifter on seasonal debut, early speed:
placed both outings last season notable when quite a dist. 4th of 9 behind Sonic Lady at
Ascot over 6f on firm.   00

-- **Majaahed** [23] 9-0
423 **Knightly Dia** [17] 8-11
-- **Finding** [12] 9-0
619 **Almutanabbi** [3] 9-0
-- **Real Moonshine** [20] 9-0
546 **Sell It Kilroy** [1] 9-0
422 **Morgiana** [26] 8-11
-- **Travel Magic** [16] 8-11
-- **Emerald Wave** [14] 8-11
218 **Jaryan** [2] 9-0
-- **Chucklestone** [5] 9-0
-- **Report Em** [22] 8-11
-- **Raf** [15] 9-0
-- **Murhaf** [18] 9-0
-- **Highly Recommended** [19] 9-0
-- **Reno Ralph** [29] 9-0
-- **Captains Jade** [27] 8-11
-- **Thunderdome** [7] 8-11
-- **Eau Courante** [24] 9-0
29 ran 3,3,¾,¾,1,½,1½ (B Hamoud) G Huffer Newmarket

807 HOLSTEN EXPORT LAGER H'CAP 3YO 0-60 £4721 1m 2f Firm 19 +18 Fast [65]

*484 **MOON MADNESS** [1] (J Dunlop) 3-8-5 P Eddery 11/10 fav: 4-11: 3 b c Vitiges - Castle Moon (Kalamoun): Fast impr colt: absolutely skated up in quite a valuable h'cap at Newmarket May 31, showing fine acceleration to go clear inside final 2f & won on the bridle: narrow winner of a maiden at Salisbury first time out & only ran once in '85: half brother to a couple of middle dist. winners: eff 10f, sure to stay at least 12f: acts on firm & yld & likes a gall trk: must not be opposed in his next few engagements. 61
654 **JANISKI** [8] (W Hern) 3-9-5(bl) W Carson 13/2: 100-42: Kept on well under press and appeared to run up to his best: likely to stay beyond 10f: see 654. 60
553 **ANDARTIS** [7] (Lord J Fitzgerald) 3-9-7 T Lucas 11/2: 002-033: Al prom & ran well under top weight: see 15, 553. 62
604 **FORCELLO** [6] (S Norton) 3-7-12 S Dawson[3] 6/1: 2-12424: Made much: btr suited by a sharp trk: see 444. 36
465 **MASHHUR** [2] 3-8-5 Paul Eddery 8/1: 2301-00: Ev ch: btr 1m? see 465. 41
234 **ATROMITOS** [5] 3-8-1 P Robinson 14/1: 041-400: Prom most: twice below 157 (yld). 35
-- **Kerry May Sing** [5] 8-0
-- **Anzere** [3] 8-5
8 ran 5,shhd,3,1½,½,2½ (Lavina Duchess of Norfolk) J Dunlop Arundel, Sussex

808 HOLSTEN DIAT PILS H'CAP 3YO 0-75 £12486 6f Firm 19 +13 Fast [72]

*516 **LATCH STRING** [13] (L Piggott) 3-7-10 B Crossley 6/1: 0024-11: 3 b f Thatch - Bentinck Hotel (Red God): Fast impr ex Irish filly: unbtn in this country & was winning 2nd race on the trot, gaining the day in a blanket fin to fast run & valuable h'cap at Newmarket May 31: first time out landed a gamble in a maiden at Thirsk: placed several times in Ireland in '85: half sister to 3 winners: eff 5f, stays 6f well: acts on firm & yld & on any trk: suited by waiting tactics. 52
496 **MERDON MELODY** [4] (R Sheather) 3-7-11 T Williams 9/1: 034-122: Dsptd lead most, just caught and ran a fine race: runs well at Newmarket: should win again soon: see 387. 52
-- **MUMMYS FAVOURITE** [10] (J Dunlop) 3-8-11 W Carson 13/2: 24111-3: Well bckd seasonal debutant, kept on strongly close home and not btn far: winner of last 3 on the trot in '85, minor events at Leicester, Goodwood & Yarmouth: half sister to several winners: very eff at 6f, may stay 7f: acts on firm & yld and on any trk: sure to run well next time. 64
600 **LUNA BID** [12] (M Blanshard) 3-9-6 R Cochrane 12/1: 30-0204: Made most and ran right up to his best: see 387. 72
+406 **SYLVAN EXPRESS** [11] 3-8-2 A Mcglone 4/1 fav: 211-010: Al well there, not btn far but probably btr over 7f in 406. 54
249 **BARCLAY STREET** [9] 3-9-1 G Starkey 33/1: 14-00: Not disgraced: ran only twice in '85, winning first time out at Leicester over 7f on firm grnd: runs well on a stiff trk. 60
534 **STRIVE** [7] 3-7-8(BL) C Rutter[1] 20/1: 00-0240: Bl first time, fin 7th: best 436 (7f) 00
691 **ROARING RIVA** [3] 3-9-7 M Wigham 8/1: 00-4400: Early speed but hmpd by tearing off a racing plate at halfway: ignore this effort: see 165. 00
387 **OH BOYAR** [5] 3-8-8 P Eddery 5/1: 300-300: Early speed: much btr 387 (C/D). 00
387 **Lochonica** [8] 9-2
624 **Bertie Wooster** [2] 7-11
443 **Au Dessus** [6] 7-9
586 **Coppermill Lad** [14] 7-10
567 **Quarryville** [1] 8-11
14 ran nk,½,hd,shhd,2½ (Mrs B R Firestone) L Piggott Newmarket

809 GINISTRELLI SELLING H'CAP 3YO 0-25 £1912 7f Firm 19 -22 SLow [32]

305 **SHARP TIMES** [2] (W Musson) 3-8-9 M Wigham 9/2: 0-021: 3 b g Faraway Times - Sharp Venita (Sharp Edge): Close up, kept on gamely to lead close home in a selling h'cap at Newmarket May 31: bought in 4,000 gns: ran well last time over 1m and is also very eff at 7f: also seems to act on firm & hvy grnd. 21
113 **MY CUP OF TEA** [8] (P Haslam) 3-7-12 T Williams 7/1: 0-032: Al prom: just failed: seems to act on firm & soft grnd & should win a seller: see 113. 08
424 **NORTHERN GUNNER** [5] (W Jarvis) 3-9-1 B Rouse 13/8 fav: 000-043: Heavily bckd, led 1 out, just failed to hold on: certain to win a seller: see 424. 24
666 **MISS TONILEE** [10] (D H Jones) 3-8-9 John Williams 8/1: 03-3224: Consistent: see 426, 627. 14
*426 **SOHO SUE** [4] 3-8-11 Paul Eddery 10/1: 0040-10: Led 6f: btr 426. 09
-- **TOUCH THE SAIL** [1] 3-8-9 R Cochrane 33/1: 0000-0: No threat: stays 7f. 03
624 **BANDYANN** [9] 3-8-6 P Eddery 10/1: 00-2000: Mkt drifter: best 113 (sharp trk). 00
620 **NANOR** [12] 3-8-9 P Cook 10/1: -003000: Best 340 (6f). 00
740 **Larches** [15] 8-9
161 **Percipio** [6] 9-1(bl)
113 **Odervy** [13] 7-11
545 **Dicks Boy** [3] 8-1
-- **Ocean Lad** [16] 8-1
-- **King Of Gems** [14] 10-3
340 **Hooray Hamilton** [7] 8-8(BL)
328 **Cheal** [11] 8-6
16 ran ½,hd,1½,4,2,1 (F W Briggs) W Musson Newmarket

810 FELIX LEACH STAKES 2YO   £2955   6f   Firm 19 -15 Slow

405 MANSOOJ [4] (N Callaghan) 2-8-11 P Eddery 8/15 fav: 31: 2 ch c Thatching - Senta's
Girl (Averof): Comfortably led 1 out, heavily bckd in a minor race at Newmarket May 31:
cost 42,000 gns: well suited by 6f, looks sure to stay further: acts well on firm grnd.   58
-- LOCKTON [5] (J Hindley) 2-8-11 M Hills 11/2: 2: Al 2nd, most promising debut: half
brother to Blue Brocade, a winner over 11f: will probably be suited by 7f, acts son firm &
should soon find a race.   55
610 ALKADI [6] (W O'gorman) 2-9-2(BL) T Ives 5/1: 3123: Made most: genuine: stays 6f: Bl 1st time 53
622 MISTER COLIN [2] (R Hannon) 2-8-13 W Carson 12/1: 12434: Btr 5f: see 622, 27.   35
-- O LA LE [1] 2-8-11 T Quinn 50/1: 0: Early speed: cost 2,800 gns.   28
5 ran   1,2½,5,½   (K Al-Said)   N Callaghan Newmarket

811 MATTHEW DAWSON MAIDEN STAKES 3YO   £3236   1m 6f Firm 19 -15 Slow

347 ACTINIUM [6] (P Cole) 3-9-0 T Quinn 3/1: 043-21: 3 br c Labus - Activity (Montevideo II
Fulfilled the promise of his seasonal debut, leading ½m out comfortably in a 3yo maiden
at Newmarket May 31: placed in 2 of his 3 outings last season and is a half brother to
several winners: eff around 12f, well suited by 15f: acts on firm & yld going: suited by a
gall trk: could win a staying h'cap soon.   46
486 ZAAJER [2] (J Dunlop) 3-9-0 P Eddery 5/1: -32: Kept on and is evidently suited by a
stamina test: appears to act on firm & yld: see 486.   40
458 MARIE GALANTE [4] (C Brittain) 3-8-11 P Robinson 12/1: 00-2323: Made much, one
paced: btr 458 (12f yld).   32
506 LAW COURT [7] (H Candy) 3-9-0 T Williams 16/1: 0-004: Prom. thro'out & probably
stays 15f: probably acts on firm & yld.   33
-- EL CONQUISTADOR [5] 3-9-0 G Starkey 11/10 fav: -0: Warm fav on racecourse debut,
ev ch: cost 290,000 gns and is out of the winning stayer Fiddle Faddle who is from a good
family herself: well bred sort who should be suited by a dist of grnd & is worth another
chance next time.   30
549 DUWANTO [1] 3-8-11 M Hills 25/1: -00: Btr 549 (10f, good).   26
619 Polecroft [3] 9-0(bl)
7 ran   2½,5,1½,3,½   (Fahd Salman)   P Cole Whatcombe, Oxon

812 RICHARD MARSH HANDICAP 3YO+ 0-35   £2467   1m   Firm 19 +04 Fast   [35]

480 AVENTINO [10] (J Sutcliffe) 3-7-9(BL) B Crossley 6/1: 0001-01: 3 ch g Cure The Blues -
Sovereign Don (Sovereign Path): Bl first time & well bckd, readily led in the final 1f in a
h'cap at Newmarket May 31: narrow winner of a Newmarket seller on final outing in '85: very
eff over 7f/1m: suited by firm grnd & a stiff trk, particularly Newmarket: well h'capped
and can follow up next time.   30
265 ALQIRM [8] (C Benstead) 4-9-7 B Rouse 14/1: 400-002: Fin well showing a return to
form: first time out winner of a minor event at Lingfield in '85: placed several times subs:
eff at 6f, seems suited by 1m nowadays: acts on heavy but probably btr on fast grnd.   33
668 FORMATUNE [9] (D Arbuthnot) 4-9-6(bl) W Carson 6/1: 3-10233: Al there and is in
good form: see 10.   30
709 DIMENSION [14] (N Smith) 4-8-3(bl) J Carter[7] 11/2: -014104: Ev ch, twice below 578.   11
129 VAGUE MELODY [13] 4-9-7 W R Swinburn 5/1 fav: 214-230: Heavily bckd, ev ch: twice
below 91 (soft).   21
453 AQABA PRINCE [19] 6-8-8 N Adams 10/1: 20-0000: Nicely bckd at long odds, kept on
well and is coming back to form: managed only a single placing from 9 outings in '85, the
previous season won at   Goodwood & Haydock: very eff around 1m on gd going but seems to
act on any trk.   05
*689 SAMHAAN [20] 4-9-0(bl)(5ex) M Hills 7/1: 40-2410: Started slowly: best 689.   00
710 Monticelli [4] 7-7   -- Wild Hope [18] 9-10   399 Spring Pursuit [6] 8-13
727 Formidable Lady [15] 8-8   452 Irish Hero [3] 9-10
-- No Credibility [1] 9-6   453 Foot Patrol [2] 8-12
-- Qualitair Prince [16] 8-4   -- Dick E Bear [7] 9-9
-- Flodabay [12] 7-13   160 Ideoligia [5] 7-9   -- Miss Monroe [11] 9-7
19 ran   4,½,1,5,1½,1½,nk   (A J Smith)   J Sutcliffe Epsom, Surrey

---

THIRSK   Saturday May 31st   Lefthand, Sharpish Track

Official Going Given as Firm

813 SKIPTON SELLING STAKES 2YO   £1178   5f   Firm 20 -18 Slow

647 SPITTIN MICK [7] (J Berry) 2-8-11 B Thomson 13/8 FAV: 121: 2 b g The Brianstan -
La Fille (Crooner): Well bckd & made ev yd, comfortably in a 2yo seller at Thirsk May 31
(sold 6,800 gns): first time out won a maiden seller at Warwick: very eff at 5f: acts on firm
& yld grnd & on any trk though well suited by forcing tactics on a sharpish one.   36
647 FIVE SIXES [13] (N Tinkler) 2-8-11 S Keightley 8/1: 01D42: Sn prom: consistent:
acts on firm & yld grnd: see 337.   26

515 GWYNBROOK [6] (M W Easterby) 2-8-11 M Birch 5/1: 003: Gambled on on first venture into selling company: al prom: impr effort from this half brother to 2 winners: should stay further than 5f: acts on firm grnd.   19

596 DORMESTONE LAD [14] (R Stubbs) 2-8-11(bl) J H Brown(5) 25/1: 004: Impr: eff 5f on firm. 18

711 HARRYS COMING [11] 2-8-11 J Callaghan(7) 8/1: 02130: Sn prom: btr 711, see 181.   17

•711 ROSE DUET [5] 2-8-8 B Mcgiff(7) 7/1: 0010: Much btr 711 (stiffer trk).   09

446 PATELS GOLD [12] 2-8-8 N Connorton 8/1: 00: Prom, ev ch: btr 446 (gall trk, gd).   00

543 THE WHITE LION [15] 2-8-8 G Duffield 7/1: 00: Op 14/1: al rear.   00

--   Chantilly Dawn [9] 8-8   --   Goldchan [8] 8-8
612 Oxford Place [2] 8-11   537 Glory Gold [3] 8-8   --   Chefitalia [10] 8-8
425 Real Rustle [4] 8-11   --   Greens Seymour [1] 8-11
15 ran   4,3,¼,¼,1½   (Mrs J M Berry)   J Berry Cockerham, Lancs

814 OVREVOLL TROPHY (H'CAP) (0-60) 3YO   £3475   6f   Firm 20 +06 Fast   [64]

586 DARK PROMISE [13] (R Hollinshead) 3-8-7 S Perks 13/2: 020-001: 3 b c Junius - Colart (Sallust): Useful colt: sn prom and led over 2f out, readily in a h'cap at Thirrsk May 31: in '85 was most consistent, winning at Wolverhampton: very eff at 6f, stays 7f: acts on soft, loves fast grnd: no trk preferences.   56

438 BREAKFAST IN BED [11] (W Haigh) 3-7-13 J Quinn(5) 16/1: 0030-32: No ch with winner but ran well: will be suited by 7f: see 438.   39

--   PREJUDICE [17] (B Mcmahon) 3-8-3(1ow) B Thomson 10/1: 30030-3: Al up there: gd seasonal debut: in '85 was a gd 3rd to Blue Eyed Boy at Doncaster: eff at 6f, stays 7f: acts on gd & firm grnd.   39

447 SEW HIGH [10] (B Mcmahon) 3-7-10 A Mackay 16/1: 1-00104: Prom, stays 6f, but btr 246.   26

671 ROVE [6] 3-7-10 J Lowe 13/2: 1-12430: Fdd final 1f: btr 671, see 6.   25

586 JARROVIAN [12] 3-8-1 C Coates(2) 20/1: 0421000: Best in 309 (soft/heavy grnd).   28

624 KIMBLE BLUE [15] 3-7-12 R Hills 11/2: 300-040: Early speed, fdd: btr 624.   00

588 GODS ISLE [8] 3-8-0 K Darley 6/1: 10-0200: Prom over 4f: btr 443: see 246.   00

628 MISS PRIMULA [14] 3-7-8 N Carlisle 9/1: 000-030: Led over 3f: btr 628 (5f non h'cap).   00

567 TUFUH [1] 3-9-7 R Carter(5) 11/2 Jt.FAV: 140-020: Eased when btn: btr 567.   00

529 Loch Form [5] 7-7(2oh)   518 Mandrake Madam [16] 8-11

670 Capeability Pound [4] 7-9   650 Jersey Maid [2] 7-7(4oh)

--   Manton Mark [3] 8-2   --   Aquarula [7] 8-7
16 ran   3,1½,2½,nk,¼,3,hd   (K H Fischer)   R Hollinshead Upper Longdon, Staffs

815 BET WITH THE TOTE HANDICAP (0-60)   £4181   7f   Firm 20 +06 Fast   [58]

+606 KNIGHTS SECRET [11] (M H Easterby) 5-7-11(6ex) A Mackay 5/1: 000-211: 5 ch h Immortal Knight - Lush Secret (Most Secret): Led final 1f, comfortably in a h'cap at Thirsk May 31: in fine form this season, last time out won at Newcastle: first time out in '85 won at Pontefract: in '83 won 3 times: eff over 6f, but well suited by 7/8f: acts on any grnd & on any trk & seems a genuine sort.   39

--   TELWAAH [9] (A Stewart) 4-9-1 M Roberts 9/2: 11010-2: Stayed on well final 1f: gd seasonal debut & should be winning soon: in fine form in '85, winning at Brighton, Folkestone (course record) and first time out at Redcar: eff at 6f, stays 7f well: acts well on fast grnd & a sharpish/undulating trk.   49

573 CREEAGER [1] (W Wharton) 4-8-4 N Carlisle 5/1: 40-0143: Nearest at fin: gd effort: needs 1m? see 573, 441.   34

--   GREETLAND DANCER [6] (S Wiles) 4-7-7(8oh) A Proud 33/1: 00000-4: Nearest fin on seasonal debut: gd effort: showed promise as a 2yo, but lost his form last season: eff at 7f, stays 1m well: acts on gd & firm grnd & on any trk: well h'capped on his best form.   23

321 IDLE TIMES [14] 4-7-10 J Lowe 4/1 FAV: 00-1000: Clear ldr 6f: abs: see 240.   25

--   SCOUTSMISTAKE [13] 7-8-5 G Duffield 20/1: 00020-0: Fdd final 1f: gd seasonal debut: in '85 won a h'cap at Pontefract & also a fine 3rd in Royal Hunt Cup: in '84 won at Pontefract, Carlisle & Ayr: eff over 7f, stays 10f: acts on firm & yld & on any trk: carries weight well.   30

616 VALLEY MILLS [8] 6-9-4 B Mcgiff(7) 8/1: 00-0300: No show: twice below form 520.   00

706 HABS LAD [12] 4-8-12 R Wernham 10/1: 00-0000: Fdd: yet to strike form: in '85 won at Brighton, Nottingham, Warwick, Salisbury & Bath: eff over 6f, stays 1m really well: acts on gd/firm & yld grnd & on any trk: genuine sort.   00

573 Moores Metal [4] 8-8   --   Major Don [7] 9-10   --   Joyful Dancer [2] 8-4
649 Air Command [3] 9-1   401 Armitage [5] 8-2(BL)   56   Farmer Jock [10] 7-7(vis)(3oh)
14 ran   3,1½,hd,¼,1½,nk   (N Westbrook)   M H Easterby Great Habton, Yorks

816 E.C. BOUSFIELD CUP (H'CAP) (0-60) 3YO   £3402   1m   Firm 20 -06 Slow   [53]

692 KNYF [5] (E Weymes) 3-9-3 E Guest(3) 7/1: 32-3201: 3 b c Kris - Kereolle (Riverman): Useful colt: held up, led inside the final 1f, ridden out in a h'cap at Thirsk May 31: deserves success after several near misses: eff at 1m, may stay further: acts on gd/firm & soft grnd & on any trk.   53

461 MILEOMETER [4] (B Hills) 3-8-3(1ow) B Thomson 7/1: 0020-02: Hmpd 2f out: ran on well: fin 3rd placed 2nd: gd effort: well suited by 1m: see 461.   35

518 IRISH PASSAGE [2] (D Barron) 3-8-4 P Waldron 5/2 FAV: 1-02D: Well bckd: went right over 2f out: stayed on under press: fin 2nd, placed 3rd: stays 1m well: see 518.   38

637 BILLS AHEAD [10] (G Moore) 3-7-9 A Mackay 20/1: 000-404: Led over 3f out: likes a
sharp track: see 14.   26
650 MRS NAUGHTY [9] 3-7-7(1oh) N Carlisle 10/1: 2000-40: Led 2f out: gd effort: see 650.   24
514 ARROW EXPRESS [7] 3-8-0(bl) M Roberts 7/2: 00-0020: Never nearer: stays 1m: see 514.   30
637 AUCTION MAN [6] 3-8-6 S Perks 9/1: -032400: Early ldr: twice below form 478 (soft/hvy). 00
674 SECLUSIVE [3] 3-8-10 M Wood 9/1: 400-040: No show: btr 674 (yld).   00
--   Try Harder [11] 9-7   650 Cumbrian Nijo [8] 8-3(vis)
--   Tour Vieille [1] 8-8
11 ran   ¾,1½,½,hd,nk   (Lady Howard de Walden)   E Weymes Leyburn, Yorks

817   DICK PEACOCK MEM. SPRINT STAKES   £2939   6f   Firm 20 -09 Slow

--   POLLY DANIELS [5] (P Cole) 4-9-7 P Waldron 4/6 FAV: 30231-1: 4 b f Clever Trick -
Policam (Pollux): First time out, well bckd & led ½way, ridden out in a stakes event at
Thirsk May 31: smart filly who in '85 won a listed race at the Curragh: has been lightly
raced: winning 2yo at Sandown and also a fine 2nd to Park Appeal in Gr.1 Cheveley Park Stakes
at Newmarket: very eff at 6f: acts on soft, but best form on gd & firm grnd.   62
--   NORTHERN CHIMES [1] (M Ryan) 4-9-3 G Duffield 8/1: 0-000-2: Ev ch over 1f out: btr
effort: lightly raced and no form in '85: showed smart form as a 2yo when trained by E Eldin,
winning at Kempton (Listed race) and York: very eff at 6f, probably stays 7f: acts well
on gd & firm grnd.   51
677 ELSOCKO [2] (B Mcmahon) 3-7-12 A Mackay 6/1: 00-3033: Prom, ran well: see 677, 309.   42
649 NO BEATING HARTS [4] (M Mccormack) 3-8-13(BL) R Wernham 5/1: 20-1304: Bl first time:
led 3f: acts on firm, but best 217 (yld).   43
628 WALLER FIELD [3] 4-9-0 M Birch 20/1: -00: Stiff task: ex Irish filly who was a
winning 2yo at Leopardstown: acts on gd grnd.   12
5 ran   2½,½,½,6,12   (Guiting Stud Ltd)   P Cole Whatcombe, Oxon

818   E.B.F. CARLTON MINIOTT FILLIES MAIDEN   £2602   5f   Firm 20 -17 Slow

--   UPPER [3] (E Weymes) 2-8-11 E Guest(3) 20/1: 1: 2 b f Cure The Blues - Meliora
(Crowned Prince): Promising filly: led final 1f, drawing clear in a 2yo fillies maiden at
Thirsk May 31: dam was a 7f winner: eff at 5f, should stay further: acts on firm grrnd &
a sharpish trk: should rate more highly.   46
450 SPANISH SLIPPER [1] (W Haigh) 2-8-11 N Day 20/1: 42: Sn prom: again ran well: acts
well on gd & firm grnd: should find a small event: see 450.   37
--   NABRAS [7] (H T Jones) 2-8-11 R Hills 10/1 FAV: 3: Well bckd debutant: al up there:
cost I.R. 340,000 ans is a half sister to 7/8f winner Edge of Town: should be suited by
further than 5f: acts on firm grnd & will do btr next time.   36
27   LADY PAT [11] (M Mccormack) 2-8-11 R Wernham 10/1: 24: Long abs: al up there: gd
effort: acts on firm & soft grnd: see 27.   35
646 GARDENIA LADY [8] 2-8-11 G Duffield 11/4: 30: Well bckd: ev ch: btr 646 (yld).   35
20   GAME FEATHERS [4] 2-8-11 N Carlisle 25/1: 00: Abs: made much: cost 12,000 gns and
is a speedily bred filly: acts well on firm grnd & a sharpish trk & should find a small event. 34
47   Emmer Green [16] 8-11   317 Sinclair Lady [2] 8-11
--   Music Star [13] 8-11   --   Dohty Baby [17] 8-11   --   Bella Georgina [15] 8-11
--   Prodigious Lady [9] 8-11   --   Croft Original [6] 8-11
627 Rivers Secret [5] 8-11   --   Abergwrle [10] 8-11
646 Bold Ad [14] 8-11   --   Treize Quatorze [12] 8-11
17 ran   3,½,nk,hd,½,1,nk   (Lady Howard de Walden)   E Weymes Leyburn, Yorks

HAMILTON   Saturday May 31st   Righthanded Undulating Track, Stiff Finish

Official Going Given as Heavy: All races started by flag: All Times Slow

819 BELLSHILL MAIDEN FILLIES STAKES 2YO   £1008   6f   Heavy 250 Slow

--   CHANTILLY LACE [1] (P Kelleway) 2-8-11 Gay Kelleway(5) 11/4: 1: 2 ch f Carwhite -
Frenchouan (Jim French): Made a successful racecourse debut, led dist and held on gamely
in a 2yo fillies maiden at Hamilton May 31: French bred filly who cost 52,000 Francs as a
yearling: eff over a stiff 6f & sure to stay further: acts on hvy grnd & on an undulating trk. 38
627 CARSE KELLY [6] (S Norton) 2-8-11 J Lowe 5/2 FAV: 02: Well bckd & just failed over
this longer trip: stayed on gamely & well clear of rem: acts on gd/firm & hvy: see 627.   38
417 SHARPHAVEN [3] (M Brittain) 2-8-11 K Darley 4/1: 3403: Led to dist, eased: best over
5f in 317 (soft): see 170.   18
450 MY SERENADE [5] (J Watts) 2-8-11 N Connorton 5/1: 04: Dist 4th on this bottomless
grnd: should be suited by this trip & will do btr on a faster surface.   02
--   MISS ACACIA [4] 2-8-11 D Nicholls 10/1: 0: Never dngr on debut: cost 82,000 gns as
a yearling and is a half sister to a couple of minor winners.   00
77   REVOLVER VIDEO [2] 2-8-11 M Fry 12/1: 00: No threat after a slow start: see 77.   00
602 Bantel Bouquet [7] 8-11(BL)
7 ran   shhd,10,8,2½,25   (R G Whalley)   P Kelleway Newmarket

820   BIRKENSHAW HANDICAP STAKES 0-35   £1786   6f   Heavy 250 Slow   [35]

594 LITTLE NEWINGTON [3] (N Bycroft) 5-7-13(bl) J Lowe 7/2 Co FAV: 4100121: 5 b m Most
Secret - Kathy King (Space King): In good form, led below dist & ran on well to win a h'cap
at Hamilton May 31: earlier this month won a similar race at Carlisle: won a seller on
similar grnd in Apr: eff over a stiff 6f, stays 1m well: acts on yld & hvy grnd & does
well on a testing course..   16
687 TANFEN [6] (T Craig) 5-9-3 N Connorton 7/2 Co FAV: 0-03102: Made most: clear of rem.   25
490 MARY MAGUIRE [7] (D Chapman) 9-9-8 D Nicholls 7/1: 0-00003: Ev ch: best in 306.   20
606 MARSILIANA [4] (Don Enrico Incisa) 4-8-0(2ow) M Beecroft 20/1: 0000-04: Ran on late:
maiden who probably needs further: stays 9f: seems to act on any grnd.   00
525 RIVERSIDE WRITER [2] 4-8-13 P D'arcy 7/2 Co FAV: 1034040: Btr on soft in 525: see 84.   09
649 ROSIE DICKINS [5] 4-8-13 R Lappin(7) 9/2: -122240: Btn dist: much btr 649 (yld):see 124   05
626 APHRODISIAC [8] 5-8-4 L Charnock 10/1: 10-0000: Fin last: see 626.   00
124 Remainder Tip [1] 7-7
8 ran   4,5,shhd,¾,1½,25   (M J Pound)   N Bycroft Brandsby, Yorks

821   QUARTER SELLING STAKES 2YO   £735   5f   Heavy 250 Slow

543 BENFIELD MORPETH [5] (J Berry) 2-8-11 M Fry 1/1 FAV: 0021: 2 b g Hills Forecast -
Running Mate (Track Spare): Made most to gamely justify fav. in a 2yo seller at Hamilton
May 31 (bought in 1,400 gns): cheaply acquired gelding who is well suited by this minimum
trip: acts on yld & hvy grnd & seems suited by forcing tactics.   18
711 FANTINE [4] (N Tinkler) 2-8-8(BL) Kim Tinkler(7) 7/2: 00442: Bl first time: with
winner most of way: acts on hvy grnd: see 543.   10
446 JULIOS LAD [1] (G Moore) 2-8-11 R P Elliott 11/2: 03: Kept on under strong press:
stoutly bred colt who will stay further in time: acts on hvy grnd & on a stiff trk.   10
696 BOOTHAM LAD [3] (M Brittain) 2-8-11 K Darley 6/1: 00004: Al up there: acts on any going.   08
696 CHOICE MATCH [2] 2-8-8 D Nicholls 12/1: 000: Slow start: dist 5th & no form yet.   00
125 KEITHS WISH [6] 2-8-8 C Dwyer 25/1: 00: Lost touch ½way: last to fin in both starts.   00
6 ran   1½,¾,¾,15,5   (J Squires)   J Berry Cockerham, lancs

822   COATBRIDGE MAIDEN STAKES 3YO   £1155   1m   Heavy 250 Slow

--   FOREMAST [10] (P Calver) 3-9-0 M Fry 12/1: 0-1: 3 br c Forli - Hey Skip (Bold Skipper):
First time out, led home turn and stayed on well to win a 3yo maiden at Hamilton May 31:
cheaply bought first foal who only ran once last season: stays 1m on hvy grnd.   46
334 EAGLE DESTINY [14] (I Balding) 3-9-0 J Matthias 7/1: -02: Kept on well under press:
beat rem decisively: stays 1m: handles heavy ground well: should find a small race.   44
615 GAY APPEAL [5] (C Nelson) 3-8-11 J Johnson 7/1: 003-03: Al well placed: no extra
dist: lightly raced last season, when showing a little promise: stays 1m: acts on gd & hvy ground 29
--   KAMPHALL [7] (Z Green) 3-8-11 S Keightley 33/1: 000-4: Never nearer on seasonal debut:
lightly raced last term: should be suited by further than 1m: acts on heavy grnd.   28
316 AMIR ALBADEIA [9] 3-9-0 N Howe 4/1 FAV: 04-220: Much btr in 316: see 253.   27
487 BREGUET [8] 3-8-11 M Beecroft 14/1: 00-20: No threat: btr over this C/D in 487.   21
423 ROSI NOA [6] 3-8-11 Gay Kelleway(5) 6/1: 0-300: Fin 7th: much btr in 315 (10f).   00
--   ARTAIUS ROSE [15] 3-8-11 A Bond 9/1: -0: No threat on racecourse debut: bred to
be suited by this trip: should impr on btr grnd.   00
--   LITTLE FIRE [4] 3-8-11 N Connorton 10/1: 0-0: Close up till home turn: btr for race:
showed promise on her only start last season, when 5th to Altiyna at Leicester: stays 7f:
much btr suited by fast grnd.   00
630 Bantel Banzai [2] 9-0(bl)   492 Blencathra Boy [3] 9-0
605 Jelly Jill [11] 8-11   328 Starboard [1] 8-11   377 Puncle Creak [13] 8-11
14 ran   1,8,¾,2½,1½,8   (P G Goulandris)   P Calver Ripon Nth Yorks

823   LIMEKILNBURN HANDICAP 3YO 0-35   £1705   1m 3f Heavy 250 Slow   [33]

*517 MIAMI IN SPRING [8] (R Stubbs) 3-8-11 K Darley 11/2: 3000-11: 3 ch g Miami Springs-
Fado (Ribero): Responded to press to lead inside dist in a 3yo h'cap at Hamilton May 31:
first time out was a comfortable winner of a seller at Thirsk: eff over 11/12f: seems to act
on any going, though certainly suited by some cut: acts on any trk.   24
491 CAROUSEL ROCKET [5] (J Wilson) 3-9-7 David Eddery(7) 8/1: 3-31042: Stumbled inside
dist, renewed effort & just held: clear of rem: see 130.   32
506 MISTS OF TIME [3] (I Balding) 3-9-4 J Matthias 7/1: 000-03: Led over 2f out: 12L
clear of rem: lightly raced last season: eff over 10/11f on firm & hvy grnd.   21
247 ALPHA HELIX [10] (K Brassey) 3-9-5 S Whitworth 4/1: -0334: Much btr in 247 (1m yld).   00
491 MARINA PLATA [2] 3-9-5 D Nicholls 15/2: -011000: Much btr over 1m here in 99 (soft).   00
609 ROCKALL [11] 3-9-3(bl) J Lowe 12/1: 0-04300: Made much: btr on gd/yld in 461 (12f).   00
674 GIBBERISH [9] 3-8-7 G Duffield 7/2 FAV: 3000-20: Fin 7th: btr on yld in 674 (1m).   00
648 STANDON MILL [7] 3-8-9 Julie Bowker(7) 10/1: 0-00040: Well btn 8th: much btr in 648.   00
648 WATERFORD WAY [3] 3-8-6 S Perks 15/2: 0-04100: Much btr over 1m here in 491.   00
631 Gunner Mac [4] 8-10
10 ran   1,5,12,4,4,2,20   (W Blakey)   R Stubbs Middleham, Yorks

824 AIRDRIE HANDICAP STAKES 0-35   £1295   1m 5f   Heavy 250 Slow   [32]

542 WESSEX [1] (N Tinkler) 4-9-7(bl) Kim Tinkler(7) 7/4 FAV: -412431: 4 b c Free State -
Bonandra (Andrea Mantegna): Consistent colt: led inside dist for a comfortable win in a
h'cap at Hamilton May 31: earlier won a similar race at Ayr and has yet to be out of the
frame this term: placed over hurdles this Winter: eff over 12f though is btr suited by a
test of stamina: acts on any going & on any trk.   34
*590 LEPRECHAUN LADY [3] (S Norton) 4-9-1(4ex) J Lowe 9/4: -200012: Made most: no ch with
winner though thrashed the rem: in gd form: acts on heavy: see 590.   22
256 BOREHAM DOWN [4] (N Bycroft) 7-7-7(1oh) S P Griffiths(5) 10/1: 00-0003: Last successful
on the Flat in '82, at Chepstow: eff over middle dists: suited by some cut in the grnd.   00
542 CAMPUS BOY [5] (J Ramsden) 5-8-4 M Fry 10/3: 32-0004: Lost touch home turn: see 542. 00
--   STAR ALLIANCE [6] 8-7-10 L Charnock 25/1: -00/3-0: Lightly raced in recent seasons:
won at Hamilton in '82, his only success to date: stays 12f: seems to act on any going.   00
630 FRASASS [2] 9-8-6(3ow) D Nicholls 8/1: 0-10040: Whipped round start, u.r. & took no
part: best in 257.   00
6 ran   3,30,12,dist   (Full Circle Thoroughbreds Ltd)   N Tinkler Malton, Yorks

---

Official Going Given as Good/Firm

825 WATERLOO APPRENTICE HANDICAP 0-35   £851   5f   Good 42 -28 Slow   [31]

626 PERGODA [6] (I Vickers) 8-9-7(bl) R Vickers(5) 6/4 FAV: 00-0001: 8 b g High Top -
Saint Joan (Grey Sovereign): On his fav. trk again made ev yd, comfortably in an app h'cap
at Edinburgh June 2: last season won twice over this C/D, incl this corresponding race:
successful 5 times previously on this sharp trk: very eff over 5f with forcing tactics,
though does stay 6f: acts on any going though is fav. by fast grnd: best on a sharp trk,
especially Edinburgh: wears bl though is a genuine sort who goes well for an app.   32
145 WESBREE BAY [5] (N Bycroft) 4-7-12(bl)(3ow) M Richardson 8/1: 004-002: Chased winner
most of way: remains a maiden: acts on any trk: see 145.   02
626 CULMINATE [8] (P Monteith) 5-7-9 G King 50/1: 000/003: All front rank: maiden sprint
h'capper who acts on fast & soft grnd: seems to have no trk preferences.   00
670 MISS TAUFAN [7] (M Brittain) 3-7-7(3oh) P Burke 20/1: 0000-04: Speed over ½way:
maiden who is a half sister to a couple of winning sprinters: should stay 6f: suited by gd
or faster ground.   00
--   Y I OYSTON [3] 4-9-6 A Wood(5) 11/1: 00004-0: Early speed: btr for race: little form
last season though in '84 won at Haydock & Pontefract: best form on fast grnd over this
minimum trip.   12
786 TRADESMAN [1] 6-7-11(bl) J Quinn 5/1: 3-00000: Never dngr: see 490.   00
198 THE BIGHT [4] 3-8-11 J Callaghan 6/1: 0100-00: Slow start: no threat: early last
season won a maiden auction race at Doncaster: best form over 5f on fast grnd with forcing
tactics: should stay 6f.   00
489 MAYBE JAYNE [2] 3-7-9 P Hill 13/2: 0-440: Early speed: btr on yld in 377.   00
8 ran   2½,2,1,1,1,4,½   (Harry Charlton)   I Vickers Sadberge, Co Durham

826 EBF ROYAL SCOTS CLUB MAIDEN STKS 2YO   £892   5f   Good 42 -28 Slow

627 BRUTUS [3] (J Wilson) 2-9-0 G Duffield 8/1: 01: 2 ch c Junius - Orangery (Realm):
Clearly benefitted considerably from his recent debut, broke well and was never hdd when
winning a 2yo maiden at Edinburgh June 2: cost 11,500 gns as a yearling: eff over 5f on
gd grnd: should stay further: well suited by forcing tactics on a sharp course.   46
473 DOMINO ROSE [5] (N Tinkler) 2-8-11 Kim Tinkler(7) 6/4 Jt FAV: 232: Had ev ch on this
faster grnd: may do btr on a more exacting course: see 236.   34
771 SWING SINGER [4] (J Watts) 2-9-0(bl) N Connorton 6/4 Jt FAV: 33: Hung right inside
dist: see 771.   36
627 MISS DISPLAY [1] (J Wilson) 2-8-11 C Dwyer 9/1: 004: Kept on well & will appreciate
another furlong: cost 6,000 gns: acts on gd & soft grnd ·& on a sharpish trk.   30
--   SING FOR THE KING [6] 2-9-0 D Nicholls 14/1: 0: Outsider: no threat after slow start:
cheaply bought gelding who should stay further in time.   00
766 ABSALOUTE HEAVEN [2] 2-8-11(BL) S Webster 6/1: 00: Bl first time: sn behind: btr in 766 00
6 ran   3,hd,1½,hd,2½   (Dowager Lady Bute)   J Wilson Ayr, Ayrshire

827 ROYAL SCOTS CUP HANDICAP 0-35   £1660   1m 4f   Good 42 +04 Fast   [35]

698 COMMANDER ROBERT [8] (J Hanson) 4-9-10 J H Brown(5) 11/2: 000-401: 4 b c Wolver Hollow-
Bernice Clare (Skymaster): Led over 2f out and held on gamely in a h'cap at Edinburgh June 2:
first success on the Flat though won twice over timber this Winter: stays 12f well: acts on
gd/firm & yld grnd & on any trk.   40
429 GOLDEN FANCY [7] (I Vickers) 9-9-4 D Nicholls 4/1 Co FAV: 1-00002: Switched below
dist, just failed to get up: gd effort: see 142.   33
631 TREYARNON [4] (S Norton) 4-8-1 J Lowe 4/1 Co FAV: 0-43433: Ev ch: flattered over
this C/D in 631.   12

EDINBURGH   Monday June 2nd   - Cont'd

80   THARALEOS [2] (F Watson) 6-7-8(1ow) A Mackay 6/1: 4200-04: Held up, no threat: has
been hurdling recently: sole success on the Flat came in '83 at Ripon: eff over 10/12f: seems
best on fast grnd: acts on any trk.   00
419   JUBILANT LADY [3] 5-7-7 S P Griffiths(5) 33/1: 00-0000: Last successful in '84,
winning twice at Catterick: stays 2m well: acts on firm & gd grnd & likes a sharp course.   00
631   NIGHT GUEST [1] 4-7-9 J Quinn(5) 8/1: 4000-00: Made much: no worthwhile form last
season & remains a maiden: suited by middle dists: suited by gd & firm grnd & likes this trk.   00
609   RUSTIC TRACK [6] 6-8-0 M Fry 4/1 Co FAV: 31-3200: Below par effort: see 281 & 131.   00
--   DONT ANNOY ME [5] 6-7-11 P Hill(7) 8/1: -0000-0: Last to fin on reapp: lightly raced
last season & last won on the Flat in '83 at Ayr: stays 12f: acts on firm & yld.   00
8 ran   nk,3,3,2½,shhd,1,4   (R Ogden)   J Hanson Sicklinghall, Yorks

828   SALAMANCA SELLING SELLING STAKES   £871   1m   Good 42 -06 Slow

163   TIT WILLOW [4] (S Wiles) 4-9-2(bl) S Keightley 2/1 FAV: 00-0221: 4 b c He Loves Me -
Willow Bird (Weeper's Boy): Led below dist, comfortably in a seller at Edinburgh June 2
(bought in 2,000 gns): first success: eff over 7/8f on fast & soft grnd: acts on any trk.   18
740   KO ISLAND [7] (J Berry) 3-8-2 M Fry 9/2: -000002: Made most: acts on gd/firm: see 259.   15
--   EISTEDDFOD [2] (W Pearce) 4-9-2 M Hindley(3) 4/1: 00000-3: Switched below dist, fin well
and not btn far: gd seasonal debut: maiden who is well suited by 1m: acts on fast & yld
grnd and likes this sharp trk.   14
822   BANTEL BANZAI [1] (I Bell) 3-8-2(bl) J Lowe 14/1: -000004: Dropped in class: longer
trip: best on this course in ,255 (5f, yld).   06
608   STEP ON [5] 3-8-2 J Bleasdale 5/1: 00-300: Btr on soft in 318 (9f).   00
788   MARTELLA [8] 4-9-2 N Connorton 12/1: 00-0300: Al mid-div: see 107.   00
673   SOPHYS FOLLY [6] 4-9-2(BL) G Duffield 10/1: 0-30000: Bl first time: trailed in last.   00
--   Brandon Grey [9] 8-13(BL)   --   Connaught Broads [10] 7-13
9 ran   1,½,5,5,1,4,½,15   (I Bell)   S Wiles Flockton, Yorks

829   GALLIPOLI MAIDEN STAKES 3YO   £547   1m   Good 42 -01 Slow

528   ADAMSTOWN [7] (M Prescott) 3-9-0 G Duffield 5/4 FAV: -31: 3 b g Hittite Glory -
Dawn Attack (Midsummer Night II): Gamely justified fav. led over 2f out and just held on in
a 3yo maiden at Edinburgh June 2: placed behind Asian Cup at Pontefract last time: stays 1m:
acts on gd/firm & soft grnd & seems well suited by a sharp trk.   37
347   TURFAH [10] (P Walwyn) 3-9-0 N Howe 11/4: 3400-02: Ran on well: gd effort & sure
to stay further: see 347.   35
--   TANYAS PRINCESS [8] (J Watts) 3-8-11 N Connorton 9/2: 03-3: Made much: btr for race:
lightly raced last season, showing some promise: will be suited by further: acts on gd &
firm grnd & on any trk.   24
--   SWEET ALEXANDRA [2] (J Shaw) 3-8-11 R Lines(3) 16/1: -4: Dwelt, fin in gd style &
will do btr next time: closely related to several middle dist winners, incl useful Deutschmark: acts on gd grnd & on a sharp course.   16
444   HITCHENSTOWN [1] 3-9-0 L Charnock 10/1: 0000-00: Had ev ch: see 444.   16
650   PAULS SECRET [5] 3-9-0 D Leadbitter(5) 16/1: 00-00000: Never beyond mid-div: rated
40 when a close 3rd to Karmo and Nap Majestica in a Pontefract maiden last term: acts on gd/
firm & yld grnd & on a sharp trk.   14
528   HAMLOUL [9] 3-9-0 P D'arcy 7/1: 0030-00: Fin 7th: rated 45 when 3rd to Priory Place
and Our Tilly at Ayr last season & is btr than this: acts on firm & soft grnd & on a gall trk.   00
667   Ortica [4] 8-11   --   Latrigg Lodge [6] 9-0   --   Miss Stanway [3] 8-11
10 ran   ½,4,5,½,½,1½,5   (Derek K Stokes)   M Prescott Newmarket

830   PONTIUS PILATE HANDICAP 0-35   £944   7f   Good 42 +02 Fast   [27]

606   YOUNG BRUSS [16] (J Etherington) 4-9-4 M Wood 6/1: 004-001: 4 b g Palco - Pamela Rose
(Vilmorin): Was well bckd when leading ½way, comfortably in a h'cap at Edinburgh June 2:
first success: half brother to several winners: well suited by 7f, stays 9f: acts on fast
& yld grnd & on any trk.   27
*700   THE MAZALL [14] (L Siddall) 6-9-12(bl)(8ex) G Gosney 4/1: 10-0012: In grand form: see 700.29
*710   GODS LAW [8] (G Reveley) 5-8-2 A Proud 3/1 FAV: 000-013: Ran on too late: btr in 710.   05
378   BARNES STAR [9] (P Monteith) 4-8-12 D Nicholls 14/1: 0-03304: Fin well: gd effort.   13
700   TRADE HIGH [1] 7-9-0 R Vickers(7) 14/1: -003000: Dwelt, never nearer: see 260.   15
606   MONINSKY [6] 5-9-1 M Richardson(7) 9/1: 332-200: Al front rank: runs well here: see 260   14
636   SANDBOURNE [10] 4-9-7 G Duffield 7/1: -00-000: Raced wide: ignore this run: see 481.   00
490   Responder [13] 8-13   700   Always Native [12] 9-3
594   High Port [7] 8-8   --   Rossett [11] 8-5   768   Skybird [3] 9-2
465   Shark Fighter [15] 8-9   606   Taj Singh [5] 9-0
--   Jokist [4] 9-1   --   Coplace [2] 8-1
16 ran   2½,shhd,1,hd,½,nk   (P D Brunt)   J Etherington Malton, Yorks

272

Official Going Given as Good

831   PULTENEY SELLING STAKES 2YO   **£853   5.5f   Good 52 -41 Slow**

482   JOSIE SMITH [3] (P Cole) 2-8-8 T Quinn 4/7 FAV: 01: 2 gr f Alias Smith - Josilu
(Caliban): Dropped to selling company & heavily bckd when a comfortable winner of a slow run
2yo seller at Bath June 2 (sold 2,900 gns): half sister to several winners & should be
suited by further than 5f: acts on gd & yld grnd & a gall trk.   30
633   ARDNACROSS [6] (J Douglas Home) 2-8-8 R Cochrane 14/1: 002: No ch with winner: should
stay 6f: acts on gd grnd & may find a similar event.   20
681   PHOEBE [4] (C Wildman) 2-8-8 Paul Eddery 10/1: 003: Best effort yet: acts on gd grnd
& a gall trk: 6L clear rest.   19
633   SAMS REFRAIN [2] (D H Jones) 2-8-8(BL) J Reid 11/2: 301D04: Led 4f: twice below 502(yld).04
596   SKY ROBBER [8] 2-8-11 A O'reilly(7) 6/1: 00: No threat: cheaply acquired: half
sister to 5f winner Ma Tante.   00
--   NUNS ROYAL [5] 2-8-8 M Miller 33/1: 0: No threat on debut.   00
717   Just Enchanting [1] 8-8   **633   Star City** [7] 8-8
633   Pullandese [10] 8-8
9 ran   4,½,6,5,1   (Richard Barber)   P Cole Whatcombe, Oxon

832   BRISTOL MAIDEN STAKES 3YO   **£1938   1m 3f   Good 52 -02 Slow**

--   WAVE DANCER [11] (W Hern) 3-8-11 W Carson 10/3: 4-1: 3 ch f Dance In Time - Pirogue
(Reliance II): Impr filly: made a winning seasonal debut, led nearing final 1f, under press
in a 3yo maiden at Bath June 2: on sole start in '85 fin 4th in a fillies maiden at Nottingham: half sister to several winners, notably the very smart stayer Longboat: should be
suited by 12f plus: acts on gd grnd & & should rate more highly.   46
--   FORT LINO [6] (I Balding) 3-9-0 Pat Eddery 5/2 FAV: 4-2: Well bckd on reapp: ev ch
final 1f: just btn: gd effort: on only outing in '85 fin 4th in a Warwick maiden: stays 11f
really well: acts on gd & firm grnd & a gall trk: should find a maiden.   48
506   SURE GROUND [10] (P Walwyn) 3-9-0 Paul Eddery 7/1: -00-03: Kept on well, showing impr:
will be suited by 12f: acts on gd grnd & a gall trk: should find a race.   43
--   FIRST RANK [15] (P Arthur) 3-9-0 S Whitworth 10/1: 00-4: Gambled on: led ½way till
over 1f out: 6L clear rem: best effort yet: highly tried on both outings in '85: half sister
to the smart sprinter Frimley Park: may stay 12f but may benefit from a drop back to 10f:
acts on gd grnd.   40
486   COLEMAN HAWKINS [5] 3-9-0 T Quinn 25/1: -000: No real threat: see 486 (yld).   30
625   FLORAL CHARGE [16] 3-9-0 B Thomson 10/1: 2-000: Mkt drifter: led 6f: yet to find
her 2yo form: see 486.   29
--   BANNEROL [13] 3-9-0 T Fahey 10/1: -0: Very active in mkt on racecourse debut: nearest
fin & impr certain: should stay 12f: acts on gd grnd.   00
570   LOBBINO [8] 3-8-11 R Cochrane 8/1: 03-00: Made no show: see 570 (10f).   00
484   Tonquin [14] 8-11   **--   Windy Hollow** [3] 9-0   **--   Tamed Shrew** [17] 8-11
218   Ebolito [7] 9-0   **420   Sales Promoter** [4] 9-0
619   Tabacos [9] 9-0   **739   Barleybree** [12] 8-11   **--   Podsnap** [19] 9-0
484   Gratify [18] 8-11   **546   Windbound Lass** [2] 8-11
479   Alceba [1] 8-11   **535   Bully Boy** [20] 9-0
20 ran   ½,3,1½,6,nk   (R D Hollingsworth)   W Hern East Ilsley, Berks

833   MONKTON FARLEIGH HANDICAP 3YO 0-50   **£2431   1m 5f   Good 52 -21 Slow**   **[50]**

--   BEIJING [2] (P Cole) 3-8-6 T Quinn 11/4: 000-1: 3 b f Northjet - Protectora (Prologo):
Well bckd & led 2f out, comfortably in a h'cap at Bath June 2: highly tried in 3 outings
in '85: bred to be suited by a dist of grnd, as she is a half sister to the smart stayer Protection
Racket and the useful Safe River: eff at 13f, should get 2m: acts on gd grnd & a gall trk:
should rate more highly.   41
459   ITTIHAAD [5] (C Benstead) 3-8-7 B Rouse 15/2: 00-0302: Made most: gd run: stays 13f:
acts on gd & soft grnd: see 117.   34
*458   NICOLA WYNN** [1] (D Elsworth) 3-9-7 Pat Eddery 6/4 FAV: -13: Held ev ch: btr 458 (yld).   44
669   BEYBARS [3] (W Hern) 3-9-0(BL) W Carson 5/1: 230-034: Bl first time: ev ch str.   35
486   DIWAAN [6] 3-9-0 Paul Eddery 12/1: 030-00: No real threat: in '85 was rated 45 when
3rd to Pactolus in a 7f maiden at Salisbury: half brother to several winners.   33
307   MOUNT SCHIEHALLION [4] 3-8-9 S Whitworth 14/1: 030-330: Abs since 307: best 171 (12f).   14
463   BRIDE [8] 3-8-7 M Miller 9/1: 00-100: Wknd 3f out: best in 123 (12f hvy).   00
458   Molucella [7] 8-3(1ow)
8 ran   4,2½,1,½,8   (Binfield Manor Farms Ltd)   P Cole Whatcombe, Oxon

834   DOWNS STAKES 2YO   **£2602   5.5f   Good 52 -12 Slow**

+536   SINGING STEVEN** [10] (R Hannon) 2-9-4 B Rouse 7/2: 2211: 2 b c Balliol - Chebs Honour
(Chebs Lad): Useful, consistent colt: ran on well to lead final 1f, driven out in a 2yo
stakes at Bath June 2: last time out was a game winner of a maiden auction at Wolverhampton:
cheaply acquired half brother to winning h'capper Minus Man: acts on gd & soft grnd & on
any trk: genuine sort who is likely to prove best over 5/6f.   51

273

-- LUCIANAGA [18] (P Walwyn) 2-8-11 Paul Eddery 3/1 FAV: 2: Gambled on on racecourse debut: led 2f out & just btn: should be winning soon: half brother to 2 winners: should be suited by 5/6f: acts on gd grnd & a gall trk.   43

531 BATTLEAXE [3] (J Toller) 2-8-11 W Carson 9/2: 33: Mkt drifter: sn prom & not btn far: 8L clear rem: acts on gd & firm grnd: should stay 6f: see 531.   43

323 CAPITAL FLOW [13] (R Hannon) 2-8-11 A Mcglone 12/1: 04: Al there: stayed: speedily bred colt who cost 6,800 gns: half brother to several winners.   27

-- BACCHANALIAN [12] 2-8-11 B Thomson 14/1: 0: Nearest fin on racecourse debut & should impr: should be suited by further than 5f: acts on gd grnd.   27

-- BAREFACED [7] 2-8-11 Pat Eddery 12/1: 0: Showed gd speed 4f on debut: cost 6,200 gns: should stay further than 5f.   25

482 YAVARRO [5] 2-8-8 P Cook 10/1: 00: Made no show: btr 482 (yld).   00

457 August Hill [17] 8-11	-- Keecagee [9] 8-11	-- Auntie Cyclone [16] 8-8
544 George Harry [8] 8-11	678 Mr Mumbles [11] 8-11	622 Highland Lodge [6] 8-11
513 Gameshow [15] 8-11	497 Flag Bearer [2] 8-11	-- Battle Heights [14] 8-11
206 Skraggs Plus Two [1] 8-11		-- Granny Takesa Trip [19] 8-8
353 Thats Motoring [4] 8-8		

19 ran   nk,shhd,8,shhd,1   (Dr S Bennett)   R Hannon East Everleigh, Wilts

---

835 MILBOURNE MAIDEN STAKES 3YO   £1555   5f   Good 52 +02 Fast

250 HIGH IMAGE [12] (I Balding) 3-8-11 Pat Eddery 4/1: -01: 3 br f High Top - Gay Shadow (Northfields): Prom filly: led approaching final 1f for an easy win in quite a fast run 3yo maiden at Bath June 22: half sister to 5f winner Follow Me Follow: eff at 5f, will be well suited by further: acts on gd grnd & a gall trk: should rate more highly.   51

677 SUPERCOOMBE [4] (P Cole) 3-9-0 M Lynch(5) 5/1: 4-302: Ran on final 1f: no ch with winner.   38

593 ACLIA [2] (N Vigors) 3-8-11 P Cook 20/1: -003: Ran on final 1f, showing impr: should stay 6f: acts on gd grnd & a gall trk.   35

516 WINSONG MELODY [17] (P Cundell) 3-8-11 A Mcglone 12/1: -44: Sn prom: acts on any trk.   34

516 KHLESTAKOV [7] 3-9-0 R Curant 33/1: -000: Never nearer: bred to be suited by further than 5f: half brother to 2 winners.   35

-- HEAVENLY CAROL [16] 3-8-11 T Williams 6/1: -0: Gambled on   racecourse debut: nearest fin & should do btr: speedily bred filly.   31

576 GREGORIAN CHANT [3] 3-9-0 Paul Eddery 10/1: -000: Lightly bckd but no show: half brother to 1m winner Palmion.   00

-- ENIGMA [9] 3-8-11 B Thomson 3/1 FAV: 204-0: Very easy to back on seasonal debut: led over 3f: showed fair form as a 2yo, first time out fin 2nd to Flyaway Bride in a fillies maiden on this trk: sister to smart Irish sprinter Princess Tracy: acts on gd & soft.   00

431 MARIES VALENTINE [21] 3-8-11 R Wernham 7/1: 04-00: Early speed, fdd: on final outing in '85 fin 4th in a stakes event at Catterick: acts on a sharp trk.   00

580 Northern Lad [22] 9-0	-- Secret Fact [6] 8-11	726 Boxers Shukee [8] 8-11
-- Moorestar [11] 9-0	-- Abutammam [1] 9-0	431 Another Western [20] 8-11
-- Lido Dancer [15] 8-11	516 Marcredea [5] 8-11	732 Miss Moth [10] 8-11
359 Private Sue [19] 8-11	624 Someway [14] 8-11	507 Sunny Match [13] 8-11
-- Some Guest [18] 9-0		

22 ran   6,hd,nk,¼,nk   (Sheikh Ali Abu Khamsin)   I Balding Kingsclere, Hants

---

836 MALMESBURY HANDICAP 0-50   £2725   5.5f   Good 52 +16 Fast   [49]

550 LOCHTILLUM [10] (J Douglas Home) 7-9-5 R Cochrane 5/1: 100-001: 7 b h Song - Spring Storm (March Past): Useful horse: fin well to lead near fin in a fast run h'cap at Bath June 2: in gd form in '85, winning valuable h'caps at Newcastle & Doncaster (Portland H'cap): very eff over 5/6f: acts on any grnd: likes a stiff trk & is a genuine sort.   51

624 CRETE CARGO [4] (M Francis) 3-9-2 Paul Eddery 16/1: 0000002: Bckd at long odds: led over 1f out: caught near line: gd effort and maybe winning soon: see 15.   56

616 DEPUTY HEAD [15] (L Holt) 6-8-13 J Matthias 14/1: 0-00003: Fin in gd style: returning to form? useful at his best: see 327.   43

550 ALL AGREED [12] (J Winter) 5-9-6 T Quinn 14/1: 204-004: Ch final 1f: not btn far: better effort: see 550.   49

*679 PINE HAWK [7] 5-7-13(2ow)(7ex) D Williams(0) 10/1: 4-41010: Another gd run: in grand form: see 679.   25

616 MANIMSTAR [11] 6-10-0(vis) B Thomson 14/1: 30-0000: Ch 1f out: gd run under top weight: useful horse who in '85 won h'caps at Newmarket (2) & Newbury: in '84 won at Bath: in '83 won at Newbury & Kempton: well suited by 6f on a stiff trk: acts on fast & yld grnd and usually comes late.   50

550 CREE BAY [9] 7-9-9 W Carson 9/2 Jt.FAV: 40-3320: Dsptd lead over 1f out: btr 550.   00

687 GEORGE WILLIAM [14] 5-8-9 R Curant 9/2 Jt.FAV: 00-2230: Wknd 1f out: btr 687: see 412.   00

*734 STONEYDALE [13] 4-8-13(7ex) Pat Eddery 8/1: 00-0010: No show: much btr 734 (5f).   00

545 Taylor Of Soham [16] 7-9		616 Bay Presto [2] 8-7(vis)
507 Websters Feast [8] 8-4		418 High Eagle [6] 7-11(BL)
525 Holt Row [5] 7-8	211 Lucky Starkist [3] 7-7(4oh)	
495 Robrob [1] 7-8(vis)		

16 ran   ½,½,nk,1,1½   (J Douglas Home)   J Douglas Home Chilton, Oxon

Official Going Given as Good/Firm: Visibility Poor

837   LEVY BOARD APP.H'CAP 3YO 0-35   £939   6f   Good 43 No Time Taken

277 LINAVOS [2] (W Brooks) 3-9-3 J Bray[5] 33/1: 000-01: 3 b c Tyrnavos - Linmill (Amber
Rama): Caused a 33/1 surprise when leading inside final 1f, narrowly, in an app. 3yo h'cap
at Folkestone June 2: first success: lightly raced previously: eff over 6f, may stay further:
acts on good grnd.   33
670 SPORTING SOVEREIGN [13] (M Jarvis) 3-9-0 P Hutton 8/1: 000-042: Just held in a driving
finish & is impr: stays 6f well: should find a small race soon: see 670.   29
657 SILVER FORM [12] (W Wightman) 3-8-12 P Johnson 33/1: 0400-03: Hdd inside final 1f:
fair effort from this maiden: see 657.   22
328 SAXON BAZAAR [9] (M Usher) 3-8-12 F Roberts[5] 25/1: 04-0004: Fair effort but btr 328.   16
438 NAWADDER [5] 3-9-7(BL) A Geran 2/1 fav: 0-240: Bl first time & heavily bckd: twice
below 205 (5f, soft).   21
--   GRISETTE [14] 3-9-3 D Meade 13/2: 030-0: Friendless in mkt on seasonal debut, likely
to impr for the race: ran only 3 times in '85 fin. a close 3rd in a minor event at Bath
(rated 42): best effort: suited by give in the grnd.   16
340 TUMBLE FAIR [6] 3-9-6 J Leech 6/1: 4014-00: Fin 7th: see 340.   18
545 LIBERTON BRAE [1] 3-8-9 M Lynch[5] 7/1: 20-4440: Fin 8th: much btr 545 (yld).   06
454 CELESTIAL DRIVE [3] 3-9-3 R Perham[5] 11/2: 3000-20: Much btr 454 (yld).   00
534 Tamalpais [4] 9-4   658 Country Craft [8] 9-1   593 Tamana Dancer [7] 8-12
564 Care In The Air [10] 7-8(vis)   498 Miss Maggie [11] 8-6(BL)
14 ran   hd,1½,3,2,nk,hd,½ '   (A Blackham)   W Brooks Lambourn, Berks

838   HAWKINGE SELLING STAKES 3 & 4-Y-O   £727   1m 2f   Good 43 -26 Slow

--   KOUS [12] (R Simpson) 3-8-1(BL) B Crossley 12/1: -1: 3 b c Huguenot - Princess Cornish
(Cornish Prince): First time out, mkt drifter, but sprinted clear in the final 1f to win
a seller at Folkestone June 2 (bought in 4,100 gns): reportedly purchased as a lead horse
for stable star Brunico: suited by 10f, likely to stay further: acts well on gd grnd:
wears bl: probably better than a plater.   20
620 ANGEL DRUMMER [9] (A Ingham) 3-8-3 A Shoults[5] 5/1: 10-0022: Hdd inside final 1f
& probably caught a tartar in this grade: should win soon: see 620: stays 10f.   14
749 FLEUR DE THISTLE [6] (A Davison) 3-8-1 N Adams 14/1: 00-0033: Ev ch: stays 10f: see 749. 09
547 FORGIVING [5] (B Stevens) 4-8-8 R Carter[5] 11/8 fav: 4000-04: Well bckd, chall inside
final 2f: rated 47 when btn only a hd in a maiden fillies race at Brighton in July '85
(trained by R Laing) but evidently has deteriorated: stays 10f: acts on firm.   01
666 SOHO SAM [4] 3-8-2(1ow) M Wigham 11/2: -0040: Btr 666 (7f soft).   07
522 NARCISSUS [10] 4-8-11 G Baxter 5/1: 0-30: Ev ch: much btr 522 (soft).   00
495 Lean Streak [11] 9-2   343 Blairs Winnie [1] 8-13
346 Winters Beta [8] 7-12   530 Deerfield Beach [3] 8-13
--   Alsace [2] 7-12
11 ran   3,3,shhd,3,10   (Tony Stafford)   R Simpson Upper Lambourn, Berks

839   BARHAM 3YO MAIDEN STAKES   £818   1m 4f   Good 43 -01 Slow

--   VAGADOR [9] (G Harwood) 3-9-0 A Clark 9/1: -1: 3 ch c Vaguely Noble - Louisa D'Or
(Indian Hemp): Prom colt: first time out, gained the day close home in a 3yo maiden at
Folkestone June 2: well suited by 12f & gd grnd: likely to stay further: scope for further
impr and is the type to win more races.   57
625 NORTHERN AMETHYST [5] (G Huffer) 3-9-0 R Carter[5] 8/13 fav: 022-32: Caught near fin:
clear of rest: possibly caught a tartar here & must find a maiden: stays 12f: see 625.   55
209 FLYING FAIRY [13] (H Cecil) 3-8-11 S Cauthen 5/1: 00-33: Mkt drifter, led over 2f
out after abs: should stay 12f: see 209.   44
619 NORTHERN SOCIETY [1] (D Murray Smith) 3-9-0 G Baxter 20/1: 0-04: Appears to be going
the right way: lightly raced colt who is a half brother to 10f winner Symphytum: stays 12f:
acts on gd grnd.   37
619 HEAD OF SCHOOL [8] 3-9-0 M Hills 25/1: 0020-00: Btr effort from this half brother
to the winning 2yo Rahash: rated 39 when a close 2nd in a maiden at Hamilton in '85, best
effort from 5 outings last term: acts well on hvy: probably also on gd: might be suited by
slightly shorter dists than 12f.   33
506 SAVAGE LOVE [10] 3-8-11 T Ives 11/1: 30-40: Has now run twice well below last years form 26
579 Naskracker [6] 9-0   --   Matbar [12] 9-0   123 Sagareme [11] 8-11
720 Azusa [14] 9-0   --   Simon Damian [4] 9-0(BL)
500 Sea Trouper [2] 9-0   423 Miss Brahms [3] 8-11(vis)
13 ran   nk,5,5,2,2½   (K Abdulla)   G Harwood Pulborough, Sussex

840   METROPOLE CHALL.CUP STAKES 2YO   £1727   5f   Good 43 +11 Fast

*614 BESTPLAN [3] (W O'gorman) 2-9-1 T Ives 4/5 fav: 0111: 2 b c Try My Best - Make Plans
(Go Marching): Very useful colt: completed his hat trick with an all the way, narrow, fast
time success in a minor race at Folkestone June 2: successful earlier at Newbury & Lingfield:
half brother to the smart Sayf El Arab and the useful Eagles Landed: speedy type who acts
on fast & yld going: very eff at 5f with forcing tactics: Royal Ascot bound.   65

*115 SIZZLING MELODY [2] (Lord J Fitzgerald) 2-9-1 M Hills 11/8: 112: Chall winner final
2f, just held: acts on gd & heavy: see 115.   64
621 STAY LOW [1] (G Blum) 2-8-12 M Rimmer 9/1: 21133: Pressed ldrs most: see 513.   53
61   CHERRYWOOD SAM [4] (H O'neill) 2-8-11 G Baxter 100/1: 404: Stiff task, no dngr after
long abs: see 27.   17
4 ran   ½,4,15   (mrs P I Yong)   W O'gorman Newmarket

841 DOVER HANDICAP 3YO+ 0-35   £1386   1m 7f Good 43 -07 Slow   [33]

430 SARFRAZ [3] (G Harwood) 3-8-11 A Clark 5/2 fav: 42-01: 3 b c Sassafras - Ziba Blue
(John's Joy): Came from behind to lead final 1f, comfortably, in a h'cap at Folkestone
June 2: placed both outings in '85: acts on firm & yld: stays 2m well: should continue to
impr & win more staying h'caps.   42
542 SMACK [9] (H Collingridge) 4-8-0 R Morse[5] 20/1: 020-002: Chall 1f out: gd effort:
showed little form last season but yet to win a race: stays 2m well & acts on gd grnd.   09
542 HARLESTONE LAKE [10] (J Dunlop) 4-8-12 G Baxter 11/1: 320-003: Prom thro'out: still
awaiting first success though placed in similar company last season: acts on gd & soft:
stays really well.   21
542 CROOK N HONEST [14] (R Holder) 4-7-11 C Rutter[4] 11/1: 40-0044: Led 3f out: see 542. 02
582 ROYAL CRAFTSMAN [7] 5-8-2 P Robinson 7/2: 10-0030: Well bckd, fin well but too late:
much btr 582 (14f).   07
712 SECURITY CLEARANCE [18] 5-9-9 M Rimmer 12/1: 0-00300: Led before ¼way, no extra
final 3f: twice below 590.   '   24
731 PALACE YARD [15] 4-8-7(1ow) S Cauthen 13/2: 0240-40: Prom most: non stayer? see 731. 00
532 LADY LIZA [6] 5-8-1 R Carter[0] 11/2: 00-3000: A gamble from 16/1, fin in rear:
trying this trip for the first time: best 202 (12f).   00

582 Chartfield [13] 7-12(3ow)   506 Music Minstrel [8] 8-0(5ow)
761 Hot Betty [1] 7-13   -- Solitaire [16] 7-9   336 Zircons Sun [12] 7-9
--   Andrea Dawn [19] 8-6(BL)(1ow)   542 American Girl [4] 8-7
504 Sylvan Joker [17] 8-9(bl)   --   Princess Jenny [5] 8-5
277 Trelawney [16] 7-9
18 ran   2,shhd,2,shhd,2,hd,nk   (K Abdulla)   G Harwood Pulborough, Sussex

842 FOLKESTONE STAKES 3YO+   £684   6f   Good 43 No Time Taken

344 MR MCGREGOR [6] (H O'neill) 4-9-0 Gay Kelleway[5] 20/1: 0-00001: 4 b g Formidable -
Mrs Tiggywinkle (Silly Season): Turned up at 20/1, holding on gamely close home in a minor
event at Folkestone June 2: has run poorly previously this season on soft grnd & probably
btr on gd or firm going: has shown form in the past though this was first win: very eff
over 6f on gd grnd & seems suited by forcing tactics.   20
481 SILENT GAIN [7] (W Jarvis) 4-8-11 S Cauthen 16/1: 0000-02: Chall winner final 1f,
just held: gd effort from this maiden: stays 6f & acts on gd grnd.   16
229 PERSIAN BALLET [13] (P Walwyn) 3-8-4 G Baxter 10/1: 0-03: Al prom: lightly raced maiden. 13
636 HILMAY [11] (W Charles) 4-8-11(bl) R Lappin[7] 33/1: 0-00304: Al prom: twice below 418. 06
501 DEPUTY GOVERNOR [4] 3-8-4 P Waldron 33/1: -00: Gd finish: needs further? unraced in
'85: half brother to 3 winning sprinters and is impr.   07
733 THE STAMP DEALER [3] 3-8-4 G Sexton 14/1: -000: Speedily bred type who ran quite well. 06
567 NORTHERN IMPULSE [9] 3-8-4 M Wigham 5/4 fav: -030: Should have hacked up on the
evidence of 567 (rated 53!).   00
--   MUBAASHIR [14] 3-8-4 M Roberts 4/1: -0: Fin 8th on debut: an 82,000 gns purchase
who may improve.   00
431 SHARP STABLE [12] 3-8-1 A Clark 9/2: 0-00: Mkt drifter, well btn: see 431.   00
656 Be So Bold [1] 8-1   -- Last Cry [8] 8-5(1ow)   500 Recapture [10] 8-1
--   Sideland [2] 9-0   592 Oeil De Tigre [5] 9-0(BL)
14 ran   ½,2,1,1,½,nk,1,hd   (C W Driscoll)   H O'neill Coldharbour, Surrey

843 WALMER HANDICAP 0-35 3YO   £1381   1m 2f Good 43 -49 Slow   [37]

615 BLACK COMEDY [9] (G Lewis) 3-9-0 P Waldron 11/4 fav: 1-00001: 3 b c Blakeney -
Laughing Goddess (Green God): Well bckd when leading under press final 1f in a 3yo h'cap
at Folkestone June 2: winner of a backend maiden at Warwick in '85: half brother to a couple
of winners: appears eff between 1m & 12f: acts on gd/firm & soft grnd & likes a sharp/easy trk 31
461 FLEET FOOTED [1] (G P Gordon) 3-9-4 W Ryan 6/1: 004-002: Every chance final 3f:
good effort: stays 10f: see 49.   32
623 SILENT RUNNING [10] (P Mitchell) 3-8-11 T Ives 12/1: 00-0003: Strong fin but too late:
appeared not to stay 12f last time but certainly suited by 10f: remains a maiden.   25
127 SIMONS FANTASY [5] (R Armstrong) 3-8-11 S Cauthen 25/1: 00-04: Ev ch: lightly raced
maiden who is a half brother to winning stayer Migoletty & also successful sprinter/miler
Linda's Fantasy: on the up grade.   23
570 MINISTRAILIS [2] 3-9-2 K Powdrell 14/1: 00-000: Ev ch: cost $375,000 as a yearling
and is a half brother to 4 winners: probably stays 10f: acts on gd.   22
480 PROBLEM CHILD [8] 3-9-1 P Robinson 12/1: 003-300: new trip: best 274 (7f, heavy).   17
422 TAIS TOI [6] 3-9-1 M Roberts 10/1: 00-40: Fin 8th: btr 422   00

491	BRAVE AND BOLD [7] 3-8-8(bl) A Shoults[5] 3/1: 1-20200: Fin 9th: btr 451 (1m).			00
*505	FAIR ATLANTA [14] 3-8-13 M Wigham 8/1: 3-24010: Mkt drifter: much btr 505 (soft).			00

716 Cheerful Times [10] 8-11   535 Roi De Soleil [13] 8-6
527 Dallona [12] 8-12   581 Miss Jade [15] 9-7   -- Cool Number [4] 9-1
14 ran   1½,hd,1,3,2   (Mrs W H Gerhauser)   G Lewis Epsom, Surrey

844 FOLKESTONE STAKES 3YO+   £684   6f   Good 43 No Time Taken

593 SATIAPOUR [6] (R J Houghton) 3-8-4(vis) S Cauthen 2/1: 043-201: 3 ch c Blushing Groom-
Safita (Habitat): Gained his first success, keeping on well under press for a clear cut 6L
win in a minor event at Folkestone June 2: only ran 3 times in '85, showing promise: eff
over 6f with forcing tactics, will stay at least 7f: suited by firm or gd grnd: often
wears a visor.   51

-- SIR ARNOLD [7] (A Stewart) 3-8-4 M Roberts 10/1: -2: Gd fin & a promising debut:
sprint bred gelding who will have no difficulty finding a maiden in the near future: acts
on good grnd.   36

600 AVALON [8] (D Murray Smith) 3-8-4 G Baxter 33/1: -03: Ev ch: seems to be going the
right way: should stay at least 7f: acts on gd.   35

564 PERSIAN PERSON [13] (G Gracey) 4-8-11 N Adams 50/1: -04: Late prog: considerable impr
here having been 8th of 10 in a seller at Brighton last time! (on belated racecourse debut):
will stay beyond 6f.   30

-671 QUINTA REEF [5] 3-8-11 T Ives 1/1 fav: 00-120: Much btr 671, 438.   39

109 ADHARI [4] 3-8-1 M Hills 20/1: -00: Prominent much on only second ever outing:
should stay beyond 6f.   17

340 WAVEGUIDE [11] 3-8-1 S Dawson[3] 8/1: 424-00: Rated 40 last term: see 340.   00

500 Golden Straw [3] 8-4(vis)   -- Al Zahyia [2] 8-1
-- Wizzard Magic [9] 8-4   733 Waverley Rose [1] 8-1   -- Celtona Peach [10] 8-11
729 Hillingdon Jim [12] 8-4
13 ran   6,½,½,½,6   (H H Aga Khan)   R J Houghton Blewbury, Oxon

---

Official Going Given as Good

845 BISHOPSTONE SELLING H'CAP (0-25)   £963   7f   Good 40 -41 Slow   [23]

-- SAHARA SHADOW [8] (D Tucker) 4-8-5 A Dicks(3) 33/1: 00000-1: 4 b f Formidable - Gay
Shadow (Northfields): First time out, caused a 33/1 surprise in a selling h'cap at Salisbury
June 3: led well over 1f out, under press: bought in 1,500 gns: placed twice in '85: eff
at 6/7f on gd & fast grnd: acts on any trk.   07

684 ON IMPULSE [14] (K Brassey) 3-8-11 S Whitworth 14/1: 000-032: Kept on well final 1f:
in gd form: should find a seller: see 684.   23

620 OSTENTATIOUS [7] (C Wildman) 4-8-13 Pat Eddery 3/1 FAV: 400-033: Well bckd (again):
ran on under press: btr 1m? see 620.   12

540 HADDON LAD [5] (M Mccourt) 3-8-8(BL) J Reid 6/1: 00-0004: Bl first time: al up there:
dropped to selling company today: eff at 7f on gd grnd.   17

749 FIRST ORBIT [4] 3-8-2 R Wernham 16/1: 0-02040: Dsptd lead 2f out: best in 346 (1m yld). 08

809 NANOR [20] 3-8-6 P Cook 12/1: 0030000: Led after ½way: best 340 (6f).   11

*568 SUPERFROST [18] 4-9-1 B Crossley 7/2: 0-00010: No show: well below form 568 (1m shrp trk 00

495 Lady Natively [3] 9-1   399 Danedancer [9] 8-5(bl)(2ow)
275 Be Positive [1] 8-4   679 Sparkford Lad [15] 9-10(bl)
335 Chepstowed [13] 8-2   -- Disting [19] 8-8   749 Blue Fantasy [10] 8-2(6ow)
578 Karamanad [2] 8-6   568 Letoile Du Palais [16] 7-13
-- Miss Comedy [6] 8-5   727 Mista Spoof [12] 8-5   709 Solstice Bell [17] 8-5(bl)
-- The Batchlor [11] 8-7(1ow)
20 ran   1,½,1,1½,nk   (Mike Tebbut)   D Tucker Frome, Somerset

846 DURNFORD HANDICAP 3YO+ (0-50)   £2758   6f   Good 40 -16 Slow   [49]

616 AL TRUI [1] (S Mellor) 6-9-11 M Wigham 11/2: 1000-01: 6 gr h Scottish Rifle - Sweety
Gray (Young Emperor): Useful horse: came fast and late to win a h'cap at Salisbury June 3:
in fine form in '85 winning valuable Stewards Cup H'cap at Goodwood: also successful in
h'caps at Lingfield (2) & Salisbury (2) incl this race: very eff at 6f on any going & on
any trk: genuine sort who carries weight well: needs to be held up.   57

616 PADRE PIO [3] (D Arbuthnot) 5-9-7 G Starkey 11/2: 1021-02: Led final 1f: caught near
finish: gd effort & may be winning soon: in '85 won valuable h'caps at Doncaster & Sandown:
in '84 won at Redcar & Beverley: equally eff at 5/6f: acts on fast & soft grnd & likes
a stiff trk.   52

748 AMEGHINO [11] (M Mccourt) 6-9-7 R Wernham 6/1: 0-00403: Led over 1f out: just btn
in close fin: gd run: see 616, 192.   52

508 CORNCHARM [4] (M Mccormack) 5-8-7 W Carson 7/2 FAV: 0-02034: Narrowly btn: see 135. 36

660 FERRYMAN [10] 10-9-2 A Mcglone 14/1: 030-000: Made most: not btn far: failed to win
in '85 but in '84 won a valuable h'cap at York and a h'cap at Brighton: in '83 won twice and
likes an undulating trk: very eff at 6f: acts on any grnd & retains his form, despite his
advancing years.   44

703 **ZULU KNIGHT** [5] 3-8-8(BL) Pat Eddery 8/1: 240-000: Tried in bl: led 2f out: btr
effort: showed fair form as a 2yo, notably when "winning" a maiden at Sandown, subs. disq:
eff at 5f, stays 6f: acts on gd & firm grnd.   47
649 **OXHEY BAY** [2] 4-8-10 John Williams 11/2: 12-0030: Prom: ev ch: see 649, 520.   00
--   **Powder Blue** [8] 9-2   --   **Snap Decision** [7] 8-0   507 **Galaxy Path** [9] 7-7(3oh)
679 **Gallant Hope** [6] 7-7(7oh)
11 ran   nk,hd,¾,½,shhd   (M S Saunders)   S Mellor Lambourn, Berks

847 TRYON HANDICAP 3YO (0-60)   **£3464**   **1m**   **Good 40 -03 Slow**   [66]

--   **SANTELLA MAC** [5] (G Harwood) 3-9-7 G Starkey 11/10 FAV: 01-1: 3 ch c Gay Fandango -
In The Clover (Meadow Mint): Smart colt: first time out, heavily bckd & led over 1f out,
readily in a 3yo h'cap at Salisbury June 3: on final outing in '85 comfortably beat Danski in
a 2yo maiden at Lingfield: eff at 1m, should stay 10f: acts on gd & firm grnd & on any
trk & will win more good races.   73
+719 **MEET THE GREEK** [7] (R Laing) 3-8-10(9ex) P Cook 6/1: 02-2112: Led 2f out: remains in
fine form & ran on only 3 shoes: see 719.   49
615 **FLOATING ASSET** [9] (P Walwyn) 3-8-5 Paul Eddery 8/1: 124-403: Ev ch final 2f: see 386.   43
723 **PORO BOY** [4] (C Williams) 3-7-13 L Jones(2) 20/1: -340004: Ev ch 2f out: btr 352 (yld).   33
615 **MUDRIK** [6] 3-9-2 B Rouse 7/1: 1-41240: No threat: btr 615: see 234.   48
659 **ASK MAMA** [3] 3-8-13 W Carson 6/1: 002-30: Fdd: btr 659 (yld/soft).   35
579 **DUFF** [1] 3-9-3 Pat Eddery 15/2: 423-340: Prom, wknd: not well h'capped: see 579, 402.   00
534 **Full Of Life** [8] 8-3   719 **Arabian Blues** [2] 7-7(7oh)
9 ran   5,½,1½,½,6   (Roy Taiano)   G Harwood Pulborough, Sussex

848 RUBBING HOUSE MAIDEN FILLIES STAKES 2YO £1487   **5f**   **Good 40 -34 Slow**

--   **PROPENSITY** [11] (G Harwood) 2-8-11 G Starkey 4/7 FAV: 1: 2 br f Habitat - Kalamac
(Kalamoun): Prom filly: first time out heavily bckd & led 1½f out, comfortably in a slow
run 2yo fillies maiden at Salisbury June 3: dam a winning 2yo: eff at 5f & should stay
further: acts on gd grnd & a gall trk: should win more races.   63
--   **DAZY** [6] (R Laing) 2-8-11 P Cook 12/1: 2: Ch final 1f: very gd racecourse debut:
22,000 gns purchase who is a half sister to Sirk & Making Hay: eff at 5f, will be suited
by further: acts on gd grnd & a gall trk: should easily find a maiden.   53
746 **BLUE TANGO** [10] (R Laing) 2-8-11 W Carson 10/1: 2433: Al up there: consistent: see 746.   51
--   **HOLD ON PLEASE** [14] (I Balding) 2-8-11 Pat Eddery 6/1: 4: Mkt drifter on racecourse
debut: ch 2f out: impr likely & should be suited by further than 5f: acts on gd grnd/gall trk.   49
--   **LADY LUCINA** [16] 2-8-11 N Howe 20/1: 0: Kept on well on debut: prom first run: cost
23,000 gns and is a half sister to several winners: will be suited by further than 5f.   40
577 **SEMIS** [2] 2-8-11 D Mckay 16/1: 000: Raced stands side: impr filly: see 577.   37
--   **FLIRTING** [8] 2-8-11 R Wernham 50/1: 0: Never nearer 7th on racecourse debut: will impr.   36
--   **LISASHAM** [9] 2-8-11 T Quinn 50/1: 0: No threat: fin 8th: half sister to 6f winner.   35
725 **BO BABBITY** [7] 2-8-11 J Reid 14/1: 30: Made running: btr 725.   34
--   **Cello Solo** [17] 8-11   --   **Dane Dolly** [12] 8-11   --   **Eastern Princess** [5] 8-11
--   **Footbridge** [18] 8-11   --   **Julia Springs** [1] 8-11
565 **Minobee** [13] 8-11   --   **Philgwyn** [4] 8-11   596 **Survival Kit** [3] 8-11
17 ran   2,½,½,3,1   hd,nk,nk   (Gerald Leigh)   G Harwood Pulborough, Sussex

849 LAVERSTOCK MAIDEN STAKES 3YO   £1837   **1m 4f**   **Good 40 +16 Fast**

--   **ALMAARAD** [2] (J Dunlop) 3-9-0 B Thomson 20/1: 00-1: 3 ch c Ela-Mana-Mou - Silk Blend
(Busted): Prom colt: made a winning seasonal debut, led over 1f out, comfortably in a 3yo
maiden at Salisbury June 3: highly tried on both outings in '85: well suited by 12f: acts on
gd grnd & a gall trk: should win more races & won in a fast time today.   60
--   **KNIGHTS LEGEND** [16] (G Harwood) 3-9-0 G Starkey 5/1: -2: Led 2f out: prom racecourse
debut from this half brother to 2 winners: stays 12f: acts on gd grnd & a stiff trk & should
easily find a maiden.   53
--   **SADEEM** [8] (G Harwood) 3-9-0 K Butler 33/1: -3: Kept on promisingly & should do btr
next time: well bred colt who is a brother to the smart 10f winner Formaz: should be winning
soon: acts on gd grnd & a gall trk.   46
--   **LINE OF CARDS** [17] (H Candy) 3-8-11 R Curant 20/1: -4: Gd late hdway on racecourse
debut: will impr: half sister to 7/8f winner: stays 12f well: acts on gd grnd & a gall trk.   40
458 **RED SHOES** [18] 3-8-11 W Carson 5/2 FAV: 0-30: Led 3f out: acts on gd & yld: see 458.   39
581 **MAGIC VISION** [20] 3-8-11 P Cook 14/1: -00: Never nearer, but is making impr: half
sister to very useful 1m winner Prince Lyph: probably stays 12f: acts on gd grnd.   30
351 **BASTINADO** [11] 3-9-0 Pat Eddery 3/1: 30: Never nearer: btr 351 (yld).   00
581 **NORDICA** [3] 3-8-11 M Banner 9/2: -00: Fdd: btr 581 (10f).   00
581 **Mighty Flash** [10] 8-11   --   **Ski Down** [13] 9-0
625 **Final Alma** [15] 9-0   347 **Billila** [19] 9-0   535 **Ikraam** [1] 9-0
--   **Jimbalou** [5] 9-0   733 **Mr Matchmaker** [12] 9-0(bl)
635 **Mystery Clock** [14] 9-0(bl)   688 **Shakeeb** [4] 9-0
635 **Shirlstar Taxsaver** [9] 9-0   535 **Son Of Sparkler** [6] 9-0
--   **Greek Swift** [7] 9-0
20 ran   3,4,1½,nk,5   (Hamdan Al-Maktoum)   J Dunlop Arundel, Sussex

850   COOMBE BISSETT HANDICAP (0-35)   £1940   1m 2f   Good 40 +05 Fast   [33]

709   PULSINGH [15] (C Benstead) 4-8-4 P Waldron 25/1: -000001: 4 br c Mansingh - Pulcini
(Quartette): Showed impr form when a 25/1 winner of a h'cap at Salisbury June 3: led over 1f
out & forged clear: showed little form previously: eff at 10f on gd grnd & a gall trk.   18
--   PEARL PET [9] (P Makin) 4-8-8 T Quinn 33/1: 00000-2: Ch 2f out on seasonal debut: ran
well: maiden who showed some form in '85: eff at 1m, stays 10f: acts on gd & firm grnd.   15
724   SPANISH REEL [1] (J Edwards) 4-9-5 B Thomson 10/1: 040-203: Nearest fin: twice below
form 420 (sharp trk).   25
*724 WELSH MEDLEY [5] (D H Jones) 4-9-9(7ex) D Williams(7) 8/1: 0-03214: Al prom: btr 724.   23
--   WHITE MILL [2] 4-8-12 R Curant 4/1: 400-0: Gambled on, but never nearer: ran only
3 times in '85, showing some promise: stays 12f & acts on gd ground   09
623   GOLDEN CROFT [12] 3-7-10 S Dawson(3) 8/1: 00-0040: Made much: btr 623 (12f).   07
*690 AUTUMN FLUTTER [3] 3-9-2(7ex) Pat Eddery 7/4 FAV: 00-3010: Fdd: well below form 690   00
709   Even Banker [13] 8-0   652 Well Meet Again [8] 9-1
618   Winter Palace [14] 9-9   --   Wizzard Art [4] 9-3
333   Lucksin [6] 8-1   --   Expletive [10] 8-2(vis)
731   Shad Rabugk [11] 8-1   727 Pamela Heaney [7] 8-5
15 ran   4,¼,3,1½,nk   (B W Hager)   C Benstead Epsom, Surrey

---

Official Going Given as Good (1st 3 races), Good/Soft remainder

851   HALL HANDICAP STAKES 3YO+ 0-35   £1951   1m 2f   Good/Yield 79 +15 Fast   [34]

652   HEART OF STONE [3] (R Akehurst) 4-8-6 W Carson 9/2: 000-001: 4 ch c Vaigly Great -
Attitude (Gratitude): Well bckd when leading inside final 3f, readily in a fast run h'cap at
Lingfield June 3: showed useful form over hurdles during the Winter and this was first
success on the Flat: stays 10f well: acts on yld but said to have been unsuited by the
heavy going in race 652: likely to win again in similar company.   23
*618 STATE BUDGET [4] (W Musson) 5-10-3(5ex) M Wigham 11/4 fav: 30-1312: Anchored by his
mammoth weight & btr judged on 618.   38
163   TEEJAY [5] (P Beavn) 7-7-12 T Williams 33/1: -03: Ev ch: off the trk in '85 & last
won in '83 at Nottingham: winning form at 1m, possibly stays further: acts on fast & gd grnd.   05
709   ELECTROPET [14] (A Pitt) 4-8-12 C Rutter[5] 15/2: 410-004: Chall inside final 2f:
winner at Windsor in '85: stays 10f well: suited by firm grnd & a sharpish trk.   16
709   DUELLING [13] 5-8-11 T Fahey 8/1: 4000000: Yet to strike form: see 7.   15
530   LINGFIELD LADY [1] 4-8-4 P Cook 50/1: 0-40000: Prom most: see 31 (6f!)   03
*683 RA NOVA [8] 7-8-13(5ex) G Dickie 7/2: 10: Never closer in 8th: much btr 683 (12f).   00
750   Dancing Barron [9] 9-4   341 Floreat Floreat [2] 7-13(1ow)
202   Assail [7] 10-0   620 Easter Rambler [12] 8-6
453   Lady Eurolink [10] 9-6   689 Pitkaithly [13] 8-12(bl)
--   Monarto [6] 8-0(1ow)
14 ran   7,hd,1½,hd,3   (M Morrison)   R Akehurst Epsom

852   EBF MANOR MAIDEN FILLIES STKS 2YO   £3211   6f   Good/Yield 79 -09 Slow

--   INVITED GUEST [10] (R Armstrong) 2-8-11 W Carson 6/1: 1: 2 ch f Be My Guest - Welcome
Break (Wollow): Prom filly: first time out, sprinted clear from the dist in a 2yo fillies
maiden at Lingfield June 3: eff over 6f, sure to be suited by further: acts on an easy
surface: sure to win more races.   52
655   RECREATION [1] (W Jarvis) 2-8-11 S Cauthen 9/4 fav: 332: Well bckd, prom thro'out:
deserves a change of luck: see 400.   40
482   JANS CONTESSA [8] (R Boss) 2-8-11 M Miller 7/2: 23: Pressed ldrs most: btr 482 (5f).   33
--   SHINING WATER [2] (R J Houghton) 2-8-11 P Hutchinson 20/1: 4: Never closer, but a
promising debut: nicely bred filly but has plenty of staying blood in her veins & is
certain to need further than 6f to be seen at her best: dam consistent & genuine, won the
Park Hill Stakes.   30
536   MY ELANE [11] 2-8-11 S Whitworth 14/1: 00: Made much: see 536.   30
--   SALINAS [3] 2-8-11 J Reid 8/1: 0: Sn prom on debut: speedily bred filly who should
benefit from the experience.   30
--   CHEVELEY CHOICE [14] 2-8-11 B Rouse 10/1: 0: Close up 4f: half sister to 4 winners,
mainly over sprint dists: sure to impr.   00
223   OUR PET [17] 2-8-11 A Mcglone 11/2: 000: Well bckd, early speed: poor draw: twice
below 73 (5f, soft).   00
--   Tufty Lady [7] 8-11   --   Churchill Lady [12] 8-11
--   Tap On Blue [16] 8-11   --   Quietly Mine [15] 8-11
533   Spanish Melody [13] 8-11   --   Deep Raptures [6] 8-11
482   Ballantrae [4] 8-11   400 Eileen A Lee 0 8-11
16 ran   4,2½,1,shhd,hd,hd   (Kinderhill Corporation)   R Armstrong Newmarket

853   GRANGE SELLING STAKES 2YO   £865   5f   Good/Yield 79 -34 Slow

681 TELEGRAPH FOLLY [3] (R Hoad) 2-8-11 B Rouse 11/2: 04331: 2 ch g Andy Rew - Jenny's
Gold (Spanish Gold): Raced by herself and gained a comfortable pillar-to-post win in a
2yo seller at Lingfield June 3: very eff at 5f with forcing tactics on a sharpish trk: acts
on gd & soft grnd.   25
717 BLOW FOR HOME [8] (D Morley) 2-8-11 S Cauthen 11/8 fav: 002: Well bckd, kept on in
his first venture into selling company: suited by 6f? acts on any surface.   13
681 SNAPSHOT BABY [4] (R Voorspuy) 2-8-8(BL) S Whitworth 33/1: 003: Dsptd lead much:
bl first time: very cheaply bought yearling.   01
261 RIBO BE GOOD [7] (J Bridger) 2-8-8 T Williams 25/1: 004: Speed to ½way but fin well btn. 00
633 SOLENT GOLD [5] 2-8-8 R Carter[5] 16/1: 00: Early speed.   00
681 ALN WATER [6] 2-8-8 R Brown[7] 5/1: 00: Sn struggling: speedily bred.   00
--   BRONZALIAS [1] 2-8-11 A Mcglone 5/2: 0: Well bckd debutant, sn behind: cost 1,200 gns.   00
7 ran   4,3,6,4,1½   (B Clark)   R Hoad Lewes, Sussex

854   LEISURE STAKES 3YO +   £8644   6f   Good/Yield 79 +11 Fast

587 HALLGATE [8] (S Hall) 3-8-3 W Carson 15/8 fav: 11-3041: 3 b c Vaigly Great - Beloved
Mistress (Rarity): Smart colt: well bckd when forcing his hd in front on the post in quite
fast run & valuable Leisure Stakes at Lingfield June 3: bl last time but btr without them
today: one of the most improved performers of '85 winning at Hamilton (2), Edinburgh, Pontefract, Redcar, Ripon & the Corn Wallis Stakes at Ascot: very eff over 5/6f, stays 7f but
possibly not 1m: acts on firm & soft & on any trk: consistent sort who has a gd turn of foot
but is not the easiest of rides as he tends to hang.   79
+691 BRIDESMAID [6] (B Hills) 3-8-6(vis) B Thomson 11/4: 30-0012: Well bckd, dsptd lead
thro'out, caught post and in terrific form: genuine filly: see 691.   81
18   ATALL ATALL [3] (M Pipe) 3-8-3 P Robinson 14/1: 2030-03: Raced by himself & battled
it out in the final 2f, only narrowly btn: proved himself a smart colt in '85, winning at
Bath (first time out) and also the Windsor Castle Stakes at Royal Ascot: later impr further
when 2nd in the Gr.3 July Stakes: very eff 5f, stays 6f: acts on firm & yld: genuine.   76
--   STALKER [7] (P Walwyn) 3-8-3 Paul Eddery 11/4: 34121-4: Made much & should benefit
from this seasonal debut: very consistent in '85 winning 4 out of 8 runs, notably Gr.1 Middle
Park Stakes at Newmarket & Gr.2 Gimcrack Stakes at York: also won at Newbury & Lingfield:
equally eff at 5 & 6f: acts on firm & yld & on any trk: genuine.   70
705 FAYRUZ [9] 3-8-3(vis) M L Thomas 12/1: 022-000: Ev ch: yet to strike best form: see 600 63
687 OUR DYNASTY [1] 4-9-0 S Cauthen 11/2: 00-0300: Twice below flattering form of 587.   60
222 Polykratis [4] 9-0   653 Vintage Port [2] 9-0   -- Puccini [5] 9-0
9 ran   shhd,½,2,2½,1   (Hoppodromo Racing Ltd)   S Hall Leyburn, Yorks

855   SUMMER HANDICAP STAKES 3YO+ 0-35   £2264   6f   Good/Yield 79 -13 Slow   [34]

748 DOWNSVIEW [3] (A Moore) 4-10-0 M Wigham 14/1: 0000-01: 4 b g Dominion - Lady Downsview
(Prince Regent): Caused a 14/1 upset making most and holding on well in a h'cap at Lingfield
June 3: scored 3 wins at Brighton last season and this was his first success away from that
switchback trk: eff over 5 & 6f & acts on firm & gd going: suited by forcing tactics &
a sharpish undulating trk.   41
--   LONELY STREET [7] (P Arthur) 5-9-3 L Johnsey[7] 10/1: 01002-2: Gd seasonal debut, just
btn in quite a close fin: winner at Goodwood in '85 and Bath in '84: equally eff at 5 & 6f
but best form on firm or hard going.   28
679 LINTON STARCHY [6] (J O'donoghue) 5-8-0(7ow)(1oh) P Hutchinson 50/1: 000-003: Ran well at
the weights, not ttn far: lightly raced maiden who showed his best form for a long time
on this occasion: evidently eff at 6f on an easy surface.   07
679 JAMES DE COOMBE [9] (M Bolton) 4-8-2 P Waldron 5/1: 0-00024: Ev ch: btr 679 (C/D).   07
748 REAR ACTION [1] 6-9-4 W Carson 5/2 fav: 01-0030: Heavily bckd: dsptd lead most:
much btr 748 (cc/firm).   13
616 BOLD REALM [5] 5-9-10 P Skelton[7] 8/1: 2100-00: Prom much: in '85 won at Newmarket &
Ripon: best form on firm or good ground on a gall. track.   18
700 CHICAGO BID [2] 5-9-11 S Cauthen 4/1: 023-020: Wk in mkt: much btr 700 (7f,firm)   00
554 FUDGE [14] 3-8-6 P Cook 5/1: 000-20 Much btr 534 (firm).   00
734 Yani [15] 7-8   399 Running Bull [8] 8-12   161 Mister March [12] 7-8
734 Pegasus Lady [13] 7-12   679 Saravanta [4] 7-13
266 Black Spout [16] 7-10 (3ow 1oh)
14 ran   ½,1,½,4,nk   (B Marsh)   A Moore Woodingdean, Sussex

856   EVENING HANDICAP 3YO + 0-35   £1853   1m 4f Good/Yield 79 -07 Slow   [33

751 THE BETSY [6] (D Elsworth) 4-7-10 P Mcentee[4] 12/1: 00-0401: 4 b f Imperial Fling -
Question Mark (High Line): Appeared well h'capped & forged clear inside final 2f for a 7L
success in a h'cap at Lingfield June 3: first success: suited by 12f: acts on firm and yield.:
seems suited by a sharpish undulating trk.   15
750 DERBY DAY [5] (D Wilson) 5-8-5(bl) B Rouse 6/1: 30-0042: Chall 2f out: gd effort and
caught a tartar: see 750.   14
--   PATRICK JOHN LYONS [14] (P Arthur) 5-8-5(2ow) L Johnsey[0] 14/1: 10030-3: Dsptd lead under
press 2f out: in '85 won at Chepstow but was not all that consistent: suited by 12f in soft. 13

663 SHUTTLECOCK STAR [19] (J Bridger) 4-7-11 T Williams 33/1: 00-0004: Ev ch: still
seeking first success: possibly best around 12f.   04
683 WILD GINGER [11] 4-8-12(bl) B Crossley 12/1: 30-0200: Ev ch: best 485 (14f, yld).   18
731 BLENDERS CHOICE [4] 4-8-9 S Whitworth 7/1: 300-030: Made much: see 358, 731.   14
683 SITAR THEME [7] 4-9-0 W Carson 7/4 fav: 003-40: Heavily bckd, fin 7th: see 683.   00
349 PICADILLY PRINCE [3] 6-9-5 S Dawson 6/1: -00: Bckd from 33/1, fin 8th: off the trk
in '85, the previous season won at Pontefract: suited by 12f on firm grnd.   00
652 THATCHINGLY [16] 5-9-4 S Cauthen 10/1: 0-10400: Ev ch in 9th: best 176 (10f).   00
761 JAZAIR [8] 4-9-9 P Cook 15/2: 00-0000: Prom most: see 761.   00
761 STARDYN [12] 4-8-7 Paul Eddery 9/1: 0-03040: Ev ch: best 569 (gd/firm).   00
721 Karamoun [2] 7-12   485 Master Francis [10] 8-10
582 Moorland Lady [9] 9-10   179 Trikkala Star [1] 8-3
731 Action Time [15] 9-5   761 Full Of Dreams [13] 7-9(bl)
578 Pandi Club [17] 8-7
18 ran   7,½,½,½,½,½,shhd   (Miss Luch Morrish)   D Elsworth Whitsbury, Hants

---

857 BEVERLEY ARMS HANDICAP STAKES 3YO 0-35   £1700   7.5f   Good/Firm 31 -18 Slow   [34]

464 PLEASURE ISLAND (8) (G Pritchard Gordon) 3-8-12 G Duffield 9/1: 0-001: 3 ch f Dalsaan -
Pleasure Boat (Be Friendly): Nicely bckd when coming from behind to lead near fin in a h'cap at
Beverley June 3: lightly raced previously: eff over a stiff 7f, sure to be suited by 1m and
probably further: well suited by fast grnd: likely to continue improving.   25
650 UNEXPLAINED (4) (R Armstrong); 3-9-6 P Struthers (7) 5/1: -4202D2: Battled with winner
final 1fL btn a whisker in a blanket fin: deserves a change of luck: see 335, 650.   32
538 MONSTROSA (1) (J Spearing) 3-8-7 D Nicholls 14/1: 300-003: Came from behind, kept on
really well and just btn: back to form & evidently handles fast & soft grnd: see 538.   17
538 RAFFIA RUN (7) (J Dunlop) 3-9-1 G Baxter 9/2 fav: 040-044: Chall final 1f: gd effort.   25
545 NEDS EXPRESSA (12) 3-9-2 M Birch 6/1: 40-0000: Dsptd lead dist: best effort this season:
winner over 7f on firm grnd at Catterick in '85.   26
487 COOL OPERATOR (6) 3-9-7 R Cochrane 9/1: 0-04040: Fin in gd style & seems to need at
least 1m, probably further: see 183.   29
700 CHABLISSE (14) 3-8-9 K Bradshaw (5) 8/1: 00-0P40: Ev ch, fin 8th: btr 700.   00
411 CASHEW KING (18) 3-9-3 J Hillis (5) 10/1: 0010-00: Fdd quickly final 2f: winner over C/D
in '85: acts on gd grnd.   00
611 IZZY GUNNER (13) 3-8-8 J Bleasdale 8/1: 002200: Fin last: twice below 491 (heavy).   00
650 Johnstan Boy (10) 8-12   -- Cloudless Sky (2) 9-2   689 Willbe Willbe (9) 8-8
451 Rapid Flight (11) 8-0   674 Molly Partridge (19) 8-6
650 Skelton (3) 8-10   529 Murryl Cannon (16) 8-2
677 Owls Way (5) 8-12
17 ran   shhd,¾,hd,shhd,1   (Seymour Bloodstock Ltd)   G Pritchard Gordon Newmarket

858 GREEN DRAGON SELLING STAKES 2YO   £928   5f   Good/Firm 31 -80 Slow

696 PRINCESS SINGH [2] (L Lightbrown) 2-8-8 R Cochrane 7/4 FAV: 0031: 2 ch f Mansingh -
Princess Story (Some Hand): Gained a pillar-to-post success, keeping on under press to win
a 2yo seller at Beverley June 3: goes well on fast grnd with forcing tactics: very eff at 5f.   20
672 SHADY BLADE [11] (K Stone) 2-8-8 C Dwyer 2/1: 02: Came from behind & looks likely to
be well suited by 6f: half sister to winning '84 juvenile Boarding House: should find a
seller before long.   14
813 REAL RUSTLE [6] (M W Easterby) 2-8-11(BL) M Birch 20/1: 0003: Pressed ldr most, showing
some impr here: may be suited by a sharper trk: eff at 5f.   16
--   PALACE RULER [3] (A Smith) 2-8-8 S Webster 14/1: 4: Never closer on debut: may be suited
by 6f: acts on fast grnd.   12
647 CARAS QUEST [4] 2-8-8 M Hindley(0) 16/1: 000: Showed some impr: quite stoutly bred
on her dam's side and may need further than 5f.   11
672 BRIARQUEEN [10] 2-8-8 K Hodgson 14/1: 0000: Showed first signs of ability here:
should stay 6f.   11
603 LATE PROGRESS [8] 2-8-8 M Fry 5/1: -0000: Early pace, wknd into 7th: rated 18 in 34.   00
--   AUSTHORPE SUNSET [5] 2-8-11 D Nicholls 7/1: 0: Al rear on debut: may need more time/dist   00
--   On The Mark [1] 8-11   543 Young Fool [9] 8-11(BL)
--   Willys Niece [7] 8-8
11 ran   2,½,½,shhd,shhd   (Jeffrey Ross)   L Lightbrown Maunby, Yorks

859   BEAVER STAKES 2YO   £1415   5f   Good/Firm 31 -47 Slow

+804 MISTER MAJESTIC [5] (R Williams) 2-9-7 R Cochrane 1/1 FAV: 12111: 2 b c Tumble Wind -
Our Village (Ballymore): Tough & useful colt: gaining his 4th win from 5 outings this season,
drawing clear in the final 1f for a 6L win in a minor 3yo race at Beverley June 3: recently
successful at Kempton, Newmarket & Beverley & met only defeat at the hands of the smart
Quel Esprit: half brother to Clotilda: very eff over 5 or 6f & acts on fast & yld going
& on any trk: genuine sort who continues to improve.   61
610   BECKINGHAM BEN [3] (J Leigh) 2-8-11 S Morris 100/1: 02: Al there, outpaced by smart
winner: sprint bred & is showing some impr.   33
--   FOUNTAINS CHOICE [4] (K Stone) 2-8-11 G Brown(5) 50/1: 3: Prom, ev ch: certain to
be suited by further than 5f: acts on fast grnd: will improve.   32
*771 SANDALL PARK [6] (M W Easterby) 2-9-4 K Hodgson 2/1: 414: Dsptd lead much: best 771.   38
728   BUDDY RICH [2] 2-8-11(bl) T Ives 4/1: 4040: Ev ch: btr 728 (wore bl).   30
--   CALLACE [1] 2-8-8 S Webster 50/1: 0: Outpcd on debut.   00
6 ran   6,nk,½,½,12   (D Johnson)   R Williams Newmarket

860   ROSE AND CROWN HANDICAP 3YO+ 0-35   £2306   1m 4f Good/Firm 31 -32 Slow   [29]

731   DON RUNI [12] (D Morley) 4-8-13 G Duffield 9/2: -000021: 4 gr g Bruni - Donnarose
(Fighting Don): Held up early, fin strongly to gain the day on the post in a h'cap at
Beverley June 3: won a maiden here last season & obviously loves this undulating trk: eff
12f, stays 2m well: acts on fast & hvy going: suited by waiting tactics.   22
721   MR LION [5] (F Carr) 4-8-8 J Carr(7) 6/1: -301222: Pressed ldrs thro'out, caught post:
in grand form & deserves another race: see 721.   17
709   DELLWOOD RENOWN [2] (W Holden) 4-7-13 J Lowe 4/1 FAV: 000-033: Prom thro'out: 04.
591   WILDRUSH [1] (W Watts) 7-9-5 C Coates(5) 15/2: 02-1034: Dsptd lead 2f out: acts on
fast & yld going: see 243.   23
184   RASHAH [10] 4-8-13 M Wood 12/1: -300-00: Close up most: lightly raced maiden.   13
712   TURI [9] 7-8-0 S Webster 14/1: 00: Made much: see 712.   00
721   MASTER CARL [7] 7-8-5(BL) D Leadbitter(3) 11/2: 0-00030: Ev ch in 7th: btr 721.   00
282   Changanoor [8] 9-7   591 Skerne Spark [4] 8-11   675 Higham Grey [3] 8-11
--   Fortune Finder [11] 9-3   609 Paris Trader [6] 9-10(bl)
36   Timurs Gift [13] 8-13
13 ran   shhd,2½,nk,2,shhd   (K Spindler)   D Morley Newmarket

861   KINGS HEAD MAIDEN STAKES   £684   1m   Good/Firm 31 +15 Fast

--   NAATELL [9] (H Cecil) 3-8-5 W Ryan 6/1: -1: 3 b c Cox's Ridge - Lisanninga (Whodunit):
Made a successful racecourse debut, fin strongly to lead final 1f comfortably in a maiden at
Beverley June 3: evidently well suited by a stiff 1m, but sure to stay 10f: acts on fast
grnd: further impr likely.   56
*388 TIMBERWOOD [7] (H T Jones) 3-8-5 A Murray 5/1: 4040-12: Tried to make all: gd effort. 48
546   MASTER THAMES [4] (M Stoute) 3-8-5 W R Swinburn 4/7 FAV: 2-43: Chall, going well
2f out, found nothing & failed to land the odds: see 546.   48
--   LYAPKIN TYAPKIN [2] (J Winter) 3-8-5 A Mackay 12/1: 04-4: Likely to impr for the
outing: 4th in a 5f maiden at Yarmouth on final of only 2 outings in '85: sure to be suited
by 1m & probably further: likely to do btr next time.   42
--   CERTAIN AWARD [12] 3-8-2 N Connorton 33/1: -0: Should impr for this first experience
of the racecourse: half brother to the winning 3yo Innes House, successful over 10f in '84:
sure to be a lot sharper next time.   24
--   COOL MUSIC [5] 3-8-2 M Wood 25/1: 000-0: Made a quiet seasonal reapp and will be
all the btr for it: showed distinct signs of ability in gd company last season, notably
when 5th to Sharrood on fast grnd at Doncaster: brother to winning '83 2yo Llandwyn: one
to keep a close eye on next time.   15
423   NAOUSSA [13] 3-8-2 G Baxter 10/1: 3-42020: Prom, wknd & much btr 423 (sharp trk).   00
--   Arras Lass [8] 9-6   713 Nap Majestica [6] 8-5   --   Mr Bennington [1] 9-9
567   Pointed Lady [10] 8-2   448 Fill Abumper [11] 9-6   --   Green Room Gambols [3] 9-6
13 ran   3,shhd,2½,8,5,6   (Sheikh Mohammed)   H Cecil Newmarket

862   ROYAL STANDARD MAIDEN 3YO FILLIES STKS   £1087   1m 2f Good/Firm 31 -09 Slow

315   MAGIC SLIPPER [9] (H Cecil) 3-8-11 W Ryan 7/4: -21: 3 b f Habitat - Glass Slipper
(Relko): Promising filly: prom & led dist readily in a 3yo fillies maiden at Beverley June 3:
unraced as a 2yo but bred in the purple, being a half sister to the top class Light Cavalry
and Fairy Footsteps: very eff 10f, should stay 12f: acts on fast & soft grnd: type to impr
further & win a decent race.   59
599   EXCEPTIONAL BEAUTY [4] (M Jarvis) 3-8-11 T Ives 6/4 FAV: 02-42: Kept on well & probably
caught a tartar here: must find a maiden soon: see 599.   52
--   NO DOUBLET [5] (B Hills) 3-8-11 A Murray 10/1: 33-3: Led 1m: 3rd on both outings in
'85 at Brighton & Goodwood over 7f & might possibly be btr suited by 1m than longer trips:
acts on fast grnd: sure to find a maiden.   52
581   CURVACEOUS [16] (M Stoute) 3-8-11 W R Swinburn 10/1: -04: Ev ch: see 581.   40

-- **ELA MAN HEE** [2] 3-8-11 M Roberts 14/1: -0: Took a long time to get the hang of things but fin in gd style & showed considerable promise: unraced as a 2yo but on this evidence is sure to pick up a race soon: likely to stay 12f.   34

-- **LINASH** [7] 3-8-11 D Gibson 20/1: -0: Showed inexperience when put under press but will benefit from the experience: should stay 10f.   31

509 **INTRINSIC** [12] 3-8-11 A Clark 6/1: -000: Prom much, fin.7th: nicely bckd: see 372.   00

720 **Swedish Princess** [10] 8-11(VIS)			-- **Dusk Approaches** [18] 8-11	
-- **Scarlet Dancer** [6] 8-11			464 **Green For Danger** [14] 8-11	
702 **Tharita** [13] 8-11	-- **Marble Moon** [15] 8-11	702 **Vikris** [1] 8-11		
779 **Ribo Melody** [17] 8-11	-- **Elbandary** [8] 8-11	-- **Arras Style** [3] 8-11		
688 **Samosa** [11] 8-11				

18 ran   3,shhd,7,3,2   (H J Joel)   H Cecil Newmarket

---

863 **KINGS HEAD MAIDEN STAKES**   £684   1m   **Good/Firm 31 +13 Fast**

402 **SHAFY** [7] (M Stoute)3-8-6(1ow)WRSwinburn2/5 FAV: 32-41: 3 b c Lyphard - I'll Be Around (Isgala): Useful colt: comfortably landed the odds in a maiden at Beverley June 3: showed plenty of promise last season when placed in both starts: stays 10f well, may stay further: suited by firm or good going.   54

402 **COCCOLUTO** [8] (J Dunlop) 3-8-5 G Baxter 13/2: 00-02: Kept on well & possibly needs 12f: half brother to winning 7f performer Hot Case: acts well on fast grnd: sure to find a maiden soon.   50

194 **FANCY PAN** [9] (W Hastings Bass) 3-8-2 R Lines(3) 25/1: 03: Unruly before start, made most in the race: did not race in '85: might possibly prove btr over 1m than longer dists.   27

452 **GREEN STEPS** [4] (G Wragg) 4-9-9 G Duffield 10/1: -04: Misbehaved before start: ev ch in the race: very well bred colt who should impr on this if his temperament does not get the better of him.   24

-- **HOT LINING** [13] 3-8-5 S Morris 100/1: 0000-0: Gd fin & will be btr for this seasonal debut: showed ability in '85: acts on gd/firm going: may stay beyond 1m.   18

-- **MAKE IT SHARP** [1] 3-8-2 M Roberts 10/1: -0: Ran on well after a slow start: should impr for this first outing: half sister to 4 winners incl very useful types Shorthouse, One Way Street and That's Your Lot: will be a different prospect next time, especially over 12f: acts on fast grnd.   13

651 **PORT PLEASE** [3] 3-8-2 J Lowe 12/1: -40: Held up, fin 7th: much btr 651 (yld).   00

-- **Trentullo Blue** [5] 9-6		594 **Johnny Frenchman** [10] 9-9	
-- **Repetitive** [11] 8-2	-- **Drumbarra** [6] 9-9	-- **Dutch Queen** [12] 8-2	
-- **Montefiasco** [2] 9-9			

13 ran   1,10,6,1,¾,2   (Sheikh Mohammed)   M Stoute Newmarket

---

Official Going Given as Good/Soft (Last 2f Soft)

864 **WASTWATER MAIDEN 2YO STAKES**   £1154   5f   **Yielding 84 -12 Slow**

536 **TAKE A HINT** [7] (M Fetherston Godley) 2-9-0 G Duffield 9/1: 441: 2 b c Pitskelly - Infanta (Intrepid Hero): Led below dist, running on strongly for a decisive win in a 2yo maiden at Carlisle June 4: well suited by a stiff 5f & sure to stay further: acts on gd & soft grnd: on the up grade.   40

-- **GOLDENDOUBLEYOU** [2] (D Barron) 2-8-11 N Carlisle 14/1: 2: Al up there, no ch with winner though will impr for this experience: half sister to 9f winner Rabirius: acts on yld grnd & on a stiff trk.   22

304 **DOCKIN HILL** [3] (M W Easterby) 2-9-0 K Hodgson 12/1: 03: Stayed on well & well suited by this stiff course: half brother to 12f winner Flashy Vynz: should stay further: acts on yielding ground.   25

672 **KATIE SAYS** [10] (J Etherington) 2-8-11 M Wood 6/1: 04: Ran on late: needs further.   16

627 **WENSLEYDALEWARRIOR** [6] 2-9-0 N Crowther 7/4 FAV: 0320: Led to ½way: clear of rem. though much btr in 627 (gd/firm, sharp trk).   17

780 **SEABURY** [12] 2-9-0 K Darley 16/1: 00: Speed to ¼way: acts on yld grnd.   01

632 **TALIESIN** [9] 2-9-0 S Perks 6/1: 00: Led/dsptd lead over 3f: fin 7th: speedily bred colt who cost 12,000 gns as a yearling: should do btr on a sharper trk: acts on yld grnd.   00

694 **SKY CAT** [11] 2-9-0 Julie Bowker(7) 3/1: 40: Early speed, eased when btn: btr 694.   00

741 **STAR PLAY** [8] 2-9-0(BL) C Dwyer 8/1: 00: Fin last: much btr on a sharp trk in 523.   00

-- **Multi Spiral** [4] 8-11   701 **Bejant Skite** [1] 9-0

11 ran   5,shhd,2½,1,8   (Philip C Nelson)   M Fetherston Godley East Ilsley, Berks

---

865 **BUTTERMERE SELLING STAKES 2YO**   £605   5f   **Yielding 84 -58 Slow**

633 **BINGO QUEEN** [7] (J Berry) 2-8-8 M Fry 5/2: 20221: 2 ch f Cajun - Star Heading (Upper Case): Gained a deserved win in a slowly run 2yo seller at Carlisle June 4: not much room inside dist though rallied well to lead final stride (no bid): eff over 5f on a stiff/gall trk: acts on gd & soft grnd: consistent filly who does well with forcing tactics.   18

633 **RUN TO WORK** [5] (G Moore) 2-8-11 D Casey(7) 4/1: 42: Led before ½way, just caught: eff over 5f in gd & yld grnd: should find a seller: see 633.   20

425 ROYAL TREATY [1] (N Tinkler) 2-8-11 J H Brown(5) 7/4 FAV: 0003: Well bckd: ev ch and
not btn far: earlier had shown promise in maiden auction races: should stay further in time:
acts on gd & soft grnd.   18
125 MILLIE DUFFER [6] (J Kettlewell) 2-8-8 R Vickers(7) 14/1: 0044: Tardy start, fin
strongly: gd effort after a fair abs & will go close next time if kept in this grade: see 125. 14
821 BOOTHAM LAD [4] 2-8-11 K Darley 8/1: 000040: Early ldr: impr of late: see 821.   10
--   RIMOVE [3] 2-8-8 G Duffield 10/1: 0: Speed to ½way on debut: should impr for this race.   01
--   HIGHLAND CAPTAIN [2] 2-8-11 S Perks 5/1: 0: Never going pace: half brother to 7/10f
winner Highland Rossie and may need further than this minimum trip.   00
7 ran   hd,¼,1,1½,2½   (Mrs H G Vernon)   J Berry Cockerham, Lancs

866 LOWESWATER HANDICAP 0-35   £1649   6f   Yielding 84 +04 Fast   [28]

745 HENRYS PLACE [1] (D Chapman) 4-8-10(bl) D Nicholls 9/2: 0020001: 4 b g Habitat -
One Over Parr (Reform): Gained his first win in convincing style, led below dist and was sn
clear in quite a fast run h'cap at Carlisle June 4: half brother to a couple of minor
winners: best form over 6f though does stay 1m: acts on any going though prefers soft
grnd: well suited by a stiff trk.   20
*820 LITTLE NEWINGTON [2] (N Bycroft) 5-8-6(bl)(7ex) M Richardson(7) 7/4 FAV: 1001212: Led/dsptd
lead over 4f: beat todays winner over this C/D in 378: see 820.   00
671 LOW FLYER [4] (G Oldroyd) 3-9-0 K Hodgson 4/1: -030243: Best in 545: see 198.   15
636 FLOMEGAS DAY [6] (B Mcmahon) 4-9-8(bl) G Duffield 5/2: 0-00034: Much btr over 7f
in 636 (good): see 369.   07
321 WILLIE GAN [5] 8-8-8 M Fry 14/1: 000-000: Dsptd lead to ½way: disapp last season
though in '84 won at Thirsk: best form over 6f on fast grnd.   00
--   POKERFAYES [3] 7-8-12(bl) A Roper(7) 6/1: 00301-0: Speed to ½way, sn btn: ended last
season with a narrow win in an app. stakes at Nottingham: best form over sprint dists though
does stay 7f: acts on any going & on any trk: btr for race.   00
6 ran   8,2,2½,5,3   (Michael Hill)   D Chapman Stillington, Yorks

867 BASSENTHWAITE H'CAP STAKES 3YO 0-35   £1861   9f   Yielding 84 -23 Slow   [27]

779 MEGANS MOVE [9] (J Jefferson) 3-9-7 A Shoults(5) 4/1 Co FAV: 004-01: 3 ch f Move Off -
River Petterill (Another River): Led below dist & stayed on well to win a 3yo h'cap at
Carlisle June 4: lightly raced last season, fin 4th to La Zingara in a Beverley maiden: eff
around 9f, stays 12f: acts on firm & yld grnd & on any trk.   32
809 MY CUP OF TEA [3] (P Haslam) 3-8-3 G French 4/1 Co FAV: 0-0322: Hung left inside dist:
stays 9f on a stiff trk: remains in gd form: see 809 & 113.   05
702 NOT A PROBLEM [6] (Denys Smith) 3-8-11 M Fry 9/2: 0-30043: Kept on under press: best 702.22
424 LA JAMBALAYA [4] (P Makin) 3-9-4 A Murray 4/1 Co FAV: 040-34: Led briefly below dist.   15
527 BOLD ANSWER [5] 3-8-6 K Darley 14/1: 000-000: Made most: first signs of form: acts
on yld grnd & on an undulating trk: seems suited by forcing tactics.   00
690 MASTER LAMB [8] 3-9-2 K Hodgson 7/1: 000-40: Btr over 10f in 690.   04
650 TEED BORE [1] 3-9-3 M Wigham 4/1 Co FAV: 0-20430: Below par effort: best over 7f in 39.   00
--   DOON VENTURE [7] 3-8-9 M Wood 9/1: 03000-0: Last to fin on seasonal debut: stoutly bred
colt who showed a little promise last season over shorter trips: acts on gd & firm grnd &
on a sharp trk.   00
--   Pink Sensation [2] 9-7
9 ran   4,½,2,2½,3   (Robert J Elliott)   J Jefferson Norton, Nth Yorks

868 ENNERDALE WATER MAIDEN STAKES 3YO   £1150   1m 1f Yielding 84 -30 Slow

--   RIVA RENALD [6] (S Norton) 3-8-11 G Duffield 25/1: -1: 3 b f Try My Best - Mellow Girl
(Mountain Call): Was a surprise winner on her racecourse debut, led below dist and ran on
well to win a 3yo maiden at Carlisle June 4: very well suited by 9f & should stay further:
acts on yld grnd & on a stiff trk.   50
216 CHINOISERIE [8] (L Cumani) 3-9-0 P Hamblett 1/3 FAV: 022-02: Just failed to land
the odds: stays 9f: should get off the mark soon: see 216.   52
765 DEAFENING [1] (P Kelleway) 3-9-0 Gay Kelleway(5) 7/1: 0-003: Kept on well: easily his
best effort to date: stays 9f: acts on fast & yld grnd & on any trk.   45
605 LUCKY BLAKE [2] (C Thornton) 3-9-0 J Bleasdale 20/1: -04: Led briefly 2f out: see 605.   33
--   COPLEYS WALK [4] 3-8-11 K Hodgson 25/1: 00-0: Stayed on late: btr for race: half sister
to very useful middle dist. winner Cannon King & will probably be btr over long distances:
acts on gd & soft grnd.   29
--   FRAME OF POWER [5] 3-9-0 A Murray 25/1: 0-0: Stayed on well from rear and impr looks
certain: full brother to minor 7f winner Pinctada: stays 9f: acts on yld grnd & on any trk.   24
--   HOME RULE [10] 3-8-11(BL) J Matthias 5/1: ----0-0: Fin 8th on reapp: wore bl today:
should be suited by middle distances.   00
539 ALICE PARRY [3] 3-8-11 M Wigham 10/1: -40: Fin last: btr in 539.   00
527 Court Ruler [9] 9-0   605 Son Of Absalom [7] 9-0
733 Saxelbye Park [11] 9-0
11 ran ½,3,7,1,5,hd   (S Taberner)   S Norton High Hoyland, Yorks

869   CRUMMOCK WATER H'CAP STAKES   0-35   £1808   1m 4f   Yielding 84 +09   [35]

-542 THE MISSISSIPPIAN [2] (M Eckley) 5-8-3 J Carter(7) 9/2: 0-421D1: 5 b g Tumble Wind -
Dolly Longlegs (Majority): Gained quick compensation for his recent disq. led over 2f out,
comfortably in quite a fast run h'cap at Carlisle June 4: narrow "winner" in a similar event
at Nottingham last month: in '84 won at Leicester: eff over 10/12f & stays 2m well: acts
on gd/firm & hvy grnd & on any trk.   25
770 MOSSBERRY FAIR [5] (W Haigh) 5-7-7(4oh) Kim Tinkler(7) 9/1: 00-0002: No ch with winner
though kept on well under press: maiden: see 770.   04
721 MENINGI [3] (N Tinkler) 5-9-4(4ex) Kim Tinkler(7) 6/4 FAV: -314143: Well bckd: remains
in good form: see 591.   26
-- TREASURE HUNTER [7] (W Pearce) 7-10-0 M Hindley(7): 10030-4: Btr for race: first
time out last season won a h'cap at Ripon: in '84 won at Nottingham, Newcastle & Chester:
well suited by a test of stamina nowadays: acts on any going & on any trk.   33
590 AULD LANG SYNE [4] 7-8-4 A Shoults(5) 15/2: 0-42400: Btr over 2m in 50.   07
675 RAMILIE [10] 4-8-7 M Wood 10/1: 0100-00: Easy winner of a seller at Thirsk last
season: eff over 10f, stays 12f well: acts on fast & yld grrnd & on any trk.   06
675 LAKINO [8] 4-9-1 A Murray 10/3: 00-1-00: No threat in 7th: see 675.   00
824 Frasass [9] 8-0   675 Country Jimmy [1] 8-11
547 Sound Work [6] 7-13(1ow)
10 ran   8,1½,2½,2,3,nk   (George Kalavanas)   M Eckley Brimfield, Salop

---

RIPON   Wednesday June 4th   Righthand, Sharpish Track

Official Going Given as Good/Firm

870   EBF APPLEYARD MOTORS 2YO STAKES   £2396   6f   Good/Firm 27 -15 Slow

*612 CROFTERS CLINE [7] (J Wilson) 2-9-3 Julie Bowker(7) 13/2: 011: 2 b c Crofter -
Modena (Sassafras): Made most, staying on well when a narrow winner of a 2yo stakes at
Ripon June 4: last time out made ev yd in a maiden auction at Beverley: seems well suited by
forcing tactics & stays 6f: acts on gd & firm grnd & on any trk.   44
-- LUZUM [4] (H T Jones) 2-8-11 A Murray 6/1: 2: Ran on final 1f & just failed to get
up: good racecourse debut & should find a race: eff at 6f, will be suited by further: acts
on gd/firm grnd   37
-- STORM HERO [5] (M Dickinson) 2-8-11 R Cochrane 5/6 FAV: 3: Well bckd: ev ch 2f out:
impr likely from this well bred colt who is a half brother to several winners, incl the
smart The Noble Player: looks sure to be suited by further than 5f.   24
-- ALBION PLACE [11] (M H Easterby) 2-8-11 K Hodgson 20/1: 4: Ev ch on racecourse debut:
cost 27,000 gns and is a half brother to 12/15f winner Bidivera: should impr.   21
544 HUNTERS LEAP [3] 2-8-11 A Mackay 9/1: 0020: Sn prom, fdd: btr 544 (yld).   13
571 MIAMI BAY [2] 2-8-11 K Darley 10/1: 00: Sn prom: btr 571 (stiffer trk).   08
*544 CONNAUGHT FLYER [12] 2-9-3 M Wood 7/1: 10: No show: much btr 544 (yld grnd).   00
685 Combermere [10] 8-11   -- Another Season [6] 8-11
-- Finlux Design [1] 8-11
10 ran   hd,5,1,3,2   (Mrs G Rees)   J Wilson Tarleton, Lancs

871   PLUMB CENTER SELLING H'CAP 3YO 0-25   £1434   6f   Good/Firm 27 -06 Slow   [26]

514 SUMMERHILL SPRUCE [11] (E Eldin) 3-9-4 A Mackay 9/2: 000-001: 3 b f Windjammer -
Sharper Still (Sharpen Up): Dropped to selling company, led 1½f out and sn clear in a selling
h'cap at Ripon June 4 (bought in 5,200 gns): showed fair form in '85, notably when 2nd in a
Kempton maiden: eff at 5f, stays 6f: acts on gd & firm grnd & a sharpish trk.   27
760 PENDOR DANCER [8] (K Ivory) 3-9-7 R Street 10/1: 000-002: Led ¼way: btr effort:
stays 6f: acts on gd & firm grnd.   10
518 POLLY WORTH [7] (R Whitaker) 3-8-7(VIS) K Bradshaw(5) 10/1: 000-003: Never nearer:
dropped to selling company here: little form previously, but is a half sister to several
winners: acts on gd & firm grnd.   00
670 WINDING PATH [9] (R Hollinshead) 3-9-0 A Whitehall(7) 9/1: 20-0004: Prom: ev ch: see 489. 00
426 GALAXY GALA [3] 3-8-11 S Keightley 9/1: 00-0040: Btr in 426 (7f).   00
666 SISTER NANCY [14] 3-8-8 J H Brown(5) 25/1: -430000: Nearest fin: needs 7f? see 195.   00
729 SAMBA LASS [17] 3-9-0 R Cochrane 7/2 FAV: 00-0320: Never nearer 7th: btr 729 (stiff trk) 00
729 CREETOWN SALLY [4] 3-8-7 I Johnson 9/2: 00-030: Well below form 729 (stiffer trk).   00
608 Balidareen [12] 8-2   -- Gutsy [16] 9-6   447 Feather Girl [5] 8-2
-- Gaywood Girl [2] 9-2   545 Rich Bitch [13] 8-0   740 Our Mumsie [6] 8-7(bl)
593 Strawberry Split [10] 9-0   426 La Manga Prince [18] 8-8
608 Miss Beswick [1] 8-6
17 ran   10,nk,2,½,½   (Summerhill Stud Ltd)   E Eldin Newmarket

872   THEAKSTONS HANDICAP 0-50   £2502   1m 4f   Good/Firm 27 -48 Slow   [40]

695 ROMIOSINI [1] (N Tinkler) 4-9-7 Kim Tinkler(7) 2/1 FAV: 103-001: 4 b c Spirit Son -
Narmeen (Le Haar): Well bckd and led 3f out, staying on gamely for a narrow win in a slow
run h'cap at Ripon June 4: winner over hurdles in the Autumn: in '85 won a maiden at Ripon
and does well here: eff over 10f, stays 12f well: best on gd & firm grnd when up with the pace 41

629 FOUR STAR THRUST [5] (R Whitaker) 4-8-9 K Bradshaw(5) 4/1: 1-00402: Ev ch final 1f:
just went under: gd effort: see 419.   28
745 GLENDERRY [4] (Hbt Jones) 4-8-2(bl) M Hills 13/2: 00-0003: Led over 1m: ran well
over this longer trip: stays 12f: see 611.   15
695 WESTRAY [6] (R Hollinshead) 4-9-2 S Perks 5/1: 30-0004: Prom, ev ch: see 225.   25
225 TOUCHEZ LE BOIS [2] 5-9-3 M Rimmer 10/1: 2-00-00: Abs: no threat: very lightly raced
in recent seasons: in '84 was trained by H Cecil, winning at Nottingham: now with M Tompkins:
stays 12f: acts on gd & firm grnd.   17
698 SHELLMAN [3] 4-9-10 C Dwyer 4/1: 0300000: Trying 12f: best in 55.   15
630 Crowfoots Couture [7] 7-7(vis)(4oh)
7 ran   nk,3,2,5,5   (Full Circle Thoroughbreds B Ltd)   N Tinkler Malton, Yorks

873 BAYER UK DORIN 2YO STAKES   £1788   5f   Good/Firm 27 -07 Slow

--   OLD EROS [5] (R Williams) 2-8-6 R Cochrane 3/1: 1: 2 ch c Bold Owl - Piccadilly Rose
(Reform): First time out, ran on well to lead inside final 1f in a 2yo stakes at Ripon
June 4: eff at 5f, should stay further: acts on gd/firm grnd & a sharpish trk.   46
632 STELBY [3] (O Brennan) 2-8-6 G Brown(5) 11/8 FAV: 022: Led over 1f out: just btn:
another gd effort: see 632: should win soon.   44
694 JOE SUGDEN [2] (R Whitaker) 2-8-6 K Bradshaw(5) 25/1: 03: Rank outsider: al up there,
showing impr form: half brother to winning 2yo Warwick Wallies: eff at 5f on gd/firm.   35
627 SILVERS ERA [1] (N Callaghan) 2-8-3 G Duffield 7/2: 0204: Ev ch, stumbled over 1f
out: best ignored: see 473, 383.   20
*473 MISS SHEGAS [6] 2-9-4 M Fry 5/1: 2210: Made much, hung right: btr 473 (soft/hvy).   32
*696 PASHMINA [4] 2-9-4 C Coates(5) 10/1: 10210: Not disgraced: see 696 (seller).   30
6 ran   ½,3,4,1,½   (P Charter)   R Williams Newmarket

874 JENNIFER BROWNING H'CAP 3YO 0-35   £2670   1m   Good/Firm 27 -07 Slow

719 STANFORD VALE [11] (C Nelson) 3-9-3 I Johnson 11/2: 0-02231: 3 b c Stanford -
Shoshoni Girl (Winning Hit): Gained a deserved success, led 2f out, comfortably in a 3yo
h'cap at Ripon June 4: has been in fine form lately: stays 1m really well: acts on gd/firm
& yld grnd & on any trk.   33
480 WHIRLING WORDS [6] (P Makin) 3-8-9 S Perks 20/1: 004-002: Ran on well final 1f: much
btr effort: lightly raced as a 2yo: eff at 1m on gd/firm & yld grnd.   20
459 NATIVE HABITAT [14] (M Jarvis) 3-9-5 T Lucas 11/2: -4133: Hmpd home turn: kept on well:
gd effort: acts on gd/firm & yld grnd: see 169.   28
258 TABLE TURNING [1] (J Watts) 3-9-0 T Ives 10/3 FAV: 00-24: Ev ch over 2f out: running well 21
--   HAYWAIN [16] 3-8-13 M Hills 14/1: 000-00: Made much on seasonal debut: highly tried
on 3 outings in '85: bred to be suited by todays trip: acts on gd/firm grnd.   15
424 BOLD ARCHER [9] 3-8-6 G Duffield 20/1: 400-000: Fdd 2f out: first time out in '85
fin 4th to Elaafuur in a Chepstow maiden: half brother to 6f winner Bold Lassie.   02
747 MR KEWMILL [19] 3-9-5 M Rimmer 15/2: 0-30140: Never nearer 7th: btr 747: see 451.   00
447 LUNAR SHAMAL GAL [17] 3-9-6 A Murray 7/1: 01-00: Fdd: see 447 (6f).   00
650 AFFAITATI [20] 3-8-13 M Beecroft 9/1: 030-020: Led/dsptd lead: fdd: much btr 650 (yld).   00
650 BALNERINO [15] 3-8-12 D Nicholls 8/1: 3140-00: Active in mkt but no show: in '85 won
a maiden at Ayr: eff at 6f, may stay further: acts on gd & yld grnd.   00
318 Jenifer Browning [18] 8-10   650 Colonial King [13] 9-3
650 Tower Fame [3] 9-1   --   Black Bank [12] 9-7   518 Uptown Randbs [7] 8-11
650 Bradbury Hall [8] 8-9   528 Cover Inn [2] 9-0   637 Saughtrees [5] 9-0(BL)
451 Katie Rhodes [10] 8-0
19 ran   1½,1,1,2,2½,1½   (Anglo Enterprises S A)   C Nelson Lambourn, Berks

875 ALLTON GROUP STAKES   £2205   1m 2f   Good/Firm 27 +18 Fast

613 TOSARA [14] (H Candy) 4-9-0 R Curant 3/1: 0-241: 4 b f Main Reef - My Fawn (Hugh Lupus):
Impr filly: well bckd & led well over 2f out, staying on well for a narrow win in a fast run
stakes event at Ripon June 4: half sister to several winners, incl the useful Border Dawn:
very eff over 10f on gd & firm grnd: should win more races.   52
625 DAARKOM [12] (A Stewart) 3-8-3 M Roberts 13/8 FAV: -22: Chall final 1f: another fine
effort & fin 10L clear 3rd: must win soon: see 625.   55
--   BUSTED FLAVOUR [8] (W Jarvis) 5-9-3 R Cochrane 20/1: -0/3: Nearest fin after a very
long abs: should be suited by 12f: acts on gd/firm grnd & should do btr next time.   34
690 GLOWING PROMISE [5] (B Hills) 3-8-5 M Hills 2/1: 02-124: Well below form 690, 452.   33
448 CHERRY LUSTRE [10] 3-8-3 T Ives 14/1: -000: Never nearer: half brother to 2 winners:
stays 10f & acts well on a sound surface.   28
651 MABEL ALICE [13] 3-8-0 A Mackay 25/1: 40-0000: Made much: btr 651 (yld).   17
528 Bollin Uncle [15] 8-3   452 Bels Angel [4] 9-0   631 Dark Cygnet [1] 9-3
491 Norcool [9] 8-3   --   Penniless Dancer [6] 9-0
--   Helen Boy [3] 8-3   689 Forever Tingo [7] 9-3   --   Barnacle Bill [11] 8-3
--   W Seafield [2] 8-3
15 ran   hd,10,2½,1½,4   (Fahd Salman)   H Candy Kingstone Warren, Oxon

Official Going Given as Good

876 WOODCOTE STAKES 2YO   £4643   6f   Good/Firm 26 -11 Slow

-- MR EATS [1] (P Kelleway) 2-8-6 C Asmussen 20/1: 1: 2 gr c Nishapour - Breathalyser
(Alcide): Prom colt: first time out, turned up at 20/1, fin strongly to lead final 1f readily
in 2yo Woodcote Stakes at Epsom June 4: half brother to 4 middle dist. winners and is stoutly
bred himself so this 6f win was something of a bonus: acts on fast grnd: sure to be suited
by much longer distances & should win more races.   60
655 REGENCY FILLE [3] (R Williams) 2-8-11 R Cochrane 5/1: 1222: Chall final 1f: gd effort
and is a model of consistency: see 655.   56
*583 SAMEEK [7] (R Armstrong) 2-9-0 W Carson 10/11 fav: 213: Prom thro'out: should be
suited by this trip but btr 583 (5f).   55
752 FAIRWAY LADY [4] (D Hughes) 2-8-11 M J Kinane 8/1: 01024: Al prom & evidently acts
on firm & soft: see 638.   52
662 PERSIAN STYLE [6] 2-8-9 C Mccarron 12/1: 00: Led almost 4f, an impr effort on this
faster going: see 662.   44
*678 FRENCH TUITION [5] 2-9-0 S Cauthen 6/1: 23310: Dsptd lead much: ran to his best.   47
230 Divine Charger [2] 8-9
7 ran   3,1½,shhd,2½,½   (Roldvale ltd)   P Kelleway Newmarket

877 NIGHTRIDER STAKES HANDICAP 0-70   £7713   5f   Good/Firm 26 +05 fast   [59]

660 CLANTIME [8] (R Whitaker) 5-9-0(VIS) D Mckeown 10/1: -022341: 5 ch h Music Boy -
Penny Pincher (Constable): Very useful sprinter: wearing a visor for the first time, set a
blistering pace & held on well to win quite a fast run & valuable h'cap at Epsom June 4:
in '85 won a similar valuable h'cap over this C/D & this is his 3rd course success in total:
best forcing the pace over a sharp 5f & is unsuited by a stiff trk or 6f.   60
705 IMPERIAL JADE [3] (A Jarvis) 4-9-9 T Ives 16/1: 030-302: Pursued winner thro'out,
closing at fin: gd effort under 9-9: deserves a race sn: see 408.   67
-660 BOLLIN EMILY [4] (M H Easterby) 5-8-11 M Birch 5/1 jt fav: 4-02423: Another good
effort but possibly btr in 660 (soft): see 428.   48
660 PERFECT TIMING [13] (D Elsworth) 4-8-11 S Cauthen 14/1: 0403-04: Reared up in stalls,
never closer in the race: won a fillies event at Newmarket in '85 from 10 outings: very eff
over 6f on fast grnd, on a stiff trk: should run well next time.   44
-- DURHAM PLACE [6] 4-9-4 S Whitworth 33/1: 00030-0: Ev ch on seasonal debut: not seen out
after mid-June in '85 & failed to win last term: in '84 won at Leicester: stays 7f: acts
on gd & heavy.   50
*477 PERION [7] 4-8-9 P Waldron 5/1 jt fav: -101110: Abs: close up thro'out: not far off
his best here: see 477.   40
705 PETROVICH [2] 4-9-10 B Thomson 7/1: 1120-30: Close 7th: btr 705 (stiff 5f).   50
616 TYROLLIE [1] 4-8-13 S Dawson[3] 9/1: 02-1220: Fin 8th: see 192.   00
477 MUSIC MACHINE [14] 5-7-8 T Williams 9/1: 10-0440: Fin 9th: see 272.   00
550 HILTON BROWN [15] 5-9-7(bl) P Eddery 10/1: 0-31300: Early speed: twice below 272 (C/D hv00
-- Axe Valley [9] 8-12   508 Native Skier [5] 8-10(VIS)
784 China Gold [16] 8-2   784 Celtic Bird [10] 7-7(5oh)
477 Little Starchy [11] 7-7(4oh)   30 Princess Wendy [12] 7-8
16 ran   ½,2½,1½,½,hd   (Clantime Ltd)   R Whitaker Wetherby, Yorks

878 GROUP ONE EVER READY DERBY STAKES 3YO   £239260   1m 4f   Good/Firm 26 +17 Fast

*574 SHAHRASTANI [10] (M Stoute) 3-9-0 W R Swinburn 11/2: 2-111: 3 ch c Nijinsky -
Shademah (Thatch): Top class colt: al prom, went on 2f out & held on well to win the Epsom
Derby June 4: unbtn this season having previously won the Guardian Classic Trial at Sandown
first time out and the Mecca-Dante at York: unlucky in running when 2nd at Newbury on sole
start in '85: eff around 10f, stays 12f well: continues to improve.   90
*407 DANCING BRAVE [6] (G Harwood) 3-9-0 G Starkey 2/1 fav: 11-112: Came from a seemingly
impossible position, just failed to get up and would have won in another few yards: looked
unlucky and clearly stays 12f well: sure to win more top class races this year.   89
*510 MASHKOUR [3] (H Cecil) 3-9-0 S Cauthen 12/1: 11-3113: Very smart colt: behind till
fin strongly and staying is certainly this one's game: looks a Leger type: see 510.   83
*476 FARAWAY DANCER [16] (H Cecil) 3-9-0 W Ryan 33/1: 111-214: 2nd most of the way, just
wknd close home: fine effort & stays 12f though may prove best at 10f: see 476.   83
*494 NISNAS [11] 3-9-0 P Waldron 40/1: 43-1310: Pressed leaders thro'out and is clearly
impr: sure to win more races if eased in class a little: see 494.   83
*640 FLASH OF STEEL [5] 3-9-0 M J Kinane 25/1: 111-110: Mid-div, never closer: evidently
stays 12f but probably btr suited by soft going than firm: see 640.   82
574 SIRK [17] 3-9-0 P Robinson 50/1: 3-13230: In last place till making up a lot of
late grnd into 7th: fine effort and has impr all season: stays 12f well: see 574, 48.   80
640 SHARROOD [1] 3-9-0 W Carson 25/1: 11-0430: spread a plate before the start, always
same place: fin 8th: see 640.   78
640 MR JOHN [2] 3-9-0 T Ives 50/1: 00-4120: Al mid-div, fin 9th: btr 640 (1m heavy).   78

*654 ALLEZ MILORD [14] 3-9-0 C Asmussen 8/1: 1-110: No threat: see 654.   77
574 NOMROOD [12] 3-9-0 T Quinn 20/1: 12-120: Pacemaker till wknd final 3f: best 10f? see 574 77
--   JAREER [4] 3-9-0 B Rouse 16/1: 210-0: Never in it on belated seasonal debut: ran only
3 times in '85 easily winning a maiden at Yarmouth: cost a mammoth $7.1m & is impeccably
bred: should be well suited by middle dists: acts on firm & gd grnd.   70
*676 THEN AGAIN [8] 3-9-0 R Guest 33/1: -01-10: Mid-div early, wknd: see 676.   65
469 BOLD ARRANGEMENT [13] 3-9-0 C Mccarron 12/1: 2D-3320: Al rear: much btr 469 (10f).   62
643 AROKAR [15] 3-9-0 Y Saint Martin 18/1: 101-120: Prom, wknd: non-stayer? see 643 (10f). 62
640 FIORAVANTI [9] 3-9-0 C Roche 33/1: 11-100: Wknd after 1m: see 466.   55
559 WISE COUNCILLOR [7] 3-9-0 P Eddery 16/1: ----120: Prom 10f, wknd quickly: see 559.   00
17 ran   ½,2½,hd,shhd,½,½,1,hd,½,hd,½,1,3,2½,shhd,10   (Aga Khan)   M Stoute Newmarket

879 SILVER SEAL STAKES H'CAP 0-70   £10191   1m 2f Good/Firm 26 +02 Fast   [65]

706 GAY CAPTAIN [16] (J Bethell) 4-8-7 C Asmussen 8/1: -000201: 4 b c Ela-Mana-Mou -
Gay Milly (Mill Reef): Useful colt: came from behind, responding gamely to strong driving
to force his head in front on the post in a valuable h'cap at Epsom June 4: only ran twice
in '85, the previous season successful at Newbury: well suited by 10f, bred to stay 12f:
acts on heavy but well at home on gd grnd.   57
445 RANA PRATAP [14] (G Lewis) 6-8-3 P Waldron 8/1: 4-04332: Came to lead final 1f,
caught death in a driving fin: due a change of luck: see 445.   52
698 TRY TO STOP ME [10] (Denys Smith) 5-8-3 T Quinn 33/1: 000-003: Led briefly dist.
just btn in a close fin: back to the form he showed last season when successful in valuable
h'caps at Thirsk & York: eff over 1m, stays 10f: acts on any going & on any trk: should
find a race soon.   50
698 BALLYDURROW [11] (R Fisher) 9-7-12(5ex) J Lowe 12/1: 13-0104: Came to chall final 1f,
narrowly btn: gd effort but btr 69 (12f).   43
--   I BIN ZAIDOON [6] 5-8-11 B Thomson 14/1: 04120-0: Led briefly 2f out on seasonal
debut though fit from a successful hurdling campaign: in '85 won twice in Ireland over 10f:
acts on firm & yld.   54
*709 MASTER LINE [3] 5-7-13(5ex) C Rutter[5] 7/2 fav: 10-0010: Ev ch, not disgraced but btr 709.40
433 TRULY RARE [4] 4-8-13 W R Swinburn 7/1: 141-030: Prom, wknd into 9th: much btr 433.   00
*652 TABARDAR [1] 4-8-11(VIS)(5ex) S Cauthen 8/1: 00-3010: Visored for the first time,
sn wkn: btr 652 (heavy).   00
511 MAILMAN [17] 7-8-7 P Eddery 10/1: 1000-00: No threat: btr 511.   00
706 Merle [2] 8-11   474 Colonel James [9] 7-7   --   Effigy [8] 9-12
706 Gilderdale [13] 8-4   221 Celebrity [5] 9-9   618 Joli Wasfi [1] 7-9(bl)(2ow)(3oh)
15 ran   hd,½,½,½,1   (John Galvanoni)   J Bethell Chilton, Oxon

880 GREAT SURREY CLAIMING STAKES 3YO   £5663   1m110y Good/Firm 26 -12 Slow

455 EMPIRE BLUE [5] (P Cole) 3-9-0(bl) T Quinn 8/1: 1240-01: 3 b c Dominion - Bold
Blue (Targowice): Prom and driven into the lead dist for a hard earned win in a valuable 3yo
claimer at Epsom June 4: winner of his first 2 races on the trot in '85 at Windsor & Bath:
stays 1m well: suited by firm or gd grnd: wears bl.   55
699 ALBERT HALL [10] (B Hills) 3-9-0 B Thomson 4/1: 02-21D2: Well bckd, wandered under
press final 1f but ran to his best: see 699.   52
386 TWICE BOLD [1] (N Callaghan) 3-9-0 P Eddery 3/1 jt fav: 01-03: Made most: ready 8L
winner of a maiden at Lingfield at the backend of '85 and only ran twice last season: half
brother to several winners: stays 7f, should be suited by 1m: acts on firm grnd.   51
459 FIRE ROCKET [7] (P Cole) 3-9-0 S Cauthen 20/1: 00-004: Showed much impr form here:
showed little in only 2 outings last season and is a half brother to the winning '81
juvenile Marquessa D'Howfen: stays 1m well & acts on firm.   39
703 BLUE BRILLIANT [6] 3-9-0 G Starkey 20/1: 00-000: Pressed ldrs most: see 276.   30
623 FIREPROOF [3] 3-9-0 A Clark 20/1: 00-0420: Dwelt, never closer: stiff task: see 623.   24
719 MAHOGANY RUN [9] 3-9-0 M Birch 10/1: 420-000: Ev ch in 7th: yet to hit form: in
'85 won at Hamilton & Redcar: front runner: showed his best form last season over 6f on firm 24
703 NATCHAKAM [8] 3-8-10(bl) P Waldron 3/1 jt fav: -42040: Prom, wknd: btr 703 (stiff trk). 00
703 Viceroy Major [11] 8-7(bl)   326 Hot Gem [2] 8-5
29   Holiday Mill [12] 7-13
11 ran   2,½,4,4,2½,hd   (G C Meyrick)   P Cole Whatcombe, Oxon

881 CRAVEN STAKES H'CAP 0-70   £7518   7f   Good/Firm 26 -03 Slow   [66]

361 MAAZI [3] (P Cole) 5-8-0 W Carson 11/2: 1001-01: 5 br h Ahonoora - Grangemore
(Prominer): Useful h'capper on his day: led dist under press in a h'cap at Epsom June 4:
in '85 won at Newbury & Catterick: eff over 6/7f on any trk but probably best on fast going. 51
433 SHMAIREEKH [4] (P Walwyn) 5-10-0 Paul Eddery 3/1 fav: 000-202: Brave attempt to defy
10-0 : see 330.   75
326 SWIFTS PAL [5] (G Lewis) 3-7-8 T Williams 8/1: 000-003: Al there: in '85 won at
Leicester & Ripon: eff 6f, probably stays 7f: acts on firm & yld.   49
687 SHARLIES WIMPY [9] (W Pearce) 7-8-1 B Rouse 8/1: 400-024: Never closer: btr 687.   43

616 SOON TO BE [2] 4-7-11 N Adams 12/1: 133-000: Made much: consistent in '85 winning at Epsom, Newbury & Lingfield (first time out): half sister to several winners: stays 7f well and acts on fast & yld going.   **39**
668 GURTEEN BOY [1] 4-7-8(1ow) D Mckay 8/1: 01-0000: No real threat: see 453.   **32**
•478 DOGMATIC [7] 3-8-7(VIS) S Cauthen 100/30: 301-410: Tried in a visor for the first time, close up 5f, fin 7th: much btr 478 (soft).   **00**
508 Vorvados [6] 8-2   **660 Young Inca** [8] 8-12
9 ran   2,2,½,hd,2   (Fahd Salman)   P Cole Whatcombe, Oxon

Official Going Given as Good

882 HEADLEY MAIDEN AUCTION STAKES 2YO   £2548   5f   Firm 20 -29 Slow

415 CREES FIGURINE [5] (M Fetherston Godley) 2-8-6 P Eddery 9/4 fav: 31: 2 b f Creetown - Figurehead (Seaepic) Justified hvy support, dsptd lead 3 out and went ahead close home in a 2yo mdn auction event at Epsom June 5: cost only 2,100 gns: very eff over 5f but should stay 6f: acts on firm and yldg: on the upgrade.   **33**
621 INFANTA MARIA [2] (N Vigors) 2-9-1 S Dawson[3] 4/1: 02: Just failed to make all: this 4,200 purchase is clearly on the upgrade and is well suited by a sharp 5f: acts on firm ground: should find a similar race.   **38**
681 ROYAL RABBLE [4] (D Elsworth) 2-8-10 A Mcglone 6/1: 020423: Never closer and may need 6f: btr 681 (good).   **28**
-- RYLANDS REEF [1] (C James) 2-8-11 W Carson 10/1: 4: Fair first eff from this half brother to winning '85 3yo Ciara's Lad: sure to appreciate 6f: will improve.   **24**
717 NERRAD [7] 2-9-4 G Baxter 10/1: 040: Every chance: btr 717 (stiff trk).   **16**
483 REVELINA [6] 2-8-6(BL) M L Thomas 11/2: 00300: Twice below 261 (soft).   **00**
701 PETROC CONCERT [3] 2-8-8 D Mckeown 8/1: 40: Btr 701.   **00**
621 Relampego [9] 8-12   **-- Whats A Guinea** [8] 8-6
9 ran   1½,2,2,5,1½   (Craig Pearman)   M Fetherston Godley East Ilsley, Berks

883 EGMONT HANDICAP 3YO 0-50   £3817   1m 4f Firm 20 -03 Slow   [50]

•648 FIRST DIVISION [7] (G P Gordon) 3-9-4(4ex) G Duffield 15/8 fav: 000-111: 3 b c Wolver Hollow - Home And Away (Home Guard) Very useful impr colt: unbtn this season and completed his hat-trick with a cantering 4L win in a h'cap at Epsom June 5: led on bit inside final 3f and sn went clear: similarly easy winner at Ripon and Doncaster (first time out): lightly raced in '85: half brother to minor winner Top of the League: well suited by 12f and acts on firm and yldg and on any trk: not one to oppose in his next few engagements.   **55**
335 UP TO UNCLE [1] (R Hannon) 3-7-12 A Mcglone 33/1: 44-0002: Prom final 3f: showed improved form here: should be winning sn: see 117.   **25**
676 AUCTION FEVER [3] (B Hills) 3-9-7 B Thomson 8/1: 33-2023: Ev ch: consistent but seems little one-paced: see 386.   **46**
459 ELAAFUUR [10] (P Walwyn) 3-9-4 Paul Eddery 11/1: 100-44: Chall 2f out: see 459.   **41**
738 OWL CASTLE [5] 3-8-13 J Reid 33/1: 3241000: Suffered interference in running and this eff can be forgotten: best 171.   **31**
648 CHEVET LADY [9] 3-8-2(vis) W Ryan 33/1: -124200: Btr 54, 461.   **20**
597 ATIG [6] 3-9-6 W Carson 10/1: 404-000: Nicely bckd, fin 8th: quite lightly raced in '85 winning 7f mdn at Salisbury on firm going: shd stay at least 10f.   **00**
609 ICARO [2] 3-8-4(1ow) Pat Eddery 5/1: 01-0220: Prom most: much btr 609 (10f gd).   **00**
738 DISCIPLE [4] 3-8-2 P Waldron 5/1: -000040: Made much: btr 738 (gd).   **00**
635 Miltescens [8] 9-3
10 ran   4,1,1½,3,hd   (William Du Pont III)   G A Pritchard Gordon, Newmarket

884 RING AND BRYMER TROPHY H'CAP 3YO 0-60   £4503   5f   Firm 20 -01 Slow   [57]

•431 RAYHAAN [12] (C Benstead) 3-8-8 B Rouse 11/1: -011: 3 b f King's Lake - Welshwyn (Welsh Saint) Useful, impr filly: fin strongly to lead well inside final 1f in quite a valuable 3yo at Epsom June 5: just prevailed in a blanket fin to a 3yo fillies stks at Kempton May 5: unraced as a 2yo: dam a smart and genuine sprinter: equally eff at 5f and 6f and acts on firm and gd going.   **49**
600 NICCOLO POLO [5] (B Hanbury) 3-9-7(BL) W R Swinburn 10/1: 00-3302: Bl first time, led final furlong and just btn: deserves a race sn: see 26.   **60**
514 WEST CARRACK [2] (A Ingham) 3-9-4(BL) G Starkey 16/1: 0-33003: Hmpd start, kept on strongly: unlucky? Grand eff: see 62: blinkered first time today.   **57**
+507 FOUNTAIN BELLS [11] (R Hannon) 3-8-5 A Mcglone 15/2: 00-2014: Gd fin and is in fine form: see 507.   **43**
760 EXCLUSIVE CAT [9] 3-8-11 Pat Eddery 3/1: fav: 4312-30: Hvly bckd, ev ch: shd find a race soon: see 760.   **45**
670 IMPALA LASS [7] 3-8-1 W Carson 8/1: 01-1100: Prom much: best 443.   **33**
507 HERMINDA [6] 3-7-9 S Dawson[3] 10/1: 024-00: No threat in 7th: placed in 2 out of only 3 outings in '85, notably when 3L 2nd to Flyaway Bride in 2yo stks at Bath: eff 5f on a galloping trk on an easy surface.

760 PLATINE [1] 3-8-3 S Whitworth 10/1: -100020: Dsptd lead much: much btr 760.   00
516 GLIKIAA MOU [8] 3-8-10 M Miller 6/1: 00-2420: No threat: btr 516 (yldg).   00
443 CRONKS QUALITY [4] 3-9-0(bl) P Waldron 10/1: 00-0000: Fin last: winner of an
early mdn at Epsom in '85: well suited by a fast 5f on gd grd.   00
624 Miss Know All [3] 8-7   580 Baliview [10] 7-7(12oh)
12 ran   ½,shthd,nk,1½,½,½   (Hamdan Al-Maktoum)   C Benstead Epsom, Surrey

885 GROUP 1 CORONATION CUP 4YO UPWARDS   £49086   1m 4f Firm 20 +29 Fast

468 SAINT ESTEPHE [10] (A Fabre) 4-9-0 Pat Eddery 20/1: 123-131: 4 b c Top Ville - Une
Tornade (Traffic) Topclass French colt: came from behind to lead final 1f and held on
by narrow margin in very fast run Group 1 Coronation Cup at Epsom June 5: first time out
winner of Group 2 Prix Harcourt at Longchamp April 6: consistent in '85 winning twice at
Saint-Cloud: stays 12f well: acts on firm and soft.   88
468 TRIPTYCH [6] (P L Biancone) 4-8-11 E Legrix 12/1: 0303-42: Led on bit 2f out,
sn ridden and rallied gamely when hdd to almost get back up again on the line: fine effort.   85
-- PETOSKI [5] (W Hern) 4-9-0 W Carson 5/2: 22011-3: Gd seasonal debut, not getting
the best of runs at the dist: in '85 was rated 97 on final outing when beating a quality
field in the King George Diamond Stks at Ascot: subsequently side-lined by injury and he
should benefit greatly from this first outing since: also won a Group 2 race at Newmarket
in '85: very well suited by 12f & firm or gd going: likes a stiff trk.   85
475 SHARDARI [7] (M Stoute) 4-9-0 W R Swinburn 1/1 fav: 1D11-24: Bckd as if defeat
was out of the question, led after ½ way but no extra final 2f: yet to regain best form.   85
641 NEMAIN [3] 4-9-0 C Roche 20/1: 3414-20: Irish chall, every chance and btr 641(10f hvy)   75
*385 PHARDANTE [4] 4-9-0 G Starkey 7/1: 230-010: Hmpd 2f out: see 385.   72
475 Gold And Ivory [2] 9-0   653 St Hilarion [9] 9-0
641 Super Move [1] 9-0   652 Boldden [8] 9-0
10 ran   shthd,3,½,10,3   (Y Houvet)   A Fabre Chantilly, France

886 LADBROKE CREDIT EXPRESS H'CAP 3YO 0-50 £4370   7f   Firm 20 -21 Slow   [51]

-- BRUISER [3] (M Prescott) 3-9-7 G Duffield 7/1 co fav: 112-1: 3 ch c Persian Bold -
Uranus (Manacle) Very useful colt: first time out, landed a gamble leading final 1f in a
valuable 3yo h'cap at Epsom June 5: winner of first 2 on the trot in '85 at Redcar & Chester
and met his only defeat when 2nd to Feisty in a Yarmouth nursery: half brother to sev
winners: very eff over 7f, should stay 1m: runs well on fast ground tho' seems to handle
any trk: shd win more races.   55
588 AMBROSINI [2] (M Jarvis) 3-9-1 T Ives 10/1: 231-102: Made much: fine effort and
stays 7f: see 454.   46
703 CHUMMYS PET [15] (N Callaghan) 3-8-0 A Mcglone 7/1 co fav: -02133: Al there and
is in gd form: see 703, 377.   26
424 FAATIK [8] (P Walwyn) 3-7-9 N Howe 12/1: 400-004: Ev ch: rated 30 in 334 (yldg)   21
616 MAJOR JACKO [7] 3-8-12(BL) S Cauthen 15/2: -014000: Bl first time: yet to reproduce
228 (6f, soft).   35
424 SEQUESTRATOR [10] 3-8-1 M Wigham 20/1: 3000-00: Sn prom: placed once in 5 outings
in '85, yet to win: acts on firm.   24
624 SOLO STYLE [6] 3-8-3 P Waldron 7/1 co fav: 000-300: Fin 9th: twice below 454 (6f yldg)   00
518 SIDONS DAUGHTER [13] 3-8-13 Pat Eddery 15/2: 3040-00: Early speed from mod draw:
placed twice from 5 races last season (rated 40): quite high in h'cap for a maiden.   00
-- ALMAROSE [4] 3-8-7 W Carson 10/1: 0012-0: Btr for race? Well bckd when winning
valuable seller at York on penultimate outing in '85: eff over 6f on gd grd: also acts soft.   00
703 WAR WAGON [12] 3-8-10 G Starkey 10/1: 000-000: Fin last: btr 703 (stiff trk).   00
480 No Jazz [9] 7-7(4oh)   624 Vaiglian [1] 8-7   -- Casbah Girl [11] 7-10
624 Delta Rose [5] 7-11   747 Light Hills [14] 8-7
15 ran   1,2,shthd,1½,shthd   (B Haggas)   M Prescott Newmarket

887 NIGHTINGALL MAIDEN STAKES 3YO   £2712   1m 2f Firm 20 -06 Slow

-- SULTAN MOHAMED [6] (J Dunlop) 3-9-0 Pat Eddery 10/1: 0242-1: 3 ch c Northfields -
Paper Sun (Match III) Made a winning seasonal reappearance, coming from behind and showed
a gd turn of foot in final 1f in a 3yo mdn at Epsom June 5: btn only a nk by Ostensible
in a backend mdn at Leicester last Nov: well suited by 10f: promises to stay 12f: acts
on fast and yldg going: is half brother to sev winners: looks certain to find further success.   62
546 PICEA [9] (M Jarvis) 3-9-0 T Ives 100/30: 42-422: Led dist, outpaced close home:
deserves a race sn: see 371.   56
224 FESTIVAL CITY USA [5] (B Hills) 3-9-0 B Thomson 5/1: 3-03: Didnot have best of runs
but not btn far and must find a mdn sn: should stay 12f: see 224.   55
384 DANSKI [7] (P Cole) 3-9-0 T Quinn 11/10 fav: 2322-24: Heavily bckd, ev ch: even his
most ardent admirers must be close to despair! Clear chance here on the form of 384.   52
-- FANAAN [3] 3-9-0 W Carson 10/1: 03-0: Led 1m on seasonal debut: rated 54 when gd
3rd to Shahaab in a Kempton mdn over 7f on firm last season, 2nd of only 2 outings: seems
suited by forcing tactics and may prove best around 1m.   44

764 ORANGE DALE [8] 3-9-0 S Cauthen 25/1: 0-000: Prom much, apparently showing impr form. 37
371 Prasina Matia [2] 9-0   625 Willow Gorge [4] 9-0   625 Next Dance [3] 9-0
9 ran   2,¼,3,4,2½.   (Dana Stud Ltd)   J Dunlop Arundel, Sussex

---

CARLISLE   Thursday June 5th   Righthand Undulating Track, Stiff Uphill Finish

Official Going Given as Good/Soft (Last 2f Soft)

888 LEVY BOARD APPRENTICE STAKES   £972   1m 1f   Good 56 -22 Slow

-- AL UQ HUWAAN [8] (H Thomson Jones) 3-8-3 A Riding(5) 7/2: 0314-1: 3 ch f Be My Guest
- Garden of Eden (Exbury) Useful filly: first time out stayed on well to lead close home
in an app race at Carlisle June 5: showed plenty of promise last season, winning a fillies
mdn at Leicester: cost $350,000 as yearling and is a half sister to sev winners: eff over
8/9f and will stay further: acts on gd and firm grd and on a stiff/gall trk.   38
+698 FORWARD RALLY [6] (M Prescott) 4-9-9 D D'arcy(5) 6/4 FAV: 021-112: Led over 2f out and
$n clear, caught near fin: remains in gd form: see 698.   42
807 FORCELLA [1] (S Norton) 3-8-6 J Murray(5) 5/2: -124243: Al up there: see 444.   34
770 THE HOUGH [2] (G Reveley) 5-8-11 G Craggs(5) 14/1: -04: Stayed on: clear of rem:
see 770.   23
772 NORDIC SECRET [3] 4-9-6 A Nixon(5) 8/1: 0-00120: Shorter trip, see 772 & 675.   16
770 NICKY DAWN [5] 4-8-8 Julie Bowker 33/1: -0000: Cl.up till home turn: no form to date   03
750 Toda Forca Avanti [4] 9-6   492 Princess Bella [7] 8-8
8 ran   ¼,2½,1½,12,½,hd   (Hamdan Al-Maktoum)   H Thomson Jones Newmarket

889 LORTON SELLING HANDICAP 3 4 & 5YO 0-25   £656   1m 1f   Good 56 -25 Slow   [18]

740 HARSLEY SURPRISE [2] (N Tinkler) 3-8-6 Kim Tinkler(7) 5/1: 040-331: 3 br f Meldrum
- Night Surprise (Articulate) Found the best grd on stands side when leading 2f out,
comfortably, in a selling h'cap at Carlisle June 5 (bght in 1,700 gns): first success: eff
over 7/9f: acts on fast and soft grd and is well suited by a stiff trk.   18
727 POCO LOCO [13] (A Davison) 4-9-11 I Johnson 4/1 FAV: 0-03402: Hung left below dist,
ev ch and seems best over this trip: acts on any trk: see 495.   09
673 RECORD HAULIER [9] (W Haigh) 4-8-11 S Lawes 9/1: 0400/43: Never nearer: stays 9f:
see 673.   00
419 CLUEDO [11] (M James) 5-9-1(bl) Sharron James 12/1: 000-004: Ran on too late: won
seller on soft grd at Wolverhampton last season and has since been hurdling: stays 12f well.   03
788 SWIFT RIVER [6] 4-9-8 J Lowe 9/2: -202030: Late prog: best in 522 (10f).   04
828 BANTEL BANZAI [12] 3-8-11(bl) S Keightley 12/1: 0000040: Not stay trip? see 828,255   00
-- DEBRIS [7] 4-9-10(vis) M Hindley(3) 8/1: 22014-0: Made much: hung left when hdd:
fin 9th: only twice out of the frame last season, when winning a selling h'cap at Edinburgh:
eff over 5f and stays 1m: acts on gd and hvy grd and on any trk.   00
-- THE GOLF SLIDE [1] 4-8-10 J Hills(5) 10/1: 00000-0: Led over 3f out: mdn who showed
little worthwhile form last season over shorter trips: acts on firm and yldg grd.   00
788 TRICENCO [8] 4-9-10 A Mackay 10/1: 000-000: No form this term and last won in '84
at Brighton and Windsor: best form over sprint dist on gd or faster ground.   00
788 RAPID STAR [4] 3-7-10(bl) N Carlisle 10/1: 3000000: Fin last: disappp: see 51.   00
718 Amplify [10] 8-3   718 Dads Gunner [5] 7-10   767 Tara Dancer [3] 8-5(bl)
13 ran   2,3,½,4,8,hd   (D Marley)   N Tinkler Malton, Yorks

890 BORROWDALE HANDICAP 0-35   £1525   5f   Good 56 +12 Fast   [35]

786 LULLABY BLUES [11] (M H Easterby) 3-8-6 M Birch 9/2: -00121: 3 br g Lochnager -
Sunset Song (Song) In fine form, broke well and was never hdd when winning fast run h'cap
at Carlisle June 5: last month won a seller at Hamilton: sprint bred gelding who is a half
brother to winning juv Sing To Me: eff over 5/6f on gd and hvy grd: acts on any trk.   35
520 GODS SOLUTION [5] (D Barron) 5-9-6(bl) E Guest(3) 7/1: 0-10402: Fin strongly: gd
effort: see 42.   34
814 MISS PRIMULA [8] (W Bentley) 3-9-0 R Guest 8/1: 00-0303: Chased winner: not btn far:
see 628.   38
784 GOLD DUCHESS [3] (M W Easterby) 4-8-7(bl) T Lucas 4/1: 4310024: Al up there:see 412   20
734 DORNEY [10] 6-8-5 I Johnson 10/1: 40-0000: Not btn far: clear rem: see 679.   16
*786 MIAMI DOLPHIN [4] 6-8-5(7ex) M Fry 3/1 FAV: -001310: Beat winner on hvy in 786.   04
866 POKERFAYES [1] 7-8-5(bl) A Roper(7) 10/1: 0301-00: Quick reappearance: fin 8th:see 866.   00
649 TASKFORCE VICTORY [7] 5-8-13 M Hindley(3) 8/1: 001-000: Al behind: fin last: fair
sprint h'capper on his day, won at Catterick last season and in '84 at Thirsk: eff over 6/7f
best form on fast grd.   00
786 Grand Celebration [9] 7-10   412 Russian Winter [2] 7-8(bl)(1ow)
10 ran   1½,nk,shthd,½,5,2,1   (P D Savill)   M H Easterby Malton, Yorks

891 KNARSDALE MAIDEN STAKES 3YO   £1103   6f   Good 56 -11 Slow

593 ROYAL FAN [13] (M H Easterby) 3-9-0 K Hodgson 5/1: -001: 3 b c Taufan - Miss Royal
(King's Company) Went on 2f out and ran on well to win a 3yo mdn at Carlisle June 5: didnot race last season: stays 6f well: acts on gd and yldg grd and on a stiff trk.   38

-787 RAAS [3] (S Norton) 3-9-0 J Quinn(5) 9/2 Jt FAV: -234022: Just held: in gd form: see 787. 35
368 BOLD SEA ROVER [1] (M H Easterby) 3-9-0 M Birch 8/1: -0303: Not clear run dist, fin
strongly and possibly unlucky: eff over 6/7f: acts on gd and hvy grd and on a stiff trk:see 82 35
677 PACKAGE PERFECTION [15] (T Fairhurst) 3-8-11 J Callaghan(7) 14/1: 320-004: Al well
placed: lightly raced last season, made the frame in her first 3 starts: eff over 5/6f
on firm and soft grd: acts on any grd. 26
--   FORETOP [11] 3-8-11 C Dwyer 12/1: -0: Kept on well on race course debut: half
sister to winning sprinter Tacheron: acts on gd/yldg grd and on a stiff course. 26
593 PRETTY GREAT [14] 3-8-11 A Shoults(5) 11/2: -3400: Best over this trip in 217. 22
787 TRY SIR [8] 3-9-0 N Connorton 8/1: -040: Fin 7th: acts on gd and yldg: see 438. 00
545 AZELLY [4] 3-8-11 M Rimmer 9/2 Jt FAV: 020-00: Fin 9th: maiden who ran up to the
useful Tarib in a small race at Beverley last season: acts on gd and yldg grd. 00
431 EMANCIPATED LADY [6] 3-8-11 P Hamblett 10/1: -00: No threat after slow start. 00
545 WINNING FORMAT [12] 3-9-0 R Guest 9/1: 00-0000: Made most, sn btn: best 545. 00
593 Whoberley Wheels [2] 9-0   -- Tenasserim [10] 9-0
605 Sana Song [7] 9-0   516 Tip Top Boy [5] 9-0   516 Eastern Heights [9] 9-0
15 ran   ½,hd,2½,shthd,1½,hd   (Ian Armitage)   M H Easterby Malton, Yorks

892 LANGDALE MAIDEN AUCTION STAKES 2YO   £1044   5f   Good 56 +04 Fast

632 STAGE [5] (K Stone) 2-8-5(1ow) C Dwyer 5/2: 001: 2 b c Taufan - Naval Artiste
(Captain's Gig) Nicely bckd when showing impr form to lead inside dist in quite a fast run
2yo maiden auction race at Carlisle June 5: half brother to winning juv Boardmans Delight:
eff over 5f on gd/yldg grd: seems suited by a stiff course. 44
536 KALAS IMAGE [8] (G Moore) 2-7-11 A Mackay 9/4 FAV: 032: Led below dist, just btn:
see 364. 35
515 BEN LEDI [4] (M H Easterby) 2-8-0 J Lowe 11/2: 03: Led over ½ way: clear rem and
should stay further: acts on gd/yldg grd and on a stiff course. 35
612 MARKET MAN [6] (D Barron) 2-8-0 N Carlisle 7/2: 04: Al up there: not quicken dist:
cheaply bought gelding who has shown ability on both starts: acts on gd and yldg. 23
766 MERE MUSIC [7] 2-8-3(BL) K Darley 20/1: 0000: Easily his best effort to date:
speedily bred colt who costs 4,300 gns as yearling: acts on gd/yldg grd. 25
548 MAZURKANOVA [10] 2-8-4 J Bleasdale 7/1: 00: Gd speed over ½ way: sprint bred filly
who cost 6,200 gns as yearling: acts on yldg grd. 14
415 Hilliard [2] 8-0   819 Bantel Bouquet [3] 7-11
--   Ski Captain [9] 8-9   --   Absolutely Free [1] 7-11
10 ran   nk,1,5,nk,5   (M Chandler)   K Stone Malton, Yorks

893 ESKDALE HANDICAP STAKES 4YO+ 0-35   £1850   1m 1f   Good 56 -03 Slow   [34]

281 QUALITY CHORISTER [3] (G Moore) 5-8-6 R P Elliott 8/1: 002-401: 5 b h Music Boy -
Blessed Beauty (Rustam) Led after 3f and held on gamely in a h'cap at Carlisle June 5:
well suited by forcing tactics, made all in a h'cap at Newcastle last season and in '84 won
at Ayr: eff over 8/10f: acts on gd and soft grd and is well suited by stiff/gall trk. 20
750 BWANA KALI [4] (M Tompkins) 4-9-5(bl) M Rimmer 9/2: -433002: Just held: see 36. 32
--   SANTOPADRE [10] (W Storey) 4-7-9 A Mackay 11/4 FAV: -0003-3: Fit from most successful
hurdling campaign, not btn far and clear rem: mdn on Flat: stays 10f and will get further:
acts on firm and soft ground. 08
698 SILLY BOY [5] (N Bycroft) 6-10-0 M Richardson(7) 9/2: 4000-04: Not quicken dist: see 698. 31
+611 PATCHBURG [6] 4-9-5(5ex) J H Brown(5) 7/2: -213010: Btr over 1m in 611. 19
745 THIRTEENTH FRIDAY [2] 4-7-11 J Lowe 12/1: 000-400: Btr over 1m in 259 (sharp trk). 00
789 MOONDAWN [8] 5-9-4 C Dwyer 15/2: 0-02000: Fin 8th: much btr 343 (sharp trk). 00
745 Kamaress [1] 8-6   --   Anitas Apple [9] 8-10   --   Sundown Sky [7] 8-3
10 ran   ½,hd,7,½,5   (G Simpson)   G Moore Middleham, Yorks

894 DUNMAIL STAKES 3YO   £952   1m 4f   Good 56 -52 Slow

*770 PLYMOUTH HOE [4] (L Cumani) 3-9-5 R Guest 4/11 FAV: -11: 3 b c Busted - Pluvial
(Habat) Had a simple task and easily landed the odds in a 3yo stks at Carlisle June 5: recent
winner of a small race at Catterick: stays 12f well: acts on firm and yldg grd and on any
trk: certain to race more highly. 34
744 DEPUTY MONARCH [3] (Denys Smith) 3-9-0 M Fry 15/2: 040-02: No chance with this easy
winner: officially rated only 12 and seems flattered in 744. 18
357 RYE HILL MARINER [2] (B Mcmahon) 3-9-0 J Lowe 7/1: 04-03: Ran on same pace: lightly
raced last season: half brother to a winning juv sprinter in Ireland tho' btr suited by
longer dist himself: acts on firm and yldg grd. 15
714 LAKISTE [5] (J Watts) 3-9-0 N Connorton 7/1: -04: Never threatened leaders: shd
be suited by middle dist: acts on gd/yldg ground. 10
379 TIEATRE [1] 3-8-11 D Casey(7) 100/1: 0000-00: Rank outsider yet to show any worthwhile form. 00
5 ran   2½,1½,3,4   (Lady Drake)   L Cumani Newmarket

BADEN BADEN	Friday May 30th	Lefthand, Sharpish Track

Official Going Given as Very Soft

895 BENAZET RENNEN LISTED 3YO+   £8475   6f   Very Soft -

*588 ELNAWAAGI (H T Jones) 3-8-3 A Murray 1: 1123-11: 3 b c Roberto - Gurkhas Band
(Lurullah): Useful colt: led well over 1f out for a comfortable win in a Listed race at
Baden-Baden May 30: first time out won a 3yo h'cap at York: consistent 2yo, winning fast run
events at Windsor & Thirsk: very eff over 6f, should stay further: acts on firm & soft grnd
& on any trk: very well bred sort who should win more races.   65
--   ROYAL ROCKS (Germany) 3-8-1 M Hofer 1: -2: Ran on, but no ch with winner: eff at 6f
on soft grnd.   58
--   HOME PLEASE (Germany) 4-8-10 S Eccles 1: -3:   48
--   LE ROC (Germany) 3-8-5(2ow) P Remmert 1: -4:   52
9 ran   ¾,2,1   (Hamdan Al-Maktoum)   H T Jones Newmarket

BADEN BADEN	Sunday June 1st	Lefthand, Sharpish Track

Official Going Given as Very Soft

896 GROUP 2 GROSSER PREIS DE BADISCHEN 4YO+ £18362   1m 3f Very Soft -

--   ACATENANGO (H Jentzsch) 4-9-4 G Bocskai 1: 111-1: 4 ch c Surumu - Aggravate
(Aggressor): Smart German colt: made it 8 wins on the trot with an easy all the way success
in Gr.2 event at Baden Baden June 1: in excellent form in '85, winning the German Derby: very
eff over 11/12f on gd & soft grnd & does well making the running: very hard to beat in his
native country.   83
--   CASSIS (Germany) 4-8-13 P Remmert 1: 41-2: No ch with winner: in '85 won a Gr.3 event
at Dusseldorf: stays 12f: acts on gd & soft.   68
*290 LOVE LETTER (Germany) 5-9-2 P Alafi 1: 32-13: Btr in 290.   61
--   DAUN (Germany) 5-9-6 E Schindler 1: -1123-4: Consistent sort in '85: very eff over
middle dists: acts on firm & soft grnd.   64
617 LEADING STAR 4-8-13 A Murray 1: 010-430: Did not act on this soft grnd & came in
last: better 617: see 251.   43
5 ran   5½,5¾,½,8   (Gestut Fahrhof)   H Jentzsch Germany

SAN SIRO	Sunday June 1st	

Official Going Given as Good/Soft

897 GROUP 1 PREMIO EMILIO TURATI   £49211   1m   Good/Soft -

598 EFISIO (J Dunlop) 4-9-3 Pat Eddery 1: 110-041: 4 b c Formidable - Eldoret (High Top)
Smart colt: led well over 1f out, easily in a Gr.1 event at San Siro June 1: in '85 won Gr.3
event at Newmarket & a Listed race at Goodwood: unbtn 2yo, winning Gr.3 Horris Hill Stakes
at Newbury after wins at Salisbury, Goodwood & Ascot: very eff at 7f/1m: acts on firm &
soft grnd & on any trk: genuine & consistent: will win more races.   78
392 KATELL (Italy) 7-9-3 M Planard 1: 22: Again ran well: see 392.   68
286 ALEX NUREYEV (Italy) 3-8-7 S Cauthen 1: -03: Ran a fine race.   70
296 GOLDEN BOY(ITA) (Italy) 5-9-3 M Jerome 1: -44: --   62
6 ran   4,1,2   (Mrs M Landi)   J Dunlop Arundel, Sussex

CAPPANELLE	Sunday June 1st	

Official Going Given as Good

898 GROUP 3 CRITERIUM DI ROMA 2YO   £12410   6f   Good -

+170 MELBURY LAD (R Mimmochi) 2-8-11 J Heloury 1: 211: 2 ch c Free State - Lucky Kim
(Whistling Wind): Much impr colt: dsptd lead final 2f, staying on gamely by a shhd in a
Gr.3 event at Cappanelle June 1: earlier trained by C Hill to win a maiden at Chepstow: eff
at 5f, stays 6f well: acts on gd & soft grnd & seems a genuine sort.   58
--   SHUTTLE COCK (Italy) 2-8-11 M Depalmas 1: 2: Duelled with winner final 1f & btn a
whisker: fine effort: eff at 6f on gd grnd.   58
--   BANDROLL (Italy) 2-8-11 B Jovine 1: 3: --   51
--   IONIO (Italy) 2-8-11 A Sauli 1: 4: --   50
*437 KHADRUF 2-8-11 A Murray 1: 10: Wknd into 6th: see 437 (5f).   38
7 ran   shhd,2½,nk   (Scuderia Azzurra)   R Mimmochi Italy

899 GROUP 3 PREMIO LAZIO 3YO   £12410   1m 2f Good -

555 LOCAL HERBERT (L Camini) 3-8-7 L Ficuciello 1: 02-4201: 3 b c Robellino - Split
Personality (Home Guard): Very useful colt: led well over 1f out, staying on well to win a
Gr.3 event at Cappanelle June 1: formerly trained by I Balding: very eff at 10f, probably
stays 11f: acts on gd & hvy grnd.   68

--   SOUISTRE (Italy) 3-8-7 G Dettori 1: -2: Ran on well to fin 2nd.   **64**
556 DANCING EAGLE (M Jarvis) 3-8-7 G Baxter 1: 01-323: Led 2f out: wknd close home:
another fine run: stays 10f: see 556, 386.   **64**
--   TAP NATIVE (Italy) 3-8-8(1ow) S Fancera 1: -4: --   **61**
4 ran   1½,shhd,2   (Scuderia Ri Ma)   L Camini

LONGCHAMP   Sunday June 1st   Righthand, Galloping Track

Official Going Given as Firm

900   GROUP 1 PRIX JEAN PRAT 3YO C & F   £58436   1m 1f Firm -

*644 MAGICAL WONDER (G Mikhalides) 3-9-2 C Asmussen 1: -111: 3 ch c Storm Bird -
Flama Ardiente (Crimson Satan): Smart French colt: maintained his unbtn record, led 1f out
when a narrow winner of Gr.1 Prix Jean Prat at Longchamp Sunday June 1: earlier a comfortable
winner of a Gr.3 event at Longchamp: first time out won in a canter at Evry: very eff at
1m, stays 9f: seems to act on any grnd: certain to win more gd races.   **83**
389 HIGHEST HONOR (P Bary) 3-9-2 A Badel 1: -122: Stayed on really well & just held:
fine effort: in grand form: stays 9f: see 156.   **82**
389 ART FRANCAIS (P Biancone) 3-9-2 E Legrix 1: 100-133: Acts on firm & hvy: see 389.   **77**
302 DOUBLE BED (F Douman) 3-9-2 G Mosse 1: 3224: In gd form.   **75**
644 CRYSTAL DE ROCHE 3-9-2 F Head 1: -030: Ev ch over 1f out: gd run: see 644.   **75**
9 ran   nk,2,½,shhd   (M Fustok)   G Mikhalides France

901   GROUP 3 PRIX DU PALAIS ROYAL 3YO+   £18330   7f   Firm -

--   COMRADE IN ARMS (P Lallie) 4-9-7 G Dubroeucq 1: 2001-21: 4 b h Brigadier Gerard -
Girl Friend (Birdbrook): Smart French horse: narrow winner in a blanket fin to Gr.3 event
at Longchamp June 1: in '85 won a Gr.3 event at M.Laffitte: very eff at 7f/1m: acts on firm   **81**
--   ELISHARP (J De Chevigny) 4-8-12 G Guignard 1: 4000-32: Just btn and ran a fine race:
very eff at 7f on firm grnd.   **71**
--   ALTDORFER (P Biancone) 5-9-1 E Legrix 1: 0-02123: Narrowly btn in close fin: earlier
won a h'cap on this trk: eff at 7f on firm grnd.   **74**
391 EPHIALTES (C Milbank) 4-9-7 A Junk 1: 3-00124: Another fine effort: acts on any grnd.   **79**
587 OROJOYA 4-9-10 M Hills 1: 13-0200: Ev ch over 1f out: not btn far & this was
a grand effort: see 413, 222.   **81**
--   ROYAL INFATUATION 3-8-6 C Asmussen 1: 130-200: --   **73**
12ran   ½,shhd,½,½,1   (D W Molins)   P Lallie France

902   GROUP 3 PRIX DE LESPERANCE 3YO   £17852   1m 7f Firm -

597 FAMILY FRIEND (W Hern) 3-8-7 W Carson 1: 240-441: 3 b c Henbit - Happy Kin (Bold
Bidder): Very useful colt: ran on strongly to win Gr.3 Prix de L'Esperance at Longchamp
June 1: in '85 made all at Sandown: very eff at 10/12f, stays 15f really well: acts on
firm & yld grnd & loves a stiff trk: genuine sort.   **69**
552 ROSEDALE USA (J Dunlop) 3-8-7 B Thomson 1: -2-2122: Left in lead after fatal fall
of Jewelled Reef: not btn far & 6L clear 3rd: in grand form: stays 15f: see 552, 347.   **68**
--   DORSOUN (A De Royer Dupre) 3-8-7 Y Saint Martin 1: -13: Ran to his best: winner at
St Cloud in April: acts on firm grnd.   **62**
--   GRETNA (J Fellows) 3-8-7 G Moore 1: -400-04: --   **60**
384 JEWELLED REEF 3-8-7 M Hills 1: 10-0P: In front, broke foreleg & tragically destroyed.   **00**
7 ran   1,6,1½   (Sir M Sobell)   W Hern East Ilsley, Berks

LEOPARDSTOWN   Monday June 2nd   Lefthand Galloping Track

Official Going Given as Good

903   GROUP 3 BALLYOGAN STAKES 3YO+   £11550   5f   Good -

639 WOLVERSTAR [9] (P Norris) 4-9-0 S Craine 12/1: 3-20101: 4 b f Wolverlife - Fotostar
(Polyfoto): Came fast & late for a narrow win in a Gr.3 event at Leopardstown June 2: earlier
won a 5f h'cap at Phoenix Park: very eff at 5f: acts on gd & hvy, possibly dislikes firm grnd.   **69**
--   MITSUBISHI VISION [13] (J Oxx) 3-8-5 P V Gilson 20/1: 442-012: Fin well: just btn:
excellent effort: last time out won over 6f at Phoenix Park: acts on gd & hvy grnd.   **68**
639 LONDON TOWER [12] (D Weld) 3-8-8(bl) M J Kinane 11/2: 2033: Fin in gd style: 6f seems
his optimum trip: acts on gd & hvy: see 293.   **71**
408 WELSH NOTE [5] (I Balding) 3-8-10 C Roche 5/1: 2214-44: Narrowly btn in a blanket fin:
gd effort: see 408.   **73**
660 DUBLIN LAD [3] 3-8-13 K Darley 14/1: 00-0000: Set fast pace 4f: ran well: coming back
to his 2yo form? one of the most impr performers of '85, winning at Wolverhampton, Thirsk,
Lingfield (2) & Catterick & never ran a bad race: very eff over 5f with forcing tactics: acts
on any trk, though is suited by a sharpish one: acts on firm & yld grnd: tough & genuine:
carries weight well.   **74**

+639 RUSTIC AMBER [1] 3-9-2 D Hogan 11/2: 210-310: Much btr in 639 (hvy grnd).   74
563 STORM WARNING [14] 4-9-5 W R Swinburn 5/2 FAV: 310-030: Below her best: btr 563.   00
705 SHARP ROMANCE [4] 4-9-8 D Gillespie 12/1: 0-23300: Btr 705: see 18.   00
14ran   hd,shhd,shhd,½,1   (L Murphy)   P Norris Ireland

CHANTILLY   Thursday June 5th

Official Going Given as Good/Soft

904 GROUP 3 PRIX DE ROYAUMONT 3YO FILLIES   £18569   1m 2f Good/Soft -

-- RELOY (J Pease) 3-8-9 C Asmussen 1: -24-311: 3 b f Liloy - Rescousses (Emerson):
Smart French filly: led over 1f out, comfortably in a Gr.3 fillies event at Chantilly June 5:
stays 10½f really well: acts on yld grnd.   72
-- LIASTRA (F. Boutin) 3-8-9 F Head 1: -212: Ran a fine race: eff at 10f on yld grnd.   69
-- ELLE SEULE (D Smaga) 3-8-12 A Lequeux 1: 32-1013: Ran on well final 1f: in fine form.   71
755 CARNATION (M Zilber) 3-8-12 G Dubroeucq 1: 414-304: Fin well, but too late: needs 12f?   71
9 ran   1½,½,nk   (N B Hunt)   J Pease France

CATTERICK   Friday June 6th   Lefthanded Tight Track

Official Going Given as Firm

905 GILLING MAIDEN FILLIES STAKES 2YO   £723   5f   Good/Firm 22 -24 Slow

818 LADY PAT [5] (M Mccormack) 2-8-11 M Wigham 3/1: 241: Broke well & made virtually ev yd
in a 2yo fillies maiden at Catterick June 6: half sister to several winners: eff over 5f
on a sharp trk, though will stay further in time: acts on firm & soft grnd: on the up grade.   40
-- GOOD GAME [8] (K Stone) 2-8-11 C Dwyer 4/1: 2: Showed plenty of speed on her racecourse
debut and would not have to impr much to win a similar race: acts on firm grnd & on a tight trk.   30
722 BROADWAY STOMP [10] (G Huffer) 2-8-11 G Sexton 7/4 FAV: 03: Nicely bckd: al up there:
half sister to winning sprinter Kamal: acts on fast grnd & on a tight trk.   24
515 GET SET LISA [6] (C Tinkler) 2-8-11 M Wood 14/1: 004: Mkt drifter: stayed on late: will
appreciate another furlong: acts on fast grnd & on a tight trk.   20
-- NEEDWOOD NUT [11] 2-8-11 B Crossley 16/1: 0: Kept on well dist on racecourse debut:
speedily bred filly who will impr for this experience: acts on gd/firm grnd & on a sharp trk.   15
818 ABERGWRLE [2] 2-8-11(BL) M Birch 16/1: 00: Early speed: sprint bred filly who is a
half sister to several winners: acts on gd/firm grnd.   13
818 MUSIC STAR [4] 2-8-11 M Roberts 10/1: 00: No threat: fin 9th.   00
425 GAME LIGHT [9] 2-8-11 Gay Kelleway(5) 7/1: 000: Early speed: fin last: btr in 425.   00
270 Pink Pumpkin [1] 8-11   -- Joyces Pet [3] 8-11   813 Chantilly Dawn [7] 8-11
376 Dear Dolly [12] 8-11
12 ran   3,2,1½,2,½   (W G Best)   M Mccormack Sparsholt, Oxon

906 SCORTON SELLING HANDICAP (0-25)   £1193   6f   Good/Firm 22 +09 Fast   [19]

355 GREY STARLIGHT [2] (L Siddall) 4-9-2(BL) G Gosney 10/1: 200-001: 4 gr g Runnymede -
Belle Mere (Tacitus): Bl first time & showed impr form, led inside dist for a comfortable win
in quite a fast run selling h'cap at Catterick June 6 (no bid): first success though twice
ran up in similar company last season: eff over 5/6f: acts on firm & yld grnd & on any trk.   16
845 LADY NATIVELY [3] (P Makin) 4-9-5 S Perks 9/1: 00-3002: Led below dist: see 160.   12
836 LUCKY STARKIST [9] (R Holder) 4-9-5 A Dicks(7) 5/1: 410-003: Fin well after slow start.   12
594 DOPPIO [6] (J Etherington) 4-9-10 M Wood 6/1: -000-04: A big gamble: never nearer:
lightly raced last season: in '84 won a small race at Nottingham: eff over 5/6f on fast
& yld grnd: acts on any trk.   13
636 SING GALVO SING [13] 5-8-9 T Williams 13/2: 44-0000: Nearest fin: won an app. selling
h'cap at Windsor last season: eff over sprint distances: stays 7f: acts on firm & yld grnd
& is well suited by a sharp trk.   00
784 LADY OF LEISURE [4] 5-9-12 R Vickers(7) 8/1: 00-0000: Made most: best in 628.   11
809 PERCIPIO [5] 3-9-3 A Shoults(5) 10/1: 00-0000: Never nearer after slow start: likes
to make the running, won in this grade at Ripon last term & later placed in none selling
company: well suited by 6f on a sharp trk: acts on gd & firm grnd.   00
310 SWEET EIRE [12] 4-9-0 N Connorton 9/1: 3400-00: Fin 8th: little form last season in
similar company: well suited by sprint distances: seems best on a sound surface.   00
594 HOPTONS CHANCE [10] 4-9-0 D Nicholls 7/2 FAV: 022-000: Dropped in class: fin 9th:
in gd form last backend, twice fin 2nd in similar company: acts on any going: seems best
on a stiff trk.   00
593 PANOVA [8] 3-8-11 M Wigham 7/1: 3000-00: Dropped in class: maiden.   00
477 Little Bori [11] 9-3   7   Coded Love [7] 9-3(BL)
12 ran   3,1,1½,1½,shhd,hd,1½   (Mrs V Ball)   L Siddall Tadcaster, Yorks

907 MERRYBENT STAKES 3YO   £684   7f   Good/Firm 22 +01 Fast

--   RAJA MOULANA [11] (M Albina) 3-8-11 A Bond 8/1: 04-1: 3 b f Raja Baba - Gallatin Valley
(Apalachee): First time out, led below dist and driven out to win a 3yo stakes at Catterick
June 6: lightly raced last season: eff over 7f & will stay further: acts on gd & fast grnd
& on a sharp trk.   39
*656 RAISINHELL [10] (W Jarvis) 3-9-3(6ex) W Ryan 6/4 FAV: 200-312: Well bckd: sustained chall
final 1f, just held: in gd form: see 656.   44
451 COUNTRY CARNIVAL [12] (W Haigh) 3-8-11 D Nicholls 33/1: 200-003: Ran on well & not
btn far: best effort to date: narrowly btn by Rockall in an Ayr maiden last season: half
sister to a couple of middle dists winners and should stay further herself: acts on gd &
firm grnd & on any trk.   37
768 HAITI MILL [2] (W Wharton) 3-8-11 N Carlsile 8/1: 303-044: Going on fin: stays 7f. see 309 36
656 CLEOFE [3] 3-8-11 R Guest 7/2: 044-00: Not btn that far: impr filly: see 656.   36
423 HARDY CHANCE [8] 3-8-11 R Hills 12/1: 0-0030: Led before ½way: running well: see 423.   35
--   ENTOURAGE [1] 3-8-11 K Bradshaw(5) 7/1: 4-0: Fin 8th on reapp: btr for race: placed
behind Palaestra in a Redcar maiden on sole start last term: eff over 7f & will stay further:
acts on fast grnd and on a gall trk.   00
674 Lady Brit [5] 8-11   431 Lone Galaxie [6] 8-11   *749 Miami Blues [4] 9-3(6ex)
733 Megadyne [9] 8-11   328 Rose Window [13] 8-11   480 Hachimitsu [7] 8-11
13 ran   hd,nk,½,shhd,½   (Mohamed Odaida)   M Albina Newmarket

908 CROFT HANDICAP STAKES (0-35) 3YO   £1331   1m 5f   Good/Firm 22 -21 Slow   [36]

648 FEDRA [4] (Lord J Fitzgerald) 3-9-7 R Hills 1/1 FAV: 00-1221: 3 b f Grundy - Zebra
Grass (Run The Gantlet): In gd form, comfortably defied top weight in a 3yo h'cap at Catterick June 6, led below dist & ran on strongly: first time out winner of a similar race
at Lingfield: showed some promise last season: stoutly bred filly who cost 41,000 gns: eff
over 10f, stays 13f really well: acts on firm & soft grnd & on any trk.   40
416 CHUMMYS OWN [6] (N Callaghan) 3-8-7 J Matthias 7/2: 0-102: Led after 1m: acts on gd/frm 22
505 SLAP BANG [3] (N Vigors) 3-8-8 S Dawson(3) 7/2: 0000-43: Kept on under press: stays 14f. 20
132 LADY ST CLAIR [5] (Denys Smith) 3-9-6 L Charnock 7/1: 404-004: Lost touch after 1m:
btr in 132 (10f, heavy).   17
--   BIG COUNTRY [2] 3-8-2 R P Elliott 25/1: 00000-0: Outsider on reapp: made early running,
sn dropped out: no form last season.   00
5 ran   2,2,15,½   (Mrs H G Cambanis)   Lord J Fitzgerald Newmarket

909 SCOTCH CORNER STAKES   £812   1m 4f   Good/Firm 22 -56 Slow

*613 LOCH SEAFORTH [2] (H Cecil) 3-8-10 W Ryan 4/5 FAV: 44-211: 3 b c Tyrnavos - Marypark
(Charlottown): In gd form, was never hdd when a comfortable winner in a slowly run race at
Catterick June 6: earlier beat subs. winner The Prudent Prince in a Beverley maiden: well
suited by 12f & will stay further: acts on gd & firm grnd & is well suited by forcing
tactics: no trk preferences: should win a h'cap.   58
*506 JUST DAVID [1] (A Stewart) 3-8-10 M Roberts 1/1: -12: Tracked winner thro'out: should
regain winning form soon in a more exacting course: stays 12f: acts on gd/firm & yld: see 506. 52
611 PETERS KIDDIE [4] (R Woodhouse) 5-9-9 A Bond 100/1: 000-003: No worthwhile form to date 00
--   TUDOR JUSTICE [3] (B Mcmahon) 4-9-9 J Hills(5) 100/1: -0-4: No threat: well btn in
sole start last term.   00
4 ran   2½,20,1½   (Sir David Wills)   H Cecil Newmarket

910 JERVAULX HANDICAP STAKES (0-35) 3YO   £1442   5f   Good/Firm 22 -08 Slow   [27]

760 CHAUTAUQUA [9] (P Haslam) 3-9-3 T Williams 2/1 FAV: 0-42141: 3 b c Stanford -
Pitmilly (Pitskelly): Made virtually ev yd, staying on well in a 3yo h'cap at Catterick
June 6: earlier used similar front running tactics to win an app. h'cap at Haydock: yet to
be out of the frame this season: very eff over 5f, stays 6f: acts on any going & on any trk.   25
--   MUSIC REVIEW [2] (W Jarvis) 3-9-7 W Ryan 6/1: 000-2: Fin strongly after slow start:
half brother to winning juvenile Record Review and showed early speed in his races last
season: well suited by fast grnd & a sharp trk: should go close next time.   26
871 PENDOR DANCER [7] (K Ivory) 3-9-6 A Shoults(5) 16/1: 00-0023: Not btn far: in gd form.   24
670 SANDITTON PALACE [10] (P Felgate) 3-9-6 M Fry 20/1: 000-004: Al up there: best in 516.   19
255 LEFT RIGHT [16] 3-9-4 Gay Kelleway(5) 11/1: 400-030: Abs: no extra dist: see 255.   15
768 THE STRAY BULLETT [14] 3-9-0 J Hills(5) 10/1: 0-00200: Nearest fin: best on soft in 529. 09
489 TAYLORS TAYLORMADE [4] 3-9-0 M Rimmer 10/1: 020-030: Never nearer in 7th: see 489.   00
593 DADS LINE [8] 3-9-6 J Bleasdale 9/2: 02-00: No threat after slow start: just btn by
Au Dessus on final start last season over this C/D (rated 34) & well h'capped on that form:
well suited by fast grnd & a tight trk.   00
--   Ever So Sharp [5] 8-13   --   Jump To It [11] 9-2
246 Mercia Gold [3] 9-1   82 Mr Coffey [1] 9-7   626 Marshall Drills [15] 8-7
784 Running Rainbow [13] 8-9   677 Hobournes Katie [12] 9-3
--   Nagem [17] 9-4   786 Musical Aid [6] 9-4
17 ran   ½,nk,2,1,½,hd   (T C Kelly)   P Haslam Newmarket

911 MERRYBENT STAKES 3YO   £648   7f   Good/Firm 22 +01 Fast

-- ARTFUL DAY [5] (J Dunlop) 3-8-11 G Baxter 9/1: 04-1: 3 ch f Artaius - Longest Day
(Lyphard): First time out, led inside dist for a narrow win in a 3yo stakes at Catterick
June 6: lightly raced last season: eff over 7f & seems certain to stay further: acts on gd/
firm grnd & on a sharp trk.   44
814 BREAKFAST IN BED [2] (W Haigh) 3-8-11 D Nicholls 4/1: 030-322: Led dist, just caught:
clearly well suited by 7f: in gd form & must win soon: see 814.   42
464 INDIAN LOVE SONG [7] (R Hollinshead) 3-8-11 W Ryan 4/1: 0400-23: Ran on well: well
suited by a tight trk: acts on fast grnd: best in 464.   38
33 NO RESTRAINT [3] (W Hastings Bass) 3-8-11 R Lines(3) 7/1: -04: Ran on well, never
nearer: gd effort after fair abs: stays 7f: acts on fast grnd & on a tight trk.   35
656 MALEIHA [8] 3-8-11 S Dawson(3) 9/4 FAV: -020: Sn led, no extra dist: much btr 656(hvy).   28
593 WATENDLATH [6] 3-8-11 E Guest(3) 16/1: 30-0300: Led early, ran on well late: stays
7f: acts on any going: see 529.   24
-- FANCY FINISH [12] 3-8-11 M Roberts 8/1: 04-0: Led/dsptd lead early on: fin 8th &
btr for race: lightly raced last season, showing some promise: half sister to several
winners: should be suited by this trip: acts on gd & fast grnd.   00
447 Tricky [11] 8-11   -- How Blue [4] 8-11   732 Raffles Virginia [10] 8-11
447 Spring Garden [9] 8-11
11 ran   hd,2,1½,4,2½,hd,1   (M Machline)   J Dunlop Arundel, Sussex

---

HAYDOCK   Friday June 6th   Lefthand, Galloping Track

Official Going Given as Good

912 INNSTOCK CASH AND CARRY HANDICAP   £2276   1m 2f Good 58 -39 Slow   [5]

547 RIMAH [7] (H T Jones) 5-12-0(bl) Mr T Thomson Jones 3/1 FAV: 0340-01: 5 b h Nishapour -
Lady Simone (Realm): Ran on well to get up last 50yds in an amateur riders h'cap at Haydock
June 6: failed to win in '85 but ran well on several occasions: in '84 won at Goodwood:
eff over 1m, stays 10f well: acts on firm & yld grnd & on any trk.   41
609 NORTH STAR SAM [10] (J Ramsden) 5-9-9 Valerie Greaves(3) 16/1: 0000402: Led/dsptd
lead: gd effort: see 333.   05
652 SALLOOM [12] (W Hastings Bass) 4-11-13 Maxine Juster 7/1: 2100-03: Ch over 1f out:
running into form: in '85 won a stakes event at Brighton when trained by G Harwood: eff at
10f on gd & firm grnd: seems to act on any trk, though likes a sharpish one.   35
782 DIPYN BACH [5] (M Camacho) 4-11-10 Mr T Reed 9/2: 000-044: Al up there: see 782.   31
827 TREYARNON [9] 4-10-2(bl) Mr T Walford 6/1: -434330: Twice below form 631 (non h'cap).   06
-- JUST A HALF [3] 4-10-4 Mr J Ryan(3) 33/1: 00000-0: Some late hdway on seasonal debut:
maiden: eff at 10f, may stay 12f: acts on gd grnd.   07
698 SIGNORE ODONE [8] 4-11-7 Mr T Easterby 13/2: 320-400: No real threat: best 594.   00
*492 PRINCE SATIRE [11] 3-11-4 Gay Arber(3) 9/2: -010: Fdd: much btr 492 (hvy grnd).   00
-- Moniar [4] 10-3   743 Annie Ra [6] 10-0   541 Celtic Quest [2] 9-9(BL)
11 ran   1½,1,½,1½,nk   (Hamdan Al-Maktoum)   H T Jones Newmarket

913 ORMSKIRK MAIDEN AUCTION STAKES 2YO   £1896   5f   Good 58 -16 Slow

-- URRAY ON HARRY [7] (R Hollinshead) 2-8-11 S Perks 12/1: 2 b c Anfield - Noorina
(Royal and Regal): First time out, mkt drifter, but ran on well to lead on line in a 2yo
maiden auction at Haydock June 6: cost 3,100 gns: eff at 5f, should be suited by further:
acts on gd grnd & a stiff trk.   40
672 MINIZEN LASS [1] (M Brittain) 2-8-5 K Darley 8/1: 0422: Nearly made all & btn a
whisker: acts on any trk & must find a small event: see 672, 548.   33
350 IMPERIAL FRIEND [2] (R Hodges) 2-7-13 A Clark 6/4 FAV: 03: Gambled on: ran on well
final 1f, but the post came too soon: half sister to 8/10f winner Frome: should be suited by
6f: acts on gd grnd & a gall trk.   24
813 GWYNBROOK [9] (M W Easterby) 2-8-2 L Charnock 8/1: 0034: Nearest fin: will be std by 6f 24
-515 CHAYOFA [5] 2-7-13 P Burke(7) 11/4: 20: Ev ch: much btr in 515 (sharper trk).   19
-785 HUGO Z HACKENBUSH [14] 2-8-8 M Wood 10/1: 40440: Dsptd lead, ev ch: see 415.   27
672 FREV OFF [6] 2-8-11 M Birch 8/1: 30: Early speed: btr 672 (yld, easier trk).   00
-- ST JOHNS BAY [13] 2-8-11 M Wigham 10/1: 0: No show on racecourse debut: cost 4,200 gns
& is a half sister to 2 winners.   00
696 Nifty Griff [10] 8-8   536 Cream And Green [4] 8-8
167 Gillot Bar [8] 8-11   612 Sound As A Pound [3] 8-8
513 Shenley Romp [15] 8-5   715 Coast Boy [12] 8-11   136 Noalimba [11] 8-8
15 ran   shhd,1½,½,½,shhd   (D Coppenhall)   R Hollinshead Rugeley, Staffs

914 BURTONWOOD BREWERY HANDICAP 3YO 0-60   £4253   7f   Good 58 +01 Fast   [54]

*659 VAGUE SHOT [7] (C Horgan) 3-9-10(6ex) S Cauthen 3/1 FAV: 300-111: 3 ch c Vaigly Great -
Cease Fire (Martial): Fast impr colt: not the best of runs, but showed a gd turn of foot to
lead well inside the final 1f in a 3yo h'cap at Haydock June 6: in excellent form, earlier
winning similar events at Goodwood & Kempton: ran well on several occasions in '85, notably
when a close up 6th to Green Desert in Gr.3 July Stakes at Newmarket: eff at 7f, stays 1m
well: acts on firm & yld/soft & on any trk. carries weight well.   63

588 KEDRON [8] (R Laing) 3-9-7 S Whitworth 6/1: 12-1132: Kept on well final 1f: in grnd form. 54
+677 HIGHEST PRAISE [3] (I Balding) 3-8-12(6ex) J Matthias 6/1: 403-013: Led over 1f out:
good effort: see 677.   43
*518 TRICK OR TREAT [10] (J Watts) 3-9-2 N Connorton 5/1: 1300-14: Prom: btr 518.   43
355 JOVEWORTH [4] 3-8-4 M Birch 16/1: 440-140: Nearest fin after abs: stays 7f: acts
on gd & heavy grnd: see 283.   31
624 BATH [9] 3-8-5 Jackie Houston(7) 16/1: 300-400: Ch 2f out: fdd: best 436.   30
615 PELLINKO [6] 3-9-1 A Mackay 8/1: 0-41200: Led briefly 2f out: btr 518, 334.   00
713 HUDSONS MEWS [2] 3-8-0 W Carson 6/1: 00-3140: Prom, fdd: btr 713, 650.   00
586 ROMANTIC UNCLE [5] 3-9-4 J H Brown(5) 10/1: 21-0200: No real threat: best 478(sft/hvy). 00
443 Runaway [1] 9-5
10 ran   1½,1,1½,hd,¾,2½,nk   (A W Anthony)   C Horgan Billingbear, Berks

915 JOHN LAWLOR STAKES 2YO   £2492   6f   Good 58 +01 Fast

*741 CHIME TIME [1] (C Tinkler) 2-8-11 M Birch 11/4: 11: 2 b c Good Times - Balnespick
(Charlottown): Useful, impr colt: ran on well under press to get up close home in a 2yo
stakes at Haydock June 6: first time out was a comfortable winner of a maiden at Redcar:
cost only 3,400 gns & appears a bargain: half brother to fair 1m/10f winner Kaukas: eff
at 6f, should be suited by further: acts on gd & firm grnd & a gall trk: should win more races 59
664 TOUGH N GENTLE [6] (L Piggott) 2-8-6 B Crossley 8/1: 32: Led inside final 1f: just
caught: fast impr & will win soon: acts on gd & soft grnd: see 664.   53
+571 QUEL ESPRIT [2] (M 'Mccormack) 2-9-7 S Cauthen 11/10 FAV: 121113: Led till wknd inside
final 1f: giving weight all round: btr 571.   65
-- GLORY FOREVER [5] (S Norton) 2-8-6 J Lowe 20/1: 4: Nearest fin on racecourse debut
and will do btr next time: should stay further than 6f: acts on gd grnd & a gall trk.   42
-- RED HERO [3] 2-8-6 T Ives 16/1: 0: Kept on & should impr: cost 11,000 gns.   38
610 CHESWOLD [4] 2-8-6 K Hodgson 11/2: 40: Much btr 610 (5f).   23
685 Regent Lad [7] 8-6
7 ran   nk,1,3,1½,6   (Red Lion Inn & Motel Ltd)   C Tinkler Malton, Yorks

916 CHIPMOBILE MAIDEN STAKES 3YO   £2997   1m 2f   Good 58 +06 Fast

479 MTOTO [2] (A Stewart) 3-9-0 M Roberts 5/4 FAV: 3-21: 3 b c Busted - Amazer
(Mincio): Useful colt: heavily bckd & led well over 1f out, readily in quite a fast run
maiden at Haydock June 6: first time out was just btn by Fleeting Affair at Salisbury: showed
promise on sole outing in '85: cost 110,000 gns & is closely related to several winners,
incl smart French filly Button Up: stays 10f really well, should get 12f: acts on gd & yld
grnd & a stiff trk: should win more races.   57
625 TOP RANGE [4] (M Jarvis) 3-9-0 T Ives 10/1: -0302: Led briefly 2f out: another gd
run: should win soon: see 625.   51
-- COMANCHERO [8] (C Thornton) 3-9-0 J Bleasdale 10/1: 3-3: Ev ch over 2f out: gd
seasonal debut: on sole outing in '85 was a promising 3rd to Comme L'Etoile in a maiden on
this trk: eff at 10f, should stay 12f: acts on gd & soft grnd.   50
739 BANANAS [12] (O Douieb) 3-9-0 R Machado 3/1: -234: Mkt drifter: fdd: btr 739.   43
699 SEATYRN [10] 3-9-0 B Crossley 25/1: 430-340: Sn prom: btr 699 (firm): see 487.   35
723 VITRY [7] 3-8-11 M Wigham 33/1: 00-000: No real threat, but an impr effort: half
sister to numerous winners: stays 10f: acts on gd grnd & a gall trk.   22
-- ADALIYAN [13] 3-9-0 S Cauthen 8/1: 00-0: Made most on seasonal debut: half brother to
several winners, incl Adiyann & Adariysa: eff at 1m, should stay 10f with more restrain:
acts on gd & soft grnd.   00

744 State Jester [11] 9-0   702 Big League [1] 9-0   699 Hello Benz [14] 9-0
-- Tempting Silver [3] 9-0   702 Jurisprudence [5] 9-0
720 Imperial Palace [9] 9-0   316 Countermine [9] 9-0
-- Patricks Star [15] 9-0
15 ran   2,½,4,4,5   (Sheikh Ahmed Al-Maktoum)   A Stewart Newmarket

917 NORTH WEST RACING CLUB HANDICAP 0-50   £3130   1m 6f   Good 58 -05 Slow   [47]

+735 TRAPEZE ARTIST [13] (N Vigors) 5-9-4(7ex) S Dawson(3) 4/1: 0400211: 5 b h High Line -
Maternal (High Top): Useful stayer who is in fine form: led 3f out, easily in a h'cap at
Haydock June 6: last time out won a fast run h'cap at Sandown: in '85 won at Newmarket:
previous season won at Chester: eff at 14f, stays further: acts on gd/firm & soft grnd &
on any trk: has worn bl: carries weight well & may complete the hat trick.   48
735 MY CHARADE [3] (B Waring) 5-7-11(vis) T Williams 8/1: 0001402: Kept on well: gd run.   21
366 MARLION [4] (S Hall) 5-8-3 W Carson 5/1: 120-003: Prom all the way: btr effort: see 366. 27
663 STERNE [2] (S Mellor) 4-9-8 M Wigham 7/2 Jt.FAV: -11-004: Led 6f out: needs further?   42
686 ROSTHERNE [5] 4-8-13 L Charnock 5/1: -421040: Never nearer: can do btr: best 215.   30
772 MOULKINS [9] 4-7-7(3oh) Julie Bowker(6) 33/1: 000-000: Prom over 1m: kept on: stays well. 09
695 DOUBLE BENZ [11] 4-9-8 M Birch 7/2 Jt.FAV: 00-0130: Wknd quickly 2f out: much
better 695, 319 (softer grnd).   00
-- Quadrillion [8] 7-7   801 Koffi [7] 9-10   541 Touch Of Luck [12] 7-9
-- Le Soir [10] 7-12
11 ran   3,hd,4,2½,½   (Intergroup Holdings Ltd)   N Vigors Lambourn, Berks

Official Going Given as Good

918   EBF FLEMINGTON MAIDEN STAKES 2YO   £2718   5f   Firm 18 -13 Slow

694 THE DOMINICAN [3] (B Hills) 2-9-0 B Thomson 5/4 fav: 3221: 2 b c Dominion - Phoebegee (Comedy Star): Gained a deserved success, leading dist. comfortably in a 2yo maiden at Epsom June 6: a 19,000 gns yearling and is speedily bred: acts on firm & yld: seems to handle any trk: very eff at 5f.   **50**

456 QUICK SNAP [5] (A Ingham) 2-9-0(bl) R Curant 7/2: 4322: Kept on well, another consistent effort & deserves a maiden race: wears bl: acts on soft/yld: eff also on firm.   **46**

728 DUTCH COURAGE [1] (D Morley) 2-9-0 S Cauthen 7/2: 4433: Made much: twice below 405. **36**

715 THE GREAT MATCH [4] (R Whitaker) 2-9-0 D Mckeown 8/1: 004: Ev ch: see 715.   **34**

614 SWIFT PURCHASE [2] 2-9-0 A Mcglone 33/1: 300: Prom most: see 434.   **28**

5 ran   1¼,4,½,2   (Mrs J M Corbett)   B Hills Lambourn, Berks

919   SUN LIFE OF CANADA H'CAP 3YO 0-50   £3908   1m 2f Firm 18 -12 Slow   [56]

538 EMRYS [1] (N Vigors) 3-8-4 W Carson 14/1: 2-10331: 3 ch c Welsh Pageant - Sun Approach (Sun Prince): Showed himself well suited by 10f, al prom & holding on under strong driving for a narrow success in quite a valuable h'cap at Epsom June 6: had previously run well over 1m/7f, winning a maiden at Leicester first time out: acts on firm & soft & on any trk.   **43**

692 SWIFT TROOPER [5] (R Williams) 3-9-7(bl) R Cochrane 1/2: 0-12142: Unable to get a clear run 3f out, flying fin & possibly unlucky: a model of consistency: acts on firm & soft & stays 10f well: see 326. carries weight well.   **59**

*716 WESHAAM [8] (B Hanbury) 3-9-3(5ex) G Starkey 6/1: 30-2013: Al there & ran right up to his best: see 716.   **51**

615 GEORGES QUAY [10] (R Hannon) 3-8-7 Pat Eddery 15/2: 0-40134: Made most, not btn far & a fine effort: see 480: stays 10f but possible btr at 8/9f.   **40**

637 LONDON CONTACT [7] 3-8-3(1ow) B Thomson 20/1: 0133-00: Not btn far in a close fin: winner of a seller at Chepstow in '84: eff around 1m, stays 10f: acts on firm & yld: has been tried in a visor but btr without.   **35**

730 CRAMMING [4] 3-8-0 P Robinson 8/1: 00-1230: Fin well, not btn far: see 318.   **31**

386 FARAG [6] 3-8-2(1ow) Paul Eddery 9/1: 031-200: Twice below 74 (1m, heavy).   **00**

*459 HOMME DAFFAIRE [2] 3-8-7 P Waldron 9/4 fav: 000-010: Well bckd, ev ch: best 459 (yld).   **00**

579 Quick Dancer [3] 7-13(1ow)   **659 Markelius** [9] 7-8

10 ran   nk,1½,nk,nk,nk   (Lady d'Avigdor Goldsmid)   N Vigors Upper Lambourn, Berks

920   GROUP 3 DIOMED STAKES   £15948   1m   Firm 18 +07 Fast

*433 PENNINE WALK [6] (J Tree) 4-9-9 Pat Eddery 4/1: 3140-11: 4 b c Persian Bold - Tifrums (Thatch): Very smart colt: well placed, comfortably led inside final 1f in Gr.3 Diomed Stakes at Epsom June 6: first time out defied top weight in valuable Jubilee H'cap at Kempton May 5: in '85 was a ready winner of a valuable 3yo h'cap at Newmarket & also collected Gr.3 Jersey Stakes at Royal Ascot: very eff over 7f/1m: acts on firm & gd grnd and on any trk: genuine & consistent & has a fine turn of foot.   **85**

-- HADEER [2] (C Brittain) 4-9-6 W R Swinburn 20/1: 0-044-2: Having his first outing for his new stable, was well bckd at long odds: led dist. & was not btn far: ran only 3 times in '85 without success: in '84 won first 2 on the trot at Windsor & Newmarket: best form on firm grnd over 7f/1m: does well when fresh: well h'capped on this performance & should be noted next time in such company.   **78**

384 CLIVEDEN [7] (G Harwood) 3-8-3 G Starkey 7/1: 213-003: Kept on well: gd effort: needs 10f? see 384.   **70**

652 ESQUIRE [8] (B Hills) 4-9-6 B Thomson 20/1: 0-21124: Made much: raised in class here and another fine effort: see 573.   **68**

598 LUCKY RING [3] 4-9-6 W Carson 7/1: 1114-00: Ev ch, wknd: in fine form in '85 winning 4 times in total at Newmarket, Goodwood, York & Doncaster: very eff over 7f/1m: acts on firm & gd grnd & is well suited by a gall trk.   **63**

*579 NINO BIBBIA [9] 3-8-3 Paul Eddery 5/2 fav: 2-110: Well bckd: appeared unsuited by the trk & btr 579.   **60**

-- EVER GENIAL [5] 4-9-4 S Cauthen 13/2: 21133-0: Slow start, no dngr: should benefit from seasonal debut: a model of consistency in '85 winning a Goodwood & Newbury (Gr.3 Hungerford Stakes): probably stays 10f but winning form over 7f/1m: acts on firm & yld & on any trk: genuine & consistent filly.   **00**

*651 English Spring [1] 9-4   **802 Sit This One Out** [4] 8-6

249 Celtic Heir [10] 8-9

10 ran   ½,2,1½,3,shhd   (Mrs Maria Niarchos)   J Tree Beckhampton, Wilts

921   NORTHERN DANCER LIM.H'CAP 4YO+ 0-70   £14854   1m 4f Firm 18 +15 Fast   [61]

-474 STATELY FORM [2] (J Tree) 4-9-3 Pat Eddery 4/1 jt fav: 140-021: 4 b c Double Form - State Pension (Only For Life): Very useful colt: well bckd led on bit 3f out & qcknd clear to win a fast run & very valuable h'cap at Epsom June 6: in gd form in '85, winning h'caps at Kempton, Goodwood & Sandown & a minor event at Windsor: half brother to several winners: eff 10f, stays 12f well: acts on soft but is well suited by firm or gd grnd: handles any trk: will win more races.   **64**

•695 POSITIVE [8] (H T Jones) 4-9-1 A Murray 7/1: 120-012: In vain pursuit of winner final
3f: met a good one here & is sure to gain compensation soon: see 363, 695.   57
743 HERRADURA [11] (M Prescott) 5-8-1 G Duffield 10/1: 3042-23: Ridden ½way, never closer.   41
474 VOUCHSAFE [6] (W Hern) 4-8-11 W Carson 14/1: 0100-04: No real threat: in '85 gamely
won a maiden at York, sole success so far: eff over 12/14f: acts on firm & yld going.   48
735 ALL IS REVEALED [4] 4-8-1(vis) T Quinn 12/1: 0-04130: Made much: best 582 (14f).   34
617 CHAUMIERE [7] 5-9-10(vis) T Ives 16/1: 3-00000: Yet to strike peak form: see 475.   54
•419 LADYS BRIDGE [9] 4-8-13 S Cauthen 4/1 jt fav: 214-10: Prom most: btr 419 (14f gd).   00
511 Pato [1] 8-13   263 Kentucky Quest [10] 8-3(1ow)
--   Tracing [5] 9-1
10 ran   2,¾,2,2½,2   (Mrs Maria Niarchos)   J Tree Beckhampton, Wilts

---

922 TOKYO HANDICAP 4YO+ 0-60   £7674   6f   Firm 18 +02 Fast   [58]

877 IMPERIAL JADE [7] (A Jarvis) 4-9-10 Pat Eddery 3/1 fav: 30-3021: 4 b f Lochnager -
Song's Jest (Song): Very useful sprinter: made a quick reapp when scoring a comfortable
pillar-to-post win in a valuable h'cap at Epsom June 6: in '85 carried top weight to victory
in a h'cap at Salisbury: eff over 5f, well suited by 6f now: acts on any trk probably on
any going though runs well on firm: genuine filly who carries weight extremely well.   67
877 HILTON BROWN [11] (P Cundell) 5-9-8 G Starkey 10/1: -313002: Quick reapp, kept on
& a btr effort: best 76 (5f, soft).   55
748 EXERT [1] (R Akehurst) 4-7-7(7oh) N Adams 20/1: -344403: Kept on well: needs 7f? see 114.23
680 AL AMEAD [3] (C Benstead) 6-8-10 B Rouse 7/1: 04-0004: Prom, ev ch: see 508.   40
742 TOBERMORY BOY [8] 9-8-9 D Mckeown 7/1: 002-000: Ev ch: see 742.   36
836 BAY PRESTO [10] 4-7-13(1ow) S Whitworth 16/1: -300000: Creditable effort but best 172 (yld)26
687 FOOLISH TOUCH [9] 4-8-1 W Carson 6/1: -003100: Never closer in 7th: best 401.   00
+660 LAURIE LORMAN [6] 4-8-12(7ex) R Wernham 6/1: 300-010: Early speed: best 660 (yld/soft). 00
550 Mendick Adventure [5] 7-8   --   Divissima [12] 7-8(1ow)(4oh)
369 Dorame [2] 7-7(15oh)   742 Gentileschi [4] 8-0
12 ran   3,1,hd,1,shhd,nk,hd   (Stanley h Kaplan)   A Jarvis Royston, Herts .

---

923 ALBERTA ROSE MAIDEN FILLIES STAKES 3YO   £2910   1m   Firm 18 -03 Slow

253 DUSTY DOLLAR [2] (W Hern) 3-8-11 W Carson 5/4 fav: 44-31: 3 b f Kris - Sauceboat
(Connaught): Justified hvy support, switched 2f out & stayed on really strongly to go 3L
clear in the final 1f in a 3yo maiden at Epsom June 6: showed promise on both starts in
'85 in gd company: half sister to the smart Kind Of Hush: acts on soft but very well suited
by fast going: eff over 1m, looks certain to be suited by 10f: can continue to improve.   50
213 EASTERN HOUSE [12] (H Cecil) 3-8-11 S Cauthen 9/1: 3022-02: Chall 1f out: placed in
3 out of 4 races in '85, notably when just touched off in a maiden at redcar in Oct: appears
to act on firm & yld: eff at 6f: stays 1m: sure to find a maiden.   44
658 STICKY GREENE [9] (B Hills) 3-8-11 B Thomson 5/1: 0-33: Fin in fine style & seems to
need 10f: acts on firm & hvy: see 658.   43
--   BLUE GUITAR [4] (J Hindley) 3-8-11 M Hills 25/1: 0430-4: Fair seasonal debut, making
most: raced only 4 times in '85, placed twice: acts on fast grnd: seems suited by forcing
tactics: probably stays 1m but may prove best around 7f.   40
570 OMANIA [7] 3-8-11 R Cochrane 33/1: 400-440: Prom, wknd: stiff task: best 570 (10f).   25
--   NUTSHAMBLES [6] 3-8-11 P Waldron 25/1: 0-0: Never closer after slow start: unplaced
only outing in '85: half sister to minor winners Dance By Night & Dominate: likely to be
suited by 10f: the type to impr as she matures.   19
658 SUMMER GARDEN [8] 3-8-11 Pat Eddery 9/2: -40: No threat in 9th: btr 658 (7f, heavy).   00
--   Hanglands [10] 8-11   624 Prissy Miss [5] 8-11   656 Pause For Applause [11] 8-11
656 Lucy Aura [1] 8-11   656 Shades Of Autumn [3] 8-11
12 ran   3,½,1,7,3,2;hd   (Maktoum Al Maktoum)   W Hern East Ilsley, Berks

---

924 AIR HANSON ACRON STAKES 2YO   £5941   5f   Firm 20 -14 Slow

•440 ABUZZ [1] (C Brittain) 2-8-11 M Roberts 4/5 fav: 111: 2 ch f Absalom - Sorebelle
(Prince Tenderfoot) Very useful filly: retained her unbtn record when completing a hat-trick
in valuable Acorn Stks at Epsom June 7: made almost all but said by her jockey.to be not
totally suited by this firm grd: earlier an easy winner of minor races at Chester and Newbury
(first time out): speedily bred sort who is very eff with forcing tactics over 5f but should
stay 6f: acts on firm, btr on gd or soft grd tho' handles any trk.   60
+450 NUTWOOD LIL [2] 2-8-11 A Mackay 5/1: 112: Pressed winner thro'out,
just held, in a driving finish: fine effort from this improving filly and she should win
again before long: acts on firm and soft: see 450.   59
•621 PLUM DROP [5] (R Armstrong) 2-8-11 W Carson 3/1: 213: Fin in gd fashion, almost
getting up in a 3-way photo: grand effort: see 621.   58
•531 DANCING DIANA [4] (R Hannon) 2-8-11 Pat Eddery 10/1: 214: Stiff task but ran close
to her best: see 531.   48

746 LADY BEHAVE [3] 2-8-7 A Mcglone   33/1: 23020: Outpaced in this gd company: see 746   43
5 ran   hd,hd,5,hd   (Mrs C Brittain)   C Brittain Newmarket

925 ALLDERS EBBISHAM H'CAP 3YO   0-70   £7687   8.5f   Firm 20 -10 Slow   [71]

*539 PRINCESS NAWAAL [9] (J Dunlop) 3-7-10 W Carson 9/4 fav: 44-11: 3 br f Seattle Slew
- Ferly (Traffic Judge) Useful filly: winner of both her races this season and on latest
success was well bckd when comfortably leading final 2f in a val 3yo fillies h'cap at
Epsom June 7: narrow winner of a fillies race at Wolverhampton May 12 (first time out):
4th in useful company on both outings in '85: very eff over 1m/9f: acts on frm and yldg:
likely to win more races.   52
575 NORMANBY LASS [1] (P Walwyn) 3-8-5 Paul Eddery 7/1: 320-002: Came back to form, overcoming difficulties in running to be narrowly btn: likes a sharp trk: shd go close next
time: see 271.   58
692 LUCKY SO SO [6] (S Norton) 3-8-3 C Rutter[5] 9/2: 34-4103: Dsptd lead 2f out: fine
effort: see 427.   53
459 POUNELTA [4] (R Hannon) 3-7-13 A Mcglone 8/1: 33-4204: Chall 2f out: best 271(hvy). 44
*713 CARRIBEAN SOUND [8] 3-7-9(7ex) M Roberts 13/2: 0-24310: Held up to get the trip but
possibly btr over 7f in 713.   38
708 SWEET ADELAIDE [5] 3-9-7 B Thomson 7/1: 30-2030: Much btr 708 (stakes).   54
656 Mirataine Venture [3] 7-8   659 Miranda Julia [2] 7-7(4oh)
8 ran   ¾,1,2,1,6   (Sheikh Ahmed Al Maktoum)   J Dunlop Arundel, Sussex

926 GROUP 1 GOLD SEAL OAKS 3YO FILLIES   £119952   1m 4f Firm 20 +23 Fast

*373 MIDWAY LADY [4] (B Hanbury) 3-9-0 R Cochrane 15/8 fav: 2111-11: 3 b f Alleged -
smooth Bore (His Majesty) Topclass filly: retained her unbtn record this season, coming
from behind to lead inside final 1f in fast run Group 1 Oaks Stakes at Epsom June 7: first
time out winner of 1,000 Guineas at Newmarket May 1: in excellent in '85, winning Gr 1
Prix Marcel Boussac at Longchamp, Gr 3 May Hill Stakes at Doncaster and a fillies mdn at
Yarmouth: eff over a stiff 1m, stays 12f really well: acts on frm and gd grd: likely to
improve further and will be a force in all the gd middle dist races this season.   88
-- UNTOLD [15] (M Stoute) 3-9-0 Paul Eddery 20/1: 0111-2: Led str, hdd final 1f and
could hardly have run btr seasonal debut: winner of her last 3 on the trot in '85 at
Yarmouth, Sandown (course record) and Gr 3 Hoover Fillies Mile at Ascot (course record):
half sister to the very useful Shoot Clear and Sally Brown: eff around 1m, stays 12f well:
acts on fast and yldg going and seems to handle any trk: sure to win a decent race
this season.   86
373 MAYSOON [11] (M Stoute) 3-9-0 W R Swinburn 12/1: 130-123: Came to chall dist, may
not have quite seen out the trip but ran a grand race and certainly stays at least 10f. 84
551 COLORSPIN [5] (M Stoute) 3-9-0 B Rouse 25/1: 11-34: No extra final 1f but ran right
up to her best tho' prove best debut 10f: see 551.   77
*372 GESEDEH [1] 3-9-0 T Ives 9/1: -110: Badly hmpd ¼ way and this effort can be forgotten. 67
*551 REJUVENATE [3] 3-9-0 B Thomson 14/1: -310: Ev ch : much btr 551 (10f).   65
754 ASTEROID FIELD [6] 3-9-0 Y Saint Martin 25/1: 14-2030: Led over 1m, fin 7th: much
btr 754 (1m, yldg).   65
551 ALA MAHLIK [8] 3-9-0 G Starkey 18/1: 11-3420: Met trouble in running, fin 8th:
much btr 551 (10f).   63
509 LAUGHTER [10] 3-9-0 W Carson 18/1: 1-20: Ev ch, wknd: btr 509 (gd).   60
*661 TRALTHEE [13] 3-9-0 Pat Eddery 9/2: 31-10: Wknd quickly, non-stayer? Best 661(10f soft) 57
*486 BROKEN WAVE [14] 3-9-0 R Curant 100/1: -10: Very stiff task: see 486.   55
*682 BONSHAMILE [7] 3-9-0 R Guest 33/1: 1-10: Best 682 (10f).   50
273 SANET [9] 3-9-0 C Asmussen 100/1: -440: Stiff task: see 273.   47
661 VOLIDA [2] 3-9-0 P Robinson 100/1: 00-4040: Sn rear: see 373, 661.   00
509 DAVEMMA [16] 3-9-0 Gay Kelleway 200/1: 0-4000: Prom 6f: see 509.   00
15 ran   1,¼,4,7,1½,shthd,2,3,2,1¼,3,3   (H Ranier)   B Hanbury Newmarket

927 STAFF INGHAM STAKES 2YO   £4350   6f   Firm 20 -10 Slow

646 JAY GEE ELL [7] (E Eldin) 2-8-6 A Mackay 11/2: 3141: 2 ch f Vaigly Gret - Calarette
(Caliban) Useful filly: showed her form last time to be all wrong, responding gamely to
strong driving to forge ahead in final 1f of a 2yo auction stks at Epsom June 7: winner of a
fillies mdn at York May 13: cheaply acquired half sister to minor 5f winner: eff at 5f,
stays 6f: acts on firm and gd, seems to give in the ground: acts any trk.   50
483 GREY WOLF TIGER [4] (R Hannon) 2-8-2 M Roberts 16/1: 022: Flying fin, too late,
but is certainly on the upgrade and is well suited by 6f, likely to stay further: acts on
firm and soft: should find a race: see 404.   39
*746 BASTILLIA [13] (D Arbuthnot) 2-8-9 G Starkey 14/1: 0013: Dsptd lead dist: fine effort:
stays 6f.   46
694 SCHUYGULLA [14] (M Jarvis) 2-8-8 T Ives 11/2: 34: Made most, fair effort: see 694:
appears to act on firm and yldg.   42
*633 CHAMBER MASTER [9] 2-8-12 P Darcy 33/1: 010: Rank outsider, ran well here and is
evidently btr than a plater: see 633: stays 6f.   46
+533 DERRING DEE [5] 2-8-6 N Adams 6/1: 010: Never closer: unsuited by trk? see 533:
stays 6f well.   40

632	HAILEYS RUN [3] 2-8-8 S Cauthen 15/2: 430: Ev ch, wknd: see 632 (5f).	00
773	LAST STAND [1] 2-8-2 P Robinson 7/1: 00: Well bckd, fin 9th.	00
664	JONLEAT [6] 2-9-4(BL) Pat Eddery 9/2 fav: 41220: Bl first time, btr 664.	00
678	KEEN EDGE [2] 2-8-8 A Mcglone 7/1: 4220: Speed 3f: best 678 (5f, gd).	00

655 Lightning Legend [8] 8-5   304 Firmly Attached [12] 8-5
596 Bloffa [11] 7-13   --   Secoot [10] 8-5
14 ran   2½,shthd,¾,hd,hd,¾,hd   (Barry Linford)   E Eldin Newmarket

928 ASHTEAD CLAIMING STAKES 3YO   £2964   7f   Firm 20 -12 Slow

886 CHUMMYS PET [9] (N Callaghan) 3-8-12 Pat Eddery 9/4 fav: -021331: 3 b g Song - Hodsock
Venture (Major Portion) Made a quick reappearance and was heavily bckd when showing improved
form to readily lead final 1f in a 3yo Claimer at Epsom June 7: won another Claimer at
Carlisle May 2: eff over stiff 5f, stays 7f well and is sure to stay 1m: acts on frm and yldg
and on any trk.   40
344 RETHYMNO [16] (C Brittain) 3-8-12 P Robinson 14/1: 000-002: Mkt drifter, prom thro'out:
best effort this season: winner of a mdn at Kempton in '85: stays 7f well, acts frm and yldg. 35
501 LOVE AT LAST [14] (W Hastings Bass) 3-8-1 Dale Gibson[7] 13/2: -33: Never closer:
unsuited by trk? Much btr 501.   23
500 PLAIN TALK [1] (A Hide) 3-8-7 R Guest 14/1: 04-04: Led over 2f out and ran
creditably here: see 500.   29
764 JAAZIEL [12] 3-8-10 S Cauthen 12/1: -000: Mkt drifter, prom much: see 764.   29
809 NORTHERN GUNNER [5] 3-8-2(BL) B Rouse 12/1: 00-0430: Bl first time: btr 809 (stiff trk) 17
835 HEAVENLY CAROL [6] 3-7-8 N Adams 7/1: -00: Nicely bckd, much btr 835 (5f, gd).   00
455 HOPEFULL DANCER [10] 3-7-9 D Mckay 10/1: 001-000: No form this season: 25/1 winner
of a Claimer at Yarmouth on final outing in '85: stays 7f and acts on gd/firm.   00
637 See No Evil [3] 7-11   275 Common Accord [15] 8-0
730 Lady Owen [2] 7-13   666 Stangrave [17] 8-1   334 Cagliostro [7] 8-10
427 Beresque [8] 8-12(bl)   402 The Quietstan [13] 7-13
229 The Lidgate Star [11] 7-13
16 ran   2,¾,hd,1½,2,¾   (C Gaventa)   N Callaghan Newmarket

929 BUNBURY HANDICAP 3YO 0-60   £6284   6f   Firm 20 +12 Fast   [62]

*593 ORIENT [3] (R Whitaker) 3-8-6 D Mckeown 9/2: 40-11: 3 b f Bay Express - Gundi
(Mummy's Pet) Useful, fast improving filly: led ½ way and qcknd well clear of her struggling
rivals to win a fast run and valuable h'cap at Epsom June 7: ready winner of a mdn at
Beverley May 16 (first time out): eff at 5 and 6f, acts on any trk and on firm & gd grd:
certain to win again next time: see 593.   60
+624 TOUCH OF GREY [1] (D Thom) 3-9-2 S Cauthen 3/1 fav: 0-00112: Caught a real tartar
here and remains in fine form: see 624.   55
387 SAFEERA [7] (M Jarvis) 3-8-9 T Ives 8/1: 1411-03: Never closer: rated 62 in '85 after
winning nurseries at Haydock and Folkestone and a mdn at Edinburgh: stays 6f well and acts
on gd and soft and on any trk.   45
447 ALEXANJO [6] (A Jarvis) 3-7-7(1oh) N Adams 20/1: 3444-04: Al prom: rated 40 when
winning a fillies mdn at Newcastle in June '85: prob stays 6f: runs well on a stiff trk.   26
443 STEPHENS SONG [9] 3-7-13 P Robinson 6/1: 00-1100: Dsptd lead most: best 233 (hvy)   31
726 COMMANDER MEADEN [10] 3-7-7(16oh) C Rutter[0] 50/1: 000-030: Very stiff task at
the weights, not disgraced: see 726.   23
580 BERNIGRA GIRL [12] 3-7-10(1ow) W Carson 7/1: 31-0000: Ev ch, fin 9th: see 496.   00
*657 PRECIOUS METAL [2] 3-9-7 G Starkey 13/2: 1200-10: Met trouble in running and btr
judged 657.   00
624 Edgewise [4] 8-13   814 Mandrake Madam [5] 8-13
657 Cresta Leap [8] 7-11(BL)
11 ran   5,1½,1½,hd,1   (Mrs R Watson)   R Whitaker Wetherby, Yorks

930 ABBOTS HILL H'CAP 3YO+ 0-50   £4181   8.5f   Firm 20 -04 Slow   [47]

668 FEI LOONG [10] (E Eldin) 5-8-3 A Mackay 7/1: 0-04421: 5 ch g Music Boy - Dimione
(Tompion) Led over 1f out, caught near and btn shthd in a h'cap at Epsom June 7 but sub
awarded race: in '85 won twice at Windsor and likes sharp trk: eff 6f, well suited by 1m now:
acts on soft, goes well on firm or gd ground.   32
762 FAIR COUNTRY [9] (D Elsworth) 4-8-12 C Asmussen 8/1: 300-032: Not btn far in a
driving fin, promoted to 2nd: gd effort: should find a race soon: see 762.   39
*481 SINGLE [5] (W Wightman) 4-8-13 Pat Eddery 4/1: -011413: Strong fin, placed 3rd
and ran up to his best: see 481.   39
652 VIRGIN ISLE [1] (P Haslam) 5-9-2 T Williams 14/1: -020004: Prom thro'out: gd effort.   42
281 VERBARIUM [12] 6-8-1 R Morse(5) 20/1: 1-23200: Abs: never closer: see 10.281.   25
481 EVERY EFFORT [8] 4-8-4 C Rutter[5] 14/1: 000-400: First past the post on merit,
getting up in the last stride but disq for almost bringing down De Rigeur earlier in race:
shd gain compensation: see 112.   33
433 PORTOGON [4] 8-9-7 D Mckay 10/1: 000-000: Made most, promoted to 6th: in '85 won
h'caps at Kempton and Brighton: eff over 7f/1m: acts on frm and yldg: front runner who
acts on any trk and carries weight well.   00
706 FLYHOME [11] 5-9-1 S Cauthen 3/1 fav: 00-2230: Heavily, bckd, ev ch: much btr 706(stiff) 00

+680 DE RIGUEUR [6] 4-9-10(5ex) W Carson 8/1: -101010: Badly hmpd ¼ way: forget this: see 680 **00**
706 **Fast Service** [13] 8-9   -- **Tarleton Elm** [3] 7-7   578 **Tamertown Lad** [7] 8-0
709 **Tip Tap** [3] 8-2
13 ran   shthd,½,hd,shthd,¼   (T H Quek)   E Eldin Newmarket

CATTERICK   Saturday June 7th   Lefthanded Tight Track

931 GAINFORD MAIDEN STAKES 2YO   £822   5f   Firm 08 -08 Slow

780 GEMINI FIRE [9] (P Felgate) 2-9-0 G Duffield 1/1 FAV: 041: 2 br c Mansingh -
Sealady (Seaepic) Easily justified fav in a 2yo maiden at Catterick June 7, led 2f out and
was sn clear: speedily bred colt who cost 18,000 gns as a yearling, and is a full brother to
useful sprinter Singing Sailor: well suited by 5f on a sharp course: acts well on fast grd.   35
780 FOURWALK [1] (N Macauley) 2-9-0 W Wharton 8/1: 002: Led over ¼ way, no chance
with winner tho' showed improvement here: half brother to a couple of winners and shd stay
further: acts on fast grd and on a tight trk.   16
--   GREY TAN [3] (D Barron) 2-9-0 C Dwyer 9/1: 3: Al up there on race course debut:
will improve: half brother to winning sprinter Jimmy Raine: acts on firm grd.   15
800 GREENS HERRING [6] (W Jarvis) 2-9-0 A Murray 7/2: 04: Dropped in class: outpaced
early and fin well: half brother to winning sprinter and useful hurdler Ballyarry: acts on
firm grd and on a sharp trk.   14
612 MAYBEMUSIC [7] 2-9-0 N Carlisle 20/1: 00: Speed to halfway: half brother to winning
juv Sing To Me: acts on firm ground.   04
--   PIT PONY [8] 2-9-0 G Gosney 20/1: 0: Unfancied on debut: never a factor: half brother
to winning sprinter Magdolin Place: cost 3,700 gns as yearling.   00
364 EUROCON [5] 2-9-0 D Nicholls 10/1: 00: Never went pace: half brother to sev winners
and looks sure to need a longer trip.   00
425 TRAFFORD WAY [4] 2-9-0 K Hodgson 7/1: 00: Sn behind: may need further.   00
--   Vaigly Yellow [2] 9-0
9 ran   6,½,hd,4,3   (J David Abell)   P Felgate Melton Mowbray, Leics.

932 ALDBROUGH SELLING STAKES 3YO   £1128   7f   Firm 08 -11 Slow

889 BANTEL BANZAI [12] (I Bell) 3-9-0(bl) S Keightley 16/1: 0000401: 3 b g Mandrake Major
- Out Mandy (Mansingh) Showed improved form when staying on well to lead cl home in a
3yo seller at Catterick June 7 (no bid): brother to winning sprinter Bantel Bondman: eff over
sprint dist: stays 1m: acts on firm and soft grd and does well on a sharp course.   26
666 COOPER RACING NAIL [3] (J Berry) 3-8-11(VIS) S Webster 8/1: -322002: Just failed to
make all: visored for first time today: see 237 & 39.   22
447 PSALM [11] (M Prescott) 3-9-0 G Duffield 5/2 FAV: 3100-03: Well bckd: had ev ch:
easy winner of a mdn at Hamilton last season when lightly raced: speedily bred colt who
acts on firm and soft grd and on any trk.   21
684 HAJ [7] (N Macauley) 3-9-0 W Wharton 6/1: 02-24: Slowly away, fin strongly: well
suited by fast grd: acts on any trk: see 864.   20
527 BAYVIEW GAL [14] 3-8-11 R P Elliott 20/1: 0-000: Dropped in class: nearest fin:
half sister to couple of middle dist winners and shd stay further herself: acts on fast grd
and on a tight trk.   13
491 MOTOR MASTER [13] 3-9-0 M Hindley(3) 20/1: 00-000: Al prom: half brother to sev
winners including fair stayer Alfie Dickins: shd stay at least 1m: acts on firm grd.   12
867 BOLD ANSWER [10] 3-9-0 K Hodgson 8/1: 00-0000: Late prog into 7th: acts on firm.   00
729 SHY MISTRESS [2] 3-8-11 J Hills(5) 6/1: -040: Slow start, fin 9th: btr 729.   00
426 DIX ETOILES [1] 3-8-11(BL) A Murray 6/1: 4-100: Bl first time: twice disapp since
305 (1m, soft).   00
774 GARY AND LARRY [8] 3-9-0(BL) E Guest(3) 15/2: 00-0000: Bl first time: no threat.   00
733 PRINCESS RYMER [15] 3-8-11 N Carlisle 8/1: 000-000: Speed over ½ way: no form this term 00
183 Noble Saxon [5] 9-0(bl)   630 Raceform Rhapsody [9] 8-11
--   Pasta Jane [4] 8-11   740 Take The Biscuit [6] 9-0(bl)
15 ran   nk,2,nk,2,2   (Barry L Bradon)   I Bell Hawick, Roxburghshire

933 MIDDLEBROOK MUSHROOMS H'CAP (0-50)   £2599   1m 7f Firm 08 +19 Fast   [43]

712 SOUND DIFFUSION [12] (R Whitaker) 4-7-13 A Shoults(4) 3/1 FAV: 030-221; 4 ch g
Grundy - Kashmir Lass (Kashmire II) In gd form, easily justified fav in a fast run h'cap
at Catterick June 7, led below dist and was sn clear: last season won at Redcar: well suited
by a test of stamina: best form on gd or faster grd: acts on any track.   26
634 JOIST [3] (M Prescott) 4-8-3 G Duffield 10/1: 010-002: Ran on well: returning to
form: quite lightly raced last season when winning a 3 runner race at Redcar: eff over 12f,
stays 2m well: acts on any going and on any trk.   22
634 RUSHMOOR [1] (R Peacock) 8-8-7 J Matthias 12/1: 30-4003: Tried to make all: see 319.   25
743 WALTER THE GREAT [6] (M H Easterby) 4-8-1(2ow) S Webster 10/1: 220-004: Going on
fin: well suited by this longer trip: last season won at Redcar and in '84 at Beverley:
stays 2m well: acts on firm and soft grd and on any trk.   16
782 BUCKLOW HILL [5] 9-9-10 C Dwyer 7/1: 0010-00: Ran on same pace: see 782.   38
686 STRATHEARN [7] 5-8-0(BL) A Murray 7/1: 00000: Bl first time: ev ch: see 686.   12

772 BUSTOFF [8] 6-7-7 S P Griffiths(5) 7/1:   0-230: Fin 7th: maiden who has been lightly
raced in recent seasons: acts on firm and yldg: see 44.   00
824 LEPRECHAUN LADY [2] 4-8-2 J Quinn(5) 7/1: 2000120: Fin 8th: btr this trip in 824 (hvy)   00
*366 MARINERS DREAM [9] 5-7-7(1oh) A Culhane(7) 8/1: 0000-10: Much btr over this C/D
in 366 (yldg).   00
462 RED DUSTER [4] 6-8-3 M Beecroft 8/1: -430000: Below par effort: btr here in 44 (yldg).   00
629 Senor Ramos [10] 8-12
11 ran   5,¼,3,1,2   (G F Pemberton)   R Whitaker Wetherby, Yorks

934 HORNBY STAKES 2YO   £1326   6f   Firm 08 -04 Slow

*785 MR GRUMPY [7] (Denys Smith) 2-9-4 D Nicholls 4/1: 0220111: 2 ch c The Brianstan -
Handy Dancer (Green God) Much improved colt: led below dist and held on gamely for a narrow
win in a 2yo stks at Catterick June 7: earlier won a fast run seller at Ripon and then
followed up with an all-the-way win in a stks at Hamilton: sprint bred colt who is equally
effective over 5 and 6f: acts on firm and hvy ground and on any trk: in fine form.   48
+483 SPARSHOLT [1] (P Cole) 2-9-4 M Lynch(5) 8/15 FAV: 312: Well bckd: sustained chall,
just failed: in gd form and stayed this longer trip well: best 146.   48
781 GALLIC TIMES [4] (I Bell) 2-9-7 G Duffield 6/1: 3113043: Kept on well under press:
stays 6f: continues to run well: best 146.   45
-- SKOLERN [5] (M W Easterby) 2-8-11 K Hodgson 11/1: 4: Ran on promisingly after slow
start: sure to do btr next time: speedily bred gelding who cost 8,800 gns as yearling and
is half brother to juv winner Torski: acts on fast grd and on a sharp trk.   34
632 SUPREME OPTIMIST [3] 2-8-11 J Matthias 11/1: 300: Twice disapp since promising debut
in 460 (5f, yldg).   16
819 SHARPHAVEN [6] 2-8-8 A Munro(7) 20/1: 34030: Early speed: best over 5f in 317(soft).   07
646 JEAN JEANIE [2] 2-8-8 S Webster 33/1: 000: Early leader: cheaply bought filly who
is a half sister to winning sprinter Dragonite Prince.   00
7 ran   shthd,2½,½,6,2   (K Higson)   Denys Smith Bishop Auckland, Co Durham

935 SWALEDALE MAIDEN FILLIES STAKES 3YO   £850   1m 4f   Firm 08 -10 Slow

-- CORRAN RIVER [7] (H Candy) 3-8-11 J Kennedy(7) 4/1: 3402-1: 3 ch f Niniski - Primrose
Bank (Charlottown) First time out, was ridden to lead cl home in a 3yo fillies maiden at
Catterick June 7: showed promise last season, being placed in 3 of her 4 starts: half sister
to a couple of winners: stays 12f well and acts on fast grd and seems well suited by sharp trk   45
779 TORREYA [3] (J Hindley) 3-8-11 A Shoults(5) 11/4 FAV: -042: Just failed to make all,
hmpd close home tho' already btn: in gd form: see 779.   43
581 BUTTERFLY KISS [6] (G Wragg) 3-8-11 G Duffield 3/1: -003: Kept on: 5l clear rem:
stays 12f: acts on fast and soft grd and on any trk: see 250.   40
702 SHINY KAY [9] (C Elsey) 3-8-11 C Dwyer 6/1: -004: Continues to improve: see 702,549.   34
779 ULTRESSA [8] 3-8-11 J Quinn(5) 20/1: 400-000: Front rank 1m: clear rem and showed
improvement here: suited by middle dist: acts on firm grd.   33
-- MOODYBINT [4] 3-8-11 E Guest(3) 20/1: 000-0: No real threat on reappearance: lightly
raced last season over shorter trips: acts on firm grd and on a tight trk.   23
452 JACQUETTE [5] 3-8-11 J Matthias 7/2: -00: Hmpd after 4f, no real threat thereafter:
better judged on her promising debut in 452: stays 10f well: acts on gd and firm ground.   00
779 Crimson Robes [1] 8-11   744 Only Flower [2] 8-11
9 ran   1½,2,5,½,8   (Lord Vestey)   H Candy Wantage, Oxon

936 LESLIE PETCH STAKES (H'CAP) (0-35)   £1951   7f   Firm 08 +17 Fast   [31]

42 MR JAY ZEE [7] (N Callaghan) 4-9-2 G Duffield 15/2: 0000-01: 4 b c Sandy Creek - Flying
Spear (Breakspear II) Despite a fair abs was al prom and led inside dist in a fast run h'cap
at Catterick June 7: showed gd form as a juv when successful at Ayr tho' was disapp last
term: stays 7f well: suited by fast ground: acts on any trk.   30
451 GOLD CHIP [6] (J Watts) 3-8-11 A Gorman(7) 5/1: 0013-42: Ev ch: gd effort: see 451.   32
*830 YOUNG BRUSS [8] (J Etherington) 4-9-3(6ex) M Wood 15/8 FAV: 04-0013: led/dsptd lead
most: see 830.   26
789 ZIO PEPPINO [3] (T Craig) 5-8-9 A Shoults(5) 7/2: -032044: Gd effort: see 606, 490.   14
830 RESPONDER [4] 4-8-9 D Nicholls 20/1: 0030000: Fin well: btr effort: see 142.   11
710 O I OYSTON [11] 10-9-3 Catherine Strickland(7) 16/1: 0-00300: Al up there: see 606.   18
135 Tiddlyeyetye [12] 8-5(bl)   689 Musical Shadow [13] 9-5
745 Sean Be Friendly [2] 7-11   -- Sir Wilmore [1] 9-10
455 Harleyford Lad [5] 8-5   281 Fair Trader [14] 7-9
-- Sharons Royale [9] 8-0
14 ran   2,shthd,2,2,½,2   (N Callaghan)   N Callaghan Newmarket

Official Going Given as Good/Firm

937 PACKWOOD MAIDEN STAKES 3YO   £857   1m   Firm 06 +02 Fast

229 FIRST DIBS [14] (M Stoute) 3-9-0 W R Swinburn 8/11 FAV: 2-31: 3 gr c J O Tobin -
Frequently (Decidedly) Sn prom and ran on well under press to lead inside final 1f in quite
a fast run 3yo mdn at Warwick June 7: has ran well on all his 3 outings: on sole start in
'85 fin a gd 2nd to Faustus at Nottingham: half brother to sev winners: stays 1m: acts on
firm and soft grd and on any trk.   47
764 SURE LANDING [13] (C Nelson) 3-9-0 J Reid 7/1: -042: Led over 2f out: kept on well
and continues to improve: eff 7f, stays 1m: acts on fast grd and a sharp trk.   45
--   FORFLITE [3] (O Douieb) 3-9-0 R Machado 14/1: -3: Nearest fin and shd improve for
this race course debut: stays 1m well: acts on fast grd and a turning trk and shd gl close
next time in similar company.   41
--   NO CAN TELL [9] (B Hills) 3-8-11 B Thomson 7/1: 0-4: Prom, ev ch: unplaced on sole
start in '85: seems to stay 1m: acts on fast grd and a sharpish trk.   30
546 CHORAL PARK [15] 3-8-11 N Carlisle 50/1: 0-00: Led over 5f, showing improved form:
may prove btr over 7f: acts on fast ground and a sharp track.   25
--   ASPARK [6] 3-8-11 A Murray 50/1: 00-0: Wknd 2f out on seasonal debut: unplaced on both
outings in '85: half sister to 7f winner El Capistrano.   19
--   NAJIDIYA [11] 3-8-11 P Hutchinson 9/1: 3-0: Easy to back on seasonal debut: never
nearer 7th: on sole start in '85 fin gd 3rd to Possedyno in Newmarket mdn: shd be suited by
1m: acts on fast grd and will do btr than this.   00
--   SHEER LUCK [16] 3-8-11 S Payne 15/2: 04-0: Mkt drifter: fdd on seasonal debut:
on final outing in '85 fin 4th in fillies mdn at Newbury: half sister to very smart 8/9f
winner King of Clubs: shd be suited by 1m+: acts on gd/firm and yldg and will do btr next time   00

-- Scented Silence [5] 8-11		764 Porte Dauphine [8] 8-11	
-- Dalsaanito [7] 9-0	-- First Summer [2] 9-0	-- Austina [19] 8-11	
-- Five Quarters [4] 8-11		-- Royal Crusader [17] 8-11	
656 Sweet Spice [10] 8-11	-- Golden Azelia [12] 8-11		

17 ran   ¾,2½,4,2,2½   (Michael Doyle Riordan)   M Stoute, Newmarket

938 MAN APPEAL MAIDEN AUCTION STAKES 2YO   £731   5f   Firm 06 -39 Slow

818 EMMER GREEN [10] (J Berry) 2-8-7 Gay Kelleway(5) 3/1 FAV: 401: 2 ch f Music Boy -
Bustellina(Busted) Well bckd when leading inside final 1f to win a 2yo mdn auction at Warwick
June 7: eff at 5f, shd stay 6f: acts on firm and hvy grd and on any trk.   35
--   MILLFAN [8] (W Musson) 2-8-8 M Wigham 6/1: 2: Lightly bckd on race course debut:
sn prom and kept on well: cost 3,100 gns and is a half sister to 3 winners, all successful
over 5f: shd stay 6f: acts on fast ground.   35
543 FALDWYN [7] (T Bill) 2-8-8 N Carlisle 7/1: 33: Made much: gd effort and looks
certain to find a seller on this run: see 543.   24
536 AFRABELA [9] (M Brittain) 2-8-4 B Thomson 6/1: 3204: Mkt drifter: al there:best 364   26
350 MARK SEAGULL [6] 2-8-10 B Crossley 4/1: 00: Sn prom: active in mkt and on upgrade:
cost 6,000 gns: acts on firm and yldg ground and seems suited by a sharpish trk.   24
533 PREMIUM GOLD [1] 2-8-2 N Howe 6/1: 4300: No threat: btr 483, 21 (easier ground).   14
--   NOT READY YET [3] 2-8-8(VIS) J Reid 13/2: 0: Hmpd early on and this run is best
forgotten: cost 4,000 gns: shd be suited by further than 5f.   00
531 BRANSTOWN SUNSET [2] 2-8-13 A Clark 6/1: 000: Mkt drifter: btr 531.   00
345 GLAMIS GIRL [4] 2-8-11 S Whitworth 15/2: -00: Never went pace: see 345.   00
612 Pearlitic [11] 8-8   834 Flag Bearer [5] 8-7(BL)
11 ran   ½,1½,shthd,3,¾,4   (Glenn Davies)   J Berry Cockerham, Lancs

939 TEA LEAF SELLING STAKES 2YO   £1597   6f   Firm 06 -57 Slow

821 FANTINE [7] (N Tinkler) 2-8-8(bl) Kim Tinkler(5) 10/3: 004421: 2 b f Hard Fought -
Dacani (Polyfoto) Mkt drifter, not the best of runs, but showed a gd turn of foot to lead
inside final 1f in a slowly run   2yo seller at Warwick June 7: shd stay further than 5f:
acts on hvy, seems well suited by fast ground and a sharpish trk.   22
696 MI OH MY [9] (K Stone) 2-8-8 G Brown 15/2: 0233402: Fin well: acts on any ground.   13
502 DEEP TAW [14] (R Hodges) 2-8-8 N Day 8/1: 043: Ev ch over 1f out: shd be suited by
further than 5f: acts on firm and yldg.   07
483 SANTO PRINCESS [5] (M Fetherston Godley) 2-8-8 R Hills 6/1: 004: Tried to make all:
fdd final 1f: dropped to selling company here: acts on firm grd and a sharp trk.   07
537 FLYING SILENTLY [1] 2-8-8 J Reid 3/1: 0330: Ev ch: btr 421 (C/D).   06
633 PIALUCI [2] 2-8-11 S Keightley 25/1: 000: Friendless in mkt: fdd.   01
543 SANDIS GOLD [3] 2-8-8 S Whitworth 9/4 FAV: 400: Very well bckd, but one of the
first btn: btr 337 (C/D yldg).   00
537 Great Stands By [8] 8-11
8 ran   3,2,hd,½,3,1   (John Allan)   N Tinkler Malton, Yorks

940 I H W GOLDEN JUBILEE HANDICAP 0-35   £1597   1m 2f   Firm 06 -03 Slow   [35]

445 THE GAMES UP [16] (P Haslam) 5-9-2 T Williams 7/2: 300-441: 5 b g Cawston's Clown
-Mandetta (Mandamus) Led final 1f, comfortably, in a h'cap at Warwick June 7: failed to win
in '85: prev season won at Windsor and Hamilton: eff at 1m, stays 10f really well: acts on
firm and soft grd and on any trk, tho' likes a sharpish one.   33

709 ANY BUSINESS [1] (W Musson) 5-9-8 M Wigham 12/1: 0-00002: Gambled on: no chance
with winner but ran well: fair hurdler but last won on the Flat in '83 at Kempton and Epsom:
eff at 1m, stays 11f: acts on firm and soft grd and likes a sharpish trk.   34
--   COMHAMPTON [7] (F Yardley) 5-8-5 I Johnson 20/1: 02022-3: Fin well on seasonal debut:
gd effort: first time out in '85 won a selling h'cap at Windsor and is a consistent performer
in that grade: very eff at 10f: acts on firm and yldg ground and likes a sharpish trk.   17
727 SANTELLA PAL [4] (L Cottrell) 5-7-13(3ow) R Hills 10/1: 00-0204: Led 2f out: see 540   07
850 SPANISH REEL [9] 4-9-3 S Dawson(3) 4/1: 40-2030: Ran on well final 1f: see 420.   25
547 RHEIN COURT [2] 6-8-0 D Williams(7) 11/2: 3000-00: No real threat: see 547.   03
812 WILD HOPE [12] 5-9-10 G Sexton 5/2 FAV: 3000-00: Well bckd: fdd: in gd form in '85,
winning h'caps at Haydock and Newmarket: in '84 won at Pontefract: eff 1m, stays 10f well:
acts on gd ground and likes a gall trk.   00

727	Macmillion [14] 9-4		636	Huytons Hope [5] 7-7(3oh)
--	Leonidas [13] 9-2		500	Lisakaty [10] 7-7(3oh)
592	Film Consultant [6] 8-1		--	Golden Triangle [8] 9-5
--	Redcross Miss [15] 8-7		--	Dinadan [11] 7-7
--	Klosterbrau [3] 7-7(5oh)		--	Le Nid [17] 7-11
17 ran	2,shthd,2,hd,2½	(Brandon Chase)	P Haslam Newmarket	

941 PACKWOOD MAIDEN STAKES 3YO   £852   1m   Firm 06 +03 Fast

-677 CHIEF PAL [13] (P Walwyn) 3-9-0 Paul Eddery 6/4 FAV: 4-21: 3 b c Kampala - Ziobia
(Tribal Chief) Well bckd and led approaching final 1f, ridden out in quite a fast run 3yo
mdn at Warwick June 7: first time out fin a gd 2nd to Highest Praise in a Pontefract maiden:
brother to useful h'capper Qualitair Flyer: eff at 6f, stays 1m: acts on firm and yldg grd
and on any track.   47
--   CARD PLAYED [1] (O Douieb) 3-8-11 R Machado 7/1: -2: Mkt drifter on race course debut:
fin well, showing promise: eff 1m, may stay further: acts on firm grd and a sharpish trk
and looks certain to find a race.   41
806 FINDING [11] (M Stoute) 3-9-0 W R Swinburn 8/1: 0-03: Ran on too late: improved effort
from this 196,000 gns yearling: shd be suited by 1m/10f: acts on fast grd and turning trk.   37
--   SARIZA [7] (H Cecil) 3-8-11 W Ryan 9/2: -4: Mkt drifter on race course debut: made
most and shd improve: very well bred filly whose dam was a very smart sort, finishing 2nd
in the 1,000 Guineas: shd have no trouble finding a race.   32
--   FACTOTUM [8] 3-9-0 B Thomson 8/1: 00-0: Ev ch in straight: unplaced on both outings
in '85, but showed promise: half brother to 3 winners including the highclass Sandhurst
Prince: should be well suited by 1m: acts on fast ground.   35
--   WELSH PAGEANTRY [5] 3-8-11 T Lucas 33/1: 0-0: No real threat on seasonal debut:
unplaced on sole start in '85: shd be suited by further than 1m.   25
--   CALVADOS [9] 3-9-0 Pat Eddery 7/1: -0: Mkt drifter on race course debut and no
threat: should do btr than this.   00

--	Captains Niece [6] 8-11		--	Rohila [4] 8-11
--	Fandango Kiss [12] 8-11		806	Sell It Kilroy [16] 9-0
733	Bears Revenge [15] 9-0		--	Fabled Monarch [19] 9-0
774	Alice Holt [2] 8-11	501 Baby Ravenna [18] 8-11		
--	Bills Belle [17] 8-11	-- Glazepta Final [3] 8-11		
656	Straightaway Star [14] 8-11		835	Some Guest [10] 9-0
19 ran	1,4,½,shthd,4,½,3	(W E Norton)	P Walwyn Lambourn, Berks	

942 SYD MERCER MEM.H'CAP 4YO+ 0-60   £3537   2m 2f   Firm 06 +06 Fast   [43]

--   TIGERWOOD [18] (R Akehurst) 5-7-7(4oh) N Adams 20/1: 0-000-1: 5 b h Lombard - Smokey
Dawn (March Past) Fit from hurdling: lightly bckd and made ev yard in quite a fast run h'cap
at Warwick June 7: little form prev on Flat: stays 2m2f really well: best out in front on
fast ground and a sharp trk.   18
569 JANUS [11] (N Smith) 8-8-5 Paul Eddery 25/1: 40-0202: No chance with winner: stays
2m2f well: see 202.   24
504 BALLET CHAMP [10] (R Holder) 8-8-4 A Proud 6/1: 042-303: Ran on too late: won this
race in '85: see 349.   22
778 OTABARI [6] (P Cole) 4-9-7 T Quinn 5/1: 14-0034: Al up there: stays 2m2f: see 778   38
462 ORANGE HILL [1] 4-8-10 Pat Eddery 7/2 FAV: 001-000: Well bckd: ev ch: on final outing
in '85 was an easy winner of a h'cap at Bath: acts on firm, likes yldg grd, stays really well 22
504 MORGANS CHOICE [13] 9-8-5 C Rutter(5) 11/1: -000000: Never nearer: in '85 won the
Chester Cup at Chester: also won at Warwick: in '83 won 5 times: stays really well: best
on gd and firm ground: game and genuine, but is not getting any younger.   14
712 JACKDAW [9] 6-8-2(1ow) W Ryan 10/1: 0000300: Never nearer 7th: best 634.   00
542 SUPER EXPRESS [17] 5-8-1(1ow) S Whitworth 8/1: 3P00-00: Much btr 542 (2m, yldg).   00
663 SAILORS REWARD [12] 4-9-3 W R Swinburn 8/1: 4-04100: Twice well below form 634(gall trk).00
724 TARS HILL [3] 5-8-5 N Carlisle 8/1: 012-020: Mkt drifter: fdd straight:bytr 724(10f)   00
675 ISHKHARA [8] 4-7-9 S Dawson(2) 4/1: 00-0030: Active in mkt, well btn: btr 675(12f)   00

--	Tinoco [14] 7-7(8oh)	801 Regent Leisure [2] 7-7(3oh)		
617	Gentle Stream [7] 9-2	663 Shiny Copper [4] 8-1	712	Pelham Line [5] 7-11
731	Castiglione [16] 7-9(bl)		590	Welsh Guard [15] 7-8(1ow)(10oh)
18 ran	6,1,¾,5,3	(Miss Anne Healy)	R Akehurst Epsom, Surrey	

943 BROOKE BOND OXO AMAT.RIDERS STAKES   £1399   1m   Firm 06 -25 Slow

812 VAGUE MELODY [13] (L Piggott) 4-11-1 Jennie Goulding 8/1: 14-2301: 4 ch g Vaigly **36**
Great - Shangara (Credo) Led inside final 1f, comfortably, in an amateur riders stks at
Warwick June 7: in '85 was trained by G Balding to win a h'cap at Leicester: eff 1m, stays
10f: acts on firm and soft and on any trk. **36**
745 SNAKE RIVER [24] (D Nicholson) 4-10-7 Princess Anne 20/1: -433102: Led over 1f out **23**
in fine form, nearly giving Princess Anne her first win under Rules: see 620.
420 KARNATAK [19] (J Spearing) 5-10-7 Miss C Reynolds(5) 33/1: 0--0-03: Al up there: **20**
maiden on Flat, but is a winner over hurdles: acts well on fast ground.
812 IRISH HERO [16] (R Sheather) 4-10-7 Maxine Juster 12/1: 42-004: Nearest fin and is **19**
running into form: showed promise on both outings in '85: half brother to a winner in France:
eff 1m on fast ground.
830 HIGH PORT [21] 7-10-7 Diana Jones 33/1: 00-0000: Ran on too late: in '85 won h'cap **13**
at Catterick: winner at Thirsk in '81: eff 7f, stays 1m: best on fast ground and sharpish trk
330 CABRAL [20] 5-10-7 Mr T Thomson Jones 14/1: -00: No real threat: very lightly raced **12**
on the Flat: has been running over hurdles.
775 MR ROSE [5] 6-10-11 Mr R Hutchinson 11/2: -000420: Much btr 775 (7f) see 636. **00**
651 INFANTRY OFFICER [1] 4-11-1 Mr T Easterby 11/8 FAV: -20: Disapp fav: slow start, **00**
no show: btr 651 (9f, yldg).
698 VINTAGE TOLL [9] 6-11-1 Mr T Walford 7/2: 0300340: No danger: btr 698, see 52. **00**

--	Fred The Tread [18] 10-7			540	Godlord [22] 11-1
651	Aqualon [12] 10-8	668	Bucks Bolt [2] 10-7	743	Castle Pool [7] 10-7
748	Catman [17] 10-12(bl)(5ow)			564	Elephant Boy [8] 10-7
--	Jimnastics [4] 10-12(5ow)			--	Kassak [3] 10-7
636	Remembrance [11] 10-7	--	Sheepscote [23] 10-7	709	Tournament Leader [15] 10-7
569	Kiki Star [10] 10-4	--	Taffys Pride [14] 10-4		
769	One For The Ditch [25] 10-4				

24 ran   2½,1,½,3,nk,1½   (A Simmons)   L Piggott Newmarket

HAYDOCK   Saturday June 7th   Lefthand Galloping Track

Official Going Given as Good/Firm

944 BASS LIGHT MAIDEN FILLIES STKS 2YO   £3036 6f   Good 60 -05 Slow

-- TWYLA [7] (H Cecil) 2-8-11 W Ryan 1/1 fav: 1: 2 ch f Habitat - Running Ballerina **70**
(Nijinsky) Smart, very promising filly: first time out, al there and cantered clear to win
a 2yo fillies mdn at Haydock June 7: sister to the useful '84 juv Defecting Dancer: eff over
6f, sure to stay further: acts on gd grd and on a gall trk: not one to oppose in her next
few engagements.
601 BINT PASHA [2] (P Cole) 2-8-11 T Quinn 5/2: 22: Made much, swerved badly 1f out **56**
tho' it made no difference to the result: caught a tartar here and shd find a race:see 601.
-- PINE AWAY [9] (J Watts) 2-8-11 N Connorton 12/1: 3: Al there, showed some inexperience **44**
but a pleasing debut from this 96,000 gns filly: sure to be suited by further than 6f:
acts on gd ground: will improve.
-- ECHO VALLEY [8] (C Brittain) 2-8-11 G Baxter 13/2: 4: Ev ch: sister to winning '85 **44**
juv My Tom Tom and half sister to 3 other winners, mostly sprinters: sure to improve
and win a race.
-- SUPERCUBE [5] 2-8-11 Wendy Carter[6] 50/1: 0: Fair race course debut from this **40**
5,200 gns filly who was bred along staying lines.
-- NATURALLY AUTUMN [3] 2-8-11 M Birch 14/1: 0: Ran on fin: shd improve considerably **36**
for this first effort: dam is a half sister to smart Wollow.

725	Edraianthus [1] 8-11	--	La Troienne [12] 8-11	819	Miss Acacia 0 8-11
--	Silver Glance [6] 8-11			685	Lack Of Pearls [11] 8-11
376	Dancing Belle [10] 8-11			--	Delite Muffin [15] 8-11
548	Bold Event [14] 8-11				

14 ran   4,4,shthd,2,2,hd   (Sheikh Mohammed)   H Cecil Newmarket

945 JOHN OF GAUNT LISTED 3YO+   £18627 7f   Good 60 +20 Fast

406 FIRM LANDING [10] (J Watts) 3-8-0 N Connorton 25/1: 310-01: 3 b c J O Tobin - **75**
Magnificent Lady (Nonoalco) Smart, improving colt: prom, led dist and held on well in a
close fin to fast run and val John of Gaunt (Listed) Stks at Haydock June 7: lightly raced
in '85 winning a minor event at Newcastle: stays 7f well, shd stay 1m: acts on firm and gd
ground and likes a gall trk.
330 HOMO SAPIEN [8] (H Cecil) 4-9-4 W Ryan 9/2: 2-132: Almost got up on the post and **81**
this was a fine effort: see 222.
433 BOLD INDIAN [1] (G Wragg) 5-8-12 J Reid 3/1 fav: -023: Met trouble in running, fin **75**
very fast and needs further than 7f now : see 433.
708 CHARGE ALONG [4] (J Winter) 4-8-9 G Baxter 20/1: 4400-04: Made much: fair effort:see 433.65
-- BREADCRUMB [5] 4-8-12 R Hills 14/1: 10010-0: Al prom, gd seasonal debut: won first
2 on the trot in '85 at Newbury and Salisbury and later picked up a h'cap at Newmarket:
very eff over 7f on firm grd and likes a stiff gall trk. **63**
361 POSTORAGE [11] 4-8-12 R Wernham 50/1: 020-000: Prom, wknd: see 361. **61**

639 MIAMI COUNT [6] 4-9-1 D Parnell 8/1: 200-440: Irish chall, fin 8th: best 267 (yldg)   00
705 GREY DESIRE [3] 6-9-4 K Darley 4/1: 1124120: Well below his best: much btr 587.   00
598 BOLLIN KNIGHT [9] 4-9-4 M Birch 4/1: -011100: Ran poorly: see 413.   00
--   Samarid [7] 8-0   587 Que Sympatica [2] 9-1
11 ran   hd,nk,2,2½,½,nk   (J L Allbritton)   J Watts Richmond, Yorks

946 STONES BEST BITTER HANDICAP 3YO 0-70   £9770   1m 2f Good 60 +13 Fast   [65]

+807 MOON MADNESS [7] (J Dunlop) 3-8-10(5ex) G Baxter 8/13 Fav: 4-111: 3 b c Vitiges -
Castle Moon (Kalamoun) Very useful colt winning 2nd val h'cap in 8 days, sprinting clear
final 1f in fast run Stones Best Bitter h'cap at Haydock June 7: hacked up in similar h'cap
at Newmarket May 31: narrow winner of a maiden at Salisbury first time and only ran once
in '85: half brother to a couple of middle dist winners and shd stay 12f himself: acts
on firm and yldg and likes a gall trk: likely to complete the hat-trick.   61
*553 LONDON BUS [4] (J Watts) 3-8-4 N Connorton 4/1: 00-112: Prom, dsptd lead dist,
outpaced by this well h'capped winner: lost nothing in defeat and shd find more races:see 553   48
411 GORGEOUS STRIKE [2] (C Nelson) 3-9-7 J Reid 16/1: 23-0203: Kept on well, gd effort
under top weight: see 191.   64
807 ANDARTIS [8] (Lord J Fitzgerald) 3-9-7 R Hills 10/1: 02-0334: Not well h'capped at
present: see 807.   57
698 MERHI [3] 3-8-0 J Lowe 10/1: 0-23430: Made most: btr 698 (firm).   34
216 LASTCOMER [11] 3-8-11 A Kimberley 8/1: 1-00: No danger: see 216.   43
370 Stage Hand [1] 8-13   386 Thalassino Asteri [9] 8-8
789 Common Farm [5] 7-7(3oh)   716 Charlton Kings [10] 8-8
10 ran   2½,hd,4,1½,1½,nk   (Lavinia Duchess of Norfolk)   J Dunlop Arundel, Sussex

947 DARESBURY HANDICAP 3YO 0-60   £4103   6f   Good 60 -14 Slow   [51]

670 GOLDEN GUILDER [3] (M W Easterby) 3-7-13(bl) L Charnock 9/2: 0212031: 3 b f Sonnen Gold
- Dutch Gold (Goldhill) Continues in fine form and led inside final 3f comfortably in a
3yo h'cap at Haydock June 7: earlier won a similar h'cap at Beverley and has performed
consistently: eff at 5 and 6f and acts on gd and soft going: wears blinkers.   33
507 USEFUL [5] (B Hills) 3-9-0 R Street 5/1: 1020-02: Not trouble winner but is back
to form: see 507.   43
*814 DARK PROMISE [1] (R Hollinshead) 3-9-13(7ex) S Perks 9/2: 20-0013: Creditable effort
under 9-13 and is in fine form: see 814.   52
814 JARROVIAN [10] (T Fairhurst) 3-9-0 C Coates[5] 14/1: 4210004: Never closer: unsuited
by firm: acts on gd and hvy: see 308.   39
671 VILTASH [6] 3-9-7 M Birch 5/1: 2000-00: Ev ch: see 671.   42
713 CUMBRIAN DANCER [4] 3-8-1 J Lowe 6/1: 2-04300: Twice below 518 (7f).   10
*545 MADRACO [9] 3-8-0 M Fry 4/1fav: 404-110: Dsptd lead, wknd and much btr 545(yldg)   00
836 Websters Feast [8] 8-11   671 Tax Roy [7] 9-1
624 Loft Boy [2] 9-1
10 ran   1½,1½,shthd,1½,8   (C Buckton)   M W Easterby Sheriff Hutton, Yorks

948 RIBBLE SELLING STAKES 2YO   £1450   5f   Good 60 -42 Slow

*589 GREENS GALLERY [6] (G Blum) 2-8-12 G Baxter 13/8 fav: 011: Heavily bckd when
picking up 2nd seller on the trot, leading final 1f at Haydock June 7 (no bid): winner at
Beverley last time: suited by a stiff or gall trk and is eff over 5f on good ground.   37
785 NATIONS SONG [4] (R Stubbs) 2-8-12(BL) J H Brown[5] 6/1: 04102: Made most, running
well: seemed unsuited by hvy last time: see 681: biinkered first time today.   31
596 SETTER COUNTRY [1] (R Hodges) 2-8-12 N Day 100/30: 0143: Never closer: see 329.   26
612 MAYSPARK [2] (P Rohan) 2-8-8 J Bleasdale 14/1: 04: Kept on well and is improving:
sure to be suited by 6f: acts on gd.   19
715 FENN TRAP [8] 2-8-11 S Morris 14/1: 00: Dropped in grade, kept on and could find
a seller at one of the smaller trks: should stay 6f.   20
694 CAUSEWAY FOOT [5] 2-8-11 L Charnock 11/1: 000: Dropped in class, unable to chall.
but showed some improvement.   19
596 DECCAN PRINCE [9] 2-8-11 M Wigham 9/1: 000: Fin 7th: see 596.   00
--   Winnies Luck [3] 8-8   813 Glory Gold [7] 8-8   646 Miss Drummond [11] 8-8
780 Master Pippin [10] 8-11
11 ran   2½,2,1½,½,nk,nk,1   (Richard Green Fine Paintings)   G Blum Newmarket

949 ENDURANCE HANDICAP 3YO 0-35   £3074   2m   Good 60 -20 Slow   [42]

*697 AGATHIST [2] (G P Gordon) 3-9-7(3ex) W Ryan 11/8 fav: 00-411: 3 ch c Bon Mot III
- We Try Harder (Blue Prince II) Winning 2nd race on the trot, keeping on well final 3f in
a slowly run 3yo h'cap at Haydock June 7: picked up similar h'cap at Redcar May 26: acts
on firm and yldg and on any trk: eff 14f, stays 2m really well.   43
331 FOUL SHOT [9] (W Musson) 3-7-7(1oh) M Fry 12/1: 00-2202: Made much: suited by front
running: see 171 (12f).   12
648 NIMBLE NATIVE [11] (S Norton) 3-8-5 J Lowe 10/1: -104003: Rear till gd late prog:
stays 2m: see 45.   23
307 PHEASANT HEIGHTS [7] (H Candy) 3-8-10 T Quinn 8/1: 0000-44: Ev ch: seems to act
on gd and hvy: see 307.   308   20

623 ROYAL EFFIGY [1] 3-8-5 N Day 25/1: 1D40000: Never closer: best 66 (10f soft)   08
730 CELTIC DOVE [8] 3-8-8 J Williams 20/1: -404000: Best 338 (1m yldg).   10
*767 FAST AND FRIENDLY [10] 3-8-1(3ex) K Darley 5/1: -004310: Well bckd, fin 7th: btr 767(12f).00
738 SWYNFORD PRINCE [6] 3-8-9 M Birch 13/2: 0012030: Much btr 738 (11f)   00
*307 COUNTLESS COUNTESS [5] 3-9-7 R Hills 7/1: -2010: Abs since much btr 307(soft/hvy)   00
648 Dors Gem [3] 8-1   769 Storm Lord [4] 7-10
11 ran   2,1,6,5,¾,4   (Wm Du Pont III)   G P Gordon Newmarket

---

Official Going Given as Good on Straight Course : Good/Firm on Round Course

950 BBC RADIO KENT STAKES 3 & 4YO   £2998   7f   Good/Firm 30 -01 Slow

*733 NATIVE OAK [9] (H Cecil) 3-8-11 S Cauthen 11/8 fav: 13-4211: 3 b c Tower Walk -
Be Royal (Royal Palm) Never hdd when gaining 2nd successive win, comfortably picking up
a minor event at Goodwood June 9: also made all in another similar race at Leicester May 27:
lightly raced in '85 winning at Yarmouth: eff 6f, well suited by 7f and shd stay 1m: acts
on firm and gd grd and is well suited by forcing tactics.   75
*546 GEORGIA RIVER [8] (O Douieb) 3-8-9 W R Swinburn 7/2: 3-12: Mkt drifter, ev ch:
stiff task: see 546.   66
--   GLIDE BY [5] (R Boss) 4-8-13 M Miller 25/1: 24200-3: Never nearer after a slow start:
placed sev times without winning in '85, the prev season successful at Yarmouth and was just
btn by Ever Genial in Gr 3 May Hill Stks at Doncaster: needs further than 7f: stays 10f:
best form on firm or gd ground.   56
--   ININSKY [3] (G Harwood) 3-8-7 G Starkey 5/2: 210-4: Al prom on seasonal debut:
lightly raced in '85, easily winning a mdn at Sandown: eff over 7f but bred to stay well:
suited by firm grd and a stiff trk: shd do better next time.   52
600 FASHADA [6] 3-8-7 W Carson 7/1: 01-030: Ev ch: btr 600 (6f).   50
762 DOLLY [4] 4-8-12 M Wigham 100/1: -004D00: Almost impossible task: see 762.   25
--   Three Bells [1] 9-0   844 Persian Person [7] 8-11
276 Wing Bee [2] 8-3(BL)
9 ran   3,1,5,1,6,10   (C d'Alessio)   H Cecil Newmarket

951 SUSSEX INDUSTRIES CLAIMING STAKES 3YO   £3120   1m 4f Good/Firm 30 -15 Slow

880 FIREPROOF [13] (D Marks) 3-9-0 W Carson 7/1: 0-04201: 3 ch c Vitiges - Marie
Mancini (Roi Soleil) Mkt drifter but was sn prom and led under press final 1f in a 3yo
claimer at Goodwood June 9: first success: well suited by 12f and firm or gd going tho' prob
acts also on soft: seems to handle any course.   30
761 WALCISIN [6] (R Hannon) 3-8-8 Pat Eddery 5/1: 0-00022: Came from behind: running
well and shd find a race in this grade: see 761.   22
625 KHETA KING [4] (W Hastings Bass) 3-8-11 W R Swinburn 12/1: 0-03: Active in mkt,
ev ch: lightly raced half brother to minor winner Prince of Kashmir: suited by 12f and a
sound surface.   24
*790 SIR BRETT [10] (P Kelleway) 3-9-2 Gay Kelleway[5] 6/1: -0414: Ev ch, btr 790 (hvy).   22
751 MELENDEZ [5] 3-9-0 G Starkey 10/1: -00: No real threat from this very lightly
raced colt: appears to be one of his powerful stables lesser lights.   18
730 BALNACRAIG [7] 3-8-7(BL) R Cochrane 10/1: 10-0000: Btr 10f? See 730.   09
908 CHUMMYS OWN [11] 3-9-7 B Thomson 10/1: 0-1020: Prom much: much btr 908 (sharp trk)   00
*838 KOUS [3] 3-9-0(bl) S Whitworth 3/1 fav: -10: Cl.up 1m: btr 838 (10f).   00
512 Last Polonaise [1] 8-6   570 Cardave [14] 9-0
613 Relatively Easy [9] 8-4   506 Vantastic [2] 8-4
535 Super Smart [8] 8-3   95 Welsh Crown [12] 8-3
14 ran   1½,½,5,1,1½   (D Marks)   D Marks Lambourn, Berks

952 JAMES LOCK PANAMA HAT HCAP 3YO+ 0-60   £4058   6f   Good/Firm 30 +21 Fast [52]

855 BOLD REALM [13] (C Horgan) 5-8-5 Pat Eddery 7/2 fav: 100-001: 5 b g Bold Lad -
Elm (Realm) Well bckd and rtnd. to form, getting up cl home in a fast run and quite valuable
h'cap at Goodwood June 9: in '85 won at Newmarket and Ripon: suited by firm or gd going
and seems to act on any trk: very eff at 6f.   41
734 MIRACLES TAKE TIME [7] (D Elsworth) 4-8-0 A Mcglone 11/2: 3-00042: Led final 1f,
caught death: shd win soon: see 734.   35
508 TRANSFLASH [10] (E Eldin) 7-9-2 R Cochrane 9/1: 0-43003: Kept on well: best effort
since 192: see 55.   45
616 GOLD PROSPECT [12] (G B Balding) 4-8-11 J Williams 10/1: 0-12204: Ev ch: see 31.   39
846 FERRYMAN [2] 10-8-13 S Cauthen 10/1: 30-0000: Ev ch: see 846.   38
*846 AL TRUI [11] 6-10-0(7ex) M Wigham 10/1: 000-000: Sn prom: btr 846.   48
508 EECEE TREE [3] 4-7-8(BL) R Street 10/1: 00-0200: Raced alone and made much,
fin 7th: bl first time: best 327 (5f soft).   00
374 ROYSIA BOY [6] 6-9-1 W Ryan 8/1: 1101-00: Early speed, fin 8th after abs: ran well
at the end of '85 winning at Kempton, Goodwood, Leicester and Nottingham: equally eff at
6 and 7f: best form on firm or gd ground: acts on any trk.   00

886 Light Hills [9] 7-9		*842 Mr Mcgregor [4] 8-4(7ex)	
-- Steady Eddie [5] 9-1		687 Brig Chop [8] 9-9	687 Stock Hill Lass [1] 8-13
13 ran hd,2,½,1½,2,hd,4		(Mrs Seamus Purcell)	C Horgan Findon, Sussex

953   BBC RADIO SUSSEX STAKES 2YO   £3056   6f   Good/Firm 30 +02 Fast

*715 CAROLS TREASURE [1] (B Hills) 2-9-1 B Thomson 5/6 fav: 211: 2 b c Balidar - Really
Sharp (Sharpen Up) Useful colt: comfortably landed the odds, coming from behind to sprint
clear final 1f in quite a fast run 2yo event at Goodwood June 9: won a mdn at Doncaster
May 26: sprint bred colt who is eff at 5f, possibly even btr at 6f: acts on firm and yldg:
sure to win more races.   64
678 SANTELLA GREY [4] (G Harwood) 2-8-11 G Starkey 10/1: 02: Mkt drifter, tried to
make all: improving sort who stays 6f and shd find a mdn shortly: see 678.   50
773 TENDER TIFF [6] (M Mccormack) 2-8-12 S Cauthen 5/2: 143: Prom, outpaced: best 655(hvy) 41
-- ROB ROY MACGREGOR [5] (J Dunlop) 2-8-11 W Carson 8/1: 4: Well bckd debutant, always
struggling for pace: half brother to '84 3yo 7f winner African Bloom: sure to benefit
greatly from the experience.   20
456 ENCHANTED TIMES [3] 2-9-1 Pat Eddery 11/1: 130: Early speed: best 187 (first time
out, 5f yldg).   20
5 ran   2½,4,8,1½   (Mrs C Lane)   B.Hills Lambourn, Berks

954   BBC RADIO SOLENT H'CAP (0-50) 3YO   £3243   1m   Good/Firm 30 -03 Slow   [44]

*812 AVENTINO [1] (J Sutcliffe) 3-8-7(bl)(6ex) Pat Eddery 8/11 fav: 001-011: 3 ch g Cure
The Blues - Sovereign Dona (Sovereign Path) Well h'capped gelding who was winning his 2nd h'cap
on the trot, going clear in final 1f for an easy win at Goodwood June 9: comfortably won
similar h'cap at Newmarket May 31: in '85 was a narrow winner of Newmarket seller on final
outing: very eff over 1m on firm or gd going: likes Newmarket tho' acts on any trk: should
complete the hat-trick.   37
514 BOWL OVER [3] (P Makin) 3-9-5(bl) B Thomson 15/2: 02-1032: Chall dist, caught a
tartar: best 157 (yldg).   41
*498 NIORO [4] (R J Houghton) 3-9-7 S Cauthen 5/1: 40-13: Ev ch: rated higher 498(7f).   31
703 STILL DREAMING [8] (N Vigors) 3-8-9 W Carson 6/1: 030-204: Chall 2f out: twice below 42418
454 HELLO BLUE [5] 3-7-13 M Roberts 33/1: 00-000: Ev ch: lightly raced mdn.   00
671 HELVICK BAY [7] 3-8-2 A Mcglone 33/1: 000-000: See 671.   01
703 Miss Venezuela [9] 8-10   538 Supreme Kingdom [6] 9-5
-- Gold Touch [2] 9-6
9 ran   4,8,½,5,1   (A J Smith)   J Sutcliffe Epsom, Surrey

955   SPECIAL OLYMPICS FILLIES H'CAP 3YO   £3902   1m 2f Good/Firm 30 -06 Slow   [50]

738 STILLOU [9] (P Mitchell) 3-7-7(1oh) T Williams 11/1: 4-34001: 3 ch f Mansingh -
Flapper (Free Range) Came from behind to get up on post in a 3yo fillies h'cap at Goodwood
June 9: in '85 won a seller at Redcar: eff 1m but nowadays well suited by 10f: seems to
act on firm and soft and on any trk.   27
688 FAREWELL TO LOVE [2] (I Balding) 3-9-6 Pat Eddery 5/6 fav: 0-21022: Appeared well
h'capped, tried to make all and caught on the post: see 315, 688.   54
682 HUSNAH [6] (L Cumani) 3-9-4 R Guest 6/1: 02-333: Mkt drifter, ev ch: best 549(stks) 42
637 TEMPEST TOSSED [7] (R Armstrong) 3-8-4 W Carson 10/1: 0003-04: Late prog: lightly
raced in '85, rated 44 when fair 3rd to Kabiyla in a fillies mdn at Leicester on final
outing: acts on firm ground.   21
232 LADY WINDMILL [5] 3-8-12 W R Swinburn 25/1: 000-400: Slow start, no danger: see 158 27
730 THEREAFTER [1] 3-7-10 N Adams 50/1: 000-000: Rank outsider, prom much: mdn with
little worthwhile form.   10
637 LADY BISHOP [8] 3-7-12(bl) A Mcglone 6/1: 00-0030: Fin 7th: much btr 637 (1m).   00
-- Fassa [4] 9-7   505 Appreciative [3] 8-3
9 ran   shthd,10,7,2,½   (Miss Linda Demetriou)   P Mitchell Epsom, Surrey

Official Going Given as Good/Firm

956   WINDERMERE HANDICAP 3YO+ 0-35   £2001   1m   Firm 02 +18 Fast   [34]

606 EASY DAY [2] (E Eldin) 4-9-3 A Mackay 14/1: 0-04101: 4 ch c Swing Easy - Break
Of Day (On Your Mark) Broke well and was never hdd when a comfortable winner of a very fast
run h'cap at Redcar June 9 (new course record): last month won a similar race at Lingfield:
eff over 7/8f: acts on any going and on any trk: well suited by forcing tactics.   36
830 GODS LAW [17] (G Reveley) 5-7-9 Julie Bowker(7) 6/1: 00-0132: Al front rank:
beat rem devisively: in gd form and btr suited by this longer trip: see 710.   08
830 MONINSKY [3] (N Bycroft) 5-8-5 M Richardson(7) 10/1: 32-2003: Never nearer: stays 1m. 13
553 HONEST TOIL [13] (R Whitaker) 3-7-9 M Fry 20/1: 0-34004: Going on fin: btr effort. 15
745 SILLITOE [10] 4-9-3 M Beecroft 16/1: 300-000: Shorter trip: ran on too late:
quite consistent last season, when successful in h'caps at Newcastle and Redcar: stays 9f:
acts on firm and yldg ground and is suited by a galloping trk.   20

521	BURAAG [11] 5-9-13 M Hindley(3) 12/1: 0-00440: Nearest fin: needs further tho' a fair effort under top weight: see 196.	29
745	RABIRIUS [8] 5-9-10 D Nicholls 7/1: -010-20: Well placed till dist: fin 8th: see 745	00
816	IRISH PASSAGE [4] 3-8-9 G Baxter 9/2 FAV: 1-02D0: Fin 9th: btr 816: see 518.	00
745	ELARIM [12] 7-9-4 C Coates(5) 10/1: 10-0000: Front rank over 5f: see 745.	00
606	BELLA BANUS [15] 4-9-6 M Birch 7/1: 0302-00: No threat: can do btr : see 606.	00
789	RUN BY JOVE [6] 3-9-0(bl)(10ex) J Lowe 10/1: 0-00120: Btr with some cut in 789.	00
*893	QUALITY CHORISTER [16] 5-8-6(7ex) R P Elliott 10/1: 02-4010: Much btr on gd 893(9f).	00

745 Swiftspender [1] 7-12   724 Highdale [9] 8-1   524 Decembre [7] 7-11(VIS)
689 Emerald Eagle [14] 8-13
16 ran   2,3,1,1½,½   (D W Rolt)   E Eldin Newmarket

---

957 GRASMERE SELLING STAKES 2YO   £955   5f   Firm 02 -04 Slow

813	FIVE SIXES [8] (N Tinkler) 2-8-11 S Keightley 2/1 FAV: 01D421: 2 br c Music Maestro - Stolen Secret (Burglar) Gained a deserved win, quickly into his stride and was never hdd in a 2yo seller at Redcar June 9 (no bid): earlier made all to "win" a similar event at Warwick tho' subsequently demoted: cost 2,600 gns and is half brother to winning miler Mitilini: eff over 5f with forcing tactics: acts on firm and yldg grd and any trk: consistent in this grade.	26
865	RUN TO WORK [2] (G Moore) 2-8-11 D Casey(7) 12/1: 422: Ran on well: continues to improve and shd pick up a simiar race soon: acts on firm and yldg: see 633.	22
717	PEGGYS TREASURE [10] (M Brittain) 2-8-8 K Darley 11/1: 003: Dropped in class: always up there and looks more at home in this grade: acts on fast ground and gall trk: half sister to a couple of winners and shd stay further in time.	17
858	REAL RUSTLE [6] (M W Easterby) 2-8-11(bl) M Hindley(3) 14/1: 00034: Ran on well from ½ way: acts on firm grd and gall trk: see 858.	14
647	MISS PISA [7] 2-8-8 A Mackay 7/1: -03030: Gd early speed: best on yldg 647.	09
376	SEATON GIRL [11] 2-8-8 G Baxter 7/1: 4200: Dropped in class: no extra dist, eased: best effort with some give in 108.	01
317	LYN RAE [4] 2-8-8 M Birch 3/1: 00: Never going well: much btr 317 (soft).	00

813 Patels Gold [3] 8-8   858 Caras Quest [1] 8-8   821 Keiths Wish [5] 8-8
515 Noble Kala [9] 8-11
11 ran   1,½,3,shthd,4   (John Binks)   N Tinkler Langton, Yorks

---

958 ULLSWATER HANDICAP 3YO 0-35   £2134   1m 4f   Firm 02 -17 Slow   [42]

*631	COMELY DANCER [2] (J Watts) 3-9-7 N Connorton 15/8 FAV: 4-311: 3 b c Northern Baby - Abordage (Luthier) In gd form, led over 3f out and ran on strongly to win a 3yo h'cap at Redcar June 9: last month won a small race at Edinburgh: eff over 10f, stays 12f well: acts on firm grd and on any trk.	46
648	PATS JESTER [5] (P Rohan) 3-8-11 M Wood 3/1: 40-4132: Stayed on well: remains in gd form: acts on fast and firm grd: good ground: see 356.	33
714	WATERDALE [4] (M W Easterby) 3-8-4(1ow) K Hodgson 5/1: 000-003: Fin well: best effort to date: stays 12f well: suited by fast grd and a gall trk.	20
688	PINTURICCHIA [6] (Don Enrico Incisa) 3-8-1 M Beecroft 16/1: 00-004: Kept on under press: stays 12f: acts on gd and firm grd and on a gall trk: see 688.	15
648	SEVEN HILLS [9] 3-8-6 M Birch 7/1: 000-000: No real threat: see 648.	12
648	LAUGH A LOT [8] 3-8-3 A Mackay 12/1: 23-3200: Twice disapp over this trip: see 54(10f)	00

823 Rockall [10] 8-8(bl)   867 Pink Sensation [3] 8-6
608 Crown Colony [1] 7-7(5oh) U   517 Fourno Trumps [7] 7-7(11oh) P
10 ran   1,4,1½,5,12   (Joe L'Albritton)   J Watts Richmond, Yorks

---

959 BUTTERMERE MAIDEN STAKES 3YO+   £768   1m 6f   Firm 02 -39 Slow

452	ASSAGLAWI [10] (H Thomson Jones) 4-9-5 R Hills 11/1: 022-001: 4 b c Troy - Queen's Counsellor (Kalamoun) Showed improved form, led below dist and ran on strongly to win a slowly run mdn at Redcar June 9: showed promise last season, notably when running up to Freedoms Choice in a Haydock mdn last backend: stays 14f well: acts on firm and soft grd and is well suited by a gall trk.	40
714	L B LAUGHS [2] (G Pritchard Gordon) 3-8-2(BL) G Duffield 10/1: 430-002: Bl first time and ran on well over this longer trip: half brother to sev middle dist winners, including useful Harry's Bar: stays 14f: acts on firm and yldg grd and on a gall trk.	36
--	DIENAUS TROVE [1] (H Collingridge) 5-9-5 M Rimmer 10/1: -3: Made most: mdn on Flat tho' showed gd form over timber this Winter, winning at Catterick: stays well: acts on any going and on any trk: could win a small h'cap.	35
770	MADISON GIRL [8] (R Whitaker) 3-7-13 D Mckeown 8/1: 300-034: Kept on: stays 14f.	30
744	DENALTO [9] 3-8-2 L Charnock 20/1: 00-00: Ran on too late: clearly well suited by a test of stamina: acts on a gall trk: see 744.	26
714	RHODE ISLAND RED [4] 3-8-2 N Connorton 11/4: -40: Btr over 12f in 714.	22
253	ZAUBARR [12] 3-8-2 M Hills 9/4 FAV: 00-00: Fin 7th: btr over 1m in 253 (soft).	00
790	NADAS [7] 3-8-2(bl) J Lowe 8/1: -4230: Fin 8th: much btr on hvy 790 (12f).	00
592	THE YOMPER [11] 4-9-5 S Webster 8/1: 200-420: Fin 9th: much btr over 12f 592(gd).	00

595 Garthman [5] 8-2   -- Messaline [13] 9-5   772 Rapidan [3] 9-5 769 Sians Pet [6] 7-13
13 ran   2½,nk,1½,7,2   (Hamdan Al-Maktoum)   H Thomson Jones Newmarket

960 THIRLMERE CLAIMING STAKES 3YO+   £1951   1m 1f   Firm 02 -04 Slow

702 TAXI MAN [1] (H Jones) 3-8-5 R Hills 5/1: 0000-01: 3 ch g Dublin Taxi - Manna
Green (Bustin) Led dist and ran on well to win a Claiming Stks at Redcar June 9: first
success: showed some promise in mdn company early on last season: eff over 9/10f: best form
on fast grd and is well suited by a gall trk.   25
650 CAPRICORN BLUE [3] (J Fitzgerald) 3-8-9(vis) D Nicholls 14/1: 000S-02: Came again
late, never nearer: closely related to a couple of winners: stays 9f: acts on fast grd
and on a gall trk.   25
745 DOMINION PRINCESS [12] (P Rohan) 5-8-11 M Birch 2/1 FAV: 00-4433: Gambled on: led
briefly 2f out: in gd form tho' remains a maiden: see 745.   12
823 GIBBERISH [8] (M Prescott) 3-8-2 G Duffield 5/1: 000-204: Led 3f out, not btn
that far: see 674.   16
366 ABBEE VALLEY [2] 4-8-13 N Connorton 50/1: -000-00: Ran on well: lightly raced last
season and has shown little worthwhile form to date: stays 9f well: acts on gd and firm.   08
452 MY HANDSOME BOY [10] 4-9-4 C Coates(5) 10/1: 30-0000: Maiden who was placed sev
times last season, notably when narrowly btn by Gilderdale in a Wolverhampton h'cap
(rated 32): half brother to sev winners, including the useful Beauvallon: eff over 8/9f and
bred to stay further: acts on gd and fast grd and on a gall trk.   11
674 KIRKELLA [6] 3-8-9(bl) M Wood 10/1: 0000-00: Chall below dist: wknd into 7th: half
brother to 8/9f winner Truculent Scholar: seems suited by fast grd.   00
527 MAWDLYN GATE [9] 3-8-9 K Hodgson 7/1: 0-00400: Hmpd 3f out: fin 9th: btr judged 414.   00
--   STANFORD ROSE [14] 3-8-1 K Darley 10/1: 02003-0: Btr for race: placed sev times
last season in selling company: stays 1m: acts on gd and firm grd and gall trk.   00
861 Mr Bennington [11] 9-0   279 Duke Of Milltimber [15] 8-4   613 Debach Revenge [4] 8-11
774 Red Zulu [17] 8-9   522 What A Line [13] 8-11   651 Green Archer [16] 8-9
651 Carlops [7] 9-1   163 Scoop The Kitty [5] 8-8
17 ran   2,nk,hd,3,½,shthd   (Mrs O K Steele)   H Jones Malton, Yorks.

961 BASSENTHWAITE HANDICAP 3YO 0-35   £2007   6f   Firm 02 +09 Fast   [37]

768 FELIPE TORO [14] (M H Easterby) 3-8-11(bl) M Birch 4/1 FAV: 0000-21: 3 b g Runnett -
Kalympia (Kalydon) Gained a pillar-to-post success in a fast run 3yo h'cap at Redcar
June 9: earlier just btn by Blue Horizon when trying to make all in a similar race at
Catterick: showed some form last season: eff over 6f on firm and yldg grd: acts on any trk.   30
447 HANSOM LAD [5] (W Haigh) 3-9-7 D Nicholls 7/1: 03-0232: Just held: clear rem:
in gd form tho' remains a maiden: see 447, 284.   39
677 QUALITAIR KING [15] (K Stone) 3-8-10 S Keightley 20/1: -030003: Ran on too late:
seems well suited by a sound surface: prob needs further: see 78.   18
768 IMPERIAL SUNRISE [1] (M W Easterby) 3-8-11 M Hindley(3) 9/1: 44-4034: Al cl.up:see 309.   18
545 NEW EVIDENCE [9] 3-8-10 A Mackay 9/1: 400-000: Ran on well : stays 6f: seems
suited by fast grd and a gall trk.   15
*837 LINAVOS [12] 3-9-2 J Bray(7) 9/1: 000-010: Never going well: much btr on gd 837.   17
784 COLWAY RADIAL [8] 3-8-1 L Charnock 8/1: 00-0440: Never nearer 8th: see 626.   00
615 CARNIVAL ROSE [11] 3-8-9 G Duffield 9/1: 300-000: Speed over ½ way: fin 9th:
nicely bckd today after being highly tried in her 2 prev starts this term: stays 6f:
acts on firm and soft grd.   00
447 DOUBLE CHAI [10] 3-9-1(bl) J Lowe 7/1: 4300-00: Jockey injured leaving stalls,
never in race and virtually p.u: closely related to sev winners and showed some promise
last season over sprint dist: acts on gd and firm grd.   00
768 Bargain Pack [17] 8-1   455 Witham Girl [3] 8-5(BL)
670 Ken Siddall [6] 8-9   --   Eastern Oasis [13] 8-4   447 Spanish Infanta [4] 7-9
784 Miss Serlby [7] 8-8(BL)   451 Daisy Star [16] 8-4   447 Henry Padwick [2] 8-1
17 ran   hd,4,hd,1,2,½,hd,shthd   (Lt-Col R Warden)   M H Easterby Great Habton.

Official Going Given as Firm - Strong Wind Behind

962 JOHN WHITE MENPHYS MAIDEN STAKES 2YO   £964   5f   Firm -9 +01 Fast

685 CUTTING BLADE [2] (L Piggott) 2-9-0 J Matthias 13/8 FAV: 31: 2 b c Sharpo - Lady
of Renown (His Majesty) Useful, impro colt: led well other 1f out, comfortably, in a 2yo
mdn at Leicester June 9: first time out fin a gd 3rd to Polemos at Doncaster: speedily bred
colt who shd stay 6f: acts on fast grd and a gall trk and looks sure to win more races.   54
777 OUR ZOUZOU [5] (M Jarvis) 2-9-0 T Ives 7/4: 42: Well bckd: made much: shd be
winning soon possibly on an easier trk: acts well on fast ground.   47
--   SINJAAB [8] (M Albina) 2-9-0 A Boond 15/2: 3: Al up there: promising race course
debut from this 14,000 gns purchase: half brother to 15f winner Shagayle: acts on fast grd.   40
--   NEW MEXICO [6] (D Morley) 2-9-0 B Rouse 15/2: 4: Prom, ev ch on debut: cost 31,000 gns
and is a half brother to sev winners, all speedy sorts: acts on firm grd.   37
--   SOMETHING EXTRA [7] 2-9-0 T Quinn 9/1: 0: No real threat on race course debut:
half brother to the smart Susa Steel and will impr on this next time: acts on firm grd.   33

632 PARKERS JOY [1] 2-9-0 W Wharton 33/1: 00: No show, but a btr effort: cheaply
acquired and shd be suited by further than 5f.   24
-- Bangkok Boy [4] 9-0   -- Hobournes Percy [9] 9-0
-- Stumble [3] 9-0
9 ran   2½,2½,1,1½,3   (Mahmoud Fustok)   L Piggott Newmarket

963 HICKLING SELLING HANDICAP (0-25)   £839   7f   Firm -9 +09 Fast   [16]

495 MAIDEN BIDDER [9] (H Beasley) 4-9-2 R Morse(5) 8/1: 000-021: 4 b f Shack -
Wolveriana (Wolver Hollow) Led 3f out, easily, in quite a fast run selling h'cap at Leicester
June 9 (bought in 2,800 gns): has improved of late: eff 6f, stays 7f well: acts on fast grd
and on any track.   12
538 RUPERT BROOKE [15] (J Spearing) 3-8-11 W Carson 7/2 FAV: 000-002: Gambled on and
al prom: showed some form in non-selling company in '85: stays 7f: acts on gd/firm and soft
grd and should find a seller.   13
689 QUALITAIRESS [2] (K Stone) 4-8-9 Pat Eddery 9/2: 0-30043: Al up there: see 101. 00
749 BLUE STEEL [10] (R Simpson) 3-9-3(VIS) S Whitworth 20/1: 00-0004: Sn prom: ev ch. 12
41 RUN FOR FRED [19] 4-8-12 Paul Eddery 20/1: 0030-00: Nearest fin after abs: eff
6/7f on gd and firm ground.   00
207 MEGANOT [13] 4-8-8 T Quinn 33/1: 000-000: Abs: sn prom: little form to date.   00
673 MISS APEX [12] 4-9-8 I Johnson 7/1: 32-0430: Made no show: much btr 673, 420(10f). 00
828 Martella [17] 8-10   906 Hoptons Chance [8] 9-3
28 Court Jewel [14] 8-9(bl)   630 Reformed Habit [18] 8-11
568 Elmcote Lad [5] 9-1   809 Larches [16] 8-13   -- Dancing Habit [3] 8-12
809 Bandyann [20] 8-10   871 Strawberry Split [11] 8-5(BL)
718 Ashraf [1] 8-4(VIS)   498 The Moon And Back [6] 8-3
426 Anderby [7] 8-1(vis)   726 Sharasar [4] 9-3(bl)
20 ran   2½,2,1½,1½,2½,   (B Sharp)   H Beasley Marlborough, Wilts

964 ALLIED DUNBAR HANDICAP (0-60) 4YO+   £4838   1m 4f   Firm -9 -14 Slow   [54]

-- SWIMMER [8] (G Huffer) 4-9-2 G Sexton 12/1: 31013-1: 4 ch c Lord Gayle - Hispanica
(Whistling Wind) First time out, led 1½f out, stayed on well, in a h'cap at Leicester
June 9: in gd form in '85, winning at Nottingham and Warwick: half brother to sev winners:
very eff at 10f, stays 12f: acts on gd and firm grd and on any trk and does well when fresh. 52
686 REGAL STEEL [3] (R Hollinshead) 8-7-7(1oh) A Culhane(7) 5/1: 3020322: Made most:
rallied final 1f: in gd form: see 686 and 474.   28
778 PEGGY CAROLYN [4] (M Ryan) 4-8-13 P Robinson 7/1: 100-003: Nearest fin: running
into form: in gd form in '85, winning h'caps at Newmarket, Nottingham and Leicester:
eff 12f: stays 2m really well: acts on gd and firm grd and on any trk: genuine filly. 45
225 ABSENT LOVER [10] (F Yardley) 5-8-11 I Johnson 16/1: 1240-04: Prom, wknd final 1f:
btr effort: last season was in fine form, winning h'caps at Warwick (2) and Wolverhampton:
in '84 won first time out again at Warwick and likes that sharp trk: eff 10f, stays 12f:
acts on any grd: genuine filly who carries weight well.   41
778 AUCHINLEA [7] 4-8-13 W R Swinburn 3/1 FAV: 000-300: Well bckd, ev ch: twice below
form 629.   29
*860 DON RUNI [6] 4-7-7(BL)(4ex)(1oh) T Williams 4/1: 0000210: Well bckd, too soon
after 860?   05
686 KUWAIT MOON [9] 4-8-8 Pat Eddery 10/1: 202-000: Prom over 1m: see 532 (sharper trk) 00
617 High Debate [5] 10-0   778 Cold Line [2] 8-8   584 Vickstown [1] 8-0
10 ran   ½,2,½,8,2   (Al Dabboos)   G Huffer Newmarket

965 SWANNINGTON CLAIMING STAKES 2YO   £2029   6f   Firm -9 -12 SLow

717 PANACHE [16] (P Haslam) 2-8-9 T Williams 9/1: 0031: 2 ch c On Your Mark - Free
Course (Sandford Lad) Improving colt: made almost all, comfortably, in a 2yo claimer at
Leicester June 9: cost 10,500 gns: stays 6f really well: acts on fast grd and a gall trk. 36
405 PACIFIC BASIN [17] (W O'gorman) 2-9-7 T Ives 16/1: 02: Al prom: gd effort under 9-7
from this 22,000 gns purchase: on the upgrade and shd find a race: stays 6f and acts on fast 43
728 MORNING FLOWER [13] (R Williams) 2-8-13 R Cochrane 8/1: 03: Lightly bckd: al prom
and is making improvement: eff 6f on firm grd and a gall trk.   33
785 INGLISTON [2] (M H Easterby) 2-8-11 B Rouse 10/1: 0334: Sn prom: remains in gd
form: stays 6f: acts on any ground.   29
*831 JOSIE SMITH [12] 2-8-3 W Carson 7/2 FAV: 010: Ev ch: btr 831 (seller).   21
834 HIGHLAND LODGE [15] 2-9-7 T Quinn 14/1: 000: Ev ch: stays 6f: see 622.   34
741 RABENHAM [5] 2-9-7 P Waldron 9/1: 0040: Early speed: btr 741.   00
728 GREAT MEMORY [10] 2-9-1 B Crossley 6/1: 000: Mkt drifter and no show: btr 728 (5f) 00
864 DOCKIN HILL [14] 2-8-13 Pat Eddery 6/1: 030: Dwelt start: btr 864 (5f yldg).   00
717 Penny Lover [8] 8-11   -- Bills Henry [7] 8-11   834 Skraggs Plus Two [9] 8-9
-- Bumptious Boy [1] 9-7   332 Mccallun [4] 9-2   -- Witham Lad [6] 8-11
-- Avenmore Star [11] 8-9(5ow)   685 Maestroman [18] 8-9(bl)
717 Musical Chorus [3] 8-8(BL)
18 ran   1½,½,½,hd,1½   (T C Ellis)   P Haslam Newmarket

966 OLD DALBY E.B.F. STAKES 3YO FILLIES   £3111   7f   Firm -9 +32 Fast

359 FLOWER BOWL [5] (J Dunlop) 3-8-7 W Carson 9/4 FAV: 22-21: 3 b f Homing - Anzeige
(Soderini) Useful filly: heavily bckd and led inside final 1f, ridden out when breaking the
course record in a 3yo fillies event at Leicester June 9: 2nd on her 3 prev outings and
this was a deserved win: eff at 7f/1m, may stay further: acts on firm and yldg/soft and
a gall trk: should win more races.   58
733 RIYDA [9] (R Johnson Houghton) 3-8-10 W R Swinburn 11/4: -122: Fin really well:
in fine form: see 733, 423.   56
776 BUTSOVA [15] (R Armstrong) 3-8-7 M Roberts 7/1: -033: Led 2f out: gd run: see 776,431   52
--   BONNET TOP [10] (O Douieb) 3-8-7 R Machado 12/1: -4: Active in mkt on race course
debut: ran on final 1f, showing promise: American bred half sister to smart 2yo filly
All For London: eff 7f on fast grd and should have no trouble finding a maiden.   48
689 NICKLE A KISS [3] 3-8-10 R Guest 9/1: 4-100: Led 3 out: in gd form: see 422.   47
--   ALCHAASIBIYEH [1] 3-8-7 A Murray 11/2: 33-0: Led 4f, fdd on seasonal debut: first
time out in '85 fin 3rd to Maysoon and Cocotte in val fillies mdn at Ascot: very well bred
filly: eff 6f, prob stays 7f: acts on gd and firm grd and should find a race.   38
--   URUGUAY [12] 3-8-7 R Cochrane 25/1: -0: Friendless in mkt: fin 7th: shd do btr next time 37
863 Fancy Pan [4] 8-7   732 Springwell [6] 8-7   -- Flash Donna [13] 8-7
480 Cracon Girl [8] 8-7   637 Centralspires Best [14] 8-7
--   Curiga [11] 8-7   764 Chardonnay [17] 8-7   732 Rodistyle [18] 8-7
--   Town Fair [7] 8-7   -- Miss Vaigly Blue [2] 8-7(bl)
17 ran   2½,nk,1½,1½,2½,nk   (J A Haverhals)   J Dunlop Arundel, Sussex

967 RAGDALE HANDICAP STAKES (0-35)   £2189   1m 2f   Firm -9 -16 Slow   [35]

609 WELL COVERED [2] (R Hollinshead) 5-9-7 S Perks 15/2: 00-0001: 5 b g Thatch -
Tirana (Ragusa) Ran on well to lead inside final 1f in a h'cap at Leicester June 9: in
'85 won a stks event at Nottingham: in '83 won at Newbury: eff over 1m, stays 10f really
well: best on fast grd and a gall track.   36
199 HARBOUR BAZAAR [10] (M Chapman) 6-7-7(viis) L Riggio(6) 7/1: 000-042: Led 4f out:
not btn far and is in gd form: acts on firm and yldg grd: see 199.   05
745 PERSHING [11] (J Leigh) 5-8-10 T Ives 4/1: 00-0203: led 2f out: stays 10f: see 611.   21
*789 LOTUS PRINCESS [8] (K Bridgwater) 5-9-1(5ex) P Darcy 7/2 FAV: 203-014: Ran well
under penalty: see 789.   25
727 BRANKSOME TOWERS [1] 6-7-7(2oh) Kim Tinkler(3) 12/1: 00-0000: Nearest fin: stays 10f.   00
--   CELTIC IMAGE [6] 4-7-9 J Carter(5) 7/1: 00042-0: No threat on seasonal debut:
maiden: on final outing in '85 fin 2nd in a selling h'cap at Nottingham: eff over 10/11f:
acts on gd and firm and on any trk.   00
--   GEM MART [13] 4-8-11 J Reid 6/1: 03020-0: Mkt drifter, fdd on seasonal debut:
trained by B Hills in '85, finishing 2nd in an app event at Leicester: now with C Holmes:
stays 12f: acts on gd and any trk.   00
*524 LILTING LAD [7] 4-8-1 N Carlisle 8/1: 0-00010: Last to fin: much btr 524 (soft).   00
689 Cuddly [9] 8-10   812 Flodabay [4] 7-13(bl)   723 Eastern Player [5] 7-7(1oh)
201 Metelski [3] 8-11
12 ran   1½,hd,½,2½,hd   (K R Tomlinson)   R Hollinshead Upper Longdon, Staffs.

HAMILTON   Tuesday June 10th   Righthanded Undulating Track, Stiff Uphill Finish

Official Going Given as Heavy. All Times Slow Except Race 971. All races started by flag.

968 HAMILTON ADVERTISER AMATS STKS 3YO+   £1387   1m 4f   Heavy Slow

823 CAROUSEL ROCKET [1] (J S Wilson) 3-10-5 Jennie Goulding 4/1: -310421: 3 ch c Whistling
Deer - Fairy Tree (Varano) Led below dist and forged clear to win an amateur riders stakes
at Hamilton June 10: earlier won a 3yo maiden at Ayr and has been placed in most starts this
term: eff over 11/12f: well suited by plenty of give in the grd tho' does act on firm:
suited by a stiff/galloping track.   32
--   FIEFDOM [6] (W Storey) 6-11-5 Fiona Storey(5) 12/1: 40400-2: Recent winner over
hurdles: stayed on late, tho' no chance with winner: quite consistent on Flat last season,
winning successive races at Folkestone and Lingfield: eff over 7/8f, stays 12f well: acts
on any going and on any track: a good mount for an apprentice.   15
772 EXCAVATOR LADY [7] (R Whitaker) 7-11-2(vis) Sandy Brook(5) 20/1: 03-0043: Ran on same
pace: see 629.   05
--   SOPHISTICATION [3] (G Moore) 6-10-11 Mr C Evans(5) 66/1: -4: Rank outsider on race
course debut: no extra straight: bred to be suited by middle dist: acts on heavy.   00
933 BUSTOFF [2] 6-11-0 Mr C Platts 14/1: -0-2300: Well placed over 1m: see 933 & 44.   00
9   COUNT COLOURS [5] 4-11-5 Mr E Mcmahon 11/2: 0204-00: Well btn after long abs: see9.   00
943 INFANTRY OFFICER [4] 4-11-5 Mr T Easterby 10/11 FAV: 104/200: Quick reappearance
and again was disappointing: much btr over 9f in 651 (yldg).   00
743 Pontyates [8] 11-0   -- Elgendon [9] 11-0
9 ran   15,7,1½,7,12   (A Saccomando)   J S Wilson Ayr, Ayrshire.

969 MECCA BOOKMAKERS MAIDEN STAKES 3YO   £1982   1m 3f   Heavy Slow

699 PAST GLORIES [6] (C Elsey) 3-9-0 C Dwyer 4/1: 200-031: 3 b c Hitite Glory - Snow
Tribe (Great Nephew) Was never hdd when a comfortable winner of a 3yo mdn at Hamilton June
10: lightly raced last season, when shthdd by Sit This One Out in a York maiden: half
brother to sev middle dist winners: eff over 10/11f and shd stay further: acts on firm and
heavy ground and on a galloping track.   **44**
-- BANASIYA [9] (M Stoute) 3-8-11 M Birch 9/4 FAV: 03-2: Uneasy fav on reappearance:
no chance with winner tho' ran a fair race: lightly raced last season when 3rd to
Chernicherva at Haydock on final start: half sister to middle dist winners Badayoun and
Burannpour: stays 11f: shd improve on btr ground next time: suited by galloping track.   **32**
631 HIDDEN MOVE [3] (W Pearce) 3-9-0 N Connorton 16/1: 00-0003: No extra dist, tho'
improved of late: brother to a winning sprinter tho' btr suited by middle dist himself:
acts on fast and heavy ground.   **34**
868 DEAFENING [7] (P Kelleway) 3-9-0 Gay Kelleway(5) 11/4: 0-0034: Late prog: best 868(9f) **32**
822 KAMPHALL [2] 3-8-11 S Keightley 10/1: 000-40: Btr here in 822 (1m).   **17**
822 JELLY JILL [10] 3-8-11 K Darley 25/1: -000: Distant 6th: no form to date: half
sister to middle dist winner Hazel Bank.   **02**
-- KASU [1] 3-8-11 J Lowe 6/1: -0: Lost place after 1m, fin 8th: half sister to sev
winners including fair stayer Wesley: shd do btr on a faster surface.   **00**
702 Manvil [5] 9-0   **790** Jessie Timmins [4] 8-11
868 Copleys Walk [8] 8-11   **--** Northern Velvet [11] 8-11
11 ran   8,½,1½,12,15   (N Hetherton)   C Elsey Malton, Yorks

970 TENNANTS HANDICAP 3YO+ 0-35   £2784   1m   Heavy Slow   [33]

690 BILLYS DANCER [4] (D Dale) 3-8-6 D Mckeown 7/1: 40-1301: 3 ch c Piaffer - Hay-Hay
(Hook Money) Led after ½ way and stayed on strongly to win a h'cap at Hamilton June 10:
first time out won a selling h'cap at Pontefract: half brother to a couple of winners: best
form around 1m: acts on any going and on any track.   **32**
745 STARS DELIGHT [6] (W Storey) 4-7-12 J Quinn(5) 9/2 FAV: 30-2342: Kept on well.   **04**
745 NIGHT WARRIOR [5] (A Robson) 4-9-4 J Bleasdale 8/1: 0040303: Late prog: see 238.   **23**
866 LITTLE NEWINGTON [11] (N Bycroft) 5-8-6(bl)(5ex) M Richardson(7) 11/2: 0012124: Best in 820.10
789 BOY SANDFORD [3] 7-7-13 N Carlisle 11/2: 220-030: Btr over 9f here in 789.   **02**
815 IDLE TIMES [7] 4-9-7 J Lowe 8/1: 0-11300: Early leader: won here in 110 (6f):see 240 **19**
*866 HENRYS PLACE [1] 4-8-10(5ex) D Nicholls 11/2: 0200010: Much btr over 6f in 866(yldg)   **00**
*630 AVRAEAS [12] 7-8-4 N Connorton 10/1: 04-0010: Fin 8th: much btr on gd/frm in 630.   **00**
789 CBM GIRL [8] 5-9-1 M Birch 6/1: 00-3200: Prom over ½ way: btr on gd in 727(7f).   **00**
9 ran   4,½,1,nk,4   (F J Phoenix)   D Dale Newmarket

971 LANGS SUPREME HANDICAP 3YO+ 0-35   £2561   5f   Heavy +12 Fast   [28]

825 CULMINATE [7] (P Monteith) 5-7-12 G King(7) 14/1: 00/0031: 5 br g African Sky -
Metrovision (Golden Vision) Quickly into his stride and made most for a decisive win in
quite fast run h'cap at Hamilton June 10: first success: eff over 5f with forcing tactics:
acts on fast and heavy ground and on any track.   **10**
+890 LULLABY BLUES [4] (M H Easterby) 3-9-6(7ex) M Birch 7/2 Co FAV: -001212: In gd form.   26
820 APHRODISIAC [9] (R Morris) 5-8-11(bl) J Quinn(5) 14/1: 0-00003: Btr effort:see 626.   **05**
830 COPLACE [10] (P Monteith) 4-8-0 S P Griffiths(5) 33/1: -000/04: Maiden sprint
h'capper who has been lightly raced: prob needs further than this minimum trip.   **00**
825 TRADESMAN [8] 6-7-13(bl)(1ow) K Darley 12/1: -000000: Front rank over ½ way:
no form this term: see 490.   **00**
890 GOLD DUCHESS [1] 4-8-13(bl) M Hindley(3) 7/2 Co FAV: 3100240: Much btr on yldg 412.   **00**
255 SONNENELLE [6] 3-8-10(vis) D Nicholls 5/1: 22-1200: Fin 7th: after abs: much btr 147 **00**
742 LADY CARA [2] 6-9-4(vis) Gay Kelleway(5) 7/2 Co FAV: 0014-00: Early last season
won at Newcastle, later visored when successful at Hamilton: eff over 5f and is at her
best on testing ground.   **00**
626 Blochairn Skolar [5] 8-0(bl)   **489** Grand Queen [11] 8-0
10 ran   6,1½,6,shthd   (P Monteith)   P Monteith Rosewall, Midlothian

972 MACTAGGART AND MICKEL HANDICAP 3YO 0-35   £2662   6f   Heavy Slow   [40]

914 HUDSONS MEWS [2] (M W Easterby) 3-9-0 K Hodgson 7/4 FAV: 0-31401: 3 b g Young
Generation - Cuba Libre (Rum) Nicely bckd when an easy winner of a 3yo h'cap at Hamilton
June 10: led before that and sn clear: earlier won a similar race at Ripon after proving
an expensive failure at Redcar first time out: eff over 6f, stays 1m well: acts on any going
and is suited by a stiff/galloping track.   **32**
871 RICH BITCH [7] (D Chapman) 3-7-7(7oh) S P Griffiths(4) 25/1: -000002: Stayed on
well under her light weight: maiden: stays 6f well: well suited by plenty of give.   **00**
787 GARDAS GOLD [8] (M Brittain) 3-8-6 K Darley 7/1: 033-033: Much btr this C/D in 787   **08**
768 DANCING TOM [4] (T Fairhurst) 3-9-5(bl) C Coates(5) 6/1: 4000004: Front rank most:
acts on heavy: see 81.   **12**
825 MAYBE JAYNE [3] 3-7-9 J Lowe 14/1: 0-4400: Led 4f, eased: best 377 (5f yldg).   **00**

315

768 MUSIC TEACHER [1] 3-7-10(bl) J Quinn(5) 13/2: 0102000: Much btr here in 489 (5f).   00
657 KENOOZ [5] 3-9-7 W Hayes(7) 2/1: 0040-20: Fin last: disapp after promising run 657.   00
874 Jenifer Browning [6] 8-3
8 ran   5,1,4,4,2½   (Hippodromo Racing)   M W Easterby Sheriff Hutton, Yorks

973 STAKIS MAIDEN STAKES 2YO   £1402   6f   **Heavy Slow**

870 HUNTERS LEAP [1] (G Moore) 2-9-0 J Lowe 13/2: 00201: 2 b c Kala Shikari - Deer
Leap (Deep Diver) led/dsptd lead thro'out, staying on gamely to win a 2yo mdn at Hamilton
June 10: cost 5,200 gns as yearling: eff over 5/6f: seems best on gd or softer ground:
acts on any track.   42
781 SILVER HAZE [2] (S Hall) 2-9-0 K Darley 11/10 FAV: 22: Led below dist, no extra
cl home: fair effort tho' btr on fast ground in 781.   40
488 U BIX COPY [4] (J S Wilson) 2-9-0 D Nicholls 3/1: 0323: Led briefly dist: not btn
far: continues to improve and shd find a small race: see 488.   40
685 DANUM DANCER [5] (M W Easterby) 2-9-0 K Hodgson 9/2: 004: Front rank till dist:see 685 34
627 PREMIER VIDEO [6] 2-8-11 M Fry 6/1: 30: Ev ch, eased cl home: shd do btr next time
on faster ground: see 627.   23
5 ran   1,shthd,3,4   (John Lishman)   G Moore Middleham, Yorks

Official Going Given as Good/Firm

974 E.B.F. JOHN HOLDRICH MAIDEN STAKES 2YO   £1046   5f   **Firm 15 -48 Slow**

685 BORN TO RACE [3] (L Piggott) 2-9-0 T Ives 15/2: 01: 2 ch c Dr Blum - Babes Sis
(Raise A Native) Impr colt: led over 1f out, ridden out in a slow run 2yo mdn at Yarmouth
June 10: eff at 5f, shd be suited by further: acts on gd and firm grd and shd rate more highly.   44
404 LAURIES WARRIOR [4] (R Boss) 2-9-0 E Guest(3) 33/1: 402: Ran on well final 1f
and will be suited by 6f: acts on gd and firm grd and a gall trk: shd find a small event   39
-- MISK [5] (H Cecil) 2-9-0 S Cauthen 1/4 FAV: 2: Long odds-on: led ½ way: well regarded
colt: should do much better than this.   39
728 BADOGLIO [2] (L Piggott) 2-9-0 B Crossley 16/1: 04: Sn prom: fdd: cost 19,000 gns
and should do better.   16
-- SUPREME NEPHEW [1] 2-9-0 P Robinson 10/1: 0: Led to ½ way on race course debut:
cost 30,000 gns and is a half brother to 3 winners, including the useful 2yo Barrack Street:
will improve.   12
5 ran   1½,ddht,10,1½   (K H Fischer)   L Piggott Newmarket

975 TOLHOUSE SELLING H'CAP 3YO+ (0-25)   £738   1m   **Firm 15 -48 Slow**   [13]

630 MARTON BOY [5] (S Wiles) 8-8-12 T Ives 12/1: 0030-01: 8 br g Tycoon II - Marton
Lady (March Past) Al prom and led under press on line in a slow run selling h'cap at Yarmouth
June 10: last won in '80: eff at 1m: acts on firm and yldg ground.   06
838 FLEUR DE THISTLE [1] (A Davison) 3-8-6 S Cauthen 3/1: 0-00332: Made almost all and
is in good form: deserves a similar event: eff 1m/10f on gd and firm ground: see 749.   13
-- BALKAN [2] (J Harris) 6-9-1 A Bond 8/1: 00010-3: Sn prom on seasonal debut: fair
effort: in '85 won this same race: eff 1m on firm and yldg ground.   07
343 UNIT TENT [6] (B Sanders) 8-9-0(bl) G Sexton 5/1: 14-0404: Ev ch over 1f out:
abs: see 201.   04
91 DALLAS SMITH [7] 5-9-4 J Williams 6/1: 0000-00: Ev ch: has been hurdling: in '85
won sellers at Brighton and Salisbury (subs disq): eff 7f/1m: acts on firm & yldg and any trk.   04
499 YOUNG BORIS [4] 4-9-10 R Cochrane 2/1 FAV: -00-000: Well bckd: no real threat:
dropped in class here: little form previously from this lightly raced gelding:acts on firm.   09
845 Letoile Du Palais [3] 8-7
7 ran   shthd,½,½,2,nk   (Mrs E K Wiles)   S Wiles Flockton, Yorks

976 CHARTER HANDICAP (0-50) 4YO+   £496   1m 2f   **Firm 15 +13 Fast**   [46]

°745 ATOKA [2] (Lord J Fitzgerald) 4-8-12(5ex) R Hills 11/4 Jt.FAV: -00011: 4 b f Kaiseradier
- Ambivalenz (Orsini) In fine form, led inside final 1f, comfortably, in quite fast run
h'cap at Yarmouth June 10: last time out won a similar event at Redcar: ex German filly
who is very eff over 9/10f: acts on fast ground and a galloping track.   40
-- RUSSIAN NOBLE [1] (M Stoute) 5-9-10 W R Swinburn 11/4 Jt.FAV: 03402-2: Not the
best of runs: ran on well final 1f: good seasonal debut: lightly raced in '85, running
consistently, but failed to win: in '84 won over 12f at Newcastle: eff 10f, stays 12f well:
acts on firm and yldg ground.   49
812 SAMHAAN [10] (B Hanbury) 4-8-3(bl)(5ex) A Geran(7) 8/1: 0-24103: Nearest fin:
gd effort: see 689.   24
652 THE HOWARD [8] (I Matthews) 4-8-10 S Cauthen 6/1: 01-0004: Prom, ev ch:eff over 1m/10f. 30
-- SAMS WOOD [9] 5-9-3 R Cochrane 11/1: 00000-0: Led 4f out: not btn far on seasonal
debut: in '85 was trained by T Fairhurst to win h'caps at Nottingham and Pontefract:
now with M Tompkins: in '84 won at Yarmouth and Pontefract: eff 1m, stays 10f well: acts
on firm and yielding ground and   is well h'capped on his best form.   36

706 ROMAN BEACH [7] 6-9-6 M Wigham 11/1: 00-0000: Al there: see 680.   38
750 BEL OSCAR [11] 4-9-3 G Duffield 9/1: 01-000: Mkt drifter: fdd: in '85 was lightly
raced, winning a mdn at Brighton: eff at 1m, stays 10f: acts on gd and firm ground.   00
--   Timber Merchant [5] 8-8   618 Levigatus [4] 7-10
709 Heathgriff [6] 7-7(1oh)   --   Breckland Lady [12] 8-0(1ow)
594 Paddystown [3] 8-2(1ow)
12 ran   ¾,1½,½,nk,nk,   (Richard Kaselowsky)   Lord J Fitzgerald Newmarket

977 GREYHOUND HANDICAP STAKES 3YO+ (0-35)   £2313   5f   Firm 15 -13 Slow   [35]

784 SILENT MAJORITY [18] (W O'gorman) 3-8-4 T Ives 7/1: 44-0301: 3 b g General Assembly
- Vexed Voter (Pontifex) Al front rank and led final 1f, ridden out in a h'cap at Yarmouth
June 10: first success: equally eff over 5/6f: acts on soft, likes fast ground.   20
64   THE MECHANIC [5] (J Sutcliffe) 3-7-13 R Hills 10/1: 0000-02: Lightly bckd and showed
improved form: unplaced in all outings as a 2yo: eff 5f on fast ground.   10
*628 SIMLA RIDGE [11] (A Hide) 4-10-0 P Robinson 5/1: -0013: Al up there: in gd form.   34
877 MUSIC MACHINE [12] (P Haslam) 5-9-4 T Williams 15/2: 0-04404: Made most, kept on:
gd run: see 272.   31
428 DAVILL [7] 4-9-10 W R Swinburn 5/1: 212-000: Al up there: running into form:see 76   25
742 SHOW HOME [10] 4-10-0 R Carter(5) 10/1: -233-00: Prom, ev ch: see 742.   27
*760 LALESTON [15] 3-9-3(7ex) W Litwin(7) 9/2 FAV: 400-210: Never showed: much btr 760.   00
520 PINETUM [14] 4-8-10 S Cauthen 10/1: -01-000: Made no show, see 520.   00
--   Godstruth [17] 8-13(bl)   910 Sanditton Palace [2] 8-4
842 Hilmay [13] 8-1(bl)   30   St Terramar [3] 7-7(bl)
877 Princess Wendy [16] 9-4   784 First Experience [1] 8-8
784 Mr Panache [9] 8-7   --   Shahreen [8] 7-7   760 Alice Hill [4] 8-4(BL) U
17 ran   1½,1½,½,1,½   (Bertram R Firestone)   W O'gorman Newmarket

978 BLACKFRIARS MAIDEN STAKES 3YO   £1242   1m 6f Firm 15 +14 Fast

--   RHYTHMIC BLUES [5] (H Cecil) 3-9-0 S Cauthen 6/1: -1: 3 ch c Cut Above - Signature
Tune (Crepello) Promising colt: first time out, mkt drifter, but led over 2f out, running
on well to win a fast run 3yo mdn at Yarmouth June 10: half brother to 2 winners, including
the smart chaser Berlin: stays 14f really well: acts on fast ground and shd win more races.   57
839 NORTHERN AMETHYST [8] (G Huffer) 3-9-0 W R Swinburn 11/10 FAV: 022-322: Heavily
bckd: ev ch final 2f and again had to settle for 2nd best: 4l clear 3rd and is certain to
win soon: stays 14f: see 839, 625.   55
315 CHALICE OF SILVER [6] (M Jarvis) 3-8-11 T Ives 15/2: 30-43: Led 1m: another gd
effort: stays 14f: should find a race: see 315.   46
409 FRENCH FLUTTER [1] (R Sheather) 3-9-0 R Cochrane 16/1: 0020-04: Led 6f out: stays
14f: acts on gd and firm ground and should find a race.   48
--   BEDHEAD [4] 3-9-0 M Roberts 40/1: 0-0: Never nearer on seasonal debut: improvement
likely: unplaced on sole outing as 2yo: stoutly bred colt who is a half brother to 13f
winner Major Setback: acts on fast ground and shd find a staying maiden.   43
714 DUNSTON [11] 3-9-0 G French 7/1: 0-0030: No real threat: stays 14f: see 714.   37
714 HANKLEY DOWN [10] 3-9-0 A Mackay 7/1: -00: Wknd straight: btr 714 (12f).   00
607 CUILLIN SOUND [12] 3-9-0 P Robinson 5/2: 0-20: Mkt drifter: much btr 607(12f)   00
738 Diva Encore [9] 8-11   --   Biafran Neville [3] 9-0
767 Miss Betel [2] 8-11   744 Bitofagirl [7] 8-11
12 ran   1,4,1,4,5   (C d'Alessio)   H Cecil Newmarket

979 HOPTON MEMORIAL STAKES 2YO   £964   6f   Firm 15 -13 Slow

--   MIDYAN [2] (H Cecil) 2-9-0 S Cauthen 2/5 FAV: 1: 2 b c Miswaki - Country Dream
(Ribot) Very promising colt: led over 1f out, readily drawing clear in a 2yo mdn at Yarmouth
June 10: eff at 6f, shd have no trouble at staying further: half brother to useful middle
distance winner Harry Hastings: acts on fast grd: shd rate more highly and win more races.   60
--   BAG ORHYTHM [1] (J Hindley) 2-9-0 M Hills 12/1: 2: Mkt drifter: al prom: gd effort:
half brother to useful miler Tea House: cost 60,000 gns and shd stay further than 6f:
acts on firm ground and will have no trouble finding a maiden.   48
777 KING BALLADEER [4] (G Pritchard Gordon) 2-9-0 G Duffield 16/1: 03: Made much:
improving: cost 28,000 gns: eff 6f on fast ground and should find a small race.   42
--   LORD COLLINS [7] (M Stoute) 2-9-0 W R Swinburn 7/2: 4: Mkt drifter: sn prom:
should improve: cost 84,000 gns and shd stay further than 6f: acts on fast ground.   33
--   BILL LAVENDER [6] 2-9-0 T Ives 16/1: 0: Showed gd speed on race course debut:
half brother to useful 2yo Misty For Me: cost 9,000 gns and shd prove eff over 5/6f:
acts on fast ground.   32
--   MOULAS [5] 2-9-0 M Roberts 16/1: 0: Speed 4f: will do btr than this.   32
--   Shaine [10] 9-0   --   Fairtown [3] 9-0   --   Oriental Dream [8] 9-0
--   Trompe Doeil [9] 8-11
10 ran   3,2,3,½,hd   (Prince A A Faisal)   H Cecil Newmarket

Official Going Given as Good/Firm

980 LEVIN DOWN 3YO MAIDEN STAKES   £2761   1m 2f   Good 72 +04 Fast

-- **ON TENTERHOOKS** [5] (J Tree) 3-9-0 Pat Eddery 6/5 fav: 43-1: 3 ch c Nodouble - Allegheny (Charlottesville) Uneasy fav on seasonal debut but responded well to press to lead cl home in a 3yo mdn at Goodwood June 10: fair 3rd to the smart Allez Milord on final of only 2 outings in '85: eff 10f, looks sure to be suited by middle dist: half brother to sev winners: acts on firm and gd ground: should come on for this race.   **41**

357 CANADIAN STAR [19] (M Jarvis) 3-9-0 T Lucas 10/1: 0-02: Dsptd lead thro'out: made no show only outing in '85, evidently an improving type: from a gd winning family which includes the successful hurdlers Star Burst and Copseand Robbers and this season's winning 2yo Gulf King: stays 10f well and acts on gd grd: sure to find a maiden.   **40**

338 AIRCRAFTIE [13] (B Hills) 3-8-11 B Thomson 20/1: -03: Showed greatly impr form, chall final 1f, not btn far: unraced in '85: well suited by 10f and gd grd: likely to improve further and win a maiden.   **36**

832 EBOLITO [16] (W Hern) 3-9-0(BL) W Carson 20/1: -004: Made much, fin cl 4th: improved effort from this son of the smart staying filly Princess Eboli: who won both the Cheshire and Lancashire Oaks: sure to stay beyond 10f and should find a maiden.   **38**

739 GODS PATH [3] 3-9-0 A Mcglone 50/1: 000-000: Kept on well in a cl fin, showing considerably improved form: well suited by 10f, shd stay 12f: see 512.   **36**

751 MISS SHIRLEY [10] 3-8-11 J Reid 13/2: 0-30: Prom, ev ch: see 751.   **32**

-720 ENSIGNE [15] 3-9-0 R Curant 4/1: -20: Ev ch, wknd: much btr 720.   **00**

-- Rattle Along [8] 8-11	-- Capulet [9] 9-0	-- Shamiyda [12] 8-11
739 Risk Another [2] 9-0	-- Home Fleet [4] 8-11	739 Full Speed Ahead [1] 9-0
739 Lucky Lad [11] 9-0	454 Noras Boy [14] 9-0	-- Out Yonder [17] 9-0
765 Ashshafak [7] 8-11	422 Pladda Princess [18] 8-11	
-- Richmond Street [6] 9-0		

19 ran   nk,½,½,1,hd   (K Abdulla)   J Tree Beckhampton, Wilts

981 BENGES SELLING STAKES 2YO   £806   5f   Good 72 -14 Slow

-- **VIVA RONDA** [5] (Pat Mitchell) 2-8-8 J Reid 9/4 jt fav: 1: 2 b f Kampala - Mary Mullen (Lorenzaccio) Made a winning debut (well bckd), leading dist and comfortably drew well clear in a 2yo seller at Goodwood June 10 (bought in 3,600 gns): half sister to the winning juv Mannerism and Lucayan Lady: eff ovr 5f, sure to stay 6f and prob further: acts on good ground.   **28**

905 PINK PUMPKIN [4] (J Douglas Home) 2-8-8 J Matthias 5/2: 002: Chall 2f out, outpaced on this first venture into selling company: sprint bred.   **13**

848 SURVIVAL KIT [6] (C James) 2-8-8 B Rouse 9/4 jt fav: 003: Wk in mkt, ev ch.   **08**

681 JANS DECISION [7] (L Holt) 2-8-11 P Waldron 8/1: 0004: Took a strong hold and made much: see 421.   **00**

-- **DONNELLYS HOLLOW** [2] 2-8-11 D Mckay 20/1: 0: May improve for the outing: sprint bred.   **00**

-- **BONZO** [3] 2-8-11 M Miller 25/1: 0: Stable companion of winner, al rear: sprint bred.   **00**

6 ran   10,2,7,nk,8   (John Li)   Pat Mitchell Folkington, Sussex

982 WEST DEAN FILLIES STAKES 3YO   £3336   1m   Good 72 +01 Fast

575 SMOOCH [10] (K Brassey) 3-9-0 S Whitworth 6/1: 103-001: 3 b f Young Generation - Buss (Busted) Very useful filly who returned to her best form when comfortably winning a minor race for fillies at Goodwood June 10, leading dist: first time out in '85. won at Salisbury and later fin 3rd in Listed Race at Newbury: suited by 1m and firm or gd ground: seems to act on any track.   **60**

656 GREAT DILEMMA [6] (P Makin) 3-8-11 B Thomson 50/1: -002: Showed remarkably improved form, keeping on under press final 2f: unraced in '85, no form prev 2 runs this season: stays 1m well and acts on gd grd; sure to win a maiden if running up to this form.   **51**

661 LAND OF IVORY [5] (I Balding) 3-9-3 Pat Eddery 4/6 fav: 4-1D433: Led on bit 3f out, found nothing when hdd: seems btr over 10f on softer ground: see 264.   **53**

-- **HANOOF** [3] (M Stoute) 3-8-11 A Kimberley 7/1: -4: Steady late prog and will benefit from this first experience of racing: first foal of Irish Oaks 2nd Little Bonny and cost $2m: should be suited by further than 1m: shd not be hard to place successfully.   **45**

-- **FORMIDABLE DANCER** [8] 3-8-11 W Carson 25/1: 000-0: Fin in style on seasonal debut: showed promise in 3 outings last season notably when a close 6th in a backend Leicester maiden over 7f on firm ground: will benefit from the outing: shd find a race.   **39**

37 SHINING POPPY [4] 3-8-13 T Quinn 6/1: 3244-20: Prom most after abs since 37.   **37**

-- Shining Skin [9] 8-11	806 Emerald Wave [8] 8-11	500 Mistral Magic [1] 8-11		
832 Alceba [2] 8-11				

10 ran   3,2,1,3,2   (A Oppenheimer)   K Brassey Upper Lambourn, Berks

983 CHARLTON HUNT STAKES H'CAP 3YO 0-60   £3642   1m 6f   Good 72 +06 Fast   [63]

*841 **SARFRAZ** [2] (G Harwood) 3-8-2(3ex) A Clark 13/8 fav: 42-011: 3 b c Sassafras - Ziba Blue (John's Joy) Impr stayer: came from behind and cleverly led final 1f in quite a fast run 3yo h'cap at Goodwood June 10: also comfortably won a similar h'cap at Folkestone June 2: placed both outings in '85: acts on firm and yldg: eff 14f, stays 2m well: good sort who is clearly improving at present and should complete the hat-trick.   **48**

*519 ONINSKY [4] (P Cole) 3-8-13 T Quinn 7/2: 410-112: Dsptd lead final 3f: fine effort
and clear of rest: should win again soon: stays 14f: see 519.   56
430 TAP EM TWICE [6] (M Jarvis) 3-7-11 W Carson 9/4: 04-233: Ev ch, looked paceless
and had a clear chance in the form of 430.   35
416 MURFAX [1] (J Glover) 3-7-12 C Rutter[5] 14/1: 04-1404: Mkt drifter, no extra final 1f.   32
597 LONGGHURST [5] 3-7-12 A Mcglone 16/1: 00-1000: Made much: disapp since 75(hvy).   12
510 NORFOLK SONATA [3] 3-9-7 M Miller 14/1: 431-300: Flattered 510? See 191.   35
6 ran   ½,5,4,20,½   (K Abdulla)   G Harwood Pulborough, Sussex

984 ROYAL SUSSEX STKS LIM.H'CAP 3YO+ 0-35   £1973   1m 4f   Good 72 -17 Slow   [6]

*743 TAXIADS [15] (C Nelson) 4-11-2(4ex) Jane Allison[5] 6/1: 200-011: 4 b c Radetzky -
Florabette (Floribunda) Winning 2nd race on the trot, leading final 2f comfortably, in an
amateur riders h'cap at Goodwood June 10: won an amateur riders stks at Redcar May 27:
first success on Flat tho' did win over hurdles in the Winter: half brother to sev winners:
eff 12f, stays 2m: acts on firm and gd ground: goes well for amateur, particularly J Allison   33
735 DOMINATE [8] (P Mitchell) 5-11-6 Mr D Benneyworth[5] 10/1: 002-002: Chall dist,
good effort: see 735.   32
530 ASTICOT [18] (C Horgan) 4-10-7 Debbie Albion[5] 33/1: 0000-03: Al there: last won
in '84 at Beverley over 1m on gd going.   12
1 SOCKS UP [2] (R J Houghton) 9-10-6 Gale Johnson Houghton 12/1: 4003-04: Al prom:
abs since running at Cagnes Mar 2: last won in '84 at Chepstow and Redcar: eff around 10/12f:
acts on any going: now into the veteran stage.   11
*869 THE MISSISSIPPIAN [14] 5-10-8(4ex) Mr B Dowling[5] 100/30 fav: -421D10: Led after
1m, wknd: much btr 869.   08
841 PALACE YARD [7] 4-10-5 Mr R Hutchinson 10/1: 240-400: Ev ch: see 731.   02
709 MARSH HARRIER [5] 5-11-1 Candy Moore 15/2: 011-000: Ev ch, fin 7th: see 709.   00
8 CORAL HARBOUR [12] 4-11-0(BL) Mr S Bullard[5] 10/1: 0300-30: Bl first time, wknd:
abs since much btr in 8 (10f, mdn).   00
9 ARGES [4] 5-11-7 Maxine Juster 7/1: 2422-20: Abs since much btr 9 (10f).   00
-- Height Of Summer [10] 10-5   731 Inchgower [9] 10-6(2ow)
675 Hyokin [16] 10-8(vis)   709 Rosanna Of Tedfold [1] 10-0
-- Paris North [11] 11-4   751 Janaab [3] 10-11   709 Trackers Jewel [13] 10-6
856 Pandi Club [6] 10-2(bl)   943 Tournament Leader [17] 10-0
18 ran   2¼,5,hd,3,2½,hd,ddht   (Silux UK Ltd)   C Nelson Lambourn, Berks

985 EAST DEAN MAIDEN STAKES 2YO   £869   6f   Good 72 -23 Slow

-- DOMINO FIRE [12] (J Dunlop) 2-8-11 W Carson 9/2: 1: 2 ch f Dominion - Enlighten
(Twilight Alley) Promising filly: made an impr winning debut, sprinting clear in final 1f
for a very ready success in a 2yo mdn at Goodwood June 10: half sister to 3 winners including
fair miler Liberty Tree: eff 6f, sure to be suited by 7f+: acts on good ground: one to
keep on the right side and is sure to win more races.   58
-- MAZILIER [14] (G Harwood) 2-9-0 G Starkey 5/4 fav: 2: Chall final 1f, possibly caught
a tartar here and should not be long in gaining compensation: half brother to 3 winners
including smart miler Crofter: sure to stay 7f+: acts on gd ground.   53
-- BAY WINDOW [2] (J Winter) 2-9-0 J Reid 9/1: 3: Chall 1f out: gd debut from this
daughter of useful staying h'capper Broken Record who has already produced smart filly
Old Domesday Book: sure to find a maiden.   44
-- LOVE TRAIN [17] (R Laing) 2-9-0 S Whitworth 9/1: 4: Led/dsptd lead much and was
just in need of the race: dam won 2 out of her 3 races as a juv at around 1m: should be
a different proposition next time.   42
-- BERYLS JOKE [1] 2-9-0 M Malham 25/1: 0: Btr for race, prom most: half brother to
a couple of winners including the successful '85 juv Black Sophie: should improve.   36
-- TROPICAL BOY [5] 2-9-0 B Thomson 33/1: 0: Shd benefit from the outing: very cheaply bght 30
-- AJANAC [13] 2-9-0 Pat Eddery 6/1: 0: Dsptd lead most, wknd into 7th: half brother
to '85 12f 3yo winner Standard Breakfast.   30
-- FOURTH LAD [15] 2-9-0 A Mcglone 12/1: 0: In need of race, early speed,fin 8th:
quite cheaply bought half brother to winning 5f performer Veeya: should improve.   30
-- Peter Moon [6] 9-0   -- Treva [16] 9-0   -- Emmas Whisper [7] 8-11
-- Persian Dynasty [4] 9-0   -- French King [10] 9-0
-- Nawwar [9] 9-0   -- Keel [3] 9-0   -- Party Match [8] 9-0
16 ran   2,3,¾,2,2,hd,shthd   (Mrs P Lewis)   J Dunlop Arundel, Sussex

986 SUSSEX MILITIA STAKES H'CAP 3YO+ 0-50   £2880   5f   Good 72 -06 Slow   [39]

-- WOODFOLD [2] (J Winter) 5-9-9 B Rouse 8/1: 02330-1: 5 br m Saritamer - Beryl's
Jewel (Silicon) Made a successful reappearance, leading final 1f in a h'cap at Goodwood
June 10: quite consistent in '85 winning a h'cap at Sandown: very eff at 5f on firm or
gd ground, prob unsuited by soft.   44
884 FOUNTAIN BELLS [4] (R Hannon) 3-9-4 G Starkey 7/2: 0-20142: Came from behind,
kept on well and is in fine form: see 507.   43
734 BROWN BEAR BOY [3] (R Armstrong) 4-9-4 W Carson 11/8 fav: 00-0233: Well bckd,
led 2f out: see 734.   32
929 COMMANDER MEADEN [1] (D O'donnell) 3-7-7(VIS)(2oh) R Street 16/1: 00-0304: Visored first
time, never closer, btr 929 (6f).   319   06

877 LITTLE STARCHY [9] 8-8-9(bl) S Whitworth 12/1: 000-000: Chall 2f out: last won
in '84 at Epsom: best at 5f on soft ground tho' also acts on good/firm.   07
884 BALIVIEW [6] 3-7-7(3oh) A Proud 50/1: 0-00000: Led 2f: maiden with no worthwhile form.   00
182 VELOCIDAD [7] 6-8-6 C Rutter[5] 8/1: 010-300: Long abs: early speed: best56 (hvy).   00
--   METEOR MISS [5] 3-8-5 Pat Eddery 6/1: 20000-0: Fin last: winner of a maiden at
Warwick early in '85: well btn most outings subsequently: half sister to 3 winners:
very eff at 5f on firm ground, on a sharp track.   00
734 Sharad [8] 7-7(vis)(4oh)
9 ran   1½,¾,5,2½,½   (Mrs J Redmond)   J Winter Newmarket

Official Going Given as Good/Firm

987 FLEGGS SELLING STAKES 2YO   £658   6f   Good 67 +03 Fast

813 DORMESTONE LAD [7] (R Stubbs) 2-8-11(bl) J H Brown(5) 7/2: 0041: 2 ch c Mansingh -
Kareela (Deep Diver) Impr colt: responded to press to lead inside final 1f in a 2yo seller
at Yarmouth June 11: cost 2,300 gns: well suited by 6f: acts on gd and fast ground.   22
681 KIND LADY [5] (J Winter) 2-8-8 T Ives 11/10 FAV: 42: Gambled on: al up there:
shd find a similar event soon: stays 6f: acts on gd ground.   15
711 ROAN REEF [3] (N Macauley) 2-8-11(BL) W Wharton 25/1: 03: Led over 5f: bl first
time today: cost 1,900 gns: eff at 6f on gd ground.   12
831 ARDNACROSS [2] (J Douglas Home) 2-8-8 R Cochrane 9/2: 0024: Never nearer: btr 831.   00
853 BLOW FOR HOME [6] 2-8-11 G Duffield 9/2: 0020: Early speed, btr 853 (5f sharper trk)   00
--   BUDSHEAD [4] 2-8-11 M Rimmer 20/1: 0: Mkt drifter, sn behind: bred to stay much
further than today's trip.   00
543 Sparkling Judy [1] 8-8
7 ran   1,2,4,5,1½   (P G Shorrock)   R Stubbs Middleham, Yorks

988 FRITTON LAKE MAIDEN FILLIES STAKES 2YO   £1180   5f   Good 67 -07 Slow

482 WABARAH [5] (H T Jones) 2-8-11 A Murray 11/4: 31: 2 b f Shirley Heights - Balista
(Baldric II) Useful filly: ran on to lead inside final 1f in a 2yo fillies mdn at Yarmouth
June 11: cost 160,000 gns as a yearling: eff 5f, sure to be suited by further: half sister
to two 5f winners: acts on gd and yldg ground.   47
848 FLIRTING [7] (R Hannon) 2-8-11 R Cochrane 20/1: 02: Led approaching final 1f:
just btn and is fast improving: should be suited by 6f: acts on gd ground and shd find
a small event.   45
--   TRIKYMIA [4] (H Cecil) 2-8-11 W Ryan 4/6 FAV: 3: Ev ch on race course debut,
sure to improve: very well bred filly, being a half sister to numerous winners, including
Tyrnavos, Tolmi and Tanaos: certain to be suited by further than 5f: shd do much btr next time. 44
--   BE CHEERFUL [2] (J Winter) 2-8-11 T Ives 10/1: 4: Nearest fin: promising debut
from this 9,600 gns purchase: half sister to sev speedy winners, incl Numismatist and
Solimile: should stay 6f: acts on gd ground.   40
--   CRISP HEART [8] 2-8-11 A Mackay 14/1: 0: Mkt drifter on debut: will improve for
the experience: cost 23,000 gns: half sister to the 5f winner Fair Test: shd stay 6f.   38
--   NANCY NONESUCH [1] 2-8-11 G Sexton 33/1: 0: Mkt drifter: never nearer: half sister
to the useful 7f winner October: will improve.   33
746 BAY WONDER [3] 2-8-11 G Duffield 8/1: 00: Gambled on, made much: see 746.   00
181 Kamstar [6] 8-11
8 ran   ½,½,1½,¾,1½   (Hamdan Al-Maktoum)   H T Jones Newmarket

989 RADIO NORFOLK HANDICAP 3YO 0-50   £2488   1m 2f Good 67 -04 Slow   [55]

868 CHINOISERIE [5] (L Cumani) 3-9-5 R Guest 6/4 FAV: 022-021: 3 b c Fluorescent Light
- From the East (Gold and Myrrh) Useful colt: well bckd and led 2f out, comfortably, in a
3yo h'cap at Yarmouth June 11: deserved success: promising 2yo: stays 10f well: acts on
gd/firm and yldg and a gall track: should win more races.   59
730 AL ZUMURRUD [1] (R Armstrong) 3-8-3 G Baxter 11/4: 400-122: Ev ch over 1f out:
in fine form: see 730, 637.   37
883 ICARO [3] (N Callaghan) 3-8-0(BL) G Duffield 15/2: 1-02203: Bl first time: gd eff.   32
--   MISAAFF [2] (H T Jones) 3-9-7 A Murray 14/1: 0213-4: Mkt drifter: made much on
seasonal debut: useful 2yo, winning a maiden at Redcar: eff 7f/1m, possibly stays 10f:
acts on firm and yldg ground.   53
572 RANELAGH [4] 3-7-8 R Morse(4) 7/1: 00-000: Prom, wknd: best 194 (yldg).   12
807 KERRY MAY SING [6] 3-8-10 P Robinson 6/1: 1031-00: Wknd straight: fair 2yo, winning
nursery h'caps at Pontefract and Nottingham: eff 1m, may not stay 10f: acts on gd and firm
ground and on any track.   27
6 ran   1½,¾,hd,8,hd   (Ivan Allan)   L Cumani Newmarket

990 WREN HANDICAP STAKES 0-35   £2005   1m 6f   Good/Firm 24 -10 Slow   [33]

778 OLD MALTON [2] (J Toller) 4-8-6 P Robinson 7/1: -4-0001: 4 ch c Whitstead - Bridestones (Jan Ekels) Mkt drifter, but led dist, driven out in a h'cap at Yarmouth June 11:
lightly raced prev: stays 14f well: acts on fast grd and a gall track.   18
801 SUGAR PALM [6] (R Hannon) 5-8-13(bl) T Ives 7/4 FAV: 0-03042: Well bckd: made
most: just btn: in gd form: see 341.   25
*824 WESSEX [4] (N Tinkler) 4-9-10(bl)(4ex) Kim Tinkler(5) 3/1: 4124313: Led 2f out,
again ran well: see 824.   34
712 LOVE WALKED IN [5] (W Holden) 5-8-10 R Morse(5) 3/1: 0013104: Btr on softer ground. 12
872 TOUCHEZ LE BOIS [1] 5-9-10 R Cochrane 16/1: -00-000: Wknd: see 872 (12f).   11
--   MISS MAGNETISM [7] 4-8-0(2ow) G Duffield 20/1: 00040-0: Fdd 3f out: winner over
hurdles in the Winter: maiden on the level: acts on fast grd and does well on a sharp trk. 00
590 Far To Go [3] 7-11
7 ran   hd,1½,6,12,2   (Alan Gibson)   J Toller Newmarket

991 MERCHANTS HOUSE MAIDEN FILLIES STKS 3YO £964   1m 3f Good/Firm 24 -07 Slow

402 KENANGA [4] (H Cecil) 3-8-11 W Ryan 11/10 FAV: -01: 3 ch f Kris - Catalpa (Reform)
Useful filly: well bckd and led approaching final 1f, comfortably, in a 3yo fillies mdn at
Yarmouth June 11: half sister to Ribblesdale winner Strigida: eff at 11f, will be suited
by 12f: acts on gd ground and on any trk: shd rate more highly and win more races.   53
739 STRIKE HOME [13] (M Stoute) 3-8-11 A Kimberley 10/3: -02: Led 2f out: not btn far
and is fast improving: half sister to numerous winners incl the highclass Ballad Rock:
stays 11f: acts on gd ground and should have no trouble finding a maiden.   50
--   LOUVECIENNES [1] (O Douieb) 3-8-11 R Cochrane 10/1: -3: Mkt drifter: kept on well
showing future promise: half sister to sev winners, including the smart filly Legend Of
France: sure to be suited by 12f: acts on gd ground and will be winning soon.   45
779 GONE OVERBOARD [20] (A Stewart) 3-8-11 M Roberts 20/1: -04: Made much and is on
the upgrade: stays 11f: acts on gd ground.   44
209 STRAW BOATER [7] 3-8-11 R Guest 10/1: -00: Mkt drifter after abs: fdd over 1f out:
may be btr suited by 10f: acts on good/firm ground.   32
661 WARM WELCOME [15] 3-8-11 B Crossley 5/1: 42-00: Fdd over 2f out: see 661.   27
720 Jubilee Jamboree [10] 8-11   765 Sokolova [19] 8-11
765 Keep Hoping [3] 8-11   379 Janie O [17] 8-11   124 My Annadetsky [5] 8-11
209 Highest Note [18] 8-11   862 Dusk Approaches [9] 8-11
770 La Cazadora [14] 8-11   769 Say Something [12] 8-11(BL)
423 Our Noora [6] 8-11   --   Absconding [2] 8-11
17 ran   ¾,2½,½,8,3   (Lord Howard de Walden)   H Cecil Newmarket

992 HEYDON HALL APPRENTICE HCAP STKS 0-35   £1450   7f   Good/Firm 24 +17 Fast   [35]

775 WINTER WORDS [1] (C Lloyd Jones) 7-8-1 Julie Bowker 10/1: 0000-01: 7 b h Wollow -
Prinia (On Your Mark) Led ½ way and ridden clear final 1f in a fast run app h'cap at Yarmouth
June 11: in '84 won at Newcastle: eff 7f, stays 1m: best on fast ground.   18
710 HOPEFUL KATIE [9] (D Leslie) 4-8-6(hd) S Gregory(5) 14/1: -430402: Al prom:
gd effort: see 65.   17
+936 MR JAY ZEE [4] (N Callaghan) 4-8-12(6ex) S Quane 9/4 FAV: 000-013: Dsptd lead:
in good form: see 936.   22
637 TROPICO [10] (P Haslam) 3-7-7 L Riggio 5/1: 02-004: Stayed on final 1f: ran well: see 318. 15
540 EUCHARIS [20] 4-7-10 M Giles 14/1: 000-000: Led stand side: eff 7f on gd/firm grd.   04
812 IDEOLIGIA [3] 4-7-9(BL) S Childs 16/1: 020-000: Never nearer: 2nd in selling h'cap
at Nottingham in '85: eff 6/7f on fast ground.   00
710 HIGHLY PLACED [16] 4-7-8 G King 10/1: 0000-00: Early speed: maiden: stays 7f:
acts on fast ground.   00
710 HOKUSAN [7] 4-8-3(bl) G Mash 8/1: -034000: Made no show: see 620.   00
657 BLACK DIAMOND [17] 3-8-3 S Meacock(5) 3/1: 000-030: Well bckd: prom 4f: btr 657 (hvy) 00
679 Sweet Andy [6] 7-7(3oh)   677 Absolute Master [12] 7-12
578 Elegant Fashion [19] 8-8   578 Singing Boy [5] 9-1
374 John Patrick [2] 10-0   975 Dallas Smith [11] 7-10
338 Naughty Nighty [18] 7-9   727 Clipsall [15] 8-8
977 Mr Panache [8] 8-7   679 Cats Lullaby [14] 8-2(bl)
19 ran   3,nk,hd,1,2   (Mrs E M Fox)   C Lloyd Jones Abergele, Clwyd.

Official Going Given as Good/Firm

993 HURN APPRENTICE SELLING H'CAP (0-25)   £1007   1m 2f Firm 18 -27 Slow   [18]

783 FOREVER YOUNG [9] (G Oldroyd) 3-7-10 P Burke(7) 25/1: 000-401: 3 br g Swing Easy -
Lizarda (Botticelli) Was a surprise winner, stayed on well to lead cl home in an app selling
h'cap at Beverley June 11 (no bid): first success: lightly raced, showing no worthwhile form
last season: stays 10f well: acts on fast and yldg ground and on a stiff track.   10

522 CADENETTE [6] (M Camacho) 4-8-13 E Guest 12/1: 30-0042: Just failed to make all:
good effort and seems well suited by forcing tactics: acts on fast ground: see 522.   10

163 ROYAL EXPORT [16] (W Watts) 6-8-9 A Shoults 16/1: 0000-03: Never nearer after abs:
stays 10f well: acts on any trk: see 163.   04

788 MURILLO [12] (F Carr) 10-9-5(bl) J Carr 20/1: -003204: Cl.up, never nearer: see 257   11

673 BUNDLING BED [14] 4-8-11 S Hustler(7) 7/1: 000-020: Late prog: see 673.   01

875 PENNILESS DANCER [2] 7-8-10 M Richardson 25/1: 0000-00: Never nearer: mdn who
has yet to show any worthwhile form: stays 10f: seems suited by fast ground.   00

788 TARLETON [17] 9-8-11 J Quinn 5/1 FAV: 0300-20: Never nearer 8th: stays 10f: see 788   00

783 VERBADING [13] 4-9-0(bl) J G Murray(7) 13/2: 00-0230: Btr over 12f in 783: see 524.   00

620 FOXCROFT [19] 3-8-11(vis) J Scally 11/2: 022-000: Well placed till run-in: see 356.   00

783 MUSICAL WILL [11] 4-9-4 C Coates 13/2: 10-0040: Btr over 12f in 783 (sharp trk).   00

609 Dubavarna [5] 9-7   889 Record Haulier [18] 8-11
872 Crowfoots Couture [1] 8-8   -- Earls Court [15] 9-3
-- Wyoming [3] 8-10   -- Monsanto Lad [8] 8-10 718 Little Dimple [7] 9-0
889 Rapid Star [10] 7-9   863 Johnny Frenchman [4] 8-11
19 ran   1½,¾,¾,2,½,5,3,shthd   (B Thomson)   G Oldroyd Malton, Yorks

994 BISHOP BURTON E.B.F. STAKES   £3168   5f   Firm 18 +14 Fast

-- IN FACT [3] (J Tree) 3-8-5 R Cochrane 1/1 FAV: 22-1: 3 b c Known Fact - Abeer
(Dewan) Useful colt: first time out made most when a game winner of a fast run stks race
at Beverley June 11: ran up to Treasure Kay and Dolka in mdns at Newbury and Newmarket
respectively last season: half brother to 12f winner Armourer: very eff over 5/6f:
acts on fast ground and on a stiff/gall track.   56

-- JOHN RUSSELL [1] (M Ryan) 3-8-5 P Robinson 8/1: -2: Al prom, just held in a tight
finish: very promising debut from this speedily bred gelding: will stay another furlong:
acts on firm ground and on a stiff track: looks sure to go one better soon.   55

550 TRUE NORA [4] (C Nelson) 3-8-8 J Reid 5/2: 110-003: Dsptd lead till dist: see 443.   50

-836 CRETE CARGO [7] (M Francis) 3-8-12 Paul Eddery 5/1: 0000024: Ran on too late: see 836   52

891 PACKAGE PERFECTION [5] 3-8-2 J Callaghan(7) 33/1: 20-0040: Speed over ¼ way: tough
task: see 891.   27

-- BURNING ARROW [6] 4-9-0 P D'arcy 100/1: -00/0: Sn outpaced: outsider and sure to
have needed this race after a lengthy abs: only ran twice in '84, showing a little promise:
sprint bred colt who is closely related to numerous winners, incl the very speedy Runnett:
acts on fast ground.   18

842 NORTHERN IMPULSE [2] 3-8-5(BL) G Duffield 25/1: -0300: Cl.up to ¼ way: clearly
flattered in 567 (6f).   00

7 ran   hd,3,1,5,4   (K Abdulla)   J Tree Marlborough, Wilts.

995 HILARY NEEDLER TROPHY 2YO   £4947   5f   Firm 18 -06 Slow

*672 GLOW AGAIN [2] (J Etherington) 2-8-8 M Wood 7/1: 311: 2 br f The Brianstan - Grey
Aglow (Aglojo) Useful filly: led dist, hung right when a comfortable winner of a val 2yo race
at Beverley June 11: last month was an easy winner of a stks race at Pontefract: half sister
to the versatile The Small Miracle: very eff over 5f and will stay further: acts on fast
and yielding ground and on any track.   54

*818 UPPER [7] (E Weymes) 2-8-8 E Guest 7/4: 12: Not much room dist, ran on well and
will improve further with experience: seems to act on any track: see 818.   48

-892 KALAS IMAGE [4] (G Moore) 2-8-4 M Birch 20/1: 0323: Made most: seems well suited by
front running tactics and shd find a small race over an easier trip: acts on firm:see 364   42

737 SAXON STAR [6] (J Winter) 2-8-8 W R Swinburn 6/4 FAV: 1444: Well bckd: denied a
clear run dist, no extra cl home: best 737: see 311.   46

766 AIR OF SPRING [1] 2-8-4 J Reid 20/1: 03020: Al up there: acts on any trk: see 766.   36

913 MINIZEN LASS [5] 2-8-4 K Darley 20/1: 04220: Ran a fair race: see 913.   35

*565 QUITE SO [8] 2-8-8 R Cochrane 7/1: -010: Much btr on similar grd in 565 (easier trk).   00

7 ran   1½, ½,shthd,2,nk   (Mrs G Liversidge)   J Etherington Malton, Yorks

996 WELTON MAIDEN STAKES 3YO   £1160   2m   Firm 18 -49 Slow

769 IN DREAMS [5] (M Prescott) 3-9-0 G Duffield 10/11 FAV: 40-21: 3 b c High Line -
Blissful Evening (Blakeney) Nicely bckd when leading 2f out and staying on well in a 3yo
mdn at Beverley June 11: stoutly bred colt who stays 2m well: acts on fast grd and on any trk.   42

769 GOODTIME HAL [8] (J Hindley) 3-9-0 M Hills 7/2: 0-432: Not clear run below dist,
going on fin and was well suited by this test of stamina: acts on gd and firm: see 430.   37

448 SNOWFIRE CHAP [6] (H Wharton) 3-9-0 G Gosney 33/1: -03: Stayed on well and clearly
suited by a dist of ground: acts on firm and on a stiff trk: lightly raced.   34

613 SIR CHESTER [2] (G Oldroyd) 3-9-0 D Nicholls 14/1: -04: Led early and again early
in straight: half brother to middle dist winner Seaway: stays 2m: acts on firm ground.   26

605 DEMON FATE [7] 3-9-0 K Darley 7/2: 04-000: Not stay this longer trip: see 605.   20
635 TUMBA [4] 3-9-0 T Lucas 16/1: -00: Pulled hard and sn went on: dropped out home turn:
acts on firm.   10
862 MARBLE MOON [1] 3-8-11 S Perks 20/1: -00: Didnot stay this longer trip.   00
7 ran   3,2,8,6,10   (B Haggas)   M Prescott Newmarket

997 RACE-A-ROUND YORKSHIRE H'CAP (0-35) 3YO £1758 1m   Firm 18 -09 Slow   [32]

*874 STANFORD VALE [15] (C Nelson) 3-9-10(6ex) J Reid 7/2 FAV: -022311: 3 b c Stanford -
Shoshoni Girl (Winning Hit) Landed some nice bets when comfortably leading inside dist in
a 3yo h'cap at Beverley June 11: recently won a similar race at Ripon: stays 1m really well:
acts on fast and yldg ground and on any trk: in fine form.   40
880 FIRE ROCKET [1] (P Cole) 3-8-10 T Quinn 4/1: 00-0042: Stayed on well and is in
good form: seems to act on any track: see 880.   20
--   FLYING BIDDY [2] (J Hindley) 3-9-2 M Hills 16/1: 000-3: Led below dist: gd effort on
her reappearance and will come on for this race: highly tried in her 3 starts last season:
stays 1m: acts on firm ground and on a stiff track.   26
*843 BLACK COMEDY [12] (G Lewis) 3-9-11(6ex) P Waldron 8/1: -000014: In good form:see 843   32
857 MONSTROSA [8] 3-8-9 D Nicholls 12/1: 00-0030: Gd eff: stays 1m: see 538.   15
868 COURT RULER [17] 3-8-8 L Charnock 33/1: 000-000: Never nearer: first signs of
form from this brother to winning sprinter Northern Ruler: stays 1m well: acts on firm grd.   14
229 LOST OPPORTUNITY [5] 3-9-2 J Lowe 11/1: 4-200: Ran on too late: best 99.   00
438 SAALIB [7] 3-9-7 P D'arcy 8/1: 40-200: Fin 8th: acts on firm: see 283.   00
857 JOHNSTAN BOY [9] 3-8-9 M Wood 7/1: 0-00000: Fin 9th: stays 1m: acts on fast grd.   00
309 PELLS CLOSE [3] 3-8-11 K Hodgson 10/1: -0000: Mkt drifter and never dangerous:
best with some give over 7f in 16.   00
*684 Hare Hill [14] 8-8(6ex)   863 Hot Lining [16] 9-6
--   Royal Rouser [11] 9-7   774 Count Almaviva [19] 9-4
874 Bradbury Hall [13] 8-10   674 Qurrat Al Ain [18] 9-2
14   Capistrano Climax [4] 8-11   --   Miss Blake [10] 9-2
451 Nippy Chippy [6] 8-13
19 ran   3,shthd,1½,½,hd,shthd,hd,½   (Anglo Enterprises)   C Nelson Upper Lambourn

998 BEVERLEY HANDICAP STAKES (0-35) 3YO   £1455 1m 4f Firm 18 -45 Slow   [35]

883 DISCIPLE [5] (G Lewis) 3-9-3(BL) P Waldron 9/4 FAV: 0000401: 3 b c Hello Georgeous -
Ex Dancer (Executioner) Bl first time: stayed on under press to lead inside dist in a slowly
run 3yo h'cap at Beverley June 11: stays 12f well: acts on firm and good ground and is
suited by a stiff/galloping track: blinkered first time today.   35
867 NOT A PROBLEM [3] (Denys Smith) 3-8-3(bl) T Quinn 4/1: -300432: Led home turn:
outstayed by winner and best over 10f in 702.   16
*823 MIAMI IN SPRING [7] (R Stubbs) 3-9-0 D Nicholls 10/3: 000-113: Clear rem: see 823.   26
635 GREAT TOPIC [2] (G Pritchard Gordon) 3-9-0(BL) G Duffield 7/1: 0-004: Bl first time:
no extra dist: half brother to a couple of 7/8f winners and may do btr when reverting to a
shorter trip: acts on fast ground.   14
823 STANDON MILL [6] 3-8-5 K Darley 10/1: -000400: Twice below form shown in 648 (yldg).   04
908 LADY ST CLAIR [4] 3-9-7(BL) L Charnock 9/1: 04-0040: Led over 1m: best on hvy 132(10f)   14
--   TIBER GATE [1] 3-8-1 P Hill(7) 20/1: 000-0: Lost touch from ½ way: btn in sellers
last season and seems of little account.   00
7 ran   3,½,8,1,6   (Mrs N Lewis)   G Lewis Epsom, Surrey.

NEWBURY   Wednesday June 11th   Lefthand Galloping Track

Official Going Given as Good - Soft

999 WEST ILSLEY FILLIES MAIDEN 2YO   £3684 5f   Good 55 -14 Slow

--   INTERVAL [3] (J Tree) 2-8-11 Pat Eddery 8/11 fav: 1: 2 ch f Habitat - Intermission
(Stage Door Johnny) Successfully landed the odds on race course debut, al there and gained
a clever nk success in a 2yo fillies mdn at Newbury June 11: dam won the Cambridgeshire:
eff 5f, sure to be suited by 6f+: acts on gd ground: has scope and will improve further
and win more races.   58
--   CHASING MOONBEAMS [13] (I Balding) 2-8-11 S Cauthen 9/1: 2: Mkt drifter, dsptd lead
final 2f, well clear rest and a maiden is a formality: half sister to the very useful
Finian's Rainbow and the winning stayer Storm Cloud: sure to be suited by further than 5f:
acts on good ground.   55
--   SEULEMENT [4] (D Arbuthnot) 2-8-11 J Williams 20/1: 3: Wk in mkt, ran green early
stages, fin well: half sister to very useful '79 2yo Varingo: will be well suited by 6f+:
acts on good: shd improve and find a race.   37
848 LADY LUCINA [5] (M Smyly) 2-8-11 N Howe 12/1: 04: Sn prom: see 848.   32
--   FIRGROVE [9] 2-8-11 W Carson 10/1: 0: Prom most: sure to improve for the experience:
sure to be suited by 6f.   30
--   NAPARIMA [2] 2-8-11 R Wernham 16/1: 0: Prom much: half sister to the winning sprinter
Song Minstrel: can improve.   28
--   KIND OF CLASS [7] 2-8-11 B Rouse 6/1: 0: Prob needed race, fin 9th: half sister to
a couple of winners incl mod stayer Worth Avenue: looks certain to be suited much longer dist.   00

--   Spotter [11] 8-11   **848 Dane Dolly** [10] 8-11   **722 Frivolous Fancy** [8] 8-11
--   Miss Lawsuit [12] 8-11
11 ran   nk,7,2,¾,¾   (K Abdulla)   J Tree Marlborough, Wilts.

1000 HIGH TOP HERMITAGE STAKES   £7869   1m   Good 55 +16 Fast

--   CONQUERING HERO [4] (M Stoute) 3-8-9 W R Swinburn 5/1: 3113-1: 3 b c Storm Bird -
Wave In Glory (Hoist The Flag) Smart colt: made a winning seasonal reappearance, responding
well to press to lead on the post in fast run Hermitage Stakes at Newbury June 11: won
2 of his 4 outings in '85 at Windsor and Doncaster (nursery): eff 6f but well suited by 1m
now and promises to stay further: acts on firm and yldg going: clearly impr and shd win again.   72
653 PRESIDIUM [2] (H Cecil) 4-9-3 S Cauthen 7/2: -03-102: Almost made all, well clear
of rest: gd effort: see 344.   65
325 BIG REEF [5] (J Dunlop) 4-9-3 W Carson 100/30: 211-003: Well bckd, no extra final
2f: flattered 221?   53
693 THE JOKER [1] (G B Balding) 6-9-3 R Weaver 50/1: -04: Looked far from easy ride
here, pushed along thro'out but nevertheless showed great improvement on only previous run on
Flat in this country: seems eff between 1m and 2m but might be best to treat this rating
with some caution: see 693.   48
736 KUFUMA [3] 4-9-3 M Miller 11/8 fav: 3220-00: Well bckd, ran mod: winner of this
event last season: also successful at Pontefract: placed on many other occasions:
best form at 1m and acts on firm and yielding.   44
5 ran   hd,8,2,2½   (R Sangster)   M Stoute Newmarket

1001 GEORGE SMITH MEMORIAL H'CAP 3YO 0-60   £4220   6f   Good 55 +06 Fast   [54]

*576 SHARPETTO [3] (M Albina) 3-9-3 A Bond 6/1: -0011: 3 ch c Sharpen Up - Morelle
(Vitello) Very useful, fast improving colt: gaining 2nd successive win, sprinting clear in
final 1f in quite a val 3yo h'cap at Newbury June 11: made all in a mdn at York May 14
over 7f: seems ideally suited by 6f: acts on gd going and likes a gall trk: plenty of scope
and is sure to win more races.   58
*844 SATIAPOUR [5] (R J Houghton) 3-9-2(vis)(7ex) S Cauthen 11/2: 43-2012: Kept on well
under strong driving and is in good form: see 844.   51
914 HIGHEST PRAISE [11] (I Balding) 3-8-13(7ex) J Matthias 7/1: 03-0133: Gd effort under
his penalty: see 677.   44
837 SILVER FORM [13] (W Wightman) 3-7-7(1oh) N Adams 16/1: 400-034: Al prom: see 657,837   20
624 TACHOMETER [10] 3-7-10(3ow) D Mckay 33/1: 00-000: Dsptd lead much: unplaced both
outings last season, this is prob best eff yet: suited by forcing tactics.   23
884 PLATINE [2] 3-8-4 S Whitworth 16/1: 1000200: Cl.up 4f: twice below 760 (5f sharp trk)   25
624 RIVIERA SCENE [14] 3-9-2 W Carson 5/1 fav: 022-00: Never closer in 7th: see 624.   00
734 MUHTARIS [8] 3-8-1 B Rouse 11/2: 0-02220: Speed 4f, fin 8th: btr 734 (5f).   00
814 ROVE [4] 3-8-6(bl) J Lowe 10/1: -124300: No danger: btr 6,671 (5f).   00
884 WEST CARRACK [12] 3-9-7(vis) R Curant 6/1: -330030: Btr 884 (5f firm).   00
836 Websters Feast 0 8-8   837 Celestial Drive [6] 7-13
--   Lydia Languish [16] 8-1   545 Merrymoles [1] 7-10
14 ran   1½,1½,1½,shthd,2½   (Mahmoud Fustok)   M Albina Newmarket

1002 BALLYMACOLL STUD STAKES 3YO   £8142   1m 2f   Good 55 -42 Slow

--   LAVENDER MIST [2] (M Stoute) 3-8-9 W R Swinburn 15/2: 12-1: 3 ch f Troy - Bold Lady
(Democratic) Useful filly: first time out al prom and comfortably led near fin in very slowly
run Ballymacoll Stks (3yo fillies) at Newbury June 11: ready first time out winner of a
maiden at Salisbury in '85, 2nd in a val event at York on only sub outing: acts on firm and
good going and likes a galloping track: stays 10f well and may stay further.   60
*744 BISHAH [1] (H Cecil) 3-8-9 S Cauthen 13/8 fav: 2-12: Made most, not btn far:
will win more races: see 744.   58
599 OLD DOMESDAY BOOK [6] (J Winter) 3-8-9 G Starkey 5/2: 0-133: Led 3f out, battled on
well and not btn far: genuine and consistent : see 444.   57
739 LOREEF [3] (J Dunlop) 3-8-6 B Thomson 20/1: -04: Kept on and seems to be going
the right way: unraced in '85 but this half sister to smart performers Loralane, On The House
(1,000 Gns winner) and Luminate is bred in the purple: looks sure to stay 12f: one
to keep on the right side from now on.   49
509 BENAROSA [5] 3-8-6 A Mcglone 20/1: -3400: Kept on under strong driving: best 372.   49
*158 MIGIYAS [7] 3-8-12 T Quinn 10/1: 1240-10: Prom, wknd: abs since btr 158 (7f yldg)   50
397 BUSTARA [9] 3-8-12 Paul Eddery 9/1: 010-040: Ran badly, much btr 397 (1m yldg)   00
59   Apprila [10] 8-6   *604 Amongst The Stars [8] 8-9
9 ran   1,nk,shthd,2½   (Maktoum Al Maktoum)   M Stoute Newmarket

1003 BERKSHIRE STAKES 2YO   £3700   5f   Good 55 -27 Slow

+728 FLOOSE [3] (P Cole) 2-8-11 T Quinn 4/5 fav: 11: 2 b c Ballad Rock - Carnival Dance
(Welsh Pageant) Highly promising colt: made it 2 wins from 2 races with a very ready success
in 4 runner Berkshire Stks at Newbury June 11: sprinted clear in the final furlong and
could have one by much further than 1l: comfortably won a mdn at Leicester first time out:
half brother to the smart 7f/1m winner Sarab: eff 5f, sure to stay further: acts well on
firm and good ground, on a stiff track: not to be lightly opposed.   68

834 LUCIANAGA [1] (P Walwyn) 2-8-6 Paul Eddery 3/1: 22: Led ½ way, murdered for foot
by the winner but should have no trouble finding a mdn soon: see 834.   53
*918 THE DOMINICAN [4] (B Hills) 2-8-11 B Thomson 4/1: 32213: Made much: see 918(sharp trk) 48
513 SAMLEON [2] (R Hannon) 2-8-11 W Carson 16/1: 41234: Outpaced final 1f, best 278(hvy) 42
4 ran   1,5,2½   (Fahd Salman)   P Cole Whatcombe, Berks

1004 NETHERAVON HANDICAP STAKES (0-50)   £3876   1m 5f Good 55 -10 Slow   [50]

778 NEWSELLS PARK [6] (J Winter) 5-9-0 W R Swinburn 7/4 fav: 12-P-21: 5 ch g Anne's
Pretender - Fernelia (Royalty) Fulfilled the promise of his seasonal reappearance when
readily winning a h'cap at Newbury June 11, leading str easily: p.u. only outing last
season but in '84 won at Beverley and was rated 55: eff 12f, stays 14f and shd stay 2m: acts
well on gd ground and also handles firm tho' because of training problems is unlikely to
be risked on such going: well h'capped and can win again.   50
--   FANDANGO LIGHT [1] (D Elsworth) 5-8-6 S Cauthen 8/1: 30100/2: Led ½ way, outpaced
by winner but a fair return to Flat: successful over hurdles during the Winter also a
winner at Ascot and Windsor on the level when last raced in this sphere in '84: well suited
by 12f on gd or firm ground but a winner in the hvy over hurdles.   35
805 JOUVENCELLE [3] (H Candy) 4-7-11 T Williams 3/1: 0244-23: Ev ch, remains mdn: see 805 19
675 DONT RING ME [7] (W Hastings Bass) 4-8-1 R Lines[3] 12/1: 3100-04: Ev ch, see 675.   20
801 NO U TURN [5] 8-9-2 M Wigham 16/1: 0200-00: No threat: winner Epsom & York '85:
has been a good stable servant over the years both on the Flat and over hurdles: eff around
12f and loves to hear his hooves rattle.   34
841 ANDREA DAWN [2] 5-7-7(5oh) R Street 33/1: 3000-00: Led to ½ way: winner over hurdles
in the Winter, lightly raced mdn on the Flat.   01
*761 MILLERS TALE [9] 4-8-8 J Matthias 7/2: 02-2010: No real threat: btr 761 (sharp trk).   00
--   Broadleaf [8] 9-9   735 King Of Comedy [4] 9-10
9 ran   3,5,2½,1,10   (D McIntyre)   J Winter Newmarket

SAN SIRO   Sunday June 8

Official Going Given as Good

1005 GROUP 1 GRAN PREMIO DI MILANO 3YO+   £78647   1m 4f Good -

*555 TOMMY WAY (J Dunlop) 3-8-6 W Carson : 021-311: 3 b c Thatch - Tilia (Dschingis
Khan) Smart, much impr colt: led 2f out, driven out for a narrow win in Gr 1 event at San
Siro June 8: last time out won the Italian Derby at Capannelle: in '85 was a runaway winner
of a mdn at Haydock: eff at 10f, stays 12f really well: acts on gd/firm and soft ground and
on any track: certain to win more gd races and has been very cleverly placed by his trainer. 82
704 SEISMIC WAVE (B Hills) 5-9-6 B Thomson : 2-03222: Chall final 1f: just btn and
continues in fine form: see 704.   79
*398 ALAN FORD (V Di Maggio) 6-9-6 V Di Maggio : 13: Another gd run: acts on gd and hvy. 73
555 BE MY MASTER (A Botti) 3-8-6 G Dettori : -324: Ev ch: gd run: see 555.   70
9 ran   shtnk,3½,2½   (Scuderia Erasec)   J Dunlop Arundel, Sussex

---

PHOENIX PARK   Saturday June 7   Left and Righand Sharpish Track

Official Going Given as Good

1006 CHERRY BLOSSOM 2YO STAKES (LISTED)   £10548   6f   Good -

558 INDEXS [4] (D Weld) 2-8-6 M J Kinane 8/11 FAV: 21: 2 b f Storm Bird - Table of
Contents (Round Table) Very promising Irish filly: ridden confidently and led nearing final
1f, easily in a val 2yo Listed race at Phoenix Park June 7: first time out proved no match
for the potential topclass filly Polonia in a mdn at Leopardstown: very eff at 6f, should
get further: acts on good ground and on any track and is certain to win more gd races.   65
--   KHARSHUF [5] (K Prendergast) 2-8-9 G Curran 10/1: 2: Mkt drifter, dsptd lead:
promising race course debut and should sn find a race: acts on good ground.   60
638 HIGH WIND [1] (J Murphy) 2-8-12 D J Murphy 5/2: 143: Dsptd lead: consistent filly:
seems to act on any ground: see 268.   63
--   RAINBOW ACRES [2] (E O'grady) 2-8-6 S Craine 10/1: 4: Stiff task on race courrse
debut: not disgraced.   45
752 WITH GODS HELP [6] 2-8-12 C Roche 10/1: 100: Twice below form 149 (hvy grd).   47
5 ran   2,hd,6,1½   (A Paulson)   D Weld Ireland

1007 KILFRUSH WHAT A GUEST STAKES (LISTED)   £21256   6f   Good -

--   KINGS RIVER [2] (D Weld) 4-9-11 M J Kinane 1/1 FAV: 0141-21: 4 ch c Irish River -
Roycon (High Top) Smart Irish colt: led approaching final 1f, ridden out in val Listed race
at Phoenix Park June 7: in '85 won a Gr 3 event at Leopardstown: also won this same race:
very eff over 1m/9f: acts well on good and firm ground.   80

466 JAZZ MUSICIAN [8] (M Kauntze) 3-8-6 P Shanahan 14/1: 00-4312: In fine form: recent
winner at Navan (1m soft).   68
--   FLEETING SNOW [7] (M O'brien) 3-8-6(bl) G Mcgrath 12/1: -1-3: Ran well in this gd co.   61
*667 HABER [9] (B Hills) 3-8-6 M Hills 4/1: -2314: English chall: stiff task but ran well   58
11 ran   1½,3,1½   (B Firestone)   D Weld Ireland

CHANTILLY   Sunday June 8 ı   Righthand Galloping Track

Official Going Given as Firm

1008 GROUP 3 PRIX DE SANDRINGHAM 3YO   £18629   1m   Firm -

--   ONLY STAR (C Head) 3-8-8 G Moore : -4-131: 3 ch f Nureyev - Rivermaid (Riverman)
Smart French filly: came fast and late for a narrow win in Gr 3 fillies event at Chantilly
June 8 : very eff at 1m on fast ground.   70
467 NORTHERN PREMIER (G Mikhalides) 3-9-0 C Asmussen : 31-0102: Just caught: grand
effort: see 288: acts on any ground and seems a genuine filly.   75
--   MADE OF PEARL (C Head) 3-8-8 G Guignard : 212-043: Not btn far: acts on fast ground   65
--   SAD AKARAD (R Collet) 3-8-11 Y Saint Martin : 40-0104: In gd form: recent winner
at Longchamp.   66
467 RIVER DANCER 3-8-11 M Philipperon 1: 124-430: Btr 467 (soft).   65
11 ran   nk,2,¾,shtnk   (R E Sangster)   C Head France

1009 GROUP 1 PRIX DU JOCKEY-CLUB LANCIA 3YO   £135409   1m 4f Firm Course Record

*562 BERING [10] (C Head) 3-9-2 G Moore 3/10 FAV: -31-111: 3 ch c Arctic Tern - Beaune
(Lyphard) Topclass French colt: all going well and led inside final 2f, easily, breaking the
course record in Gr 1 Prix du Jockey Club at Chantilly June 8: earlier won 2 Gr 2 events at
Longchamp and has yet to be severely tested: very eff at 11/12f: acts on any grd and will
be very hard to beat this season.   94
554 ALTAYAN [7] (A De Royer Dupre) 3-9-2 Y Saint Martin 1: ----122: Kept on really well
and this was a fine performance: very smart colt who first time out was an easy winner
at Evry: very eff at 12f on fast grd, also acts on good races.   88
510 BAKHAROFF [8] (G Harwood) 3-9-2 G Starkey 1: 1321-23: Ev ch in straight: another gd eff.82
--   SHARKEN [5] (A Fabre) 3-9-2 A Gibert 1: -4-314: Excellent 4th: last time out was
an easy winner at Longchamp: very eff at 12f on firm ground.   78
562 POINT DARTOIS [3] 3-9-2 F Head 1: -31-220: Remains in fine form: acts on firm & hvy.   75
*597 AL SALITE [2] 3-9-2 Pat Eddery 1: 412-110: Stiff task and ran really well: see 597   71
*554 PRADIER [13] 3-9-2 E Legrix 1: ---1110: Led entering straight: wknd: btr 554(10f soft)   00
302 ARCTIC BLAST [12] 3-9-2 M Leroy 1: -1-2030: Fin 8th: ran to his best.   00
643 MINATZIN [11] 3-9-2 G Dubroeucq 1: 431-440: See 289 (10f)   00
562 SILVER BAND [4] 3-9-2 A Lequeux 1: -1-030: Prom, wknd.   00
900 ART FRANCAIS [6] 3-9-2 D Boeuf 1: -330: Set very fast pace: see 389.   00
--   SAHARA DANCER [9] 3-9-2 C Asmussen 1: -0: -   00
597 OSTENSIBLE [1] 3-9-2 A Clark 1: 1-300: Bakharoff's pacemaker: see 435.   00
13 ran   1½,3,3,shtnk,2,1½,2½,4   (Mme A Head)   C Head France

1010 GROUP 2 PRIX DOLLAR 4YO+   £26467   1m 2f Firm -

645 IADES [7] (F Boutin) 4-9-1 F Head : 2200-41: 4 b c Shirley Heights - Isabella
Moretti (Sir Gaylord) Smart French colt: led inside final 1f, ridden out in Gr 2 event at
Chantilly June 8: consistent in '85: equally eff at 10/12f: acts on firm and yldg ground.   83
--   GRAND PAVOIS [3] (P Biancone) 4-8-12 E Legrix : 111-412: Not btn far: fine effort:
last time out won at Longchamp: formerly trained by H Cecil, winning at Royal Ascot,
Doncaster and Sandown: eff 10f, stays 12f really well: acts on gd and firm ground and
is a consistent sort.   78
391 OVER THE OCEAN [5] (G Mikhalides) 4-9-1 C Asmussen : 003-233: Cl.up 3rd: consistent.   79
298 REINE KA [1] (M Bouland) 4-8-9 M Bouland 1: 1-00424: Gd effort.   67
--   FITNAH [6] 4-9-2 G Moore : 2120-10: Long odds-on: well below her best: first time
out this season was an easy winner of a Listed race at Longchamp: in excellent form in
'85, winning 3 times at Longchamp: also btn a shthd in the Gr 1 Prix Hermes at Chantilly:
genuine filly: very eff over 10/12f: acts on any ground and is much better than this.   70
--   MA PETITE CHERIE [4] 4-8-9 M Leroy : -0: -   47
6 ran   ¾,¾,2½,2,8   (Marchese M Incisa Della Rochetta)   F Boutin France

1011 GROUP 3 PRIX DU GROS CHENE 3YO+   £17075   5f   Firm -

*563 LAST TYCOON (R Collet) 3-9-1 Y Saint Martin : 010-011: 3 b c Try My Best -
Mill Princess: In fine form, fin well to win Gr 3 event at Chantilly June 8: last time out
won a similar event at Longchamp: in '85 won again at Longchamp, also a fine 5th in the
Prix L'Abbaye: very eff at 5f: acts on gd/firm and yldg ground.   79
--   PREMIERE CUVEE (J Pease) 4-8-9 G Guignard : --030-2: Led over 1f out: not btn far:
excellent effort: formerly trained by M Prescott: winning 2yo: very eff 5f: acts on frm & yldg 62
373 ROSE OF THE SEA (G Mikhalides) 3-8-6 C Asmussen : 43-003: Led ½ way: see 155.   64

644 CRICKET BALL (J Fellows) 3-8-6 A Gibert 1: -3304: Versatile performer: see 644.   **63**
10 ran   ½,1½,nose   (R C Strauss)   R Collet France

BEVERLEY   Thursday June 12th   Righthand, Undulating Track, Stiff Uphill Finish

Official Going Given as Good/Firm

1012 ETTON SELLING STAKES 2YO   £948   5f   Firm 15 -49 Slow

957 REAL RUSTLE [4] (M W Easterby) 2-8-11(bl) M Birch 12/1: 000341: 2 gr f Enchantment -
PTS Fairway (Runnymede) Al front rank and led 2 out, under press, in a slow run 2yo seller
at Beverley June 12 (no bid): eff at 5f on fast grd: seems best in blinkers.   **26**
696 MONS FUTURE [9] (W Pearce) 2-9-1 N Connorton 7/2: 01422: Al prom: consistent:
acts on firm and soft: see 354.   **24**
865 ROYAL TREATY [2] (N Tinkler) 2-8-11 Kim Tinkler(5) 7/1: 00033: Sn prom: acts on
firm and soft: see 865.   **16**
589 PETERS BLUE [5] (J Fitzgerald) 2-8-11 A Murray 5/1: 04: Led to ½ way: acts on gd
and firm ground and may find a seller on a sharper track.   **14**
858 LATE PROGRESS [14] 2-8-8(BL) S Morris 16/1: -00000: Never nearer: bl first time today **03**
826 ABSALOUTE HEAVEN [13] 2-8-8 A Mercer 14/1: 000: Never nearer: drop in class here. **03**
858 SHADY BLADE [10] 2-8-8 C Dwyer 2/1 FAV: 020: Well bckd, no threat: much btr 858(C/D) **00**
865 MILLIE DUFFER [6] 2-8-8 R Vickers(7) 7/1: 00440: Made no show: btr 865, 125(easier grd) **00**
939 Pialuci [8] 8-11   **858** On The Mark [11] 8-11(BL)
865 Bootham Lad [7] 8-11   **957** Caras Quest [3] 8-8   -- Phils Pride [12] 8-11
858 Austhorpe Sunset [1] 8-11
14 ran   2,1½,1,3,shthd   (Mrs Anne Henson)   M W Easterby Sherrif Hutton, York.

1013 LONDESBOROUGH HANDICAP 3YO+ 0-35   £1661   7f   Firm 15 -01 Slow   [31]

-**680 SUPER TRIP** [12] (M Fetherson Godley) 5-9-9 C Rutter(5) 6/1: 00-0021: 5 b h Windjammer -
Esker Rose (Sunny Way) Led 1f, comfortably, in a h'cap at Beverley June 12: in '84 won a
h'cap at Nottingham: prev season won at Haydock and Pontefract: eff 7f: stays 10f: acts
on gd and firm ground and on any trk: in fine form.   **36**
812 FORMATUNE [4] (D Arbuthnot) 4-9-10(bl) R Cochrane 13/2: -102332: Kept on well
final 1f: most consistent: see 10.   **30**
710 GOLDEN DISC [6] (M Camacho) 4-7-11 J Lowe 7/1: 3333-43: Al prom: see 710. **00**
-- JUST A BIT [11] (M W Easterby) 4-8-9(1ow) M Hindley(3) 12/1: 03230-4: Led into straight:
wknd final 1f on seasonal debut: in gd form in '85, winning sellers at Thirsk (2) and was
subsequently placed sev times in btr company: eff 6f, stays 1m: acts on firm and yldg grd
and likes Thirsk.   **05**
680 GOLDEN BEAU [1] 4-9-1 M Birch 7/1: 0-03330: Ev ch straight: btr 680 (sharper trk). **09**
*673 CHARMING VIEW** [7] 4-8-8(6ex) W Ryan 16/1: 400-010: Nearest fin: btr 673 (1m yldg) **01**
936 RESPONDER [9] 4-8-9 D Nicholls 10/1: 0300000: Never nearer 7th: btr 936, see 142. **00**
700 BIT OF A STATE [15] 6-9-0(bl) T Ives 5/2: 0-00000: Never beyond mid-div: see 611(1m). **00**
689 ABLE MAYBOB [10] 4-8-6 M Rimmer 10/3 FAV: 000-120: Unsuited by firm? See 689, 594 (CD) **00**
775 MERRY MEASURE [5] 4-9-4 R Morse(5) 10/1: -000000: No threat: yet to strike form:
in '85 won at Pontefract, Folkestone and Beverley: eff over 6f/1m: acts on firm and yldg
ground and seems best when up with the pace.   **00**
820 Marsiliana [2] 8-2   **441** Manabel [14] 9-0   -- Hit The Button [16] 7-11(BL)
830 Always Native [8] 8-13   **540** Cindys Gold [3] 8-4(bl)
15 ran   3,2,3,1,nk,1,shthd   (Jack Maxwell)   M Fetherson Godley Godley, East Ilsley, Berks

1014 MASSEY EUROPOWER 2YO TROPHY   £4869   5f   Firm 15 +09 Fast

741 WIGANTHORPE [5] (M W Easterby) 2-8-11 T Lucas 16/1: 02201: 2 ch c Thatching -
Lustrine (Viceregal) Very useful, fast improving colt: slowly away, but showed a fine turn
of foot to lead final 1f readily drawing clear in a fast run and val 2yo event at Beverley
June 12: cost 18,500 gns: very eff at 5f, shd stay further: acts on soft, well suited
by firm ground: well regarded and should win more races.   **62**
810 ALKADI [1] (W O'gorman) 2-9-1 T Ives 11/4: 31232: Led briefly over 1f out: most
consistent: equally eff over 5/6f: tried in bl last time: see 610, 503.   **53**
*662 MANDUB** [4] (H Thomson Jones) 2-9-1(4ex) A Murray 2/5 FAV: 13: Heavily bckd: dsptd lead:
well below form 662: possibly unsuited by firm ground and definitely worth another chance. **47**
781 FLAXLEY [2] (R Hollinshead) 2-9-2 S Perks 16/1: 134: Dsptd lead: ev ch: btr 781. **39**
+**602 GLENCROFT** [6] 2-9-3 D Nicholls 10/1: 0010: Dsptd lead: beat winner 602!   **35**
5 ran   5,2,3,2   (Miss Susan E Easterby)   M W Easterby Sheriff Hutton, Yorks.

1015 101ST YEAR OF THE WATT EBF STKS 3YO+   £3778   1m 4f   Firm 15 +11 Fast

-- QUEENS SOLDIER [1] (H Cecil) 3-8-5 W Ryan 9/4: 131-1: 3 b c L'Enjoleur - Little
Lady Luck (Jacinto) Smart colt: first time out led below dist, readily, in a fast run and
quite val stks race at Beverley June 12: showed plenty of promise as a juv, winning first
time out at Yarmouth and later at Sandown: stays 12f really well: acts on gd and firm
ground and is suited by a stiff trk: should win more races.   **75**

617 RANGE ROVER [4] (J Winter) 4-9-7 T Ives 11/8 FAV: 3041-02: Tried to make all:
rallied well when hdd: should go one btr soon: see 617.   70
654 BADARBAK [2] (R Johnson Houghton) 3-8-5 K Darley 9/4: 03-3123: Ran on same pace and
seems certain to be suited by further: most consistent this term: see 654, 411.   65
613 BERNISH LADY [5] (B Mcmahon) 5-8-6 G Duffield 20/1: -04: Distant 4th: lightly raced
mare who is a half sister to a couple of winning milers: acts on fast ground.   30
875 BUSTED FLAVOUR [3] 5-8-9 R Cochrane 20/1: 30: Tough task and no threat: see 875.   28
5 ran   2,3,20,3   (Sheikh Mohammed)   H Cecil Newmarket

1016 BRANTINGHAM HANDICAP 3YO+ 0-35   £1569   2m   Firm 15 -11 Slow   [35]

519 EASY KIN [10] (R Peacock) 4-7-9(bl) J Quinn(5) 16/1: 00-0001: 4 ch g Great Nephew
- Ardneasken (Right Royal V) Showed impr form over this longer trip, led home turn and
stayed on strongly to win a h'cap at Beverley June 12: first success tho' is a half brother
to a handful of middle dist winners: stays 2m well: suited by fast grd and a stiff track.   12
841 SECURITY CLEARANCE [14] (G Blum) 5-9-10 M Rimmer 8/1: -003002: Stayed on well:
likes this stiff track: placed over this C/D in 590: acts on gd and firm.   36
860 TURI [9] (A Smith) 7-7-8 G French 12/1: 040/003: Never nearer and clear of rem:
suited by a test of stamina: acts on gd and firm ground and on a stiff track: see 712.   05
590 ALFIE DICKINS [11] (R Hollinshead) 8-7-12 P Hill(7) 6/1: 0130-04: Late prog: see 590.   01
-- ASCENMOOR [7] 7-7-7 A Proud 10/1: 40000/0: Recently successful over hurdles, tho'
lightly raced and remains a maiden on the Flat: stays well: best on gd or faster ground:
acts on any track.   00
860 WILDRUSH [8] 7-8-13 D Nicholls 8/1: 2-10340: Never nearer: stays 2m: see 243.   15
841 SMACK [6] 4-7-12 R Morse(5) 10/3 : 20-0020: Fin 7th: btr on gd in 841.   00
933 WALTER THE GREAT [13] 4-8-7 M Birch 3/1 FAV: 20-0040: Wknd run-in: btr 933 (tight trk)00
770 Perfect Double [1] 7-11   **933 Red Duster** [2] 8-11
827 Dont Annoy Me [16] 7-11   **590 Racing Demon** [4] 7-7
365 Hot Ruler [5] 7-7(11oh)   **590 La Rose Grise** [15] 8-7
731 Michele My Belle [3] 7-7(3oh)   **936 Fair Trader** [12] 7-8(1ow)(2oh)
16 ran   3,½,8,½,hd,1½   (D P McLaughlin)   R Peacock Tarporley, Cheshire

1017 GRANDSTAND HANDICAP 3YO+ 0-35   £1156   1m 2f   Firm 15 -08 Slow   [30]

584 HANDLEBAR [4] (J Watts) 4-9-8 T Ives 10/3: 031-001: 4 b c Welsh Pageant - My
Therape (Jimmy Reppin) Led over 2f out and stayed on strongly under press to win a h'cap at
Beverley June 12: successful in a mdn over this C/D last backend: stays 10f well: acts on gd
and firm ground and is well suited by this stiff track.   34
967 PERSHING [3] (J Leigh) 5-9-1 M Miller 11/2: 0-02032: Had ev ch: in gd form: see 611.   21
709 DASHING LIGHT [8] (D Morley) 5-8-13 G Duffield 9/4 FAV: 02-4043: Tried to make all:
much better over this trip in 432 (sharp track).   15
956 ELARIM [6] (T Fairhurst) 3-7-8 C Coates(5) 7/1: 0-00004: Al prom: returning to formsee 956 21
629 IVOROSKI [11] 4-8-3 L Charnock 14/1: 00-0000: Some late prog: won a h'cap at
Edinburgh last season: best form on gd or fast ground: stays 11f well: seems to act any trk.   00
946 COMMON FARM [12] 3-8-10 K Darley 16/1: -000000: Never nearer: stays 10f: see 789.   13
474 SKYBOOT [13] 7-8-10 Wendy Carter(7) 9/1: -032400: Fin 9th: suited by some give.   00
-- Rapid Lad [7] 9-10   **-- Clotilda** [1] 8-8   **827 Tharaleos** [10] 7-12
547 Boldera [2] 8-12   **893 Anitas Apple** [9] 9-0   **745 Ravens Peak** [5] 8-10(BL)
13 ran   3,2½,1½,5,2,hd   (Mrs M Haggas)   J Watts Richmond, Yorks

1018 CORK & GULLY APPRENTICES H'CAP (0-50)   £3402   1m   Good 48 -03 Slow   [46]

-- GRANNYS BANK [1] (W Hastings Bass) 4-8-11 Dale Gibson 8/1: 33211-1: 4 b f Music Boy -
Sweet Elaine (Birdbrook) Dsptd lead final 2f, holding on by the min margin in an app h'cap
at Newbury June 12: ended last season with h'cap successes at Pontefract and Doncaster: very
eff over 1m on firm or gd ground and likes a gall track.   39
709 GIBBOUS MOON [3] (D Murray Smith) 4-8-0 P Johnson 13/2: 20-002: battled with winner
final 1f, almost got up: gd eff and is prob even btr at 10f: sure to go close next time
in similar company: see 709.   28
762 GOLDEN SLADE [4] (M Mccourt) 4-8-11(6ex) A Tucker 6/1 fav: 14-0013: Al there and
is in fine form: see 762.   32
727 GAUHAR [2] (M Blanshard) 5-7-10 P Skelton[3] 16/1: 300-444: Chall dist: see 174.   16
309 SWIFT PALM [15] 9-8-2 G Watts[3] 11/1: 30-0000: Prom most: see 112.   21
724 DISPORT [8] 4-7-12(4ow) Andrea Marsh[0] 33/1: 0000-00: Rank outsider, dsptd lead
2f out, wknd: mdn who ran best races last season over 6f.   12
578 AUGUST [17] 5-8-10 J Dunne[3] 8/1: 000-000: Well there 6f, fin 7th: twice below 399   00
285 PICTOGRAPH [16] 4-9-10 P Francis 7/1: 3014-00: Abs, no threat: in gd form last
season, winning at Goodwood, Bath and Salisbury (2): very eff at 1m tho' acts on firm and
yielding on any track: high in the h'cap at present.   00
815 SCOUTSMISTAKE [12] 7-9-3 A Culhane 9/1: 0020-00: Much btr 815.   00
812 DIMENSION [10] 4-7-13(bl) Abigail Richards 8/1: 0141040: Yet to reproduce 578.   00
521 RAPID ACTION [11] 5-8-7 D Casey 11/1: -303310: Recent winner in the Isle of Mansee 521. 00

680	Hello Sunshine [5] 9-0(6ex)		775 Nicoridge [9] 9-10
--	Mia Jubes [6] 7-7(1oh)	775 Mitner [7] 7-7(5oh)	812 Aqaba Prince 0 7-11
16 ran	shthd,3,nk,hd,2½,hd	(J H James)	W Hastings Bass Newmarket

1019 E.B.F. KENNET MAIDEN STAKES 2YO   £3977   6f   Good 48 -06 Slow

777 BRAVE DANCER [16] (G Harwood) 2-9-0 G Starkey 8/11 fav: 31: 2 b c Pas de Seul - Dance Lover's (Green Dancer) Useful, impr colt: sn prom and stayed on strongly for a narrow success in a 2yo mdn at Newbury June 12: half brother to winning French colt: well suited by 6f, sure to stay 7f+: acts on gd going: attractive sort with scope: cert to win more races.   **65**

-- GELTSER [9] (J Tree) 2-9-0 Pat Eddery 9/1: 2: Fine debut, chall winner final 1f, just btn: from a good family which includes the topclass French sprinter Sigy: shd stay beyond 6f: acts on gd going and on a gall track: will have no difficulty finding a race sn.   **63**

-- WHO KNOWS [7] (W Hern) 2-9-0 W Carson 10/1: 3: Mkt drifter, dsptd lead 2f out and ran well: half brother to smart stayer Family Friend and will stay beyond 6f: acts on gd grd: should find a maiden without much trouble.   **59**

-- SANAM [14] (J Dunlop) 2-9-0 B Rouse 11/1: 4: Flying at fin and this was a promising debut: from a fair winning family which includes the smart Caro: will be well suited by 7f: sure to find a race soon.   **59**

-- NONSUCH PALACE [4] 2-9-0 W R Swinburn 11/2: 0: Prom thro'out: bred to stay very well indeed and should be well suited by 7f+.   **50**

-- BOLD GARCON [11] 2-9-0 J Reid 20/1: 0: In need of race: sure to impr on this quite creditable debut: cost 35,000 gns and is a half brother to a couple of minor winners: should stay beyond 6f.   **40**

834 BACCHANALIAN [12] 2-9-0 B Thomson 16/1: 00: Prom most, fin 7th: see 834.   **00**

664	Lord Westgate [18] 9-0		804 Cee En Cee [17] 9-0
--	Hockley [1] 9-0	804 Vaigly Blazed [10] 9-0	
777	Father Time [19] 9-0	-- Tiptree [15] 9-0	-- Hanseatic [3] 9-0
--	Ardiles [5] 9-0	-- Jonite [2] 9-0	-- Madness Not To [13] 9-0
497	Young Moreton [8] 9-0		
18 ran	½,1½,nk,1½,4	(G Zandona)	G Harwood Pulborough, Sussex

1020 COOPERS & LYBRAND SUMMERS STAKES (0-70)   £5993   1m 4f Good 48 +32 Fast   [54]

584 FIVE FARTHINGS [4] (M Stoute) 4-8-2 Paul Eddery 4/1 fav: 3100-01: 4 b f Busted - Great Tom (Great Nephew) Fast impr filly: rewarded strong support when hacking up in a very fast run h'cap at Newbury June 12: led str and sn qcknd well clear: in '85 was an easy winner of a Yarmouth mdn: eff 12f, stays 14f well: acts on firm and gd going and likes a galloping track: should run up a sequence.   **50**

485 FOLK DANCE [5] (I Balding) 4-9-0 Pat Eddery 7/1: 441-442: Came from behind, no chance with this well h'capped winner: see 189.   **48**

-- RAKAPOSHI KING [1] (H Cecil) 4-9-9 S Cauthen 9/2: 21120-3: Made much on seasonal debut: enjoyed a successful season in '85 winning h'caps at Goodwood, Sandown and Leicester: has since changed stables, originally to be lead horse to the now retired Slip Anchor: front runner who is very eff over 12/14f and is suited by firm or gd going.   **53**

584 WITCHCRAFT [2] (G Wragg) 4-8-7(BL) W Carson 5/1: 020-244: Bl first time, ev ch: twice below 225 (soft).   **33**

695 MAIN REASON [6] 4-9-3(5ex) W R Swinburn 9/1: 1002-10: Prom much: fair effort:see 695   **42**

695 BOLD REX [8] 4-9-10 B Rouse 13/2: 1-44100: No show: twice below 584 (soft)   **44**

851 STATE BUDGET [7] 5-8-12 M Wigham 9/2: 0-13120: Ran poorly, needs give? see 618.   **00**

921 KENTUCKY QUEST [3] 4-8-9 G Starkey 16/1: -002000: Poor form since 189 (soft).   **00**

8 ran   7,2½,3,½,4   (The Snailwell Stud Co Ltd)   M Stoute Newmarket

1021 KINGSCLERE STAKES 2YO FILLIES   £7713   6f   Good 48 -17 Slow

-- GENTLE PERSUASION [1] (I Balding) 2-8-6(1ow) S Cauthen 100/30: 1: 2 ch f Bustino - Harp Strings (Luthier) Promising filly who made a winning debut, qckn well in final 1f when a comfortable winner of Kingsclere 2YO Fillies Stakes at Newbury June 12: dam a winner at both 2 and 3 years: eff over 6f, sure to be suited by 7f+: open to further impr'ment   **55**

848 BLUE TANGO [2] (R Laing) 2-8-8 W Carson 33/1: 24332: Chall 1f out and this consistent mdn deserves a small race: see 746.   **52**

-- BENGUELA [6] (J Tree) 2-8-5 Pat Eddery 13/2: 3: Friendless in mkt on debut, not clear run and fin pleasingly: sound first effort: half sister to smart sprinter Al Mamoon: acts on gd ground: sure to improve and win a race soon.   **45**

•707 INDIAN LILY [5] (C Brittain) 2-8-12 P Robinson 5/6 fav: 14: Going well dist, sn btn and much better 707 (5f).   **48**

-- CANDLE IN THE WIND [4] 2-8-5 S Whitworth 25/1: 0: Ran well for much of the trip: badly in need of race and this effort bodes well for her future: cost 10,000 gns: sure to win a race at one of the smaller tracks.   **31**

•927 JAY GEE ELL [3] 2-8-12 A Mackay 13/2: 31410: Made most, hmpd final 1f, btr 927 (sharp)   **36**

6 ran   ½,1½,1½,5,2½   (The Queen)   I Balding Kingsclere, Berks

1022 CHILDREY MAIDEN STAKES 3YO   £3632   1m 5f Good 48 +12 Fast

--   **WHITE CLOVER** [15] (G Harwood) 3-9-0 G Starkey 14/1: -1: 3 gr c Danzig - Fairly
(Dancing Moss) Very promising colt: made a highly impressive race course debut when forging
clear in final 1f to win a fast run 3yo mdn at Newbury June 12: stays 13f well, looks likely
to be well suited by 2m: acts on gd ground and on a gall trk: big backward sort who has
been too weak to race previously and can   only improve further: sure to win more races.   67
555 SHIBIL [5] (M Stoute) 3-9-0 W R Swinburn 5/4 fav: 33-4432: Well bckd, led 3f out
but had no answer to the winner's pace: prob caught a tartar here and on evidence of 555
must find a maiden soon.   62
619 BOON POINT [3] (J Dunlop) 3-9-0 B Thomson 4/1: 3-03: Ev ch in what was prob a
hot contest: looks likely to stay 2m: see 619.   60
--   **DIVINE DESTINY** [10] (J Tree) 3-8-11 Pat Eddery 12/1: 0-4: Came from well off the
pace on seasonal debut and must be noted for a near at hand success: 5th in valuable race
at Ascot on only outing in '85: acts on firm and gd ground: stays 13f and likely to stay
further: attractive sort with scope who will win her share of races.   45
811 LAW COURT [6] (T Williams) 3-9-0 T Williams 20/1: 0-0040: Wknd after 3 out: shd win a mdn if
eased in class slightly: see 811.   38
--   **DARK SIRONA** [12] (J Tree) 3-8-11 P Wallace 50/1: 000-0: Rank outsider, no threat: showed
nothing in 3 outings last season but is a half sister to minor winner A Red Red Rose:
shd be suited by middle distances.   32
619 DHONI [1] (W Carson) 3-9-0 W Carson 6/1: 0-40: No threat: see 619.   00
-714 Up To Me [7] 9-0   494 Maricama [13] 9-0   723 Stop The Clock [9] 8-11
832 First Rank [11] 9-0   --   Richards Folly [14] 8-11
219 Cheetak [4] 9-0   894 Rye Hill Mariner [8] 9-0
832 Floral Charge [2] 9-0
15 ran   3,1½,8,5,1½   (Mrs A W Stollery)   G Harwood Pulborough, Sussex

1023 KENNETH ROBERTSON H'CAP (0-50) 3YO   £3746   1m 3f Good 48 -19 Slow   [55]

484 BENISA RYDER [2] (C Horgan) 3-8-8 P Cook 4/1: 03-2241: 3 ch c Stanford - Bamstar
(Relko) Al prom, wore down Satisfaction cl home by a shthd in quite a val h'cap at Newbury
June 12: first success: suited by 11f, shd stay further: acts on gd and soft going.   46
619 SATISFACTION [4] (W Hern) 3-9-7 W Carson 9/4 fav: 00-22: Led dist, caught death:
sure to win a race: see 619.   59
--   **INDIAN ORATOR** [7] (B Hills) 3-8-11 B Thomson 6/1: 22222-3: Ev ch on seasonal debut:
had a bad case of seconditis in '85, filling that spot in each of his 5 races! Eff around
1m, should stay middle distances: acts on firm and good ground: should win a race.   42
458 SHIRZAD [6] (J Tree) 3-8-11(1ow) Paul Eddery 12/1: 0-004: Made much: ran only once
in '85: half sister to fair performers Green Rock and Verdance: shd be suited by middle dist.   29
843 SILENT RUNNING [1] 3-7-7(5oh) T Williams 7/2: 0-00030: Btr 843 (10f).   18
625 MAKE PEACE [3] 3-8-8 Pat Eddery 13/2: 3-3300: Never btr placed: twice below 484(10f)   31
275 PRIOK [5] 3-7-7(8oh) L Riggio[6] 16/1: 000-030: Led ¼ way, hdd straight: absent
since better 275 (hvy).   00
7 ran   shthd,5,2,2½,1½   (Consolidate Real Est Ltd)   C Horgan Wokingham, Berks

---

Official Going Given as Good/Firm

1024 FREEMAN OF YORK APPR. HCAP 0-50   £2700   1m 4f Firm 18 -12 Slow   [45]

*872 ROMIOSINI [6] (N Tinkler) 4-9-6(7ex) Kim Tinkler(3) 8/1: 03-0411: 4 b c
Spirit Son - Narmeen (Le Haar) In fine form and gamely defied his penalty, making all in an
app h'cap at York June 13: recently a similarly narrow winner of a h'cap at Ripon: successful
over hurdles in the Autumn: in '85 won a maiden at Ripon: eff over 10f, stays 12f well:
best on good and firm ground when up with the pace.   45
827 GOLDEN FANCY [4] (I Vickers) 9-8-8 R Vickers(11) 5/1 Co FAV: -000022: Switched below
dist, ran on well and again only just failed to get up: running well: seee 142.   32
591 FENCHURCH COLONY [1] (M H Easterby) 5-8-11 J Kennedy(5) 10/1: 000/303: Al prom and
ran on well: stays 12f: well suited by a gall trk: see 429.   33
*721 PINWIDDIE [9] (P Rohan) 4-7-13 J Quinn(3) 5/1 Co FAV: -042114: Going on fin: see 721.   19
52 TRESIDDER [7] 4-9-5 L Riggio(5) 6/1: 410-040: Al up there and ran well after
lengthy absence: acts on fast grd: see 52.   38
872 FOUR STAR THRUST [3] 4-8-1(BL) K Bradshaw(3) 5/1 Co FAV: -004020: Bl first time:
ev ch: see 419.   19
*686 GULFLAND [5] 5-9-7 P Miller(11) 5/1 Co FAV: 0-13210: Dwelt, no threat: btr judged 686   00
872 GLENDERRY [2] 4-7-7(bl) S P Griffiths 16/1: 0-00030: Btr this trip in 872(sharper trk)   00
8 ran   nk,1,2,nk,¼   (Full Circle Thoroughbreds B Ltd)   N Tinkler Malton, Yorks.

1025 EBF UNIV. OF YORK TURF CLUB STKS 2YO   £3245   5f   Firm 18 -20 Slow

•905 LADY PAT [3] (M Mccormack) 2-9-1 M Wigham 5/1: 2411: 2 gr f Absalom - Miss Lollypop
(St Paddy) Impr filly: front rank till led inside dist, comfortably, in a 2yo stks at York
June 13: recently made all in a fillies mdn at Catterick: half sister to sev winners: well
suited by this minimum trip, tho' will stay further in time: acts on firm and soft ground
and on any track.   48
707 SURELY GREAT [1] (D Thom) 2-8-8 G Duffield 6/1: 0202: Kept on well: see 621.   36
905 GOOD GAME [4] (K Stone) 2-8-8 T Ives 4/1: 23: Broke well and made most: on the
upgrade and should have no trouble winning a race on a sharper course: see 905.   36
--   ANNIE NOONAN [6] (N Tinkler) 2-8-8 Kim Tinkler(5) 7/2: 4: Outpaced early tho' ran
on well cl home and looks certain to do btr next time: cost 28,000 gns as a yearling and
is a sister to winning juv Isabella Cannes: acts on firm grd and on a galloping track.   35
646 STEELOCK [5] 2-8-8 M Birch 10/3 FAV: 20: Uneasy fav: btr on yielding 646.   30
818 GARDENIA LADY [2] 2-8-8 T Quinn 5/1: 300: Speed over ½ way: best on yldg 646.   26
6 ran   1½,hd,nk,1½,1½   (W G Best)   M Mccormack Childrey, Oxon

1026 INNOVATIVE MARKETING SPRINT HCAP 0-70   £7960   6f   Firm 18 +03 Fast   [63]

687 IRISH COOKIE [7] (I Matthews) 4-7-7(1oh) G Dickie 7/1: 20-0141: 4 ch f Try My
Best (USA) - Irish Kick (Windjammer) Ran on strongly to lead on line in quite a fast run
and val sprint h'cap at York June 13: last month won at Lingfield and in '85 was placed sev
times, winning a fillies mdn at Chepstow: eff over 6/7f: acts on firm and soft grd and
on any track: in fine form.   36
192 MATOU [2] (G Pritchard Gordon) 6-8-11 W Ryan 5/1 Jt FAV: 0011-42: Strong run to
lead inside dist, caught post: fine effort after a fair abs: shd open his account for
the season soon: see 192.   54
+742 PHILIP [6] (N Tinkler) 4-9-7(bl) Kim Tinkler(5) 5/1 Jt FAV: 0003113: Led 2f out,
caught near fin and altho' running another fine race seems more eff over the minimum trip.   62
815 VALLEY MILLS [9] (D Barron) 6-8-11 T Quinn 8/1: 0-03004: Never nearer: see 520.   48
922 MENDICK ADVENTURE [4] 5-7-8(1ow)(4oh) J Lowe 16/1: -230000: Tried to make all:
btr effort: see 56.   29
616 DORKING LAD [10] 4-8-13 T Ives 10/1: 210-000: Fair fin: btr effort: very useful
sprinter on his day: last season won a val.h'cap over this C/D, after earlier winning at
Sandown: very eff over 5/6f: acts on frm and yldg and likes a galloping track.   40
817 NORTHERN CHIMES [8] 4-9-6 P Robinson 8/1: -000-20: Fin 8th: btr 817 (sharper trk).   00
742 CHAPLINS CLUB [5] 6-8-11 D Nicholls 9/1: 1-00000: Never dangerous 9th: yet to
recapture his sparkling form of last season which saw him rocket up the h'cap after successes
at York, Newcastle, Beverley (2), Hamilton, Epsom, Redcar and Ripon (2): very eff over
5/6f: acts on frm and soft ground and on any trk: genuine sort.   00
687 Fawleys Girl [1] 7-7(5oh)   815 Air Command [3] 8-7
441 Ra Ra Girl [12] 7-10   687 Sullys Choice [11] 8-2(bl)
12 ran   shthd,1,1½,1,3,nk,1,½   (Lord Mathews)   I Matthews Newmarket

1027 WINGS HOLIDAY STAKES 3YO HCAP 0-60   £4799   5f   Firm 18 +09 Fast   [57]

628 IBERIAN START [3] (D Barron) 3-8-9 T Ives 10/3: 0302-21: 3 b f King of Spain -
Lindy Ann (King's Leap) Useful filly: went on after ½ way, quickening well to win a fast
run 3yo h'cap at York June 13: first time out winner of a fillies event at Redcar last
season: very eff over this minimum trip:: acts on frm and soft grd and on any trk: can
defy a penalty.   52
814 CAPEABILITY POUND [1] (N Bycroft) 3-7-13 P Robinson 12/1: 0-10002: Ran on well:
best effort for some time and may win soon: acts on frm and soft: see 147.   34
588 CATHERINES WELL [8] (M W Easterby) 3-8-12 K Hodgson 11/2: 1011-03: Nearest fin:
does not look harshly treated on the form which saw her end last season with successive
nursery h'cap wins at Doncaster (2) after making all in a seller on that same course:
eff over 5/6f and stays 7f: acts on firm and yielding ground and is well suited by gall trk.   46
--   VENEZ TRADER [5] (J Etherington) 3-8-11 M Wood 12/1: 02214-4: Useful filly who ran
a most promising race and looks sure to go close next time: made all to defy top weight
in a nursery h'cap at Beverley last season, after a succession of placings: well suited by
sprint dist and should stay 7f: acts on gd and frm grd and is well suited by forcing tactics.   44
929 TOUCH OF GREY [2] 3-9-7 G Starkey 3/1 FAV: -001120: Al there: btr 624.   46
628 DEBBIE DO [7] 3-8-9 M Tebbutt(7) 6/1: 322-400: Gd speed over ½ way: see 588.   32
884 IMPALA LASS [4] 3-7-12 J Lowe 15/2: 1-11000: Made the early running: best in 443.   00
768 BRIDGE OF GOLD [9] 3-7-11 R Morse(5) 9/1: 120-100: Dwelt: no threat in 8th:see 529   00
814 MANTON MARK [6] 3-8-9 N Connorton 16/1: 1000-00: Prom to ½ way: last to finish.   00
9 ran   1½,½,½,3,½,½   (Mrs J Hazell)   D Barron Thirsk, Yorks.

1028 MAIL ON SUNDAY 3YO SERIES HCAP 0-60   £4337   7f   Firm 18 -23 Slow   [62]

576 PARIS TURF [1] (G Wragg) 3-8-7 P Robinson 9/2 Jt FAV: -0031: 3 ch c Northfields -
Miss Paris (Sovereign Path) Useful colt: led before ½ way and stayed on really well to win
a 3yo h'cap at York June 13: half brother to sev. winners incl the useful trio Miss Longchamp,
Miss St Cloud and Paris Match: sure to stay 1m: acts on gd and frm grd and a galloping
track: on the upgrade.   52

747 **HYMN OF HARLECH** [10] (G Pritchard Gordon) 3-8-9 G Duffield 9/2 Jt FAV: 0-00322: Ev
ch dist: hung left: likely to be bl next time and should go close: see 747, 478.   51
857 **NEDS EXPRESSA** [2] (C Tinkler) 3-7-7(5oh) L Charnock 16/1: 00-0003: Early leader,
kept on well in gd form and could pick up a small h'cap in the near future: see 857.   31
747 **ARCTIC KEN** [5] (C Nelson) 3-7-10 A Mackay 9/1: -011034: Stayed on: see 540.   30
914 **JOVEWORTH** [7] 3-7-10 A Proud 12/1: 40-1400: Al up there: see 914 & 283.   27
387 **COLWAY COMET** [12] 3-9-2(vis) T Ives 12/1: 203-000: Fair abs: ran well: see 228.   47
713 **TOP WING** [8] 3-8-10 M Hills 6/1: 2-1030: Fin 9th: btr 713: see 188.   00
891 **BOLD SEA ROVER** [3] 3-7-9 J Lowe 13/2: -03030: Btr over 6f in 891: see 82.   00
586 **ILLUMINEUX** [6] 3-9-7 A Bond 15/2: 1-000: Gd early speed: sn btn: see 586.   00
--   Scintillator [1] 7-7(15oh)   478 Toppeshamme [4] 9-3
947 Jarrovian [9] 8-3
12 ran   1,2,2,1½,shthd,1   (J L Pearce)   G Wragg Newmarket

1029 MERCHANT ADVENTURES MAIDEN STAKES 3YO   £3219   2m   Firm 18 -32 Slow

770 **MAJESTICIAN** [3] (G Pritchard Gordon) 3-9-0 G Duffield 9/2: -0021: 3 br c Honduras -
Mariova (Salvo) Impr colt: led over 2f out and won comfortably, being eased close home in
a 3yo mdn at York June 13: eff over 12f tho' seemed btr suited by this test of stamina:
acts on fast grd and on any track: German-bred colt who is being aimed at their St Leger.   44
811 **EL CONQUISTADOR** [2] (G Harwood) 3-9-0 A Starkey 1/1 FAV: -02: Again well bckd:
tried to make all tho' had no chance with easy winner: stays well: acts on frm grd and a
gall track: see 811.   35
411 **DENBERDAR** [6] (R Hollinshead) 3-9-0 S Perks 11/4: 0-203: Didnot seem to stay this
longer trip: btr with some give in 411 (10f): see 48.   20
839 **MATBAR** [1] (I Matthews) 3-9-0 A Shoults(5) 16/1: 0400-04: Btn home turn, bred to
be suited by middle dist and showed some promise in mdn company last term: may be btr
suited by an easier surface.   10
688 **SONNENDEW** [5] 3-9-0 S Keightley 33/1: 0-00: Remote 5th: no form to date.   00
592 **CAPITATION** [4] 3-9-0 E Guest(3) 16/1: 0-0P: With leader to ½ way, wknd quickly
and p.u. over 3f out: unfortunately had to be put down.   00
6 ran   4,15,10,dist   (Miss M A Wittman)   G Pritchard Gordon Newmarket

---

Official Going Given as Good/Firm

1030 JUNE MAIDEN FILLIES STAKES 2YO   £2775   5f   Firm 11 -22 Slow

--   **SEA DARA** [1] (I Balding) 2-8-11 Pat Eddery 9/4 fav: 1: 2 cj f Dara Monarch - Sea
Queen (Le Fabuleux) Promising filly: first time out, well bckd and was never hdd holding on
by the min margin in a 2yo fillies mdn at Sandown June 13: half sister to useful '79 2yo
King Hagen and smart French '80 2yo Mariacho: eff over stiff 5f: sure to be suited by 6f:
acts well on firm ground: the type to improve and win more races.   57
--   **SAUCE DIABLE** [7] (W Hern) 2-8-11 W Carson 5/2: 2: Op evens, drifted: battled with
winner final 2f: just btn and compensation awaits: evidently has plenty of speed but is
bred to stay at least 7f and prob further: acts well on firm.   57
707 **MARIMBA** [5] (J Winter) 2-9-0 W R Swinburn 15/2: 233: Prom, ev ch: see 707.   50
834 **AUNTIE CYCLONE** [2] (R Laing) 2-8-11 S Whitworth 14/1: 04: Showed impr here and
should do btr when tried over longer dist: acts on firm.   35
--   **POLLYS SONG** [4] 2-8-11 B Thomson 20/1: 0: No threat on debut from this small filly:
half sister to winning '85 2yo Swift's Pal: sprint bred.   35
--   **RED RIDING HOOD** [9] 2-8-11 B Rouse 9/1: 0: No danger on debut: related to sev minor
winners: may be btr suited by 6f+.   25
707 **PERSIAN TAPESTRY** [8] 2-8-11 Paul Eddery 5/1: 40: Wknd after ½ way, last to finish
and better 707 (C/D).   00
944 Naturally Autumn [3] 8-11   -- Gods Lil Lisa [6] 8-11
9 ran   shthd,3,4,ddht,3,nk,½,hd   (George Strawbridge)   I Balding Kingsclere, Berks.

1031 MORE LANE MAIDEN STAKES 3YO   £3309   1m 2f   Firm 11 -04 Slow

--   **MYTENS** [7] (J Tree) 3-9-0 Pat Eddery 7/4 fav: 3-1: 3 b c Spectacular Bid - Photographic
(Hoist The Flag) Promising colt: first time out, heavily bckd and led dist, holding on well
in a 3yo mdn at Sandown June 13: close 3rd behind MyTon Ton and Shahrastani in a val race
at Newbury on only outing in '85: well suited by firm grd and a stiff, gall trk: stays 10f
and should stay 12f: regarded as he powerful stable's best 3yo and is sure to impr further
and win more races.   59
384 **MILLERS DUST** [9] (H Cecil) 3-9-0 S Cauthen 5/2: -02: Prom thro'out, rallied gamely
final 1f and just held: well clear rem and a mdn is a formality, prob over 12f: see 384.   58
849 **RED SHOES** [10] (W Hern) 3-8-11 W Carson 14/1: 0-303: Never closer and will certainly
win a race in lesser company: see 458.   40
765 **ADMIRALS ALL** [12] (J Winter) 3-9-0 R Hills 33/1: 00-034: Dsptd lead str, no extra:
good effort and should win if dropped in class: see 765.   41

332

-- NOBLE FILLE [2] 3-8-11 B Rouse 33/1: -0: Kept on well and is sure to impr for this experience: half sister to sev winners and dam won the 1,000 Guineas and both English and Irish Oaks, one to keep on the right side. 38

-- SKEAN [4] 3-8-11 A Clark 14/1: -0: Some late prog and will benefit from the race: half sister to the smart Godswalk and Kabylia: well bred filly who is cerain to impr enough to at least win a maiden. 38

371 AMJAAD [6] 3-9-0 W R Swinburn 100/30: -00: Mkt drifter, fin 7th and ran much btr 371. 00

549 Veronica Ann [15] 8-11   720 Royal Dynasty [14] 9-0

714 Mr Moss [8] 9-0   916 Tempting Silver [13] 9-0

-- Cavaleuse [3] 8-11   822 Rosi Noa [11] 8-11   -- Misselfore [5] 8-11

619 Adbury [1] 9-0

15 ran   shthd,10,1½,nk,nk,1½   (K Abdulla)   J Tree Marlborough, Wilts.

1032 SURREY RACING HANDICAP (0-50) 3YO   £3522   7f   Firm 11 +08 Fast   [54]

747 PINSTRIPE [3] (R Williams) 3-8-10 R Cochrane 12/1: 0330-01: 3 b c Pitskelly - Snoozy Time (Cavo Doro) Impr colt: prom and led final 1f comfortably, in quite a fast run and val 3yo h'cap at Sandown June 13: first success: showed plenty of ability last season: well suited by 7f and firm or gd ground: runs well on a stiff track. 46

624 LADY LA PAZ [10] (P Cundell) 3-7-7 G French 12/1: 00-0402: Overcame difficulties in running and stayed on strongly: best effort yet: suited by 7f and will stay 1m: acts well on firm ground: should find a race soon: see 454. 25

423 IYAMSKI [1] (W Hastings Bass) 3-8-10 R Lines[3] 8/1: -2023: Led 2f out, hdd final 1f: running well but possibly lacks a turn of foot: see 16, 423. 40

406 BASOOF [2] (M Stoute) 3-9-7 W R Swinburn 10/1: 304-04: Never closer under top weight: lightly raced half sister to topclass Shadeed: will be suited by 1m: acts well on firm. 48

881 SWIFTS PAL [9] 3-9-4 P Waldron 8/1: 00-0030: Pulled much too hard on way to start, led 5f: see 881. 45

855 FUDGE [11] 3-7-11 S Dawson[3] 16/1: 000-200: Never closer: btr effort: see 534. 23

*703 BURHAAIN [13] 3-8-8 Paul Eddery 7/2 fav: 033-010: Disapp fav, never in it: see 703. 00

886 WAR WAGON [4] 3-8-7 S Cauthen 8/1: 00-0000: Chall dist, wknd: twice below 703(C/D). 00

455 KINGS TOUCH [8] 3-9-2 G Baxter 8/1: 01-040: Steadily wknd str: much btr 455(yld). 00

703 LITTLE PIPERS [6] 3-9-3 B Rouse 8/1: 00-0000: Al rear: active in mkt: first time out winner of a mdn at Sandown in '85: prob stays 7f: acts on fast going. 00

328 Country Gentleman [12] 8-9   925 Miranda Julia [7] 8-2

822 Gay Appeal [5] 8-8

13 ran   1½,¾,1½,shthd,½,3,½   (Michael R Jaye)   R Williams Newmarket

---

1033 SINGAPORE AIRLINES H'CAP (0-60) 3YO   £3967   5f   Firm 11 -03 Slow   [50]

660 RESPECT [6] (R Laing) 3-9-7 Pat Eddery 11/10 fav: 43-2131: 3 b c Mummy's Pet - Restive (Relic) Very useful, impr colt: heavily bckd when readily winning a 3yo h'cap at Sandown June 13, leading on bit final 1f: easy winner over same C/D May 15: placed in all 3 outings in '85: speedily bred sort who is a half brother to sev winners: very eff over a stiff 5f on firm or gd ground, possibly not so well suited by soft: shd be hard to beat next 58

-- SAY PARDON [2] (D Morley) 3-8-13 T Williams 25/1: 23220-2: Dsptd lead most for a fine seasonal debut: placed in 4 out of 5 races in '85 without winning: stays 6f, eff 5f: acts on firm and gd ground: sure to win a race shortly. 42

*884 RAYHAAN [5] (C Benstead) 3-9-8(7ex) B Rouse 7/2: -0113: Made much, gd effort under penalty and is in fine form: see 884. 49

846 SNAP DECISION [4] (R Hannon) 3-8-10 W Carson 10/1: 1300-04: Never closer: won a nursery at Windsor in '85, placed sev other times: acts on firm and yldg and on any trk: very effective at 5f but may stay further. 31

580 HELAWE [1] 3-8-8(bl) R Hills 6/1: 100-030: Early speed: btr 580 (C/D good). 22

760 NORTHERN TRUST [7] 3-9-5 J Reid 20/1: 0-33000: Dsptd lead much: best 314 (C/D soft) 28

-- Shari Louise [8] 8-8   884 Herminda [3] 8-2

8 ran   2½,½,2,2½,2,nk   (R N Richmond-Watson)   R Laing Lambourn , Berks

---

1034 ROSEMARY STAKES (H'CAP) (0-50) 3YO   £3143   1m 2f   Firm 11 -04 Slow   [56]

674 TRIPLE BLUFF [4] (B Hills) 3-8-0 R Hills 13/2: 00-031: 3 br c Pretense - Thrice Crafty (Triple Bend) Gained his first success when leading inside final 3f in a 3yo h'cap at Sandown June 13: quite lightly raced prev: suited by 10f, may stay further: acts on yldg but possibly at his best on firm. 39

275 STRAIGHT THROUGH [7] (J Winter) 3-8-3 B Rouse 11/2: 24-2122: Al prom after abs: gd effort: see 120: acts on firm and heavy. 37

739 NEEDLEWOMAN [5] (R Armstrong) 3-8-6 W Carson 7/2: -00043: Ran in snatches and better 739 (C/D good). 35

847 FLOATING ASSET [1] (P Walwyn) 3-8-10(VIS) Pat Eddery 5/1: 24-4034: Chall 2f out. 36

805 PRINCE MERANDI [3] 3-8-6 J Reid 25/1: -133000: Outsider: dsptd lead after ½ way. 28

-- SPECIAL GUEST [6] 3-7-7(1oh) T Williams 20/1: 01200-0: No danger on seasonal debut: won a nursery at Yarmouth in '85: stays at least 7f, shd stay further: acts on gd and soft. 11

919 SWIFT TROOPER [2] 3-9-7(bl) R Cochrane 2/1 fav: -121420: Dsptd lead much, wknd quickly and much better 919. 00

7 ran   2,3,2,4,4,5   (Sheikh Mohammed)   B Hills Lambourn, Berks

1035 H.W.F.A. WILLIAMS HANDICAP (0-35)   £2439   1m 6f   Firm 11 +01 Fast   [33]

801 ALSIBA [20] (C Benstead) 4-8-10 B Rouse 33/1: 4-00001: 4 gr f Northfields - Grise
(Sea Hawk II) Caused a 33/1 surprise, leading dist under press in a h'cap at Sandown June 13:
first success: eff over 14f, stays 2m: seems suited by fast going.   24
*731 DENBOY [12] (B Stevens) 4-8-13 R Carter[5] 12/1: 00-0012: Chall 1f out: gd effort
and is in fine form: see 731: stays 14f well.   24
841 ROYAL CRAFTSMAN [8] (N Smith) 5-8-6 P Cook 6/1: 0-00303: Came from well off the
pace and does not seem an easy ride: see 341.   15
541 AMIGO ESTIMADO [16] (K Brassey) 4-8-13 S Whitworth 20/1: 000-004: Al prom: stays 14f.   21
856 ACTION TIME [15] 5-9-0 B Thomson 50/1: -0U00: Never closer: best eff this season:
off the trk in '85 and has yet to win a race: stays 2m and is suited by firm ground.   22
856 SITAR THEME [13] 4-9-0 C Rutter[5] 9/1: 003-400: Nicely bckd (again) made much.   20
--   NADER [1] 5-8-7 W R Swinburn 8/1: -0: Fit from a recent spell of hurdling, well bckd
but never in it: useful over hurdles but a maiden on Flat: best form on a sound surface.   00
917 MY CHARADE [6] 5-8-9(vis) J Williams 9/1: 0014020: Prom most: much btr 917 (gd).   00
*984 TAXIADS [14] 4-9-10(4ex) J Reid 4/1 fav: 00-0110: Too soon after 984?   00
856 PATRICK JOHN LYONS [17] 5-8-3 A Clark 10/1: 0030-30: Much btr 856 (yldg).   00
--   Destroy [3] 7-10   --   Charlottes Choice [5] 7-9
735 Alacazam [18] 7-12   856 Wild Ginger [9] 8-10(bl)
590 Artesium [2] 9-1   856 Master Francis [10] 8-10
*850 Pulsingh [19] 8-8(4ex)   856 Shuttlecock Star [11] 7-11
28   Bulandshar [4] 7-9   940 Golden Triangle [7] 9-7
20 ran   1½,1½,¾,shthd,1½   (Miss A Westerdick)   C Benstead Epsom, Surrey

---

Official Going Given as Firm on the Round Course : Good/Firm on Straight Course

1036 BAKER LORENZ 3YO MAIDEN STAKES   £4489   7f   Firm -06 +17 Fast

764 MAWSUFF [18] (H T Jones) 3-9-0 R Hills 100/30: -021: 3 b c Known Fact - Last
Request (Dancers Image) Useful colt: made all at a tremendous pace and set a new course
record when holding on under strong press to win a very fast 3yo mdn at Sandown June 14:
unraced in '85: very eff with front running tactics over 7f: seems to act on any trk:
well suited by fast ground: sure to win more races.   60
--   STAR CUTTER [6] (H Cecil) 3-9-0 W Ryan 13/8 fav: -2: Heavily bckd newcomer: strong
fin and would have won in another stride: first foal of a winning miler and cost $190,000:
sure to stay 1m: acts on fast ground: will have no difficulty in winning races.   60
764 RUE ST JACQUES [8] (D Arbuthnot) 3-9-0 G Starkey 10/1: 0-333: Chall 2f out: no extra
but is certainly capable of winning a run of the mill maiden: see 764.   40
387 MARSHAL MACDONALD [17] (W Holden) 3-9-0 J Reid 20/1: 40-004: Kept on all too late:
ran only twice in '85: bred to be suited by 1m+: acts on firm.   36
--   BLAIRINGONE [3] 3-9-0 M Banner 25/1: -0: Shd benefit from this 1st effort and
shaped quite pleasingly: brother to successful '82 juv Leadenhall Lad: sprint bred:
seems to stay 7f.   31
--   PROMENADER [2] 3-9-0 Paul Eddery 20/1: 00-0: No threat on seasonal debut: no show
in 2 outings last term: half brother to winning sprinter Scintillo: speedily bred sort
who has scope for improvement.   26
624 FRUITY OROONEY [10] 3-9-0 V Smith[5] 14/1: 002-000: Prom most, fin 7th: rated 47
on final outing in '85 but has yet to run up to that form this term: best form with forcing
tactics over 6f on yielding going.   00
708 ARAB HERITAGE [11] 3-8-11 A Kimberley 6/1: -00: Prom in mkt, al rear: see 708.   00
806 Highly Recommended [5] 9-0   806 Chucklestone [13] 9-0
581 Lake Onega [1] 8-11   658 Far Too Busy [14] 8-11
--   Out Of Kindness [9] 8-11   835 Abutammam [7] 9-0
842 Deputy Governor [4] 9-0   --   North Ocean 0 9-0
--   Lydia Eva [16] 8-11   764 Umbelata [12] 9-0
18 ran   shthd,10,2,3,3   (Hamdan Al-Maktoum)   H T Jones Newmarket

1037 BAKER LORENZ SUMMER H'CAP 4YO+ 0-60   £3785   5f   Firm -06 -03 Slow   [53]

877 AXE VALLEY [3] (P Cole) 4-9-4 T Quinn 16/1: 2010-01: 4 b f Royben - Unpredictable
(Pardal) Useful filly: al well there, gained the day cl home narrowly in a blanket fin to
a val h'cap at Sandown June 14: bl for the first time when winning a h'cap at Windsor in
'85 but didnot wear them today: very eff at 5f on firm or gd grd tho' seems to act any trk:
best when up with the pace.   55
742 SPACEMAKER BOY [9] (R Nicholls) 6-8-11 Paul Eddery 14/1: 2410032: Made much,
just caught: fine effort: see 211.   47
846 AMEGHINO [8] (M Mccourt) 6-9-1 A Tucker[7] 6/1: -004033: Flying fin and is in
gd form: see 846.   50
877 DURHAM PLACE [4] (K Brassey) 4-9-10 G Baxter 9/1: 0030-04: Chall final 1f, narrowly
btn: see 877.   58
836 ALL AGREED [2] 5-9-2 B Rouse 100/30 fav: 04-0040: Fin well, gd eff: see 550.   49
748 KELLYS ROYALE [5] 4-9-3 J Reid 12/1: 0-00000: Prom thro'out: see 550.   49

836	CREE BAY [10] 7-9-5 G Starkey 10/1: 0-33200: Fin a cl 7th: see 550.		00
+836	LOCHTILLUM [6] 7-9-8(7ex) W Ryan 15/2: 00-0010: Al rear under penalty: see 836.		00
986	Brown Bear Boy [7] 8-7	854 Puccini [12] 8-12	
734	Shalbee [11] 7-7(5oh)	836 Stoneydale [1] 8-10	

12 ran   ½,nk,½,shthd,shthd,½   (Richard Barber)   P Cole Whatcombe, Oxon

---

1038 BAKER LORENZ SILVER GAVEL HCAP 3YO+ 0-60 £7986   1m 2f   Firm -06 -05 Slow   [58]

805   KALKOUR [3] (M Haynes) 4-8-10 W Ryan 12/1: -0-0101: 4 ch c General Assembly -
Crepellana (Crepello) Useful, impr colt: ran on to lead inside final 2f and forged 5l clear
in val h'cap at Sandown June 14: winner of a h'cap at Kempton May 5: lightly raced since
winning at Sandown as a 2yo and has since changed stables: very eff over 10f on firm or good
ground and said to be unsuited by soft: acts on any trk but runs well at Sandown.   55
--   AL YABIR [10] (C Benstead) 4-8-12 B Rouse 11/1: 20020-2: Gd seasonal debut: rated 62
when awarded a val 3yo h'cap at Newmarket last term: earlier successful at Salisbury:
suited by 10f and firm going and likes a stiff gallopinng track: shd run well next time.   47
*805   POCHARD [1] (P Cole) 4-9-6(5ex) T Quinn 7/4 fav: 23-3113: Made much: beat winner
decisively in 805.   53
698   CHICLET [2] (P Walwyn) 4-9-1(vis) Paul Eddery 6/1: 30-0204: Came from behind,
much closer to winner in 432 (good).   47
888   FORWARD RALLY [6] 4-8-2 C Nutter 9/2: 21-1120: Cl.up over 1m: btr 888 (gd).   33
921   PATO [7] 4-9-2 J Reid 25/1: 210-000: Ev ch: see 511.   46
--   Rusty Law [11] 9-10   724 Kates Pride [5] 7-7(VIS)(1oh)
921   Tracing [8] 9-4   706 Thats Your Lot [4] 9-0
750   Evros [9] 8-1(BL)
11 ran   5,1½,¾,½,½   (David Myers)   M Haynes Epsom, Surrey

1039 EBF SURVEYORS STAKES 2YO   £2978   5f   Firm -06 -18 Slow

918   QUICK SNAP [4] (A Ingham) 2-8-11(bl) R Curant 9/2: 43221: 2 b c Try My Best - Photo
(Blakeney) Gained a deserved success, making all comfortably in a rather slowly run minor
2yo event at Sandown June 14: placed all 4 outings prev: appears to act on firm and soft:
suited by a stiff 5f and shd stay further.   51
800   COPPER RED [1] (P Makin) 2-8-11 T Quinn 6/4 fav: 32: Mostly 2nd: needs 6f: See 800 44
876   FRENCH TUITION [3] (R Hannon) 2-9-3 L Jones[5] 11/1: 233103: Al prom: consistent.   48
800   MURAJAH [6] (C Benstead) 2-8-11 B Rouse 20/1: 04: No extra final 2f but an improved
effort: related to a couple of winning sprinters/milers: will be suited by 6f: acts on firm.   39
--   PAS DENCHERE [7] 2-8-11 P Waldron 20/1: 0: Never closer: shd benefit from the
experience: dam a winner over 7f in Ireland: will be suited by 6f+.   27
--   MISTER WIZARD [5] 2-8-11 Paul Eddery 33/1: 0: Never closer: first foal of a winning
French miler: certain to be suited by much longer distances.   25
--   TELESTO [2] 2-8-11 G Starkey 11/4: 0: Friendless in mkt, wknd ½ way: related to
sev winners in the USA and cost $255,000: speedily bred but will stay at least 6f:
certain to improve.   00
834   Keecagee [8] 8-11
8 ran   3,¾,1,4,¾,2,3   (Exors of the late S R Crowe)   A Ingham Epsom, Surrey

---

1040 VALUATION STAKES 3YO   £2973   1m 6f   Firm -06 +03 Fast

849   KNIGHTS LEGEND [4] (G Harwood) 3-8-11 G Starkey 11/8 jt fav: -21: 3 b c Sir Ivor -
Gimme Love (Dr Fager) Promising colt: led inside final 1f under press in a 4 runner 3yo minor
race at Sandown June 14: half brother to 2 winners: very eff over 12f/14f: shd stay 2m:
acts on firm and gd going and likes a stiff galloping track: the type to improve and win again.   55
*811   ACTINIUM [1] (P Cole) 3-9-2 T Quinn 11/8 jt fav: 043-212: Led 2f out, battled on
well when clear rem 2 runners: continues to impr and should pick up a h'cap soon: see 811.   57
811   ZAAJER [2] (J Dunlop) 3-8-11 B Rouse 4/1: -323: Led str, no extra final 2f: see 811.   37
832   TABACOS [3] (D Elsworth) 3-8-11 Paul Eddery 25/1: 0-4004: Made much, wknd quickly:
yet to reproduce 479 (10f, yldg).   12
4 ran   1½,10,20   (R J Shannon)   G Harwood Pulborough, Sussex

---

1041 BAKER LORENZ H'CAP 3YO+ 0-50   £3433   1m   Firm -06 +03 Fast   [47]

*954   AVENTINO [6] (J Sutcliffe) 3-7-7(bl)(5ex)(4oh) M L Thomas 11/8 fav: 01-0111: 3 ch g
Cure The Blues - Sovereign Dona (Sovereign Path) Completed a quick hat+trick when gaining
the day near the fin of a h'cap at Sandown June 14: winner of similar races at Newmarket
and Goodwood recently: narrowly won a Newmarket seller on final outing in '85: very eff
over 7f/1m and is suited by firm ground: wears bl: well h'capped and could complete a
4-timer: scheduled to move to the USA shortly.   37
775   BOLD PILLAGER [7] (J Dunlop) 4-8-7 B Rouse 8/1: 020-032: Just failed to make all
and is due a h'cap soon: see 775.   36
930   EVERY EFFORT [9] (R Holder) 4-8-4 J Reid 11/2: 0-401D3: Chall dist: fair effort
but better 930 (sharp trk).   28
680   TOM FORRESTER [4] (A Pitt) 5-8-1 C Rutter[5] 11/1: 03-0304: Ev ch: best 578 (C/D).   20
706   TALK OF GLORY [3] 5-8-6 G Baxter 10/1: 00-0200: Prom most: btr 706, 453 (yldg).   23
919   QUICK DANCER [13] 3-7-7 G French 14/1: 00-0000: There 6f: fl- :ered 579.   20

805 **Iktiyar** [2] 8-6   815 **Creeager** [12] 9-1   --   **Steeple Bell** [8] 9-10
812 **No Credibility** [5] 8-8   --   **Feydan** [1] 8-2
11 ran   nk,2,3,1,2½   (A J Smith)   J Sutcliffe Epsom, Surrey.

YORK   Saturday June 14th   Lefthand, Galloping Track

Official Going Given as Good/Firm

1042 RIDING FOR DISABLED INVITATiON STAKES   £5000   1m 4f   Firm 11 -02 Slow

688 AL KAAHIR [7] (H T Jones) 3-8-6 A Murray 7/4 FAV: 202-31: 3 ch f Valdez (USA) -
Shawn's Gal (USA) (Crimson Streak) Very useful colt: led ½ way and drew clear in str for an
easy win in a stks event at York June 14: showed a deal of promise in '85, nk 2nd to
Centrepoint at Newcastle: stays 12f well: acts on firm and yldg grd and likes a gall trk:
should win more races.   60
551 THREE TIMES A LADY [2] (P Kelleway) 3-8-3 B Thomson 7/2: -0002: Ev ch in str: stays 12f48
286 BRIGHT AS NIGHT [3] (M Ryan) 3-8-6 P Robinson 10/3: 240-303: Yet to regain his 2yo
form: prob stays 12f: see 24.   49
833 DIWAAN [1] (P Walwyn) 3-8-6 Pat Eddery 8/1: 030-004: Prom, wknd 2f out: see 833.   35
651 POWER BENDER [5] 4-9-7 G Duffield 15/2: 222-430: Wknd str: best 452 (10f).   26
917 TOUCH OF LUCK [6] 4-9-4 S Perks 20/1: 3-00000: Never in it: placed on sev occasions
in '85 when trained by H Candy: now with R Hollinshead: stays 12f: acts on gd and soft grd.   15
697 Sandmoor Prince [4] 8-6(bl)
7 ran   3,½,8,4,4   (Hamdan Al-Maktoum)   H T Jones Newmarket

1043 VERNONS FILLIES STAKES 3YO   £8792   1m   Firm 11 -01 Slow

549 ZUMURRUDAH [10] (H T Jones) 3-8-11 A Murray 20/1: -001: 3 gr f Spectacular Bid -
Royal Statute (Northern Dancer) Useful, fast impr filly: al prom and stayed on well to lead
cl home in a val 3yo fillies event at York June 14: half sister to the smart staying filly
Awaasif: eff 1m, shd be well suited by 10f+: acts well on fast grd and a stiff trk.   57
656 BALLAD ROSE [8] (P Cole) 3-8-11 T Ives 12/1: 323-432: Nearly made all: in gd form
and deserves a races soon: acts on any grd: see 359.   55
213 LIKENESS [3] (W Hern) 3-8-11 W Carson 4/1: 033-03: Abs: al up there: last season
was rated 63 when 4th to Tralthee in the Rockfel Stks at Newmarket: stays 1m: acts well on
fast ground and a gall track: shd have no trouble finding a maiden.   49
923 STICKY GREENE [6] (B Hills) 3-8-11 B Thomson 12/1: 0-334: Al up there: consistent.   43
-- ACTUALIZATIONS [1] 3-8-11 R Guest 14/1: -0: Nearest fin on race course debut and
improvement very likely: USA bred filly who cost $125,000 as a yearling: shd stay 10f:
acts on fast ground.   41
464 ABSENCE OF MALICE [7] 3-8-11 R Cochrane 12/1: -200: Twice below form 213 (7f yldg).   38
-- SHAKANA [4] 3-8-11 S Cauthen 11/2: 2-0: Never nearer 7th on seasonal debut: on sole
start in '85 fin 2nd to Northern Eternity in a val fillies mdn at Ascot: dam is a half
sister to Shergar and Shernazar: shd be well suited by 10f+: acts on yldg grd and should
do much better next time.   00
708 LADY FOR TWO [11] 3-8-11 W R Swinburn 10/3 FAV: -40: Well bckd: fdd: much btr 708.   00
576 ESFAHAN [9] 3-8-11 G Duffield 9/2: -020: Made no show: much btr 576 (7f).   00
213 SOEMBA [5] 3-8-11 Pat Eddery 10/1: 4-00: Al rear: on sole start as a 2yo fin 4th
to Dolka in val mdn at Newmarket: shd stay further than 1m: acts on gd/firm.   00
817 Elsocko [2] 8-11   **661** Gemma Kaye [12] 8-11
12 ran   ½,2½,3,1,1½,½   (Hamdan Al-Maktoum)   H T Jones Newmarket

1044 WILLIAM HILL TROPHY 3YO 0-75   £18903   6f   Firm 11 +06 Fast   [67]

+600 GOVERNOR GENERAL [3] (L Cottrell) 3-8-12(7ex) R Cochrane 6/4 FAV: 001-011: 3 b c
Dominion - Law and Impulse (Roan Rocket) Very useful colt: heavily bckd and ran on final 1f
to ddht on the post in fast run and val Wm Hill Trophy (h'cap) at York June 14: last time
out was an impressive 5l winner over Native Oak in the Hue Williams Stks at Newbury:
in '85 won a fast run mdn at Goodwood: half brother to winners: very eff at 6f on gd
and firm ground.   64
814 SEW HIGH [7] (B Mcmahon) 3-7-7 A Mackay 33/1: -001041: 3 b c Nicholas Bill-
Sew Nice (Tower Walk) Made virtually ev yard and stuck on gamely to ddht in val Wm Hill
Trophy h'cap at York June 14: earlier won a h'cap at Thirsk: in '85 won sellers at Ripon
and Haydock: equally eff over 5/6f: acts on firm and soft grd and is best when up with the
pace: only small, but seems a genuine sort.   45
947 VILTASH [1] (J Etherington) 3-8-5 M Wood 33/1: 000-003: Stayed on well final 1f:
gd effort: see 671.   51
808 MUMMYS FAVOURITE [8] (J Dunlop) 3-9-2 W Carson 7/2: 4111-34: Well bckd: never
nearer: btr 808.   57
808 LOCHONICA [11] 3-9-7 D Nicholls 33/1: 40-0000: Nearest fin: btr effort: see 245.   59

691   GOSSIPER [6] 3-8-9 T Ives 16/1: 400-000: Prom, ev ch: see 600.   45
+671 PANNANICH WELLS [5] 3-7-11(1ow)(7ex) P Robinson 9/1: 30-0210: Prom, wknd: btr 671(yld). 00
-808 MERDON MELODY [12] 3-8-2 T Williams 8/1: 34-1220: Never in it: much btr 808.   00
*895 ELNAWAAGI [2] 3-9-5(7ex) A Murray 7/1: 123-110: Prom, eased when btn: possibly better
with some give in the ground: see 895.   00
844   Quinta Reef [9] 8-4   580 Sparky Lad [13] 8-5   929 Mandrake Madam [10] 8-8
12 ran   ddht,2,1½,1,¾   (Ray Richards)   L Cottrell Cullompton, Devon
                                 (R Thornhill)   B McMahon, Tamworth, Staffs

1045 DANIEL PRENN ROYAL YORKS. STKS 3YO   £8064   1m 2f Firm 11 -41 Slow

753   HELLO ERNANI [3] (I Balding) 3-8-7 T Ives 6/1: 3-22321: 3 br c Robellino - Maple
River (Clandestine) Smart colt: gained a well deserved success, leading 2f out, staying on
well by a shthd in val but slow run Royal Yorkshire Stks at York June 14: has had sev near
misses this season in gd company: eff 1m, stays 10f: acts on any grd and on any trk:
genuine sort who should win more races.   71
476   TOP GUEST [2] (G Wragg) 3-8-7 S Cauthen 4/1: 222-122: Hmpd final 1f when ev ch:
fin 3rd, placed 2nd: in fine form: see 476, 194.   68
+806 FARAJULLAH [6] (G Huffer) 3-8-11 M Miller 11/8 FAV: -12D: Dsptd lead over 1f out:
hung left final 1f and just failed to get up: fin 2nd, placed 3rd: fine effort: will be
winning again very soon: stays 10f: see 806.   74
218   DARE SAY [4] (J Tree) 3-8-7 Pat Eddery 7/2: -24: Made much: kept on: gd effort
after abs and a mdn race is a formality: stays 10f: acts on firm and gd/yldg: see 218.   54
+723 FIRST KISS [5] 3-8-4 W Carson 6/1: -10: Stiff task: ran well: see 723.   55
806   RIVART [1] 3-8-7 B Thomson 20/1: -00: Prom, wknd 2f out: possibly stays 10f:
should have no trouble winning a mdn race: see 806.   54
6 ran   shthd,1½,2,2½,1½   (George Strawbridge)   I Balding Kingsclere, Berks

1046 OAKLEY VAUGHAN STAKES 3YO   £8792   1m   Firm 11 -02 Slow

806   MAJAAHED [4] (B Hanbury) 3-9-0 R Cochrane 14/1: -01: 3 ch c Exclusive Native -
Whydidju (Tom Rolfe) Promising colt: led inside final 1f, comfortably, in val Oakeley
Vaughan Stks at York June 14: well bred sort who cost $290,000 as yearling: eff 1m, should
stay further: acts on firm grd and will win more races.   59
887   DANSKI [9] (P Cole) 3-9-0 P Robinson 6/1: 322-242: Led over 2f out: hdd final 1f.   55
546   SEVERS [8] (H Cecil) 3-9-0 S Cauthen 5/1: -03: Al up there: gd effort: acts on
firm and yldg and will have no trouble finding a race.   53
371   AITCH N BEE [3] (J Dunlop) 3-9-0 B Thomson 14/1: -04: Ev ch over 2f out: another
good run: cost 20,000 gns as yearling: eff 1m on gd and firm ground and should find a maiden   53
--   LOCAL SILVER [10] 3-9-0 W Carson 10/1: 0-0: Nearest fin on seasonal debut: should
do better next time: half brother to very smart Local Suitor: shd be suited by 1m and   --
further: acts on fast grd and a gall track and is one to keep an eye on.   50
-861 TIMBERWOOD [6] 3-9-0(BL) A Murray 7/1: 040-120: Bl first time: made much: see 861,388   43
572   PLAXTOL [11] 3-9-0 Pat Eddery 6/1: -000: Wknd over 2f out: much btr 572 (10f)   00
806   SHERZAD [1] 3-9-0 W R Swinburn 9/4 FAV: -40: Stumbled badly after 1f: best ignored.   00
--   North Lake [5] 9-0   -- Capricorn Beau [7] 9-0
937   Sure Landing [12] 9-0   891 Whoberley Wheels [2] 9-0
12 ran   1½,½,hd,1½,3   (Maktoum Al-Maktoum)   B Hanbury Newmarket

1047 MICHAEL SOBELL HANDICAP 3YO+ 0-70   £8311   1m 1f Firm 11 -02 Slow   [58]

573   FREEDOMS CHOICE [3] (J Dunlop) 4-9-7 W Carson 11/2: 13-42D1: 4 ch c Forli (Arg) -
Full of Hope (USA) (Bold Ruler) Very useful colt: defied top weight, staying on gamely to
lead line in val h'cap at York June 14: in grand form in 2nd half of '85, winning at Newbury
and Haydock and placed many times: very eff over 1m, stays 10f: acts on gd/firm and soft
ground and on any track: genuine sort.   64
879   TRY TO STOP ME [8] (D Smith) 5-8-7 B Thomson 5/1 Jt.FAV: 00-0032: Led 3f out, caught
post: in form: see 879.   49
-706 PROMISED ISLE [7] (Lady Herries) 5-9-0 A Murray 5/1 Jt.FAV: 002-323: Stayed on well
and not btn far: is in fine form and deserves to win soon: see 706, 432.   54
--   ACCLAIMATION [4] (R Connolly) 5-8-0 A Mackay 10/1: 330-124: Irish chall: switched
over 1f out and fin well: gd effort: winner at The Curragh April 12 (1m yldg): stays 10f:
acts on firm and soft.   39
*521 SHORT SLEEVES [2] 4-8-9 W R Swinburn 11/2: 310-010: Never nearer: running well.   42
815   MOORES METAL [1] 6-8-8 S Perks 20/1: 0-00000: Kept on: see 441.   36
930   VIRGIN ISLE [9] 5-8-5 T Williams 9/1: 0200040: Btn, hmpd over 1f out: btr 930.
see 79: possibly best over 1m.   00
--   SMOKEYS SECRET [10] 4-8-12 Pat Eddery 8/1: 03113-0: Lightly bckd on seasonal debut:
fdd: better for race: in gd form in '85, winning at Chepstow and Warwick: equally eff at
1m/10f: acts on gd/firm and soft grd and on any track: seems genuine sort.   00
943   VINTAGE TOLL [6] 6-8-10 S Cauthen 10/1: 3003400: Al rear: btr 698, see 52.   00
519   Cane Mill [13] 8-1   706 Go Bananas [12] 9-7   872 Shellman [14] 8-5
433   Russell Creek [5] 8-3   -- Warplane [11] 8-1
14 ran   shthd,1,½,3,2½   (Ogden Mills Phipps)   J Dunlop Arundel, Sussex

1048 BASIL SAMUEL HANDICAP 3YO 0-70   £5271   1m 6f   Firm 11 -04 Slow   [66]

*833 BEIJING [3] (P Cole) 3-7-7(3ex)(3oh) A Mackay 7/4 FAV: 000-11: 3 b f Northjet -
Protectors (Chi) (Prologo) Impr filly: well bckd and led well over 1f out, comfortably, in
a val 3yo h'cap at York June 14: last time out won a h'cap at Bath: bred to be suited by
dist of ground as she is a half sister to the smart stayer Protection Racket and the useful
Safe River: eff at 13f, shd stay 2m: acts on gd and firm grd and a gall trk: on upgrade.   43
*908 FEDRA [6] (Lord J Fitzgerald) 3-7-7(3ex)(2oh) L Riggio(7) 6/1: 0-12212: Made much:
in grand form: stays 14f: see 908.   37
597 WAR HERO [4] (J Dunlop) 3-9-7 W Carson 7/1: 013-003: Gd effort under his big weight:
stays 14f: see 273.   65
738 HURRICANE HENRY [7] (M Stoute) 3-7-12 P Robinson 5/1: 02-004: Never in it: see 738.   30
*669 ALARM CALL [5] 3-8-4 R Cochrane 4/1: 410: Much btr 669 (yldg/soft 12f).   28
811 MARIE GALANTE [2] 3-7-8 T Williams 12/1: 0-23230: Wknd str: btr 811, see 458 (12f)   00
6 ran   3,shthd,8,5,20   (Binfield Manor Farms Ltd)   P Cole Lambourn, Berks

1049 EBF DUCHESS OF KENT STAKES 2YO   £6036   6f   Firm 11 -30 Slow

--   DARLEY KNIGHT [4] (J Dunlop) 2-9-0 W Carson 9/2: 1: 2 b c Formidable - Yelney
(Blakeney) Promising colt: switched 1½f out, led inside final 1f comfortably in a val 2yo
stks at York June 14: cost 96,000 gns as yearling and is a half brother to 12f winner
Golden Heights: eff 6f, certain to be suited by further: acts on firm grd and shd win more   56
--   SUMMERHILL STREAK [6] (E Eldin) 2-9-0 A Mackay 6/1: 2: Dsptd lead: kept on well:
promising race course debut from this half brother to winning 3yo Summerhill Spruce:
eff 6f, on firm grd and should find a maiden.   50
927 SECOOT [3] (P Cole) 2-9-0 S Cauthen 5/1: 03: Al up there: impr colt who is a half
brother to a couple of winners: shd be suited by further than 6f: acts on firm ground.   48
--   LUBRICAN [2] (J Tree) 2-9-0 Pat Eddery 3/1: 4: Led 2f out: not btn far on race course
debut: half brother to smart 9f winner Portlaw: cost $82,000: acts on fast grd and looks
sure to find a race.   48
662 BOIS DE BOULOGNE [1] 2-9-0 W R Swinburn 11/10 FAV: 20: Led/dsptd lead: btr 662.   41
--   GOLDEN TREE [7] 2-9-0 M Wood 16/1: 0: Early speed: half brother to winning stayer
Rig Steel: acts on fast ground.   39
870 ALBION PLACE [5] 2-9-0 K Hodgson 8/1: 40: Prom, fdd: see 870.   00
7 ran   1½,½,hd,2½,½   (Sheikh Mohammed)   J Dunlop Arundel, Sussex

Official Going Given as Good/Soft

1050 LONGTOWN MAIDEN STAKES 2YO   £1217   6f   Good 75 -01 Slow

864 WENSLEYDALEWARRIOR [4] (G Moore) 2-9-0 D Casey(7) 8/1: 03201: 2 ro c Alias Smith -
Foolish Heroine (Brigadier Gerard): Gained a deserved win, running on strongly to lead close
home in a 2yo maiden at Carlisle June 14: half brother to 10f winner The Villain: eff over
5/6f on fast and heavy grnd: acts on any trk: likes to be up with the pace.   42
819 CARSE KELLY [6] (S Norton) 2-8-11 J Lowe 3/1 FAV: 022: Led below dist, just caught.   37
859 FOUNTAINS CHOICE [16] (K Stone) 2-9-0 G Brown 5/1: 33: Al prom & kept on well up
this stiff finish: half brother to several middle distance winners, incl useful Yard Bird:
sure to stay further: see 859.   32
--   PHILOTAS [8] (Denys Smith) 2-9-0 D Nicholls 20/1: 4: Unfancied though always up there
on racecourse debut: cost 7,000 gns as a yearling: acts on gd grnd & on a stiff trk.   24
--   BLACK MANS BAY [2] 2-8-11 K Darley 20/1: 0: Al prom on debut & should impr: should
stay further in time: acts on gd grnd.   20
934 SUPREME OPTIMIST [7] 2-9-0(BL) J Quinn(5) 12/1: 3000: Bl first time and tried to
make all: best on a tight trk in 460.   22
873 SILVERS ERA [15] 2-8-11 M Wigham 7/1: 02040: Fin 7th: best on soft in 473 (tight trk).   00
694 BEAU BENZ [11] 2-9-0 M Birch 11/2: 000: Longer trip: fin 9th & btr in 694 (5f).   00
197 JAYS SPECIAL [1] 2-9-0 T Lucas 8/1: 40: Never dngr: abs since 197 (5f, yld).   00
--   SKINNHILL [5] 2-9-0 D Leadbitter(5) 10/1: 0: No threat on debut: half brother to fair
stayer Tresidder.   00
--   TYRED NSNOOKERED [13] 2-9-0 L Charnock 10/1: 0: Cheaply bought colt who should be
well suited by this trip.   00
685 Sergeant Meryll [3] 9-0   746 Loma Breeze [14] 8-11
603 Bantel Blazer [12] 9-0   627 Geobritony [10] 9-0
-- Betty Blue [18] 8-11   741 La Verte Gleam [9] 8-11
865 Rimove [17] 8-11
18 ran   ½,3,3,½,½,1½,hd,2   (C K Woods)   G Moore Middleham, Yorks

1051 CASTLE CARROCK HANDICAP 3YO 0-35   £1825   6f   Good 75 +08 Fast   [37]

961 QUALITAIR KING [1] (K Stone) 3-8-7 S Keightley 10/1: 0300031: 3 ch g Tumble Wind -
Maynooth Belle (Busted): Al well placed, led close home in quite a fast run 3yo h'cap at
Carlisle June 14: first success for this half brother to 10f winner Captain Webster: well
suited by a stiff 6f: acts on gd/firm & yld grnd.   25
703 GLOBAL [9] (W Musson) 3-9-2 M Wigham 11/2: 000-002: Post came just too soon: best
effort to date from this lightly raced gelding: stays 6f well: acts on gd & soft grnd
and on a stiff track.   33
961 IMPERIAL SUNRISE [16] (M W Easterby) 3-8-11 T Lucas 11/2: 4-40343: Fin well: see 768   27
947 CUMBRIAN DANCER [7] (M H Easterby) 3-9-1(vis) M Birch 6/1: -043004: Made most: btr
effort: see 518.   24
814 JERSEY MAID [8] 3-8-13 L Charnock 14/1: 20-0000: Btr effort: in gd form early last
season, made all in a maiden auction race at Beverley: eff over 5/6f: acts on gd & yld
grand and is suited by a stiff trk.   18
857 MURRYL CANNON [15] 3-7-13 Julie Bowker(7) 20/1: 00-0000: Led briefly below dist:
btr effort from this half brother to a couple of winning sprinters: acts on gd & fast grnd.   03
677 BICKERMAN [14] 3-8-3 G Duffield 7/2 FAV: 04-00: Gambled on: never dngr: lightly raced
colt who is closely related to several winning sprinters, incl the smart Tinas Pet: may do
btr on an easier course.   00
866 LOW FLYER [10] 3-9-1 M Hindley(3) 8/1: 0302430: Best in 545 (yld): see 198.   00
1001 PLATINE [2] 3-9-7 K Radcliffe(7) 10/1: 0002000: Much btr on a sharp trk in 760.   00
907 COUNTRY CARNIVAL [4] 3-8-6(BL) D Nicholls 9/2: 00-0030: Much btr over 7f in 907.   00
961 Bargain Pack [13] 8-1   830 Shark Fighter [5] 8-11
911 Spring ·Garden [3] 7-10   994 Package Perfection [11] 8-8
729 Touch Me Not [6] 7-11(bl)   891 Sana Song [17] 8-5
972 Rich Bitch [12] 7-7(4oh)
17 ran   shhd,½,2½,1½,hd,½   (Qualitair Hotels Ltd)   K Stone Malton, Yorks

1052 YOUNGERS SCOTCH BITTER HANDICAP 0-35   £1825   1m 4f   Good 75 -39 Slow   [30]

917 MOULKINS [5] (J Wilson) 4-8-7 G Duffield 11/2: 00-0001: 4 ch g Moulton - Popkins
(Romulus): Led below dist and stayed on well to win a h'cap at Carlisle June 14: first
success: eff over 12f, stays 14f: acts on gd & yld grnd and on a stiff trk.   18
860 MR LION [9] (F Carr) 4-8-9 J Carr(7) 10/3: 3012222: Again found one too good: most
consistent this term: see 860 and 721.   17
869 MENINGI [3] (N Tinkler) 5-9-10 Kim Tinkler(5) 7/2: 3141433: Again ran well: see 591.   32
869 MOSSBERRY FAIR [1] (W Haigh) 5-7-8 J Quinn(4) 3/1: 0-00024: Going on fin: see 868.   01
591 APPLE WINE [6] 9-8-12 D Nicholls 8/1: -020000: Made most: best on a sharp trk in 256.   14
872 WESTRAY [7] 4-9-7 K Darley 11/2: 0-00040: Had ev ch: see 225.   20
731 Patralan [8] 8-4(BL)   909 Peters Kiddie [4] 7-7
8 ran   ½,hd,1,2½,1½   (James Wilson)   J Wilson Preston, Lancs   --

1053 TINDALE SELLING STAKES 3YO   £599   1m 1f   Good 75 +01 Fast

608 LUCKY WEST [11] (G Moore) 3-8-8 D Casey(7) 9/2: -001: 3 ch f Lucky Wednesday -
Westergate Girl (Huntercombe): Nicely bckd and led dist, comfortably in a 3yo seller at
Carlisle June 14 (bought in 3,900 gns): did not race last season: stays 9f well: acts on gd
grnd & on a stiff trk.   22
828 KO ISLAND [3] (J Berry) 3-8-11 K Darley 4/1: 0000022: Again tried to make all: beat
rem decisively & should find a small race soon: stays 9f: see 259.   15
697 BELHILL [9] (D Chapman) 3-8-8 D Nicholls 15/8 FAV: -430003: Dropped in class: well
bckd and had ev ch: half sister to a couple of minor winners: see 100.   06
880 HOLIDAY MILL [4] (P Kelleway) 3-8-8 Gay Kelleway(5) 5/1: 300-004: Took a drop in
class: stayed on under press: placed in much btr company last season (rated 34) & should win
in this grade: well suited by soft grnd: stays 9f.   04
828 STEP ON [10] 3-8-11 J Bleasdale 9/1: 00-3000: Best on soft in 318 (sharp trk).   02
666 RAJ KUMARI [1] 3-8-8 K Radcliffe(7) 33/1: -00: Well placed over ½way: no form to date.   00
767 LADY OF HAMPTON [5] 3-8-8 S Morris 8/1: -400: Trailed in last: btr in 684 (1m).   00
871 Balidareen [2] 8-8   666 Crisp Metcalfe [7] 8-11
932 Pasta Jane [8] 8-8   969 Jessie Timmins [12] 8-8
-- Herb Robert [6] 8-11
12 ran   6,4,¾,2½,3   (G H Dawes)   G Moore Middleham, Yorks

1054 TOP OF THE NORTH RACING HCAP 0-35   £1864   1m 1f   Good 75 -08 Slow   [27]

609 MISTER POINT [4] (C Tinkler) 4-9-7 M Birch 10/1: 00-0001: 4 ch g Ahonoora - Rasmeen
(Relko): Led home turn and stayed on well to win a h'cap at Carlisle June 14: last season won
at Hamilton and Beverley and is well suited by a stiff trk: eff over 9/10f: acts on gd & hvy.   29
700 TRY SCORER [1] (Denys Smith) 4-9-5 L Charnock 14/1: 2100002: Dwelt, fin strongly: see 143.24
889 SWIFT RIVER [10] (I Bell) 4-8-7(bl) J Quinn(5) 16/1: 2020303: Stayed on well: see 522.   10
°970 BILLYS DANCER [9] (D Dale) 3-8-9 D Mckeown 7/2: 0-13014: In gd form: stayed 9f: see 970.25
943 GODLORD [7] 6-8-13 G Duffield 12/1: 00-0000: Best effort this term: see 540.   05
969 KAMPHALL [12] 3-7-12 A Mackay 10/1: 000-400: Nearest fin: stays 9f: see 822.   03

*867 MEGANS MOVE [11] 3-8-12(5ex) A Shoults(5) 7/4 FAV: 004-010: Much btr over this C/D in 867. 00
970 LITTLE NEWINGTON [6] 5-8-12(bl)(5ex) D Nicholls 8/1: 0121240: Led ober ½way: btr in 820. 00

378 Composer [2] 8-3	893 Thirteenth Friday [8] 8-1(BL)		
970 Avraeas [13] 8-10	823 Waterford Way [3] 7-12		
893 Sundown Sky [5] 8-10(bl)		789 Nugola [14] 8-12	
14 ran 1½,1,hd,6,1	(A J Duffield)	C Tinkler Malton, Yorks	

1055 GELTSDALE MAIDEN STAKES 3YO   £1242   1m 1f   Good 75 +01 Fast

861 LYAPKIN TYAPKIN [9] (J Winter) 3-9-0 A Mackay 6/1: 04-41: 3 ch g Tap On Wood -
Goirtin (Levmoss): Made virtually ev yd, comfortably in quite a fast run 3yo maiden at
Carlisle June 14: lightly raced gelding who had shown promise in his previous starts: stays
9f well: acts on gd & fast grnd & on a stiff trk.   45
334 DESERT OF WIND [3] (L Cumani) 3-9-0 R Guest 5/2 FAV: -02: Chased winner most of way:
gd effort & should find a maiden race soon: stays 9f: acts on gd grnd & on a stiff trk.   38
402 LAJNATA [11] (R Johnson Houghton) 3-8-11 P Hutchinson 13/2: -03: Kept on same pace:
lightly raced filly who is effective over 8/9f: seems to act on any trk.   32
916 HELLO BENZ [14] (M H Easterby) 3-9-0 M Birch 10/1: -4004: Al up there: see 699 & 322.   34
422 SHEREEKA [12] 3-8-11 A Murray 3/1: 2-300: Twice below form shown in 158 (7f).   25
822 BREGUET [10] 3-8-11 M Beecroft 25/1: 00-200: Never nearer: btr over 1m in 487 (yld).   18
911 INDIAN LOVE SONG [1] 3-8-11 K Darley 13/2: 400-230: No threat: much btr in 911 (7f).   00

790 The Canny Man [8] 9-0	916 State Jester [4] 9-0	829 Hitchenstown [15] 9-0	
-- Brittons Mill [5] 9-0	916 Imperial Palace [6] 9-0		
447 Larnem [2] 8-11	868 Frame Of Power [1] 9-0		
14 ran 3,1½,½,4,4	(Mrs John Winter)	J Winter Newmarket	

Official Going Given as Good to Firm

1056 JUNE SELLING HANDICAP STAKES (0-25)   £988   1m 2f   Firm 08 -09 Slow   [22]

-- ISOM DART [5] (T Hallett) 7-8-7 N Adams 16/1: -00-1: 7 b h Bold Forbes - Shellshock
(Salvo): First time out, went clear inside final 1f to win a selling h'cap at Bath June 14
(bought in 1,050 gns): first success on the Flat though a winner over hurdles in the past:
(drew a blank over jumps in 85/86): suited by 10f & firm grnd: can win again in similar company. 10
750 JENNY WYLLIE [6] (J Francome) 5-8-11 M Hills 11/2: 00-0002: Made most & should be
able to win a seller: eff over 10f on firm grnd: see 204.   09
889 POCO LOCO [9] (A Davison) 4-8-8 S Dawson[3] 6/1: -034023: Prom thro'out: see 889 (gd).   03
530 UNDER THE STARS [14] (R Akehurst) 4-8-13 R Mcghin 25/1: 300-004: Ev ch: see 343.   06
530 PURPLE [18] 5-8-11 A Clark 14/1: 0032/00: Ev ch, remains a maiden on the Flat.   01
851 LINGFIELD LADY [10] 4-9-2 P Cook 10/1: -400000: See 31 (6f).   03
532 DICK KNIGHT [11] 5-8-13 G Morgan 9/2 fav: -000000: Heavily bckd, fin 7th: see 105.   00
532 HIVE OFF [3] 5-9-6 A Mcglone 10/1: 43-2/00: Prom some: 2nd over 1m at Windsor on
sole outing in '85 and has yet to win a race: acts on fast grnd.   00

-- Porto Irene [4] 8-6	-- Double Option [16] 9-10		
333 Mr Music Man [7] 8-13	547 Top Gold [17] 8-10	851 Easter Rambler [19] 9-4(0)	
119 Shallaal [20] 8-11(vis)		845 Disting [13] 8-9	
-- East Street [15] 8-9(BL)		783 La Chula [12] 8-9	
-- Chivwain [8] 8-7	420 Gourtionist [1] 9-8		
19 ran 3,2,1½,3,3	(G H Taylor-Webber)	T Hallett Saltash, Cornwall	

1057 KELSTON TWO YEAR OLD STAKES·   £2203   5f   Firm 08 -18 Slow

*632 HARD ACT [1] (R Hannon) 2-9-4 A Mcglone 4/5 fav: 011: 2 b c Hard Fought - Excruciating
(Bold Forbes): Winning 2nd race on the trot & landed the odds, forcing his head in front on
the post under strong driving to win a minor event at Bath June 14: game winner of a maiden
at Wolverhampton last time: cost 12,000 gns: very eff over 5f, should stay 6f plus: acts
on firm & gd grnd, possibly unsuited by soft.   50
503 ABSOLUTION [7] (K Brassey) 2-8-11 S Whitworth 3/1: 32: Just failed to make all and
should find a maiden soon, possibly on a sharp trk: see 503.   42
707 BERTRADE [3] (P Makin) 2-8-8 P Cook 9/2: 403: Ev ch: possibly btr 621 (sharp trk).   35
497 MADAME FLORA [4] (H O'neil) 2-8-8 J Williams 15/2: 04: Early speed, btr 497 (sharp trk).   10
-- MUSIC DELIGHT [2] 2-8-8 G Morgan 33/1: 0: No danger from this first foal of a
maiden: sprint bred.   07
678 KINGSWOOD RESOPAL [5] 2-8-11 B Procter 33/1: 00: No threat: dam a winning plater.   02
-- Toms Little Bet [6] 8-8
7 ran   nk,1½,10,1½,4   (G Howard-Spink)   R Hannon East Everleigh, Marlborough, Wilts

1058 T.I. CREDA ELECTRIC HANDICAP (0-50)   £3386   2m 1f   Firm 08 +20 Fast   [27]

*983 SARFRAZ [2] (G Harwood) 3-9-12(6ex) A Clark 9/4 fav: 42-0111: 3 b c Sassafras -
Ziba Blue (Johns Joy): Useful, impr colt: completed a quick hat trick (well bckd), coming
from behind to lead final 1f rather cleverly in a fast run h'cap at Bath June 14: winner of
similar h'caps at Folkestone and Goodwood recently: acts on firm & yld: eff 14f, stays 2m 1f
really well: sure to win more staying h'caps.   56

*942 TIGERWOOD [4] (R Akehurst) 5-8-11(6ex) N Adams 3/1: -000-12: Tried to make all: well
clear of rest & he can gain compensation soon: in grand form: see 942.   20
801 MISS BLACKTHORN [9] (N Vigors) 4-9-4 P Cook 8/1: 1-03203: Ev ch: best 541 (14f, yld).   14
841 HARLESTONE LAKE [3] (J Dunlop) 4-9-4 S Whitworth 13/2: 20-0034: Ev ch, closer to
winner in 841 but remains a maiden.   12
712 CHEKA [7] 10-8-11 S Payne 12/1: 0-20100: Best 504 (C/D, yld).   02
634 FLYING OFFICER [1] 9-8-13(vis) J Williams 14/1: 0-04000: No form since 336 (yld).   00
841 CROOK N HONEST [6] 4-8-3 A Proud 17/2: 0-00440: Ev ch, fin 7th: best 542 (yld).   00
942 MORGANS CHOICE [8] 9-9-7 S Dawson[3] 7/1: 0000000: Fin 8th: see 942.   00
841 Zircons Sun [5] 8-1(bl)   --   Shieldaig [10] 8-6(bl)
530 Meziara [11] 8-12(bl)
11 ran   1½,10,1½,3,5.   (K Abdulla)   G Harwood Pulborough, Sussex

1059 CHARLCOMBE MAIDEN AUCTION STAKES 2YO   £1132   5.5f   Firm 08 -25 Slow

882 ROYAL RABBLE [10] (D Elsworth) 2-8-2 A Mcglone 12/1: 0204231: 2 br f Rabdan -
Consistent Queen (Queens Hussar): Fin. well to lead final 100 yds in a 2yo maiden auction
race at Bath June 14: dam a seller previously but is an impr filly who is well suited by
a stiff 5f & will be fav. by 6f plus: acts on firm & gd grnd.   38
728 TEZ SHIKARI [2] (L Cottrell) 2-8-11 M Hills 5/2: 04222: 2nd again, caught close home
& deserves a change of luck: see 728.   45
345 LAST RECOVERY [15] (M Ryan) 2-7-13 G Bardwell[7] 20/1: 303: Al prom: acts on firm &
hvy: see 206.   32
927 GREY WOLF TIGER [12] (R Hannon) 2-8-2 R Wernham 7/4 fav: 0224: Kept on under strong
driving and btr 927 (6f).   35
--   GLAMGRAM FOR GRAMS [7] 2-8-8 A Clark 14/1: 0: Led dist, no extra near fin but a
good debut: half brother to a middle dist winner & should be well suited by 6f plus: acts
on firm grnd: can win a similar race.   37
913 IMPERIAL FRIEND [1] 2-7-13 S Dawson[3] 6/1: 030: Nicely bckd (again), never went close   24
810 O LA LE [5] 2-8-2 P Cook 10/1: 00: Fin 8th: see 810 (6f).   00
--   Orient Line [4] 8-5   938 Premium Gold [6] 7-13(BL)
852 My Elane [16] 8-11   728 Young Centurion [13] 8-2
531 Akrotiri Bay [8] 8-2   --   Unity Farm Boy [9] 8-2
--   Tilloujo [14] 7-13   622 Biotin [11] 8-2   --   Scarning Shadylady [3] 7-13
16 ran   ½,½,nk,1½,1½   (Jack Joseph)   D Elsworth Whitsbury, Hants

1060 T.I.CREDA MEDALLION H'CAP 3YO+ 0-50   £3215   5.5f   Firm 08 +08 Fast   [44]

836 DEPUTY HEAD [5] (L Holt) 6-9-4 J Matthias 11/4: -000031: 6 b h Tower Walk - Ista
Jill (Gratitude): Fair sprinter: fin. strongly, leading in the last strides to win quite a
fast run h'cap at Bath June 14: failed to win in '85, previous season won at Newbury & Ascot:
eff over 5 & 9f: appears to act on any going.   45
994 CRETE CARGO [8] (M Francis) 3-9-4(BL) P Cook 9/4 fav: 0000242: Bl first time, led
½way, caught death: should find a race: see 15.   52
30   SCHULA [2] (H O'neill) 6-7-11 R Street 20/1: 400-003: Strong fin after long abs: last
won in '84 at Folkestone over 5f on soft grnd but seems to act on any going.   22
846 POWDER BLUE [7] (P Makin) 4-9-7 A Mcglone 6/1: 3101-04: Chall 1f out: in gd form in
'85 winning h'caps at Redcar & Yarmouth: very eff at 6f on firm & gd grnd.   43
817 NO BEATING HARTS [6] 3-8-12 R Wernham 10/1: 0-13040: Made much: best 217 (yld).   40
727 LYRIC WAY [10] 4-8-6 M Hills 15/2: 00-0000: No form & yet to strike form: first
time out winner of a maiden at Pontefract in '85: eff over 6f on gd grnd.   19
671 DANCING SARAH [1] 3-8-3 D Williams[7] 10/1: 10-4000: Fin 7th: twice below 443 (shp trk) 00
846 Gallant Hope [3] 7-7(5oh)   734 Silbando [9] 7-8(bl)
--   She Knows It All [4] 8-10
10 ran   ½,shhd,1,1,2½   (P Callard)   L Holt Tunworth, Hants

1061 BEDMINSTER MAIDEN STAKES 3YO   £1610   1m 2f   Firm 08 -09 Slow

--   TRAVEL MYSTERY [7] (P Walwyn) 3-8-11 M Howe 25/1: 0-1: 3 b f Godswalk - Sugar Cookie
(Crepello): First time out, caused a 25/1 surprise forging clear in final 1f in a 3yo maiden
at Bath June 14: no show on only outing in '85: half sister to 10f/hdles winner Hayakaze:
suited by 10f, may stay further: runs well on firm grnd: should be able to win more races.   51
765 FRANGNITO [6] (R J Houghton) 3-9-0 J Williams 5/2: 0-40022: Led 3f out, should find
a maiden soon: see 465.   49
--   BANQUE PRIVEE [2] (B Hills) 3-8-11 M Hills 10/1: 0-3: Chall 1f out, kept on well:
showed promise only outing in '85: dam a French middle dist maiden: should stay 12f: likely
to find a race soon.   43
599 GLITTER [12] (I Balding) 3-8-11 J Matthias 6/4 fav: -0304: Never closer: much btr
599 (good): unsuited by firm?   33
674 BOLD BORDERER [14] 3-9-0 N Adams 25/1: 00-0000: Steadily finding form: stays at
least 10f: see 674.   34
512 ANOTHER PAGEANT [16] 3-8-11 P Cook 8/1: -000: Ev ch: see 315.   27

-- RED RIVER BOY [15] 3-9-0 A Dicks[7] 8/1: -0: Well bckd, hung badly 2f out & wknd: has evidently shown ability at home.   00

-- Ribovino [8] 9-0	534 No Stopping [17] 9-0	-- La Muscade [11] 8-11
923 Lucy Aura [13] 8-11	849 Jimbalou [10] 9-0	723 Ma Feathers [5] 8-11
624 Tzu Wong [4] 8-11	625 Lockwood Prince [1] 9-0	
733 Danribo [9] 9-0		

16 ran   2¼,1½,5,1,2   (R A Patrick)   P Walwyn Lambourn, Berks

1062 BEDMINSTER MAIDEN STAKES 3YO   £1597   1m 2f Firm 08 -11 Slow

849 BASTINADO [14] (I Balding) 3-9-0 J Matthias 4/1: 301: 3 ch g Bustino - Strathspey (Jimmy Reppin): Fin strongly to gain the day near the line in a 3yo maiden at Bath June 14: unraced last term: half brother to the useful River Spey: acts on firm & yld & likes a gall trk: eff at 10f, stays 12f.   45

720 KING JACK [9] (J Dunlop) 3-9-0 S Whitworth 25/1: -002: Prom thro'out: best effort yet.   44

702 ASHINGTON GROVE [6] (D Murray Smith) 3-9-0 P Cook 5/1: 00-2233: Led 2f out, just btn in a driving fin: gd effort: see 535.   43

250 CALVINETTE [15] (B Hills) 3-8-11 M Hills 16/1: -04: Fin well, not btn far after abs: half sister to a winner in France over 1m: on the up grade & is suited by 10f & firm grnd   39

765 LORD IT OVER [7] 3-9-0 A Clark 5/4 fav: -00: Hmpd final 1f: unlucky? see 765.   41

849 MIGHTY FLASH [2] 3-8-11 A Mcglone 11/1: 00-000: Prom, ev ch: first signs of form: sister to smart performers Mighty Flutter and Mighty Fly: seems to stay 10f.   28

549 QUEENS VISIT [3] 3-8-11 N Howe 5/1: -4040: Led ½way till 2f out, fin 7th: disapp after 549 (good).   00

535 Tom Rum [5] 9-0	546 Grendel [10] 9-0	328 Guymyson [4] 9-0
-- Bedrock [11] 9-0	-- Gold Monopoly [12] 9-0	
-- Super Sihlouette [13] 8-11		535 Celtic Sword [1] 9-0
941 Some Guest [16] 9-0(BL)		

15 ran   nk,¾,1,1,6   (Paul Mellon)   I Balding Kingsclere, Berks

---

1063 TELE-ADS SELLING STAKES 3YO   £1073   7f   Firm 19 -13 Slow

625 TREMENDOUS JET [6] (M Madgwick) 3-8-11 P Hamblett 6/4 FAV: 00-0001: 3 b g Czaravich - Melissa's Jet (Sir Ivor): Landed a big gamble, running on well to lead on the post in a 3yo seller at Leicester June 14 (bought in 3,400 gns): no worthwhile form previously though had been running in btr company: stays 7f well: suited by fast grnd & a gall trk.   18

666 KLAMMERING [10] (P Haslam) 3-8-11 T Williams 10/1: -02: Led 2f out, caught final stride after showing signs of inexperience inside dist: half sister to several winners: stays 7f: acts on firm grnd & on a gall trk: should win a similar race.   --

835 BOXERS SHUKEE [9] (J Bradley) 3-8-8 R Carter(3) 20/1: -300203: Ran on too late: acts on any trk: best in 89.   04

608 ALLISTERDRANSFIELD [20] (G Moore) 3-9-2 T Ives 8/1: 010-004: Led far side thro'out: gd effort: bl when winning a seller at Redcar last term: stays 7f well: suited by firm grnd & a gall trk.   12

418 SLEEPLINE DUCHESS [5] 3-8-8 M Miller 9/1: 000-00: Never nearer: speedily bred filly who showed promise in non selling company last season & could be returning to form: acts on gd & firm grnd & on any trk.   03

932 TAKE THE BISCUIT [4] 3-8-11 A Mercer 33/1: -000000: Stayed on late: rated 23 when placed in non selling company on final start last term, though no form this season: stays 7f & suited by fast grnd.   00

907 HACHIMITSU [3] 3-8-8 B Crossley 6/1: 0-00000: Led 5f: sn btn when hdd though seems well suited by forcing tactics & should do btr over an easier trip: acts on firm grnd.   00

997 COUNT ALMAVIVA [11] 3-8-11 P Waldron 3/1: -000200: No threat: much btr in 774 (1m).   00
975 FLEUR DE THISTLE [13] 3-8-11 J Reid 8/1: -003320: Front rank over ½way: btr in 838 (10f) 00
932 HAJ [15] 3-8-11(VIS) W Wharton 6/1: 02-240: Visored first time: much btr in 932.   00
809 KING OF GEMS [16] 3-8-11 I Todd(6) 10/1: 0000-00: Mkt drifter & never dngr.   00

-- Countess Carlotti [14] 8-8		-- Au Revoir Sailor [7] 8-8
764 Sheer Class [19] 8-8	666 Bao [2] 8-8	-- Odemira [18] 8-8
684 Rose Port [17] 8-8	774 Shesingh [1] 8-8(BL)	651 Town Of Ennis [8] 8-8

19 ran   shhd,5,shhd,nk,3   (D J Willis)   M Madgwick Denmead, Hampshire

1064 TIPSTERS TABLE STAKES 3YO   £2428   1m 2f Firm 19 -07 Slow

373 LADY SOPHIE [2] (H Cecil) 3-8-7 S Cauthen 2/5 FAV: 01-201: 3 b f Brigadier Gerard - Dazzling Light (Silly Season): Smart filly: easily landed the odds, leading below dist in a 3yo stakes at Leicester June 14: last season won a fillies maiden at Yarmouth : was an excellent 2nd to Sonic Lady in Nell Gwyn Stakes at Newmarket first time out: ran below par in the Guineas though reportedly in season: half sister to '82 Lincoln winner Kings Glory: stays 10f well: acts on firm & yld grnd & is suited by a gall trk: will win much btr races.   65+

-- HABOOB BALADEE [5] (O Douieb) 3-8-7 R Cochrane 7/1: -2: Led briefly 2f out, cleverly held by winner though showed plenty of promise on his debut: cost $225,000 as a yearling: stays 10f: acts on firm grnd & on a gall trk: should open his account soon.   62
*765 LANDSKI [6] (R Simpson) 3-8-10 S Whitworth 15/2: -4013: Ran on well: in fine form.   63
706 JAZETAS [4] (N Callaghan) 3-9-2(VIS) Pat Eddery 9/2: 1140404: Fitted with a visor: ran to his best over this longer trip: see 605 & 127.   64
637 TAKE A BREAK [1] 3-8-6(vis) S Dawson(3) 50/1: 20-0100: Dist. 5th after leading till 2f out: best in 346 (1m).   04
-- SONNING [7] 3-8-4 B Crossley 100/1: 0-0: Lost touch after ½way: no form last season when she ran mostly in France: acts on firm grnd.   00
26 Arranmore Girl [3] 8-4
7 ran   1,1,3,25,8,½   (H J Joel)   H Cecil Newmarket

1065 LEICESTER MERCURY HANDICAP (0-50) 3YO   £3787   7f   Firm 19 -02 Slow   [46]

886 SOLO STYLE [19] (G Lewis) 3-8-5 P Waldron 11/1: 00-3001: 3 b c Moorestyle - Mint (Meadow Mint): Responded well; to pressure to lead close home in a 3yo h'cap at Leicester June 14: first success: sprint bred colt who was lightly raced last season: stays 7f well: acts on firm & yld grnd & is suited by a gall trk.   33
*928 CHUMMYS PET [16] (N Callaghan) 3-8-11(5ex) Pat Eddery 10/3 FAV: 0213312: Led 2f out: gd effort under his penalty and is in fine form: see 928.   38
576 BIEN DORADO [17] (B Hanbury) 3-9-0 R Cochrane 14/1: -0043: Continues to impr: acts on gd & firm grnd & on a gall trk: see 576.   37
747 MUDISHA [12] (G Huffer) 3-9-7 R Carter(5) 33/1: 130-004: Raced alone: ev ch: consistent last season, when making all in a fillies maiden at Redcar: stays 6f well: acts on fast & yld grnd & any trk: looks fairly treated on her best form.   44
335 TIME BIRD [8] 3-8-7 B Thomson 16/1: 333-00: Stayed on: placed in his 3 starts last season over shorter distances: half brother to several winners, incl the useful middle dist winner Santella King: acts on firm & yld grnd & on any trk.   22
63 ARE YOU GUILTY [3] 3-8-10 P Barnard(7) 14/1: 0003-30: Ran on late after abs: see 63.   24
857 RAFFIA RUN [15] 3-8-3(BL) W Carson 11/2: 40-0440: Fin 7th: in fair form: see 538.   00
886 AMBROSINI [1] 3-9-4 T Ives 9/2: 31-1020: Al up there: fin 8th: see 886.   00
857 UNEXPLAINED [2] 3-8-11 S Cauthen 8/1: 4202D20: Fin 9th: btr in 857.   00
628 ALKAAYED [5] 3-8-9 R Hills 7/1: 40-1040: Speed over ½way: btr in 628 (5f): see 241.   00
703 Deputy Tim [14] 8-9(bl)   438 Twicknam Garden [4] 8-4
809 Soho Sue [9] 7-11   837 Saxon Bazaar [7] 8-2   656 Absolutely Bonkers [11] 8-4
886 Faatik [6] 8-0   816 Tour Vieille [13] 9-1(BL)
17 ran   hd,2,shhd,4,½,1,shhd   (Mrs N Lewis)   G Lewis Epsom, Surrey

1066 MERCURY RACE NIGHT H'CAP (0-35) 9YO+   £1900   6f   Firm 19 +09 Fast   [34]

374 REVEILLE [12] (M Jarvis) 4-9-9 T Ives 9/2 FAV: 00-2201: 4 ch c Ahonoora - Roll Up (Roll Of Honour): Led approaching final 1f, sn clear to win a fast run h'cap at Leicester June 14: useful 2yo, winning at Carlisle & Wolverhampton: lost his form last term: very eff at 6f, stays 7f: acts on firm & soft grnd & a gall trk: should win again.   43
657 MADAM MUFFIN [8] (J Bethell) 3-8-3 W Carson 7/1: 2-2002: Ran on final 1f: gd effort: acts on soft, well suited by firm grnd: well suited by 6f: acts on any trk.   24
815 FARMER JOCK [14] (N Macauley) 4-9-0(vis) W Wharton 20/1: 40-0003: Led briefly 2f out: placed on several occasions in '85, but failed to win: eff at 6f on gd & firm grnd: acts on any trk, possibly best on a sharp one.   14
922 DORAME [11] (G Gaines) 5-8-2 A Proud 33/1: 000-004: Never nearer: btr effort: in '85 won at h'cap at Epsom: best over 6f: acts on gd & firm grnd & on any trk.   00
836 TAYLOR OF SOHAM [4] 3-8-8 D Mckay 9/1: 2340300: Prom; ev ch: twice below form 545.   11
890 DORNEY [16] 6-8-6 J Reid 11/2: 0-00000: Al up there: see 679.   00
748 SHADES OF BLUE [1] 5-9-2 N Adams 7/1: 0-20040: Early ldr: btr 748: see 160.   00
734 ROYAL BEAR [7] 4-7-7(BL) T Williams 10/1: 2043000: Led ½way, fdd: bl first time: best 266 (sharp track).   00
679 Pommes Chateau [3] 9-0(hd)   495 Fort Duchesne [13] 8-3
890 Pokerfayes [15] 8-6(bl)   760 Sequestration [10] 7-10
-- Roman Ruler [17] 9-10   594 Valrach [2] 9-4   566 Maftir [5] 9-0(bl)
966 Centralspires Best [18] 8-6   651 Ammeed [6] 7-8
17 ran   2½,4,½,2,½   (R Milsom)   M Jarvis Newmarket

1067 SPORTS FINAL MAIDEN FILLIES STAKES 2YO   £1300   6f   Firm 19 -08 Slow

-- TRY THE DUCHESS [5] (M Usher) 2-8-11 D Mckay 33/1: 1: 2 ch f Try My Best - Piece Of The Realm (Realm): Fin well to lead inside final 1f in a 2yo fillies maiden at Leicester June 14: cost 7,000 gns as a yearling: dam a 6f winner: eff at 6f, should stay further: acts on fast grnd & a gall trk.   50
-- ALBYN LADY [7] (H Cecil) 2-8-11 S Cauthen 4/7 FAV: 2: Heavily bckd debutant: ev ch final 1f: gd effort: half sister to 3yo Free Hand who stays 10f: acts on fast grnd & should find a maiden.   48

--   FLAMING EMBERS [3] (L Piggott) 2-8-11 Pat Eddery 3/1: 3: Made much: promising racecourse debut from this I.R. 36,000 purchase: eff at 6f on fast grnd & should find a race.   40
--   THANK HAVON [1] (D Morley) 2-8-11 T Williams 33/1: 4: Al prom on debut: 5L clear rem: sister to useful sprinter Blue Singh & is speedily bred: eff at 6f on firm grnd.   40
--   ACCUSTOMED [9] 2-8-11 T Ives 12/1: 0: Never nearer: should impr: half sister to a 5f winner: acts on fast grnd.   28
417   ROSE LOUBET [13] 2-8-11 P Darcy 33/1: 00: Prom, on the up grade: acts on fast grnd.   26

685	Navos [4] 8-11	--	Ribogirl [8] 8-11	--	Hush Kit [6] 8-11
852	Churchill Lady [10] 8-11			--	Fingers Crossed [2] 8-11
944	Miss Acacia [12] 8-11	--	Our Ginger [14] 8-11	--	Peerglow [15] 8-11
--	Tiklas [11] 8-11				

15 ran   ½,3,shhd,5,½   (T C Marshall)   M Usher Lambourn, Berks

1068 LATE NIGHT EXTRA E.B.F. STAKES   £2964   1m 4f   Firm 19 +05 Fast

--   TANAOS [3] (H Cecil) 3-8-6 S Cauthen 4/6 FAV: 314-1: 3 ch c Grundy - Stilvi (Derring-Do): Smart colt: first time out was a comfortable 1L winner of quite fast run 3 & 4yo stakes˜ at Leicester June 14: winning 2yo at Newmarket: on final outing finished an excellent 4th to Huntingdale in the William Hill Dewhurst at Newmarket: related to numerous winners, notably smart Tromos & Tyrnavos: well suited by 12f: acts on gd & firm grnd & a gall trk & is certain to win more good races.   75
604   SIMSIM [5] (J Dunlop) 3-8-6 W Carson 13/8 : 41-232: Chall final 1f: al held by winner, but ran really well: 20L clear of 3rd: must win soon: stays 12f: see 326.   69
693   BRIGHT BIRD [4] (C Austin) 4-9-8 B Crossley 9/1: 2103-03: Led 4f out: see 693.   29
--   GO FLAMINGO [1] (A James) 3-7-9 S Dawson(2) 100/1: 00-4: Never in it: unplaced in a seller on final outing in '85.   04
875   NORCOOL [6] 3-7-12(bl) N Howe 100/1: 00-0000: Led for 1m: impossible task.   00
--   MONTEFIASO [2] 4-9-0 J Williams 100/1: -0: Wknd straight & well btn.   00
--   Roman Track [7] 8-11
7 ran   1,20,7,25,2   (Mrs H G Cambanis)   H Cecil Newmarket

1069 EBF WILLOWBRAE MAIDEN STAKES 2YO   £868   5f   Good/Firm 23 -23 Slow

622   ORIOLE DANCER [4] (D Thom) 2-9-0 G Duffield 4/1: 000241: 2 b c Dance In Time - Famous Band (Banderilla): Led inside dist and held on gamely in a 2yo maiden at Edinburgh June 16: cheaply bought colt who is well suited by this minimum trip, though bred to stay further: acts on fast & soft grnd & likes to be up with the pace: well suited by a sharp trk.   36
826   DOMINO ROSE [9] (N Tinkler) 2-8-11(BL) Kim Tinkler(5) 5/2: 2322: BI first time, al front rank, just held: consistent filly who is due a change of luck: see 826 & 236.   32
781   DANADN [1] (R Thompson) 2-9-0 R P Elliott 9/4 FAV: 40403: Made most: not btn far: acts on any goinng and is well suited by a sharp trk: see 278.   34
892   MAZURKANOVA [2] (C Thornton) 2-8-11 J Bleasdale 9/1: 004: Al up there: clear of rem: impr with every race: acts on fast & yld grnd: see 892.   28
864   SEABURY [5] 2-9-0 J Lowe 16/1: 000: Dwelt, never nearer: acts on gd/firm & yld grnd and on any track.   18
864   BEJANT SKITE [6] 2-9-0(BL) S Webster 33/1: 0000: Early speed: see 701.   06
--   Densben [8] 9-0   785 Send It Down [7] 9-0   826 Sing For The King [3] 9-0
9 ran   nk,hd,1,5,4   (J H Bush)   D Thom Newmarket

1070 JOPPA SELLING H'CAP 3YO+ 0-25   £797   5f   Good/Firm 23 -06 Slow   [20]

211   NATIVE RULER [9] (C Austin) 5-8-8 A Mackay 8/1: 0000-01: 5 b c King Of Macedon - Noble Native (Indigenous): Broke well and was never hdd when a comfortable winner of a selling h'cap at Edinburgh June 16 (no bid): first success: half brother to several winning sprinters: eff over 5f on fast ground: suited by forcing tactics on a sharp course.   10
--   JUMP JAR [6] (D Chapman) 7-10-0 D Nicholls 12/1: 00100-2: Ran on well under top weight on seasonal debut: won a similar race at Beverley last season, after earlier winning a none selling h'cap at Nottingham: stays 12f well though is best over sprint distances: acts on firm & soft grnd & on any trk: genuine sort.   24
768   WOW WOW WOW [5] (N Tinkler) 3-9-8 Kim Tinkler(5) 7/4 FAV: 3100203: Al front rank.   22
489   THE CHALICEWELL [2] (M James) 4-8-8 Sharron James 14/1: 200-404: Kept on: best in 145.   00
266   HENRYS VENTURE [7] 4-8-6 S P Griffiths(5) 12/1: 00-0000: Never beyond mid-div: see 182.   00
977   ST TERRAMAR [1] 11-8-8(bl) G Dickie 12/1: D20-000: Never nearer: placed several times last season though last successful in '83, at Leicester & Brighton: best over 5/6f and acts well on fast ground: usually blinkered.   00
910   JUMP TO IT [10] 3-9-1 S Webster 2/1: 0030-00: Fin 8th: lightly raced last season: effective over 5f on gd & firm grnd: acts on any trk.   00
906   LADY OF LEISURE [4] 5-9-11(bl) R Vickers(7) 8/1: 0-00000: Below par effort: fin last: best in 628.   00
626   Frandie Miss [11] 8-10   910 Musical Aid [8] 9-3
825   Miss Taufan [3] 8-0
11 ran   1½,1½,nk,nk,nk,½,½   (A J Richards)   C Austin Wokingham, Berks

1071 MILLERHILL H'CAP STAKES 4YO+ 0-35   £843   1m 7f Good/Firm 23 +01 Fast   [30]

*827 COMMANDER ROBERT [8] (J Hanson) 4-10-0(4ex) J H Brown(5) 2/1: 00-4011: 4 b c Wolver
Hollow - Bernice Clare (Skymaster): In good form, comfortably defied his penalty, making all
in a h'cap at Edinburgh June 16: won a similar race on this track a fortnight ago: successful
over hurdles this Winter: effective over 12f, stays 15f well: acts on fast & yld grnd &
on any track.   40
19   SANDYLA [1] (D Thom) 5-9-3(vis) S Webster 20/1: 0--0-02: Gd effort: remains a
maiden though was placed on many occasions over hurdles and fences this Winter: stays 15f:
acts on any going and on any track.   22
1016 PERFECT DOUBLE [9] (W Pearce) 5-8-2 L Charnock 14/1: 2-00403: Stays 15f: best in 770.   05
933 JOIST [2] (M Prescott) 4-9-2 G Duffield 13/8 FAV: 10-0024: Clear of rem though btr 933.   14
827 JUBILANT LADY [5] 5-7-12 S P Griffiths(5) 12/1: 0-00000: Some late prog: see 827.   00
824 BOREHAM DOWN [6] 7-7-8 J Lowe 16/1: 0-00030: No threat: see 824.   00
366 DUKE OF DOLLIS [3] 7-8-5 J Quinn(5) 6/1: 102-000: Abs: fin 7th: successful at
Pontefract last season & in '84 won at Bath: suited by a test of stamina: best form fast grnd   00
1016 Red Duster [4] 9-2(bl)   889 Cluedo [7] 8-3(bl)
9 ran   4,2,4,15,nk   (R Ogden)   J Hanson Sicklinghall, Yorks

1072 COCKENZIE MAIDEN STAKES 3YO   £547   1m 4f Good/Firm 23 -29 Slow

--   JOHN DOREY [4] (M Prescott) 3-9-0 G Duffield 5/2: 40-1: 3 ch g Malinowski - Tuna
(Silver Shark): First time out, led over 2f out and was sn clear in a 3yo maiden at Edinburgh
June 16: closely related to several winners: brother to useful stayer Jean-Claude: stays
12f well and should be suited by further: acts on fast grnd & on a sharp trk: should
continue to improve.   32
894 DEPUTY MONARCH [5] (Denys Smith) 3-9-0 L Charnock 6/4 FAV: 040-022: Led after 4f,
ran on same pace: stays 12f: acts on any trk: see 894 & 744.   25
829 SWEET ALEXANDRA [6] (J Shaw) 3-8-11 R Lines(3) 5/1: -43: Never nearer: clear of rem:
stays 12f: acts on gd & fast grnd: on the up grade: see 829.   18
650 HIYA BUD [2] (W Bentley) 3-8-11 D Nicholls 16/1: 000-004: Well btn: no worthwhile
form to date.   00
908 BIG COUNTRY [1] 3-9-0 R P Elliott 33/1: 0000-00: Early ldr: see 908.   00
811 DUWANTO [3] 3-8-11(BL) A Shoults(5) 9/2: -000: Trailed in last: see 549.   00
6 ran   4,3,20,½,dist   (Mrs V Bourne)   M Prescott Newmarket

1073 TRANENT STAKES 3YO UPWARDS   £660   7f   Good/Firm 23 +09 Fast

837 NAWADDER [7] (B Hanbury) 3-7-13 A Geran(7) 13/2: 0-2401: 3 b f Kris - Princess
Matilda (Habitat): Led dist and ran on strongly to win a fast run stakes race at Edinburgh
June 16: below par when bl last time: half sister to useful 10f winner Trojan Prince: eff
over 5/7f: acts on fast & soft grnd & is suited by a sharp trk.   40
--   ONE TO MARK [10] (M Prescott) 3-8-2 G Duffield 5/1: 00-2: Made most on reapp: lightly
raced last season, showing a little promise and a half brother to 7f winner Stramar:
acts on fast grnd & on a sharp trk: suited by forcing tactics: may win soon.   38
*822 FOREMAST [8] (P Calver) 3-8-7 S Webster 3/1 Jt FAV: 0-13: In gd form: acts on gd/firm.   42
923 BLUE GUITAR [1] (J Hindley) 3-7-13 A Shoults(5) 3/1 Jt FAV: 0430-44: Btr over 1m in 923   22
*608 HEAVENLY HOOFER [5] 3-8-7 D Leadbitter(5) 14/1: 000-010: Gd effort in this btr
company: see 608.   22
481 KAMPGLOW [3] 4-9-0 J Lowe 10/1: -030000: No extra dist: best in 71 (1m hvy).   16
822 LITTLE FIRE [9] 3-8-1(2ow) N Connorton 7/1: 0-00: Never going well & fin last: see 822   00
--   Razzamataz Glory [6] 8-11   788 Norwhistle [2] 9-0
183 Lottie Limejuice [4] 7-13   --   The Romford Roar [11] 8-2
11 ran   2,nk,7,4,1   (Saeed Suhail)   B Hanbury Newmarket

1074 LADBROKES LAST RACE H'CAP 3YO+ 0-35   £1774   1m   Good/Firm 23 -03 Slow   [28]

-956 GODS LAW [1] (G Reveley) 5-8-5 Julie Bowker(7) 5/1: 0-01321: 5 b g Godswalk -
Fluently (Ragusa): In gd form, led inside dist for an easy win in a h'cap at Edinburgh
June 16: last month won an app h'cap at Doncaster: lightly raced last season, in '84 won
twice at Beverley: best form around 7/8f on gd or faster grnd: acts on any trk.   15
606 SHOW OF HANDS [6] (J Watts) 10-8-12 A Gorman(5) 16/1: 0000-02: Tried to make all:
fair effort: failed to win last term, though is a real Edinburgh specialist winning 7 times
on this sharp trk: eff over 7/8f on gd & firm grnd.   15
857 MOLLY PARTRIDGE [5] (Capt J Wilson) 3-7-10 S P Griffiths(5) 14/1: 03-0003: Al up there:
maiden who should be capable of winning a seller: eff over 6f, stays 1m: acts on gd/firm & yld   09
963 QUALITAIRESS [12] (K Stone) 4-8-0(vis) J Lowe 11/1: -300434: Never nearer: see 101.   00
843 BRAVE AND BOLD [13] 3-8-4 G Duffield 3/1 FAV: -202000: Nearest fin: see 451.   12
960 MY HANDSOME BOY [4] 4-8-13 C Coates(5) 20/1: 0-00000: Front rank over 6f: see 960.   04
830 TRADE HIGH [7] 7-8-13 D Nicholls 8/1: 0030000: Dwelt, never nearer 7th: see 260.   00
830 BARNES STAR [2] 4-8-11 S Keightley 8/1: -033040: Dwelt, no threat: btr in 830.   00
968 PONTYATES [3] 4-9-6 C Dwyer 8/1: 4-34000: Shorter trip: no threat: best in 519 (12f).   00
710 Petit Bot [8] 8-3(bl)   631 Cricceith [9] 9-7   830 Rossett [10] 8-4
890 Grand Celebration [11] 8-3   710 Royaber [14] 8-1
14 ran   2½,1½,nk,2,2,1   (Mrs V Robson)   G Reveley Lingdale, Cleveland

Official Going Given as Firm

1075 EBF PLUMTREE MAIDEN STAKES 2YO   £1698   5f   Firm 11 -15 Slow

728 SARIHAH [8] (H T Jones) 2-9-0 A Murray 5/6 FAV: 01: 2 b c Nodouble - Suicide Sue
(Gallant Romeo): Impr colt: heavily bckd & made ev yd, easily in a 2yo maiden at Nottingham
June 16: cost $140,000 as a yearling: eff at 5f, should be suited by 6f: acts on fast grnd
and a gall trk & can continue to impr.   46
--   GREEN GLORY [3] (B Hanbury) 2-9-0 R Cochrane 3/1: 2: Kept on well final 1f: promising
racecourse debut from this half brother to two 2yo winners: eff at 5f, should stay 6f: acts
on fast grnd & should find a race.   39
800   LIGHTNING LASER [5] (P Kelleway) 2-8-11 Gay Kelleway(5) 10/1: 003: Al up there:
continues to impr: see 800.   30
--   ALBERT HENRY [9] (A Jarvis) 2-9-0 S Cauthen 10/1: 4: Gd speed 3f: should improve.   18
--   ROCKY HORROR [7] 2-9-0 M Miller 16/1: 0: Mkt drifter: no threat on debut: cost 8,000
gns as a yearling: should be suited by further than 5f.   14
763 RING BACK [6] 2-8-11(BL) N Howe 33/1: 0040: Early speed: see 763 (seller).   11
892 Mere Music [4] 9-0(bl)   --   Danse Arabe [2] 9-0
--   Jazz Dancer [10] 9-0   --   Blue Piper [1] 9-0
10 ran   1½,2,8,1½,hd   (Hamdan Al-Maktoum)   H T Jones Newmarket

1076 YOUNGSTERS SELLING STAKES 2YOO   £873   6f   Firm 11 -33 Slow

589 BARLEY TWIST [2] (F Carr) 2-8-11 S Morris 9/4 FAV: 221: 2 ch c Creetown - Machrihanish
(King's Company): Gained a deserved win, led 2f out and held on under press in a 2yo seller
at Nottingham June 16 (no bid): 2nd in both his previous outings: effective at 5f, suited
by 6f: acts on gd & frm grnd & on any trk.   29
446 AVINASESH [1] (C Tinkler) 2-8-11 M Birch 6/1: 02: Ran on well under press: just
failed & should find a similar event: half brother to 2 winners: eff at 6f on fast grnd.   29
647 SWYNFORD PRINCESS [6] (K Stone) 2-8-8 G Brown 7/2: -04103: Prom, ev ch: stays 6f,
but best 543 (yielding).   14
957 PEGGYS TREASURE [7] (M Brittain) 2-8-8 M Wigham 5/2: 0034: Made much: see 957 (5f).   06
939 GREAT STANDS BY [3] 2-8-11 J Williams 25/1: 000: Dsptd lead, sn fdd: acts on firm.   00
865 HIGHLAND CAPTAIN [4] 2-8-11 R Adams(7) 10/1: 00: Mkt drifter: al behind: see 865.   00
939 DEEP TAW [5] 2-8-8 N Day 6/1: 0430: Prom over ½way: btr 939 (sharp trk).   00
7 ran   shhd,4,3,7,1,shhd   (Mrs Muriel Ward)   F Carr Norton, Yorks

1077 SANDIACRE HANDICAP STAKES 3YO+ 0-35   £2393   6f   Firm 11 -03 Slow   [34]

441 KEATS [4] (J Fitzgerald) 4-9-7 A Murray 9/2: 232-001: 4 br g Mummy's Pet - Fair
Sarita (King's Troop): Ran on well under press to lead near fin in a h'cap at Nottingham
June 16: first success: lightly raced in '85, placed on all 3 starts: eff at 6f, should stay
further: acts on fast grnd & on any trk.   35
679 CAPTAINS BIDD [13] (L Lightbrown) 6-7-7(bl)(2oh) G Carter(0) 8/1: 300-002: Led/dsptd lead:
just caught: gd effort: see 355.   06
846 OXHEY BAY [8] (K White) 4-9-11 J Williams 4/1 Jt.FAV: 2-00303: Stayed on well final
1f: consistent: see 649, 520.   37
--   OUT OF HAND [6] (D Dale) 7-8-8 M Banner 12/1: 00000-4: Ran on final 1f: not btn far
on seasonal debut: in '85 won a h'cap at Pontefract: in '83 won twice: eff at 6f, stays 7f:
acts on yld, likes fast grnd.   20
956 MONINSKY [12] 5-8-5 M Richardson(7) 6/1: 2-20030: Sn prom: close fin: see 956, 260.   17
734 SITEX [10] 8-7-7 R Still 11/1: 2000-00: Blanket fin: see 734.   04
952 EECEE TREE [11] 4-8-12 J Reid 4/1 Jt.FAV: 0-02000: Fdd final 1f: see 952, 327 (5f soft).   00
788 NAME THE GAME [1] 4-7-7(2oh) N Carlisle 9/1: 00-0000: Active in mkt, but no show:
seems only moderate.   00
975 Balkan [15] 7-8   906 Sing Galvo Sing [2] 7-8
710 Shirly Ann [9] 7-8   594 Grey Cree [14] 8-7   734 Paddington Belle [5] 7-13
--   Walters Wednesday [3] 7-9   820 Remainder Tip [7] 7-8
15 ran   ½,nk,shhd,shhd,½,1½   (James Roche)   J Fitzgerald Norton, Yorks

1078 BILBOROUGH HANDICAP STAKES 3YO 0-35   £1858   1m 6f Firm 11 -45 Slow   [42]

841 MUSIC MINSTREL [7] (C Nelson) 3-8-5(1ow) J Reid 11/1: 0-0001: 3 ch c Orchestra -
Victorian Era (High Hat): Showed impr form, not much room nearing final 1f: ran on well
under press: fin 2nd, placed 1st in a slow run h'cap at Nottingham June 16: first success:
little form previously: stays 14f very well: acts on gd & firm grnd.   28
607 BLOCKADE [9] (P Cole) 3-10-2 L Jones(5) 9/4 FAV: 02-1310: Led approaching final 1f,
but hung left, interfering with Music Minstrel: fin 1st, placed 2nd: grand effort under
his big weight: stays 14f well: see 239.   53
951 LAST POLONAISE [8] (M Blanshard) 3-8-3 N Adams 25/1: 000-003: Stayed on well final
1f, showing impr form: well suited by 14f: acts on fast grnd.   22
697 ARCH PRINCESS [3] (R Sheather) 3-7-7(bl) T Williams 10/1: 00-0044: Led over 3f out:
impr of late: see 697.   11
832 GRATIFY [11] 3-8-8 Paul Eddery 7/1: 00-000: Mkt drifter: made much: stoutly bred
filly who should be suited by middle distances: acts on fast grnd.   20

779 HELSANON [4] 3-8-0 N Carlisle 20/1: 00-000: Nearest fin: best effort yet & obviously
stays well: acts on firm.   11
833 MOUNT SCHIEHALLION [6] 3-9-3(BL) S Whitworth 7/1: 30-3300: Bl first time: never
nearer: best in 171 (12f yld).   00
--   DRY GIN [2] 3-8-13 C Rutter(5) 8/1: 0000-0: Active in mkt: fdd str: should be suited
by middle distances: acts on fast grnd.   00
730 Baydon Queen [1] 8-7   951 Vantastic [5] 7-7(7oh)   458 Tudor Dor [6] 8-7
11 ran   ¾,1½,nk,4,nk,shhd   (Alan Steadman)   C Nelson Upper Lambourn, Berks

1079 GUNTHORPE HANDICAP STAKES 0-35 3YO+   £1625   1m 2f Firm 11 +02 Fast   [27]

620 HARD AS IRON [5] (P Haslam) 3-8-3 T Williams 9/1: 000-41: 3 b g Ardoon - Prancer
(Santa Claus): Impr gelding: al up there and led approaching final 1f, sn clear in a h'cap
at Nottingham June 16: very lightly raced previously: eff at 1m, seems well suited by 10f:
acts well on fast grnd: appears nicely h'capped and may win again.   28
731 PRIMROSE WAY [2] (M Blanshard) 4-8-4 N Adams 14/1: 000-002: Made most: see 341.   03
710 MINUS MAN [10] (W Holden) 8-8-4 R Morse(5) 4/1 FAV: 00-0003: Well bckd: kept on well. 00
129 CAREEN [4] (M Pipe) 5-9-7 S Cauthen 9/2: 030-224: Mkt drifter: never nearer: see 129, 8. 15
850 PEARL PET [19] 4-9-0 J Reid 9/1: 0000-20: Ev ch: much btr 850.   07
838 FORGIVING [7] 4-9-1 R Carter(5) 16/1: 000-040: See 838.   00
709 FREE ON BOARD [6] 4-9-7 Paul Eddery 9/2: 00-0020: Made no show: well below form 709.   00
731 Branksome Towers [1] 7-13   875 Forever Tingo [11] 8-11
731 Monclare Trophy [17] 9-6   967 Celtic Image [14] 8-3
--   Rio Deva [16] 9-6   --   Its Good Ere [9] 9-0 851 Teejay [13] 8-5
782 Miss Morley [3] 8-4   723 Aunt Etty [12] 8-0   --   Titan King [8] 7-12
940 Huytons Hope [18] 7-13(1ow)   684 Supreme Command [15] 7-7(1oh)
19 ran   5,1½,1,½,5   (Martin Wickens)   P Haslam Newmarket

1080 LONG EATON 3YO STAKES   £1813   1m 2f Firm 11 +05 Fast

--   ORBAN [10] (H Cecil) 3-9-0 S Cauthen 4/7 FAV: -1: 3 b c Irish River - Regal Exception
(Ribot): Promising colt: first time out, heavily bckd and led 3f out, comfortably in quite
fast run 3yo stakes at Nottingham June 16: cost $150,000 & is a half brother to several
winners: eff at 10f, should be suited by 12f: well bred sort who should win more races &
rate more highly.   48
*941 CHIEF PAL [5] (P Walwyn) 3-9-7 Paul Eddery 4/1: 4-212: Ev ch final 3f: 6L clear 3rd:
in grand form: stays 10f, see 941.   50
*699 AL SHAMIKH [12] (H T Jones) 3-9-10 A Murray 8/1: 00-13: Made much: btr 699.   43
371 BURNING BRIGHT [11] (D Ringer) 3-9-0 M Wigham 50/1: 002-04: Abs: ev ch: on final
outing in '85 fin 2nd to Dancing Eagle in a maiden at Lingfield: stays 10f: acts well on
fast ground and likes a sharpish trk.   31
692 PENTLAND HAWK [2] 3-9-0 S Perks 20/1: 04-0000: Never nearer: probably stays 10f: acts
on firm, but best in 33 (soft).   19
719 TOPEKA EXPRESS [3] 3-9-0(bl) P Tulk 66/1: 00-0000: Early ldr: btr in 719 (1m).   13
--   Deniece [14] 8-11   --   Mitala Maria [1] 8-11   458 Tymbal [7] 8-11
--   Torriggia [8] 8-11   --   Knight Hunter [9] 8-11
941 Glazepta Final [4] 8-11   941 Fabled Monarch [13] 9-0
13 ran   1½,6,1,6,2½   (Prince A A Faisal)   H Cecil Newmarket

1081 RADCLIFFE APPR HANDICAP 3YO+ 0-35   £1676   1m   Firm 11 +05 Fast   [32]

439 JOHN GILPIN [8] (W Haigh) 4-8-12 B Mcgiff 5/1: 00-2121: 4 b c Comedy Star - Double
Grand (Coronation Year): Mkt drifter, but fin well to lead last 50yds in quite a fast run
app. h'cap at Nottingham June 16: in grand form this season, earlier winning at Hamilton: in
'85 won an app. selling h'cap at Windsor & a seller at Ayr: eff at 1m, stays 10f well: acts
on any ground & on any trk.   25
333 MISTER PRELUDE [6] (R Hodges) 6-8-11(hd) A Dicks 10/1: 020-002: Ev ch final 1f: gd
effort after abs: failed to win in '85, but 2nd on 3 occasions: in '84 won a seller at
Haydock and a minor event at Folkestone: eff over 7f-10f: acts on firm & soft grnd.   20
107 SWEET GEMMA [12] (D H Jones) 4-8-0 D Williams 8/1: -40-023: Led final 1f: gd effort
after abs: eff at 1m on firm & soft grnd.   07
850 EXPLETIVE [1] (M Eckley) 6-8-3(vis) J Kennedy 14/1: 0000-04: Al prom: failed to win
in '85: in '84 won at Doncaster: stays 1m well: acts on gd & firm grnd.   07
--   CAROLS MUSIC [10] 5-8-13 Nicola Dean(4) 14/1: 01020-0: Made much on seasonal debut:
has been running over hurdles: in '85 won at Hamilton and Leicester: eff at 1m, stays 10f
well: acts on any grnd & on any trk: best from the front.   13
816 MRS NAUGHTY [3] 3-8-0 J Ward(4) 10/3 FAV: 000-400: Led 2f out: fdd final 1f: btr 816. 11
724 SILVER CANNON [5] 4-9-10 S Hustler 8/1: 0-10000: Dsptd lead, wknd: best first time
out in 281 (heavy).   00
992 BLACK DIAMOND [9] 3-8-5 S Meacock(4) 8/1: 00-0300: Twice below form 657 (hvy grnd).   00
274 LABRAG [10] 3-8-10(VIS) A Corney(4) 7/1: 0300-00: Mkt drifter: al rear after abs.   00
--   Sunley Spirit [7] 7-7   993 Murillo [11] 8-5(bl)   936 Sharons Royale [2] 7-12
12 ran   1½,1,1½,2,1   (A Barker)   W Haigh Norton, Yorks

Official Going Given as Good/Firm

1082 EBF TEMPLE STAKES 2YO   £952   5f   Firm 16 -02 Slow

979 BAG ORHYTHM [7] (J Hindley) 2-8-11 M Hills 5/4 fav: 21: 2 b c Be My Guest - House
Tie (Be Friendly): Fulfilled the promise of his debut and was well bckd when comfortably
leading inside final 2f in a 2yo minor race at Windsor June 16: half brother to useful miler
Tea House: cost 60,000 gns: eff at 5f, stays 6f well: acts well on firm grnd.   52
678 KAMENSKY [5] (R Smyth) 2-8-11 W Carson 9/2: 032: Mkt drifter: outpcd final 1f: see 678.   40
*931 GEMINI FIRE [6] (P Felgate) 2-9-3 R Cochrane 7/2: 0413: Chall 2f out: gd effort.   40
531 LAZIM [13] (C Benstead) 2-8-11(BL) B Rouse 14/1: 04: Friendless in mkt: very late
progress: tried in bl here for the first time: needs 6f?   28
--   STREET LEGAL [9] 2-8-11 M Miller 25/1: 0: Friendless in mkt on debut, some late
prog: related to several winners: bred to be suited by 6f plus.   22
--   SOULEIADOU [10] 2-8-11 J Reid 20/1: 0: Never closer on debut: possibly suited by 6f.   22
678 Court Command[3]8-11   840 Cherrywood Sam[8]8-11   918 Swift Purchase[4]8-11
678 Jabe Mac   8-11[11]   --   Charmed Prince[2]8-11   --   Felsted Boy 8-11[12]
664 Baumaniere [1]8-11
13 ran   4,2,2,2,shhd   (K Al-Said)   J Hindley Newmarket

1083 HURLEY SELL. STAKES 2YO   £1103   6f   Firm 16 -25 Slow

773 FLAIR PARK [5] (D Thom) 2-8-8 T Quinn 5/2 fav: 01: 2 b f Frimley Park - Follow The
Brave (Owen Anthony): Well bckd & gamely got up under strong driving close home in a 2yo
seller at Windsor June 16 (bought in 4,500 gns): eff at 6f, looks sure to be suited by 7f:
acts well on firm grnd.   30
655 PARKLANDS BELLE [3] (M Haynes) 2-8-8 P Cook 9/2: 02402: Dsptd lead thro'out, caught
death: gd effort though rated higher in 400 (good): stays 6f.   30
-987 KIND LADY [7] (J Winter) 2-8-8 W Carson 3/1: 423: Dsptd lead most: gd effort: see 987.   27
948 DECCAN PRINCE [11] (R Hodges) 2-8-11 M Wigham 6/1: 0004: Ev ch: gd effort: stays 6f.   24
473 SAUCIER [1] 2-8-8 J Bray[7] 20/1: 000: Prom much on first venture into selling company.   00
--   JETMORE [10] 2-8-11(BL) Pat Eddery 8/1: 0: Bl on racecourse debut: dam a winning hurdler. 00
--   Glory Bee [8] 8-11   350 Record Flight [9] 8-8   633 Boxers Choice [6] 8-8
--   Donnas Darling [12] 8-8   831 Phoebe [15] 8-8
831 Pullandese [16] 8-8(BL)   939 Sandis Gold [13] 8-8
681 Floret [4] 8-8   681 Palace Fields [2] 8-8 831 Nuns Royal [14] 8-8
16 ran   shhd,½,2,12,½   (John Livock)   D Thom Newmarket

1084 JACK BARCLAY HANDICAP 3YO (0-60)   £3225   1m 2f   Firm 16 -15 Slow   [66]

586 HAWAIIAN PALM [5] (J Tree) 3-9-0 Pat Eddery 11/8 fav: 13-001: 3 b c Hawaiian -
Bold Fluff (Boldnesian): Useful colt: heavily bckd & returned to form comfortably leading
dist in a 3yo h'cap at Windsor June 16: first time out in '85 won a maiden at Salisbury:
half brother to several winners: stays 10f well, promises to stay further: well suited
by fast ground.   64
880 ALBERT HALL [6] (B Hills) 3-8-3 B Thomson 9/2: 2-21D22: Chall 1f out: see 699, 322.   48
692 FARM CLUB [7] (J Toller) 3-8-2 M Roberts 9/2: 10-0003: Made much: see 386.   43
719 PEARL FISHER [3] (J France) 3-8-0 M Hills 16/1: -13304: Ev ch: best 140 (soft).   35
919 GEORGES QUAY [2] 3-7-11 A Mcglone 9/2: -401340: Prom most: best 480 (1m yld).   29
344 FOUZ [1] 3-9-7 T Quinn 8/1: 20-3400: No threat after abs: best 60 (heavy).   48
271 La Serenata [4] 7-7(2oh)
7 ran   2,2½,4,1½,3,7   (K Abdulla)   J Tree Beckhampton, Wilts

1085 RAFFLES NIGHT CLUB HANDICAP (0-50) 3YO   £2603   1m 3f   Firm 16 -13 Slow   [50]

*751 ALDINO [3] (A Stewart) 3-9-1(bl) M Roberts 7/1: 00-0011: 3 ch c Artaius - Allotria
(Red God): Impr colt: winning 2nd race on the trot making most and rallying gamely to get
up again on the post in a 3yo h'cap at Windsor June 16: first time when making all gamely
in a maiden at Brighton May 28: well suited by 11/12f nowadays and likes fast grnd though
has also shown some form on soft: best with forcing tactics in bl on a sharpish trk.   48
659 TOBAGO DANCER [9] (R Hannon) 3-9-7 Pat Eddery 9/2: 04-0122: Led final 1f, caught death:
continues in fine form & stays 11f really well: should win again soon: see 464.   54
833 ITTIHAAD [5] (C Benstead) 3-8-7 B Rouse 6/1: 0-03023: Led 3f out, hdd final 1f: in
gd form: see 833.   36
688 LIE IN WAIT [7] (G P Gordon) 3-9-5 S Cauthen 7/2: 0-144: Close up final 4f, slightly
hmpd final 1f: stays 11f: see 448.   47
849 SHIRLSTAR TAXSAVER [2] 3-8-5(BL)(1ow) J Reid 33/1: 00-0400: Bl first time, ev ch:
stays 11f and seems to act on firm & yld.   33
1023 SILENT RUNNING [6] 3-7-8(1ow) G Carter[0] 9/1: -000300: Close up 10f: best 843 (10f).   20
*738 TEBITTO [10] 3-8-7 P Cook 11/4 fav: 000-010: Well bckd, never landed a blow: btr 738.   00
699 MOEL FAMMAU [1] 3-8-10 R Hills 14/1: -0300: Wknd after 1m: obviously flattered 527.   00
779 Lady Attiva [8] 8-0   739 Forward Move [4] 8-3
10 ran   shhd,2,1,hd,1   (A Boyd-Rochfort)   A Stewart Newmarket

1086 HOLYPORT HANDICAP (0–50) 3YO+   £2535   6f   Firm 16 +13 Fast   [47]

+952 BOLD REALM [9] (C Horgan) 5-9-4(8ex) Pat Eddery 9/4 fav: 00-0011: 5 b g Bold Lad -
Elm (Realm): In fine form at present and defied an 3lbs penalty when coming from behind to
comfortably lead inside final 1f in a fast run h'cap at Windsor June 16: won another fast run
quite valuable h'cap at Goodwood June 9: in '85 won at Newmarket & Ripon: suited by firm or
gd going though seems to act on any trk: very effective at 6f: should win again soon.   47
855 JAMES DE COOMBE [11] (M Bolton) 4-7-7(4oh) T Williams 12/1: -000242: Chall final 1f
and ran a fine race: will win a similar h'cap if reproducing this form: see 114.   19
*977 SILENT MAJORITY [5] (W O'gorman) 3-7-10(5ex) M L Thomas 9/2: 4-03013: Just failed
to make all and is in grand form: see 977.   29
-748 DELAWARE RIVER [3] (B Gubby) 4-7-13(1ow) A Mcglone 8/1: 000-024: Al there: btr 748.   15
922 AL AMEAD [10] 6-9-7 B Rouse 8/1: 4-00040: Ev ch: see 508.   36
*963 MAIDEN BIDDER [8] 4-7-7(5ex)(2oh) R Morse[4] 6/1: 00-0210: Prom most: see 963 (7f,sell.).06
922 EXERT [2] 4-7-11 N Adams 7/1: 3444030: Fin 9th: btr 922.   00
--   Tachyon Park [4] 8-10   680 Visual Identity [14] 7-12
--   Highland Image [6] 8-7   784 Jackie Blair [7] 8-5(bl)
851 Floreat Floreat (12) 7-7 (8oh)   495 Russell Flyer (1) 7-11
13 ran   ½,1,2½,½,½   (Mrs Seamus Purcell)   C Horgan Billingbear, Berks

1087 BOURNE END GUARANTEED STAKES 3YO C & G   £959   1m 2f Firm 16 +13 Fast

370 ESDALE [7] (J Tree) 3-8-11 Pat Eddery 1/2 fav: 2-201: 3 b c Fabulous Dancer -
Esdee (Hail To Reason): Despite a fair abs, started at prohibitive odds and made most
readily in a minor race for 3yos at Windsor June 16: 2nd to Zahdam at Ascot on sole start
in '85 but is a well regarded half brother to a couple of winners: eff at 1m but seems
suited by 10f & could well stay 12f: acts on firm & yld: should win more races.   57
806 NILAMBAR [1] (R J Houghton) 3-8-11 S Cauthen 3/1: 02-02: Early ldr, outpcd by
winner: probably caught a tartar & should find a maiden: see 806.   52
676 ARROW OF LIGHT [5] (O Douieb) 3-8-11 R Hills 11/1: -043: Prom 1m, one paced:
rated higher 676 (flattered?).   27
843 SIMONS FANTASY [6] (R Armstrong) 3-8-11(BL) G Sexton 50/1: 00-044: Prom 1m: see 843. 23
723 RIVER GAMBLER [8] 3-8-11 J Matthias 50/1: 0000-00: No dngr: lightly raced sort but
has scope and comes from a fair family: may improve.   08
684 BEAU DIRE [9] 3-8-11 R Cochrane 33/1: -001D0: Much btr 684 (seller).   04
941 Calvados [2] 8-11   535 Gex [10] 8-11   356 Way Above [4] 8-11
--   Aah Jim Boy [3] 8-11
10 ran   2,12,1½,10,2   (K Abdulla)   J Tree Beckhampton, Wilts

---

Official Going Given as Firm

1088 UNDERWOOD SELLING STAKES 2YO   £1111   6f   Firm 10 -13 Slow

913 NIFTY GRIFF [7] (R Whitaker) 2-8-11 K Bradshaw(5) 6/1: 001: 2 b c Ardoon - Betty
Bun (St Chad): Made almost all, holding on under press in a 2yo seller at Thirsk June 17:
cheaply acquired colt: well suited by 6f on fast ground: runs well on a sharpish track
with forcing tactics.   25
603 BOLD DIFFERENCE [2] (W Wharton) 2-8-8 I Johnson 16/1: 0002: Al up there: ran on
final 1f and just btn: very cheaply acquired: eff at 6f on fast grnd & a sharpish trk:
may find a similar event.   20
864 GOLDENDOUBLEYOU [8] (D Barron) 2-8-8 R Cochrane 7/4 FAV: 23: Dsptd lead, ev ch:
stays 6f, but better 864 (yielding ground).   12
987 ROAN REEF [10] (N Macauley) 2-8-11(bl) W Wharton 8/1: 034: nearest fin: should be
suited by 7f: acts on good and firm ground: see 987.   13
722 PINTAFORY [5] 2-8-8 A Mackay 9/2: 0000: Prom, ev ch: btr on soft in 353, 73.   07
813 HARRYS COMING [1] 2-8-11 J Callaghan(7) 12/1: 021300: Prom, fdd: btr 711 (5f): see 181. 06
589 MOONEE POND [4] 2-8-8 M Birch 10/1: 20000: Early speed: btr 317 (5f, soft).   00
646 BABY COME HOME [12] 2-8-8 J Quinn 6/1: 00: Fin 8th: much btr 646 (5f, yld).   00
446 MY MABEL [3] 2-8-8 T Lucas 10/1: 0000: Never in it: no form in 4 outings.   00
*858 PRINCESS SINGH [11] 2-8-8 Kim Tinkler(5) 5/1: 00310: Made no show: much btr 858 (5f).   00
589 Tuesday Evening [9] 8-8   701 Miss Emily [6] 8-8
12 ran   ½,3,1,1,1½   (R Griffiths)   R Whitaker Wetherby, Yorks

1089 BRICK PONDS HANDICAP STAKES (0–35) 3YO   £2267   1m 4f Firm 10 -25 Slow   [29]

1022 LAW COURT [5] (H Candy) 3-9-7 R Curant 7/4 FAV: 0-00401: 3 b c Alleged - Bay Street
(Grundy): Led approaching final 1f, driven out in a 3yo h'cap at Thirsk June 17: eff at 12f,
stays further: acts on yld, well suited by fast grnd.   30
697 REGENCY SQUARE [9] (P Feilden) 3-8-8 G Dickie 10/1: 000-32: Stayed on well final 1f:
just beaten: impr of late: see 697.   15
916 VITRY [7] (C James) 3-9-1 M Wigham 6/1: 00-0003: Ev ch over 1f out: stays 12f: see 916. 20

867 MASTER LAMB [1] (S Hall) 3-9-0 M Birch 12/1: 000-404: Led over 2f out: stays 12f:
see 690: acts on firm and yielding ground.   16
867 DOON VENTURE [4] 3-8-7 M Wood 12/1: 3000-00: Ran in snatches: stays 12f: see 867. 08
908 SLAP BANG [3] 3-9-1(vis) R Cochrane 9/2: 000-430: Fdd final 1f: eff at 12/13f on
gd/firrm and yld ground.   15
958 ROCKALL [2] 3-9-7 J Quinn(5) 10/1: 0430000: Made much, fdd: btr 461 (gd/yld): see 380. 00
883 CHEVET LADY [8] 3-9-4 S P Griffiths(5) 5/1: 1242000: Prom much: btr 461, 54.   00
769 QUEEN OF SWORDS [6] 3-9-3 S Perks 8/1: 00-0040: Never in it: btr 769: see 416.   00
9 ran   nk,1½,1½,1,¾   (D Heflin Jones)   H Candy Kingstone Warren, Oxon

1090 E.B.F. BOWNCROFT MAIDEN STAKES 2YO   £1495   5f   Firm 10 +02 Fast

800 ONGOING SITUATION [9] (D Morley) 2-9-0 G Duffield 10/11 FAV: 01: 2 br c Daring March-
Storm Crest (Lord Gayle): Well bckd and led final 1f, ridden out in quite fast run 2yo
maiden at Thirsk June 17: should be suited by 6f: acts well on fast grnd and
a sharpish trk: further impr likely.   45
995 AIR OF SPRING [7] (D Barron) 2-8-11 R Cochrane 5/2: 030202: Made much: in gd form. 38
--   ROYAL CROFTER [11] (M H Easterby) 2-9-0 M Birch 20/1: 3: Kept on well on racecourse
debut and will do btr next time: cost I.R. 3,800 and is a half brother to a winner in France:
should be suited by 6f: acts on fast grnd & should find a small event.   36
870 ANOTHER SEASON [2] (Denys Smith) 2-9-0 D Nicholls 12/1: 04: Sn prom: on the up grade:
eff at 5f on fast grnd & a sharpish trk.   30
938 FALDWYN [5] 2-8-11(bl) N Carlisle 9/1: 330: Prom over 4f: consistent: see 938, 543. 25
--   SENDIM ON SAM [10] 2-8-11 T Lucas 20/1: 0: Never nearer on racecourse debut: impr
likely from this speedily bred filly.   15
--   Lucys Melody [3] 8-11   931 Pit Pony [1] 9-0   --   Miss Management [8] 8-11
9 ran   1,2,1½,½,4   D Morley Newmarket

1091 CARR WOOD HANDICAP STAKES (0-50) 3YO   £2968   1m   Firm 10 -09 Slow   [46]

534 LJAAM [1] (H Thomson Jones) 3-9-7(bl) R Hills 7/1: 040-401: 3 b c Shirley Heights -
Think Ahead (Sharpen Up): Useful colt: defied top weight, led inside final 1f, ridden out
in a 3yo h'cap at Thirsk June 17: first time out in '85 won at Chepstow: stays 1m: acts on
gd & firm grnd.   50
814 PREJUDICE [7] (D Barron) 3-9-6 R Cochrane 7/1: 0030-32: Kept on well final 1f:
good effort: stays 1m: see 814.   46
716 GOOSE HILL [5] (M W Easterby) 3-9-4 K Hodgson 10/1: 0-10403: Ch 1f out: not btn far:
eff at 7f/1m: acts on any grnd: see 81.   43
816 BILLS AHEAD [2] (G Moore) 3-7-12 R P Elliott 7/1: 00-4044: Led/dsptd lead: see 637, 14 20
956 RUN BY JOVE [8] 3-8-9(vis) J Quinn(5) 12/1: -001200: Prom, ev ch: acts on firm,
better 789, 674 (easier grnd).   28
997 HOT LINING [12] 3-8-6 S Morris 20/1: 000-000: Nearest fin: see 863.   24
516 HARRY HULL [6] 3-8-2 L Charnock 7/2: 000-000: Well bckd, but no show: see 516, 309. 00
604 OPTIMISM FLAMED [4] 3-8-11 G Duffield 10/1: 33-2000: Made much, fdd: best first
time out in 183 (yielding).   00
816 MILEOMETER [11] 3-8-9 R Street 9/4 FAV: 020-020: Never going well: something amiss? 00
586 Golden Ancona [9] 9-2   816 Cumbrian Nijo [3] 8-8   816 Auction Man [10] 8-13
12 ran   ¾,1,1½,1½,½,1½   (Hamdan Al-Maktoum)   H Thomson Jones Newmarket

1092 FOX COVERT STAKES 4YO   £1542   1m 4f Firm 10 -05 Slow

*769 THE PRUDENT PRINCE [7] (W Jarvis) 4-9-6 R Cochrane 8/11 FAV: 32-211: 4 b c Grundy -
Ragirl (Ragusa): Useful colt who is in fine form: led approaching final 1f, comfortably in
a 4yo stakes at Thirsk June 17: last time out was an easy winner at Catterick: eff at 12f,
stays 14f and may get further: acts on firm, likes yielding grnd: no trk preferences.   42
*1071 COMMANDER ROBERT [2] (J Hanson) 4-9-6 J H Brown(5) 3/1: 0-40112: Quick reapp: made
most: in fine form: see 1071.   35
850 WHITE MILL [3] (H Candy) 4-9-0 R Curant 5/1: 400-03: Al up there: stays well: see 850. 24
--   COCKED HAT SUPREME [5] (S Hall) 4-8-11 M Birch 20/1: 03040-4: Never nearer on seasonal
debut: placed several times in '85: stays well, but lacks a turn of foot: acts on gd & firm. 17
675 TROJAN WAY [8] 4-9-0 S Perks 14/1: 030-000: Prom, ev ch: in '85 was trained by
I Balding finishing 3rd in a maiden at Bath: now with R Hollinshead: stays 12f: acts on yld. 14
1016 RACING DEMON [6] 4-9-0 S Morris 100/1: 4-30000: Never in it: see 104 (soft).   00
875 DARK CYGNET [4] 4-9-0 L Charnock 100/1: 00-0000: Impossible task.   00
7 ran   3,2½,2½,4,12   (J M Greetham)   W Jarvis Newmarket

1093 STATION WHIN HANDICAP (0-35) 3YO+   £2215   6f   Firm 10 +15 Fast   [34]

820 TANFEN [8] (T Craig) 5-9-4 N Carlisle 7/2 Jt FAV: -031021: 5 b g Tanfirion - Lady
Mary (Sallust): Made much, ridden out in quite fast run h'cap at Thirsk June 17: in gd
form this season, earlier winning a h'cap at Pontefract in '85 won h'caps at Newcastle,
Hamilton & Catterick: very eff over 6f: acts on any going & on any trk, but is best out
in front.   33

866 WILLIE GAN [3] (Denys Smith) 8-8-2 L Charnock 6/1: 00-0002: Al front rank: gd effort.   **16**
820 ROSIE DICKINS [4] (R Hollinshead) 4-8-13 R Lappin(7) 11/2: 1222403: Nearest fin: see 649.   **19**
*649 TOP THAT [2] (D Barron) 5-9-6 R Cochrane 7/2 Jt FAV: -002014: Prom, ev ch: btr 649 (yld)**25**
943 REMEMBRANCE [11] 5-8-8 J Quinn(5) 9/1: 0-04000: Sn prom: see 540.   **08**
447 AITCHANDOUBLEYOU [7] 3-8-13 B Mcghiff(7) 10/1: 0401-00: Never nearer: in '85 won
a nursery at Nottingham and a seller at Ripon: eff at 5/6f, stays 7f: best on gd & firm
grnd though acts on any trk.   **20**
649 KARENS STAR [6] 9-9-3 D Nicholls 10/1: 0-00000: Prom 4f: fin 2nd twice in '85, but
failed to win: in '84 won h'caps at Redcar (2), Hamilton and Thirsk: in '83 won 4 times:
equally eff at 5/6f: acts on any grnd.   **00**
936 Sir Wilmore [10] 9-7   626 Tollys Best [9] 7-7(1oh)
369 Monswart [5] 8-3
10 ran   nk,3,½,2,1½,1½   (William Burns)   T Craig West Barns, Dunbar

---

1094 GROUP 2 QUEEN ANNE STAKES 3YO+   £37856   1m   Firm 17 +14 Fast

*920 PENNINE WALK [4] (J Tree) 4-9-2 P Eddery 5/2: 140-111: 4 b c Persian Bold - Tifrums
(Thatch): Top class miler: maintained his unbeaten record this season, again showing a fine
turn of foot when winning Gr.2 Queen Anne Stakes at Royal Ascot June 17: came from last to
first, leading final 100yds, comfortably: won Diomed Stakes at Epsom & Jubilee H'cap at
Kempton first time out: in '85 was a ready winner of a valuable 3yo h'cap at Newmarket & also
won the Jersey Stakes at this meeting: very eff over 7f/1m: acts on firm & gd grnd, unsuited
by soft: handles any trk: genuine and consistent and has an excellent turn of foot: sure to
prove hard to beat in all the remaining top 1m races.   **86**
*897 EFISIO [3] (J Dunlop) 4-9-8 W Carson 12/1: 10-0412: Came from behind to lead final
1f, just outpcd but this was a tremendous effort at the weights and he is clearly much impr
this term: see 897.   **87**
-598 TELEPROMPTER [8] (J Watts) 6-9-8(vis) T Ives 6/4 fav: 2120-23: Led ½way, no extra
final 1f but again ran a most genuine race and retains his enthusiasm well: see 598.   **82**
920 EVER GENIAL [5] (H Cecil) 4-8-13 S Cauthen 10/1: 1133-04: Prom thro'out: see 920.   **66**
*1007 KINGS RIVER [1] 4-9-2 M Kinane 13/2: 141-210: Prom most: btr 1007 (gd).   **66**
313 YOUNG RUNAWAY [7] 4-9-5 G Starkey 14/1: 1010-40: Yet to recapture best form: see 313.   **68**
*5 MACS REEF [9] 4-9-2 P Robinson 33/1: 3202-100: No dngr in 7th: please note that he
has run unplaced in France since winning race 5.   **00**
468 FIELD HAND [2] 4-9-5 B Thomson 14/1: 21-2100: No dngr in 8th: twice well below 313(sft) **00**
598 GRAND HARBOUR [6] 6-9-2 N Connorton 250/1: 2204-00: Teleprompter's pacemaker, led
4f: won a h'cap at Chester in '85: very eff at 7f on gd grnd & runs well on a sharp trk.   **00**
9 ran   1½,3,4,1½,nk   (Mrs Maria Niarchos)   J Tree Marlborough, Wilts

1095 GROUP 2 PRINCE OF WALES STAKES 3YO+   £37183   1m 2f Firm 17 -11 Slow

920 ENGLISH SPRING [1] (I Balding) 4-8-12 Pat Eddery 14/1: 2-44101: 4 gr f Grey Dawn II-
Spring Is Here (In Reality): Smart filly who returned to her best form when winning Gr.2
Prince Of Wales Stakes at Royal Ascot June 17: came from behind to lead final 1f narrowly:
landed a minor event at Ripon previously and last season won at Epsom, Wolverhampton, Ascot &
a Gr.3 race in Italy: very eff around 9/10f: acts on any going though possible not totally
suited by soft grnd.   **80**
*736 BEDTIME [6] (W Hern) 6-9-4 W Carson 4/5 fav: 1112/12: Prom, met trouble in running
dist, kept on well but unable to get up close home: unlucky? see 736.   **86**
*641 FAIR OF THE FURZE [4] (L Browne) 4-9-5 S Cauthen 15/2: 201-413: Led dist, gd effort
though possibly suited by softer grnd: see 641 (heavy).   **80**
736 WYLFA [8] (J Shaw) 5-9-1 B Rouse 14/1: 140/224: Prom, thro'out: in fine form: see 410.   **78**
736 SUPREME LEADER [3] 4-9-4 P Robinson 5/1: 0-11330: Ev ch and has 3 times failed to
run up to the form of 325 (soft).   **78**
618 SHARP NOBLE [5] 4-8-11(BL) G Baxter 33/1: -022240: Bl first time, difficult task
and ran creditably: see 166, 263.   **61**
706 LES ARCS [9] 4-9-1 W R Swinburn 9/1: -144-00: No dngr in 8th: see 706.   **00**
+708 Purchasepaperchase [7] 8-12   653 Windsor Knot [3] 8-11
9 ran   nk,1½,¾,1¼,nk   (Paul Mellon)   I Balding Kingsclere, Berks

1096 GROUP 2 ST JAMES PALACE STAKES 3YO   £37484   1m   Firm 17 +07 Fast

407 SURE BLADE [1] (B Hills) 3-9-0 B Thomson 9/2: 113-101: 3 b c Kris - Double Lock
(Home Guard): Very smart colt: ran 2nd till leading under press inside final 1f to win Gr.2
St James's Palace Stakes at Royal Ascot June 17: in doing so reversed the form of the
2,000 Guineas with Green Desert: first time out, easily won a minor race at Thirsk: in fine
form in '85 winning at Newmarket, Royal Ascot (Coventry Stakes) and Doncaster,   just behind
Huntingdale in the Dewhurst on final outing: very eff at 1m but looks sure to stay at least
10f: acts on firm & yld going and on any trk though runs well on a stiff one: genuine and
consistent.   **86**

640 GREEN DESERT [3] (M Stoute) 3-9-0 W R Swinburn 5/2 fav: 14-1202: Adopting completely
different riding tactics, led from the start at a gd pace, no extra final 1f & was over
3L ahead of this winner in race 407 when ridden with much more restraint: see 220.   82
878 SHARROOD [5] (W Hern) 3-9-0 W Carson 9/2: 1-04303: Chall final 1f & ran up to
his best: possibly stays 12f (see 878) but is very eff at 1m: see 226, 407.   82
920 NINO BIBBIA [6] (L Cumani) 3-9-0 Pat Eddery 13/2: 2-1104: Al well there: see 579.   76
556 LUQMAN [7] 3-9-0 Paul Eddery 33/1: 114-040: No threat: looks certain to be suited
by a return to shorter distances: see 286.   69
*802 FAUSTUS [2] 3-9-0 S Cauthen 6/1: 12-1010: Prom 6f: can do btr: see 802.   63
640 HUNTINGDALE [4] 3-9-0 M Hills 5/1: 221-340: Al struggling: see 407.   00
7 ran   2,hd,4,4,3   (Sheikh Mohammed)   B Hills Lambourn, Berks

1097 GROUP 3 COVENTRY STAKES 2YO   £24928   6f   Firm 17 -27 Slow

+962 CUTTING BLADE [12] (L Piggott) 2-8-11 C Asmussen 11/1: 311: 2 b c Sharpo - Lady Of
Renown (His Majesty): Smart, improving 2yo: prom and responded gamely to strong press,
leading on the post in Gr.3 Coventry Stakes at Royal Ascot June 17: comfortably won a maiden
at Leicester June 9: speedily bred colt who is eff at 5f & stays 6f well: acts on firm grnd
& on a gall trk.   72
*685 POLEMOS [7] (H T Jones) 2-8-11 A Murray 9/1: 12: Just failed to make all: acts on
firm & gd grnd: impr sort who will win more races: see 685.   71
*781 AMIGO SUCIO [17] (K Brassey) 2-8-11 S Whitworth 20/1: 113: Dsptd lead final 2f, just
btn in a 3-way photo & continues to impr: sure to win more races: see 781.   70
915 GLORY FOREVER [14] (S Norton) 2-8-11 J Lowe 33/1: 44: Kept on really well and this
was a fine effort: sure to be suited by 7f plus: acts on firm & gd: certain to win his
maiden without any fuss: see 915.   68
*1019 BRAVE DANCER [19] 2-8-11 G Starkey 9/1: 310: Well there thro'out and was only narrowly
btn in this close fin: fine effort: see 1019.   67
*752 POLONIA [18] 2-8-8 D Gillespie 15/8 fav: 110: Al prom: gd effort for a filly but
probably btr on easier going: see 752.   60
577 SOMEONE ELSE [4] 2-8-11 T Ives 33/1: 030: Close up 7th: gd effort & should certainly
find a maiden soon: see 230: acts on firm.   60
810 LOCKTON [13] 2-8-11 M Hills 14/1: 20: Fin 8th, should find a maiden: see 810.   55
876 PERSIAN STYLE [5] 2-8-11 M Roberts 33/1: 000: Prom much, fin 9th: suited by firm.   52
915 QUEL ESPRIT [3] 2-8-11 S Cauthen 10/1: 1211130: Dsptd lead much, fin 10th: best 571.   52
*810 MANSOOJ [1] 2-8-11 Pat Eddery 10/1: 310: Early speed from a poor draw: see 810.   00
--   Al Mahamry [2] 8-11   --   Bird Dancer [8] 8-11   804 Diamond Flight [20] 8-11(BL)
*622 Munaasib [6] 8-11   --   Rich Charlie [16] 8-11
--   Search The Wind [15] 8-11   737 Whippet [10] 8-11
--   Seul Etoile [9] 8-11
19 ran   shhd,shhd,½,hd,1½ 1½,¾,1,nk   (Mahmoud Fustok)   L Piggott Newmarket

1098 GROUP 2 KING EDWARD VII STAKES 3YO   £39518   1m 4f   Firm 17 +02 Fast

324 BONHOMIE [11] (H Cecil) 3-8-8 S Cauthen 9/4 fav: 111-21: 3 ch c What A Pleasure -
Chatter Box (Ribot): Smart colt: al prom & led final 2f keeping on strongly to win Gr.2 King
Edward VII Stakes at Royal Ascot June 17: 2nd to Derby hero Shahrastani at Sandown on sole
previous outing this season but was unbtn in 3 races in '85 at Yarmouth, Lingfield & Royal
Lodge Stakes at Ascot: well suited by 12f & looks certain to stay further: acts on soft but
is very much at home on firm or gd grnd: genuine sort who finds extra when pressed and is
sure to win more top class races.   83
654 NEW TROJAN [6] (W Hern) 3-8-8 W Carson 20/1: 140-402: Al there, battled with winner
from 2f out and ran an excellent race: well suited by 12f on firm grnd though does act on
gd/soft, probably unsuited by heavy: sure to make amends soon: see 510.   79
878 NISNAS [12] (P Cole) 3-8-8 T Quinn 11/2: 3-13103: Probably the worst sufferer in quite
a rough race being hemmed on the rails final 2f: unlucky? see 494, 878.   79
*572 KADIAL [1] (R J Houghton) 3-8-8 Pat Eddery 5/1: -214: Chall dist, gd effort from
this impr colt: stays 12f: see 572.   77
*916 MTOTO [8] 3-8-8 M Roberts 14/1: 3-210: Not the best of runs & kept on strongly,
showing himself well suited by 12f & firm grnd: fast impr type who is sure to win more races.   73
--   HIGHLAND CHIEFTAIN [4] 3-8-8 B Rouse 16/1:12114-0: No threat on seasonal debut but
should come on for the race: winner at Brighton & Newmarket (2) in '85: 4th in France on
final outing in Pattern company: stays at least 10f, should be well suited by 12f: acts on
firm & yld and on any trk though likes a stiff one.   72
878 JAREER [7] 3-8-8 W R Swinburn 9/2: 210-00: Prom 10f, fin 8th: see 878.   00
442 BELDALE STAR [2] 3-8-8 G Starkey 12/1: 120-100: Ran badly & twice below 273.   00
572 Chauve Souris [13] 8-8   555 North Verdict [3] 8-8
574 Dancing Zeta [5] 8-8(vis)   887 Festival City Usa 0 8-8
476 Plaid [10] 8-8
13 ran   1½,¾,¾,1½,¾   (Sheikh Mohammed)   H Cecil Newmarket

1099 ASCOT STAKES HANDICAP 3YO+ 0-75   £9645   2m 4f   Firm 17 -11 Slow   [63]

712 RIKKI TAVI [3] (B Hills) 6-7-10 W Carson 7/2 fav: 13-0331: 6 b h Monsanto - Goosie Gantlet (Run The Gantlet): Useful stayer: heavily bckd, dsptd lead final 4f for a narrow success in valuable Ascot Stakes H'cap June 17: in '85 won h'caps at Doncaster & Ascot (again): eff 2m, well suited by extreme distances: suited by a gall trk: acts on firm & yld.   43

942 OTABARI [2] (P Cole) 5-8-1 T Quinn 10/1: 4-00342: Dsptd lead final 4f, just btn & 4L clear of rest: suited by an extreme trip nowadays & deserves a race soon: acts on firm & hvy: see 778.   47

801 MILTON BURN [9] (H O'neill) 5-7-13 S Whitworth 10/1: 0110223: Came to chall 1f out in gd form: see 312: stays 2½m.   39

693 INDE PULSE [12] (J Hindley) 4-9-10 M Hills 10/1: -010434: Led/dsptd lead much: see 280, 462.   64

462 PATHS SISTER [8] 5-7-7(1oh) J Lowe 14/1: 111-000: Fin well from rear: see 215.   31

663 FISHPOND [7] 5-7-7(1oh) D Brown 20/1: 240-200: No dngr: best 419 (14f, good).   26

*917 TRAPEZE ARTIST [4] 5-8-2(3ex) S Dawson[3] 5/1: 4002110: Fin 7th: btr 917 (14f).   00

801 ACCURACY [13] 5-8-2 J Williams 14/1: 3210100: Ev ch, fin 8th : best 663 (yld/soft).   00

801 HIGH PLAINS [11] 4-7-11 T Williams 13/2: 10-0000: Wknd into 9th: not stay 2½m? better 801 (2m): see 235.   00

-- JAMESMEAD [1] 5-8-9 Pat Eddery 9/1: 01012-0: Made much on seasonal debut: lightly raced over hurdles in 85/86, winner at Salisbury & Ascot in '85 on the Flat: acts on firm but suited by an easier surface: likes a gall trk.   00

942 Ballet Champ [6] 7-7(9oh)	856 Picadilly Prince [5] 7-7(4oh)
+933 Sound Diffusion [14] 7-7(3ex)(9oh)	801 Water Cannon [16] 8-0
712 Knights Heir [10] 7-7(19oh)	778 Northern Ruler [15] 7-8(1ow)(8oh)

16 ran   hd,4,hd,½,3   (A Boon)   B Hills Lambourn, Berks

Official Going Given as Hard

1100 MIDDLETON SELLING STAKES 2YO   £958   5f   Firm 01 -37 Slow

603 BAD PAYER [1] (M W Easterby) 2-8-8 M Birch 1/1 FAV: 431: 2 b f Tanfirion - Opening Flight (Falcon) Comfortably justified fav, making most in a 2yo seller at Beverley June 18 (no bid): cheaply bought filly who is a full sister to a winning juv: well suited by 5f, tho' will stay further: acts on fast and soft grd and is suited by a stiff track.   30

612 PERTAIN [7] (W Wharton) 2-8-11(bl) I Johnson 7/2: 04002: Dropped slightly in class: ran on well and shd win soon in this grade: cheaply bought gelding who acts on firm and soft ground: seems to act on any track.   27

-- FAIRY CHIMES [5] (R Stubbs) 2-8-8 D Nicholls 20/1: 3: Unfancied on debut: al up there and ran a fair race: suited by stayer further in time: acts on fast grd and a stiff trk.   18

-- EVERY WEDNESDAY [9] (R Thompson) 2-8-8 R P Elliott 20/1: 4: Stayed on well from ½ way on debut: acts on firm ground: should stay another furlong: likely to improve.   17

813 ROSE DUET [8] 2-9-1 B Mcghiff(7) 6/1: 00100: Ran to her best: see 711.   22

858 PALACE RULER [6] 2-8-8 S Webster 11/2: 40: Going on fin and sure to stay further.   13

711 ATHENS LADY [3] 2-8-8 S Perks 10/1: 400: Gd early speed: shd do btr on an easier course: cheaply acquired filly who is a half sister to a winning juv: acts on firm grd.   00

| -- Sorrowful [2] 8-8 | 957 Noble Kala [4] 8-11(BL) |

9 ran   1½,2,½,1,½   (C Mahoney)   M W Easterby Sheriff Hutton, Yorks

1101 HOLDERNESS STAKES (H'CAP) (0-35)   £2327   5f   Firm 01 +13 Fast   [35]

977 THE MECHANIC [15] (J Sutcliffe) 3-8-0(VIS) M Hills 11/10 FAV: 000-021: 3 b c Lochnager - Lardana (Burglar) Well bckd when leading inside dist, readily, in a fast run h'cap at Beverley June 18: first success: well suited by 5f on a sound surf, and will stay further: acts on a stiff trk: on the upgrade.   24

877 CELTIC BIRD [7] (A Balding) 6-8-10 E Guest(3) 9/1: 00-0002: Tried to make all: btr effort and loves to be out in front: suited by fast grd: see 742.   20

594 WORKADAY [12] (C Gray) 4-9-10 I Johnson 10/1: 20-0003: Fin well over this shorter trip: gd effort under her big weight: useful filly on her day, rated 55 when a comfortable winner of a h'cap over this C/D last season: in '84 won at Catterick and Beverley, and likes this stiff track: best form over 5/6f: suited by fast ground.   32

786 BAY BAZAAR [14] (M W Easterby) 4-9-1 M Hindley(3) 12/1: 2400034: Al well placed.   17

877 CHINA GOLD [3] 7-9-12 G Gosney 6/1: 00-0300: Fair effort under top weight: see 784.   27

961 KEN SIDDALL [9] 3-8-2(2ow) M Wigham 16/1: 0044000: Nearest fin: best 198 (C/D yldg)   05

1070 JUMP JAR [10] 7-8-13 D Nicholls 15/2: 0100-20: Never nearer 7th: see 1070.   00

-- DUFFERS DANCER [8] 4-8-6 N Connorton 6/1: 40004-0: Bckd from 16/1, tho' never dangerous: won a h'cap at Carlisle last season and in '84 was successful at Hamilton: eff over 5f, stays 7f well: suited by fast grd and likes a stiff track.   00

1063 Bao [5] 7-7(3oh)	742 Carpenters Boy [13] 8-10	
636 The Manor [11] 7-7(3oh)		784 Swinging Gold [3] 9-4
992 Mr Panache [8] 8-7	825 Y I Oyston [4] 9-2	906 Coded Love [1] 8-1

15 ran   2,½,2½,nk,2½,½   (Christopher Dodson)   J Sutcliffe Epsom, Surrey

1102 HUNSLEY BEACON MAIDEN STAKES   £1414   1m 4f   Firm 01 +09 Fast

720 COINAGE [3] (R Johnson Houghton) 3-8-1(2ow) R Curant 8/11 FAV: 3-231: 3 br c
Owen Dudley - Grisbi (Grey Sovereign) Useful colt: easily landed the odds,   broke the
course record when running away with an all-aged maiden at Beverley June 18: placed in all
his prev starts and deserved this win: half brother to sev winners: eff over 10f, stays 12f
well: acts on firm and yldg ground and seems to have no trk preferences.   50
959 DIENAUS TROVE [14] (H Collingridge) 5-9-0 M Rimmer 7/1: -32: Made most: no chance
with easy winner tho' again ran well: see 959.   26
--   HEADIN ON [2] (M Eckley) 6-9-0 J Williams 33/1: -3: Stayed on strongly from rear:
fair debut and shd do btr next time: stays 12f well: acts on firm grd and on a stiff trk.   25
959 NADAS [15] (S Norton) 3-8-1(vis)(2ow) G Duffield 7/1: -42304: Disapp since 669(yield/soft). 24
869 COUNTRY JIMMY [11] 4-9-0 M Birch 25/1: 00-4000: Some late prog, acts on firm:see 381   19
--   CASSANDRAS DREAM [1] 5-8-11 A Cunningham(7) 50/1: -0: Sn behind and nearer dangerous:
well btn over hurdles this Winter and seems of little account.   12
765 FAST REALM [6] 3-7-13 M Hills 7/2: -000: Fin 7th: much btr 765 (10f, sharper trk)   00
993 Dubavarna [7] 8-11   194 Fissure [4] 7-13(3ow)   -- Rolampago [13] 7-13
960 Mr Bennington [5] 9-0   990 Far To Go [10] 9-0   1068 Montefiaso [12] 9-0
13 ran   20,1,1½,1½,2½   (Mrs James A de Rothschield)   R Johnson Houghton Blewbury.

1103 ARRAM APPRENTICE STAKES (H'CAP)(0-35)   £1018   1m   Firm 01 -24 Slow   [29]

1073 HEAVENLY HOOFER [8] (Denys Smith) 3-7-8 J Quinn 7/1: 00-0101: 3 b g Dance In Time
- Heavenly Chord (Hittite Glory) Quick reappearance and was never hdd when a game winner
of an app h'cap at Beverley June 18: last month won a seller on this course: eff over 7/8f
on good and firm ground: well suited by this stiff trk and does well with forcing tactics. 15
893 KAMARESS [4] (M Brittain) 4-8-7 A Bacon(7) 14/1: -000002: Chased winner thro'out:
little form last season tho' showed some fair form as a juv, winning at Redcar: stays 1m:
suited by fast ground.   13
857 SKELTON [5] (M W Easterby) 3-8-0 A Shoults 3/1: 00-0003: Mkt drifter: fin well: see 650. 16
857 CASHEW KING [7] (B Mcmahon) 3-8-9 J Hills 13/2: 010-004: Ran well: likes this trk.   24
893 PATCHBURG [1] 4-9-7 B Mcghiff 7/2: 2130100: Best over this C/D in 611 (gd).   20
997 LOST OPPORTUNITY [6] 3-8-6 A Geran(7) 11/8 FAV: 4-2000: Well bckd: had ev ch:
best on soft in 99.   10
--   GULPHAR [9] 4-9-2 Tracy Williams(7) 8/1: -0440-0: Fin 8th: maiden who was lightly
raced last season: stays 13f and prob finds this trip inadequate: suited by fast ground.   00
517 Robbie Grant [3] 7-7(7oh)   993 Wyoming [2] 7-13
9 ran   ¾,1½,nk,1½,4   (J A Bianchi)   Denys Smith Bishop Auckland, Co Durham

1104 DERWENT STAKES (H'CAP) (0-35)   £1488   7f   Firm 01 +01 Fast   [27]

874 WHIRLING WORDS [16] (P Makin) 3-8-5(1ow) S Perks 5/2 FAV: 04-0021: 3 b f Sparkler -
Wild Words (Galivanter) Nicely bckd, led below dist for a comfortable win in a h'cap at
Beverley June 18: first success: lightly raced last season: half sister to a handful of
winners, incl useful sprinter Battle Hymn: eff around 1m on fast and yldg grd: acts on
any track: can win again.   28
874 BOLD ARCHER [8] (M Fetherston Godley) 3-8-1 P Hutchinson 16/1: 00-0002: Ran on
well: better effort and likely to be suited by further: acts on fast grd and any trk.see 874 15
*906 GREY STARLIGHT [19] (L Siddall) 4-8-13(bl)(5ex) G Gosney 12/1: 00-0013: Made most:
in gd form and stays this longer trip well: see 906.   14
992 HIGHLY PLACED [3] (E Eldin) 4-8-1 J Bleasdale 14/1: 000-004: Dwelt, never nearer.   01
--   SOHAIL [5] 3-9-8(BL) P D'arcy 6/1: 03234-0: Switched below dist, never nearer:
sure to be suited next time: maiden who was placed in 5 of his 6 outings last term:
stays 1m: acts on gd and firm ground and on any track.   32
936 MARAVILLA [1] 4-9-10 M Hindley(3) 14/1: 0300-00: Stayed on: trained by C Nelson
when placed sev times last season: stays 1m well: acts on firm & soft: now with J Etherington 22
*857 PLEASURE ISLAND [9] 3-8-13(5ex) G Duffield 9/2: 0-0010: Last: very disapp after
winning over this C/D in 857.   00
907 Rose Window [17] 9-2(BL)   -- King Cole [15] 8-12
970 Henrys Place [7] 9-0(bl)(5ex)   936 Musical Shadow [6] 9-5(BL)
--   Still Marching [18] 9-2   1013 Manabel [10] 9-4
710 Via Vitae [4] 8-1   -- Walhan [11] 8-5   733 Dress In Spring [14] 8-2
505 Sirdar Flyer [2] 8-2   972 Gardas Gold [13] 8-6
18 ran   3,1,½,¾,½   (Mrs Rodney Fitch)   P Makin Ogbourne Maisey, Wilts.

1105 SINNINGTON AUCTION STAKES 2YO   £1633   7f   Firm 01 -18 Slow

934 SPARSHOLT [10] (P Cole) 2-8-10 K Powdrell 6/4 FAV: 3121: 2 b c Miner's Lamp - Hark
Hark (Sing Sing) Heavily bckd, led/dsptd lead all the way and rallied well for a narrow
win in a 2yo Auction at Beverley June 18: most consistent: earlier winning at Salisbury:
half brother to sev winners: well suited by front running tactics: stayed today's extended
7f really well: acts on firm and soft and seems a genuine sort.   46
*722 PEN BAL LADY [13] (J Pritchard Gordon) 2-8-10 G Duffield 5/1: 12: Led over 1f out:
just btn: fine effort: stays 7f well: see 722.   45
927 LAST STAND [17] (J Hindley) 2-8-4 M Hills 11/2: 003: Sn prom, showing impr form:
cost 5,400 gns and is a sister to 3 winners: stays 7f: acts well on fast ground.   35

612 CITY FINAL [1] (R Hollinshead) 2-8-4 R Lappin(7) 14/1: 404: Fin well and was suited
by today's longer trip: will stay 1m: acts on fast ground.   27
515 GOOD BUY BAILEYS [11] 2-8-6 M Rimmer 10/1: 110: Prom, ev ch: prob stays 7f:see 186.   26
913 FREV OFF [5] 2-8-4(BL)(1ow) M Birch 14/1: 300: Never nearer: seems to stay 7f:
acts on firm and yldg ground: see 672.   16
913 CHAYOFA [9] 2-8-0 P Burke(7) 5/1: 200: Gambled on: fdd 2 out: best 515 (5f sharpish). 00
425 GALWAY EXPRESS [7] 2-8-3 M Wood 8/1: 00: Played up start and no show: active in
mkt today: cheaply acquired: may improve.   00
--   RECORD BANGLER [16] 2-8-8 M Wigham 10/1: 0: Mkt drifter: half bro. to Capeability Pound.00

962	Parkers Joy [14] 8-5(1ow)			+892	Stage [4] 8-13
252	War Child [6] 8-5	612	Cold Laser [8] 8-4	892	Hilliard [12] 8-2
--	High Cable [3] 8-4	913	Gillot Bar [2] 8-4(1ow)		
332	Wolf J Flywheel [15] 8-3				

17 ran   hd,2,4,1½,4   (W H Ponsonby)   P Cole Sparsholt, Oxon.

1106 YORK AND AINSTY STAKES (H'CAP)(0-35)   £1420   1m 2f Firm 01 -06 Slow   [33]

1017 RAPID LAD [7] (J Spearing) 8-9-7 D Nicholls 5/1: -000-01: 8 b g Rapid River -
Seacona (Espresso) On his fav trk, fin well to lead inside final 1f in a h'cap at Beverley
June 18: a course winner 7 times now at Beverley: eff 1m, stays 10f well: acts on any
ground but loves Beverley.   34
968 EXCAVATOR LADY [8] (R Whitaker) 7-7-12(vis) S P Griffiths(5) 7/1: 3-00432: Led
2f out: gd effort: see 629.   09
956 BURAAG [4] (M W Easterby) 5-10-0(BL) K Hodgson 3/1: -004403: Bl first time:
ev ch final 2f: see 196.   34
1017 ELARIM [5] (T Fairhurst) 7-9-5(BL) C Coates(5) 3/1: -000044: Made much: not btn
far: see 745.   24
1017 IVOROSKI [3] 4-8-0 M Fry 11/1: 0-00000: Never nearer: see 1017.   03
940 REDCROSS MISS [6] 4-8-9 M Birch 12/1: 3300-00: No extra final 2f: mdn: stays 12f well:
acts on gd/firm and yldg ground and likes a sharpish trk.   04
779 MISS LAURA LEE [2] 3-8-2 Gay Kelleway(2) 9/1: 40-4000: Prom 1m: best 368 (sharp trk) 00
967 HARBOUR BAZAAR [1] 6-7-9(vis) Julie Bowker(7) 11/4 FAV: 00-0420: Prom, sn wknd:
well below form 967.   00
8 ran   1,3,hd,1½,5   (Stephen Borsberry)   J Spearing Wixford, Warwickshire

1107 GR 3 JERSEY STAKES 3YO   £21020   7f   Firm 06 +08 Fast

920 CLIVEDEN [4] (G Harwood) 3-8-10 G Starkey 9/1: 13-0031: 3 b c Valdez - Rosey Ramble
(Chieftain) Smart colt: al prom and led dist comfortably in quite fast run Gr 3 Jersey Stakes
at Royal Ascot June 18: a very useful 2yo in '85 winning at Goodwood and a close 3rd
in the Coventry Stakes at this meeting: stays 10f but very eff over 7f/1m: best form on
firm or good going.   76
802 BRAVE OWEN [3] (H Cecil) 3-8-10 S Cauthen 5/1: 13-22: Prom, kept on well, gd effort. 70
802 HARD ROUND [1] (R Hannon) 3-8-10 Pat Eddery 40/1: 41-2443: Belied his S.P. leading
2f out and keeping on well: stays 1m (see 802): should win a race soon: see 159.   67
1007 JAZZ MUSICIAN [8] (M Kauntze) 3-8-10(VIS) M Kinane 50/1: 200-424: Irish chall:
visored for first time, ev ch: fair effort but prob btr on gd or soft ground: see 1007.   61
692 RESOURCEFUL FALCON [5] 3-9-2 T Quinn 25/1: 11-0220: Prom most: btr on an easier
surface: see 586.   64
605 DIGGERS REST [16] 3-8-10 Paul Eddery 33/1: 303-130: Fin well: best 216 (yldg).   57
754 LIVING ROUGH [11] 3-8-3 P Shanahan 7/1: 2-24D0: Clear chance at the weights on
form shown in 754, mod effort: unsuited by firm?   00
*803 DOLKA [10] 3-8-13 W R Swinburn 100/30 fav: 1-10: Heavily bckd: much btr 803.   00
+776 METEORIC [20] 3-8-7 W Carson 10/1: 120-010: Early speed from unfav draw: see 776(6f) 00

*586	Fleet Form [17] 9-2	501	Reignbeau [6] 8-10	925	Sweet Adelaide [2] 8-7
190	Cromwell Park [19] 8-10			+945	Firm Landing [15] 9-2
586	Vainglorious [14] 9-2	600	Home Rule Fr [12] 8-10		
--	Grey Goddess [7] 8-7	803	Sally Says So [18] 8-7		
-776	Zalatia [9] 8-7	--	Eastern Song [13] 8-6		

20 ran   2½,1,2½,1½,¾   (A Speelman)   G Harwood Pulborough, Sussex

1108 GR 3 QUEEN MARY STAKES 2YO FILLIES   £24322   5f   Firm 06 -09 Slow

*601 FOREST FLOWER [6] (I Balding) 2-8-8 Pat Eddery 9/4 fav: 11: 2 ch f Green Forest -
Leap Lively (Nijinsky) Very smart filly in the making: maintained her 100% record with
a very impressive 3l success in Group 3 Queen Mary Stakes at Royal Ascot June 18: well bckd
and was al cruising, sprinted clear, showing a rare turn of foot in final 1f: easy first
time out winner of a minor race at Newbury: well bred filly and is the first foal of
Lingfield Oaks Trial winner Leap Lively from the first crop of European Champion miler Green
Forest: very eff over 5/6f, bred to stay much further: acts on firm and gd going and on
a stiff track: not one to oppose.   78

*848 PROPENSITY [10] (G Harwood) 2-8-8 G Starkey 7/1: 12: Kept on really well, caught a
tartar here: improving filly who is sure to win more races: acts on firm and gd: see 848.   66

848 DAZY [5] (R Laing) 2-8-8 P Cook 20/1: 23: Slow start, fin strongly and she is
sure to be suited by 6f: see 848: will have no trouble winning a race.   64

+773 NATURALLY FRESH [11] (J Winter) 2-8-8 W R Swinburn 9/4 jt fav: 4114: Dsptd lead
4f: creditable effort but rated higher in 773 (made all).   62

800 GAYS FLUTTER [7] 2-8-8 J Reid 25/1: 40: Prom most: fine effort on only 2nd outing
and should have little trouble winning a maiden: see 800.   50

*1006 INDEXS [9] 2-8-8 M Kinane 8/1: 210: Never closer: much btr 1006 (6f gd).   47

621 RIPE CHRISTINA [3] 2-8-8 R Cochrane 10/1: 00: Well bckd from 33/1 (!) Outpaced
in 8th: evidently very highly regarded: see 621.   00

924 PLUM DROP [1] 2-8-8 W Carson 11/1: 2130: Btr 924 (sharp trk).   00

*924 Abuzz [12] 8-8   773 Jaisalmer [13] 8-8   924 Nutwood Lil [4] 8-8
*882 Crees Figurine [2] 8-8   852 Recreation [14] 8-8
13 ran   3,¾,¾,3,1   (Paul Mellon)   I Balding Kingsclere, Berks.

1109 ROYAL HUNT CUP H'CAP (0-75)   £28476   1m   Firm 06 +19 Fast   [74]

433 PATRIACH [12] (J Dunlop) 4-7-12 T Quinn 20/1: 411-201: 4 b c London Bells - Julip
(Track Spare) Very useful colt: al prom and led final 2f, keeping on strongly to win fast
run Royal Hunt Cup at Royal Ascot June 18: in '85 won at Leicester and Lingfield: very eff
at 1m: acts on firm and soft and likes a stiff trk: impr type who will win more decent h'caps.   61

+706 SIYAH KALEM [6] (J Dunlop) 4-8-10(7ex) W Carson 15/2: 211-412: Kept on really well
to chase up his lesser-fancied stable companion and was 3l clear rest: sure to win more
h'caps: see 706.   71

-- KINGS HEAD [22] (G Harwood) 4-8-6 G Starkey 16/1: 120-3: Made an excellent seasonal
debut, keeping on well final 1f: only ran 3 times in '85 winning first time out at Windsor:
dam a smart performer in the USA: eff over 1m but btr suited by 10f and likely to stay 12f:
acts well on firm grd: should not be missed next time.   62

*1013 SUPER TRIP [11] (M Fetherston Godley) 5-7-7(5ex)(8oh) L Charnock 50/1: 0-00214: Fin
really well and is fast improving at present: sure to pick up another h'cap or 2 in
lower grade: see 1013.   46

879 RANA PRATAP [3] 6-7-8 M L Thomas 14/1: -043320: Ev ch 2f out: btr 879 (10f sharp trk)   41

433 TREMBLANT [13] 5-9-3 Pat Eddery 8/1: 111-200: Ev ch: see 5.   62

815 TELWAAH [15] 4-7-13 M Roberts 14/1: 1010-20: Never closer in 7th: stays at least 1m.   42

879 TRULY RARE [1] 4-8-6(2ow) W R Swinburn 14/1: 41-0300: Twice below 433.   00

920 HADEER [2] 4-8-13 C Asmussen 5/1 fav: -044-20: Clear chance on the form shown in
920, ran inexplicably badly.   00

945 BOLD INDIAN [16] 5-9-10 S Cauthen 14/1: -0230: Anchored by weight: see 433.   00

706 INDIAN HAL [27] 4-7-13 N Howe 13/1: 31-0440: Badly drawn: see 248, 706.   00

879 Gilderdale [8] 7-9   706 Qualitair Flyer [20] 8-6(bl)
775 Bundaburg [23] 7-7(5oh)   *940 The Games Up [21] 7-7(5ex)(16oh)
775 All Fair [7] 7-9   1047 Moores Metal [5] 7-7(1oh)
698 Aconitum [17] 7-8   618 Running Flush [19] 7-9(VIS)(2ow)(4oh)
775 October [4] 8-0   881 Shmaireekh [29] 9-6
-- Coincidental [30] 8-3   706 Come On The Blues [32] 8-2
410 Bank Parade [25] 7-13   706 Manchesterskytrain [18] 7-11
*668 Conmayjo [31] 7-7(5ex)   706 Ready Wit [26] 7-8(1ow)(1oh)
1018 Scoutsmistake [14] 7-7(4oh) 815 Joyful Dancer [10] 7-7(5oh)
748 Xhai [28] 7-7(BL)(5oh)   521 Red Russell [24] 8-4(2ow)
573 Dorset Cottage [9] 8-5(BL)
32 ran   ¾,3,1½,2½,¾,1½   (Peter S Winfield)   J Dunlop Arundel, Sussex

1110 GR 2 CORONATION STAKES 3YO FILLIES   £34694   1m   Firm 06 -06 Slow

*754 SONIC LADY [5] (M Stoute) 3-9-4 W R Swinburn 8/15 fav: 1-1311: 3 b f Nureyev -
Stumped (Owen Anthony) Topclass filly: comfortably landed the odds, going clear in final 1f
to win Gr 2 Coronation Stakes at Royal Ascot June 18 : impressive winner of Nell Gwyn Stakes
at Newmarket first time out and the Irish 1,000 Guineas at the Curragh last time: in between
narrowly btn in the 1,000 Guineas: runaway winner of Blue Seal Stakes at Ascot on sole outing
in '85: very eff over 7f/1m: acts on frm & yldg and on a gall trk: hard to beat over this trip   85

373 EMBLA [4] (L Cumani) 3-9-4 Pat Eddery 3/1: 111-402: Kept on well under press tho'
no chance with winner: seems to be approaching her best: see 214.   77

803 SOMEONE SPECIAL [6] (P Cole) 3-9-0 T Quinn 33/1: -2133: Al well there and this
was a fine effort: see 658: stays 1m well.   70

754 CARHUE LADY [2] (P O'leary) 3-9-0 M Kinane 50/1: 142-204: Outpaced final 2f: best 269   55

926 VOLIDA [7] 3-9-0 P Robinson 66/1: 0-40400: Set the pace, hdd and wknd final 2f: see 373.   53

+59 STATELY LASS [1] 3-9-0 R Cochrane 16/1: 23-10: Long abs: no danger: see 59.   49

708 CHALK STREAM [3] 3-9-0 S Cauthen 12/1: 1124-20: No danger in 7th: race 708 is
working out poorly.   00

7 ran   2,½,7,½,2½   (Sheikh Mohammed)   M Stoute Newmarket

1111 QUEENS VASE (LISTED RACE)   £21070   2m   Firm 06 -12 Slow

720 STAVORDALE [1] (H T Jones) 3-7-10 M Roberts 33/1: 0-441: 3 b c Dance In Time - Scamperdale (French Beige) Very useful colt: showed improved form, turning up at 33/1 when a decisive winner of val Queen's Vase (Listed) at Royal Ascot June 18: lightly raced prev: obviously well suited by a stamina test and fast ground: runs well on a stiff track: should continue to improve and win more staying races.   70

*1040 KNIGHTS LEGEND [3] (G Harwood) 3-8-0 A Clark 6/1: -212: Led inside final 3f, excellent effort from this improving colt: stays 2m well: see 1040.   69

-- REASON TO BE [13] (J Morgan) 3-8-0 D Gillespie 33/1: 00-1333: Irish chall, never closer: first time out winner at Navan over 14f in hvy going: evidently stays 2m well and seems to act on any going.   64

*552 MUBAARIS [7] (P Walwyn) 3-8-0 Paul Eddery 6/1: 3-1114: Chall 2f out: btr 552 (14f)   60

654 LAABAS [9] 3-7-10 T Quinn 7/1: 04-330: Ev ch: much btr 654 (12f hvy).   46

-978 NORTHERN AMETHYST [5] 3-7-10 B Crossley 16/1: 22-3220: Made most: btr 978 (14f)   36

*778 INSULAR [6] 6-9-3 Pat Eddery 7/2 fav: 421-310: Wknd into 8th: btr 778.   00

879 I BIN ZAIDOON [10] 5-9-3 R Cochrane 13/2: 4120-00: Heavily bckd, ev ch: btr 879(10f)   00

617 AYRES ROCK [8] 5-9-3 W R Swinburn 9/1: 00-3040: Prom 10f: rated much higher 617(13f yielding) flattered?   00

*949 AGATHIST [12] 3-8-0 P Cook 8/1: 00-4110: Stiff task: btr 949 (h'cap)   00

1029 El Conquistador [11] 7-10   682 Ancilla [4] 8-10

1022 Stop The Clock [2] 7-7

13 ran   3,2½,2,5,6   (Mrs H T Jones)   H T Jones Newmarket

1112 BESSBOROUGH STKS H'CAP   (0-75)   £10051   1m 4f   Firm 06 +01 Fast   [66]

805 CONVINCED [9] (G Harwood) 4-8-11 A Clark 14/1: 00-3231: 4 b c Busted - Affirmative (Derring-Do) Very useful colt: didnot have much room in the final 1f when btn a nk by Vouchsafe in a blanket fin to val Bessborough H'cap at Royal Ascot June 18: sub awarded the race: comfortable winner at Pontefract and Goodwood in '85 when quite lightly raced: stays 12f well: suited by fast going but acts on any track.   62

-976 RUSSIAN NOBLE [3] (M Stoute) 5-8-6(2ow) W R Swinburn 4/1: 3402-22: Led dist, not much room final 1f, just btn: fin 3rd, placed 2nd: must win soon: see 976.   56

+462 WESTERN DANCER [11] (C Horgan) 5-9-2 P Cook 15/2: 124-013: Keeping on well when having to be switched inside final 1f, narrowly btn 4th, placed 3rd: versatile sort who is sure to win more h'caps: see 462.   66

+921 STATELY FORM [6] (J Tree) 4-9-5(7ex) Pat Eddery 7/2 fav: 40-0214: Led 2f out, prob held when hmpd near fin: narrowly btn: in fine form: see 921.   69

*1024 ROMIOSINI [14] 4-7-10(4ex) Kim Tinkler[5] 10/1: 3-04110: Staying on when meeting interference final 1f and is in grand form: see 1024.   44

921 VOUCHSAFE [1] 4-8-6 W Carson 9/1: 00-041D: Led final 1f but went badly right, hampering sev of his rivals and his disqualification was a mere formality: see 921.   57

698 PUBBY [12] 5-7-10(3ow)(1oh) M Roberts 14/1: 0-11200: Not the best of runs, fin 7th placed 6th: best 363 (yldg/soft)   00

879 EFFIGY [7] 4-9-11 G Starkey 10/1: 2221-00: Made much: very genuine and consistent in '85 winning 3 times and fin in the frame in all 9 starts: winner at Leicester, Goodwood and Doncaster: well suited by 10/12f and seems to act on any going and on any trk: best forcing the pace.   00

782 DUAL VENTURE [16] 4-8-6(2ow) A Murray 8/1: -42-220: Prom most: btr 782.   00

976 Samhaan [2] 7-8(bl)(1ow)(10oh)   474 Silent Journey [4] 7-7(3oh)

263 The Footman [10] 8-1   731 Moon Jester [13] 7-8(1ow)(13oh)

653 Line Of Fire [8] 9-7(VIS)   *967 Well Covered [5] 7-8(4ex)

15 ran   nk,hd,nk,nk,2   (J C Thompson)   G Harwood Pulborough, Sussex

---

SAN SIRO   Sunday June 15th

Official Going Given as Heavy

1113 GROUP 3 PREMIO PRIMI PASSI 2YO   £13134   6f   Heavy -

840 STAY LOW (G Blum) 2-8-8 T Ives 1: 211331: 2 ch f Tina's Pet - Pickled (Pitcairn) Very useful filly: gained a narrow win in a Gr 3 event at San Siro June 15: a model of consistency, earlier winning at Lingfield and Doncaster: very eff at 5f, stays 6f: seems to act on any ground and on any track: a credit to her trainer.   59

898 SHUTTLE COCK (Italy) 2-8-11 M Depalmas 1: 22: Again just btn: acts on gd & hvy.   61

876 REGENCY FILLE (R Williams) 2-8-8 R Cochrane 1: 12223: Again ran well: see 876, 655.   53

-- SMITHS PEAK (Italy) 2-8-11 S Whitworth 1: 4: Not btn far: acts on hvy.   53

*345 EASA 2-8-11 M Planard 1: 10: Not disgraced: stays 6f: acts on gd & hvy: see 345.   44

8 ran   hd,1½,1,   (G Blum)   G Blum Newmarket

1114 GROUP 3 PREMIO D'ESTATE 3YO   £13064   1m   Heavy -

286 MAX DOR (A Botti) 3-8-7 G Dettori 1: -01: 3 ch c Sassafras - Marketess (To Market) Very useful Italian colt: led final 1f, comfortably, in a Gr 3 event at San Siro June 15: smart 2yo: eff 1m, may stay further: acts well on heavy ground.   70

476 ORIENTAL SOLDIER (B Hills) 3-8-7 B Thomson 1: 2210-02: Led 2f out: kept on well:
good effort as he is much btr on firm ground: see 476.   65
803 BRAZZAKA (M Jarvis) 3-8-4 T Ives 1: 21-1123: Sn prom: another fine run: see 803,575   57
*556 SARASOTA SPRING (L D'auria) 3-8-10 M Planard 1: -14: Btr 556 (good).   62
8 ran   2,2½,nk   (Scuderia Siba)   A Botti Italy

EVRY   Saturday June 14th

Official Going Given as Good

1115 GROUP 2 GRAND PRIX D'EVRY 4YO+   £31187   1m 4f Good -

645 GALLA PLACIDIA (A Fabre) 4-8-13 C Asmussen 1: 030-101: 4 b f Crystal Palace -
Golden Gleam (Lyphard) Smart French filly: fin well for a comfortable win in a Gr 2 event
at Evry June 14: earlier won a Gr 3 event at St Cloud: in fine form in '85, winning 5 times:
acts on gd, loves soft/hvy grd: eff 10-13f: seems a genuine sort.   83
299 KING LUTHIER (A Fabre) 4-8-9 A Gibert 1: 44-1212: Stable mate of winner: gd effort.   74
*645 PREMIER ROLE (J Cunnington) 4-9-2 M Philipperon 1: 443-413: In fine form: see 645.   77
645 BABY TURK (A De Royer Dupre) 4-8-12 G Moore 1: 1004: Best 468 (soft), see 299.   69
*617 KAYTU 5-8-13 M Roberts 1: 000-310: English chall: fin 6th: btr 617.   62
7 ran   2½,2,2   (W Kazan)   A Fabre France

CHANTILLY   Sunday June 15th   Righthand, Galloping Track

Official Going Given as Firm

1116 GROUP 1 PRIX DE DIANE HERMES 3YO   £115455   1m 2f Firm -

*755 LACOVIA (F Boutin) 3-9-2(bl) F Head 1: -01-211: 3 b f Majestic Light - Hope for
All (Secretariat) Topclass French filly: long odds on and led 2f out, pushed out easily in
Gr 1 Prix de Diane Hermes at Chantilly June 15: last time out was a very impr winner of
Gr 1 Prix Saint-Alary at Longchamp: acts on hvy, very eff on fast grd: equally eff 10/12f:
runs well on a galloping trk: wears blinkers but is thoroughly gen and shd win more gd races. 86
755 SECRET FORM (P Bary) 3-9-2 G Moore 1: 11-222: Another fine eff: just stays 12f: 77
755 GALUNPE (B Secly) 3-9-2 A Gibert 1: 114-003: Fin in fine style: well suited by 12f.   77
*642 IVORS IMAGE (M Stoute) 3-9-2 W R Swinburn 1: 301-414: Ev ch str: fine eff: see 642. 76
561 RESTIVER 3-9-2 A Badel 1: -411-30: Ran well but btr 561 (10f).   68
904 CARNATION 3-9-2 A Lequeux 1: 14-3040: -   67
14 ran   2,nk,½,4,½   (G Oldham)   F Boutin France

1117 GROUP 3 PRIX BERTEUX 3YO   £17254   1m 7f Firm -

-- SATCO (P Bary) 3-8-7 F Head 1: -2-11: 3 br c Blakeney - Satwa (Nonoalco) Very useful
French colt: stayed on well to win a Gr 3 event at Chantilly June 15: obviously well
suited by 15f and shd stay 2m+: acts well on firm grd and a gall track.   70
-- GLEAM OUT (G Mikhalides) 3-8-11 C Asmussen 1: 0-30112: Ran well: eff 15f on fast grd. 71
-- SWINK (J Pease) 3-8-7 G Guignard 1: 220-323: Consistent sort: stays 15f.   66
-- ARGENT MASSIF (J P Pelat) 3-8-11 A Lequeux 1: -210114: In fine form this season.   70
*461 COMME LETOILE 3-8-7 M Hills 1: 121-310: Not btn far in 7th: prob stays 15f: see 461. 63
9 ran   2,nk,nose   (J L Bouchard)   P Bary France

1118 GROUP 3 PRIX DU CHEMIN DE FER DU NORD   £17912 1m   Firm -

*759 SARAB (P Cole) 5-9-4 T Quinn 1: 304-311: 5 b h Prince Tenderfoot - Carnival Dance
(Welsh Pageant) Smart horse: in fine form and led over 2f out, comfortably, in a Gr 3 event
at Chantilly June 15: last time out won at Baden Baden: most consistent in '85, winning
Listed races at Newcastle and Haydock: in '84 won at Goodwood, Doncaster, Newmarket, Haydock
and Beverley: very eff at 7f/1m: acts on firm and soft grd: has a fine turn of foot:
genuine sort.   78
98 ETAT MAJOR (D Prady) 4-9-0 E Legrix 1: -002002: No chance with winner: acts frm & hvy 67
*391 APELDOORN (P Barbe) 4-9-4 M Philipperon 1: 301-113: Gd eff: acts on frm: see 391(sft) 67
901 EPHIALTES (C Milbank) 4-9-4 P Schade 1: 0010244: Btr 901, see 2.   66
8 ran   3,2,shtnk   (F Salman)   P Cole Whatcombe, Berks.

Official Going Given as Good/Soft (Last furlong Soft)

1119 E.B.F. BRANDON MAIDEN STAKES 2YO   £1032   6f   Soft 134 -46 Slow

979 ORIENTAL DREAM [4] (J Hindley) 2-9-0 A Shoults(5) 7/1: 01: 2 ch c Northfields -
Jenny (Red God) Led below dist and ran on strongly to win a 2yo mdn at Hamilton June 19:
cost 50,000 gns as yearling and is a half brother to sev winners, incl useful juv Spring
Pastures: stays 6f really well: acts on soft grd and on a stiff track: on the upgrade.   35
934 SHARPHAVEN [5] (M Brittain) 2-8-11 I Johnson 9/1: 340302: Al prom, kept on under
press and seems best with plenty of give in the ground: half sister to sev winners:see 170.   23
965 DOCKIN HILL [7] (M W Easterby) 2-9-0 K Hodgson 7/2: 0303: Led briefly 2f out:
stays 6f on a stiff track: well suited by some give in the ground: see 864.   25
665 LINPAC NORTH MOOR [1] (C Elsey) 2-8-11 C Dwyer 8/1: 0024: Led over ½ way: best 665(5f)12
536 PILGRIM PRINCE [3] 2-9-0 T Williams 7/1: 000: Unruly in stalls and never in it:
should be suited by this trip: acts on yielding/soft ground.   14
627 YOUNG WARRIOR [6] 2-9-0 S Keightley 10/1: 400: Speed over ½ way: best here 488(5f).   02
--   LASCIVIOUS INTENT [2] 2-8-11 J Lowe 2/1 FAV: 0: Early speed: well bckd debutant who
should do better next time: cost $27,000 and is a half sister to a couple of winners,
including the stayer Rock Vallet.   00
7 ran   3,½,4,nk,5   (S F Hui)   J Hindley Newmarket

1120 BUSBY HANDICAP (0-35) 3YO+   £1682   6f   Soft 134 -08 Slow   [35]

1070 HENRYS VENTURE [6] (D Chapman) 4-7-7(2oh) A Proud 14/1: 0-00001: 4 b g Raise A
Native - Tudor Velvet (Tudor Grey) Outsider of the party tho' led before ½ way and was sn
clear in a h'cap at Hamilton June 19: first success: no worthwhile form prev: stays 6f:
acts on any going.   10
820 MARY MAGUIRE [5] (D Chapman) 9-9-8 D Nicholls 5/1: -000032: No chance with winner:
best in 306.   22
890 MIAMI DOLPHIN [7] (J Berry) 6-8-7 M Fry 9/2: 0013103: Best over 5f here in 786(hvy)   07
306 WARTHILL LADY [1] (M Brittain) 4-8-3 J Lowe 9/1: 0-04004: No threat after abs.   00
1001 TACHOMETER [2] 3-8-3(1ow) I Johnson 11/4 FAV: 00-0000: Btr on gd grd in 1001.   08
971 COPLACE [8] 4-7-7 S P Griffiths(5) 10/1: -040: Early leader: see 971.   00
321 JAMES PAL [4] 4-10-0 M Hindley(3) 7/2: 0211-00: Lost touch from ½ way   disapp in
both starts this season: see 321.   00
7 ran   7,shthd,2,½,8   (P D Savill)   D Chapman Stillington, Yorks.

1121 STONEFIELD SELLING STAKES 2YO   £800   5f   Soft 134 -30 Slow

957 SEATON GIRL [1] (D Barron) 2-8-8 B Mcghiff(7) 3/1: 42001: 2 b f Obac - Forest Music
(Tudor Music) Well suited by this easier grd, was never hdd when a comfortable winner of a
2yo seller at Hamilton June 19 (no bid): cheaply acquired filly who is a sister to a
juv winner: acts on a sound surf tho' seems best with some give : suited by forcing tactics
over this minimum trip.   24
1012 SHADY BLADE [4] (K Stone) 2-8-8 C Dwyer 3/1: 0202: Ran on well: acts on soft ground:
should find a seller another furlong: see 858.   14
•865 BINGO QUEEN [2] (J Berry) 2-8-13 Gay Kelleway(5) 11/4 FAV: 202213: Clear rem:
in gd form: see 865.   17
821 CHOICE MATCH [3] (J Wilson) 2-8-8 D Nicholls 20/1: 0004: Small filly who has shown
no form to date.   00
821 JULIOS LAD [5] 2-8-11(BL) R P Elliott 3/1: 030: Much btr over this C/D in 821 (hvy)   00
5 ran   3,½,12,2½   (Gordon Wilkinson)   D Barron Maunby, Yorks

1122 CARMUNNOCK HANDICAP (0-35) 3YO   £1299   1m 1f   Soft 134 +01 Fast   [34]

1017 COMMON FARM [6] (M Brittain) 3 9-7 I Johnson 12/1: 0000001: 3 b g Tachypous -
Calling High (Mountain Call) Returned to form, led below dist and ran on well to win a 3yo
h'cap at Hamilton June 19: won a nursery h'cap at Beverley last season: eff around 1m: stays
10f: acts on fast and soft ground and is suited by a stiff track.   36
997 BRADBURY HALL [4] (K Stone) 3-8-8 C Dwyer 20/1: 0000002: Made most: maiden who
ran his best race to date here: stays 9f: acts on soft ground and on a stiff track.   18
368 AUCTION TIME [3] (M Prescott) 3-9-4 C Nutter 5/2: -0333: Fair abs: no extra under
press dist and btr over 7f in 368: see 258.   16
867 MY CUP OF TEA [7] (P Haslam) 3-7-10 T Williams 9/4 FAV: 0-03224: Btr on yldg 867.
see 809 and 113.   00
762 COSMIC FLIGHT [2] 3-8-13 J Lowe 7/2: 1033400: Below par effort: much btr on gd/frm 762 00
68   RHAPSODY IN BLACK [5] 3-9-0 M Giles 13/2: -100: Trailed in last after abs: see 39.   00
6 ran   2,6,3,7,dist.   (Mel Brittain)   M Brittain Warthill, Yorks

1123 DALPATRICK MAIDEN STAKES 3YO   £1002   1m 3f   Soft 134 -20 Slow

894 TIEATRE [1] (G Moore) 3-8-11 D Casey(7) 10/1: 000-001: 3 b f Uncle Pokey - Lady
Wilder (Royal Palm) Sn in front and stayed on well to regain lead cl home in a 3yo mdn at
Hamilton June 19: little form prev, stays 11f: suited by soft grd and a stiff track.   25
188 SAFFAN [2] (M Prescott) 3-9-0 C Nutter 11/4: 03-32: Smooth prog to lead 2f out:
sn clear tho' caught cl home: stays 11f: acts on any trk: see 188.   27

935 TORREYA [5] (J Hindley) 3-8-11 A Shoults(5) 4/7 FAV: -0423: Odds on flop:
much btr 935(frm)   12
969 KASU [4] (S Norton) 3-8-11 J Lowe 8/1: -04: Led 4f out till 2 out: see 969.   06
769 FANNY ROBIN [3] (3-8-11 L Charnock 8/1: 040-00: Al last: sister to winning stayer
Bens Surprise: rated 31 when 4th to Chinchilla Boy in an Edinburgh maiden last Summer:
stays 1m: prob needs better ground.   00
5 ran   nk,8,3,20   (A Carney)   G Moore Leyburn, Yorks.

1124 EAST KILBRIDE HANDICAP (0-35) 3YO+   £1259   1m 3f Soft 134 +09 Fast   [34]

532 PERISIAN KNIGHT [5] (W Musson) 4-9-5 A Mackay 5/2 FAV: 0000-01: 4 b g Cawston's
Clown - Ivory Castle (High Top) Nicely bckd staying on strongly to lead cl home in a fast
run h'cap at Hamilton June 19: successful at Newmarket, Chepstow and Hamilton last term:
stays 12f well: suited by gd or softer ground.   32
1052 APPLE WINE [9] (D Chapman) 9-8-8 D Nicholls 15/2: 0200002: Just failed to make all:
good effort on his fav track: see 256.   20
970 NIGHT WARRIOR [10] (A Robson) 4-9-2 J Bleasdale 9/1: 0403033: Clear rem: gd effort. 24
1079 MISS MORLEY [2] (J Rowlands) 4-7-11 N Carlisle 20/1: 0000004: No extra dist:
won at Ripon and Ayr last term tho' has run below that form so far this season: best form
over 10f: suited by some give in the ground.   00
1052 MR LION [6] 4-8-5 J Carr(7) 4/1: 0122220: Btr over 12f in 1052 (gd).   04
179 ICEN [3] 8-8-9 S Webster 20/1: 400/100: Prob needed race after abs: see 28.   07
968 FIEFDOM [7] 6-9-10 T Williams 9/1: 0400-20: Btr here over 12f in 968 (hvy).   00
*968 CAROUSEL ROCKET [1] 3-8-10(5ex) Gay Kelleway(5) 11/4: 3104210: Fin 8th: much btr
on heavy here in 968 (12f).   00
542 SHERPAMAN [8] 4-7-8(1ow)(4oh) A Proud 50/1: 00-0000: Outsider and fin last:
no worthwhile form to date.   00
9 ran   ½,2,5,½,nk   (Miss Samantha Holmes)   W Musson Newmarket

---

ROYAL ASCOT   Thursday June 19th   Righthand Stiff Undulating Track

1125 GROUP 3 CORK AND ORRERY STAKES   £18950   6f   Firm -07 +14 Fast

-691 SPERRY [2] (P Walwyn) 3-8-0 Paul Eddery 5/1: 10-2021: 3 ch c Stanford - Ructions
(Rasper) Very smart colt: made all and held on with the utmost gameness breaking the course
record when gaining a shthd success in Gr 3 Cork & Orrery Stks at Royal Ascot June 19:
in '85 won at Newmarket and Salisbury (first time out): very eff at 6f, stays 7f well: acts
on yldg, but really bounces off firm grd: a most gen and consistent front runner.   80
--   CYRANO DE BERGERAC [7] (W Hastings Bass) 3-8-0 W Carson 11/4 fav: 12111-2: Well bckd
seasonal debutant, came from behind and just failed to get his hd in front cl home after
a good battle with the winner: improved with ev race in '85 winning 5 out of 6 outings at
Pontefract, Lingfield, Newbury and Newmarket (2): very eff over 5/6f & loves fast grd and a
stiff track: sure to improve for the outing and will win a decent race or two this term. 80
-854 BRIDESMAID [5] (B Hills) 3-7-11(vis) M Hills 5/1: 0-00123: Chall 1f out but found
no extra on this lightning fast going and her last 2 efforts have been on an easy surface: see 691. 68
*758 TARIB [3] (H T Jones) 3-7-11 R Hills 9/1: 112-214: Kept on, gd effort and is in
fine form: stays 6f: see 758.   66
903 RUSTIC AMBER [1] 3-8-4 Pat Eddery 9/1: 10-3100: Twice below 639 (hvy).   68
977 SIMLA RIDGE [6] 4-8-10 T Ives 66/1: -00130: Prom most: fine effort in this gd class
company and he should land a h'cap shortly: see 628.   50
*817 Polly Daniels [11] 8-7   854 Our Dynasty [9] 8-10
--   Fringe Of Heaven [10] 8-7   945 Que Sympatica [4] 8-7
10 ran   shthd,3,½,3,1½,2½,shthd   (Yahya Nasib)   P Walwyn Lambourn, Berks.

1126 GROUP 3 NORFOLK STAKES 2YO   £20086   5f   Firm -07 +01 Fast

-840 SIZZLING MELODY [2] (Lord John Fitzgerald) 2-8-11 R Hills 5/1: 1121: 2 br c Song -
Mrs Bacon (Balliol) Smart colt: gained his 3rd win from 4 races when battling on gallantly to
lead near fin of fast run Gr 3 Norfolk Stakes at Royal Ascot June 19 (set a new 2yo course
record): ready winner of his first 2 on the trot at Lingfield and Leicester, just btn by the
speedy Bestplan last time after a fair abs due to illness: very eff at 5f, shd stay 6f:
acts on firm and soft grd and on any track: game and genuine and still improving.   75
737 ZAIBAQ [4] (H T Jones) 2-8-11 A Murray 7/1: 132: Just failed to make all: battling
on gamely and loves firm ground: will win more races: see 405.   73
+800 DOMINION ROYALE [7] (R Williams) 2-8-11 R Cochrane 6/1: 413: Cl.up from 2f out and
ran a fine race: will win more races if eased slightly in class: see 800.   66
*737 RISK ME [5] (P Kelleway) 2-8-11 Pat Eddery 4/7 fav: 114: Ill at ease on this fast
going, no extra final 1f and seems to need good or softer ground: see 737.   65
804 PENSURCHIN [3] 2-8-11 S Cauthen 14/1: 13120: Found this pace too fast: see 434. 45
--   BRAZILIAN PRINCESS [6] 2-8-8 C Asmussen 14/1: 0: Stable companion of the fav:
never held a hope: lacks scope: half brother to 2 winners incl the very smart and genuine
sprinter Soba.   41
6 ran   nk,2½,½,6,shthd   (Mrs Mary Watt)   Lord John Fitzgerald Newmarket

1127 GROUP 1 GOLD CUP   £44688   2m 4f Firm -07 -07 Slow

*704 LONGBOAT [6] (W Hern) 5-9-0 W Carson 1/1 fav: 142-011: 5 b h Welsh Pageant - Pirogue
(Reliance II) Very smart stayer: comfortably justified hvy support when storming home a 5L
winner of the Ascot Gold Cup June 19: won Henry II Stakes at Sandown May 26: last season won
at Ascot and was just pipped in this race by Gildoran, gained deserved compensation today:
eff 2m, stays forever: loves fast grd and prob unsuited by soft: hard to beat in the rem Cup
races providing the ground remains on top.   83
    704 EASTERN MYSTIC [12] (L Cumani) 4-9-0 Pat Eddery 7/2: 11-4132: Made much and despite
going lame, gallantly battled on to fin 2nd: deserved btr reward after such a brave effort
but sadly may have run his last race: see 585.   77
    756 SPICY STORY [11] (I Balding) 5-9-0 S Cauthen 11/1: 214-303: Prom thr'out: just btn
in a photo for 2nd: ran right to his best and stays 2½m well: see 360.   77
    704 PETRIZZO [3] (C Brittain) 5-9-0 C Asmussen 100/1: 0000304: Led/dsptd lead much of
the way and stays really well: see 474, 585.
    704 TALE QUALE [1] 4-9-0 T Ives 9/1: 301-040: Under press some way out, kept on: stays
this trip: see 585.   69
    1005 SEISMIC WAVE [10] 5-9-0 B Thomson 10/1: -032220: May have stayed this trip but prob
btr over 1½/2m: see 704, 1005.   63
    704 Kublai [7] 9-0   704 Bourbon Boy [2] 9-0   475 Rising [9] 9-0
    704 I Want To Be [5] 8-11   -- Erydan [8] 9-0
    11 ran   5,hd,3,1½,4   (R Hollingsworth)   W Hern West Ilsley, Berks.

1128 GROUP 2 RIBBLESDALE STAKES 3YO FILLIES   £37948   1m 4f Firm -07 -07 Slow

*549 GULL NOOK [7] (J Dunlop) 3-8-8 Pat Eddery 8/1: -11: 3 b f Mill Reef - Bempton
(Blakeney) Smart, fast improving and unbtn filly: showed fine acceleration when leading final
1f in Gr 2 Ribblesdale Stakes at Royal Ascot June 19: ready winner of a slowly run fillies
race at York May 13 on race course debut: eff at 10f, stays 12f really well: acts on firm
and good ground and on a gall track: sure to win more good class races.   81
*509 MILL ON THE FLOSS [8] (H Cecil) 3-8-8 S Cauthen 9/2: 10-312: Qcknd into a good lead
3f out, no answer to winner's late burst but ran right up to her best: was withdrawn from the
Oaks last time after refusing to enter the stalls but behaved herself today: a smart filly. 78
*779 SANTIKI [9] (M Stoute) 3-8-8 W R Swinburn 8/1: 3-2413: Ev ch 2f out: grand effort
from this very useful filly: see 779.   74
    754 PARK EXPRESS [10] (J Bolger) 3-8-8 D Gillespie 20/1: 02-1304: Fin well, just failed
to snatch 3rd: stays 12f and seems to act on any going: see 148.   74
    926 GESEDEH [1] 3-8-8 T Ives 11/4 fav: -1100: Never going well on this lightning fast
ground and seems to need an easier surface: see 372.   71
    661 ALTIYNA [5] 3-8-8 G Starkey 20/1: 1-220: Prom most: prob acts on firm and soft: see 463. 71
*463 SALCHOW [2] 3-8-8 W Carson 11/2: 1112-10: Fin 8th: abs since much btr 463 (yldg). 00
    463 Sue Grundy [11] 8-8   833 Nicola Wynn [12] 8-8   509 Singletta [3] 8-8
*599 Pilot Bird [6] 8-8   373 Tender Loving Care [4] 8-8·
    12 ran   1½,1½,nk,2½,nk   (Lord Halifax)   J Dunlop Arundel, Sussex

1129 CHESHAM STAKES LISTED 2YO   £11453   6f   Firm -07 +07 Fast

    548 MINSTRELLA [12] (C Nelson) 2-8-8 J Reid 10/1: 421: 2 ro f The Minstrel - Flight
Dancer (Misty Flight) Smart, fast improving filly: set a new 2yo course record when hacking
up in Chesham Stakes (Listed) at Royal Ascot June 19: al going supremely well, qcknd clear
final 2f: related to sev winners, notably a very smart American filly called Misty Gallore:
much btr suited by 6f than 5f and shd stay 1m: seems to love fast grd and a stiff track:
will be hard to beat in the top fillies races in the next few months.   75
*915 CHIME TIME [11] (C Tinkler) 2-8-11 M Birch 16/1: 112: Northern chall, ran very
well indeed and caught me a real tartar in this winner: still improving and shd find further
success: see 915.   65
    870 LUZUM [7] (H T Jones) 2-8-11 A Murray 7/1: 23: Dsptd lead much and showed more than
enough ability to easily win a mdn soon: see 870.   64
*859 MISTER MAJESTIC [8] (R Williams) 2-8-11 R Cochrane 6/1: 121114: Made much and ran
his usual genuine race: seee 859.   61
    440 MY IMAGINATION [2] 2-8-8 S Cauthen 16/1: 1100: Bckd at long odds, prom much: best 320 51
    985 MAZILIER [6] 2-8-11 G Starkey 5/1: 20: Prom much: poss prefers an easier surface tho'
ran well here: see 985.   54
    715 SHABIB [4] 2-8-11 Pat Eddery 8/1: 40: Fin 7th: gd eff in this company and should
win a maiden at one of the minor tracks: see 715.   00
*664 GULF KING [1] 2-8-11 C Asmussen 11/2: 0210: Failed to act on this very fast ground
and best 664 (yldg/soft).   00
*777 ALBASAR [2] 2-8-11 Paul Eddery 9/2 fav: 10: Most disapp after debut win in 777 on
similar ground: much btr than this indicates.   00
*1057 Hard Act [3] 8-11   694 Tahard [10] 8-11   571 Checkpoint [9] 8-11
    350 Castle Cornet [13] 8-11
    13 ran   4,½,1,2½,nk   (Edward P Evans)   C Nelson Upper Lambourn, Berks

1130 KING GEORGE V STAKES 3YO H'CAP 0-70   £10628   1m 4f   Firm -07 -07 Slow   [61]

+946 MOON MADNESS [18] (J Dunlop) 3-9-4(7ex) C Asmussen 4/1 fav: 4-1111: 3 b c Vitiges -
Castle Moon (Kalamoun) Fast improving, smart colt who retained his unbtn record this term
when completing the four-timer in val King George V h'cap at Royal Ascot June 19: always
cruising, led 1f out and sprinted clear, turning what shd have been a competitive h'cap into
a procession: successful in val h'caps at Haydock and Newmarket and a mdn at Salisbury first
time out: only ran once in '85: eff 10f, stays 12f really well: acts on firm and yldg and
likes a stiff, galloping trk: can now make his mark in Pattern races.   75
919 WESHAAM [11] (B Hanbury) 3-8-11 M Hills 25/1: 0-20132: Led 2f out, had no chance
with this ready winner but another gd, consistent effort: stays 12f well: see 716.   52
*625 DALGADIYR [17] (M Stoute) 3-8-9 W R Swinburn 15/2: -313: Led briefly dist, outpaced
final 1f but ran well: eff 12f, better 10f? See 625.   48
*958 COMELY DANCER [14] (J Watts) 3-8-6(4ex) N Connorton 20/1: 4-3114: Came from well
off the pace, never closer and was far from disgraced in this hot race.   36
683 SAMANPOUR [8] 3-9-1 S Cauthen 11/1: 1-11130: Prom thr'out: best 547 (10f yldg) but
probably stays 12f.   44
*623 WISHLON [10] 3-9-1 Pat Eddery 9/1: -1010: Ev ch, wknd: best 623.   43
*191 TORWADA [5] 3-9-7 T Quinn 12/1: 204-10: Fin 7th, stiff task under top weight after
abs since 191 (yielding).   00
1023 SATISFACTION [13] 3-9-1 W Carson 10/1: 00-220: Led after 1m, wknd 2f out: fin 8th:
better on good in 1023.   00
*883 FIRST DIVISION [15] 3-9-0(4ex) G Duffield 6/1: 00-1110: Prom, wknd: btr 883 (sharper trk) 00
459 MUSICAL YOUTH [2] 3-8-1 P Cook 6/1: 004-20: Very heavily bckd, never sighted after
abs since 459 (10f yldg).   00

619	Dark Heritage [19] 7-13	946	Charlton Kings [12] 8-8(VIS)
983	Norfolk Sonata [1] 9-6(VIS)	510	My Ton Ton [9] 9-4
862	Exceptional Beauty [7] 8-11	*702	Llanarmon [6] 8-6
790	Target Sighted [4] 7-13(BL)	883	Owl Castle [16] 7-11
883	Atig [3] 8-7(BL)		

19 ran   5,2,6,1,½   (Lavinia, Duchess of Norfolk)   J Dunlop Arundel, Sussex

---

1131 REDBURN APPRENTICE H'CAP 3YO+ 0-35   £1308   5f   Good 62 +04 Fast   [29]

677 MURPHYS WHEELS [7] (A Jarvis) 3-9-7 I Todd(5) 4/1 Jt FAV: 3-041: 3 b c Dublin Taxi -
Lissylyn (Tower Walk): Nicely backed and stayed on well to lead close home in quite a fast
run app. h'cap at Ayr June 20: half brother to a couple of winning sprinters and is well
suited by this minimum trip himself: stays 6f: acts on gd & yld grnd & on any trk.   38
971 LADY CARA [1] (J Berry) 6-9-1 Catherine Strickland(5) 10/1: 014-002: Just failed to
make all: best effort this term and may go one better soon: well suited by forcing tactics.   22
788 FAIRGREEN [2] (D Chapman) 8-8-1(bl) M Richardson 9/1: 0040043: Al front rank: see 163.   04
1027 BRIDGE OF GOLD [4] (D Barron) 3-9-1 B Mcghiff 6/1: 20-1004: Never nearer: see 529.   22
971 SONNENELLE [9] 3-8-10(vis) E Turner 10/1: 2-12000: Dwelt, no threat: much btr early
season in 103 (soft).   11
971 BLOCHAIRN SKOLAR [5] 8-7-13 Amanda Bycroft(5) 20/1: 22-0000: Speed over ½ way: modest
sprint h'capper who won over this C/D last term: eff over 5/6f and is suited by gd or
faster ground.   00
+971 CULMINATE [8] 5-8-5(10ex) G King 5/1: -00310: Early speed: btr on heavy in 971.   00
890 RUSSIAN WINTER [3] 11-7-13(bl) J Quinn 10/1: 000-000: No threat: course specialist
who has scored here in each of the last three seasons: eff over 5/6f: acts on fast & soft grnd   00
1070 WOW WOW WOW [6] 3-8-11(BL) Kim Tinkler 4/1 Jt FAV: 1002030: Bl first time: trailed
in last: see 1070.   00
9 ran   ½,1½,1½,2½,4   (Mrs M Jarvis)   A Jarvis Royston, Herts

1132 CUNNING PARK MAIDENN FILLIES STAKES 2YO   £959   6f   Good 62 -04 Slow

1025 ANNIE NOONAN [1] (N Tinkler) 2-8-11 Kim Tinkler(5) 10/11 FAV: 41: 2 ch f Ahonoora -
Blink (Dike): Impr filly: qknd nicely below dist when a comfortable winner of a 2yo fillies
maiden at Ayr June 20: showed plenty of promise on her recent debut at York: cost 28,000 gns
as a yearling and is a sister to winning juvenile Isabella Cannes: stays 6f well: acts on
gd & firm grnd & on a gall trk.   46
-- UPSET [2] (J S Wilson) 2-8-11 D Mckeown 25/1: 2: Showed plenty of pace on her racecourse debut: half sister to 12f winner Tour De Force: stays 6f well: acts on gd grnd & on
a gall trk: can only impr.   38
1025 STEELOCK [7] (M H Easterby) 2-8-11 M Birch 7/1: 203: Made most: stays 6f: see 646.   36
944 LACK OF PEARLS [9] (R Woodhouse) 2-8-11 A Shoults(5) 9/1: 404: No extra dist: should
be well suited by this trip: acts on gd grnd & on a gall trk.   27
722 BUNDUKEYA [3] 2-8-11 R Hills 7/2: 340: Disapp effort: best on soft in 317 (5f).   15
-- OKOSAN [10] 2-8-11 L Charnock 12/1: 0: Showed gd early pace on her debut & should
impr next time: cost $25,000 as a yearling: acts on gd grnd & on a gall trk.   09

818	Rivers Secret [8] 8-11	415	Quick Sticks [5] 8-11
819	Revolver Video [6] 8-11		

9 ran   2½,½,3,4,2½   (Miss P Phoenix)   N Tinkler Malton, Yorks

1133 BELSTON HANDICAP 4YO+ 0-35   £2131   1m 3f   Good 62 -64 Slow   [27]

*•1054 MISTER POINT [7] (C Tinkler) 4-9-12(5ex) M Birch 9/2: 0-00011: 4 ch g Ahonoora -
Rozmeen (Relko): Made most when gamely defying a penalty in a slowly run h'cap at Ayr
June 20: last week won a similar race at Carlisle: in '85 successful at Hamilton & Beverley:
eff over 9/11f: acts on gd & hvy ground & is suited by a stiff track.   32
  731 THE CRYING GAME [2] (B Morgan) 4-7-13 L Charnock 12/1: 00-4002: Switched, fin strongly
but the post came just too soon: remains a maiden: stays 11f: suited by a gall trk: see 439.   04
1054 SWIFT RIVER [1] (I Bell) 4-8-8(bl) J Quinn(5) 8/1: 0203033: Ev ch: in fair form: see 522.   08
  126 BLUEBIRDINO [6] (J Ramsden) 7-8-2 D Mckeown 10/1: 000-004: Just needed race after abs.   00
  912 NORTH STAR SAM [9] 5-8-1 M Fry 9/2: 0004020: Btr over 10f in 912: see 333.   00
1016 DONT ANNOY ME [3] 6-8-1(vis) N Carlisle 12/1: 000-000: Never dngr: see 827.   00
  750 LONGSTOP [8] 5-9-7 R Hills 7/4 FAV: 4-30030: Fin last: disapp after 750 (sharp trk).   00
  830 Taj Singh [4] 8-11   1017 Boldera [5] 9-1
9 ran   nk,3,4,8,4   (A J Duffield)   C Tinkler Malton, Yorks

1134 DALMILLING SELLING STAKES 3YO   £914   1m   Good 62 -64 Slow

  960 MAWDLYN GATE [3] (M H Easterby) 3-8-9 M Birch 85/40 FAV: -004001: 3 br c Artaius -
Fiordiligi (Khalkis): Dropped in class & always looks likely to justify fav led before ½way
& stayed on strongly in a slowly run 3yo seller at Ayr June 20 (sold for 5,000 gns): half
brother to Nonabella and Ho Mi Chinh: well suited by 1m on a gall trk: acts on gd & soft grnd.   30
1063 COUNTESS CARLOTTI [5] (A Jarvis) 3-8-6 D Nicholls 9/2: 00-02: Ran on well: lightly
raced filly who looks sure to find a race in this grade: half sister to winning juvenile
Good N Sharp: stays 1m well: acts on gd grnd & on a gall trk.   24
  932 COOPER RACING NAIL [7] (J Berry) 3-8-6(vis) M Fry 5/1: 3220023: Ran well over this
longer trip: see 932.   18
  871 POLLY WORTH [8] (R Whitaker) 3-8-6 D Mckeown 8/1: 00-0034: Never nearer: stays 1m.   13
  932 SHY MISTRESS [1] 3-8-6 N Carlisle 9/2: -0400: Never dngr: see 729.   07
*•932 BANTEL BANZAI [4] 3-9-0(bl) M Hindley(3) 5/1: 0004010: Well below form shown in 932.   09
  932 NOBLE SAXON [6] 3-8-9(vis) J Quinn(5) 8/1: 00-4000: No worthwhile form to date: see 78.   00
1053 HERB ROBERT [2] 3-8-9 M Richardson(7) 16/1: 0040-00: Early ldr: trailed in last.   00
8 ran   1,3,2½,3,3   (Hippodromo Racing)   M H Easterby Great Habton, Yorks

1135 SNODGRASS MAIDEN STAKES 3YO   £959   1m 5f Good 62 -91 Slow

1023 INDIAN ORATOR [1] (B Hills) 3-9-0 R Hills 1: 2222-31: 3 br c Recitation - Icancan
(Candy Cane): Consistent colt: made ev yd at a slow pace when gaining a confidence boosting
win in a 3yo maiden at Ayr June 20: found one too good in each of his 5 starts last season:
eff around 1m, stays 13f: acts on gd & firm grnd & is suited by a gall trk: looks fairly h'capped.   38
  822 BLENCATHRA BOY [2] (C Parker) 3-9-0 D Nicholls 1: -002: In vain pursuit of winner
thro'out: lightly raced colt who seems of little account.   00
  935 ONLY FLOWER [3] (C Thornton) 3-8-11 M Tebbutt(7) 1: -003: Al last: shown nothing in
her races to date though is closely related to several winners, incl smart stayer Path of Peace.   00
3 ran   20,5   (Sheikh Mohammed)   B Hills Lambourn, Berks

1136 GOUKSCROFT H'CAP 3YO+ 0-35   £2075   7f   Good 62 -38 Slow   [24]

  970 STARS DELIGHT [3] (W Storey) 4-8-7 J Quinn(5) 9/2: 0-23421: 4 gr c John de Coombe -
Vanity Surprise (Blakeney): Gained a deserved win, led below dist, comfortably in a h'cap at
Ayr June 20: successful over timber this Winter though this was his first win on the Flat:
eff over 7/8f, stays 11f: acts on gd/firm & soft grnd & on any trk.   12
*•828 TIT WILLOW [9] (S Wiles) 4-9-3(bl) M Fry 8/1: 0-02212: Led 4f out, kept on well &
comfortably beat rem: in gd form: see 828.   18
  857 CHABLISSE [1] (R Whitaker) 3-8-5 D Mckeown 13/2: 0-0P403: Ev ch: best over 7f in 700.   09
  936 ZIO PEPPINO [5] (T Craig) 5-8-13 N Carlisle 9/2: 0320444: Kept on same pace: see 606 490.   04
1074 ROSSETT [8] 7-8-5 L Charnock 20/1: 000-000: No form this term & last won in '84,
at Edinburgh and Redcar: best form over 7/8f on gd or faster grnd: acts on any trk.   00
*•788 ABJAD [4] 5-9-0 D Nicholls 7/1: 0000-10: Well below form shown in 788 (heavy).   00
  651 ROCK SALT [2] 4-8-10 M Hindley(3) 33/1: -00-00: Yet to show any worthwhile form.   00
1013 GOLDEN DISC [10] 4-8-4(VIS) M Birch 4/1 FAV: 333-430: Btr over 7f in 1013: see 710.   00
  812 SPRING PURSUIT [6] 5-9-7 R Hills 7/1: 020-000: Last to fin: won at Lingfield &
Brighton in '84: stays 10f well: acts on gd & firm grnd & is suited by a sharpish trk.   00
9 ran   1½,4,1,nk,4   (T P Ramsden)   W Storey Consett, co Durham

---

Official Going Given as Firm - Times Slow Except Race 1141

1137 LIVERTON SELLING STAKES 2YO   £929   7f   Firm Slow

1012 ROYAL TREATY [12] (N Tinkler) 2-8-11 J H Brown(5) 6/1: 000331: 2 ch c Tower Walk -
Covenant (Good Bond) Led appr final 1f, driven out in a slow run 2yo seller at Redcar
June 20: stays today's 7f well: acts on firm and soft ground.   23

696 THE MAGUE [11] (L Siddall) 2-8-11 G Gosney 4/1: 0042: Chall final 1f: just btn:
4l clear 3rd: stays 7f and shd find a similar event: acts on fast ground and a gall track.   23
685 WESTGALE [6] (C Tinkler) 2-8-11(BL) M Wood 7/2: 003: Bl first time: al up there:
dropped to selling company today: stays 7f: acts on fast ground.   15
711 TOOTSIE JAY [10] (P Feilden) 2-8-8 N Day 2/1 FAV: 300324: Al prom: btr 711 (5f).   11
1088 MOONEE POND [2] 2-8-8 K Hodgson 11/1: 200000: Led/dsptd lead: prob stays 7f, but
best 317 (soft).   07
1050 BANTEL BLAZER [4] 2-8-11 J Lowe 8/1: 303000: Dsptd lead: best form earlier in
the season on softer ground.   09
446 NOFANDANCER [7] 2-8-8 C Dwyer 10/1: 000: Abs, ev ch: 5,000 gns purchase.   00
--   Skerne Rocket [8] 8-8   450 Miss Sherbrooke [3] 8-8
--   Super Gambler [9] 8-8   589 Millfield Blue [5] 8-11
589 Cawkell Trooper [1] 8-11(vis)
12 ran   shthd,4,nk,2,½   (Raymond Gomersall)   N Tinkler Malton, Yorks.

1138 UGTHORPE STAKES 2YO   £1735   6f   Firm Slow

+254 TEAM EFFORT [3] (Ron Thompson) 2-8-13 R P Elliott 8/1: 03011: 2 b c Stanford - Bap's
Miracle (Track Space) Useful, impr colt: despite abs, led 1f out and sprinted clear for an
easy win in a 2yo stks at Redcar June 20: earlier made ev yard in a 2yo mdn auction at
Edinburgh: cheaply acquired: acts on firm and yldg grd: stays 6f.   48
1050 FOUNTAINS CHOICE [5] (K Stone) 2-8-11 G Brown 5/1: 332: made most: still impr.   34
785 DUNLIN [6] (S Norton) 2-9-3 J Lowe 6/4 FAV: 123: Well bckd and ev ch: btr 785, 627(5f)   35
973 DANUM DANCER [2] (M W Easterby) 2-8-11 K Hodgson 2/1: 0044: Again below form 685.   27
781 MUNTAG [1] 2-8-11 S Webster 20/1: 0000: Prom, fdd: btr 781.   23
766 THEKKIAN [4] 2-9-6 S Perks 13/2: 130: Wknd: much btr 766, 415 (5f).   22
6 ran   4,2,1,1½,5   (G Mansell)   Ron Thompson Doncaster, Yorks.

1139 MOORSHOLM HANDICAP 0-35   £1850   1m   Firm   Slow   [34]

812 FOOT PATROL [11] (P Cundell) 5-8-10 G Duffield 7/4 FAV: 0-00001: 5 br g Daring
March - Molly Polly (Molvedo) Gambled on: cruised into lead final 1f, but had to be driven out
for a narrow win in h'cap at Redcar June 20: winner over hurdles during Winter: in '85 won
a h'cap at Brighton: in '84 won twice, again at Brighton: best over 1m on fast ground.   24
1013 CHARMING VIEW [1] (H Jones) 4-8-4 P Robinson 14/1: 00-0102: Led nearing final 1f:
rallied well: acts on firm and yldg grd: see 673.   16
1013 MARSILIANA [10] (D Incisa) 4-7-13 M Beecroft 20/1: 00-0403: Fin well: needs further?   07
1106 BURAAG [3] (M W Easterby) 5-9-13(bl) K Hodgson 7/1: 0044034: Made much: no extra.   34
956 BELLA BANUS [2] 4-9-6 T Lucas 8/1: 302-000: Btr eff: see 606.   22
893 BWANA KALI [8] 4-9-5(bl) R Morse(5) 6/1: 4330020: No extra final 2f: much btr 893.   20
1054 TRY SCORER [12] 4-8-12 S Perks 6/1: 1000020: Fin t.o!: see 1054 (good).   00
1074 Qualitairess [7] 7-8(vis)   861 Fill Abumper [13] 7-13
1074 Royaber [9] 7-9   1074 My Handsome Boy [6] 8-7
378 Illicit [5] 8-6(bl)   145 Malmo [4] 8-3
13 ran   ½,½,hd,2½,½,2   (Miss Lynne Evans)   P Cundell Compton, Berks.

1140 AISLABY HANDICAP 0-35   £2124   2m   Firm   Slow   [22]

225 THE CLOWN [5] (M Naughton) 5-9-7 G Duffield 9/4 Co.FAV: 2200-01: 5 ch g Green Dancer
(USA) - Eltisley (USA) (Grey Sovereign) Led appr final 2f, driven out in a h'cap at Redcar
June 20: in '85 won a h'cap at Beverley and was quite consistent: eff 12f, stays 2m: acts
on frm and yldg ground: useful hurdler.   23
942 JACKDAW [1] (R Hollinshead) 6-9-4 S Perks 9/4 Co.FAV: 0003002: Chall final 2f:
hit on head by the winner's whip and possibly unlucky: see 634.   19
959 DENALTO [4] (D Smith) 3-7-10 J Lowe 9/4 Co.FAV: 00-003: Ev ch straight: btr 959 (stks)   11
993 BUNDLING BED [3] (R Woodhouse) 4-8-10 A Proud 20/1: 00-0204: Led early: stays 2m.   06
959 RAPIDAN [6] 5-9-2 K Hodgson 12/1: 0-00000: Made much, fdd: seems mod.   02
1071 DUKE OF DOLLIS [2] 7-8-13(bl) Julie Bowker(7) 10/1: 02-0000: Wknd final 2f:see 1071   00
6 ran   ½,3,2,10,½   (Geoffrey C Greenwood)   M Naughton Richmond, Yorks

1141 COMMONDALE STAKES 3YO   £2284   1m 1f   Firm   +15 Fast

+861 NAATELL [9] (H Cecil) 3-9-7 N Day 2/5 FAV: 11: 3 b c Cox's Ridge - Lisannunga
(Whodunit) Promising colt: led 2f out, driven out in a fast run 3yo stks at Redcar June 20:
first time out was a comfortable winner of a maiden at Beverley: eff 8/9f, shd stay 10f:
half brother to numerous winners: acts well on fast ground & continues to impr/win more races   57
*937 FIRST DIBS [3] (M Stoute) 3-9-7 A Kimberley 4/1: 2-312: Just btn and 12l clear 3rd:
in fine form: stays 9f: see 937.   54
--   STORMGUARD [1] (W Jarvis) 3-9-0 G Duffield 20/1: 0-3: Led briefly over 2f out:
not pace of first 2: unplaced on only outing in '85: prob stays 9f: acts on fast ground.   22
*868 RIVA RENALD [4] (S Norton) 3-9-4 J Lowe 8/1: -14: Never in it: ridden with more
enterprise in 868 (yielding).   20
--   CHLOROPHYLL [2] 3-8-11 J Carr(7) 20/1: -0: Some late hdwy on race course debut:
should be suited by 10f: acts on firm ground.   07

REDCAR   Frriday June 20th   - Cont'd

--   EFFICIENT [8] 3-8-11 S Lawes 50/1: 0-0: Fdd final 3f on seasonal debut: half sister
to a 9f winner.   00
--   Hunting Gold [5] 8-11   875 W Seafield [6] 9-0   1042 Sandmoor Prince [7] 9-0(bl)
9 ran   ½,12,2½,2,3   (Sheikh Mohammed)   H Cecil Newmarket

1142 FLYINGTHORPE MAIDEN STAKES 3YO   £1219   6f   Firm Slow

-994 JOHN RUSSELL [15] (M Ryan) 3-9-0 P Robinson 1/1 FAV: -21: 3 ch c Palm Track - Welsh
Carol (Singing Bede) Led inside final 1f, rddn out in a 3yo mdn at Redcar June 20: first
time out was just btn by In Fact at Beverley: eff 5f, stays 6f well: acts on fast ground
and a galloping track.   46
138 ANGELS ARE BLUE [19] (M Ryan) 3-8-11 M Giles 14/1: -02: Long abs: made much and
stayed on well: half sister to the useful sprinter Polykratis: eff 6f on firm grd and
should find a race.   40
961 HANSOM LAD [16] (W Haigh) 3-9-0 N Day 3/1: 3-02323: Well bckd: ducked right
approaching final 1f: ran on: consistent: see 961.   38
911 FANCY FINISH [18] (F Durr) 3-8-11 Debbie Price(7) 20/1: 04-04: Nearest fin and
will do better: see 911.   21
997 QURRAT AL AIN [17] 3-8-11 K Hodgson 33/1: 000-000: Some late hdwy: no form prev:
eff 6f on fast ground.   02
--   CALYSTEGIA [6] 3-8-11 J Carr(7) 20/1: -0: No show on race course debut: should
do better: sister to the smart 2yo Cajun: will not be long in stepping up on this initial eff. 01
891 Tenasserim [12] 9-0   78 Clawson Thorns [8] 9-0
891 Foretop [5] 8-11   806 Report Em [11] 8-11   --   Quite Pokey [10] 8-11
928 Heavenly Carol [21] 8-11   524 Classy Scouse [1] 9-0
--   Cole Bay [14] 9-0   871 Galaxy Gala [16] 9-0   546 Mark Eden [2] 9-0
217 Angel Target [3] 8-11(BL)   --   Finlux Flair [7] 8-11
1073 Lottie Limejuice [4] 8-11
19 ran   ¾,1½,5,7,nk   (John Russell Harwood)   M Ryan Newmarket

---

ROYAL ASCOT   Friday June 20th   Righthand Stiff Galloping Track

1143 WINDSOR CASTLE STAKES 2YO   £12126   5f   Firm -17 -14 Slow

+953 CAROLS TREASURE [4] (B Hills) 2-9-4 B Thomson 6/5 fav: 2111: 2 b c Balidar - Really
Sharp (Sharpen Up) Very useful colt: completed his hat-trick with a comfortable success in
Windsor Castle Stakes at Royal Ascot June 20: easy winner of minor races at Goodwood and
Doncaster prev and prob unlucky not to be unbtn in his 4 outings: sprint bred colt who is
eff at 5f, stays 6f well: acts on firm and yldg and runs well on a galloping trk.   69
*834 SINGING STEVEN [3] (R Hannon) 2-9-4 B Rouse 10/1: 22112: Kept on well and has yet
to fin out of the first 2 in 5 races: see 834: acts on firm and soft.   64
1039 COPPER RED [8] (P Makin) 2-8-11 T Quinn 20/1: 323: Prom, ev ch: see 800.   51
834 BATTLEAXE [5] (J Toller) 2-8-11 W Carson 20/1: 334: Never closer: needs 6f? See 834. 48
1003 LUCIANAGA [2] 2-8-11 Paul Eddery 9/2: 220: Btr on gdd in 1003.   46
*1039 QUICK SNAP [10] 2-9-4(bl) R Curant 10/1: 432210: Made much: see 1039.   49
--   Joey Black [7] 8-11   1014 Alkadi [1] 9-4   962 New Mexico [9] 8-11
--   Madam Billa [6] 8-8
10 ran   1½,2,1,½,1½   (Mrs C Lane)   B Hills Lambourn, Berks

1144 GROUP 2 HARDWICKE STAKES   £31412   1m 4f   Firm -17 -12 Slow

*653 DIHISTAN [7] (M Stoute) 4-8-9 Pat Eddery 11/2: 1112-11: 4 b c Tyrnavos - Damosa
(Abdos) Very smart colt: al prom, led 2f out and held on well to win Gr 2 Hardwick Stakes
at Royal Ascot June 20: very easy first time out winner of a val Listed race at Goodwood:
in fine form in '85 winning h'caps at Leicester and Yarmouth (2)): half brother to the smart
Dazari: eff 10f, stays 12f well: acts on firm and hvy and on any track: much improved.   81
885 ST HILARION [10] (G Harwood) 4-9-0 G Starkey 8/1: 111-002: Chall final 1f, narrowly
btn and 4l clear rest: back to the form he showed abroad in '85 when winning 2 Gr 1 events
in Italy: also successful in a minor event at Kempton: very eff at 12f and is at his best
on firm ground, also acts on good: should be winning soon.   85
736 IROKO [3] (M Stoute) 4-8-9 W R Swinburn 5/1: 111-243: Ev ch dist, wknd and possibly
didnot stay the 12f: see 325.   76
475 LEMHILL [5] (M Blanshard) 4-8-9 R Cochrane 14/1: 232-134: Under press from ½ way
but kept on in his usual game fashion despite being unsuited by this very firm grd:best 251. 75
--   DUBIAN [8] 4-8-6 M Roberts 6/1: 22331-0: No real threat on seasonal debut: very
consistent in '85 winning a fillies event at Yarmouth and earlier placed in both Irish
and English Oaks: stays 12f really well: acts on firm, possibly btr on gd or yldg ground:
handles any track: sure to come on greatly for the race.   68
885 GOLD AND IVORY [4] 5-9-0 B Rouse 33/1: 00-3000: Led after 1m: see 251.   74
--   THEATRICAL [2] 4-8-12 M Kinane 11/4 fav: 10200-0: Well bckd fav on seasonal debut:
no threat in 7th: winner of first 2 on the trot in '85 at the Curragh and Leopardstown
and rated 90 when narrowly btn by Law Society in the Irish Derby: below that form
subsequently: very eff 12f and is suited by firm or gd grd: usually does well when fresh.   00

--   KIRMANN [1] 5-8-12 S Cauthen 10/1: 1-103-0: Ran himself into the grd in the first
half of the race: first time out winner of the Jockey Club Stakes at Newmarket in '85,
ran only twice more and has since changed stables: suited by 12f and firm/gd groundd.   **00**
885 Nemain (9) 8-12   **1015 Range Rover** (6) 8-9
10 ran   ¼,4,1,4,1½   (H H Aga Khan)   M Stoute, Newmarket

1145 WOKINGHAM STAKES (H'CAP) (0-75)   £19586   6f   Firm -17 +01 Fast   [60]

1027 TOUCH OF GREY [13] (D Thom) 3-8-8 M L Thomas 20/1: 0011201: 4 gr c Blakeney - Belle
(Comedy Star) Very useful sprinter: made all, hanging on gamely in a blanket fin to win val
and ultra competitive Wokingham H'cap at Royal Ascot June 20: earlier won two h'caps at
Windsor on the trot: in '85 won a nursery at Ascot: suited by 6f and firm grd and likes to
force the pace: acts on any track: genuine and consistent.   63
836 MANIMSTAR [16] (P Makin) 6-9-1 B Thomson 33/1: 0-00002: Chall strongly final 1f,
just btn: back to form and will be hard to beat next time: see 836.   59
877 PERFECT TIMING [19] (D Elsworth) 4-8-9 C Asmussen 10/1 fav: 403-043: Very well
bckd: chall under strong pressure final 1f: back to form and shd go cl next time: see 877.   50
616 OUR JOCK [2] (R Smyth) 4-9-3 W Carson 20/1: 00-0004: Prom thro'out: fine effort
from a mod draw: could be winning soon: see 361.   58
952 GOLD PROSPECT [20] 4-8-3 J Williams 33/1: -122040: Chall 2f out and ran to his best:
see 31: acts on firm and soft.   42
1060 POWDER BLUE [4] 4-8-3 A Mcglone 20/1: 101-040: Showed gd speed thro'out and looks
sure to win if eased in class: see 1060.   42
687 CORN STREET [9] 8-8-10 G Baxter 50/1: 0104000: Dsptd lead much, fin 7th: best 172(yldg)   39
687 BOOT POLISH [5] 4-8-5 N Connorton 12/1: 104-100: Late prog into 8th: best 306 (sft/hvy)   36
922 LAURIE LORMAN [8] 4-8-10 T Williams 25/1: 00-0100: No threat in 9th: best 660(yldg/sft)   36
952 AL TRUI [1] 6-9-4 M Wigham 40/1: 00-0100: Mod draw , early speed: best 846 (gd).   00
*1001 SHARPETTO [14] 3-8-8(7ex) A Bond 14/1: -00110: Much btr 1001 (gd).   00
1026 PHILIP [15] 4-9-10(bl) Pat Eddery 13/1: 0031130: Btr 1026, 7412 (5f).   00
*687 HO MI CHINH [23] 4-9-8 S Cauthen 14/1: 000-110: Early speed : abs since btr 687(gd)   00
1026 MATOU [25] 6-9-0 T Ives 14/1: 011-420: Much btr 1026.   00
846 PADRE PIO [26] 5-8-12 W R Swinburn 14/1: 021-020: Much btr 846 (gd).   00
*626 ROTHERFIELD GREYS [29] 4-8-13 J Leech[7] 13/1: 000-110: Well bckd, dsptd lead most :
abs since btr 626 but has risen considerably in the weights since then.   00

616 Prince Sky [27] 8-6   687 Sailors Song [22] 9-0(BL)
881 Young Inca [24] 9-2   1037 All Agreed [12] 8-8   1026 Dorking Lad [17] 9-2(bl)
877 Tyrollie [10] 8-13   +748 Korypheos [7] 8-11   217 Codices [30] 8-8
952 Transflash [21] 8-8   *1026 Irish Cookie [6] 8-5(10ex)
977 Show Home [3] 8-1(BL)   1037 Puccini [28] 8-5
28 ran   nk,1,shthd,¾,shthd,1½,1,nk   (T M Jennings)   D Thom Exning, Suffolk

1146 GROUP 1 KINGS STAND STAKES   £48828   5f   Firm -17 +17 Fast

*1011 LAST TYCOON [14] (R Collet) 3-8-9 C Asmussen 9/2: 10-0111: 3 b c Try My Best - Mill
Princess (Mill Reef) Very smart French sprinter: completed his hat-trick with a game success
in Gr 1 King's Stand Stakes at Royal Ascot June 20: led dist, held on well by the minimum
margin: successful prev in Gr 3 races at Chantilly and Longchamp: in '85 won again at
Longchamp and was also a fine 5th in the Prix L'Abbaye: very eff at 5f: acts on yldg but
is well suited by firm ground.   87
*705 DOUBLE SCHWARTZ [5] (C Nelson) 5-9-3 Pat Eddery 9/4 fav: 012-112: Came from behind
to chall final 1f, just held and is in tremendous form this season: see 705.   87
232 GWYDION [9] (H Cecil) 3-8-6 S Cauthen 100/30: 11-43: Dsptd lead over 3f: fine effort
after long abs and sprinting seems to be her game: see 232.   77
903 WELSH NOTE [10] (I Balding) 3-8-6 T Ives 16/1: 214-444: Prom, ev ch: see 408.   67
854 POLYKRATIS [4] 4-9-3 J Reid 66/1: 030-000: Stiff task, ran very creditably: see 222   66
903 SHARP ROMANCE [6] 4-9-3 R Cochrane 50/1: -233000: Best 18 (soft).   65
+854 HALLGATE [1] 3-8-9 W Carson 9/1: 1-30410: Taken off his feet, fin 9th: btr 854 (6f).   00
-639 NOMINATION [13] 3-8-9 T Quinn 12/1: 104-020: Unsuited by going: much btr 639(very hvy)   00
854 Fayruz [8] 8-9(vis)   903 Storm Warning [11] 9-0
854 Atall Atall [3] 8-9   587 Amigo Loco [7] 9-3(bl)
877 Petrovich [12] 9-3   854 Stalker [2] 8-9
14 ran   shthd,2½,4,½,nk   (R Strauss)   R Collet France

1147 BRITANNIA STAKES (H'CAP) (0-70) 3YO   £11720   1m   Firm -17 +13 Fast   [74]

*764 DALLAS [6] (L Cumani) 3-8-7 Pat Eddery 9/2 fav: -0211: 3 gr c Blushing Groom -
Flordelisada (Drone) Very useful, impr colt: justified strong support, comfortably leading
dist in val and fast run Britannia H'cap at Royal Ascot June 20: easily won a minor race at
Brighton last time: unraced in '85: very eff over 7f/1m: acts on soft, well suited by
fast ground: a progressive type who will win more good races.   68
--   NAVARZATO [12] (R Sheather) 3-8-8 R Cochrane 25/1: 11-2: Fine seasonal debut, keeping
on really well: winner of both his races in '85 at York and Chester: stays 1m well: acts
on fast and yldg going: will be hard to beat next time.   65

692 MISTER WONDERFUL [2] (J Dunlop) 3-9-2(VIS) T Ives 7/1: 10-3333: Visored for first
time, led briefly inside final 2f, went right under press and continues his run of 3rd
placings! Does deserve a race: see 692.   71
*465 NIGHT OUT PERHAPS [1] (G Wragg) 3-8-9 S Cauthen 12/1: 0-114: Chall 2f out: gd
effort after abs since 465: seems to act on firm and soft.   58
914 KEDRON [18] 3-8-1 J Carter[7] 20/1: 2-11320: Led ½ way: running well: see 455.   48
847 MEET THE GREEK [16] 3-8-0(2ow) P Cook 20/1: 2-21120: Far from disgraced and continues
in gd form: see 847.   46
*816 KNYF [19] 3-8-2(1ow) Paul Eddery 25/1: 2-32010: Late prog into 7th: in gd form. 45
692 HILLS BID [15] 3-8-6 B Thomson 20/1: 212-100: Fin a cl.up 8th: best 615 (yldg)   49
946 MERHI [11] 3-7-7(2oh) T Williams 33/1: -234300: Came to chall, badly hmpd 3f out,
fin 9th but this effort can be forgotten: see 143.   35
808 SYLVAN EXPRESS [25] 3-8-1 B Crossley 14/1: 11-0100: Best 406 (7f)   00
*847 SANTELLA MAC [26] 3-9-7 G Starkey 9/1: 01-10: Quite stiff task: see 847.   00
950 GEORGIA RIVER [13] 3-8-6 C Asmussen 8/1: 3-120: Early speed: much btrr 950, 546. 00
703 JOHN SAXON [20] 3-7-11 T Quinn 14/1: 33-0020: No danger, best 703.   00
1064 LANDSKI [22] 3-7-7 A Mackay 16/1: -40130: Early speed: much btr 1064 (10f) but
probably flattered.   00

703	Super Punk [5] 7-10	950	Ininsky [24] 9-4	220	Native Wizard [27] 9-1(BL)	
224	Happy Breed [3] 8-5	667	Hauwmal [23] 8-3	847	Mudrik [9] 8-2	
514	Below Zero [8] 7-7(4oh)			677	Boofy [21] 7-7(9oh)	
808	Barclay Street [14] 8-11			816	Try Harder [4] 7-10	

24 ran   1,1½,3,½,nk,1½,nk,2   (Richard L Duchossois)   L Cumani Newmarket

1148 QUEEN ALEXANDRA STAKES   £10725   2m 6f Firm -17 -05 Slow

1099 OTABARI [2] (P Cole) 4-8-8 T Quinn 7/1: -003421: 4 ch c Welsh Pageant - Milly
Lass (Bold Lad) Running for the 2nd time at this meeting, led under strong press final 1f
narrowly, setting a new course record when winning Queen Alexandra Stks at Royal Ascot
June 20: won at Leicester in '85: acts on frm & hvy and well suited by an extreme test of
stamina nowadays.   50
--   SEEHASE [8] (P Hughes) 4-8-4(2ow) J Matthias 20/1: -044202: Irish chall, challenged
and went left final 1f: ex Norwegian colt who won the St Leger in his native country in '85:
has since moved to Ireland: evidently suited by an extreme test of stamina and acts on
firm and good ground.   46
1099 JAMESMEAD [4] (D Elsworth) 5-9-3 C Asmussen 14/1: 1012-03: Making a quick reappearance,
al up there and stays extreme dist well: see 1099.   55
1099 INDE PULSE [5] (J Hindley) 4-9-3 M Hills 9/4 fav: 0104344: Running for the 2nd time
at the meeting, made much: btr 1099, 280.   55
704 BRUNICO [10] 4-8-13 G Starkey 3/1: -10100: Non-stayer? Best 475, 704.   26
1000 THE JOKER [7] 6-8-12 R Weaver 50/1: -040: Never in it: see 1000 (1m).   23
--   RAVARO [6] 6-9-0 G Curran 13/2: 3211-30: Irish mare who was 2nd in this race last
season but was unsuited by today's firm ground: enjoyed a successful hurdling campaign in
the Winter and was successful 4 times on the Flat in Ireland last season: stays well and
seems to act on any going tho' fav by gd or softer ground.   00
--   LARCHMONT [3] 5-8-12 W Carson 10/1: -0: Winner of 2 N.H. Flat races in Ireland in
Feb/Mar but   cut little ice here and was possibly unsuited by the going: acts well on soft
ground: half brother to topclass Time Charter.   00
--   LIVE IN HOPE [1] 4-8-2 Pat Eddery 7/1: -0: Winner of 2 N.H. Flat races at Plumpton
and Warwick at the end of '85/6 jump season but u.r. by swerving out of the stalls on this
first attempt under Jockey Club Rules.   00
9 ran   hd,4,hd,25,2   (Fahd Salman)   P Cole Whatcombe, Berks

---

1149 EBF ERROLL STAKES 2YO   £7515   6f   Firm -04 -19 Slow

1019 SANAM [6] (J Dunlop) 2-8-11 W Carson 5/4 fav: 41: 2 ch c Golden Act - Rose Goddess
(Sassafras) Promising colt: well bckd but had to be fairly strongly ridden to gain a narrow
success in 5 runner, val Erroll Stakes at Ascot June 21: from a gd winning family which
includes the smart Caro: eff over stiff 6f, will be suited by 7f+: acts on firm and good
ground: should continue to improve.   59
*876 MR EATS [4] (P Kelleway) 2-9-4 Pat Eddery 3/1: 12: Dsptd lead most, kept on well
fine effort: see 876.   64
1049 SUMMERHILL STREAK [1] (E Eldin) 2-8-11 A Mackay 8/1: 23: Led till ½ way: should
win a maiden if eased in class: has some scope: see 1049.   50
*694 IBNALMAGHITH [3] (H T Jones) 2-9-4 A Murray 9/2: 14: Ev ch: seems to act on firm
and yldg: stays 6f: see 694.   54
685 COMMONSIDR GIPSY [2] 2-8-11 R Cochrane 8/1: 020: Al being pushed along: unsuited
by firm? See 685.   47
5 ran   ½,2½,1,nk   (Prince A A Faisal)   J Dunlop Arundel, Sussex

1150 HIGH YIELD STEEL STKS HCAP 3YO+ 0-70   £7164   2m   Firm -04 -10 Slow   [57]

807   JANISKI [99] (W Hern) 3-8-10(bl) W Carson 9/2: 100-421: 3 b c Niniski -Seasurf
(Seaepic) Useful colt who showed himself well suited by 2m when staying on final 1f, to lead
close home in a val h'cap at Ascot June 21: first time out in '85 won at Doncaster: eff
around 10f but much btr suited by 2m nowadays: suited by firm grd and a stiff track:
should win more staying h'caps: wears blinkers.   67
1099 MILTON BURN [4] (H O'neill) 5-8-5 S Whitworth 6/1: 1102232: Well ridden to dsptd
lead final 1f, just btn: see 312, 1099.   44
1058 MORGANS CHOICE [10] (R Hodges) 9-7-7(2oh) N Adams 12/1: 0000003: Fin really strongly,
showing his best form of the season: should be winning soon: see 942.   31
801   REVISIT [5] (J Winter) 4-8-10 W R Swinburn 4/1 fav: 1-00034: Went for home 3f out,
no extra final 1f: see 58A.   45
+542 WIDE BOY [12] 4-7-12 T Quinn 9/1: 230-110: Al prom after abs since 542.   33
964   REGAL STEEL [3] 8-7-7(4oh) P Hill 25/1: 0203220: Prom most: btr 964 (12f).   18
1004 FANDANGO LIGHT [7] 5-7-13 A Mcglone 15/2: 0100/20: Wknd into 7th, btr 104 (13f gd) 00
921   ALL IS REVEALED [6] 4-8-5(vis) M L Thomas 9/1: -041300: Made much under press,
sn bt: best 582 (14f, gd).   00
942   Tars Hill [2] 7-7   474   Standard Breakfast [8] 8-3
617   Lundylux [11] 9-10   1020 Main Reason [1] 9-0
12 ran ` nk,¼,2½,hd,10   (Dowager Lady Beaverbrook)   W Hern West Ilsley, Berks

1151 STEEL PLATE VICTORY CUP HCAP 3YO 0-75   £11489   5f   Firm -04 + 34 Fast   [70]

+929 ORIENT [14] (R Whitaker) 3-8-8(10ex) D Mckeown 3/1: 40-111: 3 b f Bay Express -
Gundi (Mummy's Pet) Smart, fast impr filly: unbtn this season and completed her hat-trick
when shattering the course record in val 3yo h'cap at Ascot June 21: led inside final 2f,
won quite comfortably: easy winner of similar fast run and val h'cap at Epsom June 7 and
a maiden at Beverley first time out: equally eff at 5 and 6f and on any track: suited by
firm or good ground: now steps up in class but is still improving and should be kept on
the right side of.   70
600   TREASURE KAY [12] (P Makin) 3-9-0 B Thomson 16/1: 010-142: Fin really strongly
and was clear of rest: fine effort against this h'cap snip and is very eff over 5f tho' does
stay 6f: see 314: will be hard to beat next time.   72
903   DUBLIN LAD [7] (M Brittain) 3-9-4 A Murray 12/1: 0-00003: Set a blistering pace
over 3f: grand effort from this genuine front runner: see 903.   64
884   NICCOLO POLO [16] (B Hanbury) 3-8-8(bl) W R Swinburn 14/1: 0-33024: Ev ch, btr 884
(blinkered first time).   54
-732 FLYAWAY BRIDE [1] 3-8-8 S Cauthen 14/1: 31-0020: Sn prom: see 732 (6f).   50
*1033 RESPECT [11] 3-8-8(7ex) Pat Eddery 11/4 fav: 3-21310: Ev ch, wknd: btr 1033.   49
1027 CATHERINES WELL [13] 3-7-13 W Carson 9/1: 011-030: Fin 7th: see 1027.   00
593   RESTORE [15] 3-7-9 M L Thomas 10/1: 23-20: Abs since btr 593 (gd).   00
+808 LATCH STRING [8] 3-8-4 B Crossley 9/1: 024-110: Well below 808.   00
580   Compleat [4] 8-5   1044 Gossiper [5] 8-6(BL)   884 Glikiaa Mou [9] 8-1(1ow)
--   Wanton [2] 9-6   929 Edgewise [6] 8-5   588 Young Puggy [3] 7-10
15 ran   1,4,hd,1½,nk   (Mrs R T Watson)   R Whitaker Wetherby, Yorks.

1152 CHURCHILL STAKES 3YO   £7140   1m 4f Firm -04 -04 Slow

849   SADEEM [6] (G Harwood) 3-8-9 G Starkey 13/8: -31: 3 ch c Forli - Miss Mazepah
(Nijinsky) Promising colt: gamely led inside final 1f in val 4 runner 3yo race at Ascot
June 21: late developing sort who was unraced in '85 but is brother to the smart 10f winner
Formaz: acts on firm and gd going: suited by a stiff 12f and promises to stay further:
the type to improve and win more races.   64
*739 DANISHGAR [3] (M Stoute) 3-8-9 W R Swinburn 5/4 fav: 22-0412: Led after 1m, caught
near fin but well clear rem 2 runners: gd effort and stays 12f: see 739.   63
552   HEIGHLAD [4] (O Douieb) 3-8-9(BL) Pat Eddery 11/2: -133: Bl first time, led 1m,
fdd tamely and twice below debut win in 409.   48
*635 GOLDEN HEIGHTS [2] (P Walwyn) 3-8-9 Paul Eddery 11/2: 43-1214: Dropped out final 3f:
unsuited by going: see 635.   40
4 ran   ½,15,8   (Sheikh Mohammed)   G Harwood Pulborough, Sussex

1153 FERN HILL STAKES 3YO FILLIES HCAP 0-70   £7339   1m   Firm -04 +04 Fast   [64]

579   VIANORA [6] (G Harwood) 3-9-2 G Starkey 9/2: 3-01121: 3 ch f Ahonoora - Miss Portal
(St Paddy) Very useful filly: gaining her 3rd win of the season when leading dist under
press in quite fast run Fern Hill h'cap at Ascot June 21: earlier won 2 minor events on the
trot at Kempton and Lingfield: very eff over 7f/1m: acts on firm and yldg and on any trk:
genuine and consistent.   66
--   ROYAL LOFT [10] (W Jarvis) 3-8-9 R Cochrane 16/1: 1-2: Fin in fine style and this
was a fine seasonal debut: winner of her only race in '85, a mdn at Doncaster: eff 6f,
well suited by 1m now: acts on firm and yldg and likes a gall track: one to be on next time. 58
966   RIYDA [3] (R J Houghton) 3-9-1 S Cauthen 9/1: -1223: Chall when hmpd dist: fine
effort in the circumstances : see 423: acts on firm and good.   59

-- HOLBROOKE SUTTON [9] (B Hanbury) 3-9-7 Pat Eddery 7/2 fav: 14-4: Heavily bckd seasonal
debutant: chall 1f out: first time out winner of a fillies mdn at Newmarket in '85, 1th in
the Hyperion Stakes here on only sub start: eff over 6f, shd stay 1m: acts on firm ground.   60
575 SOMETHING CASUAL [12] 3-8-8 T Ives 20/1: 10-000: Abs: ev ch: see 386.   44
925 LUCKY SO SO [8] 3-8-9 A Murray 12/1: 4-41030: Prom much: btr 925 (sharp trk).   43
925 NORMANBY LASS [2] 3-8-12 Paul Eddery 9/2: 20-0020: Some trouble in running, fin
7th and better 925 (sharp track).   00
*925 PRINCESS NAWAAL [1] 3-8-10 W Carson 11/2: 44-110: Hmpd inside final 2f: ignore this:
best 925.   00
575 GREAT LEIGHS [11] 3-8-13 B Thomson 8/1: 02-0120: Fin last: best 359 (C/D soft).   00
656 Buthayna [5] 8-3   925 Mirataine Venture [4] 8-1
1032 Little Pipers [7] 8-7
12 ran   ¾,2½,2½,1½,¾,1,1   (J H Richmond-Watson)   G Harwood Pulborough, Sussex

1154 HALIFAX MAIDEN FILLIES STAKES 2YO   £7152   6f   Firm -04 -06 Slow

-- MOUNTAIN MEMORY [1] (P Walwyn) 2-8-11 Paul Eddery 20/1: 1: 2 b f High Top - Forgotten
Dreams (Shoemaker) Very promising filly: first time out turned up at 20/1 when running her
rivals into the grd when gaining a decisive all the way 4l success in a val event for
unraced 2yo fillies at Ascot June 21: well bred filly who is related to sev winners, notably
My Top who won the Italian Derby: dam a stayer: eff over 6f but is sure to be suited by
much longer dist: acts well on firm ground: sure to win more races.   68
-- SIMPLE TASTE [4] (I Balding) 2-8-11 Pat Eddery 11/4: 2: Mkt drifter, no extra final
1f: American bred filly who cost $1m and is the first foal of a winning miler who comes
from an outstanding winning line: should improve for the race and win a mdn at least.   56
-- RATHER HOMELY [5] (P Cole) 2-8-11 T Quinn 12/1: 3: Mkt drifter, outpaced final 1f:
half sister to winning '85 juv Sparky Lad and is bred to be speedy.   50
-- CACHONDINA [2] (B Hills) 2-8-11 B Thomson 10/11 fav: 4: Heavily bckd debutant
who had ev ch but wknd: relatively inexpensive purchase who is a half sister to a winning
'85 Irish 2yo: sprint bred.   46
-- GHANAYIM [6] 2-8-11 A Murray 9/2: 0: Prom 4f: cost $200,000 and is a half sister
to the 3yo mdn Bright As Night: likely to improve for the experience.   42
5 ran   4,2,1½,1½   (Hesmonds Stud)   P Walwyn Lambourn, Berks

1155 GRINDALE MAIDEN STAKES 2YO   £2300   6f   Firm 18 -65 Slow

931 GREENS HERRING [7] (W Jarvis) 2-9-0 T Lucas 5/2 FAV: 041: 2 ch c Mansingh - Deep
Lady (Deep River) Well bckd when leading ½ way, comfortably in a slowly run 2yo mdn at
Redcar June 21: cost 9,400 gns as a yearling and is a half brother to winning sprinter and
useful hurdler Ballyarry: stays 6f well: suited by fast grd: acts on any track.   28
973 PREMIER VIDEO [6] (J Berry) 2-8-11 M Fry 4/1: 302: Al front rank, cheaply acquired
filly who seems to act on any trk: stays 6f: see 627.   18
870 FINLUX DESIGN [1] (R Hollinshead) 2-9-0 S Perks 16/1: 03: Mkt drifter: tardy
start: some late progress: cheaply bought colt who is a half brother to winning juv Jack's
Lass: stays 6f: acts on fast ground.   18
415 THE BRAZILIAN [5] (E Alston) 2-9-0 A Proud 33/1: 04: Led/dsptd lead to ½ way:
btr effort: acts on fast ground.   17
-- EINSTEIN [3] 2-9-0 G Sexton 9/2: 0: Active in mkt on debut: kept on after a slow
start and sure to improve: cost 25,500 gns as yearling who is closely related to sev winning
sprinters: acts on fast ground.   13
979 TROMPE DOEIL [2] 2-8-11 P Robinson 14/1: 00: Half sister to sev winners in the States   02
-- JOHNNY SHARP [4] 2-9-0 J Lowe 11/4: 0: Well bckd debutant: cost $80,000 and is half
brother to sev winners: should stay further: sure to do btr than this.   00
488 MEATH PRINCESS [9] 2-8-11 A Clark 8/1: 0200: Twice well below form shown in 376(5f).   00
8 ran   2,1,½,1½,2½   (Richard Green Fine Paintings)   W Jarvis Newmarket

1156 DAILY MIRROR BELLE HANDICAP 3YO+   £1379   1m   Firm 18 -27 Slow   [14]

1041 IKTIYAR [12] (S Mellor) 4-10-6 Dana Mellor(3) 5/1: 320-001: 4 b g Corvaro - Irova
(Iron Liege) Made most to score unchall in a Lady riders h'cap at Redcar June 21: first
success: placed sev times when trained by M Stoute last term: eff over 1m, stays 10f: suited
by gd or faster grd: acts on any track.   30
943 HIGH PORT [10] (A Jones) 7-9-4 Diana Jones 7/1: 0-00002: Not reach winner: see 943.   04
*1074 GODS LAW [2] (G Reveley) 5-9-8(5ex) Geraldine Rees 2/1 FAV: -013213: Ran on too
late: see 1074.   07
448 FOLLOW THE BAND [1] (W Jarvis) 4-10-11 Jennie Goulding 8/1: 200-004: Fin strongly:
fair effort: see 448.   21
-- PRICEOFLOVE [6] 6-9-5 Mrs Jenny Moffatt 14/1: 20040-0: Never dangerous: had a
successful spell over hurdles this Winter tho' last won on the Flat in '82, at Wolverhampton
and Nottingham: stays 7f: suited by some give in the ground.   00
673 COLONEL HALL [5] 3-8-1 Valerie Greaves(3) 20/1: -000000: Late prog: stays 1m: see 237 00

860   PARIS TRADER [8] 4-10-10 Sue Burke(7) 8/1: 2-00000: Fin 7th: much btr 609 (10f gd).   00
943   IRISH HERO [3] 4-11-0 Maxine Juster 8/1: 42-0040: Fin 9th: btr 943.   00
676   Polemistis [13] 9-0(bl)   993   Tarleton [9] 9-1
1093   Remembrance [4] 10-0   --   Dreadnought [7] 10-0   960   Scoop The Kitty [11] 9-1(4ow)
13 ran   5,nk,1½,2,nk   (S P Tindall)   S Mellor Lambourn, Berks

1157 RONALDSHAY CUP (H'CAP) (0-50)   £4038   6f   Firm 18 +01 Fast   [46]

192   CANIF [10] (M Ryan) 5-9-0 P Robinson 5/1 Co.FAV: 4000-01: 5 gr g Saritamer -
Couteau (Nelcius) Despite a fair abs made virtually ev yard, gamely in a h'cap at Redcar
June 21: failed to win last season tho' in '84 won at Goodwood and Lingfield: best form over
6f on a sound surface: acts on any track.   42
947   MADRACO [11] (P Calver) 3-7-9 M Fry 7/1: 04-1102: With winner thro'out: just held:
grand effort: see 545.   22
374   INISHPOUR [4] (H Wharton) 4-9-8 M Hills 12/1: 000-003: Not btn far: returning to
form: useful on his day, won at Newmarket and Redcar last season: eff over 6/7f: suited
by fast ground.   47
922   FOOLISH TOUCH [2] (K Stone) 4-8-13(vis) C Dwyer 11/1: 0031004: Al up there: best 401.   26
1026   MENDICK ADVENTURE [8] 5-8-6 J Lowe 5/1 Co.FAV: 2300000: Btr 1026 (made most):see 56 11
1026   CHAPLINS CLUB [1] 6-10-0(BL) D Nicholls 10/1: -000000: Bl first time: ran on late:see 1026.32
+1093   TANFEN [5] 5-8-6(8ex) N Carlisle 6/1: 0310210: Fin 7th: btr 1093 (sharp trk).   00
1093   TOP THAT [6] 5-8-8 B Mcgiff(7) 6/1: 0020140: Fin 8th: best on yldg 649.   00
830   THE MAZALL [7] 6-8-9(bl) G Gosney 5/1 Co.FAV: 0-00120: Speed over ½ way, fin 9th.   00
700   Hopeful Heights [9] 9-2   1026   Air Command [3] 9-8
11 ran   nk,¾,5,3,nk,nk,¾   (T P Ramsden)   M Ryan Newmarket

1158 NEWTON SELLING H'CAP STAKES 3YO (0-25)   £1375   1m 1f   Firm 18 -10 Slow   [23]

932   BOLD ANSWER [3] (W Bentley) 3-8-6 T Lucas 10/1: 0-00001: 3 b g Bold Owl - Subtle
Answer (Stephen George) Showed impr form, stayed on well to lead cl home in a selling h'cap
at Redcar June 21 (no bid): stays 9f well: acts on firm and yldg grd and on a gall trk.   09
1055   LARNEM [2] (T Fairhurst) 3-8-8 C Coates(5) 12/1: 00-0002: Dropped in class: led
below dist, just caught: stays 9f: acts on fast grd and on a gall track.   10
969   MANVIL [4] (W Pearce) 3-9-6 M Hindley(3) 16/1: 0-0003: Eased in class: kept on
well and not btn far: stays 9f: seems well suited by top of the ground.   18
--   WOLLOW BIRD [1] (J Fitzgerald) 3-8-5 M Hills 12/1: 40000-4: Fair eff on seasonal
debut: led briefly 2f out: no worthwhile form last season.   01
422   AUSSIE GIRL [6] 3-9-3 R Carter(5) 13/2: 00-000: Active in mkt: first signs of
form: acts on fast ground.   11
740   HILL RYDE [13] 3-9-5 P Robinson 7/2: 00-0020: Btr here over 1m in 740.   11
1053   BELHILL [10] 3-8-7(bl) D Nicholls 13/2: 4300030: Fin 8th: btr on gd grd in 1053.   00
838   ANGEL DRUMMER [8] 3-9-2 C Dwyer 11/8 FAV: 0-00220: Much btr over 10f in 838 (gd).   00
1053   Balidareen [12] 8-3   958   Pink Sensation [9] 9-7
--   Planning Act [11] 8-8   1051   Spring Garden [5] 8-10
1063   Town Of Ennis [7] 8-12   545   Bonny Bright Eyes [14] 8-10
14 ran   hd,1½,¾,¾,¾,1½,3   (F R Lanni)   W Bentley Middleham, Yorks

1159 STAITHES HANDICAP STAKES (0-50)   £2695   1m 6f   Firm 18 +01 Fast   [41]

933   RUSHMOOR [8] (R Peacock) 8-8-9 S Dawson(3) 9/1: 0-40031: 8 br g Queens Hussar -
Heathfield (Hethersett) Led after 6f and held on gamely by a shthd in a h'cap at Redcar June
21: lightly raced on Flat in '85: last won in '81, but is a smart hurdler: stays 2m+: acts
on any grd: best when up with the pace.   31
917   MARLION [2] (S Hall) 5-8-9(bl) D Nicholls 5/1: 20-0032: Switched over 2f out:
just went under and was possibly unlucky: 4l clear 3rd: gd effort: see 366.   30
964   PEGGY CAROLYN [12] (M Ryan) 4-9-9 P Robinson 3/1 FAV: 00-0033: Well bckd, but never
nearer: see 964.   38
1004   NO U TURN [11] (S Mellor) 8-9-6 A Clark 6/1: 200-004: Ev ch over 1f out: btr 12f?   33
949   NIMBLE NATIVE [1] 3-7-7(3oh) J Lowe 10/1: 1040030: Nearest fin: needs 2m: acts on
firm and yielding: see 949, 45.   18
942   ISHKHARA [5] 4-7-11 A Proud 16/1: 0-00300: Never nearer: twice below form 675 (yldg)   04
693   GENTLE FAVOR [7] 5-9-6(bl) C Nutter 8/1: 210-040: Never nearer 7th: see 519.   00
933   BUCKLOW HILL [3] 9-9-10 C Dwyer 10/1: 010-000: Ev ch: see 782.   00
1024   FENCHURCH COLONY [6] 5-9-1 K Hodgson 8/1: 00/3030: Led over 6f, fdd: btr 1024 (12f)   00
1016   SECURITY CLEARANCE [13] 5-8-13 G Sexton 10/1: 0030020: Ev ch: btr 1016(2m)00
933   Strathearn [10] 8-2(bl)   860   Skerne Spark [9] 7-8
12 ran   shthd,4,1½,2½,1½,hd,nk   (Jim Ennis)   R Peacock Tarporley, Cheshire

1160 FORTY ACRE MAIDEN STAKES 3YO   £1278   1m 4f   Firm 18 +10 Fast

978   FRENCH FLUTTER [2] (R Sheather) 3-9-0 M Hills 9/1: 020-041: 3 b c Beldale Flutter -
French Princess (Prince Regent) Useful colt: led approaching final 1f, driven out in a
fast run 3yo mdn at Redcar June 21: eff 12f, stays 14f: acts on gd and firm grd and seems
a genuine sort.   51
--   LISANA [3] (M Stoute) 3-8-11 A Kimberley 11/10 FAV: 0-2: Heavily bckd on seasonal debut:
not the best of runs and just btn: possibly an unlucky loser: well bred filly who is certain
to gain compensation soon: stays 12f: acts on gd and firm ground.   47

935 BUTTERFLY KISS [4] (G Wragg) 3-8-11 P Robinson 12/1: -0033: Led/dsptd lead: another
good run: should find a race: see 935, 250.   **41**
935 SHINY KAY [1] (W Elsey) 3-8-11(BL) J Lowe 16/1: -0044: Bl first time: never nearer:
fair effort from this half sister to useful 1m/10f winner K-Battery: stays 12f: acts on gd/frm **35**
669 STORMY PROSPECT [9] 3-9-0 T Lucas 6/1: -340: Made much: twice well below form 409. **37**
1062 LORD IT OVER [5] 3-9-0 A Clark 3/1: -000: Mkt drifter: no extra final 2f: much btr 1062 **25**
-- Varsity [11] 9-0   **916 Patricks Star** [8] 9-0   **380 Dearham Bridge** [7] 9-0
-- Golflines [10] 9-0
10 ran ½,2½,3,nk,7   (J C Smith)   R Sheather Newmarket

1161 GRIBDALE GATE MAIDEN AUCTION STAKES 2YO £2004 5f   Firm 18 -23 Slow

892 BEN LEDI [12] (M H Easterby) 2-7-13 A Shoults(3) 14/1: 031: 2 b g Strong Gale -
Balacco (Balidar) Impr gelding: fin well to get up cl home in a 2yo mdn auction at Redcar
June 21: eff at 5f, shd stay further: acts on firm and gd/yldg grd and a gall track. **44**
-- KYVERDALE [1] (M Ryan) 2-8-2 P Robinson 4/1: 2: Very active in mkt on debut: led
approaching final 1f: not btn far: half sister to sev winners: eff 5f, shd stay further:
acts on fast ground and should find a small event. **45**
780 PREMIER LAD [4] (W Pearce) 2-8-8 M Hindley(0) 33/1: 03: Kept on well and is impr:
cost 8,400gns as a yealing: shd be suited by further than 5f: acts on fast ground. **45**
873 STELBY [3] (O Brennan) 2-7-13 M Wood 5/1: 0224: Made much: btr 873, 632. **30**
995 KALAS IMAGE [7] 2-7-10 J Lowe 4/1: 03230: Prom, ev ch: btr 995, see 364. **26**
882 INFANTA MARIA [9] 2-7-13 S Dawson(3) 7/2 Jt.FAV: 020: Sn prom: btr 882 (sharp trk) **24**
-- LEADING PLAYER [13] 2-8-5 S Perks 7/2 Jt.FAV: 0: A big gamble, but never nearer:
cost I.R. 8500 and is speedily bred sort: one to keep an eye on. **00**
988 Bay Wonder [8] 7-10   **905 Get Set Lisa** [2] 7-10   **882 Rylands Reef** [11] 7-13
-- Scawsby Lees [5] 8-2   **1067 Tiklas** [10] 7-10
12 ran ¾,2½,2½,hd,1½,shthd   (A A McCluskey)   M H Easterby Great Habton, Yorks

---

LINGFIELD   Saturday June 21st   Lefthanded Sharpish Undulating Track

Official Going Given as Straight Course: Firm, Round Course: Good/Firm

1162 EBF SAFFRON STAKES 2YO   £3424 5f   Good/Firm 30 +06 Fast

773 DREAM LAUNCH [3] (B Hanbury) 2-8-8 G Baxter 2/1 FAV: 01: 2 ch f Relaunch - Pleasuresome (What A Pleasure): Very useful filly: smartly away and was never hdd when an easy winner
of a fast run 2yo stakes at Lingfield June 21: cost $57,000 as a yearling and is closely
related to a couple of winners: very eff over this minimum trip with forcing tactics: acts
on fast grnd & on a sharpish trk: certain to win more races. **58**
1003 THE DOMINICAN [8] (B Hills) 2-9-4 J Carter(7) 5/1: 322132: Another gd effort: see 918. **50**
497 TAUBER [9] (Pat Mitchell) 2-8-11 R Cochrane 8/1: 03: Bckd from 33/1: ran on strongly
and should win a small race soon: half brother to the useful sprinter Camps Heath: acts on
fast grnd & on a sharpish trk. **42**
-- BOLD CRUSADER [7] (M Stoute) 2-8-11 W R Swinburn 3/1: 4: Well bckd debutant: stayed
on well & will appreciate another furlong: cost 46,000 gns & is a brother to 10f winner
F Sharp: acts on gd/firm grnd & on a sharp trk. **32**
497 JAH BLESS [5] 2-8-11 B Rouse 3/1: 220: Speed over ½way: best in 497. **30**
-- BATTLE STING [10] 2-8-11 P Cook 50/1: 0: Unfancied on racecourse debut: never reached
ldrs though likely to impr for this experience: half brother to a couple of winners: acts
on gd/firm grnd. **29**
-- Spring Forward [1] 8-11   **848 Semis** [2] 8-8
938 Not Ready Yet [6] 8-11   **-- Brainwave** [4] 8-11
10 ran 6,½,3,½,4   (Robert B Trussell jnr)   B Hanbury Newmarket

1163 SOLSTICE SELLING STAKES 2YO   £1060 6f   Good/Firm 30 -107 Slow

+987 DORMESTONE LAD [2] (R Stubbs) 2-8-11(bl) J H Brown(5) 8/13 FAV: 00411: 2 ch c
Mansingh - Kareela (Deep Diver): Impr colt: led and ran on well to win a slowly run
2yo seller at Lingfield June 21 (bought in 2,300 gns): recently won a similar event at
Yarmouth: well suited by 6f: acts on gd & fast grnd and seems suited by an easy trk. **28**
*502 CLEARWAY [4] (R Hodges) 2-8-11 J Reid 11/4: 012: Led briefly below dist: acts on
fast grnd & on a sharpish trk: see 502. **20**
-- MALACHI LAD [1] (Pat Mitchell) 2-8-11 R Cochrane 9/2: 3: Tried to make all at a
slow pace: first foal who will be btr for this run: acts on gd/firm grnd. **00**
3 ran 3,6   (P G Shorrock)   R Stubbs Coverham, Yorks

1164 WILTSHIRE BUILDERS STAKES 3YO HCAP 0-35 £2206 6f   Good/Firm 30 -11 Slow

-- KHARRANA [15] (K Brassey) 3-9-7 S Whitworth 12/1: 201-1: 3 ch f General Assembly -
Parmesh (Home Guard): Useful filly: comfortably defied top weight on her reapp, led below
dist in a h'cap at Lingfield June 21: lightly raced last term, making all in a fillies maiden
at Folkestone on her final start: stays 6f well: suited by fast grnd & a
sharpish trk: can win again. **45**

837 SPORTING SOVEREIGN [18] (M Jarvis) 3-8-9 W Woods(3) 9/1: 00-0422: Finished strongly
and should open his account soon: will stay further: suited by fast grnd: see 837.   28
545 BLOW THE WHISTLE [13] (R Sheather) 3-8-13(bl) M L Thomas 20/1: 4004-03: Made most:
best effort yet from this lightly raced maiden: suited by 6f & fast grnd: clearly does
well with forcing tactics.   32
842 PERSIAN BALLET [17] (P Walwyn) 3-8-6 Paul Eddery 7/1: 0-034: Kept on well: best
effort to date: half brother to a handful of winners, notably useful 10f performer Lucky
Wednesday: stays 6f well: seems suited by fast grnd & a sharpish trk.   25
910 PENDOR DANCER [19] 3-8-4 G Baxter 10/1: 0-00230: Ev ch: in gd form: see 871.   22
961 LINAVOS [3] 3-8-13 J Bray(7) 20/1: 00-0100: Bast on gd grnd in 837.   21
1001 MUHTARIS [4] 3-9-0 B Rouse 8/1 : -022200: Early speed: not well drawn: btr in 734.   00
*768 BLUE HORIZON [9] 3-8-13 R Cochrane 4/1: 303-010: Much btr on a tight trk in 768.   00
929 ALEXANJO [12] 3-8-13 G Starkey 5/2 FAV: 444-040: No threat: much btr in 929.   00
835 Khlestakov [16] 8-13   -- Hot Order [10] 8-12   656 Sunk Island [14] 8-7(eyeshield)
992 Naughty Nighty [6] 8-1   -- Jacqui Joy [7] 8-2
496 Dalsaan Bay [11] 8-9   -- By Chance [2] 8-7   961 Carnival Rose [8] 8-5
-- My Mutzie [20] 8-2
18 ran   ¼,shhd, • ½,½,4,1½   (Dana Stud Ltd)   K Brassey Upper Lambourn, Berks

1165 IPC WOMENS MONTHLY STAKES HCAP 0-35   £2080   7f   Good/Firm 30 -09 Slow   [26]

+992 WINTER WORDS [9] (C Lloyd Jones) 7-8-10 Paul Eddery 13/8 FAV: 000-011: 7 b h Wollow -
Prinia (On Your Mark): In gd form, was gambled on when leading over 2f out, comfortably in a
h'cap at Lingfield June 21: recently won an app. h'cap at Yarmouth: last term won at
Newcastle: eff around 7f, sure to stay at least 1m: suited by fast grnd.   18
886 NO JAZZ [4] (C Benstead) 3-8-3 B Rouse 10/1: 00-00002: Maiden who ran her best race
to date here: suited by fast grnd: stays 7f well: should win a seller.   14
-1086 JAMES DE COOMBE [12] (M Bolton) 4-8-9 J Reid 7/2: 0002423: Ev ch: best over 6f in 1086. 08
992 SWEET ANDY [11] (G Gracey) 7-7-13 W Woods(3) 14/1: -0004: Al up there: stays 7f:see 679.00
611 LONG BAY [13] 4-9-2 M Rimmer 20/1: 001-000: Made much: acts on gd/firm: see 611.   10
679 ITALIAN SPRING [2] 5-7-13 D Mckay 33/1: 000-00: Late prog: no worthwhile form last
season: stays 7f: seems suited by fast grnd.   00
750 TRUMPS [14] 6-8-3 J Carter(7) 10/1: 04-0000: Fin 8th: won at Brighton last season
though no form this term: stays 10f: acts on firm & soft grnd & likes an undulating course.   00
845 OSTENTATIOUS [8] 4-8-11 L Riggio(7) 10/1: 00-0330: Speed over ½way: btr over 1m in 620. 00
855 Black Spout [1] 7-12   1086 Visual Identity [16] 9-5
*727 Pett Velero [7] 8-7   -- Hatching [6] 8-10   30 Hampton Walk [10] 8-2
855 Chicago Bid [5] 9-7   727 Leap Year [15] 8-12   683 Overule [3] 8-2
16 ran   2,hd,1½,½,3   (Mrs E M Fox)   C Lloyd Jones Abergele, Clwyd

1166 BROOKE BOND AMATEUR RIDERS STAKES   £2057   1m 2f   Good/Firm 30 -16 Slow

*912 RIMAH [14] (H Thomson Jones) 5-11-10(bl) Mr T Thomson Jones 3/1: 340-011: 5 b h Nisha-
pour - Lady Simone (Realm): In gd form, led over 2f out and was sn clear in an amateur riders
stakes at Lingfield June 21: won a similar race at Haydock recently: unsuccessful last season
though in '84 won at Goodwood: eff over 1m, stays 10f well: acts on firm & yld grnd & on
any track.   41
943 CABRAL [7] (C Vernon Miller) 5-11-7 Mr S Bullard(5) 33/1: -002: Outsider, kept on
well and is certainly on the up grade: stays 10f: acts on fast grnd: see 943.   30
950 DOLLY [4] (A Moore) 4-11-4 Candy Moore 16/1: 004D003: Ran to her best: stays 10f.   23
*964 SWIMMER [5] (G Huffer) 4-11-10 Sue Bilborough(5) 3/1: 1013-14: Unlucky in running:
never nearer: see 964.   29
-- PACTOLUS [6] 3-10-10 Amanda Harwood(5) 7/4 FAV: 410-0: Well bckd on seasonal debut:
stayed on too late: won his maiden race at Salisbury last season, when lightly raced: stays
10f: seems suited by good or faster grnd: will impr next time.   27
850 WIZZARD ART [1] 5-11-4 Yvonne Haynes 33/1: 3130-00: Never reached ldrs: dual winner
at Folkestone last season: stays 10f well: acts on any going.   17
912 SALLOOM [10] 4-11-7(BL) Maxine Juster 6/1: 100-030: Much closer to winner in 912.   00
856 Thatchingly [15] 11-7   -- Match Master [13] 11-0
943 Aqualon [11] 11-4   -- Abbey Avenue [12] 11-0
-- Cherry Pit [2] 11-0   838 Blairs Winnie [9] 10-11
716 Dusty Diplomacy [3] 10-10   620 Night Waller [8] 11-0
15 ran   4,2,½,½,2,2   (Hamdan Al-Maktoum)   H Thomson Jones Newmarket

1167 SMUGGLERS MAIDEN STAKES 3YO   £1297   1m 4f   Good/Firm 30 +16 Fast

572 WASSL REEF [2] (J Dunlop) 3-9-0 W Carson 11/8: 22-231: 3 b c Mill Reef - Connaught
Bridge (Connaught): Useful colt: well bckd & led 3f out, gamely in a fast run 3yo maiden at
Lingfield June 21: narrowly btn by cheeky winner Armada at Brighton on his reapp & has yet
to fin out of the frame: eff over 10f, stays 12f well: acts on fast & yld grnd & on any trk:
genuine and consistent.   54
191 RUSSIAN LOGIC [4] (G Harwood) 3-9-0 G Starkey 11/10: -22: Gd effort after fair abs:
well bckd & had ev ch: stays 12f: acts on fast grnd: see 191.   51

751 GANOON [7] (P Cole) 3-9-0 J Reid 6/1: 2200-23: Ran well: see 751.   45
839 HEAD OF SCHOOL [8] (J Winter) 3-9-0 P Cook 33/1: 020-004: No extra dist: see 839.   39
1061 FRANGNITO [10] 3-9-0 J Williams 10/1: -400220: Went on ½way: best in 765 (10f).   38
570 TENDER TYPE [9] 3-9-0 R Cochrane 33/1: -000: Dwelt, never nearer: see 570.   30
--   SINDUR [5] 3-8-11 P D'arcy 33/1: 0-0: Led to ½way on reapp: also fin last on her
only outing last season.   00
7 ran   1½,4,3,hd,4,20   (Sheikh Ahmed Al Maktoum)   J Dunlop Arundel, Sussex

---

WARWICK   Saturday June 21st   Lefthand, Turning Track

Official Going Given as Good/Firm

1168 C.C.P.R. MAIDEN SELLING STAKES 2YO   £547   6f   Good/Firm 22 -84 Slow

1012 ABSALOUTE HEAVEN [3] (R Stubbs) 2-8-11 A Mercer 7/2: 0001: 2 gr f Absalom - Evvola
(Khalkis): Led final 1f, driven out in a very slowly run 2yo seller at Warwick June 21
(bought in 3,200 gns): sister to a 2yo winner: eff at 5f, stays 6f: acts on gd/firm & likes
a sharpish trk.   17
987 ARDNACROSS [5] (J Douglas Home) 2-8-11 J Matthias 13/8 FAV: 00242: Led 2f out: best
in 831 (stiff track).   12
1012 PIALUCI [4] (B Preece) 2-9-0 N Howe 15/2: 00003: Prom, ev ch: little form.   10
--   SLEEPLINE FOR BEDS [2] (R Holder) 2-9-0 A Dicks(7) 10/1: 4: Never nearer on debut:
should stay 6f plus.   07
728 SOHAMS TAYLOR [1] 2-9-0(BL) P Waldron 3/1: 0000: Bl first time: made much.   00
5 ran   1½,1½,½,4.   (W J Blakey)   R Stubbs Middleham, Yorks

1169 LIFE LEADS THE FIELD H'CAP (0-50) 3YO   £2865   7f   Good/Firm 22 +16 Fast   [50]

747 PULHAM MILLS [6] (E Eldin) 3-8-0(bl) K King(7) 16/1: 0-00001: 3 b c Morston -
Millimeter (Ribocco): Made ev yd, holding on by a hd in a fast run 3yo h'cap at Warwick
June 21: first success: placed several times previously: eff at 7f, stays 1m: seems best
forcing the pace on a sharpish trk on fast grnd.   34
1001 SATIAPOUR [12] (R Johnson Houghton) 3-9-2(vis) S Cauthen 2/1 FAV: 3-20122: Chall final
1f: just btn: in grand form: see 1001, 844: stays 7f.   49
776 NIHAD [13] (B Hanbury) 3-8-10 A Geran(7) 16/1: 0-4003: Ran on well final 1f: gd
effort: should find a h'cap: see 213: acts on gd/firm & yld.   40
929 SAFEERA [14] (M Jarvis) 3-9-7 N Ives 11/2: 411-034: Prom, ev ch: stays 7f: see 929.   47
886 SEQUESTRATOR [7] 3-8-2 R Lappin(6) 16/1: 000-000: Al there: see 886.   28
907 HAITI MILL [8] 3-8-3 A Mackay 5/1: 03-0440: Never nearer: needs 1m? see 309.   29
567 BAKERS DOUGH [11] 3-8-2 P Waldron 9/2: 011-000: Made no show: yet to hit form:
winning 2yo at Wolverhampton (nursery) at Bath (seller): eff at 7f: acts on gd & yld grnd
and a gall trk.   00

847	Full Of Life [10] 8-12	940	Klosterbrau [5] 7-7(5oh)
--	Our Children [3] 7-7(6oh)	762	Asticour [4] 9-7
451	Northern Mel·dy [9] 8-4(bl)(2ow)	954	Helvick Bay [1] 7-11(1ow)
765	Kitty Clare [2] 8-1		

14 ran   hd,1½,1½,hd,hd,2½   (P E Mills)   E Eldin Newmarket

1170 E.B.F. WARWICK OAKS 3YO   £4667   1m 4f   Good/Firm 22 +05 Fast

509 SPUN GOLD [3] (P Cole) 3-8-10 T Quinn 7/4: 14-041: 3 b f Thatch - Colourful
(Busted): Very useful filly: made ev yd, holding the odds-on Magic Slipper by ¾L in 3 runner
Warwick Oaks at Warwick June 21: earlier fin a respectable 4th to Mill On The Floss in the Oaks
Trial at Lingfield: first time out in '85 won at York: very eff at 12f, should stay further:
acts on gd & firm grnd & will win more races.   70
*862 MAGIC SLIPPER [2] (H Cecil) 3-8-10S Cauthen 4/6 FAV: -212: Heavily bckd: al 2nd:
ran very well and met a good one here: stays 12f: see 862.   65
*888 AL UQ HUWAAN [4] (H T Jones) 3-8-10 A Murray 9/1: 0314-13: Stiff task: eased when btn.   45
3 ran   ¾,12   (Conley Properties Ltd)   P Cole Whatcombe, Oxon

1171 DAILY EXPRESS HANDICAP (0-35) 3YO+   £1532   5f   Good/Firm 22 -33 Slow   [33]

977 MUSIC MACHINE [18] (P Haslam) 5-9-4 J Scally(7) 2/1 FAV: -044041: 5 b g Record Token-
Sodance (So Blessed): Well bckd and made ev yd, comfortably in a h'cap at Warwick June 21:
in gd form in '85, winning at Pontefract, Warwick & Ripon: in '84 won at Ayr: very eff at
5f, stays 6f: acts on any grnd & on any trk, though seems best forcing the pace on a
sharpish one.   33
10   MRS SAUGA [13] (M Eckley) 4-8-7 S Cauthen 14/1: 4000-02: Ran on well final 1f: gd
effort after abs: has been lightly raced & remains a maiden: eff at 5f, stays further: acts
on good/firm.   19
977 HILMAY [4] (W Charles) 4-8-0 R Lappin(4) 20/1: 0030403: Fin well: gd run: see 211.   09
977 SANDITTON PALACE [20] (P Felgate) 3-8-4 T Quinn 16/1: 0-00404: Kept on well final
1f: best in 516 (stakes).   19

855	LONELY STREET [1] 5-9-5 L Johnsey(7) 7/1: 1002-20: Prom, ev ch: btr 855 (6f).		24
+787	MARGAM [7] 3-9-8 N Howe 5/1: 0-310: Never nearer: stiff task: see 787 (6f).		35
1066	FARMER JOCK [2] 4-8-13(vis) W Wharton 10/1: 0-00030: Early speed: btr 1066.		00

855	Mister March [10] 7-10			1086	Jackie Blair [16] 9-3(bl)
620	Foxy Dyke [15] 9-1	986	Velocidad [11] 8-12	507	Choristers Dream [3] 8-7(bl)
--	Pillowing [5] 8-7	418	Miss Metal Woods [19] 8-2		
--	Sweet Salora [9] 8-0	760	Ardent Partner [12] 7-13		
910	Ever So Sharp [17] 7-13			--	Seago [6] 7-13
*726	Kelly Lindo [8] 7-13				
19 ran	¾,1,½,¾,shhd	(A Piller)		P Haslam Newmarket	

1172 NEWS OF THE WORLD 2YO STAKES   £684   7f   Good/Firm 22 -29 Slow

915 TOUGH N GENTLE [1] (L Piggott) 2-8-11 T Ives 4/5 FAV: 321: 2 b c Ginistrelli -
Added Attraction (Double Jay): Useful colt: made almost all, responding well to pressure for
a hd success in a 2yo stakes at Warwick June 21: suited by 7f: acts on gd/firm & yld grnd
and on any trk: genuine.   49
662 TRIPLE ENTENTE [3] (H Candy) 2-8-11 S Cauthen 6/4: 32: Chall final 1f: just btn:
stays 7f: acts on gd/firm & yld/soft: see 662.   48
-- BROTHER PATRICK [5] (L Piggott) 2-8-11 B Crossley 15/2: 3: Stable mate of winner:
promising debut: full brother to winning 3yo Just David & will be well suited by further
than 7f: acts on gd/firm & should have no trouble finding a race.   39
965 SKRAGGS PLUS TWO [2] (D Leslie) 2-8-11 T Quinn 100/1: 0004: Rank outsider: never
nearer: no form previously & possibly flattered by this rating: probably stays 7f: acts
on gd/firm & a sharpish trk.   29
531 ITS VARADAN [6] 2-8-11 J Matthias 100/1: 000: Prom, fdd: see 531.   23
685 HIGH CHATEAU [4] 2-8-11 N Howe 25/1: 00: Al rear: bred to stay middle distances.   19
6 ran   hd,3,2½,1½,1   (Sidney L Port)   L Piggott Newmarket

1173 DAILY MIRROR HANDICAP (0-50)   £2629   1m 2f   Good/Firm 22 +05 Fast   [49]

*943 VAGUE MELODY [6] (L Piggott) 4-8-13(7ex) T Ives 5/2: 4-23011: 4 ch g Vaigly Great-
Shangara (Credo): In fine form, led final 1f & was sn clear, readily in a h'cap at Warwick
June 21: last time out won an amateur riders event on this track and goes well here: in
'85 was trained by G Balding to win a h'cap at Leicester: eff 1m, stays 10f well: acts on
firm & soft & on any trk.   45
-- TEST OF TIME [1] (M Prescott) 5-9-7 G Duffield 14/1: 03300-2: Friendless in mkt:
made much: gd seasonal debut: lightly raced in '85, best effort when 3rd to Iroko in a
valuable h'cap at Sandown: in '84 won at Newmarket: eff at 10f, acts on gd & firm grnd.   46
1079 MONCLARE TROPHY [7] (P Bevan) 7-7-12 N Howe 16/1: 0010003: Never nearer: fair
effort: see 420.   21
919 LONDON CONTACT [2] (M Pipe) 3-7-9 B Crossley 2/1 FAV: 133-004: Well bckd: nearest
finish: better 919.   29
964 ABSENT LOVER [3] 5-9-2 I Johnson 10/3: 240-040: Chall over 1f out: see 964.   33
700 PARIS MATCH [5] 4-8-12 S Cauthen 20/1: 0000000: Little form this season: see 245.   29
686 LYSANDER [8] 4-8-13(BL) A Murray 10/1: 1-02-00: Fdd final 2f: formerly trained by
H Cecil, being lightly raced on the Flat: winning 2yo at Leicester: stays 10f: best form
to date on soft ground.   00
-- Gallois Bosquet [4] 7-10
8 ran   2½,½,1½,1½,shhd   (A Simmons)   L Piggott Newmarket

AYR   Saturday June 21st   Lefthand Galloping Track

1174 BELLEISLE STAKES 2YO   £2523   5f   Good 70 +14 Fast

*870 CROFTERS CLINE [4] (J H Wilson) 2-9-5 Julie Bowker[7] 2/1: 0111: 2 b c Crofter -
Modena (Sassafras): Very useful & speedy 2yo: completed his hat trick with comfortable pillar
to-post success in a very fast run 2yo minor race at Ayr June 21: also made all in minor
races at Ripon & Beverley previously: equally eff at 5 & 6f: acts on firm & gd grnd & on
any trk: does well forcing the pace: should win more races.   62
571 SCOTTISH FLING [3] (J S Wilson) 2-8-11 E Turner[7] 13/2: 33302: Most 2nd after abs:
seems to act on gd & yld: see 242.   42
515 WHISTLING WONDER [1] (M Brittain) 2-9-2 M Wigham 20/1: 2104303: Abs: never closer:
see 94: acts on good and soft.   40
-- CRAIGENDARROCH [6] (J S Wilson) 2-8-11 Gay Kelleway[5] 25/1: 4: Stable companion of
the 2nd, kept on: first foal of a winning sprint 2yo: should improve.   31
304 THE GRANITTON [5] 2-9-2 K Bradshaw[5] 12/1: 100: Early speed after abs: twice below 133 27
236 PRINCEGATE [2] 2-8-11 M Birch 20/1: 00: Hmpd start, never in it: first foal of a
winning sprinter: very speedily bred.   07
*646 INSHIRAH [7] 2-8-13 R Hills 6/4 fav: 10: Missed break, not recover: see 646.   00
7 ran   4,2½,1½,3,5   (D Beresford)   J H Wilson Tarleton, Lancs

1175 ROMAN WARRIOR STAKES 2YO   £1972   7f   Good 70 -27 Slow

979 KING BALLADEER [3] (G P Gordon) 2-9-0 G Duffield 15/8 fav: 031: 2 b c Dominion -
Moonlight Serenade (Crooner): Impr colt: justified strong support, forging clear final 1f in
a 2yo minor race at Ayr June 21: cost 28,000 gns: well suited by 7f, sure to stay 1m &
probably further: acts on gd grnd.   53
804 MEBHIL [1] (P Kelleway) 2-9-0 Gay Kelleway[5] 5/2: 332: Led briefly 2f out, btr 804, 614.   41
741 BE MY PROSPECT [4] (I M Bell) 2-9-0 J Quinn[5] 11/1: 03: Kept on well & is clearly
impr: half brother to the useful Verdant Boy: stays 7f, will be suited by 1m: sure to impr
& win a maiden in the North.   40
1050 BEAU BENZ [8] (M H Easterby) 2-9-0 M Birch 20/1: 0004: No real dngr: seems to stay 7f.   35
864 SKY CAT [6] 2-9-0 Julie Bowker[7] 20/1: 400: Under press when hmpd final 1f: see 694.   31
--   SOMBRERO GOLD [7] 2-9-0 K Bradshaw[5] 20/1: 0: Slow start but some late hdway: half
brother to 3 winners incl '84 juvenile Storm Burst:
should improve.   27
944 PINE AWAY [2] 2-8-11 N Connorton 3/1: 30: Wknd into 8th: much btr 944 (6f).   00
1069 Bejant Skite [9] 9-0(BL)   **-- Friends For Life** [5] 9-0
9 ran   4,½,2½,1½,1½   (Mr A Anderson)   G P Gordon Newmarket

1176 I.C.I. PETROL H'CAP 3YO+ 0-60   £3798   1m   Good 70 -05 Slow   [46]

668 WINDPIPE [6] (J Watts) 8-9-4 N Connorton 9/2: 040-041: 8 ch g Leander - Whiffle
(Kings Troop): Returned to his best, leading dist comfortably in quite a valuable h'cap at
Ayr June 21: lightly raced & failed to win in '85: in '84 won at Ayr (3) & Newcastle (2):
very eff over 7f/1m: acts on firm & soft & on any trk though a course winner 5 times at Ayr.   46
594 DARNIT [5] (E Weymes) 4-8-12 E Guest[3] 8/1: 00-0002: Came from well behind, not btn
far and is coming into form: should be winning soon: see 310.   38
•815 KNIGHTS SECRET [4] (M H Easterby) 5-9-3 M Birch 9/4 fav: 00-2113: Chall final 1f:
gd effort and is in fine form: see 815.   41
940 ANY BUSINESS [7] (W Musson) 5-8-8 M Wigham 11/2: -000024: Prom thro'out: btr 940 (10f).   29
1047 SHORT SLEEVES [2] 4-9-7 S P Griffiths[5] 9/1: 10-0100: No real threat: best 521 (yld).   37
956 EMERALD EAGLE [1] 5-8-1 R Hills 12/1: 1000300: Clear ldr over 6f: see 79 (heavy).   16
930 VERBARIUM [3] 6-7-13 R Morse[5] 17/2: -232000: No dngr in 7th: see 10, 281.   00
1047 Cane Mill [8] 8-13
8 ran   1,¾,2½,2,½   (Duke of Sutherland)   J Watts Richmond, Yorks

1177 G.A.GROUP H'CAP 3YO+ 0-50   £2515   1m 5f   Good 70 +07 Fast   [40]

805 HIGH TENSION [1] (G P Gordon) 4-9-5 G Duffield 13/8 fav: 044-241: 4 ch g Vitiges -
Montania (Mourne): Heavily bckd & led dist, just scrambling home by a hd in a h'cap at
Ayr June 21: early last season won at Yarmouth & Redcar: very eff over 12/13f: acts on
firm and yielding.   41
883 MILTESCENS [3] (A Jarvis) 3-8-13 R Hills 12/1: 3-10302: Almost gained the day close
home and was clear of rest: fine effort: stays 13f really well: see 357: should win a
h'cap soon.   51
•1052 MOULKINS [5] (J H Wilson) 4-7-9 Julie Bowker[7] 9/2: 0-00013: Led after ½way, fdd
1f out: btr 1052 (more patient tactics).   10
990 WESSEX [6] (N Tinkler) 4-9-1(bl) Kim Tinkler[5] 5/1: 1243134: Ev ch: see 824.   29
869 TREASURE HUNTER [8] 7-9-7 N Day 16/1: 0030-40: Under press thro'out: see 869.   20
686 VERY SPECIAL [7] 4-8-13 R Morse[5] 5/1: 143-030: Led till ½way, much btr 686.   12
824 Campus Boy [2] 7-7(1oh)   **745 New Barnet** [4] 7-11
8 ran   hd,5,½,15,shhd   (Lord Derby)   G P Gordon, Newmarket

1178 LONGHILL MAIDEN STAKES 3YO   £959   1m 2f   Good 70 -29 Slow

806 ASSEER [1] (H Cecil) 3-9-0 N Day 5/4 fav: -001: 3 ch c Northfields - Nagin (Pretense):
Prom colt: led on bit inside final 3f & readily drew clear in a slowly run 3yo maiden at
Ayr June 21: well suited by 10f, looks sure to stay further: acts on firm & gd grnd & on
a gall trk: should make further impr.   57
143 BOYNTON [2] (C Elsey) 3-9-0 N Connorton 25/1: 0004-02: No threat to winner though a
creditable effort after long abs: looks likely to stay beyond 10f: see 143.   45
916 COMANCHERO [5] (C Thornton) 3-9-0 J Bleasdale 5/2: 3-33: Ev ch, btr 916.   40
615 BEAUCLERC [3] (P Kelleway) 3-9-0 Gay Kelleway[5] 16/1: 000-304: Clear ldr 1m: best 427.   28
384 HAWARDEN [4] 3-9-0 R Hills 5/2: -400: Sn dropped out: has twice run badly since 218.   08
--   WHIPCRACKAWAY [6] 3-9-0 M Tebbutt[7] 100/1: -0: Started slowly & never in it:
related to several winners & should impr from this first experience.   00
6 ran   6,3,8,12,12   (Prince A A Faisal)   H Cecil Newmarket

1179 BELMONT H'CAP 3YO 0-35   £1887   1m 2f   Good 70 -61 Slow   [40]

•1079 HARD AS IRON [1] (P Haslam) 3-8-9(5ex) T Williams 85/40 fav: 000-411: 3 b g Ardoon -
Prancer (Santa Claus): In fine form & was gaining second win in 5 days, getting up close
home (despite hanging badly under press) in a very slowly run 3yo h'cap at Ayr June 21:
easy winner of similar h'cap at Nottingham June 16: very lightly raced previously: eff at
1m, well suited by 10f: acts on firm or gd grnd.   28

919 CRAMMING [6] (W Musson) 3-9-1 M Wigham 9/4: 0-12302: Led under press dist, just
caught in a close fin: see 318: consistent sort who acts on gd & soft.   33
•740 SPRING FLIGHT [5] (A Jarvis) 3-8-2 R Hills 5/1: 000-013: Well bckd, kept on strongly,
not btn far: in fine form & stays 10f: see 740.   19
935 ULTRESSA [4] (S Norton) 3-8-2 J Quinn[5] 14/1: 00-0004: Made most: rated much higher 93518
690 TAYLORMADE BOY [3] 3-9-7 D Leadbitter[5] 11/2: 0-31230: Prom much: twice below 553. 22
843 FLEET FOOTED [2] 3-9-2(BL) G Duffield 9/2: 04-0020: Bl first time, sn btn: btr 843.   15
6 ran   hd,$\frac{1}{4}$,$\frac{1}{2}$,15,1$\frac{1}{2}$ (Martin Wickens)   P Haslam Newmarket

---

PONTEFRACT   Monday June 23rd   Lefthanded Undulating Track

Official Going Given as Firm

1180 JUVENILE MAIDEN AUCTION 2YO   £1065   6f   Good 47 –08 Slow

136 MASTER POKEY [6] (M W Easterby) 2-9-0 M Birch 11/2: 01: 2 br g Uncle Pokey –
September Fire (Firestreak): Landed a gamble, al prom & despite not getting a clear run,
gained the day close home in a 2yo maiden auction race at Pontefract June 23: cheaply bought
gelding who is well suited by 6f & a sound surface: sure to stay 7f plus.   38
1090 FALDWYN [9] (T Bill) 2-8-11 N Carlisle 12/1: 3302: Led 1f out, just caught & 3L clear
of rest: consistent type who should find a small event soon: see 1090.   34
818 DOHTY BABY [8] (M W Easterby) 2-8-11 K Hodgson 25/1: 03: Came from off the pace,
strong finish: suited by 6f (dam stayed long distances): sure to be suited by further:
acts on good grnd.   26
1025 SURELY GREAT [3] (D Thom) 2-8-11 G Duffield 8/15 FAV: 02024: Led after 3f, odds on
disappointment: much btr 1025 (5f).   24
1059 PREMIUM GOLD [4] 2-8-11 T Ives 25/1: 430000: Early leader: probably stays 6f:
acts on good and soft.   22
332 TAKE EFFECT [1] 2-9-0 K Darley 10/1: 33300: Abs: no dngr: btr 136 (soft).   10
404 HAZELS GIRL [5] 2-8-11 R Morse(5) 10/1: 23040: Abs since btr 404 (5f).   00
--   Eppy Marner [2] 8-11   364 Miss Diamante [7] 8-11(VIS)
9 ran   nk,3,$\frac{1}{2}$,$\frac{1}{2}$,6   (Lord Belper)   M W Easterby Sheriff Hutton, Yorks

1181 DEWSBURY SELLING STAKES 2YO   £977   5f   Good 47 –15 Slow

931 MAYBEMUSIC [1] (W Mackie) 2-8-11(vis) N Carlisle 6/1: 001: 2 b c Vaigly Great –
Sunset Song (Song): Nicely bckd when showing impr form to gain a pillar-to-post success in a
2yo seller at Pontefract June 23 (bought in 3,500 gns): half brother to winning 2yo Sing
To Me: acts on firm & gd grnd: eff over 5f with forcing tactics. wears a visor.   30
1100 PERTAIN [6] (W Wharton) 2-8-11 I Johnson 5/2 FAV: 040022: Chall dist, no extra: see 1100. 20
1100 ROSE DUET [4] (D Barron) 2-8-13 T Ives 9/2: 001003: Prom thro'out: see 711.   18
•939 FANTINE [3] (N Tinkler) 2-8-11(bl) Kim Tinkler(5) 11/4: 0044214: Came from behind:
needs 6f? see 939.   17
913 SOUND AS A POUND [10] 2-8-11 N Connorton 13/2: 000: Prom much: first signs of form   05
632 GUNSHIP [5] 2-8-11 G Duffield 8/1: 00: Early speed: dam a winning sprint 2yo.   00
858 WILLYS NIECE [2] 2-8-8 S Webster 10/1: 00: No threat in 8th: half sister to useful
'81 2yo Mosswern.   00
1012 LATE PROGRESS [9] 2-8-8 M Fry 10/1: -000000: Dsptd lead over 3f: wore bl in 1012.   00
905 Dear Dolly [7] 8-8   1012 Bootham Lad [8] 8-11
10 ran   3,1,$\frac{1}{2}$,4,4   (M D Marshall)   W Mackie Derby Sudbury

1182 CSL TRAILER HIRE HCAP 3YO+ 0-50   £2641   6f   Good 47 +15 Fast   [45]

1037 BROWN BEAR BOY [4] (R Armstrong) 4-9-1 Pat Eddery 9/2: -023301: 4 b c San Feliou –
Gabriele (Protanto): After several placings, gained a deserved success, leading under press
final 1f in quite a fast run h'cap at Pontefract June 23: early in '85 won at Cagnes:
fair 2yo winning at Ripon: btr suited by 6f than 5f & stays 1m: acts on gd/firm & yld going.   42
1120 MARY MAGUIRE [2] (D Chapman) 9-8-11 D Nicholls 12/1: 0000322: Came from behind, fin
well & should be winning soon: see 306.   36
628 PHILSTAR [6] (A Balding) 5-8-1 A Mackay 20/1: 00-0003: Tried to make all: returning
to form: winner twice in 7 days at Edinburgh in July '85: best form at 5f on firm or gd
grnd in bl: loves Edinburgh.   22
478 EXAMINATION [9] (A Bailey) 3-8-8(bl) P Bloomfield 11/2: 0-12104: Abs: kept on: see 340.   38
881 SHARLIES WIMPY [1] 7-9-7 M Hindley(3) 11/4 FAV: 00-0240: Slow start, btr 687.   39
-890 GODS SOLUTION [10] 5-8-10(bl) T Ives 7/1: -104020: Ev ch: see 42, 890.   25
1093 ROSIE DICKINS [8] 4-8-2(bl)(1ow) W Ryan 10/1: 2224030: No extra under press final
1f, fin 8th: see 124.   00
1001 WEBSTERS FEAST [7] 3-8-3 R Wernham 7/1 : 0-00000: Well bckd, wknd 2f out: winner
of early events at Salisbury & Pontefract in '85: best form at 5f on firm grnd.   00
936 Tiddlyeyetye [3] 7-7(bl)(2oh)   863 Trentullo Blue [5] 7-7
1066 Pokerfayes [11] 7-7(bl)(1oh)
11 ran $\frac{1}{2}$,1$\frac{1}{2}$,nk,$\frac{1}{2}$,1   (F Northcott)   R Armstrong Newmarket

1183 PONTEFRACT CUP HANDICAP 4YO+ 0-35   £1741   2m 2f   Good 47 –02 Slow   [26]

-- ARBOR LANE [2] (R Boss) 5-9-7 E Guest(3) 16/1: 30440-1: 5 b m Wolverlife – Suburb's
Queen (Levanter): Made a winning seasonal reapp, leading 3f out under press in a h'cap at
Pontefract June 23: early in '85 won at Windsor: eff 12f, stays 2m2f really well: acts well
on gd grnd and likes a sharpish, turning track.   27

990 LOVE WALKED IN [3] (W Holden) 5-9-2 R Morse(5) 9/1: 0131042: Prom thro'out: stays
2m2f & acts on gd & soft: see 358.   19

1071 JOIST [6] (M Prescott) 4-9-6(BL) G Duffield 7/1: 0-00243: Bl first time: tried to
make all: see 933.   20

1016 ALFIE DICKINS [10] (R Hollinshead) 8-8-7 W Ryan 8/1: 130-044: Ev ch: see 590.   05

1099 SOUND DIFFUSION [11] 4-9-9(6ex) K Bradshaw(5) 7/2 Co FAV: 0-22100: Prom, wknd and
best 933 (15f).   15

1016 ASCENMOOR [8] 7-8-2 A Proud 10/1: 0000/00: Prom, wknd: see 1016.   00

1058 CHEKA [7] 10-8-12 Pat Eddery 7/2 Co FAV: -201000: Prom much: best 504.   00

*1016 EASY KIN [4] 4-8-7(bl)(3ex) J Quinn(5) 7/2 Co FAV: 0-00010: Btn over ½m out: best 1016. 00

358 Baluchi [9] 8-7(bl)   -- Devil To Play [1] 8-2
10 ran   1½,3,1½,6,nk   (A Papotto)   R Boss Newmarket

1184 PONTEFRACT MAIDEN MILE CHAMPIONSHIP 3YO £2407   1m   Good 47 +01 Fast

822 EAGLE DESTINY [7] (I Balding) 3-9-0 Pat Eddery 11/2: -021: 3 b g Storm Bird –
Club Savoy (Grey Dawn II): Prom gelding: cruised into lead 1f out to win a 3yo maiden at
Pontefract June 23: eff over 1m, should stay further: 2nd on heavy grnd last time but
probably much btr suited by a sounder surface: should impr further & win more races.   55

-- BOLERO MAGIC [12] (H Cecil) 3-9-0 W Ryan 9/4 Jt FAV: -2: Well bckd debutant, kept
on well & is sure to impr: first foal of an unraced dam: eff over 1m & should stay at
least 10f: sure to find a maiden.   52

719 THRESH IT OUT [4] (M Stoute) 3-9-0 M Birch 9/4 Jt FAV: 23-2303: Early ldr, rem. prom.
and ev ch: due a change of luck soon: : see 334.   52

226 PODEROSO [14] (R Boss) 3-9-0 E Guest(3) 20/1: 30-004: Abs: made much: back to the
form he showed in 2 outings as a 2yo: clearly suited by forcing tactics over 1m on gd grnd:
should find a maiden.   50

546 LYPHLAW [13] 3-9-0 G Baxter 9/2: 0-00: Abs: seemed one paced under press: see 546.   42

941 FACTOTUM [11] 3-9-0 M Hills 10/1: 00-00: Prom most: see 941.   34

-- Millracer [9] 8-11   861 Cool Music [10] 8-11   829 Pauls Secret [14] 9-0
-- Norham Castle [6] 9-0   -- Carr Wood [2] 9-0   874 Affaitati [5] 9-0
-- Sybilly [8] 8-11
13 ran   1½,shhd,¾,4,4   (Sheikh Mohammed)   I Balding Kingsclere, Berks

1185 BATLEY HANDICAP STAKES 3YO+ 0-35   £2295   1m 2f Good 47 –04 Slow   [33]

989 AL ZUMURRUD [2] (R Armstrong) 3-8-12 Pat Eddery 1/2 FAV: 00-1221: 3 ch f Be My
Guest – Mey (Canisbay): Comfortably landed the odds leading on bit dist in a 6 runner h'cap
at Pontefract June 23: very consistent this term, winning 3yo h'cap at Wolverhampton first
time out & 2nd in other 2 outings: half sister to several winners: eff over 1m, stays 10f
well: acts on firm & gd grnd.   40

-- GREED [4] (Denys Smith) 5-9-2 D Nicholls 8/1: 00304-2: Ev ch on seasonal debut: failed
to win in '85, the previous season successful at Ripon: eff 1m, stays 10f: acts on firm
& good ground.   24

1024 GOLDEN FANCY [5] (I Vickers) 9-9-10(VIS) R Vickers(7) 5/1: 0000223: Wore a visor for
the first time here, waited with, kept on but no threat: see 142, 1024.   32

-- STRICTLY BUSINESS [6] (R Whitaker) 4-8-0(1ow) D Mckeown 8/1: 0-000-4: Led after 6f,
no extra final 1f: showed nothing in 2 early season outings in '85: best form in the past over
sprint distances.   04

869 SOUND WORK [3] 4-7-9 L Charnock 12/1: 0-00000: Chall 2f out, wknd: no form this term
but winner at Newcastle, Pontefract & Ayr in '85: best form around 10f though seems to
acts on any going.   00

1054 NUGOLA [1] 4-8-6 M Beecroft 25/1: 0-00000: Led 6f: see 789.   00

6 ran   1½,shhd,2½,5,5   (Hamdan Al-Maktoum)   R Armstrong Newmarket

1186 LEVY BOARD APPRENTICE STAKES 4YO+   £1027   1m   Good/Firm23 –20 Slow

265 ROYAL HALO [7] (G Harwood) 5-9-3 S Hill 1/1 fav: 234-201: 5 b h Halo – Lady Gordon
(Royal Levee): Returned after an abs leading dist comfortably in an app race at Brighton
June 23: failed to win in '85 the previous season successful at Kempton: seems equally eff
at 1m/10f: acts on fast & soft going & on any trk.   35

-- ASH CREEK [17] (T Casey) 7-9-3 P Mcentee 25/1: 34002/2: First outing on the Flat in
this country but successful on the level in Ireland in '84 on 3 occasions: best form
around 1m/9f on fast grnd: also a winner over hurdles in Ireland.   23

1106 HARBOUR BAZAAR [18] (M Chapman) 6-8-3(vis) J Carter 16/1: 0-04203: Tried to make all.   08

992 IDEOLIGIA [15] (A Hide) 4-8-0(bl) P Brette 14/1: 20-0004: Al prom: see 992.   05

943 TAFFYS PRIDE [8] 4-8-0(bl) D Williams 50/1: 0000-00: Never closerr: placed once in
Ireland from 12 outings last season : stays at least 9f.   00
176 BOLD CONNECTION [10] 6-9-3 S Hibble[5] 6/1: 200-000: Mkt drifter after abs: see 176.   16
176 KILIMANJARO BOB [5] 4-8-3 C Barnfather 9/1: 4230-00: Long abs: prom much, fin 8th:
a maiden who was placed most outings last season & seems short of fin pace: stays 10f:
best on firm or gd grnd.   00
812 MISS MONROE [1] 4-8-0 R Perham 9/2: 3244-00: Close up 6f: lightly raced in '85,
placed in 4 or 5 outings: eff over 1m/10f on gd or firm grnd: rated 35 in '85.   00
851 Assail [13] 9-3   -- Caliph [12] 9-3   727 Turcy Boy [3] 9-3
620 Charisma Music [6] 8-0   -- Neocene [2] 8-1(1ow)
1068 Roman Track [9] 8-0   842 Oeil De Tigre [14] 8-3(bl)
15 ran   4,½,hd,3,shhd   (Mrs Doris Campbell)   G Harwood Pulborough, Sussex

1187 BEVENDEAN MAIDEN FILLIES STAKES 2YO   £959   6f   Good/Firm 23 +05 Fast

-- STRATHBLANE [9] (J Dunlop) 2-8-11 W Carson 12/1: 1: 2 ch f Castle Keep - Mother
Brown (Candy Cane): Promising filly: first time out, came from behind to lead near fin in
quite a fast run 2yo fillies maiden at Brighton June 23: both sire & dam stayed middle dists well:
Macarthurs Head and to a couple of other winners: both sire & dam stayed middle dists well:
eff over 6f, sure to be much btr suited by 7f plus: acts on fast grnd.   53
-- LINGERING [6] (J Winter) 2-8-11 W R Swinburn 5/1: 2: Looked the only winner at the
dist, caught close home but well clear of rest: fine debut from this half sister to winning
sprinter Woodfold: may prove best around sprint dists: acts on fast grnd: should find a
maiden without much trouble.   52
722 SYSTEMS GO [2] (G P Gordon) 2-8-11 J Reid 16/1: 03: Outpcd final 1f: impr filly who
is quite speedily bred & seems well at home on fast going.   37
-- RUN LITTLE LADY [11] (H Cecil) 2-8-11 S Cauthen 8/11 fav: 4: Odds on debutant, ev
ch: evidently expected to do rather btr than this and is worth another chance: should
stay beyond 6f.   28
999 SEULEMENT [3] 2-8-11 J Williams 5/1: 30: Never closer and possibly unsuited by course:
better 999 (gall trk).   26
834 YAVARRO [7] 2-8-11 P Cook 25/1: 000: Twice below 482 (5f, yld).   20
722 Shuttlecock Girl [10] 8-11   482 Downsview Lady [4] 8-11
818 Prodigious Lady [8] 8-11   848 Julia Springs [5] 8-11
10 ran   hd,6,3,¾,2½,1   (A Struthers)   J Dunlop Arundel, Sussex

1188 PEACEHAVEN HANDICAP 4YO+ 0-35   £3135   1m 2f   Good/Firm 23 No Time Taken[34]

1109 THE GAMES UP [9] (P Haslam) 5-9-8(5ex) T Williams 5/1: 0-44101: 5 b g Cawston's Clown -
Mandetta (Mandamus): In fine form at present and defied a 5lbs penalty in style when
sprinting 5L clear in the final 1f to win a h'cap at Brighton June 23: comfortable winner of
similar h'cap at Warwick June 7: failed to win in '85: well suited by 10f nowadays: acts
on soft, does well on fast going: runs well on a turning trk though probably acts on any.   40
984 MARSH HARRIER [12] (A Moore) 5-9-0 P Cook 15/2: 11-0002: Chall 1f out, outpcd but
best effort this season: could win soon: see 709.   24
1079 FORGIVING [3] (B Stevens) 4-8-3 W Carson 20/1: 00-0403: Ev ch: best effort this term. 11
*750 REDDEN [15] (M Bolton) 8-9-7 S Cauthen 7/2 fav: 4000-14: Kept on under press: see 750. 29
943 KARNATAK [14] 5-8-2 M Roberts 10/1: --0-030: No threat: flattered 943?   06
976 TIMBER MERCHANT [10] 5-9-6 T Quinn 12/1: 0304-00: Led str, fdd: lightly raced in '85,
placed twice from 5 outings: in '84 won at Warwick: possibly best over 1m: acts on firm.   22
940 LEONIDAS [8] 8-9-3 W R Swinburn 10/1: 0100-00: Fin 7th: C/D winner here last season:
best form with front running tactics on firm grnd (unsuited by soft): likes a sharp trk.   00
750 MARSOOM [4] 4-8-3 D Mckay 8/1: 0-00020: Much btr 750 (C/D).   00
1079 MINUS MAN [2] 8-7-11 M L Thomas 11/2: 0-00030: Ran poorly: see 710.   00
1165 Sweet Andy [1] 7-7(2oh)   -- Sparkler Spirit [13] 7-11
976 Heathgriff [7] 8-2   1165 Trumps [6] 7-9   341 True Weight [5] 8-12
1056 Porto Irene [11] 7-8
15 ran   5,1½,hd,2½,1   (Brandon Chase)   P Haslam Newmarket

1189 BRIGHTON MILE CHALL.H'CAP 3YO+ 0-60   £4666   1m   Good/Firm 23 No Time Taken[34]

976 SAMS WOOD [6] (M Tompkins) 5-8-12 R Cochrane 10/1: 0000-01: 5 b g Jolly Good -
Dust Sheet (Silly Season): Al prom & responded gamely to press to force his head in front
on the line in quite a valuable h'cap at Brighton June 23: in '85 was trained by T Fairhurst
to win h'caps at Nottingham & Pontefract: eff at 1m, stays 10f: acts on firm & yld: does
well at this time of year & could win again.   46
*1018 GRANNYS BANK [3] (W Hastings Bass) 4-8-6 W Carson 6/5 fav: 3211-12: Led 2f out, just
caught and is in fine form: see 1018.   39
1018 GOLDEN SLADE [1] (M Mccourt) 4-8-6 A Tucker[7] 10/1: 4-00133: Ran another fine race
on her fav. trk: see 762.   36
1041 EVERY EFFORT [5] (R Holder) 4-8-0 S Dawson[3] 5/1: -401D34: Twice below 930.   22
775 BLAZE OF TARA [4] 5-9-1 W R Swinburn 25/1: 42-0000: Led briefly ½way: placed in 3
out of 4 outings last season but has failed to run up to that form this term so far: stays
10f: best form in blinkers.   34
881 GURTEEN BOY [9] 4-8-7 L Jones[5] 8/1: 1-00000: Led briefly 3f out: see 453.   24

930 Portogon [7] 9-3		433 Really Honest [2] 9-10		
1018 Nicoridge [10] 9-3		881 Dogmatic [8] 9-5		
10 ran hd,1½,4,1½,1,shhd		(H H Wright)	M Tompkins Newmarket	

1190 MOULESCOOMB SELLING STAKES 2YO   £1702   6f   Good/Firm 23 -33 Slow

*763 GOOD TIME GIRL [4] (R Hannon) 2-8-8 A Mcglone 5/6 fav: 011: 2 b f Good Times –
Inca Girl (Tribal Chief): Gaining her 2nd successive win, leading 1f out under press in a
2yo seller at Brighton June 23 (bought in 2,300 gns): won over 5f here May 29: suited by
fast going and a sharpish, undulating trk: stays 6f well.   20
852 BALLANTRAE [6] (R Voorspuy) 2-8-8 M Roberts 33/1: 002: Early ldr, kept on & showed
a little impr here on first venture into selling company: cheaply bought, sprint bred filly.   10
1088 ROAN REEF [3] (N Macauley) 2-8-11(bl) Gay Kelleway[5] 13/2: 0343: Led ½way, outpcd
final 1f: see 1088.   13
--   LADY SUNDAY SPORT [1] (N Callaghan) 2-8-8 S Cauthen 3/1: 4: Seemed unsuited by the
fast grnd but made some late hdway & should impr for the experience: stays 6f.   08
--   THE CHIPPENHAM MAN [7] 2-8-11 R Cochrane 12/1: 0: No threat: first foal of a maid.dam.05
988 KAMSTAR [2] 2-8-8 T Quinn 33/1: 0000: Prom much: appears moderate.   00
1083 Pullandese [8] 8-8(bl)   345 Prince Mac [5] 8-11
8 ran   4,nk,½,3,1½   (D O'Brien)   R Hannon Marlborough, Wilts

1191 SHEEPCOTE H'CAP 3YO ONLY 0-35   £2197   6f   Good/Firm 23 +08 Fast   [37]

1033 HELAWE [13] (J Winter) 3-9-7(bl) W R Swinburn 13/2: 00-0301: 3 ch g Last Fandango –
Pigmy (Assagai): Ran on well under press to forge ahead in the final 1f of a quite fast
run 3yo h'cap at Brighton June 23: most consistent in '85, winning a nursery at Redcar: eff
over 5f but seems btr suited by 6f nowadays: best form on firm or gd grnd and seems to act
on any trk: wears blinkers.   40
910 MUSIC REVIEW [2] (W Jarvis) 3-8-11 R Cochrane 9/4 fav: 000-22: Chall under strong
driving final 1f: see 910 (5f).   24
*871 SUMMERHILL SPRUCE [14] (E Eldin) 3-9-6 G King[7] 5/1: 00-0013: Never closer and is
in fine form: see 871.   31
1066 TAYLOR OF SOHAM [16] (D Leslie) 3-9-0 G Starkey 14/1: 3403004: Prom, ev ch: see 38.   25
845 NANOR [12] 3-7-13 P Cook 12/1: 0300000: Waited with, gd late prog: see 340.   08
--   PERSIAN BAZAAR [4] 3-8-4 T Williams 33/1: 10000-0: Should benefit from seasonal debut:
narrow winner of a Lingfield seller in '85: very eff over 5f on gd grnd.   13
910 Left Right [7] 8-8(bl)   760 Fancy Pages [11] 8-6
886 Delta Rose [1] 8-10   637 Athletes Week [10] 8-0
1001 Lydia Languish [6] 9-4   952 Light Hills [8] 9-4
111 Harmony Bowl [9] 8-13   658 Divine Fling [3] 8-12   1066 Sequestration [5] 8-4
15 ran   2½,1,shhd,2,hd   (A R C Finn)   J Winter Newmarket

1192 HOVE MAIDEN FILLIES STAKES 3YO   £959   1m 4f   Good/Firm 23 -06 Slow

955 HUSNAH [8] (L Cumani) 3-8-11 R Guest 14/1: 02-3331: 3 b f Caro – Lovely Lovely
(Carlemont): Fin well under press to lead final 100 yds in a 3yo fillies maiden at Brighton
June 23: had looked rather one-paced previously over 10f & was clearly suited by todays 12f
trip: half sister to 4 winners: suited by firm or gd grnd & seems to act on any trk.   52
862 NO DOUBLET [10] (B Hills) 3-8-11 P Cook 8/1: 33-32: Made most, not btn far &
stays 12f: see 862.   50
991 STRIKE HOME [4] (M Stoute) 3-8-11 W R Swinburn 5/2 fav: -023: Uneasy fav. not btn
far in a close fin: see 991.   50
--   JOLIE PELOUSE [1] (G Harwood) 3-8-11 G Starkey 11/4: -4: Nicely bckd debutant, no
extra final 1f but should benefit from the race: likely to stay 12f.   40
744 ENZELIYA [7] 3-8-11 S Cauthen 12/1: 3-440: Led ½way till 3f out: rated 50 in 581 (10f).   37
479 KRISWICK [2] 3-8-11 A Clark 7/1: -00: Abs: no threat: see 479.   37
549 TRANSCENDENCE [9] 3-8-11 B Rouse 5/1: -020: Ill at east on this fast grnd: much btr 549. 00
966 ALCHAASIBIYEH [3] 3-8-11 A Murray 10/1: 33-00: Prom, fdd quickly: non-stayer: see 966.   00
581 On The Agenda [6] 8-11   351 Deruta [5] 8-11
10 ran   1½,shhd,10,2,1   (Sheikh Mohammed)   L Cumani Newmarket

Official Going Given as Firm: Last 3f Good/Firm

1193 PATTINGHAM FILLIES STAKES 3YO   £959   1m 1f   Good 46 +04 Fast

980 RATTLE ALONG [7] (P Walwyn) 3-8-11 Paul Eddery 20/1: 0-01: 3 b f Tap On Wood –
Eulalie (Queens Hussar): Impr filly: denied a clear run tho' fin strongly to lead close
home in quite a fast run 3yo fillies stakes at Wolverhampton June 23: only ran once last
term: eff over 9f & will stay further: acts on gd grnd & on a gall trk.   50
372 QUEEN OF BATTLE [4] (M Ryan) 3-8-11 P Robinson 14/1: 0-002: Fair abs though always
front rank: led 2f out till caught death: easily her best effort to date: well suited by
9f on gd grnd: acts on a gall trk: should win soon.   48

379

539 WHILE IT LASTS [3] (L Cumani) 3-8-11 P Hamblett 6/1: -333: Al up there: another gd
effort and seems equally eff on fast grnd: see 338.   42
941 ROHILA [1] (R Johnson Houghton) 3-8-11 P Hutchinson 33/1: -04: Made much: hmpd inside
dist: half sister to several middle dist winners & will stay further in time: acts on gd
grnd & on a gall trk.   39
-- PSYLLA [13] 3-8-11 N Day 3/1: -0: Nicely bckd debutant: impr to hold ev ch below dist,
not qkn: half sister to the smart miler Prismatic: acts on gd grnd & on a gall trk: likely
to improve.   38
764 GIRDLE NESS [9] 3-8-11 B Crossley 16/1: 0-400: Ran to her best: see 500.   29
937 SHEER LUCK [8] 3-8-11 J Matthias 7/1: 04-00: Active in mkt: fin 9th: see 937.   00
980 AIRCRAFTIE [15] 3-8-11 B Thomson 5/2 FAV: -030: Well bckd though never reached ldrs:
ran btr over 10f in 980.   00

862	Linash [6] 8-11	941	Welsh Pageantry [11] 8-11
--	April Fox [2] 8-11	1080	Glazepta Final [12] 8-11(BL)
--	Quite A Quest [10] 8-11	--	Sly Wheeler [14] 8-11

14 ran   nk,2½,1½,hd,3   (O F Waller)   P Walwyn Lambourn, Berks

1194 DAWLEY MAIDEN FILLIES STAKES 2YO   £996   5f   Good 46 –36 Slow

350 SPANISH SKY [2] (N Vigors) 2-8-11 R Curant 3/1: 01: 2 b f King Of Spain – Buttermilk
Sky (Midsummer Night II): Again well bckd & ran on strongly to lead inside dist in a 2yo
fillies maiden at Wolverhampton June 23: cost 8,400 gns as a yearling and is a half brother
to middle dist winner Glideaway: well suied by this minimum trip & will stay further: acts
on gd & yld grnd & on a gall trk: likes to go up with the pace.   35
1030 POLLYS SONG [7] (B Hills) 2-8-11 B Thomson 9/4 FAV: 02: Switched & fin strongly:
clearly has plenty of pace & should go one btr soon: acts on gd & firm grnd: see 1030. 30
-- NON FICTION [9] (K Brassey) 2-8-11 N Adams 7/1: 3: Made most on racecourse debut:
battled on well & should be placed to win: half sister to winning miler Dreyfus: acts on
gd grnd & on a gall trk.   28
905 NEEDWOOD NUT [3] (B Morgan) 2-8-11 B Crossley 14/1: 04: Al front rank: on the up
grade: see 905.   24
848 EASTERN PRINCESS [1] 2-8-11 M Wigham 20/1: 00: Showed impr here: sister to a couple
of modest winners: acts on gd grnd & on a gall trk.   16
-- PENBREASY [6] 2-8-11 S Perks 25/1: 0: Active in mkt on debut: no threat.   08
852 CHEVELEY CHOICE [5] 2-8-11 P Waldron 4/1: 00: Fin 7th: nicely bckd: btr in 852 (6f). 00

| 965 | Avenmore Star [4] 8-11 | -- | Gone For It [8] 8-11 |

9 ran   1½,½,1½,3,3,shhd   (Avon Industries Ltd)   N Vigors Upper Lambourn, Berks

1195 FEATHERSTONE SELL.H'CAP 3YO+ 0-25   £776   1m 6f   Good 46 –02 Slow   [18]

1035 ACTION TIME [15] (P Makin) 5-9-13 B Thomson 13/8 FAV: -0U001: 5 ch g Sagaro –
Royal Declaration (Breeders Dream): Was gaining his first win when leading over 3f out,
comfortably in a selling h'cap at Wolverhampton June 23 (sold for 3,000 gns): off the course
last season: well suited by a dist of grnd: acts well on a sound surface & on a gall trk. 26
-- UPLAND GOOSE [16] (P Rohan) 5-8-10 D Nicholls 20/1: 00304/2: Stayed on well on reapp:
maiden who did not race in '85 & seems sure to benefit from this run: stays well: acts on
gd/firm & soft grnd & on a gall trk.   01
783 TRACK MARSHALL [2] (J Davies) 4-9-7 M Wigham 4/1: 00-3223: Again ran well: stays 14f. 12
542 BEAU NAVET [14] (W Turner) 5-8-10 G Dickie 12/1: 4040/04: Bckd at long odds & al
prom: maiden who has been lightly raced in recent seasons: suited by middle distances. 00
-- GWILLIM ENTERPRISE [3] 4-8-11 A Dicks 33/1: -0000-0: Late prog: suited by a test
of stamina: maiden who showed no worthwhile form in a light season in '85.   00
1035 MASTER FRANCIS [12] 4-9-6 N Adams 12/1: 0-00000: No form this term: see 202.   00
993 VERBADING [13] 4-9-1 J G Murray(7) 15/2: 0-02300: Fin 7th: btr over 12f in 783: see 524 00
856 KARAMOUN [1] 5-8-10 P Robinson 10/1: 0-00000: Maiden who has been well btn in all
starts this term.   00

967	Flodabay [5] 8-13(vis)		727	Angies Video [7] 8-8
1071	Cluedo [4] 9-1(bl)	--	Relza Coccinea [6] 9-1(BL)
673	Video [9] 9-4	--	Hong Kong Venture [10] 8-10
--	Thatchit [8] 9-1			

15 ran   4,shhd,3,3,2½   (Action Time Ltd)   P Makin Ogbourne Maisey, Wilts

1196 TIM GORDON MEM.H'CAP 4YO+ 0-50   £2586   5f   Good 46 +02 Fast   [43]

977 FIRST EXPERIENCE [5] (P Felgate) 4-7-12 M Fry 33/1: 000-001: 4 b f Le Johnstan –
The Dupecat (Javelot): Returned to form, broke well & was never hdd in quite a fast run
h'cap at Wolverhampton June 23: won at Warwick last Summer: best form over this minimum trip:
suited by good or faster grnd: acts on any trk.   24
922 DIVISSIMA [10] (G Lewis) 4-8-4 P Waldron 13/2: 0031-02: Chased winner most of way:
gd effort & looks fairly h'capped: narrow winner of a h'cap at Folkestone last backend: half
sister to winning sprinter Eyelet: eff over 5/6f: acts on gd & fast grnd & on any trk. 24
-1101 CELTIC BIRD [4] (A Balding) 6-8-2 A Mackay 3/1: 0-00023: In gd form: see 1101.   20
1037 CREE BAY [7] (J Spearing) 7-10-0 W Carson 4/1: -332004: Never nearer: see 327.   42
1066 VALRACH [9] 4-8-9 S Perks 16/1: 100-000: Best effort this season: won her maiden at
Nottingham last season & possibly btr suited by 6f: best form on gd or faster grnnd.   17

986 SHARAD [6] 6-7-7(10oh) N Adams 33/1: 440-000: No real threat: won at Warwick in
'84 though little worthwhile form last term: best over 5f on gd or faster grnd.   00
1037 SPACEMAKER BOY [2] 6-9-7 N Howe 9/4 FAV: 410032F: Fell after leaving stalls: see 1037. 00
1093 Karens Star [3] 8-8   1131 Russian Winter [1] 7-7(bl)(8oh)
9 ran   1½,¾,1½,2½,hd   (J C Bird)   P Felgate Grimston, Leics

1197 ALDERSLEY MAIDEN STAKES 2YO   £797   7f   Good 46 –40 Slow

965 BILLS HENRY [6] (R Boss) 2-9-0 E Guest(3) 10/1: 01: 2 b g In Fijar – Danaka
(Val De Loir): Clearly benefitted considerably from his recent debut, bckd from 33/1 and
ran on strongly to lead close home in a 2yo maiden at Wolverhampton June 23: brother to a
couple of winners: stays 7f well: acts on gd grnd & on a gall trk.   47
870 STORM HERO [9] (M Dickinson) 2-9-0 R Cochrane 1/1 FAV: 32: Again heavily bckd: went
on 2f out, caught near fin though beat rem decisively & must win soon: stays 7f: acts on a
gall trk: see 870.   46
741 SILVER ANCONA [8] (E Eldin) 2-9-0 A Mackay 5/1: 3433: Never nearer: stays 7f: see 437. 32
--   TOLUCA LAKE [4] (L Piggott) 2-9-0 T Ives 5/1: 4: Attracted some support on debut:
ran green below dist & certain to impr next time: from a gd winner producing family: acts
on gd grnd & on a gall trk.   20
--   CASTLE HEIGHTS [3] 2-9-0 P Tulk 25/1: 0: Late prog on debut: will impr: stays 7f:
half brother to several winners: acts on gd/firm grnd.   08
974 BADOGLIO [10] 2-9-0 B Crossley 16/1: 040: Dwelt & no threat: btr in 974 (5f).   06
1019 BACCHANALIAN [7] 2-9-0 B Thomson 9/1: 000: Led before ½way: best in 834.   00
332 Master Knowall [1] 9-0(bl)   --   Fortyniner [5] 9-0
962 Hobournes Percy [2] 9-0
10 ran   nk,6,5,6,¾,hd   (Mrs B Dash)   R Boss Newmarket

1198 PATTINGHAM FILLIES STAKES 3YO   £959   1m 1f   Good 46 –11 Slow

--   TEMPLE WALK [11] (W Hern) 3-8-11 W Carson 1/1 FAV: 0-1: 3 b f Bustino – Temple Wood
(Sweet Revenge): Useful filly: heavily bckd on her reapp & led below dist, easily in a
3yo fillies stakes at Wolverhampton June 23: never nearer 5th behind Ivory Gull on her only
start last term: half sister to a couple of middle dist winners: will stay further than 9f:
acts on fast grnd & on a gall trk: looks one to follow.   48
423 SUNLEY SAINT [2] (P Walwyn) 3-8-11 Paul Eddery 13/2: 20-02: Kept on same pace: rated
50 when narrowly btn by Wryneck in a fillies maiden at Salisbury last summer: stays 9f:
suited by fast grnd & a gall trk.   34
464 HOT MOMMA [7] (R Boss) 3-8-11 E Guest(3) 12/1: 22-2043: Remains a maiden: see 89.   34
1055 INDIAN LOVE SONG [9] (R Hollinshead) 3-8-11 S Perks 12/1: 00-2304: Fin in gd style
& stays 9f well: acts on any trk: see 911.   31
--   CANADIAN GUEST [8] 3-8-11 T Williams 10/1: -0: Led 3f out, no extra dist: well bred
debutant who will be btr for this experience: acts on gd/firm ground & on a gall trk.   28
991 JANIE O [12] 3-8-11 P Robinson 9/1: -0300: Late prog: ran to her best: see 379.   26
422 KALANDARIYA [14] 3-8-11 P Hutchinson 7/1: 4-30: Chall 2f out, no extra & eased:
btr judged 422 (1m).   00
843 Tais Toi [6] 8-11   862 Scarlet Dancer [13] 8-11
980 Pladda Princess [3] 8-11   --   Tory Blues [10] 8-11
--   Nice Present [5] 8-11   837 Tamalpais [1] 8-11   379 Glacier Lass [4] 8-11(bl)
14 ran   5,hd,1½,1,¾   (T E Egerton)   W Hern West Ilsley, Berks

1199 DAISY BANK HANDICAP 3YO 0-50   £2777   1m   Good 46 +07 Fast   [54]

914 PELLINKO [10] (E Eldin) 3-9-1 A Mackay 7/1: -412001: 3 b c Malinowski – Cappelle
(Relko): Returned to form, led 2f out and was sn clear in quite a fast run h'cap at Wolverhampton June 23: in gd form early on, winning a stakes race at Warwick: half brother to
winning sprinter Sandy Cap: very eff over 7/8f: acts on fast & soft grnd & on any trk:
should win again.   55
713 PASTICCIO [6] (M Jarvis) 3-9-7 A Ives 9/2: 1-3222: Fin strongly: another gd effort
under top weight & is certainly due a change of luck: stays 1m well: see 68.   52
716 ON TO GLORY [7] (J Dunlop) 3-8-1 W Carson 11/2: 00-00B3: Had ev ch: stays 1m: see 716. 26
478 MY KIND OF TOWN [5] (R Williams) 3-9-5 R Cochrane 10/1: -1104: Acts on gd/firm: best 335. 43
843 MINISTRAILIS [11] 3-8-0(BL)(4ow) T Quinn 9/1: 00-0000: Bl first time: btr effort.   24
919 FARAG [8] 3-8-4(1ow) Paul Eddery 4/1 FAV: 31-2000: No extra dist: best on hvy in 74.   14
1065 ARE YOU GUILTY [3] 3-8-2 P Barnard(7) 6/1: 003-300: Made much: fin 7th: see 63.   00
880 NATCHAKAM [4] 3-8-2(1ow) P Waldron 8/1: -420400: Fin last: disapp effort: see 703 (7f). 00
1065 Twicknam Garden [2] 7-10   928 Stangrave [1] 7-10(vis)
--   Red In The Morning [9] 8-4
11 ran   4,3,½,hd,7,2½   (L Westbury)   E Eldin Newmarket

Official Going Given as Good/Firm

1200 FERRYBRIDGE FLYERS' MAIDEN APP. STAKES   £960 6f   Good 51 −11 Slow

1028 BOLD SEA ROVER [1] (M H Easterby) 3-8-7 J Kennedy(5) 13/2: -030301: 3 ch g Viking –
Sloane Ranger (Sharpen Up): Well drawn & led close home, driven out in an app maiden at
Pontefract June 14: first success: eff over 6/7f & will stay 1m: seems suited by gd or faster
grnd: acts on any trk: looks nicely h'capped.   **42**

911 RAFFLES VIRGINIA [3] (B Mcmahon) 3-8-4 A Roper 20/1: 000-402: Fin strongly, just btn:
gd effort & should do even btr over 7f: see 732.   **38**

911 BREAKFAST IN BED [8] (W Haigh) 3-8-4 B Mcgiff 7/2 FAV: 30-3223: Led ½way, no extra
inside dist & btr over 7f in 911: see 814.   **30**

891 RAAS [12] (S Norton) 3-8-7 R Lappin 8/1: 2340224: Al prom: fin 5th, placed 4th: see 787.   **32**

961 COLWAY RADIAL [5] 3-8-7 P Hill 20/1: 0-04400: No luck in running: fin 6th, placed
5th: gd effort & may win a small h'cap soon: see 626.   **26**

911 TRICKY [2] 3-8-4 Wendy Carter 14/1: 030-000: Late prog: lightly raced filly who is
a sister to smart filly Jester: eff over 6f on fast grnd.   **19**

807 ANZERE [11] 3-8-7 Alison Harper(5) 9/1: 304-00: Fin 8th: showed promise when lightly
raced last season, though probably needs further than todays trip: acts on gd & firm grnd &
on any trk.   **00**

516 FAUVE [4] 3-8-4 A Gorman 8/1: 42-00: Led to ½way: see 516.   **00**

835 SUPERCOOMBE [6] 3-8-7 S Whitelam(5) 6/1: 4-302D: Fin 4th though caused interference
below dist: disq. & placed last: acts on fast grnd: see 516.   **00**

447 La Belle Of Santo [15] 8-4		**857** Owls Way [7] 8-4	
871 Sister Nancy [17] 8-4	**871** La Manga Prince [18] 8-7		
910 Mr Coffey [16] 8-7(vis)		**830** Skybird [10] 8-7	
910 The Stray Bullett [9] 8-7		**37** Chalfont Mo [14] 8-4	
871 Our Mumsie [13] 8-4			

18 ran   hd,3,hd,2½,1½   (Lt Col R Warden)   M H Easterby Great Habton, Yorks

1201 GROVE SELLING H'CAP (0-25) 3 & 4YO   £1044 1m   Good 51 −30 Slow   [13]

963 REFORMED HABIT [8] (W Pearce) 4-9-0 M Hindley(2) 16/1: 000-301: 4 b c Reform – Fly
For Home (Habitat): Stayed on well to lead close home in a selling h'cap at Pontefract June
24 (no bid): lightly raced colt who had shown little worthwhile form previously: stays 1m
well: suited by gd or faster grnd.   **08**

889 THE GOLF SLIDE [10] (B Mcmahon) 4-9-1 G Duffield 6/1: 0000-02: Led below distance:
best effort for sometime; fav. by sharp trk: see 889.   **06**

673 GILLANBONE [2] (B Mcmahon) 4-8-12 J Hills(4) 14/1: 004-003: Fin well after slow
start: placed several times in similar company last term though yet to win: stays 1m: best
form on fast grnd.   **00**

*889 HARSLEY SURPRISE [7] (N Tinkler) 3-9-2(5ex) Kim Tinkler(5) 5/1 Jt FAV: 40-3314: Ran well
under her penalty: see 889.   **16**

1134 BANTEL BANZAI [18] 3-9-4(bl)(8ex) J Lowe 10/1: 0040100: Hmpd below dist, never
nearer: inconsistent though ran to his best here: see 932.   **18**

1065 SOHO SUE [19] 3-9-3 A Mackay 10/1: 40-1000: Early ldr: ran to her best: see 426.   **16**

1158 AUSSIE GIRL [13] 3-9-0 R Carter(5) 6/1: 00-0000: Impr of late: stays 1m: see 1158.   **00**

963 RUN FOR FRED [4] 4-9-1 Paul Eddery 5/1 Jt FAV: 030-000: Fin 8th: stays 1m: see 963.   **00**

993 CADENETTE [21] 4-9-4 N Connorton 7/1: 0-00420: Led over 2f out: best in 993 (10f firm).   **00**

960 RED ZULU [12] 3-9-0 B Thomson 10/1: 0000400: Front rank most of way: see 774.   **00**

888 Nicky Dawn [5] 9-6	**889** Tricenco [3] 9-10	**731** Cut A Caper [22] 9-7		
-- Jonney Gem [17] 9-1	**963** Meganot [9] 8-11	**828** Brandon Grey [20] 8-11		
845 Danedancer [11] 8-11(bl)		**932** Dix Etoiles [16] 8-10		
963 Martella [1] 8-8	**932** Bayview Gal [15] 8-8	**1079** Supreme Command [14] 8-7		
-- Fallonetta [6] 8-5				

22 ran   1,1½,hd,shhd,hd,1   (G N Brealy)   W Pearce Thirsk, North Yorks

1202 PLASMOR THERMALBOND H'CAP (0-50) 3YO+   £2628 1m   Good 51 +13 Fast   [39]

719 GEORDIES DELIGHT [3] (L Piggott) 3-9-4 T Ives 2/1 FAV: 0-21041: 3 b c Northern Baby –
Shout For Joy (Court Martial): Useful colt: led 2f out, gamely in a fast run h'cap at
Pontefract June 24: earlier won his maiden on heavy grnd at Epsom: stays 1m well: acts on
fast & hvy grnd & on any trk: genuine & consistent sort.   **51**

689 COUNT BERTRAND [8] (W Holden) 5-7-11 R Morse(5) 10/1: 2-00002: Slowly away, just
failed to get up: maiden who ran easily his best race of the season here: stays 1m: suited
by fast grnd.   **16**

604 PLANET ASH [7] 3-8-12 R Cochrane 8/1: 2414403: Ev ch, not btn far: see 326.   **42**

970 BOY SANDFORD [2] 7-7-9 N Carlisle 20/1: 20-0304: Al up there: fair effort.   **06**

956 SILLITOE [4] 4-8-9 M Beecroft 14/1: 00-0000: Held up, no threat: see 956.   **16**

1018 RAPID ACTION [1] 5-8-8 D Casey(7) 12/1: -303300: Nearest fin: see 1018.   **10**

862 INTRINSIC [9] 3-8-5 A Clark 5/2: -0000: Disapp 9th: should be suited by middle
distances: acts on gd & fast grnd: see 372.   **00**

+956 EASY DAY [6] 4-8-12(6ex) A Mackay 9/2: -041010: Made much: btr on firm in 956.   **00**

1013 Bit Of A State [5] 8-6(bl)	**956** Rabirius [11] 9-7	
-- Delta Wind [10] 8-8		

11 ran   shhd,½,3,2,2½   (Sheikh Mohammed)   L Piggott Newmarket

1203 YOUNGSTERS STAKES 2YO   £?260   6f   Good 51 -56 Slow

*1050 WENSLEYDALEWARRIOR [2] (G Moore) 2-9-3 D Casey(7) 7/1: 032011: 2 ro c Alias Smith –
Foolish Heroine (Brigadier Gerard): In gd form, led 2f out & ran on strongly to win a 2yo
stakes at Pontefract June 24: placed in most of his starts this term, won a maiden at
Carlisle earlier this month: half brother to 10f winner The Villain: eff over 5/6f on fast
& heavy grnd: acts on any trk: best when up with the pace.   48
*1138 TEAM EFFORT [7] (R Thompson) 2-9-3 R P Elliott 5/2 FAV: 030112: In fine form: see 1138. 44
985 PETER MOON [6] (R Armstrong) 2-8-11 B Thomson 4/1: 03: Kept on well & is clearly on
the up grade: first foal who cost $40,000 as a yearling: stays 6f: acts on gd/firm grnd.   34
*864 TAKE A HINT [4] (M Fetherston Godley) 2-9-3 R Hills 10/3: 4414: Not clear run: below
dist, never nearer: remains in gd form: stays 6f: see 864.   38
785 HARRY HUNT [8] 2-9-3 M Fry 12/1: 3100: Led over ½way: probably stays 6f though best
over the minimum trip in 488 (heavy).   32
-- BARNBY DON [3] 2-8-11 D Nicholls 25/1: 0: Unfancied on debut: speed over ½way & will
be btr for this race: brother to a couple of winning sprinters: acts on gd/firm grnd.   22
931 VAIGLY YELLOW [1] 2-8-11 G Duffield 25/1: 0U: Btn when slightly hmpd dist.   00
915 CHESWOLD [5] 2-8-11 K Hodgson 4/1: 400: Held up, no threat: twice below form in 610. 00
8 ran   1,1½,½,2½,1½,1½,hd   (C K Woods)   G Moore Middleham, Yorks

1204 RACE-A-ROUND YORKSHIRE H'CAP (0-35) 3YO £1415   1m 4f Good 51 +04 Fast   [33]

751 BLUSHING SPY [7] (M Fetherston Godley) 3-9-6(bl) R Hills 5/1: -0041: 3 b c Great Nephew-
Red Spider (Red God): Stayed on well under press to lead near fin in quite a fast run 3yo
h'cap at Pontefract June 24: lightly raced colt who is a half brother to very useful middle
dist winner Abu Kadra: stays 12f well: seems suited by fast grnd & a sharpish trk: wears bl. 34
*595 SENDER [1] (A Stewart) 3-9-7 M Roberts 5/4 FAV: -012: Just failed to make all: see 595. 32
697 BETTER BEWARE [5] (I Balding) 3-9-6 J Matthias 5/1: -343003: Al front rank: see 506 & 347 23
843 DALLONA [10] (W Musson) 3-8-10 M Wigham 14/1: 00-004: Eased below dist: lightly raced
filly who should be suited by middle dists: stays 9f: acts on gd/firm grnd.   00
699 SUNMAIDEN [2] 3-8-11 M Wood 20/1: 00-000: Half sister to a couple of useful winners
though has shown little worthwhile form herself.   00
862 RIBO MELODY [6] 3-8-11 A Shoults(5) 20/1: 000-000: Best in 779 (firm, sharp trk).   00
635 IRISH DILEMMA [9] 3-9-0(bl) P Bloomfield 8/1: -00000: Best over 10f in 535 (firm).   00
951 CARDAVE [8] 3-9-1 C Dwyer 20/1: 00-0000: No form this term.   00
782 LINTON SPRINGTIME [3] 3-8-13(BL) B Thomson 10/1: 000-000: Bl first time: trailed in last 00
9 ran   ½,5,12,1½,5   (Saeed Suhail)   M Fetherston Godley East Ilsley, Berks

1205 E.B.F. THORNE MAIDEN FILLIES STAKES 2YO £1558   5f   Good 51 -09 Slow

818 SINCLAIR LADY [5] (G Oldroyd) 2-8-11 D Nicholls 50/1: 00001: 2 gr f Absalom –
Katysue (King's Leap): Showed much impr form when causing a 50/1 surprise in a 2yo fillies
maiden at Pontefract June 24: ran on well to lead close home: cost 10,000 gns as a yearling
and her dam was successful 5 times as a juvenile: eff over 5f on fast grnd.   42
818 SPANISH SLIPPER [3] (W Haigh) 2-8-11 N Day 9/1: 422: Well bckd: led inside dist,
just caught: today's winner was well behind her in 818: see 450.   39
-- TINAS MELODY [6] (J Winter) 2-8-11 T Ives 8/1: 3: Speedily bred debutant: went on
2f out: promising effort: half sister to several winners, incl 2,000 Guineas runner up
Mattaboy: acts on gd/firm grnd.   33
-- AID AND ABET [7] (M Stoute) 2-8-11 A Kimberley 8/1: 4: Ev ch on debut: speedily bred
filly whose dam won twice as a juvenile: acts on gd/firm grnd.   32
848 HOLD ON PLEASE [2] 2-8-11 R Cochrane 4/7 FAV: 40: Led over ½way: much btr in 848.   23
1050 CARSE KELLY [1] 2-8-11 J Lowe 8/1: 0220: Lost place ½way: much btr in 1050.   21
-- PETANGO [4] 2-8-11 A Proud 50/1: 0: Slowly away on debut & al behind.   00
7 ran   1,2½,½,3,½,7   (Sinclair Developments Ltd)   G Oldroyd Malton, Yorks

1206 MEXBOROUGH STAKES 3YO   £2203   1m 2f Good 51 +03 Fast

+720 KATHY W [1] (H Cecil) 3-9-2 W Ryan 11/10 FAV: -11: 3 gr f Grey Dawn II – Pretty
Fresh (Forli): Prom filly: denied a clear run though showed a gd turn of foot to lead close
home in 3yo stakes at Pontefract June 24: ready winner of a fast run maiden at Leicester on
her debut last month: eff over 10f & will stay further: acts on fast grnd & on a gall trk. 52
219 POKEYS PRIDE [5] (R Sheather) 3-9-0 R Cochrane 7/4: 0020-02: Led inside dist, just
btn: gd effort after a lengthy abs: half brother to winning stayer Jowoody: narrowly btn by
Barclay Street in a Leicester maiden last season: stays 10f: likes fast grnd & a gall trk. 49
625 KING TEFKROS [7] (M Tompkins) 3-9-0 T Ives 33/1: -003: Stayed on well: best effort
to date: clearly well suited by 10f & fast grnd.   45
-- HIGH KNOWL [4] (B Hills) 3-9-0 B Thomson 10/1: 0-4: Led below dist: gd seasonal debut:
half brother to several winners incl useful French miler Nonoalca: lightly raced colt who
stays 10f: acts on gd/firm.   45
*969 PAST GLORIES [2] 3-9-8 J Lowe 8/1: 00-0310: Made much: in gd form: see 969.   48
-- MOLTO RAPIDO [3] 3-9-0 M Brennan(0) 100/1: -0: Al last on his racecourse debut.   00
6 ran   ½,2,shhd,2,dist   (Marvin Waldman)   H Cecil Newmarket

1207 EBF EASTBOURNE MAIDEN STAKES 2YO C & G   £1257   6f   Good/Firm 25 -20 Slow

-- WELSH ARROW [7] (J Winter) 2-9-0 W R Swinburn 4/1: 1: 2 ch c Welsh Pageant - Tripoli-
taine (Nonoalco): Made a successful debut, staying on strongly to lead final 1f, narrowly in
a 2yo maiden at Brighton June 24: dam a middle dist winner: muscular sort who is sure to be
well suited by 7f plus: acts on firm grnd: should impr further over longer dist.   42
965 MORNING FLOWER [5] (R Williams) 2-9-0 J Reid 7/2: 032: Led 2f out, narrowly btn &
3L clear of rest: should find a maiden shortly: see 965.   39
404 KIERON PRESS [2] (D Arbuthnot) 2-9-0 J Williams 33/1: 03: Stayed on well & is on
the up grade: cost I.R. 6,200: suited by 6f: looks likely to stay 7f plus.   30
497 LAST DANCE [8] (R Hannon) 2-9-0 A Mcglone 6/1: 04: Prom most: dam a middle distance
winner in Ireland.   27
-- YASIR [3] 2-9-0 T Quinn 11/4 FAV: 0: Uneasy fav on debut no real threat but impr likely   20
-- GOLDEN CAJUN [6] 2-9-0 B Rouse 100/30: 0: Early ldr: dam a middle dist winner in Ireland   13
-- Oriental Jade [4] 9-0   536 Oconnell Street [1] 9-0
8 ran ½,3,1,2½,2½   (Sheikh Ali Abu Khamsin)   J Winter Newmarket

1208 LEWES STAKES 3YO+   £1872   1m 2f Good/Firm 25 -11 Slow

*989 CHINOISERIE [2] (L Cumani) 3-9-3 R Guest 6/4: 22-0211: 3 b c Fluorescent Light -
From The East (Gold And Myrrh): Very useful, impr colt: winning 2nd race on the trot,
getting first run on the fav. & holding on well by 1L in a minor event at Brighton June 24:
comfortably won a h'cap at Yarmouth June 11: lightly raced in '85: well suited by 10f, may
stay further: acts on firm & yld.   ᴇ?
*887 SULTAN MOHAMED [7] (J Dunlop) 3-9-3 W R Swinburn 8/13 FAV: 0242-12: Came from behind,
kept on well & perhaps gave the winner too much leeway: see 887.   59
-- TOMS TREASURE [8] (R Akehurst) 4-9-5 R Mcghinn 66/1: -3: Led almost 1m: off the trk
last season, ran only once as a 2yo: may improve.   22
-- APRIL ARABESQUE [6] (L Cottrell) 4-9-5 I Johnson 66/1: -0-4: No threat: only ran
once last term.   07
838 NARCISSUS [1] 4-9-8 G Baxter 25/1: -0-300: Prom some: best 522 (soft).   07
980 OUT YONDER [4] 3-8-8 N Adams 66/1: 000-00: Ev ch, wknd: no form in the past.   04
1186 Taffys Pride [3] 9-5(bl)   -- Sweet Rascal [5] 9-5
8 ran 1,12,10,2½,1½   (Ivan Allan)   L Cumani Newmarket

1209 OPERATIC SOC. CHALL CUP HCAP 3YO+ 0-50   £3726   1m 4f Good/Firm 25 +05 Fast   [48]

*570 FLEETING AFFAIR [8] (G Harwood) 3-8-13 G Starkey 6/5 FAV: -111: 3 b f Hotfoot -
My Own II (El Relicario): Very useful, unbtn filly: completed her hat trick leading 1f out
comfortably in a h'cap at Brighton June 24: easy winner of minor races at Brighton and
Salisbury previously: unraced in '85: half sister to several winners incl the smart Haul
Knight: eff 10f, stays 12f well: acts on yld, well suited by a sound surface: looks sure
to win more races.   60
750 PELLINCOURT [4] (A Pitt) 4-8-0 T Quinn 11/1: -400202: Led 3f out, outpcd by this
useful winner but a gd effort: see 179, 532: should win soon.   28
569 VORACITY [6] (J Winter) 7-9-10 W R Swinburn 9/1: /004-23: Waited with, kept on : see 569   51
984 HEIGHT OF SUMMER [3] (D Arbuthnot) 5-7-7(2oh) N Adams 25/1: 0100-04: Led to ½way: winner
of a h'cap at Beverley in '85: eff at 12f, stays further: suited by firm grnd.   11
+851 HEART OF STONE [2] 4-8-2 G Baxter 6/1: 00-0010: Btr 851 (10f, gd/yld).   18
801 HOUSE HUNTER [9] 5-9-4 I Salmon 10/1: 00-0200: No dngr: twice below 363 (soft).   33
1020 FOLK DANCE [5] 4-9-6 P Francis‡7½ 9/1: 41-4420: Fdd quickly after 1m: unsuited by firm?   00
856 Derby Day [7] 7-7(bl)(2oh)   1035 Denboy [3] 7-12
9 ran 1½,½,6,1½,1   (Mrs S E Lakin)   G Harwood Pulborough, Sussex

1210 MONTPELIER SELLING STAKES 3YO   £823   1m   Good/Firm 25 -31 Slow

841 TRELAWNEY [10] (A Ingham) 3-9-0 R Curant 7/1: 000-0001: 3 ch c Welsh Pageant - Pilley
Green (Porto Bello): Gamely made most, holding on grimly to win a 3yo seller at Brighton
June 24 (bought in 2,000 gns): seems suited by forcing tactics & a sharpish trk over 1m:
acts on fast grnd.   14
1063 TAKE THE BISCUIT [1] (R Stubbs) 3-9-0(bl) A Mercer 4/1: 0000002: Came from well
behind, just failed to get up & 3L clear of rest: should win a similar race: see 1063.   14
749 THE UTE [11] (L Bower) 3-9-0(bl) R Guest 8/1: 0-02023: Dsptd lead 2f out: likes
this track: see 749, 564.   08
-- BEE KAY ESS [3] (R Holder) 3-9-0 I Johnson 25/1: -4: Racecourse debut, no dngr:
dam won over 7f: may improve.   01
*564 COMEDY PRINCE [6] 3-9-0 K Radcliffe‡7½ 2/1 FAV: 00-0010: Uneasy fav: no dngr & was
the subject of a stewards enquiry but was found afterwards to be lame: see 564 (C/D).   01
765 SIR SPEEDY [2] 3-9-0 P Hamblett 8/1: -0000: No dngr: no worthwile form as yet.   00
620 MISS HARLEQUIN [8] 3-8-11(0) A Mcglone 10/1: 00-0000: Fin 7th: see 620.   00
177 Thai Sky [7] 8-11   -- Testarossa [4] 8-11   839 Miss Brahms [9] 8-11(vis)
10 ran shhd,3,4,hd,2   (Exors of the late S R Crowe)   A Ingham Epsom, Surrey

1211 MID SX LIC. VICTUALLERS HCAP 4YO+ 0-35   £2072   7f   Good/Firm 25 -03 Slow   [34]

1060 LYRIC WAY [3] (B Hills) 4-9-2 M Hills 8/1: 0-00001: 4 ch c Song - Grecian Bridge
(Acropolis): Returned to form, leading inside final 1f by the minimum margin in a h'cap at
Brighton June 24: first time out winner of a maiden at Pontefract in '85: eff over 6/7f &
acts on gd & firm grnd: likes an undulating trk.   30
*845 SAHARA SHADOW [12] (D Tucker) 4-8-2(3ow) T Quinn 10/1: 0000-12: Battled with winner
final 1f, just held & is in grand form: see 845.   16
940 SANTELLA PAL [6] (L Cottrell) 5-7-9 M L Thomas 12/1: 0-02043: Tried to make all: see 540.04
1077 SITEX [9] (M Bolton) 8-7-7 S Dawson[3] 20/1: 000-004: See 734.   00
930 FAST SERVICE [4] 7-9-8 P Cook 5/1 CO FAV: 00-0000: Wk in mkt, ev ch: enjoyed a busy
but successful season in '85 winning 4 h'caps at Brighton (2), Epsom & Beverley: course
winner 4 times at Brighton & likes a sharpish, undulating trk: eff over 7f/1m: loves fast
grnd: coming back to form & can find a race soon.   27
992 DALLAS SMITH [1] 5-7-11(VIS) T Williams 33/1: 00-0000: No threat: see 975.   01
1086 EXERT [5] 4-8-10 R Rouse 5/1 CO FAV: 4440300: Fin 7th: twice below 922: see 114.   00
992 HOPEFUL KATIE [10] 4-8-4(hood) N Adams 5/1 CO FAV: 4304020: Btr 992.   00
1066 Pommes Chateau [7] 9-0(hood)   1077 Out Of Hand [11] 8-8
992 Cats Lullaby [2] 8-3(bl)   1018 Dimension 0 8-6
12 ran   shhd,2,1½,nk,½   (E D Kessly)   B Hills Lambourn, Berks

1212 MONTPELIER SELLING STAKES 3YO   £820   1m   Good/Firm 25 -23 Slow

845 ON IMPULSE [4] (K Brassey) 3-8-11 S Dawson[3] 5/6 FAV: 00-0321: 3 gr f Jellaby -
PTS Fairway (Runnymede): Well bckd & readily landed the odds, leading 2f out in a 3yo seller
at Brighton June 24 (bought in 6,600 gns): lightly raced & no form last term, impr performer
this season: suited by 1m & gd or firm grnd: may make further impr.   27
845 HADDON LAD [10] (M Mccourt) 3-9-0 R Wernham 11/2: 0-00042: Ev ch: not bl today: see 84520
-- RUN FOR YOUR WIFE [6] (G Lewis) 3-9-0 J Adams[7] 9/2: 40004-3: Prom most: rated 38
in '85 when showing more than enough ability to win a seller: stays 1m well: nicely h'capped
at present & should be noted in a selling h'cap next time.   16
963 BLUE STEEL [1] (R Simpson) 3-8-11(bl) K Radcliffe[7] 8/1: 0-00044: No real threat.   12
845 MISS COMEDY [5] 3-8-11 A Mcglone 10/1: 0000-00: Made much: maiden who showed only
modest form last term.   11
975 LETOILE DU PALAIS [8] 3-8-11 W Woods[4] 33/1: 0-04000: No threat: see 568.   09
809 Odervy [3] 9-0   -- Tinas Lad [7] 9-0   749 Splendid Magnolia [2] 9-0(BL)
9 ran   4,2,½,nk,1   (Philip Fisher)   K Brassey Upper Lambourn, Berks

1213 MARINE HANDICAP 3YO+ 0-35   £2176   6f   Good/Firm 25 +09 Fast   [35]

906 LUCKY STARKIST [5] (R Holder) 4-8-3 S Dawson[3] 16/1: 10-0031: 4 gr f Lucky Wednesday-
Starkist (So Blessed): Showed impr form, recovering from a slow start (again) &
fin strongly to cut her rivals down in the final 1f & win quite a fast run h'cap at Brighton
June 24: in '85 won a seller at Edinburgh: seems to need at least 6f nowadays & should be
suited by 7f: acts on firm & yld: runs well on a sharp trk: should win again in similar company. 21
1070 ST TERRAMAR [8] (D Jermy) 11-7-7(bl) G Dickie 33/1: 20-0002: Edged left under press
when ridden to lead briefly 1f out (causing quite a lot of interference): best effort
this season: see 1070.   05
842 SILENT GAIN [7] (W Jarvis) 4-8-11 W R Swinburn 11/2: 000-023: Chall when hmpd 1f
out: see 842.   13
1086 RUSSELL FLYER [9] (R Hoad) 4-8-9(bl) M L Thomas 33/1: -000004: Made most: best effort
this season: in '85 won at Yarmouth: suited by 6f on fast grnd.   11
1086 DELAWARE RIVER [6] 4-8-10 T Williams 10/1: 00-0240: Sn prom: hmpd 1f out: best 748 (C/D12
679 FREMONT BOY [11] 4-8-8 B Rouse 3/1 FAV: 000-230: Well bckd, no threat: much btr 679,266.06
508 BELLE TOWER [12] 4-9-2 G Starkey 7/1: 0-02100: Dsptd lead from ½way, fdd: best 266.   00
*855 DOWNSVIEW [3] 4-10-2 L Riggio [7] 4/1: 000-010: Well bckd, anchored by mammoth weight. 00
881 SOON TO BE [10] 4-9-12 G Baxter 8/1: 33-0000: Btr 881 (7f).   00
950 Three Bells [4] 9-7   845 Sparkford Lad [14] 8-7(bl)
784 Rapid Miss [1] 8-10   680 Billy Whiteshoes [3] 8-6
845 The Batchlor [2] 7-9
14 ran   2,4,ddht,shhd,2   (James Neville)   R Holder Portbury, Avon

---

Official Going Given As GOOD

1214 GROUP III PRIX DU LYS 3YO C & G   £17792   1m 4f   Good -

303 CHERCHEUR DOR [4] (C Head) 3-8-13 G Moore 1: 10-4211: 3 b c Northern Dancer -
Gold River: Very useful colt: justified fav. with a comfortable success in a Gr.3 event at
Chantilly June 20: earlier won at Longchamp: stays 12f well: acts on gd & hvy grnd.   72
-- SAND SHIP [1] (J Cunnington) 3-8-9 J C Desaint 1: -3122: Chall final 1f: gd run:
stays 12f & acts on gd grnd.   65
348 ROBBAMA [3] (J Dunlop) 3-8-9 F Head 1: 110-43: Made the running: see 348.   57
-- KLIMT [2] (A Fabre) 3-8-13 A Gibert 1: -14: Last to fin.   59
4 ran   ½,4,½   (J Wertheimer)   C Head France

ST CLOUD   Saturday June 21st

Official Going Given As GOOD

1215 GROUP 3 PRIX FILLE DE LAIR FILLIES   £19048   1m 2f   Good -

904 LIASTRA [5] (F Boutin) 3-8-3 C Asmussen 1:   -2121: 3 ch f Artaius - Lighted Glory
(Nijinsky): Smart filly: comfortable ¾L winner of a Gr.3 event at St Cloud June 21: very eff
at 10f on gd & yld grnd.   75
--   FILLE DU NORD [8] (A Fabre) 3-8-3 D Regnard 1: 0110202: Kept on well final 1f: stays
10½f well: acts on gd grnd.   72
*561 EL FABULOUS [6] (C Head) 3-8-7 G Moore 1: 01-4103: Gd effort but best 561 (soft).   72
904 ELLE SEULE [7] (D Smaga) 3-8-5 A Lequeux 1: 2-10134: Consistent sort.   68
8 Ran ½,2,¼,   (P G Goulandris)   F Boutin France

DORTMUND   Sunday June 22nd

Official Going Given As GOOD/FIRM

1216 GROUP 3 GROSSER PREIS VON DORTMUND 4YO+   £9887   1m 1f   Good/Firm -

--   AGUARICO (H Jentzsch) 4-9-1 H Horwart 1: -1: 4 b c Surumu - Antioquia (Derring-Do):
Led over 1f out, comfortably in a Gr.3 event at Dortmund June 22: eff at 9f, stays further:
acts on gd/firm grnd.   71
325 K BATTERY (W Elsey) 5-9-4 J Lowe 1: 00-1002: Another fine effort: see 325, 17.   69
--   NEW MOON (P Lautner) 5-9-1 K Woodburn 1: 34-3: ..   62
--   ANIMO (H Jentzsch) 4-9-1 A Tylicki 1: -4: Btr fancies stable mate of winner.   59
*1047 FREEDOMS CHOICE 4-9-1 W Carson 1: 3-42D10: Last to fin & this was not his form.   09
8 Ran 2¼,1½,1¼   (Gestut Fahrhof)   H Jentzsch Germany

GROENENDAEL   Sunday June 22nd

Official Going Given As FIRM

1217 GRAND PRIX DE BRUXELLES   £20704   1m 3f   Firm -

885 PHARDANTE (G Harwood) 4-9-8 G Starkey 1: 30-0101: Very smart colt: had an easy task
when a 3L winner of a valuable event at Groenendael June 22: earlier beat Slip Anchor in
Gr.2 Jockey Club Stakes at Newmarket: failed to win in '85, but was a fine 2nd to Oh So
Sharp in the St Leger at Doncaster: smart 2yo, winning 4 times: eff over 11/12f, stays 14f:
acts well on gd & firm grnd: genuine sort.   79
*1038 KALKOUR (M Haynes) 4-9-4 T Quinn 1: 0-01012: Ran very well: in fine form: see 1038.   60
--   BADINAGE (France) 6-9-4 Y De Wulf 1: -10-3: --   55
8 Ran 3,2½   (Simon Karmel)   G Harwood Pulborough, Sussex

TURIN   Tuesday June 24th

Official Going Given As GOOD/FIRM

1218 GROUP 2 PREMIO PRINCIPE AMEDEO 3YO   £15695   1m 5f   Good/Firm -

902 ROSEDALE USA (J Dunlop) 3-9-2 W Carson 1: 2-21221: 3 b c Vaguely Noble - Ivory
(Riverman): Very useful colt: easy winner of a Gr.2 event at Turin June 24: most consistent
this season, earlier winning a maiden at Bath: eff at 12f, stays 15f well: acts on any
grnd, but seems suited by a sound surface: should win more races.   71
*899 LOCAL HERBERT (L Camici) 3-9-2 L Ficuciello 1: 2-42012: Consistent sort: stays 13f.   66
--   DUCA DI BUSTED (A Botti) 3-9-2 G Dettori 1: -3: --   60
7 Ran 2¾,4   (N B Hunt)   J Dunlop Arundel, Sussex

1219 GROUP 3 PREMIO ROYAL MARES FILLIES 3YO+   £13327   1m   Good/Firm -

--   SAINT SAMBA (L Dauria) 3-8-9 W Carson 1: -1: 3 b f Thatch - St Nitouche (Riverman):
Fin well to win a Gr.3 fillies event at Turin June 24: very eff at 1m on gd/firm grnd.   73
392 MARY GUARD (M Ciciarelli) 4-8-13 A Parravani 1: 1-02: Just btn: well suited by 1m
on gd/firm.   62
--   OREADE (L Brogi) 4-8-13 S Dettori 1: 2-3: Close up 3rd.   61
*982 SMOOCH (K Brassey) 3-8-4 S Whitworth 1: 03-0010: No threat in 7th: much btr 982.   55
12 Ran 1,sh nk   (S cuderia Blu)   L Dauria Italy

Official Going Given As GOOD/FIRM

1220 BALDERSBY APPRENTICE MAIDEN STAKES 3YO   £1451   1m 1f   Firm 15 -13 Slow

941 CAPTAINS NIECE [8] (W Hastings Bass) 3-8-4 Dale Gibson(5) 25/1: -01: 3 b f Vitiges
- Captain's Girl (Captain's Gig) Lightly raced filly, led below dist, comfortably, in an
app mdn at Ripon June 25: eff over 9f and shd stay further: acts on fast grd and on a
sharpish track: on the upgrade.   34
1055 HELLO BENZ [11] (M H Easterby) 3-8-7 J Kennedy(5) 11/1: -40042: Ran on strongly
and is in gd form: well suited by fast grd: see 322.   33
874 BLACK BANK [5] (M W Easterby) 3-8-7 S Hustler(5) 33/1: 0000-03: Led early and again
3f out: best effort to date: maiden who is well suited by a sound surface: stays 9f.   30
806 REAL MOONSHINE [2] (A Stewart) 3-8-7 R Carter 10/3: -04: Well bckd: ran on same
pace: lightly raced colt who is a half brother to sev minor winners: will stay further:
acts on fast grd and on a sharpish trk.   22
776 ROYAL NUGGET [9] 3-8-4 Mark Giles(5) 2/1 FAV: 322-040: Twice hmp; early in straight:
no extra distance: proving expensive to follow: see 213.   18
371 MOORE STYLISH [12] 3-8-4 V Smith 10/1: -00: Prom when saddle slipped home turn:
no chance thereafter: lightly raced filly who is eff around 1m and will stay further:
acts on fast ground: see 371.   08
723 IS BELLO [7] 3-8-7 C Rate(5) 11/4: -0320: Disapp 7th: much btr over 10f in 723(stiff) 00
862 Eitandary [4] 8-4   937 First Summer [6] 8-7   1055 Hitchenstown [10] 8-7
862 Samosa [1] 8-4(BL)   941 Alice Holt [3] 8-4
12 ran 1½,1½,3,¾,4,nk   (N H Phillips)   W Hastings Bass Newmarket

1221 DISHFORTH SELLING STAKES 2YO   £1377   6f   Firm 15 -28 Slow

1088 BOLD DIFFERENCE [8] (W Wharton) 2-8-8 I Johnson 4/1: 00021: 2 b f Bold Owl -
Subtle Queen (Stephen George) Slowly away tho' responded well to press to lead cl home in
a 2yo seller at Ripon June 25 (no bid): recently just btn at Thirsk and clearly well suited
by a sharpish trk: stays 6f well: acts on fast grd: cheaply acquired filly who is closely
related to a couple of winners.   28
*1100 BAD PAYER [9] (M W Easterby) 2-8-8 T Lucas 15/8 FAV: 4312: Just failed to make all:
in gd form: seems to act on any trk: see 1100.   24
1067 MISS ACACIA [1] (R Stubbs) 2-8-8 A Mercer 4/1: 0003: Dropped in class: well bckd:
slightly hmpd cl home and not btn far: cost 8,200 gns and is a half sister to a couple of
minor winners: stays 6f: acts on fast ground and on a sharp course.   23
1088 PRINCESS SINGH [3] (N Tinkler) 2-8-8 Kim Tinkler(5) 10/1: 003104: Al up there:
stays 6f: see 858.   16
1088 GOLDENDOUBLEYOU [6] 2-8-8 N Carlisle 6/1: 230: Acts on fast grd: see 1088.   15
813 GOLDCHAN [5] 2-8-8 D Nicholls 13/2: 00: Very cheaply bought filly who is a half
sister to middle dist winner Wang Feihoong.   00
701 Misty Runner [10] 8-8   948 Winnies Luck [7] 8-8   -- Fidgetty Feet [4] 8-8
939 Mi Oh My [2] 8-8   1050 Rimove [11] 8-8
11 ran 1½,hd,2½,nk,6   (T H Morris)   W Wharton Melton Mowbray, Leics.

1222 HANDICAP (0-50)   £2603   6f   Firm 15 +17 Fast   [46]

992 MR JAY ZEE [5] (N Callaghan) 4-8-6 G Duffield 3/1 FAV: 00-0131: 4 b c Sandy Creek -
Flying Spear (Breakspear II) In fine form, ran on strongly to lead cl home in a fastrun
h'cap at Ripon June 25: earlier this month won a similar event at Catterick: disapp last
season tho' quite useful as a juv, winning at Ayr: eff over 6/7f: suited by fast grd:
acts on any track.   32
1157 CHAPLINS CLUB [4] (D Chapman) 6-10-0(bl) D Nicholls 9/1: 0000002: Led briefly inside
dist, just denied tho' ran his best race of the season here: now wears bl: see 1026. 53
*369 EASTBROOK [7] (S Hall) 6-7-9 L Charnock 11/1: 000-213: Game eff to make all: narrowly
btn despite a fair abs: should find a small h'cap in the near future: see 369.   19
1013 ALWAYS NATIVE [1] (D Chapman) 5-7-9 S P Griffiths(5) 33/1: 30-0004: Going on fin
and prob btr over another furlong: won a seller at Newcastle (7f yldg) last season tho' is
equally eff on fast ground: acts on any trk.   13
1157 INISHPOUR [6] 4-9-8 A Mackay 11/2: 00-0030: Al up there: see 1157.   38
1182 EXAMINATION [3] 3-8-7(bl) P Bloomfield 6/1: -121040: Quick reappearance: btr 340. 32
+1182 BROWN BEAR BOY [2] 4-9-8(8ex) V Smith(5) 9/2: 0233010: No extra below dist: too
soon after 1182?   00
1157 TOP THAT [8] 5-8-8 N Carlisle 8/1: 0201400: Early speed: best yldg 649.   00
525 CABANAX [9] 4-9-7 E Guest(3) 9/1: -220-30: Slowly away and no threat: abs since 525. 00
9 ran nk,hd,2½,½,½,1   (N A Callaghan)   N Callaghan Newmarket

1223 RIPON LADIES DERBY H'CAP (0-35)   £1003   1m 4f   Firm 15 -47 Slow   [16]

1124 FIEFDOM [16] (W Storey) 6-11-0 Fiona Storey 16/1: 400-201: 6 ch g Home Guard -
Eastwood Bounty (Bounteous) Gamely defied top weight in a h'cap for lady riders at Ripon
June 25, stayed on well to lead near fin: successful over timber this Winter and won at
Folkestone and Lingfield last season: eff around 1m, stays 12f well: acts on any going and
on any track: usually runs well in this type of race.   38
1106 EXCAVATOR LADY [18] (R Whitaker) 7-9-1(vis)(2ow) Sandy Brook 8/1: -004322: Led
dist, overhauled cl home tho' remains in gd form: well suited by fast grd: acts any trk. 10

958 **PATS JESTER** [17] (P Rohan) 3-9-8 Laura Rohan(3) 8/1: 0-41323: Fin strongly: see 958. 31

984 **ARGES** [10] (R Hollinshead) 5-10-11 Maxine Juster 10/1: 422-204: Led over 3f out: gd effort: acts on fast grd and on any trk: see 9. 31

1024 **PINWIDDIE** [12] 4-10-0 Diana Williams 11/2 FAV: 0421140: Consistent: acts on firm. 17

984 **SOCKS UP** [6] 9-9-10 Gale Johnson Houghton 13/2: 003-040: Ran on too late: see 984. 09

850 **WINTER PALACE** [15] 4-10-8 Jo Winter 7/1: 240-000: Fin 7th: trained by N Guest when winning a Sandown h'cap last season: stays 12f: acts on any going: now with C Nelson. 00

1089 **REGENCY SQUARE** [11] 3-8-9 Julia Fielden 9/1: 000-320: Well placed for 1m: btr 1089. 00

912 **Treyarnon** [14] 9-7
1016 **Walter The Great** [4] 9-12
912 **Moniar** [5] 9-6
1042 **Touch Of Luck** [9] 9-12
-- **Orvilles Song** [13] 9-5
823 **Marina Plata** [8] 9-7
1071 **Red Duster** [2] 10-2
912 **Just A Half** [7] 9-7
1156 **Dreadnought** [3] 9-12
-- **Mavitta Dee** [1] 9-3 U

18 ran ½,¾,1,1½,2 (C A Clark) W Storey Muggleswick, Co Durham

1224 RIPON CITY HANDICAP (0-50) 3YO £3615 1m Firm 15 -11 Slow [49]

880 **MAHOGANY RUN** [9] (M H Easterby) 3-9-5 M Birch 10/1: 20-0001: 3 br c Sonnen Gold - Queens Message (Town Crier) Returned to form, made most, gamely in a 3yo h'cap at Ripon June 25: last season successful at Hamilton & Redcar: stays 1m: best form on fast grd with forcing tactics. 50

886 **SIDONS DAUGHTER** [4] (A Jarvis) 3-9-1 D Nicholls 12/1: 040-002: Led dist, just btn tho' ran her best race of the season: stays 1m: suited by a sound surface: see 886. 45

1034 **SPECIAL GUEST** [7] (D Morley) 3-7-13 J Lowe 10/1: 1200-03: Ev ch: acts firm: see 1034. 23

1028 **NEDS EXPRESSA** [8] (C Tinkler) 3-8-1 L Charnock 7/2: 0-00034: Longer trip: best 1028(7f) 24

1032 **KINGS TOUCH** [1] 3-9-7 S Perks 11/2: 01-0400: Best over 7f 455 (yldg). 34

956 **IRISH PASSAGE** [5] 3-8-9(BL) N Carlisle 6/1: 1-02D00: Held up, no threat: btr 816 bl. today. 21

1091 **HARRY HULL** [6] 3-7-13 K Darley 10/3 FAV: 00-0000: Denied a clear run: see 309. 00

•774 **KEEP COOL** [2] 3-7-11 P Hill(7) 6/1: -340010: Btr 774 (seller, stiff trk). 00

666 **PHILOSOPHICAL** [3] 3-8-1 A Mackay 8/1: 041-000: Al behind: see 666. 00

9 ran nk,3,½,5,hd (P D Savill) M H Easterby Grreat Habton, Yorks

1225 E.B.F. MELMERBY MAIDEN STAKES 2YO £2109 6f Firm 15 -07 Slow

777 **MAINTAIN** [6] (L Cumani) 2-9-0 R Guest 4/5 FAV: 01: 2 ch c Main Reef - Brilliant Reay (Ribero) Promising juv: odds-on, made most for a narrow success in a 2yo mdn at Ripon June 25: showed plenty of promise behind Albasar on his recent debut at Newmarket: half brother to a couple of juv winners, notably the fairly useful Test of Time: eff over 6f on fast ground: seems to act on any trk. 50

780 **BORN FREE AGAIN** [5] (L Piggott) 2-9-0 T Lucas 12/1: 002: Much btr effort over this longer trip: ran on well and narrowly btn: stays 6f well: suited by fast grd: see 780. 48

-- **ANTINOUS** [8] (M H Easterby) 2-9-0 M Birch 9/2: 3: Nicely bckd on debut: had ev ch and will be btr for this race: half brother to useful sprint h'capper Batoni: stays 6f: acts on fast grd and on a sharp course: shd win soon. 44

944 **SUPERCUBE** [10] (E Carter) 2-8-11 Wendy Carter(7) 25/1: 04: Going on fin and will stay further: acts on gd and firm grd and on any trk: see 944. 40

1067 **THANK HAVON** [1] 2-8-11 J Lowe 6/1: 40: Al up there: see 1067. 28

701 **OUR HORIZON** [7] 2-8-11 N Carlisle 16/1: 200: Kept on from ½ way: stays 6f: see 612. 26

985 **PERSIAN DYNASTY** [4] 2-9-0 D Mckay 16/1: 00: Kept on: cost 22,000 gns and is a half brother to sev winners, incl useful sprinter Sparkling Moment: acts on fast ground. 00

780 **Kacere** [9] 9-0
1050 **Jays Special** [15] 9-0
-- **Regent Square** [3] 9-0
450 **Rose Meadow** [12] 8-11
-- **Doodlin** [14] 9-0
-- **Metroman** [13] 9-0
741 **Straight Edge** [2] 9-0
-- **Willow The King** [11] 9-0

15 ran nk,1½,½,5,hd,nk (Mrs A L Chapman) L Cumani Newmarket

1226 WATH HANDICAP STAKES (0-35) £1755 1m 4f Firm 15 -23 Slow [27]

1102 **DIENAUS TROVE** [7] (H Collingridge) 5-8-2(1ow) M Rimmer 2/1 FAV: 000/321: 5 b h Hot Grove - Dienau (Connaught) Well bckd when making most to score unchall in a h'cap at Ripon June 25: earlier twice placed in non h'cap co tho' this was his first win on the Flat: successful over timber this Winter: eff over 12/14f: acts on any going and on any trk. 09

1024 **FOUR STAR THRUST** [8] (R Whitaker) 4-9-7 D Mckeown 8/1: 0040202: Not reach winner. 25

984 **HYOKIN** [5] (D Morley) 4-9-1 G Duffield 12/1: 2-40003: Fin well: gd effort: see 282. 16

1092 **COCKED HAT SUPREME** [12] (S Hall) 4-8-12 M Birch 8/1: 3040-44: Never nearer: may need further: see 1092. 10

869 **LAKINO** [1] 4-9-4 M Hindley(3) 7/1: 0-1-000: Fin well after being denied a clear run below dist: seems to be returning to form: see 675. 15

281 **MRS CHRIS** [10] 4-9-3 K Darley 14/1: 0-04000: Fair eff after lengthy abs: see 46. 11

1124 **APPLE WINE** [4] 9-9-1 D Nicholls 11/2: 2000020: Early leader: fin 7th: see 1124. 00

772 **STRING OF BEADS** [11] 4-8-1 S P Griffiths(5) 10/1: 00-0000: Fin 8th: see 772. 00

860 **DELLWOOD RENOWN** [13] 4-8-2 R Morse(5) 6/1: 00-0330: One paced: fin 9th: see 709. 00

-- **Jipijapa** [3] 8-1
743 **Pinctada** [9] 9-1
875 **Mabel Alice** [6] 8-5
1079 **Its Good Ere** [2] 9-0

13 ran 1½,1½,1½,½,1½,¾ (Barry H Collinson) H Collingridge Newmarket

KEMPTON   Wednesday June 25th   Righthand Sharpish Track

Official Going Given As GOOD/FIRM

1227 RACAL RADIO HANDICAP STKS (0-50)   £2490   5f   Firm -03 +15 Fast   [45]

1086 SILENT MAJORITY [6] (W O'gorman) 3-8-1(1ow)(5ex) T Ives 7/2: -030131: 3 b g General Assembly - Vexed Voter (Pontefex) In fine form and defied a 5lbs pen when breaking the course rec with an all the way win in a h'cap at Kempton June 25: won similar h'cap at Yarmouth June 10: stays 6f but ideally suited by front running tactics over 5f on firm ground.   38
+1101 THE MECHANIC [8] (J Sutcliffe) 3-7-9(5ex) M L Thomas 15/8 FAV: 00-0212: Ev ch: in gd form: see 1101.   25
*986 WOODFOLD [5] (J Winter) 5-9-8(5ex) B Rouse 9/2: 2330-13: Sn prom: see 986.   39
1060 SCHULA [7] (H O'neill) 6-7-10 R Street 8/1: 00-0034: Some late prog: needs 6f:see 1060   13
775 DEALT [2] 5-7-11(4ow) M Roberts 33/1: 0000-00: No threat: lightly raced mdn.   07
1037 KELLYS ROYALE [1] 4-9-11 J Reid 10/1: -000000: Raced alone, early speed: much btr 1037   32
977 Alice Hill [4] 7-7(BL)(3oh)   412 Bincleaves [3] 8-9
8 ran   2¼,2,hd,3,1   (Bertram R Firestone)   W O'gorman Newmarket

1228 L B C FILLIES STAKES 3YO   £2175   7f   Firm -03 -29 Slow

359 ANDIKA [2] (J Tree) 3-8-8 Pat Eddery 13/2: -001: 3 b f Habitat - Anegada (Welsh Pageant) Fairly useful filly: gamely led final 1f under strong driving in a 3yo fillies stks at Kempton June 25: half sister to 2 winners, notably smart 12f performer John French: eff over 7f, will stay at least 1m: appears equally at home on firm or soft.   47
941 SARIZA [13] (H Cecil) 3-8-8 S Cauthen 11/2: -42: Tried to make all: improving filly who shd find a race soon: see 941.   45
907 CLEOFE [7] (L Cumani) 3-8-8 P Hamblett 10/1: 044-003: Never closer: suited by 1m? see 656.   40
966 BUTSOVA [12] (R Armstrong) 3-8-8 M Roberts 9/4 FAV: -0334: Ev ch, disapp after 966.   37
-- NATIJA [9] 3-8-8 B Thomson 33/1: 0-0: Ran on late: will benefit from the outing: related to a couple of winners in France: sure to app 1m+: acts well on firm: likely to improve and win a maiden.   34
-- RAAWIYEH [18] 3-8-8 A Murray 14/1: 0020-0: Prom, wknd: narrowly btn by Mummy's Favourite in Yarmouth maiden, best of 4 races in '85: eff over 6f on firm grd: should stay further: rated 47 on best outing last seasonn.   31
*907 RAJA MOULANA [8] 3-8-13 A Bond 7/1: 04-10: Much btr 907 (very sharp trk).   00
402 Bibi Khatoun [17] 8-8   501 Velvet Pearl [1] 8-8   431 Festivity [14] 8-8
-- Bella Carina [15] 8-8   -- Glade [6] 8-8   -- Hooked Bid [16] 8-8
656 My Darling [3] 8-8   -- Sancilia [10] 8-8   213 Miss Hicks [4] 8-8
-- Lady Lamb [11] 8-8
17 ran   1,2½,1½,1½,1½   (Mrs E Longton)   J Tree Beckhampton, Wilts.

1229 RACAL CHUBB HANDICAP (0-50)   £3204   1m   Firm -03 -05 Slow   [44]

1041 BOLD PILLAGER [3] (J Dunlop) 4-8-10 W Carson 5/4 FAV: 20-0321: 4 b c Formidable - Pilley Green (Porto Bello) Gained a deserved success, with a comfortable pillar to post win in a h'cap at Kempton June 25: lightly raced prev: suited by 1m and firm going: does well with forcing tactics.   39
1189 GRANNYS BANK [4] (W Hastings Bass) 4-8-13 Pat Eddery 13/8: 211-122: 2nd race in 48 hours, possibly too much tho' not discredited: see 1018.   34
750 KING OF SPEED [1] (B Wise) 7-8-9 B Rouse 12/1: -104103: Never closer: best 566.   24
1041 TOM FORRESTER [2] (A Pitt) 5-8-4 J Adams(7) 10/1: 3-03044: Ev ch: best 578 (gd)   18
815 HABS LAD [5] 4-9-10 J Reid 12/1: 0-00000: Speed 6f: see 815.   34
1018 AQABA PRINCE [6] 6-7-12 A Mcglone 33/1: -000000: No danger: see 812.   03
6 ran   4,3,½,2½,3   (Dexam International Ltd)   J Dunlop Arundel, Sussex

1230 RACAL VODAPHONE STAKES   £9723   1m 2f Firm -03 +19 Fast

+1000 CONQUERING HERO [4] (M Stoute) 3-8-6 W R Swinburn 6/1: 3113-11: 3 b c Storm Bird - Wave in Glory (Hoist The Flag) Very smart colt: came from behind to gamely force his hd in front final 1f in a cl fin to fast run Racal-Vodafone Stks (Listed Race) at Kempton June 25: first time out won fast run Hermitage stks at Newbury: won 2 of his 4 races in '85 at Windsor at Doncaster: eff 1m, stays 10f well: acts on firm and yldg: improving sort whose gameness is sure to win himmore races.   82
736 NEBRIS [7] (R Akehurst) 5-9-3 P Cook 11/1: 0-11102: Led dist, just btn and another fine effort from this much improved horse: see 511.   77
1095 WYLFA [5] (J Shaw) 5-9-3 B Rouse 11/1: 40/2243: Ev ch from 2f out: see 410, 736.   76
1094 MACS REEF [6] (M Ryan) 4-9-6 G Starkey 14/1: 02-1004: Ran to his best: see 5, 1094.   77
878 FARAWAY DANCER [1] 3-8-6 S Cauthen 4/9 FAV: 11-2140: Below his best here: see 476,878   77
384 FINAL TRY [2] 3-8-3 W Carson 20/1: 1230-00: Made much: ran only 5 times in '85, winning at York: half brother to 3 winners: stays 1m: runs well on an easy surface.   54
899 DANCING EAGLE [3] 3-8-3 T Ives 33/1: 01-3230: Al last: see 899.   00
7 ran   ¾,½,¾,nk,10   (R Sangster)   M Stoute Newmarket

389

1231 CHAMPAGNE HENRIOT TRAINERS CHALL.H'CAP   £0   1m   Firm -03 -46 Slow   [9]

851 DUELLING [10] (P Mitchell) 5-10-8(vis) R Hutchinson 10/1: 0000001: 5 ro g Vigors - Irish Sword (Irish Lancer) Well ridden to gain the day cl home in a very slowly run Trainers Challenge h'cap at Kempton June 25: in '85 won at Lingfield and also at Cagnes: eff over 1m/10f and on firm and yldg: wears a visor.   24
812 MONTICELLI [8] (C Brittain) 6-9-8 E Eldin 10/1: 404-002: Led dist, caught cl home: last succesful in '84 at Doncaster: stays 1m: acts on firm and yldg.   09
951 KOUS [11] (R Simpson) 3-9-10 C Williams 7/1: -103: Made most: fair eff: see 838(10f).   21
943 BUCKS BOLT [5] (J Berry) 4-10-1 G Oldroyd 25/1: 0030004: Some late prog: see 262.   11
*997 STANFORD VALE [7] 3-11-5 C Nelson 7/4 FAV: 0223110: Stiff task under big weight.   40
960 DOMINION PRINCESS [9] 5-10-1 Margaret Bell 10/1: 0-44330: Btr 960.   08
*955 STILLOU [2] 3-10-3 S Dow 9/2: -340010: No threat in 7th: best 955 (10f)   00
1085 SILENT RUNNING [3] 3-9-9 Brooke Sanders 8/1: 0003000: Wknd into 9th: best 843(10f gd)   00
956 Swiftspender [1] 9-7   733 Mostango [6] 10-0   1065 Saxon Bazaar [11] 9-10
1103 Gulphar [4] 11-8(14ow)
12 ran   ½,¾,2,1½,1.   (Mrs R A Johnson)   P Mitchell Epsom, Surrey

1232 RACAL DATA MAIDEN STAKES 2YO   £2770   7f   Firm -03 -45 Slow

-- BUCHAN NESS [11] (J Dunlop) 2-9-0 B Thomson 14/1: 1: 2 b c Hittite Glory - Ruddy Duck (Dicta Drake) Promising colt: first time out turned up at 14/1, fin strongly to lead on line in a slowly run 2yo mdn at Kempton June 25: closely related to 9 winners, notably smart middle dist performers Great Western and Flighting: needs at least 7f, will be well suited by 1m+: acts on firm ground: the type to improve and win more races.   56
-- LINDAS MAGIC [16] (R Armstrong) 2-8-11 W Carson 7/2: 2: Well bckd debutant, led final 1f and just caught: clear rest: related to a winner in USA: likely to stay beyond 7f: acts well on firm: should sn find a maiden.   52
741 MUBDI [17] (H T Jones) 2-9-0 A Murray 3/1 FAV: 23: Uneasy fav, made most: see 741.   45
-- ANGARA ABYSS [13] (G Harwood) 2-9-0 G Starkey 4/1: 4: Well bckd debutant, ev ch: related to USA winners: should improve for this first outing.   41
985 FOURTH LAD [3] 2-9-0 M L Thomas 14/1: 00: Prom most: prob stays 7f: see 985.   37
-- STATE BALLET [15] 2-9-0 Pat Eddery 4/1: 0: Wk in mkt (op 7/4): fdd final 1f but should benefit from race: dam a winning 2yo over 7f.   35
621 Countess Bree [12] 8-11   -- Mon Coeur [5] 9-0
804 Bold Intention [9] 9-0   694 Stars In Motion [14] 9-0
544 Caballine [1] 9-0   -- Mandalay Prince [6] 9-0
-- Mr Corman [2] 9-0   -- Spanish Connection [4] 9-0
-- Swingsign [10] 9-0   -- Sylvan Whisper [7] 9-0
-- Milcrest [8] 8-11
17 ran   nk,4,1½,1½,1   (A J Struthers)   J Dunlop Arundel, Sussex

1233 RACAL DECCA HANDICAP 3YO (0-50)   £2616   1m 4f   Fim -03 -37 Slow   [54]

1034 STRAIGHT THROUGH [5] (J Winter) 3-8-5 B Rouse 7/2: 4-21221: 3 br g Pitskelly - Queen of Time (Charlottown) Prom and led dist in a slowly run 7 horse h'cap at Kempton June 25: comfortably won a similar h'cap at Folkestone April 7: lightly raced in '85: eff 10f, stays 12f well: acts on firm and hvy: wore a visor on occasion last term but not so far this season.   41
883 UP TO UNCLE [4] (R Hannon) 3-7-8 T Williams 5/1: 4-00022: Led briefly 2f out, almost got up again near fin and was clear rest: gd effort and should find a small h'cap soon: see 117, 883: stays 12f well.   29
669 SHIPBOURNE [3] (G Harwood) 3-8-6 A Clark 6/1: -0003: Ev ch: stays 12f and acts on firm: see 430.   33
*951 FIREPROOF [1] (D Marks) 3-7-11(4ex) M L Thomas 4/1: -042014: Never closer: much btr 951   19
790 MR WHATS HIS NAME [6] 3-8-2(BL) W Woods(3) 25/1: 00-2440: Bl first time, yet to reproduce form of 25 (10f soft).   23
1045 FIRST KISS [7] 3-9-7 W Carson 3/1 FAV: -100: Set a slow pace: much btr 723 (10f)   39
720 RICMAR [2] 3-8-7 G Sexton 14/1: 00-00: Lightly raced mdn with no worthwhile form as yet.   00
7 ran   shthd,5,3,1,3   (J A N Prenn)   J Winter Newmarket

Official Going Given As GOOD/FIRM

1234 SHREWTON MAIDEN STAKES 2YO   DIV 1   £1131   7f   Firm -4 -30 Slow

-- TIMEFIGHTER [3] (J Tree) 2-9-0 Pat Eddery 2/5 FAV: 1: 2 ch c Star Appeal - Slightly Dangerous (Roberto) Promising colt: heavily bckd on debut, dsptd lead all the way and pushed clear final 1f in a 2yo mdn at Salisbury June 25: well bred colt whose dam fin. 2nd in races. the Oaks: eff at 7f, shd be suited by 1m+: acts on firm grd and gall trk and shd win more races. 50
-- MY NOBLE LORD [1] (P Cole) 2-9-0 T Quinn 4/1: 2: Dsptd lead all the way: promising debut from this $300,000 purchase: half brother to sev winners: eff 7f, shd be suited 1m: acts on fast ground and a maiden looks a formality.   43

SALISBURY   Wednesday June 25th   –Cont'd

-- FOREIGN KNIGHT [4] (M Blanshard) 2-9-0 R Cochrane 33/1: 3: Kept on well final 1f,
showing future promise: dam was winning 2yo: shd be suited by 1m and further: acts on fast
ground and should find a race.   38
1039 TELESTO [7] (G Harwood) 2-9-0(BL) G Starkey 6/1: 04: Tried in bl: improved effort:
stays 7f: acts well on fast ground: see 1039.   38
230 LEADING ROLE [2] 2-9-0 R Hills 20/1: 00: Fair effort after abs: will be suited by 1m:
half brother to sev winners and acts on fast ground.   28
-- LIGHTFOOT PRINCE [8] 2-9-0 Paul Eddery 12/1: 0: Never nearer on debut: 12,000 gns
purchase: half brother to sev winners, incl useful stayer Sir Gordon and shd be suited by
middle distances.   25
-- Hollywood Man [5] 9-0   -- Millpond Boy [6] 9-0
8 ran   2,2,shthd,5,1   (K Abdulla)   J Tree Marlborough, Wilts

1235 ALDERSHOT SPRINT H'CAP (0-60)   £4893   6f   Firm -4 +23 Fast   [59]

1145 PRINCE SKY [3] (P Cole) 4-8-7 T Quinn 4/1: 14-4301: 4 b c Skyliner - Majesta
(Majority Blue) Useful colt: well bckd and made almost all comfortably, breaking the course
record in a h'cap at Salisbury june 25: in '85 won at Brighton and Windsor: very eff over
6f: acts on firm and yldg grd and on any trk: well suited by forcing tactics and shd go
close again next time.   52
-952 MIRACLES TAKE TIME [1] (D Elsworth) 4-7-12 A Mcglone 8/1: -000422: Sn prom: in
fine form: see 952.   34
929 PRECIOUS METAL [7] (A Ingham) 3-9-0 R Curant 16/1: 200-103: Dsptd lead: gd run:
seems to act on any ground: see 657.   58
525 SUDDEN IMPACT [5] (K Brassey) 4-8-0(bl) S Whitworth 16/1: 40-1004: Al up there:
btr effort: see 65.   29
600 MEASURING [8] 3-9-0 Pat Eddery 10/1: 320-300: Held ev ch: see 59.   47
952 STEADY EDDIE [4] 4-8-8 Paul Eddery 11/1: 0010-00: Never nearer 6th, but is finding
his form: in '85 won a h'cap at Goodwood: in '84 won at Windsor and again at Goodwood:
very eff over 7f: acts on gd and firm grd and likes a sharpish trk.   30
1037 AMEGHINO [11] 6-8-9 A Tucker(7) 4/1: 0040330: No show: btr 1037, see 846.   00
+1086 BOLD REALM [10] 5-8-4(7ex) P Cook 11/4 FAV: 0-00110: Worth another chance: see 1086.   00
1145 AL TRUI [9] 6-9-5 M Wigham 8/1: 0-01000: Lightly bckd: best 846.   00
-- Green Ruby [2] 8-12   -- Glen Kella Manx [6] 8-4(1ow)
808 Coppermill Lad [14] 7-8   660 Ardrox Lad [12] 9-10
1037 Shalbee [13] 7-7(11oh)
14 ran   3,½,1½,2,nk   (Stephen Crown)   P Cole Whatcombe, Berks.

1236 GIBBS MEW BIBURY CUP H'CAP 3YO (0-50)   £3277   1m 4f   Firm -4 -23 Slow   [47]

1062 MIGHTY FLASH [4] (D Elsworth) 3-8-8 S Cauthen 10/1: 00-0001: 3 b f Rolfe - Lettuce
(So Blessed) Impr filly: led nearing final 1f, driven out in a 3yo h'cap at Salisbury June
25: closely related to smart Mighty Flutter and Mighty Fly: eff 10f, stays 12f: acts well
on fast grd and a gall track.   37
714 PEARLY KING [3] (G Harwood) 3-9-0 G Starkey 10/1: -4002: Chance final 1f: best effort
yet from this half brother to 2 winners: stays 12f: acts on firm and yldg ground.   41
*832 WAVE DANCER [7] (W Hern) 3-9-2 W Carson 6/4 FAV: 4-13: Ran on well final 1f: will
be suited by further than 12f: acts on gd and fast ground: see 832.   43
883 ELAAFUUR [5] (P Walwyn) 3-9-7 Paul Eddery 9/2: 100-444: Led/dsptd lead: consistent:
stays 12f: acts on firm and soft ground: see 459.   47
951 WALCISIN [1] 3-7-13 A Mcglone 7/1: -000220: Ev ch over 2f out: in gd form: see 951.   24
*730 MODENA REEF [6] 3-9-1 Pat Eddery 10/3: 00-3010: Not btn far, but btr 730 (10f)   38
1023 Priok [9] 7-8(1ow)   765 Bet Oliver [8] 7-10   331 Northinch [2] 7-12
9 ran   ½,shthd,½,½,1   (Mrs V A Tory)   D Elsworth Fordingbridge, Hants

1237 HERBERT AND GWEN BLAGRAVE H'CAP (0-60)   £3226   10f   Firm -4 +11 Fast   [57]

750 KALA NASHAN [6] (P Mitchell) 4-7-7(6oh) T Williams 20/1: 0-00301: 4 b f Kala Shikari -
Cry for Help (Town Crier) Showed impr form, led 2½f out and drew clear for an easy win,
breaking the course record in a h'cap at Salisbury June 25: first success: very eff at
10f: acts on any grd, but runs well at Salisbury.   33
1130 LLANARMON [3] (B Hills) 3-7-12(2ow) R Hills 2/1 JT.FAV: 0-03102: Well bckd: led
4f out: see 702.   42
-- INNISHMORE ISLAND [2] (J Dunlop) 3-9-0 Pat Eddery 3/1: 0312-3: Held in 2nd when
stumbled close home: gd seasonal debut: winning 2yo at Warwick: half brother to sev winners:
should be suited by 10f and further: acts on gd and firm ground and on any trk.   58
-- TICKFORD [1] (G Harwood) 3-8-4 A Clark 2/1 JT.FAV: 1-4: Very easy to back on seasonal
debut: no real threat: in '85 won sole start at Leicester: may stay 10f: acts on fast grd
and a galloping track and should improve on this.   44
1038 RUSTY LAW [4] 4-9-11 G Starkey 11/2: -030-00: Led over ½ way: ran over hurdles during
the Winter: lightly raced on the Flat in '85 when trained by H Cecil: very useful 2yo
winning at Wolverhampton and Newmarket: stays 10f: acts well on fast ground.   26
582 COASTAL PLAIN [5] 4-7-7(4oh) M L Thomas 33/1: --00-00: Never in it: lightly raced
colt who cost current connections 9,200 gns: formerly trained by J Dunlop.   00
6 ran   6,shthd,2,12,3   (Mrs D Brackett)   P Mitchell Epsom, Surrey

391

1238 WEYHILL MAIDEN FILLIES 2YO STAKES   £1609   5f   Firm -4 +02 Fast

1021 BLUE TANGO [14] (R Laing) 2-8-11 W Carson 4/1: 243321: 2 b f Blue Cashmere - Happy
Landing (Auction Ring) Useful filly: gained a deserved success, led/dsptd lead all the way
for a game shthd win, breaking 2yo course record in a fillies mdn at Salisbury June 25:
model of consistency in her 5 outings prev: very eff at 5f: seems to act on any grd,but likes it firm. 55
999 CHASING MOONBEAMS [4] (I Balding) 2-8-11 Pat Eddery 4/9 FAV: 22: Led well over 1f out:
caught post: 4l clear 3rd: will not be long in winning: acts on gd and firm: see 999.   55
-- KHAKIS LOVE [10] (P Walwyn) 2-8-11 Paul Eddery 5/1: 3: Active in mkt: al up there:
promising debut: 70,000 gns purchase as a yearling: dam unraced half sister to Circus Plume:
will be suited by further than 5f: acts on fast grd and shd have no trouble finding a mdn.   44
-- NORTHSHIEL [3] (H Candy) 2-8-11 T Williams 20/1: 4: Mkt drifter: never nearer but
showed promise: 20,000 gns purchase and shd be suited by further than 5f: acts on fast grd.   36
-- FINAL RUSH [16] 2-8-11 B Crossley 50/1: 0: Rank outsider: will be suited by further than 5f.
from this 21,000 gns purchase: half sister to sev winners: will be suited by further than 5f. 34
-- HINTON ROSE [8] 2-8-11 S Whitworth 20/1: 0: Never nearer: impr likely.   25
725 Lundy Isle [15] 8-11   -- Indian Jubilee [6] 8-11
-- Lady Silca Key [11] 8-11   596 Betta Win [12] 8-11
848 Cello Solo [5] 8-11   1030 Gods Lil Lisa [9] 8-11
-- Mamadora [7] 8-11   -- Must Be Magic [1] 8-11
-- Pollan Bay [2] 8-11
15 ran   shthd,4,3,½,4   (D Garfield)   R Laing Lambourn, Berks

1239 SHREWTON MAIDEN STAKES 2YO DIV 2   £1143   7f   Firm -4 -15 Slow

-- ORNE [8] (J Tree) 2-9-0 Pat Eddery 7/2: 2 b c Val De L'Orne - Northern Lullaby
(Northern Dancer) Very promising colt: first time out led inside final 1f in a 2yo mdn
at Salisbury June 25: cost $60,000 and is a half brother to a winner in Ireland: eff 7f,
bred to stay middle dist: acts on fast grd and a gall trk: sure to win more races.   60
-- OPERATIC SCORE [4] (P Cole) 2-9-0 T Quinn 8/1: 2: Led after ½ way: just btn: should
go one better soon: cost 37,000 gns as yearling: eff 7f on fast ground.   58
1019 NONSUCH PALACE [5] (I Balding) 2-9-0 S Cauthen 13/8: 03: Dsptd lead, ev ch: stays
7f: see 1019.   51
985 TREVA [1] (D Oughton) 2-9-0 B Crossley 50/1: 04: Never nearer: on the upgrade:
stays 7f and acts on fast ground.   38
-- PROSILIENT [7] 2-9-0 G Starkey 5/4 FAV: 0: Well bckd debutant: no real threat:
cost $90,000 as yearling and is a half brother to sev winners incl the smart Full Extent:
will do much better next time.   37
1057 KINGSWOOD RESOPAL [2] 2-9-0 A Mcglone 50/1: 000: Showed impr here: suited by 7f
on fast ground.   29
-- Night Visitor [9] 9-0   -- Relkoora [3] 9-0   -- Amwaj [6] 9-0
9 ran   nk,2½,5,nk,3   (K Abdulla)   J Tree Marlborough, Wilts

Official Going Given As FIRM

1240 NOEL CANNON MEM. TROPHY (H'CAP)(0-50)   £2620   1m   Firm -01 +16 Fast   [49]

812 ALQIRM [4] (C Benstead) 4-8-9 B Rouse 11/4 FAV: 00-0021: 4 b c Drone - Joie (Speak
John) Led inside final 1f, ridden out, breaking the course record in a h'cap at Salisbury
June 26: first time out in '85 won at Lingfield: eff at 6f, nowadays suited by 1m: acts on
heavy, likes fast grounnd.   42
1041 TALK OF GLORY [3] (L Cottrell) 5-8-4 G Baxter 9/1: 0-02002: Led over 2f out: good
effort: see 453.   32
930 FAIR COUNTRY [5] (D Elsworth) 4-8-11 Pat Eddery 7/2: 00-0323: Kept on well final 1f:
in gd form at present: didnot have the best of runs here: see 930, 762.   37
521 CASCABEL [7] (R Williams) 5-8-12 R Cochrane 3/1: 0012-04: Ev ch final 2f: running
into form: see 521.   33
573 STAR OF A GUNNER [9] 6-9-12 J Reid 14/1: -011000: Mkt drifter: no threat: best 248   42
724 PEANDAY [11] 5-7-9 R Morse(5) 10/1: 0-00300: Fdd final 1f: twice below form 481(7f)   10
1081 MISTER PRELUDE [6] 6-7-8(bl) S Dawson 9/1: 20-00020: Made much, fdd: btr 1081.   00
1186 Miss Monroe [2] 8-5   700 Magic Bid [12] 8-13
9 ran   2,½,2½,2½,nk   (R Miquel)   C Benstead Epsom, Surrey

1241 E.B.F. SOUTHAMPTON MAIDEN STAKES 2YO   £1424   5f   Firm -01 -02 Slow

-- MOREWOODS [11] (I Balding) 2-9-0 Pat Eddery 7/1: 1: 2 b c Northern Jove - Vogue
Folks (Reverse) Promising colt: first time out, fin well to lead inside final 1f, a shade
comfortably, in a 2yo mdn at Salisbury June 26: cost $100,000 as yearling and is a brother to
a winner in the USA: eff 5f, shd stay 6f: acts on fast ground and a gall trk: should
win more races and rate more highly.   54
953 SANTELLA GREY [14] (G Harwood) 2-9-0 G Starkey 11/10 FAV: 022: Heavily bckd: sn
prom and ran on well final 1f: must win soon: possibly btr over 6f: see 953.   50
804 SHARP REMINDER [9] (D Laing) 2-9-0 W Carson 13/2: 003: Led nearing final 1f: caught
cl home: gd effort from this improving colt: clearly well suited by fast ground and
should be winning soon: acts on a galloping track.   50
1082 CHARMED PRINCE [2] (J Bridger) 2-9-0 T Williams 33/1: 04: Sn prom: on the upgrade:
eff 5f on fast ground and a galloping track.   35
1075 GREEN GLORY [1] 2-9-0 R Cochrane 6/1: 20: Dsptd lead: see 1075.   34
1019 HANSEATIC [13] 2-9-0 S Cauthen 12/1: 00: On the upgrade: half brother to winning
sprinter Halcyon Cove: shd be suited by 6f: acts on fast ground.   28
-- YOUNG GHILLIE [16] 2-9-0 Paul Eddery 10/1: 0: Mkt drifter on debut: no threat in
7th, but should improve: half brother to the smart and speedy Stalker: shd stay 6f:
will do much better than this.   00
-- AL LUDHER [8] 2-9-0 I Johnson 33/1: 0: Fin 8th on debut: improvement likely and will
be suited by 6f+.   00

--	Going Easy [5] 9-0	--	Plague Orats [3] 9-0	678	Segovian [10] 9-0(BL)
--	Riverboat Party [4] 9-0			800	Young Lochinvar [7] 9-0
--	Summer Trip [15] 9-0	1059	Biotin [6] 9-0	--	Victory Ballard [12] 9-0

16 ran   1,hd,5,hd,2½,½,¾   (George Strawbridge)   I Balding Kingsclere, Berks

1242 VEUVE CLICQUOT CHAMPAGNE STAKES 2YO   £10331   6f   Firm -01 -07 Slow

1019 WHO KNOWS [8] (W Hern) 2-8-11 W Carson 7/4 JT FAV: 31: 2 b c Known Fact - Happy Kin
(Bold Hitter) Promising colt: made ev yard, gamely, in a val Listed race at Salisbury June
26: first time out fin a gd 3rd to Brave Dancer in a val maiden at Newbury: half brother
to the smart stayer Family Friend and should be suited by much further in time: acts on
gd and fast ground and a galloping trk: should win more races and seems a genuine colt.   60
*1049 DARLEY KNIGHT [6] (J Dunlop) 2-9-2 B Thomson 7/4 JT FAV: 12: Got loose before start:
chall final 1f and nearly got up: excellent efforts at the weights and is certain to win
more races: heavily bckd today: see 1049.   65
-- BEESHI [5] (P Cole) 2-8-11 T Quinn 5/2: 3: Nicely bckd debutant: no extra final 1f:
but seems certain to improve for the experience: half brother to numerous winners, including
Milk Heart and Chaumiere: eff 6f, will be suited by further in time: acts on fast grd and
should have no trouble finding a race.   48
-- DONT FORGET ME [7] (R Hannon) 2-8-11 A Mcglone 50/1: 4: Sn prom on race course debut
showing promise: cost 19,000 gns as yearling: dam a 12f winner in Ireland: should stay
further than 6f: acts on fast ground and should not be long in winning.   46
685 HAYTAL [4] 2-8-11 S Cauthen 8/1: 00: Fdd final 2f: fair effort in this gd company:
bred to stay further than 6f: acts on gd and fast ground.   40
-- EL ZETA [2] 2-8-11 R Cochrane 12/1: 0: Active in mkt on debut: shd improve on this
initial outing: cost I.R. 34,000 and will be suited by 7f+: acts on fast ground.   38
-- FIRES OUT [1] 2-8-8 A Proud 50/1: 0: Lost grd at start and never in it.   00
7 ran   hd,4,nk,2,½,25   (Sir Michael Sobell)   W Hern West Ilsley, Berks

1243 CARNARVON CHALL. CUP H'CAP   £994   1m 4f   Firm -01 -21 Slow   [4]

805 BEAU VISTA [6] (D Elsworth) 4-10-12 Amanda Harwood(5) 3/1 FAV: 0304-01: 4 ch c
Crimson Beau - Shanghai Lady (Crocket) Justified fav, led inside final 1f, ridden out in
an amateur's h'cap at Salisbury June 26: placed on sev occasions in '85, but this was his
first win: stays 12f: acts on gd and firm grd and a galloping track.   26
-- TOSCANA [2] (D Marks) 5-10-13 Kelly Marks 10/1: 13200-2: Led 3f out: just btn and
4l clear 3rd: fine seasonal debut: in '85 won a seller at Haydock: eff 10f, stays 12f:
acts on firm and yldg ground and does well in this type of event.   26
841 CHARTFIELD [11] (12/1) 6-9-10 Brooke Sanders 12/1: 30003: Chance over 2f out:
acts on firm and hvy: see 121.   01
1035 DESTROY [14] (D Elsworth) 7-9-11 Mr P Mcquillan(5) 6/1: 0040/04: Prom, ev ch:
maiden: acts on fast ground.   00
984 ASTICOT [16] 4-10-9 Debbie Albion(5) 7/1: 000-030: No real threat: see 984.   10
1099 FISHPOND [5] 5-11-9(BL) Sara Lawrence 9/2: 40-2000: Bl first time: never nearer:
btr 1099, see 419 (longer trips).   14
1035 TAXIADS [4] 4-12-0(7ex) Jane Allison 5/1: 0-01100: Twice below form 984.   00
1166 SALLOOM [9] 4-12-0(vis) Maxine Juster 5/1: 00-0300: Made much: best 912 (10f).   00
943 Catman [10] 10-6(bl)   912 Annie Ra [3] 10-1   -- Cindie Girl [15] 11-9
530 Viceroy Boy [7] 10-4   -- Just Candid [8] 10-10   -- Razzle Dazzle Boy [12] 10-3
724 Ricco Star [1] 9-13
15 ran   hd,4,1½,hd,5   (Vistaplan Reference Systems Ltd)   D Elsworth Whitsbury, Hants

1244 TISBURY FILLIES STAKES 3YO   £1446   7f   Firm -01 -02 Slow

1043 BALLAD ROSE [17] (P Cole) 3-8-11 T Quinn 7/4 FAV: 23-4321: 3 b f Ballad Rock -
Gracious Consent (Prince Regent) Useful filly: gained a deserved success, making ev yard,
comfortably, in a 3yo fillies mdn at Salisbury June 26: placed in all her prev outings:
half sister to 12f winner Vouchsafe: eff 7f, stays 1m: acts on any grd: runs well on a
galloping track.   48
982 GREAT DILEMMA [19] (P Makin) 3-8-11 S Cauthen 10/3: -0022: Ev ch final 3f: 4l
clear 3rd: in gd form and should be winning shortly: acts on gd and firm ground: see 982. 44
--   SATIN AND SILK [18] (A Bailey) 3-8-11 P Bloomfield 33/1: -3: Sn prom on race course
debut: gd effort: cost I.R. 9,000 as yearling and is a half sister to 3 winners including
the useful Grand Unit: shd be suited by 1m: acts on fast ground and should find a race.   36
923 HANGLANDS [1] (D Elsworth) 3-8-11 W R Swinburn 25/1: 0-04: Nearest fin and will be
well suited by 1m: half sister to 3 winners: acts well on fast ground.   34
209 PARTS IS PARTS [9] 3-8-11 R Cochrane 33/1: -000: Abs: chance 2f out: best effort
yet and acts well on firm ground: cost $75,000 as yearling: may stay 1m.   34
431 APHROSINA [7] 3-8-11 Pat Eddery 11/4: -000: Fdd final 1f after abs: prob stays 7f. 32
764 BASICALLY BETTER [10] 3-8-11 Paul Eddery 10/1: 20-400: No real threat in 8th:
best 501.   00
844 Adhari [12] 8-11   **-- Lochmar** [13] 8-11   **-- Abigails Gem** [6] 8-11
941 Baby Ravenna [5] 8-11   **-- Flitter Flutter** [2] 8-11
868 Home Rule [4] 8-11(bl)   **-- Rockville Squaw** [15] 8-11
966 Town Fair [14] 8-11   **-- Sharp Reef** [8] 8-11
16 ran   1½,4,1,shthd,¾   (N W L Abbot)   P Cole Whatcombe, Berks

1245 DOWNTON HANDICAP STAKES (0-50) 3YO   £2727   7f   Firm -01 +04 Fast   [54]

1147 BELOW ZERO [3] (A Bailey) 3-8-9 R Cochrane 25/1: 1220001: 3 ch c Northfields -
Indigine (Raise a Native) Fairly useful colt: fin well to lead cl home breaking the course
record in a 3yo h'cap at Salisbury June 26: first time out won a similar event at Kempton:
very eff at 7f, stays 1m: seems to act on any ground.   46
--   SURFING [5] (J Tree) 3-8-1 M Roberts 14/1: 003-2: Led dist, just caught: fine seasonal
debut: on final outing in '85 fin 3rd in a fillies mdn at Wolverhampton: half sister to sev
winners incl the smart Bassenthwaite: eff 7f, shd stay 1m: acts well on fast ground and
can find a h'cap.   34
1032 LADY LA PAZ [18] (P Cundell) 3-7-7 G French 6/1: 0-04023: Made most: in fine form: 24
954 BOWL OVER [4] (P Makin) 3-8-9(bl) G Baxter 5/1: 2-10324: Dsptd lead over 1f out:
btr 1m? See 157.   36
615 GIVING IT ALL AWAY [2] 3-7-11 M L Thomas 25/1: 00-3000: Kept on well final 1f:
eff 7f on gd and firm ground.   23
1065 TIME BIRD [12] 3-7-13 M Hills 20/1: 333-000: Not much room dist: see 1065.   19
861 MASTER THAMES [10] 3-9-7 W R Swinburn 6/1: 2-430: Prom, fin 7th: best 546.   41
*1065 SOLO STYLE** [16] 3-8-3(6ex) P Waldron 4/1 FAV: 0-30010: No real threat: much btr 1065. 00
808 STRIVE [1] 3-8-10 S Cauthen 13/2: 0-02400: Well bckd but no show: best 436.   00
1032 COUNTRY GENTLEMAN [8] 3-8-9 W Carson 10/1: 040-000: Never sighted: in '85 fin 4th
to Manton Dan in a maiden at Goodwood: acts on fast ground.   00
335 Artistic Champion [14] 7-8   **1001 Silver Form** [6] 7-7(1oh)
615 Lightning Wind [19] 8-5(VIS)   **886 Major Jacko** [7] 8-9(bl)
1065 Deputy Tim [13] 8-2(bl)(1ow)   **586 Bronze Opal** [20] 9-3
255 Heart Of Glass [17] 8-9   **923 Prissy Miss** [11] 7-13
847 Arabian Blues [15] 7-9(2ow)(3oh)   **928 See No Evil** [9] 7-7(8oh)
20 ran   1,1,2,½,4,hd   (T Ramsden)   A Bailey Newmarket

1246 TISBURY FILLIES STAKES 3YO   £1446   7f   Firm -01 -10 Slow

--   REALITY [3] (R Johnson Houghton) 3-8-11 S Cauthen 5/1: 0-1: 3 br f Known Fact -
Missed Blessing (So Blessed) Led over 2f out, comfortably, in a 3yo fillies stks at Salisbury
June 26: ran only once in '85: dam was a very smart miler: eff 7f, shd be suited by 1m:
acts on fast ground and a galloping track.   50
835 MARCREDEA [16] (D Murray Smith) 3-8-11 R Wernham 25/1: -002: Kept on well, but no
chance with easy winner: best effort yet: acts well on fast ground.   38
923 SUMMER GARDEN [9] (I Balding) 3-8-11 Pat Eddery 6/1: -403: Prom, ev ch: acts on
firm and heavy: may need further: see 658.   37
--   GLANGWILI [17] (H Candy) 3-8-11 T Williams 20/1: 0230-4: Nearest fin on seasonal
debut: showed some promise in '85: stays 7f: acts on firm and yldg ground.   35
--   PETRIFY [4] 3-8-11 J Williams 20/1: -0: Nearest fin on race course debut: shd
do better: half sister to winning 3yo Reyah: stays 7f: acts on fast ground.   34
498 UPHORIA [1] 3-8-11 T Quinn 4/1: 3020-40: Ev ch: abs since 498.   28
982 SHINING SKIN [8] 3-8-11 Paul Eddery 5/2 FAV: 420-00: Has not shown her 2yo form:
in '85 fin 3l 2nd to Embla in a fillies mdn at Kempton: may stay further than 7f: acts
on fast ground.   00
658 MUMTAZ MAYFLY [14] 3-8-11 W R Swinburn 10/1: 00-00: Never showed: may need
further than 7f.   00
733 HOLLY BROWN [12] 3-8-11 M Hills 10/1: -000: Mkt drifter: btr 733, see 498.   00

923 **Pause For Applause** [18] 8-11   --   **Cleavage** [15] 8-11
966 **Flash Donna** [19] 8-11   937 **Five Quarters** [7] 8-11
624 **Harmony Heights** [13] 8-11   658 **Zillebeke** [11] 8-11
--   **Celtic Bow** [6] 8-11   --   **Ivy May** [10] 8-11   1061 **Lucy Aura** [5] 8-11
18 ran   4,hd,½,½,2½,3   (T D Holland-Martin)   R Johnson Houghton Blewbury, Oxon

---

NEWCASTLE   Thursday June 26th   Lefthand, Stiff Galloping Track

1247 WALLSEND H'CAP 3YO+ 0-35   £2201   6f   Firm 05 +16 Fast   [25]

1051 CUMBRIAN DANCER [4] (M H Easterby) 3-9-3(vis) M Birch 9/1: 0430041: 3 b g Imperial
Fling - Natural Flora (Floribunda) Led after 3f, keeping on well under press and broke
the course record when narrowly winning a h'cap at Newcastle June 26: won a nursery at
Hamilton in '85: equally eff over 6/7f and handles firm and hvy going: likes a stiff trk:
wears a visor.   34
*784 SOFTLY SPOKEN [5] (P Felgate) 3-9-2 W Ryan 11/2: 100-012: Chall 1f out, kept on
under pressure and not btn far: still improving: see 784: stays 6f.   31
-1093 WILLIE GAN [6] (Denys Smith) 8-8-9 L Charnock 100/30 FAV: 0-00023: Prom ev ch.see 866. 12
1093 AITCHANDOUBLEYOU [9] (T Barron) 3-9-8 N Ives 16/1: 401-004: Came from well behind
and is running into form: see 1093.   33
-936 GOLD CHIP [1] 3-9-5 N Connorton 5/1: 013-420: Sn prom: see 451.   26
1120 WARTHILL LADY [7] 4-8-13 K Darley 14/1: -040040: Ev ch: see 56.   05
1120 MIAMI DOLPHIN [3] 6-8-13(VIS) M Fry 10/1: 0131030: Al outpaced: needs heavy? see 786. 00
890 MISS PRIMULA [13] 3-9-6 R Guest 5/1: 0-03030: Led 3f, fin 9th: btr 890 (5f gd).   00
1104 King Cole [10] 9-0   1101 Y I Oyston [11] 9-8   1093 Monswart [12] 8-12
1131 Culminate [2] 8-5(8ex)
12 ran   ½,1,½,2,2½   (Cumbrian Industrials Ltd)   M H Easterby Malton, Yorks

1248 STAGSHAW SELLING STAKES 2YO   £1263   5f   Firm 05 -22 Slow

--   KNOCKSHARRY [3] (R Hollinshead) 2-8-8 P Hill(7) 9/1: 1: 2 b f Palm Track - Octavia
(Sallust) First time out, quietly ridden and led after ½ way, cleverly winning a 2yo seller
at Newcastle June 26 (no bid): half sister to a couple of winning 2yo platers: eff 5f, will
stay 6f and prob further: acts well on firm ground.   27
948 NATIONS SONG [4] (R Stubbs) 2-8-13(bl) J H Brown(5) 7/4 FAV: 041022: Well bckd, chall
final 1f, just btn: in fine form: now wears blinkers: see 948, 681.   31
957 RUN TO WORK [5] (G Moore) 2-8-11 D Casey(7) 2/1: 4223: Al well there: deserves
a seller soon: see 957.   25
--   DUBLIN BELLE [1] (M Brittain) 2-8-8 K Darley 6/1: 4: Led till ½ way: related to a
couple of winners: quite speedily bred but should stay at least 6f.   12
415 MADDYBENNY [2] 2-8-8(BL) C Dwyer 4/1: 40000: Abs: best 20 (soft).   08
--   OKAY YAH [6] 2-8-11 S Lawes 12/1: 0: Al rear on debut.   00
6 ran   nk,1½,3,½,8.   (P J White)   R Hollinshead Rugeley, Staffs

1249 DOBSON PEACOCK H'CAP 3YO+ 0-60   £3837   1m   Firm 05 -07 Slow   [54]

1047 TRY TO STOP ME [1] (Denys Smith) 5-8-11 L Charnock 5/2: 0-00321: 5 ch h Sharpen Up
- Come Back (Bold Lad) Gained a deserved success, leading dist and holding on well when
narrowly winning val Dobson Peacock H'cap at Newcastle June 26: in '85 won h'caps at
Thirsk and York: eff over 1m, stays 10f: acts on any going and on any track.   49
719 PALAESTRA [3] (J Dunlop) 3-8-12 G Duffield 4/1: 212-002: Ran very wide into straight,
kept on well under strong driving and did well to get so close: likely to win soon: see 719 64
*1173 VAGUE MELODY [4] (L Piggott) 4-8-7(6ex) T Ives 7/4 FAV: -230113: Fair effort but
prob too soon after 1173.   36
1109 MOORES METAL [7] (R Hollinshead) 6-8-10 S Perks 12/1: 0000004: Came with a smooth
run to chall dist, sn btn: see 441.   37
815 MAJOR DON [8] 6-9-10 E Guest(3) 14/1: 0000-00: Led briefly 2f out: lightly raced
and below his best in '85, prev season won val Beeswing Stakes at Newcastle: best form on
firm ground over 7f/1m: likes a galloping track: has come down considerably in the h'cap
if refinding his old form.   45
893 SILLY BOY [5] 6-8-8 M Birch 12/1: 000-040: Not recover from a slow start: see 698. 23
789 Pacific Princess [6] 8-4(bl)   936 O I Oyston [2] 7-7(2oh)
8 ran   ½,4,1,3,3   (A L Wilkinson)   Denys Smith Bishop Auckland, Co Durham

1250 HEDDON H'CAP 3YO ONLY 0-35   £1976   1m 4f Firm 05 -67 Slow   [29]

959 MADISON GIRL [6] (R Whitaker) 3-9-5 D Mckeown 4/1: 00-0341: 3 ch f Last Fandango -
Mountain Chorus (Evening Call) Ran on to lead 2f out comfortably, in a very slowly run 3yo
h'cap at Newcastle June 26: first success: well suited by 12f, seems to stay 14f: acts
well on firm or gd going and on any trk tho' runs well on a stiff one.   28
1072 DEPUTY MONARCH [7] (Denys Smith) 3-8-11 L Charnock 7/2: 40-0222: Kept on well under
pressure, narrowly btn in a cl finish: see 1072.   19
958 WATERDALE [5] (M W Easterby) 3-9-7 K Hodgson 11/4 FAV: 00-0033: Prom, not clear
run final 1f, kept on well in a close fin: gd effort: see 958.   27
935 CRIMSON ROBES [1] (R Hollinshead) 3-8-13 S Perks 10/1: -04004: Al there: see 379:
seems to act on firm and yldg: may prove best around 10/11f.   18

1089 DOON VENTURE [3] 3-8-3 M Wood 13/2: 000-000: Held up, no danger: see 867.   05
*1123 TIEATRE [4] 3-8-3(4ex) D Casey(3) 5/1: 00-0010: Led 10f, btr 1123 (soft)   02
779 NICOLINI [2] 3-9-2(VIS) M Birch 12/1: 00-00: Visored for first time, wknd str:
very lightly raced maiden.   00
7 ran   ½,½,½,1½,2   (A K Zivanaris)   R Whitaker Wetherby, Yorks

1251 STOCKSFIELD STAYERS MAID.STAKES 3YO+   £2266   2m   Firm 05 -31 Slow

458 TEMPLE HEIGHTS [4] (J Dunlop) 3-8-5 G Duffield 6/4 FAV: -01: 3 b f Shirley Heights
- Hardirondo (Hardicanute) Impr filly: justified strong support, prom and leading dist in a
slowly run mdn at Newcastle June 26: unraced in '85: related to winning miler Redgrave
Artist: very well suited by 2m and firm ground and seems to like a stiff track: should
find a staying h'cap.   45
978 CHALICE OF SILVER [5] (M Jarvis) 3-8-5 T Ives 7/4: 30-432: Led ½ way, clear rest:
stays 2m well: see 315.   42
996 SNOWFIRE CHAP [6] (H Wharton) 3-8-8 D Nicholls 11/1: -033: Prom, ev ch: see 996.   30
1071 SANDYLA [2] (D Thom) 5-9-11(vis) M Brennan(7) 13/2: 0/0-024: No threat: see 1071.   22
959 GARTHMAN [7] 3-8-8 A Mackay 50/1: -000: Prom, wknd and may be suited by shorter dist   16
770 WRANGBROOK [8] 3-8-5 E Guest(3) 20/1: 0-300: Led till ½ way: twice below 123(12f,hvy.)   07
1089 Queen Of Swords [9] 8-5   -- Panto Girl [1] 9-8
-- Petford Chiru [3] 9-8   -- Fragrant Calamity [10] 9-8
10 ran   2,8,4,½,3   (Mrs A V Ferguson)   J Dunlop Arundel, Sussex

1252 CHESTERS STAKES 2YO   £2472   6f   Firm 05 Inapplicable

*1014 WIGANTHORPE (M W Easterby) 2-9-5 T Lucas No S.P.: -022011: Very useful colt:
walked over in a 2YO minor event at Newcastle June 26: see 1014.   00
        (Miss S E Easterby)   M W Easterby, Sheriff Hutton, Yorks.

DONCASTER   Friday June 27th   Lefthanded Galloping Track

Official Going Given As GOOD/FIRM

1253 MARGARET MAIDEN STAKES 2YO   £959   7f   Firm 18 -23 Slow

974 LAURIES WARRIOR [16] (R Boss) 2-9-0 E Guest(3) 11/4: 4021: 2 ch c Viking - Romany
Pageant (Welsh Pageant) Overcame his unfav draw, running on strongly to lead cl home in a
2yo maiden auction stks at Doncaster June 27: first foal who cost 10,000 gns as yearling:
stayys 7f well: acts on gd and fast ground and seems suited by a gall trk.   42
1019 LORD WESTGATE [2] (M Usher) 2-9-0 M Wigam 10/1: 002: Dropped in class: made most:
clearly well suited by forcing tactics and shd find a race in this grade: stays 7f: acts
on firm ground and on a gall track.   38
544 PALEFACE [18] (L Piggott) 2-9-0 T Ives 10/11 FAV: 33: Heavily bckd after fair abs:
ran on same pace: stays 7f: acts on firm and yldg: see 544.   35
1105 PARKERS JOY [7] (E Wheeler) 2-9-0 W Wharton 33/1: 0004: Btr effort: stays 7f: seems
suited by fast ground and a galloping track: half brother to middle dist winner Jai-Alai: 33
1105 CITY FINAL [21] 2-8-11 S Perks 12/1: 4040: Ran to her best: see 1105.   27
1180 DOHTY BABY [4] 2-8-11 K Hodgson 12/1: 030: Never nearer: stays 7f: acts on firm
ground and on a galloping track: see 1180.   22
780 NORTHERN DECREE [5] 2-9-0 M Hindley(3) 33/1: 000: Front rank till dist: fin 7th:
seems btr suited by this longer trip: half brother to sev winners: acts on firm ground.   24
-- PUNTA CALAHONDA [17] 2-9-0 P Robinson 33/1: 0: Never nearer 8th on race course debut:
speedily bred colt who fetched 5,200 gns at recent sales on a sound surface: will improve.   22
-- YOUNG BENZ [11] 2-9-0 M Birch 16/1: 0: Speed over ½ way, fin 9th on debut.   22
-- KANDAWGYI [20] 2-8-11 P Cook 10/1: 0: Early speed on race course debut: will
improve: cost 10,000 gns and is half sister to sev winners.   00
-- NATIVE PAWN [10] 2-9-0 M Roberts 10/1: 0: Debutant: down the field tho' should improve.   00
915 Regent Lad [12] 9-0   1175 Friends For Life [14] 9-0
-- Murphy [1] 9-0   -- Saboteur [13] 9-0   1050 Tyred Nsnookered [9] 9-0
944 Dancing Belle [8] 8-11   741 Deftly [6] 8-11
944 Delite Muffin [19] 8-11   882 Relampego [3] 8-11
913 St Johns Bay [15] 8-11
21 ran   1,1½,½,1½,2½,½,1,hd,hd   (L C James)   R Boss Newmarket

1254 LONDESBOROUGH HANDICAP (0-50)   £2650   1m 2f   Firm 18 -02 Slow   [44]

+875 TOSARA [6] (H Candy) 4-9-7 R Curant 9/4 FAV: 0-2411: 4 b f Main Reef - My Fawn (High
Lupus) Impr filly: comfortably justified fav, led 2f out in a h'cap at Doncaster Junne 27:
earlier this month won a fast run stks at Ripon: half sister to sev winners including the
useful Border Dawn: very eff around 10f on gd and fast ground: acts on any track.   48
410 ISLAND SET [4] (L Cumani) 4-9-7 S Quane(7) 4/1: 3411-02: Switched below dist,
fin strongly: gd eff after a fair abs: may go one btr soon: see 410.   46

*1133 MISTER POINT [8] (C Tinkler) 4-8-4(5ex) M Birch 6/1: -000113: Made most in this
better company: remains in good form: acts on fast ground: see 1133.   26
 429 SITTING BULL [3] (G Wragg) 4-9-3 P Robinson 6/1: 0300-04: Never nearer: abs since 429.   36
-698 MASKED BALL [2] 6-8-13 M Fry 5/1: 30-1120: Another fair eff: see 698.   29
1106 ELARIM [5] 7-8-5 C Coates(5) 16/1: 0000440: Al prom: see 745.   17
 933 Senor Ramos [9] 8-4(bl)   -- Errol Emerald [7] 7-7(bl)(1oh)
 698 Barry Sheene [1] 9-7
 9 ran   ½,1½,1½,1½,1½   (Fahd Salman)   H Candy Wantage, Oxon.

1255 GRIMTHORPE STAKES 2YO   £3345   6f   Firm 18 +03 Fast

*995 GLOW AGAIN [4] (J Etherington) 2-9-1 M Wood 11/4 FAV: 3111: 2 br f The Brianstan -
Grey Aglow (Aglojo) Useful filly: completed her hat-trick, comfortably leading at the dist
in quite a fast run 2yo stks at Doncaster June 27: earlier scored ready wins at Beverley and
Pontefract: half sister to the versatile The Small Miracle: very eff over 5/6f: acts on firm
and yielding ground and on any track: can extend her sequence.   55
*974 BORN TO RACE [6] (L Piggott) 2-8-11 T Ives 3/1: 012: Scrubbed along thr'out, led
briefly 2f out: stays 6f: should be winning again soon: see 974.   46
 898 KHADRUF [1] (H Thomson Jones) 2-9-1 A Murray 9/2: 103: Broke well and made most:
well clear rem: stays 6f: acts on a sound surface: see 437.   42
+515 KILVARNET [5] (R Hollinshead) 2-8-12 S Perks 11/2: 01314: Speed over ½ way: much
better with some give in 515 (5f sharp track): deserves another chance.   14
 953 TENDER TIFF [3] 2-8-12 S Cauthen 3/1: 1430: Has proved disapp since 655 (hvy).   12
 -- MON BALZAR [2] 2-8-11 R Cochrane 33/1: 0: Tardy start tho' soon on terms: wknd after
½ way: cost 11,000 gns and is a half brother to sev winners: will improve for this experience. 07
 6 ran   1,3,10,½,1½   (Mrs G Liversidge)   J Etherington Malton, Yorks.

1256 STOCKIL CLAIMING STAKES 3YO   £976   1m   Firm 18 +03 Fast

 861 NAP MAJESTICA [1] (M Camacho) 3-8-6 D Nicholls 9/2 JT FAV: 300-001: 3 ch g Captain
James - Semper Fi (Above Suspicion) Nicely bckd when returning to form, led below dist for
a comfortable win in a 3yo Claiming Stks at Doncaster June 27: first success tho' was placed
in most of his starts last term: stays 1m well: well suited by fast grd and a gall track.   42
 733 ROBIS [7] (N Macauley) 3-7-13 S P Griffiths(5) 20/1: 0-40002: Ev ch: best effort
this term: stays 1m: acts on fast ground and on any track: see 24.   26
 928 LOVE AT LAST [10] (W Hastings Bass) 3-8-3 R Lines(3) 9/2 JT FAV: -333: Ran on same
pace: stays 1m: acts on gd and firm ground and on any track: see 501.   26
*829 ADAMSTOWN [4] (M Prescott) 3-8-13 G Duffield 11/2: -314: Led 3f out: in gd form: see 829. 32
 464 WHAT A PARTY [9] 3-8-8 B Thomson 9/1: 2002-00: Abs: al prom: maiden who found
one too good in 3 or her 6 starts last season: stays 1m: acts on any going: has worn blinkers. 22
 494 ELEGANT GUEST [6] 3-8-6 T Ives 16/1: -00: Shown little in his 2 starts: see 494.   12
 954 STILL DREAMING [15] 3-8-9 P Cook 5/1: 30-2040: Fin 8th: best over 7f in 424 (gd)   00
 806 JARYAN [11] 3-8-11(BL) M Hills 7/1: -000: Bl first time and dropped in class:
down the field: half brother to a middle dist winner.   00
 -- Run Charlie [3] 3-8(7ow)   960 Kirkella [8] 8-11
1142 Qurrat Al Ain [2] 8-3   688 Achillean [13] 8-6   -- Avada [16] 8-11
1062 Super Silhouette [5] 8-8   -- Accumulate [14] 8-6
15 ran   3,2,2,2½,4   (D C Bramal)   M Camacho Malton, Yorks.

1257 SCURRY FILLIES H'CAP 3YO 0-35   £2239   7f   Firm 18 -03 Slow   [42]

 886 CASBAH GIRL [8] (R Smyly) 3-8-2 T Williams 20/1: 0002-01: Was a surprise winner of
a fillies h'cap at Doncaster June 27, led 2f out and stayed on well: lightly raced
last season, when running up to Aitchandoubleyou in a Nottingham nursery on her final start:
stays 7f well: suited by fast ground.   26
 961 NEW EVIDENCE [4] (E Eldin) 3-8-2 A Mackay 15/2: 00-0002: Al well placed: stays 7f: 22
 874 HAYWAIN [22] (B Hills) 3-8-3 B Thomson 13/2 FAV: 000-03: Made most stands side:
good effort: seems to act any trk: see 874.   18
 972 KENOOZ [10] (A Stewart) 3-9-3 M Roberts 12/1: 040-204: Ev ch dist: stays 7f: see 657.   30
 -- MADEMOISELLE MAGNA [3] 3-8-11 J Lowe 25/1: 30010-0: Led far side most of way: won
a Nottingham nursery last Summer and is well suited by fast ground: stays 7f: btr for race.   23
1051 COUNTRY CARNIVAL [18] 3-8-12 D Nicholls 16/1: 0-00300: Al up there: see 907.   21
 997 FLYING BIDDY [2] 3-8-9 M Hills 7/1: 000-30: Fin 7th: fair effort: see 997.   00
 929 BERNIGRA GIRL [23] 3-8-12 E Guest(3) 10/1: 1-00000: Gd early speed: see 496.   00
1103 SKELTON [14] 3-7-13 A Shoults(3) 15/2: 0-00030: Active in mkt tho' no threat: btr 1103   00
 637 Highland Tale [21] 8-1(BL)(3ow)   867 La Jambalaya [12] 8-3
 500 Opal Flower [16] 7-12   961 Daisy Star [17] 7-10
 427 Mayor [6] 9-7   806 Knightly Dia [9] 9-2   538 Annabellina [13] 8-12
 891 Azelly [1] 8-9   1032 Fudge [20] 8-7   911 How Blue [7] 8-6
 937 Choral Park [11] 8-6   997 Miss Blake [5] 8-0   -- Just The Ticket [15] 7-12
 -- Just Christened [19] 7-8
23 ran   1½,2½,½,hd,1½   (Henry Hughes)   R Smyly Lambourn, Berks

1258 GEORGE BOON APP.H'CAP 3YO 0-35   £1352   1m 4f Firm 18 -28 Slow   [34]

951 KHETA KING [5] (W Hastings Bass) 3-8-13 Dale Gibson(7) 4/1 JT FAV: 0-031: 3 b g Hittite
Glory - Matala (Misti IV) Proved a ready winner of an app h'cap at Doncaster June 27, led
2f out and sn had his race won: lightly raced half brother to minor winner Prince of Kashmir:
well suited by 12f: acts on fast ground and on a gall trk: can win again.   30
697 TEARS OF LAUGHTER [9] (C Bell) 3-8-5 J Leech(2) 16/1: 000-002: Led 3f out: best effort
to date: stays 12f: acts on fast ground and on a gall track.   16
767 ORIENTAL EXPRESS [3] (F Carr) 3-8-9 J Carr(3) 9/1: 0-01033: Never nearer: acts on
firm: see 487.   14
832 COLEMAN HAWKINS [4] (P Makin) 3-9-7 A Ball(7) 10/1: -0004: Al prom: acts on firm.   23
849 FINAL ALMA [10] 3-9-7 S Quane(5) 9/2: -0000: Well clear rem: first real signs
of form from this lightly raced colt: should be well suited by middle dist: acts on firm.   18
823 MISTS OF TIME [1] 3-9-2 A Watkins(7) 4/1 JT FAV: 000-030: Made much: btr hvy 823 (11f)   00
790 NATIVE IMAGE [2] 3-8-4 P D'arcy(7) 8/1: -0000: Fin 9th: seems to find this trip
beyond him and may do better when reverting to shorter dist.   00
767 TAP DUET [7] 3-8-11 R Carter 11/2: 00-0420: Fin last: disapp after 767 (tight trk)   00
--   Cupids Bower [6] 7-13   998 Tiber Gate [8] 7-11
10 ran   1½,4,1½,3,15   (Sir Gordon Brunton)   W Hastings Bass Newmarket

Official Going Given As FIRM

1259 ENGLISH ALE MAIDEN FILLIES STAKES 3YO   £1043   1m 4f Good/Firm 24 -02 Slow

--   APPLY [11] (J Tree) 3-8-11 Pat Eddery 9/2: -1: 3 ch f Kings Lake - Alla (Sun Prince)
Promising filly: first time out, mkt drifter, but led inside final 1f comfortably in a
3yo fillies mdn at Lingfield June 27: dam was a very useful performer: clearly stays 12f
well: acts on fast ground and an undulating track: should rate more highly.   50
--   MYTH [4] (R Johnson Houghton) 3-8-11 R Hills 20/1: 2424-2: Stayed on well on
seasonal debut: gd effort: placed on all 4 starts in '85 and should have no trouble finding
a race: well suited by 12f: acts on fast ground.   45
506 EXCELBELLE [7] (J Dunlop) 3-8-11 B Crossley 12/1: -23: Made much: stays 12f:
acts on fast and yielding: see 506.   41
581 PRELUDE [3] (W Hern) 3-8-11 J Reid 7/4 FAV: 3-34: Well bckd: stays 12f: see 581.   40
--   NEWQUAY [14] 3-8-11 G Starkey 13/2: 3-0: No real threat on seasonal debut: should
do much better next time: on sole start in '85 fin 3rd to Lavender Mist in fillies mdn
at Salisbury: should be well suited by 12f: acts on fast ground and will have no trouble
finding a race.   36
581 LA GRANDE DAME [12] 3-8-11 S Whitworth 33/1: -00: Making improvement: stays 12f:
acts on firm ground.   24
1002 BENAROSA [6] 3-8-11 A Mcglone 8/1: -34000: Fin 7th: much btr 1002, 372 (10f)   00
1002 APPRILA [10] 3-8-11 A Bond 8/1: -400: No show: lightly raced: see 59.   00
779 Elvire [7] 8-11   250 Crystal Moss [13] 8-11
980 Ashshafak [2] 8-11(BL)   765 Fidaytik [8] 8-11
923 Nutshambles [15] 8-11   1062 Queens Visit [5] 8-11(VIS)
1022 Richards Folly [16] 8-11
15 ran   2,2,nk,2½,6   (K Abdulla)   J Tree Beckhampton, Wilts

1260 GRANTS WHISKY HANDICAP STAKES (0-35)   £1906   2m   Good/Firm 24 +01 Fast   [31]

1058 HARLESTONE LAKE [10] (J Dunlop) 4-9-2 Pat Eddery 9/2: 0-00341: 4 ro f Riboboy -
January (Sigebert) Stayed on well to lead inside final 1f in a h'cap at Lingfield June 27:
first success: well suited by a stamina test: acts on firm and gd ground.   27
990 SUGAR PALM [5] (R Hannon) 5-9-2(bl) B Rouse 3/1 FAV: -030422: Led/dsptd lead:
in fine form: see 990, 341.   24
1078 GRATIFY [2] (P Walwyn) 3-7-11 N Howe 12/1: 00-0003: Sn prom: stays 2m: see 1078.   22
841 HOT BETTY [1] (P Butler) 6-7-11 N Adams 33/1: 0000004: Never nearer: see 28.   00
1099 BALLET CHAMP [7] 8-9-2 J Reid 4/1: 2-30300: Not reach leaders: btr 942, see 349.   17
663 CAPTAIN WEBSTER [8] 6-8-3(bl) S Whitworth 7/1: 0314-00: Ev ch: in '85 won a h'cap
at Folkestone: in '83 won at Goodwood: stays 2m well: acts on gd/firm and soft: likes
an undulating track.   00
839 NASKRACKER [12] 3-8-7(1ow) G Starkey 10/1: 0-000: Led/dsptd lead: fdd: no form
this season.   00
1035 SITAR THEME [11] 4-9-1 P Waldron 15/2: 03-4000: Led after 1m, wknd: btr 1035(14f).   00
1058 Crook N Honest [13] 8-1   856 Moorland Lady [3] 9-5
942 Tinoco [4] 7-11   811 Polecroft [6] 7-7(bl)(8oh)
12 ran   2,shthd,5,½,12,hd   (J L Dunlop)   J Dunlop Arundel, Sussex

398

1261 HEINEKEN REFRESHMENT STAKES 2YO   £3319   5f   Good/Firm 24 -03 Slow

1143 ALKADI [2] (W O'gorman) 2-8-11 M L Thomas 11/2: 3123201: 2 ch c Formidable -
Sa-Vegas (Star Appeal) Useful, consistent colt: led inside final 1f, ridden out in quite
val stsks event at Lingfield June 27: has only once fin out of the first 3, earlier winning
a mdn at Bath: equally eff over 5/6f: acts on firm & yldg ground and is a genuine sort.   55
+1162 DREAM LAUNCH [6] (B Hanbury) 2-9-2 Pat Eddery 2/5 FAV: 012: Heavily bckd: made
most: ran well but btr 1162.   54
1039 PAS DENCHERE [3] (G Lewis) 2-8-11 P Waldron 20/1: 03: Ev ch over 1f out: on
the upgrade: see 1039.   43
*981 VIVA RONDA [5] (Pat Mitchell) 2-8-8 J Reid 12/1: 14: Ev ch: see 981 (seller).   25
--   BLUSHER [4] 2-8-8 A Bond 12/1: 0: No show on debut: shd do btr: bred to stay 1m+.   18
737 DOUBLE TALK [7] 2-8-8 S Whitworth 50/1: 04200: Prom early: best 353 (soft)   06
6 ran   2,1½,7,2,4   (M Khalid)   W O'gorman Newmarket

1262 FREMLINS A.K. SELLING STAKES 2YO   £930   6f   Good/Firm 24 -57 Slow

1083 GLORY BEE [2] (L Holt) 2-8-11 P Waldron 4/1: 01: 2 ch c Bold Owl - Sweet Minuet
(Setay) Impr colt: landed a gamble with a comfortable win in a slow run 2yo seller at
Lingfield June 27 (bought in 1,650 gns): half brother to sev winners: eff 6f, should stay
further: acts on fast grd and an undulating track.   24
1083 JETMORE [7] (R Hannon) 2-8-11 B Rouse 9/1: 02: No chance with winner but is impr:
acts on fast ground: see 1083.   15
965 MUSICAL CHORUS [3] (G Blum) 2-8-8(bl) A Bond 10/1: 003: Made much on first venture
into selling company: acts on fast ground and a sharpish, undulating track: stays 6f.   11
1083 SAUCIER [4] (W Brooks) 2-8-8 J Bray(7) 20/1: 0004: Al prom: steadily improving:
acts on fast ground and a sharpish track.   09
853 RIBO BE GOOD [10] 2-8-8 J Williams 20/1: 0040: Al mid div: very cheaply acquired.   03
1083 PARKLANDS BELLE [9] 2-8-8 Pat Eddery 4/5 FAV: 024020: Heavily bckd: beat the 1st,
2nd and 4th in 1083 and ran very poorly here.   00
--   Magnolia Dancer [8] 8-6   985 Party Match [6] 8-11
981 Bonzo [1] 8-11   --   Flying Chapeau [5] 8-3
10 ran   2½,nk,½,2½,7,6,1   (B J Keay)   L Holt Tunworth, Hants

1263 HANDICAP (0-50) 3YO+   £4056   6f   Good/Firm 24 +03 Fast   [45]

952 FERRYMAN [4] (D Elsworth) 10-9-4 A Mcglone 10/1: 0-00001: 10 b g Forlorn River -
La Miranda (Miralgo) Genuine old horse: made almost all for a game nk success in a h'cap
at Lingfield June 27: in '84 won a val h'cap at York and a h'cap at Brighton: in '83 won
twice: very eff at 6f: likes an undulating track: acts on any grd and retains his form,
despite his advancing years.   46
1171 LONELY STREET [5] (P Arthur) 5-8-7 J Reid 5/1: 002-202: Chall final 1f: just btn:
gd effort: see 855.   34
*1060 DEPUTY HEAD [2] (L Holt) 6-9-10(7ex) P Waldron 7/1: 0000313: Mkt drifter: in gd
form: see 1060.   43
1086 AL AMEAD [1] (C Benstead) 6-9-7 B Rouse 5/2: -000404: Prom, ev ch: see 508.   39
846 CORNCHARM [6] 5-8-11 M Rimmer 15/2: -020340: Early speed: btr 846, see 135.   26
747 DARTIGNY [3] 3-8-10 S Whitworth 10/1: 01-000: No real threat: see 514.   34
808 BERTIE WOOSTER [7] 3-8-11 Pat Eddery 9/4 FAV: -031000: Well bckd: fin 7th:best 496   00
762 Thatchville [8] 7-13   952 Mr Mcgregor [9] 8-2
9 ran   nk,3,½,1,nk,nk   (W R Plummer)   D Elsworth Whitsbury, Hants

1264 APPRENTICE HANDICAP STAKES (0-35)   £1058   7f   Good/Firm 24 -19 Slow   [29]

1165 PETT VELERO [13] (S Dow) 7-8-4 P Simms 14/1: 0-00101: 7 b g Pitcairn - Naval
Artiste (Captains Gig) Mkt drifter, but led final 1f comfortably in an app h'cap at Lingfield
June 27: earlier won a h'cap at Chepstow: very eff at 7f: acts on gd and firm grd and
an undulating track.   16
1065 RAFFIA RUN [2] (J Dunlop) 3-8-9 G Foster(5) 7/1: 0-04402: Fin well: 4l clear 3rd:
in good form: see 538.   25
710 TORREY [4] (W Hern) 7-9-10(bl) T Sprake 3/1 FAV: -10-223: Dsptd lead 1f out:
better 710, see 499.   21
1165 JAMES DE COOMBE [11] (M Bolton) 4-8-6 C Rate 4/1: 0024234: Prom and ev ch:best 1086   01
1104 BOLD ARCHER [10] 3-7-11 C Kennedy 9/2: 0-00020: Much btr 1104 (stiffer trk).   00
992 EUCHARIS [12] 4-8-1(BL) P Brett 6/1: 00-0000: Made much: see 992.   00
1165 Hampton Walk [7] 7-13   679 Another Bing [8] 8-0   --   Cygne [5] 8-0
--   Bootle Jack [1] 8-6   888 Toda Forca Avanti [3] 8-6
739 Never Bee [9] 7-12(5ow)(5oh)   749 Tinsel Rose [6] 7-7(5oh)
13 ran   2½,4,1,1½,½   (Mrs Hilly Beaufort)   S Dow Bramley, Surrey

1265 FLOWERS BEST BITTER H'CAP (0-35)   £2271   1m 4f   Good/Firm 24 -01 Slow   [30]

761 TRAFFITANZI [5] (D Elsworth) 5-8-4 A Mcglone 25/1: 2-0001: 5 b g Busted - Mrs
McNicholas (Tudor Music) Made ev yard, holding on by ¾l in a h'cap at Lingfield June 27:
first success on the Flat, but is a winner over hurdles: stays 12f well: acts on firm
& yielding ground and likes an undulating track.   16

980 EBOLITO [1] (W Hern) 3-8-10(bl) Pat Eddery 7/4 JT.FAV: -0042: Sn prom: ev ch in
straight: better 980 (stakes): stays 12f.   36
*856 THE BETSY [8] (D Elsworth) 4-9-2 P Mcentee(7) 11/4: 0-04013: In gd form: see 856.   23
*1035 ALSIBA [3] (C Benstead) 4-8-12(4ex) B Rouse 7/4 JT.FAV: -000014: Well bckd:
much better 1035 (14f, gall track).   07
--   PIP [6] 6-8-10 S Whitworth 33/1: -0: Wknd in str: lightly raced on Flat: winner
over hurdles: probably stays 12f: acts on any ground.   01
--   MR CARACTACUS [7] 5-7-12 N Adams 50/1: 00044-0: Rank outsider: no extra str:
in '84 won at Leicester: eff 10f, stays 12f: acts on fast ground.   00
1166 Blairs Winnie [4] 7-7   1186 Assail [2] 10-0
8 ran   ¾,2,7,1½,¼   (Cherry Tree Stables)   D Elsworth Whitsbury, Hants

---

Official Going Given As FIRM : ALL TIMES SLOW EXCEPT RACE 1268

1266 EBF BRANDLING MAIDEN FILLIES STAKES 2YO £2021   5f   Firm Slow

--   FULL OF PRIDE [4] (M H Easterby) 2-8-11 M Birch 9/2: 1: 2 b f Lochnager - Apple
Of My Eye (Silver Cloud) Made a winning debut when readily leading dist in a 6 horse 2yo
fillies mdn at Newcastle June 27: dam a useful stayer on the Flat and over hurdles: effective
over 5f, sure to be well suited by longer dist: acts on firm ground.   45
995 MINIZEN LASS [1] (M Brittain) 2-8-11 K Darley 5/2 FAV: 042202: Made much: acts on
firm and good ground: should stay 6f: seems suited by forcing tactics: see 913.   35
--   BELLA SEVILLE [5] (T Barron) 2-8-11 R Cochrane 7/2: 3: Well bckd debutant: prom and
kept on well looking as if the 6f would suit: related to a minor 1m winner: should improve
on this next time.   31
--   LAKEDGE [3] (T Barron) 2-8-11 T Ives 5/1: 4: Prom much: half sister to minor '85
2yo winner Askagain: dam a middle dist plater.   30
--   KALEIDOPHONE [6] 2-8-11 J Lowe 9/1: 0: Ran rather green and shd benefit from the
experience: first foal of '81 2yo winner Plum Bold who was lightly raced at 3 years:
sure to be suited by 6f.   29
1090 SENDIM ON SAM [7] 2-8-11 T Lucas 6/1: 00: Never held a hope: see 1090.   09
6 ran   2½,1½,1½,hd,8   (Ian Armitage)   M H Easterby Great Habton, Yorks

1267 CAMPERDOWN SELLING H'CAP 3YO 0-25   £1280   1m 1f Firm Slow   [21]

1201 HARSLEY SURPRISE [6] (N Tinkler) 3-9-7 S Cauthen 7/2 JT FAV: 0-33141: 3 br f Meldrum -
Night Surprise (Articulate) Impr filly: well bckd when winning a selling h'cap at Newcastle
June 27: almost brought down at ½ way, recovered to quicken ahead inside final 1f: (bought
in 2400gns): comfortable winner of similar race at Carlisle June 5: well suited by 9f and
firm or gd ground tho' also acts on soft: likes a stiff trk: can win a non selling h'cap.   24
1122 BRADBURY HALL [10] (K Stone) 3-9-1 C Dwyer 11/2: 0000022: Dsptd lead final 4f and is
running well: seems to act on firm and soft: see 1122.   14
1156 COLONEL HALL [4] (J Ramsden) 3-8-7 R Cochrane 8/1: 0000003: Came from well behind
and was evidently well suited by this 9f trip, sure to stay at least 10f: acts well on firm
ground: one to note in a similar race: see 237.   01
*993 FOREVER YOUNG [2] (G Oldroyd) 3-8-12 P Burke(7) 6/1: 00-4014: Never closer: see 993.   05
993 FOXCROFT [1] 3-9-5 T Williams 8/1: 22-0000: Kept on under press: see 356: should
stay 10f.   12
1158 HILL RYDE [11] 3-9-7 M Birch 12/1: 0-00200: Made much: best 740.   12
1158 WOLLOW BIRD [5] 3-8-7 D Nicholls 10/1: 0000-40: Hmpd ½ way: see 1158.   00
1158 MANVIL [9] 3-9-0 M Hindley(3) 7/2 JT FAV: 0-00030: Tragically collapsed and died
after race.   00
868 Son Of Absalom [8] 9-5   -- Judys Desire [3] 8-9
960 Stanford Rose [12] 9-4
11 ran   1½,2½,½,hd,1½   (Andrew Marley)   N Tinkler Malton, Yorks

1268 GOSFORTH PARK CUP H'CAP 3YO+ 0-70   £6544   5f   Firm + 24 Fast   [65]

1151 DUBLIN LAD [8] (M Brittain) 3-9-1 K Darley 5/1: -000031: 3 ch c Dublin Taxi - North
Hut (Northfields) Smart sprinter: returned to his best when shattering the Course Record
in Gosforth Park Cup h'cap at Newcastle June 27: made most at a   blistering pace and
stayed on really well: very tough and genuine 2yo in '85 winning at Wolverhampton (2),
Lingfield (2), Catterick and Thirsk: best form at 5f forcing the pace: acts on any trk and
on firm and yldg ground: remarkably resilient and is a credit to his trainer.   74
*877 CLANTIME [9] (R Whitaker) 5-8-13(vis) D Mckeown 7/1: 0223412: Al chal winner: grand
effort and is possibly even btr on a sharp trk such as 877 (Epsom).   60
1037 DURHAM PLACE [15] (K Brassey) 4-8-11 G Baxter 10/1: 030-043: Fin really well after
a slow start: must find a race soon, over further than 5f: see 877.   56
1101 CHINA GOLD [12] (L Siddall) 7-7-12(4ow) M Wood 16/1: 0-03004: Prom, kept on well
and is back to form: should find a race in lesser grade: see 784.   41
1125 SIMLA RIDGE [4] 4-7-11 P Robinson 9/2 FAV: -001300: Ev ch: see 628, 977.   37
*1171 MUSIC MACHINE [13] 5-7-7(5ex)(7oh) T Williams 14/1: 0440410: Fair effort in this
higher grade: see 1171.   31

NEWCASTLE   Friday June 27th   —Cont'd

784 RAMBLING RIVER [6] 9-7-10(vis) J Lowe 16/1: 10-0200: Early pace: fin 7th: see 626,742   33
1037 LOCHTILLUM [1] 7-8-7 R Cochrane 8/1: 0-00100: Never closer after slow start,
fin 8th: best 836.   44
*1027 IBERIAN START [11] 3-8-3(2ow)(8ex) T Ives 15/2: 302-210: Ev ch, fin 9th: see 1027.   48
1146 SHARP ROMANCE [5] 4-10-0 W R Swinburn 10/1: 2330000: No danger: best 18 (soft)   00
977 Davill [14] 7-7(2oh)   1037 Stoneydale [10] 7-10(BL)
--   King Charlemagne [7] 8-3
13 ran   1¼,¼,½,½,1½,½,½,nk,shthd   (Mel Brittain)   M Brittain Warthill, Yorks.

1269 ST OSWALD MAIDEN STAKES 3YO   £3295   1m   Firm Slow

-1036 STAR CUTTER [5] (H Cecil) 3-9-0 S Cauthen 2/9 FAV: -21: 3 gr c Star de Naskra -
Azed (Al-Hattab) Readily made all against 4 mod   opponents when landing the odds in a slowly
run 3yo mdn at Newcastle June 27: first foal of a winning miler and cost $190,000: very eff
over 7f/1m, could stay further: acts on firm ground: sure to win much better races.   31
829 ORTICA [6] (J Etherington) 3-8-11 M Wood 20/1: -402: Held up, fin in very promising
style: acts on firm and soft: see 667: sure to be suited by 10f.   23
1036 NORTH OCEAN [2] (L Cumani) 3-9-0 R Guest 5/1: -03: Held up, kept on fin: first
foal of the smart Spring In Deepsea who is best around 1m: shd improve further as he gains
experience.   21
822 STARBOARD [3] (C Elsey) 3-8-11 J Lowe 66/1: 00-004: Ev ch: no worthwhile form.   15
1142 CLAWSON THORNS [7] 3-9-0 D Nicholls 40/1: 000-000: Wknd final 2f: see 78.   11
5 ran   ¾,2,¾,2½   (Sheikh Mohammed)   H Cecil Newmarket

1270 EBF ANGERTON STAKES 2YO   £2189   7f   Firm Slow

--   HIS HIGHNESS [4] (C Brittain) 2-8-11 P Robinson 6/5: 1: 2 b c High Top - Melting
Moments (His Majesty) Well bckd when making a successful debut, leading 2f out and staying
on strongly under press in a 4 horse, slowly run 2yo race at Newcastle June 27: cost
72,000 gns: eff over 7f, will be suited by 1m+: acts on firm: should improve further.   38
--   UNDERSHAFT [3] (H Cecil) 2-8-11 S Cauthen 1/1 FAV: 2: Showed signs of inexperience
and is likely to benefit greatly from the outing: half brother to sev winners, notably
Dame Foolish and Brevert: stays 7f: sure to be suited by 1m: acts well on firm grd: certain
to improve.   34
694 AFRICAN OPERA [2] (C Elsey) 2-8-11 J Lowe 20/1: 03: Made much: seems to stay 7f
and acts on firm: see 694.   22
602 JJ JIMMY [5] (M H Easterby) 2-8-11(vis) M Birch 10/1: 004: Prom most: now wears a
visor: acts on firm.   21
4 ran   1½,3,½   (Capt M Lemos)   C Brittain Newmarket

1271 JOHN OSBORNE H'CAP 4YO+ 0-35   £2225   1m 4f   Firm Slow   [31]

--   SHARP SONG [9] (T Fairhurst) 5-8-7 J Callaghan(7) 6/1: 030-3-1: 5 Sharpen Up - Mixed
Melody (Alcide) Fit from a couple of recent successes over hurdles, led inside final 1f
to comfortably win a slowly run h'cap at Newcastle June 27, despite straying off a true line:
first success on the Flat: well suited by 12f on a stiff track and likes fast going.   17
940 COMHAMPTON [3] (F Yardley) 5-8-10 I Johnson 5/2 FAV: 2022-32: Al prom, ev
chance: can win a seller soon: see 940.   17
1106 IVOROSKI [6] (Denys Smith) 4-8-2 L Charnock 8/1: -000003: Chall under press dist:
stays 12f: see 1017.   04
942 GENTLE STREAM [4] (J Toller) 4-9-7 P Robinson 17/2: 0-20004: Met some trouble in
running: best 282 (hvy).   22
860 RASHAH [1] 4-8-9 M Wood 5/1: 300-000: Prom most: see 860.   05
1159 ISHKHARA [7] 4-8-5 A Proud 17/2: -003000: 2nd 4f out, wknd: best 675 (yldg).   00
1052 MOSSBERRY FAIR [8] 5-7-13 M Fry 6/1: -000240: Fin 7th, still a maiden: see 770.   00
993 Crowfoots Couture [5] 7-8(bl)   256 Lovely Butterfly [2] 8-4
9 ran   1½,2½,½,2½,1½   (J Latham)   T Fairhurst Middleham, Yorks

CHEPSTOW   Saturday June 28th   Lefthanded, Stiff, Galloping Track

1272 SWANSEA SKETTY CLUB H'CAP (0-35) 3YO   £1520   6f   Firm -02 -04 Slow   [41]

228 YOUNG JASON [12] (G Lewis) 3-9-3 P Waldron 2/1 FAV: 011-001: 3 ch c Star Appeal -
Smarten Up (Sharpen Up) Nicely bckd after a fair abs, led inside dist in a 3yo h'cap
Chepstow June 28: in gd form last backend, winning successive nurseries at Leicester and
Newmarket: cost 62,000 gns and is a half brother to sev winners: eff over 5/6f and shd stay
further: well suited by a sound surface and a stiff track: may win again.   41
830 JOKIST [14] (J Shaw) 3-8-10 R Street 20/1: 4000-02: Led briefly below dist: won a
Warwick mdn on his race course debut last season, when trained by C Williams: eff over 5/6f:
acts on firm and hvy ground and on any track.   30
1065 ALKAAYED [4] (H Thomson Jones) 3-9-0 R Hills 5/1: 0-10403: Led dist: stays 6f:
best in 628.   30

--   MONSARAH [13] (P Cundell) 3-8-1 G French 20/1: 01000-4: Led to ½ way: fair effort
on her seasonal debut: quite lightly raced after winning a Newbury seller early on·last
term: eff over 5/6f: well suited by fast ground and a gall track.   11
713 IVORY GULL [9] 3-9-7 G Baxter 13/2: 041-000: Shorter trip: has yet to fulfill her
juv promise this term: see 514.   30
966 CRACON GIRL [2] 3-8-5 I Johnson 25/1: 000-000: Never nearer over this shorter trip:
quite lightly raced filly who has yet to trouble the judge: stays 6f well: acts on fast grd
and on a stiff track.   12
837 GRISETTE [8] 3-8-8 Paul Eddery 13/2: 030-00: Fin 7th: ground too fast?: see 837.   00
1066 MADAM MUFFIN [6] 3-8-7 T Quinn 11/2: 2-20020: Mkt drifter: fin 9th: btr 1066.   00
--   Dublinaire [3] 8-13   764 Spanish Intent [5] 7-11
1063 Boxers Shukee [1] 7-7(1oh)   699 Lauries Trojan [7] 8-9
1171 Choristers Dream [11] 8-7(bl)
13 ran   1,1½,2,½,1,nk,hd   (J L Swift)   G Lewis Epsom, Surrey

1273 SWANSEA ROYAL BRITISH LEGION H'CAP 0-35   £1641   1m   Firm -02 +02 Fast   [33]

1211 SAHARA SHADOW [4] (D Tucker) 4-8-0 T Quinn 9/2 JT FAV: 000-121: 4 b f Formidable -
Gay Shadow (Northfields) Quick reappearance and led below dist, gamely, in quite a fast run
h'cap at Chepstow June 28: earlier a surprise winner of a selling h'cap at Salisbury and only
just beaten in btr company at Brighton: eff over 7f, stays 1m well: acts on gd and firm grd
and on any track: in fine form.   13
943 SNAKE RIVER [12] (D Nicholson) 4-9-0 I Johnson 6/1: 4331022: Led after ½ way, just
held tho' remains in fine form: well suited by fast ground: see 620.   26
1081 EXPLETIVE [5] (M Eckley) 6-8-1(bl) L Riggio(7) 11/1: 000-043: Led over 4f: in fair
form: well suited by a gall trk: see 1081.   08
1041 FEYDAN [9] (L Cottrell) 5-9-2 R Hills 20/1: 4000-04: Nearest fin: failed to win last
term tho' in '84 won at Folkestone and Sandown: stays 1m well: acts on any going and has
no track preferences.   18
845 SUPERFROST [14] 4-8-3 L Jones(5) 12/1: 000100: Twice below form shown in 568 (sh. track). 01
1060 GALLANT HOPE [17] 4-7-13 T Lang(7) 33/1: 00-0000: Well placed most of way: maiden
who prob stays 1m: acts on fast ground and on a gall track.   00
1018 DISPORT [16] 4-8-5 N Adams 10/1: 000-000: Fin 8th: acts on gd and firm: see 1018.   00
1081 SWEET GEMMA [7] 4-7-13 D Williams(7) 9/2 JT FAV: 40-0230: Nicely bckd: btr 1081.   00
775 NEW CENTRAL [21] 4-8-11 P Waldron 13/2: 00-0000: Speed over ½ way: best 636 (7f gd) 00
830 Sandbourne [19] 8-12   1156 Polemistis [10] 7-9(bl)
724 Mairs Girl [3] 7-9   499 Sharp Shot [6] 9-7   1061 Tzu Wong [8] 9-2
208 Timewaster [13] 8-7   495 Bakers Double [11] 7-13
--   Dame Caroline [23] 7-12   943 Kassak [15] 7-9
727 Sue Clare [1] 7-10(1ow)   164 Lady Abinger [2] 7-11(2ow)
455 Monatation [18] 7-7   1188 True Weight [22] 8-13
22 ran   ½,2½,2½,1½,¾,2   (Mike Tebbut)   D Tucker Frome, Somerset

1274 ANDOVER CONSERVATIVE CLUB H'CAP (0-35)   £1459   1m 2f Firm -02 +07 Fast   [27]

856 BLENDERS CHOICE [10] (K Brassey) 4-9-1 N Adams 12/1: 00-0301: 4 b g Cavo Doro -
Harriny (Floribunda) Well suited by this shorter trip, made all to win unchall in quite a
fast run h'cap at Chepstow June 28: first success: stays 14f tho' seems best over 10f with
forcing tactics: suited by gd or faster ground: acts on any track.   24
--   CAPA [5] (R Holder) 6-8-2 Paul Eddery 6/1: 004-2: Stayed on well on reappearance:
nicely bckd today: lightly raced last term: eff over 10f and sure to stay further: acts
on gd and firm ground.   05
812 FORMIDABLE LADY [9] (W Wightman) 4-8-13 T Quinn 11/1: 400-003: Stayed on and seems
well suited by this longer trip: mdn who stays 10f: suited by gd or faster ground.   14
1079 CAREEN [14] (M Pipe) 5-9-7 T Sprake(7) 9/2: 30-2244: Again never nearer: see 8.   20
680 JABARABA [7] 5-9-2 R Hills 16/1: 000-000: Late prog: last successful in '83, at
Doncaster, Leicester and Redcar: stays 12f: suited by firm tho' acts on any going: ran
better here.   12
1035 PATRICK JOHN LYONS [1] 5-9-2 L Johnsey(7) 12/1: 030-300: In 2nd when veered left
2f out, not recover: acts on firm and soft ground   see 856.   08
•718 STONEBROKER [8] 4-8-7 D Williams(7) 11/2: 0-04410: Ran on: fin 7th: see 718.   00
1018 GIBBOUS MOON [3] 4-8-9 G Baxter 3/1 FAV: 20-0020: Staying when hmpd 2f out:
looked destined for a place tho' unlikely to have won: see 1018.   00
1079 PRIMROSE WAY [13] 4-8-4 P Waldron 9/2: 00-0020: Never threatened: see 341.   00
1054 Composer [2] 8-3   1173 Monclare Trophy [4] 9-6
--   Hard Oak [6] 8-1   --   Ballyowen King [11] 8-2
13 ran   3,hd,1½,2,2,2½,shthd   (Mark O'Connor)   K Brassey Lambourn, Berks

1275 E.B.F. MARLBOROUGH STAKES 2YO   £2224   6f   Firm -02 -04 Slow

614 MILEAGE BANK [1] (P Cole) 2-8-11 T Quinn 2/1: 41: 2 b c J O Tobin - Cautious Bidder
(Bold Bidder) Impr colt: made virtually ev grd, comfortably, in a 2yo stks at Chepstow
June 28: earlier had shown promise behind Bestplan and Carols Treasure on his debut at
Newbury: cost $230,000 as yearling and is a full brother to the smart juv Overtrump: stays
6f well: acts on firm and yldg ground and on a stiff track: does well with forcing tactics:
should win more races.   55

*985   DOMINO FIRE [4] (J Dunlop) 2-8-13 G Baxter 1/1 FAV: 12: Well bckd: ev ch tho' never
looks likely to peg back winner: btr on gd ground in 985.   50
*1025 LADY PAT [2] (M Mccormack) 2-9-5 M Wigham 5/1: 24113: With winner till dist: gd
effort over this longer trip: consistent filly: see 1025.   48
988 FLIRTING [3] (R Hannon) 2-8-8 L Jones(5) 12/1: 024: No threat: btr 988 (5f gd)   27
--   GUNNER STREAM [5] 2-8-11 I Johnson 33/1: 0: Mkt drifter on debut: prom over ½ way:
should improve for this initial outing.   28
5 ran   1½,2½,3,¾   (Dan J Agnew)   P Cole Whatcombe, Berks

1276 PLYMSTOCK CLUB E.B.F. STAKES 3YO   £2057   2m   Firm -02 -22 Slow

+978 RHYTHMIC BLUES [1] (H Cecil) 3-9-0 Paul Eddery 6/4: -11: 3 ch c Cut Above - Signature
Tune (Crepello) Promising colt: ran on under press to lead inside dist in quite a slowly
run 3yo stks at Chepstow June 28: first time out winner of a Yarmouth maiden: half brother
to the smart chaser Berlin: eff over 14f, stays 2m: acts on fast grd and on a stiff trk.   54
552 DUNCAN IDAHO [3] (R Johnson Houghton) 3-8-11 R Hills 7/1: -0342: Led over 2f out,
out-battled cl home: progressive colt who should find a small race: stays 2m: see 347, 231   48
983 ONISKY [2] (P Cole) 3-9-3 T Quinn 4/6 FAV: 10-1123: Kicked in the mouth by winner
before start, made most and was eased below dist: ignore this run: see 983.   39
3 ran   1,15   (C d'Alessio)   H Cecil Newmarket

1277 B'HAM SHELDON HEATH CLUB STAKES 3YO   £1507   5f   Firm -02 -12 Slow

1036 ABUTAMMAM [3] (C Benstead) 3-9-0 R Hills 10/1: -001: 3 br c Persian Bold - Tamarisk
Way (Tamerlane) Dropped slightly in class and ran on well to lead cl home in a 3yo stks
at Chepstow June 28: didnot race last season: half brother to sev winners, including prolific
juv Nagwa: eff over 5f on fast grd: acts on a stiff track.   38
835 NORTHERN LAD [4] (L Holt) 3-9-0 P Waldron 7/1: 0-00002: Al well placed: best effort
this term: suited by gd or fast ground: see 580.   30
1142 ANGELS ARE BLUE [9] (M Ryan) 3-8-11 M Giles 11/10 FAV: -023: Made most: well bckd
today: may prove btr suited by 6f: see 1142.   26
844 AVALON [2] (D Murray Smith) 3-9-0 G Baxter 5/2: -034: Well bckd: ev ch: see 844.   28
545 GLEADHILL PARK [6] 3-9-0 N Adams 11/1: 04-0000: No real threat: see 339.   23
1036 HIGHLY RECOMMENDED [8] 3-9-0 B Procter 12/1: -000: Speed over ½ way: seemed btr
suited by this shorter trip: dam won as a juv.   17
760 La Malmaison [5] 8-11   --   Ruperts Daughter [7] 8-11
8 ran   2½,nk,nk,1½,2   (Hamdan Al Maktoum)   C Benstead Epsom, Surrey

---

Official Going Given As FIRM

1278 CORPORATION MAIDEN STAKES 3 AND 4YO   £1763   1m 2f   Firm 05 +08 Fast

723 BROWN THATCH [10] (H Cecil) 3-8-8 W Ryan 9/4: -301: 3 brc Thatch - Honey Match
(Match III): Useful colt: led 2f out, comfortably in a fast run 3 & 4yo maiden at Doncaster
June 28: first time out fin a fine 3rd to Nino Bibbia in a competitive maiden at Newmarket:
eff at 1m, stays 10f well: acts on gd & firm grnd & a gall trk: should win more races.   55
883 AUCTION FEVER [11] (B Hills) 3-8-8 B Thomson 11/2: 3-20232: Ev ch final 1f: fin
5L clear 3rd: deserves a race: eff at 1m-12f: see 386.   50
863 GREEN STEPS [8] (G Wragg) 4-9-8(BL) G Duffield 10/1: -043: Bl first time: led 4f
out & is on the up grade: stays 10f: see 863.   40
980 CANADIAN STAR [4] (M Jarvis) 3-8-8 T Lucas 7/4 FAV: 0-024: Heavily bckd: no extra
final 2f: btr 980 (good).   30
--   DEBCO [13] 3-8-8 J Reid 12/1: -0: Mkt drifter: nearest fin & will do btr next
time: should be suited by 10f plus: acts on firm grnd & a gall trk.   25
916 JURISPRUDENCE [12] 3-8-8 A Mercer 33/1: -000: Never nearer, but making impr: dam
was a half sister to the very smart Bel Bolide: seems to stay 10f: acts on fast grnd.   23
1031 NOBLE FILLE [9] 3-8-5 T Ives 6/1: -00: Prom 1m: disapp after 1031.   00
--   HIGH BORN BIDDER [3] 3-8-5 B Crossley 10/1: -0: Wk in mkt & no show on debut: bred
to stay this trip: should do btr.   00
--   Carvery [6] 8-5   --   Warm Breeze [7] 8-5   916 Adaliyan [2] 8-8
1223 Mavitta Dee [1] 9-8
12 ran   1,5,5,3,1   (Sheikh Mohammed)   H Cecil Newmarket

1279 BENTLEY SELLING STAKES 2YO   £1172   6f   Firm 06 -31 Slow

*1248 KNOCKSHARRY [4] (R Hollinshead) 2-8-8 P Hill(7) 5/2 FAV: 11: 2 b f Palm Track -
Octavia (Sallust): Achieved a quick double, getting up close home in a slow run 2yo seller
at Doncaster June 28: won Newcastle, Thurs, over 5f: stays 6f and acts on fast grnd
and a gall trk.   26

1137 THE MAGUE [2] (L Siddall) 2-8-8(BL)(1ow) D Nicholls 4/1: 00422: Bl first time: led
final 1f: just caught: see 1137.   25
1137 SKERNE ROCKET [11] (H Jones) 2-8-4 G Duffield 10/1: 03: Led 2f out: just btn in
close fin: on the up grade: eff at 6f on fast grnd.   21
1221 PRINCESS SINGH [9] (N Tinkler) 2-8-8 Kim Tinkler(5) 12/1: 0031044: Nearest fin: not
btn far: stays 6f: see 858.   22
*821 BENFIELD MORPETH [12] (N Tinkler) 2-8-11(VIS) B Thomson 8/1: 00210: Made much: stays 6f & seems
to act on any grnd: visored first time today: see 821.   25
905 CHANTILLY DAWN [13] 2-8-4 D Mckeown 16/1: 000: Sn prom, showing impr form: very
cheaply acquired filly: acts on fast grnd.   13
1137 WESTGALE [1] 2-8-7(bl) M Birch 10/1: 0030: Early speed: btr 1137 (7f).   00
278 UNOS PET [6] 2-8-8(1ow) C Dwyer 5/1: 3300: Wknd after abs: see 94, 34 (soft).   00
1163 CLEARWAY [7] 2-8-11 J Reid 7/1: 0120: Never nearer: best 502 (yld).   00
728 Gold State [5] 8-7   1221 Mi Oh My [3] 8-4   -- Nicholas George [10] 8-7
-- Bank Express [8] 8-4
13 ran hd,shhd,1,hd,1½   (P J White)   R Hollinshead Upper Longdon, Staffs

1280 BELLE VUE HANDICAP (0-35) 4YO+   £2442   1m 6f Firm 06 -12 Slow   [35]

1092 WHITE MILL [11] (H Candy) 4-8-10 T Williams 5/1: 400-031: 4 b c Busted - Lowna
(Princely Gift): Led 3f out, comfortably in a h'cap at Doncaster June 28: first success:
eff at 14f, should get 2m: acts on gd & fast grnd & a gall trk.   28
*959 ASSAGLAWI [6] (H T Jones) 4-9-8 A Murray 7/2: 22-0012: Ev ch final 2f: see 959.   34
*990 OLD MALTON [5] (J Toller) 4-8-7 P Robinson 9/2: 4-00013: Not clear run: in gd form.   18
1159 MARLION [7] (S Hall) 5-9-1 E Guest(3) 7/4 FAV: 0-00324: Well bckd: btr 1159.   23
1092 TROJAN WAY [8] 4-8-11 S Perks 25/1: 30-0000: Prom, ev ch: see 1092.   14
1099 NORTHERN RULER [4] 4-8-10 A Mackay 20/1: 2000000: Wknd: best first time out in 280.   01
1140 Bundling Bed [2] 7-8   1017 Tharaleos [10] 7-7   -- Ickworth [3] 9-3
1102 Country Jimmy [1] 8-7(BL)   -- Suvadera [9] 7-8(BL)
11 ran 3,½,3,5,12   (D Hefin Jones)   H Candy Wantage, Oxon

1281 NORMAN KENDELL HANDICAP (0-35) 3YO   £2719   1m   Firm 06 +01 Fast   [39]

*1104 WHIRLING WORDS [6] (P Makin) 3-8-10(5ex) S Perks 3/1 FAV: 4-00211: 3 b f Sparkler -
Wild Words (Galivanter): In fine form, led final 1f, comfortably in a h'cap at Doncaster
June 28: last time out won a similar event at Beverley: half sister to numerous winners, incl
the useful sprinter Battle Hymn: eff around 1m: acts on yld, loves fast grnd: no track preferences. 31
829 HAMLOUL [9] (H T Jones) 3-9-0 A Murray 14/1: 030-002: Made most: gd effort: stays
1m: see 829.   29
1080 TOPEKA EXPRESS [14] (R Armstrong) 3-8-12(bl) M Roberts 10/1: 0-00003: Kept on final
1f: seems beat around 1m on fast grnd & in bl.   22
997 JOHNSTAN BOY [11] (C Tinkler) 3-8-1 L Charnock 12/1: -000004: Prom, ev ch: see 997.   07
928 PLAIN TALK [10] 3-8-10 R Guest 7/1: 04-040: Sn prom: btr 928 (7f): see 500.   12
1028 SCINTILLATOR [5] 3-8-1 G Duffield 11/1: 000-00: No real threat: little form
previously: acts on firm.   02
891 TRY SIR [12] 3-8-12 N Connorton 10/1: -0400: Made no show: btr 438 (6f).   00
982 FORMIDABLE DANCER [8] 3-9-7 T Ives 7/2: 000-00: Never in it: much btr 982 (gd, shp trk) 00
-- Broadhurst [13] 8-11   1041 Quick Dancer [1] 8-13   -- Wave Goodbye [17] 8-1
928 Common Accord [3] 8-6   318 All A Dream [4] 8-6   1079 Titan King [7] 8-0
506 Hello Georgie [16] 8-0   874 Katie Rhodes [2] 7-7(4oh)
1065 Absolutely Bonkers [15] 8-6
17 ran 2,2½,2,2,½   (Mrs Rodney Fitch)   P Makin Ogbourne Maisey, Wilts

1282 E.B.F. LONSDALE MAIDEN FILLIES STAKES   £1981   6f   Firm 06 -18 Slow

-- LALUCHE [4] (H Cecil) 2-8-11 W Ryan 40/85 FAV: 1: 2 b f Alleged - Coqueluche
(Victorian Era): Prom filly: heavily bckd & led 2f out, comfortably in a 2yo fillies maiden
at Doncaster June 28: cost $135,000: eff at 6f, should be suited by 7f plus: acts on fast grnd:
the type to win more races.   52
852 SHINING WATER [8] (R Johnson Houghton) 2-8-11 J Reid 8/1: 42: Led ½way: fast impr
and should win soon: acts on firm & yld: see 852.   45
1067 NAVOS [7] (M Leach) 2-8-11 D Nicholls 33/1: 003: Nearest fin: will be suited by 7f
plus: acts on gd & firm grnd & should find a small race.   33
-- ORDINA [5] (L Piggott) 2-8-11 T Ives 11/2: 4: Wknd final 1f on racecourse debut:
impr likely from this half sister to several winners: should be suited by further than 6f.   32
-- APRES SKI [10] 2-8-11 M Roberts 33/1: 0: Nearest fin on debut: promising run: should
be suited by 7f: cost 11,500 gns & is a half sister to 2 winners, notably useful 2yo Hilly. 24
852 JANS CONTESSA [11] 2-8-11 E Guest(3) 10/1: 230: Ev ch: best 482 (5f).   23
-- MEADOWBANK [3] 2-8-11 R Cochrane 10/1: 0: Very wk in mkt & made no show: first foal
of an unraced dam: should do btr.   00
1067 Ribogirl [1] 8-11   999 Kind Of Class [2] 8-11
-- Cinderella Derek [6] 8-11   746 Debach Deity [9] 8-11(BL)
11 ran 1½,6,½,4,nk   (Sheikh Mohammed)   H Cecil Newmarket

1283 MUNICIPAL HANDICAP (0-50) 3YO   £2637   5f   Firm 06 +06 Fast   [57]

*961 FELIPE TORO [10] (M H Easterby) 3-7-7(bl) J Lowe 4/1: 000-211: Impr gelding who is
in fine form: showed a gd turn of foot to lead final 1f in a 3yo h'cap at Doncaster June 28:
last time out made ev yd in a fast run 3yo h'cap at Redcar: equally eff over 5/6f: acts on
firm & yld grnd & on any trk: best when up with the pace.   36
*910 CHAUTAUQUA [8] (P Haslam) 3-7-7(1oh) T Williams 11/2: -421412: Set fast pace: in
fine form: see 910.   26
1227 THE MECHANIC [6] (J Sutcliffe) 3-7-7(7ex) M L Thomas 2/1 FAV: 0-02123: Consistent sort.   25
1044 PANNANICH WELLS [1] (M W Easterby) 3-8-5 M Birch 9/1: 0-02104: Not clear run ½way:
fair effort: see 671.   37
914 RUNAWAY [9] 3-8-12 S Perks 25/1: 4-00000: Sn prom: best effort this season: very
useful 2yo early last season, winning at Haydock, Catterick, Nottingham & Chester, but has
failed to regain that form: eff at 5/6f: acts on firm & hvy.   36
884 EXCLUSIVE CAT [11] 3-8-10 J Matthias 9/2: 312-300: Prom early: btr. 884, 760(sharper trk).   32
1027 VENEZ TRADER [2] 3-8-11 M Wood 7/1: 2214-40: Early speed: btr 1027.   00
1027 CAPEABILITY POUND [4] 3-7-13 P Robinson 10/1: -100020: Slow into stride: best ignored.   00
8 ran   3,nk,shhd,3,½   (Lt Col R Warden)   M H Easterby Great Habton, Yorks

---

1284 MAIL ON SUNDAY 3YO SERIES HCAP 0-60   £4422   1m 2f   Good/Firm 29 -20 Slow   [59]

*1179 HARD AS IRON [7] (P Haslam) 3-7-7(5ex)(3oh) T Williams 5/1: 00-4111: 3 b g Ardoon -
Prancer (Santa Claus): Impr gelding who completed a quick hat trick, leading dist in a 3yo
h'cap at Newmarket June 28: successful in similar h'caps at Ayr & Nottingham recently: very
lightly raced previously: eff 1m, well suited by a 10f on firm or gd grnd: continues to impr.   34
916 TOP RANGE [9] (M Jarvis) 3-8-3 T Ives 6/1: -03022: Led 3f out, consistent: see 625.   42
*535 ENBARR [5] (H Cecil) 3-8-9 W Ryan 5/2 FAV: 0-213: Prom, ev ch: see 535.   47
484 KINGS CRUSADE [2] (G Lewis) 3-7-9 M L Thomas 8/1: -4404: Rear till late prog: probably
acts on firm & yld: unraced in '85.   32
*1028 PARIS TURF [3] 3-9-1(5ex) P Robinson 9/1: -00310: Ev ch: probably stays 10f but may
prove btr over 1m: see 1028.   51
--   LA ZINGARA [8] 3-9-7 R Cochrane 33/1: 0410-0: Made much, wknd quickly & should benefit
from the outing: winner of a maiden at Beverley in '85 from only 4 outings: suited by a
stiff 1m, should stay 10f: acts on firm grnd.   42
*1034 TRIPLE BLUFF [6] 3-8-2(5ex) M Hills 100/30: 00-031P: Broke down after 3f & p.u.   00
955 Lady Windmill [4] 7-12   949 Swynford Prince [1] 7-7(3oh)
9 ran   1,nk,nk,½,15   (Martin Wickens)   P Haslam Newmarket

1285 BARCLAYS BANK H'CAP 3YO+ 0-60   £4737   6f   Good/Firm 29 +06 Fast   [56]

1145 MANIMSTAR [7] (P Makin) 6-9-5 J Reid 7/2 JT FAV: -000021: 6 b h Martinmas - Reddish
Radish (Red God): Useful sprinter on his day: waited with till sprinting clear in the
final 1f for an easy win in quite a valuable h'cap at Newmarket June 28: in '85 won this
same race, and other h'caps again at Newmarket & at Newbury: well suited by a stiff 6f:
acts on firm & yld & is best when held up: wore a visor last term but running well at
present without one.   60
922 HILTON BROWN [6] (P Cundell) 5-9-10 P Cook 10/1: 3130022: Kept on, gd effort: see 76.   56
1145 PERFECT TIMING [2] (D Elsworth) 4-8-13 A Mcglone 7/2 JT FAV: 03-0433: Much closer to
this winner in 1145: see 877.   39
1157 FOOLISH TOUCH [3] (K Stone) 4-8-1(vis) P Burke(7) 20/1: 0310044: Made much, hung
badly right final 1f: best 401 (good).   27
*1066 REVEILLE [8] 4-8-7(6ex) T Ives 11/2: 0-22010: Prom, ev ch: btr 1066.   31
1151 LATCH STRING [1] 3-8-8 R Cochrane 7/1: 24-1100: Prom most: best 808 (C/D).   39
952 ROYSIA BOY [4] 6-8-9 W Ryan 4/1: 101-000: Well bckd, no dngr: see 952.   00
952 BRIG CHOP [5] 5-9-3 T Lucas 20/1: 4-3000R: Refused to race (2nd time this season):
temperamental nowadays: see 374.   00
8 ran   3,2½,hd,1,1½   (S H J Brewer)   P Makin, Ogbourne Maisey, Wilts

1286 VAN GEEST CRITERION STAKES GR. 3   £15616   7f   Good/Firm 29 +22 Fast

1147 MISTER WONDERFUL [7] (J Dunlop) 3-8-5(BL) T Ives 8/1: 0-33331: 3 b c Mummy's Pet -
Baffle (Petingo): Very smart colt: bl for the first time when impressively winning Gr.3
Van Geest Criterion Stakes at Newmarket June 28: weaved his way through the field to sprint
clear in the final 100 yds: a deserved success after several near misses in valuable h'caps:
in '85 won a valuable maiden at Ascot: stays 1m but is very eff at 7f: acts on firm & yld &
likes a gall trk: now seems best in bl: acts on firm in more gd races.   80
1096 NINO BIBBIA [10] (L Cumani) 3-8-5 R Cochrane 6/1: 2-11042: Kept on really well final
2f: fine effort: see 579.   76
1107 BRAVE OWEN [14] (H Cecil) 3-8-5 W Ryan 5/2 FAV: 13-223: Chall dist: consistent: see 802.   73
1109 HADEER [12] (C Brittain) 4-9-2 M Roberts 7/1: 044-204: Set a fast pace, not btn
far and this was a btr effort: see 920.   73

1107 FLEET FORM [6] 3-8-5 J Reid 12/1: -122100: Fine effort from this consistent h'capper.   70
945 BREADCRUMB [1] 4-8-13 T Williams 10/1: 0010-00: Prom, ev ch: see 945.   57
--   TRUELY NUREYEV [2] 3-8-8 A Kimberley 3/1: 231-0: Well bckd seasonal debutant, fin 9th:
refused to enter the stalls on intended reapp at Kempton 4 weeks ago: in '85 ran only 3
times beating Huntingdale in a valuable event at Newmarket: suited by 7f & gd grnd: should
benefit from the outing.   00
1125 Fringe Of Heaven [11] 8-13   1107 Cromwell Park [9] 8-5
--   Filleor [4] 8-2   920 Sit This One Out [13] 8-8
1110 Stately Lass [3] 8-2   1109 Manchesterskytrain [8] 9-2
618 Thalestria [5] 8-13(BL)
14 ran   1½,1½,nk,1½,5   (Lavinia Duchess Of Norfolk)   J Dunlop Arundel, Sussex

1287 EWAR STUD FARM STAKES 2YO   £3353   6f   Good/Firm 29 -10 Slow

*944 TWYLA [6] (H Cecil) 2-8-13 W Ryan 8/11 FAV: 11: 2 ch f Habitat - Running Ballerina
(Nijinsky): Smart, very prom filly: retained her unbtn record when making all and striding
out really well in the final 1f to win quite a valuable 2yo fillies event at Newmarket
June 28: first time out, cantered up in a fillies maiden at Haydock: sister to the useful
'84 juvenile Defecting Dancer: very eff at 6f with forcing tactics but should stay further:
acts on firm & gd going & on a gall trk: should remain hard to beat.   70
--   RARELY IRISH [9] (M Ryan) 2-8-5 R Cochrane 10/1: 2: Slowly away, fin in fine fashion:
cost $65,000 and is a half sister to 3 winners, notably useful milers Exclusively Raised
and Truly Rare: sure to be suited by 7f: acts well on fast grnd & on a stiff trk: will have
no 'difficulty winning races.   56
--   IOSIFA [10] (M Stoute) 2-8-5 A Kimberley 9/1: 3: Wk in mkt on debut, started slowly
but was flying at the fin and is sure to benefit greatly from the race: from a winning 2yo:
will be a different proposition next time.   53
1021 CANDLE IN THE WIND [13] (R Laing) 2-8-5 P Cook 10/1: 04: Prom, kept on and is sure
to find a maiden if her sights are lowered a little: see 1021.   50
--   STRATCH [7] 2-8-5 J Reid 20/1: 0: No real threat but should benefit from the race:
French bred filly.   40
--   ESTA BONITA [3] 2-8-5 E Guest 20/1: 0: Fin well but much too late: sure to impr on
this next time & will be suited by another furlong.   40
*1067 TRY THE DUCHESS [12] 2-8-8 D Mckay 9/1: 10: Fin 9th: btr 1067.   00
1108 JAISALMER [11] 2-8-8 A Mcglone 12/1: 10200: Fin well btn & appears flattered in 773.   00
--   Kate Is Best [8] 8-5   1021 Jay Gee Ell [4] 8-13   --   Sad Cafe [5] 8-5
--   Caerinette [2] 8-5   417 Flapper Girl [1] 8-5
13 ran   2,1½,1,3,shhd   (Sheikh Mohammed)   H Cecil Newmarket

1288 REACH SELLING STAKES 3YO   £1954   7f   Good/Firm 29 -14 Slow

837 TAMANA DANCER [12] (F Durr) 3-8-6 P Cook 16/1: 00-0001: 3 ch f Gay Fandango -
Deflowered (Red God): Led final 1f comfortably in a 3yo seller at Newmarket June 28 (sold
7,200 gns): appreciated this drop into selling company & evidently well at home over a
stiff 7f on fast grnd.   22
992 TROPICO [13] (P. Haslam) 3-8-9 T Williams 6/1: 02-0042: Prom, led 2f out & stayed on:
good effort & looks sure to find a similar race soon: see 318.   21
857 CLOUDLESS SKY [19] (P Rohan) 3-8-6 T Ives 5/1: 3400-03: Prom, ev ch: ran only 4
times in '85: stays 7f & acts on fast grnd.   13
963 RUPERT BROOKE [18] (J Kettlewell) 3-8-9 M Roberts 10/1: 00-0024: Chall 2f out:
has changed stables since 963.   11
954 MISS VENEZUELA [17] 3-8-6 J Reid 11/1: 0-00000: Ev ch: first hint of form this term:
remains a maiden.   05
941 FANDANGO KISS [1] 3-8-6 R Cochrane 10/1: 00-00: Ev ch: lightly raced maiden.   00
842 THE STAMP DEALER [8] 3-8-9 M Miller 2/1 FAV: -0000: Heavily bckd but no threat: see 842 00
1081 MRS NAUGHTY [5] 3-8-11 A Mackay 10/1: 00-4000: Led far side till 2f out: see 650, 816.   00
--   Fast Taxi [6] 8-9   809 Ocean Lad [20] 8-9   978 Miss Betel [16] 8-6(BL)
1184 Carr Wood [2] 8-9   809 Dicks Boy [3] 8-9   --   Doubler [9] 8-9
774 Golden Bourne [11] 8-9   1200 La Manga Prince [14] 8-9(BL)
1201 Red Zulu [7] 8-9(bl)   871 Gaywood Girl [21] 8-6   1053 Holiday Mill [4] 8-6(BL)
928 Lady Owen [10] 8-6   --   Bally Fred [15] 8-9
21 ran   1½,3,3,1½,4   (D Lucie-Smith)   F Durr Newmarket

1289 PLANTATION STUD MAIDEN STAKES 2YO   £3619   7f   Good/Firm 29 -42 Slow

--   WUZO [4] (L Piggott) 2-9-0 T Ives 8/1: 1: 2 b c Storm Bird - Heathers Surprise
(Best Turn): Promising colt: first time out fin strongly to lead near line in a slowly run
2yo maiden at Newmarket June 28: comes from a useful American family: eff over 7f, sure to
stays at least 1m: acts well on fast grnd & on a stiff trk: should impr further.   50
--   SANTELLA SAM [9] (M Ryan) 2-9-0 P Robinson 12/1: 2: Led dist, caught death: fine
debut: cost $20,000 & looks quite a bargain at that price: suited by 7f on fast grnd:
will stay further: should find a maiden.   49
1049 BOIS DE BOULOGNE [1] (L Piggott) 2-9-0 T Lucas 9/4 FAV: 203: Btr fancied stable

companion of winner, led briefly 2f out: race 662 has not worked out well.   43
--   BEAT STREET [5] (C Brittain) 2-9-0 M Roberts 16/1: 4: Wk in mkt on debut, flying at
the finish & should not be long impro. on this: half brother to winning '81 2yo Ten-Traco:
stays 7f well, will stay 1m: acts on fast grnd.   42
1097 SOMEONE ELSE [6] 2-9-0 R Cochrane 100/30: 0300: Clear ch on form shown in 1097,
not stay 7f?   38
405 LACK A STYLE [11] 2-9-0 P Cook 6/1: 00: Never closer after abs: see 405.   38
1197 Master Knowall [3] 9-0   979 Shaine [2] 9-0
--   Knights Nevergreen [8] 9-0   1019 Tiptree [7] 9-0
--   Goodwood Park [10] 9-0
11 ran   nk,2,½,1½,hd   (Mrs J D Smith)   L Piggott Newmarket

1290 NAT FLATMAN MAIDEN APPR STAKES   £1965   1m 4f Good/Firm 29 -30 Slow

-875 DAARKOM [12] (A Stewart) 3-8-4 R Carter 13/8: -221: 3 b c Be My Guest - Lady Regrets
(Sir Gaylord): Very useful colt: gained a deserved success, leading ½m out & easily forging
well clear in a slowly run app. maiden at Newmarket June 28: unraced as a 2yo: type to impro further &
over 12f, promises to stay further: acts on fast going: type to impro further & win btr races.   62
-1167 RUSSIAN LOGIC [13] (G Harwood) 3-8-4 S Hill(4) 11/8 FAV: -222: Heavily bckd, not
pace of winner: see 1167.   50
991 WARM WELCOME [6] (G Wragg) 3-8-1 D Surrey(5) 10/1: 42-003: Fair effort: see 661.   43
402 SARYAN [8] (N Callaghan) 3-8-4 G King 33/1: 00-04: Abs: never closer: lightly raced
in '85 but is a half brother to several winners: suited by middle dists & fast grnd: on
the up grade.   31
--   LOUD LANDING [14] 3-8-4 Dale Gibson(5) 14/1: 0-0: Led briefly after ½way: ran only
once in '85: may improve.   26
943 FRED THE TREAD [7] 4-9-5 David Eddery(3) 33/1: -00: Prom 1m: lightly raced maiden
on the Flat & over hurdles.   23
--   Home County [2] 9-5   887 Willow Gorge [4] 8-4   --   Miss Maina [11] 9-2
991 My Annadetsky [10] 8-1   --   Katie Bridge [1] 8-1
--   Surprise Attack [3] 9-5   1160 Varsity [5] 8-4
1178 Beauclerc [9] 8-4(VIS)
14 ran   8,2½,7,3,1½   (Sheikh Ahmed Al-Maktoum)   A Stewart Newmarket

1291 FAWDON MAIDEN STAKES 3YO   £2686   1m 1f Firm 11 -09 Slow

1046 SEVERS [5] (H Cecil) 3-9-0 N Day 15/8 FAV: -031: 3 b c Ballad Rock - Courting
(Quorum): Very useful, impr colt: well bckd when scoring a comfortable pillar-to-post success
in a 3yo maiden at Newcastle June 28: unraced as a 2yo: half brother to several winners incl
useful sprinter Apollo Nine: well suited by 9f on a stiff trk, certain to stay at least 10f:
acts on firm & yld: the type to impr further & win more races.   60
370 HIGH CROWN [4] (L Cumani) 3-9-0 R Guest 5/2: -42: Mostly 2nd after abs: see 370.   55
982 HANOOF [3] (H Stoute) 3-8-11 M Birch 9/2: -43: Ev ch: see 982.   45
--   LIHBAB [6] (M Albina) 3-9-0 A Bond 25/1: -4: Kept on quite promisingly on racecourse
debut: half brother to an Irish 7f winner: likely to impr for this experience.   43
--   SMOOTH GLIDER [1] 3-9-0 A Clark 6/1: -0: Prom most on debut: half brother to 3
winners & is quite speedily bred: may be suited by shorter distances.   36
806 RAF [2] 3-9-0 G Duffield 8/1: -00: Prom much.   21
6 ran   2,3,1½,2½,8   (C St George)   H Cecil Newmarket

1292 JOURNAL GOOD MORNING H'CAP 3YO+ 0-60   £4838   7f Firm 11 +12 Fast   [52]

945 POSTORAGE [3] (M Mccormack) 4-10-0 R Wernham 12/1: 20-0001: 4 b c Pyjama Hunt -
song Of Gold (Song): Very useful colt: defied 10-0 when leading final 1f gamely in a fast
run, quite valuable h'cap at Newcastle June 28: in '85 won 4 h'caps on the trot at Sandown,
Wolverhampton, Salisbury & Warwick: very eff over 6/7f on firm or gd grnd though also acts
on yld: acts on any trk: carries weight well & is a genuine type.   64
1109 SUPER TRIP [6] (M Fetherston Godley) 5-8-8 L Charnock 2/1 FAV: -002142: Chall final 1f:
in excellent form & should win again soon: see 1013, 1109.   42
+1222 MR JAY ZEE [4] (N Callaghan) 4-8-7(6ex) G Duffield 7/2: 0-01313: Quick reapp: kept
on strongly & is in tremendous form: see 1222.   39
1176 KNIGHTS SECRET [8] (M H Easterby) 5-8-11 M Birch 7/2: 0-21134: Made most: very consistent. 42
1104 MARAVILLA [2] 4-7-10 J Lowe 12/1: 300-000: Pressed ldrs most: see 1104.   21
1026 VALLEY MILLS [9] 6-9-8 C Dwyer 9/1: -030040: Early speed: see 520.   46
1091 GOOSE HILL [7] 3-8-1 K Darley 8/1: -104030: Prom much: btr 1091 (sharpish trk).   00
1028 Jarrovian [5] 8-1   --   Lucky Song [1] 9-6
9 ran   ½,½,nk,2½,½,2   (P J Christey)   M Mccormack Wantage, Oxon

1293 NEWCASTLE BROWN ALE N'LAND PLATE H'CAP   £22724   2m   Firm 11 +11 Fast   [54]

+712 SNEAK PREVIEW [3] (H Candy) 6-8-12 S Whitworth 4/1 FAV: 043-111: 6 b g Quiet Fling -
Glimmer Of Hope (Never Say Die): Useful, much impr stayer: completed his hat trick & was
well bckd when overcoming difficulties in running to lead final 1f, comfortably in fast
run and valuable Northumberland Plate h'cap at Newcastle June 28: comfortably won h'caps at
Newmarket & Doncaster previously & is unbtn this season: in '85 won at Wolverhampton &
Salisbury (first time out): also 4th in the Cesarewitch: eff at 2m stays forever: acts on
firm & good grnd & is suited by a stiff gall trk: genuine sort who does well when fresh and has
not stopped winning yet.   52
*1004 NEWSELLS PARK [16] (J Winter) 5-9-1(3ex) K Darley 8/1: 2/P-212: Came from behind, led
2f out & ran a fine race: stays 2m really well: should win again soon: see 1004.   52
*801 SAFE RIVER [8] (L Cumani) 4-9-1(3ex) R Guest 6/1: 1-44013: Came from well behind,
fin strongly & is in grand form: see 801.   50
462 DAN MARINO [6] (M Stoute) 4-9-7 M Birch 10/1: -/11-04: Al prom after abs: won both
his races in '85, minor races at Yarmouth & York: eff 14f, stays 2m well: acts on firm
& yld & likes a gall trk.   55
462 BACKCHAT [14] 4-9-7 A Clark 14/1: 411-400: Prom, hung under press 1f out, causing
some confusion behind him: see 215 (14f, yld).   52
1150 MORGANS CHOICE [2] 9-7-8 N Carlisle 8/1: 0000030: Lost his pitch ½way, kept on fin.   23
*1099 RIKKI TAVI [1] 6-8-13 B Thomson 11/1: 3-03310: Led 3f out, hdd & hmpd 1f out, fin 7th.   43
1127 PETRIZZO [13] 5-9-1 N Day 12/1: 0003040: Ev ch, fin 8th: flattered 1127: see 474.   45
921 HERRADURA [11] 5-8-4(BL) G Duffield 15/2: 042-230: Bl first time, never closer in 9th:
btr 921 (12f).   42
917   Rostherne [4] 8-6   1177 Treasure Hunter [12] 8-8(1ow)
449   Key Royal [9] 7-7(1oh)   921 Ladys Bridge [10] 9-4   1099 Trapeze Artist [5] 8-11(3ex)
584   Singers Tryst [15] 9-3
15 ran   2,1½,½,2,1,½,½,2½   (Mrs C E Gross)   H Candy Kingston Warren, Oxon

1294 DURHAM SELLING STAKES 2YO   £2983   6f   Firm 11 -07 Slow

*1088 NIFTY GRIFF [9] (R Whitaker) 2-8-11 K Bradshaw(5) 11/1: 0011: 2 b c Ardoon - Betty
Bun (St Chad): Impr colt: led nearing final 1f, driven out, breaking the 2yo course record
in a seller at Newcastle June 28 (bought in 3,300 gns): last time out won a similar event at
Thirsk: very eff at 6f on fast grnd: acts on any trk: does well when up with the pace.   35
*1083 FLAIR PARK [11] (D Thom) 2-8-8 B Thomson 4/1 JT FAV: 012: Stayed on well: in fine form.   30
1076 AVINASESH [8] (C Tinkler) 2-8-11 L Charnock 14/1: 023: Mkt drifter: ran on all
too late: see 1076.   26
1119 SHARPHAVEN [10] (M Brittain) 2-8-8 K Darley 10/1: 3403024: Led after ½way: acts on
firm and soft: see 1119.   23
948 SETTER COUNTRY [13] 2-8-8 J Lowe 14/1: 01430: Led over ½way: stays 6f: acts on
firm and soft: see 329.   23
965 RABENHAM [1] 2-8-11 C Dwyer 10/1: 00400: Prom & ev ch: best 741.   16
1155 PREMIER VIDEO [15] 2-8-8 M Fry 7/1: 3020: Sn prom: much btr 1155: see 627.   00
913 HUGO Z HACKENBUSH [12] 2-8-11 M Wood 7/1: 404400: Dropped in class: no show: btr 913.   00
973 U BIX COPY [7] 2-8-11(VIS) D Nicholls 8/1: 03230: Friendless in mkt: no show:
much btr 973 (heavy).   00
979 FAIRTOWN [5] 2-8-11 N Day 4/1 JT FAV: 00: Springer in mkt: no show: cost 3,200 gns
and is a half sister to 2 winners: should stay further than 6f.   00
1190 Lady Sunday Sport [14] 8-8   1221 Miss Acacia [16] 8-8
1105 Frev Off [2] 8-8(bl)   1155 Finlux Design [4] 8-11
544 Benfield Newcastle [3] 8-8   1076 Swynford Princess [6] 8-8(BL)
16 ran   ½,3,shhd,shhd,4,nk,hd,hd   (Miss L Giffiths)   R Whitaker Wetherby, Yorks

1295 MONKCHESTER HANDICAP 3YO 0-35   £2098   1m 2f Firm 11 -22 Slow   [33]

451 SPACE TROOPER [2] (T Fairhurst) 3-8-3 N Day 12/1: 400-401: 3 ch g Air Trooper -
Netley (Major Portion): Sn prom & despite being held by a shhd was awarded a h'cap at
Newcastle June 28: first success: stays 10f well: acts on fast grnd & a gall trk: does
well when fresh.   16
989 ICARO [3] (N Callaghan) 3-9-7(bl) G Duffield 9/4 JT FAV: -022032: Not much room
final 1f: fin 3rd, placed 2nd: consistent: see 989, 609.   30
956 HONEST TOIL [1] (R Whitaker) 3-8-9 D Mckeown 8/1: 340041D: Led over 2f out: went
right final 1f: sht hd winner, but disq. & placed 3rd: eff at 1m, stays 10f: acts on firm
& yld grnd: see 14.   22
579 SHAHS CHOICE [6] (J Dunlop) 3-9-5 J Lowe 9/4 JT FAV: -00-04: Nicely bckd: never
nearer: lightly raced previously: half brother to several winners: should be suited by
10f plus: acts on fast grnd.   24
1089 MASTER LAMB [5] 3-8-9 M Birch 12/1: 00-4040: Led 1m: btr 1089.   11
998 NOT A PROBLEM [4] 3-8-7 L Charnock 6/1: 3004320: Fdd: btr 998: see 702.   06
*1122 COMMON FARM [8] 3-9-8(5ex) K Darley 8/1: 0000010: Well below form 1122 (9f soft).   00
997 Nippy Chippy [7] 8-7
8 ran   shhd,4,4,3,2½   (J A Turney)   T Fairhurst Middleham, Yorks

408

1304 COLWICK HALL 3YO MAIDEN STAKES   £1678   2m   Firm 10 +03 Fast

1022 DIVINE DESTINY [2] (J Tree) 3-8-11 Pat Eddery 1/1 FAV: 0-41: 3 ch f Sir Ivor - Bring
Out The Band (One For All): Useful, impr filly: led from the stalls, very comfortably in a
3yo maiden at Nottingham June 30: eff at 13f, stays 2m well: acts on gd & firm grnd & a
gall trk: attractive filly who should rate more highly & win more races.   49
978 BEDHEAD [1] (A Stewart) 3-9-0 M Roberts 8/1: 0-02: Kept on well, though no chance
with winner: 5L clear 3rd: stays 2m well: see 978.   43
839 NORTHERN SOCIETY [3] (D Murray Smith) 3-9-0(BL) S Cauthen 12/1: 0-043: Tried in bl:
ev ch str: stays 2m: acts on gd & firm: see 839.   37
959 L B LAUGHS [5] (G Pritchard Gordon) 3-9-0(bl) W Ryan 7/1: 30-0024: Never nearer: stays 2m
                                                                                            36
949 PHEASANT HEIGHTS [7] 3-8-11 T Williams 9/1: 000-440: Prom much: seems to act on
any ground: see 307.   32
996 DEMON FATE [4] 3-9-0 J Reid 25/1: 04-0000: Prom over 12f: non-stayer? see 605.   32
347 IGHTHAM [11] 3-9-0 G Starkey 7/1: -00: Abs: no threat: should do btr in time.   00
1029 DENBERDAR [10] 3-9-0 S Perks 10/1: 0-2030: Active in mkt: there 12f: see 1029, 411. 00
517 Fire Lord [6] 9-0   **347 Miranol Venture** [9] 8-11
10 ran   3,5,nk,nk,2   (K Abdulla)   J Tree Beckhampton, Wilts

1305 GINGER TOM MAIDEN AUCTION STAKES 2YO   £1257   6f   Firm 10 -16 Slow

1143 BATTLEAXE [18] (J Toller) 2-8-10 Pat Eddery 11/10 FAV: 3341: Kampala - Fine Flame :
Made all in a 2yo maiden auction at Nottingham June 30: deserved success: well suited by
6f, should stay further: acts on gd & firm grnd & a gall trk.   45
1090 ROYAL CROFTER [3] (M H Easterby) 2-8-8 M Birch 11/2: 32: Sn prom: gd effort: stays 6f. 38
-- REMAIN FREE [2] (C Williams) 2-8-3 L Jones(5) 33/1: 3: AI up there on racecourse debut:
cheaply acquired: should stay further than 6f: half sister to Duhallow Boy & Rocky's Gal.   28
931 FOURWALK [11] (N Macauley) 2-8-8 W Wharton 33/1: 0024: Dsptd lead: on the up grade:
stays 6f & acts on any trk: see 931.   33
938 AFRABELA [6] 2-8-4 K Darley 10/1: 32040: Active in mkt: sn prom: stays 6f: acts
on firm & yld: possibly best on a sharpish trk.   27
536 SNO SURPRISE [14] 2-8-7 W R Swinburn 12/1: 400: Prom much: abs: best 425 (5f).   29
1180 FALDWYN [4] 2-8-2 N Carlisle 14/1: 33020: Early speed: btr 1180.   00
-- PERFECT STRANGER [12] 2-8-11 T Williams 9/2: 0: Well bckd debutant: fin 8th: should
be suited by further than 6f: one to keep an eye on.   00
1161 Get Set Lisa [13] 8-4   **-- Reata Pass** [17] 8-5   **320 Raintree County** [8] 8-12
-- Not By Myself [15] 8-9   **1059 Young Centurion** [10] 8-7
1105 Galway Express [16] 8-6(BL)   **1194 Gone For It** [7] 8-5
-- Leg Glide [5] 8-4   **882 Whats A Guinea** [9] 8-3
17 ran   1¼,1¼,shhd,¼,hd   (C I Coleridge Cole)   J Toller Newmarket

1306 HOME ALES GOLD TANKARD (H'CAP) (0-70)   £7585   6f   Firm 10 +16 Fast   [64]

1145 OUR JOCK [1] (R Smyth) 4-8-13 C Rutter(5) 15/8 FAV: 0-00041: 4 br c Daring March -
Sweet Jane (Furry Glen): Useful sprinter: led final 1f, comfortably when breaking course
record in a 6f h'cap at Nottingham June 30: last time out a gd 4th in the Wokingham at Royal
Ascot: in excellent form in '85, winning 3yo h'caps at Windsor & Kempton (first time out):
also btn shhd in the Stewards Cup at Goodwood & Great St Winifred h'cap at Ripon in '84 won
first time out at Kempton: very eff at 5/6f, stays 7f: acts on firm & soft & on any trk.: genuine. 62
922 TOBERMORY BOY [3] (R Whitaker) 9-8-1 D Mckeown 7/2: 02-0002: Not the best of runs:
gd effort: back to form: see 742.   46
1146 POLYKRATIS [5] (M Francis) 4-9-5 Paul Eddery 7/2: 30-0003: Ch final 1f: best 1146.   59
1146 AMIGO LOCO [2] (K Brassey) 5-9-10(bl) S Whitworth 7/1: 2220004: Prom, ev ch: btr 587. 64
1125 POLLY DANIELS [6] 4-9-10 T Quinn 6/1: 231-100: Made most: see 817.   56
1145 DORKING LAD [4] 4-8-12 R Cochrane 20/1: 0-00000: Outsider: no show: see 1026.   35
6 ran   1,1½,shhd,3,3   (Lord McAlpine)   R Smyth Epsom, Surrey

1307 E.B.F. DAYBROOK STAKES 2YO COLTS   £1118   6f   Firm 10 -05 Slow

-- BUTTERFIELD ROAD [7] (M Usher) 2-8-11 M Wigham 9/1: 1: 2 b c Darby Creek Road -
Sweetladyroll (Drole Roll): Promising colt: nicely bckd on debut & led close home in a 2yo
stakes at Nottingham June 30: cost $17,000 as a yearling: eff at 6f, should stay 7f: acts
on fast grnd & should rate more highly.   49
-- WILLIESRIGHTONCUE [5] (G Huffer) 2-8-11 G Carter(3) 33/1: 2: Rank outsider: ch final
1f: gd racecourse debut from this 21,000 gns purchase: half brother to several winners incl
2m victor Harlyn Bay: eff at 6f on fast. grnd: should have no trouble finding a race.   45
+1090 ONGOING SITUATION [2] (D Morley) 2-9-2 S Cauthen 11/2: 013: Led briefly final 1f: gd
effort under 9-2: stays 6f: see 1090.   49
985 LOVE TRAIN [1] (R Laing) 2-8-11 Pat Eddery 9/4 JT.FAV: 44: Well bckd: no extra
final 1f: see 985 (easier trk).   36
685 ABIDJAN [6] 2-8-11(VIS) N Howe 33/1: 000: Visored first time: prom early: first signs
of form from this half brother to 1m winner Scotsezo.   23
1225 BORN FREE AGAIN [8] 2-8-11 T Ives 3/1: 0020: Made most: well below form 1225.   22
979 LORD COLLINS [3] 2-8-11 W R Swinburn 9/4 JT.FAV: 40: Wknd 1½f out: btr 979.   00

```
--   Ragtime Solo  [4] 8-11
8 ran   1,hd,3,5,¼,1½          (M S Burdett-Coutts)       M Usher Lambourn, Berks
```

1308 STARTING GATE 2YO FILLIES MAIDEN   £1096   5f   Firm 10 -04 Slow

773 UN BEL DI [7] (O Douieb) 2-8-11 Pat Eddery 1/1 FAV: 01: 2 b f Miswaki - Gyro Life
(Quadravan): Promising filly: bckd as if defeat was out of the question & made ev yd, easily
in a 2yo fillies maiden at Nottingham June 30: American bred filly who should stay further
than 5f: acts on fast grnd & seems suited by front running tactics: should win more races.   54
1057 BERTRADE [1] (P Makin) 2-8-11 S Cauthen 8/1: 4032: No ch with winner, but ran well.   44
1154 RATHER HOMELY [2] (P Cole) 2-8-11 T Wuinn 9/4: 33: Mkt drifter: ev ch: see 1154.   42
136 HOMING IN [4] (G Huffer) 2-8-11 M Miller 20/1: 04: Long abs: sn prom: should be
suited by a sharpish 5f: acts on fast grnd.   39
--   MISS RUNAWAY [5] 2-8-11 W R Swinburn 11/1: 0: Slow start proved fatal: should do
btr next time: half sister to Miss Silca Key: should stay 6f: acts on firm grnd.   25
1057 MUSIC DELIGHT [6] 2-8-11 W Woods(3) 50/1: 00: Prom early: stiff task: see 1057.   21
--   Musical Rhapsody [8] 8-11   1059 Scarning Shadylady [3] 8-11
8 ran   1½,½,1,7,1½   (Sheikh Mohammed)   O Douieb Newmarket

1309 RUDDINGTON HANDICAP 3YO 0-35   £1578   1m 2f Firm 10 -24 Slow   [42]

941 SELL IT KILROY [1] (G Huffer) 3-8-9 G Carter(3) 20/1: -0001: 3 b c Runnett -
Silecia (Sky Gipsy): Showed impr form to lead close home in a slow run 3yo h'cap at Nottingham June 30: no form in 3 previous outings: half brother to 3 winners: stays 10f: acts on
fast grnd.   32
941 FINDING [10] (M Stoute) 3-9-7 W R Swinburn 9/4 FAV: 0-032: Al prom: ran well: stays 10f
and acts on any trk: see 941.   40
1087 SIMONS FANTASY [9] (R Armstrong) 3-8-5(1ow) Pat Eddery 10/3: 00-0443: Nearly made
all: gd effort: may win soon on a sharper trk: see 843.   22
648 G G MAGIC [5] (D Morley) 3-8-6(4ow) M Birch 12/1: 00-0304: Prom, ev ch: stays 10f: see 38018
1173 LONDON CONTACT [6] 3-9-2 S Cauthen 11/4: 33-0040: Ev ch: twice below form 919.   26
1081 SHARONS ROYALE [2] 3-8-1(5ow) D Mckeown 33/1: 000-000: Never nearer: yet to make
the frame: probably stays 10f: acts on firm & yld grnd.   09
843 Roi De Soleil [4] 7-9   790 Idle Song [8] 8-5   1169 Klosterbrau [3] 7-9
514 Grandangus [7] 7-7(2oh)
10 ran 1½,¼,½,2½,½,½   (C R Kilroy)   G Huffer Newmarket

1310 CHISWICK SELLING HANDICAP 0-25   £970   1m 2f Firm 09 -32 Slow   [15]

*1210 TRELAWNEY [14] (A Ingham) 4-9-4(5ex) R Curant 10/1: 0-00011: 4 ch c Welsh Pageant -
Pilley Green (Porto Bello): Winning 2nd seller on the trot, leading final 1f under press at
Windsor June 30 (sold 7,100 gns): recent winner of similar seller at Brightonn: suited by a
sharpish trk: eff at 1m, stays 10f: acts on fast going.   14
1056 UNDER THE STARS [15] (A Akehurst) 4-9-6 R Mcghin 10/1: 00-0042: Led 2f out: best
effort this season & is suited by 10f: should win a seller soon: see 343.   12
625 GAY CARUSO [8] (K Brassey) 3-9-3(bl) B Procter 12/1: 00-0003: Never closer: first
signs of form & evidently appreciated the drop to selling company: may stay beyond 10f:
wears bl & acts on firm.   21
1195 GWILLIM ENTERPRISE [6] (R Juckes) 4-9-0 R Guest 33/1: 0000-04: Ev ch: see 1195: wears bl.02
1052 PATRALAN [12] 4-9-5 B Uniacke(7) 10/1: 0-00000: Not btn far: fair effort: tried
in bl last time but seems btr without them: stays 10f & acts on firm.   07
740 GROVECOTE [10] 3-8-6 B Thomson 20/1: 03-0000: Close up over 1m: see 740.   06
356 SOLENT LAD [19] 3-8-6 R Carter(4) 10/1: 000-200: Fin 9th after abs: best 139 (soft).   00
940 LISAKATY [2] 3-8-8 R Wernham 10/1: 0-00000: Dropped to a seller, no threat & evidently
flattered in 500 (7f, good).   00
1231 KOUS [7] 3-9-1(bl) S Whitworth 7/4 FAV: -1030: Heavily bckd: much btr 1231.   00
1056 EASTER RAMBLER [4] 4-9-7 Pat Eddery 7/1: -000000: Well btn in similar company previously. 00
984 Pandi Club [3] 9-2(bl)   1288 Holiday Mill [16] 9-5
1212 Odervy [17] 7-12   7   Letby [20] 9-3(vis)   856 Trikkala Star [11] 8-12(BL)
838 Lean Streak [18] 9-0   --   Montbergis [13] 8-2   666 Rebello Imp [5] 8-4(bl)
1186 Charisma Music [1] 8-13
19 ran 2,1½,1,hd,2   (S Crowe)   A Ingham Epsom, Surrey

1311 EBF MARBLE ARCH MAIDEN STAKES 2YO   £1484   5f   Firm 09 +03 Fast

1030 SAUCE DIABLE [3] (W Hern) 2-8-11 Pat Eddery 8/13 FAV: 21: 2 b f Moorestyle - Cottage
Pie (Kalamoun): Very useful filly: rewarded strong support when making all at a fast pace &
holding on by the minimum margin in a 2yo maiden at Windsor June 30: well suited by forcing
tactics over 5f on firm grnd, though bred to stay further: evidently very speedy & sure
to win more races.   60
974 MISK [8] (H Cecil) 2-9-0 S Cauthen 7/4: 22: Chall winner final 1f: caught a tartar here
& well clear of rest: a maiden is a formality: will be suited by 6f: see 974.   63

405   MELODY MARKER   [4] (B Hills) 2-9-0 B Thomson 16/1: 03: No ch with first two: related to several winners: has scope and will probably do btr over 6f: acts on firm ground.   **39**

780   JUST ONE MORE   [2] (E Eldin) 2-9-0 M L Thomas 33/1: 404: Prom much: see 678: acts on firm and good.   **37**

--   MAKE OR MAR   [7] 2-8-11 S Whitworth 33/1: 0: Early speed: first foal of a winning 2yo over 1m: may improve.   **19**

--   PETTING PARTY   [6] 2-9-0 P Waldron 25/1: 0: No threat: related to winning sprinters.   **04**

--   Cherokee Gold   [9] 8-11   --   Princess Pelham   [1] 8-11

--   Rhythm Maker   [5] 8-11   --   Sebs Mark   [10] 9-0

10 ran   shhd,8,¾,5,6   (Lord Porchester)   W Hern West Ilsley, Berks

---

1312   JACK BARCLAY HANDICAP 3YO 0-50   £2884   6f   Firm 09 +06 Fast   [53]

1065 CHUMMYS PET   [9] (N Callaghan) 3-8-10 Pat Eddery 7/2: 2133121: 3 b g Song - Hodsock Venture (Major Portion): Impr gelding who was scoring his 3rd win of the season when readily leading final 1f in quite a fast run 3yo h'cap at Windsor June 30: comfortably won claimers at Epsom & Carlisle previously & has been placed almost all other starts: unraced at 2 years: eff over a stiff 5f: stays 7f well: acts on firm & yld & on any trk: genuine, consistent & still improving.   **48**

1001 RIVIERA SCENE   [5] (J Dunlop) 3-9-1 S Cauthen 3/1 FAV: 022-002: Led dist, outpcd final 1f. see 624.   **45**

--   POSSEDYNO   [1] (D Elsworth) 3-9-5 A Mcglone 6/1: 01-3: Led ½way on seasonal debut: rated 64 when comfortably beating useful Flower Bowl in a 2yo maiden at Newmarket at the end of '85: half brother to a couple of winners: eff over a stiff 6f: should be suited by 7f plus: acts on firm grnd: looks nicely h'capped & should go well next time.   **48**

1171 MARGAM   [12] (P Walwyn) 3-8-10 Paul Eddery 7/1: 0-3104: Running consistently: see 787: acts on firm & heavy.   **35**

1235 COPPERMILL LAD   [14] 3-8-10 A Haynes(7) 33/1: -120000: Never closer: best early season in 111 (soft).   **33**

814 KIMBLE BLUE   [7] 3-8-7 R Wernham 9/1: 00-0400: Outpcd: best 624 (C/D).   **26**

*809 SHARP TIMES   [10] 3-7-9(2ow) A Mackay 8/1: 0-0210: Bckd from 14/1, fin 8th: see 809 (7f).   **00**

534 OUT OF HARMONY   [3] 3-7-13 T Williams 6/1: 010-000: Abs: no threat: see 534.   **00**

966 Nickle A Kiss   [11] 9-7   **846** Zulu Knight   [2] 8-12(BL)

1033 Herminda   [4] 7-11   **1036** Fruity Orooney   [6] 9-3

1257 Bernigra Girl   [8] 8-1(VIS)   **1151** Edgewise   [13] 9-1

14 ran   2½,nk,1½,½,1½   (C Gaventa)   N Callaghan Newmarket

1313   DERRY BACON STAKES 2YO   £2865   6f   Firm 09 -01 Slow

1143 LUCIANAGA   [7] (P Walwyn) 2-8-11 Paul Eddery 4/5 FAV: 2201: 2 b c King Of Spain - Redhead (Hotfoot): Useful colt: heavily bckd, al well there & battled home by a hd in a 2yo minor race at Windsor June 30: half brother to 2 winners: stays 6f well: acts on firm & gd ground.   **55**

985 AJANAC   [2] (J Tree) 2-8-11 Pat Eddery 100/30: 02: Duelled with winner final 1f & well clear of rest: eff at 6f, sure to stay 7f plus: will find a maiden soon: see 985: acts well on firm.   **54**

965 PACIFIC BASIN   [5] (W O'gorman) 2-8-11 T Ives 6/1: 023: Outpcd final 2f: btr 965(stiff track). **33**

332 LITTLE SACY   [8] (B Palling) 2-8-11 J Williams 50/1: 04: Rank outsider, early ldr after long abs: seems to be impr & acts well on firm.   **32**

962 BANGKOK BOY   [3] 2-8-11 S Whitworth 33/1: 00: Prom some: dam a winner in Italy.   **28**

1039 MURAJAH   [4] 2-8-11 S Cauthen 9/1: 040: Wknd ½way: btr 1039 (5f).   **28**

*717 RIMBEAU   [6] 2-9-2 A Clark 12/1: 42410: Fin a dist last & much btr judged 717 (5f).   **00**

876 Divine Charger   [1] 8-11

8 ran   hd,7,nk,1½,hd   (Mrs Rupert Hambro)   P Walwyn Lambourn, Berks

---

1314   DERRY PROVISION HANDICAP 3YO 0-50   £2620   1m 3f Firm 09 -27 Slow   [52]

1233 UP TO UNCLE   [3] (R Hannon) 3-7-11 A Mcglone 5/1: -000221: 3 ch c Saher - Roll Up (Roll Of Honour): Gained a deserved success, comfortably leading final 2f in a rather slowly run 3yo h'cap at Windsor June 30: showed ability over shorter distances last term but clearly well suited by 12f now: acts on soft, probably fav by firm grnd & likes a sharpish trk.   **33**

1130 WESHAAM   [7] (B Hanbury) 3-9-7 M Hills 2/1 FAV: -201322: Prom thro'out: see 716, 1130. **52**

1130 ATIG   [1] (J Bethell) 3-8-12 J Reid 33/1: 4-00003: Came from well behind, strong fin & is returning to form: evidently well suited by 12f & should be noted next time: see 883.   **42**

880 TWICE BOLD   [8] (N Callaghan) 3-9-2 Pat Eddery 13/2: 01-034: Made much: btr 880 (8.5f). **43**

*1102 COINAGE   [5] 3-9-8(7ex) S Cauthen 9/4: 3-2310: Led/dsptd lead much: fair effort under pen: see 1102.   **48**

843 PROBLEM CHILD   [6] 3-8-0(1ow) S Whitworth 33/1: 03-3000: Best 274 (7f, heavy).   **11**

980 GODS PATH   [4] 3-8-1(BL) S Dawson 9/1: 00-0000: Bl first time, fin 7th: race 980 is not working out well.   **00**

229 Star Shiner   [2] 7-12

8 ran   2,nk,1½,¾,15   (Nimrod Company)   R Hannon East Everleigh, Wilts

1315 KNIGHTSBRIDGE STAKES 3YO   £1019   1m 2f   Firm 09 -07 Slow

+1087 ESDALE [4] (J Tree) 3-9-3 Pat Eddery 2/5 FAV: 2-2011: 3 b c Fabulous Dancer -
Esdee (Hail To Reason): Very useful colt: gained his 2nd C/D win of the season when making
all in a virtual canter in a 3yo minor race at Windsor June 30: readily won similar race over
same C/D last time: 2nd to Zahdam at Ascot on sole start in '85: well regarded half brother
to a couple of winners who is suited by 10f & could well stay 12f: acts on firm & yld: impr
type who is capable of winning in much btr company.   61
765 MIRAGE DANCER [5] (R Smyth) 3-8-11 S Whitworth 12/1: 4-02342: Mostly 2nd but no ch
with this ready winner: best on yld/soft in 362.   45
*1198 TEMPLE WALK [13] (W Hern) 3-9-0 A Murray 9/2: 0-13: Kept on under press: stays 10f. 45
*935 CORRAN RIVER [7] (H Candy) 3-9-0 R Curant 14/1: 3402-14: No threat & btr 935 (12f). 33
1036 CHUCKLESTONE [11] 3-8-11 T Williams 66/1: 00-000: No dngr: showed some ability last
season from 2 outings: half brother to a couple of winners.   30
1061 RED RIVER BOY [2] 3-8-11 A Dicks(7) 66/1: -00: No dngr: see 1061.   23
1167 GANOON [10] 3-8-11 T Quinn 11/1: 200-230: Fin 7th: well below 751, 1167.   00
--   Speed Stick [6] 8-11   1036 Out Of Kindness [3] 8-8
688 The Godfather [12] 8-11   -- Faraway Lad [1] 8-11
1062 Gold Monopoly [9] 8-11
12 ran   3,2,8,shhd,4   (K Abdulla)   J Tree Beckhampton, Wilts

---

FOLKESTONE   Tuesday July 1st   Lefthand, Sharpish, Undulating Track

Official Going Given As FIRM

1316 MAIDSTONE HANDICAP STAKES (0-35) 3YO   £1398   7f   Firm 17 -01 Slow   [35]

1169 SEQUESTRATOR [9] (W Musson) 3-9-2 M Wigham 7/1: 00-0001: 3 b c African Sky -
Miss Redmarshall (Most Secret): Led nearing final 1f, driven out for a shhd win in a 3yo
h'cap at Folkestone July 1: first success: well suited by 7f on fast grnd: likes a sharp/
undulating trk.   32
880 BLUE BRILLIANT [7] (B Hills) 3-9-3(BL) B Thomson 9/2 FAV: 00-0002: Chall final 1f
and just btn: gd effort: eff at 7f/1m: seems suited by fast grnd: bl first time today. 33
--   CAFE NOIR [13] (R Williams) 3-9-7 R Cochrane 15/2: 0431-3: Ch final 1f: gd seasonal
debut: lightly raced 2yo: on final outing won a fillies maiden on this trk: eff at 6f, stays
7f: acts on firm & yld ground   33
276 BELLEPHERON [3] (G Lewis) 3-8-10 P Waldron 6/1: 0-044: Dsptd lead 2f out: fair effort
after abs: eff at 7f on firm & hvy: likes an undulating trk.   17
966 CHARDONNAY [8] (W Newnes) 3-9-1(BL) W Newnes 10/1: 0-30000: Nearest fin: stays 7f: best 431. 21
842 BE SO BOLD [15] 3-8-10 C Rutter(5) 25/1: -0000: Late hdway: best effort yet: will be
suited by 1m: see 501.   15
1199 ARE YOU GUILTY [2] 3-9-7 Paul Eddery 6/1: 03-3000: Prom, ev ch: see 63.   00
928 JAAZIEL [5] 3-9-1 J Reid 8/1: -0000: Fin 8th: btr 928, 764.   00
498 CHARCOAL [1] 3-9-0 S Whitworth 8/1: 00-000: Bl first time: wknd: lightly raced this
term: yet to make the frame: acts on gd grnd.   00
1104 Dress In Spring [4] 8-5   940 Le Nid [10] 8-10
907 Megadyne [14] 8-8   986 Baliview [11] 8-0   -- Our Remedy [16] 7-11
1212 Splendid Magnolia [6] 7-11(bl)   1210 Thai Sky [12] 7-8
16 ran   shhd,1½,3,nk,½   (G Nunn)   W Musson Newmarket

1317 SMEETH STAKES 3YO   £717   1m 2f   Firm 17 -01 Slow

226 LIAM [3] (M Ryan) 3-9-0 R Cochrane 7/2: 222-001: 3 b c Runnett - No Delay (Never Say Die)
Useful colt: led inside final 1f, comfortably in a 3yo stakes at Folkestone July 1: highly
tried in 2 previous outings this season: fin 2nd on all 3 starts in '85 & this was a
deserved win: stays 10f: acts well on gd & fast grnd & should win more races.   53
+1141 NAATELL [4] (H Cecil) 3-9-8 W Ryan 4/9 FAV: 112: Ev ch final 1f: in gd form: stays 10f. 57
1061 BANQUE PRIVEE [7] (B Hills) 3-8-11 B Thomson 8/1: 0-33: Led well over 1f out:
clear of rem: see 1061.   41
--   CLOUD CHASER [2] (W Brooks) 3-9-0 L Johnsey(7) 100/1: 000-4: Made much: unplaced in
3 outings in '85: may stay 10f: acts on fast grnd.   20
75   QUARTERFLASH [6] 3-9-0 M Wigham 50/1: 00-00: Prom 1m after abs: little form.   19
--   CLEVELAND BOND [1] 3-8-11 R Carter(5) 50/1: -0: Stiff task on debut.   00
--   MUSKET WET [5] 3-9-0 J Reid 50/1: -0: Al rear.   00
7 ran   1½,2½,12,nk,20   (Jack Fisher)   M Ryan Newmarket

1318 SELLINDGE 2YO'S SELLING, STAKES   £805   5f   Firm 17 -35 Slow

1082 CHERRYWOOD SAM [3] (H O'neill) 2-8-11(BL) I Johnson 11/4: 40401: 2 ch c Dublin Taxi -
Tollers Rose (Some Hand): Dropped to selling company & made ev yd, comfortably in a 2yo
seller at Folkestone July 1 (no bid): seems suited by forcing tactics over 5f: acts on
fast grnd & an undulating trk : blinkered first time today.   22
1190 THE CHIPPENHAM MAN [6] (M Tompkins) 2-8-11 R Cochrane 5/2 FAV: 02: Well bckd: sn prom:
btr effort: eff at 5/6f on fast grnd.   12
27   CAWSTONS COMEDIAN [2] (R Howe) 2-8-8 P D'arcy 25/1: 03: Rank outsider: al there: acts
on fast grnd & an undulating trk.   03

1262 BONZO [1] (Pat Mitchell) 2-8-11 L Riggio(7) 10/1: 004: Bckd at long odds: nearest fin:
should stay 6f: acts on fast grnd.   00
1163 MALACHI LAD [5] 2-8-11 J Reid 8/1: 30: Prom, ev ch: see 1163.   00
853 SNAPSHOT BABY [4] 2-8-8(bl) S Whitworth 10/1: 0030: Early speed: btr 853.   00
981 PINK PUMPKIN [7] 2-8-8(BL) J Matthias 10/3: 0020: Mkt drifter: bl first time & much
btr 981 (good).   00
7 ran   3,2½,6,nk,2½   (Mrs R A Smith)   H O'neill Coldharbour, Surrey

1319 WILLIAM YOUNGER SPRINT H'CAP (0-35)   £1206   6f   Firm 17 -05 Slow   [30]

1213 BELLE TOWER [7] (R Smyth) 4-9-7 C Rutter(5) 3/1 FAV: -021001: 4 b f Tower Walk -
Sarum Lady (Floribunda): Led inside final 2f, ridden out in a h'cap at Folkestone July 1:
earlier won a h'cap at Epsom: in '85 won a h'cap on this trk: eff over 6f, stays 7f: acts
on any grnd, but is best on a sharp/undulating trk.   32
1264 BOOTLE JACK [1] (W Brooks) 4-8-5 L Johnsey(3) 20/1: 3200-02: Fin well & nearly got
up: placed on several occasions in '85, but yet to win: stays 6f well: acts on any grnd.   15
1086 MAIDEN BIDDER [9] (H Beasley) 4-8-9 J Reid 7/1: 0-02103: Mkt drifter: led briefly 2f out. 16
620 HUNTS KATIE [10] (C Holmes) 4-8-12(bl) P Waldron 16/1: 030-004: Stayed on well: see 620.   19
760 FINDON MANOR [5] 3-8-8(bl) R Cochrane 6/1: 40-0000: Ran on too late: see 760.   19
1066 FORT DUCHESNE [3] 4-8-7 P Hamblett 20/1: 40-0000: Mkt drifter & no thrreat: last
season won a 3yo seller at Windsor: eff at 6/7f: acts on firm & gd grnd: likes a sharpish trk
but acts on any.   03
1077 PADDINGTON BELLE [6] 3-8-4 R Curant 6/1: 000-000: No show: remains a maiden: placed
on several occasions in '85 but was not that consistent: eff at 5f on gd & yld grnd.   00
1191 NANOR [2] 3-7-11 S Dawson 11/2: 3000000: Prom, fdd: best 340.   00
977 Shahreen [12] 7-10   508 Hildalarious [4] 7-7   1213 Sparkford Lad [8] 8-12(bl)
1211 Cats Lullaby [11] 8-3(bl)
12 ran   nk,½,shhd,2,2½   (Mrs G R Smith)   R Smyth Epsom, Surrey

1320 E.B.F. WESTENHANGER STAKES 2YO   £1344   6f   Firm 17 -05 Slow

1143 QUICK SNAP [2] (A Ingham) 2-9-5(bl) R Curant 6/5: 4322101: 2 b c Try My Best -
Photo (Blakeney): Useful, consistent colt: dsptd lead all the way, gaining upper hand final
1f in a 2yo stakes at Folkestone July 1: earlier won a similar event at Sandown: well suited
by a stiff 5f, stays 6f: acts on firm & soft grnd & on any trk: seems a genuine sort &
does well when up with the pace.   54
*1172 TOUGH N GENTLE [3] (L Piggott) 2-9-2 R Cochrane 5/6 FAV: 3212: Dsptd lead: 8L clear 3rd:
consistent: see 1172 (7f).   48
-- JOVICK [4] (G Lewis) 2-8-11 P Waldron 10/1: 3: Never nearer: impr likely: should be
suited by 7f: acts on fast grnd.   18
1162 SPRING FORWARD [1] (Pat Mitchell) 2-8-11 J Reid 40/1: 04: No threat: should stay 7f.   00
4 ran   1,8,6   (Exors of the late S R Crowe)   A Ingham Epsom, Surrey

1321 LYMPNE HANDICAP STAKES (0-35) 3YO+   £1197   1m 4f   Firm 17 +11 Fast   [24]

1265 THE BETSY [2] (D Elsworth) 4-9-8 P Mcentee(7) 5/2: -040131: 4 b f Imperial Fling -
question Mark (High Line): In fine form at present, led 1½f out and easily drew clear in
quite fast run h'cap at Folkestone July 1: earlier was an easy winner of a h'cap at Lingfield: well suited by 12f: acts on firm & yld grnd & likes a sharpish/undulating trk.   28
1017 DASHING LIGHT [5] (D Morley) 5-9-8 Paul Eddery 11/8 FAV: 2-40432: Heavily bckd: made
much: best 432.   18
1209 DERBY DAY [1] (D Wilson) 5-9-0(bl) W Newnes 4/1: -004203: Prom, wknd: btr 856: see 750.   00
1056 DOUBLE OPTION [3] (J Davies) 5-9-8 M Wigham 16/1: 0-20-04: No real threat: lightly
raced maiden: last season fin 2nd in a selling h'cap at Bath: stays 12f: acts on gd & firm.   00
1188 FORGIVING [4] 4-8-13 R Carter(5) 15/2: 0-04030: Fdd: btr 1188 (10f): see 838.   00
5 ran   5,7,8,10   (Miss Lucy Morrish)   D Elsworth Whitsbury, Hants

1322 EBF FILLIES MAIDEN STAKES 2YO   £1374   6f   Firm -04 +06 Fast

773 LASHING [9] (L Cumani) 2-8-11 Pat Eddery 8/15 FAV: 31: 2 b f Storm Bird - Rain Wind
(Apalachee): Very promising filly: al prom, & readily led after ½way in a 2yo fillies maiden
at Yarmouth July 1: cost almost $½m. & is from a top class family which includes smart middle
dist performer Ack Ack: well suited by 6f, will stay 7f & probably further: suited by firm
grnd: likely to win more races & rate more highly.   60
-- PELF [8] (L Cumani) 2-8-11 R Guest 16/1: 2: Stable companion of winner, kept on
promisingly: cost over 1.5m gns & is from a useful American family: will stay beyond 6f:
acts on firm grnd: will have no difficulty finding a maiden.   48
988 BE CHEERFUL [1] (J Winter) 2-8-11 W R Swinburn 10/1: 43: Bckd from 20/1, ev ch:
stays 6f well: acts on firm & gd: see 988.   47
-- MISTS OF AVALON [5] (H Cecil) 2-8-11 S Cauthen 11/4: 4: Op. 6/4, mkt drifter on debut:
outpcd final 2f: half sister to a winning French miler: sure to impr on this first effort.   41
-- TRYNOVA [7] 2-8-11 D Gibson 100/1: 0: Led/dsptd lead 3f: related to a winning 2yo
plater: quite speedily bred on the dam's side: may improve.   31

--   **ROMAN BELLE** [2] 2-8-11 G Duffield 66/1: 0: Prom much: quite cheaply acquired filly.   **29**
1067 **Churchill Lady** [6] 8-11   --   **Stylish Girl** [4] 8-11
--   **St Wendred** [3] 8-11
9 ran   3,shhd,2,3,¼,½   (Sheikh Mohammed)   L Cumani Newmarket

1323 BET WITH THE TOTE SELL. STKS 2YO   £650   5f   Firm -04 -53 Slow

1248 **NATIONS SONG** [4] (R Stubbs) 2-8-13(bl) J H Brown(5) 4/5 FAV: 0410221: 2 b f Gold Song –
Girl Commander (Bold Commander): Consistent plater: came from behind to lead final 1f
narrowly in a very slowly run 2yo seller at Yarmouth July 1 (bought in 3,800 gns): earlier
won a similar seller at Lingfield: has since worn bl: very eff over 5f on firm & yld going:
seems to act on any trk: genuine & consistent.   **27**
948 **MISS DRUMMOND** [7] (N Tinkler) 2-8-8(BL) Kim Tinkler(5) 5/1: 0002: Bl first time & a
gamble, led dist & only narrowly btn: impr effort from this speedily bred filly who is
clearly suited by bl: should stay 6f: acts on firm & should find a seller in the North.   **20**
1181 **SOUND AS A POUND** [3] (M Camacho) 2-8-11 D Nicholls 11/2: 0003: Dsptd lead most:
impr & acts on firm & gd grnd.   **17**
--   **COLLEGE WIZARD** [6] (M Tompkins) 2-8-11 R Morse(5) 50/1: 4: Sn prom on debut: spdly bred.**07**
728 **SWEET PICCOLO** [2] 2-8-11 G Carter(3) 11/2: 00: No dngr: cheaply bought colt.   **06**
987 **BUDSHEAD** [1] 2-8-11 M Rimmer 50/1: 00: Dsptd lead 3f: see 987.   **00**
1190 **ROAN REEF** [5] 2-8-11(bl) W Wharton 6/1: 03430: Hmpd start: see 1088.   **00**
7 ran   ½,2,3,nk,3,¾   (Nation Wide Racing Co Ltd)   R Stubbs Coverham, Yorks

1324 TOTE CREDIT HANDICAP 3YO+ 0-35   £2236   7f   Firm -04 +01 Fast   [29]

1165 **CHICAGO BID** [7] (R Armstrong) 5-9-4(bl) S Cauthen 5/1: 3-02001: 5 b h Bold Bidder –
Shore (Round Table): Came from behind to lead final 100 yds in a h'cap at Yarmouth July 1:
first success since winning at Newmarket in '83: stays 7f well: acts on any going though
probably fav by firm.   **27**
•1051 **QUALITAIR KING** [8] (K Stone) 3-8-11(6ex) M Birch 4/1: 3000312: Led dist, caught near
fin & is in fine form: stays 7f well: see 1051: acts on firm & gd.   **29**
1211 **HOPEFUL KATIE** [6] (D Leslie) 4-8-13 J Williams 13/2: 3040203: Dsptd lead thro'out: see 65 **18**
1186 **IDEOLIGIA** [1] (A Hide) 4-7-11(bl) G Carter(3) 8/1: 0-00044: Al there: see 992.   **01**
1104 **HIGHLY PLACED** [9] 4-7-12 A Mackay 100/30 JT FAV: 00-0040: Chall 2f out: see 992. **00**
844 **GOLDEN STRAW** [3] 3-8-2(vis) G Duffield 25/1: -0000: Early speed: no worthwhile form
this term & remains a maiden.   **04**
•1211 **LYRIC WAY** [4] 4-9-13(6ex) M Hills 100/30 JT FAV: -000010: Hmpd 2f out & this run
should be ignored: see 1211.   **00**
960 **Debach Revenge** [4] 8-1   --   **Bright Path** [2] 8-6
9 ran   ¾,1½,¼,¾,5   (Charles H Wacker III)   R Armstrong Newmarket

1325 TOTE PLACEPOT HANDICAP 3YO+ 0-50   £3152   1m 2f   Firm -04 -15 Slow   [48]

652 **MILL PLANTATION** [3] (G Wragg) 7-9-11 S Cauthen 6/1: 110-001: 7 b h Northfields –
Fairly Hot (Sir Ivor): Fair h'capper on his day: returned to form, coming from well behind
to get up on the post in a close fin to a slowly run h'cap at Yarmouth July 1: lightly raced
in '85 winning at Chepstow & Chester: best form around 10f, stays 12f: acts on firm & yld
& on any trk: does well carrying weight with waiting tactics.   **53**
-1141 **FIRST DIBS** [9] (M Stoute) 3-8-9 W R Swinburn 11/8 FAV: 2-3122: Went for home 2f out,
caught death: stays 10f: see 937.   **50**
1166 **SWIMMER** [4] (G Huffer) 4-9-11 G Carter(3) 13/2: 013-143: Chall final 1f, narrowly btn:
consistent and in fine form: see 964.   **52**
+1202 **GEORDIES DELIGHT** [1] (L Piggott) 3-9-0(5ex) T Ives 11/2: -210414: Led 6f, kept on
well & stays 10f: see 1202: in fine form.   **54**
743 **AYLESFIELD** [6] 6-8-7(bl) R Guest 33/1: 02-0000: Dsptd lead most: early in '85 was
placed in 3 out of his 4 races, notably btn a shhd by K Battery in valuable Zetland Gold Cup
at Redcar: not seen out after May: in '84 won at Newmarket & Sandown: eff at 10/11f on gd
& hvy grnd & likes a stiff trk.   **33**
1112 **THE FOOTMAN** [5] 4-9-5 A Mercer 33/1: 010-000: No real threat: winner over hurdles
in the Winter & successful on the level at Salisbury & Bath in '85: possibly unsuited by
firm & does well on gd or soft grnd: suited by 10f, should stay 12f.   **37**
997 **BLACK COMEDY** [7] 3-7-10 M L Thomas 7/1: 0000140: No dngr in 7th: best 843 (gd). **00**
989 **KERRY MAY SING** [8] 3-7-12 P Robinson 9/1: 031-000: fin 8th: see 989.   **00**
1186 **Kilimanjaro Bob** [2] 8-7
9 ran   hd,¼,shhd,nk,5,½,½   (E B Moller)   G Wragg Newmarket

1326 TOTE DUAL FORECAST HANDICAP 3YO 0-35   £2075   1m 6f   Firm -04 -13 Slow   [35]

978 **DIVA ENCORE** [6] (R Armstrong) 3-9-0 S Cauthen 14/1: 00-0001: 3 br f Star Appeal –
Regal Twin (Majestic Prince): Turned up at 14/1, leading final ½m comfortably in a 3yo h'cap
at Yarmouth July 1: first success & evidently appreciated todays extended trip: acts well
on firm grnd: suited by 14f & should stay 2m.   **30**
•1029 **MAJESTICIAN** [7] (G P Gordon) 3-9-10(4ex) G Duffield 10/11 FAV: -00212: Ev ch: needs 2m? **37**
275 **REFORM PRINCESS** [4] (M Ryan) 3-9-3(bl) P Robinson 14/1: 000-003: Came from off the
pace after long abs: seems suited by a stamina test & firm grnd: likely to stay 2m: see 275. **24**

1223 **REGENCY SQUARE** [5] (P Feilden) 3-8-2 M Hills 12/1: 00-3204: Best 1089 (12f). 08
833 **BRIDE** [1] 3-9-0 E Guest(3) 14/1: 00-1000: No extra from 3f out: best 123 (12f hvy). 10
1078 **ARCH PRINCESS** [8] 3-8-0(bl) M L Thomas 8/1: 0-00440: Made much: btr 1078. 00
•1204 **BLUSHING SPY** [3] 3-9-8(bl)(4ex) R Hills 9/2: -00410: Close up 10f: much btr 1204 (12f). 00
949 **COUNTLESS COUNTESS** [2] 3-9-7(BL) T Ives 6/1: -20100: Sn well behind: unsuited by firm? best 307 (2m, soft/heavy). 00
8 ran 1½,6,1,10,10 (Kinderhill Corporation) R Armstrong Newmarket

1327 TOTE PLACE ONLY MDN FILLIES STKS 3YO £1629 1m Firm -04 +21 Fast

849 **NORDICA** [15] (A Stewart) 3-8-11 M Roberts 10/1: -001: 3 ch f Northfields - Princess Arabella (Crowned Prince): Useful filly: al prom & led 3f out, narrowly in a fast run fillies maiden at Yarmouth July 1: unrcd in '85: eff over 1m, stays 10f but possibly not 12f: dam a sister to Oaks winner Fair Salinia: acts well on firm grnd: on the up grade & is the type to impr & win more races. 50
1193 **QUEEN OF BATTLE** [4] (M Ryan) 3-8-11 P Robinson 12/1: 0-0022: Al up there, just btn in a close fin & should find a maiden soon: see 1193. 48
1043 **ACTUALIZATIONS** [14] (L Cumani) 3-8-11 Pat Eddery 1/1 FAV: -03: Heavily bckd, ev ch final 2f, not btn far: see 1043: should win soon. 47
1043 **LADY FOR TWO** [7] (M Stoute) 3-8-11 W R Swinburn 10/1: -404: Ev ch: not btn far but twice below the form of 708. 44
250 **FLUTTERY** [11] 3-8-11 S Cauthen 6/4: -30: Long abs: not btn far: btr 250 (7f, soft) but worth another chance. 43
806 **THUNDERDOME** [3] 3-8-11 R Hills 16/1: -00: Btn less than 5L & is on the up grade: dam a winner over 7f: acts on firm grnd: should find a maiden. 40
-- **Princess Emma** [12] 8-11 7th -- **Maladetoc** [5] 8-11 8th
-- **Shujun** [1] 8-11 -- **Tern Of A Century** [13] 8-11
656 **Miss Kola** [16] 8-11 732 **Cool Gales** [2] 8-11 806 **Morgiana** [10] 8-11
-- **Freedom Line** [6] 8-11 -- **Branitska** [8] 8-11
15 ran ½,nk,1½,½,1½,2,2 (Major J H de Burgh) A Stewart Newmarket

HAMBURG Sunday June 29th Righthand, Flat Track

Official Going Given As FIRM

1328 GROUP 2 GROSSER HANSA PREIS 3YO+ £16949 1m 3f Firm

•1005 **TOMMY WAY** (J Dunlop) 3-8-5 B Thomson 1: 21-3111: 3 b c Thatch - Tilia (Dschingis Khan) Smart, tremendously improved colt who continues in excellent form: made ev yard, hacking up by 6½L in a Gr 2 event at Hamburg June 29: earlier won a Gr 1 event at San Siro and Gr 1 Italian Derby at Capannelle: in '85 was a runaway winner of a mdn at Haydock: eff at 10f, stays 12f well: acts on gd/firm and soft ground and on any trk: certain to win more good races and has been very cleverly placed by J Dunlop. 82
-- **KONIGSTRAUM** (Germany) 4-9-0 L Mader 1: -2: Ran on late. 64
896 **CASSIS** (Germany) 4-9-2 P Remmert 1: 41-23: Ev ch: see 896. 64
8 ran 6½,1 (Scuderia Erasec) J Dunlop Arundel, Sussex

THE CURRAGH Saturday June 28th Righthand, Galloping Track

Official Going Given As GOOD

1329 RAILWAY 2YO STAKES GROUP 3 £14425 6f Good +03 Fast

1097 **POLONIA** [8] (J Bolger) 2-8-10 D Gillespie 4/5 FAV: 1101: 2 b f Danzig - Moss (Round Table) Smart Irish filly: left behind her disapp Royal Ascot run with an emphatic 6L win in fast run Gr 3 Railway Stakes at the Currach June 28: highly impressive winner of her first 2 outings at the Curragh and Leopardstown and found the very firm ground against her last time out: very eff at 6f, should stay further: remains not one to oppose lightly. 70
752 **HARRY QUINN** [1] (K Prendergast) 2-8-10 G Curran 10/1: 22132: No chance with this smart winner: see 752. 52
-- **LYSHAAN** [14] (B Kelly) 2-8-7 S Craine 33/1: 23: Creditable 3rd: eff 6f on firm. 49
-- **SOLANY** [3] (J Oxx) 2-8-7 D Hogan 14/1: 34: Not disgraced: 3rd at Navan first time out. 41
9 ran 6,shthd,3 (Henryk De Kwiatkowski) J Bolger Ireland

1330 GROUP 1 BUDWEISER IRISH DERBY 3YO £299800 1m 4f Firm 13 +13 Fast

+878 **SHAHRASTANI** [10] (M Stoute) 3-9-0 W R Swinburn 1/1 FAV: 2-1111: 3 ch c Nijinsky - Shademah (Thatch) Topclass colt: al going well and led inside final 2f, rapidly drawing clear for a highly impressive 8L win in fast run Gr 1 Irish Derby at the Curragh June 28: last time out was a narrow winner of the Epsom Derby: remains unbtn this season, having previously won The Guardian Classic Trial at Sandown first time out and the Mecca-Dante at York: unlucky in running when 2nd at Newbury on sole start in '85: eff 10f, stays 12f well: acts on firm and soft ground and on any track: continues to improve and will be very hard to beat in any future engagements. 95
•1098 **BONHOMIE** [9] (H Cecil) 3-9-0 Pat Eddery 7/1: 111-212: Led after ½ way: had no answer to the easy winner, but again ran well: see 1098. 82
1009 **BAKHAROFF** [2] (G Harwood) 3-9-0 G Starkey 9/2: 321-233: Ran on too late: see 1009 80

878 MASHKOUR [3] (H Cecil) 3-9-0 S Cauthen 3/1: 1-31134: Never really threatened: better 878.   79
878 MR JOHN [11] 3-9-0 Mr T Browne 20/1: 0-41200: No extra final 3f: gd effort but best 640 (1m heavy).   75
396 WORLD COURT [6] 3-9-0 Mr T Browne 150/1: 00-1310: Rank outsider: not disgraced: stays 12f: last time out won at Leopardstown: seems to act on any ground.   71
878 Flash Of Steel 0 9-0   -- King Retain 0 9-0   1009 Ostensible 0 9-0
753 Pacific Drift 0 9-0   -- Fighting Hard 0 9-0
11 ran   8,1½,nk,2,2,1½,2½,8,4,15   (H H Aga Khan)   M Stoute Newmarket

1331 GROUP 2 PRETTY POLLY STAKES 3YO+ F & M   £23400   1m 2f   Firm 13 -22 Slow

754 FLEUR ROYALE (D O'brien) 3-8-6 C Roche 12/1: ----101: 3 b f Mill Reef - Sweet Mimosa (Levanstell) Smart Irish filly: led over 2f out, staying on well to win Gr 2 Pretty Polly Stakes at the Curragh June 28: first time out was an easy winner over 9f at Leopardstown: eff at 10f, should stay 12f: acts on firm and yldg ground and should win again.   84
754 LAKE CHAMPLAIN (D Weld) 3-8-6 M J Kinane 5/4 FAV: 2-2122: Sweated up before start: no extra final 1f: fin 3rd, placed 2nd: see 754, 560.   78
--   SIGYM (J Oxx) 3-8-6 W R Swinburn 33/1:   0-123: Fin 4th, placed 3rd: first time out this season won a 10f fillies event over this C/D: seems to act on any ground.   73
1128 PARK EXPRESS (J Bolger) 3-8-6(bl) D Gillespie 8/1: -13042D: Wandered final 1f: fin 2nd, placed 4th: see 1128, 148.   79
1095 FAIR OF THE FURZE 4-9-13 S Cauthen 9/2: 01-4130: Stiff task under 9-13: see 1095   80
470 CAROLS LUCK 3-8-6(bl) S Martinez 33/1: -1-0200: Not disgraced: see 294: acts on firm and heavy and stays 10f.   72
*753 WELSH FANTASY 3-8-13 P Shanahan 6/1: 10-0210: Disapp 7th: btr 753 (yldg).   00
*1095 ENGLISH SPRING 4-9-13 Pat Eddery 7/2: -441010: Never showed: too soon after 1095?   00
8 ran   1,1,2½,3,½   (S Niarchos)   D O'brien Ireland

1332 MCGRATH STAKES LISTED RACE 3YO+   £9968   1m   Firm 13 -17 Slow

945 SAMARID [18] (M Stoute) 3-8-7 W R Swinburn 14/1: 3140-01: 3 b c Blushing Groom - Samata (Rheffic) Smart colt: fin well to get up cl home in a Listed race at the Curragh June 28: promising 2yo, easy winner of a mdn at Doncaster: eff 1m, will be suited by further: acts on gd and firm ground and a galloping track: should win more races.   76
--   NASHAMAA [9] (J Bolger) 3-8-7 D Gillespie 15/2: 122-2: Made much: just caught: fine seasonal debut: smart 2yo, winning at Phoenix Park: full brother to the smart Park Appeal: eff 7f, stays 1m: acts on firm and yldg ground and should be winning soon.   73
754 BEES NEST [15] (M Kauntze) 3-8-4 D Manning 8/1: 4-1303: Ran well, see 754.   65
471 HUNGRY GIANT [11] (J Oxx) 3-8-7 Pat Eddery 7/1: 220-014: Recent winner over 1m at Phoenix Park.   66
-1109 SIYAH KALEM [14] 4-9-6 S Cauthen 7/4 FAV: 11-4120: Well bckd: stumbled inside final 1f and this run should be forgotten: see 1109 : fin 9th.   00
1114 ORIENTAL SOLDIER [2] 3-8-7 G Starkey 12/1: 210-020: Btr 1114, see 476: fin 12th.   00
15 ran   1½,2,¾   (H H Aga Khan)   M Stoute Newmarket

CARLISLE   Wednesday July 2nd   Righthand, Undulating Track, Stiff Uphill Finish

1333 EBF SCOTBY MAIDEN STAKES 2YO   £1262   5f   Firm 07 -49 Slow

--   FICKLE YOUNG MAN [9] (T Fairhurst) 2-9-0 C Coates(5) 7/1: 1: 2 gr c Junius - Key Of The Kingdom (Grey Sovereign) Nicely bckd on race course debut, led ¼ way, comfortably in a slowly run 2yo mdn at Carlisle July 2: cheaply acquired colt who is a half brother to middle dist winner Marnili: should stay further: acts on fast ground and on a stiff track.   40
536 LATERAL [6] (J Berry) 2-9-0 M Fry 8/1: 20002: Ran well after fair abs: acts on fast and yldg ground and on any track: should find a small race: see 43.   34
1266 BELLA SEVILLE [7] (D Barron) 2-8-11 C Dwyer 4/6 FAV: 33: Well bckd, not btn far: acts on fast ground and on a stiff track: cheaply bought: see 1266.   30
1194 PENBREASY [3] (R Hollinshead) 2-8-11 S Perks 20/1: 04: Ran on well after slow start: better effort and should stay 6f: acts on fast grd and on a stiff track.   29
254 MR BERKELEY [4] 2-9-0 M Birch 8/1: 00: Abs: al up there: may win a small race on an easier course: acts on firm and yldg: see 254.   30
1180 TAKE EFFECT [5] 2-9-0 K Darley 10/1: 333000: Front rank till dist: acts firm: see 47   28
--   Carls Pride [1] 9-0   1205 Petango [10] 8-11   -- Blaze Of Gold [2] 8-11
9 ran   1,nk,hd,¾,½   (Ian Bryant)   T Fairhurst Middleham, Yorks

1334 TENNANTS SPECIAL SELLING STAKES 3YO   £674   6f   Firm 07 -06 Slow

871 SAMBA LASS [3] (D Barron) 3-8-4 A Mackay 7/1: 0-03201: 3 ch f Roan Rocket - Cornish Lullaby (Crooner) Led below dist, gamely in a 3yo seller at Carlisle July 2 (bought in 2000 gns): first success: placed here and at Leicester earlier and likes a stiff track: stays 6f: acts on firm and yldg ground.   18
1201 BANTEL BANZAI [8] (I Bell) 3-9-0(bl) C Dwyer 10/1: 0401002: Al well placed: just btn: eff over a stiff 6f, stays 1m: acts on any trk: see 392.   27

906 PERCIPIO [14] (K Ivory) 3-9-0 A Shoults(5) 10/1: 0-00003: Not btn far: best effort
this term: acts on any trk: see 906.   25
932 PSALM [13] (M Prescott) 3-9-0 G Duffield 5/1: 100-034: In fair form: see 932.   21
1142 GALAXY GALA [12] 3-8-7(BL) D Nicholls 10/1: -004000: Dwelt, never nearer: modest
maiden who prob needs further: acts on gd and firm.   14
822 PUNCLE CREAK [9] 3-8-4 S Wood(7) 16/1: 0-40000: Dropped in class: al there: see 103. 09
1051 MURRYL CANNON [6] 3-8-7 D Leadbitter(5) 5/1: 0-00000: Led/dsptd lead till dist:
fin 7th: see 1051.   00
1134 COOPER RACING NAIL [10] 3-8-4(vis) K Darley 3/1 FAV: 2200230: Well bckd: speed
over ½ way: btr 932 (7f).   00
910 MERCIA GOLD [4] 3-8-7 S Perks 8/1: 0-30000: Bl first time in this lower grade: best 38 00

910 Marshall Drills [15] 8-4			1101 Bao [5] 8-4	
1134 Noble Saxon [7] 8-7(vis)			774 Georgian Rose [1] 8-4(VIS)	
-- Brampton Lyn [2] 8-4	1158 Bonny Bright Eyes [11] 8-4			
787 Moving Performance [17] 8-7			961 Eastern Oasis [16] 9-0	

17 ran   hd,¾,1½,shthd,¾,1   (B Bolam)   D Barron Maunby, Yorks

1335 TENNANTS LAGER CARLISLE BELL H'CAP   £3579   1m 1f Firm 07 +10 Fast   [46]

1112 SAMHAAN [7] (B Hanbury) 4-8-2(bl) A Geran(7) 8/1: 2410301: 4 ch c Niniski - Mai
Pussy (Realm) Went on 2f out and was soon clear in a fast run h'cap at Carlisle July 2:
earlier won a similar event at Doncaster: eff over 8/10f: acts on fast and heavy ground
and seems suited by a stiff track: wears blinkers.   30
584 ARISTOCRAT VELVET [14] (J Etherington) 4-9-2 K Darley 25/1: 023-002: Kept on well:
gd effort after fair abs: see 439.   39
1109 SCOUTSMISTAKE [9] (B Mcmahon) 7-9-1 J Hills(5) 10/1: 20-0003: Ran well: won this
race in '84 and likes this stiff course: see 815.   34
1185 GREED [1] (Denys Smith) 5-8-3 L Charnock 10/1: 0304-24: Nearest fin: see 1185.   21
1202 BOY SANDFORD [3] 7-7-7(7oh) J Quinn(3) 25/1: 0-03040: Never nearer: see 789.   07
1249 SILLY BOY [6] 6-9-0 M Richardson(7) 14/1: 00-0400: No extra dist: see 698.   27
1156 GODS LAW [11] 5-7-7(5ex)(3oh) Julie Bowker(7) 6/1: 0132130: Late prog, fin 7th.   00
976 THE HOWARD [2] 4-8-8 W Woods(3) 11/2 JT FAV: 1-00040: Led home turn: wknd into 8th. 00
*1091 LJAAM [10] 3-9-0(bl)(5ex) A Murray 11/2 JT FAV: 40-4010: Much btr over 1m in 1091   00
1178 BOYNTON [13] 3-7-7 A Mackay 9/1: 004-020: Much btr 1178 (gd): see 143.   00
1173 TEST OF TIME [8] 5-9-10 G Duffield 6/1: 3300-20: Al behind, fin last: much btr 1173. 00

1047 Warplane [5] 8-13		1103 Patchburg [12] 8-4	956 Quality Chorister [4] 7-10	

14 ran   2¼,2,1,1½,hd,½,2   (O Zawawi)   B Hanbury Newmarket

1336 BURGH BARONY RACES COM CUP AMAT H'CAP   £998   1m 4f Firm 07 -18 Slow   [6]

989 MISAAFF [6] (H Thomson Jones) 3-12-0 Franca Vittadini 1/1 FAV: 0213-41: 3 b c Mummy's
Pet - Honeybuzzard (Sea Hawk II) Useful colt: comfortably defied his welter burden, led home
turn and ran on strongly in an amateur riders h'cap at Carlisle July 2: showed plenty of
promise last term: when winning a Redcar mdn: eff around 1m, stays 12f well: acts on firm
and yldg ground and on any track.   56
1226 HYOKIN [7] (D Morley) 4-10-5(vis) Melanie Morley(4) 4/1: -400032: Stayed on to take
the minor honours: remains a maiden: see 282.   15
1016 TURI [8] (A Smith) 7-9-7 Mr J Wiles(3) 12/1: 40/0033: Clear rem: see 1016, 712.   00
1029 MATBAR [4] (I Matthews) 3-10-8(BL) Julia Fielden(4) 14/1: 400-044: Bl first time:
made much: see 1029.   15
1223 EXCAVATOR LADY [5] 7-9-9(vis) Sandy Brook 11/4: 0043220: Much btr 1223: see 629.   00
1223 TREYARNON [3] 4-10-3 Angela Norton(4) 12/1: 3433000: Pulled hard and btn home turn. 00

493 Porter [1] 9-5		956 Decembe [2] 9-6	

8 ran   1¼,1½,10,12,2½   (Hamdan Al-Maktoum)   H Thomson Jones Newmarket

1337 CASTLE MAIDEN 3YO FILLIES STAKES   £1507   1m 1f Firm 07 -06 Slow

991 STRAW BOATER [7] (L Cumani) 3-8-11 R Guest 9/4: -001: 3 b f Thatch - Go Surfing
(Go Marching) Nicely bckd and showing improved form to win a 3yo fillies mdn at Carlisle
July 2, led over 2f out and sn clear: cost 30,000 gns and is a half sister to sev winners:
stays 9f well: acts well on a sound surface.   48
1169 NIHAD [8] (B Hanbury) 3-8-11 A Geran(7) 7/4 FAV: 0-40032: Not pace of winner tho'
comfortably beat remainder: stays 9f: see 1169, 213.   38
1198 INDIAN LOVE SONG [12] (R Hollinshead) 3-8-11 S Perks 15/2: 0-23043: Not quicken:see 1198 30
-- MY WILLOW [11] (J Fitzgerald) 3-8-11 A Murray 10/1: -4: Made eye-catching late prog
and seems certain to improve next time: cost 30,000 gns as yearling and is a half sister to
several minor winners: stays 9f well: acts on firm ground and on a stiff track: one to
keep an eye on.   25
-- TURINA [5] 3-8-11 M Beecroft 33/1: 0-0: Unfancied on reappearance: nearest fin and
better for race: well btn on sole start last term: stays 9f: acts on fast ground.   24
1193 QUITE A QUEST [3] 3-8-11 J Hills(5) 6/1: 4-00: Well btn tho' ran well for a long
way: lightly raced filly who may be btr suited by 1m: acts on fast ground.   08
1179 ULTRESSA [13] 3-8-11 J Lowe 10/1: 0-00040: No threat in 8th: twice below 935(12f)   00

419

```
--    Giant Redwood  [9] 8-11                              1220 Samosa  [2] 8-11(vis)
1141 Hunting Gold  [6] 8-11         --   Derry  [1] 8-11   1080 Torriggia  [4] 8-11
--    Lochlairey  [10] 8-11
13 ran    5,4,3,nk,10          (B T R & B Plc)        L Cumani Newmarket
```

1338 BORDER HANDICAP STAKES (0-35)   £2018   6f   Firm 07 -04 Slow   [32]

*1120 HENRYS VENTURE [14] (D Chapman) 4-8-1(7ex) A Proud 14/1: -000011: 4 b g Raise
A Native - Tudor Velvet (Tudor Grey) Gd form, al front rank and led inside dist, gamely in a
h'cap at Carlisle July 2: decisive winner of a similar race on heavy ground at Hamilton last
month, tho' clearly equally eff on a sound surface: well suited by 6f on a stiff trk.   13
+1247 CUMBRIAN DANCER [4] (M H Easterby) 3-9-2(vis)(7ex) M Birch 6/1: 4300412: Just btn:
gd effort under his penalty, from a less than favourable draw: see 1247.   36
1157 MENDICK ADVENTURE [19] (Denys Smith) 5-9-4(bl) S Perks 15/2: 3000003: Made most:
gd effort: see 56.   25
1156 HIGH PORT [10] (A Jones) 7-8-0 N Carlisle 16/1: -000024: Al up there: in fair form.   06
1182 GODS SOLUTION [1] 5-9-9(bl) B Mcgiff(7) 14/1: 1040200: Not well drawn tho' ran well.   28
1247 WILLIE GAN [8] 8-8-2 L Charnock 5/1 FAV: -000230: Al prom: see 866.   06
-1182 MARY MAGUIRE [17] 9-9-10 D Nicholls 7/1: 0003220: Never nearer in 7th: see 1182.   00
1077 MONINSKY [11] 5-8-7 M Richardson(7) 8/1: -200300: Never beyond mid-div: see 956, 260   00
1104 GREY STARLIGHT [7] 4-8-3(bl) G Duffield 7/1: 0-00130: Broke leg and destroyed.   00
1164 ALEXANJO [16] 3-8-12 J Lowe 8/1: 44-0400: Twice below form shown in 929 (sharper trk)   00
963 Hoptons Chance [6] 7-11   1139 Qualitairess [18] 7-10(vis)
1201 The Golf Slide [9] 7-8   1247 Warthill Lady [13] 8-6(vis)
1104 Via Vitae [15] 7-10   992 Hokusan [2] 8-4   971 Aphrodisiac [3] 8-1(bl)
1101 The Manor [5] 7-7   1139 Illicit [12] 8-8(bl)
19 ran   nk,1½,½,hd,hd,1   (P D Savill)   D Chapman Stillington, Yorks
```

---

Official Going Given As GOOD/FIRM

**1339** E.B.F. ROYAL MAIDEN STAKES 2YO     £793    5f    Firm 9 -32 Slow

1057 ABSOLUTION  [5] (K Brassey) 2-9-0 S Whitworth 1/2 FAV: 321: 2 gr c Absalom - Great
Grey Niece (Great Nephew) Well bckd and made all by a nk in a slow run 2yo mdn at Warwick
July 2: just caught by Hard Act last time out at Bath: well suited by forcing tactics over
a sharpish 5f: half brother to useful winning sprinter Peckitts Well: eff at 5f on fast
and yielding ground.                                                                           43
632 MUBKIR  [2] (P Walwyn) 2-9-0 Paul Eddery 9/4: 302: Chall final 1f: just btn: should
find a small event on a sharp track: suited by gd and firm ground: see 497.                    41
864 TALIESIN  [3] (R Hollinshead) 2-9-0 P Hill(7) 12/1: 003: Prom ev ch: btr effort:
acts on firm and yielding: see 864.                                                           30
1161 RYLANDS REEF  [1] (C James) 2-9-0 M Hills 20/1: 404: Stiff task: see 882.                 22
--   MONTYS GUNNER  [4] 2-9-0 J Williams 33/1: 0: No show on debut: cheaply acquired colt
who may need further than 5f.                                                                  00
5 ran    nk,3,2¼,10          (C Wright)             K Brassey Upper Lambourn, Berks

**1340** STONELEIGH MAIDEN SELLING STAKES 3YO     £547    1m    Firm 9 -20 Slow

--   MAID OF HONFLEUR  [8] (P Cole) 3-8-11 T Quinn 2/1 FAV: -1: 3 ch f Record Token -
Spring Maiden (Silly Season) Uneasy fav, but led after 3f, forging clear in a 3yo seller at
Warwick July 2 (sold 2600 gns) : eff 1m: half sister to winning stayer Going Broke and
should be suited by further: acts on fast ground and a sharpish track.                         22
524 TYRANNISE  [5] (B Mcmahon) 3-8-11 A Roper(7) 5/1: 0-002: Op 10/1: no chance with
winner: first signs of form: stays 1m and acts on fast ground.                                 12
--   RES NON VERBA  [2] (L Siddall) 3-8-11 Paul Eddery 25/1: 0-3: Mkt drifter: never nearer:
unplaced in a Ripon seller on sole start in '85: stays 1m: acts on firm.                      10
991 LA CAZADORA  [10] (R Williams) 3-8-11 M Hills 6/1: -004: Prom, ev ch: seems modest.        10
1063 SHEER CLASS  [3] 3-8-11 R Mcghin 14/1: -000: Fdd final 1f: little form.                   00
--   SATIVA  [6] 3-8-11 R Wernham 12/1: 00-0: Wknd over 1f out on seasonal debut: ran
only twice in '85.                                                                             00
1201 FALLONETTA  [11] 3-8-11 M Rimmer 7/1: 304-00: Mkt drifter, no show: placed in sellers
in '85: acts on gd and firm.                                                                   00
937 Royal Crusader  [4] 8-11                              1053 Pasta Jane  [1] 8-11
1063 Shesingh  [9] 8-11(bl)       844 Hillingdon Jim  [7] 9-0
11 ran    3,1,shthd,4,8          (W H Ponsonby)       P Cole Whatcombe, Oxon

**1341** STRUTT & PARKER 2YO FILLIES STAKES     £2792    7f    Firm 9 -14 Slow

1105 PEN BAL LADY  [4] (G Pritchard Gordon) 2-8-11 S Cauthen 9/4: 121: 2 ch f Mummy's
Game - Northern Queen (Northfields) Useful filly: made ev yard, comfortably, in a 2yo fillies
event at Warwick July 2: first time out won a fillies mdn at Leicester: inbetween was just
btn by Sparsholt at Beverley: eff at 6f, stays 7f: acts on gd and fast ground and on any trk:
improving filly.                                                                              52
```

707 FRESH THOUGHTS [1] (H Candy) 2-8-11 W Newnes 1/1 FAV: 02: Well bckd: ran on well
final 1f and will do better on a more galloping trk: stays 7f well: should win soon:see 707   45
707 BASIC BLISS [5] (P Walwyn) 2-8-11 Paul Eddery 10/3: 303: Ev ch: stays 7f: acts on gd
and firm ground and on any track.   40
--   LUKMARIE [6] (C Brittain) 2-8-11 M Roberts 20/1: 4: Wknd inside final 2f: improvement
likely: half sister to 5/6f winner Lucky Hunter: acts on fast ground.   30
1187 YAVARRO [2] 2-8-11 S Whitworth 66/1: 0000: No show: best 482 (yldg).   00
1057 TOMS LITTLE BET [3] 2-8-11(BL) N Howe 66/1: 00: Bl first time: al struggling.   00
6 ran   2½,2,5,15,1½   (G T Park)   G Pritchard Gordon Newmarket

1342 WARWICK CASTLE H'CAP STAKES (0-60)   £3017   1m 6f Firm 09 +19 Fast   [41]

*782 KUDZ [5] (H Cecil) 3-9-10 S Cauthen 4/5 FAV: 22-2111: 3 br c Master Willie - Lucky
Ole Me (Olden Times) Very useful colt: defied top weight, led 1½f out, comfortably, in fast
run h'cap at Warwick July 2: earlier won a h'cap at Thirsk and a mdn at Beverley: half
brother to sev winners, including the smart Lucky North: eff 12f, well suited by 14f: acts
on firm and soft ground and on any track: carries weight well and should win more races.   65
1150 FANDANGO LIGHT [2] (D Elsworth) 5-9-6 A Mcglone 7/1: 202: Made most: 6l clear 3rd:
gd effort: see 1004.   40
761 PARANG [1] (P Walwyn) 5-8-4 Paul Eddery 10/1: 230-033: Prom ev ch: stays 14f:
see 761.   16
1159 NO U TURN [3] (S Mellor) 8-9-6 M Wigham 3/1: 00-0044: No real threat: btr 12f? See 1004 28
854 VINTAGE PORT [6] 4-9-1 T Quinn 8/1: -0000: Fdd straight: see 653.   08
917 KOFFI [4] 4-9-2 Pat Edder y 10/1: 00-0000: Well btn: winner over hurdles last Autumn:
formerly trained by J Hindley and was a 2yo winner at Newmarket: stays 12f well: acts
on fast ground.   00
6 ran   2,6,3,10,20   (Sheikh Mohammed)   H Cecil Newmarket

1343 WARWICK VASE STAKES 3YO   £3412   1m 2f Firm 9 +10 Fast

+1015 QUEENS SOLDIER [3] (H Cecil) 3-8-12 S Cauthen 4/6 FAV: 131-11: 3 b c L'Enjoleur -
Little Lady Luck (Jacinto) Smart colt: heavily bckd and led into straight for a clever nk
success in quite fast run Warwick Vase at Warwick July 2: first time out was an impressive
winner of quite val stks at Beverley: highly promising 2yo, winning at Yarmouth and Sandown:
eff at 10f, well suited by 12f and may get further: acts on gd and firm ground and on
any trk: the type to win more races.   70
*1045 HELLO ERNANI [1] (I Balding) 3-9-1 Pat Eddery 6/4: -223212: Dsptd lead final 1f:
just btn: most consistent: see 1045.   71
1002 BUSTARA [2] (G Wragg) 3-8-5 P Robinson 8/1: 10-0403: Fin well and this was her
best effort this season: stays 10f: see 214.   59
1032 SWIFTS PAL [4] (G Lewis) 3-8-8 P Waldron 50/1: 0-00304: Set the pace: not stay 10f?   32
4 ran   nk,¾,1,2   (Sheikh Mohammed)   H Cecil Newmarket

1344 SHOW RING H'CAP STAKES (0-35)   £1457   5f Firm 09 -09 Slow   [31]

1171 MRS SAUGA [5] (M Pipe) 4-8-9 S Cauthen 85/40 FAV: 000-021: 4 ch f Derrylin - Glencara
(Sallust) Well bckd and led inside final 1f in a h'cap at Warwick July 2: first success from
this lightly raced filly: eff at 5f, stays further: acts on gd and fast ground and goes
well on a sharpish track.   21
*1070 NATIVE RULER [6] (C Austin) 5-8-4(7ex) W Newnes 14/1: 000-012: Made almost all:
in gd form: see 1070.   10
1171 SANDITTON PALACE [16] (P Felgate) 3-8-7 T Quinn 7/1: -004043: Sn prom: in gd form.   18
1171 MISS METAL WOODS [13] (S Mellor) 4-8-4 M Wigham 16/1: 423-404: Al up there: best
effort this season: acts on firm and yldg: see 418.   06
1131 LADY CARA [14] 6-8-13(vis) P Waldron 10/1: 14-0020: Al prom: see 1131 (made running).   14

1066 AMMEED [18] 4-7-11 P Hill(7) 33/1: -00-000: Never nearer: first signs of form:
has been tried over several distances: acts on firm.   00
977 GODSTRUTH [8] 7-9-1(bl) P Darcy 9/1: 4100-00: Made no show: in '85 won h'cap at
Yarmouth, in '84 won at Wolverhampton, Brighton and Yarmouth: equally eff at 5/6f: acts on
any ground.   00
1027 IMPALA LASS [2] 3-9-4 J Hillis(5) 8/1: -110000: Prom early: best early season: see 443 00
1171 Mister March [17] 7-13   1196 Sharad [9] 7-9(vis)
1164 My Mutzie [20] 8-5(bl)   729 Dashaki Gold [15] 7-7(3oh)
1131 Fairgreen [12] 7-13(bl)   1060 She Knows It All [4] 9-9
1060 Silbando [3] 8-7(bl)   626 Last Secret [11] 8-0(bl)
871 Creetown Sally [1] 7-13(BL)   1066 Royal Bear [19] 7-10
727 Toms Nap Hand [10] 7-8
19 ran 2,¾,¾,nk,5   (Mrs V Ward)   M Pipe Brimfield, Salop

1345 KENT MAIDEN STAKES 2YO   £1374   7f   Firm 14 -46 Slow

-- WOLSEY [12] (H Cecil) 2-9-0 S Cauthen 8/15 FAV: 1: 2 b c Our Native - Sancta (Karabas)
Promising colt: landed the odds on his debut, gaining a ready pillar to post success in a
slowly run 2yo mdn at Lingfield July 2: half brother to smart middle dist colt Mashkour:
eff over 7f, sure to stay well: acts on firm ground: has scope for further improvement and
is sure to win more races.   66
-- JOHNNY ROSE [7] (P Haynes) 2-9-0 N Howe 66/1: 2: Prom thr'out: gd debut as he needed
race and showed signs of inexperience: very cheaply bought gelding who stays 7f well and
will stay 1m: acts on firm ground: should find a maiden soon.   51
1019 HOCKLEY [2] (R Hannon) 2-9-0 Pat Eddery 14/1: 03: Al prom: quite cheaply bought and
is related to sev minor winners: acts on firm.   39
1234 TELESTO [9] (G Harwood) 2-9-0(bl) G Starkey 10/1: 044: Ev ch: see 1234: wears bl.   38
206 AKII BUA [1] 2-9-0 R Cochrane 12/1: 20: Late hdwy after slow start: long abs:
stays 1m and seems to act on firm and heavy: see 206.   37
-- THE MAIN MAN [9] 2-9-0 M Roberts 25/1: 0: No threat: bred to stay well and will be
suited by 1m.   36
-- OUR TONY [4] 2-9-0 T Ives 12/1: 0: Speed most, fin 7th: related to sev winners in USA.   25
-- High Climber [3] 8-11   -- Sunset Boulevard [6] 9-0
1082 Street Legal [11] 9-0   -- Ellis Bell [10] 8-11   -- Bunches [14] 8-11
1232 Bold Intention [18] 9-0 (-- Rant On [5] 9-0
14 ran   4,3,½,½,½   (Lady Howard De Walden)   H Cecil Newmarket

1346 SECRET LEMONADE DRINKER HCAP 0-35   £1968   7.5f   Firm 14 -04 Slow   [33]

1199 NATCHAKAM [11] (G Lewis) 3-8-12(vis) P Waldron 15/2: 4204001: 3 b c Thatch - Song
In The Air (Tudor Melody) Made most, rallying to force his hd in front again on the post in
a h'cap at Lingfield July 2: first success, but unraced in '85: seems to act on firm and
soft but has shown his best form on a sharpish trk at around 7f/1m: wears a visor or blinkers
nowadays and is not all that consistent.   35
1211 FAST SERVICE [8] (C Horgan) 7-9-7 P Cook 7/2 FAV: 0-00002: Well bckd, led final 1f,
caught death: running well and should win soon: see 1211.   34
1188 SWEET ANDY [12] (G Gracey) 7-7-7(3oh) L Riggio(7) 14/1: -000403: Prom, ev ch: see 679   02
1074 BRAVE AND BOLD [3] (N Callaghan) 3-8-3(3ow) Pat Eddery 11/2: 2020004: No extra final
2f: acts on firm, best on soft? See 100.   20
1165 NO JAZZ [9] 3-7-12(1ow) R Hills 5/1: 0-00020: No threat: see 1165.   14
*1264 PETT VELERO [1] 7-8-0 P Simms(7) 11/2: -001010: Badly drawn and btr 1264 (C/D)   05
54 RED BILLY [4] 3-7-11 M Robert 9/1: 000-440: Abs since 54: see 29.   00
-- Nelsons Lady [10] 8-7   1264 Hampton Walk [5] 7-9   -- My Myra [13] 7-11(1ow)
-- Tina Rosa [6] 7-7   1035 Bulandshar [7] 7-9   832 Bully Boy [2] 7-7(1oh)
13 ran   shthd,2,1,½,½   (Mrs S Khan)   G Lewis Epsom

1347 TAYLOR WALKER BITTER HANDICAP 0-50   £2452   6f   Firm 14 +27 Fast   [42]

1263 AL AMEAD [7] (C Benstead) 6-9-10 W R Swinburn 9/4 FAV: 0004041: 6 br h Brigadier Gerard
- Hatta (Realm) Useful sprinter who returned to his best form when shattering the course
record in a very fast run h'cap at Lingfield July 2: made ev yard in impressive fashion for
a 5l win: this was his 7th course success and he has never won anywhere else: equally
effective at 6 and 7f: acts on soft, bounces off firm ground: in gd heart and may even
win somewhere other than Lingfield next time!   54
*1263 FERRYMAN [6] (D Elsworth) 10-10-0(7ex) A Mcglone 9/1: -000012: Had his winning form
of 1263 comprehensively turned around by Al Amead but a gd effort under his penalty.   46
1263 DEPUTY HEAD [8] (L Holt) 6-9-13(7ex) P Waldron 11/2: 0003133: Running most consistently.   45
1182 ROSIE DICKINS [9] (R Hollinshead) 4-8-4 R Lappin(7) 14/1: 2240304: No threat: see 124   17
922 BAY PRESTO [4] 4-8-13(bl) S Whitworth 14/1: 3000000: Plenty of early pace : yet
to reproduce form of 172 (yielding).   18
*1157 CANIF [3] 5-9-11(7ex) P Robinson 9/2: 000-010: Lost ground at start, ignore this
effort: see 1157.   20
-- MYRAS SPECIAL [1] 3-9-10 M Hills 12/1: 01010-0: Fin 7th on seasonal debut: quite
lightly raced in '85 winning at Catterick and Brighton: eff at 5 and 6f and is well suited
by firm ground: best form on a sharp track.   00
1213 DOWNSVIEW [5] 4-9-9 M Wigham 8/1: 00-0100: Fin 8th: best 855 (C/D yldg).   00
1066 MAFTIR [2] 4-8-6(bl) Pat Eddery 15/2: -000000: A gamble, fin last: best 260 (7f yldg)   00
9 ran   5,shthd,2,4,8   (Hamdan Al-Maktoum)   C Benstead Epsom, Surrey

1348 CANADA DRY HANDICAP 0-35   £2264   2m   Firm 14 -24 Slow   [30]

1035 AMIGO ESTIMADO [11] (K Brassey) 4-9-2 S Whitworth 10/1: 00-0041: 4 b g Scorpio -
House Tie (Be Friendly) Gained an all-the-way success, drawing clear under press for a 7l
win in a rather slowly run h'cap at Lingfield July 2: first success and was well suited by
today's 2m, likely to stay further: no worthwhile form in '85: acts on yldg but seems
well suited by firm ground, forcing tactics and a sharpish track.   28
1243 ASTICOT [10] (C Horgan) 4-8-9 Pat Eddery 5/1: 00-0302: Ev ch: evidently stays 2m.   12

422

984 DOMINATE [8] (P Mitchell) 5-9-10 G Starkey 6/1: 02-0023: Prom most: btr 984 (12f)   25
*1260 HARLESTONE LAKE [5] (J Dunlop) 4-9-6(3ex) B Thomson 9/2 FAV: -003414: Never closer:
btr 1260 (C/D).   20
1265 ALSIBA [9] 4-8-11(3ex) W R Swinburn 5/1: 0000140: Prom, no extra final 1f: best 1035   11
*1183 ARBOR LANE [4] 5-9-6(3ex) E Guest(3) 5/1: 0440-10: No threat: btr 1183 (gd)   19
1035 Royal Craftsman [2] 8-6   751 Broken Tackle [12] 8-5
1183 Alfie Dickins [1] 8-3   841 Solitaire [7] 7-9   -- Rufcha [3] 7-13
11 ran   7,2,¾,hd,¾   (Mrs Freda Li)   K Brassey Upper Lambourn, Berks

1349 OCS SPONSORED LADIES RACE   £1945   1m 4f Firm 14 -46 Slow

1166 PACTOLUS [14] (G Harwood) 3-9-5 Amanda Harwood 5/4 FAV: 410-01: 3 b c Lydian -
Honey Sand (Windy Sands) Ridden with supreme confidence, overcoming difficulties in running
to cleverly lead cl home from the subsequently disqualified Herradura in a very slowly run
ladies race at Lingfield July 2: lightly raced in '85 winning a maiden at Salisbury (rated
52): suited by 12f nowadays and acts well on gd or firm ground.   36
1243 TOSCANA [8] (D Marks) 5-10-2 Kelly Marks 9/1: 3200-22: Ev ch final 3f, fin a 2l 3rd
but placed 2nd: see 1243.   26
991 JUBILEE JAMBOREE [9] (A Hide) 3-8-11 Sue Brown(3) 66/1: -003: Never closer in 4th,
placed 3rd: unraced in '85: evidently well suited by middle dist and firm ground.   01
1166 DOLLY [5] (A Moore) 4-10-2 Candy Moore 10/1: 04D0034: Led 3f out, sn outpaced but
promoted from 5th to 4th: btr 1166 (10f): see 762.   06
943 CASTLE POOL [2] 4-10-5 Elizabeth Gandolfo(5) 25/1: -0400: No threat in 6th, placed
5th: flattered 743?   08
1293 HERRADURA [4] 5-10-5(vis) Maxine Juster 15/8: 2-2302D: Wore a visor today, led final
1f, just btn but disqualified from 2nd for causing interference earlier in race: see 743, 921   33
1102 Headin On [3] 10-0   -- Ribokeyes Boy [1] 10-0
-- Forewarn [6] 10-5   930 Tarleton Elm [12] 10-0
-- La Dragoniere [10] 9-11   578 Top Feather [11] 9-11
809 Hooray Hamilton [13] 9-0   275 Puppywalker [15] 8-11
1186 Roman Track [7] 9-11
15 ran   ¾,1½,8,shthd,¾   (Mrs G Harwood)   G Harwood Pulborough, Sussex

1350 CANADA DRY STAKES 3YO   £959   1m 2f Firm 14 -47 Slow

*1031 MYTENS [1] (J Tree) 3-9-5 Pat Eddery 2/13 FAV: 3-11: 3 b c Spectacular Bid - Photo-
graphic (Hoist The Flag) Promising colt who was winning 2nd race on trot when cantering in
from 3 moderate opponents in a minor race at Lingfield July 2: first time out, gamely won
a 3yo mdn at Sandown: close 3rd behind My Ton Ton and Shahrastani at Newbury on only outing
in '85: well suited by firm grd and a stiff trk: eff 10f, should stay 10f: regarded as his
powerful stable's best 3yo & likely to impr further, rate more highly & win better class races   40
1087 AAH JIM BOY [4] (R Akehurst) 3-9-0 G Baxter 12/1: 40-02: Led 3f out on sufferance
but the winner was simply toying with him: showed some ability in 2 races at backend
of '85: stays 10f and acts on firm ground.   20
1228 BELLA CARINA [3] (B Sanders) 3-8-11 P Cook 40/1: 0-03: Made most, wknd quickly:
first foal of an Irish middle distance winner.   00
-- YOURS GRENVILLE [2] (P Mitchell) 3-9-0 A Mcglone 12/1: -4: Al the whipper in on racecourse debut: half brother to minor 12f winner Hasty Mary.   00
4 ran   4,15,dist   (K Abdulla)   J Tree Beckhampton, Wilts

LONGCHAMP   Saturday June 28th   Righthand, Galloping Track

Official Going Given As GOOD

1351 GROUP 3 PRIX DU BOIS 2YO   £17374   5f   Good -

-- EXPORT PRICE (P Bary) 2-8-11 C Asmussen 1: 311: 2 b c Habitat - Martinova
(Martinmass) Very promising French colt: easy winner of a Gr 3 event at Longchamp June 28:
last time out was a comfortable winner at Chantilly: eff 5f, sure to stay further: acts on
gd ground: well regarded and should win more races.   70
-- BRICKENAY (E Bartholomew) 2-8-11 M Philliperon 1: 122: No chance with winner: first
time out winner at Saint Cloud: acts on good ground.   58
-- LIBERTINE (R Collet) 2-8-11 Y Saint Martin 1: 13: First time out winner at Chantilly:
not disgraced here.   57
9 ran   3,nk   (Ecurie Manneville)   P Bary France

1352 GROUP 3 LA COUPE 4YO+   £18091   1m 4f Good -

-885 TRIPTYCH (P L Biancone) 4-8-8 Y Saint Martin 1: 303-421: 4 b f Riverman - Trillion
(Hail to Reason) Smart filly: led 1f out and just got home in a Gr 3 event at Longchamp
June 28: last time out was an excellent shthd 2nd to Saint Estephe in Gr 1 Coronation Cup
at Epsom: trained by D V O'Brien in '85 and was in excellent form, making history when
the first filly to win the Irish 2000 Guineas: also successful in Gr 3 event at Phoenix Park
and a fine 2nd to the topclass Oh So Sharp in the Oaks: very eff at 10f, stays 12f: acts
on any ground and is thoroughly genuine.   78

--   ANTHEUS (C Head) 4-8-11 G Moore 1: 1120-12: Btn a whisker: first time out this season
won at Saint Cloud: stays 12f well: acts on gd ground.   80
1115 BABY TURK (A De Royer Dupre) 4-9-0 O Poirier 1: 10043: Btn 2 shthds: see 299.   83
6 ran   shthd,shthd.   (Alan Clore)   P L Biancone France

LONGCHAMP   Sunday June 29th   Righthand, Galloping Track

Official Going Given As FIRM

1353 GROUP 2 PRIX DE MALLERET 3YO FILLIES   £22585   1m 2f   Firm

1116 GALUNPE (B Secly) 3-8-9 A Gibert 1: 14-0031: 3 b f He Loves Me - Semantic (Tudor
Melody) Comfortable 1L winner of Gr 2 fillies event at Longchamp June 29: smart 2yo, winning
Gr 3 event on this trk: very effective over 10f: likes fast ground.   77
1116 RESTIVER (F Boutin) 3-8-9 F Head 1: 411-302: Consistent: see 561.   75
*1008 ONLY STAR (C Head) 3-8-9 G Guignard 1: 13: In gd form, stays 10f: see 1008.   70
5 ran   1,2½   (J Aubry Dumand)   B Secly France

1354 GROUP 1 GRAND PRIX DE PARIS 3YO C & F   £48215   1m 7f   Firm

1117 SWINK (J Pease) 3-8-11 W R Swinburn 1: 20-3231: 3 b c Liloy - Swiss (Vaguely Noble)
Smart French colt: narrow winner of Gr 1 Grand Prix de Paris at Longchamp June 29: stays 15f
really well: likes fast ground and is a consistent sort.   72
1048 WAR HERO (J Dunlop) 3-8-11 T Ives 1: 13-0032: Nearly got up: excellent effort and
deserves a win soon: winner at Goodwood as a 2yo: well suited by 15f: acts well on fast ground. 71
--   SILVER WORD (J Cunnington Jnr) 3-8-11 M Philliperon 1: 03-4203: Just btn in close
finish: stays really well.   71
*1117 SATCO (P Bary) 3-8-11 F Head 1: --2-114: Not btn far, but beat winner 1117.   70
1015 BADARBAK 3-8-11 Y Saint Martin 1: 3-31230: Fin 6th: stays 15f: see 1015.   62
*902 FAMILY FRIEND 3-8-11 Pat Eddery 1: 40-4410: Below his best: see 902 (C/D).   61
9 ran   shhd,shnk,½,2,5.   (N B Hunt)   J Pease France

1355 GROUP 1 PRIX DISPAHAN 3YO+ C & F   £52162   1m 1f   Firm

*468 BAILLAMONT (F Boutin) 4-9-6 F Head 1: 030-311: 4 b c Blushing Groom - Lodeve
(Shoemaker) Very smart French colt: fin well to get up cl home in Gr 1 Prix d'Ispahan at
Longchamp June 29: last time out was a narrow winner of Gr 1 Prix Ganay, again at Longchamp:
in '85 won Gr 1 Prix Jean Prat at Chantilly: very eff at 9/10f: acts on firm and soft ground
and is a genuine sort.   86
1010 FITNAH (C Head) 4-9-3 G Guignard 1: 120-102: Caught cl home and shd be winning again
very soon: see 1010.   82
759 LIRUNG (H Jentzsch) 4-9-6 S Cauthen 1: 111-123: German chall: gd eff: see 759.   81
--   LYPHARITA (A Fabre) 4-9-3 A Gibert 1: 140-114: Ev ch in 4th: winner of both her
prev starts this season at Chantilly and first time out at Maison Laffitte: very smart
French filly who last season won the Prix de Diane Hermes at Chantilly, beating Fitnah: very
effective at 10f, stays 12f: acts on firm and soft ground.   75
8 ran   shtnk,2,1½   (S Niarchos)   F Boutin France

1356 GROUP 3 PRIX DE LA PORTE MAILLOT 3YO+   £18390   7f   Firm

1008 NORTHERN PREMIER (G Mikhalides) 3-8-8 C Asmussen 1: 1-01021: 3 b f Northern Baby -
Madam Premier   Smart French filly: impressive winner of Gr 3 event at Longchamp June 29:
last time out just btn by Only Star at Chantilly: earlier won a Gr 3 event over 1m on
this track: very eff at 7f/1m: acts on any grd and seems a genuine filly.   80
*901 COMRADE IN ARMS (P Lallie) 4-9-5 G Dubroeucq 1: 000-212: In fine form: see 901.   75
--   AL RAHIB (A Fabre) 4-9-2 A Gibert 1: 000-113: Ran a fine race: winner of both his
2 prev outings this season, h'caps at Longchamp (2): very eff at 7f.   71
1008 RIVER DANCER (J Cunnington Jnr) 3-8-5 M Philliperon 1: 24-4304: Not btn far :
best 467 (soft).   71
13 ran   1½,nk,nk   (M Fustok)   G Mikhalides France

CARLISLE   Thursday July 3rd   Righthanded Undulating Track, Stiff Uphill Finish

1357 EBF WALTON STAKES 2YO   £1076   6f   Firm 07 -40 Slow

*988 WABARAH [3] (H Thomson Jones) 2-9-1 A Murray 8/13 FAV: 311: 2 b f Shirley Heights -
Balista (Baldric II) Led below dist, ridden out when landing the odds in a slowly run 2yo
stks at Carlisle July 3: narrow winner of a fillies mdn at Yarmouth last month: cost
160,000 gns as a yearling and is a half sister to useful juv Labista: stays 6f well: acts
on good and firm ground and on a stiff track.   48
--   DR BULASCO [2] (S Norton) 2-8-11 T Williams 7/1: 2: Al up there: showed signs of
inexperience and should improve: cost 7,200 gns: stays 6f: acts on fast grd and a stiff trk.   38
1161 KALAS IMAGE [1] (G Moore) 2-8-8 D Casey(7) 5/2: 032303: Led briefly 2f out:
prob stays 6f tho' best run came over the minimum trip in 995: see 364.   32

741 MUSEVENI [4] (P Calver) 2-8-11 M Fry 10/1: 4004: Led over ⅓ way, btn when hmpd
inside distance: cost 17,000 gns: eff over 6f on a sound surface.   23
4 ran   1½,1,4   (Hamdan Al-Maktoum)   H Thomson Jones Newmarket

1358 CUMREW SELLING STAKES 2YO   £764   6f   Firm 07 -43 Slow

1083 KIND LADY [2] (J Winter) 2-8-8 M Hills 1/1 FAV: 4231: 2 b f King of Hush - Jacoletta
(Artaius) Well bckd when getting up cl home in a slowly run 2yo seller at Carlisle July 3
(sold for 2,600 gns): placed in all her prev starts: stays 6f well: acts on gd and fast
ground and on any track.   25
1012 MONS FUTURE [9] (W Pearce) 2-8-12 N Connorton 11/2: 014222: Led/dsptd lead thr'out,
just denied: consistent filly who deserves another race: see 1012 & 354.   28
1279 PRINCESS SINGH [7] (N Tinkler) 2-8-12 Kim Tinkler(5) 11/2: 0310443: Kept on well
and ran to her best: see 1279 & 858.   22
*1121 SEATON GIRL [4] (D Barron) 2-8-12 B Mcgiff(7) 6/1: 420014: Al up there: stays 6f:
see 1121.   16
*1168 ABSALOUTE HEAVEN [3] 2-8-12 A Mercer 12/1: 00010: Ran in snatches and better 1168.   10
717 BROONS ANSWER [5] 2-8-12(bl) G Brown 14/1: 001300: Never nearer after fair abs:
stays 6f: see 537.   04
858 BRIARQUEEN [8] 2-8-8 K Hodgson 10/1: 00000: Fin 7th: acts on fast grd: see 858.   00
1121 Bingo Queen [1] 8-12   1100 Sorrowful [6] 8-8
9 ran   nk,2,2,2½,2½,2.   (C J Trotter)   J Winter Newmarket

1359 BRITISH SIDAC CUMBERLAND PLATE HCP 0-50 £3869   1m 4f Firm 07 -09 Slow   [42]

1336 HYOKIN [5] (D Morley) 4-7-11(vis) T Williams 5/2 FAV: 4000321: 4 br g Comedy Star -
Leylandia (Wolver Hollow) Made a quick reappearance and was nicely bckd when comfortably
leading inside dist in a h'cap at Carlisle July 3: first success: well suited by 12f:
seems best on fast ground and likes a stiff track.   20
1150 REGAL STEEL [2] (R Hollinshead) 8-8-4 A Culhane(7) 10/3: 2032202: Just failed to
make al: tough front runner who has been placed in most starts this term: loves fast grd: see 4.   22
1271 IVOROSKI [1] (Denys Smith) 4-7-7(2oh) L Charnock 8/1: 0000033: Ev ch: in fair form.   06
1206 PAST GLORIES [3] (C Elsey) 3-8-10 J Lowe 3/1: 0-03104: Chased leader most: btr 969(11f)   35
1159 BUCKLOW HILL [4] 9-9-7 C Dwyer 7/2: 10-0000: Never really threatened: see 782.   28
5 ran   1½,3,1,2   (Mrs M F D Morley)   D Morley Newmarket

1360 BORDER TV SILVER H'CAP STAKES 0-35 3YO £1870   5f   Firm 07 -09 Slow   [37]

*1131 MURPHYS WHEELS [4] (A Jarvis) 3-9-7 D Nicholls 15/8 FAV: 3-0411: 3 b c Dublin Taxi -
Lizzylyn (Tower Walk) Nicely bckd when comfortably leading cl home in a 3yo h'cap at Carlisle
July 3: also came late when winning an app h'cap at Ayr last month: half brother to a couple
of winning sprinters: eff over 5/6f: acts on firm and yldg grd and on any trk: on the upgrade.   40
1051 BARGAIN PACK [8] (G Reveley) 3-7-12 Julie Bowker(7) 7/1: 40-0002: Al front rank,
kept on well under press and this was a better effort: maiden who is eff over 5/6f: acts
on firm and soft ground and on any track.   11
814 LOCH FORM [3] (C Tinkler) 3-9-4 M Birch 13/2: -012003: Led below dist, not btn
far: acts on fast ground: see 255.   30
1131 SONNENELLE [2] (J S Wilson) 3-8-7 P Hamblett 9/1: -120004: Kept on late: best 103(soft)   09
1070 MISS TAUFAN [1] 3-7-7(4oh) J Lowe 25/1: 00-0400: Never beyond mid-div: see 825.   00
1191 SUMMERHILL SPRUCE [9] 3-9-6 G King 10/3: 0-00130: Btr 1191 (sharp trk): see 871   15
--   PORTLAND DANCER [6] 3-8-12 N Connorton 10/1: 0204-0: Early speed: fin last on
reappearance: lightly raced last term when twice placed over this trip: acts on gd and
firm ground and on any track.   00
1288 La Manga Prince [7] 7-8(bl)   910 Hobournes Katie [5] 8-3
9 ran   1½,hd,4,2,1   (Mrs M A Jarvis)   A Jarvis Royston, Herts.

1361 CARLISLE RACE CLUB STAKES   £1512   1m 1f Firm 07 +19 Fast

1055 DESERT OF WIND [12] (L Cumani) 3-8-2 P Hamblett 11/2: -021: 3 b c Lyphard -
Polynesienne (Relko) Improving colt: led home turn and stayed on well to win a fast run
stks race at Carlisle July 3: half brother to 12f winner Pyrotechnic: stays 9f well: acts
on gd and firm ground and on a stiff track.   46
*1178 ASSEER [5] (H Cecil) 3-8-9 W Ryan 8/13 FAV: -0012: Heavily bckd: sustained chall
and comfortably beat rem: see 1178.   51
1104 SOHAIL [10] (H Thomson Jones) 3-8-2 R Hills 9/2: 3234-03: Made much: stays 9f:see 1104   30
888 THE HOUGH [11] (G Reveley) 5-9-0 D Leadbitter(5) 20/1: -044: No real threat:see 770   25
*1053 LUCKY WEST [7] 3-8-6 D Casey(7) 20/1: -0010: No extra str tho' not disgraced in
this better company: won a seller over this C/D in 1053 (gd).   23
1141 RIVA RENALD [8] 3-8-6 J Lowe 7/1:   140: Never dangerous: twice disapp since
successful over this C/D in 868 (yldg).   19
--   Bell Wether [1] 8-2   -- The Rusk [9] 9-0   -- Brundean Breeze [3] 9-0
1160 Golflines [2] 8-2   -- Travel Home [4] 9-0(BL)
1139 Malmo [6] 8-11
12 ran   1,7,2½,3,1½   (M Al Maktoum)   L Cumani Newmarket

1362 BLACKHALL H'CAP STAKES (0-35) 3YO   £1912   1m 1f   Firm 07 -39 Slow   [33]

1123 SAFFAN [3] (M Prescott) 3-9-7 G Duffield 7/2: 03-321: 3 b g L'Enjoleur - Dancing
Femme (Gaelic Dancer) Was ridden to lead cl home in a 3yo h'cap at Carlisle July 3: first
success: eff over 9/11f: acts on firm and soft ground and on any trk: can defy a penalty.   34
1179 SPRING FLIGHT [4] (A Jarvis) 3-8-9 J Lowe 11/4 JT FAV: 00-0132: Led briefly below
dist: just btn and remains in gd form: see 1179 & 740.   20
874 TABLE TURNING [5] (J Watts) 3-9-0 N Connorton 11/4 JT FAV: 00-243: Ev ch: stays 9f:
acts on firm and yldg ground and on any trk: see 258.   21
874 BALNERINO [1] (Denys Smith) 3-8-7 L Charnock 7/1: 140-004: Made much, over this
longer trip: acts on fast ground: see 874.   12
1281 SCINTILLATOR [7] 3-8-7 R Hills 10/1: 000-000: Some late prog, showing first signs
of form: seems to stay 9f: acts on fast ground and on a stiff trk: see 1281.   11
1224 KEEP COOL [8] 3-8-13 S Perks 12/1: 3400100: Never in it: twice below form in 774(1m)   10
*1158 Bold Answer [11] 7-10(7ex)   1091 Hot Lining [9] 8-13
697 Mohican [10] 8-5(bl)   843 Cheerful Times [2] 8-13
10 ran   ½,2,¾,½,4   (Fahd Salman)   M Prescott Newmarket

Official Going Given As GOOD

1363 BEAU BRUMMEL 2YO MAIDEN CLAIMING STKS   £1180   6f   Good/Firm 36 -22 Slow

924 LADY BEHAVE [3] (R Hannon) 2-8-11 A Mcglone 10/3 : 30201:2 b f Crofter - In Motion
(Monsanto) Al prom and driven into lead final 1f in a slowly run 2yo Claiming mdn at Brighton
July 3: ran twice in Ireland earlier in the season: seems to act on any going and on any
track tho'has now run well twice at Brighton: stays 6f.   34
1279 MI OH MY [5] (H Whiting) 2-8-11 G Starkey 33/1: 3402002: Kept on: impr form and
was well btn twice recently in sellers: stays 6f, prob acts on any going: see 939.   31
1232 COUNTESS BREE [6] (K Cunningham Brown) 2-8-11 J Reid 10/1: 003: Led to ½ way,
dropped in class and first signs of form: seems suited by forcing tactics: stays 6f and acts
on fast ground.   30
-- SANDS OF TIME [4] (R Simpson) 2-9-0 S Whitworth 20/1: 4: Dsptd lead much: well bred
filly whose dam Sarah Siddons was a smart middle dist filly who won the Irish Oaks: should
improve on this debut effort.   27
728 SAY YOU WILL [1] 2-8-10 T Quinn 12/1: 400: Al well in rear: twice below 503 (yldg)   00
1207 MORNING FLOWER [2] 2-9-0 R Cochrane 8/11 FAV: 032F: Going well when clipping the
heels of the horse in front and coming down at the 2f mark: unlucky? See 1207.   00
6 ran   1½,nk,2,30   (Mrs E B Jackman)   R Hannon East Everleigh, Wilts

1364 RAGGETTS SELLING STAKES 3YO   £884   7f   Good/Firm 36 -25 Slow

1288 RED ZULU [4] (H Whiting) 3-9-0 G Starkey 15/2: 0040001: 3 ch g Red Johnnie - Sovereign
Sage (Sovereign Path) Came from behind to lead final 1f, narrowly, in a 3yo seller at
Brighton July 3 (bought in 3,100 gns): first success: eff around 7f/1m: acts on firm ground.   15
1210 THE UTE [3] (L Bower) 3-9-0(bl) R Guest 11/2 JT FAV: -020232: Led 2f out, narrowly btn
and running well in this grade: likes Brighton: see 564, 749.   14
1063 COUNT ALMAVIVA [12] (M Blanshard) 3-9-0 W Newnes 11/2 JT FAV: 0002003: Ran quite
well but best 774 (1m, stiff trk).   12
1212 BLUE STEEL [5] (R Simpson) 2-8-11(bl) S Whitworth 6/1: -000444: Prom most: effective
around 7f/1m on firm ground.   06
1063 HAJ [1] 3-9-0 W Wharton 6/1: 02-2400: Ev ch: see 932.   08
1244 ROCKVILLE SQUAW [8] 2-8-11 M Wigham 14/1: 0440-00: No threat: 4th in sellers at
backend of '85: prob acts on any going.   04
1212 MISS COMEDY [10] 2-8-11 A Mcglone 8/1: 000-000: Fdd into 7th: see 1212.   00
1191 SEQUESTRATION [11] 3-9-0 B Crossley 10/1: -400000: Made much, fin 8th: no form
since 203 (6f soft).   00
1210 SIR SPEEDY [6] 3-9-0(VIS) G Dickie 10/1: -00000: No threat in 9th: see 1210.   00
845 First Orbit [9] 9-0   1210 Testarossa [7] 8-11   751 Grosvenor Court [2] 9-0(VIS)
12 ran   ½,1,1½,½,½   (Jeffrey Ross)   H Whiting Costock Grange, Leics.

1365 BRIGHTON SUMMER CHALL.H'CAP 3YO+ 0-60   £3535   1m   Good/Firm 36 -05 Slow   [60]

1147 MEET THE GREEK [2] (R Laing) 3-8-0 P Cook 15/8 FAV: -211201: 3 b c Formidable -
Edellette (Edellic) Useful colt: continues in gd form and led dist rather cleverly in quite
a val h'cap at Brighton July 3: earlier won similar h'caps at Leicester and Lingfield:
very eff over 7f/1m: acts on firm and yldg: progressive sort who has been a model of
consistency this term.   55
410 ASSWAN [3] (J Francome) 6-9-4 W Newnes 11/2: 0121-02: Came from behind, fin in
fine fashion and only narrowly btn in a cl fin: fairly useful over hurdles in the Winter:
successful at Sandown and Doncaster on the level in '85: very eff over 7f/1m: best form
on firm or good going: looks sure to go close next time.   60
1189 PORTOGON [7] (M Usher) 8-8-6 D Mckay 15/2: 0-00003: Made most, narrowly btn and
clear rest: back to his best: could win soon: see 930.   47

*930 FEI LOONG [5] (E Eldin) 5-7-8 A Mackay 4/1: -044214: Ev ch: btr 930.   25
1189 GOLDEN SLADE [6] 4-7-11 A Tucker(7) 100/30: -001330: Prom most: below her best here.   23
1166 THATCHINGLY [1] 5-7-7(7oh) S Dawson 33/1: 1040000: No threat: best 176 (10f here)   14
--   Don Martino [8] 10-0   1173 Paris Match 0 8-1
8 ran   nk,¼,5,2½,2   (P G Goulandris)   R Laing Lambourn, Berks

1366 FITZHERBERT HANDICAP 3YO+ 0-50   £2728   1m 4f   Good/Firm 36 +01 Fast   [48]

1209 PELLINCOURT [1] (R Akehurst) 3-8-0 T Quinn 13/8 FAV: 4002021: 4 b c King Pellinore -
Court Barns (Riva Ridge) Al going well and led inside final 3f comfortably in a 4 runner
h'cap at Brighton July 3: first success but a deserved one after sev near misses: eff 10f,
stays 12f well: acts on firm and gd ground and runs very well at Brighton.   29
1209 VORACITY [2] (J Winter) 7-9-10 W R Swinburn 15/8: 004-232: Waited with, kept on
and ran much the same race as in 1209 (C/D)   51
1035 WILD GINGER [3] (D Oughton) 4-7-9(bl) B Crossley 14/1: -020003: Made much, sn wknd
and best 485 (14f yldg).   07
1004 MILLERS TALE [4] (I Balding) 4-8-12 G Starkey 5/2: 2-20104: Has twice run poorly
since 761 (C/D).   09
4 ran   1½,10,15   (A D Spence)   R Akehurst Epsom, Surrey

1367 BLACKMANTLE HANDICAP 3YO+ 0-35   £2047   6f   Good/Firm 36 +08 Fast   [35]

198 BEECHWOOD COTTAGE [2] (A Bailey) 3-7-8(bl) G Bardwell(7) 8/1: 010-001: 3 ch g
Malinowski Drora (Busted) Despite returning from a long abs, was well bckd and fairly
sprinted clear in the final 1f to easily win quite a fast run h'cap at Brighton July 3:
comfortably won a nursery at Hamilton in '85: equally eff at 6 and 7f, may stay further:
acts on fast and soft going: should win again if kept to this grade.   22
*729 GERSHWIN [2] (D O'donnell) 3-7-13 A Clark 10/1: 000-12: Led dist, outpaced by winner
but a good effort: see 729.   18
1213 RAPID MISS [9] (N Macauley) 6-8-10 Gay Kelleway(5) 9/1: 000-003: Chall dist: stays
6f: see 784.   19
1213 FREMONT BOY [4] (C James) 4-8-8 W R Swinburn 3/1 FAV: 00-2304: Ev ch: twice below 679.15
1213 DELAWARE RIVER [8] 4-8-10 W Newnes 9/2: 0-02400: Dsptd lead much: best 748 (C/D)   16
1066 ROMAN RULER [7] 7-9-9(bl) P Cook 8/1: 0000-00: No threat: twice a winner over
this C/D last season and has won 3 times in all at this seaside track: acts on firm and
soft: best form at 6f.   25
1213 RUSSELL FLYER [5] 4-8-9(bl) M L Thomas 8/1: 0000040: Led/dsptd lead much, fin 7th.   00
855 LINTON STARCHY [1] 5-7-12 P Hutchinson(1) 6/1: 00-0030: Led/dsptd lead some:
better 855 (yielding).   00
1213 The Batchlor [6] 7-10(bl)
9 ran   3,nk,1,¼,2   (A Bailey)   A Bailey Newmarket

1368 CHIPPENDALE MAIDEN FILLIES STAKES 3YO   £959   1m 2f   Gd/Fm 36 -04 Slow

847 ASK MAMA [2] (J Dunlop) 3-8-11 J Reid 8/1: 002-301: 3 b f Mummy's Pet - La Lidia
(Matador) Fairly useful filly: prom and battled on well final 2f for a hd success in a
3yo fillies mdn at Brighton July 3: showed promise in '85 when lightly raced: half sister
to sev winners: eff 1m, stays 10f well: and may stay further: acts on gd/firm and soft
ground: acts well on an undulating track: genuine filly.   52
1192 NO DOUBLET [5] (B Hills) 3-8-11 B Thomson 3/1: 33-322: Led ¼ way, caught death
but clear rest and is due a change of luck soon: see 862, 1192.   51
863 MAKE IT SHARP [9] (A Stewart) 3-8-11 M Roberts 7/1: -03: Al prom and is improving:
will be suited by 12f: see 863: sure to find a maiden.   43
1259 BENAROSA [1] (P Kelleway) 3-8-11(VIS) Gay Kelleway(5) 12/1: -340004: Visored for
the first time, ev ch: has been disappointing since fine effort in 372.   40
--   HELIETTA [8] 3-8-11 R Guest 5/1: -0: No threat but will be all the better for this
debut: half sister to 3 winners, notably the smart Vieille (Oaks runner-up): attractive
sort with scope and will be a different proposition next time.   39
--   CROWLEY [3] 3-8-11 S Quane(7) 33/1: -0: Quite a promising debut from this American
bred filly: should stay beyond 10f: improvement almost certain next time.   38
1031 SKEAN [7] 3-8-11 G Starkey 7/4 FAV: -00: Well bckd: chall 2f out, wknd into 8th. see 1031. 00
658 Sweepy [10] 8-11   1064 Sonning [6] 8-11   509 Flaming Dancer [4] 8-11
10 ran   hd,5,1,1,¼   (Sir Rex Cohen)   J Dunlop Arundel, Sussex

Official Going Given As FIRM

1369 RED & YELLOW CANOPY SELLING H'CAP 0-25 £895 1m 2f Good/Firm 33 -06 Slow   [19]

1136 CHABLISSE [8] (R Whitaker) 3-9-7 D Mckeown 5/2 FAV: -0P4031: 3 b f Radetzky - Late
Idea (Tumble Wind) Dropped in class and comfortably justified fav, leading inside dist in
a selling h'cap at Beverley July 4 (bought in 1050 gns): half sister to winning sprinter
Tuxford Hideaway: stays 10f well: suited by fast grd and a stiff track.   20
1267 FOREVER YOUNG [9] (G Oldroyd) 3-9-0 P Burke(7) 7/2: 0-40142: Going on fin: will stay
further: successful over this C/D in 993.   07
1201 AUSSIE GIRL [10] (A Bailey) 3-9-7 M Miller 7/2: 0-00003: Led below dist: stays 10f:
best effort to date: well suited by fast ground.   13
991 HIGHEST NOTE [4] (G Blum) 3-9-7 M Rimmer 9/1: 00-3004: Dropped in class: maiden
who has shown enough ability to suggest a seller should not be beyond her: stays 10f:
acts on firm and soft.   11
1288 MISS BETEL [7] 3-9-7(bl) M Birch 14/1: 0-04000: Led over 2f out: acts on any trk.   06
1201 BAYVIEW GAL [2] 3-9-4 R P Elliott 14/1: 0-00000: Never beyond mid-div: see 932.   00
1267 WOLLOW BIRD [5] 3-8-9 N Connorton 10/1: 000-400: Fin 7th: best over 9f in 1158.   00
-- Spare The Blushes [12] 8-10   1288 Miss Betel [7] 9-7
1056 La Chula [11] 9-6(bl)   740 Octiga [3] 9-0   828 Connaught Broads [1] 8-9
12 ran   2½,hd,1,3,2½,½,12   (E Wilkinson)   R Whitaker Scarcroft, Yorks

1370 E.B.F. SHOP WINDOW FILLIES' STAKES 2YO   £1206   5f   Good/Firm 33 -15 Slow

*1205 SINCLAIR LADY [6] (G Oldroyd) 2-9-1 D Nicholls 3/1: 000011: 2 gr f Afsalom - Katsysue
(King's Leap) In gd form, stayed on strongly to lead cl home in a 2yo fillies stks at
Beverley July 4: surprise winner of her mdn at Pontefract late last month: cost 10,000 gns
as a yearling and her dam was successful 5 times as a juv: well suited by this minimum trip
and seems certain to stay further: acts on gd and firm grd and on any track.   45
1266 MINIZEN LASS [1] (M Brittain) 2-8-8 K Darley 11/2: 0422022: Just failed to make all:
has found one too good in 4 of her last 5 starts and is certainly due a change of luck.   34
1161 SCAWSBY LEES [7] (M W Easterby) 2-8-8 K Hodgson 11/1: 03: Outpaced early tho' ran
on strongly and should appreciate another furlong: cost 7,000 gns as a yearling and is a
half sister to winning chaser Burglars Walk: dam was a prolific winning sprinter: acts
on fast ground and on a stiff track.   28
-- ALHAYAT [4] (R Boss) 2-8-8 E Guest(3) 11/4 FAV: 4: Never really looked likely to
justify fav on her race course debut, tho' should certainly improve for this experience:
speedily bred filly who seems to act on fast ground.   16
*938 EMMER GREEN [2] 2-8-11 Gay Kelleway(5) 7/2: 4010: Speed over ¼ way: btr938(easier trk) 16
1221 FIDGETTY FEET [5] 2-8-8 M Fry 33/1: 00: Early speed from this cheaply acquired filly. 10
1297 PRETTY SOON [9] 2-8-8 M Beecroft 9/1: 40: Never dangerous and better on her debut
in 1297 (sharp track).   00
1248 Dublin Belle [11] 8-8   -- Royal Special [8] 8-8
9 ran   1,2,4,1,1,½,10   (Sinclair Developments Ltd)   G Oldroyd Malton, Yorks

1371 GRANDWAYS STAKES (H'CAP)(0-50) 3YO   £5017   1m   Good/Firm 33 +02 Fast   [50]

1224 NEDS EXPRESSA [6] (C Tinkler) 3-8-3 M Wood 10/1: -000341: 3 ch g Bay Express -
Lizzie Lightfoot (Hotfoot) Quickly away and made most in a 3yo h'cap at Beverley July 4:
won at Catterick last season: stays 1m well: suited by fast ground and forcing tactics:
seems to do well on turning track.   35
1091 RUN BY JOVE [5] (S Norton) 3-8-5(vis) J Lowe 14/1: 0012002: Narrowly btn: see 789, 674 36
1147 JOHN SAXON [3] (M Stoute) 3-9-7 T Ives 6/4 FAV: 3-00203: Well bckd: stayed on well.
not btn far and ran a fair race under top weight: see 703.   51
914 TRICK OR TREAT [2] (J Watts) 3-9-4 N Connorton 3/1: 300-144: Ev ch: stays 1m: see 518 43
997 ROYAL ROUSER [7] 3-8-2 A Culhane(7) 20/1: 0000-00: Al up there: won a mdn at
Haydock last season and was subsequently placed sev times: prob stays 1m: acts on firm & hvy. 27
*891 ROYAL FAN [4] 3-8-8 M Birch 5/1: -0010: Held up, no real threat: see 891 (6f)   32
1224 SIDONS DAUGHTER [1] 3-8-11 D Nicholls 4/1: 40-0020: Last to fin: btr 1224.   00
7 ran   ½,½,2½,shthd,½,nk   (Ned Jones)   C Tinkler Malton, Yorks

1372 PRICELOW MAIDEN STAKES 3YO   £1240   1m 4f   Good/Firm 33 -04 Slow

1290 SARYAN [4] (N Callaghan) 3-9-0 M Miller 10/1: 00-041: 3 b g Try My Best - High Fidelyty
(Hautain) Continues to improve, made smooth prog to lead cl home in a 3yo mdn at Beverley
July 4: lightly raced last term: half brother to sev winners: stays 12f well: suited by
fast ground and a stiff track.   46
744 SPARTAN VALLEY [8] (B Hills) 3-9-0 R Hills 4/1: -0-232: Led below dist, narrowly
btn and ran a gd race under a fair wage: stays 12f: acts on gd/firm: shd win soon: see 448 45
1220 IS BELLO [1] (L Cumani) 3-9-0 R Guest 2/1 FAV: -03203: Well bckd: stayed on too
late tho' not btn far: stays 12f: suited by fast ground and a stiff trk: see 723.   44
699 DESERTED [6] (G Pritchard Gordon) 3-8-11 M Birch 10/1: 00-04: Going on fin and
well suited by 12f: see 699.   40
1031 ADMIRALS ALL [9] 3-9-0 T Ives 3/1: 00-0340: Led/dsptd lead most of way: see 1031, 765 36
-- GRUNDYS OWN [7] 3-9-0 S Perks 33/1: 0-0: Never nearer on seasonal debut: lightly
raced colt who should certainly improve on this effort next time: stays 12f: acts on fast
ground and on a stiff track.   28

959 RHODE ISLAND RED [2] 3-9-0 N Connorton 10/1: -400: Fin 8th: best 714.   00
1123 Kasu [13] 8-11   958 Pinturicchia [3] 8-11   1160 Patricks Star [12] 9-0
--   Pinzaureole [5] 8-11   1337 Giant Redwood [14] 8-11
991 Our Noora [10] 8-11   --   Ferry Meadows [11] 9-0
14 ran   ½,1,hd,4,6,nk,3   (K Al-Said)   N Callaghan Newmarket

1373 TROLLEY DASH STAKES 2YO   £1569   7f   Good/Firm 33 -12 Slow

1203 TEAM EFFORT [2] (R Thompson) 2-9-4 R P Elliott 9/1: 0301121: 2 b c Stanford - Bap's
Miracle (Track Spare) Consistent colt: led inside dist, gamely, in a 2yo stks at Beverley
July 4: earlier scored successive wins at Edinburgh and Redcar: cheaply acquired: stays 7f
really well: acts on firm and yldg ground and on any track: has done well with forcing tactics   52
1289 LACK A STYLE [10] (A Bailey) 2-8-6 M Miller 6/4: 002: Fin strongly and only just
denied: stays 7f well: acts on fast ground and on a stiff track: gd effort: see 405.   40
*1197 BILLS HENRY [4] (R Boss) 2-8-11 E Guest(3) 5/4 FAV: 013: Just btn in a blanket
finish: sure to stay 1m: acts on fast ground: see 1197.   45
927 LIGHTNING LEGEND [5] (P Kelleway) 2-8-3 Gay Kelleway(3) 8/1: 4404: Stayed on and
not btn far: stays 7f: see 513.   34
--   PATHERO [9] 2-8-6 J Bleasdale 66/1: 0: Showed some promise on his debut, making the
running for over 5f: will benefit from this experience: acts on fast ground.   36
870 COMBERMERE [8] 2-8-6 T Ives 25/1: 000: Seemed btr suited by this longer trip: acts
on fast ground: brother to 7f winner Life Guard.   26
--   Pharaoh Blue [1] 8-6   859 Callace [7] 8-3   --   Tubeson [3] 8-6
9 ran   shthd,shthd,1½,½,4,½   (George Mansell)   R Thompson Stainforth, Yorks.

1374 GRANDWAYS CHECKOUT STAKES (H'CAP) 0-35   £1670   1m 2f Good/Firm 33 +10 Fast   [33]

1254 SENOR RAMOS [16] (R Thompson) 4-9-1(bl) R P Elliott 25/1: 0000001: 4 b g Transworld -
Trendy (Crewman) Was a surprise winner: stayed on well to lead cl home in quite a fast run
h'cap at Beverley July 4: fair h'capper on his day, won at Thirsk last season and in '84
won twice at Edinburgh: best form over 10/12f: acts on any going and on a turning track.   28
1017 PERSHING [8] (J Leigh) 5-8-12 M Miller 7/2: -020322: Led below dist, collared close
home: deserves a race: see 611.   24
--   SMART MART [1] (M Camacho) 7-7-9(VIS) M Fry 14/1: 00000-3: Never nearer on reappearance:
visored for the first time today: last won in '84 at Beverley, placed over hurdles this
Winter: stays 12f: acts on any going: usually held up.   03
*1106 RAPID LAD [6] (J Spearing) 8-9-10 D Nicholls 3/1 FAV: 000-014: Course specialist: btr 1106. 25
1156 PARIS TRADER [10] 4-9-5(bl) M Hindley(3) 16/1: -000000: Ev ch: stays 12f: see 609.   18
993 ROYAL EXPORT [14] 6-7-8 S P Griffiths(5) 25/1: 000-030: Kept on: see 993 & 163.   00
1254 ELARIM [7] 7-9-2 J Callaghan(7) 8/1: 0004400: Fin 8th: see 745.   00
1081 CAROLS MUSIC [12] 5-8-11 A Shoults(5) 9/2: 1020-00: Fin 9th: see 1081.   00
1185 Nugola [17] 8-5   1295 Common Farm [15] 8-10(6ex)
1185 Sound Work [3] 7-9   --   Sovereign Cellar [5] 7-9
1211 Dallas Smith [2] 7-9(vis)   1195 Verbading [11] 7-13(bl)
1024 Glenderry [9] 8-2(bl)   --   Mighty Supremo [4] 8-6
1173 Gallois Bosquet [13] 8-12
17 ran   ½,2,4,1½,4,hd   (M D Marshall)   R Thompson Stainforth, Yorks.

Official Going Given As FIRM

1375 LEO ROCHE MAIDEN FILLIES STAKES 3YO   £2633   7f   Good 41 -01 Slow

1184 MILLRACER [9] (M Jarvis) 3-8-11 T Ives 20/1: 40-01: 3 b f Le Fabuleux - Marston's
Mill (In Reality) Improving filly: led inside final 1f, ridden out in a 3yo fillies maiden
at Haydock July 4: lightly raced 2yo, finishing 4th to Sonic Lady first time out in the Blue
Seal Stks at Ascot: half sister to the smart Peterhof: eff 7f, should be suited by 1m: acts
on gd and firm ground and can continue to improve.   46
1228 SARIZA [1] (H Cecil) 3-8-11 S Cauthen 15/8 FAV: -422: Led over 1f out: consistent: 44
1228 CLEOFE [5] (L Cumani) 3-8-11 R Guest 6/1: 44-0033: Chance 1f out: see 1228.   42
926 DAVEMMA [4] (P Kelleway) 3-8-11 W Carson 10/1: 0-40004: Fin well: needs further
than 7f: see 509 (12f)   41
--   SUNDAY CHIMES [1] 3-8-11 N Connorton 9/2: -0: Nicely bckd debutant: al there: half
sister to 7f winner Aulait: may stay 1m: acts on good ground.   31
1244 APHROSINA [15] 3-8-11(BL) Pat Eddery 6/1: -0000: Led 3f out: btr 1244.   29
1228 HOOKED BID [11] 3-8-11 P Robinson 20/1: -00: No threat in 7th: £600,000 purchase
who should improve, possibly over 1m+.   00
966 BONNET TOP [10] 3-8-11 R Machado 4/1: -4F: Early faller and was sadly destroyed.   00
937 Aspark [14] 8-11   33   Trixie Belle [8] 8-11   --   Atlantic Passage [3] 8-11
891 Emancipated Lady [16] 8-11   --   Famille Rose [13] 8-11   --   Pink Pyjamas [12] 8-11
--   Famille Rose [13] 8-11   776 Danesmoor [7] 8-11
1184 Sybilly [6] 8-11 S
16 ran   1,½,nk,5,1,2   (R Wilson Jnr)   M Jarvis Newmarket

1376 JOHN BARNES MAIDEN STAKES 2YO   £2618   6f   Good 41 -07 Slow

1149 SUMMERHILL STREAK [2] (E Eldin) 2-9-0 A Mackay 8/1: 231: 2 b c Imperial Fling - Sharper Still (Sharpen Up) Useful, improving colt: led over 2f out, comfortably, in a 2yo mdn at Haydock July 4: showed promise on both his prev outings, 2nd to Darley Knight at York and last time out a good 3rd to Sanam in val event at Ascot: well suited by 6f, should stay further: acts on gd and firm ground and a galloping track: should win more races.   55

1225 ANTINOUS [5] (M H Easterby) 2-9-0 M Birch 5/1: 32: Sn prom: on the upgrade and should be winning shortly: acts on any trk: see 1225.   49

-- WICHITA SPRINGS [9] (J Fitzgerald) 2-9-0 A Murray 25/1: 3: Ran on well final 1f, showing future promise: cost 900,000 gns: should be suited by further than 6f: acts on good ground and a galloping track and should be winning soon.   41

1019 GELTSER [4] (J Tree) 2-9-0 Pat Eddery 2/5 FAV: 24: Ev ch over 2f out: ran unaccountably poorly: much better 1019: deserves another chance.   38

1050 PHILOTAS [6] 2-9-0 L Charnock 20/1: 40: Led over ½ way: improving: should find a small event: see 1050.   36

1049 ALBION PLACE [8] 2-9-0 J Lowe 25/1: 400: No real threat: see 870.   25

-- PSALMODY [11] 2-9-0 S Cauthen 10/1: 0: Sn prom: fin 7th: improvement likely from this half brother to very useful 10/12f winner Galveston: acts on good ground.   00

-- Toll Bar [7] 9-0   -- Rose Of Tudor [10] 8-11
-- Overpower [1] 9-0   1203 Vaigly Yellow [3] 9-0
11 ran   2,3,1,½,4,shthd   (Summerhill Stud Ltd)   E Eldin Newmarket

1377 DEREK CRETCH HANDICAP STAKES 0-50   £3150   7f   Good 41 -05 Slow   [47]

*1229 BOLD PILLAGER [1] (J Dunlop) 4-9-3(5ex) W Carson 4/7 FAV: 0-03211: 4 b c Formidable - Pilley Green (Porto Bello) In fine form: led early and again half way for a runaway 6l success in a h'cap at Haydock July 4: last time out made ev yard easily, in a h'cap at Kempton: lightly raced prev: seems equally eff at 7f/1m: acts on gd and firm ground and does well when up with the pace: may complete the hat-trick.   50

1157 THE MAZALL [2] (L Siddall) 6-8-8 M Wood 8/1: -001202: No chance with winner: see 700   27

1222 INISHPOUR [3] (H Wharton) 4-9-7 A Mackay 9/1: 0-00303: Ev ch: best 1157 (6f firm)   36

775 BATON BOY [4] (M Brittain) 5-8-11 K Darley 10/1: 0-20004: No real threat: abs:see 55   24

-- TOP OTHLANE [6] 9-7-10 L Charnock 25/1: 00100-0: Wknd final 2f on seasonal debut: in '85 won a h'cap at Redcar and is a specialist on that trk: very eff at 7f: acts firm & yldg   01

815 GREETLAND DANCER [5] 4-7-10 A Proud 7/1: 0000-40: Made most to ½ way: abs since much better 815 (sharper track).   00

6 ran   6,2,1,4,10   (Dexam International)   J Dunlop Arundel, Sussex

1378 METROPOLE TROPHY 3YO   £6992   1m 2f   Good 41 +05 Fast

*342 ARMADA [1] (G Harwood) 3-9-5 G Starkey 4/6 FAV: -111: 3 b c Shirley Heights - If (Kashmir II) Smart colt: despite long abs, led 2f out, ridden out in quite fast run and val 3yo Metropole Trophy at Haydock July 4: remains unbtn, earlier winning at Brighton and first time out hacked up by 8l in the Wood Ditton at Newmarket: cost 1m gns as a yearling: stays 10f well: should be suited by 12f: acts on gd/firm & yldg ground and on any trk: sure to win more races: has been hobdayed.   78

1045 TOP GUEST [3] (G Wragg) 3-9-1 P Robinson 3/1: 22-1222: Kept on well final 1f: in fine form this season and has met some smart performers: see 1045.   70

1098 NORTH VERDICT [4] (M Jarvis) 3-9-1 T Ives 7/1: 210-003: Ev ch final 2f: see 555   60

*1043 ZUMURRUDAH [2] (H T Jones) 3-8-12 A Murray 8/1: -0014: Made much: stiff task:see 1043.   53

4 ran   1,5,1½   (K Abdulla)   G Harwood Pulborough, Sussex

1379 ROGER PEAKE SELLING STAKES 2YO   £1466   6f   Good 41 -28 SLow

1294 SHARPHAVEN [6] (M Brittain) 2-8-8 K Darley 7/2: 4030241: 2 ch f Sharpo - Haven Bridge (Connaught) Made ev yard for an easy 4l win in a 2yo seller at Haydock July 4 (no bid): placed sev times prev, but this was her first win: acts on firm and soft ground and does well forcing the pace.   30

913 CREAM AND GREEN [4] (K White) 2-8-11 J Williams 33/1: 0002: Al up there: dropped in class today and may find a similar event: cheaply acquired colt: stays 6f and acts good grd.   21

596 SWALLOW BAY [7] (D H Jones) 2-8-8 S Cauthen 9/1: 003: Prom, ev ch: best eff yet: half sister to 9f winner Turtle Bay: acts on gd ground.   15

826 MISS DISPLAY [5] (J S Wilson) 2-8-8 A Mackay 11/4: 0044: Ev ch: well below form 826.   03

1262 MUSICAL CHORUS [1] 2-8-8(bl) A Bond 6/1: 0030: Wknd: btr 1262 (sharper trrk).   00

1203 HARRY HUNT [3] 2-9-1 T Ives 7/4 FAV: 31000: Well bckd: there 4f: btr 1203, 488.   05

647 Sunny Gibraltar [2] 8-8
7 ran   4,1,5,1½,nk   (Mel Brittain)   M Brittain Warthill, Yorks.

1380 RAY GRIFFITHS HANDICAP 0-50   £2934   5f   Good 41 +01 Fast   [46]

947 TAX ROY [8] (B Mcmahon) 3-8-9 S Perks 14/1: 121-001: 3 b f Dublin Taxi - Loyal and Regal (Royal and Regal) Returned to her 2yo form, made almost all to come home on her own by 7l in a h'cap at Haydock July 4: in '85 won a nursery at Nottingham and a fillies mdn again at Nottingham: seems equally eff at 5/6f: well suited by forcing tactics on gd ground: should win again.   49

1268 CHINA GOLD [3] (L Siddall) 7-8-13 M Wood 3/1 JT.FAV: -030042: Prom, ev ch: see 1268.   30
1044 MANDRAKE MADAM [7] (D Smith) 3-9-2 L Charnock 25/1: 2-00003: Al up there: best effort
this season and is returning to form: consistent 2yo, winning first time out at Edinburgh:
later ran well in better company: equally eff at 5/6f: acts on firm and yldg and on any trk.   40
1151 NICCOLO POLO [2] (B Hanbury) 3-10-0(bl) S Cauthen 3/1 JT.FAV: -330244: Prom, ev ch:
twice below form 884.   47
1145 SHOW HOME [6] 4-9-1 T Ives 12/1: 33-0000: Never nearer: see 742.   22
1268 RAMBLING RIVER [4] 9-9-1(vis) J Lowe 6/1: 0-02000: No threat: best 742, see 626.   13
1283 VENEZ TRADER [5] 3-9-1 A Murray 6/1: 214-400: Fin 7th: best first time out in 1027.   00
1196 SPACEMAKER BOY [1] 6-9-5 N Howe 4/1: 10032F0: Dsptd lead early: btr 1037.   00
 8 ran   7,shthd,2,2,3   (J M Smith)   B Mcmahon Tamworth, Staffs.

SANDOWN   Friday July 4th   Righthand Stiff Galloping Track

Official Going Given As GOOD - FIRM

1381 GRE STAKES 2YO   £4201   5f   Firm 16 -48 Slow

 187 MOON INDIGO [3] (C Brittain) 2-8-11 G Baxter 33/1: 01: 2 b c Red Sunset - Lunar
Eclipse (Hot Spark) Fast improving colt: returned after long abs to comfortably lead final 1f
in a very slowly run but val minor 2yo event at Sandown July 4: a 24,000 gns yearling who
is quite highly regarded by his stable: eff over a stiff 5f, sure to stay 6f and probably
further: acts well on firm ground.   55
1207 LAST DANCE [5] (R Hannon) 2-8-11 B Thomson 20/1: 042: Chall in final 2f, narrowly
btn in a cl finish: evidently fast improving: eff over a stiff 5f, stays 6f: see 1207.   53
*1030 SEA DARA [4] (I Balding) 2-8-13 J Matthias 11/8 FAV: 13: Under press from 2f out
but stayed on well and looks as if   6f   will suit now: btr 1030 (C/D).   54
-1187 LINGERING [8] (J Winter) 2-8-8 T Quinn 9/4: 24: Made much but didnot seem to
last out this stiff 5f and should be better on a sharper track: see 1187.   48
1261 PAS DENCHERE [6] 2-8-11 P Waldron 16/1: 030: No danger but a good effort: see 1039.   45
--   BALTIC SHORE [2] 2-8-11 A Kimberley 7/1: 0: Friendless in mkt (op 5/2), no danger:
related to sev winners abroad and sired by the very promising Danzig, looks sure to improve
on this next time: will be suited by 6f+.   42
--   MONETARY FUND [4] 2-8-11 M L Thomas 33/1: 0: Sure to be btr for this first effort:
related to sev winners, notably successful miler Jade Ring: sure to be suited by 6f.   37
 927 KEEN EDGE [7] 2-8-11 A Mcglone 16/1: 42200: Early speed, fin last: twice below 678
(good): unsuited by firm?   30
 8 ran   nk,½,¾,nk,2,1,1½,2½   (Ray Richards)   C Brittain Newmarket

1382 JARDINE MAIDEN FILLIES STAKES 2YO   £4162   7f   Firm 16 -25 Slow

--   GOLDEN BRAID [10] (I Balding) 2-8-11 J Matthias 15/8: 1: 2 b f Glint of Gold - Silk
Slipper (Prince Tenderfoot) Smart filly in the making: first time out, led dist, comfortably,
in a 2yo fillies mdn at Sandown July 4: half sister to a minor winner over 1m, and dam was
useful in France: well suited by a stiff 7f, sure to stay 1m+: acts on firm ground: yet
another highly promising filly from the Ian Balding stable: sure to win more races.   65
 944 BINT PASHA [5] (P Cole) 2-8-11 T Quinn 13/8 FAV: 222: Heavily bckd, made much but
again had to settle for 2nd: has come up against 3 useful fillies and is due a change of luck:
see 601: stays 7f.   56
 707 LISIANTHUS [6] (J Winter) 2-8-11 J Reid 25/1: 03: Kept on well and is on the upgrade:
dam was moderate but comes from a good family which includes Oaks winner Ginevra: suited
by 7f, will stay at least 1m: acts on firm.   48
--   KLARARA [7] (J Dunlop) 2-8-11 P Cook 7/1: 4: Showed signs of inexperience in the
race and is sure to benefit from the outing: related to sev winners in USA and dam comes
from a prolific winning family: will improve.   43
--   GLINT OF GLORY [8] (G Baxter) 2-8-11 G Baxter 20/1: 0: Started slowly, sure to be all the btr
for this experience: related to a winner abroad: sure to be suited by 1m: has the scope to
make significant improvement on this performance.   35
--   ANORADA [1] 2-8-11 M Hills 25/1: 0: American bred filly who cost only $17,500:
should improve.   25
--   Top Wak [2] 8-11   985 Emmas Whisper [4] 8-11
--   Lady Artful [3] 8-11   400 French Plait [9] 8-11
10 ran   2½,½,4,2½,4,4   (Sir Michael Sobell)   I Balding Kingsclere, Berks.

1383 ROYAL HONG KONG JOCK.CLUB H'CAP 3YO+ 0-70 £12447 1m 2f Firm 16 +10 Fast   [62]

1047 PROMISED ISLE [10] (Lady Herries) 5-8-11 Paul Eddery 15/2: 02-3231: 5 b h Mill Reef -
Parolee (Sing Sing) Useful h'capper: gained a deserved success after sev near misses, leading
final 1f and holding on gamely in quite a fast run and val h'cap at Sandown July 4: trained
by J Dunlop in '85 and was placed on sev occasions, the prev season successful at Salisbury:
half brother to numerous winners: eff over 1m/10f: acts on firm and yldg and on any trk:
genuine and consistent.   58
1038 AL YABIR [4] (C Benstead) 4-8-12 M Hills 14/1: 0020-22: Came to chall final 1f,
just held in a driving finish: should find a decent h'cap soon: see 1038.   59
1147 HILLS BID [7] (B Hills) 3-8-5 B Thomson 12/1: 12-1003: Led 2f out, narrowly btn in
a close finish: fine effort and stays 10f well: see 615.   64

1109 RANA PRATAP [8] (G Lewis) 6-8-9 P Waldron 10/1: 0433204: Kept on well cl home:
beaten less than 1¾l: suited by 10f nowadays: see 445.   53
1130 DALGADIYR [3] 3-7-9 M L Thomas 2/1 FAV: -3130: Scrubbed along from the start, rapid
progress ½m out but failed to get a clear run final 2f: see 625.   52
432 DERRYRING [2] 4-7-11 C Rutter(4) 33/1: 10-0000: No danger after abs: in gd form in
'85 winning 2 out of his 5 races: minor events at Nottingham and Salisbury (first time out):
eff 1m, stays 10f well: acts on a galloping track and on good ground.   34
*1249 TRY TO STOP ME [11] 5-8-11(5ex) T Quinn 14/1: -003210: Ev ch, wknd into 7th: see 1249.   00
1217 KALKOUR [5] 4-9-2 W Ryan 4/1: -010120: Below his best in 9th: see 1038 (C/D)   00
1112 EFFIGY [9] 4-9-10 A Clark 7/1: 221-000: Dsptd lead much: see 1112.   00
1109 All Fair [1] 8-4   361 Fusilier [6] 7-13(bl)
11 ran   shthd,¾,¾,hd,4   (Eva lady Roseberry)   Lady Herries Littlehampton, West Sussex

1384 WAYFOONG HANDICAP 3YO 0-60   £6992   1m   Firm 16 +04 Fast   [56]

*1041 AVENTINO [7] (J Sutcliffe) 3-8-5(bl) M Hills 6/4 FAV: 1-01111: 3 ch g Cure The Blues
- Sovereign Dona (Sovereign Path) Much improved gelding: completed a four-timer when coming
from behind to comfortably lead final 1f in quite a val h'cap at Sandown July 4: earlier
completed a quick hat-trick in similar h'caps at Goodwood, Newmarket and again at Sandown:
narrowly won a Newmarket seller on final outing in '85: very eff over 7f/1m and is suited by
firm ground: wears bl but is genuine: suited by waiting tactics.   45
692 GORGEOUS ALGERNON [8] (C Brittain) 3-9-7 G Baxter 8/1: -010202: Led 1f out: gd effort:
unsuited by soft: acts on firm and yielding: see 178.   57
1107 REIGNBEAU [3] (G Lewis) 3-9-5 P Waldron 7/1: -311203: Tried to make all: seems to
act on firm and heavy: see 274.   50
1036 MARSHAL MACDONALD [6] (W Holden) 3-8-12 J Reid 8/1: 40-0044: Held up, no danger,
still seeking first win: see 1036.   38
-- MERLINS MAGIC [1] 3-8-2 P Cook 8/1: 001-0: No threat on seasonal debut: ran only 3
times at the end of '85, narrowly beating Kedron in a minor event at Folkestone: eff over
6f on firm ground tho' may stay further: acts on an easy track.   20
538 PROHIBITED [4] 3-9-3 T Quinn 15/2: 00-1100: Abs: best 316 (C/D, soft)   31
723 Turmeric [2] 8-1   880 Viceroy Major [5] 7-13
-- St James Risk [9] 8-11
9 ran   1½,2,2½,5,2   (A J Smith)   J Sutcliffe Epsom, Surrey

1385 INCHCAPE HANDICAP 4YO+ 0-60   £4448   5f   Firm 16 -09 Slow   [50]

1196 CREE BAY [7] (J Spearing) 7-9-7(bl) B Thomson 8/1: 3320041: 7 br g Bay Express -
Porsanger (Zeddaan) Fairly useful sprinter on his day: led under press final 1f, just holding
on to win a h'cap at Sandown July 4: failed to win in '85, the prev season successful at
Pontefract (2) and Warwick: stays 6f, very eff at 5f: acts on soft, best form on firm or
good going: wears blinkers.   55
1145 ALL AGREED [2] (J Winter) 5-9-4 Paul Eddery 9/2 FAV: -004002: Last for a long way:
absolutely flying at finish and would have got up in another stride: back to his best form
and should win soon: see 550.   52
1196 DIVISSIMA [9] (G Lewis) 4-7-11 M L Thomas 11/2: 031-023: Dsptd lead thr'out:
running well: see 1196.   28
-- HI TECH GIRL [5] (C Brittain) 4-9-10 M Roberts 10/1: 40340-4: Al there and a gd
seasonal debut: placed sev times without winning in '85 and was tried in bl on final outing:
in '84 won the Queen Mary Stakes at Royal Ascot and a maiden at Newbury: stays 6f: suited
by fast going and a galloping track.   52
*1037 AXE VALLEY [6] 4-9-10 T Quinn 6/1: 010-010: Made much, gd effort and likes Sandown.   51
1268 LOCHTILLUM [4] 7-9-9 W Ryan 9/1: -001000: Rear, kept on fin: best 836 (gd).   45
1145 LAURIE LORMAN [1] 4-9-6 P Cook 10/1: 0-01000: Ev ch, fin 7th: best 660 (yldg/soft)   42
1227 KELLYS ROYALE [3] 4-9-5 J Reid 14/1: 0000000: Fin 8th: see 550.   38
-1222 CHAPLINS CLUB [8] 6-9-9(bl) D Nicholls 6/1: 0000020: Sn scrubbed along: much btr 1222.   39
9 ran   shthd,1,1,hd,1½,hd,1,1   (D J Oseman)   J Spearing Alcester, Warwicks.

1386 YEAR OF THE TIGER CLAIMING STAKES 3YO   £3042   1m 6f   Firm 16 -03 Slow

1236 WALCISIN [1] (R Hannon) 3-8-9 B Thomson 11/4: 0002201: 3 ch g Balboa - Screen Goddess
(Caliban) Landed some gd bets, leading dist and just holding on in a 3yo claimer at Sandown
July 4: first success and has been running well recently: eff 12f, stays 14f: seems suited
by fast ground tho' handles any track.   28
951 MELENDEZ [4] (G Harwood) 3-9-0 A Clark 10/1: -002: Led/dsptd lead thr'out, came
again and almost got up cl home: well clear rem: evidently well suited by 14f, may stay 2m:
acts on firm ground and seems suited by forcing tactics on a stiff track: should win in
similar company.   33
996 GOODTIME HAL [5] (J Hindley) 3-8-4 M Hills 5/2 FAV: 0-4323: Well bckd, looked
very one paced in str: disapp after 996 (2m).   13
1233 FIREPROOF [3] (D Marks) 3-9-4 P Cook 4/1: 0420144: Led/dsptd lead much: ran well: 27
1031 MR MOSS [2] 3-9-0 G Baxter 8/1: -000: Prom much: see 714.   13
-- PATRIOTIC [6] 3-7-11 B Crossley 20/1: 00-0: No threat on seasonal debut: made no
show either outing last term: related to sev winners and may improve.   00
1078 LAST POLONAISE [7] 3-8-6 W Newnes 13/2: 00-0030: Wknd into 7th: disapp after 1078.   00
-- Bumi Heights [8] 7-13
8 ran   shthd,10,shthd,8,3   (C W Rogers)   R Hannon Marlborough, Wilts

Official Going Given As GOOD ON THE ROUND COURSE : GOOD/FIRM ON STRAIGHT COURSE

1387 TRAFALGAR HOUSE SPRINT STAKES (LISTED)   £11745   5f   Good/Firm 34 +20 Fast

1306 POLYKRATIS [8] (M Francis) 4-9-0 C Rutter 25/1: 0-00031: 4 b c He Loves Me - Blue
Persian (Majority Blue) Smart colt: turned up at 25/1, fin strongly to prevail cl home in
a desperate fin to a fast run, val Listed Sprint at Sandown July 5: in '85 won a h'cap at
Nottingham: stays 7f but best around 5/6f: acts on firm and gd ground and likes galloping trk.   72
1125 TARIB [5] (H T Jones) 3-8-8 R Hills 12/1: 12-2142: Fin really strongly, just btn:
fine effort: see 758, 1125.   70
-1151 TREASURE KAY [3] (P Makin) 3-8-7 F Head 9/4 FAV: 10-1423: Kept on strongly, just btn
in a blanket fin: in fine form: see 314, 1151.   68
+1268 DUBLIN LAD [4] (M Brittain) 3-8-7 K Darley 4/1: 0000314: Almost made all but this
ultra-stiff 5f found him out at the death: see 1268.   67
1146 FAYRUZ [6] 3-8-7(vis) M L Thomas 20/1: 2-00000: Dsptd lead much: fine effort: see 600   59
1227 WOODFOLD [1] 5-8-11 W Newnes 33/1: 330-130: No threat but creditable effort: see 986.   49
587 SI SIGNOR [10] 4-9-0 P Waldron 7/1: 040-420: Abs: outpaced and needs 6f: see 245.   00
691 TUSSAC [7] 3-8-7 W Ryan 4/1: 12-1130: Abs: mkt drifter, fin last: btr than this.: see 567.   00
1146 Petrovich [9] 9-0   1263 Lonely Street [2] 8-11
10 ran   hd,hd,nk,2,1½   (M Peraticos)   M Francis Lambourn, Berks

1388 COMMONWEALTH H'CAP 3YO+ 0-60   £6212   2m   Good/Firm 34 -08 Slow   [45]

1293 MORGANS CHOICE [9] (R Hodges) 9-7-12 W Carson 9/2: 0000301: 9 ch h Reliance II -
Piave (Alcide) Grand old stayer: mid-div, hdwy 2f out and stayed on strongly to lead inside
final 1f in val h'cap at Sandown July 5: in '85 won the Chester Cup and also at Warwick:
eff 2m, stays really well: best form on firm or gd ground, unsuited by soft: game and
genuine and retains his form well.   26
1260 SUGAR PALM [4] (R Hannon) 5-8-2(bl) L Jones(5) 14/1: 0304222: Just failed to make
all, well clear rem and due a change of luck: see 341.   28
1150 REVISIT [7] (J Winter) 4-9-8 T Ives 12/1: -000343: Al well there: see 58A.   43
1048 FEDRA [10] (Lord John Fitzgerald) 3-7-13 L Riggio(7) 8/1: -122124: Al prom: best 908.   34
1348 ROYAL CRAFTSMAN [6] 5-7-7(bl) D Brown 25/1: 0030300: Late prog (as usual!):see 341.   05
1150 MILTON BURN [5] 5-9-3 F Head 7/1: 1022320: No danger: much btr 1150.   29
+1058 SARFRAZ [11] 3-9-6 G Starkey 5/2 FAV: 2-01110: Ev ch, fin 7th: best 1058.   00
1099 HIGH PLAINS [2] 4-8-13 W Newnes 11/2: 0-00000: Came to chall 2f out, fdd into 8th.   00
1035 My Charade [8] 7-11(vis)   1004 King Of Comedy [1] 9-10
1280 Assaglawi [3] 8-12
11 ran   1,4,1½,5,shthd   (A Newcombe)   R Hodges Charlton Mackrell, Somerset

1389 GROUP 1 CORAL ECLIPSE STAKES   £134460   1m 2f   Good/Firm 34 +23 Fast

-878 DANCING BRAVE [5] (G Harwood) 3-8-8 G Starkey 4/9 FAV: 11-1121: 3 b c Lyphard -
Navajo Princess (Drone) Topclass colt: readily landed the odds, showing impressive turn of
foot to draw clear from the dist and win fast run Gr 1 Eclipse Stks at Sandown July 5: easy
winner of the 2,000 Guineas at Newmarket May 3 and first time out comfortably won Craven
Stakes, again at Newmarket: ready winner of both races in '85 at Newmarket and Sandown: very
eff over 1m/10f and stays 12f: acts on soft but his fine action is well suited by firm or
good ground: a rematch with Shahrastani in the King George is a mouthwatering prospect.   98
*1352 TRIPTYCH [1] (P L Biancone) 4-9-4 E Legrix 9/1: 03-4212: Led over 2f out but had no
answer to the winner's exceptional pace: grand effort from this ultra genuine and consistent
filly: see 1352.   84
1094 TELEPROMPTER [6] (J Watts) 6-9-7(vis) T Ives 9/1: 120-233: Never closer: fine effort
but possibly at his very best over 8/9f: see 598.   84
*1010 IADES [7] (F Boutin) 4-9-7(bl) F Head 28/1: 200-414: Never nearer and ran up to
his best: see 1010.   83
878 BOLD ARRANGEMENT [8] 3-8-8 M Roberts 14/1: D-33200: No danger but a fine effort and
there was a valid excuse for his poor performance at Epsom in 878: see 5, 469.   83
1095 BEDTIME [2] 6-9-7 W Carson 7/1: 112/120: Led briefly 3f out, capable of btr than
this: see 736, 1095.   77
1109 Come On The Blues [4] 9-7   1094 Grand Harbour [3] 9-7
8 ran   4,1½,nk,shthd,4   (K Abdulla)   G Harwood Pulborough, W Sussex.

1390 VICTORIA AMATEUR TURF CLUB H'CAP 0-60   £4682   7f   Good/Firm 34 -10 Slow   [54]

*1032 PINSTRIPE [4] (R Williams) 3-8-4 T Ives 7/2: 330-011: 3 b c Pitskelly - Snoozy Time
(Cavo Doro) Useful, impr colt: scoring his 2nd C/D success (well bckd) making ev yard
comfortably in a h'cap at Sandown July 5: won a 3yo h'cap over same C/D June 13: showed
ability last season: very eff over 7f on firm or gd ground and loves Sandown.   52
1109 TELWAAH [7] (A Stewart) 4-9-7(BL) M Roberts 4/1: 010-202: Bl first time, al there.   52
1028 HYMN OF HARLECH [3] (G P Gordon) 3-8-8 W Ryan 6/1: -003223: Unable to go early pace,
kept on: see 1028.   47
481 APRIL FOOL [1] (L Cottrell) 4-8-1 M L Thomas 25/1: 3020-04: Abs: dpstd lead 3f out,
wknd: placed sev times without winning in '85, prev season successful at Windsor: stays 7f:
suited by sharpish trk and firm or gd ground.   20

1109 BUNDABURG [6] 6-8-6 T Williams 3/1 FAV: -000000: Well bckd, no threat: best 775.   20
775 SAFE CUSTODY [5] 4-8-1 R Hills 25/1: 00-0000: No form this season: see 566.   15
*881 MAAZI [2] 5-9-3 W Carson 4/1: 001-010: Prom ev ch, wknd: btr 881 (sharp trk).   00
--   Gamblers Dream [8] 7-12
8 ran   4,1,7,3,hd   (M Jaye)   R Williams Newmarket

1391 LAMONT PILS H'CAP 3YO 0-50   £3069   5f   Good/Firm 34 +06 Fast   [56]

+1227 SILENT MAJORITY [6] (W O'gorman) 3-8-4(7ex) T Ives 11/8 FAV: 0301311: 3 b g General
Assembly - Vexed Voter (Pontifex) Impr sprinter who is in fine form: winning 3rd race from
last 4 outings when comfortably scoring a pillar to post success in quite a fast run 3yo
h'cap at Sandown July 5: won similar h'caps at Kempton and Yarmouth recently: stays 6f but
ideally suited by front running tactics over 5f on firm grd: could win again.   45
1033 SAY PARDON [7] (D Morley) 3-8-8 T Williams 11/2: 3220-22: Al in vain pursuit of
winner: should find a race soon: see 1033.   41
1151 COMPLEAT [5] (G Lewis) 3-9-5 P Waldron 6/1: 31-0003: Prom, outpaced final 1f:
returning to form: see 314.   48
986 FOUNTAIN BELLS [9] (R Hannon) 3-8-10 W Carson 6/1: -201424: Best 507 (yldg).   37
1164 MUHTARIS [1] 3-7-11 R Street 10/1: 0222000: Slow start, never closer: btr 734 (C/D gd)   20
--   AFRICAN REX [3] 3-9-3 R Hills 9/1: 22011-0: Early speed and should benefit from
seasonal debut: impr at end of '85 winning last 2 on the trot, minor events at Catterick
and Folkestone: well suited by 5/6f on a sharpish trk and acts on firm and yldg.   31
857 Willbe Willbe [4] 7-7(10oh)   1191 Fancy Pages [8] 7-7(6oh)
1001 West Carrack [2] 9-7
9 ran   2½,1½,1,1½,3,2   (Bertram Firestone)   W O'gorman Newmarket

1392 EBF PADDOCK MAIDEN STAKES 2YO C&G   £3248   7f   Good/Firm 34 -32 Slow

1242 DONT FORGET ME [7] (R Hannon) 2-9-0 G Starkey 8/1: 41: 2 b c Ahonoora - African
Doll (African Sky): Useful, impr colt: well bckd when gamely winning a slowly run 2yo mdn
at Sandown July 6: battled on from 2f out and responded well to press: dam a 12f winner in
Ireland: well suited by 7f, sure to stay at least 1m: acts on firm grd and on a stiff trk.   64
1129 LUZUM [6] (H T Jones) 2-9-0 R Hills 2/1: 232: Mkt drifter: led/dsptd lead most,
just btn in a cl finish: stays 7f well: see 1129, 870.   63
--   TERTIARY ZONE [4] (P Cole) 2-9-0 P Waldron 11/8 FAV: 3: Heavily bckd debutant, pressed
leaders thr'out, narrowly btn and clear rest: evidently highly regarded by connections: stays
7f well and acts on firm grd: will have no difficulty finding a race.   61
--   TROJAN WAR [3] (W Hern) 2-9-0 W Carson 5/1: 4: Unable to trouble the principals
but should benefit from the outing: half brother to 4 winners: certain to be suited by 1m+:
acts on firm: will improve and win a maiden.   46
--   STRING SECTION [2] 2-9-0 M L Thomas 50/1: 0: Outpaced thr'out: half brother to winning
'82 juv Harp Song: should be suited by this trip and further.   21
--   BOLD WORLD [1] 2-9-0 C Rutter(5) 14/1: 0: No danger: dam showed little at 2 years but
was a smart filly who at 3 winning the Princess Royal Stks at Ascot (rated 63): sure to be
suited by middle dist in time.   20
--   Bobach Boy [5] 9-0
7 ran   ½,½,7,10,½   (Jim Horgan)   R Hannon East Everleigh, Wilts

1393 ANNIVERSARY HANDICAP 3YO+ 0-35   £2733   1m 3f   Good/Firm 34 -41 Slow   [32]

1265 EBOLITO [4] (W Hern) 3-8-9(vis) W Carson 100/30: -00421: 3 b c Welsh Pageant -
Princess Eboli (Brigadier Gerard): Set a slow pace and kept on really well final 3f for a
comfortable 4l success in a slowly run h'cap at Sandown July 5: well suited by forcing
tactics over 1m 3f: wears a visor or bl: dam was a smart staying filly who won both the
Cheshire and Lancashire Oaks.   36
1112 SILENT JOURNEY [5] (J Watts) 4-9-7 T Ives 11/2: 0-12002: Al 2nd: best 256 (yldg)   27
1035 PULSINGH [3] (C Benstead) 4-8-13 P Waldron 14/1: 0000103: Al prom: see 850: stays 12f   18
+1321 THE BETSY [2] (D Elsworth) 4-9-5(5ex) P Mcentee(7) 3/1: 0401314: Quick reappearance,
no real threat: see 1321.   22
*1233 STRAIGHT THROUGH [1] 3-9-7(5ex) R Hills 7/4 FAV: -212210: Disapp fav: btr 1233.   36
5 ran   4,nk,1½,2   (Dowager Lady Beaverbrook)   W Hern West Ilsley, Berks

Official Going Given As FIRM, BASED ON TIME GOOD/FIRM

1394 LADBROKES GIVE YOU MORE H'CAP (0-35)   £1654   1m   Good/Firm 39 -04 Slow   [34]

1091 MILEOMETER [5] (B W Hills) 3-8-9 S Cauthen 7/1: 20-0201: 3 b c Taufan -Mile By Mile
(Milesian) Got up on the outside on the post in a h'cap at Nottingham July 5: first success:
half brother to sev winners incl the useful sprinter Numismatist: has been tried over longer
dist but so far best at 1m: acts on gd/firm grd: possibly needs to be held up.   35

1196 VALRACH [2] (R Hollinshead) 4-9-1 S Perks 20/1: 00-0002: Despite slow start, led
1 out and just caught: likes Nottingham, won here last year: evidently stays 1m: see 1196.   28

1264 RAFFIA RUN [1] (J Dunlop) 3-8-1 T Quinn 3/1: -044023: Unlucky in running, certainly
stays 1m and is due a change of luck: see 1264, 538.   23

1103 KAMARESS [6] (M Brittain) 4-8-4 K Darley 14/1: 0000024: Led 2 out: see 1103.   12

807 MASHHUR [7] 3-9-2 N Howe 4/1: 301-000: Was rated 43: see 465.   35

992 SINGING BOY [12] 5-9-0 G Duffield 14/1: 10-0000: No threat: returning to form?
In '85 won at Newcastle and in '84 at Doncaster: eff at 1m and stays 10f: acts on firm and
yldg: rated 32 last year.   19

1273 EXPLETIVE [11] 6-8-2(bl) J Carter(7) 9/1: 00-0430: Slowly away: see 1273.   00

*1273 SAHARA SHADOW [14] 4-8-4(5ex) B Crossley 6/1: 00-1210: Much btr 1273.   00

1273 Sandbourne [8] 8-11	56	Jo Andrew [3] 7-8	1015 Busted Flavour [9] 9-7
1338 The Golf Slide [15] 7-9(2ow)(1oh)			380 Greenhills Girl [4] 7-10
1079 Huytons Hope [10] 7-7(BL)(6oh)			1104 Musical Shadow [16] 8-9(bl)
-- Decoy Belle [13] 8-8(5ow)			

16 ran   shthd,1½,½,nk,1   (Maktoum Al-Maktoum)   B W Hills Lambourn

1395 NOTTINGHAM EVENING POST STAKES 3YO   £1951   1m   Good/Firm 39 +08 Fast

1042 BRIGHT AS NIGHT [3] (M Ryan) 3-9-0 R Cochrane 5/1: 40-3031: 3 b c Miswaki - Libras
Shining Star (Gleaming) Brought back to 1m, led 1 out, readily in quite fast run minor race
at Nottingham July 5: prob. stays 12f but so far best around 1m on sound surface.   50

-- WAAJIB [10] (A Stewart) 3-9-0 M Roberts 6/1: 02-2: Al there: placed in a Leicester maiden
last year: good seasonal debut: stays 1m and should soon find a maiden.   48

-1087 NILAMBAR [5] (R J Houghton) 3-9-0 W R Swinburn 1/1 FAV: 02-023: Hvly bkd: led 2½ out,
better 1087 (10f): should find a maiden.   47

579 RESCUE PACKAGE [2] (G Lewis) 3-9-0 G Sexton 20/1: 4-04: Led 5f, abs since 579.   42

1269 NORTH OCEAN [1] 3-9-0 R Guest 8/1: -030: Late progress: see 1269.   40

-- WILLIE THE MOON [9] 3-9-0 M Banner 33/1: -0: Half brther to 2 winners in USA: might
need further than 1m.   35

615 MISS ARON [7] 3-8-11 K Darley 33/1: 00-000: Never in it: abs since 615.   00

*- USFAN [8] 3-9-0 T Quinn 11/4: -0: Faded 2 out: £130,000 yearling: half brother to
several winners: active in mkt: should do better.   00

8 ran   1,1½,2½,1,2½.   T P Ramsden   M Ryan Newmarket

1396 JIM GOLD CLAIMING STAKES 3YO   £1329   1m 2f   Good/Firm 39 -11 Slow

960 GIBBERISH [9] (M Prescott) 3-8-7(BL) G Duffield 6/4 FAV: 00-2041: 3 ch f Final Straw
- Linguist (Mossborough) Bl for first time, led 1 out comfortably in a Claiming race at
Nottingham July 5: eff at 8/10f and seems to act on firm and yldg.   21

1081 BLACK DIAMOND [2] (A Jarvis) 3-9-0(bl) D Nicholls 10/1: 0-03002: Made most: evidently
stays 10f and seems to act on firm and soft: see 657.   23

637 CEROC [3] (J Bethell) 3-8-12 J Reid 7/1: 0-40003: Fin well after abs: stays 10f.   15

-- COLOURFIELD [1] (K Brassey) 3-9-0(BL) N Adams 9/1: 00-4: Ev ch: stays 10f.: bl. 1st time. 16

1198 PLADDA PRINCESS [4] 3-8-6 T Quinn 14/1: -0000: Al there: stays 10f.   00

-- EXPERT WITNESS [5] 3-8-9 P Robinson 33/1: -0: No threat.   00

1087 BEAU DIRE [9] 3-9-0 R Cochrane 9/2: -001D00: Disapp since 684 (seller).   00

806 MURHAF [6] 3-9-0 W R Swinburn 7/2: -00: Wk in mkt, t.o: cost $180,000 as a yearling:
should stay at least 10f.   00

1231 MOSTANGO [7] 3-9-0(BL) P Brette(7) 25/1: 0-0000: No threat: stays 10f? : bl. 1st time.   00

9 ran   2,3,½,8,½,½.   (Capt J McDonald-Buchanan)   M Prescott, Newmarket

---

1397 GEDLING STAKES 2YO   £1867   6f   Good/Firm 39 −13 Slow

1305 FOURWALK [2] (N Macauley) 2-8-11 W Wharton 11/2: 00241: 2 br c Godswalk − Vaunt (Hill Rise) Led 1 out and held on well in a minor race at Nottingham July 5 and survived a Stewards enquiry: impr sort who seems well suited by 6f and firm ground.   **38**

985   FRENCH KING [3] (W Brooks) 2-8-11 J Bray(7) 33/1: 02: Ignored in mkt but fin strongly and just btn: might be better suited by a stiff track: stays 6f well.   **36**

800   MUGHTANIM [5] (A Stewart) 2-8-11 M Roberts 7/2: 03: Well bckd, al there: cost 62,000 gns as a yearling and is a half brother to sev winners: stays 6f.   **32**

1296 GREY TAN [4] (T Barron) 2-8-11 C Dwyer 4/5 FAV: 324: Again made most but btr 1296: worth another chance.   **28**

*1155 GREENS HERRING [1] 2-9-8 T Lucas 4/1: 0410: T.o: puzzling after 1155.   **00**

5 ran   ½,1½,1½,15   (W A Fouracres)   N Macauley Sproxton, Leics.

1398 ARNOLD HANDICAP STAKES (0-35) 3YO   £2021   6f   Good/Firm 39 +10 Fast   [36]

*1257 CASBAH GIRL [11] (R Smyly) 3-8-13(5ex) T Williams 8/1: 002-011: 3 b f Native Bazaar − Avengeress (Aggressor) Despite a penalty, easily led 1 out in quite fast run h'cap at Nottingham July 5: earlier won at Doncaster (7f): well suited by fast going equally effective over 6/7f: should win again.   **30**

1063 ALLISTERDRANSFIELD [7] (G Moore) 3-7-9(bl) N Adams 10/1: 10-0042: Bkd from 25/1: made most and hmpd by a loose horse: quite wl h'capped and should find similar race: see 1063.   **03**

*1200 BOLD SEA ROVER [1] (M H Easterby) 3-9-7 M Birch 10/1: 0303013: Prom and hmpd by loose horse: see 1200.   **28**

1164 LINAVOS [3] (W Brooks) 3-9-1 J Bray(7) 12/1: 0-01004: Bkd from 25/1: prom: see 837.   **14**

1164 BLUE HORIZON [2] 3-9-4 R Cochrane 14/1: 03-0100: Best 768 (shrp track).   **15**

1272 ALKAAYED [13] 3-9-3 A Murray 5/1: -104030: See 241, 1272.   **13**

1247 AITCHANDOUBLEYOU [6] 3-9-5 T Quinn 8/1: 01-0040: Better 1247: see 1093.   **00**

1164 SPORTING SOVEREIGN [14] 3-9-0(bl) S Cauthen 9/4 FAV: 0-04220: Much better 1164.   **00**

-1247 SOFTLY SPOKEN [4] 3-9-1 W Ryan 11/2: 00-0120: Much better 1247, 784.   **00**

1191 Athletes Week [12] 8-1   871   Winding Path [16] 8-2

1257 Choral Park [5] 8-12   564   My Derya [9] 7-11(vis)

328   Man In The Moon [8] 8-7   835   Gregorian Chant [10] 8-12

961   Double Chai [15] 9-0(bl)

16 ran   2½,hd,3,1,shhd,1½.   Henry B Hughes   R Smyly Lambourn.

1399 SHERWOOD MAIDEN STAKES 3YO   £959   5f   Good/Firm 39 +10 Fast

1171 PILLOWING [2] (C Nelson) 3-8-11 J Reid 20/1: 0400-01: 3 b f Good Times − Eloped (Jimmy Reppin) Surprise, comf. winner of quite fast run maiden race at Nottinhgam July 5, made all: tried in blinkers last year: evidently well suited by a sharpish track, front running tactics and fast ground.   **31**

835   ENIGMA [13] (B Hills) 3-8-11 M Hills 3/1: 204-02: Fin well but a little disapp: was rated 44 last year: see 835.   **26**

1191 LEFT RIGHT [12] (N Macauley) 3-8-11(bl) S P Griffiths(5) 14/1: 0-03003: Not disgraced seems to acts on firm and soft and best in blinkers: see 255.   **25**

914   BATH [8] (T Toller) 3-8-11 S Cauthen 5/1: 00-4004: Disapp since 436 (rated 38).   **13**

217   SHAYI [1] 3-9-0 M Roberts 7/2: -00: Wl bckd, slow start: should do better: cost $650,000 yearling: might need further than 5f.   **15**

760   ASTARTE [7] 3-8-11 G Duffield 14/1: 30-4000: Disapp since 205 (soft).   **09**

1277 ANGELS ARE BLUE [6] 3-8-11 R Cochrane 11/4 FAV: -0230: Again a disapp fav: see 1277, 1142: so far best at 6f.   **00**

1171 Ever So Sharp [9] 9-0   −−   Era [5] 8-11(BL)   1142 Report Em [10] 8-11

1360 Hobournes Katie [3] 8-11   961   Miss Serlby [11] 8-11

1142 Cole Bay [4] 9-0(BL)   −−   Absent Lady [14] 8-11

14 ran   1½,nk,4,nk,1,½.   Lord Tavistock   C Nelson Upper Lambourn

---

BATH   Saturday July 5th   Lefthand, Stiff Galloping Track

Official Going Given As FIRM

1400 OAKHILL SELLING STAKES 3 & 4YO   £994   1m   Good/Firm 28 +03 Fast

−−   XYLOPHONE [7] (D Marks) 4-8-4 P Cook 9/4: 20003-1: 4 b f Tap On Wood − Cecily (Prince Regent): First time out, well bckd & led 2½f out, comfortably in quite fast run 3 & 4yo seller at Bath July 5 (bought in 3,000 gns): first success: placed in maidens in '85 when trained by P Walwyn: eff at 1m, stays 10f: acts on gd/firm & yld grnd.   **21**

1303 TAKE A BREAK [6] (R Laing) 3-8-0(bl)(1ow) S Whitworth 9/1: -010002: Ev ch final 1f: gd effort: likes Bath: see 346.   **22**

1195 ANGIES VIDEO [14] (R Holder) 4-8-4 I Johnson 33/1: -00003: Mkt drifter: ran on late: first signs of form: speedily bred filly, but seems to stay 1m well: acts on gd/flrm grnd.   **07**

1040 TABACOS [8] (D Elsworth) 3-7-11 A Mcglone 2/1 FAV: 0-40044: Dropped in class: best 479.   **12**

855   SARAVANTA [10] 4-8-4 N Adams 33/1: 000-000: Late hdway: little form previously: stays 1m: acts on gd/firm grnd.   **06**

1056 EAST STREET [4] 4-8-7 D Gibson(7) 33/1: 0-00-00: Led ½way: lightly raced on the Flat.

1210 TAKE THE BISCUIT [9] 3-7-12(1ow) A Mercer 4/1: 0000020: Ran wide straight: much btr 1210.00
1264 Tinsel Rose [11] 7-9(1ow)   -- Inimeg [2] 8-7
346 Hannah Reed [13] 7-8   545 Metal Woods Rule [12] 7-9(1ow)
1273 Timewaster [1] 9-0(BL)   -- Del Boy [3] 7-11
-- Silvermere Golf [5] 8-4
14 ran   2½,3,shhd,nk,3   (D Marks)   D Marks Lambourn, Berks

1401 LEVY BOARD APP. H'CAP STAKES 0-35 3YO   £1005   1m 2f   Good/Firm 28 -21 Slow   [27]

1245 ARTISTIC CHAMPION [5] (M Pipe) 3-9-7 J Carr 5/1: 00-3001: 3 b c Mummy's Pet - Wide
Of The Mark (Gulf Pearl): Impr colt: led final 1f, comfortably in a 3yo app. h'cap at Bath
July 5: lightly raced previously: seems suited by 10f: acts on yld, runs well on gd/firm &
a gall trk.   30
1066 CENTRALSPIRES BEST [2] (W Casey) 3-9-4 G King 13/2: 0-00002: Led over 2f out: best
effort this season: stays 10f: acts on gd & firm grnnd.   20
1288 TROPICO [1] (P Haslam) 3-8-12 J Scally 3/1: 2-00423: Ev ch in str: btr 1288 (7f seller).   12
997 FIRE ROCKET [4] (P Cole) 3-9-5 M Brennan 6/4 FAV: 0-00424: No extra final 2f: btr 997 88015
1036 LYDIA EVA [8] 3-9-5 R Perham(5) 8/1: 000-00: No real threat: active in mkt today:
little form previously: stays 10f: acts on gd/firm.   13
1236 BET OLIVER [7] 3-9-2 P Mcentee 14/1: -00000: Made no show: half sister to winning
hurdlers Lawnswood Miss and Lor Moss: may do btr in that sphere.   07
1079 Aunt Etty [6] 8-9   1062 Some Guest [3] 8-1(bl)
8 ran   2,1,2,1,1½   (G Demosthenous)   M Pipe Nicholashayne, Somerset

1402 KENNETH ROBERTSON H'CAP STAKES 0-50 3YO   £3225   1m 5f   Good/Firm 28 +03 Fast   [50]

959 ZAUBARR [1] (B Hills) 3-8-7(BL) S Whitworth 4/1: 00-001: 3 b c Hawaii - My Room
(Bold Lad): Impr colt: made most of the running and forged clear for a ready 8L win in quite
fast run 3yo h'cap at Bath July 5: half brother to several winners: clearly stays 13f well:
acts on gd/firm & soft grnd: ran badly on firm last time out: suited by blinkers:should defy a penalty. 44
*1085 ALDINO [5] (A Stewart) 3-9-7(bl) P Cook 6/4 FAV: 0-00112: No ch with winner: stays 13f.   44
1023 SHIRZAD [3] (J Tree) 3-7-12 J Dunne(7) 7/2: 0-0043: Bolted before start: ev ch: very
wk in mkt here & btr 1023 (11f).   20
1314 ATIG [4] (J Bethell) 3-9-0 A Mcglone 3/1: -000034: Dsptd lead: fdd straight: btr 1314.   28
171 NOBLE HILL [2] 3-8-4 J Williams 8/1: 31-40: Long abs: fdd: see 171.   14
5 ran   8,½,5,2½   (Sheikh Mohammed)   B Hills Lambourn, Berks

1403 TYSOE STAKES 2YO   £1933   5f   Good/Firm 28 -11 SLow

-- LUCRATIF [3] (I Balding) 2-8-11 P Cook 4/11 FAV: 1: 2 b c Cure The Blues - Lucaya
(Mill Reef): Well bckd colt who made a winning debut in a 4 runner stakes at Bath July 5:
led final 1f, ridden out: cost 48,000 gns as a yearling & is related to winners abroad: eff
at 5f, will be suited by 6f plus: acts on gd/firm grnd & should rate more highly.   40
*1323 NATIONS SONG [4] (R Stubbs) 2-8-8 J H Brown(5) 9/1: 4102212: Led nearing final 1f:
not btn far and is a genuine sort: in fine form: see 1323.   35
-- ANYOW [1] (C Nelson) 2-8-11 I Johnson 9/2: 3: Broke slowly: mkt drifter today and
will impr: cost 17,000 gns as a yearling & is a half sister to useful 2yo winner True Nora
and smart Mac's Reef: should be suited by further than 5f.   29
1194 NON FICTION [2] (K Brassey) 2-8-8 S Whitworth 4/1: 34: Made much: see 1194.   21
4 ran   nk,3,2   (Mrs John A McDougald)   I Balding Kingsclere, Hants

1404 SOUTHMEAD MAIDEN CLAIMING STAKES 3YO   £1984   1m 4f   Good/Firm 28 +01 Fast

951 RELATIVELY EASY [7] (M Prescott) 3-8-3 C Nutter 11/2: -001: 3 b f Relkino - Linguistic
(Porto Bello): Impr filly: led nearing final 2f, readily drawing clear in a 3yo claiming
maiden at Bath July 5: no form in two previous outings: half sister to winning stayer Castle
Douglas and should be suited by 12f: acts on gd/firm grnd & a gall trk.   35
1022 DARK SIRONA [5] (D Arbuthnot) 3-8-8 P Wallace 7/2: 000-02: Came all too late: should
find a small staying race: see 1022.   28
1062 GUYMYSON [8] (M Pipe) 3-8-9(BL) S Whitworth 6/1: -003: Bl first time & well bckd:
ev ch straight: first signs of form: probably stays 11.5f: acts on gd/firm.   23
458 PLUM BOSSY [2] (M Usher) 3-8-3 M Wigham 12/1: -04: Made much: fdd: little form lin 2
outings, but is a half sister to several winners incl the very useful French Gent: may do btr.   00
1062 BEDROCK [9] 3-8-4 B Procter 33/1: -00: Fdd str.   00
346 JEANNE JUGAN [3] 3-7-13 S Childs(7) 33/1: -00: Well btn.   00
1256 WHAT A PARTY [4] 3-8-11(VIS) Gay Kelleway(5) 7/2: 002-000: Ev ch when fell 4f out.   00
955 LADY BISHOP [6] 3-8-8(bl) A Mcglone 5/2 FAV: 0-00300: Ev ch, b.d. 1m: see 637.   00
-- Mount Wood [1] 8-0
9 ran   8,3,15,dist,12   (Lady Macdonald-Buchanan)   M Prescott Newmarket

1405 WESTON MAIDEN AUCTION STAKES 2YO   £1180   5.5f   Good/Firm 28 -33 Slow

1059 GREY WOLF TIGER [4] (R Hannon) 2-8-6 A Mcglone 9/4: 02241: 2 gr c Rolfe - Grey Twig
(Godswalk): Gained a deserved success, making most, comfortably in a slow run5 runner maiden
auction at Bath July 5: earlier a gd 2nd to Jay Gee Ell at Epsom: eff at 5.5f, stays 6f well:
acts on firm & soft grnd.   42

BATH   Saturday July 5th   -Cont'd

1059 TEZ SHIKARI [3] (L Cottrell) 2-8-12 I Johnson 11/4 FAV: 042222: Dsptd lead, ev ch, beat
winner 1059 (C/D).   40
1305 REMAIN FREE [5] (C Williams) 2-8-3 Gay Kelleway(5) 11/4: 33: Prom, ev ch: see 1305.   28
--   CONNEMARA DAWN [1] (R Holder) 2-9-0 P Cook 9/1: 4: Never in it on debut: should be
suited by 6f plus.   27
--   SAPPHARINO [2] 2-8-5 A Mercer 14/1: 0: Al rear: sister to 1m winner Music Market.   00
5 ran   2,1,4,10   (Mrs Brian Norman)   R Hannon Marlborough, Wilts

1406 JULY HANDICAP 3YO 0-50   **£2519   5.5f   Good/Firm 28 +02 Fast**   **[47]**

1344 MISTER MARCH [5] (R Hutchinson) 3-7-11(4ow)(3oh) P Hutchinson(0) 10/1: 0-00001: 3 b c
Marching On - Jewitch (Lear Jet): Impr colt: left his previous form well behind when a ready
5L winner of a 3yo h'cap at Bath July 5: seems very eff over 5.5f on gd/firm grnd: in this
form should win again.   27
1182 WEBSTERS FEAST [2] (M Mccormack) 3-8-11 M Wigham 6/1: -000002: Made much: see 1182.   27
947 USEFUL [3] (B Hills) 3-9-7 P Cook 13/8: 020-023: Prom, ev ch: btr 947: see 507.   34
1164 BY CHANCE [4] (C Wildman) 3-8-1 A Mcglone 11/2: 0130-04: Sn prom: twice a winner at
Windsor in '85: very eff at 6f: acts on gd, likes soft grnd.   03
•1164 KHARRANA [1] 3-9-9(8ex) S Whitworth 11/8 FAV: 201-10: Last to fin: much btr 1164
(sharper trk).   22
5 ran   5,¾,4,¾   (T J Blake)   R Hutchinson Reigate, Surrey

HAYDOCK   Saturday July 5th   Lefthand Galloping Track

1407 EBF JULY MAIDEN FILLIES STAKES 2YO   **£3008   6f   Good/Firm 22 -26 Slow**

--   PENANG BEAUTY [5] (E Eldin) 2-8-11 A Mackay 14/1: 1: 2 b f Gardas Revenge - Next-
of-Kin (Great Nephew): Made a winning debut, coming from off the pace to lead final 1f,
comfortably in a rather slowly run 2yo fillies maiden at Haydock July 5: sister to winning
'84 2yo Next Witness: stays 6f well, should stay 7f: acts well on fast grnd & on a gall trk:
could improve further.   46
--   YAQUT [3] (H T Jones) 2-8-11 A Murray 7/4 FAV: 2: Uneasy fav (op.4/5): ev ch but
oupcd final 1f: cost a mammoth $2¼m and is from a gd American family: will need to impr
greatly on this to justify that hefty purchase price.   37
1132 UPSET [1] (J S Wilson) 2-8-11 G Duffield 6/1: 23: Tried to make all: see 1132.   35
1030 RED RIDING HOOD [7] (J Dunlop) 2-8-11 G Baxter 11/2: 04: Prom, ev ch: see 1030.   25
1161 KYVERDALE [4] 2-8-11 P Robinson 2/1: 20: Disapp after 1161 (5f, firm).   24
--   LA PETITE NOBLESSE [6] 2-8-11 J Reid 14/1: 0: Prom, wknd: half sister to juvenile
winners Ulpha and Lovely Chimes: bred to be speedy.   04
6 ran   3,¾,3,nk,7   (K Lim)   E Eldin Newmarket

1408 GR. 3 HARP LAGER LANCASHIRE OAKS 3YO F   £31548   1m 4f Good/Firm 22 +12 Fast

1331 PARK EXPRESS [3] (J Bolger) 3-8-11 J Reid 13/2: 13042D1: 3 br f Ahonoora - Matcher
(Match III): Very smart & tough Irish filly: reversed Ascot running with Mill On The Floss
when leading 2f out comfortably in fast run Gr.3 Lancashire Oaks at Haydock July 5: first
time out winner of a minor race at Phoenix Park and has run most consistently since then:
also won first time out in '85, at Leopardstown: eff at 1m, stays 12f really well: acts on
any going & on any trk: commendably consistent.   79
1128 MILL ON THE FLOSS [6] (H Cecil) 3-8-11 S Cauthen 8/13 FAV: 10-3122: Failed to land
the odds, making most: beat the winner in 1128.   75
1128 SANTIKI [9] (M Stoute) 3-8-11 W R Swinburn 6/1: 3-24133: Prom, ev ch, not btn far in
a close fin: see 779, 1128.   75
1128 SUE GRUNDY [5] (G Wragg) 3-8-11 P Robinson 25/1: 13-1004: Al there, kept on well
and this was a fine effort: stays 12f: see 128.   73
739 BARSHAM [4] 3-8-11 G Baxter 33/1: -00: Fine effort on only second ever outing and
is clearly going the right way: well suied by 12f & fast grnd: should have no difficulty
finding a race in an easier grade.   67
•1209 FLEETING AFFAIR [2] 3-8-11 R Cochrane 13/2: -1110: Ev ch: ran well in this btr grade. 59
--   Shtaifeh [8] 8-11   **1002 Old Domesday Book** [1] 8-11
599 Bambolona [7] 8-11
9 ran   1½,hd,¾,3,5   (Patrick H Burns)   J Bolger Ireland

1409 OLD NEWTON CUP HANDICAP 3YO+ 0-75   £16206   1m 4f Good/Firm 22 +29 Fast   **[56]**

1020 RAKAPOSHI KING [10] (H Cecil) 4-9-7 S Cauthen 9/2: 1120-31: 4 b c Bustino - Supper
Time (Shantung): Very smart colt: put up a tremendous performance under 9-7, making ev yd
at a blinding pace and striding home a 5L winner of valuable Old Newton H'cap at Haydock
July 5: enjoyed a successful season in '85 winning at Goodwood, Sandown & Leicester: has
since changed stables, originally the lead horse to the now retired Slip Anchor: a smart
front runner in his own right & is very eff over 12/14f & is suited by firm or gd going:
hard to beat in h'cap company next time and is on the fringes of Group company.   67
•1177 HIGH TENSION [2] (G P Gordon) 4-8-6(3ex) G Duffield 8/1: 44-2412: Mostly 2nd but caught
a real tartar here: gd effort: in fine form & should win again soon.   42

438

1112 RUSSIAN NOBLE [6] (M Stoute) 5-9-3 W R Swinburn 9/4 FAV: 402-223: Ev ch: does not
win very often: see 976.   51
946 GORGEOUS STRIKE [4] (C Nelson) 3-9-6 J Reid 14/1: 3-02034: Hdway from rear final 2f:
see 191: not well h'capped at present.   67
1112 ROMIOSINI [3] 4-8-12 Kim Tinkler(5) 14/1: -041100: Never closer: most consistent. 43
1112 PUBBY [1] 5-8-2 P Robinson 14/1: -112000: Waited with, no threat: best 363 (soft). 28
879 BALLYDURROW [5] 9-8-5 J Lowe 6/1: 3-01040: Waited with, no threat in 7th: much btr 879. 30
946 ANDARTIS [8] 3-9-2 T Lucas 12/1: 2-03340: Ev ch, fin 8th: see 807.   00
1068 SIMSIM [9] 3-9-4 G Baxter 7/1: 41-2320: Prom, wknd into 9th: btrr 1068.   00
-921 POSITIVE [7] 4-9-7 A Murray 9/1: 0-01D20: Prom early, fdd into last: much btr 921. 00
10 ran   5,1½,½,1½,4,1½   (Lord Howard De Walden)   H Cecil Newmarket

1410 SATZENBRAU DIAT PILS HANDICAP 3YO 0-60   £3902   2m   Good/Firm 22 -25 Slow   [49]

*996 IN DREAMS [4] (M Prescott) 3-8-11 G Duffield 4/1: 40-211: 3 b c High Line - Blissful
Evening (Blakeney): Winning 2nd race on the trot, leading final 2f under press in a 5 horse
h'cap at Haydock July 5: won a maiden at Beverley last time: lightly raced previously and
is evidently a late developing sort who is well suited by 2m & will possibly stay further:
acts well on fast grnd: could complete a hat trick.   43
1042 THREE TIMES A LADY [3] (P Kelleway) 3-9-7 S Cauthen 7/2: -00022: Made most: stays 2m:
see 551: acts on firm.   48
+1160 FRENCH FLUTTER [2] (R Sheather) 3-9-7(3ex) R Cochrane 7/2: 20-0413: Prom, ev ch: btr 1160.45
*1048 BEIJING [1] (P Cole) 3-9-1 T Quinn 4/6 FAV: 000-114: Ev ch, btr 1048 (14f).   37
1233 MR WHATS HIS NAME [5] 3-8-7(bl) W Woods(3) 33/1: 0-24400: Prom much: see 1233. 25
5 ran   4,2½,2,2   (B Haggas)   M Prescott Newmarket

1411 COCK OF THE NORTH STAKES 2YO   £8116   6f   Good/Firm 22 -52 Slow

*1252 WIGANTHORPE [1] (M W Easterby) 2-9-0 T Lucas 3/1: 0220111: 2 ch c Thatching -
Lustrine (Viceregal): Very useful, much impr colt: completed his hat trick recovering from
a slow lead final 1f in a very slowly run but valuable 4 horse minor 2yo
race at Haydock July 5: walked over at Newcastle last time and earlier readly won quite a
valuable event at Beverley: cost 18,500 gns: eff at 5f, stays 6f well: acts on soft but seems
best on firm or gd grnd: tough sort who should win more races.   66
*1003 FLOOSE [4] (P Cole) 2-9-0 T Quinn 1/2 FAV: 112: Waited with, chall winner final 1f,
just btn but clear of rest: see 1003: stays 6f.   65
1014 FLAXLEY [3] (R Hollinshead) 2-8-11 S Perks 10/1: 1343: Made most: see 781, 460. 52
*1113 STAY LOW [2] (G Blum) 2-9-0 G Duffield 11/2: 2113314: Not far off her best here. 54
4 ran   nk,4,½   (Miss S E Easterby)   M W Easterby Sheriff Hutton, Yorks

1412 WHITE DOOR APPR HCAP 3YO+ 0-50   £2683   1m 2f   Good/Firm 22 -12 Slow   [41]

1084 ALBERT HALL [5] (B Hills) 3-9-2 S Dawson 3/1: -21D221: 3 ch c Monteverdi - Hortensia
(Luthier): Gained a deserved success, coming from behind to lead final 2f, narrowly, in a
h'cap at Haydock July 5: disq. after being first past the post in a maiden at Redcar
previously: quite lightly raced in '85: eff at 1m, suited by 10/11f: probably acts on any
going & on any trk.   52
1254 ISLAND SET [4] (L Cumani) 4-9-10 S Quane(7) 11/10 FAV: 411-022: Chall final 1f, just
btn & well clear of rest: deserves a race soon: see 410.   46
1179 TAYLORMADE BOY [3] (Denys Smith) 3-8-7 R Lappin(7) 10/1: -312303: Ch 2f out: fair
effort but best 553 (9f, gd).   34
1185 GOLDEN FANCY [1] (I Vickers) 9-9-0 R Vickers(7) 9/1: 0002234: No dngr, btr 1185. 22
179 MR GARDINER [2] 4-9-0 J Bray(7) 12/1: 401-200: Made much after long abs: see 92. 18
912 DIPYN BACH [9] 4-8-12 R Brown(7) 7/1: 00-0440: Prom much: much btr 912 (C/D).   15
1274 Composer [10] 7-7(6oh)   1273 Polemistis [6] 7-7(bl)(6oh)
--   Havens Pride [7] 7-7(6oh)   1079 Teejay [11] 7-7(5oh)
10 ran   ½,5,4,2½,1   (R Sangster)   B Hills Lambourn, Berks

Official Going Given As FIRM: TIMES SLOW EXCEPT RACES 1414 AND 1415

1413 LAIR GATE SELLING STAKES 2YO   £929   7f   Firm Slow

*1137 ROYAL TREATY [8] (N Tinkler) 2-9-4 D Nicholls 9/2: 0003311 2 ch c Tower Walk -
Covenant (Good Bond): In gd form, led nearing final 2f & held on gamely in a very slowly run
2yo seller at Beverley July 5 (no bid): last time out won a similar event at Redcar: stays
7f really well: acts on firm & soft grnnd.   28

741 MADAME LAFFITTE [1] (J Etherington) 2-8-8 M Wood 11/1: 02: Ev ch final 1f: just
btn: should be suited by 1m: acts on firm grnd. good effort after absence.   17
596 PETRUS SEVENTY [10] (P Haslam) 2-8-11(VIS) G French 14/1: 003: Early ldr: al prom:
visored first time today: should stay 1m: acts on fast grnd.   18
1294 FREV OFF [5] (M H Easterby) 2-8-8(bl) M Birch 3/1: 30004: Ev ch final 2f: stays 7f:
acts on firm & yld.   10
1137 SUPER GAMBLER [7] 2-8-8 J Callaghan(7) 33/1: 00: Nearest fin & should do btr next
time: should be suited by 1m plus.   09
1100 PALACE RULER [9] 2-8-8 S Webster 8/1: 400: Nearest fin: will be suited by 1m: acts
on fast ground.   01
1279 SKERNE ROCKET [12] 2-8-8 L Charnock 2/1 FAV: 030: Fin 7th: much btr 1279 (6f). 00
1105 Hilliard [2] 8-11   186 Victoria Star [4] 8-8   1105 High Cable [13] 8-11
1076 Highland Captain [3] 8-11   1137 Miss Sherbrooke [11] 8-8(BL)
1012 Phils Pride [6] 8-11
13 ran nk,¾,2½,nk,4,hd   (Raymond Gomersall)   N Tinkler Malton, Yorks

1414 MARKSMAN LAGER HANDICAP 3YO 0-35   £2649   5f   Firm +10 Fast   [42]
*1283 FELIPE TORO [3] (M H Easterby) 3-9-4(bl)(10ex) M Birch 5/4 FAV: 00-2111: 3 b g Runnett -
Kalympia (Kalydon): Useful gelding who is in fine form: readily defied a 10lbs penalty,
making most by 4L in a fast run h'cap at Beverley July 5: winner of his two previous outings,
similar events at Doncaster & Redcar: seems equally eff over 5/6f: acts on firm & yld grnd
and on any trk: best when up with the pace.   44
1060 NO BEATING HARTS [6] (M Mccormack) 3-9-7 R Wernham 9/2: -130402: Dsptd lead, ev ch:
best 217 (6f, yld).   35
*947 GOLDEN GUILDER [7] (M W Easterby) 3-9-0(bl) M Hindley(3) 7/2: 2120313: Ev ch: btr 947. 27
760 RESTLESS RHAPSODY [2] (K Brassey) 3-8-13(bl) J Bleasdale 9/1: 34-2404: Speed 3f:
best firm time out in 246 (sharp trk).   19
1164 PENDOR DANCER [4] 3-8-3 A Shoults(5) 10/1: -002300: Never nearer: btr 6f? see 1164, 871 09
837 LIBERTON BRAE [1] 3-7-13 L Charnock 11/1: 0-44400: No show: best 545 (6f, yld): see 161 00
6 ran 4,hd,2½,hd,3   (Lt Col R Warden)   M H Easterby Great Habton, Yorks

1415 THE MILLERS MILE   £3712   1m   Firm +01 Fast
912 SIGNORE ODONE [2] (M H Easterby) 4-9-6 K Hodgson 10/1: 20-4001: 4 b g Milford -
Duchy (Rheingold): Led 1½f out, comfortably in a maiden at Beverley July 5: lightly raced in
'85: stays 1m well: acts on gd & firm grnd & on any trk: does well when fresh.   38
1184 THRESH IT OUT [9] (M Stoute) 3-8-8(BL) M Birch 4/9 FAV: 3-23032: Bl first time: no
extra final 2f: should have won this and is becoming expensive to follow: see 1184, 334. 32
1198 HOT MOMMA [6] (R Boss) 3-8-5(VIS) E Guest(0) 4/1: 2-20433: Visored first time: made
much: see 89.   14
--   PELEGRIN [8] (M Mccormack) 4-9-6 R Wernham 8/1: 00000-4: Ev ch on seasonal debut:
showed little form in '85: stays 1m: acts on firm & soft.   14
875 BELS ANGEL [5] 4-9-3 R Adams(7) 20/1: -000: No threat: half sister to several winners:
should be suited by further than 1m.   01
1142 QUITE POKEY [14] 3-8-5 S Morris 50/1: -00: Prom early: lightly raced.   00
194 Glory Time [7] 8-9(1ow)   1102 Montefiaso [3] 9-6
--   Rigton Lad [1] 9-6
9 ran 3,8,1½,4,3   (B Shaw)   M H Easterby Great Habton, Yorks

1416 SWANLAND STAKES HANDICAP 0-35   £1551   1m 4f   Firm Slow   [26]
1226 MRS CHRIS [9] (M Naughton) 4-9-4 M Miller 12/1: -040001: 4 ch f Wollow - Polonaise
(Takawalk II): Led 2f out, driven out for a narrow win in a slow run h'cap at Beverley
July 5: last won in '84 at Pontefract: stays 12f: acts on soft, likes fast grnd.   23
1056 DICK KNIGHT [1] (K Ivory) 5-8-7(VIS) A Shoults(5) 12/1: 0000002: Led before ½way
and sn clear: hdd 2f out, but battled on well: visored first time here: see 105.   11
869 RAMILIE [3] (J Etherington) 4-8-10 M Wood 12/1: 100-003: Never nearer: see 869. 12
1302 APPLE WINE [8] (D Chapman) 9-9-0 D Nicholls 4/1: 0002024: Led over 5f: not btn far. 15
1186 HARBOUR BAZAAR [11] 6-8-2(vis) J Carter(7) 12/1: -042030: Ev ch: see 967, 199. 00
1226 FOUR STAR THRUST [2] 4-9-7 D Mckeown 9/4 FAV: 0402020: Well bckd: hung under press:
btr 1226: see 419.   16
1209 HEIGHT OF SUMMER [4] 5-8-11 M Birch 11/4: 100-040: Fin 8th: see 1209.   00
1226 Jipijapa [5] 8-2   770 Shandon Bells [7] 8-7   1068 Go Flamingo [10] 8-5
10 ran hd,1,hd,2,1   (CDL 44 Foods Ltd (Mr Chris))   M Naughton Richmond Yorks

1417 EAST RIDING YEOMANRY CHALL TROPHY AMATS £1484   1m 4f   Firm Slow
1223 ARGES [3] (R Hollinshead) 5-11-6 Maxine Juster 7/1: 22-2041: 5 ch h Morston - Buss
(Busted): Led 2f out, ridden out in a slow run amateur riders race at Beverley July 5:
finally lost his maiden tag after several near misses: stays 12f really well: acts on firm
& yld grnd & a gall trk.   35
968 COUNT COLOURS [10] (S Norton) 4-11-11 Angela Norton(5) 20/1: 204-002: Led after 4f:
just btn: see 9.   38

440

1112 DUAL VENTURE [2] (J Fitzgerald) 4-11-11 Mr T Fitzgerald(5) 4/7 FAV: 42-2203: Ev ch 2f
out: clear chance on the form of 782. 36
*1159 RUSHMOOR [4] (R Peacock) 8-12-2 Carmen Peacock (5) 10/1: -400314: Sn prom: in gd form. 27
1080 AL SHAMIKH [8] 3-12-0 Franca Vittadini 4/1: 00-130: Early ldr, fdd: best first time
out in 699 (10f). 34
1102 CASSANDRAS DREAM [1] 5-11-3 Mr S Whitaker(5) 33/1: -00: Never nearer: see 1102. 02
239 Justthewayyouare [13] 10-13(bl)   1015 Bernish Lady [15] 11-3
--   Straphanger [6] 11-6   968 Sophistication [14] 11-3
--   Katy Quick [11] 11-3   --   Lucky Lena [9] 11-3   968 Elgendon [12] 11-6
--   Useful Addition [5] 11-3(BL)
14 ran ½,¾,8,2½,3   (P D Savill)   R Hollinshead Upper Longdon, Staffs

1418 WOOD LANE MAIDEN STAKES 3YO   £1294   5f   Firm Slow

516 ROPER ROW [12] (M H Easterby) 3-9-0 K Hodgson 16/1: 020-01: 3 b g Lochnager -
Miss Barnaby (Sun Prince): Led close home in a 3yo maiden at Beverley July 5: lightly raced
previously and does well when fresh: 2nd in a seller in '85: eff at 5f on gd & fast grnnd. 27
1191 MUSIC REVIEW [8] (W Jarvis) 3-9-0 N Day 5/2 FAV: 000-222: Led 1f out: in gd form. 25
1200 THE STRAY BULLETT [11] (B Mcmahon) 3-9-0(bl) A Roper(7) 14/1: 0020003: Led after 2f:
not btn far & 4L clear of rem: see 529. 24
732 FOUNDRY FLYER [6] (A Bailey) 3-8-11 P Bloomfield 15/2: -04: Prom, ev ch: impr:
suited by firm grnd. 11
1164 BLOW THE WHISTLE [7] 3-9-0(bl) M Birch 11/4: 004-030: Nearest fin: btr 1164
(made running, sharper trk). 13
997 PELLS CLOSE [3] 3-9-0 M Hindley(3) 20/1: -00000: Never nearer: yet to make the frame. 11
1051 IMPERIAL SUNRISE [2] 3-8-11 D Leadbitter(5) 5/1: -403430: Prom, fdd: much btr 1051. 00
972 Maybe Jayne [9] 8-11   14 Jimmys Secret [5] 9-0 --   Belle Of Budapest [1] 8-11
862 Arras Style [10] 8-11   241 Petencore [4] 9-0
12 ran ½,hd,4,hd,¾,½   (Hippodromo Racing)   M H Easterby Great Habton, Yorks

1419 WESTWOOD STAKES HANDICAP 0-35   £1816   2m   Firm Slow   [26]

*1140 THE CLOWN [8] (M Naughton) 5-9-11(8ex) M Miller 5/2 JT.FAV: 200-011: 5 ch g Green
Dancer - Eltisely (Grey Sovereign): Led 2f out & held on gamely in a h'cap at Beverley
July 5: last time out won a similar event at Redcar: in '85 won a h'cap on this trk: eff
at 12f: stays 2m well: acts on firm & yld grnd: useful hurdler. 30
917 QUADRILLION [2] (R Hollinshead) 7-8-9 P Hill(7) 7/1: -02: Chall final 1f & just btn:
impr form: off the trk in '85: clearly stays 2m well: acts on firm grnd. 13
1183 SOUND DIFFUSION [6] (R Whitaker) 4-9-7 K Bradshaw(5) 5/2 JT.FAV: -221003: Never nearer. 22
942 WELSH GUARD [7] (M Brittain) 4-8-0 A Proud 25/1: 0000004: Ev ch straight: maiden:
stays 2m: acts on fast grnd. 01
1183 EASY KIN [3] 4-8-8(bl) J Quinn(5) 4/1: -000100: Led after ½way: twice below form 1016. 04
1223 WALTER THE GREAT [4] 4-9-0 M Birch 11/2: -004000: Wknd straight: best 933 (sharp trk). 00
1102 Far To Go [1] 7-11   769 Lineout Lady [5] 7-12
8 ran ¾,3,shhd,5,25   (Geoffrey Greenwood)   M Naughton Richmond, Yorks

---

Official Going Given As FIRM

1420 LEVY BOARD APP.STAKES 3YO   £1127   5f   Good 49 -36 Slow

*1142 JOHN RUSSELL [2] (M Ryan) 3-8-12 S Hibble(5) 2/5 FAV: -211: 3 ch g Palm Track -
Welsh Carol (Singing Bede): Appeared to have an easy task & duly landed long odds on, leading
½way in a slowly run app. 3yo stakes at Edinburgh July 7: won a maiden at Redcar June 20:
unraced in '85: eff at 5 & 6f & acts on firm & gd grnd. 38
1051 PACKAGE PERFECTION [8] (T Fairhurst) 3-8-4 J Callaghan 7/1: -004002: Led 3f: see 891. 20
1142 MARK EDEN [4] (W Jarvis) 3-8-7 R Lappin 10/1: -0003: Al there: best effort so far:
unraced in '85: may stay beyond 5f: acts on gd grnd. 22
1142 TENASSERIM [6] (I Vickers) 3-8-7 R Vickers 12/1: -004: Prom thro'out: first signs
of form: unraced in '85: acts on gd grnd: should stay 6f. 20
1418 PETENCORE [5] 3-8-9(2ow) N Rogers 66/1: -00000: Some early speed: no worthwhile form. 14
1070 MUSICAL AID [7] 3-8-4 A Whitehall 33/1: 00-0000: Wknd ½way: appears quite moderate. 07
1142 Finlux Flair [1] 8-4   --   Fur Baby [3] 8-4
8 ran 2,nk,½,2½,½   (J R Harwood)   M Ryan Newmarket

1421 EBF OLD COURSE STAKES 2YO   £884   5f   Good 49 -19 Slow

1082 GEMINI FIRE [2] (P Felgate) 2-9-4 G Duffield 4/7 FAV: 04131: 2 br c Mansingh - Sealady (Seaepic): Impr colt: gained his 2nd win, with a pillar-to-post 4L success in a 2yo minor event at Edinburgh July 7: easy winner of a maiden at Catterick June 7: speedily bred brother to useful sprinter Singing Sailor: very eff over 5f on a sharp course & acts on firm & gd grnd: impr type who should win more sprints. 50
1175 SKY CAT [4] (J S Wilson) 2-8-11 Julie Bowker(7) 15/2: 4002: Dsptd lead much, outpcd: probably acts on firm & yld: should stay 6f. 31
1069 DANADN [3] (Ron Thompson) 2-8-11 R P Elliott 4/1: 404033: prom much: btr 1069 (C/D). 22
1069 DENSBEN [7] (Denys Smith) 2-8-11 L Charnock 33/1: 04: Early speed: prom 3f: first foal of a winning miler. 16
1298 BANTEL BOUQUET [5] 2-8-9(1ow) C Dwyer 33/1: 0000020: No threat: see 1298. 08
-- CRETISE [1] 2-8-11 B Mcgiff(7) 14/1: 0: No threat from this debutant: half brother to winning '81 2yo Little Smasher: speedily bred. 07
1069 Seabury [6] 8-11   -- Pops Wilkinson [8] 8-11
8 ran   4,3,2,2,1   (J D Abell)   P Felgate Melton Mowbray, Leics

1422 IMAGE SERVICES H'CAP 3YO+ 0-35   £1654   1m 7f   Good 49 -03 Slow   [19]

590 STONE JUG [6] (S Hall) 6-9-0 K Hodgson 11/4: 401-041: 6 ch g High Line - Windmill Hill (Hul A Hul): Came with a steady run to lead dist & comfortably drew clear in a h'cap at Edinburgh July 7: loves this trk & won here twice last season as well as at Catterick: eff 12f, stays 2m2f well: acts on any going but best form on a sharp trk with waiting tactics. 14
1071 PERFECT DOUBLE [4] (W Pearce) 5-8-11 M Hindley(3) 8/1: -004032: Al with leaders: flattered in 770? stays 2m. 04
*1271 SHARP SONG [5] (T Fairhurst) 5-9-12(7ex) J Callaghan(7) 5/2 FAV: 30-3-13: Prom, ev ch: seems to stay 15f: see 1271. 18
1302 REGAL CAPISTRANO [3] (M Prescott) 4-9-7 R P Elliott 6/1: 0-20134: Ev ch, wknd: best 783 (12f, seller). 08
1177 MOULKINS [2] 4-9-7 G Duffield 7/2: -000130: Clear ldr over 12f: twice below 1052 (more patient tactics over 12f). 02
1140 DUKE OF DOLLIS [7] 7-8-10(bl) Julie Bowker(7) 14/1: 2-00000: Struggling final ½m. 00
6 ran   4,1,5,6,30   (Miss S E Hall)   S Hall Middleham, Yorks

1423 LE GARCON D'OR H'CAP 3YO+ 0-35   £846   5f   Good 49 -43 Slow   [32]

971 TRADESMAN· [4] (J Haldane) 6-7-7(bl)(1oh) M Fry 12/1: 0000001: 6 br g Workboy - Song Of May (Sing Sing): Made all, holding on close home in a slowly run h'cap at Edinburgh July 7: in '85 won at Hamilton: very eff over 5f with forcing tactics though seems to act on any trk: acts on any going. 05
825 WESBREE BAY [1] (N Bycroft) 4-7-8(bl) L Charnock 5/1: 04-0022: Al there, just held in a driving fin: likes Edinburgh: see 145, 825. 05
*1338 HENRYS VENTURE [6] (D Chapman) 4-8-0(8ex) A Proud 11/8 FAV: 0000113: Btr 1338 (6f). 07
1101 SWINGING GOLD [2] (T Barron) 4-9-4 B Mcgiff(7) 8/1: 000-004: Prom thro'out: last won in '84 at Newcastle & Thirsk & proved inconsistent last term: very eff at 5f on a sound surface. 24
*825 PERGODA [5] 8-9-7(bl) R Vickers(7) 7/4: 0-00010: Well bckd, kept on in a close fin. 27
971 GRAND QUEEN [7] 4-7-8 S P Griffiths(5) 50/1: -0-0000: Al there: remains a maiden. 00
6 ran   ½,1½,1,½,shhd,shhd   (Mrs M H Rutherford)   J Haldane St Boswells, Roxburghshire

1424 CALA HOMES SELL.H'CAP 3YO+ 0-25   £996   7f   Good 49 -03 Slow   [19]

1344 FAIRGREEN [7] (D Chapman) 8-8-11 S P Griffiths(5) 10/1: 4004301: 8 b g Music Boy - Sunny Bloom (Forlorn River): Never hdd, holding on in a close fin to a selling h'cap at Edinburgh July 7 (bought in 1,200 gns): last won in '84 at Edinburgh & Ayr: acts on gd & heavy grnd: very eff over 5f but nowadays stays 7f well. 09
1249 O I OYSTON [3] (J Berry) 10-9-12 A Woods(7) 9/1: 0030002: Fin well: now a veteran but still capable of winning a seller: see 606. 23
-- PRINGLE [10] (T Craig) 7-8-9 E Guest(2) 25/1: 10000/3: Not clear run final 1f, only narrowly btn on first outing since Nov.'84: last won in '82 at Ayr: stays 1m: acts on gd grnd. 06
1377 TOP OTHLANE [13] (N Bycroft) 9-9-10 M Richardson 8/1: 0100-04: Quick reapp: kept on. 19
1201 TRICENCO [4] 4-9-3(bl) J Quinn(5) 8/1: 0-00000: Ev ch: see 889. 11
861 ARRAS LASS [11] 6-8-9 S Webster 33/1: 0000/00: Prom most: yet to win a race. 00
906 SWEET EIRE [16] 4-8-11(BL) M Hindley(3) 8/1: 400-000: Fin 7th: see 906. 00
1334 BANTEL BANZAI [1] 3-9-9 C Dwyer 8/1: 4010020: Fin 9th: much btr 1334 (6f). 00
997 COURT RULER [8] 3-8-11 L Charnock 5/1 FAV: 00-0000: Much btr 997. 00
1201 Nicky Dawn [14] 8-11   1334 Puncle Creak [2] 7-13   1201 Martella [6] 8-2
1120 Coplace [9] 8-5   1052 Peters Kiddle [5] 8-4   1158 Balldareen [15] 7-11
943 One For The Ditch [12] 9-0
16   ½,hd,1½,½,2,½,½   (David W Chapman)   D Chapman Stillington, Yorks

1425 HONEST TOWN MAIDEN STAKES 3YO   £547   1m   Good 49 +03 Fast

861 CERTAIN AWARD [2] (J Watts) 3-8-11 A Mercer 7/2: 01: Fulfilled the promise of her debut, leading over 1f out in a 3yo maiden at Edinburgh July 7: unraced in '85, half brother to winning 10f 3yo   Innes House & should be suited by that trip herself: acts on gd & firm grnd & should impr further.   33
516 SUPER FRESCO [1] (B Hanbury) 3-9-0 A Geran(7) 5/1: 0-002: Came from behind after long abs: stays 1m well: see 516.   33
911 NO RESTRAINT [3] (W Hastings Bass) 3-8-11(BL) R Lines(3) 5/2 FAV: -043: Came to chall dist, clear of rest: stays 1m: see 911: blinkered 1st time today.   29
1091 BILLS AHEAD [9] (G Moore) 3-9-0 R P Elliott 5/1: 0-40444: Made much: see 14.   24
1269 CLAWSON THORNS [8] 3-9-0 L Charnock 20/1: 00-0000: Led briefly 2f out: see 78.   23
-- VITAL STEP [7] 3-8-11 J Callaghan(7) 33/1: 00-0: Prom much: no show in 2 races last term: dam a fairly useful 10f h'capper, has already produced 2 winners in Stephalotus and Final Step: should impr.   17
907 LADY BRIT [4] 3-8-11 E Guest(3) 5/1: 0-00000: Prom much : twice below 674 (yld).   00
414 Annual Event [6] 9-0
8 ran   1½,¾,4,½,1½,nk   (J L Albritton)   J Watts Richmond, Yorks

1426 MELROSES TEA H'CAP 3YO 0-35   £850   1m 3f   Good 49 +02 Fast   [34]

1267 BRADBURY HALL [2] (K Stone) 3-8-2 K Darley 5/1: 0000221: 3 b c Comedy Star - Grayshott Hall (Compensation): Gained a deserved success with an all the way win in a h'cap at Edinburgh July 7: 2nd in 2 sellers previously and this was first success: acts on firm & gd grnd, probably also on soft: eff 9f, stays middle dists well: impr.   16
1055 BRITTONS MILL [1] (M Prescott) 3-8-11 G Duffield 3/1 JT FAV: 00-02: Mostly 2nd, kept on & clear of rest: lightly raced maiden who was well bckd & is on the up grade: related to winners abroad: suited by 11f, will stay further: acts on gd grnd: likely to find a small h'cap soon.   22
1303 CHERRY LUSTRE [5] (J Watts) 3-9-7(vis) A Mercer 3/1 JT FAV: -00033: Sn prom: see 1303. 24
1295 NOT A PROBLEM [3] (Denys Smith) 3-8-6 L Charnock 4/1: 0043204: Prom, ev ch: twice below 998.   03
839 AZUSA [6] 3-9-0 S Hibble(7) 14/1: 0-000: Showed signs of temperament pre-race, tended to run in snatches & does not seem an easy ride: lightly raced maiden.   10
1199 TWICKNAM GARDEN [7] 3-8-13 M Fry 13/2: 20-0000: No threat: rated 32 when 2nd in a maiden at Nottingham in '85, no worthwhile form this term.   03
829 Latrigg Lodge [4] 8-1
7 ran   1,5,4,½,6   (Michael Watterson)   K Stone Malton, Yorks

---

Official Going Given As FIRM

1427 EBF WRAGBY MAIDEN FILLIES 2YO   £1417   5f   Firm 19 -12 Slow

1407 KYVERDALE [10] (M Ryan) 2-8-11 P Robinson 4/1: 201: 2 ch f Stanford - Campitello (Hornbeam): Making quick reapp. & led nearing final 1f, driven out in a 2yo fillies maiden at Pontefract July 7: half sister to several winners: eff over 5f, ran poorly over 6f last time: acts on fast grnd.   45
1308 HOMING IN [5] (G Huffer) 2-8-11 M Miller 7/2: 042: Sn prom: just btn: on the up grade: should impr a small event: see 1308.   44
-- THAT CERTAIN SMILE [8] (R Williams) 2-8-11 R Cochrane 15/2: 3: Kept on final 1f: speedily bred filly who cost 10,500 gns: acts on fast grnd & a turning trk.   40
1194 POLLYS SONG [6] (B Hills) 2-8-11 B Thomson 9/4 FAV: 024: Led/dsptd lead: see 1194.   39
-- WILLOWBANK [1] 2-8-11 J Lowe 33/1: 0: Nearest fin: bred to stay much further than 5f and will impr: half sister to 2 winners.   33
1119 LINPAC NORTH MOOR [2] 2-8-11 Pat Eddery 8/1: 00240: Prom, fdd: see 665.   21
383 QUEEN MATILDA [3] 2-8-11 G Baxter 6/1: 00: Dsptd lead to ½way: abs since 383.   00
-- Ridgiduct [7] 8-11   -- Nightdress [4] 8-11
9 ran   nk,1½,shhd,2½,6,3   (M I George)   M Ryan Newmarket

1428 SMEATON SELLING HANDICAP 3YO 0-25   £847   1m 4f   Firm 19 -29 Slow   [23]

718 MAX CLOWN [5] (W Wharton) 3-8-3 A Mackay 11/1: 000-001: 3 b g Cawston's Clown - Maxine's Here (Copte): Led 1½f out, driven out in a slow run selling h'cap at Pontefract July 7 (bought in 1,250 gns): eff at 12f on fast grnd & a turning trk.   08
949 FAST AND FRIENDLY [2] (R Hollinshead) 3-9-5 S Perks 13/8 FAV: 0043102: Ev ch in str: 7L clear 3rd: see 767.   22
1304 FIRE LORD [3] (G Moore) 3-8-5 D Casey(4) 14/1: 00-0003: Clear ldr, fdd straight: no form previously: possibly btr over 10f: acts on fast grnd.   00
1158 PINK SENSATION [4] (G Reveley) 3-9-7 D Leadbitter(5) 16/1: 00-0004: Never nearer: no form this season: trained by D Morley in '85: acts on fast grnd.   02

517   OUR ANNIE [8] 3-8-7 T Ives 33/1: 00-0000: Abs: ev ch: little form.   00
1267 SON OF ABSALOM [1] 3-9-3 J Bleasdale 8/1: 00-0000: No form in 4 outings this season.   00
740   FOLKSWOOD [10] 3-8-9 N Connorton 10/1: 000-000: Fin 7th: abs since 740.   00
718   JULTOWN LAD [9] 3-8-3 M L Thomas 6/1: 00-2040: Al trailing: abs since 718, see 93.   00
1111 STOP THE CLOCK [7] 3-9-6 N Adams 11/2: 0-0000: There 1m. 1st time in a seller.   00
365   Solent Breeze [6] 8-8
10 ran   1,7,5,3,4   (Dr W J Heffernan)   W Wharton Melton Mowbrray, Leics

1429 LIN PAC SPRINT HANDICAP 3YO+ 0-60   £5963   6f   Firm 19 +22 Fast   [55]

1145 BOOT POLISH [10] (J Watts) 4-8-10 N Connorton 6/1 CO.FAV: 04-1001: 4 gr g Godswalk -
Flirting Countess (Ridan): Stayed on well to get up near fin in fast run h'cap at Pontefract
July 11: first time out, won a similar event at Thirsk: in '85 won h'caps at Resdcar (2)
and the previous season won at Newcastle: eff at 5f, well suited by 6f: seems to act on any
grnd & on any trk.   49
1235 AL TRUI [4] (S Mellor) 6-9-9 M Wigham 8/1: -010002: Led final 1f: just caught: fine
effort: see 846.   61
1235 GREEN RUBY [6] (G Balding) 5-9-2 J Williams 8/1: 3030-03: Al up there: not btn far:
last season won a h'cap at Pontefract: in '84 won at Yarmouth, Salisbury & Hamilton (2):
very eff at 6f, stays 7f: acts on hvy, likes fast grnd.   52
1285 HILTON BROWN [2] (P Cundell) 5-9-11 C Rutter(5) 6/1 CO.FAV: 1300224: Not btn far:
gd effort under 9-11: see 1285, 76.   60
970 IDLE TIMES [8] 4-7-12 J Lowe 33/1: -113000: Led over 1f out in close fin: gd effort.   30
*1077 KEATS [13] 4-8-4 M Birch 9/1: 32-0010: Close up 6th: in fine form: see 1077.   35
-1306 TOBERMORY BOY [9] 9-8-10 D Mckeown 6/1 CO.FAV: 2-00020: Slowly away, nearest fin:
btr 1306: see 742.   00
936 YOUNG BRUSS [3] 4-7-9 S Dawson 9/1: 4-00130: Dsptd lead early: btr 936, 830 (7f).   00
1292 VALLEY MILLS [7] 6-9-4 Pat Eddery 10/1: 0300400: No threat: best 520.   00
1145 Sailors Song [5] 9-5   1285 Reveille [14] 8-10   1026 Ra Ra Girl [1] 8-1
1338 Mary Maguire [11] 8-1   1186 Caliph [12] 8-4(bl)
14 ran   nk,¾,nk,1,¾   (G B Parkinson)   J Watts Richmond, Yorks

1430 SPINDRIFTER SPRINT STAKES 2YO   £2553   6f   Firm 19 -09 Slow

1097 MUNAASIB [6] (P Walwyn) 2-9-3 Paul Eddery 7/2: 3101: 2 ch g Dara Monarch - Nagin
(Pretense): Impr colt: made ev yd, comfortably in a 2yo stakes at Pontefract July 11: earlier
won a Windsor maiden: cost I.R. 24,000 as a yearling: eff at 6f, will stay further: acts
on firm & yld grnd & on any trk: does well with forcing tactics.   58
*1203 WENSLEYDALEWARRIOR [3] (J Moore) 2-9-3 D Casey(7) 4/1: 0320112: Sn prom: gd effort.   52
*1261 ALKADI [7] (W O'gorman) 2-9-6 M L Thomas 3/1: 1232013: Ev ch: see 1261 (5f).   50
--   ON TAP [4] (M H Easterby) 2-8-11 M Birch 12/1: 4: Kept on well & should impr on this
initial effort: half brother to 3 winners incl the once very useful h'capper Glen Kella Manx:
should be suited by further than 6f: acts on fast grnd.   40
1287 KATE IS BEST [1] 2-8-8 P Robinson 7/4 FAV: 00: Very well bckd: will be suited by
further than 6f: sister to the very useful 2yo Khaki Nartak: cost 58,000 gns as a yearling
and will do btr than this: acts on fast grnd.   37
5 ran   1½,1½,nk,nk   (Hamdan Al-Maktoum)   P Walwyn Lambourn, Berks

1431 PONTEFRACT MAIDEN MILE CHAMPIONSHIP 3YO   £2222   1m   Firm 19 +01 Fast

829 TURFAH [5] (P Walwyn) 3-9-0 Paul Eddery 11/2: 400-021: 3 b c Czaravich - Hit It Rich
(Search For Gold): Led inside final 1f, driven out in a 3yo maiden at Pontefract July 7:
lightly raced previously: eff at 1m, may stay further: acts on firm & yld grnd & on any trk.   42
1281 HAMLOUL [9] (H T Jones) 3-9-0 A Murray 7/1: 30-0022: Led 4f out: 4L clear 3rd: in
gd form: should find a h'cap: see 1281, 829.   38
941 CARD PLAYED [6] (O Douieb) 3-8-11 Pat Eddery 8/11 FAV: -23: Heavily bckd: ev ch
nearing final 1f: disapp after 941 (sharp trk).   27
1055 LAJNATA [4] (R J Houghton) 3-8-11 P Hutchinson(3) 9/1: -034: Made most to ¾way: see 1055.   22
863 PORT PLEASE [7] 3-8-11 M Birch 33/1: -400: Never nearer: twice below form 651 (yld).   16
--   SWAALEF [8] 3-8-11 R Machado 33/1: -0: Never nearer: should impr: stable companion
of Card Played: $325,000 purchase who is a half sister to several winners: will do much
btr than this.   12
--   Prairie Oyster [2] 9-0   787 Mozart [1] 9-0
--   Meritmoore [10] 9-0   -- Final Amber [3] 9-0   -- Linpac Mapleleaf [11] 8-11
11 ran   1½,4,2½,3,2   (Hamdan Al-Maktoum)   P Walwyn Lambourn, Berks

1432 HOUGHTON HANDICAP 3YO+ 0-35   £1892   1m 2f   Firm 19 -14 Slow   [19]

1254 ERROL EMERALD [3] (S Norton) 5-9-3 J Lowe 16/1: 2300-01: 5 ch m Dom Racine - Calhoun
Emerald (Irish Castle): Came from behind to lead inside final 1f in a h'cap at Pontefract
July 7: in '85 won a seller at Warwick: eff at 1m, stays 10f well: acts on firrm & yld grnd:
likes a sharpish trk.   16
976 LEVIGATUS [10] (J Toller) 4-9-6 P Robinson 9/2: 240-002: Led briefly nearing final 1f:
gd effort: lightly raced in '85, fin 2nd in a fillies maiden at Salisbury: stays 10f: acts
on gd & fast grnd.   14

816 ARROW EXPRESS [4] (R Armstrong) 3-9-7 G Baxter 7/2 FAV: 0-00203: Kept on final 1f:
stays 10f but best 514 (7f).   27
993 EARLS COURT [11] (R Francis) 10-8-13 N Carlisle 16/1: 0002-04: Prom, ev ch: first
time out in '85 won a selling h'cap at Haydock: in '83 won at Thirsk: eff at 10f, stays 13f:
acts on firm & soft & is best when up with the pace.   04
1245 GIVING IT ALL AWAY [13] 3-9-5 M L Thomas 13/2: 0-30000: Led over 3f out: see 1245 (7f). 21
1185 STRICTLY BUSINESS [7] 4-8-13 D Mckeown 11/2: -000-40: No extra final 2f: see 1185.   00
1374 SMART MART [8] 7-8-9(vis) M Birch 6/1: 0000-30: Fin 8th: see 1374.   00
827 RUSTIC TRACK [12] 6-9-1 D Leadbitter(5) 8/1: 1-32000: made no show: btr 281, 131 (1m).   00
--   Biondoni [2] 8-9   1374 Mighty Supremo [5] 9-6
1055 Breguet [9] 9-6   770 Wongalilli [6] 8-9
12 ran   2¼,½,½,1,6   (Exors of the late Ian Redford)   S Norton barnsley, Yorks

---

Official Going Given As GOOD/FIRM

1433 MAIDEN FILLIES STAKES 2YO   £1043   7f   Good/Firm 29 -47 Slow

999 SPOTTER [6] (W Hern) 2-8-11 W R Swinburn 3/1: 01: 2 b f Beldale Flutter - Quest
(Welsh Pageant): Impr filly: led over 2f out, comfortably in a slow run 2yo fillies maiden at
Wolverhampton July 7: half sister to 2yo winner Creese: eff at 7f, should be suited by 1m:
acts on gd/firm grnd: should rate more highly.   40
848 PHILGWYN [2] (R Laing) 2-8-11 S Whitworth 6/1: 02: Ch final 1f: on the upgrade:
half sister to 4 winners incl the very smart Primo Dominie: stays 7f: acts on gd/firm grnd
& should impr enough to find a small event.   35
--   SO STYLISH [9] (G Pritchard Gordon) 2-8-11 W Ryan 5/2 FAV: 3: Nicely bckd debutant:
showed signs of greenness & should do btr than this: will be suited by 1m plus: half sister
to several winners incl the very useful stayer Sir Michael: acts on gd/firm.   34
1132 BUNDUKEYA [1] (H T Jones) 2-8-11(BL) R Hills 7/2: 3404: Bl first time: not the best
of runs & not btn far in the circumstances: seems suited by 7f: acts on gd/firm & soft grnd.   34
1253 KANDAWGYI [8] 2-8-11 J Reid 11/2: 00: Prom over 4f: impr: see 1253.   22
1238 LUNDY ISLE [4] 2-8-11 M Wigham 16/1: 000: Led over 4f: bred to stay 7f & further:
acts on fast grnd.   21
353 Dungehill Star [5] 8-11   -- Meeson Jose [3] 8-11
8 ran   1½,nk,shhd,6,½   (Lord Rotherwick)   W Hern West Ilsley, Berks

1434 HOPEFUL SELLING STAKES 2YO   £772   5f   Good/Firm 29 -35 Slow

1279 NICHOLAS GEORGE [1] (R Hodges) 2-8-11 J Reid 4/1: 01: 2 b c Nicholas Bill - Taw
Court (Lear Jet): Impr colt: nicely bckd & made most, comfortably in a 2yo seller at
Wolverhampton July 7 (sold 3,500 gns): eff at 5f, will be suited by further: acts on gd/
firm ground.   25
725 SAUNDERS LASS [2] (R Holder) 2-8-8 S Dawson 4/1: 02: Led briefly over 1f out:
4L clear 3rd: should find a seller: eff at 5f on gd/firm.   16
1181 LATE PROGRESS [3] (J Berry) 2-8-8 S Morris 12/1: 0000003: Sn prom, ev ch: seems moderate 06
1323 SOUND AS A POUND [6] (M Camacho) 2-8-11(VIS) N Connorton 6/4 FAV: 00034: Visored first
time: much btr 1323   00
1181 GUNSHIP [4] 2-8-11 J Hillis(5) 6/1: 000: Prom, ev ch: see 1181.   00
--   FIT THE SCRIPT [7] 2-8-8 A Mackay 33/1: 0: No show on debut.   00
--   BY THE GLEN [8] 2-8-8 M Wigham 8/1: 0: Never showed on debut: dam a winning 2yo.   00
7 ran   2,4,7,4,2,shhd   (A G Newcombe)   R Hodges Charlton Adam, Somerset

1435 JOSEPH SUNLIGHT CUP (H'CAP)(0-50) 3YO   £2477   1m 6f   Good/Firm 29 -03 Slow   [47]

1085 LIE IN WAIT [4] (G Pritchard Gordon) 3-9-7 W Ryan 9/4: 0-1441: 3 ch c Mill Reef -
Pitiless Panther (No Mercy): Led inside final 1f, ridden out in a h'cap at Wolverhampton
July 7: first time out won a maiden at Redcar: eff at 10f, seems well suited by 14f: acts
on gd & firm grnd·& on any trk.   50
1022 DHONI [3] (W Hern) 3-9-1 B Procter 4/1: 0-402: Made most: just btn & well clear rest:
stays 14f well: should find a h'cap: acts on gd/firm & yld.   43
1048 HURRICANE HENRY [2] (M Stoute) 3-8-12 W R Swinburn 2/1 FAV: 02-0043: Eased when btn:
non stayer: see 738.   30
1159 NIMBLE NATIVE [5] (S Norton) 3-8-1(VIS) J Lowe 4/1: 0400304: Visored first time: wknd.   17
1251 QUEEN OF SWORDS [1] 3-7-7 A Culhane(7) 12/1: -004000: Prom over 10f: btr 769 (shrp trk) 00
5 ran   ¾,15,1,12   (William Du Pont III)   G Pritchard Gordon Newmarket

1436 SPRINGFIELD BREWERY H'CAP (0-50) 3YO   £2977   7f   Good/Firm 29 -13 SLow   [53]

713 GAELIC FLUTTER [1] (K Brassey) 3-9-1 S Whitworth 12/1: 200-301: 3 gr c Beldale Flutter-
Elizabeth Wales (Abernant): Impr colt: made ev yd, readily in a 3yo h'cap at Wolverhampton
July 7: first success: ran well in '85 when 2nd to Beldale Star at Kempton: very eff at 7f:
acts on gd & firm grnd: & on any trk: does well with forcing tactics.   51

–1169 SATIAPOUR [3] (R Johnson Houghton) 3-9-7(vis) W R Swinburn 7/1: -201222: Al prom: most
consistent: see 1169.   51
*1199 PELLINKO [7] (E Eldin) 3-9-7(7ex) A Mackay 7/2: 4120013: Nearest fin: btr 1199 (1m).   50
1245 SURFING [6] (J Tree) 3-8-2 M Roberts 3/1 FAV: 003-24: Kept on under press: see 1245.   30
1028 ARCTIC KEN [4] 3-8-4(1ow) J Reid 12/1: 0110340: Al there: best 540 (yld).   30
*1073 NAWADDER [10] 3-8-2 M Hills 7/1: 0-24010: Prom, ev ch: much btr 1073 (sharp trk).   26
1147 SUPER PUNK [5] 3-9-3 R Hills 8/1: 31-3000: No threat in 7th: best first time out 436.   00
1051 GLOBAL [2] 3-8-2 M Wigham 9/1: 00-0020: Fdd badly: much btr 1051 (6f, gd).   00
1046 WHOBERLEY WHEELS [8] 3-7-8 N Carlisle 10/1: -0000: Tailed off last.   00
1257 Mademoiselle Magna [9] 8-0
10 ran   2½,½,½,½,½,1½   (Timothy n Chick)   K Brassey Upper Lambourn, Berks

1437 KINGSWOOD STAKES 3YO   £1354   1m 4f   Good/Firm 29 +11 Fast

*991 KENANGA [2] (H Cecil) 3-9-3 W Ryan 5/2: -011: 3 ch f Kris - Catalpa (Reform): Over-
turned the odds on Shibil in a fast run 3yo stakes at Wolverhampton July 7: led 2f out,
comfortably: first time out won a fillies maiden at Yarmouth: half sister to Ribblesdale
winner Strigida: eff at 11f, stays 12f well: acts well on a sound surface: impr filly who
should win more races.   64
1022 SHIBIL [1] (M Stoute) 3-9-0 W R Swinburn 4/6 FAV: 3-44322: Led after 5f: 5L clear 3rd,
but lacks foot: see 1022.   57
*1061 TRAVEL MYSTERY [9] (P Walwyn) 3-9-3 N Howe 10/1: 0-13: Stiff task: in gd form: stays 12f   50
1031 TEMPTING SILVER [7] (B Hills) 3-9-0 M Hills 33/1: -004: Al there, showing impr form:
well bred colt who should continue on the up grade: stays 12f: acts on gd/firm.   42
90   ROUGH PASSAGE [8] 3-9-0 M Wigham 50/1: -00: Long abs: kept on well: gd effort from
this $13,000 yearling: seems to stay 12f: acts on gd/firm.   41
1278 ADALIYAN [11] 3-9-0 J Reid 16/1: 00-000: Held up, never nearer: see 916.   33
1259 Richards Folly [5] 8-11   --   Dime And A Dollar [6] 9-0
--   Meeson More [10] 9-0   1310 Montbergis [4] 9-0   982 Alceba [3] 8-11
11 ran   ½,5,2½,nk,4   (Lord Howard de Walden)   H Cecil Newmarket

1438 HIGHGATE H'CAP STAKES (0-35) 3YO+   £1772   5f   Good/Firm 29 +01 Fast   [34]

1077 EECEE TREE [10] (J Sutcliffe) 4-8-10(bl) M Hills 11/2: -020001: 4 ch g Young Generation-
Golden Treasure (Crepello): Made ev yd, comfortably in a h'cap at Wolverhampton July 7:
in '85 won at Newmarket (seller) & Chepstow (h'cap): very eff over 5f with forcing tactics,
though does stay further: acts on firm & soft ground: wears blinkers.   27
1171 FARMER JOCK [14] (N Macauley) 4-8-12(bl) S Whitworth 16/1: -000302: Ran on under
press: see 1066 (6f).   19
1171 ARDENT PARTNER [12] (R Holder) 3-7-13 S Dawson 50/1: 40-0003: Rank outsider: sn
prom: much impr effort: eff at 5f on gd/firm.   13
910   NAGEM [5] (L Barratt) 3-8-1 R Hills 25/1: 0000-04: Raced far side: fair effort:
eff over an easy 5f on gd/firm.   15
986   COMMANDER MEADEN [13] 3-7-12(BL)(5ow) M Roberts 12/1: 0-03040: Bl first time: nearest
fin: best 929 (6f).   11
--   DJANGO [9] 6-9-10(bl) J Reid 33/1: 04-00-0: Ran on final 1f: gd effort under 9-10:
ran only twice in '85 and has been lightly raced: last won in '83 at Doncaster: very eff
at 5f: likes fast grnd: wears blinkers.   24
1077 CAPTAINS BIDD [3] 6-7-9(bl) G Carter(1) 7/1: 00-0020: Fin 7th: btr 1077 (6f).   00
*1344 MRS SAUGA [15] 4-8-13(7ex) W R Swinburn 7/4 FAV: 00-0210: Much btr 1344 (sharp trk).   00
1182 PHILSTAR [8] 5-8-12(bl) A Mackay 5/1: 0-00030: Wknd final 1f: btr 1182 (6f).   00
*1196 FIRST EXPERIENCE [1] 4-9-2(10ex) W Ryan 6/1: 00-0010: Early speed under 10lbs penalty:
btr 1196 (C/D).   00
1077 Sing Galvo Sing [11] 7-12(5ow)(1oh)   994 Burning Arrow [4] 9-2
1070 The Chalicewell [7] 7-7(1oh)   835 Private Sue [2] 7-11
--   Bold Scuffle [6] 8-10
15 ran   3,shhd,shhd,hd,2,1,hd.   (Mrs P A Garner)   J Sutcliffe Epsom, Surrey

Official Going Given As GOOD

1439 DISCOVERY BAY SELL.H'CAP 3YO+ 0-25   £1212   1m   Firm 13 +01 Fast   [16]

845   SOLSTICE BELL [14] (R Voorspuy) 4-8-7(bl) B Thomson 33/1: 40-4001: 4 br f Record Token-
Nasty Niece (Great Nephew): Al prom & got up under strong press final 1f in a selling h'cap
at Windsor July 7 (no bid): well suited by 1m on a sharpish trk on firm ground: wears blinkers.   03
963   MISS APEX [7] (F Yardley) 4-9-4 I Johnson 14/1: 2-04302: Mkt drifter, chall final
1f, not btn far: seems to act on firm & yld & is very eff over 1m: see 673.   12
1310 EASTER RAMBLER [5] (P Butler) 4-9-6(VIS) A Dicks(7) 16/1: 0000003: Tried to make all,
clear of rem: impr effort & is suited by forcing tactics & a sharp trk: stays 1m, may prove
btr over shorter dist: wore a visor for the first time here.   14
1134 COUNTESS CARLOTTI [12] (A Jarvis) 3-8-9 D Nicholls 4/1 CO FAV: 00-024: No threat: disapp
after 1134.   09

WINDSOR   Monday July 7th   -Cont'd

1288 OCEAN LAD [10] 3-8-1 L Jones(5) 8/1: 000-000: Never closer: a maiden with little
worthwhile form to recommend.   00
1346 MY MYRA [9] 4-8-13 A Mcglone 8/1: 0430-00: Never btr: maiden who showed some ability
in plating company last term.   00
1400 TAKE A BREAK [13] 3-8-8 J Carter(7) 7/1: 0100020: Quick reapp: too soon after 1400?   00
1212 RUN FOR YOUR WIFE [2] 3-8-12 P Waldron 4/1 CO FAV: 0004-30: Much btr 1212.   00
1056 POCO LOCO [8] 4-9-2 D Gibson 9/1: 0340230: Btr 1056 (10f).   00
1013 RESPONDER [1] 4-9-7 J H Brown 4/1 CO FAV: 3000000: Fin stone last: twice below 936.   00
1364 Blue Steel [3] 8-10(bl)   963 The Moon And Back [11] 8-0(BL)
832 Windbound Lass [4] 8-9   1364 First Orbit [6] 8-5
960 Duke Of Milltimber [15] 7-12
15 ran   ¾,shhd,6,½,½   (Mrs H P Kilburn)   R Voorspuy Polegate, East Sussex

1440 EBF ENCOUNTER BAY STAKES 2YO   £2005   6f   Firm 13 +01 Fast

1282 SHINING WATER [19] (R J Houghton) 2-8-8 S Cauthen 2/1: 421: 2 b f Kalaglow - Idle
Waters (Mill Reef): Impr filly: made most & forged 4L clear in the final 1f to win quite a
fast run 2yo fillies race at Windsor July 7: well bred filly whose dam was smart & genuine
& won the Park Hill Stakes: eff over 6f but sure to be suited by much longer distances:
acts on firm grnd: the type to impr & win more races.   67
-- LITTLEFIELD [23] (I Balding) 2-8-8 Pat Eddery 13/8 FAV: 2: Dsptd lead 2f out, outpcd
final stages: fair debut from this 10,000 gns purchase: half sister to '84 12f winner
Misfire: will stay beyond 6f & should impr & find a race.   55
-- CLEAR HER STAGE [21] (J Sutcliffe) 2-8-8 T Williams 25/1: 3: Apparently unfancied,
al well there & a sound debut: bred to be suited by longer distances: acts well on firm
grnd: impr looks likely.   49
1287 CAERINETTE [17] (A Bailey) 2-8-8 P Bloomfield 16/1: 04: Kept on at the one pace:
Irish bred filly: should stay beyond 6f: acts on firm.   40
-- SPARKLING BRITT [15] 2-8-8 R Weaver 33/1: 0: Showed plenty of pace on debut: speedily
bred filly who should impr for this first effort.   38
-- COPPER CREEK [1] 2-8-8 R Cochrane 20/1: 0: Prom, ev ch: a 100,000 gns purchase who
is a half sister to '81 7f winner My Sister.   38
*1059 ROYAL RABBLE [5] 2-9-1 A Mcglone 14/1: 2042310: No threat in 7th: creditable
effort: see 1059.   44
-- SHADIYAMA [25] 2-8-8 M Giles(7) 14/1: 0: Fin 8th on debut: half sister to useful
Shadiliya and Sharika and the smart Shasavaan, all of whom were very eff around 7f/1m:
sure to impr.   37
1067 ACCUSTOMED [24] 2-8-8 W Woods(3) 12/1: 00: Easy in mkt, early speed: see 1067.   00
1030 AUNTIE CYCLONE [16] 2-8-8 D Gibson 12/1: 040: No threat: see 1030.   00
1238 Lady Silca Key [4] 8-8   -- Lindas Treat [6] 8-8
-- Sunley Selhurst [2] 8-8   1194 Avenmore Star [9] 8-8
-- Blandell Beauty [8] 8-8   927 Bloffa [3] 8-8
-- Harts Lane [11] 8-8   -- Just On Time [26] 8-8   848 Lisasham [7] 8-8
1238 Must Be Magic [18] 8-8   -- Ocean Hound [13] 8-8
1067 Peerglow [12] 8-8   -- Pink Swallow [22] 8-7   -- Whos Zoomin Who [10] 8-8
621 Wind And Wave [20] 8-8   834 Granny Takesa Trip [14] 8-8
26 ran   4,2,3,½,hd,½,hd   (R Crutchley)   R J Houghton Didcot, Oxon

1441 OVERSEAS CONTAINERS H'CAP 3YO+ 0-60   £3921   1m 3f   Firm 13 -08 Slow   [56]

*909 LOCH SEAFORTH [5] (H Cecil) 3-8-6(1ow) S Cauthen 5/4 FAV: 44-2111: 3 b c Tyrnavos -
Marypark (Charlottown): Useful, impr colt: al prom & led under press dist for a narrow
success in a h'cap at Windsor July 7: earlier won minor races at Catterick & Beverley: very
eff over 11/12f on gd or firm grnd: can impr further.   59
1038 POCHARD [6] (P Cole) 4-9-10 T Quinn 4/1: 3-31132: Made most, clear of rest &
remains in good heart: see 805.   61
1209 HEART OF STONE [4] (R Akehurst) 4-7-8 W Carson 11/2: 0-00103: Never closer: best 851:
stays 11f well.   26
1209 HOUSE HUNTER [9] (C Horgan) 5-8-10 I Salmon 11/1: 0-02004: Came from off the pace:
fair effort: see 363.   41
1188 REDDEN [7] 8-7-13 T Williams 14/1: 000-140: Best at Brighton: see 750.   22
*1124 PERISIAN KNIGHT [8] 4-8-6(2ow)(5ex) Pat Eddery 4/1: 000-010: Prom most: probably acts
on firm but is btr on soft: see 1124.   28
-- Pharoahs Treasure [3] 7-8(1ow)(5oh)   964 Kuwait Moon [1] 7-11
-- Sir Blessed [2] 7-9
9 ran   ¾,4,nk,8,1   (Sir David Wills)   H Cecil Newmarket

1442 FALMOUTH BAY STAKES 2YO   £2194   5f   Firm 13 -19 Slow

+840 BESTPLAN [6] (W O'gorman) 2-9-7 T Ives 1/3 FAV: 01111: 2 b c Try My Best - Make Plans
(Go Marching): Smart colt: long odds on but only just held on to what was once a clear lead
when winning a slowly run 2yo minor race at Windsor July 7: said by his trainer to have
needed this race, his first for over one month: earlier successful at Lingfield, Newbury &
Folkestone, beating some useful types incl Royal Ascot winners Carol's Treasure & Sizzling
Melody: half brother to   smart Sayf El Arab: speedy type who is well suited by forcing
tactics over 5f though handles firm & yld going.   60

447

WINDSOR   Monday July 7th   -Cont'd

1019 **FATHER TIME** [2] (D Thom) 2-8-11 T Quinn 50/1: 0002: Chall winner thro'out final 1f, just held & this was remarkably impr form: half brother to 3 winners, notably very smart 5/7f performer Grey Desire: should find a maiden on this evidence.   **49**
-- **MASHBUB** [1] (C Benstead) 2-8-11 P Waldron 10/1: 3: Prom & chall final 1f, not btn far & well clear of rem: fine debut: dam a minor 7f winner: sprint bred & should find a maiden soon.   **47**
1019 **ARDILES** [4] (C Horgan) 2-8-11 P Cook 20/1: 04: No ch final 2f: half brother to fair h'cappers Copper Beeches & Cannon King.   **27**
725 **MY ISABEL** [5] 2-9-0 L Jones(5) 12/1: 120: Btr 482, 725.   **18**
-- **DANDY** [3] 2-8-11 S Cauthen 8/1: 0: Al in trouble: cheaply acquired half brother to 4 winners over varying distances.   **00**
6 ran hd,¾,6,4,8   (Mrs P L Young)   W O'gorman Newmarket

1443 **KOWLOON BAY H'CAP 3YO 0-50**   £2666 5f Firm 13 +09 Fast [51]

1312 **POSSEDYNO** [1] (D Elsworth) 3-9-7 Pat Eddery 100/30: 01-31: 3 b c Posse - Chit Chat (Baldric II): Looked well h'capped & duly led 2f out, ridden out to hold on by the minimum margin in a fast run 3yo h'cap at Windsor July 7: rated 64 when comfortably beating useful Flower Bowl in a 2yo maiden at Newmarket at the end of '85: half brother to a couple of winners: eff over 5f, possibly even btr over 6f & should stay 7f: acts well on firm grnd: can win again.   **54**
*1360 **MURPHYS WHEELS** [2] (A Jarvis) 3-9-0(7ex) D Nicholls 9/2: 3-04112: Ran well under his penalty, almost getting up close home: in grand form & will be winning again shortly.   **46**
884 **CRONKS QUALITY** [6] (G Lewis) 3-9-2 J Adams(7) 33/1: 0-00003: Al there & is returning to his best: see 884.   **39**
*1391 **SILENT MAJORITY** [4] (W O'gorman) 3-8-12(10ex) T Ives 6/4 FAV: 3013114: Quick reapp, led to halfway: too soon after 1391?   **33**
-- **SOUND REASONING** [7] 3-9-1 B Thomson 16/1: 22104-0: No real threat but should benefit from seasonal debut: very consistent in '85 winning a maiden at Warwick: eff over a sharp 5f on firm & yld & runs well on a sharp trk though probably acts on any: will strip fitter next time.   **24**
1164 **HOT ORDER** [13] 3-8-2 C Rutter(5) 33/1: 0000-00: Never nearer: quite lightly rcd maiden.   **11**
*1367 **BEECHWOOD COTTAGE** [10] 3-7-8(bl)(7ex)(6oh) G Bradwell(7) 6/1: 10-0010: Late prog into 7th: btr 1367 (6f).   **00**
1272 **Monsarah** [11] 7-7(2oh)   1227 **Alice Hill** [8] 7-8(1ow)(1oh)
1191 **Persian Bazaar** [12] 7-7(3oh)   1033 **Shari Louise** [3] 8-6(1ow)
11 ran shhd,3,¾,¼,shhd   (Garo Vanian)   D Elsworth Whitsbury, Hants

1444 **LIVERPOOL BAY STAKES 3YO**   £1265 1m 2f Firm 13 -02 Slow

-- **THE TALETELLER** [13] (O Douieb) 3-9-0 Pat Eddery 7/2: -1: 3 br c Fabulous Dancer - Dellear (Roi Lear): Potentially smart colt in the making: made an impressive first race-course appearance, leading 2f out, readily in a minor 3yo race at Windsor July 7: eff over 10f, looks certain to be suited by 12f: acts on firm grnd: the type to impr & win btr races than this.   **64**
*1208 **CHINOISERIE** [21] (L Cumani) 3-9-9 R Guest 5/2 JT FAV: 2-02112: Stiff task at the weights, no ch with winner but ran a gd race: see 1208.   **63**
980 **SHAMIYDA** [7] (R J Houghton) 3-8-11 S Cauthen 14/1: 0-03: Mkt drifter but led 3f out & showed considerable impr here: stays 10f: acts on firm: should find a maiden soon.   **50**
806 **BEAU SHER** [18] (B Hanbury) 3-9-0 R Cochrane 15/2: -0204: Ev ch 2f out: twice below 402 (1m).   **49**
1043 **LIKENESS** [6] 3-8-11 W Carson 5/2 JT FAV: 033-030: Early ldr, rather btr 1043 (1m).   **43**
*1193 **RATTLE ALONG** [20] 3-9-3 Paul Eddery 20/1: 0-010: Friendless in mkt, led in the middle stages of race: see 1193.   **46**
-- **Nautica** [8] 8-11   1085 **Lady Attiva** [4] 8-11   -- **Patchoulis Pet** [23] 8-11
1212 **Haddon Lad** [19] 9-0   -- **Lhirondelle** [2] 8-11   500 **Kaasib** [16] 9-0
1256 **Avada** [1] 9-0   -- **Great Gander** [3] 9-0   980 **Lucky Lad** [15] 9-0(BL)
-- **Sea Barn** [5] 9-0   838 **Alsace** [12] 8-11   937 **Golden Azelia** [22] 8-11
-- **Mary Sunley** [9] 8-11   1031 **Misselfore** [14] 8-11   855 **Pegasus Lady** [17] 8-11
-- **Return To Tara** [24] 8-11   275 **Fastway Flyer** [10] 8-11
23 ran 5,¼,2¼,3,3   (Mrs Maria Niarchos)   O Douieb Newmarket

---

CHEPSTOW   Tuesday July 8th   Lefthand, Galloping Track

Official Going Given As FIRM

1445 **E.B.F. MAPLE STAKES 2YO**   £834 5f Firm -10 -02 Slow

804 **MICRO LOVE** [1] (H O'neill) 2-8-11 Pat Eddery 6/1: 301: 2 ch c Vaigly Great - Minne Love (Homeric): Impr colt: led final 1f, breaking the 2yo course record at Chepstow July 8: lightly raced sort who seems well suited by fast grnd, though does act on yld: very eff at 5f, probably stays 6f.   **40**
*1339 **ABSOLUTION** [3] (K Brassey) 2-9-4 S Whitworth 10/11 FAV: 3212: Made much: just btn & 4L clear 3rd: in fine form: see 1339.   **45**

448

1403 ANYOW [2] (C Nelson) 2-8-11 R Hills 3/1: 33: Prom , ev ch: see 1403.   28
--   MENDIP STAR [5] (R Holder) 2-8-11 G Duffield 11/2: 4: No show on debut: should be
suited by further than 5f.   03
1242 FIRES OUT [4] 2-8-8 A Proud 50/1: 00: Rank outsider, al rear.   00
5 ran   ¼,4,12,1   (J B Stafford)   H O'neill Coldharbour, Surrey

1446 FLEUR DE LYS MAIDEN FILLIES STAKES 3YO   £1275   7f   Firm -10 +02 Fast

1246 PETRIFY [2] (G Balding) 3-8-11 J Williams 10/1: -01: 3 b f Air Trooper - Petrary
(Petingo): Impr filly: led inside final 1f & despite swerving left was a comfortable winner
of a fillies maiden at Chepstow July 8: half sister to winning 3yo Reyah: eff at 7f, may
stay 1m: acts well on fast grnd.   43
1246 GLANGWILI [3] (H Candy) 3-8-11 C Rutter(5) 9/2 FAV: 0230-42: Led over 1f out: 3L
clear 3rd: gd effort, but beat winner in 1246.   40
1153 MIRATAINE VENTURE [5] (R Akehurst) 3-8-11 S Whitworth 11/1: 2-30003: Led over 2f
out: lightly raced this term: best 271 (1m, heavy).   32
--   EASTERN COMMAND [8] (J Dunlop) 3-8-11 G Baxter 7/1: 34-4: Mkt drifter on seasonal
debut: al there: showed promise on both outings in '85 & is a half sister to several winners:
should stay 1m: acts on gd/firm & soft grnd.   30
637 FRIVOLE [13] 3-8-11 M Lynch(5) 8/1: 000-40: Led ½way: abs since 637.   28
--   KANGAROO [10] 3-8-11(bl) A Murray 9/1: 00033-0: Never nearer on seasonal debut:
should do btr: 3rd on her final 2 outings in '85 at Wolverhampton & Redcar: stays 9f: acts
on gd/firm & soft: wears bl.   23
1228 NATIJA [14] 3-8-11 A Mcglone 11/2: 0-00: Mkt drifter: no show: btr 1228.   00
--   DOUBLE TANGO [7] 3-8-11 G Duffield 7/1: -0: Active in mkt: no threat on racecourse debut
<   00
1200 RAFFLES VIRGINIA [12] 3-8-11 Pat Eddery 11/2: 00-4020: Led over 3f: much btr 1200 (6f). 00
--   Hot Twist [4] 8-11   937 Austina [6] 8-11   1244 Baby Ravenna [9] 8-11
480 Csillag [11] 8-11   --   Herne Miss Madam [1] 8-11
14 ran   1,3,¼,¼,2,2½   (J I Morrison)   G Balding Weyhill, Hants

1447 AVON STAKES (H'CAP) (0-35) 3YO+   £1371   6f   Firm -10 -01 Slow   [29]

1319 MAIDEN BIDDER [15] (H Beasley) 4-8-6 C Rutter(5) 8/1: -021031: 4 b f Shack -
Wolveriana (Wolver Hollow): In gd form, stayed on well to lead near fin in a h'cap at
Chepstow July 8: earlier was an easy winner of a seller at Leicester: eff at 6f, stays 7f
well: well suited by fast grnd: acts on any trk.   15
1273 GALLANT HOPE [5] (L Cottrell-) 4-8-3 N Carlisle 16/1: 0-00002: Led over 1f out: just
btn: eff at 6f-1m: see 1273.   11
1272 DUBLINAIRE [13] (M Pipe) 3-9-2 S Whitworth 13/2: 0303-03: Led inside final 1f: just
btn: gd effort: seems best over 6f on gd & fast grnd.   32
*1213 LUCKY STARKIST [12] (R Holder) 4-9-3(8ex) S Dawson 10/1: 0-00314: Btn ½L in tight
fin: see 1213.   24
1367 GERSHWIN [1] 3-8-5 A Shoults(5) 8/1: 000-120: Ran on well in close fin: see 729.   19
--   CONCERT PITCH [6] 7-9-5 Paul Eddery 16/1: 44200-0: Ev ch on seasonal debut: placed
several times in '85, but last won in '84 at Chepstow, Doncaster & Cagnes: eff at 6f,
suited by further & stays 11f: acts on firm & yld grnd.   22
1319 BOOTLE JACK [9] 4-8-6 L Johnsey(5) 9/1: 200-020: Never nearer 7th: btr 1319.   00
1272 IVORY GULL [3] 3-9-10 Pat Eddery 9/2 FAV: 41-0000: Fin. 8th: below her 2yo form.   00
836 High Eagle [10] 9-2   1273 Mairs Girl [2] 7-13   1182 Pokerfayes [8] 8-8(vis)
1272 Cracon Girl [11] 8-8   1060 Dancing Sarah [16] 9-1(BL)
1264 Cygne [14] 8-4(4ow)   943 Elephant Boy [7] 7-13   727 Elmdon [4] 8-12
--   Aunt Ismay [17] 7-7
17 ran   hd,nk,shhd,1,¼,2,1   (B Sharp)   H Beasley Rockley, Wilts

1448 WELSH DERBY STAKES 3YO   £9416   1m 4f   Firm -10 -43 Slow

1098 HIGHLAND CHIEFTAIN [1] (J Dunlop) 3-8-7 G Baxter 15/8: 2114-01: 3 b c Kampala -
La Primavera (Northfields): Smart colt: led over 2f out, very comfortably in slow run Welsh
Derby Stakes at Chepstow July 8: smart & consistent 2yo, winning at Brighton & Newmarket (2):
eff at 10f, seems well suited by todays 12f: acts on firm & yld & on any trk, though likes
a gall one: genuine sort who should win more gd races.   76
*1042 AL KAAHIR [2] (H T Jones) 3-8-10 A Murray 7/1: 202-312: No ch with winner but ran well. 66
*1315 ESDALE [3] (J Tree) 3-8-7 Pat Eddery 8/13 FAV: 2-20113: Set moderate pace to ½way:
led again 4f out, but hung right & is said to prefer a righthand trk: probably stays 12f.   53
1098 PLAID [4] (P Walwyn) 3-8-7 Paul Eddery 9/1: 2-31304: Led after ½way: wknd: btr 476, 348. 39
4 ran   5,6,8   (D R Honnisett)   J Dunlop Arundel, Sussex

1449 ALVESTON MAIDEN SELLING STAKES 2YO   £573   6f   Firm -10 -52 Slow

1076 DEEP TAW [1] (R Hodges) 2-8-11 N Day 7/1: 04301: 2 br f Kala Shikari - Florence
Mary (Mandamus): Led over 1½f out, comfortably in a slow run 2yo seller at Chepstow July 8:
stays 6f well: seems well suited by fast grnd, though does act on yld: bought in today 1,450 gns. 17

CHEPSTOW   Tuesday July 8th   -Cont'd

1168 SLEEPLINE FOR BEDS [6] (R Holder) 2-9-0 G Duffield 9/4 JT.FAV: 42: Prom, ev ch: should
be suited by further than 6f: acts on fast grnd.   13
1168 ARDNACROSS [2] (J Douglas Home) 2-8-11 Pat Eddery 9/4 JT.FAV: 002423: Ch over 1f out:
btr 1168: see 831.   03
831 SAMS REFRAIN [4] (D H Jones) 2-8-11 D Williams(7) 11/2: 301D044: Made much, fdd:
abs: best 502 (yld).   00
981 DONNELLYS HOLLOW [5] 2-9-0 D Mckay 6/1: 00: Ev ch: see 981.   00
1190 PULLANDESE [7] 2-8-11 R Street 40/1: 00000: Dist 6th: seems only moderate.   00
1083 Floret [3] 8-11
7 ran   1¼,2½,2,¾,8   (A G Newcombe)   R Hodges Charlton Adam, Somerset

1450 RIVER WYE STAKES (H'CAP) (0-50) 4YO+   £2435   1m 2f Firm -10 -01 Slow   [47]

+1335 SAMHAAN [9] (B Hanbury) 4-8-7(bl)(6ex) A Geran(7) 9/2: 4103011: 4 ch c Niniski -
Mai Pussy (Realm): In fine form, defied a 6lbs penalty, led nearing final 1f, ridden out in
a h'cap at Chepstow July 8: last time out won a similar event at Carlisle: earlier won
another h'cap at Doncaster: eff at 8-10f: acts on any grnd: runs well on a gall trk: best
in bl, but seems genuine enough.   36
-1240 TALK OF GLORY [3] (L Cottrell) 5-8-5 G Baxter 7/2 FAV: -020022: Kept on well: in
gd form: see 453.   30
1109 BANK PARADE [7] (J Davies) 5-9-9 Pat Eddery 7/1: 24-4403: Hmpd slightly final 1f: see 176 46
1188 LEONIDAS [13] (D Arbuthnot) 8-8-3 R Hills 10/1: 100-004: Led almost 9f: btr effort. 22
1133 LONGSTOP [12] 4-8-1 A Mcglone 11/1: -300300: Prom, ev ch: twice below form 750.   14
1150 TARS HILL [6] 5-8-2 N Carlisle 10/1: 2-02000: Ev ch str: best 724 (C/D, gd).   12
1274 FORMIDABLE LADY [10] 4-7-7 N Adams 6/1: 00-0030: Never in it: much btr 1274 (C/D). 00
968 INFANTRY OFFICER [1] 4-9-11 G Duffield 10/1: -2000: Lost pitch 3f out: disapp since 651 00
1274 Stonebroker [11] 7-7(6oh)   -- Fleet Bay [8] 7-7(9oh)
-- Tarrakan [2] 7-9   1365 Paris Match [5] 9-0
12 ran   1½,¾,2,3,1½   (O Zawawi)   B Hanbury Newmarket

1451 FLEUR DE LYS MAIDEN FILLIES STAKES 3YO   £1270   7f   Firm -10 +02 Fast

806 TRAVEL MAGIC [12] (B Hanbury) 3-8-11 G Baxter 6/1: -01: 3 b f Henbit - Quiet Harbour
(Mill Reef): Fast impr filly: led well over 1f out, readily in a fillies maiden at Chepstow
July 8: cost 10,500 gns as a yearling & is a half sister to a winner in Ireland: eff at
7f, should be suited by 1m & further: on the up grade & will rate more highly.   42
1228 FESTIVITY [13] (D Arbuthnot) 3-8-11 D Mckay 8/1: 000-002: Made much: no ch with
winner: stays 7f: see 431.   30
955 THEREAFTER [11] (W Wightman) 3-8-11(bl) A Mcglone 33/1: 00-0003: Ch nearing final 1f:
much impr form: seems best over 7f on fast grnd.   27
-- ETTAS PET [7] (R Sheather) 3-8-11 R Hills 9/2: 00-4: Nearest fin on seasonal debut:
should do btr next time: ran only twice in '85: half sister to several winners: eff at
7f, may stay 1m: acts on fast grnd & should impr enough to win a small event.   26
528 POUSSEZ [1] 3-8-11 Paul Eddery 5/1: -40: Mkt drifter, never nearer: abs since 528
and should do btr than this: acts on firm & soft: see 528.   20
-- MOGOAR [5] 3-8-11 K Powdrill 8/1: 030-0: Never nearer on seasonal debut: on 2nd outing
in '85 fin 3rd to Hofuf in a fillies maiden at Brighton: should be suited by 1m plus: acts
on fast grrnd.   16
1246 SUMMER GARDEN [2] 3-8-11 Pat Eddery 9/4 FAV: -4030: Disapp fav: btr 1246: see 658. 00
835 MARIES VALENTINE [3] 3-8-11 G Duffield 10/1: 04-000: Prom, wknd: see 835.   00
1244 Lochmar [8] 8-11   1193 April Fox [9] 8-11   1246 Five Quarters [6] 8-11
941 Straightaway Star [4] 8-11   1277 Ruperts Daughter [10] 8-11
-- Lyns Girl [14] 8-11
14 ran   4,1½,nk,3,1½   (R A Patrick)   B Hanbury Newmarket

NEWMARKET   Tuesday July 8th   Righthand Stiff Galloping Track

Official Going Given As GOOD
1452 JO STEWART MAIDEN STAKES 2YO   £4383   7f   Firm 13 -38 Slow

1097 GLORY FOREVER [2] (S Norton) 2-9-0 J Lowe 7/2: 441: 2 gr c Forever Casting -
Fager's Glory (Mr Prospector): Very useful colt: mkt drifter but made most at a moderate
pace, regaining advantage near fin in a slowly run 2yo maiden at Newmarket July 8: close up
4th in the Coventry Stakes at Royal Ascot last time: eff over a stiff 6f, suited by 7f,
sure to stay 1m plus: acts on firm & gd grnd: regarded by his trainer as one of the two best
juveniles he has trained.   55
-- NORDAVANO [7] (M Jarvis) 2-9-0 T Ives 5/1: 2: Made a fine debut, leading 2f out till
caught near fin: attractive sort with scope whose dam is a half sister to the smart Trillion:
stays 7f & acts on firm grnd & on a stiff trk: will have no difficulty winning a maiden. 53
1289 SANTELLA SAM [10] (M Ryan) 2-9-0 P Robinson 11/2: 23: Fin really well & will be
suited by 1m: see 1289.   49
-- ROUNDLET [7] (W Hern) 2-9-0 W Carson 2/1 FAV: 4: Heavily bckd debutant, dsptd lead
2f out, no extra final 100 yds: gd debut: dam a winner twice from 4 outings as a 3yo unraced
as a juvenile: stays 7f, will be suited by 1m: acts on firm: sure to impr & win a race. 48

450

-- TRY MY BRANDY [6] 2-9-0 B Thomson 20/1: 0: Prom, ev ch: may impr though does not
have much scope.   **43**
1172 BROTHER PATRICK [8] 2-9-0 R Cochrane 20/1: 30: Ev ch: see 1172.   **39**
1289 Master Knowall [4] 9-0   985 Beryls Joke [1] 9-0
1129 Checkpoint [3] 9-0   -- Alaskan [9] 9-0
10 ran nk,2,nk,1½,1½   (Prince Ahmed Salman)   S Norton High Hoyland, Yorks

1453 FAIRVIEW HOMES STAKES 2YO   £7544   5f   Firm 13 +04 Fast

-1238 CHASING MOONBEAMS [4] (I Balding) 2-8-4 T Ives 11/4 FAV: 221: 2 ch f Final Straw -
Rainbow's End (My Swallow): Very useful filly: ridden with much more restraint than
previously & showed a fine turn of foot to quicken clear in the final 1f & readily win quite
a fast run & valuable 2yo minor race at Newmarket July 8: half sister to the very useful
Finian's Rainbow & the winning stayer Storm Cloud: very eff over 5f, sure to stay further:
acts on firm & gd grnd: seems best with waiting tactics.   **63**
1113 REGENCY FILLE [2] (R Williams) 2-8-11 R Cochrane 10/1: 122232: Met trouble in running,
kept on really well and is remarkably consistent: see 223, 655: acts on any going & seems
equally eff at 5 & 6f.   **60**
1143 SINGING STEVEN [6] (R Hannon) 2-9-0 W Carson 100/30: 221123: Prom kept on well &
never runs a bad race: see 834, 1143.   **62**
-- PAGAN RITE [1] (M Stoute) 2-8-7 W R Swinburn 100/30: 4: Well regarded debutant who
was wk in mkt but led briefly dist: sure to impr for this quite gentle introduction to
racing: speedily bred half brother to useful performers Breadcrumb & Pagan Of Troy: eff 5f,
sure to stay 6f & probably further: acts on firm grnd: certain to impr & win races.   **55**
-1311 MISK [5] 2-8-7 S Cauthen 7/2: 220: Led briefly over 1f out, one paced final 100yds:
btr 1311 (sharp trk).   **55**
513 PARIS GUEST [3] 2-9-0 J Reid 50/1: 0100: Long abs, early ldr: see 404.   **40**
6 ran 2½,nk,hd,nk,8   (Lord Porchester)   I Balding Kingsclere, Berks

1454 GR 3 CHERRY HINTON STAKES 2YO FILLIES   £25776   6f   Firm 13 +07 Fast

*1108 FOREST FLOWER [1] (I Balding) 2-9-0 T Ives 4/5 FAV: 111: 2 ch f Green Forest -
Leap Lively (Nijinsky): High class filly: al well there & responded to press to lead close
home in fast run Gr.3 Cherry Hinton Stakes at Newmarket July 8: has now won all 3 of her
races, previously scoring in a minor race at Newbury & impressively in the Queen Mary Stakes
at Royal Ascot: well bred filly whose dam won the Lingfield Oaks Trial: eff 5/6f, should
stay further: acts on firm & gd going & on a stiff gall trk: only pony-sized but undoubtedly
the smartest 2yo seen so far and will take a really good one to lower her colours.   **85**
+1129 MINSTRELLA [8] (C Nelson) 2-8-12 J Reid 7/2: 4212: Swept into the lead dist, caught
near fin but a long way clear of the rest and she is indeed a smart performer who is sure
to win more good races: see 1129.   **81**
+1238 BLUE TANGO [2] (R Laing) 2-8-9 W Carson 12/1: 2433213: Prom & ran up to her best
though that was no match for the 2 high class performers ahead of her: stays 6f well:
admirably consistent: see 1238.   **58**
1108 ABUZZ [5] (C Brittain) 2-8-12 M Roberts 33/1: 11104: Led over 3f: seems to stay 6f
but may prove best at 5f: see 924.   **60**
1287 CANDLE IN THE WIND [7] 2-8-9 W Newnes 50/1: 040: No real threat but ran well in this
very good company: see 1287.   **53**
1108 DAZY [3] 2-8-9 P Cook 16/1: 230: Much closer to the winners in 1108 & can do btr.   **50**
1129 MY IMAGINATION [9] 2-8-9 W R Swinburn 50/1: 11000: Prom most, ddhtd for 7th: best
on soft in 320.   **50**
1180 SURELY GREAT [4] 2-8-9 M L Thomas 100/1: 020240: No threat, ddhtd forr 7th but,
at face value, impr form: see 1025.   **50**
1411 STAY LOW [10] 2-9-0 R Cochrane 50/1: 1133140: Quick reapp: fin 9th: needs a rest?   **50**
*1287 TWYLA [6] 2-8-12 S Cauthen 9/2: 110: Sn struggling & much btr 1287 (C/D).   **00**
10 ran ¾,7,½,1½,1½,shhd,ddht,shhd   (Paul Mellon)   I Balding Kingsclere, Berks

1455 LADBROKE BUNBURY CUP HCAP 3YO+ 0-75   £12388   7f   Firm 13 +06 Fast   [67]

+1109 PATRIACH [4] (J Dunlop) 4-9-1 T Quinn 6/1 FAV: 11-2011: 4 b c London Bells - Julip
(Track Spare): Smart, impr colt: winning his 2nd valuable h'cap on the trot when readily
leading final 2f in quite fast run Bunbury Cup at Newmarket July 8: won the Royal Hunt Cup
last time and in '85 won at Leicester & Lingfield: very eff over 7f/1m: acts on firm & soft
though probably best on the former: suited by a stiff trk: continues to impr & could well
win a Gr.3 event before the end of the season.   **71**
1286 FLEET FORM [5] (C Nelson) 3-8-12 J Reid 12/1: 1221002: Prom, 2nd from 2f out and
turned in another remarkably consistent effort: deserves another gd h'cap: see 586.   **71**
1007 HABER [6] (B Hills) 3-8-3 B Thomson 10/1: -23143: Kept on well: gd effort from this
still impr colt: see 667.   **60**
1047 VIRGIN ISLE [10] (P Haslam) 5-7-9 T Williams 11/1: 2000404: Al well there: gd eff: see 79.   **41**
1109 QUALITAIR FLYER [8] 4-8-10(bl) T Ives 20/1: 0000000: Kept on strongly: best effort
since 433: see 330.   **55**
1109 TREMBLANT [13] 5-9-10 R Cochrane 15/2: 11-2000: Last year's winner, ev ch: see 5.   **64**
1145 HO MI CHINH [16] 4-9-1 M Roberts 14/1: 00-1100: Fin a close up 7th, gd effort & is
btr over 6f: see 687.   **54**

1292 KNIGHTS SECRET [7] 5-7-10 J Lowe 9/1: -211340: Fin 8th: see 815.   33
1109 OCTOBER [2] 4-8-7 W Carson 7/1: 0-00400: Led to ½way, fin 9th: twice below 775 (C/D).   35
*747 VERDANT BOY [11] 3-9-0 W R Swinburn 8/1: 03-310: No threat, btr 747 (sharp trk).   00
1145 Young Inca [3] 8-9   1026 Northern Chimes [15] 8-10
 930 De Rigueur [1] 8-7   1235 Steady Eddie [14] 8-0 1202 Easy Day [9] 7-10
+1292 Postorage [12] 9-7(8ex)
 16 ran   2,¾,nk,nk,2½,¾,2   (Peter S Winfield)   J Dunlop Arundel, Sussex

1456 GROUP 2 PRINCESS OF WALES STAKES 3YO+   £28221   1m 4f Firm 13 +08 Fast

 885 SHARDARI [1] (M Stoute) 4-9-0 W R Swinburn 5/2: D11-241: 4 b c Top Ville - Sharmada
(Zeddaan) Top class colt: returned to his best leading dist & forging clear in the final 1f
to win Gr.2 Princess Of Wales's Stakes at Newmarket July 8: showed tremendous impr towards
the end of '85 winning Pattern races at Ascot & Newbury & minor events at Folkestone &
Sandown: also first past the post in the Great Voltigeur at York but subs. disq: very eff
over 12/13f though acts on any going & on any trk: genuine & consistent & looks sure to land
more decent races.   90
1352 BABY TURK [2] (A De Royer Dupre) 4-9-0 S Cauthen 8/1: 100432: French challenger,
ch dist: tremendous effort & is clearly eff on any going: see 299.   83
 885 PETOSKI [3] (W Hern) 4-9-5 W Carson 1/1 FAV: 2011-33: Prom, led 2f out, no extra:
rated 97 in '85: see 885.   87
1127 SEISMIC WAVE [4] (B Hills) 4-9-0 B Thomson 16/1: 0322204: No threat: see 1127.   77
*1068 TANAOS [6] 3-8-0 W Ryan 7/1: 314-10: Chall ½m out, wknd: see 1068.   73
1112 VOUCHSAFE [5] 4-9-0 B Procter 100/1: 0-041D0: Pace maker for Petoski, led over 1m.   53
 6 ran   3,1½,5,4,12   (H H Aga Khan)   M Stoute Newmarket

1457 HAMILTON HANDICAP 3YO 0-70   £5608   6f Firm 13 +13 Fast   [70]

*1312 CHUMMYS PET [5] (N Callaghan) 3-7-13(7ex) W Carson 5/2: 1331211: 3 b g Song - Hodsock
Venture (Major Portion): Very useful, much impr gelding: successfully coped with a raise in
class, leading final 1f narrowly in a fast run h'cap at Newmarket July 8: earlier won a
similar fast run h'cap at Windsor & claimers at Epsom & Carlisle: placed almost all other
starts: unrcd at 2y: eff over a stiff 5f, stays 7f: acts on firm & yld & on any trk: genuine
& consistent & looks likely to complete the hat trick.   55
1263 BERTIE WOOSTER [7] (L Piggott) 3-7-10(BL) B Crossley 16/1: 0310002: Bl first time,
led briefly final 1f & just btn: clear of rem & should gain compensation next time: acts on
firm & yld: see 496.   51
+1151 ORIENT [2] (R Whitaker) 3-9-6(7ex) D Mckeown 11/8 FAV: 40-1113: Led ½way, no extra
final 100 yds. has risen considerably in the weights & is possibly btr over an easier 6f,
ideally suited by a stiff 5f: see 1151.   65
1145 SHARPETTO [1] (M Albina) 3-8-9 A Bond 9/1: -001104: Again seemed unsuited by firm
grnd & best on good grd.   49
1065 MUDISHA [4] 3-7-10 G Carter(3) 10/1: 30-0040: Speed much: see 1065 (7f).   35
1347 MYRAS SPECIAL [6] 3-8-5 M Hills 20/1: 1010-00: Led 3f: see 1347.   42
 808 LUNA BID [3] 3-9-7 R Cochrane 9/1: 0-02400: Fin 7th: btr 808 (C/D).   00
 387 OCEAN TRADER [8] 3-8-8(bl) P Waldron 20/1: 122-000: Early speed after long abs: ran
well at the end of '85 winning twice at Folkestone: best form over 5/6f & possibly does not
stay 7f: acts on firm & gd & has shown his best form in bl.   00
 8 ran   hd,4,2,hd,1   (C Gaventa)   N Callaghan Newmarket

Official Going Given As FIRM (FIRST RACE GOOD/FIRRM)

1458 WOODINGDEAN MAIDEN STAKES 2YO   £959   7f Firm 18 -19 Slow

1232 ANGARA ABYSS [5] (G Harwood) 2-9-0 G Starkey 4/9 FAV: 41: 2 b c Far North - For
Missy (Forli) Promising, improving colt: made ev yard, very easily, in a 2yo mdn at Brighton
July 9: cost $52,000 as yearling and is a half brother to 2 winners in the USA: eff at 7f,
should be suited by 1m+: acts well on fast ground & an undulating trk: should win more
races and rate more highly.   53
1345 AKII BUA [3] (R Sheather) 2-9-0 M Rimmer 5/1: 202: No chance with winner, but seems
a consistent sort: see 1345, 206.   35
 834 BATTLE HEIGHTS [7] (K Brassey) 2-9-0 S Dawson 11/1: 03: Ev ch str: on the upgrade:
cost 20,000 as a yearling: eff 7f, bred to stay 1m: acts on fast grd and a sharpish
undulating track.   30
1313 DIVINE CHARGER [1] (G Lewis) 2-9-0 P Waldron 16/1: 0004: Fdd over 1f out: best
effort yet: acts on fast grd and should continue to improve.   25
 662 COMBINED EXERCISE [2] 2-9-0 B Crossley 14/1: 00: No show: abs since 662.   13
 -- TA WARDLE [8] 2-9-0 R Mcghin 50/1: 0: No show on debut: may improve.   01
1262 Ribo Be Good [4] 8-11
 7 ran   5,2,2,5,5   (Paul H Locke)   G Harwood Pulborough, Sussex

1459 KINGSTON SELLING H'CAP (0-25)   £918   1m 4f Firm 18 -22 Slow   [21]

1056 PURPLE [6] (F Jordan) 5-8-9 B Crossley 7/1: 032/001: 5 b g Anax - Plush (Lombard)
Led 3f out, drawing clear under press in a slow run selling h'cap at Brighton July 9 (bought
in 1,750 gns): stays 12f: acts on fast ground and seems to like a sharpish trk.   09
1321 DOUBLE OPTION [13] (J Davies) 5-9-10 M Wigham 6/1: -20-042: Led over ½m out: see 1321   19
1369 AUSSIE GIRL [7] (A Bailey) 3-8-5 P Bloomfield 15/2: -000033: Ev ch in str: stays
12f: see 1369.   14
1079 CELTIC IMAGE [15] (A Pitt) 4-8-6 T Williams 9/2: 042-004: Al there: stays 12f: see 967.   00
1265 MR CARACTACUS [10] 5-8-7 G Carter(3) 7/1: 0044-00: Never nearer: see 1265.   00
1056 SHALLAAL [8] 7-8-7 M Rimmer 33/1: 300/000: No threat: lightly raced this term:
last won in '83 at Folkestone: prob stays 12f: acts on fast ground.   00
1260 HOT BETTY [5] 6-8-7 A Proud 7/1: 0000040: Fin 7th: see 28.   00
1364 THE UTE [1] 3-8-1(bl) R Street 7/2 FAV: 0202320: Not stay 12f: see 1364.   00
1056 Top Gold [14] 8-8   1310 Pandi Club [9] 8-10(bl)
1310 Trikkala Star [3] 8-6(bl)   1056 Hive Off [12] 9-3
-- Brigadier Hawk [11] 8-7
13 ran   3,shthd,2½,1½,hd   (Peter Kenyon)   F Jordan Risbury, Hereford.

1460 JOE BLANKS MEM CHAL CUP HCAP (0-60)   £2914   1m   Firm 18 +01 Fast   [57]

1249 PALAESTRA [6] (J Dunlop) 3-8-10 W Carson 15/8 FAV: 12-0021: 3 b c Bellypha -
Hippodrome (Drone) Useful colt: stayed on well to lead cl home in a h'cap at Brighton July 9:
unlucky 2nd at Newcastle last time out: in '85 made all in a mdn at Redcar: eff 7/8f,
should stay further: likes fast ground but acts on any track.   63
1109 JOYFUL DANCER [5] (W Brooks) 6-8-2 T Quinn 20/1: 400-002: Made almost all: best
effort for a long time: formerly trained by P Cole and first time out last season fin 2nd
in the Lincoln at Doncaster: in '84 won at Sandown and Newbury: acts on soft, likes fast grd:
very eff over 1m when forcing the pace: nicely h'capped on his best form.   41
1240 CASCABEL [4] (R Williams) 5-8-4 Pat Eddery 5/1: 012-043: Not much room over 1f out
and would have finished closer: may be winning soon: see 521.   39
1346 FAST SERVICE [2] (C Horgan) 7-7-11 T Williams 5/2: -000024: Never nearer: btr 1346.   29
1365 PORTOGON [1] 8-8-9 D Mckay 7/1: -000030: Prom, wknd: btr 1365 (made running).   39
1365 ASSWAN [3] 6-9-7 W Newnes 5/1: 121-020: Well below form 1365 (C/D)   45
6 ran   nk,3,½,½,4   (Sheikh Mohammed)   J Dunlop Arundel, Sussex

1461 PRESTON PARK H'CAP (0-50)   £2870   6f   Firm 18 +03 Fast   [45]

1347 FERRYMAN [3] (D Elsworth) 10-10-0(10ex) Pat Eddery 7/2: 0000121: 10 b g Forlorn River
La Miranda (Miralgo) Grand old sprinter who is in fine form: made ev yard, holding on gamely
in a h'cap at Brighton July 9, defying a 10lbs penalty: earlier won a h'cap at Lingfield:
in '84 won at York and Brighton: very eff at 6f: likes an undulating trk: acts on any ground
and retains his form, despite his advancing years: genuine.   52
*1272 YOUNG JASON [1] (G Lewis) 3-8-11(7ex) P Waldron 10/11 FAV: 11-0012: Chance final 1f:
just btn: in fine form: see 1272.   43
1235 SUDDEN IMPACT [5] (K Brassey) 4-9-0(bl) S Whitworth 9/2: 0-10043: Al prom: not btn
far in close fin: acts on firm and soft ground and seems well suited by 6f: see 65.   36
1367 ROMAN RULER [2] (J Spearing) 7-8-10(bl) W Carson 9/1: 000-004: Eased when btn:see 1367   18
881 VORVADOS [4] 9-9-7 P Sargent(7) 14/1: 4000000: Sn outpaced: best 18 (soft)   24
5 ran   hd,hd,6,1½   (W R Plummer)   D Elsworth Fordingbridge, Hants

1462 PEVENSEY E B F STAKES 3YO   £2473   1m 2f Firm 18 -48 Slow

1208 SULTAN MOHAMED [2] (J Dunlop) 3-9-5 W Carson 1/1 FAV: 242-121: 3 ch c Northfields -
Paper Sun (Match III) Useful colt: well bckd and led 2f out, comfortably, in a slow run
4 runner stks at Brighton July 9: first time out won a competitive mdn at Epsom: in between
fin 2nd here to the much improved Chinoiserie: stays 10f well, should get 12f: acts on firm
and yielding ground and on any track: should win more races.   62
1130 SAMANPOUR [1] (R J Houghton) 3-9-5 Pat Eddery 9/4: -111302: Chance inside final 2f:
not pace of winner: consistent: see 1130, 547.   54
1147 LANDSKI [3] (R Simpson) 3-9-0 S Whitworth 5/1: -401303: Led 1m: twice below form 1064
and seems flattered in that race: see 765.   47
264 LIGHT BEE [4] (H T Jones) 3-9-2 A Murray 13/2: 2103-04: Long abs and al last:
promising 2yo, winning at Redcar and Yarmouth, but has shown little in 2 outings this season:
stays 7f well: acts on firm and soft.   39
4 ran   3,1,5   (Dana Stud Ltd)   J Dunlop Arundel, Sussex

1463 HYDRO DYNAMIC PRODUCTS STKS 3YO   £1850   6f   Firm 18 +07 Fast

+994 IN FACT [3] (J Tree) 3-9-10 Pat Eddery 1/1 FAV: 22-11: 3 b c Known Fact - Abeer
(Dewan) Very useful colt: led after 2f and just lasted home in a fast run 3yo stks at
Brighton July 9: first time out won at Beverley: 2nd on both starts in '85 in good company:
half brother to 12f winner Armourer, but only just gets 6f himself at present: well suited
by fast ground: acts on any track.   64
+1036 MAWSUFF [4] (H T Jones) 3-9-10 A Murray 11/10: -0212: Responded well to press final
1f and would have got up in another few strides: needs 7f? In fine form: see 1036.   63

657 PORTHMEOR [2] (M Bolton) 3-9-0 W Newnes 10/1: 4-42403: No chance with first 2:see 496. **39**
--   TOOTSIE ROLL [1] (J Payne) 3-8-11 P Darcy 100/1: -4: Impossible task on debut. **00**
1316 BALIVIEW [5] A Proud 100/1: 0000000: Early leader, wknd. **00**
5 ran   nk,5,12,2¼   (K Abdulla)   J Tree Beckhampton, Wilts.

NEWMARKET   Wednesday July 9th   Righthand, Stiff Galloping Track

Official Going Given As GOOD

1464 CECIL BOYD ROCHFORT 2YO MAIDEN FILLIES   £4597   6f   Firm 10 +04 Fast

--   CANADIAN MILL [11] (W Hern) 2-8-11 W Carson 6/1: 1: 2 br g Mill Reef - Par Excellance
(L'Enjoleur) Very promising filly: first time out, well bckd and led dist, keeping on
strongly to win quite a fast run and val 2yo fillies mdn at Newmarket July 9: half sister to
very useful '84 2yo Khozaam: eff 6f, will stay further: acts well on firm grd and on a stiff
galloping track: lightly to rate more highly and win more races. **64**
--   HIAAM [10] (M Stoute) 2-8-11 W R Swinburn 14/1: 2: Fin in really gd fashion showing
tremendous future promise: cost $1.5m and is related to a topclass performer in Canada:
has scope and is sure to make her mark in the near future. **62**
1232 LINDAS MAGIC [8] (R Armstrong) 2-8-11 C Asmussen 13/2: 23: Made much and ran well:
eff 6f, suited by 7f: see 1232. **52**
--   TECANA [4] (P Walwyn) 2-8-11 Paul Eddery 33/1: 4: Al prom, gd debut: cost only 11,000 gns
and is a half sister to the very useful Plaid: will stay beyond 6f: acts on firm and on a
stiff track: should soon step up on this. **44**
--   COLOR ARTIST [2] 2-8-11 T Ives 50/1: 0: Ran well, looking as if the race would do
her good: half sister to minor 1m winner Rainbow Ripple: should improve on this. **43**
--   LORAS GUEST [3] 2-8-11 J Reid 33/1: 0: Made a solid debut: related to sev winners,
notably 1,000 Guineas heroine On The House: will stay beyond 6f, acts on firm. **43**
--   HUNT BALL [7] 2-8-11 Pat Eddery 10/1: 0: Active in mkt on debut, kept on steadily
final 1f to fin 7th and will benefit from this gentle introduction: attractive sort who
should be a different proposition next time. **43**
--   MARTHA STEVENS [14] 2-8-11 S Cauthen 3/1 FAV: 0: Well touted newcomer but was sn
outpaced and will be all the better for this first ever race: comes from a useful American
family and will have no difficulty in staying further than 6f. **00**
1287 RARELY IRISH [16] 2-8-11 R Cochrane 7/2: 20: Much btr in 1287 (C/D). **00**
--   Montfort [12] 8-11   --   Ci Siamo [6] 8-11   565 Fleet Fact [5] 8-11
--   Cubby Hole [15] 8-11   --   Keen Note [9] 8-11   --   River Jig [13] 8-11
--   Moment In The Sun [1] 8-11
16 ran   1,3,2½,½,shthd,¾   (Maktoum Al-Maktoum)   W Hern West Ilsley, Berks.

1465 BERNARD VAN ,CUTSEM 2YO STAKES   £5851   7f   Firm 10 -16 Slow

--   SUHAILIE [7] (H Cecil) 2-8-8 S Cauthen 2/1: 1: 2 ch c Nodouble - Slow Hot Wind
(Canonero II) Highly promising colt: first time out, al prom and cleverly led inside final
1f to win a val 2yo minor race at Newmarket July 9: cost $310,000: well suited by 7f, sure
to stay longer dist: acts well on firm ground, on a stiff galloping track: very attractive
sort with plenty of scope and looks likes making up into a topclass performer. **63**
*1239 ORNE [6] (J Tree) 2-8-11 Pat Eddery 15/8 FAV: 12: Led dist, hdd final 100yds in a
close finish: prob caught a tartar here and should win more races: see 1239. **63**
1373 LACK A STYLE [1] (A Bailey) 2-8-8 R Cochrane 33/1: 0023: Dsptd lead thr'out, narrowly
btn and showed much improved form here: see 1373. **59**
1097 PERSIAN STYLE [5] (C Brittain) 2-8-8 C Asmussen 40/1: 0004: Made most, gd effort
and is sure to win a race if his sights are lowered slightly: see 1097, 662. **52**
*1149 SANAM [3] 2-9-2 W R Swinburn 7/1: 410: Never a threat and btr 1149 (6f). **50**
*1289 WUZO [4] 2-9-0 T Ives 9/2: 10: Raised in class here: see 1289 (C/D). **46**
--   MARDAS [2] 2-8-8 W Carson 20/1: 0: Friendless in mkt on debut, no danger: cost $135,000
and is bred to be suited by much longer distances. **00**
7 ran   ¾,hd,2,4,1   (Sheikh Mohammed)   H Cecil Newmarket

1466 GR 3 CHILD STAKES (FILLIES)   £21812   1m   Firm 10 +19 Fast

*1110 SONIC LADY [5] (M Stoute) 3-8-11 W R Swinburn 4/9 FAV: 1-13111: 3 b f Nureyev -
Stumped (Owne Anthony) Topclass filly: cruised into lead 2f out and readily put her rivals
in their place with a comfortable, fast run win in Gr 3 Child Stakes at Newmarket July 9:
impressive winner of Coronation Stks at Royal Ascot, Irish 1,000 gns at the Curragh and
first time out Nell Gwyn Stks at Newmarket: runaway winner of Blue Seal Stks at Ascot on sole
outing in '85 and met her only defeat when narrowly btn in the 1,000 Guineas: very eff
over 7f/1m: acts on firm and yielding and on a galloping trk: connections feel she is
better than ever and she will be hard to beat in all the top 1m events. **88**
*923 DUSTY DOLLAR [8] (W Hern) 3-8-5 W Carson 20/1: 44-312: Came to chall dist, lacked
the pace of the winner but ran with great credit and is fast improving: see 923. **75**
803 ARGON LASER [2] (J Dunlop) 3-8-5 B Thomson 33/1: -1003: Chall over 1f out, outpaced
final 150 yds: best effort since 250. **65**
1095 PURCHASEPAPERCHASE [1] (R Armstrong) 4-9-3 C Asmussen 25/1: 00-0104: No danger:
race 708 has worked out poorly. **62**

1110 EMBLA [6] 3-8-11 Pat Eddery 6/1: 11-4020: Cl.up ¼ way, wknd and much btr 1110.   60
1153 HOLBROOKE SUTTON [4] 3-8-5 R Guest 33/1: 14-40: Stiff task, btr in h'cap company.   50
1094 EVER GENIAL [3] 4-9-6 S Cauthen 7/1: 133-040: Made much, yet to regain best form.   00
1110 SOMEONE SPECIAL [7] 3-8-5 T Quinn 14/1: -21330: Speed most, wknd quickly & better 1110. 00
  8 ran   1½,3,1½,4,2.   (Sheikh Mohammed)   M Stoute, Newmarket

1467 GR 3 ANGLIA TELEVISION JULY STAKES 2YO £24219   6f   Firm 10 -05 Slow

1097 MANSOOJ [3] (N Callaghan) 2-8-10 C Asmussen 25/1: 3101: 2 ch c Thatching – Senta's
Girl (Averof) Smart colt: caused a 25/1 surprise, coming from behind to lead inside final 1f
in Gr 3 July Stks at Newmarket July 9: below his best in 1097 but prev won a minor race
at Newmarket and obviously likes this stiff track: very eff over 6f, shd stay further: acts
well on firm ground, on a stiff track.   71
*1242 WHO KNOWS [6] (W Hern) 2-8-13 W Carson 11/1: 312: Led over 1f out, kept on well
under press and continues to improve: likes a stiff track: see 1242.   72
+1126 SIZZLING MELODY [2] (Lord John Fitzgerald) 2-9-1 R Hills 11/2: 11213: Led briefly
2f out and ran right up to his best: a model of consistency: stays 6f, see 1126.   73
*979 MIDYAN [8] (H Cecil) 2-8-10 S Cauthen 5/1: 14: Al prom, ran as if another furlong
would suit: see 979.   68
*1143 CAROLS TREASURE [7] 2-8-13 B Thomson 5/1: 21110: Dsptd lead dist, not btn far in
tight finish: most consistent: see 1143.   69
1097 POLEMOS [5] 2-8-10 A Murray 4/1: 120: Pacemaker over 4f, much btr 1097.   58
1242 DARLEY KNIGHT [4] 2-8-13 Pat Eddery 11/4 FAV: 120: Never threatened in 7th: below
his best and much btr 1242.   00
1097 WHIPPET [1] 2-8-10 W R Swinburn 50/1: 1200: Early speed, fin last: twice below 737(5f) 00
  8 ran   1,hd,shthd,½,4   (K Al-Said)   N Callaghan Newmarket

1468 DUKE OF CAMBRIDGE HCAP 3YO (0-70)   £5872   1m 2f Firm 10 +10 Fast   [68]

946 LASTCOMER [5] (M Stoute) 3-8-6(1ow) W R Swinburn 11/1: 1-001: 3 ch f Kris – Hatter's
Dream (Buckpasser) Useful filly: returned to form, al prom and forging ahead inside final 1f
to win a fast run 3yo h'cap at Newmarket July 9: winner of a mdn at Doncaster on sole start
in '85: half sister to sev winners: well suited by 10f nowadays: acts on firm and yldg and
runs well on a galloping track: could win again.   60
1314 TWICE BOLD [11] (N Callaghan) 3-8-0 M Hills 25/1: 01-0342: Set a fast pace, hdd
final 1f: grand effort and deserves a race: eff over 9/10f with forcing tactics: see 880.   51
*1080 ORBAN [9] (H Cecil) 3-8-0 S Cauthen 15/8 FAV: -13: Al well there, not btn far:
should improve as he gains experience: see 1080.   59
1147 HAUWMAL [8] (W Hern) 3-8-9 W Carson 20/1: 20-1204: Mkt drifter, never closer: gd
effort: see 501: stays 10f well and acts on firm and good.   54
*1084 HAWAIIAN PALM [2] 3-9-3 Pat Eddery 9/2: 13-0010: Struggling final 3f: much btr 1084. 52
*1317 LIAM [3] 3-8-9 P Robinson 8/1: 22-0010: No danger: btr 1317 (sharpish trk).   39
1130 WISHLON [4] 3-8-8 R Cochrane 8/1: -10100: Fin 7th: best 623 (12f, sharp trk).   00
1153 RIYDA [7] 3-8-11 P Hutchinson(3) 10/1: -12230: Never in it: much btr 1153 (1m).   00
1130 Charlton Kings [10] 7-10(vis)   1084 Farm Club [1] 7-12
802 Top Ruler [6] 9-7(BL)
  11 ran   1½,1,2,7,3   (Sheikh Mohammed)   M Stoute Newmarket

1469 KENNETT MAIDEN STAKES 3YO   £4883   1m 2f Firm 10 +04 Fast

-- CELESTIAL STORM [16] (L Cumani) 3-9-0 R Guest 14/1: 0-1: 3 b c Roberto – Tobira Celeste
(Ribot) Very promising colt: first time out, gained an impressive success in a competitive
and quite fast run 3yo mdn at Newmarket July 9, leading dist readily: ran only once in '85:
eff over 10f, looks certain to stay 12f: acts on firm grd, on a stiff gall track: highly
regarded and sure to go on to better things.   62
409 VERITABLE [18] (P Haslam) 3-9-0 T Williams 25/1: 43-02: Led 3f out, no chance with
winner but a fine effort after fair abs: will be suited by 12f: see 409.   55
1031 MILLERS DUST [22] (H Cecil) 3-9-0 S Cauthen 11/10 FAV: -023: Heavily bckd: chall
2f out, no extra but reportedly swallowed his tongue and btr 1031.   50
1315 MIRAGE DANCER [23] (R Smyth) 3-9-0 M Hills 20/1: -023424: Al prom, gd effort and
deserves a maiden: seems to act on firm and soft: see 1315.   50
887 PICEA [1] 3-9-0 T Ives 14/1: 42-4220: Late prog: btr 887, 371.   45
1064 HABOOB BALADEE [5] 3-9-0 R Cochrane 10/1: -20: No real threat and flattered in 1064:
lacks scope.   44
1098 FESTIVAL CITY USA [11] 3-9-0 B Thomson 16/1: 3-0300: Never closer in 7th: best 887. 00
739 CIGAR [3] 3-9-0 P Cook 33/1: 00-000: Prom much, fin 8th: might prove btr at slightly
shorter distances and would benefit from being eased in class: see 619.   00
1130 SATISFACTION [13] 3-9-0 W Carson 9/1: 00-2200: Fin 9th: twice below 1023 (gd).   00
1022 BOON POINT [6] 3-9-0 Pat Eddery 8/1: 3-030: Btr 1022 (13f).   00
-- ILE DE ROI [8] 3-9-0 W Newnes 10/1: -4-0: Should benefit from this seasonal debut:
4th of 15 in Salisbury maiden on only outing in '85: should be suited by 10f: acts on fast grd 00

```
--    Comazant  [14] 9-0        1291 Lihbab  [15] 9-0          370  Moonstruck  [12] 9-0
1036 Promenader  [10] 9-0        806 Reno Ralph  [2] 9-0       528  Sahraan  [17] 9-0
739  Step In Time  [4] 9-0       --  Dawn Loch  [21] 8-11      1198 Scarlet Dancer  [20] 8-11
1043 Shakana  [9] 8-11(BL)       832 Tonquin  [7] 8-11         --   Tudorio  [19] 9-0
23 ran    3,3,hd,2½,¾          (R L Duchoissois)         L Cumani Newmarket
```

1470 REG DAY MEM.TROPHY H'CAP 4YO+ 0-70   £5280   2m   Firm 10 -98 Slow   [65]

*1092 THE PRUDENT PRINCE [6] (W Jarvis) 4-8-4 R Cochrane 11/2: 32-2111: 4 b c Grundy -
Ra Girl (Ragusa) Improving colt: al led/dsptd lead at slow pace, keeping on well final 2f
to win quite a val but very slowly run h'cap at Newmarket July 9: comfortably won minor races
at Thirsk and Catterick last month: eff at 12/14f, stays 2m really well: acts on firm and
yielding and seems to handle any track.   52
-1293 NEWSELLS PARK [1] (J Winter) 5-8-7 W R Swinburn 4/1: -P-2122: Led ½ way till 3f out:
another grand effort and deserves another race: see 1004, 1293.   52
1140 JACKDAW [4] (R Hollinshead) 6-7-7(18oh) A Culhane(7) 16/1: 0030023: Appeared to
display much improved form here but the pace was funereal & he was possibly flattered:see 634 33
1112 WESTERN DANCER [2] (C Horgan) 5-9-3 P Cook 7/4 FAV: 24-0134: Prob unsuited by this
snail's pace: better 462, 1112.   56
1293 RIKKI TAVI [7] 6-7-12 W Carson 11/2: -033100: Prom most: see 1099.   35
1150 ALL IS REVEALED [8] 4-7-11 M L Thomas 25/1: 0413000: Never in it: best 582 (14f gd)   19
1148 INDE PULSE [5] 4-9-7 M Hills 8/1: 1043440: No threat in 7th: see 1148.   00
990 Touchez Le Bois [3] 7-7(8oh)
8 ran   1½,1¼,¼,1½,15   (J M Greetham)   W Jarvis Newmarket

1471 SUMMER HANDICAP STAKES 3YO   (0-35)   £1615   1m   Good/Firm 21 -04 Slow   [38]

1401 TROPICO [15] (P Haslam) 3-8-1 G French 5/1: -004231: 3 ch g Hot Spark - Bella Canto
(Crooner) Gained his first success leading inside final 1f by the minimum margin in a h'cap
at Warwick July 9: eff over 7f/1m on fast ground tho' seems to handle any track.   20
+1169 PULHAM MILLS [2] (E Eldin) 3-9-5(bl)(5ex) G King(5) 9/2 FAV: -000012: Made much, just
failed to regain his lead on post: in fine form and loves Warwick: see 1169.   37
1061 BOLD BORDERER [12] (M Blanshard) 3-9-5 N Adams 16/1: 0-00003: Kept on well, not btn
far: needs 10f? See 1061.   35
1281 JOHNSTAN BOY [16] (C Tinkler) 3-8-3(BL)(1ow) M Birch 5/1: 0000044: Bl first time,
dsptd lead most: see 997.   18
339 STROMBERG [11] 3-7-7 G Dickie 25/1: 000-000: Long abs, never closer, showing best
form yet: evidently well suited by 1m on firm ground: may stay further.   06
1169 BAKERS DOUGH [6] 3-9-0 P Waldron 5/1: 11-0000: Ev ch in a close fin: see 1169.   26
1346 NO JAZZ [3] 3-8-2 S Whitworth 13/2: -000200: Fin a cl.up 7th: see 1169.   14
```
```
1245 Lightning Wind [13] 9-7   1081 Sunley Spirit [8] 7-10
1074 Molly Partridge [7] 7-13   720 Kookys Pet [10] 8-10
941 Bears Revenge [5] 8-11   843 Miss Jade [9] 8-9
1080 Tymbal [17] 8-4   1273 Monatation [1] 8-1   1310 Lisakaty [4] 7-13
1245 See No Evil [14] 8-1
17 ran   shthd,¾,hd,1,hd,¾   (Mrs T C Ellis)   P Haslam Newmarket
```

## 1472  JIM SLATER APP MAIDEN STAKES 3YO    £880    1m    Good/Firm 21 +09 Fast

1245 BRONZE OPAL  [12] (G Balding) 3-9-0 L Jones 6/1: 20-0001: 3 br c Guilty Conscience -
Countess Babu (Bronze Babu) Came from behind to lead on bit final 1f, comfortably, in an
app maiden at Warwick July 9: quite highly tried this season, showed a good deal of promise
in '85: half brother to 5ev winners: suited by 1m, promises to stay further: acts on firm
and yielding.                                                                                45
1315 RED RIVER BOY  [4] (R Hodges) 3-9-0 A Dicks 5/1: -002: Chall final 1f, showing
improved form: should be able to find a maiden on this evidence: acts well on firm ground
and stays 1m.                                                                                40
1036 BLAIRINGONE  [8] (A Stewart) 3-9-0 W Hayes 5/1: -03: Made most: gd effort and should
be able to win a maiden soon: see 1036.                                                      36
1327 ACTUALIZATIONS  [14] (L Cumani) 3-8-11 S Quane 11/10 FAV: -034: Disapp fav after
narrow defeat in 1327.                                                                       28
539  DASA QUEEN  [7] 3-8-11 G King 7/1: 223-020: Ev ch after abs: proving a little
exasperating: see 539.                                                                       25
1303 EASTERN PLAYER  [10] 3-9-0(bl) J Carter 50/1: 0000000: Prom most: rating looks
suspiciously high for one with such moderate form.                                           23
```
```
454  Royal Berks  [13] 9-0        966 Rodistyle  [3] 8-11       --   Gem Of Gold  [9] 8-11
--   Emma Harte  [5] 8-11         809 Cheal  [2] 9-0            1317 Cleveland Bond  [1?] 8-11
--   Cheren Hill  [6] 9-0         829 Miss Stanway  [11] 8-11
14 ran    ¾,2,2½,1½,2          (Mrs Ernest Weinstein)          G Balding Weyhill, Hants.
```

1473 JULY H'CAP STAKES (0-35)   3YO   £1343   1m 4f Good/Firm 21 -11 SLow   [35]

*1056 ISOM DART [4] (T Hallett) 7-8-3 N Adams 11/1: -00-11: 7 b h Bold Forbes - Shellshock
(Salvo) In fine form at present and came from off the pace to lead inside final 1f in a h'cap
at Warwick July 9: first time out winner of a seller at Bath June 14: a winner over hurdles
in the past: suited by 10/12f and fast ground.   19
1062 ASHINGTON GROVE [1] (D Murray Smith) 3-8-13 S Whitworth 3/1 FAV: 0-22332: Came from
well off the pace and placed for the 5th successive race, tho' yet to get his head in front.   40
851 DANCING BARRON [9] (M Blanshard) 5-9-0(bl) G Baxter 9/1: 4-00003: Made most, best
effort this term: see 750.   26
1274 JABARABA [13] (L Cottrell) 5-8-8 N Carlisle 15/2: 00-0004: Ev ch and is steadily finding
form: see 1274.   18
1271 GENTLE STREAM [2] 4-9-3(BL) G Duffield 5/1: -200040: Bl first time, prom most: 23
--   LADY KILLANE [10] 4-8-10 N Howe 12/1: 04020-0: Sn prom, fdd but will benefit from
seasonal debut: placed sev times last season without winning and remains a maiden: suited
by 12f: acts on gd and yielding.   13
940 RHEIN COURT [11] 6-7-13 D Williams(7) 4/1: 000-000: Prom most: see 547.   00
--   Hallowed [8] 7-13   1195 Relza Coccinea [6] 7-12
344 Mount Argus [3] 8-3   1017 Anitas Apple [12] 8-3(BL)
11 ran   1½,hd,1,2,1½   (G H Taylor-Webber)   T Hallett Saltash, Cornwall.

1474 BUDBROOKE MAIDEN SELLING STKS 2YO   £478   6f   Good/Firm 21 -52 SLow

1279 THE MAGUE [1] (L Siddall) 2-9-0(bl) D Nicholls 1/1 FAV: 004221: 2 br c Bold Owl -
Silvery Moon (Lorenzaccio) Comfortably led final 1f in a bad 3 runner 2yo mdn seller at
Warwick July 9 (bought in 1,500 gns): due reward for 2 recent near misses: wears blinkers:
eff over 6f on fast ground.   19
831 SKY ROBBER [2] (M Usher) 2-9-0 M Wigham 9/4: 002: Tried to make all: half brother
to '81 2yo winner Ma Tante: likely to prove best at sprint dist: acts on fast ground.   10
--   MENZIES FLYER [3] (R Simpson) 2-9-0(BL) S Whitworth 5/2: 3: Bl first time, on a race
course, wknd quickly half way and fin well beaten.   00
3 ran   2½,30   (Miss L C Siddall)   L Siddall Tadcaster, Yorks.

1475 CHANDOS MAIDEN STAKES   2YO   £684   5f   Good/Firm 21 -02 Slow

1203 PETER MOON [9] (R Armstrong) 2-9-0 P Tulk 11/2: 031: 2 b c Dewan - Smiling Through
(Personality) Improving colt: ran on to lead final 1f, comfortably, in a 2yo mdn at Warwick
July 9: first foal who cost $40,000: eff over 5f, stays 6f: acts on fast ground and on an
easy, turning track.   49
927 SCHUYGULLA [8] (M Jarvis) 2-9-0 W Woods(3) 3/1 FAV: 342: Well bckd, al well there:
consistent sort who deserves a small race: see 927.   42
1296 HAILEYS RUN [4] (G P Gordon) 2-9-0 G Diffield 11/2: 43033: Dsptd lead thr'out:
eff at 5/6f on firm ground: see 1296.   37
1059 GLAMGRAM FOR GRAMS [5] (R Boss) 2-9-0 E Guest(3) 9/2: 04: Never closer: needs further. 32
1311 JUST ONE MORE [2] 2-9-0 A Mackay 7/1: 4040: Dsptd lead most: see 1311.   30
1313 LITTLE SACY [7] 2-9-0 J Williams 20/1: 040: No threat and btr 1313 (6f)   22
--   FIRST AVENUE [1] 2-9-0 S Whitworth 5/1: 0: Well bckd debutant, cl.up from ½ way
and should benefit from the experience: half brother to '84 2yo winner Abutaia, sprint bred.   22
678 Spy Tower [3] 9-0   1305 Raintree County [6] 9-0
9 ran   2,1½,1½,½,3,nk   (Charles H Wacker III)   R Armstrong Newmarket

1476 DAVENTRY H'CAP STAKES 3YO (0-35)   £1243   5f   Good/Firm 21 +01 Fast   [34]

1344 SANDITTON PALACE [7] (P Felgate) 3-8-11 M Fry 11/2: 0040431: 3 gr g Dragonara Palace
- Petona (Mummy's Pet) Fin strongly to sprint clear in final 1f for a ready win in a 3yo
h'cap at Warwick July 9: showed little last term but evidently an improved performer:
eff 5f, should stay 6f: acts on firm & yldg & runs well on a sharpish trk particularly Warwick 28
760 JIANNA [9] (G Lewis) 3-8-8 T Lucas 12/1: 040-002: Gd late prog: lightly raced prev
and this was his best effort yet: likely to stay 6f: acts well on firm.   15
1169 OUR CHILDREN [11] (W Wharton) 3-8-3 N Carlisle 25/1: 0400-03: Chall 1f out: placed
twice from 6 outings in '85 in mod company: eff 5f, stays 6f: acts on firm and good.   08
1283 CHAUTAUQUA [5] (P Haslam) 3-9-1 J Scally(7) 7/4 FAV: 4214124: Made most: see 917.   18
1399 LEFT RIGHT [6] 3-8-8(bl) S P Griffiths(5) 10/1: -030030: Ev ch: prob flattered 1399(mdn). 10
1277 NORTHERN LAD [12] 3-9-1 N Adams 10/1: -000020: Sn prom: flattered 1277?   12
1438 ARDENT PARTNER [3] 3-8-6 C Rutter(5) 10/1: 0-00030: Quick reappearance, fin 7th:
better 1438.   00
1414 PENDOR DANCER [4] 3-8-11 A Shoults(5) 10/1: 0023000: Prom, wknd: btr 1164, 871 (6f).   00
1414 RESTLESS RHAPSODY [1] 3-9-7(bl) S Whitworth 10/1: 4-24040: Prom much: btr 1414, 246.   00
1272 Choristers Dream [10] 9-0(bl)   845 Blue Fantasy [8] 7-10(2ow)
1164 Jacqui Joy [2] 8-9
12 ran   4,½,½,nk,1½,½   (J D Abell)   P Felgate Melton Mowbray, Leics.

Official Going Given As FIRM

1477 OLD OAK HANDICAP 3YO+ 0-35   £1289   1m 7f Firm 15 -04 Slow   [24]

1422 DUKE OF DOLLIS [3] (W Storey) 7-8-5 S Whitworth 25/1: -000001: 7 b g Condorcet - Evening Primrose (Varano) Turned up at 25/1, led after 1m and driven out to win a h'cap at Catterick July 10: in '85 won at Pontefract: in '84 won at Bath: stays 2m: best form on fast ground: has been tried in bl, but seems better without.   08
1226 COCKED HAT SUPREME [1] (S Hall) 4-9-1(vis) M Birch 5/2: 040-442: Ev ch str: one paced: see 1092.   17
1280 THARALEOS [7] (F Watson) 6-8-1 J Lowe 20/1: 0-04003: Held up: nearest fin: stays 15f.   01
1260 GRATIFY [8] (P Walwyn) 3-8-5 N Howe 6/4 FAV: 0-00034: Prom, ev ch: see 1260, 1078.   21
933 MARINERS DREAM [4] 5-8-9 A Culhane(7) 9/2: 000-100: Twice below form 366 (C/D yldg).   06
1280 NORTHERN RULER [6] 4-9-7 G Carter(3) 12/1: 0000000: Never in it: yet to reproduce form 280 (hvy).   17
1302 Jubilant Lady [2] 7-13(vis)   860 Timurs Gift [5] 8-11(bl)
8 ran 1,1½,hd,3,½   (Bob Ritchie)   W Storey Consett, Co Durham.

1478 SILVER BIRCH SELLING STAKES 2YO   £1054   5f   Firm 15 -33 Slow

1012 PETERS BLUE [3] (J Fitzgerald) 2-8-11 M Roberts 8/1: 041: 2 gr g Riki-Lash - Lady Doubloon (Pieces of Eight) Impr gelding: made ev yard, comfortably, in a 2yo seller at Catterick July 10 (no bid) : seems best with forcing tactics over a sharp 5f: acts well on fast ground.   27
1181 ROSE DUET [2] (D Barron) 2-8-8 N Connorton 7/1: 0010032: Prom, ev ch: consistent.   18
1248 RUN TO WORK [5] (G Moore) 2-8-11 D Casey(7) 3/1: 42233: Saddle slipped inside final 2f: better 1248 (stiffer track).   16
1207 ORIENTAL JADE [7] (D Morley) 2-8-11 M Birch 5/1: 04: Better effort: should be suited by further than 5f: acts on fast ground and a sharp track.   09
931 EUROCON [4] 2-8-11(VIS) D Nicholls 5/1: 000: Visored first time: sn prom: see 931.   00
1333 LATERAL [8] 2-8-11 M Fry 2/1 FAV: 200020: Well below form 1333, 43 and seems non too consistent.   00
-- Katie Cuddles [1] 8-8   1181 Bootham Lad [6] 8-11
8 ran 1½,1½,2½,5,6   (Peter Rawson)   J Fitzgerald Malton, Yorks.

1479 SPREADING CHESTNUT HANDICAP 3YO 0-35   £1682 1m 5f Firm 15 -63 Slow   [27]

*1250 MADISON GIRL [5] (R Whitaker) 3-9-11(4ex) D Mckeown 5/2: 0-03411: 3 ch f Last Fandango - Evening Chorus (Mountain Call) In fine form: led final 1f, under press in a slow run h'cap at Catterick July 10: last time out won a similar event at Newcastle (first success): eff at 12f, stays 14f: best on gd and fast ground: acts on any track.   31
1309 G G MAGIC [3] (D Morley) 3-9-3 M Birch 7/2: 0-03042: Dictated the pace till final 1f: seems to stay 14f: see 380.   22
*1302 CHUMMYS OWN [2] (N Callaghan) 3-9-6(4ex) E Guest(3) 11/8 FAV: -102013: Ev ch str: better 1302.   22
969 HIDDEN MOVE [4] (W Pearce) 3-8-13 N Connorton 9/1: 0-00034: Hung under press: much better 969 (11f heavy).   12
1204 SUNMAIDEN [1] 3-9-3(BL) M Wood 20/1: 00-0000: Bl first time: no threat: see 1204.   10
5 ran 1,3,2½,5   (A K Zivanaris)   R Whitaker Wetherby, Yorks.

1480 MAPLE LEAF MAIDEN AUCTION STAKES 2YO   £684 7f Firm 15 -12 Slow

577 MY BUDDY [5] (R Williams) 2-9-0 W Newnes 11/4: 001: 2 ch c Mummy's Game - Shadow Play (Busted) Impr colt: despite long abs, led nearing final 1f, sprinting clear in a 2yo mdn auction at Catterick July 10: cost 6,000 gns: stays 7f and seems well suited by a sharp trk: acts on yielding, very eff on fast ground.   41
1050 GEOBRITONY [11] (D Moffatt) 2-8-11 J Lowe 11/1: 04002: No chance with winner: stays 7f: acts on firm and yldg ground and on any track.   28
1322 ST WENDRED [2] (D Thom) 2-8-5 G Sexton 10/1: 03: Led over 1f out, showing improvement: cheaply acquired filly: eff at 7f on fast ground and a sharp track.   20
1253 PARKERS JOY [10] (E Wheeler) 2-8-11 W Wharton 9/4 FAV: 00044: Well bckd: btr 1253.   21
1105 WOLF J FLYWHEEL [1] 2-8-8 M Wood 10/1: 02000: Sn prom: best early season 186 (5f yldg).   11
1155 THE BRAZILIAN [8] 2-8-11(BL) A Proud 8/1: 040: Bl first time: pulled hard and led over 5f: see 1155 (6f).   13
722 Philearn [6] 8-8   1294 Benfield Newcastle [3] 8-8
1050 Skinnhill [9] 8-11   1221 Misty Runner [4] 8-8   1413 Frev Off [7] 8-11
11 ran 4,½,2,3,nk   (C P Linney)   R Williams Newmarket

1481 WEEPING WILLOW MAIDEN FILLIES STKS 3YO   £684 1m 4f Firm 15 -04 Slow

779 GREAT EXCEPTION [4] (H Candy) 3-8-11 W Newnes 5/2: 0232-31: 3 ch f Grundy - Exquisite (Exbury) Well bckd and led before ½ way, ridden out in a fillies mdn at Catterick July 10: had been off the track since 3rd to Santiki at Thirsk in May and evidently does well when fresh: showed useful form as a 2yo: stays 12f well: acts on firm and soft ground and any trk.   46
1080 MITALA MARIA [3] (A Stewart) 3-8-11 M Roberts 16/1: -02: Al prom and stayed on well in str: improving filly who is a sister to winning sprinter Laurie Lorman, but seems to stay 12f herself: acts on fast ground and a sharp trk: should find a race.   43

862 CURVACEOUS [6] (M Stoute) 3-8-11 M Birch 15/2: -043: Fair eff after abs since 862: stays 12f: acts on gd and firm ground and on any track. 42
1368 HELIETTA [9] (L Cumani) 3-8-11 R Guest 10/11 FAV: -04: Heavily bckd: not the best of runs inside final 2f: 8l clear rem.: stays 12f: see 1368 41
980 HOME FLEET [10] 3-8-11 S Whitworth 12/1: 000-00: Never nearer: lightly raced filly who was highly tried in 3 outings in '85: half sister to 10f winner Cabalistic: prob stays 12f: acts on fast ground. 21
1141 EFFICIENT [2] 3-8-11 S Lawes 33/1: 0-00: No real threat: see 1141. 09
1259 CRYSTAL MOSS [1] 3-8-11 K Powdrell 8/1: -000: No show in 7th: lightly raced since best 250 (soft). 00
-- **Sweet Snugfit** [8] 8-11 932 **Raceform Rhapsody** [5] 8-11
9 ran 1½,½,nk,8,6 (T A F Frost) H Candy Wantage, Oxon

1482 RAMBLING ROSE HANDICAP 3YO+ 0-35 £1541 7f Firm 15 +08 Fast [34]

1101 WORKADAY [17] (C Gray) 4-9-10 I Johnson 10/1: 0-00031: 4 gr f Workboy - Courting Day (Right Boy) Led final 1f, comfortably, in quite fast run h'cap at Catterick July 10: in '85 won a h'cap at Beverley: winning 2yo at Catterick and Beverley: eff at 5f, stays 7f: acts on any track but likes fast ground. 38
1377 THE MAZALL [14] (L Siddall) 6-9-7 M Wood 6/1: 0012022: Stayed on well: in gd form. 30
1338 QUALITAIRESS [11] (K Stone) 4-7-8(vis) L Charnock 16/1: 0434003: Chance over 1f out: maiden: see 101. 02
1338 HIGH PORT [16] (A Jones) 7-7-12 N Carlisle 6/1: 0000244: Led over 2f out: see 943. 02
1394 KAMARESS [9] 4-8-4 M Wigham 9/1: 0000240: Nearest fin: btr 1103 (1m stiffer trk). 06
-- RESTORATION [15] 4-8-12 N Rodgers(7) 25/1: 4-000-0: Fdd final 1f on seasonal debut: ran only 3 times in '85: showed fair form as a 2yo: eff at 5/6f on gd and fast ground. 10
1299 LA BELLE OF SANTO [13] 3-7-7(2oh) A Culhane(7) 10/1: 30-0020: Never nearer 7th: better 1299. 00
1013 JUST A BIT [6] 4-8-5(bl) M Birch 9/2 FAV: 3230-40: Led 5f: fdd: see 1013. 00
1093 **Sir Wilmore** [20] 9-3 1066 **Dorame** [3] 8-0 1299 **Tanyas Princess** [19] 8-10
1299 **Uptown Randbs** [18] 7-10(vis) 1280 **Bundling Bed** [10] 7-9(bl)
1200 **Owls Way** [2] 7-13(BL) 1334 **Galaxy Gala** [4] 7-7(2oh)
1093 **Tollys Best** [1] 7-7(3oh) 1013 **Cindys Gold** [5] 7-10(bl)
1201 **Meganot** [7] 7-7(5oh) 1200 **Fauve** [8] 9-2(BL) 1104 **Manabel** [12] 8-7(BL)
20 ran 1½,hd,1½,½,2,nk (C N Wilmot-Smith) C Gray Beverley, Yorks.

NEWMARKET Thursday July 10th Righthand Stiff Galloping Track

Official Going Given As GOOD/FIRM

1483 ELLESMERE SELLING STAKES 2YO £3345 7f Firm 12 -12 Slow

717 EL BE DOUBLEYOU [9] (N Callaghan) 2-8-11 Pat Eddery 7/1: 0201: 2 b c Pitskelly - Russalka (Emerson) Returned after an abs to lead inside final 1f in a val 2yo seller at Newmarket July 10 (bought in 9,200 gns): btr suited by 7f than shorter dist, should stay 1m: acts on firm and gd ground and on a gall trk. 40
•965 PANACHE [5] (P Haslam) 2-8-11 T Williams 11/4 FAV: 00312: Well bckd: made much, kept on: stays 7f well: see 965. 36
1075 LIGHTNING LASER [16] (P Kelleway) 2-8-8 S Cauthen 8/1: 0033: Kept on final 1f and should have no trouble finding a seller: eff 5f, stays 7f well: acts on firm ground. 32
1294 FLAIR PARK [3] (D Thom) 2-8-8 T Quinn 5/1: 0124: Dsptd lead dist, no extra: running well: stays 7f: see 1083. 32
404 BRIGGS BUILDERS [13] 2-8-11 R Cochrane 25/1: 00: Long abs: prom most: dam lightly raced maiden: speedily bred but prob stays 7f: acts on firm. 28
965 JOSIE SMITH [8] 2-8-8 W Carson 20/1: 0100: Prom thr'out: best 831 (poor affair). 17
1262 JETMORE [7] 2-8-11 A Mcglone 12/1: 020: Active in mkt, no danger: btr 1262 (6f) 00
1234 **Leading Role** [15] 8-11 948 **Fenn Trap** [6] 8-11
999 **Miss Lawsuit** [11] 8-8 1059 **Unity Farm Boy** [10] 8-11
1363 **Mi Oh My** [4] 8-8 1137 **Tootsie Jay** [1] 8-8 1190 **Ballantrae** [14] 8-8
1345 **Bunches** [2] 8-8 1253 **St Johns Bay** [12] 8-8
16 ran 1½,½,hd,2½,4 (Roldvale ltd) N Callaghan Newmarket

1484 HANDK COMMISSIONS H'CAP 3YO 0-70 £5189 1m 6f Firm 12 -22 Slow [67]

•1402 ZAUBARR [6] (B Hills) 3-7-8(bl)(4ex) S Dawson 7/2: 00-0011: 3 b c Hawaii - My Room (Bold Lad) Improved colt since being fitted with bl and was winning his 2nd race in 5 days when well ridden to land a slowly run but val 3yo h'cap at Newmarket July 10: set a modest pace and stayed on strongly when chall dist for a comfortable win: made most easily in a 3yo h'cap at Bath last time: half brother to sev winners: eff over 13f, stays 15f well: acts on soft: well suited fast grd: best in blinkers with front running tactics: can complete a hat-trick. 45
+1342 KUDZ [2] (H Cecil) 3-9-3(4ex) S Cauthen 100/30: 2-21112: Ridden to chall dist: good effort: see 1342. 65
1117 COMME LETOILE [4] (J Hindley) 3-9-7 M Hills 14/1: 21-3103: Mostly 2nd: consistent: see 461: stays 15f. 64

1040 ACTINIUM [3] (P Cole) 3-8-7 T Quinn 9/4 FAV: 43-2124: Ev ch: btr 1040, 811. 50
•980 ON TENTERHOOKS [1] 3-8-4 Pat Eddery 7/2: 43-10: Waited with, ch 2f out, not given a hard time when held: see 980 (10f). 46
5 ran 2½,5,shthd,2½ (Sheikh Mohammed) B Hills Lambourn, Berks

1485 GROUP 1 NORCROS JULY CUP 3YO+ £39208 6f Firm 12 +08 Fast

1036 GREEN DESERT [2] (M Stoute) 3-8-11 W R Swinburn 7/4 FAV: 4-12021: 3 b c Danzig - Foreign Courier (Sir Ivor) Topclass colt: readily coped with this reversion to sprinting when winning quite fast run Gr 1 July Cup at Newmarket July 10: led after 2f and produced a decisive burst of speed at the 1f marker to settle the outcome: first time out winner of val Free H'cap again at Newmarket and sub was 2nd in both the 2,000 Guineas and the St James Palace Stakes at Royal Ascot, both over 1m but is prob ideally suited by 6/7f: a smart 2yo in '85 winning the Flying Childers and July Stks at Doncaster and Newmarket respectively: has pace aplenty and will prob not be inconvenienced by a return to 5f next time. 88
945 GREY DESIRE [3] (M Brittain) 6-9-6 K Darley 20/1: 1241202: Early leader: kept on in his usual game fashion and is remarkably tough and genuine: see 587. 84
1146 GWYDION [5] (H Cecil) 3-8-8 S Cauthen 15/2: 11-433: Chall dist, outpaced final 1f. see 232. 78
+1146 LAST TYCOON [1] (R Collet) 3-8-11 Y Saint Martin 9/4: 1114: Waited with, had to be switched final 2f and this run can be ignored: much better 1146 (5f). 81
-1125 CYRANO DE BERGERAC [4] 3-8-11 Pat Eddery 11/4: 2111-20: Raised in class here, not btn far in a close finish: see 1125. 79
5 ran ¾,¾,shthd,¾ (Maktoum Al-Maktoum) M Stoute Newmarket

1486 ADDISON TOOLS H'CAP 3YO 0-75 £12817 1m Firm 12 +15 Fast [71]

•1384 AVENTINO [13] (J Sutcliffe) 3-7-12(bl)(1ow)(7ex) M Hills 4/1 FAV: -011111: 3 ch g Cure The Blues - Sovereign Dona (Sovereign Path) Possibly the most impr horse in training this season and completed a nap hand of h'cap wins when hacking up in a val and fast run 3yo h'cap at Newmarket July 10: led final 1f and sprinted clear: ready winner of h'caps at Goodwood, Sandown (2) and Newmarket prev: narrowly won a Newmarket seller on final outing in '85: very eff over 7f/1m and is suited by firm grd: wears bl but is genuine: suited by waiting 57
tactics and has a fine turn of foot: looks certain to go in again next time. 57
•1390 PINSTRIPE [4] (R Williams) 3-8-4(7ex) B Thomson 6/1: 30-0112: Al prom, kept on but caught a tartar here: stays 1m well: will win more races: see 1390. 53
1080 CHIEF PAL [2] (P Walwyn) 3-8-3(1ow) Paul Eddery 12/1: 4-2123: Fin really well: almost snatching 2nd place: eff 1m, stays 10f: should win again soon: see 941. 52
•950 NATIVE OAK [8] (H Cecil) 3-9-7 S Cauthen 10/1: 3-42114: Made most: not disgraced under top weight: see 950. 70
1147 KNYF [1] 3-8-4 W Carson 20/1: -320100: Sn prom: running well: see 816. 52
•1395 BRIGHT AS NIGHT [11] 3-9-5(4ex) R Cochrane 20/1: 0-30310: Prom much, stiff task here: see 1395. 57
1107 RESOURCEFUL FALCON [9] 3-9-5 T Quinn 9/1: 1-02200: Prom thr'out, fin 7th: see 586. 00
1147 NIGHT OUT PERHAPS [12] 3-8-12 P Robinson 13/2: 0-1140: Prom much, fin 9th: btr 1147,465. 00
1384 GORGEOUS ALGERNON [14] 3-8-6 Pat Eddery 9/1: 0102020: Prom, wknd: much closer to winner in 1384 and is inconsistent. 00
•914 VAGUE SHOT [5] 3-8-13 P Cook 10/1: 00-1110: Al rear: see 914. 00
•1300 **One To Mark** [6] 7-7(4ex)(7oh) 1230 **Dancing Eagle** [10] 9-7
1044 **Elnawaagi** [15] 8-13 955 **Fassa** [7] 7-7(3oh) 1080 **Pentland Hawk** [3] 7-7(8oh)
15 ran 4,hd,hd,½,5 (A J Smith) J Sutcliffe Epsom, Surrey.

1487 BAHRAIN TROPHY H'CAP 3YO FILLIES 0-70 £8025 7f Firm 12 +07 Fast [62]

1044 MUMMYS FAVOURITE [5] (J Dunlop) 3-9-7 W Carson 5/1: 111-341: 3 b f Mummy's Pet - Woodwind (Whistling Wind) Smart filly: appreciated the step-up to 7f when readily winning quite a fast run and val 3yo fillies h'cap at Newmarket July 10, coming from behind to lead final 1f: not disgraced over 6f prev and last term won her last 3 on the trot, minor events at Leicester, Goodwood and Yarmouth: half sister to sev winners: suited by 7f now: acts on firm and yldg and on any track. 70
1153 ROYAL LOFT [8] (W Jarvis) 3-8-11 R Cochrane 9/4 FAV: 1-22: Came from well off the pace, fin strongly and her turn is merely delayed: see 1153. 53
1375 CLEOFE [2] (L Cumani) 3-7-12 P Hamblett 9/1: 4-00333: Led after ½ way, one paced and remains a maiden: see 656, 1375. 34
1065 AMBROSINI [1] (M Jarvis) 3-8-9 T Ives 16/1: 1-10204: Led to ½ way: see 454, 886. 43
925 CARRIBEAN SOUND [4] 3-8-1 Dale Gibson(7) 20/1: -243100: Prom most: best 713. 33
178 SOVEREIGN LOVE [6] 3-7-11 B Crossley 33/1: 0313230: Never closer after long abs: best 49 (hvy). 27
1244 GREAT DILEMMA [9] 3-8-5 B Thomson 10/1: -00220: Fin 7th: btr 1244 (stks). 00
271 GREY WALLS [11] 3-9-0 S Cauthen 10/1: 013-00: Fin 9th after long abs: see 271. 00
1032 BASOOF [10] 3-8-11 W R Swinburn 8/1: 304-040: No threat: btr 1032. 00
776 **Indian Summer** [7] 8-4 1316 **Cafe Noir** [12] 7-9(1ow)
1153 **Normanby Lass** [3] 9-2
12 ran 3,3,¾,¾,¾ (R More O'Ferrall) J Dunlop Arundel, Sussex.

1488 EBF FULBOURN MAIDEN STAKES 2YO C&G   £4454   6f   Firm 12 +03 Fast

--   JUST A FLUTTER [5] (M Jarvis) 2-9-0 T Ives 4/1: 1: 2 b c Beldale Flutter - Precious
Jade (Northfields) Promising colt: well bckd first time out and led final 1f in quite a fast
run 2yo mdn at Newmarket July 10: has reportedly been working well at home and is a half
brother to last year's successful juv Diamond Sky: eff over 6f on firm grd, sure to stay
further: likely to make further improvement and win more races.   66
--   CLASSIC TALE [9] (M Stoute) 2-9-0 W R Swinburn 7/4 FAV: 2: Well bckd debutant, kept on
in fine style and should not be long in going one better: half brother to 3 winners, notably
successful '85 2yo Singletta: sure to be suited by 7f+: acts on firm grd & a stiff trk.   63
--   HENDEKA [14] (H Cecil) 2-9-0 S Cauthen 7/2: 3: Wk in mkt on debut, kept on well and
is sure to benefit from this gentle introduction: cost a modest $50,000: shd be a different
proposition next time.   57
--   GILBERTO [4] (J Dunlop) 2-9-0 W Carson 10/1: 4: Promising debut, keeping on steadily
final 1f: half brother to 4 winners, notably very useful sprinter New Express: speedily bred
and looks sure to find a maiden in the near future.   56
1253 NATIVE PAWN [6] 2-9-0 B Thomson 50/1: 00: One of the outsiders, made much: gd effort
from this cheaply bought colt: stays 6f and acts on firm: can win a maiden if slightly
eased in class.   55
--   FARFURR [8] 2-9-0 Paul Eddery 12/1: 0: Active in mkt on debut, ran well for most
of the trip: cost $275,000   and is bred to be quite speedy: likely to improve.   52
--   WAHIBA [13] 2-9-0 G Duffield 50/1: 0: Apparently unfancied on debut, fin 7th: half
brother to winning miler Lady Donaro: looks certain to improve on this.   00
777   MUSICAL BELLS [12] 2-9-0 R Cochrane 12/1: 00: Abs: prom to ½ way, fin 8th: see 777.   00
--   Lord Patrick [3] 9-0   1289 Goodwood Park [10] 9-0
--   Pradel [11] 9-0   --   Crown Justice [1] 9-0
12 ran   1½,3,½,shthd,½   (F Wilson)   M Jarvis Newmarket

HAMBURG   Friday July 4th   Righthand, Flat Track

Official Going Given As FIRM

1489 GROUP 3 EVENT 3YO+ FILLIES & MARES   £9887   1m 1f Firm -

--   COMPRIDA [2] (H Jentzsch) 3-8-8 A Tylicki 1: 1-11111: 3 b f Windwurf - Colatina
(Tudor Melody) Very smart, unbtn German filly: led inside final 1f easily, in a Gr 3 event at
Hamburg July 4: earlier winner of the German 1,000 Guineas and the German Oaks: eff at 9f
stays further: will win more races.   77
--   AUENBLUME [4] (U Ostmann) 4-9-2 K Woodburn 1: 02-0012: Made much: no chance with
winner: eff at 9f on fast ground.   66
759   BOLD AND BEAUTIFUL [1] (G P Gordon) 4-9-0 G Duffield 1: D10-033: Stayed on: gd effort.   61
*1002 LAVENDER MIST [5] (M Stoute) 3-8-6(2ow) W R Swinburn 1: 12-14: Said to be unsuited by
the slow pace but not disgraced: see 1002 (10f).   61
5 ran   1½,½,½,2   (Gestut Fahrhof)   H Jentzsch Germany

HAMBURG   Saturday July 5   Righthand, Flat Track

Official Going Given As FIRM

1490 GROUP 3 POKAL SPRINTER PREIS 3YO+   £13277   7f   Firm -

1147 SYLVAN EXPRESS (P Mitchell) 3-8-5 G Carter 1: 1-01001: 3 b c Baptism - Folle Remont
(Prince Tenderfoot) Very useful, impr colt: slowly away but made up a tremendous amount of
ground to lead well inside final 1f in Gr 3 event at Hamburg July 5: earlier won a val 3yo
h'cap at Newmarket: easy winner of val nurseries at Newmarket and Ascot at the end of '85:
very eff at 7f on gd and firm grd: should win more good races and seems a progressive type.   65
895   LE ROC (Germany) 3-8-5 P Remmert 1: -42: Ran on well: gd effort from this German
trained colt: eff 7f on fast ground.   59
--   GARRICK (Germany) 6-9-0 P Schiergen 1: 43-3: Not btn far.   57
1109 SHMAIREEKH (P Walwyn) 5-9-0 Paul Eddery 1: 0-20200: Ev ch in 5th: btr 881, 330.   54
--   KELLYTALK 4-9-7 J Tandari 1: 14330-0: Fin 6th.   51
7 ran   ½,½,½,½,7   (R Johnson)   P Mitchell Epsom, Surrey.

PHOENIX PARK   Saturday July 5   Left and Righthand, Sharpish Track

Official Going Given As GOOD/SOFT

1491 MR AND MRS S D PESKOFF RACE   £9750   6f   Good/Soft -

903   LONDON TOWER [3] (D Weld) 3-8-7 M Kinane 4/1: -120331: 3 b c Habitat - Lady Seymour
(Tudor Melody) Smart Irish colt: led over 1f out, ridden out in a val event at Phoenix Park
July 5: first time out won a mdn at Naas: full brother to the very smart filly Marwell: very
eff over 6f: seems to act on any ground.   80
--   ACUSHLA [8] (V O'brien) 3-8-4 Pat Eddery 5/4 FAV: /03-012: Well bckd: ran on well:
last time out was an easy winner of a 3yo fillies event over this C/D: eff at 6f, stays
further: acts on firm and yldg ground.   74

1125 BRIDESMAID [6] (B Hills) 3-8-13 B Thomson 3/1: -001233: Ev ch: twice below form 854.   73
639 YOUNG BLADE [5] (M O'toole) 3-9-2 C Roche 4/1: 3-21104: Abs since 639 and seems best
on heavy ground: see 472.   66
7 ran ½,5,4   (Mr B Firestone)   D Weld Ireland

1492 GROUP 3 PACEMAKER INTERNATIONAL   £19530   1m   Good/Soft

*1118 SARAB [6] (P Cole) 5-9-10 Pat Eddery 7/4 FAV: 04-3111: 5 b h Prince Tenderfoot -
Carnival Dance (Welsh Pageant) Smart horse who is in excellent form this season: chall final
1f and ran on well for a nk success in a Gr 3 event at Phoenix Park July 5: earlier a winner
at Chantilly and Baden Baden: most consistent in '85, winning Listed races at Newcastle and
Haydock: in '84 won at Goodwood, Doncaster, Newmarket, Haydock and Beverley: very eff at
7f/1m: acts on firm and soft ground and has a fine turn of foot: genuine sort who will more
good races.   79
920 ESQUIRE [4] (B Hills) 4-9-5 B Thomson 8/1: -211242: Made the running and battled on
really well: excellent effort and has been in grand form this season: see 920, 573.   71
1332 NASHAMAA [1] (J Bolger) 3-8-7 D Gillespie 5/1: 122-23: Gd eff: see 1332.   64
1330 MR JOHN [5] (L Browne) 3-8-8(1ow) M Browne 6/1: -412004: Below his best: see 1330(1½m).   61
1094 KINGS RIVER [2] 4-9-5 M Kinane 100/30: 41-2100: Below form 1094, best 1007.   56
1094 YOUNG RUNAWAY [3] 4-9-10 A Clark 14/1: 010-400: Last to fin: yet to find his form.   61
6 ran nk,2½,2   (F Salman)   P Cole Whatcombe, Oxon

SAINT CLOUD   Sunday July 6th

Official Going Given As GOOD/SOFT

1493 GROUP 1 GRAND PRIX DE SAINT CLOUD   £102760   1m 4f Soft

*896 ACATENANGO [5] (H Jentzsch) 4-9-8 S Cauthen 1: 111-11: 4 ch c Surumu - Aggravate
(Aggressor) Very smart German colt: gaining his 9th successive win, led 3f out, comfortably,
in Gr 1 Grand Prix de St Cloud at St Cloud Sunday July 6: last time out a winner of a Gr 2
event at Baden Baden: in excellent form in '85, winning the German Derby: very eff over
11/12f on gd & soft grd and does well when up with the pace: virtually impossible to beat
in his home country and seems equally as good elsewhere.   89
+885 SAINT ESTEPHE [1] (A Fabre) 4-9-8 A Gibert 1: 23-1312: Kept on well and is in grand
form: see 885.   86
645 NOBLE FIGHTER [6] (M Saliba) 4-9-8 C Asmussen 1: 310-333: Another fine effort:
again going for the Turf Classic: see 299.   84
1009 ALTAYAN [4] (A De Royer Dupre) 3-8-9 Y Saint Martin 1: 1224: The only 3yo in the field
and was not disgraced: see 1009.   83
1144 ST HILARION [2] 4-9-5 G Starkey 1: 11-0020: Gd eff: see 1144 (firm).   77
-- WALENSEE [7] 4-9-5 E Legrix 1: 1141-00: Fair 6th and is finding her form: last season
was rated 88 when winning the Gr 1 Prix Vermeille at Longchamp: very eff at 12f: acts on yldg.   77
*1115 GALLA PLACIDIA [3] 4-9-5 F Head 1: 30-1010: Fin 7th: btr 1115.   00
468 MORESPEED [9] 4-9-8 D Regnard 1: 2-22010: Distant 8th.   00
-- FRENCH SCHOOL [8] 4-9-8 G Mosse 1: 4010-00: -   00
9 ran 2,1½,2,1½,nk,1½   (Gestut Fahrhof)   H Jentzsch Germany

---

LINGFIELD   Friday July 11th   Lefthand, Sharpish, Undulating Track

Official Going Given As GOOD

1494 INFANTS MAIDEN GUARANTEED STAKES   £1207   1m 4f Good 65 +03 Fast

273 EMERALD POINT [12] (I Balding) 3-8-6(1ow) S Cauthen 10/3: 3-01: 3 ch c Mill Reef -
Crown Treasure (Graustark) Useful colt: despite long abs, led after 7f, hacking up in a
3 & 4yo maiden at Lingfield July 11: on sole start in '85 fin 3rd to Mashkour in a val stks
at Goodwood: full brother to the topclasss performers Glint of Gold and Diamond Shoal: stays
12f well: acts on gd and firm grd, possibly unsuited by hvy: acts well on a sharpish trk:
should win more races.   54
1080 BURNING BRIGHT [6] (D Ringer) 3-8-5 M Wigham 14/1: 002-042: No chance with easy
winner: stays 12f: see 1080.   33
1208 TOMS TREASURE [7] (R Akehurst) 4-9-4 R Mcghin 33/1: -33: Led over 7f: in gd form:
stays 12f and seems suited by front running tactics on gd/firm and a sharpish track.   22
486 BUSHIDO [9] (G Harwood) 3-8-6(1ow) G Starkey 4/6 FAV: -24: Heavily bckd, despite abs:
never going well: prob stays 12f, but much btr 486 (yielding).   14
1087 CALVADOS [2] 3-8-5 P Waldron 25/1: -000: Never nearer: first signs of form:
half brother to a winner in France: seems to stay 12f: acts on good ground.   09
-- SEAT OF LEARNING [5] 4-9-4 G Baxter 16/1: -0: Never in it on race course debut:
half sister to sev winners: may improve.   06
832 Windy Hollow [3] 8-5   1198 Nice Present [11] 8-2   1349 Ribokeyes Boy [8] 9-7
1208 April Arabesque [10] 9-4   -- Beloved Infidel [1] 8-5
-- Trojan Splash [4] 8-5
12 ran 8,5,5,2,½   (Paul Mellon)   I Balding Kingsclere, Berks.

1495 HEVER CASTLE STUD STAKES 2YO   £959   6f   Good 65 -16 Slow

1207 KIERON PRESS [14] (D Arbuthnot) 2-8-11 S Cauthen 15/8 FAV: 031: 2 ch c Whistling Deer
- Doll Acre (Linacre) Impr colt: landed some gd bets when making nearly all, comfortably, in
a 2yo stks at Lingfield July 11: cost IR 6,200: eff at
6f, should stay 7f+: suited by a sound surf: eff with forcing tactics on a sharp track.   45
--   MUAD DIB [15] (R Akehurst) 2-8-11 R Mcghin 33/1: 2: Debutant: fin in gd style:
promising run: eff 6f, should stay another furlong: acts on gd ground and a sharpish trk.   37
1082 LAZIM [10] (C Benstead) 2-8-11(bl) B Rouse 6/1: 043: Ev ch final 2f: see 1082.   30
--   CHILIBANG [1] (J Dunlop) 2-8-11 G Baxter 8/1: 4: Hung badly left final 2f and would
have finished a lot closer if keeping a str course: impr likely from this half brother to
6/7f winner Hot Case: should stay further than 6f: acts on gd ground.   30
--   GEBLITZT [16] 2-8-11 P Tilk 10/1: 0: Al up there on debut: fair effort: cost
23,000 gns: half brother to 2 middle dist winners and should stay further than 6f.   28
--   JOCKS BROTHER [4] 2-8-11 C Rutter(5) 16/1: 0: Late hdwy on debut: full brother to
very useful sprinter Our Jock and will improve on this next time.   19
--   BLAZING HIGH [9] 2-8-11 G Starkey 5/1: 0: Mkt drifter: eased when btn and should
improve on this initial effort: Australian bred coltwhose sirewas a speedy sort.   00
1289 Tiptree [13] 8-11   --   Hey Amadeus [5] 8-11 --   Max Is Cute [6] 8-11
--   Glorious Dan [8] 8-11   --   Design Wise [17] 8-11 --   Greensward Boy [7] 8-11
1190 Prince Mac [2] 8-11   1345 Rant On [3] 8-11
15 ran   3,2½,nk,¾,5,hd   (Otterdawn Associates Ltd)   D Arbuthnot Compton, Berks.

1496 KINDERGARTEN SELLING STAKES 2YO   £872   5f   Good 65 -19 Slow

1318 PINK PUMPKIN [5] (J Douglas Home) 2-8-8 M Hills 16/1: 00201: 2 b f Tickled Pink -
Wild Pumpkin (Auction Ring) Mkt drifter, but led final 1f comfortably in a 2yo seller at
Lingfield July 11 (bought in 1,550 gns): eff at 5f on a sharpish trk: acts on gd ground,
ran poorly on firm last time out when tried in blinkers.   21
149 HEDERA HELIX [6] (M Pipe) 2-8-11 S Cauthen 1/1 FAV: 02: Ex Irish gelding: well bckd
and led 4f: unplaced on sole start in Ireland: should be suited by further than 5f: acts
on good ground.   18
1241 BIOTIN [2] (P Haynes) 2-8-11(BL) J Williams 10/1: 00003: BI first time: never nearer:
dropped to selling company today: cheaply acquired gelding who is a half brother to sev
winners: acts on gd ground.   10
1100 FAIRY CHIMES [1] (R Stubbs) 2-8-8 D Nicholls 6/4: 34: Prom, fdd: btr 1100 (firm).   00
1318 MALACHI LAD [4] 2-8-11 G Duffield 16/1: 300: Lost grd start: there 3f.   00
1308 SCARNING SHADYLADY [3] 2-8-8 G Morgan 33/1: 000: Prom early: no form to date.   00
6 ran   2,3,2½,7,5   (N C Biggs)   J Douglas Home Didcot, Oxon.

1497 LINGFIELD HOSPITAL SCHOOL HCAP 3YO 0-35 £2600   1m 4f   Good 65 -06 Slow   [40]

*1258 KHETA KING [8] (W Hastings Bass) 3-8-7 R Lines(3) 2/1 FAV: 0-0311: 3 b g Hittite
Glory - Matala (Misti IV) In gd form, led 1f out, just getting the btr of Disciple in a
3yo h'cap at Lingfield July 11: last time out was a comfortable winner of an app h'cap at
Doncaster: half brother to minor winner Prince of Kashmir: stays 12f well: acts on gd and
firm ground and on any track.   29
*998 DISCIPLE [16] (G Lewis) 3-9-5(bl) P Waldron 10/1: 0004012: Led inside final 1f:
btn a whisker and 4l clear 3rd: gd form: acts on any track: seems best in blinkers.   41
*1314 UP TO UNCLE [3] (R Hannon) 3-9-3(5ex) A Mcglone 11/2: 0002213: Al prom: another
gd effort: see 1314.   32
619 LE MOULIN [12] (K Brassey) 3-9-3 S Whitworth 20/1: 0-004: Led after 7f: first signs
of form from this lightly raced colt: prob stays 12f, but may be dtr over 10f: acts on
gd ground and a sharpish track.   30
951 SIR BRETT [9] 3-9-7 Gay Kelleway(5) 20/1: -04140: Mkt drifter: never nearer:
best 790 (heavy ground).   31
1160 LORD IT OVER [6] 3-9-2 G Starkey 10/1: -0000: Eased when btn, twice below form 1062.   16
1204 BETTER BEWARE [1] 3-8-9(BL) S Cauthen 10/1: 3430030: BI first time: led briefly in
str: better 1204.   00
1236 PRIOK [7] 3-7-12 M L Thomas 10/1: 0-03000: Active in mkt: no show: best 275 (10f hvy)   00
1258 Final Alma [14] 9-1   1401 Aunt Etty [15] 7-10(BL)
980 Capulet [11] 8-11   980 Risk Another [13] 8-11
1317 Quarterflash [4] 8-8   1386 Last Polonaise [2] 8-5
989 Ranelagh [10] 8-4   1349 Hooray Hamilton [5] 7-7
16 ran   shthd,4,1,1½,10,shthd   (Sir Gordon Brunton)   W Hastings Bass Newmarket.

1498 JULY H'CAP 4YO+ 0-60   £3142   1m 2f   Good 65 -27 Slow   [48]

*1412 ALBERT HALL [3] (B Hills) 3-8-9 M Hills 15/8: 21D2211: 3 ch c Monteverdi - Hortensia
(Fr) (Luthier) Useful colt who is in fine form: led inside final 2f, comfortably, in slow
run h'cap at Lingfield July 11: last time out won a h'cap at Haydock: earlier disqualified
after being first past the post in a mdn at Redcar: well suited by 10/11f: seems to act
on any ground and on any track: most consistent this term.   53
1284 KINGS CRUSADE [1] (G Lewis) 3-7-7 M L Thomas 11/10 FAV: -44042: Well bckd: kept on
final 1f: may be suited by 12f: see 1284.   32

879 MAILMAN [2] (I Balding) 7-9-5 A Watkins(7) 9/2: 000-403: Abs: ev ch str: see 511.   43
72 GUNDREDA [4] (C Brittain) 4-9-7 S Cauthen 10/1: 000-004: Led 1m after long abs:
in '85 was in gd form, winning at Newmarket and Nottingham (2): equally eff at 9/10f:
acts on gd but well suited by soft and hvy ground: likes a stiff track.   43
4 ran   3,¼,¾   (R E Sangster)   B Hills Lambourn, Berks

1499 PEMBURY HANDICAP 3YO 0-35   £2491   6f   Good 65 +12 Fast   [42]

1032 WAR WAGON [9] (R Armstrong) 3-9-0(VIS) P Tulk 6/1: 0-00001: 3 gr c Posse - Cadabwah
(Abwah) Equipped with a visor and made ev yard, ridden out in quite fast run 3yo h'cap at
Lingfield July 11: seems well suited by 6f with forcing tactics, does stay 7f: acts on good
and firm ground and on any track.   36
1245 SILVER FORM [6] (W Wightman) 3-8-3 N Adams 13/2: 0-03402: Kept on under press: good
effort: seems best over 6f on gd ground: see 657.   23
844 WIZZARD MAGIC [11] (M Haynes) 3-7-7(BL)(5oh) T Williams 20/1: 00-03: Abs: ran on
final 1f: bl first time here: lightly raced prev: eff at 6f on gd ground and an undulating trk   12
*1191 HELAWE [8] (J Winter) 3-9-8(bl) S Cauthen 13/8 FAV: 0-03014: Al prom: in gd form.   39
1277 GLEADHILL PARK [10] 3-8-6 S Whitworth 10/1: 4-00000: No extra inside final 2f.   15
--   AUTO ELEGANCE [5] 3-9-7 C Rutter 20/1: 00340-0: Never nearer on seasonal debut:
first time out in '85 won a 2yo mdn auction at Bath: eff at 6f: likes fast ground.   26
1443 PERSIAN BAZAAR [1] 3-7-11 A Mcglone 8/1: 000-000: Bckd at long odds: fdd final 2f.   00
1319 FINDON MANOR [4] 3-8-5(bl) M Rimmer 10/1: 0-00000: Fin 8th: btr 1319, see 760.   00
842 SHARP STABLE [3] 3-7-9(2ow)(2oh) W Woods(0) 10/1: 0-000: Never in it after abs:
lightly raced: little form in 4 outings.   00
1391 Fancy Pages [7] 8-0(1ow)   1316 Thai Sky [2] 7-7(6oh)
11 ran   1,¾,1,4,2   (Charles H Wacker III)   R Armstrong Newmarket

---

1500 WATERGATE APPRENTICE HANDICAP 0-35 3YO+ £1660   7.5f   Good/Firm 39 -04 Slow   [32]

1176 DARNIT [6] (E Weymes) 4-9-13 M Tebbutt 7/1: 0-00021: 4 br f Julio Mariner - Sew
And Sew (Hard Tack) Mkt drifter but came from behind to lead inside final 1f, comfortably,
in an app h'cap at Chester July 11: quite consistent in '85 winning at Thirsk: very eff over
7f/1m: acts on firm and soft and on any track.   40
--   HELLO GYPSY [1] (C Tinkler) 5-8-13 W Goodwin(4) 33/1: 00000-2: Gd seasonal debut,
keeping on really well: also fin 2nd on seasonal debut in '85 and sub won at Warwick (amateur
riders): stays 1m: acts on firm and gd ground and runs well on a sharp track.   24
1335 SCOUTSMISTAKE [2] (B Mcmahon) 7-10-0 A Roper 8/1: 0-00033: Led/dsptd lead much,
not btn far: in gd form at present but may need a drop in the h'cap before making the winners
enclosure: see 815.   39
1264 TORREY [12] (W Hern) 7-9-7(bl) T Sprake 6/1: 10-2234: Hmpd final bend, chall 1f
out: not btn far: see 499.   29
1018 GAUHAR [9] 5-8-10 P Skelton(5) 10/1: 00-4440: Al prom: btr 1018 (gall trk).   11
1136 ABJAD [3] 5-8-3 S Hustler 25/1: 000-000: Sn prom: twice below 780 (seller hvy).   03
*1165 WINTER WORDS [5] 7-8-11 M Brennan 5/2 FAV: 00-0110: Again well bckd: led 3f out,
wknd quickly final 1f: btr 1165.   00
1104 Walhan [16] 7-12   1394 Sahara Shadow [15] 9-0(7ex)
727 Gracious Homes [8] 8-11   594 Sky Mariner [11] 7-11
1051 Shark Fighter [7] 8-3   1156 Tarleton [14] 8-0(4ow) 1447 Mairs Girl [17] 7-10
1338 Willie Gan [18] 8-7   1424 One For The Ditch [13] 8-1
16 ran   1,shthd,1½,3,nk   (T A Smethurst)   E Weymes Leyburn, Yorks.

1501 ALICE HAWTHORN MAIDEN FILLIES STKS 2YO   £2245   5f   Good/Firm 39 -18 Slow

848 BO BABBITY [3] (D H Jones) 2-8-11 D Williams(7) 14/1: 301: 2 b f Strong Gale - Get
Ready (On Your Mark) Impr filly: prom and responded gamely to press when forcing her hd in
front on the post to win a 2yo fillies mdn at Chester July 11: half sister to In Slips and
smart sprinter Anita's Prince: very eff over 5f on fast going, will stay 6f: acts on a
sharp track.   46
533 ULTRA NOVA [1] (P Cole) 2-8-11 T Quinn 4/1: 32: Just failed to make all after abs:
suited by a sharp trk and should find a small maiden in due course: see 533.   46
1108 GAYS FLUTTER [5] (C Nelson) 2-8-11 J Reid 5/4 FAV: 403: Dsptd lead most, rather
disapp after 1108 (stiff trk).   41
1370 ALHAYAT [4] (R Boss) 2-8-11 E Guest(3) 8/1: 44: Slow start, gd fin: impr and will
benefit from a stiffer track/longer distance: see 1370.   32
1333 PENBREASY [2] 2-8-11 S Perks 14/1: 040: Ev ch: see 1333.   31
1126 BRAZILIAN PRINCESS [8] 2-8-11 Pat Eddery 4/1: 00: Early speed: flattered 1126?   26
1069 DOMINO ROSE [7] 2-8-11 T Ives 10/1: 23220: Sn btn: can do much btr: see 826.   00
--   Frimley Queen [6] 8-11
8 ran   hd,1½,3,nk,1½,2¼   (North Cheshire Trading & Storage Ltd) D H Jones Pontypridd, Glamorgan.

1502 LITEO GROUP STAKES HCAP 0-60   £3746   1m 4f   Good/Firm 39 +05 Fast   [43]

1024 GULFLAND [3] (G P Gordon) 5-9-7 S Childs(7) 11/2: -132101: 5 ch g Gulf Pearl -
Sunland Park (Baragoi) Winning for the 3rd time this season, leading dist comfortably, in a
h'cap at Chester July 11: ran poorly last time but otherwise has been most consistent
winning earlier at Doncaster and Nottingham (first time out): suited by 10/12f and seems to
act on any trk and on any going.   46
1359 REGAL STEEL [5] (R Hollinshead) 8-8-1 A Culhane(7) 10/3: 0322022: Led/dsptd lead
thr'out: see 1359.   22
***1135 INDIAN ORATOR** [1] (B Hills) 3-8-6 B Thomson 7/4 FAV: 222-313: Waited with, found little
under press final 3f: see 1135.   31
1166 CABRAL [4] (C Vernon Miller) 5-8-11 W Carson 9/2: -0024: Ev ch: flattered 1166?See 943.   18
1432 EARLS COURT [6] 10-7-7(4oh) N Carlisle 12/1: 002-040: Made most: see 1432.   00
474 RECORD WING [2] 8-8-13 D Williams(7) 8/1: -213300: Sn rear after long abs: best 92(sft)   00
6 ran   1¼,6,1½,7,6   (G A Pritchard-Gordon)   G P Gordon Newmarket

1503 HENRY GEE MAIDEN STAKES 3YO   £2154   1m 2f   Good/Firm 39 +05 Fast

-- SWEET MOVER [8] (W Hern) 3-8-11 W Carson 7/4 FAV: 22-1: 3 ch f Nijinsky - Compassion-
ately (Hail To Reason) Useful filly: heavily bckd on seasonal debut and led final 1f narrowly
in a 3yo mdn at Chester July 11: 2nd in both her outings last term: cost $1m and is a half
sister to sev winners: suited by 10f, likely to stay 12f: acts on gd/firm and yldg: the
type to win more races.   47
937 NAJIDIYA [4] (R J Houghton) 3-8-11 K Darley 12/1: 3-02: Came from well off the pace,
narrowly btn in a close fin: suited by 10f, may stay 12f: should find a mdn soon: see 937.   46
667 NORDIC PLEASURE [7] (B Hills) 3-9-0 B Thomson 6/1: -33: Waited with, gd fin and not
btn far: gd eff after abs: suited by 10f, will stay further: a mdn should come his way soon.   48
1046 SHERZAD [2] (M Stoute) 3-9-0 A Kimberley 4/1: -404: Mkt drifter, prom thr'out and
not btn far: stays 10f: best 806 (stiff trk).   47
1055 STATE JESTER [6] 3-9-0(BL) C Dwyer 33/1: 00-0000: Pressed leaders, went on 3f out,
no extra final 1f: improved effort and seems suited by this sharp trk and fast ground:
may prove best over 1m/9f.   32
1023 MAKE PEACE [3] 3-9-0 Pat Eddery 10/1: 3-33000: Never closer: disapp since 484 (yldg)   27
1147 MERHI [10] 3-9-0 J Lowe 6/1: 2343000: Prom, wknd into 7th: best 698.   27
1032 Gay Appeal [1] 8-11   **1220 Hitchenstown** [9] 9-0   **1193 Welsh Pageantry** [11] 8-11
-- Top Row [6] 9-0
11 ran   ¼,½,nk,5,2½,½   (Sheikh Mohammed)   W Hern West Ilsley, Berks.

1504 CARDINAL PUFF STAKES 2YO   £2968   7f   Good/Firm 39 -09 Slow

1373 BILLS HENRY [6] (R Boss) 2-9-3 E Guest(3) 0131: 2 b g In Fijar - Danaka (Val
de Loir) Useful, impr gelding: mkt drifter but made virtually all comfortably, in a 2yo
minor event at Chester July 11: earlier won a mdn at Wolverhampton: brother to a couple of
winners: suited by 7f, will stay at least 1m: acts on firm and gd going and on any trk:
still improving.   53
-- EMPEROR HOTFOOT [3] (R J Houghton) 2-8-11 Pat Eddery 3/1: 2: Well bckd debutant,
chall 1f out and 3l clear rem: closely related to winning 2yo Hot Girl and Hot Boy: sure to
stay at least 1m: acts on fast ground round a sharp trk and shd have little trouble finding
a maiden.   45
***1305 BATTLEAXE** [7] (J Toller) 2-9-3 W Carson 4/1: 33413: Prom thr'out: in gd form: stays 7f.   45
1050 BLACK MANS BAY [2] (J Etherington) 2-8-11 M Wood 33/1: 04: Gd fin and is improving:
suited by 7f, will stay 1m: see 1050.   38
1289 BOIS DE BOULOGNE [4] 2-8-11 T Ives 11/4 FAV: 2030: Ev ch and has yet to fulfill
initial promise in 662 which has worked out poorly.   35
***1294 NIFTY GRIFF** [9] 2-8-11 K Bradshaw(5) 7/1: 00110: Fdd quickly final 1f and btr 1294(6f)   24
503 Carjulen [5] 8-11   **1129 Tahard** [8] 8-11   **-- Gouldswood** [1] 8-11
9 ran   ¼,3,½,1½,5   (Mrs B J Dash)   R Boss Newmarket

1505 RED DEER HANDICAP 3YO 0-50   £3152   5f   Good/Firm 39 -09 Slow   [52]

1414 NO BEATING HARTS [6] (M Mccormack) 3-8-11 W Newnes 9/2: 1304021: 3 b g London Bells -
Movement (Daring Display) Gained a pillar to post success in a 3yo h'cap at Chester July 11:
first time out winner of a mdn at Newmarket April 15: seems best over 5/6f with forcing
tactics tho' acts on any trk and on firm and yielding going.   45
1438 NAGEM [3] (L Barratt) 3-7-7(3oh) P Hill(7) 9/1: 000-042: Al there: gd effort from
this maiden and could find a small race shortly: likely to stay 6f: see 1438.   22
1380 MANDRAKE MADAM [2] (D Smith) 3-9-3 L Charnock 8/1: -000033: Prom thr'out: see 1380.   45
507 THE HILCOTE CLUB [1] (R Woodhouse) 3-8-13 A Bond 10/1: 44-4004: Abs: fin well and
best effort since race 6.   35
1418 MAYBE JAYNE [9] 3-7-7(13oh) N Carlisle 50/1: -440000: Slow start, ran on fin: stiff
task and best effort since 377 (yielding).   09
1334 MARSHALL DRILLS [5] 3-7-7(14oh) A Culhane(7) 50/1: 00-0000: Slow start, never btr:
maiden who has shown little worthwhile form so far.   04
1283 RUNAWAY [4] 3-9-3 S Perks 9/1: -000000: No threat in 7th: btr 1283 (stiff trk).   26
1391 SAY PARDON [8] 3-8-12 M Birch 3/1 FAV: 220-220: Uneasy fav, early speed fin 8th:
much btr 1391 (stiff track).   20
1344 IMPALA LASS [7] 3-8-2 A Mackay 7/1: 1100000: Chall dist, fdd quickly into 9th:
little form since 443 (C/D).   00

1391 AFRICAN REX [10] 3-9-7 T Ives 9/2: 2011-00: Made no show: see 1391.   **00**
10 ran 1¼,¼,2½,2,1½,1,¾   (Tony Hart)   M Mccormack Sparsholt, Oxon.

YORK   Friday July 11th   Lefthand, Galloping Track

Official Going Given As GOOD/FIRM

1506 BLACK DUCK STAKES 2YO   £4012   6f   Firm 09 -18 Slow

1129 CHIME TIME [2] (C Tinkler) 2-9-2 M Birch 8/11 FAV: 1121: 2 b c Good Times - Balnespick (Charlottown Town) Very useful colt: readily made all, drawing 6l clear in final 1f in quite a val 2yo race at York July 11: earlier won first 2 on the trot at Redcar and Haydock and was a fine 2nd to the flying Minstrella in the Chesham Stks at Royal Ascot: half brother to fair 1m/10f winner Kaukas: very eff over 6f, sure to stay further: acts well on firm and gd grd and likes a gall track: sure to win more races.   **69**
+**1255 GLOW AGAIN** [4] (J Etherington) 2-9-2 M Wood 15/8: 31112: 2nd thr'out but had no chance with this smart winner: in grand form: see 1255.   **54**
571 PEATSWOOD SHOOTER [3] (M Brittain) 2-9-2 K Darley 12/1: 11103: Long abs: chall for 2nd 1f out, just no extra: best 278 (5f hvy).   **51**
-- **I SWEPT IN** [1] (J Kettlewell) 2-8-11 Pat Eddery 25/1: 4: Totally outpaced thr'out: cost only 900 gns and is sprint bred.   **06**
4 ran 6,1,20   (Red Lion Inn & Motel Ltd)   C Tinkler Malton, Yorks.

1507 MAIL ON SUNDAY 3YO SERIES H'CAP 0-60   £5150   1m 1f   Firm 09 +01 Fast   **[58]**

+**863 SHAFY** [3] (M Stoute) 3-9-7 W R Swinburn 9/2: 32-411: 3 b c Lyphard - I'll Be Around (Isgala) Very useful, impr colt: ran on to lead final 1f and comfortably won a 3yo h'cap at York July 11: won a mdn at Beverley June 3: showed promise both outings last term: very eff over 1m/9f and will stay 10f: acts on firm/gd going: the type to win more races.   **64**
946 LONDON BUS [2] (J Watts) 3-9-2 T Ives 2/1 FAV: 00-1122: Prom, led 3f out, outpaced near fin: fine effort from this consistent colt: see 553: acts on firm and yldg.   **55**
1220 HELLO BENZ [6] (M H Easterby) 3-7-10(VIS) A Mackay 7/2: -400423: Visored for the first time today, cl.up 3f out but looked a difficult ride in the closing stages: yet to lose his maiden tag: see 322, 1220.   **31**
1153 LUCKY SO SO [8] (S Norton) 3-9-1 J Lowe 12/1: -410304: Dsptd lead dist, not btn far and a good effort: best 925 (1m sharp trk).   **49**
1073 FOREMAST [1] 3-8-3 M Fry 14/1: 0-130: Set a gd pace over 6f: best 822 (1m hvy).   **33**
1374 COMMON FARM [5] 3-7-13 K Darley 25/1: 0001000: Never in it: needs soft: best 1122.   **19**
1130 MY TON TON [4] 3-9-2(BL) P Robinson 7/1: 10-0000: Bl first time, beat a retreat str: yet to regain last season's form: see 510.   **00**
1153 SOMETHING CASUAL [7] 3-9-0 Pat Eddery 7/1: 10-0000: Prom 6f: much btr 1153.   **00**
8 ran 1,1½,¾,2½,8,nk   (Sheikh Mohammed)   M Stoute Newmarket

1508 LIN PAC HANDICAP 3YO+ 0-70   £6170   5f   Firm 09 +19 Fast   **[62]**

1145 ROTHERFIELD GREYS [1] (C Bell) 4-8-11 J Leech(7) 11/2: 00-1101: 4 b g Mummy's Pet - Relicia (Relko) Very useful gelding: landed quite a gamble when al prom and forging ahead inside final 1f comfortably, in a very fast run, val h'cap at York July 11: easy winner of first 2 on the trot at Edinburgh and Warwick, below his best over 6f in the Wokingham last time: useful 2yo but a virus sufferer in '85: stays 6f but at his best over 5f on firm or good going: likes to be up with the pace: continues to improve.   **60**
-**1268 CLANTIME** [8] (R Whitaker) 5-9-2 D Mckeown 6/1: 2234122: Led/dsptd lead thr'out: no visor today but ran right to his best: see 818.   **60**
*922 **IMPERIAL JADE** [7] (A Jarvis) 4-9-6 Pat Eddery 5/2 FAV: 0-30213: Bolted before start, al prom in race and was staying on at the fin: needs 6f now? See 922.   **62**
1387 DUBLIN LAD [6] (M Brittain) 3-10-0(7ex) A Bacon(7) 7/1: 0003144: Made most, another grand effort under 10-0: see 1268.   **77**
994 TRUE NORA [4] 3-8-9 J Reid 12/1: 10-0030: Slow start, best in 443 (very sharp trk)   **52**
1268 KING CHARLEMAGNE [5] 7-8-6 D Leadbitter(4) 25/1: 1000-00: No threat but is slowly finding his form: easily takes sev races to hit peak form and last season won twice on the trot at Redcar and Edinburgh: 5 times a winner in '84: a 5f specialist who is at his best on gd or firm ground but seems to act on any track: another couple of races shd see him back in the winners enclosure.   **41**
1306 AMIGO LOCO [3] 5-9-10(bl) R Hills 12/1: 2200040: Al outpaced in 7th: see 1306 (6f).   **00**
1429 RA RA GIRL [2] 4-7-8 A Mackay 10/1: 0-00000: Bckd at long odds: fin 8th: winner of minor events at Pontefract and Thirsk in '85: eff between 5 and 7f and on fast and yldg going: seems to act on any track.   **00**
1385 HI TECH GIRL [9] 4-8-12 W R Swinburn 15/2: 0340-40: No threat in 9th: see 1385.   **00**
1145 PHILIP [10] 4-9-6(bl) Kim Tinkler(5) 11/1: 0311300: Fin last and appears to have lost his edge: best 687 (good).   **00**
10 ran 1½,1,hd,2,nk   (Mrs D Gleeson)   C Bell Sparsholt, Oxon.

1509 SIA MANCHESTER SINGAPORE H'CAP 0-70   £5952   1m 4f   Firm 09 +08 Fast   **[52]**

1278 AUCTION FEVER [6] (B Hills) 3-8-3(BL) B Thomson 100/30: -202321: 3 ch c Hello Gorgeous - Auction Bridge (Auction Ring) Successfully ended a frustrating sequence of placings when bl

for the first time in a val and quite fast run h'cap at York July 11: made smooth prog to
lead final 1f and drew clear: showed plenty of promise prev: eff over 1m, nowadays well
suited by 12f: acts on yldg, runs well on fast grd and on a gall trk: seems best in blinkers.   55
+1020 FIVE FARTHINGS [1] (M Stoute) 4-9-6 W R Swinburn 6/4 FAV: 100-012: Qcknd into lead
2f out, no extra final 1f but a fine effort as she has risen considerably in the
weights since 1020 (good).   52
1412 DIPYN BACH [3] (M Camacho) 4-8-1 W Carson 11/1: 0-04403: Never closer: best 912 (10f gd) 23
1147 HAPPY BREED [4] (C Brittain) 3-8-8 Pat Eddery 9/1: 31-004: Prom much: ran only twice
in '85 winning a minor event at Lingfield in Oct: eff around 7f, shd be suited by longer
dist: acts on firm ground.   44
1409 ROMIOSINI [5] 4-9-2 Kim Tinkler(5) 7/1: 0411000: Made much: see 1024.   36
1325 SWIMMER [2] 4-9-7 G Carter(5) 5/1: 13-1430: Chall 3f out, fdd and btr 1325 (10f).   39
6 ran   4,7,nk,2,1½   (R Sangster)   B Hills Lambourn, Berks

1510 PHILIP CORNES NICKEL ALLOYS 2YO MAIDEN   £3866   6f   Firm 09 +02 Fast

1097 RICH CHARLIE [4] (C Nelson) 2-9-0 J Reid 7/2: 01: 2 ch c Young Generation - Maiden
Pool (Sharpen Up) Highly promising colt: prom and forged clear in final 2f for an impr, fast
time success in a 2yo mdn at York July 11: highly tried first time out (Coventry Stks): quite
cheaply bought son of a winning 5f sprinter: speedily bred and is likely to prove most eff
at dist up to 7f: acts well on firm ground: looks sure to win more races, in btr class.   65
--   GET ON GERAGHTY [5] (G Huffer) 2-9-0 G Carter(3) 14/1: 2: Slow start, fin in grand
fashion and this was a pleasing debut: cost only 5000gns: sure to stay beyond 6f: acts on
firm ground: should have little trouble finding a maiden in the North.   50
--   GO HENRI [2] (J Dunlop) 2-9-0 W Carson 100/30: 3: Well bckd debutant, ev ch: cost
$8,000 and is speedily bred: acts on firm ground: likely to improve.   42
1242 EL ZETA [10] (P Kelleway) 2-9-0 Pat Eddery 3/1 FAV: 04: Well bckd: rather taken off
his legs by this fast pace: prob needs further than 6f: see 1242.   42
--   BOWERS FOLD [7] 2-9-0 K Hodgson 20/1: 0: No real threat but likely to benefit from the
experience: quite cheaply bought at IR 18,000: speedily bred sort.   41
--   FRENCHGATE [1] 2-9-0 M Birch 14/1: 0: Prom much: cost only IR 7,000 and is related
to a couple of winners: bred to need further than 6f and should stay middle dist in time.   33
--   ALVECOTE MAGIC [3] 2-9-0 T Lucas 11/2: 0: Well bckd debutant, fin 7th: cost 15,000 gns:
a May foal who may need more time/longer dist to reveal his true worth.   00
--   DARING DESCENT [8] 2-9-0 R Hills 10/1: 0: No threat in 9th: ran rather green and
should benefit from the experience: certain to appreciate longer dist in time.   00
1373 Pathero [6] 9-0(BL)   1266 Kaleidophone [9] 8-11   873 Joe Sugden [12] 9-0
--   Crancheter [11] 9-0
12 ran   4,3,sht hd,hd,2½   (R E A Bott Wigmore St Ltd)   C R Nelson, Lambourn

1511 MONKGATE MAIDEN STAKES 3YO   £3092   7f   Firm 09 -13 Slow

1107 EASTERN SONG [5] (C Nelson) 3-9-0 J Reid 100/30: 20-01: 3 ch c Ballad Rock - Magee
(Weaver's Hall) Heavily bckd, al prom and led dist, comfortably, in a 3yo mdn at York July
11: 2nd at Newbury on race course debut in '85, sub chipped a bone in his leg: very eff at
7f: should stay 1m: acts well on firm grd: highly regarded sort who should continue to
improve and win better races.   51
1198 KALANDARIYA [8] (R J Houghton) 3-8-11 Pat Eddery 8/1: 4-302: Tried to make all:
fine effort: seems best over 7f/1m with forcing tactics tho' acts on firm and gd going:
should find a maiden, possibly on a sharper trk: see 422.   45
844 SIR ARNOLD [7] (A Stewart) 3-9-0 M Roberts 8/1: -23: Kept on well under press:
improving and will be suited by 1m: acts on firm and good: see 844.   41
379 MRS MAINWARING [2] (S Norton) 3-8-11 T Ives 14/1: 03-04: Never closer after long abs:
best effort so far and acts well on firm ground: will stay beyond 7f.   35
699 SPINNING TURN [4] 3-9-0 M Fry 33/1: -03400: Abs: came from off the pace: prob does
not stay 12f and is eff over 1m: see 388.   35
--   PLEASING PROSPECT [6] 3-8-11 M Birch 20/1: 300-0: May improve for this seasonal debut:
ran only 3 times in '85 (rated 40 on 2nd outing): half sister to sev winners: should stay 1m.   22
702 ABADJERO [10] 3-9-0 A Murray 8/1: -020: Prom much, wknd into 7th after abs since 702.   00
1046 AITCH N BEE [11] 3-9-0 W Carson 1/1 FAV: -040: Heavily bckd: disapp 8th & much btr 1046 00
--   Snarry Hill [3] 8-11   1375 Danesmoor [9] 8-11
10 ran   1,3,1½,1½,5   (Mrs W Tulloch)   C Nelson Lambourn, Berks

Official Going Given As GOOD

1512 SUNDAY MAGAZINE STAKES 2YO £3200 6f Good/Firm 32 -05 Slow

*1320 QUICK SNAP [6] (A Ingham) 2-9-1(bl) R Curant 5/2: 3221011: 2 b c Try My Best - Photo
(Blakeney) Very useful, consistent colt: made ev yard, forging clear final 1f for a 6l win in
a 2yo stks at Lingfield July 12: earlier successful at Folkestone and Sandown and has only
once fin out of the frame: eff over a stiff 5f, suited by 6f: acts on firm and soft ground
and on any track: genuine sort who likes to force the pace and will win more races. 61
1241 HANSEATIC [3] (P Makin) 2-8-11 S Cauthen 14/1: 002: Al 2nd: kept on: on the upgrade:
acts on gd and fast ground and should find a race: see 1241. 41
1381 LAST DANCE [1] (R Hannon) 2-8-11 G Starkey 4/1: 0423: Prom, ev ch: btr 1381 (firm) 40
-- WHAT A GUY [4] (P Mitchell) 2-8-11 G Carter 33/1: 4: Never nearer on race course debut:
half brother to winning sprinter Shanouska: will prob stay 7f: should improve. 36
*1376 SUMMERHILL STREAK [2] 2-9-1 A Mackay 1/1 FAV: 2310: Never nearer: disapp after 1376. 40
382 MIGHTY BOLD [7] 2-8-11 P Tulk 20/1: 00: Long abs: prom early: possibly needed race:
cost IR 18,000 and is a half brother to winners abroad. 30
6 ran 6,nk,1½,hd,2½ (Exors of the late S R Crowe) A Ingham Epsom, Surrey

1513 SUN PAGE THREE SILVER CUP LISTED 3YO+ £15790 1m 6f Good/Firm 32 +19 Fast

+1409 RAKAPOSHI KING [6] (H Cecil) 4-8-12 S Cauthen 2/1 FAV: 120-311: 4 b c Bustino -
Supper Time (Shantung) Smart, much impr colt: made ev yard, comfortably, in a fast run Listed
race at Lingfield July 12: last time out again made all when romping home in val Old Newton
H'cap at Haydock: trained by R Armstrong in '85, winning at Goodwood, Sandown and Leicester:
bought this season as a lead horse to the now retired Slip Anchor: a smart front runner in
his own right and is very eff over 12/14f on gd and firm ground: certain to win more gd races. 78
1127 I WANT TO BE [2] (J Dunlop) 4-9-2 W Carson 16/1: 212-002: Ev ch in str: no impression:
12l clear 3rd and is finding her form: in '85 was in grand form, winning Gr 2 Park Hill Stakes
at Doncaster and a fillies h'cap at Newbury: on final outing fin 2nd to Mersey in Gr 1 Prix
Royal-Oak at Longchamp: in '84 won at York: very eff at 14f, stays 15f well: acts on firm
and yldg ground and likes a gall track. 77
*1217 PHARDANTE [4] (G Harwood) 4-9-8 G Starkey 3/1: 0-01013: No extra in str: much btr 1217 65
1128 ALTIYNA [1] (M Stoute) 3-7-11 A Mackay 9/2: 1-2204: No real threat: btr 1128 (12f). 51
1127 TALE QUALE [3] 4-9-3 W Newnes 5/1: 01-0400: Never in it: needs firm: see 1127, 585. 55
*1111 STAVORDALE [5] 3-8-3 R Hills 13/2: 0-4410: Wknd str: much btr 1111 (2m, firm). 41
6 ran 2½,12,2½,½,12 (Lord Howard de Walden) H Cecil Newmarket

1514 NEWS OF THE WORLD TROPHY 3YO+ LISTED £12661 7.5f Good/Firm 32 +04 Fast

1107 HARD ROUND [4] (R Hannon) 3-8-5 B Rouse 7/1: 1-24431: 3 ch c Hard Fought - Princess
Zeddera (English Prince) Very useful colt: enterprisingly ridden when racing alone on the
stand side for a comfortable 2½l win in a val Listed race at Lingfield July 12: last time out
fin a fine 3rd in Gr 3 Jersey Stks at Royal Ascot: in '85 won a mdn at Epsom: eff at 7f/1m:
acts on gd/firm and yldg and on any track. 71
950 GLIDE BY [8] (R Boss) 4-8-8 W Newnes 33/1: 4200-32: Led far side: fine effort:see 950 59
-1286 NINO BIBBIA [2] (L Cumani) 3-8-8 R Guest 5/4 FAV: -110423: Chance over 1f out:btr 1286 65
-1000 PRESIDIUM [11] (H Cecil) 4-9-2 S Cauthen 9/2: 03-1024: Prom, ev ch: see 1000, 344 (1m) 61
1286 SIT THIS ONE OUT [3] 3-8-5 R Curant 50/1: -303000: No extra inside final 2f: best 802 50
-- BARRACK STREET [9] 3-8-5 M Giles 33/1: 13440-0: Fair seasonal debut: ran consistently
well in '85, winning at Ascot and Doncaster: eff at 7f/1m: acts on firm & yldg, and on any trk 45
945 CHARGE ALONG [10] 4-8-13 R Hills 10/1: 400-040: Fin 7th: btr 945, see 433. 00
1332 SIYAH KALEM [6] 4-9-5 W Carson 5/1: 1-41200: No threat in 8th: twice below form 1109. 00
1186 Ash Creek [7] 8-11 1095 Windsor Knot [5] 8-11 1286 Fringe Of Heaven [1] 9-2
11 ran 2½,2,½,6,2½,nk,1½ (R J Shannon) R Hannon Marlborough, Wilts

1515 EUROPRINT FILLIES HANDICAP 3YO+ 0-50 £2560 7f Good/Firm 32 -31 Slow [36]

1036 FAR TOO BUSY [4] (R Smyly) 3-7-9 S Dawson 25/1: -0001: 3 b f Margouillat - Lakshmi
(Tribal Chief) Led 2f out, driven out in a slow run fillies h'cap at Lingfield July 12f: eff
at 7f on gd and hvy ground: seems suited by an undulating trk. 22
1257 NEW EVIDENCE [5] (E Eldin) 3-7-12 A Mackay 7/2: 0-00022: Ran on well: in fine form:
should be suited by 1m: acts on gd and firm ground and on any track. 23
1245 LADY LA PAZ [2] (P Cundell) 3-8-2 G French 5/1: -040233: Stayed on well: another good
effort: see 1245, 1032. 27
-- MORICA [8] (J Dunlop) 3-9-6 W Carson 3/1 FAV: 1-4: Uneasy fav on seasonal debut:
hmpd slightly 2f out and kept on well final 1f: will do btr next time: won sole start in
'85, a maiden at Newbury: eff at 7f, may stay 1m: acts on gd ground. 45
1346 NELSONS LADY [6] 5-8-4 I Salmon 9/2: 0310-00: Kept on: not btn far: in '85 won a
fillies h'cap over this C/D: in '84 won at Brighton: equally eff at 7f/1m: acts on gd and
firm ground and likes a sharpish undulating track. 27
1032 IYAMSKI [3] 3-9-3 S Cauthen 9/2: -20230: Chance over 1f out: see 1032. 39
874 LUNAR SHAMAL GAL [7] 3-8-3 G Carter(3) 8/1: 01-000: Made much, fdd: see 447 (6f). 00
762 BAG LADY [1] 3-9-7 G Starkey 6/1: 034-320: Ran poorly after abs: see 762. 00
8 ran ½,shthd,½,nk,½ (Mrs Mark Smyly) R Smyly Lambourn, Berks.

1516 WATMOUGHS MAIDEN FILLIES STKS 3YO   £1370   6f   Good/Firm 32 -02 Slow

787 BROOKS DILEMMA [10] (M Albina) 3-8-11 A Bond 14/1: -01: 3 b f Known Fact - Trusted
Maiden (Busted) Fast impr filly: made ev yard very easily in a 3yo fillies mdn at Lingfield
July 12: cost IR 340,000 as yearling: half sister to 3 winners: eff at 6f, looks sure to
stay 7f/1m: acts on gd/firm grd and an undulating trk: should rate more highly/win more races.   50
776 SOLO SINGER [11] (P Cole) 3-8-11 T Quinn 9/4 FAV: -0402: No chance with winner:
stays 7f: see 431.   35
732 CHART CLIMBER [7] (R Laing) 3-8-11 W Newnes 14/1: 0-03: Never nearer: btr eff from
this lightly raced filly : seems to stay 7f: should continue to improve.   25
--   CLASS ACTION [5] (R Armstrong) 3-8-11 W Carson 5/1: 0-4: Mkt drifter on seasonal debut:
sn prom: half sister to the useful 1m/10f winner Quiet Riot: should improve.   23
1272 GRISETTE [4] 3-8-11 G Starkey 12/1: 030-000: Fdd final 1f: btr 6f? See 837.   21
1228 SANCILIA [3] 3-8-11 S Cauthen 9/2: 00-00: Late hdwy: btr eff from this half sister to
winning Secret Castanheiro: should be suited by 1m: acts on good.   19
835 SECRET FACT [13] 3-8-11 B Rouse 13/2: -00: Never nearer after abs: lightly raced filly
who is a half sister to a winner in France: should be suited by 1m.   00
835 WINSONG MELODY [2] 3-8-11 J Kennedy 10/1: -440: Mkt drifter: abs since much btr 835(5f) 00
844 Al Zahyia [6] 8-11   1244 Town Fair [9] 8-11   --   Kingsfold Flame [12] 8-11
1272 Spanish Intent [1] 8-11   1368 Sonning [8] 8-11
13 ran   6,5,1,1,1   (Mahmoud Fustok)   M Albina Newmarket

1517 LAMCO VARMA HANDICAP 3YO+ 0-50   £2560   1m 2f   Good/Firm 32 -21 Slow   [45]

*1186 ROYAL HALO [4] (G Harwood) 5-9-11 G Starkey 3/1: 34-2011: 5 b h Halo - Lady Gordon
(Levee) In fine form, well bckd and led 2½f out, comfortably, in a h'cap at Lingfield July
12: last time out won an app event at Brighton: in '84 won at Kempton: seems equally eff at
1m/10f: acts on fast and soft ground and on any trk tho' likes a sharpish one.   52
*1185 AL ZUMURRUD [6] (R Armstrong) 3-8-6 W Carson 15/8 FAV: 0-12212: Ev ch inside final
2f: in fine form: see 1185.   40
1295 SHAHS CHOICE [1] (J Dunlop) 3-7-8 S Dawson 5/1: -00-043: Al up there: see 1295.   27
*1231 DUELLING [3] (P Mitchell) 5-7-13(vis) G Carter(3) 6/1: 0000014: Much btr 1231 (1m).   18
1321 DERBY DAY [5] 5-7-7(bl)(3oh) L Riggio(6) 13/2: 0042030: Led 7f: btr 856, see 750.   04
850 WELL MEET AGAIN [2] 9-8-2(1ow) B Rouse 16/1: 3000000: Al rear: best first time out 36.   03
6 ran   2½,½,nk,4,5   (Mrs Doris Campbell)   G Harwood Pulborough, Sussex

---

Official Going Given As Good/Soft

1518 QUEENPOT MAIDEN STAKES 2YO   £1938   7f   Good 57 -03 Slow

1232 STATE BALLET [15] (I Balding) 2-9-0 P Cook 2/1 FAV: 01: 2 b c Pas de Seul - Cassina
(Habitat) Clearly benefitted considerably from his recent debut, led below dist, comfortably
in a 2yo mdn at Salisbury July 12: dam won as a juv over this trip: promises to stay at least
1m: acts on gd and firm ground and on any trk: should win more races.   56
--   ASHWA [1] (P Cole) 2-9-0 M Lynch(5) 4/1: 2: Nicely bckd debutant: led/dsptd lead most
and ran a promising race: cost 200,000 gns as yearling and is a half brother to 7f winner
Feydan: stays 7f: acts on gd ground and on a stiff track: will improve and find a race.   48
--   LAENA [7] (D Oughton) 2-8-11 J Williams 33/1: 3: Unfancied on debut tho' stayed on
promisingly from dist: will benefit from this experience: should stay 1m: acts on good
ground and on a stiff track.   45
--   LOW LINE [8] (H Candy) 2-8-11 T Williams 12/1: 4: Pleasing debut: half sister to a handful of middle dist winner, notably smart Quay Line: should stay further than 7f: acts on
good ground and on a galloping track.   40
434 TASJIL [6] 2-9-0 P Waldron 16/1: 00: No extra dist tho' btr suited by this longer
trip: half brother to winning miler Senane: see 434.   35
1341 TOMS LITTLE BET [5] 2-8-11 I Johnson 33/1: 000: First signs of form: bred to stay
further: acts on gd ground and on a galloping track.   28
--   LAGTA [11] 2-8-11 G Baxter 8/1: 0: Easy to back on debut: no threat tho' sure to
improve for this experience: nicely bred filly who cost 100,000 gns.   00
--   GOLD JUSTICE [12] 2-9-0 A Mcglone 20/1: 0: Mkt drifter: al behind tho' will improve.   00
--   AMANDA JANE [17] 2-8-11 K Butler 16/1: 0: Ran green on her debut.   00
--   TARTUFFE [10] 2-9-0 A Clark 12/1: 0: Mkt drifter: veered left before ½ way and sn
no threat: cost $35,000 and is a half brother to a couple of winners in the States: should leave
         this running behind next time.   00
1239 Kingswood Resopal [20] 9-0   985 Tropical Boy [4] 9-0
1019 Cee En Cee [3] 9-0   1225 Persian Dynasty [18] 9-0
1232 Spanish Connection [2] 9-0   1039 Keecagee [13] 9-0
--   Home Jesta [14] 9-0   118 Midday Sanito [16] 9-0
1239 Treva [9] 9-0   --   Seragsbee [19] 8-11
20 ran   3,shthd,2½,4,2   (D H Back)   I Balding Kingsclere, Hants.

SALISBURY   Saturday July 12th   -Cont'd

1519 BROOKE BOND TEA CUP STKS AMATS   £1900   1m 2f Good 57 -08 Slow

1109 RUNNING FLUSH [14] (D Oughton) 4-11-7(vis) Mr G Webster(3) 6/1: 0043001: 4 ch c
Lord Gayle - Hidden Hand (Ribocco) Useful colt: led over 2f out for an easy win in an
amateur riders stks at Salisbury July 12: twice successful in h'caps at Lingfield last term:
eff around 1m, stays 10f really well: acts on any going and on any track.   50
*1349 PACTOLUS [2] (G Harwood) 3-10-10 Amanda Harwood(3) 11/10 FAV: 410-012: No extra cl.
home tho' ran a good race against older horses: acts on any track: see 1349.   44
*1166 RIMAH [7] (H Thomson Jones) 5-11-10(bl) Franca Vittadini 9/4: 40-0113: Another good
effort: see 1166.   42
959 MESSALINE [12] (J Francome) 4-11-0 Jackie Hodge(3) 20/1: -04: Ran on strongly and
certain to be suited by 12f: lightly raced half brother to 9f winner Sauvita: acts on gd
ground and on a stiff track.   25
1240 MISTER PRELUDE [13] 6-11-7 Mr M Felton(3) 33/1: 0-00200: Ran to his best: see 1081.   28
*1156 IKTIYAR [6] 4-11-7 Dana Mellor(3) 9/1: 20-0010: Made much: see 1156 (1m)   28
1274 Careen [4] 11-0   1243 Catman [16] 11-0(vis)   -- Emperor Napoleon [15] 11-0
-- Sailor Miss [1] 11-4   -- Swift Ascent [11] 11-0
1344 Toms Nap Hand [5] 10-11   1400 Timewaster [9] 11-7
1186 Neocene [8] 10-11
14 ran   4,2,4,2½,shthd   (N Capon)   D Oughton Findon, Sussex

1520 FAIR TRIAL HANDICAP 3YO 0-50   £2788   1m   Good 57 +11 Fast   [54]

1343 SWIFTS PAL [1] (G Lewis) 3-9-2 J Adams(7) 14/1: -003041: 3 b c Record Token - Polly
Oligant (Prince Tenderfoot) Returned to form, led below dist for a comfortable win in a fast
run 3yo h'cap at Salisbury July 12: won at Ripon and Leicester last season: eff over 6f tho'
btr suited by 1m nowadays: acts on firm and yldg ground and on any track.   54
1043 ABSENCE OF MALICE [13] (B Hanbury) 3-8-3(BL) A Geran(7) 5/1: -2002: Led/dsptd lead
most: bl first time today and ran her best race since 213: stays 1m: acts on gd and yldg.   38
615 TERMINATOR [2] (H Candy) 3-8-11 T Williams 5/1: 341-303: Not btn far: gd effort
after fair abs: seems well suited by a stiff trk: see 326.   45
1034 FLOATING ASSET [8] (P Walwyn) 3-8-12 N Howe 7/1: 4-40344: Ev ch: quite consistent:
see 386.   41
1147 MUDRIK [9] 3-9-4 P Waldron 11/2: 4124000: Fair effort: best on hvy in 234.   45
570 HALO HATCH [11] 3-8-13 S Whitworth 9/2 FAV: 203-030: Nearest fin after abs: see 570.   28
847 DUFF [12] 3-9-7 A Mcglone 8/1: 23-3400: Front rank to ¼ way: fin 8th and much btr 579   00
210 Song An Dance Man [5] 7-13   1281 Formidable Dancer [6] 8-6
1231 Silent Running [3] 7-8(1ow)(4oh)   880 Hot Gem [4] 8-13
1022 First Rank [14] 8-0(2ow)   480 Brent Riverside [10] 7-7(2oh)
1224 Kings Touch [7] 8-12(VIS)
14 ran   ½,½,2½,½,7   (Mrs S Khan)   G Lewis Epsom, Surrey

1521 OWEN TUDOR HANDICAP 0-35   £2641   6f   Good 57 +05 Fast   [35]

1211 OUT OF HAND [10] (D Dale) 7-8-4 M Rimmer 20/1: 000-401: 7 ch h Some Hand - Crusheen
(Typhoon) Surprise winner, made up a lot of ground to lead cl home in quite a fast run h'cap
at Salisbury July 12: won a h'cap at Pontefract last season: eff over 6/7f: acts on fast and
yldg ground and on any track: may win another small h'cap.   20
1145 GOLD PROSPECT [3] (G Balding) 4-9-13 J Williams 11/4 FAV: 1220402: Ran on well,
just btn: gd effort under top weight: see 1145 & 31.   41
1387 LONELY STREET [4] (P Arthur) 5-9-1 L Johnsey(7) 6/1: 2-20203: Made most: see 855.   25
1273 FEYDAN [8] (L Cottrell) 5-8-11 I Johnson 16/1: 000-044: Al up there: fair effort.   21
1324 HOPEFUL KATIE [14] 4-8-3(hd) Gay Kelleway(2) 7/1: 0402030: No real threat over this
shorter trip: see 65.   05
1292 MR JAY ZEE [15] 4-9-6 P Cook 9/2: -013130: Never nearer: much btr over 7f in 1292.   17
1391 MUHTARIS [17] 3-8-8 P Waldron 8/1: 2220000: Below par effort: much btr 580 (5f)   00
1319 Sparkford Lad [5] 8-4(bl)   1235 Shalbee [7] 8-0
1213 St Terramar [6] 7-7(3oh)   1171 Seago [9] 7-8
891 Winning Format [13] 7-12   1213 Soon To Be [11] 9-9(VIS)
1245 Deputy Tim [16] 8-8(bl)   1213 Three Bells [1] 9-0
1367 Linton Starchy [12] 7-12   1165 Leap Year [2] 7-12(BL)
17 ran   nk,1¼,shthd,3,2   (Mrs A Dale)   D Dale Newmarket

1522 EBF MYROBELLA STAKES 2YO   £1619   6f   Good 57 -05 Slow

*1405 GREY WOLF TIGER [4] (R Hannon) 2-9-2 A Mcglone 9/2: 022411: 2 gr c Rolfe - Grey
Twig (Godswalk) In fine form, was heavily bckd when making all, comfortably, in a 2yo stks
at Salisbury July 12: recently won a minor race at Bath, after being placed on sev occasions:
stays 6f really well: acts on firm and soft ground: suited by forcing tactics on a gall trk.   55
-- OTHET [12] (M Usher) 2-8-11 R Street 14/1: 2: Behind early tho' ran on most promisingly
inside dist and should go close next time: cost 23,000 gns: stays 6f well: acts on gd ground
and on a stiff track.   41
-- MAJD [15] (P Walwyn) 2-8-11 N Howe 9/2: 3: Showed plenty of pace on his race course
debut: cost 54,000 gns as yearling: dam won as a juv: eff over 6f on gd ground.   39
1241 GOING EASY [2] (G Balding) 2-8-11 J Williams 25/1: 04: Clearly on the upgrade: small
colt who should stay further in time: acts on gd ground and on a stiff track.   29

470

SALISBURY   Saturday July 12th   -Cont'd

1241 RIVERBOAT PARTY [1] 2-8-11 P Hutchinson(3) 33/1: 00: Never reach leaders: cheaply
acquired colt who is a half brother to winning sprinter Swinging Trio.   21
+1187 STRATHBLANE [16] 2-8-13 G Baxter 7/4 FAV: 10: Front rank over ½ way: disapp eff after
her successful debut in 1187 (easier trk): deserves another chance.   23
--   SUPREME STATE [7] 2-8-11 R Wernham 33/1: 0: Ran on well in the closing stages and will
improve on this run next time: cost 9,200 gns and is a half brother to a winning sprinter.   22
--   FIGHTING BELLE [3] 2-8-8 S Whitworth 10/1: 0: Showed gd early speed on her race course
debut: half sister to a winning sprinter: improvement looks certain.   18
--   SNOWSDOWN [6] 2-8-8 P Cook 15/2: 0: Active in mkt on debut: never reach leaders.   00
1082 Souleiadou [13] 8-11   1440 Royal Rabble [5] 8-13   1307 Ragtime Solo [11] 8-11
*1262 Glory Bee [9] 9-2   -- Birchgrove Central [14] 8-11
1039 Mister Wizard [17] 8-11   -- Straw Vote [8] 8-11
1241 Victory Ballard [10] 8-11
17 ran   2½,½,4,3,hd   (Mrs B Norman)   R Hannon East Everleigh, Wilts

1523 CRESTED LARK HANDICAP 0-50 3YO+   £2356   1m 4f Good 57 -27 Slow   [46]

*1236 MIGHTY FLASH [7] (D Elsworth) 3-7-11 A Mcglone 5/4 FAV: 0-00011: 3 b f Rolfe - Lettuce
(So Blessed) Well bckd and made ev yard, gamely, in a h'cap at Salisbury July 12: last month
won a 3yo h'cap over this C/D: closely related to smart duo Mighty Flutter and Mighty Fly:
eff over 10/12f: acts on firm and gd ground and is well suited by this gall trk.   40
1209 FOLK DANCE [1] (I Balding) 4-9-7 P Cook 4/1: 1-44202: Sustained chall : gd effort and
deserves to find a race soon: see 1020 & 189.   46
1237 TICKFORD [6] (G Harwood) 3-8-13 A Clark 4/1: 1-43: Ev ch: stays 12f: see 1237.   46
*1366 PELLINCOURT [5] (R Akehurst) 4-8-7(5ex) T Williams 4/1: 0020214: Fair eff under
his penalty: see 1366.   23
1148 THE JOKER [4] 6-9-10 R Weaver 25/1: -0400: Late prog: see 1000.   39
1335 THE HOWARD [3] 4-8-8 G Baxter 9/1: -000400: Didnot stay this longer trip: see 71.   19
1035 GOLDEN TRIANGLE [2] 5-8-4 S Whitworth 33/1: 401-000: Al last: won a minor event at
Newmarket last Summer tho' no form this term: suited by 12f: acts on firm and soft ground.   00
7 ran   2,4,2,nk,2   (Mrs V A Tory)   D Elsworth Whitsbury, Hants

YORK   Saturday July 12th   Lefthand Galloping Track

Official Going Given As GOOD/FIRM

1524 PIPER CHAMPAGNE H'CAP 3YO 0-60   £4376   6f   Firm 16 +14 Fast   [62]

+1414 FELIPE TORO [12] (M H Easterby) 3-7-7(bl)(4ex)(10h) J Lowe 7/4 FAV: 0-21111: 3 b g Runnett -
Kalympia (Kalydon): Vastly impr gelding who continued his tremendous run of success, leading
dist comfortably in fast run & valuable 3yo h'cap at York July 12: easy winner of similar
h'caps at Beverley, Doncaster & Redcar recently: equally eff over 5/6f & acts on firm & yld
& on any trk: best when up with the pace, in bl: likely to complete a nap hand.   44
947 DARK PROMISE [5] (R Hollinshead) 3-9-1 S Perks 16/1: 0-00132: Kept on well final 1f
and a fine effort: should find another race soon: see 814.   59
1151 CATHERINES WELL [9] (M W Easterby) 3-8-6 K Hodgson 8/1: 11-0303: Led/dsptd lead much.   45
*1145 TOUCH OF GREY [8] (D Thom) 3-9-7 M L Thomas 8/1: 0112014: Pressed ldrs most, hmpd dist.56
*1380 TAX ROY [2] 3-8-6(2ow)(4ex) T Ives 5/1: 21-0010: Al prom but btr 1380 (5f, gd).   39
1312 RIVIERA SCENE [6] 3-8-6 G Duffield 13/2: 22-0020: Met some trouble in running final
stages and better 1312.   39
1292 Jarrovian [10] 8-0(bl)   1283 Capeability Pound [1] 7-9
1027 Manton Mark [7] 8-1   1200 Breakfast In Bed [3] 7-13
1360 Sonnenelle [11] 7-7(11oh)   1044 Viltash [13] 8-13
12 ran   2,2,1½,½,shhd   (Lt-Col R Warden)   M H Easterby Great Habton, Yorks

1525 HOFMEISTER LAGER H'CAP 3YO+ 0-60   £4979   1m   Firm 16 +07 Fast   [54]

1109 DORSET COTTAGE [10] (W Jarvis) 4-9-10 M Hills 10/1: 1-03201: 4 b g Thatching -
Stogumber (Habitat): Useful gelding: returned to his best form leading dist & holding on
well in quite a fast run & valuable h'cap at York July 12: lightly raced gelding who in '85
broke the course record in a Beverley maiden: very eff at 1m on firm/gd grnd: acts on any trk. 62
1109 ACONITUM [2] (J Bethell) 5-8-13 J Reid 11/1: 0-03002: Steady hdway to chall dist,
just held by winner in a good last 1f battle: grand effort & should find a race soon: see 573. 50
1145 TRANSFLASH [9] (E Eldin) 7-8-12 Paul Eddery 14/1: 4300303: Held up over this new
trip, gd fin: stays 1m: see 55, 952.   44
*1377 BOLD PILLAGER [4] (J Dunlop) 4-9-4(8ex) T Ives 5/6 FAV: -032114: Made much, ran to
his best: see 1377 (7f).   49
1249 MOORES METAL [5] 6-8-9(VIS) S Perks 12/1: 0000040: Vis. for the first time, never btr.   37
1383 FUSILIER [7] 4-8-7 P Robinson 33/1: 3-30000: Well in rear till some late prog: yet
to reproduce 17 (soft).   35
706 WELL RIGGED [12] 5-9-4 M Birch 15/2: 1-21200: Dsptd lead much after abs: see 79 (hvy).   00
--   Avec Coeur [6] 8-7   1202 Rabirius [1] 8-3   1249 Pacific Princess [3] 8-4(bl)
1455 Northern Chimes [13] 9-9(VIS)   1249 Major Don [11] 9-10
1335 Silly Boy [8] 8-6
13 ran   nk,2½,1,2,hd   (Mrs S A Randall)   W Jarvis Newmarket

471

1526 JOHN SMITHS MAGNET CUP H'CAP 3YO+ 0-75   £29470   1m 2f   Firm 16 –01 Slow   [64]

921 CHAUMIERE [9] (R Williams) 5-9-5(vis) T Ives 11/1: -000001: 5 ch h Thatching -
Cafe Au Lait (Espresso): Very useful horse on his day: returned to his best when gaining 2nd
successive win in the Magnet Cup H'cap at York July 12: hdway from rear & cleverly gained
the day close home: in gd form in '85, placed several times & winning this same race: very
eff over 10f, stays 12f: acts on any going though is fav. by firm or gd grnd & a gall trk
(particularly York): best in a vis. or bl.   67
1254 MASKED BALL [1] (P Calver) 6-7-8 M Fry 14/1: 0-11202: Just failed to make all: a
gallant effort & deserves compensation: see 439: very consistent.   41
+976 ATOKA [11] (Lord John Fitzgerald) 4-7-13 M Hills 11/2: -000113: Waited with, never
closer: gd effort from this still impr filly: see 976.   42
1383 TRY TO STOP ME [7] (Denys Smith) 5-8-7(5ex) L Charnock 16/1: 0032104: Behind, never
closer: gd effort: see 1249.   48
879 MERLE [4] 4-8-8 P Robinson 25/1: 0-00000: Sn prom: best effort since 573.   49
1237 INNISHMORE ISLAND [5] 3-8-9 J Reid 10/1: 0312-30: Ev ch, wknd: see 1237.   61
1254 TOSARA [2] 4-8-7(5ex) C Rutter(5) 3/1 FAV: 0-24110: Well bckd, ch 2f out: btr 1254.   00
1383 DALGADIYR [3] 3-7-9(1ow) P Hamblett 7/2: -31300: No dngr: much btr 1383.   00
1038 CHICLET [8] 4-8-10(vis) Paul Eddery 7/1: 0-02040: Al rear: disapp since 432.   00
1216 K Battery [6] 9-10   **1098 Dancing Zeta** [10] 9-5(vis)
11 ran   ½,2,1,hd,1,1½   (C G R Booth)   R Williams Newmarket

1527 JOHN SMITHS LAGER NURSERY H'CAP 2YO   £4051   5f   Firm 16 –04 Slow   [56]

1261 DREAM LAUNCH [5] (B Hanbury) 2-9-7 M Hills 6/1: 0121: 2 ch f Relaunch - Pleasuresome
(What A Pleasure): Very useful filly: made most, holding on well final 1f in a valuable
nursery at York July 12: easy winner of a fast run minor race at Lingfield June 21: cost
$57,000 & is related to a couple of winners: speedy filly who is likely to prove best with
forcing tactics over 5f: acts well on firm grnd.   64
1132 ANNIE NOONAN [10] (N Tinkler) 2-8-6 Kim Tinkler(5) 3/1 FAV: 412: Found this trip too
short and was flying at the fin: can win a similar race over 6f: see 1132.   46
813 SPITTIN MICK [2] (M H Easterby) 2-7-12 J Lowe 4/1: 1213: Chall 1f out, no extra but
a fine effort after abs: see 813: can win a nursery.   38
766 ECHOING [12] (J Watts) 2-8-12 T Ives 13/2: 14: Al prom after abs: quite a stiff
task here: see 766.   46
927 BASTILLIA [1] 2-8-13 J Reid 14/1: 00130: Prom thro'out: stays 6f: see 746.   43
1174 WHISTLING WONDER [7] 2-8-3 K Darley 16/1: 1043030: Prom, ev ch: btr on gd or soft?   31
826 BRUTUS [3] 2-8-7 G Duffield 11/1: 010: Dsptd lead much: btr 826 (good).   00
603 Broons Addition [4] 7-11   **873 Miss Shegas** [6] 8-0
1297 Mazurkanova [8] 7-8   **701 Bothy Ballad** [9] 8-10
766 Linn Odee [11] 8-6   **1069 Oriole Dancer** [13] 8-2
13 ran   1½,hd,2,1½,½   (Robert B Trussell jnr)   B Hanbury Newmarket

1528 JERVAUX SELLING STAKES 2YO   £3917   6f   Firm 16 –06 Slow

1161 BEN LEDI [1] (M H Easterby) 2-8-11 M Birch 6/5 FAV: 0311: 2 b g Strong Gale -
Balacco (Balidar): Heavily bckd when hacking up in a 2yo seller at York July 12 (bought
in 4,200 gns): narrow winner of a maiden auction event at Redcar June 21: eff at 5f, well
suited by 6f, should stay further: acts on firm & gd going: much btr than a plater and
can win a nursery.   47
1294 LADY SUNDAY SPORT [2] (N Callaghan) 2-8-8 G Duffield 12/1: 402: Kept on and showed
impr form here: will stay further than 6f: see 1190.   31
1187 SHUTTLECOCK GIRL [11] (W Jarvis) 2-8-8 M Hills 7/1: 4303: Led stands side: see 722.   30
1294 AVINASESH [16] (C Tinkler) 2-8-11(BL) L Charnock 11/1: 0234: Bl first time, ev ch.   30
1119 DOCKIN HILL [5] 2-8-11(BL) S Perks 14/1: 03030: Bl first time, misbehaved in stalls,
dsptd lead far side much: btr 1119 (soft).   18
1181 MAYBEMUSIC [4] 2-8-11 N Carlisle 11/1: 0010: Prom most far side: btr 1181 (5f, gd).   14
1379 SHARPHAVEN [18] 2-8-8 K Darley 11/1: 0302410: No threat: btr 1379 (gd).   00
1323 Miss Drummond [14] 8-8   **1197 Fortyniner** [7] 8-11
1294 Rabenham [13] 8-11   **1480 Wolf J Flywheel** [12] 8-11
1311 Princess Pelham [8] 8-8   **1221 Winnies Luck** [9] 8-8
672 Prior Well [17] 8-8   **-- Enchanted Court** [15] 8-11
1194 Eastern Princess [6] 8-8   **-- Church Star** [10] 8-8
17 ran   5,½,1½,6,2   (A A McCluskey)   M H Easterby Great Habton, York

1529 FRIARGATE STAKES 2YO   £3178   7f   Firm 16 –45 Slow

1097 LOCKTON [3] (J Hindley) 2-8-7 M Hills 11/10 FAV: 201: 2 ch c Moorestyle - Bridestones
(Jan Ekels): Easily justified fav. drawing clear from the dist for a ready 4L success in a
very slowly run 2yo minor event at York July 12: half brother to Blue Brocade, a winner over
11f: eff 7f, sure to be suited by longer dists: acts well on firm grnd, on a gall trk:
should find further success.   57
1175 KING BALLADEER [1] (G P Gordon) 2-8-11 G Duffield 7/4: 0312: Despite only 6 runners,
managed to find plenty of trouble in running & is btr judged on 1175 (gd).   47

472

--   IN A SPIN [5] (M Brittain) 2-8-7 K Darley 25/1: 3: Made much for a creditable debut:
half brother to a 2yo minor winner: acts on firm & stays 7f.   43
--   PLANE [6] (C Brittain) 2-8-7 P Robinson 10/1: 4: Slow start, not the best of runs
final 2f: a 10,500 gns March foal whose dam was a minor winner over 7f: may improve.   39
*973 HUNTERS LEAP [4] 2-8-11 D Casey(7) 14/1: 002010: Prom most: see 973 (6f heavy).   42
1253 YOUNG BENZ [2] 2-8-7 M Birch 12/1: 00: Early ldr, stiff task for this quite cheaply
bought Jan. foal: should stay at least 7f.   30
6 ran   4,hd,1½,nk,4   (Alan Gibson)   J Hindley Newmarket

1530 FOUNTAINS MAIDEN STAKES 3YO   £3433   1m 4f Firm 16 -11 Slow

1098 CHAUVE SOURIS [1] (G Wragg) 3-9-0 Paul Eddery 6/5 FAV: 0-0201: 3 b c Beldale Flutter -
Sassalya (Sassafras): Useful colt: well bckd, al prom & easily drew clear final 1f in a
3yo maiden at York July 12: lightly raced previously but is a half brother to smart performers
Bold Indian and Assemblyman: well suited by fast going, 12f & a gall trk: should be able
to win more races.   60
1206 POKEYS PRIDE [3] (R Sheather) 3-9-0 M Hills 7/1: 020-022: Faced a stiff task here
but not disgraced: stays 12f: see 1206.   49
1410 THREE TIMES A LADY [7] (P Kelleway) 3-8-11 G Duffield 7/2: -000223: Led 3f out, no
extra when hdd: btr 1410 (2m).   36
1002 LOREEF [4] (J Dunlop) 3-8-11 J Reid 100/30: -044: No real threat: probably stays 12f but
rated much higher in 1002 (10f,good).   34
1160 SHINY KAY [8] 3-8-11 J Lowe 25/1: -00440: Led briefly str: see 1160.   33
978 HANKLEY DOWN [6] 3-9-0 M Miller 25/1: -000: Seems best at 12f: see 714.   32
--   Good Natured [2] 8-11   1372 Grundys Own [5] 9-0
8 ran   5,5,½,nk,2   (Sir Philip Oppenheimer)   G Wragg Newmarket

---

Official Going Given As GOOD

1531 ECCLESTON STAKES 2YO   £3037   6f   Good/Yield 79 -43 Slow

*1411 WIGANTHORPE [2] (M W Easterby) 2-9-2 T Lucas 1/2 FAV: 2201111: 2 ch c Thatching -
Lustrine (Viceregal): Very useful colt: had a very easy task when completing his four-timer
in a minor 3 horse race at Chester July 12: successful previously at Haydock, Newcastle
(walk over) & Beverley: a bargain buy at 18,500 gns: eff at 5f, stays 6f well: acts on soft
but best on firm or gd grnd: should continue to run very well.   63
*1075 SARIHAH [3] (H T Jones) 2-8-11 A Murray 2/1: 012: Impossible task: see 1075.   46
--   BRONZE RUNNER [1] (E Wheeler) 2-8-7 W Wharton 14/1: 3: Struggling after ½way on debut:
half brother to a minor winner over 6f.   12
3 ran   3,6   (Miss S E Easterby)   M W Easterby Sheriff Hutton, York

1532 40TH BIRTHDAY H'CAP 3YO 0-60   £4246   7.5f   Good/Yield 79 -05 Slow   [60]

1169 SAFEERA [2] (M Jarvis) 3-8-9 W Woods(3) 3/1 FAV: 11-0341: 3 b f Dalsaan - Juhayna
(Diplomat Way): Came from behind to lead dist under press in a 3yo h'cap at Chester July 12:
in '85 was rated 62 after winning nurseries at Haydock & Folkestone & a maiden at Edinburgh:
eff 6f but well suited by 7f plus nowadays: acts on gd & soft, possibly unsuited by firm:
acts on any trk.   52
1390 HYMN OF HARLECH [1] (G P Gordon) 3-8-12 W Ryan 100/30: 0032232: Chall final 1f, not
btn far: gd effort: see 1028.   53
1147 TRY HARDER [5] (J Fitzgerald) 3-8-10 A Murray 11/1: 400-003: Prom most, best effort
this term & is returning to form: made all at York in '85 & was fairly consistent: suited
by 7f, should stay 1m: acts on fast & yld going.   47
954 SUPREME KINGDOM [6] (R Hollinshead) 3-7-10 A Culhane(7) 8/1: 0320004: Ev ch: best 49.   31
406 HIDDEN BRIEF [4] 3-9-7 E Guest(3) 7/1: 00-1200: Long abs, best 37 (soft).   51
*1224 MAHOGANY RUN [7] 3-8-13(VIS) T Lucas 4/1: 0-00010: Tried to make all: btr 1224 (1m).   38
1028 Colway Comet [3] 9-2(vis)
7 ran   1,2,1,3,2½   (Mrs J Marrow)   M Jarvis Newmarket

1533 CHESTER SUMMER H'CAP 3YO+ 0-60   £3791   2m 2f Good/Yield 79 +16 Fast   [48]

-1058 TIGERWOOD [8] (R Akehurst) 5-7-10 N Adams 100/30 FAV: 000-121: 5 b h Lombard -
Smokey Dawn (March Past): In tremendous form at present & readily made all in a fast run,
valuable h'cap at Chester July 12: first time out winner of similar h'cap at Warwick June 7:
little form previously on the Flat but a fair top of the grnd hurdler: eff 2m, suited by
2m2f: best with front running tactics on a sharpish trk on fast ground, unsuited by soft.   30
933 LEPRECHAUN LADY [1] (S Norton) 4-7-10 A Culhane(7) 20/1: 0001202: Al prom: gd effort
& is suited by an easy surface, probably dislikes firm: see 590.   20
778 SPECIAL VINTAGE [4] (J Fitzgerald) 6-9-8 A Murray 6/1: 2114/03: Ev ch: see 778.   45
1348 ARBOR LANE [6] (R Boss) 5-8-2 M Roberts 9/1: 440-104: Twice below 1183 (first time out). 20

●1388 MORGANS CHOICE [9] 9-8-7 W Ryan 9/2: 0003010: Never btr: quite a stiff task: see 1388.   23
1150 STANDARD BREAKFAST [3] 4-8-6 B Thomson 12/1: 400-000: No danger: see 474.   19
712 WITHY BANK [12] 4-9-6 T Lucas 6/1: 0-11300: Prom, wknd into 9th: abs since 712: best 50.   00
712 ISLAND EXILE [10] 4-8-2 N Connorton 7/1: 344-040: Abs since btr 712.   00
1293 Treasure Hunter [11] 8-9(2ow)   1419 Sound Diffusion [2] 7-12
1293 Singers Tryst [5] 9-9   1183 Baluchi [7] 7-7(bl)(13oh)
12 ran   8,1½,5,2,2½   (Miss Anne Healy)   R Akehurst Epsom, Surrey

1534 EBF PULFORD MAIDEN STAKES 2YO   £1680   7f   Good/Yield 79 -30 Slow

1311 MELODY MAKER [7] (B Hills) 2-9-0 B Thomson 11/4: 031: 2 b c Song - Lovage (Linacre):
Led inside final 1f, comfortably in a slow run 2yo maiden at Chester July 12: related to
several winners: stayed todays 7f trip well: acts on firm & gd/yld grnd & a sharpish trk:
impr colt who should rate more highly.   46
1197 STORM HERO [1] (M Dickinson) 2-9-0 A Murray 5/6 FAV: 322: Led over 1f out: no extra
final 1f: 3L clear 3rd & must find a race: see 1197.   45
1253 CITY FINAL [2] (R Hollinshead) 2-8-11 W Ryan 16/1: 40403: Stayed on well: should be
suited by 1m plus: acts on firm & gd/yld & on any trk.   32
--   VITAL CARGO [5] (E Carter) 2-8-11 S Morris 33/1: 4: Mkt drifter: nearest fin on
racecourse debut & should impr: half sister to several winners & should be suited by 1m.   28
1155 JOHNNY SHARP [8] 2-9-0 N Day 16/1: 00: Led over 2f out, showing impr: probably
stays 7f: see 1155.   30
1175 BEAU BENZ [3] 2-9-0(BL) T Lucas 14/1: 00040: Bl first time: ev ch: see 1175.   28
1270 AFRICAN OPERA [4] 2-9-0 C Dwyer 14/1: 030: Made much: possibly does not get 7f.   23
944 Silver Glance [6] 8-11
8 ran   ½,3,1½,½,1,1½,2½   (Mrs P Shaw)   B Hills Lambourn, Berks

1535 ALDFORD MAIDEN STAKES 3YO UPWARDS   £2209   1m 5f   Good/Yield 79 -07 Slow

1259 MYTH [6] (R J Houghton) 3-8-5 W Ryan 5/1: 2424-21: 3 b f Troy - Hay Reef (Mill Reef):
Useful, impr filly: well suited by the trip & led into str, comfortably in a maiden at
Chester July 12: first time out this season was a good 2nd to Apply in a fillies maiden at
Lingfield: yet to fin out of the first 4: eff at   12f, stays 13f well: acts on firm & gd/yld
& a gall trk: should win a h'cap soon.   52
832 FORT LINO [11] (I Balding) 3-8-8 A Murray 5/1: 4-22: Made much: stays 13f: acts
on any trk: abs since 832.   43
1251 CHALICE OF SILVER [3] (M Jarvis) 3-8-5 W Woods(3) 8/1: 30-4323: Prom, ev ch: stays very
well, but seems to lack a turn of foot: see 1251, 315.   36
463 ALLATUM [7] (B Hills) 3-8-5 B Thomson 8/1: -204: Wknd str after long abs: best 351.   32
980 FULL SPEED AHEAD [1] 3-8-8 N Adams 20/1: 0-0000: Best effort yet over this lngr trip:
little form previously: stays 13f & acts on gd/yld grnd.   31
--   CRISP AND KEEN [10] 8-9-4 Mark Wood(7) 66/1: -0000-0: There 1m: little form on the Flat:
winner over hurdles: acts on firm & yld.   06
991 GONE OVERBOARD [8] 3-8-5 M Roberts 6/1: -040: Fdd over 3f out: abs since btr 991 (11f).   00
-1160 LISANA [5] 3-8-5 A Kimberley 7/4 FAV: 0-20: Hvly bckd: early ldr: disapp after 1160 (firm)   00
1208 Sweet Rascal [12] 9-4(BL)   1349 Headin On [2] 9-7
1195 Thatchit [4] 9-7   444 Showdance [13] 8-8   --   Molybdenum [9] 9-7
13 ran   6,2,2½,2½,8   (J W Rowles)   R J Houghton Blewbury, Oxon

1536 CITY WALL H'CAP 3YO+ 0-60   £3080   6f   Good/Yield 79 -05 Slow   [52]

1385 ALL AGREED [4] (J Winter) 5-9-1 B Thomson 5/2 FAV: 0040021: Fairly useful gelding: led
final 1f, comfortably in a h'cap at Chester July 12: last time out was btn a shthd by
Cree Bay at Sandown: in '85 won at Beverley & Sandown: in '83 won twice: eff over 5f,
suited by 6f: seems to act on any grnd & on any trk.   50
1338 MENDICK ADVENTURE [8] (Denys Smith) 5-7-13(bl)(1ow) M Roberts 10/1: 0000032: Made much:
3rd, placed 2nd: gd effort: see 56.   24
1461 SUDDEN IMPACT [3] (K Brassey) 4-8-5(bl) N Adams 9/2: -100433: Prom, ev ch: fin 4th,
placed 3rd: btr 1461 (firm).   27
1338 GODS SOLUTION [7] (T Barron) 5-8-1 N Connorton 12/1: 0402004: Bumped entering straight
and no chance thereafter: fin 5th, placed 4th: see 890, 42.   17
1429 YOUNG BRUSS [2] 4-7-12 M Wood 14/1: -001300: Early ldr: see 936,830(btr ground)   08
1145 MATOU [9] 6-9-10 W Ryan 5/1: 1-4202D: Ran wide in str: kept on final 1f: fin 2nd,
placed last: see 1026.   55
1182 SHARLIES WIMPY [6] 7-8-13(bl) M Hindley(3) 5/1: 0-02400: Dwelt: best 687: see 520.   00
1026 FAWLEYS GIRL [1] 4-7-11 A Culhane(7) 10/1: -002000: No show: little form since 520.   00
8 ran   1½,2½,1,2½,2½,4,12   (T M P Waterman)   J Winter Newmarket

Official Going Given As GOOD/FIRM

1537 SUTTON SELLING STAKES 2YO   £703   6f   Firm 08 -69 Slow

1358 PRINCESS SINGH [5] (N Tinkler) 2-8-13 Kim Tinkler(5) 1/1 FAV: 3104431: 2 ch f Mansingh – Princess Story (Some Hand): Tough & consistent juvenile: comfortably justified fav. making all in a slowly run 2yo seller at Leicester July 14 (no bid): all the way winner of a similar race at Beverley last month: eff over 5/6f: best form on fast grnd with forcing tactics: seems suited by a gall trk.   22

1358 ABSALOUTE HEAVEN [2] (R Stubbs) 2-8-13 A Mercer 10/1: 000102: Never threatened easy winner: acts on a gall trk: see 1168.   14

1323 SWEET PICCOLO [1] (G Huffer) 2-8-11 G Carter(3) 9/2: 003: Kept on same pace: cheaply acquired colt who stays 6f: acts on fast grnd & on a gall trk.   09

1413 HIGHLAND CAPTAIN [6] (R Hollinshead) 2-8-11 R Adams(7) 20/1: 0004: Outsider: some late prog: best effort to date: see 865.   08

1449 ARDNACROSS [3] 2-8-8 C Rutter(5) 13/2: 0024230: Never dngr: btr in 1168.   00

1262 SAUCIER [4] 2-8-8 J Bray(7) 5/1: 00040: Front rank over ½way: best in 1262 (easier trk)   00
6 ran   2¼,1,nk,2,1½   (Full Circle Thoroughbreds B Ltd)   N Tinkler Langton, Yorks

1538 MOUNTSORREL STAKES 3YO   £1951   1m 4f   Firm 08 +13 Fast

*328 **STARTINO** [4] (H Cecil) 3-8-12 S Cauthen 5/2: 2-11: 3 b f Bustino – Western Star (Alcide): Smart filly: despite a fair abs was al going easily, led dist to score cleverly in a fast run 3yo stakes at Leicester July 14: easy winner of her maiden on this trk in Apr. though subs. suffered a slight set back: narrowly btn by Entrancing on her only start at Goodwood last term: closely related to the smart Mr Fluorocarbon: stays 12f really well: acts on firm & soft grnd & on a gall trk: certain to win more races.   70

*1290 **DAARKOM** [2] (A Stewart) 3-8-7 M Roberts 6/4 FAV: -2212: Led over 2f out, no ch with winner though remains in gd form: see 1290.   58

926 **BROKEN WAVE** [7] (H Candy) 3-8-8 W Newnes 15/2: -103: Nicely bckd: fin well over this longer trip & should be winning again soon: stays 12f: see 486.   58

1409 GORGEOUS STRIKE [8] (C Nelson) 3-9-3 J Reid 4/1: -020344: Never nearer: clear of rem.   64

946 **STAGE HAND** [6] 3-9-6 Pat Eddery 25/1: 10-0000: Made much: no extra in closing stages though ran his best race this term: won a maiden at Newmarket last season: stays 10f well: suited by gd or faster grnd.   52

*839 **VAGADOR** [3] 3-8-9 G Starkey 6/1: -10: No threat & much btr in 839 (gd, easy trk).   37

--   **Rare Legend** [1] 8-4   487 **Pokeree** [5] 8-7
8 ran   1¼,½,½,1¼,8,2½   (Mrs James McAllister)   H Cecil Newmarket

1539 BELVOIR CASTLE H'CAP 3YO+ 0-50   £3345   1m 2f   Firm 08 +01 Fast   [41]

1450 LEONIDAS [6] (D Arbuthnot) 8-8-6 M Hills 7/2: 00-0041: Was never hdd when a comfortable winner of a h'cap at Leicester July 14: successful over this trip at Brighton last season: best form with forcing tactics on fast grnd, and is unsuited by soft: acts on any trk.   30

-863 **COCCOLUTO** [2] (J Dunlop) 3-9-7 Pat Eddery 7/4 FAV: 00-022: Chased winner: clear of rem & stays 10f well: acts on a gall trk: see 863.   52

1112 WELL COVERED [3] (R Hollinshead) 5-9-6 S Perks 7/1: -000103: Best over this C/D in 937. 28

1325 THE FOOTMAN [5] (R Stubbs) 4-9-7 J H Brown(5) 11/1: 10-0004: Never dngr: see 1325.   28

1335 ARISTOCRAT VELVET [4] 4-9-7 T Ives 9/4: 23-0020: Btr over 9f in 1335: see 439.   25

1079 RIO DEVA [1] 8-8-3 B Crossley 33/1: 10-2-00: Dwelt & al last: lightly raced since winning over this C/D in '84: acts on any going though is suited by fast grnd.   00
6 ran   2¼,6,¾,2,5   (George Ward)   D Arbuthnot Compton, Berks

1540 APPLEBY CLAIMING STAKES 3YO   £2862   1m   Firm 08 -07 Slow

1193 GIRDLE NESS [15] (J Dunlop) 3-7-13 T Quinn 7/1: 0-4001: 3 b f Pitskelly – Sule Skerry (Scottish Rifle): Led 2f out, comfortably in a 3yo claiming stakes at Leicester July 14: half sister to middle dist winner Jack's Island: eff over 7/9f: acts on gd & fast grnd & on any trk.   28

1191 LYDIA LANGUISH [11] (R Hannon) 3-8-6 Pat Eddery 9/2 JT FAV: 400-002: Fin strongly: returning to the form which won her a valuable seller at York last season: stays 1m well: acts on any going & on any trk.   30

1471 BOLD BORDERER [4] (M Blanshard) 3-8-11(BL) N Adams 6/1: -000033: Bl first time: al up there: see 1471.   33

776 **GRIMESGILL** [7] (J Hindley) 3-8-11 M Hills 16/1: -004: Never nearer after abs: lightly raced filly who is a half sister to a winning sprinter: stays 1m: acts on fast grnd & on a gall trk.   30

1346 BRAVE AND BOLD [9] 3-8-10(bl) G Starkey 8/1: 0200040: Ran to his best: see 100.   28

849 **SON OF SPARKLER** [3] 3-9-0(bl) A Mcglone 20/1: 043-000: Front rank to dist: btr effort maiden who was placed twice last backend: stays 1m well: acts on any going.   27

1362 KEEP COOL [13] 3-8-6 S Perks 20/1: 4001000: Fin 7th: best in 774.   00

1384 ST JAMES RISK [12] 3-9-0 B Thomson 7/1: 0100-00: Fin 9th: similarly lightly raced last season when winning a valuable seller at Sandown: stays 1m: acts well on fast grnd.   00

1303 ATROMITOS [16] 3-9-0(BL) P Robinson 8/1: 1-40000: Bl first time: best in 157 (yld).   00

*1346 **NATCHAKAM** [2] 3-9-0(vis) P Waldron 9/2 JT FAV: 2040010: Speed to ½way: much btr 1346.   00

1267 Hill Ryde [1] 8-4	1122 Cosmic Flight [20] 8-6	
1288 Fast Taxi [19] 9-0	1281 Try Sir [17] 8-9	1444 Avada [14] 9-0
-- Paper Polka [18] 8-7	1472 Cheal [10] 8-4	774 Rockhold Princess [8] 8-4
-- Ascendit [5] 8-1		
19 ran 2½,nk,2,½,2½,hd	(A J Struthers)	J Dunlop Arundel, Sussex

1541 BLABY MAIDEN STAKES 3YO FILLIES   £1216   7f   Firm 08 -05 Slow

1043 ESFAHAN [11] (J Dunlop) 3-8-11 Pat Eddery 6/4 FAV: -0201: 3 b f Persian Bold -
Press Luncheon (Be Friendly): Useful filly: made most, hdd and hmpd below dist & although
just failing to get up was promoted to 1st place in a 3yo maiden at Leicester July 14: half
sister to a couple of winners & earlier was shhd by the useful Sharpetto at York: eff over
7/8f: acts on gd & fast grnd & on a gall trk.   47
1327 LADY FOR TWO [3] (M Stoute) 3-8-11 Mark Giles(7) 5/1: -4041D: Led 2f out, just held
on though interfered with Esfahan & subsq. placed 2nd: see 708.   46
1375 SARIZA [12] (H Cecil) 3-8-11 S Cauthen 2/1: -4223: Not btn far & clear of rem: seems
a little onepaced & may do btr over 1m plus: see 941.   45
1371 SIDONS DAUGHTER [8] (A Jarvis) 3-8-11 R Hills 20/1: 0-00204: Best over 1m in 1224.   36
1257 COUNTRY CARNIVAL [7] (T Ives) 3-8-11(VIS) T Ives 20/1: -003000: Prom most of way: see 907.   32
1246 MARCREDEA [5] 3-8-11 R Wernham 10/1: -0020: No threat: best in 1246.   28
1375 Famille Rose [9] 8-11   1418 Belle Of Budapest [4] 8-11
1327 Miss Kola [10] 8-11   1142 Fancy Finish [6] 8-11   1327 Branitska [1] 8-11
11 ran nk,½,4,1½,1½   (N Avery)   J Dunlop Arundel, Sussex

1542 BURTON HANDICAP STAKES 3YO+ 0-35   £1802   5f   Firm 08 -02 Slow   [35]

1438 FARMER JOCK [3] (N Macauley) 4-8-7(bl) S Whitworth 9/2: 0003021: 4 ch c Crofter -
Some Dame (Vieux Manor): Ran on under strong press to lead inside dist in a h'cap at
Leicester July 14: first success: eff over 5/6f on gd & firm grnd: acts on any trk: wears blinkers.   22
1438 CAPTAINS BIDD [8] (H Whiting) 6-7-8 L Riggio(6) 16/1: 0-00202: Remains a maiden: see 1077   06
1347 ROSIE DICKINS [6] (R Hollinshead) 4-8-9 R Lappin(7) 12/1: 2403043: Al front rank: see 124   19
*1438 EECEE TREE [1] (J Sutcliffe) 4-9-2(bl)(7ex) M Hills 4/1 JT FAV: 0200014: Made most: fair
effort under his penalty though comfortably beat winner in 1438 (gd/firm).   20
1344 MISS METAL WOODS [5] 4-7-10 J Carter(5) 7/1: 23-4040: Al prom: see 1344 & 418.   00
1367 RAPID MISS [9] 6-8-7 Pat Eddery 7/1: 00-0030: Btr in 1367: see 784.   08
*1476 SANDITTON PALACE [13] 3-8-8(7ex) T Quinn 4/1 JT FAV: 0404310: Fin 8th: btr on gd/firm.   00
1438 DJANGO [10] 6-9-9(bl) J Reid 9/1: 4-00-00: Nicely bckd: no threat: see 1438.   00
1380 Show Home [2] 9-10(vis)   1171 Velocidad [7] 8-6
1443 Hot Order [12] 8-8   1319 Shahreen [11] 7-8(1ow)(2oh)
1423 Wesbree Bay [4] 7-7(bl)(2oh)   1013 Hit The Button [4] 7-7(bl)(2oh)
14 ran 1,½,2,½,½   (Mrs N Macauley)   N Macauley Sproxton, Leics

---

Official Going Given As FIRM

1543 MUSSELBURGH AMAT.RIDERS H'CAP 3YO+   £898   5f   Firm Slow   [8]

1423 PERGODA [15] (I Vickers) 8-11-3(bl) Maxine Juster 11/2: -000101: 8 b g High Top -
Saint Joan (Grey Sovereign): Gaining his 9th win at Edinburgh, making ev yd in an amateur
riders h'cap July 14: earlier won an app. h'cap on this trk: in '85 won twice again here:
very eff over 5f with forcing tactics, though does stay 6f: acts on any going but is fav.
by fast grnd: gd mount for an app: best on a sharp trk, especially Edinburgh.   34
1360 LOCH FORM [11] (C Tinkler) 3-10-12 Jennie Goulding 9/2 FAV: 0120032: Prom, ev ch:
in gd form: acts on any grnd: see 255.   31
1344 NATIVE RULER [4] (C Austin) 5-9-11 Yvonne Haynes 11/2: 00-0123: Al up there: see 1707.   01
1423 SWINGING GOLD [12] (D Barron) 4-11-0 Valerie Greaves 12/1: 00-0044: Never nearer: see 1423   16
1443 BEECHWOOD COTTAGE [9] (R Hollinshead) 3-10-5(bl) Sharon Murgatroyd 14/1: 0-00100: Near. fin: best 1367.   12
1344 LAST SECRET [5] 5-9-9 Sarah Hills 25/1: 000-000: Sn prom: last won in '84 at
Catterick: acts on firm & a sharp trk.   00
1344 GODSTRUTH [3] 7-10-10(bl) Franca Vittadini 15/2: 100-000: No threat: see 1344.   00
786 PARADE GIRL [8] 4-10-3 Mr T Etherington 7/1: 0100040: Abs: see 56 (heavy).   00
-- Sallustio [13] 11-7   1438 The Chalicewell [14] 9-4
1418 Jimmys Secret [7] 10-3   1338 Aphrodisiac [2] 9-11
1158 Spring Garden [6] 8-13(BL)   257 Go Spectrum [1] 9-2
14 ran 2,3,½,½,1½   (Harry Charlton)   I Vickers Sadberge, Co Durham

1544 MEADOWBANK MAIDEN STAKES 3YO   £547   1m 7f   Firm Slow

1055 THE CANNY MAN [5] (D Smith) 3-9-0 L Charnock 12/1: -0001: 3 ch g Last Fandango -
Easy Can (Tudor Music): Showed impr form, led 2f out, staying on well in a moderate 5 runner
maiden at Edinburgh July 14: half brother to a winner in Ireland: clearly stays 15f: well:
acts on fast grnd & a sharpish trk.   34
1123 TORREYA [1] (J Hindley) 3-8-11 A Shoults(5) 1/1 FAV: -04232: Ev ch 2f out: out battled
by winner & is becoming expensive to follow: best 935 (12f): see 458.   27
631 BANTEL BUSHY [4] (J Berry) 3-9-0 N Carlisle 2/1: 2222223: Made most: abs since 631.   20

1372 KASU [3] (S Norton) 3-8-11 J Lowe 5/1: -0404: Fdd str: little form: see 969.   07
1372 GIANT REDWOOD [2] 3-8-11 J Callaghan(7) 33/1: 00-000: Dist. last: seems moderate.   00
5 ran   4,10,10,30   (D Knights)   D Smith Bishop Auckland, Co Durham

1545 EBF EVEREST MAIDEN FILLIES STAKES 2YO   £976   5f   Firm Slow

1205 TINAS MELODY [6] (J Winter) 2-8-11 A Mackay 5/4 FAV: 31: 2 b f Tina's Pet - Green
Chartreuse (French Beige): Impr filly: led nearing final 1f for a comfortable 4L win in a
2yo fillies maiden at Edinburgh July 14: well bred sort, being half sister to several winners
incl 2,000 Guineas runner up Mattaboy: eff at 5f, should stay further: acts on gd & fast
grnd & a sharpish trk.   40
1294 PREMIER VIDEO [5] (J Berry) 2-8-11 M Fry 20/1: 30202: Led over 3f: fair effort:
eff at 5/6f on gd & firm grnd: likes a sharpish trk.   27
--   MISS MILVEAGH [3] (A Bailey) 2-8-11 R Cochrane 7/2: 3: Showed signs of inexperience,
should do btr next time: cost I.R. 20,000 and is a half sister to several winners: should
be suited by further than 5f.   23
1370 MINIZEN LASS [4] (M Brittain) 2-8-11 K Darley 5/2: 4220224: Prom over 3f: much btr 1370   08
1287 FLAPPER GIRL [2] 2-8-11 J Callaghan 25/1: 00000: Prom ½way: little form in 5 outings.   00
864 MULTI SPIRAL [1] 2-8-11 S Webster 16/1: 00: Abs: no form in 2 outings from this
cheaply acquired filly.   00
6 ran   4,1½,7,8,1   (Cheveley Park Stud)   J Winter Newmarket

1546 ARCHERY SELLING STAKES 3YO UPWARDS   £933   1m   Firm Slow

--   HODAKA [4] (B Cambidge) 9-9-0 N Carlisle 9/1: 14140/1: 9 b h Sir Gaylord - Chigusa
(Skymaster): Led final 1f, driven out in a seller at Edinburgh July 14 (bought in 950 gns):
last won on the Flat in '83, but successful over hurdles last Winter: eff at 1m, stays
further: best on fast grnd.   14
1412 COMPOSER [6] (M James) 8-9-0(bl) Sharron James 14/1: -000002: Led 2f out: best effort
this season: in '85 won at Haydock & Carlisle: eff at 1m, stays 10f: acts on firm & yld.   12
*1201 REFORMED HABIT [1] (W Pearce) 4-9-5 M Hindley(3) 7/1: -0-3013: In gd form: see 1201.   15
--   HALF SHAFT [5] (W A Stephenson) 5-8-9 A Shoults(5) 20/1: 3-000-4: Nearest fin: lightly
raced and a maiden on the Flat, but winning form over hurdles: acts on gd/firm & soft.   04
--   TREE FELLA [12] 9-9-0 D Nicholls 20/1: 00000-0: Ran on inside final 2f on seasonal
debut: last won in '84 at Haydock: eff at 6f, stays 1m: acts on any trk but likes fast grnd.   04
1424 O I OYSTON [9] 10-9-0 K Darley 9/4 FAV: 0300020: Never nearer: much btr 1424 (7f).   00
1074 TRADE HIGH [2] 7-9-0 R Vickers(7) 11/2: 0300000: Slow start, no show: see 260.   00
--   VILLAGE POSTMAN [3] 5-8-9 S Webster 4/1: 03430/0: Op. 20/1: led 4f out, fdd: maiden:
acts on fast ground.   00
1300 Norwhistle [11] 8-9   1200 Mr Coffey [8] 7-11(vis)
1273 Lady Abinger [7] 8-6(BL)   1201 Brandon Grey [10] 8-6(bl)
1182 Trentullo Blue [13] 8-6
13 ran   ½,¼,nk,2½,3   (B R Cambidge)   B Cambidge Shifnal, Salop

1547 COMMONWEALTH POOL H'CAP 3YO+ 0-35   £934   1m   Firm Slow   [21]

*1103 HEAVENLY HOOFER [5] (D Smith) 3-8-7 L Charnock 6/1: 0-01011: 3 b g Dance In Time -
Heavenly Chord (Hittite Glory): In fine form, led approaching final 1f, comfortably in a
h'cap at Edinburgh July 14: last time out won an app. h'cap at Beverley: earlier won a seller
again at Beverley: seems equally eff over 7/8f: acts on gd & firm grnd & on any trk.   20
1335 GODS LAW [10] (G Reveley) 5-9-4 Julie Bowker(7) 4/1 FAV: 1321302: Fin in gd style
but again left it too late: see 1074.   15
*1134 MAWDLYN GATE [1] (J S Wilson) 3-9-3 Gay Kelleway(5) 10/1: 0040013: Ev ch str:
fair effort: acts on firm & soft: see 1134.   25
1136 ROSSETT [2] (T Craig) 7-8-4 A Mackay 6/1: 00-0004: Prom, ev ch: see 1136.   00
1074 SHOW OF HANDS [9] 10-9-7 P Adams(7) 11/2: 000-020: Made much, fdd: btr 1074.   06
1017 CLOTILDA [8] 4-9-2 M Fry 12/1: 0000-00: Never in it: last won in '84 at Ayr: eff
at 6f, probably stays 1m: acts on gd & firm.   01
1136 TIT WILLOW [7] 4-9-6(bl) D Nicholls 13/2: -022120: Never nearer 7th: much btr 1136, 828   00
1424 Bantel Banzai [4] 8-12(blhd)   1054 Avraees [3] 9-0
1482 Tollys Best [6] 8-3
10 ran   2,nk,½,5,shhd,1   (J A Bianchi)   D Smith Bishop Auckland, Co Durham

1548 ATHLETES VILLAGE H'CAP 3YO+ 0-35   £1693   1m 4f Firm Slow   [29]

*1432 ERROL EMERALD [1] (S Norton) 5-8-11(4ex) J Lowe 3/1 JT.FAV: 300-011: 5 ch m Dom Racine -
Calhoun Emerald (Irish Castle): In gd form & led 1½f out, driven out in a 6 runner h'cap at
Edinburgh July 14: last time out won a h'cap at Pontefract: in '85 won a seller at Warwick:
eff at 1m, nowadays suited by 10f/12f: acts on firm & yld grnd: likes a sharpish trk.   20
1359 IVOROSKI [6] (D Smith) 4-8-0 L Charnock 3/1 JT.FAV: 0000332: Ch final 1f: see 1017.   06
1412 GOLDEN FANCY [5] (I Vickers) 9-9-10 R Vickers(7) 11/2: 0022343: Going well 2f out:
no extra: see 1024, 1412.   29
1416 APPLE WINE [3] (D Chapman) 9-8-11 D Nicholls 4/1: 0020244: Led most: btr 1302: see 1124.   12
*1426 BRADBURY HALL [4] 3-7-13(4ex) K Darley 10/3: 0002210: Wknd appr. final 1f:btr 1426(11f).   13
--   MIRPUR [2] 4-7-13 Julie Bowker(7) 33/1: -0: Rank outsider: fdd straight.   00
6 ran   1½,½,2,½,5   (Exors of the late Ian Redford)   S Norton Barnsley, Yorks

Official Going Given As GOOD

1549 NORTHFIELD APPR SELLING HCAP 3YO 0-25   £874   6f   Good/Firm 32 -14 Slow   [26]

1459 THE UTE [2] (L Bower) 3-8-10(bl) P Mcentee 8/1: 2023201: 3 ch g Hot Spark - Lantonside
(Royal Palace): Gained his first success, leading dist under press in an app. selling h'cap
at Windsor July 14: placed several times previously this season in similar company, mostly at
Brighton and runs well on a sharp trk: well suited by fast grnd & 6/7f but clearly does not
stay middle distances (see 1459): wears bl.   16
910 TAYLORS TAYLORMADE [1] (M Tompkins) 3-8-12 B Cook(5) 8/1: 20-0302: Prom thro'out: gd
effort & can win a similar race: see 489: acts on hvy, fav by firm.   14
377 SANDRON [15] (K Brassey) 3-8-11 P Simms 8/1: 20-0303: Long abs: gd fin and may go
close in a seller next time: see 237.   12
1288 MISS VENEZUELA [12] (C Horgan) 3-9-7 P Skelton(5) 4/1 FAV: -000004: Well bckd, never
closer: needs 7f? see 1288.   18
1334 BAO [6] 3-8-5 J Scally 25/1: 0000000: Chall. dist, fdd: no form since 426 (7f).   00
1364 SEQUESTRATION [8] 3-8-10 Toni Middleton(5) 25/1: 4000000: Speed much: see 1364.   01
1334 PERCIPIO [9] 3-9-1(vis) G Mash 9/2: -000030: Made most, fin 7th: flattered 1334?   04
1201 SOHO SUE [7] 3-9-2 A Whitehall 8/1: 0-10000: Prom much: best 426 (7f).   00
1367 THE BATCHLOR [5] 3-8-11(bl) P Francis 9/1: 41-0000: Well btn all outings this term.   00
837 Care In The Air [10] 8-0(vis)   1476 Blue Fantasy [4] 8-2
1444 Pegasus Lady [16] 9-1(bl)   1451 Ruperts Daughter [11] 8-2
1334 Georgian Rose [13] 8-13(bl)   835 Someway [3] 8-12
1344 Creetown Sally [14] 8-11
16 ran   2½,hd,2,1,2½,1½   (R Bastian)   L Bower Beauworth, Hants

1550 GREENACRE MAIDEN STAKES 2YO   £959   5f   Good/Firm 32 -18 Slow

1129 MAZILIER [8] (G Harwood) 2-9-0 S Cauthen 6/4 FAV: 201: 2 b c Lyphard - Marie Curie
(Exbury): Heavily bckd when gaining a pillar to post win, holding on close home in a 2yo
maiden at Windsor July 14: half brother to 3 winners incl smart miler Crofter: eff over 5f,
stays 6f & should be suited by further: acts on firm & gd grnd & seems suited by forcing
tactics & a sharpish trk.   50
1381 BALTIC SHORE [4] (M Stoute) 2-9-0 W R Swinburn 7/2: 02: Mkt drifter (op. 2/1), chall
final 1f, narrowly btn & clear of rem: sure to win a race, particularly over 6f plus: see 1381   49
1440 SPARKLING BRITT [11] (C Horgan) 2-8-11 R Weaver 10/1: 03: Prom, ev ch: see 1440.   33
834 MR MUMBLES [15] (G Balding) 2-9-0 J Williams 20/1: 004: Ev ch: best effort to date
from this first foal of a maiden: sure to stay beyond 5f.   35
252 INDIAN SET [7] 2-8-11 P Waldron 20/1: 00: Long abs: related to a couple of minor
winners: should be suited by 6f plus.   26
1297 MADAM BILLA [5] 2-8-11 G Duffield 16/1: 000: Prom most: see 1297.   23
1442 FATHER TIME [1] 2-9-0 Pat Eddery 5/1: 00020: Plenty of early pace from a poor draw,
fin 7th & much btr 1442 (C/D).   15
1305 Gone For It [18] 8-11   -- Ystrad Flower [6] 8-11
-- Rajivs Debt [2] 9-0   -- Mascalls Dream [13] 8-11
-- Dual Capacity [10] 9-0   -- Harry Em [19] 9-0
-- Bleu Celeste [3] 8-11   1445 Fires Out [12] 8-11   -- Tell Me Now [14] 8-11
-- Calypso Kid [9] 9-0   -- Baby Alex [16] 9-0
18 ran   ½,4,hd,2½,1½,4   (K Abdulla)   G Harwood Pulborough, West Sussex

1551 JACK BARCLAY HANDICAP 3YO+ 0-50   £2565   1m 4f Good/Firm 32 +10 Fast   [40]

-1468 TWICE BOLD [6] (N Callaghan) 3-9-0 Pat Eddery 13/8 FAV: 1-03421: 3 br c Persian Bold -
Grey Symphony (Track Spare): Useful colt: gained a deserved success gamely making almost all
& rallying to force his hd in front again on the post in a fast run h'cap at Windsor July 14:
ready winner of a maiden at Lingfield at the backend of '85: half brother to several
winners: very eff over 10/11f now: acts well on fast grnd: well suited by forcing tactics & a
sharp track though acts on any.   53
1409 HIGH TENSION [3] (G P Gordon) 4-9-10 G Duffield 5/2: 4-24122: Led briefly final 1f,
hdd post but well clear of rem & will be very hard to beat in a similar race next time. see 1177.   48
976 BRECKLAND LADY [10] (M Tompkins) 4-8-3 R Morse(5) 20/1: 1010-03: Mkt drifter, no ch
final 2f: winner at Wolverhampton & Folkestone (seller) in '85: eff between 9 & 13f: acts on
firm & yld and on any trk.   07
976 ROMAN BEACH [12] (W Musson) 6-9-9 S Cauthen 12/1: 0-00004: Never closer: much btr 976.   27
1441 PHAROAHS TREASURE [1] 5-8-4(bl) R Street 25/1: 0-00-00: Close up over 1m: ran only
twice last term: last won in '84 at Windsor: eff around a sharpish trk over 10f on fast grnd.   00
1176 ANY BUSINESS [7] 5-9-0 M Wigham 12/1: 0000240: No threat: much btr 1176, 940.   06
1393 PULSINGH [5] 4-8-5(BL) P Waldron 15/2: 0001030: Best 850.   00
1441 SIR BLESSED [11] 7-8-11 R Cochrane 8/1: 2410-00: Well bckd, al rear: winner of 3
h'caps at Windsor, Brighton & Carlisle in '85: very eff over 11/12f on fast grnd: acts on
any trk though runs well at Windsor.   00
1412 Mr Gardiner [9] 9-1   1473 Mount Argus [4] 7-12   832 Sales Promoter [8] 7-7(1oh)
1290 Beauclerc [2] 7-13
12 ran   hd,20,nk,8,4   (K Al-Said)   N Callaghan Newmarket

478

1552 WOODLAND STAKES 2YO   £1609   6f   Good/Firm 32 +02 Fast

1376 GELTSER [4] (J Tree) 2-8-11(BL) Pat Eddery 100/30: 241: 2 b c Sir Ivor - Sephira
(Luthier): Mkt drifter but led dist under press in quite a fast run 2yo race at Windsor
July 14, when bl for the first time: rated 63 first time out in 1019, ran very poorly in 1376:
from a good family which includes the top class French sprinter Sigy: eff 6f, should stay
further: acts on firm & gd grnd.   57
1275 DOMINO FIRE [9] (J Dunlop) 2-9-1 W Carson 4/1: 122: Fin well: gd effort: see 985.   57
1320 TOUGH N GENTLE [5] (L Piggott) 2-9-4 W R Swinburn 11/4 JT FAV: 32123: Heavily bckd,
tried to make all & ran to his best: see 1172.   55
1313 PACIFIC BASIN [1] (W O'gorman) 2-8-11 T Ives 10/1: 0234: Prom thro'out: fair effort. see 965.45
--   LINE OF SUCCESSION [6] 2-8-11 S Cauthen 12/1: 0: Should benefit from this debut:
half brother to a couple of winners incl useful Sidab, winner between 5 & 10f: impr likely
next time.   42
924 DANCING DIANA [8] 2-9-1 L Jones(5) 20/1: 2140: Ev ch: see 531.   46
1255 MON BALZAR [11] 2-8-11 R Cochrane 11/4 JT FAV: 00: Heavily bckd, early speed but fin
9th: evidently well regarded: see 1255.   00
--   Atrayu [3] 8-8   1030 Persian Tapestry [10] 8-8
--   Kims Ticket [2] 8-11   --   Woodman Weaver [7] 8-11
11 ran 1¼,2,1,1,shhd   (K Abdulla)   J Tree Marlborough, Wilts

1553 RELIANCE SECURITY HCAP 3YO+ 0-50   £2565   1m   Good/Firm 32 -11 Slow   [35]

1189 GURTEEN BOY [2] (R Hannon) 4-9-7 G Starkey 6/1: -000001: 4 ch c Tickled Pink -
Joie d'Or (Kashmir II): Returned to form, coming from behind to lead near fin in a h'cap at
Windsor July 14: winner at Newbury, Brighton, Lingfield & Nottingham in '85: very eff over
7f/1m though seems to act on any grnd & on any trk.   38
*1450 SAMHAAN [6] (B Hanbury) 4-9-7(bl)(8ex) A Geran(7) 5/2 JT FAV: 1030112: Prom final 2f,
not btn far in a close fin: in gd form: see 1450 (10f).   36
1365 FEI LOONG [7] (E Eldin) 5-9-5 A Hutchings(7) 9/2: 0442143: Tried to make all, just
btn: gd effort: see 930.   33
1309 SIMONS FANTASY [8] (R Armstrong) 3-7-13 W Carson 5/2 JT FAV: 0-04434: Led briefly dist:
fair effort: see 843, 1309.   25
1240 PEANDAY [4] 5-8-9 C Rutter(5) 12/1: -003000: Chall dist, fdd: best 481 (yld).   17
1394 SINGING BOY [5] 5-8-13 T Ives 11/2: 0-00000: Close up 6f: see 1394.   17
680 LEMELASOR [3] 6-9-4 D Williams(7) 10/1: 0323200: Prom most: abs since 680: see 441.   20
7 ran 1,nk,shhd,3,2,¾   (T Crawford)   R Hannon Marlborough, Wilts

1554 SOUTHLEA STAKES 3YO+   £1052   1m 2f   Good/Firm 32 +13 Fast

1395 NILAMBAR [3] (R J Houghton) 3-8-6(1ow) S Cauthen 11/2: 02-0231: 3 b c Shergar -
Noureen (Astec): Useful colt: gained a pillar-to-post success, setting a fast pace and
holding on well to win a minor event at Windsor July 14: only ran twice late in '85: half
brother to 3 winners, notably Nasseem: seems btr suited by 10f than 1m: does well with
forcing tactics on fast grnd.   61
1444 CHINOISERIE [11] (L Cumani) 3-9-0 Pat Eddery 6/4 FAV: -021122: Again heavily bckd, kept
on gamely and 6L clear of rem: deserves another race, possibly a h'cap: see 1208.   67
--   GALACTIC HERO [5] (M Stoute) 3-8-6(1ow) W R Swinburn 2/1: 2-3: Close up but no extra
final 1f on seasonal debut: rated 63 when just btn by Shahaab in a valuable minor race at
Kempton in Sept.'85, only previous outing: should be well suited by 10f plus: acts on
firm grnd: will strip fitter next time & should soon find a maiden.   50
1395 RESCUE PACKAGE [13] (G Lewis) 3-8-5 P Waldron 15/2: 4-044: Ev ch till fdd dist: much
closer to winner in 1395 (1m).   37
1061 LA MUSCADE [12] 3-8-2 R Hills 66/1: 0-00: No threat: lightly raced previously and
this was best effort yet: dam won over 10f: should improve.   24
--   OUR MABLE [10] 3-8-2 T Quinn 25/1: -0: Slow start, never btr: should benefit from
this racecourse debut: likely to impr.   18
1087 Way Above [8] 8-5   --   Shajar Ad Durr [1] 8-2
887 Next Dance [6] 8-5   164 Vistule [2] 9-3   806 Captains Jade [4] 8-2
--   Kings Rock [9] 9-3   --   Bang Bang [7] 9-3
13 ran 1,6,7,6,2½.   (H H Aga Khan)   R J Houghton Didcot, Oxon

1555 EBF CHRIS COWDREY MAIDEN 2YO   £1512   6f   Good/Firm 20 -42 Slow

1019 BOLD GARCON [6] (C Nelson) 2-9-0 J Reid 10/3: 01: 2 ch c Bold Lad - Motacilla
(Relko): Impr colt: mkt drifter though gamely made all in a 2yo maiden at Folkestone July 15:
showed promise when 6th behind Brave Dancer & several subsequent winners on his debut at
Newbury last month: cost 35,000 gns & is a half brother to a couple of minor winners: stays
6f well: acts on gd & fast grnd & on any trk.   50
1162 BOLD CRUSADER [3] (M Stoute) 2-9-0 W R Swinburn 10/3: 42: Well bckd: ran on strongly
under press & would have prevailed in another stride: well clear of rem & certain to win
soon: stays 6f well: see 1162.   50
834 CAPITAL FLOW [5] (R Hannon) 2-9-0 Pat Eddery 11/4 FAV: 043: Well bckd: chased winner

over ½way, sn one-paced: seems to act on any trk: acts on gd/firm: see 834.   26
1187 SYSTEMS GO [2] (G Pritchard Gordon) 2-8-11 G Duffield 14/1: 034: Ran on too late:
best over this trip in 1187.   23
--   FIRWOOD [7] 2-8-11 G Sexton 33/1: 0: Nearest fin on racecourse debut: dam successful
over 12f: may need further though should impr next time.   23
405 ON YOUR PRINCESS [14] 2-9-0 G Starkey 33/1: 00: Abs: speed over ½way: cheaply bought
colt who is closely related to several winners: should stay at least 6f: acts on gd/firm grnd.   21
1339 MUBKIR [13] 2-9-0 Paul Eddery 6/1: 3020: Early speed: much btr over 5f in 1339 (firm).   00
1495 Glorious Dan [4] 9-0   1488 Goodwood Park [3] 9-0 -- Stainsby Girl [1] 8-11
--   Shoot The Moon [8] 8-11   1187 Downsview Lady [12] 8-11
1075 Rocky Horror [9] 9-0   1313 Bangkok Boy [10] 9-0 -- The Londonderry [11] 8-11
15 ran   shhd,10,shhd,shhd,2   (Mrs J Yarnold)   C Nelson Lambourn, Berks

1556 DEREK UNDERWOOD STAKES   £689   1m 7f Good/Firm 20 -01 Slow

1111 KNIGHTS LEGEND [6] (G Harwood) 3-8-12 G Starkey 3/10 FAV: -2121: 3 b c Sir Ivor -
Gimme Love (Dr Fager): Useful colt: had a simple task, comfortably led inside dist to land
the odds in a minor race at Folkestone July 15: earlier won a similar event at Sandown &
subsq. an excellent 2nd to Stavordale in the Queen's Vase at Royal Ascot: half brother to
a couple of winners: very eff over 12/14f & stays 2m well: acts on gd & fast grnd & on any
trk: progressive colt who is certain to win more races.   54
1278 DEBCO [1] (J Dunlop) 3-8-2 Pat Eddery 9/2: -02: Led dist, no extra close home though
ran a creditable race, fin well clear of rem: clearly stays 2m well: acts on any trk: should
find a small race: see 1278.   40
1078 DRY GIN [3] (H Candy) 3-8-2 W Newnes 25/1: 0000-03: Led 6f out, well btn: see 1078.   20
1444 LUCKY LAD [2] (W Brooks) 3-8-2 G Carter(3) 66/1: 00-0004: Never threatened ldrs and
yet to show any worthwhile form.   17
--   PENTLAND BEAUTY [5] 5-8-11 P D'arcy 50/1: -0: No threat: off the trk since 84 when
she showed a little ability over middle dists: acts on gd/firm & soft grnd.   09
969 DEAFENING [4] 3-8-2 A Mcglone 14/1: 0-00340: Longer trip: much btr over 9f in 868 (yld)   16
1417 Straphanger [7] 9-0   -- Little Katrina [8] 8-11
8 ran   1,20,3,½,hd   (R J Shannon)   G Harwood Pulborough, Sussex

1557 GODFREY EVANS SELLING STAKES 2YO   £838   5f   Good/Firm 20 -50 Slow

1082 SWIFT PURCHASE [3] (R Hannon) 2-8-11(BL) Pat Eddery 13/8: 30001: 2 ch c Camden Town -
Miss Maverick (Vilmorin): Bl first time & was never hdd when a narrow winner of a slowly run
2yo seller at Folkestone July 15 (no bid): earlier had shown some ability in btr company:
cost 7,000 gns & is closely related to numerous winners: well suited by this minimum trip:
acts on gd & fast grnd & is suited by forcing tactics.   25
1323 COLLEGE WIZARD [5] (M Tompkins) 2-8-11 R Cochrane 11/2: 42: Pressed winner thro'out,
just btn though is impr & should find a seller: sprint bred colt who is suited by fast grnd
and an easy trk.   24
*1318 CHERRYWOOD SAM [2] (H O'neill) 2-8-11(bl) I Johnson 5/4 FAV: 404013: Trouble in running
& btr judged on his all-the-way success in 1318 over this C/D.   14
1458 RIBO BE GOOD [6] (J Bridger) 2-8-8(BL) R Guest 33/1: 004004: Remote 4th: no form to date.00
1318 BONZO [4] 2-8-11 J Reid 25/1: 0040: Al behind: see 1318.   00
5 ran   hd,4,15,2½   (Introgroup Holdings Ltd)   R Hannon East Everleigh, Wilts

1558 FRIENDS OF FOLKESTONE AMAT HCAP 3YO+   £1145   1m 2f Good/Firm 20 -50 Slow   [3]

1273 TRUE WEIGHT [8] (M Madgwick) 4-11-1 Mr D Madgwick(4) 16/1: 00-0001: 4 ch g True Song -
Flyweight (Salvo): Showed impr form when leading close home in an amateur riders stakes at
Folkestone July 15: won a similar race at Kempton last seeason: eff over 8/10f on gd/firm
& yld grnd: seems best on a sharpish trk.   17
1156 IRISH HERO [6] (R Sheather) 4-12-0   Maxine Juster 11/1: 2-00402: Fin well: ran to
his best here: stays 10f well: see 943.   28
1231 DOMINION PRINCESS [13] (P Rohan) 5-10-11 Laura Rohan(4) 11/2: -443303: Fin in gd style
& not btn far: however remains a mdn: stays 10f: see 310.   10
1204 IRISH DILEMMA [1] (A Bailey) 3-10-2(bl) Sharon Murgatroyd(4) 16/1: -000004: Led below
dist, not btn far: seems best over 10f on a sharpish trk: see 535.   12
1166 MATCH MASTER [15] 7-10-6 Mr J Ryan 33/1: 00/0-00: Fin well: lightly raced in recent
seasons: stays 10f: suited by fast grnd.   00
1031 ROSI NOA [11] 3-10-10 Sarah Kelleway(4) 12/1: 0-30000: Made much: best in 315 (soft/hvy)   15
1089 VITRY [10] 3-10-6 Sara Lawrence(4) 8/1: 0-00030: Fin 7th: btr in 1089 (12f): see 916.   00
1384 MERLINS MAGIC [12] 3-11-6 Debbie Albion(4) 5/2 FAV: 001-00: Wknd into 9th: see 1384.   00
1188 KARNATAK [14] 5-10-9 Cate Reynolds(4) 5/1: -0-0300: Prom 1m: clearly flattered in 943.   00
1365 Thatchingly [5] 11-7   1165 Visual Identity [9] 11-3
930 Tip Tap [2] 11-6   1243 Just Candid [4] 11-3   1349 La Dragoniere [3] 10-10(BL)
--   Ravenscraig [7] 10-3
15 ran   1,½,nk,2,½,½   (Mrs J F Cundy)   M Madgwick Denmead, Hants

1559 COLIN COWDREY HANDICAP 0-35   £1302   1m 4f Good/Firm 20 +07 Fast   [32]

*1274 BLENDERS CHOICE [11] (K Brassey) 4-9-0 S Whitworth 6/1: 0-03011: 4 b g Cavo Doro -

Harriny (Floribunda): In gd form, took command over 4f out when a comfortable winner of quite a fast run h'cap at Folkestone July 15: recently made all in a similar race at Chepstow: best form over 10/12f with forcing tactics: suited by gd or faster grnd & any trk. 28
1260 NASKRACKER [13] (G Harwood) 3-8-8 G Starkey 10/1: 0-0002: Stayed on under press: mdn who ran his best race of the season here: stays 12f: acts on gd/firm grnd. 32
1321 DASHING LIGHT [5] (D Morley) 5-8-11 B Rouse 6/1: -404323: Led over ½way: see 432. 20
•1301 KING JACK [7] (J Dunlop) 3-9-8 Pat Eddery 9/4 FAV: -00214: Stayed on too late: see 1301. 43
1416 HEIGHT OF SUMMER [9] 5-8-3 N Adams 33/1: 00-0400: Al well placed: see 1209. 09
955 TEMPEST TOSSED [10] 3-8-5 M Roberts 10/1: 003-040: Kept on: stays 12f: see 955. 24
1204 SENDER [12] 3-8-10 R Carter(5) 5/1: -0120: Not btn that far in 7th: see 1204 & 595. 00
1342 Vintage Port [4] 9-10 **849 Mystery Clock** [3] 8-5(bl)
1473 Dancing Barron [2] 9-3(bl) **1348 Broken Tackle** [8] 8-3
1416 Dick Knight [1] 8-1(vis) **856 Full Of Dreams** [6] 7-7(vis)(4oh)
13 ran 2,nk,1,hd,½,½ (Mark O'Connor) K Brassey Upper Lambourn, Berks

1560 LESLIE AMES HANDICAP 3YO 0-35 £1407 7f Good/Firm 20 -04 Slow [38]

1316 BLUE BRILLIANT [6] (B Hills) 3-9-0(bl) B Thomson 9/4 FAV: 0-00021: 3 b c Thatching - Belmont Blue (Kashmir II): Led inside dist, gamely in a 3yo h'cap at Folkestone July 15: first success: has been impr by the fitting of bl, shhd by Sequestrator over this C/D earlier this month: probably stays 1m: suited by fast grnd: runs well at Folkestone. 34
1281 TOPEKA EXPRESS [10] (R Armstrong) 3-8-10(bl) M Roberts 9/1: -000032: Led below dist, just btn & clear of rem: impr of late & may get off the mark sn: see 1281. 29
1224 SPECIAL GUEST [11] (D Morley) 3-8-8 R Guest 14/1: 200-033: Ran on too late: acts on gd/firm: see 1034. 17
1316 BELLEPHERON [12] (G Lewis) 3-8-7 G Sexton 14/1: 0-0444: Mkt drifter: ev ch: see 1316. 12
1436 ARCTIC KEN [8] 3-9-4 J Reid 15/2: 1103400: Nearest fin: best in 540 (yld). 22
997 MONSTROSA [9] 3-8-4 S Dawson 33/1: 0-00300: Late prog: needs 1m? see 538. 06
+1299 BICKERMAN [3] 3-8-9(10ex) G Duffield 11/4: 04-0010: Disapp 9th: much btr in 1299. 00
1384 VICEROY MAJOR [14] 3-9-3(bl) Pat Eddery 10/1: 0-00000: Made most though sn btn: see 703 00
1164 Persian Ballet [1] 8-9(VIS) **1191 Delta Rose** [13] 8-7
1463 Porthmeor [5] 9-7 **1231 Saxon Bazaar** [7] 8-6 **1324 Golden Straw** [2] 8-3(vis)
950 Wing Bee [15] 8-2(3oh) **1264 Never Bee** [4] 7-7(3oh)
15 ran ½,5,1½,½,1½ (A D Shead) B Hills Lambourn, Berks

1561 CITY OF HULL MAIDEN AUCTION STAKES 2YO £959 5f Firm 18 -06 Slow

1357 KALAS IMAGE [3] (G Moore) 2-8-2 A Mackay 14/1: 0323031: 2 br f Kala Shikari - Hi Friday (High Line): Gained due reward for her consistency, leading close home by a hd in a 2yo maiden auction at Beverley July 15: probably stays 6f, but seems suited by a stiff 5f: acts on firm & yld. 39
1305 ROYAL CROFTER [11] (M H Easterby) 2-8-8 M Birch 5/4 FAV: 322: Well bckd: led/dsptd lead: hung left final 2f & just caught: equally eff at 5/6f: consistent: see 1090. 44
1161 LEADING PLAYER [8] (R Hollinshead) 2-8-12 S Perks 11/2: 03: Dsptd lead: gd effort and 5L clear rem: should find a race: see 1161. 44
1370 SCAWSBY LEES [1] (M W Easterby) 2-8-8 K Hodgson 14/1: 034: Mkt drifter: al there. 28
1322 BE CHEERFUL [6] 2-8-11 T Ives 11/4: 430: Mkt drifter: never nearer: btr 1322 (6f). 31
-- VOL VITESSE [7] 2-8-7 D Mckeown 20/1: 0: Nearest fin & should impr on this initial effort: cheaply acquired colt whose dam won in France: should be well suited by further than 5f. 23
1174 CRAIGENDARROCH [5] 2-8-9 D Nicholls 8/1: 40: Prom, ev ch: see 1174. 23
1305 Reata Pass [9] 8-5 **1333 Take Effect** [14] 8-6 **813 Oxford Place** [10] 8-9
-- Stolen Star [4] 8-3 **-- Colney Heath Lad** [2] 8-6
1180 Eppy Marner [13] 8-3(1ow) **-- Culinary** [12] 8-4
14 ran hd,1½,5,hd,1½,¾ (I W Parry) G Moore Middleham, Yorks

1562 HUMBER SELLING STAKES 3YO £936 7.5f Firm 18 -14 Slow

1257 JUST THE TICKET [14] (C Booth) 3-8-11 R Lines(3) 16/1: 000-01: 3 gr f Faraway Times - Rum Year (Quorum): Led str, ridden out in a 3yo seller at Beverley July 15 (bought in 2,300 gns): little form previously: eff at 7½f, should be suited by 1m: acts on fast grrnd. 14
1288 RUPERT BROOKE [8] (J Kettlewell) 3-9-0 T Ives 7/2 JT.FAV: 0-00242: Al prom: in gd form: see 1288, 963. 15
1288 MRS NAUGHTY [6] (W Wharton) 3-9-6 M Brennan(7) 5/1: 0-40003: Kept on well: btr 1m? 20
1424 COURT RULER [1] (D Smith) 3-9-0 L Charnock 13/2: 0-00004: Nearest fin: see 997 (1m). 09
1256 QURRAT AL AIN [12] 3-8-11 M Birch 7/2 JT.FAV: 0-00000: Ch over 1f out: eff over 6/7f on fast ground. 05
1134 SHY MISTRESS [9] 3-8-11 S Perks 13/2: -04000: Wknd final 1f: best 729 (6f). 00
1288 CARR WOOD [13] 3-9-0 C Nutter 8/1: -000: Some late hdway after getting well behind: no form in 3 outings to date: should be suited by 1m plus. 00
1158 Planning Act [3] 8-11 **889 Amplify** [7] 9-0 **673 Platinum Star** [2] 8-11
1334 Brampton Lyn [11] 8-11 **1415 Glory Time** [10] 9-0(BL)
871 Miss Beswick [4] 8-11 **516 Selorcele** [5] 9-0(bl)
14 ran 1,hd,2½,nk,5 (Fred C May) C Booth Flaxton, Yorks

1563 NORTH BAR WITHIN H'CAP 3YO+ 0-50   £2398   1m 4f Firm 18 -14 Slow   [33]

1177 VERY SPECIAL [7] (W Holden) 4-9-3 R Morse(5) 3/1 FAV: 43-0301: 4 ch f Royalty -
Intrusion (Aggressor): Led final 1f, ridden out in a h'cap at Beverley July 15: in '85 won
h'caps at Sandown & Thirsk: well suited by 11/12f: best on fast grrnd: likes to be up with
the pace.   29
1416 FOUR STAR THRUST [4] (R Whitaker) 4-9-0 N Carlisle 5/1: 4020202: Ev ch final 1f: see 1416 25
*1359 HYOKIN [6] (D Morley) 4-9-1(vis)(9ex) T Williams 4/1: 0003213: Not btn far: in fine form.   25
1052 WESTRAY [2] (R Hollinshead) 4-8-13 S Perks 6/1: -000404: Dsptd lead 2f out: yet
to regain his form of '85: see 225.   22
1374 RAPID LAD [5] 8-9-10 D Nicholls 7/2: 00-0140: Ev ch over 1f out: best 1106 (10f).   .   29
1159 FENCHURCH COLONY [3] 5-9-6(vis) M Birch 6/1: 0/30300: Made most, fdd: best 1024.   22
1303 Taxi Man [1] 8-9
7 ran   1,1½,½,2½,2   (,rs E G Lambton)   W Holden Newmarket

1564 HUMBER BRIDGE H'CAP 3YO+ 0-35   £1396   2m 3f Firm 18 No Stan.Time   [20]

1336 TURI [1] (A Smith) 7-8-3 S Webster 3/1 FAV: 00331: 7 b g Welsh Pageant - Turiana
(Citation): Led 2f out, driven out in a h'cap at Beverley July 15: first success on the Flat,
but a winner over hurdles: well suited by a stamina test: loves fast grnd.   05
--   MAY BE THIS TIME [6] (J Hardy) 5-9-6 T Ives 16/1: 310-0-2: Al prom: 6L clear 3rd:
gd seasonal debut: ran only once in '85: in '84 won at Nottingham: stays 2m plus well:
probably acts on any grnd.   18
1348 ALFIE DICKINS [8] (R Hollinshead) 8-8-10 W Ryan 7/1: 0-04403: Chall 2f out: see 590.   01
*1078 MUSIC MINSTREL [3] (C Nelson) 3-8-13 M Hills 10/3: 0-00014: Ev ch str: btr 1078 (14f).   20
1419 WELSH GUARD [5] 4-8-6 M Birch 9/1: 0000040: Wknd inside final 2f: see 1419 (2m).   00
1304 PHEASANT HEIGHTS [2] 3-8-11 T Williams 9/2: 00-4400: Made most, fdd: btr 1304 (stks 2m) 03
1183 LOVE WALKED IN [4] 5-9-8 R Morse(5) 4/1: 1310420: Dist last: btr 1183 (gd).   00
1195 Beau Navet [7] 8-8
8 ran   3,6,2,8,7   (John Wiles)   A Smith Beverley, Yorks

1565 PORT OF HULL H'CAP 3YO+ 0-35   £1895   8.5f Firm 18 +13 Fast   [31]

1264 BOLD ARCHER [13] (M Fetherston Godley) 3-7-10 C Rutter(3) 8/1: -000201: 3 ch c Brave
Shot - Allander Girl (Mialgo): Led nearing final 1f, driven out in quite fast run h'cap at
Beverley July 15: first success: stays 1m well: acts on fast grnd & runs well here.   21
*1303 SURPRISE CALL [5] (M H Easterby) 3-9-10(6ex) M Birch 7/2: 10-0312: Led 2f out: in
fine form: see 1303.   45
1374 PARIS TRADER [4] (M W Easterby) 4-9-7(bl) M Hindley(3) 11/1: 0000003: Kept on in
str: btr effort: see 609.   27
1335 GREED [11] (D Smith) 5-9-4 L Charnock 10/1: 304-244: Prom, ev ch: see 1185.   21
1166 AQUALON [3] 6-8-4 A Mackay 20/1: -0000: Al there: last season won twice in Ireland:
probably stays further than 1m: acts on gd & fast grnd.   03
1335 BOY SANDFORD [12] 7-8-1 J Quinn(5) 12/1: -030400: Never nearer: see 789.   00
1139 CHARMING VIEW [2] 4-8-9 R Hills 9/1: 0-01020: Prom over 6f: btr 1139: see 673.   00
1432 SMART MART [7] 7-7-11(BL) J Lowe 9/1: 000-300: Tried in bl: see 1374.   00
-1374 PERSHING [6] 5-9-0 T Ives 9/4 FAV: 0203220: Made no show: much btr 1374 (10f).   00
1188 Porto Irene [1] 7-7(3oh)   1482 Manabel [9] 8-10
--   Velocitus [10] 8-6   1424 Peters Kiddie [14] 7-7(1oh)
1139 Fill Abumper [15] 7-11
14 ran   2,1½,1½,2,nk,1½   (Miss Jenny Rick)   M Fetherston Godley East Ilsley, Berks

1566 BOOTHFERRY PARK NURSERY H'CAP 2YO   £1429   7.5f Firm 18 -35 Slow   [37]

1357 MUSEVENI [2] (P Calver) 2-9-1(BL) M Fry 20/1: 40041: 2 b c Kampala - Deer Park
(Faraway Sun): Bl first time & led after 1f, driven out in a nursery h'cap at Beverley
July 15: clearly stays 7½f well: acts on fast grnd & a stiff trk: suited by front running.   34
*1221 BOLD DIFFERENCE [5] (W Wharton) 2-9-0 C Rutter(5) 11/2: 000212: Stayed on well:
eff at 7f & should be suited by 1m: impr filly: see 1221.   31
1172 SKRAGGS PLUS TWO [6] (D Leslie) 2-8-8 D Nicholls 7/1: 00043: Ev ch str: see 1172.   20
1197 SILVER ANCONA [3] (E Eldin) 2-9-7 A Mackay 9/4 FAV: 34334: Prom, ev ch: stays 7f: acts
on firm & soft grnd & a gall trk.   31
*1413 ROYAL TREATY [4] 2-9-0(7ex) Kim Tinkler(5) 9/2: 0033110: Ev ch str: btr 1413 (C/D).   23
913 GWYNBROOK [1] 2-9-4(BL) K Hodgson 7/1: 00340: Early ldr: bl first time after abs:
probably stays 7f: see 813.   26
1132 LACK OF PEARLS [7] 2-9-1 J Lowe 9/2: 4040: Never in it: much btr 1132 (6f, gd).   00
7 ran   ½,2½,½,hd,hd   (Lord Ronaldshay)   P Calver Ripon, Yorks

1567 WESTON SELLING STAKES 3&4YO   £1148   1m   Firm 11 -01 Slow

680 KAVAKA [14] (R Hannon) 4-9-0 W Carson 4/1 FAV: 00-0001: 4 b c Kampala - Cotoneaster (Never Say Die): Gained first success (well bkcd) when battling it out thro'out final 1f for a narrow win in a 3 & 4yo seller at Leicester July 15 (sold 1,100 gns): quite lightly raced in the past: suited by 1m & firm grnd & runs well on a stiff trk: 20

1400 ANGIES VIDEO [4] (R Holder) 4-8-11 A Proud 14/1: -000032: Mkt drifter, led final 1f, caught death: gd effort & must find a seller soon: see 1400.   16

874 SAUGHTREES [7] (P Walwyn) 3-8-0 N Howe 8/1: 000-003: Dsptd lead most: a mdn who ran her best race of the season here & is evidently suited by 1m & firm grnd.   12

578 ARMORAD [13] (P Haslam) 4-9-8(vis) T Williams 14/1: 000-004: Mkt drifter, ev ch: well btn in non-sellers previously this term & last won in '84 at Nottingham: seems to stay 1m: acts well on firm grnd.   20

1338 HOKUSAN [19] 4-9-0 R Cochrane 20/1: 3400000: Prom most: see 620.   10
1369 MISS BETEL [6] 3-8-0(bl) P Robinson 14/1: 0400000: Made much: see 767 (12f).   05
1364 COUNT ALMAVIVA [22] 3-8-3(BL) W Newnes 8/1: 0020030: Prom, ev ch: fin 7th: btr 1364.   00
1201 RUN FOR FRED [1] 4-9-0 S Websters 10/1: 30-0000: Well bckd, no dngr: see 963: a maiden.   00
1439 TAKE A BREAK [1] 3-8-5 S Whitworth 8/1: 1000200: No dngr: twice below 1400.   00

1400 Take The Biscuit [9] 8-3(bl)		1400 East Street [17] 9-0	
1054 Sundown Sky [23] 9-5(bl)		1195 Video [12] 9-5(BL)	
1394 Decoy Belle [18] 8-11		1400 Metal Woods Rule [3] 8-0	
1077 Remainder Tip [24] 8-11		1400 Saravanta [15] 8-11	
1210 Bee Kay Ess [10] 8-4(1ow)		1080 Knight Hunter [20] 8-0	
1340 Res Non Verba [8] 8-0		1369 Spare The Blushes [21] 8-1(1ow)	
-- Suntan [5] 8-0		-- Solent Dawn [16] 8-0	

23 ran   shhd,2½,½,½,1½   (R Hannon)   R Hannon East Everleigh, Wilts

1568 RADIO LEICESTER NURSERY H'CAP 2YO   £2222   5f   Firm 11 -05 Slow   [51]

1275 LADY PAT [1] (M Mccormack) 2-9-4 J Leech(7) 7/4 FAV: 241131: 2 gr f Absalom - Miss Lollypop (St Paddy): Useful filly: comfortably made all in a nursery at Leicester July 15: consistent filly who earlier won at York & Catterick: related to several winners: very eff over 5f on firm grnd with forcing tactics.   54

1059 LAST RECOVERY [2] (M Ryan) 2-8-5 R Cochrane 5/1: 3032: Ev ch: see 1059.   33

1105 GOOD BUY BAILEYS [3] (G Blum) 2-8-11 A Mackay 20/1: 1403: Sn prom: possibly btr over 5/6f than longer dists: see 186: acts on firm & yld.   35

781 COUNT TREVISIO [4] (R Sheather) 2-9-7 T Ives 10/1: 104: Pressed winner early, kept on: seems to act on firm & soft: see 523.   45

*1397 FOURWALK [6] 2-8-12(7ex) W Wharton 6/1: 002410: Pressed winner much: see 1397 (6f).   33
1313 RIMBEAU [7] 2-9-2 A Clark 10/1: 424100: No dngr: two poor efforts since 717 (C/D).   34
1050 SUPREME OPTIMIST [5] 2-7-10 A Proud 6/1: 30000: Early pace: see 1050.   13
965 INGLISTON [9] 2-8-3(1ow) M Birch 11/2: 03340: Wknd ½way: btr 965 (6f).   18

8 ran   2,1½,hd,1½,1½,½,1½   (W G Best)   M Mccormack Sparsholt, Oxon

1569 TENNANTS LAGER H'CAP 3YO+ 0-35   £2066   1m 4f   Firm 11 +11 Fast   [26]

*1326 DIVA ENCORE [6] (R Armstrong) 3-8-13(4ex) S Cauthen 9/2: 0-00011: 3 br f Star Appeal-Regal Twin (Majestic Prince): Impr filly who was winning 2nd race on the trot when comfortably leading inside final 3f in quite a fast run h'cap at Leicester July 15: won similar h'cap at Yarmouth July 1: very eff over 12/14f, may stay 2m: suited by firm grnd & a gall trk: may complete the hat trick.   36

1274 CAPA [10] (R Holder) 6-8-3 A Mackay 9/1: 004-22: 2nd final 2f: gd effort: see 1274: suited by 12f.   08

*1484 ZAUBARR [8] (B Hills) 3-9-7(bl)(4ex) M Hills 6/4 FAV: 0-00113: Again tried to make all: btr 1484 (14f).   37

1198 JANIE O [2] (M Ryan) 3-8-7 P Robinson 20/1: -03004: Late prog: a mdn who has run creditably over 1m & stays 12f: acts on firm & gd.   21

1271 COMHAMPTON [11] 5-9-1 I Johnson 16/1: 022-320: Never btr: see 940.   09
1226 LAKINO [3] 4-9-3 A Murray 4/1: -1-0000: Prom, wknd: see 675.   11
1314 STAR SHINER [4] 3-8-10 P Waldron 6/1: -00-000: Fdd ½way: lightly raced and no form since 229 (7f, soft).   00

967 Metelski [14] 9-2(bl)		783 Venture To Reform [12] 7-11	
991 Keep Hoping [13] 8-3		1099 Knights Heir [9] 8-11 1233 Shipbourne [15] 9-7	
1140 Rapidan [5] 8-7			

13 ran   2½,1½,½,½,5,nk   (Kinderhill Corporation)   R Armstrong Newmarket

1570 CARLING BLACK LABEL 2YO CLAIMER   £3574   6f   Firm 11 -15 Slow

515 CLOWN STREAKER [3] (M H Easterby) 2-8-9 M Birch 6/1: 2101: 2 ch c Cawston's Clown - Velour Streak (Firestreak): Only 2nd best on merit when awarded a 2yo claimer at Leicester July 15 after fin. ½L 2nd: early in the season won a maiden at Catterick: appears to act on yld: eff over 5/6f & seems to handle any trk: does well when fresh.   39

*1190 GOOD TIME GIRL [6] (R Hannon) 2-8-6 W Carson 4/1: 0112: Chall. when hmpd 1f out, kept on to be a close 3rd, placed 2nd: impr filly who evidently acts on any trk: see 1190.   34

1483 PANACHE [9] (P Haslam) 2-8-11(VIS) T Williams 2/1 FAV: 003121D: Led 2f out and

although a comfortable ½l winner, disq. & placed 3rd due to edging left final 1f:
improving and should find compensation: see 965 and 1483.   43
1363 SAY YOU WILL   [4] (P Makin) 2-8-7 T Quinn 20/1: 4004: Ev ch: best effort since 503.   30
261 HONEY PLUM   [5] 2-8-2 M Wigham 20/1: 440: Early pace, abs since 261 (soft).   23
1282 RIBOGIRL   [8] 2-8-6 R Cochrane 14/1: 000: No threat: first signs of form & should be
well suited by further than 6f: acts on firm.   23
1203 TAKE A HINT   [7] 2-9-0 R Hills 11/4: 44140: Prom most, fin 7th: btr 1203.   00
*1279 KNOCKSHARRY   [10] 2-8-6 R Hills 10/1: 110: Made much: btr 1279 (waiting tactics).   00
--   Ciren Jester [1] 8-9   1294 Fairtown [2] 8-9
10 ran   ½,½,3,1,1½,nk   (W Steels)   M H Easterby Great Habton, Yorks

1571 BASS FILLIES HANDICAP 3YO 0-50   £2834   7f   Firm 11 +07 Fast   [45]

1457 MUDISHA   [5] (G Huffer) 3-9-5 G Carter(3) 7/1: 0-00401: 3 b f Mummy's Pet - Armelle
(Tribal Chief): Returned to form with a pillar-to-post success in quite a fast run 3yo
fillies h'cap at Leicester July 15: consistent in '85 winning at Redcar: eff over 6/7f & is
best with forcing tactics: acts on firm & yld & on any trk.   46
1073 BLUE GUITAR   [2] (J Hindley) 3-8-9(VIS) M Hills 4/1: 430-442: Visored first time, chall
final 1f, just btn in a close fin: see 923.   35
1300 ARTFUL DAY   [8] (J Dunlop) 3-9-7 W Carson 6/1: 04-133: Kept on well in a close fin:
gd effort: see 911.   46
1257 ANNABELLINA   [11] (G Wragg) 3-8-9 S Cauthen 12/1: 0-40004: Dsptd lead much: best
effort since 162 (10f, yld).   30
168 NEW EDITION   [1] 3-8-9(bl) R Cochrane 20/1: 0000-00: Slow start, never closer after
long abs: see 168: stays at least 7f.   27
+1398 CASBAH GIRL   [4] 3-8-5(6ex) T Williams 1/1 FAV: 02-0110: Disapp well bckd fav: btr 1398.   16
*1212 On Impulse [7] 8-1   1272 Madam Muffin [10] 8-3 1446 Mirataine Venture [3] 9-1
1316 Dress In Spring [9] 7-7(1oh)   1269 Starboard [6] 7-7(5oh)
11 ran   ½,½,2,1½,4,1,2,½   (B N Hamoud)   G Huffer Newmarket

1572 WIGSTON STAKES 2YO C & G   £964   7f   Firm 11 -14 Slow

*1345 WOLSEY   [2] (H Cecil) 2-9-2 S Cauthen 4/9 FAV: 11: 2 b c Our Native - Sancta Rose
(Karabas): Very prom. colt: retained his unbtn record with an effortless win, landing the
odds in a minor 2yo race at Leicester July 15: made all in a maiden at Lingfield July 2 on
debut: half brother to smart middle dist colt Mashkour: eff over 7f, sure to stay well:
acts on firm grnd: has scope for further impr & is sure to win in btr company.   55
1253 PALEFACE   [8] (L Piggott) 2-8-11 T Ives 8/1: 332: Outpcd final 1f but a fair effort
and stays this trip well: see 1253.   40
1197 CASTLE HEIGHTS   [1] (R Armstrong) 2-8-11 P Tulk 50/1: 03: Made most: see 1197.   37
1345 SUNSET BOULEVARD   [5] (L Piggott) 2-8-11 R Cochrane 50/1: 04: Never btr: half brother
to 6/7f minor winner Reindeer Walk: on the up grade & will stay 1m.   35
1234 FOREIGN KNIGHT   [6] 2-8-11 W Newnes 33/1: 30: Ev ch: race 1234 has not worked out well. 32
965 BUMPTIOUS BOY   [7] 2-8-11 S Perks 50/1: 00: No dngr: a Feb. colt out of a dam with
no worthwhile form.   26
*1275 MILEAGE BANK   [3] 2-9-2 T Quinn 100/30: 410: Early pace, disapp after 1275 (6f).   30
--   Dam Inquisitive [4] 8-11
8 ran   2½,1,½,1,2,½   (Lady Howard de Walden)   H Cecil Newmarket

---

YARMOUTH   Wednesday July 16th   Lefthanded Fair Track

Official Going Given As GOOD/FIRM

1573 JELLICOE MAIDEN 2YO STAKES   £964   6f   Good 41 -07 Slow

--   DUTCH AUCTION   [2] (L Piggott) 2-9-0 T Ives 7/1: 1: 2 b c Taufan - Mock Auction (Auction
Ring) Made a successful race course debut, dsptd lead till went on after ½ way for a
comfortable win in 2yo maiden at Yarmouth July 16: cost 25,000 gns as a yearling: stays 6f
well: acts on gd ground and on a fair course: will improve for this experience.   48
--   GREENS OLD MASTER   [6] (W Jarvis) 2-9-0 A Murray 8/1: 2: Ev ch on debut, just held
and beat rem decisively: cost $80,000 as yearling and is a half sister to a winning sprinter:
stays 6f well.   46
--   TAFFY TEMPLAR   [8] (J Hindley) 2-9-0 M Hills 7/2 CO FAV: 3: Nicely bckd: stayed on
well from ½ way: will improve next time: cost 37,000 gns and is a half brother to dual
juv winners Gentle Gypsy and Lammastide: stays 6f well: acts on gd ground.   36
1488 MUSICAL BELLS   [5] (L Piggott) 2-9-0 T Lucas 7/2 CO FAV: 004: Btr fancied stable mate
of winner: dsptd lead to ½ way: earlier had shown promise in btr company: may do btr over
the minimum trip: acts on gd and firm ground.   28
--   ALCATRAZ   [4] 2-9-0 M Giles 9/1: 0: Active in mkt on debut tho' never dangerous: bred
to be suited by longer distances and should improve.   26
--   BE MY PRINCE   [7] 2-9-0 M Roberts 20/1: 0: Mkt drifter and never got into the race:
half brother to a couple of winning sprinters and will improve for this experience. 26
--   ALPENHORN   [1] 2-9-0 W Ryan 20/1: 0: Easy to back: early speed, not given a hard race
and should improve when tackling longer distances.   00
988 NANCY NONESUCH   [3] 2-8-11 S Cauthen 7/2 CO FAV: 00: Speed over ½ way: fin last and
better in 988 (5f).   00
8 ran   ½,4,2,1,hd   (Sheikh Mohammed)   L Piggott Newmarket

1574 FASTOLFF SELLING STAKES   £750   6f   Good 41 -01 Slow

1319 NANOR [7] (W Kemp) 3-8-0 T Williams 14/1: 0000001: 3 gr f John De Coombe - Radiant
Pearl (Gulf Pearl) Showed impr form when leading below dist, ridden out in a seller at
Yarmouth July 16 (bought in 1,900 gns): last season won a nursery selling h'cap at Lingfield:
eff over 6f, stays 1m: acts on firm and yldg ground and on any track.   20
1418 MUSIC REVIEW [4] (W Jarvis) 3-7-12(bl) R Hills 8/11 FAV: 00-2222: Heavily bckd on
first venture into selling co, tho' again found one too good: see 910.   16
1367 RUSSELL FLYER [11] (R Hoad) 4-8-12(bl) T Ives 12/1: 0000403: Dropped in class:
late prog tho' never looked likely to repeat last year's success: see 1213.   14
1549 PERCIPIO [1] (K Ivory) 3-8-3(vis) A Shoults(5) 10/1: 0000304: Led over ½way:
best in 1334.   10
1288 GAYWOOD GIRL [6] 3-7-9 B Cook(6) 20/1: 240-000: Bckd at long odds: al up there:
maiden who was placed sev times in similar company last term: stays 6f: acts on any going.   00
256 LOCHABBEY [13] 3-7-9 S Cauthen 16/1: 0000-00: Never nearer after long abs: maiden
who has yet to show any worthwhile form.   02
729 TRELALES [10] 3-7-9 G Carter(2) 8/1: 00-00: Bckd from 14/1: never nearer 7th: lightly
raced filly who is a half sister to winning miler Kuwait Palace.   00
1439 BLUE STEEL [14] 3-7-10(1ow) B Crossley 10/1: 0044400: Early speed: fin 9th: see 1364. 00
1310 Charisma Music [8] 8-4   1394 The Golf Slide [3] 8-4
--   Sly Maid [5] 7-9   --   Greenhills Boy [2] 7-12
--   Great Owing [12] 8-4
13 ran   ½,2,1,½,½,1   (T P Ronan)   W Kemp Ashford, Kent

1575 CARLTON HOTEL H'CAP 3YO (0-50)   £2599   1m   Good 41 -08 Slow   [52]

1486 PINSTRIPE [2] (R Williams) 3-9-7(5ex) S Cauthen 4/5 FAV: 0-01121: 3 b c Pitskelly -
Snoozy Time (Cavo Doro) Useful colt: cleverly made all in a 3yo h'cap at Yarmouth July 16:
earlier twice successful in h'caps at Sandown and sub ran up to the well h'capped Aventino
at Newmarket: very eff over 7/8f on gd and fast grd: acts on any trk and is well suited by
forcing tactics: should find another h'cap.   55
1325 GEORDIES DELIGHT [1] (L Piggott) 3-9-7 T Ives 11/4: 2104142: No extra cl home and
has yet to run a bad race this term: prob best over 1m tho' does stay 10f: see 1202.   50
-1327 QUEEN OF BATTLE [3] (M Ryan) 3-8-10 P Robinson 3/1: 0-00223: Much btr over this
C/D in 1327 (firm).   32
3 ran   ½,3   (Michael R Jaye)   R Williams Newmarket

1576 MARITIME CLAIMING STAKES 2YO   £1718   5f   Good 41 -33 Slow

1403 NATIONS SONG [9] (R Stubbs) 2-8-9 J H Brown(5) 7/2: 1022121: 2 b f Gold Song -
Girl Commander (Bold Commander) Most genuine and consistent filly: al cl.up and readily led
inside dist in a 2yo claiming stks at Yarmouth July 16: earlier won sellers at Lingfield and
Yarmouth and has not been out of the first 2 in her last 5 starts: very eff around 5f on
firm and yldg ground: acts on any track: wore bl when successful prev tho' clearly equally
eff without.   35
1161 BAY WONDER [11] (G Pritchard Gordon) 2-8-8 W Ryan 20/1: 0002: Led before ¼ way,
no chance with easy winner: well suited by an easy course: see 746.   24
1483 LIGHTNING LASER [13] (P Kelleway) 2-9-0 S Cauthen 5/2 FAV: 00333: Early leader:
best in 1483 (7f).   28
1323 ROAN REEF [4] (N Macauley) 2-8-10 Gay Kelleway(5) 16/1: 034304: Ran on too late see 1088.18
--   BOLD HIDEAWAY [8] 2-9-0 P Robinson 12/1: 0: Stayed on well after a slow start on
debut: first foal who should do btr next time: acts on good ground.   21
450 MARCHING MOTH [3] 2-8-11 N Connorton 4/1: 1400: Early speed after abs: best in 236(sft) 06
*1363 LADY BEHAVE [10] 2-9-2 R Perham(7) 5/1: 302010: Bolted before start: early speed:
better in 1363 (6f).   00
--   Kibara [12] 8-6   --   Tinas Beauty [7] 8-10   717 Tilting Yard [2] 8-6
1308 Music Delight [5] 8-6   --   Fu Lu Shou [1] 9-5
12 ran   2,½,2,½,5   (Nation Wide Racing Co. Ltd)   R Stubbs Middleham, Yorks.

1577 CALIFORNIA H'CAP STAKES (0-35)   £1735   1m 6f   Good 41 -01 Slow   [35]

1280 TROJAN WAY [8] (R Hollinshead) 4-8-7 W Ryan 11/1: 0-00001: 4 ch c Troy - Sea Venture
(Diatome) Put up a gutsy performance when making all in a h'cap at Yarmouth July 16: first
success: eff over 12/14f: suited by gd or faster ground and seems to act on any trk.   21
1349 CASTLE POOL [7] (D Gandolfo) 4-8-8 S Cauthen 4/1: -04002: No extra cl home over
this longer trip: best in 743.   19
1280 OLD MALTON [1] (J Toller) 4-8-7 P Robinson 2/1 FAV: -000133: Stayed on: see 990 (C/D) 17
1326 REFORM PRINCESS [3] (M Ryan) 3-8-3(vis) G Bardwell(7) 7/1: 00-0034: Al cl up: see 1326 24
66   QUICK REACTION [5] 3-7-11 P Barnard(7) 16/1: 0-000: Lack of fitness told below dist:
lightly raced colt who is closely related to sev winners: needs gd or faster ground: should
do better.   16
1388 ASSAGLAWI [6] 4-9-8 A Murray 7/2: -001200: No threat: now with G Blum: best 959.   26
44   Symbolic [4] 9-10   1290 My Annadetsky [2] 7-7(4oh)
8 ran   1½,½,2,1½,½   (J E Bigg)   R Hollinshead Upper Longdon, Staffs.

1578 STURDEE AMATEUR RIDERS MAIDEN STKS   £1323   1m 3f   Good 41 +18 Fast

25   OSRIC   [8] (M Ryan) 3-10-11 Mr J Ryan(5) 6/1: -41: 3 b g Radetzky - Jolimo (Fortissimo)
Despite a lengthy abs led ½ way and comfortably drew clear to win a fast run amateur riders
maiden at Yarmouth July 16: half brother to middle dist winner Joli's Girl: eff around 11f
and sure to stay further: acts on gd and soft ground and on any track.   42
1206 HIGH KNOWL   [7] (B Hills) 3-10-11 Mr T Thomson Jones 5/4 FAV: 0-42: Outpaced below
dist: btr in 1206 (10f).   30
1304 DEMON FATE   [4] (F Durr) 3-10-11 Jane Armytage(5) 14/1: 4-00003: Led to ½ way: best 605   25
1259 ELVIRE   [3] (S Mellor) 3-10-8 Dana Mellor(5) 9/1: -004: Never nearer: cheaply bought
filly: closely related to a couple of winners: stays 11f well: acts on gd ground.   22
1141 STORMGUARD   [2] 3-10-11 Franca Vittadini 9/2: 0-30: Hung below dist: see 1141.   25
--   TAMATOUR   [5] 3-10-11 Maxine Juster 11/2: -0: Easy to bck on race course debut: chance
2f out: should improve tho' looks to be one of M Stoute's lesser lights.   24
1416 Harbour Bazaar   [1] 11-11(vis)   1310 Letby   [9] 11-11
1303 Great Topic   [6] 10-11
9 ran   8,3,shthd,hd,½   (Richard Scott)   M Ryan Newmarket

Official Going Given As FIRM

1579 SALTFORD APPR. HCAP 0-35   £1163   1m   Firm 00 -20 Slow   [34]

1450 FLEET BAY   [3] (T Hallett) 6-7-13(2ow) B Uniacke 16/1: -000-01: 6 gr g Bay Express -
Porsanger (Zeddaan) Fin well to get up cl home in an app h'cap at Bath July 16: lightly raced
in recent seasons: last won in '83 at York: stays 1m well: acts on firm and soft ground
and a galloping track.   13
1169 FULL OF LIFE   [9] (M Pipe) 3-9-1 G Athanasiou(3) 8/1: 21-0002: Made almost all: good
effort: on final outing in '85 won a fillies mdn at Leicester: closely related to sev
winners: eff 6f, stays 1m: acts on firm and soft and a gall trk: best when making the running   37
--   ASHLEY ROCKET   [5] (M Pipe) 5-9-11 A Dicks 10/1: -0000-3: Al prom: fair seasonal debut:
lightly raced in '85: in '84 won at Pontefract and York: eff at 7f, stays 1m: acts on any grd.   36
942 CASTIGLIONE   [2] (J Francome) 4-7-10(bl) Dale Gibson 14/1: -000004: Kept on well final
1f: needs further: see 199.   03
1257 HAYWAIN   [11] 3-8-0 A Culhane 7/2: 000-030: Mkt drifter: never nearer: btr 1257.   13
*1139 FOOT PATROL   [7] 5-8-13 C Carter 11/10 FAV: -000010: Heavily bckd disapp: btr 1139.   13
1439 Windbound Lass   [10] 7-7(1oh)   1346 Hampton Walk   [1] 7-7(2oh)
--   Ciaras Lad   [12] 8-1   1079 Branksome Towers 0 7-7(3oh)
343 Fire Chieftain   [6] 8-3(10ow)(2oh)   --   With A Lot   [8] 7-8(bl)
1401 Some Guest   0 7-7(VIS)(10oh)
13 ran   ½,hd,2,2½,½   (Mrs J Wonnacott)   T Hallett Saltash

1580 LIMPLEY STOKE MAIDEN FILLIES STKS 3YO   £2053   1m 2f   Firm 00 +08 Fast

708 COCOTTE   [3] (W Hern) 3-8-11 W Carson 11/10 FAV: 224-001: 3 b f Troy - Gay Milly
(Mill Reef) Very useful filly: despite fair abs, led over 1f out, drawing clear, breaking the
course record in a 3yo fillies mdn at Bath July 16: showed a deal of promise in '85, notably
when 2nd to Maysoon in the Virginia Water at Ascot: eff at 1m/10f, may stay further: acts
on good and firm ground.   56
1193 WHILE IT LASTS   [2] (L Cumani) 3-8-11 Pat Eddery 4/1: -3332: Made much: consistent
and deserves a race: stays 10f: acts on firm and yldg ground: see 338.   41
1031 VERONICA ANN   [5] (C Nelson) 3-8-11 J Reid 14/1: -0003: Ev ch str: lightly raced this
season: eff at 10f, should stay 12f: acts on gd and firm.   32
--   STANDARD ROSE   [4] (H Candy) 3-8-11 C Rutter(5) 20/1: 0-4: Nearest fin on seasonal debut
and should do btr next time: unplaced on sole outing in '85: half sister to 2 winners,
including the useful 1m/12f winner Forest of Dean: should be suited by 12f: acts on fast grd.   30
--   SIMPLY DELICIOUS   [20] 3-8-11 W Newnes 20/1: -0: Kept on well inside final 2f on
race course debut and will be all the btr for this run: maybe suited by further than 10f:
acts on fast ground.   23
--   FRANCHISE   [18] 3-8-11 D Price 50/1: -0: Nearest fin on racecourse debut and improvement
likely: dam was a smart and genuine sort: should be suited by 10/12f: acts on fast grd and
should do much better than this.   21
1446 HOT TWIST   [17] 3-8-11 N Howe 50/1: 0-00: Late hdwy into 7th: showing steady improvement.   21
1244 HANGLANDS   [15] 3-8-11 A Mcglone 8/1: 0-040: Never nearer: much btr 1244 (7f).   00
--   MINHAH   [7] 3-8-11 B Thomson 10/1: -0: Fdd str: btr for race: US bred filly cost $100,000
                                                                                                           00

1193 Rohila   [12] 8-11   1451 April Fox   [14] 8-11   1368 Crowley   [16] 8-11
458 Cherry Glory   [6] 8-11   --   Dais   [11] 8-11   1446 Double Tango   [8] 8-11
1404 Plum Bossy   [19] 8-11   1164 Sunk Island   [9] 8-11   1198 Tory Blues   [13] 8-11
18 ran   10,2½,½,4,1½,nk   (Sir Michael Sobell)   W Hern West Ilsley, Berks

486

1581 ICI ROSECLEAR HANDICAP 0-40 3YO+   £3360   1m   Firm 00 +06 Fast   [40]

1189 EVERY EFFORT [4] (R Holder) 4-8-11 C Rutter(5) 3/1 FAV: 401D341: 4 b c Try My Best -
Quick (Jim J) Well bckd and led over 1f out, holding on by $\frac{3}{4}$l in a h'cap at Bath July 16:
earlier "won" a h'cap at Epsom, subs disq: in '85
won a maiden at Edinburgh: eff at 7f, stays 1m well: acts on firm and soft grd and on any trk.   33
724 ROCKMARTIN [6] (I Balding) 4-10-0 Pat Eddery 11/2: 20-0002: Fin really well final 1f
after a fair abs: fine eff under 10-0 and should go one btr soon: well h'capped on his best
form: see 432.   49
1199 FARAG [2] (P Walwyn) 3-8-3(1ow) Paul Eddery 10/1: 1-20003: Made much: gd eff:see 74.   31
1273 SNAKE RIVER [8] (F Jordan) 4-8-7 A Clark 5/1: 3310224: Al prom: another gd run:see 1273.   23
1500 SAHARA SHADOW [5] 4-8-5(6ex) A Dicks(5) 16/1: -121000: Never nearer: see 1273.   15
1188 MARSOOM [1] 4-7-8 D Mckay 14/1: -000200: Mkt drifter: ev ch: twice below form 750(10f)   02
1084 PEARL FISHER [9] 3-8-11 W Newnes 8/1: -133040: Ev ch in 7th: best 140 (soft).   00
1460 CASCABEL [11] 5-9-7 R Cochrane 7/2: 12-0430: Ran poorly: much btr 1460 (sharp trk)   00
1447 Gallant Hope [7] 7-7(1oh)   1211 Santella Pal [10] 7-8(1ow)(3oh)
1520 Song An Dance Man [12] 8-2   1471 Monatation [3] 7-7(5oh)
12 ran $\frac{3}{4}$,1$\frac{1}{2}$,nk,3,$\frac{3}{4}$ (M R Klein)   R Holder Portbury, Avon

1582 HAMILTON HANDICAP 0-50   £2532   2m 1f   Firm 00 +08 Fast   [33]

1388 SUGAR PALM [5] (R Hannon) 5-9-0(bl) L Jones(5) 2/1 FAV: 3042221: 5 b h Gay Fandango -
Get Ahead (Silly Season) Gained due reward for his consistency, led aftr 1m, staying on
gamely in quite a fast run h'cap at Bath July 16: 2nd on his prev 3 outings and was not
winning out of turn: in '85 won at Lingfield and Leicester: eff at 12f, stays 2m+ well:
prob acts on any ground, but goes well on firm with front running tactics.   28
1260 BALLET CHAMP [9] (R Holder) 8-9-0(bl) A Proud 5/1: -303002: Ev ch in str: 8l clear
3rd: see 349.   26
1159 GENTLE FAVOR [4] (M Prescott) 5-9-8(vis) G Duffield 9/1: 10-0403: Stays 2m, but lacks
foot: see 519.   26
1419 QUADRILLION [8] (R Hollinshead) 7-8-2 P Hill(7) 7/2: 000/024: Never nearer: btr 1419.   00
-1342 FANDANGO LIGHT [3] 5-9-10 Pat Eddery 9/4: 00/2020: Led over 1m: not stay 17f:see 1342.   11
--   RAJA KHAN [2] 5-8-10 J Williams 33/1: 000/1-0: No show: on sole outing in '85 won in
Ireland: stays 2m: acts on gd ground.   00
--   MAJUBA HILL [6] 5-9-8 Paul Eddery 10/1: 41443/0: Fdd in str: didnot race on the Flat
in '85: in '84 won at Edinburgh and Salisbury: eff 12f, stays further: acts on gd and firm.   00
375 Corston Springs [1] 8-5   1326 Countless Countess [7] 8-8(bl)
9 ran   2,8,15,2,10   (Frank J Broom)   R Hannon Marlborough, Wilts.

1583 EBF EVERSHOT MAIDEN STAKES 2YO   £1766   5.5f   Firm 00 -08 Slow

1440 LITTLEFIELD [1] (I Balding) 2-8-11 Pat Eddery 4/11 FAV: 21: 2 b f Bay Express -
Brookfield Miss (Welsh Pageant) Promising filly: heavily bckd and cruised into lead over 1f
out, sn drawing clear in a 2yo mdn at Bath July 16: first time out fin 2nd to Shining Water
in a fillies event at Windsor: cost only 10,000 gns: half sister to '84 12f winner Misfire:
should be suited by further than 6f: acts on fast grd and should continue to improve.   55
1405 TEZ SHIKARI [8] (L Cottrell) 2-9-0(BL) G Baxter 6/1: 0422222: Bl first time: made
much but no chance with winner: continues his run of 2nd: has the ability to find a race:
see 728.   38
1275 GUNNER STREAM [3] (R Holder) 2-9-0 I Johnson 8/1: 03: Never nearer: steadily improving:
should stay 7f: acts on fast ground.   32
--   TEACHERS GAME [6] (K Brassey) 2-8-11 S Whitworth 12/1: 4: Wknd over 1f out on 'race
course debut and should improve: sister to winning sprinter Teachers Pet and should be
suited by an easy 5/6f.   25
1522 GOING EASY [2] 2-9-0 J Williams 20/1: 040: Never nearer: see 1522.   28
1082 JABE MAC [9] 2-9-0 P Waldron 50/1: 000: Ev ch: lightly raced since 678.   26
662 Motor Broker [10] 9-0   -- Miami Lass [4] 8-11   853 Solent Gold [7] 8-11
--   Top Of Mai Field [5] 9-0
10 ran   7,3,2,hd,1   (Mrs R M Chaplin)   I Balding Kingsclere, Hants.

1584 BROCKHAM HANDICAP 3YO 0-35   £2064   5f   Firm 00 -22 Slow   [40]

1476 PENDOR DANCER [1] (K Ivory) 3-8-4(VIS) G Baxter 14/1: 0230001: 3 b g Piaffer -
Bounding (Forlorn River) Visored first time and made ev yard, ridden out in a 3yo h'cap at
Bath July 16: first success: eff at 5f, stays 6f: acts on gd and firm ground and seems
suited by front running in a visor.   25
1476 NORTHERN LAD [7] (L Holt) 3-8-9 P Waldron 8/1: 0000202: Sn prom: see 580.   26
1447 DANCING SARAH [4] (D H Jones) 3-8-13 J Reid 20/1: -400003: Ran on well inside final
1f: best effort since 443.   30
*1406 MISTER MARCH [5] (R Hutchinson) 3-8-0(7ex) P Hutchinson(3) 8/11 FAV: -000014: Came
all too late: btr 1406 (5.5f).   13
1499 GLEADHILL PARK [6] 3-8-8(bl) S Whitworth 10/1: -000000: Prom, ev ch: yet to make
the frame this season: see 339.   16
884 MISS KNOW ALL [10] 3-9-7 B Thomson 6/1: 10-000: Prom, fdd after abs: see 624.   23
1443 SHARI LOUISE [2] 3-9-2 Pat Eddery 10/1: 4P0-000: Al rear: no form this term: fair
early season 2yo in '85, winning at Chepstow and Nottingham: eff at 5f: acts on gd and soft.   00
1443 MONSARAH [8] 3-8-2(bl) W Carson 10/1: 000-400: Fin last: best 1272 (1st time out).

339 Skylin [3] 8-8   **1344 My Mutzie** [9] 8-4(4ow)
10 ran   1½,nk,1½,1½,2½   (Mrrs P A Brown)   K Ivory Radlett, Herts.

KEMPTON   Wednesday July 16th   Righthand Easy Track

1585 **U.S.M. NURSERY H'CAP STAKES 2YO**   £2548   5f   Firm 04 –07 Slow   [49]

918 DUTCH COURAGE [4] (D Morley) 2-9-0 C Rutter(5) 6/1: 44331: 2 br c Daring March –
Martini Time (Ardoon) Gained his first success when comfortably leading dist in a nursery at
Kempton July 16: consistent prev in mdn company: very eff over 5f and is speedily bred: acts
well on firm ground.   48
*948 GREENS GALLERY [6] (G Blum) 2-8-4 M L Thomas 5/2 FAV: 0112: Prom, led briefly 2f
out, clear rem and should find a nursery soon: acts on firm and good: see 948.   34
*1421 GEMINI FIRE [1] (P Felgate) 2-10-0(7ex) G Duffield 6/1: 041313: Early leader: anchored
by big weight: see 1421.   48
*1496 PINK PUMPKIN [5] (J Douglas Home) 2-7-8(7ex)(6oh) L Riggio(7) 10/1: 002014: Late
hdwy: see 1496.   14
1453 PARIS GUEST [2] 2-9-3 R Cochrane 10/1: 01000: Best 404 (C/D good).   34
1003 SAMLEON [8] 2-9-7 L Jones(5) 12/1: 412340: Best 200, 278 (soft/hvy).   34
*1194 SPANISH SKY [7] 2-9-4 P Cook 11/4: 010: Early pace: see 1194.   16
1261 DOUBLE TALK [3] 2-8-5 N Adams 25/1: 042000: Outpaced thr'out: disapp since 353 (sft)   00
8 ran 1½,5,shthd,1½,2,6,½   (Lord McAlpine)   D Morley Newmarket

1586 **THORN E.M.I. MAIDEN FILLIES STAKES 3YO**   £3666   7f   Firm 04 –33 Slow

982 EMERALD WAVE [7] (R Armstrong) 3-8-11 W Carson 12/1: 004-001: 3 br f Green Dancer –
Shore (Round Table) Prom and led final 1f, narrowly, in a cl fin to a slowly run 3yo fillies
mdn at Kempton July 16: reportedly almost b.d. last time at Goodwood: ran only 3 times in
'85: half sister to sev winners: suited by 7f and firm grd: should stay 1m.   47
1327 FLUTTERY. [5] (G Wragg) 3-8-11 S Cauthen 6/1: -302: Had to be switched to get a
clear run, fin wl., unlucky? Sure to stay at least 1m and appears to act on firm and soft.   46
--   CANESARA [11] (R J Houghton) 3-8-11 Pat Eddery 7/1: -3: Promising debut, meeting
trouble in running but only narrowly btn at fin: a daughter of Shergar who is almost certain
to be suited by 1m: acts well on firm ground: should sn find a maiden.   46
1487 BASOOF [3] (M Stoute) 3-8-11 W R Swinburn 3/1 FAV: 04-0404: Kept on one paced but
not btn far: see 1032.   45
1451 ETTAS PET [6] 3-8-11 G Duffield 9/1: 00-40: Prom, ev ch: improving: see 1451.   40
1198 CANADIAN GUEST [2] 3-8-11 W Newnes 7/2: -00: Heavily bckd chall dist, not btn far
in a cl finish: see 1198.   35
1375 HOOKED BID [12] 3-8-11 B Thomson 12/1: -000: Made much, fdd into 7th: see 1375.   35
--   Court Town [14] 8-11   1228 Glade [4] 8-11   1142 Calystegia [10] 8-11
--   Casa Rosada [9] 8-11   923 Omania [8] 8-11   --   Seraphino [13] 8-11
--   Fairseat Close [1] 8-11
14 ran 1,½,nk,1,1½,nk   (Mrs W J Taylor)   R Armstrong Newmarket

1587 **ECONOMIST STAKES 2YO**   £4065   7f   Firm 04 –21 Slow

*1458 ANGARA ABYSS [2] (G Harwood) 2-9-4 G Starkey 5/2: 411: 2 b c Far North – For Missy
(Forli) Useful colt: winning 2nd race on trot, scoring a pillar to post success in a rather
slowly run 2yo minor race at Kempton July 16: very easy winner of a maiden at Brighton last
time: a $52,000 yearling and is a half brother to 2 winners in USA: eff 7f, sure to be suited
by 1m+: acts on firm ground: improving type.   60
1242 BEESHI [3] (P Cole) 2-8-11 T Quinn 2/1 FAV: 32: Didnot have the best of runs final
2f, kept on well and clear rem: a maiden should come his way shortly: see 1242.   48
--   TIBER RIVER [8] (W Hern) 2-8-11 W Carson 100/30: 3: Chall 2f out, outpaced but
should benefit from the experience: dam a minor middle dist winner who was placed behind
some smart fillies in '78: will be suited by 1m: certain to improve and win a race.   38
1232 MON COEUR [7] (C Brittain) 2-8-11 P Robinson 14/1: 04: Ev ch: a 37,000 gns April foal:
should stay at least 7f.   32
1239 NONSUCH PALACE [5] 2-8-11 S Cauthen 11/2: 030: Disapp after 1239, 1019 but was
wk in mkt here and this run is perhaps best ignored.   24
1232 MANDALAY PRINCE [1] 2-8-11 B Rouse 50/1: 00: Had no sort of run 3f out: cost
IR 11,000: should stay 7f.   09
513 Sylvan Orient [4] 8-11   1019 Jonite [6] 8-11
8 ran 2,5,2½,4,7   (Paul H Locke)   G Harwood Pulborough, Sussex

1588 **CRAWLEY WARREN H'CAP STAKES (0-60) 3YO**   £4220   1m 2f Firm 04 +23 Fast   [65]

1284 ENBARR [2] (H Cecil) 3-8-3 S Cauthen 3/1: 0-2131: 3 b c King's Lake – Catherine Wheel
(Roan Rocket) Very useful colt: turned in by far his best effort so far, making ev yard and
forging clear in the str for an easy 10l success in a very fast run 3yo h'cap at Kempton
July 16: comfortable winner at Windsor May 12 and possibly needed the race last time: half
brother to Cheshire Oaks winner Hunston: well suited by 10f and front running tactics:
acts on soft but does particularly well on firm ground, on an easy track: looks certain to

win again next time.   58
1130 MUSICAL YOUTH [6] (C Horgan) 3-7-8 T Williams 6/1: 004-202: Kept on tho' no chance
with this ready winner: see 459.   33
1085 TOBAGO DANCER [1] (R Hannon) 3-8-10 P Eddery 5/1: 4-01223: Same place final 3f:
better 1085.   44
1301 PRINCELY ESTATE [4] (J Winter) 3-7-11 A Mackay 14/1: 0-22224: No threat and is
proving expensive to follow: see 259, 570.   31
1147 ININSKY [5] 3-9-7 G Starkey 14/1: 210-400: Prom, wknd str: btr 1m? See 950.   54
*1509 AUCTION FEVER [7] 3-8-9(bl)(5ex) B Thomson 2/1 FAV: 2023210: Heavily bckd, ridden
as last time but found absolutely nil when asked a question and bl didnot appear to work on
this occasion: see 1509.   30
1402 ATIG [3] 3-7-10(1ow) W Carson 10/1: 0000340: Prom, wknd: twice below 1314: need bl?
7 ran   10,5,hd,1,12,shthd   (S Niarchos)   H Cecil Newmarket   00

1589 GOLDEN HELLO MAIDEN STAKES 3YO   £2644   1m 4f Firm 04 -13 Slow

572 VERARDI [8] (W Hastings Bass) 3-9-0 Pat Eddery 13/2: -301: 3 b c Mill Reef - Val
D'Erica (Ashmore) Returned after an abs, leading ½m out and holding on well in a 3yo mdn at
Kempton July 16: below his best last time: suited by 12f and acts on firm and gd going:
should win more races.   59
--   MERANO [14] (H Cecil) 3-9-0 S Cauthen 11/8 FAV: -2: French import: came from off the
pace, fin strongly to be narrowly btn and was well clear rem: narrowly btn by French Derby
2nd Altayan at Evry in April over 9f on soft grd, only prev race: appears to act on firm
and soft: suited by 12f and should be hard to beat next time.   58
479 SLANGI VAH [11] (H Candyy) 3-9-0 W Newnes 11/2: -33: Long abs but well bckd, no
extra final 1f: this looked a gd contest and he should win a maiden soon: see 479.   50
1278 NOBLE FILLE [12] (J Dunlop) 3-8-11 B Thomson 20/1: -004: Ev ch: prob stays 12f: see 1031.   38
--   PRODIGAL DANCER [3] 3-9-0 G Starkey 13/2: -0: Belated racecourse debut for this
attractive son of Nijinsky, ran rather green and will be all the btr for the experience:
half brother to a winner in USA: sure to improve.   40
1314 GODS PATH [15] 3-9-0 A Mcglone 50/1: 0-00000: Never btr: ran poorly in bl in 1314,
better without them: see 980.   35
1259 PRELUDE [7] 3-8-11 W Carson 12/1: 3-340: Ev ch, fin 7th, twice well below 581 and
does not seem to be progressing.   30
359 TOP DEBUTANTE [10] 3-8-11 T Ives 12/1: -300: Long abs: fin 8th: needed race?
Disapp since 218 (1m, yldg).   30
926 Sanet [9] 8-11   1401 Lydia Eva [6] 8-11   -- Starlight Freddie 0 9-0
619 Burning Ambition [1] 8-11   1372 Our Noora [13] 8-11
935 Moodybint [2] 8-11   -- Mollikin [5] 8-11
15 ran   ½,5,4,¾,1,¾,hd   (F Ortelli)   W Hastings Bass Newmarket

1590 BIG BANG H'CAP STAKES (0-50)   £2616   1m   Firm 04 -04 Slow   [43]

1240 FAIR COUNTRY [9] (D Elsworth) 4-9-3 S Cauthen 11/4 JT FAV: 0-03231: 4 ch f Town &
Country - Fair Measure (Quorum) Gained a deserved success, coming from behind to comfortably
lead final 1f in a h'cap at Kempton July 16 (decisively reversing the form of 1240 with
Alqirm): in '84 won at Newbury: well suited by 1m on a fair or gall trk: acts on firm and
yielding: could win again.   42
1273 NEW CENTRAL [5] (M Blanshard) 4-8-1 W Newnes 33/1: 0-00002: Made much: best eff
since 636.   21
1179 FLEET FOOTED [7] (G P Gordon) 3-8-1(bl) G Duffield 9/1: 4-00203: Led 2f out: fair
effort: now wears blinkers: see 843.   31
1245 COUNTRY GENTLEMAN [3] (J Dunlop) 3-8-6 W Carson 11/2: 40-0004: Kept on late: needs
10f? See 1245.   33
1018 PICTOGRAPH [8] 4-9-10 Pat Eddery 11/2: 014-000: Rear, prog when not clear run 2f
out: returning to form and is worth keeping an eye on: see 1018.   40
1383 DERRYRING [4] 4-9-2 C Rutter(5) 12/1: 0-00000: Ev ch: btr 1383 (10f).   29
+1240 ALQIRM [1] 4-9-6(5ex) B Rouse 11/4 JT FAV: 0-00210: Rather disapp after 1240.   00
1415 Pelegrin [2] 8-1   1263 Mr Mcgregor [10] 8-4   481 Nicky Nick [6] 8-4
10 ran   2,hd,1½,hd,1½   (Sir Gordon Brunton)   D Elsworth Whitsbury, Hants

Official Going Given As SOFT, BASED ON TIME GOOD

1591 GROUP 3 NISHAPOUR CURRAGH STAKES 2YO   £12350   5f   Good 63 +03 Fast

1126 DOMINION ROYALE (R Williams) 2-8-10 R Cochrane 5/2 JT.FAV: 4131: 2 ch c Dominion – Bahamas Princess (Sharpen Up) Smart colt: led over 1f out, comfortably, in Gr 3   Nishapour Curragh Stakes July 12th: won his mdn at Kempton May 31 and last time a gd 3rd in Norfolk Stakes at Royal Ascot (behind Sizzling Melody): very eff over 5f on gd or fast ground: still improving and looks set for further success.   70
1097 QUEL ESPRIT (M Mccormack) 2-9-2 Pat Eddery 5/2 JT.FAV: 2111302: Gd eff from this tough colt: see 571.   68
--   AFRICAN SUNRISE (A Mcnamara) 2-8-7 W R Swinburn 5/1: 13: Most creditable 3rd having won a fillies mdn at Mallow first time out last month: acts on gd ground and is eff at 5f.   57
--   CATALONDA (L Browne) 2-8-7 S Craine 9/2: 14: Gd eff: winner of a mdn at Tipperary last month: acts on firm and gd ground: eff at 5f.   52
1329 HARRY QUINN 2-8-10 G Curran 8/1: 221320: Consistent: see 752, 1329.   51
--   ERINDALE 2-8-7 K Moses 14/1: 23210: Recent winner of a mdn at Naas (fast going, 5f)   44
--   INGABELLE 2-8-7 D Gillespie 4/1: 10: -   00
7 ran   2½,¾,2,1½,1½,4   (D Robinson)   R Williams Newmarket

1592 GROUP 1 GILLTOWN STUD IRISH OAKS 3YO   £94500   1m 4f   Good 63 –11 Slow

926 COLORSPIN (M Stoute) 3-9-0 Pat Eddery 6/1: 11-341: 3 b f High Top – Reprocolor (Jimmy Reppin) Highclass filly: was the only winner from a long way out, leading on bit final 1f and readily sprinting clear for the easiest of wins in Gr 1 Irish Oaks at the Curragh July 12: winner of both her races as a 2yo at Nottingham and Newbury (Listed race): half sister to smart Rappa Tap Tap and Bella Colora: eff 10f, stays 12f really well: prob unsuited by firm grd and acts on good: likes a gall track: given suitable underfoot conditions will be very hard to beat in any of the top middle dist races.   92
*1331 FLEUR ROYALE (D V O'brien) 3-9-0 C Roche 11/2: -012: Al prom, led str but only on sufferance and was left for dead when the easy winner went past: however a fine eff against one so smart: clearly stays 12f well: see 1331.   80
-926 UNTOLD (M Stoute) 3-9-0 W R Swinburn 8/11 FAV: 0111-23: Odds on fav and stable companion of Colorspin, never going well and fin a well btn 3rd: much btr 926 (firm).   65
--   TOO PHAR (D Weld) 3-9-0 K Moses 66/1: -104114: Not disgraced but no threat: recent winner of a couple of h'caps and this was a significant step up in class: suited by 12f and good or firm ground.   55
--   POPULARITY 3-9-0 R Cochrane 12/1: -2-110: Led after ½ way, wknd str: recent winner of minor events over 9/10f at Phoenix Park and Leopardstown: not stay 12f? Acts on gd ground.   54
1331 LAKE CHAMPLAIN 3-9-0 M J Kinane 8/1: 2-21220: No danger: non stayer? see 1331.   44
1331 Sigym 9-0   1331 Welsh Fantasy 9-0
8 ran   3,12,6,½,7,6,2   (Helena Springfield Ltd)   M Stoute Newmarket

1593 GROUP 3 ROYAL WHIP STAKES 3YO+   £12350   1m 4f   Good 63 –13 Slow

1144 DUBIAN (A Stewart) 4-9-5 Pat Eddery 5/2: 2331-01: 4 b f Highline – Melodina (Tudor Melody) Very smart and tough filly: responded with the upmost gameness to hard driving forcing her hd in front on the line to win Gr 3 Royal Whip Stks at the Curragh July 12: very consistent in '85 winning at Yarmouth and earlier placed in both the English and Irish Oaks: suited by 12f: acts on firm, possibly btr on gd or yldg going: seems to act on any track: tough and genuine.   78
--   WUTHERING HEIGHTS (D V O'brien) 3-8-5 C Roche 12/1: 144-232: Caught post: placed all 3 outings this season and deserves a change of luck: stays 12f and acts on gd and hvy ground.   77
*1144 DIHISTAN (M Stoute) 4-9-13 W R Swinburn 8/11 FAV: 112-113: Gd eff under 9-13 and is consistent: see 1144.   79
1144 LEMHILL (M Blanshard) 4-9-10 R Cochrane 5/1: 32-1344: Another fair eff from this game colt: see 1144, 251.   71
293 CURRENT WAVE 3-8-8(bl) K Moses 33/1: 0-400000:Has been well btn since 293 (hvy)   34
5 ran   hd,3,2½,15   (Mohammed Obaida)   A Stewart Newmarket

Official Going Given As GOOD

1594 GROUP 3 PRIX MESSIDOR 3YO+   £19825   1m   Good

--   GAY MINSTREL (C Head) 5-8-9 G Moore 1: 00-1211: 5 br c Gay Mecene – Gracious Smart colt: gained a narrow success in a blanket fin to Gr 3 Prix Messidor at Maisons-Laffitte July 12: 3rd win from 4 races this term: very eff over 1m on gd ground: genuine.   71
757 MAJESTIC VOICE (G Mikhalides) 3-8-1(1ow) C Asmussen 1: 431422: Just btn in a close fin: eff over 1m/10f on firm and gd ground.   74
--   NEW BRUCE (G Collet) 4-9-0 A Badel 1: 00-0203: Very cl 3rd: winner of a Gr 2 race at Deauville in '85 on hvy ground: eff 1m, stays 10f well: acts on firm, best with plenty of give.   74
--   SPECTAME (F Boutin) 4-8-9 F Head 1: -302214: Btn just over 1l and is in gd form at present: eff 1m on gd ground.   67
300 SECRET LIFE 3-7-11 Y Talamo 1: -302120: Cl.up 5th.

MAISONS-LAFFITTE   Saturday July 12th   -Cont'd

1356 AL RAHIB 4-9-0 A Gibert 1: 00-1130: Btn less than 2l in 6th: eff over 7f/1m on
firm and good: see 1356.   71
12 ran ½,nk,¾,nose,shtnk   (J Wertheimer)   C Head France

SAINT-CLOUD   Sunday July 13th   Righthand, Galloping Track

Official Going Given As GOOD/YIELDING

1595 GROUP 2 PRIX MAURICE DE NIEUIL 3YO+   £33579   1m 4f   Good/Yld

1493 ALTAYAN (A De Royer Dupre) 3-8-2(1ow) C Asmussen 1: 12241: 3 ch c Posse - Aleema
(Red God) Highclass colt: held up till leading 1f out readily in Gr 2 Prix Maurice de Nieuil
at St-Cloud July 13: easy winner at Evry first time out and ran 2nd to the topclass Bering
in the French Derby (race 1009): acts on firm and soft: eff over 9f, stays 12f really well:
likely to be aimed at the Arc.   86
389 ZAHDAM (G Harwood) 3-8-5 G Starkey 1: 11-102: Returned after an abs to run a
splendid race, keeping on well final 1f at 7f, well suited by 12f now: acts on firm and
yielding but prob unsuited by heavy (as in 389): see 159.   82
1352 ANTHEUS (C Head) 4-9-2 G Moore 1: 23: Dsptd lead 2f out, gd eff: see 1352.   78
1009 SHARKEN (A Fabre) 3-8-1 A Gibert 1: 4-3144: Dsptd lead 2f out, no extra but a gd eff. 76
6 ran 2,½,nk,¾,4   (HH Aga Khan)   A De Royer Dupre France

KREFELD (W. Germany)   Sunday July 13th

Official Going Given As FIRM

1596 GROUP 3 FILLIES STAKES 3YO   £9887   1m 3f   Firm

1002 AMONGST THE STARS (S Norton) 3-8-9 J Lowe 1: 0-10101: 3 br f Proctor - Out Of This
World (High Top) Very useful filly: an outsider when overcoming difficulties in running to
lead on the post in a Gr 3 fillies race at Krefeld July 13: earlier won a h'cap at Haydock
first time out and val XYZ h'cap at Newcastle: successful at Catterick and Wolverhampton in
'85: well suited by 10/12f nowadays tho' seems to act on any going and on any trk: genuine. 65
--   PRAIRIE NEBA (U Ostmann) 3-8-9 K Woodburn 1: -2032: German filly who led 2f out,
caught death but clear rem: stays 12f and acts on firm.   64
*470 EPICURES GARDEN (D Weld) 3-8-9 M J Kinane 1: -13-413: Irish chall: abs since btr 470 58
--   NORETTA (H Bollow) 3-8-9 P Remmert 1: -3044: --   52
599 BELICE 3-8-9 M Wigham 1: -100: Made much, wknd: fin 6th: abs since 599.   42
955 FAREWELL TO LOVE 3-8-9 A Murray 1: -210220: Dsptd lead 4f out, wknd into 8th:
said to have been unsuited by firm: see 315, 955.   32
12 ran shthd,3½,3,2½,3½   (Mrs M Keogh)   S Norton Barnsley, Yorks.

SAINT-CLOUD   Monday July 14th   Righthand Galloping Track

Official Going Given As GOOD/FIRM

1597 GROUP 2 PRIX EUGENE ADAM 3YO   £34296   1m 2f   Good/Firm

554 UN DESPERADO (A Fabre) 3-8-9 A Gibert 1: 12-031: 3 b c Top Ville - White Lightning
(Baldric) Very smart, impr colt: held up, came with a tremendous rattle to sprint clear in
the final 100yds in Gr 2 Prix Eugene Adam at St-Cloud July 14, in the process recording the
fastest time in this event for over 30 years and also giving his trainer his 4th successive
victory in the race: prev off the trk over 2 months and seems to do well when fresh: highly
regarded by his trainer and is expected to improve further next time, particularly over 12f
tho' he is evidently very eff over 10f: well suited by waiting tactics and has an excellent
turn of foot: acts on fast ground on a gall track: sure to make his presence felt whatever
company he tackles next time.   84
1096 SHARROOD (W Hern) 3-8-9 W Carson 1: -043032: Al prom: had a battle royal with the
pacemaking Directing from the dist but tapped for foot by the winner cl home: fine eff and
deserves a decent prize before season's end: see 1096, 226.   80
--   DIRECTING (Y Porzier) 3-8-12 P Johanny 1: -040113: Set a tremendous gallop and was
a clear leader at ½ way, battled on when hdd final 1f: impr colt who won a h'cap at Maison
Laffitte and a Listed race at St-Cloud in his prev 2 outings: stays 10f but with his style
of running may be best at shorter dist and winning form over 1m: acts on fast ground. 82
*1214 CHERCHEUR DOR (C Head) 3-9-0 G Moore 1: 0-24114: Ev ch final 4f: continues to
improve and is possibly even btr at 12f: see 1214.   80
+1230 CONQUERING HERO 3-8-12 W R Swinburn 1: 113-110: Prom, ev ch: btrr 1230.   72
878 NOMROOD 3-9-0 C Asmussen 1: 12-1200: Much btr 878, 574.   65
10 ran 2,nk,1½,3,5   (M F Dabaghi)   A Fabre France

Official Going Given As GOOD/FIRM ON STRAIGHT COURSE : REMAINDER FIRM

1598 HIGH STEWARD CLAIMING STKS 2YO   £1744   7f   Firm –05 –21 Slow

1373 LIGHTNING LEGEND [2] (P Kelleway) 2-9-2 Gay Kelleway(5) 5/2: 44041: 2 ch f Lord Gayle
- Mellifont (Hook Money) Nicely bckd when leading below dist, comfortably, in a 2yo Claiming
Stks at Yarmouth July 17: cost 10,500 gns and is a half sister to sev winners: eff over
shorter trips: seems best over 7f: suited by gd or faster grd: acts on any track.   43
1322 TRYNOVA [7] (G Pritchard Gordon) 2-8-6 P Robinson 5/1: 02: Went on 2f out : clear
rem and stayed this longer trip well: should find a small race: acts on fast ground: see 1322   30
1305 PERFECT STRANGER [8] (P Haslam) 2-8-11 J Scally(7) 2/1 FAV: 03: Well bckd: held up
and never nearer: stays 7f: acts on firm grd: may do better when ridden up with the pace.   29
1207 OCONNELL STREET [6] (M Tompkins) 2-9-1 R Cochrane 16/1: 0004: Al front rank: best
effort to date from this cheaply bought colt: half brother to sev minor winners: acts fast grd   32
--   ROUGH DANCE [1] 2-9-5 E Guest(3) 12/1: 0: Led ½ way: fair debut and will improve
for this experience: half brother to sev winners incl useful middle dist colt Royal   Match:
acts on fast ground.   35
1392 BOBACH BOY [10] 2-8-9 M Roberts 20/1: 00: Al mid-div: half sister to sev winners,
incl juv Jenny's Rocket.   09
1305 Leg Glide [5] 8-8   *853 Telegraph Folly [4] 9-0
1075 Danse Arabe [3] 8-6(1ow)   497 Timurtasch [9] 9-0
10 ran   1,3,hd,¼,10   (N Mandell)   P Kelleway Newmarket

1599 SPANISH PARADE SELLING STAKES 2YO   £663   6f   Firm –05 –32 Slow

1478 ORIENTAL JADE [2] (D Morley) 2-8-11(BL) R Cochrane 5/1: 041: 2 b c Kala Shikari -
Jade Girl (Bold Native) Fitted with bl,although starting slowly, led below dist for a
decisive win in a 2yo seller at Yarmouth July 17, retained for a course record 9,200 gns:
cheaply bought colt who is a half brother to winning sprinter Witham Girl: stays 6f well:
acts well on fast ground and on an easy course: may prove btr than plating class.   28
1379 MUSICAL CHORUS [1] (G Blum) 2-8-8(bl) A Bond 12/1: 00302: Tried to make all: gd
effort and is well suited by forcing tactics: see 1262.   13
1440 JUST ON TIME [3] (G Huffer) 2-8-8 M Miller 8/1: 03: Dropped in class: ran on too
late: cheaply bought filly who is a half sister to sev winners : will be suited by further in
time: acts on fast ground.   09
763 GREY ROD [5] (W Kemp) 2-8-11 R Mcghin 33/1: 004: Rank outsider: speed over ½ way
and ran his best race to date despite fair abs: acts on firm ground.   08
1537 ABSALOUTE HEAVEN [4] 2-8-8 A Mercer 4/1: 0001020: Speed over ½ way: best 1168.   04
948 CAUSEWAY FOOT [6] 2-8-11 Kim Tinkler(5) 9/4 FAV: 0000: Well bckd: early speed:
best in 948 (5f).   07
1495 GREENSWARD BOY [8] 2-8-11 W Woods(3) 14/1: 00: Dropped in class and dsptd lead to
½ way: first foal whose dam was successful in this grade.   00
1483 TOOTSIE JAY [4] 2-8-8(BL) N Day 11/2: 0032400: Bl first time: best in 711 (5f).   00
1088 PINTAFORY [9] 2-8-8(BL) W Hood 8/1: 00000: Fitted with bl: al behind: seems unsuited
by fast ground: best with some give in 73 (5f).   00
9 ran   4,1½,1½,hd,shthd,3,½,shthd   (Nicholas Rigg)   D Morley Newmarket

1600 CONWAY STAKES 3YO   £2211   1m 3f   Firm –05 –01 Slow (Course Record)

1170 MAGIC SLIPPER [2] (H Cecil) 3-8-8 S Cauthen 15/8: -2121: Very useful filly: made
most, regained lead below dist and stayed on well to win a 3yo stks at Yarmouth July 17:
ready winner of her mdn at Beverley last month and subsequently just btn by the smart Spun
Gold in Warwick Oaks: superbly bred, being a half sister to topclass duo Light Cavalry and
Fairy Footsteps: very eff over 10/12f: acts on fast and soft grd and on any trk: genuine
and consistent filly who is certain to enjoy further success.   65
1098 MTOTO [4] (A Stewart) 3-9-4 M Roberts 4/7 FAV: 3-2102: Well bckd: went on over 2f
out, rather comfortably held by winner tho' it transpired she had lost a shoe during the
race and this was a gd eff in the circumstances: sure to regain winning form sn: see 1098, 916   72
654 SIR PERCY [6] (G Wragg) 3-9-6 P Robinson 10/1: -1003: Stumbled over 2f out, no
chance with principals tho' ran a gd race after a lengthy absence: prob stays 11f: acts
on firm: see 253.   60
1469 RENO RALPH [3] (G Huffer) 3-8-7 M Miller 100/1: -004: Dwelt, never threatened leaders:
American bred colt who had been well btn in both prev starts and may be flattered by rating.   35
1538 RARE LEGEND [5] 3-8-4 M Giles 66/1: 0-00: Never dangerous: no form prev.   30
1212 TINAS LAD [1] 3-8-7 J Carter(7) 100/1: 0000-00: Wknd after ½ way, btn a long way.   00
6 ran   1,6,5,1,dist   (H J Joel)   H Cecil Newmarket

1601 EASTERN EVENING NEWS HCAP 0-50 3YO+   £2544   1m 2f   Firm –05 –39 Slow   [46]

*1498 ALBERT HALL [1] (B Hills) 3-9-3(5ex) M Hills 9/4: 1D22111: 3 ch c Monteverdi -
Hortensia (Luthier) Useful, consistent colt: was gaining his 3rd win in a fortnight when
getting up cl home in a h'cap at Yarmouth July 17: recently successful in h'caps at Haydock
and Lingfield and earlier disqualified after being first past the post in a Redcar maiden:

well suited by 10/11f: seems to act on any ground and on any trk: yet to fin out of the
first two places this term.   52
1254 SITTING BULL [3] (G Wragg) 4-9-1 S Cauthen 7/4 FAV: 300-042: Led below dist, caught
final strides: seems to be returning to form: see 429.   36
1325 AYLESFIELD [4] (A Hide) 6-8-9(bl) R Guest 7/1: 2-00003: Not btn far: see 1325.   29
1469 MOONSTRUCK [5] (M Ryan) 3-8-12 P Robinson 10/1: 0-2004: Made most, cl 4th: gd eff
and certainly seems best with out in front: prob just stays 10f: acts on firm and soft.   42
*1189 SAMS WOOD [2] 5-9-7 R Cochrane 10/3: 000-010: Trouble in running, not btn far:see 1189 39
5 ran   nk,¼,¼,shthd   (R E Sangster)   B Hills Lambourn, Berks

1602 FERRIER MAIDEN STAKES 3YO+   £964   1m   Firm -05 +11 Fast

1395 WAAJIB [1] (A Stewart) 3-8-8 M Roberts 4/11 FAV: 02-21: 3 b c Try My Best - Coryana
(Sassafras) Landed the odds with an effortless win, led over 2f out and was sn clear in a
fast run stks at Yarmouth July 17: useful colt who was just btn by Bright as Night in a
similar race at Nottingham recently: lightly raced last term when filling the same place in
a Leicester maiden: stays 1m well: suited by fast ground and an easy course.   40+
--   DONOR [5] (C Reavey) 4-9-5 I Johnson 50/1: -2: Unfanced on racecourse debut: stayed
on tho' no chance with facile winner: cost IR 230,000 gns as yearling tho' fetched only
1,550 gns when re-sold last season: stays 1m: acts on fast ground.   20
1068 NORCOOL [9] (R Nicholls) 3-8-8(vis) N Howe 50/1: 0-00003: Made much: fin 4th, placed
3rd: modest colt who has been highly tried in recent starts.   14
--   SWEET DELILAH [6] (M Ryan) 3-8-5 R Cochrane 7/1: -4: Never dangerous 5th on racecourse debut, placed 4th: half sister to 4 winners and may improve.   00
527 MR ADVISER [7] 3-8-8 G French 14/1: -00-400: No threat after fair abs: see 188.   00
1327 MALADETOC [2] 3-8-5 G Sexton 10/1: -00: Cl.up over ½ way: first foal.   00
1578 HARBOUR BAZAAR [3] 6-9-5(vis) J Carter(7) 20/1: 203003D: Bckd at long odds: fin 3rd
tho' disqualified and placed last after rider failed to weigh-in: see 967 & 199.   18
1300 Rebeccas Pet [4] 9-2(vis)
8 ran   5,1,1½,7,1½   (Hamdan Al-Maktoum)   A Stewart Newmarket

1603 FRED ARMSTRONG APPR. HCAP 3YO 0-35   £1276   6f   Firm -05 +08 Fast   [42]

1191 TAYLOR OF SOHAM [11] (D Leslie) 3-8-7 Gay Kelleway 7/2: 4030041: 3 b f Comedy Star
- Consequently (Con Brio) Ran on strongly to lead cl home in quite a fast run app h'cap at
Yarmouth July 15: first success tho' had made the frame sev times prev this season and
deserved this win: eff over 5/6f on firm and soft grd: acts on any trk.   29
1574 PERCIPIO [1] (K Ivory) 3-7-13(vis) A Shoults 6/1: 0003042: Just failed to make all:
gd eff: has been busy lately: see 1334 & 906.   20
*1574 NANOR [10] (W Kemp) 3-7-7(7ex) J Carter 8/1: 0000013: Quick reappearance and ran
a fair race under her penalty: see 1334.   10
1398 LINAVOS [3] (W Brooks) 3-8-9 J Bray(5) 13/2: -010044: Al up there: gd eff: see 837.   22
326 OUR TILLY [5] 3-9-7 E Guest 11/4 FAV: 120-000: Well bckd despite lengthy abs:
lack of fitness told below dist tho' is worth noting next time in similar grade: won his
maiden at Nottingham last summer over this trip: acts on any going tho' suited by fast grd. 34
1338 ALEXANJO [2] 3-8-9 S Meacock(8) 8/1: 4-04000: Speed over ½ way: btr eff: see 929.   20
1418 BLOW THE WHISTLE [9] 3-8-12(bl) C White(8) 5/1: 04-0300: Trailed in last and twice
disapp since 1164 (made running).   00
1164 Naughty Nighty [8] 7-9   928 The Lidgate Star [7] 8-3
1316 Our Remedy [6] 7-7(3oh)   1420 Fur Baby [4] 7-7(7oh)
11 ran   ¼,1½,1½,shthd,1   (Taylors of Soham Ltd)   D Leslie Goadby, Leics.

1604 LARCH MAIDEN FILLIES STAKES 2YO   £3309   6f   Firm 20 -25 Slow

--   DUNNINALD [16] (I Balding) 2-8-11 Pat Eddery 6/1: 1: 2 b f Mill Reef - Strathspey
(Jimmy Reppin) First time out, mkt drifter but led 2f out, narrowly, in a rather slowly
run 2yo fillies mdn at Kempton July 17: sister to useful '84 2yo River Spey: eff 6f, sure
to stay much further: acts well on firm ground: likely to improve further: yet another
useful filly from her stable's seemingly inexhaustable supply.   53
--   LUCKY STONE [3] (C Brittain) 2-8-11 G Baxter 5/1 FAV: 2: Well bckd debutant, dsptd
lead thr'out, narrowly btn and a fine eff: half sister to a minor 2yo winner: gd sort who
is sure to improve considerably for this race and should win a mdn soon.   52
--   CONNUE [9] (G Harwood) 2-8-11 G Starkey 6/1: 3: Op 2/1, mkt drifter, fin cl.up 3rd
despite looking in need of the race and showing her inexperience: sure to improve
considerably next time: half sister to very useful sprinters Meteoric and Fine Edge: acts on
firm grd: likely to prove best around 6f.   51
1308 MISS RUNAWAY [6] (J Winter) 2-8-11 R Hills 6/1: 04: Slow start, met all sorts of
trouble in running, fairly flying at the death: sure to stay beyond 6f on this evidence
and is certain to rate more highly and win a mdn very soon: see 1308.   46
--   OUT ON A FLYER [7] 2-8-11 A Mcglone 25/1: 0: Made a sound debut and will be all
the better for the experience: sprint bred filly who should improve.   41
1440 COPPER CREEK [12] 2-8-11 S Whitworth 8/1: 00: Prom most: will be suited by 7f:see 1440

-- LISA NICOLA [13] 2-8-11 W Ryan 10/1: 0: Prom much, fln 7th and will be all the btr
for this debut: a 6,000 gns April filly who may prove btr suited by 7f+: dam won over 10f:
improving sort.   30
601 LADY WESTGATE [8] 2-8-11 M Wigham 33/1: 00: Abs: no danger in 8th: cheaply bought
sister to minor winner Hymn of Harlech and a couple of winners abroad: would have
possibilities if sent up North for a small maiden.   30
601 Najaba [15] 8-11   -- Spy Glft [4] 2-8-11   1440 Auntie Cyclone [2] 8-11
1440 Harts Lane [5] 8-11   -- Ladys Mantle [14] 8-11
1308 Musical Rhapsody [1] 8-11   -- Try Dancer [11] 8-11
15 ran ¾,½,2½,2¼,1½,3,hd,½   (Paul Mellon)   I Balding Kingsclere, Berks.

1605 OAK HANDICAP 3YO 0-50   £2515   2m   Firm 20 -04 Slow   [53]

1078 BLOCKADE [1] (P Cole) 3-9-7 T Quinn 6/4: 2-131D1: 3 br c Mill Reef - Edwinarowe
(Blakeney) Fairly useful colt: led 4f out and held on well under press in a 4 runner 3yo
h'cap at Kempton July 17: disqual after being first past the post in similar h'cap at
Nottingham last time: first time out beat the useful Kudz at·Thirsk: eff 12f, well suited
by 2m: acts on firm and soft: genuine type who does well carrying weight.   55
1388 FEDRA [2] (Lord J Fitzgerald) 3-8-7 R Hills 4/5 FAV: 1221242: Ev ch final 4f: good
effort and stays the trip well: see 908.   39
714 BATTLE FLEET [4] (M Usher) 3-7-7(7oh) A O'reilly(7) 33/1: 00-0003: Abs: dsptd lead
till str: btn a long way at fin: a maiden with no worthwhile form as yet.   00
1078 MOUNT SCHIEHALLION [3] (K Brassey) 3-8-0(bl) S Whitworth 8/1: 0-33004: Led 10f, btn
out of sight at the fin: no form since 171 (12f yldg).   00
4 ran 1½,dist,not taken   (Fahd Salman)   P Cole Whatcombe, Oxon.

1606 EBF WILLOW STAKES 2YO   £3854   6f   Firm 20 -17 Slow

*1241 MOREWOODS [2] (I Balding) 2-9-4 Pat Eddery 4/7 FAV: 11: 2 b c Northern Jove - Vogue
Folks (Reverse) Smart, very promising colt: landed the odds in the easiest poss fashion when
hacking up from his 2 opponents in a minor 2yo event at Kempton July 17: first time out a
comfortable winner of a maiden at Salisbury: cost $100,000 and is a brother to a winner in
the USA: very eff over 5/6f and looks a sprinter: certain to rate more highly and win more
races, in better company.   70
*1512 QUICK SNAP [3] (A Ingham) 2-9-7(bl) R Curant 9/4: 2210112: Set the pace but had
no answer when the winner cruised past at the dist: caught a real tartar here: see 1512.   61
-- MUSTAKBIL [1] (P Walwyn) 2-8-11 Paul Eddery 10/1: 3: Kept on well and will benefit
from the outing: cost IR 94,000 gns: brother to '82 2yo winner Drumalis and half brother to
a couple of other minor winners: gd sort with scope who will improve on this next time.   36
3 ran 2½,4   (George Strawbridge)   I Balding Kingsclere, Berks.

1607 POPLAR MAIDEN STAKES 3YO   £2392   7f   Firm 20 -02 Slow

1145 CODICES [13] (G Harwood) 3-9-0 G Starkey 13/2: 340-001: 3 gr c Codex - Spice On Ice
(Grey Dawn II) Useful colt: mkt drifter (op 3/1) but came home a comfortable all the way
winner of a 3yo mdn at Kempton July 17: highly tried both prev outings this term but placed
sev times in '85: very eff over 7f on fast grd: also acts on yielding: may find a h'cap
now that he has had this confidence-booster.   59
1395 USFAN [8] (J Dunlop) 3-9-0 W Carson 10/1: -02: Kept on really well on only 2nd ever
outing and this was a fine effort: sure to stay at least 1m: acts well on firm ground and
should have little trouble finding a maiden soon.   52
1046 SURE LANDING [14] (C Nelson) 3-9-0 J Reid 7/1: -04203: Al there, one paced from
2f out: best 937 (1m sharp trk).   40
656 SYBIL FAWLTY [5] (R Laing) 3-8-11(VIS) W Newnes 10/1: 020-044: Visored first time,
abs since 656.   34
1520 DUFF [10] 3-9-0(BL) W R Swinburn 6/1: 3-34000: Bl first time, ev ch and has been
disapp since 579.   36
479 RUSSKI [7] 3-9-0 C Rutter(5) 50/1: 0-00: No danger after abs: lightly raced prev:
looks sure to be suited by longer dist than he has been attempting so far.   30
1200 SUPERCOOMBE [15] 3-9-0 T Quinn 10/1: -3022D0: Fin 8th: see 516.   00
1399 SHAYI [6] 3-9-0 R Hills 6/1: -000: Early pace: see 1399.   00
1516 CLASS ACTION [9] 3-8-11 Pat Eddery 5/1 FAV: 0-40: Well bckd, prom almost 5f: see 1516   00
1315 Speed Stick [12] 9-0   1451 Lochmar [11] 8-11   -- Anthony Gerard [1] 9-0
-- Seamere [14] 9-0   1288 Doubler [4] 9-0   -- Joker Man [2] 9-0
15 ran 3,6,1½,½,2   (Paul H Locke)   G Harwood Pulborough, Sussex

1608 PRIX HIPPODROME EVRY H'CAP 3YO+ 0-50   £2708   6f   Firm 20 +05 Fast   [49]

1145 POWDER BLUE [10] (P Makin) 4-9-2 T Quinn 9/1: 01-0401: 4 b f He Loves Me - Ridalla
(Ridan) Returned to her best when gamely getting the better of a blanket fin to quite a val
h'cap at Kempton July 17: in '85 won at Redcar and Yarmouth: best form over 6f on firm or
good ground.   48
1285 PERFECT TIMING [4] (D Elsworth) 4-9-7 Pat Eddery 9/4 FAV: 3-04332: Heavily bckd:
led dist, caught near fin: said to require exaggerated waiting tactics: see 877, 1145.   52
1429 GREEN RUBY [9] (G Balding) 5-9-5 J Williams 7/1: 030-033: Kept on really strongly,

just held: must win soon, possibly over 7f: see 1429.   49
877 PERION [1] (G Lewis) 4-9-4 P Waldron 14/1: 1011104: Al well there, narrowly btn and
remains in fine form: see 477: stays 6f and acts on firm and soft.   48
1285 ROYSIA BOY [11] 6-9-2 W Ryan 9/1: 01-0000: Slow start, gd fin: one to note next
time: see 952.   42
1347 DEPUTY HEAD [6] 6-9-7 J Reid 12/1: 0031330: Running well at present: see 1060.   43
1235 GLEN KELLA MANX [14] 5-8-11 Paul Eddery 10/1: 0000-00: Badly hmpd ½ way: fin 7th:
lightly raced and below her best last season: in '84 won 3 times at Windsor and loves that
sharp trk: best form at 6f on firm or gd ground: should not be written off just yet.   33
1268 STONEYDALE [2] 4-8-12 G Starkey 25/1: 0010000: Early speed: well btn since 734 (5f gd)   33
1447 LUCKY STARKIST [3] 4-7-7 S Dawson 10/1: -003140: No threat in 9th: see 1213.   00
1429 Sailors Song [12] 9-10(HD   1406 Useful [8] 8-11(BL)
1391 West Carrack [13] 9-6   1312 Fruity Orooney [7] 8-4(VIS)
14 ran   hd,hd,shthd,1½,1½,½,½¾   (R P Marchant)   P Makin Ogbourne Maisey, Wilts

1609 KENILWORTH APP.H'CAP 3YO+ 0-35   £1825   1m   Firm 20 -18 Slow   [21]

1346 SWEET ANDY [7] (G Gracey) 7-8-2 G Bardwell 6/1: 0004031: 7 br g Ardoon - Black Honey
(March Past) Led final 150 yds in a cl fin to an app h'cap at Kempton July 17: first success:
eff over 1m on firm or gd ground, prob also acts on soft.   02
1188 SPARKLER SPIRIT [4] (R Akehurst) 5-8-5 P Mcentee 25/1: -000-02: Just failed to make
all, narrowly btn: a maiden who was lightly raced last term: evidently eff with forcing
tactics and firm ground: stays 1m.   03
1062 TOM RUM [2] (H Candy) 3-8-6 L Riggio(7) 7/1: 0-00003: Al there, kept on well and
not btn far: a maiden who turned in his best effort so far today: eff over 1m on firm.   14
1273 SUPERFROST [9] (J Fox) 4-9-1 G King 3/1 FAV: 0001004: Came from well off the pace,
gd finish but btr 568 (needs firm handling).   09
1500 GAUHAR [3] 5-9-7 P Skelton(5) 6/1: 0-44400: Ran in snatches: best 1018.   14
1199 ON TO GLORY [1] 3-9-7 A Geran 11/2: 0-00B30: Ev ch: see 716.   24
1346 PETT VELERO [6] 7-9-0(5ex) P Simms(7) 5/1: 0010100: No danger: best 1264 (undulating trk) 00
-- STEEL PASS [5] 8-9-1 A O'reilly(7) 9/1: 30010-0: Sn in rear on seasonal debut:
in '85 won at Chepstow, the prev season at Brighton: seems suited by an undulating trk: eff
between 6f and 1m but best form on firm or gd going.   00
1229 Aqaba Prince [8] 9-2   1447 Cygne [10] 8-8
10 ran   ½,½,1½,nk,nk   (C S Harvey)   G Gracey Lower Beeding, Sussex

Official Going Given As FIRM

1610 UDDINGTON APP. H'CAP STAKES (0-35)   £953   6f   Good/Firm 34 -06 Slow   [34]

1543 BEECHWOOD COTTAGE [10] (A Bailey) 3-8-3(bl)(7ex) G Athanasiou 5/1 JT FAV: -001001: 3
ch g Malinowski - Drora (Busted) Led below dist for a comfortable win in an app h'cap at
Hamilton July 17: easy winner of a h'cap over this trip at Brighton earlier this month and
has since twice found 5f on the sharp side: last season won a nursery over this C/D: stays
7f well: acts on fast and soft ground and on any trk: in gd form.   26
1136 GOLDEN DISC [7] (M Camacho) 4-7-7(2oh) P Johnson 7/1: 33-4302: Led briefly 2f out:
ran to her best: eff over 6/7f on gd and firm ground: see 710.   03
1028 JOVEWORTH [4] (J Glover) 3-9-0 M Brennan 11/2: 0-14003: Fin well: gd effort tho'
possibly btr suited by 7f now: acts on any going: see 283.   29
42   OFF YOUR MARK [5] (G Calvert) 6-8-2(3ow) N Rodgers 12/1: 0000-04: Made much despite
long abs: won successive races at Ripon and Thirsk last summer: best form over 6f on fast
ground.   05
1482 KAMARESS [11] 4-8-4 A Bacon 5/1 JT FAV: 0002400: Best over 1m in 1103.   00
520 BOLD ROWLEY [8] 6-7-8 A Whitehall 11/1: 000-000: No real threat after abs: maiden
with no worthwhile form to his name: best over 6/7f and is suited by fast ground.   00
1429 MARY MAGUIRE [6] 9-9-10 N Leach 11/2: 0322000: Wknd into 8th under top weight:
better in 1182: see 306.   00
1344 Royal Bear [3] 7-13(6ow)(3oh)   628 Ackas Boy [9] 7-7
1131 Blochairn Skolar [1] 7-7(1oh)
10 ran   1½,1,1½,3,1½   (A Bailey)   A Bailey Newmarket

1611 BURNBANK SELLING STAKES 2YO   £834   6f   Good/Firm 34 -43 Slow

1358 MONS FUTURE [3] (W Pearce) 2-8-13 N Connorton 11/8 FAV: 0142221: 2 b f Monsanto -
Future Chance (Hopeful Venture) Consistent filly: was well bckd when comfortably making all
in a slowly run 2yo seller at Hamilton July 17: made virtually all in a similar race at
Nottingham in April and had since found one too good in 3 of her 4 subsequent starts: eff
over 5/6f: acts on fast and soft ground and is well suited by forcing tactics: likes a
stiff course.   28
1528 WOLF J FLYWHEEL [2] (C Tinkler) 2-8-11(BL) M Birch 7/1: 0200002: Bl first time:
hung under press and seems a temperamental sort: acts on fast grd tho' best in 186 (yldg):
stays 6f.   19
1434 LATE PROGRESS [1] (J Berry) 2-8-8 M Fry 14/1: 0000033: Stayed on again from dist:

improved of late: eff over 5/6f on fast ground.   10
1012 ON THE MARK [6] (J Kettlewell) 2-8-11(bl) S Webster 20/1:   004: Hmpd start, some
late prog: seems to stay 6f: acts on fast ground.   07
1298 JUST A DECOY [4] 2-8-11 M Richardson(7) 33/1: 00: Early speed: seems mod.   04
1379 MISS DISPLAY [5] 2-8-8 G Duffield 6/4: 00440: Well bckd: pressed winner till 2f
out: found nil under press: twice below form shown in 86 (5f gd).   00
1298 EVERY WEDNESDAY [7] 2-8-8 R P Elliott 10/1: 430: Tardy start and sn behind: see 1298.   00
7 ran   2,2,3,½,3,hd   (C T Lee)   W Pearce Hambleton, Yorks.

1612 E.B.F. MOTHERWELL STAKES 2YO   £943   5f   Good/Firm 34 -12 Slow

--   JUVENILEDELINQUENT [2] (A Bailey) 2-8-11 P Bloomfield 11/4: 1: 2 ch c Young Generation
- My Linnie (Frankincense) Made a successful racecourse debut, led dist and ran on well in
a 2yo stks at Hamilton July 17: cost 13,000 gns and is a half brother to winning sprinter Try
Me: clearly well suited by this minimum trip: acts on fast grd and on a stiff course.   38
1305 AFRABELA [4] (M Brittain) 2-8-8 M Wigham 4/1: 320402: Made much, kept on quite well
tho'   proving expensive to follow: see 1305.   31
1381 KEEN EDGE [1] (P Mitchell) 2-8-11 G Carter(3) 13/8 FAV: 422003: Early speed: again
well below form shown in 678 (gd ground, sharp trk).   25
1421 DENSBEN [5] (Denys Smith) 2-8-11 L Charnock 16/1: 044: Front rank over ½ way: acts
on gd and fast ground: see 1421.   16
1561 CRAIGENDARROCH [3] 2-8-11 G Duffield 9/2: 400: Twice below form shown in 1174 (gd).   04
5 ran   1,3,3,4   (Cawthorne Investments Ltd)   A Bailey Newmarket

1613 HANDICAP STAKES (0-35) 3 AND 4YO   £2330   1m 1f   Good/Firm 34 +04 Fast   [27]

+1374 SENOR RAMOS [10] (R Thompson) 4-9-12(bl)(5ex) R P Elliott 15/2: 0000011: 4 b g
Transworld - Trendy (Crewman) In fine form at present and defied his 5lbs pen, leading final
1f comfortably in a h'cap at Hamilton July 17: won similar h'cap at Beverley last time: in
'85 won at Thirsk and is also a course winner twice at Edinburgh: eff between 9 and 12f: runs
well on fast ground and prob also handles soft surface: wears blinkers.   33
1371 RUN BY JOVE [6] (P Haslam) 3-9-3(vis) T Williams 4/1: 0120022: Dsptd lead most and
is in gd form: see 674.   32
1295 ICARO [9] (N Callaghan) 3-9-2(bl) G Duffield 9/4 FAV: 0220323: Well bckd, led 4f
out, placed again: see 1295.   27
1302 TAJ SINGH [3] (Denys Smith) 4-8-6 L Charnock 20/1: -000044: Not quite get on terms
but is slowly finding form: tried in blinkers last time but ran at least as well today without   05
1439 MY MYRA [2] 4-8-2 G Carter(3) 12/1: 430-000: Remains a maiden: see 1439.   00
1362 HOT LINING [1] 3-8-9 S Morris 12/1: 0-00000: Prom much: much btr 1091 (1m).   14
1133 SWIFT RIVER [5] 4-8-9(bl) J Quinn(5) 11/1: 2030330: Waited with, eff 2f out, sn
btn and fin 7th: see 562 (seller): now wears blinkers.   00
1361 LUCKY WEST [8] 3-8-6 J Bleasdale 6/1: -00100: Badly hmpd 3f out and this run should
be forgotten: see 1053 (seller).   00
1374 Nugola [4] 8-6   1134 Herb Robert [7] 7-7(3oh)
10 ran   1,2,½,1½,1,nk   (M D Marshall)   R Thompson Stainforth, Yorks.

1614 RUTHERGLEN MAIDEN STAKES 3YO   £1136   1m   Good/Firm 34 +09 Fast

--   SAND DOLLAR [2] (M Prescott) 3-9-0 G Duffield 5/2 FAV: 00-1: 3 ch c Persian Bold -
Late Spring (Silly Season) First time out, well bckd and led dist, comfortably, in a 3yo
maiden at Hamilton July 17: ran only twice in '85: showing promise in big fields of maidens:
well suited by 1m, may stay further: acts on fast ground and on a galloping trk: should
improve further and win a small h'cap.   28
1335 BOYNTON [10] (C Elsey) 3-9-0 N Connorton 7/2: 04-0202: Made most: evidently highly
flattered in 1178.   22
1309 SHARONS ROYALE [9] (R Whitaker) 3-9-0 D Mckeown 8/1: 00-0003: Stayed on onepaced.   18
1520 SILENT RUNNING [4] (P Mitchell) 3-9-0(BL) G Carter(3) 4/1: 0300004: No threat:
disapp since 843 (10f).   12
1337 TURINA [1] 3-8-11 M Beecroft 6/1: 0-00: Waited with, never btr: btr 1337 (9f).   08
1425 VITAL STEP [8] 3-8-11 M Rimmer 12/1: 00-000: Btr 1425 (sharp trk).   05
1256 Accumulate [6] 9-0   1272 Boxers Shukee [3] 8-11
--   Berry Street [5] 8-11
9 ran   3,1½,3,½,1½   (G D Waters)   M Prescott Newmarket

1615 BLANTYRE HANDICAP STAKES (0-35) 3YO   £1303   1m 4f   Good/Firm 34 -09 Slow   [36]

1167 TENDER TYPE [6] (M Tompkins) 3-9-2 M Rimmer 10/1: -0001: 3 b c Prince Tenderfoot -
Double Type (Behistoun) Impr colt: came from behind to lead final 1f, comfortably, in a
h'cap at Hamilton July 17: unraced in '85: well suited by 12f and fast ground: on the upgrade
and can win again in similar company.   36
*1362 SAFFAN [2] (M Prescott) 3-9-0(4ex) G Duffield 6/4 FAV: 03-3212: Dsptd lead dist,
outpaced final 100 yds, clear rem: seems reasonably h'capped and is worth another chance.   28
958 SEVEN HILLS [7] (J Fitzgerald) 3-8-10(VIS) M Birch 14/1: 00-0003: Slow start, never
better: possibly needs long distances: see 648.   14
1494 BURNING BRIGHT [4] (D Ringer) 3-9-7 M Wigham 11/2: 02-0424: Prom, wknd: rated higher 1494

*1479 **MADISON GIRL** [5] 3-9-2(4ex) D Mckeown 2/1: -034110: Not the best of runs: see 1479.   18
1250 **TIEATRE** [1] 3-8-8 D Casey(7) 12/1: 0-00100: Clear leader much: wknd quickly and
best 1123 (stiff course, soft ground).   00
1372 **PINTURICCHIA** [3] 3-8-7 M Beecroft 16/1: 0-00400: Slow start, no threat: twice below 958   00
7 ran   2,5,nk,hd,6   (G H Tufts)   M Tompkins Newmarket

Official Going Given As FIRM

1616 MARLEY ROOFING H'CAP STAKES (0-35)   £1702   5f   Good/Firm 26 +02 Fast   [31]

1211 **SITEX** [3] (M Bolton) 8-7-9 G Carter(2) 4/1: 00-0041: 8 b h Record Run - Glorious Light
(Alcide) Justified his long journey North when gaining 1st win since '83, led 1f out in h'cap
at Hamilton July 8: eff at 5f, stays 7f: acts on any going.   06
1499 **WIZZARD MAGIC** [7] (M Haynes) 3-7-7(bl) T Williams 9/4 FAV: 00-032: Sn prom: ran better
when blinkered 1st time in 1499 (6f).   06
1196 **RUSSIAN WINTER** [8] (A Jones) 11-7-7(bl) Kim Tinkler(3) 14/1: 0-00003: Made most and
not btn far: course winner 5 times here: see 1131.   00
1157 **TANFEN** [4] (T Craig) 5-9-13 J H Brown(5) 5/1: 3102104: Early ldr: best 1093 (6f).   28
1610 **ROYAL BEAR** [2] 4-7-7 J Quinn(5) 16/1: 3000000: 2nd race in 24 hours: prom most: no
form recently but winner at Chepstow (5f soft) in '85, only previous success.   00
*1423 **TRADESMAN** [6] 6-8-0(bl)(7ex) M Fry 13/2: 0000010: Faded dist: see 1423 (sharp track).   00
1423 Grand Queen [1] 7-9   1338 Illicit [5] 8-0
8 ran   1½,hd,2,¾,2½.   (Mrs S P Elphick)   M Bolton East Grinstead, Sussex.

1617 MARLEY TOP OF SELLING STAKES 3YO   £873   6f   Good/Firm 26 -01 Slow

1334 **PSALM** [8] (M Prescott) 3-9-0 G Duffield 3/1: 00-0341: 3 b c Song - Arch Sculptress (Arch
Sculptor) nicely bkd and led final 1f, held on narrowly in 3yo seller at Hamilton July 18
(no bid): won maiden here last year: eff over 6/7f: acts on fir & soft: does well at Hamilton.   24
1424 **PUNCLE CREAK** [2] (G Moore) 3-8-4 J Bleasdale 10/1: 4000002 Disptd.ld all way: just
beaten and clear of remainder: best effort for long time from this maiden: see 103.   12
932 **MOTOR MASTER** [7] (W Pearce) 3-8-7 N Connorton 12/1: 00-0003: Made most: btr 932 (7f).   05
809 **TOUCH THE SAIL** [1] (M Tompkins) 3-8-4 M Rimmer 11/4 FAV: 0000-04: Diff ride?: see 809.   00
1051 **SANA SONG** [6] 3-8-7 T Williams 10/1: -200000: No form since 134 (6f, hvy).   00
1257 **HOW BLUE** [4] 3-8-4 T Ives 4/1: 00-000: Wknd ½way: no form this year.   00
1420 Musical Aid [3] 8-4   1160 Dearham Bridge [5] 8-7(BL)
8 ran   nk,4,3,1,3.   (Martin Boase)   M Prescott Newmarket

1618 MARLEY MONARCH MAIDEN STAKES 2YO   £1320   6f   Good/Firm 26 -39 Slow

1175 **PINE AWAY** [2] (J Watts) 2-8-11 T Ives 11/10 JT FAV: 301: 2 b f Shirley Heights - Piney
Ridge (Native Prince) Made all in slowly run 2yo maiden at Hamilton July 18: cost 96,000gns:
very eff over 6f with forcing tactics on fast ground: disapp over 7f but shld stay the trip.   42
1480 **THE BRAZILIAN** [1] (E Alston) 2-9-0 G Duffield 9/1: 0402: Kept on: see 1480.   15
622 **TAP THE BATON** [3] (M Tompkins) 2-9-0 M Rimmer 11/10 JT FAV: 4323: Cl up 4f: had been
absent since 622 and might be better at 5f.   12
3 ran   10,1½.   (R Sangster)   J Watts Richmond, Yorks.

1619 MARLEY ROOF TILE CO. H'CAP (0-50)   £2563   1m   Good/Firm 26 -06 Slow   [42]

1517 **DUELLING** [1] (P Mitchell) 5-8-2(vis) G Carter(3) 11/8 FAV: 0000141: 5 ro g Vigors -
Irish Sword (Irish Laughter) Won 2nd time in last 3 races: came from behind despite trouble
in running to force head in front, final 50yds in h'cap at Hamilton July 18: narrow winner of
minor h'cap at Kempton: in '85 won at Lingfield and Cagnes: stays 10f and very eff at 1m:
acts on firm and yield: wears visor and has to be held for late challenge.   24
1383 **ALL FAIR** [5] (P Haslam) 5-9-10 T Williams 11/4: 0000002: Nearly made all and just btn:
back to form and could win small h'cap soon: see 521.   43
1335 **WARPLANE** [4] (C Thornton) 6-9-0 J Bleasdale 11/4: 100-003: Led 1f out, jut btn: back
to form and in '85 won at Beverley and Hamilton: best form over 1m/9f on fast ground.   32
1546 **COMPOSER** [3] (M James) 8-7-8(bl)(1ow)(10oh) A Proud 11/1: 0000024: Better 1546(seller).   08
1302 **HONEST TOKEN** [2] 7-7-7(21oh) S P Griffiths 50/1: 0-00000: Fin well btn: see 257.   00
5 ran   ½,hd,2,20.   (Mrs R A Johnson)   P Mitchell Epsom, Surrey.

1620 MARLEY HEIGHTS STAKES   £1194   1m 3f Good/Firm 26 +02 Fast

*1372 **SARYAN** [6] (N Callaghan) 3-8-10 G Duffield 7/2: 00-0411: 3 b g Try My Best - High Fidelyty
(Hautain) Improv. gelding: won 2nd race on trot: came from behind and battled on well close
home in minor race at Hamilton: cmftly won maiden at Beverley: lightly raced previously:
½brother to sev winners: well suited by 11/12, firm ground and a stiff track:could win h'cap.   53
*1192 **HUSNAH** [4] (L Cumani) 3-8-7 R Guest 10/11 FAV: 2-33312: Led 2f out, then just failed:
clear of rem.: in good form see 1192.   49
1206 **KING TEFKROS** [5] (M Tompkins) 3-8-3 T Ives 5/2: -0033: Ev ch: better 1206 (10f).   38
951 **WELSH CROWN** [3] (M Bolton) 3-8-3 T Williams 50/1: -304: Wknd : lightly raced since 95.

1417 CASSANDRAS DREAM [2] 5-9-0 D Mckeown 20/1: -000: Led 1m: see 1102.   UO
1554 BANG BANG [1] 4-9-3 A Proud 100/1: -00: Well beaten.   00
6 ran   nk,4,20,8,30.   (K Al Said)   N Callaghan Newmarket.

1621 MARLEY ROOFUS HANDICAP STAKES (0-35)   £1811   1m 4f Good/Firm 26 -27 Slow   [32]

1223 MONIAR [1] (D Moffatt) 7-7-13 J Quinn(5) 14/1: 000/001: 7 ch g Silent Screen -
Mademoiselle Molly (Nashua) Outsider of 3 but came with late chall to win slowly run h'cap at
Hamilton July 8: 1st success on the Flat since '82 when won at Newmarket: suited by 12f
nowadays: acts well on fast ground.   10
1336 EXCAVATOR LADY [4] (R Whitaker) 7-7-13 S P Griffiths 7/4: 0432202: Made much: see 1223. 07
1393 SILENT JOURNEY [2] (J Watts) 4-9-7 T Ives 1/2 FAV: -120023: Led 4f: see 256.   28
3 ran   1½,½   (Murray Athol Investments)   D Moffatt Cartmel, Cumbria.

1622 COLIN TINKLER SELLING STKS 2YO   £1404   7f   Firm 17 -27 Slow

1413 MADAME LAFFITTE [13] (J Etherington) 2-8-8 T Ives 9/4 FAV: 021: 2 ch f Welsh Pageant
- Exciting Times (Windjammer) Impr filly: was well bckd when leading below dist, comfortably
in a 2yo seller at Thirsk July 18 (no bid): stays 7f well and should have no trouble getting
1m: well suited by fast ground and seems to act on any track.   25
1105 GILLOT BAR [12] (M W Easterby) 2-8-8 K Hodgson 14/1: 00002: Going on fin: best effort
to date from this cheaply bought filly: stays 7f well: acts on fast ground and on a sharp trk. 22
1105 WAR CHILD [3] (P Haslam) 2-8-8 T Williams 11/2: 003: Dropped in class: fin well
and could find a race if kept in this grade: will stay further: acts on firm ground and
on a sharp track.   21
957 MISS PISA [7] (W Wharton) 2-8-8 J Ward(7) 10/1: -030304: Kept on well: stays 7f.   20
1480 PHILEARN [11] 2-8-8 J Reid 16/1: 44000: Al front rank in this lower grade: stays
7f: acts on fast and yielding ground and on any track.   15
1132 RIVERS SECRET [14] 2-8-8 L Charnock 14/1: 0000: Dropped in class: al mid-div: dam
a middle distance winner: seemed btr suited by this longer trip: has some scope.   12
1181 FANTINE [4] 2-8-8(bl) Kim Tinkler(5) 7/2: 0442140: Clear leader early on, wknd
below dist: fin 7th: best over 6f in 939.   00
1358 SEATON GIRL [6] 2-8-8 B Mcgiff(7) 10/1: 4200140: Fdd into 8th: best in 1121 (5f soft) 00
957 LYN RAE [15] 2-8-8 M Birch 8/1: 000: Never dangerous 9th: much btr 317 (5f soft)   00
1480 Skinnhill [2] 8-11   1358 Broons Answer [9] 8-8 --   Rosinsky [8] 8-11
1279 Westgale [10] 8-11   -- Top Robe [5] 8-8
14 ran   1,hd,½,2½,1½,½   (Mrs P L Yong)   J Etherington Malton, Yorks.

1623 DAVID BARRON STAKES 3YO   £1625   2m   Firm 17 -01 Slow

1314 COINAGE [2] (R Johnson Houghton) 3-8-10 J Reid 1/1 FAV: 3-23101: 3 br c Owen Dudley
- Grisbi (Grey Sovereign) Useful colt: al travelling easily, led below dist and was sn clear
in a 3yo stks at Thirsk July 18: earlier a runaway winner in course record time of a Beverley
maiden: half brother to sev winners: eff over 10/12f and stays 2m really well: acts on
firm and yldg ground and has no trk preferences.   50
*1251 TEMPLE HEIGHTS [3] (J Dunlop) 3-8-7 T Ives 6/5: -012: Went on over 2f out, left
flatfooted by this easy winner: acts on a sharp course: see 1251.   36
1102 NADAS [4] (S Norton) 3-8-7 M Hills 14/1: -423043: Made much: no extra dist and
remains a maiden: stays 2m: acts on firm and soft grd and on any track.   34
1251 SNOWFIRE CHAP [5] (H Wharton) 3-8-7 D Nicholls 20/1: -0334: Early leader: remote 4th. 14
1481 SWEET SNUGFIT [1] 3-8-5(1ow) A Bond 100/1: 000-00: Sn scrubbed along, well btn as
she has been in all her prev starts: sprint bred filly who is half sister to sev minor winners 00
5 ran   5,1,20,dist   (Mrs James A de Rothschild)   R Johnson Houghton Blewbury, Oxon.

1624 JIMMY FITZGERALD HCAP 3YO+ 0-35   £2746   1m   Firm 17 -01 Slow   [31]

*1415 SIGNORE ODONE [1] (M H Easterby) 4-9-12(5ex) M Birch 5/2: 0-40011: 4 b g Milford -
Duchy (Rheingold) Comfortably defied his penalty, led over 2f out and stayed on strongly in
an all aged h'cap at Thirsk July 18: recently a comfortable winner of his maiden at Beverley:
stays 1m well: acts on gd and fast ground and on any track: in good form.   36
*1281 WHIRLING WORDS [4] (P Makin) 3-9-2 S Perks 7/4 FAV: -002112: Ran on well and beat
rem decisively: fine effort against older horses: see 1281.   32
1338 MONINSKY [6] (N Bycroft) 5-8-2 A Shoults(5) 11/2: 2003003: Slow start and never
reached leaders: usually runs his best races on sharp track: see 260.   00
1139 MARSILIANA [5] (Don Enrico Incisa) 4-8-1 M Beecroft 14/1: 0-04034: Held up, going
on fin and should improve when stepping up in dist: acts on any trk: see 820.   00
1394 JO ANDREW [7] 6-7-11 S P Griffiths 33/1: 000-000: Made much: poor h'capper whose
sole success came on heavy ground at Newcastle in '83: also acts on a sound surface:
possibly better over shorter distances.   00
1424 TOP OTHLANE [2] 9-8-12 T Ives 9/1: 100-040: Much btr over 7f in 1424 (gd).   00
1231 SWIFTSPENDER [8] 5-7-11 L Charnock 33/1: 4-00000: Fin 7th: no form this term.   00
1377 GREETLAND DANCER [3] 4-8-12 D Nicholls 8/1: 000-400: Pulled hard, wknd 2f out:
best here in 815 (7f).   00
8 ran   1½,7,½,½,1½   (B Shaw)   M H Easterby Great Habton, Yorks

498

1625 EBF CHRIS THORNTON MAIDEN 2YO   £1782   6f   Firm 17 -40 Slow

-- WORTHY PRINCE [2] (J Payne) 2-9-0 P D'arcy 7/2: 1: 2 b g Balliol - princess Vronski (The Brianstan) Landed some nice bets when making a successful race course debut in a slowly run 2yo mdn at Thirsk July 18, cruised into lead below dist and ridden out: evidently suited by 6f and seems certain to stay further: acts on fast ground and on a sharp track: can only improve.   34
-- RUSTIC EYES [3] (D Barron) 2-9-0 A Mackay 10/1: 2: Switched dist, fin well and only just denied: clearly stays 6f well: acts on a sound surface and on a sharp course.   32
1203 CHESWOLD [1] (M H Easterby) 2-9-0 K Hodgson 6/4 FAV: 4003: Not btn far: btr effort after twice disapp since promising debut in 610 (5f): acts on good and fast ground.   29
1174 PRINCEGATE [6] (S Hall) 2-9-0 M Birch 7/1: 004: Denied a clear run: however not btn that far and is certainly on the upgrade: stays 6f: acts on gd and firm ground: see 1174   26
-- MR CRICKET [5] 2-9-0 R P Elliott 12/1: 0: Gd early speed on race course debut, hdd below dist tho' will be btr for this experience: dam successful as a juv: acts on fast ground   20
-- BERTHELIER [7] 2-9-0 D Nicholls 20/1: 0: Held up: looked dangerous when chall below dist: sure to be better for this run: cheaply bought colt who is a half brother to sev winning sprinters, notably the smart Haveroid.   16
1504 CARJUJEN [8] 2-9-0 A Bond 10/1: 000: Speed to ½ way: fin 7th: cost 14,000 gns and is a half brother to sev winners: sprint bred: acts on gd and fast ground.   00
-- TOKANDA [10] 2-9-0 M Beecroft 8/1: 0: Fin 8th on debut: improvement likely.   00
-- UNCLE WILKO [4] 2-9-0 E Guest(3) 7/1:   0: Slowly away and no threat on debut.   00
-- MALACANANG [10] 2-8-11 D Garside(7) 16/1: 00: Cheaply bought filly: fin last.   00
10 ran   hd,½,1,2½,1½,½,hd,hd,½   (W O'Callaghan)   J Payne Newmarket

1626 STEVE NORTON MAIDEN 3YO   £2007   7f   Firm 17 +02 Fast

1425 BILLS AHEAD [4] (G Moore) 3-9-0 R P Elliott 12/1: -404441: 3 ch c Billion - Streets Ahead (Ovid) Broke smartly and proceeded to make all, comfortably, in quite a fast run 3yo mdn at Thirsk July 18: won a maiden auction race at Catterick last season tho' lost that race after failing a dope test: eff over 7/8f: acts on firm and yldg ground: best using forcing tactics on a sharp course.   35
1472 BLAIRINGONE [2] (A Stewart) 3-9-0 W Hayes(7) 11/4: -032: Nicely bckd: hmpd after ¼ way, never nearer: has enough ability to win a small race: see 1036.   30
1281 BROADHURST [1] (J Etherington) 3-8-11 M Wood 11/1: 2000-03: Al up there: rated 40 when narrowly btn by Falling Feather in a fillies stks at Beverley last summer: stays 1m: acts on yldg tho' seems btr suited by a faster surface.   20
1487 CLEOFE [14] (L Cumani) 3-8-11 R Guest 7/4 FAV: -003334: Longer trip: ev ch and is proving expensive to follow: see 1375 & 656.   17
1420 TENASSERIM [3] 3-9-0 S Webster 25/1: -0040: Kept on same pace: stays 1m: see 1420.   15
861 NAOUSSA [12] 3-8-11 J Reid 7/1: 03-420: Ran on too late: abs since 861: see 423.   10
1300 FORETOP [8] 3-8-11 C Dwyer 10/1: -0020: Cl.up 5f: wknd into 7th: much btr 1300.   00
-- Mark My Card [13] 9-0   972 Jenifer Browning [9] 8-11
-- Transform [6] 8-11   1463 Tootsie Roll [11] 8-11
1257 Miss Blake [10] 8-11   1375 Sybilly [7] 8-11   -- No Idea [5] 9-0
14 ran   1¼,3,1½,2½,1,4,1   (Ronald Dobson)   G Moore Middleham, Yorks.

1627 PETER EASTERBY HCAP 3YO+ 0-35   £2784   6f   Firm 17 +17 Fast   [25]

*1418 ROPER ROW [6] (M H Easterby) 3-9-5(7ex) K Hodgson 9/2 FAV: 020-011: 3 b g Lochnager - Miss Barnaby (Sun Prince) In gd form, led below dist and ridden out when defying a penalty in a fast run h'cap at Thirsk July 18: recently won his mdn at Beverley: eff over 5/6f on gd and fast ground: acts on any track.   34
1292 MARAVILLA [10] (J Etherington) 4-9-5 M Wood 10/1: 00-0002: Switched dist, ran on well and comfortably beat rem: btr effort over this shorter trip: see 1104.   23
1213 SILENT GAIN [3] (W Jarvis) 4-9-5 T Lucas 8/1: 00-0233: Kept on: acts on firm: see 842   13
1224 HARRY HULL [2] (M W Easterby) 3-8-9 M Birch 8/1: 0-00004: Al up there: see 309.   10
1476 OUR CHILDREN [11] 3-8-4 N Carlisle 14/1: 400-030: Btr over 5f in 1476.   00
1418 THE STRAY BULLETT [5] 3-8-3(bl) A Mackay 6/1: 0200030: Btr over a stiff 5f in 1418.   00
*1542 FARMER JOCK [8] 4-9-3(bl)(7ex) E Guest(3) 5/1: 0030210: Made much: wknd under his penalty into 7th: see 1542.   00
*1334 SAMBA LASS [4] 3-8-5 A Shoults(5) 9/1: -032010: Fin 8th: btr in 1334 (stiff trk)   00
1418 IMPERIAL SUNRISE [9] 3-9-1 D Leadbitter(5) 11/1: 4034300: Never dangerous 9th: btr 1051   00
1482 RESTORATION [7] 4-9-7 D Nicholls 10/1: -000-00: Early speed: see 1482.   00
1200 COLWAY RADIAL [1] 3-8-2 L Charnock 6/1: -044000: Speed to ½ way, eased: btr 1200.   00
11 ran   ¾,4,nk,2,½,nk,hd,½   (Hippodromo Racing)   M H Easterby Great Habton, Yorks.

1628 ALDBOURNE MAIDEN STAKES 3YO   £3853   1m   Good/Firm 25 +07 Fast

1046 LOCAL SILVER [6] (W Hern) 3-9-0 W Carson 7/2: 0-01: 3 b c Plugged Nickle - Home Love (Vaguely Noble) Promising colt: well bckd, led final 1f under press in quite a fast run 3yo mdn at Newbury July 18: lightly raced prev but is a half brother to the very smart Local Suitor: eff over 1m, may stay further: acts well on fast going, on a galloping track: may make further improvement .   51

1043 STICKY GREENE [5] (B Hills) 3-8-11 B Thomson 8/1: 0-3342: Came to chall 1f out, ran well and must surely find a maiden race soon: see 923.   44

579 ALECS DREAM [2] (A Stewart) 3-9-0 M Roberts 100/30 FAV: -33: Uneasy fav, led 2f out, no extra when hdd: abs since rated highly 579: needed race.   47

-- AUCHINATE [4] (G Harwood) 3-9-0 A Clark 10/1: -4: Racecourse debut: prom most: has scope: half brother to winning miler Monetarist: likely to improve in due course.   35

359 LUMIERE [12] 3-8-11 Pat Eddery 14/1: 0-00: Prom, wknd after long abs: very lightly raced maiden: quite speedily bred.   27

-- KAIYRAN [11] 3-9-0 W R Swinburn 7/2: 3-0: No threat but possibly just in need of the race: rated 40 when 3rd to Pasticcio in a backend mdn at Leicester on sole outing in '85: quite an attractive sort who should do a lot btr next time.   28

803 KICK THE HABIT [10] 3-8-11 P Robinson 12/1: 0-0000: Clear leader 6f, fin 8th:btr 803.   00

1451 Festivity [3] 8-11   -- Docksider [8] 9-0   -- Township [1] 9-0
1469 Promenader [7] 9-0   -- Lees Dominion [9] 9-0
12 ran   2,hd,7,1½,¾   (Sheikh Mohammed)   W Hern West Ilsley, Berks.

1629 EBF MAIDEN STAKES 2YO   £4081   6f   Good/Firm 25 -19 Slow

-- BELLOTTO [7] (J Tree) 2-9-0 Pat Eddery 8/11 FAV: 1: 2 b c Mr Prospector - Shelf Talker (Tatan) Smart colt in the making: heavily bckd on debut, led dist and simply slaughtered his rivals to win a 2yo mdn at Newbury July 18: reportedly stable's best 2yo and certainly created a very gd impression today: eff over 6f, sure to stay further: acts well on fast ground on a galloping trk: not one to oppose lightly, no matter what the company.   77

-- HAWAIIAN CAT [24] (I Balding) 2-9-0 S Cauthen 12/1: 2: Weak in mkt on debut: kept on well on the opposite side of the course to the winner: fine debut: half brother to useful '85 2yo Exclusive Cat: eff over 6f, should stay further: acts well on fast ground, on a galloping track: caught a real tartar today and should find a mdn without much trouble.   55

1495 MUAD DIB [5] (R Akehurst) 2-9-0 P Cook 12/1: 23: Chall 2f out, gd eff and should win a maiden if eased in class a little: see 1495.   45

-- KINGS VICTORY [8] (M Usher) 2-9-0 M Wigham 50/1: 4: Kept on, showing future promise: half brother to the very useful sprinter Music Night and to other minor winners: eff over 6f, should stay further: acts on fast ground on a galloping track: likely to find a maiden at one of the smaller tracks.   44

1465 MARDAS [10] 2-9-0 W Carson 12/1: 00: Al prom: see 1465.   43

-- PRINCESS SEMELE [15] 2-8-11 R Cochrane 50/1: 0: Late prog: this was an encouraging first effort: half sister to a couple of minor winners: should be well suited by 7f+.   38

-- LIBRAN STAR [18] 2-9-0 W Newnes 25/1: 0: Gd fin to take 7th: a 28,000 gns March foal who is bred to be quite speedy and is a half brother to 2yo winners Secret Miracle and Terminator: certain to be a different proposition next time and shd win a race soon.   40

-- MACE BEARER [17] 2-9-0 P Waldron 33/1: 0: Al prom, fin a close 8th and a promising debut: cheaply bought March foal who is a half brother to a winning stayer: should improve in due course.   38

800 CHESTER TERRACE [1] 2-9-0 N Howe 33/1: 00: Sn prom, fin 9th: on the upgrade: stays 6f: see 800.   36

985 NAWWAR [9] 2-9-0 B Rouse 12/1: 00: Made most, steadily fdd into 10th: a 36,000 gns May foal who is a half brother to 2 winners, notably smart stayer Weaver's Pin: sure to improve when tried over longer distances.   36

1241 YOUNG GHILLIE [11] 2-9-0 Paul Eddery 12/1: 00: Early speed: see 1241.   00

-- MAHAFEL [23] 2-9-0 B Thomson 12/1: 0: No show but is a rangy type who may need more time: cost IR 56,000: one for the future.   00

1019 Madness Not To 0 9-0   **1495** Jocks Brother [21] 9-0
1483 Unity Farm Boy [19] 9-0   -- Va Lute [22] 9-0
1445 Mendip Star [16] 9-0   -- Nors God [6] 9-0   -- Pewter Quarter [4] 9-0
622 Technocrat [3] 9-0   -- Warrior Brave [13] 9-0
1522 Mister Wizard [14] 8-11   **596** African Safari [2] 9-0
-- Bischero [12] 9-0
24 ran   6,3,nk,nk,½,½,½,½   (K Abdulla)   J Tree Beckhampton, Wilts

1630 ALLIED DUNBAR H'CAP 3YO FILLIES 0-60   £5408   1m 2f Good/Firm 25 -28 Slow   [63]

*1259 APPLY [5] (J Tree) 3-8-9 Pat Eddery 6/4 FAV: -11: 3 ch f King's Lake - Alia (Sun Prince) Useful, unbtn filly: heavily bckd but had nothing to spare when driven out for a narrow success in a slowly run 3yo fillies h'cap at Newbury July 18: comfortable winner of a maiden at Lingfield June 27 on only prev outing: dam was a very useful performer: eff 10f, possibly btr suited by 12f: acts on fast ground: should improve further.   56

1031 RED SHOES [7] (W Hern) 3-7-12 W Carson 4/1: 0-3032: Tried to make all and deserves

to find a race soon: see 458.   43
1507 LUCKY SO SO [8] (S Norton) 3-8-10 J Lowe 11/1: 4103043: Came from behind to chall
final 1f, not btn far and clear of rem: retains her form well and could win again soon:
see 1507, stays 10f well.   55
*1206 KATHY W [3] (H Cecil) 3-9-2 S Cauthen 11/4: -114: No extra final 2f but seemed
to run to her best: see 1206.   53
128 MYSTERIOUS DANCER [2] 3-9-2 W R Swinburn 10/1: 010-30: Slow start, no extra final
2f but should benefit from this first outing since 128: stays 10f.   52
925 POUNELTA [6] 3-8-5 B Rouse 20/1: 3-42040: Pressed leaders 1m: best 271 (1m hvy).   40
1061 Glitter [4] 8-6   --   Sunley Sinner [1] 9-7
8 ran 1,shthd,5,nk,nk   (K Abdulla)   J Tree Beckhampton, Wilts.

1631 HACKWOOD STAKES 3YO UPWARDS   £8207   6f   Good/Firm 25 +20 Fast

1485 GWYDION [3] (H Cecil) 3-8-9 S Cauthen 100/30: 11-4331: 3 b f Raise A Cup - Papamiento
(Blade) Very smart filly: showed a fine turn of foot to sprint clear at dist for a
comfortable success in fast run Hackwood Stks (Listed race) at Newbury July 18: has had
training problems previously but yet to fin out of the first 4 in any of her 6 races
including 2 wins out of 2 races in '85 at Newmarket and The Queen Mary Stks at Royal Ascot:
best form over sprint dist tho' prob stays 7f: btr suited by firm or gd grd than soft:
genuine and consistent.   81
+1387 POLYKRATIS [4] (M Francis) 4-9-3 C Rutter 16/1: -000312: Came from behind, kept
on well and continues to improve: see 1387.   78
1485 GREY DESIRE [5] (M Brittain) 6-9-7 W R Swinburn 9/1: 2412023: Didnot have the best
of runs but once again made the frame and pays a fine tribute to his trainer: see 1485.   77
1491 BRIDESMAID [10] (B Hills) 3-8-5(vis) B Thomson 12/1: 0012334: Waited with, no extra
final 1f: evidently needs give in the ground and has yet to reproduce 854.   66
1485 CYRANO DE BERGERAC [8] 3-8-5 Pat Eddery 6/5 FAV: 111-200: Heavily bckd: came to
chall dist, no extra: much btr 1485, 1125.   65
1235 MEASURING [1] 3-8-5 P Cook 33/1: 20-3000: Fdd final 1f: see 59.   63
*1044 GOVERNOR GENERAL [7] 3-8-8 R Cochrane 12/1: 01-0110: Speed much, fin 7th: see 1044.   00
1268 Durham Place [9] 9-0   1508 Imperial Jade [2] 8-11
1286 Breadcrumb [6] 9-0   +732 Dream Chaser [11] 8-5
11 ran ½,2,1½,½,shthd   (S Niarchos)   H Cecil Newmarket

1632 CHATTIS HILL MAIDEN FILLIES STAKES 2YO   £3424   5f   Good/Firm 25 -27 Slow

1311 MAKE OR MAR [8] (R Smyth) 2-8-11 S Whitworth 33/1: 01: 2 b f Daring March - Martelli
(Pitskelly) Gained a surprise success, leading dist and battling on gamely for a narrow win
in a slowly run 2yo fillies mdn at Newbury July 18: first foal of a winning 2yo over 1m:
eff 5f, sure to stay 6f+: acts well on fast going on a gall track.   51
1454 SURELY GREAT [5] (D Thom) 2-8-11 M L Thomas 12/1: 0202402: Led briefly final 1f,
just btn and should find a maiden especially if eased a little in class: see 1454.   50
1322 ROMAN BELLE [10] (G P Gordon) 2-8-11 W Ryan 25/1: 03: Ev ch, no extra: gd eff and
is certainly on the upgrade: should stay 6f: see 1322.   43
1308 BERTRADE [11] (P Makin) 2-8-11 P Cook 10/1: 40324: Prom, outpaced final 1f: eff
over 5f on fast ground: see 621.   41
--   HUNGRY GRIEBEL [12] 2-8-11 Pat Eddery 7/4 FAV: 0: Showed signs of inexperience on
debut: sure to benefit from the experience: well suited by 6f: from a stable whose 2yos
have been carrying all before them and will improve next time.   41
--   MOUNT VENUS [4] 2-8-11 R Weaver 33/1: 0: No threat tho' will benefit from the race:
will be suited by longer dist.   35
--   HURRICANE VALLEY [3] 2-8-11 M Wigham 14/1: 0: Fin strongly into 7th: cost only
IR 12,500: half sister to 3 minor winners: speedily bred and will step up on this shortly.   35
1501 ULTRA NOVA [9] 2-8-11 T Quinn 4/1: 320: Led to ½ way, fin 8th: btr 1501 (sharp trk).   35
--   ZITELLA [1] 2-8-11 S Cauthen 10/1: 0: No danger in 9th: half sister to a minor 7f
winner: should do better in due course.   35
1238 Mamadora [6] 8-11   1440 Whos Zoomin Who [2] 8-11
11 ran nk,2½,½,hd,2,shthd,hd,shthd   (Mrs G R Smith)   R Smyth Epsom, Surrey.

1633 WHITE HORSE H'CAP 3YO+ 0-50   £3915   2m   Good/Firm 25 +25 Fast   [48]

1470 JACKDAW [6] (R Hollinshead) 6-7-9 A Culhane(7) 9/2 FAV: 0300231: 6 b h Crow - Lycabette
(Lyphard) Broke a long losing sequence when running on to lead final 1f narrowly, in a fast
run h'cap at Newbury July 18: winner at Newmarket in '85 and again at that trk the previous
season, also at Beverley and Haydock: very eff over 2m tho' acts on firm and yldg: best
form on a stiff track.   25
1111 EL CONQUISTADOR [4] (G Harwood) 3-8-1 A Clark 8/1: -0202: Pressed leaders thr'out
and just held in a driving fin: best effort yet: see 1029.   44
1293 LADYS BRIDGE [8] (I Balding) 4-9-5 S Cauthen 7/1: 14-1003: Waited with, chance dist:
best effort since 419.   45
942 ORANGE HILL [2] (J Tree) 4-8-0 W Newnes 6/1: 01-0004: Led str, wknd final 1f: see 942   23
1388 MY CHARADE [5] 5-7-8(vis) J Lowe 25/1: 1402000: Ev ch: best 917 (14f gd).   07
1004 DONT RING ME [9] 4-8-3 W Carson 9/1: 100-040: Prom most: see 675.   15
--   EASTER LEE [3] 6-8-1 A Mcglone 8/1: -0122-0: Ran as if needing the race on first outing

since July '85: in gd form last term winning a h'cap at Bath and finishing 2nd in val h'caps
at Ascot and Goodwood subsequently: a useful staying hurdler: suited by fast going and a
stamina test and stays extreme dist well: should do better next time.   00
1058 MISS BLACKTHORN [1] 4-7-11 S Dawson 8/1: -032030: Fin well btn: best 541 (14f yldg).   00
1148 JAMESMEAD [11] 5-10-0 Pat Eddery 11/2: 012-030: P.U. after 6f: something amiss: see 1148 00
1470 All Is Revealed [10] 8-12(vis)   1112 Moon Jester [7] 7-10
11 ran   ½,1,2,8,½   (J E Bigg)   R Hollinshead Upper Longdon, Staffs.

RIPON   Saturday July 19th   Righthand, Sharpish Track

1634 BRADFORD MAIDEN STAKES 2YO   £2693   6f   Firm 16 -07 Slow

1376 ANTINOUS [1] (M H Easterby) 2-9-0 M Birch 10/11 FAV: 321: 2 ch g Hello Gorgeous -
Marthe Meynet (Welsh Pageant) Comfortably justified fav, making all in a 2yo mdn at Ripon
July 19: half brother to useful sprint h'capper Batoni: eff over 6f and should stay further:
acts on gd and firm ground and on any track: consistent juv who does well with forcing tactics 53
973 SILVER HAZE [6] (S Hall) 2-9-0 T Lucas 4/1: 222: Al front rank: gd eff and seems
best on fast ground: should win a similar race: see 781.   47
--   NORTON MELODY [16] (M H Easterby) 2-9-0 W Ryan 20/1: 3: Stable mate of winner:
easy to back tho' al pressing leaders and looks certain to go close next time: cost 18,500
gns and his dam was twice successful as a juv: stays 6f: acts on fast grd & a sharp course.   45
1373 CALLACE [13] (A Smith) 2-8-11 S Webster 33/1: 004: Kept on well: best eff to date:
half sister to a winning sprinter: stays 6f: seems well suited by a sound surface.   30
1132 OKOSAN [15] 2-8-11 J Lowe 20/1: 00: Al prom: on the upgrade: half sister to sev
minor winners: will stay further in time: acts on gd and firm: see 1132.   30
1143 NEW MEXICO [14] 2-9-0 C Rutter(5) 10/1: 400: Never really dangerous over this longer
trip: best over 5f in 962.   32
--   DRYGALSKI [4] 2-9-0 A Kimberley 6/1: 0: Active in mkt on debut: slow start and
not given a hard race: speedily bred colt who cost $150,000 as a yearling: certain to
improve on this eff next time.   00
1376 Overpower [9] 9-0   1282 Apres Ski [11] 8-11   1504 Tahard [2] 9-0
1376 Psalmody [10] 9-0   -- Rainbow Trout [8] 8-11
1333 Carls Pride [3] 9-0   -- Danum Lad [12] 9-0   -- Mr Chris Cakemaker [7] 8-11
-- Sunava [5] 8-11
16 ran   1½,1,4,shthd,½   (Lt Col R Warden)   M H Easterby Great Habton, Yorks.

1635 SHIPLEY SELLING STAKES 2YO   £1394   6f   Firm 16 -17 Slow

1279 CHANTILLY DAWN [5] (R Whitaker) 2-8-8 K Bradshaw(5) 8/1: 0001: 2 b f Gunner B -
Liscannor Lass (Burglar) Attracted some support when running on under press to lead cl home
in a 2yo seller at Ripon July 19 (no bid): cheaply bought filly who is well suited by 6f and
fast ground: acts on any track.   25
1180 HAZELS GIRL [2] (M Brittain) 2-8-8 S Perks 9/2: 230402: Just failed to make all:
gd effort: stays 6f: acts on any going: will win a seller: see 118.   22
1480 FREV OFF [4] (M H Easterby) 2-8-8(bl) M Birch 9/1: 3000403: Ran on same pace:
cheaply bought filly who is a half sister to sev minor winners: eff over 6/7f on firm and
yldg ground: acts on any track.   18
1339 RYLANDS REEF [9] (C James) 2-8-11   S Whitworth 9/2: 4044: Dropped in class:
al up there: stays 6f: acts on fast ground and on a sharp track: see 882.   15
1253 TYRED NSNOOKERED [1] 2-8-11 M Wood 11/2: 000: Early speed in this lower grade:see 1050 13
1478 EUROCON [7] 2-8-11 A Proud 20/1: 0000: Longer trip: no real threat: see 931.   11
1181 PERTAIN [3] 2-8-11 C Rutter(5) 6/1: 0400220: Fin 7th: btr over 5f in 1181.   00
*1012 REAL RUSTLE [4] 2-8-11(bl) T Lucas 7/2 FAV: 0003410: Never dangerous 8th: btr 1012(5f) 00
1528 DOCKIN HILL [8] 2-8-11 M Hindley(3) 5/1: 030300: Wknd into 9th: see 1528.   00
1480 Misty Runner [10] 8-8   1181 Dear Dolly [11] 8-8(BL)
11 ran   ½,1½,2½,1,½   (Mrs D Allen)   R Whitaker Scarcroft, Yorks.

1636 RIPON BELL RINGER H'CAP (0-50)   £3246   1m 2f Firm 18 -18 Slow   [47]

*1017 HANDLEBAR [4] (J Watts) 4-8-11 N Connorton 7/2: 31-0011: 4 b c Welsh Pageant - My
Therape (Jimmy Reppin) In gd form, made most and regained lead over 2f out, gamely in a
h'cap at Ripon July 19: won a similar race at Beverley last month and also successful in
a maiden on that course last season: stays 10f well: acts on gd and fast ground and on
any track.   40
1409 BALLYDURROW [1] (R Fisher) 9-9-0 D Nicholls 4/1: -010402: Post came just too soon:
gd effort tho' prob better suited by 11/12f: see 629.   42
879 MASTER LINE [6] (H Candy) 5-9-3 C Rutter(5) 3/1 FAV: 0-00103: Narrowly btn after
fair abs: creditable effort: acts on any trk: see 709.   44
1517 AL ZUMURRUD [7] (M Ryan) 3-8-5 M Roberts 7/2: -122124: Ev ch: most consistent: 39
1139 TRY SCORER [8] 4-8-1 L Charnock 25/1: 0000200: Btr over 9f in 1054 (gd): see 143.   15
1565 PARIS TRADER [3] 4-8-5(bl) T Lucas 9/1: 0000030: Led over 3f out, wknd: see 609.   18
*1416 MRS CHRIS [5] 4-8-0(5ex) M Fry 10/1: 0400010: Raised in class: btr over 12f in 1416   00
--   NONSENSE [2] 5-10-0 K Bradshaw(5) 16/1: 21230-0: Al behind: fin last on reappearance:
in gd form last season when winning amateur riders events at Ayr, Redcar, Haydock, Lingfield

RIPON   Saturday July 19th   –Cont'd

and Doncaster: stays 12f well: genuine sort who acts on any going.   **00**
8 ran   hd,nk,3,5,nk,5   (Mrs M M Haggas)   J Watts Richmond, Yorks.

1637 SKIPTON HANDICAP STAKES (0–50) 3YO   £3223   1m   Firm 16 –09 Slow   [52]

1278 CANADIAN STAR [4] (M Jarvis) 3-8-6 T Lucas 6/4 FAV: 0-0241: 3 ch c Northfields –
Pearl Star (Gulf Pearl) Heavily bckd and led over   2f out for a comfortable win in a
3yo h'cap at Ripon July 19: closely related to sev winners, including successful hurdlers
Star Burst and Copse and Robbers, and is a half brother to useful juv Gulf King: eff over
8/10f: acts on gd and fast ground and on any track.   **41**
1532 MAHOGANY RUN [2] (M H Easterby) 3-9-7 M Birch 9/2: -000102: Made much, kept on
under press and ran to his best: successful over this C/D in 1224.   **50**
1507 FOREMAST [8] (P Calver) 3-8-9 M Fry 13/2: 0-1303: Hung right str: going on fin:
acts on firm and hvy ground and on any track: best in 822.   **34**
875 BOLLIN UNCLE [5] (M H Easterby) 3-8-0 J Lowe 9/1: 00-0004: Fair abs: chance below
dist: maiden who stays 1m: acts on firm and soft ground and on a sharp track.   **22**
1295 MASTER LAMB [3] 3-7-7(6oh) L Charnock 10/1: 0-40400: Nearest fin: see 1089 & 690. **14**
1384 TURMERIC [1] 3-8-5 C Rutter(5) 12/1: 2-00000: Maiden: al mid-div: see 723.   **23**
1444 PATCHOULIS PET [7] 3-8-13 Gay Kelleway(3) 6/1: 0443-00: Early leader: fin 7th:
made the frame in last 3 starts last term tho' remains a maiden: stays 7f: acts on gd
and firm ground.   **00**
1371 ROYAL ROUSER [6] 3-8-0 A Culhane(7) 14/1: 000-000: Last to fin: btr 1371 (stiffer trk). **00**
8 ran   2,2½,½,hd,1½   (Ivan Allen)   M Jarvis Newmarket.

1638 SEE IT LIVE IN YORKSHIRE H'CAP (0–35)   £2246   5f   Firm 16 +16 Fast   [35]

1196 CELTIC BIRD [13] (A Balding) 6-8-8 N Day 5/1 FAV: -000231: 6 b m Celtic Cone –
Bird Cherry (Falcon) In gd form, made virtually ev yard for a game win in a fast run h'cap
at Ripon July 19: last season won at Thirsk and in '84 at Haydock: loves to be out in front
over this minimum trip: acts on fast and soft ground and on any track.   **24**
1380 RAMBLING RIVER [11] (W Stephenson) 9-9-9(vis) M Brennan(7) 10/1: -020002: Just held
and comfortably beat rem: best effort for some time: see 626.   **38**
1026 SULLYS CHOICE [8] (D Chapman) 5-9-13(bl) D Nicholls 14/1: 0131003: Gd eff: see 520. **35**
1542 VELOCIDAD [15] (J Glover) 6-8-6 K Bradshaw(5) 16/1: -300004: Ran on: btr eff: see 56. **13**
*1543 PERGODA [1] 8-9-9(bl)(5ex) R Vickers(7) 7/1: 0001010: Dsptd lead till dist: best 1543 **29**
1157 MADRACO [5] 3-8-11 M Fry 6/1: 4-11020: Ran on under press, never nearer: see 545. **20**
814 GODS ISLE [14] 3-9-6 M Birch 7/1: 0-02000: Fin 7th: best in 443: see 246.   **00**
1429 IDLE TIMES [12] 4-9-4 C Dwyer 8/1: 1130000: Fin 9th: best early season: see 240. **00**
1196 KARENS STAR [9] 9-9-0 S P Griffiths 10/1: 0000000: Hmpd start, no threat: see 1093. **00**
1438 First Experience [4] 8-11(bl)   1438 Philstar [6] 8-10
1344 Ammeed [3] 7-7(3oh)   1101 Carpenters Boy [2] 8-7
1101 Ken Siddall [7] 8-2   1247 Monswart [10] 7-12   1610 Blochairn Skolar [22] 7-7(2oh)
16 ran   shthd,2½,½,hd,1½,½,1,½   (J D Cooke)   A Balding Doncaster, Yorks.

1639 LEEDS MAIDEN STAKES 3YO   £2756   1m 4f   Firm 16 –31 Slow

849 LINE OF CARDS [4] (H Candy) 3-8-11 C Rutter(5) 7/4 FAV: -41: 3 b f High Line –
No Cards (No Mercy) Useful filly: well bckd and cruised into lead below dist for an easy
win in a 3yo mdn at Ripon July 19: half sister to winning miler Dabdoub: stays 12f really
well: acts on gd and fast ground and on any track: should continue to improve and looks
one to follow.   **52**
1368 NO DOUBLET [11] (B Hills) 3-8-11 W Ryan 4/1: 33-3222: Again found one too good and
remains a maiden: stays 12f: see 1368 & 862.   **45**
--   CYNOMIS [10] (W Hastings Bass) 3-8-11 R Lines(3) 14/1: -3: Easy to back on debut:
led over 2f out and kept on well when hdd: nicely bred filly by Shergar who is a half sister
to useful Range Rover: stays 12f: acts on firm grd and on a sharp course: will improve for
this run.   **45**
1259 EXCELBELLE [9] (J Dunlop) 3-8-11 T Lucas 3/1: -234: Led over 4f out: in gd form. **44**
1372 IS BELLO [6] 3-9-0 P Hamblett 8/1: -032030: Ran on same pace: see 1372 & 723. **45**
1192 JOLIE PELOUSE [3] 3-8-11 A Kimberley 8/1: -40: Btn dist: see 1192.   **31**
1080 DENIECE [7] 3-8-11 M Roberts 10/1: -00: Never dangerous 7th: lightly raced filly who
is a half sister to a couple of winners: should be suited by middle distances.   **00**
849 Shakeeb [1] 9-0   1220 Elbandary [8] 8-11   1535 Showdance [5] 9-0
--   Today Eddy [2] 9-0
11 ran   2½,shthd,nk,½,7,10   (Mrs A Johnstone)   H Candy Kingstone Warren, Oxon

503

Official Going Given As GOOD/FIRM

1640 HILLFIELDS TROPHY HCAP 3YO+ 0-60   £4090   7f   Firm 19 +01 Fast   [57]

1001 HIGHEST PRAISE [6] (I Balding) 3-8-1 P Cook 13/2: 3-01331: 3 ch g Topsider - Pride's
Promise (Crozier) Useful gelding: led final 1f, ridden out in a h'cap at Newbury July 19:
has been in fine form this season, earlier won a maiden at Pontefract: seems equally eff
at 6/7f: acts on firm and yldg ground and on any track: consistent.   51
1521 MR JAY ZEE [11] (N Callaghan) 4-7-12 A Mackay 9/2 FAV: 0131302: Not the best of
runs and fin in fine style: possibly a shade unlucky: well suited by 7f: see 1292, 1222.   38
1429 HILTON BROWN [2] (P Cundell) 5-9-7 Pat Eddery 6/1: 3002243: Chance final 1f: carries
weight well and is most consistent: see 1285, 76.   57
1018 HELLO SUNSHINE [7] (L Holt) 7-8-0 N Adams 12/1: 4-00004: Nearest fin: best effort
this season: in '85 won a h'cap over this C/D and saves his best for this trk: acts on
any ground but likes some give.   30
1390 BUNDABURG [3] 6-8-3 W Newnes 10/1: 0000000: Hmpd inside final 1f: btr effort: see 775   30
1390 MAAZI [1] 5-9-0 M Lynch(5) 10/1: 01-0100: Chance over 1f out: twice below form 881.   36
1013 FORMATUNE [12] 4-7-12(bl) D Mckay 5/1: 1023320: Made much: btr 1013.   00
1286 MANCHESTERSKYTRAIN [8] 7-8-9 I Johnson 10/1: -300000: Prom, fdd: best first time
out in 401.   00
1390 April Fool [5] 7-12   762 Black Sophie [4] 7-9   1306 Dorking Lad [9] 8-13
1455 Steady Eddie [10] 8-7(bl)
12 ran   nk,1½,2,1½,2,nk,nk   (Paul Mellon)   I Balding Kingsclere, Hants

1641 MANTON ROSE BOWL STKS 2YO FILLIES   £7934   6f   Firm 19 -09 Slow

1381 SEA DARA [3] (I Balding) 2-8-8 Pat Eddery 10/3: 131: 2 ch f Dara Monarch - Sea
Queen (Fabulous) Very useful filly: al going well and made almost all, comfortably, in a
2yo fillies Listed race at Newbury July 19: first time out won a fillies mdn at Sandown:
half sister to very useful 2yos King Hagen and Mariacho: eff over a stiff 5f, well suited by
6f: acts on fast ground and a galloping track: does well when up with the pace.   66
1154 SIMPLE TASTE [4] (I Balding) 2-8-5 P Cook 7/4 FAV: 22: Heavily bckd stable companion
of winner: ev ch final 2f: will win soon and earn a further furlong will suit: see 1154.   56
--   QUELLE FILLE [8] (P Cole) 2-8-5 T Quinn 7/1: 3: Stayed on well final 1f and improvement very likely: cost 110,000 gns and is a half sister to useful What A Riot and the very
smart Quilted: should be suited by middle dist next season and will not be long in winning:
acts on fast ground.   50
1287 SAD CAFE [7] (C Brittain) 2-8-5 G Baxter 7/1: 04: Sn prom: improving: half sister
to the useful Musical Youth and the smart sprinter Prince Sabo: acts on fast ground and
should have no trouble finding a race.   47
1287 TRY THE DUCHESS [5] 2-8-8 D Mckay 7/1: 100: Fdd final 1f: stiff task: see 1087.   46
1464 FLEET FACT [2] 2-8-5 B Thomson 16/1: 200: Prom, ev ch: lightly raced since best 565.   36
1238 KHAKIS LOVE [1] 2-8-5 Paul Eddery 7/1: 30: Mkt drifter: prom early: much btr 1238 (5f)   00
533 Clarentia [6] 8-8
8 ran   2,2½,½,2,3   (George Strawbridge)   I Balding Kingsclere, Hants

1642 MORLAND BREWERY TROPHY 3YO HCAP 0-70   £9505   1m 5f Firm 19 +17 Fast   [71]

1448 AL KAAHIR [4] (H T Jones) 3-8-6 R Hills 7/1: 02-3121: 3 ch c Valdez - Shawn's Gal
(Crimson Streak) Fast impr colt: led over 3f out, forging 8l clear for an impressive win
in fast run and val Morland Brewery Trophy (h'cap) at Newbury July 19: earlier was a ready
winner of a stks event at York: last time out was a fine 2nd to Highland Chieftain in the
Welsh Derby at Chepstow: eff at 12/13f, will be suited by 14f: acts on firm and yldg ground
and likes a gall track: should win more races and is entered in the St Leger.   70
1111 NORTHERN AMETHYST [2] (G Huffer) 3-8-6(VIS) M Miller 25/1: 2-32202: Visored first
time: no chance with winner: stays well but lacks foot: see 978.   56
*1435 LIE IN WAIT [5] (G P Gordon) 3-7-11 D Mckay 8/1: 0-14413: Led briefly over 4f out:
kept on: see 1435.   43
+714 COX GREEN [1] (G Harwood) 3-8-3 A Clark 10/3: -14: Well bckd: kept on under press
after a fair abs: stays 13f: see 714.   46
1128 NICOLA WYNN [8] 3-7-12 A Mcglone 25/1: -1300: Nearest fin: acts on firm and yldg grd:
will be suited by a stamina test: see 458.   40
1130 TORWADA [9] 3-8-4 T Quinn 9/1: 204-100: Led over 1m: lightly raced since 191.   38
1314 WESHAAM [11] 3-8-5(1ow) Pat Eddery 7/1: 2013220: Not stay 13f? See 1314, 1130.   00
+849 ALMAARAD [3] 3-8-6 B Thomson 3/1 FAV: 00-10: Heavily bckd: prom when swerved very
badly under press inside final 2f: worth another chance: see 849.   00
*1062 BASTINADO [7] 3-7-9 A Mackay 8/1: 3010: No show: btr 1062 (10f)   00
1111 MUBAARIS [10] 3-9-7 Paul Eddery 16/1: 3-11140: Slowly away, al last: btr 1111.   00
10 ran   8,2½,1½,½,6   (Hamdan Al-Maktoum)   H T Jones Newmarket.

1643 DONNINGTON CASTLE STAKES 2YO   £5471   7f   Firm 19 -33 Slow

1452 ROUNDLET [5] (W Hern) 2-8-8 P Cook 5/6 FAV: 41: 2 Roberto - Round Tower (High Top)

Very promising colt: heavily bckd and led well over 1f out, readily, in a val 2yo stks at
Newbury July 19: dam was twice a winner as a 3yo: eff at 7f, sure to stay 1m and will be
suited by middle dist next season: acts well on fast ground and a gall trk: seems certain
to win more races.   65
*1430 MUNAASIB [3] (P Walwyn) 2-8-11 Paul Eddery 9/2: 31012: Made most: no chance with
winner: most consistent: see 1430.   58
-- LEIPERS FORK [4] (I Balding) 2-8-8 Pat Eddery 6/1: 3: Chance over 1f out: promising
racecourse debut from this I R 108,000 purchase: half brother to sev winners: eff at 7f
seems sure to be suited by 1m+: acts on fast ground and will not be long in winning.   55
-- ACCOMPANIST [2] (B Hills) 2-8-8 B Thomson 9/1: 4: Kept on in gd style on race course
debut: cost $200,000 and is a half brother to the smart Irish 2yo Woodman: should be suited
by 1m+: acts on fast ground and a maiden is a formality.   55
1129 HARD ACT [6] 2-8-11 A Mcglone 12/1: 01100: Prom 5f: stiff task: see 1057: prob stays 7f   48
1289 BEAT STREET [7] 2-8-8 G Baxter 10/1: 40: Wknd inside final 2f: see 1289.   37
1518 Cee En Cee [1] 8-8
7 ran   4,shthd,shthd,5,4   (The Queen)   W Hern West Ilsley, Berks.

1644 STEVENTON STAKES 3YO+   £6596   1m 2f Firm 19 +03 Fast

249 WASSL TOUCH [4] (W Hern) 3-8-3 T Quinn 7/2: 1-01: 3 b c Northern Dancer - Queen
Sucree (Ribot) Very useful colt: despite long abs, led 1½f out, driven out in quite fast
run and val stks at Newbury July 19: has been very lightly raced, on sole start as a 2yo
hacked up in a maiden at Goodwood: cost a massive 5.1m: stays 10f: acts on firm and yldg grd.   70
896 LEADING STAR [3] (I Balding) 4-9-7 Pat Eddery 7/2: 10-4302: Led over 3f out: kept
on well: fine effort after fair abs: runs well here, his 2 prev success both coming on this
trk: seems equally eff at 10/12f: acts on firm and soft ground.   74
*1462 SULTAN MOHAMED [5] (J Dunlop) 3-8-3 B Thomson 5/2: 42-1213: Ev ch over 1f out:
raised in class here and acquitted himself well: see 1462.   65
574 FLYING TRIO [2] (L Cumani) 3-8-10 P Cook 9/4 FAV: 02-1044: Absent: best 224(soft).   63
1448 PLAID [6] 3-8-8 Paul Eddery 10/1: -313040: Wknd 2f out: see 348.   51
1068 BRIGHT BIRD [1] 4-9-5 W Newnes 50/1: -030: Led over 6f: impossible task: see 1068.   00
6 ran   1,2,5,6,15.   (Sheikh Ahmed Al Maktoum)   W Hern West Ilsley, Berks.

1645 OVERTON MAIDEN STAKES 3YO   £3866   1m 3f Firm 19 -09 Slow

572 SHIP OF STATE [5] (I Balding) 3-9-0 Pat Eddery 5/1: 23-401: 3 b c Troy - Sea Venture
(Diatome) Despite long abs, made ev yard, easily, in a 3yo mdn at Newbury July 19: eff at
11f, will be well suited by 12f: half brother to Sea Raider: acts on firm and yldg/soft
ground and should continue to improve.   60
1469 ILE DE ROI [2] (H Candy) 3-9-0 W Newnes 5/1: -4-02: Ev ch in str: should be suited
by 12f: acts on fast ground and a gall trk and should have no trouble finding a similar event.   51
739 SARONICOS [10] (C Brittain) 3-9-0 G Baxter 6/1: 00-3223: Ran on final 1f: gd effort
after abs: deserves a race: see 739.   50
1444 SHAMIYDA [7] (R J Houghton) 3-8-11 Paul Eddery 9/2 FAV: 0-034: Ev ch inside final 2f:
stays 11f: see 1444.   46
1469 BOON POINT [12] 3-9-0 A Mcglone 15/2: 3-0300: Mkt drifter: ev ch: best 1022 (13f)   46
-- CORNELIAN [3] 3-8-11 A Clark 14/1: -0: Nearest fin on racecourse debut and will improve
next time: sister to a 12f winner and will be suited by 13m herself: acts on fast ground.   31
1444 LIKENESS [13] 3-8-11(BL) T Sprake(7) 13/2: 33-0300: Visored first time, well btn:
best 1043 (1m).   00
1315 Chucklestone [14] 9-0   -- Astral [15] 9-0   1317 Cloud Chaser [8] 9-0
1031 Adbury [11] 9-0   -- Another Smokey [4] 9-0
659 Barracuda Bay [6] 9-0   1469 Comazant [17] 9-0   -- Suez [1] 9-0
409 Hopeful Line [18] 8-11   -- Tangled Love [16] 8-11
17 ran   4,½,½,1½,7   (Sir Michael Sobell)   I Balding Kingsclere, Hants.

Official Going Given As FIRM

1646 CITY GROUND MAIDEN STAKES 3YO   £959   1m 6f Good/Firm 31 -05 Slow

1372 SPARTAN VALLEY [5] (B Hills) 3-9-0 R Hills 3/1: -0-2321: 3 b c Cyane - Heavenly Valley
(Steel Heart) Useful colt: ran on well to lead inside dist, gamely in a 3yo stks at
Nottingham July 19: placed in his 3 prev starts this season and deserved this win: eff over
10/11f and stays 14f: acts on gd and fast ground and on any trk: consistent sort.   50
1259 NEWQUAY [6] (G Harwood) 3-8-11 R Cochrane 11/10 FAV: 3-02: Well bckd: made much:
just held and well clear rem: stays 14f: acts on an easy track: sure to get off the mark
soon: see 1259.   46
978 DUNSTON [7] (F Durr) 3-9-0 P Cook 10/1: 0-00303: Stayed on late: eff over 12/14f
and well suited by fast ground: seems to act on any track.   34
1192 KRISWICK [4] (J Dunlop) 3-8-11 M Wigham 8/1: -004: No extra str: see 479.   29
581 PARSONS CHILD [3] 3-8-11 R Guest 8/1: -00: Long abs: no threat: see 581.   23
1259 LA GRANDE DAME [2] 3-8-11 S Whitworth 16/1: -000: Made much: see 1259.   19

1315 The Godfather [1] 9-0   1206 **Molto Rapido** [8] 9-0 P
8 ran   ½,12,1½,6,3,2½   (Sheikh Mohammed)   B Hills Lambourn, Berks.

1647 TRENT END SELLING STAKES 2YO   £816   6f   Good/Firm 31 -52 Slow

1434 SAUNDERS LASS [3] (R Holder) 2-8-8 P Cook 7/2: 021: 2 b f Hillandale - Portella
(Porto Bello) Led below dist comfortably, in a slowly run 2yo seller at Nottingham July 19
(bought in 3,200 gns): sprint bred filly who is eff over 5/6f on fast ground: seems well
suited by an easy course.   24
1083 RECORD FLIGHT [6] (R Hodges) 2-8-8 R Curant 7/2: 0002: Nicely bckd: al well placed:
cheaply acquired filly who is a half sister to a couple of minor winners: stays 6f: acts
on fast ground.   17
1294 MISS ACACIA [4] (R Stubbs) 2-8-8(BL) J H Brown(5) 2/1 FAV: 000303: Bl first time:
al front rank tho' much btr on a sharp trk in 1221 (firm).   07
1076 PEGGYS TREASURE [2] (M Brittain) 2-8-8 W R Swinburn 11/2: 00344: Dsptd lead most
of way: prob stays 6f tho' best in 957 (5f).   02
1576 ROAN REEF [5] 2-8-11(bl) Gay Kelleway(3) 6/1: 0343040: Btr over 5f in 1576: see 1088.   04
1137 NOFANDANCER [1] 2-8-9(1ow) C Dwyer 33/1: 0000: Speed over ½ way, wknd quickly and
is moderate.   00
--   Thornyhill [7] 8-8   P
7 ran   1½,4,2,½,15   (Chris Scott)   R Holder Portbury, Avon.

1648 BRIDGEFORD END EBF STAKES 3YO   £2201   6f   Good/Firm 31 +01 Fast

387 MANTON DAN [5] (N Vigors) 3-9-8 P Cook 11/4: 012-201: 3 b c Tower Walk - Balgreggan
(Hallez): Useful colt: despite a fair abs went on over 1f out and was ridden out to win a
3yo stks at Nottingham July 19: showed gd form as a juv, winning at Goodwood: half brother to
sev winners including useful sprinter Street Market: very eff over 6f and should stay
further: acts on fast and soft ground and on any track: likes to be up with the pace.   59
1436 SATIAPOUR [2] (R J Houghton) 3-9-4(vis) W R Swinburn 2/1 FAV: 2012222: Ran on well:
narrowly btn and 4l clear rem: in fine form and deserves another win: see 1169 & 844.   52
1472 RED RIVER BOY [7] (R Hodges) 3-9-0 A Dicks(7) 11/1: -0023: Shorter trip: made much:
may prove better suited by a slightly longer trip: see 1472.   38
1263 DARTIGNY [6] (K Brassey) 3-9-6(BL) S Whitworth 8/1: 01-0004: Ran to his best: see 514   38
1524 JARROVIAN [1] 3-9-12(vis) R Lappin(7) 33/1: 0040000: Speed over ½ way: see 947 & 309   40
*1420 JOHN RUSSELL [3] 3-9-8 P Robinson 3/1: -2110: No threat: much btr over 5f in 1420.   29
1312 NICKLE A KISS [4] 3-9-1 M Guest 11/1: 4-10000: Wknd and well btn last: much btr 966.   00
7 ran   ½,4,1½,1,2½,12   (G S Tuck)   N Vigors Lambourn, Berks.

1649 NOTTINGHAM FOREST H'CAP 3YO+ 0-35   £1945   6f   Good/Firm 31 -03 Slow   [35]

1542 ROSIE DICKINS [11] (R Hollinshead) 4-8-9 R Lappin(7) 9/1: 4030431: 4 b f Blue Cashmere -
Deva Rose (Chestergate): Responded to pressure to lead on the line in a h'cap at Nottingham
July 19: has been on the go all season, being placed on many occasions since winning a
similar h'cap over this C/D in Apr: acts on fast & soft grnd & on any track.   25
*1521 OUT OF HAND [14] (D Dale) 7-8-11(7ex) M Rimmer 6/1: 00-4012: Led 1f out, caught final
stride: comfortably beat rem & is in gd form: see 1521.   27
1429 KEATS [7] (J Fitzgerald) 4-9-10 W R Swinburn 11/4 FAV: 2-00103: Ev ch: in gd form.   32
1165 OSTENTATIOUS [10] (C Wildman) 4-7-13 M Hills 20/1: 0-03304: Never nearer: needs further. 00
1319 HUNTS KATIE [9] 4-8-5(bl) P Cook 10/1: 30-0040: Nearest fin: btr in 1319: see 8.   05
1542 RAPID MISS [5] 6-8-7 S Whitworth 12/1: 0-00300: Led after ½way: btr in 1367: see 784.   02
1385 DIVISSIMA [4] 4-8-12 P Waldron 7/2: 31-0230: Wknd into 9th: btr over 5f in 1385.   00
1542 CAPTAINS BIDD [12] 6-7-8(bl) G Carter(0) 11/2: -002020: Early speed: btr in 1542 (5f).   00
--   Tagore [13] 8-3(5ow)   1066 Shades Of Blue [1] 8-12
1429 Caliph [8] 9-9   1543 Swinging Gold [15] 9-1
1380 China Gold [2] 10-0   1447 High Eagle [6] 8-10
14 ran   shhd,3,3,hd,2,1,½   (Dickins Ltd)   R Hollinshead Upper Longdon, Staffs

1650 EBF EXECUTIVE STAND MAID.FILL.STAKES 2Y £1490   6f   Good/Firm 31 -06 Slow

1464 LINDAS MAGIC [2] (R Armstrong) 2-8-11 P Tulk 11/10 FAV: 231: 2 br f Far North -
Pogonip (Jacinto): Useful juvenile: nicely bckd & was never hdd when an easy winner of a 2yo
fillies maiden at Nottingham July 19: well eff over 6/7f & is well suited by fast grnd: acts
on any trk: does well with forcing tactics.   56
--   SEEK THE TRUTH [4] (H Cecil) 2-8-11 W Ryan 6/4: 2: Nicely bckd debutant: chased winner
thro'out: seems sure to impr & should certainly find a race: half sister to several winners:
eff over 6f on gd/firm grnd.   44
1322 STYLISH GIRL [3] (L Piggott) 2-8-11 W R Swinburn 9/1: 03: Late prog though a well
btn 3rd: sprint bred filly who is eff over 6f on gd/firm grnd.   28
944 LA TROIENNE [5] (S Norton) 2-8-11 J Lowe 10/1: 04: Prom over ½way: sister to winning
miler Mona Lisa: should impr when stepping up in dist: acts on gd/firm grnd.   22
1433 LUNDY ISLE [9] 2-8-11 P Cook 150/1: 0000: Friendless in mkt: close up over ½way.   16
1161 TIKLAS [6] 2-8-11 G French 150/1: 000: Never got into race: cheaply bought filly
who seems moderate.   08
--   Able Abbe [1] 8-11   --   Rock A Little [7] 8-11
--   Highland Kate [8] 8-11
9 ran   3,7,1½,1½,2½,1,5,15   (John Bray)   R Armstrong Neewmarket

1651 RED AND WHITE H'CAP 3YO+ 0-35   £2035   1m   Good/Firm 31 +08 Fast   [28]

1245 SOLO STYLE [14] (G Lewis) 3-9-2 P Waldron 10/3 FAV: -300101: 3 b c Moorestyle -
Mint (Meadow Mint): Led dist and ran on well to win quite a fast run h'cap at Nottingham
July 19: last month gained his first win in a 3yo h'cap at Leicester: lightly raced last
term: eff over 7/8f on firm & yld grnd: likes a gall trk.   38

1432 GIVING IT ALL AWAY [13] (H Beasley) 3-8-10 R Cochrane 13/2: -300002: Just btn & remains
a maiden: well suited by a sound surface: see 1245.   29

1436 NAWADDER [3] (B Hanbury) 3-9-2 W R Swinburn 7/2: -240103: Never nearer: best 1073.   29

316 OUT OF STOCK [6] (M Blanshard) 3-8-13 W Newnes 12/1: 000-004: Led briefly below dist:
fair effort after a lengthy abs: see 140.   24

1079 FOREVER TINGO [2] 4-8-4 G Carter(3) 25/1: 0-00004: Nearest fin: ddhtd for 4th: maiden
who has been running over longer trips this term: stays 11f: acts on gd & firm.   04

1142 ANGEL TARGET [9] 3-8-9 P Robinson 16/1: 000-000: Late prog into 6th: first signs of
form: will be suited by a longer trip: acts on gd/firm grnd.   18

1394 VALRACH [11] 4-9-7 S Perks 4/1: 0-00020: Never beyond mid-div: much btr in 1394 (C/D).   00

1447 Concert Pitch [8] 9-6   1500 Sky Mariner [1] 8-1   1450 Tarrakan [5] 9-0
1204 Linton Springtime [7] 7-13(bl)   1374 Gallois Bosquet [12] 9-1
12 ran 1,3,½,ddht,1,½,3   (Mrs N Lewis)   G Lewis Epsom, Surrey

---

1652 BRITVIC STAKES (AMA. RIDERS) 3YO+   £2677   1m 4f   Good/Firm 37 -18 Slow

*1152 SADEEM [11] (G Harwood) 3-10-13 Mr T T Jones 1/3 FAV: -311: 3 ch c Forli - Miss Mazepah
(Nijinsky): Very useful colt: came home the easiest of winners, leading before ½way hacking
up by 7L in a slowly run amateur riders event at Newmarket July 19: game winner of a 3yo
minor event at Ascot June 21: late developing sort who was unraced in '85 but is a brother
to the smart 10f winner Formaz: acts on firm & gd going on a gall trk: very eff over 12f,
promises to stay further: should impr & win btr races.   51

1563 HYOKIN [3] (D Morley) 4-11-11(vis) Melanie Morley(5) 16/1: 0032132: Mkt drifter, no
ch with winner but best of the rest: in gd form: see 1359.   30

1290 LOUD LANDING [8] (W Hastings Bass) 3-10-3 Mr R Hutchinson 10/1: 0-03: Lightly raced
maiden who had a stiff task here: see 1290.   17

*1417 ARGES [9] (R Hollinshead) 5-11-8 Maxine Juster 6/1: 2-20414: Much btr 1417.   16

984 CORAL HARBOUR [1] 4-11-1 Princess Anne 25/1: 300-300: Never btr: bl last time: best 8.   04

1280 ICKWORTH [6] 4-11-1 Jane Armytage(5) 66/1: 0444-00: No threat: showed some ability
last term but has yet to win a race.   00

-- Sparklin Performer [10] 10-3   -- Highfields Lad [7] 11-1
1251 Sandyla [2] 11-1(bl)   1494 Seat Of Learning [4] 10-12
1417 Sophistication [5] 10-12
11 ran 7,1½,7,2½,4   (Sheikh Mohammed)   G Harwood Pulborough, Sussex

1653 PRIMULA MAIDEN STAKES 2YO   £3776   6f   Good/Firm 38 -17 Slow

-- LE FAVORI [13] (G Wragg) 2-9-0 P Robinson 33/1: 1: 2 b c Mummy's Pet - Miss Longchamp
(Northfields): First time out, turned up at 33/1, fin strongly to lead final 150 yds & held
on in a slowly run 2yo maiden at Newmarket July 19: dam a useful h'capper over 1m who liked
fast grnd: should stay beyond 6f: acts on gd/firm, on a stiff trk.   49

1162 TAUBER [3] (Pat Mitchell) 2-9-0 M Hills 33/1: 032: Just failed to make all: grand
effort & should win if dropped in class: seee 1162.   48

694 RIOT BRIGADE [6] (C Brittain) 2-9-0 S Cauthen 10/1: 003: Abs but quite well bckd &
fin well: suited by 6f, will stay 7f: seems btr on fast grnd than softer going: see 382.   45

-- INCINERATOR [7] (M Stoute) 2-9-0 W R Swinburn 5/2: 4: Wk in mkt on debut, showed signs
of inexperience under press and was not given a hard time when held: cost almost $½m and
is reportedly held in some regard by his powerful stable: should impr with this race under
his belt: will be suited by further than 6f.   44

-- REBEL RAISER [4] 2-9-0 R Cochrane 2/1 FAV: 0: Well bckd debutant, ev ch dist, not
btn that far: cost $275,000: sure to be suited by 7f plus: acts on fast grnd: should impr.   41

1504 BOIS DE BOULOGNE [12] 2-9-0(BL) B Rouse 9/1: 20300: Bl first time today, al prom.   40

715 JOINT SERVICES [5] 2-9-0 S Morris 9/1: 30: Prom most, fin 7th: abs since btr 715 (5f).   38

-- START RITE [11] 2-9-0 M L Thomas 7/1: 0: Well bckd at long odds, fin in rear: evidently
well regarded by connections: one to keep an eye on next time.   00

-- Slip Dancer [9] 9-0   -- Vision Of Wonder [9] 9-0
1345 Our Tony [14] 9-0   1512 What A Guy [8] 9-0   -- Tabareek [15] 8-11
-- Lightfall [10] 9-0
14 ran nk,1,1½,1½,½,1   (J Pearce)   G Wragg Newmarket

1654 FOODBROKERS CUTTY SARK H'CAP 0-60 3YO   £3876   5f   Good/Firm 38 +26 Fast   [61]

*1443 POSSEDYNO [1] (D Elsworth) 3-9-4(8ex) S Cauthen 100/30 CO FAV: 01-311: 3 b c Posse -
Chit Chat (Baldric II): Cleverly led final 100yds in valuable h'cap at Newmarket July 19:
in a fast time: earlier won at Windsor and in '85 won again at Newmarket & likes this stiff
trk: very eff at 5f & stays 6f well: suited by firm grnd: not an easy ride but fast imprving.   66

-1457 BERTIE WOOSTER [7] (L Piggott) 3-8-1 B Crossley 100/30 CO FAV: 3100022: Well backed but was under press from the start & seems a difficult ride: rated higher 1457 (6f).   44

*1505 NO BEATING HARTS [3] (M Mccormack) 3-8-10(8ex) J Leech(7) 14/1: 3040213: Made a grand
effort to make all under his pen: in fine form & deserves another race, on an easier trk.   49

1151 RESPECT [6] (R Laing) 3-9-3 R Cochrane 100/30 CO FAV: -213104: Going well on heels
of ldrs 2f out, found no extra final 1f: best 1033.   54

1235 PRECIOUS METAL [8] 3-9-7 R Curant 11/1: 00-1030: Kept on well: gd effort under
top weight: see 657.   58

1516 SANCILIA [2] 3-7-7(3oh) G Bardwell(7) 25/1: 00-000: Came from well off the pace &
needs at least 6f: see 1516.   28

1524 TAX ROY [9] 3-8-9(8ex) P Robinson 11/1: 1-00100: Prom most, fin 7th: twice below 1380.   41

1505 Say Pardon [5] 8-3   929 Stephens Song [4] 7-12
9 ran   1,1½,½,shhd,½,1   (Qmart Ltd)   D Elsworth Whitsbury, Hants

1655 FOODBROKERS TROPHY (H'CAP)(0-75) 3YO   £11920   1m   Good/Firm 38 +09 Fast   [76]

878 THEN AGAIN [7] (L Cumani) 3-9-7 R Guest 7/1: -01-101: 3 b c Jaazeiro - New Light
(Reform): Very smart colt: winner of 2 out of his 3 races this season: on latest success
defied 9-7 for an impressive win in a fast run, valuable & well contested 3yo h'cap at
Newmarket July 19: first time out won a minor event at Pontefract: last term trained in
Ireland & won at the Curragh: very eff over 1m/10f, possibly does not stay 12f (unplaced in,
the Derby): acts on gd/firm & yld: on this evidence looks sure to pick up a Gr.3 race soon.   83

*1575 PINSTRIPE [1] (R Williams) 3-8-0(3ex)(8oh) M L Thomas 4/1 JT FAV: -011212: Quick reapp:
led/dsptd lead thro'out, just btn & continues to impr: should win again soon: see 1575.   60

1507 SOMETHING CASUAL [6] (AHide)3-8-0(4oh)(BL)AShoults(5) 33/1: 0-00003: Bl first time,
made much & kept on well when hdd: fine effort: should find a h'cap soon if reproducing
this form: see 386.   58

1486 CHIEF PAL [10] (P Walwyn) 3-8-0 (3 oh), N Howe 13/2: 4-21234: Chall 2f out, no extra:
good effort: see 1486.   56

950 FASHADA [3] 3-8-7 S Cauthen 13/2: 01-0300: Kept on onepaced: gd effort: stays 1m: see600.   62

1486 BRIGHT AS NIGHT [5] 3-8-10 R Cochrane 10/1: -303100: Close up 6f: see 1395.   62

*1490 SYLVAN EXPRESS [8] 3-8-2(3ex) G Carter(3) 4/1 JT FAV: -010010: Never going well
and this run is best ignored: see 1490 (7f).   00

1455 HABER [11] 3-8-4 M Hills 5/1: -231430: Al rear: btr 1455.   00

708 Entrancing [2] 9-0   1147 Native Wizard [4] 8-10(bl)
1468 Top Ruler [9] 8-13(bl)
11 ran   ½,1,1,nk,1½   (R Shannon)   L Cumani Newmarket

1656 SELLING HANDICAP STAKES (0-25) 3YO   £1766   1m 2f   Good/Firm 38 -34 Slo   [19]

1309 GRANDANGUS [9] (K Ivory) 3-8-10(VIS) W Woods(3) 25/1: 00-0001: 3 b c Creetown -
Woolcana (Some Hand): Evidently impr by being fitted with a visor & led after 6f, keeping
on well for a narrow success in a slowly run 3yo selling h'cap at Newmarket July 19 (bought
in 2,100 gns): no worthwhile form previously: suited by 10f, a stiff trk & forcing tactics:
acts well on fast grnd.   09

1063 SLEEPLINE DUCHESS [3] (G Huffer) 3-9-4 G Carter(3) 8/1: 000-002: Prom thro'out, narrowly
btn: best effort yet: stays 10f: see 1063.   15

1369 HIGHEST NOTE [4] (G Blum) 3-9-7 M Rimmer 8/1: 0-30043: Best effort this season: see 1369.16

1439 OCEAN LAD [2] (R Hannon) 3-8-10 B Rouse 7/2 FAV: 00-0004: Prom, ev ch: see 1439.   01

774 S S SANTO [6] 3-9-6 R Cochrane 9/1: 0-22000: Never btr after abs: best 169 (yld).   08

774 PASSION PLAY [8] 3-9-5 T Williams 7/2 JT FAV: 003-030: Abs since much btr 774 (1m).   04

730 SPINNAKER LADY [10] 3-9-5 A O'reilly 6/1: 0-00000: Led 6f, fin 7th: dropped in class
here: best 538 (yld).   00

1459 AUSSIE GIRL [5] 3-9-6 R Carter(5) 5/1: 0000330: Waited with, no dngr: much btr 1459.   00

1303 Nelsonsuperyankee [7] 9-5   1497 Hooray Hamilton [1] 9-0
10 ran   ½,1,2½,1½,1½   (K Panayiotou)   K Ivory Radlett, Herts

1657 GLYNWED DURAPIPE FILLIES H'CAP (0-50)   £3069   1m 2f   Good/Firm 38 -14 Slow   [38]

1183 SHEER LUCK [7] (I Balding) 3-7-12 G French 14/1: 04-001: 3 b f Shergar - Queen Pot
(Buckpasser): Returned to form when comfortably gaining a pillar-to-post 5L success in a
fillies h'cap at Newmarket July 19: first success but lightly raced in '85: half sister to
smart miler King Of Clubs: suited by 10f & fast going & runs well on a gall trk.   32

1278 CARVERY [3] (A Hide) 3-7-13(1ow) M Hills 10/1: 40-02: Came from behind, kept on:
ran only twice last term (rated 40 on best outing): stays 10f & acts well on fast grnnd.   23

1437 TRAVEL MYSTERY [5] (P Walwyn) 3-9-0 N Howe 4/1: 0-133: Up & down like a yoyo, disapp
after 1061.   37

1526 ATOKA [4] (Lord John Fitzgerald) 4-9-10 P Darcy 13/8 FAV: 0001134: Chall on bit
2f out, no extra: much btr 1526.   32

762 ZINDELINA [1] 3-8-8 B Rouse 9/1: 40-2040: No real dngr after abs since btr 762 (1m).   25

1231 STILLOU [6] 3-8-1 T Williams 9/1: 3400100: Prom, wknd: best 955.   13

1290 WARM WELCOME [2] 3-8-10 S Cauthen 4/1: 42-0030: Much btr 1290 (12f).   00
7 ran   5,½,1½,2,3,½   (Paul Mellon)   I Balding Kingsclere, Berks

1658 LIMEKILNS STAKES 2YO   £4495   7f   Good/Firm 38 -26 Slow

*1529 LOCKTON [4] (J Hindley) 2-9-2 M Hills 10/11 FAV: 2011: 2 ch c Moorestyle - Bridestones

(Jan Ekels): Useful colt: winning 2nd race on trot, leading ¼way & cleverly gaining a narrow success in a slowly run 4 horse 2yo race at Newmarket July 19: easy winner at York July 12: half brother to Blue Brocade, a winner over 11f: eff 7f, sure to be suited by further: acts on firm grnd on a gall trk.   53
*1253 LAURIES WARRIOR [3] (R Boss) 2-8-12 E Guest(3) 7/2: 40212: Ev ch final 3f, not btn far: running well: see 1253.   45
*1270 HIS HIGHNESS [5] (C Brittain) 2-9-0 P Robinson 5/1: 13: No extra final 1f: see 1270.   43
--   KIP KEINO [2] (G Harwood) 2-8-11 S Cauthen 11/2: 4: Led 4f, but fin tailed off and there must have been something amiss: by the 2,000 Guineas winner Known Fact out of a top class Australian mare called Kip: certain to prove btr than this indicates.   00
4 ran   ¼,1,nt tkn   (Alan Gibson)   J Hindley Newmarket

Official Going Given As GOOD ON THE ROUND COURSE, GOOD/FIRM ON STRAIGHT COURSE

1659 GOAT FELL HANDICAP 3YO+ 0-35   £2260   1m 2f Good 46 -30 Slow   [31]

1133 THE CRYING GAME [2] (B Morgan) 4-7-12 J Quinn(5) 9/2: 0-40021: 4 ch f Manor Farm Boy - Molly Flo (Paveh): Gained the day close home after a final 1f battle in a slowly run h'cap at Ayr July 19: first success: well suited by 10/11f & gd going: runs well at Ayr.   09
+1237 KALA NASHAN [1] (P Mitchell) 4-9-7 T Ives 6/4 FAV: -003012: Led 2f out, touched off death: in gd form: see 1237.   31
1613 ICARO [3] (N Callaghan) 3-8-11(bl) G Duffield 58/40: 2203233: Quick reapp, ev ch. see 1613. 29
1613 SWIFT RIVER [4] (I Bell) 4-8-5(bl) J Reid 10/1: 0303304: Quick reapp: came from behind to chall 2f out, not btn far in a tight fin: see 522, 1133.   10
--   SUMMER STOP [5] 5-8-11 K Hodgson 20/1: -0: Made much: off the trk in '85, the previous season won his final outing at Warwick: very eff over 10/11f over a sharpish trk on fast grnd. 06
5 ran   hd,1½,nk,7   (Paddy Barrett)   B Morgan Burton-on-Trent, Staffs

1660 JOHNNIE WALKER RED LABEL 2YO MAIDEN   £3418   7f   Good 46 -14 Slow

1357 DR BULASCO [2] (S Norton) 2-9-0 J Reid 9/1: 21: 2 b c Sexton Blake - Bodnant (Welsh Pageant): Fast impr colt: quite well bckd, led 3f out & ran on strongly in quite a valuable 2yo maiden at Ayr July 19: well suited by 7f, sure to stay 1m plus: acts on firm & gd grnd & a gall trk: should enjoy further success.   53
1241 SANTELLA GREY [6] (G Harwood) 2-9-0 T Fahey 5/4 FAV: 0222: Dsptd lead 2f out, came off a true line: see 1241: stays 7f.   50
1465 LACK A STYLE [3] (A Bailey) 2-9-0 P Bloomfield 7/4: 00233: Held up, kept on under press but best 1465.   50
1253 MURPHY [8] (R Whitaker) 2-9-0 D Mckeown 33/1: 04: Waited with, never closer: a 6,800 gns Apr. foal who is quite speedily bred but evidently stays 7f well: acts on gd grnd: on the up grade.   38
1175 BE MY PROSPECT [7] 2-9-0 J Quinn(5) 14/1: 030: Ev ch: see 1175.   37
1289 KNIGHTS NEVERGREEN [5] 2-9-0 T Ives 9/1: 00: Made much: should be suited by this trip but may need more time.   25
43   Royal Illusion [1] 9-0   1518 Gold Justice [4] 9-0
8 ran   1½,nk,5,nk,5   (D H Brown)   S Norton Barnsley, Yorks

1661 MECCA BOOKMAKERS SCOTTISH DERBY 3YO   £13648   1m 3f Good 46 +13 Fast

*1130 MOON MADNESS [2] (J Dunlop) 3-8-9 T Ives 4/7 FAV: 4-11111: 3 b c Vitiges - Castle Moon (Kalamoun): Has developed into a very smart colt: completed his nap hand with another comfortable success, leading dist readily in fast run 4 horse Scottish Derby at Ayr July 19: won a maiden at Salisbury first time out and then picked up 3 valuable h'caps at Newmarket, Haydock & Royal Ascot: eff 10f, stays 12f & should stay further: acts on firm & yld & likes a stiff gall trk: now to be aimed at the St Leger.   82
1098 KADIAL [3] (R J Houghton) 3-8-9 J Reid 6/4: -2142: Led 3f out, outpcd by winner final 1f but caught a tartar here: see 572.   77
1124 CAROUSEL ROCKET [4] (J S Wilson) 3-8-9 G Duffield 50/1: 1042103: Outclassed by the first 2: best 968 (heavy).   22
1078 HELSANON [1] (R Whitaker) 3-8-6 D Mckeown 200/1: 00-0004: Made much, totally out of his depth: see 1078.   12
4 ran   1½,20,¾   (Lavinia Duchess of Norfolk)   J Dunlop Arundel, Sussex

1662 CAMPBELTOWN SELLING STAKES 3YO+   £1014   7f   Good 46 -06 Slow

1158 LARNEM [6] (T Fairhurst) 3-7-11 J Callaghan(7) 5/1: 0-00021: 3 br f Meldrum - Souriciere (Count Albany): Led dist under press in a 3 & 4yo seller at Ayr July 16 (no bid): first success: eff 7f, stays 9f: well suited by firm or gd grnd.   14
1482 TANYAS PRINCESS [5] (J Watts) 3-7-11 A Mercer 7/2 CO FAV: 03-3002: Chall dist, found no extra: appeared to have a clear chance here on the form shown in 829.   12
1369 OCTIGA [8] (M Brittain) 3-8-4 J Reid 14/1: 00-0003: Off the pace till late prog: first signs of form this season: should stay beyond 7f.   04
1424 BALIDAREEN [9] (J Parkes) 3-7-11 J Quinn(5) 33/1: 0000004: No threat: no worthwile form. 00
1424 MARTELLA [10] 4-8-10 A Bacon(7) 20/1: 3000000: Led 3f out, fdd: no form since 107 (soft) 00
1543 THE CHALICEWELL [4] 4-8-10(BL) Sharon James 14/1: -404000: No form since 145 (6f).

509

499 GOLD LOFT [3] 4-9-3 T Ives 7/2 COO FAV: 2-10000: Long abs, wknd & probably needed
race: best 177.
975 YOUNG BORIS [1] 4-8-10 G Duffield 7/2 CO FAV: 00-0000: A gamble, fin last: see 975.   00
1482 Galaxy Gala 0 8-0
9 ran   1,5,1½,5,1½   (R Cartwright)   T Fairhurst Middleham, Yorks

1663 JOHNNIE WALKER BLACK LABEL HCAP 0-60   £3830   1m 5f Good 46 -12 Slow   [48]

1417 DUAL VENTURE [4] (J Fitzgerald) 4-9-10 J Reid 7/2: 2-22031: 4 ch g Brigadier Gerard-
Selham (Derring-Do): Chall final 1f, did not get a clear run & although going down by a nk
was subsequently awarded a h'cap at Ayr July 19: has been running quite consistently &
last term only ran twice: very eff over 12/13f: possibly best on gd or softer grnd and
with strong handling (ran poorly for an amateur last time).   55
1523 TICKFORD [1] (G Harwood) 3-8-11 G Duffield 4/1: 1-431D: Made ev yd, hanging on
gamely by a neck but edged right under press inside final 1f, laying the grounds for his
subsequent disq: best effort this season & should gain compensation: see 1237.   57
1130 COMELY DANCER [3] (J Watts) 3-8-4 T Ives 11/10 FAV: 4-31143: Well bckd, ev ch: see 958. 46
1024 TRESIDDER [2] (M W Easterby) 4-9-1 K Hodgson 5/1: 10-0404: Waited with, no extra
final 2f: lightly raced since 52.   28
4 ran   nk,1½,15   (A Soulsby)   J Fitzgerald Malton, Yorks

1664 AILSA CRAIG HANDICAP 3YO 0-35   £2247   6f   Good 46 +19 Fast   [39]

1398 ALLISTERDRANSFIELD [4] (G Moore) 3-7-7(bl)(1oh) S Wood(7) 4/1 CO FAV: 0-00421: 3 ch g Palm
Track - Forgets Image (Florescence): Impr gelding who was nicely bckd when gaining a pillar-
to-post comfortable win in a fast run 3yo h'cap at Ayr July 19: won a seller at Redcar in
'85: eff 6f, stays 7f: acts on firm & gd grnd: best form in bl: looks likely to win again
in similar company.   17
1324 QUALITAIR KING [1] (K Stone) 3-8-8 J Bleasdale 4/1 CO FAV: 0003122: Chall dist but
was comfortably held: in fine form: see 1324.   26
1283 PANNANICH WELLS [6] (M W Easterby) 3-9-7 K Hodgson 4/1 CO FAV: -021043: Ev ch: see 671. 34
*1610 BEECHWOOD COTTAGE [2] (A Bailey) 3-8-6(bl)(7ex) J Carr(7) 6/1: 0010014: Quick reapp,
ev ch: too soon after 1610?   15
*1316 SEQUESTRATOR [5] 3-9-1 J Reid 5/1: 0-00010: Prom much: btr 1316 (7f).   20
1398 DOUBLE CHAI [3] 3-8-11(bl) T Ives 9/1: 00-0000: Nicely bckd, wknd final 2f
and remains a maiden: see 961.   15
825 The Bight [7] 8-3   1200 Tricky [8] 8-0
8 ran   2½,2½,2,2,½   (W B Marshall)   G Moore Middleham, Yorks

Official Going Given As GOOD/FIRM

1665 IRON BLUE MAIDEN STAKES 2YO   £959   5f   Good 45 -11 Slow

1320 JOVICK [9] (G Lewis) 2-9-0 P Waldron 4/1: 31: 2 br c Swing Easy - Pas De Chat
(Relko): Impr colt: led final furlong holding on grimly for a narrow win in a 2yo maiden at
Windsor July 21: eff over 5f, stays 6f: acts on firm & gd grnd.   48
1442 MASHBUB [12] (C Benstead) 2-9-0 B Rouse 6/4 FAV: 32: Well bckd, battled with winner
final 1f, just btn & 3L clear of rem: should find a mdn: see 1442.   47
--   EL DELGADO [14] (H Candy) 2-9-0 W Newnes 10/1: 3: Debutant who set the pace over 4f:
on breeding is bound to be suited by much longer distances than 5f: likely to impr,
especially over 6f plus.   38
--   FRANK THE BANK [16] (J Sutcliffe) 2-9-0 R Wernham 14/1: 4: Wk in mkt on debut, fin well:
an 18,000 gns March foal whose sire, Full Extent was a smart, fast 2yo: likely to be all
the btr for this experience & will impr.   35
1555 BANGKOK BOY [11] 2-9-0 D Gibson 33/1: 0000: No dngr: see 1313.   30
--   SKYBOLT [13] 2-8-11 M L Thomas 11/2: 0: No threat on debut: a cheaply bought sprint
bred filly who is a half sister to minor 6f winner Opal Lady.   23
1458 COMBINED EXERCISE [5] 2-9-0 S Whitworth 16/1: 000: Mkt drifter, showed plenty of
pace but was never racing on an even keal & fdd into 7th: needs soft grnd or bl? see 662.   26
1550 RAJIVS DEBT [15] 2-9-0 T Williams 12/1: 00: Never btr in 8th: sprint bred colt.   23
--   Golden Topaz [2] 9-0   1550 Tell Me Now [1] 8-11   1339 Montys Gunner [7] 9-0
--   Martian Melody [3] 8-11   --   Maureens Cavalier [10] 9-0   1550 Dual Capacity [6] 9-0
--   Johns Baby [4] 8-11
--   William Pere [8] 9-0
16 ran hd,3,1,2,1½,hd,1½   (Baker Sportswear Ltd)   G Lewis Epsom, Surrey

---

1666 **SPUR SELLING STAKES 3 AND 4YO**   £945   1m 2f   Good 45 –05 Slow

1444 HADDON LAD [2] (M Mccourt) 3-8-2(4ow) R Wernham 12/1: 0004201: 3 b g Dragonara Palace-
Gresham Girl (Right Tack): Despite carrying 4lbs o/w, gamely prevailed in a desperate finish
to a 3 & 4yo seller at Windsor July 21 (sold 3,000 gns): first success: has been tried in bl
but probably btr without them: eff 7f, stays 10f well: acts on gd grnd.   23
1195 TRACK MARSHALL [10] (J Davies) 4-8-7 M Wigham 10/1: 0-32232: Active in mkt, chall.
winner thro'out final 1f, just held: yet to fin out of the first 3 this term but remains a
mdn : eff 10f, stays 14f: acts on firm & gd grnd: should win a seller.   16
1567 TAKE A BREAK [4] (R Laing) 3-8-3(1ow) S Whitworth 33/1: 0002003: Led dist, just btn
in a driving fin & clear of rem: gd effort: see 400: eff 1m/10f.   23
1212 LETOILE DU PALAIS [11] (B Stevens) 3-7-9 A Mackay 12/1: -040004: No dngr: see 568.   09
1567 ARMORAD [14] 4-9-0 T Williams 5/1: 00-0040: Prom, ev ch: btr 1567 (1m).   12
1439 EASTER RAMBLER [1] 4-9-0(vis) Pat Eddery 9/2 JT FAV: 0000030: Well bckd, made most:
btr 1m (1439).   11
1310 GAY CARUSO [9] 3-8-1(bl)(3ow) B Proctor 6/1: 0-00030: Fin 7th: much btr 1310 (C/D).   00
1558 IRISH DILEMMA [17] 3-8-1(bl)(3ow) P Cook 9/2 JT FAV: 0000040: Btr 1558.   00
1396 PLADDA PRINCESS [5] 3-7-9 D Mckay 10/1: -00000: Appears moderate: see 1396.   00
1310 Grovecote [15] 7-10(1ow)   1400 Tinsel Rose [7] 7-9
530 Manhattan Boy [8] 9-0   1310 Odervy [6] 7-12   1404 Mount Wood [16] 7-9
1364 Testarossa [3] 7-9
15 ran   shhd,shhd,4,2½,¾   (J F Watson)   M Mccourt Letcombe Regis, Oxon

---

1667 **WINDSOR HANDICAP STAKES**   £2565   1m 3f   Good 45 –01 Slow   [49]

1441 HOUSE HUNTER [7] (C Horgan) 5-9-1 Pat Eddery 5/2 FAV: -020041: 5 ch g Dubassoff -
Sambell (Sammy Davis): Well bckd & returned to his best, leading distance comfortably in a
h'cap at Windsor July 21: winner at Brighton in '85 & 3 times in '84: eff over 10/12f: acts
on firm but ideally suited by gd or softer going: carries weight well.   46
*1310 TRELAWNEY [8] (F Yardley) 3-7-7(4oh) N Adams 9/1: -000112: Showed continued impr though
comfortably held by the winner: evidently much btr than a plater & should find a small
h'cap soon: see 1310: stays 12f.   32
1450 BANK PARADE [5] (J Davies) 5-9-7 J Reid 11/2: 4-44033: Never closer: has not won
for sometime: see 176.   45
743 CADMIUM [4] (P Cole) 4-9-6 T Quinn 9/2: 31-3034: Abs: made much: rather disapp since 215.   42
1188 MARSH HARRIER [3] 5-8-1(1ow) P Cook 11/2: 1-00020: Chall 2f out, btr 1188 (10f).   16
1166 WIZZARD ART [9] 5-8-1 T Williams 20/1: 130-000: Btr 1166 (10f).   09
*1265 TRAFFITANZI [6] 5-7-8 D Brown 5/1: 2-0001S: Slipped up & fell at ½way: see 1265.   00
1243 Cindie Girl [1] 8-3   879 Joli Wasfi [2] 8-3(bl)(1ow)
9 ran   3,1½,1,5,5   (Mrs M Campbell)   C Horgan Billingbear, Berks

---

1668 **NIMBLE STAKES 2YO**   £1687   6f   Good 45 –08 Slow

+1440 SHINING WATER [3] (R J Houghton) 2-9-2 S Cauthen 2/9 FAV: 4211: 2 b f Kalaglow - Idle
Waters (Mill Reef): Very useful filly: effortlessly landed the odds, with a 6L pillar-to-
post success in a 2yo fillies minor event at Windsor July 21: comfortably won a similar event
over the same C/D last time: well bred filly whose dam was smart & genuine & won the Park
Hill Stakes: eff 6f, sure to be suited by much longer dist: acts on firm & gd grnd: will
impr further in btr races.   66
--   GLOBAL LADY [2] (W Musson) 2-8-8 M Wigham 33/1: 2: No ch with this winner but a sound
debut: related to several winners: quite speedily bred but stays at least 6f.   38
1440 CAERINETTE [7] (A Bailey) 2-8-8 R Cochrane 13/2: 043: Ev ch: see 1440.   35
--   FRIVOLOUS LADY [4] (R Laing) 2-8-8 S Whitworth 14/1: 4: Speed most, wknd but should
benefit from this experience: very cheaply bought Feb. filly whose dam was unraced.   05
1311 CHEROKEE GOLD [1] 2-8-8 R Wernham 50/1: 00: Never in it: a 9,000 gns March filly who
is related to a couple of juv. winners: speedily bred.   01
345 PERIGRIS [5] 2-8-8 B Thomson 16/1: 00: Wknd ½way after long abs: see 345.   00
1083 PALACE FIELDS [6] 2-8-8 T Williams 50/1: 000: Al struggling: cheaply bought May foal
who has been well btn all starts (incl sellers).   00
7 ran   6,1,10,1½,1½   (R Crutchley)   R J Houghton Blewbury, Oxon

---

1669 **AGARS PLOUGH H'CAP 3YO 0-50**   £2439   6f   Good 45 +15 Fast   [57]

1272 JOKIST [4] (J Shaw) 3-7-8 R Street 10/1: 000-021: 3 ro g Orchestra - What A Picture
(My Swanee): Prom and led 2f out, comfortably in quite a fast run 3yo h'cap at Windsor
July 21: won a Warwick maiden on his racecourse debut last season, when trained by C Williams:
well suited by 6f though seems to act on any trk/going: can win again in similar company.   36
1169 ASTICOUR [2] (I Balding) 3-8-11 Pat Eddery 8/1: 124-002: Challenged distance, outpaced: needs 7f plus: see 762.   45
1246 UPHORIA [8] (P Cole) 3-8-3 T Quinn 10/1: 020-403: Gd fin needs 7f? see 498.   32
1443 SOUND REASONING [10] (B Hills) 3-8-9 B Thomson 15/2: 2104-04: Made much: running
into form: btr 5f? see 1443.   36
1524 TOUCH OF GREY [6] 3-9-12 S Cauthen 9/4 FAV: 1120140: Well there 4f: best 1145 (stiff
6f) but is a winner twice here this season.   48
1312 COPPERMILL LAD [11] 3-8-1 P Waldron 9/1: 1200000: Ev ch: see 1312.   20
808 QUARRYVILLE [3] 3-9-2 S Whitworth 9/2: -004400: Abs: speed much, fin 7th: flattered 567   00
911 MALEIHA [7] 3-7-8 S Dawson 25/1: -0200: Fin 8th: twice well below 656 (7f hvy).   00

1033 SNAP DECISION [9] 3-8-1 A Mcglone 11/2: 300-040: Well bckd, fin rear & btr 1033 (5f).
994 **Northern Impulse** [5] 8-12(VIS)   **1164 Khlestakov** [13] 7-8
1001 **Merrymoles** [12] 7-7(4oh)
12 ran   2,2,1,2,1½   (John Virgo)   J Shaw Newmarket

1670 JULY STAKES 3YO   £959   1m 2f Good 45 +01 Fast

+1554 NILAMBAR [2] (R J Houghton) 3-9-6 S Cauthen 2/9 FAV: 2-02311: 3 b c Shergar -
Noureen (Astec): Very useful colt: scored his 2nd C/D success in a row, making all very
readily in a 3yo minor race at Windsor July 21: gained a similar win in a similar race over
C/D last time: only ran twice late in '85: half brother to 3 winners, notably Nasseem:
btr suited by 10f than 1m .: does well with forcing tactics on fast grnd at Windsor.   67
1368 BENAROSA [6] (P Kelleway) 3-8-11 Pat Eddery 5/1: 3400042: No ch with this winner:
no visor today: see 1368.   40
1554 SHAJAR AD DURR [7] (J Dunlop) 3-8-11 T Quinn 11/1: -03: Btn a long way in 3rd:
American bred filly who showed a little impr here.   20
1444 RETURN TO TARA [3] (D Murray Smith) 3-8-11 P Cook 33/1: -04: No threat: related to
a winning plater.   14
1472 CLEVELAND BOND [1] 3-8-11 A Mackay 33/1: -000: No dngr: dam a mdn.   12
--   MOSSAUL [4] 3-8-11 W Woods(3) 66/1: 000-0: Prom early on seasonal debut: no form in '85. 10
1444 **Golden Azelia** [8] 8-11   -- **Popsis Pom Pom** [5] 8-11
8 ran   12,15,4,1,1   (H H Aga Khan)   R J Houghton Blewbury, Oxon

---

Official Going Given As FIRM

1671 KELLINGLEY HANDICAP STAKES 3YO 0-35   £2428   1m 2f Firm 18 -07 Slow   [35]

1486 PENTLAND HAWK [4] (R Hollinshead) 3-9-7 S Perks 12/1: -000001: 3 ch c Jaazeiro -
Catlina (Sallust): Returned to form, leading close home under press in a h'cap at Pontefract
July 21: first success: stays 10f: acts on firm & yld grnd & seems to like a turning track. 37
1615 SAFFAN [6] (M Prescott) 3-9-3(6ex) G Duffield 2/1 FAV: 3-32122: Smooth hdway to
lead nearing final 1f: outbattled by winner: see 1362.   32
1507 HELLO BENZ [3] (M H Easterby) 3-9-5(vis) M Birch 5/1: 4004233: Led over 3f out: see 1507. 28
966 CURIGA [1] (P Walwyn) 3-8-7 Paul Eddery 16/1: 000-04: Never nearer after a fair abs:
should do btr: lightly raced filly: may stay further than 10f: acts on fast grnd.   13
1337 ULTRESSA [2] 3-8-6 J Quinn(5) 16/1: -000400: Some late hdway: possibly needs 12f:
acts on gd & firm.   03
1401 CENTRALSPIRES BEST [5] 3-8-7 R Morse(5) 11/2: -000020: Well below form 1401 (gall trk). 00
1258 MISTS OF TIME [10] 3-8-9 S Cauthen 5/1: 00-0300: Fdd inside final 2f: best 823 (hvy). 00
1562 **Court Ruler** [8] 8-5   **1346 Red Billy** [11] 8-1   **1548 Bradbury Hall** [7] 8-8(6ex)
1600 **Tinas Lad** [9] 7-8
11 ran   ½,3,2,5,2   (S G Hill)   R Hollinshead Upper Longdon, Staffs

1672 ACKWORTH SELLING STAKES 2YO   £912   6f   Firm 18 -32 Slow

1363 SANDS OF TIME [2] (R Simpson) 2-8-11 S Cauthen 13/8 FAV: 41: 2 ch c Dance In Time -
Sarah Siddons (Reform): eff at 6f, driven out in a 2yo seller at Pontefract July 21
(bought in 1,350 gns): eff at 6f, will be suited by much further (dam won the Irish Oaks):
acts on fast grnd & an undulating trk: should continue to impr.   27
1305 GET SET LISA [3] (C Tinkler) 2-8-8 G Duffield 5/2: 004002: Ch over 1f out: 4L clear 3rd:
stays 6f: acts on fast grnd & does well on a turning trk.   22
1137 MOONEE POND [1] (M H Easterby) 2-8-8 M Birch 6/1: 2000003: Prom, ev ch: best in soft 317. 12
1413 HILLIARD [4] (M W Easterby) 2-8-11 M Hindley(3) 11/1: 00004: Sn prom: probably stays
further than 6f, but only moderate form to date.   05
1561 CULINARY [5] 2-8-8 N Day 8/1: 00: Fdd 2f out: cost 3,000 gns & is a half sister to
several winners: will be suited by further than 6f.   00
1279 UNOS PET [6] 2-8-11 G Brown 7/1: 33000: Sn in trouble: see 94, 34 (soft grnd).   00
6 ran   ½,4,4,6,hd   (M G Bennett)   R Simpson Upper Lambourn, Berks

1673 T B DARLEY MEM. HCAP 3YO+ 0-50   £2410   1m   Firm 18 -29 Slow   [42]

-1202 COUNT BERTRAND [3] (W Holden) 5-7-11 R Morse(5) 5/2 FAV: -000021: 5 b h Brigadier
Gerard - Gingerale (Golden Horus): Finally broke his mdn tag, leading close home under press
in a slow run h'cap at Pontefract July 21: well suited by 1m on gd & fast grnd: acts on
any trk.   19
1500 SCOUTSMISTAKE [2] (B Mcmahon) 7-9-4 S Perks 3/1: -000332: Made almost all: gd effort. 39
1565 GREED [1] (D Smith) 5-8-6 L Charnock 13/2: 04-2443: Prom, ev ch: see 1185.   23
1377 INISHPOUR [5] (H Wharton) 4-9-10 M Brennan(7) 13/2: -003034: Ev ch in str: best 1157 (6f). 40
1202 BIT OF A STATE [6] 6-8-1(bl) B Crossley 10/1: 0000000: Yet to hit form: see 611.   05
1065 UNEXPLAINED [4] 3-8-2 Paul Eddery 3/1: 202D200: Prom, wknd str: abs: best 857.   11
6 ran   nk,1½,nk,6,3   (Whitting Commodities Ltd)   W Holden Newmarket

1674 ACKTON HALL STAKES 3YO   £1753   1m 4f   Firm 18 -01 Slow

*607 PAEAN [3] (H Cecil) 3-9-0 S Cauthen 2/7 FAV: 2-1211: 3 b c Bustino - Mixed Applause
(Nijinsky): Long odds on, but had to work hard for a ¼L win in a 3 runner 3yo stakes at
Pontefract July 21: said to be hating this firm grnd: had been off the trk since an easy
winner of a similar event at Newcastle in May: first time out won a mdn at Newbury: very well
bred colt who stays 12f well & may get further: acts on firm, but is btr with some give
in the grnd: seems genuine & should win more races.   63
1152 GOLDEN HEIGHTS [1] (P Walwyn) 3-8-11 Paul Eddery 10/3: 3-12142: Led 3f out: caught
near fin: gd effort & should stay further than 12f: possibly does not act on very firm.   59
--   GREY SALUTE [2] (R Simpson) 3-8-4 G Duffield 40/1: -3: Very stiff task on debut: dam unraced. 12
3 ran   ¼,15   (Lord Howard de Walden)   H Cecil Newmarket

1675 EBF GLASSHOUGHTON MAIDEN 2YO C & G   £1434   6f   Firm 18 -03 Slow

1430 ON TAP [2] (M H Easterby) 2-9-0 M Birch 4/5 FAV: 41: 2 ch c Tap On Wood - Joshua's
Daughter (Joshua): Impr gelding: well bckd & made ev yd, hacking up in a 2yo mdn at
Pontefract July 21: half brother to 3 winners, incl the once very useful h'capper Glen
Kella Manx: eff at 6f, looks sure to stay 7f plus: acts on fast grnd & an undulating trk.   50
1534 JOHNNY SHARP [4] (S Norton) 2-9-0 N Day 16/1: 002: Sn prom: no hope with this easy
winner: eff at 6f, probably stays 7f: acts on firm & gd/yld grnd and a turning trk.   30
1232 STARS IN MOTION [1] (D Arbuthnot) 2-9-0 Paul Eddery 12/1: 0003: Al up there: best
effort yet: half brother to a winning 2yo: should stay further than 6f: acts on fast grnd. 25
1307 LORD COLLINS [9] (M Stoute) 2-9-0 M A Giles(7) 7/1: 404: Friendless in mkt: ev ch:
twice below form 979.   23
--   JUMA MONTY [10] 2-9-0 P Darcy 50/1: 0: Al there on racecourse debut: brother to
winning miler Real Monty: should be suited by further than 6f: acts on fast ground   13
1138 FOUNTAINS CHOICE [7] 2-9-0 G Brown 9/1: 3320: Stayed on late: btr 1138, 1050 (gall
trk): may need further than 6f now.   13
--   ALLOUSH [3] 2-9-0 B Crossley 5/1: 0: No show on racecourse debut: cost 19,000 gns as
a yearling & is a half brother to several winners.   00
--   Against All Odds [6] 9-0   685 Cammac Lad [5] 9-0   965 Mccallun [11] 9-0 -- Roewood [8] 9-0
11 ran   5,2½,1,5,nk   (Lt-Col R Warden)   M H Easterby Great Habton, Yorks

1676 PRINCE HANDICAP 4YO+ 0-35   £1777   6f   Firm 18 +05 Fast   [34]

1500 WILLIE GAN [5] (D Smith) 8-8-2 L Charnock 13/2: 0023001: 8 ch g McIndoe - Queen's
Bay (King's Troop): Led close home, under press in a h'cap at Pontefract July 21: failed to
win in '85, but previous season won at Thirsk: best form over 6f on fast grnd.   15
1508 RA RA GIRL [6] (B Mcmahon) 4-9-8 J Hillis(5) 4/1 FAV: -000002: Nicely bckd: led close
home, caught death: gd effort: see 1508.   34
1638 PHILSTAR [3] (A Balding) 5-8-11(vis) N Day 8/1: 0003003: Made almost all: just btn:
best effort since 1182.   22
1546 TRADE HIGH [8] (I Vickers) 7-8-7 R Vickers(7) 12/1: 3000004: Ch. final 1f: not btn far. 17
1338 WARTHILL LADY [2] 4-8-1 G Duffield 14/1: 4004000: Prom, ev ch: see 56.   03
1438 SING GALVO SING [1] 5-7-7(1oh) G Bardwell(7) 20/1: 0000000: Sn prom: see 906.   00
*1447 MAIDEN BIDDER [7] 4-8-8(6ex) S Perks 11/2: 0210310: Fin 7th: much btr 1447.   00
1610 OFF YOUR MARK [12] 6-7-13 R Morse(5) 8/1: 000-040: Lost grnd start: btr 1610.   00
1231 MONTICELLI [4] 6-7-9 D Gibson(7) 6/1: 04-0020: Al rear: much btr 1231 (1m).   00
1447 BOOTLE JACK [9] 4-8-3(vis)(4ow) L Johnsey(0) 10/1: 00-0200: Twice well below form 1319. 00
--   Tang Dancer [10] 8-9   -- Mattye Lee [11] 7-8
12 ran   hd,nk,½,3,1½   (H Hewitson)   D Smith Bishop Auckland, Co Durham

---

AYR   Monday July 21st   Lefthand, Galloping Track

Official Going Given As GOOD/FIRM

1677 ST QUIVOX MAIDEN STAKES 3&4YO   £969   1m   Good/Firm 33 -01 Slow

1541 SIDONS DAUGHTER [5] (A Jarvis) 3-8-5 D Nicholls 12/1: -002041: 3 ch f Baptism -
Sidon Star (Sidon): Led nearing final 1f, driven out in a 3 & 4yo mdn at Ayr July 21: well
suited by 1m on fast grnd: probably acts on any trk.   45
1228 BIBI KHATOUN [13] (J Dunlop) 3-8-6(1ow) B Thomson 9/1: 00-002: Led over 2f out: much
impr effort from this lightly raced filly: bred to stay further than 1m: acts on fast grnd:
may find a small h'cap if reproducing this form   44
1371 JOHN SAXON [4] (M Stoute) 3-8-8 R Cochrane 11/10 FAV: -002033: Ch final 1f: well
treated here: btr 1371.   45
1511 MRS MAINWARING [2] (S Norton) 3-8-5 J Lowe 8/1: 03-044: Kept on final 2f: will probably
be suited by further than 1m: acts on firm & soft.   35
868   LUCKY BLAKE [3] 3-8-8 J Bleasdale 20/1: -040: Abs: nearest fin: eff at 8/9f:
acts on firm & yld: see 605.   36
316   THORCASTLE [14] 3-8-8 A Murray 4/1: -40: Very long abs: ev ch str: possibly needed
this race: see 316.   33
1299 Harleyford Lad [10] 8-8   1614 Accumulate [9] 8-8(BL)   -- No More Rosies [15] 8-5
1511 Spinning Turn [12] 8-8   -- Darling Daddy [11] 8-6(1ow) 1503 State Jester [8] 8-8(bl)
888   Princess Bella [7] 9-2   -- Yellow Canary [1] 8-5
14 ran   ¾,½,4,1½,1   (Mrs M A Jarvis)   A Jarvis Royston, Herts

1678 TURNBERRY H'CAP 3YO 0-35   £2243   1m 3f   Good/Firm 33 -31 Slow   [33]

*1295 SPACE TROOPER [4] (T Fairhurst) 3-8-9 M Hills 9/1: 00-4011: 3 ch g Air Trooper -
Netley (Major Portion): In fine form & made ev yd, ridden out in a 3yo h'cap at Ayr July 21:
last time out was awarded a similar event at Newcastle: eff at 10/11f: acts on fast grnd
& a gall trk: seems well suited by forcing tactics.   22
*1615 TENDER TYPE [7] (M Tompkins) 3-9-10(5ex) R Cochrane 10/3 FAV: -00012: Fin in gd style
and is in fine form: 3L clear 3rd: see 1615 (12f).   36
1362 SPRING FLIGHT [6] (A Jarvis) 3-8-9 J Lowe 4/1: 0-01323: Prom, ev ch: consistent. 15
1220 BLACK BANK [9] (M W Easterby) 3-9-4 K Hodgson 11/2: 000-034: Chall 2f out: see 1220:
may not quite stay 11f.   21
*1267 HARSLEY SURPRISE [10] 3-9-0 B Thomson 9/1: -331410: Ev ch str: see 1267 (9f).   16
*1547 HEAVENLY HOOFER [5] 3-8-12(5ex) D Leadbitter(5) 6/1: -010110: Fdd final 1f: btr 1547 (1m).13
960 Green Archer [11] 8-4   1257 Daisy Star [3] 8-2   1432 Breguet [2] 9-5
1507 Common Farm [8] 9-7   997 Hare Hill [1] 8-6
11 ran   ½,3,2,hd,¾   (J A Turney)   T Fairhurst Middleham, Yorks

1679 TENNENT TROPHY H'CAP 3YO+ 0-70   £8504   1m 7f   Good/Firm 33 +22 Fast   [54]

*1280 WHITE MILL [1] (H Candy) 4-7-13 C Rutter(5) 5/2 FAV: 00-0311: 4 b c Busted - Lowna
(Princely Gift): Impr colt: well bckd & led final 1f, comfortably in a fast run & valuable
h'cap at Ayr July 21: last time out was a comfortable winner of a h'cap at Doncaster: eff
at 14/15f, will be suited by 2m: acts on gd & fast grnd & a gall trk: on the up grade &
sh--ld complete the hat trick.   40
*14/0 THE PRUDENT PRINCE [8] (W Jarvis) 4-9-4(3ex) R Cochrane 4/1: 2-21112: Led over 1f out:
in tremendous form: see 1470.   52
1533 SPECIAL VINTAGE [7] (J Fitzgerald) 6-9-2 A Murray 5/1: 033: Dsptd lead 1½f out:
gd effort: see 778.   50
1388 REVISIT [6] (J Winter) 4-8-13 M Hills 6/1: 0003434: Led into str: see 58A.   44
*1218 ROSEDALE USA [4] 3-9-7 B Thomson 5/1: -212210: Stiff task against older horses: see 1218. 67
1177 MILTESCENS [5] 3-8-5(VIS)(1ow) D Nicholls 11/1: -103020: Never nearer: probably
stays 15f: see 1177.   47
*1195 Action Time [3] 8-0   1348 Dominate [2] 8-1
8 ran   4,shhd,2,shhd,3   (D Hefin Jones)   H Candy Kingstone Warren, Oxon

1680 BURNS SELLING STAKES 2YO   £869   5f   Good/Firm 33 -49 Slow

1379 HARRY HUNT [4] (J Berry) 2-9-2 J Carroll(7) 6/1: 310001: 2 b c Longleat - Ardice
(Hard Tack): Ran on under press to lead on line in a blanket fin to a 2yo seller at Ayr
July 21: earlier won a mdn at Hamilton: suited by 5f, stays 6f: acts on any grnd & on any trk. 28
1088 HARRYS COMING [2] (T Fairhurst) 2-9-2 M Taylor(7) 7/1: 0213002: Btn a whisker: best over
5f on firm or soft grnd: see 181.   28
948 GLORY GOLD [8] (M Brittain) 2-8-9 J Lowe 16/1: 004003: Made most after fair abs &
btn 2 shhds: gd effort: seems suited by 5f on fast grnd.   20
1294 HUGO Z HACKENBUSH [9] (C Tinkler) 2-8-11(BL) T Lucas 4/1 CO FAV: 4044004: Led over 1f
out: just btn: eff at 5f on firm & hvy grnd : bl 1st time today.   22
1528 PRIOR WELL [7] 2-8-8(bl) K Hodgson 4/1 CO FAV: 002000: Prom, ev ch: lightly raced
since best 415.   13
--   PADDY WILL [5] 2-8-8 E Guest(3) 12/1: 0: No real threat on debut: very cheaply acquired. 07
905 JOYCES PET [3] 2-8-8 J Bleasdale 8/1: 00: Early speed: half sister to several
winners: speedily bred & may do btr on an easier trk.   00
1528 MISS DRUMMOND [1] 2-8-8(bl) Kim Tinkler(5) 4/1 CO FAV: 000200: Slowly away, fdd. 00
--   PAGODA DANCER [6] 2-8-8 A Murray 16/1: 0: Al trailing.   00
9 ran   shhd,shhd,hd,2½,2½   (J K Brown)   J Berry Cockerham, Lancs

1681 TAM OSHANTER MAIDEN STAKES 2YO   £959   6f   Good/Firm 33 -29 Slow

1241 PLAGUE ORATS [3] (R Smyly) 2-9-0 A Murray 8/1: 01: 2 b c Pitskelly - Hillbrow
(Swing Easy): Impr colt: fin well to get up near fin in a slow run 2yo mdn at Ayr July 21:
cost I.R. 9,000: eff at 6f, should be suited by further: acts on fast grnd & a gall trk. 46
3   AUTHENTIC [1] (N Tinkler) 2-9-0 Kim Tinkler(5) 6/1: 22: Led 1½f out: just caught:
fine effort after very long abs: stays 6f: acts on gd & firm grnd: see 3.   45
--   RED TWILIGHT [8] (R Whitaker) 2-9-0 D Mckeown 10/1: 3: Kept on well final 1f on
racecourse debut, showing promise: should be well suited by further than 6f: acts on fast
grnd & a gall trk.   41
--   STYLISH ENTRY [4] (J Hindley) 2-8-11 M Hills 4/1 JT FAV: 4: Chall 2f out: should
impr for this initial effort: cost $25,000 as a yearling: should stay further than 6f. 36
1510 ALVECOTE MAGIC [2] 2-9-0 T Lucas 4/1 JT FAV: 00: Led 4f: see 1510.   34
1090 ANOTHER SEASON [6] 2-9-0 D Nicholls 20/1: 040: Continues to impr: stays 6f. likes fast 32
1488 LORD PATRICK [10] 2-9-0 C Rutter(5) 13/2: 00: Prom: fin 7th & is on the upgrade:
cost 23,000 gns as a yearling: should stay further than 6f.   29
--   NAFUAT [7] 2-9-0 N Connorton 10/1: 0: Slowly away on debut: ½ brother to numerous winners.00
1205 CARSE KELLY [9] 2-8-11 J Lowe 6/1: 02200: Speed over 4f: twice below form 1050.   00
--   Savanna King [11] 9-0   1294 U Bix Copy [5] 9-0   1421 Seabury [12] 9-0
12 ran   hd,1½,¾,2,¾,1   (R F Hesketh)   R Smyly Lambourn, Berks

1682 ROZELLE H'CAP 3YO+ 0-35   £1998   5f   Good/Firm 33 -21 Slow   [35]

1616 RUSSIAN WINTER [2] (A Jones) 11-7-7(vis)(4oh) M Fry 4/1: -000031: 11 b g King Emperor-
Am Stretchin (Ambiorix): Completed a remarkable 4 timer in this race when gamely leading near
the fin in a h'cap at Ayr July 21: winner of this same event in '83, '84 & '85: very eff
over 5f, stays 6f: acts on fast & soft grnd & does very well at Ayr & Hamilton.   06
1344 LADY CARA [1] (J Berry) 6-8-7 Catherine Strickland(7) 11/2: 4-00202: Made almost all:
best forcing the pace: see 1131.   20
1443 MURPHYS WHEELS [5] (A Jarvis) 3-10-1(7ex) D Nicholls 5/2 FAV: -041123: Just btn in
close fin: see 1443.   47
742 THRONE OF GLORY [6] (D Chapman) 5-9-11 A Proud 13/2: -000044: Just btn after fair abs:
good run: see 742.   36
1101 BAY BAZAAR [7] 4-8-13 K Hodgson 11/2: 4000340: Btn 1L: acts on firm & hvy: see 42.   23
649 MELAURA BELLE [3] 5-10-0 E Guest(3) 12/1: 4004-00: Al up there after long abs: see 649.   37
1543 Last Secret [4] 7-7(bl)   516 Highland Glen [8] 8-12
8 ran   shhd,¼,nk,nk,¼   (Calmac Ltd)   A Jones Oswestry, Salop

---

Official Going Given As GOOD/FIRM: LAST MILE, GOOD

1683 WESTON FILLIES STAKES 2YO   £959   5f   Good/Firm 28 +01 Fast

*1427 KYVERDALE [9] (M Ryan) 2-8-13 P Robinson 7/1: 2011: 2 ch f Stanford - Campitello
(Hornbeam): Useful, impr filly: led dist & sn qknd clear in quite a fast run 2yo fillies
stakes at Wolverhampton July 21: just got home in a fillies mdn at Pontefract last time & is
best suited by this minimum trip at the moment: half sister to several winners: acts on fast
grnd & seems to have no trk preferences: should continue to impr.   54
*1545 TINAS MELODY [2] (J Winter) 2-8-10 Pat Eddery 6/4 FAV: 312: Well bckd: tried to make
all: impr steadily & will win more races: see 1545.   42
1501 GAYS FLUTTER [8] (C Nelson) 2-8-6 J Reid 2/1: 4033: Dsptd lead to dist: twice below
form shown at Royal Ascot 1108 and may need another furlong: see 800.   30
-- OUR NATHALIE [11] (R Sheather) 2-8-6 R Hills 16/1: 4: Stayed on well from ½way & should
impr on this run next time: half sister to a couple of winning juveniles: sure to stay
further in time: acts on fast grnd & on a gall trk.   28
-- LOUVANKAL [6] 2-8-6 G French 50/1: 0: Al prom: fair debut from this very cheaply
bought filly: speedily bred: acts on gd/firm grnd & on a gall trk: should impr.   27
1025 GOOD GAME [12] 2-8-6 C Dwyer 11/2: 230: Speed to ½way: best in 1025.   26
1333 Petango [1] 8-6   -- The Cross [7] 8-6   -- Chic Antique [4] 8-6
1427 Ridgiduct [10] 8-6
10 ran   3,2½,1,hd,nk   (M I George)   M Ryan Newmarket

1684 WORFIELD SELLING STAKES 2YO   £756   7f   Good/Firm 28 -80 Slow

1483 LEADING ROLE [7] (M Fetherston Godley) 2-8-11(BL) R Hills 11/8 FAV: 0001: 2 ch c Rolfe -
Paravant (Parthia): Dropped in class and bl first time, comfortably justified fav. when
leading over 2f out in a slowly run 2yo seller at Wolverhampton July 21 (sold for 3,000 gns):
half brother to several winners: stays 7f well: seems suited by fast grnd & a gall trk.   25
1611 LATE PROGRESS [8] (J Berry) 2-8-8 Gay Kelleway(3) 7/1: 0000332: Not qcknd dist. though
4L clear of rem & seems well suited by this longer trip: acts on a gall trk: see 1611.   14
1449 SLEEPLINE FOR BEDS [4] (R Holder) 2-8-11 J Reid 7/2: 423: Ev ch: best in 1449 (6f).   08
1168 SOHAMS TAYLOR [1] (D Leslie) 2-8-11(vis) M Rimmer 33/1: 00004: Again made much though
wknd quickly over this longer trip: yet to show any worthwhile form.   02
1121 SHADY BLADE [9] 2-8-8(bl) C Dwyer 5/1: 02020: No threat: best over 5f in 1121 (soft).   00
1434 FIT THE SCRIPT [2] 2-8-8 A Mackay 33/1: 00: Speed to ½way: cheaply bought filly who
has been well btn in both her starts to date.   00
-- RAGOVN [6] 2-8-11 Pat Eddery 9/1: 0: Slowly away & no threat on debut.   00
1083 NUNS ROYAL [3] 2-8-8 J Williams 33/1: 000: Dropped out ½way: again last to fin.   00
8 ran   3,4,2½,4,¼   (P Fetherston Godley)   M Fetherston Godley East Ilsley, Berks

1685 DUNSTALL DERBY H'CAP STAKES (0-60) 3YO   £3817   1m 4f Good/Firm 28 -19 Slow   [61]

1236 ELAAFUUR [4] (P Walwyn) 3-8-5 N Howe 2/1: 00-4441: 3 b c Seattle Slew - La Vire
(Luthier): Nicely bckd & although stumbling 2f out was sn in command when a 2L winner of a
3yo h'cap at Wolverhampton July 21: lightly raced last season when winning a mdn at Chepstow:
eff over 10/12f: acts on fast & soft grnd & is well suited by a gall trk: consistent sort   48
1408 FLEETING AFFAIR [5] (G Harwood) 3-9-7 Pat Eddery 6/4 FAV: -11102: Fin well, not
reach winner: gd effort under top weight & most consistent this term: see 1209.   60
1179 CRAMMING [6] (W Musson) 3-7-9 A Mackay 9/2: -123023: Led over 2f out: see 1179 & 318.   32
1103 CASHEW KING [7] (B Mcmahon) 3-7-7(5oh) T Williams 33/1: 10-0044: Led over 3f out:
fair effort over this longer trip though best over 1m in 1103: acts on gd & firm grnd: see 857   16
1468 CHARLTON KINGS [3] 3-8-1(vis) A Culhane(7) 16/1: -040000: Made much: see 716.   22
1284 SWYNFORD PRINCE [2] 3-7-7(5oh) P Burke(3) 20/1: 1203000: Early ldr: btr in 738 (11f gd).   13
1325 KERRY MAY SING [1] 3-7-7(1oh) P Barnard(7) 12/1: 31-0000: Behind from ½way: see 989.   00
7 ran   2,hd,8,1,½   (Hamdan Al-Maktoum)   P Walwyn Lambourn, Berks

1686 WIN WITH THE TOTE MAIDEN STAKES 3YO+   £908   1m 4f Good/Firm 28 -07 Slow

1072 SWEET ALEXANDRA [16] (J Shaw) 3-8-0(BL) M Roberts 4/1: -431: 3 br f Lord Gayle -
Santa Luciana (Luciano): Bl first time & went on over 2f out for a comfortable win in an
all aged maiden at Wolverhampton July 21: closely related to several middle dist winners,
incl useful Deutschmark: stays 12f well: acts on gd & fast grnd & on any trk.   28
--   SOLOMON LAD [10] (R Holder) 3-8-3 A Dicks(2) 20/1: -2: Mkt drifter on racecourse
debut: ran green when chall. dist & will impr: first foal: clearly stays 12f well: acts on
gd/firm grnd & on a gall trk.   25
940 DINADAN [3] (A James) 5-9-0 S Dawson 33/1: 0--0-03: Gd late prog: only ran once last
season: stays 12f: acts on fast grnd: has worn bl in the past.   20
1444 LHIRONDELLE [4] (P Cole) 3-8-1(1ow) T Quinn 4/1: -04: Eased in class: had ev ch:
closely related to several winners, incl smart French miler Prospero: stays 12f: acts on
gd/firm grnd & on a gall trk.   19
1349 JUBILEE JAMBOREE [14] 3-8-0 R Lines(3) 3/1 FAV: -0030: Led after 1m: fair effort.   16
1535 MOLYBDENUM [12] 5-9-0 G Dickie 33/1: -00: Not qckn below dist: lightly raced gelding
who may do btr over a shorter trip: acts on gd/firm grnd.   15
1251 WRANGBROOK [7] 3-8-0 R Hills 7/1: 0-3000: Led for 1m: best on heavy in 123.   00
1437 Montbergis [8] 8-3   1535 Sweet Rascal [6] 8-11   1437 Dime And A Dollar [17] 8-3
--   Boca West [15] 9-0   1244 Abigails Gem [11] 8-0   1349 Top Feather [9] 8-11
--   Johnnys Shambles [5] 9-0   --   Erics Wish [2] 9-0
--   Maestrum [1] 8-4(1ow)   --   Our Master Mark [13] 9-0
17 ran 3,1½,½,1,1   (J MacGregor)   J Shaw Newmarket

1687 SUMMER H'CAP STAKES (0-35) 3YO   £1707   5f   Good/Firm 28 +06 Fast   [28]

1542 SANDITTON PALACE [5] (P Felgate) 3-9-8(7ex) T Quinn 9/2: 4043101: 3 gr g Dragonara
Palace - Petona (Mummy's Pet): Ran on well to lead near fin in quite a fast run 3yo h'cap at
Wolverhampton July 21: recently won a similar event at Warwick: should be suited by 6f:
acts on firm & yld grnd & an easy trk: impr performer this season.   30
1476 ARDENT PARTNER [12] (R Holder) 3-8-8 S Dawson 14/1: -000302: Just failed to make all
& 3L clear of 3rd: gd effort & runs welll here: see 1438.   15
1505 NAGEM [3] (L Barratt) 3-9-0 R Hills 5/1: 00-0423: Ev ch: best in 1505 (tight trk).   13
1476 LEFT RIGHT [8] (N Macauley) 3-9-0(bl) Gay Kelleway(3) 12/1: 0300304: Always front
rank: best in 1399.   09
*1584 PENDOR DANCER [6] 3-9-9(vis)(7ex) G Baxter 8/1: 2300010: Pressed ldr 4f: in gd form.   18
1505 MAYBE JAYNE [10] 3-8-4 M Roberts 33/1: 4400000: Btr in 1505 (tight trk): see 377.   00
+1399 PILLOWING [4] 3-9-11(7ex) J Reid 10/1: 400-010: Sn outpcd: much btr in 1399.   00
1476 CHAUTAUQUA [11] 3-9-7 T Williams 3/1 FAV: 2141240: Sn behind & fin last: can do
much better: see 910.   00
1438 Private Sue [7] 8-10   1398 Choral Park [13] 9-2   1316 Charcoal [9] 9-4(bl)
1436 Whoberley Wheels [2] 9-5   1399 Hobournes Katie [1] 8-12
13 ran ½,3,1½,shhd,2   (J D Abell)   P Felgate Melton Mowbray, Leics

1688 BILBROOK MAIDEN STAKES 3YO   £821   2m 1f   Good/Firm 28 +03 Fast

1304 IGHTHAM [6] (G Harwood) 3-9-0(BL) Pat Eddery 3/1: -001: 3 b c Nijinsky - Golden Alibi
(Empery): Showed impr form when responding to press to lead dist in a 3yo mdn at Wolverhampton July 21: clearly well suited by a test of stamina: acts on gd/firm grnd & on
a gall track: bl 1st time today.   40
1304 BEDHEAD [2] (A Stewart) 3-9-0 M Roberts 4/5 FAV: 0-022: Made most: not qckn close
home though fin lame: still 5L clear of rem: see 1304 & 978.   36
1578 DEMON FATE [8] (F Durr) 3-9-0 G French 10/1: -000033: Longer trip: no extra 2f out:
undoubtedly stays beyond 1m though best over that trip in 605 (gd).   28
1564 PHEASANT HEIGHTS [10] (H Candy) 3-8-11 J Reid 6/1: 0-44004: Nearest fin: best in 1304.   21
1106 MISS LAURA LEE [3] 3-8-11 Gay Kelleway(3) 33/1: 0-40000: Made much though did not
stay this longer trip: best over 7f in 368.   11
1530 GRUNDYS OWN [4] 3-9-0 P Hill(7) 25/1: 0-000: Al mid-div: much btr in 1372 (12f).   09
839 Sagareme [1] 8-11   --   April Flutter [7] 8-11
--   Star Of Poly [12] 8-11   1437 Meeson More [5] 9-0
10 ran 2,5,3,7,4   (K Abdulla)   G Harwood Pulborough, Sussex

1689 JULY HANDICAP STAKES 3YO+ (0-35)   £2001   1m 1f   Good/Firm 28 -18 Slow   [30]

1394 EXPLETIVE [15] (M Eckley) 6-8-6(bl)(2ow) J Reid 6/1: 0-04301: 6 ch m Shiny Tenth -
Pemba (Sodium): Denied a clear run dist though burst through to lead close home in a h'cap
at Wolverhampton July 21: loves this trk, had scored 3 of her 4 previous wins here: eff
over 8/9f: acts on gd & fast grnd & on a gall trk.   16
1579 FOOT PATROL [4] (P Cundell) 5-9-3 A Mcglone 5/1: 0000102: Fin well: stays 9f: see 1139.   23
1439 MISS APEX [5] (F Yardley) 4-8-4 I Johnson 12/1: -043023: Led before ½way, caught
close home: gd effort & stays 9f: see 1439 & 673.   09
1539 RIO DEVA [8] (J Harris) 8-9-0 R Lappin(7) 33/1: 0/2-004: Fin strongly: gd effort.   18
1394 GREENHILLS GIRL [3] 3-8-1(BL) P Robinson 12/1: 001-000: Bl first time: ev ch: see 380.   13
1087 ARROW OF LIGHT [1] 3-9-3(BL) R Hills 13/2: -0430: Bl first time: in fair form: see 676.   25
1553 LEMELASOR [2] 6-9-9 D Williams(7) 10/1: 3232000: Fin 7th: see 441.   00
1079 PEARL PET [13] 4-8-10 T Quinn 10/1: 000-200: Wknd 2f out: btr over 10f in 850.   00
1274 GIBBOUS MOON [17] 4-9-2(VIS) Pat Eddery 3/1 FAV: 0-00200: Not clear run below dist,

sn btn: see 1274.   00
1274 **Primrose Way** [11] 8-2(1ow)   566 **Dicks Folly** [7] 9-2
937 **Porte Dauphine** [9] 8-3   1054 **Godlord** [6] 8-8
1223 **Orvilles Song** [16] 8-2   1274 **Ballyowen King** [10] 7-8(BL)(1ow)
-- **Riboden** [14] 7-12   1500 **Shark Fighter** [12] 8-4(VIS)
17 ran   1½,nk,½,1½,2,1½   (Mrs J G Morse)   M Eckley Brimfield, Salop

---

FOLKESTONE   Tuesday July 22nd   Lefthanded Sharpish, Undulating Track

---

1690 HOARE GOVETT STAKES 3YO   £959   1m 2f   Good/Firm 36 +10 Fast

1468 **LIAM** [6] (M Ryan) 3-9-5 P Robinson 5/2 FAV: 2-00101: 3 b c Runnett - No Delay
(Never Say Die): Useful colt: led below dist for an easy win in a fast run 3yo stakes at
Folkestone July 22: well btn at Newmarket last time though previously had been a comfortable
winner of a similar race over this C/D and is clearly well suited by this sharpish course:
eff over 10f on a sound surface: in gd form & could win in h'cap company.   54
1327 **COOL GALES** [5] (G Pritchard Gordon) 3-8-11 S Cauthen 14/1: 003-002: Mkt drifter:
made most: no ch with winner though is returning to form & looks attractively h'capped:
stays 10f: acts on any trk: see 732.   36
1372 **ADMIRALS ALL** [3] (J Winter) 3-9-0 W R Swinburn 13/2: 0-03403: Active in mkt: kept
on under press, though remains a mdn: eff over 10/12f: acts on any trk: see 1031 & 765.   38
-- **NOBLE RISE** [4] (G Harwood) 3-9-0 P Waldron 11/4: 3-4: Nicely bckd on reapp: switcheed
dist & never nearer: btr for run: placed over 7f on sole start last term: eff over 10f and
should stay further: acts on gd/firm grnd. & on any trk: should be placed to win.   38
1444 **MARY SUNLEY** [12] 3-8-11 J Williams 33/1: -00: Some late prog: btr effort from this
half sister to winning juvenile Cerise Bouquet: eff over 10f on fast grnd & on a sharp course.   35
1415 **HOT MOMMA** [10] 3-8-11 M Roberts 25/1: -204330: Never dngr: see 89.   30
1530 **LOREEF** [1] 3-8-11 B Rouse 9/2: -0440: Wknd into 8th: much btr in 1002 (gd), gall trk.   00
1350 **Aah Jim Boy** [11] 9-0   -- **Sandy Bill** [8] 9-0   -- **Cleonair** [7] 9-0
1494 **Trojan Splash** [2] 9-0   1350 **Bella Carina** [9] 8-11
12 ran   5,nk,hd,shhd,3   (Jack Fisher)   M Ryan Newmarket

1691 JONES LANG WOOTTON STAKES 3YO   £959   6f   Good/Firm 36 -10 Slow

1511 **SIR ARNOLD** [4] (A Stewart) 3-9-0 M Roberts 4/1: -231: 3 b g Mummy's Pet - Bold Polly
(Bold Lad): Responded to press to lead inside dist in a 3yo stakes at Folkestone July 22:
sprint bred gelding who is eff over 6/7f: acts on gd & fast grnd & on any trk: consistent
and impr steadily.   46
*1516 **BROOKS DILEMMA** [5] (M Albina) 3-9-2 A Bond 4/6 FAV: -012: Well bckd: made most though
no extra close home: comfortably beat rem and is in gd form: see 1516.   44
*1277 **ABUTAMMAM** [8] (C Benstead) 3-9-5 B Rouse 8/1: -0013: Ev ch: stays 6f: see 1277.   38
861 **POINTED LADY** [6] (R Armstrong) 3-8-11 S Cauthen 16/1: -0004: Fair abs: nearest fin
and showed her first signs of form here: half sister to a couple of winners in the States:
stays 6f: acts on gd/firm grnd & on a sharpish course.   15
-- **CAREER MADNESS** [3] 3-9-0 M Giles 20/1: -0: No real threat on debut: should impr for
this experience though likely to need a longer trip.   16
-- **VILEE** [1] 3-9-0 P Hutchinson(3) 50/1: -0: Friendless in mkt on debut: half brother to
useful sprinter Tina's Gold.   12
1418 **Foundry Flyer** [9] 8-11   -- **Sirtaki Dancer** [7] 9-0
-- **Heavenly Stroller** [10] 9-0   -- **Condover Silk** [2] 8-11
10 ran   1½,3,5,½,1½,hd   (Julian James)   A Stewart Newmarket

1692 MARLAR INTERNATIONAL SELLING STAKES 2YO £690   5f   Good/Firm 36 -64 Slow

1557 **COLLEGE WIZARD** [4] (M Tompkins) 2-8-11 R Cochrane 4/5 FAV: 421: 2 b c Neltino -
Baby Flo (Porto Bello): Led all the way, gamely in a slowly run 2yo seller at Folkestone
July 22 (bought in 2,100 gns): speedily bred colt who is well suited by forcing tactics: acts
on fast grnd & is well suited by this sharpish courrse.   20
1496 **BIOTIN** [2] (P Haynes) 2-8-11(bl) J Williams 6/1: 000032: Ev ch inside dist though
hung right & out-battled close home: temperamental sort: acts on gd & fast grnd: see 1496.   15
533 **PRINCESS MICHICO** [8] (R Boss) 2-8-8 M Roberts 7/1: 03: Dropped in class after a
lengthy abs: well clear of rem: cheaply bought filly who will be suited by further: acts
on gd/firm.   10
1318 **CAWSTONS COMEDIAN** [3] (R Howe) 2-8-8 G Sexton 12/1: 034: No extra dist: see 1318.   00
1495 **RANT ON** [7] 2-8-11 P Waldron 16/1: 000: Never nearer after slow start: half brother
to recent winner Nanor: will be suited by 6f.   00
1537 **SAUCIER** [6] 2-8-8 J Bray(7) 8/1: 000400: Dwelt, nearest fin: see 1262.   00
1496 **Malachi Lad** [5] 8-11(BL)   -- **My Match** [1] 8-8
8 ran   2,nk,5,1½,2   (Mrs C A Dunnett)   M Tompkins Newmarket

1693 KABC GOLDEN JUBILEE NURSERY H'CAP 2YO   £1380   5f   Good/Firm 36 -19 Slow   [46]

1568 **LAST RECOVERY** [5] (M Ryan) 2-8-10 R Cochrane 4/1: 30321: 2 gr f Final Straw -
Mercy Cure (No Mercy): Gained a deserved win, leading close home in a nursery h'cap at
Folkestone July 22: cheaply bought filly whose dam was a winning sprinter: eff around 5f &
sure to be suited by 6f: acts on gd & fast grnd & on any trk.   38
1445 **ABSOLUTION** [4] (K Brassey) 2-9-7 S Whitworth 10/3: 32122: Nicely bckd, just failed

517

to make all but remains in fine form: see 1339.   48
678 MUKHABBR [1] (C Benstead) 2-7-10 T Williams 14/1: 0303: Long abs: not btn far:
clearly well suited by fast grnd: see 270.   18
*1576 NATIONS SONG [7] (R Stubbs) 2-8-9(7ex) J H Brown(5) 4/1: 0221214: Not qcknd dist: see 1576.27
1241 SEGOVIAN [3] 2-8-7 N Adams 33/1: 200000: Nearest fin: see 230.   17
1585 GREENS GALLERY [6] 2-8-9 C Rutter(5) 15/8 FAV: 01120: Disapp fav: much btr in 1585.   13
939 SANTO PRINCESS [2] 2-7-7(6oh) L Riggio(7) 33/1: 0040: Fin last after fair abs: see 939. 00
7 ran hd,1½,1½,3,2½   (T P Ramsden)   M Ryan Newmarket

1694 KEITH SHIPTON MEM. H'CAP STAKES (0-35)   £1035   2m   Good/Firm 36 -10 Slow   [24]

1265 PIP [9] (S Woodman) 6-8-13 R Cochrane 33/1: 0000/01: 6 b g Captain James - Where
Is It (Wolver Hollow): Gained surprise win, led over 6f out & held on gamely in a h'cap at
Folkestone July 22: first success on the Flat since '83 when successful at Windsor though has
since won over hurdles: eff over 10/12f, stays 2m well: acts on any going though is well
suited by a sound surface.   15
+1569 DIVA ENCORE [4] (R Armstrong) 3-9-13(6ex) S Cauthen 7/4 FAV: -000112: Just failed to
complete her hat trick though ran a fine race under top weight: stays 2m: see 1569.   42
1243 CHARTFIELD [2] (B Sanders) 6-8-5 B Crossley 11/2: 300033: Stayed on: see 121.   02
1348 ASTICOT [10] (C Horgan) 4-9-4 W R Swinburn -10/3: 0-03024: No extra dist: see 984.   14
1459 HOT BETTY [3] 6-8-1 N Adams 33/1: 0000400: Wknd 2f out: see 28.   00
1084 LA SERENATA [6] 3-9-0 J Adams(7) 20/1: 340-000: Made most to ½way: mdn who was trying
a   longer trip here: probably btr suited by 8/10f: acts on gd/firm & yld ground.   14
1208 NARCISSUS [5] 4-8-9 G Baxter 10/1: -0-3000: Led before ½way: wknd into 7th: see 522.   00
1326 Blushing Spy [11] 9-2(bl)   1349 Forewarn [7] 9-6
984 Janaab [8] 9-2   839 Sea Trouper [1] 8-0
11 ran   ½,2,nk,7,hd   (D J Flint)   S Woodman Chichester, Sussex

1695 SUNLEY ESTATES FILLIES STAKES 3YO 0-35   £1380   7f   Good/Firm 36 +06 Fast   [37]

1446 FRIVOLE [13] (P Cole) 3-8-11 T Quinn 4/1 FAV: 000-401: 3 br f Comedy Star - Swaynes
Princess (St Chad): Led after ½way and was driven out to win quite a fast run 3yo fillies
h'cap at Folkestone July 22: lightly raced last season: cheaply bought filly who is well
suited by 7/8f & should stay further: acts on gd & firm grnd & on any trk.   30
1560 SPECIAL GUEST [4] (D Morley) 3-8-9 R Cochrane 7/1: 00-0332: Switched dist, fin strongly
& comfortably beat rem: seems to need 1m: see 1034.   24
*1603 TAYLOR OF SOHAM [9] (D Leslie) 3-8-12 W R Swinburn 13/2: 0300413: Ev ch: stays 7f.   20
1560 DELTA ROSE [11] 3-8-8 B Rouse 50/1: -000004: Bl first time: kept on
late & showed some impr here: stays 7f: suited by fast grnd & a sharp course.   16
1316 BE SO BOLD [6] 3-8-6 C Rutter(5) 11/1: -00000: Fin strongly needs further?see 501.   14
-1499 SILVER FORM [14] 3-8-7 N Adams 13/2: -034020: Led after 2f: wknd: btr in 1499 (6f).   14
1257 KENOOZ [5] 3-9-7 R Carter(5) 15/2: 40-2040: Never nearer 7th: see 657.   00
1603 NANOR [12] 3-8-2(7ex) T Williams 10/1: 0000130: Wknd into 9th: best in 1574 (seller 6f). 00
1312 Out Of Harmony [15] 8-12   1571 New Edition [1] 9-3(bl)
1245 Prissy Miss [8] 8-12   1055 Shereeka [7] 9-6(BL)   1142 Heavenly Carol [3] 8-8(BL)
1391 Willbe Willbe [2] 8-2(BL)   1158 Angel Drummer [10] 8-1
15 ran   1½,3,shhd,hd,½   (G A Chagoury)   P Cole Lambourn, Berks

---

Official Going Given As FIRM

1696 EBF ALLOWAY MAIDEN FILLIES STAKES 2YO   £1087   5f   Good 42 -14 Slow

1407 UPSET [3] (J S Wilson) 2-8-11 D Mckeown 7/4: 231: 2 b f Uncle Pokey - Set To Work
(Workboy): Impr filly: led 1f out, comfortably, in a 4 horse 2yo fillies mdn at Ayr July 22:
half sister to 12f winner Tour De Force: acts well on gd grnd: eff 5f, stays 6f.   43
1427 THAT CERTAIN SMILE [1] (R Williams) 2-8-11 M Hills 8/11 FAV: 32: Failed to land the
odds, ev ch: see 1427.   37
1427 LINPAC NORTH MOOR [2] (C Elsey) 2-8-11(BL) J Lowe 20/1: 002403: Bl first time &
showed some impr: acts on gd & soft: eff 5f.   34
1297 TOOT TOOT [4] (Denys Smith) 2-8-11 L Charnock 10/1: 34: Al outpcd: see 1297.   16
4 ran   2,½,6   (Peter Orr)   J S Wilson Ayr

1697 STRATHCLYDE STAKES 2YO   £3700   6f   Good 42 +06 Fast

*1506 CHIME TIME [5] (C Tinkler) 2-8-11 M Birch 4/9 FAV: 11211: 2 b c Good Times -
Balnespick (Charlottown): Useful colt: made it 4 wins out of 5 races with another pillar-
to-post win in a fast run, quite valuable 2yo race at Ayr July 22: easy winner at York last
time: picked up first two on the trot at Redcar & Haydock : 2nd in the Chesham Stakes at
Royal Ascot: should stay further than 6f: acts on firm and good ground on a galloping tarck:
genuiee and consistent sort: sure to win more races.   66
*1370 SINCLAIR LADY [4] (G Oldroyd) 2-8-8 D Nicholls 13/2: 0000112: Came from behind. kept
on really well & clear of rem: fast imprv filly who should soon regain the winning
thread: stays 6f well: see 1370.   58

518

*1373 TEAM EFFORT [2] (Ron Thompson) 2-8-11 R P Elliott 7/1: 3011213: Ev ch: see 1373 (7f).   51
1506 PEATSWOOD SHOOTER [1] (M Brittain) 2-8-11 M Wigham 11/1: 111034: Prom most: best 278 48
*934 MR GRUMPY [3] 2-8-11 L Charnock 16/1: 2201110: Abs but not disgraced in this company.   46
5 ran   1¼,5,1½,½   (Red Lion Inn & Motel Ltd, York)   C Tinkler Malton, Yorks

1698 SOUTER JOHNIE H'CAP 3YO+ 0-50   £2490   1m   Good 42 -03 Slow   [41]

1482 SIR WILMORE [6] (E Weymes) 4-8-10 E Guest(3) 6/1: 00-0001: 4 b c Good Counsel -
Missy Moo Mow (Dark Star): Despite uninspiring form figures, was nicely bckd & led over
2f out in a h'cap at Ayr July 22: narrow winner of a h'cap at Yarmouth in '85: eff 6f,
suited by 1m: acts on firm & gd grnd.   31
1176 EMERALD EAGLE [3] (C Booth) 5-8-3 M Hills 12/1: 0003002: Made much, rallied final
1f: see 79.   21
*1176 WINDPIPE [2] (J Watts) 8-9-13 N Connorton 11/4 FAV: 40-0413: Fin well, too much to do?
          42
1482 HIGH PORT [7] (A Jones) 7-7-7(2oh) N Carlisle 5/1: 0002444: Never btr: see 943.   08
*1619 DUELLING [4] 5-8-8(5ex) G Carter(3) 7/2: 0001410: Quick reapp, kept on under press.   20
1202 SILLITOE [5] 4-8-5 M Beecroft 11/2: 0-00000: Waited with: see 956, 1202.   07
1047 SHELLMAN [8] 4-9-5 P Burke(7) 16/1: 0000000: Al rear: disapp since 55 (heavy).   00
7 ran   1¼,2,shhd,1½,6   (K Coxon)   E Weymes Leyburn, Yorks

1699 BUTE SELLING H'CAP 3&4YO 0-25   £895   1m 2f Good 42 +05 Fast   [14]

1201 CADENETTE [6] (M Camacho) 4-9-3 N Connorton 12/1: -004201: 4 b f Brigadier Gerard -
Tremellick (Mummy's Pet): Made much, hdd but rallied gamely to forge ahead final 100 yds in
a 3 & 4yo selling h'cap at Ayr July 22 (sold 2,900 gns): first success: seems btr suited by
10f than 1m: acts on firm & gd grnd: half sister to useful hurdler Lanhydrock.   11
1547 MAWDLYN GATE [4] (J S Wilson) 3-9-10 Gay Kelleway(3) 9/2: 0400132: Led over 2f out,
no extra final 100 yds: in gd form: stays 10f, possibly best over 1m: see 1134.   26
1201 DIX ETOILES [1] (J Fitzgerald) 3-8-6 M Hills 14/1: 4-10003: Kept on onepaced: best 305:
has been tried unsuccessfully in blinkers.   03
1659 SWIFT RIVER [8] (I Bell) 4-9-8(bl) J Lowe 5/1: 3033044: 3rd race in 5 days, no threat.   00
1369 FOREVER YOUNG [7] 3-8-7 P Burke(7) 6/1: -401420: Never nrr: best 993.   00
1439 COUNTESS CARLOTTI [5] 3-9-3 D Nicholls 100/30 FAV: 00-0240: Wknd under press: twice
disapp since 1134 (1m).   00
1158 BELHILL [2] 3-7-13 A Proud 12/1: 3000300: No threat in 7th: best 1053.   00
1267 COLONEL HALL [10] 3-8-1 M Fry 11/2: 0000030: Looked a difficult ride here: see 1267.   00
8 ran   2¼,3,4,3,2,2,hd   (B P Skirton)   M Camacho Malton, Yorks

1700 KIRKOSWALD MAIDEN STAKES 3YOUPWARDS   £959   1m 5f Good 42 +08 Fast

625 RUN HIGH [11] (G Harwood) 3-8-7 A Clark 11/4: -01: 3 b c Thatch - Fleet Noble
(Vaguely Noble): Despite a lengthy abs, went clear 3f out & was eased considerably final 1f
when a comfortable & clever winner of quite a fast run mdn at Ayr July 22: unrcd in '85:
related to a couple of middle dist. winners: suited by 13f, may well stay further: acts
on good grnd: likely to rate more highly.   34
980 MISS SHIRLEY [2] (J Dunlop) 3-8-4 J Lowe 11/8 FAV: 0-302: Ev ch, probably caught a
tartar here but btr 980 (10f).   21
1140 DENALTO [5] (Denys Smith) 3-8-7 L Charnock 14/1: 00-0033: Sn prom: see 959.   14
894 LAKISTE [9] (J Watts) 3-8-7 N Connorton 20/1: -044: Prom thro'out after abs: see 894.   10
1416 JIPIJAPA [3] 5-9-4(VIS) M Beecroft 50/1: 000-000: Waited with, no dngr: little form.   00
1178 WHIPCRACKAWAY [10] 3-8-7 M Tebbutt(7) 50/1: -00: Never btr: see 1178.   00
1386 GOODTIME HAL [4] 3-8-7(BL) M Hills 15/2: 0-43230: Bl first time & set up a clear
lead till wknd str: has twice failed to reproduce 996 & has proved expensive to follow.   00
779 Nitida [6] 8-4   1386 Mr Moss [7] 8-7   702 Sunlit [8] 8-4
-- Noel Arms [1] 9-7
11 ran   1¼,4,1,3,1,6   (K Abdulla)   G Harwood Pulborough, Sussex

1701 DUMFRIES H'CAP 3YO 0-35   £2414   7f   Good 42 -04 Slow   [35]

1398 SPORTING SOVEREIGN [14] (M Jarvis) 3-9-2 W Woods(3) 15/2: -042201: 3 ch c Sovereign
Edition - Atlanta Connection (Noholme II): Gained his first success, coming from behind to
lead dist comfortably in a 3yo h'cap at Ayr July 22: New Zealand bred colt who is eff at
6f but probably btr suited by 7f: acts on gd & fast grnd: may continue to impr.   31
1247 GOLD CHIP [3] (J Watts) 3-9-3 N Connorton 6/1: 13-4202: Waited with, fin well: gd
effort: possibly needs 1m now: see 451.   30
1224 PHILOSOPHICAL [4] (W Musson) 3-8-7 M Wigham 6/1: 41-0003: Fin strongly, almost took
2nd: best effort this term & may find a small h'cap soon over 1m: see 666.   19
1664 DOUBLE CHAI [11] (A Jarvis) 3-9-1(bl) D Nicholls 20/1: 0-00004: Quick reapp, dsptd
lead most: see 1664.   25
1362 BALNERINO [12] 3-8-5 L Charnock 10/1: 40-0040: Prom, ev ch: see 874.   13
1257 FLYING BIDDY [10] 3-9-0 M Hills 9/1: 000-300: Same place final 3f: see 997.   22
1664 QUALITAIR KING [7] 3-8-12 J Bleasdale 7/2 FAV: 0031220: Well bckd, led 4f out,
fdd quickly: btr 1664 (6f).   00

1288 CLOUDLESS SKY [8] 3-8-5 A Clark 10/1: 400-030: No dngr: btr 1288 (seller).   00
498 BAXTERGATE [9] 3-8-5 P Darcy 8/1: 0-00000: Long abs since btr 498.   00
1398 Aitchandoubleyou [1] 9-7   *666 Jeldaire [2] 8-10
1541 Country Carnival [5] 9-3   1200 Skybird [13] 8-11
871 Feather Girl [6] 7-7(2oh)
14 ran   1,nk,½,1,hd   (Elisha Holding)   M Jarvis Newmarket

PONTEFRACT   Tuesday July 22nd   Lefthand Undulating, Turning Track

Official Going Given As FIRM

1702 BRADLEY EBF STAKES 3YO UPWARDS   £2750   1m 2f Firm 12 -10 Slow

--   OZOPULMIN [2] (L Cumani) 3-8-4(2ow) Pat Eddery 7/4 FAV: -10-1: 3 ch c Tap On Wood -
Oceanie (Neptunus): Promising ex Italian colt: well bckd & made ev yd, comfortably in a
stakes event at Pontefract July 22: in '85 won a Gr.3 event at Milan: eff at 10f, may stay
further: acts on gd & firm grnd.   69
1378 NORTH VERDICT [3] (M Jarvis) 3-8-4(2ow) T Ives 10/3: 10-0032: Ev ch In str: gd
effort: difficult to place: see 555.   66
--   MY GENERATION [5] (W Hastings Bass) 3-8-2 R Lines(3) 7/1: 301-3: Al prom on seasonal
debut: gd effort: on final outing in '85 won at Newmarket: brother to the very useful filly
Que Sympatica: stays 10f: likes fast grnd   but acts on any trk.   59
1409 ANDARTIS [4] (Lord J Fitzgerald) 3-8-2 R Hills 2/1: -033404: No extra inside final 2f:
much btr 807 (stiff track).   49
1514 FRINGE OF HEAVEN [1] 4-9-6 G Duffield 50/1: 01-0000: Rank outsider: no form in 4
outings this season, but has been set stiff tasks: ex Italian filly: won 4 races last season. 25
1514 ASH CREEK [6] 7-9-9 K Radcliffe(7) 100/1: 200: Never in it: stiff task: see 1186.   20
6 ran   ½,2,5,12,2½   (G Borghi)   L Cumani Newmarket

1703 ALLSORTS SELLING H'CAP 3YO+ 0-25   £1110   1m   Firm 12 -30 Slow   [16]

1412 POLEMISTIS [11] (M James) 7-8-8(bl) Sharron James 20/1: -000001: 7 b g Hittite Glory-
Swing The Cat (Swing Easy): Driven out to lead inside final 1f in a selling h'cap at
Pontefract July 22 (no bid): last won in '84 at Carlisle: well suited by 1m on fast grnd.   03
1546 MR COFFEY [6] (S Norton) 3-9-0 Paul Eddery 14/1: 0-40002: Led 2f out: btr effort:
mdn: eff at 1m on fast grnd.   17
1546 REFORMED HABIT [10] (W Pearce) 4-9-2 M Hindley(3) 4/1 FAV: 0-30133: Kept on well
final 1f: see 1546, 1201.   07
1651 SKY MARINER [1] (T Kersey) 5-8-13 J Ward(7) 20/1: 30-0004: Hmpd entering str: best
effort this seasoon: last won in '83 at Redcar: stays 1m: best on fast grnd.   00
1081 MURILLO [9] 10-9-2(bl) J Carr(7) 9/1: 0320400: Never nearer: see 257.   00
1565 PORTO IRENE [13] 6-8-5 S P Griffiths 14/1: -0-0000: Prom, ev ch: no form this
season & remains a mdn.   00
1567 RUN FOR FRED [3] 4-8-11 S Webster 15/2: 0-00000: No show in 7th: see 963.   00
--   ROYAL DUTY [6] 8-9-10 N Rogers(7) 10/1: 10000-0: Made no show on seasonal debut:
in '85 won a seller at Edinburgh: previous season won another seller at Hamilton: best
over 1m on gd & fast grnd.   00
1546 TREE FELLA [14] 9-9-2 J Reid 9/1: 0000-00: Fdd str: see 1546.   00
1424 PRINGLE [15] 7-8-12 A Mackay 9/2: 0000/30: Much btr 1424 (sharp 7f).   00
1077 BALKAN [7] 6-8-10 G Duffield 6/1: 010-300: Fdd: abs: best 975.   00
1565 Peters Kiddie [5] 8-7(bl)   522 Jalome [4] 8-12
993 Johnny Frenchman [12] 8-9(1ow)   993 Monsanto Lad [2] 8-7
1567 Remainder Tip [8] 8-6(BL)
16 ran   1½,½,1½,4,2,hd   (R R Lynn)   M James Whitchurch, Salop

1704 KING RICHARD 111 H'CAP 3YO 0-50   £2460   5f   Firm 12 +13 Fast   [48]

1044 SEW HIGH [10] (B Mcmahon) 3-9-7 J Hillis(5) 10/1: 0010411: 3 b c Nicholas Bill -
Sew Nice (Tower Walk): Useful, impr colt: made ev yd, comfortably in a fast run h'cap at
Pontefract July 22: earlier ddhtd with Governor General in valuable William Hill Trophy h'cap
at York: also won a h'cap at Thirsk: in '85 won sellers at Ripon & Haydock: equally eff over
5/6f: acts on soft, likes fast grnd: best forcing the pace: game & genuinne.   53
1033 NORTHERN TRUST [2] (C Nelson) 3-9-4(BL) J Reid 10/1: -330002: Sn prom: kept on:
bl first time here: acts on any grnd: see 233.   43
1524 CATHERINES WELL [5] (M W Easterby) 3-9-6 K Hodgson 7/2: 1-03033: Always up there.   45
1257 MAYOR [6] (M Leach) 3-8-10 N Leach(6) 12/1: -340004: Lightly bckd: kept on under
press: lightly raced this season: best first time out in 6 .   29
1283 EXCLUSIVE CAT [7] 3-8-12 Pat Eddery 10/3 FAV: 12-3000: Ev ch: best 884, 760 (sharp trk) 30
1420 PACKAGE PERFECTION [3] 3-7-9 J Callaghan(7) 10/1: 0040020: Never nearer: see 891.   07
1406 WEBSTERS FEAST [1] 3-8-5 W Newnes 6/1: 0000020: Made no show: much btr 1406: see 1182.   00
1398 BOLD SEA ROVER [8] 3-8-9 M Birch 7/2: 3030130: Al trailing: best 1200 (6f).   00
1131 Bridge Of Gold [4] 8-2   1638 Ken Siddall [9] 7-9(VIS)
10 ran   2,shhd,2½,½,2½,½   (R Thornhill)   B Mcmahon Hopwas Hill, Staffs

PONTEFRACT   Tuesday July 22nd   -Cont'd

1705 SIMONSDAY MAIDEN STAKES 3YO   £1123   1m   Firm 12 -41 Slow

937 FORFLITE [8] (O Douieb) 3-9-0 R Machado 9/4: -31: 3 b c Forli - Desert Flight
(Misty Flight): Made ev yd for an impressive win in a slow run 3yo maiden at Pontefract
July 22: on only previous outing fin 3rd at Warwick: eff at 1m, should stay further: acts on
fast grnd & a turning trk.   40
--   PERSIAN DELIGHT [6] (G Huffer) 3-8-11 M Miller 8/1: 40-2: Al up there: fair seasonal
debut: ran only twice in '85: stays 1m: acts on gd & firm.   25
1309 ROI DE SOLEIL [5] (M Blanshard) 3-9-0 W Newnes 50/1: 00-0003: Rank outsider: showed
impr form here: stoutly bred gelding: should be suited by further than 1m: acts on fast grnd.   26
822 AMIR ALBADEIA [7] (P Walwyn) 3-9-0 Paul Eddery 15/8 FAV: 04-2204: Well bckd, despite
abs: wknd over 1f out: best early season in 316, 253.   24
334 ON WATER [2] 3-9-0 G Duffield 8/1: -000: No extra in str after long abs: no form
in 3 outings to date.   00
--   LA DUSE [3] 3-8-11 Pat Eddery 13/2: -0: Mkt drifter & no show: half sister to 3
winners, incl the smart Stetchworth & should impr for this run.   00
--   Star Addie [4] 9-0
7 ran   3,½,½,15,2   (Roy Gottlieb)   O Douieb Newmarket

1706 TURN TO YORKSHIRE H'CAP (0-35) 3YO   £1305   1m 4f Firm 12 -26 Slow   [35]

1160 BUTTERFLY KISS [1] (G Wragg) 3-9-7 Pat Eddery 2/1 FAV: -00331: 2 b f Beldale Flutter-
Ready And Willing (Reliance II): Gained a deserved success, making all, readily in a 5
runner 3yo h'cap at Pontefract July 22: half sister to several winners incl the very useful
Kufuma: stays 12f well: acts on firm & soft grnd & on any trk.   44
1404 DARK SIRONA [4] (D Arbuthnot) 3-9-0 J Reid 5/2: 000-022: Ev ch in str: should stay
further than 12f: see 1404, 1022.   25
1250 WATERDALE [3] (M W Easterby) 3-9-2 K Hodgson 7/2: 0-00333: Ran in snatches: see 1250.   26
1326 REGENCY SQUARE [2] (P Feilden) 3-8-2 G Dickie 5/1: 0-32044: Fdd in str: best 1089.   04
1089 SLAP BANG [5] 3-8-7(vis) P Cook 9/1: 00-4300: No threat: abs since 1089.   00
5 ran   5,½,4,20   (H H Morriss)   G Wragg Newmarket

1707 ST JOHN PRIORY STAKES 2YO   £2036   5f   Firm 12 -04 Slow

1307 ONGOING SITUATION [3] (D Morley) 2-9-4 Pat Eddery 9/4: 0131: 2 br c Daring March-
Storm Crest (Lord Gayle): Led inside final 1f comfortably in a 4 runner 2yo stakes at
Pontefract July 22: earlier won a 2yo mdn at Thirsk & seems a consistent sort: eff at
5/6f: acts on fast grnd & seems to like a turning track: impr.   54
*1266 FULL OF PRIDE [4] (M H Easterby) 2-9-1 M Birch 11/10 FAV: 12: Well bckd: ev ch: see 1266 46
1527 ECHOING [2] (J W Watts) 2-9-1 T Ives 11/4: 143: Led over 4f: see 766.   45
--   DANCE UP [1] (Ron Thompson) 2-8-11 R P Elliott 33/1: 4: Slowly away and no show
on debut: half brother to the speedy Music Machine: should do btr.   05
4 ran   1½,½,12   (Mrs William McAlpine)   D Morley Newmarket.

OSTEND   Saturday July 19th

Official Going Given As GOOD

1708 PRIX LILYSOL 2YO   £3450   5f   Good -

1453 REGENCY FILLE (R Williams) 2-8-7 R Street 1: 1222321: 2 gr f Tanfirion- Regency Girl
(Right Boy) Very useful, consistent filly: easy winner of a 2yo event at Ostend July 19:
first time out won a fillies mdn at Newmarket and has yet to fin out of the first 3: half
sister to sev winners: seems equally eff at 5/6f: acts on any ground: genuine.   60
--   LA BRETONNE (Belgium) 2-7-13 L Mcgarrity 1: 2: No chance with winner.   35
--   CASSE COU (Belgium) 2-8-3 P Masure 1: 3: -   37
5 ran   3,½   (C P Linney)   R Williams Newmarket

OSTEND   Sunday July 20th

Official Going Given As GOOD

1709 GRAND PRIX DOSTENDE HCAP 4YO+   £11042   1m 7f Good -

--   LOUKOUM (G Franco) 4-8-5 G Couderc 1: -2-1: 4 b c Jefferson - Hanoum (Karabas)
Comfortable 5l winner of a staying h'cap at Ostend July 20: suited by a stamina test: acts
on good ground.   52
1293 TRAPEZE ARTIST (N Vigors) 5-8-8 S Dawson 1: 0211002: Kept on well: gd eff: see 917.   48
--   SANTA DOMINGA (Belgium) 4-7-11 L Mcgarrity 1: 4-3: --   29
10 ran   5,6   (Ecurre Franco)   G Franco France

1710 GRAND PRIX CASINO DOSTENDE 3YO   £4141   1m   Good -

*1460 PALAESTRA (J Dunlop) 3-8-11 J Lowe 1: 2-00211: 3 b c Bellypha - Hippodrone (Drone)
Useful colt: comfortably landed the odds in a 3yo event at Ostend July 20: last time out
won a h'cap at Brighton: in '85 made ev yard in a mdn at Redcar: seems equally eff at 7/8f
may stay further: acts on gd and fast ground and on any track.   64

521

OSTEND   Sunday July 20th   -Cont'd

--   MARCOTTE (Belgium) 3-8-1 P Vandekeere 1: -2: Led 4f.   40
--   ANTHONY (Belgium) 3-8-7 S Van Pee 1: -3:   45
6 ran   3,nk,3   (Sheikh Mohammed)   J Dunlop Arundel, Sussex

---

OSTEND   Monday July 21st

Official Going Given As FIRM

1711 PRIX MAURICE COPPEE 2YO   £2760   7f   Firm -

*1480 MY BUDDY (R Williams) 2-9-2 T Ives 1: 0011: 2 ch c Mummy's Game - Shadow Play
(Busted) Impr colt: made ev yard, readily, in a 2yo event at Ostend July 21: last time out
was a similarly easy winner of a maiden auction at Catterick: cost 6,000 gns: stays 7f well:
likes good and fast ground and does well on an easy track when up with the pace.   46
--   NUAS (Belgium) 2-8-8 P Gilson 1: 2: Well clear 3rd.   30
--   YODA (Belgium) 2-8-3 P Thoumire 1: 3:   00
5 ran   2,12   (C P Linney)   R Williams Newmarket

1712 GRAND PRIX PRINCE ROSE 3YO+   £41408   1m 3f   Firm -

--   ANATAS (H Jentzsch) 6-9-8 G Bocskai 1: 10-1231: 6 b h Priamos - Antevka (Espresso)
Smart German horse: made almost all, gamely resisting sev chall to win val Grand Prix
Prince Rose at Ostend July 21: eff at 11f, stays 12f: acts on fast grd and seems a genuine sort   79
*1448 HIGHLAND CHIEFTAIN (J Dunlop) 3-8-5 W Carson 1: 114-012: Ran on well final 1f
and would have got up in another few strides: in fine form: see 1448.   74
1513 PHARDANTE (G Harwood) 4-9-8 A Clark 1: -010133: Btn 2hds: gd eff: see 1217.   77
--   SASEBO (G Franco) 5-8-9 G Couderc 1: 1313-24: Just btn in a very cl fin: fine effort.   63
*1526 CHAUMIERE 5-9-4 T Ives 1: 0000010: Cl.up 5th: another fine run: see 1526.   69
896   DAUN 5-9-10 P V Gilson 1: 30-0400: Won this race in '85.   71
1144 IROKO 4-9-4 W R Swinburn 1: 11-2430: Fdd final 1f: best 325.   00
10 ran   hd,hd,hd,1,1½   (Gestut Ittlingen)   H Jentzsch Germany

---

EVRY   Saturday July 19th   Lefthand Fair Track

Official Going Given As GOOD

1713 GROUP 3 PRIX CHLOE 3YO FILLIES   £18749   1m 1f   Good/Firm -

--   FABULOUS NOBLE (J De Roualle) 3-8-8 C Asmussen 1: -10-331: 3 b f Fabulous Dancer -
Pleasant Noble (Vaguely Noble) Smart French filly: came home a decisive 2½l winner of
Gr 3 Prix Chloe (Fillies) at Evry July 19: evidently very eff over 9f on gd ground.   70
467   KANMARY (E Lellouche) 3-9-2 A Lequeux 1: 00-0002:   70
--   SYRIENNE (P Biancone) 3-8-8 E Legrix 1: -1203:   57
288   CARNET SOLAIRE (F Boutin) 3-8-13 F Head 1: 1-02204:   61
1153 PRINCESS NAWAAL 3-8-11 G Guignard 1: 44-1100: Fin in ruck: best 925.   39
13 ran   2½,2½,hd   (A Ben Lassin)   J De Roualle France

MAISONS-LAFFITTE   Sunday July 20th   Left and Righthand Track

1714 GROUP 1 PRIX ROBERT PAPIN 2YO   £32144   5.5f   Good -

--   BALBONELLA (F Rohaut) 2-8-9 Y Saint Martin 1: 1111: 2 br f Gay Mecene - Bamiere
(Riverman) Smart filly: maintained her unbtn record with 4th successive win in Gr 1 Prix
Robert Papin at Maisons-Laffitte July 20: set a fast pace from the stalls, never in danger:
prev won at a minor trk and recently successful here and at Evry: very fast filly who is
eff over 5f and will stay at least 6f: acts on gd grd: looks likely to win more races.   76
1351 LIBERTINE (R Collet) 2-8-9 A Lequeux 1: 132: Unable to reach this flying winner
but ran a sound race: should be suited by 6f: see 1351.   67
--   FOTITIENG (F Boutin) 2-8-11 F Head 1: 13: Good effort.   68
*1351 EXPORT PRICE (P Bary) 2-8-11 G Moore 1:   3114: Btr in 1351.   62
1351 BRICKENAY 2-8-11 M Philliperon 1:   1220: See 1351.   61
1113 SHUTTLE COCK 2-8-11 M Depalmas 1: 220: Btr 1113 (heavy).   49
--   INDIAN FOREST 2-8-11 C Asmussen 1: 10: Widely fancied before hand, fin last and
must be better than this: first time out winner at Saint-Cloud over 6f.   00
7 ran   2½,nk,2½,nk,6,1½   (Maktoum Al-Maktoum)   F Rohaut France

Official Going Given As GOOD/FIRM

1715 GROUP 3 3YO AND UPWARDS   £33192   1m 2f   Good -

759 GRAUER WICHT [2] (H Steguweit) 5-8-10 B Selle 1: -202401: 5 gr h Windwurf – Graue Welle
(Neckar) Al prom and led under press over 1f out in a Gr 3 race at Frankfurt July 20: acts
well on fast ground: suited by 10f.   75
1355 LIRUNG [1] (H Jentzsch) 4-9-5 G Bocskai 1: 11-1232: Tried to make all, another good
effort: see 759.   80
-1230 NEBRIS [4] (R Akehurst) 5-9-3 P Cook 1: -111023: Ran a good race and is a much
improved performer this term: see 511, 1230.   74
1216 NEW MOON [3] (P Lautner) 5-8-10 L Mader 1: 2232034: --   62
1109 BOLD INDIAN [7] 5-8-12 S Cauthen 1: -02300: Twice below 945: best 433.   64
1594 NEW BRUCE [5] 4-9-1 A Badel 1: 0-02030: Btr 1594 (1m).   66
-1343 HELLO ERNANI [8] 3-8-2 T Ives 1: 2232120: Fin 7th: better 1343, 1045.   00
--   Lontano [6] 8-10   *1216 Aguarico [9] 9-3
9 ran   2,2,2½,shthd,nk,1,2½,1¾   (Stall Kleeblatt)   H Steguweit West Germany

1716 EBF WALLACE MAIDEN STAKES 2YO   £919   6f   Good/Firm 33 -134 Slow

741 WIND OF PEACE [3] (J Watts) 2-8-11 N Connorton 5/4 FAV: 01: 2 b f Taufan – Miel (Pall
Mall) Despite fair abs, led dist, ridden out in a very slowly run 2yo stks at Hamilton July
23: half sister to the very useful stayer Prince of Peace and will be well suited by further
than 6f: acts on fast grd and a stiff track.   34
1440 SHADIYAMA [2] (M Stoute) 2-8-11 K Bradshaw(5) 11/8: 02: Led 4f: seems one of the
stable's lesser lights: maybe btr suited by further than 6f: see 1440.   26
1625 MR CRICKET [1] (Ron Thompson) 2-9-0 R P Elliott 4/1: 03: Not much room inside final 2f 20
3 ran   2½,3   (Sheikh Mohammed)   J Watts Richmond, Yorks.

1717 LOWTHER NURSERY HANDICAP 2YO   £1337   5f   Good/Firm 33 +08 Fast   [48]

1527 SPITTIN MICK [7] (M H Easterby) 2-8-6 K Hodgson 10/11 FAV: 12131: 2 b g The Brianstan
– La Fille (Crooner) Led nearing final 1f, ridden out in a nursery h'cap at Hamilton July
23: consistent gelding, earlier winning sellers at Thirsk and Warwick: very eff at 5f:
acts on fast and yldg ground and on any track.   35
1421 DANADN [2] (Ron Thompson) 2-8-8 R P Elliott 14/1: 4040332: Fin well and just btn:
gd effort: acts on any track: may be suited by another furlong: should find a nursery.   36
1527 BRUTUS [3] (J Wilson) 2-9-1 G Duffield 10/1: 0103: Made much: see 826 (sharp trk).   38
1478 RUN TO WORK [1] (G Moore) 2-7-7 S Wood(7) 11/2: 422334: Al there: needs 6f? See 957   14
1561 TAKE EFFECT [9] 2-8-2 M Wigham 25/1: 3300000: Slow start, never nearer: btr early
season: see 47, 20.   22
1528 AVINASESH [6] 2-8-2 M Wood 7/1: 02340: Fdd final 2f: much btr 1528 (6f).   12
1618 Tap The Baton [5] 9-2   1612 Keen Edge [8] 9-7(BL)   1528 Maybemusic [4] 8-6
9 ran   nk,1½,¾,½,4   (Sandmoor Textiles Co Ltd)   M H Easterby Malton, Yorks.

1718 HAMILTON SPRINT H'CAP (0-35)   £1648   5f   Good/Firm 33 +05 Fast   [28]

1584 MISTER MARCH [4] (R Hutchinson) 3-8-9(10ex) P Hutchinson(3) 3/1 JT FAV: 0000141: 3 b c
Marching On – Jetwitch (Lear Jet) Made almost all, defying a 10lbs penalty in a h'cap at
Hamilton July 23: earlier won a similar event at Bath: well suited by a stiff 5f: stays 5.5f:
likes fast ground.   26
1542 WESBREE BAY [3] (N Bycroft) 4-7-12 L Charnock 10/1: -002202: Prom, ev ch: gd effort.   06
1616 TRADESMAN [1] (J Haldane) 6-8-3(bl)(7ex) D Mckeown 10/1: 0000103: Ev ch over 1f
out after early trouble in running: see 1423.   05
1543 PARADE GIRL [2] (J Kettlewell) 4-8-11 N Connorton 20/1: 1000404: Sn prom: see 56 (hvy) 08
1543 LOCH FORM [7] 3-9-7 G Duffield 3/1 JT FAV: 1200320: No extra final 1f: btr 1543
(sharp track) see 255.   24
1638 CARPENTERS BOY [6] 8-9-0(bl) D Leadbitter(5) 6/1: 00-0000: Fdd final 1f: little
form this term: in '85 won a h'cap over this C/D: in '84 won 4 times: equally eff at 5/6f:
likes fast ground and Hamilton.   05
*1682 RUSSIAN WINTER [8] 11-7-10(vis)(10ex) M Fry 4/1: 0000310: Too soon after 1682?   00
1610 ACKAS BOY [5] 4-7-13 J Lowe 20/1: -00000: Early speed.   00
8 ran   ¾,2,1½,shthd,2½   (T J Blake)   R Hutchinson Epsom, Surrey

1719 BONNINGTON SELLING STAKES   £847   1m 1f   Good/Firm 33 -06 Slow

1482 BUNDLING BED [3] (R Woodhouse) 4-8-13 A Bond 5/1: 0204001: 4 ch f Welsh Pageant –
our Mother (Bold Lad (Ire)) Led over 1f out, ridden out in a seller at Hamilton July 23
(no bid): in '84 won at Nottingham: eff over 9/10f, does stay 2m: acts well on gd and firm   14
1303 CAPRICORN BLUE [6] (J Fitzgerald) 3-8-0(vis) M Fry 1/1 FAV: 0S-0242: Switched
approaching final 1f: nearly got up: possibly unlucky but should really have won this.   12
1546 NORWHISTLE [2] (T Craig) 6-8-11 E Guest(3) 16/1: -000003: Made most: little form on
the Flat.   08

1613 MY MYRA [1] (P Mitchell) 4-8-8 G Carter(3) 9/4: 30-0004: Nicely bckd, ev ch: winner
over hurdles but little form on Flat.   04
1195 CLUEDO [4] 5-8-8(bl) Sharron James 12/1: -004000: Never nearer: see 889.   00
1543 GO SPECTRUM [5] 6-8-11 J Quinn(5) 33/1: 0-00000: Al rear.   00
6 ran   hd,1½,hd,12,2   (G A Farndon Eng Co Ltd)   R Woodhouse Welburn, Yorks.

1720 COREHOUSE HANDICAP STAKES (0-35) 3YO+   £1242   1m   Good/Firm 33 -06 Slow   [24]

1500 HELLO GYPSY [3] (C Tinkler) 5-9-7 W Goodwin(7) 11/4 FAV: 0000-21: 5 b g Tumble Wind
- Shirotae (Florescence) Led well over 1f out, comfortably, in a h'cap at Hamilton July 23:
in '85 won an amateur riders event at Warwick: very eff at 1m: acts on gd and fast ground
and on any trk tho' likes a sharpish one.   24
1698 DUELLING [4] (P Mitchell) 5-10-0(vis)(8ex) G Carter(3) 3/1: 0014102: Chance final
1f: in fine form: see 1619.   30
1565 SMART MART [1] (M Camacho) 7-8-4(bl) J Lowe 7/2: 00-3003: Ev ch: see 1374.   02
1565 BOY SANDFORD [5] (W Mackie) 7-8-8 N Carlisle 7/2: 0304004: Fdd nearing final 1f:
best 789.   01
1500 ABJAD [2] 5-8-11 A Bond 7/1: 00-1000: Led over 6f: best first time out 788 (hvy).   00
5 ran   ½,1½,2½,6   (Mrs C M Tinkler)   C Tinkler Malton, Yorks

1721 ROSS MAIDEN STAKES 3YO   £906   1m 4f Good/Firm 33 -09 Slow

1600 RENO RALPH [1] (G Huffer) 3-9-0 G Carter(3) 5/4 JT FAV: -0041: 3 b c Gummo - Legere
(Lennox) Impr colt: kept on well final 1f to lead near fin in a 4 runner 3yo mdn at Hamilton
July 23: American bred colt who stays 12f well: acts on fast ground and a stiff track.   40
1535 FORT LINO [2] (I Balding) 3-9-0 G Duffield 5/4 JT FAV: 4-222: Made almost all and
just btn: see 1535, 832.   39
1544 BANTEL BUSHY [4] (J Berry) 3-9-0(BL) J Carroll(7) 7/1: 2222233: No extra final 2f:
bl first time: see 631.   19
1661 HELSANON [3] (R Whitaker) 3-8-11 D Mckeown 16/1: 0-00044: Fdd: see 1078.   14
4 ran   hd,12,½   (J A Duffel)   G Huffer Newmarket

Official Going Given As FIRM ROUND COURSE - STRAIGHT COURSE GOOD/FIRM

1722 E.B.F. COTMAN MAIDEN FILLIES STAKES 2YO   £1267   7f   Firm 04 -01 Slow

1464 MONTFORT [6] (W Jarvis) 2-8-11 R Cochrane 7/1: 01: 2 b f Red Sunset - Rubina Park
(Ashmore) Promising filly: nicely bckd and led 1½f out, readily drawing clear in a 2yo fillies
mdn at Yarmouth July 23: cost IR 27,000 as a yearling: eff at 7f, shd stay 1m: acts on fast
ground and should win more races.   58
1433 SO STYLISH [7] (G P Gordon) 2-8-11 P Robinson 7/1: 32: No chance with winner, tho'
is on the upgrade: should have no trouble finding a race: see 1433.   46
1382 LISIANTHUS [8] (J Winter) 2-8-11 T Ives 9/1: 033: Made most: see 1382.   44
--   QUEEN MIDAS [1] (H Cecil) 2-8-11 S Cauthen 4/9 FAV: 4: Well bckd debutant: ev ch:
obviously well regarded and will improve: half sister to 4 winners: bred to stay middle
distances: acts on fast ground.   44
1576 LIGHTNING LASER [2] (J Winter) 2-8-11 Gay Kelleway(3) 25/1: 003330: Sn prom: see 1483 (seller)   35
1555 FIRWOOD [4] 2-8-11 G Sexton 50/1: 00: There 5f: not disgraced: see 1555.   31
--   Miss Zola [5] 8-11   --   Atyab [3] 8-11
8 ran   4,½,shthd,4,1½   (G E Sangster)   W Jarvis Newmarket

1723 DAWSON TURNER SELLING STAKES 2YO   £643   5f   Firm 04 -36 Slow

*1478 PETERS BLUE [6] (J Fitzgerald) 2-8-11 M Roberts 4/5 FAV: 0411: 2 gr g Riki Lash -
Lady Doubloon (Pieces of Eight) Made ev yard, comfortably, in a slow run 2yo seller at
Yarmouth July 23 (bought in 3,600 gns): last time out again made all in a similar event at
Catterick: seems well suited by forcing tactics over a sharp/easy 5f: likes fast ground.   25
1318 THE CHIPPENHAM MAN [5] (M Tompkins) 2-8-11 R Cochrane 9/4: 022: Kept on final 1f.   15
1599 GREENSWARD BOY [3] (K Ivory) 2-8-11 W Woods(3) 15/2: 003: Chance 2f out: btr effort.   14
1475 RAINTREE COUNTY [1] (P Felgate) 2-8-11(BL) A Mackay 6/1: 00004: Bl first time:
slow start, no show: best 320 (soft).   00
1496 SCARNING SHADYLADY [2] 2-8-8 G Baxter 33/1: 0000: Prom 3f: no form to date.   00
1190 KAMSTAR [4] 2-8-8 Gay Kelleway(3) 20/1: 00000: Al last: only moderate.   00
6 ran   3,½,6,2½,1   (Peter Rawson)   J Fitzgerald Norton, Yorks.

1724 ROYAL WEDDING H'CAP STAKES (0-35)   £2281   1m   2f Firm 04 -18 Slow   [30]

1553 SIMONS FANTASY [3] (R Armstrong) 3-8-4 G Baxter 2/1: -044341: 3 ch c Stanford -
Loch'leven (Le Levenstell) Gained a deserved success, led inside final 1f in a h'cap at
Yarmouth July 23: half brother to 2 winners: acts on gd and fast ground and an easy track.   27
+1327 NORDICA [5] (A Stewart) 3-9-7 M Roberts 1/1 FAV: -0012: Led 2f out: 5l clear 3rd,
but better 1327 (1m).   42
751 RIVERS NEPHEW [4] (O Douieb) 3-8-2 R Hills 12/1: -0003: Abs: led 1m: half brother
to sev winners, but little form himself.   12
874 TOWER FAME [6] (E Eldin) 3-8-2 M L Thomas 11/1: 4-00004: Abs: ev ch str: lightly
raced this term: see 90.   10
1055 FRAME OF POWER [1] 3-7-12 A Mackay 12/1: 0-000: Chance 2f out: best 868 (yldg).   06
1374 DALLAS SMITH [2] 5-7-12(vis) J Carter(4) 33/1: -000000: There 5f: see 975.   00
6 ran   1,5,1,hd,20   (John Bray)   R Armstrong Newmarket

1725 APPLEGATE FILLIES H'CAP STAKES (0-50)   £2628   1m   Firm 04 +04 Fast   [41]

923 EASTERN HOUSE [2] (H Cecil) 3-9-6 S Cauthen 21/20 FAV: 022-021: 3 ch f Habitat -
Kashmir Lass (Kashmir II) Despite a fair abs, led over 1f out, ridden out in a 4 runner
fillies h'cap at Yarmouth July 23: first success after sev near misses: eff at 7f, stays 1m:
acts on firm and yldg ground and an easy track.   43
-- RARE SOUND [1] (P Kelleway) 3-9-0 Gay Kelleway(3) 9/2: 1-2: Kept on well final 1f:
encouraging seasonal debut: won sole outing in '85, maiden auction on this trk: half sister
to 3 winners including Valley Mills and Amigo Sucio: stays 1m: acts on gd and firm ground
and may win soon.   36
1515 NEW EVIDENCE [4] (E Eldin) 3-8-5 A Mackay 11/4: -000223: Chance inside final 2f:
consistent: see 1515.   25
1575 QUEEN OF BATTLE [3] (M Ryan) 3-9-7 R Cochrane 9/2: -002234: Made most: best over
this C/D in 1327.   37
4 ran   nk,¾,1½   (Louis Freedman)   H Cecil Newmarket

1726 CROME MAIDEN STAKES 3YO   £1193   1m 6f Firm 04 -06 Slow

231 FOXY PRINCE [6] (L Cumani) 3-9-0 R Guest 2/1 FAV: -01: 3 b c Nijinsky - Equanimity
(Sir Ivor) Despite long abs, led 2½f out, comfortably, in a 3yo mdn at Yarmouth July 23:
dam was a smart sort: stays 14f well: acts on fast grd and should continue to improve.   42
1670 BENAROSA [3] (P Kelleway) 3-8-11 Gay Kelleway(3) 4/1: 4000422: Ev ch final 2f:
10l clear 3rd, but lacks foot: see 1670, best 372.   37
1559 TEMPEST TOSSED [4] (R Armstrong) 3-8-11 S Cauthen 7/2: 03-0403: Led over 11f:
may stay 14f: see 955.   27
1530 HANKLEY DOWN [5] (E Eldin) 3-9-0 A Mackay 8/1: -0004: No extra final 2f: disapp
since fair debut in 714 (12f).   24
1639 SHAKEEB [1] 3-9-0 G Baxter 14/1: 00-0000: Never nearer: lightly raced and no form
to date.   17
1278 HIGH BORN BIDDER [2] 3-8-11 T Ives 7/2: -00: Active in mkt, there 10f: non-stayer?
Cost $450,000 as a yearling.   14
6 ran   1,10,5,5,hd   (Princess Lucy Ruspoli)   L Cumani Newmarket

1727 VINCENT HANDICAP STAKES (0-35)   £1749   7f   Firm 04 +07 Fast   [31]

1640 MR JAY ZEE [7] (N Callaghan) 4-9-10 R Cochrane 7/4 FAV: 1313021: 4 b c Sandy Creek -
Flying Spear (Breakspear) Not the best of runs, but fin well to lead cl home in quite fast
run h'cap at Yarmouth July 23: in tremendous form lately: earlier winning at Ripon and
Catterick: useful juv, winning at Ayr: eff at 6f, well suited by 7f: loves fast ground:
acts on any track.   39
1264 EUCHARIS [4] (A Hide) 4-7-11(bl) A Mackay 10/1: 0-00002: Led final 1f: caught
close home: best effort this season: should find a small h'cap: eff over 7f on fast ground
with blinkers.   10
1521 HOPEFUL KATIE [6] (D Leslie) 4-8-7 Gay Kelleway(3) 11/2: 4020303: Made much: see 65.   17
1324 DEBACH REVENGE [12] (M Tompkins) 4-7-9 R Morse(5) 33/1: -00004: Led ½ way: little
form prev: eff on fast ground.   02
1482 DORAME [8] 5-8-3 J Scally(4) 25/1: 0-00400: Nearest fin: see 1066.   06
*1324 CHICAGO BID [5] 5-9-7(bl) S Cauthen 4/1: -020010: Came all too late: btr 1324 (C/D)   19
1515 LUNAR SHAMAL GAL [9] 3-8-9 R Hills 8/1: 01-0000: No threat in 7th: see 447.   00
*1609 SWEET ANDY [2] 7-7-7(3oh) G Bardwell(7) 8/1: 0040310: Fdd: btr 1609 (sharper trk)   00
1455 EASY DAY [1] 4-9-12 A Hutchings 8/1: 4101000: Prom, fdd: best 956 (made all).   00
1324 IDEOLIGIA [10] 4-7-8(bl)(1ow)(2oh) M L Thomas 8/1: -000440: Last to fin: btr 1324 (C/D)   00
1290 Miss Maina [3] 9-1   00
11 ran   hd,1,1,1½,2,1½,½   (N A Callaghan)   N Callaghan Newmarket

Official Going Given As FIRM (HEAVY THUNDER STORMS THROUGHOUT MEETING)

1728 EBF SUPERSLOANE MAIDEN 2YO   £1718   5f   Good 46 +01 Fast

1143 COPPER RED [3] (P Makin) 2-9-0 T Quinn 1/1 FAV: 3231: 2 ch c Song - Najd (St Chad)
Gained a deserved success making most and holding on gamely for a ddht in a 2yo mdn at
Sandown July 23: quite a bargain buy at 9,400 gns: very eff over 5f and acts well on a
stiff track: sprint bred and unlikely to stay beyond 6f.   53
1512 LAST DANCE [4] (R Hannon) 2-9-0 Pat Eddery 15/8: 04231: 2 b c Last Fandango -
Connaught Trump (Connaught) Gamely responded to press to force a ddht on the line in a close
fin to a 2yo mdn at Sandown July 23: ran poorly over 6f last time tho' should stay the trip:
dam a middle distance winner in Ireland: acts well on firm grd and has twice performed well
at Sandown, seems to like a stiff track.   53
--   ATTEMPTING [2] (B Hills) 2-8-11 B Thomson 7/1: 3: Excellent debutant: just btn in a
desperate fin: dam a winning miler and has produced a couple of successful offspring prev:
sure to be suited by 6f+: acts well on firm ground, on a stiff track: should find a mdn soon.   49
457 OUR FREDDIE [6] (A Ingham) 2-9-0 R Curant 14/1: 444: Prom, wknd dist: abs since 457.   27
1583 MOTOR BROKER [1] 2-9-0 W Newnes 25/1: 000: Early pace: see 662.   26
1522 VICTORY BALLARD [5] 2-9-0 L Jones(5) 33/1: 000: No danger: first foal of a maiden:
sprint bred.   23
1495 Design Wise [7] 9-0(BL)   848 Minobee [8] 8-11
1238 Betta Win [9] 8-11
9 ran   ddht,nk,8,½,½   (R P Marchant)   P Makin Ogbourne Maisey, Wilts.
                                (John Norman)   R Hannon, East Everleigh, Wilts

1729 HARPERS AND QUEENS HCAP 0-50 3YO+   £3167   1m   Good 46 +01 Fast   [50]

1460 JOYFUL DANCER [4] (W Brooks) 6-8-9 T Quinn 11/2: 00-0021: 6 ch h Gay Fandango - Sheer
Joy (Major Portion) Made ev yard gamely in a h'cap at Sandown July 23: formerly trained by
P Cole and first time out last season was 2nd in the Lincoln: in '84 won at Sandown and
Newbury: acts on soft but is well suited by good or firm grd: best over 1m forcing the pace.   41
1079 FREE ON BOARD [5] (C Horgan) 4-8-1(6ow) T Williams 8/1: 0-00202: Prom, kept on well
and this was improved form: see 709: should win a small h'cap if reproducing this form.   31
+1486 AVENTINO [2] (J Sutcliffe) 3-8-6(bl)(6ex) M Hills 1/3 FAV: 0111113: Seemed entirely
unsuited by the decision not to use the stalls due to the thunderstorm in progress at start
of the race, took a long time to get going, fin really strongly but all too late: ignore
this effort: see 1486.   40
1389 COME ON THE BLUES [3] (C Brittain) 7-9-7 C Rutter(5) 15/2: 0-00004: Prom much:
has cut no ice this term but in '85 won twice in mid season at Sandown and the Royal Hunt
Cup: very eff over 1m tho' seems to act on any going and on any track: best out in front.   43
1525 NORTHERN CHIMES [1] 4-9-13 Pat Eddery 20/1: 0-20000: No threat: disapp since 817 (6f)   34
5 ran   1,4,shthd,10   (Vistaplan Ltd)   W Brooks Lambourn, Berks.

1730 SILKS OF ST JAMES HCAP 3YO+ 0-50   £3210   5f   Good 46 +15 Fast   [46]

1283 THE MECHANIC [11] (J Sutcliffe) 3-7-10(BL) C Rutter(5) 9/2 FAV: -021231: 3 b c
Lochnager - Lardana (Burglar) Bl first time and ran on well under press to lead cl home in
quite a fast run h'cap at Sandown July 23: earlier won at Beverley and has been running very
consistently: best form over 5f on a stiff trk on firm or gd ground: best visor or blinkers.   31
1521 LONELY STREET [4] (P Arthur) 5-8-4 J Reid 11/2: -202032: Led dist, caught death:
fine effort and should find a race soon: see 855.   32
1344 SILBANDO [12] (D Elsworth) 4-7-7(bl)(6oh) P Mcentee(7) 33/1: 00-0003: Outsider who
led briefly inside final 2f and ran surprisingly well: speedily bred gelding who has yet
to win a race but on this evidence can win a small event: seems best in blinkers.   17
*1461 FERRYMAN [5] (D Elsworth) 10-9-11(5ex) Pat Eddery 13/2: 0001214: Another fine effort
and is in grand form: see 1461 (6f).   47
1385 LAURIE LORMAN [6] 4-9-10 A Tucker(7) 12/1: -010000: Best effort since 660.   44
1521 ST TERRAMAR [10] 11-7-7(bl)(14oh) G Dickie 33/1: -000200: Stiff task, not totally
disgraced: see 1213.   12
1268 DAVILL [8] 4-8-9 B Rouse 5/1: 2-00000: Well bckd, fell out of the stalls, not recover : see 76. 00
1627 FARMER JOCK [7] 4-8-1(bl)(5ex) S Whitworth 13/2: 0302100: Early pace: fin 9th: best 1542 00
1380 SPACEMAKER BOY [2] 6-9-5 N Howe 10/1: 0032F00: Led to ½ way: best 1037 (C/D).   00
660 Derry River [3] 8-10   1516 Sancilia 0 7-13   233 Stanbo [9] 7-13
12 ran   nk,1½,¾,½,nk   (Christopher Dodson)   J Sutcliffe Epsom, Surrey

1731 ROYAL WEDDING STAKES 2YO   £4272   7f   Good 46 -10 Slow

1658 LAURIES WARRIOR [1] (R Boss) 2-9-1 Pat Eddery 5/1: 402121: 2 ch c Viking - Romany
Pageant (Welsh Pageant) Useful, impr colt: led dist and kept on strongly in quite a val
minor 2yo event at Sandown July 23: earlier won a mdn auction event at Doncaster: very well
suited by 7f: sure to stay at least 1m: acts on firm and gd going and likes a gall track.   57

1452 SANTELLA SAM [9] (M Ryan) 2-8-11 P Robinson 7/4 FAV: 232: Prom, ev ch: see 1452.   49
1392 STRING SECTION [8] (G Lewis) 2-8-11 P Waldron 33/1: 03: Made much: on the upgrade.   47
1232 FOURTH LAD [10] (R Hannon) 2-8-11 A Mcglone 8/1: 004: No threat: see 1232.   37
*1313 LUCIANAGA [6] 2-9-1 Paul Eddery 5/1: 22010: Mkt drifter, much btr 1313 (6f sharp trk)   31
1239 PROSILIENT [3] 2-8-11 A Clark 7/2: 00: Btr 1239.   21
 664 Makin Mischief [5] 8-11   1373 Pharaoh Blue [4] 8-11
 -- Doubly Great [7] 8-11   -- Biscuit Trader [2] 8-11
10 ran, 1½,¾,4,4,2½   (L C James)   R Boss Newmarket

1732 HOORAY HENRY CLAIMING STKS 3YO   £2914   1m 6f   Good 46 +02 Fast

1386 MELENDEZ [5] (G Harwood) 3-8-11 A Clark 4/1: -0021: 3 ch g Le Fabuleux - Touch of
Midas (Majestic Prince) Has made steady improvement and gained a deserved success, responding
gamely to lead inside final 1f in a 3yo claimer at Sandown July 23: first success: eff
over 14f, should stay 2m: acts on firm and gd ground and has twice run well at Sandown -
seems suited by a stiff track: may win a small h'cap.   42
1530 THREE TIMES A LADY [2] (P Kelleway) 3-8-8 Pat Eddery 11/8 FAV: 0002232: Heavily
bckd, led dist, no extra near fin: twice below 1410 (2m) and is proving expensive to follow.   36
1061 RIBOVINO [3] (N Vigors) 3-7-10 S Dawson 20/1: -03: Made most: on the upgrade and
is clearly suited by a good test of stamina, should stay 2m: acts well on gd ground:
brother to 4 winners including useful stayer/hurdler King's College Boy: should soon be
placed successfully.   20
1502 INDIAN ORATOR [1] (B Hills) 3-8-11 B Thomson 4/1: 22-3134: Ev ch: see 1135.   35
1410 FRENCH FLUTTER [4] 3-8-11 M Hills 4/1: 0-04130: Well below his best here: best 1160.   25
5 ran   2,2,hd,10   (Anthony Speelman)   G Harwood Pulborough, Sussex.

1733 OKAY YAH STAKES HCAP 3YO 0-35   £2324   1m 3f   Good 46 -09 Slow   [34]

1085 TEBITTO [5] (N Vigors) 3-9-7 P Cook 9/2: 00-0101: 3 b g Derrylin - Over Beyond
(Bold Lad) Never hdd, stayed on strongly for a 5l success in a 3yo h'cap at Sandown July 23:
earlier gained another C/D success and in fact these are his only victories yet: very eff
over 11f with forcing tactics on gd ground: seems to love Sandown.   38
1497 UP TO UNCLE [3] (R Hannon) 3-9-7 A Mcglone 3/1: 0022132: Never closer: running
consistently: see 1314.   31
1402 SHIRZAD [9] (J Tree) 3-9-0 Pat Eddery 2/1 FAV: 0-00433: Prom, ev ch: looked a
plodder: see 1023.   17
1130 DARK HERITAGE [11] (C Nelson) 3-9-7 J Reid 12/1: 00-004: A mdn who could only stay
on at the one pace here: lightly raced.   22
 738 THE WOODEN HUT [2] 3-8-1 S Whitworth 14/1: -120000: Abs: best 29 (soft).   01
1497 CAPULET [7] 3-9-3 M Hills 16/1: 00-000: Never in it: lightly raced mdn with no
worthwhile form.   15
1569 STAR SHINER [1] 3-8-10(BL) P Waldron 10/1: 00-0000: Fin last: see 1569.   00
1246 Pause For Applause [6] 9-0   1402 Noble Hill [4] 9-6
 832 Barleybree [10] 8-6
10 ran   5,5,1½,¾,1½   (Lady d'Avigdor-Goldsmid)   N Vigors Upper Lambourn, Berks.

Official Going Given As FIRM FOR FIRST 2 RACES, REMAINDER GOOD/FIRM.

1734 LEEDS SELLING HANDICAP (0-25) 3YO   £1086   5f   Good/Firm 39 -03 Slow   [22]

1603 PERCIPIO [16] (K Ivory) 3-9-2(vis) A Shoults(5) 7/2: 0G30421: 3 b g Alias Smith -
Frankilyn (Frankincense) Gained a deserved win after sev recent placings, leading on the post
in a selling h'cap at Catterick July 23 (no bid): does well with forcing tactics, made all
in this grade at Ripon last term: eff over 5/6f: suited by gd or faster ground: acts any trk.   18
1627 THE STRAY BULLETT [11] (B Mcmahon) 3-9-0(bl) S Perks 2/1 FAV: 2000302: Well bckd:
led below dist, caught final stride: should go one btr if kept in this grade: see 529.   16
1476 JACQUI JOY [4] (K Ivory) 3-9-4 G Morgan 12/1: 030-003: Dropped in class: made most,
not btn far: placed in similar company last season: eff over 5f on gd and fast ground.   18
1334 EASTERN OASIS [13] (E Alston) 3-8-9 A Proud 12/1: 003-004: Al up there: successful
as a juv at Hamilton on similar ground and his best form is over 5f on a sound surface.   05
1334 MURRYL CANNON [9] 3-8-5 G Craggs(7) 8/1: -000000: Never nearer after slow start.   00
1543 SPRING GARDEN [2] 3-8-6(bl) K Hodgson 25/1: 0000000: Ran on same pace: yet to show
any worthwhile form in this grade: suited by sprint distances: acts on gd/firm ground.   00
 426 PLANTER [5] 3-9-4(bl) M Beecroft 9/1: 1024000: Abs: never nearerr 7th: see 51.   00
1398 WINDING PATH [15] 3-9-2 A Whitehall(7) 8/1: -000400: Dwelt and no threat: see 489.   00
1360 MISS TAUFAN [7] 3-8-3 J Lowe 10/1: 0-04000: Early speed: see 825.   00
1420 Petencore [10] 9-4   729 Nipper Smith [8] 8-13   1617 Musical Aid [14] 9-2
1562 Selorcele [12] 9-7(bl)   545 Valdarno [6] 8-8
1603 Fur Baby [1] 8-6   1142 Classy Scouse [3] 8-7
16 ran   shthd,½,1½,nk,hd,3   (W E Patterson)   K Ivory Radlett, Herts.

1735 HUDDERSFIELD STAKES 2YO   £1343   7f   Good/Firm 39 -01 Slow

1376 TOLL BAR [3] (S Hall) 2-8-11 K Hodgson 25/1: 01: 2 b g Windjammer - Our Mother
(Bold Lad (Ire)) Impr juv: was a surprise winner, led dist and ran on well in 2yo stks at
Catterick July 23: cost 10,500 gns as a yearling and is a half brother to winning juv
Bundling Bed: stays 7f well: acts on gd/firm ground: seems well suited by a tight course.   48
1430 WENSLEYDALEWARRIOR [2] (G Moore) 2-9-7 D Casey(7) 4/1: 3201122: Al front rank: no
extra cl home but ran a fine race under top weight and is in grand form: stays 7f: see 1203.   54
1149 IBNALMAGHITH [6] (H Thomson Jones) 2-9-4 A Murray 1/1 FAV: 143: Heavily bckd: chall
strongly dist tho' didnot find much under press: prob stays 7f: needs a stiff trk? See 1149   47
1534 STORM HERO [4] (M Dickinson) 2-8-11(VIS) G Duffield 3/1: 3224: Again had ev ch and
is proving expensive to follow: see 1534 & 1197.   36
--   LINDRICK [5] 2-8-11 J Lowe 20/1: 0: Btn ½ way and should improve for this intial
effort: cost 23,000 gns as a yearling and is a half brother to a couple of winning sprinters.   20
1572 CASTLE HEIGHTS [1] 2-8-11 P Tulk 9/1: 030: Made much, btn dist: much btr using
similar tactics on a gall trk in 1572.   18
6 ran   1½,1½,2,8,1   (Hippodromo Racing)   S Hall Middleham, Yorks.

1736 DEWSBURY MAIDEN STAKES   £684   1m 4f   Good/Firm 39 -03 Slow

1503 NORDIC PLEASURE [1] (B Hills) 3-8-8 A Murray 2/9 FAV: -331: 3 b c What A Pleasure -
My Nord (Vent Du Nord) Looked to have a simple task tho' had to be driven .out after taking
command at the dist in an all aged maiden at Catterick July 23: well bred colt who is a half
brother to 2 winners, notably At Talaq: eff over 8/10f and seems to be suited by 12f:
acts on fast and soft ground and on any track.   20+
1281 WAVE GOODBYE [3] (S Hall) 3-8-8 J Lowe 9/2: 300-02: Kept on same pace tho' surely
flattered his proximity to the winner: lightly raced last term: stays 12f: suited by a
sound surface.   15
--   PALMAHALM [4] (M H Easterby) 4-9-4 K Hodgson 25/1: -3: Easy to back on debut: ran
on same pace: stays 12f: acts on gd/firm ground and on a sharp trk.   04
1546 BRANDON GREY [6] (Denys Smith) 4-9-4 L Charnock 100/1: 00-0004: Made much: yet to
show any worthwhile form and was well btn in a seller last time.   00
1361 TRAVEL HOME [5] 6-9-7(bl) S Morris 33/1: -00: Distant 5th: lightly raced on the
Flat and has shown much better form over hurdles, winning three times last winter.   00
--   BURBRIDGE KING ST [2] 5-9-7 P D'arcy 100/1: 00000/0: Well btn after lengthy abs:
no worthwhile form to his name.   00
6 ran   1½,4,2,15,12   (Sheikh Mohammed)   B Hills Lambourn, Berks.

1737 WANES OF CATTERICK H'CAP (0-35)   £1276   1m 5f   Good/Firm 39 -48 Slow   [21]

1477 NORTHERN RULER [8] (H Whiting) 4-9-5 L Riggio(7) 10/1: 0000001: 4 br g Rolfe -
Sanandrea (Upper Case) Showed impr form when leading well over 1f out, gamely in a slowly
run h'cap at Catterick July 23: successful at Redcar and Hamilton last term: eff around 12f
and stays 2m well: acts on heavy tho' best form on a sound surface.   19
1477 COCKED HAT SUPREME [1] (S Hall) 4-9-0 E Guest(3) 13/8 FAV: 40-4422: Ev ch: see 1092.   12
1636 MRS CHRIS [6] (M Naughton) 4-9-10(3ex) M Miller 5/1: 4000103: Not btn far: gd effort
over this longer trip and clearly stays well: acts on any trk: see 1416.   20
1416 RAMILIE [3] (J Etherington) 4-9-1 M Wood 5/1: 00-0034: Led 4f out: stays 13f:see 869   10
1293 KEY ROYAL [5] 5-9-7 N Rogers(7) 6/1: 00-0000: Made most: modest h'capper whose sole
win came over 1m at Ayr in '84: stays 2m: acts on gd/firm tho' prefers some cut in the ground   16
1477 THARALEOS [4] 6-8-1 J Lowe 7/1: -040030: Ran on same pace: see 827.   00
1477 JUBILANT LADY [7] 5-7-13 A Proud 25/1: 0000000: The back marker thr'out: see 827.   00
7 ran   1,1½,nk,shthd,½,1½   (R H Whiting)   H Whiting Costock Grange, Leics.

1738 BRADFORD MAIDEN FILLIES 2YO STAKES   £684   5f   Good/Firm 39 +09 Fast

1253 DANCING BELLE [1] (T Fairhurst) 2-8-11 G Duffield 5/1: 00001: 2 ch f Dance In Time
- Off The Reel (Silent Screen) Dropped in class and was produced to lead inside dist,
comfortably in quite a fast run 2yo fillies mdn at Catterick July 23: cost 9,400 gns as a
yearling: should stay further than this minimum trip: acts on yldg tho' certainly seems
best on a sound surface: seems to act on any trk.   38
1205 AID AND ABET [6] (M Stoute) 2-8-11 W R Swinburn 4/6 FAV: 42: Heavily bckd: led/
dsptd lead thr'out tho' no extra cl.home: acts on a tight course: see 1205.   35
1501 ALHAYAT [4] (R Boss) 2-8-11 E Guest(3) 5/2: 443: Led/dsptd lead most: see 1501.   26
1576 MUSIC DELIGHT [2] (K Ivory) 2-8-11(VIS) G Morgan 33/1: 0004: Al front rank: sprint
bred filly who ran her best race to date here: seems well suited by a sharp course: acts
on fast ground.   25
1370 ROYAL SPECIAL [5] 2-8-11 J Hills(5) 33/1: 00: Sn outpaced: very cheaply bought
filly who has been well btn in both her starts.   07
1405 SAPPHARINO [3] 2-8-11 A Mercer 33/1: 00: Al behind after a slow start: cheaply
bought filly who is closely related to a couple of winners.   03
6 ran   ½,3,nk,5,1   (C H Newton Jnr)   T Fairhurst Middleham, Yorks.

1739 WAKEFIELD HANDICAP (0-35) 3YO   £1598   1m 4f Good/Firm 39 -14 Slow   [28]

1569 KEEP HOPING [6] (G Huffer) 3-8-11 M Miller 16/1: 0-0001: 3 ch f Busted - Geoffrey's
Sister (Sparkler) Rank outsider and led below dist and was sn clear in a 3yo h'cap at
Catterick July 23: first success and has been well btn in all her starts prev: stays 12f
well: suited by gd/firm ground and a sharp course.   22
1615 MADISON GIRL [2] (R Whitaker) 3-9-11(4ex) D Mckeown 7/2: 0341102: Not reach winner
tho' remains in gd form and likes this tight trk: see 1479.   28
1204 DALLONA [5] (W Musson) 3-8-6 M Wigham 11/1: 00-0043: Ev ch: stays 12f: see 1204.   08
1426 BRITTONS MILL [4] (M Prescott) 3-8-13 G Duffield 2/1 FAV: 00-024: Led ½ way, btn
distance: best 1426 (11f).   14
1479 G G MAGIC [3] 3-8-12 J Lowe 9/4: -030420: Led to ½ way: btr here in 1479.   13
1540 KEEP COOL [1] 3-8-7 S Perks 7/1: 0010000: Al last: best in 774 (1m seller).   07
6 ran 4,½,½,shthd,½   (Joseph A Duffel)   G Huffer Newmarket

1740 HYNDFORD STAKES 2YO   £1347   6f   Firm 18 -42 Slow

1138 DUNLIN [2] (S Norton) 2-9-4 J Lowe 6/4: 1231: 2 ch c Miswaki - Vita Mia (Ribot)
Overturned the odds-on Pine Away, led inside final 1f, ridden out in a 2 runner 2yo stks at
Hamilton July 24: consistent colt, earlier winning an Edinburgh maiden: half brother to sev
winners in the USA: equally eff at 5/6f: acts on hvy, likes fast ground: no trk preferences.   44
*1618 PINE AWAY [1] (J Watts) 2-9-1 T Ives 4/7 FAV: 3012: Made most: see 1618.   40
2 ran nk   (Charles Buddeke)   S Norton High Hoyland, Yorks.

1741 CLYDE SELLING STAKES 2YO   £763   5f   Firm 18 -24 Slow

1680 MISS DRUMMOND [4] (N Tinkler) 2-8-8   Kim Tinkler(5) 13/2: 0002001: 2 b f The
Brianston - Miss Cindy (Mansingh) Ridden to lead last 100 yds in a 2yo seller at Hamilton
July 24 (bought in 2,700 gns): eff at 5f, may stay 6f: likes fast ground: tried in bl but
seems effective without.   20
1680 HUGO Z HACKENBUSH [8] (C Tinkler) 2-8-11(bl) M Birch 10/3 JT FAV: 0440042: Led over
1f out: see 1680.   18
1647 PEGGYS TREASURE [7] (M Brittain) 2-8-8 M Wigham 7/1: 003443: Ev ch: best 957.   06
1611 JUST A DECOY [1] (N Bycroft) 2-8-11 M Richardson(7) 20/1: 004: Little form 3 outings.   00
1225 METROMAN [6] 2-8-11 N Carlisle 8/1: 00: Led over 3f: dropped in class today: half
brother to winning 2yo Timewaster: acts on firm.   00
1478 ROSE DUET [2] 2-8-13 N Connorton 10/3 JT FAV: 0100320: Sn prom: much btr 1478 (sharp)   00
1434 SOUND AS A POUND [10] 2-8-11 T Ives 9/1: 000340: Fin 8th: twice below form 1323.   00
1611 On The Mark [9] 8-11(bl)   1180 Miss Diamante [3] 8-8 (BL)
1069 Sing For The King [5] 8-11
10 ran 1½,3,4,1,nk   (Simon Murray-Green)   N Tinkler Malton, Yorks.

1742 LEE H'CAP 3YO 0-35   £1305   6f   Firm 18 -01 Slow   [21]

*1718 MISTER MARCH [2] (R Hutchinson) 3-9-7(9ex) P Hutchinson(3) 6/4 FAV: 0001411: 3 b c
Marching On - Jetwitch (Lear Jet) In fine form, made ev yard, ridden out in a 3yo h'cap at
Hamilton July 24: yesterday won a 5f h'cap on this trk: earlier won at Bath: well suited
by a stiff 5f, stays 6f: acts on fast ground and seems to be suited by front running.   25
1312 SHARP TIMES [6] (W Musson) 3-9-7 M Wigham 11/4: 0-02102: Switched final 1f: ran on.   23
1360 BARGAIN PACK [7] (G Reveley) 3-9-0 D Leadbitter(5) 5/1: 0-00023: Prom, ev ch: see 1360   09
1664 BEECHWOOD COTTAGE [3] (A Bailey) 3-9-12(bl)(9ex) L Ford(7) 8/1: 0100144: Never nearer.   20
1664 TRICKY [4] 3-9-4 M Birch 20/1: 0-00000: Prom, fdd: bl first time: see 1200.   00
1299 GARDAS GOLD [5] 3-9-6(BL) J Lowe 20/1: -033000: Slowly away: best 787 (hvy).   00
1051 RICH BITCH [1] 3-8-3 S P Griffiths 20/1: 0000200: Earlier speed, fdd.   00
7 ran ½,2½,½,5,2½   (T J Blake)   R Hutchinson Epsom, Surrey.

1743 TRABROUN STAKES 3YO   £1009   1m   Firm 18 +13 Fast

*1431 TURFAH [5] (P Walwyn) 3-9-10 N Howe 1/1: 00-0211: 3 b c Czaravich - Hit It Rich
(Search for Gold) Overcame difficulties in running, coming from behind to narrowly win a
3yo minor event at Hamilton July 24: winner of a maiden at Pontefract recently, lightly
raced prev: very eff over 1m, may stay further: acts on firm and yldg and on any track.   46
*1184 EAGLE DESTINY [1] (I Balding) 3-9-10 T Ives 5/6 FAV: -0212: Led and went clear 2f
out, caught near finish: clear rem: better 1184 (good).   44
247 TURN EM BACK JACK [3] (A Bailey) 3-9-0(BL) P Bloomfield 25/1: -003: Prom after
long absence: very lightly raced maiden: see 134.   20
-- FLYING ZIAD [4] (A Bailey) 3-9-0 A Mackay 20/1: 000-4: Made much on seasonal debut:
showed nothing in 3 outings last term.   12
1123 FANNY ROBIN [2] 3-8-11 L Charnock 25/1: 040-000: Dsptd lead over 2f out, fdd:see 1123   07
5 ran ½,5,2½,½   (Hamdan Al-Maktoum)   P Walwyn Lambourn, Berks

1744 ORBISTON H'CAP 3YO+ 0-35   £1657   1m 3f Firm 18 -06 Slow   [34]

1636 BALLYDURROW [5] (R Fisher) 9-9-13 D Nicholls 8/13 FAV: 0104021: 9 ch g Doon - Even
Tint (Even Money) Landed the odds, coming from behind to easily lead final 1f in a h'cap
at Hamilton July 24: earlier won similar h'cap at Edinburgh and last term won 5 times in
total: equally eff over 10/12f and acts on any going and on any track: has to be held up for
a late chall: versatile sort who is a smart hurdler.   42
1621 EXCAVATOR LADY [4] (R Whitaker) 7-7-11(vis) S P Griffiths 10/1: 4322022: Tried to
make all: gd effort: see 1223.   10
1432 RUSTIC TRACK [1] (Denys Smith) 6-8-0 L Charnock 16/1: -320003: Prom, not btn far
in a close finish and well clear rem: see 131.   12
1243 SALLOOM [3] (W Hastings Bass) 4-9-8 G Duffield 11/2: 0-03004: Prom, wknd: best 912.   14
258 GENERATION GAP [6] 4-8-6(BL) A Carter(3) 20/1: -00-00: Long abs, never in it: see 258. 00
1548 APPLE WINE [2] 9-8-8 D Nicholls 11/2: 0202440: Rear thr'out: see 1124.   00
6 ran   ½,½,15,1½,1½   (N Jaffer)   R Fisher Ulverston, Cumbria

1745 LAMINGTON H'CAP 3YO+ 0-35   £1266   1m 5f Firm 18 -28 Slow   [26]

*1422 STONE JUG [3] (S Hall) 6-8-11(4ex) M Birch 10/11 FAV: 01-0411: 6 ch g High Line -
Windmill Hill (Hul A Hul) Winning 2nd race on the trot, leading final 1f, narrowly, in a
slowly run h'cap at Hamilton July 24: comfortable winner at Edinburgh July 7: twice a
winner at Edinburgh and also successful at Catterick in '85: eff 12f, stays 2m2f well:
acts on any going but best form on a sharp trk with waiting tactics.   17
1422 PERFECT DOUBLE [5] (W Pearce) 5-8-1 L Charnock 7/1: 0040322: Led from ½ way, just
btn: see 1422.   06
1473 GENTLE STREAM [2] (J Toller) 4-9-7 T Ives 6/1: 2000403: Led till ½ way, rem prom:
tried in blinkers last time, none today: best 282 (hvy).   21
1661 CAROUSEL ROCKET [1] (J S Wilson) 3-9-2 G Duffield 7/1: 0421034: Al prom: best 968 (hvy). 27
1419 EASY KIN [4] 4-8-2(VIS) J Quinn(5) 9/1: 0001000: Prom, ev ch: best 1016 (2m)   00
1195 UPLAND GOOSE [7] 5-8-2 J Bleasdale 11/1: 20: Ev ch: btr 1195.   00
860 HIGHAM GREY [6] 10-8-7 D Nicholls 14/1: 0000400: Abs: btr 675 (yldg).   00
7 ran   ½,3,2,hd,2½   (Miss S Hall)   S Hall Middleham, Yorks.

Official Going Given As STRAIGHT COURSE FIRM : ROUND COURSE HARD

1746 STAGS HEAD STAKES 2YO   £1331   5f   Firm +05 Fast

1014 MANDUB [2] (H T Jones) 2-9-0 A Murray 3/1: 131: 2 b c Topsider - Tzarina (Gallant
Romeo) Useful colt: led ½ way, ridden out in quite fast run 4 runner 2yo stks at Chepstow
July 24: first time out was an easy winner of a mdn at Goodwood: eff at 5f, should stay
further: acts on firm and yldg/soft: does well when up with the pace.   57
*1568 LADY PAT [4] (M Mccormack) 2-9-2 J Leech(7) 11/4: 2411312: Dsptd lead: in fine form. 55
*725 SUMMER SKY [1] (P Cole) 2-8-8 T Quinn 5/6 FAV: 113: Heavily bckd despite abs:
fdd final 1f: better 725.   37
1629 MENDIP STAR [3] (R Holder) 2-8-11 I Johnson 66/1: 404: Impossible task: see 1445.   00
4 ran   ¾,4,10   (Hamdan Al-Maktoum)   H T Jones Newmarket

1747 T I CREDA ECONOMY APPR HCAP 0-35 3YO+   £1343   1m 4f Firm Very Slow   [20]

1473 JABARABA [1] (L Cottrell) 5-9-6 T Lang(5) 5/2: 0-00041: 5 b g Raja Baba - Time To
Step (Time Tested) Led 3f out for a hard earned nk success in a dreadfully slow run app h'cap
at Chepstow July 24: last successful in '83 winning 3 times: eff at 10f: stays 12f: acts on
any ground but likes it firm.   19
1450 STONEBROKER [5] (D H Jones) 4-8-10 D Williams(5) 7/1: 0441002: Ran on under press:
just btn: see 718: stays 12f.   08
1309 LONDON CONTACT [7] (M Pipe) 3-9-7 J Carr(5) 5/2: 3-00403: Ev ch in str: best 919(10f) 29
1473 HALLOWED [4] (J Bosley) 4-9-0 L Riggio(5) 20/1: 000-04: Set snail's pace: little form
on Flat.   04
1567 ANGIES VIDEO [6] 4-8-1 A Dicks(2) 9/4 FAV: 0000320: Well bckd: disapp after 1567 (1m) 00
--   IM EXCEPTIONAL [2] 4-9-3 A Culhane(5) 33/1: 0-000-0: Fdd on seasonal debut: lightly
raced last season: has run in blinkers.   00
1257 Just Christened [3] 7-13
7 ran   nk,1½,2½,hd,10   (John Boswell)   L Cottrell Cullompton, Devon

1748 SIR GORDON RICHARDS HCAP 3YO 0-35   £1255   2m   Firm Slow   [36]

1569 ZAUBARR [2] (B Hills) 3-9-12(bl) B Thomson 4/9 FAV: -001131: 3 b c Hawaii - My
Room (Bold Lad) Led after 12f, comfortably, in a 4 runner h'cap at Chepstow July 24: in fine
form lately, earlier winning h'caps at Newmarket and Bath: half brother to sev winners: very
eff over 14f/2m: acts on soft, likes it firm: best in bl with front running tactics.   45
1439 RUN FOR YOUR WIFE [1] (G Lewis) 3-8-3 P Waldron 4/1: 004-302: Not get to winner:
stays 2m: see 1212.   15
1497 PRIOK [3] (W Wightman) 3-8-2 D Mckay 6/1: -030003: No extra str: best 275 (10f hvy). 00
1605 BATTLE FLEET [4] (M Usher) 3-8-3 A Mcglone 20/1: 0-00034: Made much, fdd: see 1605. 00
4 ran   3,15,25   (Sheikh Mohammed)   B Hills Lambourn, Berks

1749 T.I.CREDA ELECTRIC MAIDEN FILL.STKS 3YO   £1575   1m 2f   Firm Slow

1408 BARSHAM [2] (J Dunlop) 3-8-11 T Quinn 4/6 FAV: -001: 3 ch f Be My Guest - Bodham
(Blakeney) Well bckd and led after 7f, readily in a 3yo fillies mdn at Chepstow July 24:
last time out was an excellent 5th to Park Express in the Lancashire Oaks: eff at 10f, suited
by 12f: acts well on fast ground and a galloping track.   56
--   REMINISCING [6] (H Candy) 3-8-11 W Newnes 5/1: -2: Led over 6f: bumped over 1f out:
6l clear 3rd and looks sure to find a race: stoutly bred filly who will be well suited
by 12f, possibly further: acts on fast ground.   48
--   KEY TO THE KEEP [3] (I Balding) 3-8-11 P Cook 11/4: 20-3: No real threat on seasonal
debut and should be a lot straighter for this run: lightly raced in '85, first time out
fin 2nd to Tender Loving Care in a Sandown maiden: should be suited by 10f+: acts on fast grd 38
1198 TAIS TOI [5] (M Fetherston Godley) 3-8-11 M Hills 20/1: 00-4004: Prom 7f: best 422.   26
1580 CHERRY GLORY [1] 3-8-11 D Mckay 66/1: 00-000: Very stiff task: half sister to
numerous winners including the useful High Skies, but has shown little form herself in
4 outings.   00
941 BILLS BELLE [4] 3-8-11 J Reid 66/1: 0-00: Al rear.   00
6 ran   3,6,6,15,30   (A M Budgett)   J Dunlop Arundel, Sussex

1750 CLIFTON H'CAP 3YO 0-60   £2934   6f   Firm +15 Fast   [57]

1457 MYRAS SPECIAL [4] (J Sutcliffe) 3-9-1 M Hills 4/1: 010-001: 3 b f Pitskelly - High
Explosive (Mount Hagen) Made nearly all, ridden out in a fast run 3yo h'cap at Chepstow
July 24: in '85 won at Catterick and Brighton: eff at 5f, stays 6f well: best on fast ground:
likes a sharp/easy track.   53
1584 DANCING SARAH [2] (D H Jones) 3-7-10 D Williams(7) 7/2: 4000032: Ran on well and
just btn: runs well here: see 443.   33
-1524 DARK PROMISE [3] (R Hollinshead) 3-9-6 S Perks 6/4 FAV: -001323: Prom, ev ch:
better 1524.   53
1607 SURE LANDING [1] (C Nelson) 3-8-11(BL) J Reid 3/1: -042034: Sn prom: best 937 (1m)   32
1457 OCEAN TRADER [5] 3-9-7(bl) P Waldron 11/1: 22-0000: Early speed: yet to find 2yo form. 36
5 ran   nk,1½,6,3   (Mrs Jan Siegel)   J Sutcliffe Epsom, Surrey.

1751 SUNSET MAIDEN FILLIES STAKES 3YO   £1602   7f   Firm Slow

1273 TZU WONG [4] (M Pipe) 3-8-11 B Thomson 20/1: 24-0001: 3 ch f Manado - Tzu-Hsi
(Songedor) Stepped up on recent showings when leading 2f out, driven out in a 3yo fillies mdn
at Chepstow July 24: showed promise as a 2yo: stays 7f: acts on firm and soft ground and
a galloping track.   39
1586 CANADIAN GUEST [6] (H Candy) 3-8-11 W Newnes 5/4 FAV: -002: Well bckd: chance
final 1f: may need further than 7f: should find a small race: see 1586.   37
1446 EASTERN COMMAND [11] (J Dunlop) 3-8-11 G Baxter 3/1: 34-43: Led 5f: see 1446.   35
1451 MOGOAR [1] (P Cole) 3-8-11 T Quinn 11/2: 030-04: Prom, ev ch: see 1451.   31
1337 QUITE A QUEST [9] 3-8-11 S Perks 33/1: 4-000: Nearest fin: prob best over 1m:
acts on fast ground.   30
1327 SHUJUN [8] 3-8-11 A Murray 5/1: 0200-00: Ev ch: showed form on a couple of occasions
in '85, notably when 2nd in a fillies event at Epsom: should be suited by 1m: may favour
a sharp track: acts on good ground.   29
1451 Five Quarters [7] 8-11   1246 Harmony Heights [5] 8-11
1471 Lisakaty [2] 8-11   --   Miss Bluebell [3] 8-11
--   Revanora [10] 8-11
11 ran   1,¾,1½,nk,¾   (Mrs M Palmer)   M Pipe Nicholashayne, Somerset.

1752 EBF RAYNES PARK 2YO FILLIES MAIDEN   £3395   7f   Good/Firm 30 -01 Slow

1382 BINT PASHA [2] (P Cole) 2-8-11 T Quinn 7/4: 2221: 2 ch f Affirmed - Icely Polite
(Graustark) Useful filly who gained a deserved success making ev yard comfortably, in a 2yo
fillies mdn at Sandown July 24: has fin 2nd to 3 smart fillies recently: cost $220,000:
well suited by forcing tactics over 7f and will stay further: acts on firm and gd ground
and likes a stiff galloping trk: sure to win more races.   56
--   MISK EL KHASHAB [7] (B Hills) 2-8-11 B Thomson 10/1: 2: Fine debut, fin strongly:
half sister to winning '84 2yo Major Forum: suited by a stiff 7f, bred to be suited by
middle dist in time: sure to improve and find a race.   46
1433 PHILGWYN [3] (R Laing) 2-8-11 S Whitworth 20/1: 023: Never nrr: see 1433.   38
1021 BENGUELA [4] (J Tree) 2-8-11 Pat Eddery 11/8 FAV: 34: Ev ch, fdd, btr 1021 (6f).   36
1552 PERSIAN TAPESTRY [1] 2-8-11 R Cochrane 33/1: 4000: Disapp since 707 (5f).   35
--   WHITE JAZZ [6] 2-8-11 S Cauthen 20/1: 0: Prom much: shd benefit from this first outing:
quite cheaply bought: should improve.   31
--   KALADIOLA [9] 2-8-11 A Clark 10/1: 0: Op 4/1, friendless in mkt: fin 8th on debut:
French bred filly who is related to a winner in that country: should be capable of better.   00
852 Tufty Lady [8] 8-11   1345 Ellis Bell [5] 8-11   00

9 ran   5,4,1,$\frac{1}{2}$,1$\frac{1}{2}$ (Fahd Salman)   P Cole Whatcombe, Oxon

1753 NORMAN HILL HANDICAP 0-50 3YO   £3153   1m   Good/Firm 30 +03 Fast   [54]

*1246 REALITY [5] (R J Houghton) 3-9-4 S Cauthen 5/2 FAV: 0-11: 3 br f Known Fact -
Missed Blessing (So Blessed) Impr filly who was winning 2nd race on the trot, comfortably
leading dist in a 3yo h'cap at Sandown July 24: easy winner of a minor race at Salisbury
June 26: ran only once in '85: dam was a very smart miler: very eff over 7f/1m: suited by
firm ground and a stiff galloping track: may complete a hat-trick.   55
1575 GEORDIES DELIGHT [3] (L Piggott) 3-9-7 R Cochrane 7/2: 1041422: Made much, kept on
and ran his usual consistent race: see 1202, 1575.   54
1515 LADY LA PAZ [2] (P Cundell) 3-7-8 G French 7/2: 0402333: Chall 2f out: btr 1515 (7f)   22
1436 SUPER PUNK [1] (M Fetherston Godley) 3-8-13 C Rutter(5) 10/1: 1-30004: Chall 2f
out, no extra: disapp since 436.   38
*1228 ANDIKA [4] 3-9-4 Pat Eddery 7/2: -0010: Mkt drifter, chance dist, fdd: btr 1228 (7f)   41
5 ran   1$\frac{1}{2}$,2$\frac{1}{2}$,1$\frac{1}{2}$,1.   (T D Holland-Martin)   R J Houghton Blewbury, Oxon.

1754 MILCARS STAR STAKES 2YO   £3707   5f   God/Firm 30 -25 Slow

-1255 BORN TO RACE [3] (L Piggott) 2-8-11 R Cochrane 4/1: 0121: 2 ch c Dr Blum - Babe's
Sis (Raise A Native) Useful colt: took a long time to find his stride but responded well
to press to forge clear inside final 1f in a slowly run 4 horse 2yo minor race at Sandown
July 24: earlier won a mdn at Yarmouth: very eff over 5f, stays 6f well: acts on firm ground:
runs very lazily and may be suited by blinkers.   60
1591 QUEL ESPRIT [2] (M Mccormack) 2-9-4 S Cauthen 5/4 FAV: 1113022: Tried to make all,
no answer to winners finishing burst close home: btr 1591 (good).   60
1653 RIOT BRIGADE [4] (C Brittain) 2-8-11 M Roberts 10/1: 0033: Mkt drifter: chall dist,
kept on: see 1653.   49
*1297 GARNET [1] (R Boss) 2-8-8 Pat Eddery 2/1: 014: Dsptd lead much: see 1297.   39
4 ran   3,1$\frac{1}{2}$,3   (K H Fischer)   L Piggott Newmarket

1755 WELLINGTON APPRENTICE HCAP 0-35   £2687   1m 2f   Good/Firm 30 -14 Slow   [34]

*1220 CAPTAINS NIECE [11] (W Hastings Bass) 3-8-11 Dale Gibson(6) 2/1 FAV: -011: 3 b f
Vitiges - Captain's Girl (Captain's Gig) Impr filly: heavily bckd and winning 2nd race on
the trot, leading dist readily in an app h'cap at Sandown July 24: equally ready winner at
Ripon June 25 (maiden): lightly raced prev: very eff over 9/10f, may stay further: suited
by firm ground: looks likely to complete the hat-trick.   41
*1284 HARD AS IRON [1] (P Haslam) 3-8-10 J Scally(6) 5/2: 0-41112: Ev ch, not pace of
winner: see 1284.   34
735 FOR A LARK [12] (D Wilson) 4-9-1 L Riggio(3) 10/1: 00-0003: Made much after abs: see 312   23
575 HIGHLAND BALL [4] (G Wragg) 3-8-12 D Surrey(6) 14/1: 00-004: Long abs: see 575.   32
1559 DICK KNIGHT [10] 5-7-13(vis) G Athenasiou(3) 16/1: 0000200: No real threat: twice
below 1416 (12f).   00
1286 THALESTRIA [9] 4-9-12 Tony Middleton(6) 50/1: 00-0000: No danger, last won in '84
at York (7f yldg).   13
1609 SUPERFROST [6] 4-7-13 G King 9/2: 0010040: No threat in 7th: difficult ride: see 1609.   00
975 Unit Tent [5] 7-7(bl)(1oh)   -- Dust Conquerer [6] 8-10(bl)
1609 Aqaba Prince [7] 8-3   1274 Hard Oak [2] 7-7(3oh) -- Maskeen [3] 8-3
12 ran   3,2,shthd,12,1$\frac{1}{2}$ (N H Phillips)   W Hastings Bass Newmarket

1756 HEATH ROW MAIDEN STAKES 3YO   £2310   1m   Good/Firm 30 +05 Fast

229 EXCLUSIVE NORTH [2] (R Armstrong) 3-9-0 S Cauthen 1/1 FAV: 2330-01: 3 br g Far North -
Collection (Star Envoy) Never hdd when winning a 4 runner 3yo mdn at Sandown July 24, after
long abs: placed in 3 out of 4 races in '85: very eff over 1m with forcing tactics and acts
well on fast ground.   39
535 SILCA CHIAVI [5] (D Elsworth) 3-9-0 A Mcglone 20/1: -00-02: Long abs: no threat:
showed a little ability in only 2 races last term but is hard to assess: should stay 1m:
acts on fast ground.   34
1607 SPEED STICK [4] (P Haynes) 3-9-0 P Waldron 10/1: -003: No extra final 1f: half
brother to winning miler Star Formation.   14
-- HIGH CONDUCT [1] (J Dunlop) 3-9-0 Pat Eddery 5/4: 4-4: Slow start, ran badly and
there was something amiss: 4th behind Kedron in a backend mdn at Folkestone, sole outing '85:
half brother to 3 winners.   00
4 ran   2,8,20   (Dr Cornel Li)   R Armstrong Newmarket

1757 FOX WARREN HANDICAP 3YO+ 0-50   £3107   1m 6f   Good/Firm 30 +03 Fast   [39]

1330 OSTENSIBLE [4] (G Harwood) 3-9-10 Pat Eddery 5/4 FAV: 1-30001: 3 b c Alleged -
Proud Pattie (Noble Commander) Useful colt: well bckd and comfortably led 2f out in a h'cap
at Sandown July 24: in his last 2 outings has acted as pacemaker for Bakharoff: in '85 won
a mdn at Leicester on sole outing: well suited by 12/14f nowadays and runs well on fast ground   58
542 COLLISTO [3] (K Brassey) 5-8-1(BL) S Whitworth 12/1: 0-00002: Prom, kept on,
after long abs: fair effort: see 485.   17
1577 ASSAGLAWI [5] (G Blum) 4-9-8 S Cauthen 100/30: 0012003: Made much: see 959.   35

1348 ALSIBA [1] (C Benstead) 4-8-6 B Rouse 2/1: 0001404: Prom, wknd: disapp since 1035 (C/D)   04
--   MYTHICAL BOY [2] 5-8-4 J Williams 50/1: -0: First race on the Flat for a long time,
rear final 1m: lightly raced maiden.   00
5 ran   2,1½,15,20   (K Abdulla)   G Harwood Pulborough, Sussex

---

CATTERICK   Thursday July 24th   Lefthanded, Very Sharp Track

Official Going Given As GOOD/FIRM

1758 'A' ONE APPRENTICES' STAKES 3YO+   £932   7f   Firm 19 +03 Fast

478 HARAABAH [3] (H Thomson Jones) 3-8-8 A Riding(3) 7/1: 0200-01: 3 ch f Topsider -
Marie De Sarre (Queens Hussar) Despite a fair abs was a comfortable winner, led inside dist
and was pushed out in quite a fast run app stks at Catterick July 24: showed plenty of
promise early last season, winning her first 2 races at Leicester and Beverley: stays 7f well
acts on firm and yldg ground and on any trk.   24
1546 O I OYSTON [8] (J Berry) 10-9-7 J Carroll 25/1: 3000202: Led till cl home: looked
to face an impossible task and ran a fine race: well suited by sharp course: see 606.   24
1678 HEAVENLY HOOFER [9] (Denys Smith) 3-8-11 A Nixon(5) 25/1: 0101103: Not btn far:
good effort: see 1547.   22
1532 TRY HARDER [10] (J Fitzgerald) 3-8-11 R Brown(3) 9/1: 00-0034: Al well placed: best 1532   20
1525 MAJOR DON [7] 6-9-7 M Tebbutt(3) 3/1: 00-0000: Nicely bckd: never nearer: see 1249   20
1044 LOCHONICA [4] 3-8-11 I Todd(3) 11/4 FAV: 0-00000: Speed over ½ way: much btr 1044 (6f)   17
1084 FOUZ [2] 3-8-11 M Lynch 3/1: 0-34000: Wknd into 8th: can do much btr: seee 60.   00
1525 Moores Metal [5] 9-7(vis)   1546 Lady Abinger [6] 8-11(bl)
9 ran   1,¼,¼,¾,¾   (Hamdan Al-Maktoum)   H Thomson Jones Newmarket

1759 COLBORN SELLING H'CAP (0-25) 3YO   £977   1m 5f Firm 19 -40 Slow   [21]

1428 FAST AND FRIENDLY [10] (R Hollinshead) 3-9-7 S Perks 2/1 FAV: 0431021: 3 ch c Lord
Gayle - Raubritter (Levmoss) Again well bckd and gamely defied top weight, leading over 2f
out in a slowly run 3yo selling h'cap at Catterick July 24 (bought in 3,900 gns): earlier won
a Claimer on this course and likes a sharp/easy trk: eff over 12/14f: acts on soft ground
tho' clearly favours a sound surface and is likely to run over hurdles in the near future.   21
1428 PINK SENSATION [7] (G Reveley) 3-9-5 D Leadbitter(5) 14/1: 0-00042: Just held: maiden
who ran her best race to date here: eff over 12/14f: suited by fast ground and a sharp course.   18
1204 RIBO MELODY [3] (J Jefferson) 3-9-2 M Wood 11/2: 00-0003: Not btn far: best 779.   13
1481 RACEFORM RHAPSODY [9] (G Moore) 3-8-2 S Wood(7) 20/1: -000004: Bckd at long odds,
nearest fin: yet to show any worthwhile form tho' seems suited by 12/14f and fast ground.   00
1340 LA CAZADORA [5] 3-9-3 T Ives 7/1: -0040: Seems best over middle dist: acts on firm.   02
1567 TAKE THE BISCUIT [4] 3-9-6 David Williams(7) 12/1: 0002000: Best over 1m in 1210.   04
1267 FOXCROFT [8] 3-9-3 T Williams 5/1: 2-00000: Longer trip: wknd into 7th: see 356.   00
949 STORM LORD [6] 3-8-10 J Bleasdale 13/2: 00-0000: No threat after abs: btr over
this C/D in 769.   00
1544 Giant Redwood [1] 9-7(BL)   365 Quivering [2] 8-3
10 ran   ½,1,2½,5,¾,3,7   (J T Lawlor)   R Hollinshead Upper Longdon, Staffs.

1760 TUNSTALL STAKES 2YO   £1253   6f   Firm 19 -01 Slow

1572 MILEAGE BANK [4] (P Cole) 2-9-4 G Duffield 11/10: 4101: 2 b c J O Tobin - Cautious
Bidder (Bold Bidder) Very useful colt: led early and again below dist, for a decisive win in
a 3 runner 2yo stks at Catterick July 24: earlier comfortably made all at Chepstow: cost
$230,000 as yearling and is a full brother to the smart juv Overtrump: very eff over 6f
tho' disapp when tried over 7f last time: acts on firm and yldg ground and on any trk:
does well with forcing tactics: sure to win more races.   60
1430 ALKADI [2] (W O'gorman) 2-9-7 T Ives 4/5 FAV: 2320132: Ev ch: commendably consistent
this term and should find another winning opportunity soon: see 1261.   50
1527 MISS SHEGAS [3] (J Berry) 2-9-1 J Carroll(7) 20/1: 221003: Made most, btn dist:
acts on fast ground tho' best on an easier surface in 473 (5f).   24
3 ran   4,7   (Dan J Agnew)   P Cole Lambourn, Berks.

1761 WANE GARAGE H'CAP (0-35) 3YO+   £1613   7f   Firm 19 -01 Slow   [29]

1482 THE MAZALL [4] (L Siddall) 6-9-10 D Nicholls 11/2: 0120221: 6 br g Persian Bold -
Dance All Night (Double-U-Jay) Gained a deserved win, held up and was produced to lead in
final strides of a h'cap at Catterick July 24: earlier a comfortable all-the-way winner at
Redcar: last season won at Redcar and Carlisle and in '84 was successful at Nottingham: best
form around 6/7f: acts on firm and soft grd and any trk: does well with forcing tactics.   32
1447 POKERFAYES [5] (B Mcmahon) 7-8-4(bl) G Duffield 14/1: 1-00002: Led inside dist,
just caught: best effort for sometime: see 866.   11
1627 RESTORATION [6] (G Calvert) 4-9-3 N Rodgers(7) 25/1: 000-003: Not btn far: gd eff.   23
-1627 MARAVILLA [10] (J Etherington) 4-9-1 M Wood 4/1: 0-00024: Made much: close 4th:see 1627   20
1560 TOPEKA EXPRESS [3] 3-8-11(bl) R Guest 7/2 FAV: 0000320: In gd form: see 1560 & 1281.   21
1338 HOPTONS CHANCE [9] 4-8-0 M Fry 14/1: -000000: Nearest fin and stays 7f: see 906.   01
1547 ROSSETT [14] 7-7-10 A Mackay 8/1: 0-00040: Wknd into 7th: see 1136.   00

CATTERICK   Thursday July 24th   -Cont'd

1482 QUALITAIRESS [1] 4-7-9(vis) N Carlisle 9/1: 4340030: No threat in 9th: see 101.   **00**
1482 La Belle Of Santo [7] 7-11   **1091 Cumbrian Nijo** [13] 8-11
1222 Always Native [12] 8-10   **1156 Remembrance** [2] 8-10
1626 Miss Blake [8] 8-0   **1638 Monswart** [11] 8-4(VIS)
14 ran   shthd,¼,¼,2,shthd,2½   (Mrs Jack Fulton)   L Siddall Tadcaster, Yorks.

1762 E.B.F. LEYBURN MAIDEN STAKES 2YO   £1031   5f   Firm 19 -13 Slow

1510 JOE SUGDEN [6] (R Whitaker) 2-9-0 K Bradshaw(5) 9/2: 0301: 2 b c Music Boy – Sum
Star (Comedy Star) Nicely bckd and showed impr form, led after ¼ way and was pushed out to
win a 2yo mdn at Catterick July 24: below par over 6f last time and seems best suited by
this minimum trip at the moment: half brother to winning juv Warwick Wallies: suited by
fast ground and a sharp course.   **45**
962 SOMETHING EXTRA [1] (P Cole) 2-9-0 M Birch 7/2: 02: Led/dsptd lead thr'out: late
foal who should continue to improve: seems to act on any trk: see 962.   **40**
1475 SCHUYGULLA [2] (M Jarvis) 2-9-0 W Woods(3) 11/8 FAV: 3423: Led/dsptd lead: consistent. **35**
1475 HAILEYS RUN [8] (G Pritchard Gordon) 2-9-0 G Duffield 5/1: 430334: Clear rem tho'
better in 1475.   **29**
1625 PRINCEGATE [3] 2-9-0 K Hodgson 7/1: 0040: Speed over ½ way: btr over 6f in 1625. **15**
-- BURCROFT [7] 2-9-0 D Mckeown 25/1: 0: Mkt drifter on debut: no threat after slow
start: half brother to minor winner Bob-Double: may need a longer trip.   **00**
-- Ripster [5] 9-0   **304 Ra Raver** [4] 9-0
8 ran   ½,1½,2,5,6   (Frazer Hines)   R Whitaker Wetherby, Yorks.

1763 GROVE STAKES 3YO+   £684   1m 4f   Firm 19 -14 Slow

*****1535 MYTH** [2] (R Johnson Houghton) 3-8-8 R Hills 1: 424-211: 3 b f Troy – Hay Reef
(Mill Reef) Useful filly: was never hdd when an easy winner from sole rival Saffan in a
minor race at Catterick July 24: comfortable winner of his mdn at Chester last time and has
yet to fin out of the frame: eff over 12/13f: acts on firm and yldg grd and on any trk:
consistent.   **45**
1671 SAFFAN [1] (M Prescott) 3-8-11 G Duffield 5/2: -321222: Al in vain pursuit of winner:
see 1671 & 1362.   **34**
2 ran   7   (J W Rowles)   R Johnson Houghton Blewbury, Oxon.

CARLISLE   Friday July 25th   Righthand, Undulating Track with Stiff Uphill Finish

Official Going Given As HARD

1764 WRYNOSE MAIDEN STAKES 2YO   £1087   6f   Firm 15 -30 Slow

-- AFRICAN SPIRIT [4] (M Prescott) 2-9-0 G Duffield 3/1: 1: 2 b c African Sky – Relic
Spirit (Relic) Made a successful racecourse debut, nicely bckd and led dist, driven out in
a 2yo mdn at Carlisle July 25: speedily bred colt who is a half brother to a handful of
winners: evidently suited by a stiff 6f and a sound surface.   **48**
1555 BOLD CRUSADER [2] (M Stoute) 2-9-0 W Ryan 4/7 FAV: 422: Driven along from ½ way,
kept on well and again fin well clear rem: due a change of luck: see 1555.   **44**
1625 RUSTIC EYES [8] (D Barron) 2-9-0 A Mackay 6/1: 23: Led before ½ way, not quicken
dist: may prove more at home on an easier course: sprint bred colt: see 1625.   **28**
819 MY SERENADE [1] (J Watts) 2-8-11 N Connorton 25/1: 044: Mkt drifter afte fair abs:
front rank over ½ way : showed some improvement from abs: acts on fast grd: see 819.   **17**
1501 PENBREASY [6] 2-8-11 S Perks 20/1: 0400: Cl.up after ½ way: best 1501 (5f tight trk)
'tho the form of that race looks decidedly suspect: see 1333.   **16**
1625 TOKANDA [5] 2-9-0 J Callaghan(7) 16/1: 00: Led to ½ way: sn btn: half brother to
7/9f winner Viva Lucia.   **00**
-- Golden Air [7] 9-0   **-- Dolitino** [3] 8-11
8 ran   1,5,2½,nk,10   (B Haggas)   M Prescott Newmarket

1765 GRAHAM COMMERCIALS LTD H'CAP (0-35)   £2344   6f   Firm 15 +05 Fast   **[21]**

1101 DUFFERS DANCER [7] (W Pearce) 4-9-5 M Hindley(3) 9/1: 0004-01: 4 ch g Miami Springs
– Evening Chorus (Mountain Call) Led below dist, gamely, in quite a fast run h'cap at
Carlisle July 25: successful in a 5f h'cap on this course last term and in '84 won at
Hamilton: best form over 5/6f tho' does stay 7f well: suited by fast grd and likes a
stiff track.   **20**
1398 SOFTLY SPOKEN [1] (P Felgate) 3-9-4 W Ryan 9/4: 0-01202: Held up, ev ch and just
held: clear rem: stays 6f well: acts on any trk: see 1247 & 784.   **26**
+1664 ALLISTERDRANSFIELD [5] (G Moore) 3-8-11(bl)(7ex) D Casey(7) 13/8 FAV: -004213: Led
after 2f: no extra dist and much btr when making all in 1664.   **05**
1610 GOLDEN DISC [2] (M Camacho) 4-8-4 N Connorton 11/2: 3-43024: Slipped start, kept
on: see 1610.   **00**
1077 GREY CREE [6] 4-9-3 M Wood 14/1: -000: Early leader: rated 27 when winning successive
sellers at Catterick and Ripon in '84 tho' has been lightly raced and shown no form since:
eff over 5/6f: suited by fast ground and likes being out in front.   **00**
1338 VIA VITAE [4] 4-8-4 P Hill(7) 20/1: 40-0000: Led/dsptd lead over ½ way: maiden
who has been well btn in all her starts this term: best over 6f on gd or faster ground. **00**

534

1718 CARPENTERS BOY [3] 8-9-7 D Leadbitter(5) 12/1: 0-00000: Never dangerous: see 1718.   00
7 ran   nk,5,¼,2,3,2¼   (R Arbuthnot)   W Pearce Hambleton, Yorks.

1766 APPRENTICES' HANDICAP (0-35)   £1415   1m 1f   Firm 15 -130 Slow   [13]

1156 PRICEOFLOVE [1] (D Moffatt) 6-9-6 J Quinn(5) 7/4: 0040-01: 6 b g Blue Cashmere -
Gay Donna (Tudor Jinks) Led below dist, gamely, in a very slowly run app h'cap at Carlisle
July 25: first success on the Flat since '82, when he won at Wolverhampton and Nottingham,
tho' has won over timber since: eff over 7/9f: acts on firm and soft ground.   12
--   GOOD N SHARP [3] (G Calvert) 5-9-2 N Rogers(7) 4/1: 00000-2: Sustained chall, just
held: successful over 5f at Nottingham as a juv: stays 9f: acts on gd and fast ground.   06
1613 TAJ SINGH [2] (Denys Smith) 4-9-6 R Vickers(7) 5/4 FAV: 0000443: Had ev ch in
this poor contest: see 1613.   08
--   MANIX [5] (T Craig) 5-9-1 G King(5) 20/1: 00003/4: Made most at a funeral pace:
poor maiden who has been off the trk due to injury: acts on a sound surface.   00
--   SCOTTISH GREEN [6] 8-9-1 A Culhane(7) 12/1: 01400/0: No threat: last ran on the Flat
in '83, when successful in a selling h'cap at Yarmouth: has since shown glimpses of ability
over hurdles: stays 1m: acts on firm ground.   00
5 ran   ¾,1,1,8,shthd   (J Calvert)   D Moffatt Cartmel, Cumbria.

1767 SCANIA TRUCKS SELLING STAKES 3YO   £591   1m 1f   Firm 15 -23 Slow

1310 KOUS [1] (R Simpson) 3-8-10(bl) W Newnes 2/1: -10301: 3 b c Huguenot - Princess
Cornish (Cornish Prince) Waited with and led dist, driven out in a 3yo seller at Carlisle
July 25 (bought in 2,600 gns): easy winner of a similar race at Folkestone on his debut:
eff over 8/10f: acts on gd and firm ground and on any track.   22
1703 MR COFFEY [4] (S Norton) 3-8-3 J Lowe 6/4 FAV: -400022: Made most: improved of
late: eff over 8/9f on fast ground: seems to act on any track.   10
1759 TAKE THE BISCUIT [6] (R Stubbs) 3-8-3(bl) A Mercer 3/1: 0020003: Ev ch: best over
1m in 1210 (sharp track).   02
1428 FIRE LORD [3] (G Moore) 3-8-3 S Wood(7) 5/1: 0-00034: Kept on late: see 1428.   01
1360 LA MANGA PRINCE [5] 3-8-3 G Brown 14/1: 0000000: Longer trip: trailed in last:
no form over various distances this term: see 279.   00
5 ran   2,4,nk,25   (Tony Stafford)   R Simpson Upper Lambourn, Berks.

1768 WHINLATTER E.B.F. STAKES   £2135   1m 1f   Firm 15 -49 Slow

1462 LANDSKI [3] (R Simpson) 3-8-4 W Newnes 6/4: 4013031: 3 b c Niniski - Misacre (St
Alphage) Made virtually all for a game success in a slowly run 3 runner stks race at Carlisle
July 25: earlier won his mdn at Brighton: half brother to useful 6/8f winner Amarone: eff
over 8/10f and should stay further: acts on soft tho' favours a sound surf: no trk preferences   50
1107 SALLY SAYS SO [2] (S Norton) 3-8-2 J Lowe 4/5 FAV: 10-402: Just held: had been
highly tried in both prev starts this term: see 803.   46
411 CENTREPOINT [1] (J Etherington) 3-8-10(BL) M Wood 5/1: 001-443: Fitted with bl after
a lengthy abs: wknd quickly 2f out: see 244.   44
3 ran   hd,6   (Broderick Munro-Wilson)   R Simpson Upper Lambourn, Berks.

1769 HARD KNOTT HANDICAP (0-35)   £1383   1m 4f   Firm 15 -02 Slow   [35]

1548 IVOROSKI [3] (Denys Smith) 4-7-8 L Charnock 5/2: 0003321: 4 b g Malinowski - Fado
(Ribero) Gained a deserved win, led 1f out and just held on in a h'cap at Carlisle July 25:
won at Edinburgh last season: best form over 12f on gd or fast ground: acts on any trk.   08
1502 REGAL STEEL [2] (R Hollinshead) 8-8-9 A Culhane(7) 9/4 FAV: 3220222: Made most:
runner-up in 5 of his last 6 races: see 1359 & 4.   22
*1548 ERROL EMERALD [9] (S Norton) 5-8-13 J Lowe 4/1: 00-0113: Possibly not an easy ride:
held up as usual and ev ch.: not beaten far though may do better in blinkers: see 1548.   24
1577 SYMBOLIC [4] (R Stubbs) 6-9-10 J H Brown(5) 16/1: -2-0004: No real threat tho' a
fair effort under top weight: last successful in '84, at Lingfield and Thirsk: prob needs
further, stays 2m well: suited by gd and fast ground.   27
1280 COUNTRY JIMMY [6] 4-8-0(bl) M Wood 8/1: -400000: Best over this C/D in 381 (yldg)   02
1361 THE RUSK [5] 5-8-2 W Newnes 20/1:   03/00: Mdn on Flat tho' successful in a seller
over hurdles: suited by fast ground.   00
1054 KAMPHALL [1] 3-7-7(4oh) J Quinn(0) 10/1: 00-4000: Well btn 8th: much btr over 1m
in 822 (heavy).   00
1159 Skerne Spark [7] 7-7(VIS)   1432 Biondoni [8] 7-7(4oh)
9 ran   hd,1,5,hd,5   (P & I Darling)   Denys Smith Bishop Auckland, Co Durham.

Official Going Given As GOOD/FIRM : ALL TIMES SLOW

1770 MIDDLETON MAIDEN FILLIES STKS 2YO   £959   6f   Good/Firm Slow

1427 HOMING IN [4] (G Huffer) 2-8-11 G Carter(3) 4/6 FAV: 0421: 2 b f Homing – Rahesh
(Raffingora) Well bckd and led over 1f out, comfortably, in a 2yo fillies mdn at Ayr July 25:
stays 6f well: acts well on fast ground: no trk preferenes.   40
1333 BLAZE OF GOLD [6] (E Alston) 2-8-11 G Duffield 50/1: 02: Rank outsider: fin in gd
style: sister to fair h'capper Shellman: will be well suited by 7f and shd find a small event
in the North.   34
1296 COME ON OYSTON [1] (J Berry) 2-8-11 J Carroll(7) 9/2: 43: Sn prom: making improvement.   32
1527 MAZURKANOVA [5] (C Thornton) 2-8-11 J Bleasdale 12/1: 004204: Came all too late: see 1297.27
1090 LUCYS MELODY [3] 2-8-11 M Hindley(2) 20/1: 00: Made most, fdd: impr eff: acts gd/firm.   21
905 MUSIC STAR [8] 2-8-11 S Webster 20/1: 000: Abs: prom 4f: first signs of form:
acts on gd/firm.   12
-- TOPICAL ISSUE [7] 2-8-11 N Connorton 13/2: 0: Fdd on race course debut: very weak
in mkt here and should be btr for this run: half sister to sev winners and better things
can be expected.   00
818 Treize Quatorze [2] 8-11
8 ran   1½,½,1½,2,3   (Melvyn A Kneller)   G Huffer Newmarket

1771 MONTGREENAN SELLING STAKES   £943   6f   Good/Firm Slow

1334 COOPER RACING NAIL [5] (J Berry) 3-8-1 M Fry 8/1: 2002301: 3 b f Martinmas – Wavy
Navy (Hardicanute) Finally got her hd in front, making ev yard and holding on by a hd
in a 3 & 4yo seller at Ayr July 25 (bought in 1,750 gns): earlier placed on numerous
occasions and was not winning out of turn: acts on firm and soft: seems suited by 6/7f
with forcing tactics.   17
1617 TOUCH THE SAIL [9] (M Tompkins) 3-8-5(4ow) R Cochrane 9/1: 000-042: Chall final 1f:
just btn: eff at 6/7f on fast ground and has the ability to find a similar event.   20
*1617 PSALM [2] (M Prescott) 3-8-9 G Duffield 3/1: 0-03413: Ev ch: btr 1617.   16
1257 HIGHLAND TALE [7] (A Jarvis) 3-8-1(bl) J Lowe 2/1 FAV: 0-00004: Well bckd: al prom:
dropped in class here: little form this season: stays 7f: acts on fast ground.   06
1734 PLANTER [8] 3-9-2(bl) M Beecroft 12/1: 0240000: Never nearer: see 51.   11
1424 SWEET EIRE [4] 4-8-9(bl) N Connorton 14/1: 00-0000: There over 4f: see 906.   00
1077 SHIRLY ANN [3] 4-8-9 S P Griffiths 10/1: 00/2000: Al trailing: best first time
out in 31 (yldg/soft).   00
131 Brampton Imperial [6] 9-10   1070 Frandie Miss [1] 8-1(bl)
9 ran   hd,3,½,4,1½   (P G P Hodgson)   J Berry Cockerham, Lancs.

1772 WILLIAM THE LION HANDICAP 0-35   £1925   2m 4f Good/Firm Slow   [29]

663 TUGBOAT [4] (P Mitchell) 7-9-1 G Carter(3) 1/1 FAV: 104-021: 7 ch g Grundy – Pirate
Queen (Pirate King) Well bckd and led inside final 3f, comfortably, in a h'cap at Ayr July
25: won this same race in '85 and '84: stays all day: acts on any going and any trk but
likes Ayr: best when fresh.   26
1183 JOIST [1] (M Prescott) 4-9-0(bl) G Duffield 4/1: -002432: Chance final 2f: 8l clear
3rd: good effort: see 833.   21
1419 WALTER THE GREAT [8] (M H Easterby) 4-8-7 M Birch 10/1: 0040003: No real threat:
best 933.   06
1533 ISLAND EXILE [5] (J Watts) 4-9-7 N Connorton 12/1: 44-0404: Led 1m: not stay 2½m?   19
1737 JUBILANT LADY [2] 5-7-7(2oh) S P Griffiths 33/1: 0000000: Prom, ev ch: see 827.   00
1533 SOUND DIFFUSION [7] 4-9-2 K Bradshaw(5) 7/1: 2100300: Made no show: best 933 (15f).   10
1564 Welsh Guard [6] 7-8
7 ran   1½,8,1,2½,½   (Mrs G I Evennett)   P Mitchell Epsom, Surrey.

1773 MONKWOOD HANDICAP 3YO 0-35   £2320   1m 2f Good/Firm Slow   [27]

1678 SPRING FLIGHT [4] (A Jarvis) 3-9-2 J Lowe 9/2: -013231: 3 b c Captain James –
Late Swallow (My Swallow) Made ev yard in a 3yo h'cap at Ayr July 25: has been most
consistent, earlier winning a selling h'cap at Redcar: eff at 1m, stays 10f well: likes
fast ground and a gall track: seems suited by front running.   25
*1396 GIBBERISH [5] (M Prescott) 3-9-1(bl) G Duffield 9/2: 0-20412: Kept on well final 1f:
in gd form: see 1396.   20
*1678 SPACE TROOPER [8] (T Fairhurst) 3-9-5(4ex) R Cochrane 6/4 FAV: 0-40113: Well bckd,
ev ch: btr 1678 (made all).   21
1614 BOYNTON [3] (W Elsey) 3-9-7 G Sexton 10/1: 4-02024: Prom, ev ch: seems flattered 1178   13
*1369 CHABLISSE [1] 3-9-6 D Mckeown 10/1: 0P40310: No real threat: much btr 1369 (seller)   11
867 TEED BORE [2] 3-9-2 B Uniacke(7) 10/1: -204300: Abs: best first time out in 39 (soft)   03
1299 Watendlath [7] 8-6(1ow)
7 ran   1½,1½,5,nk,2   (Mrs M A Jarvis)   A Jarvis Royston, Herts.

1774 KELBOURNE HANDICAP 0-35 3YO+   £2439   7f   Good/Firm Slow   [33]

1624 MONINSKY [4] (N Bycroft) 5-8-0 A Shoults(4) 11/1: 0030031: 5 ch g Monsigneur –
Golden Number (Goldhill) Led final 1f, ridden out in a h'cap at Ayr July 25: placed on

sev occasions in '85 but failed to win: in '84 successful at Ayr and Pontefract: eff at 6/7f
on any ground: likes a sharpish trk,' acts on any.   13
1662 GOLD LOFT [12] (P Mitchell) 4-8-3 G Carter(3) 20/1: -100002: Ran on well final 1f:
not an easy ride: see 177.   12
1054 THIRTEENTH FRIDAY [10] (W Pearce) 4-8-3(bl)(10ow)(2oh) N Connorton 33/1: 0-40003: Kept
on: best effort since 259: acts on firm and yldg.   11
1610 KAMARESS [8] (M Brittain) 4-8-5 M Wigham 20/1: 0024004: Led 2f out: fair eff: see 1103   12
1624 MARSILIANA [13] 4-8-0(1ow) M Beecroft 16/1: -040340: Nearest fin: see 1624, 820.   06
1701 DOUBLE CHAI [5] 3-8-4(bl) J Lowe 6/1: -000040: Prom over 5f: btr 1701 (C/D).   11
1698 HIGH PORT [2] 7-7-13 N Carlisle 8/1: 0024440: Prom, fin 7th: see 943.   00
1698 EMERALD EAGLE [6] 5-8-11 R Lines 10/1: 0030020: Hmpd home turn: see 1698, 79.   00
*1500 DARNIT [9] 4-9-12 E Guest(3) 7/2 FAV: -000210: Prom, fdd: much btr 1500 (sharp trk)   00
1701 PHILOSOPHICAL [7] 3-8-0 A Mackay 5/1: 1-00030: Badly hmpd home turn: see 1701.   00
*1500 SPORTING SOVEREIGN [1] 3-8-4(9ex) W Woods(3) 13/2: 0422010: Prom when almost fell
on home turn: see 1701.   00
1247 Miss Primula [14] 8-10   1624 Jo Andrew [11] 7-9(bl)
--   Thatchered [3] 8-9
14 ran   1½,shthd,½,nk,4,½   (R Midgley)   N Bycroft York.

1775 DUNOON MAIDEN STAKES 3YO   £959   1m 3f Good/Firm Slow

1291 HANOOF [2] (M Stoute) 3-8-11 G Duffield 4/9 FAV: -431: 3 ch f Northern Dancer -
Little Bonny (Bonne Noel) Had an easy task and led final 1f, comfortably, in a 3yo mdn at
Ayr July 25: had earlier ran well in gd company at Goodwood and Newcastle: dam fin 2nd in
the Irish Oaks: cost a mammoth $2m: eff at 11f, shd be suited by 12f: acts on gd and firm
ground and should win in better company.   42
1620 KING TEFKROS [5] (M Tompkins) 3-9-0 R Cochrane 9/4: -00332: Led 10f: equally eff
at 10/11f: see 1206.   39
1614 TURINA [1] (D Incisa) 3-8-11 M Beecroft 14/1: 0-003: Ev ch in str: kept on: should
be suited by 12f: acts on gd/firm.   34
1396 EXPERT WITNESS [4] (B Morgan) 3-9-0 G Carter(3) 20/1: -04: No extra in straight.   12
1337 DERRY [3] 3-8-11 R Guest 100/1: -00: Tailed off.   00
5 ran   2,½,10,30   (Maktoum Al-Maktoum)   M Stoute Newmarket

ASCOT   Friday July 25th   Righthand, Stiff Galloping Track

1776 CRANBOURNE CHASE MAIDEN STAKES 3YO   £7421   1m 2f Good 55 +08 Fast

1469 SATISFACTION [2] (W Hern) 3-9-0 W Carson 12/1: 0-22001: 3 ch c Bustino - Conciliation
(St Paddy) Showed improvement on recent form when coming from behind to narrowly gain the
day cl home in quite a fast run 3yo mdn at Ascot July 25: lightly raced in '85: half brother
to the smart 10f performer Morcon: eff over 10/11f: seems to prefer gd or yldg ground to
firm: acts well on a stiff track.   59
1469 MILLERS DUST [5] (H Cecil) 3-9-0 S Cauthen 8/11 FAV: -0232: Raced with his tongue
tied down today, led under press dist, al held by the winner in final 1f tho' only narrowly
btn: see 1031.   58
--   PRINCE ORAC [1] (C Brittain) 3-9-0 G Baxter 33/1: -3: Led 3f out and made a sound
debut: half brother to a middle dist winner in France: may stay beyond 10f: acts on good
ground on a galloping track: should soon find a maiden.   52
1645 SHAMIYDA [3] (R J Houghton) 3-9-0 Paul Eddery 16/1: 0-0344: No extra final 2f: see 1444   47
1046 NORTH LAKE [7] 3-9-0 A Clark 12/1: -00: Same place final 3f: dam a winner in
Ireland over 9f+ and stayed well: should be suited by longer dist: on the upgrade.   48
1184 PODEROSO [9] 3-9-0 P Cook 33/1: 30-0040: Raced with his tongue tied, never better:
stays 10f: see 1184.   47
849 MAGIC VISION [10] 3-8-11 T Ives 16/1: -000: Fin 7th: abs since 849 (12f).   00
1045 DARE SAY [4] 3-9-0 Pat Eddery 4/1: -240: Prom much, fin 8th: lightly raced and
twice below 218.   00
1554 RESCUE PACKAGE [8] 3-9-0 P Waldron 33/1: 4-0440: Made much, wknd quickly: best 1395(1m) 00
9 ran   hd,4,1½,½,½   (Lord Rotherwick)   W Hern West Ilsley, Berks.

1777 ROUS MEMORIAL H'CAP 3YO+ 0-70   £7058   6f   Good 55 +09 Fast   [60]

*1385 CREE BAY [3] (J Spearing) 7-9-0(bl) W Carson 10/1: 3200411: 7 br g Bay Express -
Porsanger (Zeddan) Appears to have found a new lease of life and was winning 2nd val h'cap
on the trot when getting up cl home for a narrow success in Rous Memorial h'cap at Ascot
July 25: winner of similar h'cap at Sandown July 4: failed to win in '85, prev season
successful at Pontefract (2) and Warwick: equally eff at 6/7f: acts on firm and gd, prob
unsuited by soft: best in blinkers.   58
+1457 CHUMMYS PET [1] (N Callaghan) 3-8-5 Pat Eddery 9/4 FAV: 3312112: Came thro' to
lead briefly final 1f, just caught and is in tremendous form: see 1457.   55
1521 GOLD PROSPECT [9] (G Balding) 4-8-2 T Quinn 3/1: 2204023: Led dist, kept on well
when hdd, only narrowly btn: deserves a race: see 1521.   43
1145 TYROLLIE [2] (N Vigors) 4-8-11 P Cook 10/1: -122004: Chall 1f out, not btn far:
best effort since 192 and seems to like gd or softer ground btr than firm.   51

1455 **YOUNG INCA** [10] 8-9-0 R Hills 10/1: -000000: Never looked likely to repeat last
year's success but appears to be returning to form: won 3 times last season including
this event and has scored 4 times in all at Ascot, a course he loves: best form on firm or
good going over 6f.   44
--   SUNDEED [4] 3-9-10 A Bond 25/1: 110-0: Made a fair seasonal debut and will be all
the better for the outing: won first 2 on the trot in '85, minor events at Nottingham and
York and only raced once more: very eff around 5f tho' should stay further: acts on fast
ground and on a galloping track.   59
1669 **TOUCH OF GREY** [6] 3-9-1 S Cauthen 7/1: 1201400: Led/dsptd lead much, fin 8th: best 1145   00
1455 Ho Mi Chinh [5] 9-6   1145 Corn Street [8] 8-10   1508 Amigo Loco [7] 9-12(bl)
10 ran   ½,hd,nk,4,1½   (D J oseman)   J Spearing Wixford, Warwickshire

---

1778 **VIRGINIA WATER MAID. UNRACED 2YO FILLIE**   £8038   6f   Good 55 -05 Slow

--   GAYANE [1] (H Cecil) 2-8-11 S Cauthen 1/1 FAV: 1: 2 b f Nureyev - Roussalka (Habitat)
Very promising filly: first time out ran very green, leading dist and was ridden out to win
a val 2yo fillies Newcomers race at Ascot July 25: held in high regard by her powerful
stable and is certainly beautifully bred, her dam being a half sister to Oh
So Sharp: reportedly has proved quite highly strung on the home gallops but clearly possessed
of plenty of ability and should progress from here.   70
--   BEAUCHAMP BUZZ [5] (J Dunlop) 2-8-11 W Carson 9/2: 2: Fin really well: related to
sev winners between 6f and 1m and is held in some regard by her stable: attractive sort with
scope who will benefit enormously from this experience and should not be opposed next time.   67
--   NOT ALONE [2] (J Winter) 2-8-11 B Rouse 33/1: 3: Chall final 1f, not btn far and
belied her 33/1 S.P: excellent debut from this half sister to winning miler Beeleigh: eff
over 6f on good ground: should prove hard to beat in a maiden next time.   65
--   MUSICAL REVIEW [4] (I Balding) 2-8-11 T Ives 13/2: 4: Made much: gd debut: first
foal of a sprint winner in the USA: seems a speedy sort herself and should be able to
win a maiden soon.   58
--   ACT OF TREASON [8] 2-8-11 W R Swinburn 6/1: 0: Early pace, fin well btn but should
improve for the outing: sister to useful 6/7f winner Kedron: should win a race if her sights
are lowered slightly.   38
--   PERFECT FOIL [3] 2-8-11 B Thomson 33/1: 0: No danger: should benefit from this race:
a very late foal (June 1) who is related to middle dist winner Gillson and is likely to
need more time/longer dist to show her true worth.   33
--   Queens Lake [6] 8-11   --   Taustaff [9] 8-11   --   Miss Jasmine [7] 8-11
9 ran   1,nk,2½,8,2½   (N Philips)   H Cecil Newmarket

1779 **BROWN JACK H'CAP 3YO+ 0-70**   £7047   2m   Good 55 -08 Slow   [69]

1293 **PETRIZZO** [1] (C Brittain) 5-7-13 W Carson 6/1: 0030401: 5 b h Radetzky - Perianth
(Petingo) Broke a long leading run when leading dist keeping on strongly to win a val h'cap
at Ascot July 25: undoubtedly well h'capped on the best of his form which includes an 8l
4th to Longboat in this year's Gold Cup but has hardly been the most consistent of performers
over the seasons: last won in '84 at Chester and in that season was also disqualified after
being first past the post in the Doncaster Cup: eff over 14f, stays 2m+: acts on firm & yldg.   53
1470 **NEWSELLS PARK** [3] (J Winter) 5-8-6(2ow) W R Swinburn 7/2: P-21222: Ran his usual
consistent race: see 1470.   53
1470 **WESTERN DANCER** [2] (C Horgan) 5-8-12 P Cook 2/1 FAV: 4-01343: Ev ch: see 462.   59
--   DESTROYER [5] (K Brassey) 5-9-7 S Whitworth 20/1: 41300-4: Made most and this was
an excellent seasonal reappearance: in '85 won a Gr 3 race at Sandown and was subsequently
a fine 3rd in the Gold Cup here: acts on any ground, stays forever: looks sure to
win a race or two this term.   65
1388 **KING OF COMEDY** [8] 4-7-9 T Williams 14/1: 00-0000: Prom, fdd: best eff this term:
in '85 won at Goodwood and Lingfield: best form so far over 12f on gd or firm ground and
runs well on a sharpish track.   37
1533 **MORGANS CHOICE** [4] 9-7-7(13oh) N Adams 14/1: 0030100: Never btr: stiff task and
ran well: see 1388.   27
1388 **MILTON BURN** [6] 5-7-7 S Dawson 5/1: 0223200: No danger in 7th: much btr 1150 (C/D).   00
1111 **AYRES ROCK** [7] 5-8-13 J Reid 10/1: 0-30400: Prom, wknd: certainly flattered in 617.   00
8 ran   4,hd,3,nk,4   (Curtis Elliott)   C Brittain Newmarket

---

1780 **SANDWICH MAIDEN STAKES 2YO**   £7293   7f   Good 55 -02 Slow

-1488 **CLASSIC TALE** [2] (M Stoute) 2-9-0 W R Swinburn 8/11 FAV: 21: 2 ch c Blushing Groom -
Cambretta (Roberto) Smart, very promising colt: fulfilled his promising debut with an
impr 7l success in a val 2yo mdn at Ascot July 25: led dist and forged clear under minimal
press: half brother to 3 winners, notably successful '85 2yo Singletta: well suited by 7f,
sure to stay further: likes a stiff gall trk and acts on firm and gd ground: not one to
oppose lightly, whatever the company.   77
1587 **BEESHI** [1] (P Cole) 2-9-0 T Quinn 3/1: 322: Led/dsptd lead most, lost nothing in
defeat, coming up against a really smart one here: deserves a mdn soon: see 1242.   54
--   DEPUTY GOVERNOR USA [5] (L Piggott) 2-9-0 T Ives 7/1: 3: Well bckd debutant who
dsptd lead much: somewhat misbehaved in the paddock before hand and will benefit from this
experience: should be well suited by this trip: acts on gd ground: should improve on this.   44

538

ASCOT   Friday July 25th   -Cont'd

-- CAJUN DANCER [3] (M Francis) 2-9-0 Paul Eddery 33/1: 4: Never btr: cost a relatively
inexpensive I R 9,500: stays 7f and will stay further: should improve.   29
-- CELCIUS [7] 2-9-0 P Cook 14/1: 0: Never looked likely but this race should bring
him on: quite a well bred sort whose dam was smart over 1m/10f: certain to be suited by
longer distances than 7f.   26
1510 EL ZETA [4] 2-9-0 S Cauthen 12/1: 040: Early pace: see 1510.   26
-- TREGEAGLE [6] 2-9-0 A Clark 25/1: 0: Appeared green both before and during race:
cheaply bought filly who is a half sister to winning juv Ininsky.   00
7 ran   7,4,6,1½,dd ht   (Sheikh Mohammed)   M Stoute Newmarket

1781 CHESTER APP.H'CAP 3YO+ 0-60   £3168   1m   Good 55 -05 Slow   [50]

*1590 FAIR COUNTRY [4] (D Elsworth) 4-9-1(5ex) P Mcentee(8) 2/1 FAV: -032311: 4 ch f Town
and Country - Fair Measure (Quorum) Useful filly who is in gd form at present and was winning
2nd race on the trot when landing an app h'cap at Ascot July 25: came from behind and showed
a good turn of foot to sprint clear final 1f: equally comfortable winner at Kempton recently:
in '84 won at Newbury: very eff over 1m on a fair or gall trk: acts on firm and yldg: could
complete a hat-trick.   48
*1581 EVERY EFFORT [7] (R Holder) 4-8-6(5ex) A Dicks(7) 7/2: 01D3412: Chall final 1f,
gd effort and is in fine form: may win again soon: see 1581.   35
1041 STEEPLE BELL [8] (M Stoute) 10-9-4 M Giles(8) 7/2: 1200-03: Led briefly dist:
gd effort from this grand old campaigner who won this race last season and also another
event at Kempton: best form on firm or gd grd around 1m tho' stays 10f: genuine & consistent.   43
1390 SAFE CUSTODY [9] (M Fetherston Godley) 4-8-1 L Jones 25/1: 0-00004: Never btr: best
effort this term and seems to be returning to form: see 566.   19
1460 ASSWAN [6] 6-9-13 Dale Gibson(3) 10/1: 21-0200: Made much: twice below 1365 (sharp
trk) and seems inconsistent.   43
1519 MISTER PRELUDE [1] 6-7-7(bl)(3oh) J Carter(3) 8/1: -002000: No danger and was
flattered 1519: see 1081.   09
1390 Gamblers Dream [3] 7-13(hd)   1689 Dicks Folly [2] 7-10
1567 Count Almaviva [5] 7-7(18oh)
9 ran   1,2,4,2,shthd   (Sir Gordon Brunton)   D Elsworth Whitsbury, Hants.

WARWICK   Saturday July 26th   Lefthanded, Turning Track

Official Going Given As GOOD/FIRM

1782 GARRICK MAIDEN FILLIES STAKES 2YO   £846   5f   Firm 12 -02 Slow

1632 ULTRA NOVA [1] (P Cole) 2-8-11 T Quinn 11/4: 3201: 2 ch f Tina's Pet - Jennyjo
(Martinmas) Nicely bckd and comfortably made all in a 2yo fillies mdn at Warwick July 26:
sprint bred filly who fetched 6,600 gns as a yearling: eff over 5f on a sharpish course,
ran below par on a stiffer trk last time: suited by gd or faster ground and does well with
forcing tactics.   48
-- PARADISE COFFEE [6] (O Douieb) 2-8-11 R Machado 7/1: 2: Friendless in mkt on debut:
kept on well, running a fair race: cost 26,000 gns as yearling: is a half sister to numerous
winners: will stay further than this minimum trip: acts on firm ground.   38
-- LITTLE BOLDER [9] (A Stewart) 2-8-11 M Banner 16/1: 3: Ran on well from ⅓ way:
fair debut: cost 18,000 gns and is a half sister to a couple of 7/8f winners: will be suited
by another furlong: acts on fast ground: should improve.   32
1550 INDIAN SET [12] (G Lewis) 2-8-11 G Sexton 8/1: 004: Needs further: acts on firm : see 1550 26
1205 HOLD ON PLEASE [4] 2-8-11 A Clark 8/1: 400: Speed over ⅓ way: twice below form
shown on her debut in 848 (gd ground).   22
-- HOLTS WAY [8] 2-8-11 D Williams(7) 33/1: 0: Dwelt: nearest fin: will improve: cheaply
bought filly who is a half sister to sev winners: will stay further: acts on firm ground.   20
1282 ORDINA [13] 2-8-11 R Cochrane 5/2 FAV: 40: Early speed: much btr 1282 (6f, stiff trk)   00
1604 Try Dancer [10] 8-11   -- Irenic [2] 8-11   -- Joyful Mistress [7] 8-11
1427 Nightdress [5] 8-11
11 ran   3,2,2½,1,1   (C Shiacolas)   P Cole Whatcombe, Oxon.

1783 ENTERTAINERS HANDICAP STAKES (0-50) 3YO   £2624   1m   Firm 12 +14 Fast   [49]

1256 ADAMSTOWN [5] (M Prescott) 3-8-9 G Duffield 9/1: -3141: 3 b g Hittite Glory - Dawn
Attack (Midsummer Night II) Led below dist and was ridden out to win a fast run 3yo h'cap
at Warwick July 26: last month was a game winner of an Edinburgh mdn: best form over 1m on
gd or faster ground, tho' does act on soft: well suited by a sharp/easy course.   41
1511 KALANDARIYA [4] (R Johnson Houghton) 3-8-13 R Cochrane 9/2: 4-3022: In fine form:see 1511   43
1532 SUPREME KINGDOM [6] (R Hollinshead) 3-8-7 S Perks 10/1: 3200043: Went on ⅓ way, not
btn far: gd effort and likes to be out in front: acts on any trk: see 49.   35
*1375 MILLRACER [8] (M Jarvis) 3-8-8 W Woods(3) 5/4 FAV: 40-014: Well bckd: not quicken
dist and much btr over 7f in 1375 (gall trk).   28
1153 LITTLE PIPERS [2] 3-9-3 A Kimberley 16/1: -000000: Never nearer: btr effort: see 1032   36
1579 HAYWAIN [9] 3-7-10 R Street 16/1: 00-0300: Al mid-div: see 1257 & 874.   13
1520 HALO HATCH [11] 3-9-4 A Clark 8/1: 03-0300: Led to ⅓ way: much btr 570 (10f).   00

1384 Prohibited [3] 9-7   1669 Merrymoles [7] 7-11   1245 Strive [1] 8-12
1581 Song An Dance Man [10] 8-4
11 ran   ½,1,4,½,½   (Derek K Stokes)   M Prescott Newmarket

1784 WATERSIDE SELLING STAKES   £879   1m 2f   Firm 12 –23 Slow

1549 SOHO SUE [3] (D Ancil) 3-8-8 G Duffield 12/1: -100001: 3 ch f Red Regent - Reluctant
Maid (Relko) Well suited by this longer trip, led dist to score cleverly in a seller at
Warwick July 26 (bought in 1,900 gns) : first time out winner of a 3yo seller at Doncaster:
eff over 7/8f, stays 10f well: acts on gd and firm ground and also does well with forcing
tactics.   22
1666 ARMORAD [2] (P Haslam) 4-9-3 G French 5/1: 0-00402: Fin well: stays 10f: see 1567.   15
1747 ANGIES VIDEO [5] (R Holder) 4-9-0 A Proud 11/4 FAV: 0003203: Led 2f out: stays
10f: see 1567.   07
1316 SPLENDID MAGNOLIA [6] (S Dow) 3-8-6 P Simms(7) 33/1: 00-0004: Never nearer: maiden
who ran his best race to date here: stays 10f: suited by fast ground.   11
1231 GULPHAR [1] 4-9-3 G Baxter 7/1: 440-000: Made much: see 1103.   04
1195 MASTER FRANCIS [12] 4-9-3 R Cochrane 7/1: -000000: Btn dist: no form this term: see 202 00
1666 TRACK MARSHALL [8] 4-9-3 R Street 3/1: -322320: Fin 8th: much btr 1666.   00
1579 Ciaras Lad [15] 9-3   --   Clap Your Hands [13] 8-3
1439 The Moon And Back [11] 8-6   1416 Go Flamingo [9] 8-3
1535 Thatchit [10] 9-3   --   Low Ration [4] 8-3
13 ran   1½,2,nk,3,2   (D Ancil)   D Ancil Banbury, Oxon

1785 STRATFORD FESTIVAL NURSERY H'CAP 2YO   £3042   5f   Firm 12 –06 Slow   [40]

*1403 LUCRATIF [7] (I Balding) 2-9-6 P Cook 1/1 FAV: 11: 2 b c Cure The Blues - Lucaya
(Mill Reef) Useful juv: was heavily bckd and led dist, comfortably, in a nursery h'cap at
Warwick July 26: narrow winner of a minor race at Bath on his debut recently: cost 48,000 gns
as a yearling and is related to winners abroad: very eff over 5f and will stay further:
acts on fast ground: can defy a penalty.   46
*1445 MICRO LOVE [2] (H O'neill) 2-9-7 I Johnson 6/1: 3012: Went on below dist: no extra
cl home tho' remains in fine form: see 1445.   40
*1298 FIVE SIXES [3] (N Tinkler) 2-8-8 J Lowe 11/2: 1D42113: Led/dsptd lead most of way:
creditable effort in this btr company: see 1298.   22
*1585 DUTCH COURAGE [1] (D Morley) 2-9-13(7ex) C Rutter(5) 11/2: 443314: Had no chance
after a slow start: fin well tho' is btr judged on his comfortable win in 1585.   37
1570 SAY YOU WILL [6] 2-8-13 T Quinn 25/1: 40040: No extra dist: btr 1570 (6f stiff trk)   17
995 QUITE SO [5] 2-9-4 R Cochrane 12/1: -0100: Early speed: much btr 565.   00
596 MISS MARJORIE [4] 2-8-1 L Riggio(7) 20/1: 0100: Lost her action after ½ way,
sn behind: abs since 596: best when winning a seller over this C/D in 337 (yldg).   00
7 ran   1½,1½,1½,2,10,8   (J A McDougald)   I Balding Kingsclere, Hants.

1786 SWAN MAIDEN STAKES 3YO   £706   1m 6f   Firm 12 –25 Slow

1580 FRANCHISE [3] (R Johnson Houghton) 3-8-11 D Price(5) 8/1: -01: 3 gr f Warpath - Fee
(Mandamus) Impr filly: led under press inside final 1f in a 3yo mdn at Warwick July 26: eff
over 10f and clearly stays 14f well: acts on fast grd and seems to have no trk preferences. 44
1646 NEWQUAY [1] (G Harwood) 3-8-11(VIS) A Clark 11/10 JT FAV: 3-022: Took command 6f
out, hdd cl home: well clear of main rival: see 1646 & 1259.   42
1556 DEBCO [4] (J Dunlop) 3-9-0 T Quinn 11/10 JT FAV: -023: Wknd quickly home turn:
much better 1556 over a slightly longer trip.   00
1258 CUPIDS BOWER [2] (A James) 3-8-11 W Woods(3) 100/1: 000-04: Early leader: btn in
selling company last season and has yet to show any worthwhile form: half sister to winning
stayer/hurdler Norfolk Arrow.   00
1580 PLUM BOSSY [5] 3-8-11 C Rutter(5) 50/1: -0400: Btn home turn: see 1404.   00
5 ran   ½,25,6,4   (R F Johnson Houghton)   R Johnson Houghton Blewbury, Oxon.

1787 MARY ARDEN HANDICAP STAKES (0-35)   £1427   1m 2f   Firm 12 –03 Slow   [32]

*1559 BLENDERS CHOICE [14] (K Brassey) 4-10-1(8ex) C Rutter(5) 4/1: -030111: 4 b g Cavo
Doro - Harriny (Floribunda) In fine form, gamely defied top weight, leading over 3f out in a
h'cap at Warwick July 26: recently successful in similar races at Chepstow and Folkestone:
best form over 10/12f: suited by gd or faster ground: acts on any trk: does well with forcing
tactics.   41
1689 PEARL PET [13] (P Makin) 4-8-8 T Quinn 12/1: 00-2002: Al cl.up: ran on well: see 860.   18
1441 KUWAIT MOON [4] (J Francome) 4-9-0 R Cochrane 8/1: 2-00003: Nearest fin: best 532 (12f). 18
1559 DANCING BARRON [6] (M Blanshard) 5-9-2(bl) G Baxter 10/1: 0000304: Made much: best
here in 1473 (12f): see 750.   14
1473 RHEIN COURT [12] 6-7-11 D Williams(7) 16/1: 00-0000: Al there: best In 547 (yldg).   00
1563 RAPID LAD [1] 8-9-10 P Cook 7/2 FAV: 0-01400: Late prog: best 1106.   19
*1579 FLEET BAY [9] 6-7-13 P Mcentee(7) 9/2: 000-010: Fin 9th: btr over 1m in 1579, gall trk) 00
1535 Crisp And Keen [3] 7-10   --   Just Met [5] 8-10
1415 Bels Angel [8] 8-7   1412 Havens Pride [11] 7-8   1437 Richards Folly [7] 8-0
992 Clipsall [10] 8-9   609 Seven Swallows [2] 9-4
14 ran   ½,2½,3,½,1½   (Mark O'Connor)   K Brassey Upper Lambourn, Berks.

Official Going Given As GOOD

1788 ORLOFF DIAMOND STAKES LADIES RACE   £4285   1m   Good/Firm 24 +02 Fast

476 EVES ERROR [15] (M Stoute) 3-9-6 Maxine Juster 5/2 FAV: 112-041: 3 ch c Be My Guest
- Apple Peel (Pall Mall) Smart colt: despite a lengthy abs, al going well and sprinted clear
from the dist for a ready 7l success in quite a fast run and val Orloff Diamond Stks (Ladies
race) at Ascot July 26: a smart 2yo winning at Epsom and Nottingham and 2nd in a Gr 2 event
at the Curragh on final outing: half brother to sev winners including Apples of Gold: very
eff over 1m and acts on gd/firm and soft going.   73
1383 HILLS BID [10] (B Hills) 3-9-6 Penny Hills 9/2: 2-10032: Al prom, in gd form: see 615.   61
1463 MAWSUFF [11] (H T Jones) 3-9-6 Franca Vittadini 9/2: -02123: U.R. and bolted before
start: made much: seems ideally suited by 7f: see 1036.   54
1249 VAGUE MELODY [14] (L Piggott) 4-10-3 Jenny Goulding 9/1: 2301134: Ran a gd race at
the weights: see 1173.   49
1000 KUFUMA [3] 4-10-3(vis) Sara Cumani 9/1: 220-000: Ev ch: disapp this term: see 1000.   42
1667 MARSH HARRIER [9] 5-10-3 Candy Moore 66/1: -000200: Ran remarkably well: see 1188.   37
676 CRESTA AUCTION [17] 3-9-6 Princess Anne(3) 6/1: 3-11230: Abs, prom much, fin 9th: see 344 00
1519 Iktiyar [13] 10-3   1375 Davemma [5] 9-0   1590 Derryring [12] 10-3
1396 Mostango [1] 9-3(vis)   1517 Derby Day 0 10-3   1362 Scintillator [16] 9-3
1472 Dasa Queen [4] 9-0   -- Marine [7] 10-0   578 Big Pal [2] 10-3
16 ran   7,2½,1½,2½,½   (Sheikh Mohammed)   M Stoute Newmarket

1789 GROUP 3 PRINCESS MARGARET STKS 2YO   £10614   6f   Good/Firm 24 -03 Slow

-1464 HIAAM [1] (M Stoute) 2-8-8 W R Swinburn 4/6 FAV: 21: 2 ch f Alydar - Kamar
(Key to the Mint) Very smart filly in the making: readily landed the odds, leading inside
final 2f and forged 4l clear in Gr 3 Princess Margaret
Stks (2yo fillies) at Ascot July 26: cost $1.5m and is related to a topclass performer in
Canada: eff 6f, sure to be suited by longer dist: acts well on fast grd on a stiff trk:
not one to oppose lightly.   75
*1154 MOUNTAIN MEMORY [6] (P Walwyn) 2-8-13 Paul Eddery 9/1: 12: Led/dsptd lead most:
fine effort and will win more races: see 1154.   70
1454 BLUE TANGO [4] (R Laing) 2-8-8 W Carson 16/1: 4332133: Up there thr'out and is ultra
consistent: see 1238, 1454.   59
*1021 GENTLE PERSUASION [5] (I Balding) 2-8-13 S Cauthen 6/1: 14: Prom most: see 1021.   63
1108 NATURALLY FRESH [2] 2-8-8 Pat Eddery 7/2: 41140: Al chasing leaders, btn fully 2f
out and rather disapp since 773 (5f, made all).   46
1632 SURELY GREAT [3] 2-8-8 M L Thomas 66/1: 2024020: Outpaced final 2f: btr 1632 (5f).   36
6 ran   4,2½,½,6,5   (Maktoum Al-Maktoum)   M Stoute Newmarket

1790 GROUP 1 KING GEORGE VI DIAMOND STKS   £152468   1m 4f   Good/Firm 24 +28 Fast

+1389 DANCING BRAVE [1] (G Harwood) 3-8-8 Pat Eddery 6/4: 1-11211: 3 b c Lyphard - Navajo
Princess (Drone) Top Class colt: produced an immaculate performance when narrow but decisive
winner of very fast run King George Diamond Stks at Ascot July 26: earlier won the 2,000 Guineas
and Craven Stks at Newmarket and the Eclipse at Sandown: met his only defeat when unlucky
loser of Epsom Derby: easily won both races in '85 at Newmarket and Sandown: eff over 1m/10f,
stays 12f well: acts on soft but his fine action is well suited by firm or gd ground:
possesses tremendous acceleration and undoubtedly laid claim today to being best 3yo of '86.   99
*1456 SHARDARI [8] (M Stoute) 4-9-7 S Cauthen 14/1: 11-2412: Highclass colt: prom, led
briefly 2f out, kept on strongly under press and was 4l clear rem: right back to his very
best and will prove difficult to beat in the rem middle dist pattern races of this season:
thoroughly genuine and consistent: see 1456.   97
1389 TRIPTYCH [9] (P L Biancone) 4-9-4 Y Saint Martin 25/1: 3-42123: Outpaced early: kept
on well str and never runs a bad race: seee 1389.   86
+1330 SHAHRASTANI [3] (M Stoute) 3-8-8 W R Swinburn 11/10 FAV: 2-11114: Edgy, nervy and
looked light in the paddock: was done-with 2½f out and this was well below his best (1330)   82
1593 DIHISTAN [7] 4-9-7 A Kimberley 100/1: 12-1130: Prom, led after 1m, fdd but not
disgraced in this hot company: see 1173.   78
1456 PETOSKI [5] 4-9-7 W Carson 14/1: 011-330: Al same place and never looked likely to repeat
last year's win: much btr 1456: see 885.   76
1095 SUPREME LEADER [2] 4-9-7 A Murray 150/1: -113300: Prom over 1m, fin 7th: see 1095.   00
1456 VOUCHSAFE [4] 4-9-7 B Procter 1000/1: -041D00: Dsptd lead 7f, pacemaker for Petoski.   00
885 BOLDDEN [6] 4-9-7 P Cook 1000/1: 10-0000: Set a furious pace 1m: pacemaker for Petoski.   00
9 ran   ½,4,5,2,1½   (K Abdulla)   G Harwood Pulborough, Sussex

1791 EBF GRANVILLE MAIDEN STAKES 2YO   £7035   6f   Good/Firm 24 -36 Slow

-- NAHEEZ [1] (D Elsworth) 2-9-0 W R Swinburn 11/4: 1: 2 b c Critique - Academic World
(Arts and Letters) First time out, nicely bckd and led dist, comfortably, in Granville Maiden
Stks (unraced 2yos) at Ascot July 26: half brother to a winner in USA: dam best at up to 1m:

reportedly represents his stable's best 2yo: sure to stay beyond 6f: acts on firm ground
on a stiff track: may improve further.   54
-- ALI SMITH [6] (R Boss) 2-9-0 Y Saint Martin 7/1: 2: Al there, kept on well: half
brother to 2 winners in Italy: will stay beyond 6f: acts on fast ground.   50
-- ZARBYEV [4] (G Harwood) 2-9-0 Pat Eddery 9/4 FAV: 3: Uneasy fav, outpaced early,
met trouble in running and fin well: first foal of a sprint winner: very eff at 6f on
fast ground: should do btr next time.   50
-- KASTAMOUN [3] (R J Houghton) 2-9-0 S Cauthen 3/1: 4: Made much: first foal of a 7f
winner in France who is related to topclass performers Kozana and Karkour: bred to be suited
by middle distances in time and will need further than 6f.   38
-- FAILIQ [2] 2-9-0 Paul Eddery 9/2: 0: Early leader, fdd: cost 52,000 gns: dam a fair
middle distance winner and is related to sev decent performers: may improve.   33
5 ran   1½,hd,4,1½   (K Al-Said)   D Elsworth Whitsbury, Hants.

1792 SANDRINGHAM STAKES HCAP 0-70 3YO+   £7070   1m 2f Good/Firm 24 -09 Slow   [52]

*1517 ROYAL HALO [1] (G Harwood) 5-9-8(4ex) Pat Eddery 4/1: 4-20111: 5 b h Halo - Lady
Gordon (Royal Levee) Very useful, impr horse: completed his hat trick with a ready win in a
val h'cap at Ascot July 26, leading final 1f: comfortably won a h'cap at Lingfield and an
app race at Brighton prev: in '84 won at Kempton: seems equally eff over 1m/10f: acts on
firm and soft and on any track: looks likely to complete a four-timer.   60
+1468 LASTCOMER [4] (M Stoute) 3-9-1 W R Swinburn 11/8 FAV: 1-0012: Heavily bckd: ev ch
final 2f: clear rem: in gd form: see 1468.   60
1526 INNISHMORE ISLAND [6] (J Dunlop) 3-9-7 W Carson 8/1: 312-303: Made much: see 1237.   59
1038 PATO [5] (I Matthews) 4-9-4 C Rutter(5) 14/1: 10-0004: Prom most: see 511.   39
1526 MERLE [2] 4-9-5 S Cauthen 6/1: -000000: No danger: much btr 1526.   40
1601 SITTING BULL [3] 4-8-9 Paul Eddery 4/1: 00-0420: Sn rear: much btr 1601.   20
6 ran   1½,4,3,shthd,7   (Mrs Doris Campbell)   G Harwood Pulborough, Sussex

1793 CROCKER BULTEEL STAKES HCAP 0-70 3YO+   £7327   1m   Good/Firm 24 -01 Slow   [65]

-1292 SUPER TRIP [13] (M Fetherston Godley) 5-8-0 C Rutter(5) 8/1: 0021421: 5 b h Windjammer
- Esker Rose (Sunny Way) Useful, consistent horse: came from behind to lead 1f out, held
on well in a driving fin to a val h'cap at Ascot July 26: earlier won at Beverley and was
an excellent 4th in the Royal Hunt Cup: seems best on a stiff trk on fast ground tho' also
acts on good: genuine and consistent.   50
573 ADVANCE [5] (J Tree) 5-9-7 Pat Eddery 5/1: 101-002: Chall final 1f, just failed to
repeat last year's success under topweight and is right back to his best: should be hard to
beat next time: see 573.   70
1729 AVENTINO [1] (J Sutcliffe) 3-8-2(bl)(5ex) M Hills 7/4 FAV: 1111133: Quick reappearance:
kept on well and not btn far: seee 1486.   60
+1383 PROMISED ISLE [10] (Lady Herries) 5-8-10 A Murray 11/2: 2-32314: Chall, going well,
dist not btn far and is in gd form: see 1383.   56
1525 FUSILIER [4] 4-7-8 M L Thomas 12/1: -300000: Led 2f out, best 17 (soft).   32
1455 QUALITAIR FLYER [12] 4-8-12(bl) G Brown 14/1: 0000000: Prom much: much btr 1455 (7f). 44
*1525 DORSET COTTAGE [11] 4-9-4(5ex) S Quane(7) 7/1: -032010: Cl.up most, fin 7th: btr 1525. 00
1581 ROCKMARTIN [9] 4-8-3 P Cook 9/2: 0-00020: Al behind and much btr 1581.   00
1109 INDIAN HAL [3] 4-8-8 Paul Eddery 5/1: 1-04400: Fin last: disapp since 706.   00
1526 Dancing Zeta [8] 9-5(vis)   1514 Barrack Street [2] 9-4
1455 Postorage [6] 9-6
12 ran   hd,½,½,½,4,3   (J Maxwell)   M Fetherston Godley East Ilsley, Berks

Official Going Given As GOOD/FIRM

1794 DILSTON H'CAP 3YO 0-35   £2243   1m   Good 49 -12 Slow   [36]

1412 TAYLORMADE BOY [7] (D Smith) 3-9-7 L Charnock 5/1: 3123031: 3 b c Dominion - Ash
Gayle (Lord Gayle): Led 2f out, driven out, narrowly in a 3yo h'cap at Newcastle July 26:
earlier won a mdn at Edinburgh: eff at 1m, stays 10f: acts on gd/firm & hvy grnd & on any trk 37
1614 SHARONS ROYALE [2] (R Whitaker) 3-8-2 K Bradshaw(2) 6/1: 0-00032: Ran on under press
and just btn: in gd form: see 1309.   17
1269 ORTICA [5] (J Etherington) 3-8-12 M Wood 5/2: -4023: Hung left final 1f: see 1269.   23
1244 PARTS IS PARTS [3] (R Williams) 3-9-5 R Cochrane 4/1: -0004: Led 6f: stays 1m: see 1244. 26
1198 GLACIER LASS [1] 3-8-4(bl) B Thomson 14/1: 00-000: Ev ch str: lightly raced this
term and seems not an easy ride.   09
1418 PELLS CLOSE [9] 3-8-1(bl) A Mercer 10/1: -000000: No show: little form.   03
1371 ROYAL FAN [6] 3-9-7 M Birch 6/1: -00100: Twice below form 891 (6f).   00
613 Blue Bells Star [8] 8-7
8 ran   hd,2½,1½,1,1½   (Bryan Robson)   D Smith Bishop Auckland, Co Durham

1795 COUPLAND SELLING STAKES 2YO   £1350   7f   Good 49 -45 Slow

1622 GILLOT BAR [5] (M W Easterby) 2-8-8 K Hodgson 6/4 FAV: 000021: 2 b f Rarity -
Marfisa (Green God): Landed some good bets, making ev yd & holding on by ½L in a slow run 2yo
seller at Newcastle July 26: eff at 7f on gd & firm grnd: acts on any trk: seems suited by
front running: no bid for the winner here.   26

*1635 CHANTILLY DAWN [10] (R Whitaker) 2-8-8 K Bradshaw(5) 4/1: 00012: Chall final 1f: in
fine form: seems equally eff at 6/7f: see 1635.   25
1279 BENFIELD MORPETH [9] (J Berry) 2-8-11 J Carroll(7) 10/1: 002103: Sn prom: stays 7f:
acts on any grnd: tried in a visor last time: see 821.   21
1622 LYN RAE [4] (M H Easterby) 2-8-8 M Birch 11/1: 0004: Prominent, every chance:
stays 7f: acts on good and soft.   17
*1358 KIND LADY [6] 2-8-8 A Mercer 7/2: 42310: Ev ch: stays 7f, but btr 1358 (6f, firm).   14
1611 WOLF J FLYWHEEL [2] 2-8-11 B Thomson 7/1: 2000020: No extra inside final 2f: see 1611.   14
1088 My Mabel [8] 8-8   1622 Fantine [7] 8-8(bl)   1478 Katie Cuddles [1] 8-8
1622 Rosinsky [3] 8-11
10 ran   ½,3,½,1½,1½   (Hippodromo Racing Ltd)   M W Easterby Sheriff Hutton, Yorks

1796 GREENALLS BREWERY H'CAP 3YO+ 0-60   £4549   5f   Good 49 -03 Slow   [52]

-1638 RAMBLING RIVER [5] (W A Stephenson) 9-8-6(vis) J Lowe 4/1: 0200021: 9 b h Forlorn River-
Who-Done-It (Lucero): Came from off the pace to lead inside final 1f, driven out in a h'cap
at Newcastle July 26: in '85 won at Edinburgh and Newmarket: in '83 won 4 times: equally eff
at 5/6f: acts on any going & on any trk.   41
1638 SULLYS CHOICE [3] (D Chapman) 5-8-10(bl) M Birch 7/1: 1310032: Led briefly nearing
final 1f: in gd form: see 520.   41
1268 IBERIAN START [6] (D Barron) 3-8-12 B Thomson 11/2: 02-2103: Led 1f out: best 1029.   49
1508 KING CHARLEMAGNE [7] (G Reveley) 7-9-0 D Leadbitter(5) 4/1: 000-004: Led 2f out: see 1508.38
1682 BAY BAZAAR [4] 4-7-10 Julie Bowker(6) 12/1: 0003400: Prom, ev ch: see 1682, 42.   20
1505 MANDRAKE MADAM [2] 3-8-11 L Charnock 12/1: 0000330: Led 3f: btr 1505.   38
+1508 ROTHERFIELD GREYS [1] 4-10-2(9ex) J Leech(7) 9/4 FAV: 0-11010: Wknd over 1f out:
disapp after 1508 (firm).   00
7 ran   1½,hd,2½,shhd,1   (Miss G M Richardson)   W A Stephenson Leasingthorne

1797 SEAHOUSES MAIDEN STAKES 3YO UPWARDS   £1790   1m 1f   Good 49 +01 Fast

1178 HAWARDEN [3] (B Hills) 3-8-8(BL) B Thomson 5/2: -4001: 3 b c Hawaii - First Idea
(Forli): Bl first time & made most, driven out in a 4 runner mdn at Newcastle July 26:
first time out fin a gd 4th to Armada in the Wood Ditton at Newmarket: eff at 9f: acts on
gd & yld grnd.   51
1539 COCCOLUTO [2] (J Dunlop) 3-8-8(BL) J Lowe 1/2 FAV: 00-0222: Bl first time and well
bckd: ev ch in str: lacks foot: see 1539, 863.   49
1511 PLEASING PROSPECT [1] (M H Easterby) 3-8-5 M Birch 6/1: 300-03: Early ldr: fdd str.   00
863 DUTCH QUEEN [4] (M Brittain) 3-8-5 T Lucas 33/1: -04: Abs: al last: half sister to
several winners but has shown nothing in 2 outings to date.   00
4 ran   1,25,25   (Alan Clore)   B Hills Lambourn, Berks

1798 NORHAM STAKES 2YO   £2147   6f   Good 49 -27 Slow

1552 TOUGH N GENTLE [5] (L Piggott) 2-8-11 T Lucas 2/1: 321231: 2 b c Ginistrelli -
Added Attraction (Double Jay): Tough and genuine colt: made ev yd, gamely in a 3 runner 2yo
stakes at Newcastle July 26: earlier made almost all at Warwick and has yet to fin out of
the first 3: eff at 6f, stays 7f: acts on gd/firm & yld & on any trk: al gives his best.   55
*1357 WABARAH [4] (H T Jones) 2-8-8 P Darcy 13/8 FAV: 3112: Switched over 1f out: just btn:
in gd form: see 1357.   51
583 COLWAY RALLY [1] (J Watts) 2-8-11 A Mercer 14/1: 203: Fdd final 1f after a long abs:
fair effort: eff at 5/6f on gd & yld/soft: should find a small race soon.   48
3 ran   hd,2   (Sidney L Port)   L Piggott Newmarket

1799 BOTHAL MAIDEN STAKES 3YO UPWARDS   £2350   2m   Good 49 +07 Fast

1535 ALLATUM [5] (B Hills) 3-8-4(2ow) B Thomson 7/4 FAV: -2041: 3 b f Alleged - Star In
The North (Northern Dancer): Led 4f out, driven out in quite a fast run staying mdn at
Newcastle July 26 : clearly well suited by 2m: acts on gd & yld grnd & on any trk.   42
1372 DESERTED [8] (G P Gordon) 3-8-4(2ow) M Birch 2/1: 00-042: Ev ch str: 12L clear 3rd:
stays 2m: acts on gd & fast grnd & a stiff trk.   40
-- FALLOWFIELD LAD [4] (C Tinkler) 3-8-5 T Lucas 14/1: -3: Some late hdway & should impr
on this: probably stays 2m: acts on gd grnd.   29
1444 GREAT GANDER [3] (J Dunlop) 3-8-5 K Hodgson 4/1: -04: Kept on under driving: half
brother to several winners, incl Lohengrin: should be suited by a distance of grnd.   28
1251 PANTO GIRL [7] 5-9-2 M Wood 33/1: -00: There 10f: half sister to useful chaser
Areus and may do btr over hdles.   00
1426 CHERRY LUSTRE [2] 3-8-5(vis) A Mercer 13/2: -000330: Led 12f, wknd quickly: btr 1426.   00
-- Moonlighting [6] 9-2   -- Portly [1] 9-5
8 ran   1½,12,shhd,30,1½   (Alan Clore)   B Hills Lambourn, Berks

1800 FORD APP.H'CAP 3YO+ 0-35   £1230   1m 1f   Good 49 -07 Slow   [29]

1558 DOMINION PRINCESS [6] (P Rohan) 5-8-7 J Quinn 11/2: 4433031: 5 b m Dominion -
Eastwood Bounty (Bounteous): Made almost all and despite being btn ¼L was placed first in an
app h'cap at Newcastle July 26: first success: placed several times previously: eff over
1m/10f: acts on firm & soft & on any trk: seems suited by front running.   16

1431 PORT PLEASE [2] (M H Easterby) 3-8-7 G Hindmarch(7)8/1: 4002: Hmpd badly home turn
and rider lost irons: lost pitch, but stayed on well: possibly an unlucky loser: acts on
gd & yld grnd & a gall trk.   24
1613 LUCKY WEST [5] (G Moore) 3-8-6 D Casey(3) 11/2: 001001D: Led close home under press,
but interfered with Port Please 4f out and was placed 3rd: stays 10f: see 1053.   27
1678 HARSLEY SURPRISE [1] (N Tinkler) 3-8-7 Kim Tinkler 7/2: 3314104: Nearest fin: nicely
bckd here: see 1267.   22
1139 BELLA BANUS [4] 4-9-7 M Brennan(5) 5/1: 02-0000: Prom, ev ch: see 606.   22
1547 GODS LAW [7] 5-8-9 G Craggs(7) 3/1 FAV: 3213020: Took strong hold & much btr 1547.   00
1547 CLOTILDA [3] 4-8-8 B Mcgiff(3) 16/1: 000-000: Slow start & no threat: see 1547.   00
7 ran   ½,2½,1,1½,5   (Mrs H P Rohan)   P Rohan Malton, Yorks

---

LINGFIELD   Saturday July 26th   Lefthand, Sharpish, Undulating Track

1801 MANIFESTO MAIDEN FILLIES STKS 2YO   £998   6f   Firm 13 -09 Slow

1464 COLOR ARTIST [10] (J Winter) 2-8-11 S Cauthen 6/4 FAV: 01: 2 ch f Artaius - Color
Spectrum (Queen's Hussar): Useful, impr filly: not much room ½way, but stayed on well to lead
last strides in a 2yo fillies mdn at Lingfield July 26: first time out was a most promising
5th to Canadian Mill in a valuable fillies mdn at Newmarket: half sister to minor 1m winner
Rainbow Ripple: eff at 6f, should be suited by 7f: acts on gd & firm grnd & on any trk:
will continue to improve.   49
707 VEVILA [2] (L Cumani) 2-8-11 R Guest 13/8: 22: Led over 2f out: just caught: stays 6f: see 707.48
1604 SPY GIFT [7] (M Stoute) 2-8-11 W R Swinburn 12/1: 03: Ran on well closing stages,
fin 4L clear rem: fast impr & should have no trouble finding a race: will be suited by 7f
plus: acts on gd grnd.   44
1604 NAJABA [5] (C Benstead) 2-8-11 B Rouse 20/1: 004: Prom ev ch: see 601.   30
1440 LINDAS TREAT [8] 2-8-11 P Tulk 33/1: 00: Never nearer: on the up grade: cost
45,000 gns as a yearling: should stay further than 6f: acts on gd grnd & a sharpish trk.   22
1604 LADYS MANTLE [15] 2-8-11 P Waldron 14/1: 00: Led over ½way: American bred filly who
was cheaply acquired as a yearling.   20
1238 Final Rush [11] 8-11   1550 Bleu Celeste [1] 8-11   --   Top Cover [13] 8-11
1440 Wind And Wave [9] 8-11   --   Shirbella [14] 8-11
1440 Lisasham [12] 8-11   --   Dragusa [6] 8-11   1604 Lady Westgate [3] 8-11
14 ran   shhd,1½,4,2½,½   (D O McIntyre)   J Winter Newmarket

1802 MANIFESTO MAIDEN FILLIES STKS 2YO   £991   6f   Firm 13 -06 Slow

1440 CLEAR HER STAGE [14] (J Sutcliffe) 2-8-11 T Williams 2/1 FAV: 31: 2 b f Taufan -
Amore Mare (Varano): Made most on the stands side when a comfortable 1¼L winner of a 2yo
mdn at Lingfield July 26: first time out was a gd 3rd to Shining Water at Windsor: eff at
6f, should be suited by 7f plus: acts on fast grnd & a sharpish trk.   51
1154 GHANAYIM [5] (H Thomson Jones) 2-8-11 A Murray 13/2: 02: Al up there: gd effort &
should go one btr soon: will be suited by 7f: see 1154.   45
--   MEXICAN HONEY [6] (H Cecil) 2-8-11 S Cauthen 7/2: 3: Led far side: promising racecourse debut from this $210,000 yearling: eff at 6f, should be suited by 7f: acts on fast grnd 40
1632 MOUNT VENUS [10] (G Balding) 2-8-11 R Weaver 10/1: 04: Sn prom: see 1632.   30
--   GRANNY BIMPS [4] 2-8-11 R Guest 33/1: 0: Prom far side: fair debut: cost $100,000:
will be suited by 7f & further: acts on fast grnd.   28
--   RAHWAH [12] 2-8-11 B Rouse 20/1: 0: Early speed: cost 135,000 gns as a yearling:
will be suited by further than 6f.   23
--   TAMASSOS [11] 2-8-11 Pat Eddery 8/1: 0: Mkt drifter: no show, but should impr: half
sister to placed mdn King Tefkros: will be suited by 7f plus.   00
1604 OUT ON A FLYER [9] 2-8-11 A Mcglone 8/1: 00: Prom early: much btr 1604.   00
1632 Whos Zoomin Who [1] 8-11   1555 Shoot The Moon [2] 8-11
1440 Blandell Beauty [7] 8-11   --   Kinsham Dene 0 8-11
1555 Stainsby Girl [8] 8-11   --   Marie Baby [3] 8-11
14 ran   1½,2,3,½,2,½   (Mrs Jan Siegel)   J Sutcliffe Epsom, Surrey

1803 SIREN SELLING STAKES 2YO   £986   6f   Firm 13 -39 Slow

1576 KIBARA [3] (P Haslam) 2-8-8 T Williams 12/1: 01: 2 b f African Sky - Kanchenjunga
(Hotfoot): Mkt drifter, but led over 2f out, comfortably in a 2yo seller at Lingfield July 26
(bought in 1,450 gns): seems well suited by 6f, fast grnd & a sharpish, undulating trk.   24
1495 HEY AMADEUS [5] (P Mitchell) 2-8-11 K Butler 4/1: 02: Dropped in class: al up there:
eff at 6f on gd grnd & a sharpish trk.   21
1665 RAJIVS DEBT [10] (J Sutcliffe) 2-8-11 M Hills 2/1 FAV: 003: Well bckd: dropped in
class here: should stay 7f: acts on fast grnd.   20
1599 MUSICAL CHORUS [1] (G Blum) 2-8-8(bl) A Bond 9/1: 003024: Led over 3f: see 1599.   14
1483 JETMORE [2] 2-8-11(bl) Pat Eddery 5/1: 0200: Prom, ev ch: see 1262.   11
1253 RELAMPEGO [11] 2-8-8 G Morgan 33/1: 0000: Speed over 3f.   05
1550 GONE FOR IT [13] 2-8-8 R P Elliott 4/1: 0000: Fin 8th: nicely bckd here: half sister
to winning 2yo Auto Elegance: may impr.   00
1537 Ardnacross [4] 8-8   1059 Akrotiri Bay [7] 8-11   722 Lynda Broad [15] 8-8
--   Grenville Lass [6] 8-8   1550 Calypso Kid [8] 8-11
1583 Solent Gold [12] 8-8   --   Lantern Boy [14] 8-11
14 ran   2,nk,1,2,1   (Miss M Birkbeck)   P Haslam Newmarket

1804 RADIO MERCURY HANDICAP 0-50 3YO+   £2998   7.5f   Firm 13 +10 Fast   [48]

1245 BOWL OVER [9] (P Makin) 3-8-7(bl) Pat Eddery 5/1 JT FAV: -103241: 3 ch g Hardgreen -
Light Jumper (Red God): Ran on well to lead final 1f, driven out in a h'cap at Lingfield
July 26: first time out won a h'cap at Salisbury: very eff around 1m: acts on firm & yld grnd.   46
1109 COINCIDENTAL [15] (M Dickinson) 4-9-11 S Cauthen 8/1: 0001-02: Made most: kept on well
& just btn: fine effort under 9-11: in '85 was trained by M Lambert, winning a valuable h'cap
at Newmarket: in '84 won at Thirsk & Beverley: eff at 6f, stays 7.5f: acts on firm & yld grnd
& on any trk.   54
1640 STEADY EDDIE [6] (P Mitchell) 4-9-2 G Carter(3) 12/1: 0-00003: Al up there: best
effort this season: loves a sharp trk: see 1235.   41
1349 DOLLY [17] (A Moore) 4-7-13 L Jones(2) 8/1: 4D00344: Dsptd lead: eff over 7-10f:
best at Brighton & Lingfield: see 1166, 344.   24
1086 HIGHLAND IMAGE [4] 4-8-1 P Hutchinson(3) 16/1: 0030-00: Al there: first time out
in '85 won at Kempton: in '84 won at Thirsk: eff at 6/7f, probably stays 1m: best on fast
grnd & a sharp trk.   22
1590 NICKY NICK [14] 5-7-13 A Mcglone 33/1: 000-000: Never nearer: lightly raced this term:
remains a mdn: stays 1m: acts on gd & firm & a sharp trk.   16
1648 RED RIVER BOY [12] 3-8-5 R Curant 10/1: -00230: Mkt drifter: fin 8th: btr 1648, 1472.   00
1229 KING OF SPEED [15] 7-8-5 B Rouse 7/1: 1041030: Btr 1229, see 566.   00
1640 HELLO SUNSHINE [10] 7-8-9 P Waldron 11/2: -000040: Fin in ruck: btr 1640 (Newbury).   00
*1586 EMERALD WAVE [5] 3-8-7(6ex) W Carson 5/1 JT FAV: 04-0010: No threat: much btr 1586.   00
1649 Hunts Katie [8] 7-8(1ow)(1oh)   1165 Black Spout [11] 7-7(19oh)
--   Hautboy Lady [13] 7-7(5oh)   --   Guest Image [16] 7-7(5oh)
--   Kala Pani [1] 7-9(2ow)(10oh)   1324 Lyric Way [3] 8-6
16 ran   nk,2,shhd,1½,2,1½   (A R C Hobbs)   P Makin Ogbourne Maisey, Wilts

1805 JOHN ROGERSON HANDICAP 3YO+ 0-50   £3707   5f   Firm 13 +15 Fast   [58]

1268 MUSIC MACHINE [1] (P Haslam) 5-7-10 T Williams 7/2: 4404101: 5 b g Record Token -
Sodance (So Blessed): Made ev yd, readily in a fast run h'cap at Lingfield July 26: earlier
made all in a h'cap at Warwick: in fine form in '85, winning at Pontefract, Warwick & Ripon:
in '84 won at Ayr: very eff at 5f, does stay 6f: acts on any grnd & on any trk, but seems
best forcing the pace on a sharp one.   40
1268 SIMLA RIDGE [4] (A Hide) 4-8-6 Pat Eddery 7/4 JT FAV: 0013002: Al prom: see 628, 977.   38
587 GREEN DOLLAR [7] (B Gubby) 3-9-2 W Newnes 16/1: 210-003: Abs: never nearer: fair effort.   51
+1347 AL AMEAD [5] (C Benstead) 6-9-4 B Rouse 7/4 JT FAV: 0040414: Prom, much btr 1347 (6f).   44
477 DUCK FLIGHT [8] 4-8-8 S Cauthen 6/1: 30-0400: Abs: no threat: best 327.   24
1608 DOWNSVIEW [3] 4-8-4 A Mcglone 12/1: -010000: Al rear: best 855.   14
6 ran   4,1,1,3,2   (A Pillar)   P Haslam Newmarket

1806 LITHO TECH NIDSUMMER HCAP 3YO 0-35   £1979   1m 2f   Firm 13 -11 Slow   [36]

1657 STILLOU [11] (P Mitchell) 3-9-1 G Carter(3) 14/1: 4001001: 3 ch f Mansingh -
Flapper (Free State): Ran on well under press to lead close home in a 3yo h'cap at Lingfield
July 26: earlier was a narrow winner of a 3yo fillies h'cap at Goodwood: in '85 won a seller
at Redcar: well suited by 10f: acts on firm & soft grnd: seems suited by a sharpish trk.   31
1087 RIVER GAMBLER [2] (J Sutcliffe) 3-8-8(BL) M Hills 9/4: 000-002: Bl first time &
gambled on: led 2f out: just caught: best effort to date: eff at 10f on fast grnd & a
sharpish trk: see 1087.   23
1498 KINGS CRUSADE [3] (G Lewis) 3-9-4 P Waldron 15/8 FAV: -440423: Ev ch inside final 2f:
consistent: see 1284.   32
--   TARLETONS OAK [10] (G Harwood) 3-9-5 Pat Eddery 10/1: 000-4: Ev ch str: fair seasonal
debut: lightly raced in '85: stays 10f: acts on fast grnd & a sharpish trk.   32
--   COME TO THE BALL [13] 3-8-11 L Jones(5) 16/1: 00000-0: Ran wide in str: stays 10f:
acts on fast ground.   20
1497 FINAL ALMA [1] 3-9-0 R Guest 12/1: -000000: Never nearer: see 1258.   20
1667 TRELAWNEY [12] 3-9-1 R Curant 7/1: 0001120: There 1m: btr 1667: see 1310.   00
1431 LAJNATA [7] 3-9-2 S Cauthen 9/1: -0340: Led 1m: not stay 10f? see 1055.   00
1589 GODS PATH [4] 3-9-0 A Mcglone 15/2: -000000: Never in it: flattered 1589 (12f) ?   00
843 COOL NUMBER [15] 3-8-11 W Carson 10/1: 000-00: Fdd str after abs: lightly raced as
a 2yo: half sister to smart hurdler Janus.   00
1398 Gregorian Chant [14] 8-8   1540 Cosmic Flight [8] 8-11
1497 Le Moulin [5] 9-7   738 Matelot Royale [9] 8-10
1085 Forward Move [6] 8-7
15 ran   shhd,½,½,2,1½   (Miss Linda Demetriou)   P Mitchell Epsom, Surrey

1807 SUNSET MAIDEN STAKES 3YO   £959   2m   Firm 13 -19 Slow

1290 RUSSIAN LOGIC [6] (G Harwood) 3-9-0 Pat Eddery 1/3 FAV: -2221: 3 b c Nijinsky -
Feminine Logic (Bold Reasoning): Had a simple task, led 5f out, comfortably in a 3yo mdn
at Lingfield July 26: 2nd on his 3 previous outings this term: stays 2m well: acts on firm
& yld grnd & on any trk.   50
1368 FLAMING DANCER [4] (J Winter) 3-8-11 W Carson 9/2: 0-2002: Ev ch str: lightly raced
since 173 & seems flattered by that rating: stays 2m: acts on firm & yld.   35

1022 MARICAMA [3] (C Horgan) 3-9-0 Paul Eddery 8/1: -4003: Has been lightly raced: probably
stays 2m: see 435.   30
1315 FARAWAY LAD [1] (D Ringer) 3-9-0 M Wigham 25/1: 0000-04: Prominent over 1m: not
stay 2m: acts on gd grnd.   10
1556 LUCKY LAD [5] 3-9-0 S Cauthen 12/1: 0-00040: See 1556.   00
1304 MIRANOL VENTURE [8] 3-8-11 B Rouse 33/1: 00-0000: No form this season.   00
--   Our Generation [2] 9-0   -- Tell Em Nowt [7] 8-11
8 ran   7,5,12,10,1   (Sheikh Mohammed)   G Harwood Pulborough, Sussex

---

AYR   Saturday July 26th   Lefthand Galloping Track

Official Going Given As GOOD/FIRM

1808 AMATEUR RIDERS STAKES 3YO+   £1830   1m 2f Good 44 -25 Slow

*1336 MISAAFF [1] (H T Jones) 3-10-5 Mr T T Jones 1/4 FAV: 213-411: 3 b c Mummy's Pet -
Honeybuzzard (Sea Hawk II): Winning 2nd amateur riders race on the trot when successful at
Ayr July 26: came from behind but made hard work of gaining the day inside final 1f:
comfortably defied 12-0 in similar race at Carlisle last time: winner at Redcar in '85:
eff at 10f, suited by 12f: acts on firm & yld & on any trk: goes well for an amateur.   39
1699 MAWDLYN GATE [7] (J S Wilson) 3-10-5(VIS) Linda Perrett(5) 20/1: 4001322: Set up a
clear lead, caught final 1f but a grand effort and was clear of rem: much impr by the fitting
of a visor for the first time here: should win a h'cap next time.   35
959 THE YOMPER [3] (J Parkes) 4-10-8 Mr T Easterby 16/1: 00-4203: Abs.: ev ch: see 592.   14
1074 PONTYATES [4] (J S Wilson) 4-10-8 Mr S Mctaggert(5) 20/1: -340004: Ev ch: best 519.   09
1503 TOP ROW [2] 3-9-10 Diana Jones 20/1: 4300-00: Prom, ev ch: remains a mdn.   07
1744 EXCAVATOR LADY [8] 7-11-12(vis)(17ow) Mr F Hines 33/1: 3220220: Under massive o/w
had no ch: reportedly will now retire to the paddocks and is already in foal: see 1744.   10
1636 NONSENSE [6] 5-10-12 Sandy Brook 8/1: 1230-00: A dist last: see 1636.   00
1700 Noel Arms [5] 10-8
8 ran   1½,6,1½,1,12   (Hamdan Al-Maktoum)   H T Jones Newmarket

1809 KYLE AND CARRICK H'CAP (0-50) 3YO+   £2670   1m 5f Good 44 -05 Slow   [41]

-1551 HIGH TENSION [1] (G P Gordon) 4-9-10 W Ryan 5/4 FAV: -241221: 4 ch c Vitiges -
Montania (Mourne): Useful, consistent colt: ran on to lead final 1f & readily forged 3L clear
defying 9-10 in a h'cap at Ayr July 26: earlier won a similar h'cap over the same C/D and in
between beaten by a couple of tartars in Rakaposhi King and Twice Bold: early in '85 won at
Yarmouth & Redcar: very eff over 12/13f: acts on firm & yld & on any trk though runs well
at Ayr: most genuine.   50
1359 PAST GLORIES [4] (C Elsey) 3-8-5 C Dwyer 6/1: -031042: Made most: best 969 (heavy).   40
1563 FOUR STAR THRUST [5] (R Whitaker) 4-8-4 N Carlisle 7/1: 0202023: No extra final 2f.   23
1679 MILTESCENS [3] (A Jarvis) 3-9-4(vis) D Nicholls 9/2: 1030204: Ev ch: see 1177 (C/D).   49
*1659 THE CRYING GAME [2] 4-7-7(4ex)(1oh) P Hill(7) 5/1: -400210: Non-stayer? btr 1659 (10f). 04
5 ran   3,¾,1½,6   (Lord Derby)   G P Gordon Newmarket

1810 TOTE BOOKMAKERS SPRINT TROPHY (H'CAP)   £8886   6f   Good 44 +12 Fast   [55]

1536 MATOU [2] (G P Gordon) 6-9-7 W Ryan 7/1: -4202D1: 6 b h Mummy's Pet - Great Optimist
(Great Nephew): Very useful sprinter: defied top weight, coming from behind to lead final
100 yds in a fast run & valuable h'cap at Ayr July 26: in gd form in '85 winning h'caps at
Doncaster, Haydock & Pontefract: best form at 6f though does stay further: acts on any going:
best suited by waiting tactics.   61
1682 MURPHYS WHEELS [3] (A Jarvis) 3-8-2 M Roberts 5/1: 0411232: Al prom, chall final 1f,
narrowly btn: in fine form: see 1443.   47
+1429 BOOT POLISH [1] (J Watts) 4-8-13 N Connorton 4/1 FAV: 4-10013: Led briefly 1f out,
narrowly btn and is in grand form: see 1429.   49
1385 CHAPLINS CLUB [9] (D Chapman) 6-9-6(bl) D Nicholls 14/1: 0000204: Al well there: see 1222 52
1285 FOOLISH TOUCH [11] 4-8-0(vis) P Robinson 9/1: 3100440: Made much: best 401.   22
1429 TOBERMORY BOY [8] 9-8-9 D Mckeown 8/1: -000200: Ev ch: twice below 1306.   30
1429 VALLEY MILLS [12] 6-9-1 T Ives 14/1: 3004000: Fin 7th: best 520 (yld).   00
1338 CUMBRIAN DANCER [5] 3-7-9(vis) S P Griffiths 13/2: 3004120: Prom much, fin 8th: btr 1247. 00
1524 Capeability Pound [7] 7-7(3oh)   1157 Air Command [10] 8-9
1536 Mendick Adventure [6] 7-9   1616 Tanfen [4] 8-3
12 ran   ¼,¼,1½,4,¼,1½,¾   (Mrs T C Pick)   G P Gordon Newmarket

1811 LAND OF BURNS STAKES 3YO+   £8606   1m 2f Good 44 +24 Fast

1408 SANTIKI [3] (M Stoute) 3-7-12 P Robinson 6/5: -241331: 3 ch f Be My Guest - Sairshea
(Simbir): Smart filly: prom and led final 1f in very fast run Land Of Burns Stakes (Listed
race) at Ayr July 26: placed recently in Pattern races at Ascot & Haydock & earlier won a
mdn at Thirsk: half sister to the smart Shearwalk: eff 10f, stays 12f well: acts on gd &
firm grnd & on any trk: most consistent.   75
1526 K BATTERY [2] (C Elsey) 5-9-0 C Dwyer 20/1: -100202: Chall final 1f, ran a tremendous
race & would appear to be still impr: see 17, 325.   75

1389 TELEPROMPTER [4] (J Watts) 6-9-8(vis) T Ives 4/5 FAV: 20-2333: Led ½way, fdd final
1f & yet to recapture last seasons very best form: see 598.   81
1383 KALKOUR [5] (M Haynes) 4-9-0 W Ryan 12/1: 0101204: Fdd final 3f: best 1038.   53
1389 GRAND HARBOUR [1] 6-9-0 N Connorton 100/1: 04-0000: Pacemaker for Teleprompter,
wknd ½way: see 1094.   38
5 ran   1½,1½,20,10   (R Sangster)   M Stoute Newmarket

1812 CAMBUSDOON MAIDEN STAKES 2YO   £959   7f   Good 44 -22 Slow

741 STILLMAN [7] (M H Easterby) 2-9-0 J Bleasdale 11/4 FAV: 001: 2 br c Anfield -
Quality Blake (Blakeney): Impr colt: despite abs, al cruising and sprinted clear in the
final 2f for a very easy 4L success in a 2yo mdn at Ayr July 26: half brother to a couple of
winners incl very useful hurdler Taelos: suited by 7f, sure to stay middle dists in time:
the type to impr further & will win more races.   50
1660 MURPHY [10] (R Whitaker) 2-9-0 D Mckeown 6/1: 042: Kept on well under press & seems
to have caught a tartar here: see 1660.   40
437 DAMART [4] (E Weymes) 2-9-0 E Guest(3) 14/1: 003: Long abs: came from off the pace
and ran well: on the up grade: see 320: well suited by 7f, will stay at least 1m.   33
1397 MUGHTANIM [2] (A Stewart) 2-9-0 M Roberts 5/1: 034: Made much: see 1397.   32
1529 IN A SPIN [1] 2-8-11 T Ives 7/2: 30: Chall 2f out, fdd: btr 1529.   28
--   FRENDLY FELLOW [8] 2-9-0 N Connorton 9/1: 0: Slow start, never btr: related to several
minor winners: dam a smart middle dist filly.   30
1510 Pathero [11] 9-0   108 Area Code [5] 9-0   1534 African Opera [6] 9-0
--   Port Of Time [9] 9-0   1660 Gold Justice [3] 9-0(BL)
11 ran   4,3,nk,½,½,½   (P L Muldoon)   M H Easterby Great Habton, Yorks

1813 SPRINGSIDE HANDICAP STAKES (0-35) 3YO   £2257   1m   Good 44 -11 Slow   [25]

1701 BALNERINO [1] (Denys Smith) 3-8-12 M Fry 9/2: 0-00401: 3 b f Rolfe - Cotillion
(Gala Performance): Al prom & led inside final 3f keeping on well under press in a 6 runner
3yo h'cap at Ayr July 26: in '85 won a mdn at Ayr & obviously likes this trk: stays 1m
well: acts on gd & yld, unsuited by firm?   20
1396 BLACK DIAMOND [5] (A Jarvis) 3-9-5(bl) D Nicholls 4/1: -030022: Made much, in gd form. 22
1362 TABLE TURNING [6] (J Watts) 3-9-6(VIS) T Ives 6/4 FAV: 00-2433: Visored first time,
no extra str: see 258, 1362.   18
491 VIRAJENDRA [3] (W Pearce) 3-9-7 N Connorton 14/1: 00-0034: No threat after long abs,
since btr 491 (heavy).   12
1288 FANDANGO KISS [4] 3-8-8 P Robinson 4/1: 00-000: Al same place: see 1288.   00
1614 SILENT RUNNING [2] 3-9-4 W Ryan 10/1: 3000040: Btr 1614.   01
6 ran   2½,3,5,3,1½   (David S Nimmo)   Denys Smith Bishop Auckland, Co Durham

Official Going Given As GOOD/FIRM

1814 LARWOOD AND VOCE NURSERY H'CAP 2YO   £1505   5f   Good 65 -05 Slow   [40]

+1717 SPITTIN MICK [6] (M H Easterby) 2-9-9(7ex) M Birch 3/1: 121311: 2 b g The Brianstan -
La Fille (Crooner): In fine form, gamely defied his penalty being switched to lead close home
in a nursery h'cap at Nottingham July 28: recently won a similar race at Hamilton, after
earlier successes in sellers at Thirsk and Warwick: very eff over 5f: acts on firm & yld
grnd & on any trk: genuine & consistent gelding.   44
1501 DOMINO ROSE [1] (N Tinkler) 2-9-0 W Ryan 8/1: 232202: Just failed to make all:
consistent filly who deserves a race: eff over 5f on fast & soft grnd: acts on any trk:
clearly suited by forcing tactics.   33
*1333 FICKLE YOUNG MAN [5] (T Fairhurst) 2-9-5 A Bond 8/1: 13: Fin strongly & only just
held: in fine form & will be suited by another furlong: see 1333.   38
1205 SPANISH SLIPPER [3] (W Haigh) 2-9-7 N Day 9/4 FAV: 4224: Not btn far: see 1205 & 450. 36
1568 FOURWALK [4] 2-9-7(VIS) M Brennan(7) 12/1: 0024100: Al front rank: in fair form: see 1397. 33
*1693 LAST RECOVERY [7] 2-9-4(BL)(7ex) R Cochrane 3/1: 303210: Bl first time: btr in 1693. 28
*1434 NICHOLAS GEORGE [2] 2-8-9 J Hills(5) 12/1: 010: Speed over ½way: upped in class
after winning a seller in 1434.   00
7 ran   hd,shhd,1½,1,¾   (Sandmoor Textiles Co Ltd)   M H Easterby Great Habton, Yorks

1815 RICHMOND & BARRATT APP. SELLING STAKES   £859   6f   Good 65 -27 Slow

1627 OUR CHILDREN [2] (W Wharton) 3-8-7 J Ward 7/4 FAV: 00-0301: 3 ch f Mandrake Major -
My Audrey (Pall Mall): Dropped in class & nicely bckd when making virtually ev yd, gamely in
a 3yo app. seller at Nottingham July 28 (bought in 1,900 gns): best form over sprint dist.
on gd or faster grnd: well suited by a sharp/easy course.   12
--   STRAIGHT BAT [3] (P Haslam) 3-8-10 J Scally 8/1: -2: Pressed winner thro'out on racecourse debut: brother to 7/8f winner Smokey Shadow: eff over 6f on gd grnd: should improve. 09
1734 WINDING PATH [1] (R Hollinshead) 3-9-0 A Whitehall 13/2: 0004003: Al close up, not
btn far: see 489.   12
1549 BAO [10] (J Cosgrave) 3-8-7(vis) D Surrey 11/2: 0000004: Al front rank: best in 426 (7f). 03

1574 GREENHILLS BOY [8] 3-8-10 P Barnard 12/1: -00: Showed a little impr today: suited
by 6f & gd/firm grnd.   03
1398 MY DERYA [4] 3-9-3 A Roper 9/1: 0340300: Btr over 1m in 564: see 103.   02
608 MEDDY [11] 3-8-10 Dale Gibson 10/1: 403-000: Fin 9th after abs: see 426.   00
1574 SLY MAID [6] 3-9-0 N Leach 9/1: -00: Successful 4 times as a juvenile in Italy though
has been well btn in both her starts in this country: stays 6f.   00
--   Cascading [5] 8-7   1303 Last Jewel [7] 8-7   1369 Connaught Broads [9] 8-7
1334 Mercia Gold [12] 8-10(vis)
12 ran   1¼,¼,¼,1,3,1¼   (Ian Hunter)   W Wharton Melton Mowbray , Leics

1816 E.B.F. SAM & ARTHUR STAPLES MDN 2YO   £1473   6f   Good 65 +07 Fast

1495 CHILIBANG [6] (J Dunlop) 2-9-0 G Baxter 5/2 CO FAV: 41: 2 ro c Formidable - Chili
Girl (Skymaster): Made all for a comfortable win in quite a fast run 2yo mdn at Nottingham
July 28: half brother to 6/7f winner Hot Case: eff over 6f & should stay further: acts on gd
grnd & on a sharp/easy course: suited by forcing tactics: further impr likely.   46
1629 KINGS VICTORY [3] (M Usher) 2-9-0 M Wigham 5/2 CO FAV: 42: Hung left thro'out, ran
on strongly from dist: will impr with experience: see 1629.   41
1522 SOULEIADOU [2] (R Johnson Houghton) 2-9-0 S Whitworth 12/1: 003: With winner to ½way:
showed some impr here: cost 19,000 gns as a yearling & is eff over 5/6f on gd & firm grnd. 25
--   GENTLE DARIUS [5] (M Ryan) 2-9-0 R Cochrane 9/2: 4: Never nearer after slow start:
fair debut & will impr next time: cost 42,000 gns and is a brother to useful sprinter
Coincidental: acts on gd grnd.   24
1345 STREET LEGAL [7] 2-9-0 E Guest(3) 14/1: 000: No real threat: see 1082.   18
1606 MUSTAKBIL [4] 2-9-0 Paul Eddery 5/2 CO FAV: 30: Speed over ½way: much btr in 1606. 03
1379 Cream And Green [8] 9-0   1433 Dungehill Star [1] 8-11
--   Splashin Out [9] 9-0
9 ran   1,5,nk,2½,5   (Mrs H J Heinz)   J Dunlop Arundel, Sussex

1817 ARTHUR CARR CUP H'CAP (0-35) 3YO+   £1914   1m 6f Good 65 -72 Slow   [25]

1577 REFORM PRINCESS [3] (M Ryan) 3-9-0(vis) R Cochrane 5/4: 0-00341: 3 ch f Reform -
Bally's Princess (Salvo): Led dist and ran on strongly to win a slowly run 3 runner h'cap at
Nottingham July 28: eff around 10f though is btr suited by 14f: acts on firm & soft ground.
and likes a sharp/easy course.   32
1694 DIVA ENCORE [1] (R Armstrong) 3-9-13(6ex) V Smith(5) 5/6 FAV: 0001122: Set a slow pace,
not qcknd dist: not disgraced under top weight & remains in gd form: see 1694.   40
1223 TOUCH OF LUCK [2] (R Hollinshead) 4-8-10 S Perks 9/1: 0000003: Not qckn & remains
a mdn: probably btr suited by 12f: see 1042.   05
3 ran   3,2½   (Bill Gerhauser)   M Ryan Newmarket

1818 GEORGE AND JOHN GUNN MAIDEN STAKES 3YO   £1799   1m 2f Good 65 -03 Slow

1469 FESTIVAL CITY USA [8] (B Hills) 3-9-0(BL) R Hills 11/4: 3-03001: 3 ch c The Minstrel-
Millingdale Lillie (Tumble Wind): Eased in class & soon led, winning unchall. in a 3yo mdn
at Nottingham July 28: well bred colt who earlier had been placed in btr company, notably
when a close 3rd to Sultan Mohamed at Epsom: eff over 10f on firm & soft grnd: acts on any
trk: fitted with bl today & this win should have done his confidence some good.   48
1601 MOONSTRUCK [2] (M Ryan) 3-9-0 P Robinson 16/1: 0-20042: Early ldr: chased winner rest
of way: impr of late: see 1601.   42
991 LOUVECIENNES [3] (O Douieb) 3-8-11 R Cochrane 2/1 FAV: -33: Nicely bckd after fair
abs: had ev ch: lightly raced filly who should come good in the near future: see 991.   37
1193 LINASH [1] (G Wragg) 3-8-11 S Bridle(7) 33/1: -004: Ran on str, never nearer:
lightly raced filly who promises to be suited by a longer trip: acts on gd & fast grnd. 28
1220 REAL MOONSHINE [9] 3-9-0 Paul Eddery 20/1: -040: Al mid-div: see 1220.   25
--   OUR HERO [4] 3-9-0 G Baxter 14/1: -0: Dwelt, gd late prog & seems certain to do
btr next time: half brother to very useful French middle dist winner La Toulzanie: should
stay further than this: acts on gd grnd.   24
1503 NAJIDIYA [11] 3-8-11 S Whitworth 5/1: 3-020: Fin 7th: btr in 1503 (tight trk).   00
--   RUSSIAN RELATION [10] 3-9-0 R Guest 5/1: -0: Never dngr 8th on debut: cost I.R. 84,000
and is a half brother to several German winners: quite nicely bckd today & should do btr
than this.   00
--   MOWSOOM [7] 3-9-0 W Ryan 9/1: -0: Prom for 1m, eased & will impr for this experience:
cost $150,000 & is a ½ brother to a couple of winners: bred to be suited by middle dists. 00
--   Branch Out [6] 8-11   1578 Stormguard [12] 9-0   --   Venus Saga [5] 8-11
12 ran   2½,1,4,2½,½   (R E Sangster)   B Hills Lambourn, Berks

1819 E.MIDLANDS RACING CLUB H'CAP 3YO 0-35   £2161   1m   Good 65 -10 Slow   [36]

1651 GIVING IT ALL AWAY [2] (H Beasley) 3-8-13 R Cochrane 13/8: 3000021: 3 gr c Windjammer-
Silver Berry (Lorenzaccio): Hung left inside dist though responded to press to lead close
home in a 3yo h'cap at Nottingham July 28: first success: eff over 7/8f: suited by gd
or faster grnd & acts on any trk.   30
1581 FARAG [6] (P Walwyn) 3-9-3 Paul Eddery 11/10 FAV: -200032: Made most: well clear of
rem & is in gd form at present: suited by forcing tactics: see 74.   30

1471 LIGHTNING WIND [4] (M Usher) 3-9-7 M Wigham 5/1: 0-40003: Wknd dist: best in 514 (7f).   20
1521 SEAGO [3] (D Ancil) 3-8-2 P Robinson 16/1: 000-004: Mdn who has been well btn in all
his starts this term over various distances.   00
1309 KLOSTERBRAU [1] 3-7-9 G French 16/1: 00-0000: Never reached ldrs: modest mdn who
has shown no form this season.   00
5 ran   2,8,2½,nk   (R Daltrey)   H Beasley Lewes, East Sussex

---

NEWCASTLE   Monday July 28th   Lefthand, Galloping Track

Official Going Given As GOOD TO FIRM

1820 HOLSTEN DIAT PILS H'CAP 3YO+ 0-35   £2148   1m 2f   Good/Firm36 -07 Slow   [34]

1526 MASKED BALL [9] (P Calver) 6-9-9 M Fry 7/4 FAV: -112021: 6 b h Thatch - Miss Mahal
(Taj Dewan): In fine form, not the best of runs, but led inside final 1f, comfortably in a
h'cap at Newcastle July 28: last time out fin an excellent 2nd to Chaumiere in the Magnet
Cup at York: earlier in the season won h'caps at Haydock (2): in '85 won twice at Newcastle:
very eff at 10f, though does stay 12f: acts on firm & yld grnd & on any trk though likes
a gall one: genuine & consistent.   39
1673 GREED [4] (D Smith) 5-9-0 L Charnock 5/1: 4-24432: Led briefly final 1f: see 1185.   25
1657 CARVERY [3] (A Hide) 3-8-3(1ow) T Ives 2/1: 40-023: Ev ch final 2f: see 1657.   22
1546 HALF SHAFT [2] (W A Stephenson) 5-7-13 J Lowe 12/1: -000-44: Led over 5f, stayed prom:
eff at 1m/10f: see 1546.   04
1432 STRICTLY BUSINESS [6] 4-7-9(BL) S P Griffiths 14/1: 000-400: Bl first time: led 4f out.   00
--   MINDERS MAN [5] 4-8-0 N Connorton 33/1: 00000-0: Never nearer on seasonal debut: stays
10f: acts on fast grnd.   00
1613 Nugola [1] 8-0(1ow)   1698 Shellman [8] 9-12
8 ran   2,2,1,½,1½   (P Calver)   P Calver Ripon, Yorks

1821 DANISH LIGHT H'CAP 3YO 0-60   £4854   7f   Good/Firm 36 +01 Fast   [64]

1199 PASTICCIO [8] (M Jarvis) 3-8-11 T Ives 9/2: 1-32221: 3 b c Taufan - Karren's Pet
(Mummy's Pet): Useful colt: well ridden to lead close home in a valuable 3yo h'cap at
Newcastle July 28: most consistent this term: on final outing in '85 won a mdn at Leicester:
seems equally eff over 7f/1m: acts on firm & soft grnd & a gall trk: best when held up
for a late run.   58
1486 KNYF [1] (E Weymes) 3-8-10 E Guest(3) 7/2: 3201002: Led 2f out: just caught: gd effort
and is a consistent sort: see 816.   54
1758 LOCHONICA [4] (A Jarvis) 3-9-7 D Nicholls 11/1: -000003: Al up there: much impr
effort after dismal showing in 1758: stays 7f: may be best on a gall trk: see 245.   61
1487 CARRIBEAN SOUND [7] (C Brittain) 3-7-13 J Lowe 15/2: 2431004: Led 3f out: see 713.   35
*1451 TRAVEL MAGIC [3] 3-8-2 G Baxter 5/2 FAV: -010: Nicely bckd: ev ch: btr 1451 (very firm)   36
*1256 NAP MAJESTICA [2] 3-7-12 J Quinn(5) 8/1: 00-0010: Prom, fdd: much btr 1256 (1m, claimer)   16
1036 RUE ST JACQUES [5] 3-7-13 T Williams 10/1: 0-3330: Led 4f: abs since much btr 1036.   00
733 BON ACCUEIL [6] 3-7-12 W Carson 7/1: 42-000: Abs: prom over 4f: see 733.   00
8 ran   1,1½,1½,½,8,1,nk   (T G Warner)   M Jarvis Newmarket

1822 CARLSBERG H'CAP 3YO 0-35   £2225   1m 4f   Good/Firm 36 -26 Slow   [32]

*1404 RELATIVELY EASY [4] (M Prescott) 3-9-7 G Duffield 9/4 : -0011: 3 b f Relkino -
Linguistic (Porto Bello): Led nearing final 2f, forging clear in a 3yo h'cap at Newcastle
July 28: last time out won a claiming mdn at Bath: half sister to winning stayer Castle Douglas:
eff at 12f, will stay further: acts on gd/firm grnd & a gall trk.   36
1372 RHODE ISLAND RED [3] (J Watts) 3-9-2(BL) N Connorton 7/1: -4002: Made most: bl first
time: obviously flattered 714.   22
*1739 KEEP HOPING [1] (G Huffer) 3-9-1(5ex) M Miller 2/1 FAV: 0-00013: Acts on any trk: see 173921
1530 SHINY KAY [5] (W Elsey) 3-9-6 J Lowe 8/1: -004404: Ev ch str: best 1160 (wore bl).   23
1258 TEARS OF LAUGHTER [2] 3-8-13 J Leech(7) 4/1: 00-0020: P.u. lame: see 1258.   00
5 ran   4,hd,1½   (Lady Macdonald Buchanan)   M Prescott Newmarket

1823 GR.3 FEDERATION BREWERY BEESWING STKS   £18502   7f   Good/Firm 36 +07 Fast

1286 HADEER [6] (C Brittain) 4-9-0 S Cauthen 13/2: 44-2041: 4 ch c General Assembly -
Glinting (Crepello): Smart colt: led nearing final 2f, ridden clear in quite fast run Gr.3
Beeswing Stakes at Newcastle July 28: first time out was a fine 2nd to Pennine Walk in Gr.3
Diomed Stakes at Epsom: lightly raced in '85: very useful 2yo when trained by M Stoute, winning
at Windsor & Newmarket: very eff over 7f/1m: acts on gd & firm grnd & on any trk.   75
*1514 HARD ROUND [2] (R Hannon) 3-8-8 B Rouse 6/1: -244032: Prom all the way: in grand form.   71
1455 TREMBLANT [5] (R Smyth) 5-9-0 S Whitworth 13/2: 1-20003: Nearest fin: fair effort,
but has yet to regain his form of last season: see 5.   64
1286 CROMWELL PARK [4] (M Ryan) 3-8-5(BL) P Robinson 50/1: 1-4004: Bl first time: led
over 4f: gd effort: lightly raced this term: see 190.   62
1514 NINO BIBBIA [3] 3-8-5 R Guest 10/3: 1104230: Held ev ch: twice below form 1286.   56
*1332 SAMARID [7] 3-8-8 W R Swinburn 6/1: 140-010: Well below form 1332 (1m).   54
920 LUCKY RING [9] 4-9-3(BL) W Carson 3/1 FAV: 114-000: Bl first time: last to fin: abs
since btr 920, but seems a shadow of his former self.   00
1268 Sharp Romance [1] 9-3   384 Soughaan [8] 8-8
9 ran   3,2,½,3,2½   (W J Gredley)   C Brittain Newmarket

1824 BEST BITTER SELL.H'CAP 3YO 0-25   £1410   7f   Good/Firm 36 -12 Slow   [19]

673 DORADE [12] (D Morley) 3-9-0(BL) R Guest 20/1: 0-00301: 3 br g Windjammer - Royal
Inheritance (Will Somers): Bl first time & made almost all, readily in a selling h'cap at
Newcastle July 28 (bought in 2,100 gns): had been off the trk since May, but seems to do
well when fresh: seems very eff at 7f in bl with forcing tactics: acts on gd & firm grnd.   16
1122 MY CUP OF TEA [13] (P Haslam) 3-8-11(VIS) T Williams 3/1 FAV: -032242: Visored first
time: sn prom, but no ch with winner: see 867.   05
1617 PUNCLE CREAK [8] (G Moore) 3-8-6 D Casey(4) 6/1: 0000023: Stays 7f, but btr 1617 (6f).   00
1281 ALL A DREAM [5] (W Musson) 3-9-7(BL) M Wigham 7/2: 00-0004: Never nearer: active in
mkt: lightly raced since 318.   02
1562 RUPERT BROOKE [16] 3-9-2 R Vickers(7) 5/1: -002420: Much btr 1562.   00
*1662 LARNEM [1] 3-9-7(6ex) J Callaghan(7) 9/1: -000210: Led 4f: btr 1662.   00
1662 BALIDAREEN [11] 3-8-0 J Quinn(5) 10/1: 0000040: Fin 9th: see 1662.   00
*1562 JUST THE TICKET [9] 3-9-11(6ex) R Lines(3) 10/1: 000-010: No show: well below form 1562.   00
1562 Shy Mistress [2] 8-13   1734 Valdarno [10] 8-11   1701 Feather Girl [14] 8-7(BL)
487 Parkes Special [15] 8-10   1562 Planning Act [6] 8-7
1439 Duke Of Milltimber [7] 8-3   1574 Trelaies [3] 9-3
1734 Classy Scouse [4] 8-10
16 ran   4,2½,4,7,nk   (O Miles Pollard jnr)   D Morley Newmarket

1825 LCL PILS MAID.AUCTION STAKES 2YO   £1502   6f   Good/Firm 36 -01 Slow

1510 GET ON GERAGHTY [4] (G Huffer) 2-8-7 G Carter(3) 4/7 FAV: 21: 2 ch c Main Reef -
Gold Cypher (Pardao): Useful colt: well bckd & led nearing final 2f, sn clear in a 2yo mdn
auction at Newcastle July 28: first time out was a most prom 2nd to Rich Charlie at York:
cost only 5,000 gns: eff at 6f, sure to stay further: acts on gd & firm grnd & a gall trk:
further impr likely.   53
1376 PHILOTAS [12] (D Smith) 2-8-9 D Nicholls 20/1: 402: Raced alone: fair effort: see 1050.   37
1225 SUPERCUBE [8] (E Carter) 2-8-5 Wendy Carter(6) 10/1: 043: Sn prom: btr 1225 (shrp trk).   32
1561 VOL VITESSE [7] (R Whitaker) 2-8-5 K Bradshaw(5) 16/1: 04: Led ½way, ev ch: see 1561.   18
1570 CIREN JESTER [2] 2-8-5 M Wigham 25/1: 00: Early ldr: stayed on late: cheaply acquired
colt who may get further than 6f: acts on gd/firm.   14
927 FIRMLY ATTACHED [9] 2-8-9 B Mcgiff(7) 16/1: 0200: Abs: never nearer: lightly raced
since best 304 (soft/hvy).   18
1376 WICHITA SPRINGS [10] 2-8-11 A Murray 7/2: 30: Made no show: well below 1376.   00
--   Venherm [3] 8-9   948 Mayspark [1] 8-6   --   Leading Wren [6] 8-1
--   Brookside [11] 8-5(BL)   --   Beattys Lad [5] 8-4
12 ran   6,hd,6,1½,shhd   (M F Geraghty Ltd)   G Huffer Newmarket

Official Going Given As GOOD

1826 EBF ENGLEFIELD MAIDEN 2YO   £990   5f   Good/Firm 38 -20 Slow

1550 BALTIC SHORE [2] (M Stoute) 2-9-0 W R Swinburn 2/5 FAV: 021: 2 b c Danzig - Placid
Lake (Terrang): Readily landed the odds, leading dist & drawing 4L clear in a 2yo mdn at
Windsor July 28: related to several winners abroad & sire is probably the most promising
young stallion currently at stud: eff over 5f, sure to be suited by 6f plus: acts on firm &
gd grnd: can continue to impr.   55
1545 MISS MILVEAGH [1] (A Bailey) 2-8-11 P Bloomfield 33/1: 32: Op. 10/1, friendless in
mkt but was al there though outpaced final stages: on the up grade & should be placed
advantageously before too long: see 1545.   40
1696 THAT CERTAIN SMILE [12] (R Williams) 2-8-11 S Cauthen 11/2: 323: Quick reapp: made much.37
834 BAREFACED [3] (M Smyly) 2-9-0 Pat Eddery 14/1: 04: Abs & wk in mkt: prom much & ran
as if just needing race: can be expected to do btr next time: see 834.   31
1522 SUPREME STATE [10] 2-9-0 T Quinn 20/1: 00: Late prog: probably needs 6f: see 1522.   30
--   MA PETITE LASSIE [7] 2-8-11 J Reid 50/1: 0: Should benefit from this debut: half sister
to three winners abroad.   26
--   BU SOFYAN [9] 2-9-0 P Waldron 11/2: 0: Well bckd debutant: outpcd in 7th: half brother
to several minor winners incl successful '82 5f performer Mama Leone : seems well regarded and
should do btr next time.   20
1629 Nors God [4] 9-0   --   Jealous Lover [8] 8-11
--   Little Lochette [6] 8-11
10 ran   4,1,3,½,nk,2½   (Sheikh Mohammed)   M Stoute Newmarket

1827 READING SELLING STAKES 3YO   £925   6f   Good/Firm 38 -05 Slow

1001 CELESTIAL DRIVE [8] (R Hannon) 3-8-11(BL) B Rouse 13/2: 00-2001: 3 b f Dublin Taxi -
Balandra Star (Blast): Dropped to selling company & despite drifting in mkt, got up under
press on the post in a 3yo seller at Windsor (bought in 860 gns): first success:
half sister to several winners incl very useful stayer Another Sam: eff over 6f, sure to
stay further: acts on gd/firm & soft grnd: bl. 1st time today.   22
*1549 THE UTE [10] (L Bower) 3-9-0(bl) P Mcentee(7) 5/1: 0232012: Led final 1f, caught death
and is in fine form: loves Windsor: see 1549.   24

809 MISS TONILEE [2] (D H Jones) 3-8-11 J Williams 4/1 FAV: 3-32243: Chall dist after abs.   16
1281 ABSOLUTELY BONKERS [5] (M Smyly) 3-8-11 B Thomson 14/1: 40-0004: Prom most, outpcd
closing stages: a mdn who was dropped into selling company for the first time this season.   04
1521 WINNING FORMAT [3] 3-9-0 S Cauthen 10/1: -000000: Led ½way: best 545 (yld).   04
1549 PEGASUS LADY [7] 3-8-11 W Newnes 33/1: 0000000: No threat from this mdn.   00
1549 MISS VENEZUELA [1] 3-8-11 Pat Eddery 9/2: 0000040: Well bckd, prom to ½way: btr 1549.   00
1584 My Mutzie [4] 8-11   1364 Rockville Squaw [6] 8-11
1476 Choristers Dream [14] 9-5(bl)   1319 Paddington Belle [11] 8-11(vis)
1574 Gaywood Girl [15] 8-11   1516 Town Fair [17] 8-11
1549 Sequestration [16] 9-0   1549 Someway [9] 8-11
1444 Alsace [12] 8-11   1340 Sheer Class [18] 8-11   1400 Del Boy [13] 9-0(BL)
18 ran   hd,2,6,1½,1½   (Mrs Gerry Tremblay)   R Hannon East Everleigh, Wilts

1828 ETON NURSERY HANDICAP 2YO   £2313   6f   Good/Firm 38 -12 Slow   [55]

927 DERRING DEE [8] (P Cundell) 2-8-9 A Mcglone 8/1: 0101: 2 b f Derrylin - Insurance
(Yellow God): Returned after an abs but looked well h'capped & duly led close home in a blanket
fin to a nursery h'cap at Windsor July 28: earlier won a fast run fillies event, again at
Windsor: a bargain at only 3,000 gns: sister to fair h'capper Killyglen: eff at 5f, stays
6f & should stay 7f: acts on gd & firm grnd & likes Windsor.   47
1440 BLOFFA [2] (P Cundell) 2-7-8 N Adams 33/1: 3002: Stable companion of winner, led
dist, just went down in a driving fin: fine effort & can win a similar event: stays 6f well: see 596.   31
1483 FLAIR PARK [9] (D Thom) 2-7-12 M L Thomas 11/1: 01243: Chall final 1f, narrowly btn:
good effort: see 1483 (7f).   35
1568 GOOD BUY BAILEYS [3] (G Blum) 2-8-7 C Rutter(5) 12/1: 14034: Mkt drifter, chall final
1f in a desperate fin: gd effort: see 1568.   43
1522 GLORY BEE [6] 2-7-7(2oh) L Riggio(7) 16/1: 0100: Ev ch, kept on, not btn far: see 1262.   26
1253 LORD WESTGATE [10] 2-9-1 B Thomson 7/1: 0020: Kept on, close 6th: see 1253 (7f).   47
1570 GOOD TIME GIRL [12] 2-7-10(1ow) W Carson 9/1: 01120: Close up 7th: btr 1570 (stiff trk).   27
1050 SILVERS ERA [4] 2-7-7 G Bardwell(7) 8/1: 020400: Speed most, fin 8th: best 473 (5f).   22
*1407 PENANG BEAUTY [7] 2-9-3 A Mackay 2/1 FAV: 10: Heavily bckd, fin 9th: see 1407.   44
953 ENCHANTED TIMES [1] 2-9-7(VIS) Pat Eddery 10/1: 1300: Visored first time, made much
fin 10th: see 187 (5f).   47
927 JONLEAT [13] 2-9-2 T Lucas 10/1: 412200: Fin 11th: btr 664 (yld/soft).   38
1313 Murajah [11] 8-6   483 Sarasota [5] 7-7(5oh)
13 ran   hd,shhd,hd,1,hd,hd,½,1,shhd,nk   (Archie Hornall)   P Cundell Compton , Berks

1829 ROYAL BOROUGH HANDICAP 3YO+ 0-50   £2742   1m 3f   Good/Firm 38 -12 Slow   [41]

1192 STRIKE HOME [5] (M Stoute) 3-9-2 W R Swinburn 5/1: -0231: 3 b f Be My Guest -
True Rocket (Roan Rocket): Gained her first success, gamely leading inside final 1f in a
h'cap at Windsor July 28: a deserved success after several near misses: half sister to
numerous winners incl the high class Ballad Rock: well suited by middle dists & gd or firm.   53
*1667 HOUSE HUNTER [4] (C Horgan) 5-9-13(5ex) Pat Eddery 5/2 FAV: 0200412: Well bckd, led
str: fine effort under penalty: likes a sharp trk: see 1667.   49
1233 FIRST KISS [11] (J Dunlop) 3-9-7 T Quinn 10/1: -1003: Prom, kept on in a close fin:
gd effort: stays 12f: see 723.   55
1402 ALDINO [3] (A Stewart) 3-9-4(bl) M Roberts 5/1: -001124: Dsptd lead most: gd effort:
likes Windsor: see 1085.   52
862 SWEDISH PRINCESS [8] 3-8-3(BL) B Rouse 12/1: -0000: Bl first time, fair effort
after abs: lightly raced mdn.   29
1325 KILIMANJARO BOB [7] 4-8-7(BL) W Newnes 33/1: 30-0000: Bl first time: see 1186.   19
1223 WINTER PALACE [8] 4-8-8 J Reid 10/1: 40-0000: Prom, wknd into 9th: see 1223.   00
1139 Bwana Kali [13] 8-11   129 Gods Hope [6] 8-1   -- Mubarak Of Kuwait [10] 9-10
1551 Mr Gardiner [12] 8-11   1274 Monclare Trophy [14] 8-4
930 Tamertown Lad [16] 7-13   1694 Janaab [1] 8-4(VIS)(5ow)
--   Be My Wings [9] 7-11
15 ran   1,½,hd,5,shhd   (Maktoum Al-Maktoum)   M Stoute Newmarket

1830 STAINES HANDICAP 3YO 0-35   £1932   1m   Good/Firm 38 +19 Fast   [37]

1571 BLUE GUITAR [3] (J Hindley) 3-9-3(vis) M Hills 6/1: 30-4421: 3 b f Cure The Blues -
Mettle (Pretendre): Gained her first success, leading final 1f under press in a fast run 3yo
h'cap at Windsor July 28: ran only 4 times in '85, showing promise: acts on firm & gd grnd
& seems to act on any trk: very eff over 7f/1m: wears a visor.   38
1571 ANNABELLINA [10] (G Wragg) 3-9-0 S Cauthen 11/1: -400042: Led/dsptd lead most: in
good form: see 1571.   30
625 STARMAST [12] (W Hern) 3-9-7 W Carson 4/1 FAV: 0-403: Well bckd despite long abs,
led dist & ev ch: btr 10f? see 535.   33
1487 CAFE NOIR [4] (R Williams) 3-9-4 B Thomson 12/1: 431-304: Mkt drifter, led briefly
3f out: best 1316 (7f).   27
--   MOURADABIA [1] 3-9-6 A Mcglone 11/2: 002-0: Well bckd, ev ch but should strip fitter
for this seasonal debut: lightly raced mdn in '85 fin 2nd to the useful Primary in a backend
Lingfield mdn & could be rated 44 on that performance: should stay beyond 7f: acts on fast
grnd: should go well next time.   24

1471 KOOKYS PET [6] 3-8-8 A Mackay 33/1: -00000: No threat from this quite lightly raced mdn   11
1689 ARROW OF LIGHT [9] 3-9-7(bl) Pat Eddery 9/1: -04300: No dngr in 7th: now wears bl. see 676. 20
1753 LADY LA PAZ [8] 3-8-11 C Rutter(5) 15/2: 4023330: Fin 8th: twice below 1515.   10
*1063 TREMENDOUS JET [18] 3-8-10 P Hamblett 10/1: 0-00010: Fin in rear after abs since btr 1063 00
1471 Bakers Dough [2] 9-0   1472 Gem Of Gold [21] 8-12 1104 Pleasure Island [11] 9-0
1406 By Chance [7] 8-6   1520 Formidable Dancer [16] 9-4
982 Mistral Magic [14] 8-13   1228 Lady Lamb [13] 9-7
1540 Bold Borderer [20] 9-6   --   Chatterspark [17] 8-13
1695 Out Of Harmony [5] 8-11   1316 Jaaziel [15] 8-10
--   Cuckoo In The Nest [19] 8-5
21 ran   2¼,2,1½,3,nk,2½,shhd   (K Al-Said)   J Hindley Newmarket

1831 MAIDENHEAD STAKES 3 & 4YO   £1045   1m 2f Good/Firm 38 +10 Fast

1655 BRIGHT AS NIGHT [9] (M Ryan) 3-8-10 S Cauthen 11/2: 3031001: 3 b c Miswaki -
Libras Shiningstar (Gleaming): Very useful colt: upset the odds on fav, battling it out over
the final 3f for a narrow win in a fast run 3 & 4yo minor race at Windsor July 28: earlier
won a similar event at Nottingham and has since twice run well in gd h'caps: probably stays
12f but best form around 1m/10f: acts on fast grnd.   68
*1444 THE TALETELLER [8] (O Douieb) 3-8-10 Pat Eddery 2/7 FAV: -12: Long odds on, led
2f out, did not have a great deal of room in the final 1f but fin well clear of rem: see 1444. 67
1503 MERHI [5] (S Norton) 3-8-4 J Lowe 12/1: 3430003: Led ½way, outpcd str: best 698.   31
1558 VISUAL IDENTITY [12] (P Mitchell) 4-9-3 W R Swinburn 100/1: 0000004: No threat: no
worthwhile form this term: see 578.   17
--   VAULA [4] 3-8-1 W Carson 14/1: -0: May impr on this racecourse debut: half sister to
3 winners: may stay beyond 10f.   07
1494 RIBOKEYES BOY [10] 4-9-3 J Reid 100/1: -000: No worthwhile form as yet.   06
765 Soft Shoe Shuffle [3] 8-4   --   Tashonya [1] 9-3
1519 Messaline [2] 9-3   1315 Out Of Kindness [13] 8-1
1554 Kings Rock [6] 9-3   1607 Doubler 0 8-4   1690 Cleonair [7] 8-4(BL)
13 ran   ½,12,5,3,1½   (T Ramsden)   M Ryan Newmarket

BATH   Monday July 28th   Lefthand Galloping Track

1832 DAUNTSEY SELLING STAKES 2YO   £853   5.5f   Firm 06 -29 Slow

1583 JABE MAC [6] (L Holt) 2-8-11 P Waldron 6/4 FAV: 0001: 2 b g Windjammer - Shelton Song
(Song): Dropped into a seller & well bckd, led final 1f, comfortably, at Bath July 28
(bought in 4,200 gns): half brother to a couple of winning sprinters: very eff over a stiff
5f, should stay 6f: acts on firm & gd.   28
1647 MISS ACACIA [5] (R Stubbs) 2-8-8 J H Brown(5) 9/2: 0003032: Led dist, outpcd near fin
but clear of rem: tried in bl last time, seems btr without: see 1221.   15
1692 BIOTIN [7] (P Haynes) 2-8-11 J Williams 12/1: 0000323: Ev ch: btr 1692 (easy trk).   08
1279 CLEARWAY [8] (R Hodges) 2-9-1 J Reid 13/2: 01204: Made much: best 502 (yld).   11
1059 TILLOUJO [1] 2-8-8 D Williams(7) 11/1: 00: Slow start: cheaply bought filly.   00
--   DONNA IMMOBILE [3] 2-8-8 A Mcglone 10/1: 0: Friendless in mkt, no dngr: dam a winning
stayer & over hdls: looks certain to need longer distances.   00
1440 Avenmore Star [2] 8-8(BL)   1723 Scarning Shadylady [4] 8-8(VIS)
8 ran   3,4,½,4,5   (Mrs D Redfern)   L Holt Tunworth, Hants

1833 STAPLETON MAIDEN STAKES 3YO+   £1753   1m 4f Firm 06 -07 Slow

--   ROUBAYD [3] (R J Houghton) 3-8-8 J Reid 13/2: -1: 3 b c Exceller - Ramanouche
(Riverman): Prom colt: first time out, led dist staying on well to win a mdn at Bath July 28:
reportedly had previously suffered from a fear of starting stalls: half brother to 10f winner
Rasseema: suited by middle dists & fast grnd: likely to impr further with this first run
behind him.   48
--   NILE LARK [12] (J Dunlop) 3-8-5 Pat Eddery 8/1: 0-2: Chall 2f out for a gd seasonal
debut: fin in mid-div in a big field of mdns last Oct at Newmarket, sole previous outing:
half sister to a winner in France: well suited by middle dists & fast grnd: should find a mdn. 40
1580 MINHAH [8] (B Hills) 3-8-5 B Thomson 11/1: -03: Mkt drifter, led briefly 3f out:
impr filly who stays middle dists & acts on firm.   37
1645 CHUCKLESTONE [17] (R Laing) 3-8-8 N Adams 20/1: 0-00004: Mkt drifter, ev.ch: see 1315. 30
1437 ROUGH PASSAGE [4] 3-8-8 A Mcglone 11/1: -000: Mkt drifter, never btr: much btr 1437.   12
739 GUESSING [7] 3-8-8(BL) G Starkey 3/1 JT FAV: -00: Bl first time but an uneasy fav:
ev ch str: may prove expensive to follow.   08
1686 SOLOMON LAD [14] 3-8-8 A Dicks(7) 10/1: -20: Ev ch in 7th: btr 1686.   08
1315 GANOON [11] 3-8-8 T Quinn 3/1 JT.FAV: 00-2300: A gamble, fdd tamely str & has
twice disapp since 1157.   00
1645 Cloud Chaser [19] 8-8   1494 Windy Hollow [5] 8-8   1551 Mount Argus [2] 9-4
1346 Bully Boy [10] 8-8   1645 Suez [1] 8-8   --   Vivre Pour Vivre [9] 9-4
--   Chief Blackfoot [6] 9-4   --   Celtic Story [18] 9-4
1620 Bang Bang [15] 9-4
17 ran   2¼,1½,5,10,2,hd   (H H Aga Khan)   R J Houghton Blewbury, Oxon

                                                                                             00

1834 BET WITH THE TOTE H'CAP (0-50) 3YO+   £2691   5.5f   Firm 06 +21 Fast   [45]

+1730 THE MECHANIC [1] (J Sutcliffe) 3-8-4(bl)(7ex) C Rutter(5) 9/4 FAV: 0212311: 3 b c Lochnager -
Lardana (Burglar): In fine form & defied his pen. getting the btr of final 1f battle in a
fast run h'cap at Bath July 28: successful previously at Beverley & Sandown & has run very
consistently: best form over 5f on a stiff trk on firm/gd grnd in a visor or bl.   34
1581 GALLANT HOPE [10] (L Cottrell) 4-7-7(5oh) N Carlisle 16/1: 0000202: Prom thro'out, just
held in a driving fin: gd effort: see 1447.   16
1213 BILLY WHITESHOES [6] (L Cottrell) 4-7-7 R Street 14/1: 01-0003: Kept on under press:
best effort this term: successful at Lingfield on final outing in '85: btr suited by 7f
plus than shorter dists: acts on gd grnd.   10
1521 THREE BELLS [11] (M Mccourt) 4-8-4 R Wernham 25/1: -0-0004: Never closer: best
effort this term & ran only once in '85: remains a mdn.   18
1669 SOUND REASONING [8] 3-8-13 B Thomson 9/2: 104-040: Outpcd: see 1443.   30
1608 LUCKY STARKIST [4] 4-8-1 S Dawson 12/1: 0031400: Led briefly 2f out: best 1213 (shp trk)   07
1344 SHE KNOWS IT ALL [3] 4-8-6 Pat Eddery 3/1: 000-000: Well bckd, early ldr, fin 7th:
winner here twice last term: stays an extended 5f: best on firm grnd.   00
1608 DEPUTY HEAD [9] 6-9-10 P Waldron 11/2: 0313300: Fin last: below par effort: see 1060.   00
1519 Toms Nap Hand [7] 7-7(16oh)
9 ran   hd,2½,¾,¾,1½   (Christopher Dodson)   J Sutcliffe Epsom, Surrey

1835 KEYNSHAM HANDICAP STAKES (0-35) 3YO   £2989   1m   Firm 06 -02 Slow   [39]

1281 COMMON ACCORD [14] (J Sutcliffe) 3-8-2(VIS) M Hills 9/1: -000001: 3 b c Tyrnavos -
Carol Service (Daring Display): Visored first time, leading dist, narrowly, in a 3yo h'cap
at Bath July 28: first success & no form previously this term - evidently much impr by a
visor: stays 1m well: acts on firm.   22
1257 LA JAMBALAYA [3] (P Makin) 3-8-4 T Quinn 11/1: 40-3402: Tried to make all, clear
of rem: see 424.   23
1590 COUNTRY GENTLEMAN [7] (J Dunlop) 3-9-7 Pat Eddery 5/1: 0-00043: Again late prog: see 1590. 33
1609 TOM RUM [6] (H Candy) 3-7-13 L Riggio(7) 11/2: -000034: Prom, ev ch: see 1609.   10
1169 KITTY CLARE [10] 3-8-7 Paul Eddery 14/1: 020-000: Ev ch: a mdn who showed some
ability in '85: bred to be suited by middle dists.   17
+1565 BOLD ARCHER [16] 3-8-5(7ex) C Rutter(5) 5/1: 0002010: Btr 1565.   10
1540 LYDIA LANGUISH [2] 3-9-0 A Mcglone 6/1: 00-0020: Fin 8th: much btr 1540.   00
1651 OUT OF STOCK [5] 3-8-13 W Newnes 6/1: 00-0040: Well bckd, fin 9th: btr 1651.   00
1580 April Fox [4] 8-1   1303 Mitner [15] 8-4   1560 Saxon Bazaar [1] 8-5
1520 Brent Riverside [13] 8-6   1259 Ashshafak [11] 8-3(bl)(2ow)
1316 Chardonnay [9] 8-8   765 Home Or Away [12] 7-13
15 ran   ½,4,nk,nk,2½   (S Powell)   J Sutcliffe Epsom, Surrey

1836 RISSINGTON MAIDEN STAKES 3YO   £1372   5.5f   Firm 06 -02 Slow

1399 ANGELS ARE BLUE [3] (M Ryan) 3-8-11 M Giles 6/1: -02301: 3 ch f Stanford - Blue
Persian (Majority Blue): Fulfilled earlier promise, leading final 1f under press in a 3yo
mdn at Bath July 28: half sister to smart sprinter Polykratis: eff over a stiff, extended 5f,
stays 6f: acts on firm grnd.   31
835 SUNNY MATCH [12] (L Cottrell) 3-8-11 I Johnson 20/1: 000-002: Kept on well after
abs: quite lightly raced previously but a fair 5th behind Terminator in a backend mdn at
Lingfield in '85: bred to be suited by 7f plus: can impr on this.   27
1447 DUBLINAIRE [11] (M Pipe) 3-8-11(BL) B Thomson 2/1 JT.FAV: 303-033: Bl. 1st time: made most. 26
1472 ROYAL BERKS [8] (L Cottrell) 3-9-0 T Lang(7) 25/1: 00-0004: Never btr: best effort
so far: placed a few times in '85 over sprint dists: stays 6f & acts on firm or gd.   28
--   FIRST OPPORTUNITY [9] 3-9-0 L Johnsey(7) 25/1: 0-0: Prom, ev ch: ran only once in
'85: dam a prolific winner in Italy.   25
1375 APHROSINA [1] 3-8-11(bl) Pat Eddery 2/1 JT.FAV: -00000: Well bckd, ev ch: has
regressed since 1244: now wears bl but to no avail.   10
1584 NORTHERN LAD [5] 3-9-0 P Waldron 7/1: 0002020: Prom most: much btr 1584.   00
1691 Career Madness [4] 9-0   1669 Khlestakov [7] 9-0
1691 Sirtaki Dancer [2] 9-0   1734 Jacqui Joy [6] 8-11
1344 Dashaki Gold [10] 8-11
12 ran   1½,nk,nk,1,5   (T Ramsden)   M Ryan Newmarket

1837 AVON HANDICAP STAKES (0-50) 3YO+   £2725   1m 5f   Firm 06 -07 Slow   [42]

494 PRIMARY [12] (G Harwood) 3-9-8 A Clark 7/2: 01-441: 3 b c Green Dancer - Tertiary
(Vaguely Noble): Very useful colt: prom & led dist, readily winning a h'cap at Bath July 28:
ran only twice in '85 winning a backend mdn at Lingfield on final outing: very well suited
by middle dists & may well stay 2m: acts on fast grnd: well regarded colt who looks certain
to go in again next time now that he has found his best trip: does well when fresh.   62
1559 KING JACK [10] (J Dunlop) 3-9-0 Pat Eddery 11/4 FAV: -002142: Well bckd, led 2f out
but caught a tartar late: in fine form & stays 13f well: see 1301.   44
1450 TARS HILL [7] (L Cottrell) 5-8-7 N Carlisle 10/1: -020003: Made much: fair effort
considering it was not his fav. trk - Chepstow: see 724.   22
1388 HIGH PLAINS [5] (H Candy) 4-8-12 W Newnes 3/1: -000004: Once again found little
fin. pace & has proved expensive to follow this term: see 235.   21

1366 MILLERS TALE [9] 4-9-2 S O'gorman(7) 10/1: -201040: Ev ch: disapp since 761.   21
1523 PELLINCOURT [1] 4-8-8 C Rutter(5) 9/1: 0202140: Prom, wknd: best 1366 (sharp trk).   11
*1473 ISOM DART [6] 7-8-1 N Adams 10/1: -00-110: Btr 1473.   00
-- Coombe Spirit [3] 7-9   -- Plaza Toro [8] 7-7   -- Royal Baize [2] 8-7
1208 Taffys Pride [4] 7-7(bl)(6oh)   -- Morvern [11] 7-7(5oh)
12 ran   2,nk,4,2½,1   (K Abdulla)   G Harwood Pulborough, Sussex

---

REDCAR   Tuesday July 29th   Lefthanded Galloping Track

Official Going Given As FIRM FOR 1ST RACE: REMAINDER GOOD/FIRM

1838 TONTINE CELLAR BAR H'CAP (0-35) 3YO   £1775   1m 1f   Good/Firm 25 -05 Slow   [31]

1678 BLACK BANK [6] (M W Easterby) 3-9-6 K Hodgson 3/1 JT FAV: 00-0341: 3 ch g Julio Mariner-
La Gallia (Welsh Saint): Stayed on to lead inside dist in a 3yo h'cap at Redcar July 29:
first success: best form over 9f on fast grnd: acts on any trk: will now switch to hurdling.   31
1637 TURMERIC [1] (D Morley) 3-9-7(VIS) S Perks 16/1: -000002: Fitted with a visor: led
early & again after ½way: ran too his best: stays 9f: suited by fast grnd: see 723.   28
1362 BOLD ANSWER [3] (W Bentley) 3-8-2 J Lowe 14/1: 0000103: Best over this C/D 1158 (seller).   04
1244 ADHARI [7] (B Hanbury) 3-9-2 R Hills 8/1: -0004: Al up there: well suited by this
lngr trip: lightly raced filly who is a half sister to 5/7f winner Time Machine: acts on
gd & fast grnd.   16
1637 MASTER LAMB [4] 3-8-8 M Birch 5/1: -404000: Btr over 12f in 1089: see 690.   04
1567 MISS BETEL [9] 3-8-1(bl) J Quinn(5) 20/1: 4000000: Made most to ½way: see 767.   00
*1724 SIMONS FANTASY [2] 3-9-8(7ex) P Tulk 3/1 JT FAV: 0443410: Wknd into 8th: btr on an
easier track in 1724 (10f, firm).   00
1678 Hare Hill [8] 8-8   1563 Taxi Man [5] 9-5
9 ran   1½,2½,1,2,2   (Hippodromo Racing)   M W Easterby Sheriff Hutton, York

1839 CLEVELAND TONTINE SELLING H'CAP (0-25)   £1124   7f   Good/Firm 25 -06 Slow   [17]

1610 BOLD ROWLEY [22] (J S Wilson) 6-8-11 D Mckeown 12/1: 00-0001: 6 br g Persian Bold -
Lady Rowley (Royal Levee): Nicely bckd & showed impr form, led below dist & just held on in a
selling h'cap at Redcar July 29 (no bid): first success: best over 6/7f on a sound surface:
suited by a gall trk.   08
1761 HOPTONS CHANCE [27] (S Wiles) 4-8-12 M Fry 11/1: 0000002: Would have prevailed in
another stride: twice a r.u. in similar events last backend: stays 7f well: acts on any going.   09
1574 THE GOLF SLIDE [19] (B Mcmahon) 4-8-8 J Hills 10/1: -020003: Led over 2f out: kept
on well & narrowly btn: btr effort: eff over 7/8f: see 889.   04
1247 KING COLE [20] (G Reveley) 4-9-4 D Leadbitter(5) 12/1: 240-004: Not btn far in this
lower grade: mdn whose best form is over 6/7f: acts on fast & soft grnd.   11
1540 HILL RYDE [15] 3-8-13 M Birch 20/1: 0020000: Led over ½way: likes this trk: see 740.   09
1676 TRADE HIGH [23] 7-9-10 R Vickers(7) 11/1: 0000040: Not qckn: btr over 6f in 1676.   08
1624 TOP OTHLANE [7] 9-9-9 L Charnock 8/1: 00-0400: No threat: much btr in 1424 (sharp trk).   00
1761 ROSSETT [11] 7-8-8(bl) E Guest(3) 7/1 FAV: -000400: Prom to ½way: see 1136.   00
-- Taristeac [18] 8-11(bl)   1505 Marshall Drills [26] 8-1
1638 Ammeed [13] 8-8   1703 Run For Fred [3] 8-10   1182 Tiddlyeyetye [10] 9-2(bl)
1676 Sing Galvo Sing [9] 8-6   1774 Thatchered [6] 9-11
1703 Reformed Habit [4]-9-11   1703 Balkan [14] 8-9
1567 Sundown Sky [16] 9-1(bl)   1734 Nipper Smith [21] 8-9(BL)
1662 Martella [12] 8-0   1703 Tree Fella [1] 9-1   1542 Hit The Button [2] 8-9(bl)
1295 Nippy Chippy [8] 8-10   1703 Royal Duty [28] 9-9   1077 Name The Game [25] 8-3
1201 Jonney Gem [5] 8-9   1546 Trentullo Blue [24] 9-2
27 ran   shhd,nk,1½,3,1½   (R A Black (Airdrie) Ltd)   J S Wilson Ayr, Scotland

1840 TONTINE INN H'CAP (0-50) 3YO+   £3371   6f   Good/Firm 25 +02 Fast   [43]

1704 BOLD SEA ROVER [7] (M H Easterby) 3-8-6 M Birch 7/1: 0301301: 3 ch g Viking -
Sloane Ranger (Sharpen Up): Al close up & led inside dist, gamely in a h'cap at Redcar July 29:
earlier won an app. mdn at Pontefract: finds 5f inadequate & will probably prove btr suited
by 7f plus: acts on gd & firm grnd & on any trk.   37
1222 EASTBROOK [10] (S Hall) 6-7-12 L Charnock 4/1 JT FAV: 00-2132: Just caught: in gd form.   20
1673 INISHPOUR [2] (H Wharton) 4-9-7 M Brennan(7) 12/1: 0030343: Fin well, narrowly btn.   42
*1649 ROSIE DICKINS [9] (R Hollinshead) 4-8-9(8ex) R Lappin(7) 15/2: 0304314: Ran well under
her panelty: see 1649.   26
1810 MENDICK ADVENTURE [5] 5-8-7(bl) S Perks 8/1: 0003200: Led/dsptd lead most of way: see 56 19
1649 OUT OF HAND [11] 7-8-4(8ex) G Dickie 4/1 JT FAV: 0-40120: Nearest fin: btr in 1649.   15
1649 KEATS [3] 4-9-0 D Nicholls 9/2: -001030: Fin 7th: btr in 1649: see 1077.   00
1682 MELAURA BELLE [6] 5-9-6 E Guest(3) 10/1: 004-000: Fin last: below par effort: see 649.   00
1436 Mademoiselle Magna [8] 7-13   1608 Fruity Orooney [12] 8-10(BL)
518 Security Pacific [4] 9-0
11 ran   ½,nk,1½,1½,½,1   (Lt Col R Warden)   M H Easterby Great Habton, Yorks

1841 MCCOY BROTHERS MAIDEN STAKES 3YO+   £1935   1m   Good/Firm 25 +08 Fast

747 SWEET DOMAIN [12] (J Dunlop) 3-8-7 W Ryan 7/2: 320-001: 3 ch f Dominion - Maze
(Silly Season): Led after ½way for a comfortable win in a fast run all aged mdn at Redcar
July 29, despite a fair abs: showed promise last season: stays 1m well: acts on fast &
yld grnd & suited by a gall trk.   45

1541 LADY FOR TWO [3] (M Stoute) 3-8-7 M Giles(7) 5/4 FAV: -4041D2: Led/dsptd lead over
½way, never looked likely to peg back winner though remains in gd form: see 1541 and 708.   39
1184 FACTOTUM [4] (B Hills) 3-8-10 R Hills 4/1: 00-003: Kept on well: best effort to
date: well suited by a gall trk: see 941.   42
--   MAGIC TOWER [2] (C Brittain) 3-8-7 M Roberts 14/1: 0-4: Al up there: clear of rem:
gd seasonal debut: only ran once last term: eff over 1m on fast grnd & should stay further:
acts on a gall trk.   35
--   PEPENON [11] 4-9-7 J H Brown(5) 50/1: -0: Unfncd on debut: made gd late prog & should
impr next time: half brother to several winners: will be suited by 10f: acts on fast grnd
and on a gall trk.   22
1620 CASSANDRAS DREAM [14] 5-9-4 D Mckeown 33/1: -0000: Al mid-div: acts on firm: see 1102.   15

1626 Sybilly [16] 8-7	1444 Lady Attiva [15] 8-8(1ow)	
1482 Owls Way [13] 8-7	1614 Vital Step [9] 8-7	1511 Snarry Hill [1] 8-7
1607 Seamere [17] 8-10	-- Moloch [5] 8-10	-- Fair Zinnia [10] 8-7
-- Sica Sue [7] 8-7	164 Lush Path [8] 9-4	1602 Rebeccas Pet [6] 9-4

17 ran   2,shhd,1½,7,1½   (Mrs C J O'Sullivan)   J Dunlop, Arundel, Sussex.

1842 MCCOYS TONTINE RESTAURANT MAIDEN 3YO   £1024   1m 4f Good/Firm 25 -35 Slow

--   TOP SHOT [1] (G Wragg) 3-8-11 R Hills 6/5: 00-1: 3 ch f Grundy - Reload (Relko): Made a
successful reapp, regained lead dist for a decisive win in a 3 runner stakes race at Redcar
July 29: showed promise in both starts last term and is a half sister to several useful
winners: eff over 12f on fast grnd: acts on a galloping track: will be better for this
run and will win more races.   45
1481 HELIETTA [2] (L Cumani) 3-8-11 W Ryan 1/1 FAV: -042: Went on 3f out, not pace of
winner and is proving expensive to follow: see 1481 and 1368.   38
--   DANCING FROG [3] (W Jarvis) 3-9-0 J Bleasdale 7/1: 0-3: Outsider: led 1m, sn dropped
out: lightly raced gelding who is bred to be suited by middle dists.   00
3 ran   3,15   (E B Moller)   G Wragg Newmarket

1843 MCCOYS RESTAURANT MAIDEN AUCTION STAKES £2113   6f   Good/Firm 25 -02 Slow

1668 GLOBAL LADY [2] (W Musson) 2-8-5 M Wigham 2/1 FAV: 21: 2 b f Balliol - Princess
Nefertiti (Tutankhamen): Narrowly justified fav. led inside dist & kept on well in a 2yo
mdn auction race at Redcar July 29: chased home Shining Water at Windsor on her debut: cost
5,200 gns & is related to several winners: eff over 6f on gd & firm grnd: acts on any trk.   42
1305 SNO SURPRISE [5] (R Boss) 2-7-13 M Roberts 4/1: 4002: Led after ½way, just btn:
eff over 5/6f on gd/firm grnd: suited by a gall trk: see 425.   35
415 PAY DIRT [9] (T Fairhurst) 2-8-2(BL) R Hills 12/1: 0303: Bl first time: al front rank
despite a lengthy abs: eff over 5/6f on gd/firm & soft grnd: see 236.   32
1522 RIVERBOAT PARTY [7] (R Hutchinson) 2-7-13 P Hutchinson(3) 3/1: 004: Switched dist,
never nearer: continues to impr: eff over 6f on gd/firm grnd: see 1522.   28
1665 TELL ME NOW [4] 2-7-10 R Morse(5) 16/1: 000: Well placed over ½way: very cheaply
bought filly.   13
--   DRESS UP [1] 2-7-13 J Lowe 20/1: 0: Cheaply acquired debutant who is a half brother
to 10f winner Robertos Lady.   08

780 Cowlam Boy [10] 7-13	1561 Oxford Place [6] 8-5	-- Shannon Lady [11] 8-11
1370 Fidgetty Feet [3] 7-13		1069 Send It Down [8] 8-8

11 ran   nk,2,hd,4,3   (Global Homes Southern Ltd)   W Musson Newmarket

Official Going Given As GOOD

1844 JULY MAIDEN AUCTION STAKES 2YO   £1126   5f   Good/Firm 27 -32 Slow

1728 VICTORY BALLARD [10] (R Hannon) 2-8-8 A Mcglone 25/1: 0001: 2 ch c Ballad Rock -
Wyn Mipet (Welsh Saint): Led/dsptd lead inside final 2f and got up close home in a 2yo mdn
auction at Yarmouth July 29: speedily bred colt who was cheaply acquired as a yearling: eff
at 5f on gd/firm grnd & an easy trk.   43
1789 SURELY GREAT [4] (D Thom) 2-8-0(1ow) Gay Kelleway(0) 2/1 JT.FAV: 0240202: Ev ch final
1f: btn a whisker, best in 1632.   35
938 MILLFAN [3] (W Musson) 2-8-5 J Reid 2/1 JT.FAV: 23: Gambled on, despite abs: led
inside final 2f, just btn: see 938.   39
1665 SKYBOLT [9] (W O'gorman) 2-8-5 T Ives 4/1: 04: Led over 3f: not btn far in close
fin and is on the up grade: see 1665.   37
1552 KIMS TICKET [13] 2-8-5 M Hills 9/1: 00: Chall inside final 2f: impr: half brother to
winning plater Full Of Speed.   32
497 EBONY PRIDE [6] 2-8-3 G Duffield 9/2: 040: Long abs: prom most: eff at 5f on a snd surface 22

-- Uncle Toms Castle [7] 8-4		1059 My Elane [2] 8-5(BL)
1576 Tinas Beauty [12] 8-1(1ow)		-- Vortrack [5] 8-7(4ow)
905 Game Light [11] 7-13	1550 Fires Out [8] 7-13(VIS)	
-- Auction Groupie [1] 7-13		00

13 ran   shhd,½,½,1½,3   (St J G O'Connell)   R Hannon East Everleigh, Wilts

1845 MARINA SELLING HCAP 3YO+ 0-25   £736   1m 2f   Good/Firm 27 -17 Slow   [18]

1703 MURILLO [3] (F Carr) 10-9-0 J Carr(7) 10/1: 3204001: 10 b g Windjammer - Fuiseog
(Eudaemon): Led final 1f, ridden out in a selling h'cap at Yarmouth July 29: placed on
numerous occasions in '85: last successful in '81: acts on any grnd: eff at 7-11f: best when
coming late.   11
1056 MR MUSIC MAN [1] (C Reavey) 12-8-13 I Johnson 15/2: 0-00002: Led nearing final 1f:
fair effort for a 12yo! last season won at Beverley: in '84 won 4 times and has been a
tremendous stable servant: eff at 8/10f, stays 12f: acts on any grnd.   08
1569 METELSKI [11] (G Blum) 5-9-10(bl) M Rimmer 10/1: 00-0003: Finished well: lightly
raced since 201.   18
1724 DALLAS SMITH [10] (M Chapman) 5-8-6 J Carter(7) 16/1: 0000004: Led ½way: see 975.   00
1666 IRISH DILEMMA [14] 3-8-10(bl) P Bloomfield 6/1: 0000400: Led 3f out: best 1558.   08
1767 TAKE THE BISCUIT [8] 3-8-11 A Mercer 5/1: 0200030: Late hdway: best 1210 (sharpish 1m). 05
1656 SLEEPLINE DUCHESS [9] 3-8-7 G Carter(3) 2/1 FAV: 00-0020: Disapp fav: much btr 1656. 00
1459 Celtic Image [6] 8-7   1569 Venture To Reform [13] 8-5
1417 Useful Addition [2] 8-10(bl)   --   Majestic Star [12] 9-3
--   Bushy Bay [5] 8-8   1736 Burbridge King St [7] 8-10
13 ran ½,½,½,4,2   (F Carr)   F Carr Norton, Yorks

1846 VINCE HILL CLAIMING STAKES 2YO   £1383   7f   Good/Firm 27 -19 Slow

1598 PERFECT STRANGER [9] (P Haslam) 2-9-0 G French 4/1: 031: 2 b g Wolver Hollow -
Mrs Walmsley (Lorenzaccio): Mkt drifter, but made nearly all, driven out in a 2yo claimer
at Yarmouth July 29: eff at 7f, should stay 1m: acts on fast grnd: seems suited by front
running tactics.   35
1059 ORIENT LINE [7] (R Hannon) 2-8-12 A Mcglone 8/1: 02: Mkt drifter: ch final 1f: 4L
clear 3rd: gd effort: eff at 7f on gd/firm.   30
*1599 ORIENTAL JADE [1] (D Morley) 2-9-3(bl) R Guest 4/1: 0413: Al prom: in gd form: stays 7f. 26
1598 OCONNELL STREET [5] (M Tompkins) 2-9-3(BL) M Hills 8/1: 00044: Bl first time: no
extra final 1f: see 1598.   24
1363 COUNTESS BREE [2] 2-9-0 J Reid 12/1: 0030: Prom, ev ch: see 1363 (sharpish 6f).   19
1762 RIPSTER [6] 2-8-7 A Mercer 25/1: 00: Btr effort from this cheaply acquired colt:
half brother to winning 3yo Lyapkin - Tyapkin.   08
1598 TRYNOVA [4] 2-8-9 G Duffield 11/8 FAV: 020: Well bckd disapp: much btr 1598 (C/D). 00
1566 SKRAGGS PLUS TWO [8] 2-8-8 Gay Kelleway(3) 13/2: 000430: There 4f: btr 1566: see 1172. 00
1570 Ribogirl [3] 8-9(BL)
9 ran 1,4,½,½,1½,½,shhd,2½   (Ian A Paice)   P Haslam Newmarket

1847 SOMERLEYTON FILLIES HANDICAP 3YO 0-50   £2464   6f   Good/Firm 27 -01 Slow   [43]

1608 USEFUL [5] (B Hills) 3-9-6 M Hills 10/3: 0-02301: 3 b f Thatching - Mrs Mutton
(Dancer's Image): Mkt drifter, but led well over 1f out, readily in a 3yo fillies h'cap at
Yarmouth July 29: tried in bl last time out: in '85 won a Bath mdn: eff over 5f, stays 6f
well: acts on gd/firm & soft grnd.   46
1695 TAYLOR OF SOHAM [2] (D Leslie) 3-8-6 M Rimmer 5/2: 3004132: Nearest fin: in gd form. 25
*1571 MUDISHA [4] (G Huffer) 3-10-0(7ex) G Carter(3) 2/1: -004013: Made most: btr 1571 (7f). 39
1687 LEFT RIGHT [3] (N Macauley) 3-7-12(bl) S P Griffiths 12/1: 3003044: Ch over 2f out:
best 1399 (5f, maiden).   07
1360 SUMMERHILL SPRUCE [1] 3-8-10 G King(5) 6/1: -001300: Prom over 4f: btr 1191, 871. 12
5 ran 2½,3,¾,2½   (Mrs J M Corbett)   B Hills Lambourn, Berks

1848 MARTHAM STAKES 3YO   £1660   1m 6f   Good/Firm 27 +04 Fast

1620 HUSNAH [2] (L Cumani) 3-9-0 R Guest 5/4 FAV: -333121: 3 b f Caro - Lovely Lovely
(Carlemont): Useful filly: made ev yd, comfortably in quite fast run 3 runner stakes event
at Yarmouth July 29: earlier won a fillies mdn at Brighton & seems a consistent sort: eff
at 12f, stays 14f well: acts on gd & firm grnd & seems suited by front running.   53
458 MYCENAE CHERRY [3] (G Wragg) 3-9-0(BL) T Ives 5/2: 0-142: Bl first time: al prom:
fair effort after long abs: stays 14f: acts on gd/firm & yld: see 173.   48
1642 TORWADA [1] (P Cole) 3-9-9 P Waldron 6/4: 04-1003: Mkt drifter & ran below par:
may stay 14f: see 191.   49
3 ran 1¼,6   (Sheikh Mohammed)   L Cumani Newmarket

1849 SEASIDE HANDICAP 3YO+ 0-35   £1643   5f   Good/Firm 27 +01 Fast   [35]

+1805 MUSIC MACHINE [12] (P Haslam) 5-9-12(7ex) J Scally(7) 7/2 CO.FAV: 4041011: 5 b g Record
Token - Sodance (So Blessed): In fine form and made ev yd, readily in a h'cap at Yarmouth
July 29: impressive weekend winner at Lingfield: earlier made all in a h'cap at Warwick: in
fine form in '85, winning at Pontefract, Warwick and Ripon: in '84 won at Ayr: very eff at
5f, does stay 6f: acts on any grnd & on any trk, but best forcing the pace on a sharp/easy
one: carries weight well.   43
1649 CHINA GOLD [5] (L Siddall) 7-10-0 M Wood 14/1: 3004202: Nearest fin: best effort since 1268 37
1542 SHAHREEN [8] (G Blum) 5-9-7(5oh) S P Griffiths 33/1: 00-0003: Fin well inside final
2f: by far her best effort this season: failed to make the frame in '85: in '84 won at
Newmarket: eff at 5/6f: best on fast grnd.   01

1649 CAPTAINS BIDD [4] (H Whiting) 6-7-7(bl)(3oh) L Riggio(5) 10/1: 0020204: Prom, ev ch.   00
1676 PHILSTAR [9] 5-8-7(vis) N Day 7/2 CO.FAV: 0030030: Gambled on: sn prom: btr 1676 (6f).   11
1542 EECEE TREE [3] 4-9-1(bl) M Hills 7/2 CO.FAV: 2000140: Prom most: see 1542, 1438.   18
1347 CANIF [6] 5-9-13 T Ives 11/2: 00-0100: No show in 8th: twice disapp since 1157 (6f).   00
1649 RAPID MISS [2] 6-8-9 W Wharton 8/1: -003000: Fdd final 1f: best 1367: see 784.   00
1574 Russell Flyer [1] 8-3(bl)   1638 Velocidad [7] 8-6
1603 Alexanjo [10] 8-9(BL)   1499 Fancy Pages [13] 8-0(1ow)
1463 Baliview [11] 7-7(VIS)(3oh)
13 ran   2¼,¼,½,1,nk,nk   (A Piller)   P Haslam Newmarket

GOODWOOD.   Tuesday July 29th   Righthand Undulating Track

Official Going Given As GOOD ON THE STRAIGHT COURSE, GOOD/FIRM ON ROUND COURSE

1850 GROUP 3 MOLECOMB STAKES 2YO   £18189   5f   Good/Firm 27 -28 Slow

1585 GEMINI FIRE [1] (P Felgate) 2-8-12 S Cauthen 33/1: 0413131: 2 br c Mansingh -
Sealady (Seaepic): Very useful, impr colt: caused a 33/1 surprise when gamely making ev yd
& holding on in a close fin to rather slowly run Gr.3 Molecomb Stakes at Goodwood July 29:
earlier comfortably won minor races at Catterick & Edinburgh: speedily bred brother to
useful sprinter Singing Sailor: likely to prove best at 5f on a sharp course, making the
running: acts well on firm & gd grnd: genuine & consistent.   67
*1708 REGENCY FILLE [4] (R Williams) 2-8-7 R Cochrane 13/2: 2223212: Came from behind and
almost got up on the post: fine effort from this remarkably consistent filly: see 1708.   62
1108 NUTWOOD LIL [3] (E Eldin) 2-8-7 A Mackay 25/1: 11203: Kept on well under press:
ran right to her best: see 450, 924.   59
-1126 ZAIBAQ [2] (H T Jones) 2-8-12 A Murray 6/4 FAV: 1324: Sn under press, kept on close
home: can do btr: see 405, 1126.   64
*1308 UN BEL DI [5] 2-8-7 Pat Eddery 9/2: 010: Chall 2f out, wknd: see 1308.   58
+1311 SAUCE DIABLE [6] 2-8-7 W Carson 100/30: 210: Prom, wknd & btr 1311.   55
6 ran   shhd,1½,hd,½,1½.   (J David Abell)   Felgate Grimston, Leics

---

1851 OAK TREE STKS LISTED 3YO+ FILL.&MARES   £15738   7f   Good/Firm 27 -09 Slow

1487 ROYAL LOFT [5] (W Jarvis) 3-8-7 R Cochrane 14/1: 1-221: 3 ch f Homing - Well Off
(Welsh Pageant): Smart filly: mkt drifter but ran on to lead final 1f, holding on well to
win valuable Oak Tree Stakes (fillies & mares) at Goodwood July 29: possibly unlucky last
time, reportedly coming into season on the morning of the race: winner of her only race
in '85, a mdn at Doncaster: very eff over 7f/1m: acts on firm & yld & on any trk: certainly
on the up grade.   69
1466 HOLBROOKE SUTTON [1] (L Cumani) 3-8-7 W R Swinburn 16/1: 14-402: Came from off the
pace, not the best of runs but was just held close home: grand effort & must win soon: see 1153   69
*1153 VIANORA [11] (G Harwood) 3-8-7 G Starkey 6/1: -011213: Made most, kept on gamely
and another fine effort from this consistent filly: see 1153.   66
*1487 MUMMYS FAVOURITE [3] (J Dunlop) 3-8-7 W Carson 1/1 FAV: 11-3414: Waited with, behind
a wall of horses 2f out, no extra when finding a gap: much btr 1487 (stiff trk).   60
705 NASHIA [12] 3-8-7 Paul Eddery 25/1: 120-000: Prom thro'out, after abs: trying a
new trip today and last season was successful 3 times over 5f at Newbury, Goodwood &
Salisbury: probably stays 6f: acts on firm grnd, goes particularly well on an easy surface:
appears to act on any trk.   58
1110 CHALK STREAM [9] 3-8-7 Pat Eddery 14/1: 124-200: No threat: race 708 has worked out poorly   56
1466 PURCHASEPAPERCHASE [6] 4-9-5 C Asmussen 9/1: 0-01040: Disapp since 708.   00
1514 Charge Along [7] 9-2   1466 Ever Genial [4] 9-8   1631 Dream Chaser [8] 8-7
1514 Glide By [2] 9-2   1219 Smooch [10] 8-7
12 ran   shhd,1½,3,1,¾   (Mrs P D Player)   W Jarvis Newmarket

---

1852 WM HILL STEWARDS CUP H'CAP 3YO+ 0-75   £37824   6f   Good/Firm 27 -03 Slow   [56]

1608 GREEN RUBY [22] (G Balding) 5-8-12 J Williams 20/1: 30-0331: 5 br h Shecky Greene-
Ruby Tuesday (T V Lark): Useful sprinter: well ridden to lead final 100yds, narrowly, in
William Hill Stewards Cup H'cap at Goodwood July 29: in '85 won at Pontefract, the previous
season successful at Yarmouth, Salisbury & Hamilton (2): suited by 6f, stays 7f: acts on hvy
but is best on firm or gd going.   54
1461 YOUNG JASON [10] (G Lewis) 3-7-8 M L Thomas 10/1: 1-00122: Well bckd, came to chall
final 1f, just btn & continues in fine form: see 1272: should find another race soon.   43
1608 PERFECT TIMING [12] (D Elsworth) 4-9-0 Pat Eddery 8/1 JT FAV: -043323: Waited with,
led briefly inside final 1f in a close fin: running consistently but is not easy to win on.   53
+1235 PRINCE SKY [11] (P Cole) 4-9-3 T Quinn 8/1 JT FAV: 4-43014: Dsptd lead till went on
½way, hdd final 1f but not btn far: grand effort: still impr: see 1235.   55
+1306 OUR JOCK [7] 4-9-12(5ex) C Rutter(5) 11/1: -000410: Close up 5th, fine effort
under 9-12: see 1306.   62
1777 GOLD PROSPECT [8] 4-8-6 B Rouse 20/1: 2040230: Al prom & is in fine form: see 1777.   39
1631 MEASURING [5] 3-9-2 S Cauthen 16/1: 0-30000: Prom, fin 7th: see 59.   56
1145 PADRE PIO [18] 5-9-0 W R Swinburn 18/1: 21-6200: Close up 8th: best 846.   46
*1648 MANTON DAN [4] 3-8-12 P Cook 18/1: 12-2010: Dsptd lead most, fin 9th: see 1648.   52

-1429 AL TRUI [9] 6-9-6 M Wigham 14/1: 0100020: Ev ch in 10th: unable to repeat last
year's win & btr 1429. 50
1235 AMEGHINO [19] 6-8-9 W Newnes 11/1: 0403300: Prom, ev ch: twice below 1037 (5f stiff trk) 00
+1704 SEW HIGH [6] 3-8-5 A Mackay 12/1: 0104110: Early pace, btr 1704. 00
-1654 BERTIE WOOSTER [15] 3-8-2(bl) W Carson 9/1: 1000220: Prom much: see 1654. 00
1631 Durham Place [14] 9-6   1508 Hi Tech Girl [17] 9-4(bl)   1730 Derry River [1] 8-0(bl)
1730 Laurie Lorman [23] 9-0   1669 Quarryville [13] 8-9   1649 Shades Of Blue [28] 7-7(2oh)
1682 Throne Of Glory [25] 8-4   1608 Glen Kella Manx [21] 8-4   1676 Ra Ra Girl [2] 8-0
1521 Soon To Be [24] 8-2   1536 Sudden Impact [3] 8-1(bl)
24 ran   nk,¾,hd,¾,1½,1½,shhd,shhd,1   (Mrs Ernest Weinstein)   G Balding Fyfield, Hants

1853 GROUP 3 GORDON STAKES 3YO   £21600   1m 4f   Good/Firm 27 +16 Fast

878 ALLEZ MILORD [2] (G Harwood) 3-8-10 G Starkey 11/10 FAV: 1-1101: 3 b c Tom Rolfe -
Why Me Lord (Bold Reasoning): Very smart, impr colt: heavily bckd despite an abs of some 2 months
but justified this confidence, leading dist, ridden out to win fast run Gr.3 Gordon Stakes
at Goodwood July 29: met his only defeat so far in the Derby and reportedly pulled a muscle:
earlier won Listed races at Goodwood & Newmarket & was a runaway winner of a mdn at
Newmarket on sole outing in '85: half brother to several winners: very eff over 12f: should
stay further: acts on hvy, well suited by firm or gd grnd. 82
1330 BONHOMIE [1] (H Cecil) 3-9-2 S Cauthen 3/1: 11-2122: Made a gallant attempt to lead
thro'out, made the winner pull out all the stops in the final 1f: a most genuine front runner
who will stay the Leger trip well: see 1098. 86
878 SIRK [5] (C Brittain) 3-8-10 C Asmussen 7/1: -132303: Kept on well under press: see 878, 48 75
1098 NEW TROJAN [3] (W Hern) 3-8-10 W Carson 4/1: 40-4024: Prom, ev ch: btr 1098 (stiff trk). 73
1152 DANISHGAR [4] 3-8-10 W R Swinburn 16/1: 2-04120: Fdd inside final 2f: see 739. 61
5 ran   ¾,3,1½,8   (Jerome Brody)   G Harwood Pulborough, Sussex

1854 PAUL MASSON H'CAP 3YO 0-60   £5049   1m   Good/Firm 27 +15 Fast   [65]

*1269 STAR CUTTER [12] (H Cecil) 3-9-6 S Cauthen 7/2: -211: 3 gr c Star De Naskra -
Azed (Al Hattab): Smart, impr colt: set a fast pace from flag fall when comfortably winning
a valuable, fast run 3yo h'cap at Goodwood July 29: winner of a minor event at Newcastle last
time: unraced in '85: first foal of a winning miler & is well suited by that trip himelf:
does well forcing the pace on fast going: can win another h'cap before being reassessed &
could well be gd enough to pick up a Gr.3 race before the end of the season. 74
*1365 MEET THE GREEK [8] (R Laing) 3-8-9 P Cook 9/1: 2112012: Close up final 4f & ran
another gd race: see 1365. 55
1588 ININSKY [10] (G Harwood) 3-9-7 G Starkey 20/1: 10-4003: Fin well & ran his best
race this season: suited by 1m but did not seem to stay 10f in 1588: could win soon: see 950. 66
*1651 SOLO STYLE [5] (G Lewis) 3-7-9(5ex) M L Thomas 15/2: 3001014: Gd effort under his
pen: in grand form & should win again if eased in class: see 1651. 39
1147 BARCLAY STREET [6] 3-9-4 Pat Eddery 20/1: 14-0000: Possibly did not quite see out
the trip: see 808. 60
*1532 SAFEERA [11] 3-8-9(5ex) W Woods(3) 14/1: 1-03410: Prom most, btr 1532 (sharp trk). 41
1515 MORICA [7] 3-8-1 W Carson 3/1 FAV: 1-40: Well bckd, prom till wknd 2f out: btr 1515. 00
1520 TERMINATOR [4] 3-8-0 C Rutter(5) 7/1: 41-3030: Much btr 1520. 00
*1472 Bronze Opal [1] 8-3   1436 Pellinko [2] 8-12   1153 Great Leighs [3] 8-12
216 Town Jester [9] 8-13
12 ran   2½,½,nk,¾,½,7   (Sheikh Mohammed)   H Cecil Newmarket

1855 EBF NEW HAM MAIDEN STAKES 2YO FILLIES   £5119   7f   Good/Firm 27 -18 Slow

1287 IOSIFA [8] (M Stoute) 2-8-11 W R Swinburn 5/4 FAV: 31: 2 br f Top Ville - Cojean
(Prince John): Smart, prom filly: justified strong support, al cantering & sprinting clear
in the final 2f for a ready, impressive win in a fast run 2yo fillies mdn at Goodwood
July 29: obviously benefitted greatly from racecourse debut in 1287: dam a winning 2yo:
suited by 7f, sure to stay further: acts well on fast grnd: sure to win more races. 73
-- PORT HELENE [3] (W Hern) 2-8-11 W Carson 8/1: 2: Rear till good late prog, caught a
tartar here and this was a fine debut: suited by 7f, will stay further: should be hard to
beat in a mdn next time. 55
-- FOLLIES BERGERES [11] (M Dickinson) 2-8-11 S Cauthen 11/1: 3: Made a sound debut: half
sister to Ascot Gold Cup winner Gildoran: sure to impr for this experience but may not be
seen at her best until tackling longer dists next seasoon. 49
1464 TECANA [6] (P Walwyn) 2-8-11 Paul Eddery 6/1: 44: Ev ch, this may turn out to be a
hot race and she can win a mdn: see 1464. 48
-- CATHERINE SCHRATT [7] 2-8-11 P Cook 33/1: 0: Mkt drifter on debut, fin in very
promising style which bodes well for her future: related to a couple of minor winners:
will stay beyond 7f: should be noted next time. 48
1604 LUCKY STONE [9] 2-8-11 G Baxter 5/1: 20: Very well bckd, chall 2f out, fdd: btr 6f? 46
-- POINT OF VIEW [1] 2-8-11 Pat Eddery 10/1: 0: Rear thro'out: related to several middle
dist winners & may require lngr dists to show her true worth. 00
-- Quiet Blush [5] 8-11   1341 Fresh Thoughts [10] 8-11
-- North Pacific [2] 8-11   1382 Top Wak [4] 8-11
11 ran   7,3,½,nk,1   (Sheikh Mohammed)   M Stoute Newmarket

TIPPERARY   Thursday July 24th   Lefthand, Fair Track

Official Going Given As GOOD

1856 DAWN MILK CHALLENGE STAKES   £16028   1m 6f   Good

1150 LUNDYLUX (R Hannon) 4-8-11 S Craine 13/2: 320-001: 4 b f Grundy - Norfolk Light
(Blakeney) Useful filly: led appr final 1f driven out in a val stks at Tipperary July 24:
lightly raced prev this term: in '85 won a fillies mdn at Wolverhampton and also a fine 2nd
to Perkin Warbeck at Newmarket: stays 14f well: acts on firm and yldg ground.   58
--   GENERAL KNOWLEDGE (D Weld) 4-9-0 M J Kinane 14/1:   0342: Kept on well: gd effort.   60
--   SALUS (J Oxx) 4-8-11 D Hogan 7/1: -0023: Prom all the way.   56
1127 RISING (K Prendergast) 4-9-5 G Curran 5/4 FAV: 1034: Disapp fav: see 475.   56
6 Ran   1,hd,6   (St J G O'Connell)   R Hannon East Everleigh, Wilts.

TIPPERARY   Friday July 25th   Lefthand, Fair Track

Official Going Given As GOOD

1857 KILFRUSH COOLMORE TIPPERARY SPRINT   £15758   5f   Good

--   EDNICA (J Oxx) 4-9-8 Pat Eddery 7/4 FAV: 00-1111: 4 b g Martinmas - My Bonnie
(Highland Melody) Smart Irish gelding: led well over 1f out, holding on gamely by a nk in
a val sprint at Tipperary July 25: now unbtn in his 4 starts this term: very eff over sprint
dist: seems a genuine sort.   73
901 OROJOYA (J Hindley) 4-9-11 M Hills 7/2: 3-02002: Chall final 1f: just btn: see 413.   75
1387 PETROVICH (R Hannon) 4-9-8 S Craine 7/1: 0-30003: Not btn far: gd eff: see 705.   70
9 Ran   nk,¾   (M Garrigan)   J Oxx Ireland

PHOENIX PARK   Saturday July 26th   Left and Righthand Sharpish Track

Official Going Given As GOOD

1858 GR 3 BARODA STUD PHOENIX SPRINT   £13090   6f   Good

1491 ACUSHLA (M V O'brien) 3-8-7 C Asmussen 9/10 FAV: 03-0121: 3 b f Storm Bird -
Intrepid Lady (Bold Ruler) Smart Irish filly: well bckd and led after ½ way, readily, in a
Gr 3 event at Phoenix Park July 26: earlier was an easy winner of a fillies event over this
C/D: very eff at 6f: acts on firm and yldg ground.   77
*1491 LONDON TOWER (D Weld) 3-9-4 M J Kinane 6/1: 203312: In gd form: see 1491.   75
*1511 EASTERN SONG (C Nelson) 3-8-10 J Reid 6/1: 20-013: Ran really well in this much
better company: very eff at 6/7f: see 1511.   66
903 MITSUBISHI VISON (J Oxx) 3-8-12(bl) D Hogan 10/1: -012214: -   64
8 Ran   4,hd,1½   (R Sangster)   M V O'brien Ireland

EVRY   Saturday July 26 th

Official Going Given As GOOD

1859 GROUP 3 PRIX DAPHNIS 3YO COLTS   £19466   1m 1f   Good

--   THRILL SHOW [3] (A Fabre) 3-8-11 A Gibert 1: -111: 3 b c Northern Baby - Splendid
Girl (Golden Eagle) Smart unbtn colt: led inside final 1f, under press, in a Gr 3 event
at Evry July 26: earlier successful at Evry and Chantilly: stays 9f well: acts well on good.   74
301 SYNDROM [4] (A De Royer Dupre) 3-8-11 O Poirier 1: -103312: Dsptd lead final 1f:
just btn: last time out won at Maisons-Laffitte.   71
389 KALISTAN [9] (J Bernard) 3-8-11 M Philipperon 1: -220113: Not btn far in cl finish:
in fine form lately.   70
8 Ran   ½,nk   (R H Winn)   A Fabre France

GELSENKIRCHEN   Saturday July 26th   Righthand, Flat Track

Official Going Given As SOFT

1860 GROUP 3 OSTERMANN POKAL 3YO+   £13277   6f   Good

-1387 TARIB [10] (H Thomson Jones) 3-8-1 R Hills 1/2 FAV: 2-21421: 3 ch f Habitat -
Red Coral (Red God) Very useful, consistent filly: comfortable winner of a Gr 3 event at
Gelsenkirchen July 26: last time out was just btn by Polykratis in a val Listed race at
Sandown: earlier won a Listed race at Baden-Baden: in '85 completed a hat trick at Beverley,
Catterick and Redcar: equally eff over 5/6f: acts on firm and soft and on any trk: genuine.   70
--   ONESTO [3] (F Schlaefle) 4-8-9 K Woodburn 1: 0-20002: Not pace of winner.   64
1490 LE ROC [7] (H Bollow) 3-8-5 P Remmert 1: -004123: --   60
10 Ran   1½,2½   (Hamdan Al-Maktoum)   H Thomson Jones Newmarket

Official Going Given As GOOD

1861   GROUP 1 GROSSER PREIS VON BERLIN   £33898   1m 4f   Good

*1493 ACATENANGO [1] (H Jentzsch) 4-9-7 G Bocskai 1: 11-1111: 4 ch c Surumu – Aggravate (Aggressor) Highclass German colt: completed a magnificent 10 wins in a row, comfortably landing the odds in a Gr 1 event at Dusseldorf July 27: earlier won a Gr 1 event at St-Cloud and a Gr 2 event at Baden-Baden: in excellent form in '85, winning the German Derby: very eff over·11/12f on good and soft ground and does well when up with pace: virtually impossible to beat in his home country and seems equally as good elsewhere.   84
1144 THEATRICAL [2] (D Weld) 4-9-7 M J Kinane 1: 0200-02: Ran really well against this German wonder horse: see 1144.   78
--   ORFANO [7] (S Von Mitzlaff) 3-8-5 P Alafi 1: -133143:   67
8 Ran   2,3½   (Gestut Fahrhof)   H Jentzsch Germany

Official Going Given As GOOD/FIRM

1862   BREAKWATER SELLING STAKES   2YO   £974   7f   Firm 18 -26 Slow

317   SUE FOREVER [7] (R Whitaker) 2-8-8 D Mckeown 11/1: 01: 2 b f Riboboy – Lucy Martin (Forlorn River) Dropped in class after a long abs, led dist and was a clever winner of a 2yo seller at Redcar July 30 (no bid): very cheaply bought filly who is eff over 7f on a sound surface: acts on a galloping track.   22
1622 PHILEARN [5] (M Brittain) 2-8-8 K Darley 8/1: 440002: Led/dsptd lead thr'out: comfortably held by winner: half sister to 10f winner Foggy Glen: see 1622.   20
1622 MISS PISA [1] (W Wharton) 2-8-8 N Carlisle 85/40 FAV: 0303043: Al front rank: quite consistent in this grade tho' yet to get her head in front: eff over 5/7f: acts on firm. see 647.   18
1635 FREV OFF [10] (M H Easterby) 2-8-8(bl) M Birch 3/1: 0004034: Led/dsptd lead: clear remainder: see 1635.   16
1764 TOKANDA [9] 2-8-11 M Hills 4/1: 000: Early speed: see 1764.   04
1248 OKAY YAH [4] 2-8-11 S Lawes 25/1: 00: Cl.up to ½ way: half brother to a couple of winners, including 11f winner Tieatre.   00
1622 Top Robe   [3] 8-8   --   Soaring Eagles 0 8-8   --   Paddy Maloney [8] 8-11
9 ran   ½,1,1,7,3   (R L Hanson)   R Whitaker Wetherby, Yorks.

1863   REDCAR SILVER SALVER STAKES   2YO   £2800   7f   Firm 18 +05 Fast

*1675 ON TAP [5] (M H Easterby) 2-9-2 M Birch 4/6 FAV: 411: 2 ch g Tap On Wood – Joshua's Daughter (Joshua) Very useful juv: was never hdd when an easy winner of quite a fast run 2yo stks at Redcar July 30: recently hacked up in a Pontefract maiden: half brother to sev winners, including the once very useful h'capper Glen Kella Manx: very eff over 6/7f and will stay further: acts on fast ground and on any trk: well regarded and sure to win again.   62
*1764 AFRICAN SPIRIT [3] (M Prescott) 2-9-1 G Duffield 9/4: 12: Ev ch, lacked pace to seriously threaten this smart winner: comfortably beat rem and stays 7f well: should find another winning opportunity soon: see 1764.   46
1566 SILVER ANCONA [6] (E Eldin) 2-8-11 A Mackay 12/1: 343343: Chased winner most of way: placed in all his starts tho' lacks a turn of foot: see 1566.   30
1681 RED TWILIGHT [2] (R Whitaker) 2-8-11 D Mckeown 13/2: 34: No real threat: btr 1681 (6f)   27
1681 NAFUAT [1] 2-8-11 N Connorton 33/1: 00: Slow start, wknd after ½ way: cost IR 18,000 as a yearling and is a half brother to sev winners, including winning juv Land Without Stars.   15
1812 AREA CODE [4] 2-8-11 D Leadbitter(5) 50/1: 400: Speed to ½ way: twice below form shown in 108 (5f soft).   01
6 ran   5,5,1½,5,6   (Lt-Col R Warden)   M H Easterby Great Habton, Yorks.

1864   RED CROSS HANDICAP 3YO   (0-35)   £2674   1m   Firm 18 -38 Slow   [36]

1758 HEAVENLY HOOFER [10] (Denys Smith) 3-8-10(7ex) L Charnock 6/1: 1011031: 3 b g Dance In Time – Heavenly Chord (Hittite Glory) In fine form, gamely made all in a 3yo h'cap at Redcar July 30: won a similar race at Edinburgh earlier this month, after twice winning at Beverley: eff over 7/8f on gd and firm ground: acts on any trk.   26
1091 GOLDEN ANCONA [5] (E Eldin) 3-9-7 A Mackay 9/1: 0-10002: Just failed to get up: better effort: stays 1m well: acts on any going and on any trk: see 284.   36
1250 NICOLINI [9] (J Fitzgerald) 3-8-3 G Duffield 25/1: 00-003: Kept on late: eff over 1m tho' bred to be suited by middle dist: acts on fast grd and on a gall trk: see 1250.   15
*1425 CERTAIN AWARD [7] (J Watts) 3-9-6 N Connorton 9/2: 014: Fair eff under top weight. see 1425.27
1788 SCINTILLATOR [8] 3-8-0 M Hills 8/1: 0-00000: No extra dist: seee 1362 & 1281.   05
1626 BROADHURST [4] 3-8-11 M Wood 8/1: 000-030: Never beyond mid-div: btr 1626 (7f shp trk).   02
1431 HAMLOUL [3] 3-9-6 A Murray 9/4 FAV: 0-00220: Wknd into 7th: much btr on an easier course in 1431: now trained by K Bailey.   00
1065 FAATIK [2] 3-8-10 N Howe 7/1: 0-00400: Front rank over ½ way: fin last: see 334.   00
1761 Cumbrian Nijo   [6] 8-12(bl)   1626 Mark My Card   [1] 7-10
10 ran   shthd,1½,2½,1,7,hd   (J A Bianchi)   Denys Smith Bishop Auckland, Co Durham.

1865 SEA PIGEON HANDICAP (0-50)   £3889   1m 6f   Firm 18 -42 Slow   [35]

1280 MARLION [5] (S Hall) 5-8-13 E Guest(3) 11/4: -003241: 5 b g Julio Mariner - Rose
Mullion (Tudor Melody) Comfortably made all in a slowly run h'cap at Redcar July 30: won over
this C/D last term, when he also scored at Catterick: winning hurdler who is well suited by
a test of stamina: does well on fast ground: acts on any track.   29
+1633 JACKDAW [6] (R Hollinshead) 6-9-9(8ex) A Culhane(7) 7/1: 3002312: In gd form:see 1633. 33
 1359 BUCKLOW HILL [4] (J Fitzgerald) 9-9-7 A Murray 8/1: 0-00003: Ran on same pace: see 782   28
 1663 COMELY DANCER [3] (J Watts) 3-9-3 N Connorton 9/4 FAV: -311434: Not disgraced against
older horses: see 958.   37
 1577 OLD MALTON [1] 4-8-7 Dale Gibson(7) 4/1: 0001330: Best over this trip in 990(easier trk) 11
*1737 NORTHERN RULER [2] 4-8-10(5ex) L Riggio(7) 12/1: 0000010: Trailed in last: much
better 1737 (tight track).   00
 6 ran   4,1½,½,1,15   (Mrs M C Grant)   S Hall Middleham, Yorks.

1866 ST JOHN AMBULANCE H'CAP   (0-35)   £2670   1m 3f   Firm 18 -36 Slow   [32]

1569 LAKINO [1] (J Fitzgerald) 4-8-11 A Murray 11/4 FAV: 1-00001: 4 b g Relkino - Lake
Naivasha (Blakeney) Led below dist and held on well in an all aged h'cap at Redcar July 30:
won his only start last season, a selling h'cap at Beverley: eff over 10/12f: acts on firm
and yielding ground and on any track.   23
1548 GOLDEN FANCY [2] (I Vickers) 9-9-7 R Vickers(7) 4/1: 223432D: Ev ch, not quicken
close home and hung left: btn a nk in 2nd tho' demoted to 3rd: see 1185.   32
1671 HELLO BENZ [3] (M H Easterby) 3-8-9(BL) M Birch 7/2: 0042332: Bl first time: no
extra inside dist: fin 3rd and placed 2nd: stays 11f: see 1507 & 322.   31
1636 TRY SCORER [4] (Denys Smith) 4-9-2 L Charnock 7/1: 0002004: Made most: btr effort.   24
1739 MADISON GIRL [7] 3-9-0 D Mckeown 10/3: 3411020: Gd eff against older horses: see 1739   33
1133 BOLDERA [6] 5-8-6 S Webster 14/1: -000000: Never dangerous: no form this term:
twice successful in sellers at Thirsk last season: best form around 12/14f on gd or faster
ground: acts on any track.   00
--   LISAILY [5] 6-8-3 M Richardson(7) 20/1: -0: Early leader: well btn after long abs:
ran twice over hurdles last winter and prob will do better in that sphere: acts on yielding. 00
 7 ran   nk,1½,½,1,8   (G Horsford)   J Fitzgerald Malton, Yorks.

1867 EBF MERMAID MAIDEN 2YO FILLIES   £1311   5f   Firm 18 +10 Fast

--   NORGABIE [1] (P Calver) 2-8-11 M Fry 10/1: 1: 2 b f Northfields - Gallant Believer
(Gallant Romeo) Made a successful debut, comfortably led inside dist in a fast run 2yo
fillies mdn at Redcar July 30: cost 6,500 gns as a yearling: should be suited by further:
acts on fast ground and on a gall track.   36
1545 MINIZEN LASS [6] (M Brittain) 2-8-11 K Darley 11/2: 2202242: Again found one too good
after making virtually all the running: see 1266 & 913.   33
1583 TEACHERS GAME [2] (K Brassey) 2-8-11 S Whitworth 2/1: 43: Al front rank, not btn far:
acts on fast ground and on a gall track: see 1583.   31
1550 SPARKLING BRITT [4] (C Horgan) 2-8-11 R Weaver 1/1 FAV: 034: Well bckd: had ev ch:
eff over 5/6f on fast ground: seems to act on any ground: see 1440.   28 .
--   ILLUSTRATE [5] 2-8-11 S Webster 33/1: 0: Outpaced early, picked up ground from ½ way
and will be btr for this experience: dam successful over 1m: acts on fast ground and on a
galloping track.   27
818 BOLD AD [3] 2-8-11 J H Brown(5) 20/1: 000: Fair abs: twice below form shown in 646(yldg) 07
1050 BETTY BLUE [7] 2-8-11 Wendy Carter(7) 20/1: 00: Dwelt and never in it: half
sister to 6/9f winner Champagne Willie: well btn in both her starts to date.   00
 7 ran   ½,½,1,½,8,2   (P G Goulandris)   P Calver Ripon, Yorks.

DONCASTER   Wednesday July 30th   Lefthand, Stiff Galloping Track

Official Going Given As GOOD/FIRM

1868 TURN TO YORKSHIRE H'CAP (0-50)   £2687   7f   Good 48 +01 Fast   [42]

*1761 THE MAZALL [2] (L Siddall) 6-9-2(6ex) D Nicholls 9/2: 1202211: 6 br g Persian Bold -
Dance All Night (Double-U-Jay) In tremendous form and led most of the way drawing clear when
a ready winner of a h'cap at Doncaster July 30: last time out won at Catterick: earlier
successful at Redcar: in '85 won at Redcar and Carlisle: in '84 won at Nottingham: very
eff at 6/7f: acts on firm and soft ground and on any trk: does well with forcing tactics.   41
1810 AIR COMMAND [8] (G Reveley) 6-9-7 A Shoults(5) 10/1: -000002: Al prom: by far his
best effort this term and is returning to form: won his first 3 starts in '85, h'caps at
Chepstow, Newcastle and Ayr: very eff at 6/7f: acts on any ground: best when up with the pace. 41
1455 KNIGHTS SECRET [5] (M H Easterby) 5-9-3(6ex) K Hodgson 7/4 FAV: 2113403: Well bckd:
ev ch: see 815.   33
966 FANCY PAN [4] (W Hastings Bass) 3-8-3 R Lines(3) 8/1: -0304: Abs: sn prom: see 863.   24
1500 GRACIOUS HOMES [6] 5-8-0 D Williams(7) 25/1: 4-40000: Prom most: lightly raced
since 727, see 441.   08
649 COOL ENOUGH [1] 5-8-1 G Carter(3) 14/1: -400000: Abs: dsptd lead, fdd: see 12.   00
*1727 MR JAY ZEE [3] 4-9-4 G Duffield 9/4: 3130210: Below his best in 7th: much btr 1727.   00

--   **Jousting Boy** [9] 8-13
8 ran   1½,1½,1½,1½,5   (Mrs Jack Fulton)   L Siddall Tadcaster, Yorks.

1869 EBF DUINDIGT MAIDEN STAKES   2YO   £2138   6f   Good 48 -03 Slow

--   **SAFETY PIN** [16] (W Hastings Bass) 2-8-11 T Ives 7/1: 1: 2 b f Grundy - Safe House
(Lyphard) First time out, led over 2f out, readily drawing clear in a 2yo mdn at Doncaster
July 30: first foal: eff at 6f, will be suited by 7f+: acts on gd ground and a gall track:
most impressive here: should rate more highly.   50
1522 **OTHET** [15] (M Usher) 2-9-0 R Street 9/4 FAV: 22: Switched approaching final 1f,
but the winner had flown: should be suited by 7f and go one btr soon:see 1522.   40
--   **NORAPA** [9] (M Brittain) 2-8-11 M Wigham 33/1: 3: Al up there: promising debut:
stays 6f: acts on gd ground and a galloping trk.   35
1512 **MIGHTY BOLD** [12] (R Armstrong) 2-9-0 P Tulk 14/1: 004: Prom all the way: see 1512. 38
--   **ICHI BAN SON** [11] 2-9-0 K Hodgson 33/1: 0: Kept on promisingly and will improve on
this debut effort: cost 9,600 gns and is a half brother to 4 winners: shd be suited by 7f:
acts on good ground and a gall track.   33
544 **ARIZONA SUN** [14] 2-9-0 A Murray 10/1: 00: Long abs: al there: see 544.   28
--   **SNAAN** [6] 2-9-0 W Ryan 5/2: 0: Prom, fin 7th: bred to stay further than 6f: shd improve
for the experience   00
685 **BREWIN TIME** [10] 2-9-0 M Birch 6/1: 00: Very active mkt, but no show: brother to
fair h'capper Mashin Time.   00
--   **FLUTEAU** [8] 2-9-0 A Kimberley 9/1: 0: Ev ch 2f out: shd come on for the race: half
brother to sev winners: shd be suited by 7f+.   00
1675 **JOHNNY SHARP** [13] 2-9-0(VIS) J Lowe 9/1: 0020: Visored first time, led 4f: btr 1675. 00
1518 Home Jesta [2] 9-0   -- **Regalcroft** [3] 9-0   -- **Royal Tower** [1] 9-0
--   Northern Security [4] 9-0   1311 Sebs Mark [5] 9-0
--   Sunorius [7] 9-0
16 ran   4,½,shthd,1½,1½,nk   (Lord Porchester)   W Hastings Bass Newmarket

1870 JOHN SMITHS BREWERY HANDICAP (0-35)   £2656   1m   Good 48 +05 Fast   [34]

1558 **TIP TAP** [3] (A Hide) 4-8-11 G Baxter 16/1: 03-0001: 4 gr f Tachypous - Dashing Diana
(Silver Shark) Led well over 1f out, driven out in a h'cap at Doncaster July 30: no form
prev this season: eff over 1m, stays 10f: acts on gd and firm ground.   25
1761 **QUALITAIRESS** [9] (K Stone) 4-7-7(VIS)(3oh) L Charnock 16/1: 3400302: Ran on under
press and just btn: see 101.   05
1689 **MISS APEX** [11] (F Yardley) 4-8-2(vis) J Lowe 10/1: 0430233: Made most: consistent:
see 1689.   10
1188 **MINUS MAN** [14] (W Holden) 8-7-9 R Morse(5) 11/2: -000304: Some late hdwy: see 710. 00
1565 **CHARMING VIEW** [13] 4-8-6 W Ryan 10/1: -010200: Nearest fin: twice below 1139, see 673 09
1590 **NEW CENTRAL** [12] 4-8-6 T Ives 4/1 FAV: -000020: Prom, fdd: much btr 1590 (firm):see 636 05
1013 **ABLE MAYBOB** [16] 4-8-6 M Rimmer 10/1: 00-1200: Fdd over 1f out after abs: btr 689, 594 00
1758 **MOORES METAL** [4] 6-10-0 S Perks 9/1: 0004000: Never nearer 8th: see 1249, 441.   00
1610 **JOVEWORTH** [6] 3-8-11 M Birch 13/2: -140030: Made no show: btr 1610 (6f) see 283   00
1553 **PEANDAY** [5] 5-8-7 C Rutter 8/1: 0030000: Best 481 (yldg).   00
1774 Jo Andrew [10] 7-8   855 Running Bull [15] 8-10
1651 Forever Tingo [8] 7-12   1624 Swiftspender [1] 7-8
1676 Mattye Lee [7] 7-8   1565 Velocitus [2] 8-3
16 ran   ½,1½,1½,½,1½   (John Wilberforce)   A Hide Newmarket

1871 WEMBLEY AMATEUR RIDERS H'CAP   £1417   1m 4f Good 48 -27 Slow   [5]

1349 **TOSCANA** [8] (D Marks) 5-11-2 Kelly Marks 6/1: 200-221: 5 ch m Town & Country -
Constanza (Sun Prince) Made most, comfortably, in a amateur h'cap at Doncaster July 30: in
fine form this season: in '85 won a seller at Haydock: eff at 10f, well suited by 12f:
acts on flrm and yldg ground and does well when up with the pace: goes well for Kelly Marks. 32
1652 **ARGES** [12] (R Hollinshead) 5-11-10 Maxine Juster 13/2: -204142: Led 2f out, well
clear 3rd: see 1417.   36
1243 **TAXIADS** [13] (C Nelson) 4-11-7 Jane Allison(3) 10/1: -011003: Ev ch str: best 984. 22
1417 **COUNT COLOURS** [3] (S Norton) 4-12-0 Mr E Mcmahon 5/1 FAV: 04-0024: Btr 1417, see 9   27
1558 **VITRY** [9] 3-10-3(2ow) Sara Lawrence 25/1: -003300: Never nearer: twice below 1089. 10
1223 **PATS JESTER** [6] 3-10-8 Laura Rohan(3) 6/1: -413230: No real threat: much btr 1223. 12
1685 **KERRY MAY SING** [4] 3-10-7 Mr J Ryan 8/1: 1-00000: Nicely bckd: there 9f: non-stayer? 00
1563 **WESTRAY** [7] 4-10-13 Jennie Goulding 9/1: 0004040: Ran mod: see 1563, 225.   00
1223 **PINWIDDIE** [5] 4-10-9 Diana Williams 13/2: 4211400: Fdd str: btr 721.   00
1223 Marina Plata [1] 10-4   -- Rose Rocket [11] 10-1 1689 Godlord [10] 10-7(2ow)
19 Dawn Spirit [2] 10-7
13 ran   1,7,1,2½,1½,½   (Robert M Pegg)   D Marks Lambourn, Berks.

1872 EBF SAN SIRO STAKES   2YO   £2917   7f   Good 48 -37 Slow

--   **COUNTER ATTACK** [8] (W Hern) 2-8-7 W Carson 5/2: 1: 2 gr c Nishapour - Regain (Relko)
Ran on well to lead cl home in a 2yo event at Doncaster July 30: eff at 7f, will be well
suited by 1m+: acts on good ground and a gall trk and can only improve.   46
--   **ECHEVIN** [7] (J Fitzgerald) 2-8-7 A Murray 7/2: 2: Gambled on: led over 1f out, just

562

caught: promising effort from this half brother to 4 winners: should be suited by 1m+:
acts on good ground and a gall trk: has scope and should have no trouble finding a race.   44
1653 SLIP DANCER [3] (L Piggott) 2-8-11 B Crossley 8/1: 03: Sn prom: on the upgrade:
half brother to 3 winners: should be suited by 1m: acts on gd ground and a galloping trk.   45
--   IRISH BRIGADIER [5] (S Hall) 2-8-7 M Birch 20/1: 4: Stayed on promisingly on race
course debut: first foal whose dam was a winning miler: eff at 7f on gd ground.   40
--   ATHENS GATE [4] 2-8-7 N Connorton 12/1: 0: Led/dsptd lead on race course debut: not
btn far: American bred colt who stays 7f.   39
--'   PROSPECT PLACE [2] 2-8-7 K Hodgson 33/1: 0: No extra final 1f on debut: cheaply
acquired yearling.   37
--   NEARLY GREAT [9] 2-8-7 T Ives 11/2: 0: Fdd final 1f on debut: half brother to 2 winners.   00
1452 TRY MY BRANDY [10] 2-8-11 B Thomson 9/4 FAV: 00: Made much: hung left: disapp after 1452.00
1625 Berthelier [1] 8-11   --   Hiero Falco [6] 8-7
10 ran   ½,1,½,½,1,1   (Lord Porchester)   W Hern West Ilsley, Berks.

1873 CAEN MAIDEN STAKES   £959   1m 6f Good 48 -16 Slow

409 WHITE REEF [1] (W Hern) 3-8-7 W Carson 8/13 FAV: 3-41: 3 b c Mill Reef - Whitefoot
(Relko) Despite fair abs, led nearing final 1f comfortably, in a mdn at Doncaster July 30:
very lightly raced colt who on sole start as a 2yo fin a close 3rd to the smart Nomrood in a
backend mdn at Newmarket: half brother to sev winners, including Irish Oaks winner Swift
Foot: stays 14f well: acts on gd and firm ground: should be a lot straighter for today's
run and should win in better company.   45
1646 PARSONS CHILD [4] (L Cumani) 3-8-4 P Hamblett 6/1: -002: Led 3 out: no chance
with winner, but 10l clear 3rd: eff at 14f, may stay 2m: see 581.   37
1569 SHIPBOURNE [7] (G Harwood) 3-8-7 A Clark 7/2: -000303: Ev ch in str: best 1233 (12f)   24
1652 ICKWORTH [3] (F Durr) 4-9-7 M Birch 14/1: 444-004: Led 11f: see 1652.   19
1554 VISTULE [2] 4-9-7 M Wigham 16/1: 424-000: Prom: fdd: lightly raced this term: placed
sev times in France in '85: stays 12f, possibly not 14f.   10
1372 PINZAUREOLE [8] 3-8-4 K Bradshaw(5) 100/1: -00: Rank outsider, fdd straight.   04
1497 Last Polonaise [5] 8-4   1544 Kasu [6] 8-4(vis)
8 ran   2½,10,3,5,1½   (Lord Rotherwick)   W Hern West Ilsley, Berks.

GOODWOOD   Wednesday July 30th   Righthand Undulating Track

Official Going Given As GOOD/FIRM

1874 EBF FINDON MAIDEN FILLIES STKS 2YO   £5205   6f   Firm 16 -16 Slow

1454 CANDLE IN THE WIND [12] (R Laing) 2-8-11 W R Swinburn 11/2: 0401: 2 b f Thatching -
Her Grace (Great Nephew) Slightly dropped in class and fulfilled prev promise, battling on
well final 1f for a narrow win in quite a val 2yo fillies mdn at Goodwood July 30: looks a
bargain buy at 10,000 gns: well suited by 6f, sure to stay 7f: acts on firm and gd ground.   53
-533 SCIERPAN [4] (J Tree) 2-8-11 Pat Eddery 13/8 FAV: 22: Despite abs, heavily bckd
and led dist, no extra near fin: stays 6f: see 533. should soon find a race.   52
1238 NORTHSHIEL [2] (H Candy) 2-8-11 W Newnes 12/1: 43: Kept on stoutly final 1f and
will be suited by 7f: impr and should not be long in finding a maiden.   49
--   TOY CUPBOARD [3] (W Hern) 2-8-11 W Carson 11/1: 4: Ran rather green early, fin in
good style and will benefit greatly from the outing: first foal of an unraced half sister
to Gold Cup winner Little Wolf: sure to be suited by 7f+: will do a lot btr next time.   42
--   GREENCASTLE HILL [13] 2-8-11 T Ives 10/1: 0: Al there: sound debut: first foal of
a winner over 5-7f: should improve.   42
1632 HURRICANE VALLEY [9] 2-8-11 M Wigham 20/1: 00: Never btr: see 1632.   41
1287 STRATCH [8] 2-8-11 J Reid 11/1: 00: Led to ½ way, fin a close 7th: see 1287.   40
--   PUSHOFF [11] 2-8-11 S Cauthen 10/1: 0: Showed speed 4f on the wide outside: should
benefit from the race: related to a minor '84 juv winner and dam was a very smart 2yo: bred
to be speedy.   00
--   Stern Lass [6] 8-11   --   Achnahuaigh [7] 8-11   --   Bit Omay [14] 8-11
--   Home Device [10] 8-11   --   Jolienne [5] 8-11   --   Simply Silk [1] 8-11
14 ran   ½,1½,3,shthd,nk,nk   (Christopher Wright)   R Laing Lambourn, Berks.

1875 PIMMS GOODWOOD STAKES HCAP 0-65   £7531   2m 3f Firm 16 -08 Slow   [42]

1388 SARFRAZ [1] (G Harwood) 3-9-7 G Starkey 4/1: -011101: 3 b c Sassafras - Ziba Blue
(John's Joy) Very useful impr colt: made it 4 wins out of the last 5 races, running on from
rear to lead final 1f comfortably, in a val h'cap at Goodwood July 30: earlier completed a
hat trick at Bath, Folkestone and Goodwood: acts on firm and yldg: eff 14f, stays extreme
distances well: continues to improve.   63
-1633 EL CONQUISTADOR [10] (G Harwood) 3-8-6 A Clark 6/1: -02022: Led str, battled on well
but just run out of it by his stable companion: well suited by 2m+ and fast grd: must find
a maiden very soon: see 1029.   44
1605 FEDRA [8] (Lord John Fitzgerald) 3-8-1 R Hills 12/1: 2212423: Chall final 1f, ran
to his best and stays extreme dist: see 908, 1605.   39
1470 RIKKI TAVI [3] (B Hills) 6-9-7 W Carson 10/1: 0331004: Chall 2f out, relishes extreme
distances: see 1099.   42

1348 HARLESTONE LAKE [4] 4-8-8 Pat Eddery 8/1: 0034140: Came from rear to chall dist,
good effort: see 1260: stays extreme distances.   27
+1533 TIGERWOOD [5] 5-8-2 N Adams 9/4 FAV: 00-1210: Set the pace over 14f, one paced
str and well below the form of 1533 (very sharp trk).   09
1633 EASTER LEE [2] 6-8-7 A Mcglone 11/1: 0122-00: Prom much, fin 7th: see 1633.   00
1099 PATHS SISTER [9] 5-8-12 J Bleasdale 10/1: 11-0000: No danger in 8th and needs give. see 215.   00
1779 MORGANS CHOICE [6] 9-8-7 S Cauthen 10/1: 0301000: Rear thr'out and much btr 1779.   00
9 ran   2,shthd,1,¼,12   (K Abdulla)   G Harwood Pulborough, Sussex

1876 GROUP 2 OCL RICHMOND STAKES 2YO   £34680   6f   Firm 16 +06 Fast

+1510 RICH CHARLIE [5] (C Nelson) 2-8-11 J Reid 11/4 JT FAV: 011: 2 ch c Younng Generation –
Maiden Pool (Sharpen Up) Smart, impr colt: justified strong support gamely responding to
press to force his hd in front final 50yds of Gr 2 Richmond Stks at Goodwood July 30: easy
winner of a fast run mdn at York July 11: quite cheaply bought son of a winning 5f sprinter:
speedily bred tho' should stay 7f: acts well on fast ground: has scope for further improvement and should win more good races.   75
+1591 DOMINION ROYALE [2] (R Williams) 2-8-11 R Cochrane 7/1: 41312: Chall final 1f, just
held and continues to improve: stays 6f well: see 1591.   74
1467 CAROLS TREASURE [7] (B Hills) 2-8-11 B Thomson 6/1: 211103: Lost ground start, sn
recovered and cruised into lead dist, no extra final 150yds: stays 6f but might possibly
prove best over 5f: see 1143.   69
1467 WHO KNOWS [6] (W Hern) 2-8-11 W Carson 7/2: 3124: Prom thr'out and another good
effort: see 1467.   68
1467 WHIPPET [8] 2-8-11 S Cauthen 50/1: 12000: Led briefly 2f out: fair eff but possibly
best 5f (see 577).   62
*1097 CUTTING BLADE [1] 2-8-11 C Asmussen 11/4 JT FAV: 3110: Well bckd, outpaced most:
better 1097 (stiff trk).   57
1411 FLOOSE [3] 2-8-11 T Quinn 12/1: 1120: Sn struggling, fin 7th: see 1003.   00
1606 QUICK SNAP [4] 2-8-11(bl) R Curant 25/1: 2101120: Made much: see 1512.   00
8 ran   hd,2,nk,2½,2   (R E A Bott Ltd)   C Nelson Upper Lambourn, Berks.

1877 GROUP I SWETTENHAM STUD SUSSEX STKS   £155225   1m   Firm 16 +03 Fast

+1466 SONIC LADY [5] (M Stoute) 3-8-7 W R Swinburn 5/6 FAV: -131111: 3 b f Nureyev – Stumped
(Owen Anthony) Highclass filly: very much on her toes in the parade but settled well in the
race and showed her blistering turn of foot when sweeping into the lead 1f out for a
comfortable success in val Gr 1 Sussex Stks at Goodwood July 30: ready winner prev of Childs
Stks at Newmarket, Coronation Stks at Royal Ascot, Irish 1000 Guineas at the Curragh and
first time out, Nell Gwyn Stks at Newmarket: runaway winner of Blue Seal Stks at Ascot on
sole outing in '85 and met her only defeat when narrowly btn in the 1000 Guineas: very eff
over 7f/1m: acts on firm and yldg and on a galloping track: this was prob her finest
performance yet and she reflects great credit on her masterly trainer.   90
+598 SCOTTISH REEL [1] (M Stoute) 3-8-7 G Starkey 20/1: 240-212: Set a fast pace in
lead went down bravely to his stable companion and this was a tremendous effort on ground
too firm for him: see 598.   88
+1094 PENNINE WALK [4] (J Tree) 4-9-7 Pat Eddery 15/8: 40-1113: Hung fire when asked to
quicken at 2f mark, stayed on well cl home: not quite at his best here: see 1094 (stiff trk).   87
1389 BOLD ARRANGEMENT [3] (C Brittain) 3-8-10(BL) S Cauthen 16/1: -332004: Bl first time,
al up there and not btn far: good effort: see 1389.   85
-1094 EFISIO [2] 4-9-7 W Carson 15/2: 0-04120: Chall 1f out, fdd : much btr 1094 (stiff trk).   83
5 ran   1½,¾,nk,1   (Sheikh Mohammed)   M Stoute Newmarket

1878 SINGLETON STAKES 3YO HANDICAP 0-60   £4596   5f   Firm 16 +14 Fast   [57]

1654 RESPECT [9] (R Laing) 3-9-7 R Cochrane 6/1: 2131041: 3 b c Mummy's Pet – Restive
(Relic) Very useful sprinter: well ridden to come from behind to gain the day cl home in a
fast run and val 3yo h'cap at Goodwood July 30: reportedly short of work in race 1654 but
earlier readily won 2 similar h'caps at Sandown: speedily bred sort who is related to
numerous winners: best form over 5f on firm or gd ground: possibly unsuited by soft:
still improving.   62
*1687 SANDITTON PALACE [8] (P Felgate) 3-8-5(7ex) T Quinn 9/1: 0431012: Dsptd lead from
the dist, just btn and is greatly improved of late: must win again soon: see 1687.   45
733 MUMMYS SECRET [6] (G P Gordon) 3-8-11(bl) S Cauthen 12/1: 400-303: Chall strongly
final 1f, just btn in a close finish: seems to do well when fresh and looks sure to go close
next time: see 227.   51
1669 COPPERMILL LAD [3] (L Holt) 3-8-1 N Adams 20/1: 2000004: Prom thr'out but possibly
better on soft (111).   37
*835 HIGH IMAGE [7] 3-9-3 Pat Eddery 11/4 FAV: -010: Heavily bckd, ev ch: abs since 835.   52
1508 TRUE NORA [5] 3-9-7 J Reid 10/1: 0-00300: Made much: see 443.   50
1654 NO BEATING HARTS [2] 3-8-11(7ex) W Carson 7/2: 0402130: Pressed leaders 4f, fin 7th
and much better 1654.   00
1687 PILLOWING [4] 3-8-0(2ow) A Clark 11/1: 00-0100: Early pace: best 1399.   00
-1399 ENIGMA [1] 3-7-7 S Dawson 13/2: 204-020: Sn struggling and btrr 1399.   00
9 ran   nk,shthd,1½,¼,2   (R N Richmond-Watson)   R Laing Lambourn, Berks.

1879 HEYSHOTT STAKES 3YO HCAP 0-60   £4690   1m 6f Firm 16 -01 Slow   [53]

909 JUST DAVID [2] (A Stewart) 3-9-3 M Roberts 11/4 JT FAV: -121: 3 b c Blakeney -
Reltop (High Top) Useful, impr colt: waited with, ran on to lead final 1f and battled on
well for a narrow success in quite a val 3yo h'cap at Goodwood July 30: trotted up in a mdn
at Bath first time out and seems to do well when fresh: eff 11f, well suited by 14f and
promises to stay 2m: acts on firm and yldg going: great big strong sort who has scope for
plenty of further improvement and should be kept on the right side.   55
1642 COX GREEN [4] (G Harwood) 3-9-7 G Starkey 11/4 JT FAV: -142: Led 3f out, battled
on well when hdd and clear rem: stays 14f well: see 714: continues to improve.   58
1435 DHONI [5] (W Hern) 3-8-11 W Carson 5/1: 0-4023: Dsptd lead 3f out, no extra: see 1435.   41
1484 ACTINIUM [6] (P Cole) 3-9-7 T Quinn 8/1: 3-21244: Led briefly inside final ½m:
twice below 1040.   45
*1386 WALCISIN [7] 3-7-12 D Mckay 6/1: 0022010: No danger and btr 1386 (stiff trk)   14
*1748 ZAUBARR [3] 3-9-3(bl)(6ex) B Thomson 6/1: 0011310: Made much, fdd quickly and has
been kept very busy of late: see 1748.   32
1807 MARICAMA [1] 3-8-12 P Cook 33/1: -40030: Sn in rear, btr 1807.   00
   7 ran   nk,4,4,5,nk   (Anthony Leftwich)   A Stewart Newmarket

---

DONCASTER   Thursday July 31st   Lefthand, Galloping Track

Official Going Given As GOOD IN STRAIGHT : ROUND COURSE GOOD/FIRM

1880 WAKEFIELD MAIDEN STAKES 3YO+   £1444   1m   Good 50 +01 Fast

1628 ALECS DREAM [4] (A Stewart) 3-8-8 M Roberts 1/1 FAV: -331: 3 br c Young Generation -
Eightpenny (Pieces of Eight) Promising colt: well bckd, led nearing final 1f and despite
running green was a comfortable 4l winner of a mdn at Doncaster July 31: lightly raced this
term, due to sore shins: very well suited by 1m on a gall trk, may stay further: acts on
a sound surface: should win more races.   55
966 URUGUAY [13] (O Douieb) 3-8-5 R Cochrane //1: -02: Led 2f out: not pace of winner,
but is on the upgrade: stays 1m: acts on gd & firm ground and a gall track and should
find a small event.   42
--   NEEDLE SHARP [1] (R J Houghton) 3-8-5 J Reid 14/1: -3: Kept on well on racecourse debut,
showing future promise: half sister to the useful h'capper Telephone Man: should be suited
by further than 1m: acts on gd ground and a gall track.   39
--   HAMPER [8] (W Hastings Bass) 3-8-8 A Murray 12/1: -4: Chance 2f out: kept on well:
good racecourse debut: stays 1m well: should improve on this.   40
--   SMILING BEAR [14] 3-8-8 R Lines(3) 14/1: 00-0: Al there on seasonal debut: lightly
raced in '85 showing promise: stays 1m: acts on gd and yldg ground.   34
1511 DANESMOOR [7] 3-8-5 J H Brown(5) 50/1: -0000: Rank outsider: first signs of form:
eff at 1m on gd ground and a galloping track.   25
247 CHANCE REMARK [9] 3-8-8 M Hills 9/1: 0-40: Led 4f out, wknd after long abs: see 247.   23
--   BALANCED REALM [2] 3-8-8 W Ryan 12/1: -0: Friendless in mkt: fdd str on racecourse
debut: half brother to sev winners and should do better than this.   00
1602 Donor [5] 9-6   1602 Mr Adviser [12] 8-8   --   Birchgrove Lad [6] 9-6
--   Peace Keeper [11] 8-5   --   Discover Gold [3] 9-6   1602 Norcool [18] 8-8
1645 Another Smokey [15] 8-8   --   Mubah [10] 8-8
806 Eau Courante [17] 8-8(BL)
   17 ran   4,1½,1,3,3,½   (Maktoum Al-Maktoum)   A Stewart Newmarket

1881 YORKSHIRE DAY SELLING STAKES 2YO   £1490   6f   Good 50 No Time Taken

1379 SWALLOW BAY [11] (D H Jones) 2-8-3 D Williams(7) 5/1: 0031: 2 gr f Penmarric - Overseas
(Sea Hawk II) Impr filly: led cl home under press in a 2yo seller at Doncaster July 31: half
sister to 9f winner Turtle Bay: eff at 6f, should get 7f: acts on gd ground and a gall trk.   22
1672 GET SET LISA [8] (C Tinkler) 2-8-3 M Birch 9/2: 0040022: Led 2f out: just btn:
in good form and seems to act on any track: see 1672.   21
1801 LISASHAM [12] (P Makin) 2-8-3(bl) T Quinn 9/2: 0003: Led final 1f: not btn far in
close finish: bl first time today and showed improved form in this lower grade: half sister
to winning plater Russell Flyer: should find a seller.   20
1635 PERTAIN [10] (W Wharton) 2-8-6(bl) I Johnson 7/1: 4002204: Not the best of runs,
stayed on final 1f: seems equally eff over 5/6f: acts on firm and soft and on any track.   21
376 ROSIES GLORY [4] 2-8-3 M Wood 20/1: 00: Mkt drifter: nearest fin after long abs
and will improve on this next time out: one to bear in mind for a similar event: acts on
good and yldg: see 376.   13
1413 PALACE RULER [2] 2-8-3 S Webster 16/1: 4000: Never nearer: btr over 7f.   12
1622 SEATON GIRL [3] 2-8-8 R Cochrane 10/1: 2001400: Prom most: see 1358, best 1121(soft).   00
1680 HARRYS COMING [1] 2-8-11 M Taylor(7) 8/1: 2130020: Prom: fdd: btr 1680 (5f).   00
1427 QUEEN MATILDA [2] 2-8-3(BL) M Hills 4/1 FAV: 000: Bl first time: dsptd lead, sn wknd:
well bckd here, but has shown little in 3 outings to date: bred to be suited by a longer trip.   00
1376 Rose Of Tudor [13] 8-3   711 Sweet Ribot [6] 8-3
1075 Ring Back [9] 8-3(bl)
   12 ran   hd,nk,1,2½,hd   (Mrs T M Parry)   D H Jones Efail Isaf, Glamorgan.

565

1882 SHEFFIELD HANDICAP 3YO+ 0-50   £2494   5f   Good 50 +02 Fast   [42]

1524 MANTON MARK [4] (M Camacho) 3-8-10 N Connorton 8/1: 00-0001: 3 b g On Your Mark -
Sindy's Sister (Fidalgo) Led final 1f comfortably, in a h'cap at Doncaster July 31: little
form prev this season: in '85 won a mdn at Thirsk: very eff at 5f: acts on gd and firm ground
and on any track.   39
922 GENTILESCHI [7] (R Nicholls) 4-8-6 D Williams(7) 12/1: -000002: Made most: fair effort
after abs: useful 2yo when trained by H Cecil, winning at Haydock: eff at 5f on good ground.   25
1796 KING CHARLEMAGNE [3] (G Reveley) 7-9-10 A Shoults(5) 9/4: 00-0043: Sn prom: kept on.   43
1438 MRS SAUGA [5] (M Eckley) 7-8-1 A Mackay 2/1 FAV: 0-02104: Met trouble in running:
not btn far: see 1344.   20
1536 GODS SOLUTION [2] 5-8-11(bl) R Cochrane 5/2: 4020040: Cl.up 5th: see 890.   29
5 ran   1,hd,hd,hd   (Mrs M Pett)   M Camacho Malton, Yorks.

1883 BARNSLEY MAIDEN AUCTION STKS 2YO   £959   7f   Good 50 -57 Slow

1731 PHARAOH BLUE [4] (C Brittain) 2-8-5 M Roberts 12/1: 001: 2 ch c Blue Cashmere -
Phaedima (Darius) Dropped in class and led inside final 1f in a slowly run 2yo mdn auction at
Doncaster July 31: cheaply acquired as a yearling: dam a winning stayer: eff at 7f, should
get 1m: acts on good ground and a gall track.   32
1483 BRIGGS BUILDERS [18] (W Jarvis) 2-8-11 R Cochrane 4/1: 002: Tried to make all: gd
effort and 4l clear 3rd: improving: eff at 7f on gd and firm ground and a stiff trk.   36
1675 CAMMAC LAD [7] (C Tinkler) 2-8-11 M Wood 25/1: 00003: Stayed on well final 1f:
best effort yet and should be suited by 1m: acts on gd ground.   29
1650 TIKLAS [14] (F Durr) 2-8-2 G French 16/1: 0004: Prom, ev ch: btr eff: see 1650.   18
1345 JOHNNY ROSE [9] 2-8-2 N Howe 13/8 FAV: 20: Ev ch: well below form 1345 (frm sharper trk)15
1253 NORTHERN DECREE [3] 2-8-11 D Nicholls 14/1: 0000: Never nearer: will stay 1m: see 1253.   20
1405 REMAIN FREE [1] 2-8-2 L Jones(4) 11/2: 330: Fdd into 9th: see 1305 (6f).   00
1480 ST WENDRED [10] 2-7-10 R Morse(5) 11/2: 030: Fdd 2f out: much btr 1480 (firm sharp trk)   00
1529 Young Benz [11] 9-0   1635 Eurocon [2] 8-8   --   Miss Sarajane [12] 8-5
1504 Gouldswood [16] 8-8   186 Minizen Lad [8] 8-8   1305 Young Centurion [5] 8-8
--   Heatseeker [6] 7-13   -- Express Groupage [13] 8-5
1561 Eppy Marner [17] 7-10   1650 Rock A Little [15] 8-8
18 ran   ½,4,½,1,1½   (Mrs C Pateras)   C Brittain Newmarket

1884 LEEDS HANDICAP 3YO+ 0-35   £2327   1m 6f   Good 50 -02 Slow   [19]

1278 JURISPRUDENCE [4] (J Watts) 3-9-6 N Connorton 10/1: -0001: 3 b c Alleged - Leliza
(Gallant Romeo) Impr colt: well suited by this longer trip and led well over 1f out, drawing
clear in a h'cap at Doncaster July 31: dam is a half sister to the very smart Bel Bolide:
stays 14f well: acts on gd and firm ground and a gall trk: should continue to improve.   35
1757 COLLISTO [9] (K Brassey) 5-9-7(bl) N Adams 3/1 FAV: -000022: Led over 4f out: 6l
clear 3rd: see 1757, 485.   16
1582 QUADRILLION [2] (R Hollinshead) 7-9-3 S Perks 4/1: -0243: Ev ch str: best 1419 (2m).   04
1745 HIGHAM GREY [3] (D Chapman) 10-9-3 D Nicholls 12/1: 0004004: Early leader: ran in
snatches: see 675.   00
1700 JIPIJAPA [1] 5-8-3(vis) A Mackay 10/1: 00-0000: Never nearer: little form.   00
1226 DELLWOOD RENOWN [5] 4-8-8 R Morse(5) 13/2: 0-03300: No threat: see 709.   00
1133 BLUEBIRDINO [8] 7-8-7 M Hills 9/2: 00-0040: Fdd str: lightly raced since 126.   00
1569 Knights Heir [7] 9-4   416 Grove Tower [10] 9-6   1578 Letby [6] 8-9(vis)
10 ran   3,6,2½,nk,¾   (R E Sangster)   J Watts Richmond, Yorks.

1885 DORTMUND FILLIES HANDICAP 3YO 0-35   £2044   7f   Good 50 -23 Slow   [38]

*1695 FRIVOLE [15] (P Cole) 3-9-2(6ex) T Quinn 6/1 CO.FAV: 00-4011: 3 b f Comedy Star -
Swaynes Princess (St Chad) In fine form: led after 4f, comfortably defying her pen, in a
fillies h'cap at Doncaster July 31: last time out won a similar event at Folkestone: lightly
raced in '85: very eff at 7f, stays 1m: acts on gd and firm ground and on any trk: seems
a genuine sort.   37
1725 NEW EVIDENCE [11] (E Eldin) 3-8-8 A Mackay 13/2: 0002232: Ran on well final 1f after
not the best of runs and deserves a change of luck: see 1515.   24
1794 ORTICA [17] (J Etherington) 3-8-10 M Wood 8/1: -40233: Chance final 2f: see 1794, 1269.   24
1695 SPECIAL GUEST [5] (D Morley) 3-8-8 R Cochrane 15/2: 0-03324: Al there: see 1695, 1034.   20
1701 AITCHANDOUBLEYOU [10] 3-8-13 B Mcgiff(7) 14/1: -004000: Nearest fin: see 1093.   20
1446 RAFFLES VIRGINIA [12] 3-9-6 J Hillis(5) 12/1: 0-40200: Prom, ev ch: stays 7f: acts
on gd and firm ground and on any track.   26
1244 BASICALLY BETTER [6] 3-9-5 N Howe 10/1: 20-4000: Prom, wknd: appears flattered 501.   00
*1446 PETRIFY [1] 3-9-7 J Williams 6/1 CO.FAV: -010: Made no show: much btr 1446 (firm).   00
1446 GLANGWILI [2] 3-9-4 J Reid 6/1 CO.FAV: 230-420: Fdd and fin in ruck: well below 1446.   00
1051 Jersey Maid [7] 8-10(BL)   1560 Monstrosa' [14] 8-4
1571 On Impulse [9] 8-8   604 Soxoph [13] 9-5   575 Synthetic [4] 9-1
1761 Miss Blake [16] 8-0   650 Crownit [3] 8-0   1299 Hardy Chance [8] 8-13
17 ran   1½,1,¼,¾,3,hd   (G A Chagouty)   P Cole Whatcombe, Oxon.

1886 DARNLEY H'CAP 3YO 0-70   £8103   1m 4f   Good/Firm 25 +01 Fast   [67]

1468 HAUWMAL [10] (W Hern) 3-8-8 W Carson 11/2: 0-12041: 3 ch c Troy - Sovereign Rose
(Sharpen Up) Very useful, impr colt: showed himself well suited by 12f, leading dist and
forging 3l clear to win a val 3yo h'cap at Goodwood July 31: quite lightly raced since
winning a minor event at Lingfield first time out: acts on firm and yldg going and handles
an undulating trk well tho' acts on any: impr type who looks certain to stay beyond 12f and
is sure to win another decent race or two.   63
1526 DALGADIYR [6] (M Stoute) 3-8-2 P Robinson 6/1: -313002: Dsptd lead str, outpaced by
winner cl home: good effort: see 625: stays 12f.   51
1408 OLD DOMESDAY BOOK [7] (G Wragg) 3-9-0 W R Swinburn 25/1: 0-13303: Ridden to get the
trip: came cruising through at the 2f mark, found no extra and seems best at 10f: see 444.   61
1702 NORTH VERDICT [3] (M Jarvis) 3-9-7 T Ives 16/1: 0-00324: Fin well: see 555, 1702.   66
*1600 MAGIC SLIPPER [8] 3-9-3(4ex) S Cauthen 3/1 FAV: -21210: Well bckd, set the pace
over 9f: see 1600.   58
1315 TEMPLE WALK [5] 3-8-4 R Hills 14/1: 0-130: Prom most: stays 10f but poss. not 12f:see 1198. 43
+1167 WASSL REEF [2] 3-9-6 Pat Eddery 8/1: 22-2310: Prom, wknd final 1f and fin 7th: quite
a stiff task here: see 1167.   00
1588 MUSICAL YOUTH [9] 3-7-7(1oh) T Williams 10/1: 04-2020: Fin 8th: see 459, 1588.   00
*1523 MIGHTY FLASH [1] 3-7-8(4ex) S Dawson 31/2: -000110: Disapp 9th and much btr 1523.   00
1630 SUNLEY SINNER [4] 3-9-3 Paul Eddery 50/1: 3110-00: Fin last: won 2 minor events on
the trot in '85, both at Chepstow: best form so far over 7f on gd ground on an undulating trk.   00
10 ran   3,1½,2,4,1½   (Sheikh Mohammed)   W Hern West Ilsley, Berks.

1887 GR.3 LANSON CHAMPAGNE STAKES 2YO   £13624   7f   Good/Firm 25 -27 Slow

*1392 DONT FORGET ME [1] (R Hannon) 2-8-11 Pat Eddery 7/1: 411: 2 b c Ahonoora - African
Doll (African Sky) Smart, impr colt: gamely made all in slowly run Gr 3 Lanson Champagne Stks
at Goodwood July 31: winner of a mdn at Sandown July 6: dam a 12f winner in Ireland: very eff
over 7f with forcing tactics: sure to stay at least 1m: acts on firm grd and seems to handle
any track: genuine sort.   71
1467 MIDYAN [3] (H Cecil) 2-8-11 S Cauthen 2/1: 142: Came to chall final 1f but the winner
found extra final 100yds: see 979: stays 7f well.   70
1097 AMIGO SUCIO [5] (K Brassey) 2-8-11 S Whitworth 7/1: 1133: Kept on one pace under
press: stays 7f: see 1097.   65
1149 MR EATS [4] (P Kelleway) 2-9-0 C Asmussen 8/1: 124: Tried to chall dist, no extra:
should be suited by this trip: see 876.   67
*1643 ROUNDLET [2] 2-9-0 W Carson 11/8 FAV: 410: Well bckd, chall winner 2f out, fdd: see 1643   61
5 ran   ½,2½,hd,3   (Jim Horgan)   R Hannon East Everleigh, Wilts.

1888 GR.3 GOODWOOD CUP 3YO UPWARDS   £22350   2m 5f   Good/Firm 25 -36 Slow

*1127 LONGBOAT [2] (W Hern) 5-9-7 W Carson 1/3 FAV: 42-0111: 5 b h Welsh Pageant - Pirogue
(Reliance II) Very smart stayer: readily landed long odds on, leading final 1m and forging
ever further clear in Gr 3 Goodwood Cup July 31: a convincing 5l winner of the Ascot Gold
Cup June 19 and prev won the Henry 2 Stks at Sandown May 26: winner at Ascot and just pipped
in the Gold Cup in '85: eff at 2m, stays forever: unsuited by soft ground, loves to hear
his hooves rattle: undoubtedly the best stayer in the country at present.   83
1127 SPICY STORY [5] (I Balding) 5-9-3 S Cauthen 13/2: 14-3032: In vain pursuit of this
easy winner final 5f: closer to him in 1127: see 360.   66
*1779 PETRIZZO [3] (C Brittain) 5-9-0 C Asmussen 10/1: 0304013: Not disgraced but would
be better off in a h'cap: see 1779.   51
1513 TALE QUALE [1] (H Candy) 4-9-3 W Newnes 25/1: 1-04004: Made most over 14f: yet to
strike form this season: see 585.   51
1513 STAVORDALE [6] 3-7-10 R Hills 25/1: 0-44100: Non-stayer? Twice below 1111.   48
5 ran   10,8,3,nk   (R Hollingsworth)   W Hern West Ilsley, Berks.

1889 GR.3 KING GEORGE STAKES 3YO+   £17928   5f   Good/Firm 25 +15 Fast

-1146 DOUBLE SCHWARTZ [14] (C Nelson) 5-9-5 Pat Eddery 6/4 FAV: 12-1121: 5 b h Double Form -
Cassy's Pet (Sing-Sing) Highclass sprinter: produced a very game performance, battling on
courageously thr'out final 1f for a shthd success in fast run Gr 3 King George Stks at
Goodwood July 31: earlier won his first 2 on the trot, Palace House Stks at Newmarket and
Temple Stks at Sandown and just btn by Last Tycoon in the Kings Stand Stks at Royal Ascot:
in '85 won at Newmarket: stays 6f but particularly eff at 5f: well suited by firm or gd
ground tho' seems to handle any trk: genuine and most consistent.   87
+1631 GWYDION [9] (H Cecil) 3-8-10 S Cauthen 6/1: 1-43312: Battled it out with winner final
1f, hdd post: in tremendous form at present: see 1631.   84
1011 ROSE OF THE SEA [3] (G Mikhalides) 3-8-4(2ow) C Asmussen 16/1: 43-0033: Dsptd
lead most: fine effort: see 155.   71
-1631 POLYKRATIS [11] (M Francis) 4-9-0 C Rutter 16/1: 0003124: Ran right to his best and
should win again soon in lesser company: see 1387.   74
1146 STORM WARNING [1] 4-8-11 B Thomson 20/1: 0-03000: Prom thr'out: btr eff: see 563 (ydlg)   68
-1508 CLANTIME [2] 5-9-0(vis) P Waldron 50/1: 2341220: Led/dsptd lead most and is remarkably
consistent: see 877, 1508.   68
14 ran   sthhd,2,nk,1,½,nk,shthd,shthd,1½   (R E Sangster)   Upper Lambourn, Berks

408 PRINCE SABO [3] 4-9-8 W R Swinburn 12/1: 1020-00: Never btr 7th: abs since 408: quite
lightly raced in '85 winning the Palace House Stks at Newmarket: smart juv in '84 winning at
Doncaster, Newmarket and Epsom, stays 7f but best form over sprint dist: suited by firm or good   00
1457 ORIENT [10] 3-8-5 D Mckeown 6/1: 0-11130: Gd early pace: fin a cl.up 8th: see 1151.   00
1146 WELSH NOTE [4] 3-8-3(1ow) T Ives 16/1: 14-4440: Early speed, fin 9th: see 408.   00
1777 SUNDEED [8] 3-8-5 A Bond 33/1: 110-00: Not given a hard time and ran btr than
finishing place of 10th suggests: see 1777.   00
1508 DUBLIN LAD [13] 3-8-8 K Darley 10/1: 0031440: Showed his usual blistering early pace,
wknd: btr in h'caps under big weights: see 1268.   00
1387 Woodfold [7] 8-11   **1805 Green Dollar** [5] 8-5   **1151 Wanton** [6] 8-2
14 ran   shthd,2,nk,1,¾ nk,shhd (R Sangster)   C Nelson Upper Lambourn, Berks.

1890 DRAYTON H'CAP 3YO+ 0-60   **£4885**   **1m**   **Good/Firm 25 +01 Fast**   [57]

1729 COME ON THE BLUES [7] (C Brittain) 7-9-0 C Asmussen 25/1: -000041: 7 b g Blue Cashmere
- Floral Gift (Princely Gift) Useful h'capper on his day: returned to form, turning up at
25/1 and made all in quite a val h'cap at Goodwood July 31: in '85 won twice in mid season
at Sandown and the Royal Hunt Cup at Ascot: best form with forcing tactics over 1m tho'
prob acts on any going and on any trk: may win again.   56
1109 TRULY RARE [2] (M Stoute) 4-9-7 W R Swinburn 12/1: 1-03002: Rear, fin in fine style,
but too late: best effort since 433 and may win soon.   60
1521 FEYDAN [15] (L Cottrell) 5-7-7(4oh) N Carlisle 33/1: 00-0443: Al prom: a commendable
effort at the weights and should win soon in lower grade if reproducing this form: see 1273.   29
1525 ACONITUM [11] (J Bethell) 5-8-10 W Carson 6/1: -030024: Chall 2f out: btr 1525.   43
1525 TRANSFLASH [13] 7-8-9 N Day 33/1: 3003030: Fair eff: see 1525.   42
1640 BUNDABURG [12] 6-8-2(2ow) R Wernham 12/1: 0000000: No danger: see 775.   30
1489 BOLD AND BEAUTIFUL [10] 4-9-13 G Duffield 11/1: 10-0330: Never closer in 7th: stiff
task under 9-13: see 1489.   00
*1781 FAIR COUNTRY** [9] 4-8-8(5ex) S Cauthen 9/2: 0323110: Encountered all the trouble that
was going and this effort should be forgotten: see 1781.   00
1590 PICTOGRAPH [5] 4-8-10 Pat Eddery 11/4 FAV: 14-0000: Heavily bckd, ev ch: see 1590.   00
1781 EVERY EFFORT [8] 4-7-13(5ex) C Rutter(5) 8/1: 1D34120: Much btr 1781.   00
*1553 GURTEEN BOY** [3] 4-7-9(5ex) A Mcglone 9/1: 0000010: No threat: much btr 1553.   00
1460 Portogon [1] 8-8   **1608 West Carrack** [14] 8-6 *1729 Joyful Dancer** [4] 8-10(5ex)
1455 Virgin Isle [6] 8-5
15 ran   1¾,1¾,1¾,hd,2¼   (Mrs C Pateras)   C Brittain Newmarket

1891 LAVANT NURSERY H'CAP 2YO   **£4032**   **6f**   **Good/Firm 25 -18 Slow**   [59]

1381 PAS DENCHERE [2] (G Lewis) 2-9-0 P Waldron 12/1: 0301: 2 ch c Pas De Seul - Klewraye
(Lord Gayle) Useful, impr colt: gained his first success running on to lead well inside final
1f in a nursery h'cap at Goodwood July 31: dam a winner over 7f in Ireland: acts well on fast
ground: eff 6f, will be well suited by 7f+: the type to improve further and win more races.   58
513 WISE TIMES [6] (M Usher) 2-8-4 M Wigham 16/1: 0022: Led briefly final 1f and this
was a grand effort after a long abs: should find a similar event soon: see 252: suited by
6f tho' seems to act on any going.   45
1570 PANACHE [1] (P Haslam) 2-7-12(vis) T Williams 11/2: 03121D3: Chall 1f out and ran
well: see 1570.   37
*1522 GREY WOLF TIGER** [5] (R Hannon) 2-8-10(7ex) Pat Eddery 15/8 FAV: 0224114: Led under
press dist: fair effort but rated higher 1522 (good).   47
1126 PENSURCHIN [4] 2-9-4 S Cauthen 9/1: 131200: Not disgraced but possibly btr on
easier ground (434).   45
1693 ABSOLUTION [3] 2-8-8 S Whitworth 11/2: 321220: Clear leader much and btr 1693 (5f).   25
-1552 DOMINO FIRE** [7] 2-9-7 W Carson 11/2: 1220: Sn struggling: much btr 1552.   00
1019 VAIGLY BLAZED [8] 2-8-1 P Cook 9/1: 4000: Sn rear: best 662 (yldg/soft).   00
8 ran   1¾,¾,¾,5,6   (S G Grinstead)   G Lewis Epsom, Surrey

THIRSK   Friday August 1st   Lefthanded, Flat, Sharpish Track

Official Going Given As GOOD/FIRM : ALL TIMES SLOW EXCEPT RACES 1893 & 1896.

1892 GOLDEN FLEECE SELLING STAKES   **£1063**   **1m 4f Good/Firm Slow**

1767 MR COFFEY [8] (S Norton) 3-8-2 J Lowe 6/1: 4000221: 3 b c Sallust - Golden Stockings   15
(Home Guard) Deservedly got off the mark, led over 2f out for an easy win in a 3 and 4yo
seller at Thirsk Aug 1 (bought in 5,200 gns): over 8/9f and clearly stays 12f well:
suited by fast ground: acts on any trk: in gd form.   15
--   **STARWOOD** [4] (J Fitzgerald) 4-9-0 R Brown(7) 14/1: 000-2: Al front rank on seasonal
debut: kept on well tho' no chance with easy winner: lightly raced gelding: stays 12f: acts
on gd/firm ground and on a sharpish course.   00
993 MUSICAL WILL [3] (T Fairhurst) 4-9-0(BL) D Nicholls 5/1: 0-00403: Bl first time and
attracted some support despite fair abs: made late prog tho' btr over this C/D in 783 (firm).   06
1386 PATRIOTIC [2] (M Prescott) 3-8-0(1ow) G Duffield 6/1: 00-04: Kept on late: see 1386.   00
1737 RAMILIE [5] 4-8-11 M Wood 11/8 FAV: 0-00340: Took ld home turn, faded: better 1737   01
1700 SUNLIT [7] 3-7-13 K Darley 20/1: 0-000: Never dangerous: lightly raced filly who
is closely related to sev winners and is bred to be suited by middle distances.   00

1767 FIRE LORD [6] 3-8-2 R P Elliott 14/1: -000340: Made most to ½ way: see 1428. 00
1759 PINK SENSATION [1] 3-8-0(1ow) M Fry 7/2: -000420: Early leader: fin last: much btr 1759. 00
8 ran 8,4,shthd,1,7,hd,2½ (Mrs B Stead) S Norton High Hoyland, Yorks.

1893 NURSERY HANDICAP 2YO £2389 5f Good/Firm +10 Fast [44]

1221 BAD PAYER [7] (M W Easterby) 2-8-3 K Darley 12/1: 43121: 2 b f Tanfirion - Opening Flight (Falcon) Genuine filly: led/dsptd lead thr'out for a game win in a fast run nursery h'cap at Thirsk Aug 1: earlier made most to win a seller at Beverley and has yet to fin out of the frame: eff over 5/6f with forcing tactics: acts on fast and soft ground and on any trk: genuine sort. 30
1707 ECHOING [6] (J Watts) 2-9-7 N Connorton 8/1: 1432: Just held in a driving fin: fine effort under top weight: certain to be suited by another furlong: see 766. 45
873 PASHMINA [13] (T Fairhurst) 2-8-6 J Callaghan(7) 16/1: 102103: Abs: picked up ground from ½ way: looks on a handy mark: acts on any trk: see 696. should do better next time. 24
•1762 JOE SUGDEN [8] (R Whitaker) 2-9-1(7ex) K Bradshaw(5) 5/2 FAV: 03014: Veered left ½ way, going on fin: btr judged on his recent win in 1762. 32
1785 FIVE SIXES [11] 2-8-1 J Lowe 7/1: D421130: Early leader: btr 1785. 12
•1570 CLOWN STREAKER [5] 2-8-11 M Birch 3/1: 21010: One paced from ½ way: btr 1570 (6f). 18
1764 PENBREASY [3] 2-8-7 S Perks 10/1: 04000: Hmpd start: fin 8th: see 1764. 00
1717 BRUTUS [4] 2-9-2 G Duffield 7/1: 01030: Tardy start, no threat: see 826. 00
1370 Emmer Green [12] 8-10 1225 Kacere [9] 9-1 1576 Marching Moth [2] 8-4(VIS)
11 ran ½,2,nk,2½,1½ (C Mahoney) M W Easterby Sherriff Hutton, Yorks.

1894 JOHN BELL MEM. STAKES (H'CAP)(0-50)3YO £2561 2m Good/Firm Slow [51]

•1623 COINAGE [4] (R Johnson Houghton) 3-9-10(3ex) J Reid 13/8 JT FAV: -231011: 3 br c Owen Dudley - Grisbi (Grey Sovereign) Useful young stayer: comfortably defied his penalty, led 2f out in a 3yo h'cap at Thirsk Aug 1: easy winner of a stks race over this C/D earlier this month after winning a Beverley maiden in course record time: half brother to several winners: eff over 10/12f and stays 2m really well: acts on firm and yldg grd and any trk. 58
1706 WATERDALE [1] (M W Easterby) 3-8-0 J Lowe 12/1: -003332: Made most: kept on well under press and seemed well suited by this longer trip: acts on any trk: see 958. 29
•1410 IN DREAMS [3] (M Prescott) 3-8-13 G Duffield 13/8 JT FAV: 40-2113: Not quicken below dist: see 1410. needs stiffer track? 36
•1646 SPARTAN VALLEY [2] (B Hills) 3-9-4(3ex) M Hills 7/2: 0-23214: Longer trip: held up and no threat: see 1646 (14f). 38
4 ran 1½,6,3 (Mrs J A de Rothschild) R Johnson Houghton Blewbury, Oxon.

1895 SESSAY AUCTION STAKES 2YO £2480 7f Good/Firm Slow

•1341 PEN BAL LADY [1] (G Pritchard Gordon) 2-9-2 Abigail Richards(7) 3/1 CO FAV: 1211: 2 ch f Mummy's Game - Northern Queen (Northfields) Led after ½ way and ran on well to win a 2yo auction stks at Thirsk Aug 1: comfortable all the way winner of a fillies stks at Warwick recently: first time out won a mdn at Leicester: eff over 6/7f on gd and firm grd: acts on any trk: should continue to improve. 55
1527 BOTHY BALLAD [5] (P Calver) 2-8-5 M Fry 4/1: 102: Led briefly ½ way: kept on well over this longer trip: stays 7f well: acts on any trk: see 701. 38
612 GRECIAN JOS [4] (F Carr) 2-8-2 S Morris 25/1: 03: Abs: switched dist and never nearer: cheaply acquired colt who is a half brother to winning juv Italian Secret: stays 7f well: acts on gd/firm ground and on a sharpish course. 34
•913 URRAY ON HARRY [2] (R Hollinshead) 2-8-13 S Perks 3/1 CO FAV: 14: Led to ½ way: good effort after fair abs: stays 7f: acts on any track: see 913. 41
1527 WHISTLING WONDER [3] 2-8-0(1ow) K Darley 6/1: 0430300: No real threat: best 1174 (5f) 22
1253 DOHTY BABY [6] 2-7-10 J Lowe 3/1 CO FAV: 0300: Held up, no threat: see 1180. 17
6 ran 2,¾,1½,3,½ (G T Park) G Pritchard Gordon Newmarket

1896 THOMAS LORD H'CAP STAKES (0-50) £2544 5f Good/Firm +12 Fast [42]

+1638 CELTIC BIRD [10] (A Balding) 6-8-8(7ex) N Day 4/1 FAV: 0002311: 6 b m Celtic Cone - Bird Cherry (Falcon) Easily justified fav, led/dsptd lead and quickened dist in a fast run h'cap at Thirsk Aug 1: in gd form, recently a game winner of a similar race at Ripon: last season won over this C/D: best when out in front over this minimum trip: acts on fast and soft ground and on any track. 34
1796 IBERIAN START [9] (D Barron) 3-9-9 J Reid 9/2: 2-21032: Ran on under press: remains in good form: see 1027. 42
1638 GODS ISLE [8] (M H Easterby) 3-9-0 M Birch 11/2: -020003: Btr eff: see 443 & 246. 29
1638 PERGODA [1] (I Vickers) 8-9-1(bl) R Vickers(7) 12/1: 0010104: Led/dsptd lead over ½ way: best in 1543. 24
1849 CHINA GOLD [3] 7-9-7 M Wood 6/1: 0042020: Al cl.up: best 1268. 24
1718 PARADE GIRL [6] 4-7-7(8oh) A Proud 12/1: 0004040: Tardy start and no threat: see 56. 00
1505 AFRICAN REX [2] 3-9-7(BL) E Guest(3) 8/1: 011-000: Fin last: can do btr: see 1391. 00
1796 Bay Bazaar [4] 8-6 -- Light Angle [5] 7-13
9 ran 4,1½,nk,2,¾,1½ (J D Cooke) A Balding Doncaster, Yorks.
00

1897 COWESBY APPRENTICES' H'CAP (0-35)   £1075   2m   Good/Firm Slow   [32]

968 BUSTOFF [5] (S Hall) 6-8-0 J Callaghan 7/1: 0-23001: 6 b g Bustino - Magical
(Aggressor) Despite fair abs, led 2f out and stayed on well to win an app h'cap at Thirsk
Aug 1: first success: well suited by a test of stamina: acts on firm and yldg ground and
seems best on a sharp course.   12
*1477 DUKE OF DOLLIS [2] (W Storey) 7-7-12 J Quinn 9/2: 0000012: Made most: in gd form:see 147708
770 RAISABILLION [8] (J Wilson) 4-7-7 Jane Cottom(7) 33/1: 40-0003: Rank outsider after
fair abs: stayed on well: mdn: stays 2m: acts on gd/firm ground and on a sharp trk.   01
1737 KEY ROYAL [4] (G Calvert) 5-8-10 N Rodgers 12/1: 0-00004: Never nearer: see 1737. 16
1016 SMACK [7] 4-8-1 J Scally 9/2: 0-00200: Never beyond mid-div: see 841.   06
1772 WALTER THE GREAT [1] 4-8-4(bl) G Hindmarch(7) 4/1: 0400030: Front rank most of
way: see 933.   07
1564 ALFIE DICKINS [3] 8-7-10 P Hill 5/1: -044030: Sn behind: see 590.   00
1177 WESSEX [6] 4-9-10(bl) Kim Tinkler 5/2 FAV: 2431340: Never going well: much btr 824. 00
8 ran ½,2,1,1,2,8,4   (Miss S Hall)   S Hall Middleham, Yorks.

Official Going Given As GOOD

1898 SIDE HILL SELLING HCAP 3YO 0-25   £1295   1m 4f   Good 41 -31 Slow   [21]

1656 S S SANTO [9] (M Tompkins) 3-9-4 R Morse(5) 11/2: -220001: 3 ch f Monsanto -
Wayleave (Blakeney) Al going well and led final 1f, readily drawing clear in a 3yo selling
h'cap at Newmarket Aug 1 (bought in 5,600 gns): clearly well suited by a stiff 12f: acts on
good/firm and soft ground and a gall track.   22
1656 HIGHEST NOTE [1] (G Blum) 3-9-2 M Rimmer 11/2: -300432: Kept on well: in gd form:
stays 12f well: see 1369.   12
*1428 MAX CLOWN [14] (W Wharton) 3-8-10 A Mackay 7/2 FAV: 00-0013: Well bckd: led 2f out:
running well: see 1428.   05
1751 LISAKATY [12] (M Mccourt) 3-8-9 R Wernham 20/1: 0000004: Stays 12f: little form this
term: see 162.   00
*1656 GRANDANGUS [5] 3-8-12(vis)(4ex) W Woods(3) 9/1: 0-00010: Mkt drifter: led 3f out:
much better 1656 (10f).   00
1549 GEORGIAN ROSE [8] 3-8-7(vis) A Shoults(5) 33/1: 0400000: Fdd final 2f: little form. 00
1326 ARCH PRINCESS [6] 3-8-9(bl) R Cochrane 5/1: -004400: There 1m: btr 1078 (14f). 00
838 SOHO SAM [7] 3-9-7 M Wigham 9/1: -00400: Led 1m: abs: best 666 (7f soft).   00
1671 Tinas Lad [4] 8-8   1656 Aussie Girl [3] 9-5   1258 Tiber Gate [13] 8-4
--   Sea Venom [10] 8-7   1369 La Chula [11] 8-13   1349 Puppywalker [2] 8-7
14 ran 4,nk,2,2½,3   (Stanley Squires)   M Tompkins Newmarket

1899 PIPER CHAMPAGNE STAKES 3YO   £5095   1m 4f   Good 41 +14 Fast

1378 TOP GUEST [1] (G Wragg) 3-9-1 Pat Eddery 5/6 FAV: 2-12221: 3 ch c Be My Guest -
Topsy (Habitat) Smart, consistent colt: heavily bckd and led over 1f out, readily coming
clear in fast run and val Piper Champagne Stks at Newmarket Aug 1: first time out won a
Beverley mdn: has since fin 2nd to 3 smart types in Faraway Dancer, Hello Ernani and Armada:
eff at 10f, suited by 12f: half brother to Rye Tops and Troytops: acts on any grd and trk:
yet to run a bad race.   70
1468 ORBAN [6] (H Cecil) 3-9-5 S Cauthen 7/2: -132: Made most: no chance with winner,
but ran well: stays 12f: see 1468, 1080.   60
1674 GREY SALUTE [7] (R Simpson) 3-8-5 S Whitworth 33/1: -33: Al prom and kept on:
fine effort and is impr fast: seems well suited by a stiff 12f: acts on gd and firm grd and
should find a race.   42
1596 BELICE [3] (S Mellor) 3-8-7 M Wigham 20/1: -1004: Prom, switched and ran on final
1f: stays 12f: acts on good and hvy ground.   44
1469 CIGAR [8] 3-8-5 P Robinson 14/1: 00-0000: Late hdwy, never nearer: stable mate
of winner: clearly stays 12f and has the ability to find a race: see 619.   40
1530 POKEYS PRIDE [4] 3-8-5 R Cochrane 13/2: 20-0220: Lightly bckd: fdd 2f out: btr 1530. 36
1645 ILE DE ROI [2] 3-8-5 W Newnes 9/2: -4-020: There 10f: disapp after 1645 (11f frm). 00
--   MSHATTA PALACE [2] 3-8-5 G Baxter 25/1: -0: Stiff debut: al back marker.   00
8 ran 6,2,nk,1½,3   (E B Moller)   G Wragg Newmarket

1900 MALONEY AND RHODES HANDICAP 0-60   £4815   6f   Good 41 +17 Fast

1312 MARGAM [2] (P Walwyn) 3-7-8 A Mackay 6/1: 0-31041: 3 b c African Sky - Valley Farm
(Red God) Led 2f out and stuck on gamely to win a fast run h'cap at Newmarket Aug 1: earlier
won a Hamilton mdn: consistent sort who seems to go on any ground: well suited by 6f: acts
well on a stiff trk: genuine.   43
1044 QUINTA REEF [1] (M Jarvis) 3-8-10 T Ives 14/1: 0-12002: Chall final 1f, just btn:
fine effort: see 671, 438.   58
1777 HO MI CHINH [8] (C Brittain) 4-9-8 W Carson 12/1: -110003: Al up there: fine effort
under 9-8: see 1455, 687.   61
1777 CHUMMYS PET [6] (N Callaghan) 3-8-10 Pat Eddery 5/4 FAV: 3121124: Heavily bckd:
tremendously consistent: see 1777, 1457.   55

1377 BATON BOY [10] 5-7-12(1ow) P Robinson 33/1: -200040: Kept on final 1f: ran well: see 55. 36

1730 DAVILL [5] 4-7-11 A Mcglone 6/1: -000000: Sn prom: not btn far: see 76. 31

1750 DARK PROMISE [4] 3-8-12 S Cauthen 6/1: 0013230: Hmpd 2f out: twice below form 1524. 00

217 BONNY LIGHT [7] 3-7-9 M L Thomas 8/1: 204-30: Needed the race: btr 217 (yldg). 00

309 **Taranga** [3] 8-1   1145 **Puccini** [9] 8-3(1ow)

10 ran ½,¾,½,hd,1½,2,1 (Hamdan Al-Maktoum) P Walwyn Lambourn, Berks.

1901 BEDFORD LODGE HOTEL HCAP 0-35 3YO+ £2456 7f Good 41 -17 Slow [32]

943 MR ROSE [14] (R Hutchinson) 6-8-7 P Hutchinson(3) 9/2: 0004201: 6 b g Whistlefield - Berganza (Grey Sovereign) Despite abs, nicely bckd and led approaching final 1f, comfortably, in a h'cap at Newmarket Aug 1: earlier ran well here when 2nd to Heavy Brigade: in '85 was trained by L Lightbrown, winning at Beverley and Catterick: in '84 won at Folkestone: a 7f specialist: acts on gd and firm grd and on any trk. 22

*1560 BLUE BRILLIANT [8] (B Hills) 3-9-2(bl) B Thomson 9/2: -000212: In fine form: see 1560. 34

1774 KAMARESS [1] (M Brittain) 4-8-4 M Wigham 11/1: 0240043: Al up there: gd eff: see 1103. 12

1727 EUCHARIS [16] (A Hide) 4-7-11(bl)(1ow) W Carson 4/1 FAV: -000024: Prom, ev ch: better 1727 (firm). 02

1781 GAMBLERS DREAM [9] 9-9-3(hd) S Cauthen 12/1: 000-000: Chance inside final 2f: not btn far: last won in '84 at Ascot: suited by a stiff 1m and fast grd: usually wears bl or a hood. 20

1074 PETIT BOT [17] 4-7-12(bl)(2ow) P Robinson 20/1: 00-0000: Al up there: mdn: stays 1m: acts on good and yielding. 00

1649 **Ostentatious** [15] 8-2   1609 **Gauhar** [19] 8-8   1525 **Avec Coeur** [7] 10-0
1579 **Branksome Towers** [2] 7-7(4oh)   1227 **Dealt** [11] 8-6(bl)
1727 **Debach Revenge** [6] 7-8   -- **Dragonara Boy** [10] 9-3
1821 **Bon Accueil** [5] 9-8   424 **Buhaaz** [12] 8-4   1804 **Nicky Nick** [3] 8-11
1787 **Clipsall** [4] 8-9   1324 **Bright Path** [13] 7-13

18 ran 1½,¾,1½,¾,2½,hd (Bernard Bates) R Hutchinson Epsom, Surrey.

1902 T.I. CREDA STAKES 3YO £3490 1m Good 41 -15 Slow

806 FLASHDANCE [5] (G Harwood) 3-8-11 G Starkey 6/4 FAV: -31: 3 b f Habitat - Millvera (Mill Reef) Promising filly: led over 2f out, comfortably, in a 3yo fillies event (despite long abs) at Newmarket Aug 1: first time out fin a fine 3rd to Farajullah in a very competitive mdn on this trk: half sister to winning juv New Dimension and Prince Hab: stays 1m really well: acts on gd and firm grd and a gall trk: should continue to improve and win more races. 59

1586 FLUTTERY [6] (G Wragg) 3-8-11 S Cauthen 11/4: -3022: No chance with winner, but a long way clear of rest: should win soon: stays 1m: see 1586, 250. 53

1220 ROYAL NUGGET [7] (M Stoute) 3-8-11 W R Swinburn 9/2: 22-0403: Prom, ev ch: continues to disappoint: see 213. 41

-- LA NUREYEVA [1] (J Dunlop) 3-8-11 W Carson 10/1: 433-4: Nearest fin on seasonal debut and should be a lot straighter for this race: placed in all 3 starts in '85: half sister to the smart 2yo Cock Robin: eff at 1m, may get further: acts on gd and yldg ground and a galloping trk: should find a race. 36

1244 SATIN AND SILK [9] 3-8-11 P Bloomfield 14/1: -30: Not disgraced: stays 1m: see 1244. 36

1626 CLEOFE [4] 3-8-11 Pat Eddery 9/1: 0033340: Led 5f: see 1626. 26

1515 **Bag Lady** [3] 8-11   1516 **Secret Fact** [8] 8-11   1637 **Patchoulis Pet** [2] 8-11(bl)

9 ran 1½,7,2½,shthd,5 (Gerald Leigh) G Harwood Pulborough, Sussex.

1903 EBF BEACON MAIDEN STAKES 2YO £3918 7f Good 41 -41 Slow

-- ARABIAN SHEIK [10] (J Dunlop) 2-9-0 W Carson 6/5 FAV: 1: 2 b c Nijinsky - Arabian Miss (Damascus) Promising colt: heavily bckd and justified the confidence in impressive fashion, leading over 1f out in a 2yo mdn at Newmarket Aug 1: US bred colt who is well regarded by connections: eff at 7f, should be suited by further: acts on gd grd and a gall track and can only improve. 55

350 THE LIONHEART [7] (B Hills) 2-9-0 B Thomson 12/1: 02: Fin in gd style after long abs and his turn is near: half brother to sev winners: will be suited by 1m: acts on gd ground and a galloping track. 50

1573 ALPENHORN [9] (G P Gordon) 2-9-0 W Ryan 16/1: 03: Ran on well final 1f and is fast improving: will be suited by 1m: acts on gd ground and should find a maiden. 49

-- ESKIMO MITE [4] (P Cole) 2-9-0 T Quinn 10/1: 4: Fin really well final 1f and is bound to improve for the experience: cost IR 105,000 as a yearling: should be well suited by middle distances: acts on gd ground and a gall trk. 45

-- BIN SHADDAD [13] 2-9-0 W R Swinburn 15/2: 0: Led over 1f out on race course debut: cost 200,000 gns as a yearling: improvement likely. 43

-- FREEBYS PREACHER [5] 2-9-0 G Baxter 25/1: 0: Made most on debut: half brother to 10f winner Cold as Ice and is bred to be suited by middle distances. 41

-- ROMAN GUNNER [8] 2-9-0 Pat Eddery 5/1: 0: Prom, fin 7th: improvement likely: half brother to winning 2yo Bustara. 00

-- BOB FOREST [14] 2-9-0 T Ives 5/1: 0: Fdd final 2f on debut: nicely bred colt who will improve for the run: should be suited by 1m. 00

-- KING KRIMSON [6] 2-9-0 M Hills 8/1: 0: Wknd 1½f out: mkt drifter today and should do better in time: half brother to 2 minor winners. 00

--	Dancer To Follow [3] 9-0		--	Charlie Dickins [12] 9-0
--	Up The Ladder [2] 9-0	-- Just A Picnic [11] 8-11		
1452	Master Knowall [1] 9-0			

14 ran   1,1½,2½,½,½   (Ogden Mills Phipps)   J Dunlop Arundel, Sussex

---

EDINBURGH   Friday August 1st   Righthand, Sharpish Track

1904 CORPORATE FINANCE STAKES 3YO   £929   1m   Good 44 +08 Fast

1705 PERSIAN DELIGHT [8] (G Huffer) 3-8-8 G Carter(3) 11/4: 40-21: 3 b f Persian Bold -
Ballysnip (Ballymore) Impr filly who battled on well in final 1f for a narrow win in a
3yo minor race at Edinburgh Aug 1: ran only twice in '85: well suited by 1m, promises to
stay further: acts on firm and gd ground: certainly on the upgrade.   35
1472 ACTUALIZATIONS [7] (L Cumani) 3-8-8 R Guest 7/4 FAV: -0342: Al prom: just btn in
a close fin but has twice run below the form in 1327 (rated 47).   34
*1614 SAND DOLLAR [6] (M Prescott) 3-9-2 G Duffield 15/8: 00-13: Al there and led 3f out,
just went down in a tight fin: clear rem: improving colt who should find a h'cap sn: see 1614.   41
1743 FANNY ROBIN [1] (D Smith) 3-8-8 L Charnock 33/1: 40-0004: Chall 2f out, outpaced
but prob her best effort yet: see 1123.   21
631   STAR OF TARA [3] 3-8-9(1ow) C Dwyer 50/1: 000-000: Abs: no real danger: lightly
raced mdn.   10
1677 ACCUMULATE [2] 3-8-11 R P Elliott 33/1: 40-0000: No threat: no worthwhile form this term 00
451   Master Music [4] 8-11   1824 Parkes Special [5] 8-8
8 ran   hd,½,5,5,5   (A Afhdal)   G Huffer Newmarket

1905 SELLING STAKES 2YO   £807   7f   Good 44 -43 Slow

1684 LATE PROGRESS [4] (J Berry) 2-8-8 J Carroll(7) 11/2: 0003321: 2 ch f On Your Mark -
Trouble Pocket (In The Pocket) Gaining her 1st win, leading 2f out under press in a 2yo
seller at Edinburgh Aug 1 (bought in 2,600 gns): suited by 7f, should stay 1m: acts well on
fast ground.   19
1795 KIND LADY [7] (R Stubbs) 2-9-1 A Mercer 7/2 FAV: 423102: Prom, kept on: stays 7f:see 1358.24
1253 DELITE MUFFIN [2] (J Fitzgerald) 2-8-8 G Carter(3) 5/1: 003: Sn prom on first
venture into selling company: will be suited by 1m: acts on gd ground: abs since 1253.   13
1528 PRINCESS PELHAM [3] (N Callaghan) 2-8-8(BL) G Duffield 9/2: 004: Tried to make all:
best effort yet : blinkered first time today.   10
--   ARDAY WEDNESDAY [5] 2-8-8 R P Elliott 10/1: 0: Never btr: may impr on this 1st effort. 09
1795 WOLF J FLYWHEEL [6] 2-8-11 L Charnock 4/1: 0000200: Again displayed little enthusiasm. 04
1741 Just A Decoy [8] 8-11   1741 On The Mark [1] 8-11(bl)
8 ran   1,1½,1,nk,4   (Mrs J M Berry)   J Berry Cockerham, Lancs.

1906 HANDICAP STAKES (0-35) 3YO+   £1758   7f   Good 44 +02 Fast   [28]

1560 BICKERMAN [9] (M Prescott) 3-8-8 G Duffield 5/1: 4-00101: 3 b c Mummy's Pet - Merry
Weather (Will Somers) Al prom and gained the day near line in a cl fin to a h'cap at Edinburgh
Aug 1: winner over this me C/D June 30: lightly raced prev: related to useful sprinters
Pettingale and Tina's Pet amongst others: very eff over 7f on a sharp course, particularly
Edinburgh: acts on firm and good ground.   25
1758 O I OYSTON [3] (J Berry) 3-9-0 J Carroll(7) 9/2: 0002022: Led 2f out, just caught:
in good form: see 1758 : due a change of luck.   21
1073 KAMPGLOW [7] (Ron Thompson) 4-9-7 R P Elliott 20/1: 0300003: Prom and dsptd lead
final 1f, narrowly btn: see 71: suited by gd or soft/hvy ground: unsuited by firm? : abs. since 1073. 27
1774 THIRTEENTH FRIDAY [1] (W Pearce) 4-7-10(bl) J Lowe 4/1 FAV: -400034: Chall 1f out,
found no extra: ran btr 1774.   00
*1774 MONINSKY [11] 5-8-13(8ex) M Richardson(7) 15/2: 0300310: Waited with, not clear run
when chall dist: in gd form: see 1774.   12
1761 LA BELLE DE SANTO [5] 3-7-13 L Charnock 12/1: -002000: Ev ch: yet to reproduce 1299(C/D) 05
1761 ALWAYS NATIVE [4] 5-8-11 S Webster 7/1: -000400: Prom, wknd into 7th: best 1222(6f) 00
1547 SHOW OF HANDS [6] 10-8-10 N Connorton 6/1: 00-0200: Made much, fin 8th: best 1074. 00
1676 Warthill Lady [10] 8-7   1074 Barnes Star [2] 8-10
10 ran   ½,½,1½,1½,nk   (Major J L Green)   M Prescott Newmarket

1907 NURSERY HANDICAP STAKES 2YO   £1101   7f   Good 44 -28 Slow   [46]

1722 LIGHTNING LASER [2] (P Kelleway) 2-8-6 Gay Kelleway(3) 9/2: 0033301: 2 b f Monsigneur
- Spring Bride (Auction Ring) Impr filly: waited with, quickened to lead final 1f, readily in
a 2yo nursery at Edinburgh Aug 1: eff over 5f but is btr suited by 6/7f now: acts on firm
and good ground and on any trk: seems suited by waiting tactics: can win again in similar
modest company.   37
*1537 PRINCESS SINGH [6] (N Tinkler) 2-7-12 G Carter(3) 12/1: 1044312: Led briefly dist:
good effort: stays 7f: see 1537.   21
1528 LADY SUNDAY SPORT [1] (N Callaghan) 2-8-2 G Duffield 7/2: 4023: Chall 1f out:
fair effort but better 1528 (6f seller).   21
-1717 DANADN [3] (Ron Thompson) 2-8-7 R P Elliott 4/1: 0403324: Waited with, hdwy and
not the best of runs from dist: btr 1717 (5f): probably stays 7f.   22

1814 FICKLE YOUNG MAN [7] 2-9-1 A Bond 9/4 FAV: 130: Quick reappearance, ev ch: btr 1814 (5f)28
1697 MR GRUMPY [5] 2-9-7 L Charnock 13/2: 2011100: Made much, fdd and btr 934 (6f).   33
1528 SHARPHAVEN [4] 2-8-0(1ow) K Darley 9/1: 3024100: Early leader, fdd: twice below 1379.   00
7 ran   3,1½,2,¾,½   (N Mandell)   P Kelleway Newmarket

1908 STANECASTLE ASSETS MAIDEN STAKES 3YO+   £929   1m 4f   Good 44 -23 Slow

1317 BANQUE PRIVEE [6] (B Hills) 3-8-0(1ow) G Duffield 2/1 JT.FAV: 0-331: 3 b f Private
Account - Le Vague L'Ame (Vaguely Noble) Prom and led 2f out, comfortably, in a mdn at
Edinburgh Aug 1: lightly raced prev: dam a French middle dist mdn: well suited by 12f and
firm or gd going.   45
1337 MY WILLOW [2] (J Fitzgerald) 3-8-0(1ow) K Darley 11/2: -42: Kept on well under press,
clear rem: impr filly who is well suited by 12f and will find a mdn very soon: see 1337.   40
1481 MITALA MARIA [7] (A Stewart) 3-7-13 G Carter(3) 2/1 JT.FAV: -023: Led over 2f out,
wknd: much btr 1481 (very sharp trk).   29
164 RAGABURY [3] (R Fisher) 6-9-0 D Nicholls 33/1: -000-04: No danger after very long
abs but this will ensure he strips fit for his reappearance over hurdles: lightly raced
maiden on the Flat.   12
--   BUNRANNOCH HOUSE [1] 5-9-0 J Lowe 50/1: 00-0: Very lightly raced mdn on the Flat
but a fair top of the ground hurdler who will be all the fitter for his reappearance over
obstacles after this pipe-opener.   00
--   REKADLO [8] 4-8-11 S Webster 50/1: -0: No danger on first outing on Flat, fin 5th
in a "bumpers" at Catterick in Mar: more of a jumping type.   00
1639 IS BELLO [4] 3-8-2 P Hamblett 3/1: 0320300: Ran atrociously, and not for the first
time: see 1639.   00
--   Quality Square [5] 9-0   1424 Coplace [9] 9-0
9 ran   1½,5,8,10,2½   (Alan Clore)   B Hills Lambourn, Berks.

1909 INVESTMENT TRUST H'CAP STAKES (0-35)   £886   1m 3f   Good 44 -08 Slow   [33]

1808 PONTYATES [8] (J S Wilson) 4-8-9 C Dwyer 33/1: 3400041: 4 ch g Cawston's Clown -
No Man's Land (Salvo) Turned up at 33/1, coming from behind to force his hd in front on
the post in a h'cap at Edinburgh Aug 1: first success: well suited by 11/12f and gd or
easier going: evidently best with waiting tactics.   24
1689 GREENHILLS GIRL [2] (M Ryan) 3-7-8(VIS) G Carter(0) 5/1: 01-0002: Led ½ way, caught
death: wore visor for the first time here: see 380: stays 11f well.   20
1580 WHILE IT LASTS [5] (L Cumani) 3-8-13 R Guest 4/1: -33323: Dsptd lead final 2f, just
btn in a close fin: stays 11f: see 1580.   39
*1744 BALLYDURROW [9] (R Fisher) 9-10-1(4ex) D Nicholls 2/1 FAV: 1040214: Waited with as
usual, not reach first 3: btr 1744.   36
*1613 SENOR RAMOS [7] 4-9-11(bl)(7ex) R P Elliott 6/1: 0000110: No danger under 7lbs pen.   30
1744 RUSTIC TRACK [6] 6-7-13 L Charnock 6/1: 3200030: Ev ch, wknd and much btr 1744.   00
1744 APPLE WINE [3] 4-9-5 G Duffield 8/1: 2024400: Led to ½ way: see 1124.   00
1124 Icen [4] 8-7   1678 Common Farm [1] 8-7
9 ran   hd,hd,4,¾,4   (J J McLaren)   J S Wilson Ayr

GOODWOOD   Friday August 1st   Righthand, Undulating Track

Official Going Given As GOOD/FIRM ON STRAIGHT COURSE : FIRM ON ROUND COURSE

1910 RALPH HUBBARD MEM.NURSERY H'CAP 2YO   £9318   5f   Good/Firm 23 +03 Fast   [68]

1754 GARNET [10] (R Boss) 2-7-13 W Carson 15/2: 0141: 2 b f Thatch - Jawhara (Upper Case)
Useful, impr filly: al there and led under press final 1f in a cl fin to quite a fast run and
val nursery at Goodwood Aug 1: comfortably won a fillies mdn at Edinburgh June 30: half
sister to a minor 7f winner: very eff over 5f on fast grd & best on a sharpish track.   53
1287 JAISALMER [2] (D Elsworth) 2-7-9 A Mcglone 5/1: 102002: Fin very strongly, showing
return to the form displayed in 773: acts on firm to yldg but not on hvy: see 350: must
win a similar race next time, prob over 6f.   49
1641 CLARENTIA [5] (M Usher) 2-7-7 T Williams 7/1: 21403: Led/dsptd lead 3 out, just
btn: can find a similar event: see 400.   46
+1453 CHASING MOONBEAMS [4] (I Balding) 2-9-7 Pat Eddery 7/4 FAV: 2214: Chall dist, no
extra near fin but a fine effort under 9-7: continues to improve: see 1453.   73
1552 DANCING DIANA [3] (M Usher) 2-8-6 B Rouse 33/1: 21400: Outpaced till late prog: fine effort
and looks likely to be suited by 6f: see 531.   56
1585 SPANISH SKY [1] 2-7-9 S Dawson 14/1: 0100: Early pace: see 1194.   38
1527 BASTILLIA [8] 2-7-12 N Adams 10/1: 001300: Dsptd lead much, fin 7th: see 746.   00
1746 SUMMER SKY [7] 2-8-12 T Quinn 8/1: 1130: Early pace: twice below 725.   00
*40   Artful Maid [9] 7-7(5oh)
9 ran   hd,nk,½,¾,2½   (A Foustok)   R Boss Newmarket

1911 HOFMEISTER H'CAP 3YO+ 0-60   £5072   7f   Good/Firm 23 -07 Slow   [59]

1384 REIGNBEAU [8] (G Lewis) 3-8-7 P Waldron 5/1: 3112031: 3 b c Runnett - Queensworthy
(Capistrano) Useful h'capper: well ridden making all and staying on really strongly for a

decisive comfortable success in a val h'cap at Goodwood Aug 1: early in the season won at
Epsom (h'cap) and Brighton (minor race) : stays 1m but very eff over 7f with front running
tactics: acts on firm and hvy going and on any trk tho' fav by a sharpish one: genuine
and consistent.   58
1107 DIGGERS REST [7] (G Wragg) 3-9-6 S Cauthen 7/1: 03-1302: Behind, fin really strongly
but all too late: fine effort at the weights and looks to need 1m+ nowadays: see 216:abs since 1107 67
1640 FORMATUNE [11] (D Arbuthnot) 4-7-10(bl) T Williams 11/1: 0233203: Al there, ev ch:
consistent sort who wears blinkers: see 10.   35
1390 TELWAAH [1] (A Stewart) 4-9-2(bl) M Roberts 9/2 FAV: 10-2024: Dsptd lead 2f out,
no extra: see 815, now wears blinkers : running well.   54
1640 HILTON BROWN [9] 5-9-5 C Rutter(5) 6/1: 0022430: Ev ch: consistent: see 1640.   56
1793 FUSILIER [6] 4-7-13(bl) W Carson 11/1: 3000000: Prom much: best 17 (soft).   30
1804 HELLO SUNSHINE [10] 7-7-12 N Adams 10/1: 0000400: Active in mkt, never btr 8th:see 1640. 00
1804 STEADY EDDIE [5] 4-8-5 Pat Eddery 6/1: -000030: Much btr 1804.   00
1640 April Fool [3] 7-7(VIS)   588   King Of Spades [12] 8-9
1044 Merdon Melody [4] 8-5   1365 Don Martino [2] 9-11
12 ran   2,shthd,nk,nk,3   (Mrs B M Clarke)   G Lewis Epsom, Surrey.

1912 EXTEL H'CAP 3YO 0-75   £20712   1m 2f   Good/Firm 23 +18 Fast   [73]

-1554 CHINOISERIE [5] (L Cumani) 3-8-11 T Ives 14/1: 0211221: 3 b c Fluorescentt Light -
From the East (Gold and Myrrh) Smart, progressive colt: mid-div till qcknd up really well
to lead final 100yds and cleverly win val, fast run and very competitive Extel h'cap at
Goodwood Aug 1: earlier won at Brighton and Yarmouth and has only once been out of the first
two in sevenraces this term: very eff over 10f and acts on firm and yldg going and on any
trk: continues to improve and could win a Group 3 race.   75
*1503 SWEET MOVER [8] (W Hern) 3-8-4 W Carson 14/1: 22-12: Came to chall final 1f, not btn
far and this was a grand effort from a fast improving filly: sure to win more races: see 1503. 66
*1469 CELESTIAL STORM [12] (L Cumani) 3-9-1 W R Swinburn 3/1 FAV: 0-13: Cruised into lead
dist, lack of experience let him down cl home: btr fancied stable companion of winner and
is a most attractive sort who should go on to score in Group company: see 1469.   76
*1670 NILAMBAR [6] (R J Houghton) 3-8-5 B Thomson 8/1: -023114: Led/dsptd lead thr'out
and will not be hard put to find another race soon: see 1670.   60
1230 FINAL TRY [7] 3-9-3 C Asmussen 33/1: 230-000: Sn prom, showing much his best form
this season: prob stays 10f: seems to handle fast ground, possibly best on an easy surface:
should be noted next time: see 1230.   71
1147 SANTELLA MAC [9] 3-9-5 G Starkey 6/1: 01-100: Came to chall dist, no extra but
far from disgraced in a very good race: see 847.   72
+1588 ENBARR [13] 3-8-9 S Cauthen 9/2: 0-21310: Set a good pace over 7f: see 1588.   00
-1147 NAVARZATO [1] 3-9-3 R Cochrane 9/2: 11-20: Al in rear and is much btr than this
suggests: see 1147.   00
1325 First Dibs [11] 7-12   1657 Travel Mystery [4] 7-7(8oh)
802 Chartino [10] 9-7   1448 Esdale [3] 9-3   1645 Saronicos [2] 8-0
13 ran   ½,¾,4,nk,nk   (Ivan Allan)   L Cumani Newmarket.

1913 ALYCIDON STAKES LISTED RACE 3YO+   £15738   1m 4f   Good/Firm 23 +02 Fast

1098 NISNAS [8] (P Cole) 3-8-2 T Quinn 1/1 FAV: -131031: 3 ch c Tap on Wood - Suemette
(Danseur) Very smart colt: heavily bckd and alth' looking momentarily in trouble 3f out
showed a good turn of foot to stamp his authority on the race in final 1f when a comfortable
winner of val. Alycidon Stks (Listed race) at Goodwood Aug 1: earlier won minor races at
Lingfield and Kempton (first time out), fin 5th in the Derby and an unlucky 3rd behind
Bonhomie at Royal Ascot: needs at least 12f, should be well suited by the Leger dist:
acts on fast and yldg going and on any trk: genuine and consistent: does well when fresh. 83
+1343 QUEENS SOLDIER [2] (H Cecil) 3-8-2 W Ryan 7/1: 131-112: Tried to make all and this
was a fine effort: see 1343.   77
1230 WYLFA [5] (J Shaw) 5-8-12 B Rouse 20/1: 22433: Came from behind and kept on well:
see 410, 1230.: has faced several difficult tasks and is due a confidence-booster.   73
1009 AL SALITE [3] (J Dunlop) 3-8-5 Pat Eddery 7/1: 12-1104: Waited with, kept on strongly
final 2f and continues to improve: looks likely to stay beyond 12f: see 597.   77
*1644 WASSL TOUCH [6] 3-8-5 W Carson 6/1: 1-010: Prom thr'out: gd eff from this improving
colt: see 1644: stays 12f.   76
1098 BELDALE STAR [4] 3-8-8 A Clark 50/1: 20-1000: Came from well behind but no extra
closing stages: best effort since 273.   76
*1378 ARMADA [7] 3-8-8(3ow) G Starkey 11/2: -1110: Absolutely friendless in mkt, prom
over 10f, fin 7th: see 1378.   00
1130 Norfolk Sonata [1] 8-2
8 ran   1½,nk,shthd,shthd,¾   (Fahd Salman)   P Cole Whatcombe, Oxon.

1914 CHICHESTER CITY MAIDEN STAKES 2YO   £4753   7f   Good/Firm 23 -17 Slow

1392 LUZUM [3] (H T Jones) 2-9-0(BL) A Murray 100/30: 2321: 2 ch c Touching Wood - Velvet
Habit (Habitat) Very useful colt: gained a deserved success, bl first time, making all
readily in a slowly run 2yo mdn at Goodwood Aug 1: eff at 6f but is well suited by 7f and
sure to stay further: acts on fast grd and seems suited by bl (like his sire) & forcing tactics 64

-- BENGAL FIRE [14] (C Brittain) 2-9-0 S Cauthen 11/1: 2: Well bckd debutant, al prom
and kept on: half brother to very useful middle dist performer King's Island: has scope,
sure to benefit greatly from this race and a mdn should easily be within his reach.   55
-- MERCE CUNNINGHAM [13] (W Hern) 2-9-0 W Carson 11/8 FAV: 3: Very well bckd debutant
didnot have the best of runs but fin in a fashion which bodes very well for his future:
reportedly his stable's best 2yo: brother to highclass middle dist performer Caerleon and
sev other very useful horses: has plenty of scope and will come on a lot for this outing:
hard to beat next time.   51
-- NOBLE BID [8] (J Dunlop) 2-9-0 B Rouse 25/1: 4: Weak in mkt, made a sound debut:
half brother to sev winners, notably Glenturret, Rollahead and Sheriff Muir: likely to
prove best at up to 1m: acts on fast ground: sure to do much btr next time.   51
-- WAYAK [6] 2-9-0 G Starkey 4/1: 0: Al prom: possibly just in need of race: half brother
to a winner abroad: quite speedily bred and should soon step up on this performance.   43
-- CHAUDENNAY [19] 2-8-11 B Thomson 25/1: 0: Late prog, showing future promise: half
sister to useful Albert Hall: certain to stay beyond 1m: will improve.   39
1097 AL MAHAMRY [1] 2-9-0 C Asmussen 25/1: 00: Prom much, wknd into 7th: making improvement:
may prove btr at 6f for the time being:abs since 1097.   38
1629 CHESTER TERRACE [17] 2-9-0 Paul Eddery 50/1: 000: Prom most, fin cl 8th: see 1629.   36
-- WOOD LOUSE [10] 2-9-0 Pat Eddery 11/1: 0: Mkt drifter on debut: no show: dam a sprint
winner: sire won the Leger and Wood Louse may need more time/longer distances.   00
-- Mulhollande [9] 9-0   1458 Battle Heights [2] 9-0
1162 Brainwave [18] 9-0   -- Daunting Prospect [12] 9-0
-- Hygena Legend [11] 9-0   1289 Someone Else [16] 9-0
-- Velvet Slew [15] 9-0   -- Flight Won O Won [4] 8-11
1518 Laena [5] 8-11   915 Red Hero [7] 9-0
19 ran   3,2,sh hd,3,½,1½,sh hd   (Hamdan Al Maktoum)   H T Jones Newmarket

1915 EBF SELSEY MAIDEN STAKES 2YO   £4838   6f   Good/Firm 23 +01 Fast

1488 HENDEKA [1] (H Cecil) 2-9-0 S Cauthen 8/11 FAV: 31: 2 b c Shecky Greene - Ten Plus
(Judger) Smart colt in the making: landed the odds, prom and leading final 1f, narrowly in
quite a fast run 2yo mdn at Goodwood Aug 1: cost a modest $50,000 and looks a bargain at
today's prices: very well suited by 6f and is quite speedily bred: acts well on fast ground:
should win more races.   69
-- BALI MAGIC [3] (G Wragg) 2-9-0 Pat Eddery 5/1: 2: Fin strongly, just held and
could hardly have run a btr debut: brother to useful miler Balidancer and sev other winners:
sure to be suited by 7f+: acts well on fast ground: will have no difficulty winning a
race next time.   68
1488 GILBERTO [4] (J Dunlop) 2-9-0 W Carson 4/1: 43: Prom thr'out, fully endorsing the
promise shown on debut and will not be long in winning: see 1488.   65
1629 LIBRAN STAR [7] (H Candy) 2-9-0 W Newnes 9/1: 04: Tried to make all and was prob
unlucky to meet such talented rivals: sure to win a mdn: see 1629.   62
1488 FARFURR [2] 2-9-0 Paul Eddery 11/1: 00: Al well there and ran well, hinting at an
early success: see 1488.   52
1728 OUR FREDDIE [5] 2-9-0 R Curant 50/1: 4440: Early speed, fdd quickly: see 1728.   32
1629 Mister Wizard [10] 9-0(bl)   1241 Charmed Prince [2] 9-0
8 ran   ½,1½,½,4,10   (Sheikh Mohammed)   H Cecil Newmarket

THIRSK   Saturday August 2nd   Lefthanded, Flat, Sharpish Track

Official Going Given As GOOD/FIRM

1916 TOPCLIFFE STAKES 2YO   £2863   6f   Firm 08 +01 Fast

+1488 JUST A FLUTTER [3] (M Jarvis) 2-9-2 T Lucas 1/3 FAV: 11: 2 b c Beldale Flutter -
Precious Jade (Northfields) Smart, unbtn colt: easily landed the odds, led after ¼ way and
was sn clear in quite a fast run 2yo stks at Thirsk Aug 2: won a good class mdn at Newmarket
on his debut last month: half brother to last year's winning juv Diamond Sky: very eff over
6f and sure to stay further: acts on fast grd and on any trk: looks a fine prospect for
next season.   66+
1531 SARIHAH [6] (H T Jones) 2-9-2 A Murray 8/1: 0122: Led over ¼ way: no chance with
this smart winner: eff over 5/6f: acts on any trk: see 1075: consistent sort.   46
*1207 WELSH ARROW [5] (J Winter) 2-9-2 A Mackay 9/2: 13: Outpaced early, never nearer:
should find another winning opportunity before the season's end: see 1207.   42
523 MELGROVE [1] (J Etherington) 2-8-11 M Wood 100/1: 04: Late prog after abs: stays 6f:
acts on fast ground and on a sharpish trk: should continue to improve.   33
515 THE DEVILS MUSIC [7] 2-8-11 L Charnock 100/1: 00: Speed to ¼ way: abs since 515.   25
1225 JAYS SPECIAL [4] 2-8-11 M Hindley(3) 100/1: 4000: Slow start, no threat: best 197 (5f)   00
-- ATAKASHACK [2] 2-8-11 A Bond 100/1: 0: Early speed, trailed in last: very cheaply
bought colt.   00
7 ran   7,1,½,hd,2,15   (F C Wilson)   M Jarvis Newmarket

1917 PLAYTEX SELLING STAKES (LADIES RACE)   £1404   6f   Firm 08 -09 Slow

*1771 COOPER RACING NAIL [17] (J Berry) 3-9-4 Dana Mellor(5) 10/1: 0023011: 3 b f Martinmas - Wavy Navy (Hardicanute) Made al ev yard, in a 3yo seller at Thirsk Aug 2 (no bid) : recently just got home in a similar race at Ayr: eff over 6/7f with forcing tactics: acts on fast and soft grd and on any trk.   20

1627 IMPERIAL SUNRISE [16] (M W Easterby) 3-9-4 Christine Mccullock 6/1 FAV: 0343002: Just held: see 309.   19

1824 PUNCLE CREAK [13] (G Moore) 3-9-4 Diana Jones(5) 20/1: 0000233: Not btn far: in good form: see 1617.   17

972 MUSIC TEACHER [20] (A Robson) 3-9-4 Lyn Robson(7) 16/1: 1020004: Fair eff after abs: see 145.   14

*1824 DORADE [8] 3-9-7(bl) Miss G Arbor(2) 8/1: -003010: Had ev ch: in gd form: see 1824.   15

1524 SONNENELLE [5] 3-9-4(vis) Linda Perratt(4) 10/1: 2000400: Al front rank: best 103.   11

1603 THE LIDGATE STAR [14] 3-9-7 Franca Vittadini 8/1: -00000: Never nearer 7th: maiden who is a half brother to sev winners tho' has yet to show any worthwhile form himself: stays 6f: acts on fast ground.   00

*1734 PERCIPIO [19] 3-9-7(vis) Yvonne Haynes(2) 7/1: 0304210: Speed over ¼ way: fin 9th: best 1734 (5f).   00

1562 MRS NAUGHTY [10] 3-9-4 Kelly Marks 8/1: -400030: Early speed: btr 7f in 1562 (stiff trk)   00

1849 Alexanjo [2] 9-4	1398 Man In The Moon [21] 9-7		
1551 Beauclerc [18] 9-7(vis)		1815 Winding Path [15] 9-4	
-- Class Hopper [12] 9-7	1334 Bonny Bright Eyes [1] 9-4		
1734 Murryl Cannon [11] 9-7		997 Capistrano Climax [3] 9-7	
1839 Marshall Drills [7] 9-4		1771 Planter [9] 9-7(bl)	
1815 Sly Maid [4] 9-4	1626 Jenifer Browning [6] 9-4		
21 ran hd,1,1½,½,hd,hd,hd,1	(Peter Hodgson)	J Berry Cockerham, Lancs.	

1918 'TURN TO YORKSHIRE' H'CAP (0-50)   £2494   1m 4f   Firm 08 -28 Slow   [39]

1769 REGAL STEEL [6] (R Hollinshead) 8-8-5 A Culhane(7) 4/1: 2202221: 8 ch h Welsh Pageant - All Souls (Saint Crespin III) Ended a long losing run when gamely making all in a h'cap at Thirsk Aug 2: last successful in '84 winning twice at Doncaster: eff over 12/14f on yldg and fast ground: acts on any trk: tough front runner who has made the frame in most starts this term.   25

1726 TEMPEST TOSSED [1] (R Armstrong) 3-8-0 J Lowe 7/1: 3-04032: Kept on well: see 955.   30

*1763 MYTH [3] (R F Johnson Houghton) 3-9-11(4ex) R Hills 2/1 FAV: 24-2113: Switched below dist, not btn far and is in gd form: see 1763.   54

1124 NIGHT WARRIOR [5] (A Robson) 4-8-10 J Bleasdale 14/1: 4030334: Al cl up: see 238.   21

751 FOURTH TUDOR [7] 4-8-0 A Mackay 9/4: -200: No threat after fair abs: best 595(stiff trk)   07

1678 BREGUET [4] 3-7-10 J Callaghan(7) 50/1: -200000: Best over 1m in 487 (stiff trk yldg)   07

*1769 IVOROSKI [2] 4-7-7(4ex)(1oh) L Charnock 8/1: 0033210: Trailed in last: beat today's winner in 1769 (stiff trk).   00

7 ran   1,1,4,2½,5,12   (Steel Plate & Sections Ltd)   R Hollinshead Upper Longdon, Staffs.

1919 BURTON AGNES STUD STAKES 2YO   £2666   6f   Firm 08 +18 Fast

*1650 LINDAS MAGIC [5] (R Armstrong) 2-9-2 P Tulk 9/4 JT FAV: 2311: 2 br f Far North - Pogonip (Jacinto) Smart juv: broke the 2yo course record, led below dist for an impr win in a 2yo fillies stks at Thirsk Aug 2: recent all the way winner of a fillies mdn at Nottingham: very eff over 6/7f on fast grd: related to a winner in the USA: acts on any trk: likes to be up with the pace:'improving and should not be opposed lightly.   70

*1604 DUNNINALD [2] (I Balding) 2-9-2 A Murray 5/2: 12: Broke well and made most: lacked pace of smart winner tho' should be back in the winner's enclosure soon: see 1604.   53

995 UPPER [4] (E Weymes) 2-9-2 E Guest(3) 11/2: 123: Ran to her best despite fair abs: stays 6f: see 995 & 818.   51

*1561 KALAS IMAGE [6] (G Moore) 2-9-2 A Mackay 25/1: 3230314: Front rank most of way: not disgraced in this much btr company: see 1561.   45

*1668 SHINING WATER [1] 2-9-5 R Hills 9/4 JT FAV: 42110: Never going well: clearly well below her best today: see 1668.   36

1683 LOUVANKAL [3] 2-8-11 L Charnock 100/1: 00: Sn behind: see 1683.   08

6 ran   5,½,2,4,7   (John Bray)   R Armstrong Newmarket

1920 DIRECTORS TROPHY NURSERY H'CAP 2YO   £2624   7f   Firm 08 -25 Slow   [60]

1174 INSHIRAH [2] (H T Jones) 2-7-13 R Hills 4/1: 101: 2 gr f Caro - Endurable Heights (Graustark) Useful filly: led below dist, comfortably, in a nursery h'cap at Thirsk Aug 2: won a stks race at Ripon on her debut tho' missed the break on her subsequent start: American bred filly who cost $260,000 as a yearling: eff over 5f, stays 7f well: acts on fast and yldg ground and on any trk: should defy a penalty.   45

1735 WENSLEYDALEWARRIOR [5] (G Moore) 2-9-7 D Casey(7) 6/1: 2011222: Another fine effort under top weight, stayed on well to take the minor honours: see 1735 & 1203.   57

1307 BORN FREE AGAIN [4] (L Piggott) 2-8-7 T Lucas 7/2: 00203: Made most: stays 7f: see 1225.   42

*1483 EL BE DOUBLEYOU [1] (N Callaghan) 2-7-13 L Charnock 10/3 FAV: 02014: Btr when winning a seller in 1483 (stiff trk).   33

*1740 DUNLIN [3] 2-8-3(5ex) J Lowe 4/1: 12310: Below par eff: see 1740 (6f stiff trk)   29
1534 BEAU BENZ [6] 2-7-8(bl)(1ow)(2oh) A Mackay 7/1: 000400: Misbehaved in stalls and
no chance when stumbled below dist: best on a gall trk in 1175.   14
1478 LATERAL [7] 2-7-9 M Fry 20/1: 2000200: Twice below form shown in 1333 (5f stiff trk).   00
7 ran   4,nk,¼,4,3,12   (Hamdan Al-Maktoum)   H T Jones Newmarket~

1921 BEDALE STAKES 3YO   £2262   1m   Firm 08 -47 Slow

--   ALFARAZDQ [3] (A Stewart) 3-8-11 R Hills 5/4: -1: 3 ch c Exclusive Native - Bold
Bikini (Boldnesian) Nicely bckd and made a successful racecourse debut, led over 2f out for
an easy win in a slowly run 3yo stks at Thirsk Aug 2: cost $400,000 as a yearling and is
a half brother to numerous winners, including Irish Derby winner Law Society: eff over 1m,
will stay further: acts on firm grd and on a sharpish course: seems certain to rate more highly   38
1220 MOORE STYLISH [5] (R Armstrong) 3-8-8 P Tulk 1/1 FAV: -002: Not qckn dist: may
prove better over a slightly longer trip: see 1220 & 371.   22
1677 HARLEYFORD LAD [4] (Denys Smith) 3-8-11 L Charnock 8/1: 0-00003: Nicely bckd: early
leader: maiden who has yet to show any worthwhile form: acts on fast ground.   13
--   DIALECT [2] (Don Enrico Incisa) 3-8-8 M Beecroft 50/1: -4: Never dangerous on debut:
half sister to a couple of winners.   00
1614 BERRY STREET [6] 3-8-8 J Quinn(5) 66/1: -00: Made most, wknd quickly: half sister
to a couple of winning sprinters.   00
5 ran   5,6,6,2   (Hamdan Al-Maktoum)   A Stewart Newmarket

1922 BRADFORD STAKES (H'CAP)(0-50) 3YO   £2939   7f   Firm 08 -15 Slow   [54]

1224 IRISH PASSAGE [2] (D Barron) 3-8-1 S Webster 12/1: -02D001: 3 gr g Welsh Captain -
Honey's Queen (Pals Passage) Responded to press to lead on line in a 3yo h'cap at Thirsk
Aug 2: won his only start last season, a stks race at Ripon: eff over 6/8f: well suited by
fast grd and seems best on a sharpish course.   36
*1626 BILLS AHEAD [4] (G Moore) 3-7-9(6ex) N Carlisle 9/2: 4044412: Just failed to make
all: in gd form and likes this sharpish trk: see 1626.   30
+1627 ROPER ROW [1] (M H Easterby) 3-8-1(6ex) J Lowe 9/4 FAV: 20-0113: Well bckd: not
btn far over this longer trip: runs well here: see 1627.   34
1371 TRICK OR TREAT [3] (J Watts) 3-8-11(VIS) N Connorton 13/2: 00-1444: Close 4th,
clear rem: see 518.   42
1758 TRY HARDER [6] 3-8-13 A Murray 8/1: 0-00340: No extra dist: best 1532.   36
1664 SEQUESTRATOR [9] 3-7-13 A Mackay 9/1: -000100: Twice below form shown in 1316.   20
1524 VILTASH [7] 3-9-2 M Wood 9/1: 0-00300: Al behind: best 1044 (6f): see 671.   00
1028 TOPPESHAMME [8] 3-9-7 E Guest(3) 7/1: 311-000: No form this term: see 478.   00
*1515 FAR TOO BUSY [5] 3-7-7(2oh) M Fry 6/1: -00010: Dwelt and al behind: much btr 1515.   00
9 ran   shthd,¾,¾,4,1,2,8   (T Wilson)   D Barron Maunby, Yorks.

Official Going Given As GOOD

1923 BROOKE BOND COFFEE CUP AMATEURS   £2269   1m 4f   Good/Firm 25 -11 Slow

1538 VAGADOR [9] (G Harwood) 3-10-8 Amanda Harwood(5) 6/1: -101: 3 ch c Vaguely Noble -
Louisa D'Or (Indian Hemp) Useful colt: led after 1m for a comfortable win in an amateur
riders event at Newmarket Aug 2: first time out won a mdn at Folkestone: well suited by 12f,
may stay further: acts well on a sound surface: prob acts on any trk.   57
-1437 SHIBIL [6] (M Stoute) 3-10-4 Maxine Juster 10/11 FAV: -443222: Well bckd: held when
carried left final 1f: has had numerous chances and is proving disapp: btr 1437, see 1022.   47
--   BUCKLEY [2] (L Cumani) 3-10-4 Sara Cumani(5) 14/1: -3: Ev ch final 2f: fin 4th,
placed 3rd: promising racecourse debut from this half brother to numerous winners: stays
12f well: acts on gd/firm grd and a gall trk and should have no trouble finding a race.   46
+1578 OSRIC [4] (M Ryan) 3-10-10 Mr J Ryan 4/1: -412D: Ev ch final 2f: hung left, fin
2nd placed 4th: stays 12f: on the upgrade: see 1578.   53
1417 BERNISH LADY [8] 5-10-12 Mr E Mcmahon 66/1: -0400: Sn prom: prob stays 12f: see 1015.   27
1831 MERHI [11] 3-10-4 Mr R Hutchinson 16/1: 4300030: Ev ch: btr 1831, see 698 (10f).   25
*1620 SARYAN [14] 3-11-2 Mr T Thomson Jones 8/1: 0-04110: Well below form 1620.   00
1652 Sparklin Performer [7] 10-4   --   Well Wisher [13] 11-1
--   High Forest [5] 11-1   1590 Pelegrin [15] 11-1(BL)
1432 Arrow Express [3] 10-4   --   Liberated Girl [1] 10-12
984 Rosanna Of Tedfold [10] 10-12   --   The Berwick [12] 11-1
15 ran   2,hd,¼,8,3   (K Abdulla)   G Harwood Pulborough, Sussex

1924 MAIL ON SUNDAY 3YO SERIES HCAP 0-60   £4123   1m   Good/Firm 25 +02 Fast   [62]

1486 NIGHT OUT PERHAPS [5] (G Wragg) 3-9-7 P Robinson 11/1: 0-11401: 3 b c Cure The Blues -
Pipina (Sir Gaylord) Very useful colt: defied top weight, led inside final 1f, ridden out
in a 3yo h'cap at Newmarket Aug 22: in gd form this season: earlier winning at Chester and
again at Newmarket: stays 1m well: acts on gd/firm and soft ground, possibly unsuited by very
firm: no trk preferences: seems a genuine sort and carries weight well.   67

1487 SOVEREIGN LOVE [13] (W Hastings Bass) 3-7-9 G French 12/1: 3132302: Stayed on well
and just btn: fine effort and should win soon: see 15.   40
1613 RUN BY JOVE [2] (P Haslam) 3-7-7(vis) T Williams 10/1: 1200223: Ran on well and
just btn: in fine form: see 1371, 674.   37
1655 SOMETHING CASUAL [8] (A Hide) 3-8-5(bl) R Guest 4/1 FAV: -000034: Led over 7f:
gd effort but btr 1655 (C/D).   48
1444 BEAU SHER [7] 3-8-8 M Roberts 12/1: -02040: Never nearer: fair effort in this
competitive event: acts on firm and yldg: see 402.   49
*1245 BELOW ZERO [11] 3-8-4 R Cochrane 8/1: 2200010: Not btn far: in gd form: see 1245.   44
1655 CHIEF PAL [9] 3-8-12 Paul Eddery 8/1: -212340: Prom over 6f: btr 1655 (C/D), see 1486.   48
1637 MAHOGANY RUN [10] 3-8-8 M Birch 10/1: 0001020: Prom, fin 9th: btr 1637 (sharper trk)   43
1571 ARTFUL DAY [12] 3-8-2 T Ives 13/2: 04-1330: Never showed: btr 1571 (7f), see 911 (sharp).   00
*1753 REALITY [1] 3-9-2(6ex) W Ryan 6/1: 0-110: Well bckd but no show: well below 1753.   00
692 Dunloring [4] 8-2 7th   1520 Mudrik [3] 8-7   1586 Ettas Pet [6] 7-13
13 ran   nk,hd,½,1,½,½,1½,½   (E B Moller)   G Wragg Newmarket

1925 COLMANS OF NORWICH NURSERY HCAP 2YO   £10098   6f   Good/Firm 25 -08 Slow [63]

+1174 CROFTERS CLINE [6] (J Wilson) 2-8-12 Julie Bowker(7) 8/1: 01111: 2 b c Crofter -
Modena (Sassafras) Very useful, consistent colt: again made ev yard, ridden out in a
competitive and val nursery h'cap at Newmarket Aug 2: earlier made all in minor events at
Ayr, Ripon and Beverley: eff at 5f, stays 6f really well: acts on gd and firm grd and on
any trk: best forcing the pace when ridden by Julie Bowker: genuine.   61
*1082 BAG ORHYTHM [9] (J Hindley) 2-9-7 M Hills 11/1: 212: Ev ch over 1f out: anchored
by weight and this was a fine effort: should find a similar event: see 1082.   65
995 SAXON STAR [7] (J Winter) 2-8-8 B Rouse 14/1: 14443: Fin well after abs: gd effort:
consistent filly: stays 6f well: acts on gd/firm and soft ground: see 311.   52
*1770 HOMING IN [12] (G Huffer) 2-8-8(7ex) G Carter(3) 10/1: 04214: Nearest fin: another
good effort under 7lbs pen: see 1770.   51
1643 HARD ACT [10] 2-8-9 M Roberts 25/1: 011000: Kept on well and not btn far: see 1643,1057.   49
1707 FULL OF PRIDE [3] 2-8-3 M Birch 15/2: 120: Prom, ev ch: stays 6f: see 1266.   41
*1307 BUTTERFIELD ROAD [13] 2-8-12 M Wigham 4/1: 10: Well bckd: not go the early pace
and never nearer in 7th: should be suited by 7f: see 1307.   49
1552 PACIFIC BASIN [8] 2-8-5 T Ives 10/3 FAV: 02340: Gambled on but al ridden along:
btr 1552 (sharper trk) see 965.   36
*1381 MOON INDIGO [5] 2-8-9 R Cochrane 7/1: 010: Mkt drifter: no show: much btr 1381.   40
1891 PANACHE [2] 2-7-7(vis) T Williams 8/1: 3121D30: Nicely bckd: wknd: too soon after 1891?   22
1697 Peatswood Shooter [11] 8-12   1529 Hunters Leap [1] 7-7(2oh)
1643 Munaasib [4] 9-7
13 ran   1½,shthd,hd,1,½,nk,2½,hd,1   (D M Beresford)   J Wilson Tarleton, Lancs.

1926 EXETER STAKES 2YO   £4480   7f   Good/Firm 25 -20 Slow

*852 INVITED GUEST [4] (R Armstrong) 2-8-11 W Ryan 9/2: 11: 2 ch f Be My Guest - Welcome
Break (Wollow) Very useful filly: despite fair abs, led 1½f out and drew clear for an
impr. win in a val 4 runner 2yo event at Newmarket Aug 2: first time out was an easy winner
of a Lingfield mdn: very eff at 6/7f and should be suited by 1m: acts on gd/firm and yldg
and on any trk: sure to win more races.   66
1643 ACCOMPANIST [2] (B Hills) 2-8-8 M Hills 7/2: 42: Al up there: no chance with winner:
will be suited by 1m: see 1643.   51
1529 KING BALLADEER [3] (G P Gordon) 2-8-11 G Duffield 14/1: 03123: Made much: consistent:
see 1175.   53
1452 NORDAVANO [1] (M Jarvis) 2-8-8 T Ives 8/15 FAV: 24: Heavily bckd: well below form 1452:
something amiss? Deserves another chance.   38
4 ran   3,½,8   (Kinderhill Corporation)   R Armstrong Newmarket

1927 COBNUT CLAIMING STAKES 3YO   £3563   6f   Good/Firm 25 +01 Fast

1827 MISS TONILEE [10] (D H Jones) 3-8-0(bl) D Williams(7) 12/1: -322431: 3 b f Malinowski -
Miss Sandman (Manacle) Led nearing final 1f and forged clear in a 3yo claimer at Newmarket
Aug 2: consistent filly and this was a deserved first win: eff at 6f, stays 1m: acts on gd/
firm and soft ground and a gall trk.   24
-- BOLD FURY [17] (P Haslam) 3-8-13 T Williams 2/1 FAV: -2: Well bckd debutant: ran on
well: half brother to sev winners: will be well suited by further than 6f: acts on gd/firm
and a gall trk: should at least find a seller.   29
1256 LOVE AT LAST [7] (W Hastings Bass) 3-8-4 T Ives 9/2: -3333: Al prom: btr 1256 (1m).   19
1704 WEBSTERS FEAST [12] (M Mccormack) 3-9-7 W Newnes 13/2: 0000204: Led over 4f: see 1406.   28
1499 FINDON MANOR [16] 3-8-13 R Morse(5) 16/1: -000000: Never nearer: needs 7f? See 760.   17
971 LULLABY BLUES [2] 3-9-3 M Birch 5/1: 0012120: Sn prom: abs: see 890.   20
1734 The Stray Bullett [8] 8-3(bl)   1771 Touch The Sail [15] 8-6
1436 Global [14] 9-7   1425 Super Fresco [11] 9-7   -- Grange Farm Lady [3] 9-0
907 Lone Galaxie [5] 8-6   1701 Skybird [1] 9-7(bl)   -- No Bolder [6] 8-9
1257 Fudge [13] 8-6   -- Lady Slematic [4] 8-10
16 ran   3,hd,3,1,½   (K J Lewis)   D H Jones Efail Isaf, Glamorgan.

1928 EBF PEGASUS MAIDEN 2YO   £3476   6f   Good/Firm 25 -06 Slow

-- MOST WELCOME [12] (G Wragg) 2-9-0 P Robinson 10/11 FAV: 1: 2 ch c Be My Guest - Topsy (Habitat) Very promising colt: heavily bckd and led inside final 1f, showing a good turn of foot to draw 4l clear in a val 2yo mdn at Newmarket Aug 2: full brother to the smart 10/12f winner Top Guest and half brother to Rye Tops and Troytops: eff at 6f, should be suited by middle dist: acts on gd/firm ground and a gall trk: well regarded colt who will win more races.   65
-- CAPE WILD [2] (M Stoute) 2-9-0 A Kimberley 12/1: 2: Mkt drifter: led briefly final 1f: half brother to sev winners including useful 12f performer Marooned: will be suited by further than 6f: acts on gd/firm ground and a stiff trk: should have no trouble finding a mdn.   50
-- GREAT ACT [5] (C Brittain) 2-8-11 M Roberts 25/1: 3: Made much: kept on: promising effort from this full brother to the very speedy 2yo Vaigly Oh: stays 6f: acts on gd/firm ground and a stiff trk.   43
-- MAD MAX [10] (P Haslam) 2-9-0 T Williams 14/1: 4: Chance over 1f out: gd eff from this first foal: stays 6f: acts on a stiff trk and gd/firm ground.   46
1573 TAFFY TEMPLAR [6] 2-9-0 M Hills 6/1: 30: Nearest fin: gd effort: see 1573.   42
-- HENRIETTA PLACE [9] 2-8-11 W Ryan 33/1: 0: Unfancied: gd late hdwy and improvement very likely: cheaply acquired yearling whose sire was a smart sprinter: acts on gd/firm.   38
-- KIROWAN [4] 2-9-0 G Carter(3) 33/1: 0: Prom, fin 7th on racecourse debut: half brother to 2 winners: should be suited by further than 6f : acts on gd/firm.   40
-- UPTOTHEHILT [11] 2-9-0 G Duffield 11/2: 0: Nicely bckd: fin 8th: first foal who cost 205,000 gns as a yearling: bred to stay 1m+ and should improve.   39
-- SCHMUTZIG [1] 2-9-0 R Guest 8/1: 0: Prom, fin 10th: cost $50,000 and should do better over further than 6f.   34
-- Portentous [7] 9-0   -- Ala Hounak [3] 9-0   1653 Tabareek [8] 8-11
12 ran   4,1½,shthd,1½,nk,½,nk,1½,nk   (E B Moller)   G Wragg Newmarket

1929 CARDINAL HANDICAP 0-60 3YO+   £4090   1m 2f Good/Firm 25 +18 Fast   [54]

1042 POWER BENDER [9] (G P Gordon) 4-8-2 W Ryan 8/1: 22-4301: 4 b g Prince Tenderfoot - Spadilla (Javelot) Bckd at long odds and led well over 1f out comfortably, in a fast run and val h'cap at Newmarket Aug 2: lightly raced this term: fin 2nd on 3 occasions in '85: seems equally eff at 8/10f: acts on a sound surf and a gall trk: should win again.   42
1792 LASTCOMER [1] (M Stoute) 3-9-0 M A Giles(7) 2/1 FAV: 1-00122: Dsptd lead inside final 2f: not pace of winner: remains in gd form: see 1792, 1468.   59
*1787 BLENDERS CHOICE [2] (K Brassey) 4-8-4(5ex) S Whitworth 4/1: 0301113: Led well over 1m: btr 1787 (easier trk).   32
1526 CHICLET [5] (P Walwyn) 4-9-2(vis) Paul Eddery 13/2: -020404: Never nearer: disapp since 432.   41
1792 MERLE [4] 4-9-1 M Roberts 14/1: 0000000: Prom, twice below form 1526.   39
-1383 AL YABIR [7] 4-9-7 B Rouse 11/2: 020-220: Something amiss? Btr judged on 1383.   15
1601 AYLESFIELD [6] 6-8-0(bl) M Hills 8/1: -000030: Wknd: much btr 1601, see 1325.   00
1450 Infantry Officer [8] 8-13
8 ran   2½,3,1½,½,15   (Addison Tool Co Ltd)   G P Gordon Newmarket

---

Official Going Given As FIRM ON THE ROUND COURSE: GOOD/FIRM ON STRAIGHT COURSE

1930 BERKSHIRE ELECTRONICS MAIDEN 2YO   £4142   6f   Good/Firm 31 -23 Slow

-- STARTLE [4] (B Hills) 2-9-0 B Thomson 12/1: 1: 2 gr c Hawaii - Star Strewn (Native Dancer): Made a highly prom. debut, leading inside final 2f readily in a mdn for unrcd 2yos at Goodwood Aug.2: half brother to very smart filly Asteroid Field: eff over 6f, sure to stay much further: acts well on fast grnd: looks sure to impr further & win in btr company.   58
-- MUMMYS LUCK [5] (R Hannon) 2-9-0 W Carson 11/1: 2: Slow start, fin in gd style & should impr substantially for the outing: half brother to speedy '84 2yo Chantaco: sprint bred but is certainly suited by 6f & may well stay further: acts on fast grnd.   46
-- MISS DAISY [2] (I Balding) 2-8-11 Pat Eddery 5/2: 3: Well bckd, prom thro'out: first foal of a 4 times winner: quite speedily bred though should stay at least 7f.   33
-- EVER SHARP [6] (L Cottrell) 2-9-0 I Johnson 14/1: 4: Ran green, likely to impr for the experience: dam a sprint winner & he himself is speedily bred.   32
-- KRISTAL ROCK [3] 2-9-0 S Cauthen 4/5 FAV: 0: Gave trouble pre-race, made much, fdd tamely & must have disapp connections: first foal of a daughter of the high class Altesse Royale: has much to learn.   22
-- DYNAMIC STAR [7] 2-9-0 A Mcglone 50/1: 0: Never in it: cheaply bought colt who may well impr in time, over lngr dists.   17
-- RANKSTREET [8] 2-8-11 P Cook 50/1: 0: Outpcd from ½way: sprint bred.   00
7 ran   4,4,1½,4,2   (Mrs G Webb Bronfman)   B Hills Lambourn, Berks

1931 RACAL CHESTERFIELD CUP HCAP 3YO+ 0-75   £16466   1m 2f Good/Firm 31 +08 Fast   [59]

1498 MAILMAN [2] (I Balding) 7-8-8 Pat Eddery 11/1: 00-4031: 7 ch g Malacate - Sallail (Sallust): Grand stable servant: returned to his best, coming from behind to lead final 1f comfortably in valuable & quite fast run Chesterfield Cup h'cap at Goodwood Aug.2: lightly raced previously this term: in '85 won at Doncaster & Lingfield: eff between 1m & 11f: acts on firm & gd grnd: goes well for a boy.   52

1383 RANA PRATAP [7] (G Lewis) 6-8-11 P Waldron 6/1: 4332042: Chall under press dist, no
extra final 100yds: see 445, 1383.   52
1657 ATOKA [3] (Lord John Fitzgerald) 4-8-3 P Cook 11/1: 0011343: Hdway on bit str, ch 2f
out, no extra : see 1526.   41
*1601 ALBERT HALL [11] (B Hills) 3-8-6 B Thomson 7/1: D221114: Not the best of runs, fin
strongly & continues to impr: remarkably consistent: see 1601.   55
1792 PATO [6] 4-8-11 W Woods(3) 25/1: 0-00040: Same place final 2f: see 511.   47
1109 KINGS HEAD [5] 4-9-10 G Starkey 15/8 FAV: 120-30: Took a very strong hold, cruised
into lead 3f out but his big weight anchored him at the dist: see 1109.   60
*1519 RUNNING FLUSH [9] 4-8-6(vis) B Crossley 20/1: 0430010: Mkt drifter, fin 7th: btr 1519. 41
1644 SULTAN MOHAMED [8] 3-8-12 W Carson 8/1: 2-12130: Fin 8th after being hmpd str: see 1462 57
1636 MASTER LINE [10] 5-8-5 C Rutter(5) 10/1: -001030: Close up most, fin 9th: much btr 1636. 37
1793 PROMISED ISLE [4] 5-9-2 T Quinn 10/1: -323140: Prom much: best 1383.   00
1498 Gundreda [1] 8-9
11 ran   2,2,shhd,1,nk,1,1½,2½   (Mrs J A McDougald)   I Balding Kingsclere, Hants

1932 GROUP 2 VODAFONE NASSAU 3YO+ FILLIES   £33045   1m 2f Good/Firm 31 +07 Fast

+1408 PARK EXPRESS [7] (J Bolger) 3-8-8 J Reid 7/1: 3042D11: 3 br f Ahonoora - Matcher
(Match III): Very smart, much impr Irish filly: sn prom & led 2f out, comfortably going clear
to win Gr.2 Nassau Stakes at Goodwood Aug.2: comfortably won Gr.2 Lancashire Oaks at Haydock
July 5 & first time out winner of a minor race at Phoenix Park: also won first time out in
'85 at Leopardstown: eff at 1m, very well suited by 10/12f nowadays: acts on any going & on
any trk: continues to impr & is a credit to her trainer.   85
926 MAYSOON [3] (M Stoute) 3-8-8 W R Swinburn 4/6 FAV: 30-1232: Waited with, hdway under
strong press final 2f: fair effort, absent since better 926.   79
926 ASTEROID FIELD [2] (B Hills) 3-8-5 B Thomson 8/1: 4-20303: Chall 2f out: best 754 (1m yld) 74
*1580 COCOTTE [5] (W Hern) 3-8-5 W Carson 12/1: 24-0014: Prom, led briefly 3f out: stiff
task & ran well: see 1580.   71
1331 ENGLISH SPRING [4] 4-9-8 S Cauthen 14/1: 4410100: Ev ch: best 1095.   75
926 TRALTHEE [1] 3-8-5 Pat Eddery 5/1: 31-100: Absent since 926 and twice below 661(yld/soft). 61
1128 TENDER LOVING CARE [6] 3-8-5(BL) P Cook 33/1: 120-000: Bl first time, made much:
highly tried this season: in '85 a winner at Sandown: eff at 7f on firm grnd, on a stiff trk. 00
7 ran   3,nk,1,1,5   (Patrick H Burns)   J Bolger Ireland

1933 ALBERT STAKES HANDICAP 3YO+ 0-60   £4877   6f   Good/Firm 31 +02 Fast   [58]

*1285 MANIMSTAR [8] (P Makin) 6-9-10 J Reid 6/1: 0000211: 6 b h Martinmas - Reddish
Radish (Red God): Very useful sprinter: winning 2nd valuable h'cap on the trot, coming from
behind to lead 1f out, cleverly at Goodwood Aug.2: easy winner of similar h'cap at Newmarket June 28: in '85 won twice at Newmarket & also at Newbury: best form over 6f: acts
on firm & yld: best with waiting tactics: wore a visor last term but running well at present
without one.   67
1391 COMPLEAT [5] (G Lewis) 3-8-7 P Waldron 4/1 JT FAV: 1-00032: Well bckd, al there though
not the best of runs final 1f: only narrowly btn & is back to form: see 314.   54
1608 ROYSIA BOY [6] (G P Gordon) 6-8-5 W Carson 4/1 JT FAV: 1-00003: Well bckd, chall
1f out in a close fin & is back to his best: see 952.   43
--   NUMISMATIST [2] (M Francis) 7-8-8 R Street 25/1: 31204-4: Gd fin on belated seasonal
debut: winner at Goodwood & also a valuable h'cap at Ripon in '85: best form at 6f on gd
or firm grnd: suited by waiting tactics: should go well next time.   43
1654 PRECIOUS METAL [4] 3-9-3 R Curant 8/1: 0-10300: Led/dsptd lead most: see 657.   56
-1730 LONELY STREET [1] 5-7-7(2oh) N Adams 5/1: 2020320: Speed most: btr 5f? see 1730.   24
1730 FERRYMAN [3] 10-8-13 A Mcglone 9/1: 0012140: Made most: best 1461.   00
1151 FLYAWAY BRIDE [7] 3-8-13 Pat Eddery 7/1: 1-00200: Early speed: lightly raced and
twice below 732.   00
8 ran   ½,½,1,1,nk   (S H J Brewer)   P Makin Ogbourne Maisey, Wilts

1934 SURPLICE STAKES 3YO   £4306   1m   Good/Firm 31 -05 Slow

1854 BRONZE OPAL [2] (G Balding) 3-9-0 R Weaver 20/1: -000101: 3 br c Guilty Conscience -
Countless Babu (Bronze Babu): Useful, fast impr colt: came from behind to lead dist & readily
sprinted 6L clear to win a 3yo minor race at Goodwood Aug.2: comfortable winner of an app.mdn
at Warwick July 9: highly tried on other occasions this season: half brother to several
winners: very eff over 1m: acts on firm & yld: sure to go well in a h'cap next time.   60
--   TAVIRI [10] (G Harwood) 3-9-0 A Clark 16/1: -2: Slow start, kept on well str & will
impr greatly for the experience: related to several winners abroad: should stay beyond 1m:
acts on fast ground: likely to be a different proposition next time.   46
*1541 ESFAHAN [3] (J Dunlop) 3-9-2 Pat Eddery 9/1: -02013: Led briefly 2f out, outpcd by
the winner: stays 1m: gd effort: see 1541.   48
*1628 LOCAL SILVER [9] (W Hern) 3-9-5 W Carson 4/1: 0-014: Ev ch: see 1628.   51
1586 CANESARA [5] 3-8-11 S Cauthen 9/2: -30: Heavily bckd: fdd final 1f & btr 1586.   35
1776 PRINCE ORAC [6] 3-9-0 G Baxter 100/30 FAV: -30: Ev ch: btr 1776 (10f).   37
*1607 CODICES [11] 3-9-5 G Starkey 6/1: 40-0010: Made much, fin 7th & btr 1607 (7f).   00
*1436 GAELIC FLUTTER [7] 3-9-5 W R Swinburn 7/1: 00-3010: Prom much, fin 8th: much btr 1436. 00
438 Al Diwan [8] 9-0(BL)   -- Highblest [1] 9-0   407 Farncombe [4] 9-0(VIS)
11 ran   6,shhd,shhd,5,½   (Mrs Ernest Weinstein)   G Balding fyfield, Hants

GOODWOOD   Saturday August 2nd   -Cont'd

1935 TRUNDLE STAKES HANDICAP 3YO+ 0-60   £4752   1m 4f   Good/Firm 31 -13 Slow   [54]

1412 ISLAND SET [3] (L Cumani) 4-9-1 Pat Eddery 5/6 FAV: 11-0221: 4 b c Hawaii - Desk Set
(Tom Rolfe): Useful colt: heavily bckd & comfortably came from behind to lead 1f out in quite
a valuable h'cap at Goodwood Aug.2: a deserved success after 2 narrow defeats: winner at
Goodwood (again) & Yarmouth on final 2 outings in '85: eff 10f, possibly even btr suited
by 12f nowadays: suited by firm or gd grnd: may win again.   52
1559 VINTAGE PORT [1] (R Akehurst) 4-7-11 W Carson 12/1: -000002: Nicely bckd at long odds,
led 2f out & battled on well: best effort yet in this country & should be winning soon: see 653   30
1519 PACTOLUS [6] (G Harwood) 3-8-6 W Woods(3) 15/2: 10-0123: Ev ch: see 1349.   48
1523 THE JOKER [8] (G Dalding) 6-8-12 R Weaver 25/1: -04004: Same place final 4f: see 1000.   35
1523 FOLK DANCE [8] 4-9-1 S Cauthen 13/2: -442020: Prom much, btr 1523.   38
1755 FOR A LARK [5] 4-7-9 C Rutter(5) 13/2: 0-00030: Btr 1755 (10f).   14
1237 Rusty Law [7] 9-7   1533 Standard Breakfast [2] 7-10
8 ran   2,1½,4,hd,2½   (G Keller)   L Cumani Newmarket

WINDSOR   Saturday August 2nd   Figure 8, Sharpish Track

Official Going Given As GOOD/FIRM (STRAIGHT: GOOD)

1936 SPRINGFIELD 2YO C&G STAKES   £976   6f   Good/Firm 29 +06 Fast

--   CENTAURI [7] (B Hills) 2-8-11 B Thomson 7/1: 1: 2 b c Star De Naskra - How Charming
(What Luck): Promising colt: led below dist for an impressive debut win in a fast run 2yo
stakes at Windsor Aug.2: American bred colt who fetched $175,000 as a yearling and is a
half brother to a winner in the States: clearly very eff over 6f on gd/firm grnd: acts on
a sharpish trk: should win more races.   48
*1612 JUVENILEDELINQUENT [9] (A Bailey) 2-9-4 R Carter(5) 10/1: 12: Caught a tartar here
though is impr & should be winning again soon: stays 6f well: acts on a sharp trk: see 1612.   40
1814 FOURWALK [8] (N Macauley) 2-9-4 W Wharton 25/1: 0241003: Made most: best effort to
date & is well suited by forcing tactics: see 1397.   39
*1555 BOLD GARCON [3] (C Nelson) 2-9-4 J Reid 3/1: 014: Another gd effort: see 1555.   38
--   SPANISH CALM [13] 2-8-11 M Rimmer 20/1: 0: No extra dist though a sound debut: cost
23,000 gns & is a half brother to several winners, incl last years useful juvenile Priory
Place: acts on gd/firm grnd: can only improve.   31
--   UNIFORMITY [6] 2-8-11 W R Swinburn 7/1: 0: Late prog on debut: sprint bred colt who
cost 44,000 gns as a yearling: acts on gd/firm grnd: should make some impr next time.   21
1653 WHAT A GUY [16] 2-8-11 G Carter(3) 16/1: 400: Al prom: fin 7th: see 1512.   20
1629 MUAD DIB [4] 2-8-11 P Cook 3/1 JT FAV: 230: Nicely bckd: close up till bridle broke
2f out: btr judged on his promising run in 1629.   00
--   Whitridge [2] 8-11   1458 Ta Wardle [14] 8-11   1629 Jocks Brother [11] 8-11
--   Shannon River [5] 8-11   1162 Battle Sting [19] 8-11
*1672 Sands Of Time [12] 8-11   --   Castle Tryst [10] 8-11
--   Lyrical Lover [17] 8-11   --   Blico [15] 8-11
1552 Woodman Weaver [18] 8-11   1598 Timurtasch [1] 8-11
19 ran   4,hd,½,ddht,3,½,2,shhd   (Sheikh Mohammed)   B Hills Lambourn, Berks

1937 HARCOURT SELLING STAKES 3&4YO   £952   1m   Good/Firm 10 -10 Slow

1063 HACHIMITSU [9] (S Mellor) 3-8-3 M Wigham 16/1: -000001: 3 ch f Vaigly Great -
Spanish Ribbon (Pieces of Eight): Ran on under press to lead close home in a 3 & 4yo seller
at Windsor Aug.2 (bought in 1,450 gns): first success and had shown no worthwhile form in
this grade previously: stays 1m: acts on gd/firm grnd & seems suited by a sharp trk.   13
1521 SPARKFORD LAD [17] (D Elsworth) 4-9-0(bl) Debbie Wheatley(7) 9/1: 0000002: Btr effort
in this lower grade: led below dist, just caught: stays 1m: acts on gd & fast grnd: see 495.   13
1558 JUST CANDID [20] (D Wilson) 4-9-0 W Newnes 14/1: 000-003: Ev ch: quite lightly raced
mdn who ran her best race for sometime here: eff over 1m on gd/firm grnd.   09
1815 GREENHILLS BOY [15] (M Ryan) 3-8-6 N Day 12/1: -004: Lightly raced gelding who seems
eff over 1m on gd/firm grnd.   09
1783 SONG AN DANCE MAN [10] 3-8-11 R Wernham 9/1: 4000000: Mkt drifter despite being
dropped in class: led briefly 2f out: see 116.   13
1784 GULPHAR [1] 4-9-0 J Williams 8/1: 40-0000: Nearest fin: see 1103.   03
1319 FORT DUCHESNE [4] 4-9-5 R Carter(5) 9/1: 0-00000: Fin 7th: see 1319.   00
1567 BEE KAY ESS [8] 3-8-6 J Reid 8/1: -400: Made much: wknd into 8th: see 1210.   00
1666 EASTER RAMBLER [3] 4-9-5(vis) A Dicks(7) 7/2: 0000300: Led/dsptd lead over ½way:
best in 1439 (C/D).   00
1607 ANTHONY GERARD [16] 3-8-6 Pat Eddery 2/1 FAV: 0-00: Well bckd: led 3f out: dropped
in class here: half brother to several winners & should do btr than this.   00
1567 Saravanta [7] 8-11   1256 Run Charlie [13] 8-6   1690 Trojan Splash [18] 8-6
1549 Blue Fantasy [14] 8-3   1784 Clap Your Hands [12] 8-3
1691 Condover Silk [6] 8-3   1364 Miss Comedy [2] 8-3(BL)
17 ran   shhd,2,1,½,1½   (Mrs B Taylor)   S Mellor Lambourn, Berks

581

1938 ROBERT WILMOT NURSERY H'CAP 2YO   £2131   5f   Good/Firm 29 +11 Fast   [45]

1693 MUKHABBR [2] (C Benstead) 2-7-8 T Williams 7/2 JT FAV: 03031: 2 b c Taufan -
Ribotingo (Petingo): Comfortably made all in a fast run nursery h'cap at Windsor Aug.2:
quite cheaply bought colt who is a half brother to very useful sprinter Pampas: eff over 5f
& should stay 6f: well suited by fast grnd & a sharpish trk: does well with forcing tactics.   35
1161 INFANTA MARIA [10] (N Vigors) 2-8-13 P Cook 12/1: 0202: No ch with runaway winner
though kept on well under press: see 882.   34
1632 BERTRADE [8] (P Makin) 2-8-12 Pat Eddery 9/2: 403243: Placed again: see 1632.   30
1828 GLORY BEE [5] (L Holt) 2-7-12 W Carson 7/2 JT FAV: 01004: Speed over ½way: best in 1262. 13
1585 PINK PUMPKIN [9] 2-7-7(1oh) L Riggio(7) 4/1: 0020140: Had ev ch: best in 1496 (seller). 05
*1557 SWIFT PURCHASE [5] 2-8-8 B Rouse 12/1: 300010: Mkt drifter: never nearer: btr 1557.   10
1568 RIMBEAU [1] 2-9-1 A Clark 10/1: 4241000: Early speed: fin 7th: disapp since 717.   00
1550 MR MUMBLES [11] 2-8-13 J Williams 6/1: 0040: Fin last: much btr in 1550 (C/D).   00
1162 Jah Bless [7] 9-7   1585 Paris Guest [4] 9-1   1785 Miss Marjorie [6] 7-7
11 ran   6,1,1½,1,5,shhd,1½   (Hamdan Al-Maktoum)   C Benstead Epsom, Surrey

1939 KINGSBURY H'CAP 3YO+ 0-50   £2674   1m 3f   Good/Firm 29 -02 Slow   [39]

1468 WISHLON [1] (R Smyth) 3-9-6 Pat Eddery 5/2 FAV: -101001: 3 b c Lyphard's Wish -
swiss Swish (Wajima): Useful colt: led 2f out, comfortably in a h'cap at Windsor Aug.2:
earlier won a 3yo h'cap over this C/D & first time out won at Warwick: eff at 10f, stays 12f:
acts on firm & soft grnd & on any trk, though likes Windsor.   56
*1733 TEBITTO [7] (N Vigors) 3-8-9(5ex) P Cook 7/2: 0-01012: Led 3f out: in grand form: see 1733. 39
1481 CURVACEOUS [8] (M Stoute) 3-9-2 W R Swinburn 11/2: -0433: Ev ch str: gd effort: see 1481. 45
912 PRINCE SATIRE [3] (M Jarvis) 3-8-13 P Hutton(7) 20/1: -0104: Abs: never nearer:
stays 12f: acts on gd/firm & hvy grnd: see 492.   38
1523 GOLDEN TRIANGLE [4] 5-8-3 S Whitworth 20/1: 01-0000: Ev ch: see 1523.   06
1685 CRAMMING [10] 3-8-5 M Wigham 10/1: 1230230: Fdd final 3f: btr 1685: see 1179.   19
1085 SHIRLSTAR TAXSAVER [11] 3-8-2 W Carson 6/1: 0-04000: Nicely bckd, but no show: btr 1085. 00
1663 TICKFORD [5] 3-9-7 G Starkey 7/2: 1-431D0: Al rear: well below 1663.   00
1633 Moon Jester [2] 8-5   1240 Miss Monroe [6] 8-9(BL)
1667 Cindie Girl [12] 8-13   -- Giovanni [9] 7-10
12 ran   2,nk,2½,7,1   (K Abdulla)   R Smyth Epsom, Surrey

1940 WESTMEAD SPRINT H'CAP 3YO+ 0-35   £1557   5f   Good/Firm 29 +03 Fast   [31]

1687 PENDOR DANCER [12] (K Ivory) 3-8-10(vis) G Baxter 15/2: 3000101: 3 b f Piaffer -
Bounding (Forlorn River): In fine form & made ev yd, driven out in a h'cap at Windsor Aug.2:
earlier won a 3yo event at Bath: eff at 5f, does stay 6f: acts on gd & firm grnd & on
any trk: best out in front wearing a visor.   28
1171 HILMAY [2] (W Charles) 4-8-1(1ow) P Cook 4/1 JT FAV: 0304032: Prom all the way: see 1171. 09
1584 MISS KNOW ALL [3] (B Hills) 3-9-7 B Thomson 6/1: 10-0003: Ran on final 1f: see 624.   30
1319 HILDALARIOUS [5] (M Bolton) 4-7-7(4oh) G Carter(3) 25/1: 00-0004: Rank outsider: best
effort yet: eff at 5f on good/firm and a shrpish track.   00
*1319 BELLE TOWER [1] 4-9-9 C Rutter(5) 8/1: 0210010: Never nearer: see 1319 (6f).   23
1367 FREMONT BOY [4] 4-8-10 W Carson 4/1 JT FAV: 0-23040: Never nearer: best 679.   09
1730 FARMER JOCK [13] 4-9-1(bl) S Whitworth 8/1: 3021000: No show: best 1542.   00
1227 BINCLEAVES [6] 8-9-6 Paul Eddery 8/1: 0-01400: Fin in rear: best early season in 182. 00
1542 Miss Metal Woods [8] 7-13   1649 High Eagle [7] 8-11
1827 Paddington Belle [10] 8-4(vis)   1344 Sharad [11] 7-7(vis)(1oh)
1521 Linton Starchy [9] 7-12
13 ran   2,1½,1½,shhd,hd   (Mrs P A Brown)   K Ivory Radlett, herts

1941 LYNWOOD STAKES 3YO   £959   1m 2f   Good/Firm 29 -11 Slow

1645 BOON POINT [11] (J Dunlop) 3-8-10 Pat Eddery 4/1: 3-03001: 3 br c Shirley Heights -
Brighthelmstone (Prince Regent): Led nearing final 1f, comfortably in a 3yo stakes at
Windsor Aug.2: earlier ran well over 13f when 3rd to White Clover at Newbury: eff at 10f,
stays further: acts on gd & firm grnd & on any trk.   51
1630 RED SHOES [1] (W Hern) 3-8-7 W Carson 5/2: 0-30322: Made much: consistent but lacks
foot: see 1630, 458.   43
+1602 WAAJIB [8] (A Stewart) 3-9-3 M Roberts 4/5 FAV: 02-213: Heavily bckd: ev ch: 7L
clear of rem: stays 10f: see 1602.   50
-- PYJAMA PARTY [3] (J Dunlop) 3-8-7 G Baxter 14/1: -4: Nicely bckd: never nearer:
stable mate of winner & should impr: half sister to the useful 12f h'capper Diabolical
Liberty: should be suited by 10f plus: acts on gd/firm.   28
1444 MISSELFORE [6] 3-8-7 Paul Eddery 50/1: 00-000: Ev ch str: best effort yet from this
lightly raced filly: stays 10f: acts on gd/firm & a sharpish trk.   21
1031 CAVALEUSE [7] 3-8-7 P Cook 50/1: 0-00: Never in it: abs since 1031 & has been very
lightly raced: half sister to 2 winners.   11
1554 La Muscade [5] 8-7   1831 Soft Shoe Shuffle [4] 8-10
849 Ikraam [4] 8-10   1451 Lyns Girl [9] 8-7(BL)   1256 Super Sihlouette [10] 8-7
11 ran   2½,2,7,2½,4   (Nathan M Avery)   J Dunlop Arundel, Sussex

1942 TWISS APPRENTICES H'CAP (0-35) 3YO+   £960   7f   Good/Firm 25 +01 Fast

1013 GOLDEN BEAU [9] (D Morley) 4-9-0 Dale Gibson 4/1: -033301: 4 b g Crimson Beau - Kantado (Saulingo): Waited with, produced to lead close home in an app. h'cap at Folkestone Aug.4: failed to win last season though in '84 successful at Yarmouth, Brighton & Epsom: best form around 7/8f: acts on fast & soft grnd & on any trk, though runs well on a sharp, undulating one.   26

1165 HATCHING [5] (L Cottrell) 5-8-3 D Meade 33/1: 0000-02: Led early & again below dist: lightly raced this term: sole success came at Carlisle in '84: eff over 6/7f: acts on any going.   12

1836 ROYAL BERKS [3] (L Cottrell) 3-8-2 T Lang 6/1: 0-00043: Ev ch: stays 7f: see 1836.   15

1609 SPARKLER SPIRIT [7] (R Akehurst) 5-7-10 G Bardwell 7/2 JT FAV: 000-024: Fitted with a visor: al close up, no extra close home: see 1609.   01

1727 HOPEFUL KATIE [4] 4-8-7 S Gregory(5) 7/2 JT FAV: 0203030: Some late prog: see 65.   11

1649 TAGORE [6] 4-8-4(1ow) L Johnsey 16/1: 0000-00: Made much: no extra dist: mdn who showed no worthwhile form last term: acts on gd/firm.   07

1460 FAST SERVICE [8] 7-9-10 P Skelton(5) 5/1: 0000240: Wknd into 7th: btr in 1346.   00

1540 Son Of Sparkler [2] 8-11(VIS)   1364 Haj [1] 7-11
9 ran   1,2,shhd,nk,nk   (D R Hunnisett)   D Morley Newmarket

1943 WAKEFIELD FILLIES H'CAP (0-35) 3YO   £1375   6f   Good/Firm 25 -07 Slow   [39]

1541 MARCREDEA [9] (D Murray Smith) 3-8-13 R Wernham 6/1: -0201: 3 gr f Godswalk - Marcrest (On Your Mark): Led below dist & ridden out to win a 3yo fillies h'cap at Folkestone Aug.4: first success: eff over 6/7f on gd or faster grnd: acts on any trk.   35

1669 SNAP DECISION [6] (R Hannon) 3-9-5 L Jones(5) 9/1: 00-0402: Kept on well: stays 6f :see 1033. 33

1399 REPORT EM [8] (M Jarvis) 3-8-7 W Woods(3) 20/1: -0002: Fin in gd style, ddht for 2nd place: impr effort from this lightly raced filly: cost $25,000 and is a half sister to numerous winners: will be well suited by 7f: acts on gd/firm.   21

1476 JIANNA [12] (G Lewis) 3-8-3 M L Thomas 4/1 JT FAV: 40-0024: Al close up: stays 6f.   16

835 ACLIA [14] 3-9-2 P Cook 13/2: -0030: Abs: made most: should stay 6f though best over 5f in 835: acts on gd & firm grnd & on any trk.   23

837 TUMBLE FAIR [4] 3-8-13 S Cauthen 4/1 JT FAV: 014-000: Speed over ½way: see 340.   16

1669 UPHORIA [1] 3-9-7 M Lynch(5) 11/2: 20-4030: Early speed: much btr in 1669.   00

1695 NANOR [11] 3-8-8 C Rutter(5) 8/1: 0001300: Al behind: best in 1574 (seller).   00

1316 Megadyne [7] 8-0   1751 Five Quarters [13] 7-13
1346 Tina Rosa [5] 7-7(3oh)   1849 Fancy Pages [10] 8-0   -- Sea Shanty [3] 7-12(1ow)
1451 Straightaway Star [15] 7-10   1499 Thal Sky [2] 7-8(BL)(1ow)(7oh)
15 ran   2,ddht,nk,2,1½   (J Coleman)   D Murray Smith Upper Lambourn, Berks

1944 DUNGENESS SELLING STAKES 2YO   £961   6f   Good/Firm 25 -80 Slow

1723 THE CHIPPENHAM MAN [3] (M Tompkins) 2-8-11 R Cochrane 4/1: 0221: 2 b c Young Man - Betty's Bid (Auction Ring): Led over ½way & ralled gamely to get up in the final strides of a slowly run 2yo seller at Folkestone Aug.4 (no bid): eff over 5/6f on fast grnd: suited by a sharp/easy trk.   26

1802 OUT ON A FLYER [2] (D Elsworth) 2-8-8 A Mcglone 8/11 FAV: 002: Looked sure to land the odds when going clear dist, caught near fin: should certainly have won here on form shown in 1604.   22

1782 NIGHTDRESS [1] (D Morley) 2-8-8 B Rouse 33/1: 003: Dropped in class: ran on from ½way and more at home in this grade: cheaply bought filly who is a half sister to several winners: eff over 6f on gd/firm grnd.   17

1803 MUSICAL CHORUS [6] (G Blum) 2-8-8(bl) C Rutter(5) 10/1: 0030244: Quite consistent though remains a mdn: see 1599.   14

602 DEINOPUS [4] 2-8-11 S Cauthen 9/2: 000: No threat after fair abs: cheaply acquired colt who is bred to be suited by sprint distances.   08

1692 RANT ON [5] 2-8-11 P Waldron 20/1: 0000: Al behind: well btn in all starts: see 1692.   00
6 ran   hd,1½,½,3,15   (J M Ratcliffe)   M Tompkins Newmarket

1945 OAKLANDS HANDICAP STAKES (0-35) 3YO+   £1438   1m 4f   Good/Firm 25 +06 Fast   [24]

*1747 JABARABA [7] (L Cottrell) 5-9-0 T Lang(7) 11/2: -000411: 5 b g Raja Baba - Time To Step (Time Tested): In gd form, led below dist for an easy win in quite a fast run h'cap at Folkestone Aug.4: recently won an app h'cap at Chepstow: eff over 10/12f: acts on any grnd though suited by a sound surface: no trk preferences.   20

-- WASSEM [8] (J Jenkins) 5-8-5 J Williams 33/1: 04/00-2: Stayed on strongly, comfortably beating rem: mdn on the Flat though successful last Winter over timber & should enjoy further successes in that sphere: stays well: acts on firm & soft grnd.   05

1559 HEIGHT OF SUMMER [14] (D Arbuthnot) 5-8-7 N Adams 9/1: 0-04003: Led/dsptd lead thro'out. 00

1871 KERRY MAY SING [4] (M Ryan) 3-9-3 R Cochrane 14/1: -000004: Ran on same pace: stays 12f20

1559 NASKRACKER [3] 3-9-7 A Clark 4/1 FAV: 0-00020: No extra dist: btr in 1559 (C/D).   23

1739 G G MAGIC [11] 3-8-9 B Rouse 9/1: 0304200: Wknd below dist: see 380.   07

1290 WILLOW GORGE [1] 3-9-4 P Waldron 5/1: -0000: Dropped in class: never beyond mid-div: lightly raced colt who is a half brother to a couple of winners: bred to be suited by middle dists.   00

1694 ASTICOT [9] 4-9-4 P Cook 15/2: -030240: Wknd into 7th: see 984.   00
1273 Disport [5] 8-11   1558 Thatchingly [12] 9-6   1837 Morvern [6] 8-6
1558 Ravenscraig [13] 8-1   1686 Boca West [2] 8-5
13 ran 2,4,hd,½,2½   (John Boswell)   L Cottrell Dulford, Devon

1946 E.B.F. DEEDES MDN 2YO STAKES   £1350   5f   Good/Firm 25 -49 Slow

-- SHAIKIYA [7] (R F Johnson Houghton) 2-8-11 S Cauthen 11/10 FAV: 1: 2 b f Bold Lad -
Shaiyra (Reiko): Prom filly: showed a fine turn of foot to lead inside dist, easily in a
slowly run 2yo mdn at Folkestone Aug.4: speedily bred filly who is a half sister to a
couple of winners: will have no problem getting 6f: acts on gd/firm grnd & on a sharpish
course: can only improve.   45
1552 ATRAYU [6] (R Hannon) 2-8-11 B Rouse 7/1: 02: Led after ½way: no answer to
winners strong burst: cost 5,800 gns & is a half sister to 7/8f winner Heavenly Hoofer:
will stay 6f: acts on gd/firm.   36
1844 EBONY PRIDE [5] (Pat Mitchell) 2-8-11 R Cochrane 8/1: 0403: Ran on well & should be
suited by another furlong: acts on fast grnd & on a sharp/easy trk.   35
1668 FRIVOLOUS LADY [4] (P Cook 14/1: 44: No extra close home: see 1668.   29
1762 HAILEYS RUN [8] 2-9-0(BL) P Waldron 5/1: 4303340: Ev ch: quite consistent: see 1475. 23
1826 LITTLE LOCHETTE [2] 2-8-11 J Williams 50/1: 00: Led over ½way: cost 13,500 gns as
a yearling and is a half sister to a couple of winning sprinters.   18
746 TANGALOOMA [3] 2-8-11 B Crossley 9/2: 340: Abs: early speed: see 746.   00
1803 Gone For It [9] 8-11   -- Magnolia Express [1] 9-0
9 ran   1½,hd,2,3,½,½,1   (H H Aga Khan)   R F Johnson Houghton Didcot, Oxon

1947 HYTHE MAIDEN STAKES 3YO   £768   6f   Good/Firm 25 -43 Slow

1147 BOOFY [1] (C Nelson) 3-9-0 I Johnson 8/1: -224001: 3 b c Mummy's Pet - Home Fire
(Firestreak): Gained an overdue win, ran on strongly to lead inside dist in a 3yo mdn at
Folkestone Aug.4: half brother to several winners and had earlier made the frame on several
occasions: best form over 6f: acts on fast & soft grnd & is well suited by a sharpish trk. 42
1541 SARIZA [10] (H Cecil) 3-8-11 S Cauthen 11/8 FAV: -42232: Proving expensive to follow:
made most though no extra close home: see 1541 & 941.   30
1541 BELLE OF BUDAPEST [2] (F Durr) 3-8-11 A Clark 33/1: -003: Nearest fin: btr effort
from this lightly raced filly: cost 7,600 gns and is a half sister to fair miler Hungarian
Prince: stays 6f well: acts on gd/firm.   23
1836 FIRST OPPORTUNITY [9] (P Arthur) 3-9-0 L Johnsey 25/1: 0-04: Gd late prog: will stay
further: acts on fast grnd & on a sharpish trk: see 1836.   23
1036 UMBELATA [4] 3-9-0 P Cook 16/1: -000: Shorter trip: ev ch: see 764.   17
-1783 KALANDARIYA [8] 3-8-11 P Waldron 15/8: 4-30220: No extra dist: much btr in 1783 (1m). 06
1836 Career Madness [3] 9-0   1451 Maries Valentine [6] 8-11
-- Wykehamist [11] 9-0   1164 Dalsaan Bay [5] 9-0   1579 Some Guest [7] 9-0(bl)
11 ran   3,2,1,2,3   (R E A Bott (Wigmore St) Ltd)   C Nelson Upper Lambourn, Berks

Official Going Given As GOOD

1948 WROTTESLEY STAKES 2YO C & G   £1051   7f   Good Slow

1197 TOLUCA LAKE [6] (L Piggott) 2-8-7 T Ives 3/1 JT.FAV: 41: 2 b c Kings Lake - Zirconia
(Charlottesville): Impr colt: nicely bckd & led inside final 1f, ridden out in a 2yo stakes
at Wolverhampton Aug.4: half brother to several winners in France: eff at 7f, should be
suited by 1m: acts on gd grnd & should continue to impr.   45
1634 PSALMODY [10] (W Hastings Bass) 2-8-7 W Carson 16/1: 002: Made most, showing impr
form: half brother to the very useful 10/12f winner Galveston: stays 7f: acts on gd grnd &
should find a small event: 5L clear 3rd home.   43
1488 WAHIBA [3] (G P Gordon) 2-8-7 W Hood 10/1: 03: Nearest fin & is making impr: eff
at 7f, should stay 1m: see 1488.   34
1634 DRYGALSKI [11] (M Stoute) 2-8-7 W R Swinburn 9/1: 04: Al prom: stays 7f: see 1634. 32
1172 TRIPLE ENTENTE [5] 2-8-7 W Newnes 10/3: 320: Mkt drifter: sn prom: btr 1172 (shrp trk). 30
1863 AFRICAN SPIRIT [8] 2-9-0 G Duffield 3/1 JT.FAV: 120: No extra final 2f: see 1764 (firm) 33
1529 PLANE [12] 2-8-7 P Robinson 10/1: 40: Mkt drifter: fdd str: see 1529.   00
1653 Vision Of Wonder [1] 8-7   834 George Harry [2] 8-7
1522 Ragtime Solo [7] 8-7   1731 Makin Mischief [4] 8-7(BL)
741 Final Delight [9] 8-7
12 ran   ½,5,½,½,2   (Jack F Vollstedt)   L Piggott Newmarket

1949 BRADMORE SELLING STAKES 2YO   £748   5f   Good Slow

1478 BOOTHAM LAD [5] (M Brittain) 2-8-11 T Ives 33/1: 0400001: 2 ch c Hittite Glory -
Deagloss (Green God): Completely unfncd, but led inside the final 1f in a 2yo seller at
Wolverhampton Aug.4 (bought in 1,300 gns): only modest form previously: eff at 5f: probably
goes on any grnd: has worn bl.   24
1741 HUGO Z HACKENBUSH [4] (C Tinkler) 2-8-11(bl) G Duffield 5/2 JT.FAV: 4400422: Made almost
all: see 1741, 1680.   20

584

*1741 MISS DRUMMOND [9] (N Tinkler) 2-8-11 Kim Tinkler(5) 5/2 JT.FAV: 0020013: Never nearer:
btr 1741 (firm, stiffer track).   14
-- LIME BROOK [3] (B Morgan) 2-8-8(VIS) P Robinson 20/1: 4: Visored on racecourse debut:
nearest fin: very cheaply acquired: should stay further than 5f: acts on gd grnd.   10
1449 SAMS REFRAIN [6] 2-8-8 J Reid 4/1: 01D0440: Held ev ch: best 502 (yld).   09
1738 ROYAL SPECIAL [1] 2-8-8 J Hillis(5) 7/1: 000: Never in it: see 1738.   04
1693 SANTO PRINCESS [7] 2-8-8 R Hills 5/1: 00400: No show in 7th: best 939 (sharp trk, firm). 00
813 Greens Seymour [2] 8-11   1692 Saucier [8] 8-8
9 ran   1½,2,½,½,1½   (J I Sykes)   M Brittain Warthill, Yorks

1950 BRI EDEN CHALL TROPHY HCAP 0-50   £2452   5f   Good +16 Fast   [46]

1849 CAPTAINS BIDD [3] (H Whiting) 6-7-7(14oh) L Riggio(5) 25/1: 0202041: 6 ch g Captain
James - Muffet (Matador): Finally lost his mdn tag after several near misses, led over 1f
out, comfortably in a fast run h'cap at Wolverhampton Aug.4: very eff at 5f, stays 6f: acts
on soft, likes gd & firm grnd & is best when up with the pace.   19
1654 TAX ROY [6] (B Mcmahon) 3-9-6 T Ives 11/4 FAV: -001002: Well bckd, kept on gamely
though not reach winner: gd effort: best 1380 (made running).   46
1900 DAVILL [8] (J Winter) 4-8-9 W R Swinburn 9/2: 0000003: Kept on well: see 76.   26
1682 LADY CARA [10] (J Berry) 6-7-10 W Carson 3/1: -002024: Came all too late: btr 1682.   13
1940 FARMER JOCK [4] 4-8-0 S Whitworth 10/1: 0210000: Sn prom: best in 1542.   12
-1704 NORTHERN TRUST [5] 3-9-1(bl) J Reid 11/2: 3300020: Slow start & much btr 1704.   32
1882 GENTILESCHI [11] 4-8-2 D J Williams(7) 7/1: 0000020: Led over 3f: btr 1882.   00
1638 First Experience [1] 8-0   228 Vague Lass [9] 9-13
1662 The Chalicewell [7] 7-7(bl)(17oh)
10 ran   2,1½,shhd,1½,shhd   (R H Whiting)   H Whiting Costock Grange, Leics.

1951 THREADBARE APPR HCAP 3YO+ 0-35   £1637   1m 1f   Good Slow   [29]

1551 BRECKLAND LADY [1] (M Tompkins) 4-8-10 B Cook(5) 12/1: 010-031: 4 b f Royalty -
Clatter (Songedor): Got up on line under press in an app h'cap at Wolverhampton aug.4: in
'85 won on this trk & at Folkestone: eff at 9f, stays 13f: acts on firm & yld & a sharp/easy trk 18
*1689 EXPLETIVE [16] (M Eckley) 6-8-10(bl)(5ex) Karen Gurney(5) 6/1: -043012: Led 1f out,
caught post: in fine form: see 1689.   18
940 FILM CONSULTANT [2] (J Bosley) 4-8-4 R Perham(5) 33/1: 00-003: Ran on well final 1f:
gd effort after fair abs: first signs of form from this half brother to several winners,
notably useful h'capper Corn Street: stays 9f well: acts on gd grnd & an easy trk.   10
1231 BUCKS BOLT [4] (J Berry) 4-8-7 J Carroll 8/1: 0300044: Hmpd slightly final 1f: not
btn far: stays 9f: see 262.   13
*1546 HODAKA [10] 9-8-4 J Scally 7/1: 4140/10: Led 3f out: not btn far: see 1546.   09
1835 APRIL FOX [5] 3-8-1 A Dicks 33/1: 0-00000: Ch over 1f out: first signs of form:
probably stays 9f: acts on gd grnd & a fair trk.   12
1685 CASHEW KING [9] 3-8-10 A Roper 9/1: 0-00440: Ev ch in str: btr 1685, 1103.   00
1671 CENTRALSPIRES BEST [15] 3-8-3 J Carr 10/1: 0000200: Twice below form 1401.   00
1469 SAHRAAN [8] 3-9-7 W Hayes 5/1 FAV: -0200: Dsptd lead, fdd: lightly raced since best 528 00
1830 STARMAST [17] 3-9-5 T Sprake 7/1: 0-4030: Prom, wknd: btr 1830, 535.   00
1656 Spinnaker Lady [13] 7-13   1471 Sunley Spirit [3] 7-7
967 Lotus Princess [12] 9-6   1554 Next Dance [18] 8-8
1787 Rhein Court [14] 8-0 "   1833 Chief Blackfoot [7] 7-13
1290 Surprise Attack [6] 7-13   1273 Bakers Double [19] 7-11
1077 Walters Wednesday [11] 7-10
19 ran   shhd,½,hd,½,2   (Peter Howling)   M Tompkins Newmarket

1952 WEST MIDLANDS RACING CLUB HCAP 0-35   £1937   1m 6f   Good Slow   [30]

1035 ALACAZAM [2] (J Spearing) 4-7-12 W Carson 8/1: 0-30001: 4 gr c Alias Smith -
Repel (Hardicanute): Despite fair abs, led well over 1f out, comfortably in a h'cap at
Wolverhampton Aug.4: first success: stays 14f well: acts on gd & soft grnd & a fair trk.   07
1633 DONT RING ME [10] (W Hastings Bass) 4-9-7 R Lines(3) 6/1 JT.FAV: 00-0402: Al up there:
stays 14f: see 675.   27
1679 ACTION TIME [9] (B Mcmahon) 5-9-7 J Hillis(5) 9/1: 0U00103: Kept on final 2f:
runs well here: see 1195.   24
1688 MISS LAURA LEE [3] (P Felgate) 3-8-1 M Fry 20/1: -400004: Made early running: see 1688. 16
1260 CROOK N HONEST [12] 4-7-10 A Proud 8/1: 0044000: Ch str, wknd: best 542 (yld)   00
1745 EASY KIN [8] 4-8-0(vis) S Whitworth 12/1: 0010000: Disapp since 1016 (2m, firm).   00
*1459 PURPLE [4] 5-8-4 Paul Eddery 7/1: -0010: Fdd: btr 1459 (12f, seller).   00
1747 HALLOWED [1] 4-7-13 R Hills 10/1: 000-040: Made no show: see 1747.   00
1817 TOUCH OF LUCK [13] 4-8-5 W Ryan 9/1: 0000030: Al rear: see 1817, 1042.   00
1755 DICK KNIGHT [14] 5-8-1(vis) P Robinson 8/1: 0002000: Led after 1m, wknd: best 1416 (12f) 00
1558 DRY GIN [7] 3-8-8 W Newnes 6/1 JT.FAV: 000-030: Appears only moderate: see 1078.   00
1473 Lady Killane [11] 8-12   1884 Grove Tower [5] 8-10
-- Wonder Wood [15] 8-12   -- Shirley Grove [6] 7-12
15 ran   1½,2,hd,3,1½   (Heathavon Stables Ltd)   J Spearing Wixford, Warwicks

1953 DARLASTON FILLIES STAKES 3YO   £1299   1m 1f   Good +08 Fast

1193 PSYLLA [8] (H Cecil) 3-8-8 W Ryan 9/1: -01: 3 b f Beldale Flutter - Pris (Priamos): Led after 3f, proving a comfortable winner of a 3yo fillies stakes at Wolverhampton Aug.4: half sister to the smart miler Prismatic: stays 9f well: acts on gd grnd & seems suited by front running: should continue to impr.   **44**
1589 TOP DEBUTANTE [1] (M Jarvis) 3-8-8 T Ives 11/2: -3002: Led 3f: kept on: fair effort, but best in 218.   **39**
1586 HOOKED BID [2] (J Dunlop) 3-8-8 G Baxter 8/1: -0003: Nicely bckd: ev ch: stays 9f.   **29**
1327 PRINCESS EMMA [20] (M Stoute) 3-8-8 W R Swinburn 12/1: -04: No real threat: half sister to several winners, incl the top class dual Derby winner Shirley Heights: very wk in mkt today & should do btr than this, possibly over a lngr trip.   **28**
1690 HOT MOMMA [9] 3-8-8 E Guest(2) 20/1: 2043300: Ev ch: see 89.   **20**
-- NOHOLMINA [21] 3-8-8 R Machado 33/1: -0: Friendless in mkt on racecourse debut: should impr on this before to long: acts on gd grnd.   **17**
1628 STICKY GREENE [16] 3-8-8 B Thomson 4/1 FAV: 0-33420: Well bckd, but ran moderately: much btr 1628 (1m).   **00**
-- BELIEVE ME NOT [17] 3-8-8 W Carson 7/1: -0: Mkt drifter on racecourse debut & never showed: first foal whose dam won over 10f: should impr.   **00**

1841 Magic Tower [22] 8-8	1516 Chart Climber [18] 8-8(VIS)	
1246 Cleavage [3] 8-8	862 Ela Man Hee [15] 8-8	723 Leanders Pearl [4] 8-8
-- Mills Amend [6] 8-8	1472 Miss Stanway [11] 8-8	1677 Mrs Mainwaring [13] 8-8
1751 Quite A Quest [14] 8-8		1327 Thunderdome [10] 8-8(VIS)
1278 Warm Breeze [19] 8-8	1788 Dasa Queen [5] 8-8	1446 Kangaroo [12] 8-8(bl)
21 ran 1½,5,½,4,1½	(Peter A Shoults)	H Cecil Newmarket

1954 CHILDRENS DAY MAIDEN STAKES 3YO   £2516   1m 2f   Good/Firm 31 +09 Fast

1469 VERITABLE [3] (P Haslam) 3-9-0 G French 6/4 FAV: 43-021: 3 ch c Formidable - Ultra Vires (High Line): Uneasy fav but made most comfortably in quite a fast run 3yo mdn at Ripon Aug.4: placed both outings in '85 and is a half brother to the smart Ulterior Motive: well suited by fast grnd: eff 10f, should stay 12f: can win a h'cap.   **50**
1578 TAMATOUR [7] (M Stoute) 3-9-0 K Bradshaw(5) 12/1: -02: Prom thro'out, gd effort from this impr colt: can find a Northern mdn soon: see 1578.   **46**
1818 MOONSTRUCK [1] (M Ryan) 3-9-0 P Robinson 100/30: -200423: Prom but edged right under press final 1f: see 1818.   **42**
1046 CAPRICORN BEAU [11] (L Cumani) 3-9-0 Paul Eddery 3/1: -04: Well bckd: misbehaved before start, chall 1f out but no extra: a 35,000 gns purchase who is possibly one of his stables lesser lights: bred to be suited by middle dists: acts on fast grnd.   **41**
1530 GOOD NATURED [2] 3-8-11 K Darley 20/1: -00: Gave trouble at the stalls, never featured: half sister to a couple of winners abroad.   **08**
1589 OUR NOORA [5] 3-8-11 M Hills 33/1: -00000: Prom early, wknd & appears quite moderate.   **08**

-- Dalveen Pass [4] 9-0	-- Cherokee [9] 8-11	1072 Hiya Bud [6] 8-11
9 ran 2,2,½,20,½	(T C Ellis)	P Haslam Newmarket

1955 SEE SAW SELLING STAKES 2YO   £1505   6f   Good/Firm 31 -02 Slow

-- CRY FOR THE CLOWN [16] (A Bailey) 2-8-11 P Bloomfield 8/1: 1: 2 b c Cawston's Clown - Bayberry (Henry The Seventh): First time out, landed an old fashioned gamble, leading 2f out readily in a 2yo seller at Ripon Aug.4 (bought in 7,500 gns): dam a mdn: suited by 6f, should stay 7f: acts on fast grnd: btr than a plater & is one to bear in mind for a nursery.   **40**
1881 GET SET LISA [9] (C Tinkler) 2-8-8 J Lowe 11/2 JT FAV: 0400222: Made most stands side, 2nd again: see 1881.   **22**
1862 FREV OFF [11] (M H Easterby) 2-8-8(bl) M Birch 12/1: 0040343: Prom thro'out on far side: wears bl: see 1635.   **17**
1413 SKERNE ROCKET [14] (H Jones) 2-8-8 J H Brown(5) 9/1: 0304: Al prom: twice below 1279.   **12**
1738 MUSIC DELIGHT [15] 2-8-8(vis) G Morgan 11/2 JT FAV: 00040: Early pace, btr 1738 (5f).   **08**
1599 CAUSEWAY FOOT [7] 2-8-11(BL) Kim Tinkler(5) 12/1: 00001: Bl first time: early ldr stands side: twice well below 948 (5f).   **05**
1528 FORTYNINER [6] 2-8-11 Paul Eddery 8/1: 000: Prom, wknd into 7th: best effort yet.   **05**
1717 RUN TO WORK [10] 2-8-11 S Wood(7) 9/1: 4223340: Fin 8th: btr 1717 (5f).   **04**
•1474 THE MAGUE [8] 2-9-3(bl) D Nicholls 7/1: 0042210: Early pace: btr 1474.   **00**
-- WELSH FLITE [5] 2-8-11 A Proud 7/1: 0: Well bckd debutant, sn in rear: dam unraced.   **00**
1635 HAZELS GIRL [13] 2-8-8 K Darley 8/1: 2304020: Sn behind: much btr 1635.   **00**

367 Creole Bay [1] 8-8	1370 Dublin Belle [17] 8-8	1635 Misty Runner [4] 8-8
-- Fossard [2] 8-11	-- Mini Rose [12] 8-8	-- Start Counting [3] 8-11(BL)
17 ran 5,2,2½,2,3,shhd,½	(Mrs J Bailey)	A Bailey Newmarket

1956 TOMMY SHEDDEN CHALL.H'CAP 3YO 0-50   £2805   1m 1f   Good/Firm 31 -17 Slow   [51]

1361 SOHAIL [3] (H T Jones) 3-8-7 A Murray 7/2: 234-031: 3 ch c Topsider - Your Nuts (Creme Dela Creme): Hmpd when chall 1f out, keeping on to fin a ¾L 2nd in a 3yo h'cap at Ripon Aug.4, subsq. awarded the race by the Stewards: first success but placed in 5 out of 6 races last term: stays 9f well & acts on firm & gd grnd & probably on any trk.   **40**

*1671 PENTLAND HAWK [5] (R Hollinshead) 3-8-10(5ex) S Perks 6/1:0000011D:Led dist but
edged right 1f out & although holding on by ¾L, was disq. & placed 2nd: still impr and is
in grand form: see 1671.   44
*1797 HAWARDEN [1] (B Hills) 3-9-8(bl)(5ex) B Thomson 7/2: -40013: Led 3f out, not btn
far in a close fin,, running well: see 1797.   54
+1690 LIAM [6] (M Ryan) 3-9-12(5ex) P Robinson 7/4 FAV: -001014: Held up, never btr &
is in fine form: see 1690.   56
888 FORCELLO [2] 3-8-13 J Lowe 6/1: 1242430: Made most after abs since 888: see 444.   38
816 SECLUSIVE [4] 3-8-10 M Wood 12/1: 00-0400: Never closer after abs: see 674.   33
6 ran   ¾,nk,1,3,¼   (Hamdan Al-Maktoum)   H T Jones Newmarket

1957 ARMSTRONG MEM.CHALL.H'CAP 3YO+ 0-60   £5308   1m 4f   Good/Firm 31 -17 Slow   [58]

1809 PAST GLORIES [1] (C Elsey) 3-7-7(3oh) A Culhane(7) 4/1: 0310421: 3 b c Hittite Glory-
Snow Tribe (Great Nephew): Useful, consistent colt: recovered from a slow start & led 3f
out, staying on strongly to win quite a valuable h'cap at Ripon Aug.4: earlier won a mdn at
Hamilton: half brother to several middle dist winners & is suited by 11/12f himself: should
stay further: acts on firm & hvy: continues to impr.   47
1588 AUCTION FEVER [4] 3-8-5(bl) B Thomson 7/2: 0232102: Came cruising up to
chall 2f out, found nothing: see 1509, 1588.   54
1441 POCHARD [2] (P Cole) 4-9-10 T Quinn 11/8 FAV: -311323: Made much, wknd: btr 1441.   53
1539 WELL COVERED [3] (R Hollinshead) 5-8-2(1ow) W Ryan 9/1: 0001034: Sn under press: best 937.28
1538 STAGE HAND [5] 3-8-4(BL) Paul Eddery 9/2: 0-00000: Prom much: bl. 1st time: btr in 1538. 32
5 ran   3,8,3,10   (N Hetherton)   C Elsey Malton, Yorks

1958 TRAMPOLINE MAIDEN STAKES 2YO   £2794   5f   Good/Firm 31 -03 Slow

-- WHIPPER IN [4] (J Etherington) 2-9-0 A Murray 14/1: 1: 2 b c Bay Express - Whip
Finish (Be Friendly): Made a successful debut, coming from behind and sprinted clear in
the final 1f to win a 2yo mdn at Ripon Aug.4: related to minor winners Day Of Judgement &
Hotbee: very speedily bred & may prove best over 5f though could stay 6f: acts on fast
grnd: looks likely to win again in the North.   51
1555 ON YOUR PRINCESS [6] (J Payne) 2-9-0 P Darcy 6/1: 002: Tried to make all: gd effort
from this impr colt: see 1555.   46
1634 NORTON MELODY [14] (M H Easterby) 2-9-0 M Birch 1/1 FAV: 33: Well bckd, al there
and may need 6f: see 1634.   43
1634 RAINBOW TROUT [5] (M Camacho) 2-8-11 N Connorton 25/1: 04: Prom thro'out: impr:
dam a winning plater over 7f: should stay beyond 5f.   38
934 SKOLERN [2] 2-9-0 T Lucas 10/1: 40: Held up, gd late hdway after abs since 934:
expect impr next time.   34
934 JEAN JEANIE [8] 2-8-11 J Bleasdale 33/1: 0000: Prom thro'out after abs since 934.   30
1075 MERE MUSIC [15] 2-9-0(bl) K Darley 33/1: 000000: Speed most, fin a close 7th: seems
best in bl: see 892.   00
-- PERFUMERIE [7] 2-8-11 B Thomson 7/2: 0: Showed fine speed 4f on debut: related to
a couple of winners & dam was a useful sprinter in Ireland: sure to stay 6f: will do btr.   00
1634 OVERPOWER [3] 2-9-0 A Gorman(7) 10/1: 000: No dngr: dam a sprinter.   00
728 Touch Of Speed [11] 9-0   -- Young Snugfit [12] 9-0
-- Garcon Noir [1] 9-0   1770 Lucys Melody [16] 8-11
1090 Miss Management [13] 8-11   -- Blue Symphony [10] 8-11
-- Buy Nordan [9] 8-11
16 ran   1¼,1½,½,3,nk,½   (F R Warwick)   J Etherington Malton, Yorks

1959 MERRY GO ROUND HCAP 3YO 0-35   £1937   6f   Good/Firm 31 -04 Slow   [41]

1742 BARGAIN PACK [6] (G Reveley) 3-7-8 Julie Bowker(4) 9/1: -000231: 3 b g Silly Prices-
Coatham (Divine Gift): Made all, hanging on under press close home for a narrow win in a
3yo h'cap at Ripon Aug.4: first success: very eff over 5/6f with forcing tactics though seems
to act on firm & soft grnd & on any trk.   17
*972 HUDSONS MEWS [3] (M W Easterby) 3-9-6 T Lucas 15/2: -314012: Kept on strongly, just
held and a fine effort after abs since 972: continues to impr: should win again soon.   42
1414 GOLDEN GUILDER [15] (M W Easterby) 3-8-13 M Hindley(3) 5/1JT FAV: 1203133: Prom thro'out
on far side: consistent: see 947.   31
1840 MADEMOISELLE MAGNA [16] (S Norton) 3-8-9 J Lowe 16/1: 10-0004: Al prom on far side.   23
1765 ALLISTERDRANSFIELD [10] 3-8-2(bl)(10ex) S Wood(7) 9/1: 0042130: Best 1664 (made all). 13
1151 YOUNG PUGGY [4] 3-9-7 S Perks 11/1: -020000: Prom stands side: best effort since 138. 29
1810 CUMBRIAN DANCER [14] 3-9-3(vis) M Birch 5/1 JT FAV: 0041200: Speed much on far side,
fin 8th: best 1247 (stiff trk).   00
1917 PERCIPIO [7] 3-7-13(vis)(7ex) A Shoults(5) 10/1: 3042100: Prom, wknd: best 1734 (5f seller) 00
1257 SKELTON [9] 3-7-10 L Charnock 10/1: -000300: Saddle slipped start: see 650.   00
1664 The Bight [2] 8-1(BL)   1626 Tenasserim [5] 7-7   1734 Eastern Oasis [1] 7-7(3oh)
1399 Miss Serlby [8] 7-10   1184 Affaltati [11] 8-2   1774 Miss Primula [12] 8-11
1687 Whoberley Wheels [17] 8-3   -- Early Doors [13] 7-7(4oh)
1538 Pokeree [18] 8-1
18 ran   nk,1½,1½,1,1½   (J D Taylor)   G Reveley Saltburn , Cleveland

Official Going Given As GOOD

1960 RAOUL CLERGET SELL.STAKES 3YO   £947   1m   Good/Firm 20 -30 Slow

*1540 GIRDLE NESS [10] (N Tinkler) 3-8-11 Kim Tinkler(5) 11/10 FAV: 0-40011: 3 b f Pitskelly -
Sule Skerry (Scottish Rifle): Dropped to selling company & comfortably justified fav. leading
dist in quite a slowly run 3yo seller at Redcar Aug.5 (bought in 2,100 gns): claimed out of
J Dunlop stable after winning a minor race at Leicester last month: half sister to middle
dist winner Jack's Island: eff over 7/9f: acts on gd & firm grnd & on any trk: in gd form.   22+
1739 KEEP COOL [5] (R Hollinshead) 3-8-11 S Perks 11/1: 0100002: Went on ½way, kept on
well & comfortably beat rem: first run in selling company since successful at Newmarket in
774 & should win again if kept in this grade: suited by a gall trk.   17
1426 TWICKNAM GARDEN [6] (P Felgate) 3-9-0 W Ryan 7/1: 0-00003: Nicely bckd on first venture
into selling company: al up there: suited by fast grnd: see 1426.   10
1267 STANFORD ROSE [9] (M Brittain) 3-8-11 A Bacon(7) 20/1: 003-004: Btr effort: see 960.   06
1824 LARNEM [12] 3-8-11 J Callaghan(7) 12/1: 0002100: Led/dsptd lead most of way: best in 1662 02
1671 COURT RULER [1] 3-9-0 L Charnock 12/1: 0000400: Best over this trip in 997 (non seller)   04
1372 PATRICKS STAR [2] 3-9-0 A Murray 6/1: -0000: Dropped in class: fin 8th: lightly raced
gelding who has been well btn in mdns over longer distances.   00
1773 Watendlath [13] 8-11   --   Flamelight [11] 8-11   1815 Mercia Gold [4] 9-0(vis)
1142 Lottie Limejuice [8] 8-11   1662 Octiga [7] 8-11
1841 Moloch [3] 9-0
13 ran   1½,5,½,2,hd,1½   (Full Circle Thoroughbreds B Ltd)   N Tinkler Malton, Yorks

1961 ROBERT SARRAU MAIDEN STAKES 3YO   £823   2m   Good/Firm 20 -12 Slow

1799 FALLOWFIELD LAD [10] (C Tinkler) 3-9-0 M Birch 5/1: -31: 3 br g Anax - Gray Loch
(Lochnager): Led after home turn and stayed on well to win a 3yo mdn at Redcar Aug.5: lightly
raced gelding who is clearly well suited by a test of stamina: acts on gd/firm grnd &
on a gall trk: should have a future over hdles.   33
1304 L B LAUGHS [3] (G Pritchard Gordon) 3-9-0(bl) W Ryan 9/4 FAV: 0-00242: Not qckn & remains
a mdn: suited by a dist of grnd: seems to like this gall trk: see 959.   28
1304 DENBERDAR [4] (R Hollinshead) 3-9-0 S Perks 7/1: 0-20303: Stayed on same pace: eff
over 10/12f & stays 2m: acts on any going: see 48.   22
1645 HOPEFUL LINE [11] (B Hills) 3-8-11 A Murray 9/2: 0-004: Lngr trip: no extra 2f out:
lightly raced filly who is a half sister to several winners: should be suited by middle dists:
acts on gd/firm.   18
1721 HELSANON [1] 3-8-11 D Mckeown 16/1: -000440: Never reached ldrs: see 1078.   12
1688 DEMON FATE [9] 3-9-0 M Roberts 6/1: 0000330: Led till str: sn btn & much btr in 1688.   00
1503 Hitchenstown [6] 9-0   1700 Nitida [5] 8-11   --   French Design [2] 8-11
--   Gold Sovereign [8] 8-11   1415 Quite Pokey [7] 8-11(BL)
11 ran   3,5,1,4,25   (Mrs Hannah Marian Ballard)   C Tinkler Malton, Yorks

1962 YORKSHIRE FINE WINES CUP NURSERY H'CAP   £3158   6f   Good/Firm 20 -43 Slow   [40]

1504 NIFTY GRIFF [3] (R Whitaker) 2-9-1 K Bradshaw(5) 14/1: 001101: 2 b c Ardoon -
Betty Bun (St Chad): Al front rank & led in the final strides of a slowly run nursery at
Redcar Aug.5: earlier won sellers at Thirsk & Newcastle, breaking the 2yo course record on
the latter success: very eff over 6f & appeared not to get 7f last time: suited by fast
grnd & does well when up with the pace: acts on any trk.   37
1828 LORD WESTGATE [2] (M Usher) 2-9-7 M Wigham 9/1: 00202: Just caught: gd effort: see 1253.   42
1828 GOOD BUY BAILEYS [4] (G Blum) 2-9-1 A Shoults(5) 9/1: 140343: Picked up grnd from
½way, though not reach ldrs: quite consistent: see 1828 and 1568.   27
1893 CLOWN STREAKER [6] (M H Easterby) 2-9-1 M Birch 9/1: 210104: Ev ch dist: twice below 1570. 22
440 PANBOY [5] 2-8-9 T Ives 9/1: 312400: Long abs & needed this run: successful on soft
grnd in 108 (5f).   08
1025 GARDENIA LADY [7] 2-9-1 T Lucas 9/1: 3000: Front rank till dist: best in 646 (5f yld).   08
6 ran   hd,3,1½,3,2   (Mrs I Griffiths)   R Whitaker Wetherby, Yorks

1963 MOMMESSIN AMAT. RIDERS STKS 4YO+   £1251   1m 4f   Good/Firm 20 +12 Fast

*1502 GULFLAND [7] (G Pritchard Gordon) 5-11-10 Princess Anne(5) 5/1: 1321011: 5 ch g Gulf Pearl-
Sunland Park (Baragoi): Provided Princess Anne with her first winner, switched to lead inside
dist & was sn clear in quite a fast run amateur riders stakes at Redcar Aug.5: most consistent
this term, earlier winning at Nottingham,Doncaster & Chester: suited by 10/12f: acts on
any going & on any trk.   50
1409 POSITIVE [2] (H T Jones) 4-11-10 Mr T Thomson Jones 4/6 FAV: -01D202: Went on over
2f out, outpcd inside dist: clear of rem though twice below form shown in 921: see 695.   42
1349 HERRADURA [5] (M Prescott) 5-11-10 Maxine Juster 6/1: -2302D3: Not reach ldrs: see 1349.   30
*1223 FIEFDOM [6] (W Storey) 6-11-10 Fiona Storey 10/1: 00-2014: No real threat: btr in 1223.   28
1871 TAXIADS [3] 4-11-10 Jane Allison(5) 8/1: 0110030: No extra over 2f out: best in 984.   28
1871 COUNT COLOURS [1] 4-11-10 Angela Norton 10/1: 4-00240: Clear ldr till wknd quickly
over 2f out: btr in 1417: see 9.   12
6 ran   5,7,1,shhd,10   (Gavin A Pritchard-Gordon)   G Pritchard Gordon Newmarket

1964 CAMUSET CHAMPAGNE HCAP 3YO+ 0-35   £2169   1m 3f   Good/Firm 20 +01 Fast   [26]

1540 BRAVE AND BOLD [8] (N Callaghan) 3-8-5(bl) W Ryan 13/2: 2000401: 3 b g Brave Shot -
Kundalina (Red God): Ran on well to lead inside dist in an all aged h'cap at Redcar Aug.5:
successful on final outing last season in a nursery h'cap at Edinburgh: stays 11f well & is
eff over 7/8f: acts on firm & soft grnd & on any trk: best in bl.   24
1559 SENDER [4] (A Stewart) 3-9-2 R Carter(5) 4/1: -01202: Just failed to make all: gd
effort & clearly loves being out in front: acts on gd & firm grnd: see 595.   34
1866 GOLDEN FANCY [9] (I Vickers) 9-9-10 R Vickers(7) 6/1: 23432D3: Dwelt, ev ch: again
not btn far though yet to get his head in front this term: see 1185.   29
1820 GREED [3] (Denys Smith) 5-9-6 T Ives 11/4 FAV: -244324: Close 4th: placed again: see 1185 24
1569 JANIE O [6] 3-8-11 P Robinson 5/1: -030040: Kept on under press: see 1569.   23
1838 BOLD ANSWER [2] 3-7-9 M L Thomas 14/1: 0001030: Won a seller here in 1158 (9f).   00
1374 Elarim [1] 9-6   1724 Frame Of Power [5] 8-2
613 Mexican Mill [7] 9-0
9 ran   ½,½,½,2,6   (T A Foreman)   N Callaghan Newmarket

1965 NURSERY HANDICAP 2YO   £1730   7f   Good/Firm 20 -18 Slow   [48]

1255 KHADRUF [7] (H T Jones) 2-9-7 A Murray 4/1: 1031: 2 ch c Blushing Groom - Call Me
Goddess (Prince John): Useful colt: led ½way & held on gamely to win a nursery h'cap at
Redcar Aug.5: first time out winner of a Haydock mdn: cost $685,000 as a yearling: eff over
5f, stays 7f well: acts on gd & firm grrnd & on a gall trk.   50
1572 PALEFACE [1] (L Piggott) 2-8-10 T Ives 6/4 FAV: 3322: Dsptd lead thro'out, just held:
consistent sort who is due a change of luck: see 1253.   38
1891 WISE TIMES [5] (M Usher) 2-8-12 M Wigham 5/2: 00223: Not btn far: stays 7f: see 1891.   36
1528 RABENHAM [6] (D Barron) 2-7-13(2ow) M Roberts 14/1: 0040004: Ran on same pace: eff
over 6/7f on fast grnd: best over 6f here in 741.   17
1828 FLAIR PARK [2] 2-8-3 M L Thomas 11/2: 012430: Gd early speed: btr in 1828 (6f shrp trk)   05
1270 JJ JIMMY [3] 2-8-3(bl) M Birch 8/1: 0040: Led to ½way, wknd quickly: see 1270.   00
6 ran   hd,1½,2½,8,7   (Hamdan Al-Maktoum)   H T Jones Newmarket

Official Going Given As GOOD/FIRM

1966 EBF ALFRISTON MDN FILLIES STKS 2YO   £1803   6f   Good/Firm 24 +13 Fast

1801 VEVILA [4] (L Cumani) 2-8-11 Pat Eddery 8/13 FAV: 221: 2 b f The Minstrel - Bon Debarras
(Ruritania): Useful, impr filly: led approaching final 1f, ridden out to return a fast time
in a 2yo fillies mdn at Brighton Aug.5: last time out was btn a shhd by Color Artist in a
similar event at Lingfield: stays 6f well: seems suited by fast grnd & an undulating trk:
should win more races.   55
1604 MISS RUNAWAY [6] (J Winter) 2-8-11 W R Swinburn 7/2: 042: Kept on well: may be suited
by 7f and caught a good one here: see 1604, 1308.   47
1604 COPPER CREEK [2] (R Smyth) 2-8-11 J Reid 25/1: 003: Made much: on the up grade: half
sister to several winners incl the smart My Sister: eff at 6f on fast grrnd & should find
a small race.   44
1275 FLIRTING [7] (R Hannon) 2-8-11 B Rouse 20/1: 0244: Ev ch in str: stays 6f but best 988(5f). 37
1802 TAMASSOS [5] 2-8-11 G Starkey 12/1: 00: Fdd final 1f, but is making impr: acts on
gd/firm: see 1802.   32
1407 RED RIDING HOOD [1] 2-8-11 T Quinn 14/1: 040: Wknd final 2f: see 1030.   24
--   ITS BEEN RUMOURED [3] 2-8-11 S Whitworth 50/1: 0: Rank outsider on debut: al rear.   00
7 ran   2½,1,2½,1½,3   (William H De Burgh)   L Cumani Newmarket

1967 BURROUGHS COMPUTERS HCAP 3YO+ 0-50   £3022   1m   Good/Firm 24 -02 Slow   [44]

1689 FOOT PATROL [5] (P Cundell) 5-8-1 C Rutter(5) 7/4 FAV: 0001021: 5 br g Daring March -
Molly Polly (Molvedo): Well bckd and responded to press to lead on the line in a h'cap at
Brighton Aug 5: earlier landed a gamble in a h'cap at Redcar: winner over hdles during the
Winter: in '85 won a h'cap at Brighton and is now a winner 4 times on this trk: very eff
at 1m, stays 9f: loves fast grnd & Brighton.   27
1854 MEET THE GREEK [4] (R Laing) 3-9-6 P Cook 2/1: 1120122: Led over 1f out, caught post:
6L clear 3rd and is a model of consistency: see 1854, 1365.   56
1890 JOYFUL DANCER [3] (W Brooks) 6-9-9(5ex) T Quinn 11/2: -002103: Led over 6f: see 1729.   39
1781 STEEPLE BELL [2] (M Stoute) 10-9-10 M A Giles(7) 9/2: 200-034: Mkt drifter: wknd & btr 178136
*1439 SOLSTICE BELL [1] 4-7-7(10oh) L Riggio(5) 33/1: 0-40010: Stiff task: btr 1439 (seller).   00
5 ran   shhd,6,2,8   (Miss Lynne Evans)   P Cundell Compton, Berks

1968 DUKE OF NORFOLK MEM. NURSERY HCAP   £4534   7f   Good/Firm 24 -10 Slow   [49]

*1731 LAURIES WARRIOR [4] (R Boss) 2-9-6(6ex) Pat Eddery 8/11 FAV: 4021211: 2 ch c Viking -
Romany Pageant (Welsh Pageant): Very useful, impr colt: appeared well in at the weights and
duly made ev yd, easily in a nursery h'cap at Brighton Aug.5: last time out won a valuable
2yo stakes at Sandown: earlier won a mdn at Doncaster: well suited by 7f, sure to stay at
least 1m: acts on gd & firm grnd & a gall trk & should win more races.   68

664 OLORE MALLE [6] (R Hannon) 2-8-6 L Jones(5) 14/1: 142: Long abs: no ch with winner:
stays 7f: acts on gd/firm & hvy: see 270.   29
722 ROUMELI [5] (Lord J Fitzgerald) 2-7-12 R Hills 11/2: 4423: Prom over 5f: abs since btr 722(6f).16
*1495 KIERON PRESS [3] (D Arbuthnot) 2-9-7 S Cauthen 4/1: 0314: Fdd inside final 2f: btr 1495(6f). 35
1458 DIVINE CHARGER [1] 2-8-6 P Waldron 12/1: 00040: Never went pace: see 1458.   19
1083 DECCAN PRINCE [2] 2-7-9 N Adams 33/1: 00040: Al rear after abs: btr 1083 (6f seller).   00
6 ran   8,3,2,nk,4   (L C James)   R Boss Newmarket

1969 DOWNS SELLING STAKES 3YO+   £900   1m 2f Good/Firm 24 -12 Slow

1558 ROSI NOA [11] (P Kelleway) 3-8-7 S Cauthen 11/4 FAV: -300001: 3 gr f Kenmare -
Cabdoa (Carvin): Dropped to selling company & well bckd, led into str for a comfortable win
in a seller at Brighton Aug.5 (bought in 2,900 gns): stays 10f well: acts on gd/firm &
hvy grnd & on any trk: should win again in this grade.   22
1784 ANGIES VIDEO [12] (R Holder) 4-9-4 J Reid 4/1: 0032032: Al up there: stays 10f: see 1567. 12
1937 JUST CANDID [1] (D Wilson) 4-9-7 B Rouse 10/1: 00-0033: Ev ch 2f out: stays 10f: see 1937 11
1845 MR MUSIC MAN [5] (C Reavey) 12-9-7 I Johnson 15/2: -000024: Ev ch str: see 1845.   06
1497 AUNT ETTY [13] 3-8-7(bl) W Newnes 13/2: 0000000: Active in mkt: fdd final 2f:
dropped to selling company today: probably stays 12f: best form so far on yld grnd.   00
1845 TAKE THE BISCUIT [6] 3-8-10 A Mercer 8/1: 2000300: Never in it: best in 1210 (1m).   01
-- Himorre [7] 9-7   1666 Letoile Du Palais [4] 8-7
1845 Bushy Bay [10] 9-7(vis)   1364 Sir Speedy [8] 8-10
1786 Plum Bossy [9] 8-7(vis)   1898 Puppywalker [2] 8-7(vis)
12 ran   3,2,3,2½,shhd   (Roldvale Ltd)   P Kelleway Newmarket

1970 PIER HANDICAP 3YO 0-35   £1727   1m 4f Good/Firm 24 -46 Slow.   [34]

1671 CURIGA [7] (P Walwyn) 3-8-8 Paul Eddery 11/4: 000-041: 3 b f Kris - Parmelia
(Ballymoss): Led inside the final 1f, holding on under press in a slow run h'cap at Brighton
Aug.5: lightly raced previously: eff at 10f, stays 12f: acts on fast grnd & an undulating trk. 22
1733 UP TO UNCLE [1] (R Hannon) 3-9-7 L Jones(5) 2/1 FAV: 0221322: Heavily bckd: fin
well & nearly got up: model of consistency: stays 12f well: see 1314.   34
1544 TORREYA [4] (J Hindley) 3-9-4 M Hills 10/3: -042323: Made most: see 1544.   28
1471 MISS JADE [2] (J Winter) 3-8-6 T Quinn 25/1: 00-0004: Fdd inside final 2f: little
form this term: yet to make the frame.   00
1386 FIREPROOF [3] 3-9-3 P Cook 9/2: 4201440: Prom, fdd: much btr 1386 (14f).   00
1312 BERNIGRA GIRL [5] 3-9-2 W R Swinburn 16/1: 0000000: Al in rear: no form this term.   00
-- Solent Express [6] 8-11
7 ran   hd,1½,10,12,2   (Lord Howard De Walden)   P Walwyn Lambourn, Berks

1971 SOUTH COAST STAKES 3YO+   £2448   1m   Good/Firm 24 -04 Slow

1783 HALO HATCH [7] (K Brassey) 3-8-6(BL) S Whitworth 10/1: 3-03001: 3 b g Thatch -
Novalesa (Northfields): Bl first time & led 3f out for a comfortable 4l win in a stakes event
at Brighton Aug.5: first success, but placed several times previously: eff at 1m, stays 10f:
likes fast grnd, acts on any trk: seems suited by bl & should find a h'cap off his present mark 48
1486 DANCING EAGLE [2] (M Jarvis) 3-8-13 S Cauthen 9/4: -323002: Ev ch in str: best in 899(10f). 47
1804 HAUTBOY LADY [3] (M Madgwick) 5-8-4 P Cook 20/1: 4032-03: Stiff task: stayed on
late: placed several times previously, but has yet to win: eff over 6f, stays 1m: acts on
a sound surface & on any trk.   20
1793 BARRACK STREET [4] (M Ryan) 3-9-5(BL) G Starkey 11/4: 440-004: Bl first time, but
no threat: yet to find 2yo form: see 1514.   43
-- DAWN MIRAGE [8] 3-8-3 T Quinn 33/1: 22000-0: Made no show: seasonal debut: stiff task:
placed in sellers in '85 & is more at home in that grade: stays 7f well: acts on gd/firm
& heavy ground.   12
1626 TOOTSIE ROLL [1] 3-8-3 P D'arcy 66/1: -400: Rank outsider: led 5f.   11
407 ALSHINFARAH [6] 3-9-5 R Hills 4/1 FAV: 211-00: Very uneasy fav: fdd tamely: abs since 407 00
1609 Steel Pass [9] 9-0   1443 Alice Hill [5] 8-13
9 ran   4,4,½,5,½   (Norman Ross)   K Brassey Upper Lambourn, Berks

---

AYR   Tuesday August 5th   Lefthand Galloping Track

1972 EBF CHAPELPARK MAID.FILLIES STAKES 2YO   £1064   5f   Good 56 -19 Slow

1814 SPANISH SLIPPER [7] (W Haigh) 2-8-11 J Brown(5) 9/4 FAV: 42241: 2 b f King Of Spain-
Shoe (Shoolervile): Well bckd, al prom & led close home under press in a rather slowly run
2yo fillies mdn at Ayr Aug.5: a deserved success after a couple of near misses: cheaply
acquired filly who is a half sister to a couple of winners: acts well on gd grnd over 5f.   41
1826 MISS MILVEAGH [2] (A Bailey) 2-8-11 R Cochrane 3/1: 322: Just failed to make all:
good effort: see 1826.   40
1770 COME ON OYSTON [4] (J Berry) 2-8-11 J Carroll(7) 13/2: 433: Al there: see 1296.   33
383 LITTLE UPSTART [3] (G P Gordon) 2-8-11 G Duffield 5/2: 04: Long abs: prom till outpcd
closing stages: related to several winners & dam successful over 1m: quite speedily bred
but should stay 6f: should do btr next time.   26

1266 **SENDIM ON SAM** [1] 2-8-11 K Hodgson 14/1: 000: Prom much & appeared to show some impr here: see 1090. 25
515 **SALLY FOXTROT** [6] 2-8-11 J Lowe 33/1: 00: Outsider, no threat after long abs. 17
-- **SUESANDY** [5] 2-8-11 J Bleasdale 33/1: 0: Mostly rear on debut: related to a couple of 2yo sprint winners. 00
7 ran nk,2½,2½,nk,3,4 (R E Johnston) W Haigh Malton, Yorks

1973 AUCHENDRANE H'CAP 3YO+ 0-35 £2012 5f Good 56 -06 Slow [28]

1917 **SONNENELLE** [3] (J S Wilson) 3-8-7(vis) G Duffield 9/2: 0004001: 3 b f Sonnen Gold - Touch Of Dutch (Goldhill): Made a quick reapp getting on top under press in the final 1f to win a h'cap at Ayr Aug.5: first time out made all at Hamilton in a similar h'cap: very eff over 5f, probably stays 6f: acts on gd & soft grnd: wears a visor. 20
1222 **TOP THAT** [6] (D Barron) 5-9-10 R Cochrane 5/1: 2014002: Chall final 1f: best effort since 649 (yld) & is possibly best on good or softer grnd & unsuited by firm. 29
1718 **WESBREE BAY** [1] (N Bycroft) 4-7-12 L Charnock 3/1: 0022023: Dsptd lead 1f out and seems short of fin pace: see 1423. 00
1765 **CARPENTERS BOY** [7] (G Reveley) 8-9-0 Julie Bowker(7) 10/1: -000004: Best effort this term: see 1718. 13
1927 **LULLABY BLUES** [2] 3-9-8(VIS) J Lowe 5/2 FAV: 0121200: Made most: best 890. 25
1687 **MAYBE JAYNE** [4] 3-7-13 M Fry 10/1: 4000000: Twice below 1505 (very sharp trk). 01
1682 **HIGHLAND GLEN** [8] 3-9-6 D Nicholls 12/1: 200-000: No threat: quite a lightly raced mdn last term running best over 5f at Ripon on yld on 3rd outing. 20
7 ran 1½,1½,2,nk,nk,1 (Ben Willetts) J S Wilson Ayr

1974 CUNNINGHAME H'CAP 3YO 0-35 £2250 1m 2f Good 56 -25 Slow [37]

1773 **GIBBERISH** [6] (M Prescott) 3-8-5(bl) G Duffield 11/4 FAV: -204121: 3 ch f Final Straw-Linguist (Mossborough): Well bckd, came from behind to lead final 1f, comfortably in a rather slowly run 3yo h'cap at Ayr Aug.5: in gd form at present earlier winning a claimer at Nottingham: very eff over 10f & acts on firm & yld: best form in bl. 23
1773 **SPACE TROOPER** [3] (T Fairhurst) 3-8-10(5ex) R Cochrane 7/2: -401132: Early ldr, kept on again final 1f & probably unsuited by this slow pace: in fine form: see 1678. 23
-1520 **ABSENCE OF MALICE** [2] (B Hanbury) 3-9-7(bl) Pat Eddery 3/1: -20023: Led/dsptd lead much, one paced and is proving expensive to follow: see 1520. 32
1637 **FOREMAST** [4] (P Calver) 3-9-7 M Fry 13/2: 0-13034: Prom most: yet to reproduce 822 (hvy). 27
•1794 **TAYLORMADE BOY** [1] 3-9-11(5ex) L Charnock 7/1: 1230310: Much btr 1794 (1m) though does stay 10f. 27
•1838 **BLACK BANK** [5] 3-9-5(5ex) K Hodgson 6/1: 0-03410: Led ½way till 2f out: much btr 1838. 11
6 ran 2½,1,3,2,10 (Capt J Macdonald-Buchanan) M Prescott Newmarket

1975 HERONSLEA STAKES 2YO £2465 7f Good 56 -60 Slow

1253 **PUNTA CALAHONDA** [3] (N Bycroft) 2-8-11 D Nicholls 14/1: 01: 2 b c Moorestyle - Lolito (Busted): The outsider when gamely making almost all, narrowly, in very slowly run Heronslea Stakes (2yo) at Ayr Aug.5: well suited by forcing tactics & 7f, likely to stay at least 1m: acts well on gd grrnd. 51
1660 **LACK A STYLE** [4] (A Bailey) 2-8-11 R Cochrane 5/4 FAV: 002332: Chall winner final 2f, clear of rem: fair effort but twice below 1465. 50
1926 **KING BALLADEER** [2] (G P Gordon) 2-9-2 G Duffield 6/1: 031233: Every chance, weakened: too soon after 1926? 43
1566 **LACK OF PEARLS** [5] (R Woodhouse) 2-8-8 A Shoults(5) 25/1: 40404: Prom much: stays 7f ? 30
•819 **CHANTILLY LACE** [1] 2-8-8 Gay Kelleway(3) 5/1: 10: Abs since btr 819 (6f, hvy). 27
5 ran hd,6,2,1½ (David Faulkner) N Bycroft Brandsby, Yorks

1976 MONKTON H'CAP 3YO+ 0-35 £2292 1m Good 56 +04 Fast [34]

1774 **EMERALD EAGLE** [8] (C Booth) 5-8-10 R Lines(3) 6/1: 0300201: 5 ch m Sandy Creek - Double Eagle (Goldhill): Won a h'cap at Ayr Aug.5, for the 2nd successive year, leading 1f out & holding on well: very early in the season won at Cagnes: best at 1m: acts on firm but btr suited by gd or soft/hvy going: likes Ayr. 25
1839 **ROSSETT** [12] (T Craig) 7-7-7(2oh) J Quinn(5) 16/1: 0004002: Came from behind, kept on well to be narrowly btn & best effort for a long time: see 1136. 06
1547 **TIT WILLOW** [6] (S Wiles) 4-8-8(bl)(1ow) D Nicholls 10/1: 0221203: Ev ch: see 828 (seller). 18
1720 **BOY SANDFORD** [4] (W Mackie) 7-7-9 N Carlisle 10/1: 3040044: Kept on under press: see 789. 02
1808 **MAWDLYN GATE** [1] 3-8-6(vis) Gay Kelleway(3) 6/1: 0013220: Again made the running, wknd under press: clear ch at the weights on the form in 1808: flattered? 19
1525 **SILLY BOY** [2] 6-9-6 Pat Eddery 7/1: -040000: Waited with, late prog: see 698. 23
•1813 **BALNERINO** [3] 3-7-12(5ex) M Fry 5/2 FAV: -004010: Hvly bckd, prom most, fin 7th: btr 1813. 10
1676 **MONTICELLI** [10] 6-7-9 J Lowe 10/1: 4-00200: Slow start, fin 8th: twice below 1231. 00
1590 **FLEET FOOTED** [13] 3-8-11(bl) G Duffield 5/1: -002030: Ev ch, fin 9th: btr 1590 (firm). 00
1720 **Abjad** [9] 7-13 689 **Kings Badge** [5] 9-7 1176 **Cane Mill** [7] 9-6
1424 **Nicky Dawn** [11] 7-7
13 ran ¾,1½,1½,2,hd,½ (A Lyons) C Booth Flaxton, Yorks

00

1977 HEADS OF AYR STAKES 3YO UPWARDS   £959   1m 3f   Good 56 -09 Slow

*1589 VERARDI [1] (W Hastings Bass) 3-8-13 Pat Eddery 1/7 FAV: -3011: 3 b c Mill Reef - Val D'Erica (Ashmore): Had little more than an exercise canter, starting at unbackable odds to beat 2 rivals in a minor event at Ayr Aug.5: won a well contested 3yo mdn at Kempton last time: very eff over 12f & acts on firm & gd going: the type to win btr races.   45

-- REGAL CASTLE [3] (B Hanbury) 3-8-5 R Cochrane 6/1: -2: Belated racecourse debut for this almost 17 hands high gelding & he made much of the running: half brother to '82 2yo 5/6f winner Right Dancer: stays 11f & acts on gd going: the type to benefit greatly from this experience. 30

1703 PETERS KIDDIE [2] (R Woodhouse) 5-9-0 A Shoults(5) 33/1: 0300003: Wknd quickly str.   00

3 ran   2,dist   (F Ortelli)   W Hastings Bass Newmarket

Official Going Given As GOOD/SOFT

1978 TAMDHU WHISKY NURSERY H'CAP 2YO   £2131   6f   Yielding 92 -13 Slow   [46]

1893 EMMER GREEN [3] (J Berry) 2-8-8 Pat Eddery 15/2: 401001: 2 ch f Music Boy - Bustellina (Busted) Sn prom and led nearing final 1f, driven out in a nursery h'cap at Ayr Aug 6: earlier won a mdn auction at Warwick: eff at 5f, stays 6f: acts on any grd and on any trk.   37

1421 SKY CAT [2] (J Wilson) 2-8-10 Julie Bowker(7) 15/2: 40022: Al front rank: stays 6f: see 1421. 34

*1528 BEN LEDI [4] (M H Easterby) 2-9-7 M Birch 3/1 FAV: 03113: Stayed on: will be suited by 7f: see 1528.   44

1893 BRUTUS [7] (J S Wilson) 2-9-0 G French 14/1: 010304: Made most: stays 6f: possibly best on a sharp track: acts on gd/firm and yielding: see 826.   35

1138 DANUM DANCER [9] 2-7-13 L Charnock 7/1: 00440: Abs: prom, ev ch: yet to reproduce the form of 685 (gd).   08

1527 BROONS ADDITION [1] 2-8-4 G Brown 12/1: 4343100: Prom, fdd: lightly raced since 603. 12

1893 KACERE [6] 2-8-13(BL) M Fry 25/1: 40000: Rank outsider: fin 7th: bl first time and little form since 602.   00

1895 WHISTLING WONDER [5] 2-8-10(BL) K Darley 10/1: 4303000: Bl first time: under press when hmpd 2f out: best 1174 (5f).   00

1843 PAY DIRT [8] 2-7-10(bl) J Callaghan(7) 4/1: 03030: Wknd after ½ way: well below form 1843 (good/firm).   00

9 ran   1½,½,½,6,nk   (Glenn Davies)   J Berry Cockerham, Lancs.

1979 PINTAIL SELLING STAKES   £887   6f   Yielding 92 +16 Fast

1347 MAFTIR [2] (N Callaghan) 4-9-3(bl) Pat Eddery 5/4 FAV: 0000001: 4 gr c Godswalk - Pit's Belle (Pitskelly) Ran on under strong press to lead on the post in a 4 runner seller at Ayr Aug 6 (bought in 1,800 gns): in '85 won a h'cap at Nottingham: eff at 6f, stays 1m: acts on gd/firm and yielding and on any track: best in blinkers.   14

1562 AMPLIFY [3] (M Brittain) 3-8-5 K Darley 6/1: 0300002: Led briefly cl home: best effort since 305 and likes some give in the ground.   08

1424 TRICENCO [4] (W Storey) 4-9-3(bl) J Quinn(5) 9/4: -000003: Led ½ way, just caught: good effort: see 889.   12

1771 SWEET EIRE [1] (W Pearce) 4-8-9 N Connorton 6/1: 0-00004: Led 3f: see 906.   00

4 ran   shthd,nk,2½   (Andy J Smith)   N Callaghan Newmarket

1980 FAMOUS GROUSE H'CAP (0-35)   £2553   1m 5f   Yielding 92 -08 Slow   [35]

1897 WESSEX [7] (N Tinkler) 4-9-7 Kim Tinkler(5) 14/1: 4313401: 4 b c Free State - Bonandra (Andrea Mantegna) Made hdwy from the rear to lead final 1f in a h'cap at Ayr Aug 6: ran very poorly last time out, but earlier most consistent, winning at Hamilton and again at Ayr: eff over 12f, well suited by a test of stamina: acts on any going and on any track.   35

1517 SHAHS CHOICE [2] (J Dunlop) 3-8-5(3ow) Pat Eddery 7/2 JT FAV: 00-0432: Ran on final 1f: good effort: stays 13f: acts on fast and yldg.   28

1822 KEEP HOPING [1] (G Huffer) 3-7-7(4ex)(1oh) N Carlisle 6/1: -000133: Hmpd nearing final 1f: much btr 1822, 1739 (gd/firm).   14

1422 MOULKINS [6] (J Wilson) 4-8-1 Julie Bowker(7) 9/1: 0001304: Led 3f out, fdd: best 1052 06

1745 PERFECT DOUBLE [5] 5-7-8 M Fry 5/1: 0403220: Led over 4f out, wknd: btr 1745 (firm). 00

1226 STRING OF BEADS [3] 4-7-7(VIS)(4oh) A Culhane(6) 16/1: 0-00000: Visored 1st time: see 772. 00

1509 DIPYN BACH [9] 4-8-11 B Thomson 7/2 JT FAV: -044030: Fdd into 7th: best 912 (10f). 00

1700 DENALTO [8] 3-7-7(6oh) L Charnock 14/1: 0-00330: Fdd: btr 1700 (gd).   00

1897 DUKE OF DOLLIS [4] 7-7-9 J Quinn(5) 9/1: 0000120: Led over 1m, sn fdd: btr 1897.   00

9 ran   2,1½,2,4,nk   (Full Circle Thoroughbreds Ltd)   N Tinkler Malton, Yorks.

1981 PTARMIGAN MAIDEN STAKES   £1889   1m   Yielding 92 -22 Slow

1511 AITCH N BEE [7] (J Dunlop) 3-8-11 Pat Eddery 4/1: -0401: 3 ch c Northfields - Hot Case (Upper Case) Led well over 1f out, comfortably, in a mdn at Ayr Aug 6: earlier a good 4th to Majaahed in val event at York: stays 1m well: acts on firm and yldg and a galloping track.   46

1628 KICK THE HABIT [3] (C Brittain) 3-8-8 N Carlisle 10/1: 0-00002: Ev ch over 1f out: good effort: acts on gd/firm and yldg ground: see 803.   36

AYR   Wednesday August 6th   -Cont'd

966 SPRINGWELL [4] (G Huffer) 3-8-8 R Lines(3) 12/1: -003: Abs: nearest fin and seems
an improving sort: should stay further than 1m: half sister to 6/7f winner Reindeer Walk:
acts on yldg ground.   35
1375 SUNDAY CHIMES [8] (B Hills) 3-8-8 B Thomson 7/4 FAV: -04: Well bckd: never nearer:
seems quite well regarded: stays 1m and acts on gd and yldg ground: see 1375.   29
1628 KAIYRAN [5] 3-8-11 M Birch 5/2: 3-00: Prom, ev ch: should be suited by further than 1m. 30
1904 FANNY ROBIN [1] 3-8-8 L Charnock 33/1: 0-00040: Made most, wknd: see 1904, 1123.   24
1820 Minders Man [2] 9-7   --   Le Mans [6] 8-11
8 ran   2½,hd,3,¾,1½   (Peter S Winfield)   J Dunlop Arundel, Sussex

1982 EBF CARBIESTON MAIDEN STAKES 2YO   £1333   7f   Yielding 92 -29 Slow

1681 AUTHENTIC [3] (N Tinkler) 2-9-0 Kim Tinkler(5) 5/2: 221: 2 br c Derrylin - Crystalize
(Reliance II) Fairly useful colt: well bckd and ran on well to lead near fin in a 2yo mdn
at Ayr Aug 6: 2nd in both prev outings: brother to the smart 2yo Johnny Nobody: eff at 6f,
stays 7f well: acts on firm and yldg and a gall trk.   50
1382 KLARARA [1] (J Dunlop) 2-8-11 Pat Eddery 5/4 FAV: 42: Heavily bckd: led inside
final 1f, just caught: 4l clear 3rd and should go one btr soon: acts on firm and yldg:see 1382 46
1504 BLACK MANS BAY [9] (J Etherington) 2-8-11 M Wood 8/1: 043: Nearest fin and will
be well suited by 1m+: see 1504, 1050: acts on gd/firm and yldg.   38
1534 VITAL CARGO [7] (E Carter) 2-8-11 B Thomson 10/1: 44: Led till inside final 1f:
good effort: acts on yldg: see 1534.   37
--   FABRINA [8] 2-8-11 N Connorton 8/1: 0: Some late hdwy on racecourse debut and will
improve on this: cost 400,000 gns as a yearling: should be suited by 1m: acts on yldg ground. 36
1812 IN A SPIN [6] 2-8-11 K Darley 14/1: 300: Wknd inside final 2f: twice below form 1529.   32
1812 DAMART [2] 2-9-0 E Guest(3) 10/1: 0030: Prom most: fdd: btr 1812 (gd).   00
--   Outer Cover [4] 9-0   1812 Port Of Time [5] 9-0
9 ran   nk,4,hd,½,2   (Full Circle Thoroughbreds Ltd)   N Tinkler Malton, Yorks.

1983 HIGHLAND PARK WHISKY H'CAP (0-35)   £2281   7f   Yielding 92 -05 Slow   [28]

1976 ROSSETT [8] (T Craig) 7-7-11 J Quinn(5) 10/1: 0040021: 7 ch g Jukebox - Flo Kelly
(Florescence) Led 2f out, driven out in a h'cap at Ayr Aug 6: 2nd race in 24 hrs: last won
in '84 at Edinburgh and Redcar: equally eff over 7/8f: acts on firm and yldg ground and on
any track.   05
1870 QUALITAIRESS [9] (K Stone) 4-7-12(vis) K Darley 11/2: 4003022: Ran on well final 1f
and nearly gained the day: in gd form: see 1870, 101: stays 1m well.   04
1906 THIRTEENTH FRIDAY [5] (W Pearce) 4-8-1(5ow) N Connorton 5/1 JT FAV: 4000343: Nearest
fin: twice below 1774.   05
1906 MONINSKY [6] (N Bycroft) 5-8-11(6ex) D Nicholls 6/1: 3003104: Not the best of runs:
nearest finish: see 1774.   14
*1839 BOLD ROWLEY [3] 6-8-6(6ex) D Mckeown 8/1: 0-00010: Sn prom: btr 1839 (seller).   00
1839 KING COLE [2] 4-8-7 Julie Bowker(7) 7/1: 40-0040: No threat: btr 1839 (gd/firm seller). 00
*1976 EMERALD EAGLE [4] 5-9-2 R Lines(3) 7/1: 3002010: Quick reappearance: led 5f: see 1976. 00
1425 CLAWSON THORNS [7] 3-8-4(BL) L Charnock 16/1: 0-00000: Bl first time: prom, fdd:
better 1425 (stakes).   00
*1698 SIR WILMORE [1] 4-9-13(6ex) E Guest(3) 5/1 JT FAV: 0-00010: Fin well btn: much btr 1698. 00
9 ran   ½,¾,nk,5,hd,¾   (T Craig)   T Craig West Barns, Lothian.

PONTEFRACT   Wednesday August 6th   Lefthand, Turning, Undulating Track

Official Going Given As GOOD/FIRM

1984 E.B.F. FEATHERSTONE MAIDEN STAKES 2YO   £2567   6f   Good/Firm 36 -33 Slow

1453 MISK [4] (H Cecil) 2-9-0 W Ryan 5/4 FAV: 2201: 2 ch c Miswaki - Slow March (Queen's
Hussar) Led nearing final 1f, ridden out in a slow run 2yo stks at Pontefract Aug 6: earlier
a good 2nd to Sauce Diable at Windsor: eff at 5f, stays 6f well: acts on fast grd and any trk. 55
1798 COLWAY RALLY [1] (J Watts) 2-9-0 G Duffield 9/2: 2032: Chall final 1f: just btn
and 5l clear 3rd: fine effort and will go one btr soon: see 1798.   54
1928 MAD MAX [3] (P Haslam) 2-9-0 T Williams 3/1: 43: Not clear run after ½ way: ran on:
another good effort: see 1928.   44
1225 THANK HAVON [12] (D Morley) 2-8-11 A Mcglone 20/1: 404: Led over 2f out: sister to
useful sprinter Blue Singh and may do btr over 5f: acts on fast ground.   35
--   OH DANNY BOY [7] 2-9-0 S Webster 25/1: 0: Nearest fin on racecourse debut and should
improve on this: will be suited by further than 6f: dam was a genuine sort who stayed 2m:
acts on good/firm.   32
1762 BURCROFT [14] 2-9-0 K Bradshaw(5) 33/1: 00: Stayed on well: improving: see 1762.   24
--   Barnaby Benz [2] 9-0   1869 Johnny Sharp [8] 9-0   1634 Danum Lad [11] 9-0
--   Freddie Ashton [6] 9-0   859 Beckingham Ben [13] 9-0
1716 Mr Cricket [10] 9-0   1675 Juma Monty [5] 9-0
13 ran   nk,5,1½,2,2½   (Prince A A Faisal)   H Cecil Newmarket

593

1985 CUDWORTH CLAIMING STAKES 3YO+   £1047   1m 2f   Good/Firm 36 -42 Slow

1739 BRITTONS MILL [2] (M Prescott) 3-8-6 G Duffield 4/1: 00-0241: 3 b c Temperance Hill - Lypatia (Lyphard) Led final 1f, driven out in a slow run claimer at Pontefract Aug 6: eff at 10/11f, may not stay 12f: acts on a sound surface and a sharpish trk.   25
1800 LUCKY WEST [3] (G Moore) 3-8-7 A Mackay 7/2 FAV: 01001D2: Not clear run: in gd form.   25
1394 BUSTED FLAVOUR [5] (W Jarvis) 5-9-3 W Ryan 4/1: 3003: Ev ch over 1f out: flattered 875.   20
1719 CAPRICORN BLUE [6] (J Fitzgerald) 3-8-1(vis) J Lowe 4/1: S-02424: Ducked left 1f out:see 1719.13
615 PRIME NUMBER [10] 3-8-6 K Powdrell 9/2: 0-0000: Abs: kept on one pace: see 247.   15
-- ROYAL VALEUR [7] 6-9-4 J Burton(7) 50/1: 03040/0: Rank outsider, never nearer: last won in '82 at Ayr (6f good).   04
1412 Teejay [4] 9-4(bl)   1374 Glenderry [1] 9-7(bl)   1775 Expert Witness [9] 8-0
9 ran   ¾,2,1,1½,6   (John E Anthony)   M Prescott Newmarket

1986 POMFRET HANDICAP STAKES (0-60)   £3817   5f   Good/Firm 36 +02 Fast   [48]

*1536 ALL AGREED [3] (J Winter) 5-9-10 G Duffield 3/1: 0400211: 5 b g Jaazeiro - Tynwald Hill (Rarity) Useful sprinter: came from off the pace to lead cl home and win going away in a h'cap at Pontefract Aug 6: last time out won a h'cap at Chester and is in fine form: in '85 won at Beverley and Sandown: in '83 won twice: seems equally eff at 5/6f: acts on any ground and on any trk: carries weight well.   55
*1849 MUSIC MACHINE [4] (P Haslam) 5-8-13(7ex) J Scally(7) 15/8 FAV: 0410112: Clear leader, just caught: in fine form: see 1849.   40
1849 PHILSTAR [2] (A Balding) 5-7-8(vis) A Mackay 7/1: 0300303: Prom, ev ch: best 1676 (6f).   15
1882 KING CHARLEMAGNE [7] (G Reveley) 7-9-4 A Shoults(5) 11/2: 0-00434: Prom, ev ch: btr 1882 32
*1882 MANTON MARK [5] 3-8-12(7ex) J Lowe 6/1: 0-00010: Never nearer: btr 1882.   30
1896 LIGHT ANGLE [13] 5-7-7 S P Griffiths 25/1: 0000-00: Prom, fdd: last won in '84 at Edinburgh and Chester and likes a sharp trk: best over 5f on gd and fast ground.   00
1840 MELAURA BELLE [1] 5-9-1 S Webster 11/1: 04-0000: Yet to find her form: see 649.   00
7 ran   1½,2,3,½,5   (T M P Waterman)   J Winter Newmarket

1987 JIM GUNDILL MEM. H'CAP (0-50)   £2582   1m   Good/Firm 36 -14 Slow   [41]

1553 SINGING BOY [4] (A Hide) 5-8-5 A Mackay 10/1: -000001: 5 b g Manor Boy - Jailhouse Rock (Gulf Pearl) Led inside final 1f, driven out in a h'cap at Pontefract Aug 6: last season won at Newcastle: in '84 won at Doncaster: eff att 1m, stays 10f: acts on firm and yldg ground   28
954 NIORO [1] (R J Houghton) 3-9-0 W Ryan 7/2 CO.FAV: 40-132: Abs: hung under press, but ran well: stays 1m: see 498.   45
1870 MOORES METAL [8] (R Hollinshead) 6-9-5 S Perks 7/1: 0040003: Ev ch final 1f: see 1249,441   39
1868 KNIGHTS SECRET [2] (M H Easterby) 5-9-5 K Hodgson 7/2 CO.FAV: 1134034: Made most: not btn far: see 815.   36
1890 VIRGIN ISLE [6] 5-9-7 T Williams 7/2 CO.FAV: 0040400: Twice below 1455 (7f) see 79.   32
1906 KAMPGLOW [5] 4-8-8 R P Elliott 9/1: 3000030: Never nearer: btr 1906 (7f).   14
1047 Russell Creek [3] 9-1   1871 Godlord [9] 7-11
8 ran   1,½,1½,3,2½   (G H Eden)   A Hide Newmarket

1988 HOLIDAY TIME STAKES   £2236   1m 4f   Good/Firm 36 +11 Fast

+1437 KENANGA [1] (H Cecil) 3-8-9 W Ryan 1/1 FAV: -0111: 3 ch f Kris - Catalpa (Reform) Very useful, impr filly: heavily bckd and led well over 1f out, comfortably, in quite fast run 4 runner stks at Pontefract Aug 6: earlier won at Wolverhampton and Yarmouth: half sister to Ribblesdale winner Strigida: eff at 11f, stays 12f really well: acts on a sound surface and on any trk: continues to improve and should win more races.   70
1214 ROBBAMA [4] (J Dunlop) 3-8-6 G Duffield 11/4: 110-432: Kept on under press: best effort this season: stays 12f: see 348.   61
1354 BADARBAK [3] (R J Houghton) 3-8-9 A Mcglone 5/2: -312303: Led over 3f out: consistent: stays further than 12f: see 654, 411.   61
1092 COMMANDER ROBERT [2] (J Hanson) 4-9-10 J Lowe 20/1: -401124: Led over 1m: stiff task.   24
4 ran   3,1½,15   (Lord Howard de Walden)   H Cecil Newmarket

1989 MOTORWAY HANDICAP STAKES (0-35) 3YO   £2052   1m   Good/Firm 36 -21 Slow   [36]

1471 SEE NO EVIL [2] (G Balding) 3-8-0 T Williams 20/1: -000001: 3 gr c Bold Lad (Ire) - Rough Love (Abwah) Caused a 20/1 surprise, led nearing final 1f, holding on under press in a 3yo h'cap at Pontefract Aug 6: first success: stays 1m: acts on gd/firm and hvy ground and likes an undulating track.   16
1613 HOT LINING [8] (F Carr) 3-8-7 S Morris 20/1: -000002: Came from behind and nearly got up: good effort: well suited by 1m on gd/firm and a sharpish trk.   22
1864 NICOLINI [5] (J Fitzgerald) 3-8-4 A Shoults(5) 5/1: 00-0033: Ev ch over 1f out: in good form: see 1864.   16
1815 MY DERYA [9] (B Mcmahon) 3-7-7(bl) A Mackay 20/1: 3403004: Stayed on late: see 564, 103   02
1864 SCINTILLATOR [6] 3-8-1(BL) A Mcglone 12/1: -000000: Bl first time: ev ch: btr 1362.   02
671 DAWN LOVE [3] 3-9-1 S Perks 12/1: 0100-00: Long abs: never nearer: should do btr next time: in '85 won a 3 runner event at Redcar: prob stays 1m: acts on good ground.   11
1486 FASSA [1] 3-9-7 W Ryan 8/1: 000-000: Ev ch str: lightly raced this term: first time out in '85 won a fillies mdn at Leicester: stays 1m: acts on gd and fast ground.   00

1651 ANGEL TARGET [11] 3-8-12(vis) G Duffield 11/2: 00-0000: Prom, fdd: btr 1651.   00
1705 ROI DE SOLEIL [10] 3-7-11 C Rutter(3) 4/1: 0-00030: Fdd str: much btr 1705 (1m stks).   00
1651 NAWADDER [12] 3-9-3 A Geran(7) 3/1 FAV: 2401030: Disapp fav: btr 1651, see 1073.   00
1198 Tamalpais [5] 8-5   1446 Csillag [7] 8-0
12 ran hd,1¼,1½,4,3   (L J Strangman)   G Balding Fyfield, Hants.

BRIGHTON   Wednesday August 6th   Lefthand, Sharpish, Undulating Track

1990 STANMER SELLING H'CAP (0-25)   £958   7f   Firm 19 -12 Slow   [15]

1845 DALLAS SMITH [18] (M Chapman) 5-8-9(vis) I Johnson 14/1: 0000041: 5 b h Sir Ivor -
Sahsie (Forli) Early leader and regained advantage again 2f out, keeping on well under press
for a ¾l success in a selling h'cap at Brighton Aug 6 (sold 2,000gns): in '85 won sellers at
Brighton and Salisbury (sub disqualified): very eff over 7f/1m and acts on firm and yldg
and on any trk tho' likes Brighton.   04
1834 TOMS NAP HAND [6] (W Williams) 5-8-7 N Howe 33/1: -000002: Outsider, al well there
and not btn far: best effort yet from this maiden.   00
1609 CYGNE [7] (G Balding) 4-8-12 J Williams 16/1: 00-0003: Fin well: first venture into
selling company this term and appreciated the drop in class: mdn who showed some ability last
term: should be suited by 1m.   01
1515 NELSONS LADY [1] (C Horgan) 5-9-9 I Salmon 6/1 FAV: 310-004: Slow start, ran into
trouble 2f out and kept on strongly cl home: unlucky? See 1515.   12
1186 TURCY BOY [14] 5-9-0 R Curant 33/1: -000000: Ev ch: last won in '84 at Bath: stays
1m: acts on firm ground.   02
1781 COUNT ALMAVIVA [8] 3-8-12(bl) W Newnes 7/1: 2003000: Best 1364.   06
1567 SAUGHTREES [2] 3-8-11 Paul Eddery 13/2: 00-0030: Ev ch, fin a cl 7th: btr 1567 (stiff 1m). 05
1849 RUSSELL FLYER [9] 4-9-7(bl) G Carter(3) 10/1: 0040300: No show: twice well below 1574.   00
1447 GERSHWIN [12] 3-9-5 A Clark 7/1: 00-1200: Disapp after 1447 (6f).   00
1901 OSTENTATIOUS [4] 4-9-5 M Hills 8/1: 0330400: Early pace: see 1649.   00
1549 SANDRON [17] 3-8-13 R Wernham 15/2: 0-03030: Prom, fdd: much btr 1549 (6f).   00
1619 Composer [11] 9-0(bl)   1755 Unit Tent [3] 8-11(bl)
1404 Guymyson [16] 9-4(bl)   1827 Rockville Squaw [15] 8-12(BL)
1804 Black Spout [5] 8-7   1574 Great Owing [13] 8-7
17 ran ¾,2,¾,shthd,1,nk   (Peter A Smith)   M Chapman Clipston, Leicestershire.

1991 B T R B HANDICAP 3YO (0-50)   £3012   7f   Firm 19 +07 Fast   [50]

1640 BLACK SOPHIE [5] (R Laing) 3-8-11 P Cook 6/1: 303-001: 3 b f Moorestyle - Rockeater
(Roan Rocket) Came from behind and fin strongly to lead final 1f, comfortably, in a quite
fast run 3yo h'cap at Brighton Aug 6: surprise first time out winner of a Newbury mdn in '85
later placed in nurseries: well suited by 7f and firm or gd going, tho' seems to act on any trk 43
*1244 BALLAD ROSE [6] (P Cole) 3-9-7 T Quinn 7/4 FAV: 3-43212: Ev ch and race 1244 has
not worked out well.   48
1487 AMBROSINI [7] (M Jarvis) 3-9-7 W Carson 11/4: -102043: Kept on near fin: see 454, 886.   46
1783 MERRYMOLES [4] (M Mccourt) 3-7-10(BL) N Adams 33/1: -000004: Bl first time, made most:
by far his best effort this season: in '85 won at Salisbury: prob stays 7f but is very eff
at 6f: acts on firm and gd ground.   17
1835 LYDIA LANGUISH [2] 3-8-3 B Rouse 10/1: 0-00200: Never btr after slow start: twice
below 1540 (1m stiff trk).   24
1750 SURE LANDING [3] 3-9-4(bl) J Reid 14/1: 0420340: Prom most: best 937 (1m): now
wears blinkers but remains a maiden.   38
1499 HELAWE [1] 3-8-12(bl) G Starkey 9/2: -030140: Prom, wknd: best 1191 (6f).   00
7 ran 2½,1,2,shthd,nk   (Mrs H R Slack)   R Laing Lambourn, Berks

1992 BRIGHTON CHALLENGE CUP H'CAP (0-60)   £4331   1m 4f   Firm 19 +09 Fast   [49]

1366 VORACITY [4] (J Winter) 7-9-7 J Reid 100/30: 04-2321: 7 ch g Vitiges - Wolverene
(Relko) Broke a 2-year losing run when coming from behind to narrowly lead inside final 1f
in a h'cap at Brighton Aug 6: lightly raced in '85, prev season won a val h'cap at Haydock:
well suited by 12f and firm or gd ground: acts on any trk but runs particularly well at
Brighton: genuine and consistent.   51
1685 FLEETING AFFAIR [5] (G Harwood) 3-9-7 G Starkey 11/4 FAV: -111022: Prom, chall under
press final 1f, just btn in a close finish: retains her form very well: see 1209.   62
1667 CADMIUM [1] (P Cole) 4-9-6 T Quinn 11/2: 1-30343: Tried to make all: kept on gamely
and narrowly btn: best effort since 215 and could be winning soon.   49
1829 HOUSE HUNTER [2] (C Horgan) 5-9-4(4ex) Paul Eddery 3/1: 2004124: Prom, chall final 1f
in a cl finish: in fine form: see 1667.   46
1837 PELLINCOURT [3] 4-8-2 W Carson 9/2: 2021400: Well bckd, fdd final 2f and best 1366(C/D) 20
5 ran ¾,shthd,nk,7   (Mrs John Winter)   J Winter Newmarket

1993 BBC RADIO SUSSEX MAIDEN STAKES 2YO   £1963   6f   Firm 19 -06 Slow

1445 ANYOW [3] (C Nelson) 2-9-0 J Reid 7/2: 331: 2 b c Ya Zaman - Avereen (Averof) Rewarded
strong support, chall under press final 1f and getting up at the death to win a 2yo mdn at

Brighton Aug 6: cost 17,000 gns and is a half sister to useful 2yo True Nora and the smart
Mac's Reef: well suited by 6f, should stay further: acts on fast ground.   41
1082 KAMENSKY [1] (R Smyth) 2-9-0 S Whitworth 5/6 FAV: 0322: Just failed to make all and
is suited by a sharp trk/forcing tactics: see 678.   40
-- KING RICHARD [4] (J Dunlop) 2-9-0 W Carson 5/1: 3: Debutant who looked in need of
the race, sure to benefit from this quite gentle introduction: related to minor winners
abroad: stays 6f, should be suited by further.   36
1129 CASTLE CORNET [5] (R Hannon) 2-9-0 B Rouse 6/1: 0004: Prom most: see 187.   30
1550 HARRY EM [2] 2-9-0 P Cook 33/1: 00: Btn a long way at the fin and appears moderate.   00
5 ran   shthd,2,2,dist   (R E A Bott)   C Nelson Upper Lambourn, Berks

1994 LANES E B F STAKES   £2393   1m 2f   Firm 19 -16 Slow

*1441 LOCH SEAFORTH [4] (H Cecil) 3-8-13 Paul Eddery 11/10 FAV: 4-21111: 3 b c Tyrnavos
- Marypark (Charlottown) Very useful, impr colt who was winning his 4th race off the reel,
coming from behind to smoothly lead final 1f in a minor race at Brighton Aug 6: earlier
successful at Windsor (h'cap) and at Catterick and Beverley (minor races): very eff over
10/12f on firm or gd ground: acts on any trk tho' runs well on a sharp one: can cont to improve 62
1792 INNISHMORE ISLAND [3] (J Dunlop) 3-8-4 W Carson 6/5: 12-3032: Tried to make all:
better 1792 (stiff track).   50
*1768 LANDSKI [1] (R Simpson) 3-8-7 S Whitworth 15/2: 0130313: Hmpd dist, changed position
and fin well: see 1768.   51
1788 MARSH HARRIER [2] (A Moore) 5-9-0 P Cook 25/1: 0002004: Al prom, not btn far and
again showed remarkable improvement: see 1178, 1788.   46
-- CELTIC BELL [5] 8-8-1 N Howe 66/1: -0: Wknd final 2f on debut: possibly more of a
jumping type.   00
5 ran   1,1,hd,20   (Sir David Wills)   H Cecil Newmarket

1995 HASSOCKS STAKES   £1719   6f   Firm 13 +13 Fast

1858 EASTERN SONG [3] (C Nelson) 3-9-11 J Reid 4/6 FAV: 20-0131: 3 ch c Ballad Rock -
Magee (Weavers Hall) Very useful colt: landed the odds, leading dist, comfortably, in a
fast run minor race at Brighton Aug 6: comfortably won a mdn at York July 11 and last time
was a highly creditable 3rd in a Gr 3 race at Phoenix Park: equally eff over 6/7f and acts
on firm and good ground: progressive type who should win more races.   57
1312 ZULU KNIGHT [4] (P Walwyn) 3-9-0 Paul Eddery 10/1: 0-00002: Set a gd pace most:
creditable effort: see 846.   42
1153 BUTHAYNA [7] (H T Jones) 3-8-11 R Hills 4/1: 22-0003: Prom, outpaced final 2f after
abs: little form this season: see 431.   24
1730 STANBO [1] (D Dale) 3-9-0 B Rouse 14/1: 00-0004: Slow start, no danger: lightly
raced this term and remains a maiden.   20
1676 BOOTLE JACK [6] 4-9-0(vis) L Johnsey(7) 66/1: 0-02000: No danger from this mdn:
best 1319.   01
*1836 ANGELS ARE BLUE [5] 3-9-5 M Giles 9/1: -023010: Very stiff task: see 1836.   01
1947 SOME GUEST [2] 3-9-0(bl) J Williams 66/1: 0000000: Al rear: moderate maiden.   00
7 ran   1,4,2,3,3   (Mrs W Tulloch)   C Nelson Upper Lambourn, Berks

Official Going Given As GOOD

1996 CLIFF PARK MAIDEN FILLIES STKS 2YO   £964   6f   Good/Firm 32 -28 Slow

-- MONTERANA [3] (G Wragg) 2-8-11 P Robinson 6/1: 1: 2 b f Sallust - Aventina (Averof)
Promising filly: was a comfortable winner on her racecourse debut, qcknd inside dist in a
2yo fillies mdn at Yarmouth Aug 6: half sister to winning juv Tina's Express: eff over 6f
on gd/firm ground: likely to rate more highly.   46
-- SANAABELL [9] (M Stoute) 2-8-11 W R Swinburn 4/6 FAV: 2: Well bckd debutant: went on
below dist, ran green and no extra cl home: cost 400,000 gns as a yearling and is a half
sister to the topclass Petoski: will be suited by further: acts on gd/firm ground: a certain
future winner.   44
818 NABRAS [7] (H T Jones) 2-8-11 A Murray 5/1: 33: No extra cl home: gd effort after
fair abs and is clearly on the upgrade: stays 6f: should find a race: see 818.   40
167 SHEER ROYALTY [1] (W O'gorman) 2-8-11 T Ives 16/1: 04: Going on fin: fair effort
after a lengthy abs: promises to be suited by a longer trip: acts on gd/firm ground: see 167.   35
353 SPEEDBIRD [8] 2-8-11 N Day 33/1: 00: Rank outsider after long abs: front rank over
½ way and should improve for this run: acts on gd/firm and yldg: see 353.   33
-- ILIONA [2] 2-8-11 R Guest 12/1: 0: Easy to back on debut: kept on from ½ way and
likely to improve for this experience: half sister to middle dist winner Indian Orator: acts
on gd/firm.   26
-- Supreme Rose [6] 8-11   -- No Lie [5] 8-11   -- Sensational Lady [4] 8-11
9 ran   ½,1½,1½,½,2½,½,1½,nk   (H H Morriss)   G Wragg Newmarket

1997 BURE SELLING STAKES 2YO   £686   6f   Good/Firm 32 –45 Slow

1802 WHOS ZOOMIN WHO [2] (G Lewis) 2-8-8 P Waldron 7/4 FAV: 0001: 2 b f Kind of Hush –
Miss Twomey (WIII Somers) Dropped in class and easily justified fav, led below dist in a
slowly run 2yo seller at Yarmouth Aug 6 (bought in 6,600 gns): cost 4,000 gns as a yearling
and is a half sister to sev winners: eff over 6f on fast grd and on an easy course.   25+
1832 MISS ACACIA [3] (R Stubbs) 2-8-8 J H Brown(5) 11/2: 0030322: Led briefly below dist,
no chance with easy winner tho' remains in gd form: see 1832 & 1221.   15
1795 FANTINE [1] (N Tinkler) 2-8-13(bl) S Cauthen 5/2: 4214003: Front rank till dist: best 939   08
1803 RELAMPEGO [6] (K Ivory) 2-8-8 G Morgan 20/1: 00004: Speed over ½ way, cheaply bought
filly whose dam was successful in this grade: acts on gd/firm.   00
1803 LYNDA BROAD [4] 2-8-8 M Wigham 33/1: 0000: Early speed, no form to date.   00
1537 SWEET PICCOLO [8] 2-8-11 M Miller 5/1: 0030: Tried to make all: best 1537.   00
--   NATIONS ROSE [7] 2-8-8 A Mercer 12/1: 0: Outpaced ½ way on racecourse debut.   00
7 ran   3,4,2½,½,¾   (Mrs N Lewis)   G Lewis Epsom, Surrey.

1998 PONTINS HOLIDAY HANDICAP 3YO 0-50   £2700   1m 2f   Good/Firm 32 +18 Fast   [54]

1678 TENDER TYPE [2] (M Tompkins) 3-8-3(5ex) R Cochrane 4/1 JT FAV: -000121: 3 b c Prince
Tenderfoot – Double Type (Behistoun) In fine form, led inside dist, ridden out in a fast
run 3yo h'cap at Yarmouth Aug 6: last month won a similar race at Hamilton: eff over 10/12f
on fast ground: acts on any track.   39
1753 GEORDIES DELIGHT [10] (L Piggott) 3-9-7 T Ives 4/1 JT FAV: 0414222: Model of consistency
and deserves another race: see 1202.   54
1806 KINGS CRUSADE [3] (G Lewis) 3-8-2(1ow) P Waldron 5/1: 4404233: Led over 3f out,
no extra cl home and remains a maiden: stays 10f well: acts on any trk: see 1284.   34
1724 NORDICA [8] (A Stewart) 3-8-9 M Roberts 5/1: -00124: Late prog: best over 1m here
in 1327.   36
1690 ADMIRALS ALL [4] 3-8-3 P Robinson 14/1: -034030: Not reach leaders: btr 1690.   28
1417 AL SHAMIKH [9] 3-9-0 A Murray 10/1: 00-1300: Yet to reproduce form shown in 699.   34
1034 NEEDLEWOMAN [6] 3-8-8 W R Swinburn 9/1: -000430: Al behind: best 739 (stiff trk).   00
1384 MARSHAL MACDONALD [1] 3-8-9 S Cauthen 9/2: 0-00440: Saddle slipped home turn,
fin last: see 1036.   00
1256 Robis [5] 7-10   1724 Tower Fame [7] 7-8(1ow)(3oh)
10 ran   1½,½,3,1,3   (G H Tufts)   M Tompkins Newmarket

1999 SEACROFT HANDICAP STAKES 3YO 0-35   £2267   7f   Good/Firm 32 –14 Slow   [38]

1868 FANCY PAN [8] (W Hastings Bass) 3-9-1 T Ives 15/2: -03041: 3 b f Paavo – Fancify
(Diplomat Way) Led below dist and forged well clear for a runaway win in a 3yo h'cap at
Yarmouth Aug 6: eff over 7/8f and well suited by fast grd: acts on any trk: sure to win
again if reproducing this form.   38
1471 PULHAM MILLS [10] (E Eldin) 3-9-7(vis) G King(5) 9/2: 0000122: Tried to make all as
usual, another gd effort tho' no chance with this easy winner: see 1471 & 1169.   30
1725 RARE SOUND [6] (P Kelleway) 3-9-3 Gay Kelleway(3) 7/4 FAV: 1-23: Nicely bckd: switched
over 2f out, not qckn: lightly raced filly who deserves another chance: see 1725 (1m).   25
1742 GARDAS GOLD [1] (M Brittain) 3-8-3 M Wigham 33/1: 0330004: Best over 6f in 787 (hvy)   05
1774 SPORTING SOVEREIGN [7] 3-9-0 W Woods(3) 8/1: 4220100: Much btr 1701 (gall trk).   15
1471 BEARS REVENGE [3] 3-8-4 R Morse(5) 33/1: -00000: Al mid-div: half brother to winning
juv Dellwood Iris: didnot race last year and has yet to show any worthwhile form.   00
1673 UNEXPLAINED [7] 3-9-3(bl) S Cauthen 8/1: 02D2000: Never dangerous 8th: best 857.   00
1541 FAMILLE ROSE [2] 3-8-13(VIS) M Miller 9/2: 04-000: Visored for the first time: early
speed, wknd into 9th: lightly raced filly: eff over 7/8f on gd/firm grd.   00
1927 Lone Galaxie [4] 8-12   1603 Our Remedy [5] 7-7(3oh)
10 ran   7,nk,3,hd,5   (Mrs Mary Lou Cashman)   W Hastings Bass Newmarket

2000 BRITANNIA MAIDEN STAKES 3 & 4YO   £1288   1m 6f   Good/Firm 32 +09 Fast

1799 DESERTED [2] (G Pritchard Gordon) 3-8-5 T Ives 11/4: 00-0421: 3 b f Sassafras –
Desert Love (Amerigo) Made all in a canter when a decisive winner of quite a fast run mdn
at Yarmouth Aug 6: has improved steadily this term: eff over middle dist, stays 2m well:
acts on gd and fast ground and on any trk: does well with forcing tactics.   46
1732 THREE TIMES A LADY [4] (P Kelleway) 3-8-7(2ow) S Cauthen 7/4: 0022322: No impression
on winner: consistent tho' has had plenty of chances: see 1732 & 1410.   35
1469 TONQUIN [1] (J Toller) 3-8-5 P Robinson 33/1: -0003: Outsider: stayed on again, almost
snatching 2nd place: first signs of form: related to winning h'cappers Pubby and Air Command:
stays 14f: acts on gd/firm grd.   32
1873 PARSONS CHILD [3] (L Cumani) 3-8-5 R Guest 6/4 FAV: -0024: Disapp fav: much btr 1873.   18
714 ABYDOS [5] 3-8-8 R Cochrane 20/1: -000: Abs: back marker thr'out and seems mod.   13
5 ran   8,hd,10,4   (Wm Du Pont III)   G Pritchard Gordon Newmarket

2001 FAMILY RESORT MAIDEN STAKES 2YO   £1322   7f   Good/Firm 32 –14 Slow

--   FEARLESS ACTION [4] (H Cecil) 2-9-0 S Cauthen 4/5 FAV: 1: 2 ch c Miswaki – Rescue Party
(Roberto) Promising juv: heavily bckd on his debut and was al in command, scoring cleverly

597

in a 2yo mdn at Yarmouth Aug 6: cost $385,000 as a yearling: clearly very eff over 7f on
gd/firm ground: useful prospect who seems certain to rate more highly.   50+
--   CABOT [8] (W Holden) 2-9-0 R Morse(5) 33/1: 2: Picked up grd from ½ way: promising
debut and should improve enough to win a race: half brother to winning juv Sparkling Wit:
eff over 7f on gd/firm ground.   41
1816 GENTLE DARIUS [5] (M Ryan) 2-9-0 R Cochrane 6/1: 43: Ran on well: clear rem: stays 7f
well and should have no trouble getting 1m: acts on gd and fast ground: see 1816.   38
--   NILOJEN [1] (G Huffer) 2-9-0 M Miller 20/1: 4: Mkt drifter: some late prog and likely
to improve: cost $32,000 and is a half brother to winning juv Tax Haven: acts on gd/firm. 30
1572 SUNSET BOULEVARD [7] 2-9-0 T Ives 5/1: 040: No extra dist: see 1572.   29
1573 GREENS OLD MASTER [3] 2-9-0 A Murray 8/1: 20: Pressed winner most of way: wknd
quickly and better in 1573 (6f).   23
--   REEF OF GOLD [2] 2-9-0 P Robinson 8/1: 0: Early speed on debut: cost 30,000 gns
and is a half brother to sev winners: btr for race.   00
7 ran   1½,1,4,nk,2½   (Sheikh Mohammed)   H Cecil Newmarket

DEAUVILLE   Saturday August 2nd   Righthanded, Easy Track

Official Going Given As GOOD

2002 GROUP 2 PRIX DASPARTE F & M 3YO+   £24499   1m   Good

1215 ELLE SEULE (D Smaga) 3-8-7 A Lequeux 1: -101341: 3 ch f Exclusive Native - Fall Aspen
(Pretense) Smart French filly: caused a surprise when a ¾l winner of a Gr 2 fillies race at
Deauville Aug 2: first time out winner of val fillies race at Evry and later won a Gr 3 race
at Longchamp: very eff over 8/10f: acts on gd/firm and yldg grd and on any trk: consistent 78
1355 LYPHARITA (A Fabre) 4-8-13 C Asmussen 1: 04-1142: Hot fav: unsuited by the slow
early pace and had no luck in running: looked an unlucky loser: see 1355.   73
1356 RIVER DANCER (J Cunninyton Jnr) 3-8-7 M Philliperon 1: 4-43043: Ran a gd race:see 467 73
467 REGAL STATE (J Fellows) 3-8-8(1ow) Y Saint Martin 1: 120-404: Gd eff after long abs.   74
1713 KANMARY 3-8-7 A Badel 1: 30-0020: Ran to her best.   72
1353 RESTIVER 3-8-7 F Head 1: 11-3020: Consistent filly: see 561.   70
11 ran   ½,1½,nose,shtnk,1   (D Smaga)   D Smaga France

DEAUVILLE   Sunday August 3rd   Righthanded, Easy Track

Official Going Given As GOOD

2003 GROUP 3 PRIX MAURICE DE GHEEST 3YO+   £25336   6.5f   Good

249 LEAD ON TIME (O Douieb) 3-8-7 Pat Eddery 1: 121-21: 3 b c Nureyev - Alathea
(Lorenzaccio) Smart colt: despite a lengthy abs led 2f out for a comfortable win in a Gr 3
race at Deauville Aug 3: off the trk since being pipped by Faustus in Gr 3 Greenham Stks at
Newbury in April: won successive races in April, Goodwood (Lanson Champagne Stks) Newmarket,
Nottingham and Yarmouth last term: very eff over 6/7f and will stay further: acts on firm
and soft ground and on any trk: genuine and consistent.   85
1356 COMRADE IN ARMS (P Lallie) 4-9-0 G Dubroeucq 1: 0-21202: Sustained chall, just held
and has been in fine form this season: see 901.   81
754 BAISER VOLE (C Head) 3-8-11 G Moore 1: 31-0143: Gd eff after fair abs: see 467.   78
1011 CRICKET BALL (J Fellows) 3-8-7 C Asmussen 1: -330404: Fin strongly: fine eff: see 644 74
1857 OROJOYA 4-8-11 M Hills 1: -020020: Ran well: not btn that far: see 413.   70
1631 GREY DESIRE 6-9-0 K Darley 1: 4120230: Lack-lustre display: much btr 1631.   00
+1125 SPERRY 3-8-10 Paul Eddery 1: 0-20210: Led over ½ way, fin last: much btr 1125.   00
13 ran   ½,2½,nose,shtnk   (Maktoum Al-Maktoum)   O Douieb Newmarket

MUNICH (W. GERMANY)   Sunday August 3rd   Lefthand Galloping Track

2004 GROUP 2 EVENT 3YO+   £28249   1m 2f   Good

1712 HIGHLAND CHIEFTAIN (J Dunlop) 3-8-5 W Carson 1: 14-0121: 3 b c Kampala - La Primavera
(Northfields) Very smart colt: came from behind, led dist and comfortably forged clear to win
a Gr 2 race at Munich Aug 3: earlier comfortably won Welsh Derby at Chepstow and last time
was possibly unlucky when just failing to get up in a val listed race at Ostend: a smart and
consistent 2yo, winning at Brighton and Newmarket (2): eff over 10f, stays 12f well: acts
on firm and yldg and on any trk: genuine sort.   79
1492 ESQUIRE (B Hills) 4-9-4 B Thomson 1: 2112422: Led over 2f out, kept on well when
hdd and is most consistent: see 1492.   76
1712 DAUN (Germany) 5-9-4 E Schindler 1: 123-403: See 1712.   72
--   ALAGOS (Germany) 3-8-5 L Mader 1: 3-3:   70
--   PHILIPO 3-8-5 D Richardson 1: -110: Led briefly str, wknd: winner of German Derby.   66
9 ran   2½,2½,ddht,2   (D R Hunnisett)   J Dunlop Arundel, Sussex

VICHY (FRANCE)   Monday August 4th

2005 GROUP 3 GRAND PRIX DE VICHY 3YO+   £27125   1m 4f   Soft

-- AGENT DOUBLE (C Head) 5-9-0 G Moore 1: 10-3331: 5 b h One For All - Amya (Sanctus)
Very smart French horse: led 1f out comfortably in Gr 3 Grand Prix de Vichy Aug 4: first
success of this season but is said by his trainer to be an Autumn horse: failed to win last
term but in '84 won the Prix Royal-Oak at Longchamp: eff over 12f, stays 2m: fav by soft
ground: wears blinkers.   81
1595 ZAHDAM (G Harwood) 3-8-9 G Starkey 1: 11-1022: Came from off the pace, unable to
go with winner : possibly unsuited by this softish ground tho' ran a fine race: see 1595. 82
-- AFTER PARTY (G Mikhalides) 4-8-9 A Badel 1: 0000-23: Narrowly btn in a minor race
at St Cloud July 6: gd eff here and seems to be on the upgrade: stays 12f and acts on soft. 69
11 ran   2½,½   (J Wertheimer)   C Head France

PHOENIX PARK   Wednesday August 5th   Righthanded, Sharpish Track

Official Going Given As SOFT

2006 HARDWICK CUP LISTED RACE   £10810   7f   Soft

472 THE BEAN SIDHE (J Hayden) 3-9-1 C F Swan 4/1: 10-1301: 3 b f Corvaro - Whiskey
Mountain: Smart Irish filly: made all and kept on strongly when winning a val Listed Race
at Phoenix Park Aug 5 after a long abs: first time out turned up at 25/1 in Gr 3 1000 Guineas
trial again at Phoenix Park April 19: in '85 won at Naas nnd Phoenix Park: very eff over
6/7f on gd or heavy going: loves Phoenix Park and is best out in front when fresh.   74
1858 LONDON TOWER (D Weld) 3-9-1 M J Kinane 5/4 FAV: 2033122: Ridden 2f out but possibly
didnot see out this extra furlong in the soft going: best 1491 (6f).   69
754 KEMAGO (J Oxx) 3-9-1 D Hogan 4/1: -1-103: Gd eff after abs: likes soft ground: see 394 67
-- POKA POKA (C Collins) 4-9-6 P Shanahan 25/1: --00004:   64
1655 SYLVAN EXPRESS 3-9-4 G Carter 5/1: 0100100: Never going in the soft grd: twice
below 1490.   65
5 ran   2,½,shthd,1½,1½   (Mrs B Hayden)   J Hayden Ireland

PONTEFRACT   Thursday August 7th   Lefthanded, Sharpish Undulating Track

2007 EBF CARLETON MAIDEN STAKES 2YO   £2014   5f   Good/Firm 24 -14 Slow

-1738 AID AND ABET [9] (M Stoute) 2-8-11 W R Swinburn 5/2: 421: 2 b f Pas De Seul - Hiding
(So Blessed) Dsptd lead from start, led after ½ way and was ridden out in a 2yo mdn at
Pontefract Aug 7: sprint bred filly whose dam was successful twice as a juv: eff over 5f on
gd and fast ground: well suited by a sharp course: impr steadily.   40
1634 NEW MEXICO [1] (D Morley) 2-9-0 Pat Eddery 2/1 FAV: 4002: Al front rank: ran on
well: gd effort and seems best over this minimum trip: acts on gd and frm and on any trk.   39
1241 GREEN GLORY [4] (B Hanbury) 2-9-0 R Hills 3/1: 203: Led/dsptd lead till dist: fair
eff tho' twice below form shown on his debut in 1075.   30
94 HERR FLICK [2] (I Matthews) 2-9-0 G Carter(3) 11/1: 024: Needed race after long abs:
see 94 (soft).   18
962 STUMBLE [5] 2-9-0 K Darley 33/1: 00: Some late prog: cheaply bought colt who showed
a little improvement here.   12
1634 CARLS PRIDE [7] 2-9-0 L Charnock 20/1: 000: No threat: cheaply acquired colt who
is a half brother to 8/9f winner Hard About.   07
-- Not So Silly [3] 9-0   197 Fairburn [8] 9-0   -- Campeggio [6] 9-0
9 ran   1,3,4,2,1½   (James Wigan)   M Stoute Newmarket

2008 UPTON SELLING STAKES 3YO+   £904   1m 4f   Good/Firm 24 -24 Slow

1694 HOT BETTY [2] (P Butler) 6-8-11 Pat Eddery 7/1: 0004001: 6 b f Hotfoot - Sunstrucks
Betty (Sunstruck) Held up, stayed on to lead cl home in an all-aged seller at Pontefract
Aug 7: sold for 2,000 gns to R Thompson who trained her when she won a selling h'cap at
Brighton last summer: in '84 won at Redcar: best form over 10/12f on gd or faster ground:
acts on any track.   15
1102 DUBAVARNA [1] (C Gray) 5-8-7 I Johnson 9/1: 4-00002: Led inside dist, just caught
and remains a maiden: eff over 12f on gd/firm grd: acts on any trk.   10
-- GALAXY PRINCESS [9] (J Fitzgerald) 3-7-9 J Quinn(5) 20/1: -3: Led below dist, no
extra near fin on racecourse debut: clearly suited by 12f and gd/firm grd: acts on a sharp trk 06
1374 VERBADING [14] (S Norton) 4-8-7(vis) J Lowe 9/1: 0230004: Dwelt, ev ch: acts on
firm and soft ground and best form on a sharp course: see 524.   05
1892 MUSICAL WILL [12] 4-9-0(bl) R Hills 13/2: -004030: Al up there: see 1892 & 783.   09
838 DEERFIELD BEACH [4] 4-8-11 A Murray 16/1: 1-00000: Abs: not clear run: nvr nrr: see 202. 00
1502 EARLS COURT [6] 10-9-4 S Webster 9/1: 02-0400: Made most: wknd into 7th: see 1432.   00
1866 BOLDERA [13] 5-8-11 D Nicholls 5/1: JT FAV: 0000000: Fdd into 8th: see 1866.   00
1769 THE RUSK [7] 5-8-10 B Crossley 6/1: -000: Dropped in class: see 1769.   00
*1845 MURILLO [11] 10-9-4(bl) J Carr(7) 5/1: JT FAV: 2040010: Only beat one home: mucn btr 1845 00
1428 Our Annie [8] 7-9   1703 Johnny Frenchman [10] 8-10   00

```
--  Red Counter  [3] 8-10         1866 Lisaily  [5] 8-10
14 ran  nk,2½,½,2½,7,nk,½         (H James)          P Butler East Chiltington, Sussex
```

2009 PONTEFRACT MDN MILE C'SHIP FINAL HCAP   £3505   1m   Good/Firm 24 -06 Slow   [52]

+1743 TURFAH [2] (P Walwyn) 3-8-13(5ex) Paul Eddery 8/11 FAV: 0-02111: 3 b c Czaravich -
Hit It Rich (Search For Gold) Impr colt: heavily bckd and easily landed the odds, leading
below dist in a 3yo h'cap at Pontefract Aug 7: won a mdn over this C/D and a minor race at
Hamilton last month: very eff over 1m, should stay further: acts on firm and yldg grd and
on any track.   49
1841 FACTOTUM [5] (B Hills) 3-8-11 A Murray 7/1: 00-0032: Led early in str, no chance
with winner•tho' is in gd form: acts on any trk: see 941.   40
1776 PODEROSO [4] (R Boss) 3-9-7 Pat Eddery 5/1: 0-00403: Held up, no real threat:
better when out in front over this C/D in 1184.   42
1085 MOEL FAMMAU [1] (J Toller) 3-8-1 R Hills 12/1: -03004: Yet to reproduce form shown
over this C/D in 527.   21
1800 PORT PLEASE [3] 3-7-9 J Lowe 5/1: -4002P: Led till broke leg below dist, destroyed.   00
5 ran   2½,3,½   (Hamdan Al-Maktoum)   P Walwyn Lambourn, Berks.

2010 DIANNE NURSERY HCAP STAKES 2YO   £2569   6f   Good/Firm 24 +07 Fast   [53]

1683 TINAS MELODY [7] (J Winter) 2-8-2 R Hills 6/4 FAV: 3121: 2 b f Tina's Pet - Green
Chartreuse (French Beige) Narrowly justified fav, leading cl home in a fast run nursery h'cap
at Pontefract Aug 7: earlier a comfortable winner of a fillies mdn at Edinburgh: half sister
to sev winners, incl 2,000 Guineas runner-up Mattaboy: very eff over 5/6f: acts on gd and
firm ground and on any trk: may win again.   36
*1707 ONGOING SITUATION [2] (D Morley) 2-10-0(7ex) Pat Eddery 11/4: 01312: Persistent
late chall: just held and ran a fine race under his welter burden: genuine colt: see 1707.   61
1828 SILVERS ERA [5] (N Callaghan) 2-7-7(2oh) G Bardwell(7) 9/1: 0204003: Tried to make
all, not btn far: looks well h'capped on her early season form: stays 6f: see 473.   22
1527 LINN ODEE [3] (M W Easterby) 2-7-7(13ex) K Darley 8/1: 231404: AI front rank: stays 6f. 23
*1907 LIGHTNING LASER [4] 2-8-5(7ex) Gay Kelleway(3) 5/1: 0333010: Much btr over 7f in 1907. 15
1294 SWYNFORD PRINCESS [1] 2-7-7(11oh) L Charnock 25/1: 0410300: Best when winning a
seller in 543 (5f, yldg).   00
1155 MEATH PRINCESS [6] 2-7-7(5oh) J Lowe 20/1: 02000: Sn behind: best on yldg 376 (stiff 5f) 00
7 ran   nk,1½,1½,5,6   (Cheveley Park Stud)   J Winter Newmarket
```

**2011** STEWARDS MAIDEN AUCTION STKS 2YO    £1555    6f    Good/Firm 24 +04 Fast

```
1475 GLAMGRAM FOR GRAMS [1] (R Boss) 2-8-5(3ow) Pat Eddery 9/4 JT FAV: 041: 2 ch g Young
Generation - Super Jennie (Stephen George) Well suited by this extra furlong, made virtually
ev yard, comfortably, in quite a fast run mdn auction stks at Pontefract Aug 7: half brother
to a middle dist winner: stays 6f well: suited by fast grd and forcing tactics: seems to act
on any track.                                                                                42
1844 MILLFAN [9] (W Musson) 2-8-2(1ow) M Wigham 9/4 JT FAV: 232: Ev ch: stays 6f:see 938.    33
1883 TIKLAS [3] (F Durr) 2-7-11 G French 7/1: 00043: Smooth prog when slightly hmpd dist,
kept on again and fin clear rem: certainly improved of late: see 1650.                       22
1883 YOUNG BENZ [7] (M H Easterby) 2-8-4(1ow) M Birch 11/1: 0004: Front rank over 4f:
best over 7f in 1529.                                                                        11
1717 TAKE EFFECT [2] 2-8-0 K Darley 20/1: 3000000: Much btr early season on soft grd : see 47. 01
1883 MISS SARAJANE [6] 2-7-11 A Culhane(7) 33/1: 00: Mkt drifter and no threat: cheaply
bought filly.                                                                                00
1629 MADNESS NOT TO [4] 2-8-6 R Hills 5/1: 000: Sn scrubbed along: fin 8th: cost 5,700 gns:
should be suited by sprint dist tho' yet to show any worthwhile form.                        00
--  Champion Joker  [5] 8-10                1561 Stolen Star  [10] 7-11
1825 Brookside  [8] 8-0(bl)
10 ran  2,2,6,2,2,½        (Miss E Tully)          R Boss Newmarket
```

2012 GO RACING IN YORKSHIRE HCAP 0-35   £1850   6f   Good/Firm 24 -03 Slow   [35]

```
1810 TANFEN [7] (T Craig) 5-9-9 N Carlisle 12/1: 0210401: 5 b g Tanfirion - Lady Mary
(Sallust) Returned to form, led after ½ way and held on gamely in a h'cap at Pontefract Aug
7: earlier won similar h'caps at Thirsk and over this C/D: in '85 won at Newcastle, Hamilton
and Catterick: eff over 6f on any trk: acts on any going and does well with forcing tactics. 38
1765 SOFTLY SPOKEN [9] (P Felgate) 3-8-5 W Ryan 7/2 FAV: -012022: Just failed to get
up: in gd form and should win a small h'cap soon: see 1765.                                  26
*1765 DUFFERS DANCER [2] (W Pearce) 4-8-7(6ex) M Hindley(3) 7/1: 004-013: Ran well under
his penalty: see 1765.                                                                       18
1211 POMMES CHATEAU [1] (H Collingridge) 4-8-10(hd) M Rimmer 14/1: 00-0004: Kept on
from ½ way: returning to form: made all in a h'cap at Brighton early last season and
successful over this C/D in '84:best form over 6f on fast grd: likes a sharp course.         17
*1482 WORKADAY [3] 4-9-12 I Johnson 11/2: -000310: Ran on too late: btr 1482.                27
700  SINGLE HAND [12] 6-8-5 J Quinn(5) 20/1: 0000000: Nearest fin after fair abs: see 42.    00
1882 GODS SOLUTION [13] 5-9-2(bl) B Mcghiff(7) 9/1: 0200400: Speed over ½ way: seee 890.      00
*1676 WILLIE GAN [8] 8-8-6(6ex) L Charnock 10/1: 0230010: Much btr over this C/D in 1676.     00
1761 POKERFAYES [10] 7-7-12(bl) K Darley 4/1: -000020: Well bckd: front rank most of way
tho' wknd into 8th: btr over 7f in 1761: see 866.                                            00
```
```

1676 Off Your Mark [5] 7-12(3oh)   1765 Via Vitae [4] 7-7(3oh)
--   Nadron [6] 7-9(5oh)   1839 Sing Galvo Sing [11] 7-7(5oh)
13 ran nk,1,1½,2½,2,¾,1½   (Wm Burns)   T Craig Dunbar, Lothian, Scotland

---

YARMOUTH   Thursday August 7th   Lefthand, Fair Track

Official Going Given As GOOD/FIRM

2013 E.B.F. SCROBY SANDS FILLIES MAIDEN 2YO   £2010   7f   Good/Firm 35 -07 Slow

--   YLDIZLAR [6] (J Hindley) 2-8-11 M Hills 6/1: 1: 2 b f Star Appeal - My Therape
(Jimmy Reppin) Promising filly: mkt drifter, but led cl home in a 2yo fillies mdn at Yarmouth
Aug 7: half sister to sev winners, incl Domynsky, Dawn Star and Handlebar: eff at 7f, should
be suited by 1m+: acts on gd/firm ground: should rate more highly.   50
1322 MISTS OF AVALON [5] (H Cecil) 2-8-11 S Cauthen 2/1 FAV: 42: Made almost all: impr
filly who should go one btr soon: stays 7f: acts well on fast grd: see 1322.   48
1341 LUKMARIE [2] (C Brittain) 2-8-11 M Roberts 20/1: 43: Prom, stayed on under press:
should get 1m: see 1341.   41
1668 CAERINETTE [8] (A Bailey) 2-8-11(BL) P Bloomfield 10/1: 0434: Bl first time: prom
most: prob stays 7f: acts well on fast ground.   39
--   SKI SLOPE [4] 2-8-11 T Ives 5/1: 0: Sn prom on racecourse debut: impr likely: half
sister to 3 winners incl the smart '83 2yo Round Hill: should stay 1m.   34
--   TIPATINA [7] 2-8-11 R Guest 4/1: 0: No threat on racecourse debut: cost $270,000 as
a yearling and will do much btr than this: should be suited by .1m.   30
--   IF YOU PLEASE [1] 2-8-11 G Duffield 5/1: 0: Bckd at long odds, but no show: French
bred filly: should improve.   27
7 ran nk,3,½,2½,2,1   (K Al Said)   J Hindley Newmarket

2014 GOLDEN MILE SELLING H'CAP (0-25) 3YO+   £713   1m   Good/Firm 35 -05 Slow   [11]

1258 NATIVE IMAGE [8] (M Prescott) 3-8-10 G Duffield 4/1: -00001: 3 b c Try My Best -
Minsden's Image (Dancer's Image) Well bckd and led inside final 1f, ridden clear in a selling
h'cap at Yarmouth Aug 7 (bought in 3,200 gns): quite lightly raced prev in non-selling company:
eff at 1m, seems not to stay 12f: acts on gd/firm ground.   12
1188 HEATHGRIFF [12] (N Callaghan) 4-9-5 M Miller 11/4 FAV: -300002: Led 3f out: see 399.   05
1839 BALKAN [10] (J Harris) 6-9-1 A Proud 14/1: 0-30003: Prom, ev ch: likes Yarmouth: see 975 00
1579 HAMPTON WALK [3] (L Holt) 5-8-10 R Cochrane 13/2: -000004: Prom, ev ch: little form
this season: maiden: eff at 1m on a sound surface.   00
--   BIG LAND [4] 7-9-3 W Wharton 33/1: 00000-0: There over 5f on seasonal debut: 7yo
maiden who has shown little form in recent seasons.   00
1969 TAKE THE BISCUIT [1] 3-8-13(bl) A Mercer 14/1: 0003000: Quick reappearance: best 1210. 00
*1703 POLEMISTIS [5] 7-9-4(5ex) Sharron James 8/1: 0000010: Much btr 1703.   00
1699 COUNTESS CARLOTTI [9] 3-9-1 S Cauthen 5/1: 0-02400: Mkt drifter, no show: disapp
since 1134 (good).   00
1839 Trentullo Blue [2] 9-3   1439 Responder [7] 9-10(BL)
1288 Dicks Boy [6] 8-6(BL)
11 ran 3,3,4,½,3   (I Southcott)   M Prescott Newmarket

2015 MICHAEL BARRYMORE H'CAP (0-35) 3YO+   £2127   1m 6f   Good/Firm 35 +07 Fast   [30]

1615 SEVEN HILLS [2] (J Fitzgerald) 3-8-3(vis) M Roberts 6/1: 0-00031: 3 ch f Reform -
Campagna (Romulus) Led nearing final 1f, ridden out in a h'cap at Yarmouth Aug 7: first
success: acts on gd/firm and yldg grd: seems suited by 14f and the application of a visor.   28
1884 KNIGHTS HEIR [7] (H Whiting) 5-8-0 L Riggio(7) 16/1: 2000002: Ev ch final 2f:
best effort since 85.   08
1817 DIVA ENCORE [1] (R Armstrong) 3-9-7 S Cauthen 11/4: 0011223: Made much, in gd form.   41
1879 WALCISIN [5] (R Hannon) 3-8-8 G Duffield 9/2: 0220104: Nearest fin: see 1386.   28
*1817 REFORM PRINCESS [4] 3-8-12(vis)(4ex) R Cochrane 9/4 FAV: -003410: Well bckd: not
btn far: see 1817.   30
1535 GONE OVERBOARD [3] 3-9-1 R Carter(5) 7/1: -0400: Ev ch str: best 991 (11f).   31
1686 Jubilee Jamboree [8] 8-10
7 ran 2,¾,hd,1½,2   (Sir John Musker)   J Fitzgerald Newmarket

2016 DARKIE COSTELLO MAIDEN STAKES 2YO   £1238   6f   Good/Firm 35 +06 Fast

1754 RIOT BRIGADE [2] (C Brittain) 2-9-0 S Cauthen 1/1 FAV: 00331: 2 ch c Try My Best -
Lady R B (Gun Shot) Heavily bckd and made almost all, holding on gamely in quite fast run
2yo mdn at Yarmouth Aug 7: half brother to sev winners: eff at 6f, should be suited by 7f:
acts well on fast ground and a gall trk.   53
1653 START RITE [5] (W O'gorman) 2-9-0 T Ives 3/1: 02: Chall final 2f: btn a whisker:
gd effort and will win soon: should stay 7f: acts on fast ground.   52
--   I TRY [3] (L Cumani) 2-9-0 R Guest 13/2: 3: Mkt drifter: al there: improvement likely:
cost 52,000 gns: dam a useful 10f winner and will be suited by 7f+.   46
--   PIPSTED [6] (G Wragg) 2-9-0 P Robinson 11/2: 4: Prom, ev ch: should improve on this
initial effort: dam a useful 10f winner and will be suited by middle dist.   46

-- SLIM HOPE [1] 2-9-0 A Kimberley 8/1: 0: Friendless in mkt: never nearer: cost IR 200,000 and is a half brother to the smart Irish sprinter Exhibitioner: should improve.   41
1203 BARNBY DON [4] 2-9-0 N Leach(7) 33/1: 00: Prom ½ way, wknd: see 1203.   00
6 ran   shthd,2½,shthd,1½,15   (Philip Noble)   C Brittain Newmarket

2017 CITY OF NORWICH MAIDEN CLAIMING STAKES   £2028   1m 2f   Good/Firm 35 -12 Slow

1156 FOLLOW THE BAND [1] (W Jarvis) 4-9-8 S Cauthen 14/1: 00-0041: 4 b c Dance In Time - Yelming (Thatch) Mkt drifter, but led over 1f out, comfortably, in a Claiming Mdn at Yarmouth Aug 7: lightly raced this term: stays 10f well: acts on fast ground and on any trk.   38
1167 HEAD OF SCHOOL [9] (J Winter) 3-8-8 A Mackay 6/1: 20-0042: Led 2f out: prob best over 10f: see 839.   31
1806 COME TO THE BALL [8] (R Hannon) 3-8-3 G Duffield 2/1 FAV: 0000-03: Gambled on: stayed on tho' never nearer: maybe suited by 12f: acts on fast ground.   23
1540 GRIMESGILL [5] (J Hindley) 3-8-0 M Hills 4/1: -0044: Ev ch: btr 1540 (1m).   12
1558 IRISH HERO [7] 4-9-6 R Cochrane 5/1: -004020: Led 3f out: btr 1558 (easier trk).   18
1749 TAIS TOI [11] 3-8-0 C Rutter(3) 14/1: 0-40040: Wknd str: btr 1749, 422.   01
1220 FIRST SUMMER [2] 3-8-4(2ow) T Ives 8/1: -000: Active in mkt, no show: little form in 3 outings to date.   00
1494 NICE PRESENT [3] 3-8-5 R Curant 10/1: -000: Fin last: no form in 3 outings.   00
1831 Ribokeyes Boy [4] 9-8   1063 King Of Gems [6] 8-8 -- Regal Sam [10] 8-4
11 ran   1½,1½,4,1½,4   (Miss V Jarvis)   W Jarvis Newmarket

2018 RED FOX HANDICAP STAKES (0-35) 3YO   £2050   6f   Good/Firm 35 -05 Slow   [42]

-1810 MURPHYS WHEELS [4] (A Jarvis) 3-9-9 S Cauthen 1/3 FAV: 4112321: 3 b c Dublin Taxi - Lizzylin (Tower Walk) In fine form at present, led near fin, cleverly in a 3 runner h'cap at Yarmouth Aug 7: earlier won at Carlisle and Ayr: half brother to a couple of winning sprinters: seems equally eff over 5/6f: acts on firm and yldg grd and on any track: genuine and consistent.   45
1901 BON ACCUEIL [3] (H Whiting) 3-9-6(BL) L Riggio(7) 4/1: 2-00002: Led after 3f: caught cl home: eff at 6/7f: see 733: blinkered first time today.   39
1704 MAYOR [2] (M Leach) 3-9-2 N Leach(7) 9/2: 3400043: Led 3f: see 1704, 6.   28
3 ran   ½,2½,   (Mrs M A Jarvis)   A Jarvis Royston, Herts.

Official Going Given As FIRM

2019 EBF BLACK ROCK MAIDEN STAKES 2YO   £1903   7f   Good/Firm 28 -29 Slow

1234 MY NOBLE LORD [1] (P Cole) 2-9-0 T Quinn 2/1 JT FAV: 21: 2 b c Northern Baby - Fair (Madara) Useful colt: nicely bckd and led well over 1f out, comfortably, in a 2yo mdn at Brighton Aug 7: chased home the odds-on Timefighter at Salisbury on his debut: cost $300,000 and is a half brother to sev winners: stays 7f well: acts on fast grd and on any trk: should win more races.   53
1752 TUFTY LADY [5] (R Armstrong) 2-8-11 W Carson 14/1: 002: Led after ½ way, ran on gamely and comfortably beat rem: best eff to date: stays 7f well: acts on fast grd and sharp track: will find a race.   47
1731 STRING SECTION [11] (G Lewis) 2-9-0 P Waldron 2/1 JT FAV: 033: Early leader: ran on same pace: seems to act on any trk: acts on gd and firm: see 1392.   40
-- SEPARATE REALITIES [3] (G Harwood) 2-9-0(BL) G Starkey 12/1: 4: Bl on racecourse debut: picked up ground from ½ way and will improve for this experience: cost $425,000 and is closely related to numerous winners: sure to stay further: acts on gd/firm grd and on a sharp track.   39
1660 KNIGHTS NEVERGREEN [2] 2-9-0 W Woods(3) 14/1: 000: Nearest fin: btr eff: will be suited by 1m+: acts on gd and firm grd and on any trk: see 1660.   39
1731 FOURTH LAD [9] 2-9-0 B Rouse 8/1: 0040: Active in mkt: al prom: see 1232.   33
1752 PHILGWYN [10] 2-8-11 S Whitworth 10/1: 0230: Led/dsptd lead over ½ way: wknd and finished rear: btr on a stiff trk in 1752: see 1433.   00
1405 Connemara Dawn [4] 9-0   999 Frivolous Fancy [12] 8-11
1843 Riverboat Party [8] 9-0   1262 Magnolia Dancer [6] 9-0
1518 Tropical Boy [7] 9-0
12 ran   ½,3,½,nk,2   (Fahd Salman)   P Cole Whatcombe, Berks

2020 RINGMER SELLING STAKES 2YO   £790   5f   Good/Firm 28 -43 Slow

1944 OUT ON A FLYER [2] (D Elsworth) 2-8-8 A Mcglone 11/10 FAV: 0021: 2 b f Comedy Star - Listen To Me (He Loves Me) Made a quick reappearance and comfortably made all in a 2yo seller at Brighton Aug 7 (bought in 3,200 gns): expensive failure in a similar race at Folkestone on Monday: stays 6f but possibly btr suited by this minimum trip: acts on fast ground and on a sharp trk.   30
1496 HEDERA HELIX [4] (M Pipe) 2-8-11 B Thomson 11/8 : 022: Chased winner thr'out: will find a seller, possibly on a more galloping trk: acts on gd and firm: see 1496.   18

1803 GRENVILLE LASS [3] (M Madgwick) 2-8-8 P Hamblett 20/1: 03: Stayed on: has some scope
and will be suited by another furlong: acts on fast grd and on a sharp course.   12
1832 CLEARWAY [5] (R Hodges) 2-8-11(VIS) J Reid 9/1: 012044: Visored first time: btr
over 6f in 1163.   05
1550 BABY ALEX [1] 2-8-11 N Day 16/1: 00: Slowly into stride and never in race: dam
successful as a juvenile.   00
5 ran   4,1,3,dist   (Anthony Hunt)   D Elsworth Whitsbury, Hants

2021 BRIGHTON SPRINT H'CAP 3YO+ 0-70   £5472   6f   Good/Firm 28 +20 Fast   [60]

1852 GLEN KELLA MANX [2] (J Fox) 5-8-0 A Mcglone 13/2: 00-0001: 5 b m Tickled Pink -
Joshua's Daughter (Joshua) Returned to form, led below dist and ran on strongly in a fast
run h'cap at Brighton Aug 7: below her best last season tho' won 3 times at Windsor in '84
and loves a sharp trk: best form over 6f on firm or gd grd: said to be unsuited by large fields   44
1532 HIDDEN BRIEF [5] (R Boss) 3-8-12 E Guest(3) 14/1: 0-12002: Led 2f out: kept on well:
best effort for sometime: see 37.   59
1911 HILTON BROWN [8] (P Cundell) 5-9-4 P Cook 100/30: 0224303: Again had ev ch: see 1640.   58
*1852 GREEN RUBY [4] (G Balding) 5-9-2(7ex) J Williams 11/4 FAV: 0-03314: Well bckd:
outpaced early: ran on well from dist: comfortably beat today's winner in 1852.   54
1851 DREAM CHASER [7] 3-9-2 T Quinn 8/1: U-01000: Best on a stiff trk in 732.   51
1461 ROMAN RULER [1] 7-7-7(bl)(1oh) T Williams 14/1: 00-0040: No extra dist: btr 1367 (C/D)   12
1514 SIT THIS ONE OUT [10] 3-9-7 W Carson 10/1: 3030000: Wknd into 7th: best over 1m in 802   00
1211 EXERT [9] 4-7-7(8oh) N Adams 33/1: 4403000: Btr 922: see 114.   00
1971 BARRACK STREET [3] 3-9-7(VIS) G Starkey 20/1: 40-0040: Visored first time: dwelt and
no threat: see 1971.   00
1852 SUDDEN IMPACT [6] 4-7-13(bl) S Whitworth 8/1: 0043300: Led over ½ way: see 1461.   00
10 ran   1½,hd,1,4,3,½,½,1,shthd   (Bar Equipment & Refrigeration Co)   J Fox Amesbury, Wilts

2022 BRIGHTON SUMMER H'CAP 3YO+ 0-50   £2973   1m 2f   Good/Firm 28 +02 Fast   [41]

1788 DERBY DAY [1] (D Wilson) 5-7-7(bl)(1oh) T Williams 5/1: 4203001: 5 b g Shirley Heights
- L'Anguissola (Soderini) Made most and despite being hdd nearing final 1f, battled on gamely
for a nk success in a h'cap at Brighton Aug 7: first win this season: in '85 made all over
this C/D: very eff at 10f, stays 12f: acts on yldg, likes fast ground: best out in front
on a sharp track.   14
1497 LORD IT OVER [4] (G Harwood) 3-7-13(1ow) A Clark 9/2: -00002: Led over 1f out: out-
battled by winner: definitely best over 10f: acts on fast grd and a sharp trk: may be
suited by blinkers.   30
1223 SOCKS UP [7] (R J Houghton) 8-7-10 A Adams 13/2: 03-0403: Nearest fin: btr 12f?See 984.   13
1788 VAGUE MELODY [3] (L Piggott) 4-9-10 P Cook 2/1 FAV: 3011344: Well bckd, ev ch:
better 1788, 1173.   39
*1539 LEONIDAS [5] 8-8-13 J Reid 5/1: 0-00410: Mkt drifter: led early: see 1539 (made all).   28
1755 DUST CONQUERER [8] 5-8-3(bl) P Waldron 33/1: 3100/00: Fdd final 2f: did not race on
Flat in '85: last won in '84 at Yarmouth: has been tried over hurdles: prob best over 1m
on fast ground.   00
1321 Forgiving [6] 7-11(1ow)   1651 Tarrakan [2] 8-0
8 ran   nk,2,1,hd,2   (Nigel Spreadbury)   D Wilson Ashtead, Surrey.

2023 CLIFTONVILLE MAIDEN STAKES 3YO+   £959   1m 4f   Good/Firm 28 -15 Slow

1833 CHUCKLESTONE [3] (R Laing) 3-8-8 N Adams 25/1: -000041: 3 b c Chukaroo - Czar's
Diamond (Queen's Hussar) Fast impr colt: led inside final 2f, going well clear in a mdn
at Brighton Aug 7: stays 12f really well: acts on gd and fast ground and seems well suited
by a sharpish, undulating trk tho' prob acts on any.   37
1700 MISS SHIRLEY [5] (J Dunlop) 3-8-5 W Carson 9/2: 0-3022: No threat to winner: see 751.   24
1473 ASHINGTON GROVE [6] (D Murray Smith) 3-8-8 P Cook 7/1: -223323: Prom, ev ch:see 1473.   24
1589 PRODIGAL DANCER [4] (G Harwood) 3-8-8 G Starkey 10/11 FAV: -04: Well bckd, led 10f,
but found little when asked a question: see 1589.   22
1639 NO DOUBLET [2] 3-8-5 B Thomson 7/2: 3-32220: Ev ch str: fdd: frustrating: see 1639.   16
595 BATON MATCH [1] 6-9-6 J Williams 50/1: 000-030: Should be hurdling soon: see 595.   00
6 ran   8,3,2,3,25   (A Pettifer)   R Laing Lambourn, Berks.

2024 EDBURTON H'CAP 3YO 0-35   £1967   5f   Good/Firm 28 -08 Slow   [33]

1687 ARDENT PARTNER [4] (R Holder) 3-8-3 S Dawson 2/1 FAV: 0003021: 3 b f Native Bazaar -
Pelham Dream (Saucy Kit) Impr filly: well bckd and led 2f out, easily going clear in a h'cap
at Brighton Aug 7: last time out was a gd 2nd to the much impr Sanditton Palace at
Wolverhampton: very eff at 5f on gd and fast grd: likes a sharp/easy trk.   20
*1742 MISTER MARCH [5] (R Hutchinson) 3-9-8(7ex) P Hutchinson(3) 7/2: 0014112: Possibly
found this 5f too sharp, but kept on well & is in fine form: see 1742.   29
1476 RESTLESS RHAPSODY [7] (K Brassey) 3-9-4(bl) S Whitworth 11/2: -240403: Led over
3f: see 246.   22
1827 MY MUTZIE [2] (B Stevens) 3-8-7 N Day 20/1: 0-00004: Some late hdwy: best eff this
term: prob stays 6f: acts on fast ground.   11

1499 PERSIAN BAZAAR [1] 3-8-3 A Mcglone 12/1: 00-0000: No threat: see 1191.   04
726 LA DIVINA [3] 3-8-5 P Waldron 6/1: 004-040: Wknd over 1f out: abs since 726.   04
1849 BALIVIEW [6] 3-7-12 T Williams 33/1: 0000000: Little form to date.   00
1836 DUBLINAIRE [8] 3-9-7(bl) B Thomson 9/2: 03-0330: Mkt drifter: fin last: btr 1836(stiff trk).   00
8 ran   4,1½,½,1½,1   (H Dean)   R Holder Portbury, Avon.

HAYDOCK   Friday August 8th   Lefthand, Galloping Track

Official Going Given As GOOD

2025 MANCHESTER EVENING NEWS NURSERY HCAP   £2826   6f   Good 63 -05 Slow   [57]

1916 JAYS SPECIAL [8] (M W Easterby) 2-7-8 L Charnock 7/2: 40001: 5 b g Monsanto -
Gold Chebb (Cheb's Lad): Impr gelding: well bckd & led final 1f, easily in a nursery h'cap at
Haydock Aug.8: half brother to 2 winning sprinters: eff at 5f, stays 6f well: acts on gd
& yld grnd, possibly not firm: likes a gall trk & should find another nursery.   37
1641 FLEET FACT [2] (B Hills) 2-8-1 W Carson 9/4 FAV: 2002: Kept on final 1f, though no
threat to winner: gd effort: acts on gd & firm & on any trk: stays 6f, see 565.   36
1528 SHUTTLECOCK GIRL [5] (W Jarvis) 2-7-7(3oh) Dale Gibson(4) 8/1: 43033: Led ½way: see 722.   22
1225 OUR HORIZON [7] (D Barron) 2-7-11 J Quinn(5) 9/1: 2004: Never nearer: btr 1225: see 612.   18
1568 COUNT TREVISIO [1] 2-8-13 T Quinn 7/1: 1040: Prom, ev ch: btr 1568 (5f).   34
*1680 HARRY HUNT [6] 2-7-7(1oh) M Fry 10/1: 3100010: Dsptd lead, fdd: see 1680 (seller).   14
1555 CAPITAL FLOW [3] 2-8-4(1ow) Pat Eddery 6/1: 0430: Led 2f: btr 1555 (sharper trk).   00
1411 FLAXLEY [4] 2-9-7 S Perks 10/1: 13430: Early speed: see 781, 460.   00
8 ran   2,2,3,shhd,shhd   (T William Wilson)   M W Easterby Sheriff Hutton, Yorks

2026 WOOD PIT CLAIMING STAKES 2YO   £1515   6f   Good 63 -09 Slow

1770 MAZURKANOVA [11] (C Thornton) 2-8-5 J Bleasdale 9/2: 0042041: 2 b f Song - Red Lady
(Warpath): Led well over 1f out, ridden out in a 2yo claimer at Haydock Aug.8: first success:
eff at 5f, stays 6f well: acts on gd/firm & yld grnd & on any trk.   30
1828 GOOD TIME GIRL [10] (R Hannon) 2-8-10 W Carson 10/3 FAV: 011202: Led over 2f out:
gd run: see 1570, 1190.   29
1869 BREWIN TIME [9] (M H Easterby) 2-8-11 A Shoults(5) 7/1: 003: Kept on well: on the
up grade: should be suited by 7f: see 1869.   29
1576 BOLD HIDEAWAY [6] (R Sheather) 2-8-11 Pat Eddery 7/2: 04: Ev ch inside final 2f:
impr: will stay further than 6f: see 1576.   28
--   ISLAND LOCKSMITH [2] 2-8-11 M Hindley(3) 16/1: 0: Mkt drifter on debut: lost grnd
start & nearest fin: impr very likely from this half brother to Lakino and Fishpond: bred
to be well suited by middle dists: acts on gd grnd & a gall trk: one to keep an eye on.   23
1634 TAHARD [1] 2-8-11 S Perks 11/1: 00000: Prom most: little form since 694.   09
1675 STARS IN MOTION [4] 2-8-11 J Reid 5/1: 00030: Led 4f: btr 1675 (firm sharper trk).   00
--   Rockets Oak [5] 8-6   1955 Fossard [8] 8-11   1358 Bingo Queen [7] 8-4
10 ran   2½,½,½,3,6   (M D Marshall)   C Thornton Middleham, Yorks

2027 HAYDOCK LEISURE CO. HCAP 3YO 0-35   £4728   7f   Good 63 -01 Slow   [37]

1701 FLYING BIDDY [12] (J Hindley) 3-8-9 A Shoults(5) 12/1: 00-3001: 3 b f Affirmed -
Flying Bid (Auction Ring): Fin well to lead close home in a 3yo h'cap at Haydock Aug.8:
first success: lightly raced as a 2yo: eff at 7f, stays 1m: acts on gd & firm grnd & a
gall trk: should continue to impr.   28
1055 IMPERIAL PALACE [3] (C Tinkler) 3-8-4 L Charnock 14/1: -0002: Abs: led ½way, just
caught: best effort yet & seems to do well when fresh: ex Irish gelding who is eff at 7f
on gd ground: should find a h'cap.   21
1436 SURFING [7] (J Tree) 3-9-7 Pat Eddery 4/1: 003-243: Hmpd slightly 2f out: gd effort:
see 1245: acts on gd & firm grnd.   34
1256 STILL DREAMING [8] (N Vigors) 3-8-10 P Cook 16/1: 0-20404: Prom, ev ch: gd effort:
seems best over 7f on gd grnd: see 424.   22
*1840 BOLD SEA ROVER [11] 3-9-10(6ex) M Hindley(3) 10/1: 3013010: Ev ch str: in gd form.   35
1586 COURT TOWN [16] 3-8-11 W Carson 7/1: 04-00: Nearest fin: lightly raced filly who is
a half sister to 4 winners: eff at 7f on gd grnd & should impr on this.   19
1924 SOVEREIGN LOVE [5] 3-9-6(BL) T Lucas 6/1: 1323020: Bl first time: fin 7th: btr 1924(1m).   00
*1885 FRIVOLE [15] 3-9-7(6ex) T Quinn 10/3 FAV: 0-40110: Fdd 2f out: much btr 1885.   00
1917 Imperial Sunrise [1] 8-6   1813 Table Turning [10] 8-8(vis)
1628 Festivity [2] 9-3   1864 Broadhurst [14] 8-11   1794 Pells Close [6] 8-0(bl)
1841 Snarry Hill [13] 8-11   1637 Royal Rouser [4] 8-9   1830 By Chance [9] 8-6
16 ran   ½,2,nk,½,2,3,nk   (Guiting Stud Ltd)   J Hindley Newmarket

2028 D H WELTON STAKES 3YO+   £2582   1m 6f Good 63 -08 Slow

1538 BROKEN WAVE [6] (H Candy) 3-7-12 J Lowe 4/7 FAV: -1031: 3 b f Bustino - Britania's
Rule (Blakeney): Useful filly: landed the odds, led over 2f out. comfortably drawing clear
in a stakes event at Haydock Aug.8: first time out won a mdn at Salisbury: half sister to
smart middle dist winner Henry The Lion: eff at 12f, stays 14f well: acts on firm & yld
grnd & a gall trk: seems a genuine sort & should win more races.   59

604

*1848 HUSNAH [3] (L Cumani) 3-8-4 Pat Eddery 7/4: 3331212: Led nearly 12f: well clear 3rd: in fine form: see 1848. 53

1871 WESTRAY [4] (R Hollinshead) 4-9-0 S Perks 25/1: 0040403: Prom, ev ch: see 1563, 225. 22

-- SIRDAR GIRL [2] (D Thom) 4-8-7 G Sexton 100/1: 33--0-4: Impossible task: ran only once on the Flat in '85 & will probably be hurdling soon. 00

943 JIMNASTICS [1] 6-8-10 R Weaver 100/1: -00: Abs: no show. 00

1808 TOP ROW [5] 3-7-11 M Fry 50/1: 300-000: Prom much, wknd: mdn: clearly does not stay this trip. 00

6 ran   6,15,15,2½,1   (L N Holliday)   H Candy Wantage, Oxon

2029 EBF HERMITAGE GREEN MAIDEN STKS 2YO   £2241   6f   Good 63 +01 Fast

1512 HANSEATIC [4] (P Makin) 2-9-0 T Quinn 5/1: 0021: 2 b c Free State - Marista (Mansingh): Useful, impr colt: nicely bckd & despite changing his position nearing final 1f was a comfortable winner of a 2yo mdn at Haydock Aug.8: half brother to winning sprinter Halcyon Cove: eff at 6f, should stay 7f: acts on gd & fast grnd & on any trk: continues to impr. 51

1770 BLAZE OF GOLD [2] (E Alston) 2-8-11 J Reid 10/1: 022: Not clear run over 1f out: stayed on well: another gd effort: see 1770. 41

-- BOLD DUCHESS [12] (M Jarvis) 2-8-11 T Lucas 14/1: 3: Ch over 1f out: promising debut: cost 12,000 gns and is a half sister to a couple of winners: should be suited by 7f plus: acts on gd grnd & a gall trk. 40

-- ROLFESON [7] (B Morgan) 2-9-0 B Crossley 50/1: 4: Never nearer on debut: fair effort from this half brother to a winning 2yo: should be suited by 7f plus. 37

715 SONG N JEST [10] 2-9-0 A Murray 7/2: 320: Abs: led inside final 2f, fdd: needed race? 31

1488 NATIVE PAWN [11] 2-9-0 S Cauthen 5/4 FAV: 000: Heavily bckd: made much: btr on firm? 29

1958 SKOLERN [3] 2-9-0 M Hindley(3) 12/1: 400: Never nearer 7th: stays 6f: see 1958. 27

1427 Willowbank [9] 8-11   -- Kentons Lad [5] 9-0   1681 Savanna King [1] 9-0

-- Indian Sovereign [13] 9-0   665 Cashel View [8] 8-11

12 ran   2½,nk,2½,2½,½,½   (J P Carrington)   P Makin Marlborough, Wilts

2030 HAYDOCK PARK PONY CLUB MAIDEN 3YO+   £2461   1m 2f Good 63 +13 Fast

574 ALL HASTE [9] (H Cecil) 3-8-8 S Cauthen 2/5 FAV: -201: 3 b c Alleged - Hasty Dawn (Pronto): Very useful colt: despite long abs, heavily bckd & led final 1f, ridden out in a fast run mdn at Haydock Aug.8: first time out was an excellent 2nd to Allez Milord in a well contested stakes event at Newmarket, but ran poorly in the Mecca Dante at York in May & had been off the trk since: eff at 10f, should stay 12f: acts on gd grnd & a gall trk: should win more races. 60

1818 NAJIDIYA [11] (R J Houghton) 3-8-5 K Darley 8/1: 3-0202: Led 2f out: gd effort & 10L clear 3rd: acts on any trk & will find a mdn: see 1503, 937. 50

1645 LIKENESS [3] (W Hern) 3-8-5(bl) W Carson 15/2: 3-03003: No threat to first two: stays 10f: best 1043: now runs in blinkers. 30

1776 NORTH LAKE [2] (G Harwood) 3-8-8 A Clark 7/1: -004: Ev ch in str: much btr 1776. 23

983 TAP EM TWICE [7] 3-8-8 T Lucas 10/1: 04-2330: Fdd final 2f after abs: best 430 (12f). 18

1337 INDIAN LOVE SONG [1] 3-8-5 S Perks 33/1: -230430: Led 1m: see 1198, 911. 01

1880 Donor [8] 9-8   -- Deadly Going [6] 9-8   -- Prince Bold [10] 8-8

1686 Dime And A Dollar [5] 8-8

10 ran   2½,10,5,2½,7   (Sheikh Mohammed)   H Cecil Newmarket

---

NEWMARKET   Friday August 8th   Righthand, Stiff Galloping Track

Official Going Given As GOOD/FIRM

2031 OVERSEAS PROPERTIES H'CAP 3YO+ 0-60   £3967   2m   Good/Firm 29 -02 Slow   [43]

*1875 SARFRAZ [4] (G Harwood) 3-9-11(4ex) G Starkey 85/40 FAV: 0111011: 3 b c Sassafras - Ziba Blue (John's Joy): Very useful stayer: well bckd & led inside final 1f, gamely under 9-11 in a h'cap at Newmarket Aug.8: has been in fine form this season, earlier winning at Goodwood (2), Bath & Folkestone: eff at 14f, stays extreme dists well: acts on firm & yld grnd & continues to impr: will now step up from h'cap company. 65

1633 ORANGE HILL [6] (J Tree) 4-8-2(BL) W Newnes 11/2: 1-00042: Led over 1f out: battled on well & just btn: gd effort: bl first time today: see 942. 27

*1865 MARLION [8] (S Hall) 5-8-8(4ex) E Guest(1) 12/1: 0032413: Ch over 1f out, not btn far: in fine form: stays 2m well: see 1865. 31

1582 BALLET CHAMP [7] (R Holder) 8-8-3(bl) A Proud 9/1: 3030024: Nearest fin: needs further? 21

1848 MYCENAE CHERRY [5] 3-8-7(bl) T Ives 13/2: 0-1420: Prom much: btr 1848 (14f). 38

1865 JACKDAW [1] 6-8-6 A Culhane(7) 13/2: 0023120: Led over 14f: btr 1865, 1633. 22

1865 OLD MALTON [3] 4-7-12 R Hills 25/1: 0013300: Wknd over 2f out: best 990 (14f). 00

*1276 RHYTHMIC BLUES [2] 3-9-10 W Ryan 6/1: -110: Wknd & fin last: btr 1276. 00

8 ran   nk,1½,5,½,½   (K Abdulla)   G Harwood Pulborough, Sussex

2032 BARROW SELLING STAKES 2YO   £1786   7f   Good/Firm 29 -12 Slow

-- SHADE OF PALE [10] (P Haslam) 2-8-11 T Williams 9/1: 1: 2 b g King Of Hush - La Brigitte (Gulf Pearl): Mkt drifter, but ran on well to lead inside final 1f in a 2yo seller at Newmarket Aug.8 (bought in 6,600 gns): cost 9,200 gns: eff at 7f, should be suited by 1m: acts on gd/firm grnd & a gall trk: may prove btr than selling company. 35

1846 TRYNOVA [4] (G P Gordon) 2-8-8 W Ryan 3/1 FAV: 0202: Gd effort: see 1598, 1322: must
find a seller. 30
1844 TINAS BEAUTY [6] (G Blum) 2-8-8 P Bloomfield 33/1: 003: Dropped to selling company:
led briefly 2f out: gd effort: half sister to several winners: eff at 7f on a stiff trk:
acts on gd/firm & should find a similar event. 26
1570 HONEY PLUM [8] (M Usher) 2-8-8 M Wigham 15/2: 4404: Nearest fin: lightly raced this
season: eff at 7f, may stay further: acts on gd/firm & soft. 21
-- QUE PASA [12] 2-8-11 G French 20/1: 0: Stable companion of winner: never nearer: impr
likely on this initial effort: half brother to winning 2yo Handclap: should be suited by
1m: acts on gd/firm & is one to note for a similar event. 22
1881 PERTAIN [1] 2-8-11(bl) I Johnson 12/1: 0022040: Prom most: consistent: may stay 7f. 20
*1684 LEADING ROLE [3] 2-9-2(bl) T Ives 9/2: 00010: Made much: possibly ran too freely over
this stiff 7f: see 1684. 20
-- SWYNFORD LADY [5] 2-8-8 G Brown 6/1: 0: Early speed on debut: active in mkt today. 00
1483 St Johns Bay [11] 8-8   -- Gillys Comet [7] 8-8 1629 African Safari [9] 8-11
1881 Sweet Ribot [2] 8-8
12 ran ½,1½,2½,1,¾,2   (T C Ellis)   P Haslam Newmarket

2033 HEADLAND ESTATE AGENTS H'CAP 3YO+ 0-35   £2229 6f   Good/Firm 29 +12 Fast   [33]

1742 SHARP TIMES [3] (W Musson) 3-8-2 M Wigham 9/2 FAV: -021021: 3 b g Faraway Times -
Sharp Venita (Sharp Edge): In gd form, led inside the final 1f, ridden out in quite fast
run h'cap at Newmarket Aug.8: most consistent, earlier winning a selling h'cap again at
Newmarket: eff at 6f, stays 1m: acts on any grnd & on any trk, though likes Newmarket. 25
1608 STONEYDALE [1] (N Callaghan) 4-9-12 G Starkey 25/1: 0100002: Not the best of runs:
ran on well: returning to form: stays 6f & acts on any trk: see 734. 37
1429 REVEILLE [2] (M Jarvis) 4-10-0 T Ives 10/1: 2201003: Nearest fin: gd effort: see 1066. 39
1840 EASTBROOK [9] (S Hall) 6-8-8 K Hodgson 7/1: 0-21324: Al front rank: running well: see 369. 19
1849 SHAHREEN [10] 5-7-7(3oh) M L Thomas 7/1: 0-00030: Lost grnd start: never nearer: see 1849. 00
1840 ROSIE DICKINS [13] 4-9-0 R Lappin(7) 9/1: 3043140: Prom, not btn far: see 1649. 20
1901 EUCHARIS [14] 4-7-10(bl) A Mackay 8/1: 0000240: Led 2f out: fin 8th: best 1727. 00
2024 MISTER MARCH [7] 3-9-3(4ex) P Hutchinson(3) 7/1: 0141120: Quick reapp: btr 2024. 00
1627 Silent Gain [8] 8-9(bl)   1742 Beechwood Cottage [11] 8-7(bl)
1901 Debach Revenge [4] 7-7(2oh)   1834 Lucky Starkist [6] 8-13
1727 Ideoligia [12] 7-7(bl)(4oh)   1560 Bellepheron [5] 8-2(VIS)
14 ran 1½,shhd,shhd,1½,nk   (F W Briggs)   W Musson Newmarket

2034 MILDENHALL CLAIMING STAKES 3YO+   £2847   1m 4f Good/Firm 29 -22 Slow

1829 MUBARAK OF KUWAIT [3] (J Sutcliffe) 7-8-11 R Hills 4/6 FAV: 0/20-01: 7 b h Morston -
Dominant (Behistoun): Dropped in class & landed some heavy bets, led 2f out, ridden out in
a claimer at Newmarket Aug.8: very lightly raced in recent seasons, but formerly a very
useful h'capper, winning 4 times in '82: eff at 12f, stays 2m well: acts on gd/firm grnd
& is best on a stiff trk. 23
1829 KILIMANJARO BOB [2] (R Williams) 4-9-7(bl) T Ives 14/1: 0-00002: Led 3f out: now
wears bl: stays 12f: see 1186. 25
1578 GREAT TOPIC [10] (P Gordon) 3-8-6 W Ryan 20/1: -004003: Ev ch final 2f: best effort
yet from this mdn: stays 12f: see 998. 21
1898 HIGHEST NOTE [4] (G Blum) 3-8-3 M Rimmer 14/1: 3004324: Prom, ev ch: consistent: see 1898 12
1479 CHUMMYS OWN [12] 3-8-10 W R Swinburn 7/1: 1020130: Mkt drifter: never nearer: best
1302: may need longer than 12f. 13
1700 GOODTIME HAL [1] 3-8-4 M Hills 9/1: -432300: Never in it: lacks pace: see 1700. 01
-- SANTELLA MAN [7] 7-9-7 G Starkey 10/1: 01304/0: Made much after very long abs: formerly
a very useful stayer when trained by G Harwood, winning the Queens Vase at Royal Ascot in
'83: seems to have had many training problems & is now with P Cundell: front runner who
loves fast ground. 00
1656 Nelsonsuperyankee [11] 7-12   1690 Sandy Bill [8] 8-10
-- Not So Sharp [9] 7-9   1290 Katie Bridge [5] 8-0   1923 Rosanna Of Tedfold [6] 9-4
12 ran 3,¾,3,3,3   (Sheik Fahad)   J Sutcliffe Epsom, Surrey

2035 TUDOR GATE HOTEL NURSERY H'CAP 2YO   £4690 7f   Good/Firm 29 +02 Fast   [59]

1465 SANAM [4] (J Dunlop) 2-9-7 W R Swinburn 10/3: 4101: 2 ch c Golden Act - Rose Goddess
(Sassafras): Very useful colt: defied top weight, led 2f out, comfortably in quite fast
run nursery h'cap at Newmarket Aug.8: earlier won a valuable event at Ascot: from a gd
winning family which includes the smart Caro: well suited by 7f & will stay 1m plus: acts
on gd & fast grnd & seems well suited by a stiff trk: should win more races. 64
1920 EL BE DOUBLEYOU [3] (N Callaghan) 2-8-0 G Bardwell(7) 5/1: 020142: Al prom: in
fine form: runs well here: see 1843. 39
1925 PACIFIC BASIN [5] (W O'gorman) 2-8-9(BL) T Ives 4/1: 023403: Again well bckd: bl first
time & stayed on well: seems suited by a stiff 7f: acts on gd & firm grnd. 47
1920 BORN FREE AGAIN [2] (L Piggott) 2-8-8 R Cochrane 5/1: 002034: Ev ch 2f out: not
btn far: stays 7f well: see 1225, 780. 46
1846 OCONNELL STREET [6] 2-7-7(1oh) R Morse(3) 25/1: 000440: Dsptd lead most: best 1598. 25
1828 MURAJAH [7] 2-8-1 T Williams 12/1: 04000: Prom most: best 1039 (5f). 27

1925 HOMING IN [1] 2-9-3 G Carter(3) 5/2 FAV: 042140: Well bckd, but fin last: btr 1925(6f).   00
7 ran 1,¼,hd,3,3   (Prince A A Faisal)   J Dunlop Arundel, Sussex

2036 EBF ISLEHAM MAIDEN STAKES 2YO   £3775   7f   Good/Firm 29 -40 Slow

--   GENGHIZ [6] (L Piggott) 2-9-0 T Ives 2/1: 1: 2 ch c Sir Ivor - Royal Caprice (Swaps):
Well bdkd debutant & led nearing final 1f, comfortably in a slow run 2yo mdn at Newmarket
Aug.8: well bred sort who is obviously held in some regard: eff at 7f, should be suited by
1m plus: acts on gd/firm grnd & a stiff, gall trk: should rate more highly.   55
1791 ZARBYEV [9] (G Harwood) 2-9-0 G Starkey 5/6 FAV: 32: Heavily bckd: led 2f out:
possibly caught a tartar & should find compensation soon: stays a stiff 7f: see 1791.   52
--   CASHMERE N CAVIAR [2] (R Williams) 2-8-11 R Cochrane 33/1: 3: Gd late hdway on racecourse debut & will benefit greatly from the experience: cost 25,000 gns & will be well
suited by 1m plus: acts on gd/firm & a stiff trk: looks certain to find a mdn.   47
--   ABSINTHE [10] (D Morley) 2-8-11 R Guest 33/1: 4: Fin well from the rear on racecourse debut & will impr on this: half sister to winning 3yo Taranga: stays 7f well: acts
on gd/firm.   42
--   TORRES VEDRAS [3] 2-9-0 W R Swinburn 7/1: 0: Mkt drifter: no real threat, but seems
certain to step up on this: cost $900,000 and is a half brother to several winners: should
be suited by 1m & further: acts on gd/firm.   38
1928 TAFFY TEMPLAR [7] 2-9-0 M Hills 14/1: 300: Prom, ev ch: consistent: stays 7f: see 1928.   37
1903 UP THE LADDER [4] 2-9-0 P Bloomfield 33/1: 00: Never nearer 7th, but is making impr:
cost 17,500 gns as a yearling: stays 7f: acts on gd/firm.   00
--   Durbo [8] 9-0   1234 Lightfoot Prince [1] 9-0
--   Slippery Max [5] 9-0
10 ran ¼,¼,2½,4,nk,1   (Peter Wetzel)   L Piggott Newmarket

REDCAR   Friday August 8th   Lefthanded, Flat Galloping Track

Official Going Given As GOOD

2037 JACK COLLINS MEM. APP. H'CAP (0-35)   £1417   1m 2f   Good/Firm 32 -01 Slow   [28]

1909 RUSTIC TRACK [4] (Denys Smith) 6-8-4 R Vickers(2) 12/1: 2000301: 6 b g Palm Track -
Polly-Ann Tanja (Cletus): Led dist & ran on well to win an app h'cap at Redcar Aug.8: last
season won on this course, and also at Beverley: eff over 8/11f: suited by gd or faster grnd
& likes a gall trk.   12
*1800 DOMINION PRINCESS [8] (P Rohan) 5-8-13(5ex) Wendy Carter 6/1: 4330312: Waited with,
never nearer 3rd, placed 2nd: in gd form: see 1800.   12
1904 SAND DOLLAR [10] (M Prescott) 3-9-13 D D'arcy(5) 2/1 FAV: 00-133: Led briefly 2f out,
no extra dist: fin 4th, placed 3rd: much btr over 1m in 1904 (sharp trk).   22
1336 TREYARNON [7] (S Norton) 4-8-1 A Whitehall(5) 8/1: 4330004: Fin 5th placef 4th: best 631.   00
1964 ELARIM [2] 7-9-4 J Callaghan(5) 8/1: 0440000: Made much, btn dist: see 745.   07
611 BLACK RIVER [1] 5-7-13 G Hindmarch(3) 8/1: 40-0040: Long abs: led over 2f out: see 46.   00
1335 PATCHBURG [6] 4-9-7 B Mcghiff 8/1: 3010000: No threat: fin 8th: best in 611 (1m).   00
*1567 KAVAKA [5] 4-8-11 Kim Tinkler 13/2: -00012D: Led below dist, sn hdd: btn 1L in 2nd
though rider found guilty of careless riding & disq: see 1567.   17
1769 Biondoni [9] 7-10   1500 Tarleton [3] 8-0
10 ran 1,3,hd,4,½,1½   (D R Smith)   Denys Smith Bishop Auckland, Co Durham

2038 PAT PHOENIX HANDICAP (0-50) 3YO   £2784   7f   Good/Firm 32 -09 Slow   [46]

*1371 NEDS EXPRESSA [5] (N Tinkler) 3-8-8 M Wood 4/1: 0003411: 3 ch g Bay Express -
Lizzie Lightfoot (Hotfoot): Was never hdd when a comfortable winner of a 3yo h'cap at
Redcar Aug.8: last month employed similar front running tactics when winning at Beverley:
won at Catterick last season: eff over 7/8f: suited by fast grnd: acts on any trk.   36
1821 CARRIBEAN SOUND [6] (C Brittain) 3-9-1 S Cauthen 11/4 FAV: 4310042: Not reach winner.   39
1864 CERTAIN AWARD [3] (J Watts) 3-8-11 N Connorton 8/1: 0143: Denied a clear run below
dist, sn had ev ch: running well: see 1425.   34
1821 NAP MAJESTICA [7] (M Camacho) 3-9-2 D Nicholls 11/1: 0-00104: Al there: best in 1256.   33
1847 MUDISHA [2] 3-9-7 G Carter(3) 9/2: 0040130: No extra dist: best in 1571.   34
1885 AITCHANDOUBLEYOU [1] 3-8-5 J Quinn(5) 6/1: 0040000: Never reached ldrs: see 1093.   10
1794 ROYAL FAN [4] 3-8-11 K Hodgson 15/2: -001000: Chased winner over ½way: best in 891(6f).   00
7 ran 1½,hd,3,1½   (Ned Jones)   N Tinkler Malton, Yorks

2039 BONUSPRINT HANDICAP (0-50)   £3293   7f   Good/Firm 32 +15 Fast   [48]

1840 INISHPOUR [8] (H Wharton) 4-9-2 M Brennan 11/2: 0303431: 4 b c Nishpaour - Miss Britain
(Tudor Melody): Al close up, led below dist & sn clear in a fast run h'cap at Redcar Aug.8:
won over this C/D last term, after earlier winning at Newmarket: eff over 6/7f: well suited
by fast grnd & a gall trk.   48
1761 MARAVILLA [9] (J Etherington) 4-7-10 G Carter(3) 9/2: -000242: Comfortably beat rem
& should lose her mdn tag sn: see 1625 & 1104.   22
1638 IDLE TIMES [5] (C Elsey) 4-8-3 J Lowe 12/1: 1300003: Made most: see 240.   17

1525 WELL RIGGED [6] (M H Easterby) 5-9-9 K Hodgson 13/2: -212004: Fair effort under top
weight: best in 79 (1m, heavy).   36
1839 TOP OTHLANE [10] 9-7-7(1oh) L Charnock 25/1: 0-04000: Some late prog: see 1424.   00
1868 AIR COMMAND [7] 6-9-2 A Shoults(5) 7/1: 0000020: Speed over ½way: much btr in 1868. 13
*1864 HEAVENLY HOOFER [4] 3-7-11(8ex) J Quinn(5) 15/2: 0110310: Tardy start & no threat:
btr judged on 1864.   00
*1868 THE MAZALL [1] 6-8-13(8ex) D Nicholls 4/1 FAV: 2022110: Early speed: fin 7th: much btr 1868.00
1702 Fringe Of Heaven [2] 9-1(2oh)   1906 Always Native [11] 7-7(2oh)
1870 Running Bull [3] 7-10(VIS)
11 ran   2¼,6,nk,4,4,1½   (Peter Halsall)   H Wharton Wetherby, Yorks

2040 JOHN SMITHS BREWERY HCAP 3YO+ 0-35   £1772   2m   Good/Firm 32 -05 Slow   [35]

1772 JOIST [5] (M Prescott) 4-8-8(bl) G Duffield 6/4 FAV: 0024321: 4 ch g Malinowski -
Junella (Midsummer Night II): Well bckd & led below dist, strongly ridden & held on well
in a h'cap at Redcar Aug.8: lightly raced last season, when successful from two rivals over
this C/D: eff over middle dists, stays 2½m well: acts on any going & on any trk: wears bl. 22
712 SUN STREET [6] (C Brittain) 4-8-9 S Cauthen 9/2: 40-4002: Gd effort after fair abs:
kept on well & is suited by a test of stamina: acts on any trk: see 366.   21
1700 LAKISTE [2] (J Watts) 3-7-10 L Charnock 10/1: -0443: Led early & again home turn:
gd effort over this lngr trip: acts on fast grnd: see 894.   19
1865 BUCKLOW HILL [1] (J Fitzgerald) 9-9-7 A Murray 9/2: -000034: Smooth prog to chall
dist, no extra: not the force he once was: see 782.   28
*1897 BUSTOFF [4] 6-7-11 J Callaghan(7) 7/2: -230010: Btr on a sharp trk in 1897.   02
1745 UPLAND GOOSE [3] 5-7-7 J Quinn(5) 20/1: 304/200: Made much: well btn: see 1195.   00
6 ran   1,1½,1½,2,25   (Mrs W J Armstrong)   M Prescott Newmarket

2041 STOCKTON STALLHOLDERS SELLER 3YO   £918   1m 1f   Good/Firm 32 -13 Slow

774 PRINCESS ANDROMEDA [2] (G Pritchard Gordon) 3-8-11 G Duffield 8/1: 0-001: 3 b f Corvaro-
Frisky Matron (On Your Mark): Led dist, gamely in a 3yo seller at Redcar Aug.8 (sold for
3,500 gns): first success: lightly raced filly who had shown little ability previously: stays
9f: acts on gd/firm grnd & on a gall trk: clearly does well when fresh.   24
1540 ATROMITOS [1] (C Brittain) 3-9-0 P Robinson 5/2: -400002: Tried to make all, kept
on gamely & only just denied: gd effort: rated 47 in a Salisbury h'cap first time out
in 157 (yielding).   26
*1960 GIRDLE NESS [3] (N Tinkler) 3-8-11 Kim Tinkler(5) 4/7 FAV: -400113: Held up, ev ch. 20
1699 DIX ETOILES [4] (J Fitzgerald) 3-8-11 A Murray 8/1: -100034: Never dngr: best in 305. 06
4 ran   nk,1½,7   (Brian Pollins)   G Pritchard Gordon Newmarket

2042 DUNCAN NORVELLE STAKES 3YO   £822   1m 4f   Good/Firm 32 +10 Fast

1923 BUCKLEY [5] (L Cumani) 3-9-0 R Guest 1/1 FAV: -31: 3 b c Busted - Queensferry
(Pindari): Heavily bckd, ran on strongly final 1f when ddht in a fast run 3yo stakes at
Redcar Aug.8: half brother to numerous winners: very eff over 12f on fast grnd: well suited
by a fall trk: scope for further impr.   48
1031 ROYAL DYNASTY [2] (G Wragg) 3-9-0 S Cauthen 6/1: -0001: 3 b c Ile De Bourbon -
Popkins (Romulus): Made most when ddht in quite a fast run 3yo stakes at Redcar Aug.8: closely
related to several useful winners: stays 12f well: acts on gd & fast grnd & on a gall trk:
does well with forcing tactics.   48
1578 HIGH KNOWL [7] (B Hills) 3-9-0 B Thomson 5/1: 0-423: Gd effort: stays 12f: see 1206. 45
1690 NOBLE RISE [6] (G Harwood) 3-9-0 A Clark 4/1: 3-44: Lngr trip: wknd dist: see 1690.   33
1775 TURINA [4] 3-8-11 M Beecroft 16/1: 0-0030: Btr over 11f in 1775.   25
714 SOMETHING SIMILAR [1] 3-9-0 A Murray 11/1: 204-000: Abs: lost place halfway: much btr 613.27
823 GUNNER MAC [3] 3-9-0 D Nicholls 100/1: 0-00000: Outsider & no threat after abs: mdn
who has shown little ability to date.   00
7 ran   ddht,1½,7,3,hd   (Mrs A Chapman)   L Cumani Newmarket
                                (E B Moller)   G Wragg Newmarket

2043 EBF SINNINGTON MAIDEN FILLIES STKS 2YO   £2469   6f   Good/Firm 32 -34 Slow

1650 SEEK THE TRUTH [3] (H Cecil) 2-8-11 S Cauthen 4/6 FAV: 21: 2 b f Exclusive Native-
Royal Suspicion (Bagdad): Narrowly landed the odds in a 2yo fillies mdn at Redcar Aug.8,
made virtually ev yd in game fashion: half sister to several winners: eff over 6f & should
stay at least another furlong: acts on fast grnd & on a gall trk.   48
1802 GHANAYIM [2] (H T Jones) 2-8-11 A Murray 3/1: 022: Led briefly dist, just btn:
should get her head in front soon: see 1802.   46
-- SO KIND [12] (J Watts) 2-8-11 N Connorton 8/1: 3: Ran on promisingly on racecourse
debut: nicely bred filly who is a half sister to several winners, incl winning juvenile
Que Sera: eff over 6f on gd/firm grnd: acts on a gall trk: should find a race.   41
1825 SUPERCUBE [9] (E Carter) 2-8-11 Wendy Carter(7) 16/1: 0434: Dwelt, nearest fin: see 1225. 40
-- LISETA [13] 2-8-11 B Thomson 25/1: 0: Slowly away, going on fin & although well btn
will come on for this experience: closely related to a couple of modest winners: acts on
gd/firm grnd.   24
437 EMSLEYS HEIGHTS [8] 2-8-11 J Callaghan(7) 33/1: 00: Speed over ½way after long abs:
cost 6,000 gns and is a half sister to several winners, incl useful juvenile Emboss: acts
on gd/firm ground.   23

608

REDCAR   Friday August 8th   -Cont'd

1632 ROMAN BELLE [10] 2-8-11 G Duffield 7/1: 030: Fin in rear: much btr in 1632 (5f).   00
864 Katie Says [5] 8-11   -- Heckley Loch [6] 8-11 1650 Able Abbe [1] 8-11
1119 Lascivious Intent [4] 8-11   1722 Miss Zola [11] 8-11
1770 Treize Quatorze [7] 8-11
13 ran   nk,1½,hd,7,hd,1,shhd,1   (Wills S Farish III)   H Cecil Newmarket

LINGFIELD ,   Friday August 8th   Lefthanded, Sharpish Undulating Track

Official Going Given As GOOD

2044 HAMMERWOOD STAKES 2YO   £2264   7f   Good/Firm 29 -06 Slow

1780 DEPUTY GOVERNOR [10] (L Piggott) 2-8-11 T Ives 3/1:   31: 2 ch c Master Willie -
Regent Miss (Vice Regent): Useful colt: clearly btr for recent debut & led inside dist,
rather comfortably in a 2yo stakes at Lingfield Aug.8: showed plenty of promise behind Classic
Tale in an Ascot mdn late last month: half brother to several winners: very eff over 7f &
should stay at least 1m: suited by fast grnd: seems to act on any trk: likely to impr further
& sure to win more races.   54
*1587 ANGARA ABYSS [9] (G Harwood) 2-9-5 G Starkey 1/2 FAV: 4112: Well bckd to complete
his hat trick: outpcd inside dist though beat rem decisively & remains in gd form: see 1587. 58
1587 SYLVAN ORIENT [8] (P Mitchell) 2-8-11 A Mcglone 50/1: 0003: Stayed on late: clearly
btr suited by this lngr trip: cost 11,000 gns & is a half brother to 12f winner Beau Vista:
eff over 7f on gd/firm grnd.   30
1665 COMBINED EXERCISE [2] (R Smyth) 2-8-11 S Whitworth 50/1: 0004: Btn dist: see 1665.   28
-- ANGEL CITY [4] 2-8-11 Paul Eddery 20/1: 0: Outpcd final 1f though showed plenty of
early pace & will be btr for this experience: cost I.R. 7,600 & should be suited by a
lngr trip in time: acts on gd/firm grnd & on a sharp trk: one to keep an eye on.   27
-- BATTALION USA [11] 2-8-11 B Rouse 16/1: 0: Showed signs of inexperience on his debut
& will come on for this race.   15
1518 Low Line [3] 8-8   1587 Jonite [12] 8-11   1518 Toms Little Bet [7] 8-8
1728 Design Wise [6] 8-11   -- Glen Weaving [5] 8-11   1583 Miami Lass [1] 8-8
12 ran   1½,8,½,hd,6,5,½,½   (Prince Ahmed Salman)   L Piggott Newmarket

2045 GODSTONE SELLING STAKES 2YO   £958   6f   Good/Firm 29 -45 Slow

1262 PARKLANDS BELLE [6] (M Haynes) 2-8-8 B Rouse 7/2 FAV: 0240201: 2 b f Stanford -
Kelly's Curl (Pitskelly): Was well bckd & led under press inside dist in a 2yo seller at
Lingfield Aug.8 (bought in 1,150 gns): earlier had shown promise in btr company, rated 37
behind Clarentia at Kempton: eff over, 5/6f: acts on any going & is well suited by a sharp course. 25
939 FLYING SILENTLY [4] (D Haydn Jones) 2-8-8 D Williams(7) 12/1: 03302: Led mid-trk
from ½way, no extra inside dist though ran a gd race after fabs: eff over 5/6f on gd/firm.   18
1802 KINSHAM DENE [11] (J Douglas Home) 2-8-8 W Newnes 10/1: 03: Early ldr: showed
promise & should impr enough to win in this grade: acts on gd/firm grnd & on a sharp trk.   16
1846 RIPSTER [12] (R Stubbs) 2-8-11 A Mercer 11/2: 004: Dropped in class & sn prom:
scope for further impr: see 1846.   10
1305 WHATS A GUINEA [13] 2-8-8 W Woods(3) 20/1: 000: Led/dsptd lead till dist: cheaply
acquired filly who is a half sister to several winners: acts on gd/firm.   03
1946 GONE FOR IT [9] 2-8-8 R Curant 5/1: 000000: Dwelt, nearest fin: dropped in class
today & nicely bckd: should do btr than this.   00
-- NEIRBO LASS [10] 2-8-8 M Hills 10/1: 0: Mkt drifter on debut: fin 7th & should impr.   00
1599 ABSALOUTE HEAVEN [3] 2-8-11 David Williams(7) 10/1: 0010200: Early speed: fin 9th.   00
1803 JETMORE [8] 2-8-11(bl) G Starkey 5/1: 02000: Al behind: btr over this C/D in 1262.   00
1832 Blotin [1] 8-11(VIS)   1557 Bonzo [2] 8-11   1318 Snapshot Baby [5] 8-8(bl)
12 ran   2,½,3,1½,2½,hd,1,4   (D F Hatch)   M Haynes Epsom, Surrey

2046 COWDEN HANDICAP STAKES (0-35)   £1909   6f   Good/Firm 29 +02 Fast   [35]

1933 LONELY STREET [14] (P Arthur) 5-9-1 L Johnsey(7) 11/2: 0203201: 5 b m Frimley Park-
Abalone (Abwah): Proved a comfortable winner, led below dist & was sn clear in a fast run
h'cap at Lingfield Aug.8: most consistent this term & deserved this win: won at Goodwood in
'85 & in '84 was successful at Bath: eff over 5/6f on gd & firm grnd: likes a sharp course. 34
-1834 GALLANT HOPE [2] (L Cottrell) 4-7-12 N Carlisle 8/1: 0002022: Led inside final 2f:
in gd form: see 1834.   07
1834 THREE BELLS [16] (M Mccourt) 4-8-12 R Wernham 5/1 FAV: 0-00043: Kept on final 1f:
fair effort: seems eff over 6f on gd/firm: see 1834 : backed from 10/1 today.   19
1805 DOWNSVIEW [9] (A Moore) 4-9-11 M Wigham 14/1: 0100004: Ran well under 9-11: best 855. 32
1669 MALEIHA [10] 3-8-8 T Ives 14/1: -02000: Ch over 1f out: kept on: best 656 (hvy grnd 7f) 18
836 PINE HAWK [18] 5-8-8 D Williams(7) 8/1: -410100: Abs: better for race: see 679.   18
+1499 WAR WAGON [11] 3-9-4(vis) P Tulk 15/2: -000100: Made much, wknd: much btr 1499 (C/D). 00
1940 BELLE TOWER [15] 4-9-2 C Rutter(3) 10/1: 2100100: Made no show: best 1319.   00
1603 Naughty Nighty [3] 7-9   1581 Santella Pal [5] 7-8(VIS)
1940 Hildalarious [13] 7-7   1852 Shades Of Blue [6] 8-8
929 Cresta Leap [1] 8-9   1947 Dalssan Bay [8] 8-5   1272 Lauries Trojan [17] 8-3
1018 Mia Jubes [12] 7-13   1521 Shelbee [7] 7-12   1940 Linton Starchy [14] 7-10
18 ran   3,½,shhd,1½,nk   (Terence P Lyons III)   P Arthur Abingdon, Oxon

2047 EDENBRIDGE NURSERY HANDICAP 2YO   £2166   5f   Good/Firm 29 +12 Fast   [59]

+1938 MUKHABBR [4] (C Benstead) 2-7-7(7ex) T Williams 11/10 FAV: 030311: 2 b c Taufan -
Ribotingo (Petingo): Fast impr colt: heavily bckd & readily defied his 7lbs penalty in a
fast run nursery h'cap at Lingfield Aug.8: last time out made ev yd for a runaway win in
a similar event at Windsor: half brother to very useful sprinter Pampas: very eff over 5f,
should stay 6f: does well with forcing tactics: seems certain to complete the hat trick.   44
1910 CLARENTIA [6] (M Usher) 2-8-2 M Wigham 5/1: 214032: Dsptd lead most: in gd form:
caught a tartar: see 1910, 400.   41
1585 SAMLEON [2] (R Hannon) 2-8-5 L Jones(5) 16/1: 4123403: Kept on final 1f: fair effort.   40
1936 JUVENILEDELINQUENT [8] (A Bailey) 2-8-2 R Cochrane 6/1: 124: Prom, ev ch: btr 1936.   35
*1632 MAKE OR MAR [1] 2-8-12 S Whitworth 10/1: 010: Lost grnd start: fdd inside final 2f.   35
1910 ARTFUL MAID [9] 2-7-11 A Mackay 14/1: 0100: Some late hdway: lightly raced since 40.   19
1760 ALKADI [3] 2-9-7(bl) T Ives 7/1: 3201320: Stiff task under 9-7: see 1760.   00
1828 ENCHANTED TIMES [7] 2-9-0(VIS) Paul Eddery 10/1: 13000: Speed 3f: best early season
in 187 (yld): visored first time.   00
1557 CHERRYWOOD SAM [5] 2-7-7(VIS) C Rutter(3) 25/1: 4040130: Visored first time: best 1318   00
9 ran   2½,1½,½,4,hd,1½,1,12   (Hamdan Al-Maktoum)   C Benstead Epsom, Surrey

2048 FELCOURT MAIDEN 3YO FILLIES   £959   1m 4f Good/Firm 29 -09 Slow

1786 NEWQUAY [7] (G Harwood) 3-8-11 G Starkey 15/8 FAV: 3-0221: 3 b f Great Nephew -
Quay Line (High Line): Switched & qcknd to lead close home in a 3yo fillies mdn at Lingfield
Aug.8: eff over 12/14f: suited by fast grnd: acts on any trk.   46
--   COMMANCHE BELLE [5] (L Cumani) 3-8-11 P Hamblett 4/1: 2: Led below dist, worried out
of it close home: sure to impr for this experience & will make amends soon: half sister to
useful duo Band & Zimbalon: stays 12f well: acts on gd/firm grnd & on a sharp trk.   44
1818 LOUVECIENNES [1] (O Douieb) 3-8-11 R Cochrane 2/1: -333: Well bckd: tried to make
all: clear of rem though is proving a little disapp: stays 12f: see 1818 and 991.   42
1690 MARY SUNLEY [3] (J Francome) 3-8-11 J Williams 12/1: -004: Btn dist: btr in 1690 (10f).   22
1688 SAGAREME [8] 3-8-11(VIS) B Rouse 33/1: 0-40000: Visored for the first time: no threat.   14
--   ELOQUENCE [2] 3-8-11 D Brown 8/1: -0: Never dngr on debut though did make some late
prog & will be btr for this race: bred to be suited by middle dists.   09
1670 Shajar Ad Durr [4] 8-11   1751 Miss Bluebell [6] 8-11
8 ran   ¾,1,12,4,2½,15,3   (K Abdulla)   G Harwood Pulborough, Sussex

2049 DORMANSLAND HANDICAP STAKES [0-50]   £2742   1m 2f Good/Firm 29 -17 Slow   [47]

1441 HEART OF STONE [8] (R Akehurst) 4-8-3 S Whitworth 9/4: -001031: 4 ch c Dust
Commander - Grankie (Nashua): Led below dist, comfortably in a h'cap at Lingfield Aug.8:
clearly likes this sharp trk, won over this C/D in June: eff over 10/11f: acts on fast &
yld grnd: can win again.   34
*1368 ASK MAMA [4] (J Dunlop) 3-9-0 B Rouse 4/1: 02-3012: Made most: in gd form: see 1368.   51
1450 TALK OF GLORY [2] (L Cottrell) 5-8-6 N Carlisle 2/1 FAV: 0200223: Well bckd: again
had ev ch: running well though has not won for sometime: see 453.   30
1441 REDDEN [5] (M Bolton) 8-8-6 C Rutter(3) 8/1: 00-1404: Fair effort: best in 750.   25
1393 STRAIGHT THROUGH [1] 3-8-6 D Dunnachie(7) 4/1: 2122100: Best over 12f in 1233.   36
1787 SEVEN SWALLOWS [3] 5-8-3 M Rimmer 14/1: -100000: Much btr over this trip in 184 (yld).   10
1830 CHATTERSPARK [6] 3-7-7 P Simms(0) 33/1: 0030-00: AI rear on belated seasonal debut:
mdn who showed only modest ability in his races last term.   00
7 ran   2,½,2½,shhd,6,8   (M J Morrison)   R Akehurst Epsom, Surrey

---

REDCAR   Saturday August 9th   Lefthanded, Flat Galloping Track

Official Going Given As GOOD

2050 BEDALE SELLING STAKES 2YO   £3043   7f   Good/Firm 32 -24 Slow

1612 CRAIGENDARROCH [13] (J S Wilson) 2-8-11 C Dwyer 6/1: 4001: 2 b c Raga Navarro -
Balcanoona (Cawston's Clown) First venture into selling co was nicely bckd, gamely led
inside dist in a 2yo seller at Redcar Aug 9 (bought in 5500 gns): speedily bred colt who
stays 7f well: acts on gd and firm grd and is well suited by a gall trk.   28
1883 EUROCON [11] (D Chapman) 2-8-11 D Nicholls 20/1: 000002: Led below dist, just caught:
4l clear rem and ran his best race to date here: stays 7f: acts on gd and firm: see 931.   28
1050 SERGEANT MERYLL [10] (J Watts) 2-8-11 A Mercer 7/1: 003: Dropped in class: never
nearer: eff over 7f on gd/firm ground: acts on a gall track.   20
*1795 GILLOT BAR [15] (M W Easterby) 2-8-8 K Hodgson 9/2: 0000214: Tried to make all:see 1795.   16
1795 LYN RAE [5] 2-8-8 M Birch 14/1: 00040: Front rank thr'out: see 1795.   13
1862 PHILEARN [2] 2-8-8(BL) K Darley 14/1: 4400020: BI first time: early speed from adverse
draw: best over this C/D in 1862.   11
*1622 MADAME LAFFITTE [12] 2-8-8 M Wood 5/1: 0210: Fdd into 7th: best in 1622 (sharp trk)   00
1795 CHANTILLY DAWN [6] 2-8-8 K Bradshaw(5) 8/1: 000120: Wknd into 9th: btr in 1795.   00
1764 RUSTIC EYES [9] 2-8-11 N Day 4/1 FAV: 230: Dropped in class: btr over 6f in 1764.   00
1253 Friends For Life [14] 8-11   1795 My Mabel [1] 8-8   00

1905 Delite Muffin [4] 8-8		1955 Creole Bay [8] 8-8(BL)	
1528 Enchanted Court [7] 8-11			181 Above The Salt [3] 8-11
15 ran shthd,4,½,1½,1	(R B Morrison)		J S Wilson Ayr, Scotland.

2051 NEW MARSKE SPORTS CLUB STAKES 2YO   £2260   7f   Good/Firm 32 -24 Slow

-- ELEGANT ISLE [9] (J Watts) 2-8-6 A Mercer 5/1: 1: 2 br c Ile De Bourbon - Elegant Tern (Sea Bird II) Promising colt: comfortably made all on his debut in a 2yo stks at Redcar Aug 9: half brother to very useful 7/10f winner Elegant Air: clearly eff over 7f on gd/firm grd: acts on a gall trk: can only improve.   54

-- WOODPECKER [2] (H T Jones) 2-8-6 A Murray 6/5 FAV: 2: Heavily bckd debutant: chased winner thr'out: beat rem decisively: nicely bred colt who is a half brother to sev winners: eff over 7f on gd/firm ground: acts on a gall trk: will find a race.   45

1958 NORTON MELODY [7] (M H Easterby) 2-8-11 M Birch 4/1: 333: Friendless in mkt: outpaced below dist: best on his debut in 1634 (6f, sharp trk).   34

-- NICOPHANA [6] (Don Enrico Incisa) 2-8-3 M Beecroft 50/1: 4: Rank outsider: stayed on well after slow start and likely to improve for this experience: acts on gd/firm grd and on a gall track.   20

*1625 WORTHY PRINCE [1] 2-9-3 P D'arcy 9/1: 10: Speed over ½ way: btr 1625 (6f, sharp trk).   30

-- SPATS COLUMBO [8] 2-8-6 M Wood 10/1: 0: Fdd after ½ way: half brother to winning juv Song To Singo.   14

-- MAJESTIC MISS [4] 2-8-4(1ow) D Nicholls 33/1: 0: Mkt drifter: never reached leaders.   00

-- MILL TRIP [3] 2-8-6 G Duffield 7/1: 0: Btr for race: cost 21,000 gns as yearling: will be suited by further in time.   00

8 ran   3,8,2,2,2½   (Mrs G Weston)   J Watts Richmond, Yorks.

2052 PAUL DANIELS MAGIC NURSERY H'CAP 2YO   £4116   6f   Good/Firm 32 -33 Slow   [46]

*1296 EINSTEIN [6] (M Camacho) 2-8-11 G Sexton 11/4 FAV: 011: 2 b c Mummy's Pet - Piccadilly Etta (Floribunda) Useful colt: smooth prog to lead dist and readily drew clear in a nursery h'cap at Redcar Aug 9: well regarded, was a comfortable winner of a Newcastle mdn last month: cost 25,500 gns as a yearling and is closely related to sev winners: very eff over 6f and will stay further: acts on fast grd and on a gall trk: looks one to follow.   48

1683 GAYS FLUTTER [5] (C Nelson) 2-8-5 D Nicholls 4/1: 40332: Led after ½ way: no chance with easy winner: fair effort tho' yet to reproduce form shown in 1108 (5f): see 800.   25

1561 SCAWSBY LEES [7] (M W Easterby) 2-8-3 G Duffield 7/1: 0343: Al prom: stays 6f: see 1370.   22

1798 WABARAH [4] (H T Jones) 2-9-7 A Murray 4/1: 31124: Front rank over ½ way: btr 6f in 1357.   31

*1566 MUSEVENI [1] 2-8-6(bl) M Fry 8/1: 400410: Led over ½ way: sn btn and btr 1566.   00

1962 PANBOY [8] 2-8-3 K Darley 14/1: 3124000: Early speed: best on soft in 108 (5f).   00

1105 STAGE [2] 2-9-4 C Dwyer 12/1: 00100: Never dangerous: twice below form 892 (5f).   00

1397 GREY TAN [3] 2-8-10 N Day 8/1: 3240: Prom early: much btr 1296.   00

8 ran   5,hd,3,7,nk,½,1   (Mrs M T Burnside)   M Camacho Norton, Yorks.

2053 ASKE HANDICAP (0-50) 3YO   £4084   1m 2f   Good/Firm 32 +14 Fast   [53]

1657 WARM WELCOME [1] (G Wragg) 3-8-3(BL) G Duffield 10/1: 2-00301: 3 b f General Assembly - Fairly Hot (Sir Ivor) Responded to press to lead cl home in a fast run 3yo h'cap at Redcar Aug 9: first success: showed promise last term, notably when chasing home Sonic Lady in Blue Seal Stks at Ascot: well bred filly who is a half sister to useful duo Mill Plantation and Hot Touch: eff over 10/12f: suited by gd or faster ground.   37

1866 HELLO BENZ [5] (M H Easterby) 3-8-1(bl) A Shoults(5) 8/1: 0423322: Just held and remains a maiden: see 1866.   34

1184 LYPHLAW [7] (J Dunlop) 3-9-2 G Sexton 5/1: 0-003: Led inside dist, narrowly btn: lightly raced colt who should get off the mark soon: stays 10f: see 546.   48

1295 HONEST TOIL [6] (R Whitaker) 3-7-9 S P Griffiths 7/1: 40041D4: Led over 2f out, not btn far: see 1295.   25

1462 SAMANPOUR [3] 3-9-7 K Darley 11/4 FAV: 1113020: Well bckd: had ev ch: see 1462.   45

1511 ABADJERO [4] 3-8-9 A Murray 9/2: -01000: Made most: best over this C/D in 702.   28

1956 SECLUSIVE [2] 3-8-8   M Wood 12/1: 0-04000: Al in rear: lightly raced since 674 (1m).   00

+1361 DESERT OF WIND [8] 3-9-6 S Quane(7) 7/2: -0210: Never reach leaders: best in 1361 (9f)   00

8 ran   hd,hd,1,3,3,1½,hd   (E B Moller)   G Wragg Newmarket

2054 MEDDLETON MAIDEN STAKES 3YO+   £684   1m 6f   Good/Firm 32 -40 Slow

832 BANNEROL [8] (G Harwood) 3-8-8 A Murray 9/4: -01: 3 b c Smarten - Queen's Standard (Hoist The Flag) Impr colt: sn led and stayed on strongly to win a slowly run mdn at Redcar Aug 9: cost $41,000 as yearling and is a half brother to a couple of winners: stays 14f really well: acts on gd/firm ground and on a gall trk: on the upgrade.   48

1726 BENAROSA [5] (P Kelleway) 3-8-5 Gay Kelleway(3) 5/2: 0004222: Again found one too good and is proving expensive to follow: best over 10f in 372 tho' stays 14f well: see 1670.   38

1700 WHIPCRACKAWAY [7] (C Thornton) 3-8-8 J Bleasdale 11/1: -003: Stayed on well: clearly suited by a test of stamina : acts on gd and fast ground: see 1178.   37

1589 NOBLE FILLE [6] (J Dunlop) 3-8-5 G Duffield 15/8 FAV: -0044: Well bckd: beaten below dist: see 1031.   31

1923 BERNISH LADY [4] 5-9-4 J Hills(5) 14/1: -04000: Ran on same pace: stays 14f: see 1015.   28

1092 RACING DEMON [3] 4-9-7 J Carr(7) 33/1: -300000: Well btn: placed sev times last

REDCAR   Saturday August 9th   -Cont'd

season tho' has shown little of late: prefers some give in the ground: see 104.   00
1135 **Only Flower** [2] 8-5(BL)   1908 **Rekadlo** [1] 9-4
8 ran   4,2½,2½,1,15   (K Abdulla)   G Harwood Pulborough, Sussex

2055 FOX HUNTERS HANDICAP (0-35) 3YO   £1696   5f   Good/Firm 32 +02 Fast   [38]

*1959 **BARGAIN PACK** [9] (G Reveley) 3-8-3(6ex) Julie Bowker(7) 5/1: 0002311: 3 b g Silly
Prices - Coatham (Divine Gift) In gd form, gamely defied his penalty when making all in a
3yo h'cap at Redcar Aug 9: just held on in a similar race at Ripon recently: eff over 5/6f
with forcing tactics: acts on firm and soft ground and on any track.   22
1959 **MISS SERLBY** [8] (A Balding) 3-7-13 J Quinn(5) 20/1: 0-00002: Ran on well: best effort
to date: maiden sprint h'capper who acts on gd and fast grd and on a gall track.   15
1896 **GODS ISLE** [7] (M H Easterby) 3-9-7(BL) M Birch 4/1: 0200033: Bl first time: not btn
far: see 443.   34
1973 **HIGHLAND GLEN** [6] (F Watson) 3-8-13 D Nicholls 14/1: 00-0004: Prom most of way.   14
1810 **CAPEABILITY POUND** [5] 3-9-1 A Shoults(5) 8/1: 0020000: Front rank over ½ way:
disapp since 1027.   12
1959 **EASTERN OASIS** [3] 3-7-7(VIS)(3oh) S P Griffiths 14/1: 3-00400: Not reach leaders: see 1734   00
-1878 **SANDITTON PALACE** [1] 3-9-3 M Fry 6/4 FAV: 4310120: Disapp fav: much btr 1878.   00
1959 **THE BIGHT** [4] 3-8-0(bl) K Darley 9/1: 0-00000: Never dangerous 8th: see 825.   00
1734 **MISS TAUFAN** [2] 3-7-7(13oh) A Munro(4) 20/1: -040000: Sn outpaced: see 825.   00
9 ran   ½,1,4,1½,1½,hd,hd   (J D Taylor)   G Reveley Lingdale, Cleveland.

NEWMARKET   Saturday August 9th   Righthand, Stiff Galloping Track

2056 SACCONE AND SPEED KARAMEA MAID.STKS.2YO   £3606   6f   Good/Firm 35 -21 Slow

--   **MACROBIAN** [7] (R Shaw) 2-9-0 B Rouse 11/1: 1: 2 b c Bay Express - White Domino (Sharpen
Up) Promising colt: first time out, hdwy 2f out and led final 1f in quite a slowly run 2yo
mdn at Newmarket Aug 9: half brother to a winner abroad: dam winner over 1m: eff 6f, looks
likely to stay 7f: acts on fast grd, on a stiff trck.   56
--   **ABLE SAINT** [8] (R Armstrong) 2-9-0 B Thomson 33/1: 2: Outsider, fin in gd style
showing plenty of promise: cheaply bought colt who is related to sev winners: quite speedily
bred and clearly stays a stiff 6f well: acts on fast ground: should find a maiden soon.   53
1653 **TAUBER** [1] (Pat Mitchell) 2-9-0 M Hills 12/1: 0323: Nearly made all and deserves a
reward for his consistency: see 1653.   50
--   **RUSSIAN ROVER** [2] (M Stoute) 2-9-0 W R Swinburn 8/11 FAV: 4: Heavily bckd debutant,
under press ½ way and never closer: said to have been working well at home but this half
brother to sev winners may need 7f+ to show his true worth: sure to improve and find race soon   49
--   **CRUSADE DANCER** [9] 2-9-0 A Geran(7) 20/1: 0: Friendless in mkt, gd late prog: related
to a winner abroad: should stay beyond 6f: acts on fast ground: will do btr next time.   48
--   **GREEN VEIL** [4] 2-9-0 Paul Eddery 8/1: 0: Prom most and should benefit from the
experience: bred to be suited by longer dist than 6f: improvement likely.   47
--   **FAHAD** [10] 2-9-0 S Cauthen 6/1: 0: Plenty of early pace: half sister to '85 2yo winner
Fashada: should do better.   00
--   **Lindvaro** [6] 9-0   --   **French Sonnet** [5] 9-0 --   **Spanish Galleon** [3] 9-0
10 ran   1,1,½,½,nk   (Miss E Macgregor)   R Shaw Newmarket

2057 SWEET SOLERA STAKES LISTED 2YO FILLIES   £9853   7f   Good/Firm 35 -27 Slow

*1282 **LALUCHE** [2] (H Cecil) 2-8-8 S Cauthen 8/13 FAV: 11: 2 b f Alleged - Coqueluche
(Victorian Era) Very useful filly: comfortably landed the odds, setting her own pace thr'out
and cleverly winning slowly run Sweet Solera Stks for 2yo fillies at Newmarket Aug 9: first
time out, comfortably won a fillies mdn at Doncaster: cost $135,000: eff 6f, stays 7f well:
will be suited by 1m: acts on fast ground on a gall track: likely to improve and win more races   71
*1722 **MONTFORT** [6] (W Jarvis) 2-8-8 B Thomson 11/2: 012: Came from behind, fin well:
fine effort: see 1722.   66
*1801 **COLOR ARTIST** [7] (J Winter) 2-8-8 W R Swinburn 7/1: 013: Al there: kept on well:
stays 7f: see 1801.   63
1454 **MY IMAGINATION** [1] (P Kelleway) 2-8-8 B Rouse 33/1: 110004: Prom, ev ch: see 1454.   60
*1583 **LITTLEFIELD** [4] 2-8-8 T Ives 15/2: 210: Prom thr'out: btr 1583 (5.5f) friendless in mkt here.   56
1828 **PENANG BEAUTY** [5] 2-8-11 A Mackay 33/1: 100: No danger: see 1407 (6f).   48
1874 **HURRICANE VALLEY** [8] 2-8-8 M Wigham 33/1: 000: Early pace, wknd into 7th: see 1632.   44
1919 **UPPER** [3] 2-8-11 G Starkey 25/1: 1230: Al behind: much btr 1919 (6f).   45
8 ran   1,½,½,1½,3,½,1½   (Sheikh Mohammed)   H Cecil Newmarket

2058 AIR NEW ZEALAND H'CAP 3YO+ 0-75   £11550   1m 4f   Good/Firm 35 +19 Fast   [52]

1509 **FIVE FARTHINGS** [5] (M Stoute) 4-9-6 W R Swinburn 4/1: 00-0121: 4 b f Busted - Great
Tom (Great Nephew) Very useful filly: prom, led dist and comfortably forged clear to win a
fast run, val h'cap at Newmarket Aug 9: prob unsuited by the firm grd in 1509 but earlier
hacked up in a h'cap at Newbury on gd ground: in '85 won at Yarmouth: eff over 12/14f: unsuited
by very firm but acts on fast and gd/yldg going: suited by a gall trk: can win again.   59
+1551 **TWICE BOLD** [3] (N Callaghan) 3-8-9 M Hills 4/1: -034212: Led/dsptd lead thr'out
for another good effort: commendably consistent: stays 12f well: see 1551.   55

1020 WITCHCRAFT [4] (G Wragg) 4-8-7 B Crossley 14/1: 20-2443: Al there: tried in bl last
time but better today without them: see 225.   41
1879 COX GREEN [7] (G Harwood) 3-8-12 G Starkey 2/1 FAV: -1424: Waited with, no extra
final 3f and better 1879 (14f).   51
*1563 VERY SPECIAL [2] 4-7-13 R Morse(5) 8/1: 3-03010: Waited with, no danger: much btr 1563.   18
1343 BUSTARA [1] 3-9-7 Paul Eddery 6/1: 0-04030: Rear, no threat: flattered 1343? (10f).   45
1509 HAPPY BREED [6] 3-8-6(3ow) S Cauthen 10/1: 31-0040: Led 1m: btr 1509.   00
7 ran   2,shthd,7,8,7,8   (Snailwell Stud Co Ltd)   M Stoute Newmarket

2059 DICKENS INVITATION LIM.H'CAP 3YO+   £2642   1m   Good/Firm 35 -08 Slow   [30]

1788 IKTIYAR ⌊10] (S Mellor) 4-9-9 Brooke Sanders 13/2: -001001: 4 b g Corvaro - Irova
(Iron Liege) Returned to winning form, 'comfortably leading 1f out in an Invitation Riders
Ltd h'cap at Newmarket Aug 9: earlier made most in a lady riders h'cap at Redcar: failed to
win in '85: stays 10f but winning form at 1m, suited by gd or faster grd: seems to act any trk   36
1868 MR JAY ZEE [9] (N Callaghan) 4-10-0 B Thomson 6/1: 1302102: Fin well: gd eff: see 1727.   37
*1720 HELLO GYPSY [3] (C Tinkler) 5-9-2 Maxine Juster 8/1: 000-213: Dsptd lead dist:
in good form: see 1720.   21
1619 WARPLANE [1] (C Thornton) 6-9-8 G Starkey 3/1 FAV: 00-0034: Waited with, no extra
final 1f and better 1619.   25
*1400 XYLOPHONE [8] 4-9-2 W R Swinburn 8/1: 0003-10: never btr: see 1400 (seller).   18
1794 PARTS IS PARTS [4] 3-9-1 Diana Jones 33/1: -00040: Prom much: best 1244 (7f).   23
1720 DUELLING [6] 5-9-8(vis) Jennie Goulding 11/1: 0141020: No threat in 7th: best 1619.   00
*1967 FOOT PATROL [2] 5-9-3 Franca Vittadini 11/2: 0010210: Quick reappearance, no danger:
better 1967 (sharp track).   00
1808 The Yomper [7] 8-13   1651 Valrach [5] 9-8
10 ran   1½,2,1,½,2,¾   (S Tindall)   S Mellor Lambourn, Berks.

2060 BANK OF N.ZEALAND SELL.H'CAP 3YO 0-25   £1858   1m   Good/Firm 35 -11 Slow   [29]

1774 PHILOSOPHICAL [14] (W Musson) 3-8-13 M Wigham 5/1: -000301: 3 b f Welsh Chanter -
Stop Thinking (Divine Gift) Well bckd, al prom and led near fin, narrowly, in a 3yo selling
h'cap at Newmarket Aug 9 (bought in 7200 gns): in '85 won sellers at Haydock (nursery) and
Windsor: eff 7f, suited by 1m now: acts on any going and on any trk.   24
1521 DEPUTY TIM [16] (J Bethell) 3-9-7 S Cauthen 14/1: -400002: Came with a strong run
from rear, almost got up: appreciated this drop to selling co: can find a similar race soon:
stays 1m well: see 340.   31
1898 GRANDANGUS [11] (K Ivory) 3-8-2(vis) W Woods(3) 14/1: -000103: Prom, led dist,
caught near fin: gd effort: see 1656 (10f).   09
1917 DORADE [5] (D Morley) 3-8-9(bl)(5ex) B Rouse 7/1: 0030104: Al prom: see 1824 (7f).   13
*1471 TROPICO [10] 3-8-13 T Williams 11/4 FAV: 0042310: Well bckd, led briefly 2f out
but hung under press and btr 1471 (sharp trk).   13
1960 KEEP COOL [12] 3-8-9 S Perks 10/1: 1000020: Ev ch and btr 1960.   01
1845 SLEEPLINE DUCHESS [1] 3-8-8 G Carter(3) 20/1: 0-00200: Led 6f, fin 7th: twice below 1656   00
1927 FINDON MANOR [8] 3-9-1 R Morse(5) 6/1: 0000000: Well bckd, ev ch: see 1927.   00
1835 MITNER [2] 3-9-0 Paul Eddery 11/2: -000000: Well bckd, early pace: see 1303.   00
1788 Mostango [9] 8-9(bl)   1199 Stangrave [4] 9-1   1288 Lady Owen [6] 8-4
1813 Fandango Kiss [3] 8-5(1ow)   1516 Spanish Intent [7] 8-5(1ow)
1898 Sea Venom [13] 7-13   1824 Balidareen [15] 7-7(3oh)
16 ran   shthd,1½,1½,2,5,2½   (George L Cumming)   W Musson Newmarket

2061 KIWI MAIDEN STAKES 3YO   £3197   1m 2f   Good/Firm 35 +21 Fast

--   NORPELLA [1] (G Wragg) 3-8-11 B Crossley 33/1: 000-1: 3 ch f Northfields - Palmella
(Grundy) First time out, turned up at 33/1, fin strongly to forge clear inside final 1f in
a fast run 3yo mdn at Newmarket Aug 9: showed signs of ability over sprint dist last term
but much btr suited by 10f and looks sure to stay 12f: acts on fast grd on a stiff track:
should win more races.   54
--   AMBASSADOR [4] (W O'gorman) 3-9-0 T Ives 15/2: -2: Gd debut, coming to chall 1f out
and keeping on well: half brother to sev winners: acts on fast grd and on a stiff gall trk:
stays 10f well: sure to find a maiden.   51
1776 MILLERS DUST [3] (H Cecil) 3-9-0 S Cauthen 8/11 FAV: -02323: Made much but again
lacked final pace and is becoming expensive to follow: see 1031.   50
1031 AMJAAD [5] (M Stoute) 3-9-0 W R Swinburn 9/4: -004: Well bckd, chall 2f out, fdd:
rather disapp since 371 (1m).   42
1628 TOWNSHIP [6] 3-9-0 G French 33/1: -00: Prom much: unraced in '85 but appeared to
show some improvement here.   38
512 HIGHEST PEAK [7] 3-9-0 W Hood 11/1: 00-2320: Prom, wknd after long abs: btr 512.   28
625 MR SAVVAS [2] 3-9-0 M Wigham 33/1: 000-000: Fin well behind after long abs: no
form this term but rated 32 in '85: hard to assess.   00
7 ran   3,nk,4,1½,3   (E B Moller)   G Wragg Newmarket

2062 AUCKLAND H'CAP 3YO+ 0-60   £3843   1m 2f   Good/Firm 35 -29 Slow   [53]

+1929 POWER BENDER [1] (G P Gordon) 4-8-8(5ex) S Cauthen 2/1: 2-43011: 4 b g Prince Tenderfoot

- Spadilla (Javelot) Impr gelding who seemed well suited by this snail's pace and sprinted clear final 1f to record his 2nd successive win in h'caps at Newmarket recently: fin 2nd on 3 occasions in '85: lightly raced this term: eff 1m but is well suited by 10f and a stiff trk, particularly Newmarket: acts on fast ground: may complete the hat-trick.   46
1912 CELESTIAL STORM [3] (L Cumani) 3-9-10 W R Swinburn 4/6 FAV: 0-132: Came to chall 1f out, no extra and much btr 1912 (strong pace).   68
1931 GUNDREDA [4] (C Brittain) 4-9-1 G Carter(3) 20/1: 0-00403: Led briefly dist: see 1498.   46
940 WILD HOPE [2] (G Huffer) 5-8-3 W Litwin(7) 8/1: 000-004: Came from behind, ev ch 1f out: fair eff after abs since 940.   33
875 GLOWING PROMISE [5] 3-8-8 B Thomson 12/1: 02-1240: Made much, wknd after long absence: see 690, 452.   42
5 ran   1½,1,shthd,4   (Addison Tool Co Ltd)   G P Gordon Newmarket

---

Official Going Given As GOOD

2063 MAIL ON SUNDAY 3YO H'CAP (0-50)   £3228   7f   Good 40 -11 Slow   [50]

1924 BELOW ZERO [1] (A Bailey) 3-9-2 R Cochrane 2/1 FAV: 2000101: 3 ch c Northfields - Indigine (Raise A Native) Fair h'capper: held up and led well inside final 1f, ridden out in a 3yo h'cap at Haydock Aug 9: consistent colt, earlier winning similar events at Salisbury (course record) and first time out at Kempton: very eff at 7f, stays 1m: acts on any grd and on any track: best when coming late.   48
1821 TRAVEL MAGIC [2] (B Hanbury) 3-9-2 G Baxter 6/1: -0102: Led 2f out: caught inside final 1f: gd effort and 3l clear 3rd: see 1451.   46
1885 ORTICA [5] (J Etherington) 3-7-12 W Carson 9/4: -402333: Well bckd, but never nearer: 22
1292 GOOSE HILL [4] (M W Easterby) 3-8-11 T Lucas 11/2: 1040304: Fdd 2f out: btr 1091, 81.   27
1228 RAAWIYEH [3] 3-9-0(BL) R Hills 6/1: 0020-00: Bl first time: led 5f: see 1228.   20
1934 AL DIWAN [6] 3-9-7(bl) J Reid 25/1: 20-4000: Prom, wknd: lightly raced since 159.   15
6 ran   ¾,3,4,6,7   (T P Ramsden)   A Bailey Newmarket

2064 BURTONWOOD BREWERY SUMMER TROPHY 3YO+   £8129   1m 2f Good 40 +10 Fast

1913 WASSL TOUCH [6] (W Hern) 3-8-9 W Carson 6/1: 1-0101: 3 b c Northern Dancer - Queen Sucree (Ribot) Very smart, impr colt: held up to lead well inside final 1f, driven out in a fast run and valListed race at Haydock Aug 9: earlier this season won a val event at Newbury: has been very lightly raced, on sole start as a 2yo hacked up in a mdn at Goodwood: very eff at 10f, stays 12f: acts on firm and yldg grd and on any track: much improved.   83
*1655 THEN AGAIN [4] (L Cumani) 3-8-6 R Guest 9/4: 01-1012: Led over 1f out: just btn and is in fine form: stays 10f, but possibly at his very best over 1m/9f: see 1655.   79
1597 CONQUERING HERO [2] (M Stoote) 3-8-11 R Cochrane 6/1: 13-1103: Ran on well final 1f: fine effort: see 1230.   81
1644 LEADING STAR [3] (I Balding) 4-9-2 W Newnes 8/1: 0-43024: Led over 2f out: btr 1644.   67
1913 QUEENS SOLDIER [1] 3-8-6 W Ryan 15/8 FAV: 3i-1120: Well bckd, made most: beat winner 1913 (12f).   63
1715 NEBRIS [5] 5-9-2 P Cook 8/1: 1110230: Struck in to: best ignored: see 1715.   42
6 ran   nk,1½,4,3,12   (Sheikh Ahmed Al Maktoum)   W Hern West Ilsley, Berks.

2065 CORAL BOOKMAKERS H'CAP (0-70) 3YO+   £7843   5f   Good 40 +01 Fast   [62]

1796 SULLYS CHOICE [7] (D Chapman) 5-7-12 A Proud 7/1: 3100321: 5 b g King Pellinore - Salute The Coates (Solar Salute) Led inside final 1f, held on by ½l in a val h'cap at Haydock Aug 9: in gd form this season, earlier winning h'caps at Thirsk and Ripon: below his best in '85: in '84 won again at Ripon: very eff over 5/6f, tho' does stay 1m: acts on gd/firm and soft grd: eff with or without blinkers.   45
1852 LAURIE LORMAN [3] (M Mccourt) 4-8-6 W Carson 6/1: 1000002: Hmpd early on and sn behind: made rapid hdwy from the furlong pole and just btn: unlucky?: should be winning soon: see 660. 52
1889 CLANTIME [6] (R Whitaker) 5-9-2(vis) D Mckeown 11/4 FAV: 3412203: Led over 1f out: in fine form: see 1889.   60
1878 TRUE NORA [4] (C Nelson) 3-8-9(BL) J Reid 14/1: -003004: Bl first time: al prom: best effort this term: see 443.   54
1889 DUBLIN LAD [2] 3-9-12 A Bacon(7) 6/1: 0314400: Led over 3f: btr 1268.   68
1805 DUCK FLIGHT [1] 4-8-4 R Cochrane 20/1: 0-04000: Never nearer: lightly raced since 327.   39
1852 DURHAM PLACE [5] 4-9-0 G Baxter 7/1: -043000: Made no show: see 1268.   00
*1796 RAMBLING RIVER [8] 9-8-0(vis)(4ex) J Lowe 11/2: 2000210: No show in 8th: much btr 1796. 00
1796 MANDRAKE MADAM [9] 3-8-0 L Charnock 33/1: 0003300: Early speed: twice below 1505.   00
9 ran   ½,½,1½,1,½,½,hd,2   (Wm Chapman)   D Chapman Stillington, Yorks.

2066 HARVEY JONES HANDICAP (0-60) 3YO+   £4142   1m 2f Good 40 +04 Fast   [50]

1912 ENBARR [8] (H Cecil) 3-9-7 W Ryan 7/2: -213101: 3 b c Kings Lake - Catherine Wheel (Roan Rocket) Very useful colt: led inside final 1f, ridden out in quite a fast run h'cap at Haydock Aug 9: earlier made ev yard for a 10l win in a fast run 3yo h'cap at Kempton: also a winner at Windsor: half brother to Cheshire Oaks winner Hunston: very eff at 10f when up with

the pace, may stay 12f: acts on soft but best on gd and firm grd: seems to act on any track: consistent.   65
*1636 HANDLEBAR [6] (J Watts) 4-8-11 N Connorton 9/2: 1-00112: Led/dsptd lead: 4l clear 3rd and Is in excellent form: should win another h'cap : see 1636.   42
1923 OSRIC [4] (M Ryan) 3-8-5 P Robinson 3/1 FAV: -412D3: Well bckd: ev ch str: btr 1923 (12f)   40
*1918 REGAL STEEL [3] (R Hollinshead) 8-7-12(5ex) A Culhane(7) 7/1: 2022214: Led over 7f.   20
1468 HAWAIIAN PALM [1] 3-9-6 W Carson 4/1: 3-00100: Held ev ch: best 1084.   48
743 MIN BALADI [5] 4-8-1 J Lowe 7/1: 11-3200: Abs: no show: best 629.   13
1820 Shellman [7] 8-7   1866 Try Scorer [2] 7-10
8 ran   1,4,1,3,2½   (S S Niarchos)   H Cecil Newmarket

2067 E.B.F. LADY HILL STAKES 2YO   £3624   7f   Good 40 -26 Slow

-- GREAT ASPECT [4] (W Hern) 2-8-11 W Carson 4/5 FAV: 1: 2 b c Great Nephew - Broad Horizon (Blakeney) Heavily bckd debutant: led 2f out, readily in quite a val 2yo event at Haydock Aug 9: half brother to 9f winner   Veduta: stoutly bred and shd be well suited by middle distances next season: acts on gd ground and a gall trk: should rate more highly.   52
1872 IRISH BRIGADIER [1] (S Hall) 2-8-11 J Lowe 7/2: 42: Prom, no chance with winner:see 1872   42
-- HIGHLAND BELLE [2] (J Watts) 2-8-8 N Connorton 8/1: 3: Mkt drifter: chance over 1f out: dam a winning 2yo: eff at 7f, should be suited by 1m: acts on gd ground.   34
1598 ROUGH DANCE [3] (W Jarvis) 2-8-11 R Cochrane 8/1: 04: Stiff task: see 1598.   33
1510 CRANCHETER [6] 2-8-11 S Webster 25/1: 00: Never in it: half brother to 10f winner Homme D'Affaire: acts on gd ground.   28
-- CHICO VALDEZ [5] 2-8-11 T Lucas 9/2: 0: Led over 3f out, fdd on racecourse debut: cost $47,000 and should do better than this.   20
6 ran   4,2½,2½,2½,4.   (Sheikh Mohammed)   W Hern West Ilsley, Berks.

2068 WARRINGTON MAIDEN FILLIES STAKES 3YO   £2065   1m 4f Good 40 -18 Slow

1130 EXCEPTIONAL BEAUTY [4] (M Jarvis) 3-8-11 T Lucas 5/1: 02-4201: 3 ch f Sallust - Colonial Cousin (Tom Rolfe) Useful filly: made hdwy from the rear to lead cl home comfortably, in a 3yo fillies mdn at Haydock Aug 9: lightly raced prev, showing promise in gd company: half sister to 3 winners: eff at 10f, well suited by 12f: acts on gd and firm grd and gall trk: seems suited by waiting tactics.   52
1580 CROWLEY [9] (L Cumani) 3-8-11 R Guest 16/1: -002: Chance final 1f: best eff yet and is clearly suited by 12f: looks certain to find a maiden: see 1368.   50
1645 CORNELIAN [11] (G Harwood) 3-8-11 A Clark 5/1: -03: Led over 1f out: not btn far and is fast improving: will find a maiden: see 1645.   48
779 SECRET WEDDING [2] (W Hern) 3-8-11 W Carson 10/3: 10-2324: Abs: made much: see 779, 209 44
1639 CYNOMIS [8] 3-8-11 R Lines(3) 2/1 FAV: -30: Well bckd: ev ch str: another gd run: acts on any trk: see 1639.   43
1580 STANDARD ROSE [5] 3-8-11 W Newnes 6/1: 0-40: Some late hdwy: stays 12f: Impr: see 1580   38
1580 Tory Blues [1] 8-11   1941 Cavaleuse [7] 8-11   423 Mary Milford [3] 8-11
1444 Nautica [6] 8-11   1670 Golden Azelia [10] 8-11
11 ran   ½,¾,2,nk,3   (Mrs J Marrow)   M Jarvis Newmarket

Official Going Given As GOOD

2069 PIER MAIDEN FILLIES STAKES 2YO   £959   6f   Good/Firm 31 -08 Slow

-- GREENSWARD [6] (H Candy) 2-8-11 T Williams 12/1: 1: 2 b f Tower Walk - Early Glas (Reform) Mkt drifter tho' made a successful racecourse debut, led below dist, comfortably, in a 2yo fillies stks at Lingfield Aug 9: clearly eff over 6f on gd/firm grd, should stay at least 7f: acts on a sharp trk.   47
1683 OUR NATHALIE [4] (R Sheather) 2-8-11 M Rimmer 2/1 FAV: 42: Well bckd: fin in gd style: on the upgrade and should recoup losses soon: will be suited by 7f: see 1683.   40
999 NAPARIMA [2] (R Hannon) 2-8-11 G Starkey 11/2: 03: Not qckn inside dist, tho' ran a fair race after abs: eff over 5/6f on gd/firm: acts on any trk: see 999.   37
1801 LINDAS TREAT [10] (R Armstrong) 2-8-11 P Tulk 3/1: 004: Led over ½ way: Impr: see 1801.   37
1801 LADYS MANTLE [9] 2-8-11 R Fox 10/1: 000: Led after ½ way, one paced: see 1801.   29
1440 SUNLEY SELHURST [8] 2-8-11 Paul Eddery 14/1: 00: Stayed on from ½ way: will stay further in time: acts on gd/firm grd and on a sharp trk.   24
-- Taciturn Lady [7] 8-11   1874 Simply Silk [1] 8-11
-- Lauriston Cottage [5] 8-11   -- Tisserands [3] 8-11
621 Peroy [11] 8-11   1801 Top Cover [12] 8-11
12 ran   2½,1,shthd,3,2   (Capt M Clark)   H Candy Kingstone Warren, Oxon.

2070 PIER MAIDEN FILLIES STAKES 2YO   £959   6f   Good/Firm 31 -11 Slow

-- PERCYS LASS [12] (G Wragg) 2-8-11 P Waldron 11/10 FAV: 1: 2 b f Blakeney - Laughing Girl (Sassafras) Well bckd on racecourse debut and led after ½ way drawing away in a 2yo fillies stks at Lingfield Aug 9: half sister to middle dist winner No No Girl: eff over 6f tho' sure to appreciate a longer trip: acts on gd/firm grd and on a sharp course.   47

1345 HIGH CLIMBER [8] (R Smyth) 2-8-11 S Whitworth 20/1: 02: Broke well and led over ¼ way:
cost 12,000 gns: eff over 6f on gd/firm: on the upgrade.   38
-- RHONDALING [5] (P Walwyn) 2-8-11 Paul Eddery 6/1: 3: Nicely bckd debutant: going on
fin and seems certain to improve next time, especially over another furlong: acts on gd/firm
ground and on a sharp trk.   34
-- BELAKA [9] (R Sheather) 2-8-11 M Rimmer 12/1: 4: Nearest fin and impr likely: cost
30,000 Francs and is a half sister to a couple of winners: will be suited by 7f+: acts on
gd/firm ground.   32
-- DELPHINIA [10] 2-8-11 G Starkey 4/1: 0: Al prom on debut and likely to improve for
this run: should stay further: acts on gd/firm.   23
-- PINK FONDANT [3] 2-8-11 M Hills 20/1: 0: Friendless in mkt on debut: front rank over
¼ way: bred to be suited by a longer trip.   22
-- CHACONIA GIRL [11] 2-8-11 A Mackay 9/1: 0: No threat in 8th tho' active in mkt and
open to improvement.   00
1802 Blandell Beauty [7] 8-11   1550 Mascalls Dream [4] 8-11
1668 Perigris [2] 8-11(BL)   1632 Mamadora [6] 8-11   -- Claires Buck [1] 8-11
12 ran   3,1½,1,4,nk,½,bk,2   (E B Moller)   G Wragg Newmarket

2071 CRUISE NURSERY HANDICAP 2YO   £3308   7f   Good/Firm 31 -04 Slow   [56]

1925 HARD ACT [9] (R Hannon) 2-9-7 G Starkey 10/1: 0110001: 2 b c Hard Fought - Excruciating
(Bold Forbes) Useful colt: gamely defied top weight, led cl home in a nursery h'cap at
Lingfield Aug 9: has not been disgraced in gd company since winning minor events at
Wolverhampton and Bath: eff over 5/6f, stays 7f well: acts on firm and gd grd and on any trk:
genuine sort.   59
1675 LORD COLLINS [3] (M Stoute) 2-8-7 M Stoute 8/1: 4042: Led 2f out, caught inside dist
tho' ran his best race to date: stays 7f: looks on a handy mark: see 979.   44
1735 CASTLE HEIGHTS [8] (R Armstrong) 2-8-0 A Mcglone 25/1: 0303: Kept on well, not btn
far and ran to his best: acts on any trk: see 1197.   34
1828 BLOFFA [6] (P Cundell) 2-7-7(3oh) L Riggio(7) 8/1: 30024: Led over ¼ way: best 1828 (6f) 23
*1518 STATE BALLET [11] 2-9-1 T Ives 6/4 FAV: 010: Heavily bckd: no extra dist: btr 1518.   44
1907 LADY SUNDAY SPORT [5] 2-7-7(1oh) G Bardwell(7) 20/1: 40230: Front rank till dist: see 1907 21
*1433 SPOTTER [7] 2-8-2 M Hills 4/1: 010: Fdd into 7th: see 1433.   00
1891 VAIGLY BLAZED [1] 2-8-1 Paul Eddery 8/1: 40000: Never dangerous: best with some
give in 662.   00
1232 Caballine [10] 7-7(2oh)   1828 Sarasota [2] 7-7(9oh)
10 ran   hd,1½,2,½,½,½,5,1   (G Howard-Spink)   R Hannon East Everleigh, Wilts

2072 METROPOLE HANDICAP STAKES (0-50)   £2868   7f   Good/Firm 31 +12 Fast   [48]

1911 STEADY EDDIE [11] (P Mitchell) 4-8-13 A Mcglone 6/1: 0000301: 4 b c The Brianstan -
Roman Dawn (Neron) Useful colt on his day: strongly ridden to lead dist in quite a fast
run h'cap at Lingfield Aug 9: last term won at Goodwood and in '84 was successful at Windsor
and again at Goodwood: loves a sharp trk: very eff around 7f: acts on gd and fast ground.   45
1804 HIGHLAND IMAGE [9] (R Hutchinson) 4-8-1 P Hutchinson(3) 8/1: 030-002: Just held:
fine effort: see 1804.   32
-1804 COINCIDENTAL [8] (M Dickinson) 4-9-11 S Cauthen 2/1 FAV: 001-023: Game attempt to
make all: genuine sort who carries weight well: see 1804.   52
1854 MORICA [13] (J Dunlop) 3-8-10 B Rouse 9/2: 1-404: Ev ch: returning to form: see 1515.   40
1834 BILLY WHITESHOES [12] 4-7-7(3oh) N Carlisle 10/1: 1-00030: Fair eff in this btr
class: see 1834.   14
-- TIN BOY [7] 7-7-7(8oh) N Adams 50/1: 00020/0: Needed this race: off the trk since
Oct '84: prev season won at Bath and in '81 twice at Newmarket: stays 1m: acts on any going. 10
1189 DOGMATIC [4] 3-9-8(BL) T Ives 10/1: 1-41000: Bl first time: gd early speed: has
been below par since successful in 478 on soft ground.   00
1608 Sailors Song [3] 9-8   1109 Ready Wit [1] 9-2   1487 Indian Summer [10] 8-8
1922 Far Too Busy [6] 7-7(3oh)   1494 April Arabesque [5] 7-7(8oh)
1184 Norham Castle [2] 7-8(1ow)(13oh)
13 ran   ½,2,2½,½,1½,½,1½,nk   (N H Silbery)   P Mitchell Epsom, Surrey

2073 POLEGATE SELLING H'CAP STAKES (0-25) £897 1m 2f Good/Firm 31 -22 Slow [25]

1951 SPINNAKER LADY [1] (M Usher) 3-8-10 M Wigham 7/2: 0000001: 3 gr f Windjammer -
Easymede (Runnymede) Led dist, ridden out to win a 3yo selling h'cap at Lingfield Aug 9 (no
bid): first success tho' rated 33 when 2nd to Mayor in a York seller last backend: stays
10f: acts on gd/firm and yldg ground and on any trk.   15
1898 GEORGIAN ROSE [7] (K Ivory) 3-8-3(vis) W Woods(3) 9/2: 4000002: Led briefly 2f out:
maiden who wears a visor and has yet to show any worthwhile form: stays 10f: acts on gd/firm. 03
1061 NO STOPPING [5] (R Hannon) 3-9-7 T Ives 9/4 JT.FAV: 40-0003: Dropped in class and
nicely bckd: ran on same pace and remains a maiden: acts on gd/firm.   16
1666 ODERVY [6] (L Holt) 3-7-12(VIS) N Adams 20/1: -000004: Visored first time: outsider
and no threat: well btn previously in this grade.   00
1970 SOLENT EXPRESS [2] 3-9-6 R Wernham 9/4 JT.FAV: 0010-00: Dropped in class: btn below
dist: made all to win a seller at Wolverhampton last Summer (7f gd).   00
1827 SHEER CLASS [4] 3-8-6 T Williams 14/1: -00000: Tried to make all: inappropriately
named maiden.   00

6 ran   3,3,1½,8,6   (B H Simpson)   M Usher Lambourn, Berks.

2074 SOUTH COAST STAKES 3YO+   £2811   1m 2f   Good/Firm 31 -23 Slow

-1661 KADIAL [2] (R J Houghton) 3-8-11 S Cauthen 1/3 FAV: -21421: 3 b c Niniski - Khadaeen
(Lyphard) Smart colt: made all on a tight rein from his sole rival in a minor race at Lingfield
Aug 9: earlier an easy winner of quite a val stks race at York and has since fin a good
2nd to Moon Madness in the Scottish Derby: half brother to the smart Kalim: eff over 8/11f:
suited by fast ground: acts on any trk: consistent sort.   70
--   ITS NOW OR NEVER [3] (G Harwood) 4-9-3 G Starkey 5/2: -01-2: No threat to this effortless winner on belated reappearance: lightly raced last term, winning a fillies mdn at
Newmarket: half sister to sev winners: stays 10f well: suited by fast ground and acts on any
trk: should be placed to win.   57
2 ran   1   (H H Aga Khan)   R J Houghton Blewbury, Oxon.

2075 GATWICK HANDICAP STAKES (0-35)   £1772   2m   Good/Firm 31 +09 Fast   [28]

1694 NARCISSUS [1] (R Akehurst) 4-8-1 T Williams 16/1: 0-30001: 4 ch g Manado - White
Bunnie (Exbury) Showed impr form, led approaching home turn and held on gamely in quite a
fast run h'cap at Lingfield Aug 9: first success: half brother to the very useful miler
Petronici: stays 2m: acts on gd/firm and soft ground and seems best on a sharp course.   10
1884 COLLISTO [5] (K Brassey) 5-8-12(bl) S Whitworth 2/1 FAV: 0000222: Kept on well
under press, just held: stays 2m well: acts on gd/firm grd: see 485.   20
--   TARAS CHARIOT [4] (P Mitchell) 5-8-0 A Mcglone 33/1: 02200-3: Fair eff on reappearance:
modest h'capper who has yet to get her hd in front: suited by a test of stamina: acts on
gd and firm.   05
1748 RUN FOR YOUR WIFE [6] (G Lewis) 3-7-10 M L Thomas 5/2: 04-3024: Stays well: see 1212.   11
*1688 IGHTHAM [2] 3-9-10(bl) G Starkey 9/2: -0010: Stiff task and not disgraced: see 1688.   38
1897 SMACK [7] 4-8-5 M Rimmer 11/2: -002000: Mod late prog: see 841.   01
1726 HANKLEY DOWN [3] 3-8-8 A Mackay 7/1: -00040: Led over ½ way: best in 714 (12f).   00
7 ran   ½,3,4,½,4,½   (V Goodall)   R Akehurst Epsom, Surrey

NOTTINGHAM   Monday August 11th   Lefthand, Fair Track

Official Going Given As GOOD

2076 HUCKNALL LINBY MINERS HCAP 3YO 0-35   £2239   1m   Good 53 -30 Slow   [36]

1854 SOLO STYLE [13] (G Lewis) 3-9-7 P Waldron 7/2 JT.FAV: 0010141: 3 b c Moorestyle -
Mint (Meadow Mint): In fine form at present, switched final 1f to get up close home in a
h'cap at Nottingham Aug.11: earlier a winner of h'caps over this C/D and also at Leicester:
lightly raced last term: eff over 7f, well suited by 1m: acts on firm & yld grnd & likes a
gall trk: seems a genuine sort.   39
1864 HAMLOUL [8] (K Bailey) 3-9-7 R Hills 12/1: -002202: Led inside final 1f: just caught:
gd effort and deserves a change of luck: see 1834, 1431.   38
1830 ANNABELLINA [4] (G Wragg) 3-9-1 P Robinson 5/1: 4000423: Led over 7f: just btn in
close fin & is in fine form: see 1830, 1571.   31
1794 SHARONS ROYALE [16] (R Whitaker) 3-8-2 K Bradshaw(2) 6/1: -000324: Switched over 1f out,
nearest fin: see 1794.   13
1835 COUNTRY GENTLEMAN [15] 3-9-7(BL) J Reid 7/2 JT.FAV: -000430: Bl first time: never
nearer: needs further? see 1835.   27
1783 SUPREME KINGDOM [11] 3-9-4 A Culhane(7) 13/2: 2000430: There 2f out, fdd: btr 1783.   23
1830 Arrow Of Light [3] 9-5(bl)   1571 Mirataine Venture [12] 9-4
1819 Lightning Wind [1] 9-7   1199 Red In The Morning [14] 9-3
1645 Barracuda Bay [9] 9-3   1835 Kitty Clare [6] 8-10   1541 Miss Kola [10] 8-12
1904 Master Music [5] 7-13
14 ran   nk,½,½,3,2½,½   (Mrs N Lewis)   G Lewis Epsom, Surrey

2077 BLIDWORTH MINERS WELFARE SELLER   £806   1m 2f   Good 53 -46 Slow

1969 ANGIES VIDEO [3] (R Holder) 4-9-0 J Reid 2/1: 0320321: 4 ch f Lucky Wednesday -
Prevailing Love (Prevailing): Gained a deserved success, making all in a 3 & 4yo seller at
Nottingham Aug.11 (no bid): placed several times previously in similar company: eff at 1m/10f
may not stay 12f: acts on a sound surface & on any trk.   14
1937 RUN CHARLIE [5] (F Yardley) 3-8-7 I Johnson 3/1: 000-002: Ev ch final 2f: hung left:
first signs of form from this lightly raced colt: stays 10f: acts on gd grnd & a fair trk.   16
1902 PATCHOULIS PFT [6] (P Kelleway) 3-8-4 W Carson 11/8 FAV: 43-0003: Dropped in class &
well bckd: ev ch str: has shown precious little this term: see 1637.   10
1969 LETOILE DU PALAIS [2] (B Stevens) 3-8-4 S Whitelam(7) 14/1: 4000404: Friendless in mkt:
best in 1666 (sharp).   00
1399 COLE BAY [1] 3-8-7 W Wharton 33/1: -000: Prom most, fdd: dropped to selling company
today, but seems of little ability.   00
5 ran   ½,1½,20,8   (Stewart G Martin)   R Holder Portbury, Avon

2078 CLIPSTONE MINERS WELFARE MAIDEN 3YO   £1565   2m   Good 53 -42 Slow

1589 PRELUDE [4] (W Hern) 3-8-11 W Carson 9/4: 3-3401: 3 ch f Troy - Pas de Deux (Nijinsky):
Led approaching final 1f, comfortably in a slow run 3yo mdn at Nottingham Aug.11: half sister
to useful stayer Insular and is obviously suited by a distance of grnd: stays 2m well:
acts on gd & firm & a gall trk.   45
1875 EL CONQUISTADOR [5] (G Harwood) 3-9-0 G Starkey 8/13 FAV: -020222: Heavily bckd:
led halfway till over 1f out: 7L clear 3rd: deserves a change of luck: see 1875, 1029.   44
1733 STAR SHINER [3] (G Lewis) 3-9-0 P Waldron 50/1: 0-00003: Never nearer: seems to
stay 2m and this was a btr effort: acts on gd & soft grnd.   24
-- GINGERLAND [1] (J Dunlop) 3-9-0 T Quinn 20/1: -4: Ev ch in str: mkt drifter today:
half brother to several winners & may impr.   23
613 CORNISH PRINCE [2] 3-9-0 N Carlisle 50/1: -0000: Abs: dsptd lead 1m: little form
to date, but is a half brother to fair stayer Cavalier's Blush: may impr.   00
1833 SOLOMON LAD [6] 3-9-0 G Duffield 50/1: -200: Prom most, fdd str: best 1686 (12f).   00
849 Ski Down [7] 9-0
7 ran   1½,7,nk,20,2   (The Queen)   W Hern West Ilsley, Berks

2079 NOTTINGHAM STEWARDS CUP HCAP 0-60   £3553   6f   Good 53 +17 Fast   [47]

+1669 JOKIST [2] (R Shaw) 3-8-2 R Street 5/1: 00-0211: 3 ro g Orchestra - What A Picture
(My Swanee): In fine form, led final 1f, soon drawing clear in a fast run & valuable h'cap at
Nottingham Aug.11: last time out won a fast run h'cap at Windsor: in '85 won a Warwick mdn on
his racecourse debut, when trained by C Williams: very eff at 6f, seems to handle any trk/
going: should complete the hat trick.   42
-1950 TAX ROY [1] (B Mcmahon) 3-9-0 S Perks 11/2: 0010022: Led over 2f out: not pace of
winner, but is running well: see 1950, best 1380.   46
1852 RA RA GIRL [7] (B Mcmahon) 4-8-8 W Carson 7/1: 0000203: Al prom: see 1676, 1508.   27
1882 MRS SAUGA [5] (M Eckley) 4-7-9 T Williams 12/1: -021044: Prom, ev ch: see 1344 (shrp trk)   05
1810 TOBERMORY BOY [4] 9-9-3(VIS) N Carlisle 17/2: 0002000: Visored first time: always
there: best 1306 (C/D, firm).   21
1852 AMEGHINO [11] 6-9-4 W Newnes 7/2 FAV: 4033000: Again below form 1037 (stiff 5f).   20
1933 ROYSIA BOY [8] 6-9-2 G Duffield 4/1: -000030: Al rear: well below 1933 (easier trk).   00
1852 QUARRYVILLE [10] 3-9-3(BL) S Whitworth 10/1: 0440000: Bl 1st time: best early season 387   00
1840 Mendick Adventure [3] 8-3(bl)   2021 Exert [9] 8-2
10 ran   2½,2,3,2,½   (John Virgo)   R Shaw Newmarket

2080 MAIDEN FILLIES STAKES 2YO   £1855   6f   Good 53 -04 Slow

1869 NORAPA [13] (M Brittain) 2-8-11 K Darley 5/1: 31: 2 ch f Ahonoora - Pale Moon
(Jukebox): Impr filly: made ev yd on the stands side for a clear cut 6L success in a 2yo
fillies mdn at Nottingham Aug.11: eff at 6f, seems certain to stay 7f: acts on gd grnd &
a gall trk: well suited by front running.   48
1194 NEEDWOOD NUT [9] (B Morgan) 2-8-11 B Crossley 20/1: 042: Kept on well & continues
to impr: seems suited by 6f: acts on any trk: see 905.   35
-- PENCIL SHARPENER [4] (O Douieb) 2-8-11 Pat Eddery 4/5 FAV: 3: Heavily bckd debutant:
led on the unfav. far side & will do btr than this next time: cost $300,000 & is a half
sister to winners in the States: should stay further than 6f: acts on gd grnd.   35
-- SOME DREAM [18] (J Winter) 2-8-11 J Reid 14/1: 4: Friendless in mkt: nearest fin &
impr certain from this half sister to winning sprinter Davill.   31
1067 FINGERS CROSSED [16] 2-8-11 R Hills 25/1: 00: Prom on the stands side & is making impr:
should stay further than 6f: acts on gd grnd.   22
-- HAYGATE PARK [17] 2-8-11 P Robinson 33/1: 0: Kept on final 1f on racecourse debut &
should impr: should stay further than 6f.   22
1522 FIGHTING BELLE [8] 2-8-11 S Whitworth 8/1: 00: Mkt drifter: there 4f on far side: see 1522   00
-- MISS PONTEVECCHIO [3] 2-8-11 G Baxter 9/1: 0: Prom 4f on far side: nicely bckd here &
should do btr: first foal of a lightly raced dam: should be suited by further than 6f.   00
722 Corofin Lass [19] 8-11   350 Folly Gale [6] 8-11
1555 The Londonderry [15] 8-11(BL)   -- Dahab [1] 8-11
-- Free Skip [11] 8-11   -- Lillys Double [5] 8-11
-- Secret Teller [7] 8-11   -- Spring Tide [2] 8-11
1683 The Cross [12] 8-11
17 ran   6,shhd,2½,4,shhd   (A M Wragg)   M Brittain Warthill, Yorks

2081 LESLIE MARLER CHALL TRPY NURS HCAP   £1547   6f   Good 53 +01 Fast   [58]

1907 FICKLE YOUNG MAN [7] (T Fairhurst) 2-8-3(BL) G Duffield 6/1: 1301: 2 gr c Junius -
Key Of The Kingdom (Grey Sovereign): Impr colt: bl first time & destroyed his field, making
all on the stands side for an 8L win in a nursery h'cap at Nottingham Aug.1: first time out
won a mdn at Carlisle: cheaply acquired colt who is a half brother to a winner in Ireland:
eff at 5f, well suited by 6f: acts on gd & firm grnd & a gall trk: should win again.   49
1936 FOURWALK [2] (N Macauley) 2-7-13 R Hills 9/2: 2410032: Dsptd lead, no ch with winner:
seems suited by forcing tactics: see 1397.   29
1936 SANDS OF TIME [5] (R Simpson) 2-7-7(6oh) L Riggio(6) 16/1: 4103: Needs further: see 1672.   21
1785 DUTCH COURAGE [4] (D Morley) 2-8-10 Pat Eddery 4/1: 4433144: Prom most: twice below 1585   38
1341 BASIC BLISS [6] 2-7-12 N Howe 7/2 FAV: 3030: Sn prom: btr 1341 (7f).   25

NOTTINGHAM   Monday August 11th   -Cont'd

1612 AFRABELA [1] 2-7-8 J Lowe 6/1: 3204020: Btr 1612 (5f).   15
1570 KNOCKSHARRY [8] 2-7-7(4oh) P Hill(7) 20/1: 1100: No show in 7th: btr 1279 (seller).   00
*1573 DUTCH AUCTION [3] 2-9-7 T Ives 4/1: 10: There 4f: well below 1573.   00
8 ran 8,1,shhd,nk,3   (Ian Bryant)   T Fairhurst Middleham, Yorks

---

NEWCASTLE   Monday August 11th   Lefthand Stiff Galloping Track

Official Going Given As GOOD

2082 WANSBECK AUCTION STAKES 2YO   £1462   6f   Good/Firm 29 -08 Slow

*1825 GET ON GERAGHTY [4] (G Huffer) 2-8-5 G Carter(3) 2/5 FAV: 211: 2 ch c Main Reef -
Gold Cypher (Pardao): Winning 2nd race on the trot but had to struggle to land the odds,
leading ½way in a 2yo auction stakes at Newcastle Aug.11: easy winner over the same C/D
July 28: cost only 5,000 gns: very eff over a stiff 6f, sure to stay further: acts on firm
& gd grnd & on a gall trk: should impr further when he tackles lngr distances.   53
1161 STELBY [5] (O Brennan) 2-7-13 A Proud 10/1: 02242: Dsptd lead final 2f, just btn &
3L clear of rem: gd effort after abs: eff at 5f, probably btr at 6f now: see 632: acts on
gd and firm ground.   45
1872 PROSPECT PLACE [2] (S Hall) 2-7-13 W Carson 10/1: 03: Ev ch: see 1872.   35
1825 WICHITA SPRINGS [6] (J Fitzgerald) 2-8-8 D Nicholls 10/1: 304: Btr effort: see 1376.   38
1510 FRENCHGATE [7] 2-7-13 J Lowe 12/1: 00: Waited with, never btr: see 1510.   27
1843 SHANNON LADY [3] 2-8-8 J Quinn(5) 50/1: 00: Ev ch: quite an inexpensive half sister
to several minor winners: should stay beyond 6f.   32
1653 JOINT SERVICES [1] 2-8-2 S Morris 11/1: 300: Fin 7th: twice well below 715 (5f).   25
2043 EMSLEYS HEIGHTS [8] 2-7-10 J Callaghan(7) 33/1: 000: Led to ½way, fin last: btr 2043.   00
8 ran hd,3,2,½,1½,½   (M Geraghty Racing Ltd)   G Huffer Newmarket

2083 PRUDHOE SELLING STAKES 3YO   £1263   1m 1f   Good/Firm 29 -65 Slow

1985 CAPRICORN BLUE [4] (J Fitzgerald) 3-8-11(vis) D Nicholls 5/2 FAV: -024241: 3 b g Blue
Cashmere - Aquanimba (Acropolis): Well bckd, made most, comfortably to beat his stable
companion in a very slowly run 3yo seller at Newcastle Aug.11 (no bid): first success:
suited by forcing tactics over 9f & acts on fast going: best form in a visor.   18
1960 PATRICKS STAR [6] (J Fitzgerald) 3-8-11 J Lowe 10/1: -00002: Ev ch final 3f, showed
impr form in this slowly run affair: see 1960.   14
1701 JELDAIRE [2] (P Rohan) 3-8-13 Gay Kelleway(3) 4/1: 00-0103: Waited with, fin well:
lightly raced since best 666 (yld/soft).   15
1838 HARE HILL [1] (P Rohan) 3-8-13 J Bleasdale 12/1: 0010004: Prom, ev ch: best eff since 684 13
1960 LARNEM [8] 3-8-13 W R Swinburn 9/1: 0021000: Slow start, never btr: best 1662 (7f, gd). 03
1960 STANFORD ROSE [5] 3-8-8 K Darley 10/1: 03-0040: Prom, wknd: btr 1960 (1m).   00
1662 TANYAS PRINCESS [9] 3-8-8 N Connorton 4/1: 3-30020: Fin 7th: disapp type: see 1662.   00
1662 GALAXY GALA [3] 3-8-11 W Carson 14/1: 4000000: Early ldr, wknd into 8th: best 1334 (6f) 00
1824 RUPERT BROOKE [7] 3-8-11 S Webster 10/1: 0024200: Fin last: twice below 1562 (7.5f).   00
9 ran 2½,1,1,7,5   (P Asquith)   J Fitzgerald Malton, Yorks

2084 NORTHUMBERLAND SPRINT H'CAP 3YO 0-70   £5960   6f   Good/Firm 29 +21 Fast   [72]

1704 CATHERINES WELL [4] (M W Easterby) 3-7-9 G Carter(3) 4/1: -030331: 3 ch f Junius -
Restless Lady (Sandford Lad): Useful filly: returned to her best making most at a fast
pace in a valuable 3yo h'cap at Newcastle Aug.11: in fine form at the end of '85 winning 2
nurseries at Doncaster & a seller also on that course: stays 7f but particularly eff over 5/6f:
acts on firm & yld: suited by a gall trk: may win again.   53
1900 DARK PROMISE [6] (R Hollinshead) 3-8-5 S Perks 10/1: 0132302: Ran on halfway, went
left under press final 1f: best effort since 1524.   56
1146 HALLGATE [9] (S Hall) 3-9-7 W Carson 15/8 FAV: -304103: Well bckd, waited with: ran
on final 2f but failed to keep a str course & is not easy to win on this season: best 854. 72
-1900 QUINTA REEF [3] (M Jarvis) 3-8-3 W Woods(3) 13/2: -120024: Prom most: btr 1900.   44
1889 SUNDEED [8] 3-9-6 A Bond 7/1: 110-000: Prom, wknd: see 1777.   57
1027 DEBBIE DO [2] 3-7-7(1oh) J Lowe 20/1: 22-4000: Chall 2f out, fdd: abs since 1027 (5f). 30
1821 LOCHONICA [5] 3-8-13 D Nicholls 10/1: 0000030: No threat in 8th: much btr 1821 (7f).   00
1922 Viltash [7] 7-13   1840 Security Pacific [1] 7-7(VIS)
9 ran 2½,hd,5,2,hd   (Hippodromo Racing)   M W Easterby Sheriff Hutton, Yorks

2085 GREENHEAD MAIDEN STAKES 3YO+   £2302   1m   Good/Firm 29 -44 Slow

-- DHALEEM [9] (M Stoute) 3-8-8 W R Swinburn 5/1: -1: 3 b c Lyphard - Patia (Don II): Made
a winning debut despite drifting badly in the mkt & coming from behind to lead inside final
1f in a slowly run mdn at Newcastle Aug.11: cost $120,000: dam was a middle dist winner
in France & a half sister to the top class Pawneese: eff over 1m, certain to be suited by
10f & probably further: acts well on fast grnd on a stiff gall trk: sure to benefit from this
experience & can win more races.   47
1628 DOCKSIDER [17] (A Stewart) 3-8-8 M Roberts 14/1: -02: Left briefly 1f out: gd effort:
related to 2 winners incl very useful 2yo Count Pahlen: suited by 1m, will stay 10f: acts
on fast grnd, on a gall trk: should find a mdn soon.   45

619

NEWCASTLE   Monday August 11th   -Cont'd

1045 RIVART [1'4] (P Kelleway) 3-8-8 G&y Kelleway(3) 5/1: -003: Prom, led briefly dist:
abs since 1045.   43
1540 AVADA [8] (A Jarvis) 3-8-8 G Carter(3) 33/1: 4-0004: Made most: best effort this
term: seems best making the running over 7f/1m: acts on fast grnd.   33
1743 TURN EM BACK JACK [4] 3-8-8(bl) J Carr(7) 25/1: -0030: Prom, ev ch: now wears blinkers. 30
1091 PREJUDICE [2] 3-8-5 N Day 6/1: 030-320: Abs since much btr 1091.   25
1361 BELL WETHER [16] 3-8-8 D Nicholls 12/1: 0-00: Waited with, late prog into 7th:
ran only once in '85: should be well suited by 10f: one to keep an eye on in the near future. 25
1756 HIGH CONDUCT [1] 3-8-8 J Lowe 9/2 FAV: 4-40: Well bckd fav, sprawled on the home
turn, not recover, fin 8th: see 1756.   23
1841 PEPENON [10] 4-9-4 J H Brown(5) 9/1: -00: Well bckd, wknd under press str: see 1841. 00
1880 Birchgrove Lad [3] 9-4   -- Commitment [6] 9-4
-- Super Trucker [13] 8-8   1677 State Jester [18] 8-8(bl)
-- Henaadi [12] 8-5   -- Greek Music [5] 8-5   -- Timsolo [7] 8-8
863 Drumbarra [15] 9-4   -- Togdale [11] 8-8
18 ran   1¼,1,5,1½,½,1½,2   (Sheikh Mohammed)   M Stoute Newmarket

2086 MORPETH H'CAP 3YO+ 0-35   £2386   7f   Good/Firm 29 -14 Slow   [34]

1774 MARSILIANA [7] (Don Enrico Incisa) 4-7-12 K Darley 11/2: 0403401: 4 b f Hotfoot -
Mary Reppin (Jimmy Reppin): Needed plenty of driving before gaining the upper hand close
home in a slowly run h'cap at Newcastle Aug.11: first success: eff at 7f, stays 9f: probably
acts on any going: seems to need strong handling.   12
1959 SKELTON [9] (M W Easterby) 3-7-9 J Lowe 9/2: 0003002: Mkt drifter: al prom, caught
close home: fine effort: see 650.   16
1800 BELLA BANUS [6] (W Stephenson) 4-9-2 M Hindley(3) 7/1: 2-00003: Chall under press
1f out: see 606.   25
1774 DOUBLE CHAI [4] (A Jarvis) 3-8-6 D Nicholls 8/1: 0000404: Ev ch: twice below 1701. 18
*1983 ROSSETT [3] 7-7-12(1ow)(6ex) J Quinn(5) 11/4 FAV: 0400210: Prom most: best 1983 (yld). 00
1839 TIDDLYEYETYE [2] 5-8-0(bl)(1ow) S Webster 16/1: 0-00000: No dngr: no worthwhile form
this season: winner at Hamilton in '85: best form at 6f on gd grnd.   00
1983 KING COLE [11] 4-8-1(BL) G Carter(3) 8/1: 0-00400: Set up a clear lead, fdd quickly
final 1f: fin 7th: best 1839 (seller).   00
1870 JOVEWORTH [5] 3-9-0 M Birch 7/1: 1400300: Prom, wknd: best 1610 (6f).   00
1976 Kings Badge [10] 9-7   368 Glorlant [1] 7-7(2oh)   1885 Crownlt [8] 7-10
11 ran   hd,2,3,3,3,shhd   (Don Enrico Incisa)   Don Enrico Incisa Middleham, Yorks

2087 ELSDON H'CAP 3YO+ 0-35   £2197   2m   Good/Firm 29 -68 Slow   [34]

*1884 JURISPRUDENCE [5] (J Watts) 3-8-9(4ex) N Connorton 8/11 FAV: -00011: 3 b c Alleged -
Leliza (Gallant Romeo): Winning 2nd race on the trot & was hvly bckd, leading final 1f under
press in a very slowly run h'cap at Newcastle Aug.11: won a similar h'cap at Doncaster last
time: dam is a half sister to the very smart Bel Bolide: well suited by 14f, stays 2m:
acts on firm & gd grnd, on a gall trk: should continue to impr.   39
1663 TRESIDDER [6] (M W Easterby) 4-9-10 G Carter(3) 7/1: 0-04042: Waited with, kept on
well str: lightly raced this season: see 52.   37
2015 REFORM PRINCESS [1] (M Ryan) 3-8-7(vis)(4ex) W R Swinburn 5/1: 0034103: Led 2f out, no
extra when hdd: in gd form & probably stays 2m: see 1817.   32
1884 HIGHAM GREY [8] (D Chapman) 10-8-2(bl) S Webster 12/1: 0040044: Made much: see 675. 08
1772 SOUND DIFFUSION [7] 4-8-11 D Mckeown 8/1: 1003000: Prom, kept on: best 933.   16
1897 WALTER THE GREAT [2] 4-8-3(bl)(1ow) M Birch 9/1: 4000300: Led 4f out, fdd quickly
when hdd: see 933.   00
-- Cavalier Servente [3] 8-0   -- Broken Seal [4] 9-0
8 ran   1¼,1,2½,nk,12   (R Sangster)   J Watts Richmond, Yorks

WINDSOR Monday August 11th   Sharp Figure 8 Track

Official Going Given As GOOD, STRAIGHT COURSE: GOOD/FIRM, REMAINDER

2088 COOKHAM APP. SELLING H'CAP (0-25) 3YO   £844   6f   Good 54 -52 Slow   [19]
1990 GERSHWIN [9] (D O'Donnell) 3-9-7 R Teague 6/1: 0-12001: 3 b g Gold Song - Firey Kim
(Cannonade): Produced to lead inside dist & won going away in a slowly run 3yo app. selling
h'cap at Windsor Aug.11 (bought in 4,100 gns): first time out winner of a seller at Leicester:
best form over 6f on gd & firm grnd: acts on any trk.   22
1827 WINNING FORMAT [8] (P Makin) 3-9-5 G Landau 7/1: 0000002: Led below dist, kept on
well: mdn who is eff over 5/6f on firm & soft grnd: see 545.   13

620

1940 PADDINGTON BELLE [3] (B Stevens) 3-9-5(vis) S Whiteham(3) 33/1: -000003: Led over 1f
out: btr effort: see 1319.   12
1580 SUNK ISLAND [10] (M Blanshard) 3-9-5 L Riggio 14/1: 00-0004: Dropped in class: al
prom: quite lightly raced filly who is bred to be suited by further than sprint dists:
acts on gd/firm.   10
1827 ABSOLUTELY BONKERS [11] 3-9-0 P Johnson 8/1: 0-00040: Never reached ldrs: see 1827.   00
1827 SOMEWAY [1] 3-8-12 P Francis(3) 25/1: 0000000: Made much: placed in a Bath mdn last
term though has shown little form to date in sellers this season: eff over 5/6f on gd & fast grnd   00
1815 BAO [2] 3-8-6(vis) J Scally 8/1: 0000040: Wknd into 7th: best in 426 (7f): see 346.   00
1836 JACQUI JOY [7] 3-9-5(VIS) G Mash 6/1: 0-00300: Visored first time: fin 9th: see 1734.   00
2024 PERSIAN BAZAAR [6] 3-9-1 P Simms 11/2: 0-00000: Dropped in class: see 1191.   00
1827 MISS VENEZUELA [13] 3-9-0(VIS) P Skelton(3) 4/1 FAV: 0000400: Visored first time:
no threat: see 1288.   00
1687 Private Sue [5] 8-13   1827 Gaywood Girl [15] 8-9 --   Night Of The Comet [12] 8-4
1943 Sea Shanty [4] 9-1(BL)   --   Folly Again [14] 8-4
15 ran   2,nk,¾,2,2½,nk,½,1½   (Mrs E O'Donnell)   D O'donnell Upper Lambourn, Berks

2089 LONG ACRE MAIDEN STAKES 2YO   £959   5f   Good 54 -18 Slow

--   TISZTA SHAROK [3] (R Williams) 2-8-11 R Cochrane 12/1: 1: 2 b f Song - Tin Tessa
(Martinmas): Made a successful mdn, led on fav. far side below dist for a comfortable win
in a 2yo mdn at Windsor Aug.11: sprint bred filly who will impr for this experience: acts
on gd grnd & on a sharp trk.   46
1946 EBONY PRIDE [6] (Pat Mitchell) 2-8-11 J Reid 12/1: 04032: Ev ch: gd effort: see 1946.   38
1653 BOIS DE BOULOGNE [4] (L Piggott) 2-9-0 S Cauthen 3/1: 203003: Made most far side:
clear of rem & seems well suited by forcing tactics: likes a sharp trk: see 662.   38
73   ALWAYS A LADY [1] (L Holt) 2-8-11 N Adams 33/1: 34: Mkt drifter: needed race & will
strip fitter next time: abs since 73.   20
--   REGAL RHYTHM [5] 2-8-11 J Williams 33/1: 0: Never nearer on racecourse debut: will
be suited by 6f: acts on gd grnd.   18
1844 SKYBOLT [8] 2-8-11 T Ives 15/2: 040: No threat: much btr in 1844.   15
--   UPDATE GAL [10] 2-8-11 D Gibson 6/1: 0: Fdd into 7th: cheaply acquired filly who
attracted some support today & is likely to impr.   00
1665 FRANK THE BANK [9] 2-9-0 Pat Eddery 5/4 FAV: 40: Heavily bckd: raced on unfav.
stands side, showing gd speed till no extra below dist: deserves another chance: see 1665 (C/D)   00
1936 Shannon River [2] 9-0   --   Kept Waiting [11] 8-11
10 ran   2,1,5,½,1,hd,½,1   (Tedwood Bloodstock Ltd)   R Williams Newmarket

2090 JUNIORS NURSERY HANDICAP 2YO   £1590   6f   Good 54 +04 Fast   [58]

1522 STRATHBLANE [5] (J Dunlop) 2-9-0 Pat Eddery 9/2: 101: 2 ch f Castle Keep - Mother Brown
(Candy Cane): Useful filly: gamely made all on fav far side to win quite a fast run nursery
h'cap at Windsor Aug.11: narrow winner of a Brighton mdn on her debut: half sister to smart
miler Macarthurs Head and to a couple of other winners: very eff over 6f & bred to be suited
by much further: suited by gd or faster grnd: likes being out in front on a sharp trk.   55
715 TIMESWITCH [7] (W O'gorman) 2-8-1 M L Thomas 4/1 JT FAV: 2002: Al front rank, rallied
gamely inside dist though hung badly left: gd effort after lengthy abs & can win a nursery: see 531.   40
1910 SPANISH SKY [2] (N Vigors) 2-8-5 P Cook 5/1: 01003: Not btn far: stays 6f: see 1194.   42
2047 JUVENILEDELINQUENT [4] (A Bailey) 2-8-3 P Bloomfield 4/1 JT FAV: 1244: Best over this
C/D in 1936.   34
1910 DANCING DIANA [3] 2-9-2 B Rouse 6/1: 214000: No extra dist: btr over 5f in 1910.   43
1731 LUCIANAGA [1] 2-9-7 Paul Eddery 9/2: 220100: Gd speed over ½way: twice below form
shown in 1313 (C/D).   28
1938 Mr Mumbles [6] 8-0(VIS)   +86 Goldorina [8] 8-6
8 ran   ½,½,2,1½,8,10,15   (A J Struthers)   J Dunlop Arundel, Sussex

2091 RACECOURSE ROUNDABOUT H'CAP (0-50)   £2687   1m   Good 54 +22 Fast   [41]

*1637 CANADIAN STAR [1] (M Jarvis) 3-8-7(VIS) T Lucas 9/4 FAV: 0-02411: 3 ch c Northfields-
Pearl Star (Gulf Pearl): In gd form, led well over 2f out & ran on strongly to win a fast
run h'cap at Windsor Aug.11: last month won a 3yo h'cap at Ripon: half brother to useful
juvenile Gulf King, and also closely related to winning hurdlers Star Burst & Copse And
Robbers: eff over 8/10f: acts on gd & fast grnd & on any trk.: wore a visor today.   40
1514 WINDSOR KNOT [10] (P Walwyn) 4-9-10 Paul Eddery 12/1: 00-4002: Slightly impeded by
winner inside dist, though btn on merit: still a gd effort under top weight: see 653.   44
530 HIT THE HEIGHTS [6] (M Pipe) 5-7-13 T Williams 7/1: 000-223: Not btn far: gd effort
after lengthy abs: should be noted if dropping back to selling company: see 530.   17
1901 AVEC COEUR [3] (A Bailey) 4-9-5 M Miller 14/1: 400-004: Came from a long way back:
last successful in '84 at Brighton & Leicester: stays 1m well: acts on gd/firm & soft grnd
and on any track.   33
1942 FAST SERVICE [8] 7-8-13 P Cook 12/1: 0002400: Never nearer: best in 1346.   24
1870 NEW CENTRAL [11] 4-8-3 W Newnes 10/1: 0000200: Made much: btr in 1590: see 636.   11
*1673 COUNT BERTRAND [7] 5-8-1 R Morse(5) 13/2: 0000210: Dwelt, no threat in 7th: btr in 1673   00
1553 FEI LOONG [9] 5-8-13 A Mackay 6/1: 4421430: Wknd into 8th: btr over this C/D in 1553.   00
1890 BUNDABURG [2] 6-9-2 R Wernham 9/2: 0000000: Fdd into 9th: little form this term: see 775   00
1755 Aqaba Prince [4] 7-7   1890 Portogon [5] 9-10
11 ran   ¾,½,2½,½,1,hd,shhd,nk   (Ivan Allan)   M Jarvis Newmarket
                                                                                                                            00

2092 SKYPORT STAKES 3YO   £959   1m 2f   Good 54 -08 Slow

*1941 BOON POINT [1] (J Dunlop) 3-9-6 Pat Eddery 9/4: -030011: 3 br c Shirley Heights -
Brighthelmstone (Prince Regent): Useful colt: led 2f out, ridden out in a minor race at
Windsor Aug.11: recently won a similar event over this C/D: very eff over 10f, stays further:
acts on gd & firm grnd & on any trk: on the up grade.   61
1934 PRINCE ORAC [8] (C Brittain) 3-9-0 G Baxter 8/1: -302: Led 3f out, kept on well
under press: best over 10f: acts on any trk: should win soon: see 1776.   52
1912 NILAMBAR [9] (R F Johnson Houghton) 3-9-9 S Cauthen 1/2 FAV: 0231143: Odds on: tried
to make all, not qckn : slightly below par today: see 1912 & 1670.   53
1941 PYJAMA PARTY [7] (J Dunlop) 3-8-11 B Rouse 16/1: -44: Late prog, though well btn.   16
1927 NO BOLDER [3] 3-9-0 R Wernham 66/1: 00-00: Never dngr over this lngr trip: closely
related to several winners though has yet to trouble the judge himself.   00
1953 CLEAVAGE [5] 3-8-11 R Weaver 66/1: -000: Al behind: half sister to winning juvenile
Marita: bred to be suited by middle dists.   00
1670 Return To Tara [4] 8-11   1540 Rockhold Princess [2] 8-11
1244 Sharp Reef [6] 8-11
9 ran   1,4,15,8,7   (Nathan M Avery)   J Dunlop Arundel, Sussex

2093 SENIOR HANDICAP STAKES (0-35) 3YO+   £1923   1m 4f   Good 54 -32 Slow   [30]

*1686 SWEET ALEXANDRA [12] (R Shaw) 3-8-1(bl) A Mackay 5/1: -4311: 3 br f Lord Gayle -
Santa Luciana (Luciano): Strongly ridden to lead close home in an all aged h'cap at Windsor
Aug.11: last month won a mdn at Wolverhampton: closely related to several middle dist winners,
incl useful Deutschmark: eff over 11/12f: acts on gd & fast grnd & on any trk: in gd form.   24
1535 FULL SPEED AHEAD [13] (R Smyly) 3-8-6 Pat Eddery 13/2: 0-00002: Led over 2f out,
kept on well and is impr of late: likes a sharp trk: see 1535.   25
1970 UP TO UNCLE [9] (R Hannon) 3-9-3 A Mcglone 7/2 FAV: 2213223: Most consistent: see 1314.   34
1829 GODS HOPE [2] (R Akehurst) 4-8-12 P Cook 13/2: 00-0004: Btr effort: lightly raced
mdn: eff at around 10f on gd & soft grnd.   16
--   LISMORE [5] 4-9-2 B Rouse 16/1: 20004-0: Needed this race: rated 40 when 2nd to
Glas Y Dorlan in a Lingfield mdn last term: stays 12f: acts on gd/firm & yld: could win a h'cap   19
1837 ISOM DART [11] 7-8-13 A Clark 12/1: 00-1100: Btn dist: best over 12f in 1473.   11
2022 SOCKS UP [10] 9-8-7 D Kent(7) 15/2: 3-04030: Fin 7th: modest nowadays: see 984.   00
1787 KUWAIT MOON [4] 4-9-2 G Cochrane 15/2: -000030: Never nearer 8th: see 532.   00
1952 Hallowed [8] 7-13   -- Il Pontevecchio [7] 9-7
1470 Touchez Le Bois [15] 9-3   8   Rustling [3] 9-3
851 Pitkaithly [1] 9-1   1733 Capulet [16] 8-1(VIS)   --   Homeward [4] 7-12
1670 Mossaul [6] 7-7
16 ran   1½,¾,½,hd,3,nk,½   (J A MacGregor)   R Shaw Newmarket

---

2094 SANDLING SELLING H'CAP (0-25)   £704   1m 2f   Good/Firm 26 -14 Slow   [15]

1074 GRAND CELEBRATION [11] (R Simpson) 4-8-13 S Whitworth 5/1: -040001: 4 ch c Monteverdi -
Blackfly (Mount Marcy) Dropped in class after fair abs and led below dist, comfortably, in a
selling h'cap at Folkestone Aug 12 (no bid): first success: eff around 10f on gd/firm ground:
acts on a sharp track.   10
1063 FLEUR DE THISTLE [5] (A Davison) 3-8-8(vis) R Fox 9/2: 0033202: Tried to make all:
remains a mdn: eff over 8/10f: see 749.   06
1990 BLACK SPOUT [3] (H O'neill) 5-8-7   S Cauthen 3/1 JT FAV: 2000003: Longer trip:
ran on same pace: has shown a little ability over sprint dist: acts on gd/firm and soft: 00
1969 JUST CANDID [7] (D Wilson) 4-9-10 B Rouse 3/1 JT FAV: 0-00334: Late prog: see 1937.   06
1567 SOLENT DAWN [1] 3-7-11 A Mcglone 20/1: 0000-00: Wknd 2f out: quite lightly raced
filly who has yet to show any worthwhile form: acts on gd/firm.   00
1989 CSILLAG [2] 3-8-10(BL) J Williams 16/1: 00-0000: Bl first time: dropped in class
here tho' wknd home turn: no form prev over shorter distances.   00
--   FULL OF SPEED [4] 5-9-9 P Cook 12/1: 0-100-0: Never dangerous on belated seasonal
debut: won in this grade at Windsor last term: eff over 1m on fast ground.   00
1567 HOKUSAN [8] 4-9-2 N Day 5/1: 4000000: Al rear: see 620.   00
1265 BLAIRS WINNIE [3] 5-8-7 P Bradwell (BL) 10/1: 000000: Bl first time: well behind from
½ way: see 201.   00
9 ran   4,1½,1,8,1   (Tony Stafford)   R Simpson Upper Lambourn, Berks.

2095 IVYCHURCH JUVENILE MAIDEN AUCTION 2YO   £959   6f   Good/Firm 26 -66 Slow

1846 ORIENT LINE [2] (R Hannon) 2-8-10 Pat Eddery 5/4 FAV: 021: 2 gr c Capricorn Line -
Rue Taima (Vigo) Comfortably led inside dist when a well bckd winner of a slowly run mdn
auction race at Folkestone Aug 12: cost 3,400 gns and is closely related to sev minor winners:
eff over 6/7f on gd/firm ground: seems to like a sharp/easy course.   34
1825 CIREN JESTER [4] (W Musson) 2-8-8 M Wigham 7/1: 002: Made most: btr eff: see 1825.   22
715 GYPSYS BARN RAT [7] (W Holden) 2-8-2 R Morse(5) 13/2: 03: Long abs: nearest fin:
cheaply bought filly who is a half sister to sev winners: will stay further: acts on gd/firm
ground and on a sharp course.   10

1883 REMAIN FREE [6] (C Williams) 2-8-2 G Baxter 6/1: 3304: Al prom: best 1405 (gall trk).   10
1665 WILLIAM PERE [5] 2-8-5 P Cook 33/1: 00: Never nearer: very cheaply bought colt whose
dam won over sprint distances.   00
1253 SABOTEUR [10] 2-8-5 G Dickie 11/2: 00: Early speed: half brother to sev winners.   00
1483 Ballantrae [1] 8-2   1067 Hush Kit [9] 8-2   1928 Ala Hounak [11] 9-0
1883 Rock A Little [3] 8-7
10 ran   3,2,nk,8,shthd   (J Lizzari)   R Hannon East Everleigh, Wilts.

2096 APPLEDORE STAKES 3YO+   £959   1m 7f Good/Firm 26 +07 Fast

--   CAP DEL MOND [4] (G Harwood) 3-8-8 G Starkey 4/1: -1: 3 b c Troy - Rainbow's End
(My Swallow) Made a successful debut, led dist and ridden out in quite a fast run stks race
at Folkestone Aug 12: fetched 400,000 gns as yearling and is a half brother to winning stayer
Storm Cloud: clearly well suited to a test of stamina himself: acts on gd/firm grd and on a
sharp track: seems sure to improve.   44
*1786 FRANCHISE [7] (R F Johnson Houghton) 3-8-10 S Cauthen 4/7 FAV: -012: Went on home
turn, strongly ridden and not quicken: see 1786.   42
1494 TOMS TREASURE [6] (R Akehurst) 4-9-4 R Mcghin 16/1: -333: Made most: fair eff: see 1494. 30
*1721 RENO RALPH [5] (G Huffer) 3-8-13 M Miller 9/2: -00414: Not qckn over this longer trip.   35
1652 SEAT OF LEARNING [1] 4-9-4 Pat Eddery 16/1: -000: Never dangerous: see 1494.   00
1799 PORTLY [2] 5-9-7(BL) A Murray 50/1: -00: Early leader: lightly raced gelding: wore bl today. 00
6 ran   2,2½,2,dist,dist   (Prince Ahmed Salman)   G Harwood Pulborough, Sussex

2097 PRIX DU TOUQUET (NURSERY H'CAP) 2YO   £1646   6f   Good/Firm 26 -51 Slow   [47]

1938 GLORY BEE [2] (L Holt) 2-7-10 N Adams 6/1: 010041: 2 ch c Bold Owl - Sweet Minuet
(Setay) Led inside final 1f, ridden out in a slowly run nursery h'cap at Folkestone Aug 12:
earlier won a seller at Lingfield: half brother to sev winners: best form over 6f on a
sharp, undulating trk, suited by fast ground.   28
*47   NAIVE CHARM [1] (R Boss) 2-8-12 Pat Eddery 7/4 JT FAV: 12: Well bckd despite a
lengthy abs: led after ½ way, not qckn inside dist: eff over 5/6f: acts on gd/firm: see 47.   34
1916 SARIHAH [5] (H T Jones) 2-9-7 A Murray 7/4 JT FAV: 01223: Made much under top weight:
best in 1916.   34
1938 SWIFT PURCHASE [4] (R Hannon) 2-7-7(bl)(3oh) G French 10/1: 3000104: Best over 5f here
in 1557 (seller).   00
1598 TELEGRAPH FOLLY [3] 2-8-13(bl) L Riggio(7) 25/1: 433100: Lightly raced since 853 (5f,yld)
1518 MIDDAY SANITO [7] 2-8-3 A Mcglone 33/1: 3000: Never went pace: placed over 5f here
in 27 (soft).   00
1345 TELESTO [3] 2-8-13 G Starkey 7/1: 0440: Sn behind: much btr 1435 (7f).   00
7 ran   3,3,2,5,3   (B Keay)   L Holt Basingstoke, Hants

2098 LITTLESTONE H'CAP STAKES (0-35) 3YO+   £1305   1m 4f Good/Firm 26 +01 Fast   [27]

1450 LONGSTOP [6] (P Makin) 4-9-4 Pat Eddery 4/1: 3003001: 4 b g On Your Mark - Shade
(Gratitude) Led dist, comfortably, in a h'cap at Folkestone Aug 12: loves a sharp, undulating
trk especially Brighton, where he won twice last season: also successful at Goodwood and
Wolverhampton: best form over 12f on gd or faster ground: may win again.   26
1935 VINTAGE PORT [2] (R Akehurst) 4-9-10 P Cook 4/1: 0000022: In gd form: see 1935 & 653.   28
1559 DASHING LIGHT [3] (D Morley) 5-9-2 B Rouse 5/2 FAV: 4043233: Well bckd: led/dsptd
lead thr'out on her fav trk: quite consistent: see 432.   15
1745 GENTLE STREAM [4] (J Toller) 4-9-4 S Cauthen 7/1: 0004034: Nearest fin: see 1745.   16
1686 WRANGBROOK [8] 3-7-12(BL) L Riggio(7) 33/1: 0-30000: BI first time: al there: see 123.   05
1964 JANIE O [10] 3-8-10(BL) G Starkey 9/1: 0300400: BI first time: led/dsptd lead till
home turn: see 1569.   13
1945 HEIGHT OF SUMMER [7] 5-8-4 N Adams 6/1: -040030: Wknd into 7th: see 1209.   00
1970 Miss Jade [9] 8-1   1951 Sunley Spirit [5] 7-7   1829 Winter Palace [1] 9-8(BL)
10 ran   1½,3,½,1½,2   (K Luebke)   P Makin Ogbourne Maisey, Wilts.

2099 DYMCHURCH 3YO STAKES   £959   7f   Good/Firm 26 -08 Slow

1934 CODICES [6] (G Harwood) 3-9-0 G Starkey 5/1: 0-00101: 3 gr c Codex - Spice On Ice
(Grey Dawn) Useful colt: burst through to lead cl home in a 3yo stks at Folkestone Aug 12:
earlier comfortably made all in a mdn at Kempton: best form over 7f on fast grd, tho' does
acts on yldg: likes a sharp trk.   59
1607 USFAN [4] (J Dunlop) 3-8-7 Pat Eddery 9/2: -022: Led well over 1f out, caught final
strides: lightly raced colt who is on the upgrade and must win soon: see 1607.   51
*1691 SIR ARNOLD [5] (A Stewart) 3-9-0 M Roberts 7/1: -2313: Early leader, kept on well
and not btn far: continues to improve: see 1691.   54
*1934 BRONZE OPAL [3] (G Balding) 3-9-0 R Weaver 2/1 FAV: 0001014: Not btn far tho' btr
over 1m in 1934.   50
*1756 EXCLUSIVE NORTH [1] 3-9-0 S Cauthen 9/4: 330-010: Led before ½ way, kept on: see 1756.   49
1947 CAREER MADNESS [2] 3-8-7 M Giles(7) 33/1: -0000: Outpaced, late prog: see 1691.   00
1880 MUBAH [7] 3-8-7 Julie Pyne(7) 50/1: -00: Outsider: slow start and never in race:
cheaply bought colt who is a half brother to winning juv Regal Mate.   00

7 ran hd,1½,2,½,4 (P Locke) G Harwood Pulborough, Sussex.

BEVERLEY Tuesday August 12th Righthand Undulating Track with Uphill Finish

2100 WOODHALL WAY AUCTION STAKES 2YO £1631 5f Good/Firm 36 +18 Fast

•1782 **ULTRA NOVA** [10] (P Cole) 2-8-8 T Quinn 9/4 FAV: 32011: 2 ch f Tina's Pet - Jennyjo (Martinmas) Impr filly: winning 2nd race on the trot, making all readily in a fast run auction race at Beverley Aug 12: also made all in a fillies mdn at Warwick July 26: sprint bred filly who fetched 6,000 gns as a yearling: very eff at 5f with forcing tactics: acts on firm and good ground: seems equally at home on a sharp or stiff trk: should pick up a nursery very soon. 55
1561 **ROYAL CROFTER** [7] (M H Easterby) 2-8-5 M Birch 5/2: 3222: Mostly 2nd, not the pace of winner: see 1561 (C/D). 42
+1738 **DANCING BELLE** [13] (T Fairhurst) 2-8-8 G Duffield 11/2: 000013: Al prom, kept on and is in good form: will be suited by 6f. 40
1561 **LEADING PLAYER** [5] (R Hollinshead) 2-8-8 S Perks 13/2: 034: Pressed winner much:see 1561 40
1919 **KALAS IMAGE** [2] 2-8-4 A Mackay 11/1: 2303140: Prom, ev ch: best 1561 (C/D). 33
1333 **MR BERKELEY** [12] 2-8-5 M Wood 9/1: 000: Prom much: see 1333. 32
1958 **GARCON NOIR** [4] 2-8-5 S Webster 20/1: 00: Speed most, fin 7th: will be suited by an easier track: a 3,900 gns yearling who is a half brother to a couple of minor winners including fair middle dist performer Sagamore. 30
1088 **MISS EMILY** [14] 2-7-12 S P Griffiths 33/1: 000: Kept on to fin 8th: best eff yet from this small filly: half sister to winning stayer Alpha Omega. 20
1916 **THE DEVILS MUSIC** [6] 2-8-5 L Charnock 15/2: 000: Outpaced ½ way: flattered 1916? 00
1825 **Vol Vitesse** [9] 8-1 -- **Overnite Sensation** [8] 8-5(4ow)
1955 **Hazels Girl** [15] 7-12 -- **Park Frolics** [1] 7-12 1825 Leading Wren [3] 7-12
1825 **Mayspark** [11] 8-5
15 ran 4,2,shthd,1½,½,nk,2 (C Shiacolas) P Cole Whatcombe, Oxon.

2101 LADYGATE SELLING H'CAP 3YO+ 0-25 £925 1m 4f Good/Firm 36 -24 Slow [14]

1952 **DICK KNIGHT** [2] (K Ivory) 5-9-3(vis) A Shoults(5) 5/1: 0020001: 5 ch g Owen Dudley - Illumination (St Paddy) Gained his first win of the season, leading ½ way and forging clear under strong driving in a slowly run selling h'cap at Beverley Aug 12 (no bid): in '85 won at Warwick and Hamilton: very eff over 11/12f: acts on firm and soft. 11
2008 **MUSICAL WILL** [3] (T Fairhurst) 4-9-6(bl) G Duffield 8/1: 0040302: Prom, ev ch: see 1892 07
2008 **EARLS COURT** [1] (R Francis) 10-9-0 S Webster 10/1: 2-04003: Waited with, fin well: usually a front runner: see 1432. 00
1845 **METELSKI** [9] (G Blum) 5-9-7(bl) M Rimmer 4/1: 0-00034: Gd chance at the weights on the form shown in 1845, ev ch 3f out, no extra: inconsistent: see 1845. 03
1898 **MAX CLOWN** [10] 3-8-5 C Rutter(5) 7/2 FAV: 0-00130: Misbehaved before start, prom, wknd: best 1428. 00
2008 **THE RUSK** [11] 5-9-9 A Clark 14/1: -0000: Led to ½ way: see 1769. 01
1772 **JUBILANT LADY** [8] 5-8-3 Julie Bowker(7) 17/2: 0000000: Never closer in 7th: see 827. 00
2008 **DUBAVARNA** [5] 5-9-11 N Connorton 7/1: -000020: Fin 8th: much btr 2008. 00
2040 **UPLAND GOOSE** [4] 5-9-0 D Nicholls 7/1: 2000: See 1195. 00
1985 **Royal Valeur** [13] 9-5 1845 **Majestic Star** [12] 9-7
1969 **Bushy Bay** [6] 8-12(vis)
12 ran 7,2,3,3,1 (Wallace Farms Stud Ltd) K Ivory Radlett, Herts.

2102 WEDNESDAY MARKET H'CAP 3YO+ 0-35 £2341 1m 2f Good/Firm 36 -18 Slow [33]

1835 **BOLD ARCHER** [4] (M Fetherston Godley) 3-8-2 C Rutter(3) 8/1: 0020101: 3 ch g Brave Shot - Allander Girl (Miralgo) Continued his gd recent form, leading dist but was all out to hold on by a shthd on the line in a h'cap at Beverley Aug 12: winner over 1m here July 15: likes this stiff uphill finish: stays 10f well: suited by firm ground and Beverley. 26
1951 **CASHEW KING** [8] (B Mcmahon) 3-8-5 S Webster 10/1: -004402: Came with a storming late run, just failed: best eff this season and can win soon: stays 10f well: see 857. 29
1941 **MISSELFORE** [2] (P Walwyn) 3-7-7 A Mackay 10/1: 00-0003: Kept on at the one pace, possibly flattered in 1941 (stks, sharp track). 13
1773 **CHABLISSE** [16] (R Whitaker) 3-8-0 D Mckeown 14/1: P403104: Prom, ev ch: fair eff: see 1369 19
2037 **BLACK RIVER** [7] 5-7-8 J Lowe 10/1: 0-00400: Prom 1m: see 46 00
1565 **PERSHING** [13] 5-8-12 T Ives 5/1 JT FAV: 2032200: Slow start, never btr: best 1374 (C/D) 16
1787 **RAPID LAD** [1] 8-9-9 D Nicholls 5/1 JT FAV: -014000: Waited with, eff 3f out, no extra, fin 7th: best 1106 (C/D). 26
•1699 **CADENETTE** [10] 4-8-4 P Robinson 10/1: 0042010: Made most, fin 8th: see 1699 (seller) 06
1720 **SMART MART** [5] 7-7-7(bl) M Fry 10/1: 0-30030: Led briefly 2f out, sn in retreat: see 1374. 00
1761 **RESTORATION** [12] 4-8-11 A Bond 8/1: 00-0030: Well bckd, no danger: btr 1761 (7f). 00
1987 **Godlord** [6] 8-0(BL) 1985 **Teejay** [11] 7-10 1951 **Lotus Princess** [9] 9-2
1964 **Mexican Mill** [15] 8-7 1871 **Dawn Spirit** [14] 8-7
15 ran shthd,2½,½,1,1½,1½,1½ (Miss Jenny Rick) M Fetherston Godley East Ilsley
00

BEVERLEY   Tuesday August 12th   -Cont'd

2103 HENGATE CLAIMING STAKES 3YO   £1811   1m   Good/Firm 36 -21 Slow

1960 WATENDLATH [6] (E Weymes) 3-7-11(BL) M Fry 16/1: 3000001: 3 br f Skyliner - North
North West (Northfields) Bl for the first time and showed greatly impr form, fin strongly to
forge clear in final 1f in a slowly run 3yo claimer at Beverley Aug 12: evidently well suited
by a stiff 1m and acts on fast ground.   13
2060 TROPICO [11] (P Haslam) 3-8-8(VIS) T Williams 3/1: 0423102: Led briefly over 1f out,
wearing a visor for the first time: best 1471.   19
1705 ON WATER [12] (M Prescott) 3-8-10 G Duffield 8/1: -0003: Kept on one paced final 2f:
improved form from this lightly raced maiden: may appreciate further than 1m: should be borne
in mind in a seller/claimer.   20
1701 CLOUDLESS SKY [8] (P Rohan) 3-8-1 S Morris 10/1: 00-0304: Made most: mdn , best 1288. 06
*1969 ROSI NOA [1] 3-8-11 Gay Kelleway(3) 5/1: 3000010: Chall 3f out, fdd: btr 1969 (10f shp) 16
1540 ST JAMES RISK [9] 3-8-10 T Quinn 11/4 FAV: 100-000: Well bckd, ev ch: see 1540.   13
74   QUICKEN THE BID [4] 3-8-11 A Mackay 8/1: 0400-00: Ev ch, wknd into 8th: long abs:
showed a little ability last term.   00
1841 LADY ATTIVA [2] 3-8-1 A Clark 11/2: 0-00000: Slow start, no threat in 9th: only poor
form this term.   00
1838 Taxi Man [10] 8-11   448 Taufast [5] 8-2   1999 Lone Galaxie [3] 8-5(BL)
1841 Fair Zinnia [7] 8-1
12 ran 4,¼,5,nk,2   (T Barker)   E Weymes Leyburn, Yorks.

2104 MANOR ROAD H'CAP 3YO+ 0-35   £1581   7.5f   Good/Firm 36 -21 Slow   [35]

1901 KAMARESS [7] (M Brittain) 4-8-1 K Darley 9/1: 2400431: 4 br f Kampala - I'm The
Latest (Polyfoto) Prom and led dist under press in a slowly run h'cap at Beverley Aug 12:
winner at Redcar in '84, below her best last season: well suited by 7f/1m and fast ground. 16
*1624 SIGNORE ODONE [18] (M H Easterby) 4-10-0 M Birch 5/2 FAV: -400112: Early leader,
kept on again final 1f: gd effort under 10-0 and is in fine form: see 1624.   41
1885 MONSTROSA [1] (J Spearing) 3-7-12(2ow) R Hills 12/1: 0030003: Waited with: came to
chall dist: best effort this season: see 538.   18
1839 HOPTONS CHANCE [6] (S Wiles) 4-7-8 M L Thomas 10/1: 0000024: Led 2½f out, hdd and
wknd: better 1839 (easy 7f).   00
1743 FLYING ZIAD [3] 3-8-5 J Carr(7) 20/1: 000-40: Never nearer and is one to bear in
mind for a small h'cap/seller, possibly over 1m+.   13
1202 RAPID ACTION [12] 5-8-8 J Bleasdale 14/1: 3033000: See 521, 46.   05
1701 GOLD CHIP [13] 3-8-9 N Connorton 9/2: 3-42020: Much btr 1701 and is worth another chance 00
1870 CHARMING VIEW [11] 4-8-2 S Morris 9/1: 0102000: Misbehaved start, no threat: best 1139 00
518 IMPROVISE [19] 3-8-11 S Webster 10/1: 10-2000: Long abs, no danger: best first time
out in 81.   00
2039 Top Othlane [8] 8-5   1839 The Golf Slide [17] 7-8(1ow)(6oh)
1761 Remembrance [10] 8-8(4ow)   1864 Mark My Card [14] 7-7(3oh)
--   Carousel Nougat [5] 7-8(1ow)(2oh) 1800 Clotilda [2] 7-12(vis)
1438 Burning Arrow [16] 8-11   1101 Mr Panache [15] 8-4(1ow)
1765 Grey Cree [9] 8-3
18 ran 1,hd,6,2,1¼   (M Brittain)   M Brittain Warthill, Yorks.

2105 MINSTER MOORGATE MAIDEN STAKES 2YO   £1017   7.5f   Good/Firm 36 -09 Slow

1452 BROTHER PATRICK [8] (L Piggott) 2-9-0 T Ives 5/1: 301: 2 b c Blakeney - Reltop
(High Top) Impr colt: well bckd, battled it out in the final 2f for a shthd success in a
2yo mdn at Beverley Aug 12: full brother to winning 3yo Just David: suited by a stiff 7f,
sure to be suited by longer dist: acts well on fast ground.   50
1587 MON COEUR [15] (C Brittain) 2-9-0(BL) P Robinson 12/1: 042: Bl first time, almost
made all and well clear rem: evidently suited by bl and forcing tactics: should find a mdn. 49
1801 SPY GIFT [11] (M Stoute) 2-8-11 W R Swinburn 6/4 FAV: 033: Well bckd: only the one
pace final 2f: should have been well suited by this trip but much btr 1801 (sharp 6f).   34
1675 ALLOUSH [10] (L Piggott) 2-9-0 B Crossley 33/1: 04: Prom much, showing some improvement. 34
1440 ACCUSTOMED [12] 2-8-11 W Woods(3) 33/1: 000: Prom, ev ch: see 1067.   30
1903 THE LIONHEART [19] 2-9-0 B Thomson 7/2: 020: Ev ch: btr 1903.   33
1903 ALPENHORN [4] 2-9-0 W Ryan 5/1: 030: Never btr in 7th: see 1903.   00
780 LAMB BECK [1] 2-9-0 L Charnock 10/1: 30: Long abs but lightly bckd, wknd final 2f:
will benefit from the race: see 780.   00
--   Falling Leaf [5] 9-0   1984 Thank Havon [16] 8-11   -- Flaunting [17] 8-11
1296 Sparkler Boy [2] 9-0   1175 Sombrero Gold [13] 9-0
1681 Carse Kelly [3] 8-11   1376 Albion Place [6] 9-0   -- Oriental Dancer [14] 9-0
1561 Colney Heath Lad [18] 9-0   1916 Melgrove [9] 9-0
1872 Hiero Falco [7] 9-0
19 ran shthd,7,1½,½,shthd,2   (Anthony Leftwich)   L Piggott Newmarket

NOTTINGHAM   Tuesday August 12th   Lefthand, Fair Track

Official Going Given As GOOD

2106 LAMBLEY HANDICAP STAKES 3YO 0-35   £1291   5f   Good 63 +09 Fast   [36]

1847 LEFT RIGHT [10] (N Macauley) 3-8-3(1ow) Paul Eddery 8/1 : 0030441: 3 br f
Marching On -`Beryl's Gift (Sayfar) Led 1f out, ridden out in quite fast run 3yo h'cap at
Nottingham Aug 17: placed sev times prev and was not winning out of turn: eff at 5f, does
stay further: acts on firm and soft ground and seems best when held up: has worn bl in past.   20
1584 GLEADHILL PARK [8] (K Brassey) 3-8-9(bl) S Whitworth 14/1: 0000002: Led 4f: kept
on well and just btn: best eff this term: see 339.   25
1927 WEBSTERS FEAST [13] (M Mccormack) 3-9-1(BL) W Newnes 9/2: 0002043: Bl first time:
ran on too late: see 1406.   28
1691 FOUNDRY FLYER [9] (A Bailey) 3-8-12(BL) P Bloomfield 8/1: -0404: Bl first time:
never nearer: see 1418.   19
1940 MISS KNOW ALL [7] 3-9-7 A Culhane(7) 7/1: 0-00030: Sn prom: in gd form: see 624.   28
545 TOLLYS ALE [1] 3-8-4 G Carter(3) 12/1: 04-4300: Never nearer after abs: seems
flattered 175 (sharpish track).   03
1574 MUSIC REVIEW [4] 3-8-9 R Cochrane 7/1: 0-22220: Early speed: see 1574, 910.   00
*2024 ARDENT PARTNER [2] 3-8-10(7ex) S Dawson 5/2 FAV: 0030210: There over 3f: btr 2024 (shrp).00
1687 Choral Park [5] 8-6(VIS)   1687 Hobournes Katie [6] 7-13
2046 Lauries Trojan [11] 8-9(BL)   1704 Package Perfection [3] 8-5
12 ran   ½,1,2,shthd,3,1,1   (Mrs Peggy Cowey)   N Macauley Melton Mowbray, Leics.

2107 COLWICK PARK SELLING STKS 2YO   £963   6f   Good 63 -01 Slow

1949 MISS DRUMMOND [3] (N Tinkler) 2-8-8 Kim Tinkler(5) 9/2: 0200131: 2 b f The Brianstan
- Miss Cindy (Mansingh) Al prom and ran on well to lead post in a 2yo seller at Nottingham
Aug 12 (bought in 3400 gns): earlier won a similar event at Hamilton: eff at 5f, stays 6f:
acts on gd and fast ground.   21
1881 ROSIES GLORY [1] (C Tinkler) 2-8-8 T Lucas 3/1: 002: Made virtually all and caught
post: 4l clear 3rd: see 1881: should certainly find a seller.   21
1647 RECORD FLIGHT [10] (R Hodges) 2-8-8 R Curant 7/4 FAV: 00023: Led stands side:see 1647.   12
2026 BINGO QUEEN [4] (J Berry) 2-8-8 J Carroll(7) 20/1: 2213004: Prom far side: best 865 (5f)   06
1723 RAINTREE COUNTY [9] R Cochrane 12/1: 000040: Best early season in 320 (soft)   03
1684 SLEEPLINE FOR BEDS [11] 2-8-11 J Reid 8/1: 4230: Led stands side: best 1449.   00
1832 Tilloujo [6] 8-8   -- Ragtime Party [2] 8-11
-- Max Star [5] 8-11   -- Lane Patrol [8] 8-8
10 ran   shthd,4,2,2,1   (Simon Murray-Green)   N Tinkler Malton, Yorks.

2108 EBF NOTTINGHAMSHIRE MAIDEN 2YO   £1725   6f   Good 63 +05 Fast

1762 SOMETHING EXTRA [5] (P Cole) 2-9-0 T Quinn 8/1: 021: 2 ch c Enchantment - Extra
La (Exbury) Impr colt: mkt drifter, but made most, comfortably, in quite a fast run 2yo
mdn at Nottingham Aug 12: half brother to the smart Susa Steel: eff at 5f, stays 6f well:
acts on gd and firm ground and on any track.   48
1984 MAD MAX [6] (P Haslam) 2-9-0 T Williams 7/2: 432: Dsptd lead: consistent colt:see 1984.   45
1928 KIROWAN [9] (G Huffer) 2-9-0 G Carter(3) 8/1: 03: Hung left over 1f out: gd eff: see 1928   42
1869 SUNORIUS [2] (J Glover) 2-9-0 D Mckeown 50/1: 04: Nearest fin and is fast improving:
half brother to fair 3yo winner Straw Boater: should be suited by further than 6f: acts
on gd ground and a fair track.   39
1936 WOODMAN WEAVER [3] 2-9-0 W Newnes 50/1: 000: Dsptd lead ½ way: showed impr form here:
cheaply acquired colt: eff at 6f on gd ground.   37
-1816 KINGS VICTORY [8] 2-9-0 M Wigham 7/4 FAV: 420: Well bckd: ev ch: btr 1816, 1629.   32
1149 COMMONSIDR GIPSY [7] 2-9-0 M Brennan 4/1: 0200: Abs: best 685.   00
-- DOLLAR SEEKER [4] 2-9-0 R Cochrane 6/1: 0: Slow start on debut: should impr on this:
cost $140,000 as yearling: should be suited by further than 6f.   00
1915 Mister Wizard [1] 9-0(bl)   1869 Regalcroft [10] 9-0
10 ran   1,1,1,½,2,½   (Guiting Stud Lttd)   P Cole Whatcombe, Oxon.

2109 STRETTON AUTOMATICS HCAP 0-35   £3078   1m 2f Good 63 -08 Slow   [29]

1706 REGENCY SQUARE [6] (P Feilden) 3-7-9(2ow) A Mackay 20/1: -320441: 3 b c Red Regent
- Sequoia (Sassafras) Showed impr form, led inside final 1f in a h'cap at Nottingham Aug 12:
placed sev times prev, this was his first win: half brother to 7f winner Travelguard: eff at
10/12f, does stay further: acts on gd and fast grd and on any track.   16
1956 PENTLAND HAWK [2] (R Hollinshead) 3-9-7 S Perks 5/2 FAV: 00011D2: Well bckd: led 2f
out and just btn: 4l clear 3rd: in excellent form: see 1956, 1671.   40
1671 MISTS OF TIME [17] (I Balding) 3-8-0(BL)(1ow) W Newnes 14/1: 0-03003: Made much
1m: bl first time: see 823.   11
1806 GREGORIAN CHANT [15] (P Walwyn) 3-8-4 Paul Eddery 20/1: 000004: Some late hdwy:
best eff yet: eff 10f on good ground.   15
1951 FILM CONSULTANT [9] 4-8-4 I Johnson 11/1: 00-0030: Stays 10f but btr 1951 (9f)   02
1985 BUSTED FLAVOUR [12] 5-9-10 R Cochrane 20/1: 30030: Nearest fin: should benefit from
12f: acts on gd and firm ground.   21
1258 COLEMAN HAWKINS [8] 3-8-11 T Quinn 8/1: -00040: Never nearer 8th: acts firm & yldg.   00
1838 ADHARI [1] 3-8-7 Pat Eddery 8/1: -00040: Mkt drifter, never showed: btr 1838.   00

626

1838 SIMONS FANTASY [11] 3-8-7 G Baxter 7/1: 4434100: Prom, fdd: twice below 1724 (firm).   00
1565 Manabel [3] 8-9   1104 Sirdar Flyer [13] 7-10
1820 Strictly Business [16] 8-0(vis)   1804 Guest Image [4] 8-7
--   Catch The Thatch [14] 9-0   1923 High Forest [7] 9-5
1830 Mistral Magic [18] 8-10
16 ran   ¾,4,shthd,1,¼   (A S Helaissi)   P Feilden Newmarket

2110 HEMLOCK STONE MAIDEN STKS 3YO   £1372   1m 2f   Good 63 -09 Slow

916 BANANAS [10] (O Douieb) 3-9-0 Pat Eddery 2/1 FAV: -2341: 3 b c Alleged - Little Nana
(Lithiot) Despite fair abs, led 1f out, ridden out in a mdn at Nottingham Aug 12: placed in
his 3 prev outings: first time out a fine 2nd to Top Guest at Beverley: eff at 10f on gd
and yldg ground: likes a gall track.   47
1953 MAGIC TOWER [2] (C Brittain) 3-8-11 G Baxter 25/1: 0-402: Led briefly over 1f out:
good eff: seems suited by 10f: acts on gd and firm ground and a gall trk: should find a race.   42
1954 MOONSTRUCK [12] (M Ryan) 3-9-0 R Cochrane 8/1: 2004233: Led 3f out: consistent:see 1954   41
1818 LINASH [9] (G Wragg) 3-8-11 Paul Eddery 3/1: -0044: Chance over 1f out: needs 12f.   35
592 BAYTINO [3] 3-8-11 M Rimmer 33/1: -030: Long abs: see 592.   30
1818 OUR HERO [6] 3-9-0 W Carson 6/1: -00: Prom, ev ch: see 1818.   24
599 LOST IN FRANCE [8] 3-8-11 B Thomson 7/2: 0-000: Well bckd, despite long abs: there 1m:
prob needed race: little form in 3 outings this season, but seems quite well regarded:
half sister to sev winners abroad and should improve.   23
1602 Maladetoc [4] 8-11   1841 Sybilly [5] 8-11   1589 Starlight Freddie [7] 9-0
1540 Ascendit [11] 8-11   --   Hillison [1] 9-0
12 ran   ¾,2,1½,2½,5,shthd   (Arno Scheffer)   O Douieb Newmarket

2111 BYRON HANDICAP 3YO+ 0-35   £1381   2m   Good 63 -27 Slow   [23]

1873 SHIPBOURNE [9] (G Harwood) 3-9-6 A Clark 9/1: 0003031: 3 b c Ille de Bourbon - Fleet
Girl (Habitat) Led over 2f out, comfortably, in a h'cap at Nottingham Aug 12: obviously well
suited by 2m: acts on gd and firm grd and a gall trk.   38
1577 QUICK REACTION [7] (M Ryan) 3-8-5 R Cochrane 10/1: 0-0002: No chance with winner,
but is improving: stays 2m: see 1577.   19
1884 QUADRILLION [6] (R Hollinshead) 7-8-11 P Hil(7) 8/1: -02433: Ev ch in str: see 1419.   08
1564 MUSIC MINSTREL [4] (C Nelson) 3-8-9 J Reid 5/1: -000144: Led 14f: best 1078.   19
1952 CROOK N HONEST [10] 4-8-3 A Proud 10/1: 0440000: Held ev ch: best 542 (yldg)   00
19   DEW [13] 5-9-0 A Dicks(7) 33/1: 0/00-00: Very long abs: there 13f: very lightly
raced on the Flat: winner over hurdles in 85/86.   07
2040 SUN STREET [12] 4-9-7 Pat Eddery 7/2 FAV: 0-40020: Fin 7th: btr 2040.   00
2015 KNIGHTS HEIR [3] 5-8-7 W Woods(3) 6/1: 0000020: Fdd str: much btr 2015 (14f)   00
1897 ALFIE DICKINS [11] 8-8-5 W Ryan 10/1: 0440300: Made no show: see 590.   00
1569 Comhampton [1] 9-3   --   Franciscus [8] 8-5   1071 Boreham Down [2] 8-4(8ow)
--   Nashood [5] 8-9
13 ran   1¼,2,1,nk,1½,1,1½   (K Abdulla)   G Harwood Pulborough, Sussex

---

PHOENIX PARK   Sunday August 10th   Left and Righthand, Sharpish Track

Official Going Given As YIELDING/SOFT

2112 SHANBALLY HOUSE STUD STAKES (LISTED)   £11113   1m 2f   Good 72 -09 Slow

1886 NORTH VERDICT (M Jarvis) 3-8-10 R Cochrane 10/1: -003241: 3 b c Far North - Best
Dressed List (Buckpasser) Very useful colt: led over 1f out and battled on gamely for a nk
success in a Listed race at Phoenix Park Aug 10: has been running consistently all season:
winning 2yo at York and also a good 6th to Bakharoff in Gr I Futurity Stks at Doncaster: half
brother to sev winners: eff at 10f, prob stays 12f: acts on firm and yldg ground and on any
track: genuine colt.   70
--   SPENDING CONTINUES (J Oxx) 3-8-10 Pat Eddery 2/1 JT FAV: -2-112: Battled with winner
final 1f and just went under: excellent effort: a winner of his prev 2 starts this season,
both at Phoenix Park : acts on gd & yielding.   69
1538 GORGEOUS STRIKE (C Nelson) 3-8-3 J Reid 10/1: 0203443: Stayed on well under press
and not btn far in cl finish: well clear rem: running consistently: eff at 10f, stays 12f:
deserves a change in fortune: see 191.   66
--   ADORAMUS (J Bolger) 3-8-10 D Gillespie 12/1: -4: Stiff task on racecourse debut,
not disgraced.   54
1715 HELLO ERNANI 3-8-13 B Rouse 11/2: 2321200: Fdd final 2f: btr 1343, 1045.   00
--   DON DIEGE 3-8-13 C Roche 2/1 JT FAV: -10-10: Well bckd: fdd: first time out this
season won at Down Royal : eff at 10f, stays 12f: acts on gd and yielding.   00
--   OUT AND ABOUT 5-9-7 M Lynch 16/1: -031020: Last to fin: winner early this season
at the Curragh: acts on yielding and heavy.   00
7 ran   nk,nk,8   (Elisha Holdings Ltd)   M Jarvis Newmarket

2113 GROUP 1 HEINZ '57' PHOENIX STAKES 2YO   £127500   6f   Good 72 +19 Fast

-1454 MINSTRELLA (C Nelson) 2-8-11 J Reid 5/1: 42121: 2 rof The Minstrel - Flight Dancer
(Misty Flight) Very smart filly: led over 1f out, going well and just held   the late

chall of Forest Flower to win fast run Gr 1 Phoenix Stks at Phoenix Park Aug 10: gaining her
revenge here for a ¾l beating by Forest Flower in Gr 3 Cherry Hinton at Newmarket: earlier
set a 2yo course record when an easy winner of Chesham Stakes (Listed) at Royal Ascot: related
to sev winners, notably very smart American filly Misty Gallore: very eff at 6f, should
be suited by further: acts on gd/yldg and fast ground and on any trk: best when held up
for a late chall and will be hard to beat in any future engagements.   83
+1454 FOREST FLOWER (I Balding) 2-8-11 Pat Eddery 9/4 FAV: 1112: Never going as well as
the winner on this rain-softened ground, but ran on most gamely and was just btn: another
excellent effort and is a most courageous filly: sure to win more races: see 1454.   82
*1329 POLONIA (J Bolger) 2-8-11 D Gillespie 5/2: 11013: Dsptd lead: tapped for speed over
1f out, but kept on well and was closing again towards the finish: another fine effort:
will be suited by further than 6f and a more gall trk: see 1329.   78
*1531 WIGANTHORPE (M W Easterby) 2-9-0 T Lucas 12/1: 2011114: Not btn that far and was
first of the colts home: still improving: should be suited by further than 6f: see 1531.   76
1467 SIZZLING MELODY 2-9-0 R Hills 16/1: 112130: Not btn that far: gd effort: see 1467.   75
--   FLAWLESS IMAGE 2-9-0 C Roche 5/1: 10: By no means disgraced in this tough company:
first time out was a most impr 6l winner of a maiden over this C/D.   00
1453 SINGING STEVEN 2-9-0 B Rouse 100/1: 2211230: Stiff task here: see 1453.   00
--   SNOW FINCH 2-8-11 M J Kinane 33/1: 0110: Fin 8th: winner earlier at Leopardstown
and the Curragh: eff at 6f, stays 7f: acts on gd/firm and soft.   00
-1876 DOMINION ROYALE 2-9-0 R Cochrane 12/1: 413120: Btr on firm in 1876.   00
--   ADVENTURINE 2-8-11 G Curran 100/1: 2120: Rank outsider: fin last: earlier won a
minor race at Leopardstown (5f, gd/firm).   00
10 ran   shthd,1,1¾,hd   (E Evans)   C Nelson Upper Lambourn, Berks.

DEAUVILLE   Sunday August 10th   Righthand Track

Official Going Given as GOOD/FIRM

2114 GROUP 2 PRIX KERGORLAY 3YO+   £23183   1m 7f Good/Firm .

1115 KING LUTHIER [9] (A Fabre) 4-9-4 C Asmussen 1: -121201: 4 ch c Luthier - Lighted Lamp
(Sir Gaylord) Chall over 1f out and readily drew clear in a Gr 2 event at Deauville Aug 10:
earlier a winner at St Cloud and Maisons Laffitte: in '85 was trained by G Lewis, winning at
Epsom and Warwick (sub disq): eff 12f, well suited by 15f: acts on any ground and on any trk.   78
*1354 SWINK [11] (J Pease) 3-9-2 Y Saint Martin 1: 11013: Grand eff against older horses
and is fast impr: St Leger bound and on this form looks sure to give a gd account: see 1354.   84
1493 FRENCH SCHOOL [5] (P L Biancone) 4-9-4 E Legrix 1: 10-0003: Best eff this season:
clearly stays 15f well: acts on gd/firm.   71
+1513 RAKAPOSHI KING [10] (H Cecil) 4-9-4 S Cauthen 1: 20-3114: Again tried to make all:
far from disgraced in this very gd company: see 1513.   70
390 GRANDCOURT [6] 4-9-4 F Head 1: -333010: Ran well in 5th: last time out won at
Longchamp: stays 15f.   68
1354 SILVER WORD [8] 3-8-7 M Philipperon 1: 3-42030: Another gd run: see 1354.   70
1354 FAMILY FRIEND [7] 3-8-12 W Carson 1: 0-44100: Fdd str: best 902.   65
12 ran   4,½,½,1½,¾,6   (J Atrib)   A Fabre France

OSTEND   Sunday August 10th

Official Going Given As FIRM

2115 PRIX MONA 2YO   £2760   7f   Firm .

*1711 MY BUDDY (R Williams) 2-9-4 T Ives 1: 00111: 2 ch c Mummy's Game - Shadow Play
(Busted) Proved a very easy winner of a 4 runner minor event at Ostend Aug 10: has been
well placed by his trainer, earlier winning again at Ostend and also successful in a mdn
auction at Catterick: stays 7f well: likes gd and fast ground: does well on an easy trk
when up with the pace.   52
--   TAFFYS DELIGHT (Belgium) 2-8-5 P Vandekeere 1: 2: No chance with winner.   20
--   MISS CONSTABLE (Belgium) 2-8-2 Y De Wulf 1: 3: --   15
--   IRISH BLARNEY   2-8-1 P D'arcy 1: 4: --   10
4 ran   8,1,2   (C P Linney)   R Williams Newmarket

2116 PRIX DE PRESIDENT MAX DUGNIOLLE (H'CAP) £16563   1m 3f Firm .

--   BALKAN PRINCE (G Franco) 5-8-1 G Couderc 1: -1: 5 b c King of Macedon - Hone (Sharpen
Up) Narrow winner of a val h'cap at Ostend Aug 10: stays 11f well: acts on fast ground.   48
--   QUINOA DE SAISY (L Cacquevel) 4-8-5 W Martin 1: -2: French chall, just btn.   51
1712 CHAUMIERE (R Williams) 5-9-10 T Ives 1: 0000103: Btn 2 hds: in fine form: see 1712.   69
1659 KALA NASHAN (P Mitchell) 4-7-7 G Carter 1: 0030120: Fin 6th: see 1659, 1237.   00
7 ran   hd,hd   (Ecurie Franco)   G Franco --

2117 GROUP 3 FILLIES RACE 3 AND 4YO   £11299   1m 2f   Good .

1128 SINGLETTA (M Stoute) 3-8-7 W R Swinburn 1: 12-301: 3 b f Nodouble - Cambretta
(Roberto) Smart, impr filly: made ev yard, hacking up by 9½l in a Gr 3 fillies event at
Neuss Aug 10: has been lightly raced this term: in '85 was an easy winner first time out
at Ascot: eff at 10f, stays 12f: acts on gd and firm ground and on any trk: seems certain
to win more races, both home and abroad.   75
1596 NORETTA (German) 3-8-7 P Remmert 1: 42: No chance with winner.   57
*1489 COMPRIDA (German) 3-8-7 A Tylicki 1: 13: Below her best: see 1489.   56
  6 ran   9½,½   (Sheikh Mohammed)   M Stoute Newmarket

Official Going Given As GOOD/SOFT

2118 AMPORT MAIDEN 2YO STAKES   £1457   5f   Good 40 -17 Slow

1407 LA PETITE NOBLESSE [6] (D H Jones) 2-8-11 J Reid 25/1: 01: 2 b f Thatching - Karella
(Juke Box) Fast impr filly: al there and led inside final 1f, comfortably, in a 2yo mdn at
Salisbury Aug 13: speedily bred sort who is a half sister to juv winners Ulpha and Lovely
Chimes: very eff at 5f, prob stays 6f: acts on gd ground and a gall trk: well regarded and
should rate more highly.   49
1665 MASHBUB [5] (C Benstead) 2-9-0 B Rouse 3/1: 322: Made much: kept on well and is
most consistent: acts on any trk: see 1665, 1442.   47
1629 HAWAIAN CAT [4] (I Balding) 2-9-0 Pat Eddery 11/8 FAV: 23: Well bckd: al niggled along
and stayed on well: needs 6f+: see 1629.   47
1728 MOTOR BROKER [1] (R Laing) 2-9-0 W Newnes 33/1: 0004: Sn prom: best eff yet: eff
at 5f, but is a half brother to 10f winner Marsoom and should stay further: acts on gd ground
and a galloping track.   41
1936 LYRICAL LOVER [8] 2-9-0 P Waldron 50/1: 00: Kept on well inside final 2f and is
on the upgrade: should stay 6f: acts on gd ground and a gall track.   35
938 FLAG BEARER [3] 2-9-0 R Wernham 33/1: 0000: Fair abs: no real threat: however
an improved eff and seems suited by a stiff trk: cheaply acquired gelding who acts on gd ground 35
1632 ZITELLA [14] 2-8-11 J Matthias 16/1: 00: Friendless in mkt, slow start, fin 7th:
will need further than 5f to show her true worth: see 1632.   28
1550 YSTRAD FLOWER [9] 2-8-11 J Williams 50/1: 00: Rank outsider: never nearer 8th but
is making improvement: very cheaply acquired.   26
1930 EVER SHARP [10] 2-9-0 I Johnson 5/1: 40: Bckd from 10/1: prom most, fin 9th: see 1930 25
1936 Battle Sting [7] 9-0   1915 Charmed Prince [13] 9-0
1802 Marie Baby [12] 8-11   --   Imperial Way [11] 9-0 --   Helens Hero [2] 9-0
14 ran 1,shthd,2½,2½,shthd,2½,½,hd   (North Cheshire Trading & Storage Ltd) D H Jones, Glam

2119 E B F ROCKBOURNE STAKES 2YO   £3662   6f   Good 40 +02 Fast

-- NETTLE [5] (W Hern) 2-8-8 W Carson 7/1: 1: 2 ch f Kris - Sans Blague (The Minstrel)
Very promising filly: first time out, led 2f out and sprinted clear in final 1f for an
impr 5l win in quite fast run 2yo stks at Salisbury Aug 13: first foal whose dam was a useful
12f winner: eff at 6f, sure to be suited by 7f and further: acts on gd grd and a gall trk:
can only improve and looks sure to win more races.   61
-1728 LAST DANCE [1] (R Hannon) 2-9-1 B Thomson 6/1: 042312: Giving weight all round:
kept on well and is in fine form: stays 6f well: see 1728.   55
1791 ALI SMITH [10] (R Boss) 2-8-11 Pat Eddery 11/8 FAV: 23: Well bckd: ev ch: should
be suited by further than 6f: acts on gd and fast ground: should find a race: see 1791. 50
-- PALM REEF [3] (C Horgan) 2-8-11 S Cauthen 6/1: 4: Prom most on racecourse debut,
showing promise: half brother to the very useful, but lightly raced 3yo winner Hollow Hand:
eff at 6f, will be well suited by much further: acts on gd grd and a gall trk: should have
no trouble finding a race.   43
-- SCATTERED SHOWERS [4] 2-8-8 A Mcglone 16/1: 0: Bckd at long odds: never nearer:
half sister to 2 winners and should improve on this initial effort: stoutly bred filly who
will stay 1m.   31
-- CHARLIE ME DARLING [8] 2-8-11 P Cook 33/1: 0: No threat on racecourse debut, but
should improve: cost 20,000 gns: dam placed sev times as a 2yo in modest company.   29
-- SHARP VICTOR [2] 2-8-11 G Starkey 11/2: 0: Mkt drifter: slowly away and never made
up the ground.   28
1518 TASJIL [7] 2-8-11 B Rouse 11/1: 400: Led 4f: fin 8th: see 1518, 434.   26
1802 Stainsby Girl [9] 8-8   --   Buy Mums Act [6] 8-11
10 ran 5,hd,3,4,2,nk,1   (The Queen)   W Hern West Ilsley, Berks.

2120 HOMINGTON HANDICAP STKS 3YO   £1912   6f   Good 40 +14 Fast   [36]

1991 MERRYMOLES [4] (M Mccourt) 3-8-7(bl) R Wernham 12/1: 0000041: 3 b g Tyrnavos - Sovereign
Help (Sovereign Lord) Made ev yard, staying on gamely for a narrow win in quite fast run 3yo
h'cap at Salisbury Aug 13: in '85 won again on this trk and runs here: very eff at 6f,
prob does best out in front on gd and firm ground and seems suited by blinkers.   25
2033 BEECHWOOD COTTAGE [1] (A Bailey) 3-8-11(bl) Pat Eddery 13/2: 0014402: Al prom and
kept on well: just btn and 4l clear 3rd: another gd eff: see 1610.   28

1277 HIGHLY RECOMMENDED [14] (P Cundell) 3-8-8 B Rouse 14/1: -0003: Al up there after
abs: eff over 5/6f: acts on gd ground and a gall trk.   17
1431 MOZART [2] (B Hanbury) 3-8-7 G Baxter 33/1: -0004: Prom all the way: lightly raced
colt who ran his best race here: dam the topclass sprinter Marwell: eff at 6f on good.   15
1695 SILVER FORM [16] 3-8-5 N Adams 8/1: 0340200: Twice below 1499 (sharpish trk).   06
1836 SUNNY MATCH [17] 3-8-4 I Johnson 11/2 FAV: 00-0020: No threat in 6th: race 1836
looks very moderate.   04
*2088 GERSHWIN [13] 3-8-6 J Carter(7) 8/1: -120010: Too soon after 2088 (seller)?   00
*1947 BOOFY [12] 3-10-0(7ex) J Reid 10/1: 2240010: Made no show: much btr 1947 (stks, sharpish) 00
1943 SNAP DECISION [10] 3-9-5 L Jones(5) 10/1: 0-04020: Speed early: btr 1943 (sharpish trk)   00
886 VAIGLIAN [11] 3-9-5 W Carson 10/1: 3-40000: No show after abs: no form since 436.   00
-1750 DANCING SARAH [6] 3-9-1 D Williams(7) 6/1: 0000320: Well in rear: see 1750.   00
1032 Miranda Julia [3] 9-3   1447 Cracon Girl [5] 8-6   1581 Monatation [15] 7-11
1943 Aclia [9] 9-5   1830 Gem Of Gold [8] 8-13
16 ran nk,4,hd,3,nk,3,½   (A J Bingley)   M Mccourt Letcombe Regis, Oxon.

2121 H S LESTER MEMORIAL HANDICAP 0-50   £2342   1m 2f Good 40 -14 Slow   [47]

1553 SAMHAAN [6] (B Hanbury) 4-8-10(bl) A Geran(7) 15/8 FAV: 0301121: 4 ch c Niniski -
Mai Pussy (Realm) In tremendous form, led inside final 1f, under press in a h'cap at Salisbury
Aug 13: earlier a winner of similar events at Chepstow, Carlisle and Doncaster: eff at 1m,
well suited by 10f: acts on any grd and on any trk tho' likes a gall one: best in blinkers,
but seems thoroughly genuine.   40
1729 FREE ON BOARD [2] (C Horgan) 4-7-13 T Williams 11/2: -002022: Led 2f out: just btn
and 6l clear 3rd: running well: see 1729.   28
1755 SUPERFROST [8] (J Fox) 4-7-7(7oh) N Adams 33/1: 0100403: Kept on one pace: see 1609, 568.   10
1788 DERRYRING [9] (R Laing) 4-8-8 C Rutter(3) 10/1: 0000004: Late hdwy: best 1383.   24
2049 TALK OF GLORY [4] 5-8-6 G Baxter 6/1: 2002230: Chance over 2f out: see 2049, much
closer to winner in 1450.   18
1929 CHICLET [5] 4-9-9(BL) Paul Eddery 11/2: 0204040: Tried in bl: disapp since 432.   33
-- FIRE BAY [3] 5-8-13(vis) B Rouse 10/1: 32130-0: Fin 7th on seasonal debut: late
last season won a h'cap at Brighton: in '84 won at Haydock: eff at 10f, stays 12f: acts
on gd and firm ground: could be hurdling soon.   00
850 WELSH MEDLEY [1] 4-8-5 D Williams(7) 8/1: -032140: Prom much after abs: needed race.   00
1539 THE FOOTMAN [7] 4-8-12 J H Brown(5) 10/1: 0-00040: Led 6f: see 1324.   00
9 ran ½,6,nk,2,1,2½,shthd,½   (O Zawawi)   B Hanbury Newmarket

2122 MANTON E B F STAKES 3YO   £2616   1m 4f Good 40 -34 Slow

1886 WASSL REEF [2] (J Dunlop) 3-9-3 W Carson 8/15 FAV: 2-23101: 3 b c Mill Reef - Connaught
Bridge (Connaught) Useful colt, dictated the pace much and led again final 1f, ridden out
in a 3 runner stks at Salisbury Aug 13: earlier was a game winner of a mdn at Lingfield:
consistent sort: eff over 10f, stays 12f well: acts on fast and yldg grd and on any track:
seems a genuine sort.   53
*894 PLYMOUTH HOE [1] (L Cumani) 3-9-3 Pat Eddery 15/8 : -112: Led over 1f out: stiff
task at these weights: gd effort after abs: see 894.   51
-- IN CONTENTION [3] (D Oughton) 3-8-10 P Cook 40/1: -3: Chance over 2f out: stiff task
on racecourse debut: should improve for this run.   14
3 ran ½,12   (Sheikh Ahmed Al Maktoum)   J Dunlop Arundel, Sussex

2123 BOURNEMOUTH HANDICAP 0-50   £2488   7f   Good 40 +16 Fast   [45]

1890 FEYDAN [10] (L Cottrell) 5-8-0 W Carson 4/1 FAV: 0-04431: 5 ch g Double Form -
Baby Brew (Green God) Led 2f out for a clear cut success in quite fast run h'cap at Salisbury
Aug 13: failed to win in '85: prev season won at Folkestone and Sandown: eff at 7f, stays 1m
well: acts on any grd and on any trk: may win again in similar company.   31
1640 MANCHESTERSKYTRAIN [11] (D Elsworth) 7-9-4 Pat Eddery 7/1: 3000002: Ran on well
final 1f, showing a return to form: see 401.   40
1890 GURTEEN BOY [14] (R Hannon) 4-9-0 G Starkey 7/1: 0000103: Ran on final 1f: gd
effort: see 1553.   34
1651 CONCERT PITCH [6] (B Palling) 7-8-1 J Williams 14/1: 200-004: Chance 2f out: see 1447.   21
1901 GAUHAR [7] 5-7-8 N Adams 33/1: 4440000: Never nearer: best 1018, see 174.   10
*1901 MR ROSE [9] 6-8-1(7ex) P Hutchinson(3) 7/1: 0042010: Not clear run to ¼ way:
worth another chance: see 1901.   12
1648 SATIAPOUR [2] 3-9-7(vis) S Cauthen 6/1: 0122220: Led 5f, fin 7th: over the top? See 1648   00
1109 CONMAYJO [4] 5-9-7 D Williams(7) 10/1: 0330100: Abs: needed race: see 668.   00
1519 Catman [5] 7-7(vis)(3oh)   1579 Ashley Rocket [3] 9-0
1901 Nicky Nick [8] 7-12(BL)   1365 Golden Slade [13] 8-10
1942 Hatching [1] 7-7(5oh)   1911 April Fool [15] 8-10(vis)
1901 Gamblers Dream [12] 8-4
15 ran 2½,½,½,hd,2,3,3   (Mrs Henry Seymour)   L Cottrell Cullimpton, Devon

CATTERICK   Wednesday August 13th   Lefthand, Very Tight Track

Official Going Given As GOOD

2124 LEVY BOARD APP H'CAP 0-35   £953   5f   Good/Firm 25 +14 Fast   [28]

1950 LADY CARA [1] (J Berry) 6-9-0 J Carroll(3) 8/1: 0020241: 6 br m Lochnager – Gold Cheb
(Cheb's Lad) Led inside final 2f, comfortably, in fast run app h'cap at Catterick Aug 13:
deserved success: in '85 won at Newcastle and Hamilton: 5f specialist: acts on any grd and
on any trk: best when up with the pace.   25
1638 KARENS STAR [12] (D Chapman) 9-9-4 N Leach(5) 20/1: 0000002: Ran on well final 1f:
best effort this term: see 1093.   22
1682 LAST SECRET [3] (D Chapman) 5-7-12(bl) J Callaghan(5) 33/1: 0-00003: Al up there:
likes this trk: see 1543.   00
+1950 CAPTAINS BIDD [14] (H Whiting) 6-8-4(7ex) L Riggio(3) 4/1: 2020414: Late hdwy from
an adverse draw: in gd form: see 1950.   06
1917 PUNCLE CREAK [19] 3-7-7(1oh) S Wood(5) 12/1: 0002330: Poorly drawn: kept on: btr 1917.   00
1718 TRADESMAN [16] 6-8-0 J Quinn 14/1: 0001030: Sn prom: best 1423.   00
1718 ACKAS BOY [2] 4-7-9 P Burke(7) 25/1: -000000: Late hdwy into 7th: little form prev.   00
1896 BAY BAZAAR [6] 4-9-4 S Hustler(5) 14/1: 0340000: Fin 8th: see 1682, 42.   00
1986 LIGHT ANGLE [4] 5-8-13(vis) N Rodgers(5) 33/1: 000-000: Dsptd lead, saddle slipped: see 1986. 00
1986 MUSIC MACHINE [9] 5-10-5(7ex) J Scally(3) 3/1 FAV: 4101120: Dsptd lead, below his
best: see 1986.   00
1986 PHILSTAR [8] 5-9-1(vis) J Leech(5) 10/1: 3003030: Early speed: best 1676 (6f).   00
1896 Pergoda [10] 10-0(bl)   1730 Silbando [11] 8-11   1973 Wasbree Bay [7] 7-12
1638 Blochairn Skolar [13] 7-8(1ow)   1896 Parade Girl [17] 8-7
1979 Tricenco [15] 8-5(bl)   1616 Grand Queen [18] 7-9
18 ran 2,1,hd,½,½,1½,hd,shthd   (Mrs V O'Brien)   J Berry Cockerham, Lancs.

2125 TILTON HOUSE SELLING STAKES 3YO   £952   1m 5f Good/Firm 25 -37 Slow

1892 PATRIOTIC [4] (M Prescott) 3-8-11 G Duffield 10/11 FAV: 00-041: 3 b f Hotfoot – Poppy
Day (Soleil II) Stayed on under press to lead final 1f in a slow run and mod. selling stks at
Catterick Aug 13 (bought in 3,600 gns): related to sev winners: stays 14f well: acts on
fast ground and a sharpish track.   07
1892 FIRE LORD [1] (G Moore) 3-9-0 S Wood(7) 12/1: 0003402: Led to ½ way: stays 14f:
best on fast grd and a sharp track.   08
1666 GROVECOTE [3] (P Makin) 3-8-11 W R Swinburn 3/1: -000003: Al up there: stays 14f:
acts on fast ground and a sharp trk.   04
139 ANDREAS PRIDE [7] (A Smith) 3-9-0 S Webster 15/2: 004-404: Long abs: chance 1f out:
lightly raced colt who stays 14f on a sharp trk: acts on gd/firm and soft.   06
1892 SUNLIT [6] 3-8-11 J Bleasdale 10/1: 0-0000: Led ½ way to over 1f out.   00
1898 TIBER GATE [5] 3-9-0 S Perks 12/1: 00-0000: Fdd str: see 998.   00
1734 FUR BABY [2] 3-8-11 Jane Eades(7) 66/1: 00-0000: Fin t.o.   00
7 ran 1½,½,¾,½,4,2,dist   (Mrs C R Phillipson)   M Prescott Newmarket

2126 TURN TO YORKSHIRE HANDICAP 0-35   £2376   7f   Good/Firm 25 -06 Slow   [35]

1839 TRADE HIGH [5] (I Vickers) 7-8-5(1ow) D Nicholls 20/1: 0000401: 7 br g Tower Walk –
Lucky Deal (Floribunda) Led inside final 2f, driven out in a h'cap at Catterick Aug 13: in
'85 won a selling h'cap at Pontefract: in '83 won at Carlisle: eff at 5f, suited by 7f: acts
on gd and firm grd and likes a turning track.   21
1774 DARNIT [3] (E Weymes) 4-10-0 M Tebbutt(7) 12/1: 0002102: Just btn under 10-0: fine
effort and seems well suited by a sharp track nowadays: see 1500.   43
1870 FOREVER TINGO [6] (H Whiting) 4-7-9 L Riggio(7) 25/1: 0000003: Ev ch str: eff at
7f, stays further: acts on gd and firm ground.   08
2012 POKERFAYES [18] (B Mcmahon) 7-8-1(bl)(3ow) G Duffield 10/1: 0000204: Kept on final 1f:
best 1761 (C/D): see 866.   04
1536 YOUNG BRUSS [17] 4-8-13 M Wood 10/1: 0013000: Al prom: best 936, 830.   15
1906 LA BELLE OF SANTO [10] 3-7-7(1oh) L Charnock 33/1: 0020000: Prom 5f: best 1299.   00
1136 ZIO PEPPINO [9] 5-8-0 Julie Bowker(7) 13/2: 3204440: Prom most after abs: see 606, 490.   00
2012 WORKADAY [12] 4-9-12 N Connorton 13/2: 0003100: Twice below 1482 (C/D).   00
1987 KNIGHTS SECRET [7] 5-9-11 G Hindmarsh(7) 6/1 JT FAV: 1340340: Made no show: btr 1987.   00
1983 SIR WILMORE [8] 4-9-5 E Guest(3) 10/1: -000100: Never in it: twice well below 1698.   00
1922 BILLS AHEAD [16] 3-8-10 R P Elliott 6/1 JT FAV: 0444120: Fdd in str: btr 1922, 1626.   00
1766 Good N Sharp [11] 7-8   2012 Pommes Chateau [14] 8-10(hood)
1999 Gardas Gold [2] 7-13(1ow)   1765 Golden Disc [13] 7-7(3oh)
1839 Tree Fella [1] 7-11   1917 Class Hopper [15] 7-9 1839 Nippy Chippy [4] 7-8(bl)(1ow)
18 ran ½,1,5,½,1½,nk,½   (Northumbria Leisure Ltd)   I Vickers Seahouses, Northumberland

2127 PADDOCK HOUSE MAIDEN 2YO FILLIES   £797   5f   Good/Firm 25 +08 Fast

1030 MARIMBA [2] (J Winter) 2-8-11 W R Swinburn 5/2 FAV: 2331: 2 b f Music Boy – Double
Finesse (Double Jump) Fin well under press to lead cl home in quite fast run 2yo fillies mdn
at Catterick Aug 13: had been off the trk since a gd 3rd to Sea Dara at Sandown in June and
clearly does well when fresh: speedily bred filly who is a half sister to the useful 6/8f
winner Larionov: very eff at 5f: acts on gd and firm grd and on any trk.   45
1576 BAY WONDER [12] (G P Gordon) 2-8-11 G Duffield 16/1: 00022: Held clear lead over
1f out: caught near fin: fine eff in this better company and runs very well on a sharp trk.   41
631

1782 PARADISE COFFEE [7] (O Douieb) 2-8-11 T Quinn 4/1: 23: Al prom: see 1782.   37
1867 TEACHERS GAME [14] (K Brassey) 2-8-11 S Whitworth 14/1: 434: Al up there: acts on
any trk: see 1583.   37
-1867 MINIZEN LASS [17] 2-8-11 K Darley 16/1: 2022420: Prom most: consistent: see 1867.   33
473 VERYAN BAY [1] 2-8-11 J Lowe 9/1: 00: Never nearer after abs: acts on gd/firm: see 473.   28
1958 RAINBOW TROUT [20] 2-8-11 N Connorton 10/1: 040: Prom, fin 7th: btr 1958.   23
717 STARCH BROOK [21] 2-8-11 S Perks 25/1: 400: Abs: never nearer 8th: has been very
lightly raced: acts on gd/firm and heavy.   20
--   BINGDON BUILDERS [3] 2-8-11 J Hills(5) 25/1: 0: Fin 9th on racecourse debut: cheaply
acquired filly who is a half sister to sev winners.   20

1545 Premier Video [8] 8-11		1972 Sendim On Sam [16] 8-11	
1650 Stylish Girl [10] 8-11		1958 Miss Management [11] 8-11	
-- Monfem [5] 8-11	1683 Petango [13] 8-11	610 Rosies Image [9] 8-11	
-- Jean Jeannie [15] 8-11		-- Lewista [18] 8-11	
-- Oak Field [19] 8-11	1187 Prodigious Lady [4] 8-11		
1881 Rose Of Tudor [6] 8-11			

21 ran   1¼,1½,shthd,1½,2,1½,1½,shthd   (Mrs P D Rossdale)   J Winter Newmarket

2128 SKYRAM HANDICAP STAKES 3YO   0-35   £1708   1m 5f Good/Firm 25 -15 Slow   [32]

*2015 SEVEN HILLS [2] (J Fitzgerald) 3-9-2(vis)(4ex) M Roberts 11/4: -000311: 3 ch f Reform -
Campagna (Romulus) In gd form and stayed on well under press to lead final 1f in a h'cap at
Catterick Aug 13: last time out won a similar event at Yarmouth: stays 14f well: acts on
gd/firm and yldg ground and a sharp/easy trk: best in a visor.   30
*1822 RELATIVELY EASY [10] (M Prescott) 3-9-11(4ex) G Duffield 2/1 FAV: -00112: Led into str:
6l clear 3rd and is in gd form: stays 14f: see 1822: acts on any track.   36
1961 NITIDA [12] (E Weymes) 3-8-5(BL) S Webster 33/1: -000003: Stayed on under press:
little form this term: see 130.   09
1871 MARINA PLATA [3] (D Chapman) 3-9-4 D Nicholls 12/1: 1000004: No real threat: best
early season in 99.   14
1822 RHODE ISLAND RED [9] 3-9-2(vis) N Connorton 8/1: -40020: Prom, ev ch: btr 1822 (12f)   11
1898 TINAS LAD [6] 3-7-10 J Quinn(5) 33/1: 0-00000: Made much, wknd: see 1600.   00
1396 COLOURFIELD [11] 3-8-10(vis) S Whitworth 10/1: 00-40: Wknd str: btr 1396 (10f)   00
1054 MEGANS MOVE [4] (D Garraton) 5/1: 04-0100: No show after abs: best 867 (9f)   00

1089 Chevet Lady [8] 8-13	1945 G G Magic [5] 8-13(bl)	
1615 Pinturicchia [7] 8-6	1961 Hitchenstown [1] 8-10(BL)	

12 ran   2,6,8,1,3   (Sir John Musker)   J Fitzgerald Malton, Yorks

2129 STOCKWELL MAIDEN STAKES 3YO   £822   1m 4f Good/Firm 25 -33 Slow

1645 ASTRAL [2] (P Cole) 3-9-0 T Quinn 2/1 JT FAV: 0-01: 3 ch c Ela-Mana-Mou - Red Val
(Red God) Impr colt: led inside final 1f, ridden out to win slow run 3yo mdn at Catterick Aug
13: ran only once in '85: half brother to 4 winners incl the very useful h'capper Carpet
General: clearly stays 12f well: acts on gd/firm and a sharpish trk.   37
2030 INDIAN LOVE SONG [10] (R Hollinshead) 3-8-11 S Perks 11/2: 2304302: Ran on final 1f:
stays 12f on a sharp trk: yet to lose her mdn tag and clearly flattered 464.   31
1705 LA DUSE [8] (L Cumani) 3-8-11 R Guest 8/1: -03: Chance over 1f out: btr eff,
stays 12f: see 1705.   29
1998 ADMIRALS ALL [4] (J Winter) 3-9-0 W R Swinburn 2/1 JT FAV: 0340304: Dsptd lead over
1f out: see 1690.   29
1336 MATBAR [9] 3-9-0(bl) G Dickie 14/1: 00-0440: Led 4f out: btr eff: see 1029.   21
--   MARETH LINE [7] 3-9-0 M Roberts 20/1: -0: Prom, fdd inside final 2f on racecourse debut.   13

1842 Dancing Frog [11] 9-0	2028 Top Row [5] 9-0	937 Dalsaanito [1] 9-0
969 Jelly Jill [6] 8-11	-- Lucky Tas [3] 8-11	

11 ran   1¼,1,1¼,4,4   (Fahd Salman)   P Cole Whatcombe, Oxon.

2130 MIDDLEBROOK MUSHROOM TRAINERS RACE   £0   1m 4f Good/Firm 25 -88 Slow

*1980 WESSEX [3] (N Tinkler) 4-12-0 N Tinkler 8/11 FAV: 3134011: 4 b c Free State - Bonandra
(Andrea Mantegna) In gd form: stayed on well to lead cl home in a very slowly run trainers
invitation race at Catterick Aug 13: earlier a winner at Ayr(2) & Hamilton and has been most
consistent this term: eff over 12f, suited by a test of stamina: acts on any going and on
any track.   35
1918 NIGHT WARRIOR [7] (A Robson) 4-11-7 A Robson 11/2: 0303342: Led 2f out, just caught:
stays 12f: see 238.   25
1964 GOLDEN FANCY [1] (I Vickers) 9-12-0 I Vickers 7/2: 3432D33: Never nearer: see 1964.   26
1799 MOONLIGHTING [4] (J Parkes) 6-12-4(14ow) J Parkes 33/1: -04: Clear leader over 10f:
may be hurdling soon.   10
*1766 PRICEOFLOVE [6] 6-11-11 D Moffatt 7/1: 040-010: Fdd str: btr 1766 (9f).   00
--   ASCOT AGAIN [2] 10-11-7(bl) J P Smith 50/1: -0: No show: maiden under Rules.   00
491 Van Der Pup [5] 11-3

7 ran   1,3,8,3,1½   (Full Circle Thoroughbreds Ltd)   N Tinkler Malton, Yorks.

Official Going Given As GOOD

2131 UPAVON EBF STAKES 3YO FILLIES   £3052   1m 2f   Good 46 -03 Slow

1981 KICK THE HABIT [8] (C Brittain) 3-8-7 G Baxter 20/1: -000021: 3 bf Habitat - Supremely
Royal (Crowned Prince) Impr filly: led inside final 1f, comfortably, in a 3yo fillies stks at
Salisbury Aug 14: first success: half sister to sev winners, notably smart miler Capricorn
Belle: eff at 1m, stays 10f well: acts on gd/firm and yldg ground: on the upgrade.   46
1444 RATTLE ALONG [3] (P Walwyn) 3-8-12 Paul Eddery 20/1: 0-0102: Al up there: consistent
filly who stays 10f well: see 1193.   48
1941 RED SHOES [4] (W Hern) 3-8-7 W Carson 5/1: -303223: Made running: placed again: see 1941.   43
1002 BISHAH [1] (H Cecil) 3-8-12 S Cauthen 8/13 FAV: 2-124: Heavily bckd, despite abs:
stayed on at the one pace and will be suited by 12f: see 1002, 744.   44
1829 FIRST KISS [9] 3-8-12 Pat Eddery 6/1: -10030: Wknd inside final 2f: btr 1829 (12f).   43
1487 GREY WALLS [5] 3-8-12 P Robinson 8/1: 013-000: Lightly raced since 271: prob stays 10f.
          39
-- SHEER NECTAR [7] 3-8-7 J Williams 50/1: -0: No threat in 7th, but should improve:
half sister to 1m winner Lady Liza.   00
1971 Dawn Mirage [2] 8-7   --   Farceuse [6] 8-7
9 ran   1,shthd,2,nk,2,1   (Capt M Lemos)   C Brittain Newmarket

2132 NETTON APPR HCAP 3YO+ 0-35   £1210   1m   Good 46 -08 Slow   [34]

1619 ALL FAIR [1] (P Haslam) 5-10-0(BL) J Scally 9/2 FAV: 0000021: 5 b h Free State -
Be Honest (Klairon) Made ev yard and forged clear in the final 2f for an impr 7l win in an
app h'cap at Salisbury Aug 14: in '85 was trained by R Whitaker, winning h'caps at York and
Ripon: in '84 won at Newbury and Haydock: eff over 1m, stays 10f: acts on firm and soft grd
and a gall trk: does well when up with the pace and should go close again next time:
bl first time today.   46
1579 FULL OF LIFE [8] (M Pipe) 3-9-2 J Carr 10/1: 1-00022: In vain pursuit final 2f: see 1579.   30
1804 DOLLY [5] (A Moore) 4-8-13 S Hill(3) 8/1: D003443: Chance 2f out: see 1804.   13
*1987 SINGING BOY [18] (A Hide) 5-9-3(5ex) S Bridle(3) 9/1: 0000014: Al prom: btr 1987.   13
1787 FLEET BAY [11] 6-8-2 B Uniacke(3) 16/1: 00-0100: Twice below 1579.   00
1830 TREMENDOUS JET [6] 3-8-3 P Francis(0) 10/1: -000100: Best 1063 (7f seller).   08
1827 THE UTE [9] 3-7-13(bl) P Mcentee(3) 15/2: 2320120: Prom much, btr 1827 (sharp trk)   00
1581 SNAKE RIVER [15] 4-8-13 W Hayes 7/1: 3102240: Prom 6f: much btr 1581, see 1273.   00
1951 Centralspires Best [3] 7-13(4ow)   1969 Mr Music Man [14] 7-11
--   The Upstart [16] 8-12   1581 Sahara Shadow [2] 8-6   1607 Russki [12] 8-11
1375 Aspark [13] 8-4   --   Silver Empress [7] 8-0(bl)
499 Rest And Welcome [10] 7-11   1686 Top Feather [4] 7-11
17 ran   7,2,2,shthd,nk   (S A B Dinsmore)   P Haslam Newmarket

2133 WHITSBURY MANOR STUD STKS 2YO   £5653   7f   Good 46 -06 Slow

1097 BRAVE DANCER [6] (G Harwood) 2-9-0 G Starkey 8/13 FAV: 3101: 2 b c Pas De Seul -
Dance Lovers (Green Dancer) Very useful colt: despite fair abs, heavily bckd and led 1½f out,
ridden clear in val 2yo stks at Salisbury Aug 14: earlier won a competitive mdn at Newbury
and in between was a fine 5th to Cutting Blade in Gr 3 Coventry Stks at Royal Ascot: half
brother to winning French colt: well suited by 7f and will stay further: acts on gd and firm
ground and a stiff track: certain to win more races.   69
1658 HIS HIGHNESS [4] (C Brittain) 2-9-0 Pat Eddery 11/2: 132: Made much, no chance with
winner but 5l clear 3rd and is still improving: should be suited by 1m: acts on gd and firm
ground: see 1270.   58
1641 TRY THE DUCHESS [5] (M Usher) 2-8-11 D Mckay 20/1: 1003: Ev ch: stays 7f: see 1067.   45
-- FAIRY GOLD [2] (M Dickinson) 2-8-6(1ow) S Cauthen 7/1: 4: Some late hdwy on debut
and will improve: half sister to 3 winners including smart middle dist colt Infantry: sure
to be suited by 1m+ and is one to keep an eye on.   38
1936 WHITRIDGE [1] 2-8-8 Dominic Gibson 50/1: 00: Stiff task and was not disgraced:
improving colt who is a half brother to 4 winners: stays 7f: acts on gd grd and a gall trk.   40
1780 CAJUN DANCER [3] 2-8-8 J Reid 9/1: 40: Speed most: see 1780.   30
-- KIREEN [7] 2-8-8 N Howe 25/1: 0: There 4f on debut: American bred colt who cost
26,000 gns: highly tried today and should do better.   00
7 ran   4,5,1,shthd,5,7   (G Zandona)   G Harwood Pulborough, Sussex

2134 VIOLET APPLIN CHALL CUP HCAP 0-35   £2193   1m 6f   Good 46 +08 Fast   [35]

*1952 ALACAZAM [12] (J Spearing) 4-7-11(4ex) W Carson 13/2: -300011: 4 gr c Alias Smith -
Repel (Hardicanute) In gd form and led inside final 2f in a h'cap at Salisbury Aug 14:
last time out won a similar event at Wolverhampton: well suited by 14f and a gall trk: acts
on good and soft ground.   13
2031 BALLET CHAMP [2] (R Holder) 8-8-12(bl) Pat Eddery 7/1: 0300242: Chance over 1f out:
good eff but possibly btr over 2m+: see 349.   26
1952 WONDER WOOD [15] (R Holder) 7-8-7 A Dicks(6) 33/1: 3030/03: Kept on: best eff on
the Flat for a long time: last successful on the Flat in '84 at Doncaster: has been lightly
raced over both Flat and hurdles (useful h'capper in that sphere): stays 2m+ well: acts on
good and firm ground.   20

1837 TARS HILL [9] (L Cottrell) 5-9-0 N Carlisle 9/1: 0200034: Made much: in gd form: see 1837.   21
1918 FOURTH TUDOR [16] 4-8-4 A Geran(7) 20/1: -2000: Prom, fdd final 2f: best 595.   10
1236 PEARLY KING [8] 3-8-13 G Starkey 13/8 FAV: -40020: Well bckd: fdd final 2f: btr 1236(12f).   30
1733 SHIRZAD [5] 3-8-0 W Newnes 8/1: -004330: Prom much, fdd: see 1733.   00
126 Librate [4] 7-12   2015 Walcisin [7] 8-3   1939 Golden Triangle [10] 8-7
--   High Morale [11] 10-0   1757 Alsiba [13] 8-10   535 Noble Viking [3] 7-9
1559 Broken Tackle [14] 7-9(VIS)(2ow)   1757 Mythical Boy [6] 8-8
1633 My Charade [1] 8-3(vis)
16 ran   1½,½,4,½,2   (Heathavon Stables Ltd)   J Spearing Wixford, Warwicks.

2135 AMESBURY EBF STAKES 3YO   £3142   1m   Good 46 +12 Fast

982 LAND OF IVORY [7] (I Balding) 3-9-1 Pat Eddery 11/10: -1D4331: 3 b f The Minstrel -
Ivory Wand (Sir Ivor) Very useful filly: well bckd despite abs and led inside final 1f a
shade comfortably in quite fast run 3yo stks at Salisbury Aug 14: first time out "won" a
listed race at Epsom but was sub disqualified and placed 4th: in '85 won a fillies mdn at
Sandown: half sister to the smart Gold and Ivory: very eff at 1m: prob stays 10f: acts on
good and soft ground and on any trk: seems to do well when fresh.   70
1486 NATIVE OAK [3] (H Cecil) 3-9-4 S Cauthen 10/11 FAV: -421142: Made much: just btn
and well clear rem: genuine and consistent: see 1486, 950.   71
1208 OUT YONDER [5] (W Wightman) 3-8-11 J Williams 66/1: 000-003: No chance with first
two: best eff yet, but possibly flattered: eff 1m on gd ground.   14
1836 SIRTAKI DANCER [2] (W Wildman) 3-8-11 J Reid 200/1: -004: Impossible task.   04
1061 DANRIBO [4] 3-8-11 I Johnson 200/1: 0-0000: Abs: no threat.   00
1451 THEREAFTER [6] 3-8-8(bl) A Mcglone 28/1: 0-00030: There ½ way: well below 1451 (7f firm)   00
6 ran   nk,15,6,8,3   (Paul Mellon)   I Balding Kingsclere, Hants.

2136 OGBOURNE NURSERY HCAP 2YO   £2075   6f   Good 46 -04 Slow   [58]

1925 PANACHE [3] (P Haslam) 2-7-12 T Williams 8/1: 121D301: 2 ch c On Your Mark - Free
Course (Sandford Lad) Led 2f out, comfortably, in a nursery h'cap at Salisbury Aug 14:
earlier won a Claimer at Leicester and also successful in a similar event at Leicester, but
sub disqualified: very eff at 6f, stays 7f: acts on gd and firm grd and does well on a gall
track, tho' seems to act on any.   39
-1910 JAISALMER [2] (D Elsworth) 2-8-5 A Mcglone 1/1 FAV: 1020022: Not the best of runs:
ran on well final 1f and should win soon: see 1910.   45
1968 OLORE MALLE [7] (R Hannon) 2-7-11 W Carson 11/4: 1423: Nicely bckd: needs 7f? See 1968   31
944 EDRAIANTHUS [6] (R Laing) 2-8-3 N Adams 33/1: 0404: Chance 2f out: abs: stays 6f: see 533   36
1938 PARIS GUEST [4] 2-8-2(BL) T Quinn 20/1: 010000: Led 4f: best 404 (5f sharpish):bl 1st time.   31
1555 MUBKIR [1] 2-8-10 Pat Eddery 9/1: 30200: Prom much: best 1339 (sharp 5f).   32
1925 MOON INDIGO [5] 2-9-7 S Cauthen 8/1: 0100: Twice below 1381.   00
7 ran   ½,2,nk,1½,2½   (T C Ellis)   P Haslam Newmarket

2137 CHRISTMAS MORNING NURSERY H'CAP 2YO   £1693   6f   Good 44 +09 Fast   [35]

2025 SHUTTLECOCK GIRL [8] (W Jarvis) 2-8-12 R Cochrane 5/1: 430331: 2 gr f Absalom -
Margaret's Ruby (Tesco Boy) Ran on strongly to lead cl home in quite a fast run nursery
h'cap at Catterick Aug 14: first success tho' has made the frame sev times in various company:
half sister to sev winners: eff over 6f on fast and soft grd: acts on any track.   27
1962 CLOWN STREAKER [1] (M H Easterby) 2-9-6 M Birch 10/1: 2101042: Al front rank:
just held: good effort and likes this tight trk: see 1570.   34
1893 PASHMINA [2] (T Fairhurst) 2-9-1 M Hills 7/2 FAV: 1021033: Led/dsptd lead thr'out,
narrowly btn in a tight fin: clearly suited by this extra furlong: see 1893.   28
2010 SILVERS ERA [10] (N Callaghan) 2-8-10 M Miller 7/1: 2040034: Dsptd lead: not btn
far: see 2010.   17
*1647 SAUNDERS LASS [5] (2) 2-8-12 G Duffield 8/1: 0210: Fair eff in this better grade: see 1647.   18
1843 SNO SURPRISE [4] 2-9-6 E Guest(3) 6/1: 40020: Best on a gall trk in 1843: see 425.   25
*1978 EMMER GREEN [7] 2-9-12 J Carroll(7) 8/1: 4010010: Stiff task: wknd dist: see 1978.   00
1978 Broons Addition [3] 9-1   1978 Whistling Wonder [6] 9-7
1893 Penbreasy [9] 9-2
10 ran   hd,nk,2,½,nk   (H J Steckmest)   W Jarvis Newmarket

2138 GASTLY GUEST SELLING STAKES 2YO   £1065   7f   Good 44 -19 Slow

1795 BENFIELD MORPETH [7] (J Berry) 2-8-11 J Carroll(7) 7/1: 0021031: 2 b g Hills Forecast -
Running Mate (Track Space) Made early running and led again dist, gamely, in a 2yo seller at
Catterick Aug 14 (no bid): consistent since winning a similar race at Hamilton in May: cheaply
bought gelding who is eff over 5/7f: acts on any going and on any trk and is well suited
by forcing tactics.   23
1955 THE MAGUE [2] (L Siddall) 2-8-11(bl) D Nicholls 8/1: 0422102: Just failed: stays 7f: see 1474.   22
2050 PHILEARN [12] (M Brittain) 2-8-8 K Darley 13/2: 4000203: Sn in front, no extra
close home: in fair form: see 1862.   15

1622 RIVERS SECRET [14] (Denys Smith) 2-8-8 L Charnock 9/2: 00004: Ev ch dist: see 1622.   12
1862 MISS PISA [6] 2-8-8 J Ward(7) 13/2: 3030430: Al up there: see 1862 & 647.   11
1905 KIND LADY [5] 2-8-8 J H Brown(5) 13/2: 4231020: Nearest fin: see 1358.   03
1944 NIGHTDRESS [4] 2-8-8 M Birch 7/2 FAV: 0030: Never dangerous: see 1944 (6f)   00
2050 Creole Bay [1] 8-8   1984 Danum Lad [3] 8-11   2050 Friends For Life [8] 8-11
1298 Ryesong [9] 8-11   1862 Soaring Eagles [10] 8-8
2050 Above The Salt [13] 8-11   813 The White Lion [11] 8-8
14 ran hd,2,1,½,4,½   (J Squires)   J Berry Cockerham, Lancs.

2139 STUFFED TURKEY H'CAP STAKES (0-35) 3YO   £2211   6f   Good 44 +11 Fast   [41]

2027 ROYAL ROUSER [10] (R Hollinshead) 3-8-6(1ow) S Perks 16/1: 0-00001: 3 b g He Loves Me -
Royal Sensation (Prince Regent) Returned to form, qcknd to lead inside dist in quite a fast
run 3yo h'cap at Catterick Aug 14: began last season in gd form, winning a Haydock mdn and
later placed sev times: best form over sprint dist: acts on firm and hvy grd and on any trk:
could win again.   30
1959 CUMBRIAN DANCER [7] (M H Easterby) 3-9-3(vis) M Birch 11/4 FAV: 0412002: Good effort.   36
2018 BON ACCUEIL [8] (H Whiting) 3-9-7 L Riggio(7) 13/2: -000023: Gd run under top weight.   39
972 DANCING TOM [4] (T Fairhurst) 3-9-2 M Hills 9/2: 0000044: Fair eff after abs: see 81   30
961 SPANISH INFANTA [6] 3-7-7(6oh) A Mackay 20/1: 000-000: Not reach leaders: maiden
sprint h'capper who has shown only a little ability.   06
*1815 OUR CHILDREN [9] 3-7-8 A Culhane(5) 9/1: 0-03010: No extra dist: btr 1815.   04
1648 DARTIGNY [2] 3-9-3(bl) S Whitworth 9/2: 1-00040: Tried to make all: see 514.   00
2055 HIGHLAND GLEN [11] 3-8-10(BL)(1oh) D Nicholls 10/1: 0-00040: Bl first time: fin
last: see 1973.   00
1917 Music Teacher [5] 7-7(1oh)   1973 Maybe Jayne [3] 7-7(6oh)
1613 Herb Robert [1] 7-7(10oh)
11 ran 1½,hd,1½,hd,1,1½   (F H Lee)   R Hollinshead Upper Longdon, Staffs.

2140 PORT & STILTON MDN. AUCTION STAKES 2YO   £822   7f   Good 44 -09 Slow

1812 MURPHY [12] (R Whitaker) 2-8-11 D Mckeown 4/1: 0421: 2 ch c Touch Paper - Iamstopped
(Furry Glen) Nicely bckd and led over 1f out, comfortably, in a 2yo mdn auction race at
Catterick Aug 14: eff over 7f on gd/firm ground and seems sure to be suited by 1m: acts
on any trk.   40
-- BRIMUR [10] (J Watts) 2-8-11 N Connorton 14/1: 2: Slow away, stayed on well from ½ way
and would not have to improve much to win a small race: cost IR 10,000: eff over 7f on
good ground: acts on a tight course.   36
1895 GRECIAN JOS [7] (F Carr) 2-8-8 S Morris 10/1: 033: Ev ch: see 1895.   31
2050 EUROCON [6] (D Chapman) 2-8-8 D Nicholls 9/1: 0000024: Improved of late: see 2050.   28
1561 REATA PASS [11] 2-8-5 M Roberts 25/1: 000: Early leader: remained prom: first signs
of form from this cheaply bought filly: eff over 7f on gd ground, and on a tight trk.   25
2052 SCAWSBY LEES [4] 2-8-8 K Hodgson 13/2: 03430: Al prom: prob stays 7f: see 1370.   27
965 GREAT MEMORY [3] 2-8-11 B Crossley 9/1: 0000: Fin 7th after fair abs: best 728 (5f)   00
1883 BRIGGS BUILDERS [1] 2-8-8 R Cochrane 3/1 FAV: 0020: Led/dsptd lead over 5f: best 1883   00
1982 VITAL CARGO [5] 2-8-8 Wendy Carter(7) 11/2: 440: No threat: btr 1982 (gall trk).   00
852 QUIETLY MINE [2] 2-8-5 E Guest(0) 7/1: 00: Fin in rear after abs: cost 3,700 gns
and is a half sister to useful miler I'll See You.   00
2019 Connemara Dawn [9] 8-8   1920 Lateral [8] 8-8(bl)
12 ran 1½,½,1½,shthd,¾,nk,shthd   (Mrrs S R Brook)   R Whitaker Wetherby, Yorks.

2141 COMATOSE H'CAP STAKES (0-35) 3YO+   £1297   1m 7f   Good 44 -06 Slow   [31]

1477 MARINERS DREAM [7] (R Hollinshead) 5-8-0 A Culhane(7) 5/1: 00-1001: 5 br h Julio
Mariner - My Ginny (Palestine) Led below dist and was sn clear in a h'cap at Catterick
Aug 14: first time out successful over this C/D: stays 2m well: acts on firm and soft grd
and on any track: winning hurdler.   12
1980 STRING OF BEADS [9] (J Etherington) 4-7-7(vis) J Lowe 12/1: -000002: Led over 5f
out, no chance with winner and remains a mdn: eff around 12f, stays 2m: seems to act on any grd.   00
1884 JIPIJAPA [2] (Don Enrico Incisa) 5-7-9(vis)(2ow)(2oh) A Mackay 12/1: 0-00003: Al up there:
mdn who is suited by a test of stamina tho' has shown little ability.   00
*1745 STONE JUG [12] (S Hall) 6-8-6(4ex) M Birch 6/4 FAV: 1-04114: Well bckd to complete
his hat-trick: no extra below dist and btr 1745.   03
-- SECRET FINALE [8] 7-8-1 J Bleasdale 25/1: 2-200-0: Al mid-div and will be btr for
this run: stays well: acts on any going: quite useful h'cap hurdler.   00
2040 BUCKLOW HILL [11] 9-9-11 M Hindley(3) 7/2: 0000340: Btn home turn: see 2040.   11
1897 Key Royal [6] 8-11   -- Special Settlement [5] 7-11
1736 Brandon Grey [10] 7-7(4oh)   312 Bellanoora [4] 8-13
10 ran 5,3,1½,2½,5   (Dennis Newton)   R Hollinshead Upper Longdon, Staffs.

2142 QUEENS SPEECH E.B.F. STAKES 3YO   £2040   1m 5f   Good 44 -08 Slow

1908 MY WILLOW [2] (J Fitzgerald) 3-8-0 M Roberts 11/2: -421: 3 ch f Tap on Wood - Nye
(Sanctus II) Outsider of the party tho' comfortably made ev yard in a stks race at Catterick
Aug 14: cost 30,000 gns as a yearling and is a half sister to sev minor winners: eff around

12/14f on good and firm grd: acts on any trk: on the upgrade.   45
1837 KING JACK [1] (J Dunlop) 3-8-4 G Baxter 6/4: 0021422: Consistent colt: see 1837, 1301   44
1674 GOLDEN HEIGHTS [3] (P Walwyn) 3-8-9 Paul Eddery 10/11 FAV: -121423: Chall after 1m,
found little under press and clearly below form shown in 1674 (12f): see 635.   35
3 ran   3,10   (Mrs A Scott-Harden)   J Fitzgerald Malton, Yorks

---

NEWBURY   Friday August 15th   Lefthand, Stiff, Galloping Track

Official Going Given As GOOD

2143 POLAR VEST APPRENTICE H'CAP (0-50) 3YO   £2792   6f   Good/Firm 23 -24 Slow   [50]

624 EASY LINE [9] (P Haslam) 3-8-0 L Riggio(3) 14/1: -1001: 3 ch g Swing Easy - Impromptu
(My Swanee) Led 1f out, comfortably, in an app h'cap at Newbury Aug 15: first time out won
a mdn on soft grd at Nottingham: half brother to a couple of winners: very eff over 6f,
should stay further: acts on gd/firm ground and a gall trk: does well when fresh.   33
1245 MAJOR JACKO [17] (R Hannon) 3-8-10 L Jones 16/1: 1400002: Kept on well final 1f
and 4l clear 3rd: gd eff: has been fairly lightly raced since 228: acts on gd/firm and soft.   41
1847 TAYLOR OF SOHAM [5] (D Leslie) 3-8-0(4ow) Gay Kelleway 10/1: 0041323: Al prom:
another gd eff: seems equally eff at 6/7f: see 1603.   23
1900 TARANGA [14] (M Tompkins) 3-9-2 A Shoults 12/1: -110204: Mkt drifter: never nearer:
very lightly raced since 309, see 134.   39
1878 NO BEATING HARTS [8] 3-9-2 J Leech(5) 12/1: 4021300: Led over 2f out: fair eff
but best 1654 (5f).   38
1750 OCEAN TRADER [13] 3-9-7(bl) G Kennedy(7) 20/1: 2-00000: Ran well under top weight:
best eff this season: see 1457: possibly best on a sharpish trk.   38
*1847 USEFUL [16] 3-9-4 G Carter 5/1 FAV: -023010: Well below 1847.   00
-1669 ASTICOUR [4] 3-9-2 M Marshall(7) 8/1: 24-0020: Much btr 1669 (sharper trk).   00
1878 COPPERMILL LAD [7] 3-8-6 P Mcentee(5) 9/1: 0000040: Active in mkt: slow start:
better 1878.   00
-2120 BEECHWOOD COTTAGE [2] 3-7-9(bl) P Barnard(5) 9/1: 0144020: No show: too soon after 2120? 00
1959 Young Puggy [15] 8-12   1730 Sancilia [18] 7-9   1406 Kharrana [10] 9-3
1044 Sparky Lad [11] 9-3   2072 Indian Summer [1] 9-0   1516 Solo Singer [3] 8-13
1751 Mogoar [12] 8-2   1995 Stanbo [6] 7-13(BL)
18 ran   ¾,4,hd,nk,2½   (B Lasala)   P Haslam Newmarket

2144 TOM CAXTON HOME BREW H'CAP (0-60)   £6555   1m   Good/Firm 23 +20 Fast   [60]

1229 GRANNYS BANK [2] (W Hastings Bass) 4-8-1 W Carson 6/1: 11-1221: 4 b f Music Boy - Sweet
Eliane (Birdbrook) Impr filly who has been in fine form all season: led final 1f, under
press in fast run and won an app h'cap at Newbury Aug 15: first time out won over
this C/D: in '85 won her last 2 starts, h'caps at Pontefract and Doncaster: very eff over
1m on gd and fast ground: acts on any trk but seems best on gall one especially Newbury: genuine 45
1987 MOORES METAL [9] (R Hollinshead) 6-7-12 A Culhane(7) 16/1: 0400032: Chance final 1f:
just btn and this was his best eff for a long time: should win if reproducing this form: 40
1240 STAR OF A GUNNER [10] (R Holder) 6-8-11 J Reid 11/1: 0110003: Led over 1f out:
narrowly btn in a close fin: runs well here: see 248.   53
1854 ININSKY [6] (G Harwood) 3-9-2 G Starkey 8/1: 0-40034: Led 3f out: another gd eff.   63
1890 ACONITUM [12] 5-8-10 W R Swinburn 12/1: 0300240: Ev ch str: see 1525.   45
1793 INDIAN HAL [4] 4-8-9 Paul Eddery 14/1: -044000: Came from behind: see 706.   42
1793 ADVANCE [1] 5-10-1 Pat Eddery 7/2 FAV: 01-0020: Well bckd: never nearer 7th: btr 1793.   00
2072 COINCIDENTAL [8] 4-8-13 S Cauthen 9/1: 01-0230: Made much: btr 2072, 1804 (7f)   00
2072 Ready Wit [5] 8-4   1852 Al Trui [13] 9-2   1929 Merle [7] 8-6(BL)
1890 Every Effort [3] 7-9   1911 Hello Sunshine [11] 7-8
13 ran   ½,hd,3,1,1   (John H James)   W Hastings Bass Newmarket

2145 GR.3 TRUSTHOUSE FORTE HUNGERFORD STAKES £21705   7f   Good/Firm 23 +17 Fast

*1823 HADEER [5] (C Brittain) 4-9-3 S Cauthen 11/2: 4-20411: 4 ch c General Assembly -
Glinting (Crepello) Smart colt who is at the peak of his form: ran on well final 1f, under
press for a narrow win in a fast run Gr 3 Hungerford Stks at Newbury Aug 15: last time out
was a comfortable winner of Beeswings Stks at Newcastle: lightly raced in '85: very useful
2yo when trained by M Stoute winning at Windsor & Newmarket: very eff at 7f, stays 1m: acts
on gd and firm grd and on any trk: game and genuine and should win more races.   80
1286 TRUELY NUREYEV [10] (M Stoute) 3-8-6 W R Swinburn 5/1 FAV: 231-02: Al going well:
led 2f out till inside final 1f: just btn and looks sure to find a decent race: acts on
gd and fast ground: see 1286.   76
1823 TREMBLANT [7] (R Smyth) 5-9-0 Pat Eddery 6/1: -200033: Ran on well final 1f, after
having trouble getting a run: best effort this term and should be winning soon: see 5.   72
*1851 ROYAL LOFT [8] (W Jarvis) 3-8-3 R Cochrane 6/1: 1-2214: Kept on well: in grand form.   67
1823 HARD ROUND [1] 3-8-6 B Rouse 8/1: 2443120: Al up there: most consistent: see 1823, 1514 68
2003 GREY DESIRE [4] 6-9-3 K Darley 8/1: 1202300: Never nearer: twice below 1631 (6f).   65
945 BOLLIN KNIGHT [11] 4-9-0 M Birch 8/1: 0111000: Wknd final 2f after abs: best 413 (yldg)   00

*2006 THE BEAN SIDHE [9] 3-8-6 C F Swan 9/1: 0-13010: Made much: btr 2006 (soft, sharper trk)   00
1851 Chalk Stream [3] 8-3   897 Alex Nureyev [2] 8-6   641 Lidhame [6] 9-3
11 ran   nk,2½,½,1,3   (W J Gredley)   C Brittain Newmarket

2146 WASHINGTON SINGER STAKES (LISTED) 2YO   £7401   7f   Good/Firm 23 -21 Slow

*2044 DEPUTY GOVERNOR USA [7] (L Piggott) 2-8-11 T Ives 5/2: 311: 2 ch c Master Willie -
Regent Miss (Vice Regent) Smart, fast impr colt: well bckd and led inside final 2f, going
clear for an impr win in Washington Singer Stks (Listed race) at Newbury Aug 15: last time
out was a comfortable winner from the very useful Angara Abyss at Lingfield: half brother
to sev winners: very eff over 7f and looks sure to stay at least 1m: acts well on fast grd:
seems to go on any trk: most definitely on the upgrade and is certain to win more gd races.   74
1887 ROUNDLET [6] (W Hern) 2-9-3 W Carson 10/1: 4102: Ran on well final 1f and will be
suited by 1m: runs well at Newbury and likes a gall trk: see 1643.   71
*1660 DR BULASCO [4] (S Norton) 2-8-11 J Reid 9/2: 213: Dsptd lead 2f out: fine effort
in this smart company and is still improving: see 1660.   63
1465 ORNE [2] (J Tree) 2-8-11 Pat Eddery 7/2: 124: Hmpd start: chance over 1f out,
but no extra: consistent colt who should be suited by 1m: see 1239.   62
1643 LEIPERS FORK [3] 2-8-8 S Cauthen 8/1: 30: Hmpd start: no show: see 1643.   47
*1914 LUZUM [1] 2-9-0(bl) A Murray 9/4 FAV: 23210: Well bckd: made much, but sn fdd when
hdd: well below 1914 (sharper trk).   50
1129 ALBASAR [5] 2-9-0 Paul Eddery 20/1: 100: Abs: prom 5f: twice below 777.   00
7 ran   2½,½,½,8,1½   (Prince Ahmed Salman)   L Piggott Newmarket

2147 SEVEN BARROWS MAIDEN FILLIES STAKES   £4484   6f   Good/Firm 23 -36 Slow

-- TAHILLA [21] (J Tree) 2-8-11 Pat Eddery 6/1: 1: 2 b f Moorestyle - Woodwind (Whistling
Wind) Promising filly: first time out, led approaching final 1f, comfortably, in a 27 runner
2yo fillies mdn at Newbury Aug 15: half sister to the very useful 6/7f performerr Mummy's
Favourite, amongst sev others: eff 6f, looks sure to stay 7f: acts on gd/firm grd and a
gall trk: looks sure to win more races.   58
1874 TOY CUPBOARD [14] (W Hern) 2-8-11 W Carson 3/1 FAV: 42: Well bckd: ran on well
final 1f and will be suited by 7f: should win soon: see 1874.   52
-- STREET PARTY [26] (G Wragg) 2-8-11 P Robinson 5/1: 3: Nicely bckd: chance over 1f out:
promising racecourse debut: dam was a most consistent sort who stayed 12f well: sure to
be suited by 7f and further: acts on gd/firm and a gall trk: must find a maiden.   51
-- JUST KALA [15] (P Walwyn) 2-8-11 Paul Eddery 20/1: 4: Fin best of all, will step
up on this next time: half sister to a couple of winners: should be suited by 7f/1m: acts
on gd/firm and a gall track and can get off the mark in the near future.   47
-- GREENHIL JAZZ TIME [11] 2-8-11 S Whitworth 33/1: 0: Al up there on racecourse debut,
showing promise: half sister to very useful hurdler/chaser Mr Moonraker: eff at 6f on gd/
firm ground and should find a race.   46
-- HOORAY LADY [19] 2-8-11 T Quinn 7/1: 0: Made much on racecourse debut: half sister
to winning 2yo Run With The Wind: quite speedily bred and may benefit from an easier trk:
acts on gd/firm.   45
-- ETONNANTE [25] 2-8-11 B Thomson 16/1: 0: Fin 7th and looks certain to improve:
half sister to a winner in France: one to keep an eye on.   42
-- SUPER SURPRISE [27] 2-8-11 R Hills 33/1: 0: Never nearer 8th on debut: half sister
to winning 2yo Super Punk.   42
-- COLDWATER CANYON [9] 2-8-11 R Cochrane 20/1: 0: Never nearer 9th: cost 20,000 as
a yearling and is a half sister to 2yo winner Rowanberry: should be suited by 7f.   35
-- TAHGREBA [16] 2-8-11 L Jones(5) 25/1: 0: Has scope and should improve: half sister
to numerous winners including the Cesarewitch victor Kayudee : certain to stay 7f+.   34
-- SHELDON MILLS [2] 2-8-11 J Matthias 10/1: 0: Active in mkt: prom most.   32

-- Barbary Court [18] 8-11   -- Sunbridge [7] 8-11
1440 Lady Silca Key [22] 8-11   -- Indian Flare [1] 8-11
446 Belle Of Stars [8] 8-11   383 Call For Taylor [6] 8-11
1855 Catherine Schratt [24] 8-11   533 Go My Pet [12] 8-11
-- Hidden Asset [4] 8-11   -- Lavandou Legend [13] 8-11
-- London Cries [10] 8-11   -- Millennia [23] 8-11
-- Moonshine [3] 8-11   2070 Pink Fondant [20] 8-11
2069 Taciturn Lady [6] 8-11   -- Watered Silk [17] 8-11
27 ran   2,nk,2½,hd,nk,1½,hd,3,½   (Lady Derby)   J Tree Beckhampton, Wilts.

2148 NEWTOWN MAIDEN STAKES 3YO   £3619   1m 4f   Good/Firm 23 +07 Fast

1589 MERANO [2] (H Cecil) 3-9-0 S Cauthen 4/5 FAV:-321: 3 ch c Tip Moss - Association
(Margouillat) Very useful colt: justified strong support, led over 1f out, easily in quite
fast run 3yo mdn at Newbury Aug 15: last time out was just btn by Verardi at Kempton: ex
French colt who showed gd form when not far behind French Derby 2nd Altayan on his sole outing
at Evry: well suited by 12f: acts on gd/firm and soft grd and looks sure to win more races.   63
1554 GALACTIC HERO [12] (M Stoute) 3-9-0 W R Swinburn 11/2: 2-32: Led inside final 2f:
caught a tartar and should go one btr soon: see 1554: stays 12f.   51
1642 NORTHERN AMETHYST [5] (D Elsworth) 3-9-0 B Rouse 5/1: -322023: Nicely bckd: chance
inside final 2f: has changed stables since race 1642.   49

1646 DUNSTON [13] (F Durr) 3-9-0 Pat Eddery 33/1: -003034: Made most 1m and fin 7l clear
rem: this was much impr form and if not flattered here, should find a h'cap before being
reassessed: see 1646.   48
1939 SHIRLSTAR TAXSAVER [3] 3-9-0(bl) B Thomson 66/1: -040000: Stiff task: see 1085.   32
1899 GREY SALUTE [15] 3-9-0 S Whitworth 33/1: -330: Led over 3f out, fdd: btr 1899.   23
1589 SLANGI VAH [6] 3-9-0 W Newnes 16/1: -330: Mkt drifter: btr 1589.   00
832 Sure Ground [8] 9-0   -- Castle Rock [17] 9-0   1645 Adbury [18] 9-0
1087 Gex [10] 9-0   -- Lord Capilano [9] 9-0   -- Masnoon [4] 9-0
1954 Good Natured [14] 8-11   1481 Home Fleet [1] 8-11
1941 La Muscade [7] 8-11   1395 Miss Aron [11] 8-11   1830 Cuckoo In The Nest [16] 9-0
18 ran   4,¼,hd,7,5   (C A B St George)   H Cecil Newmarket

RIPON   Saturday August 16th   Righthanded, Sharpish Track

Official Going Given As GOOD

2149 NEWBY HANDICAP STKS 3YO 0-50   £2914   1m 1f Good/Firm 25 -27 Slow   [49]

2053 HONEST TOIL [6] (R Whitaker) 3-8-0(1ow) D Mckeown 5/1: 0041D41: 3 br c Anax - Be
Honest (Klairon): Waited with, ran on strongly to lead inside dist in a 3yo h'cap at Ripon
Aug.16: narrow "winner" of a similar race at Newcastle in June though subsq. disq: half
brother to several winners: eff over 8/10f on gd/firm grnd: acts on any trk.   31
*1971 HALO HATCH [9] (K Brassey) 3-9-3(bl)(5ex) R Hills 6/1: -030012: Led briefly dist,
no extra close home though remains in gd form and may win again soon: see 1971.   44
1685 CHARLTON KINGS [11] (R Hollinshead) 3-8-7(1ow) S Perks 7/1: 0400003: Early ldr, not
btn that far & seemed btr suited by this shorter trip: see 716.   32
1199 MY KIND OF TOWN [2] (R Williams) 3-9-7 T Ives 7/1: -11044: Gd effort after abs:
stays 9f: carries weight well: see 335.   46
2037 SAND DOLLAR [7] 3-8-3 G Duffield 5/2 FAV: 00-1330: Well bckd though again below
form shown in 1904 (1m).   24
1299 BIEN DORADO [8] 3-8-8(bl) M Hills 7/1: -004340: Abs: led/dsptd lead till dist: see 1065 22
1848 TORWADA [1] 3-9-7 P Waldron 6/1: 4-10030: Shorter trip: best over 11f in 191 (yld). 00
874 COLONIAL KING [4] 3-7-13(1ow) K Darley 16/1: 400-000: No threat after long abs:
quite lightly raced colt who has shown some ability over 7/8f: acts on gd/firm grnd.   00
1956 FORCELLO [3] 3-9-1 J Lowe 7/1: 2424300: Wknd into 9th: see 444.   00
1773 BOYNTON [10] 3-7-8 A Culhane(7) 10/1: -020240: Yet to reproduce form shown in 1178 (10f) 00
10 ran   1½,½,shhd,2,3   (D I Buckley)   R Whitaker Wetherby, Yorks

2150 WOOL SELLING STAKES 2YO   £1377   5f   Good/Firm 25 -11 Slow

1958 MERE MUSIC [10] (M Brittain) 2-8-11(bl) K Darley 6/1: 0000001: 2 ch g Music Boy -
Mrs McNicholas (Tudor Music): Dropped in class & gamely made ev yd in a 2yo seller at Ripon
Aug.16 (bought in 4,700 gns): cheaply acquired gelding who had earlier shown some ability in
btr company: eff over 5f on gd/firm & yld grnd: suited by forcing tactics: acts on any trk:
best in blinkers.   28
1881 HARRYS COMING [14] (T Fairhurst) 2-8-11 M Hills 5/1: 1300202: Kept on well: see 1680. 25
1949 HUGO Z HACKENBUSH [7] (C Tinkler) 2-8-11(vis) M Birch 9/2: 4004223: Al front rank,
not btn far & must win soon if kept in this grade: acts on any trk: see 1680.   24
1955 CAUSEWAY FOOT [4] (N Tinkler) 2-8-11(bl) Kim Tinkler 16/1: 000004: Al up there: cheaply
bought colt who is a half brother to several minor winners: eff over 5f on gd/firm: suited
by an easy course.   15
2026 BOLD HIDEAWAY [6] 2-8-11 D Nicholls 3/1 FAV: 040: Nearest fin: btr in 2026 (stiff 6f). 11
1825 VENHERM [2] 2-8-11 M Fry 10/1: 00: Dropped in class: prom most of way: brother to
winning sprinter Maftir.   10
1680 PADDY WILL [3] 2-8-8 N Day 5/1: 00: Al rear, fin last: see 1680.   00
1741 Metroman [12] 8-11   1576 Fu Lu Shou [1] 8-11   2100 Overnite Sensation [11] 8-11
1843 Send It Down [5] 8-11   1958 Buy Nordan [9] 8-8   1421 Bantel Bouquet [8] 8-8
13 ran   ¾,½,3,1½,hd   (Mel Brittain)   M Brittain Warthill, Yorks

2151 GREAT ST WILFRID HCAP 0-70   £7877   6f   Good/Firm 25 +23 Fast   [57]

+2084 CATHERINES WELL [3] (M W Easterby) 3-8-11(7ex) G Carter(3) 10/3: 0303311: 3 ch f Junius -
Restless Lady (Sandford Lad): Useful filly who is in tremendous form: never looked likely to
be caught when winning a very fast run h'cap at Ripon Aug.16: in fine form last back end, winning nurseries at
Doncastter & Newmarket, after
earlier scoring in a seller on the former course: very eff over 5/6f, stays 7f: acts on
firm & yld grnd on any trk: looks set to complete her hat trick.   60
1852 PADRE PIO [2] (D Arbuthnot) 5-8-11 M Hills 7/2: 1-02002: No ch with winner though
ran well, beating rem decisively: should go one btr soon: see 846.   42
1852 SEW HIGH [9] (B Mcmahon) 3-8-8 J Hills(5) 11/2: 1041103: Best over 5f in 1704.   33
-- PLAYTEX [7] (D Barron) 6-7-13 R Street 20/1: 33400-4: Fair effort on belated reapp:
has been successful at Thirsk for the past 3 seasons, and has yet to win anywhere else:
eff over 6/8f: well suited by fast ground & a sharp trk.   17

1852 PRINCE SKY [6] 4-9-5 P Waldron 11/4 FAV: -430140: Early speed: much btr in 1852.   33
*2065 SULLYS CHOICE [12] 5-9-1(10ex) D Nicholls 8/1: 1003210: Much btr over 5f in 2065 (gall trk) 25
2039 Idle Times [8] 7-8   2079 Mendick Adventure [10] 7-7(bl)(3oh)
2065 Duck Flight [5] 8-6   1655 Fashada [4] 9-4(BL)
10 ran   4,4,¼,1½,1¼,hd,1½,hd   (Hippodromo Racing)   M W Easterby Sheriff Hutton, York:

2152 COCKED HAT MAIDEN CLAIMING STKS   £2644   1m 4f   Good/Firm 25 -48 Slow

1706 DARK SIRONA [8] (D Arbuthnot) 3-8-3 K Darley 8/1: 00-0221: 3 b f Pitskelly -
Step-You-Gaily (King's Company): Led dist, comfortably in a slowly run claiming stakes at
Ripon Aug.16: half sister to minor winner A Red Red Rose: well suited by 12f & should stay
futher: acts on gd & firm grnd & on any trk.   24
1737 COCKED HAT SUPREME [5] (S Hall) 4-8-13 E Guest(3) 9/1: 0-44222: Led 3f out, kept
on same pace: remains a mdn: well suited by a sharp trk: see 1092.   18
1589 SANET [3] (P Kelleway) 3-8-9 D Nicholls 9/4 FAV: -44003: Faced her easiest task of
the season: well bckd though no extra inside dist: best in 273 (heavy).   22
2017 HEAD OF SCHOOL [7] (J Winter) 3-8-12 G Duffield 4/1: 0-00424: Btr over 10f in 2017.   22
1361 THE HOUGH [15] 5-9-7 D Leadbitter(7) 12/1: -0440: Ran on same pace: see 770.   17
1497 BETTER BEWARE [6] 3-8-12(bl) T Ives 7/1: 4300300: Best early season with some give: see 506.18
2034 KILIMANJARO BOB [12] 4-9-7(bl) M Hills 8/1: -000020: Fdd into 8th: btr in 2034 (stiff trk)   00
1873 Last Polonaise [13] 8-6   1479 Hidden Move [9] 8-7
--   Separate Lives [10] 8-7   356 Belvel [16] 8-3
1554 Way Above [4] 8-3   1337 Torriggia [14] 8-9   2008 Lisaily [1] 8-11(BL)
1736 Wave Goodbye [11] 8-7(BL)   2054 Rekadlo [2] 8-9
2008 Red Counter [17] 8-11 P
17 ran   2½,1½,1½,1½,½   (Miss C A Allsopp)   D Arbuthnot Compton, Berks

2153 EBF STUDLEY STAKES 2YO   £3029   6f   Good/Firm 25 -12 Slow

1996 SHEER ROYALTY [9] (W O'gorman) 2-8-8 T Ives 5/2 FAV: 041: 2 b f Dara Monarch -
Organdy (Blakeney): Stumbled below dist though ran on strongly to lead near fin in a 2yo stakes
at Ripon Aug.16: cost 62,000 gns as a yearling: eff over 5/6f & seems sure to stay further:
acts on gd/firm grrnd & on a sharp/easy course: should continue to improve.   40
+1867 NORGABIE [5] (P Calver) 2-9-1 M Fry 10/3: 12: Just failed to make all: well clear of
rem and is on the up grade: see 1867.   45
2029 BLAZE OF GOLD [4] (E Alston) 2-8-8 G Duffield 10/3: 0223: Outpcd below dist: much
btr in 2029 (gall trk).   20
--   GOOD WOMAN [7] (R Boss) 2-8-8 E Guest(3) 7/1: 4: Speed over ½way: likely to improve.   17
1464 KEEN NOTE [1] 2-8-8 M Birch 5/1: 00: Early speed: cost 66,000 gns and is a half
sister to winning sprinter Restless Rhapsody.   12
1972 SUESANDY [8] 2-8-8 J Bleasdale 25/1: 00: Prom over ½way: see 1972.   10
1634 Callace [6] 8-8   -- Hytak Pet [3] 8-8   -- Sweet Mary Lou [10] 8-8
9 ran   hd,6,1,1½,½   (T R Capehart)   W O'gorman Newmarket

2154 WHARFE HANDICAP STAKES 0-35 3YO+   £2418   1m 2f   Good/Firm 25 -26 Slow   [27]

*1773 SPRING FLIGHT [2] (A Jarvis) 3-8-10 D Nicholls 11/4 FAV: 0132311: 3 b c Captain James-
Late Swallow (My Swallow): In gd form, led 4f out for an easy win in a h'cap at Ripon Aug.16:
last month made all in a 3yo h'cap at Ayr: earlier won a seller at Redcar: eff over 8/10f
on fast grnd: acts on any trk: suited by forcing tactics: may win again.   30
*1951 BRECKLAND LADY [7] (M Tompkins) 4-8-12 T Ives 10/3: 10-0312: Fin well: see 1951.   14
1689 PRIMROSE WAY [10] (M Blanshard) 4-8-1 M Hills 12/1: -002003: Early ldr, ev ch: little
form this term: see 341.   01
1820 NUGOLA [3] (Don Enrico Incisa) 4-8-2 M Beecroft 20/1: 0000004: Nearest fin: see 789.   00
1671 BRADBURY HALL [5] 3-8-1 K Darley 10/1: 0221000: Led/dsptd lead over ½way: best in 1426.   08
1535 HEADIN ON [6] 6-8-12 Karen Gurney(7) 33/1: -3000: Best over 12f in 1102 (stiffer trk).   06
1964 GREED [13] 5-9-5 L Charnock 5/1: 2443240: Never nearer 7th: see 1185.   00
1870 MISS APEX [8] 4-8-9(vis) I Johnson 15/2: 4302330: Never dngr 9th: btr in 1689.   00
1781 SAFE CUSTODY [1] 4-9-7 P Waldron 8/1: -000040: Much btr over 1m in 1781 (stiff trk).   00
1124 Mr Lion [12] 8-8   1624 Greetland Dancer [4] 8-8
1985 Glenderry [9] 8-6
12 ran   2½,½,1½,shhd,1½,½   (Mrs M Jarvis)   A Jarvis Royston, Herts

---

Official Going Given As GOOD/FIRM

2155 LADBROKES RACING H'CAP (0-60) 3YO   £4253   7f   Good/Firm 24 -18 Slow   [61]

*1821 PASTICCIO [10] (M Jarvis) 3-9-5 R Cochrane 14/1: -322211: 3 b c Taufan - Karens Pet
(Mummy's Pet): Very useful, fast impr colt: not the best of runs, but fairly flew inside the
final 1f to get up close home & win going away in a valuable 3yo h'cap at Newbury Aug 16:
last time out led close home in a similar event at Newcastle: most consistent this term: on
final outing in '85 won a mdn at Leicester: very eff at 7f, stays 1m: acts on firm &
soft grnd & a gall trk: needs to be held up for a late run & has a fine turn of foot.   65

•1725 EASTERN HOUSE [12] (H Cecil) 3-8-2 W Ryan 13/2: 22-0212: Led inside final 2f: just
caught & 3L clear 3rd: in grand form & should win again soon: see 1725.   46
1753 ANDIKA [15] (J Tree) 3-8-7 W Carson 10/1: -00103: Ch final 2f: seems best over 7f: see 1228   45
1486 ELNAWAAGI [16] (H T Jones) 3-9-7 A Murray 14/1: 3-11004: No extra final 1f: fair
effort: stays 7f: see 895.   56
•1991 BLACK SOPHIE [5] 3-8-3(6ex) P Cook 8/1: 03-0010: No real threat, but is in gd form.   36
•692 AL BASHAAMA [3] 3-9-4 R Guest 10/1: -01310: Mkt drifter after fair abs: steady hdway
into 6th & looks certain to run well next time: eff at 7f/1m: acts on gd/firm & yld.   49
1486 GORGEOUS ALGERNON [2] 3-8-12(BL) S Cauthen 9/1: 1020200: Bl first time: see 1486, 1384.   00
•1640 HIGHEST PRAISE [4] 3-8-10 J Matthias 7/1: -013310: Fin 9th: btr 1640 (C/D).   00
•1999 FANCY PAN [14] 3-7-12(6ex) R Lines(3) 11/2 FAV: -030410: Well bckd: fin rear: much btr 1999. 00
1691 Abutammam [7] 8-6   1889 Green Dollar [9] 9-2   --   Into The Gap [6] 8-10
1947 Kalandariya [1] 8-4   1821 Rue St Jacques [18] 8-0
1032 Burhaain [13] 8-0   2139 Bon Accueil [11] 7-13
16 ran nk,3,1½,½,1½   (T G Warner)   M Jarvis Newmarket

2156 ASSOCIATED TYRE SPEC. H'CAP (0-70) 3YO   £9957   1m 4f   Good/Firm 24 +27 Fast   [63]

--   EL CUITE [10] (H Cecil) 3-9-6 S Cauthen 6/1: 1-1: 3 b c Vaguely Noble - Assez Cuite
(Graustark) : Smart colt: first time out, led approaching final 1f, easily run: well suited by 1½m: acts on gd & fast grnd & a gall trk: most impressive today
& should find a Gr.3 event.   71
•1886 HAUWMAL [3] (W Hern) 3-9-1(3ex) W Carson 85/40 FAV: -120412: Led inside final 2f:
caught a tartar: see 1886.   60
+1998 TENDER TYPE [11] (M Tompkins) 3-8-2(3ex) R Cochrane 8/1: 0001213: Fin in gd style and
is in grand form: should find another h'cap soon & stays 12f well: see 1998.   42
1484 ON TENTERHOOKS [12] (J Tree) 3-8-4 S Whitworth 12/1: 43-104: Ch final 2f: stays 12f,
but possibly not 14f: see 980.   40
•1023 BENISA RYDER [2] 3-8-3 P Cook 16/1: 3-22410: Nearest fin after abs: stays 12f: see 1023   36
1886 MIGHTY FLASH [7] 3-8-2 A Mcglone 20/1: 0001100: Led into str: twice below 1523.   31
1276 ONISKY [5] 3-9-3 T Quinn 10/1: 0-11230: Led 3f out: best 983 (14f).   00
•1923 Vagador [6] 9-5(3ex)   •1685 Elaafuur [1] 8-7   •619 Senor Tomas [8] 9-5
•1645 Ship Of State [4] 9-7
11 ran 2½,3,2,1½,2   (Sheikh Mohammed)   H Cecil Newmarket

2157 GROUP 2 GEOFFREY FREER STAKES   £36882   1m 5f   Good/Firm 24 +11 Fast

1330 BAKHAROFF [2] (G Harwood) 3-8-3 W Carson 6/4 FAV: 21-2331: 3 b c The Minstrel -
Qui Royalty (Native Royalty): Very smart colt: heavily bckd & led over 1f out, comfortably
for a deserved success in Gr.2 Geoffrey Freer Stakes at Newbury Aug.16: earlier placed in
both Irish & French Derbys: the officially top rated 2yo last season after winning the
Futurity Stakes at Doncaster: earlier successful at Royal Ascot & Sandown & also 2nd to
Huntingdale in the Dewhurst: eff at 12/13f, should be suited by 14f: acts on gd & firm
grnd & a gall trk: almost certainly going for the St Leger: most consistent.   84
1853 SIRK [4] (C Brittain) 3-8-3 P Robinson 10/3: 1323032: Led over 2f out: battled on
well when hdd by winner & has been in excellent form this season: sure to be suited by the
Leger trip and is a genuine colt: see 878, 48.   81
1513 I WANT TO BE [6] (J Dunlop) 4-9-2 B Thomson 11/1: 12-0023: Ran on well final 1f: in
fine form & should win soon: see 1513.   77
1712 PHARDANTE [5] (G Harwood) 4-9-8 G Starkey 11/1: 0101334: Ev ch str: see 1217.   75
1888 SPICY STORY [6] 5-9-2 S Cauthen 12/1: 4-30320: Made much: see 1127 (2½,).   66
•1593 DUBIAN [3] 4-8-13 W R Swinburn 9/2: 331-010: Fdd 2f out: not stay 13f? see 1593.   60
6 ran 1,2,4,1½,1½   (K Abdulla)   G Harwood Pulborough, Sussex

2158 GOFFS ST HUGHS STAKES (LISTED) 2YO FILL   £8896   5f   Good/Firm 24 -19 Slow

1454 ABUZZ [2] (C Brittain) 2-8-8 M Roberts 11/2: 111041: 2 ch f Absalom - Sorebelle
(Prince Tenderfoot): Very useful filly: returned to her best form, led over 1f out, driven
out in a 2yo Listed race at Newbury Aug.16: won her first 3 outings at Epsom, Chester &
Newbury: speedily bred filly who is very eff over this min. trip, though does stay 6f: acts
on firm grnd: likes some give in the grnd: no trk preferences & is a genuine sort.   68
1850 REGENCY FILLE [3] (R Williams) 2-8-8 R Cochrane 5/1: 2232122: Ran on well final 1f &
again just btn: thoroughly genuine & consistent: see 1850, 1708.   67
1910 CHASING MOONBEAMS [7] (I Balding) 2-8-8 P Cook 11/4 FAV: 22143: Slowly away & held
up in rear: not clear run nearing final 1f & fin best of all: possibly a shade unlucky:
will win again soon: see 1910, 1453.   67
•1527 DREAM LAUNCH [4] (B Hanbury) 2-8-8 G Baxter 7/2: 01214: Prom all the way & not btn
far: another gd effort: see 1527.   64
1850 UN BEL DI [1] 2-8-8 Paul Eddery 14/1: 0100: Gd effort in this hot company: see 1308.   60
1850 SAUCE DIABLE [8] 2-8-8 A W Carson 12/1: 2100: Made much, fdd: best 1311 (sharper trk).   52
•1501 BO BABBITY [5] 2-8-8 J Reid 33/1: 3010: Stiff task: see 1501.   00
1874 SCIERPAN [9] 2-8-5 B Thomson 5/1: 220: Nicely bckd: speed most: btr 1874 (easier trk).   00
8 ran ½,nk,1,1½,3   (Mrs C E Brittain)   C Brittain Newmarket

2159 E.B.F. YATTENDON MAIDEN STAKES 2YO   £4490   7f   Good/Firm 24 -22 Slow

-- NEW ATTITUDE [8] (G Harwood) 2-9-0 G Starkey 12/1: 1: 2 b c Sallust - Sarus (Amber Rama):
Very promising colt: mkt drifter, but led nearing final 1f, comfortably in a 27 runner mdn
at Newbury Aug.16: cost 30,000 gns as a yearling: eff at 7f, should stay at least 1m: acts
on gd/firm grnd & a gall trk: should win more races.   70
-- ZAIZOOM [27] (P Cole) 2-9-0 T Quinn 9/4 FAV: 2: Heavily bckd debutant who was al prom
on the stands side: 4L clear 3rd & seems sure to open his account soon: cost $30,000 and
is a half brother to several winners in the States: sure to be suited by 1m: acts on gd/
firm & a gall trk.   66
1914 BENGAL FIRE [3] (C Brittain) 2-9-0 G Baxter 7/1: 23: Made most far side: another gd run.   59
-- THAMEEN [24] (H T Jones) 2-9-0 A Murray 8/1: 4: Al up there on racecourse debut:
will be suited by 1m & further: cost $600,000 as a yearling & should have no trouble
finding a maiden.   53
1914 WOOD LOUSE [5] 2-9-0 J Matthias 16/1: 00: On the up grade: see 1914.   50
1914 NOBLE BID [16] 2-9-0 B Thomson 7/1: 40: Ev ch, btr 1914.   43
1791 KASTAMOUN [12] 2-9-0 S Cauthen 8/1 : 40: Mkt drifter: prom much: seee 1791.   00

-- Silk Topper [15] 9-0	-- Hello Trouble [21] 9-0	
1241 Young Lochinvar [13] 9-0		1583 Gunner Stream [9] 9-0
-- Convincing [18] 9-0	-- Tenth Dimension [23] 9-0	
614 Mahrajan [14] 9-0	1452 Beryls Joke [17] 9-0	1442 Ardiles [19] 9-0
-- Box The Compass [7] 9-0		-- Cock Sparrow [6] 9-0
1442 Dandy [25] 9-0	1914 Daunting Prospect [26] 9-0	
-- Flutter Money [20] 9-0		1518 Kingswood Resopal [10] 9-0
-- Ninth Saga [4] 9-0	-- Nipikan [1] 9-0	1629 Pewter Quarter [11] 9-0
-- Rarely At Odds [22] 9-0		-- Tamourad [2] 9-0

27 ran 1,4,3,1½,4   (H H Prince Yazid Saud)   G Harwood Pulborough, Sussex

2160 SHRIVENHAM HANDICAP (0-50) 3YO+   £4045   5f   Good/Firm 24 -24 Slow   [49]

1852 DERRY RIVER [10] (L Cottrell) 5-8-4(VIS) C Rutter(3) 25/1: 0000001: 5 br g Irish
River - Duboff (So Blessed): Gained his first success in 3 seasons, with a very comfortable
¾L win in a h'cap at Newbury Aug.16: in '83 won at Wolverhampton: very eff at 5f: acts on
gd/firm & yld grnd & runs well here : wore a visor today.   37
1852 PERFECT TIMING [12] (D Elsworth) 4-9-11 W R Swinburn 9/2: 0433232: Held up in rear:
fin fast but not get to winner: most consistent: see 1852, 1608.   54
1834 DEPUTY HEAD [6] (L Holt) 6-9-4 J Matthias 25/1: 3133003: Another gd effort: see 1060.   43
*2046 LONELY STREET [9] (P Arthur) 5-8-9(8ex) L Johnsey(5) 9/1: 2032014: Dsptd lead final
1f: in grand form: see 2046.   33
+2021 GLEN KELLA MANX [4] 5-9-2(8ex) R Cochrane 6/1: 0-00010: Ch over 1f out: running well.   38
1608 PERION [14] 4-9-3 J Adams(7) 6/1: 0111040: Led after 3f: see 477.   35
1033 RAYHAAN [15] 3-9-4 B Rouse 10/1: -01130: Abs: prom much: needed race: see 1033.   00
2065 LAURIE LORMAN [13] 4-9-4 W Carson 4/1 FAV: 0000020: Trouble in running: see 2065.   00
1805 SIMLA RIDGE [8] 4-8-13 P Robinson 10/1: 0130020: Dsptd lead, wknd: see 628, 977.   00

1950 Northern Trust [5] 8-13(bl)		808 Oh Boyar [11] 9-10
1900 Puccini [7] 8-11	1654 Stephens Song [1] 8-4	1950 Farmer Jock [3] 7-9

14 ran ½,1½,nk,½,1½   (Mrs N Duffield)   L Cottrell Cullompton, Devon

---

Official Going Given As GOOD, STRAIGHT COURSE: GOOD/FIRM, ROUND COURSE

2161 WARDROBE PLACE 3YO FILLIES STAKES   £1025   1m 2f   Good/Firm 23 -02 Slow

*1841 SWEET DOMAIN [6] (J Dunlop) 3-9-3 B Thomson 4/1: 20-0011: 3 ch f Dominion - Maze
(Silly Season): Useful filly: stayed on well to lead inside dist in a 3yo fillies stakes at
Lingfield Aug.16: earlier won mdn at Redcar: eff over 1m, clearly stays 10f well: acts
on firm & yld grnd & on any trk: in gd form.   50
1974 ABSENCE OF MALICE [4] (B Hanbury) 3-8-11(bl) G Starkey 9/2: -200232: Tried to make
all: gd effort though remains a mdn: see 1974 & 1520.   38
1924 ETTAS PET [1] (R Sheather) 3-8-11 T Quinn 16/1: 00-4003: Al close up: stays 10f: see 1451   33
1902 FLUTTERY [3] (G Wragg) 3-8-11 S Cauthen 10/1: 300224: Well bckd: found nothing
under press and is proving expensive to follow: best over 1m in 1902.   31
1751 SHUJUN [2] 3-8-11 A Murray 16/1: 200-000: Some late prog: see 1751.   24
1690 COOL GALES [8] 3-8-11 P Cook 20/1: 03-0020: Much btr in 1690: see 732.   20

1639 Deniece [5] 8-11(BL)	-- Carange [7] 8-11	

8 ran 1,4,2,4,2   (Mrs C O'Sullivan)   J Dunlop Arundel, Sussex

2162 LHW HOLDINGS STAKES 2YO   £2034   5f   Good/Firm 23 +06 Fast

*780 COME ON CHASE ME [6] (J Etherington) 2-9-2 M Wood 4/1: 311: 2 ch c Sharpo - Dragonist
(Dragonara Palace): Useful colt: despite long abs was smartly away when a comfortable all
the way winner of a fast run 2yo stakes at Lingfield Aug.16: earlier won a mdn at Thirsk:
speedily bred colt who cost 12,500 gns as a yearling: very eff over 5f with forcing tactics:
acts on gd & firm grnd & is well suited by a sharpish trk.   61

+1728 COPPER RED [1] (P Makin) 2-9-2 T Quinn 5/2 JT FAV: 32312: Kept on well to ddht for 2nd
place: genuine & consistent colt who acts on any trk: see 1728.   52
+1746 MANDUB [4] (H T Jones) 2-9-7 A Murray 4/1: 1312: Ddhtd for 2nd: consistent: see 1746.   57
-1746 LADY PAT [5] (M Mccormack) 2-9-4 S Cauthen 5/2 JT FAV: 4113124: Chased winner over 3f. 39
1803 HEY AMADEUS [3] 2-8-11 S Cauthen 50/1: 020: Upped in class: no threat: see 1803.   24
1629 NAWWAR [2] 2-8-11 B Rouse 9/1: 000: Sn outpcd: btr over 6f in 1629 (gall trk).   22
6 ran   3,ddht,4,2,1½   (Duncan Norvelle)   J Etherington Norton, Yorks

2163 LADY S.WORTLEY SELL.HCAP 3YO 0-25   £832   1m 4f   Good/Firm 23 -33 Slow   [17]

2034 HIGHEST NOTE [5] (G Blum) 3-9-7 R Cochrane 5/4 FAV: 0043241: 3 ch f Music Boy -
Alchorus (Alcide): Finally got off the mark, led 2f out and was sn clear in a 3yo selling
h'cap at Lingfield Aug.16 (bought in 6,100 gns): first success though had been placed in
most starts this term: eff over 10/12f: acts on firm & soft grnd & on any trk.   20
1428 JULTOWN LAD [3] (H Beasley) 3-8-3 R Morse(5) 11/1: 0-20402: No ch with winner: mdn :
stays 12f: acts on gd/firm & soft grnd: see 93.   00
1759 LA CAZADORA [6] (R Williams) 3-9-5 S Cauthen 5/1: -00403: Led ½way till 2f out: see 1759. 06
1666 TESTAROSSA [4] (J Davies) 3-8-6 N Howe 33/1: 0-0004: Rank outsider: no form to date.   00
1607 JOKER MAN [2] 3-9-3 N Adams 6/4: -00: Dropped in class & gambled on: led to ½way, sn
btn: half brother to several winners, incl smart hurdler/chaser Sula Bula: lightly raced &
should do btr than this.   00
2034 NELSONSUPERYANKEE [1] 3-9-2 G French 14/1: 0-00000: Al in rear.   00
6 ran   10,2,6,15,6   (Mrs B Blum)   G Blum Newmarket

2164 LHW H'CAP 3YO+ 0-50   £2763   1m 6f   Good/Firm 23 +03 Fast   [45]

1935 PACTOLUS [8] (G Harwood) 3-9-1 G Starkey 2/1 FAV: 0-01231: 3 b c Lydian - Honey Sand
(Windy Sands): Useful colt: well suited by this lngr trip, led over 1f out for a comfortable
win in an all aged h'cap at Lingfield Aug.16: earlier an easy winner of a Ladies race over
12f here: lightly raced in '85, winning a Salisbury mdn: eff over 10/12f, stays 14f really
well: suited by good or faster grnd & acts on any trk.   55
1709 TRAPEZE ARTIST [1] (N Vigors) 5-9-8 S Dawson 5/1: 2110022: Just held on to 2nd place:
gd effort under top weight: see 917.   46
*2023 CHUCKLESTONE [5] (R Laing) 3-8-0(4ex) N Adams 100/30: 0000413: Never nearer: stays
14f: see 2023.   36
1623 TEMPLE HEIGHTS [4] (J Dunlop) 3-8-9 B Rouse 8/1: -0124: Al prom: gd effort: see 1623.   40
1935 FOR A LARK [9] 4-8-3 T Williams 10/1: -000300: Lngr trip: made most: see 312.   17
1779 MILTON BURN [3] 5-9-2 S Cauthen 6/1: 2232000: No extra 2f out: best in 1150 (stiff 2m) 26
1939 PRINCE SATIRE [7] 3-8-7 P Hutton(7) 10/1: -01040: Btr over 11f in 1939: see 492.   00
--   Italian Sunrise [2] 8-9   263 Marley Roofus [6] 9-1
9 ran   2½,shhd,4,5,4   (Mrs G Harwood)   G Harwood Pulborough, Sussex

2165 LHW FUTURES H'CAP 3YO+ 0-70   £6399   7.5f   Good/Firm 23 +06 Fast   [60]

1911 FUSILIER [3] (C Brittain) 4-7-11(BL) T Williams 10/1: 0000001: 4 b c Habitat -
Formentera (Ribot): Returned to form, led below dist & ran on well to win quite a fast run
h'cap at Lingfield Aug.16: first success: eff over 7/8f: stays 10f: acts on firm & soft grnd
& on any trk : wore blinkers today.   42
1455 VERDANT BOY [6] (M Stoute) 3-9-10 M Giles(7) 4/1: 03-3102: Kept on well under top
weight: fine effort & likes a sharp, undulating trk: see 747.   73
1114 BRAZZAKA [8] (M Jarvis) 3-9-1 R Cochrane 11/2: 1-11233: Tried to make all: gd effort
after fair abs: most consistent filly: see 803 & 575.   62
1788 CRESTA AUCTION [1] (G P Gordon) 3-9-3 S Cauthen 13/2: -112304: Raced alone far side,
prom thro'out: gd effort on this fast ground: see 210.   61
1854 GREAT LEIGHS [4] 3-8-5 B Thomson 14/1: -012000: Prom most: best on soft in 359.   48
+2072 STEADY EDDIE [2] 4-8-7(6ex) A Mcglone 6/1: 0003010: Ran well under his penalty: see 2072. 41
2059 MR JAY ZEE [5] 4-7-12 C Rutter(5) 100/30: 3021020: No threat after slow start: see 1727 00
-1743 EAGLE DESTINY [7] 3-8-1 P Cook 4/1: -02120: Speed over ½way: much btr in 1184.   00
8 ran   2,½,2,nk,½,½,hd   (Ray Richards)   C Brittain Newmarket

2166 BROKERS NURSERY HCAP   £1816   6f   Good/Firm 23 -16 Slow   [52]

+2047 MUKHABBR [3] (C Benstead) 2-7-10(7ex) T Williams 8/15 FAV: 0303111: 2 b c Taufan -
Ribotingo (Petingo): Much impr colt: comfortably completed his hat trick, led below dist &
qcknd clear in a nursery h'cap at Lingfield Aug.16: earlier scored easy all the way wins in
nurseries at Windsor & again at Lingfield: half brother to very useful sprinter Pampas:
very eff over 5/6f & does well with forcing tactics: suited by fast grnd: should extend his
winning sequence.   39
*1798 TOUGH N GENTLE [4] (L Piggott) 2-9-7 R Cochrane 9/4: 3212312: Led before ½way, outpcd
by winner inside dist though yet to fin out of the frame: see 1798.   52
1717 KEEN EDGE [2] (P Mitchell) 2-8-0 A Mcglone 6/1: 2200303: Early ldr: ran on same pace:
best early season: see 678 and 577.   24
2032 LEADING ROLE [1] 2-7-7(1oh) N Adams 33/1: 000104: Al behind: best over 7f in 1684.05
4 ran   3,2,5   (Hamdan Al-Maktoum)   C Benstead Epsom, Surrey

642

Official Going Given As GOOD

2167 CUB SCOUTS MAIDEN STAKES 2YO   £851   5f   Good/Firm 29 -02 Slow

1381 LINGERING [13] (J Winter) 2-8-11 R Hills 6/5 FAV: 241: 2 bf King Of Hush - Beryl's
Jewel (Siliconn): Useful filly: readily made ev yd in a 2yo mdn at Wolverhampton Aug.16:
first time out was just btn by Strathblane at Brighton: half sister to winning sprinter
Woodfold: well suited by fast grnd: very eff over 5f with forcing tactics, stays sharpish 6f:
should find a nursery.   50
2089 BOIS DE BOULOGNE [6] (L Piggott) 2-9-0 T Lucas 13/2: 2030032: Sn prom: not pace
of winner, but is consistent: see 2089, 662.   40
1495 BLAZING HIGH [4] (L Piggott) 2-9-0 B Crossley 12/1: 03: Prom all the way & is making
impr: seems suited by 5f on fast grrnd: see 1495.   40
-- ROCK MACHINE [7] (N Callaghan) 2-9-0 M Miller 14/1: 4: Nearest fin on racecourse debut &
looks certain to impr: cost 21,000 gns as a yearling: should be suited by 6f: acts on gd/firm and
can find a race.   33
1782 HOLTS WAY [8] 2-8-11 D Williams(7) 8/1: 00: Ev ch: needs further? see 1782.   24
1946 ATRAYU [3] 2-8-11 L Jones(5) 7/1: 020: Mkt drifter: btr 1946.   21
1958 Touch Of Speed [5] 9-0   -- Hazel Bee [11] 8-11
2007 Green Glory [2] 9-0(BL)   1801 Dragusa [9] 8-11
-- Charming Gracie [12] 8-11   -- Miss Atwell [10] 8-11
1573 Nancy Nonesuch [1] 8-11
13 ran   3,shhd,3,2,1   (Warren Elñs)   J Winter Newmarket

2168 VENTURE SCOUTS SELLING STAKES 2YO   £1205   7f   Good/Firm 29 -55 Slow

*1905 LATE PROGRESS [5] (J Berry) 2-8-8 J Carroll(7) 7/1: 0033211: 2 ch f On Your Mark -
Trouble Pocket (In The Pocket): Mkt drifter, but made much, ridden out in a 2yo seller at
Wolverhampton Aug.16 (bought in 2,700 gns): impr filly who last time out won a similar event
at Edinburgh: eff at 7f: should stay 1m: acts on gd & fast grnd & a sharp/easy trk.   25
-- ROOF GHOST [12] (A Bailey) 2-8-11 P Bloomfield 6/5 FAV: 2: Gambled on debutant: led
inside final 2f: just btn & 4L clear 3rd: looks certain to find a similar event: eff at 7f
on good/firm.   27
*1944 THE CHIPPENHAM MAN [2] (M Tompkins) 2-8-11 M Rimmer 5/1: 02213: Early ldr, remained prom:
stays 7f: see 1944.   20
2045 KINSHAM DENE [6] (J D Home) 2-8-8 W Newnes 7/1: 034: Prom, ev ch: btr 2045 (6f).   07
1832 DONNA IMMOBILE [10] 2-8-8 L Jones(5) 14/1: 00: Never nearer: see 1832.   02
1684 SOHAMS TAYLOR [9] 2-8-11(VIS) Gay Kelleway(3) 33/1: 000040: Prom, wknd: see 1684.   01
1294 FINLUX DESIGN [7] 2-8-11 S Perks 15/2: 0300: Never nearer 7th: best 1155.   00
1905 Princess Pelham [4] 8-8(bl)   1944 Rant On [1] 8-11(BL)
1181 Willys Niece [8] 8-8   2019 Magnolia Dancer [11] 8-11
11 ran   ½,4,5,3,2   (Mrs J M Berry)   J Berry Cockerham, Lancs

2169 CONI GILBERT & SANKEY H'CAP (0-35)   £2070   2m 1f Good/Firm 29 -13 Slow   [33]

1875 HARLESTONE LAKE [10] (J Dunlop) 4-9-3 W Carson 3/1: 0341401: 4 ro f Riboboy -
January (Sigebert): Led over 1f out, ridden out in a h'cap at Wolverhampton Aug.16: earlier
won a similar event at Lingfield: eff at 2m, stays 2m3f: acts on soft, suited by fast grnd
& a sharpish/easy trk: half sister to smart hurdler Janus.   32
2031 ORANGE HILL [5] (J Tree) 4-8-13(bl) W Newnes 9/4 FAV: -000422: Ran on final 1f:
in gd form: see 2031.   27
2031 MARLION [1] (S Hall) 5-9-3 T Lucas 7/2: 0324133: Led over 2f out: consistent: see 2031. 28
1952 ACTION TIME [3] (B Mcmahon) 5-9-2 J Hillis(5) 12/1: U001034: Ev ch str: stays 2m: see 1952 24
2075 COLLISTO [2] 5-8-7(bl) S Whitworth 11/2: 0002220: Ev ch: btr 2075.   11
2078 STAR SHINER [7] 3-7-7(3oh) M L Thomas 6/1: -000030: Op.10/1: stumbled after 5f: btr 2078. 08
1945 Boca West [6] 7-10   1533 Singers Tryst [4] 10-0
1807 Faraway Lad [8] 8-4   1952 Shirley Grove [9] 7-9
10 ran   1,3,2½,4,2   (J Dunlop)   J Dunlop Arundel, Sussex

2170 PAINS LANE TROPHY STAKES 3YO   £1725   1m 1f Good/Firm 29 +01 Fast

*1953 PSYLLA [7] (H Cecil) 3-9-0 W Ryan 7/4 FAV: -011: 3 b f Beldale Flutter - Pris
(Priamos): Useful filly: comfortable made all in a 3yo stakes at Wolverhampton Aug.16:
earlier this month ran a fillies stakes over this C/D: half sister to the smart miler Prismatic:
very eff over 9f & will stay further: acts on gd/firm grnd & is well suited by forcing tactics:
should win a h'cap.   49
*1981 AITCH N BEE [9] (J Dunlop) 3-9-6 W Carson 5/1: -04012: Kept on well & is in fine
form: stays 9f well: lightly raced & will win more races: see 1981.   51
1912 SARONICOS [3] (C Brittain) 3-8-11 P Robinson 13/2: -322303: Never nearer over this
slightly shorter trip: consistent though remains a mdn: see 739.   40
1954 CAPRICORN BEAU [2] (L Cumani) 3-8-11 Paul Eddery 11/4: -044: Slightly hmpd below dist:
fin well clear of rem: see 1954.   39
1776 SHAMIYDA [4] 3-8-8 J Reid 15/2: 0-03440: Much btr over 10f in 1444.   16

1830 BOLD BORDERER [5] 3-8-11 W Newnes 33/1: 0003300: Below par effort: see 1471.   14
1902 Satin And Silk [10] 8-8   1446 Austina [8] 8-8
1833 Cloud Chaser [6] 8-11   868 Alice Parry [11] 8-8
10 ran   1¼,¾,1,12,2¾   (P F Shoults)   H Cecil Newmarket

2171 J.SAVILLE GORDON H'CAP (0-35) 3YO   £2070   1m   Good/Firm 29 +03 Fast   [32]

2027 IMPERIAL PALACE [11] (C Tinkler) 3-8-9 T Lucas 4/1 JT.FAV: -00021: 3 b g Jaazeiro -
Persian's Glory (Prince Tenderfoot): Led over 2f out for a comfortable win in a 3yo h'cap at
Wolverhampton Aug.16: ex Irish gelding who is well suited by 7/8f: acts on gd/firm grnd &
on a gall trk.: may win again.   27
1761 TOPEKA EXPRESS [15] (R Armstrong) 3-9-1(bl) W Ryan 9/2: 0003202: Another gd effort &
deserves a race: see 1560 & 1281: 7L clear of 3rd today.   27
874 NATIVE HABITAT [3] (M Jarvis) 3-9-6 W Woods(3) 4/1 JT.FAV: -41333: Stayed on well
after long abs: btr for race: see 874 and 169.   20
2027 TABLE TURNING [13] (J Watts) 3-8-11 N Connorton 12/1: -243304: Al up there: see 1813.   10
1835 OUT OF STOCK [1] 3-9-2 W Newnes 16/1: 0-00400: Some late prog: acts on gd/firm: see 140   14
1989 DAWN LOVE [8] 3-9-5 S Perks 11/1: 100-000: Al mid-div: see 1989.   13
1819 FARAG [14] 3-9-7(VIS) Paul Eddery 13/2: 2000320: Made much: wknd into 9th: wore a
visor for the first time today: btr without in 1819.   00
1830 PLEASURE ISLAND [5] 3-8-12 J Reid 9/1: -001000: Speed to halfway: best in 857.   00
1300 LOST OPPORTUNITY [10] 3-8-12(bl) W Carson 10/1: -200040: Never in race: much btr in 99.   00
*2014 NATIVE IMAGE [9] 3-8-5(6ex) G Duffield 8/1: -000010: Fin last: best in 2014 (seller).   00
1942 Son Of Sparkler [7] 9-1   1226 Mabel Alice [6] 8-10
1603 Linavos [12] 9-3   2009 Moel Fammau [2] 9-7
14 ran   1½,7,¾,¾,2   (Mrs C Tinkler)   C Tinkler Malton, Yorks

2172 SWISH PRODUCTS NURSERY H'CAP 2YO   £2070   5f   Good/Firm 29 -01 Slow   [48]

-1893 ECHOING [6] (J Watts) 2-9-7 N Connorton 9/2: 14321: 2 b f Formidable - Siren Sound
(Manado): Useful filly: gamely defied top weight, led below dist & just held on in a nursery
h'cap at Wolverhampton Aug.16: has not been out of the frame since winning a minor race on
her debut at Catterick in May: eff over 5f, should stay 6f: suited by fast grnd & a sharp/
easy trk: genuine & consistent.   51
1938 INFANTA MARIA [2] (N Vigors) 2-8-10 W Carson 7/2 FAV: 02022: Fin well, just held:
in gd form & may get off the mark soon: see 1938.   39
1814 DOMINO ROSE [9] (N Tinkler) 2-8-3 W Newnes 11/2: 2322023: Led over ½way: see 1814.   24
*376 SHADES OF NIGHT [5] (J Winter) 2-8-8 W Ryan 5/1: 2214: Al up there despite long abs:
should come on for this run: see 376.   26
2047 CLARENTIA [3] 2-8-13 M Wigham 9/2: 2140320: Front rank most of way: see 2047.   25
1814 NICHOLAS GEORGE [7] 2-7-9(1ow) A Mackay 16/1: 0100: Best over this C/D in 1434 (seller).   00
1573 MUSICAL BELLS [1] 2-9-3 T Lucas 6/1: 0040: No threat in 7th: see 1573.   00
1717 Tap The Baton [4] 8-9   1938 Pink Pumpkin [10] 7-8(1ow)(4oh)
1760 Miss Shegas [8] 8-5(BL)
10 ran   hd,3,1,2½,4,nk,2½   (C C Campbell Golding)   J Watts Richmond, Yorks

2173 MEASHAM HANDICAP STKS 3YO+ 0-35   £2410   1m 2f   Good 50 -06 Slow   [33]

2093 SOCKS UP [16] (R F Johnson Houghton) 9-8-4 D Price 9/1: -040301: 9 ch g Sharpen Up -
Mrs Moss (Reform): Led dist for a comfortable win in a h'cap at Leicester Aug.18: last
successful in '84, at Chepstow & Redcar: eff around 10/12f: acts on any going & on any trk:
still retains some ability despite his advancing years.   16
1951 EXPLETIVE [8] (M Eckley) 6-8-6(bl) J Reid 9/1: 0430122: Kept on well & remains in
fine form: stays 10f well: suited by a gall trk: see 1689.   14
1747 IM EXCEPTIONAL [15] (R Hollinshead) 4-7-13 A Culhane(7) 50/1: -000-03: Good late prog:
lightly raced gelding who stays 10f well: acts on gd/firm grnd & on a gall trk: see 1747.   06
2037 TREYARNON [1] (S Norton) 4-7-10 J Lowe 50/1: 3300044: Al close up: best in 631 (12f).   03
1909 COMMON FARM [4] 3-8-8 K Darley 20/1: 1000000: Never nearer: btr effort: best in 1122.   24
2037 KAVAKA [19] 4-8-6 L Riggio(7) 16/1: 00012D0: Tried to make all: see 2037.   11
1899 CIGAR [9] 3-9-1 Pat Eddery 9/4 FAV: 0-00000: Fdd into 7th: best over 12f in 1899.   00
1806 RIVER GAMBLER [14] 3-8-3(bl) T Ives 3/1: 00-0020: No real threat: much btr in 1806.   00
1254 Mister Point [18] 9-10   1829 Bwana Kali [2] 9-2
2102 Godlord [10] 8-0(BL)   1998 Tower Fame [5] 7-9   1983 Qualitairess [13] 7-8(vis)
2008 Deerfield Beach [17] 7-10   1503 Welsh Pageantry [12] 8-9
1951 Starmast [11] 9-0   2037 Elarim [3] 8-13   *1719 Bundling Bed [6] 7-10
1038 Evros [7] 9-6
19 ran   1½,¾,shhd,¾,¾,nk   (R F Johnson Houghton)   R F Johnson Houghton Blewbury

2174 REARSBY SELLING STAKES 3YO   £1054   7f   Good 50 -16 Slow

2060 DEPUTY TIM [10] (J Bethell) 3-8-11 S Cauthen 13/8 FAV: 4000021: 3 ch g Crofter -
Kindle (Firestreak): Comfortably justified fav, led inside dist in a 3yo seller at Leicester
Aug.18 (sold 6,250 gns): first success though earlier placed in non-selling company: eff
over 6/8f: acts on gd & firm grnd & on any trk: should win again if kept in this grade.   22
1917 ALEXANJO [7] (A Jarvis) 3-8-8 D Nicholls 12/1: 4000002: Led 2f out, kept on well &
clearly stays 7f: has enough ability to win a seller: see 929.   16
1288 THE STAMP DEALER [16] (G Huffer) 3-8-11 G Sexton 6/1: -00003: Abs: ran on same pace:
eff over 6/7f on gd & fast grnd: seems to act on any trk.   15
1815 LAST JEWEL [15] (C Spares) 3-8-8 N Day 33/1: 00-0004: Al up there, showing first
signs of form: eff over 7f on gd grnd: has been tried in bl.   10
1990 SANDRON [13] 3-8-11 Pat Eddery 15/2: -030300: Kept on late: stays 7f: see 237.   08
1815 STRAIGHT BAT [19] 3-8-11 T Williams 5/1: -20: Front rank most: see 1815 (6f).   05
1990 SAUGHTREES [5] 3-8-8 N Howe 8/1: 0-00300: Made much: btr 1567 (1m).   00
2088 Sunk Island [9] 8-8   1917 Man In The Moon [20] 8-11(bl)
2126 Class Hopper [11] 8-11   -1979 Amplify [3] 8-11
1917 Capistrano Climax [6] 8-11   1959 Pokeree [4] 8-11
2085 Timsolo [17] 8-11   -- Abscilla [1] 8-8   1937 Clap Your Hands [8] 8-8(vis)
726 Eastern Lass [18] 8-8   1953 Leanders Pearl [2] 8-8
2103 Lone Galaxie [12] 8-8(bl)
19 ran   1,1½,1,2½,1½   (P Trant)   J Bethell Chilton, Oxon

2175 LEICESTER TIGERS HANDICAP 3YO+ 0-35   £2547   1m 4f Good 50 +07 Fast   [29]

1160 STORMY PROSPECT [5] (M Jarvis) 3-9-0(VIS) T Lucas 7/1: -3401: 3 b g Hello Gorgeous -
Sea Horse (Sea Bird II): Visored first time & led 3f out, staying on well to win quite a
fast run h'cap at Leicester Aug.18: rated 54 when 3rd to Heighlad at Newmarket in May, though
subsq. disapp & has been gelded: half brother to useful winners Felthorpe Mariner & Footshore:
stays 12f well: acts on gd & firm grnd & seems suited by a stiff trk.   36
282 PENTHOUSE C [1] (G Balding) 5-8-6   J Williams 33/1: -0/0-02: Fin well: gd effort
after lengthy abs: lightly raced gelding: eff over 12f on gd grnd: acts on a gall trk.   12
1909 ICEN [13] (J Parkes) 8-8-11 S Webster 33/1: 0/10003: Ran on same pace: best effort
since his first time out success in 28: seems to act on any trk.   12
2023 BATON MATCH [7] (M Chapman) 6-7-13 L Riggio(7) 20/1: 00-0304: Nearest fin: mdn on
the Flat & has more chance of breaking his duck over hdles: stays 12f well: acts on gd grnd.   00
1806 LE MOULIN [17] 3-8-13 S Whitworth 16/1: 0-00400: Best in 1497 (sharp trk).   19
2042 TURINA [2] 3-7-8 J Lowe 20/1: 0-00300: Stayed on late: best in 1775 (11f).   00
*2098 LONGSTOP [14] 4-9-6(5ex) Pat Eddery 7/3 FAV: 0030010: Al mid-div: btr in 2098 (easier trk)00
2028 WESTRAY [12] 4-8-13 S Perks 10/1: 0404030: Fdd into 8th: only modest form this term.   00
2093 GODS HOPE [9] 4-8-6 T Williams 11/2: 0-00040: Fin 9th: best in 2093 (sharp trk).   00
1935 STANDARD BREAKFAST [4] 4-9-7 R Hills 9/1: 0-00000: Wknd over 2f out: see 474.   00
1964 SENDER [6] 3-9-0 R Carter(5) 9/2: -012020: Best when out in front: see 1964.   00
*2101 DICK KNIGHT [8] 5-8-6(vis)(4ex) A Shoults(5) 7/1: 0200010: Made much: wknd 3f out.   00
1556 Straphanger [3] 8-7   983 Murfax [11] 9-4   998 Standon Mill [10] 7-10
-- Skinny Dipper [15] 7-7(1oh)
16 ran   2,2½,nk,3,½,1½   (K H Fischer)   M Jarvis Newmarket

2176 CAPTAINS EBF STAKES 3YO   £2616   1m 4f Good 50 -22 Slow

*1833 ROUBAYD [3] (R F Johnson Houghton) 3-8-12 J Reid 5/4: -11: 3 b c Exceller -
Ramanouche (Riverman): Useful colt: led dist & comfortably held the odds-on Ambassador in a
3yo stakes at Leicester Aug.18: won a mdn at Bath late last month: half brother to 10f
winner Rasseema: very eff over 12f on gd & firm grnd: on the up grade & should win more races. 58
2061 AMBASSADOR [4] (W O'gorman) 3-8-7 T Ives 4/6 FAV: -22: Tried to make all, kept on well
over this lngr trip: should be winning soon: see 2061.   50
2068 NAUTICA [1] (S Mellor) 3-8-4 M Wigham 28/1: -003: No ch with principals: lightly
raced filly who is a half sister to winning hurdler Intrepida: would appreciate a drop in
class: seems to act on gd & firm grnd.   23
-- MERSEYSPEED [2] (J Parkes) 3-8-4 S Webster 100/1: -4: Sn well behind on racecourse
debut: closely related to several winners, being a full sister to fair stayer Hydrangea.   00
4 ran   ¾,12,15   (H H Aga Khan)   R F Johnson Houghton Blewbury, Oxon

2177 METROPOLE CLAIMING STAKES 2YO   £3162   7f   Good 50 No Time Taken

2032 TRYNOVA [16] (G Pritchard Gordon) 2-8-9 G Duffield 8/1: 02021: 2 gr f Tyrnavos -
Alicia Markova (Habat): Led below dist & held on gamely to win a 2yo claiming stakes at
Leicester Aug.18: half sister to winning juvenile Sauvita: eff over 6/7f on gd & firm grnd:
acts on any trk.   34
1363 MORNING FLOWER [10] (R Williams) 2-9-3 R Cochrane 11/2: 032F2: Just held: gd effort
after a fair abs: seems certain to win a similar race in the near future: see 1363 & 1207 : stays 7f. 41
1738 ALHAYAT [20] (R Boss) 2-8-8 Pat Eddery 9/2: 4433: Consistent filly: stays 7f: see 1501.   28
1993 CASTLE CORNET [4] (R Hannon) 2-8-8 S Webster 7/1: 0004: Ev ch: stays 7f: see 187.   30
2010 LIGHTNING LASER [14] 2-9-0 Gay Kelleway(3) 9/1: 3330100: Never nearer: best in 1907.   30
1883 YOUNG CENTURION [18] 2-8-10(BL) D Mckay 14/1: 00000: Al front rank: btr effort from
this cheaply bought colt: half brother to winning juvenile Mr Panache: acts on good ground and
seems best when up with the pace.   20

1802 **MOUNT VENUS** [9] 2-8-7 R Weaver 11/4 FAV: 040: Fdd into 8th: btr in 1802 (6f).   00

938 **Pearlitic** [5] 8-10	965 **Penny Lover** [12] 8-8	2019 **Frivolous Fancy** [7] 8-7
1598 **Danse Arabe** [6] 9-3	1555 **Glorious Dan** [11] 9-3	-- **Market Spirit** [1] 9-3
-- **Running Money** [8] 9-3	1782 **Joyful Mistress** [2] 9-0	
1599 **Just On Time** [19] 9-0	-- **Mytyme** [13] 8-12	2044 **Miami Lass** [3] 8-8(VIS)
864 **Star Play** [15] 8-8	-- **Ive No Idea** [17] 8-5	
20 ran hd,1½,1,1,2½	(Mrs A P Allen)	G Pritchard Gordon Newmarket

---

2178 **LEICESTER TIGERS CUP NURSERY HANDICAP**   £1940   7f   Good 50 -33 Slow   [42]

1965 **PALEFACE** [1] (L Piggott) 2-9-7 T Ives 4/1 JT FAV: 33221: 2 b c Treboro - Jetador
(Queens Hussar): Consistent juvenile: gamely defied top weight when an all the way winner of
a nursery h'cap at Leicester Aug.18: certainly deserved this win after a succession of
placings: very eff over 6/7f: acts on firm & yld grnd & is well suited by a gall trk:
does well with forcing tactics.   46
2071 **SPOTTER** [5] (W Hern) 2-9-2 W Carson 11/1: 0102: Fin well: gd effort: see 1433.   36
1483 **JOSIE SMITH** [17] (R Holder) 2-8-2 A Proud 33/1: 01003: Al front rank & ran surprisingly
well: stays a gall trk: see 831.   21
1785 **SAY YOU WILL** [2] (P Makin) 2-8-4 T Quinn 20/1: 400404: No extra close home: not btn
that far & ran well over this lngr trip: acts on gd/firm & yld: see 503.   22
2071 **LORD COLLINS** [10] 2-9-7 W R Swinburn 11/2: 40420: Nearest fin: best in 2071.   38
1197 **BADOGLIO** [8] 2-8-9 R Cochrane 16/1: 0400: Never nearer after abs: stays 7f: see 974.   22
*1716 **WIND OF PEACE** [6] 2-9-5 S Cauthen 5/1: 010: Prom to ½way: btr in 1716 (6f).   00
-2035 **EL BE DOUBLEYOU** [4] 2-9-3 Pat Eddery 33/1: 0201420: Pressed winner 4f, wknd: btr in 2035   00
1968 **ROUMELI** [11] 2-8-5 R Hills 9/1: 44230: Early speed: best over 6f here in 722.   00

1717 **Avinasesh** [9] 8-6	2013 **Caerinette** [16] 8-13(bl)	
2032 **Honey Plum** [13] 7-13	2081 **Knocksharry** [12] 8-2	1675 **Mccallun** [3] 8-10
1305 **Faldwyn** [7] 8-6	2010 **Meath Princess** [15] 8-0(VIS)	
*1881 **Swallow Bay** [14] 7-13(7ex)		
17 ran 1½,nk,nk,nk,2,1½,½	(Mrs S Rudolf)	L Piggott Newmarket

Official Going Given As GOOD/FIRM

2179 **NEWHOLME STAKES 2YO C & G**   £1020   6f   Good/Firm 38 -12 Slow

1936 **UNIFORMITY** [1] (M Stoute) 2-8-11 W R Swinburn 6/1: 01: 2 ch c Formidable - Antilla
(Averof): Fast impr colt: made ev yd, ridden out in a 2yo stakes at Windsor Aug.18: first time
out fin 6th to Centauri over this same C/D: cost 44,000 gns as a yearling: dam a 2yo winner:
seems well suited by forcing tactics over a sharpish 6f: acts on gd/firm grnd: further
improvement likely.   50
+1936 **CENTAURI** [3] (B Hills) 2-9-3 B Thomson 5/4 FAV: 12: Well bckd: ran on well under press
& 7L clear 3rd: should be suited by 7f: see 1936.   52
1522 **BIRCHGROVE CENTRAL** [6] (B Palling) 2-8-11 J Williams 33/1: 03: Kept on, though no ch with
first 2: on the up grade: cheaply acquired half brother to 3 winners: should stay further than 6f and
can continue to improve.   31
-- **WONDERFUL WILLIAM** [7] (R Laing) 2-8-11 R Cochrane 16/1: 4: Ch 2f out: impr likely from
this 8,000 gns purchase: quite speedily bred: eff at 6f on gd/firm.   30
1234 **MILLPOND BOY** [2] 2-8-11 J Reid 33/1: 00: Never nearer but is impr: half brother to
3 winners: may stay further than 6f.   29
-2016 **START RITE** [5] 2-8-11 T Ives 11/4: 020: Wk in mkt & ran well below 2016: worth another ch.   26
+2029 **HANSEATIC** [4] 2-9-6 T Quinn 8/1: 00210: Friendless in mkt: ran well below form 2029.   00
1993 **KING RICHARD** [9] 2-8-11 B Rouse 8/1: 30: Early speed: see 1993.   00

-- **Zen West Three** [13] 8-11		513 **Marquee Cafe** [12] 8-11
-- **Born A Star** [8] 8-11	1930 **Dynamic Star** [11] 8-11	
-- **Karabat** [10] 8-11		
13 ran 1½,7,½,½,1½	(Mrs I Phillips)	M Stoute Newmarket

2180 **STRATFIELDSAYE SELLING STAKES 2YO**   £853   5f   Good/Firm 38 -46 Slow

2118 **FLAG BEARER** [8] (M Mccourt) 2-8-11 R Wernham 11/2: 00001: 2 br c Runnett - Royal
aunt (Martinmas): Seemed a fortunate winner of a 2yo seller at Windsor Aug.18 (bought in
3,500 gns): looked held by Lucky Starch when that horse fell approaching final 1f: speedily
bred colt who is eff at 5f, but seems to act on any trk: acts on gd grnd.   26
1949 **SAMS REFRAIN** [6] (D H Jones) 2-8-8 D Williams(7) 16/1: 1D04402: Ran on final 1f:
better effort: see 502.   15
981 **SURVIVAL KIT** [4] (C James) 2-8-8 B Rouse 8/1: 0033: Abs: al up there: best effort
yet: eff at 5f on gd grnd.   14
1832 **AVENMORE STAR** [9] (E Wheeler) 2-8-8 W Newnes 33/1: 00004: Never nearer: no form
previously: acts on gd/firm.   07
2020 **HEDERA HELIX** [5] 2-8-11 B Thomson 6/1: 0220: Mkt drifter: no threat: see 2020.   10
1955 **MUSIC DELIGHT** [13] 2-8-8(vis) Pat Eddery 5/1: 000400: Mkt drifter: twice below 1738.   06
-- **LUCKY STARCH** [2] 2-8-11 G Starkey 10/3 FAV: 0: Well bckd & led till swerved violently
left, hit rails & fell nearing final 1f: unlucky: brother to 3 winning sprinters & seems
quite speedy himself: eff over a sharpish 5f on gd/firm & if his confidence is not badly
effected should win a similar event.   00

1680 GLORY GOLD [1] 2-8-8 W Carson 6/1: 0040030: Early speed: btr 1680.   00
2118 Ystrad Flower [11] 8-8   1434 By The Glen [14] 8-8
1545 Flapper Girl [3] 8-8(BL)   2032 Gillys Comet [7] 8-8
1966 Its Been Rumoured [12] 8-8   -- Pimms Party [10] 8-8
14 ran   2,nk,2½,hd,½   (Intercraft)   M Mccourt Letcombe Regis, Oxon

2181 LOUDWATER NURSERY HANDICAP 2YO   £2721   6f   Good/Firm 38 +12 Fast   [51]

2047 SAMLEON [4] (R Hannon) 2-8-13 W Carson 8/1: 1234031: 2 gr c Kind of Hush - Perlesse
(Bold Lad)(USA): Made ev yd staying on well under press to win fast run nursery h'cap at
Windsor Aug.18: consistent colt who earlier in the season who on soft grnd at Folkestone:
eff at 5f, stays 6f well: acts on gd/firm, likes some give: possibly best making the
running on a sharpish trk.   48
1936 BOLD GARCON [7] (C Nelson) 2-9-7 J Reid 8/1: 0142: Ch final 1f: in gd form: see 1555.   51
1294 SETTER COUNTRY [1] (R Hodges) 2-7-8 N Adams 20/1: 014303: Al there: see 1294, 329.   24
1925 SAXON STAR [3] (J Winter) 2-9-6 W R Swinburn 2/1 FAV: 144434: Well bckd: never nearer:
better 1925 (stiff).   47
2007 NEW MEXICO [6] 2-8-6 B Rouse 5/1: 40020: Nearest fin: stays 6f, but btr 2007 (5f).   29
*1828 DERRING DEE [5] 2-9-0(BL) A Mcglone 11/2: 01010: BI first time: btr without in 1828.   36
1693 GREENS GALLERY [8] 2-8-3 M L Thomas 12/1: 011200: Slow into stride: twice below 1585.   00
1826 THAT CERTAIN SMILE [2] 2-8-6 Pat Eddery 6/1: 3230: Prom much, wknd: much btr 1826 (5f). 00
8 ran   1½,shhd,1½,2,½   (G Howard-Spink)   R Hannon East Everleigh, Wilts

2182 BINFIELD H'CAP 3YO+ FILLIES & MARES   £1959   1m 3f   Good/Firm 38 -74 Slow   [23]

*1970 CURIGA [3] (P Walwyn) 3-9-0(6ex) Paul Eddery 5/1: 00-0411: 3 b f Kris - Parmelia
(Ballymoss): Impr filly: set a slow pace & made ev yd, ridden out in a h'cap at Windsor Aug.18:
last time out won a 3yo h'cap at Brighton: eff at 10f, stays 12f well: acts on gd & fast
grnd & a sharp/easy trk: seems suited by front running.   29
2022 FORGIVING [7] (B Stevens) 4-9-0 W Newnes 16/1: 0403002: Ch 2f out: kept on: btr
effort: stays 12f: see 1188, 838: best on a sharpish trk.   14
1918 TEMPEST TOSSED [6] (R Armstrong) 3-9-3 W Carson 5/1: -040323: Ev ch in str: btr 1918.   24
1830 FORMIDABLE DANCER [1] (J Dunlop) 3-9-3 B Rouse 8/1: 0-00004: Ran on from the rear:
little form since 982, but should impr on this next time: stays 12f.   23
2037 DOMINION PRINCESS [4] 5-8-13 Pat Eddery 7/4 FAV: 3303120: Well bckd: btr 2037 (10f).   07
36   LADY FIREPOWER [9] 4-8-6 R Fox 20/1: 002-000: Long abs & no threat: very lightly
raced on the Flat: placed several times over timber.   00
*1806 STILLOU [8] 3-9-6 G Carter(3) 5/1: 0010010: No show: much btr 1806 (10f).   00
1923 Liberated Girl [5] 8-5   967 Gem Mart [10] 9-7
 -- Kilmington Castle [2] 8-10
10 ran   1½,2,½,hd,10   (Lord Howard de Walden)   P Walwyn Lambourn, Berks

2183 RAYS STAKES 3 & 4YO   £959   1m 2f   Good/Firm 38 -23 Slow

1923 SHIBIL [1] (M Stoute) 3-8-8(BL) W R Swinburn 8/11 FAV: 4432221: 3 b c Shergar -
Hilo Girl (Pago Pago): Tried in bl & finally got his hd in front, led 3f out, ridden out in
a 3 & 4yo stakes at Windsor Aug.18: placed numerous times previously, notably 3rd in the
Italian Derby: eff at 10f, stays 13f: acts on gd & firm grnd & on any trk: seems suited by
the application of blinkers.   55
980 ENSIGNE [8] (H Candy) 3-8-8 W Newnes 5/1: -202: Kept on well after fair abs: will be
suited by 12f: acts on gd/firm grnd & should find a race.   48
1953 NOHOLMINA [3] (O Douieb) 3-8-5 R Machado 12/1: -03: Stays 10f: see 1953.   35
2099 EXCLUSIVE NORTH [5] (R Armstrong) 3-9-0 T Quinn 5/1: 30-0104: There over 7f: well
below 2099 (7f).   24
1301 AIRCRAFTIE [4] 3-8-5 B Thomson 8/1: -03030: Fdd 3f out: btr 1301.   10
1444 KAASIB [7] 3-8-8 B Rouse 33/1: 00-000: No threat: very lightly raced colt who is a
half brother to 4 winners: may do btr over a shorter trip.   01
1831 Kings Rock [6] 9-2   1840 Fruity Orooney [2] 8-8
8 ran   2,6,12,3,7.   (Sheikh Mohammed)   M Stoute Newmarket

2184 MANTON HANDICAP 3YO 0-35   £1941   1m   Good/Firm 38 -03 Slow   [32]

2060 GRANDANGUS [16] (K Ivory) 3-7-13(vis) W Woods(2) 14/1: 0001031: 3 b c Creetown -
Woolcana (Some Hand): In fine form, sn prom & stayed on well to lead inside final 1f in a
3yo h'cap at Windsor Aug.18: earlier won a selling h'cap at Newmarket: eff at 1m, stays 10f
well: acts on gd & fast grnd & on any trk: best when up with the pace in a visor.   12
1399 BATH [8] (J Toller) 3-8-11 P Robinson 9/1: 0-40042: Led over 2f out: caught near fin:
best effort since 436: stays 1m.   23
*2027 FLYING BIDDY [18] (J Hindley) 3-9-8(8ex) M Hills 7/1: 0-30013: Nearest fin & is
in fine form: may stay further than 1m: see 2027.   31
1830 KOOKYS PET [6] (E Eldin) 3-8-10(BL) A Mackay 7/1: -000004: BI first time: prom most:
has been quite lightly raced previously: stays 1m & acts on a sound surface.   14
1695 BE SO BOLD [10] 3-8-11 P Cook 8/1: -000000: Wknd inside final 2f: little form: see 501.   12
1783 HAYWAIN [3] 3-8-10(VIS) B Thomson 14/1: 0-03000: Made much, wknd: btr 1257 (7f): see 874   10
1830 CAFE NOIR [5] 3-9-6 Paul Eddery 7/1: 31-3040: No show in 7th: btr 1830: see 1316.   00

647

2017 COME TO THE BALL [12] 3-9-0 G Starkey 9/2 FAV: 000-030: Again well bckd: fdd 2f out.   00
1609 ON TO GLORY [13] 3-9-4 W R Swinburn 10/1: -00B300: Made no show: best 1199: see 716.   00
1989 Roi De Soleil [4] 8-8   1885 Synthetic [15] 9-7(VIS)
2061 Mr Savvas [7] 9-4   1830 Out Of Harmony [21] 8-13
1695 Delta Rose [17] 8-10(bl)   980 Noras Boy [20] 8-10(BL)
1941 Ikraam [14] 8-6   1824 All A Dream [1] 8-5   1841 Sica Sue [11] 8-1
--   Golden Handcuff [9] 7-13
19 ran   ½,1½,2½,1½,½,2   (K Panayiotou)   K Ivory Radlett, Herts

---

FOLKESTONE   Tuesday August 19th   Righthanded, Sharpish Undulating Track

Official Going Given As GOOD/FIRM

2185 E.B.F. DANES MAIDEN FILLIES STAKES 2YO   £1311   6f   Good 50 -55 Slow

1728 ATTEMPTING [6] (B Hills) 2-8-11 M Hills 10/3: 31: 2 ro f Try My Best - Attanagh
(Dancer's Image): Useful filly: fulfilled the promise of her debut, led below dist & ran on
well to win a 2yo fillies mdn at Folkestone Aug.19: cost 9,000 gns as a yearling & is closely
related to several winners: very eff over 6f & will stay further: acts on gd & firm grnd &
on any trk.   48
1782 LITTLE BOLDER [8] (A Stewart) 2-8-11 M Roberts 6/1: 32: Ran on well under press fin
well clear of rem: on the up grade & will be winning soon: stays 6f well: acts on gd & firm.   46
1108 RIPE CHRISTINA [7] (A Bailey) 2-8-11 P Bloomfield 9/1: 003: Abs: not reach ldrs though
a fair effort & seemed well suited by this extra furlong: acts on gd & firm: see 621.   28
2070 DELPHINIA [5] (J Dunlop) 2-8-11 P Robinson 12/1: 04: Front rank over ½way: see 2070.   26
2080 FINGERS CROSSED [3] 2-8-11 R Hills 50/1: 000: Led till below dist: see 2080.   14
999 LADY LUCINA [9] 2-8-11 N Howe 16/1: 040: Gd speed over ½way: needed race after long
abs & will do btr next time: acts on any trk: see 848.   12
1322 PELF [13] 2-8-11 Paul Eddery 9/4 FAV: 20: Well bckd: prom most, fdd into 7th: btr on
fast ground in 1322.   00
1874 STRATCH [14] 2-8-11 P Cook 5/1: 000: Hmpd ½way, not recover: fin 9th: see 1287.   00
--   Debach Delight [15] 8-11   2043 Able Abbe [12] 8-11 F
--   Bugberry [10] 8-11   --   Carlton Glory [11] 8-11 F
1802 Shoot The Moon [4] 8-11   --   Sunley Projects [2] 8-11
14 ran   ½,7,½,5,½,½,hd   (Mrs J Corbett)   B Hills Lambourn, Berks

2186 WARREN MAIDEN STAKES 3YO   £812   6f   Good 50 -32 Slow

-1995 ZULU KNIGHT [16] (P Walwyn) 3-9-0 Paul Eddery 5/4 FAV: -000021: 3 br g African Sky -
Benicia (Sir Ivor): Well bckd & comfortably made ev yd in a 3yo mdn at Folkestone Aug.19:
showed some useful form last season, notably when "winning" a Sandown mdn, though subs. disq:
eff over 5/6f on gd & fast grnd: acts on any trk: does well with forcing tactics.   42
1607 SYBIL FAWLTY [14] (D Laing) 3-8-11(vis) W Newnes 9/1: 20-0442: Chased winner thro'out:
kept on well & fin 4L clear of rem: eff over 6/7f on firm & hvy grnd: see 656.   34
1927 GRANGE FARM LADY [11] (M Tompkins) 3-8-11 M Rimmer 33/1: -03: Al prom: clearly all
the btr for her recent debut: sister to winning sprinter Grange Farm Lad: eff over 6f on
good ground.   22
923 SHADES OF AUTUMN [15] (M Haynes) 3-8-11 T Williams 33/1: -0004: Abs: no extra dist:
cheaply bought filly who showed her first signs of ability here, though had been keeping
better company.   16
656 COLLYWESTON [10] 3-8-11 G Duffield 16/1: -00: Stayed on from ½way: fair effort
after a lengthy abs: half sister to several winners, incl fair sprinter Red Letter: should
stay 7f: acts on gd grnd.   14
1228 MISS HICKS [12] 3-8-11 P Robinson 25/1: -000: Al mid-div: ½ sister to several winners
in the States though has yet to show any worthwhile form herself: quite speedily bred.   07
1277 AVALON [2] 3-9-0 P Cook 7/1: -0340: Early speed: fin 9th: best over this C/D in 844.   00
1804 RED RIVER BOY [9] 3-9-0 A Dicks(7) 8/1: -002300: Front rank over ½way: btr in 1648.   00
1947 BELLE OF BUDAPEST [5] 3-8-11 G French 13/2: -0030: Soon in rear and much better
over this C/D in 1947.   00
1943 REPORT EM [8] 3-8-11 W Woods(3) 10/1: -00020: Early speed: much btr in 1943 (C/D).   00
842 Last Cry [13] 9-0   1947 Wykehamist [7] 9-0   1942 Royal Berks [6] 9-0
1586 Casa Rosada [4] 8-11   1815 Cascading [1] 8-11
15 ran   1½,4,2½,1,2½,shhd,hd,1   (Mrs Lionel Wigram)   P Walwyn Lambourn, Berks

2187 LEAS SELLING STAKES 3 AND 4YO   £735   1m 2f   Good 50 -10 Slow

2076 KITTY CLARE [2] (P Walwyn) 3-8-3(VIS) Paul Eddery 9/2: 0-00001: 3 ch f Milford -
Sleekit (Blakeney): Dropped in class & was never hdd when a decisive winner of a 3 & 4yo
seller Aug.19 (sold for 3,100 gns):
first success though was placed in a Bath mdn last term: eff over 8/10f & likely to stay
further: acts on firm & soft grnd & seems to have no trk preferences. visored 1st time today.   20

2094 JUST CANDID [6] (D Wilson) 4-9-0 T Williams 15/2: -003342: Never looked likely to
catch this winner though is in gd form: stays 10f: see 1937.   10
1806 COOL NUMBER [10] (J Dunlop) 3-8-3 P Robinson 3/1: 000-003: Took a drop in class:
stayed on too late: see 1806.   04
2073 SOLENT EXPRESS [5] (B Stevens) 3-8-3 C Rutter(3) 16/1: 010-004: Prom 1m: see 2073. 00
1719 MY MYRA [7] 4-8-11 A Mcglone 4/1: 0-00040: Btn below dist: see 1719.   00
*1767 KOUS [9] 3-8-6(bl) W Newnes 5/2 FAV: -103010: Dwelt & never in race: has been hurdling
since his win in 1767.   00
1937 Condover Silk [3] 8-3   --   Chief Runner [1] 9-0
8 ran   5,3,5,1½,2   (Mrs S Cayzer)   P Walwyn Lambourn, Berks

2188 CHERITON HANDICAP STAKES (0-35) 3YO+   £1257   1m 4f   Good 50 +05 Fast   [30]

*1945 JABARABA [5] (L Cottrell) 5-9-2(4ex) T Lang(7) 2/1: 0004111: 5 b g Raja Baba -
Time To Step (Time Tested): In fine form & comfortably completed his hat trick, led below
dist & was pushed out to win quite a fast run h'cap at Folkestone Aug.19: recently successful
over this C/D, after earlier winning at Chepstow: eff over 10/12f: suited by gd or faster
grnd: acts on any trk.   28
1980 SHAHS CHOICE [1] (J Dunlop) 3-8-9 G Duffield 13/8 FAV: 0-04322: Ev ch: in gd form
though remains a mdn: acts on any trk: see 1980.   26
856 JAZAIR [6] (C Horgan) 4-9-7 P Cook 16/1: 0-00003: Clear of rem: gd effort under
top weight after a long abs: see 761.   25
2098 DASHING LIGHT [2] (D Morley) 5-8-13(bl) T Williams 9/2: 0432334: Set a gd pace over
10f: sn btn & btr over this C/D in 2098: see 432.   08
1829 MR GARDINER [4] 4-9-1(BL) J Bray(7) 14/1: -200000: Bl first time: no threat: see 92. 05
1580 HOT TWIST [3] 3-8-5 Paul Eddery 16/1: 0-000: Never dngr: best over 10f in 1580.   00
1652 CORAL HARBOUR [7] 4-9-1(BL) P Robinson 16/1: 00-3000: Bl first time: rear from ½way. 00
7 ran   2,1,6,2½,6   (John Boswell)   L Cottrell Cullompton, Devon

2189 CANTERBURY H'CAP (0-35) 3YO+   £1515   7f   Good 50 +06 Fast   [32]

2046 WAR WAGON [2] (R Armstrong) 3-9-7(bl) P Tulk 12/1: 0000101: 3 gr c Posse - Cadabwah
(Abwah): Gamely defied top weight, making ev yd in quite a fast run all aged h'cap at
Folkestone Aug.19: last month was an all the way winner of a 3yo h'cap at Lingfield: very
eff over 6/7f with forcing tactics: acts on gd & firm grnd & is well suited by a sharp trk:
genuine sort who carries weight well.   40
*1942 GOLDEN BEAU [13] (D Morley) 4-8-12 T Williams 9/2: 0333012: Just failed to peg back
winner: in gd form & runs well on this sharp course: see 1942.   22
2123 APRIL FOOL [15] (L Cottrell) 4-9-6(vis) T Lang(7) 14/1: -040003: Ran on well & seems
to be returning to form: see 1390.   26
1901 BLUE BRILLIANT [1] (B Hills) 3-9-3(bl) M Hills 4/1 FAV: 0002124: In fine form: see 1560. 29
1971 HAUTBOY LADY [14] 5-8-4 P Cook 6/1: 032-030: Btr over 1m in 1971.   07
2046 NAUGHTY NIGHTY [12] 3-7-12 W Woods(2) 33/1: -000000: First signs of ability: bred
to stay beyond sprint dists: acts on gd/firm grnd.   07
*1943 MARCREDEA [8] 3-9-4(5ex) R Wernham 8/1: -002010: Much btr over 6f here in 1943.   00
2091 COUNT BERTRAND [4] 5-8-10 R Morse(5) 8/1: 0002100: Some late prog: best in 1673 (1m). 00
2123 MR ROSE [7] 6-9-1(8ex) P Hutchinson(3) 13/2: 0420100: Never nearer & much btr in 2123. 00
2104 Flying Ziad [9] 8-5   1273 Sharp Shot [5] 9-6   2126 Pommes Chateau [10] 8-13(hd)
907 Miami Blues [11] 8-7   1942 Tagore [3] 8-7(BL)(6ow)
1971 Steel Pass [16] 8-0
15 ran   ½,2,½,1,nk,1,2   (Charles H Wacker III)   R Armstrong Newmarket

2190 RADNOR HANDICAP STAKES (0-35) 3YO+   £1394   1m 2f   Good 50 -19 Slow   [28]

1994 MARSH HARRIER [12] (A Moore) 5-9-7 P Cook 7/2: 0020041: 5 b h Raise A Cup - Belle
De Jour (Speak John): Looked well h'capped & duly led below dist, comfortably in an all
aged h'cap at Folkestone Aug.19: last season won h'caps at Folkestone & Lingfield, & a
Ladies race at Brighton: eff over 10/12f: acts on gd & firm grnd & best on a sharp,
undulating trk: should defy a penalty.   34
1870 MINUS MAN [15] (W Holden) 8-8-0 R Morse(5) 10/1: 0003042: Kept on well under press
& is in fair: stays 10f: see 710.   06
1602 HARBOUR BAZAAR [3] (R Simpson) 6-8-1 N Adams 16/1: 03003D3: Kept on: best in 1602 (1m)00
1733 THE WOODEN HUT [14] (R Voorspuy) 3-7-9 D Brown 33/1: 1200004: Never nearer: best
over 12f on soft grnd here in 29.   02
1733 PAUSE FOR APPLAUSE [4] 3-8-2 W Newnes 33/1: 0-00000: Fin well: stays 10f: see 656.   09
1838 TURMERIC [7] 3-9-0(vis) T Williams 12/1: 0000020: Led ½way, wknd dist: btr 1838 (9f). 17
1401 FIRE ROCKET [6] 3-8-8 M Hills 5/1: -004240: Fdd into 8th: see 997.   00
2022 LORD IT OVER [10] 3-8-12 A Clark 11/4 FAV: -000020: No luck in running btr judged on 2022 00
1787 Dancing Barron [9] 9-3(bl)   2093 Pitkaithly [8] 9-3
2085 Turn Em Back Jack [2] 8-9(bl)   2109 Gregorian Chant [13] 8-4(VIS)
1830 Jaaziel [1] 8-4   1837 Taffys Pride [5] 8-1(bl)
--   Pat On The Back [11] 8-0
15 ran   1½,4,¼,shhd,2,1   (F Hill)   A Moore Woodingdean, Sussex
                                                                                         00

FOLKESTONE   Tuesday August 19th   -Cont'd

2191 E.B.F. DANES MAIDEN FILLIES STAKES 2YO   £1311   6f   Good 50 -20 Slow

1641 KHAKIS LOVE [11] (P Walwyn) 2-8-11 Paul Eddery 9/2: 301: 2 b f Dominion - Fettle
(Relkino): Useful filly: sn in front when scoring an easy win in a 2yo fillies mdn at
Folkestone Aug.19: 70,000 gns purchase as a yearling whose dam was an unrcd half sister to
Circus Plume: very eff over 6f & will stay further: acts on gd & firm grnd & on any trrk:
certain to win more races.   50
-- EXOTIC SOURCE [14] (P Cole) 2-8-11 G Baxter 5/4 FAV: 2: Hvly bckd debutant: chased
winner thro'out, beat rem decisively & looks a certain future winner: half sister to very
useful 8/10f winner Alydar's Best: sure to stay further: acts on gd grnd & on any sharp trk. 42
1996 NO LIE [8] (G Pritchard Gordon) 2-8-11 G Duffield 20/1: 03: Al up there, showing
some impr: will stay further than 6f: acts on gd grnd & on a sharp trk.   28
1440 PINK SWALLOW [13] (D Dale) 2-8-11 G Dickie 33/1: 04: No extra dist: half sister
to 8/10f winner Seven Swallows & will be suited by a lngr trip in time.   24
1930 RANKSTREET [1] 2-8-11 T Williams 33/1: 00: Gd early speed: half sister to very useful
sprinter Frimley Park & 12f winner Firm Foundations.   06
1382 EMMAS WHISPER [10] 2-8-11 A Mcglone 20/1: 000: Abs: prom over ½way: cost 17,000 gns
and is a half sister to 10f winner Beau Fils.   00
1958 PERFUMERIE [7] 2-8-11 M Hills 15/2: 00: Fin 7th: see 1958.   00
1778 PERFECT FOIL [2] 2-8-11 R Hills 15/2: 00: Sn outpcd: btr in 1778 (stiff trk).   00
1716 SHADIYAMA [5] 2-8-11 E Guest(3) 9/2: 020: Btr in 1716 (stiff trk).   00
-- Battle Queen [4] 8-11   852 Spanish Melody [6] 8-11
-- For You And Me [9] 8-11   1433 Kandawgyi [3] 8-11
2069 Tisserands [12] 8-11
14 ran   3,4,1½,6,2,1,4   (Yahya Nasib)   P Walwyn Lambourn, Berks

CURRAGH   Saturday August 16th   Righthand, Galloping Track

Official Going Given As GOOD/YIELDING

2192 TARA SIRES DESMOND STKS GROUP 3   £11550   1m   Good/Yielding -

878 WISE COUNSELLOR (M V O'brien) 3-8-8 Pat Eddery 4/5 FAV: -1201: 3 b c Alleged -
Quarrel (Raise A Native): Smart colt: despite fair abs well bckd & led inside final 2f,
comfortably in a Gr.3 event at the Curragh Aug.16: first time out was an easy winner again
at the Curragh: later unplaced in the Epsom Derby & seems at his best over todays 1m trip:
acts on gd & yld grnd, possibly not firm.   78
1492 MR JOHN (L Browne) 3-8-13 M T Browne 5/1: 4120042: Made much: gd effort: see 1330, 640 76
-- BERMUDA CLASSIC (P Mullins) 3-8-10 S Craine 10/1: 02110-3: Never nearer 3rd: fair
effort: in '85 won 2 Gr.3 events on this trk: stays 1m: acts on gd/firm & yld.   69
2112 ADORAMUS (J Bolger) 3-8-8 K Manning 20/1: -44: Again ran well in gd company: eff
at 1m/10f on gd/yld.   66
2006 KEMAGO 3-8-10 D Hogan 12/1: -1-1030: Ran to her best & seems to stay 1m: see 394.   68
471 FORLAWAY 4-9-3(bl) C Roche 4/1: 2202-30: Long abs: needed race? much btr 471.   62
1492 Kings River 9-8   2006 Poka Poka 9-3   -- Majestic Monarch 8-8
945 Miami Count 9-3(bl)
10 ran   2,2,nk,shhd,2   (S Niarchos)   M V O'brien Ireland

DEAUVILLE   Friday August 15th   Righthand Track

Official Going Given As GOOD

2193 GROUP 2 PRIX DE LA COTE NORMANDE 3YO   £26412   1m 2f   Good -

900 DOUBLE BED (F Doumen) 3-8-9 G Mosse 1: -223441: 3 b c Be My Guest - Claire's Slipper
(Welsh Saint): Smart French colt: gained his first success, led final 1f & sprinted clear in
a Gr.2 event at Deauville Aug.15: consistent colt who seems well suited by 10f on gd grnd:
likely to win more gd races.   80
900 CRYSTAL DE ROCHE (F Boutin) 3-8-9 F Head 1: -030022: Had no answer to the winners
foot: consistent sort.   70
-- LESOTHO (C Head) 3-8-9 C Asmussen 1: -4-1113: Odds on flop: winner of his 3 previous
outings this season, at Deauville & Maison Laffitte (2).   70
1009 MINATZIN (G Bonnaventure) 3-8-9 G Guignard 1: 31-4404: See 289.   65
7 ran   6,shhd,2½   (R Reeves)   F Doumen France

650

Official Going Given As GOOD

2194 PRIX GONTAUT BIRON 4YO+   £17672   1m 2f **Good** -

1010 OVER THE OCEAN (G Mikhalides) 4-8-11 A Badel 1: 1-23301: 4 gr c Super Concorde - Lost Virtue (Cloudy Dawn): Smart, consistent French colt: narrow winner of a Gr.3 event at Deauville Aug.16: has had several near misses since winning the European Free H'cap at Newmarket in '85 when trained by O Douieb: stays 10f well: acts on fast & yld grnd.   80
1389 IADES (F Boutin) 4-9-4 F Head 1: 00-4142: Fine effort & is most consistent: see 1010.   85
1456 BABY TURK (A De Royer Dupre) 4-9-1 C Asmussen 1: 1004323: Not btn far: in fine form.   82
299 SIRIUS SYMBOLI (P L Biancone) 4-8-8 E Legrix 1: 003-04: Lightly rcd this season.   71
-1811 K BATTERY 5-8-11 C Dwyer 1: 1002020: Again ran well: see 1811.   72
1851 PURCHASEPAPERCHASE 4-8-8 P Tulk 1: -010400: Fin 8th: best 708.   64
10 ran ¾,shnk,2   (M Fustok)   G Mikhalides France

Official Going Given As GOOD

2195 GROUP 1 PRIX DU JACQUES LE MAROIS   £65483   1m **Good** -

1715 LIRUNG [12] (H Jentzsch) 4-9-2 S Cauthen 1: 1-12321: 4 ch c Connaught - Liranga (Literat): Very smart German colt: al prom & led ½way, comfortably in Gr.1 Prix Jacques le Marois at Deauville Aug.17: most consistent, first time out winning at Cologne: German 2,000 Guineas winner last season: very eff at 1m/10f, does stay 12f: acts on gd & firm grnd: best up with the pace & is certain to win more good races.   85
2002 REGAL STATE [1] (J Fellows) 3-8-7(1ow) Y Saint Martin 1: 20-4042: Ran on well final 1f, his best effort this season: back to his smart 2yo form: see 288.   82
1877 EFISIO [11] (J Dunlop) 4-9-2 W Carson 1: -041203: Another gd effort: consistent : see 1094.   79
1597 DIRECTING [13] (Y Porzier) 3-8-9 P Johanny 1: 0401134: In grand form: see 1597.   81
2002 LYPHARITA [10] 4-8-13 C Asmussen 1: 4-11420: Not btn far in 5th: gd effort : see 2002.   76
313 VIN DE FRANCE [1] 4-9-2 E Legrix 1: 3140-00: Ran well in 6th: see 313.   78
*1355 BAILLAMONT [7] 4-9-2 F Head 1: 30-3110: No luck in running & beat winner in 1355: unlucky? 00
*900 MAGICAL WONDER [9] 3-8-9 A Badel 1: 4-1110: Fin 8th: abs since 900.   00
*2002 ELLE SEULE [5] 3-8-6 A Lequeux 1: 1013410: Hmpd in running: btr 2002.   00
1118 Apeldoorn [2] 9-2   878 Arokar [3] 8-9   -- Gallop Dyna [6] 9-2
641 Vertige [8] 9-2
13 ran 1,1½,nse,nse,shnk,1,nk   (Gestut Fahrhof)   H Jentzsch Germany

2196 GROUP 3 PRIX DE PSYCHE 3YO FILLIES   £18689   1m 2f **Good** -

-- DARARA (A De Royer Dupre) 3-8-9 Y Saint Martin 1: --121: Smart French filly: 1¾L winner of Gr.3 Prix de Psyche at Deauville Aug.17: lightly raced sort who first time out won at St Cloud: last time btn 1L by Fille Du Nord at Evry: stays 10f well: has scope for further improvement.   76
1932 COCOTTE (W Hern) 3-8-9 W Carson 1: 4-00142: Made much of the running and is in grand form: see 1932, 1580.   72
*904 RELOY (J Pease) 3-9-2 C Asmussen 1: 4-31103: Stiff task at the weights: ran very well indeed: see 904.   77
-- RIVERBRIDE (P L Biancone) 3-8-9 E Legrix 1: 4100000: Best effort since winning at Evry in April.   67
754 GAILY GAILY 3-8-9 M Kinane 1: 41-0010: Recent winner in Ireland: fin 6th , pl. 5th: see 560.   64
2002 RESTIVER 3-8-9 F Head 1: 1-30200: Fin 7th: btr 2002: see 561.   63
1768 SALLY SAYS SO 3-8-9 J Lowe 1: 10-4020: Very stiff task: see 1768, 803.   00
12 ran 1½,¾,1½,¼,1   (S A Aga Khan)   A De Royer Dupre France

---

Official Going Given As GOOD/FIRM

2197 GROUP 1 ARAL POKAL 3YO+   £26554   1m 4f **Good/Firm** -

*1861 ACATENANGO (H Jentzsch) 4-9-7 G Bocskai 1: 11-1111: 4 ch c Surumu - Aggravate (Aggressor): Gained his 11th win in a row with a comfortable success in Gr.1 Aral-Pokal at Gelsenkirchen-Horst Aug.17: likely to extend the sequence even further: see 1861.   80
-- EL SALTO (H Jentzsch) 3-8-8 A Tylicki 1: -2: No ch with this top class wnr but ran well   73
1861 ORFANO (H Jentzsch) 3-8-8 P Alafi 1: 33: --   71
1328 CASSIS (H Bollow) 4-9-7 P Remmert 1: 41-234: --   72
8 ran 1½,1,½   (Gestut Fahrhof)   H Jentzsch Germany

651

Official Going Given As GOOD

2198 EGLINTON NURSERY HCAP 2YO   £4253   7f   Good/Firm 25 -29 Slow   [56]

1129 GULF KING [6] (P Kelleway) 2-9-4 B Rouse 13/2: 02101: 2 ch c King's Lake - Pearl
Star (Gulf Pearl): Useful colt: returned after a 2 month abs, keeping on strongly to gain
the day near the line in a close fin to a rather slowly run nursery h'cap at York Aug.19:
ready winner of a minor race at Goodwood earlier: half brother to 5 winners incl useful
hurdlers Star Burst & Copse And Robbers: eff at 6f, well suited by 7f: will stay at
least 1m: unsuited by very firm grnd but acts on fast going though probably ideally suited
by give in the grnd.   60
*2025 JAYS SPECIAL [12] (M W Easterby) 2-8-1(BL)(6ex) W Carson 9/2 JT FAV: 400012: Waited with, fin
very well & was just btn in a tight fin: in grand form and can win another nursery soon:
see 2025: suited by 7f.   41
*1895 PEN BAL LADY [1] (G P Gordon) 2-9-1(6ex) Abigail Richards(7) 12/1: 12113: Mkt drifter, led
dist till close home: in terrific form & should win more races: see 1895.   55
1984 COLWAY RALLY [5] (J W Watts) 2-8-12 T Ives 8/1: 20324: Prom thro'out: probably stays
7f, best 6f? see 1798.   48
1895 URRAY ON HARRY [14] 2-8-6 S Perks 16/1: 140: Chall 2f out: gd effort: see 1895, 913.   42
1506 GLOW AGAIN [7] 2-9-7 M Wood 9/1: 311120: Found top weight just too much but a
most creditable effort & probably stays 7f: see 1255.   54
2052 GAYS FLUTTER [11] 2-7-9 J Lowe 9/1: 403320: Active in mkt: see 2052 (6f).   00
+2081 FICKLE YOUNG MAN [8] 2-8-6(bl)(6ex) Pat Eddery 9/2 JT FAV: 13010: Made most, fdd
quickly: best 2081 (6f).   00

870 Connaught Flyer [10] 8-4(1ow)		2057 Penang Beauty [13] 8-13	
1566 Bold Difference [4] 7-8		*1735 Toll Bar [9] 9-4	
1675 Fountains Choice [3] 7-12		2019 Fourth Lad [2] 9-6	
14 ran ½,shhd,2,shhd,1½	(Roldvale ltd)	P Kelleway Newmarket	

2199 ACOMB STAKES 2YO   £8714   7f   Good/Firm 25 -26 Slow

*1629 BELLOTTO [6] (J Tree) 2-9-4 Pat Eddery 3/1: 11: 2 b c Mr Prospector - Shelf Talker
(Tartan): Very smart colt in the making: retained his unbtn record with a very impressive
win in valuable Acomb Stakes at York Aug.19: made steady hdway to lead on bit at the dist
& readily forged clear: first time out slaughtered a big field of mdns at Newbury July 19:
reportedly his stable's best 2yo: eff 6f, suited by 7f & sure to stay 1m & further: likes
fast grnd & a gall trk: should not be opposed in his future engagements.   80
1914 MERCE CUNNINGHAM [1] (W Hern) 2-8-11 W Carson 7/2: Al well there, dsptd lead
dist & was unlucky to meet one so smart at this winner: a race awaits him: see 1914.   66
*1812 STILLMAN [2] (M H Easterby) 2-9-4 M Birch 25/1: 0013: Waited with, kept on well and
this was a most creditable effort: sure to win more races.   65
2146 DR BULASCO [7] (S Norton) 2-9-4 J Reid 20/1: 2134: Quick reapp, led over 5f & acquitted
himself well in this high class company: see 1660.   63
*1780 CLASSIC TALE [5] 2-9-4 W R Swinburn 6/5 FAV: 210: Going easily ½way, ridden & btn
3f out and this is clearly not his form: see 1780.   53
*1930 STARTLE [3] 2-9-4 B Thomson 10/1: 10: Prom much: stiff task: see 1930.   44
-- GOMEZ [4] 2-8-11 I Johnson 20/1: 0: Stiff task on debut, no threat: evidently highly
regarded: related to winning sprinters Relatively Sharp and Lady Donna: should be seen to
btr effect in mdn company.   00
7 ran   2,3,½,8,6   (K Abdulla)   J Tree Beckhamptonn, Wilts

2200 GROUP 1 MATCHMAKER INTERNATIONAL   £117018   1m 2f   Good/Firm 25 +27 Fast

-1790 SHARDARI [4] (M Stoute) 4-9-6 W R Swinburn 13/8 FAV: 1-24121: 4 b c Top Ville -
Sharmada (Zeddaan): Top class colt: well served by his pacemaker Dihistan, running in mid-div
till forging on 3f out & won a shade comfortably in very fast run Gr.1 Matchmaker International at York Aug.19: winner of Gr.2 Princess of Wales Stakes at Newmarket July 8 & last
time a superb ½L 2nd to Dancing Brave in the King George at Ascot: winner at Sandown,
Folkestone & Pattern races at Newbury & Ascot in '85, also first past the post in the Great
Voltigeur at York but subs disq: very eff over 12/13f: acts on any going & on any trk.   92
1790 TRIPTYCH [7] (P L Biancone) 4-9-3 J Reid 5/1: -421232: Came from behind to chall final
1f, al held by the winner but clear of rem & she is a remarkably genuine & consistent filly: see 1389 86
641 DAMISTER [1] (J Tree) 4-9-6 Pat Eddery 9/1: 13-3043: Returned after a long abs,
never btr placed: has not recaptured his very best form of '85 but this was an encouraging
run & he appears on the way back: ran poorly in bl on hvy grnd in 641: probably unsuited
by both.   80
2192 MR JOHN [3] (L Browne) 3-8-10 G Starkey 33/1: 1200424: Quick reapp: prom thro'out
and ran right to his best: probably best over 1m/10f: see 640 (heavy).   78
1877 BOLD ARRANGEMENT [8] 3-8-10(bl) T Ives 12/1: 3320040: Never landed a blow & btr 1877.   78
1913 WYLFA [11] 5-9-6 B Rouse 50/1: 224330: Brought over to the stands side to race
alone in the str, fdd final 1f: most consistent: see 1913.   73
1389 BEDTIME [6] 6-9-6 W Carson 12/1: 12/1200: Twice below 1095 which has not worked
out well: see 736.   00
1355 FITNAH [2] 4-9-3 G Moore 7/1: 20-1020: No dngr: see 1010.   00

1790 Dihistan [9] 9-6		1932 Asteroid Field [5] 8-7	
1790 Fioravanti [12] 8-10		*2074 Kadial [10] 8-10	
12 ran ½,6,½,hd,3	(H H Aga Khan)	M Stoute Newmarket	

                                                        00

2201 MELROSE HANDICAP 3YO 0-70   £8636   1m 6f   Good/Firm 25 +03 Fast   [68]

*1757 OSTENSIBLE [10] (G Harwood) 3-8-13 G Starkey 7/1: -300011: 3 b c Alleged - Proud
Pattie (Noble Commander): Very useful, impr colt: waited with, ran on to lead final 1f in
valuable Melrose H'cap at York Aug.19: comfortable winner of a h'cap at Sandown July 24 &
prior to that had acted as pacemaker for Bakharoff: in '85 won a mdn at Leicester on sole
outing: well suited by 12/14f nowadays & likes a gall trk & fast grnd: may well win again.   68
1679 ROSEDALE USA [2] (J Dunlop) 3-9-7 B Thomson 12/1: 2122102: Led 2f out, hdd final
1f: grand effort under top weight: very genuine & consistent: see 1218.   74
1642 LIE IN WAIT [8] (G P Gordon) 3-8-4 W Ryan 20/1: -144133: Came from off the pace, fine
effort & can win again soon in slightly lower grade. : see 1435.   54
1410 BEIJING [9] (P Cole) 3-7-10 A Mackay 12/1: 00-1144: Dsptd lead dist, not btn far
in quite a close fin: likes York: see 1048.   46
1600 SIR PERCY [6] 3-8-12 S Cauthen 12/1: -10030: Waited with, unable to land a blow:
see 253, 1600: seems to stay 14f.   60
-2058 TWICE BOLD [11] 3-8-6 Pat Eddery 7/1: 0342120: Led/dsptd lead most: possibly best
12f: see 1551, 2058.   49
*1873 WHITE REEF [12] 3-8-3 W Carson 4/1 FAV: --3-410: Well bckd, fin 7th: see 1873.   00
*1957 PAST GLORIES [7] 3-7-13(7ex) A Culhane(7) 10/1: 3104210: Prom, wknd into 8th: btr
in 1957 (12f).   00
*1799 ALLATUM [5] 3-7-9 R Fox 8/1: -20410: Prom, wknd into 9th: btr 1799 (2m).   00
*1894 COINAGE [3] 3-8-10(4ex) J Reid 8/1: 2310110: Prom, wknd: btr 1894 (2m).   00
*1304 DIVINE DESTINY [1] 3-8-0 B Rouse 8/1: 0-410: Led 10f: abs since btr 1304.   00
2028 Husnah [4] 8-4   2053 Abadjero [13] 7-8
13 ran   ¾,1½,hd,1,3   (K Abdulla)   G Harwood Pulborough, Sussex

2202 GROUP 1 YORKSHIRE OAKS 3YO FILLIES   £42672   1m 4f   Good/Firm 25 +14 Fast

1592 UNTOLD [9] (M Stoute) 3-9-0 G Starkey 5/1: 111-231: 3 ch f Final Straw - Unsuspected
(Above Suspicion): Very smart filly: returned to her best, coming from off the pace to
gamely gain the day final 150yds in a close fin to fast run Gr.1 Yorkshire Oaks Aug.19:
btn only 1L on seasonal debut in the Oaks by Midway Lady & well below her best at the
Curragh last time: winner of her last 3 on the trot in '85 at Yarmouth, Sandown (course
record) & Gr.3 Hoover Fillies Mile at Ascot (course record): half sister to the very useful
Shoot Clear & Sally Brown: suited by 12f now: acts on firm grnd unsuited by soft.   86
*1932 PARK EXPRESS [6] (J Bolger) 3-9-0 J Reid 9/2: 042D112: Prom, went on 3f out till
hdd inside final 1f: another grand effort from this much impr, most genuine filly: see 1932.   85
1116 IVORS IMAGE [2] (M Stoute) 3-9-0 S Cauthen 16/1: 01-4143: Stable companion of
winner, came from well off the pace & was btn only just over 1L at the line: tremendous
effort from this impr filly & she should be winning again soon: see 642.   84
*1592 COLORSPIN [7] (M Stoute) 3-9-0 W R Swinburn 9/4 FAV: 11-3414: Came cruising up to
chall 3f out, btn in a matter of strides & this cannot be her form: see 1592 (good).   78
1592 FLEUR ROYALE [8] 3-9-0 C Roche 9/1: -0120: Prom, ev ch: best 1331.   75
755 QUEEN HELEN [1] 3-9-0 W Carson 12/1: 21-00: Long abs, no extra final 3f: should do
btr next time with this outing behind her: see 755.   67
*1128 GULL NOOK [3] 3-9-0 Pat Eddery 100/30: -110: Heavily bckd despite abs, waited with
and never in it: see 1128.   00
926 Rejuvenate [5] 9-0   1128 Gesedeh [11] 9-0   2000 Three Times A Lady [10] 9-0
*1170 Spun Gold [4] 9-0
11 ran   ¾,½,4,1½,8   (Sheikh Mohammed)   M Stoute Newmarket

2203 LONSDALE STAKES 3YO+   £7492   2m   Good/Firm 25 -02 Slow

*360 VALUABLE WITNESS [6] (J Tree) 6-9-6 Pat Eddery 8/11 FAV: 1111-11: 3 b g Val De L'Orne-
Friendly Witness (Northern Dancer): Very smart stayer: returned after a long abs to come
from behind and easily win Lonsdale (Listed) Stakes at York Aug.19: first time out, gained
a hard earned win in Gr.3 Sagaro Stakes at Ascot: unbtn in 4 races in '85 at Sandown,
Haydock, Royal Ascot & Gr.2 Goodwood Cup: eff at 14f, stays extreme dists well: seldom risked
on firm grnd nowadays & is at his best with give under foot: does well when fresh and
is a credit to his trainer.   76
1326 MAJESTICIAN [2] (G P Gordon) 3-8-0 W Ryan 33/1: -002122: Made most, no ch with
winner but a fine effort in this company: runs well here: this was impr form & he can win
a h'cap soon if reproducing it: see 1029.   62
1593 LEMHILL [4] (M Blanshard) 4-9-4 R Cochrane 6/1: 2-13443: Chall 2f out, rather hmpd
by the winner which may have cost him 2nd place: stays 2m well: see 251.   67
2157 SPICY STORY [1] (I Balding) 5-9-4 S Cauthen 9/2: -303204: Quick reapp, below his
best here & was rated 79 in 1127 (2½m).   62
--   BRIGHTNER [3] 5-8-13 G Starkey 16/1: 01110/0: Steadily fdd str. on first outing since
Oct '84: that season was rated 66 after winning at Bath (2) & Edinburgh: acts on firm & gd
grnd & is eff over 11/13f: should strip much fitter next time.   42
1779 DESTROYER [5] 5-9-4 S Whitworth 7/1: 1300-40: Prom much, wknd quickly: see 1779.   27
6 ran   2½,¾,½,5,10,20.   (S Niarchos)   J Tree Beckhampton, Wilts

2204 HAREWOOD HANDICAP 3YO+ 0-60   £5423   6f   Good/Firm 25 +13 Fast   [57]

2021 GREEN RUBY [1] (G Balding) 5-9-4 J Williams 6/1: -033141: 5 br h Shecky Greene -
Ruby Tuesday (T V Lark): Very useful sprinter: prom & led final 100 yds in a close fin to
a fast run valuable h'cap at York Aug.19: recent winner of the Stewards Cup H'cap at Goodwood:
in '85 won at Pontefract: very eff over 6f, stays 7f: acts on hvy but is best on firm or gd.   60

228 CARELESS WHISPER [4] (I Matthews) 3-7-12 G Carter(3) 33/1: 010-302: Al prom, dsptd
lead final 1f, just btn: tremendous effort after very long abs: should be difficult to
beat next time in a similar race: see 168.   44
1922 ROPER ROW [2] (M W Easterby) 3-7-7 J Lowe 15/2: 0-01133: Nicely bckd, led/dsptd lead
thro'out, just went down in a close fin: in grand form: see 1627.   37
1900 BATON BOY [7] (M Brittain) 5-7-12 K Darley 20/1: 2000404: Dsptd lead from dist in
a tight fin: see 55.   35
1810 BOOT POLISH [10] 4-8-11 N Connorton 11/2: -100130: Kept on well under press: running well. 47
+1810 MATOU [8] 6-9-10 W Ryan 7/1: 4202D10: Never closer: much btr 1810 (good).   48
*1777 CREE BAY [6] 7-9-3(bl) W Carson 5/1 FAV: 2004110: Fin 8th: much btr 1777 (stiff trk). 00
2065 True Nora [3] 8-13(bl)   1852 Throne Of Glory [9] 8-0
-2124 Karens Star [5] 7-7(4oh)   2079 Tobermory Boy [13] 8-5
2065 Rambling River [12] 8-7(vis)(1ow)   2033 Rosie Dickins [15] 7-7(3oh)
2084 Lochonica [11] 9-6   2084 Debbie Do [14] 8-1
15 ran   ½,¾,hd,nk,6   (Mrs Ernest Weinstein)   G Balding Fyfield, Hants

---

LINGFIELD   Wednesday August 20th   Lefthand, Sharpish, Undulating Track

Official Going Given As GOOD/FIRM

2205 E.B.F. FINDON STAKES 2YO   £1612   6f   Good/Firm 38 -33 Slow

2056 ABLE SAINT [5] (R Armstrong) 2-8-11 P Tulk 10/11 FAV: 21: 2 ro c Welsh Saint -
Magnanimous (Runnymede): Useful, impr colt: hvly bckd & led over 1f out, readily in a stakes
at Lingfield Aug.20: first time out was a promising 2nd to Macrobian at Newmarket: quite
cheaply bought colt who is related to several winners: well suited by 6f & should stay
further: acts on fast grnd & on any trk: further impr likely.   54
1936 MUAD DIB [1] (R Akehurst) 2-8-11 A Clark 5/2: 2302: Made much till swamped for
foot by the winner: runs well here & should find a small race: see 1629.   40
-- IRISH SAILOR [4] (Pat Mitchell) 2-8-11 P Bradwell 50/1: 3: Al up there on racecourse
debut, showing promise: cost I.R. 10,000 as a yearling: is a half brother to 3 winners,
incl useful Irish hurdler Yankee's Princess: stays 6f: acts on gd/firm & a sharpish trk. 37
962 SINJAAB [8] (M Albina) 2-8-11 A Bond 4/1: 34: Prom most after abs: stays 6f: see 962. 36
2025 CAPITAL FLOW [2] 2-8-11(BL) B Rouse 16/1: 04300: Bl first time: seems best on a
sharpish trk: see 1555, 834.   31
-- ZANUSSI LINE [9] 2-8-11 P Wallace 50/1: 0: No real threat on debut: cost 15,000 gns:
half brother to 5f winner Young Angel but is bred to stay much further.   29
-- The Grifter [7] 8-11   -- Say You [10] 8-11   2159 Daunting Prospect [6] 8-11
9 ran   4,½,nk,1½,½,1,½   (Dr Cornel Li)   R Armstrong Newmarket

2206 UPHAM STAKES 3YO+   £2519   1m 4f   Good/Firm 38 +17 Fast

2064 LEADING STAR [1] (I Balding) 4-9-0 A Clark 3/1: -430241: 4 b c Homing - Christchurch
(So Blessed): Smart colt: led after 1m, staying on well under press to win fast run stakes
event at Lingfield Aug.20: last season won at Newbury & in '84 won again on that trk:
eff at 10f, stays 12f well: acts on firm & soft grnd & on any trk, but likes Newbury.   70
*1702 OZOPULMIN [3] (L Cumani) 3-8-7 R Guest 9/4 FAV: -10-12: Led 1m: stays 12f & is in
good form: see 1702.   69
1913 NORFOLK SONATA [6] (R Boss) 3-8-3 N Adams 33/1: -300003: Hdway from rear in the str
and kept on well: best effort this season & has seemed difficult to place: stays 12f well: see 191. 65
1853 DANISHGAR [8] (M Stoute) 3-8-10 B Rouse 6/1: -041204: Ev ch in str: gd effort: see 739. 70
654 WINDS OF LIGHT [5] 3-8-7 R Fox 5/1: 1-0100: Prom most after abs: see 435.   65
*2122 WASSL REEF [7] 3-8-7 A Murray 6/1: -231010: Prom, ev ch: not disgraced: see 2122. 60
654 KOLGONG HEIGHTS [2] 3-8-3 B Crossley 10/1: 00-0200: Never threatened after abs: best 597 00
7 ran   2½,shhd,1,¾,2½,12   (The Queen)   I Balding Kingsclere, Hants

2207 ARUNDEL HANDICAP STAKES (0-50) 3YO+   £2725   7f   Good/Firm 38 -11 Slow   [49]

2072 SAILORS SONG [6] (N Vigors) 4-9-7 S Dawson 14/1: 0000001: 4 ch g Song - Balgreggan
(Hallex): Led nearing final 1f, holding on under press in a blanket fin to a h'cap at
Lingfield Aug.20: had been below his best previously this season: in '85 was most consistent,
winning at Pontefract: eff at 6/7f: acts on gd & firm grnd & may prefer a turning trk.   52
1852 BERTIE WOOSTER [9] (L Piggott) 3-8-11(bl) B Crossley 4/1: 0002202: Not much room
over 1f out: just btn: gd effort & seems best over 6/7f: see 1654, 1457.   48
2123 GOLDEN SLADE [7] (M Mccourt) 4-8-6 R Wernham 9/1: 0133003: Hmpd appr. final 1f &
just btn: unlucky? runs really well at Lingfield & Brighton: see 1189, 762.   36
2033 LUCKY STARKIST [2] (R Holder) 4-7-9 R Teague(1) 20/1: 3140004: Al prom & not btn
far: stays 7f: see 1213.   24
1805 AL AMEAD [8] 6-9-10 B Rouse 7/2 FAV: 0404140: Made much: btn 1L: see 1347 (6f).   52
+1804 BOWL OVER [1] 3-8-11(bl) A Murray 9/2: 1032410: Not btn far in close fin: see 1804. 45
2165 STEADY EDDIE [5] 4-9-4(6ex) R Guest 13/2: 0030100: Not clear run nearing final 1f: see 2072.00
1804 LYRIC WAY [10] 4-8-2(BL) A Clark 10/1: 0001000: Fin 9th: best 1211: tried in blnkers today. 00
1228 Raja Moulana [11] 8-12   -- Friends For Ever [4] 7-7(2oh)
10 ran   nk,shhd,nk,nk,½,1   (Introgroup Holdings Ltd)   N Vigors Upper Lambourn, Berks

2208 SIDEWALK APP. SELLING H'CAP (0-25)   £873 1m 2f   Good/Firm 38 -33 Slow   [15]

*2094 GRAND CELEBRATION [3] (R Simpson) 4-9-4(5ex) G Landau 1/1 FAV: 0400011: 4 ch c Monteverdi ⊄
Blackfly (Mount Marcy): In gd form, hvly bckd & gained the day close home, under press in an
app selling h'cap at Lingfield Aug 20 (no bid): last time out won a selling h'cap at
Folkestone: eff around 10f on a sharpish/undulating trk: likes fast grnd.   15
2094 BLAIRS WINNIE [2] (Pat Mitchell) 4-8-4 R Teague 33/1: 0000002: Led 3 out till caught
close home: 10L clear 3rd: much impr effort compared to 2094: see 201.   00
-- TROJAN GOD [8] (R Akehurst) 4-9-7 P Mcentee 10/1: -0000-3: Ev ch str: lightly raced
and little form last season: stays 10f: acts on gd/firm & a sharpish trk.   00
2073 SHEER CLASS [5] (J Long) 3-8-1(VIS) J Stenning(5) 50/1: -000004: Led 7f, ran wide: see 2073. 00
1264 TODA FORCA AVANTI [4] 4-9-1 I Jupp(5) 4/1: 2D00000: Abs: no form since 262.   00
-- ESS JAY ESS [7] 3-8-4 S Whitelam(5) 16/1: 0000-0: Ev ch on seasonal debut: lightly
raced & little form in '85.   00
*2077 ANGIES VIDEO [1] 4-9-10(5ex) A Dicks 11/2: 3203210: Prom much: well below 2077.   00
2073 GEORGIAN ROSE [6] 3-8-3(vis) G Mash 11/2: 0000020: Hmpd early on: see 2073.   00
8 ran   ½,10,½,2,12,12   (T Stafford)   R Simpson Epsom, Surrey

2209 PULBOROUGH NURSERY H'CAP 2YO   £1997 7f   Good/Firm 38 -20 Slow   [49]

1746 MENDIP STAR [1] (R Holder) 2-7-7(BL)(3oh) S Dawson 25/1: 4041: 3 ch c Sparkler -
sa Fille (Mon Fils): Outsider, but seemed much impr by the application of bl, making ev yd,
driven out in a nursery h'cap at Lingfield Aug.20: seems well suited by 7f, forcing tactics
& a sharpish trk: acts on gd/firm.   24
1965 WISE TIMES [5] (M Usher): 2-8-11 M Wigham 11/4: 002232: Prom, ev ch: twice below 1891 (6f) 39
434 STRIKE RATE [4] (R Hannon) 2-9-7 B Rouse 5/1: 123: Abs: nearest fin: stays 7f: see 180. 48
*1920 INSHIRAH [2] (H T Jones) 2-9-1(5ex) A Murray 6/5 FAV: 1014: Well bckd: ev ch & btr 1920. 41
2071 CASTLE HEIGHTS [6] 2-8-12 P Tulk 7/1: 03030: No extra final 3f: btr 2071 (C/D).   28
1518 TREVA [3] 2-8-6 B Crossley 25/1: 0400: Sn outpcd: flattered 1239?   00
6 ran   1,½,½,5,12   (Mrs B M L Davis)   R Holder Portbury, Avon

2210 LEWES MAIDEN FILLIES STAKES 3YO   £959 5f   Good/Firm 38 -06 Slow

1151 GLIKIAA MOU [4] (R Boss) 3-8-11 N Adams 10/3: -242001: 3 b f Young Generation -
Snow Chief (Tribal Chief): At last opened her account, making ev yd, driven out in a 3yo
fillies mdn at Lingfield Aug.20: has had several near misses previously: in '85 was a nk 2nd
to the Queen Mary winner Gwydion: eff at 5/6f on firm or soft grnd: seems best forcing the
pace & likes a sharpish trk: goes well when fresh.   32
1516 GRISETTE [7] (P Walwyn) 3-8-11(bl) N Howe 12/1: 30-0002: Al prom & kept on under
press: eff at 5/6f on gd/firm & soft grnd.   28
1399 ASTARTE [12] (G Pritchard Gordon) 3-8-11 A Murray 12/1: 0-40003: Kept on well final
1f, but best 205 (soft).   25
-- ZIADS ALIBY [1] (M Albina) 3-8-11 A Bond 12/1: -4: Ran on well on racecourse debut
& should impr much next time: dam a winning sprinter & is quite speedily bred.   22
2046 CRESTA LEAP [2] 3-8-11 S Dawson 8/1: 3024000: Lightly raced since best 431(6f).   21
1947 MARIES VALENTINE [3] 3-8-11 R Wernham 25/1: 4-00000: Lightly raced filly: see 835.   17
2143 SOLO SINGER [5] 3-8-11 A Clark 2/1 FAV: -040200: Disapp 7th: better 1516(6f): see 431.   00
1516 WINSONG MELODY [6] 3-8-11(bl) B Rouse 7/1: -4400: Never went pace: lightly rcd since 835 00
2106 FOUNDRY FLYER [11] 3-8-11(bl) J Carr(7) 8/1: -04040: Made no show: btr 2106.   00
2088 Jacqui Joy [10] 8-11(vis)   2088 Private Sue [8] 8-11
1516 Kingsfold Flame [9] 8-11   1943 Thai Sky [13] 8-11(bl)
13 ran   1,1,1,hd,1½,½   (Mrs Andry Muinos)   R Boss Newmarket

---

Official Going Given As GOOD/FIRM

2211 BOTTOM BROTHERS H'CAP (LADIES)(0-35)   £1324 1m 6f   Firm 05 -52 Slow   [18]

2111 QUICK REACTION [2] (M Ryan) 3-8-12 Celia Radband(3) 6/1: 0-00021: 3 b c Main Reef -
Swift Response (No Argument): Nicely bckd & led 3f out, ridden out in a Ladies h'cap at
Yarmouth Aug.20: impr of late & has been fairly lightly raced: half brother to several
winners: eff at 14f, stays 2m well: acts on gd & fast grnd.   22
1963 HERRADURA [6] (M Prescott) 5-11-0(vis) Maxine Juster 7/2: 2302D32: Ran on well final
2f but never looked likely to reach winner: see 1349.   37
*2048 NEWQUAY [4] (G Harwood) 3-10-11(4ex) Amanda Harwood 3/1 FAV: 3-02213: Ev ch in str:
in gd form: see 2048.   42
1923 SPARKLIN PERFORMER [5] (B Sanders) 3-8-7 Tina Pile 14/1: 00-004: Al prom, showing best
form to date: stays 14f & acts on fast grnd.   07
1652 HYOKIN [3] 4-9-13(vis) Melanie Morley(3) 7/2: 0321320: Came too late: btr 1652 (12f).   14
2087 HIGHAM GREY [9] 10-9-0 Lynne Robson(3) 14/1: 0400440: Led 4f out: see 675.   00
1963 TAXIADS [10] 4-10-7 Jane Allison 8/1: 1100300: No threat: best 984 (12f).   00
1589 Moodybint [8] 8-12   1744 Generation Gap [7] 9-1
1833 Windy Hollow [1] 9-4
10 ran   1½,2,1½,½,2   (T P Ramsden)   M Ryan Newmarket

2212 PLEASURE BEACH SELLING STAKES 2YO   £640   5f   Firm 05 -47 Slow

2138 NIGHTDRESS [2] (D Morley) 2-8-8(BL) G Duffield 7/2: 00301: 2 ch f Pyjama Hunt -
Coppice (Pardao): Made much, staying on well to win slow run 2yo seller at Yarmouth Aug.20
(bought in 2,500 gns): cheaply acquired filly who is a half sister to several winners: eff
at 5/6f, may not stay 7f: likes fast grnd: improved by blinkers today.   18
2150 CAUSEWAY FOOT [4] (N Tinkler) 2-8-11 A Murray 5/1: 0000042: Led inside final 2f, just
caught: in gd form: see 2150.   20
1741 PEGGYS TREASURE [5] (M Brittain) 2-8-8 M Wigham 4/1: 0034433: Sn prom: best 957.   05
1997 NATIONS ROSE [1] (R Stubbs) 2-8-8 A Mercer 10/1: 04: Never nearer: eff at 5f on firm.   02
1723 GREENSWARD BOY [3] 2-8-11 W Woods(3) 11/4 FAV: 0030: Prom, wknd: btr 1723 (C/D).   00
2045 ABSALOUTE HEAVEN [6] 2-8-8 D Nicholls 7/1: 0102000: Al under press: best 1168.   00
1844 GAME LIGHT [7] 2-8-8(BL) W Wharton 12/1: 00000: Bl first time: prom early.   00
7 ran   nk,4,½,1½,7   (J Carroll)   D Morley Newmarket

2213 LONGSHORE HANDICAP (0-35)   £2060   7f   Firm 05 +08 Fast   [33]

1942 HOPEFUL KATIE [6] (D Leslie) 4-9-1 J Williams 12/1: 2030301: Mkt drifter, but led
final 1f, comfortably in a h'cap at Yarmouth Aug.20: placed several times previously this
season: in '85 was in gd form, winning at Yarmouth, Folkestone & Ripon: eff at 6f, stays
7f well: acts on firm & soft ground.   31
1691 POINTED LADY [2] (R Armstrong) 3-9-3 R Hills 12/1: -00042: Not pace of winner: still
impr & stays 7f: see 1691.   30
2033 EUCHARIS [3] (A Hide) 4-8-7(bl) W Woods(3) 13/2: 0002403: Al up there: gd effort: see 1727 12
*2143 EASY LINE [12] (P Haslam) 3-9-7 G French 9/2 FAV: -10014: Led most stands side: in
good form: stays 7f: see 2143.   32
1423 HENRYS VENTURE [4] 4-9-2 A Proud 8/1: 0001130: Made most far side: stays 7f: see 1338.   14
2033 SHAHREEN [15] 5-8-1 M L Thomas 5/1: -000300: Prom most: see 1849 (5f).   00
*2104 KAMARESS [9] 4-9-5(6ex) P Robinson 8/1: 4004310: Early speed: btr 2104.   00
2126 POKERFAYES [16] 7-8-12(bl) G Duffield 5/1: 0002040: Never beyond mid-div: best 1761.   00
2014 Balkan [8] 8-0   1880 Norcool [10] 8-1(bl)   2033 Ideoligia [14] 8-0(bl)
1999 Our Remedy [13] 7-13(bl)   1676 Tang Dancer [5] 9-4
217 Low Key [11] 9-4   658 Humble Beauty [1] 9-5
15 ran   4,½,½,3,1½,2½   (M A Cawthorne)   D Leslie Billesdon, Leics

2214 FRANK STONE E.B.F. STAKES 3YO   £3173   6f   Firm 05 +28 Fast

691 PILOT JET [6] (R Williams) 3-8-12 P Robinson 5/6 FAV: 41-341: 3 ch c Hot Spark -
Captive Flower (Manacle): Very useful colt: despite fair abs, well bckd & led close home
under press in a fast run 3yo stakes at Yarmouth Aug.20: has been lightly raced: in '85 was
a ready winner of a Newmarket mdn: half brother to several winners: eff at 6/7f on firm &
yld grnd: should be straighter for this run & can win more races.   64
227 ALKAASEH [4] (H T Jones) 3-8-12 R Hills 7/2: 210-42: Very long abs: led inside
final 2f, just caught: gd effort & should find another race: see 227.   62
2155 GREEN DOLLAR [5] (B Gubby) 3-8-11(bl) R Curant 8/1: -003003: Led over 4f: see 401.   50
1885 RAFFLES VIRGINIA [2] (B Mcmahon) 3-8-4 G Duffield 25/1: -402004: Early speed: stiff task.
: see 1885.   30
1933 FLYAWAY BRIDE [1] 3-8-9(BL) J Matthias 9/2: -002000: Speed over ½way: best in 732
but has failed to regain her 2yo form: see 59: tried in blinkers today.   20
1073 THE ROMFORD ROAR [3] 3-8-7 D Nicholls 200/1: -00: Rank outsider: impossible task.   00
6 ran   ½,3,4,5,15   (Tedwood Bloodstock Ltd)   R Williams Newmarket

2215 HALL QUAY MAIDEN FILLIES STAKES 2YO   £964   7f   Firm 05 -13 Slow

944 ECHO VALLEY [7] (C Brittain) 2-8-11 P Robinson 16/1: 41: 2 b f Good Times - Singing
Witch (Sing Sing): Impr filly: despite fair abs, led 1½f out, ridden out in a 2yo fillies
mdn at Yarmouth Aug.20: full sister to the very useful 2yo, but subs. disapp My Ton Ton: stays
7f well & should get 1m: acts on fast grnd.   52
1855 FOLLIES BERGERES [2] (M Dickinson) 2-8-11 G Duffield 3/1 FAV: 32: Chall final 1f:
will be suited by 1m & is sure to win soon: see 1855.   50
-- SAINTE JOIE [6] (L Piggott) 2-8-11 M Fozzard 11/1: 3: Bckd at long odds on racecourse
debut: good late hdway: French bred filly who seems certain to impr & find a race soon:
should be suited by 1m: acts on fast grnd.   49
2013 MISTS OF AVALON [12] (H Cecil) 2-8-11 N Day 7/1: 424: Made most: consistent: see 2013.   48
1996 NABRAS [8] 2-8-11 R Hills 9/1: 330: Al up there: gd effort & stays 7f: see 1996, 818.   46
1464 HUNT BALL [13] 2-8-11 J Matthias 6/1: 00: Ch over 1f out: not btn far in close fin:
should be suited by 1m: see 1464.   44
-- IVORY FIELDS [5] 2-8-11 A Kimberley 7/1: 0: Prom 4f on debut: cost $820,000 & is
bred to stay middle dists: will impr.   00
1752 MISK EL KHASHAB [9] 2-8-11 R Street 7/1: 20: Mkt drifter & well below form 1752.   00
1996 Iliona [15] 8-11 7th   1996 Speedbird [11] 8-11 8th -- Sportin Honors [1] 8-11
-- Lizzy Hare [3] 8-11   1287 Esta Bonita [10] 8-11   -- Approaching Star [4] 8-11
1464 Moment In The Sun [14] 8-11
15 ran   ½,½,½,½,1,hd,1   (Mrs P Lemos)   C Brittain Newmarket

2216 EVE MAIDEN STAKES 3YO   £1315   1m   Firm 05 -10 Slow

1425 NO RESTRAINT [7] (W Hastings Bass) 3-8-11 Dale Gibson 6/1: -0431: 3 b f Habitat - Censorship (Prince John): Impr filly: led final 1f, drawing clear in a 3yo app. mdn at Yarmouth Aug.20: lightly raced sort who stays 1m well and may get further: acts on gd & fast grnd.   40

1991 SURE LANDING [4] (C Nelson) 3-9-0 C Rosier(5) 6/1: 4203402: Led ½way: see 1991, 937.   33

1431 PRAIRIE OYSTER [2] (B Hanbury) 3-9-0 A J Geran 8/1: -03: Dsptd lead: kept on & is fast impr: dam a winner over 10f: eff at 1m on fast grnd.   32

2017 GRIMESGILL [10] (J Hindley) 3-8-11 Alison Harper 12/1: -00444: Ev ch over 1f out: see 1540   21

--   HOROWITZ [3] 3-9-0 S Quane 5/4 FAV: 02-0: Uneasy fav on seasonal debut: prom most: must have needed this outing: on final start in '85 split Allez Milord & On Tenderhooks in a mnd at Newmarket: half brother to useful filly Mary Davies: should leave this form well behind.   18

1998 ROBIS [1] 3-8-11 J Scally 25/1: 4000200: Led over 3f: impossible task: see 1256, 24.   08

907 ENTOURAGE [8] 3-8-11 M Giles 6/1: 4-00: Abs: no threat: see 907.   00

--   Dancer Do [5] 8-11   **1880 Mr Adviser** [9] 9-0(BL)

2099 Mubah [6] 9-0

10 ran   4,hd,4,3,3   (G Strawbridge)   W Hastings Bass Newmarket

2217 COBHOLM FILLIES' H'CAP (0-35) 3YO+   £1710   1m 3f   Firm 05 -13 Slow   [25]

1909 WHILE IT LASTS [6] (L Cumani) 3-9-8 P Hamblett 10/1: -333231: 3 ch f Foolish Pleasure- Prom Date (Arts And Letters): Gained a deserved success, led final 1f, pushed out in a fillies h'cap at Yarmouth Aug.20: most consistent this season, yet to fin out of the first 3: eff at 10/11f & should get 12f: acts on yld, seems suited by gd & fast grrnd: should go close again next time.   40

2015 GONE OVERBOARD [10] (A Stewart) 3-9-8 R Carter(5) 14/1: -04002: Made most: gd effort and seems suited by forcing tactics: runs well here: acts on gd & fast grnd.   35

1820 CARVERY [3] (A Hide) 3-8-12 W Woods(3) 8/1: 0-0233D: Fin 3rd, but rider failed to weigh in and was disq & placed last: stays 11f: see 1657.   24

1755 HIGHLAND BALL [2] (G Wragg) 3-9-7 G Duffield 8/1: 00-0043: Held when hmpd nearing final 1f: fin 4th, placed 3rd: fair effort: see 575.   32

1909 GREENHILLS GIRL [4] 3-8-3(vis) P Robinson 13/2: 1-00024: Chased ldr, fdd over 2f out: fin 5th, placed 4th: btr 1909 (sharper trk).   03

•1657 SHEER LUCK [11] 3-9-7 J Matthias 7/4 FAV: 04-0010: Well bckd: faded str: btr 1657(10f).   19

2182 TEMPEST TOSSED [1] 3-9-1 P Struthers(4) 10/1: 0403230: Never looked likely: too soon after 2182?   00

•1870 TIP TAP [7] 4-9-10 L Riggio(7) 12/1: 3-00010: Never showed: well below 1870 (1m).   00

•2163 Highest Note [8] 8-6   **2109 Adhari** [5] 8-8   **2008 Boldera** [9] 8-7

11 ran   2,nk,nk,7,1½,shhd   (Alan Clore)   L Cumani Newmarket

---

Official Going Given As GOOD

2218 ROUS SELLING STAKES 2YO   £5680   6f   Firm 13 -25 Slow

--   DERWENT VALLEY [19] (J Hanson) 2-8-11 J Brown(5) 25/1: 1: 2 gr c Frimley Park - Rykneld (Warpath): Easy to back on racecourse debut though impr to lead inside dist, comfortably in a 2yo seller at York Aug.20 (sold for 6,600 gns): speedily bred colt who is clearly well suited by 6f: acts on fast grnd & on a gall trk: can only improve.   35

2081 SANDS OF TIME [13] (R Simpson) 2-8-11 S Whitworth 10/1: 41032: Led/dsptd lead thro'out, no extra close home though a fine effort: acts on any trk: see 1672.   31

1984 BURCROFT [11] (R Whitaker) 2-8-11 K Bradshaw(5) 10/1: 003: Fin well: on the up grade & certain to find a rader in the near future: eff over 6f, should stay 7f: see 1762.   28

2108 WOODMAN WEAVER [8] (J Douglas Home) 2-8-11 W Newnes 7/1: 0004: Dropped in class: made most: no extra close home though not btn far: sure to find a race if kept in this grade: see 2108.   28

1522 ROYAL RABBLE [12] 2-8-8 S Cauthen 13/2 JT FAV: 4231000: Ev ch: gd effort: best in 1059.   23

61   WINDMEDE [5] 2-8-11 K Darley 10/1: 230: Dropped in class after long abs: al prom & certain to come on for this race: stays 6f: acts on firm & soft: see 34.   16

2050 RUSTIC EYES [15] 2-8-11 B Mcgiff(7) 20/1: 2300: Mkt drifter: never nearer 7th: see 1764.   16

2080 COROFIN LASS [9] 2-8-8 M Birch 14/1: 0000: Took a drop in class & prom till dist: fdd into 8th: cheaply bought filly who is a half sister to several winners: eff over 6f on fast ground.   10

1261 BLUSHER [3] 2-8-8 W Carson 10/1: 00: Abs: fin 9th: see 1261.   06

2071 LADY SUNDAY SPORT [2] 2-8-8 Pat Eddery 13/2 JT FAV: 402300: Gd early pace: best over this C/D in 1528.   00

2097 Swift Purchase [18] 8-11(bl)   **1975 Lack Of Pearls** [1] 8-8

2007 Stumble [7] 8-11   **2016 Barnby Don** [14] 8-11   **1762 Princegate** [6] 8-11

1528 Church Star [21] 8-8(BL)   **2127 Starch Brook** [17] 8-8

1660 Royal Illusion [20] 8-11   **2056 Spanish Galleon** [18] 8-11(BL)

612 Broom Star [10] 8-11

20 ran   1,1,shhd,¾,5,nk,1½,2   (J Hanson)   J Hanson Sicklinghall, Yorks

2219 ANDY CAPP HANDICAP 0-70   £8974   1m 1f   Firm 13 +06 Fast   [61]

1702 MY GENERATION [17] (W Hastings Bass) 3-8-13 W R Swinburn 12/1: 301-31: 3 ch c Young Generation - High Finale (High Line): Smart colt: broke the course record, led dist & ran on strongly to win valuable Andy Capp H'cap at York Aug.20: lightly raced this term, showed plenty of promise when winning at Newmarket on his final start in '85: brother to the very useful filly Que Sympatica: very eff over 9/10f: well suited by fast grnd & acts on any trk.   70

1600 MTOTO [1] (A Stewart) 3-9-7 M Roberts 8/1: 3-21022: Led below dist, kept on well when hdd: fine effort under top weight against older horses: genuine & consistent: see 1098.   73

*2121 SAMHAAN [12] (B Hanbury) 4-8-1(bl)(5ex) Paul Eddery 12/1: 3011213: Ran on well: in grand form & should win again soon if eased slightly in class: see 2121.   42

1931 PATO [10] (I Matthews) 4-8-4 G Carter(3) 25/1: -000404: In gd form: see 511.   41

1931 RANA PRATAP [14] 6-8-9 P Waldron 8/1: 3320420: Hmpd below dist, going on fin: in gd form though has not won for sometime: see 1931.   44

1931 SULTAN MOHAMED [8] 3-9-3 T Ives 14/1: -121300: Nearest fin: gd effort: see 1462.   60

*2132 ALL FAIR [7] 5-8-1(bl) T Williams 7/1: 0000210: Set a strong pace: fdd into 7th: see 2132.   00

1912 NAVARZATO [16] 3-9-6 R Cochrane 14/1: 11-200: Picked up ground from below dist: fin 8th though surely would have been closer with a btr run: stays 9f well: see 1147.   00

1047 ACCLAIMATION [6] 5-7-13 A Mackay 10/1: -124200: Trouble in running & never seen with a ch: btr than this: see 1047.   00

*1776 SATISFACTION [11] 3-8-9 W Carson 10/1: -220010: Much btr over 10f in 1776 though the form of that race is looking decidedly suspect.   00

*1350 MYTENS [4] 3-8-12 Pat Eddery 7/2 FAV: 3-110: Hvly bckd: said to be unsuited by the fast pace, met trouble in running & never beyond mid-div: certainly deserves another ch.   00

1931 Atoka [3] 8-0   2066 Shellman [9] 7-9(bl)   879 Tabardar [15] 9-0
1507 My Ton Ton [13] 7-12   1987 Russell Creek [2] 7-9   1698 Windpipe [5] 8-6
17 ran   2,½,2,1½,nk   (Michael Doyle Riordan)   W Hastings Bass Newmarket

2220 TOTE EBOR HANDICAP 0-75   £42860   1m 6f   Firm 13 +11 Fast   [59]

*1837 PRIMARY [2] (G Harwood) 3-8-7 G Starkey 6/1: 01-4411: 3 b c Green Dancer - Tertiary (Vaguely Noble): Smart colt: landed a massive ante-post gamble, took command over 3f out & ran on strongly for a comfortable win in valuable & fast run Tote Ebor h'cap at York Aug.20: highly regarded though showed signs of a wayward temperament before hacking up in a h'cap at Bath last month: lightly raced last season, winning a backend mdn· at Lingfield: very eff over middle dists & seems sure to stay 2m: suited by fast grnd & a gall trk: should now make his presence felt in Group company.   67

*1530 CHAUVE SOURIS [4] (G Wragg) 3-9-3 Paul Eddery 16/1: 0-02012: No ch with this well h'capped winner though kept on doggedly & ran a fine race: stays 14f well: clearly likes this gall trk: see 1530.   69

-1538 DAARKOM [15] (A Stewart) 3-8-11 M Roberts 20/1: -22123: Ran on well: has been in tremendous form this season & should get his head in front again soon: stays 14f: see 1290.   62

1779 NEWSELLS PARK [10] (J Winter) 5-9-1 K Darley 25/1: -212224: Out and out stayer who was putting in his best work at the death: commendably consistent this term & a credit to his trainer: see 1470.   52

*1809 HIGH TENSION [1] 4-8-8 W Ryan 10/1: 2412210: Ran his usual consistent race: see 1809.   45

1409 RUSSIAN NOBLE [13] 5-9-0 W R Swinburn 14/1: 02-2230: Held up to get this lngr trip, made gd late prog: stays 14f: see 976.   50

1484 KUDZ [9] 3-9-1 S Cauthen 14/1: -211120: Never nearer 7th: gd effort: see 1342.   61

1293 SAFE RIVER [17] 4-9-0 R Cochrane 16/1: -440130: Late prog into 8th: needs further.   48

*1663 DUAL VENTURE [14] 4-9-1(4ex) J Reid 25/1: -220310: Creditable 9th: see 1663.   48

*1879 JUST DAVID [20] 3-8-6(4ex) W Carson 25/1: -1210: Al mid-div: see 1879.   51

*1935 ISLAND SET [5] 4-9-0(4ex) T Ives 16/1: 1-02210: Al about same pace: see 1935.   45

+1679 WHITE MILL [19] 4-7-11(7ex) T Williams 5/1 FAV: 0-03110: Hvly bckd though never got into the race & fin in rear: much btr in 1679 & deserves another ch.   00

2164 Milton Burn [6] 8-4   *1856 Lundylux [8] 9-10(7ex)
+2058 Five Farthings [22] 9-6(7ex)   1679 Special Vintage [18] 8-13
1988 Badarbak [7] 9-5(BL)   1633 Ladys Bridge [12] 8-7   1112 Stately Form [13] 9-10
1509 Romiosini [16] 8-5   1779 King Of Comedy [21] 8-5
1988 Commander Robert [3] 8-5
22 ran   4,½,2,hd,nk,1½,shhd,nk,nk,½   (K Abdulla)   G Harwood Pulborough, Sussex

2221 GRP 2 SCOTTISH EQUITABLE GIMCRACK STKS 2YO £33318 6f   Firm 13 +04 Fast

2113 WIGANTHORPE [2] (M W Easterby) 2-9-0(BL) W Carson 9/2: 0111141: 2 ch c Thatching - Lustrine (Vice Regal): Smart, much impr colt: bl for the first time & was al prom, led final 1f & held on under driving to win Gr.2 Gimcrack Stakes at York Aug.20: earlier completed a 4 timer at Chester, Haydock, Newcastle (walk over) & Beverley: last time out was an excellent 4th to Minstrella in Gr.1 Phoenix Stakes at Phoenix Park: stays 6f really wcll & will get further: acts on yld, loves fast grnd: seems suited by bl, but is extremely tough and will win more good races.   75

*1467 MANSOOJ [7] (N Callaghan) 2-9-3 R Cochrane 9/1: 31012: Made hdway from the rear to chall final 1f & btn the minimum dist: excellent effort, giving the winner 3lbs: genuine colt who will win more gd races: see 1467.   77

+1697 CHIME TIME [4] (C Tinkler) 2-9-0 M Birch 7/1: 112113: Prom, led over 1f out, no
extra final 1f but ran extremely well: in grand form this season & has yet to run a bad race.   70
*1606 MOREWOODS [9] (I Balding) 2-9-0 Pat Eddery 100/30 FAV: 114: Never got in the race
despite attracting strong support: worth another ch: see 1606.   60
+1916 JUST A FLUTTER [3] 2-9-0 T Ives 9/2: 110: Never nearer after being taken off his
feet early on: will be suited by 7f: see 1916.   58
1887 AMIGO SUCIO [1] 2-9-0(VIS) S Whitworth 12/1: 11330: Set fast pace over 4f: btr 1887, 1097   54
+1876 RICH CHARLIE [10] 2-9-5 J Reid 9/2: 0110: Wknd after ½way & this was not his form:
worth another ch: see 1876.   00

*1826 Baltic Shore [5] 9-0   *1925 Crofters Cline [6] 9-0
1920 Wensleydalewarrior [8] 9-0   2029 Song N Jest [11] 9-0
11 ran   shhd,1½,4,½,1½   (R E Sangster)   M W Easterby Sheriff Hutton, Yorks

2222 GR 2 GREAT VOLTIGEUR STAKES 3YO   £33706   1m 4f Firm 13 -13 Slow
*1913 NISNAS [5] (P Cole) 3-8-7 T Quinn 6/1: 1310311: 3 ch c Tap On Wood - Suemette
(Danseur): Very smart colt: al prom & led 2f out, staying on gamely in a thrilling fin to
Gr.2 Great Voltigeur Stakes at York Aug.20: tremendously consistent, earlier winning the
Alycidon Stakes (Listed race) at Goodwood & minor races at Lingfield & Kempton (first time
out): also a fine 5th in the Derby & an unlucky 3rd to Bonhomie at Royal Ascot: stays 12f
really well & will be suited by the Leger trip: acts on firm & yld grnd & on any trk:
genuine & consistent & must run well in the final Classic.   83
1330 MASHKOUR [4] (H Cecil) 3-8-7 S Cauthen 7/2: -311342: Chall final 1f & narrowly btn: fine
effort and the extra 2f of the Leger trip will be well in his favour: see 878, 510.   83
+1661 MOON MADNESS [2] (J Dunlop) 3-8-7 Pat Eddery 7/2: -111113: Took a step up in class
here, but ran on most gamely final 1f & btn 2 hds: lost nothing in defeat & remains on
course for the Leger: see 1661.   82
+2064 WASSL TOUCH [3] (W Hern) 3-8-7 W Carson 12/1: 1-01014: Ch inside final 2f: in
grand form & is a much impr performer: equally eff at 10/12f: see 2064.   81
+1853 ALLEZ MILORD [1] 3-8-7 G Starkey 5/2 FAV: 1-11010: Chall over 1f out after not the
best of runs: not btn far: see 1853.   81
2064 CONQUERING HERO [7] 3-8-7(VIS) W R Swinburn 16/1: 3-11030: Vis. 1st time: see 2064.   76
--   AUTHAAL [6] 3-8-7 C Roche 13/2: -110: Led 10f: Irish colt who had won both his previous
starts at Leopardstown & Phoenix Park: acts on firm & soft.   00
7 ran   hd,hd,1½,shhd,5,hd   (Fahd Salman)   P Cole Whatcombe, Oxon

2223 ROSES STAKES LISTED RACE 2YO   £7895   5f   Firm 13 -04 Slow
1876 CAROLS TREASURE [2] (B Hills) 2-9-2 B Thomson 15/8 FAV: 2111031: 2 b c Balidar -
Really Sharp (Sharpen Up): Smart, most consistent colt: ridden to lead final 1f in a Listed
race at York Aug.20: earlier completed a hat trick at Royal Ascot, Goodwood & Doncaster:
sprint bred colt who is very eff at 5f, though does stay 6f (3rd to Rich Charlie in Gr.2
Richmond Stakes at Goodwood): acts on fast & yld grnd & on any trk: has a fine turn of foot
and has not stopped winning yet.   73
1925 BAG ORHYTHM [4] (J Hindley) 2-8-11 M Hills 5/1: 2122: Nicely bckd & was al to the
fore: in grand form & seems equally eff over 5/6f: should win again soon: see 1082, 1925.   65
1876 WHIPPET [1] (C Brittain) 2-8-11 S Cauthen 11/1: 120003: Dsptd lead all the way
& was not btn far: another gd effort & is probably at his best over todays trip: see 1876, 577   64
1754 QUEL ESPRIT [8] (M Mccormack) 2-8-11 Pat Eddery 5/1: 1130224:Prom, kept on well: see 1591.   60
2158 DREAM LAUNCH [3] (G Baxter) 2-8-11 P Cook 13/2: 012140: Quick reapp: front
rank till gave best final 1f: consistent: see 2158, 1527.   57
1893 JOE SUGDEN [5] 2-8-11 D Mckeown 25/1: 030140: Stiff task: not disgraced: see 1762.   42
*1754 BORN TO RACE [7] 2-8-11 R Cochrane 11/2: 01210: No show in 7th: much btr 1754.   00
1850 Nutwood Lil [9] 8-8   --   Fox Path [6] 8-8
9 ran   ½,hd,1½,hd,6   (Mrs C lane)   B Hills Lambourn

2224 WYKEHAM HANDICAP 3YO 0-60   £3824   5f   Firm 13 +16 Fast   [60]
1852 MANTON DAN [4] (N Vigors) 3-9-1 P Cook 6/1: 2-20101: 3 b c Tower Walk - Balgreggan
(Hallez): Very useful colt: led 1½f out, readily by 4L in fast run 3yo h'cap at York Aug.20:
earlier a winner of a 3yo stakes at Nottingham: winning 2yo at Goodwood: half brother to
several winners incl useful sprinters Street Market & Sailors Song: very eff at 5/6f:
acts on firm & soft grnd & on any trk: has a fine turn of foot.   67
+1878 RESPECT [5] (R Laing) 3-9-7 Pat Eddery 10/30 FAV: 1310412: Hdway on bit 1f out:
most consistent, but does not find much when let down: see 1878.   60
1151 RESTORE [9] (G Lewis) 3-8-1 P Waldron 11/2: 23-203: Al up there: fair effort
after 4m: may be btr over 6f: see 593.   32
1718 LOCH FORM [3] (C Tinkler) 3-7-7(1oh) L Charnock 20/1: 2003204: Made much: fair
effort: see 1543, 255.   23
1878 MUMMYS SECRET [1] 3-8-8(bl) S Cauthen 5/1: 00-3030: Prom, ev ch: much btr 1878 (shrp trk). 34
1664 PANNANICH WELLS [8] 3-7-12 W Carson 7/1: 0210430: Never nearer: see 671 (6f).   20
2079 TAX ROY [10] 3-8-8 S Perks 6/1: 0100220: Ran fast 3f: btr 2079.   00
1896 IBERIAN START [11] 3-8-10 R Cochrane 8/1: -210320: Speed early on: btr 1896 (shrp trk).   00
2018 Mayor [6] 7-10   1986 Manton Mark [2] 8-5(7ex)
2106 Websters Feast [7] 7-7(bl)(2oh)   2055 Gods Isle [12] 7-13(bl)
12 ran   4,2½,nk,1½,1½   (G B Tuck)   N Vigors Upper Lambourn, Berks

2225 WELLINGTON PIER MAIDEN STAKES 2YO   £964   7f   Good/Firm 32 -21 Slow

2105 FALLING LEAF [17] (M Prescott) 2-9-0 G Duffield 20/1: 01: 2 b c Auction Ring -
Autumn Flush (Rustam): Impr colt: ran on strongly from rear to lead inside dist in a 2yo mdn
at Yarmouth Aug.21: cost 32,000 gns as a yearling & is closely related to several winners:
well suited by 7f & sure to stay at least 1m: acts on gd/firm grnd & on an easy course.   45

-- TROJAN SONG [4] (W Hern) 2-9-0 N Day 13/2: 2: Prom debut: al front rank & kept on
well: half brother to several winners, incl very useful middle dist filly Sing Softly: sure
to be suited by lngr trips next season: acts on gd/firm grnd.   40

1914 RED HERO [19] (M Jarvis) 2-9-0 T Lucas 25/1: 003: Al up there: best effort to date
& should continue to impr: eff over 7f on gd/firm grnd.   38

1573 ALCATRAZ [3] (M Ryan) 2-9-0 M Giles 33/1: 04: Made most far side: on the up grade:
acts on gd/firm grnd: see 1573.   37

-- KALGOORLIE [9] 2-9-0 T Ives 9/2: 0: Active in mkt on debut: al prom & will come on
for this experience: well bred colt who fetched 105,000 gns & is a half brother to a couple
of winners: should stay further than 7f: acts on gd/firm grnnd.   35

-- KRIBENSIS [15] 2-9-0 A Kimberley 6/1: 0: Switched below dist, never nearer: prom
run by this 125,000 gns son of Henbit: half brother to useful sprinter Cooliney Prince & a
couple of middle dist winners: acts on gd/firm: seems sure to impr.   34

-- MUGATH [1] 2-9-0 M Roberts 10/1: 0: Active in mkt on debut: kept on well to fin 7th:
fetched $275,000 as a yearling: should stay at least 1m: acts on gd/firm.   33

2051 WOODPECKER [16] 2-9-0(BL) A Murray 10/3 FAV: 20: Fitted with bl & well bckd:
made most of the running, wknd into 8th: btr over this trip in 2051.   30

2001 NILOJEN [14] 2-9-0 G Carter(3) 10/1: 40: Gd speed over ½way: btr over this C/D in 2001.   00

777 GOOD POINT [7] 2-9-0 M Hills 11/2: 020: Early speed: needed race: abs since 777 (6f).   00

-- Select Company [18] 9-0   2105 Alloush [20] 9-0

404 Calibogue [5] 9-0   -- Cuvee Charlie [13] 9-0   -- Regal Raider [2] 9-0

2108 Dollar Seeker [11] 9-0   2019 Tropical Boy [6] 9-0

1452 Alaskan [10] 9-0   612 Squiggle [12] 9-0

1984 Juma Monty [8] 9-0

20 ran   1½,½,nk,1,½,shhd,1,nk   (B Haggas)   M Prescott Newmarket

2226 YARMOUTH INDUSTRIAL H'CAP (0-35) 3YO+   £1780   1m 2f   Good/Firm 32 +09 Fast   [34]

•2062 POWER BENDER [7] (G Pritchard Gordon) 4-9-13(5ex) A Murray 2/1 FAV: -430111: 4 b g Prince
Tenderfoot - Spadilla (Javelot): In tremendous form, made smooth prog to lead inside final
1f, readily in a fast run h'cap at Yarmouth Aug.21: earlier won successive h'caps at Newmarket: eff over 1m though seems best over 10f: suited by fast grnd: acts on any trk:
carries weight well : may extend his sequence.   44+

1636 AL ZUMURRUD [6] (R Armstrong) 3-9-4 P Tulk 11/1: 1221242: Sn in front: no extra close
home though ran her usual consistent race: acts on any trk: see 1185.   38

•1974 GIBBERISH [3] (M Prescott) 3-8-4(bl)(5ex) G Duffield 13/2: 2041213: Stayed on well
under press & remains in gd form: see 1974.   22

•2109 REGENCY SQUARE [1] (P Feilden) 3-7-7(5ex)(4oh) A Mackay 8/1: 3204414: Late prog: see 210910   24

1792 SITTING BULL [4] 4-9-8 M Hills 6/1: 0-04200: Al in mid-div: btr over this C/D in 101.   03

2154 BRECKLAND LADY [10] 4-8-5 W Woods(3) 9/1: 0-03120: Best over 9f in 1951.

1581 Marsoom [8] 7-11   1468 Farm Club [5] 9-3   1299 Mr Kewmill [2] 8-5

1951 Sahraan [9] 9-2   •1964 Brave And Bold [11] 8-4(bl)(5ex)

11 ran   1½,1,hd,2½,2,1½,½   (Addison Tool Co Ltd)   G Pritchard Gordon Newmarket

2227 LES DENNIS NURSERY H'CAP 2YO   £2425   7f   Good/Firm 32 -14 Slow   [48]

2137 SNO SURPRISE [7] (R Boss) 2-8-5 R Cochrane 14/1: 400201: 2 ch c Tina's Pet -
My Portavia (Porto Bello): Well suited by this extra furlong, stayed on really well to
lead close home in a nursery h'cap at Yarmouth Aug.21: quite speedily bred colt though
relished this lngr trip & seems certain to stay at least 1m: acts on gd & firm grnd &
on any trk.   36

-2090 TIMESWITCH [3] (W O'gorman) 2-8-11 T Ives 6/4 FAV: 20022: Hvly bckd: led below dist,
caught near fin: stays 7f & certainly deserves a race: see 2090 & 531.   40

1105 LAST STAND [5] (J Hindley) 2-8-7 M Hills 7/2: 0033: No extra dist: clear of rem: see 1105.   31

2035 OCONNELL STREET [8] (M Tompkins) 2-8-1 W Woods(3) 16/1: 0004404: Front rank most:
best over this C/D in 1598.   13

1846 ORIENTAL JADE [4] 2-8-1(bl)(1ow) G Duffield 9/1: 04130: Wknd 2f out: btr over this
C/D in 1846.   10

2081 FOURWALK [2] 2-8-9 W Wharton 7/1: 4100320: Tried to make all: btr 2081 (6f): see 1397.   12

2035 HOMING IN [6] 2-9-7 G Carter(3) 6/1: 0421400: Btn 2f out, eased: much btr in 1925 (6f)   00

7 ran   1,2,6,1½,3   (Mrs Judi Gold)   R Boss Newmarket

2228 JOHN BECKETT MAIDEN STAKES 3YO+   £828   1m 6f   Good/Firm 32 +03 Fast

1954 TAMATOUR [3] (M Stoute) 3-8-7 A Kimberley 1/1 FAV: -021: 3 b c Caro - Taduska
(Daring Display): Hvly bckd & went on 2f out when a comfortable winner of quite a fast run
mdn at Yarmouth Aug.21: eff over 10f, stayed this lngr trip well: acts on gd & firm grnd
on a sharp/easy course: should continue to impr.   44½

1833 GUESSING [2] (G Harwood) 3-8-7 A Clark 5/2: -002: Led ½way, stayed on same pace &
well suited by this lngr trip: acts on gd & firm: stays 14f well: lightly raced & should
impr further.   42

2000 PARSONS CHILD [5] (L Cumani) 3-8-4 P Hamblett 7/1: -00243: Kept on well & not btn far: well clear of rem: see 1873 & 581. 38
2000 TONQUIN [4] (J Toller) 3-8-4 G Duffield 12/1: -00034: Much btr over this C/D in 2000. 18
1818 MOWSOOM [1] 3-8-7 N Day 7/1: -00: Led to ½way, sn behind: see 1818. 00
5 ran   1,hd,15,30   (H H Aga Khan)   M Stoute Newmarket

2229 E.B.F. PEDDARS CROSS MAIDEN STAKES 2YO   £1335   6f   Good/Firm 32 -06 Slow

1928 CAPE WILD [7] (M Stoute) 2-9-0 A Kimberley 3/1: 21: 2 ch c Bold Lad (Ire) - Short Rations (Lorenzaccio): Useful colt: fulfilled the promise of his debut, broke well & was never hdd when winning a 2yo mdn at Yarmouth Aug.21: half brother to several winners, inc useful 12f colt Marooned: very eff over 6f & will stay further: acts on gd/firm grnd & seems to have no trk preferences: scope for further impr. 54
2056 CRUSADE DANCER [3] (B Hanbury) 2-9-0 M Hills 7/1: 02: Ran on really well, just failed to peg back winner: will app another furlong: should win soon: see 2056. 49
-- GHAWWAS [4] (H T Jones) 2-9-0 A Murray 5/2 FAV: 3: With winner most of way, not btn far & this was a promising debut: well bred colt who cost 280,000 gns as a yearling, and is a half brother to winning juvenile Bright Domino: eff over 6f on gd/firm: will impr & should recoup losses in the near future. 48
-- BECCADELLI [2] (H Cecil) 2-9-0 N Day 7/1: 4: Al up there: fair debut: cost 120,000 gns & is a half brother to winning juvenile Great Reef: acts on gd/firm grnd: should be placed to win. 45
-- MACS MAESTRO [9] 2-9-0 T Ives 16/1: 0: No extra inside dist: should come on for this experience: fetched 14,500 gns & should be suited by lngr dists in time. 40
-- QUIET HERO [5] 2-9-0 R Cochrane 4/1: 0: Nicely bckd on debut: al in touch, showing plenty of promise: half brother to several winning juveniles, & also very useful 6/7f winner Don Martino: one to keep an eye on. 34
-- LORJ GARBACZ [6] 2-8-11 E Guest(3) 16/1: 0: Given a tender introduction: fin 7th though certainly could have fin closer: impr certain on next start: acts on gd/firm. 32
-- Degenerale [8] 9-0   565 Inthar [1] 9-0   1665 Golden Topaz [3] 9-0
1984 Freddie Ashton [10] 9-0
11 ran   1,½,1,1½,2,½   (J Greetham)   M Stoute Newmarket

2230 MAGDALEN ESTATE H'CAP (0-35) 3YO   £1912   1m   Good/Firm 32 -04 Slow   [34]

1695 WILLBE WILLBE [12] (C Brittain) 3-7-13 G Carter(3) 25/1: 0000001: 3 ch f Music Boy - K-Sera (Lord Gayle): Showed much impr form & gamely made all in a 3yo h'cap at Yarmouth Aug.21: no form previously this season though showed some promise last term: eff over sprint dists, stays 1m well: acts on gd & fast grnd on any trk: clearly well suited by forcing tactics. 12
1794 GLACIER LASS [11] (B Hills) 3-8-2(bl) R Fox 20/1: 00-0002: Prom run to chall dist, out battled & remains a mdn: stays 1m: acts on gd/firm: see 1794. 12
*2060 PHILOSOPHICAL [1] (W Musson) 3-8-10(5ex) M Wigham 15/2: 0003013: Given too much to do: fin well & deserves another ch: see 2060 (seller). 14
2149 CHARLTON KINGS [10] (R Hollinshead) 3-9-7 S Perks 5/1: 4000034: Ev ch: btr over 9f in 2149 21
1818 REAL MOONSHINE [9] 3-9-5 M Roberts 16/1: -0400: Shorter trip: btr 1818 (10f): see 1220. 17
1885 NEW EVIDENCE [8] 3-8-12 A Mackay 4/1 FAV: 0022320: Prom most: btr over 7f in 1885. 07
2085 AVADA [4] 3-8-7 T Lucas 5/1: 4-00040: Fdd into 9th: best in 2085 (stiff trk). 00
*1819 GIVING IT ALL AWAY [7] 3-9-5 R Cochrane 9/2: 0000210: Outpcd ½way, eased: much btr 1819 00
1281 Plain Talk [5] 8-13   1554 Captains Jade [3] 8-1   1089 Rockall [6] 8-11
183 Final Curtain [2] 9-6
12 ran   1,2½,2½,nk,1½   (Mrs C Brittain)   C Brittain, Newmarket

Official Going Given As GOOD/FIRM

2231 CITY OF YORK STAKES 3YO+   £4861   7f   Firm 03 +08 Fast

1514 PRESIDIUM [8] (H Cecil) 4-9-4 S Cauthen 100/30: 3-10241: 4 b c General Assembly - Doubly Sure (Reliance II): Smart colt: al prom & led ½way, ridden out, breaking the course record in City Of York Stakes at York Aug.21: first time out won at Brighton: subsq. a fine 2nd to Conquering Hero at Newbury: lightly raced in '85, due to a back problem: very smart 2yo, winning at Yarmouth & 2nd to Local Suitor in Mill Reef Stakes at Newbury: very eff at 7f/1m: acts on yld but is best on gd & fast grnd: genuine sort who is a full brother to top class miler Kris. 70
1125 QUE SYMPATICA [9] (R Boss) 4-9-4 J Reid 16/1: 3300002: Failed to qckn final 2f, but kept on well: gd effort after fair abs: see 18. 64
-- RACKSTRAW [4] (B Hills) 3-9-0 B Thomson 12/1: 130-3: Stayed on well on belated seasonal debut & should impr on this next time out: ran only 3 times as a 2yo: first time out won a valuable mdn at Ascot, subsq 3rd to Moorgate Man in Gr.3 event at Newcastle: should be suited by 1m: acts on fast & yld grnd & a gall trk. 65

1851 HOLBROOKE SUTTON [2] (L Cumani) 3-8-8 W R Swinburn 11/4: 14-4024: Nvr nrr: btr 1851.   59
754 TANOUMA [1] 3-8-8 W Carson 9/4 FAV: 1-3000: Well bckd, despite abs: needs give
in the grnd? see 467, 232.   54
1983 EMERALD EAGLE [7] 5-9-4 J Matthias 50/1: 0020100: Kept on well & ran remarkably well
in this gd class company: would win another h'cap if reproducing anything like this form: see 1976.   47
1854 BARCLAY STREET [5] 3-8-11 Pat Eddery 10/1: 4-00000: Fdd final 2f: see 808.   00
1823 Soughaan [3] 9-0
8 ran   2½,1½,hd,3,2½   (Lord Howard De Walden)   H Cecil Newmarket

2232 MOORESTYLE CONVIVIAL MAIDEN STKS 2YO   £5353   6f   Firm 03 -18 Slow

-1915 BALI MAGIC [13] (G Wragg) 2-9-0 S Cauthen 1/1 FAV: 21: 2 b c Habitat - Miss Bali
(Crepello): Prom colt: hvly bckd & despite being rousted along from ½way, responded well to
lead inside final 1f & win a val. maiden at York with something in hand: first time out was
a fine 2nd to Hendeka at Goodwood: brother to the useful miler Bali Dancer & several other
winners: eff at 6f, sure to be btr suited by 7f/1m: acts on fast grnd & will win more races.   55
--   YOUNG JUDGE [15] (J Watts) 2-9-0 N Connorton 16/1: 2: Led 2f out: caught well inside
final 1f: excellent racecourse debut from this 40,000 gns purchase: half brother to very
useful 2yo winner Takfa Yahmed: should be suited by 7f: acts on fast grnd & will win soon.   52
1522 MAJD [12] (P Walwyn) 2-9-0 Paul Eddery 12/1: 33: Ch 1f out: not btn far in close
fin & is fast impr: acts on gd & fast grnd & should have no trouble finding a mdn: see 1522.   51
2119 ALI SMITH [3] (R Boss) 2-9-0 W R Swinburn 12/1: 234: Dsptd lead inside final 2f:
consistent : see 2119.   50
--   SUNERTA [10] 2-8-11 W Carson 6/1: 0: Stayed on well on racecourse debut & impr very
likely from this good looking US bred filly: half sister to several winners, notably the
very smart Hatim: should be well suited by 7f/1m: acts on fast grnd & can win soon.   46
--   ROCK CHANTEUR [4] 2-9-0 P Cook 25/1: 0: Al there: gd racecourse debut from this
I.R. 28,000 gns yearling: quite speedily bred colt who is a half brother to a winner in
Ireland: acts on fast grnd & can find a race.   45
--   ALBANY PARK [7] 2-9-0 J Reid 8/1: 0: No real threat on racecourse debut, though active
in mkt today: cost 18,000 gns & is a half brother to 2 winners, incl Derrygold: speedily bred.   00
--   WOOD CHISEL [5] 2-9-0 B Thomson 11/1: 0: Made no show on racecourse debut, but will
benefit from the experience: half brother to 3 winners.   00
1049 LUBRICAN [11] 2-9-0 Pat Eddery 6/1: 40: Prom most after abs: needed race? see 1049.   00
--   Rumboogle [9] 9-0   1867 Illustrate [1] 8-11   1984 Barnaby Benz [2] 9-0
1869 Ichi Ban Son [8] 9-0   --   Pagitek [6] 9-0
14 ran   ½,nk,½,½,1½   (J L C Pearce)   G Wragg Newmarket

2233 GROUP 1 WILLIAM HILL SPRINT C'SHIP   £49518   5f   Firm 03 +25 Fast

1485 LAST TYCOON [4] (R Collet) 3-9-2 Y Saint Martin 7/2: 11141: 3 b c Try My Best -
Mill Princess (Mill Reef): Top class sprinter: settled in behind the ldrs & showed a fine
turn of foot to lead inside the final 1f for a ready win in very fast run Gr.1 William Hill
Sprint Championship at York Aug.21: had no luck in running when 4th last time out in the
July Cup, but earlier was a game shhd winner of Gr.1 King's Stand Stakes at Royal Ascot, again
beating Double Schwartz: also successful previously this season in Gr.3 events at Chantilly &
Longchamp: in '85 won again at Longchamp & was a close up 5th in the Prix L'Abbaye: very
eff at 5f, stays further: acts on yld but is well suited by fast grnd: not one to oppose.   90
+1889 DOUBLE SCHWARTZ [2] (C Nelson) 5-9-6 Pat Eddery 5/2: 2-11212: Led ½way till hdd by
winner last 100yds: kept on gamely & is tremendously consistent: certain to win more races.   87
*1485 GREEN DESERT [3] (M Stoute) 3-9-2 W R Swinburn 9/4 FAV: -120213: Al up there: another
fine effort & met 2 top class sprinters here: see 1485.   85
-1889 GWYDION [5] (H Cecil) 3-8-13 S Cauthen 9/2: -433124: Prom, much closer to Double
Schwartz in 1889, but again ran well.   72
408 MAROUBLE [8] 3-9-2 J Reid 33/1: 4023-00: Showed gd speed to ½way after long abs: see 408   65
1631 BRIDESMAID [1] 3-8-13(vis) B Thomson 40/1: 0123340: Never nearer: see 1631, 854.   62
2145 GREY DESIRE [6] 6-9-6 K Darley 20/1: 2023000: Never threatened: btr 1631, 1485 (6f).   00
1889 ORIENT [7] 3-8-13 D Mckeown 33/1: _111300: Led to ½way: see 1889, 1151.   00
8 ran   ½,1½,4,3,hd   (R C Strauss)   R Collet Chantilly, France

2234 BRADFORD AND BINGLEY HCAP 0-75 3YO+   £20582   1m   Firm 03 -13 Slow   [60]

1911 DIGGERS REST [2] (G Wragg) 3-9-4 S Cauthen 15/2: 3-13021: 3 b c Mr Prospector -
Loraine (Habitat): Smart colt: ran on well to lead final 1f in a blnkt fin to a valuable
h'cap at York Aug.21: first time out won another valuable h'cap at Newmarket: well bred sort
whose dam is a half sister to 1,000 Guineas winner On The House: eff at 7f, suited by
1m: acts on gd/firm & yld grnd & a gall trk: seems best when held up for a late run.   73
*2009 TURFAH [3] (P Walwyn) 3-8-5(5ex) Paul Eddery 12/1: -021112: Chall final 1f & just
btn: has risen steeply in the weights and is in excellent form: should win another h'cap
very soon: see 2009.   58
1890 TRULY RARE [14] (M Stoute) 4-9-4 W R Swinburn 12/1: -030023: Led 2f out & just
btn in close fin: in grand form: see 1890, 433.   61
1793 AVENTINO [6] (J Sutcliffe) 3-8-12(bl) C Rutter(5) 10/1: 1111334: Under press all
the way up the str, but fin like a train & would have btn them all in another 50yds:
commendably consistent: see 1793, 1486.   63

662

1931 KINGS HEAD [10] 4-9-9 G Starkey 5/1 FAV: 120-300: Chall Inside final 2f: not btn
far & again ran well: see 1931, 1109.   65
1890 BOLD AND BEAUTIFUL [12] 4-9-10 Pat Eddery 12/1: 0-03300: Nearest fin & btn less
than 2L: fine effort under top weight & may be winning soon: see 759.   66
2104 SIGNORE ODONE [1] 4-8-3 M Birch 10/1: 4001120: Hmpd over 3f out & did well to
fin so close: remains in fine form: see 2104, 1624.   00
*1890 COME ON THE BLUES [11] 7-8-12(5ex) W Carson 8/1: 0000410: Made most 6f: btr 1890. 00
-2144 MOORES METAL [7] 6-7-12 A Culhane(7) 10/1: 4000320: Made no show & is extremely
difficult to catch: btr 2144: see 441.   00
*1793 SUPER TRIP [13] 5-8-9 R Hills 10/1: 0214210: Never in it: below his best: btr 1793. 00
1655 Top Ruler [8] 8-12   1486 Resourceful Falcon [4] 9-7
1793 Qualitair Flyer [9] 9-0(bl)   1332 Oriental Soldier [5] 9-5
14 ran   ½,nk,¾,hd,shhd,1   (Sir Philip Oppenheimer)   G Wragg Newmarket

2235 GROUP 2 LOWTHER STAKES 2YO FILLIES   £15336   6f   Firm 03 +08 Fast

2113 POLONIA [7] (J Bolger) 2-9-0 J Reid 5/2: 110131: 2 b c Danzig - Moss (Round Table):
Smart Irish filly: gaining her 4th success from 6 races when gamely winning fast run, Gr.2
Lowther Stakes at York Aug.21: led over 2f out & held on really well final 1f: eaarlier
successful 3 times in Ireland at the Curragh (2) & Leopardstown: btn only by the top class
Minstrella & Forest Flower at Phoenix Park last time & ran her only poor race when unstd by
the very firm grnd at Royal Ascot: very eff at 6f, will stay further: acts on fast & soft
grnd: most genuine & consistent.   78
*999 INTERVAL [1] (J Tree) 2-8-11 Pat Eddery 7/2: 12: Well bckd despite lengthy abs,
responded well to press to make the winner pull out all the stops final 1f: fast impr filly
who acts on firm & gd grnd & stays 6f well: see 999.   74
+1919 LINDAS MAGIC [8] (R Armstrong) 2-8-11 S Cauthen 8/1: 23113: Outcpd, kept on well
final stages & ran really well: see 1919.   69
1021 INDIAN LILY [9] (C Brittain) 2-8-11 G Starkey 25/1: 144: Sn prom, fine effort after
abs & seems to do well when fresh (won first time out in 707).   68
*1641 SEA DARA [2] 2-8-11 J Matthias 14/1: 1310: Pacemaker till past ½way: see 1641.   68
*1789 HIAAM [4] 2-9-0 W R Swinburn 2/1 FAV: 210: Below her best here: see 1789.   68
-1697 SINCLAIR LADY [3] 2-8-11 D Nicholls 25/1: 0001120: No ch from ½way, fin 7th but
a stiff task: see 1370, 1697.   00
2158 CHASING MOONBEAMS [5] 2-8-11 P Cook 12/1: 221430: Quick reapp: early speed, fin 8th. 00
1778 BEAUCHAMP BUZZ [6] 2-8-11 W Carson 12/1: 20: No dngr, much btr 1778.   00
9 ran   ½,2½,nk,hd,1½   (Henryk De Kwiatkowski)   J Bolger Ireland

2236 GALTRES STAKES LISTED FILLIES & MARES   £7843   1m 4f   Firm 03 -11 Slow

+1538 STARTINO [4] (H Cecil) 3-8-7 S Cauthen 85/40 FAV: 2-111: 3 b f Bustino - Western Star
(Alcide): Smart, progressive filly who is unbtn this season: completed her hat trick (hvly
bckd), leading 3f out comfortably from her stable companion in valuable Galtres Stakes at
York Aug.21: winner of minor events at Leicester (2) previously: narrowly btn at Goodwood
on only start in '85: closely related to the smart Mr Fluorocarbon: very well suited by 12f,
should stay further: acts on firm & soft & on a gall trk: can impr further.   75
+1988 KENANGA [6] (H Cecil) 3-8-7 W Ryan 11/2: -01112: Came from rear, fine effort this
this stable companion of the winner: see 1988.   70
926 BONSHAMILE [8] (A Hide) 3-8-7 R Guest 20/1: 1-103: Long abs: gd performance: stays 12f. 68
*1596 AMONGST THE STARS [10] (S Norton) 3-8-11 J Lowe 20/1: -101014: Never btr, most
creditable effort from this genuine filly: see 1596.   67
*1630 APPLY [12] 3-8-7 Pat Eddery 9/1: -110: No dngr but not disgraced in this btr company. 53
1513 ALTIYNA [1] 3-8-7 W R Swinburn 10/1: 1-22040: No dngr: twice below 1128.   52
926 LAUGHTER [2] 3-8-11 W Carson 6/1: 1-200: Well bckd, fin 7th after abs: see 509.   00
*1749 BARSHAM [5] 3-8-7 T Quinn 9/1: -0010: Prom, wknd into 9th: see 1749.   00
1408 SUE GRUNDY [11] 3-8-7 P Robinson 13/2: 3-10040: Led/dsptd lead till 3f out: btr 1408. 00
*2078 Prelude [3] 8-7(BL)   2074 Its Now Or Never [7] 9-4
1918 Myth [9] 8-7   1378 Zumurrudah [13] 8-11
13 ran   3,1,2½,7,¾   (Mrs James McAllister)   H Cecil Newmarket

2237 GREAT YORKSHIRE HANDICAP 0-60 3YO+   £3986   1m 4f   Firm 03 -29 Slow   [55]

2058 WITCHCRAFT [8] (G Wragg) 4-8-4 Pat Eddery 5/1: 0-24431: 4 b c Grundy - Broomstick
Corner (Bustino): Gained a deserved success, al prom & leading 3f out in a slowly run h'cap
at York Aug.21: early in '85 won a mdn at Haydock: eff 10f, suited by 12f now: acts on
firm & hvy & likes a gall trk: has been tried in bl but btr without them.   43
+1963 GULFLAND [5] (G P Gordon) 5-9-3(4ex) S Childs(7) 11/2: 3210112: Came from behind,
ch dist: gd effort from this ultra-consistent gelding: see 1963.   53
1909 BALLYDURROW [1] (R Fisher) 9-8-8 D Nicholls 10/1: 0402143: Waited with, smooth hdway
to chall 2f out, no extra closing stages: gd effort: see 1744.   42
*1818 FESTIVAL CITY USA [6] (B Hills) 3-8-10(bl) B Thomson 6/1: -030014: Made much: probably
stays 12f: see 1818.   52
582 NAFTILOS [10] 4-8-11 P Robinson 14/1: 0-02000: Never btr after long abs: best 215 (14f). 40
*1142 CONVINCED [4] 4-9-10 G Starkey 4/1: 0-32310: Prom most: abs since btr 1112.   53
1293 ROSTHERNE [3] 4-8-2 L Charnock 10/1: 2104000: Prom, ev ch, wknd into 7th: best 215 (14f) 00

1790 VOUCHSAFE [7] 4-9-4 W Carson 7/2 FAV: 041D000: Ev ch, fin 8th: see 921, 112. Disapp. fav.   00
964 Vickstown [9] 7-7(1oh)   1866 Madison Girl [2] 7-7(3oh)
10 ran 2,1½,2,1,nk,shhd   (E Moller)   G Wragg Newmarket

NEWMARKET   Friday August 22nd   Righthand Stiff Galloping Track

2238 BEAUFORT SELLING HANDICAP 3YO 0-25   £1998   7f   Good 42 -14 Slow   [26]

1571 DRESS IN SPRING [8] (G Blum) 3-8-6 M Rimmer 33/1: -000001: 3 ch f Northfields -
Sweet Spark (Hot Spark): Came from behind to lead dist for a narrow success in a 3yo selling
h'cap at Newmarket Aug.22 (no bid): won final start in '85, also at Newmarket & evidently
likes this gall trk: suited by fast or gd grnd & 6/7f.   14
1960 OCTIGA [9] (M Brittain) 3-8-0 P Robinson 33/1: -000302: Fin well & may need 1m
though looks likely to find a seller soon: see 1662.   06
2060 SLEEPLINE DUCHESS [4] (G Huffer) 3-8-11 G Carter(3) 12/1: -002003: Prom, ev ch:
best effort since 1656 (10f).   11
2174 MAN IN THE MOON [10] (P Feilden) 3-8-13(bl) G Duffield 20/1: 0-00004: Never closer,
showing first form this term: wears bl: looks likely to be suited by 1m.   13
1771 HIGHLAND TALE [3] 3-8-2 J Lowe 10/1: -000040: Prom most: see 1771.   00
2060 DORADE [5] 3-9-1(bl) R Cochrane 7/1: 0301040: Ev ch: see 1824.   09
1937 SONG AN DANCE MAN [12] 3-9-1 R Wernham 15/2: 0000000: No threat in 7th: btr 1937.   00
1824 MY CUP OF TEA [6] 3-8-4(BL) T Williams 6/1: 0322420: Made most, fin 8th: btr 1824.   00
1471 JOHNSTAN BOY [11] 3-9-0(VIS) M Birch 7/2 FAV: 0000440: Prom most, fin 9th: abs
since btr 1471 (sharp trk).   00
2189 NAUGHTY NIGHTY [7] 3-8-11 W Woods(3) 10/1: 0000000: Prom some: see 2189.   00
2027 STILL DREAMING [1] 3-9-7 S Dawson 5/1: -204040: Prom, wknd: btr 2027.   00
1917 Winding Path [2] 8-5   1937 Anthony Gerard [13] 8-5
13 ran ½,2½,shhd,2,½,2½,nk,½   (Spring House Dresses Ltd)   G Blum Newmarket

2239 LOCKWOODS AND SMEDLEYS MDN STKS 2YO   £4484   7f   Good 42 -23 Slow

1903 ROMAN GUNNER [10] (G Wragg) 2-9-0 P Robinson 3/1 FAV: 01: 2 ch c Grundy - Romara
(Bold Lad): Prom colt: overcame great difficulties in running, fin strongly to win going
away in a slowly run 2yo mdn at Newmarket Aug.22: half brother to winning 2yo Bustara: eff
over a stiff 7f, bred to be suited by middle dists in time: acts on gd grnd on a gall trk:
will impr further.   60
--   ARDEN [3] (H Cecil) 2-9-0 W Ryan 7/1: 2: Prom, led 1f out, outpcd close home: fine r,
debut: half brother to fair h'capper Knif: certain to be suited by lngr dists: acts on
gd grnd, on a gall trk.   51
--   BUCKRA MELLISUGA [12] (J Toller) 2-9-0 G Duffield 20/1: 3: Prom 3 out, not btn far
in a tight fin: gd debut: an 11,000 gns purchase who stays 7f & acts on gd grnd/on a gall trk. 50
--   WOOD CHANTER [17] (J Dunlop) 2-9-0 T Ives 10/1: 4: Mkt drifter, fin in gd style &
will benefit from the race: brother to the smart middle dist colt Moon Madness: probably
well suited by further & should find a mdn in the near future.   48
1307 WILLIESWRIGHTONCUE [8] 2-9-0 G Carter(3) 10/1: 20: Led/dsptd lead 3 out: gd effort
& should be up to find a mdn if dropped slightly in class: see 1307.   46
--   RED TIMBER [14] 2-9-0 M Rimmer 20/1: 0: Prom, ev ch: cost 15,500 gns: related to
several winners incl useful 7f/1m performer El Gitano.   42
1872 SLIP DANCER [1] 2-9-0 R Cochrane 6/1: 030: Prom most, fin 7th: see 1872.   00
--   BRENTANO [15] 2-9-0 Paul Eddery 14/1: 0: Mkt drifter, fin a close up 8th: quite a
cheaply bought May foal who is related to several winners, incl successful '85 2yo Softly
Spoken: should stay 7f.   00
1232 MR CORMAN [7] 2-9-0 J Reid 14/1: 00: Bckd at long odds, fin close 9th: quite cheaply
bought foal: may impr.   00
--   JAMES STANLEY [11] 2-9-0 G Baxter 20/1: 0: Made much & should impr for the experience:
cost I.R. 20,000: may prove best over 6f at present.   00
--   GLORY LINE [9] 2-9-0 T Quinn 10/1: 0: Wk in mkt: prom much: cost I.R. 160,000 and
is a half brother to winning stayer Brave The Reef: may do btr in time/over lngr dists.   00
--   Infanta De Castile [4] 8-11   --   Surf Board [6] 9-0
1903 Dancer To Follow [16] 9-0   --   Jack Straw [13] 9-0
777 Highland Laird [9] 9-0
16 ran ½,½,1,1,2,nk,shhd   (E Moller)   G Wragg Newmarket

2240 HARRIS GROUP HANDICAP 0-50   £3256   1m 6f   Good 42 -22 Slow   [43]

2098 VINTAGE PORT [6] (R Akehurst) 4-8-12 T Quinn 15/2: 0000221: 4 b c Blood Royal -
Port Au Pass (Pass): Gained a deserved success leading under press dist & keeping on strongly
in a slowly run h'cap at Newmarket Aug.22: was successful at Down Royal & Irish this term:
in '85: eff 12f, btr suited by 14f & should stay 2m: acts well on gd grnd.   35
--   BENS BIRDIE [5] (M Tompkins) 6-7-8 A Mackay 25/1: 30413-2: Came from off the pace, gd
fin & a prom seasonal debut: winner of a h'cap at Hamilton in '85: eff over 12f, stays 14f
well: probably unsuited by firm but acts on gd & hvy: likes a gall trk: will strip fitter
next time.   14
2058 VERY SPECIAL [2] (W Holden) 4-8-8 R Morse(5) 9/1: -030103: Chall 2 out, ran well: see 1563 26

2031. JACKDAW [4] (R Hollinshead) 6-8-12 A Culhane(7) 12/1: 0231204: Led 3f out will no extra
final 2f: see 1633 (2m).   28
*1700 RUN HIGH [3] 3-8-11 A Clark 9/4 FAV: -010: Well bckd, ev ch: see 1700.   36
*1726 FOXY PRINCE [7] 3-8-12 R Cochrane 4/1: -010: Prom most: see 1726.   35
1111 AGATHIST [9] 3-9-0 G Duffield 7/1: 0-41100: Abs: wknd into 7th: best 949.   00
-- KINGSWICK [1] 6-9-7 M Miller 25/1: 20100-0: Belated seasonal debut & will be btr
for it: lightly raced on the Flat in '85 winning a h'cap at Warwick: a very useful staying
hdlr who was at Wincanton in that sphere in 85/86: acts on gd & soft grnd: eff 12f, stays 2m well   00
1879 DHONI [8] 3-8-9 T Ives 13/2: 0-40230: Made much, wknd quickly: see 1435.   00
9 ran   2,nk,1,2,1   (Mrs Mary Wickins)   R Akehurst Epsom, Surrey

2241 HILLSDOWN HOLDINGS HOPEFUL STKS LISTED   £9396   6f   Good 42 +27 Fast

2084 HALLGATE [3] (S Hall) 3-9-3 J Reid 7/4 FAV: 3041031: 3 b c Vaigly Great - Beloves
Mistress (Rarity): Smart sprinter: hvly bckd waited with quickened lead final 100yds in a
fast run, valuable minor race at Newmarket Aug.22: earlier won a similar event at Lingfield:
very tough & genuine in '85 winning at Hamilton (2), Edinburgh, Pontefract, Redcar, Ripon
& Ascot (Cornwallis Stakes): stays 7f but best form at sprint dists: acts on firm & soft
& on any trk: has a gd turn of foot but tends to hang under press & is not the easiest of rides   80
1387 TREASURE KAY [6] (P Makin) 3-8-8 B Thomson 9/4: 0-14232: Led 1f out, caught near
fin: stays 6f: in fine form: see 1387.   69
1107 METEORIC [4] (W Hern) 3-8-8 T Ives 11/2: 20-0103: Set a gd pace for 5f, after abs:
best 776.   60
1851 CHARGE ALONG [1] (J Winter) 4-8-11 P Robinson 16/1: 0-04004: Prom, ev ch: best 645 (7f).   51
1286 FILLEOR [7] 3-8-8 G Duffield 12/1: 132-00: Chall dist, wknd: ex Irish filly who was
at Phoenix Park & the Curragh in '85, on both occasions over 5f on yld.   53
-2021 HIDDEN BRIEF [5] 3-8-5 Paul Eddery 12/1: -120020: Prom much: much btr 2021 but
had a stiff task here.   35
2021 SIT THIS ONE OUT [2] 3-9-0(BL) R Cochrane 25/1: 0300000: Continues to run poorly.   00
7 ran   ½,3,2,hd,5   (Hippodromo Racing Ltd)   S Hall Middleham, Yorks

2242 BUXTED HANDICAP 3YO 0-60   £4233   6f   Good 42 +02 Fast   [59]

+2151 CATHERINES WELL [3] (M W Easterby) 3-9-0(6ex) G Carter(3) 10/11 FAV: 3033111: 3 ch f Junius-
Restless Lady (Sandford Lad): Very useful sprinter: completed a quick hat-trick in valuable
h'caps when sprinting .clear final 1f for an easy success at Newmarket Aug.22: recently won
similar h'caps at Ripon & Newcastle: in fine form last backend, winning at Doncaster &
Newmarket & earlier on a seller on the former course: stays 7f but very eff at 5/6f:
acts on any trk and on firm & yld going: can win again.   58
886 ALMAROSE [6] (J Sutcliffe) 3-7-10 R Fox 13/2: 0012-02: Did not have the best of runs,
gdfin: fine effort after long abs & she should run a good race next time: see 886.   36
2021 DREAM CHASER [9] (P Cole) 3-9-7(BL) L Johnsey(7) 20/1: -010003: Led 2f out, outpcd
final stages: bl first time today & ran best race since 732: likes a stiff trk.   58
1911 MERDON MELODY [7] (R Sheather) 3-8-10 M L Thomas 16/1: -122004: Early pace, kept on:
lightly raced since best 808 (C/D).   38
+1900 MARGAM [1] 3-8-3 Paul Eddery 6/1: -310410: Prom much: btr 1900 (C/D).   25
2084 DARK PROMISE [4] 3-9-2 S Perks 5/1: 1323020: Made most, wknd: btr 2084.   34
1060 Crete Cargo [8] 9-4   1521 Muhtaris [5] 7-7(2oh)   1868 Jousting Boy [2] 8-3
9 ran   1,½,3,2½,1½   ippodromo Racing Ltd)   M W Easterby Sheriff Hutton, Yorks

2243 EBF BLUE PETER STAKES 2YO   £3398   6f   Good 42 -32 Slow

*2036 GENGHIZ [3] (L Piggott) 2-9-6 T Ives 5/6 FAV: 11: 2 ch c Sir Ivor - Royal Caprice
(Swaps): Retained his unbtn record, easily leading 1f out in a slowly run 2yo minor race at
Newmarket Aug.22: comfortably won a mdn on the same trk Aug.8: well bred sort who is eff
over 6/7f & will stay 1m plus: acts on gd & fast grnd & runs well at Newmarket: should win again   64
-- HOW VERY TOUCHING [5] (J Hindley) 2-8-11 M Hills 11/2: 2: Led briefly dist: fair
debut from this May foal: bred to be suited by further & should impr over 7f plus.   50
-- BLANTON RESERVE [4] (B Hills) 2-8-11 B Thomson 12/1: 3: Never closer: should benefit
from the experience: quite a cheaply bought colt who seems quite well regarded by his stable:
should stay behind 6f.   42
-- MOORE BRASS [7] (C Brittain) 2-8-11 G Baxter 10/1: 4: Made most: related to several
winners, notable useful h'capper My Tony: should impr when tried over lngr dists.   38
-- SUPER LUNAR [6] 2-8-11 R Cochrane 25/1: 4: Ddhtd for 4th: will be suited by lngr dists.   38
-- GRAND TOUR [1] 2-8-11 J Reid 25/1: 0: Early pace: sired by Derby hero Troy & will
probably need lngr dists.   30
-- MILITARY ATTACHE [2] 2-8-11 W Ryan 13/2: 0: Wk in mkt, no dngr: rather a disapp
debut from this half brother to top class Green Desert.   00
7 ran   1½,3,1,ddht,3   (Peter Wetzell)   L Piggott Newmarket

Official Going Given As

2244 TOTE BOOKMAKERS STAKES (H'CAP)(0-60)   £3200   1m   Good 56 +04 Fast   [55]

2144 ININSKY [3] (G Harwood) 3-9-8 G Starkey 9/2: -400341: 3 ch c Niniski - Buckhurst
(Gulf Pearl): Useful colt: easy to back though proved a decisive winner under top weight,
led over 2f out & ran on strongly in quite a fast run h'cap at Goodwood Aug.22: lightly raced
last season, winning a Sandown mdn: bred to be suited by further though 1m seems his best
trip: suited by gd or faster grnd & acts on any trk: carries weight well.   70
1890 PICTOGRAPH [2] (I Balding) 4-8-9 Pat Eddery 15/8 JT FAV: 4-00002: Looked dangerous dist:
kept on well & is clearly returning to form: likes this sharp trk though does act on any.   42
930 FLYHOME [1] (P Cundell) 5-8-7 P Cook 8/1: 0-22303: Rear, some late prog though in
need of this race after a fair abs: should be straighter next time: see 706.   34
1934 LOCAL SILVER [4] (W Hern) 3-8-1(BL) W Carson 15/8 JT FAV: 0-00144: Fitted with bl:
made running over ½way, dropped out tamely when hdd: can do much btr than this: see 1628.   31
1967 STEEPLE BELL [5] 10-8-7 W R Swinburn 6/1: 00-0340: Btn over 2f out, eased: see 1781.   08
5 ran   2½,3,3,10   (Prince Yazid Saud)   G Harwood Pulborough, Sussex

2245 APPRENTICES' HANDICAP (0-40)   £3200   5f   Good 56 -04 Slow   [39]

1443 SILENT MAJORITY [7] (W O'gorman) 3-9-6 R Carter 9/4 FAV: 0131141: 3 b g General Assembly-
Vexed Voter (Pontifex): Narrowly justified fav. after a fair abs, made most & just got home
in an app h'cap at Goodwood Aug.22: much impr this season, earlier won h'caps at Yarmouth,
Kempton & Sandown: eff over 5/6f on gd & firm grnd: well suited by front running tactics.   44
2210 ASTARTE [5] (G Pritchard Gordon) 3-7-12 Abigail Richards(3) 8/1: -400032: Outpcd to ½way
fin in fine style & only just denied: in gd form & deserves a small h'cap: see 205.   20
1171 JACKIE BLAIR [6] (M Mccormack) 4-8-7(bl) J Leech(3) 12/1: 0300003: Narrowly btn: fine
effort after a lengthy abs: well h'capped on her best form: see 211.   24
2012 DUFFERS DANCER [9] (W Pearce) 4-8-4 G King(3) 5/1: 04-0134: Strong late chall though
the post came just too soon: another gd effort though probably best over another furlong.   20
1902 CLEOFE [8] 3-9-0(16!oh) S Quane(3) 8/1: 0333400: Some late prog: see 1626.   18
1940 SHARAD [4] 6-7-7(vis)(11oh) S Whitelam(5) 33/1: -000000: Al in mid-div: see 1196.   00
1834 SHE KNOWS IT ALL [2] 4-8-10 J Carr(3) 10/1: 00-0000: Speed to ½way: see 1834.   00
1950 FIRST EXPERIENCE [10] 4-8-5(VIS) L Riggio(3) 12/1: 0010000: Visored first time: best 1196   00
2055 CAPEABILITY POUND [3] 3-8-10 M Richardson(3) 10/1: 0200000: Never dngr 9th: see 1027.   00
2124 MUSIC MACHINE [1] 5-9-9 J Scally(3) 7/2: 1011200: Showed his usual gd early pace
though fizzled out very quickly & can do much btr than this: has been very busy lately.   00
10 ran   nk,nk,nk,4,1,½,½   (Bertram R Firestone)   W O'gorman Newmarket

2246 GR.3 WATERFORD CANDELABRA STAKES 2YO   £19654   7f   Good 56 -08 Slow

*1926 INVITED GUEST [4] (R Armstrong) 2-8-7 S Cauthen 4/1: 111: 2 ch f Be My Guest -
Welcome Break (Wollow): Smart juvenile: waited with & showed a fine turn of foot to lead
inside dist, comfortably in Gr.3 Waterford Candelabra Stakes at Goodwood Aug.22: earlier
successful in a Lingfield mdn in a valuable stakes race at Newmarket: very eff over 6/7f,
certain to be suited by 1m plus: acts on gd/firm & yld grnd & on any trk: potentially top
class & certainly looks one to follow.   78
*1382 GOLDEN BRAID [6] (I Balding) 2-8-7 Pat Eddery 8/1: 12: Tried to make all: caught a
real tartar & lost nothing in defeat: fin well clear of rem: fine effort after abs & looks
certain to be back in the winners enclosure soon: acts on any trk: see 1382.   68
*1855 IOSIFA [2] (M Stoute) 2-8-7 W R Swinburn 4/5 FAV: 313: Hvly bckd: ran too freely &
not qckn below dist: highly regarded & certainly deserves another ch: see 1855 (C/D).   58
+2119 NETTLE [1] (W Hern) 2-8-7 W Carson 6/1: 14: Front rank till paced qcknd dist:
creditable effort though probably already needs a lngr trip: see 2119.   54
2057 MY IMAGINATION [3] 2-8-7 B Rouse 40/1: 1100040: Rank outsider & faced a seemingly
impossible task: far from disgraced: ran right up to her best: eff over 5/7f on firm & soft.   52
*1874 CANDLE IN THE WIND [5] 2-8-7 W Newnes 25/1: 04010: Easy to back: prom most over this
lngr trip & ran a fair race in this hot company: see 1874.   52
6 ran   2½,5,2,½,shhd   (Kinderhill Corporation)   R Armstrong Newmarket

2247 TAYLOR WOODROW TEAM H'CAP (0-60) 3YO   £3200   1m 4f   Good 56 +13 Fast   [58]

1829 ALDINO [4] (A Stewart) 3-9-0(bl) M Roberts 10/1: 0011241: 3 ch c Artaius - Allotria
(Red God): Very useful colt: led below dist & drew well clear of an easy win in a fast run
3yo h'cap at Goodwood Aug.22: much impr this season, earlier won a similar race at Windsor
& a Brighton mdn: very eff over 11/12f: suited by gd or faster grnd, though does act on
soft: suited by forcing tactics: best form on a sharp trk: should win again.   60
1886 DALGADIYR [7] (M Stoute) 3-8-12 W R Swinburn 4/1: 3130022: Al front rank, took 2nd
close home: in gd form: see 1886 & 625.   42
2122 PLYMOUTH HOE [3] (L Cumani) 3-9-1 Pat Eddery 2/1 FAV: -1123: Well bckd: led 3f out,
onepaced: consistent colt who acts on any track: see 894.   44
1630 POUNELTA-(1) (R Hannon) 3-8-7 (bl) W Carson 20/1: -420404: Absent, never dngr &
has been rather disapp since early season (271,hvy): does act on fast ground: see 63   31
1939 TEBITTO [6] 3-8-8 P Cook 10/1: -010120: Made most: btr in 1939 (11f).   26
1630 KATHY W [5] 3-9-3 S Cauthen 7/2: -1140: Below par effort over this lngr trip: much
btr over 10f in 1630 (gall trk): see 1206.   26

666

*1808 MISAAFF [2] 3-9-7 A Murray 13/2: 13-4110: Stiff task under top weight: see 1808.   00
7 ran 10,hd,3,4,6   (A Boyd-Rochfort)   A Stewart Newmarket

2248 HANNINGTONS CHARITY FILLIES MDN. 3YO   £2070   1m   Good 56 -07 Slow

-- DARING DOONE [8] (A Stewart) 3-8-11 M Roberts 11/1: -1: 3 b f Daring March - Doogali
(Doon): Promising filly: made a successful debut, smooth prog to lead below dist, readily in
a 3yo fillies mdn at Goodwood Aug.22: first foal of useful 8/10f winner Doogali: clearly well
suited by 1m & seems certain to stay further: acts on gd grnd & on a sharp trk: has plenty
of scope & looks one to follow.   52
1368 SKEAN [7] (G Harwood) 3-8-11 G Starkey 9/4 FAV: -002: Had ev ch: no threat to winner
though beat rem fairly decisively: eff over 8/10f on gd & firm grnd: acts on any trk: should
find a race: see 1031. had been absent since 1368.   46
1842 HELIETTA [5] (L Cumani) 3-8-11 Pat Eddery 4/1: -0423: Mkt drifter: tried a shorter
trip though again.lacked pace at the business end of the race: see 1842 (12f).   37
1677 BIBI KHATOUN [3] (J Dunlop) 3-8-11 W Carson 4/1: 00-0024: Easy to back: led over
½way: in gd form: see 1677.   35
1586 GLADE [4] 3-8-11 A Mcglone 50/1: -000: Abs: rank outsider & showed her first signs
of ability here: eff over 1m on gd grnd: acts on a sharp trk.   33
1981 SUNDAY CHIMES [2] 3-8-11 S Cauthen 7/2: -040: Looked dngr 2f out, wknd quickly.   29
1516 Al Zahvia [9] 8-11   2048 Eloquence [1] 8-11   -- Popthorn [6] 8-11
9 ran 1½,4,¾,1,2.   (Mrs W McAlpine)   A Stewart Newmarket

2249 MAIDEN STAKES 2YO   £1370   6f   Good 56 -12 Slow

1930 MUMMYS LUCK [8] (R Hannon) 2-8-11 Pat Eddery 4/5 FAV: 21: 2 ch c Mummy's Game -
Catherine Howard (Tower Walk): Impr colt: produced a tremendous late surge to lead on the
line in a 2yo mdn at Goodwood Aug.22: half brother to speedy juvenile Chantaco: very eff
over 6f & should do even btr when tackling lngr trips: acts on gd & fast grnd & on a
sharp trk: should continue to improve.   52
-- TROJAN MISS [3] (W Hern) 2-8-8 W Carson 7/2: 2: Led 2f out, caught final stride:
sound debut from this first foal of useful 8/10f winner Sally Rose: eff over 6f, sure to stay
further: acts on gd grnd & on a sharp trk: will impr for this experience & sure to go
one btr soon.   48
2016 SLIM HOPE [1] (M Stoute) 2-8-11 W R Swinburn 11/2: 03: Easy to back: impr after ½way,
not btn far & well clear of rem: on the up grade: see 2016.   45
1874 HOME DEVICE [6] (B Hills) 2-8-8 S Cauthen 4/1: 04: No extra dist: bred to be suited
by 1m plus: acts on gd grnd & on a sharp trk.   24
2069 LADYS MANTLE [4] 2-8-8 B Rouse 16/1: 0000: Mkt drifter: no threat: see 1801.   20
2089 ALWAYS A LADY [2] 2-8-8 P Waldron 12/1: 340: Lightly raced since prom debut in 73 (5f).   14
-- TREBLE TOP [5] 2-8-11 P Cook 20/1: 0: Led over ½way: fdd into 7th: strong looking
colt who will be all the btr for this race & can be expected to impr.   00
-- GOLD MINORIES [7] 2-8-11 A Mcglone 33/1: 0: Dwelt & never in race: cheaply bought colt
who attractive little mkt support today though can only impr.   00
8 ran shhd,1½,7,1½,2   (R I Khan)   R Hannon East Everleigh, Wilts

Official Going Given As GOOD

2250 MAIL ON SUNDAY 3YO SERIES HCAP 0-60   £4259   7f   Good 56 +06 Fast   [57]

*1904 PERSIAN DELIGHT [7] (G Huffer) 3-7-12 A Mackay 9/1: 40-211: 3 b f Persian Bold -
Ballysnip (Ballymore): Impr filly: ran on well to lead last 100yds in a 3yo h'cap at
Newmarket Aug.23: last time out won a minor event at Edinburgh: eff at 7f, stays 1m well
and may get further: acts on gd & firm grnd & on any trk: lightly raced & can continue to impr. 40
1655 PINSTRIPE [12] (R Williams) 3-9-7 T Ives 6/1: 0112122: Led inside final 1f: another
fine effort & is a model of consistency: eff at 7f/1m: see 1655.   60
1880 SMILING BEAR [6] (W Hastings Bass) 3-7-12 Dale Gibson(7) 13/2: 00-03: Not clear run
over 1f out & stayed on well: gd effort & should find a h'cap: see 1880.   36
1924 SOMETHING CASUAL [2] (A Hide) 3-8-10(bl) R Guest 11/2 JT.FAV: 0000344: Made most: in
gd form but twice below 1655.   46
1804 EMERALD WAVE [4] 3-8-4 A Mcglone 20/1: 4-00100: Front rank all way: see 1804.   40
1911 KING OF SPADES [10] 3-9-2 P Cook 20/1: 3-10000: Never nearer: not btn far & has
been lightly raced this season: stays 7f: see 26.   48
2038 CARRIBEAN SOUND [11] 3-8-4 T Williams 9/1: 3100420: Prom, fin 7th: not btn far: see 713. 35
907 RAISINHELL [9] 3-8-10(BL) R Cochrane 6/1: 00-3120: Bl first time: no threat after
abs since 907 (sharp trk).   38
2143 MAJOR JACKO [8] 3-8-3 B Rouse 11/2 JT.FAV: 4000020: Well below 2143 (6f).   00

1991 AMBROSINI [1] 3-8-11 P Hutton(7) 9/1: 1020430: Prom much, fdd: btr 1991.   00
2155 Bon Accueil [3] 8-1   1950 Vague Lass [14] 9-0   1896 African Rex [5] 8-7
13 ran 1,½,¼,hd,1½,1½,1½   (A Afdhal)   G Huffer Newmarket

2251 DANEPAK BACON STAKES 2YO LISTED   £9068   1m   Good 56 -09 Slow

1975 LACK A STYLE [4] (A Bailey) 2-8-8 R Cochrane 16/1: 0023321: 2 b c Moorestyle -
Noor (Mill Reef): Very useful colt: led nearing final 1f, readily by 4L in valuable Listed
race at Newmarket Aug.23: runs well here, earlier a fine 3rd to Suhailie last month: eff at
7f, seems well suited by 1m: acts on gd & firm grnd & seems best at Newmarket.   65
*1968 LAURIES WARRIOR [2] (R Boss) 2-9-2 J Reid 4/1: 0212112: Led early: kept on: in
gd form: stays 1m: see 1968.   ̃64
*2133 BRAVE DANCER [1] (G Harwood) 2-9-2 A Clark 15/8 FAV: 31013: Made much: stays 1m, but
btr 2133 (7f).   63
--   IBN BEY [5] (P Cole) 2-8-8 G Duffield 5/1: 4: Active in mkt on racecourse debut: sn
behind & stayed on well closing stages: impr certain from this well regarded colt: cost
210,000 gns as a yearling & is a half brother to winning 2yo Cerise Bouquet: bred to stay
middle dists: acts on gd grnd & will have no trouble finding a mdn.   52
*1975 PUNTA CALAHONDA [3] 2-8-11 P Cook 25/1: 010: Prom, ev ch: stiff task: see 1975.   53
1903 BIN SHADDAD [6] 2-8-8 T Ives 11/4 : 00: Active in mkt: fdd final 2f: see 1903.   47
6 ran 4,hd,1½,1,1½   (T P Ramsden)   A Bailey Newmarket

2252 PHILIP CORNES NICKEL ALLOYS NURSERY   £10316   6f   Good 56 +08 Fast   [64]

*1928 MOST WELCOME [10] (G Wragg) 2-9-7 Paul Eddery 2/1 FAV: 11: 2 ch c Be My Guest -
Topsy (Habitat): Smart, most prom colt: bckd as if defeat was out of the question & led
over 1f out, comfortably defying top weight in a fast run nursery h'cap at Newmarket Aug.23:
first time out was again hvly bckd when a ready 4L winner of a valuable 2yo mdn over this
C/D: full brother to the smart 10/12f winner Top Guest & half brother to Rye Tops & Troytops:
eff at 6f, bred to stay middle dists: acts on gd & fast grnd & a gall trk: held in high
regard and is certain to win more good races: not one to oppose lightly.   75
-2010 ONGOING SITUATION [12] (D Morley) 2-8-13 B Rouse 11/1: 013122: Ch over 1f out: caught a
tartar and is in grand form: deserves to win again soon: see 2010, 1707.   61
*2052 EINSTEIN [8] (M Camacho) 2-8-0(7ex) M Hills 9/2: 0113: Not clear run 1f out &
would have fin closer: in fine form & can find another nursery: see 2052.   44
*1869 SAFETY PIN [7] (W Hastings Bass) 2-8-6 T Ives 11/2: 14: Al up there: gd effort: see 1869. 47
2166 TOUGH N GENTLE [5] 2-8-9 R Cochrane 14/1: 2123120: Sn prom & is most consistent.   49
2119 LAST DANCE [9] 2-9-0 J Reid 14/1: 0423120: Never nearer 6th: consistent: see 2119, 1728   54
*1785 LUCRATIF [11] 2-8-1 P Cook 10/1: 110: Prom, fin 7th: see 1785 (firm).   38
*1802 Clear Her Stage [4] 8-6   *353 Four Laffs [2] 7-7(2oh)
2097 Naive Charm [1] 7-9   *1814 Spittin Mick [3] 7-11
2136 Moon Indigo [6] 9-1(BL)
12 ran 1,2,1,hd,shhd,1   (E B Moller)   G Wragg Newmarket

2253 LAGRANGE SELLING STAKES 3YO   £1626   1m 4f   Good 56 -36 Slow

1503 GAY APPEAL [4] (C Nelson) 3-8-8 J Reid 3/1 FAV: 3-03001: 3 ch f Star Appeal -
Summer Madness (Silly Season): Dropped to selling company when an easy 5L winner of a 3yo
seller at Newmarket Aug.23 (bought in 6,000 gns): quite lightly raced previously: stays
12f well: acts on hvy, suited by gd grnd & a gall trk.   28
2073 NO STOPPING [3] (R Hannon) 3-8-11(BL) B Rouse 13/2: 0-00032: Bl first time: led 4f
out: no ch with winner: in gd form & stays 12f: should find a seller: see 2073.   18
1898 LISAKATY [2] (M Mccourt) 3-8-8 R Wernham 10/1: 0000043: Stayed on: best effort this term.
: see 162   07
2152 LAST POLONAISE [5] (M Blanshard) 3-8-8 G Sexton 13/2: 0300004: Prom, ev ch: best 1078 (14f)01
1799 CHERRY LUSTRE [1] 3-8-11 R Carter(4) 9/2: 0003300: Fdd 3f out: twice below 1426.   00
2034 NOT SO SHARP [8] 3-8-8 T Williams 12/1: -00: There 1m.   00
2017 FIRST SUMMER [9] 3-8-11(BL) T Ives 5/1: -0000: Dist last: see 2017.   00
1818 Venus Saga [7] 8-8   2163 Joker Man [6] 8-11(BL)
9 ran 5,4,3,15,10   (Arne Larsson)   C Nelson Upper Lambourn , Berks

2254 MIDWICH THAME MAIDEN STAKES 2YO   £3763   6f   Good 56 -30 Slow

1903 KING KRIMSON [2] (J Hindley) 2-9-0 M Hills 8/1: 01: 2 br c Indian King - Clear Belle
(Klairon): Impr colt: led over 2f out, staying on well to win a slow run 2yo mdn at Newmarket Aug.23: half brother to 2 minor winners: eff at 6f, should stay 7f: acts on gd grnd
& a gall trk.   47
2056 GREEN VEIL [1] (G Wragg) 2-9-0 G Duffield 5/4 FAV: 02: Hvly bckd: al prom: should be
suited by further than 6f: see 2056.   45
2118 LYRICAL LOVER [9] (C Benstead) 2-9-0 B Rouse 10/1: 003: Al up there & continues to
impr: suited by 6f: see 2118.   44
1872 NEARLY GREAT [3] (M Jarvis) 2-9-0 T Ives 7/2: 04: Ch over 1f out: half brother to 2
winners: suited by 6f & gd grnd.   37
--   MUHIM [5] 2-9-0 Paul Eddery 7/1: 0: Prom most on debut: half brother to winning
miler Aristocrat Velvet: acts on gd grnd.   33
1928 PORTENTOUS [4] 2-9-0 G Sexton 14/1: 00: Held ev ch: eff at 6f on gd grnd.   29

-- RUWI VALLEY [8] 2-8-11 T Williams 25/1: 0: Never nearer 7th on racecourse debut:
cost 14,000 gns & is a half sister to several winners, all who stayed well.   23
1629 Technocrat [6] 9-0   1162 Semis [7] 8-11
9 ran 1,¼,2½,1½,1½,1½   (K Al-Said)   J Hindley Newmarket

2255 STANLEY HOUSE HANDICAP 3YO+ 0-60   £4006   1m   Good 56 -19 Slow   [41]

1551 ROMAN BEACH [7] (W Musson) 6-9-3 M Wigham 11/2: -000041: 6 b h Averof - Lovage
(Linacre): Hdway to lead inside final 1f, ridden out in quite slow run h'cap at Newmarket
Aug.23: last won in '84 at Doncaster: well suited by 1m: acts on firm & yld grnd & on any trk.   41
2063 TRAVEL MAGIC [6] (B Hanbury) 3-9-0 J Reid 9/2: -01022: Led final 1f: continues in
fine form: eff at 7f/1m: see 2063, 1451.   45
1395 NORTH OCEAN [4] (L Cumani) 3-9-2 R Guest 13/2: -0303: Ch over 1f out: fair effort, see 1269 44
1028 TOP WING [2] (J Hindley) 3-9-5 M Hills 11/1: 2-10304: Dsptd lead inside final 2f:
gd effort after abs: does well when fresh: see 188.   45
1590 ALQIRM [1] 4-9-7 B Rouse 11/1: -002100: Prom, ev ch: twice below 1240.   36
2149 MY KIND OF TOWN [5] 3-9-6 T Ives 11/2: -110440: Btr 2149: see 335.   41
*1705 FORFLITE [9] 3-8-13 Paul Eddery 7/2 FAV: -310: Made much: btr 1705 (turning trk).   00
*2165 FUSILIER [8] 4-9-6(bl)(5ex) T Williams 7/1: 0000010: Early ldr: fdd & much btr 2165.   00
8 ran 1,1½,1,1,1½   (R Canham)   W Musson Newmarket

2256 BERESFORD HANDICAP STAKES 3YO+ 0-35   £2072   5f   Good 56 +14 Fast   [35]

2124 CAPTAINS BIDD [8] (H Whiting) 6-8-1 W Woods(3) 8/1: 0204141: 6 ch g Captain James -
Muffet (Matador): Led inside final 1f, driven out in quite fast run h'cap at Newmarket Aug.23:
earlier won a similar event at Wolverhampton: placed several times previously: very eff at
5f, stays 6f: acts on soft, likes gd & firm grnd: in fine form.   18
1810 FOOLISH TOUCH [6] (K Stone) 4-9-4(vis) C Dwyer 11/2: 1004402: Sn prom: went right
over 1f out, but stayed on well & just btn: not the easiest of rides: see 401.   34
1940 FREMONT BOY [1] (C James) 4-8-4 B Rouse 10/1: -230403: Nearest fin: fair effort. best 679. 17
2120 MOZART [7] (B Hanbury) 3-8-4 M Hills 6/1: -00044: Led over 1f out: eff at 5/6f: may
find a race on a sharper trk: see 2120.   19
-2033 STONEYDALE [5] 4-9-10 G Duffield 11/2: 1000020: No luck in running: see 2033.   33
1950 DAVILL [4] 4-9-4 T Ives 7/2 FAV: 0000030: Speed over 3f: see 1950, 76.   25
1947 Umbelata [10] 8-10   1584 Skylin [9] 8-5   2143 Sancilia [3] 8-6(BL)
2160 Farmer Jock [12] 8-9(vis)   2160 Puccini [11] 9-6
977 Princess Wendy [2] 9-1
12 ran nk,1,¾,1,¾   (R Whiting)   H Whiting Costock Grange, Leics

---

GOODWOOD   Saturday August 23rd   Righthand Undulating Track

Official Going Given As GOOD/FIRM ON ROUND COURSE: GOOD FOR THE REST

2257 MARCH STAKES LISTED RACE - 3YO   £11394   1m 6f   Good/Firm 24 -08 Slow

2062 CELESTIAL STORM [6] (L Cumani) 3-8-11 W R Swinburn 3/1: 0-1321: 3 b c Roberto -
Tobira Celeste (Ribot): Smart, progressive colt: waited with, smooth hdway to lead dist when
comfortably winning valuable March Stakes (Listed race) at Goodwood Aug.23: first time out,
impressively won competitive mdn at Newmarket & also fin a close 3rd to stable companion
Chinoiserie in the valuable Extel H'cap again at Goodwood: eff over 10f but certainly seems
btr suited by lngr dists & stays 14f really well: acts on any trk & on firm & gd going:
his turn of foot must give him a leading ch in the St Leger.   78
*1652 SADEEM [7] (G Harwood) 3-9-1 G Starkey 11/8 FAV: -3112: Hvly bckd, chall dist, not
pace of winner: fine effort from this impr colt: stays 14f well: see 1652.   75
1992 FLEETING AFFAIR [2] (G Harwood) 3-8-8 B Thomson 12/1: 1110223: Led briefly 2f out,
kept on well & staying on to impr: stays 14f: see 1209.   66
+1642 AL KAAHIR [5] (H T Jones) 3-9-1 A Murray 7/2: 2-31214: Led ½way, no extra final 2f:
btr 1642 (gall trk).   63
1642 MUBAARIS [1] 3-8-11 W Ryan 14/1: -111400: Not disgraced but best 552.   58
1642 NICOLA WYNN [4] 3-8-8 T Quinn 33/1: -13000: Out of her depth: see 458.   45
1988 ROBBAMA [3] 3-8-11 W Carson 14/1: 10-4320: Led to ½way: btr 1988.   00
7 ran 3,¾,10,1,5   (Richaard L Duchossois)   L Cumani Newmarket

2258 LISMORE H'CAP 3YO+ 0-75   £12681   6f   Good/Firm 24 +15 Fast   [60]

1933 PRECIOUS METAL [2] (A Ingham) 3-9-0 R Curant 11/1: -103001: 3 b c Mummy's Pet -
Golden Treasure (Crepello): Al prom & just got the btr of a driving, blanket fin in a fast
run valuable h'cap at Goodwood Aug.23: won an app h'cap over the same C/D: in '85 won at
Salisbury: very eff at 6f: acts on fast & hvy going.   64
1145 IRISH COOKIE [7] (I Matthews) 4-8-1 G Dickie 25/1: -014102: Dsptd lead final 3f,
just btn: fine effort after abs: see 1026.   44
1777 YOUNG INCA [4] (L Cottrell) 8-8-13 I Johnson 12/1: 0000003: Kept on well: just btn &
must be noted next time: see 1777.   56
1852 OUR JOCK [16] (R Smyth) 4-9-5 W Carson 11/4 FAV: 0004104: Hvly bckd: led 2f out, just
failed to last home: loves Goodwood: see 1306.   61

2160 GLEN KELLA MANX [6] 5-8-2(5ex) J Williams 7/1: -000100: Waited with, not quite
get on terms but in gd form: see 2021.   4½
1443 CRONKS QUALITY [3] 3-7-12 R Fox 11/1: -000030: Held up, gd fin: again showed he
is returning to form: one to note in the near future: see 884.   42
--   HANDSOME SAILOR [12] 3-9-7 B Thomson 20/1: 10412-0: Ran well 5f, fin 7th & a fine
seasonal debut: has changed stables since last season when proving most consistent, winning
at Windsor, Newcastle & Haydock: best form at 5f though acts on any going & on any trk:
certain to go close next time, especially over 5f.   61
1911 FORMATUNE [17] 4-7-8(bl) R Street 11/1: 2332030: Ev ch, fin 8th: see 10, 1911. 28
1777 AMIGO LOCO [8] 5-9-7(bl) S Whitworth 25/1: 0004000: Speed most, fin 9th: see 70, 245. 53
+1750 MYRAS SPECIAL [10] 3-8-10 R Hills 10/1: 10-0010: Fdd into 10th: see 1750.   48
*1933 MANIMSTAR [11] 6-9-11 G Baxter 8/1: 0002110: Anchored by top weight: see 1933 (C/D). 00
660 BRIDGE STREET LADY [14] 5-9-2 G Starkey 10/1: -201200: Led to ½way, after long abs. 00
1777 TYROLLIE [1] 4-8-11 S Dawson 9/1: 1220040: Early pace: btr 1777.   00
2079 AMEGHINO [15] 6-8-4 K Darley 8/1: 0330000: Dsptd lead 2f out, fdd: best 1037 (stiff 5f). 00
1235 Ardrox Lad [5] 9-3   2021 Barrack Street [9] 9-1(bl)
2079 Exert [13] 7-7(BL)(8oh)
17 ran   nk,shhd,½,1,½,1½,hd,¾,hd   (G Moore)   A Ingham Epsom, Surrey

2259 GR.2 WATERFORD CRYSTAL MILE   £38440   1m   Good/Firm 24 +07 Fast

-2064 THEN AGAIN [7] (L Cumani) 3-8-7(1ow) G Starkey 8/1: 1-10121: 3 b c Jaaziero -
New Light (Reform): Very smart colt: well ridden to lead 1f out, holding on close home in a
tight fin to Gr.2 Waterford Crystal Mile at Goodwood Aug.23: defied 9-7 in a valuable h'cap
at Newmarket July 19 & first time out won a minor event at Pontefract: last season trained in
Ireland & won at the Curragh: just about stays 10f but definitely seems best over 1m: acts
on gd/firm & yld: progressive colt.   84
1597 SHARROOD [1] (W Hern) 3-8-6 W Carson 13/2: 0430322: Waited with, stayed on strongly
final 1f: seems to need 10f now: see 1597.   82
1514 SIYAH KALEM [5] (J Dunlop) 4-9-0 B Thomson 50/1: -412003: Fin strongly showing
further impr: see 706, 1109.   79
1790 SUPREME LEADER [6] (C Brittain) 4-9-0 P Robinson 10/1: 1133004: Prom thro'out. see 1095 78
1877 SCOTTISH REEL [4] 4-9-4 W R Swinburn 4/5 FAV: 40-2120: Hvly bckd, led/dsptd lead
till no extra final 1f: btr 1877 (C/D).   79
*1492 SARAB [2] 5-9-0 T Quinn 9/1: 4-31110: Chall on bit 2f out, no extra: btr 1492 (yld). 75
+2145 HADEER [3] 4-9-0 G Baxter 9/1: -204110: Fdd final 2f, fin 7th: much btr 2145 (7f). 65
2233 GREY DESIRE [8] 6-9-0 K Darley 33/1: 0230000: Made much: stiff task but has just
lost his edge: see 1631.   00
8 ran   ½,½,nk,2,hd,5   (R J Shannon)   L Cumani Newmarket

2260 RICHMOND BRISSAC AMAT.H'CAP 0-45   £3830   1m 2f   Good/Firm 24 -17 Slow   [23]

1929 BLENDERS CHOICE [7] (J King) 4-10-11 Mr T T Jones 5/2 FAV: 3011131: 4 b g Cavo Doro -
Harriny (Floribunda): Prog colt: scoring his 4th win in last 5 outings, leading 4f out.
readily in a slowly run amateur riders h'cap at Goodwood Aug.23: earlier completed a hat
trick at Warwick, Chepstow & Folkestone: below his best at Newmarket last time: seems best
on a sharpish/easy trk: eff over 10/12f & does well up with the pace.   48
*1931 MAILMAN [8] (I Balding) 7-11-7 Mr T Reed 7/2: 0-40312: 2nd final 2f & btr 1931 (C/D). 48
*2059 IKTIYAR [5] (S Mellor) 4-10-9(7ex) Mr R Hutchinson 7/2: 0010013: Prom thro'out:
in gd form: see 2059.   36
1931 RUNNING FLUSH [9] (D Oughton) 4-10-10(vis) Mr F Grasso Caprioli 9/2: 4300104: better 1519. 27
2121 DERRYRING [1] 4-10-4 Mr A Schultz 16/1: 0000040: Ev ch: best 1383.   16
2049 SEVEN SWALLOWS [4] 5-9-12 Mr J Ryan 16/1: 1000000: No threat: little form since 184(yld) 00
2132 Dolly [2] 9-7   1497 Ranelagh [3] 9-12(5ow) 1788 Big Pal [6] 10-7
9 ran   8,hd,8,3,15   (Mark O'Connor)   J King Uffcote, Wilts

2261 FED.OF BRITISH RACING CLUBS NURSERY   £2876   5f   Good/Firm 24 +09 Fast   [53]

*2166 MUKHABBR [3] (C Benstead) 2-8-8(7ex) W Carson 11/8 FAV: 3031111: 2 b c Taufan -
Ribotingo (Petingo): Well h'capped colt who landed his 4th nursery off the reel, comfortably
leading dist in a fast run nursery at Goodwood Aug.23: similarly easy winner at Lingfield (2)
& Windsor recently: half brother to very useful sprinter Pampas: very eff over 5/6f with
forcing tactics on fast grnd: may even win again.   45
2136 JAISALMER [4] (D Elsworth) 2-9-0(BL) W R Swinburn 7/2: 0200222: Bl first time today:
waited with, gd fin but becoming a little frustrating to follow: see 1910 (C/D). 47
+1683 KYVERDALE [7] (M Ryan) 2-9-7 P Robinson 11/2: 20113: Al there, fin effort: see 1683. 54
1938 JAH BLESS [6] (P Haynes) 2-8-12 B Thomson 25/1: 22004: Chall 2f out: best effort
since 497 & likes an undulating trk.   39
1891 ABSOLUTION [8] 2-9-2 S Whitworth 5/1: 3212200: Made much & likes a sharp 5f. see 1693. 39
2127 MINIZEN LASS [5] 2-8-0(2ow) T Quinn 10/1: 0224200: Early pace: btr 1867.   11
1867 Sparkling Britt [1] 7-11   1261 Viva Ronda [2] 8-0
8 ran   1,shhd,2,1½,8   (Hamdan Al-Maktoum)   C Benstead Epsom, Surrey

2262 SHIPS DECANTER STAKES 3YO   £2758   1m   Good/Firm 24 -08 Slow

1823 CROMWELL PARK [1] (M Ryan) 3-9-8(bl) P Robinson 7/4: 1-40041: 3 b c Moorestyle -
Appleby Park (Bay Express): Useful colt: never hdd, holding on gamely final 1f in a 4 horse

3yo minor race at Goodwood Aug.23: won only race in '85, a 26 runner Newmarket mdn: well
suited by forcing tactics over 7f/1m though seems to act on any trk: likes fast grnd: best
form in bl this season.   65
1655 ENTRANCING [3] (J Dunlop) 3-9-2 W Carson 11/10 FAV: 12-0002: Going easily 3f out,
hung badly under press final 2f: best 7f? see 264.   57
1971 DANCING EAGLE [2] (M Jarvis) 3-9-3 W R Swinburn 5/1: 3230023: Ev ch: yet to reproduce 899 48
1890 WEST CARRACK [4] (A Ingham) 3-9-8 R Curant 10/1: 0300004: Has run badly since 884.   28
4 ran   1,10,25   (G W Mills)   M Ryan Newmarket

2263 COWDRAY STAKES 2YO   £2658   7f   Good/Firm 24 -49 Slow

+1915 HENDEKA [11] (H Cecil) 2-9-3 W Ryan 4/7 FAV: 311: 2 b c Shecky Greene - Ten Plus
(Judger): Prom colt: scoring his 2nd course win on the trot, cleverly leading dist in a
very slowly run 2yo minor race at Goodwood Aug.23: earlier won a fast run mdn on the same
trk Aug.1: cost a modest $50,000 & looks a bargain at todays prices: eff over 6/7f, looks
likely to stay 1m: acts on fast grnd & an undulating trk though also ran well at Newmarket
first time out: should impr further.   67
--   RANDOM ROVER [6] (B Hills) 2-8-11 B Thomson 20/1: 2: Chall final 1f, fine first
effort and has the scope to impr & win a mdn very soon: first foal of a middle dist winner:
certain to stay at least 1m.   57
--   WHITSTABLE [5] (G Harwood) 2-8-11 G Starkey 8/1: 3: Tried to make all & this was
a prom debut, considering he looked just in need of the race: American bred colt who is
sure to impr on this first effort.   52
--   ARTFUL DODGER [8] (W Hern) 2-8-11 W Carson 5/1: 4: Never btr & showed signs of
inexperience on this racecourse debut: cost I.R. 57,000 gns: should impr greatly for this race 49
2044 ANGEL CITY [1] 2-8-11 T Quinn 11/1: 00: No real threat: see 2044.   37
1307 LOVE TRAIN [10] 2-8-11 S Whitworth 33/1: 440: Last away after abs since btr 1307.   36
2001 REEF OF GOLD [4] 2-8-11 P Robinson 14/1: 00: Ran well: should impr: see 2001.   35
--   Arrowknight [3] 8-11   1234 Hollywood Man [7] 8-11
--   Goodnight Master [9] 8-8   -- Charity Day [2] 8-11 U
11 ran   nk,2,1,4,nk,nk   (Sheikh Mohammed)   H Cecil Newmarket

---

NEWCASTLE   Saturday August 23rd   Lefthanded, Stiff Galloping Track

Official Going Given As GOOD/SOFT

2264 ACOMB APPRENTICE HANDICAP 0-35   £1518   1m   Good 60 -28 Slow   [27]

2173 QUALITAIRESS [8] (K Stone) 4-8-0(vis) P Burke(5) 16/1: 0302201: 4 b g Kampala -
Leapallez (Hallez): Stayed on well to lead near fin in an app h'cap at Newcastle Aug.23:
first success, previously had found one too good on several occasions: eff over 6/8f on
fast & soft grnd: runs well on a gall trk: wears a visor.   08
1906 O I OYSTON [6] (J Berry) 10-9-1 J Carroll(3) 6/1: 0020222: Sn in front, again just
denied: retains plenty of enthusiasm despite his advancing years: see 1758.   21
2126 ZIO PEPPINO [3] (C Lloyd Jones) 5-8-8 Julie Bowker(3) 16/1: 2044403: Al up there: see 490 12
2076 SHARONS ROYALE [12] (R Whitaker) 3-8-6 K Bradshaw 5/1 FAV: 0003244: Nearest fin:
remains a mdn though may get off the mark when tackling a slightly lngr trip: see 1309.   18
1671 ULTRESSA [7] 3-8-2(VIS) J Quinn 16/1: 0004000: Visored first time: fair effort though
probably found this trip too short: see 1671 & 935.   12
2126 GOOD N SHARP [19] 5-8-3(1ow) N Rodgers(0) 25/1: 000-200: Late prog: see 1766.   00
2059 HELLO GYPSY [15] 5-9-5 W Goodwin(5) 6/1: 00-2130: Big weight & no threat: much
btr in 1760.   00
2086 BELLA BANUS [16] 4-9-7 B Mcgiff(3) 9/1: -000030: Dwelt & al behind: btr here in 2086.   00
1841 Cassandras Dream [13] 8-4   *2126 Trade High [20] 9-3(6ex)
1976 Balnerino [4] 8-6   2012 Single Hand [18] 8-13   2104 Gold Chip [9] 9-2
1565 Fill Abumper [1] 8-1(4ow)   2104 Rapid Action [5] 9-2
2039 Heavenly Hoofer [2] 9-0   1054 Little Newington [10] 8-12
2076 Master Music [17] 7-11   1766 Manix [4] 7-11
19 ran   ½,½,nk,½,2½,shhd,nk   (Qualitair Engineering Ltd)   K Stone Malton, Yorks

2265 ARMADA NURSERY HANDICAP 2YO   £2031   5f   Good 60 +15 Fast   [49]

1925 FULL OF PRIDE [1] (M H Easterby) 2-9-7 M Birch 11/2: 1201: 2 b f Lochnager - Apple
Of My Eye (Silver Cloud): Useful filly: comfortably defied top weight, made all in a fast time
to win a nursery h'cap at Newcastle Aug.23: earlier made a successful debut in a fillies mdn
over this C/D: dam a useful stayer on the Flat & over hdles: very eff over 5f, though
does stay further: acts on gd & firm grnd & well suited by a stiff trk.   56
*1972 SPANISH SLIPPER [3] (W Haigh) 2-8-7(BL) J H Brown(5) 9/2: 422412: Chased winner thro'out,
kept on well & remains in fine form: acts on any trk: see 1972: bl 1st time today.   36
2137 PASHMINA [12] (T Fairhurst) 2-8-1 J Callaghan(7) 13/2: 0210333: Clear of rem: running well
see 2137 and 1893.   26
1696 LINPAC NORTH MOOR [11] (C Elsey) 2-8-2(bl) N Connorton 12/1: 0024034: Al prom: best 1696.15
+1893 BAD PAYER [2] 2-8-3 G Carter(3) 7/2 FAV: 431210: No extra dist: btr in 1893 (shrp trk).   14
1681 ANOTHER SEASON [4] 2-8-8(BL) D Nicholls 20/1: 0400: Bl first time: short lived
effort ½way, never reached ldrs: btr over 6f in 1681: see 1090.   15

1978 BRUTUS [10] 2-9-2 M Fry 9/1: 0103040: Led stands side over ½way: fin 8th: see 1978.   00
1825 Firmly Attached [13] 8-9   1174 The Granitton [6] 8-1
2137 Penbreasy [8] 8-0   1475 Just One More [5] 8-9   2137 Broons Addition [9] 8-1
2047 Artful Maid [7] 8-7
13 ran   1½,1¼,4,¾,1¼,hd,1½   (Ian Armitage)   M H Easterby Great Habton, Yorks

2266 NORTHERN HANDICAP 3YO 0-70   £5781   1m   Good 60 -27 Slow   [67]

1974 TAYLORMADE BOY [3] (Denys Smith) 3-7-7 L Charnock 13/2: 2303101: 3 b c Dominion -
Ash Gayle (Lord Gayle): Gsmely made all in a 3yo h'cap at Newcastle Aug.23: 1ast month won
a similar event over this C/D, after earlier winning an Edinburgh mdn: stays 10f though all
his winning form is over 1m: acts on gd/firm & hvy grnd & on any trk, though clearly has
a liking for Newcastle: does well with forcing tactics.   44
+2091 CANADIAN STAR [1] (M Jarvis) 3-7-9(vis)(4ex) M L Thomas 5/4 FAV: -024112: Well bckd: just
failed to peg back winner & remains in fine form: see 2091.   44
1912 CHARTINO [6] (G Huffer) 3-9-7 G Carter(3) 9/2: 112-003: Held up, going on fin:
lightly raced this term & is quite high in the h'cap after showing smart form as a juvenile:
seems to be returning to that form: see 802.   66
1864 GOLDEN ANCONA [4] (E Eldin) 3-7-7 J Quinn(5) 5/1: -100024: No extra inside dist: see 1864   32
2076 SUPREME KINGDOM [2] 3-7-7(3oh) P Hill(7) 16/1: 0004300: Fdd below dist: best in 1783
(sharper track): see 49.   22
2027 BOLD SEA ROVER [5] 3-7-8 M Fry 8/1: 0130100: No real dngr: much btr in 1840 (6f).   13
6 ran   nk,2,2,5,5   (Bryan Robson)   Denys Smith Bishop Auckland, Co Durham

2267 THOMAS LONSDALE GALLAGHER HCAP 0-35   £4454   1m 2f   Good 60 -28 Slow   [35]

*2149 HONEST TOIL [4] (R Whitaker) 3-8-8(5ex) D Mckeown 7/1: 041D411: 3 br c Anax -
Be Honest (Klairon): In fine form, confidently ridden to lead close home in a h'cap at
Newcastle Aug.23: recent winner of a 3yo h'cap at Ripon & earlier first past the post in a
similar race over this C/D though subs. disq: half brother to several winners: eff over 8/10f
on firm & yld grnd: acts on any trk.   35
2066 HANDLEBAR [6] (J Watts) 4-9-12 N Connorton 8/1: -001122: Just failed to make all:
grand effort under top weight & should regain winning form soon: see 1636.   40
*2154 SPRING FLIGHT [11] (A Jarvis) 3-8-7(5ex) D Nicholls 85/40 FAV: 1323113: Dsptd lead
over ½way, not qckn close home though ran another gd race: see 2154.   28
2154 GREED [2] (J Fitzgerald) 5-8-12 L Charnock 16/1: 4432404: Placed again: see 1185.   19
1974 FOREMAST [12] 3-8-9 M Fry 14/1: -130340: Best on hvy in 822 (1m).   26
2149 BOYNTON [1] 3-7-12(BL) P Hill(7) 25/1: 0202400: Bl first time: disapp since 1178.   14
*1866 LAKINO [10] 4-8-12 R Brown(6) 15/2: -000010: Fdd into 7th: best in 1866 (11f).   00
893 SANTOPADRE [8] 4-7-8 J Quinn(5) 10/1: 0003-30: Long abs: fin 8th: see 893.   00
*2102 BOLD ARCHER [13] 3-8-4(5ex) C Rutter(3) 7/1: 0201010: Fin last: much btr in 2102.   00
2173 Common Farm [3] 8-6   2130 Golden Fancy [7] 9-2   1581 Pearl Fisher [5] 8-12
12 ran   nk,1½,2,shhd,nk   (D I Buckley)   R Whitaker Wetherby, Yorks

2268 GALLOWGATE SELLING STAKES 3YO   £1383   6f   Good 60 -01 Slow

*1917 COOPER RACING NAIL [16] (J Berry) 3-8-9 J Carroll(7) 7/1: 0230111: 3 b f Martinmas-
Wavy Navy (Hardicanute): In fine form & was completing a hat trick when comfortably making all
in a 3yo seller at Newcastle Aug.23 (no bid): earlier a narrow winner of similar races at
Ayr & Thirsk: eff over 6/7f with forcing tactics: acts on firm & soft grnd & on any trk:
a good mount for an app.   22
2124 PUNCLE CREAK [4] (G Moore) 3-8-9 D Casey(7) 10/1: 0023302: Led far side, just held on
to 2nd place & remains a mdn: see 1617 & 103.   15
2027 IMPERIAL SUNRISE [3] (M W Easterby) 3-8-9 T Lucas 9/4: 4300203: Clear of rem: mdn: see 309.15
1841 VITAL STEP [5] (T Fairhurst) 3-8-9 M Rimmer 16/1: 00-0004: Wknd dist: see 1425.   00
1927 BOLD FURY [12] 3-8-12 G French 7/4 FAV: -20: Disapp fav: much btr on his debut in 1927
and worth another ch if kept in this grade.   01
2106 HOBOURNES KATIE [1] 3-8-9 S Perks 20/1: 0000000: Prom most: has shown little worthwhile form this term: see 246.   00
2174 ALEXANJO [10] 3-9-0 D Nicholls 7/1: 0000020: Wknd quickly dist: btr in 2174 (7f).   00
1885 Miss Blake [13] 8-9   1959 Tenasserim [8] 8-12(BL)
1200 Sister Nancy [2] 8-9   1824 Duke Of Milltimber [14] 8-12
2139 Music Teacher [6] 8-9   1917 Marshall Drills [11] 8-9
1960 Moloch [9] 8-12(bl)   1734 Spring Garden [7] 8-9(bl)
1617 Motor Master [15] 8-12
16 ran   1½,shhd,5,¾,2½,shhd,¾   (Peter G Hodgson)   J Berry Cockerham, Lancs

2269 NEWGATE MAIDEN STAKES   £1566   1m 4f   Good 60 -12 Slow

2042 HIGH KNOWL [4] (B Hills) 3-8-3 C Rutter(3) 3/1: 0-4231: 3 ch c High Line - Madina
(Beau Prince): Useful colt: well bckd & was never hdd when a comfortable winner of an all
aged mdn at Newcastle Aug.23: half brother to several winners, incl useful French miler
Nonoalca: eff over 10/12f on gd & fast grnd: acts on any trk: consistent & clearly well
suited by front running tactics.   52
--   SHERGOR [3] (H Cecil) 3-8-3 N Day 5/2 FAV: -2: Chased winner thro'out: 140,000 gns
son of Shergar whose dam also possessed plenty of ability: eff over 12f on gd grnd: acts
on a gall trk: should be placed to win.   46

1899 POKEYS PRIDE [5] (R Sheather) 3-8-3 M Rimmer 11/4: 0-02203: Seems one paced: see 1530.   42
2030 TAP EM TWICE [2] (M Jarvis) 3-8-3 M L Thomas 4/1: 4-23304: Well btn & yet to reproduce
form shown in 430.   20
-- KARAKTER REFERENCE [1] 4-9-0 D Nicholls 33/1: -0: Btn a dist. on racecourse debut: bred
to be suited by middle dists.   00
-- AUERSBERG [7] 3-8-3 S Webster 16/1: 30040-0: Al behind on belated reapp: twice placed
in mdn company last term over 7/8f: acts on gd & firm grnd: clearly needed this race.   00
6 ran   3,2½,15,dist,25   (K Abdulla)   B Hills Lambourn, Berks

---

WINDSOR   Saturday August 23rd   Left & Righthand, Sharpish Track

Official Going Given As GOOD/SOFT

2270 E.B.F. GREAT PARK STAKES 2YO   £1372   6f   Good 41 +11 Fast

*1955 CRY FOR THE CLOWN [14] (A Bailey) 2-8-11 R Cochrane 4/1: 11: 2 b c Cawston's Clown-
Bayberry (Henry The Seventh): Useful, fast impr colt: again well bckd & led 1½f out, readily
in a fast run 2yo stakes at Windsor Aug.23: first time out landed a big gamble when an easy
winner of a seller at Ripon: very eff at 6f, should stay 7f: acts on gd & fast grnd & a
sharpish trk: should complete the hat trick.   56
1629 UNITY FARM BOY [1] (P Cundell) 2-8-11 N Adams 33/1: 0002: Al up there, showing much
impr form: seems well suited by gd grnd, 6f & a sharpish trk: cost only 3,000 gns as a yearling 40
1826 SUPREME STATE [6] (P Makin) 2-8-11 D Price 33/1: 003: Front rank most: best effort
yet & seems suited by an easy 6f: acts on gd & fast grnd: see 1522.   39
1915 LIBRAN STAR [17] (H Candy) 2-8-11 W Newnes 5/4 FAV: 044: Dsptd lead most: well below
fine effort in 1915 & deserves another ch: see 1629.   34
*2080 NORAPA [7] 2-9-4 K Darley 11/2: 310: Dsptd lead most: btr 2080.   31
773 RUSSIAN WALTZ [18] 2-8-8 P Tulk 16/1: 00: Prom most after fair abs: U.S. bred filly
who acts on gd grnd.   15
-- TAIANA [12] 2-8-8 G Baxter 20/1: 0: Nearest fin in 7th: mkt drifter today & will impr.   00
1869 FLUTEAU [2] 2-8-11 A'Kimberley 9/1: 00: No real threat: see 1869.   00
1238 Pollan Bay [8] 8-8   -- Odiaxere [20] 8-8   -- San Juan Song [16] 8-11
1665 Montys Gunner [3] 8-11   1869 Home Jesta [5] 8-11
13 Dear Glenda [11] 8-8   -- Pathias [19] 8-11   -- Suivez Moi [15] 8-11
-- Lord Of Canewdon [13] 8-11
17 ran   5,hd,2,3,2,2   (Mrs J Bailey)   A Bailey Newmarket

2271 SUMMER SELLING STAKES   £971   1m   Good 41 -5¼ Slow

1937 SPARKFORD LAD [8] (D Elsworth) 4-8-8(bl) Debbie Wheatley(7) 5/1: 0000021: 4 b g Hot Spark-
Callidice (Worden II): Made most, ridden out in a seller at Windsor Aug.23 (bought in
3,100 gns): first success: seems suited by 1m & a sharpish trk: acts on gd & fast grnd.   17
1937 BLUE FANTASY [15] (B Stevens) 3-7-11 A Mackay 14/1: -000002: Kept on well, showing
impr form: suited by an easy 1m & gd grnd: see 749.   11
2187 JUST CANDID [10] (D Wilson) 4-8-8 T Williams 9/2 FAV: 0033423: Ev ch final 2f:
consistent: see 2187.   11
2132 THE UTE [2] (L Bower) 3-8-6(bl) P Mcentee(7) 15/2: 3201204: Al up there: see 1827 (6f).   15
1990 COUNT ALMAVIVA [14] 3-8-0(bl) W Newnes 10/1: 0030000: No extra final 1f: see 1364 (7f).   07
1439 POCO LOCO [5] 4-8-8 G Baxter 7/1: 3402300: Prom most: see 1056 (10f), 889.   00
-- UP TOWN BOY [16] 4-9-0 N Adams 10/1: 14443-0: Mkt drifter on seasonal debut: speed 5f:
in '85 won a seller at Brighton & is consistent in this grade: eff at 1m, stays 10f: likes
a sharpish, undulating trk.   00
2017 NICE PRESENT [4] 3-7-12(1ow) R Hills 8/1: -0000: Made no show: see 2017.   00
344 MIND THE TIME [19] 4-8-8 J Williams 5/1: 0202-00: Mkt drifter & no threat: long abs
& maybe been hurdling season: placed in Ireland last season.   00
2132 Top Feather [13] 8-5   2094 Csillag [3] 7-11(bl)   -- Shelley Marie [9] 8-11
1819 Seago [7] 8-0   2187 Chief Runner [11] 8-8   568 Equipped For Duty [18] 8-8
1937 Fort Duchesne [1] 9-0   -- Mr Fizycal [17] 8-0   1340 Hillingdon Jim [20] 8-0
1694 Sea Trouper [12] 8-0
19 ran   1½,1,1½,¾,3,4   (A G Wheatley)   D Elsworth Fordingbridge, Hants

2272 NEL BRITANNIA NURSERY H'CAP 2YO   £2905   6f   Good 41 -02 Slow   [54]

2095 REMAIN FREE [3] (C Williams) 2-7-7(BL)(7oh) R Morse(5) 20/1: 33041: 2 b f Kampala -
Mallow Isle (Young Emperor): Bl first time & showed impr form, dspt lead final 2f & staying
on well in a nursery h'cap at Windsor Aug.23: well suited by 6f & gd & fast grnd: half
sister to Duhallow Boy and Rocky's Gal: acts on any trk, but seems suited by an easy one.   27
1972 MISS MILVEAGH [6] (A Bailey) 2-8-1 A J Geran(7) 9/1: 3222: Led over 1f out: in gd
form: stays 6f: see 1972, 1826.   32
*1832 JABE MAC [2] (L Holt) 2-7-8 N Adams 14/1: 00013: Kept on well: stays 6f: see 1832.   22
2035 BORN FREE AGAIN [1] (L Piggott) 2-8-13 R Cochrane 9/2: 0020344: Ch when hmpd final 1f:
unlucky? see 2035.   40
2166 KEEN EDGE [12] 2-7-12 R Fox 7/1: 2003030: Prom, ev ch: see 2166.   24
2071 BLOFFA [7] 2-7-10 J Lowe 14/1: 300240: Led over 3f: best 1828 (C/D).   14
1891 GREY WOLF TIGER [10] 2-8-13 L Jones(5) 4/1 FAV: 2241140: Speed most: twice below 1522.   00

1968 KIERON PRESS [5] 2-8-9 J Reid 6/1: 03140: Never showed: best 1495.   00
1735 IBNALMAGHITH [4] 2-9-7 A Murray 7/1: 1430: Speed most: see 1735.   00
+1816 CHILIBANG [11] 2-9-0(BL) G Baxter 7/1: 410: Well below 1816 (made running): wore bl. today. 00
2071 SARASOTA [8] 2-7-7(8oh) T Williams 33/1: 0024000: No show: lightly raced since 354.   00
*1665 JOVICK [9] 2-8-13 P Cook 5/1: 310: Sn in trouble: well below 1665: something amiss?   00
12 ran   ¾,¾,½,½,3,¾,nk,shhd   (Mrs C L Nixon)   C Williams Buckhold, Berks

2273 BRITANNIA ARROW H'CAP (0-60)   £3066   1m 3f Good 41 -72 Slow   [46]

1409 PUBBY [3] (J Toller) 5-8-8 W Carson 6/4 FAV: 1120001: 5 b m Doctor Wall - Snotch
(Current Coin): Landed some gd bets, led inside final 1f, ridden out in a very slow run h'cap
at Windsor Aug.23: won her first 2 starts this season, at Ascot & Newmarket: in fine form
in '85, winning at Haydock & Yarmouth: eff at 10f, well suited by 12f: acts on gd & firm,
likes soft grnd: genuine mare.   35
2066 MIN BALADI [7] (S Norton) 4-8-5 J Lowe 9/2: 1-32002: Led inside final 2f: fair eff: see 629. 30
1939 MOON JESTER [8] (M Usher) 6-7-7(2oh) D Mckay 9/1: 2400003: Made most: best eff since 349. 15
1935 FOLK DANCE [2] (I Balding) 4-9-7 P Cook 7/1: 4420204: Mkt drifter: best 1523.   38
2121 THE FOOTMAN [4] 4-8-13 A Mercer 20/1: -000400: Ev ch in str: see 1324.   27
2015 DIVA ENCORE [5] 3-8-9 R Hills 13/2: 0112230: Needs further? see 1817, 1694.   33
1441 PERISIAN KNIGHT [1] 4-8-11 M Wigham 5/1: 00-0100: There over 9f: see 1441: best 1124.   00
2121 WELSH MEDLEY [6] 4-8-6 D Williams(7) 14/1: 0321400: Mkt drifter: the first btn: best 724   00
8 ran   ½,1½,3,1½,1½,¾,3   (A J Morrison)   J Toller Newmarket

2274 BRITANNIA UNIT TRUSTS H'CAP (0-35)   £2673   1m   Good 41 -09 Slow   [27]

2076 COUNTRY GENTLEMAN [10] (J Dunlop) 3-9-7 W Carson 7/1: 0004301: 3 b c Skyliner -
Killyhevlin (Green God): Adopted new tactics & made ev yd, comfortably in a h'cap at
Windsor Aug.23: first success: eff at 1m on gd & firm grnd: seems suited by front running on
an easy trk: has worn bl.   40
2091 HIT THE HEIGHTS [2] (M Pipe) 5-8-13 T Quinn 9/2: 00-2232: No ch with winner, consistent.   16
2091 AQABA PRINCE [1] (P Cundell) 6-8-5 N Adams 20/1: 0000003: Ev ch str: best effort since 812   06
2171 TOPEKA EXPRESS [12] (R Armstrong) 3-8-11(bl) R Hills 2/1 FAV: 0032024: Hvly bckd:
fdd final 1f: btr 2171.   18
1953 THUNDERDOME [9] 3-8-8(vis) Paul Eddery 7/1: -0000: Al there: tried in a visor last
time: stays 1m & acts on gd & fast grnd.   11
1927 FUDGE [15] 3-8-3 S Dawson 20/1: -200000: Mkt drifter: lightly raced this term:
probably stays 1m: see 534.   04
1976 MONTICELLI [3] 6-7-12 J Lowe 10/1: -002000: No threat: best 1231.   00
843 FAIR ATLANTA [11] 3-9-0 R Street 10/1: -240100: Abs: need race? see 505 (yld).   00
1901 Dragonara Boy [8] 9-4   2184 Ikraam [4] 8-0   2132 Rest And Welcome [13] 8-4(BL)
1245 Arabian Blues [7] 8-8   2094 Full Of Speed [5] 8-11
1940 Miss Metal Woods [6] 8-1
14 ran   3,1,1½,1½,¾   (CGA Horseracing Ltd)   J Dunlop Arundel, Sussex

2275 RED SPINNER STAKES 3YO   £959   1m 2f Good 41 -44 Slow

2030 NAJIDIYA [2] (R J Houghton) 3-8-8 J Reid 5/2 JT FAV: 3-02021: 3 ch f Riverman -
Nawazish (Run The Gauntlet): Useful filly: gained a deserved success, led nearing final 1f,
driven out in quite slow run stakes at Windsor Aug.23: very eff at 10f: acts on gd & fast
grnd & on any trk.   46
*2110 BANANAS [5] (O Douieb) 3-9-4 Paul Eddery 5/2 JT FAV: -23412: Ev ch inside final 2f:
consistent: see 2110: acts on any trk.   54
2053 LYPHLAW [10] (J Dunlop) 3-8-11 G Baxter 7/2: 0-0033: Stayed on under press: gd effort.   47
--   FINAL SELECTION [14] (W Hern) 3-8-11 W Carson 10/3: 30-4: Nicely bckd on seasonal
debut: led 2f out: gd effort: ran only twice in '85 & has been very lightly raced: half
brother to 14f winner Musical Box and the smart miler Soprano: acts on gd & yld & should
find a race.   41
1   VILLAGE HERO [6] 3-8-11 R Lines(3) 50/1: 00: Very long abs: showed impr form here:
stays 10f: acts on gd grnd & an easy trk.   35
1503 MAKE PEACE [9] 3-8-11 P Cook 20/1: -330000: Fdd final 2f: best 484 (yld).   25
1835 Chardonnay [13] 8-8   2030 Prince Bold [4] 8-11   357 Tanagon [1] 8-8
2183 Kaasib [8] 8-11   --   Moonlight Madness [7] 8-8
1751 Revanora [3] 8-8   2024 Baliview [11] 8-8   --   Progo [12] 8-11
14 ran   ¾,shhd,3,2½,5   (Aga Khan)   R J Houghton Didcot, Oxon

NEWCASTLE   Monday August 25th   Lefthanded, Stiff Galloping Track

Official Going Given As GOOD

2276 LANGLEE NURSERY H'CAP 2YO   £2851   7f   Good/Firm 33 -07 Slow   [53]

1978 BEN LEDI [4] (M H Easterby) 2-9-6 K Hodgson 12/1: 031131: 2 b g Strong Gale -
Balacco (Balidar): Useful juvenile: well suited by this extra furlong and made all, easily
in a nursery h'cap Aug.25: earlier successful in a mdn auction race at Redcar & a seller
at York: eff over 5/6f, stays 7f really well: acts on gd & firm grnd & is well suited by
a gall trk: does well with forcing tactics: genuine sort who carries weight well: should win again,   58
*1883 PHARAOH BLUE [7] (C Brittain) 2-8-0 W Carson 7/1: 0012: Stayed on well though no ch
with easy winner: in gd form & will be suited by 1m: see 1883.   22
2198 JAYS SPECIAL [11] (M W Easterby) 2-8-6(8ex) T Lucas 5/4 FAV: 4000123: Well bckd: led
stands side, pipped for 2nd place close home: worth another ch: see 2198 & 2025.   27
1925 HUNTERS LEAP [10] (G Moore) 2-8-1 K Darley 20/1: 0201004: Dsptd lead stands side:
gd effort over this lngr trip: acts on gd/firm & hvy: see 973.   20
1625 CHESWOLD [9] 2-7-11 J Lowe 11/1: 40030: Abs: never nearer: stays 7f: see 1625.   08
2108 COMMONSIDR GIPSY [5] 2-8-10 A Proud 14/1: 02000: Prom most: best over 6f in 685.   15
*2140 MURPHY [3] 2-9-0(5ex) K Bradshaw(5) 8/1: 04210: Upped in class: speed to ½way: see 2140.   00
1555 Systems Go [1] 8-4   2198 Toll Bar [8] 9-7
1685 Swynford Prince [2] 7-7(10oh)   *2050 Craigendarroch [6] 7-7(8ex)(1oh)
11 ran   4,½,½,3,2,1,½   (A A McCluskey)   M H Easterby Great Habton, Yorks

2277 CHEVIOT H'CAP STAKES (0-60) 3YO+   £4032   6f   Good/Firm 33 +12 Fast   [40]

1849 CANIF [2] (M Ryan) 5-9-6 W R Swinburn 8/1: 0-01001: 5 gr g Saritamer - Couteau
(Nelcius): Al front rank on fav. far side, led dist for a comfortable win in a fast run h'cap
at Newcastle Aug.25: earlier made most in a similar race at Redcar: failed to win last season
though in '84 won at Goodwood & Lingfield: best form over 6f on gd or faster grnd: acts on any trk   44
2204 ROPER ROW [1] (M H Easterby) 3-8-10 K Hodgson 10/3 FAV: -011332: Made much, hung over
to stands side & no extra close home: most consistent this term: see 2204 & 1627.   35
1959 GOLDEN GUILDER [8] (M W Easterby) 3-8-6(bl) W Carson 7/2: 2031333:Led nearside: see 947.   28
2204 BATON BOY [6] (M Brittain) 5-8-13 K Darley 4/1: 0004044: Dwelt, no extra close home
though not btn far: may find a small h'cap as the grnd eases: see 55.   28
2204 DEBBIE DO [7] 3-9-4 J Lowe 16/1: -400000: Nearest fin: fair effort: see 588.   39
2151 PLAYTEX [3] 6-9-2 R Street 6/1: 3400-40: Prom far side over 4f: see 2151.   26
1247 MIAMI DOLPHIN [4] 6-7-9 M Fry 20/1: 1310300: Gd early speed after abs: see 786.   00
2033 REVEILLE [5] 4-9-7 T Lucas 6/1: 2010030: Front rank to ½way: btr in 2033: see 1066.   00
8 ran   ½,1,½,hd,1½,½   (T P Ramsden)   M Ryan Newmarket

2278 VIRGINIA STAKES (LISTED) 3YO+ FILLIES   £7778   1m 2f   Good/Firm 33 -09 Slow

*2117 SINGLETTA [4] (M Stoute) 3-8-13 W R Swinburn 6/4: 12-3011: 3 b f Nodouble - Cambretta
(Roberto): Smart filly: made ev yd for a decisive win in valuable Virginia Stakes at Newcastle Aug.25: quite lightly raced this term, recently trotted up in a Gr.3 fillies race
at Neuss: in '85 was an easy first time out winner at Ascot: very eff over 10/12f: acts on
gd & firm grnd & on any trk: well suited by front running tactics & certain to win more races.   76
-1912 SWEET MOVER [3] (W Hern) 3-8-4 W Carson 10/11 FAV: 22-122: Chased winner thro'out,
ridden home turn & no impression: comfortably beat rem though btr in 1912.   56
*2068 EXCEPTIONAL BEAUTY [5] (M Jarvis) 3-8-4 T Lucas 10/1: 2-42013: Raised in class &
never threatened the principals: probably btr suited by 12f: see 2068.   48
1630 LUCKY SO SO [1] (S Norton) 3-8-7(VIS) J Lowe 12/1: 1030434: Abs: visored for the
first time today: held up & no real threat: best over this trip in 1630.   39
1111 ANCILLA [2] 4-8-9 Gay Kelleway 33/1: -2-200: No real threat after abs: see 682.   00
5 ran   5,4,7,7   (Sheikh Mohammed)   M Stoute Newmarket

2279 LEAF SELLING STAKES 2YO   £2973   6f   Good/Firm 33 -07 Slow

2025 HARRY HUNT [11] (J Berry) 2-8-11 J Carroll(7) 6/1: 1000101: 2 b c Longleat -
Ardice (Hard Tack): Stayed on well to lead near fin in a 2yo seller at Newcastle(no bid):
last month won a similar race at Ayr, after earlier winning a Hamilton mdn: eff over 5/6f:
acts on any grnd & likes a stiff track.   30
1907 SHARPHAVEN [9] (M Brittain) 2-8-8 K Darley 12/1: 0241002: Dropped back to selling
company: led ½way till caught close home: gd effort & quite useful in this grade: see 1379.   25
2107 ROSIES GLORY [1] (C Tinkler) 2-8-8 W Carson 15/8 FAV: 0023: Early ldr, kept on well
& should win a seller on a lesser trk: acts on gd/firm & yld: see 1881.   19
1604 MUSICAL RHAPSODY [3] (G Pritchard Gordon) 2-8-8 W R Swinburn 7/1: 004: Abs: dropped in
class & showed first signs of form: speedily bred filly who is eff over 6f on gd/firm grnd.   18
2050 GILLOT BAR [5] 2-8-8 T Lucas 9/2: 0002140: Best over 7f here in 1795.   06
2050 ENCHANTED COURT [6] 2-8-11 A Proud 20/1: 000: Prom over ½way: cheaply bought colt
who is a half brother to several winning sprinters: may do btr in time.   01
2025 OUR HORIZON [10] 2-8-8 R Street 11/2: 20040: Fin 7th: best in 1225 (6f): see 612.   00
*2212 NIGHTDRESS [8] 2-8-8(bl) J Lowe 8/1: 003010: Sn lead, hdd ½way: fin 9th: btr 2212 (5f).   00
2080 Lillys Double [4] 8-8   2032 Swynford Lady [2] 8-8 1955 Frev Off [7] 8-8(bl)
11 ran   ½,2,hd,4,3   (J K Brown)   J Berry Cockerham, Lancs

675

NEWCASTLE   Monday August 25th   -Cont'd

2280 PERKINS MEM. CUP H'CAP (0-35) 3YO+   £2257   2m   Good/Firm 33 -69 Slow   [23]

*2111 SHIPBOURNE [8] (G Harwood) 3-9-10(3ex) W R Swinburn 1/1 FAV: 0030311: 3 b c Ilede Bourbon-
Fleet Girl (Habitat): Impr colt: easily justified fav, led below dist & was pushed clear to
win a slowly run h'cap at Newcastle: recent winner of a similar race at Nottingham: well
suited by 2m: acts on gd & firm grnd & on a gall trk: should complete his hat trick.   45
1980 DENALTO [4] (Denys Smith) 3-8-1 M Fry 12/1: -003302: Stayed on well & is suited by
a test of stamina: mdn who acts on gd & firm: see 744.   14
2040 BUSTOFF [7] (S Hall) 6-8-12 J Callaghan(7) 10/1: 2300103: Gd effort: see 1897.   08
2141 STRING OF BEADS [3] (J Etherington) 4-8-1(vis) J Lowe 7/1: 0000024: Made most: see 2141.   00
1700 MR MOSS [2] 3-8-10 W Carson 11/1: -00000: Lngr trip: fair effort: see 714.   12
2211 HIGHAM GREY [1] 10-8-9 A Proud 14/1: 4004400: Little form this term: see 675.   00
1497 SIR BRETT [6] 3-9-6 Gay Kelleway(3) 6/1: -041400: Abs: fin 7th: best in 790 (hvy).   00
1961 Helsanon [9] 8-0   1615 Tieatre [5] 8-8
9 ran 1¼,2½,1½,3,shhd   (K Abdulla)   G Harwood Pulborough, Sussex

2281 E.B.F. HEDGEHOPE MAIDEN STAKES 2YO   £1807   5f   Good/Firm 33 +10 Fast

2127 PARADISE COFFEE [10] (O Douieb) 2-8-11 W R Swinburn 9/2: 231: 2 ch f Sharpo - St Isabel
(Saint Crespin III): Mkt drifter though sn in front & held on gamely to win a fast run 2yo
mdn at Newcastle Aug.25: cost 26,000 gns & is a half sister to numerous winners: eff over
5f & sure to stay further in time: acts on gd & fast grnd & on any trk: clearly does well
with forcing tactics.   45
2127 RAINBOW TROUT [6] (M Camacho) 2-8-11 W Carson 5/1: 0402: Early ldr, going on fin &
will be suited by another furlong: acts on gd/firm grnd & on any trk: see 1958.   39
2105 LAMB BECK [5] (J Jefferson) 2-9-0 A Proud 7/2 JT FAV: 303: Kept on well: see 2105.   38
701 JAMES OWL [8] (W Pearce) 2-9-0 K Darley 8/1: 024: Fair effort after a lengthy abs &
should do btr next time: best in 701.   34
--   PETICOV SHADES [11] 2-9-0 M Fry 14/1: 0: Never nearer on racecourse debut: acts on
gd/firm grnd & on a gall trk.   30
--   ALTOBELLI [7] 2-9-0 K Hodgson 5/1: 0: Nicely bckd debutant: dwelt & had little luck
in running: should do btr next time: speedily bred colt who cost 8,000 gns: acts on gd/firm.   27
1958 YOUNG SNUGFIT [12] 2-9-0 T Lucas 7/2 JT FAV: 00: Raced along nearside: eased inside
dist: half brother to several winners incl Grand National 2nd Mr Snugfit: likely to need
a lngr trip & more time.   00
2007 Not So Silly [3] 9-0   1958 Overpower [2] 9-0   602 Queens Connection [1] 8-11
1916 Atakashack [4] 9-0   2100 Vol Vitesse [9] 9-0(VIS)
12 ran 1½,1½,1½,1½,1½,1½   (Joe Arriola)   O Douieb Newmarket

CHEPSTOW   Monday August 25th   Lefthand, Galloping Track

Official Going Given As FIRST RACE GOOD: REM. GOOD/SOFT. RAINED THRO'OUT THE AFTERNOON.

2282 CAERWENT APPRENTICE HCAP 0-35 3YO+   £1002   1m   Good/Soft 96 -16 Slow   [30]

1901 PETIT BOT [4] (W Musson) 4-7-11(bl) R Price 14/1: 0-00001: 4 ch f Vitiges - Calibina
(Caliban): Gained her first success, staying on well to lead inside final 1f in quite slow run
app h'cap at Chepstow: stays 1m well: acts on gd & yld grnd & a gall trk.   07
1747 STONEBROKER [1] (D H Jones) 4-8-0 J Lake 4/1: 4410022: Led inside final 2f: just
caught: in gd form at present: see 1747, 718.   09
2171 NATIVE HABITAT [12] (M Jarvis) 3-8-13 P Hutton 3/1 FAV: -413333: Ran on well final 1f:
consistent filly: see 2171 : best in 169(10f,yld)   27
1990 CYGNE [11] (G Balding) 4-8-0(3ow) J O'sullivan 12/1: 0-00034: Came too late: stays 1m.   00
2132 FULL OF LIFE [14] 3-9-7 J Scally 11/2: -000220: Fdd final 1f: best 1579.   28
2014 POLEMISTIS [10] 7-7-12(bl) R Teague 16/1: 0000100: No threat: best 1703 (firm).   00
1830 BAKERS DOUGH [9] 3-8-9 G Kennedy 11/2: -000000: Mkt drifter: fin 7th: best 1471.   00
--   Warily [6] 8-5(7ow)   2132 Mr Music Man [2] 8-1 2175 Skinny Dipper [8] 7-8(1ow)
2132 Sahara Shadow [13] 8-10 2189 Steel Pass [15] 8-2   2190 Taffys Pride [5] 8-0(1ow)
2060 Keep Cool [7] 7-12   1953 Miss Stanway [3] 7-8(1ow)(3oh)
15 ran ½,2,3,1,4,hd   (E A Badger)   W Musson Newmarket

2283 EBF CASTLE MDN FILLIES STKS 2YO DIV I   £1278   7f   Good/Soft 96 -04 Slow

2070 RHONDALING [3] (P Walwyn) 2-8-11 N Howe 5/1: 31: 2 b f Welsh Pageant - Touch Of Class
(Luthier): Fast impr filly: led nearing final 2f, gamely holding on by ¾L in a 2yo fillies Chepstow
mdn: dam stayed 12f: eff at 7f & will stay 1m: acts on gd/firm & yld grnd & can cont. to impr.   50
1778 MUSICAL REVIEW [8] (I Balding) 2-8-11 J Matthias 10/11 FAV: 42: Chall final 1f: just
btn & 8L clear 3rd: stays 7f well: acts on yld: see 1778 (gd).   48
2191 RANKSTREET [10] (M Haynes) 2-8-11 W Ryan 20/1: 003: No ch with first 2, but an
impr effort: stays 7f & acts on gd & yld grnd: see 2191.   34
2215 SPEEDBIRD [5] (M Ryan) 2-8-11 G Duffield 8/1: 0004: Prom, ev ch: quite consistent:
stays 7f: half sister to middle dist winner Joli's Belt: acts on firm & yld.   33
548 INDIRAJI [2] 2-8-11 G Baxter 8/1: 00: Mkt drifter after abs: made much: see 548.   28
2105 FLAUNTING [7] 2-8-11 R Hills 10/1: 00: Speed most: btr effort from this half sister to the

676

smart & much impr Hadeer:should be suited by 7f/1m & rate more highly, possibly on better ground.   22
1382 Lady Artful [1] 8-11   1855 Quiet Blush [12] 8-11   1282 Kind Of Class [4] 8-11
1844 My Elane [9] 8-11   1997 Lynda Broad [6] 8-11   2070 Perigris [11] 8-11(bl)
12 ran ½,8,½,2½,3,4   (Mrs Rupert Hambro)   P Walwyn Lambourn, Berks

2284 JOHN HYLTON WATTS MEM NURSERY HCAP   £2444   5f   Good/Soft 96 +13 Fast   [51]

1948 AFRICAN SPIRIT [9] (M Prescott) 2-9-4 G Duffield 10/3 FAV: 1201: 2 b c African Sky -
Relic Spirit (Relic): Useful colt: led inside final 1f for a ready win in fast run nursery
h'cap at Chepstow: below his best over 7f last time out: made a winning debut at Carlisle:
half brother to several winners: very eff at 5f, stays 6f: acts on firm & yld grnd:
should win again: does well on a stiff track.   55
-2181 BOLD GARCON [7] (C Nelson) 2-9-7 J Reid 11/2: 01422: Sn prom: no ch with winner, but
remains in gd form: acts on firm & yld: see 2181, 1555.   50
2158 BO BABBITY [3] (D H Jones) 2-8-12 D Williams(7) 7/2: 30103: Kept on well final 1f:
may be suited by 6f: acts on yld, best 1501 (gd/firm).   36
2178 FALDWYN [1] (T Bill) 2-7-11(bl) W Woods(0) 12/1: 3302004: Made most: see 1180.   20
1782 INDIAN SET [8] 2-8-1 M L Thomas 4/1: 0040: Ev ch: acts on yld but btr 1782 (sharp trk). 19
2172 PINK PUMPKIN [2] 2-7-7(7oh) R Teague(0) 16/1: 2014000: Gd early speed: acts on gd
& yld: see 1496.   10
2172 CLARENTIA [6] 2-8-13 R Hills 6/1: 1403200: Speed 3f: btr 2047, 1910 (gd/firm).   00
*1844 VICTORY BALLARD [5] 2-8-12 L Jones(5) 10/1: 00010: Made no show: see 1844 (gd/firm). 00
2047 Cherrywood Sam [4] 7-7(3oh)   1339 Taliesin [10] 8-3
10 ran   3,2,nk,2½,nk,1½,shhd   (B Haggas)   M Prescott Newmarket

2285 DIAMOND JUBILEE HANDICAP 3YO+ 0-60   £4705   1m 4f   Good/Soft 96 -02 Slow   [43]

*2049 HEART OF STONE [3] (R Akehurst) 4-8-12(5ex) T Quinn 6/4 FAV: 0010311: 4 ch c Dust Com-
mander - Grankie (Nashua): In fine form & led 1½f out, easily in a h'cap at Chepstow: last time
out won comfortably in a h'cap at Lingfield: earlier won again at Lingfield & likes that trk:
eff over 10f, stays 12f well: acts on firm & yld grnd and on a undulating track.   37
*2173 SOCKS UP [4] (R J Houghton) 9-7-13(5ex) R Hills 3/1: 0403012: No threat to winner:
in good form: see 2173.   15
1935 THE JOKER [5] (G Balding) 6-9-7 R Weaver 4/1: -040043: Made much: see 1000.   35
1502 RECORD WING [2] (D H Jones) 8-8-11 D Williams(7) 3/1: 2133004: No extra final 3f: best 92. 13
4 ran 4,½,7   (M J Morrison)   R Akehurst Epsom, Surrey

2286 FERRY STAKES 3YO FILLIES   £3309   1m 2f   Good/Soft 96 +02 Fast

*2170 PSYLLA [5] (H Cecil) 3-9-0 W Ryan 4/5 FAV: -0111: 3 b f Beldale Flutter - Pris
(Priamos): Useful, impr filly: well bckd & led inside final 3f, easily in a 3yo fillies
stakes at Chepstow: winner of her 2 previous starts at Wolverhampton (2): half sister to
the smart miler Prismatic: very eff over 9/10f, may stay further: acts on gd/firm & yld grnd
& runs well from the front: should win more races.   54
1912 TRAVEL MYSTERY [6] (P Walwyn) 3-9-0 N Howe 10/1: 0-13302: Stayed on, though no
ch with winner: gd effort: acts on firm & yld grnd: see 1061: consistent sort, prob. stays 12f 44
2110 MAGIC TOWER [4] (C Brittain) 3-8-11 G Baxter 9/1: 0-4023: Led 7f: rated higher 2110 (gd). 35
*581 SMASHING MILLIE [2] (P Cole) 3-9-3 T Quinn 11/4: 0-14: Mkt drifter after long abs:
needed race? see 581 (good).   40
2062 GLOWING PROMISE [7] 3-9-0 R Hills 5/1: 2-12400: No threat: btr early season in 690, 452 34
2170 AUSTINA [3] 3-8-11(BL) D Williams(7) 33/1: 00-0000: Bl first time: no threat:
stiff task here & little form in 3 previous starts this term.   19
6 ran 3,3,½,1½,4   (P F Shoults)   H Cecil Newmarket

2287 EBF CASTLE MDN FILLIES STKS 2YO DIV II   £1334   7f   Good/Soft 96 -07 Slow

1874 NORTHSHIEL [3] (H Candy) 2-8-11 W Newnes 6/5 FAV: 431: 2 ch f Northfields - Coryana
(Sassafras):Useful filly: well bckd & made nearly all, comfortably in a 2yo fillies stakes
at Chepstow: a gd 3rd to Candle In The Wind last time out at Goodwood: well suited by 7f,
should stay 1m: acts on firm & yld grnd & seems suited by forcing tactics: can continue to improve. 50
-- RARE MEMORIES [6] (P Cole) 2-8-11 T Quinn 3/1: 2: Al up there on debut & 5L clear 3rd:
promising effort from this half sister to winners in USA: eff at 7f & yld grnd &
can find a maiden.   45
2105 ACCUSTOMED [2] (M Jarvis) 2-8-11 W Woods(3) 10/1: 0003: Sn prom & 10L clear rem:
stays 7f well: acts on firm & yld grnd.   35
-- DAWN ROMP [7] (R Smyly) 2-8-11 W Ryan 12/1: 4: Never nearer on debut, but impr likely
from this half sister to very useful middle dist winner Romper: will be suited by 1m: acts
on yielding ground.   17
2147 GO MY PET [13] 2-8-11 N Howe 16/1: 0000: Speed most: best in 383 (5f gd/firm).   02
1440 OCEAN HOUND [5] 2-8-11 R Weaver 20/1: 00: Never nearer: little form in 2 outings,
but is a half sister to 5 winners.   00
-- ALJAW [12] 2-8-11 R Hills 5/1: 0: Mkt drifter on racecourse debut & never in it: half
sister to 12f winner Timsah: bred to stay middle dists: should do btr in time.   00
2167 HOLTS WAY [4] 2-8-11 D Williams(7) 10/1: 000: Never in it: see 2167 (gd/firm).   00
2080 Folly Gale [9] 8-11   1634 Apres Ski [8] 8-11   852 Our Pet [10] 8-11
11 ran 1½,5,10,8,1   (H R Mould)   H Candy Wantage, Oxon

677

Official Going Given As GOOD FOR FIRST 2 RACES, GOOD/SOFT FOR REMAINDER

2288 RANMORE H'CAP 3YO+ 0-50   £3048   8.5f   Firm +10 Fast   [42]

2076 HAMLOUL [1] (K Bailey) 3-8-4 M Hills 9/2: 0022021: 3 ch c Mansingh - Elegante
(Frankincense): Gained a deserved first win, making all & fighting off the runner-up in
the final 2f for a narrow win in quite a fast run h'cap at Epsom: placed several times previously
in mdn/h'cap company: very eff over 1m & is best up with the pace: acts on gd & firm grnd.   38
+2123 FEYDAN [4] (L Cottrell) 5-8-10(4ex) I Johnson 7/2 JT FAV: -044312: Chall winner final 2f,
just held & is in grand form: see 2123.   33
1852 YOUNG JASON [9] (G Lewis) 3-8-13 P Waldron 7/2 JT FAV: -001223: Kept on, prob. stays 1m.   41
2059 FOOT PATROL [3] (P Cundell) 5-8-5 C Rutter(3) 15/2: 0102104: Never closer: best 1967.   20
2091 FAST SERVICE [6] 7-8-9 P Cook 9/1: 0024000: Best 1346.   21
1942 SPARKLER SPIRIT [7] 5-7-7(8oh) P Barnard(7) 25/1: 00-0240: See 1942.   02
1934 GAELIC FLUTTER [5] 3-9-10(VIS) B Rouse 16/1: 0-30100: Fin 7th: best 1436 (7f).   00
1967 JOYFUL DANCER [8] 6-9-6 S Cauthen 6/1: 0021030: Best 1729 (stiff track, made all).   00
8 ran   ½,2½,2½,1½,1½   (Mrs K Bailey)   K Bailey East Ilsley, Berks

2289 PADDOCK H'CAP 3YO+ 0-60   £7271   5f   Firm +10 Fast   [52]

2160 PERFECT TIMING [6] (D Elsworth) 4-9-8 S Cauthen 6/4 JT FAV: 4332321: 4 b f Comedy Star-
Eridantini (Indigenous): Useful sprinter: gained an overdue success, leading final 150yds
in quite a fast run & valuable h'cap at Epsom: placed most outings this term incl in the
Stewards Cup: in '85 won at Newmarket from 10 outings: best form at 5/6f on fast grnd:
has to be held up for a very late chall & is not an easy ride : carries weight well.   58
--   MEESON KING [2] (B Mcmahon) 5-8-12 J Hills(5) 10/1: 01000-2: Just failed to make all:
excellent seasonal debut: in '85 won h'caps at Sandown, Nottingham & Chester: eff at 5/6f
though seems to act on any going & on any trk: must go close next time.   44
2065 CLANTIME [3] (R Whitaker) 5-9-12(vis) D Mckeown 6/4 JT FAV: 4122033: Slow start, needs
to be in front: see 877, 1508.   54
2065 DURHAM PLACE [5] (K Brassey) 4-9-8(bl) B Rouse 11/2: 0430004: See 877, 1268.   46
1543 NATIVE RULER [1] 5-7-7(10oh) A Lappin(7) 33/1: 0-01230: Well btn: best 1070 (seller).   00
5 ran   1,1½,1½,15   (R J Vines)   D Elsworth Whitsbury, Hants

2290 MOET AND CHANDON AMAT. H'CAP 3YO+ 0-50   £5231   1m 4f   Good 37 -02 Slow   [20]

*2164 PACTOLUS [7] (G Harwood) 3-11-3(2ex) Mr Henri Van De Vuer 9/2: -012311: 3 b c Lydian -
Honey Sand (Windy Sands): Impr colt: al there & led inside final 3f, comfortably, in a
valuable amateur riders h'cap at Epsom Aug.25: recently won a h'cap at Lingfield & a
Ladies race, again at Lingfield: lightly raced in '85 winning at Salisbury: well suited by
12/14f now: acts on gd & firm grnd & on any trk though runs well on an undulating one.   59
2066 OSRIC [5] (M Ryan) 3-10-7 Mr J Ryan 11/4 FAV: -412D32: Prom, ev ch: gd effort but
twice below rating in 1923 (stakes): consistent sort.   45
1342 NO U TURN [11] (S Mellor) 8-10-9 Mr R Hutchinson 4/1: 0-00443: Fit from a recent win
over hdles but wk in the mkt here & one paced   final 2f: see 1004.   30
*1992 VORACITY [10] (J Winter) 7-11-10 Mr T T Jones 11/2: 4-23214: Held up, no threat: see 1992.   42
1992 CADMIUM [6] 4-11-6 Mr F Grasso Caprioli 15/2: -303430: Made much: much btr 1992.   33
976 BEL OSCAR [2] 4-10-10 Mr T Reed 25/1: 01-0000: No dngr after long abs since 976.   21
2066 REGAL STEEL [9] 8-10-0 Mr A Hollinshead 8/1: 0222140: Ev ch: best 1918.   00
2101 Metelski [3] 10-0(bl)   1992 Pellincourt [12] 10-0
9 ran   1½,6,3,5,1½   (Mrs G Harwood)   G Harwood Pulborough, Sussex

2291 BRIDGET FILLIES H'CAP 3YO   £4058   7f   Good 37 -01 Slow   [46]

1934 ESFAHAN [7] (J Dunlop) 3-9-2 A Murray 6/1: -020131: 3 b f Persian Bold - Press Luncheon
(Be Friendly): In fine form at present & was winning 2nd time from last 3 outings, comfortably
leading dist in a 3yo fillies h'cap at Epsom: awarded a mdn at Leicester July 14: half sister
to a couple of winners: very eff at 7f on gd or fast grnd: seems to act on any trk.   45
2027 FRIVOLE [4] (P Cole) 3-8-13 P Waldron 8/1: -401102: Kept on well: gd effort: see 1885.   40
+1830 BLUE GUITAR [5] (J Hindley) 3-9-1(vis) M Hills 15/2: 0-44213: Not btn far: gd effort.   42
2143 ASTICOUR [8] (I Balding) 3-9-6 P Cook 12/1: 4-00204: Ev ch: see 762, 1669.   42
2155 EASTERN HOUSE [2] 3-9-3 S Cauthen 10/11 FAV: 2-02120: Led 2 out: btr 2155(stiff track).   37
2120 MIRANDA JULIA [1] 3-8-7 P Mcentee(7) 20/1: 1300000: Made much: best 276 (C/D, hvy).   23
1191 Divine Fling [6] 7-13   2038 Mudisha [3] 9-7   2143 Kharrana [9] 9-7
9 ran   1,shhd,2,1,2   (Nathan M Avery)   J Dunlop Arundel, Sussex

2292 SHERWOOD STAKES 2YO FILLIES   £2306   6f   Good 37 -02 Slow

*2191 KHAKIS LOVE [10] (P Walwyn) 2-8-12 P Cook 9/4: 3011: 2 b f Dominion - Fettle (Relkino):
Useful filly: gained her 2nd win off the reel, leading dist comfortably in a 2yo fillies race
at Epsom: easy winner of mdn at Folkestone last time: 70,000 gns purchase whose dam is
from a gd family: very eff at 6f, should stay 7f: acts on firm & gd grnd & on any trk though
certainly runs well on an undulating one.   50
--   ABHAAJ [2] (H T Jones) 2-8-6(1ow) A Murray 7/1: 2: Mkt drifter on debut, led halfway
& kept on well: first foal of a 2yo 5f winner who is a half sister to prolific stallion Danzig:
sure to impr & find a mdn.   40

2185 RIPE CHRISTINA [7] (A Bailey) 2-8-8 C Rutter(3) 6/1: 0033: Al prom: improving: see 2185.   42
+2127 MARIMBA [1] (J Winter) 2-8-12 S Cauthen 15/8 FAV: 23314: Chall 2f out: see 2127: stays 6f.   46
2127 BINGDON BUILDERS [9] 2-8-9 J Hills(5) 20/1: 00: Kept on: impr: see 2127.   40
1801 BLEU CELESTE [4] 2-8-8 P Hutchinson(3) 33/1: 000: Dwelt: first foal of a winner over 5-7f   19
1238 Indian Jubilee [5] 8-8   1604 Harts Lane [3] 8-8
2069 Peroy [8] 8-8   -- Oh My Joy [6] 8-5
10 ran   2,hd,hd,1,8   (Yahya Nasib)   P Walwyn Lambourn, Berks

2293 CICERO CLAIMING STAKES 3YO   £2465   1m 2f Good 37 -26 Slow

2190 JAAZIEL [3] (D Murray Smith) 3-8-6(BL) R Wernham 9/1: 0000001: 3 b c Jaazeiro - Sweet
Pleasure (Sweet Revenge): Bl first time & showed impr form, leading str & drawing 3L clear
to win a slowly run 3yo claimer at Epsom: ran quite well here earlier in the season: seems
to like a sharpish, undulating trk: stays 10f well: acts on gd: best in bl.   21
2092 NO BOLDER [6] (R Hannon) 3-8-7 B Rouse 9/1: 00-002: Ev ch: see 2092.   17
1985 PRIME NUMBER [5] (P Cole) 3-9-0(BL) S Cauthen 7/2 FAV: 0-00003: Bl first time, made much.16
1690 AAH JIM BOY [4] (R Akehurst) 3-9-0 P Cook 11/2: 40-0204: Ev ch: flattered 1350.   06
2170 BOLD BORDERER [7] 3-9-0 M Hills 4/1: 0033000: Disapp since 1471.   01
2077 RUN CHARLIE [2] 3-8-9(VIS) I Johnson 9/2: 00-0020: Visored first time, btr 2077.   00
2034 SANDY BILL [1] 3-8-11 A Murray 6/1: -000: A gamble, fin last.   00
7 ran   3,4,5,3,4   (John E Guest)   D Murray Smith Upper Lambourn, Berks

2294 REDHILL MAIDEN STAKES 3YO   £2278   7f   Good 37 +07 Fast

1841 LADY FOR TWO [5] (M Stoute) 3-8-11 M Giles(7) 9/4 FAV: 4041D21: 3 b f Storm Bird-
Very Special Lady (Buckpasser): Gained a deserved success (hvly bckd) comfortably leading
dist in quite a fast run 3yo mdn at Epsom: unrcd in '85: eff over 7f/1m on gd & firm grnd:
seems to handle any trk.   46
1880 URUGUAY [1] (O Douieb) 3-8-11 M Hills 8/1: -022: Led over 2f out, should win mdn: see 1880. 42
1776 RESCUE PACKAGE [10] (G Lewis) 3-9-0 P Waldron 7/1: 4-04403: A gamble, ev ch: see 1554.   41
2027 COURT TOWN [13] (R Hannon) 3-8-11 R Wernham 10/1: 04-004: Late prog: impr: see 2027.   38
600   ROYAL TROUBADOR [2] 3-9-0 S Cauthen 10/1: 0-000: Made much after long abs: very
lightly raced colt who is a half brother to the very useful miler The Noble Player & several
other winners: should be btr next time with this race under his belt: will stay beyond 7f.   41
1246 SHINING SKIN [11] 3-8-11 P Cook 20/1: 420-000: Abs: mkt drifter: see 1246.   34
1902 LA NUREYEVA [6] 3-8-11 B Rouse 6/1: 433-40: Mod. eff: rated 48 in 85: see 1902.   00
658   SUNNY LIZ [7] 3-8-11(BL) A Murray 6/1: 2-200: Bl first time after long abs, proving
disappointing: see 498 when rated 46.   00
1756 Speed Stick [12] 9-0   2186 Wykehamist [3] 9-0   2155 Rue St Jacques [9] 9-0
1669 Northern Impulse [8] 9-0(vis)   764 Alburuj [4] 9-0(BL)
13 ran 2,1½,hd,shhd,1½   (John C Mabee)   M Stoute Newmarket

RIPON   Monday August 25th   Righthanded Fair Track

Official Going Given As GOOD

2295 BONUSPRINT HANDICAP STAKES 0-50   £3563   6f   Good/Firm 28 +04 Fast   [39]

2033 EASTBROOK [6] (S Hall) 6-8-4 L Charnock 9/2 FAV: -213241: 6 br g Lochnager - Lush Gold
(Goldhill): Well bckd, made all in a h'cap at Ripon: has run consistently since winning at
Catterick: in '85 won at Hamilton: very eff at 5/6f & seems to act on gd/firm & soft grnd:
well suited by a sharp trk & front running tactics.   23
2143 TAYLOR OF SOHAM [7] (D Leslie) 3-8-1 D Mckay 12/1: 0413232: Just btn despite bad
luck in running: very consistent since 1603 & is eff at 5-7f: due a change of luck.   25
2213 HENRYS VENTURE [14] (D Chapman) 4-7-13 S Webster 14/1: 0011303: Al prom, just btn
in a close fin & remains in fine form: ran well last time over 7f but possibly best over 6f.   16
1906 WARTHILL LADY [9] (M Brittain) 4-7-7 A Munro(4) 25/1: 0400004: Dsptd lead, just btn,
best effort this year: eff over 6f but won over 5f last year at Ayr: acts on firm & yld.   09
1840 OUT OF HAND [10] 7-8-5 R Morse(5) 10/1: -401200: Fin well: see 1521.   20
1536 SHARLIES WIMPY [4] 7-9-10 D Nicholls 10/1: -024000: Not btn far under top weight: see 520 38
2046 THREE BELLS [15] 4-8-8 B Thomson 7/1: -000430: Only btn 2L in 7th: see 2046.   00
1222 BROWN BEAR BOY [5] 4-9-9 P Tulk 9/1: 2330100: Abs since 1222: see 1182.   00
-2139 CUMBRIAN DANCER [3] 3-8-9(vis) M Birch 13/2: 4120020: Best 1247 (stiff trk).   00
1973 TOP THAT [1] 5-8-13 N Connorton 10/1: 0140020: Btr 1973 (good).   00
2038 Royal Fan [2] 8-11   1959 Allisterdransfield [12] 7-10(bl)(3ow)(2oh)
1868 Cool Enough [11] 8-3   1995 Angels Are Blue [8] 8-13
2039 Always Native [3] 7-11
15 ran   nk,nk,½,nk,½,½   (Hippodromo Racing)   S Hall Middleham, Yorks

2296 ICI PETROL RIPON ROWELS HCAP 3YO+ 0-60   £6399   1m   Good/Firm 28 +12 Fast   [58]

2219 ALL FAIR [3] (P Haslam) 5-8-4(vis) G French 4/1 FAV: 0002101: 5 b h Free State -
Be Honest (Record Token): Tried in a visor, won this race for the 2nd year running, led   2
out in a valuable h'cap at Ripon: earlier bl when winning an app. h'cap at Salisbury: in '85
was trained by R Whitaker, winning at York & Ripon: in '84 won at Newbury & Haydock: eff
over 1m & stays 10f: does well when up with the pace: best now in bl or visor.   45

2062 WILD HOPE [11] (G Huffer) 5-7-12 G Carter(3) 11/2: 00-0042: Fin well, returning to
form and is one to note on a stiffer trk: see 940.   37
1941 WAAJIB [5] (A Stewart) 3-8-11 M Roberts 11/2: 02-2133: Kept on well, not btn far &
is very consistent: ran well last time over 10f: see 1602.   59
+2039 INISHPOUR [12] (H Wharton) 4-9-2(10ex) J H Brown(5) 10/1: 3034314: Gd eff over 1m under
a penalty: probably even better on a gall. track: see 2039.   50
*1710 PALAESTRA [13] 3-9-3 R Fox 7/1: 0021100: Gd effort under big weight, unplaced last
time in Spain: consistent sort: see 1710.   59
2126 SIR WILMORE [1] 4-7-9 J Quinn(5) 20/1: 0001000: Best effort since 1698.   27
1793 DORSET COTTAGE [8] 4-9-10 B Thomson 9/1: 0320100: Best 1525 (gall trk).   00
2091 BUNDABURG [7] 6-7-12 R Morse(5) 10/1: 0000000: Fdd 2 out: little form this year: see 775   00
1924 MAHOGANY RUN [10] 3-8-3(vis)(2ow) M Birch 9/1: 0010200: Likes Ripon but ran disapp.
today when tried in a visor: possibly needs to make it all: see 1224.   00
2091 Portogon [14] 8-5   1539 Aristocrat Velvet [6] 8-6(bl)(2ow)
2219 Shellman [9] 8-0(2ow)   789 Rocabay Blue [15] 8-4   1976 Silly Boy [2] 7-7
14 ran   ¾,shhd,2½,nk,¼   (S A B Dinsmore)   P Haslam Newmarket

2297 BONUSPRINT CHAMPION 2YO TROPHY 1986   £8038   6f   Good/Firm 28 +02 Fast

2133 TRY THE DUCHESS [2] (M Usher) 2-8-8 D Mckay 14/1: 10031: 2 ch f Try My Best - Piece Of
The Realm (Realm): Brought back to 6f, surprise winner of a valuable event at Ripon, coming
with a strong late run to win going away: first time out winner at Leicester on firm grnd:
cost 7,000 gns as a yearling: probably stays 7f but very eff at 6f on fast grnd: best when
held up & goes well for D Mckay.   57
+1910 GARNET [7] (R Boss) 2-8-8 R Guest 6/1: 01412: Led & looked the winner 2 out: gd
effort over 6f & is a very consistent filly: see 1910.   53
2113 SINGING STEVEN [8] (R Hannon) 2-9-0 M Roberts 1/1 FAV: 2112303: Disapp. fav.:   below
his best & had had a busy time: possibly best at 5f: see 834, 1143.   55
2043 SO KIND [3] (J Watts) 2-8-8 N Connorton 11/2: 34: Al prom: another gd effort: see 2043.   47
*1982 AUTHENTIC [5] 2-8-11 Kim Tinkler 14/1: 2210: Running consistently: see 1982.   50
1925 BUTTERFIELD ROAD [4] 2-8-11 R Fox 10/1: 100: Set fast pace 4f: see 1307.   46
2029 NATIVE PAWN [6] 2-8-11(BL) G Carter(3) 14/1: 0000: Disapp after rated 55 in 1488.   00
*1634 ANTINOUS [1] 2-9-0(BL) M Birch 6/1: 3210: Much btr 1634 (made all).   00
8 ran   1½,1½,½,shhd,1½   (T C Marshall)   M Usher Lambourn, Berks

2298 STAINLEY SELLING NURSERY HANDICAP   £1937   6f   Good/Firm 28 -39 Slow   [28]

1955 GET SET LISA [11] (C Tinkler) 2-9-1 B Thomson 6/1: 4002221: 2 ch f On Your Mark -
Prima Bella (High Hat): Prom, gamely led near fin for a well deserved win in a selling nursery
at Ripon: has been running very consistently over 6f & well suited by a turning trk & a
sound surface: no bid.   24
2227 ORIENTAL JADE [4] (D Morley) 2-9-6(bl) S Perks 15/2: 041302: Led 1½ out, just failed:
well suited by 6f but has also run well over 7f: see 1599: consistent: carries weight well.   28
2050 LYN RAE [5] (M H Easterby) 2-8-12 M Birch 9/1: 000403: Not much luck in running, fin
well, possibly btr over 7f & should find a seller: acts on gd/firm & soft.   17
*1692 COLLEGE WIZARD [17] (M Tompkins) 2-8-8 R Morse(5) 13/2: 4214: Just failed to last 6f.   12
2168 SOHAMS TAYLOR [18] 2-8-9(vis) D Mckay 25/1: 0000400: Showed impr in a visor: see 1684.   12
2138 PHILEARN [16] 2-9-3 A Bacon(7) 12/1: 0002030: Running consistently: see 2138, 1832.   14
*1803 KIBARA [15] 2-8-13 G French 5/1 FAV: 010: Disapp fav: much btr 1803.   00
2150 HARRYS COMING [2] 2-9-7 J H Brown(5) 10/1: 3002020: Best 1680 (5f).   00
1965 RABENHAM [13] 2-9-4 M Roberts 10/1: 0400040: Much btr 1965, 741 (gall trk).   00
1944 Musical Chorus [10] 8-6(bl)   2032 Pertain [12] 8-13(bl)
1717 Maybemusic [7] 9-4   1949 Santo Princess [6] 8-2
1537 Highland Captain [14] 8-2(BL)   1012 Millie Duffer [9] 8-2
1566 Gwynbrook [1] 9-7   1905 Just A Decoy [3] 8-6   1105 Chayofa [19] 8-10
1672 Hilliard [8] 8-6
19 ran   hd,1½,hd,nk,2½   (Walter Bulmer)   C Tinkler Malton, Yorks

2299 PATELEY MAIDEN FILLIES STKS 3YO   £2511   1m 4f   Good/Firm 28 -46 Slow

2068 CROWLEY [6] (L Cumani) 3-8-11 R Guest 5/2: -0021: 3 b f Vaguely Noble - Funny Funny
Ache (Jester): Led 3 out, very readily in a mdn race at Ripon: clearly well suited by 12f,
may stay further & should win a btr race.   48
1198 SUNLEY SAINT [10] (P Walwyn) 3-8-11 L Charnock 10/1: 20-022: Mkt drifter: despite an
abs, chall 3 out & ran well over this 12f trip: should sn find a mdn: see 1198: stable in grand form. 41
1586 CALYSTEGIA [12] (C Brittain) 3-8-11 G Carter(3) 20/1: -003: Tried over 12f, set the
pace & showed sufficient ability to secure a mdn race.   37
2023 NO DOUBLET [5] (B Hills) 3-8-11 B Thomson 8/1: -322204: A little frustrating, rtd 45 in 1639 32
2068 CYNOMIS [8] 3-8-11 R Lines(3) 9/2: -300: Disapp: closer to winner in 2068 (much stiffer trk) 26
1939 CURVACEOUS [4] 3-8-11 A Kimberley 9/2: -04330: Much btr 1939 on a sharp track.   22
1833 NILE LARK [3] 3-8-11 R Fox 7/2: 0-20: Disapp after 1833 (lefthand trk).   00
1908 MITALA MARIA [2] 3-8-11 M Roberts 10/1: -0230: Made some, might do btr in bl: see 1481.   00
1327 Tern Of A Century [9] 8-11   1694 La Serenata [1] 8-11
--   Suede Lady [11] 8-11   --   Fair Cadette [7] 8-11
12 ran   3,2,2½,3,2,nk   (N B Hunt)   L Cumani Newmarket

00

RIPON   Monday August 25th   -Cont'd

2300 TOPCLIFFE HANDICAP STAKES 3YO 0-35   £2060   1m 2f   Good/Firm 28 -16 Slow   [42]

1998 KINGS CRUSADE [5] (G Lewis) 3-8-13 G Sexton 11/2: 4042331: 3 ch c Reform - Crusader's
Dream (St Paddy): Led 3 out, gamely in a h'cap at Ripon, first success: very eff over 10f &
acts on firm & yld & probably on any trk: consistent sort who should stay 12f.   36
2154 BRADBURY HALL [8] (K Stone) 3-7-10 R Morse(4) 16/1: 2210002: Not btn far with a
strong late chall: made all the running when successful in 1426: goes well on a sharp trk.   18
*1309 SELL IT KILROY [4] (G Huffer) 3-9-1 G Carter(3) 8/1: -0013: Stayed on well after
abs: should be dr next time & is usually held up.   29
1652 LOUD LANDING [11] (W Hastings Bass) 3-8-4 R Lines(3) 8/1: 0-034: Kept on well &
probably btr suited by 12f: should find a small race on a stiffer trk.   16
751 SWISS NEPHEW [2] 3-9-2 M Roberts 15/2: 00-300: Late prog after long abs: will
probably be btr suited by 12f & should do btr next time: see 512.   27
2109 PENTLAND HAWK [14] 3-9-7 S Perks 7/1: 0011D20: Much btr 2109, 1956.   28
1974 SPACE TROOPER [13] 3-8-6(BL)(1ow) D Nicholls 4/1 FAV: 4011320: Well bckd, tried in bl:
led 4 out: possibly best when able to make all the running: see 1678.   00
1921 MOORE STYLISH [9] 3-8-7 P Tulk 8/1: -0020: Btr 1921.   00
2103 Taxi Man   [6] 8-6   2217 Greenhills Girl [12] 8-1(bl)
1578 Elvire   [7] 8-1   2027 Pells Close [15] 7-7(bl)(1oh)
1426 Not A Problem [16] 7-8   1580 Dais [3] 7-12
1481 Efficient   [17] 8-1   2128 Megans Move [1] 8-11 1974 Black Bank [10] 8-11(bl)
17 ran ½,4,1½,hd,2,shhd   (H R Mould)   G Lewis Epsom, Surrey

WOLVERHAMPTON   Monday August 25th   Lefthand, Fair Track

Official Going Given As GOOD/SOFT: LAST 2 RACES SOFT: RAINED THRO'OUT THE AFTERNOON

2301 EBF ASTON MAIDEN STAKES 2YO   £763   5f   Yielding 97 +07 Fast

777 VIVALDI [13] (W Jarvis) 2-9-0 E Guest(3) 33/1: 01: 2 ch c Music Boy - Two Stroke
(Malicious): Despite a long abs, caused a 33/1 surprise, led ½way & held on in a close fin
to a 2yo mdn at Wolverhampton: first foal who is quite speedily bred: eff at 5f on yld grnd. 45
-- PRINT [11] (W Hastings Bass) 2-9-0 T Ives 5/1: 2: Ran on well final 1f & nearly got up:
fine debut from this half brother to 3yo mdn Likeness: will stay 6f: acts on yld grnd.   44
1936 SPANISH CALM [1] (R Sheather) 2-9-0 M Rimmer 8/1: 03: Front rank all the way & just
btn in a tight fin: 4L clear 4th: eff at 5/6f on gd/firm & yld: see 1936.   43
-- DAYS LIKE THESE [12] (P Bailey) 2-9-0 J Williams 25/1: 4: Al there on debut: 13,000 gns
yearling who is quite speedily bred: acts on yld.   31
-- MALIBU TOAST [4] 2-8-11 R Cochrane 9/1: 0: Late hdway on racecourse debut: mkt drifter
today & will impr: American bred filly who is a half sister to several winners in the States:
will be suited by further than 5f.   24
1874 BIT OMAY [3] 2-8-11 Paul Eddery 5/1: 00: Speed over 3f: ½ sister to 10f winner Moorland Lady 04
1376 VAIGLY YELLOW [10] 2-9-0 A Mackay 10/1: 0000: Springer in mkt, but no threat: little
form to date: abs since 1376.   00
1946 FRIVOLOUS LADY [8] 2-8-11 J Carter(7) 10/1: 00000: Much btr 1946, 1668 (btr grnd).   00
1958 ON YOUR PRINCESS [7] 2-9-0 D Gibson 2/1 FAV: 0020: Led to ½way: much better 1958(gd/fm) 00
1966 TAMASSOS [9] 2-8-11 G Starkey 10/1: 000: Prom over 2f: btr 1966 (gd/firm).   00
1665 EL DELGADO [6] 2-9-0 R Curant 7/1: 30: A dist last: much btr 1665 (gd).   00
-- Paparelli [2] 9-0   -- Nevada Mix [5] 9-0
13 ran hd,nk,4,1½,7   (Mrs P Payne)   W Jarvis Newmarket

2302 SPINNEY SELLING STAKES   £799   1m   Yielding 97 -58 Slow

1989 MY DERYA [1] (B Mcmahon) 3-8-7(bl) A Mackay 4/5 FAV: 4030041: 3 b g Mandalus - Rose
Of Norscot (On Your Mark): Ran on under press to lead inside final 1f in a slow run & modest
3 & 4yo seller at Wolverhampton Aug.25 (no bid): early last season won a seller at Warwick:
stays 1m: acts on gd/firm & soft grnd & likes a sharp/easy trk.   10
2184 ALL A DREAM [5] (W Musson) 3-8-7(bl) R Cochrane 7/4: -000402: Made most: see 318.   06
1976 NICKY DAWN [6] (J H Wilson) 4-9-3(BL) Paul Eddery 8/1: 0000003: Prom most: bl first
time: form here previously.   00
1917 BONNY BRIGHT EYES [3] (R Hollinshead) 3-8-7 T Ives 10/1: -000004: No real threat: modest. 00
2174 ABSCILLA [4] 3-8-7 E Guest(1) 25/1: -00: Al in rear.   00
-- BINNEYS LASS [2] 4-9-3 J Williams 33/1: -0-0: Fdd on seasonal debut: very lightly raced.   00
6 ran 1½,8,2,10,1½   (Mrs H Akyve)   B Mcmahon Tamworth, Staffs

2303 MIDLAND CAMBRIDGESHIRE HANDICAP 0-60   £4480   1m 1f   Yielding 97 -12 Slow   [49]

*2076 SOLO STYLE [6] (G Lewis) 3-8-7(5ex) J Adams(7) 6/1: 0101411: 3 b c Moorestyle -
Mint (Meadow Mint): Useful colt who is in fine form: dsptd lead in str & stayed on most gamely
for a ¾L win in a valuable h'cap at Wolverhampton: last time out won a h'cap at Nottingham:
earlier won h'caps again at Nottingham & Leicester: very eff at 1m, stays 9f: acts on firm
& yld grnd & likes a gall trk: game & genuine.   46
2173 KAVAKA [10] (H Whiting) 4-7-3(3oh) J Carter(6) 16/1: 0012D02: Dsptd lead in the str
& stayed on well: fine effort: see 2037, 1567: acts on firm & yld.   21
2062 GUNDREDA [5] (C Brittain) 4-8-12 N Day 9/4 FAV: -004033: Prom, stayed on under
press & not btn far: in gd form: see 2062, 1498: due a change of luck & likes it soft.   40

1047 SMOKEYS SECRET [11] (W Wharton) 4-9-7(VIS) R Cochrane 7/1: 3113-04: Visored first
time: stayed on well after fair abs & ran well: see 1047.   46
1176 VERBARIUM [7] 6-7-8 P Hill(7) 20/1: 2320000: Abs: never nearer: see 10, 281.   11
2059 WARPLANE [8] 6-8-3 J Bleasdale 8/1: 0-00340: No show: twice below 1619 (1m gd/firm).   18
2144 INDIAN HAL [12] 4-9-6 Paul Eddery 7/1: 0440000: Btr 2144: see 706.   00
1935 RUSTY LAW [9] 4-9-4(BL) G Starkey 8/1: 30-0000: Bl first time: there 7f: see 1237.   00
2132 SINGING BOY [2] 5-8-0 A Mackay 9/1: 0000140: Al rear: twice below 1987.   00
--   Open Hero [4] 9-4   2154 Miss Apex [1] 7-7(6oh)
11 ran ¾,shhd,1½,5,hd   (Mrs N Lewis)   G Lewis Epsom, Surrey

2304 TETTENHALL MAIDEN FILLIES STAKES 3YO   £952   1m 4f Yielding 97 +05 Fast

--   HOTEL STREET [12] (H Cecil) 3-8-11 N Day 7/2: -1: 3 b f Alleged - Native Street
(Native Dancer): Very prom filly: was an effortless winner on her racecourse debut, led over
3f out & was sn clear in quite a fast run 3yo mdn at Wolverhampton Aug.25: cost $285,000 as
a yearling & is a half sister to numerous winners in the States: clearly very eff over 12f
& seems certain to stay further: acts on yld grnd & on an easy trk: looks one to follow.   65
2131 RED SHOES [4] (W Hern) 3-8-11 T Ives 4/1: 3032232: Caught a real tartar here &
remains a mdn: has just the one pace & may need even further to get off the mark: see 1630, 458   35
2048 COMMANCHE BELLE [11] (L Cumani) 3-8-11 R Cochrane 7/2: 23: Al prom: better 2048.(gd/fm) 32
2023 MISS SHIRLEY [2] (J Dunlop) 3-8-11 R Curant 14/1: 0-30224: Late prog: see 751.   26
2131 SHEER NECTAR [8] 3-8-11 J Williams 33/1: -00: Never nearer: stays 12f: see 2131.   24
2148 LA MUSCADE [6] 3-8-11(BL) S Horsfall(0) 33/1: 0-00000: Bl first time: stayed on late:
clearly has some ability though would app a drop in class: see 1554.   21
2068 CORNELIAN [1] 3-8-11 G Starkey 6/4 FAV: -030: Bckd from 7/2: never going well &
had no ch from ½way: much btr in 2068 & worth another ch: see 1645: unsuited by yld?   00
1259 Queens Visit [5] 8-11   --   Skevena [10] 8-11   1953 Ela Man Hee [13] 8-11
1078 Baydon Queen [9] 8-11   2048 Sagareme [7] 8-11(vis)
2170 Alice Parry [3] 8-11
13 ran 20,1½,4,¾,1½   (Robert N Clay)   H Cecil Newmarket, Suffolk

2305 STEWARDS H'CAP STAKES (0-35) 3YO+   £1956   1m 6f Yielding 97 -54 Slow   [23]

2148 DUNSTON [5] (F Durr) 3-9-7 G Starkey 9/4: 0030341: 3 b c Valdez (USA) - Donut's Bunnie
(Donut King): Comfortably defied top weight, led below dist, ridden out in a slowly run h'cap
at Wolverhampton Aug.25: first success: half brother to several winners: well suited by
12/14f: acts on fast & yld grnd & on any trk: should defy a penalty now he has struck form.   42
*2211 QUICK REACTION [4] (M Ryan) 3-8-13(5ex) R Cochrane 7/4 FAV: -000212: Led over 2f out,
outpcd by winner though easily beat the rem: in gd form & should win again soon: on the up
grade: see 2211.   25
1833 MOUNT ARGUS [8] (M Mccourt) 4-8-8 R Curant 33/1: 0000003: Made most: ex Irish gelding
who has yet to show any worthwhile form in this country: eff around 11/12f: acts on gd/firm
& yielding ground.   00
2175 STANDON MILL [9] (J Wilson) 3-8-2 Julie Bowker(7) 33/1: 0040004: Btr over 12f in 648.   00
1678 GREEN ARCHER [1] 3-8-0 P Hill(7) 33/1: -30000: Little form since 524 (10f soft).   00
2078 CORNISH PRINCE [6] 3-9-0 W Wharton 20/1: -00000: No dngr: see 2078.   00
*2182 CURIGA [7] 3-9-4(5ex) Paul Eddery 9/4: 0-04110: Led early in str: wknd into 7th &
did not seem to stay this lngr trip: btr in 2182 (11f).   00
1177 Campus Boy 0 8-7   *1784 Soho Sue 0 8-9
9 ran 5,10,2,12,3   (K Abdulla)   F Durr Newmarket, Suffolk

2306 COPPICE MAIDEN STAKES   £822   2m 1f Yielding 97 -46 Slow

1688 BEDHEAD [9] (A Stewart) 3-8-5 R Cochrane 2/1 FAV: 0-0221: 3 b c Shirley Heights -
Bedfellow (Crepello): Led home turn & again inside dist, ridden out to win quite a slowly run
mdn at Wolverhampton: stoutly bred colt who is a half brother to middle dist winner Major
Setback: stays 2m really well: acts on firm & yld grnd & on an easy course.   46
1535 CHALICE OF SILVER [1] (M Jarvis) 3-8-5(3ow) T Ives 9/2: 0-43232: Led 2f out: consistent.   39
1048 MARIE GALANTE [10] (C Brittain) 3-8-2 R Curant 6/1: -232303: Abs: led early in str,
not qckn below dist: clearly stays well though best over 12f in 458: see 128.   28
1799 GREAT GANDER [5] (J Dunlop) 3-8-5 Paul Eddery 11/1: -044: Late prog & fin clear
of rem: stays well: acts on gd & yld grnd: lightly raced & should impr: see 1799.   30
833 MOLUCELLA [7] 3-8-2 J Williams 25/1: 000-000: Long abs: made up some late grnd though
has yet to show any worthwhile form: half sister to very useful miler Fair Season: acts on yld   12
--   KAFARMO [12] 3-8-7(2ow) G Starkey 9/2: -0: No extra str: cost 32,000 gns as a
yearling: dam was a fair sprinter though he promises to be btr suited by a distance of grnd.   15
1469 DAWN LOCH [11] 3-8-2 M Priddey(7) 5/1: 00: Wknd into 8th after abs: attracted plenty
of mkt support today & should be open to impr: half sister to several winners.   00
2183 AIRCRAFTIE [3] 3-8-2 N Day 10/1: -030300: Led to ½way: best in 1301 (11f): see 980.   00
1952 Grove Tower [14] 8-5   2109 High Forest [13] 9-4   1786 Cupids Bower [8] 8-2
--   Cash To Burn [4] 8-8(3ow)   1472 Cheren Hill [2] 8-5
1688 Grundys Own [6] 8-5
14 ran 5,6,¾,15,¾   (Louis Freedman)   A Stewart Newmarket, Suffolk

2307 MEREVALE NURSERY HANDICAP   £1735   5f   Yielding 97 -41 Slow   [59]

2172 INFANTA MARIA [4] (N Vigors) 2-8-0 S Dawson 5/4 FAV: 020221: 2 b f King Of Spain -
Pearling (Ribero): Well bckd & gained a deserved win, led before ½way & just held on in an

WOLVERHAMPTON   Monday August 25th   -Cont'd

nursery at Woverhampton: quite cheaply bought filly who had found one too good in 3 of her
last 4 starts: well suited by this minimum trip: acts on fast & yld grnd & is suited by
a sharp/easy course.   38
2150 HUGO Z HACKENBUSH [3] (C Tinkler) 2-7-7(9oh) A Richards(3) 14/1: 0042232: Just held after
being "bumped" inside dist: fine effort in this btr grade & should be noted when reverting
to selling company: see 2150.   30
*1949 BOOTHAM LAD [9] (M Brittain) 2-7-7(6oh) L Riggio(6) 14/1: 4000013: Upped in class: stayed
on really well & not btn far: likes this trk: see 1949.   27
2172 NICHOLAS GEORGE [8] (B Mcmahon) 2-7-9(BL)(2ow)(10oh) A Mackay 20/1: 01004: Bl first time:
impeded below dist & not recover: still ran well at the weights: likes Wolverhampton: see 1434   27
2090 JUVENILEDELINQUENT [6] 2-8-5(BL)(3ow) R Cochrane 11/2: 12440: Bl first time: best in 1936 34
1693 NATIONS SONG [2] 2-7-9 J P O'reilly(2) 11/2: 2212140: Early speed: best in 1576.   17
1527 ORIOLE DANCER [7] 2-7-10 J Carter(2) 20/1: 0024100: Led to ½way, fin 7th: see 1069.   00
1876 QUICK SNAP [5] 2-9-9(bl) R Curant 11/2: 1011200: Stiff task under top weight: see 1512 00
1978 SKY CAT [4] 2-8-4 Julie Bowker(7) 11/2: 400220: Nicely bckd but much btr in 1978 (6f). 00
9 ran   hd,1½,½,½,2½   (George Johnson)   N Vigors Upper Lambourn, Berks

---

WARWICK   Monday August 25th   Lefthand, Sharp Track

2308 TOTE CREDIT FILLIES STAKES 2YO   £919   5f   Yielding 100 +07 Fast

--   SUSAN HENCHARD [3] (J Francome) 2-8-8 M Miller 33/1: 1: 2 b f Auction Ring - Let Slip
(Busted): First time out, came home at 33/1, got up near the fin in a fast run, minor race
at Warwick: half sister to Branksome Towers a winner at 5 & 7f who also seemed to like
softish grnd: looks sure to be suited by 6f plus.   45
-2127 BAY WONDER [10] (G P Gordon) 2-8-8 P Robinson 11/1: 000222: Loves a sharp trk &
front running tactics, just failed & due a change of luck: continues to impr & acts
on firm and yld.   43
1778 ACT OF TREASON [1] (R Laing) 2-8-8 B Crossley 11/2: 03: Well bckd, late prog & also
ran well last time over 6f: should find a mdn.   42
+2104 ULTRA NOVA [2] (P Cole) 2-9-1 Pat Eddery 11/10 FAV: 320114: Acts on yld: btr 2100(gd/fm). 49
--   EVENING PRAYERS [4] 2-8-8 A Shoults(5) 11/1: 0: Fin well, prom debut: impr likely &
should be suited by 6f.   32
--   INSHAD [16] 2-8-8 M Banner 6/1: 0: Early speed, very active in the mkt & might do
btr next time.   32
*2069 GREENSWARD [5] 2-9-1 T Williams 6/1: 10: Much btr 2069 (6f, gd/firm).   36
--   SINGING PARTNER [13] 2-8-8 A Mcglone 33/1: 0: No threat, fin 8th: should stay 6f.   27
1238 HINTON ROSE [6] 2-8-8 S Whitworth 16/1: 00: Fin 9th: might do btr over 6f.   25
2185 Bugberry [11] 8-8   1826 Jealous Lover [17] 8-8
2167 Miss Atwell [14] 8-8   1650 Lundy Isle [9] 8-8   -- Sussarando [7] 8-8
1928 Tabareek [12] 8-8   1647 Thornyhill [15] 8-8   1501 Frimley Queen [8] 8-8
17 ran   ½,½,½,3,hd,1½,½,1   (Mrs P W Harris)   J Francome Sheepcote, Berks

2309 TOTE PLACEPOT SELL.H'CAP 3YO+ 0-25   £786   1m 2f Yielding 100 -01 Slow   [12]

2190 HARBOUR BAZAAR [9] (R Simpson) 6-9-3(vis) S Whitworth 7/2: 3003D31: 6 gr g Native Bazaar-
Overseas (Sea Hawk II): Made much & kept on well in a selling h'cap at Warwick (no bid):
well suited by 10f, forcing tactics & soft grnd but does act on firm: best in a visor.   13
2077 LETOILE DU PALAIS [1] (B Stevens) 3-8-4 P Bloomfield 16/1: 0004042: Kept on & not
btn far, goes well on a sharp trk & acts on firm & soft: see 568: well clear of rem.   09
2008 MURILLO [4] (F Carr) 10-9-8(bl) J Carr(7) 11/2: 0400103: Late prog: running well: see 1845. 08
2088 NIGHT OF THE COMET [14] (A King) 3-8-3 N Adams 25/1: 000-04: Last ran over 6f: stays 10f.00
1990 NELSONS LADY [10] 5-9-10 I Salmon 3/1 FAV: 10-0040: Much btr 1990 (7f).   05
1990 UNIT TENT [6] 8-8-12(bl) B Crossley 8/1: 0404000: Won this race last year: see 201.   00
2037 TARLETON [3] 9-9-2 Wendy Carter(7) 10/1: -200000: Fin 7th, first sign of form since 788. 00
1951 HODAKA [2] 9-9-5 N Carlisle 8/1: 100: Btr over 1m on fast grnd in 1546.   00
2068 Golden Azelia [7] 8-6   1990 Composer [5] 9-1(bl)   1394 Huytons Hope [13] 8-9
1670 Cleveland Bond [12] 8-11   1870 Swiftspender [11] 8-13
13 ran   ½,6,4,nk,1½,½   (M Courtney)   R Simpson Lambourn, Berks

2310 TOTE NURSERY H'CAP 2YO   £1820   1m   Yielding 100 -01 Slow   [43]

2001 SUNSET BOULEVARD [13] (L Piggott) 2-9-4(BL) Pat Eddery 9/2 JT FAV: 0401: 2 b c Red Sunset-
Carcajou (High Top): Bl for the first time, made a gd deal of the running when a comfortable
winner of a nursery h'cap at Warwick on yld: acts on firm & evidently well suited by forcing
tactics, a sharpish trk & softish going: gets 1m well.   45
1816 CREAM AND GREEN [3] (K White) 2-7-10 G Dickie 33/1: 000202: Btn in a 6f seller in
1379 but ran well over this lngr trip on softer grnd.   17
2178 ROUMELI [12] (Lord John Fitzgerald) 2-8-4 N Carlisle 9/1: 442303: Probably stays 1m
but rated 36 in 722 (6f).   25
2011 TIKLAS [2] (F Durr) 2-7-12 9/2 Jt Fav 9/2 JT FAV: 000434: Well bckd but not recover
from a slow start: evidently expected to be suited by 1m and on the up grade: see 1650, 2011. 14
2198 BOLD DIFFERENCE [11] 2-8-9 C Dwyer 14/1: 0021200: Late prog: see 1566: stays 1m.   18
*1119 ORIENTAL DREAM [15] 2-8-13 A Shoults(5) 6/1: 010: Abs since 1119: stays 1m?   21

683

1622 WAR CHILD [7] 2-8-1 T Williams 6/1: 0030: Btr 1622 (7f seller, firm).   00
2105 CARSE KELLY [9] 2-8-5(VIS) P Robinson 7/1: 0220000: Disapp since rated 37 in 1050 (6f).   00
2209 WISE TIMES [6] 2-9-7 M Wigham 9/1: 0022320: Led 5 out: best 1891 (6f).   00
1253 Regent Lad [14] 8-8   2178 Caerinette [5] 9-2(bl)
1846 Countess Bree [1] 8-5   1828 Jonleat [8] 9-6   2071 Caballine [10] 8-4
1914 Battle Heights [4] 8-8
15 ran   3,hd,2¼,4,nk,hd   (C T Heard)   L Piggott Newmarket

2311 WARWICK CESAREWITCH H'CAP   0-60   £2940   2m 2f Yielding 100 +08 Fast   [53]

1875 FEDRA [4] (Lord John Fitzgerald) 3-7-8 N Carlisle 3/1: 2124231: 3 b f Grundy - Zebra
Grass (Run The Gantlet): Consistent filly: first or second most of the way & stayed on well
in quite a fast run h'cap at Warwick: won over shorter dists of 10f at Lingfield & 13f at
Catterick & is evidently suited by an extreme test of stamina: acts on firm & soft & on any
trk but goes well on a sharp one.   42
1875 TIGERWOOD [3] (R Akehurst) 5-7-8 N Adams 100/30: 0-12102: Loves a sharp trk & as
usual set a fast pace: see 1533.   24
1633 JAMESMEAD [1] (D Elsworth) 5-9-6 Pat Eddery 7/4 FAV: 12-0303: Very well bckd, a
little disapp: btr on a more gall trk: see 1099.   47
2164 CHUCKLESTONE [5] (R Laing) 3-7-7(6ex)(1oh) T Williams 5/1: 0004134: Btr 2164 (14f).   19
1779 AYRES ROCK [2] 5-9-10 A Clark 11/1: -304000: Very disapp following 617, 360.   21
5 ran   3,2,15,15   (Mrs H G Cambanis)   Lord John Fitzgerald Newmarket

2312 TOTE DUAL F'CAST MAIDEN STAKES   £684   5f   Yielding 100 +05 Fast

1654 SAY PARDON [18] (D Morley) 3-8-10 T Williams 4/1: 0-22001: 3 b c Malinowski - Primrose
(Primera): Consistent sort who at last found a race, led 1 out under press in quite a fast
run mdn at Warwick: earlier ran well twice on the much stiffer Sandown trk: eff at 5 & 6f
and acts on firm & yld: could pick up a h'cap.   33
--   DURASINGH [10] (A Hide) 4-9-0 P Brette(7) 10/1: -2: Bckd from 20/1, put up a fine
debut: eff at 5f on a sharp trk on yld grnd & should pick up a mdn.   30
846 GALAXY PATH [15] (L Cottrell) 3-8-10 N Carlisle 14/1: 0-00403: After a lengthy abs,
fin well & impr likely: should stay further than 5f & goes well on yld.   27
2210 GRISETTE [1] (P Walwyn) 3-8-7(bl) Pat Eddery 3/1 FAV: 0-00024: Led over 3f: see 2210.   22
2106 TOLLYS ALE [20] 3-8-7 G Dickie 14/1: 4-43000: Late prog: probably btr at 6f: see 175.   19
1940 HILMAY [17] 4-8-11 R Lappin(7) 8/1: 3040300: Likes Warwick: see 1171, 211.   19
2055 MISS SERLBY [13] 3-8-7 P Bloomfield 10/1: -000020: Fin 8th, btr 2055.   00
2186 AVALON [4] 3-8-10 A Mcglone 7/1: -03400: A well bckd disapp. best 844 (6f).   00
2033 SILENT GAIN [8] 4-8-11(bl) M Wood 10/1: -023300: Wk in mkt: much btr 1627.   00
2106 GLEADHILL PARK [12] 3-8-10(bl) S Whitworth 10/1: 0000020: Much btr 2106 (gd).   00
2186 Miss Hicks [9] 8-7   1959 Whoberley Wheels [19] 8-10
1541 Fancy Finish [11] 8-7   1695 Heavenly Carol [14] 8-7
1399 Ever So Sharp [16] 8-10   2104 Burning Arrow [6] 9-0
1901 Bright Path [2] 8-11   2024 Dublinaire [7] 8-7   1742 Tricky [3] 8-7
2210 Winsong Melody [5] 8-7
20 ran   1,1,¼,1,shhd,4   (Lord McAlpine)   D Morley Newmarket

2313 TOTE BOOKMAKERS HCAP 3YO 0-35   £1631   7f   Yielding 100 -11 Slow   [34]

*2171 IMPERIAL PALACE [9] (C Tinkler) 3-9-0(7ex) M Wood 11/4 JT FAV: -000211: 3 b g Jaazeiro
- Persian's Glory (Prince Tenderfoot): Led 1½ out, readily in a h'cap at Warwick, defying a
7lb penalty for a similar success at Wolverhampton: ex Irish gelding who is well suited by
7/8f & seems to act on gd/firm & yld: might make it a hat trick.   29
2186 ROYAL BERKS [14] (L Cottrell) 3-8-4 T Lang(7) 20/1: 0004302: Gd effort from this mdn
who ran well earlier over 5/6f: acts on firm & yld.   16
2213 EASY LINE [7] (P Haslam) 3-9-2 T Williams 7/2: -100143: Al prom: consistent: stays
7f: possibly btr on a more gall trk: see 2143.   25
1818 STORMGUARD [11] (W Jarvis) 3-8-10(BL) E Guest(3) 12/1: 0-3004: Late prog: best 1141 (9f).   17
2120 SUNNY MATCH [2] 3-9-3 A Clark 14/1: 0-00200: Not recover from slow start: see 1836.   23
2214 RAFFLES VIRGINIA [10] 3-9-7 A Roper(7) 25/1: 4020040: So far best 1200.   22
2076 ANNABELLINA [12] 3-9-5 Pat Eddery 11/4 JT FAV: 0004230: Early ldr, much btr 2076 &
is probably unsuited by soft grnd: worth another chance.   00
2126 Gardas Gold [4] 8-2   1922 Sequestrator [3] 9-3   1943 Tina Rosa [5] 7-7(3oh)
1943 Megadyne [13] 8-0   2135 Out Yonder [6] 8-2   1885 Hardy Chance [8] 9-0(BL)
1885 Glangwili [1] 9-5
14 ran   1½,1½,1,nk,2½,3   (Mrs C M Tinkler)   C Tinkler Malton, Yorks

2314 TOTE MAIDEN FILLIES STAKES 3YO   £1031   1m   Yielding 100 -09 Slow

1885 BASICALLY BETTER [18] (P Walwyn) 3-8-11(VIS) N Carlisle 20/1: 0-40001: 3 b f Derrylin -
Oudalia (Gala Performance): Tried in a visor, showed her gd effort in 501 was no fluke with
an easy win in a mdn race at Warwick: led 3 out unchall: very eff at 7/8f: acts on firm &
yld & much impr by a visor: could win a h'cap.   40
--   CONCORDES DEMON [23] (G Huffer) 3-8-11 M Miller 14/1: -2: No ch with easy winner but
most prom debut: will probably stay further than 1m: acts on yld & should pick up a mdn.   30

1830 LADY LA PAZ [11] (P Cundell) 3-8-11 N Adams 4/1: 0233303: Bckd from 14/1, stays 1m
& is due a change of luck following several consistent efforts: acts on firm & yld.   27
1880 PEACE KEEPER [16] (W Jarvis) 3-8-11(BL) E Guest(3) 20/1: -04: Bl for the first time,
fin well: should be suited by 10f & a stiffer trk.   25
1880 NEEDLE SHARP [15] 3-8-11 A Bond 7/2 FAV: -30: Btr 1880 on a more galloping track.   23
2161 ETTAS PET [3] 3-8-11 A Shoults(5) 14/1: 0-40030: Stays 10f: see 1451.   23
1953 MRS MAINWARING [19] 3-8-11(VIS) M Wood 7/1: 3-04400: Bckd from 25/1, btr 1677.   00
1751 EASTERN COMMAND [8] 3-8-11 P Robinson 6/1: 34-430: Not well drawn: see 1446.   00
1902 BAG LADY [2] 3-8-11(bl) A Mcglone 5/1: 4-32000: Active in mkt but disapp since 762.   00
1751 CANADIAN GUEST [14] 3-8-11 T Williams 5/1: -0020: Btr 1751 (firm).   00
--   FOX STEEP [4] 3-8-11 A Clark 5/1: -0: Drifted from 5/2, can probably do btr than this.   00
1953 Chart Climber [24] 8-11   1368 Sweepy [20] 8-11
1690 Bella Carina [21] 8-11(BL)   379 Armour Of Light [5] 8-11
1749 Cherry Glory [12] 8-11   -- Everyinchalady [13] 8-11
2085 Henaadi [17] 8-11   -- Hillgate Lady [1] 8-11
1446 Natija [10] 8-11   1257 Opal Flower [6] 8-11   937 Scented Silence [9] 8-11
22 ran   5,1½,1½,1,nk,1   (Bloodstock & Stud Investment Co Ltd)   P Walwyn Lambourn

Official Going Given As SOFT: ALL TIMES SLOW EXCEPT RACE 2319

2315 FOREST SELLING STAKES   £605   1m 2f   Soft Slow

*2208 GRAND CELEBRATION [4] (R Simpson) 4-9-12 S Whitworth 11/4: 4000111: 3 ch c Monteverde-
Blackfly (Mount Marcy): Easy to back but comfortably completed his hat trick, led 3f out
& eased close home when winning a seller at Chepstow (bought in 4,000 gns): earlier won
selling h'caps at Folkestone & Lingfield: eff over 10f on firm & soft grnd: seems to act
on any trk: in fine form & should win a small h'cap.   22
347 GRAND FLING [8] (D Laing) 3-8-11 R Cochrane 14/1: 000-402: Mkt drifter after long
abs: lost a lot of ground when slipped start, ran on strongly though comfortably held by
winner: lightly raced colt who stays 10f & seems best on soft grnd.   05
2271 POCO LOCO [2] (A Davison) 4-9-7 J Reid 8/1: 4023003: Al prom: see 889 & 495.   00
1733 NOBLE HILL [5] (D Arbuthnot) 3-9-2 T Quinn 11/10 FAV: 31-4004: Dropped in class:
nicely bckd though never got into race: lightly raced this term: see 171.   00
1656 PASSION PLAY [6] 3-8-11 T Williams 3/1: 03-0300: Made much: best over 1m in 774 (firm)   00
1303 MAHABAD [7] 3-8-8 N Adams 33/1: -0000: Abs: dropped in class though wknd quickly 3f
out & seems of little account: bred to be well suited by this trip.   00
2208 ESS JAY ESS [3] 3-8-11 A Mackay 20/1: 0000-00: Mkt drifter: well btn: see 2208.   00
7 ran   1,2½,7,1,15,15   (Tony Stafford)   R Simpson, Upper Lambourn

2316 RIVER MAIDEN STAKES 3YO (DIV 1)   £900   1m   Soft Slow

1953 TOP DEBUTANTE [6] (M Jarvis) 3-8-11 T Ives 2/9 FAV: -30021: 3 b f Monteverdi -
Vaguely Deb (Vaguely Noble): Had a simple task & easily landed the odds when making all in
a 4 runner mdn at Chepstow: eff over 8/9f on gd & soft grnd: seems well suited by a stiff
trk & likes to force the pace.   30
2135 DANRIBO [5] (L Cottrell) 3-9-0 A Mcglone 6/1: 0-00002: Pressed winner over ½way,
sn outpcd: well btn in all his starts previously.   00
-- KINGS RING [7] (D Hanley) 3-9-0 J Williams 10/1: 00-3: Outpcd from ½way: only ran
twice last season, fin well btn on both occasions.   00
-- LINRIBO [1] (L Cottrell) 3-8-11 N Carlisle 9/1: -P: Sn behind, p.u. after 2f:
broke a leg and had to be put down.   00
4 ran   15,10.   (Tjo Tek Tan)   M Jarvis Newmarket

2317 LYSAGHT AMA. RIDERS STAKES (H'CAP)   £2540   2m   Soft Slow   [6]

1879 ACTINIUM [5] (P Cole) 3-11-9 Mr A Schutz 3/1: -212441: 3 br c Labus - Activity
(Montevideo II): Useful colt: led over 3f out & held on well in an amateur riders h'cap at
Chepstow: earlier a comfortable winner of a Newmarket mdn: half brother to several winners:
eff over 12/14f, stays 2m well: acts on firm & soft grnd & well suited by a gall trk: carries
weight well.   48
*1564 TURI [4] (A Smith) 7-9-9 Mr J Wiles(1) 9/4 JT FAV: 003312: No extra close home: see 1564.   04
2075 IGHTHAM [8] (G Harwood) 3-11-5 Mr T Thomson Jones 9/4 JT FAV: -00103: Made most,
kept on well under strong driving & remains in gd form: 7L clear of rem: carries weight well.   40
2148 ADBURY [7] (D Laing) 3-9-13 Mr J Ryan 20/1: -00004: Lngr trip, no extra dist: mdn
who has shown little worthwhile form: stays well: acts on soft grnd.   10
2129 MATBAR [9] 3-10-9(bl)(7ow) Mr E Mcmahon 20/1: 0-04400: No extra str: see 1029.   05
1873 VISTULE [6] 4-10-3 Mr T Mitchell(5) 5/1: 24-0000: Led/dsptd lead till home turn : see 1873.   00
-- Oakdale [3] 8-9   -- Royal Condor [1] 9-12(4ow)
8 ran   ½,½,7,10,10,15,dist   (Fahd Salman)   P Cole Whatcombe, Oxon

2318 LIONS LODGE STAKES (H'CAP)(0-35) 3YO+   £1284   5f   Soft Slow   [29]

2245 SHARAD [4] (B Stevens) 6-7-9(bl)(2ow)(1oh) A Mackay 14/1: 0000001: 6 b h Mummy's Pet -
Autumn Breeze (King's Bench): Gained a surprise win on this rain softened grnd, made all,

ridden out in a h'cap at Chepstow Aug.26: last successful in '84 at Warwick: best form over
this minimum trip: acts on fast & soft grnd & on any trk: does well with forcing tactics.   04
2046 GALLANT HOPE [5] (L Cottrell) 4-8-10 N Carlisle 9/4: 0020222: Ev ch: acts on soft.   16
2160 LONELY STREET [6] (P Arthur) 5-10-1(8ex) L Johnsey(7) 7/4 FAV: 0320143: Not btn far:
acts on soft: see 2046.   34
*1827 CELESTIAL DRIVE [3] (R Hannon) 3-9-2(bl) B Rouse 7/2: 0-20014: Mkt drifter: in gd form.   20
2046 HILDALARIOUS [2] 4-7-7(2oh) T Williams 11/2: -000400: Not qcknd dist: see 1940.   00
1839 AMMEED [1] 4-7-7 P Hill(7) 14/1: -000000: Speed to ½way: well btn: see 1344.   00
6 ran   ½,nk,2,1½,6   (John A Nicholson)   B Stevens Bramley, Surrey

2319 BERKELEY STAKES (H'CAP)(0-35) 3YO+   £1551   7f   Soft +12 Fast   [31]

2123 CONCERT PITCH [9] (B Palling) 7-9-1 R Cochrane 9/2 FAV: 00-0041: 7 ch g Royal Match -
Ballychord (Ballymoss): Returned easily the fastest time of the day when leading 2f out,
comfortably in a h'cap at Chepstow: last successful in '84, at Chepstow, Doncaster & Cagnes:
versatile sort who is probably best over 6/7f though does stay 12f: acts on firm & soft grnd
& is well suited by a stiff trk.   27
436 SITZCARRALDO [1] (R Hannon) 3-8-12 B Rouse 10/1: 00-2002: Long abs: ran on well &
seems to do well when fresh: likes some cut under foot: see 62.   25
*1751 TZU WONG [15] (M Pipe) 3-9-6 A Clark 12/1: -000013: In gd form: see 1751.   32
850 PAMELA HEANEY [4] (H Beasley) 4-8-3 T Williams 10/1: 0-00304: Gd effort after long abs.   05
2123 GAUHAR [11] 5-8-6 N Adams 9/1: 4400000: Nearest fin: see 174.   05
2046 MIA JUBES [21] 4-8-3 S Whitworth 14/1: 000-000: Ran on too late: lightly raced this
term & last successful in '84 at Kempton: eff over 6/7f on fast & soft grnd: acts on any trk.   00
2072 BILLY WHITESHOES [19] 4-8-5(VIS) I Johnson 10/1: -000300: Fitted with a visor: clear
ldr, wknd into 7th: see 1834.   00
1947 FIRST OPPORTUNITY [20] 3-8-11 L Johnsey(7) 10/1: 0-040: Fin 8th: see 1947 & 1836.   00
*1616 SITEX [13] 8-8-0 G Duffield 13/2: 0-00410: Btr over 5f in 1616 (gd/firm).   00
1122 RHAPSODY IN BLACK [11] 3-8-5 Paul Eddery 10/1: -1000: Abs: early speed: best in 39.   00
1609 PETT VELERO [8] 7-8-4 P Simms(7) 6/1: 0101000: Last to fin: best in 1264 (gd/firm).   00
1136 Spring Pursuit [16] 8-11   2123 Catman [18] 8-4
2123 Hatching [6] 8-2   2072 April Arabesque [12] 8-2
1833 Bang Bang [2] 7-11
16 ran   2,hd,1½,1½,1,2,hd   (Bryn Palling Ltd)   B Palling Cowbridge, Sth Glam

2320 BREAM CLAIMING STAKES 2YO   £2094   6f   Soft Slow

2090 DANCING DIANA [10] (R Hannon) 2-8-1 B Rouse 2/1 JT FAV: 2140001: 2 gr f Raga Navarro-
Lovely Diana (Supreme   Sovereign): Led below dist & ran on well to win a 2yo claiming stakes
at Chepstow: earlier a narrow winner of a mdn at Windsor: eff over 5/6f on firm & soft
grnd: acts on any trk.   44
2067 ROUGH DANCE [3] (W Jarvis) 2-8-4 R Cochrane 9/2: 042: Al prom, kept on well & is
on the up grade: eff over 6/7f on firm & soft grnd: see 1598.   40
2051 MILL TRIP [2] (M Prescott) 2-8-1 G Duffield 2/1 JT FAV: 03: Nicely bckd: dwelt, ev
ch though no extra close home: btr effort & should find a small race in due course: acts
on gd/firm & soft: see 2051.   35
621 PINEAPPLES PRIDE [8] (M Blanshard) 2-7-12 N Adams 10/1: 04: Long abs: made much though
just needed race: speedily bred filly who acts on firm & soft grnd: see 621.   22
*2180 FLAG BEARER [1] 2-7-13 A Tucker(7) 12/1: 000010: Al prom: btr in 2180 (5f, gd/firm).   15
1665 JOHNS BABY [14] 2-7-10 D Mckay 33/1: 00: Ran on strongly though too much to do:
will be suited by further: acts on soft grnd & on a stiff trk.   09
1778 Miss Jasmine [11] 8-11   2218 Starch Brook [5] 7-10
1955 Fortyniner [4] 7-13(BL)   938 Mark Seagull [9] 7-13
--   Charlous Choice [6] 9-0   --   White Of Morn [13] 9-0
12 ran   2½,1,4,3,1½   (G A Bosley)   R Hannon Marlborough, Wilts

2321 RIVER MAIDEN STAKES 3YO (DIV 2)   £928   1m   Soft Slow

2085 DOCKSIDER [3] (A Stewart) 3-9-0 M Roberts 7/4 FAV: -021: 3 ch c Hotfoot - Tanara
(Romulus): Impr colt: led over 2f out, readily in a 3yo mdn at Chepstow: half brother to very
useful 2yo Count Pahlen: very eff over 1m, will stay further: acts on fast & soft grnd
& on a gall trk.   48
891 PRETTY GREAT [8] (I Matthews) 3-8-11 G Dickie 33/1: -34002: Kept on well after a
long abs: stays 1m well: acts on gd & soft grnd: see 217 & 33.   38
1628 AUCHINATE [5] (G Harwood) 3-9-0 A Clark 7/1: -43: Led briefly over 2f out, not qckn:
should do btr when stepping up in dist: acts on gd/firm & soft: see 1628.   35
1607 DUFF [7] (D Elsworth) 3-9-0 A Mcglone 7/1: -340004: Led over ½way: disapp since 579 (gd).   27
--   LOWARA [2] 3-8-11 J Reid 8/1: -0: Easy to back on debut: chased ldrs most of way
and will come on for this race: likely to stay at least 10f: acts on soft grnd.   20
--   ZAGAZIG [10] 3-9-0 B Rouse 16/1: -0: Mkt drifter on debut: not given a hard race &
should impr in due course.   15
887 PRASINA MATIA [12] 3-9-0 Paul Eddery 9/2: -0000: Speed over ½way but needed race:
lightly raced since showing promise on his debut in 218.   00
937 Sweet Spice [4] 8-11   1446 Herne Miss Madam [11] 8-11
9 ran   2,3,4,2½,4,8   (A Villar)   A Stewart Newmarket

RIPON   Tuesday August 26th   Righthand, Sharpish Track

Official Going Given As SOFT: BASED ON TIMES SOFT & DETERIORATING: SLOW EXCEPT 2322 & 2325

2322 CURFEW HANDICAP STAKES 3YO+ 0-35   £2330   5f   Soft +10 Fast   [35]

+2124 LADY CARA [16] (J Berry) 6-8-5 J Carroll(7) 10/3 FAV: 0202411: 6 br m Lochnager -
Gold Cheb (Chebs Lad): In fine form: al prom & led final 1f, driven out in quite fast run
h'cap at Ripon Aug.26: last time out won an app h'cap at Catterick: winner in '85 at Newcastle & Hamilton: 5f specialist: acts on any grnd & on any trk: best when up with the pace:
genuine.   21
2033 DEBACH REVENGE [11] (M Tompkins) 4-7-7(5oh) R Morse(1) 33/1: 0004002: Led 2f out:
kept on well & just btn: gd effort: clearly handles soft grnd well: eff at 5-7f: see 1727.   08
971 GOLD DUCHESS [21] (M W Easterby) 4-8-6(bl) B Thomson 12/1: 1002403: Abs: led far side
& just btn in close fin: fine effort: see 412.   20
1543 GODSTRUTH [14] (H T Jones) 7-8-8(bl) A Riding(7) 20/1: 00-0004: Sn prom & stayed on:
best effort this term: see 1344.   18
*1940 PENDOR DANCER [2] 3-8-11(vis) G Baxter 12/1: 0001010: Led stands side: acts on
soft, but btr 1940 (gd/firm).   20
2224 LOCH FORM [17] 3-8-13 W Goodwin(5) 10/1: 0032040: Never nearer: see 1543, 255.   17
1973 LULLABY BLUES [3] 3-8-13 M Birch 7/1: 1212000: Fin 7th: best 890 (stiff 5f).   00
2124 BAY BAZAAR [9] 4-8-9 G Carter(3) 10/1: 3400000: No threat: see 1682, 42.   00
2079 RA RA GIRL [10] 4-9-4 J Hillis(5) 10/1: 0002030: Unsuited by soft? see 2079 (gd).   00
2124 Parade Girl [1] 7-10   2124 Wesbree Bay [5] 7-7(4oh)
1917 Sly Maid [13] 7-7   2124 Last Secret [12] 7-7(bl)(2oh)
2204 Karens Star [18] 8-11   2124 Pergoda [4] 9-6(bl)   1927 The Stray Bullett [6] 7-13(bl)
1136 Rock Salt [22] 7-10   2124 Tradesman [19] 7-7(bl)
1734 Petencore [20] 7-8   1973 Carpenters Boy [7] 8-4
1704 Bridge Of Gold [8] 8-9
21 ran   hd,nk,2,3,2½,½   (Mrs V O'Brien)   J Berry Cockerham, Lancs

2323 BOROUGHBRIDGE SELLING STAKES 2YO   £1461   5f   Soft Slow

1895 DOHTY BABY [13] (M W Easterby) 2-8-8(BL) B Thomson 9/2: 03001: 2 ch f Hittite Glory-
Ventrex (Henry The Seventh): Bl first time & led inside final 2f, ridden out in a 2yo
seller at Ripon (bought in 2,400 gns): eff at 5f, stays 7f: acts on firm & soft grnd &
on any trk: seems suited by bl.   24
2100 MISS EMILY [9] (D Chapman) 2-8-8 D Nicholls 16/1: 0002: Al up there & kept on:
will need further than 5f: acts on gd/firm & soft & can find a similar event: see 2100.   19
741 LEVEN LASS [16] (I Vickers) 2-8-8 R Vickers(7) 20/1: 003: Abs: al prom: dropped to
selling company today: cheaply acquired filly who handles soft grnd well.   15
1955 RUN TO WORK [14] (G Moore) 2-8-11 D Casey(5) 12/1: 2233404: Stayed on: consistent,
but yet to win: acts on firm & soft trk: see 1717, 957.   17
1279 GOLD STATE [12] 2-8-11 R Fox 12/1: 0000: Abs: ran on final 1f, showing marked impr
on this soft grnd: half brother to a winning 2yo.   16
1862 TOKANDA [8] 2-8-11(BL) R Hills 14/1: 0000: Kept on final 2f: acts on firm & soft
and will do btr over 6/7f: see 1764: bl 1st time today.   15
1881 SEATON GIRL [7] 2-8-8 G Carter(3) 10/1: 0014000: Prom stands side most: see 1358.   00
2212 CAUSEWAY FOOT [4] 2-8-11(bl) W R Swinburn 5/1: 0000420: Much btr 2212 (firm grnd).   00
2212 GREENSWARD BOY [11] 2-8-11(VIS) G Baxter 8/1: 00300: Dsptd lead far side: visored
first time: best 1723 (firm).   00
-- CAWSTONS PREJUDICE [1] 2-8-8 A Roper(4) 10/1: 0: No threat on debut.   00
2100 HAZELS GIRL [2] 2-8-8 K Darley 4/1 FAV: 0402000: Bckd from 20/1 but fdd after a
slow start: see 1635: see 118.   00
2150 Metroman [18] 8-11(BL)   2127 Rosies Image [3] 8-8
2127 Jean Jeanie [19] 8-8   2150 Venherm [5] 8-11   146 Swift Challenger [10] 8-11
1905 Arday Wednesday [17] 8-8   2107 Ragtime Party [6] 8-11
-- Beena Star [15] 8-8
19 ran   1½,1½,nk,½,½   (Lady Hesketh)   M W Easterby Sheriff Hutton, Yorks

2324 STEVE NESBITT CHALL TROPHY HCAP 0-50   £2695   1m 4f   Soft Slow   [41]

-- MALADHU [8] (J Fitzgerald) 7-8-7 D Nicholls 7/1: 03240-1: 7 b g Malacate - Mhairi Dhyu
(Great Nephew): First time out, waited with & led over 1f out, comfortably in a h'cap at
Ripon Aug.26: in '85 ran consistently, winning this same race: in '84 won h'caps at Ripon
& Edinburgh: eff at 10f, stays 12f well: acts on gd & soft grnd & on any trk.   32
1621 SILENT JOURNEY [1] (J Watts) 4-8-11 N Connorton 6/1: 1200232: Made most: 5L clear 3rd:
gd effort & likes some give in the grnd, though does act on gd/firm: see 256.   30
2164 PRINCE SATIRE [2] (M Jarvis) 3-8-12 W Woods(3) 9/2: -010403: Ch over 2f out: see 1939, 492   35
*1908 BANQUE PRIVEE [3] (B Hills) 3-9-4 B Thomson 11/4 FAV: 0-3314: Chall in str, wknd:
better 1908 (good).   35
778 LEON [6] 4-9-2 Kim Tinkler 7/1: -220240: No threat after abs: see 778, 80.   20
*1481 GREAT EXCEPTION [7] 3-9-7 W Newnes 9/2: 232-310: Fdd str: well below 1481 (shp trk firm)   31
1980 MOULKINS [4] 4-7-8 Julie Bowker(6) 7/1: 0013040: Lightly bckd, fdd 2 out: best 1052.   00
7 ran   3,5,4,1½,3   (Mrs A C Robson)   J Fitzgerald Malton, Yorks

2325 WENSLEY AUCTION STAKES 2YO   £2810   6f   Very Soft +08 Fast

1925 PEATSWOOD SHOOTER [7] (M Brittain) 2-8-11 K Darley 4/1: 1103401: 2 gr c Windjammer-
Raffinata (Raffingora): Useful colt: appreciated the soft grnd when making ev yd on the stands
side by an easy 10L in a 2yo auction at Ripon: winner of his first 3 outings, at Pontefract,
Beverley & Leicester (first time out): eff at 5f, stays 6f well: well suited by yld & hvy
grnd with front running tactics: acts on any trk & should win more races while the grnd is soft   61
2011 MISS SARAJANE [3] (R Hollinshead) 2-7-12 A Culhane(7) 12/1: 002: Prom, no threat to
winner: bckd at long odds here & showed impr form: eff at 6f on soft grnd.   28
1454 STAY LOW [9] (G Blum) 2-8-8 M Rimmer 1/1 FAV: 1331403: Well bckd & ev ch: needed race?   38
1225 WILLOW THE KING [2] (E Weymes) 2-8-1 S Webster 33/1: 04: Abs: kept on final 2f: half
brother to My Aisling: acts on soft grnd.   28
2082 STELBY [16] 2-8-1 A Proud 4/1: 022420: Prom, much btr 2082 (gd/firm).   25
1161 PREMIER LAD [17] 2-8-6(1ow) D Nicholls 20/1: 030: Abs: gd late hdway & will step up
on this next time: stays 6f & acts on firm & soft: see 1161.   29
2147 Call For Taylor [21] 7-12   1634 Mr Chris Cakemaker [14] 7-12
2011 Champion Joker [6] 8-3   1665 Dual Capacity [20] 8-1
1090 Pit Pony [10] 8-1   2029 Savanna King [18] 8-1   2082 Frenchgate [4] 8-1
2153 Suesandy [1] 7-12   931 Trafford Way [22] 8-1   2026 Fossard [11] 8-1
1825 Beattys Lad 0 8-1   685 Banks And Braes [5] 8-1
-- Melody Liner [19] 8-1   2100 Park Frolics [8] 7-12
20 ran   10,hd,1½,1½,nk   (G G Ashton)   M Brittain Warthill, Yorks

2326 WAKEMAN STAYERS HANDICAP 3YO+ 0-35   £2138   2m 2f   Very Soft Slow   [31]

2111 SUN STREET [5] (C Brittain) 4-8-13 G Baxter 6/1: -400201: 4 br f Ile De Bourbon-
Polly Packer (Reform): Led fully 7f out & stayed on dourly to win a h'cap at Ripon Aug.26:
in '85 won a mdn at Catterick: well suited by a stamina test nowadays: acts on gd/firm &
soft grnd & on any trk, though likes an easy one.   25
2111 KNIGHTS HEIR [1] (H Whiting) 5-7-13 L Riggio(7) 12/1: 0000202: Led till 7f out:
stayed: see 85.   08
1952 DONT RING ME [3] (W Hastings Bass) 4-9-6 R Lines(3) 11/4: 0-04023: Prom, ev ch:
stays 2m2f: see 675.   23
2087 TRESIDDER [4] (M W Easterby) 4-9-13 G Carter(3) 2/1 FAV: -040424: Well bckd: btr 2087.   29
1688 PHEASANT HEIGHTS [8] 3-7-9 J Lowe 6/1: -440040: Fdd str: best 1304 (firm): see 307.   01
2111 ALFIE DICKINS [7] 8-7-7(1oh) A Culhane(7) 12/1: 4403000: No show: see 590.   00
*1544 THE CANNY MAN [6] 3-8-11 L Charnock 8/1: -00010: Abs since much btr 1544 (15f, firm).   00
2087 Cavalier Servente [2] 8-3   2087 Broken Seal [11] 9-3 P
9 ran   3,6,nk,10,2   (J Ward Hill)   C Brittain Newmarket

2327 HARROGATE MAIDEN STAKES 3YO   £2478   1m 2f   Very Soft Slow

1677 NO MORE ROSIES [5] (C Thornton) 3-8-11 J Bleasdale 25/1: -01: 3 gr f Warpath -
Rosie Wings (Telegram II): Impr filly: came from a long way back to lead close home & win
going away in a 3yo mdn at Ripon Aug.26: sister to 2 staying winners, notably Flying Officer
who also must have soft grnd: eff at 10f, will stay further: acts on very soft grnd.   37
1953 PRINCESS EMMA [3] (M Stoute) 3-8-11 W R Swinburn 10/3: -042: Led over 1f out:
caught close home: stays 10f: handles very soft grnd: may win a small event on btr going.   34
2129 INDIAN LOVE SONG [7] (R Hollinshead) 3-8-11 S Perks 10/1: 3043023: Ev ch in str: see 2129   32
2183 NOHOLMINA [6] (O Douieb) 3-8-11 R Machado 11/2: -034: Acts on gd/firm & soft.   31
1797 COCCOLUTO [16] 3-9-0 R Fox 5/2 JT.FAV: 0-02220: Made much: wandered final 3f in this
very poor grnd: see 1797.   32
1797 PLEASING PROSPECT [2] 3-8-11 M Birch 20/1: 300-030: Ev ch str: fdd: btr 1m? see 1511.   26
1749 REMINISCING [12] 3-8-11 W Newnes 5/2 JT.FAV: -20: Nicely bckd: fin 9th: much btr 1749.   00
-- Fiesta Dance [4] 9-0   1954 Dalveen Pass [14] 9-0   2171 Out Of Stock [13] 9-0
1921 Dialect [1] 8-11   1361 Golflines [10] 9-0   -- Lindon [15] 8-11
13 ran   1½,1½,¾,1½,2   (Guy Reed)   C Thornton Middleham, Yorks

Official Going Given As SOFT

2328 LADAS MAIDEN STAKES 2YO   £2106   6f   Good/Yielding 76 -19 Slow

1583 TEZ SHIKARI [4] (L Cottrell) 2-9-0(VIS) G Starkey 7/4 FAV: 4222221: 2 b c Kala Shikari -
Eagle's Quest (Legal Eagle): Equipped with a visor & finally got off the mark, led inside
dist, comfortably in a 2yo mdn at Epsom: had fin 2nd in his 5 previous races & deserved this
win: cheaply bought colt who is a half sister to winning sprinter Legalize: eff over 5/6f
on firm & soft grnd: acts on any trk.   41
1381 MONETARY FUND [2] (G Lewis) 2-9-0 P Waldron 2/1: 02: Led below dist, outpcd close
home though a gd effort after fair abs: eff over 5/6f on firm & yld: see 1381.   35
2147 WATERED SILK [3] (M Francis) 2-8-11 C Rutter(3) 13/2: 03: Never nearer: will be
suited by further: acts on yld ground & on a sharp trk: should continue to impr.   27
1475 SPY TOWER [6] (D Murray Smith) 2-9-0 P Robinson 10/1: 004: Abs: no extra dist: quite
cheaply bought colt who is closely related to a couple of minor winners: will be suited by
7f in time: acts on gd & soft grnd.   29

-- **CLOUDY LIGHT** [1] 2-8-11 A Murray 6/1: 0: Broke well & made most on her racecourse debut: acts on yld grnd & on a sharp course: should impr for this run. 22
2089 **SHANNON RIVER** [7] 2-9-0 P Cook 12/1: 000: Early speed: down the field in both his previous races. 05
6 ran 2,2,nk,1½,6 (Clement M Brown) L Cottrell Dulford, Devon

2329 EBF RUBBING HOUSE STAKES 2YO £3472 7f Good/Yielding 76 +08 Fast

1948 PSALMODY [2] (W Hastings Bass) 2-8-11 A Murray 4/1: 0021: 2 b c Hittite Glory - Happy Music (Hethersett): Useful colt: led dist, easily in a fast run 2yo stakes at Epsom: half brother to the very useful 10/12f winner Galveston: very eff over 7f, should stay at least 1m: acts on gd & yld grnd & on a sharp/easy course. 51
2019 TUFTY LADY [3] (R Armstrong) 2-8-8 W Carson 5/2: 0022: Tried to make all: gd effort & certain to get off the mark soon: acts on gd/firm & yld: see 2019. 42
2105 MON COEUR [6] (C Brittain) 2-8-11(bl) P Robinson 7/4 FAV: 0423: Hvly bckd: al front rank: sure to be suited by 1m: acts on gd/firm & yld: see 2105. 41
1345 HOCKLEY [4] (R Hannon) 2-8-11 S Cauthen 6/1: 034: Outpcd below dist: abs since 1345 (frm) 26
1495 LAZIM [1] 2-8-11(bl) P Waldron 10/1: 0430: Abs: btr over 6f in 1495. 11
5 ran 2,2,7,7 (Lord Derby) W Hastings Bass Newmarket

2330 STEVE DONOGHUE APP.H'CAP 3YO+ 0-35 £3116 1m 4f Good/Yielding 76 -25 Slow [35]

1209 DENBOY [4] (B Stevens) 4-8-11 R Carter 15/2: -001201: 4 ch g On Your Mark - Petal (Whistler): Fair abs though led inside dist, holding on well to win an app. h'cap at Epsom: earlier won a h'cap at Leicester: eff over 12/14f on firm & soft grnd: acts on any trk. 26
•410 BEN ADHEM [1] (H Candy) 4-9-11 C Rutter 100/30: 3014-12: Just btn: fine effort after a lengthy abs: stays 12f well: acts on firm & yld: see 410. 39
•2188 JABARABA [6] (L Cottrell) 5-9-1(4ex) T Lang(3) 9/2: 0041113: Tried to make all, not btn far & remains in fine form: see 2188. 28
1945 WILLOW GORGE [2] (G Lewis) 3-8-3 R Crowden(7) 20/1: -00004: Btr effort: see 1945. 22
2154 MR LION [5] 4-8-0 J Carr(3) 3/1 JT FAV: 2222000: Best in 1052 (stiff trk): see 860, 721 07
•2217 WHILE IT LASTS [3] 3-9-2(4ex) S Quane(3) 3/1 JT FAV: 3332310: Btr on fast grnd in 2217. 31
6 ran nk,½,4,¾,3 (Martin Coles) B Stevens Winchester, Hants

2331 CHALK LANE H'CAP 3YO+ 0-50 £3500 1m 2f Good/Yielding 76 -14 Slow [50]

2219 RANA PRATAP [2] (G Lewis) 6-9-7 P Waldron 3/1: 3204201: 6 b h Faliraki - Dodo S (Nagea): Fair h'capper: gained a deserved success, led 2f out, ridden out in a h'cap at Epsom: has had several near misses this term: last season won a h'cap at York: twice a winning 2yo: eff at 1m, nowadays suited by 10f: acts on firm & soft grnd & on any trk. 53
2219 SAMHAAN [1] (B Hanbury) 4-8-11(bl)(4ex) A Geran(7) 7/2: 0112132: Ch final 1f: continues in fine form: see 2219, 2121. 42
2053 SAMANPOUR [6] (R J Houghton) 3-9-0 S Cauthen 11/4 FAV: 1130203: Ch final 2f: fair effort, see 1130, 547. 54
•919 EMRYS [5] (N Vigors) 3-8-4 P Cook 4/1: -103314: Prom most after abs: needed race? 40
•1792 ROYAL HALO [7] 5-10-2 G Starkey 4/1: -201110: Mkt drifter: led 1m: btr 1792 (gd/firm). 48
5 ran ½,½,4,8 (Mrs Georgie Thornberry) G Lewis Epsom, Surrey

2332 HEATHCOTE NURSERY H'CAP 2YO £2949 7f Good/Yielding 76 +05 Fast [71]

2044 ANGARA ABYSS [2] (G Harwood) 2-9-7 G Starkey 7/4 FAV: 41121: 2 b c Far North - For Missy (Forli): Smart colt: hvly bckd & made ev yd, very easily in quite fast run nursery h'cap at Epsom: earlier an easy winner at Kempton & Brighton: last time out lost nothing in defeat when 2nd to the smart Deputy Governor at Lingfield: cost only $52,000 as a yearling & is a half brother to 2 winners in the : very eff at 7f, should be suited by 1m: acts on firm & yld grnd: suited by forcing tactics on an easy trk, probably acts on any. 75
•1891 PAS DENCHERE [1] (G Lewis) 2-8-6 P Waldron 9/4: 03012: Caught a tartar: acts on gd/firm & yld: stays 7f: see 1891. 47
2209 STRIKE RATE [4] (R Hannon) 2-7-13 W Carson 15/8: 1233: Btr 2209 (gd/firm): see 180. 37
1936 WHAT A GUY [3] (P Mitchell) 2-7-7(3oh) S Dawson 14/1: 4004: Prom most: stiff task. 28
4 ran 6,1½,1½ (Paul H Locke) G Harwood Pulborough, Sussex

2333 CHESSINGTON MAIDEN STAKES 3YO £2058 8.5f Good/Yielding 76 +14 Fast

2092 PRINCE ORAC [7] (C Brittain) 3-9-0 S Cauthen 6/4 JT FAV: -3021: 3 ch c Good Times - Hannah Darling (Match III): Well bckd & made ev yd, comfortably in a fast run 3yo mdn at Epsom: last time out was a gd 2nd to Boon Point at Windsor: half brother to a middle dist winner in France: eff at 1m, well suited by 10f: acts on gd & yld grnd & on any trk: seems suited by front running. 50
1657 ZINDELINA [3] (R Hannon) 2-8-11 W Carson 9/1: 0-20402: Kept on well final 2f: gd effort: see 505: may find a h'cap shortly. 42
1775 KING TEFKROS [4] (M Tompkins) 3-9-0 P Robinson 12/1: -003323: Ev ch in str: consistent: acts on firm & yld: see 1775, 1206. 45
1934 TAVIRI [1] (G Harwood) 3-9-0 G Starkey 6/4 JT FAV: -24: Well bckd: much btr 1934 (gd/firm) 35
2076 MIRATAINE VENTURE [6] 2-8-11 P Cook 33/1: 0003000: Outsider: fdd final 2f: see 1446. 31

EPSOM   Tuesday August 26th   -Cont'd

2170 CAPRICORN BEAU [5] 3-9-0 T Lucas 6/1: -0440: Fdd over 2f out: btr 2170 (gd/firm).   31
1864 FAATIK [2] 3-9-0(VIS) N Howe 25/1: -004000: Visored first time: prom over 5f: see 334.   00
7 ran   2½,shhd,10,nk,3   (Dimitris M Lemos)   C Brittain Newmarket

BEVERLEY   Wednesday August 27th   Righthanded Undulating Track, Stiff Uphill Finish

2334 KIRKELLA CLAIMING STAKES 2YO   £1250   5f   Yielding 86 -34 Slow

--   AEGEAN DANCE [6] (M Prescott) 2-8-5 G Duffield 8/1: 1: 2 b g Tyrnavos - Dance In Rome
(Dancing In Time): Made a successful debut, went on ½way & held on gamely in a 2yo claiming
stakes at Beverley: clearly eff over a stiff 5f & seems certain to be suited by further: acts
on yld grnd: genuine filly who can only improve.   28
2032 QUE PASA [8] (P Haslam) 2-8-11 T Williams 13/2: 02: Sustained chall inside dist,
just held: impr colt who may prove btr over a lngr trip: acts on yld: see 2032.   33
1683 CHIC ANTIQUE [3] (P Makin) 2-8-11 T Quinn 14/1: 03: Dropped in class: al front rank:
half sister to much impr sprinter Jokist & 5f winner Penchetta: eff over 5f on yld grnd.   27
1568 INGLISTON [4] (M H Easterby) 2-8-11 M Birch 13/2: 033404: Al up there: see 965.   25
*2150 MERE MUSIC [14] 2-9-0(bl) K Darley 9/2: 0000010: Early ldr: no extra dist: best in 2150. 18
1707 DANCE UP [10] 2-8-10 R P Elliott 16/1: 40: Nearest fin: acts on yld: see 1707.   12
2026 TAHARD [12] 2-8-12(BL) S Perks 8/1: 000000: Bl first time: fin 7th: speedily bred
colt who cost 8,000 gns: little form since showing promise in 694.   00
2265 BAD PAYER [7] 2-8-7 T Lucas 4/1 FAV: 4312100: Gd early speed: fin 8th: btr in 1893.   00
717 BALIDUCK [11] 2-8-7 M Wood 11/2: 3020: Abs: needed race: see 717 (gd/firm).   00
2168 Kinsham Dene [1] 8-6   2007 Fairburn [5] 8-9   -- Lady Of Riga [13] 8-11
--   I Promised [9] 8-11(BL)
13 ran   shhd,2½,¾,4,1   (Major General Sir George Burns)   M Prescott Newmarket

2335 TOLL GAVEL SELLING HANDICAP 0-25   £950   1m   Yielding 86 -08 Slow   [12]

1562 CARR WOOD [9] (M Prescott) 3-8-7 G Duffield 2/1 FAV: -0001: 3 b g Formidable -
Grovette (Derring-Do): Was very well bckd & led dist, comfortably in a selling h'cap at
Beverley (bought in 4,400 gns): did not race last season & had shown little in his previous
starts this term: eff around 1m, should stay further: suited by yld grnd & a stiff trk.   12
1428 FOLKSWOOD [16] (M Camacho) 3-8-7 N Connorton 25/1: 00-0002: Led early & again below
dist: gd effort after a fair abs: lightly raced gelding who is eff over 1m on yld grnd.   02
1639 SHOWDANCE [5] (R Hollinshead) 3-8-8 S Perks 25/1: 0-0003: Dropped in class & made
most: lightly raced gelding who had been well btn previously in mdn races: stays 1m: acts on yld 00
1917 MRS NAUGHTY [11] (W Wharton) 3-9-2 G Carter(3) 7/1: 4000304: Bt here in 1562 (firm).   05
*2103 WATENDLATH [12] 3-8-12(bl)(7ex) E Guest(3) 7/2: 0000010: Saddle slipped: ignore
this run: see 2103.   00
1567 RES NON VERBA [15] 3-8-7 S Webster 20/1: 0-300: Abs: gd late prog: lightly raced
filly who acts on firm & yld grnd: see 1340.   00
2104 THE GOLF SLIDE [10] 4-9-0 J Hills(5) 8/1: 2000300: No threat: fin 9th: see 1839.   00
1482 JUST A BIT [8] 4-9-11 D Leadbitter(5) 13/2: 230-400: Abs: prom early: see 1013 (7f firm) 00
1703 Jalome [2] 8-13   1699 Belhill [1] 8-0   1904 Accumulate [13] 8-12
1200 Our Mumsie [14] 8-9   2174 Amplify [4] 9-2   1064 Arranmore Girl [17] 8-13
1415 Montefiaso [18] 9-0   2085 Drumbarra [3] 9-2   -- Keyanloch [6] 9-12
2104 Carousel Nougat [7] 9-0
18 ran   4,3,shhd,5,nk   (Edward St George)   M Prescott Newmarket

2336 BEVERLEY SILVER SALVER NURSERY H'CAP   £2649   7f   Yielding 86 -08 Slow   [56]

*2227 SNO SURPRISE [6] (R Boss) 2-8-0(7ex) G Duffield 7/1: 4002011: 2 ch c Tina's Pet -
My Portavia (Porto Bello): In fine form, led dist & held on well to win a nursery h'cap at
Beverley: recently won a similar event at Yarmouth: very eff around 7f, sure to stay at
least 1m: acts on firm & yld grnd & on any trk.   40
2199 STILLMAN [1] (M H Easterby) 2-9-7 M Birch 10/11 FAV: 00132: Ran a gd race under top
weight: could not qckn close home: in fine form: acts on gd/firm & yld: see 1812.   60
2105 THANK HAVON [7] (D Morley) 2-8-2 J Lowe 11/1: 40403: Led over 2f out, narrowly btn:
stays 7f: acts on yld: see 1984.   40
1978 DANUM DANCER [8] (M W Easterby) 2-7-7(3oh) L Charnock 14/1: 004404: Made much: not
btn far & ran his best race for sometime: seems suited by some give: see 685.   29
*1846 PERFECT STRANGER [3] 2-7-13 T Williams 11/2: 0310: Unlucky in running, going on fin
& only btn 2L: acts on gd/firm & yld: see 1846.   34
1907 PRINCESS SINGH [2] 2-7-7(4oh) Kim Tinkler 20/1: 0443120: Ran to her best: see 1907 & 1537. 22
*1862 SUE FOREVER [5] 2-7-7(3oh) A Culhane(7) 14/1: 010: Btn 2f out: btr in 1862 (firm slr).   00
2178 BADOGLIO [4] 2-7-9 M Fozzard 10/1: 04000: No threat after slow start: probably needs
faster grnd: see 974.   00
8 ran   nk,nk,1,½,2   (Mrs Judi Gold)   R Boss Newmarket

690

2337 CHARLES ELSEY MEM CHALL TROPHY HCAP 0-5   £2607   1m 4f   Yielding 86 +09 Fast   [41]

2201 PAST GLORIES [5] (C Elsey) 3-9-4 J Lowe 6/4 FAV: 1042101: 3 b c Hittite Glory -
Snow Tribe (Great Nephew): Gamely justified fav, regained lead close home in quite a fast
run h'cap at Beverley Aug.27: consistent colt who earlier won a Hamilton mdn & a valuable
h'cap at Ripon: half brother to several middle dist winners: well suited by 11/12f & should
stay further: acts on firm & hvy grnd & on any trk.   45
1980 DIPYN BACH [3] (M Camacho) 4-8-1 G Duffield 4/1: 0440302: Moved smoothly into lead
dist, out battled close home: well clear of rem & likes this stiff trk: see 782.   16
--   TROMEROS [1] (Denys Smith) 5-7-9 L Charnock 14/1: 10000-3: No ch with front pair:
sole success on the Flat came in a h'cap at Catterick last season, though subs. successful over
hdles: eff around 1m, stays 14f well: acts on gd & firm grnd & on any trk.   00
429 LUMINATE [2] (J Leigh) 5-9-4 M Birch 20/1: -000-04: Cong abs & no threat: lightly
raced since showing gd form when winning at Beverley & Lingfield in '84: stays 12f well:
acts on firm & yld grnd.   00
1909 APPLE WINE [6] 9-7-7(2oh) A Proud 8/1: 0244000: In front to ½way: see 256.   00
2276 SWYNFORD PRINCE [4] 3-7-11 N Carlisle 8/1: 0300000: Well btn: much btr in 738: see 331. 00
964 AUCHINLEA [7] 4-9-7 A Murray 9/2: 00-3000: Fin last after long abs: see 629.   00
7 ran   nk,30,1½,6,15   (N Hetherton)   C Elsey Malton, Yorks

2338 BEVERLEY AMATEUR RIDERS STAKES   £937   2m   Yielding 86 -23 Slow

*1674 PAEAN [7] (H Cecil) 3-11-0 Franca Vittadini 4/5 FAV: 2-12111: 3 b c Bustino -
Mixed Applause (Nijinsky): Smart colt: landed the odds with consumate ease, led ½way and
pushed out to win an amatuer riders stakes at Beverley: first time out winner of a Newbury
mdn, later won minor events at Newcastle & Pontefract: very well bred colt who is eff around
12f & clearly stays 2m well: acts on firm though prefers some give in the grnd: genuine &
consistent & looks a high class stayer in the making.   70
1408 SHTAIFEH [5] (H T Jones) 3-10-8 Mr T Thomson Jones 13/2: 1-02: No ch with winner though
kept on well: fin well clear of remainder: lightly raced , last season won her only start,
a back end minor race at Nottingham: well bred filly who stays 2m well: acts on firm &
yld grnd & on a stiff trk: should find a race soon.   52
2156 ONISKY [6] (P Cole) 3-11-0 Mr T Easterby 7/2: -112303: Seems btr over a slightly
shorter trip: see 983 (14f).   38
1417 RUSHMOOR [1] (R Peacock) 8-11-13 Carmen Peacock(5) 16/1: 4003144: Abs: best in 1159 (14f) 24
2211 HERRADURA [2] 5-11-13(vis) Maxine Juster 14/1: 302D320: Much btr in 2211 (14f firm). 19
363 JOLIS GIRL [9] 4-11-7 Mr J Ryan 20/1: -030300: Al behind after long abs: see 72.   03
--   Radwhaw [8] 11-10   1963 Count Colours [4] 11-10(VIS)
9   Cri De Grace [3] 11-6
9 ran   8,20,10,3,6   (Lord Howard De Walden)   H Cecil Newmarket

2339 NORTH BAR MAIDEN STAKES 3YO   £873   1m   Yielding 86 -01 Slow

210 GERAGHTY AGAIN [1] (A Bailey) 3-9-0(BL) K Hodgson 10/1: 00-041: 3 b c Hard Fought -
Ottoline (Brigadier Gerard): Fitted with bl after a lengthy abs, led over 2f out, decisively
in a 3yo mdn at Beverley Aug.27: lightly raced colt who is a half brother to winning juvenile
Standing Order: eff around 1m on gd or softer grnd: acts on a stiff trk: should win again
in this form.   46
2216 PRAIRIE OYSTER [16] (B Hanbury) 3-9-0 A J Geran(7) 13/2: -032: Stayed on well from
½way to take the minor honours: acts on fast & yld grnd: gd form: see 2216.   32
1880 HAMPER [9] (W Hastings Bass) 3-9-0 A Murray 11/8 FAV: -43: Hvly bckd: not qckn below
dist: should be suited by a lngr trip: acts on gd/firm & yld: see 1880.   31
1677 LUCKY BLAKE [10] (C Thornton) 3-9-0 J Bleasdale 14/1: -0404: Al prom: see 1677 & 605. 29
1705 AMIR ALBADEIA [7] 3-9-0(VIS) N Howe 13/2: 4-22040: Much btr in 316: see 253: vis. today 25
2173 WELSH PAGEANTRY [2] 3-8-11 T Lucas 20/1: 0-00000: Late prog: acts on firm & yld: see 941 21
1981 KAIYRAN [12] 3-9-0(BL) M Birch 6/1: 3-000: Bl first time: made much, fdd into 8th.   00
1701 Country Carnival [4] 8-11   2085 Super Trucker [6] 9-0
1841 Owls Way [13] 8-11   2214 The Romford Roar [14] 9-0
1921 Harleyford Lad [15] 9-0   --   Nomad Boxer [3] 9-0
891 Tip Top Boy [11] 9-0   1797 Dutch Queen [5] 8-11   --   Dublin Daygo [8] 8-11
16 ran   7,nk,¾,2,nk,hd,1½   (M F Geraghty Racing Ltd)   A Bailey Newmarket

2340 WM HILL FIRST FOR PRICES HANDICAP 0-35   £2088   7.5f   Yielding 86 -04 Slow   [27]

1835 LA JAMBALAYA [15] (P Makin) 3-8-12 T Quinn 7/1 FAV: 0-34021: 3 b f Reform -
Gay Tamarind (Tamerlane): Led over 2f out & sprinted clear to gain her first success in a
h'cap at Beverley: eff around 7/8f on firm & yld grnd: usually up with the pace: should defy
a penalty.   32
2109 MANABEL [5] (S Bowring) 4-8-11 J Quinn(5) 33/1: 0000002: No threat to winner though
showed impr form: placed several times last year but seemed to have lost her form: best
around 7f on an easy surface.   09
*2213 HOPEFUL KATIE [2] (D Leslie) 4-8-13(5ex) J Williams 9/1: 0303013: Ran on too late: see 2213 10
1976 TIT WILLOW [3] (S Wiles) 4-8-13(bl) M Fry 14/1: 2212034: Never nearer: see 828.   08
*2086 MARSILIANA [4] 4-8-10(5ex) M Beecroft 12/1: 4034010: Ran on strongly: best in 2086. 00
2213 KAMARESS [8] 4-8-12(5ex) K Darley 12/1: 0043100: Best over this C/D in 2104 (gd/firm). 00

2039 MARAVILLA [16] 4-9-2(VIS) G Carter(3) 8/1: 0002420: Visored first time: btr in 2039.   00
2213 POKERFAYES [17] 7-8-7(bl) G Duffield 10/1: 0020400: Al in rear: best in 1761 (firm).   00
1885 SPECIAL GUEST [6] 3-8-10 J Lowe 10/1: -033240: Can do much btr: see 1695 (gd/firm).   00

2104 Charming View [12] 8-11	710 Janes Brave Boy [1] 8-12
1771 Brampton Imperial [18] 8-11	1673 Bit Of A State [7] 8-12
1987 Kampglow [9] 9-7 1950 Gentileschi [10] 9-5	2104 Improvise [14] 9-6
2102 Restoration [19] 9-3 2264 Little Newington [11] 8-12(bl)	
2104 Top Othlane [13] 8-9	

19 ran   6,nk,1,4,nk,½   (Mrs P Makin)   P Makin Ogbourne Maisey, Wilts

---

Official Going Given As GOOD

2341 FEE FARM MAIDEN STAKES 2YO   £964   7f   Good 50 -06 Slow

--   RUSSIAN STEPPE [2] (H Cecil) 2-9-0 S Cauthen 1/2 FAV: 1: 2 b c Nijinsky - Jump Seat
(Hasty Road): Prom colt: well bckd on debut & despite running rather green got up close home
in a 2yo mdn at Yarmouth: half brother to several winners incl the smart Diaglyphard: eff
at 7f, will be suited by 1m & further: acts on gd grnd & will rate more highly/win btr races.   54
2225 KALGOORLIE [11] (L Piggott) 2-9-0 T Ives 5/2: 02: Bckd from 7/1 & nearly landed
the gamble: led over 2f out & just caught: compensation awaits: see 2225.   53
--   MOMENTS OF SILVER [4] (M Albina) 2-9-0 A Bond 14/1: 3: Al up there on racecourse
debut, showing a deal of promise: dam a 5f winner: eff at 7f, should be suited by 1m:
acts on gd grnd & can find a mdn.   47
--   FASHIONABLY FORBES [5] (R Armstrong) 2-9-0 R Hills 40/1: 4: Wk in mkt: kept on well
on racecourse debut: half brother to very useful stayer Prince Crow: will be suited by 1m
& further: sure to impr.   40
--   BEST O BUNCH [10] 2-9-0 W R Swinburn 20/1: 0: Prom most on racecourse debut: stays
7f: acts on gd grnd.   38
1844 VORTRACK [3] 2-9-0 W Wharton 40/1: 00: Led over 4f, showing impr: cheaply acquired
colt whose dam was a 5f winner: eff at 7f on gd.   36

-- Taweel [1] 9-0	-- Optional Choice [14] 9-0	
2225 Alcatraz [9] 9-0	-- Amadeus Rock [12] 9-0 --	Near Heaven [6] 9-0
-- General Meilland [7] 9-0		-- Obidos [8] 9-0
1289 Shaine [13] 9-0		

14 ran   nk,3,4,½,½   (Sheikh Mohammed)   H Cecil Newmarket

2342 HOLIDAY PLAYGROUND SELL HCAP 0-25   £679   1m   Good 50 -21 Slow   [11]

2126 NIPPY CHIPPY [5] (M W Easterby) 3-8-12(bl) G Baxter 15/2: 0000001: 3 b g Manor Farm
Boy - Square Note (High Top): Mkt drifter, but cruised into lead 2f out, comfortably in a
3 & 4yo selling h'cap at Yarmouth Aug.27 (bought in 1,100 gns): no form previously this term:
on final outing in '85 won a 2yo seller at Beverley: stays 1m well: acts on gd & firm
& a gall trk.   11
1937 GREENHILLS BOY [8] (M Ryan) 3-9-0 R Cochrane 4/1: -0042: Nearest fin: may stay further.   09
2014 HEATHGRIFF [6] (N Callaghan) 4-9-5 M Miller 5/2: 3000023: Not clear run inside final 2f.   04
2060 MOSTANGO [3] (A Hide) 3-9-4(bl) W R Swinburn 20/1: 0000004: Ev ch when hmpd final
1f: unlucky? stays 1m: acts on gd grnd.   02
786 PORT MIST [1] 4-9-0 R Hills 10/1: 0-00000: Abs: prom much: see 679.   00
--   TOLLYS TONIC [7] 4-9-10 G King(5) 20/1: 3000-0: There 5f on seasonal debut: off the
trk since last July: first time out in '85 fin 3rd on hvy grnd at Nottingham but has shown
little form since.   00
2208 TODA FORCA AVANTI [4] 4-9-5 S Cauthen 2/1 FAV: D000000: Bckd from 6/1: led 6f:
has shown little since 262.   00

7 ran   1¼,nk,5,5,½,2   (P D Savill)   M W Easterby Sheriff Hutton, Yorks

2343 CASTLEMAINE XXXX HCAP   3YO   0-60   £3090   6f   Good 50 +30 Fast   [60]

+2079 JOKIST [2] (J Shaw) 3-8-2(6ex) R Street 7/2: 0-02111: 3 ro g Orchestra - What A
Picture (My Swanee): In grand form, led 2f out, easily in very fast run 3yo h'cap at Yarmouth:
fast time winner of h'caps previously at Nottingham & Windsor: in '85 won first time out at
Warwick when trained by C Williams: very eff at 6f: seems to handle any trk/going: much
impr & can win again.   49
2143 USEFUL [10] (B Hills) 3-8-8 B Thomson 14/1: 0230102: Nearest fin: gd effort: see 1847.   42
1995 BUTHAYNA [3] (H T Jones) 3-7-12 R Hills 33/1: 2-00033: Kept on & ran her best race
this season: has failed to find her 2yo form: see 431.   31
2207 BERTIE WOOSTER [1] (L Piggott) 3-8-7(bl) B Crossley 3/1 FAV: 0022024: Ran in snatches.   39
1933 COMPLEAT [7] 3-8-13 P Waldron 4/1: -000320: Never nearer: much btr 1933.   44
1457 SHARPETTO [4] 3-9-3 A Bond 12/1: 0011040: Made most 4f: best 1001.   47
2143 TARANGA [5] 3-8-4 R Cochrane 6/1: 1102040: Prom much, wknd: see 2143, 134.   00

1999 Pulham Mills [6] 7-13(vis)	1900 Bonny Light [8] 7-12
2258 Barrack Street [9] 9-7(bl)	

10 ran   3,nk,nk,½,½   (John Virgo)   J Shaw Newmarket

00

2344 IND COOPE SALES CLAIMING STKS 3YO   £1276   1m 2f   Good 50 -26 Slow

*2083 CAPRICORN BLUE [1] (J Fitzgerald) 3-8-7(vis) M Roberts 2/1: 0242411: 3 b g Blue
Cashmere - Aquanimba (Acropolis): In gd form & made ev yd, pushed out in a 3yo claimer at
Yarmouth Aug.27: last time out was a comfortable winner of a seller at Newcastle: well
suited by front running tactics over 9/10f on gd & fast grnd: best form in a visor.   25
2226 GIBBERISH [3] (M Prescott) 3-8-9(bl) C Nutter 8/11 FAV: 0412132: Well bckd but
no ch with winner: see 2226 (C/D) 1974.   19
1989 ANGEL TARGET [2] (G Wragg) 3-9-0 P Robinson 7/1: 0-00003: No threat: probably stays 10f.   16
2230 ROCKALL [4] (N Macauley) 3-8-12(bl) S Cauthen 12/1: 3000004: Faded straight and
well beaten: better 461, 380.   00
4 ran   4,4,25   (P Asquith)   J Fitzgerald Malton, Yorks

2345 EBF PEREBROWN MAIDEN 2YO STAKES   £1711   6f   Good 50 -06 Slow

2179 START RITE [1] (W O'gorman) 2-9-0 T Ives 6/1: 0201: 2 b c Comedy Star - Fahrenheit
(Mount Hagen): Useful colt: made ev yd, comfortably in a 2yo mdn at Yarmouth: earlier a fine
2nd to Riot Brigade over this C/D, but subs. ran below form at Windsor: eff with forcing
tactics over 6f, should stay further: acts on gd & fast grnd.   54
--   LUCAYAN KNIGHT [6] (M Stoute) 2-9-0 W R Swinburn 8/1: 2: Mkt drifter on debut: ran
on well, but no ch with winner: impr certain from this 50,000 gns purchase: looks sure to
be suited by 7f plus: acts on gd grnd & will find a mdn soon.   49
--   AT RISK [3] (H Cecil) 2-8-11 S Cauthen 8/11 FAV: 3: Well bckd debutant: came from
behind & will do btr next time: half sister to a couple of winners: will be suited by 7f/1m
& should have no trouble finding a mdn.   40
--   GIROTONDO [2] (L Cumani) 2-9-0 R Guest 11/1: 4: Prom, ev ch: cost 17,000 gns as a
yearling and is a half brother to the very useful 3yo Salchow: will do btr than this,
possibly over a lngr trip.   40
1495 GEBLITZT [7] 2-9-0 P Tulk 25/1: 00: Prom most: improving: see 1495.   35
--   HYDRAULIC POWER [5] 2-9-0 A Bond 9/2: 0: Fdd final 1f on racecourse debut: btr for
race: cost 115,000 gns as a yearling & is a half brother to 6f winner Fawley's Girl.   33
2016 PIPSTED [4] 2-9-0 P Robinson 8/1: 40: Friendless in mkt: prom most: much closer to
winner in 2016 & can do btr.   00
7 ran   1½,3,¾,1½,¾,5   (A Foustok)   W O'gorman Newmarket

2346 EAST COAST HANDICAP 0-35   £1766   1m 6f   Good 50 -20 Slow   [32]

*2128 SEVEN HILLS [8] (J Fitzgerald) 3-8-4(vis)(4ex) M Roberts 1/1 FAV: 0003111: 3 ch f Reform-
Campagna (Romulus): In grand form: hvly bckd & smooth hdway to lead 2f out, easily in a
h'cap at Yarmouth Aug.27: winner of her 2 previous starts, h'caps at Catterick & again
at Yarmouth: stays 14f really well: acts on gd/firm & yld grnd & an easy trk: best form
in a visor: much improved.   32
2169 COLLISTO [5] (K Brassey) 5-8-10(bl) S Whitworth 6/1: 0022202: Led 4f out: fair
effort: see 2075, 485.   18
2075 RUN FOR YOUR WIFE [11] (G Lewis) 3-7-12 M L Thomas 14/1: 4-30243: Made much: kept
on: see 2075, 1212.   16
2175 STANDARD BREAKFAST [9] (B Hills) 4-9-4(BL) B Thomson 14/1: -000004: Bl first time:
late hdway: stays 14f, but little form this term: see 474.   22
1633 ALL IS REVEALED [1] 4-9-10(vis) M Brennan(7) 8/1: 1300000: Led early: stayed on
again: btr 582.   27
1945 KERRY MAY SING [6] 3-8-4 R Cochrane 15/2: 0000040: Probably stays 14f: see 989.   18
2228 PARSONS CHILD [10] 3-9-2 W R Swinburn 15/2: -002430: Mkt drifter: no show: btr 2228.   00
1873 ICKWORTH [7] 4-8-8 G Starkey 6/1: 44-0040: Fdd str: see 1652.   00
1829 Swedish Princess [2] 8-9(vis)   88   Arrow Beak [3] 9-4
2211 Generation Gap [4] 8-1
11 ran   3,2,1½,1,1   (Sir John Musker)   J Fitzgerald Malton, Yorks

Official Going Given As GOOD TO SOFT

2347 GROUP 3 PRIX DE MEAUTRY 3YO+   £17912   6f   Good/Soft Slow

2003 CRICKET BALL (J Fellows) 3-8-7 G Moore 1: 3304041: 3 b c Olden Times - Caterina
(Princely Gift): Smart French colt: came from behind to lead near fin in a Gr.3 race at
Deauville: a late foal who reportedly is just coming to hand now: very eff over 6f, stays
further: acts on gd & yld: may make further impr.   77
563   BATAVE (P L Biancone) 4-8-11 E Legrix 1: /11-122: Dsptd lead 3 out, caught death:
grand effort after long abs & does well when fresh (winner first time out): see 563.   75
2003 COMRADE IN ARMS (P Lallie) 4-9-2 G Dubroeucq 1: -212023: Chall final 2f, narrowly
btn & in grand form: see 2003.   79
--   PARIOLI (J Cunnington Jnr) 5-8-8 M Philipperon 1: 10413-4: Fine effort on seasonal
debut: winner of Gr.3 races at Maisons Laffitte, Chantilly & Longchamp in '85: very eff over
5/6f on gd or hvy going.   63
1889 POLYKRATIS 4-9-0 C Rutter 1: 0031240: Ran much btr in 1889 (5f, gd/firm).   64
+1654 POSSEDYNO 3-8-10 A Mcglone 1: 01-3110: Fin in rear but was found afterwards to
have been slightly injured & this run can be ignored: see 1654.   50
11 ran   shhd,hd,3   (R Scully)   J Fellows France

Official Going Given As YIELDING/SOFT

2348 EUROPEAN RACEHORSE TRIAL 3YO+   £4450   1m 3f   Good/Yld 77 -16 Slow

--   LEADING COUNSEL (V O'brien) 4-9-7 Pat Eddery 2/5 FAV: 01021-1: 4 br c Alleged -
Society Column (Sir Gaylord): First time out, after 10 month abs, cantered up in a minor event
at Phoenix Park Aug.23: also won twice at Phoenix Park last term & fin the season with a
decisive success in the Irish St Leger at the Curragh: eff around 1m though much btr
suited by 11f plus & stays 14f really well: suited by give in the grnd: now likely to run
in a Group race in France.   75
2112 SPENDING CONTINUES (J Oxx) 3-9-3 D Hogan 5/1: 2-1122: No ch with this easy winner.   70
559 INISHEER (D Weld) 3-8-10(bl) D Parnell 5/1: 3-23313: See 559.   56
6 ran   2½,4   (R Sangster)   V O'brien Ireland

2349 LISTED HANDICAP 3YO+   £13969   7f   Good/Yld 77 +23 Fast

--   IRISH FOLLY (J Oxx) 5-9-8 Pat Eddery 6/1: -003211: 5 ch h Irish River - Insulaire
(Aureole): Very well ridden to lead on the post & win a valuable h'cap at Phoenix Park
in easily the fastest time of the day: winner of another valuable h'cap at the Curragh
recently and is in fine form: very eff over 7f & seems to appreciate some give in the grnd.   56
--   AMONIQUE (R Connolly) 3-7-11 R Hillis(5) 20/1: -100412: Caught at the death: recent
winner of a h'cap at Sligo: suited by forcing tactics & yld/hvy going.   37
--   NOORA ABU (J Bolger) 4-8-9(bl) C Roche 6/1: 1210013: Close up 3rd & is in fine form
having recently won a h'cap at Phoenix Park over 5f: seems to stay 7f.   39
--   CLOVEN DANCER (J Harty) 4-7-11 P Mcloughlin(5) 20/1: 0000204: --   26
*1911 REIGNBEAU 3-9-1 P Waldron 7/4 FAV: 1120310: A hot fav but fin in rear & btr 1911.   00
17 ran   shhd,1½,nk   (M Fustok)   J Oxx Ireland

2350 OLDTOWN STUD DEBUTANTE STKS LISTED 2YO   £10842   6f   Good/Yld 77 -18 Slow

--   DOWN AGAIN (J Oxx) 2-8-9(bl) Pat Eddery 5/1: -121: 2 b f Encino - Dawn Is Breaking
(Import): Very useful Irish filly: led over 2f out & kept on under strong driving to win a
2yo fillies Listed race at Phoenix Park Aug.23: first time out winner of a mdn at Naas &
last time fin strong, just failing to get up in a valuable Listed event at Leopardstown:
eff over 6f, stays 7f well: acts on fast & yld going.   60
2113 SNOW FINCH (J Bolger) 2-9-0 C Roche 12/1: 01102: Fin 3rd, placed 2nd after a stewards
inquiry: see 2113.   60
149 SNAPPY DRESSER (P Doyle) 2-8-9 S Martinez 33/1: 3022123: Fin 4th, placed 3rd:
consistent filly who seldom finishes out of the frame & recently won a minor event at Tipperary   54
--   NORTH TELSTAR (P Canty) 2-8-12 D Manning 9/4 FAV: 12D: Strongly ridden to fin 2nd
but disq. & placed 4th after a stewards inquiry: winner of a fillies mdn at Phoenix Park
recently on only previous outing: acts on soft: eff at 6f.   63
1919 DUNNINALD 2-8-12 J Matthias 10/1: 120: English challenger: btr 1919, 1604.   03
11 ran   1½,hd,hd   (N Schibbye)   J Oxx Ireland

2351 ORCHARDSTOWN STUD STAKES 3YO+ LISTED   £11753   6f   Good/Yld 77 -06 Slow

--   NORTHERN EXPRESS (T Stack) 3-8-10 Pat Eddery 10/3: -011: 3 b c Northern Guest -
Tough Lady (Bay Express): Smart, impr colt: held on gamely for a narrow success in a valuable
Listed race at Phoenix Park: unraced last season, recently won a mdn at Phoenix Park &
obviously likes this trk: very eff over 6/7f & is well suited by give in the grnd: impr type
who should win more races.   72
2192 BERMUDA CLASSIC (P Mullins) 3-8-7 C Roche 5/2 FAV: 110-032: See 2192 (1m).   68
1857 PETROVICH (R Hannon) 4-9-2 S Craine 3/1: -300033: English chall who ran close
to his best: see 1857, 705.   67

1096 LUQMAN (P Walwyn) 3-8-10 N Howe 6/1: 14-0404: English chall, not btn far in 4th
after long abs: see 286.   67
2006 LONDON TOWER 3-9-3 D Parnell 7/1: 0331220: Twice below 1858 (C/D).   69
--   KNESSET 3-8-10 D Gillespie 10/1: -10: --   61
1852 MEASURING 3-8-7 J Matthias 10/1: -300000: See 59, 1852.   00
7 ran   nk,1½,shhd,2,hd   (Mrs T Stack)   T Stack Irelaand

OSTEND   Sunday August 24th

Official Going Given As GOOD TO FIRM

2352 PRIX NEGRESCO 2YO   £4141   7f   Good/Firm -

*1948 TOLUCA LAKE (L Piggott) 2-8-9 T Ives 1: 411: 2 b c King's Lake - Zirconia: Gained a
first success abroad for Lester Piggott as a trainer when readily winning a minor event at
Ostend: recent winner of a minor event at Wolverhampton: half brother to several winners in
France & cost over 1m. French francs: very eff over 7f, sure to be suited by further: acts
on firm & gd grnd & is certainly on the up grade.   52
1711 NUAS (Belgium) 2-8-5 P Gilson 1: 22: German chall. but had no ch with this winner.   34
102 GAELIC CROSS (Belgium) 2-8-11 L Mcgarrity 1: 003: --   .30
*2082 GET ON GERAGHTY (G Huffer) 2-8-13 G Carter 1: 2114: Ran much btr in 2082 (6f).   29
2032 TINAS BEAUTY 2-8-5 P Bloomfield 1: 0030: Out of her depth: see 2032 (seller).   14
5 ran   8,5,1½,4   (J Vollstedt)   L Piggott Newmarket

2353 PRIX BAYEUX 3YO   £5521   1m 2f   Good/Firm -

-1998 GEORDIES DELIGHT (L Piggott) 3-8-7 T Ives 1: 4142221: 3 b c Northern Baby - Shout
For Joy (Court Martial): Responded gamely to lead inside final furlong in a minor event at
Ostend Aug.24: has been a model of consistency all season: earlier won a h'cap at Pontefract & a mdn at Epsom: eff 1m, stays 10f: acts on firm & hvy & on any trk: genuine.   56
1994 INNISHMORE ISLAND (J Dunlop) 3-8-7 Pat Eddery 1: 2-30322: Hdd inside final 1f but
held on to ddht for 2nd: see 1792, 994.   55
--   DEL MONDO (Belgium) 3-8-7 P Gilson 1: -3: German chall, fin well to force a ddht for 2nd 55
5 ran   ½,ddht   (Sheikh Mohammed)   L Piggott Newmarket

2354 GRAND INTERNATIONAL DOSTENDE 3YO+   £13803   1m 3f   Good/Firm -

*2092 BOON POINT (J Dunlop) 3-8-5 Pat Eddery 1: 0300111: 3 br c Shirley Heights - Bright-
elmstone (Prince Regent): In gd form at present & completed his hat trick with an all the
way success in a valuable minor event at Ostend Aug.24: recently won 2 minor events at
Windsor: very eff over 10/11f with forcing tactics: acts on gd & firm grnd & on any trk.   65
1712 SASEBO (G Franco) 5-9-2 G Couderc 1: 313-242: French chall & seems to run well over
this C/D: see 1712.   63
2116 CHAUMIERE (R Williams) 5-9-10 T Ives 1: 0001033: Fin well to take 3rd: see 1526.   68
2004 DAUN (Germany) 5-9-10 P Gilson 1: 23-4034: See 1712.   66
1811 KALKOUR 4-9-8 T Quinn 1: 1012040: Does not seem quite up to this grade: best 1038.   54
6 ran   1,1½,1,5   (N M Avery)   J Dunlop Arundel, Sussex

2355 PRIX KLOOSTERS 4YO+   £3106   1m 1f   Good/Firm -

2022 VAGUE MELODY (L Piggott) 4-9-4 T Ives 1: 0113441: 4 ch c Vaigly Great - Shangara
(Credo): Gamely won a minor event at Ostend: has been in fine form all season & earlier won
twice at Warwick: eff 1m, stays 10f: acts on firm & soft & on any trk: genuine.   49
--   PERSIAN EAGLE (Belgium) 4-8-9 P Vandekeere 1: -2: Just btn in a driving fin.   39
--   MR PAGANINI (Belgium) 6-8-7 P Masure 1: -3: --   29
6 ran   snk,4.   (A Simmons)   L Piggott Newmarket

2356 PRIX BORGIA HANDICAP 4YO+   £1725   1m 1f   Good/Firm -

1667 WIZZARD ART (M Haynes) 5-8-5 T Quinn 1: 30-0001: 5 b m Wolver Hollow - My Sweetie
(Bleep-Bleep): Gained a narrow success in a h'cap at Ostend: lightly raced this term, won
at Folkestone in '85: very eff over 9/10f though seems to act on any going.   22
--   GABBLE (Belgium) 5-7-7(4oh) P Vandekeere 1: -2: Not btn far in a tight fin.   09
--   KASKADEUR (Belgium) 7-8-3 L Mcgarrity 1: -3: --   05
9 ran   ½,8   (D Myers)   M Haynes Epsom

DEAUVILLE	Saturday August 23rd	Righthand Fair Track

Official Going Given As HEAVY

2357 GROUP 2 PRIX DE POMONE 3YO+ FILLIES   £22944   1m 5f   Heavy -

-- PERSONA (P Bary) 4-9-2 A Gibert 1: 0003011: 4 b f Sanhedrin - Angelina (Shantung): Smart filly: fin strongly to lead final 100yds in Gr.2 Prix de Pomone (fillies & mares) at Deauville: has only recently changed stables: recent winner of a minor event at Claire Fontane in the French Provinces: suited by 12/14f: acts well on hvy.   75

1493 GALLA PLACIDIA (A Fabre) 4-9-9 C Asmussen 1: 0-10102: The fav, just btn in a driving finish: see 1115.   81

-- BLUE BELLY (A De Royer Dupre) 4-9-2 Y Saint Martin 1: -100133: Has been in gd form recently fin 3rd behind todays winner at Clairefontaine & picked up a h'cap at Saint Cloud prior to that: well suited by middle dists & give in the grnd.   70

-- CITY FORTRESS (D Smaga) 3-8-7 A Lequeux 1: 2220114: Had his bid for a hat-trick thwarted: recent winner of minor races at Deauville & Evry: well suited by middle dists & acts on softish grnd.   73

-1408 MILL ON THE FLOSS 3-8-7 S Cauthen 1: 0-31220: English chall, beat only one home: much btr 1408 (gd/firm).   48

1493 WALENSEE 4-9-2 E Legrix 1: 141-000: Fin last: see 1493.   44

9 ran   ½,2½,nose   (J L Bouchard)   P Bary France

DEAUVILLE	Sunday August 24th	Righthand Fair Track

Official Going Given As HEAVY

2358 GROUP 1 PRIX MORNY 2YO   £35133   6f   Heavy -

-- SAKURA REIKO (P Biancone) 2-8-8 E Legrix 1: 111: 2 gr f Kenmare - Primula (Petingo): Smart French filly: retained her unbtn record when completing a hat trick in Gr.1 Prix Morny at Deauville: waited with, came with a gd late run to lead inside final 1f: recent winner of minor races at Deauville & Evry: suited by 6f, looks sure to stay further: handles heavy ground well: certainly impr.   78

-- SHY PRINCESS (J Cunnington Jnr) 2-8-8 M Philipperon 1: 312: Just held on to 2nd place: recent winner of a fillies race at St Cloud: seems to act on gd & hvy grnd: stays 6f.   75

-- MIESQUE (F Boutin) 2-8-8 F Head 1: 13: Fin well, almost snatching 2nd place near the fin: earlier in the month won a minor fillies race at Deauville on soft grnd: looks likely to stay beyond 6f.   75

*1714 BALBONELLA (C Head) 2-8-8 Y Saint Martin 1: 1-11114: Set a fast pace but was unable to sustain the effort in this hvy going & btr 1714 (gd).   68

8 ran   1,nose,3   (E Zen)   P Biancone France

DEAUVILLE	Wednesday August 27th	Righthand Easy Track

Official Going Given As HEAVY

2359 GROUP 3 PRIX QUINCY 3YO+   £20064   1m   Heavy -

2195 APELDOORN (P Barbe) 4-9-4 A Badel 1: 23-1301: 4 b c R B Chesne - Grey Magic (Zeddaan): Much impr colt: well ridden to come with a gd late run & comfortably win Gr.3 Prix Quincey at Deauville Aug.27: a mdn at the beginning of this season but first time out won a Gr.3 race at St Cloud: very eff over 1m & seems to revel in soft or hvy going: suited by waiting tactics.   79

330 NORTHERN ASPEN (O Douieb) 4-8-10 A Lequeux 1: 1001-02: British chall, leading at the dist but had no answer to the winners fine burst: fine effort after abs since 330: rated 83 in '85 but very lightly raced this term: see 330.   67

389 SPLENDID MOMENT (R Collet) 3-8-13 Y Saint Martin 1: 10-4403: See 389.   76

2195 VIN DE FRANCE (P Biancone) 4-9-0 E Legrix 1: 140-004: Made much, went clear but was hdd dist: btr 2195 (gd).   67

2145 ALEX NUREYEV 3-8-8 J Reid 1: -0300: Ex Italian colt now trained in England: see 897   00

1490 SHMAIREEKH 5-9-0 Paul Eddery 1: -202000: Dsptd lead 6f: best 330 (first time out).   00

6 ran   2,1½,hd   (G Coscas)   P Barbe France

BEVERLEY	Thursday August 28th	Righthanded Undulating Track, Stiff Uphill Finish

Official Going Given As GOOD/SOFT

2360 SATURDAY MARKET STAKES (H'CAP)(0-35)   £1680   1m 2f   Good 77 -01 Slow   [33]

2102 CASHEW KING [2] (B Mcmahon) 3-8-2 S Webster 9/2 FAV: 0044021: 3 b c Faraway Times-Sinzinbra (Royal Palace): Led below dist, comfortably in an all aged h'cap at Beverley: loves this quite testing course: gained his sole previous win here last season & only just btn over this C/D last time: stays 10f really well: acts on firm & yld grnd & on a stiff trk.   26

2102 PERSHING [6] (J Leigh) 5-8-12 M Miller 8/1: 0322002: Stayed on well on his fav trk: stays 10f well: acts on fast & yld grnd: see 611.   20

2109 BUSTED FLAVOUR [8] (W Jarvis) 5-9-0 R Cochrane 10/1: 300303: In gd form: see 2109.   22

2102 CHABLISSE [12] (R Whitaker) 3-7-13 A Culhane(7) 12/1: 4031044: Likes this trk: see 1369.   14

1133 NORTH STAR SAM [13] 5-7-9 N Carlisle 20/1: 0040200: Abs: tried to make all, wknd
dist: mdn who loves to be out in front: stays 10f: see 333.   00
1963 FIEFDOM [3] 6-9-12 S Whitworth 10/1: 0-20140: Best over 12f in 1220 (firm).   24
*2037 RUSTIC TRACK [18] 6-7-11 M Fry 9/1: 0003010: Late prog into 9th: btr in 2037.   00
2102 RAPID LAD [15] 8-9-7 D Nicholls 10/1: 0140000: Much btr over this C/D in 1106 (firm). 00
2182 DOMINION PRINCESS [4] 5-8-3 A Clark 10/1: 3031200: Prom early: best in 1800.   00
2132 Centralspires Best [10] 7-9   2037 Patchburg [9] 9-2
2154 Nugola [17] 7-10   2109 Sirdar Flyer [19] 7-7   2300 Pells Close [14] 7-8(bl)(1ow)(2c
2129 Top Row [11] 7-13   2190 Gregorian Chant [7] 7-13
2173 Evros [5] 9-6   1964 Bold Answer [16] 7-7(6oh)
1361 Riva Renald [1] 9-3
19 ran   2½,nk,1½,hd,3,2½,½   (J Harrop & Co Ltd)   B Mcmahon Hopwas Hill, Staffs

2361 AUGUST SELLING STAKES 3YO   £979   7.5f   Good 77 -27 Slow

857 IZZY GUNNER [11] (A Robson) 3-8-6 J Bleasdale 4/1: 0022001: 3 ch c Gunner B -
Nanking (Above Suspicion): Nicely bckd depite a lengthy abs & led over 2f out, gamely in a
3yo seller at Beverley (bought in 4,400 gns): first success though earlier this season twice
fin 2nd in non-selling company: eff over 7/8f & seems best on gd or softer grnd: acts on any trk   20
2268 VITAL STEP [15] (T Fairhurst) 3-8-3(BL) M Rimmer 9/1: 0-00042: Just held, gd eff: see 1425. 15
1927 SKYBIRD [7] (M Brittain) 3-8-6 K Darley 20/1: 0000003: Not btn far: btr effort: last year
showed some promise when placed over sprint dists: stays 7f: acts on gd/firm & yld grnd:
has been blinkered.   16
2174 SUNK ISLAND [9] (M Blanshard) 3-8-3 N Adams 14/1: -000404: Made most: stays 7f: see 2088. 10
*2302 MY DERYA [13] 3-8-11(bl) G Duffield 10/1: 0300410: Al prom: in gd form: see 2302. 17
2103 CLOUDLESS SKY [8] 3-8-3 S Morris 9/1: 0-00042: Ch dist: acts on yld: see 1288.   05
-- GODOUNOV [16] 3-8-6 S Whitworth 8/11 FAV: -0: Attracted strong mkt support on his
debut: had been working well at home though did not reproduce that form here: half brother
to a couple of winners: should be well suited by this trip: worth keeping an eye on.   00
545 AMBER CLOWN [5] 3-8-6 N Carlisle 9/1: 0-24000: Needed race: much btr in 6 (5f).   00
2174 Class Hopper [14] 8-6   1543 Jimmys Secret [12] 8-6
2139 Herb Robert [10] 8-6   -- Jay Bee Windows [17] 8-3
2174 Capistrano Climax [2] 8-6(BL)   2238 Octiga [4] 8-13
1256 Kirkella [1] 8-6(bl)   1824 Planning Act [6] 8-3
16 ran   nk,1,1½,½,2,1½,shhd   (T Leahy)   A Robson Stockton, Cleveland

2362 MAX JAFFA SPRINT H'CAP STAKES (0-60)   £4084   5f   Good 77 +14 Fast   [51]

*2242 CATHERINES WELL [8] (M W Easterby) 3-9-8(10ex) G Carter(3) 1/1 FAV: 0331111: 3 ch f Junius -
Restless Lady (Sandford Lad): Much impr filly who comfortably completed her four timer,
led dist & pushed out to win a fast run quite valuable h'cap at Beverley: tremendous form
recently, winning h'caps at Ripon, Newcastle & Newmarket in less than a fortnight: last backend won nurseries at Doncaster & Newmarket, after winning a seller on the former course:
eff over 5f though probably btr over 6/7f: acts on firm & yld grnd & on any track: has shot
up the h'cap though could still win again in this form.   65
2204 TRUE NORA [3] (C Nelson) 3-9-7 J Reid 9/1: 0300402: Al front rank, kept on well to
take the minor honours: gd effort: see 443.   52
+1896 CELTIC BIRD [6] (A Balding) 6-8-9 N Day 11/2: 0023113: Made most: in gd form: see 1896. 35
1959 MISS PRIMULA [2] (W Bentley) 3-7-7 J Lowe 25/1: 3030004: Gd early speed: see 628.   17
1691 BROOKS DILEMMA [7] 3-9-5 A Bond 8/1: -0120: Prom most: best in 1516 (6f).   42
2151 SEW HIGH [4] 3-9-2 J Hills(5) 6/1: 0411030: Showed gd early pace: see 1704.   37
1878 HIGH IMAGE [1] 3-9-3 T Ives 10/1: -0100: There to ½way: lightly rcd since 835.   00
2224 MANTON MARK [5] 3-8-7 N Connorton 25/1: 0001000: Best over this trip in 1882.   00
8 ran   2,nk,2,nk,½,2   (Hippodromo Racing)   M W Easterby Sheriff Hutton, Yorks

2363 WALKINGTON MAIDEN STAKES 3YO+   £822   2m   Good 77 -27 Slow

2228 GUESSING [3] (G Harwood) 3-8-8 A Clark 6/5 FAV: -0021: 3 ch c Be My Guest - Miss
Reasoning (Bold Reasoning): Impr colt: cruised into lead over 2f out when an easy winner of
a mdn at Beverley: clearly well suited by a test of stamina: acts on gd/firm & yld grnd
& on a stiff trk: should rate more highly.   46
2054 WHIPCRACKAWAY [9] (C Thornton) 3-8-8 J Bleasdale 11/4: -0032: Had ev ch: stays 2m. 35
2128 NITIDA [6] (E Weymes) 3-8-5(bl) S Webster 16/1: 0000033: One paced: stays 2m: see 130. 20
1961 DENBERDAR [5] (R Hollinshead) 3-8-8 S Perks 13/2: -203034: No extra str: see 1961. 15
1961 HOPEFUL LINE [2] 3-8-5 M Hills 8/1: 0-0040: Made most: acts on yld: see 1961.   08
2054 BERNISH LADY [1] 5-9-6 G Duffield 10/1: -040000: Well btn: btr in 2054 (14f): see 1015. 00
1884 Letby [4] 9-9(vis)   2028 Sirdar Girl [8] 9-6   1961 French Design [7] 8-5
9 ran   6,8,6,2½,15,15   (K Abdulla)   G Harwood Pulborough, Sussex

2364 WIN WITH THE TOTE MAIDEN STAKES 2YO   £879   7.5f   Good 77 -22 Slow

2159 ARDILES [8] (C Horgan) 2-9-0 T Ives 9/4: 0401: 2 b c Windjammer - Primmy (Primera):
Nicely bckd & stayed on gamely to lead close home in a 2yo mdn at Beverley: half brother to
fair h'cappers Copper Beeches & Cannon King: had shown promise over shorter trips though
probably will prove best over 7/8f: acts on gd & firm grnd & on any trk.   36

2198 FOUNTAINS CHOICE [5] (K Stone) 2-9-0 G Brown 6/1: 332002: Led over 2f out, just
caught: stays 7f well: deserves a small race: see 1050.   35
2026 ISLAND LOCKSMITH [9] (M W Easterby) 2-9-0 M Birch 4/1: 03: Hung under press up this
stiff fin: should prove well suited by 7/8f & has scope for impr: see 2026.   27
2153 BLAZE OF GOLD [1] (E Alston) 3-8-11 J Reid 7/4 FAV: 02234: Well bckd: no extra dist
& has twice failed to reproduce the form shown in 2029 (6f).   22
1067 ROSE LOUBET [7] 3-8-11 D Gibson 14/1: 000: Abs: btn dist: quite cheaply bought filly
who is bred to be well suited by this lngr trip: see 1067 (6f firm).   17
1088 BABY COME HOME [10] 3-8-11 A Clark 14/1: 000: Never nearer after abs: best in 646 (5f). 16
1846 Ribogirl [11] 8-11   741 Step By Step [4] 9-0   1155 Trompe Doeil [6] 8-11
2218 Church Star [3] 8-11   -- Raymonds Star [2] 9-0
11 ran   hd,4,¾,2½,½   (Mrs D McKinley)   C Horgan Billingbear, Berks

2365 ROUTH MAIDEN FILLIES 2YO STAKES   £1093   5f   Good 77 -05 Slow

1996 SUPREME ROSE [16] (W Musson) 2-8-11 M Wigham 10/1: 01: 2 b f Frimley Park - Ragtime
Rose (Ragstone): Clearly all the btr for her recent debut & qknd well to lead inside dist
in a 2yo fillies mdn at Beverley: speedily bred first foal who is clearly well suited by
gd grnd & a stiff trk: should continue to improve.   44
2043 LISETA [1] (M W Easterby) 2-8-11 G Carter(3) 16/1: 02: Stayed on well: on the up grade
& should find a race over a lngr trip: see 2043.   38
1966 MISS RUNAWAY [17] (J Winter) 2-8-11 R Hills 7/4 FAV: 0423: Well bckd: went on ½way,
not qkn & seems to need further than this minimum trip: worth another ch: best in 1966 (6f). 32
1067 OUR GINGER [5] (Ron Thompson) 2-8-11 R P Elliott 33/1: 04: Abs: ran on same pace:
closely related to several winners: likely to need more time & lngr trip.   20
--   SILVERCOAST [2] 2-8-11 A Murray 6/1: 0: Broke well & led over ½way: cost I.R. 115,000 &
is a half sister to a smart German juvenile: acts on gd/yld grnd: will impr & should do
better on a sharper trk.   14
1782 ORDINA [7] 2-8-11 R Cochrane 13/2: 400: Never nearer: best in 1282 (6f, firm).   08
2153 GOOD WOMAN [13] 2-8-11 J Reid 3/1: 40: Early speed: fin 8th: half sister to very
useful juvenile Moorgate Man: should do btr on a sounder surface.   00
1782 HOLD ON PLEASE [10] 2-8-11(BL) T Ives 7/1: 4000: Close up over ½way: disapp since 848. 00
--   Oxstalls Lady [12] 8-11   -- Riverstyle [3] 8-11
--   Salop Rouge [11] 8-11   2127 Lewista [9] 8-11   1867 Bold Ad [15] 8-11
--   Springwell Lady [6] 8-11   544 Mission Bird [18] 8-11
2127 Miss Management [14] 8-11
16 ran   1½,2,4,2,2½   (E Badger)   W Musson Newmarket

2366 FREEMENS MAIDEN STAKES   £822   1m 4f   Good 77 -05 Slow

1977 REGAL CASTLE [7] (B Hanbury) 3-8-8 R Cochrane 5/2: -21: 3 b g Tachypous - Right Mall
(Pall Mall): Clearly benefitted from his recent debut & ran on well under press to lead near
fin in a mdn at Beverley: cost 8,200 gns & is a half brother to useful juvenile Right Dancer:
eff over 11/12f on gd/yld grnd: acts on a stiff trk: can continue to improve.   42
1721 FORT LINO [2] (I Balding) 3-8-8 T Ives 7/4 FAV: 4-2222: Again made most of the running
& again found one too good!: well clear of rem: see 1535 & 832.   40
--   TOUKSHAD [3] (R F Johnson Houghton) 3-8-8 K Darley 7/1: -3: Took sometime to find
his stride: late prog & should leave this running behind next time: bred to be suited by
middle dists.   20
2129 MARETH LINE [1] (J Fitzgerald) 3-8-8 M Roberts 10/1: -04: No extra str: bred to
be well suited by this trip: acts on gd/firm & yld.   10
832 PODSNAP [9] 3-8-8 A Clark 8/1: -00: Long abs & no threat: half brother to winning
miler Regent Cat: lightly raced & should do btr in time.   00
669 MILFORD QUAY [4] 3-8-8 D Nicholls 5/1: -00: Well btn after long abs: see 669.   00
1954 Hiya Bud [8] 8-5(BL)   1258 Tap Duet [6] 8-8(vis)
8 ran   ¾,20,7,6,15   (H Turney McKnight)   B Hanbury Newmarket

BRIGHTON   Thursday August 28th   Lefthand, Sharpish, Undulating Track

Official Going Given As FIRM

2367 SEAGULLS MAIDEN STAKES 3YO   £1775   6f   Good/Firm 31 +15 Fast

2245 CLEOFE [4] (L Cumani) 3-8-11 G Starkey 2/1 FAV: 3334001: 3 ch f Grey Dawn II -
Astro Lady (Skymaster): Finally found her best trip, finishing well to lead close home in a
fast run 3yo mdn at Brighton: placed several times previously over 7f & has been tried over
1m: eff at 6f on a sharpish trk, though probably acts on any: likes fast grnd.   33
1878 ENIGMA [2] (B Hills) 3-8-11 B Thomson 9/2: 04-0202: Made most & caught near fin:
4L clear 3rd & should find a small event: eff at 6f on fast grnd: see 835.   32
1246 ZILLEBEKE [6] (W Brooks) 3-8-11 S Cauthen 20/1: -003: Abs: prom & stayed on, showing
improved form: very lightly raced filly who is a half sister to a 12f winner: should stay
further than 6f: acts on gd/firm.   20
1560 PERSIAN BALLET [3] (P Walwyn) 3-9-0 Paul Eddery 6/1: 0-03404: Every chance straight:
lightly raced since 1164.   22
1971 TOOTSIE ROLL [8] 3-8-11 G Baxter 33/1: -4000: Best effort yet from this half sister
to several winners in the States: should stay 7f: acts on gd/firm.   15

1607 SUPERCOOMBE [11] 3-9-0 T Quinn 7/2: 3022D00: Only modest form since 516 (5f gd/yld).   17
2186 GRANGE FARM LADY [1] 3-8-11 A Mackay 9/1: -030: Fdd into 7th: btr 2186.   00
2186 Last Cry [10] 9-0   2186 Shades Of Autumn [7] 8-11
2216 Dancer Do [9] 8-11   2210 Kingsfold Flame [5] 8-11
11 ran   ½,4,nk,1½,hd   (Mrs D Zurcher)   L Cumani Newmarket

2368 SADDLESCOMBE FILLIES STAKES 2YO   £1909   7f   Good/Firm 31 -06 Slow

1454 DAZY [5] (R Laing) 2-8-8 B Thomson 6/4 FAV: 2301: 2 b f Persian Bold - Belle Viking
(Riverman): Very useful filly: eased in class & led over 1f out, easily in a 2yo fillies
event at Brighton Aug.28: earlier a fine 3rd to Forest Flower in Gr.3 Queen Mary Stakes at
Royal Ascot: half sister to smart middle dist performer Sirk & also Making Hay: eff at 7f,
sure to stay 1m: acts on gd & firm grnd & on any trk: the type to win more races.   57
1874 ACHNAHUAIGH [2] (P Walwyn) 2-8-8 Paul Eddery 8/1: 02: Active in mkt: not the best
of runs & kept on well: fast impr & can find a race soon: half sister to useful h'capper
Bettyknowes: will be suited by 1m: acts on gd/firm & a sharpish trk.   49
2070 HIGH CLIMBER [1] (R Smyth) 2-8-8 P Cook 20/1: 023: Made much: another gd run &
continues to impr: stays 7f & runs well on a sharpish trk: can find a race: see 2070.   45
*2043 SEEK THE TRUTH [6] (H Cecil) 2-9-3 S Cauthen 13/8: 214: Well bckd: led early:
stiff task at these weights & ran very well: stays 7f: see 2043.   52
2215 HUNT BALL [3] 2-8-8 J Matthias 10/1: 000: Mkt drifter: ch str: will do btr: see 1464.   40
2013 LUKMARIE [4] 2-8-8 G Baxter 25/1: 430: Mkt drifter: see 2013, 1341.   35
2177 Alhayat [8] 8-8   2191 Pink Swallow [9] 8-8   --   Brolga [7] 8-8
9 ran   2,2,1,2,2   (Tony Stratton Smith)   R Laing Lambourn, Berks

2369 GEORGE ROBEY CHALL TROPHY HCAP 0-50   £3017   7f   Good/Firm 31 +04 Fast   [49]

2021 HILTON BROWN [1] (P Cundell) 5-10-0 P Cook 4/1: 2243031: 5 b h Daring March -
Holiday Season (Silly Season): Useful, consistent h'capper: made ev yd, ridden out in a
h'cap at Brighton: early in the season won a h'cap at Kempton & has been in the frame on
numerous occasions: in '84 won at Ascot & Newmarket: eff at 5f, stays 7f: acts on firm or
soft grnd: genuine & carries weight really well.   59
*2099 CODICES [5] (G Harwood) 3-9-7(6ex) G Starkey 4/1: -001012: Ran on final 1f: in
grand form: see 2099.   57
2189 GOLDEN BEAU [2] (D Morley) 4-8-2 B Rouse 7/1: 3330123: Ev ch str: in fine form: see 2189. 29
2189 BLUE BRILLIANT [4] (B Hills) 3-8-0(bl) W Carson 5/2 FAV: 0021244: Nicely bckd:
consistent: see 2189, 1560.   29
2207 GOLDEN SLADE [3] 4-8-6 R Wernham 4/1: 1330030: Switched 2f out: no extra: btr 2207.   27
1640 MAAZI [6] 5-9-5 S Cauthen 12/1: 1-01000: Fdd inside final 2f: best in 881.   36
6 ran   1,1,2½,½,2   (Lord McAlpine)   P Cundell Compton, Berks

2370 BRIGHTON LADIES HANDICAP 0-35 3YO+   £1713   6f   Good/Firm 31 -04 Slow   [17]

2274 MISS METAL WOODS [1] (S Mellor) 4-8-11 Dana Mellor 16/1: 4040001: 4 b f Piaffer (USA) -
Catherine Rose (Floribunda): Al front rank & led inside final 3f, staying on well in a
Ladies h'cap at Brighton: placed several times previously, but this was her first win:
suited by front running on a sharpish trk: acts on gd/firm & yld.   09
2271 THE UTE [11] (L Bower) 3-9-6(bl) Celia Radband 10/1: 2012042: Nicely bckd, chall final
1f & just btn: another fine effort: see 1827, 1549.   23
1870 PEANDAY [13] (H Beasley) 5-9-7 Clare Nicholas(5) 16/1: 0300003: Stayed on well:
best effort since 481.   14
-624 GYPSYS PROPHECY [5] (G Harwood) 3-10-8 Amanda Harwood 2/1 FAV: 230-324: Long abs:
ch over 1f out: gd effort: see 624.   35
2120 BOOFY [12] 3-11-0 Joanna Winter 20/1: 2400100: Ran well under top weight: see 1947.   40
2139 DARTIGNY [3] 3-10-7 G Armytage 20/1: -000400: Ev ch str: see 514.   30
1367 DELAWARE RIVER [4] 4-9-12 Franca Vittadini 5/1: -024000: Nicely bckd despite abs: best 748.00
2046 DOWNSVIEW [16] 4-11-0 Candy Moore 7/2: 1000040: Led over ½way: btr 2046: see 855.   00
1066 Dorney [2] 9-7   1943 Tumble Fair [7] 9-12 2213 Ideoligia [10] 8-7
--   Friendly Lass [6] 9-7   1990 Russell Flyer [14] 9-3(bl)
2282 Steel Pass [17] 9-1   1943 Fancy Pages [8] 8-10
15 ran   ½,1½,shhd,½,1   (Metal Woods Ltd)   S Mellor Lambourn , Berks

2371 NEWHAVEN SELLING HANDICAP 3YO 0-25   £825   1m   Good/Firm 31 -15 Slow   [20]

2238 MY CUP OF TEA [2] (P Haslam) 3-8-10 T Williams 11/10 FAV: 3224201: 3 b g Porto Bello-
Aravania (Rarity): Well bckd & gained a deserved success, led inside final 1f under press
in a 3yo selling h'cap at Brighton (sold 3,800 gns): placed several times previously in
similar company: eff at 7f, stays 9f: acts on firm & soft & on any trk.   09
2238 SONG AN DANCE MAN [5] (M Mccourt) 3-9-7(BL) R Wernham 4/1: 0000002: Bl first time:
led 2f out: 5L clear 3rd: see 1937, 116.   18

BRIGHTON Thursday August 28th —Cont'd

2094 FLEUR DE THISTLE [6] (A Davison) 3-9-0(vis) R Fox 10/3: 0332023: Made most: btr 2094. 02
1937 TROJAN SPLASH [7] (P Haynes) 3-8-9 W Carson 15/2: -0004: Ev ch str: lightly raced
& little form previously. 00
2060 FANDANGO KISS [4] 3-8-9 W Newnes 8/1: 0-00000: No threat: little form. 00
1827 ALSACE [3] 3-8-6 I Jupp(7) 33/1: 0-0000: Rank outsider: there 3f. 00
6 ran 1,5,8,2½,10 (W J Hall) P Haslam Newmarket

2372 ROTTINGDEAN HANDICAP 3YO+ 0-35 £2061 1m 4f Good/Firm 31 -04 Slow [25]

2217 TEMPEST TOSSED [1] (R Armstrong) 3-8-13(bl) B Thomson 9/1: 4032301: 3 ch f Our Native-
Witchy Woman (Strate Stuff): Mkt drifter: but led over 2f out, ridden out in a h'cap at
Brighton: consistent filly who gained her first win here, though placed several times
previously: stays 12f well: acts on gd & fast grnd & on any trk: suited by bl. 31
2175 LONGSTOP [9] (P Makin) 4-9-10(4ex) S Cauthen 15/8 FAV: 0300102: Kept on: gd effort
under 9-10: see 2098. 26
1366 WILD GINGER [2] (D Oughton) 4-8-13(vis) B Crossley 9/1: 0200033: Led ½m: abs: see 485. 11
2226 REGENCY SQUARE [4] (P Feilden) 3-8-4(7ex) A Mackay 4/1: 2044144: Came too late:
needs stiffer trk? see 2109. 11
2152 KILIMANJARO BOB [8] 4-9-4 W R Swinburn 12/1: 0000200: No threat: btr 2034 (stiff trk). 12
2182 FORGIVING [5] 4-8-12 W Newnes 9/2: 4030020: Fdd str: much btr 2182. 04
2182 FORMIDABLE DANCER [3] 3-9-1 B Rouse 6/1: -000040: Mkt drifter: prom early: btr 2182. 00
2173 Bwana Kali [7] 9-10(bl)
8 ran 2½,2,1,1,1 (W J C Hancock) R Armstrong Newmarket

2373 LANCING MAIDEN STAKES 3YO £959 1m 2f Good/Firm 31 -07 Slow

1588 PRINCELY ESTATE [7] (J Winter) 3-9-0 W R Swinburn 6/1: -222241: 3 b c Northfields-
Princess Redowa (Prince Regent): Gained a deserved win, led 1½f out, holding on by a hd
in a 3yo mdn at Brighton: fin 2nd on his first 4 outings this term: eff at 10f, stays further:
acts on firm & yld grnd & on any trk, though may prefer a sharpish one. 36
2184 ON TO GLORY [4] (J Dunlop) 3-8-11 W Carson 25/1: 00B3002: Fin well & just btn:
best effort yet & was suited by this lngr trip: acts on gd & fast grnd & likes a sharpish trk. 32
1394 RAFFIA RUN [2] (R Akehurst) 3-9-0 R Mcghin 16/1: 0440233: Never nearer after abs:
fair effort: stays 10f: see 1394. 30
2183 ENSIGNE [1] (H Candy) 3-9-0 W Newnes 11/8 FAV: -2024: Made most till over 1f out:
disapp after 2183. 30
1806 TARLETONS OAK [3] 3-9-0 G Starkey 10/3: 000-40: No extra final 2f: btr 1806. 24
2110 LOST IN FRANCE [6] 3-8-11 B Thomson 7/2: 0-0000: Nicely bckd but needs to impr to
win a race: see 2110. 19
2216 MR ADVISER [5] 3-9-0 P Cook 33/1: -400000: Outsider: al rear. 00
7 ran hd,2,hd,3,1 (Lady Clague) J Winter Newmarket

CHESTER Friday August 29th Lefthanded, Very Sharp Track

2374 WIRRAL APPRENTICE H'CAP 0-35 £1554 1m 2f Yielding 102 +12 Fast [33]

2173 MISTER POINT [8] (C Tinkler) 4-9-10 W Goodwin 7/2 FAV: 0011301: 4 ch g Ahonoora -
Rozmeen (Relko) Made ev yard for an easy win in a fast run app h'cap at Chester: earlier won
successive h'caps at Carlisle and Ayr: last season successful on Hamilton and Beverley: eff
around 9/11f with forcing tactics: acts on firm tho' prefers some give under foot: genuine
sort who has no trk preferences: carries weight well and can win again. 40
1951 RHEIN COURT [2] (D Haydn Jones) 6-7-7(1oh) J Lake(2) 12/1: -000002: Al cl up, no
chance with this easy winner tho' did show signs of a return to form on this easier
ground: see 547. 00
2173 TREYARNON [7] (S Norton) 4-7-10 J Ward 11/2: 3000443: Ran on same pace: best 631. (12f) 00
2101 EARLS COURT [4] (R Francis) 10-7-8(1ow)(1oh) A Whitehall 6/1: -040034: No threat:
clear rem: see 1432. 00
2282 POLEMISTIS [1] 7-7-8 G Athanasiou 12/1: 0001000: Well btn and much btr on firm 1703(1m) 00
2102 DAWN SPIRIT [10] 4-7-7 A Culhane 33/1: 00-0000: Never dangerous: maiden tho' fin
down the field in all his starts. 00
1829 MONCLARE TROPHY [6] 7-8-9 A Munroe 9/1: 0003000: Fin 7th: best 420. 00
1766 SCOTTISH GREEN [3] 8-8-1(bl)(8ow)(2oh) D Meade 33/1: 1400/00: Wknd into 8th: see 1766 00
1951 BUCKS BOLT [9] 4-8-3 A Woods(3) 4/1: 3000440: Al in rear: btr over 9f in 1951. 00
2046 SANTELLA PAL [5] 5-7-8 T Lang 7/1: 2043000: Little form this term: see 540. 00
10 ran 7,3,2½,15,2 (M Battle) C Tinkler Malton, Yorks.

2375 E B F COMBERMERE MAIDEN 2YO STAKES £1749 5f Yielding 102 -24 Slow

1681 STYLISH ENTRY [2] (J Hindley) 2-8-11 A Shoults(5) 6/4 FAV: 41: 2 b f Super Concorde -
Ball Gate (Snow Ball) Well bckd and led inside dist, driven out in a 2yo fillies mdn at
Chester: cost $25,000 as a yearling: eff over a sharp 5f tho' should prove btr over longer
dist: acts on gd/firm and yldg ground and on any trk. 38
2153 KEEN NOTE [4] (C Brittain) 2-8-11 M Roberts 7/1: 002: Going on fin and showed
improved form on this easier ground: should do even btr over 6f: acts on a sharp trk: see 2153 32

700

1403 NON FICTION [10] (K Brassey) 2-8-11 S Whitworth 11/1: 343: Led below dist, no
extra near fin: acts on gd and yldg ground and on any trk: see 1194.   26
1972 LITTLE UPSTART [11] (G Pritchard Gordon) 2-8-11 G Duffield 8/1: 044: Nearest fin:
acts on yldg: see 1972.   26
818 GAME FEATHERS [6] 2-8-11 N Carlisle 20/1: 000: Tried to make all tho' wknd dist:
fair effort after a lengthy abs: acts on yldg: see 818.   25
2080 MISS PONTEVECCHIO [8] 2-8-11 G Baxter 7/1: 00: On the upgrade: acts on yldg: see 2080.   24
2127 STYLISH GIRL [1] 2-8-11 B Crossley 13/2: 0300: Dwelt and no threat in 8th: see 1650.   00
2167 ATRAYU [7] 2-8-11 Paul Eddery 6/1: 0200: Mkt drifter: fin 9th: best 1946 (gd/frm)   00
1370 Pretty Soon [3] 8-11   2080 The Cross [9] 8-11
10 ran   1¼,2,shthd,nk,nk   (Guiting Stud Ltd)   J Hindley Newmarket

2376 BLACK FRIARS HANDICAP 0-50   £3241   2m   Yielding 102 -10 Slow   [46]

1886 TEMPLE WALK [6] (W Hern) 3-8-8 W Newnes 6/1: 0-1301: 3 b f Bustino - Temple
Wood (Sweet Revenge) Well suited by this longer trip, led 2f out for a facile win in a
h'cap at Chester: useful filly who earlier won a fillies stks over 9f at Wolverhampton:
half sister to a couple of middle dist winners and very well suited by a test of stamina
herself: acts on fast and yldg ground and on any trk: certain to win again in this form.   54
1533 LEPRECHAUN LADY [7] (S Norton) 4-8-1 B Crossley 17/2: 0012022: Abs: gd eff: see 1533   24
2203 MAJESTICIAN [5] (G Pritchard Gordon) 3-8-11 G Duffield 11/8 FAV: 0021223: Well bckd:
tried to make all: h'cap "good thing" after his fine run in 2203, gall trk: see 1029. needs firm?   43
1679 REVISIT [2] (J Winter) 4-9-7 Paul Eddery 5/1: 0034344: Stiff task under top weight. see 58A.   32
2134 BALLET CHAMP [4] 8-7-13(bl) A Proud 11/2: 3002420: Much btr in 2134 (stiff trk)   02
2240 JACKDAW [3] 6-8-9 A Culhane(7) 17/2: 2312040: Held up no threat: best 1633 (stiff trk)   00
319 LHASA [1] 4-8-13 D Nicholls 25/1: 3200-00: Long abs and sn behind: quite consistent
last season when successful at Haydock: suited by a test of stamina: acts on gd/firm
and soft ground.   00
7 ran   6,4,6,6,10   (T E Egerton)   W Hern West Ilsley, Berks.

2377 GREY FRIARS MAIDEN STAKES 2YO   £1780   7f   Yielding 102 +08 Fast

--   RIO PIEDRAS [3] (A Bailey) 2-8-11 M Miller 9/2: 1: 2 b f Kala Shikari - Glory Isle
(Hittite Glory) Nicely bckd on racecourse debut, led inside dist, comfortably, in quite a
fast run 2yo mdn at Cheste: clearly well suited by 7f, tho' shoul stay further: acts on
yldg ground and on a tight trk: can only improve.   45
2056 FRENCH SONNET [1] (C Brittain) 2-9-0 M Roberts 3/1 JT FAV: 02: Tried to make all,
snatched up cl home tho' btn on merit: cost 185,000 gns and is a half brother to very useful
Lucayan Princess: eff over 7f on yldg grd: acts on a sharp trk and seems suited by forcing
tactics: on the upgrade.   40
2225 ALLOUSH [4] (L Piggott) 2-9-0 B Crossley 5/1: 0403: Ev ch: cost 19,000 gns and is
a half brother to sev winners: will be suited by further in time: acts on gd/firm and
yldg and on any trk.   32
2105 ALBION PLACE [9] (M H Easterby) 2-9-0 K Hodgson 20/1: 40004: Al prom: acts on yldg.   24
1869 ARIZONA SUN [5] 2-9-0 D Nicholls 8/1: 000: Prom most of way: best 1869 (6f).   18
--   ONE TO NOTE [10] 2-9-0 M Birch 6/1: 0: Never nearer after slow start and seems
certain to improve on this run next time: half brother to winning juv Mickey Go: stays 7f:
acts on yldg grd and on a sharp trk.   17
1634 OKOSAN [7] 2-8-11 Paul Eddery 10/1: 000: Fin 7th after abs: best 1634 (6f, firm).   00
2215 MISK EL KHASHAB [6] 2-8-11 G Duffield 3/1 JT FAV: 200: Fdd into 8th: twice
below 1752 (stiff track, good/firm).   00
1088 Tuesday Evening [2] 8-11   -- Major Oakey [8] 9-0
10 ran   2,4,4,3,¾   (T P Ramsden)   A Bailey Newmarket

2378 MOSTYN HANDICAP 0-60   £3412   6f   Yielding 102 +01 Fast   [56]

2242 MERDON MELODY [11] (R Sheather) 3-8-7(BL) A Shoults(5) 8/1: 1220041: 3 b c Mummy's
Pet - Singing (Petingo) Useful colt: bl first time and qcknd first time to lead inside dist,
comfortably, in a h'cap at Chester: first time out won a val h'cap at Newmarket: in '85 won
a Sandown mdn: half brother to the useful Durham Place: eff over 5/6f on fast and soft grd:
acts on any track.   52
2258 ARDROX LAD [10] (M Blanshard) 6-9-7 W Newnes 14/1: 0000002: Dwelt, led below dist
and ran his best race for some time: may win soon: see 550.   56
*1986 ALL AGREED [7] (J Winter) 5-9-7 G Duffield 4/1: 4002113: Came late as usual: see 1986   56
1536 FAWLEYS GIRL [6] (R Hollinshead) 4-7-7(3oh) A Culhane(7) 12/1: 0020004: Abs: likes
this trip trk: see 520.   22
2084 VILTASH [13] 3-8-6(VIS) M Wood 12/1: 0030000: Visored first time: best 1044 (firm).   33
*2012 TANFEN [4] 5-8-4 N Carlisle 13/2: 2104010: Ran on too late: best 2012 (gd/frm).   20
2224 PANNANICH WELLS [5] 3-7-10 A Proud 7/2 FAV: 2104300: Fdd into 7th: best 671 (gall trk)   00
2242 CRETE CARGO [8] 3-9-1 Paul Eddery 10/1: 0024200: Al in rear: much btr 1060 (frm).   00
2224 Gods Isle [12] 7-10(bl)   2021 Sudden Impact [9] 8-1(bl)(3ow)
2046 Pine Hawk [2] 7-7(7oh) 1505 Runaway [1] 8-1 1951 Bakers Double [3] 7-8(BL)(1ow)(28oh)
13 ran   1¼,shthd,2¼,3,2   (J C Smith)   R Sheather Newmarket

2379 GREY FRIARS MAIDEN STAKES 2YO   £1780   7f   Yielding 102 -29 Slow

2239 MR CORMAN [7] (M Blanshard) 2-9-0 W Newnes 11/4 FAV: 001: 2 ch c Homing - Rosy Lee
(Le Haar) Well bckd and led inside dist, ridden out in a 2yo mdn at Chester: quite cheaply
bought colt who is eff over 7f and will be suited by further next season: acts on gd and
yldg ground and on any trk: improving steadily.   42
2029 WILLOWBANK [1] (S Norton) 2-8-11 Paul Eddery 6/1: 002: Led/dsptd lead thr'out,
narrowly btn and is on the upgrade: stays 7f: acts on firm and yldg and well suited by a
sharp trk: see 1427.   38
1510 KALEIDOPHONE [6] (C Elsey) 2-8-11 C Dwyer 10/1: 003: Abs: stayed on well and not
btn far: stays 7f: acts on firm and yldg grd and on any trk: see 1266.   38
--   CRESTED [4] (W Hern) 2-9-0 B Procter 7/2: 4: Mkt drifter on racecourse debut:
showed gd speed till wknd dist: acts on yldg grd and on a sharp trk:
should improve.   33
1534 CITY FINAL [3] 2-8-11 S Perks 3/1: 404030: Dsptd lead till dist: best 1534 (C/D).   22
1480 GEOBRITONY [8] 2-9-0 G Duffield 8/1: 040020: Abs: prom most: best 1480(firm).   20
2177 Running Money [5] 9-0   -- Nova Lad [2] 9-0   -- Try Hills Supplies [9] 9-0
9 ran   nk,shthd,4,4,2½   (G H Atkinson)   M Blanshard Lambourn, Berks.

2380 EASTGATE NURSERY HANDICAP 2YO   £3086   5f   Yielding 102 -12 Slow   [40]

2272 MISS MILVEAGH [4] (A Bailey) 2-9-1 J Carr(7) 5/1: 32221: 2 b f Pas De Seul -
Milveagh (Milesian) Gained a deserved win, improved to lead dist and ran on well in a nursery
h'cap at Chester: had just failed to make all her two prev starts and does well with forcing
tactics: half sister to sev winners: eff over 5/6f on firm and yldg grd: suited by a sharp
trk: consistent filly.   38
*2007 AID AND ABET [3] (M Stoute) 2-9-5 Paul Eddery 11/4 FAV: 4212: Made most: acts on
yldg: see 2007.   35
*2272 REMAIN FREE [5] (C Williams) 2-8-0(bl)(7ex) C Rutter 5/1: 330413: Ev ch: beat today's
winner over 6f in 2272: acts on firm and yldg ground.   08
2100 ROYAL CROFTER [6] (M H Easterby) 2-9-4 M Birch 9/2: 32224: Dsptd lead most: btr 2100.   24
2010 LINN ODEE [7] 2-8-7 L Charnock 5/1: 2314040: No chance when hmpd dist: best 665 (gall trk)   05
2100 DANCING BELLE [2] 2-9-7 G Duffield 6/1: 0000130: Gd early speed tho' btr 2100 (stiff).   00
2284 FALDWYN [1] 2-8-8(bl) N Carlisle 12/1: 3020040: Outpaced from ½ way: btr 2284 (gall trk)   00
7 ran   2,2½,¾,3,8   (Cawthorne Investments Ltd)   A Bailey Newmarket

Official Going Given As ROUND COURSE GOOD : STRAIGHT GOOD/SOFT

2381 HOOK APPRENTICE HANDICAP 0-35   £2666   1m 1f Good/Firm 24 No Stan Time [27]

1733 DARK HERITAGE [3] (C Nelson) 3-9-4 S Horsfall(3) 14/1: 00-0041: 3 b c Scorpio -
Mother of the Wind (Tumble Wind) Led over 2f out, ridden out in an app h'cap at Sandown
Aug 29: first success: lightly raced prev: eff at 9f, stays 11f: acts on gd and fast grd
and seems suited by front running on a gall track.   34
1998 NEEDLEWOMAN [7] (R Armstrong) 3-9-7 V Smith(3) 11/1: 0004302: Ev ch final 2f:
gd effort and runs well here: see 739.   34
2190 MINUS MAN [17] (W Holden) 8-8-1 R Morse(3) 5/1 FAV: 0030423: Ran on final 1f:
gd effort: see 2190.   04
1520 FIRST RANK [14] (P Arthur) 3-8-12 L Johnsey(6) 14/1: 00-4004: Made much after abs:
lightly raced since 832.   14
2109 SIMONS FANTASY [9] 3-8-6(bl) M Lynch 11/1: 4341000: Never nearer: best 1724 (firm)   03
1327 MORGIANA [11] 3-8-4 P Price(7) 25/1: -0000: No threat: lightly raced filly who
seems to stay 9f: acts on gd/firm.   00
2059 XYLOPHONE [10] 4-9-3 Gay Kelleway 7/1: 003-100: Ev ch str: twice below 1400 (seller)   00
2027 SOVEREIGN LOVE [5] 3-9-8 Dale Gibson(7) 13/2: 3230200: Best over 1m in 1923.   00
2173 Starmast [1] 9-5   2154 Primrose Way [19] 8-1 1727 Sweet Andy [8] 7-13
--   Main Star [13] 9-4   2123 Gamblers Dream [4] 9-3
--   Okaadh [20] 9-3   2171 Son Of Sparkler [15] 8-10
2121 Superfrost [16] 8-10   -- Farm Lane [6] 8-5   2109 Film Consultant [12] 8-4
*2073 Spinnaker Lady [18] 8-2
19 ran   1½,nk,6,3,1   (John E Guest)   C Nelson Upper Lambourn, Berks.

2382 TERRY RAMSDEN BLISS HCAP 3YO 0-60   £7986   5f   Good/Firm 24 -02 Slow   [86]

*2245 SILENT MAJORITY [11] (W O'gorman) 3-8-2(5ow) T Ives 4/1 FAV: 1311411: 3 b c General
Assembly - Vexed Voter (Pontifex) Useful sprinter who is in fine form: despite 5lbs ow made
ev yard and was sn clear for a comfortable win in a val h'cap at Sandown Aug 29: successful
in h'caps prev at Goodwood (appr), Yarmouth, Kempton and Sandown: very eff at 5f with
forcing tactics: stays 6f: best on gd and firm grd: much improved this season and can win again. 53
2224 RESTORE [4] (G Lewis) 3-7-9 W Carson 6/1: 23-2032: Ran on final 1f: in gd form:
needs 6f? See 2224, 593.   42
2258 HANDSOME SAILOR [12] (M Dickinson) 3-9-7 B Thomson 9/2: 0412-03: Ev ch far side:
another gd effort: see 2258. carries weight well: should soon find a race.   64
2224 RESPECT [9] (R Laing) 3-9-1 R Cochrane 9/2: 3104124: Ev ch: btr 2224, see 1878. consistent. 52

SANDOWN   Friday August 29th   -Cont'd

2160 NORTHERN TRUST [7] 3-7-12(bl) J Lowe 25/1: 0002000: Nearest fin: best 1704, see 233   35
1991 HELAWE [1] 3-7-7(bl) A Mackay 20/1: 0301400: Prom most: best 1191 (6f).   29
+2258 PRECIOUS METAL [8] 3-9-7(7ex) R Curant 7/1: 1030010: No show and well below 2258 (6f)   00
2143 Coppermill Lad [2] 7-7(3oh)   2210 Cresta Leap [5] 7-8(1ow)(6oh)
2160 Rayhaan [3] 8-5   593 Pas De Regrets [10] 7-12
1391 Fountain Bells [6] 7-11
12 ran   1¼,1½,2½,hd,nk,½   (Bertram R Firestone)   W O'gorman Newmarket

2383 ME AND MY GIRL NURSERY HANDICAP 2YO   £4045   1m   Good/Firm 24 -09 Slow [51]

2336 PERFECT STRANGER [10] (P Haslam) 2-8-6 T Williams 6/1: 03101: 2 b g Wolver Hollow -
Mrs Walmsley (Lorenzaccio) Impr colt: unlucky earlier in the wk at Beverley and gained
compensation, leading inside final 1f most gamely in a nursery h'cap at Sandown: earlier a
winner of a claimer at Yarmouth: eff at 7f, stays 1m really well: acts on firm and yldg grd
and likes a gall trk: genuine.   41
*2178 PALEFACE [2] (L Piggott) 2-9-3(4ex) T Ives 5/1: 332212: Made much: kept on well
and is in grand form: suited by 1m: see 2178.   50
2044 COMBINED EXERCISE [6] (R Smyth) 2-8-10 S Cauthen 20/1: 00043: Chance 1f out: not
btn far and was suited by today's longer trip: eff at 1m on gd/firm grd and a gall trk and
can find a race.   41
*1681 PLAGUE ORATS [7] (R Smyly) 2-9-1 A Murray 6/1: 014: Stays 1m: gd eff: see 1681.   42
2136 OLORE MALLE [5] 2-8-4 A Mcglone 14/1: 14230: Ev ch str: stays 1m: consistent:see 1968   29
2035 MURAJAH [8] 2-8-2 B Rouse 20/1: 040000: Prom most: stays 1m, but best 1039 (5f)   25
1722 LISIANTHUS [4] 2-8-13 G Starkey 8/1: 0330: Never threatened: btr 1722, 1382 (7f)   00
*1872 COUNTER ATTACK [9] 2-9-6 W Carson 10/3 FAV: 10: Wkning when hmpd inside final 2f.   00
2071 VAIGLY BLAZED [3] 2-8-1 P Cook 25/1: 400000: Outsider: al rear: best 662 (yldg/soft)   00
*2013 YLDIZLAR [1] 2-9-7 M Hills 7/2: 10: Nicely bckd but p.u. lame half way: see 2013.   00
10 ran   ½,1,2,1,1   (I Paice)   P Haslam Newmarket

2384 GLENN INTERN. SOLARIO STKS GR 3 2yo   £20193   7f   Good/Firm 24 +03 Fast

1919 SHINING WATER [4] (R J Houghton) 2-8-8 S Cauthen 20/1: 421101: 2 b f Kalaglow -
Idle Waters (Mill Reef) Very useful filly: made ev yard, readily, in quite fast run Gr 3
Solario Stks at Sandown : below her best last time out, but earlier hacked up twice at
Windsor: well bred filly whose dam was smart and genuine and won the Park Hill Stks: eff
at 7f, seems sure to stay 1m: acts on gd and firm ground and seems suited by front running:
sure to win more races.   75
+2035 SANAM [9] (J Dunlop) 2-9-2 W Carson 12/1: 41012: Kept on well: another fine effort after 2035 77
*1658 LOCKTON [10] (J Hindley) 2-9-0 M Hills 8/1: 20113: Hmpd over 1f out: ran on well
and can win again soon: see 1658.   74
*1760 MILEAGE BANK [3] (P Cole) 2-8-11 T Quinn 33/1: 41014: Al prom: gd effort from this
consistent colt: seems to stay 7f: see 1760.   69
2232 ROCK CHANTEUR [8] 2-8-11 J Reid 20/1: 00: Fin best of all and is fast improving:
sure to be suited by 1m and can win soon: see 2232.   69
*2159 NEW ATTITUDE [6] 2-9-0 G Starkey 10/11 FAV: 10: Heavily bckd: drifted right when
ridden over 1f out: slightly disapp after 2159, but was facing btr class here.   70
*1452 GLORY FOREVER [2] 2-9-0 J Lowe 17/2: 4410: Hmpd over 2f out: best ignored: see 1452.   00
1887 MR EATS [7] 2-9-0(BL) B Rouse 11/1: 1240: Bl first time: much btr 1887, 876 (easier trks) 00
*2251 LACK A STYLE [5] 2-9-2 R Cochrane 15/2: 0233210: Slow start: much btr 2251 (1m).   00
*2071 HARD ACT [1] 2-8-11 B Thomson 20/1: 1100010: Badly hmpd inside final 2f: see 2071.   00
1731 SANTELLA SAM [11] 2-8-11 P Robinson 33/1: 2320: Mkt drifter: fdd quickly str: see 1731   00
11 ran   2,¾,¼,hd,¾   (R Crutchley)   R J Houghton Blewbury, Oxon.

2385 B.B.A. ATALANTA STAKES   £7934   1m   Good/Firm 24 +10 Fast

2194 PURCHASEPAPERCHASE [6] (R Armstrong) 4-9-7 W Carson 16/1: 0104001: 4 b f Young Generation
- Tin Goddess (Petingo) Smart filly on her day: made ev yard, comfortably, in fast run
and val Listed race at Sandown Aug 29: earlier in season won another fast run event over
this C/D and clearly loves this trk: in '85 won first time out at Ascot and later an excellent
2nd to Fitnah in Gr 1 event at Longchamp: eff at 1m, stays 10f well: acts on gd and firm
ground and a gall trk.   73
*1064 LADY SOPHIE [8] (H Cecil) 3-8-7(1ow) S Cauthen 2/1 FAV: 01-2012: Ran in snatches
when asked to qckn: abs since 1064: best 214 (yldg grd).   64
1924 REALITY [4] (R J Houghton) 3-8-6 J Reid 14/1: 0-1103: Al prom and ran a fine race:
on this form can win a h'cap soon: stays Sandown: see 1753.   60
2155 BLACK SOPHIE [3] (R Laing) 3-8-6 R Cochrane 50/1: 3-00104: Kept on really well:
fine effort in this much btr company and should be able to win a h'cap next time out:
suited by 1m: see 1991.   59
+2135 LAND OF IVORY [1] 3-8-6 P Cook 9/2: 1D43310: Never nearer: btr 2135 when fresh.   58
1851 VIANORA [7] 3-8-9 G Starkey 13/2: 0112130: Ev ch str: btr 1851, 1153.   57
1107 DOLKA [2] 3-8-12 W R Swinburn 11/4: 1-100: Sweating: fin 8th: abs: twice below 803.   00
*1902 Flashdance [9] 8-6   2145 Chalk Stream [10] 8-6(BL)
1999 Rare Sound [5] 8-6
10 ran   2,1,hd,nk,2   (John Bray)   R Armstrong Newmarket

00

703

SANDOWN   Friday August 29th   -Cont'd

2386 EARLY AUTUMN CLAIMING STAKES 3YO   £2683   1m 3f   Good/Firm 24 -14 Slow

1589 LYDIA EVA [2] (R Hannon) 3-8-1 A Mcglone 12/1: 00-0001: 3 b f Connaught - Syltung
(Shantung) Gained her 1st success, led 3f out, staying on really well in 3yo Claimer at
Sandown: well suited by a gall trk and will get 12f: acts on gd/firm grd and does well when fresh.   24
*1898 S S SANTO [3] (M Tompkins) 3-8-3 R Cochrane 9/4: 2200012: Chance final 1f: 6l clear 3rd:
in fine form: see 1898.   23
2109 COLEMAN HAWKINS [9] (P Makin) 3-9-0 T Quinn 9/1: -000403: Prom, ev ch: seems to
lack a turn of.foot: stays 12f and acts on firm and yldg.   24
2190 TURMERIC [1] (D Morley) 3-9-0 B Rouse 16/1: 0000204: Twice below 1838 (9f).   21
--   GHOFAR [4] 3-8-5(1ow) B Thomson 20/1: -0: Sn rear: stayed on and will be all the
better for this racecourse debut: stoutly bred colt who may be seen to btr eff over timber.   02
1970 FIREPROOF [6] 3-9-4 W Carson 9/1: 2014400: Fdd inside final 3f: btr 1386 (14f), 951.   00
1923 MERHI [5] 3-9-0 S Cauthen 2/1 FAV: 3000300: Led 1m: eased when btn: much btr 1831 (10f)   00
2248 Eloquence [8] 8-11   2098 Miss Jade [7] 8-3   --   Hang Loose [10] 8-9
10 ran   1½,6,1½,7,10   (C A Blackwell)   R Hannon East Everleigh, Wilts.

CHESTER   Saturday August 30th   Lefthanded, Very Sharp Track

Official Going Given As SOFT

2389 BERRY MAGICOAL SUREFIRE H'CAP 3YO+ 0-60   £3116   1m 4f   Yielding 99 -10 Slow   [54]

2237 GULFLAND [5] (G Pritchard Gordon) 5-9-8 Abigail Richards(7) 4/1: 2101121: 5 ch g Gulf
Pearl - Sunland Park (Baragoi) In tremendous form: easily led 1 out in a h'cap at Chester,
5th success this year following wins at Redcar, Nottingham, Doncaster and again at Chester:
suited by 10/12f and acts on any going and on any trk: goes well for an amateur: genuine sort
who should win yet again and carries weight well.   60
2164 TRAPEZE ARTIST [2] (N Vigors) 5-8-13 S Dawson 4/1: 1100222: Gd eff over 12f: possibly
btr suited by 14f: running well: see 917.   45
2290 REGAL STEEL [4] (R Hollinshead) 8-7-7(2oh) A Culhane(7) 6/1: 2221403: Dsptd lead much.   20
2201 TWICE BOLD [1] (N Callaghan) 3-8-9 M Hills 9/4 FAV: 3421204: Made most, best 1551 (gd/frm)   40
*2176 ROUBAYD [3] 3-9-7(6ex) J Reid 10/3: -110: Ran badly: unsuited by soft?   00
5 ran   3,2½,5,30   (G A Pritchard-Gordon)   G Pritchard Gordon Newmarket

2390 BERRY MAGICOAL SUN SEEKER H'CAP 0-60   £3636   7.5f   Yielding 99 +07 Fast   [50]

1316 ARE YOU GUILTY [13] (M Ryan) 3-7-8 G Bardwell(7) 8/1: 3-30001: 3 b f Runnett -
Gullistan (Sharpen Up) Despite a lengthy abs and a slow start, led 1 out comfortably(bkd from 20/1), in
quite a fast run h'cap at Chester: first success: tried in bl last year: seems best around 7f
on a sharp trk and goes well on soft ground: could win again. improving filly.   36
2144 STAR OF A GUNNER [5] (R Holder) 6-9-7 J Reid 7/1: 1100032: Fin well on this sharp trk,
btr suited by a stiff one: see 248: back to his best and goes well on soft.   49
2234 MOORES METAL [11] (R Hollinshead) 6-8-9 A Culhane(7) 16/1: 0003203: Kept on well: see 441   34
2126 KNIGHTS SECRET [14] (M H Easterby) 5-8-6 A Mackay 16/1: 3403404: Led 2 out, returning
to form? In grand form earlier this season and acts on any going: see 815.   30
2189 APRIL FOOL [15] 4-7-12 T Lang(5) 20/1: 0400030: Much btr 2189 (gd).   08
2126 DARNIT [18] 4-8-13 M Tebbutt(7) 16/1: 0021020: Not well drawn: btr 2126.   23
2264 O I OYSTON [3] 10-7-7(1oh) J Quinn(3) 10/3 FAV: 0202220: Dsptd lead 4f, well bckd.   00
1854 SAFEERA [2] 3-9-0 W Woods(3) 9/1: -034100: Disapp since 1532 (C/D).   00
2255 Top Wing [12] 8-12   2151 Idle Times [10] 7-13(vis)
1777 Corn Street [9] 9-4   2155 Burhaain [1] 8-4   *1758 Haraabah [8] 9-2
1041 Creeager [17] 8-11   2104 Remembrance [16] 7-7(6oh)
914 Romantic Uncle [7] 8-12   2258 Formatune [6] 8-4(bl)
2126 Young Bruss [4] 7-10
18 ran   2½,1½,hd,7,shthd   (T P Ramsden)   M Ryan Newmarket

2391 BERRY MAGICOAL MATCHLESS NURSERY H'CAP   £5119   7f   Yielding 99 +08 Fast   [51]

2026 BREWIN TIME [3] (M H Easterby) 2-7-10 A Mackay 10/1: 0031: 2 b g Palm Track - Baggin
Time (Pinsun) Despite being btn in a Claiming race last time, made all unchall by 6f in a
nursery at Chester: evidently well suited by 7f, soft grd and a sharp trk: best out in front:
brother to far h'capper Mashin Time.   36
*2032 SHADE OF PALE [8] (P Haslam) 2-8-2 G French 7/1: 12: Forced wide into str, gd eff
after winning a seller last time on firm ground.   28
2198 PEN BAL LADY [2] (G Pritchard Gordon) 2-9-7 Abigail Richards(7) 3/1 FAV: 121133: Consistent
but btr 1895 (gd/firm).   45
1916 WELSH ARROW [6] (J Winter) 2-9-5 G Duffield 13/2: 134: Prob stays 7f: see 1207.   42
2276 PHARAOH BLUE [10] 2-7-13 M Roberts 13/2: 00120: Btr on gall trk in 1883.   02
2081 DUTCH AUCTION [7] 2-9-4 B Crossley 11/1: 100: So far best 6f in 1573.   20
*2115 MY BUDDY [5] 2-9-5 M Hills 4/1: 001110: Ran very wide into str: can do much better.   00
*2026 MAZURKANOVA [1] 2-7-10 N Carlisle 8/1: 0420410: Btr 2026, stiff trk, 6f, gd/firm.   00
1138 Thekkian [9] 8-9   1764 My Serenade [4] 7-10
10 ran   6,1,nk,10,hd   (P Baillie)   M H Easterby Malton, Yorks.   00

704

2392 LINENHALL STAKES 2YO   £2788   6f   Yielding 99 -32 Slow

2232 RUMBOOGIE [1] (C Brittain) 2-8-11 M Roberts 3/1: 01: 2 ch c Sharpo - Santa Musica
(Luthier) Led 1 out comfortably, in a 4 runner event at Chester: evidently goes well on a
sharp trk on soft ground: might stay further than 6f.   58
2232 MAJD [4] (P Walwyn) 2-8-11 Paul Eddery 5/4 FAV: 332: Ran wide into str and is
certainly worth another chance: prob acts on yldg: see 1522, 2232.   52
*1984 MISK [3] (H Cecil) 2-9-5 W Ryan 7/4: 22013: Consistent, prob acts on yldg: see 1984.   58
1568 SUPREME OPTIMIST [2] (R Peacock) 2-8-11(bl) S Dawson 20/1: 300004: Does well on a
sharp trk, tried to make all but ran wide in str: goes well on soft: see 460.   30
4 ran   1¼,1,5   (A J Richards)   C Brittain Newmarket

2393 ROUGE ROSE MAIDEN FILLIES STAKES 3YO   £1927   1m 2f   Yielding 99 -07 Slow

1725 QUEEN OF BATTLE [1] (M Ryan) 3-8-11 N Day 7/1: 0022341: 3 b f Relkino - Worthy Venturer
(Northfields) Made all unchall in a mdn race at Chester: earlier ran well over 1m but now
seems suited by 10f: seems to act on firm and soft: goes well on a sharp trk and has also
run well at Yarmouth: could pick up a h'cap.   48
2170 SATIN AND SILK [7] (A Bailey) 3-8-11 M Miller 10/3: -3002: Al 2nd: well bckd: eff
at 7/10f and seems to act on firm and soft: should find a maiden.   34
2110 LINASH [4] (G Wragg) 3-8-11 Paul Eddery 5/1: -00443: No threat: btr 12f? See 1818.   28
723 EYE SIGHT [8] (R Johnson Houghton) 3-8-11 J Reid 3/1 FAV: -34: Mkt drifter following
a lengthy abs: worth another chance and rated 43 in 723.   26
2314 MRS MAINWARING [5] 3-8-11 B Crossley 16/1: -044000: Best 1677 (1m).   08
1368 MAKE IT SHARP [6] 3-8-11 M Roberts 4/1: -030: Abs since 1368.   08
1626 Transform [2] 8-11   2161 Shujun [3] 8-11(BL)
8 ran   7,4,1½,10,hd   (B Gerhauser)   M Ryan Newmarket

2394 PARADISE MAIDEN CLAIMING STAKES 3YO   £1640   7.5f   Yielding 99 -48 Slow

2186 COLLYWESTON [5] (M Prescott) 3-8-7 G Duffield 10/3: -001: 3 br f Thatching - Kentucky
Robin (Falcon) Very well bckd when winning a Claiming race at Chester, led final 1f under
strong press: half sister to sev winners including fair sprinter Red Letter: well suited by
7f and seems to act on gd and soft ground: goes well on a sharp trk.   24
2268 BOLD FURY [7] (P Haslam) 3-8-0(VIS) G French 7/2: -202: Tried in a visor, made
much: prob stays 7f but btr 1927 (6f).   11
928 NORTHERN GUNNER [1] (W Jarvis) 3-9-0 A Mackay 9/1: 0-04303: Kept on well after
lengthy abs: gd effort without bl this time: acts on yldg: see 928, 809.   22
2275 CHARDONNAY [11] (D Laing) 3-8-11 J Reid 14/1: 0000004: Tried over 10f last time.   18
2085 STATE JESTER [2] 3-8-8 J Lowe 16/1: 0000000: Early leader: see 1503.   14
-2319 SITZCARRALDO [4] 3-8-8 M Roberts 5/2 FAV: 0-20020: Not much luck in running and
worth another chance on a more gall trk following 2319.   12
2216 GRIMESGILL [6] 3-8-5 M Hills 6/1: -004440: So far best 1540 (1m).   00
1981 Le Mans [3] 8-8   2312 Ever So Sharp [10] 8-6
1989 Scintillator [8] 9-0(bl)   1927 Lady Siematic [9] 7-9(BL)
11 ran   2½,1½,½,nk,1½   (Lady Macdonald Buchanan)   M Prescott Newmarket

---

RIPON   Saturday August 30th   Righthand Sharpish Track

Official Going Given As SOFT (HEAVY PATCHES)

2395 SUNSHINE COACHES H'CAP (0-35)   £1725   1m 4f   Yielding 82 -45 Slow   [33]

1569 RAPIDAN [9] (M H Easterby) 5-7-7 G Carter(0) 16/1: 0000001: 5 ch Mississippi -
Tragedy (Milesian) Abs tho' showed impr form, led below dist, ran on strongly to gain his
1st success in a h'cap at Ripon: little worthwhile form prev: stays 12f well: acts on soft
ground and on a sharpish track.   06
*1956 SOHAIL [4] (H T Jones) 3-9-2 A Murray 5/2 FAV: 34-0312: Ran on well over this longer
trip: acts on yldg/soft ground and clearly likes this sharpish course: see 1956.   34
2324 LEON [3] (N Tinkler) 4-9-10 Kim Tinkler 11/2: 2202403: Ran on too late: suited by
some give under foot and may gain a deserved win in the near future: see 80.   30
2217 CARVERY [1] (A Hide) 3-8-6(2ow) W R Swinburn 7/2: -0233D4: Led over 2f out, could
not qckn on this sticky ground: has shown her best form on a sound surface: see 2217, 1657.   18
2175 DICK KNIGHT [5] 5-8-5(vis) A Shoults(5) 12/1: 2000100: No extra dist: best 2101 (gd/firm).   01
2154 GLENDERRY [7] 4-8-0(bl) S Morris 20/1: 0300000: Made much: wknd 2f out: btr here 872.   00
2110 BAYTINO [10] 3-8-8 M Rimmer 8/1: -0300: Wknd into 8th: btr over 10f in 2110 (gd).   00
2059 THE YOMPER [2] 4-8-8 S Webster 8/1: -420300: Best early season in 592 (stiff trk)   00
1918 Breguet [8] 7-8   1865 Northern Ruler [6] 8-9
10 ran   3,½,3,3,3,1   (Mrs D Brewster)   M H Easterby Malton, Yorks.

2396 VARIETY CLUB SELLING STAKES 2YO   £1380   6f   Yielding 82 -25 Slow

1488 CROWN JUSTICE [19] (N Callaghan) 2-8-11 A Murray 3/1 FAV: 01: 2 b c High Top -
Justicia (Nonoalco) Despite fair abs, was well bckd and led over 1f out, comfortably, in a
2yo seller at Ripon (bought in 12,800 gns): speedily bred colt who is clearly eff over 6f on
yldg/soft ground: acts on a sharpish trk: likely to prove btr than plating class.   32

2323 MISS EMILY [12] (D Chapman) 2-8-8 D Nicholls 11/2: 00022: Al front rank, kept on
well over this longer trip: 4l clear rem and sure to win in this grade: likes this sharp trk.   22
2323 VENHERM [2] (P Calver) 2-8-11 M Fry 16/1: 0003: Led stand side over 4f: eff over
5/6f on gd/firm and yldg ground: acts on a sharp trk: see 2150. ran well from unfav. draw.   15
1221 GOLDCHAN [4] (H Wharton) 2-8-8 J H Brown(5) 10/1: 004: Abs: al up there: acts on
yldg/soft: see 1221.   02
1681 U BIX COPY [11] 2-8-11 C Dwyer 13/2: 0323000: Never nearer: best 973 (hvy).   01
2050 CHANTILLY DAWN [15] 2-9-1 K Bradshaw(5) 12/1: 0001200: Best on fast grd over this
C/D in 1635.   03
701 RHABDOMANCER [5] 2-8-8 N Connorton 7/1: 3330: Long abs: fin 9th: btr 701 (5f firm).   00
2279 SHARPHAVEN [10] 2-9-1 K Darley 15/2: 2410020: Early speed: btr on gd/firm in 2279 (stiff)   00
2298 Pertain [16] 8-11(bl)   2298 Just A Decoy [17] 8-11
1955 Skerne Rocket [6] 8-8   1248 Maddybenny [20] 8-8   186 Medallion Man [8] 8-11
948 Master Pippin [21] 8-11   2218 Corofin Lass [24] 8-8
957 Patels Gold [9] 8-8   2180 Music Delight [14] 8-8(vis)
763 Pipers Enterprise [18] 8-11   -- Holyrood [23] 8-8
425 Miss Bolero [13] 8-8   1972 Sally Foxtrot [7] 8-8   2325 Trafford Way [1] 8-11
1650 Highland Kate [22] 8-8
23 ran   1½,4,4,1½,¾,3   (K Al-Said)   N Callaghan, Newmarket.

2397 BUXTED TURKEY H'CAP (0-35)   £1380   6f   Yielding 82 -03 Slow   [35]

1839 THATCHERED [14] (J Berry) 5-8-3 M Fry 25/1: 000-001: 5 b g Thatch - Derrede (Derring-Do)
Showed much impr form, led inside dist for a decisive win in a h'cap at Ripon: sole success
prev came in a Salisbury mdn in '84, tho' had shown little form since: eff over 6/8f on
firm and yldg/soft ground: acts on any trk.   22
2295 ROYAL FAN [6] (M H Easterby) 3-8-13 M Birch 7/1: 0100002: Led dist: gd eff: see 891.   28
2277 GOLDEN GUILDER [18] (M W Easterby) 3-8-11(vis) T Lucas 10/3 FAV: 0313333: V.consistent   24
2295 HENRYS VENTURE [1] (D Chapman) 4-8-3 A Proud 11/2: 0113034: Made most: see 2295(gd/frm)06
2295 WARTHILL LADY [4] 4-7-12(1ow) K Darley 10/1: 4000040: Impr of late: see 2295 (gd/frm)   01
2264 SINGLE HAND [16] 6-8-3 J Callaghan(7) 33/1: 0000000: Nearest fin: see 42.   03
2295 TOP THAT [12] 5-9-3 S Webster 10/1: 1400200: No threat in 9th: see 1973, 649.   00
1120 JAMES PAL [10] 4-9-11 D Nicholls 10/1: 211-000: Btn when hmpd dist: abs since 1120.   00
2340 MARAVILLA [11] 4-8-8(vis) M Wood 8/1: 0024200: Much btr in 2039 (7f gd/firm).   00
2204 ROSIE DICKINS [9] 4-8-11 R Lappin(7) 10/1: 4314000: Btr on gd/firm in 1649.   00
2322 Wesbree Bay [17] 7-7(bl)(5oh)   2103 Quicken The Bid [5] 8-1
2124 Ackas Boy [2] 7-7(8oh)   1885 Jersey Maid [19] 8-5(vis)
-- Costock Bunny [15] 7-7   2335 Just A Bit [8] 8-4(bl)(2ow)
2342 Port Mist [20] 7-7(3oh)   1839 Name The Game [7] 7-9(2ow)(12oh)
1438 Bold Scuffle [13] 8-5   651 Sing Out Loud [3] 8-11
20 ran   4,1,2,shthd,1½,1   (J Fry)   J Berry Cockerham, Lancs.

2398 BAYFORD FUELS HORN BLOWER STAKES 2YO   £4480   5f   Yielding 82 +10 Fast

*1958 WHIPPER IN [2] (J Etherington) 2-8-11 A Murray 3/1: 11: 2 b c Bay Express - Whip Finish
(Be Friendly) Promising colt: led on bit below dist, readily, in a fast run and quite val
2yo stks at Ripon: comfortable winner of a mdn over this C/D recently: half brother to
surprise Acomb Stks winner Hotbee: clearly very eff over 5f   tho' should stay further: acts
on fast and yldg/soft ground and does well on a sharp trk: should complete his hat trick.   62
+2265 FULL OF PRIDE [4] (M H Easterby) 2-9-0 M Birch 3/1: 12012: Tried to make all,
rallied well when hdd and remains in fine form: acts on frm and yldg ground: see 2265.   60
2223 WHIPPET [5] (C Brittain) 2-8-11 W R Swinburn 10/11 FAV: 1200033: Al front rank and
not btn far: would prob have preferred a sounder surf tho' clearly does act on yldg ground.   56
918 THE GREAT MATCH [3] (R Whitaker) 2-8-6 D Mckeown 33/1: 0044: Abs: no threat: see 715.   34
2052 PANBOY [6] 2-8-11(BL) M Rimmer 50/1: 1240000: Outclassed: best on soft in 108.   31
826 SWING SINGER [1] 2-8-6 D Nicholls 33/1: 330: Sn under press and well btn: abs since 826   00
6 ran   1½,nk,6,1½,12   (F Warwick)   J Etherington Malton, Yorks

2399 PLAYTIME POLLYNUT H'CAP (0-35) 3YO   £1725   1m   Yielding 82 -18 Slow   [39]

2184 BATH [1] (J Toller) 3-8-6(2ow) W R Swinburn 11/4 FAV: -400421: 3 b f Runnett - Break
Of Day (On Your Mark) Nicely bckd and led 4f out, comfortably in a 3yo h'cap at Ripon:
eff over 7/8f on gd/firm and yldg ground: acts on any trk.   28
1989 NICOLINI [10] (J Fitzgerald) 3-8-0 M L Thomas 7/1: 0-00332: Ran on well: acts on
yldg: see 1864.   16
2266 GOLDEN ANCONA [5] (E Eldin) 3-9-7(VIS) E Guest(3) 10/1: 1000243: Visored first time:
ran well: see 1864, 284.   36
1169 HAITI MILL [7] (W Wharton) 3-8-11 A Shoults(5) 12/1: 3-04404: Abs: never nearer: see 309   25
1841 SEAMERE [3] 3-7-9 G Carter(2) 11/1: 0-000: Half brother to sev winners tho' lightly
raced himself and yet to show any worthwhile form: acts on yldg grd and on a sharp trk.   05
*2313 IMPERIAL PALACE [12] 3-9-1 M Wood 7/2: 0002110: Remains in gd form: see 2313.   25
*2184 GRANDANGUS [9] 3-7-11(vis) M Fry 7/1: 0010310: Led/dsptd lead most: best in 2184 (gd/frm) 00
2313 Gardas Gold [6] 7-13   1628 Promenader [14] 8-9(VIS)
*2041 Princess Andromeda [14] 8-8   1999 Bears Revenge [8] 7-12   00

2230 Charlton Kings [13] 9-2(vis)				1184 Pauls Secret [4] 7-12	
874 Cover Inn [15] 8-3	1959 Affaitati [2] 8-2(2ow)				
15 ran 2½,nk,nk,1½,hd,1½	(Lady Aitken)			J Toller Newmarket	

2400 THRUST PETROLEUM MAIDEN STAKES 3YO   £1398   1m 2f   Yielding 82 +09 Fast

2275 LYPHLAW [12] (J Dunlop) 3-9-0 G Sexton 11/8 FAV: 0-00331: 3 b c Lyphard - New Lawn
(Herbager) Well bckd and gained a deserved win, led over 2f out and ran on strongly in quite
a fast run mdn at Ripon: eff over 8/10f and likely to stay further: acts on gd/firm and
yldg ground and on any trk.   50
2085 RIVART [2] (P Kelleway) 3-9-0 Gay Kelleway(3) 7/2: -0032: Ran on same pace: lightly
raced colt who should soon find a maiden   : eff over 8/10f on gd/firm and yldg: see 1045.   46
1981 SPRINGWELL [7] (G Huffer) 3-8-11 G Carter(3) 13/2: -0033: Longer trip: stayed on
well and may do even better over 12f: acts on any trk: see 1981.should win a maiden.   40
2048 LOUVECIENNES [11] (O Douieb) 3-8-11 W R Swinburn 9/2: -3334: Again made most: see 2048. 36
2327 PLEASING PROSPECT [4] 3-8-11 M Birch 14/1: 00-0300: Led briefly 3f out: see 1511.   24
1167 SINDUR [5] 3-8-11 M Wigham 50/1: 0-00: Late prog after abs: see   08
-- Rideside [3] 8-11   -- Santo Boy [6] 9-0   1104 Still Marching [1] 8-11
2042 Something Similar [10] 9-0   2176 Merseyspeed [13] 8-11
2085 Togdale [9] 9-0
12 ran   1½,1½,2½,6,7   (Sheikh Mohammed)   J Dunlop Arundel, Sussex

2401 LEVY BOAD APPRENTICES' STAKES   £1142   1m 1f   Yielding 82 -36 Slow

2339 HAMPER [7] (W Hastings Bass) 3-8-6 D Gibson(5) 7/2: -431: 3 ch g Final Straw -
Great Care (Home Guard) Made a quick reappearance and led below dist, pushed out in an app
stks at Ripon: eff over 8/9f on gd/firm and yldg grd: acts on any track.   34
2061 HIGHEST PEAK [11] (G Pritchard Gordon) 3-8-6 S Childs 5/4 FAV: 0-23202: Well bckd:
led briefly 2f out, not quicken: could win small maiden race: see 512, 140.   30
2093 RUSTLING [3] (D Arbuthnot) 4-8-11 J Leech 25/1: 320-003: Stayed on well and seems
to be returning to form: eff over 9/10f on any going.   25
2340 MANABEL [1] (S Bowring) 4-8-11 N Carson(5) 16/1: 0000024: Led 3f out: stays 9f:see 2340. 22
2126 FOREVER TINGO [4] 4-9-0 A Corney(5) 20/1: 0000030: Some late prog: see 2126.   10
1830 LADY LAMB [6] 3-8-3 S Williams(5) 11/1: 000-000: Lightly raced filly who was rated 35
as a juv tho' has shown little this term.   05
1953 KANGAROO [13] 3-8-3(bl) A Riding(5) 5/1: 033-000: Made most: sn btn: see 1446.   00
993 Record Haulier [14] 9-0   1951 Surprise Attack [9] 9-0   -- The Fink Sisters [12] 8-3
379 Zeelandia [5] 8-3   -- Golden Secret [2] 8-11   1703 Sky Mariner [10] 9-6
-- Moon Melody [8] 9-9
14 ran   1,½,½,5,1,1½   (Mrs M McCalmont)   W Hastings Bass Newmarket

---

SANDOWN   Saturday August 30th   Righthand, Stiff, Galloping Track

Official Going Given As GOOD

2402 LADBROKE HOLIDAYS HANDICAP 4YO+ 0-50   £3158   5f   Good/Firm 25 +07 Fast   [50]

836 GEORGE WILLIAM [8] (M Mccourt) 5-8-7 B Thomson 16/1: 0-22301: 5 b h Import - Bloomsbury
Girl (Weepers Boy) Fair h'capper: despite fair abs, led inside final 1f, ridden out in quite
fast run h'cap at Sandown Aug 30: in gd form in '85 winning h'caps at Wolverhampton (2),
Doncaster and Ripon: very eff at 5f, stays 6f well: acts on firm and yldg grd and on any trk:
seems a genuine sort and does well when fresh.   40
2245 JACKIE BLAIR [2] (M Mccormack) 4-7-10(bl) R Street 14/1: 3000032: Made most: kept
on: running well: see 2245, 211: acts on any going and does well at Warwick.   26
2258 BRIDGE STREET LADY [7] (J Bosley) 5-9-12 G Baxter 20/1: 2012003: Chance final 1f:
not btn far under 9-12 and carries weight really well: see 477, 327.   53
1385 LOCHTILLUM [9] (J D Home) 7-9-6 R Cochrane 14/1: 0010004: Hdwy, not much room
final 1f: gd effort after abs: see 836.   47
2160 DEPUTY HEAD [3] 6-9-3 P Waldron 11/1: 1330030: Going on fin: another gd effort: see 1060 44
*2160 DERRY RIVER [5] 5-8-10(vis)(7ex) C Rutter(3) 6/1 JT.FAV: 0000010: Sn prom: running
well: see 2160.   36
2204 CREE BAY [12] 7-9-10 W Carson 6/1 JT.FAV: 0041100: Hdwy when shut in final 1f:see 1777.   00
1889 WOODFOLD [6] 5-9-2 B Rouse 15/2: 0-13000: Fdd final 1f: fin 8th: see 986.   00
2258 GLEN KELLA MANX [11] 5-9-1 A Mcglone 8/1: 0001000: Not btn that far in 9th: see 2021.   00
2289 DURHAM PLACE [13] 4-9-9 G Starkey 7/1: 4300040: Speed over 3f: see 877, 1268.   00
2151 Duck Flight [10] 8-13   1385 Axe Valley [4] 9-8   +2256 Captains Bidd [1] 7-7(5ex)(7oh)
13 ran   ½,1,shthd,nk,½,½,1,nk,½   (Clarence Naden)   M Mccourt Letcombe Regis, Oxon.

2403 SPORTSMAN CLUB HANDICAP 3YO+ 0-35   £3776   1m 6f   Good/Firm 25 +05 Fast   [35]

782 ELPLOTINO [10] (R Williams) 4-10-0 A Kimberley 20/1: 100-301: 4 br c Bustino -
Explosiva (Explodent) Fair h'capper: despite abs, made most gamely under 10-0 in quite fast
run h'cap at Sandown Aug 30: in '85 won at Sandown, Yarmouth (2) and Ayr: eff at 14f, stays
14f well: acts on firm: likes some give: seems suited by forcing tactics on a gall trk: does well fresh 46
-- FLOYD [3] (D Elsworth) 6-9-12 S Cauthen 7/1: 04200-2: Led/dsptd lead: kept on well

and just btn: fine seasonal debut: in '85 won h'caps at Newbury and Kempton (first time out):
also a very useful hurdler: eff at 14f, stays 17f: acts on fast and soft grd and on any trk:
best out in front and does well when fresh.   43
1085 ITTIHAAD [1] (C Benstead) 3-8-11 B Rouse 14/1: -030233: Abs: al up there and ran
on well: gd effort and was suited by today's 14f trip: acts on gd/firm and soft and a
galloping trk: may gain his first success soon.   38
*2240 VINTAGE PORT [4] (R Akehurst) 4-9-12(6ex) T Quinn 8/1: 0002214: Cl.up 4th: in
grand form: see 2240.   40
2093 LISMORE [15] 4-8-11 B Thomson 11/1: 0004-00: Ran on well and not btn far: well
suited by today's 14f: see 2093: acts on any track.   24
2211 HYOKIN [5] 4-8-10(vis) T Williams 25/1: 3213200: Ev ch 3f out: see 1359.   19
2134 PEARLY KING [12] 3-9-0 G Starkey 15/2: -400200: Fdd str: twice below 1236 (12f).   00
*2134 ALACAZAM [2] 4-8-1(4ex) W Carson 11/4 FAV: 3000110: Well bckd disappointment: btr 2134. 00
2134 Alsiba [17] 8-8   *2152 Dark Sirona [16] 8-8(6ex)
2164 Italian Sunrise [13] 9-5   -- Barnbrook Again [8] 9-4
2087 Reform Princess [9] 8-7(bl)   1945 Asticot [7] 8-5
1871 Pinwiddie [11] 8-5   2111 Music Minstrel [14] 7-11
2075 Taras Chariot [6] 7-7
17 ran   nk,1,¾,¾,2½   (Michael Thomas)   R Williams Newmarket

2404 INTERNATIONAL LEIS. GRP HCAP 3YO 0-60   £5926   1m 2f Good/Firm 25 -08 Slow   [54]

2131 RATTLE ALONG [7] (P Walwyn) 3-8-9 S Cauthen 13/2: 0-01021: 3 b f Tap On Wood - Eulalle
(Queen's Hussar) Useful filly: al prom and led inside final 2f under press, in a val 3yo h'cap
at Sandown Aug 30: earlier won a 3yo fillies event at Wolverhampton: eff at 10f, should
be suited by 12f: acts on a sound surf and a gall trk: genuine.   46
1755 HARD AS IRON [10] (P Haslam) 3-8-4 T Williams 11/2 FAV: -411122: Prom, kept on
well: in grand form this season: likes a gall trk: see 1284.   39
1998 MARSHAL MACDONALD [1] (W Holden) 3-8-9 B Thomson 11/1: -004403: Ran on really well
final 1f, despite having to change his position: stays 10f well: can find a h'cap, but
seems a tricky ride: acts on fast grd and likes Sandown. might appreciate 12f.   43
2049 STRAIGHT THROUGH [3] (J Winter) 3-8-8 B Rouse 16/1: 1221004: Kept on well: not btn
far: see 1233.   41
*2131 KICK THE HABIT [2] 3-8-6(6ex) G Baxter 13/2: 0000210: Beat the winner in 2131.   36
1713 PRINCESS NAWAAL [6] 3-9-4 W Carson 6/1: 4-11000: Well bckd: made most: best 925 (8.5f)   47
+2053 WARM WELCOME [9] 3-8-5(bl) R Hills 7/1: -003010: Well below 2053 and had ev ch.   00
919 HOMME DAFFAIRE [4] 3-8-6 P Waldron 15/2: 00-0100: No show after abs: best 459 (yldg)   00
1956 Liam [8] 9-7   2331 Emrys [5] 8-10   2182 Stillou [11] 8-0
11 ran   ¾,¾,¾,1½,¾,nk   (O Waller)   P Walwyn Lambourn, Berks.

2405 BERNARD SUNLEY SELLING STAKES 2YO   £3662   7f   Good/Firm 25 -27 Slow

2218 SWIFT PURCHASE [10] (R Hannon) 2-9-1 G Starkey 20/1: 0010401: 2 ch c Camden Town -
Miss Maverick (Vilmorin) Showed impr form, led over 2f out, under press for a hd success in a
2yo seller at Sandown (bought in 4000 gns): earlier won a similar event at Folkestone: related
to sev winners: stays a stiff 7f: acts on gd and fast ground: has won in blinkers:
best when up with the pace.   35
2177 MOUNT VENUS [16] (G Balding) 2-8-8 S Cauthen 12/1: 0402: Ran on well final 1f but
the post came just too soon: certain to find a seller: will be suited by 1m: acts on fast
ground and likes a galloping track.   27
*2045 PARKLANDS BELLE [2] (M Haynes) 2-8-12 P Cook 14/1: 2402013: Chance final 1f: in
good form: stays 7f: see 2045: seems to act on any track.   27
2334 QUE PASA [17] (P Haslam) 2-8-11 T Williams 9/4 FAV: 024: Heavily bckd: ridden to
chall 2f out: fdd final 1f: btr 2334, see 2032.   21
2178 JOSIE SMITH [14] 2-8-12 W Carson 10/1: 010030: Ev ch str: fair eff: see 2178.   18
1495 TIPTREE [5] 2-8-11 P Robinson 16/1: 0000: Abs: nearest fin: dropped to selling
company today: will be suited by 1m and can be backed to find a similar event.   17
2177 MORNING FLOWER [4] 2-8-11 R Cochrane 11/4: 032F20: Heavily bckd: came to chall
when badly hmpd over 1f out: unlucky! See 2177.   00
2218 ROYAL RABBLE [6] 2-8-12 A Mcglone 10/1: 2310000: Mkt drifter, no show: btr 2218.   00
2270 Pathias [7] 8-11   2177 Young Centurion [1] 8-11(bl)
2097 Telegraph Folly [3] 9-1   1803 Akrotiri Bay [8] 8-11
1119 Pilgrim Prince [11] 8-11(VIS)   2159 Rarely At Odds [13] 8-11
2045 Ripster [15] 8-11   -- Willy Jump [18] 8-11   2180 Avenmore Star [12] 8-8
2020 Grenville Lass [9] 8-8
18 ran   hd,2,2½,2,shthd   (Introgroup Holdings Ltd)   R Hannon East Evereleigh, Wilts

2406 LADIES MEMORIAL STAKES   £1761   1m 2f Good/Firm 25 -12 Slow

1383 EFFIGY [4] (G Harwood) 4-10-3 Amanda Harwood 7/4: 21-0001: 4 b c Busted - Lady Segrave
(Tudor Music) Useful colt: returned to form, making ev yard, readily, in a ladies race at
Sandown: in excellent form in '85, winning at Leicester, Goodwood and Doncaster and never
fin out of the frame: eff at 10f, stays 12f well: acts on any ground and on any trk: best
out in front: genuine and may win a h'cap.   61
*1994 LOCH SEAFORTH [1] (H Cecil) 3-10-0 Franca Vittadini 8/13 FAV: -211112: Chased leader
final 2f: 12l clear 3rd and is most consistent: see 1994.   61

*2190 MARSH HARRIER [7] (A Moore) 5-10-6 Candy Moore 12/1: 0200413: Not disgraced: in fine
form: see 2190 (h'cap).   39
2273 THE FOOTMAN [6] (R Stubbs) 4-10-3 Linda Stubbs(3) 50/1: 0004004: Prom, ev ch: see 1325.   29
2098 WINTER PALACE [2] 4-10-3 Joanna Winter 50/1: -000000: Mostly 2nd: best eff this term
and likes Sandown: see 1223.   28
2182 LIBERATED GIRL [5] 6-10-0 Kate Morris(2) 100/1: -000: Impossible task for this
lightly raced mare.   05
2017 Irish Hero [8] 10-3   1941 Soft Shoe Shuffle [9] 9-7
--   Corn Noil [3] 9-4
9 ran   4,12,2,shthd,8   (K Abdulla)   G Harwood Pulborough, Sussex

2407 EBF HEART OF VARIETY STKS 2YO   £3616   1m   Good/Firm 25 +09 Fast

1855 PORT HELENE [1] (W Hern) 2-8-8 W Carson 9/4: 21: 2 ch f Troy - Docklands (On Your
Mark) Very promising filly: made almost all, staying on well for a hd win in a fast run
2yo stks at Sandown: first time out a fine 2nd to Oisifa at Goodwood: stays 1m really well,
will be suited by further: cost 400,000 gns as a yearling and is a half sister to lightly
raced 3yo Thorcastle: seems suited by front running on a gall trk: sure to rate more highly
and win more races.   59
*2105 BROTHER PATRICK [12] (L Piggott) 2-9-1 R Cochrane 15/2: 3012: Ran on most gamely,
but was al held by the winner: grand effort and 6l clear 3rd: well suited by 1m and sure
to win again soon: see 2105.   65
--   REFERENCE POINT [14] (H Cecil) 2-8-11 S Cauthen 11/10 FAV: 3: Very heavily bckd debutant:
kept on well final 2f and will improve greatly for this run: highly regarded colt who is
a half brother to 3yo winner Top Range: should be suited by middle dist: acts on gd/firm
and a gall trk: will retrieve losses very soon. well clear rest.   52
2225 ALASKAN [7] (C Brittain) 2-8-11 G Baxter 33/1: 004: Stayed on final 2f, tho' no
threat: steadily improving colt who should be suited by 1m and further: acts on gd/firm
ground: on the upgrade and can find a race.   32
2239 DANCER TO FOLLOW [9] 2-8-11 P Bloomfield 50/1: 000: Prom most: best effort yet
from this quite cheaply acquired colt: prob stays 1m: acts on gd/firm.   31
1587 MANDALAY PRINCE [11] 2-8-11 B Rouse 50/1: 000: Never nearer, but is making improvement:
half brother to a staying winner and will be suited by 1m and further: on the upgrade.   28
--   OLD MAESTRO [5] 2-8-11 G Starkey 16/1: 0: Slow start and nearest fin on debut: looks
sure to improve: American bred colt who cost $275,000.   00
1518 Spanish Connection [2] 8-11   --   Crespin [3] 8-11
1518 Keecagee [6] 8-11(BL)   2036 Lightfoot Prince [13] 8-11
--   Marley Monarch [8] 8-11   1914 Laena [4] 8-8
1801 Wind And Wave [10] 8-8
14 ran   hd,6,10,½,1½,½   (Sheikh Mohammed)   W Hern East Ilsley, Berks

2408 VARIETY CLUB MAIDEN STAKES 3YO   £1959   1m 2f   Good/Firm 25 -06 Slow

1284 TOP RANGE [6] (M Jarvis) 3-9-0 R Cochrane 4/1: -030221: 3 b c High Top - Home On
The Range (Habitat) Gained a deserved success, led over 1f out, gamely, in a 3yo mdn at
Sandown Aug 30: placed sev times prev: very eff at 10f: acts on soft, likes good and firm grd:
suited by a gall trk: genuine. does well when fresh.   50
2148 NORTHERN AMETHYST [3] (D Elsworth) 3-9-0 S Cauthen 11/4 FAV: 3220232: Well bckd:
ev ch final 2f, but again found one too good: see 2148, 1642.   48
806 SEA POWER [12] (W Hern) 3-8-11 W Carson 13/2: 03-03: Abs: al there: fair effort:
stays 10f: see 806.   43
739 KEEPCALM [9] (G Wragg) 3-9-0 P Waldron 20/1: -0404: Abs: nearest fin and will do
better next time: seems suited by a stiff 10f: acts on gd/firm grd and a gall trk.   43
2170 SARONICOS [7] 3-9-0 P Robinson 6/1: 3223030: Led 4f out: see 170, 739.   39
1469 MIRAGE DANCER [4] 3-9-0 S Whitworth 5/1: 0234240: Ev ch str: abs since btr 1469.   33
1886 MUSICAL YOUTH [5] 3-9-0 P Cook 10/1: 4-20200: No show in 7th: btr 1588, see 459.   00
1291 Raf [1] 9-0   2054 Benarosa [8] 8-11   806 Almutanabbi [11] 9-0
847 Poro Boy [2] 9-0   -- La Shaka [10] 8-11   937 No Can Tell [13] 8-11
13 ran   1,1,2,2,3,½   (V Rabin)   M Jarvis Newmarket

Official Going Given As GOOD

2409 PLUMBCENTER GRUNDFOR PUMP MDN 3YO　　£685　5f　Good/Firm 36 -06 Slow

1627 HARRY HULL [7] (M W Easterby) 3-9-0 T Lucas 8/11 FAV: -000041: 3 ch c Sagaro - Polly
Peacham (Singing Strand): Reverted to the minimum trip & landed some gd bets, led close home
under press in a 3yo mdn at Hamilton: half brother to useful sprinter Able Albert: has run
several times over 1m but seems best over 5/6f: acts on gd/firm & soft grnd & on any trk.　22
2367 GRANGE FARM LADY [11] (M Tompkins) 3-8-11 M Rimmer 5/1: -0302: Led 2f out, caught close
home though 5L clear of rem: seems to act on any trk: see 2186.　16
2268 HOBOURNES KATIE [9] (R Hollinshead) 3-8-11 S Perks 20/1: 0000003: Late prog: see 2268.　02
2312 TOLLYS ALE [8] (I Matthews) 3-8-11 G Dickie 8/1: -430004: No real threat: see 2312.　00
2139 MAYBE JAYNE [6] 3-8-11 C Dwyer 20/1: 0000000: Never beyond mid-div: btr in 1505.　00
1678 DAISY STAR [10] 3-8-11 M Fry 14/1: 0-00000: Close up over ½way: has been tried over
various dists this term though has yet to trouble the judge: seems best on gd/firm grnd.　00
2210 FOUNDRY FLYER [5] 3-8-11 J Carr(7) 9/1: -040400: Wknd into 9th: much btr in 2106.　00
2268 Motor Master [1] 9-0(BL)　　　　1734 Musical Aid [3] 8-11
2268 Spring Garden [8] 8-11(bl)　　　2322 Petencore [4] 9-0(VIS)
11 ran　½,5,½,1½,2,½　　(M W Easterby)　　M W Easterby Sheriff Hutton, Yorks

2410 PLUMBCENTER MYSON HEATING MDN 2YO　　£685　5f　Good/Firm 36 -16 Slow

-2301 PRINT [10] (W Hastings Bass) 2-9-0 Paul Eddery 11/10 FAV: 21: 2 ch c Sharpo - Picture
(Lorenzaccio): Comfortably justified fav. led dist & ran on strongly to win a 2yo mdn at
Hamilton: just denied by Vivaldi on his recent debut at Wolverhampton: speedily bred colt
who acts on gd/firm & yld grnd & on a stiff trk.　40+
2270 SUPREME STATE [1] (P Makin) 2-9-0 D Price 4/1: 0032: Led below dist, not qckn close
home: in gd form: seems to act on any trk: see 2270.　32
-- ENTIRE [2] (M Prescott) 2-9-0 G Duffield 7/2: 3: Led over ½way, hmpd below dist &
ran on again close home: cost 11,000 gns & is a half brother to several winners incl winning
juvenile Padro: will stay further: acts on gd/firm grnd & on a stiff trk: seems sure to impr.　24
2323 LEVEN LASS [7] (I Vickers) 2-8-11 R Vickers(7) 20/1: 0034: Front rank most: see 2323.　16
2100 MR BERKELEY [6] 2-9-0 M Birch 8/1: 0000: Al up there: see 1333 & 254.　17
1612 DENSBEN [3] 2-9-0 S Perks 20/1: 0440: Never nearer after slow start: see 1612.　16
2281 Not So Silly [9] 9-0　1611 Miss Display [5] 8-11　1872 Berthelier [8] 9-0　627 Arishan [4] 9-0
10 ran　1½,2,1½,½,nk　　(Lord Porchester)　　W Hastings Bass Newmarket

2411 SOUTER OF STIRLING HANDICAP 3YO+ 0-35　　£1973　6f　Good/Firm 36 -09 Slow　[35]

2397 WARTHILL LADY [17] (M Brittain) 4-8-0(3ow) K Darley 14/1: 0000401: 4 b f Hittite Glory -
Suffice (Faberge II): Was having her third race in a week & led 2f out, gamely in a h'cap at
Hamilton: sole success previously came in a similar race at Ayr last term: best form over
5/6f on firm & yld grnd: well suited by a testing course.　15
2204 THRONE OF GLORY [9] (D Chapman) 5-9-8 D Nicholls 10/1: 0044002: Fin well: just btn.　35
2340 TIT WILLOW [14] (S Wiles) 4-8-5(bl) Paul Eddery 16/1: 2120343: Not btn far: gd run: see 828　16
-2256 FOOLISH TOUCH [11] (K Stone) 4-9-4(vis) C Dwyer 5/1 FAV: 0044024: Another gd effort.　28
2264 TRADE HIGH [7] 7-8-8 R Vickers(7) 25/1: 0040100: Had ev ch: best in 2126 (7f tight trk)　13
2256 STONEYDALE [20] 4-9-10 G Duffield 13/2: 0000200: Al up there: see 2033 & 734.　29
2295 SHARLIES WIMPY [6] 7-10-0 J Carroll(7) 10/1: 0240000: Sn in rear: btr in 2295: see 520.　28
2397 GOLDEN GUILDER [10] 3-8-12(bl) T Lucas 7/1: 313333U: Under press when stumbled &
u.r. inside dist: see 1959 & 947.　00
1648 Jarrovian [13] 9-5　　　2126 Tree Fella [4] 7-7　　2277 Miami Dolphin [5] 8-0
2295 Cumbrian Dancer [3] 9-0(vis)　-- Royal Aries [2] 7-9　1983 Bold Rowley [19] 8-0(4ow)
2086 Tiddlyeyetye [12] 7-8(bl)　　2086 King Cole [8] 7-10(bl)　2322 Tradesman [16] 7-8(1ow)(3oh)
2124 Grand Queen [15] 7-8(1ow)(5oh) 2012 Off Your Mark [18] 7-8　2154 Greetland Dancer [1] 8-0
20 ran　½,½,½,2,shhd,1½,hd　　(M Brittain)　　M Brittain Warthill, Yorks

2412 PLUMBCENTER PEGLER/SUNVIC SELLER　　£784　1m 3f　Good/Firm 36 -08 Slow

2360 CHABLISSE [4] (R Whitaker) 3-8-2 D Mckeown 7/4 JT FAV: 0310441: 3 b f Radetzky -
Late Idea (Tumble Wind): Dropped in class & led over 2f out, readily in a seller at
Hamilton (bought in 3,000 gns): earlier won a selling h'cap at Beverley: half sister to
winning sprinter Tuxford Hideaway: best form over 10/11f on gd or faster grnd: likes a stiff trk　22
+1979 MAFTIR [6] (N Callaghan) 4-9-1(bl) T Lucas 15/2: 000012: Led briefly over 2f out,
no ch with winner though ran a gd race over this much lngr trip: a winner over 6f in 1979.　17
1617 SANA SONG [3] (C Parker) 3-8-1(1ow) S Webster 25/1: 2000003: Ran on same pace:
probably stays 11f though best when 2nd to Taranga (rated 28) in 134 (6f, hvy).　06
2008 OUR ANNIE [1] (E Carter) 3-7-11 N Carlisle 33/1: -000004: Yet to show any worthwhile form　00
2335 SHOWDANCE [5] 3-9-0 A Culhane(7) 14/1: 0-00030: Led briefly 3f out: see 2335 (1m).　00
2101 MUSICAL WILL [7] 4-9-1(bl) G Duffield 6/1: 0403020: Never dngr: btr in 2101 (12f).　00
1839 REFORMED HABIT [2] 4-9-1 N Connorton 10/1: 3013300: No threat in 7th: btr in 1703 (1m).　00
-- NORTHERN RIVER [8] 4-9-4(bl) C Dwyer 7/4 JT FAV: 00000-0: Clear ldr till wkn quickly
early in str: formerly trained by J Dunlop, won a valuable stakes at Newbury in '84 &
kept good company thro'out last term: well suited by middle dists: acts on gd/firm & yld
grnd: wears bl: should certainly win a seller with this race under his belt.　00
8 ran　2½,½,4,6,nk,8　　(E Wilkinson)　　R Whitaker Scarcroft, Yorkshire

2413 WIN WITH THE TOTE MAIDEN 3YO+   £863   1m   Good/Firm 36 +09 Fast

2264 SHARONS ROYALE [4] (R Whitaker) 3-8-6 K Bradshaw(5) 9/2: 0032441: 3 ch g Royal Match -
Rose Amber (Amber Rama): Gained a deserved win after a succession of placings, led below dist
& driven out in quite a fast run mdn at Hamilton: eff over 8/10f on firm & yld grnd: runs
well on a stiff trk.   26
2394 NORTHERN GUNNER [2] (W Jarvis) 3-8-6 A Mackay 5/1: -043032: Fin well: stays 1m: see 239422
2027 BROADHURST [6] (J Etherington) 3-8-3(vis) M Wood 7/1: 0-03003: Led over 3f out, no
extra when let down: seems to act on any trk: see 1626.   14
1677 DARLING DADDY [3] (C Thornton) 3-8-3 J Bleasdale 12/1: -04: Ran on same pace: lightly
rcd filly who promises to stay further than 1m: acts on gd/firm grnd & on an undulating trk.   06
2152 THE HOUGH [11] 5-9-0 A Shoults(5) 6/1: -04400: Needs further: see 770.   09
2085 COMMITMENT [8] 4-9-0 D Nicholls 14/1: 0000-00: Rated 38 early last season & has
been lightly raced this term: eff over 7/8f on firm & yld grnd & acts on any trk.   05
2189 FLYING ZIAD [13] 3-8-6 Paul Eddery 5/2 FAV: 00-4000: Fdd into 9th: see 2104.   00
2401 Zeelandia [7] 8-3   1981 Minders Man [1] 9-0(bl)
1677 Princess Bella [14] 8-11(BL)   --   Reliable Vynz [10] 9-0
2264 Manix [9] 9-0   2141 Brandon Grey [5] 8-11(bl)
487 Cricket House [12] 8-6
14 ran 1½,1½,4,shhd,1½   (W Birch)   R Whitaker Scarcroft, Yorkshire

2414 PLUMBCENTER BARTOL PLASTICS HCAP 0-35   £2043   1m   Good/Firm 36 +12 Fast   [27]

2264 HELLO GYPSY [20] (C Tinkler) 5-9-4 W Goodwin(7) 12/1: 0-21301: 5 b g Tumble Wind -
Shirotae (Florescence): Made steady prog to lead inside dist in quite a fast run h'cap at
Hamilton: earlier won a similar race over this C/D & clearly loves this testing course: in
'85 won an amateur riders event at Warwick: very eff over 1m on gd & firm grnd: acts on
any trk, though runs particularly well at Hamilton.   27
*2264 QUALITAIRESS [18] (K Stone) 4-8-0(vis) P Burke(7) 9/1: 3022012: In fine form: see 2264.   06
2104 HOPTONS CHANCE [3] (S Wiles) 5-8-0 M Fry 10/1: 0000243: Never nearer: see 1839.   04
2264 GOOD N SHARP [7] (G Calvert) 5-8-0 J Lowe 12/1: 00-2004: Led after ½way: see 1766.   01
2282 NATIVE HABITAT [12] 3-9-3 W Woods(3) 7/1 FAV: 4133330: Al up there: see 2282.   25
2340 BIT OF A STATE [16] 6-8-12 D Mckeown 16/1: 0000000: Ran on too late: see 611.   11
1800 GODS LAW [13] 5-8-11 Julie Bowker(7) 10/1: 2130200: No threat in 9th: see 1417.   00
2184 KOOKYS PET [15] 3-8-7(bl) A Mackay 8/1: 0000040: Al mid-div: btr in 2184 (sharp trk).   00
2066 Try Scorer [9] 9-1   2303 Warplane [17] 9-9   1698 Sillitoe [1] 9-1
2102 Cadenette [19] 8-7   2309 Swiftspender [2] 7-12   2109 Strictly Business [8] 7-11
2274 Arabian Blues [4] 8-9   1813 Virajendra [5] 8-7(bl)
2340 Janes Brave Boy [6] 8-12   2342 Tollys Tonic [10] 8-8(BL)
606 Nipknowes [11] 8-9(1ow)   2076 Barracuda Bay [14] 8-13(BL)
20 ran ½,1½,1½,hd,nk,hd   (M Battle)   C Tinkler Malton, Yorks

2415 PLUMBCENTER SELKIRK FLUE HCAP 0-35   £1467   1m 4f Good/Firm 36 -26 Slow   [25]

2240 BENS BIRDIE [4] (M Tompkins) 6-8-12 A Mackay 11/8 FAV: 0413-21: 6 ch g Track Spare -
Gold Topaz (Goldhill): Landed some good bets, led below dist, comfortably in a h'cap at
Hamilton: successful over this C/D in '85 & in '84 won at Hamilton: eff over 12f, stays 14f
well: acts on gd/firm & hvy grnd & likes a stiffish trk: should win again.   16+
2267 GREED [7] (Denys Smith) 5-9-7 L Charnock 10/1: 4324042: Rarely out of the money this
term but has not won for sometime: see 1185.   22
2273 MOON JESTER [5] (M Usher) 6-8-12 D Mckay 9/2: 4000033: Not btn far: gd effort: see 349.   12
697 LUCKY HUMBUG [8] (W Pearce) 3-8-7 N Connorton 20/1: 00-2224: Abs: onepaced: see 697 & 365.14
2054 RACING DEMON [6] 4-7-13 J Carr(3) 25/1: 3000000: Late prog: see 2054.   00
2175 WESTRAY [10] 4-9-3(BL) S Perks 7/1: 4040300: Bl first time: al mid-div: see 225.   11
2175 ICEN [3] 8-8-12 Paul Eddery 8/1: /100030: Led briefly 2f out: fin 7th: see 2175.   00
282 Wise Cracker [1] 9-3   1271 Ishkhara [9] 8-7   2267 Common Farm [11] 9-2
2337 Apple Wine [12] 8-9
11 ran ½,nk,1½,½,nk   (Mrs Anna Tompkins)   M Tompkins Newmarket

Official Going Given As GOOD

2416 ADDITIONAL APP. H'CAP (0-35) 3YO   £916   5f   Good/Firm 25 -05 Slow   [41]

2024 RESTLESS RHAPSODY [11] (K Brassey) 3-8-7(bl) A Whitehall 10/1: 2404031: 3 ch g Young
Generation - Bohemian Rhapsody (On Your Mark): Made much, ridden out in a 3yo app. h'cap at
Windsor: placed several times previously this term: in '85 was most consistent, winning at
Catterick: very eff at 5f on a sharp trk: acts on firm & yld grnd & seems best in bl,
making the running.   28
1571 MADAM MUFFIN [14] (J Bethell) 3-8-3 B Lynch(3) 12/1: 2002002: Al up there: btn ½l:
lightly raced since 1066 & seems equally eff at 5/6f.   23
2106 MUSIC REVIEW [6] (M Tompkins) 3-8-2 B Cook(5) 11/1: -222203: Dsptd lead: gd effort:see 910.18
2382 CRESTA LEAP [10] (R Hannon) 3-8-12 R Perham(5) 20/1: 2400004: Ran on final 1f: best 431.   22
2245 ASTARTE [2] 3-8-0 Abigail Richards 9/4 FAV: 4000320: Prom, much btr 2245.   06

*2312 SAY PARDON [5] 3-9-7(7ex) Dale Gibson 15/2: -220010: Well below 2312 (yld).   26
2256 MOZART [15] 3-8-0 A Riding 6/1: -000440: Mkt drifter: no show in 7th: see 2256, 2120.   00
1836 NORTHERN LAD [9] 3-8-2(BL) P Francis 11/2: 002020U: Saddle slipped, u.r. over 1f out:
bl first time: best 1584.   00

2210 Jacqui Joy [3] 7-7(5oh)		2106 Ardent Partner [8] 8-7
2313 Tina Rosa [4] 7-7(8oh)	1971 Alice Hill [13] 7-11	2224 Websters Feast [7] 8-8
2046 Dalsaan Bay [1] 7-11	2088 Persian Bazaar [12] 7-7(BL)(6oh)	
15 ran ½,1½,2,1½,½,shhd,nk	(Mrs M Haggas)	K Brassey Upper Lambourn, Berks

2417 BELMEAD SELLING H'CAP (0-25) 3YO   £907   6f   Good/Firm 25 -05 Slow   [22]

2055 EASTERN OASIS [2] (E Alston) 3-8-4 T Williams 9/1: -004001: 3 b g Anax - Casbar Lady
(Native Bazaar): Sn prom & led final 1f under press in a selling h'cap at Windsor (bought
in 820 gns): winning 2yo at Hamilton: eff over 5f, stays 6f: best on gd & fast grnd though
acts on any trk.   06
2370 THE UTE [10] (L Bower) 3-9-7(bl) R Guest 6/1: 0120422: Led over 1f out: just btn &
4L clear of rem: in fine form: see 2370.   22
2238 NAUGHTY NIGHTY [18] (M Tompkins) 3-8-13 R Curant 14/1: 0000003: Dsptd lead: see 2189.   04
845 CHEPSTOWED [13] (D H Jones) 3-8-10(bl) D Williams(7) 12/1: 0-12004: Ch inside final
2f: abs: see 93 (soft).   01
2088 PADDINGTON BELLE [19] 3-8-9(vis) S Whitelam(7) 7/1: 0000030: Kept on under pressure.   00
2060 FINDON MANOR [15] 3-9-5(bl) R Cochrane 9/1: 0000000: Prom most: see 1927, 760.   06
2027 BY CHANCE [5] 3-9-1 A Mcglone 8/1: 0-04000: Fin 8th: see 1406.   00
2033 BELLEPHERON [14] 3-9-3 P Waldron 11/2: -044400: Dropped in class: best 1316 (7f).   00
2088 WINNING FORMAT [9] 3-8-12 Pat Eddery 5/1 FAV: 0000020: Prom most: btr 2088 (C/D).   00

2120 Cracon Girl [7] 9-3	2088 Absolutely Bonkers [17] 8-7	
2060 Spanish Intent [4] 8-5		2370 Fancy Pages [16] 8-11
-- Young Lucy [6] 8-11	2024 La Divina 0 8-7	2088 Someway [11] 8-6
2060 Sea Venom [8] 7-11(bl)		2210 Thai Sky [12] 8-3(bl)
18 ran nk,4,shhd,½,1	(John Crossfield)	E Alston Preston, Lancs

2418 POTENTIAL STAYERS STAKES 2YO   £959   6f   Good/Firm 25 +09 Fast

-- SHADY HEIGHTS [16] (R Armstrong) 2-8-11 P Tulk 6/1: 1: 2 b c Shirley Heights -
Vaguely (Bold Lad): Very prom colt: nicely bckd & led well over 1f out, very easily in a fast
run 2yo stakes at Windsor: cost 110,000 gns as a yearling & is a half brother to the useful
2yo winner Top Ruler: eff at 6f, sure to be suited by 7f plus: acts on gd/firm grnd & an
easy trk & is certain to win more races.   64
2243 HOW VERY TOUCHING [5] (J Hindley) 2-8-11 M Hills 11/8 FAV: 22: Well bckd: led over
2f out: caught a tartar: can win soon: see 2243.   50
-- CASTLE IN THE AIR [6] (J Dunlop) 2-8-8 B Thomson 20/1: 3: Nearest fin & impr certain
from this stoutly bred filly: half sister to useful Rollrights & Rollfast: sure to be
suited by 7f plus: acts on a sound surface & can win soon.   45
-- NOBLE MINSTREL [2] (O Douieb) 2-8-11 R Machado 12/1: 4: Al front rank on racecourse
debut: will impr: cost $100,000: acts on gd/firm & can find a race.   47
2229 CRUSADE DANCER [8] 2-8-11 R Cochrane 7/2: 020: Made much: btr 2229.   39
-- POLLENATE [11] 2-8-11 Pat Eddery 8/1: 0: Never nearer: will come on for this racecourse debut: well bred sort who acts on gd/firm.   37
-- ROCK OF AGES [13] 2-8-8 W Carson 12/1: 0: Prom most on debut: sister to useful staying
winner Rough Stones: should be suited by middle dists next term: acts on gd/firm.   33
-- MILAN FAIR [14] 2-8-11 M Roberts 14/1: 0: Prom, fin 8th on racecourse debut: cost
92,000 gns as a yearling & should be suited by 7f/1m.   35

2089 Regal Rhythm [12] 8-8	2056 Fahad [1] 8-11	-- Yamrah [10] 8-8
2013 Ski Slope [9] 8-8	383 Mariko Gold [4] 8-8	-- Grunidad [3] 8-11
-- La Carabine [7] 8-8	-- Bamar Lad [15] 8-11	
16 ran 4,¾,½,4,1,½,nk	(George Tong)	R Armstrong Newmarket

2419 WINTER HILL E.B.F. STAKES   £2781   1m 2f   Good/Firm 25 +01 Fast

1823 SAMARID [2] (M Stoute) 3-8-13 W R Swinburn 7/1: 40-0101: 3 b c Blushing Groom -
Samata (Rheffic): Led final 1f, driven out to ddht in a stakes event at Windsor: earlier won
a Listed race at the Curragh: winning 2yo at Doncaster: eff at 1m, stays 10f: acts on gd
& firm grnd & on any trk.   76
1912 ESDALE [5] (J Tree) 3-8-5 Pat Eddery 13/8 FAV: 2011301: 3 b c Fabulous Dancer -
Esdee (Hail To Reason): Hvly bckd: made most & came again final 1f to ddht in a stakes event
at Windsor: earlier was an easy winner of 2 minor events over this C/D & clearly likes this
trk: half brother to a couple of winners: very eff at 10f, probably stays 12f: acts on firm
& yld grnd.   68
2206 OZOPULMIN [8] (L Cumani) 3-8-13 G Starkey 3/1: -10-123: Ev ch str: btr 2206, see 1702.   64
2404 LIAM [3] (M Ryan) 3-8-5 P Robinson 14/1: 0101404: Quick reapp: gd effort: see 1690.   54
-- GALESA [1] 3-7-11 T Williams 16/1: 00-0: No extra final 2f on seasonal debut: very
lightly raced filly who was a gd 5th to Janiski at Doncaster first time out: half sister to
2 winners: eff at 1m, probably stays 10f: should find a race.   38
653 KHOZDAR [7] 4-9-5 W Carson 10/3: 0120-30: Long abs: there 1m: see 653.   51

698 Quiet Riot [4] 9-5	2303 Kavaka [6] 9-0	935 Jacquette [9] 8-5(8ow)
9 ran ddht,7,½,4,hd	(H H Aga Khan)	M Stoute Newmarket
	(K Abdulla)	J Tree Beckhampton

2420 QUORTINA CHALL. CUP H'CAP (0-50) 3YO   £2675   1m 3f   Good/Firm 25 -27 Slow   [57]

*1939 WISHLON [5] (R Smyth) 3-9-8 Pat Eddery 4/1: 1010011: 3 b c Lyphard's Wish - Swiss
Swish (Wajima): Useful h'capper: defied top weight, led close home, gamely in a 3yo h'cap at
Windsor: earlier a winner of 2 h'caps again over this C/D & first time out won at Warwick:
eff at 10f, stays 12f: acts on firm & soft grnd & on any trk, though runs well on an easy
trk, especially Windsor.   62

*2093 SWEET ALEXANDRA [2] (J Shaw) 3-7-7(3oh) G Carter(0) 6/1: -43112: Led over 2f out, just
btn: in fine form & runs well here: see 2093.   32

2331 SAMANPOUR [8] (R J Houghton) 3-9-1(BL) S Cauthen 4/1: 1302033: Bl first time: running
consistently, but has been very busy this term: see 1130, 547.   51

2156 TENDER TYPE [6] (M Tompkins) 3-8-4 R Cochrane 11/10 FAV: 0012134: Hvly bckd: not
btn far but slightly disapp after 2156 (stiffer trk).   40

1315 CORRAN RIVER [3] 3-8-10 W Newnes 12/1: 402-140: Abs: fdd final 1f: fair effort.   40

2093 FULL SPEED AHEAD [7] 3-7-7(2oh) N Adams 11/1: -000020: Led after 7f: fdd: btr 2093 (C/D).17

2247 POUNELTA [1] 3-8-8 B Rouse 4/1: 4204040: Mkt drifter: made much: see 2247.   00

7 ran   nk,1½,hd,3,3   (K Abdulla)   R Smyth Epsom, Surrey

2421 RUSSELL NURSERY H'CAP 2YO   £1685   5f   Good/Firm 25 +03 Fast   [53]

2272 CHILIBANG [12] (J Dunlop) 2-8-6 W Carson 7/1: 4101: 2 ro c Formidable - Chili Girl
(Skymaster): Made ev yd, comfortably in a nursery h'cap at Windsor: disapp when tried in bl
last time, but earlier made all in a mdn at Nottingham: half brother to 6/7f winner Hot Case:
eff at 5f, stays 6f well: acts on gd & firm grnd & sharp/easy trk: seems best out in front.   42

2261 KYVERDALE [13] (M Ryan) 2-9-7 P Robinson 5/1: 201132: Al prom & is most consistent:
see 2261, 1683: carries weight well.   54

*2020 OUT ON A FLYER [14] (D Elsworth) 2-7-7(7oh) D Brown 14/1: 00213: Ch over 1f out:
gd run: see 2020 (seller).   20

2089 EBONY PRIDE [8] (Pat Mitchell) 2-8-5(1ow) J Reid 8/1: 040324: Late hdway: needs 6f?   32

-2011 MILLFAN [1] 2-8-6 M Wigham 14/1: 2320: Al up there: see 2011, 938.   27

2272 JABE MAC [10] 2-7-9 N Adams 9/1: 000130: Prom most: btr 2272 (6f): see 1832.   15

2167 BOIS DE BOULOGNE [17] 2-8-11(bl) T Ives 8/1: 0300320: Speed most: fin 7th: see 2167.   31

2081 DUTCH COURAGE [4] 2-9-1 Pat Eddery 9/1: 4331440: Ev ch in 8th: best 1585.   33

*2089 TISZTA SHAROK [15] 2-8-13 R Cochrane 4/1 FAV: 1P: P.u ½way: something amiss? see 2089.   00

2307 Nations Song [11] 8-1   2047 Make Or Mar [5] 8-13   2172 Tap The Baton [2] 8-4
2261 Jah Bless [9] 8-12   1576 Lady Behave [3] 8-13   2090 Goldorina [7] 8-2
2047 Enchanted Times [6] 9-1(vis)   1693 Segovian [16] 7-7
17 ran   ½,2½,hd,2½,nk,shhd,1   (Mrs H J Heinz)   J Dunlop Arundel, Sussex

2422 BRACKNELL STAKES   £959   1m 3f   Good/Firm 25 -46 Slow

+2030 ALL HASTE [14] (H Cecil) 3-9-3 S Cauthen 4/9 FAV: -2011: 3 b c Alleged - Hasty Dawn
(Pronto): Very useful colt: hacked up by 10L in a 3 & 4yo stakes at Windsor: will win much
btr races: see 2030.   66

690 SOLVENT [7] (M Jarvis) 3-8-9 T Ives 16/1: 4-2002: Long abs: kept on, but was never
going to get near the winner: seems to have had training problems: see 116.   28

1939 GIOVANNI [4] (S Mellor) 4-9-0 M Wigham 100/1: 3000-03: Rank outsider: prom most:
quite lightly raced mdn on the Flat who was formerly trained by M Prescott: acts on yld   10

2182 GEM MART [3] (C Holmes) 4-8-11 A Clark 100/1: 020-004: Impossible task: lightly rcd since967 00

1899 MSHATTA PALACE [8] 3-8-9 G Baxter 25/1: -00: Nearest fin: should do btr than this:
bred to be suited by 10/12f: acts on gd/firm.   00

-- LOCH BLUE [11] 4-9-0 P Simms(7) 100/1: 00-0: Some late hdway on seasonal debut: ran
only twice in '85.   00

1830 MOURADABIA [9] 3-8-9 Pat Eddery 5/1: 002-00: Wknd str: not stay trip: see 1830 (1m).   00

2275 FINAL SELECTION [6] 3-8-9 W Carson 4/1: 30-40: Mkt drifter: ran moderately: btr 2275.   00

2184 Mr Savvas [10] 8-9   2092 Sharp Reef [13] 8-6   978 Cuillin Sound [1] 8-9
845 Be Positive [12] 8-9   2072 Norham Castle [5] 8-9   1400 Silvermere Golf [2] 8-11
14 ran   10,4,2½,4,2   (Sheikh Mohammed)   H Cecil Newmarket

HAMILTON   Tuesday September 2nd   Righthanded, Undulating Track, Stiff Uphill Finish

Official Going Given As GOOD

2423 E.B.F. HALLEATH STAKES 2YO   £1223   6f   Good/Firm 26 -19 Slow

2325 PREMIER LAD [4] (W Pearce) 2-8-11 D Nicholls 8/1: 0301: 2 b c Tower Walk - Wigeon
(Divine Gift) Useful colt: led inside distance, gamely   in a 2yo stks at Hamilton: cost
8,400 gns as yearling and is a half brother to winning juv Ma Pierrette, who later won over
8/10f: very eff over 5/6f and should stay further in time: acts on firm and yldg ground and
is suited by a stiffish track.   50

-- SHARBLASK [19] (N Vigors) 2-8-11 P Cook 7/2 JT FAV: 2: Well bckd debutant: led below
dist, caught cl home tho' ran a sound race and looks a certain future winner: cost 10,500 gns
and is a half brother to sev winners: will stay further than 6f: acts on gd/firm and a stiff trk   48

2001 GREENS OLD MASTER [8] (W Jarvis) 2-8-11 R Cochrane 14/1: 203: Fin well: not btn
far: see 1573.   44
2167 ROCK MACHINE [10] (N Callaghan) 2-8-11 W Ryan 7/2 JT FAV: 44: Al up there and kept
on well over this extra furlong: on the upgrade and should win a small race soon: see 2167.   43
2043 SUPERCUBE [9] 2-8-8 Wendy Carter(6) 12/1: 04340: Ran on well: consistent: see 1225.   39
1972 COME ON OYSTON [18] 2-8-8 J Carroll(7) 25/1: 4330: Again al prom: eff over 5/6f: see 1296   34
--   ANAKA [11,] 2-8-8 K Darley 50/1: 0: Unfancied on debut: showed gd speed over ½ way
and will improve for this experience: acts on gd/firm ground.   30
1232 MUBDI [1] 2-8-11 A Murray 5/1: 230: Made much, hung right half way and hdd dist:
fin 8th and still a fair effort after a lengthy abs: will prob prefer a sharper trk: see 741   00
*2225 FALLING LEAF [12] 2-9-4 G Duffield 11/2: 010: Mkt drifter and much btr over 7f in 2225   00
1863 RED TWILIGHT [3] 2-8-11 D Mckeown 8/1: 340: Lost place after ¼ way: best 1681.   00
--   Long View [16] 8-8   --   Stray No More [13] 8-11
1225 Straight Edge [5] 8-11   2229 Golden Topaz [7] 8-11
2153 Sweet Mary Lou [20] 8-8   1764 Dolitino [15] 8-8
--   Happy Harriet [2] 8-8   2127 Oak Field [17] 8-8
18 ran   ¾,1,nk,½,2,1½   (Premier Properties Ltd)   W Pearce Hambleton, Yorks.

2424 ROYAL SCOTS DRAGOON GUARDS H'CAP 0-35   £1914   6f   Good/Firm 26 -04 Slow   [42]

2313 EASY LINE [6] (P Haslam) 3-8-8 T Williams 3/1 FAV: 1001431: 3 ch c Swing Easy -
Impromptu (My Swanee) Consistent sprinter: led below dist, comfortably, in a 3yo h'cap at
Hamilton: last month won an app h'cap at Newbury and first time out won a Nottingham maiden:
half brother to a couple of winners: very eff over 6/7f on fast ground, tho' does act on
yielding: suited by a stiff trk.   32
2143 BEECHWOOD COTTAGE [14] (A Bailey) 3-8-7(bl) R Cochrane 11/2: 1440202: Had ev ch:see 2120.23
+2139 ROYAL ROUSER [9] (F Lee) 3-8-8   (8ex) S Perks 10/1: -000013: Never nearer: see 2139.   23
*2268 COOPER RACING NAIL [7] (J Berry) 3-8-7   (5ex) J Carroll(7) 8/1: 2301114: Made most:
in grand form: see 2268.   22
*2055 BARGAIN PACK [10] 3-8-1 Julie Bowker(7) 8/1: 0023110: Going on fin: see 2055.   13
2038 AITCHANDOUBLEYOU [8] 3-8-6 T Quinn 16/1: 0400000: Dwelt: gd late prog: see 1093.   15
2322 LULLABY BLUES [13] 3-8-10 M Birch 10/1: 2120000: Al mid-div: fin 8th: best 890 (5)   09
2139 Dancing Tom [3] 9-1   518 Vendredi Treize [16] 9-7
1989 Tamalpais [12] 7-8(BL)   2126 La Belle Of Santo [1] 7-7(2oh)
1981 Fanny Robin [5] 7-12   1742 Rich Bitch [11] 7-7(14oh)
2086 Gloriant [2] 7-8(BL)(1ow)(6oh)   1864 Cumbrian Nijo [15] 8-1(bl)
*1973 Sonnenelle [4] 8-4
16 ran   2½,nk,shthd,1½,1½,nk,1½   (B Lasala)   P Haslam Newmarket

2425 LORD HAMILTON OF DALZELL NURSERY H'CAP   £1788   5f   Good/Firm 26 -04 Slow   [46]

2137 SILVERS ERA [2] (N Callaghan) 2-7-12 G Bardwell(7) 7/1: 0400341: 2 b f Balidar - Toccatina (Bleep-Bleep) Led ½ way and ran on strongly to win a nursery h'cap at Hamilton: speedily
bred filly who is a half sister to sev winners: eff over 5/6f on firm and soft ground: acts
on any track: may win again.   28
2265 JUST ONE MORE [7] (E Eldin) 2-8-12 A Mackay 12/1: 404002: Kept on well: see 1311, 678.   30
*2107 MISS DRUMMOND [1] (N Tinkler) 2-7-13 Kim Tinkler 8/1: 2001313: Never nearer: gd eff
and likes this stiff trk: see 2107.   16
2265 LINPAC NORTH MOOR [9] (C Elsey) 2-8-5(bl) J Lowe 12/1: 0240344: Led to ½ way: see 1696.   18
2081 AFRABELA [3] 2-8-6 J H Brown(5) 16/1: 2040200: Stayed on too late: best 1612 (C/D)   18
2279 ROSIES GLORY [12] 2-7-13 M Wood 12/1: 00230: Dwelt, nearest fin: see 2279 (6f)   10
2307 BOOTHAM LAD [13] 2-8-0 K Darley 7/1: 0000130: Fdd into 7th: best 2307 (yldg): see 1949.   00
2265 PASHMINA [10] 2-8-4 J Callaghan(7) 9/2: 2103330: Fin 9th: btr 2265.   00
*1696 UPSET [5] 2-9-1 D Mckeown 7/2 FAV: 2310: Never in the hunt: abs since 1696.   00
2298 COLLEGE WIZARD [4] 2-7-7(3oh) R Morse(2) 8/1: 42140: Al behind, fin last: best 1692 (sharp) 00
1962 Gardenia Lady [6] 8-6   1907 Mr Grumpy [14] 9-7
12 ran   4,hd,1½,nk,½,shthd   (J Cresswell)   N Callaghan, Newmarket

2426 PLUMCENTER H'CAP (0-50) 3YO   £2788   1m 1f   Good/Firm 26 +07 Fast   [37]

2404 HARD AS IRON [1] (P Haslam) 3-9-7 T Williams 13/8 FAV: 4111221: 3 b g Ardoon - Prancer
(Santa Claus) Made a quick reappearance and proved a very easy winner, led over 2f out and
was sn clear in quite a fast run 3yo h'cap at Hamilton: earlier won successive h'caps at
Nottingham, Ayr and Newmarket and has made tremendous improvement this season: very eff over
8/10f on gd and firm grd: well suited by a stiff trk: carries weight well and sure to win again. 45
1659 ICARO [8] (N Callaghan) 3-9-0(bl) G Duffield 10/1: 2032332: Abs: no chance with
winner tho' stayed on well to take the minor honours: rarely out of the frame: see 1295.   24
2264 BALNERINO [10] (Denys Smith) 3-8-5 L Charnock 14/1: 0401003: Best over 1m in 1813.   14
*2413 SHARONS ROYALE [5] (R Whitaker) 3-8-3(5ex) K Bradshaw(5) 13/2: 0324414: Won over
1m here yesterday but did not stay to that form here: see 2413.   11
2173 TOWER FAME [6] 3-8-1(BL) A Mackay 20/1: 0004000: Stayed on late: eff over 8/9f: see 90.   08
2041 GIRDLE NESS [3] 3-8-6 Kim Tinkler 9/1: 4001130: Btr 1960 (seller).   10
2300 BRADBURY HALL [2] 3-8-1 K Darley 7/1: 2100020: Early leader, fin 7th: see 2300.   00
1989 FASSA [9] 3-9-1 T Lucas 10/1: 00-0000: Fdd into 9th: see 1989.   00

2339 Lucky Blake [11] 8-13   2226 Mr Kewmill [7] 8-12   2190 Turn Em Back Jack [4] 8-10
11 ran 2,nk,¾,nk,1½   (Martin Wickens)   P Haslam Newmarket

2427 PLUMBCENTER CLAIMING STAKES 3YO   £896   1m   Good/Firm 26 +06 Fast

2103 TROPICO [5] (P Haslam) 3-8-4(bl) T Williams 7/1: 4231021: 3 ch c Hot Spark - Bella
Canto (Crooner) In gd form: led 2f out and just held on in quite a fast run 3yo Claiming stks
at Hamilton: earlier won a h'cap at Warwick: eff around 7/8f on fast ground: acts on any trk.   23
*2394 COLLYWESTON [6] (M Prescott) 3-8-10 G Duffield 11/4 FAV: -0012: Strong fin, just
failed: stays 1m well: in gd form and likely to win again soon: see 2394.   28
2038 NAP MAJESTICA [10] (M Camacho) 3-9-3 D Nicholls 4/1: -001043: Al prom: best 1256.   30
2282 KEEP COOL [11] (R Hollinshead) 3-8-4 W Ryan 12/1: 0002004: Led briefly over 2f out.   13
2361 VITAL STEP [1] 3-8-4 M Rimmer 12/1: -000420: Ran on same pace: btr 2361.   05
1976 MAWDLYN GATE [9] 3-9-3 Gay Kelleway(3) 7/1: 0132200: Twice below form in 1808 (10f)   13
2335 WATENDLATH [3] 3-7-12(bl) M Fry 9/2: 0000100: Wknd and fin last: best 2103.   00
2264 Master Music [8] 8-13   2083 Hare Hill [12] 8-6(bl)
2083 Stanford Rose [4] 8-2   2129 Jelly Jill [2] 8-2   2152 Torriggia [7] 9-0
12 ran hd,2,1½,4,3   (Mrs T Ellis)   P Haslam Newmarket

2428 PLUMBCENTER STELRAD BOILER STAKES   £685   1m 4f Good/Firm 26 -12 Slow

1535 LISANA [5] (M Stoute) 3-8-1 M A Giles(7) 9/2: 0-201: 3 b f Alleged - Licara (Caro)
Useful filly: despite fair abs responded to press to lead cl home in a 3 & 4yo stks at
Hamilton: lightly raced since looking an unlucky loser when pipped by French Flutter at Redcar:
well bred filly who is very eff over 12f: acts on a stiff trk: should improve and win
more races.   45
+2042 BUCKLEY [6] (L Cumani) 3-8-11 R Guest 8/11 FAV: -312: Heavily bckd: tried to make
all: no extra inside dist: 4l clear rem and should win again soon: see 2042.   50
2148 GREY SALUTE [1] (R Simpson) 3-8-4 S Whitworth 5/2: -3303: Dwelt: late prog: best 1899.   37
1970 TORREYA [2] (J Hindley) 3-8-1 M Hills 12/1: 0423234: No extra dist: one paced and
yet to break her duck: see 1544.   24
--   MAJOR WALLER [4] 4-9-0 A Mackay 14/1: -0: Slowly away on racecourse debut: no threat
tho' attracted some support today and should improve: half brother to a handful of winners
and should be well suited by this trip: acts on gd/firm.   15
--   MARINERS STAR [3] 4-9-0(VIS) Julie Bowker(7) 66/1: 22340-0: Visored for first time
on his belated seasonal debut: only fin out of the frame once in 7 starts last season but
yet to win: stays 2m: should do better on an easier surface.   13
6 ran 2½,4,6,5,shthd   (Aga Khan)   M Stoute Newmarket

2429 SPTEMBER SELLING STAKES   £953   1m   Good 46 -15 Slow

2174 SAUGHTREES [3] (P Walwyn) 3-8-4(bl) Paul Eddery 14/1: -003001: 3 ch f Young Generation
- Djimbaran Bay (Le Levanstell) Stayed on strongly to lead inside dist for her first win, in
a seller at Bath (bought in 2100 gns): half sister to 10f winner Bettyknowes: eff around 1m
on gd and firm ground: likes a gall track.   14
2271 COUNT ALMAVIVA [1] (M Blanshard) 3-8-7(bl) R Cochrane 16/1: 0300002: Led below dist,
just btn and ran his best race for some time: likes a gall trk: best in 774.   15
*2271 SPARKFORD LAD [4] (D Elsworth) 4-9-0(bl) Debbie Wheatley(7) 9/2 JT FAV: 0000213: Ev ch:
in gd form: see 2271: acts on any track.   10
2271 UP TOWN BOY [10] (L Holt) 4-9-0 N Adams 6/1: 4443-04: Ran on under press: see 2271.   09
1273 SWEET GEMMA [2] 4-8-11 D Williams(7) 9/2 JT FAV: 0-02300: Abs: bckd from 10/1:
ev ch: see 1081.   02
2088 MISS VENEZUELA [11] 3-8-4 R Fox 20/1: 0004000: Some late prog: see 1288.   00
2103 ST JAMES RISK [13] 3-8-7(BL) B Thomson 5/1: 00-0000: Bl first time: led over 2f
out: see 1540.   00
2371 SONG AN DANCE MAN [5] 3-8-7 R Wernham 9/1: 0000020: Wknd 2f out: btr 2371 (sharp trk). 00
2017 TAIS TOI [7] 3-8-4 G Duffield 13/2: -400400: Only beat one home: best 422 (sharper trk)   00
2131 Dawn Mirage [12] 8-4   2271 Chief Runner [16] 9-0   2208 Trojan God [8] 9-0
1995 Bootle Jack [15] 9-0(vis)   1835 Saxon Bazaar [14] 8-7
2319 Bang Bang [6] 9-0(BL)
15 ran ½,2,nk,2,1½   (H Keswick)   P Walwyn Lambourn, Berks.

2430 PENNSYLVANIA MAIDEN STAKES 3YO   £1580   1m 4f Good 46 +05 Fast

2408 NORTHERN AMETHYST [15] (D Elsworth) 3-9-0(bl) Pat Eddery 1/1 FAV: 2202321: 3 b c
Imperial Fling - Abielle (Abwah) Finally got off the mark, ridden with supreme confidence
to lead cl home in a 3yo mdn at Bath: earlier trained by G Huffer and has only once finished
out of the money this term: eff between 10 & 15f: suited by gd or faster grd and likes a
galloping track: this win should have boosted his confidence.   45+
2129 ADMIRALS ALL [14] (J Winter) 3-9-0 G Duffield 20/1: 3403042: Went on 3f out, caught
cl home tho' finished 8l clear rem: should win a race on this form: acts on any trk: see 1690   38

2228 TONQUIN [17] (J Toller) 3-8-11(BL) R Cochrane 33/1: -000343: Bl first time: mkt
drifter: al cl up and beat the rem decisively: acts on a gall trk: see 2000.   22
576 SHAREEF [20] (W Hern) 3-9-0 B Proctor 20/1: -004: Active in mkt after long abs:
led home turn, not qckn: lightly raced colt who is a half brother to smart French middle dist
winner Fitnah: should improve with experience.   14
2092 PYJAMA PARTY [16] 3-8-11 R Fox 20/1: -440: Mkt drifter: best 1941 (sharp trk).   06
2275 MAKE PEACE [19] 3-9-0 J Matthias 20/1: 3300000: Never dangerous: best 484 (10f yldg).   08
1833 MINHAH [9] 3-8-11 B Thomson 13/2: -030: Never beyond mid-div: much btr over this
C/D in 1833 (firm).   00
2054 NOBLE FILLE [12] 3-8-11 B Rouse 9/1: -00440: Mkt drifter: below par effort: see 1031.   00
2042 NOBLE RISE [10] 3-9-0 G Starkey 11/2: 3-440: Nicely bckd: prom to ½ way: see 1690.   00
--   Moma [11] 8-11   2148 Home Fleet [1] 8-11   1833 Bully Boy [6] 9-0(BL)
1042 Diwaan [4] 9-0   1061 Jimbalou [10] 9-0   1428 Solent Breeze [17] 8-11
--   Aspatia 0 8-11   1614 Boxers Shukee [5] 8-11
2061 Township [3] 9-0   2314 Hillgate Lady [7] 8-11
2048 Miss Bluebell [18] 8-11
20 ran   hd,8,7,3,1   (Mrs M Cooper)   D Elsworth Whitsbury, Hants

2431 BE HOPEFUL MEMORIAL HANDICAP 0-60   £3496   1m   Good 46 +05 Fast   [51]

1034 PRINCE MERANDI [10] (M Francis) 3-7-12 C Rutter(3) 25/1: 1330001: 3 b c Blakeney -
Copt Hall Princess (Crowned Prince) Easy to back after a fair abs but ran on strongly to
lead near fin in a h'cap at Bath: first time out winner of a Leicester mdn: eff around 8/10f
and seems best on a gall trk: acts on gd/firm and soft ground.   40
-2091 WINDSOR KNOT [9] (P Walwyn) 4-9-4 Paul Eddery 6/1: 0-40022: Prog to lead below dist,
just caught: in fine form and deserves a win: see 2091, 653.   51
1967 MEET THE GREEK [8] (D Laing) 3-8-12 P Cook 11/4 FAV: 1201223: Well bckd: did not have
the best of runs and was not btn far: most consistent this term: see 1854, 1365.   51
*2063 BELOW ZERO [4] (A Bailey) 3-8-12 R Cochrane 7/2: 0001014: Nearest fin: in fine form.   50
1793 ROCKMARTIN [2] 4-9-4 Pat Eddery 9/1: -000200: Had ev ch: see 1581 & 432.   44
2123 MANCHESTERSKYTRAIN [3] 7-8-13 A Mcglone 13/2: 0000020: Hmpd below dist: see 2123 & 40137
2123 Ashley Rocket [11] 8-6   2296 Portogon [13] 8-11
2296 Bundaburg [12] 8-4   2288 Joyful Dancer [1] 8-12
+2319 Concert Pitch [7] 8-2(7ex)   1525 Bold Pillager [6] 9-7
112 Westerham [5] 8-2
13 ran   nk,1¼,shthd,2,½   (Merandi Bloodstock Ltd)   M Francis Lambourn, Berks

2432 MENDIP HANDICAP STAKES 0-35   £2926   1m 5f   Good 46 +04 Fast   [29]

1875 EASTER LEE [13] (D Elsworth) 6-8-13 Pat Eddery 7/2 FAV: 122-001: 6 b g Idiot's Delight
- Stacey Lee (French Beige) Held up, steady prog to lead below dist for a comfortable win in
a h'cap at Bath: gained his only prev win on the Flat on this course last season, later
fin 2nd in val h'caps at Ascot and Goodwood: eff over 13f, stays extreme dist well: suited
by good or faster ground: will now be aimed at the Cesarewitch.   25
*2309 HARBOUR BAZAAR [7] (R Simpson) 6-8-6(6ex) S Whitworth 8/1: 003D312: Led home turn:
kept on well under strong driving and is in gd form: acts on a gall trk: see 2309.   12
2093 UP TO UNCLE [6] (R Hannon) 3-9-4 A Mcglone 9/2: 2132233: Model of consistency: see 1314   34
1732 INDIAN ORATOR [1] (B Hills) 3-9-7 A Culhane(7) 9/1: 2-31344: Going on fin: fair
effort: see 1135.   35
541 GWYN HOWARD [10] 4-8-10 R Mcghin 16/1: 0-04000: Long abs: onepaced: see 121.   12
2148 SHIRLSTAR TAXSAVER [15] 3-8-8 B Thomson 5/1: 0400000: No extra dist: see 1085 (sharp trk)18
2403 ITTIHAAD [2] 3-9-4 B Rouse 4/1: 0302330: Fdd into 7th: btr 2403.   00
850 Golden Croft [3] 8-2   2169 Faraway Lad [5] 8-10   955 Appreciative [8] 8-6(VIS)
2109 Catch The Thatch [9] 8-9   2134 Librate [11] 8-4(BL)
2304 Baydon Queen [14] 8-3(BL)   2093 Il Pontevecchio [12] 9-3
2078 Solomon Lad [4] 8-9(BL)
15 ran   2½,¾,1,½,2   (Anthony Hunt)   D Elsworth Whitsbury, Hants.

2433 TOG HILL FILLIES STAKES 2YO   £1260   5f167y Good 46 +01 Fast

*2147 TAHILLA [12] (J Tree) 2-9-1 Pat Eddery 4/9 FAV: 11: 2 b f Moorestyle - Woodwind
(Whistling Wind) Very useful filly: easily landed the odds, led dist and was sn clear in a
fast run 2yo fillies stks at Bath: made a successful debut in a fillies mdn at Newbury
recently: half sister to sev winners, notably very useful 6/7f performer Mummy's Favourite:
very eff around 5/6f on gd/firm ground: acts on a gall trk: should complete a hat trick.   64
--   CHORIZTO [14] (R Williams) 2-8-8 R Cochrane 14/1: 2: Ran on promisingly and will be
all the better for this experience: will stay further: acts on gd ground and on a gall trk:
sure to find a race.   48
2147 GREENHIL JAZZ TIME [10] (K Brassey) 2-8-8 S Whitworth 8/1: 03: Led briefly below
dist: seems well suited by a gall trk: see 2147.   40
2301 BIT OMAY [5] (P Walwyn) 2-8-8 Paul Eddery 33/1: 004: Unfancied: al up there and
fin clear rem: speedily bred filly who showed improvement here: see 2301.   32
--   LUCK BE A LADY [4] 2-8-8 P Cook 20/1: 0: Never nearer on debut: will be suited by
further: half sister to 7f winner Kuwait Desert: acts on gd grd and on a gall trk.   12+
--   MAY BELFORT [13] 2-8-8 R Street 20/1: 0: Gd late prog and certain to do btr next
time: cost 9,800 gns as a yearling: should stay 6f+: acts on gd ground and on a gall trk.   11+
716

-- WOODBERRY [15] 2-8-8 C Rutter(3) 25/1: 0: No threat tho' btr for experience: cheaply
bought filly who will stay further in time.   00
2069 NAPARIMA [16] 2-8-8 G Starkey 10/1: 030: Gd early speed: btr 2069 (sharp trk).   00

1665 Martian Melody [7] 8-8	2292 Bleu Celeste [11] 8-8
2249 Ladys Mantle [8] 8-8(BL)	2292 Peroy [3] 8-8
2308 Lundy Isle [1] 8-8(BL)	2270 Dear Glenda [9] 8-8
2308 Frimley Queen [2] 8-8	2180 Flapper Girl [6] 8-8(bl)

16 ran   2½,2½,3,7,nk   (Lady Derby)   J Tree Beckhampton, Wilts.

2434 TOG HILL FILLIES STAKES   2YO   £1255   5f167y Good 46 -09 Slow

*2185 ATTEMPTING [1] (B Hills) 2-9-1 B Thomson 9/2: 311: 2 ro f Try My Best - Attanagh
(Dancer's Image) Very useful filly: denied a clear run tho' showed a gd turn of foot to lead
cl home comfortably, in a 2yo fillies stks at Bath: last month won a fillies mdn at Folkestone:
cost 9,000 gns and is closely related to sev winners: very eff over 5/6f and will stay
further: acts on gd and firm ground and on any trk: on the upgrade.   58
2185 LITTLE BOLDER [4] (A Stewart) 2-8-8 M Roberts 7/2: 322: Just failed to make all:
clear rem and must win soon: clearly well suited by forcing tactics: acts on any trk: see 2185   48
2147 JUST KALA [11] (P Walwyn) 2-8-8 Paul Eddery 7/4 FAV: 43: Had ev ch: may need further.   38
2147 SHELDON MILLS [13] (I Balding) 2-8-8 J Matthias 6/1: 04: Al prom: speedily bred
filly who acts on gd/firm ground and on a gall trk: should improve further.   30
938 GLAMIS GIRL [9] 2-8-8 S Whitworth 33/1: -000: Mkt drifter after abs: no real
threat: speedily bred filly who cost 10,000 gns: acts on gd ground.   29
2147 MILLENNIA [6] 2-8-8 S Raymont 16/1: 00: Mkt drifter: al mid-div: will be suited by
further in time and has plenty of scope.   27
-- RITZS PEARL [2] 2-8-8 P Cook 25/1: 0: Easy to back: stayed on from dist and will
be btr for this run.   00

2147 Hidden Asset [10] 8-8	-- Lady Westown [5] 8-8	+2308 Susan Henchard [7] 9-1
-- Borotown [3] 8-8	-- Hail A Cab [15] 8-8	2118 Marie Baby [12] 8-8
-- Fair Moon [8] 8-8	2070 Mascalls Dream [14] 8-8	

15 ran   nk,4,3,nk,¾   (Mrs J Corbett)   B Hills Lambourn, Berks

2435 LADBROKE NURSERY HANDICAP   2YO   £2746   5f167y Good 46 -06 Slow   [50]

+2270 CRY FOR THE CLOWN [7] (A Bailey) 2-8-13(7ex) R Cochrane 4/5 FAV: 111: 2 b c Cawston's
Clown - Bayberry (Henry The Seventh) Useful colt: again heavily bckd and duly completed his
hat trick, led over 1f out and was driven out to win a nursery at Bath: earlier won a
seller at Ripon and a fast run stks at Windsor: very eff around 6f on gd and fast ground:
acts on any trk: expected to win again.   52
2179 CENTAURI [12] (B Hills) 2-9-3 B Thomson 6/1: 122: Ran on strongly, clear rem and
should win again soon: acts on a gall trk: see 1936.   52
2137 SAUNDERS LASS [5] (R Holder) 2-7-9 S Dawson 33/1: 02103: Nearest fin: in gd form: see 1647. 18
2252 LUCRATIF [10] (I Balding) 2-9-1 J Matthias 7/1: 1104: Al up there: acts any trk: see 1785   37
2081 BASIC BLISS [2] 2-8-6 Paul Eddery 33/1: 30300: Ran on too late: best 1341 (7f)   26
2090 SPANISH SKY [11] 2-9-3 P Cook 20/1: 010030: Front rank till dist: see 2090 & 1194.   34
2272 JOVICK [9] 2-9-3 Pat Eddery 8/1: 3100: Cl up over ½ way, fin last: best 1665 (sharp trk)   00

2307 Oriole Dancer [4] 8-5	*2097 Glory Bee [3] 8-1	2177 Castle Cornet [6] 8-11
2127 Teachers Game [1] 8-5	1891 Pensurchin [8] 9-7	

12 ran   ¾,4,shthd,¾,1   (Mrs J Bailey)   A Bailey Newmarket

Official Going Given As GOOD/SOFT

2436 E B F AVONDALE NEW ZEALAND STKS   2YO   £4149   6f   Good/Yld 83 -46 Slow

1855 LUCKY STONE [1] (C Brittain) 2-8-8 J Reid 7/1: 201: 2 b f Shirley Heights -
Brightelmstone (Prince Regent) Useful filly: sn prom and led ½ way, driven out in a slow
run 2yo stks at York Sept 3: half sister to a winning 2yo and also full sister to useful
middle dist colt Boon Point: eff at 6f, should be suited by further in time: acts on firm
and yldg ground.   53
*1996 MONTERANA [6] (G Wragg) 2-8-12 P Robinson 3/1 JT.FAV: 12: Kept on well under press
and should appreciate 7f: acts on gd/firm and yldg ground and is on the upgrade.   54
-- MISCHIEVOUS MISS [11] (S Hall) 2-8-3 M Birch 14/1: 3: Fin well from the rear and
improvement certain: half sister to 12f winner Willow Twig: will be suited by further than
6f: acts on yldg ground and can find a race soon.   40
2147 HOORAY LADY [7] (P Cole) 2-8-3 T Quinn 3/1 JT.FAV: 04: Well bckd: al up there:
acts on gd/firm and yldg grd: see 2147.   44
-- SCIMITARRA [10] 2-8-3 W Ryan 4/1: 0: Wk in mkt: dsptd lead most: half sister to
sev winners notably topclass sprinter Double Form: eff at 6f: acts on yldg grd and will improve   38
-- SMART SALUTE [5] 2-8-3 R Hills 14/1: 0: Kept on well on debut and should do btr next
time: half sister to a winning stayer: should be suited by 7f+: acts on yldg ground.   37
-- LUCKY PICK [4] 2-8-3 W Carson 13/2: 0: Prom most on racecourse debut, fin 7th:
improvement very likely from this full sister to the smart Lucky Ring.   30

-- Lullaby Baby [8] 8-3	-- Talland Bay [2] 8-3	882 Petroc Concert [9] 8-8

2232 Illustrate [3] 8-8
11 ran   1,2,nk,nk,¾,2½   (Robert Holmes A Court)   C Brittain Newmarket

2437 QUINTIN GILBEY SILVER TROPHY H'CAP 0-60   £3501   7f   Good/Yld 83 +05 Fast   [59]

2255 TRAVEL MAGIC [8] (B Hanbury) 3-8-0 M Hills 6/1: -010221: 3 b f Henbit - Quiet Harbour
(Mill Reef) In fine form and fin well to lead cl home in quite a val h'cap at York Sept 3:
most consistent this term, earlier winning a fillies mdn at Chepstow: half sister to a
winner in Ireland: seems equally eff at 7f/1m: acts on firm and yldg grd and does well
on a galloping track: genuine filly.   48
2039 AIR COMMAND [2] (G Reveley) 6-8-2 Julie Bowker(7) 11/1: 0000202: Made most: hung
right over 1f out and caught near fin: unlucky? see 1868.   43
2277 BATON BOY [1] (M Brittain) 5-7-8 J Lowe 13/2: 0040443: Ev ch, out battled final 1f:
beaten only 1l: see 2277, 55.   34
1793 POSTORAGE [7] (M Mccormack) 4-9-10 C Asmussen 10/1: 0001004: Nearest fin: gd eff
under his big weight: see 1292.   62
2231 EMERALD EAGLE [4] 5-7-7(5oh) G Bardwell(7) 14/1: 0201000: Al prom: see 2231 (C/D stks)   27
2234 SIGNORE ODONE [9] 4-8-4 M Birch 7/2 FAV: 0011200: Prom, see 2234, 1624 (1m fast grd).   33
2039 THE MAZALL [3] 6-7-13 M Wood 10/1: 0221100: Prom most: twice below 1868.   00
2250 MAJOR JACKO [12] 3-7-10(1ow) W Carson 15/2: 0000200: No threat in 8th:twice below 2143(6f). 00
1890 TRANSFLASH [6] 7-8-6 N Day 7/1: 0030300: Never showed: best 1525, see 55.   00
17   Hay Street [11] 8-12   2296 Shellman [5] 7-7(2oh)   2340 Improvise [10] 7-9(2ow)(7oh)
12 ran   ½,½,1,2,2½,nk   (Mrs M H D Madden)   B Hanbury Newmarket

2438 SUN LIFE OF CANADA HANDICAP 3YO 0-70   £7934   1m 2.5 Good/Yld 83 +06 Fast   [66]

2219 SULTAN MOHAMED [8] (J Dunlop) 3-8-13 W Carson 10/3 FAV: 1213001: 3 ch c Northfields -
Paper Sun (Match III) Very useful colt: well bckd and led 1f out, driven out in a val 3yo
h'cap at York Sept 3: in fine form this season earlier winning at Brighton and first time
out a gd mdn at Epsom: eff at 9/10f, may get further: acts on firm and yldg grd and any trk:
genuine and consistent.   65
*2066 ENBARR [5] (H Cecil) 3-9-7 S Cauthen 7/2: 2131012: Made most and kept on really
well: fine effort under 9-7 and is still improving: carries weight well: see 2066.   71
*1924 NIGHT OUT PERHAPS [2] (G Wragg) 3-9-5 P Robinson 7/2: -114013: Waited with over
this new trip: not much room over 2f out and stayed on: in fine form and seems equally
eff over 1m/10f: see 1924.   66
1994 LANDSKI [4] (R Simpson) 3-8-3 W Newnes 10/1: 1303134: Prom, not the best of runs
inside final 3f: see 1768.   46
1886 OLD DOMESDAY BOOK [1] 3-9-1 J Reid 7/1: -133030: Waited with: acts on yldg, but
btr 1886 (gd/firm) see 444.   57
1702 ANDARTIS [7] 3-8-10(BL) R Hills 14/1: 0334040: Bl first time: prom over 1m: best 807(firm). 51
*1046 MAJAAHED [3] 3-9-5 C Asmussen 13/2: -010: Never nearer after abs: see 1046.   00
*2183 SHIBIL [6] 3-9-2(bl) W R Swinburn 9/1: 4322210: There over 7f: btr 2183.   00
8 ran   ¾,2,2½,½,½   (Dana Stud Ltd)   J Dunlop Arundel, Sussex

2439 UK OPTICAL NURSERY HANDICAP 2YO   £5708   1m   Good/Yld 83 -09 Slow   [56]

*2067 GREAT ASPECT [8] (W Hern) 2-9-7 W Carson 2/1 FAV: 11: 2 b c Great Nephew - Broad
Horizon (Blakeney) Promising colt: uneasy fav, but led over 1f out and kept on gamely for
a shthd success in a val nursery h'cap at York Sept 3: first time out was a ready winner of
a 2yo event at Haydock: half brother to 9f winner Veduta: stays 1m really well and will be
suited by middle dist next season: acts on gd and yldg grd and a gall trk: further
improvement to come.   61
*2051 ELEGANT ISLE [7] (J Watts) 2-9-1 S Cauthen 3/1: 12: Al up there: led briefly final
1f: beaten a whisker and can find a similar event: stays 1m well and acts on gd/firm & yldg.   54
1914 SOMEONE ELSE [4] (R Hannon) 2-8-4(BL) C Asmussen 6/1: 030003: Kept on under press:
bl first time today: stays 1m and acts on firm and yldg, but mainly disapp since 1097.   38
*2276 BEN LEDI [1] (M H Easterby) 2-9-8(6ex) M Birch 7/1: 0311314: Made most: see 2276 (7f)   52
2105 ALPENHORN [2] 2-8-12 W Ryan 9/1: 0300: Bckd at long odds, no real threat: twice
below 1903 (good).   40
2140 EUROCON [3] 2-7-10 A Proud 25/1: 0000240: Stiff task: see 2140 (7f), 2050.   16
2364 FOUNTAINS CHOICE [6] 2-7-7 P Burke(3) 10/1: 3320020: Held up, no threat: btr 2364.   12
2198 Connaught Flyer [5] 8-3
8 ran   shthd,2½,2,1,4,nk   (Sheikh Mohammed)   W Hern, West Ilsley

2440 STRENSALL STAKES (LISTED) 3YO FILLIES   £7830   7f   Good/Yld 83 +01 Fast

2262 ENTRANCING [7] (J Dunlop) 3-8-4 W Carson 6/1: 2-00021: 3 ch f Posse - Red Ruby (Tudor
Melody) Useful filly: ran on well to get up cl home in a Listed race at York: last season won
first time out at Goodwood: prob stays 1m but is very eff at 7f: acts on gd/firm and yldg
ground and on any trk.   59

1286 STATELY LASS [4] (J Winter) 3-9-0 S Cauthen 6/1: 23-1002: Led over 2f out: just btn:
fine effort after abs and is definitely best with some give in the ground: see 59.   67
2161 FLUTTERY [3] (G Wragg) 3-7-12 P Robinson 11/1: -302243: Led briefly final 1f:
just btn: disapp last time out over 10f and seems best over 7f/1m: see 1902.   51
2231 QUE SYMPATICA [1] (R Boss) 4-9-8 J Reid 5/1: 3000024: Switched and chall 1f out:
not btn far in cl finish: see 2231, 18.   68
2231 HOLBROOKE SUTTON [5] 3-8-8 W R Swinburn 7/4 FAV: 4-40240: Heavily bckd: not the
best of runs but twice below 1851.   58
2314 SWEEPY [6] 3-7-12 A Mackay 50/1: -0000: Rank outsider: prom most, showing improved
form: lightly raced prev and is a half sister to 3 winners: acts on yldg ground.   23
1002 MIGIYAS [8] 3-9-0 T Quinn 10/1: 240-100: Led over 4f: needed race? Best 158.   00
1107 ZALATIA [9] 3-8-8 R Hills 13/2: 2-10200: Chance over 2f out, fdd: needed race?   00
2294 URUGUAY [2] 3-7-13(1ow) M Hills 14/1: -0220: Prom most: stiff task: see 2294, 1880.   00
9 ran   ¾,shthd,nk,1½,8   (Lavinia Duchess of Norfolk)   J Dunlop Arundel, Sussex

2441 HESLINGTON MAIDEN STAKES 3YO   £3362   1m 4f Good/Yld 83 -07 Slow

613 CALL TO HONOR [5] (O Douieb) 3-9-0(bl) W R Swinburn 4/1: -431: 3 b c Sir Ivor -
Plankton (Quack) Despite long abs, led over 1f out, driven out in a 3yo mdn at York Sept 3:
lightly raced colt who stays 12f really well: acts on gd and soft grd and seems best in
blinkers on a stiff trk.   49
2148 CASTLE ROCK [7] (J Dunlop) 3-9-0 W Carson 15/8: 0-02: Well bckd: ev ch final 1f:
best effort yet from this lightly raced colt: stoutly bred, being a half brother to Gold Cup
winner Ragstone and the very smart stayer Castle Keep: should be suited by further than 12f
and can find a race: acts on yldg ground.   43
2176 AMBASSADOR [6] (W O'gorman) 3-9-0 T Ives 13/8 FAV: -223: Led after 1m: btr 2176, 2061.   39
714 SNOW WIZARD [1] (O Douieb) 3-9-0(bl) R Machado 20/1: -004: Led 1m after long abs:
stable mate of winner: half brother to a winner in Ireland but has shown only modest form
in 3 outings: wears blinkers.   27
916 SEATYRN [2] 3-9-0 J Reid 10/1: 30-3400: Abs: prom most: best 699 (10f firm): see 487   21
1471 MOLLY PARTRIDGE [4] 3-8-11 A Bond 25/1: -000300: No threat: lightly raced since 1074   00
2339 NOMAD BOXER [3] 3-9-0 N Day 50/1: -00: Rank outsider and t.o.   00
7 ran   3,2,6,3,15   (Joseph Allen)   O Douieb Newmarket

2442 KOWLOON MAIDEN STAKES 3YO   £3479   1m   Good 44 -15 Slow

2099 USFAN [3] (J Dunlop) 3-9-0 W Carson 9/4: -0221: 3 br c Riverman - Essie BS Venture
(Intentionally) Useful colt: well suited by this extra furlong and led 2f out, comfortably,
in a 3yo mdn at York: very eff over 7/8f and should stay further: acts on gd and firm grd
and on any track: lightly raced and should continue to improve.   50
1431 MERITMOORE [7] (R Armstrong) 3-9-0 S Cauthen 25/1: 00-02: Abs: slowly away, ran
on same pace: lightly raced colt who showed improved form here: eff over 1m on gd ground:
acts on a gall trk: should win a small h'cap on this form.   42
2255 NORTH OCEAN [4] (L Cumani) 3-9-0 Pat Eddery 7/4 FAV: -03033: Heavily bckd: early
leader, not qckn dist: eff over 1m on gd and firm grd: likes a gall trk: see 1269.   38
1953 STICKY GREENE [2] (B Hills) 3-8-11 B Thomson 8/1: -334204: Led briefly 3f out: best 1628   29
2401 HIGHEST PEAK [10] 3-9-0(BL) G Duffield 9/1: -232020: Bl first time: onepaced: see 2401.   29
733 VITAL FORM [6] 3-9-0(bl) W R Swinburn 9/1: -000: Mkt drifter after abs: no threat:
lightly raced colt who is a half brother to sev winners, including smart 12f winner Head
for Heights: eff over 7/8f on gd and firm grd: should do btr next time.   25
2314 CONCORDES DEMON [5] 3-8-11 M Miller 10/1: -20: Fin last: btr on yldg in 2314 (sharp trk)   00
2314 Scented Silence [9] 8-11   2216 Sure Landing [1] 9-0
9 ran   2¼,1½,3,1½,1½   (Prince A Faisal)   J Dunlop Arundel, Sussex

2443 DUBAI STAKES (H'CAP) (0-60) 3YO+   £3334   1m 1f Good 44 +01 Fast   [46]

2219 ATOKA [5] (Lord J Fitzgerald) 4-9-1 R Hills 4/1 CO FAV: 1134301: 4 b f Kaiseradler -
Ambivalenz (Orsini) Useful filly: led below dist and was sn clear in an all aged h'cap at
York: earlier won similar races at Redcar and Yarmouth and subs. 3rd in the Magnet Cup here:
ex German filly who is very eff over 9/10f: acts on gd and firm grd and is well suited by
a gall track: should win again in this form.   49
2303 GUNDREDA [2] (C Brittain) 4-9-7 G Moore 4/1 CO FAV: 0040332: Led 3f out, no chance
with this easy winner: remains in gd form: see 2303, 1498.   40
2144 ACONITUM [3] (J Bethell) 5-9-7 J Reid 4/1 CO FAV: 3002403: Had ev ch: best here 1525 (1m)   39
2390 ROMANTIC UNCLE [4] (H Wharton) 3-9-1 D Nicholls 10/1: -020004: Btn dist: should
improve as the ground eases: best in 478 (7f, soft).   34
1922 TRY HARDER [8] 3-8-11 M Hills 8/1: -003400: Best in 1532 on a tight track.   18
2219 RUSSELL CREEK [6] 4-8-6 J Matthias 14/1: -000000: Yet to recapture her gd form
of last season when winning at Ayr and Ascot: suited by 1m: best form on soft grd and
on a galloping track.   00

-- KILLARY BAY [7] 4-9-6 Pat Eddery 10/1: 31300-0: Sn well behind on belated reappearance:
last season won a mdn at Newcastle and later made all in a Windsor h'cap: stays 11f well:
acts on firm and soft ground and on any trk: clearly needed this race.   00
2183 EXCLUSIVE NORTH [1] 3-9-0(BL) S Cauthen 5/1: 0-01040: Bl first time: clear leader
over ½ way: see 1756.   00
8 ran   8,nk,4,7,5   (Richard Kaselowsky)   Lord J Fitzgerald Newmarket

2444 E.B.F. SAUDI ARABIA STAKES 2YO   £4428   7f   Good 44 +02 Fast

2159 BENGAL FIRE [2] (C Brittain) 2-8-11 C Asmussen 11/4: 231: 2 br c Nishapour - Gerardmer
(Brigadier Gerard) Very useful colt: well bckd and led 2f out, gamely, in a val 2yo stks at
York: half brother to very useful middle dist performer King's Island: very eff over 7f and
should stay further: acts on gd and firm grd and on any trk: well regarded and should win again   62
*2263 HENDEKA [8] (H Cecil) 2-9-4 S Cauthen 10/11 FAV: 3112: Heavily bckd to complete his
hat-trick: ran on gamely and beat rem decisively: consistent sort: see 2263.   67
2276 COMMONSIDR GIPSY [4] (O Brennan) 2-8-11 J Carroll(7) 33/1: 020003: Ran on same pace:
stays 7f: seems best on a gall trk: see 685.   42
1926 NORDAVANO [7] (M Jarvis) 2-8-11(VIS) T Ives 11/2: 244: Visored first time: led early
in str, outpaced below dist: twice below form shown in 1452.   41
1984 OH DANNY BOY [6] 2-8-11 E Guest(3) 25/1: 00: Prom most: on the upgrade: see 1984.   40
2251 PUNTA CALAHONDA [1] 2-9-1 D Nicholls 12/1: 0100: Led 3f, sn no extra: btr 1975.   39
2239 Highland Laird [3] 8-11   2379 Try Hills Supplies [5] 8-11
8 ran   ½,7,¾,nk,3   (N H Phillips)   C Brittain Newmarket

2445 PEAK STAKES (H'CAP) (0-60) 3YO+   £3366   1m 6f   Good 44 -22 Slow   [49]

2206 WASSL REEF [4] (J Dunlop) 3-9-7 W Carson 5/1 FAV: 2310101: 3 b c Mill Reef - Connaught
Bridge (Connaught) Led below dist, ridden out in quite a val h'cap at York: useful colt
who earlier won a Lingfield mdn and a minor race at Salisbury: eff over 10/12f, clearly stays
14f well: acts on fast and yldg ground and on any trk: genuine and consistent sort.   60
2237 ROSTHERNE [8] (K Stone) 4-8-8 L Charnock 8/1: 1040002: Held up, stayed on well:
btr effort and is well suited by some give in the ground: see 215.   31
2376 REVISIT [5] (J Winter) 4-9-4 W R Swinburn 6/1: 0343443: Led briefly 2f out: fair
effort: see 58a.   40
2220 DUAL VENTURE [12] (J Fitzgerald) 4-9-9 J Reid 6/1: 2203104: Ran on same pace: best 1663   44
1875 PATHS SISTER [11] 5-7-13 J Lowe 11/2: 1-00000: Stayed on too late: see 215.   17
2326 TRESIDDER [7] 4-8-9 G Carter(3) 6/1: 0404240: Suited by some give: see 2087.   25
2171 LOST OPPORTUNITY [10] 3-7-7(9oh) R Fox 8/1: 2000400: Made most: fin 7th: stays 12f:
best in 99.   00
*2130 WESSEX [6] 4-8-13 Kim Tinkler 7/1: 1340110: Al in rear: fin 8th: much btr 2130.   00
2237 NAFTILOS [2] 4-9-3 P Robinson 8/1: -020000: Fdd into 9th: best in 215.   00
2337 LUMINATE [9] 5-8-10 M Birch 33/1: 000-00: Btn 2f out: see 2337.   00
10 ran   2,¾,½,2,¾,1½,8,½,1½   (Sheikh Ahmed Al Maktoum)   J Dunlop Arundel, Sussex

2446 HONG KONG MARLBORO' CUP H'CAP (0-70)   £16596   6f   Good 44 +09 Fast   [61]

+2224 MANTON DAN [13] (N Vigors) 3-9-2(7ex) P Cook 6/1: -201011: 3 b c Tower Walk - Balgreggan
(Hallez) Very useful sprinter: ran on gamely to lead inside dist in a fast run and val h'cap
at York: earlier successful in a stks race at Nottingham and a h'cap at York: last season won
at Goodwood: half brother to sev winners, including useful sprinters Street Market and
Sailors Song: very eff over 5/6f: acts on firm and soft grd and on any trk: has a fine
turn of foot: in grand form.   67
2258 OUR JOCK [12] (R Smyth) 4-9-4 W Carson 11/2: 0041042: Fin well: just btn: see 2258.   62
2151 PADRE PIO [5] (D Arbuthnot) 5-8-7 W R Swinburn 9/2 FAV: -020023: Led 2f out, not
btn far: see 2151.   50
+1995 EASTERN SONG [1] (C Nelson) 3-8-9 J Reid 5/1: 0-01314: No extra cl home: see 1995.   51
2378 VILTASH [2] 3-8-2(vis) M Wood 20/1: 0300000: Al front rank: gd eff: see 1044.   41
2402 CREE BAY [11] 7-8-13 B Thomson 12/1: 0411000: Ran on late: best 1777.   42
-2204 CARELESS WHISPER [3] 3-7-9 G Dickie 10/1: 10-302U: Stumbled and u.r. ½ way: see 2204.   00
2155 Elnawaagi [8] 9-2   2343 Sharpetto [6] 8-11   2258 Manimstar [10] 9-10
2390 Idle Times [9] 7-7(5oh)   2250 Bon Accueil [4] 7-7(1oh)
2151 Sullys Choice [7] 8-3
13 ran   nk,½,2½,1,2   (G S Tuck)   N Vigors Upper Lambourn, Berks

2447 SHA TIN STAKES 2YO   £6128   5f   Good 44 +07 Fast

2221 CROFTERS CLINE [1] (J Wilson) 2-9-2 Pat Eddery 9/2: 0111101: 2 b c Crofter - Modena
(Sassafras) Very useful colt: returned to winning form, led under strong press inside dist
for a narrow win in a fast run and val 2yo stks at York: most genuine and consistent, earlier
made all in minor events at Ayr, Ripon and Beverley and later a val nursery at Newmarket:
very eff over 5/6f on gd and firm grd: acts on any trk: does well with forcing tactics:
sure to win more races.   68
*2158 ABUZZ [5] (C Brittain) 2-8-13 M Roberts 13/8 FAV: 1110412: Heavily bckd fav: ran
on strongly under press and is in gd form: see 2158.   64
+2162 COME ON CHASE ME [3] (J Etherington) 2-8-11 M Wood 5/2: 3113: Tried to make all,
no extra cl home: acts on any trk and is in fine form: see 2162.   57

2221 BALTIC SHORE [2] (M Stoute) 2-8-11 W R Swinburn 4/1: 02104: Ran to his best: see 1826.   55
2325 STELBY [4] 2-8-7 W Carson 33/1: 0224200: Outsider and no extra dist: best 2082 (6f)   40
5 ran ½,1½,½,1½   (D M Beresford)   J Wilson Sollom, Lancs

BADEN-BADEN   Friday August 29th   Lefthand, Sharpish Track

Official Going Given As SOFT

2448 KRONIMUS RENNEN LISTED 2YO   £3390   6f   Soft -

2043 GHANAYIM (H T Jones) 2-8-3 R Hills 1: 0221: 2 cj f Sharpen Up - Libra's Shiningstar
Gained a deserved success with a comfortable win in a Listed 2yo event at Baden-Baden Aug 29:
narrowly btn by Seek The Truth at Redcar last time: eff at 6f, should be suited by 7f: half
sister to useful 3yo Bright As Night: acts on firm and soft.   50
--   ZAMPANO (H Jentzsch) 2-8-12 G Bocskai 1: 12: Ran well at weights.   54
--   TOPAS (N Sauer) 2-8-7 K Woodburn 1: 3: --   40
5 ran 1½,3½   (Hamdan Al-Maktoum)   H T Jones Newmarket

2449 GROUP 3 OETIINGEN RENNEN 3YO+   £12712   1m   Soft -

*1788 EVES ERROR (M Stoute) 3-8-5 A Kimberley 1: 12-0411: 3 ch c Be My Guest - Apple Peel
Smart colt: led well inside final 1f in a Gr 3 event at Baden-Baden: last time out was a ready
winner of a val Ladies race at Ascot: smart 2yo, winning at Epsom and Nottingham and 2nd
in Gr 2 company at the Curragh: half brother to sev winners: very eff over 1m: acts on gd/
firm and soft ground: genuine sort.   72
2266 CHARTINO (G Huffer) 3-8-5 G Carter 1: 12-0032: Fin in gd style and is back to his
best: can win soon: see 2266, 802.   70
2165 BRAZZAKA (M Jarvis) 3-7-10 M L Thomas 1: -112333: Made much: not btn far: yet to
run a bad race: see 2165.   60
--   LILIOM (H Jentzsch) 4-9-0 G Bocskai 1: 1400104: --   62
1492 YOUNG RUNAWAY 4-9-4 A Clark 1: 10-4000: Tried in bl today: lightly raced and below
his best this season: see 313.   65
8 ran ½,hd,3,hd   (Sheikh Mohammed)   M Stoute Newmarket

THE CURRAGH   Saturday August 30th   Righthand, Galloping Track

Official Going Given As GOOD/YIELDING

2450 GROUP 3 MELD STAKES 3YO+ F & M   £11550   1m 4f   Good/Yld -

2157 I WANT TO BE (J Dunlop) 4-9-11 Pat Eddery 8/11 FAV: 2-00231: 4 b f Roberto -
Frontonian (Buckpasser) Smart filly: in grand form and was ridden confidently to lead inside
final 1f, easily, in Gr 3 Meld Stks at the Curragh: last time out a fine 3rd to Bakharoff in
Gr 2 Geoffrey Freer Stks at Newbury: smart 3yo, winning Gr 2 Park Hill Stks at Doncaster and
a fillies h'cap at Newbury: on final outing fin 2nd to Mersey in Gr 1 Prix Royal Oak at
Longchamp: in '84 won at York: eff at 12f, stays 15f really well: acts on firm and soft
ground and a gall track: certain to win more races.   77
148 CATHERINE MARY (L Browne) 3-8-7 S Craine 8/1: -312: No chance with winner but ran
well: last month won over 10f at Phoenix Park: stays 12f and acts on yldg and heavy.   62
1596 EPICURES GARDEN (D Weld) 3-8-12 D Gillespie 10/1: 13-4133: Lightly raced since best 470   60
1592 POPULARITY (D Weld) 3-8-12 D Parnell 6/1: -2-1104: See 1592.   55
468 RAMICH JOHN 4-9-7 M T Browne 7/1: 0113200: Abs: btr early season: see 360, 325.   51
9 ran 2½,4,2½,¾   (Sheikh Mohammed)   J Dunlop Arundel, Sussex

2451 GROUP 3 TATTERSALLS ANGLESEY STKS 2YO   £11550   6f   Good/Yld -

--   ISLAND REEF (K Prendergast) 2-8-10 K Moses 12/1: -12411: 2 ch c Main Reef - Helba
(Habat) Very useful colt but perhaps a trifle lucky to win a Gr 3 2yo stks at the Curragh
Aug 30: fin 3rd but promoted to 1st after being slightly hmpd in final 2f: winner prev at
Tipperary and Navan: eff at 6f, stays 7f: acts on gd and yldg.   65
2223 QUEL ESPRIT (M Mccormack) 2-8-10 S Craine 9/2: 1302242: Dsptd lead inside final 2f
but drifted left into Island Reef: very tough colt: see 1591.   66
--   DARCYS THATCHER (M Kauntze) 2-9-0 Pat Eddery 6/4 FAV: 111D: Well bckd to keep his
unbtn record: led over 1f out, but drifted left, causing minimal interference: the winner
on merit: earlier successful at Phoenix Park and over this C/D: acts on gd and soft grd
and should gain compensation.   73
2350 SNOW FINCH (J Bolger) 2-8-11 D Gillespie 10/3: 011024: In gd form: see 2350, 2113.   63
--   CURRAGH DANCER 2-8-10 D Manning 10/1: 140: First time out winner at Phoenix Park:
acts on yldg and heavy.   55
*638 KEEN CUT 2-9-0(bl) D Parnell 13/2: 110: Abs: btr 638.   49
1006 Kharshuf 8-10
7 ran 1,¾,1½,3,5   (Mrs M O'Connell)   K Prendergast Ireland

Official Going Given As HEAVY

2452 GROUP 3 PRIX DE LA NONETTE 3YO FILLIES   £17912   1m 2f   Heavy -

*1353 GALUNPE (B Secly) 3-8-13 A Gibert 1: 4-00311: 3 b f He Loves Me - Semantic (Tudor Melody) Smart French filly: seems to revel in this hvy grd when a ready 2½l winner of a Gr 3 fillies event at Deauville: last time out won a Gr 2 fillies event at Longchamp: smart 2yo: very eff over 10f: seems to act on any ground.   80

2196 RIVERBRIDE (P Biancone) 3-8-9 E Legrix 1: 0000422: Caught a tartar: running well.   70

+1811 SANTIKI (M Stoute) 3-8-9 W R Swinburn 1: 2413313: Gd eff on this hvy ground: see 1811   66

*1215 LIASTRA (F Boutin) 3-8-11 F Head 1: -212104: Acts on gd and hvy: see 1215.   67

7 ran   2½,2,shtnk   (J M Aubry-Dumand)   B Secly France

2453 GROUP 2 GRAND PRIX DE DEAUVILLE 3YO+   £33579   1m 5f   Heavy -

2194 BABY TURK (A De Royer Dupre) 4-9-3 Y Saint Martin 1: 0043231: 4 ch c Northern Baby - Vielle Villa (Kashmir II) Very smart French colt: well ridden, dictating a slow pace and quickening final 3f for a narrow win in a Gr 2 event at Deauville: earlier a fine 2nd to Shardari in Gr 2 Princess of Wales Stks at Newmarket: early in the season won a Gr 3 event at Longchamp: very eff at 12f, stays 13.5f: acts on any grd and is sure to win more races.   83

-- FABUROLA (P Biancone) 5-9-2 E Legrix 1: 2421-22: Just btn in a blanket fin: fine effort on only 2nd outing this term: last season fin 2nd to Leading Counsel in the Irish St Leger and is again on target for that race: stays really well and acts on gd and hvy ground   81

-- NIGHT LINE (P Lautner) 3-8-3 P Robinson 1: 2102203: Tremendous eff from this German filly: stays 13.5f well and acts on hvy ground.   79

-- PUB ROYAL (G Collet) 3-8-5 P Bruneau 1: 0100134: Just btn in cl fin and is clearly eff over 13.5f on hvy ground.   80

-2157 SIRK 3-8-5 W Carson 1: 3230320: Seemed unsuited by this slowish pace and did well to finish a cl.up 5th: remains in fine form: see 2157.   79

390 DENEL 7-9-3 A Badel 1: /43-120: Long abs: see 153.   78

2357 GALLA PLACIDIA 4-9-2 E Lequeux 1: -101020: Cl.up 7th: see 2357, 1115.   77

10 ran   shtnk,shthhd,nk,nk,nk,nose   (Mme A M D'Estainville)   A De Royer Dupre France

---

Official Going Given As GOOD

2454 GROUP 3 FURSTENBERG RENNEN 3YO   £12712   1m 3f   Good -

2197 EL SALTO (H Jentzsch) 3-9-0 G Bocskai 1: -21: 3 br c Surumu - Escada (Luciano) Smart German colt: made ev yard and stayed on gamely to win Gr 3 3yo event at Baden-Baden: eff at 11f, stays 12f well: acts on a sound surf and best out in front.   77

-- TIBERIUS (S Von Mitzlaff) 3-8-9 P Alafi 1: -2: Just held by the winner.   71

-- ARC (P Lautner) 3-8-9 R Suerland 1: -3: Completed a German 1-2-3.   70

2112 GORGEOUS STRIKE (C Nelson) 3-8-9 J Reid 1: 2034434: Kept on well and was best of the British: see 2112.   67

2005 ZAHDAM 3-8-11 G Starkey 1: 1-10220: Below his best: btr 2005, 1595 (12f).   66

*2112 NORTH VERDICT 3-8-9 R Cochrane 1: 0032410: Btr on softer ground: see 2112.   60

2117 Comprida 8-9

7 ran   ½,½,1¾,1½,2,½   (Gestut Fahrhof)   H Jentzsch Germany

---

Official Going Given As GOOD/SOFT

2455 GLADIATEUR DOSTENDE HANDICAP 4YO+   £6901   2m 4f   Good/Soft -

*2169 HARLESTONE LAKE (J Dunlop) 4-9-4 B Thomson 1: 3414011: 4ro f Riboboy - January (Sigebert) Impr staying filly: romped home by a dist in a h'cap at Ostend: earlier won h'caps at Wolverhampton and Lingfield: eff at 2m, well suited by 2½m: acts on soft and fast ground and likes an easy trk: half sister to smart hurdler Janus: clearly on the upgrade.   38

*1772 TUGBOAT (P Mitchell) 7-8-7 G Carter 1: 04-0212: No chance with winner: see 1772.   00

-- LE PRIVILEGE (France) 4-9-11 D Vincent 1: -3: --   14

14 ran   dist,½   (J Dunlop)   J Dunlop Arundel, Sussex

Official Going Given As FIRM

2456 GRADE 1 BUDWEISER ARLINGTON MILLION   £419580   1m 2f   Firm -

-- ESTRAPADE [7] (C Whittingham) 6-8-10 F Toro 1: -232101: 6 ch m Vaguely Noble - Klepto (No Robbery) Highclass American mare: sent clear entering the str and was never going to be hdd when an easy 5l winner of Grade 1 Arlington Million at Arlington: formerly a high-class filly in Europe: very eff at 10f.   90

-- DIVULGE [1] (G Moschera) 4-9-0 J Cruguet 1: 2-12102: Outsider but ran well.   85

1877 PENNINE WALK [10] (J Tree) 4-9-0 Pat Eddery 1: 0-11133: First time over 10f and
ran really well: a credit to his trainer: see 1094.   85
--   UPTOWN SWELL [4] (R Lundy) 4-9-0 W Guerra 1: -010124: Stayed on well: gd eff in
this top company.   84
--   PALACE MUSIC [3] 5-9-0 G Stevens 1: -312040: Stable mate of winner.   83
--   FLYING PIDGEON [8] 5-9-0 J Santos 1: -101340: 3rd in this race last season and
again ran well.   82
1811 TELEPROMPTER [9] 6-9-0 T Ives 1: 0-23330: Never allowed to reach the running rail
after a slowish start: fin 7th: see 598.   79
*2194 OVER THE OCEAN [6] 4-9-0 C Asmussen 1: 3-23310: Never btr than 6th: see 2194.   00
1861 THEATRICAL [14] 4-9-0 S Cauthen 1: 200-020: No show after very slow start: see 1861.   00
1932 MAYSOON [13] 3-8-2 C Mccarron 1: 0-12320: Ev ch in str, but ran well below her best:
said to have broken a blood vessel last time out and was given the drug Lasix here: see 926.   00
14 ran   5,hd,½,hd,½,1½   (A Paulson)   C Whittingham America

---

BADEN-BADEN   Wednesday September 3rd   Lefthand, Sharpish Track

Official Going Given As GOOD

2457 GROUP 3 GOLDENE PEITSCHE 3YO+   £12712   6f   Good -

1011 PREMIERE CUVEE (J Pease) 4-8-13 G Guignard 1: 030-201: 4 b f Formidable - Clicquot
(Bold Lad (Ire)) Smart filly: led final 1f, readily, in a Gr 3 event at Baden-Baden: lightly
raced this season: formerly trained by M Prescott and was a winning 2yo: eff at 5f, stays
6f well: acts on firm and yldg ground.   74
*1860 TARIB (H T Jones) 3-8-7 A Murray 1: -214212: Had no answer to winner final 1f:
remains in fine form: see 1860.   67
--   SIMON SACC (K Engan) 4-9-3 C Gauntlett 1: 4420133: --   66
2241 FILLEOR (G P Gordon) 3-8-7 G Carter 1: 132-004: Ran quite well: see 2241: stays 6f.   55
1851 NASHIA 3-8-7 N Howe 1: 20-0000: See 1851.   54
2144 AL TRUI 6-9-3 M Wigham 1: 0002000: Fin 9th: see 1429.   00
10 ran   2½,2½,2¾,½   (D Hicks)   J Pease France

KEMPTON   Friday September 5th   Righthanded, Sharpish Track

Official Going Given As GOOD

2458 GEOFFREY HAMLYN H'CAP (0-50) 3YO   £2842   1m   Firm 13 -09 Slow   [57]

1998 NORDICA [7] (P Walwyn) 3-7-11 M Roberts 7/2: -001241: 3 ch f Northfields - Princess
Arabella (Crowned Prince) Back over her best trip and led over 2f out, ridden out to win a
3yo h'cap at Kempton: earlier won a fillies mdn at Yarmouth: eff over 1m, stays 10f tho'
possibly not 12f: dam a sister to Oaks winner Fair Salinia: acts on gd and firm grd and
does well on a sharp/easy course: in gd form.   40
2234 TURFAH [1] (P Walwyn) 3-9-1 Paul Eddery 3/1 FAV: 0211122: Held up, had ev ch: see 2234   54
1284 PARIS TURF [3] (G Wragg) 3-9-3 P Robinson 10/1: -003103: Abs: ev ch and fin clear
rem: gd effort and is racing off quite an attractive mark: stays 1m well: see 1028.   52
2170 AITCH N BEE [5] (J Dunlop) 3-9-4 W Carson 9/1: -040124: Prom most: btr over 9f in 2170   39
*2085 DHALEEM [9] 3-8-9 W Swinburn 7/2: -10: Ran on same pace: btr 2085 (stiff trk).   29
--   SHANNON VALE [2] 3-9-8(3oh) G Foster(7) 25/1: 01-0: In need of race and never posed
a threat: only ran twice last season, winning a Leicester mdn on his latter start: eff over
7f and will stay further: acts on gd and firm grd: should improve next time.   40
*2399 BATH [6] 3-7-7(3oh) Jackie Houston(7) 9/1: 4004210: Made much: fdd into 7th:see 2399   00
2294 RESCUE PACKAGE [10] 3-8-9 P Waldron 10/1: -044030: Cl.up 6f: fin 8th: best 1395.   00
1520 Hot Gem [8] 8-4   2294 Northern Impulse [4] 8-9
10 ran   ¾,2,8,nk,1   (Major J H de Burgh)   P Walwyn Newmarket

2459 HILLFIELDS FILLIES H'CAP (0-60) 3YO   £3454   1m   Firm 13 -06 Slow   [49]

2314 LADY LA PAZ [3] (P Cundell) 3-7-10 N Adams 9/1: 2333031: 3 br f King of Spain -
Selham (Derring-Do) Gained a deserved win, ran on strongly to lead on the post in a 3yo fillies
h'cap at Kempton: rarely out of the money this term tho' this was her first win: half sister
to sev winners, including fair middle dist performer Hazel Bush: eff between 6f and 1m:
acts on firm and yldg ground and seems suited by a sharp/easy course.   20
2184 FLYING BIDDY [12] (J Hindley) 3-8-6 A Shoults(5) 9/1: -300132: Btn a whisker: see 2184.   30
2274 FAIR ATLANTA [4] (M Usher) 3-8-1 R Street 33/1: 2401003: Led over 2f out, just caught.   25
2250 SOMETHING CASUAL [10] (A Hide) 3-9-4(bl) S Cauthen 6/1: 0003444: Just btn: see 2250.   42
1953 HOT MOMMA [1] 3-8-1 Paul Eddery 20/1: 0433000: Held up, ran on same pace: see 89.   21
2250 CARRIBEAN SOUND [8] 3-8-12 M Roberts 14/1: 1004200: Late prog: stays 1m: see 713.   28
2291 FRIVOLE [5] 3-8-7 T Quinn 11/2 JT FAV: 4011020: Al mid-div: fin 7th: see 1885.   00
2165 GREAT LEIGHS [7] 3-9-7 R Hills 16/1: 0120000: No threat in 8th: best 359 (soft).   00

2294 COURT TOWN [2] 3-7-11 A Mcglone 11/2 JT FAV: 04-0040: Fdd into 9th: see 2027.   00
*2316 TOP DEBUTANTE [11] 3-9-3(5) W Swinburn 6/1: -300210: Made most: wknd: see 2316 (soft)   00
2250 EMERALD WAVE [9] 3-8-12 W Carson 10/1: -001000: Wknd 2f out: btr 2250 (7f): see 1804. 00
2319 TZU WONG [6] 3-8-9 Pat Eddery 8/1: 0000130: Al rear: best over 7f in 1751   00
12 ran   shthd,hd,shthd,1½,2½   (G Herridge)   P Cundell Compton, Berks.

2460 BONUSPRINT SIRENIA STAKES 2YO   £7908   6f   Firm 13 -05 Slow

*1778 GAYANE [5] (H Cecil) 2-9-0 S Cauthen 2/1 JT FAV: 11: 2 b f Nureyev - Rousalka (Habitat)
Smart filly: quickly into her stride and was never hdd when an impressive winner of val Sirenia
Stks at Kempton: earlier won a val newcomers race at Ascot: beautifully bred, dam is a half
sister to last years triple Classic winner Oh So Sharp:: clearly very eff over 6f and
certain to stay further: acts on gd and firm grd and on any trk: suited by front running
tactics: well regarded by her omnipotent stable and looks a very exciting prospect for
next season.   77
1467 DARLEY KNIGHT [7] (J Dunlop) 2-9-3 W Carson 7/1: 1202: Ran a fine race after a
fair abs: caught a real tartar here: will be winning again soon: see 1242.   68
2221 MOREWOODS [8] (I Balding) 2-9-0 Pat Eddery 2/1 JT FAV: 1143: Heavily bckd, never
travelling that well tho' did run on well from dist: twice rather disapp since 1606 (C/D).   61
2162 MANDUB [4] (H T Jones) 2-8-11 R Hills 20/1: 13124: No extra dist: genuine sort: see 1746 56
876 SAMEEK [1] 2-8-11 W Swinburn 14/1: 2130: Abs: nearest fin: see 876.   46
*2118 LA PETITE NOBLESSE [3] 2-8-8 B Rouse 20/1: 010: Came to chall below dist, sn btn:
may prove best over the minimum trip for the time being: see 2118.   42
*2392 RUMBOOGIE [2] 2-8-11 M Roberts 10/1: 010: Prom over ¼ way: see 2392.   00
1789 BLUE TANGO [6] 2-8-8 G Starkey 9/1: 3321330: Cl up over ¼ way: see 1454 & 1238.   00
8 ran   2½,1½,½,4,hd   (N Phillips)   H Cecil Newmarket

2461 BONUSPRINT SEPTEMBER STAKES   £17210   1m 3f   Firm 13 +15 Fast

2200 DIHISTAN [5] (M Stoute) 4-9-2 W R Swinburn 6/1: -113001: 4 b c Tyrnavos - Damosa
(Abdos) Very smart colt: under press early in str but rallied gamely to lead on the line
in very fast run Gr 3 September Stks at Kempton: earlier won Gr 2 Hardwicke Stks at Royal
Ascot and was a very easy first time out winner of a val Listed race at Goodwood: in fine
form last season, winning h'caps at Leicester and Yarmouth (2): half brother to the smart
Dazari: very eff over 10/12f: acts on any going and on any trk: most genuine and consistent
colt who has also proved a fine pacemaker for his stable's stars.   82
+2157 BAKHAROFF [3] (G Harwood) 3-8-6 G Starkey 11/8 FAV: 1-23312: Heavily bckd: sn
niggled along but ran on gamely to lead cl home only to be pipped on the post: another
fine effort: see 2157.   82
2114 RAKAPOSHI KING [6] (H Cecil) 4-9-0 S Cauthen 9/2: 0-31143: Set a strong pace and
kept on most determindly when hdd inside dist: only just btn and is enjoying a fine season: see 1513. 79
2145 TREMBLANT [1] (R Smyth) 5-9-0 Pat Eddery 14/1: 2000334: Looked dangerous below dist,
not quicken: fine effort over this longer trip against highclass opposition: see 2145 & 5.   73
*2004 HIGHLAND CHIEFTAIN [7] 3-8-6 W Carson 7/2: 4-01210: Would surely have fin closer
but for being bumped below dist: not given a hard race and worth another chance: see 2004.   71
2200 WYLFA [2] 5-9-0 B Rouse 14/1: 2243300: Wknd 2f out: see 2200 & 1913.   61
2194 K BATTERY [4] 5-9-0 M Roberts 50/1: 0020200: Outsider and the first btn: see 1811.   00
7 ran   shthd,hd,3,2,5   (H H Aga Khan)   M Stoute Newmarket

2462 TWICKENHAM FILLIES STAKES 3YO   £7362   1m 2f   Firm 13 -07 Slow

2202 GESEDEH [4] (M Jarvis) 3-9-0 Pat Eddery 2/1: -110001: 3 ch f Ela-Mana Mou - Le
Melody (Levmoss) Smart filly who returned to her best form here, qcknd to lead inside dist
in a val 3yo fillies stks at Kempton: began the season with impressive wins in a Salisbury
mdn and val Pretty Polly Stks (Listed race) at Newmarket: very well bred, being a half sister
to sev winners including topclass middle dist performer Ardross: very eff over 10f: acts on
fast ground tho' prefers some cut under foot: acts on any trk: should win again before
season's end.   75
1468 RIYDA [3] (R F Johnson Houghton) 3-8-11 S Cauthen 14/1: -122302: Abs: stayed on
really well to snatch 2nd cl home: stays 10f well: grand effort and must win again soon: see 1153. 69
2196 COCOTTE [1] (W Hern) 3-8-11 W Carson 6/5 FAV: -001423: Heavily bckd and tried to
make all: no extra cl home tho' remains in fine form: see 1932, 1580.   68
+2061 NORPELLA [6] (G Wragg) 3-8-11 P Robinson 7/1: 000-10: Raised in class and although
never threatening principals ran a gd race: acts on any trk: see 2061.   62
1489 LAVENDER MIST [2] 3-9-0 W R Swinburn 6/1: 12-140: Btn 2f out: abs since 1489.   49
2381 SPINNAKER LADY [5] 3-8-11 A Mcglone 200/1: 0000100: A forlorn hope: see 2073.   00
6 ran   1,nk,2½,10,15   (Sheikh Ahmed Al Maktoum)   M Jarvis Newmarket

2463 EUCLID HANDICAP STAKES (0-50) 3YO   £2981   7f   Firm 13 -25 Slow   [52]

2120 HIGHLY RECOMMENDED [13] (P Cundell) 3-7-7(3oh) N Adams 12/1: -00031: 3 b g Daring
March - Rosette (Red Alert) Well suited by this longer trip and made most, comfortably, in
a 3yo h'cap at Kempton: eff over 5/6f tho' clearly btr over 7f and should stay 1m: acts
on gd and firm ground and on any trk: on the upgrade and should win again.   28
2313 STORMGUARD [9] (W Jarvis) 3-7-7(1oh) M L Thomas 20/1: 0-30042: Fin strongly: will
be suited by a return to a longer trip: acts on any trk: see 1141.   20

*2294 LADY FOR TWO [10] (M Stoute) 3-9-1(6ex) M A Giles(7) 15/2: 041D213: Had ev ch:
in gd form: see 2294.   40
2313 SEQUESTRATOR [6] (W Musson) 3-7-13 P Robinson 20/1: 0010004: Al up there: best 1316. 23
2120 GERSHWIN [4] 3-7-7(VIS)(6oh) J Carter(7) 33/1: 1200100: Visored first time: al prom: see 2088.17
2343 BERTIE WOOSTER [3] 3-9-2(bl) Pat Eddery 6/1: 0220240: Never nearer: see 2207.   40
2369 CODICES [7] 3-9-7 G Starkey 10/3: 0010120: Well bckd: below-par eff: see 2099.   00
2242 ALMAROSE [1] 3-8-3 W Carson 2/1 FAV: 012-020: Never looked likely to justify fav:
better over 6f in 2242 (stiff trk): see 886.   00
234 Misnaad [14] 9-7   2120 Vaiglian [12] 8-0   2250 King Of Spades [8] 9-7
928 Hopefull Dancer [11] 7-11(bl)(3ow)   2135 Sirtaki Dancer [2] 7-7(3oh)
1970 Bernigra Girl [5] 7-9
14 ran   2½,1,½,shthd,hd   (Lord McAlpine)   P Cundell Compton, Berks

---

HAYDOCK   Friday September 5th   Lefthand, Galloping Track

Official Going Given As GOOD

2464 MERSEYSIDE POLICE MAIDEN STAKES 3YO   £2054   1m 6f   Good 56 -18 Slow

2148 SURE GROUND [4] (P Walwyn) 3-9-0 N Howe 8/1: 00-0301: 3 ch c Grundy – Lareyna (Welsh
Pageant) Led over 2f out, running on under press in a 3yo mdn at Haydock: lightly raced colt
who stays 14f well: acts on gd grd and a gall trk.   40
2175 LE MOULIN [14] (K Brassey) 3-9-0 T Williams 16/1: -004002: Ev ch final 1f: best
effort yet and is clearly suited by today's 14f trip: acts on gd grd and on any trk.   35
2269 TAP EM TWICE [5] (F Lee) 3-9-0(VIS) T Lucas 12/1: -233043: Visored first time: al prom:
has changed stables recently: best in 430.   34
2306 DAWN LOCH [9] (J Shaw) 3-8-11 T Ives 7/1: 004: Active in mkt: chance inside final
2f: improved effort from this lightly raced filly: stays 14f well: acts on gd ground: see 2306. 28
2269 SHERGOR [13] 3-9-0 W Ryan 4/6 FAV: -20: Heavily bckd: not stay 14f? See 2269.   30
996 MARBLE MOON [11] 3-8-11 S Perks 50/1: -000: Abs: nearest fin and should do better
next time: very lightly raced filly who is a half sister to the smart Marble Run: stoutly
bred and should be suited by this trip, possibly further.   22
--   WINTER HAVEN [12] 3-9-0 G Duffield 8/1: -0: Fdd str on racecourse debut: half brother
to sev winners and should improve.   00
1645 Comazant [7] 9-0   2275 Prince Bold [8] 9-0   2148 Lord Capilano [1] 9-0
2280 Mr Moss [6] 9-0   2030 Dime And A Dollar [2] 9-0
--   Tancred Sand [10] 9-0   2400 Merseyspeed [3] 8-11
14 ran   2½,nk,2,hd,3   (Salisbury Farms Ltd)   P Walwyn Lambourn, Berks.

2465 ST ANNES NURSERY HANDICAP 2YO   £3456   6f   Good 56 +08 Fast   [56]

+2391 BREWIN TIME [16] (M H Easterby) 2-8-0(10ex) A Mackay 9/4 FAV: 00311: 2 b g Palm
Track – Baggin Time (Pinsun) Impr gelding who is in fine form: comfortably defied 10lbs pen
in nursery h'cap at Haydock: easy winner of a similar event at Chester recently: eff at 6f
stays 7f well: acts on gd and soft ground and on any trk: runs well when up with the pace:
brother to fair h'capper Mashin Time.   38
*2136 PANACHE [11] (P Haslam) 2-8-2 T Williams 10/1: 21D3012: Al prom: in gd form: see 2136. 35
*2380 MISS MILVEAGH [9] (A Bailey) 2-8-9(10ex) J Carr(7) 7/1: 322213: Led over 1f out:
in fine form: acts on any trk: see 2380.   42
2310 CREAM AND GREEN [4] (K White) 2-7-7(10oh) G Dickie 25/1: 0002024: Stayed on well,
despite being 10lbs out of the h'cap: in gd form and seems equally eff over 6f/1m: acts on
gd and yielding.   20
2272 BORN FREE AGAIN [10] 2-8-11(bl) T Lucas 11/1: 0203440: Nearest fin: btr 7f? See 2035. 37
2198 GLOW AGAIN [1] 2-9-7 M Wood 12/1: 3111200: Slow start, fair eff under 9-7: see 2198, 1255 45
2398 PANBOY [2] 2-7-7(bl)(3oh) N Carlisle 25/1: 2400000: Dsptd lead most: see 108 (soft)   17
1895 BOTHY BALLAD [5] 2-8-1 M Fry 12/1: 1020: Led most: see 1895 (7f).   25
2307 Hugo Z Hackenbush [8] 7-7(8oh)   2082 Joint Services [3] 8-5
2284 Bo Babbity [13] 8-7   2265 Penbreasy [6] 7-7(4oh) 1599 Tootsie Jay [9] 7-7(15oh)
2137 Ermine Green [14] 8-7   2284 Taliesin [20] 8-3   1480 Parkers Joy [12] 8-1
2137 Whistling Wonder [15] 7-13(5ow)   2364 Blaze Of Gold [18] 7-8
2218 Lady Sunday Sport [17] 7-7(2oh)   *2209 Mendip Star [7] 7-7(bl)
20 ran   1½,hd,2½,½,1,shthd,shthd   (P Baillie)   M H Easterby Great Habton, Yorks

2466 BIRKDALE SELLING STAKES 2YO   £1249   1m   Good 56 -35 Slow

2364 RIBOGIRL [11] (R Sheather) 2-8-8 M Rimmer 10/1: 000001: 2 b f Riboboy – Green
Diamond (Green God) Made almost all, ridden out in a 2yo seller at Haydock Sept 5 (bought
in 2,200 gns): stays today's 1m trip well: acts on gd and firm grd and a galloping trk.   20
--   GAELIC LOVER [12] (C Tinkler) 2-8-11 M Wood 16/1: 2: Chance final 1f: just btn on
racecourse debut and 6l clear 3rd: can find a similar event: cheaply bought: stays 1m and
acts on gd ground.   22
2405 PATHIAS [8] (J D Home) 2-8-11 W Newnes 9/2: 003: Disp. lead: best eff yet and
seems suited by 1m and gd ground.   11
1413 VICTORIA STAR [1] (G Reveley) 2-8-8 R P Elliott 16/1: 004: No extra final 1f:
best effort yet after abs: very lightly raced filly who is a half sister to middle dist
winner Vickstown.   05

2166 LEADING ROLE [13] 2-9-1 A Dicks(7) 4/1 FAV: 0001040: Best over 7f in 1684.   10
2298 GWYNBROOK [9] 2-8-11(bl) L Charnock 9/2: 0034000: Ev ch str: lightly raced since 1566.   00
1635 TYRED NSNOOKERED [5] 2-8-11 M Birch 11/2: 0000: Prom early: fin 8th.   00
1413 SUPER GAMBLER [3] 2-8-8 J Callaghan(7) 11/2: 000: No show after abs: see 1413.   00
2140 LATERAL [2] 2-8-11 J Carroll(7) 15/2: 0020000: Wknd and fin last: disapp since 1333   00
1905 On The Mark [4] 8-11   2377 Tuesday Evening [7] 8-8
2177 Star Play [10] 8-11   1373 Tubeson [14] 8-11   1997 Relampego [6] 8-8
14 ran   ½,6,1½,½,3   (Mrs E N Pyle)   R Sheather Newmarket

2467 HEPWORTH SUPERSLEVE HANDICAP 0-35   £5039   1m 4f   Good 56 +06 Fast   [33]

--   MISRULE [9] (D Arbuthnot) 4-9-7 K Darley 25/1: 0120-1: 4 b g Dominion - Miss McLairon
(Klairon) First time out, led over 1f out, ridden out in a h'cap at Haydock Sept 5: lightly
raced on the Flat last term, winning a Bath mdn: eff at 12f, stays further and has useful
form over hurdles: acts on firm and soft ground and on any trk.   37
--   FIRST BILL [12] (H Candy) 3-8-9 W Newnes 20/1: 00000-2: Led till 1f out on belated
seasonal debut: gd effort: lightly raced in '85: bred to be suited by this trip and further:
acts on a sound surface and may find a small h'cap.   31
*2324 MALADHU [3] (J Fitzgerald) 7-9-5(4ex) D Nicholls 8/1: 3240-13: In gd form: see 2324.   28
2188 MR GARDINER [7] (W Brooks) 4-8-5 T Ives 33/1: 2000004: Prom most: stayed: tried
in blinkers last time out: best in 92.   10
*2395 RAPIDAN [4] 5-7-11(4ex) G Carter(3) 15/2: 0000010: Came too late: see 2395 (sharpish trk)   01
*2330 DENBOY [15] 4-8-13 R Carter(5) 8/1: 0012010: Ev ch str: btr 2330.   16
2300 LOUD LANDING [17] 3-8-3 R Lines(3) 10/1: 0-0340: There 1m: much btr 2300 (10f).   00
*2315 GRAND CELEBRATION [2] 4-8-6(4ex) R Curant 13/2 FAV: 0001110: Op 10/1: btr 2315(10f,sell) 00
2337 DIPYN BACH [20] 4-8-9(BL) G Duffield 7/1: 4403020: Bl first time but found little: see 2337.   00
*2175 STORMY PROSPECT [10] 7-13 (vis) T Lucas 7/1: -34010: Much btr 2175.   00
2173 Im Exceptional [8] 7-13   1569 Capa [11] 8-3
2285 Socks Up [6] 8-9   2406 Irish Hero [1] 9-6(BL)
--   Career Bay [16] 8-12   2346 Standard Breakfast [14] 8-11(bl)
1651 Gallois Bosquet [13] 8-3   2337 Swynford Prince [19] 8-6(vis)
2217 Boldera [18] 7-8(1ow)
19 ran   2,1½,2,½,hd   (T D Holland-Martin)   D Arbuthnot Newbury.

2468 JACK RUBIN TROPHY STAKES 2YO   £3175   1m   Good 56 +01 Fast

2384 SANTELLA SAM [5] (M Ryan) 2-8-7 N Day 12/1: 23201: 2 b c Balzac - Summertime Lady
(No Robbery) Useful colt: gained his first win, led over 1f out, cmftbly in quite val 2yo
stks at Haydock Sept 5: clearly stays 1m well: acts on gd and fast grd and goes well on a
gall track.   56
2199 DR BULASCO [17] (S Norton) 2-9-1 J Reid 8/1: 21342: Kept on well final 1f and 4l
clear 3rd: consistent colt who deserves another win: see 2199, 1660: stays 1m.   60
2239 RED TIMBER [15] (R Sheather) 2-8-7 M Rimmer 20/1: 03: Ev ch in str: gd effort and
stays 1m: acts on gd ground and a gall trk and can find a race: see 2239.   44
*1572 WOLSEY [18] (H Cecil) 2-8-11 W Ryan 9/4: 114: Hmpd slightly over 2f out: abs since 1572:
stays 1m, looks to need further.   47
2001 CABOT [8] 2-8-7 W Newnes 12/1: 20: Nearest fin : another gd effort and stayed today's
1m trip well: one to keep an eye on: see 2001.   42
--   LORD JUSTICE [10] 2-8-7 G Duffield 9/1: 0: Prom most on racecourse debut, showing
promise: first foal of the very smart filly Star Pastures who stayed 10f well: should
be suited by today's trip: acts on gd ground, will improve.   34
+2332 ANGARA ABYSS [3] 2-9-1 A Clark 5/4 FAV: 411210: Heavily bckd: led till over 1f out,
folding disapp quickly: not stay 1m? See 2332 (easier trk).   00
2218 Lack Of Pearls [16] 8-4   *1504 Bills Henry [1] 9-1
2379 Running Money [4] 8-7   1345 The Main Man [11] 8-7 -- Prince Zamaro [12] 8-7
2051 Nicophana [13] 8-4   1296 Golden Tree [7] 8-7   2270 Montys Gunner [14] 8-7
2325 Call For Taylor [2] 8-4   1812 Pathero [9] 8-7
1735 Lindrick [6] 8-7
18 ran   2,4,½,nk,¾   (Roy Taiano)   M Ryan Newmarket

2469 CLAUDE HARRISON MEM TRPHY HCAP 0-60   £3402   5f   Good 56 +01 Fast   [55]

2378 ARDROX LAD [12] (M Blanshard) 6-9-8 J Reid 11/2 FAV: 0000021: 6 ch h Roi Soleil -
Petalina (Mummy's Pet) Remains a useful sprinter: showed a gd turn of foot to lead near the
finish in a h'cap at Haydock: in gd form in the first half of last season winning h'caps at
Sandown, Goodwood and Haydock (first time out): in '84 won at York and Haydock: eff at 5/6f:
acts on any going and on any trk: genuine horse who has dropped down the h'cap and may
go in again.   60
2322 PENDOR DANCER [5] (K Ivory) 3-7-7(vis)(1oh) N Carlisle 12/1: 0010102: Made almost all:
fine effort and is in grand form: below his best in 2322(soft): see 1940.   31
1810 CHAPLINS CLUB [14] (D Chapman) 6-9-4(bl) D Nicholls 8/1: 0002043: Came too late:
gd effort: see 1222, 1026.   53
877 BOLLIN EMILY [9] (M H Easterby) 5-9-4 M Birch 13/2: -024234: Sn prom and ran well
after fair abs: deserves a win: see 660, 428.   51
2160 STEPHENS SONG [13] 3-7-10 S Dawson 14/1: 1100000: Al there and not btn far: lightly
raced since 233 and ran a fair race here: see 233.   30

+2322 LADY CARA [6] 6-7-12(6ex) M Fry 7/1: 2024110: Cl.up 6th: in grand form: see 2322. 29
2143 NO BEATING HARTS [15] 3-8-6 W Newnes 7/1: 0213000: Prom most, fin 7th: best 1654, 1505 00
2362 CELTIC BIRD [7] 6-8-5 N Day 7/1: 0231130: Below her best: see 1896. 00
1986 KING CHARLEMAGNE [10] 7-8-8 Julie Bowker(7) 10/1: -004340: Never showed: yet to
find best form: see 1508. 00
1896 CHINA GOLD [1] 7-8-4 M Wood 9/1: 0420200: Stumbled at the start: see 1268. 00
2378 Runaway [4] 8-5(vis)   1704 Ken Siddall [17] 7-7(10oh)
1347 Bay Presto [11] 7-10(bl)   1730 Spacemaker Boy [3] 8-8
2124 Philstar [2] 7-7(8oh)   2256 Princess Wendy [8] 7-9
16 ran   1,hd,½,¼,shthd,1   (Sheikh Hazza bin Zahed Al Nahayan)   M Blanshard Lambourn

2470 BIRKDALE SELLING STAKES 2YO   £1241   1m   Good 56 -25 Slow

2150 FU LU SHOU [7] (P Haslam) 2-8-11 T Williams 8/1: 001: 2 gr c Godswalk - Perdliance
(Reliance) Showed impr form over this longer trip, led inside final 2f, driven out in a
2yo seller at Haydock Sept 5 (no bid): half brother to sev winners: clearly stays 1m well,
acts on gd ground and a gall trk. 23
1622 WESTGALE [10] (C Tinkler) 2-8-11 M Wood 12/1: 003002: Abs: led briefly over 2f out:
gd effort and seems best over 7f/1m: see 1137. 19
2298 LYN RAE [11] (M H Easterby) 2-8-8 M Birch 9/4 JT.FAV: 0004033: Nicely bckd: ev ch
2f out: consistent: stays 1m: see 2298. 16
2364 BABY COME HOME [6] (P Rohan) 2-8-8 A Clark 9/4 JT.FAV: 0004: Nicely bckd: stays 1m:
half sister to middle dist winner Timminion: acts on gd and yldg: may find a seller. 14
2050 DELITE MUFFIN [13] 2-8-8 J Quinn(5) 14/1: 00300: Never nearer: stays 1m, see 1905. 06
1305 GALWAY EXPRESS [4] 2-8-11 G Duffield 15/2: 0000: Made much after abs: dropped to
selling company today: tried in bl last time: see 1105. 05
-- MISS PRECARIOUS [9] 2-8-8 T Ives 8/1: 0: Never nearer 7th on racecourse debut and
should do better: sister to middle dist winner General Concorde: should be suited by today's trip 00
603 SAWDUST JACK [5] 2-8-11 T Lucas 10/1: 0000: Long abs: there 5f: should strip fitter
next time: see 515. 00
1862 Paddy Maloney [12] 8-11   2168 Willys Niece [8] 8-8
1738 Sappharino [1] 8-8(BL)   2168 Finlux Design [3] 8-11
-- Johnsons Pride [2] 8-8
13 ran   2,shthd,1,4,2,5   (M H Yong)   P Haslam Newmarket

2471 BIRKDALE SELLING STAKES 2YO   £1241   1m   Good 56 -49 Slow

*2177 TRYNOVA [9] (G P Gordon) 2-8-8 G Duffield 5/4 FAV: 020211: 2 gr f Tyrnavos - Alicia
Markova (Habat) In gd form and led final 1f, driven out in the slowest div of a 2yo seller
at Haydock: last time out was a game winner of a Claimer at Leicester: eff at 7f, stays 1m:
acts on gd and firm ground and on any trk: sold today for 7,400 gns. 28
1883 CAMMAC LAD [5] (C Tinkler) 2-8-11 M Wood 5/1: 000032: Fin well and just btn: seems
certain to find a similar event and suited by today's trip: see 1883. 30
-- MISS MARIPOSA [4] (D H Jones) 2-8-8 J Reid 12/1: 3: Chance final 1f on racecourse
debut: cheaply acquired filly who stays 1m on a gall trk: should find a seller. 24
2279 GILLOT BAR [7] (M W Easterby) 2-8-12 T Lucas 9/1: 0021404: Al up there: ran well:
best over 7f/1m: see 1795. 24
2168 DONNA IMMOBILE [2] 2-8-8 B Thomson 10/1: 000: Led over 2f out, showing improved form:
stays 1m: see 1832. 19
2050 MADAME LAFFITTE [13] 2-8-12 T Ives 7/1: 02100: Hmpd over 1f out: prob stays 1m: see 1622 20
2178 HONEY PLUM [3] 2-8-8 M Wigham 6/1: 440400: Nicely bckd: pulled hard in lead: best 2032 00
1121 Julios Lad [12] 8-11   -- Sampreki [10] 8-11   1105 Record Bangler [1] 8-11
2396 Miss Bolero [8] 8-8   2323 Rosies Image [6] 8-8   1881 Palace Ruler [11] 8-8
13 ran   ½,1½,2,½,2,6   (Mrs A P B Allen)   G P Gordon Newmarket

Official Going Given As GOOD

2472 FLEETWOOD CLAIMING STAKES 2YO   £5475   6f   Good 54 +01 Fast

2301 SPANISH CALM [12] (R Sheather) 2-8-9 M Rimmer 4/1 FAV: 031: 2 gr c King Of Spain -
Tranquility Base (Roan Rocket) Impr colt: led ½ way on standside and readily drew clear in a
2yo Claimer at Haydock Sept 6: claimed for 20,000 today: half brother to sev winners,
including last years useful juv Priory Place: eff at 5f, stays 6f well: acts on gd/firm
and yldg ground and does well on a gall trk. 49
-2265 SPANISH SLIPPER [6] (W Haigh) 2-8-6(bl) J H Brown 9/1: 4224122: Led far side over
1f out: seems equally eff over 5/6f: see 2265, 1972. 36
*2320 DANCING DIANA [9] (R Hannon) 2-8-9 G Starkey 5/1: 1400013: Chance far side final 1f:
running well: see 2320. 38
2067 CRANCHETER [18] (J Etherington) 2-8-9(BL) S Webster 33/1: 004: Bl first time: led
3f standside: improving: see 2067. 36
2364 ISLAND LOCKSMITH [15] 2-8-4 M Wigham 14/1: 030: Nearest fin: claimed by D Garraton
here: see 2026. 31
2100 KALAS IMAGE [11] 2-8-5 J Bleasdale 20/1: 3031400: Prom most far side: see 1561 (5f). 22

2162 LADY PAT [7] 2-9-2 J Reid 9/1: 1131240: Early speed: btr 5f? See 1746, 1568 (firm)   00
2308 EVENING PRAYERS [5] 2-8-1 A Shoults 8/1: 00: No threat: btr 2308 (yldg).   00

1920 Beau Benz [3] 8-4	2179 Marquee Cafe [22] 9-0	2323 Cawstons Prejudice [20] 7-13
2080 Needwood Nut [8] 8-4	*1163 Dormestone Lad [13] 8-8(bl)	
2043 Treize Quatorze [23] 7-13		2297 Native Pawn [1] 9-0
2249 Home Device [17] 8-11	-- Sixty Minutes [10] 8-9	
2334 Mere Music [14] 8-7(bl)		-- Everloft [16] 8-4
-- Via Veritas [19] 8-1	1625 Malacanang [21] 8-5(5ow)	
1949 Lime Brook [2] 7-13	2380 Remain Free [4] 8-4(bl)	
23 ran 5,hd,½,shthd,5	(J C Smith)	R Sheather Newmarket

2473 HOYLAKE STAKES 3YO   £3589   7f   Good 54 -15 Slow

2241 HIDDEN BRIEF [5] (R Boss) 3-9-1 E Guest(3) 13/8 FAV: 1200201: 3 ch f Pyjama Hunt -
Himalia (High Line) Fairly useful filly: led 2f out, cmftbly, in a 3yo stks at Haydock: first
time out won on soft grd at Leicester: in '85 won at Redcar and also 4th in Gr 3 Hoover Fillie
Mile at Ascot: eff at 6f - 1m: acts on firm and soft and a gall trk.   49
295 MYSTICAL MAN [9] (E Eldin) 3-8-12 T Lucas 7/1: -030402: Led over 2f out: ex Irish
colt who was a winner on soft grd in '85: stays 7f: acts on gd - soft.   39
2295 TAYLOR OF SOHAM [10] (D Leslie) 3-8-8 D Mckay 5/1: 4132323: Nearest fin: another
good run: see 2295.   30
-- BOLD CELT [2] (C Booth) 3-8-11 J Reid 33/1: 0-4: Belated seasonal debut: chance over
1f out: fair effort from this very lightly raced colt: eff at 7f on gd grd and should
further improve.   28
-- BRITWYDD [6] 3-8-11 D Nicholls 33/1: 00-0: Never nearer on seasonal debut: ran only
twice in '85 and has scope for improvement: half brother to 2yo winner Kellys Reef: acts
on a sound surface.   23
2288 GAELIC FLUTTER [7] 3-9-4 W R Swinburn 10/3: -301000: Made much: best 1436.   29

2313 Raffles Virginia [8] 8-8	2126 Bills Ahead [4] 9-2	
2360 Top Row [11] 8-11	2174 The Stamp Dealer [3] 8-11	
1312 Edgewise [1] 9-2		
11 ran 2,1½,1½,1½,nk	(K Bethel)	R Boss Newmarket

2474 GROUP 2 VERNONS SPRINT CUP 3YO+   £41154   6f   Good 54 +17 Fast

2233 GREEN DESERT [1] (M Stoute) 3-8-12 W R Swinburn 5/4 FAV: 1202131: 3 b c Danzig -
Foreign Courier (Sir Ivor) Very smart colt: waited with, led 1f out and ridden out cl home
for a narrow win in Gr 2 Vernons Sprint Cup at Haydock: in tremendous form this season:
earlier winning Gr 1 July Cup at Newmarket, Free H'cap again at Newmarket (first time out) and
also 2nd in both the 2,000 Guineas and the St James' Palace Stks at Royal Ascot : stays 1m
on fast grd but is prob ideally suited by 6/7f (found 5f a little sharp last time): smart
2yo, winning the Flying Childers at Doncaster and July Stks at Newmarket: has a blistering
turn of foot and certain to win more highclass races.   87
+2241 HALLGATE [2] (S Hall) 3-8-12 G Starkey 11/2: 0410312: Kept on really well final 1f
and narrowly btn: in peak form and looks sure to win again soon: see 2241.   85
2347 POLYKRATIS [6] (M Francis) 4-9-3 C Rutter 25/1: 0312403: Dsptd lead 1f out: fine
effort: see 1889, 1387.   76
-2233 DOUBLE SCHWARTZ [8] (C Nelson) 5-9-3 J Reid 6/4: -112124: Chance over 1f out:
at his best over 5f: see 2233, 1889.   74
2233 BRIDESMAID [5] 3-8-9(vis) B Thomson 16/1: 1233400: Never nearer: see 1631, 854.   68
808 ROARING RIVA [3] 3-8-12 M Wigham 50/1: 0-44000: Led after ¼ way: fair effort after
long abs: now trained by W Musson: see 165.   65

2259 Grey Desire [4] 9-3	2347 Possedyno [7] 8-12	
8 ran nk,4,1,1½,2½,2,10	(Maktoum Al Maktoum)	M Stoute Newmarket

2475 JOHN SMITHS BREWERY H'CAP (0-70) 3YO+   £5908   1m   Good 54 -03 Slow   [59]

2234 ORIENTAL SOLDIER [5] (B Hills) 3-9-7(VIS) B Thomson 20/1: 0-02001: 3 b c Far Out
East - La Militante (Faraway Son) Very useful colt: visored first time and returned to form,
led over 1f out, ridden out in a val h'cap at Haydock: earlier a gd 2nd in a Gr 3 event in
Italy: most consistent 2yo winning at Salisbury and Haydock and placed on sev occasions:
eff at 7f, stays 1m well: acts on any grd: likes a gall trk, especially Haydock.   71
2144 READY WIT [8] (R Hannon) 5-8-1 D Mckay 20/1: 1000002: Chance final 1f: fine effort:
by far his best run since 361.   41
2437 SHELLMAN [9] (K Stone) 4-7-7(2oh) P Burke(5) 50/1: 0000003: Ran on well final 1f:
best effort for a long time: runs well here: see 55.   33
2296 INISHPOUR [6] (H Wharton) 4-8-11 J H Brown(5) 6/1: 0343144: Came too late: in
fine form: stays 1m: see 2039.   49
1912 SANTELLA MAC [13] 3-9-8 G Starkey 3/1 FAV: 01-1000: Well bckd: ev ch over 1f out:
btr 1912, 847.   62
+1520 SWIFTS PAL [2] 3-8-9 J Adams(7) 8/1: 0030410: Abs: never nearer: see 1520.   48
*2266 TAYLORMADE BOY [12] 3-8-1(8ex) L Charnock 12/1: 3031010: Fdd inside final 2f under
penalty: better 2266 (made all).   38
2258 YOUNG INCA [1] 8-9-0 J Reid 7/1: 0000030: Not his best trip: see 2258 (6f).   00
1507 LONDON BUS [11] 3-8-10 W R Swinburn 4/1: 0-11220: Abs: no threat: needed race?: see 1507. 00

2039 WELL RIGGED [3] 5-8-10 M Birch 7/1: 2120040: Made some: best 79.   00
2234 Come On The Blues [7] 9-3   2399 Golden Ancona [10] 7-7(vis)
12 ran   ¾,shthd,1,3,¼,1,2,1   (Sheikh Mohammed)   B Hills Lambourn, Berks

2476 E.B.F. BIRKENHEAD MAIDEN STAKES 2YO   £2824   5f   Good 54 -25 Slow

2301 PAPARELLI [14] (D Barron) 2-9-0 G Carter(3) 33/1: 01: 2 br c King of Spain - Davinia
(Gold Form) Fast impr colt: caused a 33/1 surprise, led inside final 2f cmftbly in quite
slow run 2yo mdn at Haydock: speedily bred colt who seems very eff over the minimum trip:
acts on gd grd and a gall track.   48
2301 ON YOUR PRINCESS [19] (J Payne) 2-9-0(BL) G Starkey 7/1: 00202: Visored first time:
chance final 1f: should find a race: below his best on yldg last time: see 1958.   43
780 BALKAN LEADER [7] (J Fitzgerald) 2-9-0 D Nicholls 4/1: 023: Sn prom after long abs:
fair effort: see 780, 583.   36
2167 TOUCH OF SPEED [16] (R Hollinshead) 2-9-0(BL) S Perks 25/1: 000004: Bl first time:
made much and kept on under press: best effort since 728 and seems suited by front running.   35
2191 PERFUMERIE [17] 2-8-11 B Thomson 14/1: 000: Al there, showing improvement: see 1958   27
1550 FATHER TIME [6] 2-9-0(BL) W R Swinburn 11/1: 000200: Bl first time after abs: prom
most: best 1442.   29
1928 GREAT ACT [3] 2-8-11 M Roberts 5/2 FAV: 30: Prom, fdd: disapp after 1928.   00
2254 NEARLY GREAT [8] 2-9-0 T Lucas 7/1: 040: Early speed: btr 2254.   00
-- UNSELFISH [12] 2-9-0 J Reid 10/1: 0: Early speed on debut: half brother to 7f winner
Dogmatic and should improve.   00
2232 Barnaby Benz [11] 9-0   2118 Motor Broker [9] 9-0   2281 Young Snugfit [15] 9-0
2320 White Of Morn [5] 9-0   2095 Gypsys Barn Rat [2] 8-11
-- Westpark Princess [20] 8-11   236 Dream Ticket [4] 9-0
-- Hopping Around [1] 9-0   -- Introvert [8] 9-0
18 ran   1½,2½,nk,1½,hd   (Colin Webster)   D Barron Thirsk, Yorks

2477 SOUTHPORT HANDICAP (0-60) 3YO+   £4155   1m 2f Good 54 +01 Fast   [56]

-2296 WILD HOPE [1] (G Huffer) 5-7-13 G Carter(3) 7/2 CO.FAV: 0-00421: 5 ch g Great Nephew -
Grove Star (Upper Case) Waited with and led inside final 1f, cmftbly in a h'cap at Haydock:
won this same event in '85 and also successful at Newmarket: in '84 won at Pontefract: eff at
1m, stays 10f well: acts on a sound surface and likes a gall trk.   38
2331 ROYAL HALO [4] (G Harwood) 5-9-10 G Starkey 5/1: 2011102: Led over 2f out: fine
effort under 9-10: definitely best on a sound surface: see 1792.   60
2331 SAMHAAN [9] (B Hanbury) 4-8-8(bl) W R Swinburn 7/2 CO.FAV: 1121323: Tremendously
consistent: see 2331.   42
2415 GREED [7] (D Smith) 5-7-7(4oh) L Charnock 12/1: 3240424: Never nearer: see 2415, 1185.   19
2219 PATO [2] 4-8-8 J Reid 13/2: 0004040: Chance 2f out: btr 2219 (9f), see 511.   32
1167 FRANGNITO [10] 3-7-11 G French 14/1: 4002200: Prom, fdd: long abs: best 765.   28
2123 CONMAYJO [3] 5-8-5 D Williams(7) 14/1: 3301000: Fin 7th: best 668.   00
2303 SMOKEYS SECRET [6] 4-9-0(vis) E Guest(3) 10/1: 113-040: Led over 3f out: best 2303 (9f) 00
+2374 MISTER POINT [5] 4-7-13 C Rutter(3) 7/2 CO.FAV: 0113010: Made much: well below 2374(yld). 00
9 ran   ¾,1,4,1,1,3,2,7   (John Wright)   G Huffer Newmarket

THIRSK   Saturday September 6th   Lefthand Sharpish Track

Official Going Given As GOOD

2478 FALCON CLAIMING STAKES 3YO   £2442   1m 4f Good/Firm 22 -21 Slow

2366 MARETH LINE [13] (J Fitzgerald) 3-7-11 J Lowe 12/1: -041: 3 ch g Royal Palace - Oceania
(Aureole) Prog to lead over 2f out and ran on strongly to win a 3yo Claimer at Thirsk: lightly
raced gelding who is bred to be well suited by middle dist: acts on gd/firm and yldg grd and
on a sharp trk: now to be trained by M Pipe and will eventually go hurdling.   18
2305 STANDON MILL [8] (J Wilson) 3-7-12 Julie Bowker(7) 20/1: 0400042: Ran on well: maiden
filly who seems to do best over 12f: acts on gd/firm and soft grd and on any trk.   12
1732 FRENCH FLUTTER [11] (R Sheather) 3-9-1 T Ives 15/2: -041303: Best on firm in 1160 (gall) 27
2300 SPACE TROOPER [12] (T Fairhurst) 3-9-0 M Hills 15/2: 0113204: Had ev ch: see 2300, 1678. 25
2128 RELATIVELY EASY [14] 3-8-12 G Duffield 11/4 FAV: -001120: Btr over 13f in 1822: see 1822 15
1809 MILTESCENS [7] 3-9-4(vis) W Ryan 5/1: 0302040: No threat: much btr 1177 (gall trk).   18
*2129 ASTRAL [6] 3-9-1 R Hills 9/2: 0-010: Front rank over 1m: best 2129(tight track).   00
2399 Princess Andromeda [19] 8-2   2300 Taxi Man [16] 8-3
1952 Miss Laura Lee [5] 7-12   1258 Oriental Express [10] 8-1
2152 Way Above [9] 7-11   1250 Doon Venture [2] 7-13(2ow)
2363 Nitida [4] 7-8(bl)   2152 Belvel [18] 7-12(1ow)   -- Floater [1] 7-13(2ow)
2366 Tap Duet [20] 7-11(vis)   -- Raffles Rogue [15] 8-1
194 Redally [17] 7-12
19 ran   3,1,nk,5,1½   (A Hutchins)   J Fitzgerald Malton, Yorks.

2479 RUSH AND TOMPKINS TROPHY NURSERY HCAP   £3720   7f   Good/Firm 22 -15 Slow [61]

*1180 MASTER POKEY [10] (M W Easterby) 2-7-7(2oh) A Proud 10/1: 011: 2 br g Uncle Pokey -

September Fire (Firestreak) Despite a lengthy abs led over 2f out, driven out to win a
nursery h'cap at Thirsk: earlier a well bckd winner of a mdn auction race at Pontefract:
cheaply bought gelding who is eff over 6/7f and should stay at least 1m: acts on gd and firm
ground and on a sharpish course.   36
2391 SHADE OF PALE [5] (P Haslam) 2-7-7(1oh) T Williams 7/4 FAV: 122: Heavily bckd:
ran on strongly under press, just held: in fine form: acts on fast and yldg ground and on
any trk: see 2032.   34
2209 INSHIRAH [6] (H T Jones) 2-8-6 R Hills 12/1: 10143: Narrowly btn: see 1920 (C/D).   46
+2011 GLAMGRAM FOR GRAMS [8] (R Boss) 2-8-5 G Duffield 14/1: 0414: In gd form: stays 7f.   42
2198 COLWAY RALLY [9] 2-8-10(BL) N Connorton 7/1: 203240: Bl first time: made much: see 2198 43
2227 TIMESWITCH [4] 2-8-3 T Ives 5/1: 200220: Well bckd: sn niggled along, stayed on
well and never nearer: see 2227 & 531.   32
2297 AUTHENTIC [15] 2-8-5 Kim Tinkler 6/1: 22100: Al mid-div: fin 7th: best 1982 (yldg)   33
2051 NORTON MELODY [16] 2-7-7(1oh) J Lowe 10/1: 3330: Never nearer in 8th: see 2051.   00
2105 SPY GIFT [11] 2-8-9 M A Giles(7) 10/1: 0330: Best over 6f in 1801.   00
2172 Musical Bells [1] 8-4   1697 Team Effort [7] 9-7   2310 Caerinette [14] 7-7(bl)(1oh)
612 Oyster Gray [13] 7-7(9oh)   2105 Melgrove [3] 8-1
2043 Katie Says [12] 7-7(1oh)   685 Boy Singer [2] 7-7(3oh)
16 ran   ½,nk,1½,2,3,nk,1   (Lord Belper)   M W Easterby Sherrif Hutton, Yorks

2480 GOLDEN GRAIN HAMBLETON CUP HCAP 0-60   £4259   2m   Good/Firm 22 -07 Slow   [47]

2201 ALLATUM [2] (B Hills) 3-8-2 M Hills 11/2: -204101: 3 b f Alleged - Star in The
North (Northern Dancer) Useful young stayer: led home turn and was sn clear for an easy win
in quite a val h'cap at Thirsk: earlier won a mdn at Newcastle over this trip and is clearly
well suited by a test of stamina: acts on gd/firm and yldg grd and on any trk: likely to
go for the Cesarewitch and should run well off her light weight.   46
1533 WITHY BANK [8] (M H Easterby) 4-9-4 K Hodgson 7/1: -113002: Abs: staying on fin tho'
no chance with winner: may win a h'cap as the ground eases: see 50.   44
*2326 SUN STREET [9] (C Brittain) 4-7-13(3ex) J Lowe 5/1: 4002013: Nicely bckd in this btr
class: al prom and is in gd form: see 2326.   22
2220 SPECIAL VINTAGE [6] (J Fitzgerald) 6-9-7 T Ives 5/1: 03304: Ran on same pace: see 778.   40
2326 DONT RING ME [3] 4-8-1 R Lines(3) 6/1: -040230: Wknd over 2f out: see 675.   15
2240 AGATHIST [4] 3-8-10 W Ryan 6/1: -411000: Led till home turn, rather disapp since 949.   28
2169 Singers Tryst [7] 8-2   1223 Red Duster [5] 7-7(4oh)
--   General Concorde [1] 9-2
9 ran   4,1½,3,4,8   (Alan Clore)   B Hills Lambourn, Berks

2481 MAIL ON SUNDAY 3YO SERIES HCAP 0-60   £3571   1m   Good/Firm 22 -03 Slow   [61]

2291 BLUE GUITAR [5] (J Hindley) 3-8-0(vis) M Hills 3/1 FAV: -442131: 3 b f Cure The Blues
- Mettle (Pretendre) In gd form, ran on well to lead inside dist in a 3yo h'cap at Thirsk:
earlier gained her first win in a similar race at Windsor: very eff over 7/8f on firm and
gd ground: well suited by a sharpish trk.   44
2266 BOLD SEA ROVER [9] (M H Easterby) 3-7-13 M Wood 10/1: 1301002: Led 2f out: stays 1m: 38
2165 CRESTA AUCTION [6] (G Pritchard Gordon) 3-9-7 G Duffield 7/2: 1123043: Kept on well:
gd effort under top weight and has only once fin out of the frame this term: see 2165, 210.   55
*2361 IZZY GUNNER [8] (A Robson) 3-7-7(6ex)(15oh) A Culhane(7) 12/1: 0220014: Upped in
class: led before ½ way, kept on: fine effort at the weights: see 2361.   22
1922 TRICK OR TREAT [4] 3-8-3(vis) N Connorton 5/1: 0-14440: No real threat: best over
this C/D in 518 and seems best when fresh.   31
2149 HALO HATCH [3] 3-8-7(bl) R Hills 5/1: 0300120: Held up, no threat: btr 2149 (9f)   28
2085 PREJUDICE [2] 3-8-1 T Williams 6/1: 30-3200: Al rear: fin 8th: see 1091 (C/D)   00
2266 Supreme Kingdom [1] 7-7   1626 Foretop [7] 7-8
9 ran   1½,2½,2½,½,4,1½   (K Al-Said)   J Hindley Newmarket

2482 HIGHFLYER STAKES 2YO   £3324   5f   Good/Firm 22 +02 Fast

2252 NAIVE CHARM [10] (R Boss) 2-8-8 G Duffield 10/1: 1201: 2 b f Milford - Proper Madam
(Mummy's Pet) Useful filly: showed impr form, led below dist and ran on strongly to win quite
a fast run 2yo stks at Thirsk: first time out winner of a mdn auction race at Haydock: very
eff over 5/6f on gd/firm and hvy ground: acts on any trk.   55
2162 COPPER RED [2] (P Makin) 2-8-11 T Ives 9/2: 323122: Al front rank: in gd form: see 2162 52
2153 NORGABIE [8] (P Calver) 2-8-8 M Fry 13/2: 123: Hung under press when chall after ½ way,
going on fin and possibly unlucky: certain to improve further and should win again soon.   49
2158 UN BEL DI [9] (O Douieb) 2-8-8 G Baxter 9/4 FAV: 01004: Tried to make all: see 1308.   47
-2398 FULL OF PRIDE [6] 2-9-6 K Hodgson 5/2: 120120: Al up there: clear rem: see 2398.   54
2097 SARIHAH [5] 2-8-11 R Hills 15/2: 012230: Front rank over ½ way: best here in 1916 (6f)   27
2375 Game Feathers [1] 8-8   1907 Danadn [7] 8-11   2281 Atakashack [4] 8-11
1869 Northern Security [3] 8-11
10 ran   2,shthd,½,2,7,2,hd   (K Bethel)   R Boss Newmarket

2483 SAXTY WAY STAKES 3YO   £2301   6f   Good/Firm 22 +09 Fast

2343 BONNY LIGHT [4] (R Sheather) 3-8-10(BL) T Ives 4/1 JT FAV: 04-3001: 3 b c Welsh
Saint - Daring Choice (Daring Display) Bl first time and landed some gd bets, led ½ way,

ridden out in quite a fast run 3yo stks at Thirsk: quite lightly raced colt whose best form
is over 6f: acts on firm and yldg grd and on any trk: may now win a small h'cap.   40
1043 ELSOCKO [11] (B Mcmahon) 3-8-7 J Hills(5) 14/1: -303302: Led 3f: fair eff: see 677, 309   30
2210 ZIADS ALIBY [12] (M Albina) 3-8-7 W Ryan 5/1: -43: Ran on well: stays 6f: see 2210.   25
*2409 HARRY HULL [10] (M W Easterby) 3-9-1 G Baxter 6/1: 0000414: Ran on same pace: in gd
form: see 2409.   32
2063 ORTICA [8] 3-8-7(VIS) M Wood 12/1: 4023330: Visored first time: onepaced: see 1794,   18
2339 SUPER TRUCKER [13] 3-8-10 N Day 20/1: -000: Nearest fin: speedily bred gelding who
showed his first signs of form here: acts on gd/firm grd and on a sharpish trk.   18
-2367 ENIGMA [7] 3-8-7 M Hills 4/1 JT FAV: 4-02020: Fin 8th: btr 2367: see 835.   00
2416 SAY PARDON [2] 3-9-1 T Williams 13/2: 2200100: Speed over ½ way: best over 5f in 2312   00

658 Free Clare [9] 8-7	2063 Raawiyeh [3] 8-7(bl)	2446 Bon Accueil [5] 8-10(bl)
2085 Greek Music [6] 8-7	1426 Latrigg Lodge [15] 8-10	
109 Faline [1] 8-7	2268 Imperial Sunrise [14] 8-7	
15 ran 1¼,2,hd,2½,1,shthd,nk	(Dr K Owusu-Nyantekyi)	R Sheather Newmarket

---

Official Going Given As GOOD/FIRM

2484 PRICE WATERHOUSE CHERTSEY LOCK STKS 2YO   £3200   7f   Good/Firm 28 -19 Slow

2263 WHITSTABLE [10] (G Harwood) 2-8-11 A Clark 9/4 FAV: 31: 2 b c Our Native - Carolina
Moon (Grey Dawn II): Very prom colt: hvly bckd & led over 1f out, soon drawing clear in a
2yo stakes at Kempton: first time out fin 3rd to Hendeka at Goodwood: U.S. bred colt who
should be well suited by 1m plus in time: acts on a sound surface & an easy trk: sure to
impr further & win btr races.   60
--   ROUSHAYD [20] (R J Houghton) 2-8-11 S Cauthen 10/1: 2: Made much on racecourse debut
and looks a certain future winner: half brother to a 10f winner: eff at 7f, should stay 1m:
acts on gd/firm grnd & an easy trk.   53
2263 ARTFUL DODGER [2] (W Hern) 2-8-11 W Carson 4/1: 43: Mkt drifter: dsptd lead: another
gd effort and can win soon: see 2263.   49
--   MARIENBOURG [18] (J Dunlop) 2-8-11 B Rouse 20/1: 4: Kept on well on racecourse debut:
promising effort from this first foal: dam a winner in France: should be suited by 1m plus
and have no trouble finding a race.   48
2239 BUCKRA MELLISUGA [14] 2-8-11 P Robinson 6/1: 30: Ev ch in str: another gd run: see 2239.   47
2179 KARABAT [6] 2-8-11 W Newnes 50/1: 00: Rank outsider: kept on & is fast impr: half
brother to 1m winner Franca Puzzle: acts on gd/firm & an easy trk.   43
2341 FASHIONABLY FORBES [8] 2-8-11 T Quinn 13/2: 40: Nicely bckd: fin 8th: see 2341.   00

-- Shantaroun [13] 8-11	-- Clopton [17] 8-11	2341 Optional Choice [16] 8-11
2205 Zanussi Line 0 8-11	-- Bonafortune [1] 8-11	-- Jubilee Again [9] 8-11
-- Bee Bee Cee [5] 8-11	-- Phaetons Glory [12] 8-11	
-- Apiarist [4] 8-11	2270 Lord Of Canewdon [3] 8-11	
2263 Arrowknight [7] 8-11	-- Torrance [15] 8-11	
19 ran 2¼,2,nk,nk,1½	(Anthony Speelman)	G Harwood Pulborough, Sussex

2485 CONTINENTAL AIRLINES NURSERY HCAP 2YO   £2560   6f   Good/Firm 28 -13 Slow   [62]

2172 SHADES OF NIGHT [2] (J Winter) 2-7-8 R Fox 20/1: 22141: 2 b f Red Sunset - Purple
Princess (Right Tack): Fin well to lead close home in a blnkt fin to a nursery h'cap at
Kempton: lightly raced since winning a fillies mdn at Carlisle in May: half sister to useful
2yo Running Princess: eff at 5f, stays 6f: acts on gd/firm & yld grnd & on any trk: well
suited by waiting tactics: consistent.   40
2252 ONGOING SITUATION [1] (D Morley) 2-9-7 B Rouse 12/1: 0131222: Under top weight &
just failed to get up: in grand form: see 2252.   66
-2261 JAISALMER [8] (D Elsworth) 2-8-3(bl) A Mcglone 13/2: 2002223: Ev ch inside final 2f: see 226147
+2016 RIOT BRIGADE [17] (C Brittain) 2-8-7 S Cauthen 15/2: 003314: Made much & stuck on
gamely: just btn: see 2016.   51
*2153 SHEER ROYALTY [4] 2-8-2 M L Thomas 12/1: 0410: Ch final 1f: not btn far: in fine form.   44
1869 MIGHTY BOLD [18] 2-7-11 W Carson 3/1 FAV: 0040: Hvly bckd: led ½way till close home:
btn just over 1L & can find a nursery: see 1512.   38
+2137 SHUTTLECOCK GIRL [5] 2-7-7(3oh) Dale Gibson(6) 33/1: 4303310: Stayed on well into 7th:
in fine form: see 2137.   30
*1843 GLOBAL LADY [6] 2-7-12 A Mackay 8/1: 210: Close up 8th: see 1843.   35
2181 GREENS GALLERY [16] 2-7-7(3oh) G Carter(1) 14/1: 0112000: Never nearer 9th: best 1585 (5f)24

2272 Grey Wolf Tiger [14] 8-5		2181 Derring Dee [10] 8-2	
1785 Micro Love [12] 8-1(1ow)		1604 Auntie Cyclone [9] 7-7	
1550 Madam Billa [11] 7-7(8oh)		1816 Souleiadou [7] 7-7(BL)(3oh)	
1504 Battleaxe [15] 8-10	2162 Hey Amadeus [3] 7-7	2070 Mamadora [13] 7-8(1ow)(8oh)	
18 ran hd,nk,shhd,½,hd,½,shhd,2	(P K B Nurse)	J Winter Newmarket	

2486 ANDERSON HANDICAP STAKES 3YO+ 0-70   £6400   1m 4f Good/Firm 28 +13 Fast   [57]

2220 STATELY FORM [2] (J Tree) 4-9-10 S Cauthen 3/1: -021401: 4 b c Double Form - State
Pension (Only For Life): Very useful colt: comfortably defied top weight, leading over 3f out

in a valuable h'cap at Kempton: earlier an easy winner of a valuable h'cap at Epsom: in gd
form in '85, winning at Kempton, Goodwood & Sandown & a minor event at Windsor: very eff
over 12f: acts on soft, best form on gd & firm grnd: acts on any trk, but well at home
on a sharpish one when up with the pace.   67
2220 ISLAND SET [3] (L Cumani) 4-9-5 R Cochrane 4/1: -022102: Stayed on well final 2f after
coming under press early in the str: fine effort: see 1935.   59
2237 CONVINCED [5] (G Harwood) 4-9-8 A Clark 7/1: -323103: Ev ch final 2f: not btn far &
well clear rest: lightly raced since 1112.   62
*1977 VERARDI [1] (W Hastings Bass) 3-8-9 Paul Eddery 5/2 FAV: -30114: Well bckd: fdd
final 2f: much btr 1977, 1589 (C/D).   51
*2273 PUBBY [6] 5-8-3 W Carson 6/1: 1200010: Fdd str: see 2273.   34
1923 SARYAN [7] 3-8-6(BL) G Bardwell(7) 20/1: -041100: Bl first time: slowly away:
twice below 1620.   47
2240 Kingswick [4] 8-7
7 ran   ¾,shhd,8,1,hd   (Mrs Maria Niarchos)   J Tree Marlborough, Wilts

---

2487 ROBERT FLEMING FILLIES STAKES 2YO   £2560   7f   Good/Firm 28 -26 Slow

2249 TROJAN MISS [5] (W Hern) 2-8-8 W Carson 7/4 FAV: 21: 2 b f Troy - Sally Rose (Sallust):
Useful filly: hvly bckd & stayed on well to lead inside dist in a 2yo fillies stakes at
Kempton: first time out pipped by the useful Mummys Luck at Goodwood: very eff over 6/7f &
will do even btr when tackling longer trips: acts on gd/firm grnd & on a sharp trk: seems
certain to rate more highly.   51
2287 RARE MEMORIES [11] (P Cole) 2-8-8 T Quinn 3/1: 22: Well bckd: tried to make all &
only just denied: on the up grade & will be winning soon: acts on gd/firm & yld & on any trk.   50
--   GOLDEN PLEASURE [7] (M Stoute) 2-8-8 A Kimberley 8/1: 3: Easy to back on debut: stayed
on most promisingly under minimum pressure & looks a certain future winner: well bred filly
who is a half sister to useful 8/12f winner Trakady: sure to stay at least 1m: acts on
gd/firm grnd & on a sharp trk.   50
--   GALA NIGHT [8] (I Balding) 2-8-8 J Matthias 10/1: 4: Ran on same pace: fair debut:
cost 76,000 gns as a yearling & is a half sister to winning sprinter Debutina Park: acts
on gd/firm grnd: should impr.   42
--   CAS EN BAS [9] 2-8-8 B Rouse 20/1: 0: Al mid-div on racecourse debut: should impr in
stayer: should impr in time, especially over a slightly lngr trip: acts on gd/firm grnd.   36
--   KENTUCKY AIR [4] 2-8-8 S Cauthen 7/1: 0: Mkt drifter on debut: prominent most &
sure to impr for this experience: acts on gd/firm grnd.   31
--   Soothing Word [10] 8-8   --   Castle Melody [3] 8-8
--   Heavenly Harmony [2] 8-8   --   Patient Dreamer [1] 8-8
--   Ladiz [6] 8-8 P
11 ran   ¾,1,4,2½,2   (Sir Michael Sobell)   W Hern West Ilsley, Berks

---

2488 TEBC FILLIES STAKES 3YO   £2070   6f   Good/Firm 28 -03 Slow

2186 SYBIL FAWLTY [11] (R Laing) 3-8-11(vis) W Newnes 16/1: 0-04421: 3 b f Be My Guest -
Veronica Heron (Crooner): Gained a deserved win, stayed on well to lead close home in a
3yo fillies stakes at Kempton: eff over 6/7f on firm & hvy grnd: well suited by a sharp course   41
1051 PLATINE [14] (R Simpson) 3-8-11 S Cauthen 14/1: 0020002: Led below dist, caught near
fin: gd effort after a fair abs: likes a sharp trk: see 760 & 111.   37
2343 USEFUL [8] (B Hills) 3-9-3 P Cook 6/1: 2301023: Remains in gd form: see 1847.   38
*2210 GLIKIAA MOU [15] (R Boss) 3-8-11 Paul Eddery 6/1: 2420014: Led after ½way: see 2210.   26
+2367 CLEOFE [1] 3-9-0 R Cochrane 7/1: 3340010: Ran on too late: see 2367.   29
431 CORRALS JOY [13] 3-8-11 B Rouse 14/1: 200-100: Long abs: led early, wknd dist: see 205.   25
2242 DREAM CHASER [5] 3-9-11(bl) L Johnsey(7) 7/1: 0100030: Fin 7th: btr in 2242 (stiff trk)   33
-2362 TRUE NORA [10] 3-9-3 A Clark 4/1 FAV: 3004020: Speed over ½wayy: fin 8th: btr in 2362.   25
2362 Brooks Dilemma [4] 8-13   2155 Into The Gap [9] 9-3
*2106 Left Right [12] 8-13   1586 Omania [2] 8-11   1312 Kimble Blue [3] 9-3
2370 Tumble Fair [6] 9-0(BL)   --   Passo Finale [7] 8-11
15 ran   1¼,2,3,hd,nk,2½,nk   (Christopher Wright)   R Laing Lambourn, Berks

---

2489 CHARTERHOUSE HANDICAP 3YO 0-50   £2070   1m 3f   Good/Firm 28 +05 Fast   [52]

2286 TRAVEL MYSTERY [12] (P Walwyn) 3-8-10 Paul Eddery 11/2 JT FAV: -133021: 3 b f Godswalk -
Sugar Cookie (Crepello): Led under press inside dist for a narrow win in a 3yo h'cap at
Kempton: first time out winner of a Bath maiden & has run consistently since: eff over
10/12f on firm & yld grnd: acts on any trk: genuine sort.   45
2148 SLANGI VAH [9] (H Candy) 3-8-10 W Newnes 9/1: -3302: Led 2f out, just btn: see 1589.   44
2404 STRAIGHT THROUGH [6] (J Winter) 3-8-10 B Rouse 11/2 JT FAV: 2210043: Stayed on: see 1233.38
1469 STEP IN TIME [1] (P Makin) 3-8-5 T Quinn 12/1: -0004: Held up, steady late prog &
should impr on this next time: stays 11f: acts on gd & firm: see 371.   30
2053 DESERT OF WIND [10] 3-9-2 R Cochrane 14/1: -02100: Made most: fair effort over this
longer trip: acts on any trk: see 1361.   41
1642 BASTINADO [7] 3-8-12 J Matthias 12/1: 30100: Abs: best over 10f in 1062 (gall trk).   34
*2372 TEMPEST TOSSED [4] 3-8-2(bl)(5ex) A Mcglone 11/2 JT FAV: 0323010: Al mid-div: fin 7th.   00
2049 ASK MAMA [5] 3-9-7 W Carson 11/2 JT FAV: 2-30120: No threat in 8th: btr in 1368 (10f).   00

1833 Ganoon [3] 8-0   2327 Out Of Stock [8] 7-9   2324 Banque Privee [2] 9-4
11 ran   ½,4,2,nk,3   (Mrs M D Madden)   P Walwyn Lambourn, Berks

2490 SSAFA APPR HANDICAP 3YO+ 0-35   £2082   1m 1f   Good/Firm 28 −03 Slow   [35]

2267 SPRING FLIGHT [12] (A Jarvis) 3-8-13 S Meacock(7) 11/2 FAV: 3231131: 3 b c Captain James-
Late Swallow (My Swallow): Nicely bckd & led 1f out, ridden out in an all aged app. h'cap
at Kempton: in fine form, earlier won a seller at Redcar & later h'caps at Ayr & Ripon: eff
over 8/10f on gd or faster grnd: acts on any trk: does well with forcing tactics: genuine
& consistent colt.   35
2401 RUSTLING [3] (D Arbuthnot) 4-8-7 J Leech(5) 10/1: 20-0032: Post came just too soon:
running well & should win a small h'cap soon: does well on a sharp trk: see 2401.   20
2340 SPECIAL GUEST [16] (D Morley) 3-8-1 Dale Gibson(5) 10/1: 0332403: Not btn far: gd run.   20
2319 CATMAN [15] (R Mitchell) 5-7-13 G King 50/1: 0000004: Gd late prog: much impr effort:
stays 9f: acts on gd/firm grnd & on a sharp trk.   09
2171 FARAG [7] 3-8-7 D Meade(5) 10/1: 0003200: Led till dist: fair effort: see 1819.   24
2474 FLYHOME [11] 5-9-13 C Carter(7) 13/2: -223030: No real threat: see 2244 & 706.   33
--   MOUNT TUMBLEDOWN [20] 5-9-7 L Jones 50/1: -0000-0: Some late prog & btr for race:
lightly raced last season & last won in '84, at Pontefract, Beverley & Ayr: eff around
1m on gd/firm & soft grnd: acts on any trk.   00
1636 PARIS TRADER [18] 4-9-1 Vicki Garner(7) 33/1: 0000300: Never nearer in 8th: see 609.   00
--   POLYNOR [10] 5-7-11 P Barnard(5) 10/1: 0-440-0: Active in mkt but no show: very lightly
raced on the Flat & remains a maiden: stays 10f & acts on yld grnd.   00
2404 STILLOU [17] 3-8-10 R Carter 6/1: 1001000: Nicely bckd but never in it: best in 1806.   00
--   Slydonbye [9] 8-3   2381 Sweet Andy [21] 7-7(2oh)
2282 Warily [1] 8-5(12ow)   2282 Cygne [19] 7-7(1oh)   2030 Donor [8] 9-1
2381 Primrose Way [4] 7-7   2260 Dolly [14] 8-9   2381 Okaadh [5] 8-9
2230 Captains Jade [13] 7-7(1oh)   2381 Gamblers Dream [6] 8-9
2288 Fast Service [2] 9-2
21 ran   ½,1,½,nk,1½,shhd,hd,½,½   (Mrs M A Jarvis)   A Jarvis Royston, Herts

---

NOTTINGHAM   Monday September 8th   Lefthanded, Flat Oval Track

2491 DELIRIUM MAIDEN STAKES 2YO   £959   6f   Firm 19 −16 Slow

2345 LUCAYAN KNIGHT [3] (M Stoute) 2-9-0 W R Swinburn 1/2 FAV: 21: 2 b c Dominion -
Riverine (Riverman): Fulfilled the promise of his debut when comfortably landing the odds in
a 2yo mdn at Nottingham: cost 50,000 gns as a yearling: eff over 6f though seems certain to
do btr over lngr distances: acts on gd & firm grnd & on an easy course: should rate more highly.   45
2108 SUNORIUS [6] (J Glover) 2-9-0 D Mckeown 14/1: 042: Led/dsptd lead thro'out, cleverly
held by winner but is making steady impr & should go one btr soon: acts on gd & firm: see 2108   42
2341 GENERAL MEILLAND [10] (L Piggott) 2-9-0 B Crossley 14/1: 03: Led/dsptd lead till
dist, not qckly: cheaply bought colt who is a half brother to winning juvenile Sandford Rose:
will be suited by further: acts on firm grnd & on an easy trk: on the up grade.   36
2179 WONDERFUL WILLIAM [5] (D Laing) 2-9-0 R Cochrane 7/2: 44: Not reach ldrs: see 2179.   22
2225 REGAL RAIDER [14] 2-9-0 E Guest(3) 16/1: 00: Nearest fin & will be suited by further
in time: cost 5,000 gns as a yearling and is a half brother to winning juvenile Rapid Glory:
acts on fast ground.   17
2308 JEALOUS LOVER [8] 2-8-11 T Quinn 50/1: 000: Picked up grnd from ½way, showing her
first signs of form: cheaply bought filly who is likely to do btr when stepping up in dist:
acts on firm ground.   14
--   IN FAT CITY [13] 2-9-0 R Hills 14/1: 0: Showed gd speed over ½way on racecourse debut:
half brother to very useful 8/10f winner Baronet: should impr for this experience: acts on firm.   16
--   MAKING HISTORY [15] 2-8-11 A Bond 12/1: 0: No real threat on her debut: speedily bred.   10
--   GULF OF GOLD [11] 2-9-0 D Nicholls 33/1: 0: Stayed on late & should do btr next time.   11
2325 Banks And Braes [7] 9-0   2325 Melody Liner [4] 9-0
2364 Church Star [1] 8-11   -- My Promised Land [9] 8-11
2334 I Promised [12] 9-0(bl)
14 ran   ½,2½,6,1½,shhd,hd,1½ ½   (Lady Hayward)   M Stoute Newmarket

2492 STRATHSPEY HANDICAP (0-35) 3YO+   £2259   1m 6f   Firm 19 +03 Fast   [35]

•2054 BANNEROL [16] (G Harwood) 3-9-10 G Starkey 7/1: -011: 3 b c Smarten Up - Queens
Standard (Hoist The Flag): Useful colt: comfortably defied top weight, progress   to lead
inside dist in quite a fast run h'cap at Nottingham: lightly raced, earlier won a mdn at
Redcar: cost $41,000 as a yearling & is a half brother to a couple of winners: very eff
over 14f & will stay 2m: acts on gd & firm grnd & on a gall trk: should impr further &
win more races.   52
2188 SHAHS CHOICE [19] (J Dunlop) 3-8-10 W Carson 4/1: -043222: Led 2f out, kept on well:
again found one too good & is certainly due a change of luck: see 2188 & 1980.   34

2395 **LEON** [4] (N Tinkler) 4-9-8 Kim Tinkler 9/1: 2024033: Not btn far: in gd form: see 2395. **34**

2031 **OLD MALTON** [8] (J Toller) 4-8-4 P Robinson 16/1: 0133004: Going on fin: best in 990. **12**

2141 **BUCKLOW HILL** [9] 9-9-3 A Murray 16/1: 0003400: Ran on same pace: see 2040. **23**

1477 **GRATIFY** [18] 3-7-8 N Carlisle 11/1: -000340: Abs: btn dist: see 1260, 1078. **03**

2305 **QUICK REACTION** [13] 3-7-13 G Bardwell(7) 10/3 FAV: 0002120: Fdd into 9th: btr in 2305. **00**

2346 Run For Your Wife [6] 7-7(bl)(1oh)
2141 Jipijapa [5] 7-8(vis)(1ow)(7oh)
2305 Mount Argus [7] 7-9
2098 Height Of Summer [12] 7-7(3oh)
2280 Denalto [2] 7-7(2oh)
2280 Higham Grey [3] 7-7
2305 Campus Boy [17] 7-8
2326 Cavalier Servente [14] 7-7
2403 Music Minstrel [11] 7-12
1879 Maricama [10] 8-12
2326 Knights Heir [15] 7-10(vis)
1564 May Be This Time [1] 8-9 P

19 ran ¾,¾,2½,1½,5,1½,shhd (K Abdulla) G Harwood Pulborough, Sussex

2493 DELIRIUM MAIDEN STAKES 2YO £959 6f Firm 19 -09 Slow

2345 **GIROTONDO** [9] (L Cumani) 2-9-0 Pat Eddery 4/1: 41: 2 b c Young Generation - Spin (High Top): Useful colt: qcknd well to lead close home in a 2yo mdn at Nottingham: fetched 17,000 gns as a yearling: is a half brother to the very useful 3yo Salchow: eff over 6f though should do btr when tackling 7f plus: acts on gd & firm grnd: should continue to impr. **48**

2080 **PENCIL SHARPENER** [14] (O Douieb) 2-8-11 Paul Eddery 7/4 FAV: 32: Hvly bckd: led below dist, caught near fin though well clear of rem: should recoup losses in the near future: acts on gd & firm: see 2080. **42**

-- **MOORESTYLE GIRL** [4] (L Piggott) 2-8-11 W R Swinburn 12/1: 3: Chased ldrs: no extra dist though will be btr for this run: speedily bred filly who clearly acts on fast grnd & has plenty of pace: certain to impr. **22**

2229 **MACS MAESTRO** [7] (W O'gorman) 2-9-0 T Ives 7/2: 04: Nicely bckd: not qckn dist: btr 2229. **21**

2056 **LINDVARO** [12] 2-9-0 P Tulk 16/1: 00: Al prom: speedily bred colt who seems well suited by fast grnd & an easy course. **20**

-- **LILARDIA** [2] 2-8-11 W Ryan 33/1: 0: No threat on debut: cheaply acquired filly who is a half sister to a couple of middle dist winners: likely to need a longer trip & more time. **11**

-- **PANAMA JACK** [13] 2-9-0 M Fry 33/1: 0: Outpcd early, stayed on well closing stages & seems certain to do btr next time: speedily bred colt who acts on fast grnd. **00**

2328 **MONETARY FUND** [11] 2-9-0 P Waldron 6/1: 020: Unsuited by the fast grnd: see 2328 (yld). **00**

2177 Market Spirit [10] 9-0
2118 Imperial Way [6] 9-0
2218 Barnby Don [8] 9-0(BL)
-- Dreaming River [5] 8-11
2398 Swing Singer [3] 9-0
-- Gallant Ribo [1] 9-0

14 ran ½,8,2,hd,2½,2 (C D'Alessio) L Cumani Newmarket

2494 DELIRIUM MAIDEN STAKES 2YO £959 6f Firm 19 -16 Slow

-- **A PRAYER FOR WINGS** [4] (J Sutcliffe) 2-9-0 M Hills 9/1: 1: 2 ro c Godswalk - Late Swallow (My Swallow): Made a successful debut, nicely bckd & made gd prog to lead inside dist in a 2yo mdn at Nottingham: speedily bred colt who cost 19,000 gns: clearly eff over 6f on firm grnd: can only improve. **45**

2225 **MUGATH** [12] (A Stewart) 2-9-0 M Roberts 13/8 FAV: 02: Well bckd: led briefly dist, ran on well & should go one btr soon, especially over a longer trip: acts on gd & firm. **42**

2229 **QUIET HERO** [2] (L Cumani) 2-9-0 Pat Eddery 5/2: 03: Hvly bckd: had ev ch: see 2229. **34**

2080 **HAYGATE PARK** [3] (M Ryan) 2-8-11 P Robinson 16/1: 04: Led ½way, no extra when hmpd dist: acts on gd & firm grnd: on the up grade: see 2080. **26**

2341 **VORTRACK** [14] 2-9-0 Paul Eddery 33/1: 000: Nearest fin: best in 2341 (7f). **22**

-- **BILLY CONNOLLY** [11] 2-9-0 K Darley 33/1: 0: Unfancied on debut: led/dsptd lead, btn when bumped 1f out: cheaply acquired colt who should stay further in time: acts on fast ground: seems suited by forcing tactics. **22**

-- **HEAVEN ONLY KNOWS** [7] 2-8-11 J Lowe 33/1: 0: Mkt drifter on debut: early speed & should improve. **00**

2080 **SOME DREAM** [5] 2-8-11 J Reid 7/1: 40: Denied a clear run: btr in 2080 (C/D). **00**

-- **ELEVEN LIGHTS** [1] 2-9-0 G Starkey 10/1: 0: Easy to back on debut: dwelt & not given a hard race: cost 400,000 gns as a yearling: seems certain to do btr next time. **00**

2301 Nevada Mix [10] 9-0
2080 Free Skip [13] 8-11
2105 Sparkler Boy [8] 9-0
2287 Holts Way [15] 8-11
-- King Among Kings [6] 9-0
-- Flaxon Worrior [9] 9-0

15 ran ¾,3,2½,3,shhd,1½,2,nk (Miss T Flynn) J Sutcliffe Epsom, Surrey

2495 OYSTER MAID SELLING STAKES 3 AND 4YO £940 1m 2f Firm 19 -23 Slow

2406 **SOFT SHOE SHUFFLE** [4] (B Sanders) 3-8-6 P Waldron 3/1 JT FAV: 0-00001: 3 b c Hard Fought-Carroldance (Lyphard): Dropped in class & was nicely bckd, led 2f out & ridden out to win a seller at Nottingham (bought in 3,800 gns): stays 10f well: suited by fast grnd & shp/easy trk **22**

2412 **MAFTIR** [7] (N Callaghan) 4-9-0(bl) Pat Eddery 3/1 JT FAV: 0000122: In gd form: see 2142. **18**

2188 **HOT TWIST** [3] (P Walwyn) 3-8-3(BL) Paul Eddery 4/1: 0-0003: Tried to make all, kept on under strong pressure & well clear of rem: mdn who is well suited by 10f & fast grnd. **12**

2429 **COUNT ALMAVIVA** [10] (M Blanshard) 3-8-6(bl) W Newnes 11/2: 3000024: Nearest fin: btr 2429. **01**

-- **COLONEL POPSKI** [2] 4-9-0(bl) N Carlisle 20/1: 00-0: Lightly rcd mdn who has yet to show any worthwhile form on the Flat or over hdles: acts on firm grnd. **00**

2335 **RES NON VERBA** [8] 3-8-3 S Webster 14/1: 0-3000: Btn early in str: see 2335, 1340. **00**

2014 COUNTESS CARLOTTI [5] 3-8-3 J Lowe 10/1: -024000: Fdd into 9th: best in 1134 (1m gd).   00
2427 VITAL STEP [1] 3-8-3(bl) J Callaghan(7) 5/1: 0004200: Al behind: best in 2361 (stiff 7f)   00
1364 Grosvenor Court [11] 8-6   2286 Austina [6] 8-3(bl)
-- Fire Hazard [9] 9-0
11 ran   1½,2,10,shhd,2   (Miss Brooke Sanders)   B Sanders Epsom, Surrey

2496 FINAL SCORE E.B.F. STAKES 3 AND 4YO   £2918   1m 2f   Firm 19 -01 Slow

1788 KUFUMA [3] (G Huffer) 4-9-0(vis) G Carter(3) 5/1: 20-0001: 4 b c Habitat - Ready And
Willing (Reliance II): Smart colt: returned to form, led below dist & ran on strongly to
win a well contested stakes race at Nottingham: in fine form last season, winning at Pontefract & Newbury & later finished 2nd in the Cambridgeshire - but has since suffered from
the virus: very eff over 8/10f on firm & yld grnd: acts on any trk : clearly back to his best.   70
2200 KADIAL [5] (R F Johnson Houghton) 3-9-0 Pat Eddery 1/1 FAV: 2142102: Well bckd: see 2074.   70
*1954 VERITABLE [2] (P Haslam) 3-8-10 T Williams 5/1: 43-0213: Made most: in fine form: see 1954.58
1851 SMOOCH [6] (K Brassey) 3-8-7 S Whitworth 25/1: -001004: Mkt drifter: stayed on same
pace & seems to be returning to form: stayed 10f: best in 982.   54
2346 ICKWORTH [1] 3-8-0 W Carson 20/1: 4-00400: Bckd from 100/1, no threat: see 1652.   07
-2385 LADY SOPHIE [7] 3-8-11(BL) S Cauthen 7/2: 1-20120: Bl first time: never seen with
a chance & has proved disapp since running up to Sonic Lady in the Nell Gwyn Stakes at
Newmarket in 214.   16
2419 Kavaka [11] 9-4   2264 Fill Abumper [8] 7-11   -- Why Tumble [4] 9-0
487 Bills Daughter [9] 7-11   2327 Dialect [10] 7-11
11 ran   4,4,nk,12,¾,nk   (B N Hamoud)   G Huffer Newmarket

2497 STEROPE HANDICAP (0-35) 3YO   £2404   1m   Firm 19 +20 Fast   [38]

*2274 COUNTRY GENTLEMAN [4] (J Dunlop) 3-9-10(10ex) W Carson 4/1: 0043011: 3 b c Skyliner-
Killyhevlin (Green God): In fine form, easily defied his penalty, led well over 2f out &
was pushed out to win a very fast run 3yo h'cap at Nottingham: recently made all in a h'cap
at Windsor: very eff around 1m on gd & fast grnd: does well with forcing tactics: suited by
a sharp/easy course: looks certain to win again.   48
*1906 BICKERMAN [7] (M Prescott) 3-8-6 G Duffield 6/1: -001012: Gd effort: stays 1m: see 1906.   20
2230 GIVING IT ALL AWAY [3] (H Beasley) 3-8-12 J Reid 12/1: 0002103: Best over this C/D in 181920
1904 ACTUALIZATIONS [10] (L Cumani) 3-8-10 Pat Eddery 7/2 FAV: -03424: Ev ch str.: btr 1904.   10
2149 BIEN DORADO [11] 3-8-12 W R Swinburn 10/1: 0043400: Best over 7f in 1065 (gall trk).   08
2399 CHARLTON KINGS [9] 3-9-0(vis) S Perks 14/1: 0003400: Led ½way: best in 2149 (9f).   09
2230 PHILOSOPHICAL [17] 3-8-5 M Wigham 8/1: 0030130: Best in 2060 (seller, stiff trk).   00
2360 Centralspires Best [12] 7-11(BL)   2230 Real Moonshine [16] 8-12
1469 Scarlet Dancer [2] 8-6   2186 Report Em [18] 7-11
2319 First Opportunity [5] 8-8   1394 Scarlatti [8] 9-7(vis)
1787 Just Met [6] 8-9   2230 Avada [1] 8-0   2339 Harleyford Lad [13] 7-13
2184 Roi De Soleil [14] 7-7(BL)(4oh)   1671 Red Billy [15] 7-8(1ow)(2oh)
18 ran   4,3,4,2½,½   (C G A Horseracing 1984 Ltd)   J Dunlop Arundel, Sussex

2498 TULYAR NURSERY HANDICAP 2YO   £1706   1m   Firm 19 -11 Slow   [62]

1984 JOHNNY SHARP [9] (S Norton) 2-7-7(3oh) J Lowe 14/1: 002001: 2 ch c Sharpen Up -
Crimson Flame (Stage Door Johnny): Returned to the form of race 1675 when making most from 3f
out, driven out in a nursery h'cap at Nottingham: seems well suited by 1m: acts well on
firm grnd: appears to handle any trk.   32
2136 MUBKIR [2] (P Walwyn) 2-7-13 N Howe 6/1: 302002: Led briefly 1f out: btn a whisker:
gd effort over this lngr trip & seems to act on any trk: best on fast grnd: see 497.   38
2310 TIKLAS [7] (F Durr) 2-7-7(5oh) G French 9/2: 0004343: Ev ch final 1f: not btn far
in a blnkt fin: seems suited by 1m & acts on firm & yld grnd & on any trk.   30
2468 LACK OF PEARLS [6] (R Woodhouse) 2-7-7(5oh) K Darley 10/1: 0404004: 6lbs o/w & btn 1L:
stays 1m well: acts on gd & firm grnd & may find a nursery.   35
1975 CHANTILLY LACE [3] 2-7-13(6ow)(4oh) T Williams 6/1: 100: Al up there: close up 5th:
stays 1m & acts on any trk.   34
2329 MON COEUR [1] 2-9-7 P Robinson 4/1 FAV: 04230: Led 4f: kept on: giving lumps of
weight all round and ran well: stays 1m: see 2329.   56
2136 EDRAIANTHUS [4] 2-7-9 N Adams 5/1: 04040: Not clear run 2f out: stays 1m? see 533.   00
2178 WIND OF PEACE [5] 2-8-0(BL)(1ow) N Connorton 10/1: 0100: Bl first time: never threatened.   00
2140 CONNEMARA DAWN [11] 2-7-7(4oh) A Proud 8/1: 4000: Prom most: lightly rcd since 1405.   00
2439 Eurocon [8] 7-7(3oh)   2177 Just On Time [10] 7-7(21oh)
11 ran   shhd,¾,nk,¾,shhd   (Peter Wetzel)   S Norton Barnsley, Yorks

2499 DELIRIUM MAIDEN STAKES 2YO   £959   6f   Firm 19 -14 Slow

2392 MAJD [11] (P Walwyn) 2-9-0 Paul Eddery 9/4: 3321: 2 b c Young Generation - Eightpenny
(Pieces Of Eight): Gained a deserved success, led inside final 2f, ridden out in a 2yo mdn
at Nottingham: placed on all 3 previous starts: cost 54,000 gns as a yearling: very eff over
6f, should get further: acts on fst & yld grnd & on any trk.   50
2281 PETICOV SHADES [4] (P Calver) 2-9-0 M Fry 25/1: 02: Ran on well final 1f & narrowly btn:
impr & should go one btr soon: related to 3 sprint winners: acts on fast grnd & a gall trk.   48

2229 BECCADELLI [13] (H Cecil) 2-9-0 S Cauthen 4/5 FAV: 43: Hvly bckd: made most: 4L
clear 4th: see 2229.   42
2029 ROLFESON [12] (B Morgan) 2-9-0 B Crossley 25/1: 44: Prom, ev ch: another gd run:
will be suited by further than 6f: acts on gd & fast grnd.   34
1782 IRENIC [10] 2-8-11 W Woods(3) 33/1: 00: Fdd final 1f but is making impr: half sister
to several winners incl the very useful Forzando: acts on fast grnd.   24
--   HUNTING COUNTRY [7] 2-9-0 M Banner 16/1: 0: Prom most on racecourse debut: impr likely
from this 5,000 gns purchase: should be suited by further than 6f.   24
--   THE TAIN [5] 2-9-0 W R Swinburn 10/1: 0: Made no show on racecourse debut: cost
115,000 gns & should do btr than this.   00
2167 Charming Gracie [14] 8-11   --   Floreat Tina [1] 8-11
--   Fireiron [9] 8-11   --   Dalby Dancer [2] 8-11 --   Main Brand [8] 8-11
--   Mitral Magic [3] 8-11
13 ran   nk,2¼,4,3,1¼   (Hamdan Al-Maktoum)   P Walwyn Lambourn, Berks

---

BADEN BADEN (W.G.)   Friday September 5th   Lefthand Sharpish Track

Official Going Given As GOOD

2500 PREIS DER STADT BADEN BADEN LISTED   £5650   1m 2f   Good -
--   TRIPWIRE (P Lamotte Dargy) 3-8-6 J Lowe   : 32010-1: 3 b c Homing - Ambuscade (Relko):
Came from off the pace when easily winning quite a valuable Listed race at Baden Baden: suited
by 10f & good ground.   67
2004 ALAGOS (B Schutz) 3-8-10 L Mader : 3-32: --   65
*2353 GEORDIES DELIGHT (L Piggott) 3-8-4 R Cochrane : 1422213: Started fav. ran another
fine race: see 2353.   56
--   BABY BID (Germany) 4-9-2 E Schindler : -4: --   53
11 ran   3,1½,3½   (E Landi)   P Lamotte Dargy France

2501 GROUP 2 ZUFUNKTS RENNEN 2YO   £18362   6f   Good -
2221 AMIGO SUCIO [10] (K Brassey) 2-9-2 S Whitworth : 113301: 2 gr c Stanford - Haunting
(Lord Gayle): Smart colt: despite being poorly drawn, came to lead after ½way & forged clear
for a comfortable win in a valuable Gr.2 event at Baden Baden: earlier won two minor events
at Salisbury (first time out) & Thirsk: has since been placed in the Coventry & Champagne
Stakes at Royal Ascot & Goodwood & has proved a bargain buy at 17,000 gns: half brother to
several winners incl useful sprinter Valley Mills: eff over 5/6f & acts on firm & yld &
on any trk: genuine & consistent.   71
--   CROFTITO [4] (F Doumen) 2-9-2 J C Desaint : 2230232: French trained colt who ran well
but remains a mdn after 7 outings.   65
2223 BAG ORHYTHM [5] (J Hindley) 2-9-2 M Hills : 21223: Al prom: stays 6f, possibly
btr 5f: see 1082, 2223.   61
1129 MISTER MAJESTIC [1] (R Williams) 2-9-2 R Cochrane : 1211144: Long abs, ran creditably
in the circumstances: see 859, 1129.   60
--   SIR DAVID [6] 2-9-2 A Tylicki : 2104210: --   59
1467 POLEMOS [3] 2-9-2 A Murray : 1200: Early ldr, wknd: twice well below 1097.   52
10 ran   2½,1½,nk,½,3½   (J Li)   K Brassey Lambourn

BADEN BADEN (W.G.)   Sunday September 7th   Lefthand Sharpish Track

Official Going Given As GOOD

2502 GROUP 1 GROSSER PREIS VON BADEN 3YO+   £46610   1m 4f   Good -
*2197 ACATENANGO (H Jentzsch) 4-9-7 G Bocskai : 1-11111: 4 ch c Surumu - Aggravate
(Aggressor): Top class German colt: gained his 12th consecutive victory when making all
readily to win Gr.1 Grosser Preis von Baden at Baden Baden: won another Gr.1 event at
Gelsenkarchen-Horst Aug.17: see 1861: remarkably consistent & deserves a crack at the Arc.   88
1493 ST HILARION (G Harwood) 4-9-7 G Starkey : 1-00202: Al chasing this easy winner:
twice below 1144.   74
2354 DAUN (T Grieper) 5-9-7 P Remmert 1: 3-40343: Ev ch: see 1712.   71
--   VIF ARGENT (P Lautner) 3-8-9 L Mader : -1-414: --   66
2157 PHARDANTE 4-9-7 A Clark : 1013340: Wknd 3f out: see 1217.   66
5 ran   5,1,1½,¾   (Gestut Farhof)   H Jentzsch Germany

736

Official Going Given As GOOD (PROBABLY FAST GROUND BASED ON TIME)

2503 GLEN INTERNATIONAL FLYING FIVE LISTED   £32402   5f   Good -

*1858 ACUSHLA (V O'brien) 3-9-7 Pat Eddery 9/4 FAV: 3-01211: 3 b f Storm Bird - Intrepid
Lady (Bold Bidder): Smart Irish filly: strongly ridden final 1f to get up close home in a
blnkt fin to a valuable Listed sprint at Phoenix Park: set a new course record in the process:
ready winner of a Gr.3 event on the same trk July 26: earlier won a fillies race again at
Phoenix Park: eff at 5f, probably btr suited by 6f: acts on firm & yld but probably fav
by the former.   78
1889 STORM WARNING (W Hastings Bass) 4-9-5 A Murray 7/1: -030002: Just failed to make
all, caught death: see 563.   72
2233 MAROUBLE (C Nelson) 3-9-2 C Roche 4/1: 023-003: Just btn in a very close finish but
reportedly fin feelingly and may have been slightly unlucky: see 708.   72
*903 WOLVERSTAR (P Norris) 4-9-5 S Craine 10/1: 1012034: Not btn far in a tight fin: see 9   69
2158 REGENCY FILLE 2-7-11 R Street 14/1: 2321220: Tremendous effort against older rivals
and she just does not know how to run a bad race: see 2158.   68
*1857 EDNICA 4-9-10 D Hogan 4/1: 0-11110: Fine effort: see 1857.   72
2351 London Tower 9-7   472 Steel Commander 9-5(bl)
2351 Knesset 9-5
9 ran   ½,shhd,½,nk,½   (R Sangster)   V O'brien Ireland

Official Going Given As GOOD

2504 GOFFS SILVER FLASH STKS 2YO FILLIES L   £20352   7f   Good -

1641 SIMPLE TASTE (I Balding) 2-8-5 P Cook 4/1: 221: 2 b f Sharpen Up - Trove (USA): Useful
filly: well suited by this lngr trip, led dist & ran on well to win a valuable Listed race
at Phoenix Park: American bred juvenile who cost $1m and is closely related to a host of
winners: very eff over 6/7f & will be suited by 1m: acts on gd & firm grnd & on any trk.   62
1591 ERINDALE (K Prendergast) 2-8-10 G Curran 20/1: 2321012: Gd effort: recent winner of
a Nursery at Leopardstown (6f, good): stays 7f: acts on any trk: see 1591.   64
2057 MONTFORT (W Jarvis) 2-9-0 R Cochrane 4/1: 0123: Ran to her best: see 1722.   67
-- TREK (D Weld) 2-8-8 D Parnell 8/1: 104: Not btn far: lightly rcd since winning a
fillies mdn at Leopardstown & will be eff over 6/7f on gd grnd.   60
2246 CANDLE IN THE WIND 2-9-0 W Newnes 20/1: 040100: Fin 7th though not btn very far.   62
*2350 DOWN AGAIN 2-9-0(bl) Pat Eddery 7/2 FAV: --1213D: Fin a close 3rd though bumped
several horses inside dist & subsq. disq & placed last: wears bl & seems a difficult ride.   68
13 ran   ½,shhd,nk,½,1,nk,hd,2,½   (Mrs R Kirk)   I Balding Kingsclere, Berks

2505 BARRONSTOWN STUD STAKES LISTED 3YO+   £18504   7f   Good -

-- BRAVO FOX (D Weld) 3-8-9(BL) D Parnell 12/1: 44-0101: 3 b c Northern Baby - Fantastic
Girl: Smart colt: bl for the first time & proved a game winner, led on the line in a valuable
Listed race at Phoenix Park Sept.7: lightly raced this season, earlier won a minor race at
Naas: best form over 6/7f on gd or faster grnd: seems to act on any trk.   73
-- REDEEM HERSELF (J Oxx) 4-8-12 Pat Eddery 5/2: -111022: Caught post: in fine form
this season, winning 3 of her 6 races: eff over 5/7f on gd & soft grnd: acts on any trk.   69
1851 MUMMYS FAVOURITE (J Dunlop) 3-8-6 W Carson 7/4 FAV: 1-34143: Gd effort: see 1487.   66
2351 LUQMAN (P Walwyn) 3-8-9 Paul Eddery 5/1: 4-04044: Btn less than 2L: see 286.   68
7 ran   shhd,1½,shhd,2½,3   (D B Firestone)   D Weld Ireland

2506 GROUP 1 PHOENIX CHAMPION STAKES 3YO+   £261500   1m 2f   Good -

-2202 PARK EXPRESS [4] (J Bolger) 3-8-8 J Reid 11/2: 42D1121: 3 br f Ahonoora - Matcher:
Very smart Irish filly: qcknd clear over 2f out & stayed on strongly to win Gr.1 Phoenix
Champion Stakes at Phoenix Park: much impr this season, first time out won a minor race on
this course & rather lost her form until winning Gr.2 Lancashire Oaks & Gr.2 Nassau Stakes at
Haydock & Goodwood respectively: subsq. just btn by Untold in Gr.1 Yorkshire Oaks at York:
in '85 won at Leopardstown: eff over 1m though best over 10/12f nowadays: acts on any going
& on any trk: most genuine filly who is a credit to her trainer.   88
*2193 DOUBLE BED [6] (F Doumen) 3-8-11 Paul Eddery 33/1: 344D212: French challenger: stayed
on well to take the minor honours & is in fine form: see 2193.   86
-2200 TRIPTYCH [10] (P Biancone) 4-9-3 A Cordero 3/1 FAV: 4212323: Held up, ev ch below
dist: tremendously consistent filly who has not run a bad race this season: see 2200 & 1389. 78
2157 DUBIAN [12] (A Stewart) 4-9-3 M Roberts 25/1: 31-0104: Ran on well: fine effort: see 1593. 71
2200 MR JOHN [1] 3-8-11 M Browne 33/1: 2004240: Another creditable effort in top class company. 74
2195 BAILLAMONT [11] 4-9-6 F Head 5/1: 0-31100: Held up, ran on too late: see 1355.   74
2259 SHARROOD [7] 3-8-11 W Carson 10/1: 4303220: Fin 7th: see 2259 & 1597.   00
2259 SUPREME LEADER [2] 4-9-6 R Cochrane 20/1: 1330040: Fin 8th: see 1095.   00
*2192 WISE COUNSELLOR [5] 3-8-11 Pat Eddery 6/1: -12010: Never going well on this fast
ground & much btr over 1m in 2192 (gd/yld).   00
2202 COLORSPIN [9] 3-8-8 A Murray 12/1: 1-34140: Seems to need softer grnd these days: see 1592. 00

2351 Bermuda Classic [3] 8-8   2450 Ramich John [8] 9-3
--   Gayle Gal [9] 8-8
13 ran   2½,2½,4,hd,hd,1½,½   (P H Burns)   J Bolger Ireland

LONGCHAMP   Sunday September 7th   RH Galloping Track

2507 GROUP 1 PRIX DU MOULIN DE LONGCHAMP   £100258   1m   Good/Firm -

*1877 SONIC LADY [9] (M Stoute) 3-8-8 W R SWinburn: 1311111: 3 b f Nureyev - Stumped (Owen
Anthony): High Class filly: proved herself Europe's top mile filly, staying on bravely to
win in Gr.1 Prix du Moulin de Longchamp Ecurie Fustok at Longchamp: earlier won the Sussex
Stakes at Goodwood, Child Stakes at Newmarket, Coronation Stakes at Royal Ascot, Irish
1,000 Guineas at the Curragh & first time out Nell Gwyn Stakes at Newmarket: easy winner of
Blue Seal Stakes at Ascot on her sole outing in '85 & met her only defeat when narrowly btn
in the 1,000 Guineas: very eff over 7/8f: acts on firm & yld grnd & on a gall trk: admirably
consistent and a great credit to her trainer : not one to oppose.   87
*1859 THRILL SHOW [4] 3-8-11 C Asmussen :   -1112: Battled on gamely & lost
nothing in defeat: had won his 3 previous races & certain to enjoy further successes.   88
*2195 LIRUNG [5] (H Jentzsch) 4-9-2 S Cauthen : 23213: Tried to make all, no extra close
home though ran another fine race: see 2195.   80
2195 MAGICAL WONDER [3] (G Mikhalides) 3-8-11 J Velasquez : 4-11104: Gd effort: loves
this track: see 900.   83
2195 ELLE SEULE [2] 3-8-8 A Lequeux : 0134100: Ran to her best: see 2002.   80
*2359 APELDOORN [6] 4-9-2 M Philipperon : 3-13010: Much impr this season: see 2359.   76
2195 DIRECTING [8] 3-8-11 P Johanny : 4011340: Fin 7th: see 1597.   77
2359 NORTHERN ASPEN [12] 4-8-13 A Badel : 001-020: Creditable 8th: see 2359.   75
2200 BOLD ARRANGEMENT [7] 3-8-11 G Moore : 3200400: Below his best: see 1389 & 469.   00
1715 New Bruce (13) 8-13   2195 Gallop Dyna (1) 9-2   2359 Vin De France (14) 9-2
2195 Regal State (11) 8-8   --   Petrol Blue (10) 9-2
14 ran   ½,2½,hd,shhd,2,½,shhd   (Sheikh Mohammed)   M Stoute Newmarket

---

PONTEFRACT   Tuesday September 9th   Lefthand, Turning, Undulating Track

Official Going Given As GOOD/FIRM

2508 ILKLEY HANDICAP STAKES (0-35) 3YO   £1692   1m   Firm 14 -07 Slow   [39]

2171 DAWN LOVE [2] (R Hollinshead) 3-8-9 S Perks 16/1: 00-0001: 3 b f He Loves Me -
Fog (English Prince): Led over 1f out, ridden out in a 3yo h'cap at Pontefract Sept.9: in
'85 won a 3 runner event at Redcar: stays 1m well: acts on gd & fast grnd.   29
*1922 IRISH PASSAGE [7] (D Barron) 3-9-7 S Webster 14/1: 02D0012: Ch final 1f: in grand form. 39
2399 GRANDANGUS [8] (K Ivory) 3-7-12(vis) W Woods(1) 14/1: 0103103: Prom, stayed on: gd effort 07
1989 HOT LINING [17] (F Carr) 3-8-7 S Morris 14/1: 0000024: Never nearer: beat winner 1989 (C/D) 13
2314 OPAL FLOWER [10] 3-8-0(2ow) M Rimmer 25/1: 32-0000: Kept on under press: very lightly
raced this season: showed promise as a 2yo: acts on gd & fast grnd & likes an easy trk.   06
2399 NICOLINI [18] 3-8-0 J Quinn(5) 8/1: -003320: Prom, btr 2399 (yld): see 1864.   00
*2390 ARE YOU GUILTY [11] 3-9-3(5ex) G Bardwell(7) 7/2 FAV: -300010: Fin 7th: btr on
yld grnd in 2390.   00
2149 COLONIAL KING [13] 3-8-4(VIS) M Wood 8/1: 00-0000: Visored first time & bckd at
long odds: fdd str: see 2149.   00
1924 RUN BY JOVE [1] 3-9-3(vis) T Williams 5/1: 2002230: Prom most, fdd: much btr 1924.   00
2230 GLACIER LASS [21] 3-7-11(blnd) R Fox 10/1: 0-00020: Difficult to win on: btr 2230.   00
2264 Ultressa [14] 7-13(bl)   1880 Danesmoor [4] 8-7
2171 Moel Fammau [12] 8-6   *1989 See No Evil [15] 8-1   2361 Herb Robert [9] 7-7(8oh)
1953 Quite A Quest [20] 8-3   2264 Gold Chip [5] 8-9(BL)
2427 Torriggia [19] 8-0(2ow)   1885 Soxoph [18] 9-1
1941 Super Silhouette [6] 7-7(1oh)   1824 Feather Girl [3] 7-7(9oh)
21 ran   ¾,5,1½,shhd,3,½   (J R Rees)   R Hollinshead Upper Longdon, Staffs

2509 CASTLE SELLING STAKES 3 AND 4YO   £956   1m 2f   Firm 14 -16 Slow

2413 NORTHERN GUNNER [7] (W Jarvis) 3-8-3(3ow) R Cochrane 1/1 FAV: 0430321: 3 b c Northern
Guest-Jukella (Jukebox): Dropped to selling company & led final 1f, readily in a 3 & 4yo seller
at Pontefract (bought in 6,800 gns): deserved success: stays 10f well: acts on fast &
yld grnd & on any trk.   25
2271 JUST CANDID [1] (D Wilson) 4-8-9 T Williams 5/1: 0334232: Led into str: in gd form.   10

2427 KEEP COOL [9] (R Hollinshead) 3-8-2 A Culhane(7) 6/1: 0020043: Kept on final 1f:
stays 10f: see 1960, 774.   09
2441 MOLLY PARTRIDGE [10] (R Woodhouse) 3-7-11 A Proud 12/1: 0003004: Led 4f out: lightly
raced since 1074.   00
1892 RAMILIE [4] 4-8-11 T Ives 11/2: -003400: Active in mkt: twice below 1737 (13f).   00
2412 MUSICAL WILL [8] 4-9-0(bl) J Callaghan(7) 12/1: 4030200: Prom str, fdd: see 2101 (12f).   00
2174 Timsolo [2] 8-0   891 Eastern Heights [9] 8-0
673 Empire Sands [5] 8-9(bl)   -- Vintage Lady [11] 8-9
10 ran   6,1½,7,5,3   (A Gunn-Forbes)   W Jarvis Newmarket

2510 PHIL BULL TROPHY (STAKES) 3YO+   £2469   2m 2f Firm 14 +14 Fast

2220 KUDZ [1] (H Cecil) 3-8-8 S Cauthen 4/5 FAV: 2111201: 3 br c Master Willie - Lucky
Ole Me (Olden Times): Very useful stayer: led 2f out, ridden out close home in a fast run   4
runner stakes at Pontefract: tremendously consistent this term, earlier winning h'caps at
Warwick & Thirsk & a Beverley mdn: half brother to several winners incl the smart Lucky North:
eff at 14f, stays 2m2f well: acts on firm & soft grnd & on any trk: carries weight well.   60
2220 SAFE RIVER [4] (L Cumani) 4-9-2 R Cochrane 9/4: 4401302: Kept on well under press:
stays really well & will be suited by 2½m Cesarewitch trip: see 801.   52
2203 BRIGHTNER [2] (G Harwood) 5-9-2 G Starkey 4/1: 1110/03: Mkt drifter: made much: see 2203.   37
2395 THE YOMPER [3] (J Parkes) 4-8-9 D Nicholls 50/1: 4203004: Impossible task: there ½way.   00
4 ran   1½,10,dist   (Sheikh Mohammed)   H Cecil Newmarket

2511 JUNIOR STAKES 2YO   £2597   6f   Firm 14 -02 Slow

+1863 ON TAP [3] (M H Easterby) 2-9-6 M Birch 1/1 FAV: 4111: 2 ch g Tap On Wood - Joshua's
Daughter (Joshua): Very useful 2yo: heavily bckd & led 2f out, readily drawing clear in a 2yo
stakes at Pontefract: earlier a similarly easy winner at Redcar & again at Pontefract: half
brother to several winners incl useful h'capper Glen Kella Manx: very eff over 6/7f and
looks sure to stay further: acts well on fast grnd: well regarded & will win more races.   67
2252 TOUGH N GENTLE [11] (L Piggott) 2-9-6 T Ives 14/1: 1231202: No ch with winner, but
ran his usual game race: see 2166, 1798.   50
*2179 UNIFORMITY [5] (M Stoute) 2-9-3 W R Swinburn 9/2: 013: Waited with & no real threat.   46
1430 KATE IS BEST [9] (M Ryan) 2-8-8 R Cochrane 9/1: 004: Abs: never nearer: will do btr
next time: see 1430.   33
2235 SINCLAIR LADY [12] 2-9-0 D Nicholls 11/1: 0011200: Prom much: well below 1697.   36
2460 SAMEEK [7] 2-9-6(BL) S Cauthen 6/1: 21300: Bl first time: made much: yet to regain
early season form: see 583 (5f).   36
870 Miami Bay [14] 8-11   2229 Freddie Ashton [2] 8-11
-- Honeyway Mist [1] 8-11   2301 Vaigly Yellow [6] 8-11
1883 Express Groupage [10] 8-8   2364 Raymonds Star [4] 8-11
2007 Campeggio [13] 8-11   913 Noalimba [8] 8-11
14 ran   7,nk,2,1½,3,nk   (Lt Col R Warden)   M H Easterby Great Habton, Yorks

2512 THORPE NURSERY HANDICAP 2YO   £2429   1m   Firm 14 -21 Slow   [54]

2310 ROUMELI [8] (Lord J Fitzgerald) 2-7-7(2oh) N Carlisle 9/1: 4423031: 2 b f Blakeney -
Lefki (Red God): Gained a deserved success, running on under press to lead close home in a
nursery h'cap at Pontefract: stays 1m well: acts on soft, likes fast grnd: seems a
genuine filly.   28
2178 AVINASESH [13] (C Tinkler) 2-7-7 P Burke(4) 20/1: 0234002: Kept on well final 2f:
suited by 1m: has been fitted with bl: see 1076.   25
2383 PALEFACE [12] (L Piggott) 2-9-7 T Ives 2/1 FAV: 3322123: Made almost all: fine
effort under 9-7 and is a genuine colt: see 2383, 2178.   53
2336 THANK HAVON [11] (D Morley) 2-8-3(2ow) R Cochrane 4/1: 404034: Prom, ev ch: stays 1m.   35
2050 SERGEANT MERYLL [10] 2-7-7(3oh) L Charnock 16/1: 0030: Nearest fin: suited by 1m.   25
2310 BOLD DIFFERENCE [1] 2-7-12 J Quinn(5) 20/1: 0212000: Never nearer: consistent & stays 1m   23
1982 BLACK MANS BAY [4] 2-8-3 M Wood 11/2: 0430: Prom most: btr 1982 (7f, yld).   00
2310 War Child [16] 7-7(3oh)   2011 Young Benz [2] 7-10
2336 Badoglio [3] 7-13(BL)   2336 Princess Singh [6] 7-7(2oh)
2276 Hunters Leap [5] 8-0   2298 Highland Captain [9] 7-7(17oh)
1566 Royal Treaty [14] 7-7(1oh)   2140 Grecian Jos [15] 8-1
15 ran   1½,hd,shhd,hd,3   (Mrs H G Cambanis)   Lord J Fitzgerald Newmarket

2513 WENTWORTH HANDICAP (0-35) 3YO+   £1658   6f   Firm 14 -04 Slow   [35]

2245 DUFFERS DANCER [8] (W Pearce) 4-8-8 N Connorton 4/1 JT.FAV: 4-01341: 4 ch c Miami
Springs - Evening Chorus (Mountain Call): In grand form: well bckd & got up close home in a
h'cap at Pontefract: earlier won a h'cap at Carlisle: in '85 won again at Carlisle & in
'84 at Hamilton: eff at 5f, well suited by 6f & stays 7f: best on gd & fast grnd: probably
acts on any trk.   24
2397 MARAVILLA [14] (J Etherington) 4-8-8 M Wood 16/1: 0242002: Al up there: gd run:
definitely best on fast grnd: see 2039.   23
2411 THRONE OF GLORY [6] (D Chapman) 5-9-6 D Nicholls 9/2: 0440023: Led over 1f out: just btn
and is in fine form at present: seems equally eff at 5/6f: see 742.   34

2322 BAY BAZAAR [4] (M W Easterby) 4-8-8(bl) G Baxter 20/1: 4000004: Made most: see 1682, 42.   18
2213 POINTED LADY [3] 3-8-9(3ow) S Cauthen 4/1 JT.FAV: -000420: Making hdway when hmpd 1f
out: see 2213 (7f).   23
*2397 THATCHERED [9] 5-8-10(7ex) M Fry 7/1: 00-0010: Hmpd over 1f out: unlucky? see 2397.   16
*2411 WARTHILL LADY [7] 4-8-7(10ex) K Darley 14/1: 0004010: Never nearer 7th: in gd form.   00

2189 Pommes Chateau [2] 8-7(hd)		2469 Philstar [15] 8-5(vis)
2340 Gentileschi [17] 8-11	2397 James Pal [10] 9-11	2397 Jersey Maid [16] 8-6
2186 Belle Of Budapest [12] 8-11		2256 Skylin [5] 8-4(vis)
2397 Sing Out Loud [1] 8-11		1701 Qualitair King [13] 8-5
710 Bubs Boy [18] 8-7		

17 ran   ½,½,1½,½,2,shhd   (Robin Arbuthnot)   W Pearce Hambleton, Yorks

---

FOLKESTONE   Tuesday September 9th   Lefthand, Sharpish, Undulating Track

Official Going Given As FIRM

2514 REED CORRUGATED CASES 2YO STAKES   £1578   5f   Firm 18 -14 Slow

2301 DAYS LIKE THESE [14] (P Bailey) 2-8-11 Pat Eddery 11/4 FAV: 41: 2 b c The Brianstan-
Sally Ann II (Port Corsair): Well bckd & led over 1f out, driven out in a 2yo stakes at
Folkestone: cost 13,000 gns: speedily bred & is well suited by this minimum trip: acts on
fast & yld grnd & an easy trk.   43
2089 KEPT WAITING [20] (W Musson) 2-8-8 A Mackay 33/1: 02: Friendless in mkt: stayed on
well: quite cheaply acquired filly who should be placed to find a small event: eff at 5f,
should stay further: acts on fast grnd & an easy trk.   38
2229 INTHAR [2] (R Armstrong) 2-8-11 P Tulk 14/1: 003: Al up there: kept on: has been
very lightly raced this season: will be suited by 6f: acts well on fast grnd.   41
2167 BLAZING HIGH [15] (L Piggott) 2-8-11 B Crossley 9/2: 034: Made much: btn 1L: see 2167, 149540
*2365 SUPREME ROSE [4] 2-9-1 M Wigham 9/2: 010: Prom, just btn in close fin: acts on gd & fast   41
1552 MON BALZAR [17] 2-8-11 M Miller 14/1: 000: Abs: sn prom: best effort yet & has
been lightly rcd: half brother to several winners incl Longstop: acts on fast grnd.   36
+2301 VIVALDI [12] 2-9-4 E Guest(3) 5/1: 010: Friendless in mkt: prom, close up 7th: see 2301.   42
2127 VERYAN BAY [11] 2-8-8 Pat Eddery 12/1: 000: Prom, fin 8th: best effort yet: lightly
raced filly who seems best on fast grnd.   32
2089 FRANK THE BANK [19] 2-8-11 M Hills 10/1: 400: No show: twice below 1665.   00

2177 Frivolous Fancy [9] 8-8		2191 Kandawgyi [16] 8-8(BL)
2108 Mister Wizard [18] 8-11(vis)		2308 Bugberry [6] 8-8
-- Feasible [5] 8-11	2249 Treble Top [8] 8-11	882 Revelina [7] 8-8
-- Starsign [13] 8-8	2308 Sussarando [3] 8-8	1803 Lantern Boy [10] 8-11
1844 Auction Groupie [1] 8-8		

20 ran   ½,hd,hd,1,nk,½,½   (P Davies)   P Bailey Salisbury

2515 HASTINGS SELLING STAKES 3 & 4YO   £965   1m 2f Firm 18 +08 Fast

2190 PAUSE FOR APPLAUSE [6] (S Woodman) 3-8-3 P Cook 4/1: -000001: 3 b f Rolfe - Jemquo
(Quorum): Dropped to selling company: well bckd & led near fin, driven out in quite fast
run seller at Folkestone: first success: very eff at 10f: acts on hvy, suited by fast grnd
& an undulating track: bought in for 3,000 gns.   20
2103 ROSI NOA [7] (P Kelleway) 3-8-3 Paul Eddery 2/1 FAV: 0000102: Made almost all:
4L clear 3rd: gd effort: see 1969.   19
2187 COOL NUMBER [3] (J Dunlop) 3-8-5(2ow) Pat Eddery 6/1: 00-0033: Ev ch over 1f out:
may need further than 10f as she is a half sister to Janus and Harlestone Lane.   15
2429 ST JAMES RISK [13] (P Makin) 3-8-6 T Quinn 8/1: 0-00004: Prom str, fdd: not stay 10f?   12
2429 UP TOWN BOY [1] 4-9-1 P Waldron 5/1: 443-040: Ev ch str: see 2429, 2271.   07
1937 GULPHAR [10] 4-9-1 J Williams 16/1: 0-00000: Never nearer: see 1103.   03
2208 BLAIRS WINNIE [2] 4-8-12 R Teague(7) 8/1: 0000020: Fin 7th: btr 2208.   00

1960 Flamelight [5] 8-3	1437 Alceba [9] 8-3	2208 Sheer Class [11] 8-3(vis)
2271 Hillingdon Jim [8] 8-6(VIS)		-- Rocky Royale [4] 8-6

12 ran   ½,4,2,3,2½   (Miss Jane Lane)   S Woodman Chichester

2516 HIGHLAND COURT APPLE HCAP 3YO+ 0-35   £1775   1m 2f Firm 18 +11 Fast   [31]

2373 ON TO GLORY [11] (J Dunlop) 3-8-6 B Thomson 6/1: 0B30021: 3 ch f Welsh Pageant -
Glebehill (Northfields): Impr filly: fin well to get up close home in quite fast run h'cap
at Folkestone: gd 2nd in a Brighton mdn last time & clearly likes a sharpish, undulating trk:
stays 10f well: acts on gd & fast grnd.   27
1229 TOM FORRESTER [2] (M Mitchell) 5-9-2 C Rutter(3) 12/1: -030442: Ch final 1f: fine
effort after abs: stays 10f: see 453.   25
2188 DASHING LIGHT [5] (D Morley) 5-8-7 B Rouse 8/1: 4323343: Sn clear leader: caught
close home: see 2098, 432.   15
1325 BLACK COMEDY [9] (M Ryan) 3-8-11 P Robinson 14/1: 0001404: Abs: kept on: gd effort.   26
2022 LEONIDAS [3] 8-9-8 M Hills 9/1: .004100: Not btn far: see 1539 (made all).   26
*2381 DARK HERITAGE [4] 3-9-0 J Reid 9/2 FAV: 00-0410: Ev ch str: see 2381 (stiffer trk).   27
2406 MARSH HARRIER [15] 5-9-11 P Cook 10/1: 2004130: Never nearer 7th: much btr 2190 (C/D).   00
2173 RIVER GAMBLER [10] 3-8-6(vis) Pat Eddery 5/1: 0-00200: No threat: twice below 1806.   00

FOLKESTONE   Tuesday September 9th   -Cont'd

2190 LORD IT OVER [6] 3-8-13(BL) A Clark 10/1: 0000200: Bl first time: fdd 3f out &
twice below 2022.   00
2184 Cafe Noir [1] 8-10   2161 Cool Gales [14] 8-9   2422 Gem Mart [8] 8-8
2176 Nautica [7] 8-5   2132 Tremendous Jet [13] 8-4
-- Faaris [12] 8-13
15 ran 1,hd,1,1½,nk,1½   (James Barber)   J Dunlop Arundel, Sussex

2517 WINDSOR HOTEL AMAT RIDERS STKS 3YO+   £1014   1m 7f Firm 18 -20 Slow

*2096 CAP DEL MOND [3] (G Harwood) 3-10-13 Amanda Harwood(5) 11/8 FAV: -11: 3 b c Troy -
Rainbow's End (My Swallow): Impr young stayer: led over 3f out & kept on well under press
for a narrow win in an amateur riders stakes at Folkestone: first time out won again over this
C/D: cost 400,000 gns as a yearling & is a half brother to winning stayer Storm Cloud & also
the useful Finian's Rainbow: stays really well: acts on fast grnd and an undulating trk: can
improve further.   46
*2228 TAMATOUR [6] (M Stoute) 3-10-13 Maxine Juster 9/4: -0212: Chall final 1f: just denied:
stays 15f well: in fine form: see 2228.   45
2403 TARAS CHARIOT [11] (P Mitchell) 5-11-5 Mr D Benneyworth(5) 33/1: 200-303: Kept on well
final 2f, showing marked impr in this non-h'cap company: yet to win & possibly flattered
by this rating: see 2075.   32
2211 SPARKLIN PERFORMER [13] (B Sanders) 3-10-9 Tina Pile(5) 50/1: 00-0044: Led over 10f
out till over 3f out: much impr effort in this non-h'cap company: see 2211.   29
2290 OSRIC [7] 3-11-2 Mr J Ryan 11/4: 412D320: Prom most: much btr 2290 (12f): see 1923. 28
1923 WELL WISHER [10] 4-11-5 Princess Anne 25/1: -00: Fdd in str: very lightly rcd under
Rules: acts on fast grnd.   17
-- Solar Light [12] 11-5(vis)   -- Rendsley Girl [8] 11-2
2169 Boca West [4] 11-5   448 Al Misk [5] 11-5   -- Vaguely Artistic [1] 11-5
-- Dassells [14] 11-5   2381 Farm Lane [9] 11-2 -- Kalimpong [2] 11-2
-- Tears Of Gold [15] 11-2
15 ran nk,2,2½,8,2   (Prince Ahmed Salman)   G Harwood Pulborough, Sussex

2518 ICI CULTAR ALL AGED STAKES   £1387   6f   Firm 18 -35 Slow

2370 GYPSYS PROPHECY [8] (G Harwood) 3-9-7 A Clark 9/4: 30-3241: 3 ch c Tilt Up -
Scurry Along (Hurry To Market): Gained a deserved win, responding to press to lead inside
final 1f in quite slow run all aged stakes at Folkestone: very eff at 6f, does stay 7f:
acts on firm & yld grnd: runs well on an undulating trk.   42
*2186 ZULU KNIGHT [4] (P Walwyn) 3-9-7 Paul Eddery 8/11 FAV: 0000212: Hvly bckd: made most. 38
2367 ZILLEBEKE [7] (W Brooks) 3-9-4 J Reid 11/1: -0033: Prom, ev ch: in gd form: see 2367. 20
1990 TOMS NAP HAND [6] (W Williams) 5-9-8 N Howe 50/1: 0000024: Speed most: abs since 1990. 00
776 FORLIS FAIR [3] 3-9-4 R Machado 6/1: -000: Long abs: wknd over 1f out: has been
very lightly rcd & appears to have had training problems: see 567.   00
1691 VILEE [2] 3-9-7 P Hutchinson(3) 50/1: -00: Ev ch: see 1691.   00
831 Just Enchanting [5] 7-9   2270 San Juan Song [1] 7-12
8 ran 1½,2½,5,½,1½   (Spyros Niarchos)   G Harwood Pulborough, Sussex

2519 BOWRING HANDICAP 3YO+ 0-35   £1712   6f   Firm 18 -29 Slow   [35]

2012 SOFTLY SPOKEN [9] (P Felgate) 3-8-8 W Ryan 5/1: 0120221: 3 b f Mummy's Pet - Tender
Answer (Prince Tenderfoot): In fine form & led nearing fin in quite slow run h cap at
Folkestone: earlier won a h'cap at Thirsk: in '85 won at Edinburgh: very eff at 6f: acts on
yld, best on fast grnd: no trk preferences: genuine.   29
2171 LINAVOS [16] (W Brooks) 3-8-5(1ow) J Reid 20/1: 1004402: Ch final 1f: gd effort:
runs well here: see 837.   23
2318 GALLANT HOPE [2] (L Cottrell) 4-8-0 M Hills 15/2: 0202223: Al front rank: another
good run: see 2318, 1834.   08
2319 HATCHING [12] (L Cottrell) 5-7-9(vis) T Lang(3) 16/1: 0-02004: Led over 1f out: best
effort since 1942.   03
2242 MUHTARIS [20] 3-8-10 B Rouse 20/1: 2000000: Raced alone far side: best effort since 734. 22
2318 LONELY STREET [10] 5-9-7 L Johnsey(7) 9/1: 3201430: Led 2f out: see 2046.   26
2079 ROYSIA BOY [4] 6-9-12 G Duffield 10/1: 000300: Never nearer 7th: twice below 1933. 00
2295 THREE BELLS [15] 4-8-12 Pat Eddery 9/2 FAV: 0004300: Again well bckd: fin 8th: see 2046. 00
2411 STONEYDALE [11] 4-9-10 P Robinson 10/1: 0002000: No threat: btr 2033: see 734.   00
2120 SILVER FORM [7] 3-7-12 M L Thomas 9/1: 3402000: Nicely bckd: best 1499.   00
2033 Mister March [5] 8-11   2271 Fort Duchesne [8] 7-13(VIS)
1676 Maiden Bidder [13] 8-3   1086 Tachyon Park [14] 9-1
2370 Downsview [6] 9-10(VIS)   2258 Exert [1] 8-7(bl)
2370 Russell Flyer [3] 7-13(vis)   2370 Dartigny [18] 9-0
2120 Aclia [17] 8-12   2370 Friendly Lass [19] 8-3
20 ran ½,2,shhd,nk,½,1,hd   (J David Abell)   P Felgate Melton Mowbray, Leics

2520 ST GEORGES MAIDEN FILLIES STKS 3YO   £959   1m 4f Firm 18 +16 Fast

2304 MISS SHIRLEY [1] (J Dunlop) 3-8-11 Pat Eddery 11/2: -302241: 3 b f Shirley Heights-
Miss Carina (Caro): Led ½m out & came home unchall by 6L in a fast run 3yo fillies mdn at

741

Folkestone: placed several times previously: stays 12f really well: well suited by fast grnd
& an undulating trk: runs well from the front: half sister to smart French miler Mendez &
can find a h'cap.   40
2306 AIRCRAFTIE [13] (B Hills) 3-8-11(BL) B Thomson 16/1: 0303002: Ev ch in str: lacks
foot: stays 12f & acts on gd & fast grnd.   30
2327 PRINCESS EMMA [6] (M Stoute) 3-8-11 A Kimberley 4/1: -0423: Stayed on too late: gets 12f. 30
2299 SUNLEY SAINT [10] (P Walwyn) 3-8-11 Paul Eddery 4/1: 20-0224: Prom, ev ch: btr 2299.   28
1192 ON THE AGENDA [11] 3-8-11 B Rouse 20/1: 0-000: Long abs: fair effort: very lightly
rcd filly who seems to have had training problems: half sister to 3 winners: stays 12f
& acts on fast grnd.   21
2129 LA DUSE [4] 3-8-11 R Guest 3/1 FAV: -030: Well bckd: no threat: see 2129.   18
2217 GONE OVERBOARD [7] 3-8-11 M Roberts 5/1: -040020: Fdd final 3f: much btr 2217 (11f).   00
2314 Armour Of Light [9] 8-11   2304 La Muscade [2] 8-11(bl)
2184 Be So Bold [3] 8-11   1686 Lhirondelle [5] 8-11   2401 The Fink Sisters [8] 8-11
1639 Jolie Pelouse [12] 8-11(BL)   2299 La Serenata [14] 8-11
14 ran   6,nk,1½,5,2½   (Sheikh Mohammed)   J Dunlop Arundel, Sussex

---

DONCASTER   Wednesday September 10th   Lefthanded, Galloping Track

Official Going Given As GOOD

2521 PRINCE OF WALES NURSERY H'CAP 2YO   £4084   1m   Firm 17 -03 Slow   [67]

*2352 TOLUCA LAKE [1] (L Piggott) 2-9-0(8ex) T Ives 6/4 FAV: 4111: 2 b c King's Lake -
Zirconia (Charlottesville) Very useful colt: held up, took command at dist for an easy win
in a nursery h'cap at Doncaster: earlier won a minor race at Wolverhampton and then quite a
val event at Ostend: cost over 1m French Francs and is a half brother to sev winners: very
eff over 7/8f on gd and firm grd: acts on a gall trk: should win btr races.   66
2439 SOMEONE ELSE [5] (R Hannon) 2-7-10(BL)(3ow) W Carson 11/4: 0300032: Tried to make
all, no chance with winner but fin well clear rem: seems impr by blinkers: see 2439 & 1097. 40
2383 PLAGUE ORATS [6] (R Smyly) 2-7-13 N Howe 10/3: 0143: Wknd over 2f out: best 1681 (6f)   28
2377 ALBION PLACE [2] (M H Easterby) 2-7-8(VIS) J Lowe 14/1: 400044: Visored first time
over this longer trip: front rank over ½ way, btn 2f out: acts on firm and yldg: see 870.   22
*2019 MY NOBLE LORD [3] 2-9-7 T Quinn 6/1: 210: Well btn: much btr over 7f in 2019 (sharp trk) 38
5 ran   2,8,shthd,7   (Jack F Vollstedt)   L Piggott Newmarket

2522 E.B.F. QUEEN'S OWN DRAGOONS STAKES 2YO   £7408   7f   Firm 17 -24 Slow

2239 BRENTANO [10] (L Cumani) 2-8-11 R Guest 12/1: 01: 2 b c Thatch - Tender Answer
(Prince Tenderfoot) Useful colt: easy to back tho' btr for recent debut and gamely made all
in a val 2yo Stks at Doncaster: cost 9,400 gns as a yearling and is closely related to sev
winners, including the recently successful Softly Spoken: very eff over 7f and should be
suited by 1m: acts on gd and firm grd and on a gall trk: on the upgrade.   56
-- LOVE THE GROOM [13] (J Dunlop) 2-8-7 Pat Eddery 9/2: 2: Ran on well: sound debut
from this $325,000 yearling: well bred colt who is sure to be suited by longer dist: acts
on firm grd and on a gall trk: sure to find a race.   50
2341 KALGOORLIE [14] (L Piggott) 2-8-11 T Ives 3/1: 023: Al up there, not btn far: see 2341. 52
-- DUCKINGTON [15] (M H Easterby) 2-8-7 M Birch 20/1: 4: Outpaced early: ran on promisingly
and should improve on this next time: will be suited by 1m+: acts on fast grd and a gall trk. 44
-- FINAGLE [5] 2-8-7 W Ryan 20/1: 0: Stayed on well from rear, promisingly debut: half
brother to very useful 10/14f winner Range Rover: sure to stay further in time: acts on
firm grd and on a gall trk: should improve.   39
-- PITCHFORK [3] 2-8-7 N Howe 20/1: 0: Prom most of way on debut: quite cheaply bought
colt who is bred to be suited by 1m+: acts on firm grd: likely to do btr.   37
2232 YOUNG JUDGE [2] 2-8-11 S Cauthen 9/4 FAV: 20: Heavily bckd: fin 7th: btr 2232 (6f).   39
2239 SURF BOARD [12] 2-8-11 M Hills 11/1: 00: Some late prog into 8th: half brother to
winning juv Holly Patch: acts on fast grd: should continue to improve.   38
-- APPEALING DANCER [8] 2-8-4 W Carson 12/1: 0: Fdd into 9th after showing gd speed over
½ way: acts on fast grd: should be better for this experience.   33
-- ZAREEF [2] 2-8-7 W R Swinburn 9/1: 0: Al mid-div on racecourse debut: half brother
to 7f winner Zariya: acts on firm grd: will be better for this run.   35
-- Star North [6] 8-7   2243 Moore Brass [1] 8-11   -- Charlie Milord [11] 8-7
-- Larloch [7] 8-7   -- Home To Tara [9] 8-7
15 ran   ¾,¾,2,3,¾,1,hd,½,nk   (C A B St George)   L Cumani Newmarket

2523 UNIPART HANDICAP 3YO+   £20015   1m 6f   Firm 17 +02 Fast   (54)

1293 BACKCHAT [4] (G Harwood) 4-9-6 G Starkey 7/2: 11-4001: 4 b c Stage Door Johnny
- Dos A Dos (Advocator) Useful colt: despite fair abs led early and again home turn for a
game win in a val h'cap at Doncaster: similarly lightly raced last season when winning at
Newmarket and Bath: very eff over 14/16f and should stay 2m: acts on fast and yldg ground
and likes a gall trk.   60
2220 DAARKOM [10] (A Stewart) 3-9-3 M Roberts 5/1: -221232: Sustained chall, hung left
and just outstayed cl home: another fine effort and deserves another race: see 2220 & 1290. 65

1894 SPARTAN VALLEY [3] (B Hills) 3-8-4 B Thomson 20/1: -232143: Ran on same pace: see 1646.   44
2220 NEWSELLS PARK [7] (J Winter) 5-9-7 Pat Eddery 6/1: 2122244: Most consistent: see 2220, 1470 50
2445 REVISIT [2] 4-8-13 T Ives 12/1: 3434430: No extra str: see 58a.   38
2220 CHAUVE SOURIS [1] 3-9-9 S Cauthen 3/1 FAV: -020120: Heavily bckd: much btr 2220.   47
2220 RUSSIAN NOBLE [9] 5-9-5 W R Swinburn 13/2: 2-22300: Al rear: fin 8th: see 2220 & 976.   00
2290 Cadmium [6] 9-1(BL)   2389 Trapeze Artist [8] 8-13
2376 Lhasa [5] 8-7(2ow)
10 ran   1¼,4,shthd,3,12   (K Abdulla)   G Harwood Pulborough, Sussex

2524 SCARBOROUGH STAKES   £9224   5f   Firm 17 +02 Fast

-2241 TREASURE KAY [7] (P Makin) 3-9-5 Pat Eddery 11/10 FAV: -142321: 3 b c Mummy's Pet
- Welsh Blossom (Welsh Saint) Smart sprinter: heavily bckd and confidently ridden to lead
inside dist, readily, in val Scarborough Stks at Doncaster: has been placed in useful company
since his first time out success in a h'cap at Sandown: in '85 won a mdn at Newbury: very
eff over 5/6f: acts on firm and hvy ground: well suited by a gall trk: genuine and consistent
sort who is certain to win more good races.   72
1889 WELSH NOTE [8] (I Balding) 3-9-9 T Ives 7/2: 4-44402: Made most: gd effort: see 408.   64
2398 WHIPPET [3] (C Brittain) 2-8-0 M Roberts 6/1: 2000333: Al front rank: fine effort
against other horses: should win soon: see 2398 & 577.   64
2457 FILLEOR [1] (G Pritchard Gordon) 3-9-1 W Ryan 16/1: 32-0044: Not btn far: acts on
firm: see 2241.   60
+2289 PERFECT TIMING [5] 4-9-10 S Cauthen 7/2: 3323210: Had ev ch: consistent sort: see 2289.   59
--   ALL IS FORGIVEN [2] 6-9-9 G Sexton 33/1: 02030/0: Sn outpaced after a lengthy abs:
useful sprinter in '84, winning a val race at Chester: in '83 won at Yarmouth, York and
Newmarket (2) : suited by gd or fast ground and acts on any trk.   00
2254 SEMIS [6] 2-7-7 D Mckay 100/1: 000000: Gd early speed: outclassed: see 577.   00
7 ran   1½,½,½,shthd,2½,10   (G W Yates)   P Makin Ogbourne Maisey, Wilts.

2525 GROUP 2 PARK HILL STAKES 3YO FILLIES   £28194   1m 6f   Firm 17 +06 Fast

2202 REJUVENATE [6] (B Hills) 3-8-9 B Thomson 8/1: -31001: 3 b f Ile De Bourbon - Miss
Petard (Petingo) Smart filly: returned to her best form, led below dist and gamely held on
in fast run Gr 2 Parkhill Stks at Doncaster: earlier a similarly narrow winner of Gr 3
Musidora Stks at York: half sister to sev winners: very eff over 10/14f: acts on firm and
soft ground and on any trk: genuine filly.   76
1128 SALCHOW [9] (W Hern) 3-8-9 W Carson 6/1: 112-102: Well bckd despite a lengthy abs:
ran a fine race, kept on gamely and only just denied: stays 14f well: should win soon: see 463.   75
2236 ALTIYNA [10] (M Stoute) 3-8-9 W R Swinburn 20/1: -Led over 2f out: ran on
same pace: best effort for sometime: stays 14f: acts on any trk: see 463.   68
*2236 STARTINO [2] (H Cecil) 3-8-9 S Cauthen 6/4 FAV: 2-1113: Heavily bckd over this longer
trip: unable to qckn below dist and ddhtd for 3rd: best in 2236 (12f).   68
*2028 BROKEN WAVE [7] 3-8-9 W Newnes 16/1: -10310: Ran on late: gd eff: see 2028.   60
2156 MIGHTY FLASH [4] 3-8-9 J Reid 50/1: 0011000: No extra over 2f out tho' a creditable
effort in this hot company: should find a h'cap if reproducing this form: see 1523.   55
2236 KENANGA [12] 3-8-9 W Ryan 7/2: -011120: Well bckd: trailed in last and btr 2236 (12f)   00
1128 Pilot Bird [5] 8-9   *2000 Deserted [3] 8-9   2236 Bonshamile [8] 8-9
2202 Spun Gold [1] 8-9   2257 Fleeting Affair [11] 8-9
12 ran   ½,3,ddht,5,1½   (K Abdulla)   B Hills Lambourn, Berks.

2526 ELECTRO COPY UBIX H'CAP (0-60) 3YO+   £4272   7f   Firm 17 -09 Slow   [54]

2437 THE MAZALL [11] (L Siddall) 6-8-4 M Wood 11/1: 2211001: 6 br g Persian Bold - Dance
All Night (Double-U-Jay) Returned to form, broke well and was never hdd when a 2l winner of
quite a val h'cap at Doncaster: earlier won a similar race over this C/D and earlier won
smaller h'caps at Catterick and Redcar: in '85 won at Redcar and Carlisle: very eff over
6/7f and does well with forcing tactics: acts on firm and soft grd and on any trk.   42
2390 KNIGHTS SECRET [9] (M H Easterby) 5-8-2 J Lowe 8/1: 4034042: Ran on well: see 2390 & 815 36
*2155 PASTICCIO [12] (M Jarvis) 3-9-10 T Ives 5/1: 3222113: Had no luck in running, flying
at the fin and looked an unlucky loser: in fine form and should gain compensation soon:
carries weight well: see 2155.   63
2155 AL BASHAAMA [8] (L Cumani) 3-9-3 Pat Eddery 9/4 FAV: -013104: Held up, denied a
clear run, going on fin: btr than his final placing indicates: should prove btr over 1m : see 2155.   56
2437 AIR COMMAND [2] 6-8-7 Julie Bowker(7) 8/1: 0002020: Ran to his best: see 1868.   37
2390 CREEAGER [7] 4-8-7 N Carlisle 20/1: 0143000: Late prog: btr eff: see 441.   32
732 SKEEB [4] 3-8-13 W R Swinburn 8/1: 114-030: Long abs: fin 7th: see 732.   00
2277 Playtex [14] 8-0   1041 No Credibility [10] 7-11
2378 Fawleys Girl [6] 7-7(1oh)   2390 Corn Street [1] 9-0
814 Tufuh [3] 9-8   1727 Easy Day [5] 8-1
13 ran   2,½,nk,½,2   (Mrs Jack Fulton)   L Siddall Colton, Yorks.

SALISBURY Wednesday September 10th Righthand, Stiff, Galloping Track

Official Going Given As FIRM

2527 **E B F QUIDHAMPTON MAIDEN 2YO FILLIES** **£2026 7f Firm 12 -03 Slow**

-- **IBTIDAAR** [6] (H T Jones) 2-8-11 A Murray 6/1: 1: 2 b f Danzig - Shivering (Etonian) Very promising filly: first time out, led final 1f readily in a 2yo fillies mdn at Salisbury: cost $700,000 as a yearling and is related to sev winners: eff at 7f, looks sure to be suited by 1m: acts on fast grd and a gall trk: certain to win more races and rate more highly. 60

1641 **QUELLE FILLE** [17] (P Cole) 2-8-11 P Waldron 13/8 FAV: 32: Stayed on under press: caught a tartar here: stays 7f well and will be suited by 1m: can win soon: see 1641. 52

2215 **IVORY FIELDS** [8] (M Stoute) 2-8-11 A Kimberley 10/1: 03: Led 6f: fine effort and looks sure to find a maiden: stays 7f: acts on fast ground: see 2215. 48

-- **KNOWN LINE** [10] (H Candy) 2-8-11 T Williams 14/1: 4: Al up there on debut, showing future promise: half sister to winning 3yo Newquay: eff at 7f, looks sure to be suited by 1m+: acts on fast ground and can find a race. 45

1282 **MEADOWBANK** [2] 2-8-11 G Duffield 25/1: 00: Mkt drifter after abs: dsptd lead over 1f out: gd effort: further improvement likely: eff at 7f on fast ground. 39

1778 **TAUSTAFF** [20] 2-8-11 Paul Eddery 12/1: 00: Never nearer after abs: half sister to a winning sprinter and is on the upgrade: stays 7f: acts on fast ground. 38

2283 **MUSICAL REVIEW** [3] 2-8-11 J Matthias 4/1: 420: Early speed: unsuited by firm? See 2283 (yielding): twice below 1778 (good). 00

1030 **Naturally Autumn** [9] 8-11 -- **Answers Please** [11] 8-11
1464 **Cubby Hole** [15] 8-11 1518 **Lagta** [12] 8-11 1518 **Amanda Jane** [18] 8-11
-- **Camillas Girl** [5] 8-11 2270 **Odiaxere** [4] 8-11
2418 **Regal Rhythm** [13] 8-11 -- **Main Rocket** [19] 8-11
2292 **Harts Lane** [7] 8-11 -- **Meldon Hill** [1] 8-11 852 **Deep Raptures** [16] 8-11
19 ran 2½,2,1½,3,nk,3,shthd,½ (Hamdan Al-Maktoum) H T Jones Newmarket

2528 **DANEBURY SELLING STAKES** **£1149 1m 4f Firm 12 -08 Slow**

2282 **MR MUSIC MAN** [10] (C Reavey) 12-9-3 N Day 14/1: 0024001: 12 b g March Past - Merry Melody (Counsel) Grand old gelding: stuck on well to lead inside final 1f in a seller at Salisbury (no bid): in '85 won at Beverley, in '84 won 4 times and has been a tremendous stable servant: eff at 8/10f: stays 12f well: acts on any grd and on any trk: genuine. 16

2395 **DICK KNIGHT** [4] (K Ivory) 5-9-3(vis) A Shoults(5) 12/1: 0001002: Led 3f out: just btn: see 2101. 15

1769 **SYMBOLIC** [7] (R Stubbs) 6-9-3 J H Brown(5) 11/2: 2-00043: Ev ch final 2f: disapp after 1769 11

2306 **HIGH FOREST** [1] (M Hinchliffe) 4-8-11(vis) B Procter 14/1: 00-0004: No threat: little form on the Flat: prob stays 12f: acts on fast ground. 00

2173 **DEERFIELD BEACH** [12] 4-9-0 J Williams 33/1: 0000000: Never in it: see 202. 00

2253 **LAST POLONAISE** [13] 3-8-8(BL) N Adams 12/1: 3000040: Bl first time: led over 5f out: best 1078 (14f). 00

*2034 **MUBARAK OF KUWAIT** [5] 7-9-3 R Hills 1/1 FAV: -20-010: Fin 7th: has bad legs and cannot stand much racing: see 2034. 00

-- **CONNAUGHT PRINCE** [11] 5-8-11 T Williams 6/1: 03432/0: Gambled on but never looked likely: off the trk last season: placed sev times in '84 but has yet to win: stays 12f: acts on fast and yldg ground but appears to have regressed. 00

-- **Mist Over Pendle** [3] 8-8 2317 **Oakdale** [2] 8-8
2309 **Cleveland Bond** [8] 8-8 2094 **Solent Dawn** [6] 8-8
1686 **Molybdenum** [9] 8-11(BL)
13 ran ½,2,3,1,4,2½ (Mrs C J Reavey) C Reavey Maidenhead, Berks.

2529 **HIURSTBOURNE NURSERY HANDICAP 2YO** **£2506 6f Firm 12 -05 Slow** **[52]**

*2070 **PERCYS LASS** [12] (G Wragg) 2-9-4 P Robinson 7/4 FAV: 11: 2 b f Blakeney - Laughing Girl (Sassafras) Impr filly: well bckd and stayed on well to lead inside final 1f in a nursery h'cap at Salisbury: first time out was an easy winner of a fillies mdn at Lingfield: half sister to middle dist winner No No Girl: eff at 6f, sure to be suited by 7f/1m: acts on fast ground and on any track: may win again. 54

2272 **KEEN EDGE** [9] (P Mitchell) 2-7-10 G Carter 12/1: 0030302: Led over 1f out: just caught: gd effort: deserves a race after sev near misses: well suited by 6f and fast ground : see 577. 29

2185 **LADY LUCINA** [11] (R Smyly) 2-7-13(BL) R Fox 16/1: 0403: Made most: gd effort: eff at 6f on fast ground: see 848: bl 1st time today. 27

1966 **COPPER CREEK** [5] (R Smyth) 2-8-10 S Whitworth 14/1: 0034: Al up there: in gd form. 36

-2108 **MAD MAX** [8] 2-8-9 T Williams 11/2: 4320: Chance over 2f out: btr 2108, see 1984. 34

2071 **STATE BALLET** [7] 2-9-3(VIS) J Matthias 11/1: 0100: Visored first time: twice below 1518(7f). 37

2090 **LUCIANAGA** [14] 2-9-7 Paul Eddery 20/1: 2201000: Prom, fin 7th: btr eff: see 1313. 40

*1997 **WHOS ZOOMIN WHO** [1] 2-7-10 P Hill(7) 9/2: 00010: Fin 8th: see 1997 (seller). 00

2435 **GLORY BEE** [13] 2-7-8 N Adams 10/1: 1004100: Stiff task: fin 9th: twice below 2097 (sharp) 00

2329 **Lazim** [6] 8-5(bl) 2265 **Artful Maid** [10] 8-1(2ow)
2181 **Setter Country** [2] 7-7 2097 **Telesto** [3] 8-3(bl)
13 ran ¾,1½,¾,nk,1½,nk,hd,2 (E B Moller) G Wragg Newmarket

2530 **HUNTSMAN ALES HANDICAP 0-60** **£3128 5f Firm 12 +10 Fast** **[51]**

2402 **AXE VALLEY** [6] (P Cole) 4-9-7(bl) G Duffield 5/1: 0-01001: 4 b f Royben - Unpredictable (Pardal) Useful filly: made almost all, dirven out in a fast run h'cap at Salisbury: earlier

won a val h'cap at Sandown: in '85 won at Windsor: very eff at 5f on gd and fast ground:
seems to act on any trk: suited by front running in blinkers.   55
2402 WOODFOLD [10] (J Winter) 5-9-1 B Rouse 5/1: -130002: Chance final 1f: gd eff: see 986.   44
2120 SNAP DECISION [1] (R Hannon) 3-7-12(BL) R Fox 9/1: -040203: Bl first time: kept
on final 1f: gd eff: see 1033.   29
2160 SIMLA RIDGE [4] (A Hide) 4-8-8 G Baxter 8/1: 1300204: Ev ch final 2f: see 977, 628.   34
2402 GLEN KELLA MANX [5] 5-8-12 A Mcglone 11/4 FAV: 0010000: Going well 2f out: best 2021.   33
2382 NORTHERN TRUST [2] 3-8-9(bl) A Clark 10/1: 0020000: Never nearer: best 1704, see 233.   33
2143 OCEAN TRADER [3] 3-9-0(bl) P Waldron 10/1: -000000: Mkt drifter: fin 9th: btr 2143 (6f) 00
2160 OH BOYAR [9] 3-9-6 P Cook 7/1: 0-30000: Came in last: lightly raced since 228.   00
2312 Dublinaire [8] 7-8   952 Stock Hill Lass [7] 8-11
10 ran   1¼,1,shthd,1½,¾   (Richard Barber)   P Cole Lambourn, Berks

2531 E B F QUIDHAMPTON MAIDEN 2YO FILLIES   £3065   7f   Firm 12 +01 Fast

1996 SANAABELL [10] (M Stoute) 2-8-11 A Kimberley 2/1 FAV: 21: 2 b f Persepolis - Sushila
(Petingo) Promising filly: stayed on well to lead cl home in a 2yo fillies mdn at Salisbury:
first time out just btn at Yarmouth: cost 400,000 gns as a yearling and is a half sister to
topclass Petoski: eff at 7f, sure to be suited by 1m and further: acts on fast grd and a
gall trk: certain to win more races.   56
2147 STREET PARTY [12] (G Wragg) 2-8-11 P Robinson 5/2: 32: Made virtually all and just
caught: 4l clear 3rd and will not be long in gaining compensation: stays 7f: see 2147.   55
1855 NORTH PACIFIC [9] (P Cole) 2-8-11 P Waldron 33/1: 03: Mkt drifter: kept on final 2f:
fast improving: cost $120,000: should be suited by 1m: acts on fast grd and can find a race. 48
--   FATAL CHARM [4] (M Dickinson) 2-8-11 A Murray 20/1: 4: Mkt drifter on debut: no
extra final 1f, but improvement very likely: American bred filly who should be suited by 1m:
acts on fast ground and should have little trouble finding a maiden.   46
--   AGLOWING [16] 2-8-11 A Clark 10/1: 0: Friendless in mkt, but ran a promising race:
dam unraced: bred to stay 1m and further: acts on fast ground and will improve.   39
2147 COLDWATER CANYON [6] 2-8-11 R Cochrane 14/1: 00: Prom most: stays 7f: see 2147.   38
2368 ACHNAHUAIGH [11] 2-8-11 Paul Eddery 6/1: 020: Fin 7th: rated higher 2368 (sharper trk). 33
2433 Bleu Celeste [8] 8-11   --   Dream Dollar [7] 8-11   2287 Dawn Romp [13] 8-11
--   Lurex Girl [14] 8-11   1752 Kaladiola [5] 8-11   2292 Oh My Joy [15] 8-11
--   Dance A Jig [19] 8-11   --   Sarietta [20] 8-11   --   Trivia [1] 8-11
1801 Najaba [17] 8-11   --   Employ Force [18] 8-11
18 ran   nk,4,1½,4,nk,2½,nk,nk,nk   (Maktoum Al Maktoum)   M Stoute Newmarket

2532 FLEET MAIDEN STAKES   3YO   £996   1m   Firm 12 +04 Fast

1953 HOOKED BID [8] (J Dunlop) 3-8-11 G Baxter 8/1: -00031: 3 gr f Spectacular Bid -
Barb's Bold (Bold Forbes) Impr filly: led final 1f, ridden out in quite a fast run 3yo mdn at
Salisbury: very eff at 1m, does stay further: acts well on gd and fast ground and runs
well on a gall trk: may find a h'cap now she has struck form.   41
--   MAIYAASAH [1] (L Cumani) 3-8-11 R Cochrane 4/5 FAV: -2: Heavily bckd debutant:
ran on well cl home and nearly landed the odds: half sister to 5f winner Fair Charter:
clearly stays 1m well: acts on fast ground, but may enjoy some give: will find a race.   40
183 MR PASTRY [4] (G Wragg) 3-9-0 P Robinson 14/1: -03: Very long abs: kept on well
final 1f: fine effort: half brother to sev winners: eff at 1m, prob will stay further:
acts on fast ground and a gall trk.   41
2030 LIKENESS [12] (W Hern) 3-8-11(bl) J Matthias 8/1: -030034: Chance over 1f out: see 2030. 33
2321 AUCHINATE [13] 3-9-0 A Clark 11/2: -430: Made most: consistent: see 2321, 1628.   35
2314 NEEDLE SHARP [14] 3-8-11 R Fox 12/1: -300: Twice below 1880 (good).   17
1228 Velvet Pearl [3] 8-11   2339 Welsh Pageantry [6] 8-11
2373 Lost In France [7] 8-11   2186 Red River Boy [2] 9-0(BL)
2314 Cherry Glory [15] 8-11   2313 Out Yonder [10] 9-0(bl)
2253 Venus Saga [11] 8-11
13 ran   nk,¾,2,hd,8,1   (Sheikh Mohammed)   J Dunlop Arundel, Sussex

2533 WOODFORD APPRENTICE HANDICAP 0-35   £1269   1m 2f   Firm 12 -22 Slow   [32]

2432 UP TO UNCLE [2] (R Hannon) 3-9-3 L Jones 3/1 JT.FAV: 1322331: 3 ch c Saher - Roll
Up (Roll Of Honour) Most consistent h'capper: in fine form this season and led 2f out, readily
in a slow run app h'cap at Salisbury: earlier won a 3yo h'cap at Windsor and has made the
frame in his last 9 starts: eff at 10f - 13f: acts on soft, likes gd and fast ground:
no trk preferences.   39
1787 PEARL PET [11] (P Makin) 4-8-8 D J Williams 5/1: 0-20022: No chance with winner:
fair effort: see 860.   14
2330 WILLOW GORGE [12] (G Lewis) 3-8-8 R J Crowden(7) 16/1: -000043: Al up there: improved
of late: half brother to a couple of winners: seems eff at 10/12f on fast and yldg.   21
2190 DANCING BARRON [8] (L Cottrell) 5-8-9(vis) T Lang(5) 14/1: 0030404: Made some:
best 1473 (12f): see 750.   09
*1401 ARTISTIC CHAMPION [5] 3-8-8 J Carr(3) 3/1 JT.FAV: 0-30010: No real threat: loser over
hurdles since 1401.   16
2490 POLYNOR [7] 5-8-0 P Barnard(3) 12/1: -440-00: Prom most: see 2490.   00
1551 PULSINGH [3] 4-8-10 J Adams(3) 8/1: 0010300: Fin 7th: abs: best 850 (C/D).   00

2093 ISOM DART [9] 7-8-3 P Mcentee(3) 15/2: 0-11000: Made no show: best over 12f in 1473.   00
2094 Hokusan [13] 7-11   2282 Taffys Pride [10] 7-7(2oh)
2381 Main Star [6] 8-13   1472 Rodistyle [4] 7-13   2406 The Footman [1] 9-10
13 ran   3,¾,2,¾,shthd,¾   (Nimrod Company)   R Hannon Marlborough, Wilts

2534 FLEET MAIDEN STAKES   3YO   £1375   1m   Firm 12 -02 Slow

-- ELBURY PARK [1] (G Harwood) 3-9-0 A Clark 7/4 FAV: -1: 3 b c Young Generation -
Sandfornia (Sandford Lass) Made a winning debut, heavily bckd, in a 3yo mdn at Salisbury:
led nearing final 1f, driven out: dam a 7f winner: eff at 1m, should get further: acts
on fast ground and a gall trk.   38
2314 NATIJA [3] (P Makin) 3-8-11 R Cochrane 16/1: 0-0002: Fin well: gd eff: lightly raced
this term: definitely best on fast ground and may stay further than 1m: see 1228.   31
2381 STARMAST [6] (W Hern) 3-9-0(BL) T Sprake(7) 10/1: 4030003: Tried in bl: led 2f out:
best effort since 1830.   32
2294 ROYAL TROUBADOR [12] (B Hills) 3-9-0(L) R Hills 4/1: 0-0004: Led over 3f out: well
clear rem, but btr 2294 (easy trk).   29
2314 EASTERN COMMAND [4] 3-8-11 B Rouse 5/1: 34-4300: Never nearer: only modest form
this term: see 1446.   06
2408 PORO BOY [8] 3-9-0 P Waldron 16/1: 4000400: Held ev ch: lightly raced since best 352(yld). 07
2321 LOWARA [9] 3-8-11 R Fox 10/1: -00: Fdd final 3f: disapp after 2321 (soft).   00
-- Lost Island [2] 9-0   -- Hello Sam [5] 9-0   2076 Lightning Wind [13] 9-0
2314 Everyinchalady [7] 8-11   1284 Lady Windmill [10] 8-11
-- Parijoun [11] 8-11   1749 Bills Belle [14] 8-11
14 ran   1½,¾,¾,1½,10,¾   (J B Austin)   G Harwood Pulborough, Sussex

Official Going Given As GOOD

2535 DEVONSHIRE SELLING STAKES 2YO   £4125   6f   Good/Firm 21 -25 Slow

2265 FIRMLY ATTACHED [1] (T Barron) 2-8-7 G Carter 12/1: 020001: 2 br c Tina's Pet -
Izobia (Mansingh) Quickly into his stride and gamely made all in a 2yo seller at Doncaster
(bought in 9200 gns)): speedily bred colt who cost 6600 gns as a yearling and was placed in
non-selling company early season: eff over 5/6f on gd/firm and soft ground: acts on any trk. 32
2472 MERE MUSIC [5] (M Brittain) 2-8-11 M Birch 20/1: 0001002: Ran on well: stays 6f: see 2150. 34
2308 SINGING PARTNER [20] (R Smyly) 2-8-4 W Ryan 7/1: 03: Stayed on well and not btn far:
half sister to 7f winner Far Too Busy: should stay 7f+: acts on gd/firm ground and on a
gall trk: should continue to improve and sure to find a seller.   27
2279 MUSICAL RHAPSODY [23] (G Pritchard Gordon) 2-8-4 P Robinson 16/1: 0044: Not btn far. 26
2396 MISS EMILY [15] 2-8-4 A Proud 14/1: 000220: AI front rank: in gd form: see 2396.   20
*2334 AEGEAN DANCE [11] 2-8-8 G Duffield 6/1: 10: AI up there: stays 6f: see 2334.   23
2185 FINGERS CROSSED [8] 2-8-4 R Cochrane 10/1: 0000: Never nearer 7th: acts on gd/firm: see 2080.17
2472 EVENING PRAYERS [14] 2-8-4 A Shoults(5) 9/1: 000: AI prom: fin 8th: eff over 5/6f
on gd/firm and yldg ground: acts on any trk: see 2308.   17
1373 COMBERMERE [22] 2-8-7 N Connorton 10/1: 0000: No threat after abs: see 1373.   00
2172 DOMINO ROSE [19] 2-8-7(3ow) S Cauthen 11/2 FAV: 3220230: Well bckd: speed over ½ way:
best in 1814 (5f).   00
2405 ROYAL RABBLE [18] 2-8-8 C Asmussen 10/1: 3100000: No danger: best in 1059.   00
2045 Flying Silently [2] 8-4   2425 Bootham Lad [21] 8-11
2472 Malacanang [12] 8-4   2011 Take Effect [6] 8-7(bl)
2320 Starch Brook [3] 8-4   2476 Dream Ticket [7] 8-7 2396 Patels Gold [4] 8-4
2307 Nicholas George [16] 8-11(bl)   2177 Glorious Dan [9] 8-7
2138 Soaring Eagles [17] 8-4   2375 Pretty Soon [13] 8-4
685 Thatch Avon [10] 8-7
23 ran   ¾,shthd,nk,2½,hd,1,shthd   (Mrs J Ramsden)   T Barron Maunby, Yorks.

2536 BET WITH THE TOTE H'CAP (0-60) 3YO+   £5205   1m 2f Good/Firm 21 +09 Fast   [47]

*2017 FOLLOW THE BAND [1] (W Jarvis) 4-8-8 R Cochrane 14/1: 0-00411: 4 b c Dance In Time -
Yelming (Thatch) In fine form, ran on strongly to lead cl home in quite a fast run and
val h'cap at Doncaster: last month got off the mark in a claiming mdn at Yarmouth: eff
around 10f on fast ground: acts on any trk.   37
2149 FORCELLO [8] (S Norton) 3-8-3 J Lowe 16/1: 4243002: Just failed to make all: best
effort for sometime and may win soon: see 444 and 106.   39
2237 FESTIVAL CITY USA [6] (B Hills) 3-9-6(bl) B Thomson 8/1: 0300143: No extra cl home
tho' another gd effort: eff over 10/12f and is well suited by a gall trk: see 1818.   53
*1820 MASKED BALL [2] (P Calver) 6-9-0 M Fry 13/2: 1120214: Boxed in: unlucky: see 1820. 38
2237 BALLYDURROW [16] 9-9-1 D Nicholls 7/1: 4021430: Had ev ch: see 2237 & 1744.   34
2438 ANDARTIS [11] 3-9-6(bl) T Lucas 12/1: 3340400: Nicely bckd: in gd form: see 807.   46
2009 FACTOTUM [3] 3-8-7 A Shoults(5) 9/1: 0-00320: Never nearer 8th: stays 10f: see 941. 00
*2477 WILD HOPE [13] 5-9-1(7ex) W Litwin(7) 8/1: -004210: No threat: much btr 2477.   00
+2333 PRINCE ORAC [10] 3-9-6(4ex) S Cauthen 8/1: -30210: Wknd early in str: much btr 2333. 00

2296 Aristocrat Velvet [9] 9-1   1854 Pellinko [5] 9-4
1983 Moninsky [4] 7-7(2oh)   2445 Lost Opportunity [15] 7-7(11oh)
1509 Swimmer [12] 9-7   2300 Pentland Hawk [7] 8-7 2443 Killary Bay [14] 9-5
16 ran   ¾,1½,½,2,1½   (Miss V Jarvis)   W Jarvis Newmarket

2537 PORTLAND HANDICAP (0-75) 3YO+   £13149   5f   Good/Firm 21 Flag Start   [65]

+1524 FELIPE TORO [2] (M H Easterby) 3-8-2(bl) J Lowe 11/2 FAV: -211111: 3 b c Runnett -
Kalympia (Kalydon) Very useful, much impr sprinter: completed his nap hand, was quickly away
and made all at a good pace in val Portland h'cap at Doncaster: earlier won successive h'caps
at Beverley, Doncaster, Redcar and York: very eff over 5/6f on firm and yldg ground: acts
on any trk: best when up with the pace: wears blinkers tho' is a genuine sort: now goes
for the Ayr Gold Cup.   58
2469 BOLLIN EMILY [8] (M H Easterby) 5-8-8 M Birch 14/1: 0242342: Chased winner thr'out:
kept on well and comfortably beat rem: must win soon: see 2469.   50
2160 PERION [12] (G Lewis) 4-7-13 M L Thomas 10/1: 1110403: Fin well: best in 477.   32
2402 DERRY RIVER [3] (L Cottrell) 5-7-7(vis) C Rutter(0) 20/1: 0000104: Never nearer: see 2160 26
2160 LAURIE LORMAN [20] 4-8-2 R Wernham 11/1: 0000200: Gd speed over ½ way: best in 2065.   34
*1608 POWDER BLUE [23] 4-8-8 T Quinn 16/1: 1-04010: Front rank over 3f: best 1608 (6f).   36
2402 LOCHTILLUM [16] 7-8-5 R Cochrane 10/1: 0100040: Gd early speed, wknd: see 2402.   00
2258 TYROLLIE [19] 4-8-6 P Cook 20/1: 2200400: Bolted after false start, withdrawn: 00
-2289 MEESON KING [14] 5-7-13 W Carson 10/1: 1000-20: Bolted after false start, withdrawn. 00
*2402 GEORGE WILLIAM [18] 5-7-13(7ex) R Fox 16/1: -223010: Bolted after false start, withdrawn. 00
2469 CHINA GOLD [5] 7-7-8 A Mackay 25/1: 4202000: Bolted after false start, withdrawn:see 1268 00
2513 THRONE OF GLORY [6] 5-7-7(3oh) A Culhane(7) 25/1: 4400230: Bolted before start, withdrawn 00
2402 Deputy Head [21] 8-2(2ow)   2378 Tanfen [1] 7-9
2469 Chaplins Club [15] 8-8(bl)   2446 Sullys Choice [13] 7-13
1933 Ferryman [4] 8-5(1ow)   *2469 Ardrox Lad [9] 9-5(7ex)
2474 Bridesmaid [7] 10-0(vis)   +616 Dawns Delight [17] 9-3
2012 Gods Solution [11] 7-7(bl)(11oh)   2469 King Charlemagne [22] 7-12
2446 Careless Whisper [10] 7-10
23 ran   4,4,shthd,shthd,1½,1,1   (Lt Col R Warden)   M H Easterby Great Habton, Yorks.

Note: Following stalls breakdown, the above race was started by Flag.

2538 GROUP 3 KIVETON PARK STAKES 3YO+   £21600   7f   Good/Firm 21 +02 Fast

2259 HADEER [7] (C Brittain) 4-9-4 T Ives 10/1: 2041101: 4 ch c General Assembly -
Glinting (Crepello) Very smart colt: easy to back but produced a fine late burst when leading
on line in Gr 3 event at Doncaster: earlier game winner of Gr 3 Hungerford Stks at Newbury:
comf. winner of Beeswing Stks at Newcastle: very eff over 7/8f: acts on good and firm ground
and on any track: game and genuine.   83
214 MOONLIGHT LADY [1] (P Kelleway) 3-8-4 C Asmussen 33/1: 0320-02: Led 1f out, just caught:
grand effort after lengthy absence and must win soon: very useful filly who was placed several 74
times in Pattern company after winning valuable stakes race at Sandown, last year: suited by
7/8f: acts on firm and yielding and goes well on a galloping track.   74
2233 GWYDION [2] (H Cecil) 3-8-4 W Ryan 9/2: 4331243: Nt qkn close home: good effort but does
seem best over sprint dists: see 1889 and 1631.   73
2259 SARAB [9] (P Cole) 3-9-0 T Quinn 10/1: -311104: Fin well: best in 1492 (1m).   76
*2234 DIGGERS REST [11] 3-8-7 S Cauthen 10/1: -130210: Remains in fine form: see 2234.   70
*1107 CLIVEDEN [6] 3-8-11 A Clark 6/1: 3-00310: Late prog after absence: see 1107.   72
-2145 TRUELY NUREYEV [10] 3-8-7 W R Swinburn 7/4 FAV: 231-020: Hvly bkd but not clear run and
did not challenge: just btn by Hadeer in 2145.   00
1631 Governor General [4] 8-7   2440 Que Sympatica [3] 8-11
1823 Sharp Romance [5] 9-0   1107 Firm Landing [8] 8-7 1851 Glide By [12] 8-11
12 ran   shhd,¾,2½,nk,¾   (W J Gredley)   C Brittain Newmarket.

2539 GROUP 3 DONCASTER CUP 3YO+   £19407   2m 2f   Good/Firm 21 +03 Fast

*1888 LONGBOAT [5] (W Hern) 5-9-6 W Carson 1/5 FAV: 2-01111: 5 b h Welsh Pageant - Pirogue
(Reliance II) Very smart stayer: looked to have a simple task, led over 2f out but hard ridden and
pipped on the post in quite fast run Gr 3 Doncaster Cup at Doncaster, tho' adjudgedly bumped
inside dist and awarded   race: earlier scored convincing wins in Gr 3 Goodwood Cup, the
Ascot Gold Cup and the Henry II Stks at Sandown: last season won at Ascot: very eff over 2m,
stays forever: loves fast grd and seems unsuited by soft: below his best today tho' remains
the best stayer in the country at present.   68
1888 PETRIZZO [2] (C Brittain) 5-8-9 C Asmussen 9/1: 040131D: Sustained chall final 2f,
got home by a whisker but bumped the runner-up inside dist and disqualified: suffered a
similar fate in this race 2 seasons ago: see 1779.   56
1679 THE PRUDENT PRINCE [1] (W Jarvis) 4-8-9 R Cochrane 9/1: -211123: Abs: took a
big step up in class and was far from disgraced: progressive young stayer: see 1470.   48
2376 MAJESTICIAN [4] (G Pritchard Gordon) 3-7-10 J Lowe 14/1: 0212234: Made most: btn
2f out: see 2376.   44

4 ran   shthd,7,3   (R D Hollingsworth)   W Hern West Isley, Berks

2540 GROUP 3 MAY HILL STAKES 2YO FILLIES   £13896   1m   Good/Firm 21 -13 Slow

*2057 LALUCHE [1] (H Cecil) 2-8-9 S Cauthen 7/4 FAV: 111: 2 b f Alleged - Coqueluche
(Victorian Era) Very useful filly: sn led and held on bravely when completing her hat-trick
in Gr 3 May Hill Stks at Doncaster: earlier a comfortable winner of a fillies mdn at Doncaster,
subsequently made all in Sweet Solera Stks at Newmarket: cost $135,000 as a yearling: very
eff over 6/8f and   sure to stay further: suited by fast grd and a gall trk: genuine filly
who is certain to win more races.   70
2215 SAINTE JOIE [7] (L Piggott) 2-8-6 T Ives 8/1: 32: Easy to back: ran on strongly and
only just denied: certain to be suited by further than 1m: acts on a gall trk: on the upgrade
and certain to go one btr soon: see 2215.   67
2246 MY IMAGINATION [4] (P Kelleway) 2-8-6 R Cochrane 25/1: 1000403: Switched dist, ran
on well and seemed well suited by this longer trip: should win soon if dropped slightly
in class: see 2246.   63
1329 LYSHAAN [3] (B Kelly) 2-8-6 G Duffield 16/1:23104: Irish chall.: ev. ch.: winner of
a minor race at Roscommon: eff over 7/8f on gd and fast grd.   57
1914 CHAUDENNAY [5] 2-8-6 B Thomson 10/1: 00: Denied a clear run over 2f out, onepaced:
better effort and will stay further: see 1914.   56
+2407 PORT HELENE [9] 2-8-6 W Carson 9/4: 210: Lost place ¼ way, ran on late: btr when
out in front in 2407.   55
*1752 BINT PASHA [2] 2-8-6 T Quinn 10/1: 22210: Fdd into 7th: best 1752 (7f).   00
*2368 DAZY [6] 2-8-6 W R Swinburn 12/1: 23010: Fin 8th: btr over 7f in 2368.   00
--   LIGHTNING DISC [8] 2-8-6 C Asmussen 12/1: 0: Early leader, lost place over 2f out
and not given a hard time: cost 21,000 gns as a yearling and is a half sister to winning
miler Foremast : will improve.   00
*2215 ECHO VALLEY [10] 2-8-6 P Robinson 10/1: 410: Never going well: much btr 2215 (7f).   00
 10 ran   shthd,1½,2½,shthd,1   (Sheikh Mohammed)   H Cecil Newmarket

---

SALISBURY   Thursday September 11th   Righthand, Stiff, Gall Trk

Official Going Given As FIRM

2541 MARLBOROUGH MAIDEN STAKES DIV I 2YO   £1204   7f   Firm 02 -19 Slow

2159 NOBLE BID [1] (J Dunlop) 2-9-0 B Rouse 13/8 FAV: 401: 2 b c Kings Lake - First Round
(Primera) Waited with, led nearing final 1f, readily, in the slowest division of a 2yo mdn at
Salisbury: half brother to sev winners, notably Glen Turret, Rollahead and Sheriff Muir: eff
at 7f, should stay 1m: acts well on fast grd and prob handles any trk.   52
2232 WOOD CHISEL [2] (B Hills) 2-9-0 M Hills 9/4: 02: Al up there: led inside final 2f:
not foot of winner: stays 7f and can win soon: acts well on fast ground: see 2232.   45
--   HABCAN [12] (P Cole) 2-9-0 P Waldron 12/1: 3: Stayed on well on racecourse debut and
should improve for the experience: cost only $13,000 as a yearling and is a half brother to
a winner in the States: should be suited by 1m: acts on fast grd and a gall trk and can
find a maiden.   43
1780 TREGEAGLE [3] (G Harwood) 2-9-0 G Starkey 12/1: 04: Al up there, making improvement:
eff at 7f on fast grd: half brother to useful miler Ininsky.   38
2254 MUHIM [4] 2-9-0 Paul Eddery 7/1: 00: Led over 2f out: another gd run: stays 7f: see 2254 36
2159 BOX THE COMPASS [5] 2-9-0 W Newnes 33/1: 00: Made gd late hdwy and can improve further:
first foal who acts well on fast ground.   35
1239 NIGHT VISITOR [11] 2-9-0 G Baxter 33/1: 00: Made much after abs: half brother to
sev winners including King Jack: bred to stay further than 7f: acts on fast ground.   34
2159 DANDY [6] 2-9-0 J Reid 20/1: 000: Fin 8th, but is making impr: half brother to sev
winners and acts on fast ground: maybe placed to advantage at one of the minor trks.   31
--   STARK REALITY [10] 2-9-0 J Matthias 16/1: 0: Friendless in mkt on debut: fin 9th:
US bred colt who cost $120,000: should improve.   30
--   Phelioff [8] 9-0   1914 Brainwave [7] 9-0   -- Master Comedy [13] 9-0
12 ran   2½,½,2½,½,½,½,1½,nk   (A Stirling)   J Dunlop Arundel, Sussex

2542 MARLBOROUGH MAIDEN STAKES DIV I 2YO   £1193   7f   Firm 02 -03 Slow

1518 TARTUFFE [10] (G Harwood) 2-9-0 G Starkey 10/1: 01: 2 ch c Golden Act - Tarop (Dr
Fager) Very promising colt: set a 2yo course record, leading inside final 1f, readily, in
a 2yo mdn at Salisbury: appears something of a bargain at only $35,000 and is a half brother
to 2 winners in the States: eff at 7f, should be suited by 1m: acts well on fast grd and
a galloping trk: certain to win more races.   67
1392 TERTIARY ZONE [1] (P Cole) 2-9-0 P Waldron 11/10 FAV: 32: Well bckd, despite abs:
led ½ way till inside final 1f: caught a tartar and 4l clear 3rd: compensation awaits:see 1392 61
2263 RANDOM ROVER [6] (B Hills) 2-9-0 M Hills 7/4: 23: Came from behind: will be suited
by 1m and can win soon: see 2263.   53
2418 FAHAD [7] (R J Houghton) 2-9-0 J Reid 33/1: 004: Prom, kept on: friendless in mkt
today, but showed improved form: half brother to 2yo winner Sashada: eff at 7f on fast grd
and can find a race.   51
2036 DURBO [8] 2-9-0 W Newnes 33/1: 00: Made some: fair effort: cost 30,000 gns: dam
was a genuine sort who stayed 12f well: acts on fast ground.   41

SALISBURY   Thursday September 11th   -Cont'd

1552 LINE OF SUCCESSION [2] 2-9-0 A Murray 20/1: 00: Mkt drifter: abs since 1552.   40
2205 THE GRIFTER [9] 2-9-0 N Adams 33/1: 00: Never nearer 7th: improving: prob stays 7f:
acts on fast ground.   39
2159 Mahrajan [5] 9-0   --   Gwynras [4] 9-0   --   Wink Gulliver [3] 9-0
--   For The Crack [11] 9-0   --   No Concern [13] 9-0
2133 Kireen [12] 9-0
13 ran   1¼,4,1,5,½,¼   (D J Saxby)   G Harwood Pulborough, Sussex

2543 DICK POOLE STAKES 2YO FILLIES   £4175   6f   Firm 03 -01 Slow

+2433 TAHILLA [3] (J Tree) 2-8-11 Pat Eddery 10/11 FAV: 111: 2 b f Moorestyle - Woodwind
(Whistling Wind) Very useful, unbtn filly: led over 1f out, comfortably landing the odds
in val 2yo fillies stks at Salisbury Sept 11: earlier successful in fillies events at Bath
and Newbury: half sister to sev winners, notably very useful 6/7f performer Mummy's Favourite:
eff at 6f, should stay further: acts on fast ground and a gall trk: on the upgrade.   71
1108 PROPENSITY [6] (G Harwood) 2-8-8 G Starkey 13/8 : 122: Well bckd, despite abs:
not the best of runs and ran on well: another fine effort and certain to win again soon:
stays 6f well: see 1108, 848.   62
2057 LITTLEFIELD [1] (I Balding) 2-8-8 J Matthias 10/1: 2103: Led 2f out: kept on well:
below her best over 7f last time out, but stays 6f well: see 1583.   59
--   CORVIGLIA RUN [2] (R Hannon) 2-8-3 B Rouse 50/1: 4: Very tough debut but ran a
promising race: cost only IR 6000 as a yearling: acts well on fast ground and should find a race 46
*2292 KHAKIS LOVE [5] 2-8-8 Paul Eddery 16/1: 30110: Led 4f: see 2292 (easy trk).   43
+2377 RIO PIEDRAS [4] 2-8-8 M Miller 16/1: 10: Never in it: stiff task: see 2377 (7f yldg)   40
6 ran   1,¼,3,3,1   (Lady Derby)   J Tree Beckhampton, Wilts

2544 FONTHILL HCAP 3YO+ 0-50   £3390   7f   Firm 02 -05 Slow   [46]

2431 ASHLEY ROCKET [7] (M Pipe) 5-8-10 T Williams 14/1: 00-3001: 5 b h Roan Rocket -
City Sound (On Your Mark) Ran on well to lead inside final 1f in a h'cap at Salisbury: lightly
raced in '85: in '84 won at Pontefract and York: eff at 7f/1m: acts on any ground.   38
*2207 SAILORS SONG [1] (N Vigors) 4-9-12 S Dawson 8/1: 0000012: Led briefly final 1f: in
grand form: see 2207.   53
-2288 FEYDAN [2] (L Cottrell) 5-8-6 R Hills 3/1 JT.FAV: 0443123: Ran on final 1f: just
btn in close fin: remains in excellent form: see 2288, 2123.   33
2189 MR ROSE [6] (A Hutchinson) 6-7-12 P Hutchinson(2) 12/1: 4201004: Led inside final 3f: 23
2431 MANCHESTERSKYTRAIN [3] 7-9-3 B Rouse 3/1 JT.FAV: 0000200: Well bckd and al prom:see 2123.'42
930 SINGLE [4] 4-9-0 D Mckay 10/1: 0114130: Not btn far after abs: gd eff: see 481.   36
2369 GOLDEN SLADE [10] 4-8-9 J Reid 8/1: 3300300: There 5f: twice below 2189 (sharp).   00
2369 BLUE BRILLIANT [9] 3-8-2(bl) M Hills 7/1: 0212440: No show in 8th: below his best :see 1560   00
2319 Pett Velero [12] 7-7(4oh)   2207 Steady Eddie [11] 9-5
950 Persian Person [8] 7-11
11 ran   ½,shthd,1,shthd,1¼   (Mrs Wendy Fine)   M Pipe Nicholashayne, Somerset

2545 WINTERBOURNE HANDICAP 3YO+ 0-50   £2947   1m   Firm 02 +22 Fast   [45]

2490 FLYHOME [10] (P Cundell) 5-9-3 N Adams 14/1: 2230301: 5 ch g Home Guard - Western Gem
(Sheshoon) Mkt drifter, but made ev yard, readily, breaking the course record in a h'cap at
Salisbury: deserved success: in '85 won at Sandown: prev season won at Bath and Wolverhampton:
very eff at 1m, stays 10f: well suited by fast ground and goes well on a gall trk: carries
weight well.   47
764 ASIAN CUP [9] (G Harwood) 3-9-9 G Starkey 4/1: 02-102: Came too late: fine effort
after abs: can find a h'cap: see 528.   53
2288 YOUNG JASON [7] (G Lewis) 3-8-11 P Waldron 7/4 FAV: 0012233: Heavily bckd: kept on
under press: stays 1m and is in gd form: see 1852, 1272.   40
2217 TIP TAP [1] (A Hide) 4-8-2 G Baxter 16/1: -000104: Al up there: seems best over 1m.   18
2437 HAY STREET [11] 5-9-12 J Reid 20/1: 000-000: Prom most under top weight: very lightly
raced this term:in gd form last term when trained by Mrs C J Reavey, but failed to win:
in '84 won twice at Thirsk: eff at 6/7f, may stay 1m: acts on fast and yldg ground.   40
2144 EVERY EFFORT [5] 4-8-8 Paul Eddery 14/1: 3412000: No extra over 1f out: btr 1781, 1581.   22
2099 BRONZE OPAL [2] 3-9-3 R Weaver 4/1: 0010140: Prom much: inconsistent: well below 1934   00
2255 ALQIRM [4] 4-9-3 B Rouse 7/1: 0021000: No show: best 1240 (C/D).   00
--   Grumble [6] 9-7   --   Fast Dealer [3] 7-7(8oh)
10 ran   4,¼,2½,1,shthd   (Colin G Southgate)   P Cundell Compton, Berks

2546 NETHERAVON MAIDEN FILLIES STKS 3YO   £1160   1m 2f Firm 02 -23 Slow

2248 HELIETTA [8] (L Cumani) 3-8-11 R Guest 5/2: -04231: 3 b f Tyrnavos - Hurdy-Gurdy
(Espresso) Adopted different tactics, making ev yard and driven out final 1f in the slower div
of a 3yo fillies mdn at Salisbury: half sister to 3 winners, notably the smart Vieille, 2nd
in the Oaks: does stay 12f, but seems suited by 10f with forcing tactics: acts well on fast grd   39
2068 CAVALEUSE [7] (J Bethell) 3-8-11(VIS) Paul Eddery 16/1: 0-0002: Visored first time
and showed improved form, staying on well final 1f: quite lightly raced filly who is a half
sister to 2 winners: clearly suited by a stiff 2f on fast ground.   37
2393 EYE SIGHT [6] (R J Houghton) 3-8-11 J Reid 9/4 FAV: -343: Prom, ev ch: lightly raced
since 723, a race that has not worked out too well.   31

2333 MIRATAINE VENTURE [5] (R Akehurst) 3-8-11 G Baxter 33/1: 0030004: Prom most: see 271 (hvy) 26
--   GREENHILLS JOY [1] 3-8-11 N Day 25/1: -0: Never nearer on debut: improvement likely
and was friendless in mkt today: stays 10f: acts on fast ground.   21
1062 CALVINETTE [9] 3-8-11 C Booth(7) 7/1: -040: Prom much after abs: see 1062.   11
1690 LOREEF [10] 3-8-11 B Rouse 7/2: -04400: Fin 7th: mainly disapp since 1002.   00
2131 Farceuse [4] 8-11(VIS)   1751 Harmony Heights [3] 8-11
2422 Sharp Reef [2] 8-11   2386 Eloquence [12] 8-11(BL)
1670 Popsis Pom Pom [11] 8-11
12 ran   ¾,3,2½,2½,5,½   (Fittocks Stud Ltd)   L Cumani Newmarket

2547 MARLBOROUGH MAIDEN STAKES DIV II 2YO   £1670   7f   Firm 02 -06 Slow

2119 SHARP VICTOR [12] (G Harwood) 2-9-0 G Starkey 6/4 FAV: 01: 2 ch c Sharpen Up - Elegant
Victress (Sir Ivor) Very promising colt: justified heavy support, led over 1f out and readily
drew clear in a 2yo mdn at Salisbury: brother to a winner in the States: eff at 7f, looks
sure to be suited by 1m: clearly acts well on fast grd and does well on a stiff trk: will
improve further and win more races.   60
--   SERGEYEVICH [3] (J Dunlop) 2-9-0 B Rouse 13/2: 2: Fin in fine style and will be all
the better for the experience: half brother to useful middle dist performer Diabolical Liberty:
will be well suited by 1m and further: acts on fast grd and a gall trk: a certain future winner   52
1869 OTHET [5] (M Usher) 2-9-0 A Mcglone 8/1: 223: Kept on well final 1f and met 2
useful performers here: stays 7f and will win when dropped slightly in class: see 1869.   46
1791 FAILIQ [10] (P Walwyn) 2-9-0 Paul Eddery 14/1: 04: Kept on well and is on the upgrade:
should be suited by 1m: see 1791: acts on fast ground.   45
1518 ASHWA [6] 2-9-0 G Baxter 7/1: 20: Led ½ way after abs: another gd run: see 1518.   44
--   KIKUYU [15] 2-9-0 S Raymont 10/1: 0: Late hdwy into 6th and will improve: cost
31,000 gns as a yearling and is a half brother to winning stayer The Bedford: will be suited
by further than 7f: acts on fast ground.   41
1510 GO HENRI [11] 2-9-0 J Reid 7/2: 30: Fin 7th after abs: prob stays 7f: see 1510.   39
1629 Mace Bearer [9] 9-0   --   Sahood [1] 9-0   1510 Daring Descent [14] 9-0
1936 Jocks Brother [13] 9-0   --   Solent Knight [7] 9-0
--   Profit A Prendre [2] 9-0
13 ran   4,2,½,nk,1½,½   (Marvin Malmuth)   G Harwood Pulborough, Sussex

2548 NETHERAVON MAIDEN FILLIES STKS 3YO   £1154   1m 2f   Firm 02 -04 Slow

2393 SATIN AND SILK [4] (A Bailey) 3-8-11 M Miller 8/1: -30021: 3 b f Persian Bold-
Silken Topper (High Hat) Impr filly: led over 3f out, ridden out in a 3yo fillies mdn at
Salisbury: half sister to 3 winners including the useful Grand Unit: acts on yldg, seems
suited by fast ground and 10f: acts on any trk.   44
2304 RED SHOES [10] (W Hern) 3-8-11 J Reid 7/4 FAV: 0322322: Again found one too good: see 2304.   41
2048 MARY SUNLEY [7] (J Francome) 3-8-11 W Newnes 12/1: -0043: Al up there, stayed:
seee 1690, acts on any track.   35
2304 CORNELIAN [1] (G Harwood) 3-8-11 G Starkey 10/3: -0304: Op 6/4: twice well below 2068.   29
2314 ETTAS PET [3] 3-8-11 M Rimmer 12/1: -400300: Prom most: stays 10f: see 1451.   25
2109 MISTRAL MAGIC [5] 3-8-11 G Baxter 33/1: 0-00000: No show, but nevertheless an
improved effort: little form prev: acts on fast ground.   23
2248 BIBI KHATOUN [2] 3-8-11 B Rouse 9/2: 0-00240: Led 6f: much btr 2248, 1677 (1m).   00
2304 Sheer Nectar [9] 8-11   --   Sparkling Hock [6] 8-11
1954 Our Noora [11] 8-11
10 ran   1½,3,3,2,½   (T P Ramsden)   A Bailey Newmarket

DONCASTER   Friday September 12th   Lefthanded, Galloping Track

Official Going Given As GOOD

2549 CHARITY DAY SELLING H'CAP (0-60) 3YO+   £3200   1m   Firm 13 -12 Slow   [23]

-2414 QUALITAIRESS [20] (K Stone) 4-8-6(vis) P Burke(7) 9/1 CO FAV: 0220121: 4 b f Kampala -
Leapallez (Hallez) In fine form and made smooth prog to lead cl home for an easy win in a
selling h'cap at Doncaster (no bid): quite consistent this season, last month got off the
mark in an app h'cap at Newcastle: eff over 6/8f on fast and soft grd: goes well on a gall trk:
wears a visor.   12
2390 O I OYSTON [3] (J Berry) 10-9-5 J Carroll(7) 12/1: 2022202: Game attempt to make all:
the bridesmaid in five of his last 7 races and certainly due a change of luck: see 2264 & 1758   20
2335 MRS NAUGHTY [14] (W Wharton) 3-8-6 Pat Eddery 12/1: 0003043: Fin well: gd eff: see 650.   14
2401 MANABEL [5] (S Bowring) 4-8-10 J Quinn(5) 12/1: 0000244: running well: see 2340.   05
2123 NICKY NICK [17] 3-8-6 P Cook 33/1: -00000: Gd late prog: see 1804.   10
2340 KAMARESS [10] 4-8-13 K Darley 20/1: 0431000: Stayed on: best 2104.   07
*2238 DRESS IN SPRING [19] 3-8-4 M Rimmer 16/1: 0000010: Fin 7th: stays 1m: see 2238.   00
2303 VERBARIUM [24] 6-9-3 R Hills 9/1 CO FAV: 3200000: Never nearer 8th: see 281 & 10.   00
*2344 CAPRICORN BLUE [16] 3-9-8(vis) W R Swinburn 10/1: 2424110: Fin 9th: btr over 10f in 2344   00
*2335 CARR WOOD [22] 3-8-5 G Duffield 10/1: -00010: Much btr with some give in 2335.   00
2496 KAVAKA [6] 4-9-7 W Carson 9/1 CO FAV: 2D02000: Prom most: can do btr: see 2303.   00

2274 Aqaba Prince [7] 8-9	2360 North Star Sam [15] 8-5
1880 Discover Gold [13] 9-1	2411 Trade High [1] 9-6
2414 Strictly Business [8] 8-1(vis)	2335 Jalome [23] 7-12
2374 Monclare Trophy [2] 9-5	2264 Zio Peppino [18] 8-11
2374 Rhein Court [11] 8-2	2374 Polemistis [21] 8-4(bl)
2360 Pells Close [4] 8-4(bl)(3ow)	2490 Gamblers Dream [9] 9-7(bl)
23 ran 1,¼,2½,½,hd,nk,hd,nk	(Qualitair Engineering Ltd) K Stone Malton, Yorks.

2550 SWETTENHAM STUD STAKES 3YO   £3200   7f   Firm 13 -07 Slow

733 ICHNUSA [6] (J Dunlop) 3-8-11 W Carson 5/2 FAV: -41: 3 b f Bay Express - Skiboule
(Boulou) Well bckd despite a long abs, led over 2f out for a game win in a 3yo stks at
Doncaster: half sister to sev winners, including useful stayer Rollrights: eff over 7f
and should stay further: acts on fast ground and on a gall trk: seems fully recovered from
her setback and should go on from here.   46
2248 SKEAN [4] (G Harwood) 3-8-11 A Clark 5/1: -0022: Just held in a driving fin: should
get off the mark soon, prob over a slightly longer trip: see 2248 & 1031.   45
1431 CARD PLAYED [8] (O Douieb) 3-8-11 Pat Eddery 10/3: -233: Very well bckd despite
abs: looked dangerous dist, found little under press tho' not btn far: see 941.   44
--   JUNGLE BEAT [5] (W Jarvis) 3-8-11 A Murray 20/1: 0-4: Al prom, onepaced: very lightly
raced filly who should come on for this race: half sister to 5/8f winner Formatune: acts
on fast ground and a gall track.   34
1586 BASOOF [2] 3-8-11 W R Swinburn 5/1: 4-04040: Outpaced below dist: abs since 1586.   26
2027 FESTIVITY [9] 3-8-11 K Darley 16/1: -002000: Wknd 2f out: see 1451 & 431.   25
2483 ZIADS ALIBY [3] 3-8-11 A Bond 9/1: -430: Longer trip: btn 2f out: see 2210.   00
2248 SUNDAY CHIMES [7] 3-8-11(BL) S Cauthen 10/1: -040Q: Bl first time: made much,
wknd and last to finish: see 1981 & 1375.   00
1472 EMMA HARTE [1] 3-8-11 D Williams 50/1: 00-0P: P.U. lame after 2f: lightly raced
filly who has clearly proved difficult to train.   00
9 ran   shthd,¾,6,4,nk   (Mrs Manuelita Landi)   J.Dunlop Arundel, Sussex.

2551 MECCA BOOKMAKERS H'CAP STAKES (0-60)   £3200   1m 4f   Firm 13 +15 Fast   [49]

2220 HIGH TENSION [4] (G Pritchard Gordon) 4-9-4 T Ives 9/2 FAV: 4122101: 4 ch g Vitiges -
Montania (Mourne) Useful, consistent h'capper: switched and qcknd well to lead dist,
comfortably, in a fast run h'cap at Doncaster: in fine form this season, earlier twice
successful in h'caps at Ayr: early in '85 won at Yarmouth and Redcar: very eff around 12/13f:
acts on firm and yldg ground and on any track: most genuine and should win again in this form.   52
2247 TEBITTO [13] (N Vigors) 3-8-2 P Cook 14/1: 0101202: Led 3f out: fine eff: see 1733.   38
2389 TWICE BOLD [11] (N Callaghan) 3-8-13 Pat Eddery 10/1: 4212043: Had ev ch: see 1551.   45
2408 SARONICOS [2] (C Brittain) 3-8-7 P Robinson 16/1: 2230304: Stayed on: maiden: see 739.   38
1939 TICKFORD [8] 3-8-10 A Clark 8/1: -431D00: No extra 2f out: best 1663 (13f).   40
2273 MIN BALADI [14] 4-8-2 J Lowe 7/1: -320020: Nicely bckd: btr 2273.   17
2201 SIR PERCY [6] 3-9-4 S Cauthen 11/2: -100300: Fin 8th: btr 1600: see 253.   00
2237 VOUCHSAFE [1] 4-9-7 W Carson 10/1: 41D0000: Btn when bumped 2f out: see 921.   00
2337 AUCHINLEA [7] 4-8-6(VIS) M Birch 10/1: 0-30000: Visored first time: btr 629.   00
2300 SELL IT KILROY [9] 3-7-11 G Carter 9/1: -000130: No threat, fin last: best in 1309.   00
2389 Regal Steel [12] 7-10   1865 Comely Dancer [3] 8-7(VIS)
2441 Seatyrn [10] 7-12   2467 Swynford Prince [5] 7-7(vis)(8oh)
14 ran   3,2,¾,nk,3   (Lord Derby)   G Pritchard Gordon Newmarket

2552 GR.2 LAURENT PERRIER CHAMPAGNE STAKES   £36108   7f   Firm 13 +02 Fast

*1887 DONT FORGET ME [2] (R Hannon) 2-9-0 Pat Eddery 6/1: 4111: 2 b c Ahonoora - African
Doll (African Sky) Smart colt: gamely completed his hat trick, led below dist and ran on
strongly to win Gr 2 Champagne Stks at Doncaster: earlier made all in Gr 3 Lanson Champagne
Stks at Goodwood, after winning a Sandown mdn: very eff over 7f, sure to stay at least 1m:
acts on firm ground and seems to act on any trk: genuine sort who does well with forcing
tactics: highly regarded and improving with every race.   76
*2146 DEPUTY GOVERNOR USA [7] (L Piggott) 2-9-0 T Ives 7/4 FAV: 3112: Again heavily bckd:
battled on gamely and lost nothing in defeat: genuine and consistent colt: see 2146.   75
1876 WHO KNOWS [9] (W Hern) 2-9-0 W Carson 7/1: 31243: Al up there, going on in fin and
certain to be suited by a 1m+: consistent sort: see 1242.   72
2221 CHIME TIME [4] (C Tinkler) 2-9-0 M Birch 11/1: 1121134: Tried to make all, not btn
far: another fine effort and is a credit to his trainer: see 2221 & 1697.   70
*2232 BALI MAGIC [6] 2-9-0 S Cauthen 9/1: 210: Stayed on late: gd eff tho' seems certain
to do even better when stepping up in dist: well suited by a gall trk: see 2232.   69
+2221 WIGANTHORPE [3] 2-9-0(bl) W R Swinburn 4/1: 1111410: Never going well and is prob
due a rest after an arduous season: see 2221.   59
--   CEDRICO [8] 2-9-0 A Lequeux 11/1: 0: French chall: showed gd speed over ¼ way: dual
winner at Maisons Laffitte: may prove best over sprint dist: acts on firm and soft ground.   58
*2056 MACROBIAN [5] 2-9-0 B Rouse 11/1: 10: Prom to ½ way: see 2056 (6f).   00
2479 TEAM EFFORT [1] 2-9-0 R P Elliott 50/1: 1121300: Rank outsider: first btn: see 1373.   00
9 ran   ½,1½,nk,½,5,shthd   (Jim Horgan)   R Hannon East Everleigh, Wilts.

2553 TROY STAKES 3YO   £3200   1m 4f Firm 13 -04 Slow

*2422 ALL HASTE [3] (H Cecil) 3-8-9 S Cauthen 5/6 FAV: -20111: 3 b c Alleged - Hasty Dawn
(Pronto) Smart colt: heavily bckd and comfortably made all in quite a val 3yo stks at
Doncaster: recently trotted up in a minor race at Windsor and first time out was an excellent
2nd to Allez Milord in a val stks race at Newmarket: very eff over 10/12f: acts on gd and
firm ground and on any trk: does well with forcing tactics: should rate more highly and
win more races.   68
+1022 WHITE CLOVER [6] (G Harwood) 3-9-0 A Clark 3/1: -12: Stayed on well after a fair abs:
fine effort and certain to be winning again soon: acts on gd and firm: see 1022.   68
2206 KOLGONG HEIGHTS [4] (B Hanbury) 3-9-0 W R Swinburn 20/1: 0-02003: Kept on well: gd eff:
highly tried this term and sure to win if eased in class: see 597.   64
+2247 ALDINO [5] (A Stewart) 3-9-0(bl) Pat Eddery 4/1: 0112414: No extra 2f out tho' a
creditable effort in this btr class: acts on a gall trk: see 2247.   60
2206 NORFOLK SONATA [1] 3-9-0 E Guest 20/1: 3000030: Btr 2226 (sharp trk).   52
2389 ROUBAYD [2] 3-9-0 K Darley 14/1: -1100: Twice fin last since 2176.   51
6 ran   2,2½,1½,4,hd   (Sheikh Mohammed)   H Cecil Newmarket

2554 LAURENT PERRIER CHAMPAGNE STAKES 2YO   £2550   6f   Firm 13 -07 Slow

--   AJDAL [7] (M Stoute) 2-8-7 W R Swinburn 5/4 FAV: 1: 2 b c Northern Dancer - Native
Partner (Raise A Native) Very promising colt: heavily bckd and made an impr debut, led ½ way
and readily drew clear in quite a val 2yo stks at Doncaster: well bred colt who is a half
brother to very useful duo Formidable and Serheed: clearly very eff over 6f on fast ground:
seems sure to stay further: acts on a gall trk: very well regarded and looks an exciting prospect   65
1915 GILBERTO [2] (J Dunlop) 2-8-11 Pat Eddery 4/1: 432: Mkt drifter: stayed on well
but caught a real tartar: placed behind some smart juv and must win soon: see 1488.   56
1653 REBEL RAISER [3] (M Ryan) 2-8-11 P Robinson 11/1: 03: Just pipped for 2nd place:
gd eff after fair abs: should continue to improve: see 1653.   56
--   FLIP THE BIRD [6] (M Francis) 2-8-4 T Ives 25/1: 4: Ran on very promisingly from
below dist and certain to improve for this experience: cost IR 24,000 and is a half sister
to winning juv Leslie Stone: acts on fast ground and on a gall trk: one to keep an eye on. 44
2232 ALI SMITH [9] 2-8-11 G Duffield 11/1: 2340: Ev ch: consistent sort: see 2119.   46
--   JADE HUNTER [5] 2-8-7 S Cauthen 5/2: 0: Well bckd debutant: tardy start, sn prom
but not qckn dist: cost $700,000 and is closely related to a host of winners: acts on firm
ground and on a gall trk: sure to improve.   40
--   Sergeant Smoke [4] 8-7   -- Benz Belle [1] 8-4
2334 Dance Up [8] 8-11
9 ran   3,shthd,2½,1½,½   (Sheikh Mohammed)   M Stoute Newmarket

---

Official Going Given As GOOD/FIRM

2555 CARNES SEAT FILLIES STAKES 2YO   £2308   6f   Firm 04 +01 Fast

1874 GREENCASTLE HILL [6] (I Balding) 2-8-8 J Matthias 5/1: 01: 2 b f High Top - Fairy Tern
(Mill Reef) Promising filly: despite 6 week abs, led over 1f out, gamely in a 2yo fillies
stks at Goodwood: dam a 5 & 7f winner: will be suited by much further than 6f: acts on
fast ground and an undulating trk: will continue to improve.   53
2185 PELF [1] (L Cumani) 2-8-8 R Cochrane 5/1: 202: Made most: kept on: gd eff and can
win soon: goes well on an easy trk: see 3122.   50
2308 INSHAD [2] (A Stewart) 2-8-8 M Roberts 2/1 FAV: 03: Behind, kept on final 2f:
on the upgrade: quite speedily bred filly who acts on firm and yldg ground.   44
2147 LAVANDOU LEGEND [8] (G Lewis) 2-8-8 P Waldron 33/1: 04: Chance final 2f: gd eff:
improving filly who is a half sister to winning 2yo Rushad: eff at 6f on firm grd and an
undulating trk.   40
2147 INDIAN FLARE [9] 2-8-8 Paul Eddery 16/1: 00: No real threat, but is making improvement:
American bred filly who is a half sister to winning 2yo River Scape: should stay further
than 6f: acts on fast ground.   32
2433 MAY BELFORT [4] 2-8-8 R Street 9/2: 00: Never showed: needs further than an easy 6f:
will do better: see 2433.   28
--   SENSITIVE MATERIAL [7] 2-8-8 G Starkey 7/1: 0: Friendless in mkt: never threatened:
cost IR 80,000 as a yearling and can improve.   00
2185 Stratch [3] 8-8   2365 Good Woman [5] 8-8(VIS)
9 ran   1,2,1½,3,2   (Paul Mellon)   I Balding Kingsclere, Hants

2556 SE PERFORMANCE NURSERY HCAP   £3179   7f   Firm 04 -24 Slow   [62]

2328 SPY TOWER [9] (D Murray Smith) 2-7-7(2oh) C Rutter(0) 20/1: 0041: 2 b c Tower Walk -
Up And At It (Tamerlane) Impr colt: made ev yard off bottom weight, driven out in a slow
run nursery h'cap at Goodwood: quite cheaply bought colt who is closely related to a couple
of minor winners: well suited by forcing tactics over an easy 7f: acts on firm and yldg ground   38
2133 HIS HIGHNESS [5] (C Brittain) 2-9-7 G Baxter 8/1: 1322: Fin well under 9-7 and
nearly got up: excellent effort and will be suited by 1m: see 2133, 1270.   65

+2090 STRATHBLANE [3] (J Dunlop) 2-9-0 J Reid 4/1: 1013: Ev ch inside final 3f: ran on
and just btn in a tight finish: in fine form: stays 7f: see 2090.   57
-2465 PANACHE [6] (P Haslam) 2-7-10 T Williams 9/4 FAV: 1D30124: Switched 2f out: never
nearer: see 2136 (6f).   33
1938 BERTRADE [2] 2-8-0 T Quinn 16/1: 4032430: Never nearer: prob stays 7f: see 621.   34
2332 STRIKE RATE [4] 2-8-10 G Starkey 8/1: 12330: Prom most: twice below 2209, see 180.   34
1993 KAMENSKY [7] 2-8-7 S Whitworth 8/1: 03220: No show in 7th: btr 1993 (6f, made running).   00
2044 SYLVAN ORIENT [8] 2-8-1 A Mcglone 8/1: 00030: Prom, fdd over 2f out: btr 2044.   00
2239 SLIP DANCER [1] 2-8-6 (BL) R Cochrane: 15/2: 0300: Bl 1st time: twice
below 1872.   00
9 ran   nk,nk,3,1½,5   (Sir Anthony Page-Wood)   D Murray Smith Upper Lambourn, Berks.

2557 GRP 3 SCOTTISH EQUITABLE SELECT STKS   £14128   1m 2f   Firm 04 +15 Fast

+1790 DANCING BRAVE [4] (G Harwood) 3-8-13 G Starkey : -112111: 3 b c Lyphard - Navajo
Princess (Drone) Outstanding colt: waited with and led 2f out, easily drawing 10l clear to
break the course record in Gr 3 Scottish Equitable Select Stks at Goodwood: last time out
was a decisive winner of very fast run King George Diamond Stks at Ascot: earlier won the
2,000 Guineas and Craven Stks at Newmarket and the Eclipse at Sandown: has met defeat only
once when a desperately unlucky 2nd in the Epsom Derby: easy winner of both starts in '85
at Newmarket and Sandown: very eff at 1m/10f, stays 12f well: acts on soft, but his fine
action is well suited by firm or gd ground: has a brilliant turn of foot and in our view
is the best 3yo for a long time: must go very cl in the Arc if the ground is gd or better.   99
2419 OZOPULMIN [3] (L Cumani) 3-8-6(BL) R Cochrane : 10-1232: Bl first time and led 1m.   64
--   KAZAROUN [5] (M Stoute) 4-9-5 A Kimberley : 11210-3: Al there: stayed: gd seasonal
debut: smart colt who in '85 won the Gr 3 Gordon Stks here: also successful at Sandown and
Carlisle: eff at 12f, stays 14f well: acts on firm and yldg ground and shd be btr next time.   65
1931 PROMISED ISLE [6] (Lady Herries) 5-9-2 Paul Eddery : 3231404: Impossible task:see 1383. 58
2404 KICK THE HABIT [2] 3-8-3 G Baxter : 0002100: Fdd final 2f: not disgraced: see 2131.   46
--   LADINA [1] 3-8-4(1ow) B Thomson : 0-0: Broke blood vessel and t.o: Irish filly who
recently won over 9f at Phoenix Park: acts on gd ground and a sharpish trk.   00
6 ran   10,1½,2,4,dist   (K Abdulla)   G Harwood Pulborough, Sussex

2558 EXSEL PLUS STAKES HANDICAP 0-60   £4045   1m 4f   Firm 04 +03 Fast   [53]

2290 VORACITY [7] (J Winter) 7-9-1 J Reid 6/1: -232141: 7 ch g Vitiges - Wolverene (Relko)
Grand old horse: waited with and well produced to lead cl home in a val h'cap at Goodwood:
earlier won a similar event at Brighton: lightly raced in '85, prev season won val h'cap at
Haydock: very eff at 12f on gd and fast ground: acts on any trk but particularly suited by
an undulating one: genuine and consistent and retains his form really well.   53
2058 COX GREEN [1] (G Harwood) 3-8-11 G Starkey 3/1 FAV: -14242: Led over 2f out:
jٖٖ·ٖt caught and 8l clear 3rd: fine effort and should win a h'cap soon: runs well here: see 1879 58
2131 FIRST KISS [5] (J Dunlop) 3-8-13 R Cochrane 12/1: -100303: No chance with first two:
stays 12f: see 723 (10f).   48
2330 JABARABA [6] (L Cottrell) 5-8-0 T Lang(7) 7/2: 0411134: Well bckd: btr 2330, 2188.   19
2156 ELAAFUUR [8] 3-8-4 Paul Eddery 11/2: -444100: Made much: twice below 1685.   28
2273 FOLK DANCE [4] 4-8-8 J Matthias 6/1: 4202040: Fdd over 2f out: not that consistent: see 1523 16
1929 AL YABIR [3] 4-9-7 M Hills 8/1: 20-2200: Al trailing: twice well below 1383 and
seems best watched at present.   00
1667 Joli Wasfi [2] 7-7(bl)(1oh)
8 ran   nk,8,4,3,4   (Mrs John Winter)   J Winter Newmarket

2559 REFLEX STAKES 3YO+   £3921   1m   Firm 04 -07 Slow

*2244 ININSKY [4] (G Harwood) 3-8-6 G Starkey 11/8 FAV: 4003411: 3 ch c Niniski - Buckhurst
(Gulf Pearl) Heavily bckd and made ev yard, ridden out in a 4 runner stks at Goodwood: last
time out won again over this C/D: lightly raced 2yo, winning a Sandown mdn: very eff over
1m, tho' should stay further: acts on gd and firm ground and on any trk: seems suited by
front running.   70
2231 RACKSTRAW [2] (B Hills) 3-8-9 B Thomson 5/2: 130-32: Ev ch in str: kept on well:
another gd run and stays 1m well: see 2231.   69
+1147 DALLAS [1] (L Cumani) 3-9-2 R Cochrane 5/2: -02113: Chance final 1f: possibly just
in need of race and ran really well: should strip more fitter next time: see 1447.   76
2359 ALEX NUREYEV [3] (J Dunlop) 3-8-6(BL) J Reid 10/1: -03004: Held up: not much room
2f out: no extra: bl first time today: ex Italian colt: stays 1m: acts on fast and yldg ground 62
4 ran   2,hd,2   (H H Prince Yazid Saud)   G Harwood Pulborough, Sussex

2560 HARVEST SELLING STAKES 3YO   £1197   1m 2f   Firm 04 -41 Slow

2189 MIAMI BLUES [4] (M Francis) 3-8-13 C Rutter(3) 5/1: -001001: 3 b f Palm Track - Blue
Empress (Blue Cashmere) Led inside final 2f, comftbly in a slow run 3yo seller at Goodwood
(bought in 2100 gns): had been lightly raced since winning a similar event at Brighton in May:
eff at 1m, stays 10f well: well suited by fast ground and a sharpish track.   24
2381 SON OF SPARKLER [2] (M Usher) 3-8-11(bl) M Wigham 6/1: 0000002: Led 1m: kept on
and 7l clear 3rd: dropped in class today: eff at 1m, stays 10f: prob acts on any ground.   17

2253 NO STOPPING [5] (R Hannon) 3-8-11(bl) L Jones(5) 3/1 FAV: -000323: Prom most: btr 2253   05
--   NAME THE DAY [6] (J D Home) 3-8-8 W Newnes 14/1: 0-4: No real threat on belated seasonal
debut: ran only once last season and appears difficult to train: may stay 10f: acts on firm.   00
2302 ALL A DREAM [8] 3-8-11(bl) B Uniacke(7) 9/2: 0004020: There 1m: see 2302 (1m yldg).   00
2253 LISAKATY [1] 3-8-8 R Wernham 10/1: 0000430: there over 7f: btr 2253 (stiff 12f).   00
2238 MAN IN THE MOON [3] 3-8-11(bl) A Mcglone 9/2: -000040: Fin well btn: much btr 2238 (7f)   00
2208 GEORGIAN ROSE [7] 3-8-8(vis) W Woods(3) 12/1: 0000200: Fin t.o: best 2073.   00
8 ran   2,7,2,3,4   (Mrs M Francis)   M Francis, Lambourn, Berks.

2561 JOHN WOOTON MAIDEN STAKES 2YO   £1292   6f   Firm 04 -04 Slow

1241 SHARP REMINDER [4] (R Laing) 2-9-0 S Whitworth 10/1: 0031: 2 b c Sharpo - Fallen Rose
(Busted) Useful colt: despite fair abs, led well over 1f out, cmftbly in a 2yo mdn at
Goodwood: very eff at 6f on fast grd: seems to act on any trk but seems well suited by
a sharpish one.   57
--   WAR BRAVE [2] (J Dunlop) 2-9-0 T Quinn 2/1 FAV: 2: Well bckd debutant: ev ch 2f out:
stayed on well and can go one btr soon: cost 160,000 gns as a yearlings and is a half brother
to winning 2yo Dancer's Shadow: eff at 6f, should stay 7f: acts on fast grd and undulating trk   52
--   NATIVE DRESS [10] (I Balding) 2-9-0 J Matthias 16/1: 3: Mkt drifter: stayed on well
on debut and improvement certain: cost 26,000 gns as a yearling and is a half brother to
sev winners: also full brother to winning 2yo Illumineux: quite speedily bred: eff at 6f
on fast ground and should have no trouble finding a maiden.   48
1313 AJANAC [5] (J Tree) 2-9-0 S Raymont 5/1: 024: Kepton well after fair abs: gd eff
and should strip fitter next time: will be suited by 7f: see 1313.   45
2476 ON YOUR PRINCESS [17] 2-9-0(vis) G Starkey 12/1: 002020: No extra final 1f, but
is in gd form: stays 6f: see 2476.   42
1311 PETTING PARTY [16] 2-9-0 P Waldron 20/1: 00: Prom most: gd eff after abs: quite
speedily bred colt who is a half brother to winning 2yo Little Pipers: acts on fast ground
over 6f: seems suited by an easy trk.   40
834 GAMESHOW [12] 2-9-0 R Cochrane 33/1: 000: Not btn far in 7th after a long abs:
gd effort and should improve on this next time: half brother to winning 2yo Nagajaya: maybe
suited by 7f: acts on fast ground.   38
2254 LYRICAL LOVER [11] 2-9-0 B Thomson 14/1: 0030: Prom, fin 8th: btr 2254 (gall trk).   37
--   WUJUD [3] 2-9-0 Paul Eddery 11/1: 0: Never nearer 9th on debut and should do much
better next time: half sister to 2 winners and maybe suited by 7f: acts on firm ground.   36
2249 SLIM HOPE [9] 2-9-0 A Kimberley 11/4: 030: Never going well: much btr 2249 (C/D gd)   34
2205 Irish Sailor [1] 9-0   --   Achill Bay [8] 9-0   --   George James [13] 9-0
2287 Go My Pet [15] 8-11   2205 Say You [7] 9-0   2044 Design Wise [14] 9-0
16 ran   1¼,2,1½,1,¾,¾,hd,nk,¾   (R T Jacobson)   R Laing Lambourn, Berks.

Official Going Given As GOOD/FIRM

2562 HOLSTEN FOR LADIES STAKES 3YO+   £4253   7f   Firm 00 -17 Slow

2165 VERDANT BOY [8] (M Stoute) 3-9-9 Maxine Juster 5/1: 3-31021: 3 br g Green Dancer -
Favourite Prospect (Mr Prospector) Smart colt: al prom and led over 2f out, cmftbly in a
Ladies race at Doncaster: lightly raced sort who earlier won a h'cap at Brighton: very eff
over 7f, stays 1m: acts on yldg, well suited by fast grd: acts on any trk and carries weight
well: genuine.   70
*2473 HIDDEN BRIEF [9] (R Boss) 3-9-6 Jennie Goulding 14/1: 2002012: Kept on well and
is in grand form: see 2473.   60
-2135 NATIVE OAK [12] (H Cecil) 3-9-6 Franca Vittadini 5/4 FAV: 4211423: Heavily bckd:
made much: see 2135 (1m), 950.   59
2473 BOLD CELT [7] (C Booth) 3-9-3 Linda Harris(3) 50/1: 0-44: Prom much: another gd run: 36
2427 MAWDLYN GATE [3] 3-9-3(bl) Linda Perratt(0) 50/1: 1322000: Again ran well in non-h'cap
company: see 1808, 1134.   35
2431 BELOW ZERO [1] 3-9-9 Sharon Murgatroyd 16/1: 0010140: Never nearer: btr 2431, 2063.   41
2234 KINGS HEAD [2] 4-9-11 Amanda Harwood 2/1: 20-3000: Well bckd: fdd 2f out: well below 2234 00
2370 Boofy [10] 9-3   1064 Jazetas [5] 9-3   775 Reindeer Walk [11] 9-11
--   Deadbolt [6] 9-2   2338 Cri De Grace [4] 9-11
12 ran   2,hd,5,nk,shthd,1   (Sheikh Mohammed)   M Stoute Newmarket

2563 HOLSTEN MORAVIA NURSERY H'CAP 2YO   £8766   6f   Firm 00 -19 Slow   [52]

*2479 MASTER POKEY [5] (M W Easterby) 2-8-5(5ex) M Birch 7/2: 0111: 2 br g Uncle Pokey -
September Fire (Firestreak) In grand form: sn front rank and led inside final 2f, gamely, in
a val nursery h'cap at Doncaster: earlier won a nursery at Thirsk and a mdn auction at
Pontefract: cheaply acquired gelding who seems equally eff at 6/7f and may stay further: acts
on gd and firm grd: best when up with the pace, but seems to act on any trk.   40
*2229 CAPE WILD [1] (M Stoute) 2-9-7 W R Swinburn 10/3: 212: Cruising over 1f out: ran on
under press and just btn: in fine form: see 2229.   55
-2421 KYVERDALE [7] (M Ryan) 2-9-6 P Barnard(7) 6/1: 2011323: Ev ch over 1f out: had
very little room in the closing stages and may have been a shade unlucky? : genuine filly.
who stays 6f well: deserves another race: see 2421.   53

2292 RIPE CHRISTINA [2] (A Bailey) 2-9-0 R Cochrane 7/1: 00334: Nicely bckd: ev ch: in
gd form: acts on any trk: see 2292, 2185.   43
*2218 DERWENT VALLEY [4] 2-8-5 W Carson 8/1: 10: Made much: fair eff: see 2218 (seller)   30
2391 THEKKIAN [6] 2-8-8 S Perks 20/1: 13000: Early speed: lightly raced since 415.   23
2252 EINSTEIN [3] 2-9-6 Pat Eddery 11/4 FAV: 01130: Well bckd, but never going well:
something amiss? See 2252.   00
7 ran   nk,½,1½,1½,4   (Lord Belper)   M W Easterby Sherrif Hutton, Yorks

2564 GROUP 2 B.SWIFT FLYING CHILDERS STAKES   £16776   5f   Firm 00 +02 Fast

2113 SIZZLING MELODY [4] (Lord J Fitzgerald) 2-9-0 R Hills 6/4 FAV: 1121301: 2 br c Song -
Mrs Bacon (Balliol) Smart colt: al up there and qcknd well to lead over 1f out cmftbly in
quite fast run Gr 2 Flying Childers Stks at Doncaster: a model of consistency, earlier winning
Gr 3 Norfolk Stks at Royal Ascot and his first 2 on the trot at Lingfield & Leicester: very
eff at 5f, stays 6f: acts on firm and soft grd and on any trk: game and genuine and a
credit to his trainer.   78
*1946 SHAIKIYA [7] (R J Houghton) 2-8-11 S Cauthen 4/1: 12: Active in mkt: chance 2f out:
ran on well, fine effort: : a very speedy filly who looks certain to win again soon:
acts on any trk: see 1946.   69
*2223 CAROLS TREASURE [2] (B Hills) 2-9-0 B Thomson 5/2: 1110313: Ev ch 2f out: another
gd run: see 2223.   69
-2447 ABUZZ [5] (C Brittain) 2-8-11 M Roberts 6/1: 1104124: Stayed on under press: genuine
filly who is at her best on softer ground: see 2158.   61
2447 COME ON CHASE ME [3] 2-9-0 Pat Eddery 17/2: 31130: Led over 3f: most consistent: see 2162 59
2485 MICRO LOVE [1] 2-9-0 C Asmussen 33/1: 301200: Ran well 3f: not btn far in this
smart company: should find a nursery on this form: seems very eff at 5f on fast ground.   54
6 ran   2,1,1½,1½,1½   (Mrs Mary Watt)   Lord J Fitzgerald Newmarket

2565 GROUP 1 HOLSTEN PILS ST LEGER STAKES   £110592   1m 6f   Firm 00 +01 Fast

2222 MOON MADNESS [6] (J Dunlop) 3-9-0 Pat Eddery 9/2: 1111131: 3 b c Vitiges - Castle
Moon (Kalamoun) Very smart colt: crowned a magnificent season with a ready success in Gr 1
St Leger Stks at Doncaster: waited with and gained a lovely run on the rails to draw clear
inside final 1f: started this season with a mdn success at Salisbury: sub successful in 3
val h'caps at Newmarket, Haydock and Royal Ascot: later cmftbly won the Scottish Derby at Ayr
and last time out looked an unlucky 3rd to Nisnas in Gr 2 Great Voltigeur: eff at 12f,   89
stays 14f well: acts on firm and yldg ground and is at his best on a stiff, gall trk:
will remain in training as a 4yo and will prove hard to beat.   89
*2257 CELESTIAL STORM [5] (L Cumani) 3-9-0 S Cauthen 6/1: 0-13212: Held up, qcknd to lead
over 2f out, but had no answer to the winner: lost nothing in defeat here and is a very
smart colt: see 2257.   81
+2202 UNTOLD [7] (M Stoute) 3-8-11 W R Swinburn 5/2 FAV: 11-2313: Heavily bckd: waited
with and ran on under press: stays 14f, but possibly at her best over 12f: see 2202.   74
2114 SWINK [1] (J Pease) 3-9-0 C Asmussen 8/1: -323124: Not much room over 3f out:
stayed on: possibly needs a stiffer test of stamina: see 2114, 1354.   73
*2222 NISNAS [2] 3-9-0 T Quinn 11/2: 3103110: Seemed to hold ev ch: btr 2222 (12f)   71
2453 SIRK [3] 3-9-0 M Roberts 18/1: 2303200: Prom most: btr 2453, 2157.   65
2114 FAMILY FRIEND [9] 3-9-0 W Carson 66/1: -441000: Made most over 11f: see 902.   52
2222 ALLEZ MILORD [4] 3-9-0 G Starkey 4/1: -110100: Led 3f out, not stay 14f: see 2222, 1853   52
8 ran   4,2,2½,1,3,8,shthd   (Lavinia, Duchess of Norfolk)   J Dunlop, Arundel, Sx.

2566 BATTLE OF BRITAIN H'CAP (0-75) 3YO+   £13149   1m   Firm 00 +08 Fast   [68]

1890 FAIR COUNTRY [8] (D Elsworth) 4-7-10 G Carter 10/1: 3231101: 4 ch f Town and Country
- Fair Measure (Quorum) Useful filly: despite a 6 wks abs, ran on well to lead inside final
1f, cmftbly, in a fast run and val h'cap at Doncaster: earlier a ready winner of an app h'cap
at Ascot and a h'cap at Kempton: winning 2yo at Newbury: very eff over 1m on a fair or
gall trk: acts on firm and yldg grd: has a gd turn of foot.   50
2296 WAAJIB [10] (A Stewart) 3-8-3 M Roberts 15/2: 2-21332: Led briefly final 1f, another
fine effort and deserves another win: see 2296, 1602.   62
2267 HANDLEBAR [4] (J Watts) 4-7-10 L Charnock 7/1: 0011223: Made most and is in grand
form: seems equally eff at 1m/10f: see 2267, 1636.   43
2144 ADVANCE [5] (J Tree) 5-9-7 Pat Eddery 13/2: 1-00204: Chance over 1f out: gd effort
under topweight: see 1793.   63
2241 SIT THIS ONE OUT [2] 3-8-9 B Thomson 33/1: 3000000: No extra over 1f out: btr eff:
best in 802.   56
2443 ACONITUM [1] 5-7-13 R Fox 16/1: 0024030: Fair eff but best in 1525.   37
2255 FUSILIER [6] 4-7-7(bl) A Proud 25/1: 0000100: Prom most, fin 7th: twice below 2165.   30
+2144 GRANNYS BANK [15] 4-7-10 J Lowe 9/2 FAV: 1-12210: Well bckd: never nearer and ddhtdd
7th: well below 2144 and is worth another chance.   33
1216 FREEDOMS CHOICE [3] 4-9-1 W Carson 9/1: -42D100: Abs: no threat: see 1047.   00
2390 STAR OF A GUNNER [11] 6-8-5 C Asmussen 8/1: 1000320: Fdd in str: well below 2390, 2144.   00

2390 **Moores Metal** [13] 7-7(3oh)		2475 **Inishpour** [7] 8-4(bl)
2296 **Dorset Cottage** [12] 8-11		2234 **Qualitair Flyer** [9] 8-4
2437 **Transflash** [16] 7-11	2354 **Kalkour** [14] 8-11(VIS)	
16 ran 1,2,2½,1½,½,nk,ddht	(Sir Gordon Brunton)	D Elsworth Whitsbury, Hants.

2567 HOLSTEN DIAT PILS H'CAP (0-70) 3YO   £8259   1m 2f   Firm 00 -02 Slow   [74]

2438 ENBARR [3] (H Cecil) 3-8-13 S Cauthen 1/1 FAV: 1310121: 3 b c Kings Lake - Catherine
Wheel (Roan Rocket) Smart colt: made ev yard, gamely, in a val 3yo h'cap at Doncaster: has
been in grand form this season, earlier winning h'caps at Haydock and Kempton and also a
winner at Windsor: half brother to Cheshire Oaks winner Hunston: very eff with front running
tactics over 10f, may stay further: acts on soft, but best form on gd and fast grd: seems
to act on any trk: genuine and consistent.   73
2500 GEORDIES DELIGHT [5] (L Piggott) 3-8-6 W Carson 11/2: 4222132: Chased winner in str:
just btn and continues to improve: yet to run a bad race: see 2353.   64
2438 MAJAAHED [1] (B Hanbury) 3-8-11 C Asmussen 20/1: -0103: Al up there: gd eff: stays 10f.   64
2219 MYTENS [6] (J Tree) 3-8-3 Pat Eddery 7/2: 3-1104: Ev ch 2f out: see 1350.   54
1823 NINO BIBBIA [2] 3-9-7 R Cochrane 5/1: 1042300: New trip: no threat: twice below 1286.   68
2462 LAVENDER MIST [4] 3-8-12 W R Swinburn 9/1: 12-1400: Fdd final 2f: lightly raced
since 1002.   53
6 ran   ½,2½,1½,1½,3   (S S Niarchos)   H Cecil Newmarket

2568 SCEPTRE STAKES (LISTED) 3YO+ FILLIES   £11862   1m   Firm 00 +28 Fast

2200 ASTEROID FIELD [11] (B Hills) 3-8-6 B Thomson 5/2: 2030301: 3 b f Forli - Star Strewn
(Native Dancer) Smart filly: regained her best form when a ready winner of Sceptre Stks
(Listed) at Doncaster: easily led over 1f out and qcknd away, breaking the course record:
earlier a gd 3rd in the Irish 1,000 Guineas: first time out fin 2nd in Gr 3 Fred Darling at
Newbury: smart 2yo, winning Gr 3 event at Goodwood and a fillies mdn at Sandown: eff at 7f,
well suited by 1m: acts on hvy, likes fast ground: can win again before season's end.   77
-1466 DUSTY DOLLAR [1] (W Hern) 3-8-2 W Carson 13/8 FAV: 44-3122: Well bckd, despite fair
abs: chance over 1f out, not foot of winner: see 1466, 923.   68
2234 BOLD AND BEAUTIFUL [7] (G P Gordon) 4-8-10 Pat Eddery 7/1: -033003: Al front rank
and kept on well: another fine effort and deserves a win: see 2234, 759.   66
*2437 TRAVEL MAGIC [4] (B Hanbury) 3-8-2 M Roberts 14/1: 0102214: Not btn far in this hot
company: in excellent form: see 2437.   65
*2443 ATOKA [9] 4-8-10 R Hills 12/1: 1343010: Ev ch 2f out, not btn far: fine eff: see 2443.   64
2440 HOLBROOKE SUTTON [10] 3-8-3(1ow) R Cochrane 11/1: -402400: Never nearer: best 1851.   61
2385 REALITY [6] 3-8-2 K Darley 11/1: 0-11030: Made much: another gd run: see 2385, 1753.   59
+2385 PURCHASEPAPERCHASE [3] 4-9-0 S Cauthen 8/1: 1040010: Prom, wknd: much btr 2385.   56
2440 **Migiyas** [8] 8-6(BL)   2278 **Lucky So So** [5] 8-2
10 ran   2,½,½,½,2,hd,2   (Sheikh Mohammed)   B Hills Newmarket

---

Official Going Given As FIRST 2 RACES GOOD/FIRM : REM GOOD

2569 HORSE RACING ABROAD H'CAP 3YO 0-60   £4032   1m 4f   Good 56 -07 Slow   [56]

2462 NORPELLA [5] (G Wragg) 3-9-7 P Robinson 2/1 FAV: 000-141: 3 ch f Northfields -
Palmella (Grundy) Very useful filly: defied top weight, led inside final 1f, cmftbly, in a
val h'cap at Goodwood: first time out a fast time winner of a 3yo mdn at Newmarket: eff at
10f, stays 12f: acts on gd and fast grd and on any trk: seems a genuine filly and should
win more races.   62
2211 NEWQUAY [4] (G Harwood) 3-8-11 A Clark 9/4: -022132: Cruised into lead over 2f
out: failed to find as much as the winner: in gd form: see 2048.   49
*2299 CROWLEY [2] (L Cumani) 3-9-6 R Guest 3/1: -00213: Ev ch in str: fair eff: see 2299.   51
2058 HAPPY BREED [3] (C Brittain) 3-8-4 T Ives 10/1: 1-00404: Led 6f: see 1509.   27
2420 CORRAN RIVER [1] 3-8-11 C Rutter(3) 15/2: 02-1400: Led ½ way to over 2 out: see 935   34
5 ran   1,5,8,½   (E B Moller)   G Wragg Newmarket

2570 MAIL ON SUNDAY 3YO SERIES H'CAP 0-60   £3993   7f   Good 56 +03 Fast   [67]

2291 EASTERN HOUSE [5] (H Cecil) 3-7-13 W Ryan 100/30: -021201: 3 ch f Habitat - Kashmir
Lass (Kashmir II) Fair filly: led inside final 2f, readily, in quite val 3yo h'cap at Goodwood:
earlier won a fillies h'cap at Yarmouth and just btn by Pasticcio at Newbury: very eff
at 7f: acts on gd and fast grd and prob on any trk: may win again.   49
2313 SUNNY MATCH [2] (L Cottrell) 3-7-7(10oh) C Rutter(3) 20/1: -002002: Led over 2f out:
gd eff, being 10lbs out of the h'cap here: suited by an easy 7f: see 1836.   36
*2291 ESFAHAN [4] (J Dunlop) 3-8-0 B Rouse 6/5 FAV: 0201313: Well bckd: btr 2291 (beat winner)   39
1991 BALLAD ROSE [3] (P Cole) 3-8-3(1ow) T Ives 100/30: -432124: Made most: see 1991.   35
2457 NASHIA [1] 3-9-7 M Lynch(5) 7/1: 0-00000: Prom most, fdd: btr 1851 (C/D).   50
5 ran   4,2,5,2   (L Freedman)   H Cecil Newmarket

2571 CHROMACOPY STAKES 2YO   £6273   1m   Good 56 -17 Slow

1780 BEESHI [3] (P Cole) 2-8-11 P Waldron 7/1: 3221: 2 b c Red Sunset - Cafe Au Lait

(Espresso) Useful colt: gained a deserved success, led over 2f out, ridden out in quite slow
run but val 2yo Chromacopy Stks at Goodwood: earlier placed behind the smart trio Classic
Tale, Angara Abyss and Who Knows: half brother to numerous winners, incl Milk Heart and
Chaumiere: well suited by 1m on gd and fast grd: acts on any trk: should win more races.   61
+2468 SANTELLA SAM [1] (M Ryan) 2-9-3 N Day 6/1: 232012: Made most: ran on gamely inside
final 1f: well clear 3rd and is in fine form: acts on any trk and seems suited by front
running: see 2468.   63
*2239 ROMAN GUNNER [5] (G Wragg) 2-9-3 P Cook 7/2: 013: Never nearer on this rain softened
ground: prob stays 1m and deserves another chance: see 2239.   48
*2484 WHITSTABLE [2] (G Harwood) 2-9-3 A Clark 8/11 FAV: 314: Well bckd: carried head
high when asked to qckn over 2f out: deserves another chance after impr win in 2484 (gd/frm).   48
2263 REEF OF GOLD [6] 2-8-11 P Robinson 33/1: 000: No extra over 1f out: can improve
further: see 2001.   39
2159 CONVINCING [4] 2-8-11 S Whitworth 11/1: 00: Prom most, fdd: half brother to 12f
winner Romantic Feeling and should do better than this.   19
2407 Crespin [7] 8-11
7 ran   2,10,shthd,¾,10   (F Salman)   P Cole Whatcombe, Oxon.

2572 OXO STAKES AMATEUR RIDERS   £2351   1m 2f Good 56 -30 Slow

2333 TAVIRI [1] (G Harwood) 3-10-6 Amanda Harwood(5) 7/2: -241: 3 b c Irish Tower - Rikki
Tikki Tavi (Mongo) Found the best grd on the standside and led inside final 2f, cmftbly, in
a slow run amateur riders stks at Goodwood: first time out was a gd 2nd on this trk and runs
well here: related to sev winners abroad: stays 10f well: acts on gd and fast grd and an
undulating trk.   40
1956 HAWARDEN [3] (B Hills) 3-10-11(bl) Mr T T Jones 7/4 FAV: -400132: Led well over 2f
out: btr 1956.   42
1831 VISUAL IDENTITY [6] (P Mitchell) 4-11-2 Mr D Benneyworth 50/1: 0000043:Never nearer:
better eff: see 1831, 578.   28
2300 ELVIRE [5] (S Mellor) 3-10-3 Dana Mellor(5) 33/1: -00404: Chance over 2f out: see 1578.   20
2327 COCCOLUTO [8] 3-10-6(bl) Mr J Ryan 7/2: -022200: In lead 3f out: see 1797.   11
-- VODKATINI [9] 7-11-2 Mr D Madgwick(5) 50/1: -0: May be seen jumping shortly.   02
-- DON PIPER [13] 4-11-2 Mr R Hutchinson 5/1: 2113-00: Springer in mkt, but t.o!
Ex Irish gelding who was a winner 3 times last season: stays 10f and goes well in the mud.   00
-- The Foodbroker [11] 11-12   2406 Liberated Girl [10] 10-13
-- Jameena [4] 10-13   -- Staghound [7] 11-2   2517 Kalimpong [2] 10-13
12 ran   ¾,4,1½,8,5   (K J Buchanan)   G Harwood Pulborough, Sussex

2573 COURT HILL HANDICAP 3Y+ 0-50   £2763   6f   Good 56 +19 Fast   [48]

2382 COPPERMILL LAD [1] (L Holt) 3-8-0 C Rutter(3) 8/1: 0004001: 3 ch c Ardoon - Felin
Geri (Silly Season) Led inside final 1f, ridden out in a fast run h'cap at Goodwood: well
suited by some give in the grd: first time out a winner on soft at Leicester: eff at 5f,
stays 6f: prob acts on any trk.   37
2151 PRINCE SKY [11] (P Cole) 4-9-12 T Ives 13/2: 4301402: Led over 1f out: fine eff under
9-12: runs very well here: see 1852, 1235.   55
2258 CRONKS QUALITY [9] (G Lewis) 3-8-9 P Waldron 13/2: 0000303: Kept on well and not
btn far: may win soon: see 2258, 884.   41
2207 AL AMEAD [8] (C Benstead) 6-9-10 B Rouse 14/1: 4041404: In front 3f out: see 1347 (frm)   45
*2378 MERDON MELODY [6] 3-9-7(bl)(7ex) A Shoults(5) 10/1: 2200410: Not disgraced under 7lbs
pen: see 2378.   45
+2277 CANIF [7] 5-9-3 P Robinson 7/1: -010010: Fdd final 1f: btr 2277 (gd/firm).   32
1524 RIVIERA SCENE [4] 3-8-13 P Cook 6/1: 2-00200: Abs: no threat: best 1312, see 624.   00
1933 NUMISMATIST [10] 7-9-3 R Street 9/2 FAV: 1204-40: Well bckd: fin rear: much btr 1933   00
2312 Galaxy Path [3] 8-1   2258 Myras Special [5] 9-7
10 ran   1,¾,3,¾,2   (Mrs J K Sargood)   L Holt Basingstoke, Hants

2574 EBF GOLDINGS MAIDEN STAKES 2YO   £3983   7f   Good 56 -11 Slow

-- TRUE GENT [15] (J Dunlop) 2-9-0 P Robinson 9/1: 1: 2 b c Lord Gaylord - Glamour
Girl (Riverman) Promising colt: ran on well to lead inside final 1f in a 2yo mdn at Goodwood:
cost $75,000 and is a half brother to the smart stayer Ilium: should be suited by 1m and
further: acts on gd grd and an undulating trk.   66
-- BALAKIREV [9] (I Balding) 2-9-0 T Ives 11/8 FAV: 2: Well bckd: led over 1f out:
gd debut and can go one btr soon: Canadian bred colt who should be suited by 1m: acts on
gd ground and an undulating trk.   62
-- MOUNTAIN ISLE [2] (W Hern) 2-8-11 P Cook 8/1: 3: Led standside 3f out: improvement
likely from this half sister to winners in France: bred to stay 1m and further: acts on
gd ground and can find a race.   53
-- BOLD TANGENT [13] (M Usher) 2-9-0 W Ryan 33/1: 4: Fdd final 1f on debut: quite cheaply
bought yearling who should improve enough to find a race: eff over 7f on gd ground.   50
-- ARADU [14] 2-9-0 M Hills 33/1: 0: Nearest fin on racecourse debut and impr looks certain:
cost 11,500 gns: dam a winning 2yo: bred to stay 1m.   40
-- CAMMARINO [1] 2-9-0 T Lucas 12/1: 0: Chance 2f out: should impr on this: cost IR 720,000
and is a half brother to 7/8f winner Precis.   36

GOODWOOD   Saturday September 13th   -Cont'd

-- THREE TAILS [7] 2-8-11 B Rouse 10/1: 0: Friendless in mkt tho' should improve: cost
290,000 gns as yearling and is a half sister to the smart 3yo Maysoon, amongst others.   00
-- ANUBI [3] 2-9-0 R Guest 10/1: 0: Mkt drifter: will do btr: American bred colt who
cost $25,000.   00
-- Marble Rock [12] 9-0   -- Strelliiane [5] 8-11   -- Beaulieu Bay [8] 9-0
-- Time Odyssey [4] 9-0   -- Spitzablt [6] 9-0   -- Green Laleek [16] 9-0
-- Sallys Won [11] 9-0
15 ran 1½,2,2,5,2   (Sheikh Mohammed)   J Dunlop Arundel, Sussex

2575 PILLEY GREEN MAIDEN STAKES 3YO   £822   5f   good 56 +11 Fast

2519 MUHTARIS [4] (C Benstead) 3-9-0(BL) B Rouse 5/1: 0000001: 3 b c Song - Penny Blessing
(So Blessed) Tried in bl and was in the lead over 2f out and held on under press in quite
fast run 3yo mdn at Goodwood: runner up earlier in the season in h'caps at Sandown (2) and
Bath: this was his first win: very eff at 5f: acts on gd and yldg ground and an easy trk.   31
2143 STANBO [9] (D Dale) 3-9-0 T Ives 14/1: -000402: Chance hung 1f: just btn: gd eff:
eff at 5/6f on gd and fast ground and a sharpish, undulating trk.   30
2416 ASTARTE [6] (G P Gordon) 3-8-11 Abigail Richards(7) 7/2: 0003203: Kept on: runs well
here: see 2245.   21
1191 HARMONY BOWL [3] (M Jarvis) 3-9-0(BL) T Lucas 15/2: 00-0004: Long abs: bl first time
and prom most: very lightly raced gelding who had shown little form prev: eff at 5f on good.   22
500 MRS WADDILOVE [1] 3-8-11 Gay Kelleway(3) 2/1 FAV: 04-0020: Well bckd despite long abs:
kept on: btr 500 (7f).   18
2409 GRANGE FARM LADY [7] 3-8-11 M Rimmer 9/2: -03020: Fdd final 1f: see 2409.   12
2416 Dalsaan Bay [2] 9-0   835 Moorestar [5] 9-0   2312 Gleadhill Park [8] 9-0(bl)
9 ran hd,2,½,nk,2   (Hamdan Al Maktoum)   C Benstead Epsom, Surrey

CHEPSTOW   Saturday September 13th   Lefthanded, Galloping Track

Official Going Given As GOOD/FIRM (FIRST RACE): GOOD (REMAINDER)

2576 BRECON APPRENTICE STAKES DIV I 3YO+   £967   1m 2f   Good/Firm 28 -66 Slow

2419 LIAM [6] (M Ryan) 3-8-5 S Hibble(1) 4/7 FAV: 1014041: 3 b c Runnett - No Delay
(Never Say Die): Useful colt: well bckd & led ¼way, comfortably in a slowly run app. stakes
at Chepstow: earlier twice successful over this trip at Folkestone: very eff over 10f on
gd & firm grnd: seems to act on any trk.   30+
2489 ASK MAMA [1] (J Dunlop) 3-8-2 G Foster(7) 9/4: -301202: Led/dsptd lead to ½way: ran
on well under press & comfortably beat rem: acts on any trk: best in 1368.   25
2282 STONEBROKER [3] (D Haydn Jones) 4-8-11 D Williams(3) 8/1: 4100223: Ran on same pace.   14
1579 WINDBOUND LASS [2] (R Holder) 3-7-11 R Price(7) 33/1: 0-00004: Never dngr after abs:
maiden filly who has been well btn in selling company this term.   08
2170 CLOUD CHASER [5] 3-8-0 R Morse 33/1: 0-40000: Mkt drifter: early ldr: see 1317.   00
2401 LADY LAMB [4] 3-7-11 S Williams(7) 14/1: 00-0000: Raced wide home turn, well btn.   00
6 ran ½,4,hd,6,10   (Jack Fisher)   M Ryan Newmarket

2577 BLACK CAT STAKES 2YO   £3124   7f   Good/Firm 28 +01 Fast

*2283 RHONDALING [14] (P Walwyn) 2-8-8 Paul Eddery 9/2: 311: 2 b f Welsh Pageant -
Touch Of Class (Luthier): Useful filly: led inside dist, gamely in quite a valuable 2yo stakes
at Chepstow: last month won a fillies mdn over this C/D: very eff over 7f & will stay 1m:
acts on gd/firm & yld grnd & is well suited by a gall trk: should continue to impr.   52
2052 WABARAH [6] (H T Jones) 2-8-8 A Murray 6/1: 311242: Led briefly dist, kept on well
over this lngr trip: eff over 6/7f: may win again soon: see 1357.   50
*2287 NORTHSHIEL [10] (H Candy) 2-8-8 W Newnes 11/4 FAV: 4313: Led ½way: in gd form: see 2287A6   43
1891 DOMINO FIRE [3] (J Dunlop) 2-8-8 G Baxter 8/1: 12204: Had ev ch: best over 6f in 1552.   43
2147 SUNBRIDGE [12] 2-8-8 G Duffield 7/2: 00: Gambled on: front rank over ½way: half
sister to 12f winner Auction Fever: acts on gd/firm grnd & on a gall trk.   35
2377 MISK EL KHASHAB [13] 2-8-8(BL) J Matthias 20/1: 2000: Bl first time: showed gd speed
over ½way though again below form shown on her debut in 1752.   31
2147 TAHGREBA [2] 2-8-8 A Mcglone 8/1: 00: Early speed: fin 8th: see 2147.   26
1629 PRINCESS SEMELE [1] 2-8-8 N Adams 10/1: 00: Led to ½way, sn btn: abs since 1629 (6f).   00
2019 Philgwyn [4] 8-8   2057 Hurricane Valley 0 8-8
2434 Borotrem [11] 8-8   2308 Miss Atwell [9] 8-8   -- Della Robbia [15] 8-4
-- Chukatalk [8] 8-4   2080 Fighting Belle [7] 8-8
15 ran ½,2,1½,4,2,2,2,nk   (Mrs Rupert Hambro)   P Walwyn Lambourn, Berks

2578 HORSESHOE STAKES HANDICAP 3YO+ 0-50   £2893   1m 2f   Good/Firm 28 +06 Fast   [44]

1939 CRAMMING [3] (W Musson) 3-8-0 A Mackay 9/2: 2302301: 3 b g Viking - Damaring
(Saidam): Nicely bckd & led 2f out, easily in quite a fast run h'cap at Chepstow: first time
out winner of a seller at Ripon & has only twice fin out of the frame since: eff over 9/10f,
stays 12f: acts on fast & soft grnd & on any trk: consistent sort who should win again
in this form.   38

758

2260 DERRYRING [9] (D Laing) 4-8-5 J Reid 9/1: 0000402: No ch with winner: see 1383.   18
1274 PATRICK JOHN LYONS [5] (P Arthur) 5-7-11(3ow) A Mcglone 16/1: 30-3003: Abs: made most.   09
2431 WINDSOR KNOT [7] (P Walwyn) 4-9-10(VIS) Paul Eddery 7/2: -400224: Visored first time:
better in 2431 (1m).   35
2490 MOUNT TUMBLEDOWN [1] 5-8-12 L Jones(5) 11/1: 0000-00: Ran on too late: see 2490.   20
2273 WELSH MEDLEY [8] 4-8-3 D Williams(7) 11/1: 3214000: Led briefly 2f out: best in 724.   10
*2360 CASHEW KING [6] 3-8-3 T Williams 11/2: 0440210: Fin 7th: btr in 2360.   00
2121 TALK OF GLORY [2] 5-8-8 G Baxter 7/1: 0022300: Wknd 2f out: much btr in 1450 (C/D).   00
*2161 SWEET DOMAIN [4] 3-9-1 A Murray 2/1 FAV: 0-00110: Well bckd: led over 3f out, sn btn:
much btr in 2161 & worth another chance.   00
9 ran   8,shhd,nk,2,hd,4,2   (Mrs Catherine Perkins)   W Musson Newmarket

2579 CLOVER STAKES NURSERY HANDICAP 2YO   £1535   5f   Good/Firm 28 -01 Slow   [43]

+2261 MUKHABBR [5] (C Benstead) 2-9-5 T Williams 13/8 FAV: 0311111: 2 b c Taufan -
Ribotingo (Petingo): Useful, much impr colt: comfortably completed his nap hand, led below
dist & sprinted clear in a nursery h'cap at Chepstow: earlier won similar events at Lingfield
(2), Windsor & Goodwood: half brother to very useful sprinter Pampas: very eff over 5/6f
with forcing tactics: acts on gd & fast grnd: difficult to oppose in this mood.   50
2421 OUT ON A FLYER [2] (D Elsworth) 2-7-12 D Brown 5/1: 002132: Lacked foot of winner:
in fair form & seems to act on any trk: see 2020.   14
2218 WOODMAN WEAVER [1] (J Douglas Home) 2-8-8 W Newnes 3/1: 00043: Led over ½way: see 2218. 23
2284 VICTORY BALLARD [4] (R Hannon) 2-8-11 A Mcglone 16/1: 000104: Ran on same pace: best 1844. 22
2485 GREENS GALLERY [8] 2-8-9 M L Thomas 11/2: 1120000: Bckd from 14/1: never nearer:
well h'capped on her best form & worth keeping an eye on: see 1585 & 948.   20
2301 FRIVOLOUS LADY [3] 2-8-10 S Whitelam(7) 10/1: 4400: Speed to ½way: see 1946 & 1668.   16
2320 Flag Bearer [6] 8-8   2435 Spanish Sky   [7] 9-7(VIS)
8 ran   5,½,1½,sh hd,2,4,nk   (Hamdan Al-Maktoum)   C Benstead Epsom, Surrey

2580 HEATHER SELLING STAKES 2YO   £909   7f   Good/Firm 28 -29 Slow

1948 VISION OF WONDER [13] (M Usher) 2-8-11 M Wigham 6/1: 001: 2 b c Tyrnavos - Valeur
(Val de Loir): Dropped in class and ran on strongly to lead dist in a 2yo seller at Chepstow
(bought in 4,500 gns): cost 6,200 gns as a yearling & is a half brother to a couple of
winners: eff over 7f & will be suited by 1m plus: acts on gd/firm grnd & on a gall trk.   22
2310 CABALLINE [7] (M Haynes) 2-8-11 A Murray 14/1: 0300002: Took a drop in class: ev ch:
showed enough ability early season to win in this grade: acts on gd/firm & soft: see 200.   18
2396 MEDALLION MAN [4] (W Mackie) 2-8-11 J Matthias 25/1: 003: Made most far side: cheaply
bought colt who has been lightly rcd this term: stays 7f: acts on gd/firm grnd & on a gall trk 17
1948 RAGTIME SOLO [10] (P Makin) 2-8-11 G Baxter 16/1: 0004: Not btn that far in this
lower grade: cheaply acquired colt who is eff over 7f on gd/firm grnd.   16
2044 JONITE [18] 2-8-11 R Mcghin 9/1: 0000: Led stands side most: soundly btn in all his
previous starts: acts on gd/firm grnd.   11
2405 AVENMORE STAR [12] 2-8-8 A Mackay 11/2 FAV: 0000400: Close up till dist: see 2180.   06
2471 HONEY PLUM [1] 2-8-8 R Curant 7/1: 4404000: Led far side 2f out: wknd into 8th.   00
2471 DONNA IMMOBILE [16] 2-8-8 L Jones(5) 10/1: 0000: Fdd into 9th: btr in 2471 (1m).   00
--   PASS THE CATCHUP [9] 2-8-8 A Mcglone 7/1: 0: Active in mkt on debut: some late hdway
after slow start: fetched 4,500 gns as a yearling: bred to be suited by further.   00
2433 DEAR GLENDA [11] 2-8-8 T Williams 8/1: 2000: Speed to ½way: best in 13 (yld).   00
2020 Clearway [15] 9-2   --   Red Sky At Night [14] 8-8
2107 Sleepline For Beds [17] 8-11(bl)   2334 Kinsham Dene [6] 8-8(vis)
2095 Rock A Little [3] 8-8   2405 Young Centurion [8] 8-11(bl)
1083 Phoebe [2] 8-8   2107 Max Star [5] 8-11
18 ran   1½,½,hd,2½,1,½,2,3   (C A Cyzer)   M Usher Lambourn, Berks

2581 RABBITS FOOT HANDICAP 3YO+ 0-35   £2270   1m   Good/Firm 28 +02 Fast   [35]

2288 SPARKLER SPIRIT [5] (R Akehurst) 5-7-7(1oh) N Adams 20/1: 0-02401: 3 b g Mandamus -
Swallow Street (My Swallow): Quickly into his stride & was never hdd on far side when a game
winner of a h'cap at Chepstow: first success: eff over 7/8f on gd & firm grnd: acts on
any trk: best when out in front.   09
2022 TARRAKAN [8] (C Wildman) 4-8-0(1ow) W Newnes 25/1: 31-0002: Fin well, only just held:
last season won selling h'caps at Goodwood & Brighton & is worth noting if dropping back
to that grade: eff over 8/10f: suited by fast grnd: acts on any trk.   15
*2230 WILLBE WILLBE [10] (C Brittain) 3-7-11(1ow) M L Thomas 10/1: 0000013: In gd form: see 2230 15
*2282 PETIT BOT [2] (W Musson) 4-7-10(bl) R Price(7) 10/1: -000014: Fin well: likes this trk. 05
2390 APRIL FOOL [15] 4-8-13(vis) T Lang 12/1: 4000300: Al up there: stays 1m: see 1390.   20
2282 FULL OF LIFE [20] 3-9-2 R Brid 8/1: 0002200: Never nearer: see 1579.   30
2431 CONCERT PITCH [6] 7-9-3 J Williams 10/1: -004100: Fdd into 7th: best here in 2319 (7f).   00
1689 GIBBOUS MOON [14] 4-8-8 R Wernham 10/1: -002000: Abs: fin 8th: best in 1018.   00
2260 IKTIYAR [23] 4-9-7 M Wigham 8/1: 0100130: Prom over ½way: best in 2059.   00
1202 INTRINSIC [22] 3-8-9 A Murray 10/1: -00000: Needed race after abs: see 372.   00
2149 SAND DOLLAR [17] 3-8-9 G Duffield 9/2 FAV: 0-13300: Bckd from 10/1: no threat: best 1904 00
2319 Pamela Heaney [9] 7-11   2397 Quicken The Bid [11] 7-13   00

2313 **Royal Berks** [18] 7-11
2189 **Sharp Shot** [4] 9-0
1471 **No Jazz** [19] 7-9
2319 **April Arabesque** [13] 7-8
2490 **Farag** [21] 8-7
2497 **Just Met** [16] 8-7
2187 **Solent Express** [12] 7-7(5oh)
1500 **Mairs Girl** [7] 7-7(3oh)
2211 **Windy Hollow** [1] 7-10
22 ran hd,2½,1,½,hd,1,1 (Sparkler Filters (Great Britain) Ltd) R Akehurst Epsom, Surrey

2582 **BRECON APPR STAKES DIV II 3YO+ £965 1m 2f Good/Firm 28 -19 Slow**

2353 **INNISHMORE ISLAND** [5] (J Dunlop) 3-8-5 G Foster(7) 4/5 FAV: -303221: 3 ch c Great Nephew - Makura (Pampered King): Useful colt: gained a deserved win when landing the odds in an app. race at Chepstow: led 3f out, comfortably: quite consistent last season when winning at Warwick & has only once been out of the money this term: half brother to several winners: very eff around 10f: acts on gd & firm grnd & on any trk. 30+
2462 **SPINNAKER LADY** [2] (M Usher) 3-8-2 L Jones 20/1: 0001002: Stayed on well without troubling winner: should win again when dropped back to selling company: see 2073. 20
1951 **NEXT DANCE** [1] (H Candy) 3-8-0 R Teague(3) 20/1: -00003: Early ldr, ran on same pace: closely related to a couple of winners though has shown little form himself since 625. 16
2438 **SHIBIL** [3] (M Stoute) 3-8-5 M A Giles(3) 11/8: 3222104: Went on before ½way, btn dist: has ability but has proved most frustrating: see 2183. 18
-- **PENLLYNES PRIDE** [6] 5-8-9 J Hills 20/1: 02204-0: Never dngr on belated seasonal debut: mdn who was placed several times last season when trained by W Hastings-Bass: stays 10f: acts on any going. 00
-- **UNCORNERED** [7] 4-8-6 L Johnsey(3) 14/1: 00020-0: Needed race after long abs: rated 38 when 2nd in a fillies mdn at Haydock late last season: stays 10f well: suited by some give in the ground. 00
2401 **SKY MARINER** [4] 5-8-11 J Ward(7) 50/1: -000400: Al behind: see 1703. 00
7 ran 2½,1,1½,20,dist,dist (Mrs A V Ferguson) J Dunlop Arundel Sussex

EDINBURGH Monday September 15th Righthand, Sharpish Track

Official Going Given As GOOD/FIRM

2583 **BET WITH THE TOTE STAKES 3YO+ £1001 1m 4f Good/Firm 28 -25 Slow**

2430 **ADMIRALS ALL** [6] (J Winter) 3-8-10 A Mackay 1/3 FAV: 4030421: 3 br g Julio Mariner - Double Finesse (Double Jump): Had an easy task & led over 1f out, pushed out in quite slow run 2yo stakes at Edinburgh: placed several times previously in mdn company: half brother to the smart miler Larionov: stays 12f well: acts on gd & fast grnd & on any trk. 15
2374 **TREYARNON** [5] (S Norton) 4-9-5 J Lowe 6/1: 0004432: Made most: runs well over this C/D, normally in non-h'cap company: see 631. 08
2267 **BOYNTON** [1] (W Elsey) 3-8-10(bl) K Darley 7/1: 2024003: Ev ch str: disapp since 1178 (10f) 03
2085 **BIRCHGROVE LAD** [2] (G Oldroyd) 5-9-5 K Hodgson 16/1: -004: Never nearer: lightly raced gelding who has displayed little ability on the Flat to date. 00
2413 **MINDERS MAN** [7] 4-9-5 N Connorton 16/1: 00-0000: No show: only moderate: see 1820. 00
-- **LOCH AVICH** [4] 3-8-10 N Carlisle 33/1: -0: Prom much on racecourse debut. 00
-- **PHILCLASS** [3] 3-8-10 C Dwyer 25/1: -0: Fdd str on debut. 00
7 ran 2,3,8,1½,4,1½ (Mrs D H Clifton) J Winter Newmarket

2584 **TOTE EACH WAY MAIDEN STAKES 2YO £1114 1m Good/Firm 28 -20 Slow**

2043 **MISS ZOLA** [10] (J Fitzgerald) 2-8-11 M Birch 66/1: 001: 2 ch f Raga Navarro - Stardom (Hornbeam): Caused a 66/1 surprise, al prom & stayed on gamely for a narrow win in a slow run 2yo mdn at Edinburgh: half sister to several winners incl useful 10/11f winner Tolstoy: eff at 1m, should be suited by further: acts on fast grnd & aa sharpish trk. 36
2364 **TROMPE DOEIL** [14] (J Payne) 2-8-11(BL) A Mackay 50/1: 0002: Made much: hdd inside final 1f & rallied well: bl first time today & showed much impr form: evidently suited by forcing tactics over 1m on a sharpish trk: acts on fast grnd. 35
1948 **DRYGALSKI** [3] (M Stoute) 2-9-0 Paul Eddery 7/2 JT.FAV: 043: Prom, ev ch:stays 1m: see 1634. 37
2283 **FLAUNTING** [13] (M Dickinson) 2-8-11 A Shoults(5) 10/1: 004: Prom, kept on: on the up grade & stays 1m: acts on gd/firm: see 2283. 33
1914 **AL MAHAMRY** [2] 2-9-0 Gay Kelleway(3) 4/1: 000: Ev ch in str: seems to stay 1m: see 1914 35
1948 **WAHIBA** [12] 2-9-0 G Carter 7/2 JT.FAV: 030: No extra final 1f: stays 1m: see 1948. 34
1812 **FRENDLY FELLOW** [1] 2-9-0 N Connorton 8/1: 00: Never beyond mid-div: btr 1812. 00
2423 **COME ON OYSTON** [5] 2-8-11 K Darley 10/1: 43300: Btr over 6f: see 2423. 00
2494 **Sparkler Boy** [11] 9-0
1982 **Damart** [6] 9-0
-- **Winged Pharaoh** [15] 9-0
-- **Amiable Amy** [16] 8-11
2511 **Honeyway Mist** [7] 9-0
-- **Mixedup Mhairi** [8] 8-11
2080 **The Londonderry** [4] 8-11(vis)
2410 **Arishan** [9] 9-0(BL)
16 ran nk,½,½,½,½. (Lady Musker) J Fitzgerald Malton, Yorks

2585 TOTE PLACE ONLY SELLING STKS 3 & 4YO   £897   7f   Good/Firm 28 +05 Fast

2509 MOLLY PARTRIDGE [7] (R Woodhouse) 3-8-2 A Proud 10/1: 0030041: 3 gr f Sexton Blake -
Coquette (St Paddy): Adopted different tactics & made ev yd, cmftbly in a 3 & 4yo seller at
Edinburgh (bought in 1,250 gns): eff at 7f, stays 1m: acts on gd/firm grnd: runs well here.   11
2361 CLOUDLESS SKY [10] (P Rohan) 3-8-4(2ow) M Birch 7/1: -030402: Fin well, but too late.   07
2411 KING COLE [11] (G Reveley) 4-8-10 D Nicholls 8/1: 0040003: Al there: see 1839.   06
334 SAIYYAAF [12] (D Thom) 3-8-5 J Curant 6/4 FAV: -0004: Hvly bckd, despite !ong abs:
prom & ev ch: lightly rcd gelding who was running in selling company today for the first
time: half brother to several winners & one to keep an eye on in this grade.   06
1574 LOCHABBEY [9] 4-8-10 Paul Eddery 12/1: 000-000: Prom much: abs since 1574.   03
1979 SWEET EIRE [5] 4-8-7(bl) R Hull(6) 20/1: -000040: No real threat: see 906.   00
2174 LAST JEWEL [13] 3-8-2 G Carter 5/1: 0-00040: Fin 7th: much btr 2174.   00
2124 TRICENCO [1] 4-9-3(bl) S Webster 8/1: 0000300: Fdd str: best 1979 (6f).   00
2374 BUCKS BOLT [4] 4-9-3 J Carroll 7/1: 0004400: Prom, fdd: twice below 1951 (9f).   00
2427 STANFORD ROSE [6] 3-8-2 K Darley 9/1: -004000: Best 1960: see 960.   00
2361 Class Hopper [3] 8-5   2335 Carousel Nougat [2] 8-7
673 The Dabber [8] 8-2
13 ran   3,½,½,1½,2½,3   (G A Farndon Eng Co Ltd)   R Woodhouse Whitwell, Yorks

2586 TOTE CREDIT SPRINT HCAP 3YO+ 0-50   £2767   5f   Good/Firm 28 +06 Fast   [40]

2537 CHINA GOLD [10] (L Siddall) 7-9-5 M Wood 12/1: 2020001: 7 b h Blue Cashmere - China
Girl (Shantung): Sn prom on the far side & led 1f out, driven out in a h'cap at Edinburgh: in
'85 won at Carlisle & in '84 won at Edinburgh (2) & Ripon: very eff at 5f, does stay 6f:
best on fast grnd when up with the pace: probably acts on any trk.   42
2469 LADY CARA [3] (J Berry) 6-8-7 J Carroll(7) 6/1: 0241102: Prom stands side, fin well
& just btn: remains in grand form: see 2322.   29
2469 PENDOR DANCER [8] (K Ivory) 3-8-5(vis) N Carlisle 7/2 FAV: 0101023: Led most stands
side: see 2469, 1940.   25
2322 PERGODA [12] (I Vickers) 8-9-0(bl) R Vickers(7) 10/1: 0104004: Made most far side: see 1543. 30
2204 TOBERMORY BOY [11] 9-9-6 K Bradshaw(5) 10/1: 0200000: Prom far side: best in 1306(6f).   28
2469 SPACEMAKER BOY [1] 6-9-9 Paul Eddery 16/1: 32F0000: Prom stands side: best 1037: see 211   26
2322 LOCH FORM [2] 3-8-7 M Birch 8/1: 0320400: Fdd over 1f out: btr 1543 (C/D): see 255.   00
2537 KING CHARLEMAGNE [4] 7-9-9 A Shoults(5) 9/1: 0434000: There over 3f: below best:see 1508. 00
2151 Mendick Adventure [5] 8-7(bl)   2411 Tradesman [14] 7-8(1ow)(9oh)
--   Blessit [6] 9-2(bl)   2224 Iberian Start [9] 9-10
12 ran   nk,1½,nk,3,2,1   (Mrs D Ibbotson)   L Siddall Appleton Roebuck, Yorks

2587 TOTE PLACEPOT HANDICAP 3YO+ 0-35   £989   1m 7f   Good/Firm 28 -13 Slow   [18]

1435 NIMBLE NATIVE [6] (S Norton) 3-9-1 J Lowe 8/1: 4003041: 3 ch f Our Native - Fleeting
Vision (Pronto): Led well over 2f out, driven out final 1f in a h'cap at Edinburgh: gd
effort after a fair abs: first time out won a fillies mdn at Catterick: well suited by 15f
& stays 2m: acts on firm & yld grnd & probably on any trk: has worn a visor: does well when fresh. 24
2141 STONE JUG [7] (S Hall) 6-9-7 M Birch 2/1 FAV: -041142: Ev ch final 3f: just btn:
well clear 3rd: see 1745.   17
860 MASTER CARL [2] (G Reveley) 7-9-2 D Nicholls 9/1: -000303: Long abs: never nearer: see 590.00
1548 MIRPUR [8] (G Reveley) 4-8-3 A Shoults(5) 14/1: 0000/04: Abs: led 6f out, wknd:
mdn on the Flat.   00
*2125 PATRIOTIC [5] 3-8-5 C Nutter 7/1: 00-0410: Fdd str: btr 2125 (seller).   00
2300 DAIS [1] 3-8-5(VIS) Paul Eddery 10/1: 00-000: Visored 1st time: never nearer: lightly
rcd filly who is a half sister to winning stayer Fitzpatrick but has shown little herself.   00
2040 LAKISTE [4] 3-8-12(BL) N Connorton 3/1: -04430: Bl first time: led 9f: btr 2040.   00
--   Mount Ephraim [3] 8-0
8 ran   nk,12,7,nk,3   (Bahman Abtahi)   S Norton Barnsley, Yorks

2588 TOTE DUAL FORECAST NURSERY 2YO   £1270   5f   Good/Firm 28 +02 Fast   [46]

*1723 PETERS BLUE [11] (J Fitzgerald) 2-8-3 M Birch 4/1: 04111: 2 gr g Riki Lash - Lady
Doubloon (Pieces Of Eight): Despite a 7 week abs, made ev yd, cmftbly in a nursery h'cap at
Edinburgh: earlier employed similar tactics to win sellers at Yarmouth & Catterick: very eff
with front running over sharp/easy 5f: loves fast grnd.   31
2425 LINPAC NORTH MOOR [9] (W Elsey) 2-8-4(bl) K Darley 12/1: 2403442: Chased winner: gd
effort: seems well suited by an easy 5f: likes fast grnd.   25
2410 DENSBEN [17] (D Smith) 2-7-13 L Charnock 20/1: 04403: Prom, kept on: eff at 5f on
fast grnd: see 1421.   17
2172 MISS SHEGAS [13] (J Berry) 2-8-7 C Dwyer 25/1: 2100304: Kept on final 1f: tried in
bl last time: best in 473 (soft/hvy).   19
2465 HUGO Z HACKENBUSH [14] 2-8-4 Abigail Richards(7) 16/1: 4223200: Never nearer: twice
below 2307 (yielding).   13
2435 ORIOLE DANCER [16] 2-8-3 S Webster 14/1: 2410000: Prom most: best 1069 (C/D).   11
2465 MISS MILVEAGH [10] 2-9-8(10ex) J Carroll(7) 10/3 FAV: 3222130: Btr 2465, 2380.   30
1920 DUNLIN [4] 2-8-12 J Lowe 10/1: 123100: Prom stands side: see 1740.   00
2425 Gardenia Lady [15] 8-6(BL)   2227 Fourwalk [5] 8-13   00

2323 Greensward Boy [12] 7-7(vis)   2180 Glory Gold [1] 7-7
2425 Mr Grumpy [7] 9-7   2465 Tootsie Jay [3] 7-7(5oh)
2323 Run To Work [2] 7-10   2298 Harrys Coming [8] 7-10
2435 Basic Bliss [6] 8-10
17 ran   2,1,2½,1,nk,1½   (Peter Rawson)   J Fitzgerald Malton, Yorks

---

WOLVERHAMPTON   Monday September 15th   Lefthanded, Fair Galloping Track

2589 HAGLEY MAIDEN FILLIES STAKES 2YO   £822   5f   Good/Firm 30 -18 Slow

2301 MALIBU TOAST [6] (L Cumani) 2-8-11 R Cochrane 5/2: 01: 2 ch f Raise A Cup -
California Girl (California Kid): Btr for her recent debut & was nicely bckd when qckning
to lead inside dist in a 2yo fillies mdn at Wolverhampton: American bred filly who is a half
sister to several winners in the States: eff over 5f on gd/firm & yld grnd: will stay
further: seems well suited by a fair trk.   45
1874 PUSHOFF [12] (C Brittain) 2-8-11 T Ives 4/1: 02: Tried to make all: gd effort & is
clearly on the up grade: acts on gd/firm grnd: see 1874.   36
2167 HAZEL BEE [2] (P Calver) 2-8-11 M Fry 50/1: 03: Al up there: btr effort from this
speedily bred filly: acts on gd/firm grnd & on a fair trk.   30"
--   JUST CLASS [11] (S Norton) 2-8-11 G Baxter 20/1: 4: Quite a promising debut: picked up
grnd from below dist & seems sure to impr next time: will be suited by another furlong: acts
on gd/firm grnd.   26
2514 KEPT WAITING [10] 2-8-11 M Wigham 8/1: 020: Btr on a sharp trk in 2514.   20
2308 ACT OF TREASON [3] 2-8-11 W R Swinburn 15/8 FAV: 030: Well bckd: onepaced: best in 2308 19
--   FLITTERISS PARK [4] 2-8-11 D Mckeown 50/1: 0: Late prog on debut: speedily bred filly
who should be btr for this experience.   13
2070 BELAKA [9] 2-8-11 M Rimmer 7/1: 40: Mkt drifter: no threat: btr in 2070 (6f). 12
--   Millfields House [1] 8-11   2434 Hall A Cab [5] 8-11
2325 Park Frolics [8] 8-11
11 ran   2½,2,1½,2,nk,3,hd   (Fittocks Stud Ltd)   L Cumani Newmarket

2590 BEWDLEY SELLING STAKES 3YO   £731   1m 4f   Good/Firm 30 -42 Slow

2560 LISAKATY [6] (M Mccourt) 3-8-11 R Wernham 6/4 FAV: 0004301: 3 b f Condorcet -
Galtee Princess (Valdano): Led 2f out & was hard ridden to justify fav. in a slowly run 3yo
seller at Wolverhampton (no bid): well suited by 10/12f nowadays: acts on fast & yld grnd
& seems to like a gall trk.   10
2478 REDALLY [5] (W Wharton) 3-9-0 G Duffield 10/1: -002: Led early: stayed on well under
press & only just held: lightly rcd gelding who is eff over 12f on gd/firm grnd.   12
2495 COUNTESS CARLOTTI [1] (A Jarvis) 3-8-11 J Reid 2/1: 0240003: Made much: best in 1134 (1m) 02
1784 GO FLAMINGO [2] (A James) 3-8-11 S Dawson 33/1: 00-4004: Rank outsider & no threat. 00
1985 EXPERT WITNESS [3] 3-9-0 P Robinson 4/1: -0400: Short lived effort 3f out.   00
2125 TIBER GATE [4] 3-9-0 P Dalton(7) 10/1: 0-00000: Trailed in last: see 998.   00
6 ran   ½,4,2½,½,20   (M J McNamee)   M Mccourt Letcombe Regis, Oxon

2591 MIDLAND CESAREWITCH (H'CAP)(0-60) 3YO+   £4721   2m 1f   Good/Firm 30 +15 Fast   [47]

*2290 PACTOLUS [2] (G Kindersley) 3-9-7 J Reid 8/1: 0123111: 3 b c Lydian - Honey Sand
(Windy Sands): Useful colt: made a successful debut for his new connections, led below dist &
stayed on gamely to win a fast run & quite valuable h'cap at Wolverhampton: earlier won twice
at Lingfield & more recently a valuable h'cap at Epsom for G Harwood: lightly rcd in '85,
winning at Salisbury: eff over 12/14f, clearly well suited by a test of stamina: acts on
gd & fast grnd & on any trk: in grand form.   62
2311 TIGERWOOD [8] (R Akehurst) 5-8-1 N Adams 10/1: -121022: Made most, kept on gamely
& remains in gd form: see 1533.   27
*2280 SHIPBOURNE [7] (G Harwood) 3-8-9 G Starkey 2/1 Fav: 0303113: Not btn far: much impr of late. 47
2376 BALLET CHAMP [3] (R Holder) 8-8-0 S Dawson 16/1: 0024204: Never nearer: see 2134. 25
2169 ORANGE HILL [13] 4-8-2(bl) R Fox 4/1: 0004220: Led early in str: in gd form: see 2031. 26
2346 ALL IS REVEALED [6] 4-8-8(vis) M L Thomas 20/1: 3000000: Al prom: best over 14f in 582. 26
2445 ROSTHERNE [5] 4-8-7(1ow) W R Swinburn 9/1: 0400020: Never dngr: much btr in 2445 (14f). 00
375 Tom Sharp [4] 8-1   1875 Morgans Choice [15] 7-13
2432 Harbour Bazaar [14] 7-7(9oh)   2376 Jackdaw [1] 8-7
--   Mandown Lad [11] 7-8(1ow)(7oh)   942 Janus [12] 8-2
--   Puget [9] 8-5
14 ran   2,hd,nk,½,4,2,½,½   (Robert B De Lisser)   G Kindersley Lambourn, Berks

2592 APPRENTICES' H'CAP STAKES 3YO+ (0-35)   £976   5f   Good/Firm 30 -12 Slow   [29]

2312 HILMAY [3] (W Charles) 4-8-1 R Lappin 10/1: 0403201: 4 b f Creetown - Gold Ribbon
(Blast): Lost her mdn tag, led dist & ran on strongly to win an app h'cap at Wolverhampton:

well suited by this minimum trip & has made the frame several times this season: acts on fast & yld grnd & is well suited by a sharp/easy trk. 10
2519 **TACHYON PARK** [7] (P Arthur) 4-9-7 L Johnsey 14/1: 000-002: Led briefly below dist, kept on well: lightly rcd this term & remains a mdn: eff over 5/6f: acts on any going. 25
2322 **GODSTRUTH** [5] (H T Jones) 7-9-0(bl) A Riding 5/1: 0-00043: In gd form: see 1344. 16
1687 **NAGEM** [4] (L Barratt) 3-8-10 P Hill 10/1: 0-04234: Abs: al prom: best in 1505. 10
2416 **ARDENT PARTNER** [8] 3-9-2 A Dicks 14/1: 3021000: Made most: best in 2024. 14
2416 **JACQUI JOY** [9] 3-7-11 G Bardwell 16/1: 0300000: Had ev ch: best in 1734. 00
2402 **CAPTAINS BIDD** [15] 6-8-10 L Riggio 3/1 FAV: 0414100: Fdd into 7th: best in 2256. 00
2245 **FIRST EXPERIENCE** [14] 4-8-12 A J Geran 9/1: 0100000: Much btr over this C/D in 1196. 00
1438 **COMMANDER MEADEN** [2] 3-7-12(bl) J Carter 13/2: -030400: Abs: dwelt & no threat:best 929. 00
2469 **Ken Siddall** [13] 8-9 2245 **She Knows It All** [12] 9-3
2397 **Wesbree Bay** [1] 7-8(bl) 2394 **Ever So Sharp** [11] 8-2
2361 **Amber Clown** [6] 8-10
14 ran 1½,1,1½,1,¾,2½,shhd (Mrs P P Dunn) W Charles Warwick, Warwickshire

2593 NEWPORT STAKES 3YO £1275 1m 1f Good/Firm 30 -17 Slow

2009 **PODEROSO** [7] (R Boss) 3-8-11 W R Swinburn 10/3: -004031: 3 b c Artaius - Twelve O'Clock (Hardicanute): Stayed on well to lead inside dist in a 3yo stakes at Wolverhampton: eff over 8/10f on gd & fast grnd: well suited by a sharp/easy course. 46
-- **NINOTCHKA** [4] (W Hern) 3-8-8 W Carson 3/1 FAV: 4-2: Easy to back on her belated reapp: tried to make all: gd effort & should win a small race soon: half sister to useful sprinter Novello, amongst others: stays 9f: acts on gd/firm grnd & on a gall trk. 40
1580 **SIMPLY DELICIOUS** [8] (H Candy) 3-8-8 W Newnes 4/1: -03: Ev ch & well clear of rem: gd effort after a fair abs & should continue to impr: see 1580. 36
-- **SAVE IT LASS** [3] (R Hollinshead) 3-8-8 S Perks 25/1: -4: Slowly into her stride, ran on late & should do btr next time: acts on gd/firm grnd. 08
-- **WATERSIDE LODGE** [10] 3-8-11 R Hills 33/1: -0: Easy to back on debut: never threatened leaders: closely related to several winners, notably useful 8/9f performer Miner's Lamp. 06
-- **WORTH DEBATING** [5] 3-8-8 R Fox 50/1: -0: Cheaply bought filly who is a half sister to several winners, incl very useful 7/12f performer Brandon Hill. 00
-- **Horton Glory** [1] 8-8 -- **Gardinia Lad** [11] 8-11
-- **Bombalong** [6] 8-8 2110 **Hillison** [2] 8-11(VIS)
10 ran 1,1½,15,3,3 (Mrs Andry Muinos) R Boss Newmarket

2594 BLOWWICH H'CAP STAKES (0-35) 3YO £2466 1m Good/Firm 30 +06 Fast [41]

2339 **KAIYRAN** [18] (M Stoute) 3-8-7 W R Swinburn 9/1: 3-0001: 3 gr c Dalsaan - Carota (Caro): Sn led & held on gamely in quite a fast run 3yo h'cap at Wolverhampton: lightly rcd colt who seems best when out in front: eff around 1m on fast & yld grnd: suited by an easy course. 28
2497 **GIVING IT ALL AWAY** [14] (H Beasley) 3-8-8 J Reid 14/1: 0021032: Ran on well: see 1819. 25
2497 **BICKERMAN** [8] (M Prescott) 3-8-6 G Duffield 4/1: 0010123: Fin well: in gd form: see 1906. 20
2086 **DOUBLE CHAI** [13] (A Jarvis) 3-8-2(vis) M Roberts 33/1: 0004044: Visored first time: best in 1701 (7f). 15
2267 **PEARL FISHER** [12] 3-8-9 W Newnes 20/1: 3304000: Best on soft grnd in 140 (10f). 21
2481 **SUPREME KINGDOM** [5] 3-8-12 S Perks 33/1: 0430000: Ran on same pace: best in 1783. 22
2250 **SMILING BEAR** [4] 3-8-13 T Ives 9/4 FAV: 00-030: Denied a clear run & btr in 2250 (7f). 00
•2339 **GERAGHTY AGAIN** [7] 3-9-7(bl) R Cochrane 6/1: 00-0410: Dwelt & no show: best in 2339. 00
2190 **FIRE ROCKET** [2] 3-8-4(BL) T Quinn 9/1: 0042400: Bl first time: early ldr: see 997. 00
2104 **MONSTROSA** [11] 3-7-13 W Carson 10/1: 0300030: No dngr: best in 2104: see 538. 00
2282 **Bakers Dough** [19] 8-3 2463 **Gershwin** [16] 7-12(vis)
2294 **Rue St Jacques** [6] 8-7 2497 **First Opportunity** [17] 8-5
2426 **Mr Kewmill** [9] 8-4(BL) 2132 **Aspark** [15] 8-2(bl)
2473 **The Stamp Dealer** [20] 7-13 •1937 **Hachimitsu** [3] 7-10
2508 **Hot Lining** [10] 8-5
19 ran 1½,1½,nk,¾,¾,¾,hd (H H Aga Khan) M Stoute Newmarket

2595 FORDHOUSES NURSERY H'CAP STAKES 2YO £1372 7f Good/Firm 30 -44 Slow [49]

1962 **LORD WESTGATE** [4] (M Usher) 2-9-2 M Wigham 9/2: 002021: 2 br c Hello Gorgeous - Riverlily (Green Dancer): Went on 2f out, sn hdd but rallied gamely to ddht in a nursery h'cap at Wolverhampton: very eff over 6/7f on gd & fast grnd: does well with forcing tactics & seems best on a gall trk. 48
2439 **FOUNTAINS CHOICE** [2] (K Stone) 2-8-2(2ow) G Brown 16/1: 3200201: 2 ch c Vitiges - Final Orders (Prince John): Led below dist & plugged on gamely when ddht in a nursery h'cap at Wolverhampton: half brother to several middle dist winners, incl useful Yard Bird: stays 7f well: acts on gd & fast grnd & on any trk. 34
2225 **RED HERO** [6] (M Jarvis) 2-9-7 T Lucas 7/1: 0033: Going on fin: gd effort under top weight 50
2391 **PHARAOH BLUE** [7] (C Brittain) 2-8-3 M Roberts 12/1: 001204: Ran on same pace: see 1883. 28
2377 **ALLOUSH** [3] 2-9-0 T Ives 5/1: 04030: Al mid-div: see 2377. 35
2178 **SPOTTER** [9] 2-9-4 W Carson 5/2 FAV: 01020: Well bckd: best over this C/D in 1433. 36
2435 **TEACHERS GAME** [8] 2-8-2(2ow) S Whitworth 12/1: 43400: No extra 2f out: see 2127 & 1583. 00
•2168 **LATE PROGRESS** [1] 2-7-7(2oh) M Fry 12/1: 0332110: Made most: best over this C/D in 2168. 00
2485 **AUNTIE CYCLONE** [10] 2-8-6 N Adams 6/1: 040000: Dwelt & no threat: see 1030. 00
9 ran ddht,1½,2,2,1½ (K H Jaffa) M Usher, Lambourn, Berks.
(Trevi Holdings Ltd) K Stone, Malton, Yorks.

2596 E.B.F. NUTFIELD FILLIES MAIDEN 2YO   £1337   5f   Good 65 -04 Slow

2292 ABHAAJ [4] (H T Jones) 2-8-11 A Murray 5/1: 21: 2 br f Kris - Ibtihaj (Raja Baba):
Quickly into her stride when a comfortable all the way winner of a 2yo fillies mdn at
Lingfield: first foal of a juvenile winner, who is a half sister to prolific stallion Danzig:
eff over 5/6f on gd grnd: clearly well suited by forcing tactics on a sharp trk: should
continue to impr.   50
2433 CHORITZO [2] (R Williams) 2-8-11 Pat Eddery 11/10 FAV: 22: Uneasy fav: ran on under
press but probably found this trip on the sharp side: worth another ch: see 2433.   44
2421 EBONY PRIDE [10] (Pat Mitchell) 2-8-11 B Thomson 14/1: 0403243: Al up there: quite
consistent though yet to get her head in front: see 1946.   38
2249 ALWAYS A LADY [8] (L Holt) 2-8-11 N Adams 25/1: 3404: Al front rank, kept on same pace
& will be suited by another furlong: acts on gd & soft grnd: best in 73.   28
2147 SUPER SURPRISE [11] 2-8-11 S Cauthen 10/3: 00: Hvly bckd: dwelt & never reached
ldrs: will probably prove btr suited by 6f plus: see 2147.   26
-- AUNT FRANCES [6] 2-8-11 B Rouse 25/1: 0: Kept on well from ½way on debut: speedily bred
filly who should impr on this next time: acts on gd grnd & on a sharp trk.   20
2433 Luck Be A Lady [9] 8-11   167 Johnkeina [7] 8-11
2167 Dragusa [14] 8-11   -- Godford [5] 8-11   2433 Lundy Isle [13] 8-11(vis)
2191 Tisserands [3] 8-11   -- Mayfair Doll [12] 8-11
13 ran   1,2½,4,½,2   (Hamdan Al-Maktoum)   H T Jones Newmarket

2597 GO HURDLING SELLING STAKES 3YO   £900   1m 2f   Good 65 -04 Slow

2163 LA CAZADORA [10] (R Williams) 3-8-8 B Thomson 14/1: -004031: 3 br f Faraway Times -
Hunting Call (Averof): Mkt drifter but led inside dist & kept on well to win a 3yo seller at
Lingfield (sold for 1,850 gns): first success: seems best over 10/13f: acts on gd & firm
grnd & on a sharp trk.   15
2560 NO STOPPING [3] (R Hannon) 3-8-11(bl) Pat Eddery 3/1: 0003232: Quick reapp: al prom,
not qckn: remains a mdn: see 2253 & 2073.   14
2300 GREENHILLS GIRL [1] (M Ryan) 3-9-0(viss) S Cauthen 6/4 FAV: 0002403: Dropped in class:
well bckd & tried to make all: clear of rem though best in 1909: see 380.   14
2309 LETOILE DU PALAIS [5] (B Stevens) 3-8-8 P Bloomfield 10/1: 0040424: Late prog: btr in 2309   00
2432 BAYDON QUEEN [4] 3-8-8 S Whitworth 7/1: 0-00000: Dropped to selling company for the
first time: outpcd after ½way & has been well btn in all her starts this term.   00
2560 NAME THE DAY [11] 3-8-8 W Newnes 8/1: 0-40: No dngr: see 2560.   00
2515 Sheer Class [9] 8-8(vis)   2315 Ess Jay Ess [6] 8-11
2417 Thai Sky [12] 8-8   -- Patsy Kelly [2] 8-11   2515 Alceba [7] 8-8
2271 Sea Trouper [8] 8-11(BL)
12 ran   2,1½,15,4,3   (Mrs L Sherrard)   R Williams Newmarket

2598 CELLAMAN BURR STAKES 2YO   £5972   7.5f   Good 65 -29 Slow

*1465 SUHAILIE [7] (H Cecil) 2-9-4 S Cauthen 11/10 FAV: 11: 2 ch c Nodouble - Slow Hot
Wind (Canonero): Smart, unbtn colt: justified hvy support, shaken up to lead inside dist for
an easy win in a valuable 2yo stakes at Lingfield: earlier a clever winner of a similar race
at Newmarket: clearly very eff around 7f & sure to stay 1m plus: acts on gd & firm grnd &
on any trk: very attractive sort with plenty of scope & looks a top class prospect for
next season.   75
2221 JUST A FLUTTER [8] (M Jarvis) 2-9-1 W Carson 11/4: 1102: Led below dist: caught a
real tartar: seemed well suited by this lngr trip: see 1916.   66
2146 ORNE [2] (J Tree) 2-8-11 Pat Eddery 5/1: 1243: Rr ch: consistent sort: see 2146, 1239.   62
2251 LAURIES WARRIOR [6] (R Boss) 2-9-1 M Hills 7/1: 2121124: Made most: consistent: see 1968.   64
2384 HARD ACT [5] 2-8-11 B Rouse 20/1: 1000100: Front rank most: likes this trk: see 2071.   56
+2329 PSALMODY [4] 2-8-11 A Murray 12/1: 00210: Fair effort in this btr class: see 2329.   50
1928 UPTOTHEHILT [3] 2-8-11 J Reid 33/1: 00: Mkt drifter: ch over 2f out: not disgraced: see 1928.47
7 ran   2,shhd,1,2,2½,1   (Sheikh Mohammed)   H Cecil Newmarket

2599 RON ASHDOWN HALF CENTURY STAKES 3YO   £2547   1m 4f   Good 65 +19 Fast

*2269 HIGH KNOWL [3] (B Hills) 3-9-4 B Thomson 5/1: 0-42311: 3 ch c High Line - Madina
(Beau Prince): Useful colt: in gd form & led below dist, comfortably in a fast run 3yo stakes
at Lingfield: earlier made all in a Newcastle mdn: half brother to several winners, incl useful
French miler Nonoalca:very eff over 10/12f on gd & fast grnd: acts on any trk: consistent sort   51
*2430 NORTHERN AMETHYST [2] (D Elsworth) 3-9-4(bl) Pat Eddery 1/1 FAV: 2023212: Again hvly bckd:
snatched up close home though btn on merit: in gd form & can win again soon: see 2430.   47
+2520 MISS SHIRLEY [7] (J Dunlop) 3-9-1 B Rouse 4/1: 3022413: Early ldr: in gd form: see 2520.   36
2152 HEAD OF SCHOOL [10] (Pat Mitchell) 3-8-11 J Reid 20/1: -004244: Led home turn, see 2017.   28
*2386 LYDIA EVA [4] 3-9-1 A Mcglone 20/1: 0-00010: No extra 2f out: see 2386: stays 12f.   26
1953 BELIEVE ME NOT [1] 3-8-8 W Carson 11/1: -00: Led after 4f, btn when hmpd dist: see 1953   14
2275 Village Hero [6] 8-11   -- Bradmores Girl [11] 8-8
823 Alpha Helix [9] 8-11   1813 Silent Running [5] 8-11
-- Sit In The Dark [8] 8-11
11 ran   2½,4,1½,2½,3   (K Abdulla)   B Hills Lambourn, Berks

00

2600 EBF NUTFIELD MAID.STKS DIV.2 2YO F   £1268   5f   Good 65 -24 Slow

2514 VERYAN BAY [9] (M Dickinson) 2-8-11 S Cauthen 12/1: 0001: 2 b f Storm Bird -
Queen Of Cornwall (Cornish Prince): Impr filly: al front rank & led below dist, ridden out
in a 2yo fillies mdn at Lingfield: well suited by this minimum trip: acts on gd & fast
grnd & seems best on a sharp trk.   40
2375 KEEN NOTE [2] (C Brittain) 2-8-11 Pat Eddery 10/3 FAV: 0022: Ran on well: see 2375 & 2153 36
2375 ATRAYU [4] (R Hannon) 2-8-11 B Rouse 14/1: 02003: Not btn far: gd effort: see 1946.   36
-2308 BAY WONDER [8] (G Pritchard Gordon) 2-8-11 W Ryan 7/2: 0002224: Made most: best in 2308. 33
2365 MISS RUNAWAY [11] 2-8-11 J Reid 7/2: 04230: Al prom: best in 1966 (6f): see 2365.   27
852 SALINAS [10] 2-8-11 M Hills 13/2: 00: Long abs: kept on late & should do btr next time:
acts on gd & yld grnd & on a sharp trk: see 852.   25
2375 MISS PONTEVECCHIO [5] 2-8-11 W Carson 6/1: 000: Never going pace: btr in 2375 (yld).   00
1946 Little Lochette [6] 8-11   --   Verbier [3] 8-11
2070 Blandell Beauty [7] 8-11   800   Ring Of Pearl [1] 8-11
11 ran   ¾,shhd,1,2,1   (R E Sangster)   M Dickinson Manton, Wilts

2601 MIDDLESEX HANDICAP 3YO+ F & M 0-35   £2628   7f   Good 65 -12 Slow   [34]

2184 HAYWAIN [8] (B Hills) 3-8-1(vis)(2ow) M Hills 25/1: -030001: 3 b f Thatching -
Contention (Connaught): Led below dist & held on well for her first win in a fillies h'cap at
Lingfield: eff over 7/8f on gd & fast grnd: acts on any trk: best when up with the pace.   19
2459 COURT TOWN [3] (R Hannon) 3-9-2 B Thomson 16/1: 4-00402: Fin. well, just held: see 2027. 33
2230 NEW EVIDENCE [7] (E Eldin) 3-8-6 M L Thomas 12/1: 0223203: Never nearer: mdn: see 1885. 20
2291 MIRANDA JULIA [1] (D Elsworth) 3-8-11 A Mcglone 25/1: 3000004: Gd late prog: stays 1m:
best form on a sharp trk: see 276.   23
2513 POINTED LADY [2] 3-8-8(1ow) S Cauthen 9/1: 0004200: Led 2f out: best in 2213 (7f).   20
2534 LADY WINDMILL [6] 3-8-11 G Morgan 50/1: -400000: No extra dist: prob stays 1m: see 158.   22
1581 CASCABEL [17] 5-9-10 R Guest 10/1: 2-04300: Trouble in running & never nearer: see 1460.   00
2340 HOPEFUL KATIE [14] 4-8-11 J Williams 15/2: 3030130: No threat & much btr over 7f in 2213 00
2490 SLYDONBYE [19] 4-8-4 A J Geran(7) 10/1: 0040-00: Speed over ½way: lightly rcd filly
who has yet to show any worthwhile form: stays 1m: acts on gd & firm.   00
2313 ANNABELLINA [4] 3-8-11 Pat Eddery 10/3 FAV: 0042300: Much btr over this trip in 2076.   00
2207 LUCKY STARKIST [20] 4-8-9 S Dawson 8/1: 1400040: Led briefly ½way: btr here in 2207 (7f) 00
2309 Nelsons Lady [11] 8-1   1991 Lydia Languish [10] 8-9
2184 Bertse Rose [5] 8-0   2210 Solo Singer [9] 8-7   2143 Indian Summer [18] 9-8
1246 Mumtaz Mayfly [12] 8-8(BL)   2519 Maiden Bidder [13] 8-4
2367 Shades Of Autumn [15] 8-3
19 ran   hd,1¼,1,shhd,hd,½   (D J Deer)   B Hills Lambourn, Berks

---

Official Going Given As GOOD/FIRM

2602 TURN TO YORKSHIRE H'CAP (0-35) 3YO+   £2413   7f   Firm 12 -14 Slow   [34]

2549 ZIO PEPPINO [22] (C Lloyd Jones) 5-8-0 A Shoults(3) 12/1: 4440301: 5 ch g Thatch -
Victorian Habit (Habitat): Led over 1f out, cmftbly in a 30 runner h'cap at Redcar: in '85
made ev yd to win at Ayr: eff at 6/7f, stays 1m: acts on hvy, likes fast grnd.   15
2038 CERTAIN AWARD [25] (J Watts) 3-9-3(BL) N Connorton 11/1 CO.FAV: 01432: Al prom:
bl first time today: remains in gd form: see 2038, 1425.   31
2414 HOPTONS CHANCE [27] (S Wiles) 4-7-7 M Fry 11/1: 0002433: Kept on final 1f:
running well: stays 1m: see 1839.   00
2513 JERSEY MAID [21] (C Tinkler) 3-8-7(vis) M Birch 16/1: 0000004: Made much: best effort
since 1051: seems to stay 7f: now wears a visor: see 1051.   15
2401 FOREVER TINGO [19] 4-7-8 L Riggio(6) 14/1: 0000300: Nearest fin: see 2401 (9f).   00
2264 CASSANDRAS DREAM [30] 5-7-8 A Culhane(7) 16/1: -000000: Al prom: see 1102.   00
2226 SAHRAAN [14] 3-9-1 M Roberts 12/1: -020000: Never beyond mid-div: best 528(1m,soft)   00
1500 WINTER WORDS [10] 7-8-9 G Duffield 12/1: 0-01100: Stable mate of winner: needed race?   00
2340 POKERFAYES [28] 7-7-9(bl) J Lowe 11/1 CO.FAV: 0204000: Early speed: best 1761.   00
2411 Bold Rowley [20] 8-1(4ow)   1165 Long Bay [17] 8-7(1ow)   2427 Master Music [15] 7-7(5oh)
2340 Top Othlane [1] 7-13(2ow)   2513 Sing Out Loud [29] 8-12   2101 Majestic Star [24] 7-9(1ow)
--   Recollect [26] 9-2   2513 Bubs Boy [7] 8-8   2424 Vendredi Treize [8] 9-10
1263 Corncharm [13] 9-6   2340 Marsiliana [2] 8-3   2513 Qualitair King [16] 8-6
1051 Low Flyer [18] 8-10   2039 Running Bull [23] 8-5   1983 Thirteenth Friday [3] 7-8(bl)
2367 Persian Ballet [11] 8-5   2397 Just A Bit [12] 8-1(bl)   2139 Spanish Infanta [9] 7-7(4oh)
2295 Cool Enough [4] 8-3   1824 Just The Ticket [6] 7-12 2497 Harleyford Lad [5] 7-12
30 ran   3,1½,1½,4,½   (M Vettraino)   C Lloyd Jones Clwyd

2603 RUNSWICK BAY CLAIMING STAKES 3YO   £976   1m 2f Firm 12 +05 Fast

2427 COLLYWESTON [5] (M Prescott) 3-8-5 G Duffield 9/4 FAV: -00121: 3 br f Thatching -
Kentucky Robin (Falcon): In fine form & led over 2f out, driven out in a 3yo claimer at

Redcar: earlier won a mdn claimer at Chester: half sister to several winners: eff at 7f,
seems to stay 10f well: acts on firm & soft grnd & on any trk.   27
2427 NAP MAJESTICA [4] (M Camacho) 3-9-0 D Nicholls 11/2: 0010432: Chall final 2f: just
btn: stays 10f: see 1256.   35
*2412 CHABLISSE [7] (R Whitaker) 3-8-3 D Mckeown 5/1: 3104413: Nearest fin: in gd form : see 2412.16
2103 LADY ATTIVA [2] (P Rohan) 3-8-8(5ow) C Dwyer 10/1: -000004: Never placed to chall:
best effort this term from this mdn: suited by 10f: acts on fast grnd & should be noted
for a seller.   19
2399 PAULS SECRET [12] 3-8-6 L Charnock 12/1: 0000000: Prom, ev ch: lightly rcd since 829.   11
2339 COUNTRY CARNIVAL [1] 3-8-7(BL) M Wood 12/1: 3000000: Fdd over 2f out: bl first time:
little form since 907 (sharp trk).   11
2497 CHARLTON KINGS [6] 3-9-0 S Perks 11/2: 0034000: Mkt drifter: no show: best in 2149 (9f) 00
2360 Bold Answer [11] 8-4   2478 Taxi Man [10] 8-8   2327 Dalveen Pass [9] 9-0
2110 Sybilly [3] 8-11   2508 Torriggia [8] 8-11
12 ran ½,4,1½,3,½,nk   (Lady Macdonald-Buchanan)   M Prescott Newmarket

2604 LESLIE PETCH MEM. H'CAP (0-35) 3YO+   £2537   1m 3f Firm 12 +09 Fast   [26]

2414 KOOKYS PET [2] (E Eldin) 3-8-6(bl) A Mackay 16/1: 0000401: 3 b c Baptism - Great
Aunt II (Mourne): Al there & led inside final 2f, driven out in a h'cap at Redcar: clearly
suited by this lngr trip: acts well on fast grnd: stays 11f well: seems to have no trk preferences. 21
2267 GOLDEN FANCY [15] (I Vickers) 9-9-6 D Nicholls 8/1: 32D3302: Held up: stayed on well.   25
2386 S S SANTO [1] (M Tompkins) 3-8-11 R Morse(5) 7/T CO.FAV: 2000123: Ch over 1f out: not
btn far: in fine form: see 1898.   24
2128 CHEVET LADY [14] (R Whitaker) 3-8-7 K Bradshaw(5) 20/1: 4200004: Kept on under press:
lightly rcd since 461: see 54.   12
2360 BUSTED FLAVOUR [8] 5-9-7 G Starkey 7/1 CO.FAV: 3003030: Ch over 2f out: see 2109.   17
2467 IM EXCEPTIONAL [12] 4-8-6 A Culhane(7) 12/1: 00-0300: Never nearer: best 2173: see 1747. 00
2175 SENDER [3] 3-9-4 M Roberts 7/1 CO.FAV: 0120200: Made some: fdd: btr 1964 (C/D).   00
2372 REGENCY SQUARE [9] 3-8-4 J Lowe 7/1 CO.FAV: 0441440: Dsptd lead 3f out: best in 2109.   00
2467 LOUD LANDING [17] 3-8-10 G Duffield 10/1: 0-03400: Twice below form 2300 (10f).   00
*1909 PONTYATES [13] 4-9-5 C Dwyer 9/1: 4000410: Fdd str: abs since btr 1909 (sharper trk).   00
*2008 Hot Betty [6] 8-12   2360 Nugola [7] 8-3   2173 Elarim [16] 9-2
2395 Glenderry [18] 8-2(vis)   2053 Seclusive [4] 9-6
2413 The Hough [10] 9-5   1918 Ivoroski [11] 8-6   2428 Mariners Star [5] 9-3(vis)
18 ran ½,nk,4,shhd,2   (T H Quek)   E Eldin Newmarket

2605 MULGRAVE MAIDEN STAKES 3YO+   £706   1m 6f Firm 12 -32 Slow

2269 POKEYS PRIDE [5] (R Sheather) 3-8-8 M Rimmer 9/4 FAV: -022031: 3 b c Uncle Pokey -
Strawberry Ice (Arctic Storm): Gained a deserved success (well bckd), leading close home in
a slow run mdn at Redcar: suited by todays 14f trip as he is a half brother to winning stayer
Jowoody: well suited by fast grnd & a gall trk: may even stay 2m.   38
2441 SNOW WIZARD [7] (O Douieb) 3-8-8(bl) Paul Eddery 7/1: -0042: Led 3f out, just caught:
impr colt who seems suited by todays lngr trip: acts on firm & yld: see 2441.   37
2306 KAFARMO [2] (G Harwood) 3-8-8 G Starkey 11/4: -03: Easy to back: ch over 2f out:
acts on firm & yld grnd: may stay 2m: see 2306.   33
2422 MSHATTA PALACE [8] (J Dunlop) 3-8-8 J Lowe 8/1: -004: Probably stays this 14f trip.   17
2464 WINTER HAVEN [4] 3-8-8 G Duffield 9/2: -00: Prom, no extra final 3f: see 2464.   16
2327 FIESTA DANCE [1] 3-8-8 M Birch 20/1: -00: Led over 11f: non-stayer?   10
2306 Grundys Own [10] 8-8   -- Boschendal [6] 9-6   1251 Garthman [9] 8-8
744 Spansyke [3] 8-8
10 ran ½,2½,10,nk,4   (Mrs M Mann)   R Sheather Newmarket

2606 DAVE MCHALE NURSERY H'CAP 2YO   £951   5f Firm 12 +02 Fast   [41]

2281 LAMB BECK [9] (J Jefferson) 2-8-4 L Charnock 9/2: 3031: 2 ch g Move Off - River Peterill
(Another River): Turned the tables with Paradise Coffee, making ev yd, cmftbly in a nursery
h'cap at Redcar: first success: half brother to a winning 2yo: seems well suited by front
running over 5f: likes fast grnd.   30
+2281 PARADISE COFFEE [10] (O Douieb) 2-8-8 Paul Eddery 6/4 FAV: 2312: Well bckd: 2nd most
of way: see 2281.   30
2261 MINIZEN LASS [5] (M Brittain) 2-8-4 K Darley 14/1: 2242003: Stayed on, nvr nrr: see 1867 21
2380 DANCING BELLE [12] (T Fairhurst) 2-9-6 G Duffield 10/1: 0001304: Al there: needs 6f?   34
1984 BECKINGHAM BEN [7] 2-8-13 S Morris 20/1: 0200: Prom most: lightly rcd since 859:
eff over 5f on fast grnd.   26
2334 BAD PAYER [3] 2-8-13 T Lucas 10/1: 3121000: Never nearer: best 1893 (sharpish trk).   26
2252 SPITTIN MICK [4] 2-9-6 M Birch 8/1: 2131100: Fin 7th: twice below 1814.   00
2398 THE GREAT MATCH [6] 2-9-6 D Mckeown 10/1: 00440: Lightly bckd: there 3f: lightly rcd.   00
2010 Swynford Princess [8] 7-9   2425 Miss Drummond [2] 7-13
2482 Danadn [11] 9-7   2425 Rosies Glory [1] 7-13
12 ran 1½,1½,1,nk,shhd,½   (Miss Beverley Oliver)   J Jefferson Malton, Yorks

2607 ROBIN HOOD BAY MAIDEN AUCTION STAKES   £822   1m Firm 12 -28 Slow

2325 MISS SARAJANE [3] (R Hollinshead) 2-7-10 A Culhane(7) 8/1: 0021: 2 b f Skyliner -
Taffeta (Shantung): Impr filly: led inside final 2f under press in a 2yo mdn auction at

Redcar: quite cheaply bought: eff at 6f, stays 1m: acts on firm & soft grnd & probably
on any track.   30
--   ZEUS [21] (W Hastings Bass) 2-7-13 M Roberts 9/1: 2: Stayed on well under press on
racecourse debut: half brother to 7f winner Penllyne Trooper: may stay further than 1m:
acts on fast grnd & a gall trk.   31
2471 CAMMAC LAD [22] (C Tinkler) 2-8-2 M Wood 5/1: 0000323: Ch over 1f out: in fine form. 32
2036 SLIPPERY MAX [4] (G P Gordon) 2-7-13 G Duffield 11/2: 04: Stayed on final 2f: on the
up grade & suited by this 1m trip: quite cheaply acquired gelding who can impr further:
brother to 10f winner Surprise Call.   26
2491 REGAL RAIDER [23] 2-8-5 E Guest(3) 9/2 FAV: 000: Prom, hung left inside final 2f:
stays 1m: see 2491.   27
2177 MYTYME [7] 2-8-2 M Rimmer 20/1: 00: Impr effort over this lngr trip: eff at 1m
on fast grnd: half brother to winners abroad.   21
2140 REATA PASS [14] 2-7-13 A Mackay 10/1: 0000: No threat: much btr 2140 (sharp 7f).   00
2379 GEOBRITONY [13] 2-7-13 J Lowe 10/1: 0400200: Quite lightly rcd since best 1480 (7f, firm) 00
2325 FRENCHGATE [5] 2-8-8 K Hodgson 10/1: 0000: Quite lightly rcd since initial promise
in 1510: should be capable of much btr than this.   00

2310 Regent Lad [9] 8-5		2466 Tyred Nsnookered [19] 7-13(VIS)	
1843 Dress Up [15] 7-13		-- Primetta Prince [17] 9-0	
2491 Gulf Of Gold [6] 8-5		2491 Melody Liner [16] 8-5	2470 Sawdust Jack [11] 8-2
2468 Call For Taylor [8] 7-13			2535 Pretty Soon [12] 7-13(BL)
2466 Victoria Star [10] 7-13			2511 Express Groupage [18] 7-10
-- Tower Bay [1] 7-10		2491 Banks And Braes [2] 8-11	
22 ran ½,½,1½,2½,1½	(G Smyth)	R Hollinshead Upper Longdon, Staffs	

Official Going Given As GOOD

2608 BROOKE SELLING STAKES 2YO   £893   6f   Good/Firm 20 -09 Slow

2405 PILGRIM PRINCE [6] (M Usher) 2-8-11 M Wigham 33/1: 00001: 2 ch g Mr Fluorocarbon -
Hasta (Skymaster): Turned up at 33/1, leading halfway & again close home in a 2yo seller at
Yarmouth (bought in 2,600 gns): first success: lightly rcd previously & was tried in a visor
last time but ran btr today without that aid: eff over 6f, should stay 7f: probably acts on
soft, well suited by fast grnd.   25
2150 BOLD HIDEAWAY [1] (R Sheather) 2-8-11(BL) P Robinson 7/2 FAV: 0402: Bl first time,
led/dsptd lead 3 out, no extra close home but clear of rem: rated 28 in 2026.   23
2323 CAUSEWAY FOOT [5] (N Tinkler) 2-8-11(bl) T Williams 14/1: 0004203: Ev ch: see 2150 (5f).   15
2465 LADY SUNDAY SPORT [4] (N Callaghan) 2-8-8(BL) W R Swinburn 7/1: 0230004: Blinkered
first time, ev ch: see 1907.   10
1881 LISASHAM [12] 2-8-8(bl) G Baxter 6/1: 00030: Prom most: much btr 1881 (gd).   05
1647 ROAN REEF [3] 2-8-11 Gay Kelleway(3) 20/1: 3430400: Abs, early speed: see 1088.   06
2218 RUSTIC EYES [9] 2-8-11 G Carter 6/1: 23000: AI rear: btr 2218.   00
2279 ENCHANTED COURT [8] 2-8-11 R Hills 8/1: 0000: Early pace: see 2279.   00

1598 Leg Glide [2] 8-8		1997 Miss Acacia [10] 8-8	2177 Pearlitic [11] 8-11
2547 Solent Knight [7] 8-11			
12 ran 1,4,1,2½,1	(C Cyzer)	M Usher Lambourn, Berks	

2609 BROOKE SELLING STAKES 2YO   £887   6f   Good/Firm 20 -06 Slow

2180 ITS BEEN RUMOURED [3] (R Simpson) 2-8-8 J Carr(7) 11/1: 001: 2 br f Red Sunset -
Love Child (Roi Soleil): Landed a gamble, leading final 1f in a 2yo seller at Yarmouth
(bought in 3,400 gns): first success but had only run twice previously: half sister to
winners abroad: sire smart & fast 2yo: eff over 6f, may stay further: suited by fast grnd.   23
2410 LEVEN LASS [2] (I Vickers) 2-8-8 T Ives 11/4 FAV: 00342: Tried to make all: acts
on firm & soft & stays 6f: may find a seller sooner: see 2323.   20
2168 THE CHIPPENHAM MAN [5] (M Tompkins) 2-9-2 R Cochrane 5/1: 022133: AI prom: see 1944.   22
1997 FANTINE [12] (N Tinkler) 2-8-13 P Robinson 14/1: 2140034: Mkt drifter, rcd alone: best 939   09
2323 HAZELS GIRL [6] 2-8-8(hd) W R Swinburn 5/1: 4020000: Wandered under press: see 2323.   00
2212 NATIONS ROSE [1] 2-8-8(BL) R Hills 12/1: 040: Prom most: see 2212: bl 1st time today.   00

596 Highfalutin Lymey [8] 8-11		2298 Sohams Taylor [9] 8-11	
2279 Nightdress [4] 8-13(bl)		-- Four Crowns [7] 8-11	
1665 Maureens Cavalier [10] 8-11		-- Little Law [11] 8-8	
12 ran 1½,3,6,3,2½	(T Ramsden)	R Simpson Upper Lambourn, Berks	

2610 LAVENDER LINEN MAIDEN STAKES 3YO   £1231   1m 6f   Good/Firm 20 -23 Slow

2464 TAP EM TWICE [4] (M Jarvis) 3-9-0(vis) G Carter 12/1: 2330431: 3 ch g Tap On Wood -
Twice A Month (Jammed Lucky): Gained an overdue success, dsptd lead final 2f & winning
narrowly in a slowly run 3yo mdn at Yarmouth : placed most other outings this season: wears
a bl nowadays: well suited by 14f, should stay 2m: likes fast grnd.   43

2441 AMBASSADOR [8] (W O'gorman) 3-9-0(BL) T Ives 6/4 FAV: -2232: Led 2 out but despite
the strongest driving, just failed to hold on: well clear of rem: proving rather exasperating.   42
2299 CURVACEOUS [6] (M Stoute) 3-8-11 W R Swinburn 5/1: -043303: Ran in snatches: twice
well below 1939 (11f).   27
2299 CYNOMIS [1] (W Hastings Bass) 3-8-11 P Robinson 11/1: -3004: Led 4f out, wknd qckly
final stages: best 2068 (12f).   27
2428 GREY SALUTE [7] 3-9-0 T Williams 10/1: -33030: Prom much, btr 2428 (12f).   29
2520 LA DUSE [3] 3-8-11 R Cochrane 20/1: -0300: Mkt drifter, no dngr: best 2129 (12f).   23
2202 THREE TIMES A LADY [2] 3-8-11 Gay Kelleway(3) 8/1: 2232200: Led 10f: btr 2000 (C/D):
has proved expensive to follow.   00
2464 DAWN LOCH [5] 3-8-11 R Hills 13/2: 0040: Nicely bckd, sn btn: see 2464.   00
8 ran   nk,12,hd,½,1½,2   (F Lee)   M Jarvis Newmarket, Suffolk

2611 JACK LEADER MEM.NURSERY HCAP   £5799   7f   Good/Firm 20 +01 Fast   [56]

2436 MONTERANA [10] (G Wragg) 2-9-7 P Robinson 13/2: 121: 2 b f Sallust - Aventina (Averof):
Very useful filly: winning for the 2nd time in 3 races, al prom & leading final stages, under
top weight, in a valuable nursery at Yarmouth Sept.16: first time out winner on the same trk:
well suited by fast grnd: eff 6f, suited by 7f & should stay 1m: likes Yarmouth.   62
1975 KING BALLADEER [6] (G P Gordon) 2-9-5 G Carter 14/1: 0312332: Mkt drifter, tried to
make al: consistent: see 1175.   57
2485 GLOBAL LADY [7] (W Musson) 2-8-4 M Wigham 16/1: 2103: Al there: in gd form: see 1843.   41
2479 SHADE OF PALE [5] (P Haslam) 2-7-11(BL) T Williams 11/4 FAV: 1224: Bl first time,
well bckd & dsptd lead most: see 2479.   29
2485 SHEER ROYALTY [1] 2-8-8 T Ives 10/1: 04100: Ev ch: btr 2153 (6f).   36
2485 RIOT BRIGADE [8] 2-8-13 G Baxter 13/2: 0033140: Btr 2485, 2016 (6f).   41
2283 SPEEDBIRD [3] 2-8-4 G Bardwell(7) 12/1: 00040: Ev ch in 7th: see 2283.   32
*873 OLD EROS [9] 2-8-6 R Cochrane 9/1: 10: Long abs, early pace: see 873.   34
*2249 MUMMYS LUCK [2] 2-9-1 D Mckay 9/2: 210: Prom most: btr 2249 (6f).   00
2391 WELSH ARROW [4] 2-9-0 W R Swinburn 8/1: 1340: Prom, wknd: see 1207.   00
10 ran   1½,½,2½,2,hd,shhd,½   (H Morriss)   G Wragg Newmarket

2612 BRIAN TAYLOR MEMORIAL EBF STAKES   £4635   1m   Good/Firm 20 +07 Fast

*2562 VERDANT BOY [3] (M Stoute) 3-9-3 W R Swinburn 13/8: -310211: 3 br g Green Dancer -
Favorite Prospect (Mr Prospector): Smart gelding: gained his second win inside 4 days, making
all & keeping on strongly in a 4 runner minor race at Yarmouth: comfortable winner of a well
contested Ladies race at Doncaster recently & earlier won a h'cap at Brighton: very eff over
7f/1m & acts on yld but is well suited by fast grnd: handles any trk: carries weight well:
in grand form.   73
1924 CHIEF PAL [4] (P Walwyn) 3-8-4 N Howe 5/1: 2123402: Despite only 4 runners, failed to
get a clear run though it probably made little difference: see 1486, 941.   56
2219 NAVARZATO   [1] (R Sheather) 3-8-13 R Cochrane 5/4 FAV: 11-2003: Disappointed
connections here: see 1147, 2219.   60
*2576 LIAM [2] (M Ryan) 3-8-6(BL) P Robinson 7/1: 0140414: Quick reapp: prom most: see 2576.   46
4 ran   2,3,4   (Sheikh Mohammed)   M Stoute Newmarket

2613 BECCLES MAIDEN CLAIMING STAKES 3YO   £1291   1m 3f Good/Firm 20 -53 Slow

2216 HOROWITZ [2] (L Cumani) 3-9-3 R Cochrane 4/5 FAV: 02-01: 3 b c Beldale Flutter -
Lady Minstrel (Tudor Music): Waited with, needed plenty of driving to gain the day close home
in a very slowly run 3yo claiming mdn at Yarmouth: rated 53 last season when splitting Allez
Milord & On Tenterhooks in a mdn at Newmarket: half brother to useful filly Mary Davies: stays
12f well: acts on fast grnd.   30
2386 TURMERIC [1] (D Morley) 3-9-3 T Williams 12/1: 0002042: Trouble in running, no extra
final stages, though only narrowly btn: ran to his best: see 1838.   28
2015 JUBILEE JAMBOREE [3] (A Hide) 2-8-2 P Robinson 14/1: -003003: Led 3f out, hdd final stages 11
1256 ELEGANT GUEST [5] (W O'gorman) 3-9-3 T Ives 12/1: -004: Waited with, no extra final 1f:
fair effort after long abs: see 494.   26
2293 NO BOLDER [4] 3-9-3 L Jones(5) 7/1: 00-0020: Ev ch: see 2092.   19
2083 PATRICKS STAR [6] 3-8-7 R Hills 5/1: -000020: Prom most: btr 2083 (9f).   02
2128 Tinas Lad [7] 8-7
7 ran   ½,1½,hd,3,4   (C St George)   L Cumani Newmarket

2614 NORTH DENES HANDICAP 3YO 0-35   £2250   6f   Good/Firm 20 +10 Fast   [38]

*2424 EASY LINE [1] (P Haslam) 3-9-7(7ex) T Williams 5/1: 0014311: 3 ch g Swing Easy -
Impromptu (My Swanee): In fine form & was winning second h'cap on the trot, leading ½way,
comfortably, at Yarmouth: won similar h'cap at Hamilton last time: earlier successful at
Newbury & Nottingham (first time out): half brother to a couple of winners: very eff over
6/7f on fast grnd, though does act on yld: can complete his hat trick in this mood.   41
2473 TAYLOR OF SOHAM [3] (D Leslie) 3-8-10 D Mckay 9/2: 1323232: Al there, btr 2473 (7f).   23
2424 TAMALPAIS [4] (H Collingridge) 3-7-12 B Crossley 33/1: 3000003: Ran by far her best
race since 283 (hvy).   08
2424 AITCHANDOUBLEYOU [10] (D Barron) 3-8-10 T Ives 14/1: 4000004: Never btr: see 1093.   19

768

2343 BUTHAYNA [8] 3-9-4(BL) R Hills 4/1 FAV: -000330: Bl first time, ev ch: btr 2343.   22
2424 BEECHWOOD COTTAGE [9] 3-8-11(bl) R Cochrane 9/2: 4402020: No threat: btr 2424.   10
2488 CORRALS JOY [2] 3-9-7 W R Swinburn 8/1: 00-1000: Led to ½way: see 205.   00
2416 CRESTA LEAP [5] 3-8-9(VIS) L Jones(5) 8/1: 4000040: Early pace: btr 2416 (5f).   00
1999 Famille Rose 0 8-8(vis)   1917 The Lidgate Star 0 8-3
10 ran   2½,1,nk,2,2   (B Lasala)   P Haslam Newmarket

BRIGHTON   Wednesday September 17th   Lefthand, Sharpish Undulating Track

Official Going Given As FIRM

2615 TOP TWENTY PHONOMATICS MAIDEN STKS 2YO £2166   7f   Firm 13 -10 Slow

2016 I TRY [11] (L Cumani) 2-9-0 Pat Eddery 11/10 FAV: 31: 2 b c Try My Best - Amenity
(Luthier) Impr colt: heavily bckd and led inside final 1f, ridden out in a 2yo mdn at Brighton
Sept 17: cost 52,000 gns: dam a winner over 10f: stays 7f well, should get 1m: acts on
fast ground: on the upgrade.   49
1903 FREEBYS PREACHER [7] (C Brittain) 2-9-0 T Quinn 9/2: 02: Well bckd: led 2f out:
not btn far and 6l clear 3rd: should gain compensation soon: will be suited by 1m: acts on fast grnd   47
1869 SNAAN [6] (H Cecil) 2-9-0 N Day 6/1: 03: Wk in mkt: ev ch from 2f out: improving
but seems one of his stable's lesser lights: eff at 7f on fast ground.   37
1762 SCHUYGULLA [5] (M Jarvis) 2-9-0 W Woods(3) 12/1: 34234: Nvr nrr: prob stys 7f: see 1475   32
2019 SEPARATE REALITIES [1] 2-9-0(bl) A Clark 7/1: 40: Friendless in mkt: ran on late:
better 2019 (C/D): will be suited by 1m.   31
2225 GOOD POINT [9] 2-9-0(BL) M Hills 12/1: 0200: Tried in bl: lightly raced since fine
effort in 777 and seems to have had a training setback.   23
2179 KING RICHARD [8] 2-9-0 B Rouse 10/1: 300: Never nearer 7th: prob stays 7f: see 1993.   00
1816 Mustakbil [10] 9-0   2225 Separate Boy [4] 9-0(BL)
1936 Ta Wardle [2] 9-0(BL)   1993 Harry Em [3] 9-0   1495 Prince Mac [12] 9-0
12 ran   ½,6,2½,½,4,shthd   (Dr M Boffa)   L Cumani Newmarket

2616 LICENSED TRADE CHARITY SELL HCAP 3YO 0- 25 £865 1m   Firm 13 -28 Slow   [22]

2342 MOSTANGO [1] (A Hide) 3-8-12(bl) B Rouse 9/2: 0000041: 3 ch g Last Fandango - Most
Appealing (Majority Blue) Gained his first win, led over 1f out, ridden out in a 3yo selling
h'cap at Brighton: well suited by 1m on gd and fast ground: runs well on an undulating trk.   15
1937 BEE KAY ESS [8] (R Holder) 3-8-10 J Reid 6/1: -4002: Made much: stays 1m: see 1216.   06
2174 SANDRON [9] (B Stevens) 3-8-6(vis) P Bloomfield 10/3: 0303003: Never nearer: btr 2174 (7f)   00
2417 FINDON MANOR [2] (M Tompkins) 3-9-5(bl) R Curant 15/2: 0000004: Fdd over 1f out.   05
2394 CHARDONNAY [4] 3-9-7 W Newnes 9/4 FAV: 0000040: Dropped in class: disapp since 431(6f)   02
2429 DAWN MIRAGE [5] 3-9-1 T Quinn 15/2: 00-0000: Fdd final 2f: see 1971.   00
963 Ashraf [3] 8-3(vis)   2597 Thai Sky [7] 8-3
8 ran   4,3,2,2½,8   (Mrs B Wilkinson)   A Hide Newmarket

2617 W & A GILBEY HANDICAP 0-50   £2847   1m 2f Firm 13 +02 Fast   [46]

2066 HAWAIIAN PALM [2] (J Tree) 3-9-10 Pat Eddery 4/1 FAV: -001001: 3 b c Hawaii - Bold
Fluff (Boldnesian) Useful colt: defied 9-10, led inside final 2f and again cl home gamely in
a h'cap at Brighton: earlier won a 3yo h'cap at Windsor: first time out last season won a
Salisbury mdn: half brother to sev winners: very eff at 10f: acts well on fast grd and
seems suited by a sharpish trk, tho' acts on any: carries weight well.   61
2516 MARSH HARRIER [9] (A Moore) 5-8-10 P Cook 8/1: 0041302: Led over 1f out: just caught:
another gd eff: see 2190.   38
2288 FOOT PATROL [7] (P Cundell) 5-8-0 A Mcglone 9/2: 1021043: Ran on final 1f: stays 10f.   23
2121 FIRE BAY [1] (P Haynes) 5-8-11 B Rouse 8/1: 2130-04: Nearest fin: finding his form.   30
2516 LORD IT OVER [14] 3-7-13 A Clark 11/1: 0002000: Stayed on final 2f: tricky ride:see 2022.   21
2516 LEONIDAS [12] 8-8-7 M Hills 12/1: 0041000: Led over 1m: see 1539.   18
2049 REDDEN [8] 8-8-5 W Newnes 8/1: 0-14040: Fdd inside final 2f: best first time out in 750.   00
2189 COUNT BERTRAND [5] 5-7-8 R Morse(3) 5/1: 0021000: Fin 9th: again below form 1673 (1m).   00
2481 HALO HATCH [3] 3-9-0(bl) S Whitworth 10/1: 3001200: Prom most: twice below 2149 (9f)   00
2190 The Wooden Hut [11] 7-7(14oh)   -- French Emperor [13] 7-7(6oh)
2374 Santella Pal [10] 7-7(12oh)   *2356 Wizzard Art [4] 8-0(1ow)
-- Summers Darling [6] 8-5
14 ran   nk,3,2,2½,1½   (K Abdulla)   J Tree Beckhampton, Wilts

2618 PHOENIX BREWERY NURSERY H'CAP 2YO   £3267   6f   Firm 13 +07 Fast   [56]

2435 LUCRATIF [2] (I Balding) 2-8-11 Pat Eddery 4/1: 11041: 2 b c Cure The Blues - Lucaya
(Mill Reef) Useful colt: made ev yard, cmftbly in quite fast run nursery h'cap at Brighton:
earlier won a similar event at Warwick and first time out a minor race at Bath: cost 48,000
gns as a yearling and is related to winners abroad: very eff at 5/6f with forcing tactics:
loves fast grd: no trk preferences.   51
2529 WHOS ZOOMIN WHO [1] (G Lewis) 2-7-8(1ow)(1oh) R Fox 8/1: 000102: No chance with winner,
tho' ran well: see 1997.   25
2511 TOUGH N GENTLE [7] (L Piggott) 2-9-7 B Crossley 11/4 FAV: 2312023: Al prom: another
gd run: see 2511.   51

2292 MARIMBA [4] (J Winter) 2-8-13 B Rouse 5/1: 233144: Never nearer: btr 2292, 2127:   37
2205 MUAD DIB [5] 2-8-3 P Cook 4/1: 23020: Nicely bckd: well below 2205: see 1629.   24
2026 STARS IN MOTION [8] 2-7-7(2oh) N Adams 20/1: 000300: There 4f: best 1675.   03
*1993 ANYOW [6] 2-9-0 J Reid 7/1: 3310: Early speed: abs since btr 1993.   00
2095 Ballantrae [3] 7-7(10oh)
8 ran   3,nk,2½,1,4,3   (Mrs John A Mac Dougald)   I Balding Kingsclere, Hants

2619 CLUB MIXER E B F STAKES   £2959   6f   Firm 13 +19 Fast

-2214 ALKAASEH [3] (H T Jones) 3-9-3 R Hills 5/4 FAV: 210-421: 3 b c Ela-Mana-Mou -
Tigeen (Habitat) Useful colt: well fav by the weights and led over 1f out, cmftbly, in a
fast run stks at Brighton: very lightly raced this term: winning 2yo at Yarmouth: half brother
to a useful Irish sprinter: very eff at 6f on fast ground.   57
2312 DURASINGH [9] (A Hide) 4-8-5 P Brette(6) 6/1: -22: Chance over 1f out: stiff task
and ran well: stays 6f and acts on firm and yldg ground: see 2312.   32
2258 AMIGO LOCO [6] (K Brassey) 5-9-12(bl) S Whitworth 5/2: 0040003: Led over ½ way:
has had a busy season: see 245, 70.   47
2370 DELAWARE RIVER [7] (B Gubby) 4-9-1 P Cook 33/1: 0240004: Al there: stiff task:see 748.   20
2319 BILLY WHITESHOES [4] 4-9-1 J Reid 33/1: 0003000: Very stiff task: see 1834.   08
2575 MOORESTAR [10] 3-8-6 N Adams 50/1: -000: Never nearer: very lightly raced colt
who has shown little in 3 outings.   02
2530 OCEAN TRADER [1] 3-9-8(bl) J Adams(7) 9/1: 0000000: Never went pace: twice below 2143.   00
2518 Toms Nap Hand [2] 8-2   2488 Kimble Blue [5] 9-5   2046 Linton Starchy [8] 8-5
10 ran   3,2,4,3,nk   (Hamdan Al Maktoum)   H T Jones Newmarket

2620 HOLSTEN PILS MAIDEN STAKES   £959   1m 4f   Firm 13 -20 Slow

2366 FORT LINO [6] (I Balding) 3-8-8 Pat Eddery 13/8 FAV: 4-22221: 3 ch c Bustino - Forliana
(Forli) Gained a deserved success, well bckd, led ½m out and stayed on well in quite slow
run 3yo mdn at Brighton: 2nd on all 4 starts prev this season: stays 12f well: acts on firm
and yldg ground and on any track.   45
2408 MIRAGE DANCER [7] (R Smyth) 3-8-8 M Hills 4/1: 2342402: Twice below 1469: lacks foot.   41
2422 SOLVENT [1] (M Jarvis) 3-8-8 P Cook 6/1: 4-20023: Ev ch in str: has been gelded since
early season: see 116.   31
2517 SPARKLIN PERFORMER [4] (B Sanders) 3-8-8 R Mcghin 33/1: 0-00444: Made some: stiff
task: in gd form: see 2517.   25
2299 NILE LARK [8] 3-8-5 B Rouse 8/1: 0-200: No threat: twice well below form 1833 (gall trk)   20
1494 BUSHIDO [3] 3-8-8(BL) A Clark 5/2: -240: Bl first time: mod 6th: twice well below
form 486 and appears difficult to train.   15
2366 Podsnap [5] 8-8   1831 Out Of Kindness [2] 8-5
8 ran   2,5,3,1,4   (Sheikh Mohammed)   I Balding Kingsclere, Hants

Official Going Given As GOOD

2621 NEWTOWN SELLING H'CAP STAKES (0-25)   £1007   7f   Firm 12 -06 Slow   [16]

2238 HIGHLAND TALE [14] (A Jarvis) 3-8-4 M Roberts 25/1: 0000401: 3 ch f Crofter - Tell
The Truth (Monseigneur) Was a surprise winner, led below dist for a runaway win in a selling
h'cap at Yarmouth (no bid): first success and little worthwhile form prev: eff over 6/7f on
fast ground.   10
2592 JACQUI JOY [17] (K Ivory) 3-8-8 G Bardwell(7) 25/1: 3000002: Dropped in class: led/
dsptd lead most: stays 7f tho' best over 5f in 1734 (tight trk).   02
2509 KEEP COOL [18] (R Hollinshead) 3-8-10 S Perks 6/1: 0200433: Al up there: see 2509.   03
1927 TOUCH THE SAIL [5] (M Tompkins) 3-8-4 M Rimmer 10/1: 0-04204: Best over 6f in 1771.   00
2342 GREENHILLS BOY [16] 3-8-13 R Cochrane 9/1: -00420: Btr here in 2342 (1m).   03
2342 HEATHGRIFF [13] 4-9-0 A Murray 4/1 FAV: 0000230: Ran on too late: btr here in 2014 (1m)   00
*2342 NIPPY CHIPPY [12] 3-9-0(bl) Gay Kelleway(3) 13/2: 0000010: Dsptd lead: wknd into
8th: best 2342 (1m).   00
2213 SHAHREEN [2] 5-8-4 G Duffield 13/2: 0003000: Early speed: btr over 5f here in 1849.   00
2411 Tiddlyeyetye [15] 8-13(bl)   2370 Ideoligia [4] 8-3(1ow)
--   Arnab [9] 9-11   2519 Russell Flyer [11] 9-4(bl)
2271 Shelley Marie [10] 9-4   2335 Montefiaso [3] 8-4
2319 Spring Pursuit [8] 9-9(bl)
15 ran   6,½,1,½,1,2,½   (Mrs M A Jarvis)   A Jarvis Royston, Herts.

2622 DE COURCY CHAMPAGNE MAIDEN STAKES   £1433   1m   Firm 12 +17 Fast

714 SAKER [1] (L Cumani) 3-8-8 R Guest 7/1: -0401: 3 ch c Coastal - Sarsar (Damascus) Useful
colt: despite long abs sn held a clear lead and held on gamely in a fast run mdn at Yarmouth:
cost $100,000 as a yearling: eff over 8/10f on gd and firm grd: acts on a gall trk: clearly
well suited by forcing tactics.   55
1184 BOLERO MAGIC [11] (H Cecil) 3-8-8 W Ryan 9/4 FAV: -22: Long abs: stayed on strongly,
not quite reach winner: will be suited by further: acts on gd and firm grd: should win soon.   54

2532 AUCHINATE [13] (G Harwood) 3-8-8 A Murray 12/1: -4303: Ran on same pace: see 2321.	40
2400 RIVART [10] (P Kelleway) 3-8-8 Gay Kelleway(3) 7/1: -00324: Btr over 10f in 2400 (yldg)	34
2490 DONOR [12] 4-9-2 M Wigham 50/1: -20000: Prom most: btr eff: see 1602.	31
2532 MR PASTRY [2] 3-8-8 P Robinson 4/1: -030: Much btr 2532 (stiff trk).	27

-- FOUNTAIN OF YOUTH [7] 3-8-8 R Cochrane 3/1: -0: Heavily bckd debutant: going on fin
and sure to improve next time: cost 100,000 gns as a yearling and is a half brother to smart
duo Katies and Millfontaine: acts on fast grd: one to keep an eye on.   00

2497 Bien Dorado [6] 8-8	2408 No Can Tell [14] 8-5	1586 Fairseat Close [9] 8-5	
2442 Highest Peak [3] 8-8	-- Makalu [5] 8-5	-- Bledsoe [8] 8-8	
2186 Cascading [4] 8-5			
14 ran ½,6,2½,1½,1½	(Sheikh Mohammed)	L Cumani Newmarket	

2623 EAST COAST LIFEBOAT H'CAP (0-50) 3YO+   £2704   1m 3f   Firm 12 -24 Slow   [45]

1642 WESHAAM [7] (B Hanbury) 3-9-4 G Duffield 6/1: 0132201: 3 b c Fappiano - Priceless
Asset (What A Pleasure) Useful colt: led ½ way and qcknd clear over 2f out for an easy win
in a h'cap at Yarmouth: most consistent this term, earlier won a 3yo h'cap at Doncaster and
has only once been out of the frame since: very eff over 10/12f: acts on hvy tho' best form
on fast ground: seems to act on any trk: can win again.   58
*2355 VAGUE MELODY [9] (L Piggott) 4-9-5 T Ives 5/1: 1134412: Not reach winner:in gd form
and saw out this longer trip well: should find a h'cap: see 2355.   42
2478 FRENCH FLUTTER [1] (R Sheather) 3-8-8 R Cochrane 9/1: 0413033: Best over 12f in 1160.   34
2286 MAGIC TOWER [4] (C Brittain) 3-8-7 G Baxter 14/1: 0-40234: Quite consistent: stays 11f.   32
2217 HIGHLAND BALL [3] 3-8-2 P Robinson 14/1: 0-00430: Led over 4f: much btr this C/D 2217   19
2420 SWEET ALEXANDRA [5] 3-7-7(bl) A Mackay 11/4 FAV: -431120: Much btr 2420: see 2093.   09
*1775 HANOOF [6] 3-9-0 W R Swinburn 3/2: -4310: Fdd into 8th: abs since 1775.   00

2415 Westray [11] 7-7	-- Carillon [8] 9-10	2516 Black Comedy [10] 7-11
2467 Irish Hero [12] 8-8(bl)		919 Markelius [2] 7-7(4oh)
12 ran 5,4,½,6,½,3,½	(Abdullah Ali)	B Hanbury Newmarket

2624 GOLDEN JUBILEE CHALL. TROPHY (H'CAP)   £7895   1m 2f   Firm 12 -102 Slow   [67]

2406 LOCH SEAFORTH [1] (H Cecil) 3-9-7 W Ryan 4/1: 2111121: 3 b c Tyrnavos - Marypark
(Charlottown) Very useful and much impr colt: regained winning form, led early and again dist, cmftbly,
in slow run, val 3yo h'cap at Yarmouth: earlier won minor races at Catterick, Beverley and
Brighton and a h'cap at Windsor: very eff over 10/12f on firm or gd ground: acts on any trk
tho' runs well on a sharp/easy one: in fine form.   72
*2426 HARD AS IRON [6] (P Haslam) 3-7-10 T Williams 11/4 FAV: 1112212: Just btn: in fine
form: see 2426.   45
2438 NIGHT OUT PERHAPS [4] (G Wragg) 3-9-4 P Robinson 7/2: 1140133: Led ½ way till dist: 64
2155 GORGEOUS ALGERNON [3] (C Brittain) 3-8-4 G Baxter 9/1: 0202004: Late prog: best 1384.   48
2303 OPEN HERO [2] 3-8-7 M Roberts 7/1: 4211-00: Btn below dist: lightly raced this term:
showed useful form in '85, winning nurseries at Warwick & Yarmouth: very eff over 1m on good/
firm and yldg ground: acts on any track.   48
2404 MARSHAL MACDONALD [5] 3-7-10 A Mackay 9/2: 0044030: No threat: best 2404 (stiff trk)   32
6 ran   nk,1½,1½,1½,3   (Sir David Wills)   H Cecil Newmarket

2625 DENIS BUSHBY CLAIMING STAKES 2YO   £2495   7f   Firm 12 -21 Slow

2227 LAST STAND [10] (J Hindley) 2-9-0 P Robinson 11/2: 00331: 2 b f Mandrake Major -
Siouxsie (Warpath) Led 2f out and just held on in a 2yo claiming stks at Yarmouth: cost
5,400 gns and is a sister to sev winners: seems best over 7f on fast grd: runs well at
Yarmouth.   35
2191 NO LIE [17] (G Pritchard Gordon) 2-8-10 G Duffield 9/1: 032: Just failed: stayed on
well over this longer trip and should be suited by 1m: acts on gd and firm grd: on the upgrade.   30
1946 HAILEYS RUN [6] (G Pritchard Gordon) 2-9-3 W Ryan 16/1: 3033403: Not btn far: stays
7f: see 1475.   36
2320 ROUGH DANCE [15] (W Jarvis) 2-9-3(BL) R Cochrane 7/2 FAV: 0424: Bl first time: nicely
bckd: stayed on well and btn less than 1l: see 2320 & 1598.   35
2425 COLLEGE WIZARD [4] 2-8-7 M Rimmer 33/1: 421400: Stays 7f: see 1692.   21
2435 CASTLE CORNET [18] 2-9-3 A Murray 13/2: 0004000: Prom most: eff over 6/7f: see 187.   25
2405 QUE PASA [4] 2-8-9(VIS) T Williams 4/1: 0240: Visored first time: btr 2334 (5f yldg)   00
*2323 DOHTY BABY [8] 2-9-0 R Guest 10/1: 030010: No threat: btr 2323 (5f soft)   00

1572 Bumptious Boy [2] 9-3	2352 Tinas Beauty [19] 8-4	2499 Main Brand [14] 8-4
-- Raunchy Rita [13] 8-2	2177 Ive No Idea [16] 8-5(3ow)	
-- Taylor Cares [11] 8-3(1ow)		1692 Princess Michico [7] 8-4
2298 Musical Chorus [3] 8-4		-- Choisun [5] 8-9
2405 Telegraph Folly [1] 9-3		-- Sicilian Tony [12] 9-3
19 ran shthd,½,nk,2,1½,1½,½,nk	(Charles Philipson)	J Hindley Newmarket

2626 E.B.F. HASTINGS MAIDEN STAKES 2YO   £3162   6f   Firm 12 +20 Fast

2345 HYDRAULIC POWER [2] (M Albina) 2-9-0 A Bond 10/1: 01: 2 ch c Northfields - Princess
Biddy (Sun Prince) Btr for recent debut and went on 2f out for a cmftble win in a very fast
run 2yo mdn at Yarmouth: cost 115,000 gns as a yearling and is a half brother to winning
sprinter Fawley's Girl: eff over 6f on gd and firm grd: on the upgrade.   54

-- IMPERIAL FRONTIER [5] (L Cumani) 2-9-0 R Cochrane 6/4 FAV: 2: Heavily bckd debutant: stayed on well after slow start and sure to improve: cost $300,000 as a yearling and is bred to be suited by further: acts on fast grd.   41

777 FORESIGHT [4] (L Piggott) 2-9-0 T Ives 6/1: 03: Long abs: ran on same pace: should improve when tackling a longer trip: acts on firm grd: see 777.   38

-- OFFICER KRUPKE [13] (H Cecil) 2-9-0 W Ryan 7/1: 4: Kept on promisingly and should do better next time: cost $30,000 as a yearling: should stay 7f+: acts on firm grd.   30

-- LOUD APPEAL [11] 2-9-0 W R Swinburn 6/1: 0: Early speed: not given a hard race and sure to improve next time: half brother to sev winners, incl useful juv Mums: acts on fast grd   22

-- KNOCKIN EXPRESS [6] 2-9-0 G Carter 33/1: 0: Friendless in mkt: prom over ½ way: cheaply bought colt who is a half brother to a winning sprinter in States.   18

-- MOLASSES MAN [10] 2-9-0 P Robinson 9/2: 0: Fin 7th on debut: active in mkt and should do better than this: cost 26,000 gns as a yearling: should stay to 7f winner Ghika.   16

2320 MILL TRIP [8] 2-9-0 G Duffield 17/2: 030: Bckd from 12/1: btr 2320 (6f soft)   00

-- Alajib [9] 9-0	-- Prescription [14] 9-0	-- Crown Ridge [7] 9-0
2223 Fox Path [3] 9-0	2444 Try Hills Supplies [12] 9-0	
2484 Apiarist [1] 9-0 R		

14 ran   4,1,3,4,1½,½,½,½   (Muttar Salem)   M Albina Newmarket

---

AYR   Wednesday September 17th   Lefthanded, Fair Galloping Trk

Official Going Given As GOOD/FIRM

2627 KILKERRAN AMAT RIDERS STAKES   £1451   1m 7f   Firm 10 +03 Fast

*2201 OSTENSIBLE [1] (G Harwood) 3-10-13 Amanda Harwood 13/8: 3000111: 3 b c Alleged - Proud Pattie (Noble Commander) Very useful, impr colt: al prom: qcknd well to lead cl home in an amateur riders race at Ayr: earlier won val h'caps at York and Sandown, after being employed as a pacemaker for Bakharoff: last season won a Leicester mdn on his sole outing: very eff over 12/15f: suited by fast grd and a gall trk: may well extend his winning sequence.   70

*2338 PAEAN [3] (H Cecil) 3-10-13 Franca Vittadini 11/8 FAV: -121112: Led/dsptd lead thr'out: no extra cl home: most consistent this season: see 2338.   69

2338 HERRADURA [5] (M Prescott) 5-11-0(vis) Maxine Juster 20/1: 02D3203: Ran to his best: 49

2338 SHTAIFEH [2] (H T Jones) 3-10-4(4ow) Mr T T Jones 5/1: 1-024: Made much: btn 2f out: better in 2338.   40

1745 CAROUSEL ROCKET [9] 3-10-3 Sandy Brook 50/1: 4210340: Abs: best with some give: see 968   19

2326 THE CANNY MAN [7] 3-9-0 Geraldine Rees 66/1: -000100: Much btr over this trip in 1544   00

-- Biras Creek [11] 11-0(bl)	827 Night Guest [8] 10-13(6ow)
2093 Touchez Le Bois [1] 11-0	2480 Red Duster [6] 11-0
2562 Cri De Grace [1] 10-7	

11 ran   ½,4,10,20,6   (K Abdulla)   G Harwood Pulborough, Sussex

2628 E B F SANDGATE MAIDEN STAKES 2YO   £3733   1m   Firm 10 -12 Slow

2225 KRIBENSIS [9] (M Stoute) 2-9-0 A Kimberley 5/1 CO FAV: 01: 2 gr c Henbit - Aquaria (Double-U-Jay) Useful colt: showed a gd turn of foot when leading below dist in a 2yo mdn at Ayr: cost 125,000 gns and is a half brother to useful sprinter Cooliney Prince and a couple of middle dist winners: eff over 7/8f and should stay further: acts on fast ground and on a gall track: broke the 2yo course record here.   49

1982 FABRINA [6] (J Watts) 2-8-11 N Connorton 10/1: 02: Ran on well: acts on fast grd: on the upgrade and should win a small race soon: see 1982.   44

2468 LORD JUSTICE [8] (M Dickinson) 2-9-0 G Starkey 5/1 CO FAV: 03: Kept on well: acts on firm: see 2468.   43

2263 ANGEL CITY [4] (J Dunlop) 2-9-0 W Carson 7/1: 004: Al prom: on the upgrade: see 2044.   43

2468 GOLDEN TREE [11] 2-9-0 K Darley 33/1: 0000: Btr eff: stays 1m: see 1049.   40

2019 STRING SECTION [7] 2-9-0 P Waldron 5/1 CO FAV: 0330: Led/dsptd lead most: see 2019 (7f)   40

2067 IRISH BRIGADIER [10] 2-9-0 M Birch 6/1: 420: Fin 7th: acts on gd and firm: see 1872.   00

1587 NONSUCH PALACE [2] 2-9-0 S Cauthen 9/1: 0300: Abs: led/dsptd lead over ½ way: best 1239   00

-- STAR AFFAIR [5] 2-9-0 D Nicholls 10/1: 0: No threat on debut: cost 6,000 gns and is a brother to winning juv Starjay: likely to improve next time.   00

| -- Trojan Legend [1] 9-0 | 2468 Prince Zamaro [12] 9-0 |
| -- Strong Sea [3] 9-0 | |

12 ran   1,2,hd,1½,nk,4,½,½   (Sheikh Mohammed)   M Stoute Newmarket

2629 DICK PEACOCK HANDICAP 0-60   £4624   1m   Firm 10 -18 Slow   [44]

+2296 ALL FAIR [11] (P Haslam) 5-9-7(vis) G French 6/1: 0021011: 5 b h Free State - Be Honest (Klairon) In grand form, led below dist and stayed on strongly to win quite a val h'cap at Ayr: earlier won similar races at Ripon & Salisbury: in '85 won at York & Ripon when trained by R Whitaker: very eff over 1m, stays 10f well: acts on fast grd tho' is suited by some give: best when up with the pace: wears a visor.   48

2526 KNIGHTS SECRET [3] (M H Easterby) 5-8-12 M Birch 7/2 FAV: 0340422: Well bckd: just held on to 2nd place: see 2390 & 815.   37

2296 SIR WILMORE [6] (E Weymes) 4-8-7 E Guest(3) 10/1: 0010003: Fin well and not btn far: returning to form and can win a small h'cap: see 1698.   32

*2303 SOLO STYLE [10] (G Lewis) 3-9-4 P Waldron 13/2: 1014114: Al there: in grand form: see 2303. 48
2437 EMERALD EAGLE [2] 5-8-3 R Lines(3) 12/1: 2010000: Stayed on well: see 2231 & 1976.   25
2264 HEAVENLY HOOFER [7] 3-7-11(5oh) L Charnock 33/1: 1031000: Tried to make all: gd eff
against older horses and should win again when dropped in class: see 1864.   23
2475 READY WIT [8] 5-9-2 D Mckay 7/1: 0000020: Fin 8th: btr 2475: see 361.   00
2475 SHELLMAN [13] 4-8-6 P Burke(7) 7/1: 0000030: Dwelt and no threat: btr 2475: see 55.   00
2414 Sillitoe [5] 7-10   2549 Kamaress [3] 7-7(BL)(1oh)
1109 Xhai [12] 9-2   2536 Moninsky [4] 7-8   2086 Kings Badge [9] 8-7
13 ran   1,shthd,1,½,1½,1,1½,1½   (S A B Dinsmore)   P Haslam Newmarket

2630 DOONSIDE CUP   £10571   1m 3f Firm 10 +23 Fast

2452 SANTIKI [1] (M Stoute) 3-8-3(1ow) A Kimberley 11/4: 4133131: 3 ch f Be My Guest -
Sairshea (Simbir) Smart filly: chall over 1f out and despite going slightly left led cl home,
breaking the course record in val Doonside Cup (Listed) at Ayr: earlier successful in another
Listed race at Ayr and a mdn at Thirsk: also placed in Group races at Ascot and Haydock:
eff at 10f, stays 12f well: acts on hvy, very well suited by gd and fast grd: no track
preferences, game and consistent.   77
2461 RAKAPOSHI KING [5] (H Cecil) 4-9-0 S Cauthen 10/11 FAV: -311432: Led till near fin:
lost nothing in defeat: remains in grand form: see 2461.   78
*2354 BOON POINT [3] (J Dunlop) 3-8-5 W Carson 13/2: 3001113: Chance 2f out: gd eff in
this company and remains in fine form: see 2354.   68
*2331 RANA PRATAP [2], (G Lewis) 6-8-11 P Waldron 20/1: 2042014: Stayed on under pressure
and ran very well in this company: stays 11f: see 2331.   60
+2206 LEADING STAR [4] 4-8-11 G Starkey 6/1: 4302410: Not much room over 2f out: much btr 2206 59
2175 TURINA [6] 3-7-13 J Lowe 200/1: -003000: Impossible task: best 1775.   06
6 ran   nk,2½,shthd,1½,30   (R E Sangster)   M Stoute Newmarket

2631 EGLINTON & WINTON MEM HANDICAP   0-60   £3818   2m 1f Firm 10 -05 Slow   [47]

*2492 BANNEROL [3] (G Harwood) 3-9-1(3ex) G Starkey 11/10 FAV: -0111: 3 b c Smarten -
Queen's Standard (Hoist The Flag) Promising young stayer: well bckd and led over 1f out
very cmftbly in a 3 runner h'cap at Ayr: earlier successful in a h'cap at Nottingham and
a mdn at Redcar: cost $41,000 as a yearling and is a half brother to 2 winners: eff at 14f,
stays 2m+ well: acts on gd and fast grd and a gall trk: looks sure to win more staying races.   55
2480 SPECIAL VINTAGE [2] (J Fitzgerald) 6-9-7(BL) S Cauthen 5/2: 033042: Led over 2m:
gd effort: see 778 : tried in blinkers today.   46
*2087 JURISPRUDENCE [1] (J Watts) 3-7-13 W Carson 9/4: -000113: Dsptd lead 1m out: well
below 2087.   26
3 ran   1½,8   (K Abdulla)   G Harwood Pulborough, Sussex

2632 KILBRIDE HANDICAP   0-35   £2369   5f Firm 10 +09 Fast   [35]

2513 WARTHILL LADY [12] (M Brittain) 4-8-4(7ex) K Darley 16/1: 0040101: 4 b f Hittite Glory
Suffice (Faberge II) In fine form lately and fin well to lead cl home in a h'cap at Ayr:
earlier won a similar event at Hamilton: in '85 won again at Ayr: very eff at 5f, stays 6f:
acts on yldg, loves fast grd and a gall trk: genuine.   21
2586 PENDOR DANCER [14] (K Ivory) 3-8-11(vis) A Shoults(5) 9/2 JT FAV: 1010232: Made
almost all: retains his form really well: see 2586.   27
2245 CAPEABILITY POUND [13] (N Bycroft) 3-8-11(BL) R Lines(3) 25/1: 2000003: Not clear
run 2f out: fin well when getting some daylight: unlucky? Best eff since 1027 and may win soon.   26
2537 THRONE OF GLORY [10] (D Chapman) 5-9-6 D Nicholls 7/1: 4002304: Al there: another gd
eff: see 2513.   32
2411 FOOLISH TOUCH [1] 4-9-6(vis) C Dwyer 12/1: 0440240: Nearest fin: running well: see 2256   30
2289 NATIVE RULER [3] 5-8-0 A Carlisle 20/1: -012300: Not btn far: gd eff: see 1070 (seller)   08
2513 BAY BAZAAR [2] 4-8-5(bl) M Birch 10/1: 0000040: Much btr 2513 (6f).   00
-2322 DEBACH REVENGE [8] 4-7-7 M Fry 7/1: 0040020: Dwelt start: much btr 2322.   00
2402 JACKIE BLAIR [11] 4-9-1(bl) S Cauthen 9/2 JT FAV: 0000320: Early speed, sn fdd: well
below 2402.   00
2362 Miss Primula [5] 8-11   2204 Rambling River [7] 9-12(vis)
2586 Mendick Adventure [9] 8-12   2586 King Charlemagne [6] 10-0
1718 Russian Winter [4] 7-9(vis)
14 ran   1,nk,nk,½,½   (Mel Brittain)   M Brittain Warthill, Yorks.

THE CURRAGH   Saturday September 13th   Righthand Galloping Track

Official Going Given As GOOD/FIRM

2633 GROUP 3 BROWNSTOWN MATRON STKS 3YO+   £11550   1m   Good/Firm .

1107 GREY GODDESS (E O'grady) 3-8-7 S Craine 10/1: 03-1011: 3 gr f Godswalk - Thialla
(Busted) In a rough race, came from behind to lead inside final 1f cmftbly in a Gr 3 race at
the Curragh: has met defeat only once in 4 races this term, earlier scoring at Gowran and the
Curragh: acts on fast and yldg going: very eff over 7f/1m.   75
1592 LAKE CHAMPLAIN (D Weld) 3-8-10 D Parnell 5/2 FAV: -212302: Best eff since 1331 and
prob does not stay 12f.   74
2505 MUMMYS FAVOURITE (J Dunlop) 3-8-10 D Gillespie 6/1: -341433: Badly bumped at the dist:
gd eff: see 1487.   68
2145 ROYAL LOFT (W Jarvis) 3-8-12 C Roche 6/1: 1-22144: Gd eff in this btr company and
continues to improve: see 1851.   69
2192 ADORAMUS 3-8-10 K J Manning 14/1: -4400: Gd eff: see 2192.   66
2145 THE BEAN SIDHE 3-8-12 C F Swan 12/1: -130100: Btr on soft in 2006.   67
2506 BERMUDA CLASSIC 3-8-12 P V Gilson 3/1: 0-3204D: Barged his way thr' at the dist,
fin 4th but disqualification was a formality: see 2351.   00
1592 Welsh Fantasy 9-1   2192 Kemago 8-12   -2349 Amonique 8-7
-- Shardah 8-7
11 ran   1½,2½,hd,½,nk   (Mrs K Watts)   E O'grady Ireland

THE CURRAGH   Sunday September 14th   Righthand Galloping Track

2634 GROUP 1 MOYGLARE STUD STKS 2YO FILLIES   £65600   6f   Good/Firm

+2113 MINSTRELLA (C Nelson) 2-8-11 J Reid 9/10 FAV: 421211: 2 ro f The Minstrel - Flight
Dancer (Misty Flight) Very smart filly: al prom, qcknd clear inside final 1f to win Gr 1
Moyglare Stud Stks at the Curragh: last time won val Gr 1 Heinz 57 Phoenix Stks and earlier
won Chesham Stks (Listed) at Royal Ascot setting a new 2yo course record: related to sev
winners, notably very smart American filly Misty Gallore: very eff at 6f, should be suited
by further: acts on fast and gd/yldg and on any trk: best when held for a late chall and
will remain very hard to beat.   83
+2235 POLONIA (J Bolger) 2-8-11 Pat Eddery 6/4: 1101312: Tried to make all, lost nothing
in defeat against this brilliant winner: see 2235.   76
2235 INDIAN LILY (C Brittain) 2-8-11 M Roberts 20/1: 1443: Someway behind the first 2 but
confirmed the improvement shown in 2235.   62
-- ANGELS SHARE (E O'grady) 2-8-11 S Craine 10/1: 4: Winner of a mdn at Phoenix Park
earlier in the month: eff over 6f and gd ground.   56
1108 INDEXS 2-8-11 D Parnell 20/1: 2100: See 1006.   52
+2482 NAIVE CHARM 2-8-11 G Curran 66/1: 12010: Stiff task: see 2482 (5f).   46
638 Kalorama 8-11   1591 African Sunrise 8-11
8 ran   2½,5,2½,1½,2½   (E Evans)   C Nelson Lambourn

2635 GROUP 1 NATIONAL STAKES 2YO C & F   £66050   7f   Good/Firm

2384 LOCKTON (J Hindley) 2-9-0 M Hills 7/2: 201131: 2 ch c Moorestyle - Bridestones
(Jan Ekels) Very useful colt: got the btr of a sustained battle in final 1f when a hd winners
of Gr 1 National Stks at the Curragh: earlier won at Newmarket and York: half brother to Blue
Brocade, winner over 11f: very eff at 7f, sure to be suited by 1m+: acts on fast grd and
on a gall trk.   71
-- BABA KARAM (D Cordell Lavarack) 2-9-0 D Gillespie 12/1: 2012: Fought a sustained dual
with the winner in final stages, just touched off: winner of a mdn at Naas recently over 7f
on fast grd: useful sort in the making.   70
2384 ROCK CHANTEUR (C Nelson) 2-9-0 J Reid 5/1: 003: Not btn far in a cl fin: fine eff
and continues to improve: must win soon: see 2384.   68
2460 MOREWOODS (I Balding) 2-9-0 Pat Eddery 3/1 JT FAV: 11434: Best 1606 (6f).   66
-- BEST SOLUTION 2-9-0 D Parnell 8/1: 10: Winner of his only prev race, a mdn over
this C/D last month: suited by give in the ground.   58
-2377 FRENCH SONNET 2-9-0 M Roberts 20/1: 020: Stepped up considerably in class here.   57
2113 FLAWLESS IMAGE 2-8-11 C Roche 3/1 JT FAV: 100: Fin 7th: see 2113.   00
-- Rictorious 9-0   -- Kamplight 9-0
9 ran   hd,½,1,4,½   (A Gibson)   J Hindley Newmarket

LONGCHAMP   Sunday September 14th   Righthand Galloping Track

Official Going Given As GOOD/SOFT

2636 GR 3 PRIX DE LA ROCHETTE 2YO   £18031   1m   Good/Soft

-- GRAND CHELEM [2] (R Collet) 2-8-9 Y Saint Martin : 11: 2 b c Be My Guest - Racquette
(Ballymore) Promising French colt: fav, when gaining a narrow success in Gr 3 Prix La Rochette
at Longchamp: winner of his only prev race: well suited by 1m, should stay further: acts
well on soft ground.   70
-- DON MARIO [6] (C Head) 2-8-9 G W Moore 12: Just btn: gd eff on only 2nd ever outing.   70

774

-- ZINBEAU [1] (R Touflan) 2-8-6 A Badel   : 34423: Creditable 3rd and evidently acts on soft.   62
-- TREMPOLINO [7] (A Fabre) 2-8-9 C Asmussen : 14: -   62
7 ran   shthd,2,1½   (R Strauss)   R Collet France

2637 GROUP 3 PRIX FOY 4YO+ COLTS & FILLIES   £17314   1m 4f   Good/Soft

468 MERSEY [3] (P L Biancone) 4-8-8 Y Saint Martin : 3111-21: 4 gr f Crystal Palace -
Martingale (Luthier) Smart French filly:: prevailed in a blanket fin to Gr 3 Prix Foy at
Longchamp: has been off the trk since narrowly btn in Gr 1 Prix Gany at Longchamp May 4: in
fine form last Autumn winning at Evry, Longchamp and Gr 1 Prix Royal Oak again at Longchamp:
eff between 10 & 15f and acts on firm and soft grd tho' prob prefers the latter: runs well
at Longchamp.   78
2194 SIRIUS SYMBOLI [1] (P L Biancone) 4-8-12 M Philipperon : 3-03042: Just btn in a
very tight fin: best eff yet in Europe from this Japanese horse: eff over 12f on soft grd.   80
1595 ANTHEUS [6] (C Head) 4-8-12 G W Moore : 0-12303: Very cl 3rd: see 1352.   80
*2348 LEADING COUNSEL [5] (M V O'brien) 4-8-11 C Asmussen : 1021-14: Also involved in
this very cl fin: see 2348.   79
*2357 PERSONA [4] 4-8-12 A Gibert : 0030110: 3l 5th behind the bunched finishers: see 2357.   74
2195 VERTIGE [2] 4-8-13 D Boeuf : 2100000: Best 98.   74
6 ran   nk,shtnk,shtnk,3,½   (D Wildenstein)   P L Biancone France

2638 GR 1 PRIX VERMEILLE 3YO FILLIES   £71095   1m 4f   Good/Soft

*2196 DARARA [2] (A De Royer Dupre) 3-9-2 Y Saint Martin : 11211: 3 b f Top Ville -
Delsy (Abdos) Very smart, impr French filly: qcknd clear for an easy 5l win in a Gr 1 Prix
Vermeille at Longchamp: first time out winner at St Cloud and last time won at Deauville:
eff 10f, well suited by 12f: acts on gd and soft grd: fast impr filly who is rather diminutive
but can certainly gallop: sure to win more topclass races.   84
2196 RELOY [3] (J Pease) 3-9-2 C Asmussen : -311032: No answer to the winner's finishing
burst but a gd effort: see 904.   75
*1116 LACOVIA [4] (F Boutin) 3-9-2 F Head : 01-2113: Below her best: unsurprisingly as
she broke a blood vessel and damaged her off-fore tendon and is unlikely to race again.   74
2452 RIVERBRIDE [8] (P L Biancone) 3-9-2 G W Moore : 0004224: See 2452.   72
*2452 GALUNPE [7] 3-9-2 A Gibert : -003110: Btr 2452 (10f).   70
2202 GULL NOOK [1] 3-9-2 S Cauthen   -1100: Made much: see 1128 (firm).   67
8 ran   5,nk,½,1,2   (Aga Khan)   A De Royer Dupre France

2639 GROUP 3 PRIX NIEL 3YO C & F   £17314   1m 4f   Good/Soft

*1009 BERING [2] (C Head) 3-9-4 G W Moore : 31-1111: 3 ch c Artic Tern - Beaune (Lyphard)
Topclass colt: reappeared after a 3 month abs to easily defeat minimal opposition in a Gr 3
Prix Niel at Longchamp: earlier won Gr 1 Prix du Jockey-Club at Chantilly and two Gr 2
events at Longchamp: very eff over 11/12f: seems to act on any going but likes a gall trk:
remains fav to defeat Dancing Brave in the Arc.   85
302 MALAKIM [1] (A De Royer Dupre) 3-8-11 Y Saint Martin : -2-1422: No chance with
this winner.   70
1009 ARCTIC BLAST [4] (C Head) 3-8-11 G Guignard : 2030143.   66
-- VALIOS [5] (A Fabre) 3-8-11 C Asmussen : -214: Made much.   65
1009 POINT DARTOIS [3] 3-8-11 A Lequeux : 1-22000.   63
5 ran   2½,2,½,½   (Mme A Head)   C Head France

Official Going Given As GOOD

2640 GROUP 2 PREMIO FEDERICO TESIO 3YO+   £18179   1m 1f   Yielding

1000 BIG REEF (L Camici) 4-9-1 M Jerome : 11-0031: 4 b c Mill Reef - Lady Habitat
(Habitat) Very useful ex English colt: ran on under press to lead final strides in a Gr 2
event at San Siro: formally trained by J Dunlop: winning 3yo at Newcastle and York: eff at
9f: acts on firm and soft grd and a gall trk.   73
2419 ESDALE (J Tree) 3-8-11 M Planard : 0113012: Having last run for J Tree: caught on
the post after making almost all: fine eff: see 2419.   76
*2449 EVES ERROR (M Stoute) 3-8-11 W R Swinburn : 2-04113: Narrowly btn in a cl fin:
stays 9f : see 2449.   75
-- WHITE WATER (France) 5-8-12 O Poirier : -4: Ran well in this gd company.   65
13 ran   shthd,nk,2   (Allevamento White Star)   L Camici Italy

775

Official Going Given As GOOD/SOFT

2641 SCANDINAVIAN GROUP 1 SPRINT   £21958   5.75f   Good/Soft

2457 SIMON SACC (K Engan) 4-8-8 C Gauntlett : 31: 4 b c Colombian Friend - Kreta
Got up in the last strides to win a Scandanavian Gr 1 sprint at Taby: most eff around 6f:
acts well on gd and yldg ground.   65
1490 KELLYTALK (T Hansen) 4-9-0 J Tandari : 4330-02: Ex English colt who was hdd on
the post: gd effort.   70
--   LE MANS SWE (S Ostgard) 5-9-1 A Auld :   -3: Just btn in a very cl fin.   70
--   MANDARIN (O Stenstrom) 6-8-6 R Guest : -4.   53
2351 PETROVICH 4-9-9 B Rouse : 3000330: Fin 7th: best 2351.   60
2289 CLANTIME 5-9-7 D Mckeown : 1220330: Well below his best: see 1508, 877.   37
11 ran . Nose,½,2½   (Stall Flash)   K Engan Norway

2642 STOCKHOLM CUP (SCANDINAVIAN GROUP 1)   £21958   1m 4f Good/Soft

+1899 TOP GUEST (G Wragg) 3-8-2 P Robinson : -122211: 3 ch c Be My Guest - Topsy (Habitat)
Very useful colt: in grand form and led inside final 1f, cmftbly in a Scandanavian Gr 1 event
at Taby: last time out won val Piper Champagne Stks at Newmarket: made a winning seasonal
debut in a Beverley mdn: in between fin 2nd to 3 smart types in Faraway Dancer, Hello Ernani
and Armada: eff at 10f, suited by 12f: half brother to Rye Tops and Troytops: acts on any
ground and on any trk: yet to run a bad race.   64
2220 LUNDYLUX (R Hannon) 4-9-3 B Rouse : 0-00102: Led over 2f out: fine eff: see 1856.   65
--   GYLLEN (L Reuterskiold) 3-8-2 Jenny Moller : -3.   55
1214 SAND SHIP (T Dahl) 3-8-5 C Cordrey : 24.   54
2354 CHAUMIERE 5-9-11 T Ives : 0010330: Nearest fin: see 2354, 1526.   60
2438 LANDSKI 3-8-3 S Whitworth : 3031340: Very stiff task: see 1768.   41
14 ran 1,2,2,3   (E B Moller)   G Wragg Newmarket

Official Going Given As GOOD/SOFT

2643 GR 3 FORD HENTSCHEL POKAL 3YO FILLIES   £11299   1m 4f Good/Soft

1596 PRAIRIE NEBA (U Ostmann) 3-9-2 W Newnes : 21: 3 b f Nebos - Prairie Bar
Al prom and qcknd into lead entering str, holding on by a nk in a Gr 3 3yo fillies event at
Hanover: clearly eff at 12f on yldg grd, tho' also acts on firm.   65
2117 NORETTA (H Bollow) 3-9-2 P Remmert : 422: Fin well and just btn: in fine form.   64
--   LOMELA (A Wohler) 3-9-2 P Schiergen : -3.   59
2236 AMONGST THE STARS (S Norton) 3-9-2 J Lowe : 1010144: Ev ch entering str: below
her best: see 2236.   56
2453 NIGHT LINE 3-9-2 G Starkey : 30: Odds-on fav: unsuited by this slow pace and well
below form shown in 2453 (hvy).   40
8 ran nk,2½,1½   (W Vischer)   U Ostmann Germany

Official Going Given As SOFT

2644 GROUP 3 PRIX DAUMALE 2YO FILLIES   £17374   1m   Soft

--   PRINCESSE DU BOURG [5] (R Touflan) 2-8-9 D Vignali : 11: 2 ch f Sharpman - Instancia
(Le Fabuloux) Very useful French filly: led cl home to win a Gr 3 2yo fillies event at
Longchamp: first time out won at Deauville and is unbtn in both her outings now: clearly stays
1m well: acts on soft.   64
--   TOUCHING LOVE [3] (C Head) 2-8-9 C Asmussen : 2132: Made most and just caught:
gd effort: earlier a winner in the Provinces: eff at 1m on soft.   63
--   CADEAUX DAMIE [2] (C Head) 2-8-9 G W Moore : 13: Just btn in a cl fin: first time
out ddhtd at Deauville: acts on soft.   63
--   THREE GENERATIONS [9] (G Mikhalides) 2-8-9 J Velasquez : 14: Btn less than 1l in
4th: first time out ddhtd with the 3rd at Deauville.   62
8 ran ½,shthd,hd   (Adolf Bader)   R Touflan France

2645 SHADWELL MAIDEN STAKES 2YO   £964   7f   Firm 10 -06 Slow

2225 TROJAN SONG [10] (H Cecil) 2-9-0 S Cauthen 7/4 FAV: 21: 2 b c Troy - Melody Hour
(Sing Sing) Well bckd and gamely made all in a 2yo mdn at Yarmouth: earlier chased home Falling
Leaf over this C/D: half brother to sev winners, including very useful middle dist filly
Sing Softly: sure to be suited by 1m+ next season: acts on gd and fast grd and is well
suited by this fair course: on the upgrade.   50
2341 BEST O BUNCH [9] (L Piggott) 2-9-0 T Ives 10/1: 02: Sustained chall from dist,
just held: clearly impr and should win a similar race soon: should stay 1m: see 2341.   50

-- GRIMESGILL USA [6] (M Stoute) 2-9-0 W R Swinburn 11/2:   3: Nicely bckd debutant:
ev ch and ran a promising race: should be suited by 1m and further: acts on firm ground
should improve and win a race.   46
2341 MOMENTS OF SILVER [12] (M Albina) 2-9-0 B Thomson 5/1: 34: Ran on same pace: see 2341. 42
-- SOUTHERN COMFORT [4] 2-9-0 R Cochrane 20/1: 0: Mkt drifter on debut: no extra dist
and fin well clear rem: will be suited by 1m+ next season: acts on firm grnd and on a fair trk   40
2254 PORTENTOUS [3] 2-9-0 R Hills 20/1: 000: Prom over ½ way: see 2254 (6f).   26
-- ABU MUSLAB [5] 2-9-0 G Duffield 5/1: 0: Fdd into 8th on debut: should do btr next
season when stepping up in distance.   00
2484 Clopton [14] 9-0   2341 Taweel [1] 9-0   -- Chantry Boy [13] 9-0
1903 Master Knowall [7] 9-0'   -- Higham Broke [11] 9-0
-- Taylors Revenge [8] 9-0   -- Sauce Of The Sea [2] 9-0
14 ran   hd,2,1½,½,8   (H J Joel)   H Cecil Newmarket

2646 SHADWELL MAIDEN STAKES 2YO   £964   7f   Firm 10 -13 Slow

-- ARRASAS [9] (H T Jones) 2-9-0 R Hills 11/4 FAV: 1: 2 ch c Irish River - Dish Dash
(Bustino) Useful colt: made a successful debut, led before ½ way for a ready win in aa 2yo
mdn at Yarmouth: cost $550,000 as a yearling, dam won the Ribblesdale: clearly very eff over
7f and sure to stay further: acts on fast grd and seems well suited by forcing tactics:
will win more races.   50
2243 SUPER LUNAR [2] (R Sheather) 2-9-0 A Clark 6/1: 42: Al front rank: cmftbly beat
rem and is on the upgrade: suited by 7f and will stay further: acts on fast ground.   40
2225 DOLLAR SEEKER [4] (M Ryan) 2-9-0 R Cochrane 20/3: 003: Nicely bckd: gd late prog:
suited by 7f and should stay at least 1m: acts on gd and firm grd: see 2108.   34
2493 MACS MAESTRO [7] (W O'gorman) 2-9-0 T Ives 6/1: 044: Early leader: best here in 2229 (6f) 32
-- PRINCE NEWPORT [12] 2-9-0 G Duffield 33/1: 0: Kept on same pace: fair debut and
should improve: cost 9200 gns and is a half brother to a couple of winners, including juv
Ahona: acts on firm ground.   31
-- RIJISTAN [3] 2-9-0 W R Swinburn 4/1: 0: No extra 2f out: attracted some support today:
likely to improve next time: acts on firm grd.   26
2484 FASHIONABLY FORBES [8] 2-9-0 S Cauthen 8/1: 400: Fin 8th: best over this C/D in 2341 00
-- Lovenko [10] 9-0   1555 Rocky Horror [1] 9-0   -- Great Caesar [11] 9-0
-- Corleon [6] 9-0   1488 Pradel [5] 9-0   -- Quassimi [13] 9-0
13 ran   3,3,1,½,2½   (Hamdan Al Maktoum)   H T Jones, Newmarket

2647 GREAT YARMOUTH STAYERS H'CAP (0-50)   £2700   2m 2f Firm 10 -05 Slow   [37]

2317 IGHTHAM [10] (G Harwood) 3-9-0 A Clark 12/1: -001031: 3 b c Nijinsky - Golden
Alibi (Empery) In fine form and led 4 out, gamely, in a stayers h'cap at Yarmouth: earlier
won a mdn at Wolverhampton: well suited by a test of stamina: acts on fast and soft grd and
does well on a gall trk: carries weight well: has worn blinkers but is a genuine sort.   46
2220 JUST DAVID [13] (A Stewart) 3-9-10 M Roberts 8/1: -12102: Led briefly inside dist,
just btn: tremendous eff under topweight: clearly well suited by 2m+: genuine and consistent:
see 1879.   56
*2346 SEVEN HILLS [2] (J Fitzgerald) 3-8-5(vis) T Ives 4/1: 0031113: In fine form:
stays 2m+: see 2346.   33
*2311 FEDRA [5] (Lord J Fitzgerald) 3-9-3 R Hills 7/1: 1242314: Another gd eff: see 2311. 42
2480 SUN STREET [14] 4-8-13 A Mackay 25/1: 0020130: Running well: see 2326.   23
*2480 ALLATUM [3] 3-9-3(3ex) B Thomson 3/1 FAV: 2041010: Longer trip: btr over 2m in 2480. 32
*2040 JOIST [12] 4-8-8(bl) G Duffield 10/1: 0243210: No threat: much btr 2040 (2m).   00
-- High Renown [1] 8-6(1ow)   2403 Reform Princess [9] 8-5(bl)
-- Our Bara Boy [8] 7-8(vis)(1ow)(2oh)   2031 Mycenae Cherry [7] 9-2(bl)
2403 Italian Sunrise [11] 8-12   1056 Lingfield Lady [6] 7-11
2164 Temple Heights [15] 9-1   *2306 Bedhead [16] 9-4
15 ran   hd,3,2½,2,7,5   (K Abdulla)   G Harwood Pulborough, Sussex

2648 ALBERT BOTTON MEM. NURSERY H'CAP 2YO   £3785   1m   Firm 10 +01 Fast   [57]

*2383 PERFECT STRANGER [3] (P Haslam) 2-8-9(5ex) T Williams 7/2: 031011: 2 b g Wolver Hollow
- Mrs Walmsley (Lorenzaccio) In fine form and led/dsptd lead thr'out, running on gamely to win
quite a fast run nursery at Yarmouth: earlier won a claimer over 7f here and last month again
made most in a nursery at Sandown: stays 1m really well, acts on firm and yldg ground and
likes a gall trk: genuine sort.   45
*2512 ROUMELI [9] (Lord J Fitzgerald) 2-7-12(5ex) R Hills 16/1: 4230312: Dsptd lead,
rallied gamely and only just btn: fine eff under her penalty: see 2512.   32
2479 CAERINETTE [10] (A Bailey) 2-7-10 Abigail Richards(6) 50/1: 4340003: Fin strongly and
narrowly btn: btr effort and clearly stays 1m well: runs well here: see 2013.   30
2178 LORD COLLINS [8] (M Stoute) 2-8-12 W R Swinburn 10/1: 404204: Not btn far: fine
effort: see 2071.   46
1050 LOMA BREEZE [11] 2-7-7(4oh) W Woods(4) 50/1: -30000: Abs: gd late prog and likely
to do better next time: stays 1m: acts on gd and firm: see 345.   23
2479 TIMESWITCH [6] 2-8-6 M L Thomas 6/1: 2002200: No luck in running: see 2227 & 531.   36
-2407 BROTHER PATRICK [1] 2-9-7 T Ives 7/4 FAV: 30120: Well bckd: fdd dist under topweight:
fin 8th: best in 2407 (stiff trk): see 2105.   00

777

*2336 SNO SURPRISE [2] 2-8-1 R Cochrane 6/1: 0020110: Fin 9th: btr over 7f in 2336 (yldg).   00
2391 MY BUDDY [4] 2-8-13 S Cauthen 9/1: 0011100: Dwelt and no threat: much btr 2115 (7f)   00
2383 Olore Malle [5] 7-9   2198 Penang Beauty [7] 8-12
11 ran   ½,shthd,shthd,1½,½   (Ian A Paice)   P Haslam Newmarket

2649 NORFOLK FILLIES E.B.F. STAKES 3YO   £5624   1m 2f   Firm 10 -25 Slow

581 TASHTIYA [1] (M Stoute) 3-8-7 W R Swinburn 5/1: 0-21: 3 b f Shergar - Tremogia
(Silver Shark) Useful filly: despite a lengthy abs cruised into lead 2f out and qcknd well to
win a val 3yo fillies stks at Yarmouth: first time out a gd 2nd to Smashing Millie at Sandown:
very eff over 10f and likely to stay further: acts on gd and fast ground and on a gall trk:
lightly raced and seems certain to win more races.   60
*2304 HOTEL STREET [5] (H Cecil) 3-8-10 S Cauthen 8/13 FAV: -12: Heavily bckd: led 3f out,
lacked foot of winner: may prove btr over longer dist: acts on firm and yldg: see 2304 (12f)   52
*1337 STRAW BOATER [6] (L Cumani) 3-8-12 R Cochrane 12/1: -0013: Gd eff after a long break:
eff over 9/10f and seems sure to be suited by further: see 1337.   48
2286 SMASHING MILLIE [3] (P Cole) 3-9-0 T Ives 9/1: 0-144: Held up, ran on same pace:
lightly raced since beating today's winner in 581, acts on gd and firm ground.   44
*2393 QUEEN OF BATTLE [4] 3-8-13 N Day 10/1: 0223410: Led over ½ way: btr 2393 (sharp trk).   41
2131 GREY WALLS [2] 3-8-8(VIS) P Robinson 10/1: 13-0000: Visored first time: well btn : see 271.   16
6 ran   5,3,3,½,12   (H H Aga Khan)   M Stoute Newmarket

2650 HARBOUR E.B.F. STAKES 3YO   £2624   7f   Firm 10 +14 Fast

2099 SIR ARNOLD [6] (A Stewart) 3-8-11 M Roberts 11/1: -23131: 3 b g Mummy's Pet - Bold
Polly (Bold Lad) Led dist and ran on strongly to win a fast run 3yo stks at Yarmouth: in gd
form, earlier won a minor race at Folkestone: speedily bred gelding who is very eff over 6/7f:
acts on gd and fast ground and on any trk: consistent.   45
2518 ZULU KNIGHT [8] (P Walwyn) 3-8-11 S Cauthen 6/1: 0002122: Tried to make all, kept
on well when hdd: deserves another race: stays 7f: see 2186.   42
2488 CLEOFE [10] (L Cumani) 3-8-12 R Cochrane 14/1: 3400103: Narrowly btn: fine eff: see 2367.   42
2459 SOMETHING CASUAL [1] (A Hide) 3-8-4(vis) A Shoults(5) 6/1: 0034444: Not btn far: see 1655   33
2314 HENAADI [9] 3-8-4 G Duffield 33/1: -000: Gd late prog from this lightly raced filly:
mkt drifter but ran much btr today: stays 7f well: acts on fast grd.   30
1932 TENDER LOVING CARE [12] 3-8-4(bl) B Thomson 2/1 FAV: 20-0000: Heavily bckd: looked
dangerous below dist, found nothing under press: should have won this on her juv form: see 1392   28
2458 SHANNON VALE [5] 3-8-7 W R Swinburn 6/1: 01-00: Front rank 5f: see 2458.   00
2463 BERTIE WOOSTER [11] 3-9-6(bl) T Ives 8/1: 2202400: Onepaced from ½ way: see 2207.   00
2207 Raja Moulana [7] 8-7   2143 Sparky Lad [2] 8-7   2473 Mystical Man [3] 8-7
2321 Zagazig [4] 8-7(VIS)
12 ran   ½,hd,hd,1½,1   (Julian James)   A Stewart Newmarket

2651 GORLESTON MAIDEN FILLIES STAKES 2YO   £1590   6f   Firm 10 +12 Fast

2345 AT RISK [1] (H Cecil) 2-8-11 S Cauthen 4/7 FAV: 31: 2 gr f Mr Prospector - Misgivings
(Cyane) Useful filly: heavily bckd, led early and rallied gamely to get up cl home in a
fast run 2yo fillies mdn at Yarmouth: placed behind Start Rite in a well contested mdn over
this C/D last month: half sister to a couple of winners: eff over 6f and sure to stay further:
acts on gd and firm grd: should continue to improve.   46
2563 RIPE CHRISTINA [8] (A Bailey) 2-8-11 P Bloomfield 12/1: 003342: Ran on gamely, just
btn: gd eff and should go one better soon: acts on gd and firm: see 2185.   45
2365 SILVERCOAST [9] (H T Jones) 2-8-11 R Hills 10/1: 03: Led before ½ way, narrowly btn:
on the upgrade and looks certain to win soon: eff over 5/6f on gd and firm: suited by
forcing tactics: see 2365.   44
2511 KATE IS BEST [2] (M Ryan) 2-8-11 R Cochrane 10/1: 0044: Active in mkt: al up there:
should do better when stepping up in dist: see 1430.   36
-- TARSA [6] 2-8-11 B Thomson 14/1: 0: Showed gd speed over ½ way: btr for race:
cost 40,000 gns and is a half sister to sev winning sprinters: acts on fast grd.   35
-- SKIPAWAY [3] 2-8-11 N Day 33/1: 0: Btr for this run: cost $320,000 as a yearling and
is a half sister to a couple of winning sprinters: acts on firm grd: will improve.   27
-- NAMARAI BAY [18] 2-8-11 W R Swinburn 9/1: 0: Gd speed over ½ way on debut: cost $700,000
as yearling and is out of a very smart winner in the States: should be btr for this experience   20
-- ANOTHER GUEST [13] 2-8-11 A Shoults(5) 50/1: 0: Prom over ½ way: quite cheaply bought
filly who is a half sister to winning juv Shaves You Close.   16
-- SPECULATE [17] 2-8-11 T Ives 10/1: 0: No threat on racecourse debut tho' likely to
improve next time: cost IR 72,000 and is a half brother to winning juv Silent Flutter.   14
988 Crisp Heart [10] 8-11   -- Viens Vite [5] 8-11   -- Known Point [15] 8-11
-- Gloire De Dijon [7] 8-11   -- Camallino Rose [4] 8-11
-- Sara Lane [11] 8-11   -- Aglasini [19] 8-11   2487 Patient Dreamer [12] 8-11
-- Aerial Ballet [14] 8-11   -- Debutante Ball [16] 8-11
19 ran   hd,nk,3,nk,3,2½,1½,½,1½   (Mrs John W Hanes)   H Cecil Newmarket

BRIGHTON   Thursday September 18th   Lefthand, Sharpish,Undulating Track

Official Going Given As FIRM

2652 HENFIELD MAIDEN FILLIES STAKES 2YO   £959   7f   Firm 10 +02 Fast

2013 TIPATINA [12] (L Cumani) 2-8-11 G Starkey 7/1: 01: 2 b f Northern Baby - Princess
Sucree (Roberto) Fast impr filly: mkt drifter, but led inside final 2f, readily drawing clear
in quite fast run 2yo fillies mdn at Brighton: cost $270,000 as yearling: eff at 7f, looks
sure to be suited by 1m and further: acts well on fast ground and an undulating trk: should
win more races.   58
2487 RARE MEMORIES [11] (P Cole) 2-8-11 T Quinn 7/4 FAV: 222: Al prom: met a gd one here
and deserves a win: see 2487.   46
2527 MEADOWBANK [6] (M Dickinson) 2-8-11 Pat Eddery 9/2: 003: Al up there: gd eff: see 2527. 41
2191 PERFECT FOIL [10] (W Jarvis) 2-8-11 J Reid 25/1: 004: Ev ch in str: fair eff: stays 7f. 37
-2329 TUFTY LADY [8] 2-8-11 P Tulk 7/2: 00220: Made most: much btr 2329, 2019 (C/D).   31
2276 SYSTEMS GO [13] 2-8-11 W Ryan 20/1: 03400: Never nearer: see 1187 (6f)   27
--   SHEER AUDACITY [5] 2-8-11 A Kimberley 11/2: 0: Mkt drifter: fin 7th and should improve:
quite stoutly bred filly who is a half sister to sev winners.   22
722 Our Lucky Native [3] 8-11   2364 Rose Loubet [9] 8-11
2527 Meldon Hill [1] 8-11(BL)   2434 Fair Moon [7] 8-11
2191 For You And Me [4] 8-11   1483 Miss Lawsuit [2] 8-11
13 ran 7,2,2,3,2,2½   (Miss Caroline R Alexander)   L Cumani Newmarket

2653 LITTLEHAMPTON FILLIES STAKES 3YO   £1898   1m   Firm 10 -06 Slow

*2248 DARING DOONE [8] (A Stewart) 3-9-7 J Reid 7/4 JT.FAV: -11: 3 b f Daring March -
Doogali (Doon) Well bckd and led inside final 1f, cmftbly, in a 3yo fillies stks at Brighton:
first time out was a ready winner of a similar event at Goodwood: first foal of useful 8/10f
winner Doogali: clearly well suited by 1m and should stay further: acts on gd and fast grd
and a sharpish trk: can improve further.   53
1192 ALCHAASIBIYEH [5] (H T Jones) 3-8-11(BL) P Darcy 10/1: 33-002: Bl first time after abs
and nearly made all: gd eff: stays 1m but prob not any further: see 966.   41
*2532 HOOKED BID [6] (J Dunlop) 3-9-4 G Baxter 5/1: -000313: Eff over 1f out: in fine form.   44
338 FIREAL [12] (H Cecil) 3-8-11 W Ryan 7/4 JT.FAV: 4-24: Well bckd, despite long abs:
prom, ev ch: should be straighter for this run: see 338.   34
2210 MARIES VALENTINE [2] 3-8-11 J Leech(7) 33/1: -000000: Chance 2f out: showed improved
form over this longer trip and does well on a sharp trk: likes fast ground: officially rated
only 11.   30
1061 ANOTHER PAGEANT [10] 3-8-11 R Fox 12/1: -0000: Abs: no threat: lightly raced: 16
2256 Sancilia [3] 8-11   2408 La Shaka [7] 8-11   1471 Tymbal [9] 8-11(BL)
--   Aggie [1] 8-11   2275 Moonlight Madness [4] 8-11
--   Papun [11] 8-11
12 ran nk,1½,1,1,7   (Mrs Wm McAlpine)   A Stewart Newmarket

2654 QUEENS PARK APP.SELL.H'CAP 3Y+ 0-25   £832   1m 4f   Firm 10 -55 Slow   [9]

1459 SHALLAAL [6] (A King) 7-9-1 A Riding(4) 10/1: 0001: 7 ch g Honest Pleasure - Grass
Court (Herbager) Bckd at long odds and led inside final 2f, cmftbly, in a slow run app
selling h'cap at Brighton: last successful in '83 at Folkestone and does well on a sharpish,
undulating trk: stays 12f, likes fast ground: no bid for the winner today.   06
2309 UNIT TENT [7] (B Sanders) 8-8-11(bl) J Adams 10/1: 4040002: Led ½ way: see 201.   00
2429 TROJAN GOD [1] (R Akehurst) 4-9-10 P Mcentee 10/1: 000-303: Stays 12f: see 2208.   05
2128 G G MAGIC [2] (D Morley) 3-9-8 Dale Gibson 5/2 JT.FAV: 0420004: Led to ½ way:
dropped in class today: best 1479, see 380.   06
*2528 MR MUSIC MAN [5] 12-9-8(4ex) J Carr 5/2 JT.FAV: 0240010: Well below form shown 2528.   00
2517 SOLAR LIGHT [3] 6-9-8(vis) A Dicks 11/2: 2403-00: Fdd over 2f out: maiden who was
placed in similar events last season: has also made the frame over timber in selling co:
likes a sharp trk: acts on fast and soft.   00
1898 AUSSIE GIRL [4] 3-9-6 G Athanasiou(4) 5/1: 0033000: Al rear: best 1459 (C/D)   00
7 ran 5,1,3,shthd,8,1½   (David L Davies)   A King Wilmcote, Warwickshire

2655 FRIEND JAMES MEM.H'CAP 3YO+ 0-60   £3262   7f   Firm 10 +02 Fast   [52]

2519 DOWNSVIEW [7] (A Moore) 4-8-7 M Wigham 16/1: 0004001: 4 b c Dominion - Lady Downsview
(Prince Regent) Led most and stayed on well to win a val h'cap at Brighton: has been below
his best recently, but earlier won a h'cap at Lingfield: a winner 3 times at Brighton in '85
and loves this switchback trk: eff at 5/6f: stays 7f: acts on yldg: likes fast ground:
best out in front around Brighton.   43
2544 MANCHESTERSKYTRAIN [8] (L Cottrell) 7-8-11 B Rouse 11/2: 0002002: Fin in gd style:
running well at present: see 2123, 401.   44
2250 PINSTRIPE [9] (R Williams) 3-9-7 J Reid 9/2: 1121223: Hmpd slightly final 1f: ultra
consistent: see 2250.   57
2431 BOLD PILLAGER [10] (J Dunlop) 4-9-5 Pat Eddery 3/1 FAV: 3211404: Well bckd: chance
2f out: not btn far: see 1377.   49
2530 STOCK HILL LASS [6] 4-8-10 G Starkey 25/1: 0-00000: Led before ½ way: prom when
not much room dist: very lightly raced this term and this was a much btr effort: in '85 was
trained by M Blanshard to win a val h'cap at Newbury: winning 2yo at Nottingham and Salisbury:
very eff at 6f, stays 7f: acts on fast and yldg grd and prob on any trk: well in on best form. 38
                                          779

1515 IYAMSKI [1] 3-8-1 R Lines(3) 5/1: -202300: Ev ch when hmpd over 1f out: unlucky?
Gd eff after a fair abs: consistent sort: see 423, 16.   33
2369 GOLDEN BEAU [5] 4-7-13(1ow) A Mcglone 7/1: 3301230: Ev ch in 7th: btr 2369 (C/D)   23
2214 GREEN DOLLAR [4] 3-9-2 P Cook 10/1: 0030030: No show: much btr 2214 (stks 6f).   00
2091 FEI LOONG [11] 5-8-1 G King(5) 10/1: 4214300: Fdd over 2f out: lightly raced and
twice below 1553.   00
2619 Toms Nap Hand [3] 7-7(18oh)   2473 Edgewise [2] 8-6
11 ran   1½,½,nk,1,½,½   (B Marsh)   A Moore Woodingdean, Sussex.

2656 WIN WITH THE TOTE MAIDEN STAKES 3YO+   £808   1m 2f Firm 10 +02 Fast

1615 BURNING BRIGHT [4] (D Ringer) 3-8-3 M Wigham 11/2: 2-04241: 3 b c Star Appeal -
Lead Me On (King's Troop) Led after 2f and came home unchall by 5l in a 3yo mdn at Brighton:
eff at 10f, stays 12f: acts on gd, likes fast ground and a sharpish trk: seems to do well
when fresh.   35
2534 PORO BOY [7] (C Williams) 3-8-3 G Baxter 10/1: 0004002: Ev ch in str: best 352 (yldg) 26
2572 VISUAL IDENTITY [8] (P Mitchell) 4-9-0 Pat Eddery 7/2: 0000433: Chance 2f out:
in gd form: see 2572.   28
2373 RAFFIA RUN [3] (R Akehurst) 3-8-3 P Cook 15/8 FAV: 4402334: Much btr 2373 (C/D)   21
2422 MR SAVVAS [6] 3-8-3(BL) W Newnes 14/1: -000000: Bl first time but no threat:
little form this term: stays 10f and acts on fast ground.   19
--   LIGHT THE WAY [1] 3-8-0 A Mcglone 9/4: 0-0: Very well bckd on seasonal debut:
prom over 7f: ran only once in J85, fin down the field in a gd fillies mdn at Newmarket:
sure to strip fitter next time: acts on firm ground.   07
1257 Knightly Dia [5] 8-0.   2519 Friendly Lass [9] 8-11
--   Stampy [2] 9-0
9 ran   5,shthd,2½,1,5   (Mrs E M English)   D Ringer Newmarket

2657 EBF WITHDEAN MAIDEN STAKES 2YO   £1086   1m   Firm 10 -08 Slow

2547 FAILIQ [7] (P Walwyn) 2-9-0 Paul Eddery 5/1: 041: 2 b c Bustino - Salvationist
(Mill Reef) Impr colt: led inside final 1f, driven out in a 2yo mdn at Brighton: stoutly bred
colt who was well suited by today's 1m trip and will get further: acts well on fast ground
and seems to have no trk preferences: genuine.   49
2407 OLD MAESTRO [1] (G Harwood) 2-9-0 G Starkey 10/11 FAV: 02: Well bckd: led ½ way
not much room final 1f and just btn: should go one better soon: stays 1m and acts well on fast. 48
1239 OPERATIC SCORE [4] (P Cole) 2-9-0 T Quinn 5/2: 23: Well bckd, despite long abs:
no real threat and will strip fitter next time: stays 1m: can find a race soon: see 1239. 44
2270 FLUTEAU [2] (M Stoute) 2-9-0 A Kimberley 20/1: 004: No extra final 2f: best eff yet
and prob stays 1m: half brother to sev winners and acts on fast ground.   32
2283 KIND OF CLASS [5] 2-8-11 B Rouse 20/1: 0000: No show: lightly raced since 999.   16
--   ROYAL ASTRONAUT [3] 2-9-0 J Reid 20/1: 0: Mkt drifter on debut and no threat:
American bred colt who cost $77,000: should be suited by 1m and further.   15
2287 Ocean Hound [6] 8-11   2493 Gallant Ribo [8] 9-0
8 ran   nk,2,8,7,1½   (Hamdan Al Maktoum)   P Walwyn Lambourn, Berks

2658 HENFIELD MAIDEN FILLIES STAKES 2YO   £959   7f   Firm 10 -04 Slow

2215 ILIONA [12] (L Cumani) 2-8-11 G Starkey 8/1: 001: 2 gr f Al Nasr - Icancan (Candy
Cane) Impr filly: led early and again over 1f out, readily, in a 2yo fillies mdn at Brighton:
half sister to middle dist winner Indian Orator: eff at 7f: should be suited by 1m+: acts
on fast ground and an easy trk.   49
2434 JUST KALA [4] (P Walwyn) 2-8-11 Paul Eddery 4/1: 432: New trip: stayed on well
and can win soon: acts on any trk: see 2147.   44
2270 RUSSIAN WALTZ [5] (R Armstrong) 2-8-11 P Tulk 20/1: 003: Stayed on well and should
be suited by 1m: acts on gd and fast ground and can continue to improve.   39
2434 SHELDON MILLS [1] (I Balding) 2-8-11 Pat Eddery 4/1: 044: Led 2f out: impr filly
who stays 7f: acts on any trk: see 2434.   37
1966 FLIRTING [2] 2-8-11 A Mcglone 14/1: 02440: Never nearer: prob stays 7f: best 988 (5f) 35
2036 ABSINTHE [9] 2-8-11 R Guest 7/1: 40: Al mid-div: btr 2036 (stiff trk)   27
2229 LORI GARBACZ [7] 2-8-11 E Guest(3) 12/1: 00: Fin 7th: should do btr than this: see 2229 25
2433 GREENHIL JAZZ TIME [6] 2-8-11 S Whitworth 12/1: 030: Led most 5f: btr 2433, 2147.   25
2531 NORTH PACIFIC [10] 2-8-11 T Quinn 10/3 FAV: 030: Disapp run after 2531 (stiff 7f)   24
--   DALROUMA [8] 2-8-11 A Kimberley 8/1: 0: Prom to over 2f out on debut: sister to
middle dist winner Dalgadiyr: should do btr than this.   00
1966 Red Riding Hood [1] 8-11   2185 Carlton Glory [11] 8-11
2518 Just Enchanting [13] 8-11
13 ran   2,3,1,1,4,½,shthd,nk   (Studcrown Ltd)   L Cumani Newmarket

2659 JIM TAYLOR MEM.H'CAP 3YO 0-35   £2222   6f   Firm 10 +12 Fast   [40]

2382 HELAWE [4] (J Winter) 3-9-5 Pat Eddery 9/2: 3014001: 3 ch c Last Fandango - Pigmy
(Assagai) Led over 1f out, driven out in a fast run 3yo h'cap at Brighton: earlier won a
similar event again at Brighton: consistent sort in '85 winning a nursery at Redcar: well
suited by 6f: best on gd and fast grd, however acts on any trk: wears blinkers but seems genuine 41

BRIGHTON   Thursday September 18th   -Cont'd

*2463 HIGHLY RECOMMENDED [13] (P Cundell) 3-8-12(10ex) N Adams 4/1 FAV: -000312: Led
4f: ran on well and just btn: in grand form: seems equally eff at 6/7f: see 2463.   33
2614 BEECHWOOD COTTAGE [6] (A Bailey) 3-8-9(bl) G Bardwell(7) 9/1: 4020203: Led briefly
1f out: has been very busy this season: retains his form well: see 1610.   24
2184 COME TO THE BALL [15] (R Hannon) 3-8-3 B Rouse 12/1: 00-0304: Ev ch inside final 2f:
tried over a much shorter trip today: see 2017.   17
2592 COMMANDER MEADEN [12] 3-7-9(bl)(2ow)(3oh) R Fox 14/1: 0304000: Nearest fin: best 929   08
2519 LINAVOS [14] 3-8-4 W Newnes 10/1: 0044020: No real threat: btr 2519.   13
*2518 GYPSYS PROPHECY [11] 3-9-12(7ex) G Starkey 7/1: 0-32410: Fdd inside final 2f:
better 2518.   30
2416 NORTHERN LAD [2] 3-8-3(bl) C Rutter(3) 13/2: 02020U0: There 4f: see 2416, 1584.   00
*2416 RESTLESS RHAPSODY [7] 3-8-8(bl) A Whitehall(7) 10/1: 4040310: P.U. lame: see 2416.   00
1607 Shayi [10] 8-5   2367 Tootsie Roll [9] 7-9(BL)
2532 Cherry Glory [1] 7-9   2562 Boofy [3] 9-7   2135 Thereafter [5] 8-8(bl)
2120 Monatation [8] 7-7(3oh)
15 ran ½,2½,nk,½,1½,   (A R C Finn)   J Winter Newmarket

AYR   Thursday September 18th   Lefthanded, Flat Galloping Track

Official Going Given As GOOD/FIRM

2660 SHAW MEMORIAL HANDICAP 3YO 0-35   £2281   6f   Firm 14 -05 Slow   [42]

2382 RESTORE [7] (G Lewis) 3-9-3 P Waldron 5/2: 3-20321: 3 ch c Habitat - Never So Lovely
(Realm) Well suited by this extra furlong, sn led altho' hanging badly inside final 2f just
held on in a 3yo h'cap at Ayr: earlier placed sev times over 5f tho' seems btr suited by
6f: acts on gd and fast ground and is well suited by a galt trk: seems well suited by
forcing tactics and should do better when fitted with blinkers.   42
2411 GOLDEN GUILDER [9] (M W Easterby) 3-8-9(bl) L Charnock 12/1; 13333U2: Just hld:see 1959.   33
-2277 ROPER ROW [10] (M H Easterby) 3-9-1 K Hodgson 13/8 FAV: 0113323: Well bckd: fin well.   35
2483 ORTICA [11] (J Etherington) 3-8-3(vis) M Wood 12/1: 0233304: Remains a mdn: see 1269.   20
2424 DANCING TOM [5] 3-8-13 M Hills 14/1: 0004400: Prom most: little form this term: see 81   24
2424 GLORIANT [2] 3-7-7(bl)(6oh) J Lowe 33/1: 0340000: Yet to show any worthwhile form:
suited by sprint dist: acts on fast and soft ground.   00
2483 ELSOCKO [4] 3-9-1 W Carson 10/1: 3033020: Early speed, wknd into 8th: btr 2483.   00
2295 Allisterdransfield [6] 7-8(bl)   2469 Runaway [8] 9-7
2409 Maybe Jayne [1] 7-7(BL)(7oh)   2411 Royal Aries [3] 7-7
11 ran nk,1½,3,2½,1,1,1,2½   (Mrs C Khan)   G Lewis Epsom, Surrey

2661 HARRY ROSEBERRY CHALL TROPHY LISTED 2YO £10532   5f   Firm 14 +01 Fast

2297 SINGING STEVEN [4] (R Hannon) 2-8-11(BL) W Carson 4/1: 1123031: 2 b c Balliol
- Cheb's Honour (Cheb's Lad) Very useful colt: bl first time and gamely made all in a val
and quite fast run 2yo Listed race at Ayr: has retained his form well, earlier won minor races
at Wolverhampton & Bath and has since been placed at Royal Ascot: bargain buy who is a half
brother to h'capper Minus Man: very eff over 5/6f: acts on fast and soft ground
and on any. trk: genuine sort who does well with forcing tactics.   63
+2398 WHIPPER IN [6] (J Etherington) 2-9-0 A Murray 5/4 FAV: 112: Heavily bckd: ran on
gamely and lost nothing in defeat: certain to win more races: acts on any trk: see 2398.   62
2447 STELBY [2] (O Brennan) 2-8-7 D Nicholls 25/1: 2242003: Slowly into his stride:
close 3rd and sure to win soon if reproducing this form: well suited by a gall trk: see 2082   51
2501 BAG ORHYTHM [3] (J Hindley) 2-8-11(VIS) M Hills 9/4: 212234: Visored first time:
had ev ch: see 2223.   54
2100 THE DEVILS MUSIC [5] 2-8-7 L Charnock 100/1: 0000: Rank outsider: never dangerous
and almost certainly flattered by this rating: eff over 5/6f on fast and yldg grd: see 515   40
*2172 ECHOING [1] 2-8-8 N Connorton 8/1: 143210: Btn over 1f out: btr 2172 (5f)   39
6 ran 1,1,shthd,2,1½   (Dr Steve Bennett)   R Hannon East Everleigh, Wilts

2662 GOODSIDE CUP 3YO+ 0-60   £4854   1m 5f Firm 14 +06 Fast   [50]

*2445 WASSL REEF [8] (J Dunlop) 3-9-11(4ex) W Carson 7/4 FAV: 3101011: 3 b c Mill Reef -
Connaught Bridge (Connaught) Very useful colt: held up and responded to press to lead inside
dist in quite a fast run and val h'cap at Ayr: recently won a similar race at York, after
earlier successes at Salisbury and Lingfield: very eff over 10/14f: acts on fast and yldg
ground and on any trk: genuine and consistent sort.   69
*2337 PAST GLORIES [1] (W Elsey) 3-8-13 J Lowe 9/2: 0421012: Led/dsptd lead most: kept
on gamely and should be winning again soon: stays 13f well: see 2337.   55
*2237 WITCHCRAFT [6] (G Wragg) 4-9-0 P Waldron 11/4: -244313: Not btn far: stays 13f:see 2237.   44
*2415 BENS BIRDIE [4] (M Tompkins) 6-7-7(3oh) G Carter 7/1: 413-214: Stayed on: see 2415.   19
2237 MADISON GIRL [2] 3-7-7 N Carlisle 12/1: 1102000: Early leader: onepaced: see 1615, 1479   24
2445 TRESIDDER [9] 4-8-5(BL) J Bleasdale 9/1: 4042400: Bl first time: found nil over 2f
out: see 2087.   20
6 ran ½,½,2½,4,3   (Sheikh Ahmed Al Maktoum)   J Dunlop Arundel, Sussex

781

2663 JACK JARVIS MEM NURSERY HCAP 2YO   £4862   1m   Firm 14 -17 Slow   [60]

2479 BOY SINGER [8] (K Stone) 2-7-12(VIS)(5ow)(2oh) A Mercer 25/1: 0430001: 2 b c Alias
Smith - Mum's Song (Saintly Song) Caused a 25/1 surprise, making most and staying on well
in a nursery h'cap at Ayr: lightly raced since early season and has worn a hood: clearly very
eff over 1m with forcing tactics on fast ground.   40

2332 PAS DENCHERE [10] (G Lewis) 2-9-5 P Waldron 6/1: 030122: Consistent colt who kept
on well: suited by 1m: see 1891.   58

2276 CHESWOLD [1] (M H Easterby) 2-7-7(BL)(6oh) G Carter 9/1: 400303: Chance over 1f out:
ran well: suited by today's 1m trip: bl first time today: see 1625.   31

2439 ELEGANT ISLE [3] (J Watts) 2-8-11(BL) W Carson 10/11 FAV: 124: Bl first time:
ev ch over 1f out: btr 2439 (yldg)   48

*2498 JOHNNY SHARP [5] 2-7-11(5ex) J Lowe 8/1: 0020010: Al prom: in good form: see 2498.   32

2276 CRAIGENDARROCH [7] 2-7-7 M Fry 14/1: 400100: Not the best of runs and never nearer:
seems to stay 1m: see 2050.   24

1914 CHESTER TERRACE [6] 2-7-7(1oh) L Charnock 7/1: 0000: Pulled hard, fdd str: active in
mkt today despite a fair abs: btr 1914 (7f).   00

2444 Punta Calahonda [4] 9-7   1296 Muntag [9] 7-7(8oh)
9 ran   1½,hd,nk,½,1½   (Gordon Stead)   K Stone Malton, Yorks

2664 EBF HALL FARM STUD MDN FILLIES STKS 2YO. £3882   7f   Firm 14 -34 Slow

2232 SUNERTA [5] (W Hern) 2-8-11 W Carson 7/4 FAV: 01: 2 b f Roberto - Sunday Purchase
(T V Lark) Heavily bckd and made ev yard, running on well in a slow run 2yo fillies mdn at
Ayr: US bred filly who is a half sister to sev winners, notably the very smart Hatim: eff
at 7f, should be suited by further: eff with forcing tactics on fast ground and can further
improve.   46

2365 LISETA [11] (M W Easterby) 2-8-11 J Bleasdale 16/1: 022: Kept on well under press
and got today's 7f well: improving filly who can find a race: see 2043.   43

2185 DEBACH DELIGHT [1] (M Tompkins) 2-8-11 G Carter 14/1: 03: Al there: backed at long
odds today and showed improved form: cost 18,500 gns: stoutly bred and will be well suited
by 1m and further: acts on fast ground.   42

2379 KALEIDOPHONE [6] (W Elsey) 2-8-11 D Nicholls 16/1: 0034: Al prom: appeared held
when carried left clear closing stages: ran well: see 2379, 1266.   41

2436 MISCHIEVOUS MISS [4] 2-8-11 M Birch 11/4: 30: Not the best of runs and came too
late: eff at 7f and should be suited by 1m: see 2436.   40

852 TAP ON BLUE [7] 2-8-11 A Murray 14/1: 00: Prom most after fair abs: gd eff: half
brother to 1m winner Pearl Blue: stays 7f: acts on fast ground.   37

2067 HIGHLAND BELLE [8] 2-8-11 N Connorton 15/2: 30: Never nearer 7th: needs 1m? See 2067.   00

--   Kilauea [10] 8-11   2436 Petroc Concert [3] 8-11
2379 Willowbank [9] 8-11   1187 Seulement [12] 8-11   --   Emsley Heights [2] 8-11
12 ran   1,½,½,nk,1,2½   (K Abdulla)   W Hern West Ilsley, Berks.

2665 SAM HALL EBF STAKES 3YO   £3184   1m 7f Firm 14 -01 Slow

*2376 TEMPLE WALK [6] (W Hern) 3-8-10 W Carson 9/4 FAV: 0-13011: 3 b f Bustino - Temple
Wood (Sweet Revenge) In fine form: held up and led well inside final 1f, ridden out in a
3yo stks at Ayr: last time out an easy winner of a Chester h'cap: earlier won a fillies event
at Wolverhampton: half sister to a couple of middle dist winners and is clearly well suited
by a test of stamina: acts on fast and yldg grd and on any trk: improving filly.   54

2142 GOLDEN HEIGHTS [7] (P Walwyn) 3-8-10 N Howe 14/1: 1214232: Led over 1f out: stays
15f: acts on firm and yielding ground: see 635.   50

2096 FRANCHISE [9] (R J Houghton) 3-8-7 K Darley 10/1: -0123: Held up: kept on final 1f:
stays well, but lacks turn of foot: see 1786.   46

*2305 DUNSTON [3] (F Durr) 3-8-10 M Birch 8/1: 0303414: Led 2½f out: stays 15f and is in
grand form: see 2305.   48

*2142 MY WILLOW [2] 3-8-10 A Murray 13/2: -4210: Chance over 2f out: stays 15f: see 2142.   43

2142 KING JACK [1] 3-8-10 J Lowe 6/1: 0214220: Led early: possibly does not stay 15f : see 1837.   38

*1494 EMERALD POINT [5] 3-8-10(VIS) J Matthias 3/1: 3-010: Abs: took a strong hold and
made most 12f: visored first time today: much btr 1494 (easy 12f).   00

2422 Cuillin Sound [8] 8-5(BL)
8 ran   1,½,nk,3,3   (T E S Egerton)   W Hern West Ilsley, Berks.

2666 KEITH ASPLAND MEM. E.B.F. STAKES 3YO+   £3464   1m 5f Firm 15 +11 Fast

2236 MYTH [1] (R F Johnson Houghton) 3-8-6 K Darley 5/1: -211301: 3 b f Troy - Hay Reef
(Mill Reef) Useful filly: led below dist and held on well in a fast run and quite val stks
race at Ayr: earlier won a Chester mdn and a minor event at Catterick: very eff over 12/13f
on firm and yldg ground: acts on any trk: genuine and consistent.   52

-2042 ROYAL DYNASTY [5] (G Wragg) 3-8-5 P Robinson 5/1: -00012: Led over 2f out: kept on
gamely and is in gd form: stays 13f well: see 2042.   49

2627 HERRADURA [6] (M Prescott) 5-9-1(vis) M Birch 10/1: 2D32033: Quick reappearance and
ran another gd race: see 1349 & 743.   45

*2582 INNISHMORE ISLAND [3] (J Dunlop) 3-8-5 R Fox 11/8 FAV: 3032214: Heavily bckd to
follow up his recent win: outstayed over this longer trip: see 2582 (10f).   40
2247 MISAAFF [2] 3-8-5(BL) R Hills 6/1: 3-41100: Bl first time: much btr here in 1808 (10f)   35
1980 PERFECT DOUBLE [8] 5-7-12 T Williams 50/1: 4032200: Btn over 2f out: best in 770 (sharp)   06
2492 JIPIJAPA [7] 5-7-12(vis) A Mackay 50/1: 0000300: Made most: see 2141.   00
2085 PEPENON [4] 4-8-1 J H Brown(1) 33/1: -000: Al behind: btr over 1m in 1841.   00
8 ran   ½,2,2½,3,4,nk,1½   (J W Rowles)   R F Johnson Houghton Blewbury, Oxon

2667 LADBROKES LANTON LEISURE STAKES 2YO   £3928   6f   Firm 15 -09 Slow

*2491 LUCAYAN KNIGHT [4] (M Stoute) 2-9-0 P Robinson 11/4: 211: 2 b c Dominion - Riverine
(Riverman) Useful colt: nicely bckd and sn in front and held on gamely in a tight fin to quite
a val 2yo stks at Ayr: earlier a cmftbly winner of a Nottingham mdn: cost 50,000 gns as a
yearling: very eff over 6f and sure to stay further: acts on gd and fast ground and on a
gall trk: genuine sort who is clearly well suited by forcing tactics.   55
2418 HOW VERY TOUCHING [5] (J Hindley) 2-8-11 R Hills 5/1: 222: Ev ch, ran on well but
again found one too good: due a change of luck & sure to win sn: acts on gd and firm
ground and on any trk: see 2423.   50
1510 BOWERS FOLD [7] (S Hall) 2-8-11 G Carter 12/1: 03: Abs: fin fast and only narrowly
btn: sure to be suited by another furlong: acts on fast grd and on a gall trk: will win a
race: see 1510.   50
2561 WAR BRAVE [1] (J Dunlop) 2-8-11 R Fox 13/8 FAV: 24: Again heavily bckd: led briefly
below dist, no extra cl home: not btn far and sure to be placed to win at one of the lesser
trks: see 2561.   49
1936 BLICO [3] 2-8-11 G Sexton 66/1: 00: Stayed on from dist and is clearly on the upgrade:
very cheaply bought colt who will be suited by further: acts on firm grd and on a gall trk.   44
2444 OH DANNY BOY [2] 2-8-11 E Guest(3) 20/1: 000: Pressed leaders till no extra dist.   39
2499 PETICOV SHADES [6] 2-8-11 M Fry 12/1: 020: Wknd below dist: best 2499.   37
2514 MON BALZAR [9] 2-8-11 R Cochrane 20/1: 0000: Speed to ½ way: fin 8th: see 2514.   00
2423 HAPPY HARRIET [8] 2-8-8 J Lowe 100/1: 00: Never went pace: half sister to sev winners,
incl useful 8/9f performer Steelworks: should improve when tackling longer dist next term.   00
9 ran   ½,shthd,½,1½,1½,½   (Lady Hayward)   M Stoute Newmarket

2668 LADBROKES AYR GOLD CUP (H'CAP)(0-75)   £22470   6f   Firm 15 +12 Fast   [67]

+2204 GREEN RUBY [17] (G Balding) 5-8-11(3ex) J Williams 25/1: 0331411: 5 br h Shecky Greene
- Ruby Tuesday (T V Daly) Very useful sprinter: al prom on stands side and led inside dist for
a narrow win in fast run and val Ayr Gold Cup at Ayr: enjoying a fine season, earlier a
similarly narrow winner of the Stewards Cup H'cap at Goodwood and has since taken another val
prize at York: in '84 won at Pontefract: very eff over 6f, stays 7f: best form on fast ground
tho' does act on heavy: genuine sort who seems to have no trk preferences.   62
*2537 FELIPE TORO [29] (M H Easterby) 3-8-6(7ex) J Lowe 5/1 FAV: 2111112: Caused sev over-
drafts! Fin strongly but just failed to justify hvy mkt support: much impr this term: see 2537   60
2204 BOOT POLISH [23] (J Watts) 4-8-1 N Connorton 20/1: 1001303: Fin well and only
narrowly btn: fine eff and should be winning again soon: see 1429.   50
2573 NUMISMATIST [11] (M Francis) 7-7-12 N Carlisle 33/1: 204-404: Ev ch: grand eff: see 1933   43
-2258 IRISH COOKIE [16] 4-7-8 G Dickie 20/1: 0141020: Led centre, not btn far: see 1026.   38
2446 OUR JOCK [15] 4-8-12 S Whitworth 9/1: 0410420: Well bckd: al front rank: in gd form.   55
*2446 MANTON DAN [22] 3-8-11(7ex) P Cook 10/1: 2010110: Cl 7th: another gd eff: see 2446.   57
2446 PADRE PIO [25] 5-8-1 K Darley 16/1: 0200230: Never nearer 8th: in gd form: see 2151.   42
2537 POWDER BLUE [5] 4-8-6 P Robinson 40/1: -040100: Won his race on the far side: fine
effort: see 1608.   41
+2362 CATHERINES WELL [6] 3-8-13(BL)(7ex) G Carter 12/1: 3311110: Bl first time: made most
far side: see 2362.   00
2204 MATOU [1] 6-9-0 W Ryan 40/1: 202D100: Not well drawn, late prog: see 1810.   00
+2343 JOKIST [27] 3-7-8 R Street 15/2: -021110: Well bckd to complete his four-timer,
squeezed start and never reached front rank: btr judged on his effortless win in 2343.   00

2537 Lochtillum [3] 8-3   2204 Lochonica [4] 8-11   2537 Ferryman [13] 8-2(BL)
2632 Rambling River [19] 7-8(vis)   2524 All Is Forgiven [7] 9-7(bl)
2537 Bollin Emily [12] 8-6   2457 Al Trui [10] 8-9   2545 Hay Street [20] 8-4
*2369 Hilton Brown [18] 8-10   2537 Dawns Delight [8] 9-1(vis)
2446 Viltash [28] 7-11(vis)   2343 Compleat [26] 8-2
2537 Chaplins Club [2] 8-6(bl)   2475 Young Inca [9] 8-6
2537 Sullys Choice [14] 7-11   1777 Touch Of Grey [24] 8-10
2526 Air Command [21] 7-8
29 ran   nk,½,1½,nk,nk,nk,hd,½   (Mrs J Everitt)   G Balding Fyfield, Hants.

2669 LADBROKE HOTELS NURSERY H'CAP 2YO   £4688   6f   Firm 15 -01 Slow   [51]

2479 AUTHENTIC [4] (N Tinkler) 2-9-7 Kim Tinkler 12/1: 221001: 2 br c Derrylin - Crystallize
(Reliance II) Useful colt: returned to form when gamely making most in a nursery h'cap at
Ayr: earlier successful in a mdn on this course: brother to the smart juv Johnny Nobody: eff
over 6/7f: acts on fast and yldg ground and is well suited by this gall trk.   56
*2423 PREMIER LAD [3] (W Pearce) 2-8-11 D Nicholls 10/3 FAV: 03012: Led briefly dist, ran
on well under press and only just denied: cmftbly beat rem and is in gd form: see 2423.   46

2276 JAYS SPECIAL [9] (M W Easterby) 2-8-10 M Birch 9/2: 0001233: Never nearer: see 2276.   38
2472 KALAS IMAGE [8] (G Moore) 2-7-12 A Mackay 11/1: 0314004: Fin well: best 1561.   24
1825 PHILOTAS [7] 2-8-12 L Charnock 16/1: 4020: Outpaced early, fin well: see 1050.   38
2307 JUVENILEDELINQUENT [6] 2-8-5(bl) R Cochrane 8/1: 124400: Al mid-div: see 1936 & 1612.   25
2479 NORTON MELODY [12] 2-8-2 G Carter 10/1: 33300: Fdd into 7th: see 2051 & 1634.   22
*1962 NIFTY GRIFF [5] 2-8-9 K Bradshaw(5) 9/1: 0011010: Fin 9th: btr 1962.   00
2391 MAZURKANOVA [11] 2-7-9 J Lowe 17/2: 4204100: Speed to ½ way: best 2026 (claimer).   00
1965 Flair Park [1] 8-1   2535 Miss Emily [2] 7-7(1oh)
2465 Emmer Green [10] 8-12
12 ran   shthd,3,1,shthd,2½,shthd,1½   (Full Circle Thoroughbreds B Ltd)   N Tinkler Malton

2670 AYRLINE TROPHY (FILLIES STAKES) 3YO   £3204   7f   Firm 15 -19 Slow

*2314 BASICALLY BETTER [5] (P Walwyn) 3-8-12(vis) N Carlisle 5/2: -400011: 3 b f Derrylin -
Oudalia (Gala Performance) Nicely bckd and led below dist, ridden out in a 3yo fillies stks
at Ayr: last month was an easy winner of a Warwick mdn: eff over 7/8f: acts on firm and yldg
ground and on any trk: seems much improved by a visor and could win a h'cap.   36
2440 FLUTTERY [4] (G Wragg) 3-8-5 P Robinson 1/1 FAV: 3022432: Looked to have a simple
task but again lacked foot at the business end of the race: has had plenty of chances to
break her duck: see 2440 & 1902.   24
2086 SKELTON [6] (M W Easterby) 3-8-12 M Birch 12/1: 0030023: Tried to make all: fine
effort but almost certainly flattered by her proximity to the first two: see 650.   30
2277 DEBBIE DO [2] (C Thornton) 3-8-12 J Bleasdale 6/1: 4000004: Longer trip: btr 2277 (6f).   24
1727 LUNAR SHAMAL GAL [3] 3-8-12 W Ryan 14/1: 1-00000: Abs: held up and no threat: see 447.   18
2299 FAIR CADETTE [1] 3-8-5 N Connorton 100/1: -00: Wknd over 2f out: lightly raced filly.   00
6 ran   1½,shthd,2½,2½,5   (Bloodstock & Stud Investment Co Ltd)   P Walwyn Lambourn

2671 WEIR MEMORIAL TROPHY (H'CAP)(0-60) 3YO   £4149   1m 2f   Firm 15 -12 Slow   [41]

2408 KEEPCALM [3] (G Wragg) 3-9-7 P Robinson 9/2: -04041: 3 b c Auction Ring - Old Kate
(Busted) Defied topweight in a 3yo h'cap at Ayr, led inside dist and ran on strongly: well
suited by 10f and fast ground: seems best on a gall trk: lightly raced and should imp further.   45
*2490 SPRING FLIGHT [4] (A Jarvis) 3-8-13 D Nicholls 5/2 FAV: 2311312: Led 3f out, ran
on well: in grand form and can win again soon: see 2490.   35
2478 SPACE TROOPER [2] (T Fairhurst) 3-8-6 A Mackay 11/2: 1132043: Made most: consistent.   23
2339 PRAIRIE OYSTER [7] (B Hanbury) 3-9-4 R Hills 10/1: -0324: Running well: stays 10f.   31
2404 HOMME DAFFAIRE [8] 3-9-3 G Lewis 8/1: 0-01000: Best with some give in 459.   26
2426 BALNERINO [6] 3-9-0 L Charnock 14/1: 4010030: Best here in 1813 (gd).   06
*2267 HONEST TOIL [5] 3-9-4 D Mckeown 9/2: 41D4110: Held up, no threat: much btr 2267.   00
2508 RUN BY JOVE [1] 3-9-1 T Williams 8/1: 0022300: Much btr over 1m in 1924: see 674.   00
8 ran   ½,2½,2,2,1½,1   (E B Moller)   G Wragg Newmarket

Official Going Given As GOOD

2672 MARLBOROUGH STAKES 3YO   £4581   5f   Good/Firm 31 +02 Fast

2524 FILLEOR [10] (G P Gordon) 3-8-11 G Duffield 8/1: 2-00441: 3 b f Wolverlife - Woo
(Stage Door Johnny) Led final 1f, readily, in a val 3yo stks at Newbury: ex Irish filly who
in '85 won at Phoenix Park and the Curragh: very eff at 5f, does stay 6f: acts on fast & yldg.   66
2474 POSSEDYNO [9] (D Elsworth) 3-9-0 S Cauthen 6/1: -311002: Ran on well final 1f: another
gd effort: see 1654.   63
1387 FAYRUZ [1] (W O'gorman) 3-9-0(vis) Pat Eddery 7/1: -000003: Led 4f: gd eff after
abs: see 600.   58
1228 BUTSOVA [7] (R Armstrong) 3-8-2 W Carson 25/1: -03344: Nearest fin: ran well after
fair abs: best 966 (7f).   41
2524 WELSH NOTE [6] 3-9-0 T Ives 7/2: -444020: Ev ch inside final 2f: beat winner 2524.   50
2488 GLIKIAA MOU [4] 3-8-11 N Adams 33/1: 4200140: Speed over 3f: in fine form: see 2210.   43
2503 MAROUBLE [3] 3-9-2 J Reid 3/1 FAV: 23-0030: Prom over 3f: well below 2503.   44
2084 SUNDEED [8] 3-9-0 Paul Eddery 8/1: 10-00000: No show: stiff task: see 1777.   00
2224 Tax Roy [2] 8-11   -- Individualist [5] 9-0
10 ran   2,1½,1½,½,½   (Warner L Jones Jnr)   G P Gordon Newmarket

2673 HAYNES HANSON AND CLARK STAKES 2YO   £5676   1m   Good/Firm 31 -08 Slow

2159 THAMEEN [9] (H T Jones) 2-8-11 A Murray 6/1: 41: 2 ch c Roberto - Secreterial Queen
(Secretariat) Very promising colt: al front rank and led inside final 3f, cmftbly, in val
2yo stks at Newbury: first time out fin 4th to New Attitude on this trk: cost $600,000 as
yearling: well suited by 1m and should prove eff over middle dist next season: acts well on
gd/firm ground and a gall track: will improve further and win more good races.   64
-- ZERO WATT [5] (G Harwood) 2-8-11 G Starkey 20/1: 2: Came from off the pace and fin
in fine style: excellent racecourse debut from this $72,000 purchase: half brother to Ayr
Gold Cup and Stewards Cup winner Green Ruby: eff at 1m, will be well suited by middle dist:
acts on gd/firm ground and will win races.   63

2199 MERCE CUNNINGHAM [11] (W Hern) 2-8-11 W Carson 4/6 FAV: 323: Heavily bckd: ev ch
over 1f out but could only stay on at the one pace: already needs further than 1m: see 2199
2484 ROUSHAYD [6] (R J Houghton) 2-8-11 S Cauthen 10/1: 24: Al up there: another fine eff:
stays 1m: see 2484.   60
--   DRY DOCK [3] 2-8-11 B Procter 25/1: 0: Chance 2f out: not given a hard time and is   56
certain to improve on this debut effort: from a very gd winning family that includes Oaks
winner Bireme: dam lightly raced and won over 1m as a 2yo: should be suited by 10/12f:
acts on fast ground and a gall trk: one to follow.   55
1903 ESKIMO MITE [4] 2-8-11 T Quinn 11/1: 40: Stiff task, but ran well: eff at 1m and
should get further: see 1903.   47
--   LAVROSKY [13] 2-8-11 Pat Eddery 7/1: 0: Fin 7th on racecourse debut and improvement
very likely: US bred colt who cost $1.3m: bred to stay 10f+: acts on gd/firm.   44
--   KADAN [1] 2-8-11 M Hills 33/1: 0: Prom most on racecourse debut and will be btr for
the run: German bred colt who has scope.   42
2159 Flutter Money [7] 8-11   2159 Beryls Joke [8] 8-11
2407 Alaskan [10] 8-11   2044 Glen Weaving [12] 8-11
12 ran ¾,1,2,¾,4,1¼,¾   (Hamdan Al Maktoum)   H T Jones Newmarket

2674 SCHWEPPES AUTUMN HANDICAP 0-70 3YO+   £7189   7f 6oy Good/Firm 31 +06 Fast   [59]

1852 GOLD PROSPECT [1] (G Balding) 4-8-4 B Rouse 13/2: 0402301: 4 b c Wolverlife -
Golden Darling (Darling Boy) Useful colt: led inside final 1f cmftbly, in val Autumn H'cap
at Newbury: in fine form this season, winning early on at Folkestone and subs being narrowly
btn in many val h'caps: eff at 6f, stays 7f well: acts on firm and soft grd and on any trk:
genuine and consistent.   47
2562 BELOW ZERO [14] (A Bailey) 3-8-6 T Ives 8/1: 0101402: Dsptd lead over 1f out, but
hung left: running very well at present: see 2063.   50
2155 HIGHEST PRAISE [17] (I Balding) 3-8-4 M Marshall(7) 9/1: 0133103: Not the best of
runs and stayed on well: likes this trk: see 1640.   44
2144 HELLO SUNSHINE [3] (L Holt) 7-7-7 N Adams 14/1: 0040004: Ran on well under press on
his fav trk: see 1640.   26
2234 RESOURCEFUL FALCON [12] 3-9-10 T Quinn 16/1: 0220000: Anchored by his big weight,
but ran a fine race: see 692, 586.   57
2390 TOP WING [2] 3-8-2(VIS) M Hills 14/1: 1030400: Visored first time: led 1½f out:
better 2255 (1m) see 188.   33
2488 USEFUL [16] 3-8-2 W Carson 6/1 FAV: 3010230: Made no show: btr 6f? See 1847.   00
2382 PRECIOUS METAL [8] 3-9-5 R Curant 10/1: 0300100: Twice well below 2258 (6f).   00
2526 Corn Street [4] 8-6   2250 Ambrosini [10] 8-1   2343 Taranga [5] 7-12
2544 Steady Eddie [9] 8-6   2537 Careless Whisper [13] 8-0
2431 Joyful Dancer [7] 7-12   2566 Sit This One Out [15] 9-7
2562 Reindeer Walk [19] 8-9   2562 Deadbolt [18] 8-4
2382 Pas De Regrets [11] 7-11   2463 King Of Spades [6] 8-7
19 ran 1½,2½,¾,2½,¾   (Harvey Spack)   G Balding Fyfield, Hants.

2675 STABLE STUD AND FARM EAST WEST STKS 2YO £6679   7f   Good/Firm 31 +02 Fast

--   MILLIGRAM [9] (M Stoute) 2-8-8 W R Swinburn 13/2: 1: 2 ch f Mill Reef - One In A
Million (Rarity) Very promising filly: first time out, easy to back, but led over 1f out,
ridden out to win a val and competitive fillies mdn at Newbury in a gd time: impeccably bred
filly whose dam won the 1,000 Guineas: eff at 7f, will be suited by 1m: acts on gd/firm grd
and a gall trk: has scope for improvement and looks certain to win more races.   66
--   MAMOUNA [23] (M Stoute) 2-8-8 A Kimberley 33/1: 2: Lesser fancied stable mate of
winner but made most on the stands side and kept on really well: US bred filly who should be
well suited by 1m and further: acts on gd/firm grd and a gall trk: has scope for improvement
and will not be long in winning.   64
--   GOLD FEE [12] (L Cumani) 2-8-8 Pat Eddery 5/2 FAV: 3: Very heavily bckd debutant:
ev ch over 1f out and was not given a hard time: looks certain to repay that kindness in
the near future: bred to stay middle dist: acts on gd/firm ground.   60
--   SUMMER POSY [24] (I Balding) 2-8-8 T Ives 16/1: 4: Made gd late hdwy on her debut
and should be noted next time: half sister to numerous winners, including the useful Cistus
and the very smart Lancastrian: should be suited by 1m: acts on gd/firm ground.   56
--   HEIGHT OF ELEGANCE [17] 2-8-8 Paul Eddery 25/1: 0: Al there: impr very likely:
dam a very useful sprinter, but should stav 1m: acts on gd/firm ground and will find a rce.   56
2418 CASTLE IN THE AIR [25] 2-8-8 T Quinn 13/2: 30: Stayed on well but never nearer:
will be well suited by 1m and can win soon: see 2418.   55
--   HEAD OF VICTORY [20] 2-8-8 W Carson 12/1: 0: Not btn far in 7th on debut: American bred
filly whose dam was the topclass stayer Shoot A Line: should be suited by 1m, acts on gd/
firm ground and will improve.   55
2543 CORVIGLIA RUN [18] 2-8-8 B Rouse 20/1: 40: Prom most: again ran well in hot company
and will win when dropped slightly in grade: prob stays 7f: see 2543.   50
--   LA VIE EN ROSE [1] 2-8-8 M Hills 20/1: 0: Prom on the far side most of the way: gd
racecourse debut as she was unfavoured by the draw: should stay 1m.   48
--   SANNOX BAY [4] 2-8-8 S Cauthen 10/1: 0: Prom most far side and should do btr next time:
dam a winner at 2 years at sprint dist: acts on gd/firm.   48
--   BLUE GRASS FIELD [21] 2-8-8 A Murray 33/1: 0: Never beyond mid-div on debut: half
sister to 3 winners and should finish a lot closer next time.   46

-- PETSARIA [19] 2-8-8 J Reid 12/1: 0: Fin 12th: has scope for improvement: cost 62,000 gns
as a yearling and is a half sister to 10f winner Gibberish.   41

-- Kind Of Glitter [5] 8-8		-- Mainmast [13] 8-8
2292 Bingdon Builders [2] 8-8		2029 Bold Duchess [16] 8-8
-- Lipreader [6] 8-8	-- Arriviste [22] 8-8	2368 Brolga [8] 8-8
-- Mayroni [27] 8-8	-- Miss Lalie [10] 8-8	-- Mount Holyoke [3] 8-8
2531 Najaba [7] 8-8	1752 Persian Tapestry [14] 8-8	
252 Sonoco [26] 8-8	-- Tale Of Intrigue [15] 8-8	
-- Vestal Flame [11] 8-8		

27 ran   ¾,2½,2½,hd,nk,shthd,2½,1½,shthd,1,shthd   (H Springfield Ltd)   M Stoute, Newmarket

2676 MAIL ON SUNDAY 3YO SERIES HCAP 3YO 0-50 £4344   1m 2f Good/Firm 31 +05 Fast   [47]

2385 BLACK SOPHIE [2] (R Laing) 3-9-6 M Roberts 15/2: -001041: 3 b f Moorestyle - Rockeater
(Roan Rocket) Useful filly: in fine form and ran on gamely to lead cl home in quite fast run
and val 3yo h'cap at Newbury: last time out an excellent 4th to Purchasepaperchase over 1m
at Sandown: earlier won a 3yo h'cap over 7f at Brighton, but now seems eff over 1m/10f:
acts on any trk: runs well on gd and fast ground: genuine.   51
2217 SHEER LUCK [7] (I Balding) 3-8-8 Pat Eddery 4/1 FAV: 4-00102: Well bckd: very nearly
made all: fine effort and should find another h'cap soon: definitely best out in front:see 1657   37
1337 NIHAD [1] (B Hanbury) 3-9-1 G Baxter 20/1: -400323: Abs: chance over 1f out and btn
1l in a cl fin: grand effort: deserves a win: suited by 10f: see 1169, 213.   43
*2548 SATIN AND SILK [3] (A Bailey) 3-9-0(6ex) P Bloomfield 7/1: -300214: In gd form: see 2548   35
2072 MORICA [5] 3-9-2 W Carson 8/1: 1-4040: Nearest fin: lightly raced this term: prob
stays 10f: see 1515.   37
2333 ZINDELINA [4] 3-8-10 A Mcglone 16/1: -204020: Chance over 2f out: btr 2333 (easy 1m).   30
*2404 RATTLE ALONG [10] 3-9-7 Paul Eddery 13/2: -010210: There 1m: well below 2404.   00
*2459 LADY LA PAZ [14] 3-8-9(6ex) N Adams 12/1: 3330310: Fdd over 2f out: much btr 2459 (1m)   00
2459 FLYING BIDDY [15] 3-8-8 M Hills 7/1: 3001320: No show: btr 2549 (1m).   00

2546 Mirataine Venture [9] 8-2		1628 Lumiere [11] 8-7
2548 Mary Sunley [12] 8-0	642 Dunoof [8] 9-7	1580 Veronica Ann [13] 8-6
2248 Glade [6] 8-8		

15 ran   ½,½,4,shthd,½   (Mrs H R Slack)   R Laing Lambourn, Berks

2677 FAIRHURST NURSERY HANDICAP 2YO   £4344   7f 60y Good/Firm 31 -07 Slow   [57]

*2095 ORIENT LINE [13] (R Hannon) 2-7-7(1oh) G French 4/1 FAV: 0211: 2 gr c Capricorn Line
- Rue Talma (Vigo) Impr colt: well bckd and ran on well to lead inside final 1f, cmftbly, in
a nursery h'cap at Newbury: last time out was a ready winner of a mdn auction at Folkestone:
cost only 3,400 gns and is closely related to sev minor winners: eff at 6f, stays 7f well
and should get 1m: acts on any trk.   35
2521 PLAGUE ORATS [1] (R Smyly) 2-8-10 A Murray 11/1: 01432: Led inside final 2f: caught
near finish: stays 7f, but didnot get home over 1m last time: see 1681.   46
*2205 ABLE SAINT [2] (R Armstrong) 2-9-7 S Cauthen 6/1: 213: Anchored by weight final 1f:
another fine effort: see 2205: stays 7f.   51
2529 KEEN EDGE [9] (P Mitchell) 2-7-11(2ow) A Mcglone 7/1: 0303024: Ev ch final 2f:
consistent: stays 7f: see 2529.   22
2272 KIERON PRESS [5] 2-8-3 Paul Eddery 20/1: 031400: Never nearer: stays 7f: see 1495.   24
1097 DIAMOND FLIGHT [3] 2-9-1 B Rouse 20/1: 014400: Abs: nearest fin and should do
btr next time: stays 7f: see 804, 261: acts on gd/firm and soft.   30
2511 UNIFORMITY [4] 2-9-4 W R Swinburn 9/2: 0130: Led 2f out, fdd: see 2179 (sharpish 6f).   00
2383 COMBINED EXERCISE [12] 2-8-9 W Carson 10/1: 000430: No show: much btr 2383 (1m).   00
*2556 SPY TOWER [6] 2-8-1(6ex) T Quinn 8/1: 00410: Led 5f: btr 2556 (easy trk)   00
2270 UNITY FARM BOY [10] 2-8-0 N Adams 15/2: 00020: Wknd in str: much btr 2270 (6f sharp)   00

*2379 Mr Corman [8] 8-12	2418 Crusade Dancer [11] 9-0	
2383 Murajah [7] 7-9		

13 ran   1¼,3,2½,2,3,½   (A J Lazzari)   R Hannon Marlbourugh, Wilts

Official Going Given As GOOD/FIRM

2678 .E.B.F. ASKRIGG STAKES 2YO   £2434   5f   Firm 19 -07 Slow

2606 MINIZEN LASS [10] (M Brittain) 2-8-8 M Wigham 10/1: 2420031: 2 b f Hittite Glory -
Derrinthea (Derring-Do) Finally got off the mark, sn led and ran on strongly in a 2yo stks
at Catterick: prev had fin 2nd on 5 occasions and has retained her form well in a busy
campaign: well suited by forcing tactics over this minimum trip: acts on fast and yldg grd
and on any trk.   36
2215 MISTS OF AVALON [1] (H Cecil) 2-8-8 W Ryan 2/5 FAV: 4242: Heavily bckd over this shorter
trip: pressed winner thr'out but seems to find this trip on the sharp side: much btr over 7f
in 2215: see 2013.   30
2301 TAMASSOS [4] (G Harwood) 2-8-8 A Clark 14/1: 0003: Al front rank: see 1802.   28
2494 HAYGATE PARK [5] (M Ryan) 2-8-8 N Day 5/1: 044: Ran on same pace: see 2494.   26
2607 PRETTY SOON [3] 2-8-8(bl) M Beecroft 50/1: 400000: Yet to improve on her debut in 1297.   16

-- .M KELLY [6] 2-8-8 M Rimmer 10/1: 0: Some late prog on debut: cost 5200 gns as yearling
and should impr on this next time: acts on fast ground.   15
1545 Multi Spiral [2] 8-8   1680 Joyces Pet [7] 8-8   2499 Firelron [11] 8-8
1782 Try Dancer [12] 8-8   -- Intellect [8] 8-8   -- The Victor Girls [9] 8-8
12 ran 2,¾,½,4,nk,shthd,4,1   (Minizen-Ltd)   M Brittain Warthill, Yorks.

2679 BEDALE SELLING STAKES 3YO   £1052   1m 6f Firm 19 -27 Slow

2515 COOL NUMBER [1] (J Dunlop) 3-8-11 G Sexton 7/2: 0-00331: 3 gr f Swing Easy - January
(Sigebert) Well suited by this longer trip, led below dist, cmftbly in a 3yo seller at
Catterick (sold for 3500 gns): half sister to Janus and Harlestone Lake: eff over 10f, stays 14f well:
suited by fast grd and a sharp trk.   14
2654 G G MAGIC [3] (D Morley) 3-9-0 G Duffield 2/1 FAV: 4200042: Quick reappearance and
nicely bckd: tried to make all, out stayed cl home: gd eff and likes this trk: see 380.   12
2478 DOON VENTURE [9] (J Etherington) 3-9-0 M Birch 7/2: 0-00003: Outstayed over this
longer trip: see 867.   06
2590 REDALLY [8] (W Wharton) 3-9-0 A Shoults(5) 6/1: -0024: Best over 12f in 2590 (gall trk)   01
2125 ANDREAS PRIDE [4] 3-9-0 S Webster 7/1: 04-4040: No real threat: see 2125.   00
2495 GROSVENOR COURT [6] 3-9-0 W Ryan 33/1: 0-0000: Yet to show any worthwhile form:
never dangerous over this longer trip.   00
2590 Tiber Gate [2] 9-0   2478 Tap Duet [7] 9-0(vis)   2412 Sana Song [5] 9-0
9 ran 1½,3,3,3,3,1½,6,8   (J L Dunlop)   J Dunlop Arundel, Sussex

2680 LONDON & NORTHERN GROUP NURSERY H'CAP   £4805   7f   Firm 19 -03 Slow   [50]

2512 THANK HAVON [9] (D Morley) 2-8-9 M Wigham 9/1: 4040341: 2 ch f Mansingh - Great Blue
White (Great Nephew) Led well over 1f out, gamely, in a nursery h'cap at Catterick: sister to
useful sprinter Blue Singh: eff between 6f and 1m: well suited by fast grd and a sharp trk.   40
2472 BEAU BENZ [13] (M H Easterby) 2-8-1 A Shoults(5) 20/1: 0040002: Ran on well: gd eff
and seems best over 7f: acts on gd and firm grd and on any trk: see 583.   30
2479 GLAMGRAM FOR GRAMS [12] (R Boss) 2-8-7 G Duffield 11/4: 04143: Not btn far: in gd
form: see 2011.   35
2498 TIKLAS [8] (F Durr) 2-7-7(2oh) G French 9/1: 0043434: Best over 1m in 2498.   19
2498 EUROCON [2] 2-8-1(1ow) S Webster 20/1: 0024000: Stayed on well: gd eff: see 2050.   25
*1611 MONS FUTURE [7] 2-7-9 A Proud 12/1: 1422210: Abs: late prog: best 1611 (6f).   17
2479 COLWAY RALLY [11] 2-9-4(bl) A Mercer 8/1: 2032400: Never nearer 7th: can do btr: see 1798 00
2425 PASHMINA [6] 2-8-5 M Rimmer 16/1: 1033300: Longer trip, fin 8th: btr 2265 (5f) see 1893   00
*2563 MASTER POKEY [5] 2-8-11(9ex) M Birch 7/4 FAV: 01110: Made much: wknd into 9th: btr 2563 00
2276 TOLL BAR [4] 2-9-7 E Guest(3) 10/1: 01000: Prom over ½ way: best over this C/D in 1735.   00
1812 Mughtanim [3] 8-11   2287 Accustomed [1] 8-8   2493 Swing Singer [10] 7-7(2oh)
13 ran ½,½,½,½,1,1,½,½,hd   (Mrs C Van C Anthony)   D Morley Newmarket

2681 JOHN SMITHS STAKES H'CAP (0-35)   £2273   7f   Firm 19 +09 Fast   [35]

2343 PULHAM MILLS [12] (E Eldin) 3-9-3(vis) E Guest(3) 12/1: 0012201: 3 b c Morston -
Millimeter (Ribocco) Sn led when a cheeky winner of a fast run h'cap at Catterick: earlier
gamely made all in a 3yo h'cap at Warwick: very eff over 7/8f with forcing tactics: suited by
fast grd and a sharpish trk.   38
2508 ARE YOU GUILTY [1] (M Ryan) 3-9-5 G Bardwell(7) 10/1: 3000102: Fin well: gd eff and
likes a tight trk: acts on fast and soft ground: see 2390.   38
1987 VIRGIN ISLE [14] (P Haslam) 5-9-11 G French 12/1: 0404003: Ran on: not btn far: see 79   38
2490 SPECIAL GUEST [10] (D Morley) 3-7-13 W Woods(3) 12/1: 3324034: Cl 4th: running well.   16
1695 KENOOZ [4] 3-9-1 W Hayes(7) 16/1: 0-20400: No luck in running: not btn very far
and certainly would have finished in the money with a clear run: will be suited by 1m: see 657   32
2513 MARAVILLA [2] 4-8-3(bl) G Duffield 4/1: 2420020: Ran on same pace: btr 2513 (6f)   13
*2601 HAYWAIN [5] 3-7-12(vis)(6ex) S Whitworth 10/3 FAV: 0300010: Fin 7th: best 2601.   00
2544 MR ROSE [7] 6-8-9 P Hutchinson(3) 9/1: 2010040: No threat: best 1901 (stiff trk)   00
*2295 EASTBROOK [18] 6-8-11 A Shoults(5) 17/2: 2132410: Early leader: btr over 6f in 2295.   00
1616 WIZZARD MAGIC [9] 3-8-2(bl)(7ow) A Clark 10/1: 00-0320: Al rear after abs: btr 1499 (6f)   00
2390 Young Bruss [8] 8-7   2463 Sequestrator [17] 8-8   2602 Just A Bit [19] 7-13
2424 Royal Rouser [11] 8-9   2414 Janes Brave Boy [15] 7-12
2583 Minders Man [6] 7-12(bl)(2ow)   2437 Improvise [3] 8-9
2340 Brampton Imperial [13] 7-12   2274 Dragonara Boy [20] 8-8
19 ran nk,½,½,hd,½,1½,nk,nk   (P E Mills)   E Eldin Newmarket

2682 MIDDLEHAM MAIDEN STAKES 3YO   £959   2m   Firm 19 -01 Slow

2492 SHAHS CHOICE [8] (J Dunlop) 3-9-0 G Sexton 4/9 FAV: 0432221: 3 b c Persian Bold -
Royal Display (Right Royal V) Well bckd and had a simple task, cruised into lead home turn
and was sn clear in a 3yo mdn at Catterick: deserved this win after a succession of placings:
eff around 12/14f, clearly stays 2m well: acts on fast and yldg grd and on any trk.   35
2464 COMAZANT [4] (G Harwood) 3-9-0 A Clark 6/1: -0002: No chance with this easy winner:
cost $265,000 as yearling and is a half brother to sev winners tho' has shown only modest
form himself to date: stays well: acts on fast ground.   14
2551 SEATYRN [3] (S Norton) 3-9-0 M Wigham 12/1: -340003: Best over 10f in 699: see 487.   06

2400 RIDESIDE [9] (M W Easterby) 3-8-11 J Bleasdale 14/1: -04: Mkt drifter: held up and
never nearer: half sister to 8/10f winner Rose Glow and is bred to be well suited by middle
distances: acts on fast ground.   02
1873 PINZAUREOLE [1] 3-8-11 K Bradshaw(5) 33/1: -000: Well btn after abs: no form.   00
2464 MARBLE MOON [7] 3-8-11 S Perks 12/1: -0000: Led over 6f out, wknd: btr 2464 (14f).   00
2520 ON THE AGENDA [5] 3-8-11 G Duffield 15/2: 0-0000: Dropped out after ½ way: see 2520.   00
2042 Gunner Mac [6] 9-0   2400 Togdale [2] 9-0 P
9 ran   10,7,1½,10,10,6   (Lord Granard)   J Dunlop Arundel, Sussex

2683 RALPH LAWSON MEM. HANDICAP (0-35) 3YO+   £2088   1m 4f   Firm 19 +01 Fast   [26]

*1072 JOHN DOREY [11] (M Prescott) 3-9-2 G Duffield 5/2 FAV: 40-11: 3 ch c Malinowski -
Tuna (Silver Shark) Nicely bckd after a long abs and ran on well to lead cl home in an all
aged h'cap at Catterick: first time out an easy winner of an Edinburgh mdn and clearly does
well when fresh: closely related to sev winners, including useful stayer Jean-Claude: stays
12f well and will be suited by further: acts on fast grd and on a sharp trk: should defy
a penalty.   36
1809 FOUR STAR THRUST [2] (R Whitaker) 4-9-3 D Mckeown 9/1: 2020232: Led below dist,
caught near fin: gd eff tho' has yet to get her hd in front this term: see 419.   24
1884 DELLWOOD RENOWN [9] (W Holden) 4-7-11 D Mckay 12/1: -033003: Led after ½ way: see 709.00
2330 MR LION [9] (F Carr) 4-8-5 J Carr(7) 16/1: 2220004: Late prog: see 860 & 721.   04
2432 INDIAN ORATOR [10] 3-9-10 S Whitworth 13/2: -313440: Ran on same pace: see 1135.   28
2426 TOWER FAME [13] 3-8-1(bl) J Bleasdale 12/1: 0040000: No extra 2f out: see 2426 & 90.   00
2477 GREED [17] 5-9-5 M Birch 8/1: 2404240: Wknd into 7th: see 2415, 1185.   00
449 TIMMINION [4] 4-8-11 C Dwyer 5/1: 0-30000: Long abs: fdd into 8th: btr here 44.   00
2572 ELVIRE [6] 3-8-3 M Wigham 15/2: -004040: Btr over 11f in 1578 (gd).   00
2467 Boldera [7] 8-0   2101 Jubilant Lady [14] 7-7(6oh)
2152 Cocked Hat Supreme [8] 9-2   2400 Santo Boy [5] 8-7
449 Bamdoro [3] 8-2   381 Paravane [15] 8-12   2327 Golflines [12] 7-12
2106 Choral Park [16] 8-4
17 ran   1½,3,2,2,5   (Mrs V Bourne)   M Prescott Newmarket

2684 LADBROKE STRATHCLYDE H'CAP 3YO 0-60   £4409   1m   Firm 10 +02 Fast   [55]

2508 IRISH PASSAGE [6] (D Barron) 3-8-5 D Nicholls 5/1: 2D00121: 3 gr g Welsh Captain -
Honeys Queen (Pals Passage) In gd form, held up and ran on strongly to lead near fin in a
3yo h'cap at Ayr: last month won a similar race at Thirsk: successful on sole start last
season in a stks race at Ripon: very eff over 6/8f: suited by fast grd and acts on any trk.   43
2629 SOLO STYLE [4] (G Lewis) 3-9-0 P Waldron 11/2: 0141142: Just failed to make all:
genuine sort who is in fine form and should win again soon: see 2303.   50
2458 TURFAH [1] (P Walwyn) 3-9-7 N Howe 9/4 FAV: 2111223: Not btn far: in grand form: see 2234.56
2399 IMPERIAL PALACE [2] (C Tinkler) 3-7-13 M Wood 8/1: 0021104: Ran on same pace: see 2313.   26
2400 PLEASING PROSPECT [8] 3-7-7 J Lowe 6/1: 0-03000: Ran on too late: see 1511.   19
2481 IZZY GUNNER [5] 3-7-7(8oh) T Williams 16/1: 2200140: No extra 2f out: see 2481 & 2361.   18
2165 EAGLE DESTINY [7] 3-9-0 J Matthias 8/1: -021200: Al behind: btr 1743: see 1184.   00
2475 TAYLORMADE BOY [3] 3-8-7 L Charnock 10/1: 0310100: Wknd and fin last: best 2266 (gd)   00
8 ran   ½,nk,4,¼,¼,¼   (T Wilson)   D Barron Maunby, Yorks

2685 HOLSTEN DIAT PILS H'CAP 3YO+ 0-70   £5665   7f   Firm 10 +04 Fast   [58]

2629 EMERALD EAGLE [2] (C Booth) 5-7-7(4oh) T Williams 8/1: 0100001: 5 ch m Sandy Creek -
Double Eagle (Goldhill) Made a quick reappearance and returned to her best form, cmftbly making
all in course record time in a h'cap at Ayr: last month won a similar race over 1m on this
course and early in the season was successful at Cagnes: very eff over 7/8f: acts on firm
and hvy ground and is well suited by a gall trk, especially Ayr: should win again.   33
*2526 THE MAZALL [4] (L Siddall) 6-8-5(7ex) M Wood 5/2 JT FAV: 2110012: Dwelt, stayed on:
remains in gd form tho' best when out in front: see 2526.   42
2437 POSTORAGE [1] (M Mccormack) 4-9-10 G Baxter 5/2 JT FAV: 0010043: Another gd eff: see 1292.59
2481 BOLD SEA ROVER [5] (M H Easterby) 3-7-11 J Lowe 5/1: 3010024: Ran to his best: see 1840. 36
2458 RESCUE PACKAGE [6] 3-8-1 K Darley 9/1: 0440300: Never reached leaders: see 579.   36
2602 RECOLLECT [3] 4-7-7(1oh) N Carlisle 7/1: 0230-00: No extra below dist: placed sev
times last season over 7/8f, when showing his best form with some give in the ground.   23
-- Gouverno [7] 9-1   668 Mels Choice [8] 7-7(4oh)
8 ran   2½,1½,½,½,shthd   (A Lyons)   C Booth Flaxton, Yorks

2686 LADBROKES AYRSHIRE H'CAP 3YO+ 0-70   £7431   1m 3f   Firm 10 -13 Slow   [53]

2630 RANA PRATAP [1] (G Lewis) 6-9-7 P Waldron 8/1: 0420141: 6 b h Falikari - Dodo S
(Nagea) Useful h'capper: led over 2f out and held on gamely in c val h'cap at Ayr: last month
won a similar race at Epsom: in '85 won a h'cap at York and seems to like a gall track:
suited by 10/11f nowadays: acts on firm and soft ground and on any trk.   58
+2551 HIGH TENSION [8] (G P Gordon) 4-9-3(3ex) P Waldron 9/4 FAV: 1221012: Kept on well:
just held: in tremendous form this season and can win again soon: see 2551.   53

2536 BALLYDURROW [3] (R Fisher) 9-8-9 D Nicholls 9/1: 0214303: Held up, kept on well:see 1744.   42
2496 VERITABLE [3] (P Haslam) 3-9-2 T Williams 9/2: 3-02134: Led briefly over 2f out: see 1954   54
*1325 MILL PLANTATION [5] 7-9-6 P Robinson 8/1: 10-0010: Gd eff after long abs: see 1325.   49
2536 MASKED BALL [7] 6-8-8 M Fry 9/2: 1202140: No extra 2f out: see 1820 (10f)   35
*2300 KINGS CRUSADE [2] 3-7-11 J Lowe 10/1: 0423310: Made most: wknd into 7th: see 2300.   00
2412 NORTHERN RIVER [6] 4-7-7(3oh) N Carlisle 100/1: 0000-00: Rank outsider: al rear: see 2412   00
8 ran   ½,1½,2½,shthd,2   (Mrs G Thornberry)   G Lewis Epsom, Surrey

2687 FIRTH OF CLYDE STAKES 2YO FILLIES   £8855   6f   Firm 10 +01 Fast

2235 LINDAS MAGIC [12] (R Armstrong) 2-8-8 P Tulk 6/5 FAV: 231131: 2 br f Far North - Pogonip
(Jacinto) Very useful, consistent filly: led below dist and ran on strongly to win quite a
fast run Listed race at Ayr: earlier an easy winner of a fillies stks at Thirsk and a mdn at
Nottingham: related to a winner in the States: very eff over 6/7f on fast grd: acts on any
trk: likes to be up with the pace.   62
*2434 ATTEMPTING [13] (B Hills) 2-8-8 M Hills 7/1: 3112: Met a smart filly here and will
be back in the winners enclosure herself soon: sure to stay further: see 2434.   58
2563 KYVERDALE [7] (M Ryan) 2-8-8 P Robinson 9/1: 0113233: Al front rank: most consistent
filly who is sure to win more races when dropped slightly in class: see 2563 & 2421.   57
2297 SO KIND [10] (J Watts) 2-8-3 N Connorton 14/1: 344: Trouble in running and never
nearer: continues to improve and will be winning soon: see 2043.   51
2482 NORGABIE [3] 2-8-8 M Fry 16/1: 1230: Nearest fin: consistent: see 2482.   52
2391 PEN BAL LADY [12] 2-8-8 P Waldron 16/1: 1211330: Consistent filly: al prom: see 1895.   50
*2448 GHANAYIM [9] 2-8-8 A Murray 10/1: 02210: Didn't have the best of runs but put up
another gd eff to fin 7th: clearly acts on any trk: see 2448.   48
-2555 PELF [5] 2-8-3 P Hamblett 10/1: 2020: Made most, fin 8th: see 2555, 1322.   40
2543 LITTLEFIELD [11] 2-8-8 J Matthias 10/1: 21030: Dsptd lead most: see 2543 & 1583.   00
2465 Glow Again [4] 8-11   2270 Norapa [6] 8-8   2425 Upset [2] 8-8
2310 Wise Times [1] 8-3
13 ran   1½,nk,½,1½,½,½,½,½   (John Bray)   R Armstrong Newmarket

2688 CRAIGMORE SELLING STAKES 3YO   £939   6f   Firm 10 -02 Slow

2483 IMPERIAL SUNRISE [2] (M W Easterby) 3-8-2(BL) P Robinson 9/2: 0020301: 3 b f Kala
Shikari - Reflected Glory (Double Jump) Bl for the first time and stayed on strongly to lead
cl home in a 3yo seller at Ayr (bought in 1900 gns): first success tho' had been placed on
many occasions prev: eff over 6/7f on firm and soft grd: acts on any trk.   20
2497 AVADA [1] (A Jarvis) 2-8-5 D Nicholls 10/1: 0004002: Led below dist: gd eff and
has shown enough ability to win in this grade: suited by a gall trk: see 2085.   19
2065 MANDRAKE MADAM [7] (Denys Smith) 2-8-7 L Charnock 5/2 FAV: 0033003: Dropped in class:
nicely bckd and led/dsptd lead till dist: would have won this on her juv form: see 1380.   18
2361 GODOUNOV [8] (W Storey) 2-8-7(BL)(2ow) A Murray 4/1: -04: Bl first time and again
well bckd: had traffic problems and fin strongly: see 2361.   15
2416 WEBSTERS FEAST [9] 3-8-10(bl) M Hills 9/2: 2043000: Led/dpstd lead most: see 1406.   14
2361 SKYBIRD [6] 2-8-5 K Darley 16/1: 0000030: Btr over 7f in 2361 (gd).   05
2585 Class Hopper [3] 8-5   2424 Cumbrian Nijo [4] 8-10(bl)
2424 Sonnenelle [5] 9-1   2409 Motor Master [10] 8-5(bl)
10 ran   1½,3,2½,2,2½,hd,shthd,2½   (A Dickman)   M W Easterby Sherriff Hutton, Yorks

2689 TOP FLIGHT LEISURE NURSERY HANDICAP   £2758   5f   Firm 10 -07 Slow   [40]

+2421 CHILIBANG [2] (J Dunlop) 2-9-6 G Baxter 3/1: 41011: 2 ro c Formidable - Chili Girl
(Skymaster) Speedy colt who is in fine form: again made all, cmftbly, in a nursery h'cap at
Ayr: recently employed similar tactics to win a nursery at Windsor and a mdn at Nottingham:
half brother to 6/7f winner Hot Case: very eff over 5f, stays 6f well: acts on gd and frm grd
and on any trk: loves being out in front and should not be opposed lightly in this form.   44
2579 WOODMAN WEAVER [1] (J Douglas Home) 2-8-11 P Robinson 10/1: 000432: Kept on well:
without troubling winner: running well at present: see 2218 & 2108.   30
2588 GREENSWARD BOY [2] (K Ivory) 2-7-13(vis) G Dickie 33/1: 0030003: Al front rank: should
win a race if dropped back to selling company: eff over 5f on fast grd: see 1599.   18
2606 SPITTIN MICK [8] (M H Easterby) 2-9-7 K Hodgson 8/1: 1311004: Fin well: btr eff: see 1814   37
859 SANDALL PARK [7] 2-9-4 A Murray 5/2 FAV: 4140: Long abs: heavily bckd fav: would
have finished closer with a clear run: worth another chance: see 771.   34
1844 SURELY GREAT [9] 2-8-9(BL) N Connorton 9/1: 2402020: Bl first time: denied a clear
run and never nearer: likes a gall trk: see 1632 & 1454.   24
*2375 STYLISH ENTRY [3] 2-9-7 M Hills 11/2: 410: Gd early speed: much btr 2375 (sharp trk yld)   00
2410 Miss Display [10] 7-7(6oh)   2421 Nations Song [12] 8-5
2535 Bootham Lad [5] 8-1   2396 Venherm [4] 8-2   2185 Able Abbe [11] 8-7(VIS)
12 ran   2,shthd,1,shthd,½,½,½   (Mrs H J Heinz)   J Dunlop Arundel, Sussex

2690 BRODICK STAKES 3YO   £1874   1m 2f   Firm 10 -16 Slow

*2400 LYPHLAW [5] (J Dunlop) 3-9-3 G Baxter 8/11 FAV: -003311: 3 b c Lyphard - New Lawn
(Herbager) Useful colt: cmftbly landed the odds, led over 2f out in a 3yo stks at Ayr: last

month was a well bckd winner of a Ripon mdn: eff over 8/10f and should stay further: acts
on fast and yldg grd and on any trk: in gd form and can win a h'cap.   50
*2546 HELIETTA [2] (L Cumani) 3-9-0 R Guest 5/4: -042312: Tried to make all: outpaced by
winner: in gd form: see 2546.   41
2300 NOT A PROBLEM [6] (Denys Smith) 3-8-12 D Nicholls 33/1: 4320403: No threat to principals
but showed signs of a return to form here: eff over 10/12f on a gall trk: see 702.   29
2424 FANNY ROBIN [3] (Denys Smith) 3-8-9 L Charnock 50/1: 0004004: Never dangerous: see 1904 14
1425 ANNUAL EVENT [7] 3-8-12 N Carlisle 50/1: 400-000: Abs: btn 2f out: placed in sellers
over sprint dist last season: prob stays 1m: acts on firm and hvy grd.   16
--   OUR JAMIE [4] 3-8-12 P Hamblett 50/1: -0: No threat on racecourse debut: cheaply bought
gelding who is a half brother to a couple of juv winners: should be btr for this experience. 08
2508 DANESMOOR [1] 3-8-9 J H Brown(5) 33/1: -000000: Best over 1m in 1880 (gd).   00
7 ran   3,4,6,½,4   (Sheikh Mohammed)   J Dunlop Arundel, Sussex

NEWBURY   Saturday September 20th   Lefthand, Galloping Track

Official Going Given As GOOD

2691 ARLINGTON STAKES 3YO+   £4682   1m   Good/Firm 22 -06 Slow

2385 LAND OF IVORY [5] (I Balding) 3-8-11 T Ives 11/8 FAV: D433101: 3 b f The Minstrel -
Ivory Wand (Sir Ivor): Very useful filly: al prom & led close home, under press, in quite
a valuable stakes at Newbury: earlier won a 3yo stakes at Salisbury: first time out "won"
a Listed race at Epsom but subs. disq: in '85 successful in a fillies mdn at Sandown: half
sister to the smart Gold & Ivory: very eff at 1m: prob. stays 10f: acts on gd/firm & soft
grnd & on any trk.   65
1147 GEORGIA RIVER [1] (O Douieb) 3-8-8 Paul Eddery 7/2: 3-1202: Fair abs: switched over 1f
out & fin well: fine effort & should be winning again soon: see 546.   61
1655 HABER [4] (B Hills) 3-8-8 B Thomson 3/1: 2314303: Led over 2f out: just btn in close
fin: gd effort after abs: see 1455, 667.   60
2255 MY KIND OF TOWN [6] (R Williams) 3-8-8 S Cauthen 8/1: 1104404: Led over 5f: ran well:
in fine form this season: probably acts on any grnd: see 335.   46
--   DIRECTLY [2] 3-8-4 J Williams 25/1: -0: Ch 2f out on racecourse debut: prom effort from
this half brother to fair stayer Accuracy & very useful filly So True: acts on gd/firm.   32
1934 FARNCOMBE [3] 3-8-4 R Curant 66/1: 0-00R00: Slowly away: impossible task.   00
6 ran   shhd,nk,5,4,30   (Paul Mellon)   I Balding Kingsclere, Hants

2692 CORAL AUTUMN CUP H'CAP (0-70) 3YO+   £12315   1m 5f Good/Firm 22 +21 Fast   [69]

2525 BROKEN WAVE [5] (H Candy) 3-8-3 W Newnes 10/1: -103101: 3 b f Bustino - Britannia's
Rule (Blakeney): Very useful filly who is in grand form: led over 1f out, running on gamely
for a narrow win in very fast run & valuable Coral Autumn Cup (H'cap) at Newbury: earlier a
winner at Haydock & first time out a mdn at Salisbury: half sister to smart middle dist
winner Henry The Lion: eff at 12f, stays 14f well: acts on firm & yld grnd & a gall trk:
game & genuine filly who should win more races.   68
2156 HAUWMAL [9] (W Hern) 3-8-4 W Carson 8/1: 1204122: Led 2f out: ran on well & jst btn
in a tight fin: excellent effort: stays over 13f: see 1886.   68
1642 ALMAARAD [7] (J Dunlop) 3-7-12 R Fox 9/1: 00-103: Found little room inside the final
1f: switched outside but the post came too soon: unlucky?: fine effort after fair abs.   61
not the easiest of rides, but 12l clear of rem here & can find a h'cap: stays 13f well: see 849. 61
+2220 PRIMARY [6] (G Harwood) 3-8-12 G Starkey 33/8 FAV: 1-44114: Hvly bckd: led over 4f
out: fdd tamely & well below form 2220: worth another chance.   60
2523 REVISIT [2] 4-7-8 M L Thomas 12/1: 4344300: Ev ch in str: better 2445: see 58A.   29
2278 EXCEPTIONAL BEAUTY [13] 3-7-10 C Rutter(3) 20/1: -420130: Nvr nrr: stays 13f: see 2068. 37
*2403 ELPLOTINO [1] 4-7-11(1ow) R Hills 10/1: 00-3010: Led over 9f: well below 2403.   00
2486 Kingswick [4] 7-7(1oh)   2420 Tender Type [10] 7-7(8oh)
2203 Lemhill [11] 10-0   721 Holyport Victory [8] 7-7(3oh)
*2285 Heart Of Stone [12] 7-7   2219 Tabardar [14] 8-2(vis)
13 ran   ½,½,12,1½,2   (L B Holliday)   H Candy Kingstone Warren, Oxon

2693 COURAGE STAKES LIMITED H'CAP (0-75)   £21430   1m 2f Good/Firm 22 -04 Slow   [65]

*2226 POWER BENDER [2] (G P Gordon) 4-8-1 T Quinn 5/2 FAV: 4301111: 4 b c Prince Tenderfoot-
Spadilla (Javelot): Useful, impr gelding: completed the 4 timer, cruised into lead 2f out &
despite idling in front was a comfortable winner of valuable Courage Stakes (Limited H'cap) at
Newbury: earlier won h'caps at Yarmouth & Newmarket (2): eff over 1m, well suited by 10f:
acts on any trk: loves fast grnd: must have a leading chance in the Cambridgeshire.   52
2260 MAILMAN [4] (I Balding) 7-8-7 T Ives 8/1: -403122: Ran on most gamely final 1f:
fine effort from this grand old horse: see 1931.   54
2419 KHOZDAR [5] (W Hern) 4-9-7 W Carson 11/1: 120-303: Ch 2f out: gd effort but prob.
best over 12f: back to form: see 653.   61
2303 INDIAN HAL [3] (P Walwyn) 4-8-1 P Cook 12/1: 4400004: Nearest fin: fair effort: stays 10f. 39
2419 QUIET RIOT [9] 4-8-11 A Mcglone 33/1: 4-01000: Ch 2f out: no extra: lightly rcd since 48
2477 SAMHAAN [8] 4-8-0(bl) A J Geran(7) 10/1: 1213230: Al prom: another gd run: see 2477, 2331 36
2220 FIVE FARTHINGS [10] 4-8-10 Paul Eddery 6/1: -012100: Nvr nrr 7th: needs further? see 2058 46
2330 BEN ADHEM [11] 4-8-0 L Riggio(7) 9/1: 014-120: Made most 1m: see 2330.   34

2454 Gorgeous Strike [12] 9-2   1034 Swift Trooper [13] 8-5(bl)
*879 Gay Captain [7] 8-11   2566 Qualitair Flyer [1] 8-9(bl)
2558 Al Yabir [6] 8-9
13 ran ¾,4,1,½,hd,½,1½   (Addison Tool Co Ltd)   G P Gordon Newmarket

2694 HIGHCLERE NURSERY H'CAP 2YO   £10222   5f   Good/Firm 22 -06 Slow   [68]

*2410 PRINT [10] (W Hastings Bass) 2-7-10 W Carson 3/1: 211: 2 ch c Sharpo - Picture
(Lorenzaccio): Fast impr colt: led inside the final 1f & readily drew clear for an easy win
in a valuable nursery h'cap at Newbury: last time out won cmftbly in a mdn at Hamilton:
speedy sort who is very eff over this minimum trip though should stay 6f: acts on gd/firm &
yld grnd & a gall trk: should defy a penalty.   50
2284 CLARENTIA [8] (M Usher) 2-7-7(1oh) C Rutter(1) 33/1: 4032002: Led over 1f out: no ch
with winner, but ran well: below her best on yld last time: see 1910, 400.   35
*2561 SHARP REMINDER [5] (R Laing) 2-9-3(7ex) D Williams(7) 10/1: 00313: Ch over 1f out:
kept on well & is in grand form: see 2561.   59
2350 DUNNINALD [1] (I Balding) 2-8-7 T Ives 14/1: 1204: Ch over 1f out: gd run: see 1919 (6f). 48
2252 MOON INDIGO [13] 2-8-4(bl) M Roberts 25/1: 00000: Dspt lead: best effort since 1381
& seems at his best over the minimum trip.   40
2380 AID AND ABET [12] 2-7-7(4oh) M L Thomas 13/2: 42120: Made most: see 2007 (sharper trk). 26
2421 MAKE OR MAR [6] 2-7-7(3oh) L Riggio(7) 20/1: 01000: Prom most: best 1632 (C/D).   24
*2579 MUKHABBR [9] 2-8-3(7ex) R Hills 85/40 FAV: 3111110: Hvly bckd: al mid-div: btr 2579. 34
2308 ULTRA NOVA [4] 2-8-5 T Quinn 10/1: 3201140: No threat: twice below 2100.   00
1108 Plum Drop [7] 9-7   2434 Susan Henchard [3] 8-3
*2307 Infanta Maria [2] 7-8   +2181 Samleon [11] 8-2
13 ran   4,hd,nk,1½,1,2,hd,½   (Lord Porchester)   W Hastings Bass Newmarket

2695 GROUP 2 MILL REEF STAKES 2YO   £27312   6f   Good/Firm 22 -01 Slow

-2113 FOREST FLOWER [7] (I Balding) 2-8-8 T Ives 4/7 FAV: 11121: 2 ch f Green Forest -
Leap Lively (Nijinsky): Very smart filly: readily landed the odds in Gr.2 Mill Reef Stakes at
Newbury: squeezed through to lead over 1f out & was always holding the chall of Shady Heights:
met her only defeat when a courageous shhd 2nd to Minstrella in the Gr.1 Phoenix Stakes at
Phoenix Park last time out: earlier beat that filly in Gr.3 Cherry Hinton Stakes at Newmarket: also an easy winner of the Queen Mary Stakes at Royal Ascot & first time out a minor
race on this trk: dam won the Lingfield Oaks trial: eff at 6f, should stay the 1,000 Guineas
Mile: acts on yld, well suited by good & fast grnd & a gall trk: only small, but is a real battler
who is certain to win more good races.   81
+2418 SHADY HEIGHTS [2] (R Armstrong) 2-8-11 S Cauthen 7/2: 12: Smart colt: kept on really
well final 1f: never going to beat the winner but a long way clear of the rest: will be much
btr suited by 7f/1m & is sure to win a decent prize soon: acts on any trk: see 2418.   81
2460 RUMBOOGIE [3] (C Brittain) 2-8-11 M Roberts 33/1: 0103: Prom most: kept on well
final 1f: fine effort: acts on gd/firm & yld grnd & on any trk: should win more races.   66
2564 CAROLS TREASURE [1] (B Hills) 2-8-11 B Thomson 14/1: 1103134: Got very worked up at
the start: no real threat: has had a busy season: see 2223.   66
2451 QUEL ESPRIT [4] 2-8-11 J Reid 25/1: 3022420: Prom, ev ch: fair effort: see 2451.   66
2554 REBEL RAISER [5] 2-8-11 R Cochrane 20/1: 030: Led over 2f out: gd effort in this
smart company: can win soon: see 2554, 1653.   63
2460 DARLEY KNIGHT [8] 2-8-11 W Carson 9/1: 12020: Fin 7th: well below 2460: see 1242.   48
*2499 MAJD [9] 2-8-11 Paul Eddery 25/1: 33210: Led over 3f: stiff task: see 2499.   45
2501 MISTER MAJESTIC [6] 2-8-11 R Hills 20/1: 2111440: Reared up badly in the stalls
and was withdrawn under starters orders: see 2501.   00
9 ran   ½,5,hd,shhd,1,7,1½   (Paul Mellon)   I Balding Kingsclere, Hants

2696 E.B.F. HARWELL MAIDEN STAKES 2YO   £3372   5f   Good/Firm 22 -44 Slow

350 IMAGINARY SKY [3] (M Blanshard) 2-9-0 W Newnes 7/1: 01: 2 b c African Sky - Imagination
(Relko): Despite long abs, led inside final 1f, cmftbly in a slow run 2yo mdn at Newbury:
cost 16,000 gns as a yearling: eff at 5f, should stay 6f: well suited by gd/firm grnd &
a gall trk.   45
2589 PUSHOFF [10] (C Brittain) 2-8-11 T Ives 5/2 FAV: 022: Well bckd: ch final 1f: in
fine form: see 2589.   38
-- TIMES ARE HARD [7] (J Sutcliffe) 2-9-0 R Hills 14/1: 3: Al up there on racecourse
debut: cost 17,000 gns as a yearling & is very speedily bred: may find a race on a sharper
trk: acts on gd/firm.   34
1915 OUR FREDDIE [13] (A Ingham) 2-9-0 R Curant 20/1: 44404: Made most: half brother to
several winners who is eff over 5f on gd/firm & yld grnd.   33
311 BECHEMAL [5] 2-8-11 B Thomson 6/1: 330: No threat after long abs: should do btr
next time: acts on gd/firm & yld: see 223.   28
-- SHAFT OF SUNLIGHT [4] 2-8-11 Paul Eddery 10/1: 0: No show on debut: impr likely:
half sister to 4 winners incl 14f winner Solamente: acts on gd/firm.   20
2476 UNSELFISH [1] 2-9-0 S Cauthen 9/1: 00: Early speed: see 2476.   00
2232 LUBRICAN [14] 2-9-0(BL) R Cochrane 6/1: 400: Bl first time & ran poorly: twice well
below debut promise in 1049.   00
-- Daring Damsel [6] 8-11   -- Captain Holly [11] 9-0
-- Runlad [8] 9-0   -- Dallors Conquest [9] 9-0
-- Flopet [2] 9-0   2179 Zen West Three [12] 9-0
14 ran   ½,2½,shhd,½,4   (R Mohammed)   M Blanshard Upper Lambourn

Official Going Given As GOOD/FIRM

2697 AUTUMN SELLING STAKES 3 AND 4YO   £1014   1m   Firm 15 +02 Fast

2303 MISS APEX [5] (F Yardley) 4-8-11 John Williams 12/1: 0233001: 4 ch f Wolverlife -
Camarina (Aureole): Dropped in class, tardy start but stayed on well to lead inside dist,
comfortably in quite a fast run seller at Bath (bought in 1,050 gns): quite a consistent filly
who was a first time out winner of a Haydock seller last season: eff around 1m, stays 10f
well: acts on firm & soft grnd & on any trk: can win a small h'cap.   18
2516 TREMENDOUS JET [7] (M Madgwick) 3-8-8 R Guest 4/1 JT FAV: 0010002: Led below dist,
no extra close home: gd effort & should win soon if kept in this grade: see 1063.   18
2560 SON OF SPARKLER [13] (M Usher) 3-8-8 B Thomson 6/1: 0000023: Led briefly 2f out:
another gd effort and is capable of winning a seller: see 2560.   14
2515 ST JAMES RISK [17] (P Makin) 3-8-8 G Baxter 10/1: -000044: Ev ch: in fair form: see 1540. 14
--   FAIR CHARTER [4] 4-9-0 A Mcglone 20/1: 00000-0: Led/dsptd lead till dist: seems sure
to benefit from this run & is worth noting in this grade next time: successful over 5f at
Brighton last season, though seems sure to stay at least 1m: suited by fast grnd.   09
2429 SPARKFORD LAD [1] 4-9-0(bl) Debbie Wheatley(7) 8/1: 0002130: Ran on same pace: see 2271. 04
2515 UP TOWN BOY [3] 4-9-0 P Waldron 8/1: 43-0400: Never nearer 7th: see 2429 & 2271.   00
943 KIKI STAR [6] 4-8-11 A Dicks 14/1: 1-00000: Long abs: wknd into 8th: trained by
M Usher when successful at Newmarket (2) and Leicester last season: stays 12f well: suited
by fast grnd: now trained by R Hodges.   00
*2616 MOSTANGO [18] 3-8-8(bl) B Rouse 4/1 JT FAV: 0000410: Wknd into 9th: much btr 2616.   00
2616 CHARDONNAY [16] 3-8-5(VIS) J Reid 7/1: 0000400: Visored first time: disapp since 431 (6f) 00
2533 Hokusan [9] 4-9-0   2335 The Golf Slide [8] 8-11(bl)
2518 Vilee [10] 8-8   1937 Saravanta [12] 8-11   2271 Top Feather [15] 8-11(BL)
2597 Alceba [11] 8-5
16 ran   1½,2,shhd,2,3,2½,nk,½,1½   (R H Griffiths)   F Yardley Boreley, Worcs

2698 TORMARTON MAIDEN STAKES 2YO   £1917   5f   Firm 15 -31 Slow

2535 SINGING PARTNER [7] (R Smyly) 2-8-11 B Thomson 6/1: 031: 2 b f Song - Lakshmi
(Tribal Chief): Making prog when left clear over 1f out in a slowly run 2yo mdn at Bath:
half sister to 7f winner Far Too Busy: eff over 5/6f & should stay further: acts on gd &
fast grnd & on a gall trk: on the up grade.   32
--   EAGLES NEST [5] (C Austin) 2-8-11 J Williams 16/1: 000002: Ran on under press: French
import who failed to make the frame in her native country: certain to be suited by further:
acts on fast grnd & on a gall trk.   22
2433 LADYS MANTLE [2] (J Dunlop) 2-8-11 (bl) R Fox 14/1: 000003: Dropped in class: al prom
and kept on same pace: certainly one of her stables lesser lights: see 1801.   20
2476 WHITE OF MORN [8] (M Mccormack) 2-9-0(BL) N Howe 25/1: 004: Mkt drifter: al prom:
cost 7,000 gns as a half brother to useful 8/12f winner Bay Empress: should impr over
lngr dists next term.   22
73 FOWL PLAY [14] 2-8-11 G Dickie 20/1: 00: Late prog: sure to benefit from this race
after a long break: cost 13,000 gns and is a half sister to 1m winner Absheer: should be
suited by 6f plus: acts on fast grnd & on a gall trk.   14
2596 JOHNKEINA [6] 2-8-11 J Reid 12/1: 4000: Best on her debut in 73 (soft).   12
2600 ATRAYU [12] 2-8-11(BL) B Rouse 7/2: 020030: Bl first time: fdd into 9th & she can
do much btr than this: see 1946 (sharp 5f).   00
2514 BLAZING HIGH [1] 2-9-0 B Crossley 11/8 FAV: 034U: Nicely bckd & looked set for victory
when swerved and hit rails below dist: see 2167 and 1495.   00
2433 Martian Melody [9] 8-11   2499 Charming Gracie [4] 8-11
2579 Frivolous Lady [15] 8-11(BL)   --   Farmers Gamble [11] 9-0
--   Hautboyslittlegirl [10] 8-11
13 ran   4,nk,nk,1½,1,3,nk,hd,1½   (Mrs Mark Smyly)   R Smyly Lambourn, Berks

2699 VICTORIA HOUSE H'CAP STAKES (0-50) 3YO+   £3203   1m 2f   Firm 15 +07 Fast   [44]

2226 FARM CLUB [10] (J Toller) 3-8-7 B Thomson 7/1: 0003001: 3 ch c Kris - Touraine
(Luthier): Returned to his best form, led 4f out and was sn clear for an easy win in a fast
run h'cap at Bath: sole success last season also came on this trk: eff over 8/10f on fast
& yld grnd: well suited by a gall trk, especially Bath: should win again in this form.   44
2578 TALK OF GLORY [3] (L Cottrell) 5-8-8 G Baxter 8/1: 0223002: Kept on well without
troubling winner: has found one too good on 4 occasions this season: see 453.   28
--   STORM HOUSE [4] (K Brassey) 4-8-5 N Adams 16/1: 32230-3: Belated reapp: stayed on
from dist & should do btr next time: placed in most of his starts last season: seems best
over 9/10f on gd & firm grnd: acts on any trk.   22
*2293 JAAZIEL [2] (D Murray Smith) 3-7-8(bl) C Rutter(0) 9/2: 0000014: Running well: see 2293. 15
2303 RUSTY LAW [13] 4-9-5 G Starkey 15/2: 0-00000: Ran on same pace: see 1237.   30
2558 JOLI WASFI [1] 5-8-1 R Fox 16/1: -000000: Made much: disapp this term & yet to
show the form which won him a valuable prize at Epsom last summer: suited by 10/12f: acts
on fast & soft grnd & does well with forcing tactics.   07
2578 DERRYRING [9] 4-8-6 J Reid 5/2 FAV: 0004020: Fdd into 7th: see 1383.   00
2533 PULSINGH [8] 4-7-12 A Mcglone 10/1: 0103000: No threat: fin 8th: best in 850 (good). 00
--   Waafi [12] 9-13(2oh)   2533 Isom Dart [7] 7-9(2ow)(2oh)
2132 The Upstart [6] 7-12   1058 Mezlara [5] 7-12(bl)(3ow)
12 ran   4,2,1½,½,½,3,½,hd   (G E Sangster)   J Toller Newmarket

---

2700 STEPHEN LITTLE NURSERY H'CAP 2YO   £2687   1m   Firm 15 -06 Slow   [41]

2287 OUR PET [5] (R Hannon) 2-7-13 A Mcglone 25/1: 00001: 2 b f Mummy's Pet - My Candy (Lorenzaccio): Showed impr form when qckning well to lead inside dist, comfortably in a nursery h'cap at Bath: cost 21,000 gns and is a half sister to several winners: ran well on soft grnd at Kempton on her debut but until now had failed to reproduce that form: clearly stays 1m well: acts on fast & soft grnd & on any trk: should defy a penalty.   24

2465 MENDIP STAR [1] (R Holder) 2-8-6(bl) B Thomson 8/1: 404102: Made most: rallied gamely to snatch 2nd place close home: stays 1m: acts on any trk: see 2209.   23

2521 SOMEONE ELSE [12] (R Hannon) 2-9-7 B Rouse 2/1 FAV: 3000323: Led below dist: see 2521.   38

2407 MANDALAY PRINCE [9] (D Morley) 2-9-6 R Guest 25/1: 0004: Came from well behind and is sure to do btr when stepping up in dist: acts on firm & gd grnd & on a gall trk: impr.   35

2556 BERTRADE [2] 2-9-5 J Reid 8/1: 0324300: Led over 2f out: probably stays 1m: see 621.   30

2498 MUBKIR [11] 2-9-6 N Howe 11/2: 3020020: No extra dist: btr in 2498: see 497.   27

2283 RANKSTREET [10] 2-8-12 G Starkey 9/1: 0030: Fdd into 9th: best in 2283 (7f, yld).   00

2368 LUKMARIE [8] 2-8-10 G Baxter 8/1: 4300: Mkt drifter & no threat: see 2013, 1341.   00

2287 Folly Gale [4] 8-6   2310 Countess Bree [3] 8-2   2421 Segovian [7] 7-10
2405 Josie Smith [6] 8-11   2498 Connemara Dawn [13] 8-10(BL)
13 ran   2,shhd,1½,1½,2,shhd,1,2½   (Mrs M Horgan)   R Hannon East Everleigh, Wilts

---

2701 SHERSTON STAKES 3YO   £1604   1m 5f   Firm 15 -10 Slow

+2599 HIGH KNOWL [7] (B Hills) 3-9-7 B Thomson 7/2: -423111: 3 ch c High Line - Madina (Beau Prince II): Useful colt: comfortably completed his hat trick, led over 2f out in a 3yo stakes at Bath: recently beat Northern Amethyst in a similar race at Lingfield, after making all in a Newcastle mdn: half brother to several winners, incl useful French miler Nonoalca: very eff over 10/13f & will stay further: acts on gd & fast grnd & on any trk: consistent and is in fine form.   54

2599 NORTHERN AMETHYST [3] (D Elsworth) 3-9-7(bl) B Rouse 4/1: 0232122: Ev ch: see 2599, 243050

2489 SLANGI VAH [5] (H Candy) 3-9-0 C Rutter(3) 7/2: -33023: Made much: onepaced: see 1589.   39

2408 SEA POWER [2] (W Hern) 3-8-11 B Procter 5/2 FAV: 03-034: Stayed on well over this lngr trip & promises to be suited by even further: acts on gd & firm grnd & on a gall trk: should win a stayers mdn: see 806.   36

1646 KRISWICK [6] 3-8-11 R Fox 20/1: -0040: Led till running very wide after 3f, no ch thereafter: abs since 1646.   30

2430 SHAREEF [1] 3-9-0 J Reid 12/1: -0040: Never dngr: see 2430.   24

--   Caesar Imperator [4] 9-0   1646 La Grande Dame [8] 8-11(BL)
8 ran   1½,2,hd,3,4,nk,10   (K Abdulla)   B Hills Lambourn, Berks

---

2702 LYEGROVE HANDICAP STAKES (0-35) 3YO+   £2973   5f   Firm 15 +06 Fast   [35]

2592 TACHYON PARK [9] (P Arthur) 4-9-1 R Guest 8/1: 00-0021: 4 b c Frimley Park - Frimley's Alana (Lear Jet): In gd form and gamely made all when losing his mdn tag in quite a fast run h'cap at Bath: eff over 5/6f on any going: well suited by forcing tactics & likes a gall trk.   31

2594 GERSHWIN [17] (D O'donnell) 3-8-2(vis) A Clark 25/1: 0010002: Fin well: gd effort:see 2088. 18

2519 GALLANT HOPE [1] (L Cottrell) 4-8-4 C Rutter(3) 3/1 FAV: 2022233: Well bckd: ev ch.   14

2416 MADAM MUFFIN [16] (J Bethell) 3-8-7 R Fox 10/1: 0020024: Running well: see 2416.   18

2079 MRS SAUGA [14] 4-8-6 J Reid 13/2: 0210440: Hmpd below dist, not recover: best in 1344.   14

2619 BILLY WHITESHOES [19] 4-7-12 N Carlisle 10/1: 0030000: Al up there: likes this trk.   00

2258 AMEGHINO [4] 6-9-12 G Baxter 4/1: 3300000: Al front rank: fin 7th: see 1037.   00

2592 SHE KNOWS IT ALL [10] 4-8-11 J Carr(7) 8/1: -000000: Dsptd lead to ½way, wknd: see 1834. 00

2592 Ardent Partner [13] 8-9   2120 Dancing Sarah [8] 9-5
2318 Celestial Drive [15] 8-12(bl)   2601 Miranda Julia [2] 8-13(BL)
+2575 Muhtaris [5] 9-5(bl)(7ex)   2417 Cracon Girl [18] 7-13
2530 Dublinaire [12] 8-5   2316 Kings Ring [11] 9-2   2519 Mister March [7] 9-0
2313 Hardy Chance [3] 8-6   2519 Aclia [6] 9-1(BL)
19 ran   ½,1½,hd,½,2½,hd,½,1   (Terence P Lyons II)   P Arthur Abingdon, Berks

---

Official Going Given As FIRM

2703 FILBERT MAIDEN FILLIES STAKES 2YO   £964   1m   Firm 18 +05 Fast

2574 THREE TAILS [17] (J Dunlop) 2-8-11 G Duffield 9/2: 01: 2 b f Blakeney - Triple First (High Top): Promising filly: bckd from 20/1 for a comfortable win in quite fast run 2yo fillies mdn at Leicester: obviously needed the race first time out at Goodwood: cost 290,000 gns as a yearling & is a half sister to the smart 3yo Maysoon amongst others: stoutly bred & will be suited by middle dists: acts well on firm grnd & a gall trk: the type to impr further & win more races.   52

2527 KNOWN LINE [16] (H Candy) 2-8-11 W Newnes 11/4 FAV: 42: Well bckd: led over 2f out: met a good one here & fin 4L clear 3rd: can go one btr soon: stays 1m: see 2527.   50

--   PEARL BAY [6] (B Hills) 2-8-11 R Hills 16/1: 3: No real threat on racecourse debut though showed a deal of promise: half sister to numerous winners incl the smart middle dist stayer Seismic Wave: will be suited by 9/10f: acts on firm grnd & will find a race.   43

--   EMILYS PRIDE [14] (M Stoute) 2-8-11 W R Swinburn 11/1: 4: Switched over 2f out: never
nearer on debut, but impr very likely: cost 6,000 gns as a yearling: dam a 9f winner in
Ireland: bred to stay middle dists: acts on firm grnd & can find a mdn.   39
2491 MAKING HISTORY [4] 2-8-11 T Ives 33/1: 00: Friendless in mkt: prom most: on the
up grade: stays 1m but may prove btr over 7f: acts on fast grnd.   36
2215 APPROACHING STAR [2] 2-8-11 M Rimmer 12/1: 00: Prom most: impr effort from this quite
cheaply bought filly who is a half sister to 3 winners.   35
2531 FATAL CHARM [15] 2-8-11 A Murray 4/1: 40: There 6f: below form 2531 (7f): well below 241800
2418 ROCK OF AGES [7] 2-8-11 W Carson 9/1: 00: Well below form 2418: worth another chance.   00
2472 Via Veritas [8] 8-11   400   Water Of Love [10] 8-11
2433 Woodberry [5] 8-11   2418 La Carabine [12] 8-11   2434 Millennia [9] 8-11
--   Oh Wiggy [11] 8-11   --   Orangeade [3] 8-11   2069 Sunley Selhurst [1] 8-11
16 ran   ¼,4,2½,1½,½,3   (Sheikh Mohammed)   J Dunlop Arundel, Sussex

2704 HEADLAND OVERSEAS APP. STAKES 3YO+   £1240   1m 2f   Firm 18 +06 Fast

*2216 NO RESTRAINT [14] (W Hastings Bass) 3-8-3 Dale Gibson 5/2 JT.FAV: -04311: 3 b f Habitat-
Censorship (Prince John): In grand form and led 2f out, readily in quite fast run app. stakes
at Leicester: last time out a 4L winner in a mdn at Yarmouth: lightly rcd previously: eff
at 1m, stays 10f well: acts on gd & fast grnd & goes well for Dale Gibson: may find a h'cap.   45
519   SOLAR CLOUD [5] (D Nicholson) 4-8-8 D Meade 16/1: -002: Not get to winner but a gd
effort after a long abs: see 519.   37
2486 SARYAN [13] (N Callaghan) 3-8-12 M Denaro 7/1: 0411003: Came too late: best 1620 (11f).   47
2442 SURE LANDING [3] (C Nelson) 3-8-0 C Rossier 9/1: 0340204: Btr 2216 (1m).   27
2612 LIAM [8] 3-8-13 S Hibble 5/2 JT.FAV: 1404140: Uneasy fav: led inside final 3f, fdd:
has been very busy lately: see 2576.   36
2516 GEM MART [10] 4-8-5 S Meacock 33/1: 0-00400: Prom much: stiff task: see 967.   15
1989 NAWADDER [17] 3-8-0 A Whitehall 8/1: 4010300: Abs: prom over 7f: best 1073 (7f).   00
2363 Sirdar Girl [1] 8-5   2401 Surprise Attack [15] 8-8
2576 Lady Lamb [12] 7-11(VIS)   --   Court Appeal [19] 8-8
1976 Abjad [7] 9-2   2173 Bundling Bed [4] 9-0   2622 Bledsoe [16] 8-0
2432 Solomon Lad [6] 8-0 F   2426 Turn Em Back Jack [18] 8-0(bl)
1951 April Fox [9] 7-11 F   --   Malin Fleet [11] 7-11   2413 Zeelandia [2] 7-11(BL)
19 ran   2½,1½,4,2,2½,1½   (George Strawbridge)   W Hastings Bass Newmarket

2705 GOLDEN HAND SELLING STAKES 3YO   £976   1m 2f   Firm 18 -14 Slow

2495 HOT TWIST [8] (P Walwyn) 3-8-8(bl) Paul Eddery 15/8 FAV: 0-00031: 3 br f Hotfoot -
Maiden's Walk (Tower Walk): Led inside the final 1f, ridden out in a 3yo seller at Leicester
(sold 1,700 gns):seems well suited by the appl. of bl: eff over 10f on fast grnd & a gall trk.   13
2597 GREENHILLS GIRL [4] (M Ryan) 3-9-1(vis) S Cauthen 9/4: 0024032: Led 3f out: consistent.   17
--   RYMOS [2] (R Simpson) 3-8-11(bl) S Whitworth 7/2:   00-3: Ex Irish gelding who made his
racecourse debut here: ev ch over 1f out: recent runner over hdles but ran out: wore bl
& a hood today & seems a tricky ride.   07
2581 SOLENT EXPRESS [7] (B Stevens) 3-8-8 T Williams 11/1: 0-00404: Prom most: see 2073.   00
2412 SHOWDANCE [5] 3-8-11 S Perks 14/1: -000300: Led 7f: see 2335 (1m).   00
2335 ARRANMORE GIRL [3] 3-8-8 D Nicholls 33/1: 00-0000: Fdd final 2f: very lightly rcd
this term & little form.   00
2495 VITAL STEP [6] 3-8-8(bl) M Hills 8/1: 0042000: There 7f: best 2361 (7f).   00
--   High Bazaar [1] 8-11
8 ran   1½,3,5,10,1   (P J McCalmont)   P Walwyn Lambourn, Berks

2706 HEADLAND OVERSEAS HCAP STKS 3YO+ 0-50   £3061   1m 2f   Firm 18 +01 Fast   [43]

619   BILLET [5] (H Candy) 3-7-12 T Williams 11/2: 0-001: 3 ch c Nicholas Bill - Cosset
(Comedy Star): Despite long abs, well bckd & led 1½f out, very cmftbly in a h'cap at
Leicester: very lightly rcd previously: eff at 10f on fast grnd: should impr further & win
another h'cap.   34
2226 AL ZUMURRUD [3] (R Armstrong) 3-9-0 S Cauthen 9/4 FAV: 2212422: Made most: see 2226,1185.43
2623 VAGUE MELODY [2] (L Piggott) 4-9-7 Pat Eddery 5/2: 1344123: Never nearer: see 2623 (11f).   40
1880 CHANCE REMARK [7] (B Hills) 3-7-12(1ow) R Hills 11/2: 0-404: Very lightly rcd colt
who prob. stays 10f: acts on firm & yld grnd.   23
1278 GREEN STEPS [4] 4-9-5(bl) P Robinson 4/1: -0430: Ch over 2f out: fdd: needed race?   35
2549 KAVAKA [1] 4-8-1 L Riggio(7) 25/1: D020000: Early ldr: best 2303.   00
--   Tudor Bob [6] 7-7(13oh)
7 ran   2,¼,½,¼,10   (Commander G G Marten)   H Candy Kingstone Warren, Oxon

2707 LEICESTERSHIRE CLAIMING STAKES 2YO   £2589   7f   Firm 18 -09 Slow

2225 CALIBOGUE [1] (R Sheather) 2-9-3 R Cochrane 7/2: 001: 2 b c Taufan - Montana Moss
(Levmoss): Impr colt: showed a gd turn of foot to lead inside final 1f in a 2yo claimer at
Leicester: lightly rcd previously this season: cost 5,400 gns as a yearling: eff at 7f,
should stay 1m: acts on fast grnd & a gall trk.   44
2626 MILL TRIP [2] (M Prescott) 2-8-12 G Duffield 9/1: 0302: Ev ch over 1f out: stays
1m & acts on firm & soft grnd: should at least find a seller.   35

2611 SHADE OF PALE [11] (P Haslam) 2-8-11 T Williams 7/4 FAV: 12243: Led 2f out: again
well bckd: see 2611, 2479.   29
-- CORAL HALL [7] (R Hannon) 2-8-12 W Carson 9/1: 4: Al prom on racecourse debut: cost
only 3,900 gns: half brother to 1m winner De Rigueur : acts on fast grnd.   26
-- TYRIAN PRINCESS [6] 2-9-0 T Quinn 8/1: 0: Prom most on debut: cost 14,000 gns as aa
yearling and is a half sister to 7/8f 2yo winner Tyrian Noble: acts on fast grnd & should
do better.   23
-- AMBER ESPANA [8] 2-8-11 M Rimmer 33/1: 0: Slow away & should impr for this initial
outing: half brother to 2yo 5f winner Bold Roll.   18

2542	No Concern	[10]	8-12		1665	Bangkok Boy	[4]	9-3	2577	Miss Atwell	[12]	8-6
2471	Samprekl	[13]	8-7		2580	Medallion Man	[5]	8-8	2646	Corleon	[14]	9-2
--	Sunset Sam	[15]	8-7		2625	Bumptious Boy	[3]	9-3	--	Sagres	[9]	9-0

15 ran   2,2½,2,2½,¾   (M D Scott)   R Sheather Newmarket

2708 LEICESTERSHIRE CLAIMING STAKES 2YO   £2589   7f   Firm 18 -15 Slow

2493 IMPERIAL WAY [7] (J Sutcliffe) 2-8-9 R Hills 8/1: 001: 2 b c Runnett - Barefoot
Contessa (Homeric): Dropped in class & showed impr form, led inside final 1f narrowly in a
2yo claimer at Leicester: cost 4,800 gns as a yearling: clearly well suited by 7f, fast
ground & a gall trk.   36
2529 MAD MAX [1] (P Haslam) 2-9-2 T Williams 9/4 FAV: 43202: Chall final 1f & just btn:
looks certain to find a similar event: stays 7f: first foal who runs well on fast grnd
& a gall trk.   42
2625 NO LIE [10] (G P Gordon) 2-8-7 G Duffield 5/2: 0323: Led over 2f out: in gd form.   27
2625 MAIN BRAND [15] (W O'gorman) 2-8-4 T Ives 20/1: 004: Nearest fin, showing first signs
of form: cost 8,000 gns as a yearling & should be suited by another furlong: acts on fast grnd   21
2178 KNOCKSHARRY [8] 2-8-4 P Hill(7) 25/1: -110000: Mkt drifter: ran on late: stays 7f.   20
2095 SABOTEUR [2] 2-9-3 M Rimmer 33/1: 000: Never nearer, but an impr effort from this
half brother to several winners: should be suited by 1m: acts on fast grnd.   28
*2405 SWIFT PURCHASE [14] 2-9-3 W Carson 9/2: 0104010: Made most over 4f: well below 2405.   00
-- PRINCE SWIFTFOOT [4] 2-9-3 T Lucas 10/1: 0: Never showed on debut: may impr.   00
2320 JOHNS BABY [12] 2-8-9 D Mckay 10/1: 000: Active in mkt: early speed: btr 2320 (soft).   00

2471	Madame Laffitte	[13]	8-9		--	Power Of Love	[9]	9-0
2472	Sixty Minutes	[3]	9-2		1846	Skraggs Plus Two	[11]	8-7
2574	Sallys Won	[6]	8-12		1801	Lady Westgate	[5]	8-9

15 ran   nk,3,1½,½,2½   (Anglo Enterprises (SA))   J Sutcliffe Epsom, Surrey

2709 HEADLAND ESTATE AGENTS HCAP 3YO 0-35   £2954   1m 4f   Firm 18 +07 Fast   [39]

*2253 GAY APPEAL [10] (C Nelson) 3-8-10 M Hills 20/1: -030011: 3 ch f Star Appeal -
Summer Madness (Silly Season): In fine form and ridden to lead inside final 1f in quite fast
run h'cap at Leicester: last time out was an easy winner of a 3yo seller at Newmarket: well
suited by a stiff 12f: acts on hvy, likes gd & fast grnd.   32
2395 SOHAIL [9] (H T Jones) 3-9-7(BL) A Murray 8/1: 4-03122: Bl first time, nearly done
ev yd: fine effort: stays 12f & acts on fast & yld grnd: see 1956.   39
*2604 KOOKYS PET [7] (E Eldin) 3-8-5(bl)(6ex) A Mackay 8/1: 0004013: Al there: in gd form:
stays 12f: see 2604.   18
2267 FOREMAST [1] (P Calver) 3-8-12 M Fry 10/1: 1303404: Ch over 2f out: best in 822 (1m hvy).   24
2102 MISSELFORE [15] 3-7-11 W Carson 7/1: 0-00030: Prom most: flattered 1941 (10f)?   01
2467 FIRST BILL [2] 3-8-13 W Newnes 9/4 FAV: 0000-20: Prom much: disapp after 2467 (gd).   17
2305 CURIGA [5] 3-8-12 Paul Eddery 10/1: -041100: Twice below 2182 (easy trk, made all).   00
1739 DALLONA [4] 3-7-13 J Lowe 10/1: 0-00430: Abs, no show: see 1739.   00
2420 FULL SPEED AHEAD [8] 3-8-7 Pat Eddery 9/1: 0000200: Twice well below 2093.   00

2274	Ikraam	[6]	7-7(2oh)		1061	Ma Feathers	[14]	8-3(BL)
2516	Nautica	[11]	8-6		2381	Simons Fantasy	[3]	8-2(bl)
1259	Fidaytik	[12]	8-3					

14 ran   2,2½,hd,4,hd   (Arne Laarsson)   C Nelson Lambourn, Berks

2710 FILBERT MAIDEN FILLIES STAKES 2YO   £964   1m   Firm 18 -09 Slow

-- ICE HOUSE [14] (W Hern) 2-8-11 W Carson 8/1: 1: 2 ch f Northfields - Knighton House
(Pall Mall): First time out, al prom & led inside final 1f, narrowly in a 2yo fillies mdn
at Leicester: nicely bred filly who is a sister to smart middle dist winner Open Day &
a half sister to numerous other winners: eff at 1m, may stay further: acts on fast grnd
& a gall trk & can only impr.   48
2487 KENTUCKY AIR [6] (H Cecil) 2-8-11 S Cauthen 9/2: 02: Led 2f out: came again final
1f & just btn: impr filly who should go one btr soon: stays 1m & acts well on fast grnd.   47
-- CHEVREFEUILLE [3] (M Stoute) 2-8-11 W R Swinburn 7/1: 3: Friendless in mkt on debut:
not the best of runs & finished in fine style: well bred filly who should be suited by
middle dists next season: acts on fast grnd & a gall trk & should be winning soon.   46
2487 CAS EN BAS [7] (J Dunlop) 2-8-11 G Duffield 3/1: 04: Bckd from 6/1: al there: stays 1m.   42
-- CORVALENT [10] 2-8-11 R Hills 20/1: 0: Kept on well on racecourse debut & should
benefit from the experience: half sister to 10f winner Kelro: should stay further than 1m:
acts on fast ground.   40
601 ZILDA [15] 2-8-11 R Cochrane 12/1: 00: Long abs: never nearer & should strip fitter
next time: eff at 1m & acts well on fast grnd.   36

-- ROYAL RESPECT [5] 2-8-11 Pat Eddery 13/8 FAV: 0: Hvly bckd debutant: prom, fin 8th: clearly held in some regard: well bred filly who is a half sister to winning 2yos Millbow and Piney Ridge: one to keep an eye on. 00
2434 **Lady Westown** [16] 8-11 2577 **Borotown** [8] 8-11
2418 **Mariko Gold** [9] 8-11 -- **Iron Dance** [13] 8-11 2140 **Quietly Mine** [2] 8-11
2153 **Hytak Pet** [11] 8-11 2283 **Lady Artful** [12] 8-11
14 ran hd,¾,2,1,2½ (Sir Michael Sobell) W Hern West Ilsley, Berks

LEICESTER Tuesday September 23rd Righthanded, Galloping Track

2711 E.B.F. KEGWORTH MAIDEN STAKES (DIV 1) £2794 7f Firm 14 +05 Fast

2418 **NOBLE MINSTREL** [9] (O Douieb) 2-9-0 Pat Eddery 7/4 FAV: 41: 2 ch c The Minstrel - Noble Natisha (Noble Commander): Useful colt: easily justified fav. led below dist & pushed out to win a fast run 2yo mdn at Leicester: cost $100,000 as a yearling: eff over 6/7f & will stay further: acts on gd & fast grnd & on any trk: should make his presence felt in btr company. 52
2044 **BATTALION USA** [2] (J Dunlop) 2-9-0 G Baxter 12/1: 02: Clearly all the btr for his recent debut: tried to make all and stuck on well: cost $200,000 & is bred to be suited by 1m plus: acts on fast grnd & on a gall trk: sure to find a race. 44
2036 **TORRES VEDRAS** [3] (M Stoute) 2-9-0 W R Swinburn 7/2: 03: Al prom, stayed on well & will be suited by another furlong: acts on fast grnd & on a gall trk: see 2036. 44
2595 **RED HERO** [14] (M Jarvis) 2-9-0 T Lucas 10/1: 00334: Al up there: running well: see 2225. 38
-- **SPOILED BRAT** [16] 2-9-0 T Ives 12/1: 0: Ran on promisingly & should impr on this next time: cost 14,000 gns & is brother to winning juvenile Good N Sharp: stays 7f: acts on firm grnd & on a gall trk. 38
-- **CHESHAM SQUIRE** [7] 2-9-0 Paul Eddery 10/1: 0: Easy to back on debut: prom most & will be btr for this experience: cost 30,000 gns and is a half brother to several useful winners, incl Kampala and Stately Form: acts on fast grnd. 36
-- **MAGIC FLUTTER** [11] 2-9-0 W Ryan 11/2: 0: Fdd into 7th on debut: very well bred colt who should do btr next time: acts on fast grnd. 32
497 **BOLD MOJACQUES** [10] 2-9-0 M Giles 40/1: 00: Never nearer after a long abs: cost IR£ 16,500 and is a half brother to several winners: stays 7f: acts on fast grnd: should strip fitter next time. 28
2574 **BEAULIEU BAY** [5] 2-9-0 B Crossley 40/1: 00: Gd speed over ½way: fin 9th: easy to back today but showed some impr: half brother to several winners: acts on fast grnd. 28
2465 **Cream And Green** [4] 9-0 2036 **Up The Ladder** [15] 9-0
2542 **The Grifter** [13] 9-0 -- **Mansio** [8] 9-0 -- **Penny Forum** [6] 9-0
-- **Escudero** [1] 9-0
15 ran 1½,shhd,2½,½,½,1½,1½,hd (Allen E Paulson) O Douieb Newmarket

2712 RANCLIFFE NURSERY SELLING H'CAP 2YO £1004 1m Firm 14 -31 Slow [24]

2405 **AKROTIRI BAY** [15] (L Holt) 2-8-9 N Adams 8/1: 00001: 2 b c Ya Zaman - Felin Geri (Silly Season): Gambled on & showed impr form to lead dist, comfortably in a nursery selling h'cap at Leicester (no bid): cheaply bought colt who is a half brother to winning sprinter Coppermill Lad: stays 1m well: acts on fast grnd & on a gall trk. 14
2580 **RAGTIME SOLO** [3] (P Makin) 2-8-13 G Baxter 10/3 FAV: 00042: Al front rank: ran on same pace: stays 1m: running well: see 2580. 12
2298 **MAYBEMUSIC** [16] (W Mackie) 2-9-4 D Nicholls 20/1: 0010003: Al prom: showed signs of a return to form over this lngr trip: best over 5f in 1181. 16
2396 **COROFIN LASS** [13] (C Tinkler) 2-8-13(BL) M Birch 8/1: 000004: Bl first time & trying a lngr trip: led before ½way, no extra dist: see 2218. 08
2470 **FINLUX DESIGN** [10] 2-8-9 S Perks 20/1: 030000: Ran on too late: best in 1155 (6f). 02
2580 **AVENMORE STAR** [18] 2-8-12 W Newnes 10/1: 0004000: Lngr trip: fdd dist: see 2180. 00
2466 **LEADING ROLE** [14] 2-9-6 M Wigham 8/1: 0010400: Fin 8th: best in 1684 (7f). 00
2168 **PRINCESS PELHAM** [12] 2-8-4(bl) Pat Eddery 11/2: 00400: Nicely bckd but no threat: best in 1905 (7f, sharp track). 00
2298 **Santo Princess** [17] 8-5(3ow) 2609 **Sohams Taylor** [2] 8-12(vis)
2396 **Music Delight** [9] 9-0 2320 **Fortyniner** [1] 8-12(bl)
2625 **Musical Chorus** [5] 8-6(bl) 2284 **Cherrywood Sam** [6] 9-3
1168 **Plaluci** [11] 8-10 2466 **Relampego** [8] 8-6(VIS)
2471 **Miss Bolero** [4] 8-4 2423 **Straight Edge** [7] 9-7
18 ran 2,½,1½,1½,1½,4,1½ (Bernard Bates) L Holt Tunworth, Hants

2713 WREN E.B.F. STAKES 3YO £3301 1m Firm 14 -42 Slow

2672 **INDIVIDUALIST** [1] (M Jarvis) 3-8-13 T Lucas 10/3: 0002001: 2 b c Viking - Lusaka (Wolver Hollow): Led 3f out and just held on in a slowly run 3yo stakes at Leicester: successful twice in Ireland as a juvenile: showed some fair form there before joining his new stable: eff over 7/8f on gd & fast grnd: acts on a gall trk. 42

2562 JAZETAS [4] (N Callaghan) 3-9-2 Pat Eddery 1/1 FAV: 4040402: Just held in a driving
fin: lightly rcd of late & would have won this on his early season form: see 605 & 127.   45
2534 ROYAL TROUBADOR [3] (B Hills) 3-8-7(bl) R Hills 2/1: 0-00043: Narrowly btn in a
desperate fin: eff over 7/8f on gd & fast grnd: see 2294.   36
2441 NOMAD BOXER [2] (M Chapman) 3-8-7 J Williams 150/1: -004: Led over ½way, sn btn.   00
4 ran   shhd,shhd,30   (Miss C J McCulloch)   M Jarvis Newmarket

2714 CHARNWOOD CLAIMING STAKES 3 AND 4YO   £1965   1m 4f Firm 14 +08 Fast

984 TRACKERS JEWEL [14] (J Dunlop) 4-8-8 Pat Eddery 7/2: -00-001: 4 ch f Posse - More
Treasure (Ballymore): Despite a long abs proved an easy winner, cruised ahead dist in a
fast run claimer at Leicester: lightly rcd filly who does not seem to stand much racing: eff
over 12f on fast grnd: acts on a gall trk.   15
2492 RUN FOR YOUR WIFE [4] (G Lewis) 3-8-2(bl) M L Thomas 3/1 FAV: 3024302: Sn led & qcknd
clear early in str: no extra dist & remains a mdn: see 2075 & 1212.   12
2613 ELEGANT GUEST [12] (W O'gorman) 3-8-12 T Ives 11/2: -0043: Nearest fin: see 2613.   18
2509 JUST CANDID [10] (D Wilson) 3-8-9 W Newnes 7/1: 3342324: Ran on same pace: mdn: see 2187.14
2605 GRUNDYS OWN [5] 3-8-12(VIS) S Perks 25/1: -000000: Visored first time: best in 1372.   10
2217 HIGHEST NOTE [9] 3-8-5 M Rimmer 9/2: 4324100: Btn over 2f out: best in 2163 (sharp trk)   02
1892 STARWOOD [11] 4-9-3 M Birch 8/1: 000-20: Fdd into 7th: best in 1892 (sharp trk).   00
2613 JUBILEE JAMBOREE [13] 3-7-11 G Carter 8/1: 0030030: Wknd into 9th: see 1349.   00
2190 Pitkaithly [1] 9-7   1705 Star Addie [7] 8-12   2528 High Forest [3] 8-9
11 ran   1½,2½,shhd,4,¾   (A W Gooda)   J Dunlop Arundel, Sussex

2715 APOLLO HANDICAP STAKES (0-35) 3YO+   £3016   6f   Firm 14 -06 Slow   [35]

2601 HOPEFUL KATIE [12] (D Leslie) 4-8-10(hd) J Williams 12/1: 0301301: 4 ch f Full Of
Hope - Katie Gay (Royben): Ran on strongly to lead near fin in an all-aged h'cap at Leicester:
earlier a comfortable winner of a similar race at Yarmouth: in gd form last season, winning at
Yarmouth, Folkestone & Ripon: eff over 6/7f on firm & soft grnd: acts on any trk.   25
2277 REVEILLE [10] (M Jarvis) 4-9-10 T Lucas 7/1: 0100302: Led inside dist, just caught:
another gd effort & may win again soon: see 1066.   38
2397 HENRYS VENTURE [16] (D Chapman) 4-8-2 A Proud 12/1: 1130343: Again made most: see 2295 12
2416 MUSIC REVIEW [2] (M Tompkins) 3-8-3 A Mackay 16/1: 2222034: Al front rank: consistent.   16
2526 FAWLEYS GIRL [15] 4-8-11 A Culhane(7) 25/1: 2000400: Had ev ch: gd effort: see 520.   19
2411 JARROVIAN [8] 3-9-4(bl) R Hills 33/1: 4000000: Fin well: see 947 & 309.   29
2581 CONCERT PITCH [20] 7-9-1 Pat Eddery 9/1: 0041000: No real threat: best in 2319 (soft).   00
-2575 STANBO [23] 3-8-7 G Duffield 11/2 FAV: 0004020: Disapp fav: much btr in 2575 (5f gd).   00
2519 Three Bells [7] 8-11   2602 Corncharm [3] 9-5   2519 Roysia Boy [1] 9-12
2463 Vaigllan [18] 8-13(BL)   2594 Monstrosa [13] 8-1
1603 Our Tilly [6] 9-8   2526 Playtex [11] 9-5   2602 Qualitair King [17] 8-6
2619 Delaware River [22] 8-4   606 Pentoff [21] 8-3
2312 Burning Arrow [9] 8-3   2124 Silbando [19] 8-1(bl)   961 Witham Girl [4] 8-0
22 ran   hd,1½,nk,nk,nk,½,nk,nk   (N A Cawthorne)   D Leslie Goadby, Leics.

2716 E.B.F. KEGWORTH MAIDEN STAKES (DIV 2)   £2808   7f   Firm 14 -09 Slow

--   ASSULTAN [7] (H T Jones) 2-9-0 A Murray 7/4 FAV: 1: 2 ch c Troy - Plum Run (Run The
Gantlet): Well bckd & made a successful debut, led over 2f out and ran on well in a 2yo
mdn at Leicester: clearly eff over 7f & should stay at least 1m: acts on fast grnd & on
a gall trk: can only improve.   48
2494 QUIET HERO [12] (L Cumani) 2-9-0 Pat Eddery 4/1: 032: Ran on well & only just denied:
on the upgrade & sure to go one btr soon: stays 7f: see 2229.   44
2491 GENERAL MEILLAND [10] (L Piggott) 2-9-0 B Crossley 20/1: 033: Another gd effort:
stays 7f: see 2491.   40
2239 WILLIESWRIGHTONCUE [3] (G Huffer) 2-9-0 G Carter 4/1: 204: Fin well: see 2239 & 1307.   39
2499 BECCADELLI [9] 2-9-0 W Ryan 11/2: 430: Not qckn dist: best in 2229 (6f).   35
2547 ASHWA [14] 2-9-0 G Baxter 16/1: 200: Prom most: best in 1518 (gd).   32
--   FEARLESS MAN [8] 2-9-0 W R Swinburn 14/1: 0: Never nearer on racecourse debut: cost
17,500 gns & is closely related to a couple of winners: stays 7f: acts on fast grnd:
should do better.   30
--   SPRUCE BABY [5] 2-9-0 J Lowe 50/1: 0: Unfancied on debut but made a lot of the running,
showing future promise: half brother to several winners & is likely to stay 1m plus in time:
acts on fast ground.   28
2499 Hunting Country [4] 9-0   --   Forums Folly [6] 9-0
2646 Pradel [1] 9-0   2423 Greens Old Master [2] 9-0
--   Roches [13] 9-0
13 ran   ½,1½,¾,1½,1½,½,1,hd   (Hamdan Al-Maktoum)   H T Jones Newmarket

Official Going Given As GOOD/FIRM

2717 EBF HEATHER MAIDEN STAKES 2YO   £1970   5f   Firm 19 -07 Slow

2423 ROCK MACHINE [13] (N Callaghan) 2-9-0 R Cochrane 11/2: 441: 2 ch c Ballad Rock -
Move Over (Galivanter): Impr colt: stayed on well to lead inside final 1f in a 2yo mdn at
Sandown: cost 21,000 gns as a yearling: eff over a stiff 5f, stays 6f well: acts on gd &
fast grnd & a gall trk.   47
1826 MA PETITE LASSIE [10] (M Francis) 2-8-11 J Reid 20/1: 02: Finished well and is on
the up grade: half sister to 3 winners in the USA: will be suited by 6f: acts on fast grnd.   36
2561 ON YOUR PRINCESS [5] (J Payne) 2-9-0(vis) P D'arcy 8/1: 0020203: Ch over 1f out:
consistent: see 2561.   37
2514 INTHAR [1] (R Armstrong) 2-9-0 S Cauthen 7/2: 0034: Al up there: needs 6f? see 2514.   37
2476 FATHER TIME [8] 2-9-0(bl) T Quinn 20/1: 0002000: Made most: yet to reproduce form 1442
but should find a small race on a sharp trk: wears bl now.   35
460 RUN BY [6] 2-9-0 R Weaver 16/1: 00: Nearest fin after abs: should be btr next time:
has changed stables since early season: should be suited by 6f: acts on fast grnd.   34
2561 PETTING PARTY [12] 2-9-0 P Waldron 11/4 FAV: 000: Prom, fdd: much btr 2561 (easy 6f).   00
2493 LINDVARO [15] 2-9-0 P Tulk 8/1: 000: Never showed: see 2493 (6f).   00
--   Swiss Connection [4] 9-0   2484 Torrance [3] 9-0
2514 Feasible [2] 9-0   2574 Spitzabit [9] 9-0   --   Whatta Business [7] 9-0
13 ran   3,¾,shhd,¾,nk   (K Al-Said)   N Callaghan Newmarket

2718 WILLOW STAKES NURSERY HCAP 2YO   £2532   1m 1f   Firm 19 No Stan Time   [49]

2648 OLORE MALLE [2] (R Hannon) 2-8-5 B Rouse 7/1: 1423001: 2 ch c Camden Town - Grace
Poole (Sallust): Led over 2f out, driven out closing stages in a nursery h'cap at Sandown:
consistent colt: earlier a winner on hvy grnd at Epsom: stays 9f well: probably acts on any
ground and any track.   36
2341 ALCATRAZ [4] (M Ryan) 2-9-1 R Cochrane 7/2: 0402: Ran on well final 1f: well suited
by this 9f trip: acts well on gd & firm.   42
2405 PARKLANDS BELLE [6] (M Haynes) 2-8-6 P Cook 9/1: 4020133: Ch inside final 2f: gd effort:
in fine form & stays 9f: no trk preferences: see 2045.   32
*2310 SUNSET BOULEVARD [3] (L Piggott) 2-9-7(bl) J Reid 9/4 FAV: 04014: Hvly bckd: made
most: stays 9f & acts on any trk: see 2310.   46
2580 CABALLINE [1] 2-7-7(1oh) T Williams 7/1: 3000020: Led 3f out: btr 2580 (7f, seller).   08
2310 ORIENTAL DREAM [7] 2-8-4(VIS) M Hills 15/2: 0100: Wknd final 2f: lightly rcd since 1119(6f). 18
acts on firm and soft grnd: tried in a visor today.
2556 SYLVAN ORIENT [5] 2-9-3 R Carter(5) 10/1: 000300: Never in it: twice below 2044.   00
7 ran 1½,hd,hd,6,½   (Mrs J Reglar)   R Hannon East Everleigh, Wilts

2719 STELLITE HANDICAP 3YO FILLIES 0-50   £3620   1m   Firm 19 +10 Fast   [47]

*2458 NORDICA [16] (A Stewart) 3-8-11(4ex) M Roberts 15/2: 0012411: 3 ch f Northfields -
Princess Arabella (Crowned Prince): Impr filly who is in fine form: led 2f out & stayed on
gamely for a shhd success in quite fast run & valuable 3yo fillies h'cap at Sandown: last time
out won a 3yo h'cap at Kempton & earlier a fillies mdn at Yarmouth: very eff over 1m, though
does stay 10f: dam a sister to Oaks winner Fair Salinia: acts well on gd & fast grnd, though
probably acts on any trk.   43
*2481 BLUE GUITAR [6] (J Hindley) 3-9-6(vis) M Hills 12/1: 4421312: Chall final 1f & btn
the min. dist: fine effort under her 6lbs penalty & acts on any trk: in grand form: see 2481.   51
2404 PRINCESS NAWAAL [2] (J Dunlop) 3-9-7 W Carson 7/1: -110003: Never nearer: best 925.   45
2534 NATIJA [12] (P Makin) 3-8-0 T Quinn 7/1: 0-00024: Nearest fin after slow start:
needs further? see 2534.   21
1451 SUMMER GARDEN [17] 3-8-7 B Rouse 25/1: -40300: Abs: late hdway & should strip fitter
next time: should be well suited by this trip & further: acts on fast grnd: see 658.   28
1043 SOEMBA [14] 3-8-7 P Robinson 10/1: 4-000: Abs: lightly rcd & little form this term
but this was a btr effort: see 1043.   27
2459 CARRIBEAN SOUND [5] 3-8-12 S Cauthen 16/1: 0042000: Led 3f out: fin 7th: see 713 (7f).   00
2385 FLASHDANCE [13] 3-9-6 G Starkey 13/2: -3100: Twice below form 1902: can do btr.   00
2568 TRAVEL MAGIC [15] 3-9-7 J Reid 6/1 FAV: 1022140: Bumped ½way & no chance thereafter:
worth another chance on form displayed in 2568.   00
2459 FAIR ATLANTA [11] 3-8-0 A Clark 10/1: 4010030: No threat: much btr 2459: see 505.   00
2649 Grey Walls [18] 9-5   2676 Glade [1] 8-8   2385 Rare Sound [3] 8-7
2488 Omania [8] 8-2   *2560 Miami Blues [10] 7-10
2184 Out Of Harmony [9] 7-7(1oh)   2304 Alice Parry [4] 7-7(4oh)
2314 Bella Carina [7] 7-7(bl)(5oh)
18 ran shhd,4,1½,shhd,hd,hd   (J De Burgh)   A Stewart Newmarket

2720 COOMBE HANDICAP 3YO 0-50   £3473   1m 2f   Firm 19 -11 Slow   [52]

2536 PRINCE ORAC [6] (C Brittain) 3-9-6 S Cauthen 10/1: -302101: 3 ch c Good Times -
Hannah Darling (Match III): Useful colt: made ev yd & kept on well under press in a 3yo h'cap
at Sandown: clearly best out in front, earlier employed similar tactics to win a fast run
3yo mdn at Epsom: half brother to a winner in France: eff at 1m, stays a stiff 10f: acts on
firm & yld grnd & on any trk: best from the front.   54
2442 NORTH OCEAN [9] (L Cumani) 3-8-12 R Cochrane 3/1 FAV: -030332: Hvly bckd: under press
early on & hung right inside the final 2f: just btn & is in gd form: see 2442, 1269.   45

798

2599 HEAD OF SCHOOL [7] (Pat Mitchell) 3-8-0(3ow) M Roberts 12/1: 0042443: Ev ch over 1f
out: in fair form: eff over 10f, probably stays an easy 12f: acts on gd & fast grnd. 28
2489 STEP IN TIME [11] (P Makin) 3-8-5 T Quinn 4/1: -00044: Ev ch in str: half brother to
the fair stayer & smart hurdler Pike's Peak: maybe btr over 12f: acts on fast grnd. 30
2536 FACTOTUM [2] 3-8-11 B Thomson 9/1: -003200: Ev ch over 2f out: btr 1m? see 2009. 32
2173 CIGAR [1] 3-8-6 P Robinson 10/1: -000000: No show: best over 12f in 1899. 20
2422 FINAL SELECTION [8] 3-8-7 W Carson 10/1: 30-400: Prom most: twice well below 2275. 00
2576 ASK MAMA [4] 3-9-7 J Reid 10/1: 3012020: Fdd over 2f out: best 1368. 00
2656 RAFFIA RUN [10] 3-7-12 T Williams 10/1: 4023340: Twice below form 2373: see 1394. 00
2604 Regency Square [3] 7-7(6oh)   2267 Bold Archer [5] 7-11
11 ran   shhd,2½,1½,2,4   (D M Lemos)   C Brittain Newmarket

2721 DORKING STAKES 2YO   £3052 1m   Firm 19 +18 Fast

2407 REFERENCE POINT [9] (H Cecil) 2-8-11 S Cauthen 4/5 FAV: 31: 2 b c Mill Reef -
Home On The Range (Habitat): Highly promising colt: made almost all & was eased clear inside
the final 2f for a very impressive win, breaking the 2yo course record in quite valuable stakes
at Sandown: half brother to 3yo winner Your Range: eff at 1m: will be well suited by middle
dists next season: acts on fast grnd & a gall trk: held in very high regard by his powerful
stable & should play a part in next year's Derby. 80
1914 MULHOLLANDE [3] (P Cole) 2-8-11 T Quinn 25/1: 02: Ch over 2f out: not foot of winner
but showed easily enough ability here to find a race: cost $200,000 & is a half brother to
several winners in the States: eff at 1m, should stay further: acts on fast grnd & a gall trk. 56
1392 TROJAN WAR [4] (W Hern) 2-8-11 W Carson 6/1: 43: Abs: never nearer: should stay
further than todays 1m trip & will strip fitter next time: see 1392. 46
--   VIGLIOTTO [2] (G Harwood) 2-8-7 G Starkey 8/1: 4: Easy to back on debut & never
nearer: impr very likely from this half brother to several winners: cost $310,000 & should
stay middle dists next term: one to keep an eye on. 38
*2522 BRENTANO [5] 2-9-2 R Guest 5/1: 010: Dsptd lead most: btr 2522 (7f). 42
--   QUESSARD [7] 2-8-7 M Roberts 12/1: 0: Prom much: stiff introduction & should impr:
first foal whose dam was a 2yo winner. 26
--   Gallions Point [8] 8-7   2542 Wink Gulliver [1] 8-11
8 ran   8,3,2½,3,4   (L Freedman)   H Cecil Newmarket

2722 LEATHERHEAD CLAIMING STAKES 3YO   £1758   1m 6f Firm 19 -22 Slow

2599 VILLAGE HERO [7] (W Hastings Bass) 3-9-0 R Lines(3) 8/1: 0001: 3 b g Blakeney -
Thereby (Star Moss): Made ev yd, staying on under press in quite slow run 3yo claimer at
Sandown: first success: eff at 10f, clearly stays 14f: acts on gd & fast grnd & on any trk. 31
2134 WALCISIN [4] (R Hannon) 3-9-8 B Thomson 8/1: 2010402: Ev ch inside final 2f: stays
well: see 1386. 35
2613 TURMERIC [9] (D Morley) 3-9-0 R Cochrane 8/1: 0020423: Ch over 1f out: stays 14f. 26
2386 COLEMAN HAWKINS [8] (P Makin) 3-9-0(BL) W Carson 6/1: 0004034: Bl first time: never
nearer: see 2386. 23
2478 ASTRAL [3] 3-9-5 T Quinn 8/1: 0-0100: No threat: twice below 2129 (sharp 12f). 27
2478 MILTESCENS [12] 3-9-5 M Roberts 3/1 FAV: 3020400: Hvly bckd but again ran moderately:
has lost his form: see 1177, 357. 25
2363 WHIPCRACKAWAY [2] 3-8-9 J Bleasdale 4/1: -00320: Well below form 2363 (2m): see 2054. 00
1733 Barleybree [5] 8-3   2317 Adbury [1] 9-0   2478 Way Above [13] 8-4(BL)
2599 Alpha Helix [14] 9-0   2430 Bully Boy [6] 0-0(bl)   2478 Belvel [11] 8-4
13 ran   2,nk,2,½,1½   (Sir Gerard Newman)   W Hastings Bass Newmarket

2723 E.B.F. GARROWBY MAIDEN STAKES 2YO   £1832   1m 100y Firm -05 +03 Fast

2239 ARDEN [7] (H Cecil) 2-9-0 W Ryan 8/13 FAV: 21: 2 b c Ardross - Kereolle (Riverman)
Useful colt: heavily bckd & qcknd into lead dist, cmftbly winning quite a fast run 2yo mdn
at Beverley: half brother to winning miler Knyf: clearly stays 1m really well: acts on gd
and fast ground and on a gall trk: should win more races. 54
2239 GLORY LINE [4] (P Cole) 2-9-0 T Quinn 14/1: 02: Al prom: much closer to winner than
he was on his recent debut and is clearly on the upgrade: stays 1m well: acts on gd and
firm ground: should win a race: see 2239. 46
2225 WOODPECKER [15] (H T Jones) 2-9-0(bl) R Hills 10/1: 203: Early leader, remained
prom thr'out: eff over 7/8f on gd and fast grd: see 2051. 42
2001 GENTLE DARIUS [11] (M Ryan) 2-9-0 R Cochrane 7/2: 434: Made most: stays 1m: see 2001. 36
2522 SURF BOARD [3] 2-9-0 M Hills 12/1: 000: Prom till no extra dist: see 2522. 32
--   BRANDY BOTTLE [2] 2-9-0 R Lines(3) 12/1: 0: Slow start, fdd below dist: quite well
btn but should improve next time: acts on fast ground. 20
2541 TREGEAGLE [5] 2-9-0 A Clark 12/1: 040: Fdd into 7th: btr 2541 (7f). 00
2468 Pathero [12] 9-0   1675 Against All Odds [14] 9-0
2607 Banks And Braes [17] 9-0(BL)   2067 Chico Valdez [8] 9-0
2468 Lindrick [10] 9-0   2535 Thatch Avon [6] 9-0(BL) 00

2626 Try Hills Supplies [13] 9-0   **2584 Winged Pharaoh** [9] 9-0
15 ran 2½,1½,2½,2,7,1   (Lord Howard de Walden)   H Cecil Newmarket

2724 LEVEN NURSERY SELLING H'CAP 2YO   £1111   1m 100y Firm -05 -31 Slow   [30]

1413 PETRUS SEVENTY [16] (P Haslam) 2-8-7(vis) T Williams 3/1 FAV: 0031: 2 b c Treboro -
Bold Pioneer (Wolver Hollow) Despite a far abs gamely made all in a nursery selling h'cap at
Beverley: quite cheaply bought yearling who seems to be impr with ev race: stays 1m well:
suited by forcing tactics on a sound surface.   18
987 BLOW FOR HOME [13] (D Morley) 2-7-10 J Lowe 7/1: 00202: Ran on well: gd eff after
a long break: stays 1m: acts on fast and yldg ground: best in 853 (5f).   02
2138 CREOLE BAY [12] (T Fairhurst) 2-8-3 M Hills 20/1: 000003: Ran on same pace: seems
to be improving slightly as she steps up in dist: stays 1m: acts on fast ground.   08
2470 DELITE MUFFIN [8] (J Fitzgerald) 2-8-0(BL) J Quinn(5) 7/1: 003004: Nearest fin: see 1905. 05
2625 QUE PASA [7] 2-9-7 G French 5/1: 02400: Never nearer over this longer trip: see 2334. 22
2663 CRAIGENDARROCH [11] 2-9-7 J Carroll(7) 5/1: 4001000: Al prom: stays 1m: see 2050. 21
2470 GALWAY EXPRESS [5] 2-8-7(bl) G Duffield 9/1: 00000: Fdd into 7th: see 2470.   00
2466 STAR PLAY [2] 2-8-2(vis) K Darley 10/1: 000000: Visored first time: dwelt and no
threat: see 523.   00
2588 Tootsie Jay [15] 8-4   2405 Ripster [9] 8-6(1ow)   2512 Highland Captain [1] 7-13
2298 Hilliard [3] 8-0   2471 Palace Ruler [10] 8-6   2466 Tuesday Evening [6] 8-3
2470 Willys Niece [4] 7-9
15 ran 2,nk,½,1½,hd,2½,1½,½   (T C Ellis)   P Haslam Newmarket

2725 RAFFINGORA E.B.F. SPRINT STAKES 2/3YO   £3106   5f   Firm -05 +04 Fast

2382 HANDSOME SAILOR [4] (M Dickinson) 3-10-1 G Duffield 5/6 FAV: 412-031: 3 ch c Some Hand
- Found At Sea (Pieces of Eight) Very useful sprinter: easily landed the odds, led inside dist
in quite a fast run stks race at Beverley: most consistent last season when trained by
R Thompson, winning at Windsor, Newcastle and Haydock: very eff over 5f: acts on any going
tho' is well suited by some give: acts on any trk: genuine sort who carries weight well. 62
2511 SAMEEK [5] (R Armstrong) 2-8-5 T Quinn 15/8: 213002: Tried to make all: gd eff against
older horses: loves to be out in front: see 583.   46
2483 BON ACCUEIL [1] (H Whiting) 3-9-3 J Bleasdale 20/1: 2300003: Btr over 6f in 2018. 30
2668 VILTASH [2] (J Etherington) 3-10-1(vis) E Guest(3) 6/1: 0000004: Btn below dist:
stiff task: see 671.   35
-- GOLDEN GAME [3] 2-7-10 A Mercer 33/1: 0: Slowly away and never going pace: half
brother to winning miler Foolish Ways and should be btr for this experience.   00
5 ran 2½,2½,2,8   (R E Sangster)   M Dickinson Manton, Wilts.

2726 BURTON AGNES STUD CO. FILLIES MDN. 3YO   £1658   1m 2f Firm -05 -20 Slow

2294 SHINING SKIN [8] (P Walwyn) 3-8-11 Paul Eddery 8/1: 20-0001: 3 b f Fappiano -
Extreme Turbulence (Swaps) Qcknd into lead dist and ran on strongly to win a 3yo fillies mdn
at Beverley: eff over 1m but seemed much btr suited by today's longer trip: likes fast grd
and seems to act on any trk.   38
2304 COMMANCHE BELLE [11] (L Cumani) 3-8-11 R Cochrane 13/8 FAV: 232: Heavily bckd: led
below dist, kept on well: eff over 10/12f and seems to act on any trk: best in 2048 (12f). 34
1431 SWAALEF [4] (O Douieb) 3-8-11 R Machado 9/1: -03: Stayed on well: gd eff after a
long break: eff over 10f and should stay further: seems well suited by fast grd: see 1431. 30
1102 FISSURE [9] (J Leigh) 3-8-11 D Nicholls 33/1: 00-004: Never nearer after a long abs:
should do btr over a longer trip: acts on firm grd: should benefit from this run.   22
2304 ELA MAN HEE [3] 3-8-11 M Hills 14/1: -0000: Wknd 2f out: best over this C/D in 862. 16
2299 TERN OF A CENTURY [5] 3-8-11 G Duffield 20/1: -000: Late prog: lightly raced filly
who showed her first signs of form here: stays 10f: acts on firm ground.   14
2327 REMINISCING [6] 3-8-11 T Williams 7/2: -200: Led early and again 2f out: fdd into 7th:
twice below form shown over this trip in 1749.   00
2314 PEACE KEEPER [2] 3-8-11(bl) R Hills 5/1: -040: Made most: fin 8th: see 2314 (1m yldg). 00
2682 RIDESIDE [1] 3-8-11 M Birch 10/1: -040: Held up, fin last: see 2682.   00
2497 Report Em [7] 8-11   2508 Ultressa [10] 8-11(vis)
11 ran 2,1½,5,3,½,nk,4,2½   (Maktoum Al Maktoum)   P Walwyn Lambourn, Berks.

2727 CHERRY BURTON H'CAP STAKES (0-35) 3YO+   £1882   1m 4f Firm -05 -02 Slow   [30]

2492 HEIGHT OF SUMMER [7] (D Arbuthnot) 5-7-9 A Mackay 10/1: 4003001: 5 b g Shirley Heights
- Midsummertime (Midsummer Night II) Led below dist and ran on well to win an all aged h'cap
at Beverley: his only prev success came in this corresponding race last year: best form
over 12f on fast grd: runs well at Beverley.   06
2403 HYOKIN [5] (D Morley) 4-8-12(vis) T Williams 6/1: 2132002: Ev ch: gd eff: see 1359. 20
2604 IM EXCEPTIONAL [12] (R Hollinshead) 4-8-2 W Ryan 16/1: 0-03003: Held up, fin well:
seems well suited by 12f: see 2173 & 1747.   09
2372 LONGSTOP [3] (P Makin) 4-9-5 T Quinn 3/1 FAV: 3001024: Not btn far after being denied
a clear run: in gd form and may win again soon: see 2098.   25
2578 CASHEW KING [2] 3-8-12 S Webster 7/1: 4402100: Had ev ch: best here in 2360 (10f gd). 24
2536 LOST OPPORTUNITY [10] 3-7-13 J Lowe 8/1: 0040000: Made most: gd eff: see 99.   10
2604 S S SANTO [14] 3-8-7 R Cochrane 5/1: 0001230: Ran on too late: fin 7th: see 1898. 00

2528 **DICK KNIGHT** [4] 5-8-5(vis) A Shoults(5) 10/1: 0010020: Btn 2f out: btr 2528: see 2101. 00
2492 **Campus Boy** [8] 7-7(2oh) 1563 **Fenchurch Colony** [9] 9-4
2604 **Chevet Lady** [6] 8-3 2415 **Apple Wine** [13] 7-12 2445 **Luminate** [1] 9-10
13 ran 1½,nk,½,1½,nk,shthd (R Crutchley) D Arbuthnot Compton, Berks.

2728 **WEEL HANDICAP STAKES (0-35) 3YO+ £2013 1m 100y Firm -05 +03 Fast [31]**

2414 **WARPLANE** [18] (C Thornton) 6-9-3 J Bleasdale 5/1: 0034001: 6 b g Warpath - Glider (Buisson Ardent) Didnot have the best of runs but squeezed through inside dist to win an all-aged h'cap at Beverley: won this same race last year when also successful at Hamilton: best form over 8/9f on fast grd: likes a gall trk. 29
2360 **PERSHING** [14] (J Leigh) 5-9-0 J Carr(7) 10/1: 3220022: Led over 1f out: course specialist who is running well at present: see 2360 & 611. 22
992 **ELEGANT FASHION** [6] (E Weymes) 4-8-12 E Guest(3) 14/1: 00-0003: Fin well: gd run after a long abs: maiden filly who has shown her best form around 1m on gd or faster ground. 18
2426 **SHARONS ROYALE** [5] (R Whitaker) 3-8-7 K Bradshaw(5) 12/1: 3244144: Kept on: best 2413. 17
2413 **FLYING ZIAD** [13] 3-8-2 R Hills 20/1: 0-40000: Never nearer: best here in 2104. 11
2629 **MONINSKY** [19] 5-8-7 A Shoults(5) 14/1: 3104000: No extra dist: see 1774. 07
2594 **BICKERMAN** [10] 3-8-9 G Duffield 5/1: 0101230: Trouble in running, fin 7th: see 1906. 00
•2340 **LA JAMBALAYA** [9] 3-9-2 T Quinn 4/1 FAV: -340210: Longer trip: much btr here 2340 (yldg) 00
2581 **WILLBE WILLBE** [2] 3-8-1 J Lowe 9/1: 0000130: Btn when hmpd below dist: see 2230. 00
2545 **TIP TAP** [8] 4-9-2 R Cochrane 10/1: 0001040: Btn 2f out: best 1870 (gd). 00
2397 **Single Hand** [11] 8-4 2602 **Forever Tingo** [16] 7-11
2681 **Janes Brave Boy** [7] 8-2 2602 **Running Bull** [12] 8-8
•1990 **Dallas Smith** [3] 7-11(vis) 2526 **No Credibility** [15] 9-6
-- **Mal Y Pense** [4] 9-7 1727 **Dorame** [1] 8-1 2312 **Whoberley Wheels** [17] 8-2
19 ran 1½,1,1½,½,½,½,1½,1½ (A Wilson) C Thornton Middleham, Yorks

SANDOWN Wednesday September 24th Righthand, Galloping Track

Official Going Given As GOOD/FIRM

2729 **OXSHOTT APP NURSERY H'CAP 2YO £2302 5f Firm 12 -02 Slow [61]**

2158 **SAUCE DIABLE** [11] (W Hern) 2-9-7 T Sprake(11) 4/1 JT.FAV: 21001: 2 b f Moorestyle - Cottage Pie (Kalamoun) Useful filly: gamely defied top weight, led inside final 1f, holding on by a hd in an app nursery h'cap at Sandown: earlier a fast time winner of a 2yo mdn at Windsor: very eff over this minimum trip but should stay further: acts well on fast ground tho' prob on any trk. 60
2579 **VICTORY BALLARD** [10] (R Hannon) 2-7-9 R Perham(2) 10/1: 0001042: Led inside final 2f: narrowly btn: fine effort: seems suited by a stiff 5f: see 1844. 33
2485 **HEY AMADEUS** [6] (P Mitchell) 2-7-8(1ow)(16oh) G Carter 9/1: 02003: Ran on well final 1f: well out of the h'cap and ran well: stays a sharpish 6f: likes fast ground. 27
2579 **OUT ON A FLYER** [5] (D Elsworth) 2-7-7(13oh) Debbie Wheatley(4) 10/1: 0021324: Al prom and is in gd form: 13lbs out of the h'cap here: see 2579, 2020. 23
2435 **JOVICK** [8] 2-8-1(BL) J Adams(5) 10/1: 31000: Bl first time: best 1665. 28
2159 **YOUNG LOCHINVAR** [13] 2-8-0 L Jones 12/1: 0000: No threat: quite lightly raced colt who is a half brother to winning sprinter Today and Tomorrow: acts on fast ground: prob needs further than 5f. 25
2100 **LEADING PLAYER** [4] 2-7-7(1oh) A Culhane(7) 11/2: 0340: Led over 3f: well below 2100. 00
2588 **MISS MILVEAGH** [7] 2-8-2 G Athanasiou(9) 4/1 JT.FAV: 2221300: No show: btr 2465, 2380. 00
2588 **Oriole Dancer** [1] 7-7(4oh) 1583 **Going Easy** [3] 7-8
2090 **Mr Mumbles** [9] 7-7(2oh)
11 ran hd,2,¾,1,¾ W Hern (Lord Porchester)

2730 **WEY HANDICAP STKS 0-50 £3753 1m Firm 12 +05 Fast [45]**

+2545 **FLYHOME** [4] (P Cundell) 5-9-6(4ex) N Adams 9/2 JT.FAV: 2303011: 5 ch g Home Guard - Western Gem (Sheshoon) In fine form, making most and again cl home gamely in a h'cap at Sandown: last time out was a ready all the way winner in course record time in a h'cap at Salisbury: in '85 won at Sandown: prev season won at Bath and Wolverhampton: very eff with forcing tactics over 1m, stays 10f: loves fast grd and a gall trk: genuine sort who carries weight well. 47
2266 **CANADIAN STAR** [8] (M Jarvis) 3-8-11(vis) T Lucas 6/1: 0241122: Led over 1f out: outbattled by winner: consistent: see 2266. 44
-- **SPRING IN MY STEP** [5] (M Prescott) 4-9-5 C Nutter 25/1: -1110-3: Ev ch inside final 2f: gd seasonal debut: won her first 3 outings in '85, Hamilton, Goodwood and Chester (first time out): very eff at 1m: prob acts on any grd and on any trk: carries weight well and is a genuine filly. 36
2594 **GIVING IT ALL AWAY** [6] (H Beasley) 3-7-11 W Carson 9/2 JT.FAV: 0210324: Prom, ev ch: quite consistent: see 1819. 21
2544 **SINGLE** [7] 4-9-1 D Mckay 11/2: 1141300: No threat: see 481. 32
2526 **SKEEB** [1] 3-9-7 M A Giles(7) 12/1: 14-0300: Never nearer: lightly raced since 732 (6f) 36
2526 **CREEAGER** [9] 4-8-13 Pat Eddery 7/1: 1430000: Active in mkt: fin 7th: btr 2526 (7f). 00

2566 **Moores Metal** [9] 8-13   2091 **New Central** [3] 7-8   2475 **Swifts Pal** [11] 9-10
2490 **Sweet Andy** [10] 7-7(14oh)
11 ran   nk,5,shthd,shthd,5   (Colin G Southgate)   P Cundell Compton, Berks.

2731 **WEST END STKS HANDICAP** 0-50   £3429   5f   Firm 12 +07 Fast   [49]

2537 **TYROLLIE** [11] (N Vigors) 4-9-5 P Cook 14/1: 2004001: 4 br f Balidar - Segos (Runnymede)
Useful filly: led 1f out, under press in a h'cap at Sandown: first time out won a h'cap at
Kempton: in '85 won at Sandown and Newbury: also a "winner" at Epsom (sub disq): winning 2yo
at Folkestone: seems equally eff at 5/6f: acts on firm and soft ground: thoroughly genuine. 51
2537 **DEPUTY HEAD** [9] (L Holt) 6-9-2 P Waldron 10/1: 3003002: Fin really well: enjoying a
gd season: see 1060. 44
2530 **SNAP DECISION** [8] (R Hannon) 3-8-1(bl) A Mcglone 16/1: 0402033: Chance final 1f:
another gd run: see 2530, 1033. 30
2586 **TOBERMORY BOY** [1] (R Whitaker) 9-8-11 N Carlisle 20/1: 2000004: Not btn far: best
effort since 1306. 38
*2382 **SILENT MAJORITY** [10] 3-9-8 Pat Eddery 11/4 FAV: 3114110: Led 4f: not btn far: another
gd effort from this consistent colt: see 2382. 51
2469 **STEPHENS SONG** [16] 3-8-3 S Dawson 20/1: 1000000: Cl.up 6th: see 2469, 233. 32
2256 **DAVILL** [4] 4-8-2 B Rouse 12/1: 0000300: Ran on into 7th: see 1950, 76. 28
2537 **GEORGE WILLIAM** [17] 5-8-12 J Reid 6/1: 2230100: Fin 8th: not btn far: see 2402. 37
2446 **CREE BAY** [7] 7-9-9(bl) W Carson 9/1: 4110000: Btr 2446, see 1777 (6f). 00
2378 **ALL AGREED** [3] 5-10-0 B Thomson 10/1: 0021130: Btr 2378, 1986. 00
2668 **Ferryman** [2] 9-6   2378 **Crete Cargo** [14] 9-7(VIS)
*2318 **Sharad** [12] 7-8(vis)(1ow)(16oh)   2469 **No Beating Harts** [15] 8-13
2488 **Platine** [6] 8-4   2319 **Sitex** [13] 7-8(1ow)(14oh)
855 **Yani** [5] 7-8(1ow)(16oh)
17 ran   1½,nk,shthd,hd,hd,nk,nk   (Lady d'Avigdor Goldsmid)   N Vigors Lambourn, Berks.

2732 **GRANBY STAKES** 2YO   £3514   7f   Firm 12 -07 Slow

2522 **LOVE THE GROOM** [6] (J Dunlop) 2-8-11 W Carson 3/1: 21: 2 b c Blushing Groom - Nell's
Briquette (Lanyon) Impr colt: switched early in the str and squeezed through to lead final
1f by a shthd in quite val 2yo stks at Sandown: first time out was a fine 2nd to Brentano at
Doncaster: cost $325,000 as a yearling: eff at 7f, looks sure to be suited by 1m: acts on
fast ground and a gall trk: on the upgrade. 58
*2001 **FEARLESS ACTION** [4] (H Cecil) 2-9-1 S Cauthen 8/11 FAV: 12: Made almost all: rallied
when hdd and btn a whisker: fine effort: can win again soon: see 2001. 61
1653 **INCINDERATOR** [3] (M Stoute) 2-8-11 W R Swinburn 12/1: 43: Chance over 1f out:
fine effort after a fair abs: suited by 7f and can get off the mark soon: see 1653. 52
-- **BAY BOULEVARD** [2] (R Armstrong) 2-8-4 Pat Eddery 14/1: 4: Mkt drifter and never nearer:
improvement very likely this half sister to 12f winner Law Court and 10f winner Bird Point:
looks sure to be suited by 1m+: acts on fast ground. 39
2146 **LUZUM** [1] 2-9-4(bl) A Murray 10/1: 232100: Fdd over 1f out: twice below 1914 (made all) 45
2418 **MILAN FAIR** [5] 2-8-11 M Roberts 33/1: 00: Prom most: should be suited by this trip and
further: acts on firm ground: see 2418. 30
6 ran   shthd,2,3,4,4   (Mrs V Gaucci del Bono)   J Dunlop Arundel, Sussex

2733 **DITTON STAKES H'CAP** 0-50   £3930   1m 6f   Firm 12 +04 Fast   [47]

*2523 **BACKCHAT** [4] (G Harwood) 4-10-4(5ex) G Starkey 5/1: 1-40011: 4 b c Stage Door Johnny -
Dos A Dos (Advocator) Very useful colt who is in fine form: led inside final 2f, running on
well under press in a h'cap at Sandown: last time out was a game winner of a val h'cap at
Doncaster: lightly raced in '85, winning at Newmarket and Bath: very eff over today's 14f trip:
acts on fast and yldg ground and a gall trk: genuine sort who carries weight really well. 63
2599 **MISS SHIRLEY** [14] (J Dunlop) 3-8-2(3ex) W Carson 11/2: 0224132: Led 12f: in fine
form and stays 14f: acts on any trk: see 2520. 39
2517 **TAMATOUR** [3] (M Stoute) 3-8-11 W R Swinburn 4/1 JT.FAV: -02123: Ev ch over 1f out:
remains in fine form: see 2517, 2228. 46
2403 **ALSIBA** [11] (C Benstead) 4-7-8(1ow)(1oh) R Fox 25/1: 1404004: Kept on final 1f:
gd eff and goes well over this C/D: best 1035. 18
2311 **CHUCKLESTONE** [5] 3-8-1 N Adams 14/1: 0041340: Nvr nrr: stays 14f: see 2023. 31
2656 **VISUAL IDENTITY** [13] 4-7-8(1ow) G Carter 16/1: 0004330: No threat: btr 2656 (10f). 13
*2432 **EASTER LEE** [10] 6-8-0(1ow) A Mcglone 4/1 JT.FAV: 22-0010: Chance 2f out: much btr 2432. 00
1837 **HIGH PLAINS** [1] 4-8-3 W Newnes 8/1: 0000400: Ev ch over 2f out, wknd: see 1837. 00
2240 **Very Special** [7] 8-4   2523 **Trapeze Artist** [9] 9-7
2572 **Staghound** [8] 8-6   541 **Avebury** [12] 8-5   --   **Baraoora** [2] 8-2
1388 **Royal Craftsman** [6] 7-7(4oh)
14 ran   2½,¾,nk,2½,½   (K Abdulla)   G Harwood Pulborough, Sussex

2734 **MITRE MAIDEN STAKES** 3YO   £1976   1m 2f   Firm 12 -14 Slow

1776 **MAGIC VISION** [1] (J Dunlop) 3-8-11 B Thomson 16/1: -0001: 3 gr f Shergar - As You
Desire Me (Kalamoun) Despite an abs, led over 2f out, readily, in a 3yo fillies mdn at Sandown:
lightly raced filly who is a half sister to very useful 1m winner Prince Lyph : very eff
over 10f, prob stays 12f: likes fast ground. 50

2419 GALESA [7] (P Kelleway) 3-8-11 J Williams 7/2 JT.FAV: 00-02: Ran on inside final 2f
but no chance with easy winner: 6l clear 3rd: see 2419.   42
2304 SKEVENA [10] (W Hern) 3-8-11 W R Swinburn 10/1: -03: Never nearer: very lightly
raced filly: prob stays further than 10f: acts on fast ground and can improve further.   32
2548 RED SHOES [6] (W Hern) 3-8-11(BL) W Carson 7/2 JT.FAV: 3223224: Made much: no extra
final 2f: tried in blinkers today but these made little difference: frustrating: see 2304. 32
2550 JUNGLE BEAT [9] 3-8-11 A Murray 12/1: 0-40: Prom, ev ch: stays 10f? See 2550.   27
2653 FIREAL [8] 3-8-11 S Cauthen 5/1: 4-240: Led ½ way, fdd, not stay 10f? See 2653, 338.   26
-- MADRAMA [3] 3-8-11 M Roberts 16/1: -0: Fin 7th on racecourse debut: half sister to
sev winners and seems certain to come on for this race.   25
2068 STANDARD ROSE [11] 3-8-11 W Newnes 8/1: 0-400: Prom over 7f: btr 2068.   24
430 Davallia [2] 8-11   2059 Parts Is Parts [4] 8-11
2248 Popthorn [5] 8-11
11 ran   5,6,hd,3,½,shthd,¾   (Col F R Hue-Williams)   J Dunlop Arundel, Sussex

BELMONT PARK   Saturday September 20th

Official Going Given As FIRM

2735 GRADE 1 TURF CLASSIC 3YO+   £295909   1m 4f Firm -

-- MANILA (L Jolley) 3-8-7 J Santos : 2211111: 3 b c Lyphard - Dona Ysidra (Le
Fabuleux) Very smart American colt: in a slowly run race, led 3f out and gamely held on for
a narrow win in val Grade 1 Turf Classic at Belmont: has only once fin out of the first 2
in 12 outings winning 7 times: stays 12f well and acts on firm ground: genuine.   85
2200 DAMISTER (J Tree) 4-9-0 Pat Eddery : 3-30432: Battled with winner thr'out final 2f
and possibly got his hd in front briefly at one stage, just btn and lost nothing in defeat. 82
-- DANGERS HOUR (M Miller) 4-9-0 J Bailey : 2100113: Btn only a nk for 2nd place:
stays 12f, acts on firm.   81
2456 DIVULGE (G Moschera) 4-9-0 J Cruguet : -121024: Creditable eff but rated higher 2456 78
9 ran   nose,nk,1½   (B M Shannon)   L Jolley USA

LONGCHAMP   Sunday September 21st   Righthand Galloping Track

Official Going Given As GOOD/SOFT

2736 GROUP 3 PRIX DU PRINCE D'ORANGE 3YO+   £18689   1m 2f Good/Soft -

2200 FITNAH (C Head) 4-8-10 G Moore : 0-10201: 4 ch f Kris - Greenland Park (Red God)
Smart French filly: well treated at the weights when leading in the final 1f to win Gr 3
Prix du Prince d'Orange at Longchamp: reportedly didnot travel well when racing at York last
time but first time out was an easy winner of a Listed race at Longchamp: in excellent form
in '85, winning 3 times at Longchamp and loves this trk: very eff over 10/12f tho' acts
on any going.   79
1493 SAINT ESTEPHE (A Fabre) 4-9-6 C Asmussen : 3-13122: Chall in final 1f: narrowly
btn and now takes his chance in the Arc: most consistent: see 885.   86
*643 FAST TOPAZE (G Mikhalides) 3-9-2 J Velasquez : -1113: Returning after long abs,
led 4f out but just fdd cl home: this was an excellent trial for the Arc tho' that
will be a new trip for him: see 643.   90
2507 NEW BRUCE (G Collet) 4-8-10 G Guignard : 0030104: See 1594.   75
7 ran   1,shthd,hd,6,15   (Mlle H Al-Maktoum)   C Head, France

2737 GROUP 1 PRIX DE LA SALAMANDRE 2YO   £42369   7f   Good/Soft -

2358 MIESQUE [3] (F Boutin) 2-8-8 F Head : ----131: 2 b f Nureyev - Passadoble (Prove
Out) Smart French filly: decisively reversed the form of the Prix Morny with Sakura Reiko
when cmftbly winning Gr 1 Prix de la Salamandre at Longchamp: first time out won a minor
fillies race at Deauville on soft grd and evidently likes an easy surface: eff 6f, stays 7f
well and should stay at least 1m: improving.   82
*2358 SAKURA REIKO [4] (P L Biancone) 2-8-8 Y Saint Martin : 1112: Had no luck in running
and was not given a hard time once clearly held: prob stays 7f: see 2358 (6f hvy).   77
-- WHAKILYRIC [9] (F Boutin) 2-8-8 E Saint Martin : 1214123: Stable companion of winner
and has proved most consistent so far winning or being placed in her last 7 races: most
recent success was in   Gr 3 Prix du Calvados at Deauville.   71
1126 RISK ME [8] 2-8-11 C Asmussen : 1144: Long abs: far from disgraced and
likes this easy surface: see 737.   72
-- FLEUR DORANGER [10] 2-8-8 J Velasquez : -120300:   68
*2198 GULF KING [7] 2-8-11 R Cochrane : 021010: Raised in class here but not disgraced
in a fair 6th place: see 2198.   70
*2243 GENGHIZ [1] 2-8-11 T Ives : 110: Beat only 1 other home and was well below his best. 00
10 ran   1½,3,1,nk,hd   (S Niarchos)   F Boutin France

2738 GROUP 3 PRIX DE LUTECE 3YO   £17672   1m 7f Good/Soft -

-- ANAZID [3] (A De Royer Dupre) 3-8-11 Y Saint Martin : -10211: 3 gr c Nishapour - Andalgala

(Abdos) Smart colt: easy all the way winner of Gr 3 Prix du Lutece at Longchamp: recent
winner of a minor event at Deauville and also successful first time out: evidently well suited
by forcing the pace: stays 15f really well: acts on an easy surface.   72
-- ALESSO [4] (D Smaga) 3-8-11 A Lequeux : -1412: Ran well here and is in fine form
at present, recently winning at Deauville: likes softish ground and a test of stamina.   68
643 MISTER BIG LOUIE [5] (P L Biancone) 3-8-7 D Boeuf : 0-40003: Close, creditable 3rd
showing that he stays 15f and acts on soft.   62
1354 SATCO [7] (P Bary) 3-9-1 F Head : -2-1144: Best 1117 (firm)   68
2453 PUB ROYAL [6] 3-8-11 P Bruneau : 1004340: Disapp after much btr eff in 2453(13f,hvy)   59
*1556 KNIGHTS LEGEND [2] 3-8-7 G Starkey : -21210: Below his best in 6th: see 1556 (fast)   43
8 ran   1½,¾,1,3,8   (H H Aga Khan)   A De Royer Dupre France

---

Official Going Given As FIRM

2739 GROUP 3 SILKEN GLIDER STAKES 2YO   £14535   1m   Firm -

-- INANNA (J Oxx) 2-8-7 D Hogan 5/1: 11: 2 gr f Persian Bold - Callixena (Kalamoun)
Promising Irish filly who retained her unbtn record leading inside final 2f under press in
Gr 3 Silken Glider Stks (2yo fillies) at Leopardstown Sept 20: first time out winner on the
same trk in June: stays 1m well, acts on firm ground.   61
-- CECINA (L Browne) 2-8-4 D Gillespie 10/1: 2202: Kept on well to be a close 2nd: a
mdn who has been 2nd in 3 out of her 4 races so far, including a Listed race at the Curragh:
stays 1m, acts on firm and yldg.   56
2504 TREK (D Weld) 2-8-7 M J Kinane 7/2 FAV: ---1043: Fav on the strength of her close 4th
in 2504 but had to give best to Inanna who is in the same ownership: see 2504.   55
-- CONNAUGHT ROSE (L Browne) 2-8-4 P Shanahan 20/1: 04: --   49
10 ran   1,2½,1½   (Miss E Laidlaw)   J Oxx Ireland

2740 GROUP 3 GLENCAIRN STAKES 3YO+   £11610   1m 1f   Firm -

*2219 MY GENERATION (W Hastings Bass) 3-8-9 C Asmussen 7/1: 301-311: 3 ch c Young Generation
- High Finale (High Line) Smart impr colt: came from well behind to lead inside final 1f,
gamely, in Gr 3 Glencairn Stks at Leopardstown: broke course record when winning val h'cap
at York last time: in '85 won at Newmarket on final outing: brother to very useful filly
Que Sympatica: well suited by 9/10f and fast ground: genuine and impr colt who is sure to
win more races.   75
*2496 KUFUMA (G Huffer) 4-8-13(bl) G Carter 8/1: 0-00012: Met trouble in running, absolutely
flying at the fin and just failed to get up in a blanket fin: definitely back to his best
and should win again soon: see 2496.   71
2633 LAKE CHAMPLAIN (D Weld) 3-8-6 M J Kinane 3/1: 2122023: Btn only ½l for 2nd: best 1331   69
-- ISTORIATO (D V O'brien) 3-8-6 D Gillespie 14/1: -2114: Cl.up 4th: recent winner here
and at Tipperary over 7f/1m but clearly stays 9f well: acts on gd and firm grd.   68
*2419 SAMARID 3-9-0 W R Swinburn 9/4 FAV: 0-01010: Cl 5th and ran to his best: see 2419.   76
2200 FIORAVANTI 3-9-0 C Roche 11/2: 1-10000: See 466: has failed to fulfill the high
regard in which he was held.   73
-- Stop The Fighting 8-6   2633 Bermuda Classic   8-11
8 ran   nk,¼,nk,shthd,1½,1,10   (M Riordan)   W Hastings Bass Newmarket

---

Official Going Given As GOOD

2741 GROUP 1 GRAN PREMIO D'ITALIA 3YO   £64798   1m 4f   Good/Soft -

+2156 EL CUITE (H Cecil) 3-9-1 S Cauthen : 1-11: 3 b c Vaguely Noble - Assez Cuite
(Graustark) Smart, impr colt who retained his unbtn record when coming from behind to lead
final 100 yds in Gr 1 Gran Premio d'Italia at San Siro: first time out, ready winner of val,
very fast run h'cap at Newbury: winner of his sole outing in '85 a 27 runner event at Newbury:
very well suited by 12f and promises to stay further: acts on gd and fast grd and on a gall
trk: likely to stay in training next season and should have further impr in him.   80
*1328 TOMMY WAY (J Dunlop) 3-9-1 W Carson : 1-31112: Led 4f out, battled on well and
was btn only a nk in a close fin: thoroughly consistent and genuine: see 1328.   79
555 TONY BIN (L Camici) 3-9-1 W R Swinburn : 33-1413: Set a mod pace for over 1m,
kept on well and was btn less than a nk by the winner: much impr form and poss flattered by
the slow pace: stays 12f well and acts on gd going.   78
1218 DUCA DI BUSTED (A Botti) 3-9-1 G Dettori : 1113114: Distant 4th: see 1218.   66
4 ran   nk,shthd,8   (Sheikh Mohammed)   H Cecil Newmarket

Official Going Given As GOOD - SOFT

2742 GROUP 3 PRIX DE SEINE-ET-OISE 3YO+   £17971   7f   Good/Soft -

2347 PARIOLI (J Cunnington Jnr) 5-8-10 M Philliperon : 0413-41: 5 b m Bold Bidder -
Rumbling Roman (Roman Line) Very smart French mare: came with a strong late run to win Gr 3
Prix de Seine-et-Oise at Maisons-Laffitte: has run only once before this season in 2437 and
has been trained with the Prix de L'Abbaye in mind: winner of 3 Gr 3 races last term: very
eff over 5/6f and acts on gd and hvy going.   80
2003 BAISER VOLE (C Head) 3-8-9 G Moore : 1-01432: Led 1f out, hdd near fin: grand eff
from this versatile filly who is eff between 6f and 1m: see 467.   81
2347 COMRADE IN ARMS (P Lallie) 4-9-0 G Dubroeucq 1: 2120233: Fin really strongly and
is btr suited by longer dist: see 2003.   80
155 GLIFHADA (C Head) 3-8-8 A Lequeux : -400024: See 155.   73
2474 ROARING RIVA 3-8-11 M Wigham : -440000: Ran well for most of the trip: fine eff.   75
13 ran   ½,nose,2½,nk   (D Arnold)   J Cunnington Jnr France

2743 DRIFFIELD ALL-AGED STAKES 2YO+   £1092   5f   Firm 02 -10 Slow

2621 JACQUI JOY [16] (K Ivory) 3-9-0 G Bardwell(7) 8/1: 0000021: 3 b f Music Boy - Superb
Lady (Marcus Superbus) Led below dist and just held on for her first win in an all-aged seller
at Beverley Sept 25 (no bid): stays 7f tho' seems best over 5f: suited by fast grd and seems
to act on any track.   08
--   GENOTIN [7] (M Prescott) 3-9-3 G Duffield 5/4 FAV: 000-2: Heavily bckd on belated
reappearance: fin well but the post came just too soon: lightly raced colt who is sure to
do btr over 6f+: acts on fast grd: can win a seller.   10
2585 SWEET EIRE [19] (W Pearce) 4-9-2 R Hull(7) 25/1: 0000403: Btr eff: see 906.   02
2417 NAUGHTY NIGHTY [1] (M Tompkins) 3-9-0 M Rimmer 14/1: 0000034: Led briefly 2f out:see 2189. 00
2107 RAINTREE COUNTY [11] 2-8-0 A Mackay 20/1: 0000400: Never nearer: acts on firm and soft. 01
2592 KEN SIDDALL [20] 3-9-3 M Birch 12/1: 0000000: Rated 29 in h'cap here in 198 (yldg)   00
2322 KARENS STAR [17] 9-10-1 N Leach(7) 5/1: 0002000: Never nearer 8th: best 2124 (sharp trk) 00
2365 OUR GINGER [6] 2-7-11 R P Elliott 15/2: 040: Late prog: btr here 2365 (gd).   00
2608 CAUSEWAY FOOT [14] 2-8-0(bl) P Robinson 10/1: 0042030: Btr over 6f in 2608: see 2150   00
2295 Always Native [4] 10-1   537 Brookhead Girl [2] 7-11
2688 Motor Master [13] 9-3(bl)   1684 Shady Blade [15] 7-11(bl)
2411 Tree Fella [8] 10-1   2548 Mistral Magic [9] 7-11
2621 Montefiaso [12] 9-5   2322 The Stray Bullett [3] 9-3(vis)
2514 Bugberry [5] 7-11(BL)   871 Gutsy [18] 9-0
19 ran   nk,1½,1½,1½,nk,hd,2½,nk   (Mrs I Reichler)   K Ivory Radlett, Herts.

2744 BROMPTON NURSERY H'CAP 2YO   £1667   5f   Firm 02 +04 Fast   [40]

2380 LINN ODEE [9] (M W Easterby) 2-8-4(1ow) M Birch 8/1: 3140401: 2 b f King of Spain -
Heavenly Chorus (Green God) Led below dist, cmftbly in a fast run nursery h'cap at Beverley:
later won a fillies mdn at Haydock: speedily bred filly who fetched 8,200 gns as a yearling:
best over 5f tho' does stay 6f: acts on fast and soft grd and on any trk.   28
2410 SUPREME STATE [8] (P Makin) 2-9-2 G Baxter 9/2: 00322: Going on fin: in gd form: see 2270 34
2421 TAP THE BATON [13] (M Tompkins) 2-8-8(BL) A Mackay 14/1: 3230003: Bl first time:
ev ch: bckd at long odds today: best on a sharp trk in 622.   20
2606 MISS DRUMMOND [5] (N Tinkler) 2-8-5 Kim Tinkler 20/1: 0131304: Fin strongly: btr
over 6f? See 2107.   14
2689 WOODMAN WEAVER [5] 2-8-11 W Newnes 5/1: 0004320: Led before ½ way: btr 2689.   18
+2606 LAMB BECK [7] 2-8-13(7ex) L Charnock 9/4 FAV: 30310: Early leader: wknd dist:btr 2606 19
2535 MERE MUSIC [12] 2-8-4 J Lowe 11/2: 0010020: No threat: btr over 6f in 2535.   00
2279 Our Horizon [14] 8-7   2535 Nicholas George [10] 8-2(bl)
2606 Beckingham Ben [4] 9-0   2625 Dohty Baby [3] 8-7
2606 Swynford Princess [11] 7-10   2606 The Great Match [2] 9-7
2051 Worthy Prince [6] 9-2   2618 Stars In Motion [1] 8-7
15 ran   1½,2½,1,¾,shthd,½,4,1½   (C F Spence)   M W Easterby Sherrif Hutton, Yorks.

2745 SNOWY GRAY MEM. H'CAP (0-35) 3YO+   £2600   2m   Firm 02 +05 Fast   [32]

*2141 MARINERS DREAM [10] (R Hollinshead) 5-8-3 A Culhane(7) 15/2: 0-10011: 5 br g Julio Mariner
- My Ginny (Palestine) Broke the course record when trotting up in a h'cap at Beverley:
last month gained a similarly easy win at Catterick, where he also won first time out: stays
2m really well: acts on firm and soft grd and on any trk: will go hurdling when the ground
eases.   20
2403 DARK SIRONA [9] (D Arbuthnot) 3-8-6 W Newnes 11/2: -022102: No chance with winner
but ran to her best: stays 2m well: see 2152.   25
2647 JOIST [12] (M Prescott) 4-8-13(bl) G Duffield 6/1: 2432103: Gd eff: best 2040.   18
*2363 GUESSING [4] (G Harwood) 3-9-10 A Clark 10/11 FAV: -00214: Well bckd, ev ch, not
quicken below dist: btr over this C/D in 2363 (gd).   38
2306 MARIE GALANTE [7] 3-8-10 G Baxter 8/1: 2323030: Led home turn, btn dist: see 2306.   21

2087 SOUND DIFFUSION [8] 4-8-10 D Mckeown 10/1: 0030000: No extra over 2f out: best 933   04
2509 Ramille [5] 8-3   2686 Northern River [6] 8-11
2492 Knights Heir [3] 8-1   2647 Our Bara Boy [1] 7-10(vis)
2111 Boreham Down [2] 7-7(7oh)
11 ran   5,2,1½,2½,4,4   (Dennis Newton)   R Hollinshead Upper Longdon, Staffs.

2746 CRUSADERS HORN H'CAP STAKES (0-35) 3YO+   £1754   1m 2f   Firm 02 +01 Fast   [29]

2274 THUNDERDOME [5] (O Douieb) 3-8-5 G Duffield 7/2: -00001: 3 br f Lyphard - Mr P's
Girl (Mr Prospector) Showed impr form, led below dist and was sn clear in an all-aged h'cap
at Beverley: eff over 1m, clearly stays 10f well: acts on gd and fast grd and seems to have
no trk preferences: wore a visor last time, but not today.   26
2399 SEAMERE [8] (M Tompkins) 3-7-11 A Mackay 8/1: 0-0002: Led briefly 2f out, no chance
with easy winner: beginning to show a little form: eff over 8/10f on firm and yldg: see 2399   08
2533 PEARL PET [4] (P Makin) 4-8-11 G Baxter 10/3: -200223: Remains a mdn: see 850.   12
2623 BLACK COMEDY [6] (M Ryan) 3-9-0 P Robinson 3/1 FAV: 0140404: Dwelt, never nearer:
best 843.   20
2622 DONOR [11] 4-9-7 M Wigham 20/1: -200000: Btr over 1m in 2622: see 1602.   14
2260 SEVEN SWALLOWS [2] 5-9-2 M Wigham 20/1: 0000000: Led 1m: best over this C/D in 184(yld).05
2654 MR MUSIC MAN [10] 7-8-4(6ex) N Day 13/2: 2400100: Fin 7th: twice well below 2528 (12f)   00
2604 ELARIM [3] 7-8-13 M Birch 15/2: 0000000: Fdd into 8th: see 745.   00
2508 Colonial King [9] 8-6(vis)   2497 Red Billy [1] 7-9
10 ran   5,¾,2,3,2½,hd,nk,1½   (Edward Seltzer)   O Douieb Newmarket

2747 SANCTON STAKES 3YO+   £1645   1m 4f   Firm 02 -125 Slow

-- OWN UP [2] (R Whitaker) 4-9-4 D Mckeown 20/1: -000-1: 4 gr g Alias Smith - Be Honest
(Klairon) A surprise winner on his reappearance: qcknd clear home-turn to come home
unchallenged in a very slowly run stks race at Beverley: no form last season when trained by
R Hollinshead: half brother to sev winners, including useful h'capper All Fair: stays 12f:
acts on fast grd: likely to go hurdling.   32
2372 FORMIDABLE DANCER [3] (J Dunlop) 3-8-8 G Duffield 11/8: 0000402: Held up, was never
going to peg back winner: see 2182 & 982.   22
2620 SOLVENT [1] (M Jarvis) 3-8-11 T Lucas 8/11 FAV: -200233: Odds-on flop: unsuited by
very slow pace and remains a maiden: see 2620 & 116.   18
2593 WORTH DEBATING [5] (G Gaines) 3-8-8 J Quinn(5) 33/1: -04: Set snail's pace: wknd
str: see 2593.   12
4 ran   5,4,1½   (R M Whitaker)   R Whitaker Wetherby, Yorks

2748 E.B.F. WILLERBY FILLIES MAIDEN 2YO   £1602   1m 100 Firm 02 -18 Slow

2658 ABSINTHE [1] (D Morley) 2-8-11 R Guest 6/1: 401: 2 br f Tyrnavos - Emblazon (Wolver
Hollow) Slowly away but made smooth prog to lead near fin in a 2yo fillies mdn at Beverley:
half sister to winning sprinter Taranga: stays 1m well: acts on gd and firm grd and likes
a stiff trk.   42
1407 YAQUT [6] (H T Jones) 2-8-11 R Hills 1/1 FAV: 22: Well bckd despite a long break:
led below dist, caught cl home: stays 1m: should win a race: see 1407.   40
2527 NATURALLY AUTUMN [3] (C Brittain) 2-8-11 G Baxter 6/1: 0003: Tried to make all over
this longer trip: gd eff: stays 1m: acts on gd and firm: see 944.   36
2584 FLAUNTING [7] (M Dickinson) 2-8-11 G Duffield 10/3: 0044: Slightly impeded below dist,
ran on same pace: see 2584 & 2283.   36
2664 WILLOWBANK [4] 2-8-11 J Lowe 10/1: 00200: No extra 2f out: best 2379 (7f yldg)   26
2153 CALLACE [2] 2-8-11 S Webster 16/1: 00400: Btn 2f out: best 1634 (6f sharp trk).   16
2254 RUWI VALLEY [5] 2-8-11(VIS) T Williams 3/1: 00: Visored first time: slowly into
her stride and never seen with a chance: should do much btr than this: see 2254.   00
7 ran   ½,2,shthd,6,5,½   (Lord Fairhaven)   D Morley Newmarket

ASCOT   Thursday September 25th   Righthand, Stiff, Galloping Track

Official Going Given As GOOD/FIRM

2749 SWINLEY FOREST HANDICAP 0-70   £7538   1m   Good/Firm 26 +07 Fast   [58]

*2566 FAIR COUNTRY [1] (D Elsworth) 4-8-13(7ex) G Carter 3/1: 2311011: 4 ch f Town and
Country - Fair Measure (Quorum) Useful filly: in grand form and led inside final 1f cmftbly
in quite fast run and val h'cap at Ascot: last time out won a similar event at Doncaster:
earlier a ready winner of an app h'cap at Ascot and a h'cap at Kempton: winning 2yo at Newbury:
very eff over 1m on a fair or gall trk: acts on firm and yldg grd and has a gd turn of foot:
genuine.   55
2629 READY WIT [9] (R Hannon) 5-8-2 A Mcglone 10/1: 0000202: Led over 1f out: another
gd eff and runs well here: see 2475, 361.   41
2475 COME ON THE BLUES [8] (C Brittain) 7-9-0 S Cauthen 7/1: 0041003: Led 7f: gd eff: see 1890 52
2545 ASIAN CUP [3] (G Harwood) 3-8-11 G Starkey 5/2 FAV: 02-1024: Well bckd: prom, switched
1f out and kept on: not btn far: another gd run: see 2545, 528.   56
2567 MAJAAHED [2] 3-9-4 R Cochrane 13/2: -01030: Never nearer: best 2567 (10f)   57

ASCOT   Thursday September 25th   -Cont'd

2234 SUPER TRIP [7] 5-8-11 C Rutter(3) 8/1: 2142100: No extra over 1f out: twice below 1793   39
2545 Alqirm [6] 8-2   2668 Hay Street [10] 8-10   1644 Plaid [4] 9-9
9 ran   1,hd,¼,3,1¼   (Sir Gordon Brunton)   D Elsworth Whitsbury, Hants.

2750 EBF CLARENCE HOUSE MAIDEN STKS 2YO   £7351   6f   Good/Firm 26 +02 Fast

--   ZAJAL [2] (M Stoute) 2-9-0 W R Swinburn 3/1: 1: 2 b c Seattle Slew - Rainbow Connection
(Halo) Very promising colt: first time out, led over 1f out, easily, in quite a fast run
and val 2yo mdn at Ascot: cost $2.6m and dam was a topclass filly in Canada: eff at 6f, looks
sure to be suited by 7f/1m : acts well on fast grd and a gall trk and looks sure to win more
gd races.   66
--   ROSE REEF [6] (I Balding) 2-9-0 Pat Eddery 11/1: 2: No chance with winner, but kept
on well for a most promising racecourse debut: half brother to very useful Golden Bowl who
stays 12f: will be suited by further than today's 6f trip: acts on gd/firm grd and a gall trk:
sure to win a race.   58
800   ROCKFELLA [10] (R J Houghton) 2-9-0 S Cauthen 7/2: 23: Long abs: chance over 1f out:
fine effort: suited by today's 6f and will stay further: dam is a half sister to Irish St Leger
M-Lolshan: acts on gd/firm grd and seems certain to open his account soon.   55
2626 FORESIGHT [8] (L Piggott) 2-9-0 T Ives 12/1: 034: Made much: gd eff in this company:
on the upgrade: see 2626, 777.   47
--   INAAD [7] 2-9-0 A Murray 9/4 FAV: 0: Well bckd debutant: prom most: brother to 1m
winner Al-Aabir: bred to stay further than today's 6f trip: will do btr than this. 35
--   MAKSAB [1] 2-9-0 W Carson 14/1: 0: Made no show on racecourse debut but will come
on for the race: cost 200,000 gns as a yearling and is a full brother to the very smart Irish 2,000
Guineas winner WassL: will be suited by further than 6f and should leave this form well behind. 34
--   Good Cause [4] 9-0   2232 Albany Park [5] 9-0   -- Genobra [9] 9-0
9 ran   2,1,3,5,hd   (Maktoum Al-Maktoum)   M Stoute Newmarket

2751 GROUP 2 HOOVER FILLIES MILE 2YO   £25185   1m   Good/Firm 26 -08 Slow

*2246 INVITED GUEST [5] (R Armstrong) 2-9-0 S Cauthen 8/11 FAV: 1111: 2 ch f Be My Guest -
Welcome Break (Wollow) Smart filly: maintained her unbtn record when winning Gr 2 Hoover
Fillies Mile at Ascot: came from off the pace to lead inside final 1f under press: last time
out was an impressive winner of Gr 3 Waterford Candelabra Stks at Goodwood: earlier won a
Lingfield mdn and a val stks at Newmarket: eff at 7f, stays 1m well and should get middle dist
next term: acts on gd/firm and yldg grd and on any trk: looks certain to win more gd races. 79
1789 MOUNTAIN MEMORY [12] (P Walwyn) 2-8-10 Paul Eddery 16/1: 122: Led 1f out: fine eff
after a 2 month break: well suited by today's 1m trip and will stay further: can win again sn. 73
+2384 SHINING WATER [10] (R J Houghton) 2-9-0 A Murray 12/1: 4211013: Made much and kept
on well when hdd: game and genuine filly who is still improving: stays 1m: see 2384. 75
2540 BINT PASHA [8] (P Cole) 2-8-10 T Quinn 33/1: 222104: Al up there: excellent effort
in this smart company: stays 1m: see 1752.   66
2540 MY IMAGINATION [11] 2-8-10 B Rouse 33/1: 0004030: No real threat but continues to
run well: see 2540, 2246.   60
*2504 SIMPLE TASTE [3] 2-8-10 T Ives 12/1: 2210: Ev ch in str: stays 1m and ran to her best. 59
2540 DAZY [9] 2-8-10 B Thomson 33/1: 230100: No threat in 7th: not disgraced: stays 1m: see 2368. 56
2057 COLOR ARTIST [2] 2-8-10 W R Swinburn 33/1: 0130: Never nearer 8th: prob stays 1m
but faced a stiff task here: see 1801.   57
2246 GOLDEN BRAID [1] 2-8-10 Pat Eddery 13/2: 120: Bumped on the home turn and that
effectively put her out of the race: best ignored: see 2246.   00
2540 Port Helene [6] 8-10   *2436 Lucky Stone [7] 8-10   2504 Montfort [4] 8-10
12 ran   ¾,1,2½,3,½,½,hd   (Kenderhill Corporation)   R Armstrong Newmarket

2752 GROUP 3 CUMBERLAND LODGE STAKES 3YO+   £17750   1m 4f   Good/Firm 26 -28 Slow

2557 KAZAROUN [2] (M Stoute) 4-9-3 W R Swinburn 7/2: 1210-31: 4 b c Alleged - Korinetta
(Petingo) Smart colt: well ridden to make ev yard, cmftbly, in Gr 3 Cumberland Lodge Stks at
Ascot: in '85 won the Gr 3 Gordon Stks at Goodwood and also successful at Sandown & Carlisle:
eff at 12f, stays 14f well: acts on flrm and yldg grd: can win more races.   82
2461 HIGHLAND CHIEFTAIN [4] (J Dunlop) 3-8-10 W Carson 7/2: -012102: 2nd most: came again
final 1f to snatch 2nd: another gd run from this genuine colt: see 2004.   79
-2461 BAKHAROFF [3] (G Harwood) 3-8-10 G Starkey 8/11 FAV: -233123: Heavily bckd but again
showed his inability to quicken: not an easy ride: see 2461.   78
2557 KICK THE HABIT [1] (C Brittain) 3-8-2 Pat Eddery 33/1: 0021004: Al last: see 2131. 40
4 ran   2,½,12   (Aga Khan)   M Stoute Newmarket

2753 GOLDEN GATES NURSERY HANDICAP 2YO   £7538   6f   Good/Firm 26 +01 Fast   [64]

2485 DERRING DEE [3] (P Cundell) 2-8-0 N Adams 33/1: 0101001: 2 b f Derrylin - Insurance
(Yellow God) Caused a 33/1 surprise, staying on well to lead cl home in a val nursery h'cap
at Ascot: earlier won a similar event at Windsor and also a fast run fillies event at
Windsor: cost a bargain 3,000 gns: sister to fair h'capper Killyglen: stays a stiff 6f:
acts on gd and firm grd and on any trk: has been tried in bl but seems btr without. 47
2611 SHEER ROYALTY [7] (W O'gorman) 2-8-3(BL)(3ow) T Ives 10/1: 041002: Bl first time:
led inside final 1f and just caught: below her best over 7f last time: see 2153: acts any trk. 49

807

ASCOT   Thursday September 25th   -Cont'd

2472 DANCING DIANA [6] (R Hannon) 2-8-4 B Rouse 16/1: 4000133: Stayed on well final 2f:
remains in fine form: see 2472, 2320.   44
2198 FICKLE YOUNG MAN [1] (T Fairhurst) 2-8-2(bl) M Hills 13/2: 130104: Set a fast pace
over 5f: kept on when hdd: takes a good hold and maybe suited by an easier 6f: see 2081.   41
2485 MIGHTY BOLD [10] 2-7-9 C Rutter(2) 5/1: 00400: Never nearer: btr 2485.   28
2618 MUAD DIB [8] 2-7-10(BL)(1ow) B Crossley 20/1: 230200: Bl first time: no show: btr 2205   28
2563 CAPE WILD [2] 2-8-9 W R Swinburn 7/4 FAV: 2120: Heavily bckd but never looked likely:
well below 2563.   00
2284 BOLD GARCON [5] 2-8-11 J Reid 9/1: 014220: No show: btr 2284, 2181.   00
2504 CANDLE IN THE WIND [4] 2-9-7 Pat Eddery 9/1: 0401000: Better suited by 7f: see 2246.   00
2600 KEEN NOTE [9] 2-7-7 G Carter 10/1: 00220: Fin last: btr 2600 (easy 5f).   00
10 ran   nk,2½,nk,2½,nk,nk   (Archie Mornall)   P Cundell Compton, Berks.

2754 GORDON CARTER HANDICAP 3YO+ 0-70   £8100   2m   Good/Firm 26 -52 Slow   [60]

*2031 SARFRAZ [1] (G Harwood) 3-9-3 G Starkey 7/2 FAV: 1110111: 3 b c Sassafras - Siba
Blue (John's Joy) Smart, much impr colt: led under press over 1f out and ran on well to
the line for a game win in a slow run but val h'cap at Ascot: in excellent form this season,
last time out winning a h'cap at Newmarket and earlier successful at Goodwood (2), Bath and
Folkestone: eff at 14f, stays extreme dist well: acts on firm and yldg grd: game and
genuine colt.   70
*2467 MISRULE [11] (D Arbuthnot) 4-7-12(1ow)(3ex) K Darley 9/2: 0120-12: Chall final 1f:
beaten a whisker and is in grand form: stays 2m: see 2467.   40
+2510 KUDZ [4] (H Cecil) 3-9-4(3ex) S Cauthen 4/1: 1112013: Waited with: stayed on well
under press and has yet to run a bad race: see 2510.   70
2591 ORANGE HILL [5] (J Tree) 4-7-7(4oh) J Dunne(5) 20/1: 0042204: Never nearer: remains
in gd form: see 2031, 942.   30
2539 PETRIZZO [8] 5-9-10 Pat Eddery 9/2: 40131D0: Not btn far under 9-10: see 2539.   60
1875 RIKKI TAVI [10] 6-8-4 W Carson 9/2: 3310040: 2nd most but was prob unsuited by this
slow pace: btr 1099 (2½m).   39
1150 WIDE BOY [3] 4-7-9 M Marshall(7) 10/1: 30-1100: Bckd at long odds: fdd str: lightly
raced since 542.   00
11   Ibn Majed [6] 7-7(6oh)
8 ran   shthd,1,2½,½,½   (K Abdulla)   G Harwood Pulborough, Sussex

2755 BISHOPSGATE APPR HANDICAP 3YO+ 0-60   £3225   1m   Good/Firm 26 -42 Slow   [42]

*1755 CAPTAINS NIECE [3] (W Hastings Bass) 3-9-3 Dale Gibson(6) 7/4 FAV: -0111: 3 b f
Vitiges - Captain's Girl (Captain's Gig) Useful, impr filly: very heavily bckd and cruised
into lead over 1f out for a ready win in an app h'cap at Ascot: earlier a cmftble winner of a
similar event at Sandown and a mdn at Ripon: quite lightly raced: eff over 1m, stays 10f
well: loves fast grd and has not stopped winning yet.   50
*2549 QUALITAIRESS [4] (K Stone) 4-7-7(vis)(5ex) P Burke(4) 10/3: 2201212: Ran on final 1f
but no chance with the winner: wears a visor but is a genuine filly who is in fine form: see 2549. 13
2550 BASOOF [10] (M Stoute) 3-9-2 M A Giles(6) 12/1: -040403: Kept on final 1f: gd eff:
may stay further than 1m: see 1032.   40
2370 PEANDAY [5] (H Beasley) 5-7-8 C Rutter 14/1: 3000034: Nearest fin: in fair form: see 2370   08
2578 MOUNT TUMBLEDOWN [2] 5-9-0 L Jones(3) 14/1: 000-000: Ev ch: see 2490.   27
2319 GAUHAR [11] 5-7-7 P Hill(3) 33/1: 4000000: Chance 2f out: btr 7f? See 174.   04
2516 DARK HERITAGE [12] 3-8-11 S Horsfall(3) 9/1: -004100: Led 3f out: twice below 2381 (9f)   00
2617 COUNT BERTRAND [7] 5-7-12 R Morse(3) 10/1: 0210000: Never showed: disapp since 1673   00
1601 Sams Wood [6] 9-10   2490 Fast Service [1] 8-7   2578 Welsh Medley [8] 8-5
1211 Dimension [9] 7-9(bl)
12 ran   1,1½,1½,½,1   (N H Phillips)   W Hastings Bass Newmarket

---

REDCAR   Friday September 26th   Lefthanded, Galloping Track

2756 NEWBY NURSERY HANDICAP 2YO   £2371   7f   Firm 14 -06 Slow   [48]

2611 SPEEDBIRD [5] (M Ryan) 2-8-12 P Robinson 10/1: 000401: 2 b f The Brianstan - Jolimo
(Fortissimo) Led dist and ran on strongly to win a nursery h'cap at Redcar: half sister to
middle dist winner Joli's Girl: eff over 7f and will stay at least 1m: acts on fast & yldg
ground and on a galloping track.   42
2595 PHARAOH BLUE [6] (C Brittain) 2-8-4 M Roberts 6/1: 0012042: Ran on well: best 1883.   26
2479 INSHIRAH [11] (H T Jones) 2-9-7(BL) R Hills 4/1 CO FAV: 101433: Bl first time:
led well over 1f out, no extra inside dist: gd eff under top weight: see 1920.   43
2677 KIERON PRESS [2] (D Arbuthnot) 2-8-9(BL) K Darley 4/1 CO FAV: 0314004: Wore bl today:
ev ch: see 1495.   31
2336 DANUM DANCER [8] 2-8-2(1ow) M Wigham 4/1 CO FAV: 0044040: Led/dsptd lead most:
running well: see 2336.   24
2281 OVERPOWER [4] 2-7-8 M Fry 8/1: 00000: Al mid-div: speedily bred colt who cost
IR 16,000 as a yearling: prob stays 7f: acts on fast ground.   15

808

2663 CHESWOLD [7] 2-7-13(bl) J Lowe 6/1: 4003030: Fin 7th: btr over 1m in 2663.   00
*2298 GET SET LISA [1] 2-7-13 M Wood 10/1: 0022210: Speed over ½ way: best 2298 (6f seller)   00
2512 Princess Singh [10] 7-8   2511 Freddie Ashton [3] 8-7(BL)
2007 Carls Pride [9] 7-13
11 ran 3,hd,shthd,shthd,½,4,½,4   (M J Baxter)   M Ryan Newmarket

2757 SCARBOROUGH SELLING STAKES 2YO   £1240   7f   Firm 14 -26 Slow

2479 MELGROVE [14] (J Etherington) 2-8-11(VIS) S Webster 7/1: 04001: 2 br c Marching On -
Annie-Jo (Malicious) Fitted with a visor, gamely made all on the stands side to win a slowly
run 2yo seller at Redcar (no bid): eff over 6/7f: suited by fast grd and forcing tactics:
seems to have no trk preferences.   30
2689 VENHERM [13] (P Calver) 2-8-11 M Fry 14/1: 000302: Al front rank: best eff to date
and can win if kept in this grade: stays 7f: acts on any trk: see 2396 & 2150.   25
2479 KATIE SAYS [9] (J Etherington) 2-8-8(BL) M Wood 9/1: 04003: Bl first time in this
lower grade: al up there: eff over 6/7f and likely to stay 1m: suited by fast ground.   20
2584 AMIABLE AMY [19] (D Barron) 2-8-8 D Nicholls 8/1: 04: Dropped in class: al prom and
kept on same pace: stays 7f: acts on fast grd and on a gall trk.   19
2535 DREAM TICKET [18] 2-8-11(BL) A Clark 20/1: 0000: Al prom over this longer trip: quite
cheaply bought gelding who seems well suited by fast ground: wore blinkers today.   18
2607 VICTORIA STAR [6] 2-8-8 R P Elliott 16/1: 00400: Stayed on late: see 2466.   14
2465 TALIESIN [4] 2-8-11 S Perks 10/1: 003000: Fdd into 9th: see 1339 & 864.   00
2580 HONEY PLUM [8] 2-8-8 M Wigham 8/1: 4040000: No show: best 2032.   00
892 MARKET MAN [11] 2-8-11 T Ives 7/2 FAV: 040: Long abs and no threat: see 892 (5f gd)   00
2466 Gwynbrook [20] 8-11(bl)   2396 Skerne Rocket [12] 8-8
2323 Tokanda [3] 8-11(bl)   2472 Treize Quatorze [15] 8-8
2609 Fantine [16] 9-1   2365 Salop Rouge [7] 8-8   2298 Chayofa [17] 8-8
2396 Holyrood [21] 8-8   2279 Lillys Double [10] 8-8
1955 Dublin Belle [5] 8-8   1012 Austhorpe Sunset [1] 8-11
2466 On The Mark [2] 8-11(vis)
21 ran 1½,½,nk,1½,nk,1,shthd,nk   (J R Rowbottom)   J Etherington Norton, Yorks.

2758 PARSON AND CROSLAND STAKES 3YO+   £2599   5f   Firm 14 +26 Fast

2619 DURASINGH [2] (A Hide) 4-8-9 P Brette(7) 5/1: -221: 4 b g Mansingh - Milduras
(Vilmorin) Led ½ way and ran on strongly to win a fast run stks race at Redcar: closely
related to sev winning sprinters: eff over 5/6f on firm and yldg ground: acts on any trk.   0
2402 DURHAM PLACE [4] (K Brassey) 4-9-0 T Ives 11/10 FAV: 3000402: Well bckd: had ev ch.   40
2614 TAYLOR OF SOHAM [1] (M Leslie) 3-8-6 J Williams 8/1: 3232323: Al front rank: another
gd effort and has retained her form well in a busy season: see 2473.   32
2715 STANBO [6] (D Dale) 3-8-4 G Duffield 14/1: 0040204: Al up there: best 2575.   22
2143 YOUNG PUGGY [3] 3-8-9 S Perks 10/1: 2000000: Best first time in 138 (6f soft)   26
1380 VENEZ TRADER [5] 3-8-6(BL) K Darley 5/1: 14-4000: Bl first time: gd early speed
after a long break: should be btr next time: see 1027.   21
2322 BRIDGE OF GOLD [7] 3-8-6 D Nicholls 11/1: 1004000: Led to ½ way, sn btn: see 529.   00
7 ran 1½,½,3,½,1,5   (T G Warner)   A Hide Newmarket

2759 GUNNERGATE MAIDEN STAKES 3YO+   £959   1m 4f Firm 14 -63 Slow

2373 ENSIGNE [3] (H Candy) 3-8-8 W Newnes 1/1 FAV: -20241: 3 ch c Master Willie - Holiday
Regrets (Silly Season) Well bckd and showed the btr turn of foot to lead dist in a slowly
run mdn at Redcar: cost 160,000 gns as a yearling: eff over 10f tho' seems btr suited by
12f: acts on gd and fast ground and on any track.   44
2464 SHERGOR [1] (H Cecil) 3-8-8 W Ryan 11/10: -202: Led over 2f out: ran on same pace and
is proving expensive to follow: see 2269.   42
1250 DEPUTY MONARCH [2] (Denys Smith) 3-8-8 L Charnock 6/1: 0-02223: Gd eff after a long
abs: see 1072 & 744.   22
2630 TURINA [4] (Don Enrico Incisa) 3-8-5 M Beecroft 33/1: 0030004: Made most at a sedate
pace: see 1775.   18
4 ran 1,4,½   (Fahd Salman)   H Candy Kingstone Warren, Oxon.

2760 GLAISDALE HANDICAP (0-35) 3YO   £1923   2m 115 Firm 14 -14 Slow   [42]

*2683 JOHN DOREY [3] (M Prescott) 3-9-0(5ex) G Duffield 7/4 FAV: 40-111: 3 ch g Malinowski -
Tuna (Silver Shark) Prog to lead below dist and stayed on well when completing his hat-trick
in a 3yo h'cap at Redcar: first time out was an easy winner of an Edinburgh mdn and last week
returned from a long break to win a h'cap at Catterick: closely related to sev winners,
including useful Jean-Claude: eff around 12f, clearly stays 2m well: suited by fast ground:
acts on any trk: can win again.   38
2492 DENALTO [6] (Denys Smith) 3-7-7(1oh) M Fry 14/1: 0330202: Led home turn, kept on
well: running well but has yet to get his hd in front: see 2280 & 744.   15
2492 GRATIFY [7] (P Walwyn) 3-7-8 L Charnock 9/2: 0003403: Remains a mdn: see 1260, 1678.   12
2587 LAKISTE [2] (J Watts) 3-8-0 N Connorton 11/1: -044304: Ran on same pace: see 2040.   11
2478 ORIENTAL EXPRESS [1] 3-7-12 J Carr(7) 20/1: 0103300: Pulled hard, btn home turn: see 487   01
2603 TAXI MAN [8] 3-8-4(1ow) G Sexton 14/1: 0000000: No form since winning here in 960(9f)   07

*2647 IGHTHAM [4] 3-9-12(5ex) A Clark 9/4: 0010310: Made most, wknd str: much btr 2647.   00
1435 QUEEN OF SWORDS [5] 3-7-7(2oh) A Culhane(7) 20/1: 0040000: Abs: wknd str: best 769 (14f) 00
8 ran   ½,3,4,7,8,shthd,½   (Mrs V Bourne)   M Prescott Newmarket

2761 E.B.F. CARLTON MAIDEN STAKES 2YO   £2067   1m   Firm 14 -07 Slow

1872 ATHENS GATE [11] (J Watts) 2-9-0 N Connorton 6/1: 01: 2 ch c Lydian - Pago Miss
(Pago Paago) Impr colt: qcknd to lead inside dist and ran on well to win a 2yo mdn at Redcar:
half brother to sev winners in the States: stays 1m well and will be suited by middle dist
next season: acts on gd and fast ground and on a gall trk.   45
2646 DOLLAR SEEKER [3] (M Ryan) 2-9-0 R Cochrane 3/1 JT FAV: 0032: Led below dist, kept
on same pace: continues to improve and should find a small race: stays 1m: see 2646.   40
--   YAHEEB [8] (H T Jones) 2-9-0 R Hills 3/1 JT FAV: 3: Uneasy fav on racecourse debut:
went on over 2f out, ran on same pace tho' should improve for this experience: cost $240,000
and should be suited by middle dist in time: acts on fast grd and on a gall trk.   36
2484 BONAFORTUNE [5] (D Morley) 2-9-0 R Guest 20/1: 04: Ran on same pace: brother to
smart middle dist performer Highland Chieftain and is likely to improve when tackling longer
trips next season: acts on fast ground.   28
2484 OPTIONAL CHOICE [12] 2-9-0 W Ryan 15/2: 000: No extra dist: cost IR 20,000 as yearling:
stays 1m: acts on fast ground.   26
2626 APIARIST [4] 2-9-0 M Roberts 16/1: 0R0: Made most, wknd quickly below dist: half
brother to sev winners, notably 10f performers Hatched and Brown Thatch: acts on fast ground. 18
2615 SEPARATE REALITIES [2] 2-9-0(bl) A Clark 4/1: 400: Fdd into 7th: best 2019 (7f sharp trk 00
1572 FOREIGN KNIGHT [10] 2-9-0 W Newnes 8/1: 300: Abs: no show: best 1234 (7f)   00
--   Lindis Gold [1] 9-0   -- Westajames [7] 9-0   -- The Price is Right [9] 9-0
2494 Flaxon Worrior [6] 9-0
12 ran   1½,2½,3,½,5,1½   (R E Sangster)   J Watts Richmond, Yorks

2762 REDCAR APPRENTICES' H'CAP (0-35) 3YO+   £1289   1m   Firm 14 +01 Fast   [34]

*2602 ZIO PEPPINO [17] (C Lloyd Jones) 5-8-5(5ex) J Carroll(3) 13/2: 4403011: 5 ch g Thatch
- Victorian Habit (Habitat) In gd form and led below dist, cmftbly, in an app h'cap at Redcar:
recently successful in a h'cap at Redcar: last season won at Ayr: eff over 6/8f: acts on
fast and hvy grd and likes to be up with the pace.   18
2490 PARIS TRADER [7] (J Payne) 4-9-2 G Bardwell(3) 12/1: 0003002: Fin well: gd eff: see 609   25
2260 RANELAGH [6] (W Holden) 3-7-9 I Glindoni(7) 20/1: -000003: Had ev ch: not btn
far and ran his best race for some time: acts on firm and yldg: see 194.   10
2715 JARROVIAN [3] (T Fairhurst) 3-9-2(bl) M Taylor(7) 12/1: 0000004: Sn in front, hung
left below dist and sn hdd: seems to be returning to form: see 309.   30
2360 RUSTIC TRACK [13] 6-7-13 J Quinn 9/1: 0030100: Nearest fin: see 2037.   03
2655 GOLDEN BEAU [8] 4-9-1 Dale Gibson 8/1: 3012300: Ran on same pace: stays 1m: see 2189,192 15
2414 GODS LAW [18] 5-8-2 Julie Bowker(5) 6/1 FAV: 1302000: Early speed: best on a sharp
trk in 1074.   00
2549 VERBARIUM [2] 6-8-6 D D'arcy(5) 9/1: 200000U: Unseated rider start, took no part.   00
2728 Single Hand [1] 8-1   1571 Starboard [11] 7-7(6oh)
2621 Nippy Chippy [10] 7-8(bl)   2296 Silly Boy [12] 8-13
2602 Marsiliana [15] 8-3   2309 Murillo [19] 7-13(bl) 2602 Long Bay [9] 8-6
2728 Janes Brave Boy [14] 7-13   2602 Master Music [5] 7-7(7oh)
1839 Royal Duty [4] 8-2   815 Armitage [16] 9-10
19 ran   1½,½,nk,1½,2,3,nk,2   (Mrs C Lloyd Jones)   C Lloyd Jones Abergele, Clwyd

---

Official Going Given As GOOD/FIRM

2763 TERRY RAMSDEN STAKES HANDICAP 3YO 0-70   £8012   1m 2f Good/Firm 34 -26 Slow [65]

*2275 NAJIDIYA [7] (R J Houghton) 3-8-2 P Cook 6/1: -020211: 3 ch f Riverman - Nawazish
(Run the Gantlet) Useful filly who is in fine form: fin well to lead final 1f in a slow run
but val h'cap at Ascot: last time out won a stks at Windsor: very eff at 10f: acts on gd
and fast ground and on any trk: on the upgrade.   51
2219 SATISFACTION [5] (W Hern) 3-8-10 W Carson 12/1: 2200102: Ran on well over 1f out:
just btn: runs well over this C/D: see 1776.   58
2536 FESTIVAL CITY USA [4] (B Hills) 3-8-8(bl) B Thomson 7/1: 3001433: Ev ch over 1f out:
in fine form at present: see 2536, 1818.   52
*2676 BLACK SOPHIE [8] (R Laing) 3-8-7(5ex) D J Williams(7) 11/2: 0010414: Chance 2f out:
kept on under press and is in fine form.   50
2624 GORGEOUS ALGERNON [2] 3-8-6 J Reid 20/1: 2020040: Ev ch in str: best 1384 (1m).   45
2624 HARD AS IRON [9] 3-7-12 T Williams 7/2 FAV: 1122120: Well bckd: made most: btr 2624.   37
2567 GEORDIES DELIGHT [3] 3-9-1 W R Swinburn 6/1: 2221320: Fdd final 2f: btr 2567.   00
2624 NIGHT OUT PERHAPS [1] 3-9-7 Pat Eddery 15/2: 1401330: Fdd final 2f: btr 2624, 2438.   00
2642 Landski [6] 8-4   2594 Geraghty Again [10] 8-2(bl)
10 ran   hd,2,hd,2,shthd,nk   (Aga Khan)   R J Houghton Blewbury, Oxon

2764 WILLIAM HILL STAKES HANDICAP 0-70   £8142   5f   Good/Firm 34 +03 Fast   [70]

2474 POLYKRATIS [7] (M Francis) 4-10-1 C Rutter(3) 12/1: 3124031: 4 b c He Loves Me - Blue
Persian (Majority Blue) Very smart sprinter: defied 10-1 in impressive fashion, bursting through
to lead inside final 1f, cmftbly in a val h'cap at Ascot: in excellent form this season,
earlier winning a Listed sprint at Sandown and also placed in Gr company: in '85 won a h'cap
at Nottingham: very eff at 5/6f: acts on gd and firm grd and a gall trk: genuine sort.   82
2524 PERFECT TIMING [11] (D Elsworth) 4-8-8 S Cauthen 13/2: 3232102: Ev ch final 1f:
caught a tartar: tremendously consistent: see 2289.   55
2537 DERRY RIVER [1] (L Cottrell) 5-7-7(vis)(5oh) N Carlisle 16/1: 0001043: Led over 4f:
fine effort and runs well when up with the pace: see 2160.   39
*2660 RESTORE [9] (G Lewis) 3-7-10(BL)(7ex) M L Thomas 7/1: -203214: Bl first time: went
left after 1f: never nearer: not an easy ride but is in fine form: see 2660 (6f).   41
2668 LOCHTILLUM [3] 7-7-12 W Carson 7/1: 0004000: Kept on final 1f: see 2402, 836.   40
2731 DEPUTY HEAD [4] 6-7-9 N Adams 13/2: 0030020: Quick reappearance: btr 2731.   36
-2530 WOODFOLD [8] 5-7-7 A Mackay 6/1: 1300020: Prom, fin 7th: btr 2530, see 986.   34
2382 RESPECT [5] 3-8-9 Pat Eddery 11/2 FAV: 1041240: Fdd quickly final 1f: btr 2224: see 1878   00
2731 Tobermory Boy [6] 7-7(3oh)   **2537** Ardrox Lad [10] 8-11
2382 Rayhaan [2] 7-10
11 ran   2,nk,1,hd,nk,nk   (M C Praticos)   M Francis Upper Lambourn, Berks

2765 TAYLOR WOODROW HANDICAP 3YO F 0-75   £11569   1m   Good/Firm 34 +21 Fast   [68]

692 KABIYLA [8] (M Stoute) 3-9-1 W R Swinburn 7/1: 1-1201: 3 b f Busted - Karera (Kalamoun)
Smart filly: despite a long abs, destroyed her field with a 7l win in a fast run and val
3yo fillies h'cap at Ascot: led over 1f out and sauntered clear: first time out was an easy
winner of a val h'cap at Newmarket: subs a gd 2nd to Pilot Bird in a Listed race at Newbury:
won sole start at '85 at Leicester: very eff at 1m, tho' does stay 10f: acts on gd and firm
ground and a gall trk: has a leading chance in the Cambridgeshire.   71
*2440 ENTRANCING [6] (J Dunlop) 3-9-2 W Carson 15/2: -000212: Kept on: caught a tartar:see 2440 57
2562 HIDDEN BRIEF [7] (R Boss) 3-8-8 E Guest(3) 15/2: 0020123: Took a gd hold and made
much: btr 2562 (stks 7f).   43
2385 VIANORA [1] (G Harwood) 3-9-7 G Starkey 10/1: 1121304: Kept on final 2f: best 1851.   55
2650 SOMETHING CASUAL [3] 3-7-13(vis) A Shoults(3) 9/1: 0344440: Led/dsptd lead: yet
to reproduce form shown in 1655 and has had plenty of chances to do so.   25
2496 SMOOCH [2] 3-8-7 S Whitworth 12/1: 0010040: Prom, ev ch: much btr 2496 (10f stks)   29
*2670 BASICALLY BETTER [10] 3-7-11(vis)(4ex) N Carlisle 4/1 FAV: 4000110: Well bckd:
much btr 2670.   00
*338 DONNAS DREAM [4] 3-9-2 Pat Eddery 10/1: 40-310: No show after very long abs: see 338   00
*2488 SYBIL FAWLTY [9] 7-7   **2674** Careless Whisper [5] 7-10
10 ran   7,3,nk,4,2   (Aga Khan)   M Stoute Newmarket

2766 EWAR STUD FARMS APPR HCAP 0-60   £4261   1m 4f   Good/Firm 34 -20 Slow   [54]

*2428 LISANA [8] (M Stoute) 3-8-5 M A Giles 4/1 JT.FAV: 0-2011: 3 b f Alleged - Licara
(Caro) Impr filly: well bckd and led over 1f out, cmftbly, in a val app h'cap at Ascot: last
time out won a stks event at Hamilton and earlier was unlucky when 2nd at Redcar: well bred
filly who is very eff over 12f: acts well on fast grd and a stiff, gall trk: can continue
to improve.   53
2536 SWIMMER [3] (G Huffer) 4-9-0 W Litwin(7) 14/1: -143002: Led inside final 3f: gd
eff: lightly raced since 1325, see 964.   48
*2533 UP TO UNCLE [9] (R Hannon) 3-8-0 L Jones 5/1: 3223313: Ran his usual consistent race.   38
2517 OSRIC [2] (M Ryan) 3-8-3 P Barnard(3) 13/2: 12D3204: Led after 3f: stayed: btr 2290, 1923   37
1837 MILLERS TALE [5] 4-8-1 F Arrowsmith6) 16/1: 2010400: Behind, late hdwy: best 761.   25
1111 INSULAR [10] 6-9-11 S O'gorman(3) 6/1: 21-3100: Long abs: led early: best 778.   41
2558 JABARABA [6] 5-7-13 T Lang(3) 9/1: 4111340: Fdd final 2f: twice below 2330, see 2188   00
2156 ON TENTERHOOKS [1] 3-8-1 J Dunne(7) 4/1 JT.FAV: 43-1040: Well bckd: led after 3f
but fdd tamely: disapp after 2156: see 980.   00
2623 Carillon [4] 9-1
9 ran   2,3,2,hd,4   (Aga Khan)   M Stoute Newmarket

2767 EBF MORNINGTON STAKES 2YO   £8088   7f   Good/Firm 34 +10 Fast

*2554 AJDAL [2] (M Stoute) 2-8-11 W R Swinburn 8/13 FAV: 11: 2 b c Northern Dancer - Native
Partner (Raise A Native) Potentially topclass colt: heavily bckd when a highly impressive
winner of a fast run and val 2yo stks at Ascot: cruised into lead final 1f, winning very
easily: first time out a ready winner of a 2yo stks at Doncaster: well bred colt who is a half
brother to very useful duo Formidable and Serheed: very eff at 7f, will have no trouble staying
1m and should be suited by middle dist next season: acts very well on fast grd and a gall trk:
not one to oppose lightly, whatever the opposition and looks Classic standard.   81
*2547 SHARP VICTOR [5] (G Harwood) 2-8-11 G Starkey 11/4: 012: Made much but caught a real
tartar: lost nothing in defeat and can win again soon: see 2547.   68
*2646 ARRASAS [3] (H T Jones) 2-8-11 A Murray 8/1: 13: Ev ch 2f out: no extra final 1f:
met 2 smart performers here and was by no means disgraced: see 2646.   52
1465 PERSIAN STYLE [1] (C Brittain) 2-8-11 Pat Eddery 25/1: 00044: Never in it:absent since
better in 1465 and possibly needed today's race.   37

-- **SPARSHOLT BREEZE** [4] 2-8-11 S Cauthen 12/1: 0: Very tough debut: early speed: cost
31,000 gns as a yearling and is related to sev winners: should improve.   00
5 ran   2,6,8,dist   (Sheikh Mohammed)   M Stoute Newmarket

2768 EBF KENSINGTON PALACE STKS 2YO FILLIES   £8310   7f   Good/Firm 34 -19 Slow

-- **BOURBON GIRL** [5] (B Hills) 2-8-8 G Starkey 10/1: 1: 2 b f Ile De Bourbon - Fleet Girl
(Habitat) Promising fillyy: bckd at long odds and fin well to lead cl home in val Kensington
Palace Stks at Ascot: full sister to 2m winner Shipbourne: eff at 7f, looks sure to be suited
by middle dist next term: acts on gd/firm ground and a gall trk: can only improve.   63
-- **MISS STORM BIRD** [3] (M Stoute) 2-8-8 W R Swinburn 6/4 FAV: 2: Heavily bckd debutant:
nearly made all and looks sure to go one btr soon: cost $210,000 as a yearling and is a half
sister to 3 winners in the States: stays a stiff 7f: acts on gd/firm ground.   61
2574 **MOUNTAIN ISLE** [9] (W Hern) 2-8-8 W Carson 14/1: 33: Slowly away and fin in gd style:
fast improving filly who can win very soon over 1m: see 2574.   59
-- **QUEENS BRIDGE** [10] (I Balding) 2-8-8 Pat Eddery 14/1: 4: Ev ch inside final 2f: sure
to come on for the race and this was a promising effort: half sister to middle dist winner Lady's
Bridge: looks sure to be suited by 1m: acts on gd/firm and will have no trouble finding a mdn.   57
-- **GLINT OF VICTORY** [8] 2-8-8 M Hills 14/1: 0: Kept on final 1f, showing a deal of future
promise: half sister to a winner in France: looks sure to be suited by an extra furlong:
acts on gd/firm and a stiff trk.   56
2540 **CHAUDENNAY** [2] 2-8-8 B Thomson 10/1: 000: Ran well in this gd class company: possibly
btr over 1m: see 2540, 1991.   54
*2527 **IBTIDAAR** [7] 2-8-12 A Murray 5/2: 10: Well bckd: prom 5f: disapp 8th and this could
not have been her true form: worth another chance: see 2527.   00
-- **OVERDRIVE** [6] 2-8-8 S Cauthen 9/1: 0: Mkt drifter on debut: prom much: half sister
to sev winners, notably smart 2yo filly Mill On The Floss: looks sure to be suited by 1m
and further and will do btr than this.   00
-- **Shanama** [4] 8-8   -- **Prydwen** [1] 8-8
10 ran   1,1,½,½,½   (K Abdulla)   B Hills Lambourn, Berks

Official Going Given As GOOD/FIRM

2769 RED DEER STAKES (H'CAP) (0-70) 3YO+   £7503   1m 4f   Good/Firm 23 +11 Fast   [59]

2692 **ALMAARAD** [10] (J Dunlop) 3-8-9 Pat Eddery 7/4 FAV: 00-1031: 3 ch c Ela-Mana-Mou -
Silk Blend (Busted) Very useful colt: well suited by the strong pace and made steady hdwy to
lead 1f out, cmftbly, in a fast run and val h'cap at Ascot: last time out appeared rather
unlucky when a close 3rd to Broken Wave in the Autumn Cup at Newbury: first time out was a
ready winner of a fast run mdn at Salisbury: eff over a stiff 12f, stays 13f+: acts on gd
and fast ground and a gall trk: can win again.   65
*2623 **WESHAAM** [7] (B Hanbury) 3-8-8(4ex) R Hills 6/1: 1322012: Led 4f out: kept on well
when hdd and is in grand form: can win another h'cap: see 2623.   58
2486 **CONVINCED** [9] (G Harwood) 4-9-5 G Starkey 8/1: 3231033: Chance over 1f out: kept
on well and is a most consistent colt: genuine sort: see 1112.   60
2551 **SARONICOS** [4] (C Brittain) 3-7-8 T Williams 12/1: 2303044: Led briefly inside final
2f, not btn far and well clear rem: remains a mdn, but should certainly find a h'cap on
this form: stays 12f and acts on fast & yldg ground: see 194.   44
*2558 **VORACITY** [2] 7-8-13(4ex) W R Swinburn 10/1: 2321410: No show after slow start:btr 2558   24
2551 **VOUCHSAFE** [3] 4-8-11 W Carson 11/1: 1D00000: No threat: best 1112 (C/D).   21
2662 **PAST GLORIES** [8] 3-8-3 J Lowe 10/1: 4210120: Fdd over 2f out: much btr 2662 (13f).   00
*2489 **Travel Mystery** [1] 8-1(2ow)   2486 **Pubby** [5] 7-12   1957 **Pochard** [6] 9-7
10 ran   2,hd,shthd,25,½   (Hamdan Al-Maktoum)   J Dunlop Arundel, Sussex

2770 GROUP 2 QUEEN ELIZABETH STAKES 3YO+   £31280   1m   Good/Firm 23 +11 Fast

*1096 **SURE BLADE** [2] (B Hills) 3-8-11 B Thomson 6/5 FAV: 13-1011: 3 b c Kris - Double Lock
(Home Guard) Very smart colt: despite a fair abs, was heavily bckd when winning Gr 2 Queen
Elizabeth II Stks at Ascot: ran on well final 2f to lead cl home in a fast time: earlier won
Gr 2 St James' Palace Stks at Royal Ascot and first time out a minor race at Thirsk: highclass
2yo winning at Newmarket, Royal Ascot (Coventry Stks) and Doncaster: very eff at 1m, will
be well suited by 10f and possibly further: acts on firm & yldg ground and likes a stiff trk:
genuine and consistent and will win more gd races.   87
2456 **TELEPROMPTER** [4] (J Watts) 6-9-7(vis) T Ives 13/2: -233302: Led from the stalls at
a fast pace and only gave best cl home: excellent eff from this most genuine horse: clearly
right back to his best: see 598.   89
2195 **EFISIO** [7] (J Dunlop) 4-9-7 W Carson 8/1: 0412033: Squeezed through on the rails
over 1f out and kept on well: fine effort and never runs a bad race: see 1094, 897.   84
2219 **MTOTO** [1] (A Stewart) 3-8-7 M Roberts 25/1: -210224: Sn prom: fine eff in this company
and is tremendously consistent: see 2219, 1098.   75
2538 **TRUELY NUREYEV** [6] 3-8-7 W R Swinburn 6/1: 31-0200: Ev ch: best 2145 (7f).   71
*2538 **HADEER** [5] 4-9-0 Pat Eddery 11/2: 0411010: Much btr over 7f in -2538.   65

ASCOT   Saturday September 27th   -Cont'd

2538 MOONLIGHT LADY [3] 3-8-4 J Velasquez 12/1: 320-020: Stiff task: much btr 2538 (7f)   00
7 ran   ½,2½,2,1½,3   (Sheikh Mohammed)   B Hills Lambourn, Berks.

2771 GROUP 2 ROYAL LODGE STAKES 2YO   £27015   1m   Good/Firm 23 -17 Slow

+2444 BENGAL FIRE [6] (C Brittain) 2-8-11 M Roberts 14/1: 2311: 2 br c Nishapour - Gerardmer
(Brigadier Gerard) Smart, impr colt: led final 1f and stuck on gamely to lead again cl home
in rather slow run Gr 2 Royal Lodge Stks at Ascot: last time out a narrow winner of a val
2yo event at York: half brother to smart middle dist performer King's Island: very eff over
7f, stays a stiff 1m well: acts on gd and firm grd and on any trk: well regarded and is a
genuine sort: will win more races.   77
-2552 DEPUTY GOVERNOR USA [4] (L Piggott) 2-8-11 T Ives 7/4 FAV: 31122: Heavily bckd: led
inside final 1f hdd near post: another fine effort and has yet to run a bad race:
stays 1m: see 2552.   76
2574 BALAKIREV [2] (I Balding) 2-8-11 Pat Eddery 5/2: 23: Well bckd in this smart company:
ev ch over 1f out: grand eff in only his 2nd ever race: well regarded sort who must win
soon: stays 1m and acts on any trk: see 2574.   72
2384 MR EATS [9] (P Kelleway) 2-8-11 J Velasquez 33/1: 12404: Made much: ran well: disapp
in blinkers last time: stays 1m: see 876.   67
2159 ZAIZOOM [1] 2-8-11 T Quinn 15/2: 20: Chance 2f out: fine eff: stays 1m: see 2159.   66
2552 WHO KNOWS [3] 2-8-11 W Carson 15/2: 312430: Prom most: much btr 2552 (7f)   58
2571 SANTELLA SAM [8] 2-8-11 P Robinson 20/1: 2320120: No threat: btr 2571, made running.   00
2635 ROCK CHANTEUR [5] 2-8-11 W R Swinburn 8/1: 0030: Prom over ½ way: well below 2635 (7f) 00
2542 GWYNRAS [7] 2-8-11 J Williams 200/1: 00: Impossible task and no show.   00
9 ran   hd,2,2,nk,4   (N H Phillips)   C Brittain Newmarket

2772 GROUP 3 DIADEM STAKES 3YO+   £18620   6f   Good/Firm 23 +10 Fast

-2474 HALLGATE [10] (S Hall) 3-8-12 G Starkey 11/4 JT.FAV: 4103121: 3 b c Vaguely Great -
Beloved Mistress (Rarity) Very smart colt: fin really well to lead cl home in fast run Gr 3
Diadem Stks at Ascot: last time out narrowly btn by Green Desert in Gr 2 Vernon Sprint Cup at
Haydock: earlier a winner of val events at Newmarket and Lingfield: very tough and genuine
2yo, winning at Hamilton (2), Edinburgh, Pontefract, Redcar, Ripon and Ascot (Cornwallis Stks):
best form over sprint dist: acts on firm, likes some give in ground: no trk preferences:
has a fine turn of foot and should made a bold bid in the Prix de L'Abbaye.   85
2538 GWYDION [2] (H Cecil) 3-8-9(BL) W Ryan 7/2: 3312432: Bl first time: looked a certain
winner when qckning clear over 1f out but tired badly cl home and was just caught: nevertheless
another gd effort: see 2538.   80
2538 FIRM LANDING [8] (J Watts) 3-8-12 T Ives 33/1: 0-01003: Ran on well final 1f, showing
a return to form displayed in race 945: lightly raced colt who can win again soon: see 945. 81
*2503 ACUSHLA [11] (M O'brien) 3-8-9 Pat Eddery 11/4 JT.FAV: -012114: Well bckd Irish chall:
led 2f out: in fine form: see 2503.   71
2538 SHARP ROMANCE [5] 4-9-2 R Cochrane 50/1: 0000000: No extra final 1f: fine eff: see 18:
now trained by J Bethell.   68
1146 NOMINATION [12] 3-9-2(BL) T Quinn 20/1: 04-0200: Bl first time: there 4f after a
long abs: needs give: best 639.   60
2003 SPERRY [7] 3-8-12 Paul Eddery 12/1: -202100: Led over ½ way: see 1125 (C/D)   56
2672 Possedyno [3] 3-8-12   2668 Touch Of Grey [9] 8-12
2241 Meteoric [6] 8-9   2731 George William [4] 9-2
*557 Tinterosse [1] 9-2
12 ran   nk,½,3,2,6,shthd   (Hippodromo Racing)   S Hall Middleham, Yorks.

2773 BALMORAL STAKES (H'CAP) (0-75) 3YO+   £10394   7f   Good/Firm 23 +06 Fast   [66]

1455 DE RIGUEUR [8] (J Bethell) 4-8-5 Pat Eddery 20/1: 0101001: 4 b c Derrylin - Northern
Lady (The Brianstan) Useful colt: despite an abs, fin well to lead cl home in quite a fast
run and val h'cap at Ascot: early in season was in fine form, winning h'caps at Lingfield,
Salisbury and Warwick: in '85 won at Wolverhampton: very eff at 7f, stays 1m: acts on firm
and soft ground and on any trk: genuine sort who does well when fresh.   54
*2674 GOLD PROSPECT [11] (G Balding) 4-8-3(6ex) B Rouse 5/1 FAV: 4023012: Dsptd lead final
1f: just caught: in grand form: see 2674.   50
2566 FUSILIER [1] (C Brittain) 4-7-9(bl) T Williams 25/1: 0001003: Made most and only
just btn: seems sulted by front running: see 2165.   41
2674 BELOW ZERO [3] (A Bailey) 3-7-13 C Rutter(3) 7/1: 1014024: Ev ch when hung right
final 1f: not an easy ride but remains in gd form: see 2674.   47
2390 FORMATUNE [12] 4-7-7(bl)(9oh) N Carlisle 25/1: 3203000: Nearest fin: see 1911, 10.
9lbs out of the h'cap here and this was a gd effort.   34
2544 SAILORS SONG [14] 4-8-6 S Dawson 10/1: 0000120: Chance 2f out: btr 2544.   45
2655 MANCHESTERSKYTRAIN [13] 7-7-10 G Carter 6/1: 0020020: Prom, ev ch: btr 2655.   00
2655 PINSTRIPE [9] 3-8-7 T Ives 8/1: 1212230: Early speed: over the top? See 2655.   00
2655 BOLD PILLAGER [10] 4-8-3 W Carson 8/1: 2114040: Prom most: btr 2655.   00
2668 IRISH COOKIE [6] 4-7-11 G Dickie 10/1: 1410020: Btr 2668, 2258 (6f)   00
2545 YOUNG JASON [7] 3-7-7 M L Thomas 13/2: 0122330: Prom, fdd: btr 2545.   00
2619 Amigo Loco [2] 8-12(bl)   2359 Shmaireekh [4] 9-10(vis) 00

813

2566 **Transflash** [5] 7-11
14 ran   1,shthd,1½,½,½   (Mrs Christopher Heath)   J Bethell Didcot, Oxon

2774 BLUE SEAL STAKES 2YO FILLIES   £9661   6f   Good/Firm 23 -12 Slow

-- WHITE MISCHIEF [2] (L Cumani) 2-8-3 R Cochrane 14/1: 1: 2 ch f Dance In Time - Nyeri (Saint Crespin III) Very promising filly: first time out, led final 1f and readily drew clear in val Blue Seal Stks (2yo fillies) at Ascot: half sister to a couple of winners over 10f and further: eff at 6f, looks sure to stay 1m and further, next season: acts on gd/firm ground and a gall trk: certain to win more races and rate more highly.   65
-- UNITE [10] (M Stoute) 2-8-5(2ow) W R Swinburn 4/6 FAV: 2: Heavily bckd debutant: led 2f out till outpaced by winner final 1f: cost 310,000 gns as a yearling and is held in some regard: eff at 6f on gd/firm ground: looks sure to win races.   61
-- AZYAA [3] (H T Jones) 2-8-3 R Hills 7/1: 3: Nearest fin and will be well suited by 7f+: half sister to useful winning stayer Otabari: acts on gd/firm grd and should have no trouble finding a race.   54
-- PECKING ORDER [5] (I Balding) 2-8-3 T Quinn 33/1: 4: Kept on well final 1f on racecourse debut and improvement very likely: bred to be suited by much further than today's 6f: acts on gd/firm grd and a gall trk.   54
2531 DREAM DOLLAR [1] 2-8-8 G Baxter 33/1: 00: Al prom and is fast improving: cost only 14,000 gns as a yearling and is a speedily bred filly: eff at 6f on gd/firm grd and can win soon on a sharper track.   59
2540 LIGHTNING DISC [9] 2-8-8 J Velasquez 20/1: 00: Made most: gd eff: see 2540.   58
2554 FLIP THE BIRD [6] 2-8-8 B Thomson 10/1: 40: Fin 7th: will do btr: see 2554.   00
-- BRIDGET OBIRD [4] 2-8-4(1ow) Pat Eddery 9/1: 0: Slow start and no threat on debut: cost $425,000 and is a half sister to sev winners in the States: should stay further than 6f.   00
-- SEVENTH SONG [11] 2-8-3 Paul Eddery 8/1: 0: There over 4f on debut: half sister to sev winners and will come on for this run: quite speedily bred.   00
2493 MOORESTYLE GIRL [7] 2-8-8 T Ives 14/1: 30: Stiff task: see 2493.   00
10 ran   3,2½,hd,hd,½   (J Becher)   L Cumani Newmarket

REDCAR   Saturday September 27th   Lefthand, Flat, Galloping Track

2775 JOHN LIVINGSTON HANDICAP 0-35   £2432   5f   Firm 03 +13 Fast   [33]

2715 MUSIC REVIEW [13] (M Tompkins) 3-8-7 A Mackay 10/1: 2220341: 3 ch g Music Boy - Right View (Right Tack) Gained a deserved win, stayed on strongly to lead near fin in a fast run all-aged h'cap at Redcar: first success tho' has only once fin out of the frame this season: half brother to winning juv Record Review: eff over 5/6f on gd and firm grd: acts on any trk.   22
2668 RAMBLING RIVER [15] (W Stephenson) 9-10-0(vis) M Brennan(7) 9/1: 2100002: Fin well, only just held: genuine old sprinter who is in gd form at present: see 1796.   40
2632 NATIVE RULER [18] (C Austin) 5-8-2 W Newnes 10/1: 0123003: Just failed to make all: gd eff and may win again soon on a sharp trk: loves being out in front: see 1070.   14
2592 GODSTRUTH [14] (H T Jones) 7-8-10(bl) A Riding(7) 7/1: -000434: Not btn far: fine effort: see 1344.   21
*2632 WARTHILL LADY [6] 4-8-11(7ex) K Darley 7/1: 0401010: Gd eff under her penalty: see 2632.   18
2592 CAPTAINS BIDD [12] 6-8-6 W Woods(3) 11/1: 4141000: Stayed on well: best 2256.   09
2632 CAPEABILITY POUND [9] 3-8-13 R Lines(3) 5/1 FAV: 0000030: Never beyond mid-div: better 2632: see 1027.   00

2586 Pergoda [10] 9-7(bl)	2394 Le Mans [17] 8-3	2513 Philstar [3] 8-4(vis)
2632 Miss Primula [2] 8-10	2743 Karens Star [1] 8-9	2409 Tollys Ale [5] 8-3
2378 Gods Isle [16] 9-7	2586 Tradesman [11] 7-8(bl)(1ow)(2oh)	
2513 Gentileschi [4] 8-8(BL)		2322 Last Secret [8] 7-7(bl)(2oh)

17 ran   hd,shthd,½,1,1½,½,½,½,shthd   (Coronet Bingo Newmarket)   M Tompkins Newmarket

2776 RED MOUNTAIN COFFEE CUP AMATEURS STKS   £2918   1m 4f   Firm 03 +06 Fast

2666 HERRADURA [12] (M Prescott) 5-10-12(vis) Maxine Juster 6/1: 320331: 5 b h Malinowski - Blakeney Belle (Blakeney) Held up and led dist, cmftbly, in a fast run amateur riders race at Redcar: first win this term tho' only twice fin out of the money previously: most consistent in this type of race, last season won at Pontefract and Thirsk: in '84 won 7 times: eff over 10/12f: stays 2m well: acts on gd and fast grd and on any trk: genuine sort who carries weight well.   42
2551 TWICE BOLD [6] (N Callaghan) 3-9-13 Jennie Goulding 3/1: 2120432: Led home turn, not pace of winner: remains in gd form: see 1551.   28
2604 GOLDEN FANCY [2] (I Vickers) 9-10-12 Mr T Thomson Jones 11/1: 2D33023: Placed again.   28
2551 MIN BALADI [7] (S Norton) 4-10-12 Franca Vittadini 14/1: 3200204: No extra dist: fair effort: see 629.   28
2665 GOLDEN HEIGHTS [5] 3-9-13 Princess Anne(5) 9/2: 2142320: Early leader: much btr 2665   19
2727 HYOKIN [10] 4-11-1(vis) Melanie Morley(5) 20/1: 1320020: Wknd over 2f out: best 1359   00
2156 VAGADOR [11] 3-9-13 Amanda Harwood 2/1 FAV: -10100: Made most till saddle slipped, dropped out early in str: best over this trip in 1923.   00

| 2122 In Contention [3] 9-7 | 2478 Floater [8] 9-12(5ow) | 772 Wandering Walter [5] 10-12 |
| 2627 Touchez Le Bois [4] 10-12 | | 2562 Mawdlyn Gate [1] 9-13 |

12 ran   5,1¼,shthd,2½,12,¾   (P D Savill)   M Prescott Newmarket

2777 NORTHERN MACHINE TOOLS NURSERY HCAP 2YO   £3698   6f   Firm 03 -24 Slow   **[49]**

2472 SPANISH SLIPPER [1] (W Haigh) 2-8-13(bl) J H Brown(5) 7/2 CO FAV: 2241221: 2 b f
King of Spain - Shoe (Shoolerville) Consistent filly: made steady prog to lead inside dist,
ridden out in a nursery h'cap at Redcar: early last month won a fillies mdn at Ayr and has
yet to fin out of the frame: cheaply bought filly who is a half sister to a couple of winners:
eff over 5/6f on gd and fast grd: likes a gall trk: wears bl now.   44
2396 SHARPHAVEN [5] (M Brittain) 2-7-9 A Proud 10/1: 4100202: Tried to make all: gd eff
and should win again if dropped back to selling company: see 2279 & 1379.   20
2680 COLWAY RALLY [4] (J Watts) 2-9-5 G Duffield 7/2 CO FAV: 0324003: Shorter trip:
kept on late: see 1798.   40
2472 DORMESTONE LAD [6] (R Stubbs) 2-7-12(bl) A Mackay 10/1: 0041104: Ev ch: lightly raced
since 1163 (seller).   12
2272 IBNALMAGHITH [2] 2-9-7 A Murray 7/2 CO FAV: 14300: No extra dist: best 1735 (7f sharp) 30
2297 ANTINOUS [3] 2-9-6 M Birch 6/1: 32100: Some prog when hmpd dist: see 1982.   28
2476 PERFUMERIE [7] 2-8-6 P Hill(7) 6/1: 0000: Wknd below dist, after showing gd speed :see 1958. 00
7 ran   2,1½,2½,2,nk,2   (R E Johnston)   W Haigh Malton, Yorks

2778 REYNARD SELLING HANDICAP 3YO 0-25   £960   1m 2f   Firm 03 -16 Slow   **[21]**

2603 LADY ATTIVA [8] (P Rohan) 3-8-11 C Dwyer 5/6 FAV: 0000041: 3 b f Red Regent - Manx
Image (Dancer's Image) Dropped in class and was well bckd when leading dist, cmftbly, in a
3yo selling h'cap at Redcar: first success: well suited by 10f: acts on fast grd and gall trk. 12
2603 CHABLISSE [2] (R Whitaker) 3-9-7 D Mckeown 9/2: 1044132: Kept on well: in gd form: see 2412.00
2621 KEEP COOL [1] (R Hollinshead) 3-9-0 S Perks 9/2: 2004333: Led 2f out: see 1960 & 774   10
2679 DOON VENTURE [5] (J Etherington) 3-8-9 M Wood 7/1: -000034: Made most: stays 10f: see 867.01
2679 ANDREAS PRIDE [3] 3-8-7 S Webster 14/1: 4-40400: Btn 2f out: see 2125.   00
1824 VALDARNO [4] 3-8-2 A Proud 33/1: 0000000: Mkt drifter and well btn: has been
running over shorter dist tho' yet to show any worthwhile form.   00
2083 Galaxy Gala [6] 8-3   2508 Herb Robert [7] 8-3
8 ran   ¾,1½,2,1½,25,6,3   (Peter O'Sullevan)   P Rohan Malton, Yorks

2779 BOULAND MACHINERY STAKES 3YO+   £2149   1m6.7f Firm 03 -43 Slow

2324 GREAT EXCEPTION [1] (H Candy) 3-8-10 W Newnes 2/11 FAV: 32-3101: 3 ch f Grundy -
Exquisite (Exbury) Easily made all from her sole rival in a slowly run stks race at Redcar:
earlier won her mdn at Catterick after being placed behind Santiki at Thirsk: eff over 12/15f:
acts on firm and soft grd and on any trk.   25+
2141 KEY ROYAL [2] (G Calvert) 5-9-11 D Nicholls 4/1: 0000402: No chance with winner:see 1737. 12
2 ran   7   (T A Frost)   H Candy Kingston Warren, Oxon.

2780 WIN WITH THE TOTE MAIDEN STKS 3YO+   £1137   1m   Firm 03 -11 Slow

2413 BROADHURST [3] (J Etherington) 3-8-7(vis) A Murray 6/4 FAV: -030031: 3 b f Workboy -
Simbirica (Simbir) Cruised into lead over 1f out and was sn clear in an all-aged mdn at Redcar:
well suited by 1m: acts on yldg tho' seems btr suited by fast grd: acts on any trk.   20
1701 BAXTERGATE [1] (J Payne) 3-8-10 P D'arcy 7/2: -000002: Abs: al prom, not pace of
winner: acts on fast and soft grd: see 498.   10
2367 DANCER DO [6] (A Jarvis) 3-8-7 D Nicholls 16/1: 00-003: Made most: first signs of
form from this lightly raced filly: stays 1m: acts on fast grd.   06
2496 FILL ABUMPER [5] (R Hollinshead) 4-9-0 R Lappin(7) 9/1: 0000004: Nicely bckd: no form. 00
2704 ZEELANDIA [4] 3-8-7(bl) J Callaghan(7) 13/2: -400000: Prom over ½ way: no form since 53 00
2583 BIRCHGROVE LAD [2] 5-9-3(BL) K Hodgson 11/2: -0040: Bl first time: lost touch
from ½ way: see 2583.   00
--   PATTOMMY [7] 6-9-0 R P Elliott 25/1: -0: Outsider and sn lost touch.   00
7 ran   6,hd,5,4,½   (Les Baker)   J Etherington Malton, Yorks.

2781 TRANSMORE VAN HIRE AUCTION STAKES 2YO   £1463   5f   Firm 03 +09 Fast

47 LUCEDEO [9] (R Hollinshead) 2-8-11 S Perks 20/1: 001: 2 ro g Godswalk - Lucy Limelight
(Hot Spark) Gained a surprise win after a lengthy abs, led below dist and ran on well to win
a fast run 2yo Auction Stks at Redcar: cost IR£ 8,500 & his dam was a winning juv: seems
well suited by this min. trip : acts on fast ground   and a gall trk: further improvement
likely.   34
-2687 ATTEMPTING [5] (B Hills) 2-8-12 P Hill(7) 8/15 FAV: 31122: No extra cl home: prob
now finds this mimum trip too sharp: much btr over 6f in 2687: see 2434.   29
2689 NATIONS SONG [12] (R Stubbs) 2-8-12 J H Brown(5) 16/1: 2140003: Btr eff: see 1576.   28
2744 TAP THE BATON [3] (M Tompkins) 2-8-11(bl) A Mackay 6/1: 2300034: Bl first time and
made most: better effort and seems suited by forcing tactics: best 622 (sharp trk).   26
892 SKI CAPTAIN [1] 2-8-11 M Wood 25/1: 00: Long abs: prom over ½ way and should be
better for this run: cost 7400 gns as a yearling: acts on gd and firm ground.   14
2334 TAHARD [7] 2-8-11 A Culhane(7) 50/1: 0000000: Front rank to ½ way: see 2334 & 694.   12
2365 Riverstyle [8] 8-8   -- Hittite Ruler [11] 8-11   00

2472 Everloft [6] 8-11   1978 Pay Dirt [10] 8-11(bl)
2323 Jean Jeanie [2] 8-8
11 ran   1¼,hd,nk,4,½,2½,1½   (J R Good)   R Hollinshead Upper Longdon, Staffs.

GOODWOOD   Monday September 29th   Righthand Undulating, Sharpish Track

Official Going Given As GOOD

2782 EBF HAT HILL MAIDEN STAKES 2YO   £2334   6f   Good/Firm 29 -21 Slow

2561 NATIVE DRESS [6] (I Balding) 2-9-0 Pat Eddery 7/4 FAV: 31: 2 b c Mummy's Pet -
Sarong (Taj Dewan): Fulfilled debut promise, al prom and gamely leading dist in a close fin
to a 2yo mdn at Goodwood: cost 26,000 gns as a yearling and is a half brother to several
winners: quite speedily bred & is effective at 6f: acts on fast grnd: runs well at Goodwood.   51
2547 MACE BEARER [16] (L Holt) 2-9-0 P Waldron 20/1: 002: Front rank from ½way, showing
impr form & is progressing along the right lines: will be suited by 7f: see 1629.   50
2056 TAUBER [13] (Pat Mitchell) 2-9-0 J Reid 9/1: 03233: Came from behind, kept on well
to be narrowly btn in a close fin: see 2056: deserves a race.   50
2491 IN FAT CITY [18] (J Sutcliffe) 2-9-0 R Hills 8/1: 04: Prom thro'out, btn only 1L
in 4th: impr & will be suited by further: see 2491.   48
2574 BOLD TANGENT [1] 2-9-0 M Wigham 4/1: 40: Unlucky in running, strong fin: eff over
6/7f: will stay at least 1m: looks certain to find a mdn soon: see 2574.   46
2263 LOVE TRAIN [10] 2-9-0 N Adams 20/1: 4400: Kept on well under press: best effort since 1307 44
2554 SERGEANT SMOKE [14] 2-9-0 W R Swinburn 12/1: 00: Plenty of pace, fin 7th: impr effort
from this half brother to several winners abroad: scope for impr & possibly the sort to do
btr as a 3yo.   40
--   TILTING COURT [3] 2-9-0 B Rouse 33/1: 0: Close up 8th on debut: dam a winner up to
1m but sire was a smart stayer & stamina may be the game for this one.   39
--   CARPET CAPERS [4] 2-9-0 S Whitworth 33/1: 0: No threat in 9th: quite an inexpensive
foal who has plenty of stamina in his pedigree.   38
--   BIRWAZ [9] 2-9-0 T Quinn 12/1: 0: Fin 10th on debut: cost I.R. 90,000 gns: dam a winner
over 5f: bred to be speedy.   36
2561 WUJUD [5] 2-9-0 Paul Eddery 14/1: 00: Fin 11th: see 2561.   34
1936 Castle Tryst [7] 9-0   2646 Quassimi [15] 9-0   2696 Dallors Conquest [11] 9-0
2205 Capital Flow [2] 9-0   -- Fourth Protocol [12] 9-0
2541 Phelloff [8] 9-0   -- Tumble Time [17] 9-0
18 ran   nk,hd,½,½,½,1,½,½,½   (Mrs J A McDougald)   I Balding Kingsclere, Hants

2783 PORTSMOUTH F.C. H'CAP 3YO+ 0-60   £3047   5f   Good/Firm 29 +06 Fast   [57]

1796 ROTHERFIELD GREYS [12] (A Hide) 4-9-8 J Leech(7) 7/1: -110101: 4 b c Mummy's Pet -
Relicia (Reiko): Very useful sprinter: returned after an abs narrowly leading final stages in
a h'cap at Goodwood: earlier won 3 out of his first 4, valuable h'cap at York & small h'caps
at Edinburgh & Warwick: useful 2yo but a virus sufferer in '85: stays 6f but at his best
over 5f on firm or gd grnd: usually up with the pace : goes best for J Leech.   62
*2483 BONNY LIGHT [11] (R Sheather) 3-8-1(bl) A Shoults(5) 12/1: 4-30012: Chall final 1f,
narrowly btn in a photo finish: in grand form & has been impr by bl: see 2483.   40
2537 PERION [10] (G Lewis) 4-8-7 P Waldron 6/1: 1104033: Gd fin: see 477.   44
2632 PENDOR DANCER [6] (K Ivory) 3-7-7(vis) N Carlisle 10/1: 0102324: Made much, running well. 26
580 STEEL CYGNET [3] 3-8-5(1ow) J Reid 20/1: 2-00340: Fin well after long abs: one to
keep an eye on next time: see 62.   36
2731 SILENT MAJORITY [8] 3-9-0 T Ives 13/2: 1141100: Had possibly just peaked, best 2382.   45
*2702 TACHYON PARK [2] 4-8-1(4ow)(7ex) S Whitworth 8/1: 0-00210: Plenty of early pace:
difficult task: see 2702.   00
2537 MEESON KING [5] 5-8-7 W Carson 9/2 FAV: 000-200: Sn in trouble & btr 2289.   00
2702 Ameghino [7] 8-4   2245 Music Machine [1] 8-4   2362 High Image [14] 8-10
2458 Northern Impulse [13] 7-8   2586 Spacemaker Boy [15] 8-4
2731 Sharad [4] 7-8(bl)(1ow)(24oh)
14 ran   ½,shhd,2½,1,shhd   (Mrs D Gleeson)   A Hide Newmarket

2784 MEAD WORMAN JUBILEE H'CAP 3YO 0-60   £3316   1m   Good/Firm 29 -09 Slow   [64]

2458 AITCH N BEE [8] (J Dunlop) 3-8-9 W Carson 5/1: 0401241: 3 ch c Northfields - Hot
Case (Upper Case): In gd form at present & led over 2f out, narrowly, in a 3yo h'cap at
Goodwood: recent winner of a mdn at Ayr: very eff over 1m & seems to act on firm & yld &
on any trk: continues to impr.   56
*2321 DOCKSIDER [4] (A Stewart) 3-8-1 M Roberts 10/3 FAV: -0212: Strong fin & is in fine form. 47
2420 POUNELTA [2] (R Hannon) 3-7-11(2ow) A Mcglone 12/1: 2040403: Made much: best effort
for sometime: see 2247.   41
1520 FLOATING ASSET [3] (P Walwyn) 3-8-1(1ow) Paul Eddery 16/1: -403444: Abs: ev ch: see 386. 43
*1507 SHAFY [1] 3-9-7 W R Swinburn 9/2: 32-4110: Prom, ev ch: has changed owners/stables
since winning in 1507.   62
2713 ROYAL TROUBADOR [7] 3-7-8(VIS) R Fox 6/1: -000430: See 2713: vis 1st time today.   30
2321 PRETTY GREAT [6] 3-7-7(3oh) G Dickle 14/1: -340020: No dngr: much btr 2321 (soft).   26

1486 VAGUE SHOT [5] 3-9-5 S Cauthen 4/1: 0-11100: Prom, wknd after abs: best 914 (gd).   00
8 ran   ½,1,½,½,3,2½,6   (P Winfield)   J Dunlop Arundel, Sussex

2785 HARROWAYS STAKES 3YO+   £12076   7f   Good/Firm 29 +04 Fast

2538 SARAB [1] (P Cole) 5-9-1 T Quinn 7/4 FAV: 3111041: 5 b h Prince Tenderfoot -
Carnival Dance (Welsh Pageant): Very smart horse: rewarded strong support, leading dist till
hdd inside final 1f but gamely regained advantage on the line in a valuable Listed race at
Goodwood: earlier completed a hat trick abroad at Phoenix Park, Chantilly & Baden Baden
in valuable events: in '85 won at Newcastle & Haydock: very eff over 7f/1m though acts on
any going: genuine sort who is a credit to his trainer.   81
2145 BOLLIN KNIGHT [4] (M H Easterby) 4-8-12 M Birch 7/1: 1110002: Led under press final
1f, caught post but a grand effort, wearing only 3 shoes: back to his best: see 413.   77
*2612 VERDANT BOY [8] (M Stoute) 3-8-4 Pat Eddery 3/1: 3102113: Not the best of runs, fin
well: in fine form: see 2612.   69
1823 LUCKY RING [6] (W Hern) 4-8-12 W Carson 8/1: 14-0004: Led 3f out, wknd: best effort
this term: see 1823.   67
2241 CHARGE ALONG [10] 4-8-6 T Ives 25/1: -040040: No dngr, creditable effort: see 645.   55
2731 ALL AGREED [3] 5-8-12 W R Swinburn 20/1: 0211300: No dngr: see 1986 (5f).   56
+2619 ALKAASEH [7] 3-8-4 R Hills 12/1: 10-4210: Fin 7th: see 2619 (6f).   00
2505 LUQMAN [5] 3-8-4(vis) Paul Eddery 15/2: -040440: Well btn last, much btr 2505.   00
*2519 Softly Spoken [2] 8-1   2538 Governor General [9] 8-7
10 ran   hd,3,1½,1½,½,hd   (F Salman)   P Cole Whatcombe, Oxon

2786 GOODWOOD PARK HOTEL STAKES 3YO+   £3066   1m 4f   Good/Firm 29 -09 Slow

2558 COX GREEN [1] (G Harwood) 3-8-7 G Starkey 7/4 JT FAV: -142421: 3 ch c Cox's Ridge -
Love You Dearly (Sadair): Made almost all, cmftbly in a stakes event at Goodwood: most
consistent this term, first time out a ready winner of a mdn at Doncaster & yet to fin out
of the first 4: eff at 12f, stays 14f well: acts on gd & fast grnd & on any trk, though
likes Goodwood.   61
370 NADEED [3] (M Stoute) 3-8-3 B Rouse 7/4 JT FAV: -02: Well bckd, despite long abs:
chall over 2f out: 7L clear 3rd & ran very well: should strip fitter next time: stays 12f:
acts on gd/firm grnd & on any trk: can win soon.   53
2438 OLD DOMESDAY BOOK [6] (J Winter) 3-8-10 W R Swinburn 4/1: 1330303: Btr 10f? see 2438.   49
2676 DUNOOF [4] (D Laing) 3-8-3 W Carson 10/1: 12-0004:   Ev ch over 2f out: very
lightly rcd this term: see 642.   33
2578 PATRICK JOHN LYONS [5] 5-9-3 J Reid 100/1: 0-30030: Impossible task: see 1274.   00
2467 MR GARDINER [2] 4-8-11 T Ives 100/1: 0000040: Prom much: see 2467, 92.   00
6 ran   1½,7,6,4,6   (K Abdulla)   G Harwood Pulborough, Sussex

2787 COCKED HAT SELLING H'CAP 3YO 0-25   £2211   1m 2f   Good/Firm 29 -51 Slow   [21]

2702 GERSHWIN [7] (D O'donnell) 3-9-4(vis) A Kimberley 12/1: 0100021: 3 b c Gold Song -
Firey Kim (Cannonade): Mkt drifter, but made ev yd, cmftbly in a 3yo selling h'cap at
Goodwood (bought in 3,200 gns): in gd form lately, earlier winning an app. selling h'cap at
Windsor: first time out won another seller at Leicester: eff at 6f, clearly stays 10f well:
acts on gd/firm grnd & on any trk, though does well forcing the pace on a sharpish one.   20
2597 NO STOPPING [11] (R Hannon) 3-9-7 L Jones(5) 7/1: 0032322: Ev ch in str: consistent,
but lacks a turn of foot: see 2597.   19
2597 LETOILE DU PALAIS [12] (B Stevens) 3-8-5 R Fox 14/1: 0404243: Ch over 1f out: twice
below 2309 (yielding).   02
2361 MY DERYA [3] (B Mcmahon) 3-8-11(bl) N Carlisle 8/1: 3004104: Al there: btr 2361 (7.5f).   04
2549 DRESS IN SPRING [6] 3-9-0 W Newnes 7/1: 0000100: Twice below form 2238 (7f).   00
*1340 MAID OF HONFLEUR [8] 3-9-2 A Clark 6/1: -10: Abs: no show: see 1340.   00
2582 SPINNAKER LADY [2] 3-9-0 D Mckay 11/4 FAV: 0010020: Well bckd: fdd final 2f: btr 2582.   00
2093 CAPULET [4] 3-9-5(vis) J Matthias 8/1: 0-00000: There over 7f: flattered 1733?   00
2092 Cleavage [10] 9-4   2463 Sirtaki Dancer [1] 9-4
2515 Flamelight [9] 8-6   1310 Solent Lad [5] 8-11
12 ran   1,½,2,10,1,shhd   (Mrs E O'Donnell)   D O'donnell Upper Lambourn, Berks

2788 SETTRINGTON MAIDEN FILLIES STAKES 2YO   £1430   6f   Good/Firm 29 +06 Fast

2436 SCIMITARRA [23] (H Cecil) 2-8-11 S Cauthen 7/4 FAV: 01: 2 ch f Kris - Fanghorn
(Crocket): Very promising filly: attracted hvy support & made ev yd to come home on her own
by 6L in a fast run fillies mdn at Goodwood: half sister to several winners, notably the top
class sprinter Double Form: very eff over an easy 6f: acts on gd/firm & yld grnd & does
well making the running on a sharpish trk: looks certain to win more races & is a speedy sort. 65
2596 CHORITZO [6] (R Williams) 2-8-11 W R Swinburn 11/2: 222: Al prom: deserves a change
of luck and caught a tartar here: stays 6f: see 2433.   48
-- BRONZEWING [4] (J Dunlop) 2-8-11 T Quinn 13/2: 3: Stayed on well final 2f on racecourse debut: eff at 6f: should be suited by another furlong: acts on gd/firm grnd & can
find a race.   42
-- AUNTIE SYBIL [18] (J Francome) 2-8-11 W Newnes 33/1: 4: Kept on well closing stages
& looks certain to impr: cost 26,000 gns & is a half sister to several winners: will be
suited by 7f: acts on gd/firm.   38

2527 TAUSTAFF [19] 2-8-11 Paul Eddery 16/1: 000: Needs 7f? see 2527.   32
2531 BLEU CELESTE [24] 2-8-11 P Hutchinson(3) 33/1: 000000: Sn prom: impr of late:
dam a winner over 5 & 7f: acts on gd/firm.   31
--   GOOD SAILING [16] 2-8-11 A Shoults(5) 20/1: 0: Fin 7th: will impr: quite cheaply
acquired & is a sister to winning 3yo Dark Heritage.   30
2555 LAVANDOU LEGEND [12] 2-8-11 P Waldron 16/1: 040: Fin 8th: btr 2555 (C/D).   29
2436 LUCKY PICK [2] 2-8-11 W Carson 8/1: 00: Prom early: btr 2436 (yld).   00
1930 MISS DAISY [10] 2-8-11 Pat Eddery 11/1: 30: Abs: btr in 1930 (C/D).   00

2577 Hurricane Valley [17] 8-11		-- Balinese Dancer [9] 8-11
-- Dont Knock It [7] 8-11		2147 Barbary Court [11] 8-11
2263 Goodnight Master [8] 8-11		2308 Hinton Rose [14] 8-11
2710 Lady Westown [13] 8-11		2433 Naparima [3] 8-11(BL)
-- Piplola [22] 8-11	2577 Princess Semele [15] 8-11	
1522 Snowsdown [25] 8-11	2514 Starsign [21] 8-11	2418 Yamrah [26] 8-11
23 ran 6,2½,1½,2½,nk,nk,nk	(Baroness H H Thyssen)	H Cecil Newmarket

---

NOTTINGHAM   Monday September 29th   Lefthanded, Flat Oval Track

Official Going Given As FIRM: ALL TIMES SLOW EXCEPT RACE 2790.

2789 ALVERTON SELLING H'CAP (0-25) 3&4YO   £833   1m 6f Firm Slow   [14]

2679 G G MAGIC [8] (D Morley) 3-9-2 R Cochrane 5/1: 2000421: 3 b g Strong Gale - King's
Chase (King's Leap): Ran on under press to lead inside dist in a selling h'cap at Nottingham
(bought in 3,400 gns): half brother to several minor winners & won a seller at Catterick last
season: eff around 1m, stays 14f well: acts on fast & yld grnd & on any trk.   19
2403 ASTICOT [6] (C Horgan) 4-9-9 R Weaver 11/4: 3024002: Dropped in class: led 2f out,
no extra close home: eff over 12/14f: acts on gd & fast grnd: see 984.   15
2683 TIMMINION [2] (K Stone) 4-9-9 C Dwyer 9/4 FAV: -300003: Took a drop in class & nicely
bckd: stayed on and not btn far: see 44.   14
2549 JALOME [3] (R Whitaker) 4-8-7 A Cunningham(7) 25/1: 0000004: Mkt drifter: denied a
clear run: not btn far & possibly unlucky: suited by 10f & fast grnd.   00
2125 GROVECOTE [9] 3-8-4(1ow) B Thomson 8/1: 0000030: Led over 3f out: onepaced: see 2125. 02
2528 DEERFIELD BEACH [7] 4-8-10 J Williams 9/1: 0000000: Little form this term: see 202.   00
2679 Tiber Gate [5] 7-8   888 Nordic Secret [4] 9-10
2163 Nelsonsuperyankee [1] 8-2
9 ran ½,½,1,1,2½   (A Glass)   D Morley Newmarket

2790 BENTINCK E.B.F. STAKES 3 AND 4YO   £3517   1m 2f Firm +20 Fast

1912 FINAL TRY [1] (J Dunlop) 3-8-7 B Thomson 8/11 FAV: 30-0001: 3 ch c Try My Best -
Clarina (Klairon): Very useful colt: easily landed the odds, led below dist in a fast run
stakes race at Nottingham: half brother to several winners: showed useful form as a juvenile,
winning at York & last month was a fine 5th to Chinoiserie in the Extel h'cap at Goodwood: very
eff over 10f: acts on fast & soft grnd & on any trk: sure to win btr races.   56
2649 STRAW BOATER [6] (L Cumani) 3-8-9 R Cochrane 3/1: -00132: Tried to make all, not foot
of winner but clear of rem & remains in gd form: see 2649 & 2304.   48
2305 SOHO SUE [2] (C Williams) 3-8-4 M L Thomas 40/1: 0000103: Ran on same pace: see 1784 (sir)22
1831 VAULA [3] (W Hern) 3-7-13(BL) G Carter 7/2: -04: Bl first time & nicely bckd: never
reached ldrs & clearly did not run as well as expected: see 1831.   16
2495 MAFTIR [5] 4-9-0(bl) Sharron James 50/1: 0001220: Out of his depth: see 2412 (seller). 09
--   BRIMSOL [4] 3-7-13 P Robinson 50/1: -0: Easy to back on racecourse debut: no threat:
cost I.R. 4,300 & is a half sister to a couple of minor winners.   01
6 ran 1½,10,½,8,nk   (Sheikh Ahmed Al Maktoum)   J Dunlop Arundel, Sussex

2791 EXTON PARK STAKES 2YO C & G   £1674   6f Firm Slow

2667 WAR BRAVE [5] (J Dunlop) 2-9-0 B Thomson 1/1 FAV: 241: 2 gr c Indian King - Kizzy
(Dancer's Image): Useful colt: hvly bckd & proved an easy winner, led below dist & qcknd clear
in a 2yo stakes at Nottingham: cost 160,000 gns as a yearling & is a half brother to winning
2yo Dancer's Shadow: eff over 6f, should stay further: acts on fast grnd & on any trk:
consistent sort who should win more races.   55
2423 SHARBLASK [9] (N Vigors) 2-9-0 P Cook 7/4: 22: Made most: see 2423.   44
--   BEAU NASH [3] (M Prescott) 2-9-0 C Nutter 20/1: 3: Mkt drifter on debut: ev ch &
kept on well: fetched I.R. 60,000 as a yearling & is a half brother to several winners: will
be suited by 7f plus: acts on fast grnd.   42
2561 GEORGE JAMES [16] (J Dunlop) 2-9-0 P Robinson 20/1: 04: Never nearer & is clearly on
the up grade: cost 35,000 gns as a yearling: sure to be suited by 7f: acts on firm.   41
2541 MUHIM [2] 2-9-0 R Cochrane 16/1: 000: Mkt drifter: never nearer & possibly already
needs further than todays trip: acts on gd & fast grnd: see 2254.   40
--   LAST CHORD [17] 2-9-0 C Dwyer 33/1: 0: Easy to back on debut: no show but should
benefit from this run: cost 20,000 gns & is closely related to several useful sprinters:
acts on firm grnd.   26
--   Musical Dancer [13] 9-0   -- To Monakrivo Mou [8] 9-0   00

2680 Swing Singer [6] 9-0 -- **Night Club** [7] 9-0 -- **Linebacker** [15] 9-0
2320 Charlous Choice [4] 9-0 -- **Sprats Brat** [1] 9-0
13 ran 4,½,nk,nk,5,¾,½,½,2½ (Sheikh Mohammed) J Dunlop Arundel, Sussex

2792 WINTHROPE FILLIES NURSERY H'CAP 2YO £1861 6f Firm Slow [43]

2425 AFRABELA [12] (M Brittain) 2-8-2 P Robinson 14/1: 0402001: 2 b f African Sky - Lobela (Lorenzaccio): Led below dist, ridden out in a fillies nursery h'cap at Nottingham: cheaply bought filly who is a half sister to 7f winner Baton Boy: stays 6f well & should be suited by further next season: acts on firm & soft grnd & on any trk. 28
2498 EDRAIANTHUS [16] (D Laing) 2-8-13 B Thomson 5/1 JT FAV: 040402: Made most: gd effort. 34
2708 KNOCKSHARRY [5] (R Hollinshead) 2-7-10 P Hill(7) 16/1: 1100003: Close 4th, promoted to 3rd: both her wins have come in sellers: see 1279. 14
2435 SAUNDERS LASS [8] (R Holder) 2-8-2 S Dawson 8/1: 021034: Fin 5th, placed 4th: see 1647. 15
2579 SPANISH SKY [7] 2-9-7 P Cook 16/1: 1003000: Faded: fin 6th, placed 5th: see 2090, 1194. 34
2588 GARDENIA LADY [10] 2-8-3(bl) G Carter 12/1: 3000000: Promoted to 6th: best in 646 (5f). 11
2191 EMMAS WHISPER [4] 2-8-4 L Riggio(7) 25/1: 0003D: Fin a close 3rd, disq. after causing interference & placed last: eff over 6f on fast grnd: see 2191. 25
2089 SKYBOLT [1] 2-8-5 M L Thomas 10/1: 0400: Prom most: best in 1844 (5f): see 1665. 00
2529 LADY LUCINA [13] 2-8-10(bl) A Murray 5/1 JT FAV: 04030: No threat: best in 2529. 00
2680 Pashmina [15] 8-10 **2421 Lady Behave** [14] 9-0 **2700 Bertrade** [6] 9-3
2375 Stylish Girl [2] 8-2 **2595 Teachers Game** [11] 8-6(VIS)
2535 Fingers Crossed [9] 8-8 **2708 Lady Westgate** [3] 7-11(VIS)(1ow)
16 ran 1½,hd,¾,1½,shhd,1½,nk,nk,nk (A M Wragg) M Brittain Warthill, Yorks

2793 FISKERTON MAIDEN FILLIES STAKES 3YO £959 6f Firm Slow

2659 COME TO THE BALL [13] (R Hannon) 3-8-11 B Thomson 9/1: 0-03041: 3 br f Daance In Time - Moment To Remember (Assagai): Showed impr form when comfortably making all in a 3yo fillies mdn at Nottingham: has been placed over 10f this term but seems btr suited by sprint dists: likes fast grnd & a sharp/easy trk: clearly does well with forcing tactics. 27
2672 BUTSOVA [4] (R Armstrong) 3-8-11 P Tulk 4/5 FAV: -033442: Looked to have a simple task & was hvly bckd to open her account: not qckn & much btr early season: see 776, 431. 23
2660 ORTICA [2] (J Etherington) 3-8-11(vis) A Murray 10/1: 2333043: Kept on same pace: see 1269. 22
2614 TAMALPAIS [11] (H Collingridge) 3-8-11(bl) M Rimmer 20/1: 0000034: Never nearer: see 283. 14
2575 GRANGE FARM LADY [14] 3-8-11 R Cochrane 10/1: -030200: Front rank most: see 2409,2186. 12
2550 ZIADS ALIBY [9] 3-8-11 W Ryan 15/2: -4300: Ran on same pace: see 2210. 10
-- LACED [12] 3-8-11 P Robinson 10/1: -0: Bckd at long odds on her debut: made late prog into 7th & should be more prom next time: sister to a couple of winners. 00
2312 Fancy Finish [5] 8-11 -- **Pink N Perky** [7] 8-11 **2719 Bella Carina** [6] 8-11(bl)
2622 Cascading [1] 8-11 **1375 Emancipated Lady** [10] 8-11
-- Gretas Song [3] 8-11 **2534 Parljoun** [8] 8-11
14 ran 1,hd,3,¾,½,1,¾,1 (Jim Horgan) R Hannon East Everleigh, Wilts

2794 VICTORIA CENTRE H'CAP STAKES (0-35) £2133 2m Firm Slow [21]

2430 PYJAMA PARTY [1] (J Dunlop) 3-9-1 B Thomson 7/2: -4401: 3 ch f Pyjama Hunt - Rexana (Relko): Well suited by this lngr trip & led inside dist, gamely in a h'cap at Nottingham: lightly rcd filly who is a half sister to the useful 12f h'capper Diabolical Liberty: eff around 10f, stays 2m well: acts on gd & fast grnd & is suited by a sharp/easy trk 27
2722 WALCISIN [5] (R Hannon) 3-9-3 R Wernham 3/1 FAV: 0104022: Just btn: in gd form: see 1386. 28
2111 QUADRILLION [4] (R Hollinshead) 7-8-11 P Hill(7) 6/1: -024333: Led 3f out: last successful in '83 at Beverley: suited by a test of stamina nowadays: see 1419. 08
2492 OLD MALTON [6] (J Toller) 4-9-2 P Robinson 7/2: 1330044: Made most: best in 990. 06
2745 SOUND DIFFUSION [8] 4-9-7 K Bradshaw(5) 9/1: 0300000: Btn 2f out: best in 933 (tight trk) 06
2111 DEW [3] 5-8-11 S Dawson 5/1: /00-000: No threat from ½way: see 2111. 00
126 GAINVILLE LAD [7] 5-9-3 P Burke(7) 33/1: -000: Long abs: dropped out quickly str. 00
7 ran nk,2½,5,3,10,20 (Mrs Douglas Riley-Smith) J Dunlop Arundel, Sussex

---

HAMILTON Monday September 29th Righthand, Undulating Track, Stiff Uphill Finish

Official Going Given As GOOD/FIRM

2795 FINE FARE SELLING STAKES 3YO £756 1m 1f Good/Firm 21 -19 Slow

2621 GREENHILLS BOY [2] (M Ryan) 3-8-7 G Duffield 4/1 FAV: -004201: 3 ch c Manor Farm Boy - Saucy Pirate (Le Pirate): Led 1½f out, ridden out in a 3yo seller at Hamilton (bought in 1,700 gns): first success: eff at 1m/9f: acts on gd & firm grnd. 15
2690 FANNY ROBIN [3] (D Smith) 3-8-4 L Charnock 9/2: 0040042: Ev ch over 1f out: eff at 9/10f on gd & firm grnd. 08
2705 RYMOS [5] (R Simpson) 3-8-7(bl hd) T Williams 9/2: --00-33: Not much room inside final 2f: see 2705. 07
2654 AUSSIE GIRL [9] (A Bailey) 3-8-4 P Bloomfield 7/1: 0330004: Ev ch over 2f out: best 1459. 00
2585 STANFORD ROSE [1] 3-8-4 K Darley 12/1: 0040000: No extra final 2f: best 1960 (1m). 00
2184 SICA SUE [7] 3-8-4 J Quinn(5) 14/1: 000-000: Led after ½way, hdd. 00
2690 ANNUAL EVENT [4] 3-8-7 D Mckeown 8/1: 00-0000: Chall 3f out: non-stayer? see 2690. 00

2361 OCTIGA [6] 3-8-11 A Bacon(7) 8/1: 0030200: Sn behind: best 2238 (7f).   00
2705 Showdance [8] 8-7
9 ran   1¼,2,6,3,nk   (L Audus)   M Ryan Newmarket

2796 EBF PALMOLIVE MAIDEN 2YO STAKES   £1953   1m   Good/Firm 21 +01 Fast

2243 GRAND TOUR [8] (W Hastings Bass) 2-9-0 R Lines(3) 7/2: 01: 2 b c Troy - Peculiar One
(Quack): Impr colt: well bckd & led inside final 1f, narrowly in a 2yo mdn at Hamilton: well
suited by todays 1m trip & should stay middle dists next term: acts on gd & firm grnd &
a stiff trk: on the up grade.   48
2439 ALPENHORN [1] (G P Gordon) 2-9-0 G Duffield 7/1: 03002: Led inside final 2f: just
btn in a close fin: stays 1m & should go one btr in similar company: see 1903.   47
2484 MARIENBOURG [7] (J Dunlop) 2-9-0 G Baxter 2/1 FAV: 43: Made smooth hdway to chall 2f
out: ran on under press & just btn in a tight fin: 6L clear 4th & stays 1m well: see 2484.   46
2664 KALEIDOPHONE [4] (W Elsey) 2-8-11 J Lowe 8/1: 00344: Ev ch inside final 2f: btr 2664 (7f)   31
2341 AMADEUS ROCK [14] 2-9-0 M Hills 10/1: 00: Made much: impr: half brother to 3 winners:
probably stays 1m: acts on gd/firm grnd.   31
2341 NEAR HEAVEN [3] 2-9-0 N Crowther(7) 10/1: 00: Ev ch in str: btr effort: should be
suited by todays 1m trip: acts on gd/firm.   27
2487 SOOTHING WORD [10] 2-8-11 W Woods(3) 6/1: 00: Wknd over 1f out: cost $27,000 as a
yearling & is a half sister to several winners: should do btr than this.   00
--   Elsenham Star [2] 8-11   2711 Escudero [5] 9-0
2711 Bold Mojaques [6] 9-0   2584 Mixedup Mhairi [12] 8-11
2607 Tower Bay [11] 8-11   --   Holy Willie [13] 9-0
13 ran   hd,nk,6,1½,2   (Mr L Schott)   W Hastings Bass Newmarket

2797 FINE FARE SCOTTISH HANDICAP 0-35 3YO+   £2659   1m   Good/Firm 21 +16 Fast   [32]

+2414 HELLO GYPSY [13] (C Tinkler) 5-9-6 W Goodwin(7) 7/1: -213011: 5 b g Tumble Wind -
Shirotae (Florescence): In grand form & led final 1f, readily in a fast run h'cap at
Hamilton: earlier twice successful this season over this C/D: in '85 won an amateur riders
event at Warwick: very eff over 1m on gd & firm grnd: always runs well at Hamilton.   37
1038 FORWARD RALLY [14] (M Prescott) 4-9-12 G Duffield 7/1: 1-11202: Long abs: led inside
final 3f: no ch with winner but a gd effort: should go close next time: see 698.   33
*2762 ZIO PEPPINO [1] (C Lloyd Jones) 5-8-7(5ex) J Carroll(7) 5/1 FAV: 4030113: Stays in fine form. 12
2602 HOPTONS CHANCE [12] (S Wiles) 4-7-10(1ow) M Fry 8/1: 0024334: Stayed on final 2f:
eff at 7f, stays a stiff 1m: probably acts on any grnd.   00
2339 AMIR ALBADEIA [9] 3-8-11(bl) N Howe 12/1: -220400: Never nearer: has now been tried
in bl & a visor: btr early season in 316: see 253.   18
2414 GOOD N SHARP [7] 5-7-12(4ow) A Mercer 14/1: 0-20040: Ev ch in str: see 1766.   00
*2728 WARPLANE [3] 6-9-7(5ex) J Bleasdale 8/1: 0340010: Fin 7th: btr 2728.   00
2705 GREENHILLS GIRL [4] 3-8-0(vis) J Lowe 13/2: 0240320: Gambled on, btn 3f out: btr 2705.   00
2629 Kamaress [11] 8-4   2414 Try Scorer [6] 8-9   2012 Via Vitae [2] 7-9(2ow)(4oh)
2469 Bay Presto [5] 9-3(bl)   2602 Bold Rowley [10] 7-13
2508 Glacier Lass [8] 7-11(bl hd)
14 ran   5,¾,nk,2,7,¾   (M Battle)   C Tinkler Malton, Yorks

2798 COLGATE JUNIOR NURSERY HANDICAP 2YO   £1459   1m   Good/Firm 21 -07 Slow   [46]

2138 RIVERS SECRET [7] (D Smith) 2-7-8(1ow)(3oh) L Charnock 16/1: 000041: 2 b f Young Man-
Pendle's Secret (Le Johnstan): Showed impr form to win a nursery h'cap at Hamilton: led
inside final 1f, under press: clearly suited by this lngr trip today: acts on gd & firm grnd.   20
*2470 FU LU SHOU [1] (P Haslam) 2-8-1 T Williams 5/1 CO.FAV: 0012: Met much trouble in
running & was probably an unlucky loser: may find a similar event: in gd form: see 2470.   26
2663 CHESTER TERRACE [8] (P Walwyn) 2-8-6 N Howe 12/1: 00003: Ev ch when switched 1f out:
unlucky? stays 1m: acts on gd & fast grnd.   30
2584 TROMPE DOEIL [15] (J Payne) 2-7-8(bl)(1ow)(4oh) A Mackay 5/1 CO.FAV: 00024: Ch 2f out:
well below 2584 (sharp).   14
2512 SERGEANT MERYLL [13] 2-8-0(2ow) N Connorton 5/1 CO.FAV: 00300: Led inside final 3f:
stays 1m: see 2050.   19
2615 SCHUYGULLA [11] 2-8-13 W Woods(3) 12/1: 342340: Probably stays 1m: best 1475.   28
*2728 HARRY HUNT [10] 2-8-2 J Carroll(4) 8/1: 0001010: Prom most: btr 2279 (6f).   00
2663 JOHNNY SHARP [9] 2-8-7 J Lowe 15/2: 0200100: Made much: btr 2663, 2498.   00
2498 CHANTILLY LACE [14] 2-8-10 Gay Kelleway(3) 8/1: 1000: Fdd in str: btr 2498.   00
*2471 TRYNOVA [4] 2-8-7 E Guest(2) 10/1: 0202110: No threat: has changed stables: see 2471.   00
2325 Pit Pony [5] 7-11   2468 Running Money [3] 8-7 2680 Eurocon [6] 8-6(3ow)
2680 Mons Future [2] 7-13
14 ran   ¾,¾,1¼,hd,2   (James Simpson)   D Smith Bishop Auckland, Co Durham

2799 INTEGRATION YEAR EBF STAKES 3YO   £2131   1m 3f Good/Firm 31 -12 Slow

2330 WHILE IT LASTS [6] (L Cumani) 3-9-1 P Hamblett 5/1: 3323101: 3 ch f Foolish Pleasure-
Prom Date (Arts And Letters): Useful filly: led over 1f out, comfortably in a 3yo stakes at
Hamilton: below her best on yld last time but earlier a model of consistency, winning at
fillies h'cap at Yarmouth: eff at 10/11f, should get 12f: acts on gd & fast grnd & on any trk.   50

2676 NIHAD [5] (B Hanbury) 3-8-3 A Geran(7) 13/8 FAV: 4003232: Well bckd: led over 2f out:
consistent but btr 2676 (10f).   36
2558 FIRST KISS [3] (J Dunlop) 3-8-8 G Baxter 5/2: 1003033: Led over 1m: btr 2558: see 723.   39
2623 FRENCH FLUTTER [7] (R Sheather) 3-9-0 M Hills 6/1: 4130334: Ev ch: best in 1160.   40
*2613 HOROWITZ [1] 3-9-0 G Duffield 8/1: 02-010: Has changed stables: see 2613.   28
--   CASUAL PASS [2] 3-8-11 J Lowe 33/1: -0: Al rear: ex Irish colt who was a winner earlier
at Navan and Ballinrobe.   09
2690 Our Jamie [4] 8-6
7 ran   ½,½,3,7,8   (Alan Clore)   L Cumani Newmarket

2800 COLGATE FAMILY FAVOURITE HCAP 3YO+ 0-35   £1541   1m 3f   Good/Firm 21 -26 Slow   [24]

2134 FOURTH TUDOR [9] (B Hanbury) 4-8-9(BL) A Geran(7) 7/2 FAV: -20001: 4 ch g Horatius -
Fourth Dimension (Time Tested): Bl first time & well bckd: led over 2f out for a ready win in
a slow run & rather moderate h'cap at Hamilton: first success: eff at 11/12f: acts on gd &
fast grnd & seems suited by bl.   17
1976 BOY SANDFORD [6] (W Mackie) 7-8-3 J Quinn(5) 9/2: 0400442: Recent winner over hdles:
no ch with winner: in gd form: see 789: stays 11f.   01
2683 GREED [4] (D Smith) 5-9-7 L Charnock 11/2: 4042403: Al there: see 2415, 1185.   18
2324 MOULKINS [10] (J Wilson) 4-8-8 G Duffield 6/1: 0130404: Nearest fin: best 1052.   01
2432 APPRECIATIVE [3] 3-8-7(vis) N Howe 10/1: 00-0000: Led early: lightly rcd sister to
the fair stayer Bloodless Coup.   08
2604 NUGOLA [5] 4-8-4(VIS) M Beecroft 7/1: 0004000: Visored first time: some late hdway:
little form this term: see 789.   00
2604 PONTYATES [8] 4-9-7 T Williams 10/1: 0004100: Fin 7th: twice below 1909 (sharpish trk).   00
2426 GIRDLE NESS [11] 3-8-7 A Mackay 7/1: 0011300: Btr in selling company in 1960 (1m).   00
2415 Wise Cracker [7] 8-13(BL)   2520 The Fink Sisters [2] 8-12
2604 Mariners Star [1] 9-5
11 ran   5,½,2,hd,¼   (B Hanbury)   B Hanbury Newmarket

Official Going Given As FIRM

2801 SIBTHORPE SELLING STAKES 2YO   £1120   1m   Good/Firm 31 -29 Slow

2712 COROFIN LASS [13] (C Tinkler) 2-8-8(bl) M Wood 4/1 JT FAV: 0000041: 2 b f Junius -
Tanzanite (Marino): Never hdd, comfortably winning a 2yo seller at Nottingham (bought in
13,000 gns): first success: has impr since fitted with bl: seems suited by forcing tactics
over 1m & promises to stay further: acts on fast grnd.   15
2434 MASCALLS DREAM [5] (P Makin) 2-8-8 T Ives 5/1: 0002: Ev ch: impr effort over this
lngr trip: acts well on fast grnd: dam winner over middle dists: should stay 10f+ next season.   08
2707 NO CONCERN [11] (M Blanshard) 2-8-11 W Newnes 4/1 JT FAV: 003: Showed a little impr
here: stays 1m: related to several minor winners: acts on firm.   06
2609 NATIONS ROSE [3] (R Stubbs) 2-8-8 J H Brown(5) 11/1: 0404: Never btr: tried in bl
last time, btr without: stays 1m & acts on firm.   03
2580 MAX STAR [1] 2-8-11 N Carlisle 33/1: 000: No dngr: related to winning middle dist plater   00
2724 CREOLE BAY [2] 2-8-8 M Hills 11/2: 0000030: Prom, wknd: btr 2724 (same trip).   00
2138 MISS PISA [12] 2-8-8 J Ward(7) 9/2: 030430F: Fell early: btr 1862.   00
--   Cajun Moon [7] 8-8   1672 Culinary [10] 8-8(BL)   --   Acertainhit [6] 8-11
2757 Lillys Double [9] 8-8(BL) B   2724 Willys Niece [4] 8-8 B
12 ran   2,2,nk,4,½   (J Ryan)   C Tinkler Malton, Yorks

2802 NOTTINGHAM GOOSE FAIR HANDICAP 3YO 0-35   £2010   1m 6f   Good/Firm 31 +03 Fast   [36]

2497 REAL MOONSHINE [1] (A Stewart) 3-9-0 M Roberts 12/1: -040001: 3 b c Known Fact -
Shebeen (Saint Crespin III): Showed impr form coming from behind to lead dist in a 3yo h'cap
at Nottingham: first success: appreciated this 14f trip & promises to stay 2m: half brother
to several minor winners: acts well on fast grnd: may win again.   32
*2682 SHAHS CHOICE [4] (J Dunlop) 3-9-12(5ex) W Carson 9/4: 4322212: Led 2f out, outpcd but
in good form: see 2682 (2m).   38
2516 RIVER GAMBLER [5] (J Sutcliffe) 3-8-8 M Hills 7/1: -002003: Ev ch: best 1806 (10f, bl).   16
2727 LOST OPPORTUNITY [6] (J Bethell) 3-8-9 W Newnes 10/1: 0400004: Made much: mdn: see 99.   16
*2760 JOHN DOREY [3] 3-9-6(5ex) G Duffield 11/10 FAV: 40-1110: Below his best: see 2760.   18
2701 LA GRANDE DAME [2] 3-8-10 S Whitworth 25/1: -00000: Remains a mdn: see 1259.   00
6 ran   2,2½,½,5,8   (Brook Bloodstock plc)   A Stewart Newmarket

2803 CARLTON MAIDEN FILLIES STAKES 2YO   £1120   6f   Good/Firm 31 -23 Slow

2652 TUFTY LADY [1] (R Armstrong) 2-8-11 P Tulk 11/2: 002201: 2 b f Riboboy - War Talk

(Assagai): Mkt drifter but was never hdd when comfortably winning a 2yo fillies mdn at
Nottingham: very eff with forcing tactics over 6f & possibly does not quite stay 7f as
yet: acts on fast & yld going.   46
2687 SO KIND [2] (J Watts) 2-8-11 T Ives 4/7 FAV: 3442: Long odds on, chall on bit 1f
out, no extra: rated higher 2687 (flattered?).   44
1282 JANS CONTESSA [3] (R Boss) 2-8-11 M Hills 8/1: 2303: Dsptd lead much, after long abs. 32
2185 DELPHINIA [4] (J Dunlop) 2-8-11 W Carson 5/1: 044: No dngr: btr 2185.   16
4 ran   ½,4,8   (Mrs S Hinde)   R Armstrong Newmarket

2804   TRENT AUCTION STAKES 2YO   £2282   6f   Good/Firm 31 -03 Slow
2588 FOURWALK [6] (N Macauley) 2-9-6 R Hills 16/1: 0032001: 2 br c Godswalk - Vaunt
(Hill Rise): Caused a 16/1 surprise when making ev yd, comfortably, in an auction race at
Nottingham: earlier won over the same C/D & obviously likes Nottingham: needs to be out in
front & is suited by 6f & firm grnd.   45
2494 BILLY CONNOLLY [1] (M Brittain) 2-8-11 K Darley 10/1: 02: Prom thro'out: gd effort. 30
2716 GENERAL MEILLAND [9] (L Piggott) 2-8-11 T Ives 3/1: 0333: Sn driven along: much btr 2716. 26
2140 BRIMUR [7] (J Watts) 2-8-11 W Carson 5/1: 24: Mkt drifter, never btr: btr 2140 (7f). 24
*2608 PILGRIM PRINCE [3] 2-9-1 M Wigham 20/1: 000010: Never closer: see 2608.   26
-2482 COPPER RED [8] 2-9-2 S Perks 13/8 FAV: 3231220: Dsptd lead some: much btr 2482 (5f). 24
2580 Young Centurion [10] 8-11(VIS)   2025 Flaxley [4] 9-8
2434 Glamis Girl [2] 8-8   2708 Power Of Love [5] 8-8
10 ran   1½,1½,1,½,½   (W A Fouracres)   N Macauley Sproxton, Leics

2805 EBF STAUNTON MAIDEN STAKES 2YO C & G   £963   5f   Good/Firm 31 -02 Slow
--   GALLANT GALLOIS [10] (C Booth) 2-9-0 R Hills 10/1: 1: 2 b c Mummy's Game - La Gallia
(Welsh Saint): Made a successful debut (bckd at long odds) comfortably winning a 2yo mdn at
Nottingham: half brother to 9f winner Black Bank & a couple of other minor winners: dam
successful over middle dists & over hdles: a June foal who can only impr further, especially
over longer distances.   50
2554 ALI SMITH [13] (R Boss) 2-9-0 T Ives 13/8 FAV: 23402: Kept on, not trouble winner:
proving expensive to follow: see 1791.   44
2661 STELBY [12] (O Brennan) 2-9-0 J Carroll(7) 7/2: 2420033: Led 2f out: flattered 2661? 41
2696 OUR FREDDIE [5] (A Ingham) 2-9-0 R Curant 11/1: 444044: Al prom: appears on the up grade. 38
1207 GOLDEN CAJUN [9] 2-9-0 G Duffield 11/1: 00: Long abs & should be btr for race: see 1207 33
2476 TOUCH OF SPEED [7] 2-9-0(bl) S Perks 12/1: 0000040: Led to ½way: see 2476.   29
--   Mont Arthur [1] 9-0   2396 Pertain [6] 9-0(bl)   2100 Garcon Noir [11] 9-0
1076 Great Stands By [8] 9-0   2323 Metroman [2] 9-0(BL)
2301 El Delgado [4] 9-0
12 ran   1,1,1,2,1½   (J L Acklam)   C Booth Flaxton, Yorks

2806 FOSTON NURSERY HANDICAP STAKES 2YO   £1832   1m   Good/Firm 31 +03 Fast   [47]
*2712 AKROTIRI BAY [11] (L Holt) 2-7-10(10ex) R Fox 6/1: 000011: 2 b c Ya Zaman - Fellin
Geri (Silly Season): Nicely bckd, came from behind & overcame difficulties in running to
lead on the line in quite a fast run nursery at Nottingham: in fine form at present having
recently won a selling nursery at Leicester: well suited by 1m, promises to stay middle
dists next season: suited by firm grnd & runs well on a gall trk: may complete the hat trick. 25
-2648 ROUMELI [5] (Lord J Fitzgerald) 2-8-3 R Hills 11/4 FAV: 2303122: Led 1f out, caught
death in a driving fin: in fine form: see 2512.   30
2648 LOMA BREEZE [1] (P Kelleway) 2-8-0 M Hills 12/1: -300003: Kept on in a close finish. 25
2512 AVINASESH [7] (C Tinkler) 2-8-2 M Wood 17/2: 2340024: Slow start, never btr: see 2512. 23
2444 COMMONSIDR GIPSY [8] 2-8-10 J Carroll(7) 7/1: 0200030: Ev ch: rated higher 2444 (7f). 30
2700 MUBKIR [12] 2-8-12 N Howe 11/1: 0200200: Led 3f out: twice below 2498.   31
2556 SLIP DANCER [4] 2-9-7 T Ives 9/1: 30000: Fin 7th: yet to reproduce 1872.   00
2700 LUKMARIE [9] 2-8-4 M Roberts 8/1: 43000: Dsptd lead much, fin 8th: see 1341, 2013. 00
2595 SPOTTER [10] 2-9-4 W Carson 5/1: 010200: Trouble in running: best 1433.   00
1672 Unos Pet [3] 7-7(2oh)   1307 Abidjan [6] 8-13   2444 Highland Laird [2] 8-7(BL)(4ow)
12 ran   shhd,½,2,hd,nk,½   (Bernard Bates)   L Holt Tunworth, Hants

Official Going Given As GOOD
2807 GEORGE TODD APP. CHALL TROPHY (H'CAP)   £2526   1m 2f Good 46 -07 Slow   [31]
2381 MINUS MAN [15] (W Holden) 8-7-13 R Morse(6) 7/1: 0304231: 8 b g Firestreak - Cheb's
Honour (Cheb's Lad): Ran on well final 1f to get up close home in an app h'cap at Goodwood:
in fair form lately: in '85 won a h'cap at Kempton & in '84 won again at Kempton: eff over 1m,
stays 10f well: acts on firm & yld grnd & on any trk.   10
*2401 HAMPER [4] (W Hastings Bass) 3-9-6 A Dicks(5) 9/1: -4312: Led over 1f out: just caught. 38
-2516 TOM FORRESTER [2] (P Mitchell) 5-9-2 R Carter(8) 5/1 FAV: 0304423: Led over 3f out:
just btn: running well: see 2516, 453.   25
2671 SPRING FLIGHT [10] (A Jarvis) 3-9-7 S Meacock(12) 8/1: 3113124: Not much room final
1f: tremendously consistent: see 2671, 2490.   36

2533 DANCING BARRON [17] 5-8-8(vis) T Lang(10) 20/1: 0304040: Ev ch in str: best 1473 (12f).   11
2576 WINDBOUND LASS [12] 3-7-7(1oh) S Dawson 14/1: -000040: Ev ch: see 2576.   03
851 ELECTROPET [19] 4-8-13 A Shoults 20/1: 10-0040: Long abs: nearest fin: should do
btr next time: see 851.   00
*2578 CRAMMING [24] 3-9-4(4ex) B Uniacke(12) 11/2: 3023010: No show: well below 2578.   00

2490 Primrose Way	[18] 7-8	1017 Skyboot	[9] 8-7	2623 Irish Hero	[3] 9-3(bl)	
-- Foche	[23] 9-5	2490 Dolly	[20] 8-11	-- Scarlet Trouper	[21] 7-11	
1806 Cosmic Flight	[6] 8-4	*2187 Kitty Clare	[13] 8-5	2617 Redden	[22] 9-6	
2260 Big Pal	[16] 9-6	2395 Carvery	[5] 8-7	2372 Forgiving	[1] 8-6	
1362 Cheerful Times	[11] 8-2			2381 Morgiana	[8] 7-13	
22 ran	nk,hd,1,2,nk,½	(Whitting Commodities Ltd)		W Holden Newmarket		

2808 FOUNDATION STAKES (LISTED RACE) 3YO+   £7661   1m 2f   Good 46 -01 Slow

+1912 CHINOISERIE [7] (L Cumani) 3-8-6 R Cochrane 9/2: 2112211: 3 b c Fluorescent Light -
From The East (Gold And Myrrh): Smart, much impr colt: despite a fair abs, led 1f out, ridden
out in a valuable Listed race at Goodwood: last time out was a clever winner of the valuable
& fast run Extel h'cap on this trk: earlier a winner at Brighton & Yarmouth & has only once
been out of the first two in 8 races this term: very eff over 10f: acts on firm & yld grnd
& on any trk: sure to win more races & is a progressive sort.   74
1597 NOMROOD [5] (P Cole) 3-8-9 T Quinn 10/3: 2-12002: Abs: ev ch final 1f: fine effort
& is probably at his best over 10f: see 578.   78
2630 BOON POINT [1] (J Dunlop) 3-8-9 J Reid 14/1: 0011133: Made most & kept on well:
remains in grand form: see 2630, 2354.   72
2740 SAMARID [6] (M Stoute) 3-8-9 W R Swinburn 6/1: -010104: Mkt drifter: kept on under
press: consistent: see 2419.   70
2740 KUFUMA [4] 4-9-0(vis) Pat Eddery 11/4 FAV: -000120: Well bckd: no extra final 1f:
better 2740, 2496.   65
1715 BOLD INDIAN [2] 5-9-0(BL) S Cauthen 15/2: -023000: Bl first time, fdd over 2f out:
again below 945: see 433.   53
2559 RACKSTRAW [3] 3-8-6 B Thomson 11/2: 130-320: Not stay 10f? see 2559.   53
7 ran   1,1,1,1,7,15   (Ivan Allan)   L Cumani Newmarket

2809 AJAX ENGINEERING H'CAP (0-60) 3YO+   £3115   2m 3f   Good 46 No Time Taken   [50]

2510 BRIGHTNER [12] (G Harwood) 5-10-0 G Starkey 11/1: 110/031: 5 ch g Sparkler - Smarten Up
(Sharpen Up): Very useful gelding: defied 10-0 in game fashion to win a h'cap at Goodwood:
led inside final 1f, ridden out: in '84 was rated 66 after winning at Bath (2) & Edinburgh:
stays 2m3f well: acts on gd & firm grnd & on any trk: genuine sort.   61
2591 BALLET CHAMP [2] (R Holder) 8-7-8 S Dawson 3/2: 0242042: Led inside final 2f: just btn:
another good effort & deserves a win: see 349.   26
*2455 HARLESTONE LAKE [6] (J Dunlop) 4-8-10 Pat Eddery 11/4 FAV: 4140113: Another gd effort.   37
*2317 ACTINIUM [9] (P Cole) 3-8-8 T Quinn 8/1: 2124414: Ev ch inside final 2f: remains in
gd form & probably stays 2m3f: see 2317.   45
*569 DETROIT SAM [11] 5-8-9 R Cochrane 16/1: 00-2210: Led over 2f out after a long abs:
tried over a much lngr trip today & ran quite well: see 569.   34
2480 WITHY BANK [4] 4-9-3 A Shoults(5) 10/3: 1130020: No extra final 2f: see 2480.   41

2647 Sun Street	[8] 7-10	462 Contester	[5] 8-8	1099 Accuracy	[7] 8-13	
2647 Italian Sunrise	[10] 7-10(VIS)			-- Rig Steel	[13] 7-7(9oh)	
663 Aldo King	[1] 8-2	-- Fleeting Knight	[3] 8-8			
13 ran	½,5,2,hd,½	(K Abdulla)		G Harwood Pulborough, Sussex		

2810 JOURNAL (PORTSMOUTH) H'CAP (0-60) 3YO   £3145   7f   Good 46 -05 Slow   [54]

-2659 HIGHLY RECOMMENDED [3] (P Cundell) 3-8-0 N Adams 7/2: 0003121: 3 b g Daring March -
Rosette (Red Alert): In fine form & made ev yd gamely in quite a valuable 3yo h'cap at
Goodwood: last time out just btn at Brighton & earlier won a 3yo h'cap at Kempton: eff at
6f, stays 7f well: acts on gd & firm grnd & on any trk, but is well suited by forcing tactics
on a sharpish one: seems a genuine sort.   37
*2442 USFAN [9] (J Dunlop) 3-9-3 Pat Eddery 5/2 FAV: -02212: Not the best of runs & kept
on under press: another gd effort: see 2442.   52
2702 MISTER MARCH [5] (R Hutchinson) 3-7-8 G French 16/1: 1120003: Gd effort: see 2024, 1742.   25
2655 IYAMSKI [10] (W Hastings Bass) 3-8-4 R Lines(3) 13/2: 2023004: Not clear run, nearest fin.   34
1783 STRIVE [2] 3-8-1 A Mcglone 20/1: 0240000: Mkt drifter: ev ch: quite lightly rcd this
term: best 436.   26
2390 BURHAAIN [1] 3-8-3 P Cook 14/1: -010000: Fdd final 1f: lightly rcd: best 703.   24
2570 SUNNY MATCH [8] 3-7-10 C Rutter(3) 6/1: 0020020: Prom most: well below 2570 (C/D).   14
2463 CODICES [4] 3-9-7 G Starkey 13/2: 0101200: There 5f: twice below 2369.   00
2422 MOURADABIA [11] 3-7-12 G Carter 10/1: 002-000: Active in mkt: disapp: see 1830.   00

2534 Lightning Wind	[7] 7-7(1oh)	2394 Sitzcarraldo	[6] 7-7(1oh)
11 ran	1,2,hd,2½,2,hd	(Lord McAlpine)	P Cundell Compton, Berks

2811 LIMEKILN STAKES 2YO   £7643   7f   Good 46 -21 Slow

*2542 TARTUFFE [4] (G Harwood) 2-8-13 G Starkey 1/2 FAV: 011: 2 ch c Golden Act - Tarop
(Dr Fager): Promising colt: hvly bckd: not entirely suited by the slow pace but led inside

final 1f, under press in a valuable 2yo stakes at Goodwood: last time out broke the 2yo course
record when a ready winner of a 2yo mdn at Salisbury: cost only $35,000 & is a half brother to
2 winners in the States: eff at 7f, will be well suited by 1m & further: acts on gd & fast
grnd & on any trk: certain to win more races.   58
2677 ABLE SAINT [2] (R Armstrong) 2-9-0 S Cauthen 7/2: 2132: Set moderate pace: just btn
& is most consistent: see 2677, 2205.   57
--   CASTLE WARD [3] (J Dunlop) 2-8-8 B Thomson 12/1: 3: Mkt drifter on debut: never nearer
& impr certain: quite stoutly bred colt who should be well suited by 1m & further: half brother
to the smart Silly Steven: acts on gd grnd.   33
2522 MOORE BRASS [5] (C Brittain) 2-8-11(BL) Pat Eddery 16/1: 404: Bl first time: fdd
final 2f: best 2243.   26
--   WHITE MINSTREL [1] 2-8-8 B Rouse 16/1: 0: Prom most on debut: half brother to several
winners, notably the smart 2yo R B Chesne.   19
5 ran   ¼,12,5,2   (D J Saxby)   G Harwood Pulborough, Sussex

2812 SOLENT STAKES 2YO   £959   6f   Good 46 +06 Fast

2696 CAPTAIN HOLLY [6] (P Makin) 2-8-11 T Quinn 20/1: 01: 2 ch c Absalom - Top Stream
(Welsh Pageant): Impr colt: led inside final 1f, comfortably in quite fast run 2yo stakes at
Goodwood: cost $31,000 as a yearling & is quite a speedily bred sort: eff over an easy 6f
on gd grnd: should impr further.   52
2589 ACT OF TREASON [4] (R Laing) 2-8-8 B Thomson 7/1: 0302: Ran on well final 1f: gd
effort: stays 6f well: sister to winning h'capper Kedron: acts on gd & yld grnd: can find a race   48
2554 GILBERTO [1] (J Dunlop) 2-8-11 Pat Eddery 4/9 FAV: 4323: Hvly bckd: led inside final
2f but ran disappointingly: much btr 2551, 1915 (C/D).   47
2345 GEBLITZT [5] (R Armstrong) 2-8-11 S Cauthen 7/1: 004: Prom most: fair effort: see 1495.   35
2717 SPITZABIT [9] (J Reid 66/1: 000: Led over 4f, showing impr form: cheaply
acquired colt who seems suited by front running tactics on a sharpish trk: can win a seller.   30
--   SAXON MIRCEL [3] (P Cook 33/1: 0: No threat on debut: stable mate of winner &
should do btr: half brother to winning hurdler/chaser Garfunkel.   24
2561 Say You [2] 8-11   2249 Gold Minories [8] 8-11
--   Castillito [10] 8-8   2484 Lord Of Canewdon [7] 8-11
10 ran   nk,1¼,5,2,3   (S H J Brewer)   P Makin Ogbourne Maisey, Wilts

2813 KINRARA NURSERY STAKES HANDICAP 2YO   £3052   1m   Good 46 -02 Slow   [52]

2405 MORNING FLOWER [9] (R Williams) 2-8-4 T Quinn 7/1: 032F201: 2 b c Hittite Glory -
Flora Leigh (Floribunda): Led inside final 1f cmftbly in a nursery h'cap at Goodwood: first
success, though a deserved one: eff at 7f, suited by 1m: acts on gd & firm grnd & on any trk.   41
2485 GREY WOLF TIGER [4] (R Hannon) 2-8-8 P Cook 10/1: 4114002: Led over 1f out: gd
effort: stays 1m but best in 1522 (6f).   40
2625 CASTLE CORNET [7] (R Hannon) 2-7-8 G French 8/1: 0044003: Led over 2f out, stays 1m.   22
2700 MENDIP STAR [1] (R Holder) 2-7-9(bl) S Dawson 5/1: 4041024: Made most: btr 2700.   14
1570 TAKE A HINT [10] 2-8-2 C Rutter(3) 12/1: 441400: No show: abs: best 864 (yld).   16
2677 MR CORMAN [6] 2-9-3 J Reid 12/1: 00100: Twice below 2379 (7f, yld).   21
2512 PALEFACE [5] 2-9-7 Pat Eddery 9/4 FAV: 3221230: Below his best: see 2512.   00
2700 MANDALAY PRINCE [3] 2-8-9 S Cauthen 13/2: 00040: Btr 2700 (stiffer trk).   00
2433 Peroy [8] 7-7   2527 Harts Lane [2] 7-8(1ow)
10 ran   1½,2,4,2½,5   (John Harding)   R Williams Newmarket

Official Going Given As GOOD

2814 STRATHCLYDE MAIDEN FILLIES STAKES 2YO   £812   6f   Good/Firm 20 -03 Slow

2652 MEADOWBANK [13] (M Dickinson) 2-8-11 D Nicholls 10/1: 0031: 2 b f Northfields -
Reesooka (Godswalk): Comfortably made all in a 2yo fillies mdn at Hamilton: probably stays 7f
though may prove best over todays trip: acts on gd & firm grnd & on any trk: clearly suited
by forcing tactics.   46
1187 RUN LITTLE LADY [6] (H Cecil) 2-8-11 W Ryan 11/4 JT FAV: 42: Al prom & kept on well:
gd effort after a long break: acts on gd/firm: should win a small race: see 1187.   38
2658 JUST KALA [4] (P Walwyn) 2-8-11 Paul Eddery 11/4 JT FAV: 4323: Hvly bckd: would have
fin closer had her saddle not slipped below dist: deserves a race: see 2658 & 2147.   36
-2651 RIPE CHRISTINA [9] (A Bailey) 2-8-11 P Bloomfield 3/1: 0033424: Btn dist: much btr 2651.   22
2499 IRENIC [7] 2-8-11 T Lucas 14/1: 000: With winner .till wknd dist: see 2499.   18
2678 HAYGATE PARK [11] 2-8-11 P Robinson 14/1: 0440: Tardy start & never nearer: see 2494.   12
2465 Blaze Of Gold [5] 8-11   2698 Fowl Play [8] 8-11
--   Dark Winter [1] 8-11   2423 Oak Field [10] 8-11   2678 Fireiron [3] 8-11
2423 Dolitino [12] 8-11   2334 Lady Of Riga [2] 8-11
13 ran   2,½,6,1½,2,5   (R E Sangster)   M Dickinson Manton, Wilts

2815 ROYAL CALEDONIAN HUNT NURSERY H'CAP 2YO   £2004   6f   Good/Firm 20 -08 Slow   [55]

2588 DUNLIN [5] (S Norton) 2-8-3 J Lowe 12/1: 1231001: 2 ch c Miswaki - Vita Mia (Ribot):
Stayed on under press to lead close home in a nursery h'cap at Hamilton: earlier won a 2

runner race over this C/D & first time out won an Edinburgh mdn: half brother to several
winners in the States: eff over 5/6f on fast & hvy grnd: acts on any trk.   38
2465 WHISTLING WONDER [10] (M Brittain) 2-7-7 A Proud 20/1: 3000002: Led inside dist, btn
a whisker: btr effort & may win soon: acts on firm & soft: see 94.   27
2652 ROSE LOUBET [9] (J Payne) 2-7-7(8oh) A Mackay 33/1: 00003: Led after ½way: gd effort.   23
2529 LUCIANAGA [4] (P Walwyn) 2-8-13 Paul Eddery 6/1: 2010004: Kept on late: see 1313.   41
2265 BRUTUS [6] 2-8-6 N Connorton 16/1: 1030400: Led over ½way: quite consistent: see 1893.   32
2669 JUVENILEDELINQUENT [8] 2-8-1 T Williams 6/1: 1244000: Slow start & no threat.   15
2556 STRATHBLANE [2] 2-9-7 P Robinson 9/4 FAV: 10130: Fdd into 7th: much btr in 2556 (7f).   00
1893 FIVE SIXES [7] 2-7-7(3oh) J Quinn(5) 12/1: 4211300: Fin 8th: won a seller in 1298.   00
2608 BOLD HIDEAWAY [3] 2-7-7(bl)(3oh) M Fry 10/1: 04020: Never going pace: btr in 2608 (slr).   00
9 ran shhd,1½,½,½,5,hd   (Charles Buddeke)   S Norton Barnsley, Yorks

2816 ROYAL CALEDONIAN HUNT CUP H'CAP (0-35)   £2122   6f   Good/Firm 20 +05 Fast   [34]

*2513 DUFFERS DANCER [17] (W Pearce) 4-8-13 N Connorton 7/1 FAV: -013411: 4 ch g Miami
Spring - Evening Chorus (Mountain Call): Stayed on strongly to lead near fin in quite a fast
run h'cap at Hamilton: in grand form this term, earlier won h'caps at Pontefract & Carlisle:
in '85 again successful at Carlisle: well suited by 6f, stays 7f: suited by gd & fast grnd
& acts on any trk.   28
2411 TIT WILLOW [18] (S Wiles) 4-8-6(bl) G Baxter 14/1: 1203432: Led below dist, hdd
close home: very consistent this season & deserves another win: see 828.   16
2632 THRONE OF GLORY [19] (D Chapman) 5-9-8 D Nicholls 8/1: 0023043: Not btn far: see 2513.   31
2537 GODS SOLUTION [7] (D Barron) 5-8-13(bl) W Ryan 20/1: 0040004: Never nearer: see 42.   18
2775 WARTHILL LADY [5] 4-8-13(10ex) A Bacon(7) 10/1: 4010100: Quick reapp: again ran
creditably under her penalty: see 2632.   17
2411 OFF YOUR MARK [11] 6-7-8(1ow)(3oh) L Charnock 33/1: -040000: Nearest fin: see 1610.   00
2659 BEECHWOOD COTTAGE [14] 3-8-11(bl) P Bloomfield 8/1: 0202030: Wknd into 7th: btr in 2659.   00
2537 TANFEN [8] 5-9-8 M Birch 9/1: 0401000: Fin down the field: best in 2012.   00
2715 HENRYS VENTURE [12] 4-8-3 A Proud 9/1: 1303430: Early speed: btr in 2715: see 2295.   00
2513 THATCHERED [2] 5-8-12 M Fry 10/1: 0-00100: No dngr: best in 2397 (yld).   00
1959 Mademoiselle Magna [13] 8-9   2585 King Cole [6] 7-7
628 Its Heaven [15] 7-7(4oh)   2084 Security Pacific [20] 9-7
2728 No Credibility [4] 8-13   2483 Free Clare [1] 8-5(bl)
2575 Harmony Bowl [10] 8-8(bl)   2775 Tradesman [3] 7-7(bl)(3oh)
2659 Tootsie Roll [16] 7-11(bl)   2728 Moninsky [9] 8-4
20 ran 1½,nk,1½,nk,1½,½,1½   (Robin Arbuthnot)   W Pearce Hambleton, Yorks

2817 REDERECH SELLING STAKES 2YO   £854   1m 40y Good/Firm 20 -40 Slow

2466 GAELIC LOVER [3] (C Tinkler) 2-8-11 M Birch 13/8 JT FAV: 21: 2 b g He Loves Me -
Argalie (Ace Of Aces): Well bckd & led below dist, comfortably in a slowly run 2yo seller at
Hamilton (bought in 1,300 gns): cheaply bought gelding who stays 1m well: acts on gd & fast
grnd & on a gall trk: should continue to impr.   25
2512 WAR CHILD [2] (P Haslam) 2-8-8 T Williams 13/8 JT FAV: 003002: Had ev ch: stays 1m.   16
2724 RIPSTER [6] (R Stubbs) 2-8-11 D Nicholls 16/1: 004003: Made most: probably stays 1m.   14
2310 CARSE KELLY [5] (S Norton) 2-8-8 J Lowe 13/2: 220004: Btn dist: best in 1050 (6f).   04
2396 U BIX COPY [4] 2-8-11 P Robinson 8/1: 3230000: Best here in 973 (6f, hvy).   04
2609 LITTLE LAW [1] 2-8-8 A Proud 50/1: 00: Rank outsider & dropped out quickly ½way.   00
6 ran 2,1½,3,1½,15   (E Hutchinson)   C Tinkler Malton, Yorks

2818 AVONDALE CLAIMING STAKES 3YO+   £684   1m 1f Good/Firm 20 +08 Fast

*2603 COLLYWESTON [4] (M Prescott) 3-8-6 C Nutter 11/8 FAV: -001211: 3 br f Thatching -
Kentucky Robin (Falcon): Well bckd & led below dist, ridden out in a fast run claimer at
Hamilton: in fine form recently, winning similar races at Redcar & Chester: half sister to
several winners: eff over 7/10f: acts on fast & soft grnd & on any trk.   24
2583 TREYARNON [8] (S Norton) 4-8-9 J Lowe 12/1: 0044322: Remains a mdn: see 2583.   16
2394 SCINTILLATOR [6] (C Booth) 3-7-13 T Williams 16/1: 0000003: Led 3f out: best in 2319 (7f)   08
2656 PORO BOY [1] (C Williams) 3-8-7 G Baxter 13/2: 0040024: Rated 40 in 352 (1m yld).   16
2414 NIPKNOWES [5] 5-8-4(BL) A Mackay 33/1: 00-0000: Bl first time: no form this term.   00
2604 BUSTED FLAVOUR [2] 5-9-0 T Lucas 5/2: 0030300: Btr in 2109: see 875.   00
1091 OPTIMISM FLAMED [7] 3-8-2(2ow) M Beecroft 8/1: 3-20000: Abs: made most: best in 183 (1m).00
2603 TORRIGGIA [3] 3-7-13 Julie Bowker(7) 100/1: 0000000: Outsider: btr early in str: no form.   00
8 ran ½,2½,shhd,4,6   (Lady Macdonald Buchanan)   M Prescott Newmarket

2819 CAPTAIN J.C. STEWART MEM. H'CAP (0-35)   £1402   1m 5f Good/Firm 20 -01 Slow   [23]

2683 FOUR STAR THRUST [1] (R Whitaker) 4-9-6 D Mckeown 4/1: 0202321: 4 ch f Derrylin -
Smiling (Silly Season): Gained an overdue win, led below dist, comfortably in a h'cap at
Hamilton: won a minor event at Edinburgh last season & had made the frame in most of her
starts this term: best form around 12/14f on gd & fast grnd: consistent filly who acts
on any trk.   25
2727 IM EXCEPTIONAL [2] (R Hollinshead) 4-8-7 W Ryan 3/1: -030032: Fin well: see 2727 & 1747.   09
2403 LISMORE [7] (J Dunlop) 4-9-7 J Lowe 2/1 FAV: 004-003: Held up, led on bit over 2f
out but found little when led down: see 2403 & 2093.   20

825

2415 ISHKHARA [4] (G Reveley) 4-8-6 P Robinson 6/1: 0300004: Ran on same pace: see 449.   01
2666 PERFECT DOUBLE [6] 5-8-6 N Connorton 8/1: 0322000: No extra 2f out: see 770.   00
2745 BOREHAM DOWN [3] 7-7-9 L Charnock 50/1: 0030000: Never dngr: see 824.   00
2666 Jipijapa [8] 7-12(vis)   2727 Apple Wine [5] 8-5
8 ran   1¼,1½,2,2,5,2½,7   (Mrs Jean Turner)   R Whitaker Wetherby, Yorks

---

MAISONS-LAFFITTE   Thursday September 25th   Fair Track

Official Going Given As SOFT

2820 GROUP 3 LA COUPE DE MAISONS LAFFITTE   £19526   1m 2f   Soft -

2637 ANTHEUS (C Head) 4-9-0 G Moore   -123031: 4 b c Northern Dancer - Apachee (Sir
Gaylord) Smart colt: al prom and cmftbly led 2f out in Gr 3 La Coupe de Maisons-Laffitte:
first time out this season won at St-Cloud: eff over 10/12f on gd and soft grd.   82
2359 SPLENDID MOMENT (R Collet) 3-8-5 A Lequeux   310-432: Ev ch dist, gd effort: see 389.   75
2195 AROKAR (J De Chevigny) 3-8-11 C Asmussen   1-12003: Ev ch dist: best 10f: see 289.   79
2736 NEW BRUCE (G Collet) 4-8-10 P Bruneau   0301044: Btr 2737.   67
8 Ran   2½,1,2   (J Wertheimer)   Mme. C Head France

THE CURRAGH   Saturday September 27th   Righthand Galloping Track

Official Going Given As FIRM

2821 GROUP 3 FERRANS FUTURITY STAKES 2YO   £14455   1m   Firm -

-2384 SANAM (J Dunlop) 2-9-2 S Cauthen 5/4 FAV: 410121: 2 ch c Golden Act - Rose Goddess
(Sassafras)   Smart, consistent colt: showed a fine turn of foot to draw clear in the final
1f in a Gr 3 race at the Curragh: earlier won a val event at Ascot and a nursery at Newmarket
and was 2nd in the Solario Stks behind Shining Water: very eff over 7f/1m, promises to stay
further: acts on gd and fast grd and likes stiff track: genuine, consistent & continues to impr.   75
2451 DARCYS THATCHER (M Kauntze) 2-9-2 S Craine 3/1: --111D2: Ev ch 2f out: rated higher
2451 (6f).   67
--   WAIT TILL MONDAY (D Weld) 2-8-10 M Kinane 8/1: 2133: Fin in fine style: just failed
to make all in a valuable Listed race at Leopardstown in mid July and this was his first
outing since: earlier won a mdn at Phoenix Park: eff 6f, clearly stays 1m well: appears to
act on any going.   60
--   BOBSBENT (C Collins) 2-8-10 P Shanahan 10/3: 4314: Dsptd lead 2f out, no extra:
easy winner in the heavy at Tralee recently: stays 1m.   56
--   OREMBO 2-8-10 D Manning 25/1: 0210: Not disgraced in 5th: easy all the way winner
of a mdn at Dundalk recently: stays 1m: acts on gd: suited by front running tactics and
a sharp track.   54
2451 KHARSHUF 2-8-10 K Moses 14/1: 2122010: Best 1006 (6f).   52
6 ran   4,nk,2,¾,1   (Prince A A Faisall)   J Dunlop Arundel, Sussex

2822 GROUP 2 BLANDFORD STAKES   £21625   1m 4f   Firm -

1144 NEMAIN (D V O'brien) 4-9-8 C Roche 12/1: 14-2001: 4 b c Alleged - Gulls Cry (Sea
Bird II) Smart Irish colt who returned to his best when winning Gr 2 Blandford Stks at the
Curragh: enterprisingly ridden from the front and held on well in the final stages: reportedly
was jarred up on the firm grd at Epsom and Ascot and has been lightly raced this season:
in '85 won this same race again and was also 4th in the St Leger: eff between 10 & 14f and
on fast and heavy ground: genuine sort who does well from the front.   81
*2506 PARK EXPRESS (J Bolger) 3-8-12 J Reid 4/6 FAV: 2D11212: Stayed on well but the
winner had flown and is capable of better: see 2506.   79
2222 MASHKOUR (H Cecil) 3-8-11 S Cauthen 6/4: 3113423: Waited with, stayed on strongly
and was not btn far: see 2222.   77
2506 MR JOHN (L Browne) 3-8-11 D Gillespie 12/1: 0042404: Has had a very busy season.   65
--   MASTER SWORDSMAN 3-8-4 D Hogan 25/1: -10140: Last of the 5 runners.   50
5 ran   ½,½,6,2   (P Wetzel)   D V O'brien Ireland

2823 GROUP 3 ELITE PREIS 3YO+   £16949   1m   Good -

2507 LIRUNG (H Jentzsch) 4-9-8 G Bocskai   232131: 4 ch c Connaught - Liranga (Literat)
Very smart German colt: easily made all in a Gr 3 race at Cologne: fine
3rd behind Sonic Lady in the Prix du Moulin at Longchamp last time: earlier successful at
Deauville and Cologne: winner of the German 2000 Guineas last season: stays 10/12f but
extremely eff over 1m with forcing tactics: does well on firm and gd grd: tough genuine and
consistent and a credit to his trainer.   85
2259 SIYAH KALEM (J Dunlop) 4-9-4 P Cook   4120032: In vain pursuit of winner, btr 2259   73
1860 ONESTO (F Schlaefle) 4-8-12 K Woodburn   23: See 1860.   63
7 Ran   3½,1½   (Gestut Fahrhof)   H Jentzsch West Germany

2824 GROUP 1 PUMA EUROPA PREIS 3YO+   £66384   1m 4f   Good .

2565 ALLEZ MILORD [5] (G Harwood) 3-8-10 G Starkey   1101001: 3 b c Tom Rolfe - Why
Me Lord (Bold Reasoning) Bounced back to form leading 3f out and held on for a narrow win
in Gr 1 Puma Europa Preis at Cologne, thoroughly overturning the form with Moon Madness from
the St Leger: earlier won at Newmarket (2), Goodwood and the Gordon Stks at Goodwood:
reportedly pulled a muscle in the Derby and was said not to stay the Leger trip: evidently
ideally suited by 12f and firm or gd ground tho' has shown form on heavy.   82
*2453 BABY TURK [8] (A De Royer Dupre) 4-9-7 S Cauthen   0432312: Made much, kept on
well when hdd and only btn ¾l in a cl finish: see 2453.   83
*2565 MOON MADNESS [1] (J Dunlop) 3-8-10 Pat Eddery   1111313: Ran below his St Leger
form and was said to have been unsuited by the slow pace and the shorter trip: see 2565.   78
2197 ORFANO [2] (S Von Mitzlaff) 3-8-10 P Alafi   3314334: -   73
2454 TIBERIUS [4] 3-8-10 L Mader   2100120: See 2454.   72
2197 CASSIS [6] 4-9-7 P Remmert   41-2340: -   67
2502 Daun [3] 9-7   2643 Night Line [7] 8-6
8 ran   ½,¾,1½,shthd,3,½   (J Brody)   G Harwood Pulborough, Sussex

---

Official Going Given As GOOD

2825 GROUP 3 PRIX MENERVE 3YO FILLIES   £18689   1m 4f   Good -

--   SHARANIYA (A De Royer Dupre) 3-8-8 Y Saint Martin   -21: 3 b f Alleged - Shanizadeh
(Baldric II) Smart French filly: on only her 2nd ever outing was an easy winner of a Gr 3
fillies event at Evry: first time out was a gd 2nd at Deauville: stays 12f well, acts on
gd and soft ground and looks certain to win more races.   77
--   SHARP GIRL (D Smaga) 3-8-11 A Lequeux   1014302: No chance with winner: gd effort:
earlier a winner at Longchamp (2): acts on gd and soft and stays 12f.   72
--   KRUGUY (B Secly) 3-8-8 M De Smyter   -113: Another gd eff: winner of her first 2
outings in the Provinces: stays 12f and acts on good.   67
--   LUTH DOR (J Cunnington Jr) 3-8-11 M Philipperon 1: 0010104: Ran to her best.   66
2462 COCOTTE 3-8-8 F Head 1: 0014230: Made much: best 10f? See 1932.   62
2525 BONSHAMILE 3-8-8 R Guest 1: 1-10300: Fin 7th: twice below 2236.   52
11 Ran   3,¾,2,¼   (Aga Khan)   A De Royer Dupre France

Official Going Given As GOOD/SOFT

2826 GROUP 3 PRIX DES CHENES 2YO   £18749   1m   Good/Soft -

1714 FOTITIENG (F Boutin) 2-8-9 F Head   3---131: 2 br c Nureyev - Dry Fly (Mill Reef)
Highly promising French colt: led well over 1f out for an emphatic 3l win in Gr 3 Prix des
Chenes at Longchamp: first time out was a winner at Chantilly: eff at 6f, well suited by
1m: acts on gd and yldg ground and looks sure to win more races.   77
1714 LIBERTINE (R Collet) 2-8-6 A Lequeux   --13202: No chance with winner: a reversal
of the form in 1714.   66
--   WILLESDON (A Fabre) 2-8-9 C Asmussen   13: Ran to his best: first time out winner
on this track.   68
8 Ran   3,nk   (S Niarchos)   F Boutin France

2827 GROUP 3 PRIX DU ROND POINT 3YO+   £19885   1m   Good/Soft -

2507 MAGICAL WONDER (G Mikhalides) 3-9-3 J Velasquez   -111041: 3 ch c Storm Bird -
Flama Ardiente (Crimson Satan) Very smart French colt: led final 1f, narrowly in a Gr 3 event
at Longchamp: in fine form this season, earlier winning Gr 1 Prix Jean Prat at Longchamp,
also a Gr 3 event at Longchamp and first time out successful at Evry: very eff at 1m/9f:
acts on any ground: always runs well at Longchamp.   83
757 ISTIKAL (A De Royer Dupre) 3-8-10 Y Saint Martin   2122: Long abs: just btn and
ran a very good race: earlier a winner at St-Cloud: seems very eff at 1m on gd/soft ground. 74
*1594 GAY MINSTREL (C Head) 5-9-2 G Moore   -121103: Just btn in a cl fin: see 1594.   72

1118 EPHIALTES (C Millbank) 4-9-2 C Asmussen   0124404: Btr early season: see 391, 2.   69
9 Ran nk,shtnk,1¼   (M Fustok)   G Mikhalides France

2828 GROUP 3 PRIX GLADIATEUR 4YO+   £16955   2m 4f   Good/Soft -

-- SILVER GREEN (A De Royer Dupre) 5-8-7 Y Saint Martin   100-011: 5 b h Green Dancer -
St Colline (Sanctus) Smart French stayer: winner of Gr 3 event at Longchamp, justifying fav:
recent winner at Evry: stays forever, acts on gd and soft.   74
298 ROBERTOS FIGHTER (R Collet) 4-8-4 E Saint Martin   3441002: Al prom.   69
-- EXACTLY RIGHT (P L Biancone) 4-8-7 G Mosse   0432403: Stays 2½m: running quite
consistently but yet to win this season.   70
7 Ran 2,1½   (Marquise S de Moratalla)   A De Royer Dupre France

---

NEWMARKET   Wednesday October 1st   Righthand, Stiff, Galloping Track

Official Going Given As GOOD/FIRM

2829 LONSDALE SELLING STAKES 2YO   £3132   7f   Firm 14 -32 Slow

2707 TYRIAN PRINCESS [11] (P Cole) 2-8-9(1ow) S Cauthen 15/2: 01: 2 b f Comedy Star -
Chasten (Manacle) Impr filly: waited with and led inside final 1f, under press in a val 2yo
seller at Newmarket (bought in 7000 gns): half sister to 7/8f 2yo winner Tyrian Noble: eff at
7f, looks sure to stay 1m: acts well on fast grd and a gall track.   31
2625 HAILEYS RUN [13] (G P Gordon) 2-8-11 W Ryan 15/2: 0334032: Led 3f out: just caught
and ran well: looks certain to win in similar company: stays a stiff 7f and acts well on fast.   31
2580 JONITE [15] (R Akehurst) 2-8-11 W Carson 12/1: 00003: Ran on well final 1f and is
much improved of late: should be suited by 1m: acts well on fast grd and a gall track:
can find a seller.   29
2292 INDIAN JUBILEE [7] (R Hannon) 2-8-8 M Hills 7/2 FAV: 004: Heavily bckd in this
lower grade: chance final 1f: cost 15,000 gns as yearling: eff at 7f on fast grd: can find
a similar race.   22
1816 STREET LEGAL [22] 2-8-11 Pat Eddery 8/1: 0000: Abs: al there: stays 7f and acts well
on fast ground: half brother to sev winners: should be suited by 1m.   18
2625 CHOISUN [4] 2-8-11 J Scally(7) 25/1: 00: Chance 2f out: btr eff from this half
brother to a sprint winner: acts on fast ground.   17
2708 MAIN BRAND [19] 2-8-8 T Ives 10/1: 0040: Mkt drifter: much btr in 2708.   00
2491 JEALOUS LOVER [10] 2-8-8 B Thomson 10/1: 0000: No show: btr 2491.   00
2707 MILL TRIP [6] 2-8-11 G Duffield 8/1: 03020: Prom much: well below 2707.   00
2708 SIXTY MINUTES [1] 2-8-11 T Williams 10/1: 000: No form in 3 outings to date: half
brother to a 6f winner and may improve.   00

1345 Bold Intention [5] 8-11		2700 Countess Bree [16] 8-8
-- Omen [9] 8-11	1948 George Harry [14] 8-11	
2625 College Wizard [8] 9-2		1803 Calypso Kid [21] 8-11(BL)
2707 Corleon [3] 8-11	985 Keel [2] 8-11	2608 Pearlitic [12] 8-11(BL)
2712 Sohams Taylor [20] 8-11(vis)		2596 Godford [17] 8-8
2600 Little Lochette [18] 8-8		

22 ran ½,¼,1½,3,hd   (W H Ponsonby)   P Cole Watcombe, Oxon.

2830 ROWLEY MILE NURSERY HANDICAP 2YO   £4721   1m   Firm 14 -21 Slow   [69]

2252 LAST DANCE [6] (R Hannon) 2-8-8 B Thomson 7/1: 4231201: 2 b c Last Fandango -
Connaught's Trump (Connaught) Useful colt: got up cl home, gamely, in a very cl finish to
val 2yo nursery h'cap at Newmarket: consistent sort who earlier ddhtd when winning a 2yo
mdn at Sandown: eff at 5f, clearly stays a stiff 1m: acts really well on fast ground and
loves a gall trk: genuine sort.   58
2663 ELEGANT ISLE [1] (J Watts) 2-8-9 T Ives 6/1: 1242: Made almost all and btn a whisker:
below his best in bl last time and this was a fine effort: see 2539.   59
2498 MON COEUR [2] (C Brittain) 2-8-9(bl) S Cauthen 10/1: 042303: Al prom, just btn:
consistent colt who deserves a win: stays 1m well: acts on firm and yldg ground and runs
well in blinkers.   58
*1534 MELODY MAKER [7] (B Hills) 2-7-11 R Hills 9/2: 0314: Ran well after a fair abs:
stays 1m: acts on firm and yldg grd and on any track: see 1534.   41
-2468 DR BULASCO [3] 2-9-7 J Reid 6/1: 213420: No extra final 1f under 9-7: never runs
a bad race and carries weight well: see 2468.   64
2383 COUNTER ATTACK [5] 2-7-13 W Carson 4/1 JT.FAV: 100: Wknd over 1f out: see 1872.   42
2571 ROMAN GUNNER [4] 2-9-1 Pat Eddery 4/1 JT.FAV: 0130: Twice below form 2239.   00
2648 Caerinette [8] 7-7(12oh)
8 ran shthd,hd,2½,hd,ddht   (John Norman)   R Hannon East Everleigh, Wilts.

2831 GR 1 TATTERSALLS CHEVELEY PARK STKS 2YO £41110   6f   Firm 14 +06 Fast

+2634 MINSTRELLA [2] (C Nelson) 2-8-11 J Reid 11/10 FAV: 4212111: 2 ro f The Minstrel - Flight Dancer
(Misty Flight) Highclass filly: fin 2nd but later awarded Gr 1 Cheveley Park Stks at Newmarket
on appeal to the Jockey Club, a fortnight later: on the day was given a hefty bump by Forest
Flower inside final 2f but an recovered to lead over 1f out, however probably hit the
front too soon and could not quicken inside final 1f: reportedly returned with heavy bruising
and can do btr than this: see 2634.   80

*2695 FOREST FLOWER [1] (I Balding) 2-8-11 T Ives 13/8: 111211D: 2 ch f Green Forest
Leap Lively (Nijinsky) Highclass filly: held up, pulled out inside final 2f and led final 1f
ridden clear in fast run Gr 1 Cheveley Park Stks at Newmarket: last time out a ready winner
of Gr 2 Mill Reef Stks at Newbury: earlier completed a hat trick in Gr 3 Cherry Hinton Stks at
Newmarket, Queen Mary Stks at Royal Ascot and first time out a minor event again at Newbury:
has met her only defeat when a shthd 2nd to the runner-up today in the Gr 1 Phoenix Stks
at Phoenix Park on easy ground: dam won the Lingfield Oaks Trial: eff at 6f, should stay
the 1,000 Guineas Mile: acts on yldg, well suited by gd and fast ground and a gall track:
only small but is a real battler who is certain to win more gd races. later demoted to 2nd place.   85
+1464 CANADIAN MILL [5] (W Hern) 2-8-11 W Carson 7/1: 13: Led 2f out: fine effort after
a long abs and was btn by 2 very smart fillies: sure to win more races: see 1464.   73
-2564 SHAIKIYA [4] (R J Houghton) 2-8-11 S Cauthen 14/1: 124: Wknd final 1f: see 2564 (5f)   66
2634 INDIAN LILY [3] 2-8-11 Pat Eddery 40/1: 14430: Made much, stiff task: see 2634, 2235.   58
5 ran   2½,2½,2½,3   (Paul Mellon)   I Balding Kingsclere, Hants.

2832 NEVER SO BOLD FILLIES HANDICAP 0-70   £5993   7f   Firm 14 -01 Slow   [56]

2650 CLEOFE [4] (L Cumani) 3-7-7(2oh) T Williams 7/2: 4001031: 3 ch f Grey Dawn II -
Astro Lady (Skymaster) Impr filly: ran on well under press to lead cl home in a val fillies
h'cap at Newmarket: earlier won a fast run 3yo mdn at Brighton and has been placed on numerous
occasions: eff at 6/7f, may stay 1m: acts on any trk, but is well suited by fast ground.   37
2449 BRAZZAKA [2] (M Jarvis) 3-9-7 T Ives 11/2: 1123332: Sn well clear only to be caught
cl home: another fine effort from this tremendously consistent filly: see 2449.   63
-2719 BLUE GUITAR [4] (J Hindley) 3-8-6(vis) M Hills 5/2 FAV: 4213123: Btr suited 1m? see 2719. 40
2440 ZALATIA [5] (W Jarvis) 3-9-7 Pat Eddery 9/2: -102004: Rather lightly raced: btr 776,213   54
2602 CERTAIN AWARD [6] 3-7-10(bl) W Carson 4/1: 014320: Upped in class: btr 2602.   22
2755 QUALITAIRESS [1] 4-7-7(vis)(19oh) P Burke(7) 12/1: 2012120: 19lbs out of h'cap:
not disgraced: see 2755.   14
6 ran   ½,4,nk,3,shthd   (Mrs D Zurcher)   L Cumani Newmarket

2833 ROUS STAKES   £6129   5f   Firm 14 +26 Fast

2672 FAYRUZ [7] (W O'gorman) 3-8-5(bl)(2ow) Pat Eddery 4/1: 0000031: 3 b c Song - Friendly
Jester (Be Friendly) Smart sprinter: regained his best form when an all the way winner of val
Rous Stks at Newmarket in a very fast time: in '85 won at Newbury, Lingfield, Kempton, Ripon, Thirsk
and Windsor: subs off the trk for sometime after chipping a bone but returned on final outing
to be a fine nk 2nd to Hallgate in Gr 3 event at Ascot: very eff over 5f: acts on firm and
yldg ground: game and genuine sort.   72
2503 STORM WARNING [4] (W Hastings Bass) 4-8-2 W Carson 10/11 FAV: 0300022: Very heavily
bckd: chall final 1f and just btn: in fine form lately and deserves a win: see 563.   67
2641 PETROVICH [6] (R Hannon) 4-8-5 B Thomson 8/1: 0003303: Chance over 1f out: running
well in gd company this season and has been rather difficult to place: see 705.   60
2764 ARDROX LAD [2] (M Blanshard) 6-8-11 J Reid 11/1: 0021004: Stiff task: ran well:see 2469   61
2668 ALL IS FORGIVEN [3] 6-8-5(bl) G Sexton 14/1: 030/000: Early speed: see 2524.   50
2530 SIMLA RIDGE [5] 4-8-9 T Ives 50/1: 3002040: Prom 3f: see 977, 628.   49
1146 STALKER [1] 3-8-3 Paul Eddery 5/1: 121-400: Long abs: chance 2f out: needed race? see 854   00
7 ran   nk,3,1,1,1   (A Foustok)   W O'gorman Newmarket

2834 STAYERS 3YO HANDICAP 0-60   £4924   2m 24y Firm 14 -21 Slow   [62]

*2517 CAP DEL MOND [4] (G Harwood) 3-8-11 A Clark 5/1: -111: 3 b c Troy - Rainbow's End
(My Swallow) Unbtn, impr colt: led inside final 1f, driven out in a val 3yo h'cap at Newmarket:
earlier successful twice at Folkestone: cost 400,000 gns as a yearling and is a half brother
to winning stayer Storm Cloud and also the useful Finian's Rainbow: stays 2m really well:
acts on fast grd and on any trk: very much on the upgrade.   57
2610 AMBASSADOR [3] (W O'gorman) 3-8-8(bl) T Ives 8/1: -22322: Led final 1f and just held:
suited by 2m and on this evidence should find a staying handicap: see 2610.   53
2523 SPARTAN VALLEY [5] (B Hills) 3-8-6 B Thomson 11/2: 2321433: Nvr nrr: stays 2m: see 1646.   45
2201 COINAGE [1] (R J Houghton) 3-9-1 S Cauthen 9/2 JT.FAV: 3101104: Led over 1f out: see 1894   53
2558 ELAAFUUR [7] 3-8-5 Paul Eddery 20/1: 4441000: Al prom: fair eff over this longer trip
and prob stays 2m: see 1685.   40
*2662 WASSL REEF [2] 3-9-12(5ex) Pat Eddery 9/2 JT.FAV: 1010110: No show and below his
best: see 2662 (13f).   60
*2665 TEMPLE WALK [9] 3-9-5(5ex) W Carson 8/1: -130110: Mkt drifter: fair effort: see 2665.   53
2569 HAPPY BREED [8] 3-7-12 T Williams 33/1: -004040: Made much: best 1509 (12f).   00
2647 SEVEN HILLS [6] 3-7-7(vis)(1oh) J Lowe 13/2: 0311130: Btr 2647, 2346.   00
9 ran   ½,4,nk,2½,½,shthd,1   (Prince Ahmed Salman)   G Harwood Pulborough, Sussex

BRIGHTON   Wednesday October 1st   Lefthand, Sharpish, Undulating Track

Official Going Given As FIRM : NO TIMES TAKEN DUE TO BAD VISIBILITY

2835 RACE HILL STAKES 2YO   £1766   5f 66y Firm No Time Taken

2694 ULTRA NOVA [2] (P Cole) 2-9-4 T Quinn 7/2: 2011401: 2 ch f Tina's Pet - Jennyjo
(Martinmas) Speedy filly: made ev yard, unchall in a 2yo stks at Brighton: earlier made all
at Beverley and Warwick: very eff over 5f with forcing tactics: acts on gd and firm ground:
prob acts on any trk but goes really well on a sharp one.   58
*2514 DAYS LIKE THESE [5] (P Bailey) 2-9-3 W R Swinburn 3/1: 412: Not get to winner:
gd effort: see 2514.   50
2661 BAG ORHYTHM [4] (J Hindley) 2-9-3(vis) P Robinson 4/5 FAV: 2122343: Uneasy fav and ran
well below his best: should have won this easily on form displayed in 2223 and appears to
have gone backwards.   44
2320 MISS JASMINE [1] (D Marks) 2-8-8 P Cook 66/1: 004: Prom over 3f: stiff task: half sister
to sev winners: seems suited by an easy 5f.   20
2514 MISTER WIZARD [3] 2-8-11 C Rutter(3) 66/1: 0000000: Al last: little form: see 1039.   20
5 ran   2½,3,3,¾   (C Shiacolas)   P Cole Whatcombe, Oxon

2836 WATERHALL SELLING HANDICAP 0-25   £1023   1m   Firm No Time Taken   [18]

2102 TEEJAY [6] (P Bevan) 7-8-6 G Bardwell(7) 25/1: 0300001: 7 b g Jimmy Reppin - Billingsgate
(High Perch) Led inside final 1f, ridden out in a selling h'cap at Brighton (no bid): off the
trk last season: in '83 won at Nottingham: eff over 1m, may stay 10f: best on fast ground.   04
2697 TREMENDOUS JET [14] (M Madgwick) 3-9-2 R Guest 7/2: 0100022: Led 1f out: another
gd run: see 2697.   15
2621 HEATHGRIFF [15] (N Callaghan) 4-8-12 G Starkey 13/2: 0002303: Led over 1f out: see 2014   02
2762 LONG BAY [9] (H Collingridge) 4-9-8 M Rimmer 12/1: -000004: Lightly raced: see 611.   10
2697 UP TOWN BOY [8] 4-9-0 N Adams 10/1: 3-04000: See 2429, 2271.   00
2490 CYGNE [13] 4-8-9 J Williams 16/1: 0003400: See 2282, 1990.   00
2601 NELSONS LADY [11] 5-9-3 I Salmon 8/1: -004000: Fin 7th: best 1990 (7f)   00
2697 SPARKFORD LAD [4] 4-9-2(bl) Debbie Wheatley(7) 10/1: 0021300: Fin 8th: best 2271.   00
2616 BEE KAY ESS [17] 3-8-8 A Dicks(7) 7/1: -40020: Much btr 2616 (C/D)   00
2309 Composer [16] 8-4(bl)   2621 Spring Pursuit [7] 9-7
2490 Catman [10] 9-2   2581 Windy Hollow [12] 9-1   2582 Sky Mariner [2] 8-9(bl)
2619 Linton Starchy [5] 8-6(BL)   2370 Steel Pass [3] 8-8
2655 Toms Nap Hand [1] 8-9 U
17 ran   3,2,1,1½,nk,1½,nk   (D Waldron)   P Bevan Kingstone, Staffs.

2837 ERIC SIMMS MEMORIAL HANDICAP 0-50   £2977   1m   Firm No Time Taken   [36]

2617 MARSH HARRIER [5] (A Moore) 5-9-4 P Cook 5/2 FAV: 0413021: 5 b g Raise A Cup - Belle
de Jour (Speak John) Consistent h'capper: well bckd when a 2½l winner of quite a val h'cap at
Brighton: in fine form this season, earlier winning at Folkestone and also running well in
stks company: in '85 won h'caps at Folkestone and Lingfield and a Ladies race at Brighton:
eff at 1m, stays 12f: acts on gd and firm grd and loves a sharp, undulating trk.   37
2617 FOOT PATROL [3] (P Cundell) 5-8-10 C Rutter(3) 7/2: 0210432: Loves Brighton: see 2617,1967 25
2155 FANCY PAN [6] (W Hastings Bass) 3-9-5 G Starkey 13/2: 0304103: Fair eff: see 1999.   38
2581 FULL OF LIFE [10] (M Pipe) 3-9-3 S Whitworth 14/1: 0022004: Mkt drifter: see 1579.   35
*2581 SPARKLER SPIRIT [4] 5-7-10(5ex)(2oh) N Adams 9/1: -024010: Btr 2581.   00
2255 FORFLITE [1] 3-9-2 G Baxter 8/1: -3100: Twice below 1705.   25
2655 Fei Loong [11] 9-3(VIS)   2674 Joyful Dancer [8] 9-7
1744 Salloom [9] 9-0   2601 Lucky Starkist [2] 8-7
2189 Hautboy Lady [7] 7-12
11 ran   2½,1,¾,8,¾   (F L Hill)   A Moore Woodingdean, Sussex

2838 E B F KEMP TOWN STAKES 2YO   £2314   7f   Firm No Time Taken

2695 REBEL RAISER [2] (M Ryan) 2-8-11 P Robinson 7/4 FAV: 0301: 2 ch c Raise A Native - Lady
Oakley (Gulf Pearl) Cmftble winner of a 2yo stks at Brighton: last time out a fine 6th to
Forest Flower in Gr 2 Mill Reef Stks at Newbury: cost $275,000 as a yearling: stays 7f: acts
on any trk, goes well on fast grd and should win more races.   57
*2541 NOBLE BID [6] (J Dunlop) 2-9-2 B Rouse 10/3: 4012: 6l clear 3rd: in fine form: see 2541. 55
2645 BEST O BUNCH [3] (L Piggott) 2-8-11 W R Swinburn 9/4: 023: Btr 2645.   38
--   BETTY JANE [5] (J Dunlop) 2-8-8 P Cook 14/1: 4: Mkt drifter on debut: may improve:
cheaply acquired, will be suited by 1m+.   29
2577 SUNBRIDGE [7] 2-8-8 C Mcnamee 10/1: 000: Btr in 2577.   27
1320 SPRING FORWARD [1] 2-8-11 M Roberts 50/1: 040: Long abs: lightly raced.   15
2645 SAUCE OF THE SEA [4] 2-8-11 N Day 50/1: 00: Mkt drifter: fin last.   00
7 ran   2½,6,2½,6,7   (T P Ramsden)   M Ryan Newmarket

2839 TELSCOMBE HANDICAP (0-35)   £2872   1½m
Abandoned due to Sea Mist

2840 STEINE STAKES 3 yos   £959   1m 2f
Abandoned due to Sea Mist

830

Official Going Given As GOOD/FIRM

2841 BOSCAWEN SELLING STAKES 2YO   £2637   1m   Firm 13 -38 Slow

2341 OBIDOS [14] (J Hindley) 2-8-11 M Hills 10/1: 01: 2 b c Tap On Wood - Bru Ri (Sir
Gaylord) Dropped in class and made virtually ev yard, cmftbly, in a 2yo seller at Newmarket
(bought in 11,200 gns): stays 1m really well and should be suited by middle dist next season:
acts on fast ground and on a stiff trk: suited by forcing tactics: looks btr than selling class   32
2748 RUWI VALLEY [2] (P Haslam) 2-8-8 T Williams 10/1: 002: Easy to back: kept on well
to take the minor honours: sure to win a seller: stays 1m: acts on gd and firm: see 2254.   20
2680 TIKLAS [3] (F Durr) 2-8-8 W Newnes 5/1 FAV: 0434343: Trouble in running, fin well:
will be suited by middle dist next season: best in 2498.   19
2512 BOLD DIFFERENCE [7] (W Wharton) 2-8-13 C Dwyer 10/1: 2120004: Ev ch: consistent:see 1566 23
2703 WOODBERRY [6] 2-8-8 S Whitworth 10/1: 000: Kept on well: btr eff: stays 1m: acts on
firm ground and on a gall track: see 2433.   18
2723 AGAINST ALL ODDS [10] 2-8-11 K Darley 9/1: 000: No extra dist: quite well bckd in
this lower grade and would not have to improve much to win a seller: acts on fast ground.   21
2711 PENNY FORUM [13] 2-8-11 R Hills 10/1: 00: Fdd into 7th: half brother to 6/7f winner
Kayus: acts on fast grd: should do btr in time.   00
2159 KINGSWOOD RESOPAL [12] 2-8-11(BL) A Mcglone 10/1: 000000: Bl first time: fin 8th:
best in 1239 (7f)   00
2405 TIPTREE [9] 2-8-11 G Starkey 6/1: 00000: Fin 9th: btr over 7f in 2405.   00
2580 PASS THE CATCHUP [11] 2-8-9(1ow) S Cauthen 10/1: 00: Fin down the field: see 2580.   00
2646 Rocky Horror [1] 8-11   2518 San Juan Song [4] 8-11
2225 Squiggle [8] 8-11   2625 Ive No Idea [5] 8-8
14 ran   3,nk,hd,hd,nk,½   (Mrs H F Demetriou)   J Hindley Newmarket

2842 STALKER H'CAP STAKES (0-60) 3YO   £5298   6f   Firm 13 +11 Fast   [64]

1571 CASBAH GIRL [12] (R Smyly) 3-7-7 G Carter 14/1: 2-01101: 3 b f Native Bazaar -
Avengeress (Agressor) Returned to winning form despite a long break, produced a strong late
burst to lead cl home in a fast run and val 3yo h'cap at Newmarket: earlier won successive
h'caps at Doncaster & Nottingham: very eff over 6/7f: suited by fast grd and a gall trk:
seems fully recovered from her setback and can win again.   40
+2614 EASY LINE [7] (P Haslam) 3-8-1(7ex) T Williams 9/1 FAV: 0143112: Well bckd to complete
his hat-trick: led under press inside dist, caught near fin: remains in grand form: see 2614.   44
2573 MERDON MELODY [2] (R Sheather) 3-8-9(bl) A Shoults(5) 14/1: 2004103: Al prom: in
gd form: see 2378.   50
2526 TUFUH [17] (A Stewart) 3-9-0 M Roberts 33/1: 0-02004: Made most: gd eff: see 567.   51
2772 POSSEDYNO [10] 3-9-7 S Cauthen 11/1: 1100200: Fair eff under top weight: see 1654.   56
1028 ILLUMINEUX [3] 3-9-0 Pat Eddery 10/1: 1-0000: Nearest fin: gd eff after a long abs
and he can be expected to improve on this next time: won here last year: see 586.   49
-2650 ZULU KNIGHT [13] 3-8-1(2ow) Paul Eddery 9/1: 0021220: No extra dist: fin 7th: see 2650, 218600
2573 CRONKS QUALITY [6] 3-7-12 W Carson 11/2: 0003030: Wknd into 8th: see 2258, 884   00
2758 Young Puggy [11] 7-8   2670 Fluttery [8] 8-11   947 Loft Boy [15] 7-13
2573 Riviera Scene [4] 8-2   2772 Touch Of Grey [1] 9-3   2655 Green Dollar [14] 8-9
2731 Crete Cargo [9] 8-8(vis)   2715 Our Tilly [5] 7-11
16 ran   1½,½,1½,½,shthd,½,shthd   (Henry B Hughes)   R Smyly Lambourn, Berks

2843 NURSERY HANDICAP 2YO   £6118   5f   Firm 13 +09 Fast   [66]

2694 CLARENTIA [16] (M Usher) 2-7-10 C Rutter(3) 12/1: 0320021: 2 ch f Ballad Rock -
Laharden (Mount Hagen) Led after ½ way and ran on strongly to win a fast run and val nursery
h'cap at Newmarket: earlier won a fillies mdn at Kempton: speedy filly who is very eff over
this minimum trip: likes gd or faster ground tho' seems to have no trk preferences.   46
*2689 CHILIBANG [8] (J Dunlop) 2-8-1(7ex) W Carson 4/1: 410112: Heavily bckd: had ev ch
and kept on gamely: in tremendous form and may win again soon: see 2689.   46
2514 VIVALDI [14] (W Jarvis) 2-8-6 M Hills 25/1: 0103: Al prom and kept on well: gd eff:
acts on fast and yldg ground: see 2301.   47
2689 SANDALL PARK [5] (M W Easterby) 2-7-8(1ow)(1oh) G Carter 9/4 FAV: 41404: Heavily bckd:
ev ch: see 2689, 771.   32
2694 MOON INDIGO [1] 2-8-4(bl) G Baxter 25/1: 0100000: Led to ½ way: running well: see 1381   41
2223 NUTWOOD LIL [13] 2-9-7 J Reid 20/1: 1120300: Nearest fin: fine eff under top weight.   58
2634 NAIVE CHARM [10] 2-8-12 Pat Eddery 9/1: 120100: Not btn that far in 7th: see 2482.   00
-2753 SHEER ROYALTY [6] 2-7-12(bl) M L Thomas 10/1: 0410020: Fin 9th: see 2753 & 2153.   00
*1550 MAZILIER [2] 2-9-5 G Starkey 10/1: 2010: Early speed: needed race: abs since 1550.   00
2753 FICKLE YOUNG MAN [3] 2-7-10(bl) A Mackay 10/1: 1301040: Early speed, fin in rear:
much better in 2753 (6f).   00
*2425 Silvers Era [12] 7-7(9oh)   2447 Baltic Shore [9] 9-4
2661 Echoing [15] 8-10   1683 Good Game [7] 7-13 2729 Oriole Dancer [4] 7-8(1ow)(11oh)
15 ran   1½,1½,1,nk,shthd,nk,nk,shthd   (Mrs Nicolas Kairis)   M Usher Lambourn, Berks.

2844 GROUP 3 JOCKEY CLUB CUP 3YO+   £18884   2m   Firm 13 -06 Slow

*2203 VALUABLE WITNESS [4] (J Tree) 6-9-5 Pat Eddery 4/5 FAV: 111-111: 6 b g Val D L'Orne -
Friendly Witness (Northern Dancer) Very smart stayer: heavily bckd despite the unsuitably fast

grd and led dist, pushed out for a narrow win in Gr 3 Jockey Club Cup at Newmarket: earlier won
Lonsdale (Listed) Stks at York and first time out Gr 3 Sagaro Stakes at Ascot: also unbtn last season,
winning at Sandown, Haydock, Royal Ascot and Gr 2 Goodwood Cup: eff over 14f, stays extreme
dist well: seldom risked on fast grd nowadays and is at his best with give underfoot: well
suited by a gall trk: tremendously consistent and is a credit to his trainer.   **78**
2502 PHARDANTE [3] (G Harwood) 4-9-7 G Starkey 11/4: 0133402: Ran right up to his best:
led 2f out and only failed by the minimum margin: stays 2m well: see 1217.   **78**
2203 SPICY STORY [1] (I Balding) 5-9-3 S Cauthen 6/1: 3032043: Made most: wknd 2f out:
best in 1127.   **62**
1888 TALE QUALE [2] (H Candy) 4-9-3 W Newnes 7/1: -040044: Abs: below-par this term: see 585 **58**
4 ran   shthd,12,3   (S S Niarchos)   J Tree Beckhampton, Wilts.

2845 CHOKE JADE STAKES 3YO+   £6243   1m 4f Firm 13 -13 Slow

494 VERD ANTIQUE [5] (H Cecil) 3-8-11 W Ryan 11/2: -121: 3 b c Shirley Heights - Vejana
(Braccia Da Montone) Smart colt: despite a long abs was a most impr winner, led over 2f out
and was sn clear for an easy win in a val stks race at Newmarket: one-time Derby-hope who won a
val Listed race over 10f here on his debut and subs narrowly btn by the smart Nisnas: very eff
over 12f: acts on gd and fast grd and is well suited by a gall trk: highly regarded and
should win a Group race.   **80**
2693 KHOZDAR [3] (W Hern) 4-8-11 W Carson 2/1 FAV: 20-3032: Heavily bckd: no chance with
winner but put up another gd eff: should be back in the winner's ensloure soon: see 653.   **61**
2642 CHAUMIERE [7] (R Williams) 5-9-5(vis) T Ives 16/1: 0103303: Ran on well: fine eff: see 1526 **68**
2257 ROBBAMA [2] (J Dunlop) 3-8-5(BL)(2ow) Pat Eddery 12/1: 0-43204: Bl first time: no extra
dist: see 1988.   **59**
1913 BELDALE STAR [6] 3-8-11 G Starkey 3/1: 0-10000: Well bckd: led over 3f out: abs 1913.   **62**
2553 NORFOLK SONATA [4] 3-8-3 P Cook 33/1: 0000300: Outsider and no danger: best in 2206   **43**
2064 QUEENS SOLDIER [1] 3-8-9 S Cauthen 5/1: 1-11200: Stable mate of winner: reportedly
had been working well at home but dropped out quickly after making most of the running: see 1343   **00**
7 ran   5,½,1½,1½,7   (Sheikh Mohammed)   H Cecil Newmarket

2846 EBF ALINGTON MAIDEN FILLIES STKS 2YO   £4981   6f   Firm 13 -22 Slow

2675 GOLD FEE [11] (L Cumani) 2-8-11 G Starkey 6/4 FAV: 31: 2 b f Glint of Gold - Green
Fee (Green Dancer) Very useful filly: heavily bckd and duly fulfilled the promise of her debut,
led below dist for an easy win in a 2yo fillies mdn at Newmarket: tenderly-ridden when placed
behind Milligram at Newbury last month: well bred and cost 2m Francs a yearling: eff over
6/7f and bred to be suited by middle dist next term: acts on gd and fast grd and on a gall trk:
should rate more highly and go on to better things.   **64**
2651 TARSA [1] (M Albina) 2-8-11 Pat Eddery 13/2: 02: Tried to make all: caught a tartar
and should go one btr soon: see 2651.   **54**
--   PICNICING [17] (H Cecil) 2-8-11 S Cauthen 5/1: 3: Well bckd debutant: could not quicken
inside dist tho' certain to improve for this experience: half sister to numerous winners,
including the smart juv Precocious and Krayyan and highclass middle dist stayer Jupiter Island:
acts on fast grd: sure to win a race.   **48**
--   ICE CHOCOLATE [13] (W Jarvis) 2-8-11 W Newnes 50/1: 4: Ignored in the mkt but showed
plenty of promise here: cost 10,000 gns as a yearling: sure to improve, especially over longer
trips: acts on fast ground.   **47**
--   NURYANA [14] 2-8-11 P Robinson 11/2: 0: Nicely bckd on debut: al prom and showed plenty
of promise for the future: half sister to 7f winner Digger's Rest: acts on fast grd: one
to keep an eye on.   **46**
2328 WATERED SILK [21] 2-8-11 C Rutter 50/1: 030: With leaders over ½ way: see 2328.   **32**
--   VALENTINE SONG [19] 2-8-11 A Mackay 50/1: 0: Fin 7th on debut: prom most of way and
should do btr next time: cost 32,000 gns and is a half sister to sev winners: acts on firm grd.   **30**
--   CAVENDISH QUEEN [20] 2-8-11 T Ives 50/1: 0: Mkt drifter on debut: showed gd speed
over ½ way before fading into 8th: half sister to winning sprinter Latch String and should be
btr for this experience: acts on firm grd and on a gall track.   **29**
2696 SHAFT OF SUNLIGHT [2] 2-8-11 Paul Eddery 25/1: 00: No extra dist: fin 9th: see 2696.   **25**
--   KASHAPOUR [18] 2-8-11 P Hamblett 50/1: 0: Unfancied debutant from the Cumani-stable
and altho' never dangerous kept on encouragingly and should do better next time.   **24**
--   SWEPT AWAY [8] 2-8-11 W Carson 7/1: 0: Nicely bckd on debut: lost her place after
½ way but should be all the btr for this experience: half sister to sev winners, including
useful miler Seven Bore.   **19**
--   Courtwood [7] 8-11   -- Dianes Best [5] 8-11   1903 Just A Picnic [3] 8-11
--   Just Mine [16] 8-11   -- Lake Tana [12] 8-11   2436 Lullaby Baby [22] 8-11
--   Penelope Strawberry [6] 8-11   -- Pour Litalle [4] 8-11
--   Sirius River [10] 8-11   -- Tabellina [15] 8-11
21 ran   2,2,hd,hd,4,1,hd,1½,shthd,nk   (Antonio Balzarini)   L Cumani, Newmarket

Official Going Given As GOOD/FIRM

2847 WESTLEY MAIDEN STAKES DIV I 2YO   £5208   7f   Firm 18 -15 Slow

2418 POLLENATE [26] (J Tree) 2-9-0 Pat Eddery 5/1: 01: 2 b c High Line - Fine Honey (Drone) Useful colt in the making: al prom and led below dist, ridden out in a 2yo mdn at Newmarket: well bred sort who is clearly well suited by 7f and should stay middle dist next term: acts on gd and fast ground and on any trk: should continue to improve.   60

-- TIQUEGREAN [27] (J Dunlop) 2-8-11 R Fox 50/1: 2: Ignored in the mkt on her debut but was al cl.up and kept on promisingly: closely related to sev winners, incl highclass stayer Harly: sure to be suited by middle dist in time: acts on fast grd and on a stiff trk.   52

-- MAGICAL LACE [23] (M Albina) 2-8-11 B Thomson 20/11: 3: Fin best of all, showing plenty of promise for the future: fetched 36,000 gns as a yearling and is a half sister to 7f winner Bobby Dazzler: will be suited by 1m+: acts on fast grd and on a stiff trk: sure to improve.   49

2561 IRISH SAILOR [22] (Pat Mitchell) 2-9-0 R Wernham 33/1: 304: Mkt drifter: al prom and seemed well suited by this extra furlong: acts on gd and fast grd and on any trk: see 2205   50

2522 PITCHFORK [18] 2-9-0 Paul Eddery 9/1: 00: Well bckd: al front rank: see 2522.   47

-- SIR JAMESTOWN [20] 2-9-0 N Connorton 12/1: 0: Backed from 33/1 on his debut: picked up ground from below dist and sure to improve: half brother to 6/7f winner Firm Landing: should stay at least 1m: acts on fast ground.   44

-- BRONZE BUCK [25] 2-9-0 B Rouse 33/1: 0: Easy to back: prom most, fdd into 7th: first foal who cost 60,000 gns as a yearling: acts on fast grd: btr for race.   43

-- STAFILIO [15] 2-9-0 R Cochrane 10/1: 0: Active in mkt on debut: never nearer 8th and should leave this running behind next time: half brother to useful 6f juv Miscrown: acts on fast grd: one to keep an eye on.   40

-- PICK OF THE PACK [19] 2-9-0 R Hills 33/1: 0: No real threat in 9th: quite speedily bred gelding who is a brother to 7f winner Highly Recommended: acts on fast grd: open to impr.   00

-- OXYMERON [2] 2-9-0 S Cauthen 7/1: 0: Btr fancied of Cecil's 2 runners but fdd qckly after showing gd speed over ½ way: should do btr than this.   00

-- SILHOUETTE DANCER [8] 2-9-0 J Reid 7/2 FAV: 0: Heavily bckd debutant: broke well and led far side over ½ way but ran green in the later stages and fin well btn: American bred colt who is certain to improve for this experience: acts on fast ground.   00

-- Rushluan [4] 9-0	2675 Mayroni [17] 8-11	2468 Cabot [13] 9-0
1464 Ci Siamo [21] 8-11	-- Arquati Redwood [1] 9-0	
-- Manly Boy [3] 9-0	-- Riot Squad [9] 9-0	2019 Riverboat Party [6] 9-0
-- Running Steps [24] 9-0		2270 Sulvez Moi [5] 9-0
-- Talus [16] 9-0	-- Trapper [14] 9-0	-- Wing Park [10] 9-0
-- Panienka [11] 8-11	-- Penny Practice [12] 8-11	
-- Piffle [7] 8-11		

27 ran   2,1½,½,½,1,shthd,nk,1½   (K Abdulla)   J Tree Beckhampton, Wilts.

2848 UNIDARE HANDICAP 3YO 0-60   £5322   1m 2f Firm 18 +15 Fast   [56]

2567 MYTENS [4] (J Tree) 3-9-5 Pat Eddery 6/1: 3-11041: 3 b c Spectacular Bid - Photographic (Hoist the Flag) Useful colt: easy to back but led over 2f out and was sn clear in a fast run and val 3yo h'cap at Newmarket: first time out winner of a Sandown mdn and then trotted up in a minor event at Lingfield: very eff over 10f on fast grd: seems best on a stiff trk tho' does act on a sharp one: should win again in this mood.   60

2749 ASIAN CUP [7] (G Harwood) 3-9-7 G Starkey 4/1: 2-10242: Plugged on well over this longer trip: in gd form and should win again soon: stays 10f: see 528.   54

2489 BASTINADO [10] (I Balding) 3-8-6 T Ives 14/1: 301003: Well clear rem: gd eff: see 1062   38

*2763 NAJIDIYA [1] (R F Johnson Houghton) 3-9-3(5ex) P Cook 5/1: 0202114: Not qckn: much btr 2763.33

2624 MARSHAL MACDONALD [11] 3-8-6 W Newnes 14/1: 0440300: No real threat: best 2404.   18

*2720 PRINCE ORAC [2] 3-9-7(5ex) S Cauthen 11/1: 3021010: Led almost 1m: much btr 2720.   32

*2706 BILLET [9] 3-7-13(5ex) T Williams 5/2 FAV: 0-0010: Heavily bckd to follow up his recent win: no extra below dist and fin well btn: see 2706.   00

| 2720 Cigar [6] 8-4 | 2426 Icaro [3] 7-10(bl) | 850 Autumn Flutter [5] 8-9 |

10 ran   2½,hd,10,2,nk   (K Abdulla)   J Tree Beckhampton, Wilts.

2849 SOMERVILLE TATTERSHALL STKS LISTED   £10098   7f   Firm 18 -01 Slow

2626 IMPERIAL FRONTIER [6] (L Cumani) 2-8-8 G Starkey 15/8 FAV: 21: 2 ch c Lyphard - Hartebeest (Vaguely Noble) Very promising colt: again heavily bckd and was sn in command, qckn clear at dist to win a val Listed race at Newmarket: lost his chance with a slow start when btn by Hydraulic Power in a Yarmouth mdn last month: cost $300,000 as a yearling and is very well regarded: sure to be suited by 1m+: acts on fast grd and on a gall trk: certain to win again.   65

*1903 ARABIAN SHEIK [8] (J Dunlop) 2-8-11 T Ives 2/1: 12: Heavily bckd: fin in gd style and was pegging back the winner at the death: still learning and is certain to impr further and win more races: see 1903.   65

*1791 NAHEEZ [5] (D Elsworth) 2-9-2 W R Swinburn 14/1: 13: Easy to back after a fair abs: ran a gd race to fin 4th but hmpd inside dist and placed 3rd: stays 7f: see 1791.   65

2598 ORNE [2] 2-8-11(BL) Pat Eddery 15/2:12433D: Bl first time: al cl.up, fin 3rd but subsequently demoted to 4th: yet to run a bad race and should win again when dropped slightly in class: see 2146 & 1239.   60

-2444 HENDEKA [7] 2-9-2(BL) S Cauthen 7/2: 31120: Bl first time: no extra 2f out and ran almost a stone below the form shown in 2444: see 2263.   55

2384 LACK A STYLE [3] 2-9-2 R Cochrane 33/1: 2332100: Mkt drifter: twice below form shown 225151
2146 ALBASAR [4] 2-8-11 Paul Eddery 50/1: 1000: Early leader: has proved disapp since
his debut-success here in 777 (6f)   00
7 ran   1½,1½,shthd,6,2   (Sheikh Mohammed)   L Cumani Newmarket

2850 TOLLY COBBOLD HANDICAP 0-60 3YO+   £5688   1m 4f   Firm 18 +21 Fast   [59]

-2486 ISLAND SET [7] (L Cumani) 4-9-3 R Cochrane 10/3 FAV: 0221021: 4 b c Hawaii - Desk Set
(Tom Rolfe) Useful colt: well bckd and returned to winning form, led dist and stayed on well
to win a fast run and val h'cap at Newmarket: most consistent this season, earlier won a
similar race at Goodwood: won his final two starts at Goodwood & Yarmouth last season: very
eff over 10/12f on gd and firm grd: acts on any trk.   60
2486 VERARDI [5] (W Hastings Bass) 3-8-5 T Ives 11/1: -301142: Didnot have the best of
runs, fin strongly and looked a trifle unlucky: nicely h'capped at present and can gain
consolation soon: see 1977.   55
2692 TENDER TYPE [15] (M Tompkins) 3-7-11 A Mackay 12/1: 1213403: Ev ch: gd eff: see 2156.   42
2551 TEBITTO [2] (N Vigors) 3-7-9 S Dawson 10/1: 1012024: Made most: in fine form: see 1733   36
2693 BEN ADHEM [10] 4-8-4 W Newnes 12/1: 14-1200: No extra dist but another gd eff: see 2330. 36
2536 WILD HOPE [12] 5-7-13 G Carter 12/1: 0042100: Stayed on: best over 10f in 2477.   29
2551 SIR PERCY [9] 3-8-6(BL) J Reid 10/1: 1003000: Bl first time: fin 7th: btr 1600: see 253   00
+2666 MYTH [11] 3-8-10(5ex) S Cauthen 10/1: 2113010: No extra 2f out: fin in rear: much btr 2666 00
1159 Peggy Carolyn [1] 8-1   2704 Saryan [14] 8-0   2642 Lundylux [6] 9-7
--   Thorny Rose [4] 8-6   2188 Jazair [13] 7-10   *1393 Ebolito [3] 7-9
2480 General Concorde [8] 7-8
15 ran   1,1½,2,½,1½   (Peregrine Moncrieffe)   L Cumani Newmarket

2851 PETITION STAKES 3YO   £5362   1m   Firm 18 -18 Slow

1466 EMBLA [1] (L Cumani) 3-8-5 R Cochrane 8/11 FAV: 1-40201: 3 b f Dominion - Kaftan
(Kashmir II) Smart filly: heavily bckd despite a long break and qcknd to lead cl home for a
narrow win in a val 3yo stks at Newmarket: highclass juv, winning at Kempton & Ripon and on
her final outing, Gr 1 Cheveley Park Stks on this trk: half sister to the very useful 3yo
Tantino: very eff over 7/8f: suited by fast grd and a stiff trk.   64
2475 SANTELLA MAC [4] (G Harwood) 3-9-0 G Starkey 9/2: 1-10002: Led dist, hdd near fin:
fine eff against this smart filly and should win again soon: see 1912 & 847.   70
2674 RESOURCEFUL FALCON [3] (P Makin) 3-8-8 T Quinn 9/2: 2200003: Led briefly below dist.   58
2674 SIT THIS ONE OUT [7] (D Laing) 3-8-8 B Thomson 11/1: 0000004: Made most: best 802.   48
2713 JAZETAS [5] 3-8-13 S Cauthen 20/1: 0404020: No danger: see 2713 & 127.   48
2196 SALLY SAYS SO [2] 3-8-5(VIS) Paul Eddery 33/1: 0-40200: Visored first time: al last: see 803. 36
6 ran   nk,2½,5,3,2   (Sheikh Mohammed)   L Cumani Newmarket

2852 WESTLEY MAIDEN STAKES DIV II 2YO   £5156   7f   Firm 18 -16 Slow

--   TWEETER [11] (G Harwood) 2-9-0 G Starkey 6/1: 1: 2 b c Northern Baby - Kilmona (Bold
Bidder) Promising colt: made a successful debut, burst thro' to lead cl home in a 2yo mdn at
Newmarket: fetched 3,200,000 francs as a yearling and is bred to be well suited by middle dist:
acts on fast grd and on a stiff trk: sure to improve and win more races.   60
--   BASHAYER [16] (M Stoute) 2-9-0 W R Swinburn 3/1: 2: Well bckd debutant: led 2f out,
just denied: cost 560,000 gns as a yearling: clearly very eff over 7f and should stay at
least 1m: acts on fast grd and on a gall trk: sure to find a race.   58
--   BRACORINA [17] (J Dunlop) 2-8-11 R Fox 33/1: 3: Ran on promisingly: not btn far on
her debut and certain to win a race: will be suited by 1m+: acts on fast ground.   55
--   INDIAN SKIMMER [3] (H Cecil) 2-8-11 S Cauthen 6/1: 4: Al front rank on debut: kept
on well and not btn far: 350,000 gns yearling who is a half sister to a winner in the States:
sure to stay further than 7f: acts on a sound surface.   53
--   PILLAR OF WISDOM [12] 2-9-0 Pat Eddery 5/2 FAV: 0: Much touted debutant: picked up
gd ground from below dist and should recoup losses in the near future: cost $325,000 and is
a half brother to sev winners: sure to stay 1m: acts on firm ground.   50
--   FLORAL CHARMS [2] 2-8-11 M Roberts 50/1: 0: Never nearer: ignored in mkt today but
this was a fair first effort: first foal who fetched $110,000 as yearling: bred to stay at
least 1m: acts on firm.   44
--   ARDASHIR [4] 2-9-0 J Reid 33/1: 0: Front rank most of way: fin 7th: acts on fast ground:
should be all the btr for this run.   41
--   TRAPEZE DANCER [20] 2-9-0 T Ives 8/1: 0: Quickly into his stride and made most:
hmpd below dist and should improve on this next time: cost $1,500,000 and is closely related
to sev winners: will be suited by middle dist next term: acts on fast ground.   41
--   KNOCKANDO [10] 2-9-0 R Cochrane 11/1: 0: Backed from 25/1: never reached leaders tho'
clearly held in some regard and should improve on this next time: half brother to sev winners:
will be suited by further.   40
--   Big Red [6] 9-0   --   Boy Jamie [15] 9-0   2646 Fashionably Forbes [21] 9-0
2673 Flutter Money [13] 9-0   --   Glass Castle [5] 9-0
--   Kirpan [8] 9-0   685 Mark Angelo [9] 9-0   --   Mighty Glow [1] 9-0
2646 Prince Newport [14] 9-0   --   Rathdrum [19] 9-0
--   Dapping [7] 8-11   --   Traniski [18] 8-11
21 ran   ½,shthd,½,3,1½,nk,shthd,nk   (J Garcia-Roady)   G Harwood Pulborough, Sussex

Official Going Given As Firm

2853 KNUTSFORD MAIDEN FILLIES STAKES 3YO   £2512   1m2.5f Firm 14 -17 Slow

2430 NOBLE FILLE [9] (J Dunlop) 3-8-11 G Duffield 10/1: -004401: 3 b f Known Fact - Altesse
Royale (Saint Crespin III) Gained her first success when leading inside final 1f in a 3yo
fillies mdn at Haydock: beautifully bred filly who is a half sister to sev winners and whose
dam was a topclass performer who won the 1,000 Guineas and both English & Irish Oaks: stays
10f well, acts on firm ground.   40
1600 RARE LEGEND [2] (M Ryan) 3-8-11 N Day 16/1: 0-002: Kept on well under press: gd
eff after long abs and is clearly on the upgrade: eff 10f, should stay 12f: seems suited
by fast ground: can win a mdn soon.   36
1788 DAVEMMA [1] (P Kelleway) 3-8-11 S Whitworth 7/1: 4000403: Abs, led 3f out: eff over
10/12f: see 509.   36
2593 NINOTCHKA [8] (W Hern) 3-8-11 W Carson 13/8 FAV: 4-24: Well bckd: chall 3f out, no
extra: ran better 2593 (9f).   30
2327 INDIAN LOVE SONG [15] 3-8-11 S Perks 10/1: 0430230: No extra final stages: see 2129.   29
2393 MRS MAINWARING [10] 3-8-11 C Rutter(3) 14/1: 0440000: Ev ch: see 1677.   29
-- SIT ELNAAS [3] 3-8-11 A Murray 10/1: 0-0: Didnot enjoy the best of runs on belated
seasonal debut: in mid-div in a backend Newmarket mdn on only outing last season and appears
to have been slow to come to hand: one to keep an eye on.   25
-- LEI [11] 3-8-11 R Hills 9/1: -0: Racecourse debut, came from off the pace to fin 8th
and will be all the btr for the experience: dam a smart filly on her day around 1m.   24
2532 NEEDLE SHARP [13] 3-8-11 K Darley 10/1: -3000: Prom, wknd: disapp since 1880 (1m gd).   00
2546 LOREEF [5] 3-8-11(BL) A Clark 10/1: -044000: No danger: mainly disapp since 1002.   00
2653 Maries Valentine [6] 8-11   2653 Papun [14] 8-11
2747 Worth Debating [4] 8-11   -- Little Token [12] 8-11
14 ran   1½,hd,3,½,hd,½,1½   (F Hue Williams)   J Dunlop Arundel, Sussex

2854 ALTRINCHAM SELLING STAKES 3YO   £1530   6f   Firm 14 -18 Slow

2688 WEBSTERS FEAST [11] (M Mccormack) 3-9-2 W Wharton 9/1: 0430001: 3 gr c Dragonara Palace
- Feast-Rite (Reform) Dsptd lead thr'out, hanging on in a cl fin to a 3yo seller at Haydock
(no bid): first success of the season tho' in '85 won at Salisbury and Pontefract: eff over
5/6f with forcing tactics on firm ground.   18
*2743 JACQUI JOY [8] (K Ivory) 3-8-13 G Bardwell(7) 13/2: 0000212: Dsptd lead from dist,
narrowly btn and is in gd form: stays 6f: see 2743.   13
2602 SPANISH INFANTA [16] (P Feigate) 3-8-8 J Williams 25/1: 0-00003: Kept on well, narrowly
btn and seems best in sellers: see 2139.   08
2601 LYDIA LANGUISH [17] (R Hannon) 3-8-13 A Murray 9/2: 0020004: Ev ch: twice well below 1991.05
2495 AUSTINA [1] 3-8-8(bl) D J Williams(7) 20/1: -000000: Ev ch: see 2286.   00
2424 COOPER RACING NAIL [7] 3-8-13 J Carroll(7) 10/3 FAV: 3011140: Dsptd lead much: see 2268 00
2602 LOW FLYER [5] 3-9-2(vis) K Hodgson 8/1: 0243000: Best 545 (yldg).   00
2099 CAREER MADNESS [13] 3-8-11 N Day 6/1: -00000: No improvement since 1691.   00
*2585 MOLLY PARTRIDGE [5] 3-8-13 A Proud 10/1: 0300410: Much btr 2585 (7f)   00
2702 Cracon Girl [15] 8-8   2775 Le Mans [9] 8-11   2743 Gutsy [12] 8-8
1824 Shy Mistress [2] 8-8   2743 Ken Siddall [4] 8-11
14 ran   ½,hd,3,½,3   (L Oxenham)   M Mccormack Sparsholt, Oxon

2855 OUTLAND HANDICAP (0-60) 3YO+   £4194   1m 4f Firm 14 +15 Fast   [54]

2769 CONVINCED [7] (G Harwood) 4-9-10   A Clark 2/1 JT FAV: 2310331: 4 b c Busted -
AAffirmative (Derring-Do) Useful colt: defied top weight, coming from behind to lead final
stages in a cl fin to a fast run h'cap at Haydock: quite lightly raced this season, earlier
was awarded val Bessborough H'cap at Royal Ascot after being btn a nk: cmftble winner at
Pontefract & Goodwood in '85: very eff over 12f on fast going and runs well on a gall trk.   61
2766 OSRIC [3] (M Ryan) 3-8-4 N Day 8/1: 2D32042: Led dist, hdd near line in a tight fin:
gd eff: see 1578.   47
2686 HIGH TENSION [4] (P Pritchard Gordon) 4-9-4 G Duffield 2/1 JT FAV: 2210123: Waited
with, fin well and only narrowly btn: in fine form: see 2551.   53
2623 HANOOF [2] (M Stoute) 3-8-0 W Carson 15/2: -43104: Didnot have much luck in running,
only narrowly btn and may gain compensation soon: see 1775.   43
2551 REGAL STEEL [1] 8-7-7(3oh) A Culhane(7) 16/1: 2140300: Made most: see 1918.   23
2776 MIN BALADI [4] 4-7-8(vis) J Lowe 8/1: 2002040: Waited with, no extra when asked to qckn   22
2553 ROUBAYD [6] 3-9-0(BL) K Darley 12/1: -11000: Prom, wknd: rather disapp since 2176.   00
7 ran   ½,hd,shthd,2½,½   (J C Thompson)   G Harwood Pulborough, Sussex

2856 NORTH LANCS. MAIDEN STAKES DIV 1) 3YO   £1799   1m 40y Firm 14 -13 Slow

2622 AUCHINATE [7] (G Harwood) 3-9-0 A Clark 10/1: -43031: 3 b c Auction Ring - Elated
(Sparkler) Came from behind to cmftbly lead final 1f in a 3yo mdn at Haydock: quite lightly
raced prev: eff over 1m, may stay further: acts on soft, runs well on fast grd: may improve.   43
2532 MAIYAASAH [3] (L Cumani) 3-8-11 R Guest 8/13 FAV: -22: Heavily bckd to odds-on,
led dist, caught near fin but 3l clear rest and should gain compensation: see 2532.   38
2534 STARMAST [2] (W Hern) 3-9-0(bl) W Carson 10/1: 0300033: Difficult to restrain,
no extra final 2f: see 2534.   34

2442 STICKY GREENE [8] (B Hills) 3-8-11 J Lowe 8/1: 3342044: Proved disapp: see 1628.   26
2653 ALCHAASIBIYEH [5] 3-8-11(bl) A Riding(7) 6/1: 33-0020: Mkt drifter, made much: btr 2653   20
(sharp track); bl first time.
1626 NAOUSSA [1] 3-8-11 G Duffield 14/1: 03-4200: Abs: early leader, wknd: see 423.   19
--   PETE MARSH [6] 3-9-0 R Hills 20/1: -0: Belated debut, sn in trouble: first foal of
a 10f winner.   20
7 ran   ½,3,3,2½,½,½   (J Vanner)   G Harwood Pulborough, Sussex

2857 NORTH LANCS. MAIDEN STAKES (DIV 2) 3YO   £1897   1m 40y Firm 14 +06 Fast

2622 BIEN DORADO [4] (B Hanbury) 3-9-0 A Geran(7) 20/1: 4340001: 3 ch c Silent Screen -
Borine Note (Bon Mot III) Turned up at 20/1, showing impr form when readily leading 2f out
in a 3yo mdn at Haydock: seems best over 7f/1m on firm grd: can win again on this form.   45
2550 SKEAN [2] (G Harwood) 3-8-11 A Clark 5/2 JT FAV: -00222: Waited with: fin well but
all too late: possibly a difficult ride: see 2550.   32
2333 CAPRICORN BEAU [1] (L Cumani) 3-9-0 R Guest 11/2: -04403: Waited with, some hdwy str
but found no extra final stages: see 1954.   35
2532 LIKENESS [6] (W Hern) 3-8-11(bl) W Carson 5/1: 0300344: Continues to disapp: now
wears blinkers: best 1043.   29
2653 ANOTHER PAGEANT [7] 3-8-11 G Duffield 20/1: -00000: Never btr: see 315.   19
2706 CHANCE REMARK [5] 3-9-0 R Hills 12/1: 0-4040: Btr 2706 (10f).   16
733 BOLD ADMIRAL [9] 3-9-0 M A Giles(7) 5/2 JT FAV: -30: Well bckd, led 4f out, wknd:
prob needed race after abs since 733.   00
2497 Roi De Soleil [10] 9-0(bl)   2683 Golflines [8] 9-0(bl)
9 ran   5,shthd,1½,6,3   (Mrs Allen Manning)   B Hanbury Newmarket

2858 BRYN HANDICAP (0-50) 3YO+   £3424   5f   Firm 14 -07 Slow   [42]

-2775 RAMBLING RIVER [11] (W Stephenson) 9-9-3(vis) G Duffield 9/2 FAV: 1000021: 9 b h
Forlorn River - Who-Done-It (Lucero) Gamely led cl home in a h'cap at Haydock: earlier won
similar h'caps at Newcastle: last season won at Edinburgh and Newmarket: equally eff at 5/6f
and acts on any going and on any trk: best form nowadays in visor or bl: grand stable servant
over the years.   40
2816 WARTHILL LADY [12] (M Brittain) 4-8-2 K Darley 9/1: 0101002: Dsptd lead thr'out,
just touched off cl home and is in grand form: see 2632.   24
2586 IBERIAN START [13] (D Barron) 3-9-6(BL) W Carson 7/1: 1032003: Made most: see 1027.   39
2702 GALLANT HOPE [7] (L Cottrell) 4-7-9 N Carlisle 9/1: 0222334: Lacks finishing pace:see 1834 12
*2592 HILMAY [1] 4-7-9(2ow) R Lappin(0) 10/1: 4032010: Al there, not btn far: in gd form : see 2592.10
2469 CELTIC BIRD [8] 6-9-2 N Day 9/1: 2311300: Prom most: see 1896.   30
*2586 CHINA GOLD [4] 7-9-7 M Wood 8/1: 0200010: Ev ch: see 2586.   00
2816 THRONE OF GLORY [10] 5-9-0 D Nicholls 8/1: 0230430: Btr 2816.   00
2702 MRS SAUGA [2] 4-7-13 J Lowe 10/1: 2104400: Early pace: best 1344.   00
2586 LADY CARA [5] 6-8-9 J Carroll(7) 8/1: 2411020: Fin last: much btr 2586.   00
2362 Manton Mark [3] 9-2   2397 Rosie Dickins [9] 7-13
2291 Kharrana [6] 9-7
13 ran   nk,1½,hd,1,nk   (Miss G Richardson)   W Stephenson Bishop Auckland, Co Durham

2859 BUGGINS FARM NURSERY H'CAP 2YO   £4740   6f   Firm 06 +03 Fast   [45]

2729 VICTORY BALLARD [8] (R Hannon) 2-8-6 A Mcglone 3/1 FAV: 0010421: 2 ch c Ballad Rock -
Wyn Mipet (Welsh Saint) In gd form and was al front rank, when a game winner of quite a fast
run nursery h'cap at Haydock: earlier won a mdn auction at Yarmouth: speedily bred colt who
only cost 5,000 gns as a yearling: eff over 5/6f on gd and fast grd: acts on any trk:
best when up with the pace.   32
2792 SAUNDERS LASS [7] (R Holder) 2-8-0 S Dawson 8/1: 0210342: Ran on well under press,
only just held: gd eff: seems to act on any trk: see 1647.   25
*2535 FIRMLY ATTACHED [5] (D Barron) 2-8-8 N Carlisle 8/1: 0200013: Not btn far: in gd
form: see 2535.   31
+2744 LINN ODEE [6] (M W Easterby) 2-8-5(7ex) M Birch 7/2: 1404014: Best over 5f in 2744.   20
2577 PHILGWYN [4] 2-8-11 D J Williams(7) 14/1: 023000: Prom most: btr 1752: see 1433.   18
2577 DOMINO FIRE [9] 2-9-7 J Lowe 9/2: 122040: Never going pace: much btr 1552: see 985.   22
2744 Beckingham Ben [3] 8-3   2563 Thekkian [1] 8-8
2744 Miss Drummond [2] 8-0
9 ran   nk,½,3,3,2½,1½,shthd,1½   (St J G O'Connell)   R Hannon East Everleigh, Wilts.

2860 HAYDOCK DREAM MILE STAKES 2YO   £7390   1m 40y Firm 06 +01 Fast

*2598 SUHAILIE [1] (H Cecil) 2-9-5 W Ryan 4/9 FAV: 111: 2 ch c Nodouble - Slow Hot Wind
(Canonero) Smart, unbtn colt: easily landed the odds in quite a fast run and val 2yo stks at
Haydock, led over 2f out and steadily drew clear: earlier scored easy wins in similar races
at Lingfield & Newmarket: very eff over 7/8f and sure to be suited by middle dist next
season: acts on gd and fast grd and on any trk: very attractive sort with plenty of scope:
looks Classic-material.   78

HAYDOCK   Saturday October 4th   -Cont'd

2542 TERTIARY ZONE [2] (P Cole) 2-8-11 P Waldron 5/2: 322: Not the pace of winner: see 2542.   56
2721 QUESSARD [3] (C Brittain) 2-8-11 S Perks 12/11: 03: Led over ½ way: acts on firm:see 2721   32
3 ran   6,10   (Sheikh Mohammed)   H Cecil, Newmarket

2861 AMATEUR RIDERS FINAL (H'CAP) 3YO+   £3782   1m2.5f Firm 06 -25 Slow   [26]

1763 SAFFAN [11] (M Prescott) 3-9-9 Maxine Juster 7/1: 3212221: 3 b c L'Enjoleur - Dancing
Femme (Gaelic Dancer) Despite a fair abs proved an easy winner, held up and led on bit cl home
in an amateur riders h'cap at Haydock: yet to fin out of the frame this season and earlier won
a 3yo h'cap at Carlisle: very eff around 9/12f: acts on fast & soft grd and on any trk:
consistent sort.   38
*2406 EFFIGY [10] (G Harwood) 4-12-0 Amanda Harwood 6/4 FAV: 1-00012: Well bckd: led over
2f out till near fin: gd eff under a big weight and should win again soon: see 2406.   60
2666 INNISHMORE ISLAND [9] (J Dunlop) 3-11-4 Princess Anne(3) 9/1: 0322143: Kept on
well: see 2582.   55
*1226 DIENAUS TROVE [4] (H Collingridge) 5-9-0 Mr J Ryan 12/11: -3214: Tried to make all:
onepaced below dist but ran a gd race after a long break: see 1226.   12
2467 MALADHU [12] 7-9-13 Mr A Robson(0) 6/1: 240-130: Late prog: see 2324.   22
2572 LIBERATED GIRL [1] 6-7-9 Kate Morris(2) 100/1: -00000: Some late prog: no form: see 2406   00
*1871 TOSCANA [7] 5-9-12 Kelly Marks 7/1: 00-2210: Fdd into 9th: btr over 12f 1871 (gd)   00
*1892 MR COFFEY [2] 3-9-1 Franca Vittadini 10/1: 0002210: Dwelt and al behind: abs since 1892   00
2715 Three Bells [3] 9-4   --   The Lodge Prince [5] 9-9
2017 King Of Gems [8] 8-12(3ow)   2496 Why Tumble [13] 9-4
-- Aesculapius [6] 8-4
13 ran   1½,½,2,1½,4   (Fahd Salman)   M Prescott Newmarket

2862 BUCKLOW HILL HANDICAP (0-70) 3YO+   £7876   6f   Firm 06 +22 Fast   [61]

2715 ROYSIA BOY [5] (G Pritchard Gordon) 6-7-11 Abigail Richards(7) 10/1: 0030001: 6 b g
African Sky - For Keeps (Track Spares) Returned to his best form, made all cmftbly when setting
a new course record in a val h'cap at Haydock: ended last season in gd form, winning at Kempton,
Goodwood, Leicester and Nottingham: very eff over 6/7f with forcing tactics: best form on
fast or gd ground: acts on any trk: can win again.   45
2764 TOBERMORY BOY [4] (R Whitaker) 9-7-10 N Carlisle 10/1: 0000402: Fin well: gd eff: see 130634
2668 YOUNG INCA [8] (L Cottrell) 8-9-0 R Guest 8/1: 0003003: Switched, fin well: see 1777.   46
2715 FAWLEYS GIRL [10] (R Hollinshead) 4-7-7(10oh) A Culhane(7) 25/1: 0004004: Al front
rank, fine effort at the weights and seems to be returning to form: see 2500.   23
2668 NUMISMATIST [6] 7-8-4 C Rutter(3) 9/2: 04-4040: No extra dist: see 1933.   33
*2731 TYROLLIE [3] 4-8-12(5ex) P Cook 7/2 FAV: 0040010: Well bckd: front rank most: best 2731   40
2530 GLEN KELLA MANX [7] 5-7-13(BL) J Williams 8/1: 0100000: Bl first time: btr than this.   00
2446 MANIMSTAR [12] 6-9-7 W Ryan 9/1: 0211000: Fin 8th: best 1933.   00
2573 CANIF [2] 5-8-2 N Day 10/1: 0100100: Fdd into 9th: best 2277.   00
2475 Golden Ancona [9] 7-7(vis)   2668 Lochonica [1] 9-2
2783 Ameghino [13] 8-0   2655 Stock Hill Lass [11] 7-9
13 ran   3,2,½,hd,nk   (P Martin)   G Pritchard Gordon Newmarket

2863 SALE SELLING STAKES   £1440   1m 40y Firm 06 -40 Slow

2778 KEEP COOL [6] (R Hollinshead) 3-8-8 S Perks 8/1: 0043331: 3 ch f Northern Treat - Douce
Grece (Timmy My Boy) Stayed on well to lead cl home in a slowly run seller at Haydock (no
bid): earlier won a similar event at Newmarket and is consistent in this grade: best around 1m
on gd or faster ground tho' does handle heavy: well suited by a gall trk.   15
2549 MRS NAUGHTY [7] (W Wharton) 3-8-8 N Carlisle 11/2: 0030432: Just btn: see 650.   14
2268 ALEXANJO [9] (A Jarvis) 3-8-8 J Lowe 12/1: 0000203: Led 2f out, not btn far: see 2174   12
2429 SWEET GEMMA [1] (D Haydn Jones) 4-8-10 D J Williams(7) 12/1: -023004: Remains a mdn.   04
2688 SKYBIRD [4] 3-8-6 K Darley 16/1: 0000300: Made most: best over 7f in 2361 (gd)   05
2585 BUCKS BOLT [12] 4-9-4 J Carroll(7) 16/1: 0044000: Prom most: btr over 9f in 1951.   07
*2697 MISS APEX [14] 4-9-1(vis) J Williams 11/2: 2330010: No threat in 9th: btr 2697.   00
2381 XYLOPHONE [2] 4-9-1 P Cook 3/1 FAV: 03-1000: Yet to reproduce form shown in 1400.   00
2603 COUNTRY CARNIVAL [3] 3-8-3(bl) J H Brown(3) 6/1: 0000000: Held up, no threat: btr 907.   00
2762 Janes Brave Boy [5] 9-4   2429 Song An Dance Man [10] 8-11
2681 Brampton Imperial [3] 9-4   2126 Golden Disc [11] 8-10
2790 Maftir [13] 9-4
14 ran   nk,½,1½,½,1½,shthd,3,shthd,hd,nk   (Mrs J E Bigg)   R Hollinshead Upper Longdon,

2864 PRESTON HANDICAP (0-50) 3YO   £3434   1m 6f Firm 06 -50 Slow   [53]

2428 BUCKLEY [6] (L Cumani) 3-9-7 R Guest 5/2: -3121: 3 b c Busted - Queensferry (Pindari)
Useful colt: gamely defied topweight when making all in a slowly run h'cap at Haydock: earlier
ddhtd with Royal Dynasty in a stks race at Redcar: half brother to numerous winners: eff
over 12/14f on gd and fast grd: suited by a gall trk and front running tactics: on the upgrade   56
2546 EYE SIGHT [1] (R F Johnson Houghton) 3-7-13 K Darley 9/2: -3432: Stays 14f: see 2546.   29
2201 BEIJING [5] (P Cole) 3-8-10 P Waldron 2/1 FAV: 0-11443: Onepaced: see 2201 & 1048.   40
2599 LYDIA EVA [2] (R Hannon) 3-7-8 C Rutter(1) 9/2: -000104: Much btr over 11f in 2386.   09
2662 MADISON GIRL [4] 3-8-1(1ow) D Mckeown 12/1: 1020000: Chall winner4f out: see 1615, 1479   12

837

2682 MARBLE MOON [3] 3-7-7 A Culhane(7) 33/1: -00000: Outsider: al behind: see 2464.   00
6 ran   3,shthd,10,3,12   (Mrs A L Chapman)   L Cumani Newmarket

---

NEWMARKET   Saturday October 4th   Righthand, Stiff Galloping Track

Official Going Given As GOOD/FIRM

2865 CARLSBERG TROPHY NURSERY HANDICAP 2YO   £8701   6f   Good/Firm 22 -01 Slow   [59]

*2494 A PRAYER FOR WINGS [6] (J Sutcliffe) 2-8-12 Pat Eddery 3/1: 11: 2 ro c Godswalk - Late
Swallow (My Swallow) Fast impr colt: well bckd and led over 1f out, readily, in a val nursery
h'cap at Newmarket: first time out won a mdn at Nottingham: speedily bred colt who cost 19,000
gns: eff over 6f, should stay 7f: acts well on fast grd and a gall trk: clearly on the upgrade
and can win more races.   62
*2493 GIROTONDO [7] (L Cumani) 2-8-13 R Cochrane 15/8 FAV: 412: Heavily bckd: caught a tartar
and 3l clear 3rd: can find a similar event: see 2493.   55
2563 DERWENT VALLEY [9] (R Hannon) 2-7-7 G French 14/1: 103: Kept on well final 1f: in
gd form: see 2218.   23
*2485 SHADES OF NIGHT [8] (J Winter) 2-8-0 R Fox 16/1: 221414: Led 1½f out: btr 2485.   28
2485 JAISALMER [3] 2-8-7(bl) W R Swinburn 12/1: 0022230: Not clear run 2f out: btr 2485.   33
2687 KYVERDALE [1] 2-9-1 P Robinson 11/2: 1132330: Below her best: see 2687.   41
*2729 SAUCE DIABLE [10] 2-9-7 W Carson 12/1: 210010: Made much, fin 7th: btr 2729 (5f)   00
2552 Macrobian [5] 9-7   2669 Flair Park [4] 7-7(2oh)
2618 Marimba [11] 8-7   2694 Dunninald [2] 9-2
11 ran   2,3,½,½,shthd   (Miss Tracey Flynn)   J Sutcliffe Epsom, Surrey

2866 GROUP 1 TATTERSALLS MIDDLE PARK STAKES   £33184   6f   Good/Firm 22 -07 Slow

2695 MISTER MAJESTIC [5] (R Williams) 2-9-0 R Cochrane 33/1: 1114401: 2 b c Tumble Wind -
Our Village (Ballymore) Smart colt: showed much impr form when making ev yard, gamely, for a
narrow win in Gr 1 Middle Park Stks at Newmarket: in fine form early in the season, winning
4 of his first 5 starts at Beverley (2), Kempton & Newmarket: stays a stiff 6f really well and
will get 7f: acts on fast & yldg grd and on any trk: tough and genuine sort who shd win again. 74
2737 RISK ME [3] (P Kelleway) 2-9-0 S Cauthen 10/1: 11442: Al there: kept on well and just
btn in a cl finish: fine effort on ground that was a shade too firm for him: see 2737, 737.   73
2737 GENGHIZ [4] (L Piggott) 2-9-0 T Ives 9/1: 1103: Chance final 1f: narrowly btn and
is a smart colt: should be suited by 7f+: see 2243.   73
-2221 MANSOOJ [1] (N Callaghan) 2-9-0 Pat Eddery 7/4: 310124: Well bckd: prom and ev ch
over 1f out: below form shown in 2221.   72
*2252 MOST WELCOME [7] 2-9-0 Paul Eddery 11/8 FAV: 110: Very heavily bckd: slow start and
never looked likely: worth another chance over a longer trip: see 2252.   70
2524 WHIPPET [6] 2-9-0 P Robinson 33/1: 0003330: No threat: btr 2524 (5f)   58
+2447 CROFTERS CLINE [2] 2-9-0 J Reid 16/1: 1111010: Speed over 3f: stiff task: see 2447.   00
7 ran   nk,hd,½,½,4   (D A Johnson)   R Williams Newmarket

2867 WILLIAM HILL CAMBRIDGESHIRE HCAP 0-75   £37280   1m110y Good/Firm 22 +02 Fast   [68]

2559 DALLAS [16] (L Cumani) 3-9-6 R Cochrane 10/1: -021131: 3 gr c Blushing Groom - Flordelisada
(Drone) Smart colt: led inside final 1f, cmftbly, in val and highly competitive Cambridgeshire
H'cap at Newmarket: earlier a ready winner of the Britannia H'cap at Royal Ascot and a minor
event at Brighton: very eff over a stiff 1m: acts on gd, well suited by fast grd: a
progressive type who has not stopped improving and can win a Gr race.   81
*2693 POWER BENDER [21] (G P Gordon) 4-8-3(5ex) T Quinn 9/1: 3011112: Led over 1f out and
was narrowly denied his nap hand: tremendous eff: see 2693.   56
+2765 KABIYLA [31] (M Stoute) 3-9-0(5ex) W R Swinburn 7/1: 1-12013: Ev ch 2f out: in
grand form: see 2765.   71
2461 TREMBLANT [27] (J Tree) 5-9-10 Pat Eddery 6/1 FAV: 0003344: Nearest fin: sound eff
under 9-10: most consistent: see 2461.   70
2526 PASTICCIO [23] 3-8-10 T Ives 20/1: 2221130: Ran on well final 1f: gd eff over this
longer trip and has yet to run a bad race : see 2526, 2155.   60
2762 PARIS TRADER [25] 4-7-7(11oh) G Bardwell(7) 66/1: 0030020: Al there: ran very well
and looks certain to pick up a small h'cap on this form: see 2762, 609.   33
2566 WAAJIB [7] 3-8-5 M Roberts 22/1: -213320: Prom, fin 7th: see 2566.   49
*2559 ININSKY [26] 3-9-1 G Starkey 22/1: 0034110: Sn prom: fin 8th: beat winner 2559.   59
2612 NAVARZATO [3] 3-9-0 S Cauthen 20/1: 11-2000: Fin 9th: fair eff, best 1147.   57
2568 ATOKA [10] 4-7-11(4ow)(2oh) R Hills 16/1: 3430100: Prom much: well below 2568 (stks)   00
*2749 FAIR COUNTRY [13] 4-8-1(5ex) G Carter 15/1: 3110110: Prom most: below her best: see 2749 00
2612 Chief Pal [9] 7-12   2431 Meet The Greek [1] 8-3
2557 Promised Isle [12] 8-7   2749 Alqirm [4] 7-8(BL)(1ow)(1oh)
2526 Al Bashaama [17] 8-5   2461 K Battery [6] 9-8   2684 Turfah [19] 8-2
2773 Formatune [28] 7-8(bl)(1ow)(9oh)   *2730 Flyhome [29] 7-12(5ex)
2536 Andartis [30] 8-2   2773 Manchesterskytrain [11] 7-9
2693 Swift Trooper [8] 8-5(bl)(1ow)   2693 Qualitair Flyer [20] 8-4(VIS)
2458 Paris Turf [14] 8-0(VIS)   2676 Lady La Paz [5] 7-7(17oh)00

2755 Sams Wood [24] 7-12	2691 Georgia River [2] 8-5	*2629 All Fair [22] 7-11(vis)
2629 Xhai [18] 7-7(1oh)	2763 Gorgeous Algernon [15] 7-11(bl)	
31 ran ½,1,3,¾,2,1,nk,¾	(Richard L Duchossios)	L Cumani Newmarket

2868 GROUP 2 SUN CHARIOT STAKES   £23487   1m 2f   Good/Firm 22 +08 Fast

-2568 DUSTY DOLLAR [4] (W Hern) 3-8-7 W Carson 7/2: 4-31221: 3 b f Kris - Sauceboat
(Connaught) Smart filly: well bckd and squeezed through to lead inside final 1f in fast run
Gr 2 Sun Chariot Stks at Newmarket: lightly raced filly who earlier won a 3yo mdn at Epsom:
later a fine 2nd to Sonic Lady in Gr 3 Child Stks here and last time out 2nd to record-breaking
Asterord Field in a Listed race at Doncaster: eff at 1m, well suited by 10f: loves fast grd
and is certain to win more races.   78
*2462 GESEDEH [3] (M Jarvis) 3-8-7 Pat Eddery 10/3: 1100012: Led 1f out: ran on well under
press and is in grand form: see 2462.   76
*2278 SINGLETTA [1] (M Stoute) 3-8-7 W R Swinburn 7/4 FAV: 2-30113: Heavily bckd: led
over 2f out and ran on well when hdd: another fine eff: see 2278.   76
2202 QUEEN HELEN [5] (W Hern) 3-8-7 T Ives 20/1: 21-004: Ev ch 2f out: fair eff: see 755.   68
2770 MOONLIGHT LADY [7] 3-8-7 R Cochrane 14/1: 20-0200: Twice below form 2538 (7f)   64
2568 PURCHASEPAPERCHASE [6] 4-9-0 S Cauthen 20/1: 0400100: Made most: best 2385.   52
1331 FAIR OF THE FURZE [2] 4-9-4 G Starkey 13/2: 1-413010: Al rear: winner at Phoenix Park
last month: much btr 1331, 1095.   00
7 ran   1,shthd,4,2,6   (Maktoum Al Maktoum)   W Hern West Ilsley, Berks.

2869 SOLTYKOFF MAIDEN STAKES 2YO   £5196   1m   Good/Firm 22 -35 Slow

2673 DRY DOCK [3] (W Hern) 2-9-0 W Carson 7/2: 01: 2 b c High Line - Boathouse (Habitat)
Very promising colt: well bckd and led 2f out, ridden out in a slow run but val 2yo mdn at
Newmarket: from a very gd winning family that includes Oaks winner Birene: dam lightly raced
and was a winner over 1m as a 2yo: stays a stiff 1m: will be suited by middle dist next season:
acts on fast grd and a gall trk: further improvement likely and is the type to win again.   60
--   ALTOUNTASH [18] (M Stoute) 2-9-0 W R Swinburn 3/1 FAV: 2: Heavily bckd debutant:
ran on well final 1f and will not be long in going one btr: half brother to 4 winners
including the very useful Altiyna: eff at 1m, will be suited by further: acts on fast grd
and a gall track.   57
--   KING OF MERCIA [6] (L Cumani) 2-9-0 P Hamblett 33/1: 3: Fin in fine style on his
debut: stoutly bred colt whose dam was placed in Gr company: eff at 1m, certain to be suited
by 10/12f: acts on fast grd and is the type to win races.   55
571   RODOMONT [8] (J Fitzgerald) 2-9-0 M Roberts 20/1: 04: Long abs: led 6f and kept on
well: fine effort: cost 105,000 gns as yearling and is a brother to the useful Kolgong Heights:
stays 1m well: acts on gd/firm grd and a gall track: sure to find a race.   54
--   NORMAN INVADER [5] 2-9-0 R Cochrane 12/1: 0: Stable mate of 3rd: chance inside final
2f: encouraging debut from this half brother to a minor winner: eff at 1m on gd/firm grd
and should have no trouble in finding a maiden.   51
2484 KARABAT [17] 2-9-0 W Newnes 33/1: 000: Ran on final 1f: another gd eff and is suited
by 1m: acts on a gall trk and should win a race: see 2484.   50
--   VESTRIS [12] 2-9-0 G Starkey 4/1: 0: Op 6/4: fin 7th: impr likely from this first
foal: dam a very smart French filly: sure to improve.   48
--   BREAKOUT [11] 2-9-0 G Baxter 25/1: 0: Hmpd 1½f out and fin 8th: will do btr next
time: should be suited by 1m and further: acts on gd/firm.   00
--   MOMENT OF TRUTH [1] 2-9-0 P Robinson 10/1: 0: Backd at long odds: fdd final 1f:
cost 54,000 gns as a yearling and is a half brother to sev winners, who all stayed well:
should find a race when dropped slightly in class.   00
2541 HABCAN [14] 2-9-0 T Quinn 11/2: 30: Much btr 2541.   00
--   Calapaez [19] 9-0   --   Faceview [16] 9-0   2721 Gallions Point [9] 9-0
2418 Grunidad [4] 9-0   --   Hubba [10] 9-0   --   Interest Rate [7] 9-0
--   Leavenworth [2] 9-0   2574 Marble Rock [15] 9-0   2468 Red Timber [13] 9-0
19 ran ¾,¾,shthd,1¼,shthd,¾   (R D Hollingsworth)   W Hern West Ilsley, Berks.

2870 SEVERALS HANDICAP 3YO 0-70   £6732   7f   Good/Firm 22 -09 Slow   [67]

2765 HIDDEN BRIEF [5] (R Boss) 3-9-2 W R Swinburn 5/1: 0201231: 3 ch f Pyjama Hunt -
Himalia (High Line) Very useful filly: led inside final 1f, ridden out in a val 3yo h'cap at
Newmarket: earlier a winner at Haydock and Leicester (first time out): in '85 won at Redcar
and also 4th in Gr 3 Hoover Fillies Mile at Ascot: stays 1m but her best form is over today's
7f trip: acts on firm and soft grd and a gall track.   65
2674 TARANGA [4] (M Tompkins) 3-7-9 A Mackay 8/1: 0204002: Backed from 14/1 and tried to
make all: gd effort: stays 7f: see 2143.   41
+2650 SIR ARNOLD [3] (A Stewart) 3-8-12(6ex) M Roberts 4/1: -231313: Chance 2f out, in
grand form: see 2650.   57
2773 BELOW ZERO [6] (A Bailey) 3-8-4(1ow) Pat Eddery 7/4 FAV: 0140244: Heavily bckd:
consistent: see 2773.   46
692   PRINCE PECADILLO [1] 3-9-7 R Cochrane 20/1: 000-000: Long abs: fdd final 1f: fair
effort as he prob needed this run: very lightly raced this term: very useful 2yo, winning
at Haydock, Beverley & Ripon: eff at 6f, stays 7f: acts on gd and fast grd and a gall trk.   62
2362 SEW HIGH [8] 3-8-2 G Duffield 9/1: 4110300: Chance 2f out: btr 5/6f? See 1704.   38

2562 **Bold Celt** [9] 8-2   **2762 Jarrovian** [2] 7-7(bl)(3oh)
1854 **Town Jester** [7] 8-2
9 ran   1¼,hd,1½,¾,2½   (K Bethel)   R Boss Newmarket

WOLVERHAMPTON   Monday October 6th   Lefthanded, Galloping Track

2871 EBF DUDLEY MAIDEN STAKES DIV.1 2YO   £717   5f   Good/Firm 25 -01 Slow

2651 ANOTHER GUEST [4] (R Sheather) 2-8-11 A Shoults(5) 20/1: 01: 2 ch f Anfield -
Sharpway (Good Bond): Easy to back & showed impr form, led 2f out & ran on well in a 2yo mdn
at Woverhampton: cheaply bought filly who is a half sister to winning juvenile Shaves You
Close: eff over 5/6f on gd & firm grnd: acts on a galal trk.   42
--   WANTAGE PARK [3] (M Ryan) 2-8-11 P Robinson 14/1: 2: Mkt drifter on debut: al prom
& should impr for this experience: cheaply bought filly: acts on gd/firm grnd.   36
--   ARAMOR [8] (G Huffer) 2-9-0 G Carter 11/4: 3: Nicely bckd debutant: ran on well &
never nearer: half brother to several winning juveniles, including Fayruz: acts on gd/firm
grnd: would not have to impr much to win a race.   38
2805 GARCON NOIR [2] (D Moorhead) 2-9-0 S Webster 20/1: 0004: Switched, one-paced: see 2100.   32
2687 PELF [9] 2-8-11 R Guest 7/4 FAV: 20200: Much btr over 6f in 2555: see 1322.   28
2221 SONG N JEST [5] 2-9-0 M Birch 5/1: 32000: Hmpd 2f out: ran on late: see 715.   29
2158 SCIERPAN [1] 2-8-11(BL) T Ives 7/2: 2200: Bl first time: led over ½way: much btr in 1874   00
--   Olympic Challenger [7] 9-0   --   Frimley Parkson [6] 9-0
9 ran   1½,¾,2,nk,1   (D O McIntyre)   R Sheather Newmarket

2872 SEDGELEY NURSERY SELL.H'CAP 2YO   £853   1m   Good/Firm 25 -22 Slow   [26]

*2724 PETRUS SEVENTY [5] (P Haslam) 2-9-2(vis)(5ex) T Williams 6/4 FAV: 00311: 2 b c Treboro -
Bold Pioneer (Wolver Hollow): Well bckd and again gamely made ev yd in a nursery selling h'cap
at Wolverhampton (bought in 5,200 gns): recent winner of a similar race at Beverley: stays 1m
well: suited by forcing tactics on a sound surface: continues to improve.   22
2757 VICTORIA STAR [3] (G Reveley) 2-8-8 R P Elliott 12/1: 004002: Fin well, just btn: see 2466   12
2625 PRINCESS MICHICO [6] (R Boss) 2-8-0 G Duffield 12/1: 0303: Not btn far: stays 1m: see 1692   03
2724 BLOW FOR HOME [10] (D Morley) 2-8-0 S Dawson 5/1: 002024: Close 4th: in gd form: see 2724.01
2608 LEG GLIDE [11] 2-8-11 T Ives 10/1: 0000: Nearest fin: cheaply well suited by this
longer trip: cheaply bought filly who stays 1m & acts on gd/firm grnd.   09
*2801 COROFIN LASS [8] 2-9-2(bl)(5ex) W Goodwin(7) 6/1: 0000410: Fair effort under her penalty.   13
2712 FINLUX DESIGN [4] 2-8-7 S Perks 7/1: 0300000: Prom most: fin 8th: see 1155 (6f).   00
2724 **Delite Muffin** [7] 8-4(bl)   2724 **Highland Captain** [9] 8-3(bl)
2712 **Santo Princess** [12] 8-0   2127 **Rose Of Tudor** [1] 8-8
11 ran   ½,nk,¾,1½,shhd,nk   (T C Ellis)   P Haslam Newmarket

2873 WEST MIDLAND H'CAP 3YO+ 0-50   £3174   1m 6.5 Good/Firm 25 -54 Slow   [50]

+1293 SNEAK PREVIEW [7] (H Candy) 6-9-11 R Curant 2/1 FAV: 43-1111: 6 b g Quiet Fling -
Glimmer of Hope (Never Say Die): Remains unbtn this season, despite a long break was produced
to lead close home in a slowly run h'cap at Wolverhampton: useful, much improved stayer who had
earlier won h'caps at Newmarket and Doncaster and the Northumberland Plate h'cap at Newcastle: last season won at Wolverhampton & Salisbury & was also 4th in the Cesarewitch , a race
he will again take his chance in: eff around 2m, stays forever: acts on firm & gd grnd &
is suited by a stiff, gall trk: genuine sort who does well when fresh: needs to be held up.   52
--   TANCRED WALK [4] (C Jackson) 7-7-9 M L Thomas 33/1: 02210/2: Led below dist, collared
close home: ran surprisingly well: last ran on the Flat in '83, when successful at Edinburgh:
has since proved himself useful over timber: stays 2m well: acts on gd & fast grnd & on any trk   20
2273 DIVA ENCORE [3] (R Armstrong) 3-8-3 G Baxter 6/1: 1122303: Led 4f out: see 1817, 1694.   35
*2776 HERRADURA [2] (M Prescott) 5-8-10(vis)(4ex) G Duffield 5/2: 3203314: Not btn far but
better in 2776.   32
2794 SOUND DIFFUSION [5] 4-7-7(1oh) N Carlisle 12/1: 3000000: Made much: close 5th: see 933.   14
2403 ALACAZAM [6] 4-7-7(7oh) P Hill(7) 12/1: 0001100: Wknd home turn: btr in 2134.   00
2733 TRAPEZE ARTIST [1] 5-9-2 S Dawson 8/1: 0222000: Well btn: not running well: see 2389, 917   00
735 OWENS PRIDE [8] 4-8-3 T Williams 10/1: 0-13000: Long abs: fin last: see 236 (soft).   00
8 ran   nk,1,¾,1½,25,¾   (Mrs C E Gross)   H Candy Kingstone Warren, Oxon

2874 PERTON CLAIMING STAKES 3YO   £1746   1m 4f Good/Firm 25 +09 Fast

2722 TURMERIC [9] (D Morley) 3-9-0 T Williams 5/1: 0204231: 3 ch c Alias Smith -
Hot Spice (Hotfoot): Gained an overdue win but needed the steward's help, led below dist till
close home but was subs. awarded the race, a 3yo claimer at Wolverhampton: eff around 1m,
stays 14f: seems best on fast grnd & likes a gall trk.   26
2714 ELEGANT GUEST [2] (W O'gorman) 3-9-0 T Ives 4/1: -00431D: Denied a clear run, squeezed
through to lead near fin but after an objection was demoted to 2nd: should gain consolation
if kept in this grade: stays 12f: acts on gd & firm: see 494.   27

2714 RUN FOR YOUR WIFE [7] (G Lewis) 3-9-0(bl) M L Thomas 10/3 FAV: 0243023: Made most.   23
2722 ASTRAL [3] (P Cole) 3-9-0 G Duffield 7/2: 0-01004: Best in 2129 (tight trk).   20
2778 DOON VENTURE [10] 3-8-2 S Webster 12/1: 0000340: Some late prog: see 867.   00
2722 BULLY BOY [8] 3-9-0(bl) S Whitworth 20/1: 0000000: Btn 2f out: no form.   08
2787 NO STOPPING [6] 3-8-4 P Cook 5/1: 0323220: Fin 7th: btr in 2787 (10f): see 2597.   00
-2603 Dalveen Pass [5] 9-0   2714 Star Addie [1] 8-2   2593 Waterside Lodge [4] 8-8
10 ran ½,2,1½,6,1,2   (Christopher Spence)   D Morley Newmarket

2875 EBF DUDLEY MAIDEN STAKES DIV.2 2YO   £724   5f   Good/Firm 25 -07 Slow

2589 KEPT WAITING [3] (W Musson) 2-8-11 M Wigham 13/2: 0201: 2 b f Tanfirion - Lady Bequick
(Sharpen Up): Mkt drifter but stayed on strongly to lead close home in a 2yo mdn at Wolverhampton: cheaply bought filly who is eff over 5f & should stay further: acts on fast grnd
& seems to have no trk preferences.   40
2717 INTHAR [9] (R Armstrong) 2-9-0 P Tulk 3/1: 00342: Led below dist, just caught: see 2514.   42
--   ANOTHER RHYTHM [10] (R Hutchinson) 2-9-0 T Lucas 9/2: 3: Made much: not btn f. &
5L clear of rem: cheaply acquired colt who should prove best over sprint dists: acts on
gd/firm grnd: should be placed to win a small race.   40
2476 BALKAN LEADER [1] (J Fitzgerald) 2-9-0 M Birch 5/2 FAV: 0234: Uneasy fav: fdd: best 780.   28
2667 MON BALZAR [6] 2-9-0(BL) T Ives 5/1: 00000: Btn dist: time: speed over ½way: see 2514.   26
2491 MY PROMISED LAND [2] 2-8-11 J Williams 33/1: 00: Wknd below dist: sprint bred filly.   16
2375 The Cross [4] 8-11   2805 Touch Of Speed [5] 9-0
2678 The Victor Girls [8] 8-11   --   Medrian [7] 8-11
10 ran hd,½,5,1,2   (Mrs R F Beckwith)   W Musson Newmarket

2876 OAKEN LODGE H'CAP 3YO 0-35   £2354   1m 1f   Good/Firm 25 +01 Fast   [41]

2728 BICKERMAN [1] (M Prescott) 3-8-7 G Duffield 9/2 FAV: 1012301: 3 b c Mummy's Pet -
Merry Weather (Will Somers): Al prom & led below dist, comfortably in a 3yo h'cap at
Wolverhampton: quite consistent this term, earlier won twice at Edinburgh: related to useful
sprinters Pettingale & Tina's Pet amongst others though seems btr suited by 7/9f himself:
acts on gd & firm grnd & on any trk.   28
2594 PEARL FISHER [8] (J Francome) 3-8-8 T Ives 7/1: 3040002: Gd effort: may win soon: see 140   25
2719 FAIR ATLANTA [4] (M Usher) 3-8-9 R Street 12/1: 0100303: Kept on well: see 2459 & 505.   22
2293 PRIME NUMBER [12] (P Cole) 3-8-1 G Baxter 10/1: -000034: Had ev ch: mdn: see 247.   12
1787 RICHARDS FOLLY [11] 3-8-3(2ow) J Williams 25/1: 0-00000: Abs: nearest fin: no form
previously: stays at least 9f: acts on gd/firm.   13
2681 SPECIAL GUEST [9] 3-8-4 M Wigham 6/1: 3240340: Made most: consistent: see 1695.   11
2404 EMRYS [10] 3-9-7 P Cook 6/1: 0331400: Btn over 2f out: little form since 919 (sharp trk)   00
2442 SCENTED SILENCE [14] 3-7-8 G Carter 8/1: 0-0000: Yet to show any worthwhile form.   00
2582 Next Dance [13] 7-7(1oh)   2360 Sirdar Flyer [3] 7-7(BL)(2oh)
2728 Flying Ziad [5] 7-13   2676 Mirataine Venture [15] 8-8
2746 Red Billy [2] 7-7(BL)(8oh)   2602 Persian Ballet [7] 7-13
2381 First Rank [6] 8-7
15 ran 1½,2,1,½,1½,3,½,shhd,½   (Major J Green)   M Prescott, Newmarket

Official Going Given As
2877 ALDIE APPRENTICE H'CAP 3YO+ 0-35   £2018   1m 2f   Firm 16 -05 Slow   [32]

2755 MOUNT TUMBLEDOWN [6] (R Hannon) 5-9-8 R Perham(3) 9/2: 00-0001: 5 b h Tumble Wind -
Dowdy (Sea Hawk II): Ran on strongly to lead close home, gamely in an app h'cap at Bath:
lightly rcd in recent seasons and last successful in '84, at Pontefract, Beverley & Ayr:
eff over 8/10f on fast & soft grnd: acts on any trk.   30
*2654 SHALLAAL [5] (A King) 7-8-0(1ow)(7ex) A Riding 4/1: 00012: Strong late burst, just
failed: running well at present: acts on any trk: see 2654.   08
2807 DANCING BARRON [3] (L Cottrell) 5-8-7(vis) T Lang 4/1: 3040403: Led below dist, narrowly
btn in a desperate fin: gd effort: acts on any trk: see 750.   14
2766 MILLERS TALE [1] (I Balding) 4-9-9 P Francis 9/4 FAV: 0104004: Made most: best in 761.   27
2533 POLYNOR [7] 5-7-12 P Barnard 9/2: 440-000: Not btn very far: see 2490.   01
2546 FARCEUSE [2] 3-7-9(vis)(1ow) A Whitehall 33/1: 000-000: Early ldr: well btn: poor mdn.   00
6 ran shhd,shhd,1½,nk,25   (Mrs J Collins)   R Hannon East Everleigh, Wilts

2878 EBF DONNINGTON STAKES 2YO   £2454   1m 8yd Firm 16 -15 Slow

-2711 BATTALION USA [16] (J Dunlop) 2-8-11 B Thomson 3/1: 021: 2 b c Vaguely Noble -
Blazon (Ack Ack): Made steady progress to lead inside dist, ridden out in a 2yo stakes at
Bath: cost $200,000 as a yearling & is impr steadily: eff over 7/8f on fast grnd & on a
gall trk: further impr likely.   45
1826 NORS GOD [8] (M Usher) 2-8-11 Paul Eddery 50/1: 002: Friendless in mkt after a fair
break: made most & kept on well when hdd: much btr effort & should find a race on a sharper
trk: half brother to 6/7f winner Blue Emmanuelle: acts on fast grnd.   42
1802 RAHWAH [4] (C Benstead) 2-8-8 P Waldron 16/1: 03: Stepped up on her debut run here:
fin well & not btn far: stays 1m: acts on fast grnd & on a gall trk: see 1802.   37

2721 **VIGLIOTTO** [5] (G Harwood) 2-8-11 G Starkey 13/8 FAV: 44: Well bckd: never nearer: see 2721 **40**
2574 **GREEN LALEEK** [9] 2-8-11 T Quinn 16/1: 00: Ran on same pace: btr effort from this
$20,000 yearling: half brother to several winners & should continue to impr: stays 1m:
acts on firm.   **35**
*2748 **ABSINTHE** [7] 2-8-13 B Rouse 10/1: 4010: Mkt drifter: no real threat: see 2748.   **36**
2541 **STARK REALITY** [15] 2-8-11(BL) Pat Eddery 9/1: 00: BI first time: fdd into 7th: see 2541.   **00**
2159 **COCK SPARROW** [17] 2-8-11 W Carson 7/1: 00: AI mid-div: fin 9th: closely related to
several winners incl Bespoke & Santella Boy: should be suited by middle dists next term.   **00**

2542 Durbo [18] 8-11	2657 Ocean Hound [1] 8-8	2159 Gunner Stream [12] 8-11
2698 Charming Gracie [6] 8-8		2541 Master Comedy [10] 8-11
1696 Toot Toot [14] 8-8	— Stubble Fire [3] 8-11	2698 Martian Melody [13] 8-8
2716 Roches [11] 8-11(BL)		

17 ran   1,¾,hd,2,½,½   (Sheikh Mohammed)   J Dunlop Arundel, Sussex

2879 MORRIS DANCER H'CAP 3YO 0-50   £2289   1m 8yd Firm 16 +17 Fast   [57]

1753 **SUPER PUNK** [1] (M Fetherston Godley) 3-8-6 C Rutter(3) 20/1: -300041: 3 ch c Hot
Spark - Super Lady (Averof): Returned to form, came from well off the pace when ddht in a fast
run 3yo h'cap at Bath: on final outing last season won a Nottingham mdn: eff around 7/8f &
should stay further: acts on fast & yld grnd & on any trk.   **47**
*2534 **ELBURY PARK** [3] (G Harwood) 3-8-6(1ow) G Starkey 6/5 FAV: -11½.3 b c Young Generation-
Sandforinia (Sandford Lad): Hvly bckd, led below dist & just held on when ddht in a 3yo
h'cap at Bath: recent winner of a Salisbury mdn: eff over 1m on fast grnd & seems to
like a gall trk.   **47**
*2704 **NO RESTRAINT** [2] (W Hastings Bass) 3-8-2 W Carson 7/2: -043113: Ev ch: see 2704.   **40**
2784 **FLOATING ASSET** [4] (P Walwyn) 3-8-7 Paul Eddery 12/1: 4034444: Consistent sort: see 386.   **41**
+2288 **HAMLOUL** [9] 3-8-3 W Newnes 11/1: 0220210: Ran on same pace: best in 2288.   **34**
2702 **MIRANDA JULIA** [13] 3-7-7(VIS)(2oh) G French 25/1: 0000400: Visored first time: btn
dist: see 2601, 276.   **18**
*2699 **FARM CLUB** [8] 3-8-9(7ex) B Thomson 9/1: 0030010: Led over 2f out, fin 7th: btr here 2699.   **00**
*2681 **Pulham Mills** [14] 8-8(vis)(1ow)(7ex)   1758 Fouz [12] 9-7
2837 **Full Of Life** [11] 8-1   2730 **Swifts Pal** [6] 9-4   1924 **Mudrik** [7] 8-8(BL)
2728 **Mal Y Pense** [10] 8-2
13 ran   ddht,1½,2,1½,3   (J B Austin)   M Fetherston Godley East Ilsley, Berks

2880 COUNTY H'CAP 3YO 0-50   £2826   1m 3f Firm 16 -01 Slow   [45]

2525 **MIGHTY FLASH** [4] (D Elsworth) 3-9-7 J Reid 11/4: 0110001: 3 b f Rolfe - Lettuce
(So Blessed): Fairly useful filly: led early, stayed prom & led over 1f out, under press in
a h'cap at Bath: last time out a fine 6th to Rejuvenate in Gr.2 Park Hill Stakes at Doncaster:
earlier a winner of 2 h'caps at Salisbury: closely related to the smart duo Mighty Flutter
& Mighty Fly: eff at 12/14f: acts well on gd & firm grnd & likes a gall trk.   **47**
2430 **MAKE PEACE** [3] (I Balding) 3-8-1(BL) W Newnes 7/1: 3000002: Made most & kept on well:
best effort for a long time:˜eff at 10/12f: acts on firm & yld grnd: bl for the first time today   **25**
2766 **ON TENTERHOOKS** [2] (J Tree) 3-9-5 Pat Eddery 6/4 FAV: 3-10403: Ev ch inside final 2f.   **41**
2393 **MAKE IT SHARP** [6] (A Stewart) 3-8-8 M Roberts 9/2: -0304: No extra str: lightly
raced since 1368.   **26**
2533 **ARTISTIC CHAMPION** [1] 3-8-3 Paul Eddery 13/2: -300100: Fdd over 2f out: best 1401 (10f)   **09**
2719 **OMANIA** [5] 3-7-13 A Mcglone 12/1: 4400000: AI near: best 570.   **00**
6 ran   ½,¾,1½,12,8   (Mrs V Tory)   D Elsworth Whitsbury, Hants

2881 BLATHWAYT FILLIES STAKES 2YO   £1401   5f   Firm 16 -14 Slow

*2596 **ABHAAJ** [2] (H T Jones) 2-8-13 A Murray 4/6 FAV: 211: 2 br f Kris - Ibtihaj (Raja Baba):
Useful, impr filly: hvly bckd & made ev yd, comfortably in a 2yo fillies stakes at Bath:
last time out led all the way in a fillies mdn at Lingfield: first foal of a juvenile winner,
who is a half sister to prolific stallion Danzig: very eff at 5f, stays 6f: acts on gd &
fast grnd & on any trk: well suited by forcing tactics & should rate more highly.   **52**
+2555 **GREENCASTLE HILL** [4] (I Balding) 2-8-13 Pat Eddery 9/4: 012: Ev ch over 1f out: btr 2555.   **45**
2698 **LADYS MANTLE** [5] (J Dunlop) 2-8-8(bl) W Carson 33/1: 000033: Sn prom: see 2698, 1801.   **30**
2792 **LADY LUCINA** [3] (M Smyly) 2-8-8 Paul Eddery 33/1: 040304: Stiff task: see 2529.   **28**
— **FRENSHAM MANOR** [1] 2-8-8 B Rouse 11/2: 0: Never went pace on debut: sister to 3
winners incl the smart 2yo Cat O'Nine Tails & should leave this form behind.   **07**
5 ran   2,3,½,7   (Hamdan Al-Maktoum)   H T Jones Newmarket

2882 WESTMORLAND H'CAP 3YO+ 0-50   £2923   2m 1f Firm 16 +14 Fast   [39]

2078 **EL CONQUISTADOR** [1] (G Harwood) 3-9-7 G Starkey 13/8 FAV: 0202221: 3 b c Shirley Heights-
Fiddle Faddle (Silly Season): Useful stayer: well bckd & led final 1f, under press in a fast
run h'cap at Bath, a deserved first win after four 2nds: well suited by dists in excess of
2m: acts well on fast grnd & probably on any trk: seems a genuine sort.   **53**
-2591 **TIGERWOOD** [2] (R Akehurst) 5-8-11 N Adams 11/4: 1210222: Clear ldr, caught final 1f:
in fine form this season: see 2591, 1533.   **29**
1243 **FISHPOND** [7] (P Jones) 5-8-10 G French 12/1: 0-20003: Abs: no ch with first 2: see 419.   **20**
2733 **ALSIBA** [3] (C Benstead) 4-8-0 R Fox 7/1: 4040044: Late hdway: btr 2733 (14f).   **05**

2647 TEMPLE HEIGHTS [4] 3-9-1 W Carson 10/1: -012400: Btr 2164, 1251.   30
2754 WIDE BOY [5] 4-9-2 Pat Eddery 11/2: 0-11000: Fdd final 2f: see 2754, 542.   18
*1694 PIP [6] 6-8-1 W Newnes 12/1: -010: No show: winner over hdles since 1694.   00
7 ran   ½,8,5,2½,½   (J Garcia-Roady)   G Harwood Pulborough, Sussex

---

EDINBURGH   Monday October 6th   Righthand, Sharpish Track

Official Going Given As GOOD/FIRM

2883 INGLISTON FILLIES STAKES 2YO   £547   5f   Firm 19 -14 Slow

*2589 MALIBU TOAST [1] (L Cumani) 2-9-1 R Cochrane 4/11 FAV: 011: 2 ch f Raise A Cup -
California Girl (California Kid): Useful filly: well bckd & led over 1f out, easily in a
2yo fillies stakes at Edinburgh: last time out was a comfortable winner of a fillies mdn
at Wolverhampton: half sister to several winners in the States: very eff over 5f, will stay
further: acts on fast & yld grnd: does well on an easy trk.   52
*2600 VERYAN BAY [4] (M Dickinson) 2-9-1 D Nicholls 5/1: 00012: Mkt drifter: led till
swamped for foot by the winner: see 2600.   38
-2588 LINPAC NORTH MOOR [7] (W Elsey) 2-8-8(bl) J Lowe 12/1: 4034423: Prom, ev ch: consistent:
runs well here: see 2588.   21
2436 ILLUSTRATE [5] (A Smith) 2-8-8 J Quinn(5) 12/1: 0004: No extra final 2f: see 1867.   20
2127 PREMIER VIDEO [2] 2-8-8 J Carroll(7) 20/1: 3020200: Sn prom: best 1545 (C/D).   15
2678 INTELLECT [3] 2-8-8 N Connorton 50/1: 00: Never in it: sister to fair sprinter Lonely
Street: may improve.   00
--   Bilup [6] 8-8
7 ran   4,3,hd,1½,5   (Fittocks Stud Ltd)   L Cumani Newmarket

2884 GULLANE SELLING HCAP 3 & 4YO 0-25   £840   5f   Firm 19 -39 Slow   [15]

2397 ACKAS BOY [2] (D Moffatt) 4-8-5 J Lowe 6/1: 0000001: 4 ch g Town And Country -
Ackabarrow (Laser Light): Led final 1f, driven out in a very slow run & moderate selling h'cap
at Edinburgh (bought in 1,150 gns): first success & little form previously: seems eff at 5f
on fast grnd & a sharp trk.   01
2743 SWEET EIRE [5] (W Pearce) 4-8-3(bl) L Charnock 4/1 FAV: 0004032: Chall final 1f &
btn a whisker: in gd form: see 906.   00
2592 EVER SO SHARP [12] (J Smith) 3-8-12 J Carroll(7) 33/1: 0000003: Prom, not btn far:
no form previously outside selling company: eff at 5f on fast grnd & a sharp trk.   06
2775 TOLLYS ALE [4] (I Matthews) 3-9-8(BL) C Dwyer 8/1: 3000404: Bl first time: fin 5th,
placed 4th: best 2312 (yld).   10
2688 CLASS HOPPER [11] 3-8-2(BL) J Quinn(5) 12/1: 0000000: Bl first time: ev ch: fin 6th,
placed 5th: placed in sellers as a 2yo, but no form this season: acts on fast grnd.   00
2335 OUR MUMSIE [8] 3-8-10 D Nicholls 10/1: 0040000: Led 2f out: best 103.   00
1662 YOUNG BORIS [1] 4-8-12(BL) M Hills 8/1: 0-00000: Bl first time after abs: see 975.   00
2743 NAUGHTY NIGHTY [3] 3-9-0 R Cochrane 7/1: 0000340: Btr 2417 (6f): see 2189.   00
*2417 EASTERN OASIS [9] 3-8-13 A Proud 7/1: 040014D: Fin 4th but rider failed to weigh in
and was disq. & placed last: see 2417.   00
2743 Motor Master [6] 8-7(bl)   -- Star Crimson [10] 8-12
2335 Keyanloch [7] 9-4
12 ran   shhd,½,1½,½,½   (G Atkinson)   D Moffatt Cartmel, Cumbria

2885 REGENCY HANDICAP 0-35 3YO+   £1539   1m 4f   Firm 19 -05 Slow   [26]

*2819 FOUR STAR THRUST [1] (R Whitaker) 4-9-8(5ex) D Mckeown 11/4 FAV: 2023211: 4 ch f Derrylin
Smiling (Silly Season): In gd form: hdway on bit 2f out & led final 1f, readily in a h'cap
at Edinburgh: last time out won a similar event at Hamilton: in '85 was a winner on this trk:
placed also on numerous occasions: seems equally eff at 12/14f on gd & fast grnd: consistent.   29
2400 SOMETHING SIMILAR [4] (J Fitzgerald) 3-8-13 D Nicholls 12/1: 4-00002: Led 2f out:
wandered under pressure: stays 12f & acts on fast & yld grnd.   24
2818 TREYARNON [12] (S Norton) 3-8-3 J Lowe 11/2: 0443223: Al up there: see 2818.   06
2604 IVOROSKI [8] (D Smith) 4-8-6 L Charnock 9/1: 3321004: Not clear run over 1f out:
best in 1769.   06
2414 CADENETTE [2] 4-8-5 J Quinn(5) 14/1: 4201000: Stays 12f: best 1699 (seller)   00
2727 CAMPUS BOY [11] 5-7-9 M Fry 10/1: 0400000: Led/dsptd lead: see 542.   00
*2709 GAY APPEAL [5] 3-9-9(8ex) M Hills 7/2: 030011U: Slipped up home turn: see 2709.   00
2779 Key Royal [3] 8-12   2627 Birss Creek [9] 9-2(bl)
2819 Boreham Down [6] 7-8(1ow)(1oh)   2685 Recollect [7] 9-7
--   Strathconon [10] 7-11
12 ran   1½,shhd,2½,2,hd   (Mrs J Turner)   R Whitaker Wetherby, Yorks

2886 PORTOBELLO MAIDEN STAKES 2YO   £657   1m   Firm 19 +02 Fast

2798 TROMPE DOEIL [3] (J Payne) 2-8-11(bl) A Mackay 10/1: 000241: 2 b f Longleat -
Just Kidding (Jester): Led/dsptd lead & came again under press to lead close home in a
2yo mdn at Edinburgh: runs very well here (disapp. at Hamilton last time): well suited by
forcing tactics over 1m on a sharpish trk: acts on fast grnd & runs well in bl.   35

2377 OKOSAN [2] (S Norton) 2-8-11(VIS) J Lowe 16/1: 0002: Tried in a visor: led over 2f
out & just caught: half sister to several winners: stays 1m: seems best on fast grnd & a
sharpish track.   34
2716 QUIET HERO [6] (L Cumani) 2-9-0 R Cochrane 4/11 FAV: 0323: Ev ch inside the final 2f
but seemed unwilling: see 2716.   31
2796 AMADEUS ROCK [7] (J Hindley) 2-9-0 R Hills 8/1: 004: Btr in 2796 (stiffer trk).   19
2651 KNOWN POINT [5] 2-8-11 W Woods(3) 8/1: 00: Prom most: half sister to 4 winners
& should be capable of btr than this.   10
1382 ANORADA [1] 2-8-11 A Geran(7) 7/1: 00: Abs: there 5f: should do btr next time: see 1382 00
2511 Campeggio [4] 9-0
7 ran   hd,3,6,3,5   (N Yiasoumi)   J Payne Newmarket

2887 FISHERROW MAIDEN STAKES 3YO+   £547   1m   Firm 19 -06 Slow

2585 CLOUDLESS SKY [5] (P Rohan) 3-7-7 L Charnock 7/2: 0304021: 3 b f He Loves Me -
Nuaguese (Prince Regent): Broke her mdn tag, led 2f out & driven out in a mdn claimer at
Edinburgh: eff at 7f, stays 1m: acts on fast & yld grnd & on any trk.   15
2728 ELEGANT FASHION [8] (E Weymes) 4-8-3 K Darley 2/1 FAV: 0-00032: Kept on under press
& is in gd form: see 2728.   18
2807 IRISH HERO [1] (R Sheather) 4-8-4 W Woods(3) 7/2: 2000003: Stayed on late: little
form since 1558 (10f).   13
2762 MASTER MUSIC [6] (M Brittain) 3-8-0 A Proud 20/1: 0000004: Made much: little form.   05
2795 FANNY ROBIN [2] 3-7-7(BL) J Lowe 11/2: 0400420: Bl first time: btr 2795 (stiffer trk). 00
2409 DAISY STAR [3] 3-7-7 M Fry 14/1: -000000: Sn prom, fdd: see 2409.   00
2414 Swiftspender [4] 8-2   2818 Nipknowes [7] 8-2(bl)
8 ran   ½,3,5,1½,½   (Mrs H P Rohan)   P Rohan Malton, Yorks

2888 QUEENSFERRY NURSERY HANDICAP 2YO   £1295   7f   Firm 19 +03 Fast   [40]

2423 MUBDI [7] (H T Jones) 2-9-1 R Hills 3/1 JT.FAV: 2301: 2 br c Star de Naskra -
Manal (Luthier): Well bckd & made most, readily in a nursery h'cap at Edinburgh: lightly rcd
sort who seems suited by front running over an easy 7f: best form on fast grnd & may win
again in similar company.   42
2595 FOUNTAINS-CHOICE [10] (K Stone) 2-9-0(VIS) G Brown 11/2: 2002012: Visored first time:
no ch with winner but is in gd form: see 2595.   30
2757 VENHERM [5] (P Calver) 2-8-2 M Fry 20/1: 0003023: Led after 2f: kept on under press.   15
2095 CIREN JESTER [4] (W Musson) 2-8-1 A Mackay 3/1 JT.FAV: 0024: Well bckd: ev ch: btr 2095. 09
2724 CRAIGENDARROCH [1] 2-8-11 C Dwyer 14/1: 0010000: Ev ch in str: btr 2724.   14
2611 OLD EROS [9] 2-9-4 R Cochrane 6/1: 100: Never nearer: lightly rcd since 873.   20
2680 ACCUSTOMED [8] 2-9-4 W Woods(3) 10/1: 000300: Prom, fdd: best in 2287 (yld grnd).   00
2383 LISIANTHUS [3] 2-9-7 K Darley 8/1: 03000: Wide straight & no show: btr 1722, 1382.   00
2607 Geobritony [2] 8-8   2798 Mons Future [6] 8-5
10 ran   3,1,2,2½,½   (Hamdan Al-Maktoum)   H T Jones Newmarket

---

NEWCASTLE   Tuesday October 7th   Lefthand, Galloping Track

Official Going Given As FIRM

2889 E.B.F. POLWARTH MAIDEN STAKES 2YO   £3330   7f   Good 48 -25 Slow

2036 ZARBYEV [2] (G Harwood) 2-9-0 G Starkey 4/11 FAV: 321: 2 ch c Nureyev - Grand Bonheur
(Blushing Groom): Promising colt: hvly bckd, dsptd the lead & went on inside final 2f for a
very cheeky ½L success in a mdn at Newcastle: last time out a fine 2nd to Genghiz at Newmarket: first foal of a sprint winner: stays a stiff 7f & looks sure to be suited by 1m:
acts on gd & fast grnd & a gall trk: should win more races & rate more highly.   52
1928 SCHMUTZIG [1] (L Cumani) 2-9-0 R Cochrane 6/1: 02: Al up there: flattered by ½L defeat
but ran well: improving colt who cost $50,000 as a yearling: stays 7f: acts on gd & fast grnd
and should find a race.   42
2716 SPRUCE BABY [5] (S Norton) 2-9-0 J Lowe 16/1: 03: Stayed on well closing stages aand
can continue to improve: will be suited by 1m: see 2716.   36
2468 THE MAIN MAN [11] (C Brittain) 2-9-0 W Carson 16/1: 004: Dsptd lead most: gd effort:
rather lightly rcd colt who should improve: acts on gd grnd.   34
--   CUSHINA [13] 2-8-11 G Duffield 25/1: 0: Late hdway on debut & looks sure to improve:
appears certain to be suited by another furlong.   28
1872 TRY MY BRANDY [7] 2-9-0 S Cauthen 10/1: 000: Abs: twice well below 1452.   26
2029 KENTONS LAD [14] 2-9-0 M Wood 20/1: 00: Never nearer 7th & looks sure to do btr
than this: brother to winning 2yo Kenton's Girl: one to keep an eye on.   24
--   MARQUETERIE [9] 2-8-11 N Connorton 16/1: 0: Never nearer on debut: half sister to
several winners in the States: will do much btr than this.   22

2756 Freddie Ashton [8] 9-0(eyeshield)   -- Will Raine [3] 9-0
-- Danensian [15] 9-0   2177 Danse Arabe [10] 9-0   2667 Happy Harriet [6] 8-11
-- Grossen [12] 9-0
14 ran   ½,2½,1½,2,2,1,¾   (Jerome Brody)   G Harwood Pulborough, Sussex

2890 NEWLANDS CLAIMING STAKES 3YO   £1314   1m 2f Good 48 +04 Fast

2549 CAPRICORN BLUE [3] (J Fitzgerald) 3-9-0(vis) S Cauthen 3/1: 4241101: 3 b g Blue Cashmere-
Aqua Nimba (Acropolis): In gd form and led over 3f out, ridden out final 1f in a 3yo claimer
at Newcastle: earlier won a similar event at Yarmouth (made all) and a seller at Newcastle:
well suited by forcing tactics over 9/10f on gd & fast grnd: wears a visor.   28
1813 BLACK DIAMOND [4] (A Jarvis) 3-9-0 J Lowe 7/1: 0300222: Abs: al prom & kept on:
gd effort & should certainly find a seller: see 1396, 657.   24
2603 NAP MAJESTICA [7] (M Camacho) 3-9-0 D Nicholls 9/4 FAV: 0104323: Uneasy fav & btr 2603. 18
-- NOZET [6] (W Jarvis) 3-9-1 G Starkey 6/1: 0031004: Never nearer: ex French filly who
is a winner in the Provinces: seems to stay 10f: acts on good ground.   12
2734 DAVALLIA [5] 3-8-11 R Cochrane 11/2: 3-000: Fdd over 2f out: lightly rcd: see 430.   06
2818 OPTIMISM FLAMED [1] 3-8-10 M Beecroft 16/1: -200000: Made much, faded : best in 183.   00
2760 TAXI MAN [2] 3-8-12 M Birch 20/1: 0000000: Fdd in str: best 960.   00
7 ran   2,3,4,nk,10   (P Asquith)   J Fitzgerald Malton, Yorks

2891 BBC RADIO NEWCASTLE H'CAP (0-35) 3YO+   £2663   1m   Good 48 +01 Fast   [33]

2728 SHARONS ROYALE [8] (R Whitaker) 3-8-6 K Bradshaw(5) 10/1: 2441441: 3 ch g Royal Match -
Rose Amber (Amber Rama): In gd form this season and led over 2f out, cmftbly in a h'cap at
Newcastle: earlier a winner of a mdn at Hamilton: very eff at 1m, does stay further: acts
on gd & fast grnd & does well on a stiff trk.   26
2581 SHARP SHOT [4] (J Dunlop) 5-8-9 W Carson 16/1: 0-00002: Had difficulty finding a run
& finished very well: unlucky? lightly raced and by far his best effort this season: stays
1m well: last successful in '84 at Leicester & Brighton: acts on any grnd but likes it
good or firm.   20
2581 SAND DOLLAR [10] (M Prescott) 3-8-9 G Duffield 15/2: -133003: Not clear run & ran
on well: good effort: see 1614.   24
2797 GOOD N SHARP [5] (G Calvert) 5-7-7 J Lowe 10/1: -200404: Prom, hmpd closing stages.   01
1177 NEW BARNET [19] 4-7-11 Abigail Richards(7) 25/1: 40-0000: Ch over 2f out: abs &
remains a mdn: stays 1m & acts on gd ground.   01
2797 ZIO PEPPINO [15] 5-8-8 Julie Bowker(7) 10/1: 0301130: Al there: see 2762.   10
2549 O I OYSTON [20] 10-8-9 J Carroll(7) 10/1: 0222020: Made most, fdd: btr 2549 (seller).   00
2832 QUALITAIRESS [2] 4-8-0(vis) P Burke(7) 5/1 FAV: 0121200: Not clear run: see 2755.   00
2264 Bella Bañus [16] 9-1   2780 Baxtergate [11] 7-10   2730 Moores Metal [9] 9-10
2536 Aristocrat Velvet [3] 9-10   2762 Single Hand [13] 8-2
2797 Kamaress [17] 8-1   2629 Heavenly Hoofer [14] 8-7
2086 Rossett [7] 7-9   2816 Henrys Venture [12] 8-4
-- Norton Warrior [18] 7-12   2322 Rock Salt [1] 7-8
19 ran   1½,¾,hd,2,1   (W W Birch)   R Whitaker Wetherby, Yorks

2892 HEATHFIELD HANDICAP STAKES (0-35) 3YO   £2264   2m   Good 48 -09 Slow   [38]

*2587 NIMBLE NATIVE [6] (S Norton) 3-8-9 J Lowe 4/1: 0030411: 3 ch f Our Native - Fleeting
Vision (Pronto): Overcame difficulties in running to lead inside the final 1f by the minimum
margin in a 3yo h'cap at Newcastle: winner of a similar event at Edinburgh last time and first
time out successful in a fillies mdn at Catterick: very eff around 15f/2m: seems to acts on
firm & yld & on any trk: has worn a visor though not when/winning last 2 outings.   28
2760 DENALTO [4] (Denys Smith) 3-7-10 M Fry 11/4 FAV: 3302022: Led dist, hdd but battled
back well & was just denied: clear of rem: deserves a win soon: see 2760.   14
2605 MSHATTA PALACE [1] (J Dunlop) 3-8-12 W Carson 6/1: -0043: Ran in snatches but seemed
to appreciate this 2m trip and is evidently a staying sort: acts on fast grnd.   26
2760 GRATIFY [5] (P Walwyn) 3-7-12 N Howe 7/1: 0034034: Ev ch, one paced: see 2760.   10
2683 INDIAN ORATOR [7] 3-9-7 S Cauthen 9/2: 3134400: Set the pace: see 1135.   28
2682 COMAZANT [2] 3-8-11 G Starkey 11/2: -00020: Led briefly 2f out: see 2682.   16
2760 LAKISTE [3] 3-8-1(1ow) N Connorton 12/1: 0443040: Wknd str: see 2040.   00
7 ran   shhd,4,1½,4,1½   (Bahman Abtahi)   S Norton High Hoyland, Yorks

2893 NEWCASTLE UNIV. TURF CLUB STAKES 3YO   £1450   1m 1f Good 48 -25 Slow

-2622 BOLERO MAGIC [6] (H Cecil) 3-9-0 S Cauthen 1/2 FAV: -221: 3 b c Overskate - Firebird
(Nijinsky): Promising colt: landed the odds with the minimum of fuss in a minor event at
Newcastle: 2nd on previous 2 outings and unraced in '85: eff over 1m/9f on gd & firm grnd:
open to further improvement.   50
*2550 ICHNUSA [1] (J Dunlop) 3-9-4 W Carson 4/1: -412: Mkt drifter, well clear of rem but
no ch with winner: stays 1m: see 2550.   48
*2726 SHINING SKIN [4] (P Walwyn) 3-9-4 N Howe 11/2: 0-00013: Outpcd final 2m: see 2726 (10f). 34
2409 MUSICAL AID [5] (T Craig) 3-8-11 A Mackay 100/1: 0000004: Chall 2f out: well btn in
sellers previously.   10
1626 NO IDEA [3] 3-9-0 M Birch 33/1: -00: No threat on only second ever outing: related to
minor winners here and abroad.   00

2483 LATRIGG LODGE [2] 3-9-0 L Charnock 100/1: 00-0000: Rank outsider, no dngr: moderate mdn   00
6 ran   1½,7,7,4,8   (M Samlalsingh)   H Cecil Newmarket

2894 E.B.F. PRINCES MAIDEN STAKES 2YO   £3134   1m   Good 48 +05 Fast

2761 DOLLAR SEEKER [5] (M Ryan) 2-9-0 R Cochrane 9/2: 00321: 2 b c Buckfinder - Syrian
Song (Damascus): Well bckd when gaining first success, showing a gd turn of foot to draw
clear final 1f in quite a fast run 2yo mdn at Newcastle: has made steady improvement as he has
tackled longer dists and will stay 10f plus next season: acts on firm & gd grnd & runs
well on a stiff trk: the type to continue improving.   50
2628 ANGEL CITY [3] (J Dunlop) 2-9-0 W Carson 7/1: 0042: Not the best of runs, kept on
well and is suited by 1m, likely to benefit from lngr dists next season: see 2044.   42
2628 GOLDEN TREE [7] (J Etherington) 2-9-0 K Darley 14/1: 00003: Led briefly dist and has
shown improved form since being tried 'over 1m: see 1049.   38
2761 BONAFORTUNE [2] (D Morley) 2-9-0 R Guest 16/1: 044: Onepaced but making improvement
aand is suited by 1m: see 2761.   34
2615 SNAAN [13] 2-9-0 S Cauthen 8/1: 030: Made much: see 2615.   34
2657 OLD MAESTRO [12] 2-9-0 G Starkey 10/11 FAV: 020: Hvly bckd, ev ch, wknd: much btr 2657.   33
2571 Reef Of Gold [4] 9-0   1965 Ji Jimmy [11] 9-0   --   Daffodil [10] 8-11
1075 Jazz Dancer [6] 9-0   2628 Strong Sea [1] 9-0   2423 Stray No More [9] 9-0
12 ran   3,1½,2,hd,½   (T Ramsden)   M Ryan Newmarket

BRIGHTON   Tuesday October 7th   Lefthand, Sharpish, Undulating Track

Official Going Given As FIRM

2895 E.B.F. SOMPTING MAIDEN STAKES (DIV 1)   £1031   6f   Firm 18 +08 Fast

2788 CHORITZO [2] (R Williams) 2-8-11 J Reid 1/2 FAV: 2221: 2 b f Runnett - Magee
(Weaver's Hall): Useful filly: gained a deserved success with an easy all the way win in a
fast run 2yo mdn at Brighton: second on her three previous outings and was not winning out
of turn: half sister to the useful sprinter Eastern Song: eff at 6f, should stay 7f: acts
on any trk, but seems suited by front running on a sharpish one: goes well on fast grnd.   52
1501 BRAZILIAN PRINCESS [1] (P Kelleway) 2-8-11 T Williams 7/1: 002: Abs: sn prom but
was easily outpcd by the winner: lightly rcd: see 1126: stays 6f.   29
2600 SALINAS [4] (J Winter) 2-8-11 P Robinson 6/1: 003: Prom, kept on: stays 6f: see 2600.   27
2529 LAZIM [6] (C Benstead) 2-9-0(bl) B Rouse 16/1: 043004: Never nearer: may stay further
than 6f: acts on gd & fast grnd & a sharpish trk.   30
2229 DEGENERALE [5] 2-9-0 W Woods(3) 20/1: 00: Prom, ev ch: 8,000 gns purchase who showed
some impr here: acts on fast grnd.   26
2118 BATTLE STING [8] 2-9-0 P Cook 66/1: 0000: No extra final 2f: rated 29 in 1162 (5f).   10
2812 Spitzabit [1] 9-0   2788 Goodnight Master [3] 8-11
8 ran   8,½,shhd,1½,8   (Christopher Wright)   R Williams Newmarket

2896 SALTDEAN HANDICAP (0-35) 3YO+   £2617   1m 2f   Firm 18 -04 Slow   [34]

*2807 MINUS MAN [13] (W Holden) 8-7-10 R Morse(5) 4/1: 3042311: 8 b g Firestreak -
Cheb's Honour (Cheb's Lad): In fine form & led over 1f out, ridden out for a narrow win in
a h'cap at Brighton: last time out just got up in an app. h'cap at Goodwood: in '85 won a
h'cap at Kempton & in '84 won again at Kempton: eff over 1m, stays 10f well: acts on firm
& yld grnd on any trk: retains his form well.   11
2837 FOOT PATROL [8] (P Cundell) 5-8-11 C Rutter(3) 9/2: 2104322: Ran on well final 1f &
just btn: seems equally effective over 1m/10f & loves it here: see 1967.   25
1945 NASKRACKER [3] (G Harwood) 3-8-12 A Clark 15/2: -000203: Abs: ev ch final 2f: see 1559.   27
2728 WILLBE WILLBE [1] (C Brittain) 3-7-13(1ow) M Roberts 16/1: 0001304: Best in 2230(1m).   02
2617 LEONIDAS [11] 8-9-3 J Reid 14/1: 0410000: Led over 1m: see 1539.   12
+2516 ON TO GLORY [6] 3-8-10 B Rouse 3/1 FAV: B300210: Well below form 2516.   02
2617 FIRE BAY [10] 5-9-8(bl) T Williams 4/1: 130-040: Fin 7th: btr 2617 (C/D).   00
2416 Tina Rosa [12] 7-7(VIS)(8oh)   2807 Cosmic Flight [2] 8-2
2837 Salloom [4] 9-2   *1558 True Weight [5] 8-9   2617 French Emperor [9] 7-12
12 ran   hd,3,8,½,7,shhd   (Whitting Commodities Ltd)   W Holden Newmarket

2897 BRIGHTHELMSTONE NURSERY H'CAP 2YO   £2641   1m   Firm 18 -35 Slow   [45]

2529 STATE BALLET [6] (I Balding) 2-9-7(vis) J Matthias 7/1: 01001: 2 b c Pas De Seul -
Cassina (Habitat): Fairly useful colt: defied top weight when making most, ridden out in a
slow run nursery h'cap at Brighton: earlier a winner of a mdn at Salisbury: well suited by
1m: acts on gd & firm grnd & on any trk: carries weight well.   49
1561 BE CHEERFUL [3] (J Winter) 2-8-7 P Robinson 10/1: 4302: Abs: ran on well & nearly
got up: good effort: clearly stays 1m well: half sister to several winners incl the useful
sprinter Numismatist: acts well on gd & fast grnd & should find a winner.   34
2718 PARKLANDS BELLE [1] (M Haynes) 2-8-4 P Cook 3/1: 0201333: Ev ch: see 2718 (9f).   26
2178 SAY YOU WILL [5] (P Makin) 2-8-6 M Roberts 12/1: 4004044: Prom, ev ch: stays 1m: see 2178   22
*2580 VISION OF WONDER [2] 2-7-13 C Rutter(3) 10/1: 0010: No threat: btr 2580 (seller).   11
2798 FU LU SHOU [4] 2-8-2 T Williams 7/4 FAV: 00120: Hvly bckd disapp: btr 2798, 2470 (gall trks).   09

2756 KIERON PRESS [7] 2-8-12(bl) J Reid 6/1: 3140040: Prom, wknd: btr 2756 (7f).   00
7 ran   hd,2½,3,2,2½   (D H Back)   I Balding Kingsclere, Hants

2898 STEYNING SELLING H'CAP (0-25) 3YO   £888   7f   Firm 18 -33 Slow   [24]

2417 THE UTE [4] (L Bower) 3-9-6(bl) T Williams 4/1: 1204221: 3 ch g Hot Spark - Lantonside
(Royal Palace): Consistent performer in this grade: led inside the final 1f, driven out in a
slow run 3yo selling h'cap at Brighton (sold 3,000 gns): in fine form this season, earlier
winning an app. selling h'cap at Windsor & placed on numerous occasions: very eff at 6/7f,
stays 1m: acts on gd & fast grnd & loves a sharp trk, especially Brighton: genuine sort.   23
1560 GOLDEN STRAW [5] (C Reavey) 3-8-13(bl) J Reid 10/1: -000002: Led after 2f: led again
final 1f & just btn: gd effort after an abs: effective over 7f on fast grnd & should
find a similar event.   15
2836 TREMENDOUS JET [1] (M Madgwick) 3-9-2 E Guest(3) 4/1: 1000223: Fin very well & was
just btn: in fine form and ran well at Brighton: see 2697.   17
2312 MISS HICKS [7] (M Ryan) 3-9-0 P Robinson 3/1 FAV: -00004: Ev ch in str: dropped to
selling company today: should note race 2186.   11
2429 MISS VENEZUELA [2] 3-8-3 R Fox 20/1: 0040000: Mkt drifter, never nearer: see 1288.   00
2238 DORADE [8] 3-8-13(bl) B Rouse 6/1: 3010400: Early ldr: fdd: best 1824 (made all).   01
2621 TOUCH THE SAIL [3] 3-7-13 W Woods(1) 5/1: -042040: No show: best in 1771 & appears
none too consistent.   00
2312 HEAVENLY CAROL [10] 3-8-12 C Rutter(3) 6/1: -000000: Fin 9th: active in mkt but
little form to recommend: see 835 (5f).   00
2312 Winsong Melody [11] 9-0   1827 Sequestration [6] 8-4
10 ran   nk,nk,2,2½,2   (R Bastian)   L Bower Beauworth, Hants

2899 E.B.F. SOMPTING MAIDEN STAKES (DIV 2)   £1019   6f   Firm 18 -20 Slow

2555 INSHAD [5] (A Stewart) 2-8-11 M Roberts 8/15 FAV: 031: 2 b f Indian King - Glancing
(Grundy): Hvly bckd & made ev yd, very easily in a 2yo maiden at Brighton: quite a speedily
bred filly who seems effective with forcing tactics over a sharpish 6f: acts on fast &
yld ground: should rate more highly.   35
2744 STARS IN MOTION [3] (D Arbuthnot) 2-9-0 J Reid 25/1: 0030002: Nearest fin but had
no ch with the easy winner: best effort since 1675.   24
2596 AUNT FRANCES [2] (J Winter) 2-8-11 B Rouse 9/4: 03: Sn 2nd: eased when btn: see 2596.   11
2527 DEEP RAPTURES [4] (R Laing) 2-8-11 B Procter 16/1: 004: No show: lightly rcd filly
who is a half sister to a winning 2yo: needs to improve.   00
1692 MALACHI LAD [1] 2-9-0 P Bradwell 66/1: 30000: Abs: al last: little form.   00
5 ran   2½,7,2½,10   (Hamdan Al-Maktoum)   A Stewart Newmarket

2900 AMATEUR RIDERS STAKES 3YO+   £1649   1m 4f   Firm 18 -48 Slow

2699 STORM HOUSE [6] (K Brassey) 4-11-0 Mr T Thomson Jones 10/11 FAV: 2230-31: 4 ch g Streak-
Nelski (Skymaster): Well bckd & led over 2f out, under press in a very slow run amateur riders
event at Brighton: first success on the Flat but is a winning hurdler: stays 12f: acts on
soft, likes fast grnd.   10
2110 OUR HERO [2] (J Dunlop) 3-10-9 Mr R Hutchinson 2/1: -002: Ev ch final 2f: stays 12f
but seems of only modest ability: see 1818.   08
*2727 HEIGHT OF SUMMER [1] (D Arbuthnot) 5-11-11 Mr M Armytage 7/1: 0030013: Prom, kept on:
impossible task at these weights but ran well: see 2727.   15
2372 WILD GINGER [4] (D Oughton) 4-11-6(vis) Mr G Webster(5) 9/1: 2000334: Led after 4f.   09
-- HAWSER [5] 4-11-0 Mr D Madgwick(3) 25/1: -0004-0: Fdd final 4f: dual winner over hdles,
but a mdn on the Flat: acts on fast grnd.   00
1969 HIMORRE [3] 7-11-3 Mr S Cowley(5) 66/1: -000-00: Al rear.   00
2572 Kalimpong [8] 10-11
7 ran   2,shhd,½,12,12   (Mrs Nicole Myers)   K Brassey Upper Lambourn, Berks

Official Going Given As GOOD/FIRM IN STRAIGHT, REMAINDER FIRM

2901 EBF BUSHBURY MAIDEN FILLIES STKS 2YO   £1145   1m 1f   Good/Firm 22 -08 Slow

1464 RIVER JIG [3] (P Cole) 2-8-11 T Quinn 10/1: 01: 2 b f Irish River - Baranova
(Nijinsky): Impr filly: despite a long break recovered from a tardy start to lead 2f out,
comfortably in a 2yo fillies mdn at Wolverhampton: cost $220,000 as a yearling and is a half
sister to winning juvenile Miranda: already stays 9f well & seems certain to be suited by
middle distances next season: acts on gd/firm grnd & on a gall trk: should rate more highly.   48
2664 DEBACH DELIGHT [6] (M Tompkins) 2-8-11 G Carter 8/1: 032: Led briefly over 2f out:
continues to impr as she steps up in dist: sure to win a race: see 2664.   45
2710 CAS EN BAS [2] (J Dunlop) 4-11-6(bl) G Baxter 7/2 JT FAV: 043: Ran on same pace, though
not btn far: improving steadily: eff over 8/9f on gd & fast grnd: see 2487.   44
-- SUTOSKY [10] (I Matthews) 2-8-11 G Dickie 33/1: 4: Mkt drifter on debut: stayed on from
below dist & likely to impr next time: 30,000 gns yearling who is bred to be suited by
middle dists: acts on gd/firm grnd.   38

--   RUSSIAN LULLABY [8] 2-8-11 T Ives 20/1: 0: Never nearer on racecourse debut and almost
certain to step up on this next time: first foal whose dam was a winning stayer: stays 9f:
acts on gd/firm grnd.   30
2215 NABRAS [11] 2-8-11 A Murray 10/1: 3300: Front rank most, eased: much btr in 1996 (6f).   10
2703 EMILYS PRIDE [13] 2-8-11 W R Swinburn 7/2 JT FAV: 40: Made most: wknd into 8th: btr 2703 00
--   JOARA [5] 2-8-11 S Whitworth 7/1: 0: Prom over ½way: quite well bckd debutant who will
be all the better for this experience: 16,000 gns yearling who should be suited by middle
dists in time.   00
2675 LA VIE EN ROSE [7] 2-8-11 M Hills 4/1: 00: Friendless in the mkt: prom to ½way, sn
btn & trailed in last: disapp after showing promise on her debut in 2675 (7f) : found to be lame. 00
--   Karonga [12] 8-11   2527 Cubby Hole [4] 8-11   --   Luckley [9] 8-11
2788 Lady Westown [14] 8-11   --   Going Greek [1] 8-11
14 ran   ½,nk,3,5,10   (Fahd Salman)   P Cole Whatcombe, Berks

2902 FINAL FLING SELLING STAKES 3YO   £693   1m6.5f Good/Firm 22 -80 Slow

--   LOVE YOU ROSY [3] (G Reveley) 3-8-8 Paul Eddery 14/1: -1: 3 b f Derring Rose -
Elizabeth Jane (Andrea Mantegna): Made a successful racecourse debut, led below dist,
comfortably in a slowly run 3yo seller at Wolverhampton (bought in 3,000 gns): clearly suited
by a distance of grnd & is now likely to go hurdling: acts on gd/firm grnd & on a gall trk.   20
2299 MITALA MARIA [8] (A Stewart) 3-8-8 W R Swinburn 10/11 FAV: -02302: Dropped in class
and made odds-on to win this modest contest: led briefly 2f out, kept on well: stays 14f
: officially rated 32 & should be up to winning a seller.   16
*2789 G G MAGIC [7] (D Morley) 3-9-2 A Murray 11/4: 0004213: Made most: in gd form: see 2789. 18
2590 GO FLAMINGO [6] (A James) 3-8-8 L Riggio(7) 14/1: 0-40044: Wknd str: no worthwhile form. 00
*2590 LISAKATY [5] 3-8-13 R Wernham 5/1: 0043010: Best over 12f here in 2590.   00
2789 TIBER GATE [1] 3-8-11 P Dalton(7) 20/1: 0000000: Wknd home turn: no form to his name.   00
--   CHARIOTS OF FIRE [4] 3-8-11 A Dicks(7) 33/1: -0: Mkt drifter on debut & appears of
little ability.   00
7 ran   1½,4,10,8,2,10   (P D Savill)   G Reveley Saltburn, Guisborough, Yorks

2903 STAFFORDSHIRE NURSERY H'CAP 2YO   £1965   5f   Good/Firm 22 +05 Fast   [46]

2781 NATIONS SONG [9] (R Stubbs) 2-8-0(1ow) J H Brown(0) 5/1: 1400031: 2 b f Gold Song -
Girl Commander (Bold Commander): Genuine filly: stayed on strongly to lead close home in
quite a fast run nursery h'cap at Wolverhampton: earlier won sellers at Lingfield & Yarmouth
and then won a claimer, again at Yarmouth: very eff over 5f on firm & yld grnd: acts on
any trk: does not seem to need blinkers now.   28
2729 OUT ON A FLYER [5] (D Elsworth) 2-7-7 D Brown 4/1: 0213242: Led briefly inside dist,
caught near fin: remains in gd form: see 2729 & 2020.   18
2843 SILVERS ERA [7] (N Callaghan) 2-8-4 G Bardwell(7) 7/1: 0034103: Ev ch: in gd form.   26
2698 BLAZING HIGH [6] (L Piggott) 2-9-7 T Ives 33: 034U4D: Tried to make all, wknd
inside dist: fin 4th but rider failed to weigh in, disq. & placed last: see 2698 & 1495.   39
2729 MR MUMBLES [8] 2-8-4 N Adams 33/1: 0040000: Ev ch: fin 5th, placed 4th: best in 1550.   22
2744 MERE MUSIC [10] 2-8-10 W R Swinburn 16/1: 0100200: Al prom: fin 6th, placed 5th: see 2535 25
+2588 PETERS BLUE [4] 2-8-7 G Carter 7/2 FAV: 041110: Fdd into 7th: btr in 2588 (sharp trk).   00
2261 ABSOLUTION [1] 2-9-3 S Whitworth 8/1: 2122000: Front rank: fin 8th: see 1693.   00
2717 ON YOUR PRINCESS [3] 2-9-5(vis) P D'arcy 10/1: 0202030: Fdd into 9th: can do btr.   00
2698 Johnkeina [11] 8-8   2579 Flag Bearer [2] 8-0
11 ran   ½,1,1½,shhd,1,½,½,1¾   (Nation Wide Racing Co Ltd)   R Stubbs Leyburn, Yorks

2904 EBF BUSHBURY MAIDEN FILLIES STKS 2YO   £1132   1m 1f Good/Firm 22 -29 Slow

2527 IVORY FIELDS [11] (M Stoute) 2-8-11 W R Swinburn 11/8 FAV: 031: 2 ch f Sir Ivor -
Norette (Northfields): Useful filly: well suited by this longer trip, led over 2f out and
was pushed clear in a 2yo fillies mdn at Wolverhampton: cost $820,000 and is certain to be
suited by middle dists next term: stays 9f well: acts on gd & fast grnd & on a gall trk:
the type to impr further.   48
2119 SCATTERED SHOWERS [4] (D Elsworth) 2-8-11 A Mcglone 12/1: 02: Stayed on well without
troubling winner: clearly stays 9f well: acts on gd/firm grnd & on a gall trk: sure to win
a race: see 2119.   40
2522 APPEALING DANCER [9] (M Jarvis) 2-8-11 T Lucas 6/1: 03: Made most: stays 9f: see 2522.   35
2133 FAIRY GOLD [5] (M Dickinson) 2-8-11 B Thomson 3/1: 44: Led early: one paced: bred to
be suited by middle dists & should do btr than this: see 2133.   32
2527 LAGTA [2] 2-8-11 G Baxter 16/1: 000: Al mid-div over this longer trip: eff over 7/9f
& gd/firm grnd: see 1518.   26
--   TRIBAL PAGEANT [10] 2-8-11 G Carter 33/1: 0: Easy to back on debut: should improve.   24
2675 VESTAL FLAME [8] 2-8-11 T Ives 7/1: 00: Dropped in class: easy to back & no real
threat: half sister to 10f winner Tiber Creek & should do btr than this.   00
2531 Trivia [6] 8-11   2287 Aljaw [1] 8-11   --   Miss Penguin [7] 8-11
2577 Della Robbia [3] 8-11
11 ran   2,2,1½,2,1   (Mana Al Maktoum)   M Stoute Newmarket

2905 BOCOBEL OAK FILLIES H'CAP 3YO 0-35   £2166   7f   Good/Firm 22   -24 Slow   [38]

2810 IYAMSKI [4] (W Hastings Bass) 3-9-6 W R Swinburn 8/1: 0230041: 3 b f Baldski -
Cannoness (Cannonade): Was gaining an overdue win when getting up in the final strides of
a 3yo fillies h'cap at Wolverhampton: placed several times previously and needs to be held
up to the last minute: eff over 7/8f on fast & soft grnd: seems well suited by a gall trk.   40
2314 CANADIAN GUEST [3] (H Candy) 3-9-0 W Newnes 12/1: -00202: Led inside dist, just caught:
should find a small h'cap: seems best over 7f at the moment: see 1198.   32
2601 ANNABELLINA [1] (G Wragg) 3-8-6 R Hills 8/1: 0423003: Made most: gd effort: see 2076.   21
2681 HAYWAIN [9] (B Hills) 3-8-4(vis) B Thomson 9/1: 3000104: One paced: best in 2601.   15
2550 FESTIVITY [16] 3-9-0 G Carter 20/1: 0020000: Ran on too late: see 1451, 431.   22
1447 IVORY GULL [17] 3-9-7 G Baxter 12/1: 1-00000: Nearest fin: abs since 1447.   25
2719 NATIJA [10] 3-8-13 T Quinn 6/1: -000240: Fdd into 9th: best over 1m in 2534.   00
*2832 CLEOFE [11] 3-9-8(9ex) P Hamblett 3/1 FAV: 0010310: No threat under top weight: best 2832.   00
2670 SKELTON [12] 3-8-3 Paul Eddery 4/1: 0300230: Clearly flattered in 2670: see 650.   00
2459 TZU WONG [5] 3-9-1(BL) S Whitworth 10/1: 0001300: Bl first time: prom to ½way: see 1751   00
2594 Supreme Kingdom [14] 8-13   1885 Petrify [7] 9-4
2816 Mademoiselle Magna [13] 8-9   2614 Altchandoubleyou [8] 8-8
2702 Celestial Drive [15] 8-11
15 ran ½,1½,1½,2,1½,1½,½,1½   (Mrs Mary Lou Cashman)   W Hastings Bass Newmarket

2906 AUTUMN H'CAP 3YO 0-35   £1853   5f   Good/Firm 22   +04 Fast   [39]

2783 BONNY LIGHT [7] (R Sheather) 3-9-7(bl) A Shoults(5) 9/4 FAV: -300121: 3 b c Welsh Saint-
Daring Choice (Daring Display): In grand form and led below dist, comfortably when defying
top weight in quite a fast run 3yo h'cap at Wolverhampton: last month was a well bckd winner
of a stakes race at Thirsk and is much impr by blinkers: very eff over 5/6f on fast & yld
grnd: acts on any trk: carries weight well & can win again.   44
2592 NAGEM [1] (L Barratt) 3-8-1 P Hill(7) 12/1: -042342: Quite consistent: best in 1505.   16
+2120 MERRYMOLES [1] (M Mccourt) 3-8-8(bl) R Wernham 8/1: 0000413: Running well: see 2120.   22
2854 JACQUI JOY [2] (K Ivory) 3-7-8(7ex) G Bardwell(7) 10/1: 0002124: Not qcknd: btr 2854.   04
2488 LEFT RIGHT [15] 3-8-0 R Hills 14/1: 3044100: Ran on same pace: best in 2106.   04
2702 MUHTARIS [11] 3-8-10(bl) W R Swinburn 12/1: 0000100: Led over ½way: best in 2575.   08
*2793 COME TO THE BALL [8] 3-8-11(7ex) B Thomson 4/1: -030410: No show & disapp after 2793.   00
2659 Northern Lad [6] 7-13(bl)   2758 Stanbo [13] 8-7(bl)
1505 Impala Lass [12] 8-13   2702 Ardent Partner [5] 8-7
2702 Kings Ring [9] 9-0   2513 Skylin [4] 7-13   2758 Bridge Of Gold [10] 8-5
2793 Tamalpais [3] 7-12(bl)(3ow)
15 ran 2½,hd,1½,2,2,1½,nk   (Dr K Owusu-Nyantekyi)   R Sheather Newmarket

---

Official Going Given As GOOD

2907 GROUP 3 PRIX ECLIPSE 2YO COLTS & FILL.   £18808   6.5f   Good

--   HOLST [1] (A Fabre) 2-8-7 C Asmussen : 2211: 2 b c Explodent - Angel Rouge: Very
useful French colt: led early and again cl home in Gr 3 Prix Eclipse at St-Cloud: yet to fin
out of the first two and last month won at Longchamp: eff over 6/8f on gd ground: acts on a
gall trk: genuine and consistent sort who is open to further improvement.   68
--   HARLEM SHUFFLE [10] (F Boutin) 2-8-7 F Head : 102: Just held in a desperate fin:
first time out winner at Deauville and is clearly a smart colt in the making: stays 6f well.   66
2485 ONGOING SITUATION [5] (D Morley) 2-8-11 B Rouse : 1312223: Al front rank: no extra
cl home but this was another fine effort: see 2485 & 2252.   66
2435 CENTAURI [2] (B Hills) 2-8-7 B Thomson : 1224: Led dist: fine eff: see 2435.   61
2695 RUMBOOGIE [12] 2-8-7 Y Saint Martin 1: 01030: Cl 5th: running well: see 2695.   60
2552 CEDRICO [6] 2-9-2 A Lequeux : 21100: Not btn very far: see 2552.   66
12 ran nose,1½,nose,shthd,1   (K Abdullah)   A Fabre France

Official Going Given As GOOD

2908 GROUP 2 ST LEGER ITALIANO 3YO   £26630   1m 6f   Firm

1484 COMME LETOILE (J Hindley) 3-9-2 M Hills : 1-31031: 3 b c Star Appeal - The Yellow
Girl: Smart colt: led over 2f out and ran on strongly to win Gr 2 St Leger Italiano at San
Siro: earlier won a val h'cap at Chester: useful juv, winning at Doncaster and Haydock last
season: very eff over 12/14f on firm and soft grd: acts on any trk: genuine sort who clearly
does well when fresh.   74
2201 ROSEDALE USA (J Dunlop) 3-9-2 A Murray : 1221022: Held up, looked dangerous dist
but could not quicken: fine eff nevertheless from this consistent colt: see 2201.   70
2741 DUCA DI BUSTED (A Botti) 3-9-2 J Heloury : 1131143: Fin clear rem: see 1218.   67
6 ran 1½,2,12   (Prince K Al Said)   J Hindley Newmarket

Official Going Given As GOOD

2909 GROUP 1 PREMIO LYDIA TESIO 3/4YO FILL.   £31024   1m 2f   Good

2506 **DUBIAN** (A Stewart) 4-8-13 M Roberts   : 1-01041: 3 b f High Line – Melodina : Smart
filly: took command over 2f out and held on gamely in Gr 1 Premio Lydia Tesio at Capannelle:
earlier just got up in the Gr 3 Royal Whip Stks at the Curragh: very consistent last season,
winning at Yarmouth after being placed in both the English & Irish Oaks: very eff over 10/12f:
acts on firm, tho' possibly btr on gd or yldg ground: tough and genuine filly who acts on
any trk.   75
+2630 **SANTIKI** (M Stoute) 3-8-10 W Carson   1331312: Sustained chall and only just denied:
in grand form at present: see 2630.   78
642 **DANZICA** (E Borromeo) 3-8-10 B Thomson   : 123: Ran to her best: see 642.   69
2638 **RIVERBRIDE** (P L Biancone) 3-8-10 D Boeuf : 0042244: Remains in gd form: see 2452.   67
11 ran ½,4,1,1   (Mohammed Obaida)   A Stewart Newmarket

Official Going Given As FIRM

2910 GROUP 3 C.L. WELD PARK STAKES 2YO FILL   £17350   7f   Firm

2235 **SEA DARA** (I Balding) 2-9-1 J Matthias 5/1: 13101: 2 b f Dara Monarch – Sea Queen
Smart juv: led below dist and just held on under strong press in Gr 3 C L Weld Park Stks at
Phoenix Park: first time out winner of a fillies mdn at Sandown, later made most in a fillies
Listed race at Newbury: half sister to very useful juvs King Hagen & Marlacho: eff over a
stiff 5f, stays 7f well: suited by a sound surface: acts on any trk and is best when up with pace   70
--   **SKY NINSKI** (D Weld) 2-8-7 M J Kinane 3/1: 2: Much touted debutant and only just failed
to make a winning start to her career: clearly stays 7f well: half sister to winning stayer
Water Bailiff and sure to be suited by mid dist next season: acts on fast ground.   61
+2577 **RHONDALING** (P Walwyn) 2-8-13 N Howe 8/1: 3113: Cl 3rd: fine eff: see 2577.   65
--   **PALLASS BLUE** (J Oxx) 2-8-10 S Craine 20/1: 4214: Cl 4th: last month won a fillies mdn
at the Curragh: eff over 7/8f: seems to act on fast & soft grd and on any trk.   62
2635 **FLAWLESS IMAGE** 2-8-13 C Roche 10/1: 1000: Gd eff: stays 7f: see 2113.   61
--   **DIAMOND SEAL** 2-8-10 D Hogan 7/1: 130: Recent winner at Leopardstown: eff over 6/7f
on firm grd.   56
2504 **ERINDALE** 2-8-10 K Moses 10/1: 3210120: Prob unsuited by this very fast grd: see 2504   00
+2687 **LINDAS MAGIC** 2-9-1 P Tulk 2/1 FAV: 2311310: Disapp fav: reportedly ran much too
freely and this run can be ignored: much btr 2687.   00
8 ran nk,½,shthd,1½,½,3,3½   (G Strawbridge)   I Balding Kingsclere, Hants

2911 BALLYSHEEHAN FAIRY KING STAKES 3YO+   £10941   1m 2f   Firm

--   **COCKNEY LASS** (D Weld) 3-9-3 M J Kinane 9/4 FAV: 20-1111: 3 ch f Camden Town – Big
Bugs Bomb: Smart Irish filly: remains unbtn this season after making smooth prog to lead inside
dist in a val fillies Listed race at Phoenix Park: first time out winner at Tipperary and
has since won val races at Leopardstown and again at Phoenix Park: very eff over 8/10f on gd
and firm grd and on any trk: much improved and likely to win more races.   76
2462 **RIYDA** (R J Houghton) 3-8-8 C Roche 10/3: 1223022: Cmftbly beat rem: has not stopped
improving this season and deserves to get her head in front again: see 2462 & 1153.   66
*2633 **GREY GODDESS** (E O'grady) 3-9-3 S Craine 11/4: 3-10113: Consistent filly: stays 10f :see 2633. 68
2633 **ADORAMUS** (J Bolger) 3-9-0 K J Manning 12/1: -44004: Another gd eff: see 2912.   64
2557 **LADINA** 3-9-0 P Shanahan 14/1: -020100: Ran well, fin clear rem: see 2557.   63
2676 **SHEER LUCK** 3-8-8 J Matthias 7/1: -001020: Last to fin but not disgraced: see 2676.   39
9 ran ½,4,hd,½,6,1½,1½   (J O'Morrissey)   D Weld Ireland

Official Going Given As GOOD/FIRM

2912 GROUP 1 SIEMENS OSLO CUP 3YO+   £18332   1m 4f   Good/Firm

2642 **SAND SHIP** (T Dahl) 3-8-7 T Joergensen   : 241: 3 gr c Ela Mana Mou – Desert Nymph
Very useful colt: ran on well for a 2l success in Gr 1 Siemens Oslo Cup at Ovrevoll: clearly
very eff over 12f on gd/firm grd.   68
2693 **GORGEOUS STRIKE** (C Nelson) 3-8-5 J Reid : 3443402: Another gd eff: much travelled
and altho' yet to win this term has picked up plenty of place-money: see 2112.   62
--   **KEEP ME WAITING** 6-9-6 C Gauntlett : -3: Clearly a useful horse.   68
*2389 **GULFLAND** (G P Gordon) 5-8-11 W Ryan : 1011214: Another gd eff: see 2389.   57
11 ran 2,½,1   (Mrs A Larsson)   T Dahl Norway

Official Going Given As GOOD

2913 GROUP 2 DEUTSCHES ST LEGER 3YO   £16949   1m 6f   Good

*2643 PRAIRIE NEBA (U Ostmann) 3-8-11 W Newnes : 211: Very useful German filly: led 2f out
and just held on in a very fast run Gr 2 German St Leger at Dortmund: last month was a
similarly narrow winner of a Gr 3 fillies race at Hanover: very eff over 12/14f on fast &
yldg ground.   68
2643 NORETTA (H Bollow) 3-8-11 P Remmert : 4222: Again had to settle for the minor
honours behind this ultra-game filly: eff over 12/14f on gd & yldg grd: see 2643.   67
2502 VIF ARGENT (P Lautner) 3-9-1 P Waldron : 43: Not btn far.   71
*2454 EL SALTO (H Jentzsch) 3-9-1 G Bocskai : -214: Best over 11f in 2454.   66
2539 MAJESTICIAN 3-9-1 G Duffield : 2122340: Led 1m, fin last: best 2376.   00
8 ran   ½,shthd,3,5½,6,7½   (Walter Vischer)   U Ostmann Germany

Official Going Given As FIRM

2914 GROUP 3 PRIX SAINT-ROMAN 2YO   £17912   1m 1f   Firm

--   CONMAICHE [5] (A Fabre) 2-8-11 C Asmussen : 211: 2 b c King's Lake - Connaught Bridge
(Connaught) Promising French colt: fin well to be btn a shtnk in a close & rather rough fin to
Gr 3 Prix Saint-Roman at Longchamp: subs awarded the race: won a minor event at Deauville in
Aug: eff over 7f, stays 9f well and should be suited by mid dist next season: acts on fast grd   70
--   HARD LEAF [2] (C Head) 2-8-11 G Moore : 212: Fin a very cl 3rd, placed 2nd: recent
winner of a minor event on this trk: appears to act on firm & soft: stays 9f well.   69
--   STEAMSHIP [8] (A Fabre) 2-8-11 D Regnard : 213: The worst sufferer being continually hmpd
by the disqualified Tiger Run in the final 2f: fin 4th, placed 3rd: recently won over 7f
at Evry: acts on firm & soft.   69
--   TIGER RUN [4] (G Mikhalides) 2-8-11 J Velasquez : 11D: Battled hard thr'out final 2f,
first past the post by the narrowest of margins but disqualified and placed 4th for causing
interference.   71
8 ran   shtnk,nk,shthd,hd,nk,ddht,4   (Sheikh Mohammed)   A Fabre France

Official Going Given As FIRM

2915 GROUP 1 PRIX MARCEL BOUSSAC 2YO FILLIES £39618   1m   Firm

*2737 MIESQUE [4] (F Boutin) 2-8-9 F Head : 1311: 2 b f Nureyev - Pasadoble (Prove Out)
Very smart French filly: showed a remarkable turn of foot, coming from well off the pace to
strike the front near the fin of Gr 1 Prix Marcel Boussac at Longchamp: cmftbly beat Sakura
Reiko again in Gr 1 Prix de La Salamandre on the same trk Sept 21: first time out won a minor
fillies race at Deauville: acts on firm & soft grd: eff 6f, stays 1m: certainly looks a
1000 Guineas prospect and her turn of foot should stand her in gd stead no matter what the company. 82
+2675 MILLIGRAM [3] (M Stoute) 2-8-9 W R Swinburn : 12: Led dist, just unable to   match
the winner's astonishing final pace but this was a fine effort   from a fast impr filly and
she certainly looks a classic prospect for next season: see 2675.   80
2737 SAKURA REIKO [6] (P L Biancone) 2-8-9 Y Saint Martin : 11123: Stayed on well to fin
a cl 3rd and very consistent: see 2737, 2358.   79
*2644 PRINCESSE DU BOURG [11] (R Touflan) 2-8-9(14) D Vignali : 114: Met her first defeat
but lost nothing in this topclass company: seems to act on firm & soft: see 2644.   75
2644 THREE GENERATIONS [3] 2-8-9 J Velasquez :   140: Creditable 5th and seems to act
on firm & soft: see 2644.   74
2634 POLONIA [3] 2-8-9 C Asmussen : 1013120: Cl.up most, wknd: perhaps feeling her long
busy season: see 2235 (6f).   73
2358 SHY PRINCESS [8] 2-8-9 M Philipperon :   3120: Cl 7th: gd eff: seems to act firm & hvy   72
2737 WHAKILYRIC [9] 2-8-9 E Saint Martin : 2141230: Stable mate of winner and by no means
disgraced in 8th: stays 1m: acts on firm & yldg: see 2737.   00
--   Bint Alnasr [5] 8-9   2644 Cadeaux Damie [1] 8-9 2739 Connaught Rose [10] 8-9
11 ran   ½,nk,2,½,½,½   (S Niarchos)   F Boutin France

2916 GROUP 1 PRIX DE L'ABBAYE DE LONGCHAMP £34499   5f   Firm

2474 DOUBLE SCHWARTZ [1] (C Nelson) 5-9-10 Pat Eddery 6/4 FAV: 1121241: 5 b h Double Form -
Cassy's Pet (Sing Sing) Very smart, impr sprinter: reverted to 5f and led after ½ way,
holding on gamely in a driving fin to Gr 1 Prix L'Abbaye: earlier won 3 out of his first 4,
Temple Stks at Sandown, Palace House Stks at Newmarket and Gr 3 King George Stks at Goodwood:
below his best over 6f last time and undoubtedly is a 5f specialist: well suited by firm or
gd ground: most genuine and a credit to his trainer.   87
*2742 PARIOLI [8] (J Cunnington Jnr) 5-9-7 M Philipperon : 413-412: Chall winner hard
final 1f, right back to his best: acts on firm & heavy: see 2742.   83
+2772 HALLGATE [13] (S Hall) 3-9-10 G Starkey : 1031213: Ran a tremendous race in defeat,
on ground faster than he really liked: see 2772.   86

851

+2474 GREEN DESERT [10] (M Stoute) 3-9-10 W R Swinburn : 2021314: Stayed on too late and
doesnot have the pace for 5f: see 2474 (6f).   81
2742 COMRADE IN ARMS [13] 4-9-10 C Asmussen : 1202330: Started slowly, gd fin: see 2003.   79
2347 BATAVE [5] 4-9-7 Y Saint Martin : 11-1220: Speed over 3f: see 563, 2347.   74
2772 Sharp Romance [4] 9-10   1889 Rose Of The Sea [12] 9-7
2742 Balser Vole [3] 9-7   *2347 Cricket Ball [7] 9-10
*2457 Premiere Cuvee [2] 9-7   --   Proudest Hour [9] 9-10
*2351 Northern Express [11] 9-10
13 ran   nk,hd,2,shthd,½   (R Sangster)   C Nelson Upper Lambourn, Berks

2917 GROUP 1 PRIX DE L'ARC DE TRIOMPHE   £367985   1m 4f Firm Course Record

+2557 DANCING BRAVE [15] (G Harwood) 3-8-11 Pat Eddery 11/10 FAV: 1121111: 3 b c Lyphard -
Navajo Princess (Drone) Established his claim to being considered the best colt seen this
decade when defeating one of the strongest fields seen in the Arc de Triomphe at Longchamp:
waited with, then displayed a sparkling turn of foot to win in most authorive fashion: met
his only defeat this season when a most unlucky loser of the Epsom Derby: winner of a Gr 3
race at Goodwood last time and earlier impressive winner of the King George Diamond Stks at
Ascot, the Eclipse at Sandown and the 2000 Guineas and Craven Stks at Newmarket: easy winner of
both outings in '85: very eff over 1m/10f really well: acts on soft but his
fine action is well suited by firm or gd ground: has a brilliant turn of foot: a tremendous
credit to his trainer who has kept him in peak form from the early stages of the season.   101
*2639 BERING [14] (C Head) 3-8-11 G Moore : 1-11112: Waited with, came to lead briefly
1f out, unable to hold Dancing Brave's late surge but confirmed himself a highclass midle
distance colt: see 2639: later found to have fractured a shin bone during the race.   97
2506 TRIPTYCH [2] (P L Biancone) 4-9-1 A Cordero : 2123233: Fin well to be placed
yet again in top company and arguably produced her finest performance of the season here.   91
1790 SHAHRASTANI [9] (M Stoute) 3-8-11 W R Swinburn : -111144: Al just behind the leaders,
chall 1f out and ran right up to his best: see 1330.   95
+2200 SHARDARI [5] 4-9-4 G Starkey : -241210: Sn prom, kept on bravely final 2f but was
closer to winner in 1790: see 2200.   93
*2638 DARARA [12] 3-8-8 Y Saint Martin : 112110: Dsptd lead early, stayed up with the
leaders and ran a fine race: see 2638.   88
*2502 ACATENANGO [1] 4-9-4 S Cauthen : -111110: Well there till outpaced final 2f, fin 7th:
first defeat for 13 races: see 2502.   88
*2637 MERSEY [6] 4-9-1 F Head : 111-210: No danger in 8th: see 2637.   84
2736 SAINT ESTEPHE [7] 4-9-4 C Asmussen : -131220: No danger in 9th: gd eff: see 2736.   85
+2461 DIHISTAN [4] 4-9-4 A Kimberley : 1130010: Fin 10f: see 2461.   83
2194 IADES [3] 4-9-4 A Lequeux : 0-41420: Fin 11th: see 2194, 1010.   82
2824 BABY TURK [11] 4-9-4 A Gibert : 4323120: Made much: see 2824, 2453.   79
*2822 NEMAIN [13] 4-9-4 C Roche : 4-20010: Prom, wknd: see 2822.   77
2637 SIRIUS SYMBOLI [8] 4-9-4 M Philipperon : 03-0420: Al rear: see 2637.   75
--   MARIA FUMATA [10] 4-9-0 F Diaz : -0: Chilean chall, fin last.   69
15 ran   1¼,¾,shthd,nk,1½,2,nk,1½,nk,1,2,1½,2,1¼   (K Abdulla)   G Harwood Pulborough, Sx.

2918 GROUP 2 PRIX DE L'OPERA 3/4YO FILLIES   £28500   1m 1f Firm

1116 SECRET FORM [6] (P Bary) 3-8-9 C Asmussen : 11-2221: 3 b f Formidable - Secretive
(Secretariat) Smart French filly: gained a deserved success when winning Prix De L'Opera
(fillies) at Longchamp: runner-up in her prev 3 races, notably when 2l 2nd to Lacovia in the
Gr 1 Prix de Diane at Chantilly: very eff over 9/10f and acts on firm grd.   81
2507 ELLE SEULE [4] (D Smaga) 3-9-0 A Lequeux : 1341002: Ran well to be 2nd and is a
genuine and consistent filly: see 2002.   82
391 BLUE TIP [8] (P L Biancone) 4-9-0 Y Saint Martin : -324013: Cl 3rd: recent winner
of a minor event at Maisons Laffitte: see 98: acts on firm & hvy.   75
--   MANGAYAH [2] (C Head) 3-8-9 G Mosse : 2210104: Creditable 4th: recently won over
12f at Longchamp tho' seems eff at shorter dist: acts on gd & firm grd and likes righthanded trk 75
*2736 FITNAH [5] 4-9-2 G Moore : -102010: Fair eff but btr 2736 (yldg)   75
2638 RELOY [7] 3-8-12 W R Swinburn : 3110320: Fairly close 6th: see 904, 2638.   76
8 ran   1¼,½,nk,½,nk   (P Goulandris)   P Bary France

YORK   Wednesday October 8th   Lefthand, Galloping Track

Official Going Given As GOOD/FIRM

2919 BBC RADIO SHEFFIELD SELLING STAKES 2YO £4172   6f   Good/Firm 26 -16 Slow

2698 WHITE OF MORN [10] (M Mccormack) 2-8-11(bl) W Wharton 12/1: 0041: 2 b c Smoggy - Not
Mistaken (Mill Reef) Impr colt: active in mkt and led after ¼ way, driven out in a 2yo seller
at York (bought in 4200 gns): cost 7000 gns as a yearling and is a half brother to a 12f
winner: eff at 6f, will be suited by further: acts on fast grd and gd trk.   27
965 HIGHLAND LODGE [11] (P Cole) 2-8-11 T Quinn 5/1 JT.FAV: 0002: Well bckd, despite abs:
stayed on well final 1f and looks certain to find a similar event: stays 6f well: see 622.   25
2804 PILGRIM PRINCE [16] (M Usher) 2-9-3 M Wigham 14/1: 0000103: Kept on well final 2f:
another gd run and should be suited by 7f: see 2608.   30

*2609 ITS BEEN RUMOURED [14] (R Simpson) 2-9-0 S Whitworth 6/1: 0014: Led stands side: not btn far: in fine form: see 2609.   26
2815 WHISTLING WONDER [17] 2-9-3 A Munro(7) 12/1: 0000020: Al there: see 2815.   26
2396 RHABDOMANCER [20] 2-8-8 T Ives 14/1: 33300: Sn prom: prob stays 6f: acts on firm & yldg   16
2218 BURCROFT [22] 2-8-11 D Mckeown 5/1 JT.FAV: 0030: Never nearer 7th: btr 2218 (C/D).   13
--   EDENTHORPE [15] 2-8-11 M Hindley(3) 25/1: 0: Mkt drifter: late hdwy on racecourse debut: brother to winning plater Tricenco and is one to watch for a similar event.   08
2609 LEVEN LASS [18] 2-8-8 R Hills 7/1: 003420: No show: btr 2609.   00
2792 LADY BEHAVE [8] 2-9-0 Pat Eddery 7/1: 2010000: Prom, fdd: best 1363 (sharp trk)   00

2792 Gardenia Lady [5] 8-8(bl)			-- Ling Gold [4] 8-8	
2410 Mr Berkeley [13] 8-11(BL)			2744 Our Horizon [6] 8-8	
2138 The Mague [23] 9-3	2744 Swynford Princess [2] 9-0			
2757 Gwynbrook [1] 8-11(bl)			-- Harryaker [21] 8-11	
2535 Take Effect [7] 8-11	2781 Jean Jeanie [3] 8-8(BL)			
2625 Raunchy Rita [12] 8-8	2757 Salop Rouge [9] 8-8(BL)			
2743 Shady Blade [19] 8-8(bl)				

23 ran   ½,nk,nk,1,hd,2,1   (P F Durkan)   M Mccormack

2920 BBC RADIO YORK MAIDEN AUCTION STKS 2YO   £4357   1m   Good/Firm 26 +01 Fast

2159 SILK TOPPER [10] (W Hastings Bass) 2-8-11 Pat Eddery 5/2 FAV: 01: 2 b c Blakeney - Silk Stocking (Pardao) Fast impr colt: led inside final 2f, staying on under press but hmpd slightly on the line and just caught: fin 2nd, placed 1st in a fast run 2yo mdn auction at York: cost 20,000 gns as a yearling and is related to sev winners: eff at 1m, looks sure to stay further: acts on fast grd and a gall trk: on the upgrade.   55
--   BOCATOWER [6] (G Harwood) 2-8-8 G Starkey 11/4: 1D: Stayed on well under press and got up on the line: however disq and placed 2nd for marginal interference: quite cheaply acquired colt who can gain compensation very soon: will stay further than 1m: acts on fast ground and a gall track: 8l clear rem here.   52
1643 BEAT STREET [15] (C Brittain) 2-8-5 T Williams 12/1: 403: Abs: nvr nrr: stays 1m:see 1289.   33
2198 FOURTH LAD [7] (R Hannon) 2-8-5 W Carson 14/1: 004004: Made much: prob stays 1m: acts on gd and fast ground.   30
2484 BUCKRA MELLISUGA [14] 2-8-8 G Duffield 10/1: 300: Much btr 2484, 2239 (7f).   30
2782 BOLD TANGENT [1] 2-8-5 C Rutter(3) 8/1: 400: Btr than this: see 2782 (sharper trk)   24
2804 BRIMUR [4] 2-8-5 B Thomson 10/1: 240: Early leader, fin 7th: twice below 2140 (sharp 7f)   22
2711 SPOILED BRAT [13] 2-8-9(1ow) S Cauthen 9/2: 00: Nicely bckd: never nearer: btr 2711 (7f)   25

2812 Say You [3] 8-5	2147 London Cries [8] 8-2	2541 Night Visitor [12] 8-11	
2607 Dress Up [9] 8-5	2646 Macs Maestro [5] 8-8(BL)		
2703 Making History [2] 8-8		1982 In A Spin [16] 8-2	
2325 Mr Chris Cakemaker [11] 8-2			

16 ran   shthd,8,1½,1½,1½,½,½   (H M Herbert)   W Hastings Bass Newmarket

2921   BARCLAYS UNION TROPHY H'CAP 0-60   £4149   5f   Good/Firm 26 +27 Fast   [59]

*2783 ROTHERFIELD GREYS [9] (A Hide) 4-9-13(7ex) J Leech(7) 10/3 FAV: 1101011: 4 b c Mummy's Pet - Relicia (Relko) Very useful sprinter who is in excellent form: readily defied his 7lbs penalty in very fast run and val h'cap at York: led final 1f, ridden out: in superb form this season, last time out won a h'cap at Goodwood and earlier won 3 of his first 4, val h'cap at York and small h'caps at Edinburgh and Warwick: useful 2yo, but a virus sufferer in '85: stays 6f but is best over 5f on firm or gd ground: usually up with the pace: goes best for J Leech.   68
2772 GEORGE WILLIAM [10] (M Mccourt) 5-8-4(2ow) B Thomson 8/1: 3010002: Ran on well final 1f: gd eff and is a consistent sort: see 2402.   40
2668 BOLLIN EMILY [7] (M H Easterby) 5-9-1(VIS) M Birch 9/2: 4234203: Tried in a visor: led/dsptd lead: another gd eff: see 2537.   50
2783 STEEL CYGNET [4] (Pat Mitchell) 3-8-5(2ow) J Reid 9/1: -003404: Behind, fin well: btr 6f? see 2783.   40
2862 TOBERMORY BOY [5] 9-7-12 N Carlisle 11/2: 0004020: Al there: see 2862 (6f)   30
2858 CHINA GOLD [3] 7-8-4 M Wood 10/1: 2000100: Sn prom: see 2586.   32
2858 IBERIAN START [12] 3-8-3(bl) W Carson 11/2: 0320030: No show: btr 2858, 1027.   00
2858 CELTIC BIRD [8] 6-7-13 A Mackay 10/1: 3113000: Early speed: see 1896.   00
--   Be Lyrical [6] 8-6   2775 Pergode [2] 7-8(bl)   2833 All Is Forgiven [1] 9-10(bl)
2783 Music Machine [11] 8-2
12 ran   1½,nk,nk,½,1½   (Mrs D Gleeson)   A Hide Newmarket

2922 BBC RADIO LEEDS NURSERY H'CAP 2YO   £3724   7f   Good/Firm 26 -17 Slow   [48]

*2677 ORIENT LINE [1] (R Hannon) 2-8-11(10ex) Pat Eddery 6/4 FAV: 02111: 2 gr c Capricorn Line - Rue Talma (Vigo) Fast impr colt: completed his hat-trick, led over 2f out readily, in a nursery h'cap at York: last time out won a similar event at Newbury and first time out a mdn auction at Folkestone: cost only 3400 gns and is closely related to sev minor winners: well suited by 7f and should get 1m: acts on any trk, but is well suited by fast ground: may complete the four-timer.   44
2491 SUNORIUS [10] (J Glover) 2-9-7 D Mckeown 16/1: 0422: Kept on under press and again ran well: met a gd one here: stays 7f: see 2491.   46

2625 ROUGH DANCE [5] (W Jarvis) 2-8-9 R Cochrane 8/1: 04243: Stayed on under press,
went badly left inside final 1f: wore bl in race 2625.   33
2680 BEAU BENZ [8] (M H Easterby) 2-8-3 J Lowe 8/1: 0400024: Badly hmpd final 1f: see 2680.   26
2108 KINGS VICTORY [3] 2-8-10 C Rutter(3) 7/1: 4200: Ev ch: best 1629 (6f)   30
-2137 CLOWN STREAKER [2] 2-8-11 M Birch 8/1: 1010420: Made some: btr 2137 (sharp 6f)   28
*2254 KING KRIMSON [7] 2-9-2 M Hills 5/1: 010: Prom much: btr 2554 (6f).   00
  2218 Windmede [9] 8-1   2476 Young Snugfit [6] 8-7   2648 Penang Beauty [4] 9-1
10 ran   2¼,nk,¾,1,1,hd   (J A Lazzari)   R Hannon Marlborough, Wilts

2923 BBC RADIO HUMBERSIDE STAKES 3YO   £3278   1m 6f   Good/Firm 26 -09 Slow

*2605 POKEYS PRIDE [5] (R Sheather) 3-9-3 M Rimmer 5/1: 0220311: 3 b c Uncle Pokey -
Strawberry Ice (Arctic Storm) In fine form and led over 2f out easily, in a 3yo stks at York:
last time out was a narrow winner at Redcar: well suited by 14f, will prob stay 2m: loves
fast grd and a gall trk: half brother to winning stayer Jowoody and may find a h'cap.   50
2734 GALESA [4] (P Kelleway) 3-8-11 S Cauthen 10/3: 00-022: Led over 2f out: 8l clear 3rd:
stays 14f: see 2734, 2419.   36
2701 CAESAR IMPERATOR [2] (R Akehurst) 3-9-0 A Clark 14/1: -03: Some late hdwy and is
making improvement: half brother to 3 winners in France: stays 14f: acts on fast grd.   27
2605 KAFARMO [7] (G Harwood) 3-9-0 G Starkey 9/2: -034: Much closer to winner in 2605.   23
2776 IN CONTENTION [6] 3-9-0 G Duffield 33/1: -300: No threat: lightly raced gelding who
may be seen over hurdles.   00
2441 CASTLE ROCK [8] 3-9-0 W Carson 11/8 FAV: 0-020: Prom, fdd: disapp: see 2441 (yldg).   00
 -- Febrino [1] 9-0   2759 Turina [3] 8-11
8 ran   4,8,2,15,7   (Mrs M Mann)   R Sheather Newmarket

2924 BBC RADIO CLEVELAND HANDICAP 0-60   £2972   1m 2.5f Good/Firm 26 -11 Slow   [52]

*2690 LYPHLAW [3] (J Dunlop) 3-9-0(5ex) W Carson 15/8 FAV: 0033111: 3 b c Lyphard - New Lawn
(Herbager) Useful, impr colt: heavily bckd and led inside final 1f, ridden out in a h'cap at
York: earlier successful at Ayr and Ripon: stays 10f well, may get further: acts on firm &
yldg grd and on any trk.   55
2693 SAMHAAN [5] (B Hanbury) 4-8-11(bl) R Cochrane 9/2: 2132302: Kept on well final 1f
and just btn: never runs a bad race: see 2477, 2331.   43
2623 MAGIC TOWER [4] (C Brittain) 3-7-12 T Williams 11/2: -402343: Led 2f out: consistent,
but seems to lack a turn of foot: should stay 12f: see 2110.   34
2686 MILL PLANTATION [2] (G Wragg) 7-9-7 Pat Eddery 3/1: 0-00104: Lost place 3f out:
btr 2686, 1325.   40
2572 HAWARDEN [1] 3-8-13(bl) B Thomson 11/2: 4001320: Led over 1m: twice below 1956.   38
2861 THE LODGE PRINCE [6] 4-7-11 P Burke(7) 33/1: 0000-00: No threat: maiden who at one
stage last season was rated 48 but has shown little form since then: acts on fast grd and
stays a stiff 10f.   00
6 ran   ¼,1½,7,½,20   (Sheikh Mohammed)   J Dunlop Arundel, Sussex

Official Going Given As GOOD/FIRM ON STRAIGHT COURSE, FIRM ON ROUND COURSE

2925 LINGFIELD PARK H'CAP STAKES (0-35) 3YO+   £2236   1m 2f Firm 06 +02 Fast   [35]

*2746 THUNDERDOME [3] (O Douieb) 3-8-7(7ex) B Thomson 3/1 FAV: -000011: 3 br f Lyphard -
Mr P's Girl (Mr Prospector) In gd form and was well bckd when leading at the dist, cmftbly in
quite a fast run h'cap at Lingfield: recently won a similar race at Beverley: eff over 1m tho'
seems btr suited by 10f and shd stay further: acts on gd & fast grd and on any trk: may
win again.   30
2431 PORTOGON [14] (M Usher) 8-9-9 D Mckay 16/1: 3000002: Led home turn: see 1365 & 930.   32
2727 DICK KNIGHT [6] (N Ivory) 5-8-8(vis) A Shoults(5) 33/1: 0100203: Gd eff: see 2101.   15
2746 PEARL PET [13] (P Makin) 4-8-5 T Quinn 12/1: 2002234: Placed again: see 850.   12
2896 NASKRACKER [7] 3-8-11 G Starkey 10/1: 0002030: Quick reappearance: never nearer: see 1559 24
2699 TALK OF GLORY [10] 5-8-12 G Baxter 10/1: 2230020: Late prog: btr 2699.   16
2720 HEAD OF SCHOOL [12] 3-8-7 J Reid 10/1: 0424430: Never nearer 7th: see 2720.   00
2807 TOM FORRESTER [11] 5-8-12 C Rutter(3) 6/1: 3044230: Fdd: btr 2807: see 453.   00
*2837 MARSH HARRIER [9] 5-10-2(7ex) Candy Moore(7) 7/1: 4130210: Much btr over 1m in 2837.   00
  2699 Jaaziel [4] 8-4(bl)   2360 Rapid Lad [5] 9-2   2520 Sunley Saint [15] 9-0
  2807 Redden [2] 8-13   735 Tana Mist [8] 8-9
14 ran   3,¾,shthd,nk,¾,1   (Edward Seltzer)   O Douieb Newmarket

2926 E.B.F. BROKERS STAKES 2YO   £1931   6f   Good/Firm 35 +04 Fast

*2791 WAR BRAVE [4] (J Dunlop) 2-9-2 B Thomson 13/8 FAV: 2411: 2 gr c Indian King - Kizzy
(Dancer's Image) Useful colt: heavily bckd and led below dist, driven out in quite a fast
run 2yo stks at Lingfield: recently an easy winner of a similar race at Nottingham: cost

160,000 gns as a yearling and is a half brother to winning juv Dancer's Shadow: very eff
over 6f on fast grd: acts on any trk: consistent sort who will win more races.   58
--   DUNENNY [2] (R Akehurst) 2-8-11 A Clark 50/1: 2: Made a most promising debut: al front
rank and only gave best cl home: half brother to winning juv Beechwood Cottage: clearly very
eff over 6f on fast grd: acts on a sharp trk: sure to win a race on this evidence.   50
2750 FORESIGHT [6] (L Piggott) 2-8-11 W R Swinburn 4/1: 0343: Made most: in gd form:see 2626.   44
--   SERVE N VOLLEY [9] (M Usher) 2-8-8 C Rutter(3) 33/1: 4: Came to chall below dist,
not quicken but this was still a promising debut: cheaply acquired filly who is closely related
to sev winners: acts on gd/firm grd and on a sharp trk: should improve.   38
--   EL REY [15] 2-8-11 R Lines(3) 20/1: 0: Al cl up on his racecourse debut: 12,000 gns
yearling who is a half brother to sev winners: will stay further: acts on gd/firm ground.   32
2675 CORVIGLIA RUN [8] 2-8-8 B Rouse 10/1: 400: Late prog: btr over 7f in 2675.   23
2717 LINDVARO [5] 2-8-11(BL) P Tulk 33/1: 0000: Bl first time: speed most: see 2493.   00
2788 DONT KNOCK IT [10] 2-8-8 R Fox 25/1: 00: Never nearer 8th: half sister to sev minor
winners and should improve further when stepping up in dist: acts on gd/firm grd.   00
*2782 NATIVE DRESS [3] 2-9-2 J Matthias 7/1: 310: Speed over ½ way: fin 9th: much btr 2782.   00
2846 CAVENDISH QUEEN [18] 2-8-8 J Reid 9/1: 00: Early speed: fin in rear: see 2846.   00
--   Thornfield [7] 8-11   2782 Dallors Conquest [11] 8-11
2119 Buy Mums Act [19] 8-11   2791 Linebacker [1] 8-11
2711 The Grifter [16] 8-11   2717 Torrance [20] 8-11 2782 Tumble Time [12] 8-11
2717 Whatta Business [14] 8-11   --   Rectory Girl [13] 8-8
2119 Stainsby Girl [17] 8-8
20 ran   ½,2,½,4,2½,2,½,2½   (Sheikh Mohammed)   J Dunlop Arundel, Sussex

2927 GRE SELLING NURSERY HANDICAP 2YO   £1033   6f   Good/Firm 35 -39 Slow   [27]

2804 YOUNG CENTURION [7] (M Usher) 2-8-7(vis) D Mckay 7/1: 0000001: 2 ch c Roman Warrior -
Becalmed (Right Tack) Wore a visor for the first time and led below dist, gamely, in a selling
nursery h'cap at Lingfield (no bid): cheaply bought colt who is a half brother to winning juv
Mr Panache: best over 6f on gd and fast grd: acts on any trk: seems best when up with pace.   15
2608 MISS ACACIA [6] (R Stubbs) 2-8-6(bl) R Hills 8/1: 3032202: Just held: consistent: see 1997   12
2272 SARASOTA [14] (R Akehurst) 2-8-10 B Rouse 14/1: 0240003: Led after ½ way: ran on
same pace: eff over 5/6f on fast & soft ground: seems suited by a sharp/easy trk: see 354.   15
2580 DONNA IMMOBILE [3] (R Hannon) 2-8-4 A Mcglone 10/1: 00004: Kept on well: best 2471 (1m) 04
2298 KIBARA [15] 2-8-12 T Williams 7/2 FAV: 0100: Led over ½ way: best over this C/D 1803.   10
2829 LITTLE LOCHETTE [10] 2-9-7 J Williams 16/1: 00000: Never nearer: stays 6f: see 1946.   18
1692 CAWSTONS COMEDIAN [13] 2-7-8 N Adams 10/1: 0340: Abs: no show: see 1318.   00
2815 BOLD HIDEAWAY [8] 2-9-4(bl) A Shoults(5) 6/1: 040200: Much btr 2608 when up with pace.   00
2608 LISASHAM [12] 2-8-10(bl) T Quinn 6/1: 000300: Best 1881 (gall trk).   00
1528 Eastern Princess [2] 8-10   2600 Blandell Beauty [1] 9-4
2792 Lady Westgate [4] 8-12   1938 Miss Marjorie [11] 8-8
2580 Phoebe [5] 8-6   2045 Snapshot Baby [9] 8-0(bl)
15 ran   ½,½,2,½,nk,nk,½   (T C Marshall)   M Usher Lambourn, Berks

2928 GRE PROPERTY H'CAP (0-50) 3YO   £3279   7.5f   Good/Firm 35 -04 Slow   [45]

2674 AMBROSINI [2] (M Jarvis) 3-9-6(VIS) T Lucas 14/1: 2043001: 3 ro f Drone - Mother Nature
(Restless Wind) Fitted with a visor and returned to her best form when leading cl home in a
3yo h'cap at Lingfield: has been placed sev times since her first time out success in an
app h'cap at Salisbury: last season won a backend mdn at Redcar: half sister to sev winners:
very eff over 6/8f: acts on any going and on any trk: genuine filly who carries weight well.   46
*2810 HIGHLY RECOMMENDED [9] (P Cundell) 3-9-0(5ex) N Adams 13/8 FAV: 0031212: Heavily
bckd to defy his penalty and just failed to make all: in grand form: see 2810.   40
2393 LINASH [1] (G Wragg) 3-8-9 Paul Eddery 10/1: -004433: Another gd eff tho' prob found
this trip too short: seems to act on any trk: see 1818.   28
*2787 GERSHWIN [12] (D O'donnell) 3-7-12(vis)(5ex) N Carlisle 8/1: 1000214: Late prog:
much better 2787 (10f).   16
2810 MISTER MARCH [8] 3-8-3 D Mckay 10/1: 1200030: Never reached leaders: see 2024, 1742.   20
2730 GIVING IT ALL AWAY [11] 3-8-7 T Williams 10/1: 2103240: Hung left below dist, no extra   20
2207 BOWL OVER [10] 3-9-7(bl) G Baxter 10/1: 0324100: Chance when hmpd 2f out, not recover.   20
2810 STRIVE [3] 3-8-10 B Rouse 10/1: 2400000: Fdd into 8th: best in 436.   00
2473 BRITWYDD [4] 3-8-8 R Hills 6/1: 00-00: Speed over ½ way: wknd: see 2473.   00
1540 Natchakam [7] 8-13(bl)   1499 Auto Elegance [6] 9-1
11 ran   shthd,4,hd,½,2½,1½,nk   (Ananda Krishnan)   M Jarvis Newmarket

2929 GRE BLUE PLAN MAIDEN STAKES 3YO   £957   7.5f   Good/Firm 35 -06 Slow

2367 KINGSFOLD FLAME [3] (M Haynes) 3-8-11 B Rouse 33/1: -0001: 3 ch f No Loiterer -
Kingsfold Flash (Warpath) Showed impr form when leading inside dist, cmftbly in a 3yo mdn at
Lingfield: well btn in her prev starts over shorter trips and clearly btr suited by this
extended 7f: acts on gd/firm grd and on a sharp track.   22
2681 WIZZARD MAGIC [16] 3-9-0(bl) T Williams 25/1: 0-03202: Stable mate of
winner: led briefly 2f out, ran on same pace: eff over 6/7f on gd & firm: runs well here:see 1499. 18
2715 VAIGLIAN [11] (J Bethell) 3-9-0 J Reid 10/1: 0000003: Tried to make all: btr eff
tho' yet to reproduce his juv-promise: see 64.   16

2274 TOPEKA EXPRESS [8] (R Armstrong) 3-9-0(bl) P Tulk 7/2: 0320244: Ev ch: best 2171 (1m).   15
2534 EASTERN COMMAND [10] 3-8-11(BL) R Fox 7/1: 4-43000: Bl. 1st time: nvr nrr: see 1446.   04
2601 LADY WINDMILL [4] 3-8-11 G Morgan 14/1: 4000000: Prom most: btr over this C/D 2601.   00
2857 BOLD ADMIRAL [12] 3-9-0 W R Swinburn 2/1 FAV: -300: Heavily bckd: with leaders most
of way, wknd quickly below dist: lightly raced since showing promise in 733.   00
2674 PAS DE REGRETS [1] 3-9-0 G Starkey 6/1: 04-4000: Gd speed over ½ way: little form
since 593.   00

2581 Royal Berks [5] 9-0	2697 Vilee [13] 9-0	--	Royal Native [7] 8-11
-- Barbershop Quartet [15] 9-0		2186	Casa Rosada [14] 8-11
2659 Cherry Glory [6] 8-11	-- Peggy Drive [9] 8-11	--	Whos That Girl [2] 8-11
16 ran 2½,½,hd,5,3	(Mrs B Nye)	M Haynes	Epsom, Surrey

2930 GRE TRADEPAK STAKES 3YO   £959   1m 4f Firm 06 -01 Slow

*2572 TAVIRI [6] (G Harwood) 3-9-2 G Starkey 4/5 FAV: -2411: 3 b c Irish Tower - Rikki Tikki
Tavi (Mongo) Useful, fast impr colt: was heavily bckd and proved an easy winner, going on 2f
out in a 3yo stks at Lingfield: last month won an amateur riders race at Goodwood: related to
sev winners abroad: very eff over 10/12f and should make a nice stayer next season: acts on
gd and fast grd and on a sharp, undulating track.   54
-- LAKE ERIE [1] (M Stoute) 3-8-11 W R Swinburn 5/1: -2: Made a promising debut: chall
winner below dist and kept on well: bred to be suited by middle dist: acts on fast grd and
on a sharp, undulating track: sure to win a race.   42
2701 NORTHERN AMETHYST [3] (D Elsworth) 3-9-2(bl) B Rouse 7/2: 2321223: Set off in front,
onepaced when hdd: consistent colt tho' is very hard to win on: see 2599 & 2430.   44
2464 PRINCE BOLD [4] (J Dunlop) 3-8-11(BL) B Thomson 14/1: -0004: Bl first time: lacked
the pace to chall over this shorter trip and looks a staying sort: brother to 12f winner
Bold Rex: acts on gd & firm.   14
2620 MIRAGE DANCER [7] 3-8-11(BL) Paul Eddery 7/1: 3424020: Fitted with bl but didnot run
his race and is proving disapp: see 1469 & 1315.   00
2623 MARKELIUS [2] 3-8-11 J Reid 50/1: 0-00000: Wknd home turn: no form since 659.   00
1317 MUSKET WET [5] 3-8-11 J Williams 50/1: -00: Abs: well behind from ½ way.   00
7 ran   2,2,8,7,6   (K H Buchanan)   G Harwood Pulborough, Sussex

2931 GRE BLUE PLAN MAIDEN STAKES 3YO   £957   7.5f   Good/Firm 35 +04 Fast

2857 SKEAN [7] (G Harwood) 3-8-11 G Starkey 8/11 FAV: -002221: 3 ch f Kris - Kate's Intent
(Intentionally) Gained a deserved win when landing sev big bets in quite a fast run 3yo mdn
at Lingfield, led on bit 2f out and was sn clear: seems best over 7/8f tho' should stay
further: acts on gd & fast grd and on any trk: half sister to the smart duo Godswalk & Kabylia:
may win again after this confidence booster.   36+
2601 POINTED LADY [4] (R Armstrong) 3-8-11 G Baxter 9/1: 0042002: No chance with this easy
winner but kept on well to take the minor honours: see 2213 & 1691.   26
2622 MAKALU [1] (M Jarvis) 3-8-11 T Lucas 12/1: 2340-03: Well clear rem: lightly raced
this term but was placed in 3 of her 4 starts as 2yo & is probably open to further improvement:
eff over 7/8f on fast & soft grd.   24
2548 BIBI KHATOUN [13] (J Dunlop) 3-8-11 B Thomson 6/1: -002404: Chance 2f out: sn btn:
can do much better than this: see 2248 & 1677.   08
2601 DELTA ROSE [5] 3-8-11 B Rouse 25/1: 0004000: Late prog: see 1695.   08
2508 OPAL FLOWER [3] 3-8-11 W R Swinburn 10/1: 2-00000: Never nearer: see 2508.   04

2653 La Shaka [15] 8-11	-- Dom Edino [12] 9-0	2602 Sahraan [10] 9-0	
576 Downtown Brown [16] 9-0		2807 Cheerful Times [11] 9-0	
2534 Lost Island [8] 9-0	-- Rare Wind [9] 9-0	2653 Aggie [2] 8-11	
-- Jewel Mist [14] 8-11	2546 Popsis Pom Pom [6] 8-11		
16 ran 2½,½,8,hd,2½	(Mrs J A Chandler)	G Harwood Pulborough, Sussex	

YORK   Thursday October 9th   Lefthand, Galloping Track

Official Going Given As GOOD/FIRM

2932 AINSTY SELLING STAKES HCAP 3YO 0-60   £2944   1m2.5f Good/Firm 25 -35 Slow   [19]

2394 STATE JESTER [6] (W Elsey) 3-9-4(bl) Pat Eddery 5/1: 0000001: 3 b c Free State -
Mirthful (Will Somers) Dropped to selling company and hard ridden to lead cl home in a slow
run 3yo selling h'cap at York: stays 10f: acts on fast grd and is best in bl: no bid for
the winner today.   16
2604 LOUD LANDING [4] (W Hastings Bass) 3-9-7 W Carson 11/4 FAV: -034002: Made most: just
caught: should find a similar event: eff around 10f on fast grd.   18
2818 SCINTILLATOR [3] (C Booth) 3-8-11 M Hills 7/2: 0000033: Led 4f out till over 1f out:
btr 2818 (9f).   01
2489 OUT OF STOCK [5] (M Blanshard) 3-9-5 W Newnes 11/2: 0400004: Never nearer: little
form: prob stays 10f: acts on gd/firm and soft.   04
2797 GREENHILLS GIRL [7] 3-9-4(vis) S Cauthen 7/2: 2403200: Twice well below 2705.   00
1651 LINTON SPRINGTIME [2] 3-8-12 D Mckeown 8/1: 0-00000: Al rear: abs: little form.   00
6 ran   ¼,4,3,12,1½   (Eric Barber)   W Elsey Malton, Yorks.

2933 EBF MALTON STAKES 2YO FILLIES   £5312   7f   Good/Firm 25 -09 Slow

2540 SAINTE JOIE [8] (L Piggott) 2-8-8 T Ives 13/8 FAV: 321: 2 b f Akarad - Sainte Gemme
(Dancer's Image) Very useful filly: well bckd and got up well inside final 1f, under press in
a val 2yo fillies event at York: last time out was btn a whisker by Laluche in Gr 3 May Hill
Stks at Doncaster: French bred filly who seems equally eff at 7f/1m and should get further:
acts on fast grd and a gall track: can win more races.   65
2675 SUMMER POSY [6] (I Balding) 2-8-8 S Cauthen 7/2: 42: Well bckd: made almost all:
fine effort and will not be long in winning: see 2675.   63
-2531 STREET PARTY [3] (G Wragg) 2-8-8 Pat Eddery 4/1: 323: Prom, stayed on under press:
consistent filly who will be suited by another furlong: see 2531, 2147.   57
2703 APPROACHING STAR [4] (R Sheather) 2-8-8 M Rimmer 12/1: 004: Took a strong hold: stayed
on final 1f and is fast improving: eff at 7f/1m and acts well on fast ground: looks sure
to find a maiden.   55
+2652 TIPATINA [1] 2-8-13 R Cochrane 4/1: 010: Wk in mkt: stiff task at these weights and
is in gd form: see 2652.   58
-- MISS MARTINIQUE [2] 2-8-8 M Hills 20/1: 0: Stiff task on debut and was not disgraced:
cost IR 26,000 as a yearling and is a half sister to 3 winners: should stay 1m: acts gd/firm.   38
2589 Millfields House [7] 8-8   -- Turtur NI [5] 8-8
8 ran   ½,3,hd,1,5,nk   (K Al-Said)   L Piggott Newmarket

2934 ALLIED DUNBAR HANDICAP 3YO+ 0-60   £4688   1m   Good/Firm 25 -04 Slow   [47]

2810 USFAN [4] (J Dunlop) 3-9-4 W Carson 11/4 FAV: -022121: 3 br c Riverman - Essie B S
Venture (Intentionally) Useful colt who is in grand form: led inside final 2f, driven out in
a val h'cap at York: last time out was just btn at Goodwood and earlier won a mdn over this
C/D: very eff over 7/8f, may get further: acts on gd & firm grd and on any trk: improving sort   54
2566 GRANNYS BANK [1] (W Hastings Bass) 4-9-1 Pat Eddery 5/1: -122102: Not much room over
1f out: stayed on well and is a most consistent filly: can win another h'cap: see 2144.   44
2624 OPEN HERO [10] (A Stewart) 3-9-5 M Roberts 15/2: 211-003: Ran on well final 1f and
was just btn: may win soon: see 2624.   54
2730 SPRING IN MY STEP [5] (M Prescott) 4-9-3 G Duffield 8/1: 1110-34: Stayed on final 1f
and was not btn far in a cl finish: can win soon: see 2730.   45
1768 CENTREPOINT [3] 3-9-0 K Darley 25/1: 01-4430: Abs: nearest fin: very lightly raced
this season and wore bl last time: see 244.   43
2566 HANDLEBAR [2] 4-9-4 T Ives 11/2: 0112230: Led/dsptd lead: consistent: see 2566.   39
2437 SIGNORE ODONE [6] 4-9-0 M Birch 6/1: 0112000: Fin 7th: btr 2104, 1624.   33
2867 Sams Wood [7] 9-5   2295 Brown Bear Boy [11] 8-13
2404 Warm Welcome [9] 8-3(bl)   1109 Red Russell [8] 9-7
11 ran   ½,hd,½,3,1,1   (Prince A A Faisal)   J Dunlop Arundel, Sussex

---

2935 DICK TURPIN NURSERY HANDICAP 2YO   £3563   6f   Good/Firm 25 +13 Fast   [48]

2687 NORAPA [1] (M Brittain) 2-8-13 K Darley 9/1: 31001: 2 ch f Ahonoora - Pale Moon
(Jukebox) Led from the stalls, ridden out in a fast run nursery h'cap at York: earlier made
all for an easy win in a fillies mdn at Nottingham: very eff at 6f with forcing tactics:
acts on gd and fast grd and a gall track.   45
2514 SUPREME ROSE [2] (W Musson) 2-9-7 M Wigham 11/1: 0102: Al prom: fine effort under 9-7:
stays 6f and acts on gd and fast ground: see 2365.   49
2026 GOOD TIME GIRL [5] (R Hannon) 2-7-10 G French 5/1: 0112023: Sn prom: btr 2026.   16
2669 KALAS IMAGE [6] (G Moore) 2-8-1 P Robinson 11/1: 3140044: Ev ch over 1f out: best 1561   20
*2777 SPANISH SLIPPER [9] 2-9-7(bl)(10ex) J H Brown(5) 5/1: 2412210: Never nearer: btr 2777.   38
2689 SPITTIN MICK [4] 2-8-10 J Lowe 4/1: 3110040: Prom, ev ch: btr 2689 (5f)   17
2753 MIGHTY BOLD [8] 2-8-10(BL) W Carson 7/2 FAV: 004000: Tried in bl: tricky ride: best 2485   00
2748 CALLACE [10] 2-7-8 J Quinn(5) 20/1: 004000: Outsider: best 1634 (sharpish trk)   00
2514 FRANK THE BANK [7] 2-9-0 Pat Eddery 5/1: 4000: Well bckd: lost much grd at start and
virtually p.u. closing stages: best 1665.   00
9 ran   1½,3,½,½,4,½   (A M Wragg)   M Brittain Warthill, Yorks

---

2936 GREEN HOWARDS CUP CLAIMING STKS 2YO   £3646   1m 1f   Good/Firm 25 -23 Slow

2521 ALBION PLACE [13] (M H Easterby) 2-8-4 M Birch 16/1: 4000441: 2 b c Try My Best -
Veronica Heron (Crooner) Showed Impr form, led 2f out, driven clear in solitle slow run 2yo
Claimer at York: half brother to middle dist winner Bidivera and was suited by this 9f trip:
acts on firm & yldg ground and a gall track.   35
2584 WAHIBA [1] (G P Gordon) 2-8-3 G Duffield 10/1: 0302: Stayed on well final 1f: in gd
form: stays 9f and acts on gd & firm ground.   31
*2813 MORNING FLOWER [3] (R Williams) 2-9-3 T Ives 8/1: 32F2013: Came from off the pace
and fin very well: stays 9f and is in fine form: see 2813.   43
2716 FORUMS FOLLY [14] (J Sutcliffe) 2-8-4(1ow) Pat Eddery 7/2 CO.FAV: 04: Well bckd:
al there and stayed on under press: improved effort from this brother to a winner in Ireland:
stays 9f and acts on gd/firm.   25
2813 CASTLE CORNET [16] 2-8-6 R Cochrane 16/1: 0440030: Stays 9f: acts on fast & yldg grd
and should find a seller.   22
2829 OMEN [7] 2-8-3 G French 14/1: 00: Never nearer: btr eff from this cheaply bought
colt: stays 9f: acts on gd/firm.   15

```
2723 BRANDY BOTTLE [4] 2-8-3 W Carson 15/2: 00: Prom, fin 9th: btr 2723.                        00
*2841 OBIDOS [8] 2-8-12 M Hills 7/2 CO.FAV: 010: Made much, btr 2841 (1m).                      00
2841 RUWI VALLEY [17] 2-8-1 J Scally(4) 10/1: 0020: No show and well below 2841 (1m).           00
2664 LISETA [2] 2-7-12 L Charnock 7/2 CO.FAV: 0220: Well bckd but al rear and well btn:
something amiss? See 2664 (7f)                                                                  00
2798 Eurocon [11] 7-11            2336 Sue Forever [9] 7-13      2051 Majestic Miss [12] 7-12
2798 Running Money [5] 8-11                                       780 Bennetthorpe [10] 8-6
2607 Mytyme [15] 8-1              2607 Gulf Of Gold [6] 8-1
17 ran   1½,1,2,2½,2            (Hippodromo Racing Ltd)         M H Easterby Great Habton, Yorks.
```

2937 LITTLE GO APPRENTICE STAKES   £2548   1m 4f   Good/Firm 25 +01 Fast

```
*2701 HIGH KNOWL [5] (B Hills) 3-8-10 P Hill(3) 6/4 FAV: 4231111: 3 ch c High Line - Madina
(Beau Prince) Useful colt who is in fine form: heavily bckd and led 3f out, gamely, in an
app stks at York: unbtn now in his last 4 outings, earlier successful at Bath, Lingfield and
Newcastle: half brother to sev winners including useful French miler Nonoalca: very eff over
10f/13f and may get further: acts on gd & fast grd and on any trk: genuine sort.               49
2558 FOLK DANCE [7] (I Balding) 4-9-0 S O'gorman(6) 9/1: 2020402: Chall final 2f and
just btn: 5l clear 3rd and this was one of his btr efforts: see 1020, 189.                      43
2569 CROWLEY [3] (L Cumani) 3-8-6 S Quane(3) 7/2: -002133: Ev ch over 2f out: btr 2569, 2299    35
-2666 ROYAL DYNASTY [2] (G Wragg) 3-8-2 D Surrey(3) 5/2: -000124: Wknd over 2f out: well
below 2666.                                                                                     28
2754 IBN MAJED [4] 4-8-10 N Carson(6) 16/1: 000-000: Fdd final 2f: lightly raced performer
on the Flat: showed useful form over timber, winning 3 times last season: acts on firm & yldg.  18
*2747 OWN UP [6] 4-9-0 K Bradshaw 14/1: -000-10: Led inside final 4f: see 2747 (non event).     00
2604 SENDER [1] 3-8-2 G Clarke(1) 11/1: 1202000: Led 1m: btr 1964, 595.                         00
7 ran   ½,5,1½,4,20            (K Abdulla)                      B Hills Lambourn, Berks
```

Official Going Given As GOOD/FIRM

2938 WYNDHAM STAKES HANDICAP 0-70 3YO+   £7234   2m   Good 41 -17 Slow   [55]

```
*2834 CAP DEL MOND [9] (G Harwood) 3-8-11(3ex) G Starkey 7/4 FAV: -1111: 3 b c Troy -
Rainbow's End (My Swallow) Useful, impr colt: maintained his unbtn record, staying on well
to lead inside final 1f in rather slow run, but val, h'cap at Ascot: last time out won a
similar event at Newmarket: earlier successful twice at Folkestone: cost 400,000 gns as a
yearling and is a half brother to winning stayer Storm Cloud and also useful Finian's Rainbow:
stays 2m really well and will get further: acts on gd & fast grd and on any trk: on the upgrade  59
2809 BALLET CHAMP [5] (R Holder) 8-7-7(4oh) S Dawson 11/2: 2420422: Led 2f out, kept on:
consistent sort but lacks finishing pace: see 2809, 349.                                        27
2766 INSULAR [3] (I Balding) 6-9-10 Pat Eddery 6/1: 1-31003: Switched inside final 2f:
nearest fin: see 778.                                                                           57
2809 DETROIT SAM [1] (R Akehurst) 5-8-5(1ow) J Reid 13/2: 0-22104: Prom, another gd run.        38
2754 RIKKI TAVI [8] 6-8-9 W Carson 12/1: 3100400: Not btn far: see 1099 (2½m).                  41
2692 REVISIT [6] 4-8-4 T Ives 8/1: 3443000: Made much, fdd: btr 2445 (14f) see 58a.             29
2733 EASTER LEE [2] 6-7-8(1ow)(3oh) G Carter 8/1: 2-00100: Led ½ way: fdd: twice below 2432     00
7 ran   2,½,shthd,½,5          (Prince Ahmed Salman)            G Harwood Pulborough, Sussex
```

2939 DUKE OF EDINBURGH STAKES 2YO   £7492   6f   Good 41 -08 Slow

```
--   RAAHIA [8] (B Hanbury) 2-8-11 R Cochrane 7/2: 1: 2 ch f Vice Regent - Full Marks
(Round Table) Very promising filly: led 2f out for an impressive 4l win in a val 2yo mdn at
Ascot: cost $400,000 as a yearling and is a half sister to a winner in the States: eff at 6f,
sure to be suited by 7f/1m: acts on gd grd and a gall track: held in high regard and certain
to go on to better things.                                                                      65
--   HENRYK [7] (R Simpson) 2-9-0 S Whitworth 33/1: 2: Made much: kept on: fine effort
in this gd class company: cost only 5,000 gns as a yearling: half brother to middle dist
winner Clouds Daughter: should be suited by further than 6f: acts on gd grd and can
find a race.                                                                                    54
--   ALWASMI [3] (H T Jones) 2-9-0 A Murray 13/2: 3: Wk in mkt: stayed on well closing stages
and looks sure to improve on this: well bred colt whose dam was a smart sort winning Gr 2
Princess of Wales Stks: will be suited by 7f/1m: acts on gd grd and a gall trk: a certain
future winner.                                                                                  52
--   CANANGO [4] (M Stoute) 2-9-0 W R Swinburn 15/8 FAV: 4: Well bckd: ev ch over 1f out:
first foal who cost 115,000 gns as a yearling: bred to stay much further than 6f: acts on gd
ground and should improve.                                                                      51
--   KERALI [2] 2-8-11 Pat Eddery 3/1: 0: Well bckd: chance 2f out: half sister to smart
Irish miler Field Dancer and also Ricura: eff at 6f on gd grd: should do btr next time.         46
--   ROYAL ROB [5] 2-9-0 G Starkey 11/1: 0: Wk in mkt: improvement likely: American bred
colt who is a half brother to a winner in France: will be suited by further than today's 6f:
acts on gd ground.                                                                              44
```

-- GAME THATCHER [1] 2-9-0 B Rouse 14/1: 0: Slow start and never nearer: cost 15,000 gns
as a yearling and is a half brother to sev winners incl smart Last Fandango: will do better   00
-- MORTAL SIN [6] 2-8-11 B Thomson 12/1: 0: Speed most: U.S. bred filly whose dam unraced.   00
8 ran   4,1,shthd,1,2,hd   (Hamdan Al-Maktoum)   B Hanbury Newmarket

2940 GRAND METROPOLITAN STAKES 3YO FILLIES   £7661   1m   Good 41 -24 Slow

*2653 DARING DOONE [5] (A Stewart) 3-8-11 M Roberts 8/1: -111: 3 b f Daring March - Doogali
(Doon) Very useful, fast impr filly: retained unbtn record when game winner of a slow run 3yo
fillies Listed race at Ascot: al prom and led cl home under press: earlier successful at
Brighton & Goodwood: first foal of useful 8/10f winner Doogali: very eff at 1m and should stay
further: acts on gd & fast grd and on any track: genuine filly who is very much on the upgrade   66
*2870 HIDDEN BRIEF [1] (R Boss) 3-8-11 Pat Eddery 11/4 FAV: 2012312: Well bckd: led over
1f out till no extra cl home: another fine effort but is prob at her very best over 7f:see 2870   65
2231 TANOUMA [6] (J Dunlop) 3-8-8 W Carson 9/2: 1-30003: Chance 2f out: btr eff, see 467   59
2385 DOLKA [3] (M Stoute) 3-9-4 W R Swinburn 7/1: 1-1004: Hdwy 2f out: no extra final 1f:
fair effort but best 803.   68
2752 KICK THE HABIT [4] 3-8-11 T Ives 20/1: 0210040: Al prom and not btn far: much improved
form, but possibly flattered by this slow pace: see 2131.   59
2868 MOONLIGHT LADY [2] 3-8-8 J Reid 3/1: 0-02000: Heavily bckd: made much, but fdd tamely:
yet to reproduce form 2538 (7f).   55
2719 TRAVEL MAGIC [7] 3-8-11 M Hills 8/1: 0221400: No extra final 2f: twice well below 2568   00
7 ran   nk,1½,shthd,½,shthd   (Mrs Wm McAlpine)   A Stewart Newmarket

2941 HOLSTEN PILS NURSERY HANDICAP 2YO   £7409   7f   Good 41 +02 Fast   [60]

*2529 PERCYS LASS [1] (G Wragg) 2-9-7 P Robinson 9/2: 111: 2 b f Blakeney - Laughing Girl
(Sassafrass) Smart, fast improving filly: well bckd and led 1½f out, forging well clear in a
fast run and val nursery h'cap at Ascot: winner of her only 2 prev outings, nursery h'cap at
Salisbury and first time out a fillies mdn at Lingfield: half sister to middle dist winner
No No Girl: eff at 7f, looks sure to stay middle dist next term: acts on gd & fast grd
and on any trk: certain to win more races.   72
2677 DIAMOND FLIGHT [6] (R Hannon) 2-8-9 B Rouse 15/2: 0144002: Active in mkt: hdwy 2f out
but went left under press: caught a tartar here and can find a similar event: see 2677.   46
2547 OTHET [5] (M Usher) 2-8-1 A Mcglone 6/1: 2233: Never nearer: btr 2547.   35
2611 RIOT BRIGADE [7] (C Brittain) 2-8-10 Pat Eddery 10/1: 0331404: Prom and going well:
no extra inside final 2f: btr 2485 (6f).   37
2611 GLOBAL LADY [10] 2-7-13 A Mackay 9/2: 21030: Ev ch 2f out: btr 2611.   21
2753 MUAD DIB [4] 2-7-7(bl)(1oh) N Adams 25/1: 2302000: Made much: btr 2753 (6f), 2205   14
*2645 TROJAN SONG [8] 2-9-0 S Cauthen 7/2 FAV: 210: Heavily bckd: held when hmpd 1f out:
better 2645 (firm).   31
2663 PAS DENCHERE [11] 2-9-0 P Waldron 8/1: 0301220: Sn prom: well below 2663 (1m firm)   30
*2803 TUFTY LADY [3] 2-8-13(5ex) W Carson 10/1: 0022010: Early speed: see 2803 (6f).   00
2813 TAKE A HINT [2] 2-7-8 C Rutter(1) 20/1: 4414000: Outsider: no show: best 864 (yldg)   00
10 ran   5,1½,4,2½,½,2,shthd   (E B Moller)   G Wragg Newmarket

2942 MECCA BOOKMAKERS STAKES HANDICAP 0-70   £8285   1m 2f   Good 41 -06 Slow   [57]

2766 SWIMMER [7] (G Huffer) 4-8-9 G Carter 10/1: 1430021: 4 ch c Lord Gayle - Hispanica
(Whistling Wind) Useful colt: fin well to lead cl home in a val h'cap at Ascot: first time
out won a h'cap at Leicester: in gd form in '85, winning at Nottingham & Warwick: half brother
to sev winners: seems equally eff at 10/12f: acts on gd & fast grd and on any trk: genuine
sort who does well when fresh.   51
*2755 CAPTAINS NIECE [2] (W Hastings Bass) 3-8-2 M Roberts 9/4 JT.FAV: -01112: Led 2f
out: just caught: another fine eff: see 2755.   50
+2848 MYTENS [1] (J Tree) 3-9-3(7ex) Pat Eddery 9/4 JT.FAV: -110413: Well bckd: led 1m:
in fine form: see 2848.   62
*2438 SULTAN MOHAMED [3] (J Dunlop) 3-9-7 W Carson 10/1: 2130014: Never nearer: gd eff under
9-7: see 2438.   64
2477 PATO [5] 4-8-3 C Rutter(3) 20/1: 0040400: Ev ch in str: not btn far: see 2219, 511.   37
2766 UP TO UNCLE [9] 3-7-13 A Mcglone 20/1: 2233130: Never nearer: most consistent: see 2533   37
2706 VAGUE MELODY [4] 4-8-8 T Ives 16/1: 3441230: Fdd inside final 2f: see 2355.   00
2693 MAILMAN [6] 7-9-3 S Cauthen 13/2: 4031220: Slow start, no show: well below 2693.   00
*2536 FOLLOW THE BAND [8] 4-8-3 R Cochrane 10/1: -004110: T.O: something amiss: see 2536.   00
9 ran   nk,1½,¾,¾,1½   (Quality Castings Slough Ltd)   G Huffer Newmarket

2943 RITZ CLUB APPRENTICES STAKES 3YO+   £4254   1m   Good 41 +15 Fast

*527 ABSHEER [5] (S Norton) 3-8-5 A Culhane(3) 7/1: -011: 3 b c Double Form - Milaire
(Tudor Melody) Smart colt: despite a long abs, led inside final 1f, cmftbly, in a fast run
app stks at Ascot: beat the Cambridgeshire winner Dallas in a 3yo mdn at Pontefract in May:
has subs had back trouble and has also changed stables: very eff over 1m, should stay further:
acts on gd and soft grd and on any trk: certain to win more races.   70
2785 VERDANT BOY [4] (M Stoute) 3-8-11 W R Swinburn 5/4: 1021132: Led ½ way: ran on well
when hdd and is a most consistent colt: see 2785, 2612.   74

2808 KUFUMA [1] (G Huffer) 4-8-11(vis) G Carter(3) 6/5 FAV: 0001203: Heavily bckd:
disapp effort: twice below 2740.   48
--   KEYNES [2] (J Jenkins) 6-9-0 L Riggio(3) 20/1: 41044/4: Ex Irish gelding: prom to
¼ way: in '84 won 3 times: stays further than 1m and maybe seen hurdling soon: acts on any grnd. 00
2617 SUMMERS DARLING [6] 4-8-8 C Rutter 50/1: 0-00000: Impossible task: has been running
in Ireland early this season: showed fair form as a 3yo when trained by L Cumani: best over
this trip on fast ground.   00
2319 MIA JUBES [3] 4-8-8 L Johnsey(6) 100/1: 00-0000: Led 4f: see 2319.   00
6 ran   nk,10,25,5,2   (M Abdulateef)   S Norton High Hoyland, Yorks

---

2944 SAM HALL MEM. TROPHY (H'CAP)(0-60)   £4643   1m 6f   Good/Firm 26 -42 Slow   [45]

2169 MARLION [6] (S Hall) 5-8-3 G Duffield 5/2 JT FAV: 3241331: 5 b g Julio Maariner -
Rose Mullion (Tudor Melody) Consistent h'capper: made virtually ev yard, gamely, in a slowly
run h'cap at York: earlier employed similar front running tactics to win a h'cap at Redcar:
last season again won at Redcar and also at Catterick: winning hurdler who is well suited by
14/16f: does well with forcing tactics on a sound surface: acts on any track.   28
*2885 FOUR STAR THRUST [2] (R Whitaker) 4-8-5(4ex) D Mckeown 5/2 JT FAV: 0232112: Heavily
bckd to complete her hat-trick: held up and only just denied: in fine form: see 2885. 29
2850 PEGGY CAROLYN [7] (M Ryan) 4-9-1 P Robinson 7/2: -003303: Not btn far: gd eff and
seems almost back to her best: likes a gall trk: see 964.   38
2134 MY CHARADE [4] (B Waring) 5-7-7(vis)(3oh) J Lowe 25/1: 0200004: Clear rem: see 485. 15
2873 TRAPEZE ARTIST [5] 5-9-7 S Dawson 14/1: 2220000: Btn below dist: see 2389 & 917. 28
11   COOL DECISION [8] 9-8-1 N Carlisle 14/1: /432-00: No extra 2f out: off the trk since 11 08
2492 LEON [3] 4-8-12 Kim Tinkler 9/2: 0240330: Btr over this trip in 2492: see 2395. 00
2745 OUR BARA BOY [1] 9-7-8(vis)(1ow)(10oh) J Carter(0) 100/1: 000/000: Dwelt, no danger:
modest stayer on the Flat nowadays and has been lightly raced since winning a h'cap at Ascot
in '81: acts on any going.   00
8 ran   hd,nk,¼,10,shthd,1   (Mrs M C Grant)   S Hall Middleham, Yorks

2945 CARLING BLACK LABEL LAGER H'CAP (0-70)   £6063   7f   Good/Firm 26 +01 Fast   [53]

2668 BOOT POLISH [7] (J Watts) 4-9-3 N Connorton 11/4 FAV: 0013031: 4 gr g Godswalk -
Flirting Countess (Ridan) Useful h'capper: well bckd and qcknd into lead at dist to win a
val and quite fast run h'cat at York: close 3rd to Green Ruby in the Ayr Gold Cup last time,
earlier won h'caps at Thirsk and Pontefract: in '85 won twice at Redcar: very eff over 6/7f:
seems to act on any going and on any trk: in gd form.   52
2842 ILLUMINEUX [5] (M Albina) 3-9-7 B Thomson 12/1: 1-00002: Al prom: kept on well: fine
effort and should win a similar h'cap soon: likely to stay 1m: see 2842 & 586.   57
2773 SAILORS SONG [12] (N Vigors) 4-9-6 S Dawson 8/1: 0001203: Ran on late: gd effort:see 2207 47
2674 REINDEER WALK [8] (G Huffer) 4-8-10 G Carter 16/1: 03-0004: Nearest fin: best effort
this term: a winner at Folkestone & Beverley last season: suited by 7f on gd & fast ground. 36
2867 FORMATUNE [2] 4-7-11(bl) R Street 9/1: 0300000: Not clear run: fin strongly: see 2773 22
*2685 EMERALD EAGLE [4] 5-8-5 T Williams 8/1: 1000010: Sn in front: qcknd ½ way but no
extra when chall dist: running well at present: see 2685.   30
2566 INISHPOUR [1] 4-9-3 J H Brown(5) 10/1: 4314400: Never nearer 7th: see 2475 & 2039. 00
2685 THE MAZALL [9] 6-8-11 D Nicholls 5/1: 1100120: Front rank: fdd into 8th: see 2685. 00
2810 CODICES [10] 3-9-4 A Clark 15/2: 1012000: Another disapp effort: see 2369.   00
*2715 Hopeful Katie [11] 7-9   2685 Mels Choice [6] 7-7(2oh)
2730 Creeager [3] 8-2
12 ran   ¼,2½,hd,½,hd,nk   (G B Parkinson)   J Watts Richmond, Yorks.

2946 'MAIL ON SUNDAY' 3YO H'CAP (0-70)   £8285   1m 1f   Good/Firm 26 -04 Slow   [64]

2807 HAMPER [2] (W Hastings Bass) 3-7-7(2oh) Dale Gibson(7) 7/2 FAV: -43121: 3 ch g
Final Straw - Great Care (Home Guard) Proved a narrow winner off his feather-weight, led
below dist and held on well in a val 3yo h'cap at York: lightly raced gelding who earlier won
an app race at Ripon and looked unlucky when just touched off by Minus Man at Goodwood last
time: eff over 8/9f on fast & yldg grnd: acts on any trk.   42
2719 PRINCESS NAWAAL [4] (J Dunlop) 3-8-3 P Robinson 11/2: 1100032: Had ev ch, just held:
back to form and may get her hd in front before the season's end: acts on any trk: see 925. 50
2763 GEORDIES DELIGHT [3] 3-9-4 J Reid 8/1: 2213203: Led early and again 3f
out, not btn far and is tremendously consistent: see 2567 & 2353.   62
*2684 IRISH PASSAGE [1] (D Barron) 3-7-13 S Webster 8/1: D001214: Not the best of runs,
fin full of running and may win again soon: stays 9f well: see 2684.   42
*2431 PRINCE MERANDI [9] 3-7-10 N Carlisle 14/1: 3300010: Running well: see 2431.   34
2442 MERITMOORE [7] 3-8-2 G Baxter 9/1: 00-020: Ran on same pace: stays 9f: see 2442. 40
2867 NAVARZATO [11] 3-9-7 M Birch 6/1: -200000: Fin 7th: is proving rather disappp: see 1147. 00
2763 FESTIVAL CITY USA [5] 3-8-12(VIS) B Thomson 7/1: 0014330: Visored first time, fdd
into 8th: see 2763.   00
2749 MAJAAHED [6] 3-9-5 G Duffield 9/1: -010300: Wknd into 9th: best over 10f in 2567. 00
2870 TOWN JESTER [10] 3-8-6(1ow) P Tulk 33/1: 10-0000: Made much, wknd early in straight. 00

YORK   Saturday October 11th   -Cont'd

2686 VERITABLE [8] 3-8-10 T Williams 6/1: -021340: Led early in str, wknd quickly: see 1954.   00
11 ran   nk,1½,nk,3,shthd,1½,1   (Mrs M McCalmont)   W Hastings Bass Newmarket

2947 CORAL BOOKMAKERS SPRINT H'CAP 0-70   £8779   6f   Good/Firm 26 -02 Slow   [59]

*2725 HANDSOME SAILOR [5] (M Dickinson) 3-9-9 G Duffield 5/1: 12-0311: 3 ch c Some Hand -
Found At Sea (Pieces of Eight) Very useful colt: showed a fine turn of foot to lead inside
dist in Coral Bookmakers Sprint Trophy at York: found to be lame after race: recently an easy
winner of a stks race at Beverley: much improved last season when trained by R Thompson,
winning at Windsor, Newcastle and Haydock: very eff over 5/6f: acts on any going and on any
trk: genuine sort who carries weight well.   69
2793 BUTSOVA [1] (R Armstrong) 3-8-9 J Reid 25/1: 0334422: Led over ¼ way, rallied well
cl home and this was a fine effort: maiden, but certain to win a race on this form: see 431.   52
-2668 FELIPE TORO [9] (M H Easterby) 3-9-4(bl) M Birch 10/11 FAV: 1111123: Heavily bckd:
al front rank, kept on well under press and not btn far: remains in fine form: see 2668 & 2537   60
2668 CATHERINES WELL [6] (M W Easterby) 3-9-10 G Carter 5/1: 3111104: Led over ¼ way, kept
on well under top weight and has been in tremendous form of late: see 2362.   65
1640 DORKING LAD [3] 4-8-8 R Morse(5) 25/1: 0000000: Ran on well: gd eff after abs: see 1026   45
2862 NUMISMATIST [2] 7-8-6 R Street 10/1: 4-40400: Dwelt, not btn very far: see 1933.   43
2785 SOFTLY SPOKEN [7] 3-7-7(4oh) N Carlisle 10/1: 2022100: Has twice been highly tried
since winning in 2519.   00
2668 MATOU [8] 6-9-5 W Ryan 10/1: 02D1000: Held up, no threat: see 1810.   00
2550 CARD PLAYED [4] 3-8-6 B Thomson 14/1: -2330: Speed over ¼ way, fin last: see 2550 & 941   00
9 ran   ½,nk,½,½,ddht,hd,3,½   (R E Sangster)   M Dickinson Manton, Wilts.

2948 COLDSTREAM GUARDS ASSOC. STAKES 3YO   £3804   1m 1f   Good/Firm 26 -13 Slow

2719 SOEMBA [6] (G Wragg) 3-8-11 P Robinson 3/1 FAV: 4-0001: 3 b f General Assembly -
Seven Seas (Riverman) Nicely bckd and showed improved form when trotting up in a 3yo fillies
mdn at York, went on over 1f out and was sn clear: has been difficult to train but is clearly
quite useful: eff over 9f and should stay further: acts on fast grd and on a gall track.   38
2734 JUNGLE BEAT [10] (W Jarvis) 3-8-11 M Hills 9/1: 0-402: Led over 2f out, no chance
with winner and only just held on to 2nd place: stays 9f: see 2550.   26
2546 GREENHILLS JOY [2] (M Ryan) 3-8-11 N Day 12/1: -03: Ev ch: lightly raced filly who
should improve further when stepping up in dist: acts on a gall trk: see 2546.   26
2300 MOORE STYLISH [4] (R Armstrong) 3-8-11 J Reid 10/1: -00204: Al prom: stays 9f: see 1921   24
2734 FIREAL [8] 3-8-11 W Ryan 11/2: 4-2400: Much btr on yldg in 338 (1m).   20
2857 ANOTHER PAGEANT [3] 3-8-11 B Thomson 9/1: -000000: Wknd below dist: little form.   16
2548 ETTAS PET [11] 3-8-11 A Shoults(5) 8/1: 4003000: Fdd into 7th: see 2548 & 1451.   00
2719 SUMMER GARDEN [9] 3-8-11 J Matthias 6/1: -403000: Dwelt and al in rear: btr 2719 (1m)   00
-- ALYDARS PROMISE [1] 3-8-11 A Kimberley 5/1: -0: Fin last on her racecourse debut, after
leading for most of the way: $530,000 yearling whose dam was very smart over slightly shorter
trips: should do better than this.   00
2653 Sancilla [12] 8-11   1602 Sweet Delilah [13] 8-11
2496 Dialect [5] 8-11   2400 Still Marching [7] 8-11
13 ran   6,hd,1,2,2½   (Sir Philip Oppenheimer)   G Wragg Newmarket

2949 ROCKINGHAM STAKES LISTED RACE 2YO   £7765   6f   Good/Firm 26 +18 Fast

1887 MIDYAN [2] (H Cecil) 2-8-11 W Ryan 7/2: 1421: 2 b c Miswaki - Country Dream (Ribot)
Smart colt: took command 2f out and ran on strongly for an impressive win in fast run Rockingham
Stks at York: first time out winner of a Yarmouth mdn and had been off the trk since chasing
home Don't Forget Me in Gr 3 Lanson Champagne Stks at Goodwood in July: half brother to useful
middle dist winner Harry Hastings: very eff over 6/7f on gd & fast grd: acts on any trk.   75
*2511 ON TAP [4] (M H Easterby) 2-8-11 M Birch 8/11 FAV: 41112: Heavily bckd to complete
his four-timer: given quite a hard race and was never going to catch this smart winner:
promises to do btr when stepping up in dist: see 2511.   66
2552 CHIME TIME [7] (C Tinkler) 2-9-0 T Lucas 9/2: 1211343: Led over ¼ way, rallied well
and remains in fine form: see 2552 & 1697.   65
+2618 LUCRATIF [3] (I Balding) 2-8-11 J Matthias 20/1: 110414: Gd eff in this btr class: see 2618.   56
+2325 PEATSWOOD SHOOTER [1] 2-8-11 K Darley 33/1: 1034010: Prom most of way: best 2325 (soft)   52
2223 BORN TO RACE [5] 2-8-11 J Reid 20/1: 012100: Slow start and no threat: best 1754.   51
2843 NUTWOOD LIL [6] 2-8-8 G Duffield 25/1: 1203000: Sn outpaced: has joined R Hannon since
her last run: can do btr than this: see 924 & 450.   00
7 ran   2½,1½,2,1½,nk   (Prince A A Faisal)   H Cecil Newmarket

2950 EBF BRAMHAM MOOR STAKES 2YO   £3342   5f   Good/Firm 26 -16 Slow

*2805 GALLANT GALLOIS [5] (C Booth) 2-9-4 M Hills 6/4 FAV: 11: 2 b c Mummy's Game -
La Gallia (Welsh Saint) Gamely justified fav, responded well to press to lead on post in a
2yo stks at York: recently made a winning debut in a Nottingham mdn: half brother to 9f winner
Black Bank: dam successful over mid dist and over hurdles: may already find today's trip on
the sharp side and should do btr over longer dist: acts on fast grd and a gall trk.   52
2717 MA PETITE LASSIE [4] (M Francis) 2-8-8 J Reid 5/1: 022: Just failed to make all and
is clearly well suited by forcing tactics: on the upgrade and sure to win a race: see 2717   41

861

2696 PUSHOFF [1] (C Brittain) 2-8-8 T Williams 13/8: 0223: Not btn far: consistent: see 2589.   38
2805 GOLDEN CAJUN [2] (W Jarvis) 2-8-11 G Duffield 9/1: 004: Ran on late: will be suited
by another furlong: acts on fast grd and on a gall trk: see 1207.   33
2281 ALTOBELLI [6] 2-8-11 J Matthias 11/1: 00: Front rank most: see 2281.   33
2723 TRY HILLS SUPPLIES [3] 2-8-11 J Williams 100/1: 00000: Rank outsider and never went
pace: very cheaply bought gelding who has only btn two horses in his 5 races to date.   00
6 ran   shthd,1,2,shthd,8   (J L Acklam)   C Booth Foston, Yorks.

ASCOT   Saturday October 11th   Righthand, Stiff, Galloping Track

Official Going Given As GOOD/FIRM

2951 HYPERION STAKES 2YO   £9645   7f   Good/Firm 27 -19 Slow

*2811 TARTUFFE [1] (G Harwood) 2-9-6 G Starkey 10/3: 0111: 2 ch c Golden Act - Tarop (Dr Fager)
Smart colt: giving weight all round, but qcknd to lead final 1f for a decisive win in val 2yo
Hyperion Stks at Ascot: last time out won a val event at Goodwood: earlier broke the 2yo course
record when readily winning a 2yo mdn at Salisbury: cost only $35,000 and is a half brother
to 2 winners in the States: eff at 7f, will be well suited by 1m and further: acts on gd and
fast ground and on any track: improving colt who will win more races.   71
-2750 ROSE REEF [4] (I Balding) 2-8-11 S Cauthen 8/13 FAV: 22: Heavily bckd: ev ch inside
final 2f: another gd effort and is certain to get off the mark soon: stays 7f: see 2750.   60
--   CATHEDRAL PEAK [6] (M Usher) 2-8-11 M Wigham 12/1: 3: Made most and ran on well when
hdd: excellent racecourse debut from this half brother to a 12f winner: eff at 7f, looks
sure to stay 1m and further: acts on gd/firm and a stiff trk: certain to find a race.   58
--   TROYES [3] (W Hern) 2-8-8 W Carson 8/1: 4: Easy to back: some late hdwy and will be
all the better for this debut effort: full sister to the smart New Trojan who was a winner
over this trip as a 2yo: will be well suited by 1m and further: acts on gd/firm grd and
can find a race.   45
--   HONEY DANCER [2] 2-8-11 R Cochrane 33/1: 0: Never nearer: stiff debut and by no means
disgraced: cheaply acquired colt who is a half brother to sev winners including the useful
middle dist performer Positive: will be suited by another furlong: acts on gd/firm.   45
2852 MIGHTY GLOW [5] 2-8-11 P Cook 33/1: 00: Prom most: on the upgrade: half brother to
a couple of minor winners and should be btr in time.   44
6 ran   1,1,5,1½,hd   (D J Saxby)   G Harwood Pulborough, Sussex

2952 GROUP 3 PRINCESS ROYAL STAKES 3YO+   £16790   1m 4f   Good/Firm 27 -09 Slow

*2649 TASHTIYA [6] (M Stoute) 3-8-9 W R Swinburn 5/4 FAV: 0-211: 3 b f Shergar - Tremogia
(Silver Shark) Smart, fast impr filly: bckd as if defeat was out of the question and led final
1f under press for a game win in Gr 3 Princess Royal Stks at Ascot: rather lightly raced prev,
last time out was an easy winner of a 3yo fillies event at Yarmouth: eff 10f, stays 12f well:
acts on gd & fast grd and on a gall trk: certain to win more races.   78
2357 MILL ON THE FLOSS [5] (H Cecil) 3-8-9 S Cauthen 11/2: -312202: Led till hdd final 1f:
came again and just btn: fine effort and is a genuine filly: see 1128, 509.   77
2525 SALCHOW [2] (W Hern) 3-8-9 W Carson 3/1: 12-1023: Came from off the pace but had
ev ch final 1f: another fine effort: see 2525, 463.   73
2525 STARTINO [3] (H Cecil) 3-8-9 R Cochrane 5/1: 2-11144: Chance over 2f out: best 2236.   70
2649 HOTEL STREET [1] 3-8-6 Paul Eddery 16/1: -120: Fdd final 2f: stiff task: see 2649, 2304   55
2525 SPUN GOLD [4] 3-8-6 P Waldron 33/1: -041000: Outsider: best 1170.   45
6 ran   hd,2,1½,8,6   (H H Aga Khan)   M Stoute Newmarket

2953 BOVIS STAKES (H'CAP) (0-75) 3YO+   £10736   5f   Good/Firm 27 +12 Fast   [64]

2764 PERFECT TIMING [10] (D Elsworth) 4-9-0 S Cauthen 13/2: 2321021: 4 b f Comedy Star -
Eridantini (Indigenous) Very useful filly: well bckd: slowly away but led over 1f out and
held on cl home in fast run and val Bovis H'cap at Ascot: tremendously consistent filly,
earlier winning a similar event at Epsom and has been placed on numerous occasions: in '85 won
at Newmarket: best form at 5/6f on fast grd: has to be held up for a late chall: carries weight
well and is a credit to her trainer.   61
2783 PERION [3] (G Lewis) 4-8-1(1ow) P Waldron 7/1: 1040332: Behind, ran on well final 1f
and nearly gained the day: another fine effort and handles any ground: should win again soon.   47
2463 ALMAROSE [4] (J Sutcliffe) 3-7-9 R Fox 12/1: 12-0203: Reverting to 5f and ran well:
disapp over 7f last time: see 2242, 886.   34
-2758 DURHAM PLACE [8] (K Brassey) 4-8-5(bl) S Whitworth 20/1: 0004024: Dsptd lead inside
final 2f: fair effort: see 877.   42
2764 DERRY RIVER [16] 5-7-8(vis) C Rutter(1) 7/1: 0010430: Ran on final 1f, closer to
winner 2764.   30
2668 MANTON DAN [14] 3-9-7 P Cook 15/2: 0101100: Led 2f out: see 2446 (6f)   56
2764 DEPUTY HEAD [6] 6-8-11 W Carson 10/1: 0300200: Kept on under press: see 2731.   00
2862 YOUNG INCA [5] 8-8-6 R Cochrane 6/1 FAV: 0030030: Not clear run inside final 2f:
btr 6f? See 1777.   00
2668 PADRE PIO [15] 5-8-4 Paul Eddery 9/1: 2002300: Ev ch over 1f out, eased and reportedly
broke a bone in his hind leg: see 2151.   00

2731 **Cree Bay** [1] 8-5(bl)	2764 **Woodfold** [13] 7-13	2833 **Ardrox Lad** [2] 9-3
2783 **Meeson King** [9] 8-0	2785 **All Agreed** [11] 8-10	660 **Broadwater Music** [7] 8-9
2764 **Lochtillum** [12] 8-4		
16 ran shthd,3,hd,hd,½,½,1	(R J Vines)	D Elsworth Fordingbridge, Hants.

2954 GROUP 3 CORNWALLIS STAKES 2YO   £13984   5f   Good/Firm 27 +07 Fast

+2661 SINGING STEVEN [10] (R Hannon) 2-8-11(bl) B Rouse 7/1: 1230311: 2 b c Balliol - Cheb's
Honour (Cheb's Lad) Tough and smart colt: sn prom and led well over 1f out, running on under
press to win quite fast run Gr 3 Cornwallis Stks at Ascot: has retained his form really well
after being on the go all season: last time out won a 2yo Listed race at Ayr, earlier successful
in minor races at Wolverhampton & Bath: bargain buy who is a half brother to winning h'capper
Minus Man: very eff over 5/6f: acts on firm & soft grd and on any trk: genuine sort who
has shown further improvement with the application of blinkers.   70
-2661 WHIPPER IN [8] (J Etherington) 2-8-11 R Cochrane 7/1: 1122: Stayed on well under press
final 1f and is in grand form: see 2661, 2398.   69
+2843 CLARENTIA [3] (M Usher) 2-8-8 C Rutter 20/1: 3200213: Prom, ev ch when edged right
final 1f: an amazingly gd effort from this speedy filly: has an official rating of only 34!
Should win again soon: see 2843.   63
1714 INDIAN FOREST [4] (G Mikhalides) 2-9-1 J Velasquez 6/4 FAV: -101014: Heavily bckd
French colt: made most but was held when carried right inside final 1f: recently won a Gr 3
event at Longchamp: earlier successful at Deauville and St Cloud: speedy sort who is eff
over 5f on fast ground.   65
2694 SHARP REMINDER [6] 2-8-11 W Carson 9/1: 003130: Chance 2f out: most consistent: see 2694 56
*2501 AMIGO SUCIO [1] 2-9-1(vis) S Whitworth 5/1: 1133010: Prom most: below his best: see 2501 49
2235 CHASING MOONBEAMS [2] 2-8-8 S Cauthen 8/1: 2214300: Fin last: well below 2158.   00
2460 Mandub [5] 8-11   1789 Naturally Fresh [7] 8-8
9 ran ½,1,1½,1½,4   (Dr Steve Bennett)   R Hannon Marlborough, Wilts

2955 CORINTHIAN STAKES (AMA.RIDERS) H'CAP   £3293   1m 4f   Good/Firm 27 -46 Slow   [14]

*2260 BLENDERS CHOICE [4] (J King) 4-11-11 Mr T Thomson Jones 7/4 FAV: 0111311: 4 b c Cavo
Doro - Harriny (Floribunda) Useful colt: landed some hvy bets, led 2f out, easily, in a slow
run amateur riders h'cap at Ascot: recent winner over hurdles: in tremendous form on the level
winning 5 of his last 6 outings, earlier a similar event at Goodwood & also ran up a hat-trick
at Warwick, Chepstow & Folkestone: seems equally eff at 10/12f: does well when up with the pace
and acts on any trk: genuine.   50
2290 NO U TURN [2] (S Mellor) 8-10-11 Mr R Hutchinson 5/1: -004432: No chance with winner
but ran well: see 1004.   26
-- VELESO [11] (J King) 8-9-7 Mr A Forte 50/1: 44340/3: Stable mate of winner: belied
his 50/1 S.P: btr known as a 3m chaser!   06
2861 MALADHU [9] (J Fitzgerald) 7-10-11 Mr A Robson 12/1: 40-1304: Hmpd early: styd: see 2324. 34
-2855 OSRIC [7] 3-11-2 Mr J Ryan 7/2: D320420: Led to ½ way: much btr 2855.   34
1052 MENINGI [8] 5-10-10 Mr T Mitchell 16/1: 1414330: Abs: no threat: see 591.   12
2523 CADMIUM [10] 4-11-6 Mr T Reed 10/1: 0343000: Fdd str: tried in bl last time: best 1992.   00
2722 Adbury [1] 9-7   2467 Socks Up [3] 10-1(3ow) 2845 Norfolk Sonata [5] 12-0
2733 Chucklestone [12] 10-8(VIS)   2467 Dipyn Bach [6] 10-0
12 ran 5,1,½,nk,4,   (Mark O'Connor)   J King Swindon, Wilts.

2956 BROCAS STAKES (H'CAP) (0-70) 3YO+   £7947   1m   Good/Firm 27 -07 Slow   [65]

2867 FLYHOME [10] (P Cundell) 5-8-4 N Adams 8/1: 0301101: 5 ch g Home Guard - Western Gem
(Sheshoon) In terrific form and made ev yard, gamely, in a val h'cap at Ascot: unplaced in the
Cambridgeshire last time but earlier won h'caps at Sandown & Salisbury (course record): in
'85 won again at Sandown, in '84 won at Bath & Wolverhampton: very eff with forcing tactics
over 1m, stays 10f: loves fast grd and a gall trk: genuine sort who carries weight well.   52
2867 ININSKY [6] (G Harwood) 3-9-4 G Starkey 3/1 FAV: 0341102: Well bckd: chall final 1f
and narrowly btn: another gd effort and should win again soon: see 2559.   71
2867 ALL FAIR [7] (P Haslam) 5-8-5(vis) G French 9/1: 2101103: Al prom: in grand form: see 2629 49
*2773 DE RIGUEUR [2] (J King) 4-8-11(5ex) S Cauthen 4/1: 1010014: Heavily bckd: chance
over 1f out: gd effort: see 2773.   50
2867 QUALITAIR FLYER [4] 4-7-12 A Mackay 14/1: 0000000: Never nearer: best run since 1455.   29
2545 GRUMBLE [9] 4-7-12 A Mcglone 20/1: 1300-00: Never nearer: only his 2nd outing this term:
twice a winner over 1m at Windsor in '85: acts on firm & yldg grd and on any trk.   25
2567 NINO BIRRIA [5] 3-9-7 R Cochrane 7/2: 0423000: Well bckd but fdd 2 out: has lost
his form: see 1286, 579.   00
2668 DAWNS DELIGHT [8] 8-9-0 W Woods(3) 25/1: 0001000: No show: lightly raced since 616 (6f)   00
2568 REALITY [1] 3-8-4 P Cook 6/1: -110300: Prom 6f: well below 2385 (stks form).   00
9 ran nk,1½,2½,4,2,shthd   (Colin G Southgate)   P Cundell Newbury, Berks.

Official Going Given As FIRM: NO TIMES TAKEN

2957 E.B.F. BRINKLOW MAIDEN STAKES (DIV 1)   £1057   1m   Firm No Time Taken

2598 UPTOTHEHILT [9] (J Dunlop) 2-9-0 W Carson 4/1: 001: 2 b c Kris - Karine (Habitat): Led
below dist & was driven out to win a 2yo mdn at Warwick: 205,000 gns yearling who had earlier
shown promise in much btr company & is sure to impr further with experience: stays 1m well
& will be suited by middle dists next season: acts on gd & fast grnd & on any trk.   46
2847 TALUS [3] (H Cecil) 2-9-0 S Cauthen 9/4 FAV: 02: Stayed on well under press: cmftbly
beat rem: half brother to several winners: eff over 1m on fast grnd: will win a race.   44
--   DRAW LOTS [8] (P Cole) 2-9-0 T Quinn 7/1: 3: Friendless in mkt on debut: al prom,
not qckn dist: cost I.R. 130,000 as a yearling & is a half brother to middle dist winner
No-U-Turn: should stay further than 1m: acts on fast grnd.   36
2522 STAR NORTH [7] (L Piggott) 2-9-0 E Guest(3) 14/1: 04: Set off in front, kept on
same pace: bred to be suited by middle dists next term: acts on fast grnd.   36
2761 APIARIST [6] 2-9-0 M Roberts 25/1: 0R00: One-paced but put up his best effort to
date here: will be suited by lngr dists: seems to act on any trk: see 2761.   34
2542 FOR THE CRACK [4] 2-9-0 R Wernham 25/1: 00: Never beyond mid-div: acts on fast grnd.   26
1658 KIP KEINO [2] 2-9-0 G Starkey 6/1: 40: Long abs: no threat: see 1658.   00
2852 BOY JAMIE [5] 2-9-0 C Nutter 8/1: 00: Some late prog: fin 8th: 16,500 gns yearling
who is a half brother to winning juvenile Stanley The Baron.   00
2646 GREAT CAESAR [10] 2-9-0 T Ives 10/1: 00: Close up 6f: fdd into 9th: cost $24,000 and
is bred to be well suited by this trip.   00
--   RIBOBAMBINO [1] 2-9-0 N Adams 10/1: 0: Dwelt & always behind on his debut: first foal
whose dam was successful over middle dists.   00
2561 Achill Bay [11] 9-0   979 Bill Lavender [12] 9-0
12 ran   ½,4,shhd,½,3,shhd,1½   (Prince Ahmed Salman)   J Dunlop Arundel, Sussex

2958 ARDEN E.B.F. STAKES 3YO+   £2555   1m 3f Firm No Time Taken

*1278 BROWN THATCH [3] (H Cecil) 3-8-10(3ow) S Cauthen 9/4: -3011: 3 br c Thatch - Honey
Match (Match III): Very useful colt who proved an easy winner despite a long abs, led below
dist in a stakes race at Warwick: earlier won a mdn at Doncaster, & first time out was a
fine 3rd to Nino Bibbia in a competitive Newmarket mdn: very eff around 10f on gd & fast
grnd: seems to act on any trk: has been lightly raced due to breathing problems.   60
+2790 FINAL TRY [1] (J Dunlop) 3-9-3 W Carson 7/4 FAV: 0-00012: Ran on well, but cmftbly
held by winner: in gd form: seems to act on any trk: see 2790.   60
2121 CHICLET [8] (J Jenkins) 4-9-0 Pat Eddery 5/1: 2040403: Previously trained by P Walwyn:
kept on well under strong press and made most as a gd effort: now likely to go hurdling: see 432.   46
*2593 PODEROSO [2] (R Boss) 3-8-7 W R Swinburn 12/1: 0040314: Made most: in gd form: see 2593. 46
2726 SWAALEF [9] 3-7-11 N Howe(0) 7/1: -030: No extra 2f out: see 2726 & 1431.   22
--   SWEETWATER LASS [5] 4-7-11 N Adams 50/1: 00030-0: Front rank over ½way on belated reappearance: little form last season & has since changed stables: best form over 10f.   00
2790 Soho Sue [7] 8-4   -- Sousaga [10] 7-11   -- National Image [4] 9-0
164 Ryans Dove [6] 7-11
10 ran 2,1,¾,7,5   (Sheikh Mohammed)   H Cecil Newmarket

2959 KINSBURY HANDICAP (0-35) 3YO+   £1808   1m 4f Firm No Time Taken   [31]

2699 ISOM DART [4] (T Hallett) 7-8-2 N Adams 25/1: 1100001: 7 b h Bold Forbes - Shellshock
(Salvo): Returned to form when gaining a surprise win in a h'cap at Warwick: made steady
progress to lead inside dist & ran on well: earlier successful in a seller at Bath & another
h'cap over this C/D: a winner over hdles in the past: suited by 10/12f & fast grnd: runs
well here.   16
*2714 TRACKERS JEWEL [9] (M Ryan) 4-8-11 G Starkey 4/1 FAV: 00-0012: In gd form: see 2714.   20
2346 KERRY MAY SING [3] (M Ryan) 3-8-4(BL) W Carson 8/1: 0000403: Bl first time: led below
dist, no extra close home: see 989.   16
2900 HEIGHT OF SUMMER [6] (D Arbuthnot) 5-7-11 C Rutter(3) 8/1: 0300134: Btr in 2727.   01
2874 ELEGANT GUEST [8] 3-8-6 T Ives 5/1: 00431D0: Btr in 2874 (gall trk).   12
2880 ARTISTIC CHAMPION [13] 3-8-10(1ow) S Cauthen 16/1: 3001000: No extra below dist: best 140113
2709 SOHAIL [10] 3-9-10(bl) P D'arcy 6/1: -031220: Fdd into 8th: btr in 2709 (gall trk).   00
2623 HIGHLAND BALL [2] 3-8-12 Pat Eddery 11/2: -004300: Made most: fin 9th: see 2217.   00
2023 ASHINGTON GROVE [7] 3-9-2 T Quinn 9/1: 2233230: Beaten 2f out: much better over
this C/D in 1473.   00
2861 Toscana [1] 9-7   2685 Rescue Package [5] 9-8
2727 Fenchurch Colony [12] 8-12
12 ran 2,3,shhd,3,1½,2   (G H Taylor-Webber)   T Hallett Carkeel, Cornwall

2960 GUYS CLIFFE SELLING H'CAP (0-25) 3/4YO   £964   1m   Firm No Time Taken   [13]

2836 HEATHGRIFF [7] (N Callaghan) 4-9-1 G Starkey 7/2: 0023031: 4 b g Balliol - Gilstee
(Crocket): Mkt drifter but got a lovely run on the rails to lead dist, cmftbly in a selling
h'cap at Warwick (bought in 2,600 gns): won a seller on fast grnd at Pontefract last season:
eff over 8/10f: best form on a sound surface & likes a sharp trk.   08
1771 SHIRLY ANN [10] (N Macauley) 4-8-12 N Adams 33/1: 0/20002: Abs: ran on well & clearly
does well when fresh: rated 22 behind Gold Prospect first time out (6f, soft): also acts on firm   00

2594 HACHIMITSU [8] (S Mellor) 3-9-0 M Wigham 12/1: 0000103: Chall dist: best in 1937.   06
2621 IDEOLIGIA [12] (A Hide) 4-8-3 W Newnes 8/1: 4000004: Ran on late: see 992.   00
2898 MISS VENEZUELA [2] 3-8-8(vis) R Guest 10/1: 0400000: Ran on same pace: see 1288.   00
2836 CYGNE [9] 4-9-0 J Williams 14/1: 0034000: Some late prog: see 2282 & 1990.   00
2836 SPARKFORD LAD [3] 4-9-7(bl) Debbie Wheatley(7) 10/1: 0213000: Made most: fin 7th.   00
2581 PAMELA HEANEY [11] 4-9-2 Pat Eddery 3/1 FAV: 0030400: Wknd into 9th: see 727.   00
2024 MY MUTZIE [1] 3-8-12 C Rutter(3) 10/1: -000040: Dwelt & al rear: btr in 2024 (5f).   00
2898 MISS HICKS [6] 3-9-5 S Hibble(7) 6/1: -000040: Started slowly: btr in 2898: see 2186.   00
--   Ginas Match [5] 9-1   2104 Mr Panache [14] 9-4   963 Elmcote Lad [4] 9-1(bl)
13 ran   2,nk,shhd,2½,nk,1½,½,½   (D A Griffiths)   N Callaghan Newmarket

2961 BRINKLOW MAIDEN (DIV 2) 2YO C & G   £1075   1m   Firm No Time Taken

--   HEYSHOTT [9] (G Harwood) 2-9-0 G Starkey 5/4 FAV: 1: 2 b c Persepolis - Agujita
(Vieux Manore): Promising colt: made a winning debut, well bckd & impr to lead at the dist,
cmftbly in a 2yo mdn at Warwick: cost $575,000 as a yearling & is a half brother to Arc
winner All Along: sure to be suited by middle dists next season: acts on fast grnd & on
a sharpish trk: can only improve.   50+
2811 CASTLE WARD [10] (J Dunlop) 2-9-0 W Carson 3/1: 32: Rallied well inside dist: on
the up grade & sure to find a race: certain to stay further: acts on gd & fast grnd: see 2811.   44
2095 ALA HOUNAK [6] (F Durr) 2-9-0 Pat Eddery 14/1: 003: Showed impr form, staying on
well under press & was not btn very far: cheaply bought colt who is a half brother to the
smart Ala Mahlik, who fin 4th in the 1,000 Guineas: stays 1m well: acts on fast grnd.   40
2232 PAGITEK [5] (S Wiles) 2-9-0 Paul Eddery 50/1: 04: Friendless in the mkt but was al
prom over this lngr trip: very cheaply bought gelding who is bred to be suited by middle
dists: acts on firm grnd.   38
2878 GREEN LALEEK [2] 2-9-0 T Quinn 6/1: 000: Ran on same pace: see 2878.   34
2878 NORS GOD [1] 2-9-0 W R Swinburn 6/1: 0020: Not qckn: btr in 2878 (made most).   33
--   CEDAR CREEK [3] 2-9-0 C Nutter 12/1: 0: Op. 4/1: no threat after slow start: should impr   00
2657 Gallant Ribo [4] 9-0   --   Goodwyns Lad [11] 9-0 2791 Charlous Choice [7] 9-0
--   Marcovich [8] 9-0   --   Ulysses [12] 9-0
12 ran   1,1½,½,2,½   (K Abdulla)   G Harwood Pulborough, Sussex

2962 OCTOBER NURSERY HANDICAP 2YO   £1362   5f   Firm No Time Taken   [42]

2792 SKYBOLT [6] (W O'gorman) 2-8-6(BL) T Ives 7/1: 04001: 2 gr f Absalom - Hum (Crooner):
Bl first time & showed impr form when leading over 1f out in a nursery h'cap at Warwick:
speedily bred filly who is a half sister to minor 6f winner Opal Lady: best form over 5f on
fast ground.   30
-2903 OUT ON A FLYER [3] (D Elsworth) 2-8-1 A Mcglone 3/1: 2132422: Placed again: see 2903.   18
2694 AID AND ABET [2] (M Stoute) 2-9-3 W R Swinburn 5/2: 421203: Led after ½way: see 2007.   32
2792 SPANISH SKY [4] (N Vigors) 2-9-7 P Cook 9/1: 0030004: Led over ½way: see 2090, 1194.   28
2744 WOODMAN WEAVER [7] 2-8-7 Pat Eddery 9/4 FAV: 0043200: Fdd: much btr in 2689.   12
2284 PINK PUMPKIN [5] 2-7-8 N Adams 20/1: 0140000: Mkt drifter: al behind: see 2284, 1496.   00
6 ran   2,½,3,½,2   (Mrs Linda Yong)   W O'gorman Newmarket

Official Going Given As FIRM

2963 OCTOBER APPR HANDICAP 3YO 0-35   £1583   1m   Good/Firm 26 -20 Slow   [32]

2230 PLAIN TALK [3] (A Hide) 3-8-12 P Brette 8/1: 4-04001: 3 b g The Brianstan - Claymore
Honey (Levanter): Despite an abs, led over 1f out, under press in an app h'cap at Pontefract:
first success: eff at 7f, stays 1m: acts on gd & fast grnd & a turning trk.   24
2581 FARAG [1] (P Walwyn) 3-9-2 D Meade 3/1: 0320002: Made much: gd run: see 1819.   24
2863 MRS NAUGHTY [8] (W Wharton) 3-8-5 Abigail Richards 4/1: 0304323: Al there: in gd form.   10
*2863 KEEP COOL [2] (R Hollinshead) 3-8-4(6ex) A Whitehall 10/3: 0433314: Slow start, btr 2863.   06
2143 MOGOAR [7] 3-9-3 G Thompson(4) 6/1: 30-0400: Sn prom: lightly rcd: see 1451.   15
2060 LADY OWEN [6] 3-7-9 I Glindoni(4) 16/1: -000000: Abs: fdd str: lightly rcd & no
form this term: see 356.   00
2879 MAL Y PENSE [9] 3-9-7 B Murtagh(4) 10/1: 010-000: Fdd quickly str: lightly rcd this
term & little form: last season won a fillies event at Catterick: eff at 7f on gd & fast grnd
and a sharp trk.   00
2509 Timsolo [5] 7-7   --   Floreamus [4] 8-8
9 ran   2,1½,1½,2,1   (Sir Gordon Brunton)   A Hide Newmarket

2964 NOSTELL SELLING STAKES   £965   1m 2f Good/Firm 26 -09 Slow

2902 G G MAGIC [13] (D Morley) 3-8-7 R Cochrane 6/1: 0042131: 3 br c Strong Gale -
King's Chase (King's Leap): In gd form lately: switched final 1f & got up close home in a
seller at Pontefract (bought in 2,700 gns): last mnth won a selling h'cap at Nottingham: in
'85 won another seller at Catterick: eff at 10f, stays 14f: acts on firm & yld grnd & on any trk   19
2925 DICK KNIGHT [14] (K Ivory) 5-9-3(vis) A Shoults(5) 4/1: 1002032: Led over 3f out &
sn clear: fdd & caught near fin: 5L clear 3rd: gd effort: see 2925, 2101.   21

2395 **BAYTINO** [5] (H Collingridge) 3-8-4 M Rimmer 9/4 FAV: -03003: Early ldr: ev ch:
flattered in 2110?   05
2836 **COMPOSER** [9] (M James) 8-9-3(bl) D Nicholls 25/1: 0240004: Stayed on late: best
effort since 1546.   09
2008 **VERBADING** [2] 4-8-11(vis) L Ashworth(7) 14/1: 2300040: Never nearer: see 2008, 524.   02
2374 **EARLS COURT** [8] 10-9-3 S Webster 16/1: 0400340: No threat: see 1432.   04
2836 **NELSONS LADY** [1] 5-9-0 I Salmon 9/1: 0040000: Some late hdway: best 1990 (7f).   00
2604 **HOT BETTY** [11] 6-8-11 R P Elliott 8/1: 0400100: Twice well below 2008 (12f).   00
2714 **JUST CANDID** [12] 4-9-0 T Williams 15/2: 3423240: Can do btr: see 2714, 2187.   00
2762 Murillo [4] 9-3(bl)   *2836 Teejay [6] 9-3   -- Frisky Hope [15] 9-0
2549 Polemistis [10] 9-0(bl)   2780 Birchgrove Lad [7] 9-0(vis)
2621 Arnab [3] 9-3
15 ran   nk,5,1,shhd,2,nk   (A Glass)   D Morley Newmarket

2965 STAYERS EBF STAKES 3YO+   £2845   2m 2f   Good/Firm 26 -59 Slow

*2809 **BRIGHTNER** [1] (G Harwood) 5-9-10 A Clark 1: 10/0311: 5 ch g Sparkler - Smarten Up
(Sharpen Up): Easily disposed of his sole rival in a staying event at Pontefract and there
were no Started Prices returned: see 2809.   41
*2679 **COOL NUMBER** [2] (H Whiting) 3-8-7(3ow) D Nicholls 1: -003312: Btn over 3f out: see 2679.   15
2 ran   10   (K Abdulla)   G Harwood Pulborough, Sussex

2966 BARNSLEY HANDICAP STAKES 3YO+ 0-50   £2817   5f   Good/Firm 26 +06 Fast   [47]

1263 **THATCHVILLE** [5] (I Matthews) 4-7-7 G Bardwell(7) 25/1: 0440001: 4 ch f Thatch -
Miss Filbert (Compensation): Despite a long abs, outpcd to ½way but fin really well to get
up close home in a h'cap at Pontefract: lightly rcd filly who won a h'cap at Catterick in
'85: eff at 5/6f, stays 1m: acts on gd/firm & soft grnd: seems to like a turning track.   20
2731 **DAVILL** [7] (J Winter) 4-8-2 G Carter 9/2: 0003002: Led 1f out: caught near line:
7L clear 3rd: gd effort: see 1950, 76.   28
2715 **SHARLIES WIMPY** [6] (W Pearce) 7-8-5(bl) S Buckton 10/1: 4000003: Not much room over 1f
out: best 2295.   17
2775 **PHILSTAR** [4] (A Balding) 5-7-8(bl)(1ow)(3oh) J Lowe 12/1: 0300000: Sn prom: best 1676.   01
+2530 **AXE VALLEY** [3] 4-9-13(bl) J Reid 15/8 FAV: -010010: Met troubling in running: see 2530.   34
2758 **VENEZ TRADER** [9] 3-8-13(bl) A Murray 16/1: 4-40000: Best first time out in 1027.   21
2783 **SPACEMAKER BOY** [10] 6-8-13 D Nicholls 10/1: F000000: Prom most: best 1037: see 211.   00
2921 **CHINA GOLD** [1] 7-9-2 M Wood 11/2: 0001000: Front rank most: best 2586.   00
2906 **LEFT RIGHT** [2] 3-7-7(2oh) G French 10/1: 0441000: Led over 3f: best 2106.   00
2775 **MISS PRIMULA** [8] 3-7-11 T Williams 12/1: 0004000: Early speed: flattered 628.   00
10 ran   hd,7,2½,hd,hd   (Lord Matthews)   I Matthews Newmarket

2967 EBF WHITLEY STAKES 2YO FILLIES   £2078   6f   Good/firm 26 -02 Slow

+2895 **CHORITZO** [4] (R Williams) 2-9-0 J Reid 5/1: 22211: 2 b f Runnett - Magee (Weaver's Hall):
Very useful, impr filly: made ev yd, readily in a 2yo fillies event at Pontefract: last time
out again made all when an 8L winner of a fast run 2yo mdn at Brighton: fin 2nd on her first
3 starts: half sister to the useful sprinter Eastern Song: very eff at 6f, should stay 7f:
acts on any trk, but seems suited by front running tactics: loves fast grnd: on the up grade.   60
-- **ZUAETREH** [7] (H T Jones) 2-8-8 A Murray 12/1: 2: Mkt drifter: switched inside final 2f
and ran on well: impr very likely from this American bred filly who cost $75,000: should be
suited by 7f plus: acts on gd/firm grnd & should go one btr soon.   48
2774 **AZYAA** [6] (H T Jones) 2-8-8 R Hills 5/6 FAV: 33: Hvly bckd: sn prom & ev ch: 6L clear
4th & is worth another ch: may need further than 6f: see 2774.   47
2651 **SKIPAWAY** [8] (H Cecil) 2-8-8 W Ryan 13/2: 04: Prom, ev ch: btr effort: see 2651.   35
2215 **FOLLIES BERGERES** [1] 2-8-8 D Nicholls 5/1: 320: Sn prom: well below 2215 (7f).   35
2589 **JUST CLASS** [9] 2-8-8 J Lowe 16/1: 40: Prom most: on the up grade: see 2589.   32
-- Kumzar [2] 8-8   2710 Hytak Pet [3] 8-8
8 ran   2½,shhd,6,shhd,1½   (Christopher Wright)   R Williams Newmarket

2968 MINOR NURSERY HANDICAP 2YO   £2793   1m   Good/Firm 26 +02 Fast   [57]

*2707 **CALIBOGUE** [6] (R Sheather) 2-8-6 R Cochrane 7/4 FAV: 0011: 2 b c Taufan - Montana Moss
(Levmoss): In gd form and led over 1f out: held on under press in a nursery h'cap at
Pontefract: last time out won a 2yo claimer at Leicester: cost only 5,400 gns as a yearling:
eff at 7f, stays 1m: acts on fast grnd & probably on any trk.   43
2756 **PHARAOH BLUE** [9] (C Brittain) 2-7-7(2oh) G Carter 10/1: 0120422: Ran on well final
1f under press & nearly got up: 6L clear 3rd & deserves another win: best 1883.   29
2657 **FLUTEAU** [10] (M Stoute) 2-7-8(BL) D Gibson(7) 8/1: 0043: Bl first time: al there: btr 2657 18
2615 **MUSTAKBIL** [5] (P Walwyn) 2-7-7(1oh) T Williams 11/1: 3004: No real threat: lightly
raced since 1606: prob. stays 1m.   05
*1965 **KHADRUF** [7] 2-9-7 A Murray 6/1: 10310: Led after ½way: needed race? see 1965 (7f).   27
2798 **JOHNNY SHARP** [2] 2-7-8(1ow)(1oh) J Lowe 20/1: 2001000: Twice below 2663: see 2498.   00
2792 **KNOCKSHARRY** [3] 2-7-7(11oh) P Hill(6) 25/1: 1000030: Not clear run in str: see 2792.   00
2806 **AVINASESH** [4] 2-7-7(1oh) G French 10/1: 3400240: Well below form shown in 2806, 2512 (C/D)00
2748 **FLAUNTING** [11] 2-8-10 D Nicholls 10/1: 00440: Led over 4f: btr 2748.   00

2888 FOUNTAINS CHOICE [8] 2-7-11(vis) P Burke(7) 8/1: 0020120: Fdd quickly str: not stay 1m?   00
2830 CAERINETTE [1] 2-7-8 Abigail Richards(4) 12/1: 4000300: Very slowly away: best 2648.   00
11 ran   hd,6,7,3,nk   (M D Scott)   R Sheather Newmarket

AYR   Monday October 13th   Lefthand Galloping Track

2969 EBF ARRAN STAKES 2YO FILLIES   £1818   5f   Good 40 -08 Slow

223 TOP AND TAIL [4] (M Ryan) 2-8-8 P Robinson 9/4 FAV: 01: 2 b f Tilt Up - Roast Duck
(Sea-Bird II): Impr filly who was well bckd when cmftbly leading 2f out in a minor race for
2yo fillies at Ayr: only ran once previously, very early in the season: related to a winning
stayer in France: eff 5f, should stay 6f: acts on gd grnd.   38
-- SLEEPERS [6] (C Booth) 2-8-8 N Howe 7/1: 2: Nicely bckd on debut, chall 1f out & ran
well: sprint bred filly who cost only 4,600 gns: should stay 6f: acts on gd grnd: sure to
impr on this first effort.   35
2127 SENDIM ON SAM [3] (M W Easterby) 2-8-8 M Birch 33/1: 00003: Prom, ev ch: btr effort.   31
2043 ROMAN BELLE [2] (G P Gordon) 2-8-8 M Hills 7/1: 0304: Kept on, never btr: see 1632.   29
2375 NON FICTION [7] 2-8-8 S Whitworth 7/1: 3430: Early ldr: btr 2375 (sharp trk).   17
2423 ANAKA [8] 2-8-8 G Brown 7/2: 00: Outpcd: btr 2423 (6f).   11
2678 JOYCES PET [5] 2-8-8 J Bleasdale 33/1: 0000: No threat in 7th: no worthwhile form.   00
-- TITANIAS STAR [1] 2-8-8 G Duffield 7/1: 0: Early pace on debut: cost 27,000 gns: quite
speedily bred & should be capable of btr than this.   00
8 ran   ¾,1½,½,4,2   (T Ramsden)   M Ryan Newmarket

2970 AYR SPRINT H'CAP 3YO+ 0-50   £2750   6f   Good 40 +15 Fast   [41]

2725 VILTASH [6] (J Etherington) 3-9-2 M Birch 9/1: 0000041: 3 ch c Tachypous - Swynford's
Pride (Rapid River): Returned to his best, never hdd when cmftbly winning a fast run h'cap at
Ayr: in gd form early last season winning at Ayr & Thirsk: equally eff at 5/6f & acts on
any going & on any trk though has now won twice at Ayr: can win again.   46
2660 GOLDEN GUILDER [10] (M W Easterby) 3-8-9(bl) L Charnock 6/1: 3333U22: Prom, ev ch:
does not win often but is consistent: see 947.   30
2858 WARTHILL LADY [1] (M Brittain) 4-8-3 P Robinson 11/2 JT FAV: 1010023: Kept on well &
is in fine form: see 2632.   20
2816 TIT WILLOW [5] (S Wiles) 4-7-13(bl) M Fry 11/2 JT FAV: 2034324: Never btr: see 828, 2816.   15
2670 DEBBIE DO [8] 3-8-12 J Bleasdale 9/1: 0000040: Prom: see 2277.   26
2816 GODS SOLUTION [3] 5-8-6(bl) G Duffield 7/1: 0400040: See 42.   12
2891 HENRYS VENTURE [7] 4-7-9 N Carlisle 14/1: 0343000: Slow start, fin 7th: see 2295.   00
2518 ZILLEBEKE [11] 3-8-4 S Whitworth 10/1: -00330: Prom, wknd into 8th: see 2367.   00
2446 Idle Times [9] 8-5   2715 Pentoff [4] 7-7   -- Kathred [2] 9-7
2413 Manix [12] 7-8(bl)(1ow)(16oh)
12 ran   3,nk,hd,2,2,½,1½   (J Marshall)   J Etherington Malton, Yorks

2971 CLYDE COAST NURSERY H'CAP 2YO   £5127   1m   Good 40 +09 Fast   [57]

2658 NORTH PACIFIC [8] (P Cole) 2-7-12 A Culhane(7) 5/1: 0301: 2 ch f Hawaii - Ivory
Smooth (Sir Ivor): Appeared well h'capped & duly came from behind to lead 1f out in a fast
run nursery at Ayr: cost $120,000: btr suited by 1m than shorter dists & should appreciate
10/12f next season: acts on firm & gd grnd: can win another nursery over 1m.   40
2796 KALEIDOPHONE [6] (C Elsey) 2-8-3 G Duffield 14/1: 003442: Prom, kept on well: btr
effort & stays 1m: see 1266, 2664.   41
2894 GOLDEN TREE [1] (J Etherington) 2-8-11 A Mackay 5/1: 000033: Waited with, ch 2f out.
disapp after 2830.   47
2830 MON COEUR [2] (C Brittain) 2-9-0(bl) P Robinson 9/4 FAV: 0423034: Dsptd lead 3f out,
disapp after 2830.   50
2439 BEN LEDI [5] 2-9-7 M Birch 8/1: 3113140: Dsptd lead 2f out, wknd: best 2276 (7f).   54
2888 CRAIGENDARROCH [7] 2-7-7(7oh) N Carlisle 20/1: 0100000: No threat: see 2050 (seller).   20
*2663 BOY SINGER [4] 2-7-13(vis) A Mercer 11/2: 4300010: Made much: btr 2663 (C/D).   00
*2584 MISS ZOLA [3] 2-8-13 M Hills 14/1: 0010: Prom, wknd: best 2584.   00
8 ran   1½,½,hd,1½,3   (F Salman)   P Cole, Whatcombe, Oxon

2972 PRESTWICH SELLING STAKES 3 & 4-Y-O   £905   1m   Good 40 -10 Slow

2863 COUNTRY CARNIVAL [8] (W Haigh) 3-7-13(bl) P Robinson 8/1: 0000001: 3 b f Town And
Country - Fairabunda (Floribunda): Gaining first success, making most to win a seller at
Ayr (no bid): early in the season a close up 3rd in a minor event at Catterick, subsq. disapp:
seems best over 7f/1m forcing the pace: acts on gd & firm grnd: wears bl now.   11
2656 LIGHT THE WAY [7] (M Prescott) 3-8-0(1ow) G Duffield 11/8 FAV: 0-02: Rear, never btr:
well bckd in this first venture into selling company: see 2656.   07
2863 MAFTIR [2] (M James) 4-9-8(bl) J Bleasdale 25/1: 0122003: Held up, late prog: see 2419.   19
2893 MUSICAL AID [3] (T Craig) 3-7-13 A Mackay 7/1: 0000044: Ch 2f out, no extra: flattered 2893 00
2863 SKYBIRD [6] 3-8-2 A Proud 7/1: 0003000: Sn prom: btr 2863.   00
2704 LADY LAMB [5] 3-7-13(vis) N Howe 6/1: -000000: Prom, wknd: now wears a visor:
seems totally moderate.   00
2424 LA BELLE OF SANTO [1] 3-7-13 L Charnock 6/1: 2000000: Fin 7th: mainly disapp since 1299 00

2509 EASTERN HEIGHTS [14] 3-8-2(VIS) M Fry 33/1: 00-0000: Fin last: very lightly raced
and no form.   00
8 ran   2¼,1½,1,2½,3,hd   (R Lloyd)   W Haigh Malton, Yorks

2973 BALLANTRAE FILLIES STAKES 3YO   £959   1m   Good 40 -04 Slow

2755 BASOOF [3] (M Stoute) 3-8-8 M Birch 7/4 FAV: 0404031: 3 b f Believe It - Continual
(Damascus): At last gained an elusive success, hvly bckd & showed a turn of foot to lead
inside final 1f in a 3yo fillies event at Ayr: placed several times previously: suited by
1m, may stay further: acts on firm & gd grnd & seems best with waiting tactics: half sister
to the top class miler Shadeed.   46
2653 HOOKED BID [4] (J Dunlop) 3-9-1 G Baxter 85/40: 0003132: Led briefly 1f out: gd
effort at the weights & may win a h'cap soon: see 2532.   50
862 GREEN FOR DANGER [6] (J Hindley) 3-8-8 M Hills 14/1: -3003: Made most: gd effort
after long abs: best effort since 213 (first time out) & evidently does well when fresh.   41
1487 GREAT DILEMMA [1] (P Makin) 3-8-8 B Thomson 5/2: -002204: Never closer: gd effort
after abs: see 1244.   41
2854 MOLLY PARTRIDGE [5] 3-9-1 S Hustler(7) 33/1: 3004100: No ch final 2f but not disgraced
at the weights: see 2858 (seller).   28
2086 CROWNIT [7] 3-8-8 N Howe 33/1: 0-00000: Abs: well btn here & no worthwhile form.   01
2762 STARBOARD [2] 3-8-8 G Duffield 20/1: -004000: Al rear: no form.   00
7 ran   ¾,1,hd,7,8   (Maktoum Al Maktoum)   M Stoute Newmarket

2974 AUCHINCRUIVE H'CAP 3YO+ 0-35   £2401   1m 7f   Good 40 -02 Slow   [28]

2445 PATHS SISTER [8] (C Thornton) 5-9-2 M Tebbutt(7) 7/2 FAV: -000001: 5 gr m Warpath -
Turtle Dove (Gyr): Returned to form, coming from behind to cmftbly lead final 1f in a h'cap
at Ayr: has not had the necessary soft grnd this season but last term won at Doncaster,
Haydock (2), Newcastle & Ayr: eff 14f, stays 2m2f: acts on any going but is fav by good
or softer grnd: may win again.   25
2701 KRISWICK [11] (J Dunlop) 3-8-13 G Baxter 6/1: -00402: Prom, led 2f out, narrowly btn
& clear of rem: remains a mdn but clearly suited by a stamina test & can find a small
event soon over a dist of grnd: see 479.   30
2306 CHALICE OF SILVER [2] (M Jarvis) 3-9-7 T Lucas 10/1: -432323: Ev ch, once again
lacked finishing pace: see 2306, 315.   31
2627 CAROUSEL ROCKET [9] (R Whitaker) 3-9-2 K Bradshaw(5) 20/1: 2103404: Fair effort: see 968. 24
2346 COLLISTO [4] 5-8-9(vis) S Whitworth 6/1: 0222020: Made much: btr 2346.   05
2647 REFORM PRINCESS [10] 3-8-13(vis) N Day 9/1: 4103000: Prom, wknd: disapp since 2087.   15
2267 LAKINO [7] 4-9-1 M Birch 8/1: 0000100: Prom, wknd: twice below 1866 (11f).   00
2722 COLEMAN HAWKINS [3] 3-8-9(bl) B Thomson 8/1: 0040340: Wknd ¼way: btr 2722.   00
2603 Pauls Secret [5] 7-8   **1016 Hot Ruler** [1] 7-11   **1737 Tharaleos** [6] 7-8(1ow)
11 ran   ¾,5,1½,2,4   (Miss Betty Duxbury)   C Thornton Middleham, Yorks

---

Official Going Given As FIRM
2975 E.B.F. CAPTAIN COOK MAIDEN STAKES 2YO   £2677   7f   Firm 16 +05 Fast

-- AFTERNOON WINNER [11] (G Harwood) 2-8-11 G Starkey 1/1 FAV: 1: 2 gr f Text - Morning
Games (Grey Dawn II): Promising filly: first time out, well bckd & led over 1f out, easily
in fast run 2yo mdn at Redcar: half sister to the smart Alphabatim: eff at 7f, looks sure to
be suited by 1m & further: acts on fast grnd & can only impr.   51
2646 SUPER LUNAR [3] (R Sheather) 2-9-0 M Rimmer 11/4: 422: Kept on under press & met a
good one here: 4L clear 3rd: can find a race: see 2646.   42
2626 ALAJIB [12] (H T Jones) 2-9-0 A Murray 6/1: 03: Made much: btr effort from this
I.R. 22,000 gns purchase: half brother to a winner in Ireland: should be suited by this
trip: acts on fast grnd.   34
2606 DANADN [1] (Ron Thompson) 2-9-0 R P Elliott 25/1: 3324004: Dsptd lead: fair eff: see 1907. 29
1869 ROYAL TOWER [2] 2-9-0 W Newnes 25/1: 00: Abs: prom much: btr effort from this half
brother to 4 winners: acts on fast grnd.   21
-- MARIE ZEPHYR [10] 2-8-11 C Dwyer 50/1: 0: Rank outsider on debut: slowly away &
never nearer: very cheaply acquired filly who acts on firm grnd.   13
-- NORWICH CASTLE [9] 2-8-11 G Duffield 8/1: 0: Mkt drifter on debut: made no show:
American bred filly who should impr on this.   11
2725 Golden Game [5] 9-0   **2761 Westajames** [7] 9-0   **2482 Northern Security** [6] 9-0
10 ran   2½,4,2,4,2½,¾   (Jerome Brody)   G Harwood Pulborough, Sussex

2976 AIRY HILL STAKES 2YO   £1196   1m   Firm 16 +01 Fast

2829 CHOISUN [11] (P Haslam) 2-8-11 T Williams 2/1 FAV: 001: 2 ch g Viking - Miss Season
(Silly Season): Impr gelding: well bckd & led inside final 2f for a ready win in quite fast
run 2yo seller at Redcar: half brother to a winning sprinter but stays 1m well himself:
suited by a gall trk & fast grnd: may win outside selling company & was bought in for
5,200 gns today.   33

*2757 MELGROVE [3] (J Etherington) 2-9-2(bl) S Webster 7/1: 040012: Al front rank: stays
1m and is in fine form: can find another seller: see 2757.   29
2179 DYNAMIC STAR [12] (M Usher) 2-8-11 M Wigham 10/1: 003: Abs: al prom: dropped in class
today & can find a similar event: eff over 1m on firm grnd.   22
2841 BOLD DIFFERENCE [13] (W Wharton) 2-8-13 A Culhane(7) 9/2: 1200044: Made most: quite
a consistent filly who stays 1m: see 1221.   16
2138 DANUM LAD [14] 2-8-11 R P Elliott 20/1: 0000: Al there: first signs of form & seems
eff at 1m on fast grnd.   08
2801 CREOLE BAY [9] 2-8-8 C Dwyer 16/1: 0000300: Sn prom: best 2724.   02
2757 MARKET MAN [18] 2-8-11 S Perks 12/1: 0400: Mkt drifter: fin 7th: probably stays 1m:
acts on gd & firm grnd.   00
2757 AMIABLE AMY [8] 2-8-8 M Fry 7/1: 040: Never nearer 8th: can do btr: see 2757.   00
2894 JAZZ DANCER [4] 2-8-11(BL) G Starkey 8/1: 000: Bl first time: dropped in class today
but has shown little form in 3 outings: may do btr.   00
2894 STRAY NO MORE [10] 2-8-11 R Lappin(7) 10/1: 000: Active in mkt but made no show:
cost I.R. 6,000 as a yearling and is a half brother to a winning juvenile.   00
2757 Skerne Rocket [5] 8-8   2323 Swift Challenger [1] 8-11
1413 Phils Pride [2] 8-11   2470 Paddy Maloney [7] 8-11
2757 Austhorpe Sunset [19] 8-11   -- Linco King [15] 8-11
  -- Only Joking [17] 8-8   1816 Splashin Out [6] 8-11
18 ran   2¼,¼,4,3,1½,1½,2½   (Harvey Hill)   P Haslam Newmarket

2977 BROTTON SEAFOODS H'CAP (0-35) 3YO+   £2194   6f   Firm 16 +01 Fast   [32]

2870 JARROVIAN [7] (T Fairhurst) 3-9-6(bl) G Starkey 8/1: 0000401: 3 ch c Moorestyle -
Shady Desire (Meldrum): Al prom & led final 1f, under press in a h'cap at Redcar: in gd
form early in the season, winning at Thirsk: eff at 6f, does stay 1m: acts on any grnd
and on any trk.   35
1520 KINGS TOUCH [11] (P Makin) 3-9-10 S Perks 8/1: -040002: Abs: al prom: lightly rcd
colt & has shown his best effort since 455.   35
2858 ROSIE DICKINS [4] (R Hollinshead) 4-8-9 R Lappin(7) 8/1: 1400003: Waited with: fin well. 13
2513 POMMES CHATEAU [10] (H Collingridge) 4-8-7(bl) M Rimmer 12/1: 0040004: Led 4f:see 2012.   10
2602 COOL ENOUGH [13] 5-7-13 T Williams 10/1: 0000000: Ev ch: little form: see 12.   00
2614 BUTHAYNA [1] 3-9-5(bl) A Murray 11/2: 0003300: Prom, wknd: btr twice below 2343.   13
2793 ORTICA [9] 3-8-7(bl) G Duffield 4/1 FAV: 3330430: Prom, wknd: btr 2793.   00
2905 AITCHANDOUBLEYOU [5] 3-8-9 M Roberts 8/1: 0000400: No show in 8th: see 1093.   00
2816 OFF YOUR MARK [12] 6-7-7(1oh) M Fry 10/1: 0400000: Dsptd lead, fdd: see 1610.   00
2594 DOUBLE CHAI [6] 3-8-8(bl) C Dwyer 8/1: 0040440: Prom to ½way: best 1701 (7f).   00
2854 Low Flyer [2] 8-8   2743 Always Native [3] 8-1   2884 Keyanloch [8] 8-1
13 ran   1½,1½,hd,2½,2½   (A J Le Blond)   T Fairhurst Middleham, Yorks

2978 HANGING STONE HANDICAP 3YO+ 0-35   £2733   1m 3f   Firm 16 -04 Slow   [34]

2850 WILD HOPE [9] (G Huffer) 5-9-10 R Carter(5) 5/2 JT.FAV: 0421001: 5 ch g Great Nephew -
Grove Star (Upper Case): Led inside final 1f for a narrow win in a h'cap at Redcar: earlier
successful in a h'cap at Haydock: in '85 won again at Haydock & also at Newmarket: in '84
won at Pontefract: eff at 1m, stays 11f: acts well on gd & fast grnd & a gall trk: usually
comes late .   38
*2861 SAFFAN [8] (M Prescott) 3-9-9(9ex) G Duffield 5/2 JT.FAV: 2122212: Well bckd: held
up: finished really well but the post came too soon: fine effort under a 9lbs penalty: see 2861. 44
2746 ELARIM [3] (T Fairhurst) 7-8-1(BL) W Newnes 9/1: 0000003: Led after 1f & nearly made
all: bl first time today & produced an impr effort: see 745.   13
2885 IVOROSKI [1] (D Smith) 4-7-12 A Culhane(7) 10/1: 3210044: Ev ch over 1f out: best 1769.   06
2776 GOLDEN FANCY [10] 9-9-0 G Starkey 9/2: D330230: Waited with, never nearer: btr 2776 (12f). 18
2300 EFFICIENT [4] 3-7-9 P Burke(5) 33/1: 0-0000: Prom most, fdd: lightly rcd & little
form to recommend: see 1141.   00
1737 MRS CHRIS [5] 4-8-11 M Wigham 9/1: 0001030: Fdd str: has been hurdling: see 1737 (13f).   00
2800 Nugola [6] 7-7(vis)(2oh)   -- Craigs Venture [2] 7-7
2027 Snarry Hill [7] 8-2
10 ran   nk,nk,1½,1½,6   (John Wright)   G Huffer Newmarket

2979 SALTBURN EBF STAKES 3YO+   £2368   2m115y Firm 16 -69 Slow

2776 GOLDEN HEIGHTS [1] (P Walwyn) 3-8-5 N Howe 5/2: 1423201: 3 b c Shirley Heights -
Yelney (Blakeney): Fair stayer: led over 1f out, under press in a very slow run 4 runner
stakes event at Redcar: in gd form early in the season, winning at Wolverhampton & Bath:
eff at 15f, stays 2m: acts on fast & yld grnd & on a gall trk.   50
2665 MY WILLOW [4] (J Fitzgerald) 3-8-2 M Roberts 7/2: -42102: Kept on well & stays 2m:
consistent: see 2142.   45
*2779 GREAT EXCEPTION [2] (H Candy) 3-8-2 W Newnes 9/4 JT.FAV: 2-31013: Set slow pace:
prob. stays 2m: see 2779.   44
2873 HERRADURA [3] (M Prescott) 5-9-5(vis) G Duffield 9/4 JT.FAV: 2033144: Al last: see 2776. 50
4 ran   1½,¾,¾   (P G Goulandris)   P Walwyn Lambourn, Berks

2980 BOULBY HANDICAP 3YO 0-35   £2096   1m 1f   Firm 16 -04 Slow   [38]

2690 HELIETTA [5] (L Cumani) 3-9-7 G Starkey 3/1: 0423121: 3 b f Tyrnavos - Hurdy-Gurdy
(Espresso): Fairly useful filly: led 2f out, readily in a 3yo h'cap at Redcar: in fine form
lately, earlier making all in a fillies mdn at Salisbury: half sister to 3 winners incl the
smart Vieille: probably stays 12f but seems very eff over 9/10f when up with the pace:
likes fast grnd & may win another h'cap.   43
2890 BLACK DIAMOND [6] (A Jarvis) 3-8-7 C Dwyer 5/1: 3002222: Led/dsptd lead: hung right
under press: another gd run: see 2890.   24
2508 NICOLINI [3] (J Fitzgerald) 3-8-0 M Roberts 13/2: 0033203: Never nearer: stays 10f:
acts on firm & yld grnd.   12
*2508 DAWN LOVE [4] (R Hollinshead) 3-9-3 S Perks 11/2: 0-00014: Ch over 2f out: btr 2508 (1m). 21
2603 BOLD ANSWER [2] 3-7-7(2oh) T Williams 16/1: 1030000: Ev ch: best over this C/D in 1158. 00
*2876 BICKERMAN [1] 3-9-3(7ex) G Duffield 13/8 FAV: 0123010: Well bckd, but well below 2876. 14
1983 CLAWSON THORNS [7] 3-7-11 M Fry 20/1: -000000: Led after 3f: fdd: abs: see 78.   00
7 ran   1,2,4,2,1½,1½   (Fittocks Stud Ltd)   L Cumani Newmarket

---

FOLKESTONE   Tuesday October 14th   Righthand, Sharpish, Undulating Track

Official Going Given As FIRM

2981 BREDE APP. H'CAP STAKES (0-35) 3YO+   £1094   6f   Good/Firm 32 -20 Slow   [35]

2715 REVEILLE [12] (M Jarvis) 4-9-11 P Hutton 3/1 FAV: 1003021: 4 ch g Ahonoora - Roll Up
(Roll Of Honour): Led 2f out, ridden out in quite slow run app. h'cap at Folkestone: earlier
a ready winner of a h'cap at Leicester: useful 2yo winning at Carlisle & Wolverhampton but
lost his form in '85: very eff at 6f, does stay further: acts on fast & soft grnd & on any trk 40
2581 APRIL FOOL [1] (L Cottrell) 4-8-11(vis) S O'gorman 10/1: 0003002: Al prom & kept on
well: in gd form: eff at 6f-1m: see 1390: runs well here.   24
2519 HATCHING [6] (L Cottrell) 5-7-8(vis) T Lang 5/1: -020043: Nearest fin: see 1942.   04
2837 HAUTBOY LADY [11] (M Madgwick) 5-7-13 R Price 14/1: 2-03004: Sn prom: rated 20 in 1971(1m) 00
2715 CORNCHARM [7] 5-9-2 P Brette 6/1: 0340000: Led 4f: lightly rcd since early season:see 135. 16
2594 FIRST OPPORTUNITY [5] 3-9-2(12ow) L Johnsey 14/1: -040000: Prom most: best 1947 (stakes). 16
1943 JIANNA [2] 3-8-1 J Adams 13/2: 0-00240: Slowly away: abs: btr 1943, 1476.   00
2546 Harmony Heights [8] 8-1   2312 Silent Gain [9] 8-3(bl)
2417 Paddington Belle [3] 7-10(vis)(3ow)(3oh)   2429 Chief Runner [10] 7-8
2619 Moorestar [4] 8-8
12 ran nk,1,4,hd,1½   (Sqdn Ldr R A Milsom)   M Jarvis Newmarket

2982 E.B.F. ASHFORD MAIDEN STAKES 2YO FILL.   £1378   5f   Good/Firm 32 -07 Slow

2814 RUN LITTLE LADY [2] (H Cecil) 2-8-11 W Ryan 1/1 FAV: 421: Impr filly: well bckd &
made ev yd, easily in a 2yo fillies mdn at Folkestone: has been rather lightly rcd since
her debut at Brighton in June: stays 6f but seems well suited by forcing tactics over an
easy 5f: likes fast grnd.   40
2651 SPECULATE [1] (L Piggott) 2-8-11 B Crossley 3/1: 02: Prom, kept on well but had
no ch with the winner: see 2651.   30
2698 EAGLES NEST [7] (C Austin) 2-8-11 J Williams 12/1: 23: Prom, ev ch: see 2698.   24
2927 LITTLE LOCHETTE [8] (D Wilson) 2-8-11 S Whitworth 33/1: 000004: Some late hdway:
btr 6f? see 1946.   18
-- JOHNS LAST [5] 2-8-11 M Giles 14/1: 0: Mkt drifter on debut & was never nearer: should
be suited by further than 5f: acts on fast grnd.   16
2788 BALINESE DANCER [9] 2-8-11 A Mcglone 7/1: 00: Early speed, fdd: cost 6,400 gns.   12
2600 Verbier [4] 8-11   2875 Medrian [3] 8-11   -- Olive Leaf [6] 8-11
9 ran   1½,2½,2½,½,1½   (Mrs Mark Burrell)   H Cecil Newmarket

2983 E.B.F. HURST GREEN MAIDEN STAKES 2YO   £1664   6f   Good/Firm 32 -13 Slow

2711 BEAULIEU BAY [8] (L Piggott) 2-9-0 B Crossley 5/1: 001: 2 b c Longleat - Peta's Boy
(I Say): Made most, driven out for a narrow win in a 2yo mdn at Folkestone: half brother to
several winners: eff at 6f on fast grnd & an easy trk.   52
2791 GEORGE JAMES [2] (J Dunlop) 2-9-0 R Fox 6/5 FAV: 042: Well bckd: kept on well under
press final 1f & 3L clear 3rd: should find a race: see 2791.   50
-- UNWISE [6] (H Cecil) 2-9-0 W Ryan 4/1: 3: Sn prom on racecourse debut & was easy
to back here: cost $150,000 & should stay further than 6f: acts on gd/firm grnd.   41
2782 QUASSIMI [5] (F Durr) 2-9-0 A Clark 16/1: 004: Al prom: impr effort: eff at 6f on
good/firm ground.   37
2875 MON BALZAR [4] 2-9-0(bl) J Carr(7) 16/1: 000000: Fdd final 1f: best 2514 (5f).   21
979 MOULAS [1] 2-9-0 J Williams 12/1: 00: Abs, no show: probably needed the race:
first foal whose dam won over middle dists.   20
-- Shuko [9] 9-0   2547 Profit A Prendre [7] 9-0
2895 Battle Sting [3] 9-0(VIS)
9 ran   ½,3,1½,3,½   L Piggott Newmarket

2984 SEDLESCOMBE SELLING STAKES 3/4YO   £724   1m 4f   Good/Firm 32 -27 Slow

2478 MISS LAURA LEE [2] (P Feigate) 3-8-4 W Ryan 4/1: 0000401: 3 ch g On Your Mark -

Strawberry Blonde II (Red God): Led over 1f out for a decisive ¼L win in a seller at
Folkestone (bought in 2,200 gns): first success from this half sister to 2 winners: stays 12f
& acts on gd/firm & yld grnd.   12
2795 RYMOS [10] (R Simpson) 3-8-7(hd) S Whitworth 11/2: 00-332: Ran on final 1f: stays 12f.   13
2515 GULPHAR [1] (J Jenkins) 4-9-0 J Williams 10/1: -000003: Made much: fdd final 1f: see 1103   06
2490 OKAADH [9] (M Tompkins) 4-9-0 W Woods(3) 9/1: 000-004: Led early, remained prom:
dropped in class here: 2nd in a Warwick mdn last term but has shown little form since &
also been tried in blinkers.   02
2697 KIKI STAR [7] 4-8-11 A Mcglone 6/1: -000000: Prom, ev ch: see 2697.   00
2787 SOLENT LAD [4] 3-8-7 P Bloomfield 20/1: 0-20000: Fdd final 2f: best 1st time out in 139   00
459 ROAMING WEIR [3] 3-8-7   A Clark 5/2 FAV: 00-0000: Well bckd, despite long abs:
no show: lightly rcd & no form this term: rated 31 as a 2yo but seems to have lost most
of that ability: acts on gd/firm.   00
1666 Tinsel Rose [8] 8-4   2789 Deerfield Beach [5] 8-11
2776 Wandering Walter [6] 9-0
10 ran   ½,3,2,1½,8   (Mrs Anita Quinn)   P Felgate Grimston, Leicestershire

2985 ROBERTSBRIDGE HANDICAP STAKES (0-35)   £1649   1m 4f Good/Firm 32 +12 Fast   [31]

2900 WILD GINGER [14] (D Oughton) 4-8-2(vis) B Crossley 14/1: 0003341: 4 ch c Wollow -
Anadyomene (Sea Hawk II): Led after 4f & driven out to win a h'cap at Folkestone: quite
lightly rcd this term: in '85 won at Beverley: eff at 12f, stays 14f: acts on fast & yld grnd
and likes a stiff trk, though acts on any: wears bl or a visor.   16
2699 PULSINGH [3] (C Benstead) 4-8-7 Paul Eddery 14/1: 1030002: Ch over 1f out: 4L clear 3rd:
staays 12f: see 850.   17
*2515 PAUSE FOR APPLAUSE [9] (S Woodman) 3-8-1 W Woods(3) 12/1: 0000013: Mkt drifter: btr 2515   12
2766 JABARABA [8] (L Cottrell) 5-9-7 T Lang(7) 10/1: 1113404: Late hdway: see 2330, 2188.   22
2373 TARLETONS OAK [15] 3-9-2 A Clark 13/2: 000-400: Ev ch in str: best 1806 (10f).   22
*2853 NOBLE FILLE [10] 3-9-4(7ex) R Fox 4/1 JT FAV: 0044010: Well below 2853(10.5f).   17
2864 LYDIA EVA [5] 3-8-8 A Mcglone 10/1: 0001040: No show in 7th: best 2386.   00
2776 HYOKIN [1] 4-8-11(vis) Dale Gibson(7) 10/1: 3200200: Prom, fin 8th: best 1359 (stiff).   00
2746 SEAMERE [16] 3-7-9 R Morse(4) 5/1: 0-00020: Prom, fdd: btr 2746 (10f).   00
2885 GAY APPEAL [7] 3-9-2 W Ryan 4/1 JT FAV: 30011U0: Well below form: possibly remembering
her fall in race 2885: see 2709.   00
2704 Sirdar Girl [4] 7-11   1004 Andrea Dawn [13] 8-4   2900 Himorre [12] 7-11
1577 My Annadetsky [2] 7-10
14 ran   2,4,1½,1½,4   (Alan Ross)   D Oughton Findon, Sussex

2986 NORTHIAM NURSERY H'CAP 2YO   £1281   5f   Good/Firm 32 +01 Fast   [55]

2729 JOVICK [6] (G Lewis) 2-7-9 R Fox 5/1: 310001: 2 br c Swing Easy - Pas de Chat
(Reiko): Behind early but fin well to lead inside final 1f, under press in a nursery h'cap
at Folkestone: earlier a narrow winner at Windsor & seems suited by an easy 5f: acts on gd
& fast grnd & wears bl.   30
*2167 LINGERING [8] (J Winter) 2-9-7 A Mcglone 3/1 FAV: 2412: Prom, in fine form: see 2167.   52
2843 ORIOLE DANCER [2] (D Thom) 2-7-7(6oh) Dale Gibson(7) 33/1: 0000003: Led 2f out: best
effort since 1069 & does well on a sharp/easy trk.   18
2781 TAP THE BATON [7] (M Tompkins) 2-7-7(bl) R Morse(5) 9/2: 3000344: Ev ch: btr 2781.   17
2743 RAINTREE COUNTY [5] 2-7-7(19oh) G Bardwell(7) 33/1: 0004000: Rated 24 earlier in the
season on soft grnd but has shown little form since then.   12
2883 VERYAN BAY [1] 2-8-3 Paul Eddery 11/2: 000120: Led 3f: btr 2883, 2600.   21
2564 MICRO LOVE [4] 2-8-7 S Whitworth 10/3: 3012000: Early speed: clearly flattered 2564.   00
2678 TAMASSOS [3] 2-7-7(2oh) K Butler 7/1: 00030: Soon behind: well below 2678.   00
8 ran   1½,2,nk,1½,hd   (Baker Sportswear Ltd)   G Lewis Epsom, Surrey

---

WARWICK   Tuesday October 14th   Lefthanded, Turning Track

2987 MARKET SQUARE MAIDEN AUCTION STKS 2YO   £684   5f   Firm 07 -24 Slow

2875 ANOTHER RHYTHM [13] (R Hutchinson) 2-8-7 W Carson 5/4 FAV: 31: 2 b c Music Boy -
Just You Wait (Nonoalco): Well bckd & despite running green in the lead, just held on in
a 2yo mdn auction stakes at Warwick: cheaply bought colt who is likely to prove best over
sprint dists: acts on fast grnd & seems suited by forcing tactics: will impr with experience.   35
2626 KNOCKIN EXPRESS [5] (G Huffer) 2-8-11 G Carter 9/4: 02: Took a drop in class: outpaced early but flying at the finish and would have won in another stride: sure to win a
race, probably over another furlong: acts on fast grnd: see 2626.   38
2812 GOLD MINORIES [1] (P Mitchell) 2-8-4(1ow) R Cochrane 12/1: 003: Al up there & ran
his best race to date here: seems suited by sprint dists: acts on firm grnd: see 2249.   21
2927 SARASOTA [11] (R Akehurst) 2-8-3 B Rouse 16/1: 2400034: Never nearer: see 2927.   19
2600 BAY WONDER [7] 2-8-8 P Waldron 10/1: 0022240: Best over this C/D in 2308 (yld).   22
2743 BROOKHEAD GIRL [4] 2-8-0 Julie Bowker(7) 50/1: 0000: Ran on late: acts on firm & yld.   13
2472 LIME BROOK [12] 2-8-0(VIS) P Hill(7) 50/1: 400: Visored first time: never nearer 7th
after slow start: may do btr when reverting to selling company: see 1949.   00
2698 FRIVOLOUS LADY [9] 2-8-0 A Mackay 7/1: 440000: Fdd into 8th: see 1946 & 1668.   00

2675 Sonoco [10] 8-4   2805 Metroman [2] 9-0(bl)   2608 Roan Reef [14] 8-7
2045 Biotin [8] 8-3   -- Al Laventa [6] 8-11   2950 Try Hills Supplies [3] 8-3
14 ran   shhd,3,nk,½,hd,1½,½   (P Byrne)   R Hutchinson Epsom, Surrey

2988 ANN HATHAWAY HANDICAP 3YO 0-35   £1358   2m   Firm 07 -07 Slow   [42]

2864 BEIJING [8] (P Cole) 3-9-7 T Quinn 4/1: -114431: 3 b f Northjet - Protectora
(Prologo): Consistent filly: well suited by this test of stamina & cmftly defied top weight ,
led 6f out & was eased close home in a h'cap at Warwick: earlier successful in h'caps at
Bath & York: half sister to very useful stayers Protection Racket & Safe River: effective
around 14f, clearly stays 2m well: acts on gd & fast grnd & is suited by a gall tr,
though appears to act on any.   46
2745 DARK SIRONA [5] (D Arbuthnot) 3-8-7 R Cochrane 6/1: 0221022: Stayed on well under
press: flattered by proximity to winner but is in fine form and deserves a win: see 2745 & 2152   29
2733 MISS SHIRLEY [1] (J Dunlop) 3-9-5 W Carson 5/2 FAV: 2241323: Uneasy fav: early ldr,
stayed on same pace: clearly suited by a test of stamina: see 2733 and 2520.   38
2794 WALCISIN [4] (R Hannon) 3-8-11 B Rouse 4/1: 1040224: Another gd effort: see 1386.   28
2874 RUN FOR YOUR WIFE [9] 3-7-11(bl) G Carter 13/2: 2430230: Fdd: btr over 12f in 2874.   08
2682 ON THE AGENDA [6] 3-8-0 A Mackay 25/1: 0-00000: Yet to trouble the judge: see 2520.   10
2620 SPARKLIN PERFORMER [2] 3-7-7(5oh) C Rutter(0) 5/1: -004440: Led around ½way, fin lame. 00
2743 Mistral Magic [10] 7-11   -- Water Musick [3] 7-7(1oh)
2546 Sharp Reef [7] 7-7(6oh)
10 ran   ½,3,1½,6,½   (Binfield Manor Farms Ltd)   P Cole Whatcombe, Oxon

2989 WARMINGTON NURSERY HANDICAP 2YO   £1612   1m   Firm 07 +08 Fast   [48]

+2648 PERFECT STRANGER [8] (P Haslam) 2-9-3 G French 6/1: 0310111: 2 b g Wolver Hollow -
Mrs Walmsley (Lorenzaccio): In grand form and was gaining his 4th win in 5 starts when
leading at the dist, gamely in a fast run nursery h'cap at Warwick: earlier successful at
Sandown & Yarmouth (2): very eff over 7/8f: acts on firm & yld grnd & likes a gall trk:
genuine & consistent sort who keeps on improving.   48
2648 TIMESWITCH [10] (W O'gorman) 2-8-10(1ow) S Cauthen 5/1: 0022002: Ran on strongly &
only just held: has yet to get his head in front but certainly deserves a race: stays 1m: see 2227.   40
2615 KING RICHARD [1] (J Dunlop) 2-8-7 W Carson 20/1: 3003: Led below dist, not btn far
& clearly stays 1m well: acts on fast grnd & seems suited by an easy trk: see 1993.   35
2479 SPY GIFT [12] (M Stoute) 2-9-1 W R Swinburn 10/1: 03304: Al prom: stays 1m: see 1801. 41
2658 FLIRTING [3] 2-8-7 B Rouse 12/1: 024400: Seems to stay 1m though best in 988 (5f).   30
2368 ALHAYAT [2] 2-7-10 C Rutter(3) 25/1: 443300: Ran on same pace: stays 1m: see 1501.   18
*2708 IMPERIAL WAY [4] 2-8-8 T Quinn 4/1 FAV: 0010: Fin 8th: btr over 7f in 2708 (gall trk). 00
-2806 ROUMELI [14] 2-8-5 R Hills 8/1: 3031220: Made most: fdd into 9th: btr in 2806.   00
2651 KATE IS BEST [6] 2-8-9(BL) R Cochrane 8/1: 00440: Prom over ½way: btr in 2651 (6f).   00
2675 Persian Tapestry [9] 8-4   2341 Shaine [13] 7-7(1oh)
2628 String Section [15] 9-7   2806 Mubkir [11] 8-4(VIS)
2541 Brainwave [7] 7-11   2878 Ocean Hound [5] 7-7(1oh)
15 ran   nk,½,½,1½,nk,shhd,nk,2   (Ian A Paice)   P Haslam, Newmarket

2990 MOP APPR MAIDEN SELLING STAKES 2YO   £550   1m   Firm 07 -34 Slow

2829 MAIN BRAND [9] (W O'gorman) 2-8-11(BL) J Leech 7/2 FAV: 00401: 2 ch f Main Reef -
Brandon Creek (Be My Guest): Fitted with bl & although failing to keep a straight course,
got up close home in an app mdn seller at Warwick (bought in 3,000 gns): cost 8,000 gns as
a yearling: eff over 7/8f on fast grnd: seems to act on any trk.   20
2829 COUNTESS BREE [10] (K Cunningham Brown) 2-8-11 R Perham 8/1: 0300002: Led well over 1f
out, caught near fin: stays 1m: suited by fast grnd & a sharp/easy trk: see 1363.   18
2580 RED SKY AT NIGHT [1] (C Wildman) 2-8-11 A Riding 33/1: 03: Made rapid late progress
after a slow start and is worth noting next time in similar company: cheaply bought filly
who stays 1m well: acts on firm grnd.   15
2561 DESIGN WISE [16] (A Ingham) 2-9-0(bl) R Teague 33/1: 00004: Led after ½way: first
signs of form from this cheaply bought colt who has already changed stables this season:
stays 1m: acts on fast grnd: wears bl.   16
2724 TOOTSIE JAY [5] 2-8-11(VIS) Jane Eades(5) 16/1: 4000000: Visored first time: never
nearer: stays 1m: showed enough ability over sprint dists early-season to win a seller: see 711 08
2817 WAR CHILD [4] 2-8-11 P Johnson 4/1: 003020: Btr in 2817: see 1622.   05
2177 JOYFUL MISTRESS [13] 2-8-11(BL) P Francis 6/1: 000: Bl first time on her first
venture into selling company: prom most & fin 7th: cheaply bought filly who acts on firm. 00
2801 NO CONCERN [6] 2-9-0 M Giles 7/1: 0030: Fin 9th: best in 2801.   00
2801 NATIONS ROSE [12] 2-8-11 T Parkes 10/1: 00400: Never dngr: see 2801.   00
2707 BANGKOK BOY [14] 2-9-0 A Tucker 8/1: 000000: Dropped in class but no threat: see 1313. 00
2901 GOING GREEK [8] 2-8-11 G Thompson 10/1: 00: Dropped in class: never went pace.   00
1083 Donnas Darling [7] 8-11   2801 Cajun Moon [11] 8-11
2609 Four Crowns [18] 9-0   2168 Magnolia Dancer [17] 9-0
-- Magnolia Princess [3] 8-11   2927 Phoebe [15] 8-11
2580 Rock A Little [19] 8-11   2045 Whats A Guinea [2] 8-11
19 ran   ½,1½,½,3,1½,1½,½,1½   (Rockhouse Stud)   W O'gorman Newmarket

2991 QUEEN BESS EBF STAKES 3YO   £2124   1m   Firm 07 +05 Fast

-- WATER CAY [1] (H Cecil) 3-9-9 S Cauthen 2/13 FAV: 14123-1: 3 br c J O Tobin - Waterloo (Bold Lad) (Ire): Had a simple task on his belated seasonal debut & easily landed the odds, making all in a 3yo stakes at Warwick: one of last seasons top juveniles, winning at Doncaster (2) & Newbury before being placed in the Group 2 Royal Lodge Stakes at Ascot and the Group 1 Futurity Stakes at Doncaster: very well bred colt whose dam won the 1,000 Guineas: very eff over 1m & will stay further: acts on gd & fast grnd & is suited by a gall trk: genuine & consistent colt who seems to have recovered well from his set back & should now go on to win some nice prizes.   50++

2274 FUDGE [8] (P Jones) 3-8-4 G French 12/1: 2000002: Posed no threat to this effortless winner but did run one of her btr races to finish clear of rem: see 2274 and 534.   14

2853 PAPUN [6] (J Payne) 3-8-4 P D'arcy 25/1: -003: Ex Italian filly who has shown little ability in her starts in this country: bred to be suited by middle dists in time.   04

-- DO RUN DO [3] (J Bosley) 3-8-4 C Rutter(3) 50/1: 0-4: Btn 2f out: only ran once last season, fin. down the field in a Doncaster mdn.   01

2534 HELLO SAM [5] 3-8-7 W Wharton 25/1: -00: Never dngr.   00

2534 EVERYINCHALADY [2] 3-8-4 N Adams 50/1: 0-000: Yet to show any worthwhile form.   00

2853 LITTLE TOKEN [4] 3-8-4 R Hills 8/1: -00: Bckd from 20/1 but was al behind & fin last: half sister to several winners & is clearly expected to do btr than this.   00

7 ran   2½,5,1½,1½,½,½   (Peter Burrell)   H Cecil Newmarket

2992 PRINCE RUPERT HANDICAP STAKES 3YO+ 0-35   £1487   5f   Firm 07 -07 Slow   [35]

2775 NATIVE RULER [7] (C Austin) 5-7-12 A Mackay 4/1 FAV: 1230031: 5 b g King Of Macedon-Noble Native (Indigenous): In gd form & responded well to pressure to lead close home in a h'cap at Warwick: placed several times since an all-the-way winner of a selling h'cap at Edinburgh: half brother to several winning sprinters: best form over 5f on fast grnd: does well with forcing tactics on a sharp trk.   13

2858 GALLANT HOPE [2] (L Cottrell) 4-8-2 W Carson 6/1: 2223342: Led after ½way, just caught & remains a mdn: rarely out of the frame: see 1834.   16

2906 NAGEM [15] (L Barratt) 3-8-4 P Hill(7) 9/1: 0423423: Ran on well: in gd form: see 1505.   15

2775 GODSTRUTH [13] (H T Jones) 7-8-7(bl) A Riding(7) 8/1: 0004344: Fin well: see 1344.   15

2783 TACHYON PARK [1] 4-9-6 C Rutter(3) 6/1: -002100: Al prom: best in 2702.   25

2906 SKYLIN [8] 3-8-7(vis)(5ow) W Wharton 33/1: -000000: Ran on too late but showed her best form of the season here: winner over this minimum trip at Leicester in '85: does well on fast ground.   09

+2775 MUSIC REVIEW [16] 3-8-12(7ex) R Cochrane 6/1: 2203410: Fdd into 7th: btr in 2775 (gall trk)   00

2921 MUSIC MACHINE [9] 5-9-12 J Scally(7) 10/1: 1200000: Led over ½way, wknd qckly: see 2245   00

2256 Fremont Boy [11] 8-4   727 Fairdale [14] 7-7(1oh)   2702 Dublinaire [4] 8-1

2614 Corrals Joy [10] 9-6   1730 St Terramar [3] 7-8(bl)(1ow)(5oh)

-- Lady Songe [12] 7-7(5oh)   1836 Dashaki Gold [6] 7-7(1oh)

-- Dippy [5] 9-0

16 ran shhd,1½,1,1,1½,½,½,2,1½   (A J Richards)   C Austin, Wokingham, Berks

---

2993 ENTERKINE NURSERY H'CAP 2YO   £3179   5f   Good 42 -06 Slow   [48]

-2843 CHILIBANG [4] (J Dunlop) 2-9-2 B Thomson 8/11 FAV: 4101121: 2 ro c Formidable - Chili Girl (Skymaster): Useful, impr colt: easily landed the odds, never hdd or chall. when a 6L winner of a nursery h'cap at Ayr: successful previously in similar nurseries at Ayr (again), Windsor & a mdn at Nottingham: half brother to 6/7f winner Hot Case: very eff at 5f, stays 6f well: acts on gd & firm grnd & on any trk: best out in front: now likely to step up in class   51

*2476 PAPARELLI [7] (D Barron) 2-9-7 D Nicholls 9/1: 012: Waited with, fin well, though much too late: see 2476.   41

2687 UPSET [6] (J S Wilson) 2-8-7 N Carlisle 12/1: 231003: Prom, ev ch: see 1696 (C/D).   26

2588 DENSBEN [2] (Denys Smith) 2-7-8(1ow) L Charnock 16/1: 044034: Al prom: see 1421, 2588.   12

2815 FIVE SIXES [1] J Quinn(5) 33/1: 2113000: Speed much: best 1298 (seller).   09

2843 MOON INDIGO [3] 2-9-7 P Robinson 12/1: 1000000: Ev ch: btr 2843.   29

-2281 RAINBOW TROUT [5] 2-7-13 J Lowe 6/1: 04020: Sn under press: btr 2281.   00

7 ran   6,¾,1,3,2   (Mrs H J Heinz)   J Dunlop Arundel, Sussex

2994 MIDSANDS SELLING STAKES 2YO   £1054   6f   Good 42 -44 Slow

2817 U BIX COPY [3] (J S Wilson) 2-8-11(bl) E Guest(3) 14/1: 2300001: 2 b c Absalom - Oh Well (Sahib): Al prom & led final 1f under press in a 2yo seller at Ayr (no bid): probably did not stay 1m last time & seems best at 6f though appears to act on gd & hvy grnd: seems best in blinkers.   20

603 GLORIAD [5] (M Brittain) 2-8-8 P Robinson 33/1: 00002: Led ½way, hdd final 1f but a grand effort after long abs: acts on gd & yld: stays 6f.   13

2535 MALACANANG [8] (M Camacho) 2-8-8 N Connorton 5/1: 0003: Al prom & showed some impr here: stays 6f & acts on good.   12

2708 MADAME LAFFITTE [19] (J Etherington) 2-9-0 M Birch 12/1: 0210004: Prom, kept on: see 1622, 2471.   15

2298 RABENHAM [11] 2-8-11(BL) D Nicholls 9/1: 4000400: Ch when hmpd final 1f: see 1965, 741.   11
2396 JUST A DECOY [6] 2-8-11 J Lowe 33/1: 0040000: Probably best effort yet: acts on good.   11
2919 RHABDOMANCER [18] 2-8-8 B Thomson 3/1 FAV: 333000: Dsptd lead much, btr 2919.   00
2927 MISS ACACIA [17] 2-8-8(bl) M Hills 7/1: 0322020: Outpcd, btr 2927.   00

892 Absolutely Free [14] 8-8		2470 Sappharino [12] 8-8	
2919 Salop Rouge [16] 8-8(bl)		2756 Carls Pride [13] 8-11	
2919 Raunchy Rita [4] 8-8	2364 Step By Step [9] 8-11	2678 Pretty Soon [10] 8-8(bl)	
2707 Medallion Man [7] 8-11		2325 Suesandy [15] 8-8	
1795 Katie Cuddles [2] 8-8	2279 Swynford Lady [1] 8-8		
19 ran 1½,nk,1½,½,hd	(J B Russell)	J S Wilson Ayr	

2995 LOCHRANZA HANDICAP 3YO+ 0-50   £3532   1m 2f   Good 42 +07 Fast   [36]

*2800 FOURTH TUDOR [5] (B Hanbury) 4-8-2(bl)(5ex) A Geran(7) 9/4 FAV: -200011: 4 ch g Horatius -
Fourth Dimension (Time Tested): In fine form at present & was winning 2nd race on the trot,
landing some good bets when easily leading inside final 3f in a h'cap at Ayr: ready
winner of a h'cap at Hamilton last time: very eff over 10/12f: acts on firm & gd grnd & has
impr since being fitted with bl: could complete the hat trick.   22
2415 COMMON FARM [10] (M Brittain) 3-8-3 P Robinson 20/1: 0000002: Fin well from rear
showing signs of a return to form: best effort since 1122: stays 10f.   18
2800 GREED [4] (Denys Smith) 5-8-4 L Charnock 7/1: 0424033: Placed again, seldom wins: see 1185.   11
2578 SWEET DOMAIN [1] (J Dunlop) 3-9-7 B Thomson 9/1: -001104: Held up, late prog:
twice below 2161.   35
*2890 CAPRICORN BLUE [9] 3-9-0(vis)(5ex) M Hills 10/1: 2411010: Prom, wknd: see 2890.   24
2800 BOY SANDFORD [11] 7-7-7(2oh) N Carlisle 14/1: 4004420: See 2800.   00
2536 FORCELLO [7] 3-9-4 J Lowe 9/2: 2430020: Made much, wknd into 7th: btr 2536.   26
2130 Night Warrior [2] 8-12   1822 Shiny Kay [8] 8-8
2327 Noholmina [6] 8-12   2885 Recollect [3] 8-11
11 ran   7,nk,nk,4,½,1½   (B Hanbury)   B Hanbury Newmarket

2996 GLENBURN MAIDEN STAKES 3YO+   £1051   1m 3f   Good 42 +02 Fast

1469 PICEA [3] (M Jarvis) 3-9-0 T Lucas 13/8 FAV: 2-42201: 3 b c Mummy's Pet - May Hill
(Hill Clown): Returned after an abs to justify fav. cmftbly leading 2f out in quite a close
fin to a mdn at Ayr: placed in useful company previously and this was undoubtedly his easiest
task so far: dam a smart middle dist performer: eff around 1m, probably btr suited by
10/11f: acts on gd grnd: should certainly win more races.   48
--   MEVAGISSEY [8] (B Hanbury) 3-9-0 G Baxter 3/1: -2: Very promising racecourse debut,
leading 2f out and only narrowly btn: half brother to several winners: eff over 11f on gd
grnd: should have little difficulty finding a mdn very soon.   45
1818 RUSSIAN RELATION [12] (L Cumani) 3-9-0 R Guest 9/1: -03: Fin in fine style, clearly
appreciating this trip & should stay further: acts on gd grnd: likely to find a mdn very
soon: see 1818.   44
2853 RARE LEGEND [10] (M Ryan) 3-8-11 P Robinson 6/1: 0-0024: Kept on well in a close fin:
should stay 12f: see 2853.   40
1736 PALMAHALM [4] 4-9-5 M Birch 20/1: -30: Abs, never btr & a much impr effort on only
second ever outing: see 1736.   36
744 MOUNT OLYMPUS [7] 3-9-0 N Connorton 16/1: 04-0320: Ev ch after long abs & should
benefit from the outing: see 744.   32
2759 SHERGOR [11] 3-9-0 N Day 7/1: -2020: Mkt drifter, prom, wknd: possibly one to
avoid: see 2759 (rated 42).   00
2201 Abadjero [9] 9-0   --   Miss Becca [6] 8-11   2496 Ickworth [2] 9-8
--   Funny Lass [14] 8-11(bl)   2816 Its Heaven [1] 9-5
--   Connaught Queen [5] 9-5   2688 Godounov [13] 9-0
14 ran   ½,½,½,2,4   (T G Warner)   M Jarvis Newmarket

2997 FAIRLIE MAIDEN STAKES 2YO   £1187   1m   Good 42 -34 Slow

1681 ALVECOTE MAGIC [9] (C Tinkler) 2-9-0 M Birch 12/1: 001: 2 gr c Anfield - Sawk
(Sea Hawk II): Showed impr form when cmftbly leading dist in rather slowly run 2yo mdn at
Ayr: clearly suited by todays 1m trip, should stay middle dists next season: acts on gd
grnd: can continue to impr.   45
2806 COMMONSIDR GIPSY [11] (O Brennan) 2-9-0 D Nicholls 16/1: 2000302: Tried to make most:
consistent but one-paced: see 685, 2444.   42
2889 SPRUCE BABY [4] (S Norton) 2-9-0 J Lowe 3/1: 033: Kept on well & suited by 1m: see 2889.   40
2648 LORD COLLINS [1] (M Stoute) 2-9-0 N Connorton 7/2: 4042044: Al prom, btr 2648.   39
2711 RED HERO [6] 2-9-0 T Lucas 7/1: 003340: Ev ch: twice below 2595.   32
2522 FINAGLE [8] 2-9-0 P Robinson 15/8 FAV: 00: Ev ch: btr 2522 (7f).   30
--   Nicholas Mark [3] 9-0   --   Mamamere [2] 8-11   1914 Hygena Legend [7] 9-0
2628 Prince Zamaro [5] 9-0   --   Which Direction [10] 8-11
11 ran   1½,½,nk,2½,1   (D Collins)   C Tinkler Malton, Yorks

2998 MILLBRAE HANDICAP 3YO+ 0-35   £2645   1m   Good 42 -01 Slow   [33]

*2857 BIEN DORADO [3] (B Hanbury) 3-9-3(5ex) A Geran(7) 13/8 FAV: 3400011: 3 ch c Silent Screen

AYR   Tuesday 14th October   -Cont'd

-Bonne Note (Bon Mot III): In fine form & was well bckd when winning 2nd race on the trot,
leading under press final 1f in a h'cap at Ayr: readily won a 3yo mdn at Haydock previously:
very eff over 1m on firm & gd grnd: may complete the hat trick.   41
2650 HENAADI [10] (O Douieb) 3-8-4 B Thomson 8/1: -0002: Led over 3f out, caught near
fin: might prove best at 7f: see 2650.   26
2762 SILLY BOY [4] (N Bycroft) 6-9-1 D Nicholls 25/1: 0000003: Fin really strongly showing a
return to form: probably worth noting next time: see 698.   17
*2780 BROADHURST [15] (J Etherington) 3-8-5(bl)(5ex) M Birch 8/1: 0300314: Waited with, not
get on terms: in gd form: see 2780.   23
2887 ELEGANT FASHION [2] 4-8-11 E Guest(3) 12/1: -000320: Held up, late prog: see 2728.   18
2797 HOPTONS CHANCE [11] 4-7-7(1oh) N Carlisle 9/1: 0243340: Ev ch: see 2797.   00
2414 Native Habitat [9] 8-13   2854 Career Madness [16] 8-5(bl)
2629 Sillitoe [5] 8-4   2715 Qualitair King [12] 8-3
2876 Flying Ziad [1] 8-1(2ow)   2891 New Barnet [7] 7-11
1081 Silver Cannon [3] 9-7   2660 Gloriant [6] 7-8(1ow)(3oh)
--   Christmas Cottage [13] 9-6(bl)
15 ran ½,1½,hd,3,shhd   (Mrs Allen Manning)   B Hanbury Newmarket

PHOENIX PARK   Saturday October 11th   Left and Righthanded, Sharpish Track

Official Going Given As GOOD/FIRM

2999 IRISH NATIONAL STUD STAKES (LISTED) 2YO £15076   7f   Good/Firm -

2768 QUEENS BRIDGE [9] (I Balding) 2-8-8 T Ives 7/4 FAV: 41: 2 ch f Spectacular Bid -
Colony Club Promising filly: ran on under press to lead at dist, holding on well in a val
Listed race at Phoenix Park: half sister to middle dist winner Lady's Bridge: very eff over
7f and will be suited by 1m+ next season: acts on gd/firm grd and on any trk: has plenty of
scope and seems certain to rate more highly.   60
2687 GHANAYIM [6] (H T Jones) 2-9-1 A Murray 8/1: 022102: Well suited by this longer trip
and was only just denied: acts on fast & soft ground: sure to win more races: see 2448.   65
--   FINAL MOMENT [5] (J Oxx) 2-8-8 D Hogan 13/2: 23: Narrowly btn, and cmftbly beat rem:
clearly very eff over 7f on gd/firm grd, and is certain to win races.   57
--   PUMPING IRON [1] (D Weld) 2-8-8 M J Kinane 7/2: 24: Gd eff: acts on gd/firm.   49
--   RUSTY LADY [3] 2-8-11 D Gillespie 14/1: 10200: --   50
2910 PALLASS BLUE [4] 2-8-11 S Craine 14/1: 42140: Btr over this C/D in 2910.   49
9 ran nk,hd,4,1,nk   (P Mellon)   I Balding Kingsclere, Hants.

3000 BREEDERS CUP PREP MILE (LISTED) 3YO+   £33285   1m   Good/Firm -

-2770 TELEPROMPTER [5] (J Watts) 6-9-2(bl) T Ives 1/3 FAV: 2333021: 6 b g Welsh Pageant -
Ouija (Silly Season) Highclass gelding who had a simple task when gaining a well deserved win
in a val Listed race at Phoenix Park: sn in front and was never off the bridle: only just
pegged back by Sure Blade in Gr 2 Queen Elizabeth Stks at Ascot last time and is right back to
his best: in excellent form last season, winning a Gr 3 race on this course, after making all
in the Gr 1 Arlington Million at Arlington Park, USA: in '84 won Pattern races at Deauville,
the Curragh and Phoenix Park: best form over 8/9f tho' does stay 10f: acts on fast & yldg
ground and is best out in front: wears blinkers but is thoroughly genuine.   86
2740 ISTORIATO [2] (D O'brien) 3-8-10 C Roche 8/1: 21142: No chance with this easy winner
but ran to his best and seems a consistent sort: see 2740.   70
2192 FORLAWAY [1] (D O'brien) 4-9-2(bl) D Gillespie 12/1: 2-30323: Stable mate of runner-up. 66
*2505 BRAVO FOX [4] (D Weld) 3-8-10(bl) M J Kinane 7/1: 4-01014: Btr over 7f here in 2505.   61
--   CUMUTE [3] 3-8-13 A Murray 10/1: 2111030: Trained by F Durr when winning a Newmarket mdn
last season: now trained in Norway and was their 2000 Guineas winner: eff over 7/8f on gd
and fast ground.   44
5 ran 8,2,2½,8   (Lord Derby)   J Watts Richmond, Yorks

3001 BREEDERS CUP CLASSIC TRIAL(LISTED) 3YO+ £32025   1m 3f Good/Firm -

1492 NASHAMAA [4] (J Bolger) 3-8-10 C Roche 6/1: 122-231: Smart colt: off the trk for
some time but returned in style, running on gamely to win the Breeders Cup Classic Trial at
Phoenix Park: also lightly raced last season when winning a val race over 6f on this course:
now much btr suited by middle dist: acts on fast & yldg ground and does well on this sharpish
trk: genuine sort.   75
2752 HIGHLAND CHIEFTAIN [2] (J Dunlop) 3-9-1 Pat Eddery 11/8 FAV: 0121022: Just out-
battled but ran right up to his best: see 2752 & 2004.   79
2808 NOMROOD [3] (P Cole) 3-8-13 T Quinn 7/4: -120023: Not btn far: see 2808 & 578.   75
2450 POPULARITY [1] (D Weld) 3-8-7 M J Kinane 12/1: --11044: Far from disgraced: see 1592.   62
2845 CHAUMIERE [5] 5-9-4(bl) T Ives 8/1: 1033030: Again ran well in defeat: see 1526.   65
5 ran nk,1,2½,nk   (Maktoum Al-Maktoum)   J Bolger Ireland

3002 TAYLOR MADE STAKES (LISTED) 3YO+ FILL.   £15604   1m   Good/Firm -

2740 LAKE CHAMPLAIN [11] (D Weld) 3-9-4 M J Kinane 4/1 FAV: 1220231: 3 b f Kings Lake -

875

Sensibility Smart filly: gained a deserved win when running on strongly in a val Listed race
at Phoenix Park: has been placed sev times in Pattern company since winning val fillies race
at Leopardstown in May, notably when 2nd to Sonic Lady in the Irish 1000 Guineas: very eff
over 8/9f on fast & soft ground: acts on any trk.   71
2911 LADINA [8] (M Kauntze) 3-9-4 P Shanahan 14/1: 0201002: Another gd eff: see 2557.   67
--   ANY SONG [1] (E O'grady) 3-9-4 S Craine 11/2: 1031113: Much improved filly who lost
nothing in defeat: recently completed a hat-trick in a val h'cap at Leopardstown: eff over
8/9f on gd & firm ground.   65
--   ALDER ROSE [5] (M Grassick) 4-9-10 D Gillespie 20/1: 0010004: Ran well under top weight.   59
--   PHEOPOTSTOWN [2] 3-8-8 P Lowry 16/1: 0222220: Consistent sort.   47
+2719 NORDICA [6] 3-9-4 M Roberts 6/1: 0124110: Continues to improve: see 2719.   55
2196 GAILY GAILY [10] 3-9-6 D Parnell 10/1: 1-00100: Fin 7th: see 2196 & 560.   55
*2691 LAND OF IVORY [7] 3-9-4 T Ives 5/1: 4331010: Rather disapp in 8th: see 2691.   51
12 ran   1½,1,2½,½,1,½,1   (Mrs B Firestone)   D Weld Ireland

---

THE CURRAGH   Sunday October 12th   Righthanded, Galloping Track

Official Going Given As GOOD

3003 GROUP 2 BERESFORD STAKES 2YO   £28950   1m   Good -

2737 GULF KING [3] (P Kelleway) 2-9-0 S Cauthen 7/1: 0210101: 2 ch c Kings Lake - Pearl
Star (Gulf Pearl) Smart colt: led just inside the final 1f and ran on strongly to win Gr 2
Panasonic Beresford Stks at the Curragh: earlier successful in a minor race at Goodwood and
later a nursery h'cap at York: half brother to sev winners, including useful hurdlers Star
Burst and Copse & Robbers: very eff over 7/8f and likely to stay further: acts on fast
and soft ground and likes a gall trk.   72
2821 WAIT TILL MONDAY [6] (D Weld) 2-9-0 M J Kinane 10/1: --21332: Al front rank: most
consistent colt who loves to be up with the pace and is sure to win more races: see 2821.   68
2821 BOBSBENT [10] (C Collins) 2-9-0 P Shanahan 16/1: --43143: Fine eff: see 2821.   65
*2673 THAMEEN [7] (H T Jones) 2-9-0 A Murray 3/1: 414: Ran well in defeat: see 2673.   64
*2451 ISLAND REEF [1] 2-9-0 G Curran 14/1: -124120: Ran to his best: stays 1m: see 2451.   64
--   ANCIENT TIMES [2] 2-9-0 Pat Eddery 4/7 FAV: 10: Made odds-on after his impressive win
at Leopardstown last month but was never going well and fin a well btn 7th: surely btr than
this and is worth another chance.   00
9 ran   1½,1½,nk,hd,4   (Roldvale Ltd)   P Kelleway Newmarket

3004 GROUP 1 IRISH ST LEGER 3YO+   £55700   1m 6f   Good -

2222 AUTHAAL [5] (D O'brien) 3-8-12 C Roche 8/1: -11011: 3 b c Shergar - Galletto
(Nijinsky) Very smart colt: sn out in front, held a clear lead at ½ way and won unchall in
Gr 1 Irish St Leger at the Curragh: last to fin in the Great Voltigeur at York but remains
unbtn in Ireland, winning at Naas, Phoenix Park and Leopardstown: eff over 9f but btr suited
by 12/14f: acts on gd/firm and soft grd and clearly is well suited by forcing tactics:
genuine and consistent.   84
2453 FABUROLA [6] (P Biancone) 5-9-4 E Legrix 7/2: 21-2202: Stayed on well to take the
minor honours in this race for the 2nd successive season: smart middle dist mare who has
yet to run a bad race: see 2453.   73
*2450 I WANT TO BE [4] (J Dunlop) 4-9-4 S Cauthen 6/4 JT.FAV: -002313: Remains in gd form.   71
2637 LEADING COUNSEL [1] (M O'brien) 4-9-7 Pat Eddery 6/4 JT.FAV: 021-144: Never looked
likely to repeat last year's win in this race but ran creditably under topweight: see 2438.   73
--   ELEMENTARY [2] 3-8-12 S Craine 50/1: -0: Pitched in at the deepend on his racecourse
debut and is hard to assess accurately on this run: half brother to useful 7/9f winner
Santa Roseanna.   53
2506 RAMICH JOHN [3] 4-9-4 M J Kinane 50/1: 3200000: Has lost her form: much btr with
some give in the ground: see 360 & 325.   40
6 ran   5,1½,1,10,5   (Sheikh Mohammed)   D O'brien Ireland

LONGCHAMP   Sunday October 12th   Righthand Galloping Track

Official Going Given As FIRM

3005 GROUP 1 GRAND CRITERIUM 2YO   £57479   1m   Firm -

--   DANISHKADA [2] (A De Royer Dupre) 2-8-8 Y Saint Martin : 131: 2 b f Thatch - Demo
(Abdos) Smart, improving filly: cmftbly made almost all in Gr 1 Grand Criterium at Longchamp:
below her best last time out first time out winner: well suited by 1m and should stay further:
acts on fast grd and on a gall track: does well forcing the pace.   78
*2635 LOCKTON [1] (J Hindley) 2-8-11 M Hills : 2011312: Fin strongly and didnot have
the best of runs: certainly fast improving at present and the further they go the btr he is:
looks certain to be suited by middle distances next term: see 2635.   78
*2826 FOTITIENG [6] (F Boutin) 2-8-11 F Head : 313: Dpstd lead 3f out, lost 2nd place
cl home: trainer thought him unsuited by the slowish pace: see 2826.   77
--   GRECIAN URN [5] (D Smaga) 2-8-8 A Lequeux : -321204: Cl up 4th: winner of a minor
event at Deauville in Aug over extended 6f, stays 1m well.   73

2826 WILLESDON [4] 2-8-11 C Asmussen :   -130: Fair eff in 5th: see 2826.   71
2636 DON MARIO [7] 2-8-11 G Mosse : -120: Creditable eff and prob acts on firm & yldg.   70
8 ran 1,¼,shthd,2½,½   (H H Aga Khan)   A De Royer Dupre France

3006 GROUP 3 PRIX DE ROYALLIEU 3YO+ FILLIES   £18330   1m 4f Firm

*2825 SHARANIYA [7] (A De Royer Dupre) 3-8-11 Y Saint Martin :   -2111: 3 br f Alleged -
Shanizadeh Completed her hat-trick when readily winning a Gr 3 fillies event at Longchamp:
successful in Gr 3 races here and at Evry prev: unraced as a 2yo: well suited by 12f and acts
on firm & soft: certainly improving.   79
2825 KRUGUY [4] (B Secly) 3-8-8 J L Kessas :   -1132: No chance with this easy winner.   69
2825 LUTH DOR [5] (J Cunnington Jnr) 3-8-8 M Philipperon : 0101043: See 2825.   68
2452 LIASTRA [8] (F Boutin) 3-8-11 F Head : 2121044: See 1215.   70
2825 SHARP GIRL [3] 3-8-8 A Lequeux : 0143020: Closer to winner in 2825.   64
2828 ROBERTOS FIGHTER [10] 4-8-13 E Saint Martin : 4410020: Btr 2828 (2½m)   58
2643 AMONGST THE STARS [2] 3-8-11 J Lowe : 0101440: English chall, fin 7th, not far of
her best: see 2236.   00
10 ran 2,nk,hd,1½,1½,½   (H H Aga Khan)   A De Royer Dupre France

---

DUSSELDORF (W. GERMANY)   Sunday October 12th

Official Going Given As GOOD

3007 GROUP 2 GROSSER PREIS 3YO+   £14124   1m 100y   Good

2640 EVES ERROR (M Stoute) 3-8-11 W R Swinburn : -041131: 3 ch c Be My Guest - Apple
Peel (Pall Mall) Smart, improving colt: al prom and led over 1f out, cmftbly, in a Gr 2 race
at Dusseldorf: prev won a Gr 3 race at Baden-Baden and a val ladies race at Ascot: smart 2yo
winning at Epsom & Nottingham: half brother to sev winners: very eff over 1m/9f: acts on
firm & soft ground: genuine and improving.   78
2823 SIYAH KALEM (J Dunlop) 4-9-4 B Thomson : 1200322: Waited with, gd prog str but was
cmftbly held by the winner: rated 79 in 2259 but twice below that.   75
2449 CHARTINO (G Huffer) 3-8-9 G Carter : 2-00323: Never closer: see 2449.   69
--   OLDTIMER (H Bollow) 3-8-11 P Remmert : -4: Proved best of local German horses in 4th.   69
9 ran 1½,1½,1   (Sheikh Mohammed)   M Stoute Newmarket

FLORENCE (ITALY)   Sunday October 12th

Official Going Given As GOOD

3008 GROUP 3 PREMIO CASCINE 3YO+   £11293   1m 2f Good

2640 ESDALE (F Turner) 3-8-6 M Planard : 1130121: 3 b c Fabulous Dancer - Esdee (Hail
To Reason) Smart ex English colt: made all, staying on strongly to win a Gr 3 event at Florence:
prev trained by J Tree to win 3 minor events at Windsor: very eff over 10f, prob stays 12f:
acts on firm & yldg.   76
--   RIVER HAWK (L Brogi) 3-8-4 M Paganini : -2: Locally trained colt who ran well to be 2nd   69
--   OBIRA JARA (D Pessi) 3-8-4 A Rovetto : -3: --   67
2808 BOON POINT (J Dunlop) 3-8-8 R Fox : 0111330: Below his best here and may have had
enough for the present: see 2808.   62
1095 SHARP NOBLE 4-8-7 Paul Eddery : 0222400: Fin last after long abs: see 1095.   49
7 ran 2½,1,4,½,2,hd   (K Abdulla)   F Turner Italy

SAN SIRO   Sunday October 12th

Official Going Given As GOOD

3009 GROUP 1 GRAN CRITERIUM 2YO   £33024   1m   Good

*2821 SANAM (J Dunlop) 2-8-11 W Carson : 4101211: 2 ch c Golden Act - Rose Goddess
(Sassafras) Smart, impr colt: stayed on well to lead final 1f, narrowly, in Gr 1 Gran Criterium
at San Siro: earlier won a Gr 3 race at the Curragh, a val event at Ascot and a nursery at
Newmarket: very eff over 7f/1m, promises to stay further: acts on gd & fast grd and likes a
stiff gall track: most genuine and consistent.   73
*898 MELBURY LAD (B Agriformi) 2-8-11 R Cochrane : 2112: Chall inside final 2f, just held
in a driving fin: evidently much improved since moving to Italy: see 898.   72
2522 KALGOORLIE (L Piggott) 2-8-11 T Ives : 0233: Very cl 3rd: quite a remarkable effort
from this mdn: see 2341.   71
*2571 BEESHI (P Cole) 2-8-11 T Quinn : 32214: Led inside final 2f, run out of it near fin:
btn less than ¾l and continues to improve: see 2571.   71
16 ran nk,nk,ddht,6,3   (Prince A A Faisal)   J Dunlop Arundel, Sussex

3010 GROUP 3 PREMIO OMENONI 3YO+   £15152   5f   Good Course Record

-2833 STORM WARNING (W Hastings Bass) 4-8-4 T Ives : 3000221: 4 b f Tumble Wind - Maggie

Nine (Native Prince) Smart sprinter: lowered course record leading 2f out and holding on well
from fellow English chall Polykratis in a Gr 3 event at San Siro: has returned to form recently
tho' this was her first success since picking up a Listed race at Doncaster and another event
at Nottingham in '85: prob best at 5f tho' acts on firm & yldg going.   75
*2764 POLYKRATIS (M Francis) 4-8-7 C Rutter   : 1240312: Just held in a cl fin: another gd
effort from this most consistent sprinter: see 2764.   77
--   DUPLORI (L D'auria) 3-8-7 V Panici : -3: Best of the home-trained contingent in 3rd   70
557 SESIN (A Botti) 5-8-7 S Dettori : -1-44.   69
8 ran   shtnk,2½,nose   (K Fischer)   W Hastings Bass Newmarket

---

HAYDOCK   Wednesday October 15th   Lefthanded, Galloping Track

Official Going Given As GOOD/FIRM

3011 WHITBEAM MAIDEN STAKES 2YO   £2630   1m 40y Good 58 -05 Slow

2251 IBN BEY [14] (P Cole) 2-9-0 T Quinn 4/5 FAV: 41: 2 ch c Mill Reef - Rosia Bay (High Top)
Useful colt: missed the break and had to make up a lot of ground to gamely lead cl home in a
2yo mdn at Haydock: 210,000 gns yearling who is a half brother to winning juv Cerise Bouquet:
stays 1m well and should go on to btr things over middle dist next season: acts on gd/firm
grd and on a gall track.   50
2860 QUESSARD [1] (C Brittain) 2-9-0 J Lowe 9/1: 032: Game attempt to make all: worn down
near finish but cmftbly beat rem: on the upgrade and sure to find a race: stays 1m: acts
on gd ground and on a gall track: see 2721.   48
--   AIM TO PLEASE [9] (R F Johnson Houghton) 2-8-11 J Reid 25/1: 3: Mkt drifter on debut:
al prom, not qckn below dist: half sister to a couple of winners and should be suited by
middle dist next season: acts on gd ground and on a gall track.   34
--   CRYSTAL HAWK [3] (M Jarvis) 2-9-0 R Cochrane 14/1: 4: Made steady late prog on debut
and looks one to keep an eye on: acts on gd grd and on a gall track: certain to improve for
this run.   32
1903 CHARLIE DICKINS [4] 2-9-0 S Perks 33/1: 00: Stayed on from ½ way, showing some improvement: bred to be suited by further: acts on a gall trk.   24
--   GOLD SCEPTRE [11] 2-9-0 G Duffield 20/1: 0: Ran in snatches on debut and will be all
the btr for this experience: cost $90,000 as a yearling and is a half brother to a couple
of winners abroad: bred to be well suited by this trip.   20
2531 EMPLOY FORCE [8] 2-8-11 W Carson 14/1: 00: Fin 7th: well bred filly who fetched
$205,000 as yearling and looks certain to do btr next season, prob over middle dist.   15
2675 TALE OF INTRIGUE [7] 2-8-11 Pat Eddery 6/1: 00: Fin 8th: daughter to the highclass
Mrs Penny who fetched $700,000 as a yearling: seems quite well regarded and should do much
btr than this.   15
2133 Whitridge [5] 9-0   2140 Vital Cargo [6] 8-11   2571 Crespin [13] 9-0
2781 Everloft [2] 9-0   2499 Rolfeson [15] 9-0   1050 La Verte Gleam [12] 8-11
14 ran   hd,6,2½,4,2½,½,shthd   (Fahd Salman)   P Cole Whatcombe, Oxon.

3012 WALNUT STAKES   £2607   5f   Good 58 +13 Fast

2953 DURHAM PLACE [8] (K Brassey) 4-8-9(bl) S Whitworth 11/2: 0040241: 4 b c Homing - Singing
(Petingo) Was gaining an overdue win when leading inside dist and ridden out in a fast run
stks race at Haydock: last successful as a juv at Leicester: best over sprint dist, tho' does
stay 7f: acts on any going and is well suited by a gall trk.   51
+2833 FAYRUZ [7] (W O'gorman) 3-9-2(bl) Pat Eddery 2/5 FAV: 0000312: Odds-on to follow up
his recent win, sn in front but hung left from half way and wknd quickly inside dist: much
better in 2833 and has not regained his juvenile consistency since a knee operation.   50
2488 TRUE NORA [9] (C Nelson) 3-8-6 J Reid 8/1: 0040203: Best in 2362: see 443.   34
2725 BON ACCUEIL [1] (H Whiting) 3-8-4 J Bleasdale 50/1: 3000034: Prom most: btr 2018 (6f)   26
2921 BE LYRICAL [6] 4-8-6 G Duffield 12/1: 3000-00: Hmpd start and never near leaders:
has been lightly raced this season: successful at Warwick & Brighton as a juv: this is
was awarded a h'cap at Epsom after being btn by Tyrollie: best form over 5f on fast & yldg.   17
2966 PHILSTAR [10] 5-8-9(bl) J Lowe 16/1: 3000040: Quick reappearance: early speed: see 1676   11
2256 Farmer Jock [4] 9-2(bl)   2660 Maybe Jayne [3] 8-1(bl)
1101 Coded Love [5] 8-6   1337 Lochlairey [2] 8-1
10 ran   3,2,2½,4,3,4   (Mrs Nicole Myers)   K Brassey Upper Lambourn, Berks

3013 OAK HANDICAP 0-60   £4058   2m 28y Good 58 -08 Slow   [39]

*2938 CAP DEL MOND [5] (G Harwood) 3-10-2(6ex) G Starkey 10/11 FAV: -11111: 3 b c Troy -
Rainbow's End (My Swallow) Useful, impr colt: made a quick reappearance and gamely completed
his nap-hand, leading under press cl home in a val h'cap at Haydock: began his winning run at
Folkestone (2), subs won val h'caps at Newmarket & Ascot: cost 400,000 gns as a yearling and
is a half brother to winning stayer Storm Cloud and also useful Finian's Rainbow: stays 2m
really well and will get further: acts on gd & fast grd and on any trk: most genuine.   60
2591 TOM SHARP [1] (W Wharton) 6-8-5 Pat Eddery 85/40: 00-0002: Set off in front, kept on
gamely but was worn down cl home: lightly raced on the Flat this season and last successful in
'84 at Newmarket (2), the latter success coming in the Cesarewitch: stays really well: acts
on any grd and is best out in front.   24

2733 **VERY SPECIAL** [2] (W Holden) 4-8-10 R Morse(5) 9/1: 3010303: Cl up most, eased: trying a longer trip here and ran to her best: see 1563. 21
2873 **SOUND DIFFUSION** [3] (R Whitaker) 4-8-3 A Culhane(7) 16/1: 0000004: Best early-season in 933 (sharp trk). 07
474 **BOLLIN PALACE** [4] 4-9-0 M Birch 12/1: 000-300: Trailed in last: after long abs: see 308 00
5 ran ½,8,6,dist (Prince Ahmed Salman) G Harwood Pulborough, Sussex

3014 WHITEBEAM MAIDEN STAKES 2YO £2687 1m 40y Good 58 -05 Slow

-2703 **KNOWN LINE** [12] (H Candy) 2-8-11 W Newnes 5/2 FAV: 421: 2 br f Known Fact - Quay Line (High Line) Useful filly: went on over 2f out and was ridden out to win a 2yo mdn at Haydock: half sister to winning 3yo Newquay: eff over 7/8f and likely to stay further: acts on gd & fast grd and on a gall track. 50
2547 **DARING DESCENT** [5] (R F Johnson Houghton) 2-9-0 J Reid 33/1: 002: Led ½ way: kept on well when hdd and this was a much btr effort: stays 1m well and should be suited by middle distances next term: acts on gd ground and on a gall track: should find a race. 48
2019 **KNIGHTS NEVERGREEN** [5] (M Jarvis) 2-9-0 W Woods(3) 20/1: 0003: Al prom, ran on same pace: eff over 7/8f and will be suited by further: see 2019 & 1660. 39
2878 **VIGLIOTTO** [3] (G Harwood) 2-9-0(BL) G Starkey 9/2: 444: Bl first time: led to ½ way, onepaced and seems to need further: see 2721. 38
2847 **RUSHLUAN** [18] 2-9-0 T Quinn 7/2: 00: Nicely bckd: short-lived eff 3f out: 30,000 gns yearling who is bred to be well suited by this trip and should do btr than this. 30
-- **IJAZAH** [1] 2-8-11 A Murray 10/1: 0: Made steady late prog on debut and should do btr next time: bred to be suited by middle dist next season: acts on gd grd. 26
2628 **TROJAN LEGEND** [2] 2-9-0 J Lowe 33/1: 00: Never nearer 7th: half brother to sev winners, including 12/14f filly Diva Encore: sure to do btr when stepping up in dist next season. 24
2869 **KARABAT** [10] 2-9-0 S Whitworth 7/1: 0000: Fin 8th: much btr 2869. 23
2522 **Home To Tara** [8] 9-0 2607 **Call For Taylor** [15] 8-11 2675 **Brolga** [7] 8-11
2723 **Lindrick** [9] 9-0 2377 **One To Note** [17] 9-0 -- **Bentham Bazaar** [11] 9-0
1883 **Heatseeker** [16] 9-0 -- **Strange Music** [13] 8-11 1883 **Gouldswood** [4] 9-0
17 ran 1½,5,½,4,½,2½,½,½ (R Barnett) H Candy Kingstone Warren, Oxon

3015 HAWTHORN HANDICAP 0-50 £3801 6f Good 58 +03 Fast [47]

+2862 **ROYSIA BOY** [15] (G Pritchard Gordon) 6-9-4(7ex) Abigail Richards(7) 11/2 FAV: 0300011: 6 b g African Sky - For Keeps (Track Spare) Took command after ½ way and altho' hanging left held on well to win quite a fast run h'cap at Haydock: recently made all to set a new course record in a seller race at Haydock: ended last season in gd form, winning at Kempton, Goodwood, Leicester & Nottingham: very eff over 6/7f with forcing tactics: likes gd or faster grd: acts on any trk: in fine form and may complete his hat-trick. 46
2758 **TAYLOR OF SOHAM** [7] (D Leslie) 3-7-13 D Mckay 10/1: 2323232: Al front rank: see 2758 24
2731 **SNAP DECISION** [9] (R Hannon) 3-8-1(bl) A Mcglone 9/2: 4020333: Fin well, in gd form. 26
2668 **POWDER BLUE** [6] (P Makin) 4-9-10 T Quinn 8/1: 0401004: Ran on well: see 1608. 46
2397 **ROYAL FAN** [4] 3-8-4 M Birch 16/1: 1000020: Not btn very far: running well: see 891. 27
2842 **RIVIERA SCENE** [16] 3-8-13 W Carson 9/1: 0020000: Btr eff but has proved disapp: see 1312 35
•2858 **RAMBLING RIVER** [13] 9-9-4(vis)(7ex) G Duffield 12/1: 0000210: Gd eff under pen:see 2858. 40
2668 **AL TRUI** [11] 6-9-12 M Wigham 11/1: 0200000: Never nearer 8th: see 1429. 47
2862 **FAWLEYS GIRL** [3] 4-7-11 A Culhane(7) 9/1: 0040040: Speed over ½ way: btr over this C/D in 2862. 00
2378 **Pine Hawk** [14] 7-9 2862 **Golden Ancona** [1] 8-7(BL)
2870 **Sew High** [17] 9-5 2659 **Gypsys Prophecy** [8] 9-0
378 **Stevejan** [10] 7-7(12oh) 1810 **Valley Mills** [5] 9-7
2921 **Tobermory Boy** [2] 8-12 2084 **Quinta Reef** [12] 9-9
17 ran 1,shthd,½,shthd,½,1½,hd,hd (P Martin) G Pritchard Gordon Newmarket

3016 MAPLE SELLING NURSERY HANDICAP 2YO £1576 7f 40y Good 58 -37 Slow [30]

2470 **LYN RAE** [11] (M H Easterby) 2-8-10 M Birch 8/1: 0040331: 2 ch f Derrylin - Donrae (Don II) Stayed on well from the rear to lead near fin in a selling nursery h'cap at Haydock (no bid): quite consistent in this grade and deserved this win: eff over 6/8f on fast & soft ground: seems well suited by a gall trk. 20
2801 **MASCALLS DREAM** [1] (P Makin) 2-9-1 T Quinn 9/1: 00022: Led below dist, caught cl home: much improved of late and can win a seller: see 2801. 24
2757 **TOKANDA** [4] (T Fairhurst) 2-8-9(bl) G Duffield 20/1: 000003: Ran well: stays 1m:see 2323 13
2919 **ITS BEEN RUMOURED** [8] (R Simpson) 2-9-0 S Whitworth 2/1 FAV: 00144: Well bckd: slow start and found no extra when she moved into a chall position: prob stays 1m tho' best 2609 (6f) 17
2535 **FLYING SILENTLY** [10] 2-8-9 D J Williams(7) 14/1: 0330200: Never nearer: stays 1m. 11
2919 **THE MAGUE** [6] 2-9-4(bl) D Nicholls 20/1: 2210200: Not clear run below dist, not recover 17
2817 **CARSE KELLY** [13] 2-8-12(vis) J Lowe 14/1: 2000040: Trouble in running, fin 7th: best 1050 00
2609 **THE CHIPPENHAM MAN** [16] 2-8-12 R Cochrane 11/2: 0221330: No danger: best over 6f 1944. 00
1635 **RYLANDS REEF** [7] 2-8-12 W Carson 8/1: 40440: Led ½ way, wknd: abs since 1635 (6f) 00
2723 **Thatch Avon** [2] 9-1 2391 **My Serenade** [5] 9-1 2757 **Dream Ticket** [9] 8-13(bl)
2757 **Katie Says** [12] 9-7(bl) 2757 **Chayofa** [15] 9-0 00
2465 **Parkers Joy** [3] 9-6 2712 **Maybemusic** [14] 9-0
16 ran ½,2,½,½,1½,1½,nk,½ (B S Hawkeswell) M H Easterby Great Habton, Yorks.

Official Going Given As GOOD

3017 BUCKENHAM SELLING STAKES 2YO   £3061   6f   Good/Firm 32 -40 Slow

2615 GOOD POINT [16] (J Hindley) 2-8-11 M Hills 4/1: 02001: 2 b c Try My Best - Point
Gammon (Bold Lad): Regained something like his form of race 777 when an all-the-way winner
of a 2yo seller at Newmarket (sold 11,500 gns): quite a speedily bred sort who cost
I.R. 50,000 as a yearling: well suited by a stiff 6f, fast grnd & forcing tactics: btr
than selling class.   33

2829 BOLD INTENTION [20] (A Ingham) 2-8-11 R Curant 7/2 FAV: 00002: Gambled from 10/1:
ev ch final 2f & just btn: form previously but is sure to find a seller: eff at
6f, probably stays 7f: acts on gd/firm grnd & a gall trk.   31

2919 WHISTLING WONDER [6] (M Brittain) 2-9-2 A Munro(7) 14/1: 0000203: Ev ch final 2f &
not btn far in a close fin: gd effort under top weight: see 2919, 2815.   35

2883 ILLUSTRATE [15] (A Smith) 2-8-8 S Webster 10/1: 00044: Ch 2f out: fair effort:
should be capable of finding a seller: see 1867: stays 6f well.   20

2994 SAPPHARINO [10] 2-8-8 J Brown(7) 14/1: 00000: Kept on final 1f: best effort yet
from this half sister to a couple of winners & seems eff over a stiff 6f on gd/firm.   17

2865 FLAIR PARK [4] 2-8-13 T Quinn 14/1: 2430000: No real threat: btr in 1483 (7f).   12

2888 CIREN JESTER [18] 2-8-11 M Wigham 6/1: 00240: Never nearer: twice below 2095 (easy 6f).   00

2696 UNSELFISH [2] 2-8-11(BL) S Cauthen 9/1: 000: Tried in bl: prom much: see 2476.   00

-- Neighnay [17] 8-8	2609 Highfalutin Lymey [1] 8-11	
2011 Madness Not To [7] 8-11		2325 Beattys Lad [5] 8-11
2829 George Harry [9] 8-11	2609 Maureens Cavalier [19] 8-11	
-- Mendels Law [14] 8-11	-- Canebrake Lady [11] 8-8	
2045 Neirbo Lass [11] 8-8	987 Sparkling Judy [8] 8-8(BL)	
2180 Survival Kit [13] 8-8		

19 ran   ½,hd,2½,½,4,1½,nk   (R E Sangster)   J Hindley Newmarket

3018 EBF CHESTERTON MAIDEN STAKES 2YO   £4643   1m   Good/Firm 32 -46 Slow

-- LADY BENTLEY [1] (L Piggott) 2-8-11 B Crossley 33/1: 1: 2 b f Bellypha - Strike It
Rich (Rheingold): Promising filly: first time out, caused a 33/1 surprise in a slow run
2yo mdn at Newmarket: led inside the final 1f, under press: cost I.R.100,000 as a yearling:
eff at 1m, should be suited by middle dists next term: acts on gd/firm & a gall trk: can
rate more highly.   63

2771 ZAIZOOM [5] (P Cole) 2-9-0 T Quinn 2/1 FAV: 202: Well bckd, led inside final 1f:
ran on well & just btn: deserves a win: see 2771, 2159.   64

-- WATER BOATMAN [3] (B Hills) 2-9-0 R Street 6/1: 3: Ev ch final 1f: promising debut
from this 19,000 gns purchase: should be suited by middle dists next season: acts on gd/
firm grnd & will have no trouble finding a race.   59

2645 SOUTHERN COMFORT [7] (W Jarvis) 2-9-0 R Cochrane 14/1: 04: Ran on well final 1f &
is fast impr: well suited by this stiff 1m: should do well next season: see 2645.   58

-- SONG OF SIXPENCE [2] 2-9-0 Pat Eddery 13/2: 0: Ran on well final 2f for an eye-
catching debut: American bred colt who is a half brother to the smart miler Clare Bridge:
will be suited by further than 1m & will have no trouble winning races.   56

2782 WUJUD [12] 2-9-0 Paul Eddery 20/1: 000: Led 2f out & this was his best effort yet:
half brother to 2 winners & seems well suited by a stiff 1m: acts on fast grnd.   52

-- GENNARO FR [10] 2-9-0 G Starkey 11/1: 0: Prom most on debut: wk in mkt here & should
impr: acts on gd/firm.   44

2936 OMEN [14] 2-9-0 T Williams 25/1: 000: No show in 8th but this was a good effort
in this company: can win a small event: see 2936.   38

2522 DUCKINGTON [6] 2-9-0 A Mcglone 6/1: 40: Fin 9th: btr in 2522: worth another chance.   38

2782 CARPET CAPERS [16] 2-9-0 S Whitworth 33/1: 00: Made much: fin 10th: see 2782.   38

| 2484 Arrowknight [13] 9-0 | -- Burly Native [11] 9-0 | 2345 Pipsted [8] 9-0 |
| -- Sun Fleece [9] 9-0 | -- Jane Marple [15] 8-11 | -- Lily Mab [17] 8-11 |

16 ran   nk,2,hd,½,1½,2½,2,shhd,shhd   (Mohammed Suhail)   L Piggott Newmarket

3019 A R DENNIS NURSERY HANDICAP 2YO   £8714   6f   Good/Firm 32 +06 Fast   [61]

*2694 PRINT [3] (W Hastings Bass) 2-9-2 W Carson 6/4 FAV: 2111: 2 ch c Sharpo - Picture
(Lorenzaccio): Very useful, fast impr colt: led inside the final 1f, running on
well to record a gd time in a valuable nursery h'cap at Newmarket: last time out was a ready
4L winner of a similar event at Newbury: also won a mdn at Hamilton: eff at 5f, stays 6f well:
acts on gd/firm & yld grnd & a stiff trk: speedy colt who is certain to win more gd races.   65

2865 JAISALMER [2] (D Elsworth) 2-8-6(bl)(1ow) W R Swinburn 14/1: 0222302: Chall final 1f:
another gd effort & would find a nursery on this form but has not won since race 350.   52

2865 GIROTONDO [5] (L Cumani) 2-8-11 R Cochrane 3/1: 4123: Led well over 1f out: in fine form.
: see 2493.   55

*1475 PETER MOON [9] (R Armstrong) 2-8-8 B Thomson 33/1: 0314: Long abs & ran on closing
stages: fine effort: clearly handles any trk: see 1475.   46

+2010 TINAS MELODY [8] 2-7-13 T Williams 33/1: 31210: Ch inside final 2f: in gd form: see 2010   36

2865 KYVERDALE [8] 2-9-2 P Robinson 12/1: 1323300: Prom much: twice below 2687 & has
been very busy lately.   46

*2595 LORD WESTGATE [7] 2-8-7 M Wigham 33/1: 0020210: Prom 4f: not disgraced: see 2595.   37

*2717 ROCK MACHINE [11] 2-8-5 Pat Eddery 15/2: 4410: No show: well below 2717.   00

+2859 **Victory Ballard** [6] 7-13(7ex)   *2669 **Authentic** [12] 9-4
2308 **Greensward** [10] 8-1   2949 **Born To Race** [1] 9-7
12 ran   ½,½,2½,½,3,shhd   (Lord Porchester)   W Hastings Bass Newmarket

3020 GROUP 3 RICARD CHALLENGE STAKES 3YO+   £23306   7f   Good/Firm 32 +13 Fast

2785 LUCKY RING [5] (W Hern) 4-9-0 W Carson 20/1: 4-00041: 4 b c Auction Ring - La Fortune
(Le Haar): Very smart colt: returned to his best when a 20/1 winner of fast run Gr.3 Ricard
Challenge Stakes at Newmarket: led well over 1f out, staying on under press: in grand form
in '85, winning 4 times at Newmarket, Goodwood, York & Doncaster: very eff over 7f, stays
1m: acts on gd & fast grnd & likes a stiff trk.   83
*2785 SARAB [10] (P Cole) 5-9-0 T Quinn 12/1: 1110412: Not much room 1f out: ran on:
fin 3rd, placed 2nd: in fine form, but beat the winner in race 2785.   79
-945 HOMO SAPIEN [12] (H Cecil) 4-9-0 S Cauthen 5/1: -2-1323: Sn prom: badly hmpd over 1f out
& had no chance to recover: fin 4th, placed 3rd: fine effort after a long abs: see 945, 222.   77
1466 ARGON LASER [8] (J Dunlop) 3-8-7 B Rouse 33/1: -10034: Abs: kept on well: fin 5th,
placed 4th: very gd effort & is even btr over 1m: acts on fast & soft grnd: see 250.   71
2770 TRUELY NUREYEV [6] 3-8-10 W R Swinburn 14/1: 1-02000: Ch 2f out: fin 6th, placed 5th.   72
*2231 PRESIDIUM [9] 4-9-0 Paul Eddery 20/1: -102410: Led over 5f, fin 7th, placed 6th:
in fine form this season: see 2231.   69
2770 HADEER [7] 4-9-0 A Murray 12/1: 4110100: Not much room over 1f out: best 2538.   00
2770 EFISIO [1] 4-9-0 B Thomson 3/1: 4120330: Well bckd: much btr 2770 (1m).   00
2867 PASTICCIO [4] 3-8-10 Pat Eddery 8/1: 2211300: Nicely bckd, stiff task: see 2867.   00
*2259 THEN AGAIN [11] 3-8-10 G Starkey 11/4 FAV: 101212D: Held up: made gd hdway inside
the final 2f but hung badly left across several of his rivals & his disq. was a formality: see 2259.   81
2474 Grey Desire [2] 9-0   +2214 Pilot Jet [3] 8-10
12 ran   nk,1½,1½,nk,½,1½   (Sir Michael Sobell)   W Hern West Ilsley, Berks

3021 EMBLA HANDICAP STAKES 0-70 3YO+   £6027   7f   Good/Firm 32 -07 Slow   [57]

2867 MEET THE GREEK [14] (R Laing) 3-8-11 B Thomson 10/1: 0122301: 3 b c Formidable -
Edelliette (Edellic): Useful colt: regained the winning thread in a valuable h'cap at
Newmarket: led inside the final 1f, under press in a close fin: most consistent, earlier
successful in h'caps at Brighton, Leicester & Lingfield: very eff over 7f/1m: acts on firm
& yld grnd & on any trk: genuine sort.   54
2668 HILTON BROWN [10] (P Cundell) 5-9-8 P Cook 14/1: 4303102: Ran on well under press
final 1f & just btn: fine effort: see 2369.   61
2945 SAILORS SONG [6] (N Vigors) 4-9-2 S Dawson 12/1: 0012033: Led over 1f out: just btn
in a close fin: another gd run: see 2945, 2207.   54
2773 GOLD PROSPECT [12] (G Balding) 4-8-11 B Rouse 11/2: 0230124: Btn under 1L: most
consistent: see 2773, 2674.   48
2674 HIGHEST PRAISE [9] 3-8-5 M Marshall(7) 6/1: 1331030: Prom, ev ch: not btn far: see 2674   43
2155 ABUTAMMAM [1] 3-8-3 P Waldron 33/1: -001300: Ran on final 1f: gd effort: lightly
raced since 1277: stays 7f.   36
2765 ENTRANCING [8] 3-9-10 W Carson 12/1: 0002120: Fair 7th under 9-10: see 2765, 2440.   56
+2622 SAKER [7] 3-9-7 R Cochrane 4/1 FAV: -04010: No real threat: btr 2622 (1m, made running)   00
2207 Lyric Way [4] 7-7(1oh)   2749 Come On The Blues [11] 9-0
*2928 Ambrosini [5] 8-8(vis)(6ex)   2945 The Mazall [3] 8-7
*2655 Downsview [13] 8-6   2674 Deadbolt [15] 8-3   2165 Mr Jay Zee [2] 7-12
15 ran   nk,nk,nk,1,2½,nk   (P G Goulandris)   R Laing Lambourn, Berks

3022 PARK PADDOCKS STAKES HANDICAP 3YO 0-60   £5431   1m 7f Good/Firm 32 +21 Fast   [67]

2236 PRELUDE [14] (W Hern) 3-8-2 W Carson 14/1: -340101: 3 ch f Troy - Pas De Deux
(Nijinsky): Useful filly: under press over 1f out, but led inside final 1f in very fast
run & valuable at Newmarket: earlier successful in a 3yo. mdn at Nottingham: half sister
to useful stayer Insular and is well suited by 14f/2m: acts well on gd & firm grnd & a
gall trk.   54
*2864 BUCKLEY [11] (L Cumani) 3-8-12(5ex) R Cochrane 5/1: -31212: Led 4f out: kept on well
and is in excellent form: genuine colt: see 2864.   62
2525 FLEETING AFFAIR [7] (G Harwood) 3-9-4 G Starkey 16/1: 1022303: Ch over 1f out: gd
run: consistent filly: see 2257, 1209.   66
*2569 NORPELLA [15] (W Wragg) 3-9-3 P Robinson 15/2: 00-1414: Ch final 1f: well clear of
rem & stays 14f: in fine form this season: see 2569.   64
*2880 MIGHTY FLASH [1] 3-8-4(5ex) A Mcglone 8/1: 1100010: Led 5f out: fdd: btr 2880.   41
2523 DAARKOM [9] 3-9-3 M Roberts 7/2 FAV: 2212320: Hvly bckd: well below 2523.   53
2236 APPLY [2] 3-8-10 Pat Eddery 9/1: -1100: No threat: see 2236, 1630.   00
2156 BENISA RYDER [3] 3-7-11 C Rutter(3) 7/1: -224100: Nicely bckd, no show: see 2156, 1023.   00
604 Sprowston Boy [12] 8-0   2834 Wassl Reef [5] 9-7
2220 Badarbak [10] 9-1(bl)   2769 Past Glories [4] 8-7   *32 Truely Billy [6] 8-4
2834 Elaafuur [8] 7-13   2480 Agathist [16] 8-0(2ow) 2834 Happy Breed [13] 7-7(7oh)
16 ran   ½,1½,1,10,nk   (The Queen)   W Hern West Ilsley, Berks

3023 EBF CHESTERTON MAIDEN STAKES 2YO   £4610   1m   Good/Firm 32 -32 Slow

2159 NINTH SAGA [14] (M Francis) 2-9-0 C Rutter 66/1: 01: 2 br c Nain Bleu - Bridge

Master (Iron Ruler): Fast impr colt: turned up at 66/1 in a 2yo mdn at Newmarket: made ev
yd & never really looked in dngr: dam successful over 5f: well suited by front running
tactics over a stiff 1m & acts on gd/firm grnd.   59
2484 SHANTAROUN [15] (M Stoute) 2-9-0 W R Swinburn 14/1: 02: Ev ch 1f out: impr colt who
should have no trouble finding a race: will be suited by further than 1m: acts on gd/firm
grnd & a gall trk.   53
2768 OVERDRIVE [8] (H Cecil) 2-8-11 S Cauthen 12/1: 03: Sn prom: gd effort: see 2768.   47
2675 BLUE GRASS FIELD [4] (W Jarvis) 2-8-11 A Murray 66/1: 04: Ch 2f out: no extra close
home: another gd run: see 2675.   45
--   OUR ELIASO [17] 2-9-0 J Matthias 33/1: 0: Promising late hdway on his debut: cost
46,000 gns & is a full brother to the smart '84 2yo Kala Dancer: one to keep an eye on.   45
--   ISLAND KING [13] 2-9-0 M Hills 20/1: 0: No real threat on debut but should impr: cost
155,000 gns as a yearling: acts on gd/firm grnd & a gall trk.   40
2869 VESTRIS [2] 2-9-0 G Starkey 6/4 FAV: 00: Very hvly bckd: never nearer 7th: clearly
well regarded, but btr in 2869 (C/D).   00
2847 SIR JAMESTOWN [16] 2-9-0 B Rouse 7/1: 00: Prom, fin 8th: btr 2847.   00
2852 KNOCKANDO [11] 2-9-0 R Cochrane 11/2: 00: Never in hunt: see 2852.   00
2847 MAGICAL LACE [10] 2-8-11 B Thomson 9/2: 30: Well below form displayed 2847 (7f).   00
2852 Ardashir [12] 9-0   --   Coup De Foudre [5] 9-0
--   Fe [1] 9-0   --   Highland Bounty [6] 9-0
--   Northern Alliance [9] 9-0   --   Barmera [3] 8-11
16 ran   2½,1½,1,1½,2½   (Mrs Virginia Kraft)   M Francis Lambourn, Berks

---

Official Going Given As GOOD STRAIGHT COURSE: REM. GOOD/FIRM

3024 SYCAMORE SELLING STAKES 3YO   £1511   6f   Good 53 -14 Slow

2793 GRANGE FARM LADY [12] (M Tompkins) 3-8-8 A Mackay 8/1: 0302001: 3 br f Faraway Times-
Sweet Helen (No Mercy): Made ev yd, clear over 1f out but just lasted home in a 3yo seller at
Haydock (sold 2,900 gns): sister to winning sprinter Grange Farm Lad: eff at 5f, just stays
6f: acts on gd & firm grnd: acts on any trk but her style of running would seem suited by a
sharpish one.   21
1927 LOVE AT LAST [7] (W Hastings Bass) 3-8-8 R Lines(3) 5/1: -33332: Abs: al prom &
nearly got up: gd effort and is a consistent filly: see 1256 (1m).   21
2884 TOLLYS ALE [10] (I Matthews) 3-8-8 C Dwyer 14/1: 0004043: Prom, stayed on: in gd form:
stays 6f & acts on gd/firm & soft grnd.   18·
2928 BRITWYDD [4] (C Booth) 3-8-11 D Nicholls 4/1: 00-004: Behind, stayed on too late:
lightly rcd: see 2473 (7f): should find a seller.   20
2409 HOBOURNES KATIE [5] 3-8-8 S Perks 16/1: 0000030: Ran on under press: see 2268.   10
2854 SPANISH INFANTA [9] 3-8-8 J Williams 20/1: -000030: Nearest fin: in fair form: see 2854   08
2312 AVALON [13] 3-8-11 G Duffield 6/1: -034000: Active in mkt: lightly rcd since best 844.   00
2702 MADAM MUFFIN [2] 3-8-8 J Reid 11/4 FAV: 0200240: Sn prom, fdd: btr 2702 (5f).   00
2884 Ever So Sharp [14] 8-11   2854 Le Mans [11] 8-11
2854 Shy Mistress [15] 8-8   2463 Hopefull Dancer [8] 8-13
2906 Jacqui Joy [1] 8-13   2854 Ken Siddall [3] 8-11   --   Cals Symphony [6] 8-8
15 ran   hd,1½,nk,2½,½   (R Bates)   M Tompkins Newmarket

3025 THE POPLAR STAKES 2YO FILLIES   £3224   7f 40y Good 53 -06 Slow

+2788 SCIMITARRA [5] (H Cecil) 2-8-8 W Ryan 1/4 FAV: 011: 2 ch f Kris - Fanghorn
(Crocket): Highly promising filly: easily landed the long odds-on in 2yo fillies event at
Haydock: led over 1f out, readily: last time out made ev yd when a 6L winner of a fast run
fillies mdn at Goodwood: half sister to several winners, notably the top class sprinter
Double Form: very eff over 6f, stays 7f: acts on yld, suited by gd & firm grnd: looks
certain to win more races & is a very speedy filly.   62
*2658 ILIONA [4] (L Cumani) 2-8-8 R Guest 7/1: 0012: Led ½way till over 1f out: well clear
of rem. & caught a tartar here: see 2658.   55
--   MRS PISTOL [1] (R Simpson) 2-8-8 J Reid 33/1: 3: Stiff task on debut & had no ch with
the leading pair: cheaply acquired filly who is a half sister to 3 winners incl the very
speedy 2yo Katysue: should impr enough to find a small race: acts on gd grnd.   35
2675 BOLD DUCHESS [2] (M Jarvis) 2-8-8 W Woods(3) 33/1: 304: Sn prom: see 2029.   32
2675 MOUNT HOLYOKE [12] 2-8-8 M Kettle 25/1: 00: Waited with: never nearer: half sister to
a winner in Ireland & is on the up grade: acts on gd grnd & should impr further.   31
2847 PANIENKA [3] 2-8-8 R Fox 33/1: 00: Never nearer: should stay 1m.   25
--   Dark Rosaan [6] 8-8   2859 Philgwyn [8] 8-8   2476 Westpark Princess [9] 8-8
--   Royal Meeting [7] 8-8   2703 Via Veritas [10] 8-8
11 ran   1½,8,1½,½,½,2   (Baroness H H Thyssen)   H Cecil Newmarket

3026 HORNBEAM HANDICAP (0-60) 3YO+   £4422   1m 4f Good 53 +15 Fast   [41]

2769 SARONICOS [8] (C Brittain) 3-9-1 M Birch 11/2: 3030441: 3 b c Dalsaan - Gulf Bird
(Gulf Pearl): Gained an overdue success in a fast run h'cap at Haydock: led over 1f out,
under press: placed numerous occasions previously & was not winning out of turn: stays 12f:
well: acts on firm & yld grnd & does well on a stiff, gall trk.   46

2855 REGAL STEEL [4] (R Hollinshead) 8-8-3 A Culhane(7) 16/1: 1403002: Led till over 1f out:
retains his form really well: see 1918.   23
2799 FIRST KISS [7] (J Dunlop) 3-9-7 R Fox 9/1: 0030333: Al there: see 2558, 723.   47
2848 NAJIDIYA [6] (R J Houghton) 3-9-12(7ex) J Reid 11/2: 2021144: Stayed on: gd effort:
see 2763: seems equally eff at 10/12f.   50
2855 HANOOF [2] 3-9-0 G Duffield 2/1 FAV: -431040: Well bckd: fdd over 1f out: btr 2855 (C/D)   37
2569 NEWQUAY [1] 3-9-7 A Clark 6/1: 0221320: No threat: btr 2569: see 2048.   43
*2759 ENSIGNE [9] 3-9-3(4ex) W Newnes 6/1: -202410: Slowly away & no show: btr 2759.   00
2924 The Lodge Prince [5] 8-8(vis)   2873 Diva Encore [3] 9-0
9 ran   1½,¾,1½,¼,1½   (M Lemos)   C Brittain Newmarket

3027 ROWAN NURSERY HANDICAP 2YO   £2378   5f   Good 53 -13 Slow   [60]

2717 FATHER TIME [9] (D Thom) 2-7-12(bl) A Mackay 13/2: 0020001: 2 ch c Longleat -
Noddy Time (Gratitude): Showed impr form, leading ½way & holding on well in a nursery at
Haydock: first success: very eff over 5f on gd & firm grnd: seems best in bl.   41
2843 SANDALL PARK [7] (M W Easterby) 2-7-12 L Charnock 2/1 FAV: 414042: Uneasy fav,
fin well under press, just failed & well clear of rem: should win a nursery soon: see 771, 2689.   40
2843 FICKLE YOUNG MAN [1] (T Fairhurst) 2-8-2(bl) R Hills 10/1: 3010403: Set pace on the
far side to ½way: twice below 2753: see 2081.   29
2875 INTHAR [8] (R Armstrong) 2-8-5 P Tulk 13/2: 003424: Early pace: well below 2875.   22
2476 MOTOR BROKER [2] 2-7-8(VIS) N Adams 16/1: 000400: Prom much: several times below 2118.   10
1910 BASTILLIA [3] 2-8-5(1ow) J Reid 10/1: 0013000: Outpcd after abs: see 746.   20
2835 DAYS LIKE THESE [5] 2-8-7 G Duffield 9/4: 4120: Misbehaved start, no dngr: btr 2835.   00
2744 DOHTY BABY [4] 2-7-7(6oh) G Bardwell(7) 33/1: 3001000: Sn rear: best 2323 (seller,soft)   00
8 ran   hd,6,4,nk,½,2½,1½   (Mrs Angela Hollest)   D Thom Newmarket

3028 SILVER BIRCH STAKES 3YO+   £2977   1m 2f   Good 53 -02 Slow

2786 NADEED [4] (M Stoute) 3-8-0 G Duffield 21/20 FAV: -021: 3 b c Nijinsky - Palmistry
(Forli): Useful colt: al prom & readily went clear from the dist for a very easy win in a
minor event at Haydock: has only run once recently since fin a close & creditable 5th behind
the very smart Allez Milord at Newmarket in May: did not race as a 2yo: well suited by 10f,
should stay 12f: acts well on gd grnd & on a gall trk: should find a h'cap soon.   48
2876 RICHARDS FOLLY [5] (P Bailey) 3-7-11 N Adams 50/1: -000002: Prom thro'out: no ch with
winner but displayed impr form: can win a race if reproducing this form: eff over 9/10f on
gd & firm grnd: see 2876.   30
*2893 BOLERO MAGIC [1] (H Cecil) 3-8-7 W Ryan 6/5: -2213: Made much, one-paced & btr 2893 (9f).40
2776 FLOATER [8] (S Wiles) 3-8-0 M Wood 100/1: -004: Early ldr: lightly rcd: 1st signs of form   26
2467 CAREER BAY [3] 4-8-7 D Wiliams(7) 33/1: 0300-00: Hard to settle, prom much: very
lightly rcd mdn.   17
2683 PARAVANE [2] 4-8-4 M Beecroft 50/1: 000-000: Waited with, no dngr: lightly rcd mdn.   09
2856 Pete Marsh [7] 8-0   2800 Moulkins [6] 9-0
8 ran   6,shhd,3,5,2   (Sheikh Mohammed)   M Stoute Newmarket

3029 THE BEECH HANDICAP (0-50) 3YO+   £3488   1m 40y Good 53 +17 Fast   [39]

2797 FORWARD RALLY [8] (M Prescott) 4-9-5 G Duffield 13/2: -112021: 4 b f Formidable-
Rally (Relko): Impr filly: nicely bckd, al prom & forged clear in the final 2f for a
decisive win in a fast run h'cap at Haydock: earlier in the season won first 2 on the trot
at Beverley & valuable Zetland Gold Cup at Redcar: off the trk subsequently for some time:
: very eff over 1m/10f on a gall trk: appears to act on any going, runs well on firm
or gd: genuine filly who will be hard to beat again next time.   45
2629 KNIGHTS SECRET [6] (M H Easterby) 5-9-5 M Birch 6/1: 3404222: Dsptd lead most & is
in grand form: see 2629.   37
2836 LONG BAY [17] (H Collingridge) 4-8-2(1ow) M Rimmer 25/1: 0000043: Apparently unfncd,
made most, showing best form yet this season: see 611, her turn could well be near.   17
*2891 SHARONS ROYALE [2] (R Whitaker) 3-8-6(5ex) K Bradshaw(5) 10/1: 4414414: Prom, not
the best of runs closing stages & is in grand form: see 2891: could win again soon.   26
2905 SUPREME KINGDOM [11] 3-8-7 S Perks 25/1: 3000000: Prog from ½way :btr effort but
seems inconsistent: see 1783.   26
+2797 HELLO GYPSY [14] 5-9-4(5ex) W Goodwin(7) 4/1 FAV: 2130110: Waited with, gd fin: see 2797. 31
2891 QUALITAIRESS [7] 4-7-8(vis) P Burke(7) 8/1: 1212000: No threat: best 2549.   00
2601 COURT TOWN [3] 3-8-11 R Fox 9/1: -004020: No threat: much btr 2601 (sharp trk).   00
2629 SIR WILMORE [9] 4-9-0 E Guest(3) 10/1: 0100030: Much btr 2629.   00
2755 Welsh Medley [13] 8-6   2837 Fancy Pan [12] 9-3   2443 Try Harder [1] 9-5
2891 Bella Banus [16] 8-9   2891 Zio Peppino [4] 8-2   1999 Sporting Sovereign [15] 8-6
2173 Godlord [10] 7-7(bl)(3oh)
16 ran   3,1½,shhd,¾,nk   (Lady Macdonald-Buchanan)   M Prescott Newmarket

Official Going Given As FIRM

3030 CRAVEN APPRENTICE STAKES 3YO+   £1279   1m 4f   Good/Firm 25 -27 Slow

2937 CROWLEY [5] (L Cumani) 3-8-3 S Quane 7/4 FAV: 0021331: 3 b f Vaguely Noble - Funny
Funny Ache (Bold Jester): Well bckd, stayed on well under press to lead cl home in an app stks
at Catterick: earlier an easy winner of a mdn race at Ripon: very eff around 12f on gd & fast
ground: consistent filly who seems to act on any track.   42
2489 BANQUE PRIVEE [2] (B Hills) 3-8-3 P Hill 5/1: -331402: Made most, slightly hmpd near
fin, but btn on merit: gd eff from this consistent filly: see 1908.   40
372 SHEHANA [10] (P Cole) 3-8-3 G Thompson 4/1: 4431-03: Al prom, ran on same pace:
off the trk since May and clearly has proved very difficult to train since showing considerable
promise as a juv, when making all in a fillies mdn at Wolverhampton (rated 56): stays 12f:
acts on fast & yldg ground and on any track.   33
2985 HYOKIN [4] (D Morley) 4-9-0(vis) W Hollick(7) 20/11: 2002004: Well btn in h'cap company
last time, ran much btr here but prob flattered by this rating: acts on any trk: see 1359.   36
*2900 STORM HOUSE [6] 4-9-0 A Whitehall 9/1: 230-310: Running well, but prob flattered here.   35
2893 SHINING SKIN [1] 3-8-3 D Meade 7/1: -000130: Unruly before start, onepaced: best 2726.   26

2536 Pentland Hawk [7] 8-6	2789 Jalome [3] 8-11	2760 Oriental Express [8] 8-6
-- Rosies Member [11] 9-0	2745 Ramille [9] 8-11
11 ran nk,3,½,½,3,nk,nk	(N B Hunt)	L Cumani Newmarket

3031 HORNBY CASTLE SELLING STAKES 2YO   £1082   5f   Good/Firm 25 -01 Slow

2919 GARDENIA LADY [7] (D Barron) 2-8-8(bl) D Nicholls 5/2 FAV: 0000001: 2 b f Mummy's Game
- Mallow (Le Dieur d'Or) Well bckd and was al prom, ran on well under press to lead in final
strides of a 2yo seller at Catterick (no bid): half sister to winning sprinter Meneghini Rose
and had earlier run with credit in btr company (rated 45 early-season on yldg): best form
over 5f: acts on fast & yldg grd and on any track.   25
2712 MUSIC DELIGHT [5] (K Ivory) 2-8-8(vis) A Shoults(5) 12/1: 0400002: Game attempt to
make all, caught post: well suited by a return to this minimum trip and likes this tight trk: see 1738.24
2465 PENBREASY [14] (R Hollinshead) 2-8-8 S Perks 7/1: 0000003: Ran on late: see 1764.   15
2969 JOYCES PET [8] (C Thornton) 2-8-8 J Bleasdale 20/1: 00004: Al up there: see 1680.   09
2806 HIGHLAND LAIRD [11] 2-8-11 R Guest 7/1: 00000: Kept on late: 20,000 gns yearling
who had been well btn on all his prev starts, albeit in considerablybtr. class:may need further   09
2323 GOLD STATE [10] 2-8-11 N Carlisle 12/1: 00000: Prom most: best 2323 (soft).   07
2994 MISS ACACIA [15] 2-8-8(bl) R Hills 6/1: 3220200: Has been busy lately: btr 2927 (6f)   00
2608 LADY SUNDAY SPORT [1] 2-8-8 G Duffield 4/1: 2300040: Wknd quickly after ½ way: see 2608   00

2588 Glory Gold [2] 8-8	1528 Winnies Luck [6] 8-8	2883 Intellect [12] 8-8
2712 Miss Bolero [3] 8-8	329 Scarning Sparkler [9] 8-11
2499 Mitral Magic [4] 8-8	2817 Little Law [13] 8-8
15 ran shthd,3,2,½,½,1,2,½	(W G Spink)	D Barron Thirsk, North Yorks.

3032 HORNBY CASTLE SELLING STAKES 2YO   £1075   5f   Good/Firm 25 -03 Slow

2743 OUR GINGER [1] (Ron Thompson) 2-8-8 R P Elliott 4/1: 0401: 2 ch f Le Johnstan -
Summersoon (Sheshoon) Dropped in class and was quickly into her stride, cmftbly making all in
a 2yo seller at Catterick (no bid): closely related to sev winners: eff over a sharp 5f and
is sure to stay further next season: acts on gd/firm grd and does well with forcing tactics.   24
2883 PREMIER VIDEO [3] (J Berry) 2-8-8 J Carroll(7) 9/2: 0202002: Al up there: best 1545.   12
2781 TAHARD [5] (R Hollinshead) 2-8-11 S Perks 8/1: 0000003: Al prom: see 2334 & 694.   12
2212 PEGGYS TREASURE [11] (M Brittain) 2-8-8 A Munro(7) 10/1: 0344334: Consistent, but
onepaced: best 957.   `03
2987 FRIVOLOUS LADY [4] 2-8-8(vis) R Guest 13/2: 4400000: Visored first time: well bckd
and showed gd speed over ½ way: btr 1946 (maiden): see 1668.   01
612 CHUNKY SUPREME [6] 2-8-11 M Hindley(3) 33/1: 000: Long abs: prom most: very cheaply
bought gelding who showed a little improvement here: acts on gd/firm grd.   00
2580 DEAR GLENDA [9] 2-8-8 G Duffield 5/2 FAV: 20000: Well bckd: fin 7th: best in 13 (yldg)   00
2927 EASTERN PRINCESS [12] 2-8-8 M Wigham 8/1: 00000: No threat in 8th: see 1194.   00
2805 PERTAIN [2] 2-8-11(bl) R Curant 8/1: 0400000: Hmpd early, sn no threat: see 1881.   00

1785 Quite So [10] 8-12	2814 Oak Field [8] 8-8	2757 Dublin Belle [14] 8-8
12 ran 4,1,2,½,1½,1½,hd	(Ronald Thompson)	Ron Thompson Doncaster, S. Yorks.

3033 MOULTON HANDICAP (0-35) 3YO   £2206   7f   Good/Firm 25 +09 Fast   [41]

2681 KENOOZ [2] (A Stewart) 3-8-12 W Hayes(7) 9/2 JT FAV: -204001: 3 b f Mummy's Pet -
Topling (High Top) Led below dist and ran on strongly to gain her first win in quite a fast
run 3yo h'cap at Catterick: eff over 6/7f and likely to get 1m: acts on gd/firm and hvy grd
and seems well suited by a sharp track.   34
2928 MISTER MARCH [3] (R Hutchinson) 3-8-7 G French 9/2 JT FAV: 2000302: Kept on well.   24
2681 SEQUESTRATOR [15] (W Musson) 3-8-5 M Wigham 9/1: 1000403: Had ev ch: best 1316.   20
2905 HAYWAIN [1] (B Hills) 3-8-1 P Hill(7) 7/1: 0001044: Best 2601.   13
2905 IVORY GULL [9] 3-9-4 G Sexton 13/2: -000000: Never nearer: needs 1m? See 154.   28
2602 JUST THE TICKET [4] 3-7-7(3oh) G Bardwell(7) 16/1: 0-01000: Nearest fin: best 1562   02
*2688 IMPERIAL SUNRISE [13] 3-8-2(bl) L Charnock 10/1: 0203010: Never beyond mid-div: btr 2688   00

2858 Manton Mark [5] 9-1		2268 Miss Blake [17] 7-7(6oh)	
2681 Royal Rouser [6] 8-6		2713 Nomad Boxer [12] 7-7(6oh)	
2481 Foretop [7] 8-6		2816 Security Pacific [8] 8-12	
2963 Mal Y Pense [16] 8-12(VIS)			2339 Owls Way [10] 7-9
15 ran 1½,1,1½,1,½,hd	(Mohamed ,Suhail)		A Stewart Newmarket

3034 E.B.F. ILKLEY STAKES 2YO   £1736   7f   Good/Firm 25 -25 Slow

2748 YAQUT [5] (H T Jones) 2-8-8 R Hills 10/11 FAV: 221: 2 ch f Northern Dancer - Christmas
Bonus (Key To The Mint) Well bckd and cmftbly landed the odds, leading inside dist in a 2yo
fillies stks at Catterick: cost a mammoth $2½m as a yearling: eff over 6/8f on gd & fast
ground: acts on any track.   38
2678 TRY DANCER [1] (J Winter) 2-8-8 J Lowe 20/1: 0002: Led below dist, not pace of
winner but showed improved form here: closely related to sev winners: stays 7f: acts on
gd/firm ground.   32
2846 KASHAPOUR [3] (L Cumani) 2-8-8 R Guest 5/4: 03: Led/dsptd lead most: see 2846.   26
1843 TELL ME NOW [6] (D Thom) 2-8-8 G Sexton 20/1: 0004: No extra 2f out: abs since 1843.   13
2757 HOLYROOD [2] 2-8-8 J H Brown(5) 100/1: 000: Early leader: no worthwhile form.   10
5 ran   1½,3,6,½   (Hamdan Al Maktoum)   H T Jones Newmarket

3035 ZETLAND STAKES 3YO+   £684   2m   Good/Firm 25 -19 Slow

2802 SHAHS CHOICE [3] (J Dunlop) 3-9-0 G Sexton 11/10 FAV: 3222121: 3 b c Persian Bold -
Royal Display (Right Royal V) Consistent colt: led over 2f out and stayed on strongly to
win a minor race at Catterick: earlier broke his duck in a mdn over today's C/D and clearly
likes this tight course: rarely out of the frame this season: eff around 12/14f, stays 2m well:
acts on fast & yldg ground and on any track.   38
613 SAGAX [5] (S Hall) 4-9-5 M Birch 16/1: -00/002: Long abs: no extra cl home but cmftbly
beat rem and is clearly well suited by a distance of ground: see 448.   31
2620 BUSHIDO [6] (G Harwood) 3-8-10 G Baxter 13/8: -2403: Led over 4f out, onepaced:
has proved very disapp since 486, when rated 54 behind Broken Wave at Salisbury (10f, yldg).   26
-- MASTER VINCE [2] (M Tompkins) 8-9-5 M Rimmer 66/1: -0/4: Put up a fair effort on
only his 2nd start on the Flat: winning jumper who is suited by a dist of grd: acts gd/firm.   25
2734 STANDARD ROSE [4] 3-8-7 R Curant 5/1: 0-4000: Wknd after home turn: see 1580.   18
-- PADYKIN [7] 6-9-2 G Duffield 66/1: -00/0: Wknd home turn: only lightly raced on Flat
but showed gd form to win twice over hurdles last season.   11
1748 BATTLE FLEET [1] 3-8-7 M Wigham 50/1: -000340: Made much: abs since 1748.   00
7 ran   1½,4,nk,3,5   (Lord Granard)   J Dunlop Arundel, Sussex

3036 BRETTANBY HANDICAP (0-35) 3YO+   £1576   1m 6f   Good/Firm 25 -05 Slow   [27]

2944 FOUR STAR THRUST [11] (R Whitaker) 4-9-9(4ex) D Mckeown 5/2 FAV: 2321121: 8 ch f
Derrylin - Smiling (Silly Season) In grand form and was well bckd when leading inside dist
for a cheeky win in a h'cap at Catterick: rarely out of the frame this season and recently
successful in h'caps at Hamilton & Edinburgh: in '85 also won at Edinburgh: equally eff over
12/14f on gd & fast grd: consistent sort who acts on any track.   30
2819 PERFECT DOUBLE [8] (W Pearce) 5-7-12 A Proud 11/1: 3220002: Led over ½ way and again
below dist: kept on well: stays 14f: see 770.   03
*2874 TURMERIC [3] (D Morley) 3-9-4(4ex) S Perks 8/1: 2042313: In fine form: see 2874.   28
2789 TIMMINION [1] (K Stone) 4-8-6 C Dwyer 10/1: 3000034: Not btn very far: see 2789, 44.   07
2337 TROMEROS [5] 5-8-7 L Charnock 5/1: 0000-30: Four times a winner over hurdles this
Autumn: stayed on well but never reached leaders: see 2337.   07
2861 DIENAUS TROVE [2] 5-8-13 M Rimmer 3/1: -32140: Well bckd: ev ch: see 2861 & 1226.   10
2346 Parsons Child [6] 9-7   2726 Rideside [7] 8-7   2128 Pinturicchia [10] 7-11
2861 Mr Coffey [4] 8-13   2681 Minders Man [9] 8-0(bl)
11 ran   ¾,1½,½,nk,2,1½,hd   (Mrs Jean Turner)   R Whitaker Wetherby, North Yorks.

Official Going Given As GOOD

3037 SNAILWELL MAIDEN STAKES 2YO   £5293   6f   Good 58 -13 Slow

2651 AGLASINI [22] (F Durr) 2-8-11 Pat Eddery 11/2: 01: 2 ch f Ahonoora - Inis Ealga
(Sallust) Fast impr filly: well bckd and led inside final 1f, ridden out in a val 24 runner
2yo mdn at Newmarket: cost IR 55,000 and is a first foal of an unraced dam: seems very eff
over a stiff 7f: acts on gd ground and is the type to win more races next term.   58
-- SARSHARA [21] (M Stoute) 2-8-11 W R Swinburn 5/1: 2: Led 2f out: ran on and just btn:
fine debut from this half sister to the topclass performer Shardari: looks sure to be suited
by 1m: acts on gd grd and a gail track and should win races next season.   57
1930 KRISTAL ROCK [7] (H Cecil) 2-9-0 W Ryan 20/1: 03: Abs: kept on well & this was a
much better effort: can find a race: see 1930: stays 7f and acts on gd ground.   56
-- PRINCE BOCA [15] (A Stewart) 2-9-0 M Roberts 20/1: 4: Al up there on debut, showing
future promise: should be suited by 1m: acts on gd grd and a stiff track.   55
-- PENELOPE STRAWBERY [10] 2-8-11 R Cochrane 10/1: 0: Mkt drifter: stayed on well closing
stages and is sure to improve on this: quite cheaply acquired at 12,500 gns and is a half
sister to a couple of minor winners: should be suited by 1m+ next season: acts on gd ground.   46

-- JARRETIERE [19] 2-8-11 P Cook 20/1: 0: Ran on well final 1f on debut: half sister to
a couple of winners: should be suited by another furlong and acts on gd ground: one to
keep an eye on.   45
2645 MOMENTS OF SILVER [18] 2-9-0 B Thomson 14/1: 340: Prom, fin 7th: another gd eff: see 2341 47
2782 TAUBER [20] 2-9-0 J Reid 16/1: 032330: Never nearer 8th: see 2782 (6f)   47
2554 JADE HUNTER [13] 2-9-0 S Cauthen 11/4 FAV: 00: Heavily bckd: fdd over 1f out:see 2554 00

-- Shahdji [16] 9-0	-- Lotus Island [24] 9-0	2645 Abu Muslab [3] 9-0
2869 Calapaez [4] 9-0	-- Cross Bencher [1] 9-0	1225 Doodlin [23] 9-0
2626 Fox Path [2] 9-0	2732 Milan Fair [8] 9-0	-- Puppet Show [5] 9-0
-- Raise A Flyer [6] 9-0	2696 Runlad [14] 9-0	-- Salopard [11] 9-0
2522 Young Judge [12] 9-0(BL		-- Domineering [17] 8-11
-- Saffron Light [9] 8-11		

24 ran   nk,1½,hd,3,1,hd,shthd   (K Abdulla)   F Durr Newmarket

3038 FAKENHAM HANDICAP 3YO+ 0-70   £6108   1m 4f   Good 58 +11 Fast   [63]

2701 SLANGI VAH [7] (H Candy) 3-7-7 T Williams 14/1: -330231: 3 b c Riva Ridge - La
Atrevida (Bold Bidder) Gained his first win, sent on 2f out and held on under press in a
fast run and val h'cap at Newmarket: placed sev times prev: eff at 10/12f on firm & yldg grd
and prob acts on any trk.   47
+2850 ISLAND SET [8] (L Cumani) 4-9-4(5ex) R Cochrane 13/2: 2210212: Ran on well under press
and is in grand form: genuine and consistent: see 2850.   64
2834 AMBASSADOR [9] (W O'gorman) 3-8-5(bl)(1ow) Pat Eddery 12/1: -223223: Ev ch final 2f:
another gd effort from this consistent colt: eff at 12f/2m: see 2834, 2610.   55
2733 TAMATOUR [10] (M Stoute) 3-7-12 P Robinson 15/2: -021234: Kept on well final 2f:
consistent: see 2517.   47
2850 TENDER TYPE [2] 3-7-8 A Mackay 16/1: 2134030: Another gd run: see 2850, 2156.   39
2769 VOUCHSAFE [4] 4-8-3 W Carson 12/1: D000000: Nicely bckd: never nearer: best 1112.   35
-2850 VERARDI [11] 3-8-2 M Roberts 11/2 FAV: 3011420: Disapp 7th and well below 2850 (C/D) 00
*2937 HIGH KNOWL [3] 3-8-7 B Thomson 10/1: 2311110: Led after ½ way: below his best: see 2937 00
*2733 BACKCHAT [14] 4-9-10 G Starkey 7/1: -400110: P.U. over 1f out: something amiss? See 2733 00
2692 Tabardar [15] 8-3(vis)   +2855 Convinced [1] 9-7(5ex)
2749 Plaid [5] 9-2   *2686 Rana Pratap [16] 9-1   2845 Robbama [12] 8-12(bl)
1130 First Division [13] 8-6   208 Lobkowiez [17] 7-7(1oh)
698 Tivian [6] 7-7(vis)(3oh)
17 ran   nk,1½,nk,2,3,1½   (F Salman)   H Candy Wantage, Oxon.

3039 GROUP 1 WILLIAM HILL DEWHURST STKS 2YO   £45717   7f   Good 58 +01 Fast

+2767 AJDAL [3] (M Stoute) 2-9-0 W R Swinburn 4/9 FAV: 111: 2 b c Northern Dancer - Native
Partner (Raise A Native) Very smart colt: very heavily bckd when a cmftbly winner of Gr 1
Dewhurst Stks at Newmarket: showed a fine turn of foot to lead final 1f and despite idling
when he hit the front showed Classic potential here: remains unbtn, earlier an effortless
winner at Ascot & Doncaster: half brother to sev winners: very eff at 7f, looks sure to be
suited by 1m and further next season: acts on gd & fast grd and a gall trk: undoubtedly the
best 2yo colt seen this season and is not one to oppose lightly, whatever the opposition. 85
2695 SHADY HEIGHTS [4] (R Armstrong) 2-9-0 S Cauthen 5/2: 122: Not entirely suited by
the slow early pace but ran on well final 1f: another fine effort and will be even btr over
1m: see 2695, 2418.   81
2866 GENGHIZ [1] (L Piggott) 2-9-0 W Carson 18/1: 11033: Held up: ran on final 1f: suited
by 7f and will stay 1m: continues to improve: see 2866, 2243.   77
*2866 MISTER MAJESTIC [5] (R Williams) 2-9-0 R Cochrane 20/1: 1144014: Led 6f: another gd
run: see 2866.   73
2907 RUMBOOGIE [2] 2-9-0 Pat Eddery 50/1: 010300: Very stiff task: prom 5f: see 2695.   61
5 ran   ½,1½,1½,4   (Sheikh Mohammed)   M Stoute Newmarket

3040 GR 3 CHEVINGTON STUD ROCKFEL STKS 2YO F   £13320   7f   Good 58 -05 Slow

+2651 AT RISK [2] (H Cecil) 2-8-9(1ow) S Cauthen 4/1: 311: 2 gr f Mr Prospector - Misgivings
(Cyane) Smart filly: led over 1f out and was al holding the chall of White Mischief when a
decisive ½l winner of Gr 3 Rockfel Stks at Newmarket: last time out was a narrow winner of
a fillies mdn at Yarmouth: half sister to a couple of winners: eff at 6/7f looks sure to
be suited by 1m: acts on gd & firm grd: held in high regard by her powerful stable: certain
to win more races and rate more highly.   72
*2774 WHITE MISCHIEF [8] (L Cumani) 2-8-8 R Cochrane 9/4 FAV: 12: Heavily bckd: led inside
final 2f and ran on gamely: 3l clear 3rd and is a smart filly: stays 7f well: see 2774.   69
2732 BAY BOULEVARD [1] (R Armstrong) 2-8-8 B Thomson 33/1: 43: Gd late hdwy: fin 4th,
placed 3rd: fast improving filly who looks certain to win races over 1m and further: acts
on gd & fast ground: see 2732.   61
1789 GENTLE PERSUASION [12] (I Balding) 2-8-8 Pat Eddery 12/1: 144: Mkt drifter after abs:
ev ch 2f out: another gd run: see 1021.   59
2751 COLOR ARTIST [13] 2-8-8 G Starkey 33/1: 01300: Never nearer: fin 6th, placed 5th:
again ran well in smart company: see 2751, 1801.   57
2901 DEBACH DELIGHT [5] 2-8-8 A Mackay 33/1: 0320: Made much: fin 7th, placed 6th: ran
very well here and seems eff over 7/9f: see 2901, 2664.   55

886

2768 MISS STORM BIRD [6] 2-8-8 W R Swinburn 9/2: 20: Pulled hard, prom most: btr 2768
and needs to settle better. 54
+2611 MONTERANA [3] 2-8-8 P Robinson 8/1: 1210: Badly hmpd after ½ way: best ignored see 2611 00
2768 GLINT OF VICTORY [4] 2-8-8 M Hills 8/1: 03D: Hmpd when looking for room inside final
3f: ran on well but was disq and placed last for interfering with Monterana: nevertheless
a fine effort and will be suited by 1m: looks sure to win races: see 2768. 63
2710 Zilda [10] 8-8   -2297 Garnet [11] 8-8   1464 Loras Guest [9] 8-8
*2664 Sunerta [7] 8-8
13 ran   ½,3,1,½,½,½,nk   (Mrs John W Hanes)   H Cecil Newmarket

3041 EBF NURSERY HANDICAP 2YO   £11359   7f   Good 58 -01 Slow   [62]

*2615 I TRY [7] (L Cumani) 2-8-8 R Cochrane 6/1: 311: 2 b c Try My Best - Amenity (Luthier)
Useful, impr colt: ran on gamely to lead cl home in a val nursery h'cap at Newmarket: last
time out won a mdn at Brighton: cost 52,000 gns and dam was a winner over 10f: eff at 7f,
will be suited by 1m: acts on gd & fast grd and on any track: on the upgrade. 57
+2711 NOBLE MINSTREL [14] (O Douieb) 2-9-4 Pat Eddery 7/1: 412: Very heavily bckd:
led on bit 2f out but was caught cl home: fin 3l clear 3rd and compensation awaits: fast
improving: see 2711. 68
*2951 TARTUFFE [15] (G Harwood) 2-9-10(7ex) G Starkey 11/2: 01113: Al there: kept on under
press: fine effort under 9-10: see 2951. 66
*2756 SPEEDBIRD [9] (M Ryan) 2-8-4 P Robinson 14/1: 0004014: Ev ch over 1f out: in fine
form: see 2756. 45
2485 BATTLEAXE [10] 2-8-3(BL) W Carson 16/1: 3341300: Bl first time: sn prom: lightly
raced since 1305, stays 7f. 37
2140 BRIGGS BUILDERS [13] 2-7-7 A Mackay 33/1: 00200: Rank outsider, prom most: best 1883. 18
*2667 LUCAYAN KNIGHT [2] 2-9-7 W R Swinburn 10/1: 2110: There 4f: btr 2667 (6f) 00
2811 ABLE SAINT [5] 2-9-3 S Cauthen 8/1: 21320: Early speed: below his best: see 2811. 00
2561 Lyrical Lover [3] 7-13   2696 Bechemal [12] 8-0
2598 Psalmody [11] 9-5   +1966 Vevila [1] 9-7   2865 Macrobian [8] 9-5
-2611 King Balladeer [4] 8-13   2815 Lucianaga [6] 8-5(BL)
15 ran   ½,3,hd,3,4,1½,hd   (Dr M Boffa)   L Cumani Newmarket

3042 MELBOURN HANDICAP 3YO 0-70   £6372   1m   Good 58 -13 Slow   [67]

*2934 USFAN [3] (J Dunlop) 3-8-10(5ex) W Carson 3/1 FAV: 0221211: 3 br c Riverman - Essie
B S Venture (Intentionally) Very useful colt who is in excellent form: led inside final 1f,
under press for a narrow win in a val h'cap at Newmarket: last time out won a similar event
at York and earlier won a mdn again at York: very eff over 7f/1m and may get further: acts
on firm, suited by gd grd and should prefer some give: acts on any trk: game & genuine and
has not stopped improving. 61
2459 GREAT LEIGHS [10] (B Hills) 3-8-0 M Hills 20/1: 1200002: Led inside final 2f: ran
on well under press and just btn: best effort for a long time and doesnot seem suited by firm
ground: can win before season's end: see 359. 50
2763 NIGHT OUT PERHAPS [12] (G Wragg) 3-9-2 Pat Eddery 5/1: 4013303: Ran on final 1f:
stays 10f but is eff over a stiff 1m: see 2438, 1924. 63
2934 CENTREPOINT [5] (J Etherington) 3-8-0(bl) A Mackay 12/1: 1-44304: Sn prom: gd effort. 43
2870 PRINCE PECADILLO [1] 3-9-7 R Cochrane 33/1: 00-0000: Fin in fine style under 9-7:
clearly stays a stiff 1m: returning to his best: see 2870. 63
2867 TURFAH [4] 3-8-10 Paul Eddery 11/1: 1122300: Prom most: see 2234, 2009. 51
2784 DOCKSIDER [2] 3-7-12 M Roberts 7/2: -02120: Ev ch 2f out: much btr 2784, 2321. 00
+2879 SUPER PUNK [9] 3-8-1(5ex) C Rutter(3) 8/1: 3000410: No show: well below 2879. 00
1655 Native Wizard [11] 8-13(bl)   1231 Stanford Vale [8] 8-0
2851 Sit This One Out [6] 9-1   600 Pop The Cork [7] 8-11
12 ran   hd,1½,2,nk,½   (Prince A A Faisal)   J Dunlop Arundel, Sussex

3043 NEWMARKET CHALLENGE CUP 2YO   £0   7f   Good 58 -21 Slow

--   NESHAD [4] (M Stoute) 2-9-0 W R Swinburn 7/2: 1: 2 gr c Sharpen Up - Nasseem (Zeddan)
Promising colt: first time out led 1½f out, readily, in a 2yo mdn at Newmarket: half brother
to 7f winner Nioro: eff over 7f on gd grd and a gall trk: can only improve. 58
2847 PIFFLE [1] (J Dunlop) 2-8-11 W Carson 12/1: 02: Led over 2f out: not pace of winner:
stoutly bred filly who will be well suited by middle dist next term: half sister to useful
stayer L Conquistador: acts on gd grd and can find a race. 46
`-- HAATIF [2] (H T Jones) 2-9-0 A Murray 8/13 FAV: 3: Heavily bckd: ev ch inside final 2f
but could not quicken: evidently highly regarded: half brother to the smart '84 2yo Foulaad:
should do better than this. 47
-2796 ALPENHORN [6] (G P Gordon) 2-9-0 W Ryan 8/1: 030024: Led over 4f: see 2796. 43
2869 MARBLE ROCK [5] 2-9-0 Paul Eddery 14/1: 000: Mkt drifter: there 4f: should be well
suited by middle dist next term and staying could be his game. 23
2651 GLOIRE DE DIJON [3] 2-8-11 M Hills 20/1: 00: No show: quite stoutly bred filly who
is a half sister to sev winners and should do btr in time. 08
6 ran   3,1,2,10,6   (H H Aga Khan)   M Stoute Newmaarket

CATTERICK   Saturday October 18th   Lefthanded, Very Sharp Track

Official Going Given As FIRM FOR FIRST 3 RACES : GD/FIRM FOR REMAINDER

3044 E.B.F. NORTH RIDING MAIDEN STAKES 2YO   £2078   5f   Good/Firm 24 +04 Fast

2805 STELBY [2] (O Brennan) 2-9-0 B Crossley 11/8 FAV: 4200331: 2 ch c Stetchworth - Little Trilby (Tyrant) Gained an overdue win when leading under press cl home in quite a fast run 2yo mdn at Catterick: cheaply bought colt who is well suited by sprint dist: likes fast ground tho' seems to act on any trk. 44

2875 BALKAN LEADER [5] (J Fitzgerald) 2-9-0 D Nicholls 4/1: 02342: Led after ½ way, caught close home but cmftbly beat rem: deserves a small race: acts on any trk: see 780, 583. 40

2791 LAST CHORD [3] (I Matthews) 2-9-0 C Dwyer 9/4: 03: Well bckd: led/dsptd lead over ½ way, not quicken: may have found this trip too sharp and should do btr than this: see 2791 28

2651 PATIENT DREAMER [6] (H Collingridge) 2-8-11 G Sexton 20/1: 004: No chance from ½ way: 8000 gns yearling who is a half sister to sev winners but has yet to show any worthwhile form herself over various distances. 00

2781 HITTITE RULER [1] (R Hollinshead) 2-9-0 K Darley 14/1: 00: Sn pushed along and no threat: half brother to sev winners, tho' is likely to need longer dist and more time. 00

3027 MOTOR BROKER [4] 2-9-0(vis) G Duffield 9/1: 0004000: Quick reappearance: led early. 00

2982 OLIVE LEAF [7] 2-8-11 D Mckay 33/1: 00: Dwelt and never went pace: half sister to a number of winners, including 8/12f filly Marie Cath: will be suited by middle dist in time. 00

7 ran   1,4,10,3,2½,shthd   (Victor Sassie)   O Brennan Kelham, Notts.

3045 BATLEY SELLING H'CAP (0-25) 3YO   £1069   1m 4f   Good/Firm 24 -130 Slow   [27]

2874 DOON VENTURE [1] (J Etherington) 3-8-1 S Webster 9/4 JT FAV: 0003401: 3 ro c Ardoon - Happy Adventure (Credo) Led after ½ way and just held on in a very slowly run selling h'cap at Catterick (sold for 4000 gns) : stoutly bred colt who stays 12f on a sharp trk: acts on gd and firm ground. 05

2705 SOLENT EXPRESS [4] (B Stevens) 3-8-3(2ow) P Bloomfield 7/1: -004042: Just held: stays 12f: see 2073. 06

2587 DAIS [6] (P Walwyn) 3-8-3 R Curant 7/2: 00-0003: Led briefly ½ way: see 2587. 00

2890 DAVALLIA [5] (D Morley) 3-9-7 G Duffield 9/4 JT FAV: 3-0004: Prom most: acts on gd/firm. 10

2366 HIYA BUD [3] 3-8-11 C Dwyer 16/1: -004000: Dropped in class: see 1072. 00

1759 STORM LORD [8] 3-7-11 L Charnock 10/1: 0-00000: Abs: wknd home turn: best here 769. 00

2902 Tiber Gate [7] 7-7(10oh)   2590 Expert Witness [2] 7-12

8 ran   hd,6,2,1½,5   (P D Brunt)   J Etherington Norton, Yorks.

3046 FAVERDALE HANDICAP (0-35) 3YO+   £1875   5f   Good/Firm 24 +10 Fast   [32]

3024 JACQUI JOY [10] (K Ivory) 3-8-1 A Shoults(5) 8/1: 0212401: 3 b f Music Boy - Superb Lady (Marcus Superbus) Quick reappearance and stayed on strongly to lead on post in a fast run h'cap at Catterick: earlier a similarly narrow winner of a seller at Beverley: stays 7f tho' seems best over 6f: well suited by fast grd: acts on any track. 14

2906 STANBO [5] (D Dale) 3-8-8 G Duffield 8/1: 4020402: Led inside dist, caught final strides: gd eff but remains a maiden: see 2575. 20

2775 CAPTAINS BIDD [9] (H Whiting) 6-8-4 G Sexton 13/2: 1410003: Narrowly btn: best 2256. 15

2797 VIA VITAE [8] (R Hollinshead) 4-7-7(8oh) A Culhane(7) 33/1: 0000004: Ran on just too late: see 1765. 03

2816 TRADESMAN [2] 6-7-7(2oh) M Fry 20/1: 0000000: Not btn far: best 1423. 01

2688 MANDRAKE MADAM [1] 3-9-2 L Charnock 15/2: 0330030: Made most: in fair form: see 2688. 20

2775 KARENS STAR [7] 9-8-3 K Darley 8/1: 0200000: Fdd into 7th: best 2124 (C/D): see 1093. 00

2659 RESTLESS RHAPSODY [4] 3-9-5(bl) A Whitehall(7) 5/1: 0403100: Wknd into 8th: best 2416 00

2833 SIMLA RIDGE [11] 4-9-10 J Leech(7) 2/1 FAV: 0020400: Never dangerous 9th: see 977, 628 00

2775 Last Secret [3] 7-7(bl)(7oh)   2992 Lady Songe [12] 7-7(2oh)

2313 Megadyne [6] 7-13   1849 Velocidad [13] 8-3

13 ran   shthd,nk,½,½,1½,hd,2,2   (Mrs I Reichler)   K Ivory Radlett, Herts.

3047 OGDEN SPACEMAKER STAKES 2YO   £2840   7f   Good/Firm 24 -56 Slow

+2926 WAR BRAVE [1] (J Dunlop) 2-9-2 G Sexton 4/9 FAV: 24111: 2 gr c Indian King - Kizzy (Dancer's Image) Useful colt: landed the odds over this longer trip, held up and pushed into lead cl home in a slowly run 2yo stks at Catterick: earlier successful at Nottingham and Lingfield: cost 160,000 gns as a yearling and is a half brother to winning juv Dancer's Shadow: very eff over 6/7f on fast grd: consistent sort who acts on any trk and is sure to win again. 52

2791 BEAU NASH [2] (M Prescott) 2-8-11 G Duffield 3/1: 32: Went on below dist, outpaced by winner near finish: sure to find a race: will be suited by further: see 2791. 42

2667 OH DANNY BOY [5] (E Weymes) 2-8-11 E Guest(3) 12/1: 0003: Made much: kept on well when hdd: eff over 6/7f, should be suited by 1m+ next term: see 1984. 40

2889 FREDDIE ASHTON [3] (D Morley) 2-8-11(bl) S Perks 25/1: 000004: Appeared to put up an improved effort but may have been flattered by proximity to winner in this slowly run race: has improved since stepping up to 7f and should be suited by 1m+ next term: acts on gd/firm. 40

-- SAINTS ABOVE [4] 2-8-11 S Webster 25/1: 0: Dropped out quickly before ½ way in this slow run race: cheaply bought colt. 00

5 ran   1,½,shthd,dist   (Sheikh Mohammed)   J Dunlop Arundel, Sussex

3048 OTLEY STAKES 2YO   £1469   5f   Good/Firm 24 -06 Slow

2843 MAZILIER [3] (G Harwood) 2-9-1 G Duffield 5/4 FAV: 20101: 2 b c Lyphard - Marie Curie
(Exbury) Useful colt: well bckd and responded to strong press to lead near fin in a 2yo stks
at Catterick: earlier a game all-the-way winner of a mdn at Windsor: half brother to sev
winners, including smart miler Crofter: eff over 5/6f on gd & fast grd: likes to be up with
the pace and does well on a sharp track.   49
2781 SKI CAPTAIN [1] (J Etherington) 2-8-11(bl) M Wood 11/2: 002: Broke well and only just
failed to make ev yard: fine effort and certain to go one btr soon: likes a sharp trk: see 2781   44
2903 BLAZING HIGH [5] (L Piggott) 2-8-11 B Crossley 7/4: 034U4D3: Al up there: consistent.   40
2983 QUASSIMI [6] (F Durr) 2-8-11 G Baxter 7/1: 0044: Prom most: see 2983.   28
3031 MUSIC DELIGHT [4] 2-8-8(vis) A Shoults(5) 25/1: 4000020: Gd early speed, wknd 2f out.   20
--   CAROLS HEIGHTS [2] 2-8-11 S Webster 100/1: 0: Never went pace on debut.   00
2150 Send It Down [8] 8-11   -- Ash Dee Royale [7] 8-11
8 ran   shthd,1½,4,2,12,2   (K Abdulla)   G Harwood Pulborough, Sussex

3049 RIPLEY HANDICAP (0-35) 3YO+   £1490   2m   Good/Firm 24 -40 Slow   [30]

2802 LOST OPPORTUNITY [2] (J Bethell) 3-7-13(VIS) J Lowe 11/4: 4000041: 3 ch c Final Straw -
Chalumeau (Relko) Fitted with a visor and led home turn, cmftbly, in a slowly run h'cap at
Catterick: first success: eff around 1m tho' seems btr suited by a dist of ground: acts on
fast and soft ground and seems suited by a sharp/easy trk.   18
1533 TREASURE HUNTER [1] (W Pearce) 7-9-10 D Nicholls 6/1: 0-40002: Abs: see 869.   26
*2745 MARINERS DREAM [4] (R Hollinshead) 5-8-13 A Culhane(7) 4/5 FAV: -100113: Ev ch: see 2745. 14
2885 KEY ROYAL [3] (G Calvert) 5-8-8 A Mercer 8/1: 0040204: Made most: see 1737.   05
2819 JIPIJAPA [5] 5-7-7(vis)(7oh) M Fry 12/1: 0030000: Trailed in last: see 2141.   00
5 ran   5,1,3,dist   (Sheikh Mohamed Al Sabah)   J Bethell Chilton, Oxon

---

3050 MACE WORTH APPRENTICES H'CAP 0-60   £4597   1m 2f   Good 62 -08 Slow   [52]

2850 BEN ADHEM [1] (H Candy) 4-8-9 R Teague(5) 8/1: 4-12001: 4 b g Hotfoot - Heaven Chosen
(High Top) Led over 1 out readily, in an app h'cap at Newmarket: seems to do well when fresh
and also won at Newmarket first time out in May: in '85 won at Lingfield: eff at 10/12f and
acts on firm and good and on any track: goes well for a boy.   46
1189 NICORIDGE [4] (G Wragg) 4-8-13 D Surrey(5) 33/1: -000002: Gd late prog after lengthy abs
however has yet to win and seems eff at 7/10f: should find a race.   46
2867 POWER BENDER [2] (G P Gordon) 4-9-6 S Childs(5) 7/4 FAV: 0111123: Ev ch: too soon
after 2867: remarkably consistent: see 2693.   46
2458 DHALEEM [8] (M Stoute) 3-8-7 M A Giles(5) 12/1: -104: Trying 10f for the first time,
fin well: does well when fresh: see 2085.   34
*2877 MOUNT TUMBLEDOWN [5] 5-8-7(5ex) L Jones 16/1: 0-00010: Late prog: see 2877.   24
2693 QUIET RIOT [12] 4-9-6 P Struther(5) 16/1: -010000: Al there: lightly raced since 429.   35
2867 PARIS TRADER [7] 4-7-12 G Bardwell(5) 9/1: 0300200: Much btr over 1m in 2867.   00
2879 NO RESTRAINT [13] 3-8-8 Dale Gibson 10/1: 0431130: Prom 7f, bdr 2704.   00
2566 Dorset Cottage [16] 9-10   2942 Vague Melody [10] 8-12
-2790 Straw Boater [11] 9-4   2925 Tom Forrester [14] 7-10
2879 Farm Club [9] 8-7   1976 Fleet Footed [15] 7-7(2oh)
2945 Reindeer Walk [6] 8-11(9)   2699 Rusty Law [3] 8-7
16 ran   2,4,3,2,½,shthd   (G Kidd)   H Candy Kingstone Warren, Oxon.

3051 GROUP 1 DUBAI CHAMPION STAKES 3YO+   £86750   1m 2f   Good 62 +17 Fast

2917 TRIPTYCH [5] (P Biancone) 4-9-0 A Cruz 4/1: 1232331: 4 b f Riverman - Trillion (Hail
to Reason) Highclass filly: showed remarkable turn of foot to lead 1 out and held on gamely
in Dubai Champion Stks at Newmarket: earlier fin 3rd behind Dancing Brave in the Arc: yet to
fin out of the frame this year, all in Gr races following a win in a Gr 3 race at Longchamp
over 12f: in '85 made history when the first filly to win the Irish 2,000 Guineas and also won
a Gr 3 race at Phoenix Park and fin a fine 2nd in the Oaks: prob acts on any going but fav
by some cut in the ground: remarkably genuine and consistent.   91
2565 CELESTIAL STORM [7] (L Cumani) 3-8-10 R Cochrane 9/1: -132122: Fin strongly, just btn
fine eff. over this shorter trip: continues to improve: see 2565.   91
2822 PARK EXPRESS [9] (J Bolger) 3-8-7 J Reid 3/1 FAV: D112123: Out in front for 1m: another
gd effort but best 2506.   81
2506 BAILLAMONT [10] (F Boutin) 4-9-3 F Head 25/1: -311004: Ran well and prob appreciated
the btr going: in gd form outside this year: see 1355.   83
2735 DAMISTER [2] 4-9-3 Pat Eddery 9/1: -304320: Al there: consistent: see 2735.   82
2565 UNTOLD [4] 3-8-7 W Swinburn 5/2: 1-23130: 2nd 2 out: btr 2202 (firm).   71
2506 DOUBLE BED [1] 3-8-10 Paul Eddery 14/1: 44D2120: Well there 2 out but much btr 2506.   00
+2770 SURE BLADE [8] 3-8-10 B Thomson 100/30: 3-10110: Wk in mkt, fdd: so far best 1m 2770.   00
2867 Tremblant [11] 9-3   3007 Siyah Kalem [3] 9-3   463 Mona Lisa [6] 8-7
11 ran   ¾,4,½,shthd,4,3½   (Alan Clore)   P Biancone Chantilly, France

3052 TOTE CESAREWITCH H'CAP 3YO+   £31128   2m 1f   Good 60 00   [54]

2754 ORANGE HILL [20] (J Tree) 4-7-9(bl) J Fox 20/1: 0422041: 4 b f High Top - Carrot Top
(High Hat) Evidently benefitted from btr grd, led 1 out gamely in the Cesarewitch at Newmarket:
in '85 won at Bath: acts on firm, suited by yldg grd and a gd test of stamina: best in blinkers. 33
*2944 MARLION [21] (Miss S Hall) 5-7-10 N Carlisle 25/1: 2413312: Led 3 out, just btn:
a genuine and consistent sort who stays really well. 32
2754 MISRULE [10] (D Arbuthnot) 4-8-0 A Mackay 11/2 FAV: 120-123: Kept on well, just went
down in a cl fin: stays very well and is running most consistently: see 2467. 35
2809 ACCURACY [24] (G Balding) 5-8-9 J Williams 33/1: 1010004: Led over 2 out, back to her early-
season best: loves soft grd and a test of stamina: see 663. 43
*2974 PATHS SISTER [1] 5-7-8 T Williams 12/1: 0000010: Fin well: see 2974. 27
2944 PEGGY CAROLYN [5] 4-8-6(BL) P Robinson 20/1: 0033030: Running well: see 2944, 964. 35
2809 WITHY BANK [7] 4-8-11 M Birch 16/1: 1300200: Creditable 7th: likes it soft: see 50. 00
+2591 PACTOLUS [22] 3-9-3(4ex) J Reid 17/2: 1231110: Much btr 2591. 00
*2873 SNEAK PREVIEW [18] 6-9-7 W Newnes 17/2: 3-11110: Disapp after 2873. 00
+2882 EL CONQUISTADOR [13] 3-8-7 G Starkey 12/1: 2022210: Best on firm in 2882. 00
2403 FLOYD [3] 6-8-7 A Mcglone 10/1: 4200-20: 2nd 14f, btr 2403. 00
2591 SHIPBOURNE [8] 3-8-5 Pat Eddery 11/1: 3031130: Well bckd: best 2280. 00
2623 Sweet Alexandra [23] 7-7(9oh)   2809 Actinium [2] 8-7
2647 Fedra [9] 8-3   2631 Special Vintage [11] 9-0(bl)
2937 Ibn Majed [15] 7-7   2882 Fishpond [12] 7-9   2311 Ayres Rock [16] 9-2
2220 Milton Burn [6] 8-5   2809 Contester [17] 8-4   58A Meadowbrook [4] 8-7
2809 Harlestone Lake [25] 8-5   2665 Dunston [14] 8-0
2539 The Prudent Prince [19] 9-7
25 ran   ½,hd,1,1,4,hd   (R G McCreery)   J Tree Beckhampton, Wilts.

3053 HOUGHTON STAKES 2YO   £8974   7f   Good 60 -28 Slow

--   SCARLET BLADE [4] (H Cecil) 2-8-11 S Cauthen 100/30: 1: 2 ch c Kris - Red Velvet
(Red God) Made all and held on in a cl fin to the Houghton Stks at Newmarket, first time out:
half brother to 4 winners incl Redcross and Red Rufus: stays 7f well, goes well with forcing
tactics: should stay 1m and does well when fresh. 60
2852 BASHAYER [10] (M Stoute) 2-8-11 W Swinburn 2/1 FAV: 22: Mkt drifter: al there and
just btn: gd effort and sure to find a race soon: see 2852. 59
--   FLOOD MARK [5] (H Cecil) 2-8-11 Paul Eddery 25/1: 3: Outsider but kept on gamely and
just held: dam is a half sister to Royal Palace but only ran once: gd eff over 7f but
looks certain to be suited by much longer dist and should easily find a mdn race. 58
--   INFAMY [9] (L Cumani) 2-8-8 R Cochrane 10/1: 4: Al there, promising first effort from
this daughter of Shirley Heights: will be suited by longer dist than 7f. 48
--   PONDERED BID [12] 2-8-11 J Reid 33/1: 0: Wknd 2 out: seems quite highly regarded and
should stay at least 1m. 50
2782 BIRWAZ [7] 2-8-11 T Quinn 33/1: 00: Will benefit from a drop in class: see 2782. 43
2847 PICK OF THE PACK [6] 2-8-11 M Hills 12/1: 00: Fin creditable 7th: see 2847. 00
--   DOWSING [8] 2-8-11 Pat Eddery 11/4: 0: Well bckd on debut and fin a disapp 10th:
should do btr: cost $400,000. 00
--   Shooting Party [13] 8-11   2847 Wing Park [1] 8-11
--   My Best Lady [3] 8-8   --   Icarus [11] 8-11
12 ran   hd,nk,3,nk,3,1,shthd   (Sheikh Mohammed)   H Cecil Newmarket

3054 BENTINCK STAKES LISTED RACE 3YO+   £9115   5f   Good 60 +19 Fast

-2772 GWYDION [9] (H Cecil) 3-8-12(bl) S Cauthen 8/13 FAV: 3124321: 3 b f Raise A Cup -
Papmiento (Blade) Came with a strong late run when winning a fast run Listed race at Newmarket:
has been running consistently in gd class company since winning over 6f at Newbury: in '85
won at Newmarket and Royal Ascot (Queen Mary Stks): yet to fin out of the frame: stays 7f
but best at 5/6f: btr suited by firm or gd ground than soft: consistent sort who is now best
in blinkers. 73
3012 FAYRUZ [2] (W Ogorman) 3-8-10 Pat Eddery 9/1: 0003122: Nearly made all: much btr effort
after defeat in 3012: see 2833. 70
2947 BUTSOVA [7] (R Armstrong) 3-8-3 W Carson 16/1: 3344223: Kept on, yet to win a race
but is surely due a change of luck: see 431: eff at 5 & 6f. 58
2953 BROADWATER MUSIC [10] (M Tompkins) 5-8-10 R Cochrane 40/1: 0100004: Ran a fine race,
leading 1 out: back to his early season form in 165: needs some cut nowadays? 64
2457 TARIB [6] 3-8-12 A Murray 15/2: 2142120: Btr 2457, 1860 (6f). 59
2672 WELSH NOTE [1] 3-8-3 P Cook 10/1: 4440200: Best 2524, see 408. 42
2833 PETROVICH [5] 4-8-6 B Rouse 8/1: 0033030: Disapp after 2833: see 705. 00
2641 Clantime [3] 8-10   2992 Music Machine [8] 8-10(0)
2672 Glikiaa Mou [4] 8-7(9ex)
10 ran   nk,1½,hd,2,2½   (S S Niarchos)   H Cecil Newmarket

3055 PHANTOM HOUSE H'CAP 3YO+ 0-60   £6591   6f   Good 60 +03 Fast   [60]

+2953 PERFECT TIMING [11] (D Elsworth) 4-9-11(7ex) S Cauthen 8/1: 3210211: 4 b f Comedy Star 69

- Eridantini (Indigenous) Made light of a 7lbs pen when coming with a late run to win a
h'cap at Newmarket under 9-11: earlier won at Ascot & Epsom and has only once been out of the
frame: in '85 also won at Newmarket: best form at 5/6f on gd or fast grd and needs to be held
up: carries weight well and is a credit to her trainer.   69
2668 OUR JOCK [4] (R Smyth) 4-9-5 S Whitworth 10/1: 4104202: Appreciated the easier grd,
led 2 out and continues in gd form: see 2258.   61
2832 ZALATIA [9] (W Jarvis) 3-9-2 Pat Eddery 14/1: 1020043: Fin well, not btn far: back to
her best early season form of 213: seems to prefer some cut in the ground.   59
2437 BATON BOY [13] (M Brittain) 5-7-8(0) A Proud 33/1: 0404434: Cl 4th: due change of luck. 33
2947 DORKING LAD [1] 4-8-7 R Cochrane 25/1: 0000000: Again fin well, back to form: see 1026   42
2947 MATOU [18] 6-9-5 W Carson 14/1: 2D10000: Cl 6th: see 1810.   52
2953 ALMAROSE [5] 3-7-12 R Hills 11/2 FAV: 2-02030: Well bckd fav and btr 2953 (5f).   00
2842 MERDON MELODY [23] 3-8-10(bl) M Rimmer 14/1: 0041030: Chance 2 out: see 2378.   00
*3015 ROYSIA BOY [2] 6-8-5(7ex) Abigail Richards(7) 10/1: 3000110: Quick reappearance after 3015 00
2773 YOUNG JASON [20] 3-7-13 (BL) R Fox :8/1: 223300: Well bckd but fin in the ruck: see 2545. 00
2862 Manimstar [17] 9-8   2956 Dawns Delight [22] 9-5
+2842 Casbah Girl [3] 8-2(9ex)   2921 All Is Forgiven [10] 9-4(bl)
2764 Respect [6] 9-2   1911 Telwaah [14] 9-0(bl)   2731 Ferryman [19] 8-6
2842 Loft Boy [12] 8-1   992 John Patrick [8] 8-1   +2659 Helawe [16] 8-0(bl)
2921 Steel Cygnet [21] 8-0   2842 Zulu Knight [7] 7-13   2981 Corncharm [24] 7-7(2oh)
2256 Puccini [15] 7-7(3oh)
24 ran ½,hd,½,1½,1,shthd,nk   (R Vines)   D Elsworth,Whitsbury, Hants.

Official Going Given As GOOD/SOFT

3056 MURDOSTOUN MAIDEN FILLIES STAKES 2YO   £685   5f   Good 70 -08 Slow

2881 LADYS MANTLE [10] (J Dunlop) 2-8-11 B Thomson 7/1: 0000331: 2 ch f Sunny Clime -
Alchimella (Quadrangle): Made virtually ev yd, holding on well to win a 2yo fillies mdn at
Hamilton: American bred filly who is a half sister to several minor winners in the States:
well suited by this minimum trip, should stay 6f plus next term: acts on gd & fast grnd &
on any track.   34
-- MRS DARLING [11] (W Hastings Bass) 2-8-11 R Lines(3) 11/4 FAV: 2: Well bckd debutant:
chall. on bit below dist, but inexperience cost her the race: half sister to several winners
over a variety of dists & seems certain to be suited by further herself: acts on gd grnd:
should impr & win a race.   30
2781 RIVERSTYLE [12] (M Brittain) 2-8-11 K Darley 14/1: 003: Very cheaply bought filly
who showed her first signs of form here: ran as if another furlong would suit: acts on gd grnd 22
1282 CINDERELLA DEREK [4] (M Mccormack) 2-8-11 N Wharton 5/1: 04: Abs: nicely bckd &
stayed on well fin: cheaply acquired filly who should impr over another furlong: acts on gd grnd 19
-- DEJOTE [8] 2-8-11 G Duffield 6/1: 0: Nicely bckd on debut: prom most & likely to
impr for this run: quite speedily bred filly.   18
3032 PREMIER VIDEO [9] 2-8-11 J Carroll(7) 16/1: 2020020: Close up over ½way: best in 1545. 10
2846 VALENTINE SONG [7] 2-8-11 A Mackay 3/1: 00: Fdd into 7th: btr in 2846 (6f, firm).   00
-- SPRING SUNSET [6] 2-8-11 M Wigham 10/1: 0: Dwelt & never went pace on debut: speedily
bred filly who cost I.R. 22,000 & is sure to do btr than this.   00
1881 Ring Back [2] 8-11   -- Trickle [1] 8-11   2987 Brookhead Girl [5] 8-11
3032 Frivolous Lady [3] 8-11(vis)
12 ran 1,2,1,½,3   (Duke of Marlborough)   J Dunlop Arundel, Sussex

3057 BLACKWOOD SELLING H'CAP (0-25) 3/4YO   £1206   6f   Good 70 -18 Slow   [25]

2981 PADDINGTON BELLE [20] (B Stevens) 3-8-1(vis) G French 14/1: 0003001: 3 b f London Bells -
Grey Fleck (Sing Sing): Nicely bckd & went on 2f out, holding on gamely for her first win in a
selling h'cap at Hamilton (no bid): eff over 5/6f: acts on fast grnd though is well suited by
some give: seems to act on any trk.   08
2602 JERSEY MAID [14] (C Tinkler) 3-9-2(bl) M Birch 7/1 JT FAV: 0000042: Took a drop in
class: ran on well & is capable of winning a seller off her present mark: see 2602 & 1051. 20
3024 LE MANS [18] (J H Wilson) 3-8-8(bl) Julie Bowker(7) 50/1: -000003: Al front rank &
not btn far: easily his best effort this season & seems suited by some give.   12
2816 KING COLE [6] (G Reveley) 4-7-13 M Fry 10/1: 000304D: Never nearer 4th, but disq.
after rider failed to weigh in: probably needs further nowadays: see 1839.   00
2417 WINNING FORMAT [3] 3-8-6(2ow) B Thomson 12/1: 0000200: Fin 5th, placed 4th: best in 2088. 00
2960 SHIRLY ANN [15] 4-8-0 G Bardwell(7) 10/1: /200020: In fair form, but btr in 2960 (1m firm) 00
2863 GOLDEN DISC [11] 4-7-10 L Charnock 8/1: 3024000: Fin 8th: little form since 1610 (C/D). 00
3015 STEVEJAN [16] 4-8-3 J Quinn(5) 10/1: -330400: Fdd into 9th: lightly rcd since early
season: see 65.   00
*2884 ACKAS BOY [1] 4-8-0(5ex) J Lowe 7/1 JT FAV: 0000010: Btr over 5f in 2884 (sharp trk). 00

2681 **Just A Bit** [9] 8-5(bl)(1ow) 2335 **Amplify** [13] 8-1
2884 **Naughty Nighty** [19] 8-3(BL) -- **Sparkling Wit** [10] 10-0
2424 **Rich Bitch** [7] 7-8 1607 **Lochmar** [4] 9-12 2793 **Pink N Perky** [8] 9-2
1627 **Samba Lass** [12] 8-9 2509 **Vintage Lady** [17] 8-1 2884 **Our Mumsie** [5] 7-13
1029 **Sonnendew** [2] 8-2
20 ran ¾,shhd,3,1,shhd,hd (Miss Denise Jarvis) B Stevens Winchester, Hants

3058 BRIADWOOD NURSERY H'CAP 2YO £1629 6f Good 70 -04 Slow [46]

2421 **MILLFAN** [12] (W Musson) 2-8-4 M Wigham 10/1: 23201: 2 b c Taufan - Modern Millie (Milesian): Made virtually ev yd, cmftbly in a nursery h'cap at Hamilton: cheaply bought colt who is a half brother to several winning sprinters: stays 6f well: acts on gd & fast grnd & clearly does well with forcing tactics: seems to act on any trk. 35
•2396 **CROWN JUSTICE** [16] (N Callaghan) 2-8-3 G Duffield 11/2: 012: Dwelt, going on well at the fin & may win a similar event before the seasons end: will stay 7f: see 2396. 27
2281 **JAMES OWL** [15] (W Pearce) 2-7-8 L Charnock 5/1 JT FAV: 0243: Well bckd: al front rank: has been lightly rcd so far & is quite capable of winning a nursery off his present mark: stays 6f: see 701. 12
•2815 **DUNLIN** [4] (S Norton) 2-9-1 J Lowe 16/1: 2310014: Ran on too late: see 2815. 32
•2792 **AFRABELA** [1] 2-8-6 K Darley 16/1: 4020010: Nearest fin: in gd form: see 2792. 22
2392 **SUPREME OPTIMIST** [11] 2-7-8(bl) A Proud 20/1: 3000040: Al up there, kept on well: see 2392. 08
2729 **HEY AMADEUS** [14] 2-8-0 R Lines(3) 8/1: 020030: Never nearer 8th: see 2729. 00
2903 **MR MUMBLES** [13] 2-7-10 M Fry 10/1: 0400000: Fin 9th: best over 5f in 1550 (sharp trk). 00
2859 **FIRMLY ATTACHED** [7] 2-8-7 N Carlisle 10/1: 2000130: No threat: btr in 2859 & 2535. 00
2465 **BORN FREE AGAIN** [9] 2-9-0(bl) E Guest(3) 8/1: 2034400: Btr over 7f in 2035: see 1225, 780 00
•2814 **MEADOWBANK** [18] 2-9-7 D Nicholls 5/1 JT FAV: 00310: Dsptd lead early, eased & fin last: did not run her race here & is worth another ch: see 2814 (C/D). 00
2425 **Just One More** [6] 8-12 3017 **Flair Park** [8] 8-1
2815 **Rose Loubet** [17] 8-2 2919 **Mr Berkeley** [3] 7-13(bl)
2994 **Just A Decoy** [10] 7-7(9oh) 2815 **Brutus** [5] 8-13
17 ran 2,2,nk,hd,¾,1½,¾,½ (G A Wright) W Musson Newmarket

3059 THANKERTON AUCTION STAKES 2YO £685 1m Good 70 -26 Slow

2894 **ANGEL CITY** [7] (J Dunlop) 2-8-11 B Thomson 4/6 FAV: 00421: 2 gr c Carwhite - Kumari (Luthier): Well bckd & led below dist, cmftbly in a 2yo Auction stakes at Hamilton: cheaply bought colt who seems to be impr as he steps up in dist & is certain to stay further than 1m: acts on gd & fast grnd & on any trk. 45
2920 **IN A SPIN** [2] (M Brittain) 2-8-8 K Darley 12/1: 30002: Led after ½way: btr effort: effective over 7/8f on gd & fast grnd: best in 1529. 34
2607 **PRIMETTA PRINCE** [3] (W Pearce) 2-8-11 D Nicholls 14/1: 03: Going on fin & looks certain to be suited by middle dists next season: cost 8,000 gns & is a half brother to a host of winners: seems suited by some give. 30
2522 **CHARLIE MILORD** [6] (E Eldin) 2-8-11 A Mackay 10/3: 04: Eased in class: fin clear of rem but might have done btr with a stronger pace: likely to impr. 29
-- **ANOTHER NONSENSE** [4] 2-8-11 G Duffield 7/1: 0: No real threat on debut: cost 8,200 gns & is a half brother to several winners: stoutly bred & should do btr than this. 16
-- **MIDBADGE** [9] 2-8-11 D D'arcy(7) 20/1: 0: Never went pace & well btn on debut. 00
•2919 **WHITE OF MORN** [8] 2-9-7(bl) W Wharton 10/1: 00410: Btn 2f out: btr over 6f in 2919 (slr) 00
2026 **ROCKETS OAK** [1] 2-8-11 J Quinn(5) 50/1: 00: Led over ½way, sn btn. 00
8 ran 2½,3,nk,7,10 (Cyril Humphris) J Dunlop Arundel, Sussex

3060 SYMINGTON HANDICAP (0-35) 3YO+ £2192 1m Good 70 +15 Fast [34]

•2998 **BIEN DORADO** [9] (B Hanbury) 3-9-5(8ex) A Geran(5) 9/4 FAV: 4000111: 3 ch c Silent Screen - Bonne Note (Bon Mot II): Cmftbly completed his hat trick, led almost 3f out and ran on strongly to win a fast run h'cap at Hamilton: earlier won his mdn at Haydock & a h'cap at Ayr: very eff over 1m on fast & gd grnd: likes a gall trk: in fine form. 41
2497 **ACTUALIZATIONS** [2] (L Cumani) 3-8-10 R Guest 11/2: -034242: Remains a mdn but ran one of her btr races here, keeping on in good style: see 1904 & 1327. 30
2360 **PATCHBURG** [14] (W Haigh) 4-8-12 G Duffield 16/1: 1000003: Btr effort: see 611. 22
2059 **DUELLING** [1] (P Mitchell) 5-9-2(vis) R Carter(5) 12/1: 1410204: Runs well here: see 1619. 22
2671 **RUN BY JOVE** [13] 3-9-0(vis) G French 12/1: 0223000: Quite well bckd but seems to have gone off the boil: much btr over this trip in 1924. 17
2998 **SILLY BOY** [7] 6-8-10 D Nicholls 11/2: 0000030: No luck in running: see 2998. 07
2497 **PHILOSOPHICAL** [10] 3-8-4 M Wigham 8/1: 0301300: Fdd into 7th: best in 2060 (slr). 00
2130 **Priceoflove** [15] 8-1 2887 **Master Music** [6] 7-7(6oh) 2102 **Black River** [16] 7-9(bl)(2ow)(3oh)
2684 **Izzy Gunner** [8] 8-5 2998 **Silver Cannon** [5] 9-5(bl) 2998 **Sillitoe** [18] 8-3
2513 **James Pal** [3] 9-7 2762 **Rustic Track** [4] 7-12 2998 **Flying Ziad** [11] 8-0
2602 **Thirteenth Friday** [17] 7-8(bl)(1ow)(2oh) 2998 **Christmas Cottage** [12] 9-5
18 ran ½,2½,2,4,hd,½ (Mrs Allen Manning) B Hanbury Newmarket

3061 ABINGTON MAIDEN STAKES 3YO £751 1m 4f Good 70 -01 Slow

2996 **RUSSIAN RELATION** [4] (L Cumani) 3-9-0 R Guest 3/1 JT FAV: -031: 3 b c Niniski -

HAMILTON   Monday October 20th   -Cont'd

Fair Cousin (Great Nephew): Impr colt: took command at the dist & qcknd well clear in a
3yo mdn at Hamilton: half brother to several winners abroad: eff over 10/12f & likely to
stay further: acts on gd grnd & on a gall trk: should continue to impr.   46
2520 AIRCRAFTIE [11] (B Hills) 3-8-11 B Thomson 10/1: 3030022: No ch with winner: see 2520.   28
2691 DIRECTLY [3] (G Balding) 3-9-0 J Williams 9/1: -03: Probably stays 12f: see 2691.   28
2734 RED SHOES [1] (W Hern) 3-8-11 R Lines(3) 9/2: 2232244: Well bckd: led over 3f out
but found no extra when hdd: has had plenty of chances: see 2734 & 2304.   25
2520 PRINCESS EMMA [6] 3-8-11 M Birch 10/1: -04230: No extra 2f out: see 2327.   24
2996 MEVAGISSEY [9] 3-9-0 A Geran(5) 3/1 JT FAV: -20: Beat today's winner on his recent
debut and this was obviously not his true running: worth another ch: see 2996 (11f).   21
2900 OUR HERO [8] 3-9-0 G Duffield 9/1: -0020: Front rank 9f: fin 7th: see 2900, 1818.   00
619 DUNAN HILL [10] 3-9-0 J Matthias 11/2: -30: Long abs & needed race: see 619.   00
2853 Mrs Mainwaring [12] 8-11   2395 Breguet [2] 8-11
2152 Sanet [7] 8-11(BL)   2008 Galaxy Princess [5] 8-11
12 ran   8,2,hd,nk,4   (Sheikh Mohammed)   L Cumani Newmarket

CHEPSTOW   Monday October 20th   Lefthand, Galloping Track

Official Going Given As GOOD

3062 GAINSBOROUGH STAKES DIV.1 3YO   £1783   1m   Good/Firm 32 +08 Fast

*2905 IYAMSKI [11] (W Hastings Bass) 3-8-11 G Starkey 13/8 FAV: 2300411: 3 b f Baldski -
Cannoness (Cannonade): In gd form & led inside the final 1f, narrowly in quite fast run
3yo claimer at Chepstow: last time out won a fillies h'cap at Wolverhampton: placed several
times previously: seems equally eff over 7/8f on firm & soft grnd: well suited by a gall trk:
needs to be held up for a late chall.   44
2879 FOUZ [7] (P Cole) 3-9-0(BL) P Waldron 4/1: 3400002: Bl first time: ev ch final 1f:
lightly rcd & has regressed since race 60.   46
2879 FULL OF LIFE [3] (M Pipe) 3-8-1(BL) A Mcglone 6/1: 2200403: Led inside final 3f:
well clear rem: see 1579.   32
2932 OUT OF STOCK [10] (M Blanshard) 3-8-6 J Reid 20/1: 4000044: Never nearer: see 2932.   12
1472 EASTERN PLAYER [5] 3-8-2 C Rutter(3) 33/1: 0000000: Abs: see 1472.   05
2867 LADY LA PAZ [8] 3-8-11 N Adams 10/1: 3031000: Made no show: best in 2459.   14
2473 GAELIC FLUTTER [6] 3-8-12 S Whitworth 13/2: 3010000: Prom over 5f: best in 1436 (7f).   00
2085 HIGH CONDUCT [1] 3-8-2 R Fox 9/1: 4-400: Never in it: see 1756.   00
--   Olympic Eagle [4] 8-2   2414 Arabian Blues [9] 8-4   3029 Court Town [12] 8-6
1350 Yours Grenville [2] 8-6
12 ran   ½,½,10,1,hd   (Mrs Mary Lou Cashman)   W Hastings Bass Newmarket

3063 ASTON PARK H'CAP 3 & 4-Y-O 0-35   £1719   1m 4f Good/Firm 32 -21 Slow   [33]

2937 FOLK DANCE [2] (I Balding) 4-9-9 S O'gorman(7) 10/3: 0204021: 4 b g Alias Smith -
Enchanting Dancer (Nijinsky): Led over 2f out in a 3 & 4yo h'cap at Chepstow: in '85 won a
h'cap at Leicester & Lingfield: very eff at 12f: acts on gd/firm & yld grnd & on any trk.   38
2175 GODS HOPE [13] (R Akehurst) 4-8-4 A Clark 12/1: -000402: Ev ch from 2f out: ran on
& just btn: 4L clear 3rd: stays 12f & acts on gd/firm & soft.   18
2925 NASKRACKER [14] (G Harwood) 3-8-13 G Starkey 11/2: 0020303: Ch over 1f out: see 1559.   26
2671 HOMME DAFFAIRE [11] (G Lewis) 3-9-2 P Waldron 3/1 FAV: -010004: Kept on: stays 12f.   26
2959 ARTISTIC CHAMPION [9] 3-8-8(BL) S Whitworth 14/1: 0010000: Bl first time: best in 1401. 00
2709 MISSELFORE [12] 3-7-7(1oh) S Dawson 10/1: -000300: Led/dsptd lead: seems flattered 1941. 00
2620 NILE LARK [1] 3-8-12 R Fox 9/1: 0-2000: Little form since 1833.   00
-2985 PULSINGH [3] 4-8-5 W Ryan 9/1: 0300020: Led/dsptd lead over 9f: see 2985.   00
2458 Hot Gem [5] 8-13   2879 Miranda Julia [7] 8-7(vis)
2818 Poro Bay [15] 8-0   2164 Marley Roofus [8] 9-4   2988 Sharp Reef [6] 7-7(4oh)
13 ran   hd,4,1½,10,hd   (Mrs John A McDougald)   I Balding Kingsclere, Hants

3064 BIDDESTONE STAKES 2YO UPWARDS   £1651   5f   Good/Firm 32 -03 Slow

2785 ALKAASEH [1] (H T Jones) 3-9-1 R Hills 10/11 FAV: 0-42101: 3 b c Ela-Mana-Mou -
Tigeen (Habitat): Very useful colt: led over 1f out, readily in a 3yo stakes at Chepstow:
earlier won a minor event at Brighton & has been very lightly rcd this term: winning 2yo at
Yarmouth: half brother to a useful Irish sprinter: very eff at 5/6f on fast grnd.   60
3055 RESPECT [4] (D Laing) 3-9-4(BL) G Starkey 11/10: 4124002: Ev ch over 1f out: see 2224, 1878. 50
*2992 NATIVE RULER [2] (C Austin) 5-8-12 A Clark 10/1: 2300313: Led over 3f: gd effort :see 2992. 36
3 ran   4,1.   (Hamdan Al-Maktoum)   H T Jones Newmarket

3065 CALOR GAS LADIES H'CAP 3YO+ 0-35   £2054   6f   Good/Firm 32 -08 Slow   [18]

2715 CONCERT PITCH [9] (B Palling) 7-10-0 Celia Radband(5) 8/1: 0410001: 7 ch g Royal Match -
Ballychord (Ballymoss): Stayed on well to lead close home in a ladies h'cap at Chepstow:
earlier won a h'cap again at Chepstow: in '84 won at Chepstow, Doncaster & Cagnes: eff at
6/7f, but does stay 1m plus: acts on firm & soft grnd & runs well here.   25
2837 LUCKY STARKIST [3] (R Holder) 4-9-5 Dawn Harris(5) 14/1: 0004002: Led well over 1f
out: just caught: gd effort: see 2207, 1213.   12

                                        893

2970 ZILLEBEKE [2] (W Brooks) 3-10-0 Kim Allison(5) 16/1: -003303: Sn prom: quite
consistent: may stay further than 6f: see 2367.   17
2960 HACHIMITSU [1] (S Mellor) 3-9-0(1ow) Alison Begley(0) 20/1: 0001034: Al there: best 1937. 02
2294 WYKEHAMIST [11] 3-10-0 Sue Brown(5) 16/1: -0000: Late hdway: lightly rcd & no
form previously: eff at 6f on gd/firm.   16
2842 CRONKS QUALITY [20] 3-10-13 Princess Anne(5) 9/1: 0030300: Led over 4f: best 2258(easy trk).23
*2981 REVEILLE [5] 4-11-8 Gay Arber(5) 3/1 FAV: 0030210: Prom, btr 2981.   00
2929 WIZZARD MAGIC [12] 3-9-4(bl)(5ow) Yvonne Haynes 9/1: -032020: Late hdway: see 2929 (stks). 00
*2370 MISS METAL WOODS [10] 4-8-12 Dana Mellor 5/1: 0400010: Abs since much btr 2370.   00
2544 PERSIAN PERSON [15] 4-8-10 Miss Z Davison(5) 9/1: -04000: Active in market:
lightly raced since 844.   00
2898 Winsong Melody [7] 9-4   2601 Maiden Bidder [13] 9-3
2282 Sahara Shadow [16] 9-5   993 Little Dimple [4] 9-3(7ow)
2575 Gleadhill Park [6] 9-2(bl)   2715 Monstrosa [19] 9-2(1ow)
2906 Come To The Ball [18] 10-0   2836 Bee Kay Ess [8] 8-9
*2966 Thatchville [14] 10-2(8ex)   2981 Hatching [17] 8-11(vis)
20 ran   1,2,½,shhd,2½   (D Egan)   B Palling Cowbridge

3066 GAINSBOROUGH STAKES DIV.2 3YO   £1872   1m   Good/Firm 32 +01 Fast

2684 EAGLE DESTINY [12] (I Balding) 3-8-4 A Clark 5/1: 0212001: 3 br g Storm Bird -
Club Savoy (Grey Dawn II): Led over 1f out, under press in a 3yo claimer at Chepstow: earlier
successful in a Pontefract mdn: best form over 1m & probably acts on any grnd.   44
2879 SWIFTS PAL [9] (G Lewis) 3-9-0(BL) P Waldron 8/1: 0410002: Bl first time & made most.   48
2617 HALO HATCH [11] (K Brassey) 3-8-12(bl) S Whitworth 8/1: 0012003: Al there: best in 1971. 40
2593 GARDINIA LAD [1] (D Haydn Jones) 3-8-4 D Williams(7) 12/1: -04: Sn prom: btr effort
from this very lightly rcd gelding: brother to a winning plater: acts on gd/firm.   22
2851 JAZETAS [4] 3-9-0 G Starkey 11/8 FAV: 4040200: Well bckd: again below his early
season best: see 2713.   26
2810 SITZCARRALDO [2] 3-8-4 L Jones(4) 10/1: 2002000: Stiff task: best 2319 (soft).   12
*880 EMPIRE BLUE [6] 3-9-0(bl) K Powdrell 6/1: 240-010: Very long abs & t.o: see 880.   00
2991 Everyinchalady [10] 8-3   2928 Auto Elegance [5] 8-1
2929 Whos That Girl [8] 8-4   2931 Rare Wind [7] 8-5
2931 Popsis Pom Pom [3] 7-13   2793 Parijoun [13] 8-6(3ow)
13 ran   2½,2½,5,3,2½   (Sheikh Mohammed)   I Balding Kingsclere, Hants

3067 WHITSBURY MANOR STAKES 2YO   £1415   7f   Good/Firm 32 +03 Fast

2645 GRIMESGILL USA [16] (M Stoute) 2-8-11 A Kimberley 6/1: 31: 2 b c Northern Baby -
Mild Deception (Buckpasser): Promising colt: led over 2f out, readily in quite fast run 2yo
stakes at Chepstow: eff at 7f, should be well suited by 1m & further: acts on a sound surface
& a gall trk: on the up grade.   55
-- JUILLIARD [18] (M Dickinson) 2-8-6 J Reid 10/1: 2: Ev ch inside final 2f: prom debut
from this $925,000 yearling: dam a prolific winner: eff at 7f, should stay 1m: acts on gd/
firm grnd & should certainly find a race.   40
*2716 ASSULTAN [12] (H T Jones) 2-9-4 R Hills 5/1: 13: Al there: gd effort: see 2716.   46
*2889 ZARBYEV [9] (G Harwood) 2-9-4 G Starkey 11/10 FAV: 3214: Hvly bckd but found no
extra final 1f: much btr in 2889.   40
2574 ARADU [7] 2-8-11 T Lucas 5/1: 00: Never nearer, but is making impr: quite cheaply
acquired colt who should be suited by 1m & further: acts on a sound surface.   32
-- SPLASH ON [15] 2-8-6 M A Giles(7) 16/1: 0: Gd late hdway on racecourse debut: looks
sure to impr & was wk in mkt here: expensive purchase who should be suited by 1m: acts on gd/firm 22
2961 GOODWYNS LAD [5] 2-8-11 W Woods(3) 20/1: 00: Speed most: impr effort: acts on gd/firm.   26
1531 Bronze Runner [8] 8-11   2407 Marley Monarch [11] 8-11
2547 Sahood [13] 8-11   2179 Birchgrove Central [3] 8-11
2771 Gwynras [4] 8-11   2983 Moulas [17] 8-11   1948 Triple Entente [14] 8-11
-- Scarlet Crest [2] 8-6   2869 Grunidad [6] 8-11   2782 Phelioff [10] 8-11
17 ran   3,3,3,shhd,2½   (Marshall W Jenney)   M Stoute Newmarket

---

LEICESTER   Monday October 20th   Righthand, Stiff, Galloping Track

Official Going Given As GOOD/FIRM

3068 HARE MAIDEN FILLIES STAKES 2YO DIV I   £964   7f   Good/Firm 29 -06 Slow

2215 LIZZY HARE [6] (L Cumani) 2-8-11 R Cochrane 15/2: 01: 2 b f L'Enjoleur - Fleur De
Mont (Graustark): Impr filly: led over 4f & again inside final 1f, ridden out in a 2yo
fillies mdn at Leicester: related to several winners: eff at 7f, should be suited by 1m:
acts on gd/firm grnd & a gall trk.   47
2574 STRELLILANE [14] (L Piggott) 2-8-11 B Crossley 7/1: 2: Led after 4f & kept on well:
impr filly who is clearly effective over a stiff 7f: acts on gd/firm grnd & should find a race. 44
-- HOLD DEAR [9] (H Cecil) 2-8-11 S Cauthen 11/4 FAV: 3: Uneasy fav: slowly away but
had ev ch final 1f: half sister to 3 winners, notably the smart French performer River Mist:
should be suited by 1m & can impr: acts on gd/firm.   43
-- RUWIYDA [2] (A Stewart) 2-8-11 M Roberts 14/1: 4: Al prom, stayed: U.S. bred filly who
acts on gd/firm grnd & a gall trk: will be well suited by another furlong.   42

-- JOANIES STYLE [10] 2-8-11 Gay Kelleway(3) 5/1: 0: Ch 2f out: U.S. bred filly who
should do btr: acts on a sound surface & stays 7f.   41
2494 SOME DREAM [11] 2-8-11 P Robinson 14/1: 400: No show: best 2080 (6f).   25
-- TROPICAL FLOWER [3] 2-8-11 W Carson 9/2: 0: Early speed on debut: half sister to
winning 3yo Artful Day & is bred to stay todays trip.   00
2118 ZITELLA [2] 2-8-11 Pat Eddery 6/1: 000: Prom over 4f: needed race? see 2118, 1632.   00
1883 St Wendred [12] 8-11   -- Petalouda [5] 8-11   2095 Hush Kit [7] 8-11
722 Our Lena [8] 8-11   -- Tuneful Flutter [15] 8-11
-- Dreemskerry [4] 8-11
14 ran   1,hd,½,shhd,10   (Fittocks Stud Ltd)   L Cumani Newmarket

3069 STOAT SELLING STAKES 2YO   £850   1m 2f   Good/Firm 29 -32 Slow

2700 FOLLY GALE [14] (C Reavey) 2-8-8 G Dickie 10/1: 000001: 2 b f Strong Gale - Sans
Sabot (Whistler): Dropped to selling company: led well over 1f out, readily in a slow run
2yo seller at Leicester (no bid): lightly rcd & little form previously but was well suited
by todays 10f trip: half sister to several winners: acts on gd/firm grnd & a gall trk.   20
2806 UNOS PET [2] (K Stone) 2-8-11 P Burke(7) 33/1: 3300002: Ev ch over 1f out: gd effort
& stays 10f: best effort since 94.   17
2990 NATIONS ROSE [11] (R Stubbs) 2-8-8 J H Brown(5) 16/1: 040403: Kept on final 1f
& showed impr form over todays lngr trip: see 2801.   13
2817 RIPSTER [10] (R Stubbs) 2-8-11(BL) S Cauthen 12/1: 0040034: Bl first time & led 1m:
seems to stay 10f: acts on gd/firm grnd: see 1846.   14
2841 PENNY FORUM [6] 2-8-11 M Hills 10/3: 000: Led 2f out: best effort yet: suited by 10f
& gd/firm: see 2841.   10
-- HEMMINGFORD GREY [7] 2-8-8 P Brette(7) 6/4 FAV: 0: Gambled from 5/1: no extra over
1f out on debut: quite cheaply acquired filly who is a half sister to several winners: bred
to be suited by middle dists & is one to keep an eye on in this grade.   05
2872 BLOW FOR HOME [18] 2-8-11 R Cochrane 11/2: 0020240: Ev ch inside final 2f: btr 2724.   00
2841 IVE NO IDEA [13] 2-8-8 T Williams 8/1: 0000: Fdd over 2f out: no form in 4 outings
from this sister to fair h'capper Travelguard.   00
2814 Fireiron [16] 8-8   2872 Finlux Design [1] 8-11(BL)
2270 Home Jesta [15] 8-11   2801 Acertainhit [4] 8-11   2990 Magnolia Dancer [17] 8-11
2990 No Concern [3] 8-11   3016 Tokanda [8] 8-11(bl)   2990 Going Greek [12] 8-8
2990 Magnolia Princess [9] 8-8   2990 Tootsie Jay [5] 8-8(VIS)
18 ran   2½,½,1,2,1,2½   (Mrs A M Upsdell)   C Reavey Holyport, Berks

3070 BADGER EBF STAKES 3YO   £3713   1m   Good/Firm 29 +08 Fast

2867 WAAJIB [9] (A Stewart) 3-8-11 M Roberts 8/11 FAV: 2133201: 3 b c Try My Best -
Coryana (Sassafras): Useful colt: hvly bckd & led 2f out, not extended in quite fast run
3yo stakes at Leicester: last time out a gd 7th in the Cambridgeshire from a poor draw &
has been tremendously consistent this season: won his mdn at Yarmouth in July: very eff
at 1m & stays 10f: well suited by fast grnd & a gall trk.   50
2784 ROYAL TROUBADOR [12] (B Hills) 3-8-11(vis) M Hills 11/1: 0004302: Mkt drifter: ev ch
over 1f out: gd effort at the weights & wears a visor nowadays: see 2294.   44
2867 CHIEF PAL [3] (P Walwyn) 3-8-11 Paul Eddery 9/2: 2340203: Sn prom: btr 2612.   40
2650 SHANNON VALE [6] (J Dunlop) 3-9-2 W Carson 9/2: 01-004: Led over 6f: twice below 2458.   35
334 RETRIEVE [4] 3-8-11 S Cauthen 7/1: -00: Very long abs: prom most & almost certainly
needed race: see 334.   25
2810 SUNNY MATCH [7] 3-8-8 R Cochrane 25/1: 0200200: Very stiff task: best in 2570.   19
2931 Cheerful Times [8] 8-11   2650 Sparky Lad [10] 9-2
2408 Almutanabbi [5] 8-11   2991 Papun [13] 8-8   -- Time Warp [11] 8-8
2793 Gretas Song [2] 8-8   -- High Velocity [1] 8-8
13 ran   1½,2,5,2,1   (Hamdan Al-Maktoum)   A Stewart Newmarket

3071 RABBIT HANDICAP STAKES 3YO+ 0-35   £2550   1m 4f Good/Firm 29 -14 Slow   [32]

2959 HEIGHT OF SUMMER [4] (D Arbuthnot) 5-7-11(1ow) B Crossley 8/1: 3001341: 5 b g Shirley
Heights - Midsummer Time (Midsummer Night II): In gd form & led over 2f out, winning rather
cleverly by a head in a h'cap at Leicester: earlier won a h'cap at Beverley: in '85 won again
at Beverley: very eff at 12f on gd & fast grnd & a stiff trk.   09
2699 JOLI WASFI [2] (M Haynes) 5-8-6(bl) T Williams 8/1: 0000002: Made most: came again
final 1f & just btn: best effort this term: see 2699.   17
2591 HARBOUR BAZAAR [9] (R Simpson) 6-8-3 W Newnes 15/2: 3D31203: Nearest fin: see 2432 (13f).09
2676 MORICA [8] (J Dunlop) 3-9-7 W Carson 5/2: 1-40404: Ev ch 2f out: btr in 2676 (10f).   27
2746 DONOR [7] 4-8-13(VIS) N Day 25/1: 2000000: Dsptd lead over 2f out: visored first
time today: see 2622 (1m).   05
2549 MANABEL [1] 4-8-0 L Riggio(7) 16/1: 0002440: Fdd over 2f out: btr 2549 (1m).   00
2985 Andrea Dawn [5] 8-3   356 Resha [6] 8-0(3ow)
8 ran   hd,3,4,4,1½   (R Crutchley)   D Arbuthnot Compton, Berks

3072 HEDGEHOG STAKES 2YO   £3542   6f   Good/Firm 29 +01 Fast

2941 RIOT BRIGADE [4] (C Brittain) 2-9-0 Pat Eddery 11/4: 3314041: 2 ch c Try My Best -
Lady R B (Gunshot): Useful colt: led after 2f & cmftbly made rest in a 2yo stakes at

Leicester: earlier successful in a mdn at Yarmouth: very eff over todays 6f trip & does not
seem to stay 7f at present: half brother to several winners: suited by fast grnd & a gall trk.   50
*2804 FOURWALK [6] (N Macauley) 2-9-7 S Cauthen 4/1: 0320012: Early ldr & kept on well:
fine effort at the weights & is in grand form: see 2804: can win again soon.   52
2859 DOMINO FIRE [2] (J Dunlop) 2-8-10 W Carson 10/3: 1220403: Prom most, ev ch: see 985.   29
2618 TOUGH N GENTLE [7] (L Piggott) 2-9-4 R Cochrane 2/1 FAV: 3120234: Hvly bckd: below
his best: has been very busy this season: see 2511.   35
2871 FRIMLEY PARKSON [1] 2-8-11 D Price 50/1: 00: Rank outsider, no show.   00
+136 LAWNSWOOD LAD [5] 2-8-13 S Perks 14/1: 410: Dwelt: no show: abs since 136.   00

834 Thats Motoring   [3] 8-8
7 ran   1,5,½,12,10   (Philip Noble)   C Brittain Newmarket

3073 HARE MAIDEN FILLIES STAKES 2YO DIV II   £1244   7f   Good/Firm 29 +02 Fast

-- AMBER COOKIE [4] (H Candy) 2-8-11 W Newnes 14/1: 1: 2 ch f Master Willie - Maryland
Cookie (Bold Hour): Promising filly: first time out, led appr. final 1f when a ready 3L winner
of a 2yo fillies mdn at Leicester: dam was a very speedy sort: well suited by 7f, should stay
1m: acts on gd/firm grnd & a stiff trk: can rate more highly.   52
2788 BRONZEWING [10] (J Dunlop) 2-8-11 Pat Eddery 8/11 FAV: 32: Hvly bckd: switched over
1f out but no ch with winner: stays 7f & is sure to find a race: see 2788.   46
2774 BRIDGET OBIRD [18] (I Balding) 2-8-11 M Hills 14/1: 03: Ch over 1f out: on the up grade:
stays 7f: see 2771.   44
2531 ACHNAHUAIGH [3] (P Walwyn) 2-8-11 Paul Eddery 20/1: 0204: Made much: gd effort:
handles any trk: see 2368.   43
-- SPIRE [8] 2-8-11 W Carson 14/1: 0: Al prom on debut: promising effort from this half
sister to numerous winners incl. the smart Church Parade & Leading Star: sure to be well
suited by middle dists next season & is the type to win races.   39
2658 LORI GARBACZ [12] 2-8-11 W R Swinburn 33/1: 000: Gd late hdway: should be suited by
1m: acts on gd/firm grnd & a gall trk.   36
-- WORKING MODEL [7] 2-8-11 T Quinn 14/1: 0: Mkt drifter: never nearer & impr expected:
cost 30,000 gns as a yearling & is a half sister to several winners: will be suited by 1m
& further.   00
-- PRIDE OF PARIS [14] 2-8-11 R Cochrane 9/1: 0: Never nearer on debut: half sister to
numerous winners & bred to stay 1m plus.   00
-- GUARD ROOM [16] 2-8-11 S Cauthen 6/1: 0: Op. 5/2: no threat: half sister to a
winning 2yo.   00
-2812 ACT OF TREASON [13] 2-8-11 M Roberts 8/1: 03020: Fdd inside final 2f: well below 2812(6f). 00
-- Fah So Lah [5] 8-11   2308 Tabareek [1] 8-11   -- Alhamiya [9] 8-11
2707 Amber Espana [19] 8-11   -- First Applause [2] 8-11
-- Just Something [17] 8-11   2967 Kumzar [6] 8-11
-- Lady Lax [20] 8-11   -- Redwood Eve [11] 8-11 3034 Tell Me Now [15] 8-11
20 ran   3,1,½,1½,1½   (R Barnett)   H Candy Kingstone Warren, Oxon

3074 HARE MAIDEN FILLIES STAKES 2YO DIV I   £964   7f   Good/Firm 29 +01 Fast

2675 SANNOX BAY [1] (H Cecil) 2-8-11 S Cauthen 10/11 FAV: 01: 2 b f Shirley Heights -
Sunderland (Dancer's Image): Useful, impr filly: well bckd & led inside final 1f, cmftbly
in a 2yo fillies mdn at Leicester: dam a winner at 2 years over sprint dists: eff at 7f,
should be suited by 1m: acts on gd/firm grnd & a stiff trk: on the up grade.   49
2838 BETTY JANE [8] (J Dunlop) 2-8-11 P Cook 14/1: 42: Ran on well final 2f & is fast
impr: will be well suited by 1m & further: cheaply acquired but looks sure to find a race.   47
2651 SILVERCOAST [6] (H T Jones) 2-8-11 A Murray 10/3: 033: Made most: stays 7f: see 2651.   44
2989 SPY GIFT [11] (M Stoute) 2-8-11(VIS) W R Swinburn 17/1: 033044: Visored first time:
ch over 1f out: see 2989.   40
1752 BENGUELA [10] 2-8-11 Pat Eddery 5/1: 340: Abs: no extra over 1f out: see 1021 (6f).   36
2894 DAFFODIL [5] 2-8-11 C Nutter 16/1: 00: Speed most: btr effort: half sister to smart
2yo Picatrix & also useful h'capper Forward Rally: on the up grade.   24
-- Cryptic [13] 8-11   2878 Rahwah [7] 8-11   -- Canary Wharf [3] 8-11
2494 Heaven Only Knows [2] 8-11   2703 Water Of Love [9] 8-11
2080 Dahab [14] 8-11   2803 Jans Contessa [4] 8-11
13 ran   ½,1,1½,2,6   (Dr Carlo Vittadini)   H Cecil Newmarket

Official Going Given As GOOD/FIRM

3075 EBF SOAR MAIDEN STAKES DIV.1 2YO   £2008   7f   Firm 16 +04 Fast

2878 STUBBLE FIRE [2] (J Dunlop) 2-9-0 W Carson 25/1: 01: 2 ch c Thatch - Explosive
(Explodent): Tailed off on his recent debut & showed much impr form here, gamely making all
in quite a fast run 2yo mdn at Leicester: half brother to fair middle dist winner Elplotino:
stays 7f well & will be suited by 1m plus next season: acts on fast grnd & on a gall trk:
clearly does well with forcing tactics & is likely to impr further.   46
2847 IRISH SAILOR [10] (Pat Mitchell) 2-9-0 J Reid 11/1: 3042: Another gd effort: al prom
& was only just denied: stays 7f well: see 2847 & 2205.   44

2119 TASJIL [7] (C Benstead) 2-9-0 B Rouse 25/1: 4003: Not btn far: stays 7f well & will
be suited by further next season: see 1518 & 434.   42
2574 ANUBI [8] (L Cumani) 2-9-0 R Cochrane 11/2: 04: Fin best of all & is certain to
rate more highly: will be suited by middle dists next season: acts on fast grnd: see 2574.   39
2804 GENERAL MEILLAND [3] 2-9-0 W R Swinburn 10/1: 03330: Al prom: consistent sort: see 2716   36
--   RAW ENERGY [9] 2-9-0 B Thomson 25/1: 0: Prom most on debut: ignored in the mkt but
this was quite a promising debut from this full brother to useful French sprinter Sigy:
acts on fast grnd & on a gall trk: likely to impr.   35
--   SHER SHAH [11] 2-9-0 S Cauthen 4/6 FAV: 0: Hvly bckd debutant: front rank till no
extra below dist: $80,000 yearling who is bred to be suited by middle dists: clearly quite
well regarded & should do much btr than this.   30+
1780 CELCIUS [12] 2-9-0 Pat Eddery 8/1: 00: Fdd into 8th: abs since 1780.   00
2852 Prince Newport [6] 9-0   2847 Riverboat Party [4] 9-0
--   Alynzona [13] 9-0   2494 King Among Kings [5] 9-0
1731 Doubly Great [14] 9-0   2179 Millpond Boy [1] 9-0
14 ran   hd,¾,1½,1½,nk,1½   (Duke of Marlborough)   J Dunlop Arundel, Sussex

3076 WHISSENDINE SELL.H'CAP 3&4-Y-O 0-25   £784   1m 2f Firm 16 -40 Slow   [8]

2984 KIKI STAR [3] (R Hodges) 4-9-7 W Carson 10/1: 0000001: 4 b f Some Hand - Princess Story
(Prince de Galles): Led below dist & was pushed out to win a slowly run selling h'cap at
Leicester (bought in 1,500 gns): successful at Newmarket (2) & Leicester last season, when
trained by M Usher: best form over 10/12f on fast grnd: well suited by a stiff, gall trk.   10
2317 VISTULE [2] (R Simpson) 4-9-7 S Whitworth 12/1: 4-00002: Ran on well: see 1873.   06
2800 APPRECIATIVE [11] (P Walwyn) 3-9-5(vis) Paul Eddery 11/2: 0-00003: Led early, ran
on same pace: beginning to show a little form: eff over 10/11f on gd/firm: see 2800.   06
2787 LETOILE DU PALAIS [12] (B Stevens) 4-9-7 S P Bloomfield 20/1: 4042434: Still a maiden:see 2309. 00.
3030 JALOME [16] 4-8-8 D Mckeown 3/1 FAV: 0000400: Well bckd: one-paced: see 2789.   00
2863 SWEET GEMMA [7] 4-9-7 D J Williams(7) 10/1: 0230040: Not the best of runs: see 1081.   00
2714 JUBILEE JAMBOREE [5] 3-9-4 P Robinson 10/1: 0300300: Led after ½way: fdd into 7th.   00
2238 SLEEPLINE DUCHESS [19] 3-9-5 M Miller 10/1: 0020030: Never nearer 8th: see 2238 (7f)
and 1656 (10f).   00
2017 Regal Sam [6] 9-10   2787 Sirtaki Dancer [14] 9-3
2342 Toda Forca Avanti [8] 9-3   2876 Sirdar Flyer [13] 9-4(bl)
727 Maundy Gift [10] 9-5   1686 Montbergis [1] 9-2   2597 Name The Day [4] 8-13
1340 Tyrannise [15] 8-12   2560 Georgian Rose [9] 8-10(vis)
17 ran   1½,2,½,½,½,3,1½   (J Hoare)   R Hodges Charlton Adam, Somerset

3077 WREAKE FILLIES EBF STAKES 3YO   £3267   1m   Firm 16 +17 Fast

*2931 SKEAN [14] (G Harwood) 3-8-7, G Starkey 5/2 FAV: 0022211: 3 ch f Kris - Kate's Intent
(Intentionally): Ran on well under press to lead close home in a fast run 3yo fillies stakes
at Leicester: recently broke her duck in a mdn at Lingfield: seems best over 7/8f though
should stay further: acts on gd & fast grnd & on any trk: half sister to the smart duo
Godswalk and Kabylia: in gd form & should go on to win a h'cap.   49
2765 SOMETHING CASUAL [13] (A Hide) 3-8-8(vis) R Guest 9/1: 3444402: Made most: btr effort
but has proved expensive to follow this season: see 1655 and 386.   47
2973 HOOKED BID [2] (J Dunlop) 3-8-8 W Carson 4/1: 0031323: Kept on well & cmftbly beat
the rem: in gd form at present: see 2973 & 2532.   44
2856 MAIYAASAH [4] (L Cumani) 3-8-5 R Cochrane 11/4: -224: Never nearer after a slow
start: btr than this & is worth another ch: see 2856 & 2532.   26
2905 ANNABELLINA [9] 3-8-5 Pat Eddery 10/1: 4230030: Front rank most, wknd: see 2076.   18
2704 MALIN FLEET [10] 3-8-5 M Hughes(7) 33/1: -00: Lightly rcd filly: al mid-div.   17
1469 SHAKANA [6] 3-8-5 J Reid 8/1: 2-000: Abs: fdd into 8th: has been very lightly rcd
this term & has yet to reproduce her juvenile form: see 1043.   00
2550 Sunday Chimes [12] 8-6(1ow)   2991 Do Run Do [1] 8-5
2406 Corn Noil [3] 8-7   2973 Molly Partridge [7] 8-7
2593 Horton Glory [11] 8-5
12 ran   1,1½,8,4,hd,1½,nk   (Mrs J A Chandler)   G Harwood Pulborough, Sussex

3078 STEWARDS HANDICAP STAKES 3YO+ 0-35   £3034   1m   Firm 16 -10 Slow   [35]

3029 SHARONS ROYALE [18] (R Whitaker) 3-8-10 (5ex) K Bradshaw(5) 12/1: 4144141: 3 ch g Royal Match-
Rose Ambler (Amber Rama) In gd form & went on 2f out, running on strongly to win a h'cap at
Leicester: has been busy lately, a fortnight ago won a similar event at Newcastle: earlier won
his mdn at Hamilton: best form over 1m on gd & fast grnd: likes a stiff, gall trk.   30
2867 XHAI [23] (M Tompkins) 4-9-9 M Rimmer 16/1: 0200002: Ran on well: best effort for
sometime & is well h'capped on this basis: best form: see 649 & 171.   34
2816 NO CREDIBILITY [14] (B Richmond) 4-8-7 M Roberts 33/1: -000003: Ran his best race
this season here: al prom & not btn far: won a small race at Lingfield last season: eff
over 7/8f & is at his best on a sound surface.   16
2545 EVERY EFFORT [22] (R Holder) 4-9-1 B Thomson 11/1: 4120004: Not btn that far: see 1781.   23
2876 FAIR ATLANTA [2] 3-8-7 R Street 12/1: 1003030: Running well: see 2459 & 505.   19
2762 GOLDEN BEAU [13] 4-8-11 R Cochrane 33/1: 0123000: Late prog: best in 2189 (sharp trk).   17
2726 REMINISCING [7] 3-8-2 W Newnes 20/1: -2000: Fin 7th: best over 10f in 1749.   00

-2072 HIGHLAND IMAGE [21] 4-9-1 J Reid 10/1: 30-0020: Wknd into 8th: btr over 7f in 2072.   00
2945 FORMATUNE [11] 4-9-1(bl) Pat Eddery 11/2: 3000000: Front rank early: btr over 7f in 2773   00
2891 SHARP SHOT [1] 5-8-7 W Carson 7/2 FAV: -000020: Much closer to todays winner in 2891.   00

-- Lady Coombe [5] 9-8	2861 Three Bells [20] 8-9	-- Flower Of Tintern [3] 10-0
*2544 Ashley Rocket [12] 9-11		2945 Creeager [8] 9-6
2381 Sovereign Love [16] 9-3		2928 Strive [9] 8-12
970 Cbm Girl [15] 8-11	2719 Rare Sound [19] 8-11	2797 Bay Presto [6] 8-9
2876 First Rank [4] 8-8(BL)		1885.On Impulse [17] 8-3
2581 Tarrakan [10] 8-3		
23 ran 1½,1,hd,½,½,shhd,nk	(W W Birch)	R Whitaker Wetherby, Yorks

3079 WYMESWOLD CLAIMING STAKES 2YO   £2491   6f   Firm 16 +01 Fast

-2989 TIMESWITCH [2] (W O'gorman) 2-9-3 Pat Eddery 11/8 FAV: 0220021: 2 ch c Mechizado-
On Second Thought (Raise A Native): Finally got off the mark, again well bckd & cmftbly made
all in a 2yo claiming stakes at Leicester: had found one too good 4 times previously over
various dists & seems equally eff between 5/6f & 1m: half brother to winning juvenile Indigo
Jones: acts on gd & fast grnd & on any trk: the type to impr now he has got his head in front
& can win again.   45
3017 WHISTLING WONDER [20] (M Brittain) 2-8-9 A Munro(7) 7/1: 0002032: Clear of rem: see 3017.34
2829 MILL TRIP [17] (M Prescott) 2-8-13 C Nutter 12/1: 030203: Ran on too late: best
over 7f here in 2707.   26
2927 BOLD HIDEAWAY [9] (R Sheather) 2-8-3 Dale Gibson(7) 33/1: 0402004: Never nearer: see 2608 15
2899 STARS IN MOTION [5] 2-8-7 J Reid 14/1: 0300020: Btr over 6f in 2899: see 1675.   13
2935 GOOD TIME GIRL [8] 2-8-10 G Starkey 9/1: 1120230: Prom over ½way: fin 7th: see 2922.   15
2922 ROUGH DANCE [13] 2-9-3(bl) R Cochrane 10/1: 042430: No show: btr over this trip in 2341.   00
2494 VORTRACK [4] 2-9-3 Paul Eddery 8/1: 0000: Active in mkt: fin 9th: best 2341(7f).   00

3031 Highland Laird [10] 9-3(bl)		3032 Tahard [15] 8-3
2698 Atrayu [7] 8-10	2272 Bloffa [11] 8-6	-- Recorded Time [6] 8-6
2872 Princess Michico [3] 8-4		2889 Danse Arabe [16] 8-3
2829 Pearlitic [1] 8-3(bl)	2511 Vaigly Yellow [12] 8-3	
858 Young Fool [14] 8-4(1ow)		2178 Meath Princess [18] 8-2
2812 Castillito [19] 8-0		
20 ran 1,4,nk,2½,½	(Times of Wigan)	W O'gorman Newmarket

3080 EBF SOAR MAIDEN STAKES DIV II 2YO   £1969   7f   Firm 16 -08 Slow

-- PRIMITIVE RISING [9] (H Cecil) 2-9-0 S Cauthen 3/1 FAV: 1: 2 b c Raise A Man -
Periquito (Olden Times): Uneasy fav on his debut but scored an impressive win, led dist &
sn qcknd clear in a 2yo mdn at Leicester: cost $17,500 gns as a yearling: clearly very eff
over 7f & seems sure to stay further: acts on fast grnd & on a gall trk: can only impr &
should go on to btr things.   48
2108 KIROWAN [2] (G Huffer) 2-9-0 M Miller 6/1: 032: Broke well & made most: not pace of
winner but fin clear of rem: stays 7f: should find a small race: see 1928.   42
2645 CLOPTON [7] (M Ryan) 2-9-0 P Robinson 25/1: 003: Showed impr form here: al close up:
seemed well suited by this stiffer trk: half brother to a couple of winning sprinters: eff
over 7f on fast grnd.   34
2479 MUSICAL BELLS [16] (L Piggott) 2-9-0 B Crossley 20/1: 004004: No extra below dist: see 1573 30
1239 RELKOORA [4] 2-9-0 W Newnes 33/1: 00: Long abs & lack of fitness told below dist:
12,000 gns yearling who is closely related to several winners abroad: acts on fast grnd:
should do better.   27
-- MAKSOUD [5] 2-9-0 M Roberts 7/1: 0: Front rank most on debut: quietly fancied & should
be btr for this run: 70,000 gns yearling who seems suited by fast grnd.   23
-- TRANBY CROFT [13] 2-9-0 R Cochrane 7/1: 0: Prom over ½way on racecourse debut: half
brother to winning juvenile No Fluke: should do btr than this.   16
-- HAJJI BABA [14] 2-9-0 W Carson 5/1: 0: Did not run as well as expected but should impr
for this initial effort: 14,000 gns yearling who is a half brother to several winners: likely
to be suited by middle dists next term.   00
1948 PLANE [6] 2-9-0(BL) Pat Eddery 7/1: 400: Bl first time: front rank most, eased: see 1529.   00

577 Bold As Bold [12] 9-0	2957 Boy Jamie [8] 9-0	2646 Lovenko [15] 9-0
2645 Higham Broke [11] 9-0	2878 Roches [3] 9-0	2841 San Juan Song [10] 9-0
-- St Clair Charger [1] 9-0		
16 ran 2½,4,2,1½,2,½,½,hd,2	(S S Niarchos)	H Cecil Newmarket

3081 WYMESWOLD CLAIMING STAKES 2YO   £2488   6f   Firm 16 -14 Slow

3032 DEAR GLENDA [16] (M Pipe) 2-8-0(BL) M Roberts 16/1: 200001: 2 br f Gold Song -
Kinngdom Prize (Key To The Kingdom): Showed impr form when leading at the dist, cmftbly in a
2yo claiming stakes at Leicester: 2nd in a seller on yld grnd at Doncaster on her debut: eff
over 5/6f: also acts on fast grnd: seems to like a gall trk : wore blinkers today.   22
2847 MANLY BOY [12] (M Jarvis) 2-9-3 T Lucas 12/1: 02: Took quite a drop in class: led 2f
out: should win a race if kept in this grade: eff over 6f on fast grnd.   31
2777 SHARPHAVEN [15] (M Brittain) 2-8-10 A Munro(7) 12/1: 1002023: Al up there: see 2777 & 1379.20
*2990 MAIN BRAND [8] (W O'gorman) 2-8-5(bl)(1ow) Pat Eddery 13/8 FAV: 004014: Hvly bckd:
no impression from below dist & btr over 1m in 2990 (easier trk).   14

3047 FREDDIE ASHTON [17] 2-9-3(bl) R Guest 16/1: 0000040: Prom most: flattered in 3047 (7f).   23
2987 ROAN REEF [19] 2-8-3(bl) Gay Kelleway(3) 25/1: 3040000: Stayed on too late: see 1088 & 987 05
2484 BEE BEE CEE [9] 2-8-13 J Reid 8/1: 00: Took a drop in class & nicely bckd: late prog
into 7th: 7,000 gns yearling who is effective over 6f on firm.   14
--   CODED MESSAGE [10] 2-8-13 S Whitworth 10/1: 0: Prom over ½way on debut: should impr.   00
2792 PASHMINA [6] 2-8-6 R Hills 5/1: 3330000: Wknd 2f out: btr 2265 (5f): see 1893.   00

2982 Balinese Dancer [5] 8-10		2927 Lisasham [2] 8-3	
2205 Daunting Prospect [13] 9-3		2535 Musical Rhapsody [18] 8-10	
2919 Take Effect [20] 8-9	-- Netzer [7] 8-7	3017 Highfalutin Lymey [4] 8-5	
2796 Escudero [11] 8-3	2757 Taliesin [1] 8-3	3016 The Chippenham Man [3] 8-3	
-- Baileys Topline [14] 8-0			

20 ran   2½,1½,½,1,1½,nk,1,1   (Richard Green)   M Pipe Nicholashayne, Somerset

---

HAMILTON   Tuesday October 21st   Righthand, Undulating Track, Stiff Uphill Finish.

Official Going Given As SOFT

3082 BIRNIEHILL MAIDEN STAKES 2YO   £773   6f   Yld/Soft 106 -05 Slow

2926 EL REY [3] (W Hastings Bass) 2-9-0 R Lines(3) 9/2: 01: 2 b c King Of Spain - Powderhall
(Murrayfield): Held up: switched to race on the btr grnd & led over 1f out, cmftbly, in a
2yo mdn at Hamilton: cost 12,000 gns as a yearling & is a half brother to several winners:
eff at 6f, should stay 7f: acts on gd/firm & soft grnd & a stiff trk: can impr further.   45
2967 JUST CLASS [8] (S Norton) 2-8-11 J Lowe 16/1: 402: Ran on well under press & continues
to impr: will be suited by 7f: acts on gd/firm & soft grnd & a stiff trk: should find a
small race.   36
2804 BILLY CONNOLLY [5] (M Brittain) 2-9-0 K Darley 10/1: 023: Made much: in gd form &
acts on gd/firm & yld/soft grnd: see 2494.   33
2717 RUN BY [7] (G Balding) 2-9-0 J Williams 6/1: 004: Held up: fin well: acts on firm
& soft & stays 6f well: can impr further: see 2717.   33
2889 KENTONS LAD [4] 2-9-0 M Wood 7/1: 000: Stayed on under press: acts on gd & soft.   26
2774 DREAM DOLLAR [12] 2-8-11 W Wharton 5/1: 000: Dsptd lead, wknd: either unsuited by
this soft grnd or totally flattered in race 2774.   21
2410 ENTIRE [11] 2-9-0 G Duffield 7/2 FAV: 30: There ½way: btr 2410 (5f, gd/firm).   00
--   SNOWKIST [13] 2-8-11 D Nicholls 8/1: 0: Mkt drifter on debut: prom much: well bred
filly who is bred to stay 1m & further & should impr on this, possibly on btr grnd.   00
2987 Gold Minories [6] 9-0   2476 Hopping Around [1] 9-0
2423 Long View [9] 8-11   2499 Floreat Tina [10] 8-11
2127 Petango [2] 8-11
13 ran   2,2,½,4,½   (Sir Gerard Newman)   W Hastings Bass Newmarket

3083 FINAL SPRINT HANDICAP 3YO+ 0-35   £1791   5f   Yld/Soft 106 +06 Fast   [31]

2632 DEBACH REVENGE [9] (M Tompkins) 4-7-9 A Mackay 11/2 JT.FAV: 0400201: 4 b f Balboa -
Miss Deed (David Jack): Made ev' yd, holding on by ¾L in a h'cap at Hamilton: first success:
seems suited by forcing tactics over 5f & handles soft grnd well: possibly even btr on a
sharper trk.   07
2966 SPACEMAKER BOY [3] (D Leslie) 6-9-11 G G Duffield 16/1: 0000002: Al led on stands
side & stayed on well: best effort since 1037: see 2011.   35
2592 WESBREE BAY [2] (N Bycroft) 4-7-8(1ow)(5oh) L Charnock 20/1: 2300003: Ran on well
under press: btr effort on this easier grnd: see 1423.   00
679 ALNASHME [8] (D Thom) 4-8-12 A Murray 10/1: 4-40144: Long abs: slow start & stayed
on well: will do btr next time: see 495.   16
2970 WARTHILL LADY [1] 4-8-11 K Darley 7/1: 0100230: Well clear rem: see 2970 (6f): acts
on firm & yld/soft: consistent.   14
*2854 WEBSTERS FEAST [12] 3-8-12(7ex) W Wharton 7/1: 4300010: Prom, wknd: btr 2854 (firm).   01
2463 BERNIGRA GIRL [11] 3-8-9 C Rutter(3) 10/1: 0000000: Lightly bckd: fin 7th: see 1970.   00
2688 SONNENELLE [4] 3-8-5(vis) N Carlisle 10/1: 4001000: No threat: best 1973.   00
2424 LULLABY BLUES [5] 3-9-5 M Birch 10/1: 1200000: Prom early: best in 890.   00
2970 DEBBIE DO [13] 3-9-11 M Tebbutt(7) 8/1: 0000400: Prom to ½way: btr 2970 (gd): see 2277.   00
2858 HILMAY [10] 4-8-4 R Lappin(7) 11/2 JT.FAV: 0320100: Dislikes soft? much btr 2858, 2592.   00
3046 Tradesman [6] 7-7(1oh)   2124 Blochairn Skolar [7] 7-8(1ow)(6oh)
13 ran   ¾,1½,1,nk,8   (Mrs Celia Miller)   M Tompkins Newmarket

3084 RIGHEAD SELLING STAKES 3 & 4YO   £1144   1m 40y Yld/Soft 106 -15 Slow

2972 LIGHT THE WAY [4] (M Prescott) 3-8-5 G Duffield 2/1 FAV: 0-021: 3 b f Nicholas Bill -
Conway Bay (Saritamer): Hvly bckd & came from behind to lead inside final 2f, ridden out in a
3 & 4yo seller at Hamilton (bought in 2,600 gns): lightly rcd previously: eff at 1m, probably
stays further: acts on firm & yld/soft grnd.   12
2697 HOKUSAN [11] (B Stevens) 4-9-0 S Whitelam(7) 8/1: 0000002: Made most: 4L clear 3rd:
best effort for a long time & may be best on soft grnd: see 620.   12
2963 KEEP COOL [6] (R Hollinshead) 3-8-10 S Perks 6/1: 4333143: Gd hdway over 2f out:
best in 2863.   06
3057 SPARKLING WIT [1] (D Tucker) 4-8-11 A Dicks(7) 33/1: 0-00-04: Al there: kept on under
press: very lightly rcd since successful as a 2yo at Yarmouth on soft grnd.   00

2960 MISS VENEZUELA [12] 3-8-5(vis) J Williams 8/1: 4000000: Stayed on from rear: see 1288.   00
3057 JERSEY MAID [10] 3-8-5 M Birch 9/2: 0000420: Fdd final 2f: btr 3057 (6f).   00
2898 TOUCH THE SAIL [7] 3-8-5(BL) A Mackay 8/1: 0420400: Bl first time: disapp: see 2898.   00
3057 SHIRLY ANN [9] 4-8-11 T Williams 10/1: 2000200: Well below 2960 (firm grnd).   00
2863 Janes Brave Boy [2] 9-0   1336 Decembre [3] 9-0
2495 Res Non Verba [13] 8-5
11 ran   1½,4,2,nk,hd   (C H & D W Stephenson Ltd)   M Prescott Newmarket

3085 WHITEMOSS NURSERY HANDICAP 2YO   £1616   1m 40y Yld/Soft 106 -10 Slow   [37]

2897 BE CHEERFUL [14] (J Winter) 2-9-1 G Duffield 11/2 JT.FAV: 43021: 2 b f Sayyaf -
Mile By Mile (Milesian): In gd form & came from behind to lead near fin in a nursery h'cap
at Hamilton: last time out just btn in a similar event at Brighton: half sister to several
winners incl the useful sprinter Numismatist but stays 1m well herself: acts on fast & yld/
soft grnd & probably on any trk: genuine.   33
*2817 GAELIC LOVER [2] (C Tinkler) 2-8-11 M Wood 7/1: 212: Led inside final 1f: just caught:
running well & acts on gd/firm & yld/soft grnd: see 2817.   28
2718 ORIENTAL DREAM [4] (J Hindley) 2-8-10(vis) A Shoults(5) 15/2: 01003: Led inside final
2f, just btn in close fin & 4L clear rem: stays 1m & seems best on soft grnd: see 1119.   26
*2798 RIVERS SECRET [5] (D Smith) 2-8-6 L Charnock 10/1: 0000414: Led ½way: in gd form &
acts on gd/firm & soft: see 2798.   15
2718 SYLVAN ORIENT [6] 2-9-7 A Mcglone 20/1: 0003000: Nearest fin: stays 1m well: acts
on firm & soft: see 2044.   27
2922 BEAU BENZ [1] 2-9-4 M Birch 10/1: 4000240: Never nearer: probably stays 1m but best
over 7f in 2680 (firm).   20
+2886 TROMPE DOEIL [7] 2-8-6(5ex) A Mackay 13/2: 0002410: Disapp after 2886 & has twice
run very poorly here: see 2886 (sharp trk, firm).   00
2897 FU LU SHOU [3] 2-8-12 T Williams 11/2 JT.FAV: 001200: Fdd final 2f: btr 2798, 2470 &
was probably unable to act on this softer grnd.   00
2989 ALHAYAT [11] 2-8-7 C Rutter(3) 8/1: 4433000: Prom most: btr 2989 (sharp trk, firm).   00
2968 Knocksharry [8] 8-5   2669 Miss Emily [16] 8-6   2512 Black Mans Bay [17] 9-4(BL)
2968 Caerinette [12] 9-0(bl)   3016 Carse Kelly [9] 7-12(bl)
2178 Mccallun [10] 8-10   2512 Hunters Leap [13] 8-11
16 ran   hd,½,4,1½,2   (T M P Waterman)   J Winter Newmarket

3086 MURRAY HANDICAP 3YO 0-35   £986   1m 1f Yld/Soft 106 +01 Fast   [33]

2548 SHEER NECTAR [12] (G Balding) 3-8-9 J Williams 3/1 FAV: -0001: 3 b f Piaffer - Liza
Paul (Ron): Well bckd when a comfortable winner of a h'cap at Hamilton: lightly rcd filly
who had earlier shown promise in mdn company: half sister to 1m winner Lady Liza: eff at 9/10f
& acts on gd & yld grnd.   28
1773 TEED BORE [8] (W Musson) 3-8-4 M Wigham 10/1: 2043002: Abs: led 3f out till caught
near fin: gd effort: well suited by soft grnd & may find a race before season's end:see 39.   21
2980 NICOLINI [11] (J Fitzgerald) 3-8-5 M Birch 7/1: 0332033: Ev ch inside final 2f : see 2980.   17
2400 RINGWELL [1] (G Huffer) 3-9-10 R Carter(5) 5/1: -00334: Nearest fin: needs further.   34
2414 VIRAJENDRA [7] 3-8-5(bl) L Charnock 10/1: -003400: Never nearer: lightly rcd since 491.   10
2998 ELEGANT FASHION [9] 4-9-1 E Guest(3) 6/1: 0003200: No extra final 2f: see 2728 (firm).   01
2985 SEAMERE [6] 3-8-2 A Mackay 10/1: -000200: Fdd str: best 2746 (firm).   00
2996 Its Heaven [3] 7-9   2925 Pearl Pet [4] 8-12(bl)
2985 Sirdar Girl [2] 8-0   -- Lord Sun [13] 8-12   2973 Crownit [5] 8-1
2496 Bills Daughter [10] 7-13   2931 Opal Flower [14] 8-2
14 ran   ¾,3,¾,3,8   (L R Turland)   G Balding Fyfield, Hants

3087 WHIRLIES HANDICAP 3YO+ 0-35   £2085   1m 4f Yld/Soft 106 +01 Fast   [34]

2978 IVOROSKI [5] (D Smith) 4-7-12 L Charnock 8/1: 2100441: 4 b g Malinowski - Fado
(Ribero): Bckd from 12/1 when winning a h'cap at Hamilton: brought over to the stands side
in the straight & led close home: earlier successful in a h'cap at Carlisle: in '85 won at
Edinburgh: best form over 12f: acts on firm, handles yld/soft grnd, no trk preferences.   12
1980 KEEP HOPING [18] (G Huffer) 3-8-2 R Lines(3) 14/1: 0001332: Abs: led 3f out: just
btn: fine effort: acts on gd/firm & soft & on any trk: see 1739.   22
*2995 FOURTH TUDOR [6] (B Hanbury) 4-8-13(bl)(6ex) A Geran(5) 6/4 FAV: 2000113: Hvly bckd:
ev ch over 1f out & 4L clear rem: gd effort under his penalty: see 2995: acts on firm &
yld/soft.   23
2877 MILLERS TALE [3] (I Balding) 4-9-7 J Matthias 10/1: 1040044: Well behind: late hdway.   25
2415 ICEN [8] 8-8-1 S Webster 50/1: 1000300: Ev ch 2f out: btr 2175: see 28.   03
3028 PARAVANE [7] 4-7-11 A Proud 50/1: 00-0000: Nearest fin: see 3028.   00
2995 COMMON FARM [15] 3-8-5 K Darley 10/1: 0000020: No threat in 7th: btr 2995 (10f gd).   00
2467 RAPIDAN [14] 5-7-11 J Lowe 9/1: 0000100: Never nearer: best 2395 (sharper trk).   00
-3026 REGAL STEEL [20] 8-8-10 A Culhane(7) 8/1: 4030020: Led 9f: btr 3026 (good).   00
2727 S S SANTO [12] 3-8-3 G Duffield 10/1: 0012300: No threat: best 1898.   00
2995 Night Warrior [2] 9-0   1871 Pats Jester [16] 8-9   675 Christmas Holly [9] 8-0
2885 Cadenette [1] 7-11   2415 Lucky Humbug [19] 7-13
2709 Foremast [4] 8-9   2709 Kookys Pet [11] 8-3(bl)
2478 Standon Mill [10] 7-13   3028 Moulkins [13] 7-10
-- Made For Life [17] 7-11
20 ran   nk,1½,4,¾,5   (P & I Darling)   D Smith Bishop Auckland, Co. Durham

SAINT CLOUD   Friday October 17th   Righthanded, Galloping Track

Official Going Given As GOOD/FIRM

3088 GROUP 3 PRIX THOMAS BRYON 2YO   £19885   7.5f   Good/Firm -

2384 GLORY FOREVER (S Norton) 2-8-7 J Velasquez 1: 44101: 2 gr c Forever Casting - Fagers
Glory Smart colt: set off in front and fought back bravely to lead again cl home in Gr 3
Prix Thomas Bryon at St-Cloud: earlier again made most when winning his mdn at Newmarket:
stays 7f really well and will be suited by 1m+: acts on gd & firm grd and is well suited by a
gall trk: highly regarded by his trainer and seems a most genuine sort.   71
2826 LIBERTINE (R Collet) 2-8-4 C Asmussen 1: -132022: Odds on fav: went on below dist,
but just out-battled: consistent sort who stays 7f well: see 1714 & 1351.   67
2907 HARLEM SHUFFLE (F Boutin) 2-8-7 F Head 1: 1023: Another gd eff and seems well suited
by this longer trip: sure to win more races: see 2907.   65
-- MAGISTROS (G Bonnaventure) 2-8-11 G Dubroeucq 1: 340104: Gd eff: earlier successful
over a similar trip at Deauville and seems likely to be suited by middle dist next term.   68
7 ran   nk,2½,shtnk   S Norton (A Salman)

LYON-PARILLY   Saturday October 18th   -

Official Going Given As GOOD/SOFT

3089 GROUP 3 PRIX ANDRE BABOIN 3YO+   £24379   1m 3f   Good/Soft -

-- YAKA (A Chelet) 3-8-7 A Badel 1: -1: 3 b g Margouillat - Atlante du Cadran Smart French
gelding: extended his winning sequence when getting up cl home in Gr 3 Prix Andre Baboin at
Lyon: earlier completed a hat-trick of wins in the Provinces: very eff over mid dist on fast
and yldg grd: genuine and consistent.   75
-- STAR MAITE (A De Royer Dupre) 3-8-7 P Coppin 1: -2: Just btn and is in fine form:
last time out a narrow winner of quite a val race at Deauville: very eff around 11/14f.   74
-- BLACK DANCER (A Lyon) 5-8-10 M Cesandri 1: -3: Ran on gamely: not btn far.   68
1597 CHERCHEUR DOR (C Head) 3-8-10 G Moore 1: 10-4144: Fine eff after abs: see 1597.   75
2845 BELDALE STAR 3-8-7 A Clark 1: -100000: Never going well and was btn at ½ way:
unlikely to be seen out again this season: best in 273.   00
10 ran   nk,½,shthd   (Mme A Dewez)   A Chelet France

LONGCHAMP   Sunday October 19th   Righthanded, Galloping Track

Official Going Given As FIRM

3090 GROUP 3 PRIX DE CONDE 2YO   £18928   1m 1f   Firm -

-- GROOM DANCER (T Clout) 2-8-13 D Boeuf 1: 1101: 2 b c Blushing Groom - Featherhill
Smart French colt: was an impressive winner of a Gr 3 race at Longchamp: began his career with
wins at Chantilly and Evry but put up a lack-lustre effort last time: very eff around 8/9f,
looks likely to make a smart mid.dist. colt next term: acts well on fast grd and a gall trk.   75
-- RIVER MEMORIES (R Collet) 2-8-8 A Lequeux 1: 312: Ran a fine race and caught a real
tartar here: won a fillies race on this course last time and is improving with ev race:
stays 9f well: acts on fast ground.   62
-- BOLD SHARK (F Boutin) 2-8-11 F Head 1: 103: Gd eff: first time out winner of a colts
race at Deauville: eff over 8/9f on fast ground.   59
2914 STEAMSHIP (A Fabre) 2-8-11 J L Kessas 1: 2134: Consistent sort: see 2914 (C/D).   58
5 ran   3,3,nk,4   (M L Warner Jnr)   T Clout France

3091 GROUP 2 PRIX DU CONSEIL DE PARIS 3YO+   £33937   1m 4f   Firm -

*1595 ALTAYAN (A De Royer Dupre) 3-9-2 A Poirier 1: 122411: 3 ch c Posse - Aleema Highclass
colt: took command at the dist, staying on strongly in a Gr 2 event at Longchamp: earlier won
a Gr 2 event at St-Cloud at was successful first time out at Evry: chased home the topclass
Bering in the French Derby: eff over 9f, tho' seems best around 12f: acts on fast & soft grd
and likes a gall track: consistent sort.   88
289 BAROOD (A Fabre) 3-8-9 A Lequeux 1: 3203112: Stayed on well to take the minor honours:
winner of his last 2 starts at Evry and Maisons-Laffitte: very eff over mid dist: acts on fast   74
2824 DAUN (T Grieper) 5-9-0 D Richardson 1: 4034303: German chall, no extra cl home: this
was a creditable effort: see 1712.   71
2917 SIRIUS SYMBOLI (F Palmer) 4-9-0 M Philipperon 1: 3-04204: Made much: best 2637 (C/D).   69
2822 MASHKOUR 3-9-0 S Cauthen 1: 1134230: Led over 4f out, no extra inside dist:
consistent sort: see 2222.   75
2738 SATCO 3-9-0 E Saint Martin 1: 2-11440: Ran well: see 1117.   73
10 ran.   2,½,½,½,½   (Aga Khan)   A De Royer Dupre France

3092 GROUP 3 PRIX DU PETIT COUVERT 2YO+   £17971   5f   Firm -

2916 PARIOLI (J Cunnington Jnr) 5-9-11 M Philipperon 1: 13-4121: 5 b f Bold Bidder -
Rumbling Roman Very smart French sprinter: cmftbly landed the odds in a fast run Gr 3 race
at Longchamp: has been lightly raced this season, last month won a Gr 3 event at Maison-Laffitte
and then chased home Double Schwartz in the Prix de l'Abbaye over this C/D: winner of three
Gr 3 races last term: very eff over 5/6f on fast & hvy grd: seems to act on any trk.   81

2916 BAISER VOLE (C Head) 3-10-0 F Head 1: 0143202: Went on ½ way, kept on well but was
al being held by winner: genuine & consistent filly: good effort at weights: see 2742   81
2916 PREMIERE CUVEE (J Pease) 4-9-11 G Guignard 1: 30-2103: Gd eff: see 2457.   71
2916 SHARP ROMANCE (J Bethell) 4-9-11 S Cauthen 1: 0000004: Ran to his best: see 18.   70
  -- **MUSIC STREAK** 8-9-11 O Larsen 1: 23000-0: Danish chall: ran well. 69
*2672 FILLEOR 3-9-8 G Duffield 1: -004410: Whipped in her face below dist: ran really
well in circumstances: see 2672.   61
8 ran   1,2½,shtnk,nk,2   (D Arnold)   J Cunnington Jnr France

---

SAN SIRO, MILAN   Saturday October18th   -

Official Going Given As GOOD

3093 GROUP 2 PREMIO VITTORIO DI CAPUA 3YO+   £18138   1m   Good -

+1854 STAR CUTTER (H Cecil) 3-8-9 W Ryan 1: -2111: 3 gr c Star De Naskra - Axed Smart, much
improved colt: sn in front and qcknd clear at the dist to win a Gr 2 event at San Siro: off
the trk since an easy winner of a fast run h'cap at Goodwood in July: earlier won a minor
race at Newcastle: very eff around 1m on fast grd: does well forcing the pace: has prob not
stopped improving and should win more gd races.   79
2867 KABIYLA (M Stoute) 3-8-6 A Kimberley 1: -120132: Another fine eff: see 2765.   73
2820 SPLENDID MOMENT (R Collet) 3-8-9 A Lequeux 1: 10-4323: Gd eff over this shorter trip:
most consistent this season: see 389.   72
  -- **GOLDEN BOY(ITA)** (A Aiello) 5-8-11 M Planard 1: ------4: Italian challenger.   66
2909 DANZICA 3-8-6 A Parravani 1: 1230: Consistent filly: see 642.   63
11 ran   1,1½,½,1   (Sheikh Mohammed)   H Cecil Newmarket

SAN SIRO, MILAN   Sunday October 19th   -

3094 GROUP 3 PREMIO BAGUTTA 3YO+ FILLIES   £11108   1m   Good -

*1219 SAINT SAMBA (L D'auria) 3-8-9 V Panici 1: -11: 3 b f Thatch - Ste Nitouche Smart
Italian filly: ran on strongly to win a Gr 3 race at San Siro: earlier won a similar race at
Turin: very eff over 1m on gd & fast grd.   75
1353 ONLY STAR (C Head) 3-8-9 G Moore 1: 132: Fine effort: eff over 8/10f: see 1008.   73
2633 MUMMYS FAVOURITE (J Dunlop) 3-8-6 W Carson 1: 3414333: Much-travelled of late but
has retained her form really well: not btn that far here: see 1487.   67
2640 WHITE WATER (A De Royer Dupre) 5-8-8 P Coppin 1: -44: Another gd effort.   62
1219 MARY GUARD 4-8-11 S Dettori 1: 1-020: Not btn very far: see 1219.   64
2568 BOLD AND BEAUTIFUL 4-8-8 Pat Eddery 1: 0330030: Fin 7th: below form shown 2568 (frm)   52
12 ran   ½,1½,½,shthd,2,3   (Scuderia Blu Fir)   L D'auria Italy

3095 GROUP 2 PREMIO DORMELLO 2YO FILLIES   £15745   1m   Good -

+2703 THREE TAILS (J Dunlop) 2-8-11 W Carson 1: 011: 2 b f Blakeney - Triple First Smart,
improving filly: came from off the pace to lead cl home in a Gr 2 fillies race at San Siro:
earlier a cmftbly winner of her mdn at Leicester: 290,000 gns yearling who is a half sister
to the smart 3yo Maysoon, amongst others: stoutly bred and is sure to be suited by middle dist
next season: acts on fast grd and on a gall trk: sure to win more races.   70
  -- **ALIMATHA** (L D'auria) 2-8-11 S Dettori 1: 2: Ran on well: fine effort.   67
  -- **SWEETTUC** (J Fellows) 2-8-11 G Moore 1: 3: Al up there and not btn far.   66
  -- **CUNIZZA DA ROMANO** (L D'auria) 2-8-11 Pat Eddery 1: 4: Cmftbly beat the rem.   62
12 ran   1,shtnk,1½,4   (Sheikh Mohammed)   J Dunlop Arundel, Sussex

3096 GROUP 1 GRAN PREMIO DEL JOCKEY-CLUB   £86747   1m 4f   Good -

*2820 ANTHEUS (C Head) 4-9-3 G Moore 1: 1230311: 4 b c Northern Dancer - Apachee Smart,
French colt: led below dist for an easy win in a Gr 1 event at San Siro: equalling the course
record in the process: last month won a Gr 3 race at Maison-Laffitte and first time out was
successful at St-Cloud: very eff over 10/12f on gd & soft grd.   84
2741 TONY BIN (L Camici) 3-8-11 M Depalmas 1: 3-14132: Ran on too late: this was another
fine effort: clearly not flattered last time: see 2741.   79
2917 DIHISTAN (M Stoute) 4-9-3 Pat Eddery 1: 1300103: Al cl up but could not qckn at the
business-end: very consistent colt who has been on the go all season: see 2461.   77
2502 ST HILARION (G Harwood) 4-9-3 G Starkey 1: -002024: Not btn that far: best 1144.   76
  -- **FIRE OF LIFE** 4-9-3 M Jerome 1: 0-24010: Stable mate of 2nd and ran well.   74
2741 TOMMY WAY 3-8-11 W Carson 1: -311120: Kept on under press: see 2741 & 1328.   75
*2640 BIG REEF 4-9-3 V Panici 1: 0032110: Trailed in last and this is nothing like his
true form: much better over 9f here in 2640 (yldg).   00
7 ran   2,nk,½,1,ddht,20   (J Wertheimer)   C Head France

WOODBINE, CANADA   Sunday October 19th   -

Official Going Given As FIRM

3097 GRADE 1 ROTHMANS INTERNATIONAL CHAMP.   £209702   1m 5f   Yielding -

-- SOUTHJET (A Penna) 3-8-6 J Santos 1: 1421221: 3 Northjet - Syzygy Highclass American
colt: produced a fine late burst to lead cl home in Grade 1 Rothmans International Championship
at Woodbine: earlier successful in Grade 1 Secretariat Stks at Arlington and is in fine
form at present: very eff over 12/13f on fast grd: most genuine.   94
2917 SHARDARI (M Stoute) 4-9-0 W R Swinburn 1: 2412102: Looked home & hosed at dist but
could not cope with the winner's late burst: nevertheless a fine effort on ground softer
than he would have liked: most consistent: well clear rest: see 2200, 1790   93
-- ROYAL TREASURER (J Day) 3-8-6 J Lauzon 1: -12123: Ran well in this smart company.   83
2917 MERSEY (P L Biancone) 4-8-11 A Cordero Jr 1: 11-2104: Consistent French filly: see 2637   79
2565 SIRK 3-8-6 E Maple 1: 3032000: Fin 8th: seems to have gone off the boil, not
surprisingly after a long and busy season: see 2453 & 2157.   68
9 ran   1,6,hd,1½,5½,hd,nk   (Dogwood Stable)   A Penna U.S.A.

3098 GRADE 2 E P TAYLOR STAKES 3YO+ FILL.   £92716   1m 2f   Yielding -

2202 IVORS IMAGE 0 (M Stoute) 3-8-5 W R Swinburn 1: 1-41431: 3 b f Sir Ivor - Embryo (Busted)
Smart filly: proved an easy winner of Grade 2 E P Taylor Stks at Woodbine: has been lightly
raced since winning Gr 1 Italian Oaks at San Siro in May, but ran another fine race last
time when a cl 3rd to Untold in Gr 1 Yorkshire Oaks at York: last season again won a Pattern
race at San Siro and also a fillies mdn at Yarmouth: very eff over 10/12f: acts on fast &
yldg ground and on any track: retains her form really well and is a credit to her trainer.   85
-- CAROTENE 0 (R Attfield) 3-8-5 R Platts 1: -2: Fine eff from this ½ sister to the
Cesarewitch winner Orange Hill: very eff over 10f on an easy surface.   81
2918 BLUE TIP 0 (P L Biancone) 4-8-11 A Cordero Jr 1: 3240133: Ran to her best: see 2918.   77
-- DEVALOIS [1] (W Stephens) 4-8-11 E Maple 1: 14231-4: Ex French filly who ran a fine race   76
10 ran   1½,2½,hd   (S Fraser)   M Stoute Newmarket

REDCAR   Thursday October 23rd   Lefthanded, Flat Galloping Track

3099 RUSWARP MAIDEN STAKES 2YO   £2168   1m   Good/Firm 30 -17 Slow

2761 YAHEEB [9] (H T Jones) 2-9-0 A Murray 7/1: 31: 2 b c Alleged - Rissa (Nijinsky)
Useful colt: al front rank and led almost 2f out, gamely, in a 2yo mdn at Redcar: $240,000
yearling who stays 1m well and should do even btr when tackling middle dist next term: acts
on fast grd and likes this flat, galloping track: on the upgrade.   55
2710 CHEVREFEUILLE [12] (M Stoute) 2-8-11 W R Swinburn 3/1 FAV: 32: Chall below dist, ran
on gamely and only just held: stays 1m really well and will have no trouble winning a race
next season: see 2710.   50
2869 RODOMONT [19] (J Fitzgerald) 2-9-0 M Birch 4/1: 043: Al up there: best 2869.   48
1802 GRANNY BIMPS [11] (R Sheather) 2-8-11 R Guest 20/1: 04: Ran really well after a long
break: bred to be suited by middle dist: scope for further improvement: see 1802.   44
1270 UNDERSHAFT [6] 2-9-0 W Ryan 5/1: 20: Well bckd despite a long abs: stayed on well
from mid div and looks certain to improve on this rating: seems sure to be suited by middle
dist next season: has plenty of scope: see 1270.   40
2936 MAJESTIC MISS [24] 2-8-11 G Brown 100/1: 000: Showed much improved form here, having
been well btn in her prev starts in considerably lesser company: saw this 1m trip out well:
acts on gd/firm grd and on a gall track.   36
2723 GENTLE DARIUS [18] 2-9-0 G Duffield 8/1: 4340: Fdd into 7th: consistent sort: see 2001.   00
-- LORD THATCH [10] 2-9-0 M Wood 33/1: 0: Made steady late prog and will be btr for this
experience: half brother to useful middle dist colt El-Fayez: likely to be suited by 10f+
himself next season: acts on gd/firm grd and on a gall trk.   00
2159 WOOD LOUSE [1] 2-9-0 J Matthias 5/1: 000: Speed to ½ way: rather disapp: see 1914.   00
2889 The Main Man [14] 9-0   2997 Nicholas Mark [21] 9-0
-- Busted Harmony [4] 8-11   2664 Kilauea [15] 8-11
2841 Against All Odds [23] 9-0   2869 Faceview [22] 9-0
577 Comedy Sail [13] 9-0   2894 Strong Sea [16] 9-0(BL)
2663 Muntaq [17] 9-0   2889 Danensian [20] 9-0   -- Rebel Grey [3] 9-0
3011 La Verte Gleam [2] 8-11   3014 Bentham Bazaar [5] 9-0
2961 Cedar Creek [7] 9-0 F
23 ran   hd,2½,½,2½,shthd,hd,2   (M Al-Maktoum)   H T Jones Newmarket

3100 CUB HUNTERS SELLING STAKES 3YO   £576   1m 4f   Good/Firm 30 -01 Slow

3028 FLOATER [8] (S Wiles) 3-9-0 M Wood 8/1: -0041: 3 b c Vaguely Noble - Need a Dime
(Three Bagger) Dropped in class and led 2f out, battling on gamely to ddht in a 3yo seller at
Redcar (no bid): cost $35,000 as a yearling but was re-sold earlier this season fetching only
600 gns: eff over 10/12f on gd/firm grd: seems suited by a gall trk.   25
*2984 MISS LAURA LEE [2] (P Felgate) 3-8-11 W Ryan 8/1: 0004011: Narrow advantage inside
dist and kept on gamely to ddht in a 3yo seller at Redcar (no bid): in gd form, recently
gained her first win in a similar race at Folkestone: half sister to a couple of winners:
stays 12f: acts on gd/firm and yldg ground and would appear to have no trk preferences.   22

903

2778 CHABLISSE [3] (R Whitaker) 3-8-11 D Mckeown 5/2 FAV: 0441323: Ran on late: consistent.   17
2902 MITALA MARIA [6] (A Stewart) 3-8-11 W R Swinburn 3/1: -023024: Led 3f out, fdd: see 2902. 10
2984 RYMOS [9] 3-9-0(bl) W Newnes 8/1: 00-3320: Still a mdn: see 2705.   12
*2964 G G MAGIC [1] 3-9-0 R Guest 9/2: 0421310: Fdd: btr 2964 (easier trk).   10
--   Angel Dust [11] 8-11   2890 Taxi Man [10] 9-0   2984 Solent Lad [4] 9-0
2412 Our Annie [7] 8-11   2963 Timsolo [5] 9-0
11 ran   ddht,3,4,½,1½,1½   (Bill Benson)(Mrs A Quinn) S Wiles, Flockton: P Felgate, Melton Mowbray

3101 REDCAR. OCTOBER HANDICAP 3YO 0-35   £2234   1m 2f Good/Firm 30 +22 Fast   [40]

*2925 THUNDERDOME [2] (O Douieb) 3-9-6(7ex) W Ryan 3/1 FAV: 0000111: 3 br f Lyphard - Mr P's
Girl (Mr Prospector) Well bckd and cmftbly completed her hat-trick, quickening inside dist
in a fast run 3yo h'cap at Redcar: recently won similar races at Beverley & Lingfield: eff
over 1m, tho' seems btr suited by 10f and is likely to stay further: acts on gd & fast grd
and on any trk: in grand form.   44
2978 SAFFAN [6] (M Prescott) 3-9-9(7ex) G Duffield 11/2: 1222122: Ran on well, but just
too late: commendably consistent and should get his hd in front again soon: see 2978 & 2861   44
2885 SOMETHING SIMILAR [9] (J Fitzgerald) 3-8-7 M Birch 8/1: -000023: Led over 2f out,
no extra cl home: running well and seems to act on any trk: see 2885.   24
2709 FIRST BILL [1] (H Candy) 3-8-12 W Newnes 6/1: 000-204: Had ev ch: best 2467.   27
2286 GLOWING PROMISE [4] 3-9-7 W R Swinburn 14/1: -124000: Ran on same pace: btr 690: see 452   31
2152 WAVE GOODBYE [12] 3-7-9 J Lowe 20/1: 00-0200: Stayed on late: needs 12f: see 1736.   04
*2980 HELIETTA [14] 3-9-12(7ex) G Starkey 9/2: 4231210: Much btr over 9f here in 2980:
worth another chance.   00
2622 MR PASTRY [15] 3-9-2 A Murray 7/1: -0300: No show: twice well below form 2532 (1m).   00
2776 Mawdlyn Gate [8] 8-6   2762 Ranelagh [5] 7-10   2727 Chevet Lady [16] 8-2
2671 Space Trooper [11] 8-7   2719 Miami Blues [3] 8-4
2891 Heavenly Hoofer [7] 8-6   2948 Ettas Pet [10] 8-7
2103 Fair Zinnia [13] 7-7(4oh)
16 ran   ½,2,1,½,1,nk   (Edward Seltzer)   O Douieb Newmarket

3102 ELLERBY STAKES 3YO   £1786   2m115y Good/Firm 30 -08 Slow

2923 KAFARMO [9] (G Harwood) 3-9-0 G Starkey 9/4: -0341: 3 b c High Line - Fashion Club
(Tribal Chief) Led below dist and stayed on well under press to win a 3yo stks at Redcar: dam
was a fair sprinter, but staying seems to be his game: acts on fast & yldg grd and seems well
suited by a gall trk.   34
2974 KRISWICK [7] (J Dunlop) 3-8-11 G Duffield 1/1 FAV: -004022: Led 4f out, kept on same
pace: fin well clear rem and is in gd form: see 2974.   28
2923 IN CONTENTION [5] (J Wilson) 3-9-0 Julie Bowker(7) 25/1: -3003: No chance with front
pair: has shown little form to date: see 2923.   14
2682 PINZAUREOLE [4] (R Whitaker) 3-8-11 K Bradshaw(5) 25/1: -0004: Well btn in all starts.   10
619 LANDMARK [6] 3-9-0 J Matthias 9/2: -000: Long abs: trying a much longer trip here
and altho' bred to stay, never looked likely to figure in the finish: well bred colt who is
a half brother to several winners, including the smart trio Church Parade, Castle Rising & Leading
Star: only lightly raced and should do much btr than this.   09
1952 DRY GIN [2] 3-9-0 W Newnes 13/2: 00-0300: Made much: no form: see 1078.   00
--   GLYNCORRWG [1] 3-9-0 S Perks 20/1: 00-0: Al behind: lightly raced and no form.   00
7 ran   1½,15,shthd,2,10   (M E Kayall)   G Harwood Pulborough, Sussex

3103 EBF EGTON MAIDEN STAKES 2YO   £3148   6f   Good/Firm 30 -10 Slow

2777 COLWAY RALLY [5] (J Watts) 2-9-0 G Starkey 10/1: 3240031: 2 ch c Final Straw - Boswellia
(Frankincense) Useful colt: returned to form, bursting clear inside dist in a 2yo mdn at
Redcar: eff over 5/6f on fast & yldg grd: half brother to sev winners and on breeding should
stay at least 7f: best when held up for a late chall.   48
2626 LOUD APPEAL [7] (M Stoute) 2-9-0 W R Swinburn 3/1: 02: Made most: well bckd today and
is clearly on the upgrade: sure to find a race: see 2626.   40
2716 GREENS OLD MASTER [9] (W Jarvis) 2-9-0 A Murray 20/1: 20303: Al up there: best 1573.   36
2871 SONG N JEST [6] (J Fitzgerald) 2-9-0 M Birch 14/1: 320004: Dsptd lead most: btr effort
and seems to be returning to his early season form: see 715 & 583.   36
2774 FLIP THE BIRD [4] 2-8-11 W Newnes 12/1: 400: Ran on well: see 2554.   30
2846 TARSA [3] 2-8-11 A Mackay 11/4 FAV: 020: Heavily bckd despite a poorish draw: kept
on same pace and should do btr when allowed to make the running: see 2846 & 2651.   29
2926 DONT KNOCK IT [2] 2-8-11 G Duffield 12/1: 000: Al prom: fin 7th: btr eff: see 2926.   00
2922 SUNORIUS [26] 2-9-0 D Mckeown 9/2: 04220: Well bckd: no danger: much btr 2922 (7f).   00
2982 Johns Last [8] 8-11   2919 Burcroft [20] 9-0   2894 Reef Of Gold [21] 9-0
2814 Blaze Of Gold [16] 8-11   2889 Grossen [24] 9-0
--   Autobahn [25] 9-0   2922 Young Snugfit [22] 9-0
--   Eranthe [17] 8-11   2919 Harryaker [13] 9-0   2919 Edenthorpe [12] 9-0
2325 Willow The King [18] 9-0   --   Tiger River [14] 9-0
2281 Queens Connection [10] 8-11   2871 Olympic Challenger [1] 9-0
1225 Rose Meadow [23] 8-11   2791 Musical Dancer [19] 9-0
24 ran   2½,1½,shthd,½,hd,1   (R Coleman)   J Watts Richmond, Yorks.

3104 REDCAR AUTUMN HANDICAP 3YO+ 0-35   £2673   6f   Good/Firm 30 +01 Fast   [34]

2992 NAGEM [18] (L Barratt) 3-8-4 P Hill(7) 10/1: 4234231: 3 b f Headin' Up - Eleonora
(Falcon) Was gaining an overdue win when making virtually ev yard, gamely, in an all-aged
h'cap at Redcar: placed in her last six starts: eff over 5/6f: acts on any trk: does well
with forcing tactics.   20
2945 HOPEFUL KATIE [24] (D Leslie) 4-9-0 J Williams 10/1: 0130102: Not clear run: only
just failed to peg-back winner: in grand form and can win again soon: see 2715.   27
*2977 JARROVIAN [12] (T Fairhurst) 3-10-1(bl)(9ex) M Brennan(7) 16/1: 0004013: Al up there:
in fine form: see 2977.   43
2970 GOLDEN GUILDER [2] (M W Easterby) 3-9-3(bl) G Starkey 10/1: 333U224: Most consistent.   28
2977 ROSIE DICKINS [6] 4-8-7 R Lappin(7) 6/1 FAV: 4000030: Bckd from 14/1 but never really
looked likely to land the gamble: has had a gd season: see 1649.   15
2602 CASSANDRAS DREAM [16] 5-7-7(2oh) J Quinn(5) 25/1: 0000000: Al prom: not btn that far.   00
2970 GODS SOLUTION [5] 5-8-11 W Ryan 14/1: 4000400: Cl 7th: gd eff: see 42.   00
3024 BRITWYDD [20] 3-9-3 D Nicholls 25/1: 00-0040: Not btn far in 8th: see 3024 & 2473.   00
3015 ROYAL FAN [19] 3-9-4 M Birch 8/1: 0000200: Fdd into 9th, but not btn that far: see 981   00
2681 EASTBROOK [22] 6-8-10 B Hart(7) 10/1: 1324100: Speed over ½ way, fdd: see 2295.   00
*2816 DUFFERS DANCER [23] 4-9-4 N Connorton 13/2: 0134110: Won a hat-trick but fdd quickly
below dist: see 2816.   00
2870 TARANGA [8] 3-9-9 G Duffield 8/1: 2040020: Disapp eff: much btr 7f in 2870.   00

3012 Bon Accueil [11] 8-13	2977 Low Flyer [10] 8-7	2980 Clawson Thorns [25] 7-13	
3033 Manton Mark [13] 9-6	1610 Mary Maguire [3] 9-6	2816 Thatchered [26] 8-10	
2411 Miami Dolphin [14] 7-12		2966 Sharlies Wimpy [4] 9-4(bl)	
-- Park Mill [15] 7-11	2970 Pentoff [9] 8-0	2816 Beechwood Cottage [7] 8-11(bl)	
135 Tollymore [17] 7-12		2728 Whoberley Wheels [21] 8-1(BL)	
3033 Security Pacific [1] 9-3			

26 ran   shthd,nk,1,½,½,nk,nk,½   (Doug Brereton)   L Barratt Oswestry, Salop.

NEWBURY   Thursday October 23rd   Lefthand, Stiff Galloping Track

Official Going Given As GOOD/SOFT

3105 READING MAIDEN FILLIES STAKES 3YO   £3795   1m 2f   Good/Soft 92 -05 Slow

2610 CYNOMIS [13] (W Hastings Bass) 3-8-11 A Kimberley 15/2: -30041: 3 b f Shergar -
Coyote (Welsh Pageant) Al there and ran on well to lead cl home in a 3yo fillies mdn at Newbury:
has been tried over longer trips but seems suited by a stiff 10f: half sister to the useful
Range Rover: acts on fast & yldg grd and on any trk.   42
2701 SEA POWER [1] (W Hern) 3-8-11 B Procter 11/2 JT.FAV: 03-0342: Led final 1f, just btn:
gd effort and should find a mdn: acts on firm & yldg ground: see 2701, 806.   41
2799 NIHAD [4] (B Hanbury) 3-8-11 R Wernham 8/1: 0032323: Led 3f out: consistent but seems
to lack finishing pace: best 2676 (C/D): acts on gd/firm & yldg.   36
2948 JUNGLE BEAT [6] (W Jarvis) 3-8-11 N Carlisle 16/1: 0-4024: Kept on under press:
continues to improve and stays 10f: acts on gd/firm & yldg ground: see 2550.   36
2299 NO DOUBLET [2] 3-8-11 R Street 16/1: 3222040: Led 7f: abs since 2299.   28
1246 HOLLY BROWN [12] 3-8-11 B Crossley 33/1: -0000: Long abs: nearest fin and should do
better next time: lightly raced filly who should be suited by 10f & further: acts on yldg grd. 24
1630 GLITTER [14] 3-8-11 R Curant 11/2 JT.FAV: -030400: Wknd final 2f after abs: best 599.   00
2726 COMMANCHE BELLE [11] 3-8-11 P Hamblett 8/1: 2320: No threat: btr on firm 2726, 2048.   00
2853 LEI [3] 3-8-11 G Sexton 8/1: -00: Active in mkt but fdd in str: see 2853.   00

2734 Skevena [15] 8-11	2790 Brimsol [8] 8-11	1589 Burning Ambition [19] 8-11	
2546 Cavaleuse [20] 8-11(vis)		2929 Cherry Glory [7] 8-11	
2442 Concordes Demon [21] 8-11		2853 Davemma [10] 8-11	
-- Horns Lodge [22] 8-11	1134 Polly Worth [9] 8-11	-- Roberts Flower [5] 8-11	
2958 Sousaga [17] 8-11	2948 Summer Garden [16] 8-11		
2676 Zindelina [18] 8-11			

22 ran   nk,2½,shthd,4,2½,1½   (Lord Derby)   W Hastings Bass Newmarket

3106 HOGG ROBINSON H'CAP (0-60) 3YO+   £4907   5f   Good/Soft 92 +03 Fast   [53]

*2906 BONNY LIGHT [10] (R Sheather) 3-9-3(bl)(8ex) A Shoults(5) 14/1: 3001211: 3 b c
Welsh Saint - Daring Choice (Daring Display) In grand form, led inside final 1f and sn clear
in a val h'cap at Newbury: recently a winner of a h'cap at Wolverhampton & a stks event at
Thirsk and has been much improved by the appl of blinkers: very eff over 5/6f on firm & yldg
ground, acts on any track: carries weight well and may complete a hat-trick.   55
2668 CHAPLINS CLUB [2] (D Chapman) 6-9-3(bl) Pat Eddery 6/1: 2043002: Ev ch final 1f:
gd eff: see 1222, 1026.   48
3055 STEEL CYGNET [12] (Pat Mitchell) 3-8-9 J Reid 20/1: 0340403: Ran on well final 1f
under press: runs as if he needs 6f: may win before season's end: see 62.   39
2966 DAVILL [4] (J Winter) 4-7-10 R Street 14/1: 0030024: Kept on well: another gd run.   26
+2758 DURASINGH [16] 4-8-13 P Brette(7) 11/1: -2210: Led 2f out: in fine form: see 2758.   39
3054 BROADWATER MUSIC [5] 5-9-6 R Cochrane 9/2 FAV: 1000040: Ev ch: flattered in 3054.   44
2402 BRIDGE STREET LADY [6] 5-9-7 G Baxter 8/1: 0120030: Early speed: best 2402.   00
-2921 GEORGE WILLIAM [3] 5-8-6 R Fox 9/1: 0100020: No show: well below 2921 (gd/firm)   00

2731 STEPHENS SONG [14] 3-7-13 S Dawson 10/1: 0000000: Below his best: see 2731, 233.   00
2953 Derry River [15] 8-11(vis)   2537 Laurie Lorman [13] 9-0
2731 Platine [8] 7-13   +3012 Durham Place [11] 9-10(8ex)
2262 West Carrack [9] 9-1(bl)   3012 Be Lyrical [7] 8-12
2953 Deputy Head [1] 8-10
16 ran   2½,hd,shthd,1½,1   (Dr K Owusu-Nyantekyi)   R Sheather Newmarket

3107 GROUP 3 MATCHMAKER HORRIS HILL STAKES   £33480   7f 60y Good/Soft 92 -09 Slow

2849 NAHEEZ [1] (D Elsworth) 2-9-0 Pat Eddery 5/2: 131: 2 b c Critique - Academic World
(Arts and Letters) Smart colt: led over 2f out and responded gamely to lead again cl home in
Gr 3 Horris Hill Stks at Newbury: first time out won a val mdn at Ascot: in between was unlucky
in running when 3rd to Imperial Frontier at Newmarket: half brother to a winner in the USA:
eff at 7f, looks sure to stay 1m and further: acts on fast & yldg grd and on a gall trk:
a genuine sort.   71
2711 CHESHAM SQUIRE [2] (P Walwyn) 2-8-9 Paul Eddery 16/1: 02: Led inside final 2f: ran
on gamely and just btn in a driving finish: acts on firm & yldg grd and
compensation awaits him: genuine: will be suited by 1m: clearly fast improving: see 2711   65
2648 BROTHER PATRICK [7] (L Piggott) 2-9-0 M Roberts 20/1: 301203: Made most 4f: stayed
on under press and ran well: possibly btr over 1m: acts on gd/firm & yldg ground: see 2407.   61
2907 CENTAURI [8] (B Hills) 2-9-0 B Thomson 12/1: 12244: Prom and ev ch: a consistent
colt who stays 7f and acts on gd/firm & yldg ground: no trk preference: see 1936.   60
3037 MILAN FAIR [6] 2-8-9 W Carson 100/1: 0000: Rank outsider: not disgraced: eff over
7f on gd/firm & yldg ground.   35
*2849 IMPERIAL FRONTIER [4] 2-9-0 R Cochrane 4/6 FAV: 210: Heavily bckd disapp: pulled hard:
going well 3f out but found nothing when asked a question: beat the winner in 2849.   32
*2838 REBEL RAISER [3] 2-9-0 P Robinson 14/1: 03010: Fdd 2f out: much btr 2838 (firm).   00
7 ran   hd,5,½,10,4,1   (K Al-Said)   D Elsworth Whitsbury, Hants.

3108 NEWBURY STAKES (LISTED) 2YO FILLIES   £9910   7f 60y Good/Soft 92 -12 Slow

2246 NETTLE [6] (W Hern) 2-8-8 W Carson 4/1: 141: 2 ch f Kris - Sans Blague (The Minstrel)
Very useful filly: suited by the easier grd and led 2f out, running on gamely to get up again
cl home in a Listed race at Newbury: first time out was a ready winner at Salisbury: first
foal whose dam was a useful 12f winner: eff at 7f, looks sure to be suited by 1m: acts on
gd & yldg ground and a gall track: a genuine filly who looks certain to win more gd races.   68
*2846 GOLD FEE [2] (L Cumani) 2-8-12 R Cochrane 4/1 FAV: 312: Heavily bckd: led 1f out:
ran on well but was just out-battled by the winner: 4l clear 3rd: lost nothing in defeat:
acts on firm & yldg: see 2846.   71
--   CASTLE CREEK [1] (I Balding) 2-8-5 Pat Eddery 6/1: 3: Easy to back on debut: ev ch
over 1f out and was not given too hard a race: a gd sort who is certain to improve on this:
dam a very smart filly, winning the Irish 1000 Guineas and Oaks: eff at 7f and should be
suited by 1m: acts on yldg grd and will win races.   57
1855 TECANA [4] (P Walwyn) 2-8-5 Paul Eddery 16/1: 444: No real threat after abs but
by no means disgraced in this company: should be suited by 1m: acts on firm & yldg: see 1464.   51
2527 MUSICAL REVIEW [9] 2-8-5 P Cook 16/1: 4200: Chance over 2f out: ran poorly on firm
ground last time and seems best with some give: see 2283, 1778.   46
3040 ZILDA [8] 2-8-5 M Hills 50/1: 0000: Fdd 2f out: acts on firm & yldg: see 2710.   40
3040 COLOR ARTIST [3] 2-8-8 P Robinson 9/1: 013000: Led over 5f: btr on gd in 3040.   00
--   Sunley Park Street [7] 8-5   2788 Auntie Sybil [5] 8-5
9 ran   ½,4,3,2½,3,1½   (The Queen)   W Hern West Ilsley, Berks.

3109 E.B.F. THEALE MAIDEN STAKES 2YO   £4315   6f   Good/Soft 92 -18 Slow

2939 GAME THATCHER [10] (R Hannon) 2-9-0 B Rouse 12/1: 01: 2 b c Thatching - Welsh Game
(Pall Mall) Impr colt: led inside final 1f for a decisive win in a 2yo mdn at Newbury: cost
15,000 gns as a yearling and is a half brother to sev winners, including the smart Last
Fandango: eff at 6f, should stay 7f: acts on gd & yldg ground and a stiff trk: on the upgrade.   51
3037 ABU MUSLAB [12] (B Hanbury) 2-9-0 G Baxter 6/1 FAV: 002: Bckd from 14/1: led over
1f out, showing improved form: clearly acts well on yldg ground: cost 80,000 gns as a yearling
and should stay further than 6f: can find a race.   45
2852 KIRPAN [20] (G Wragg) 2-9-0 P Robinson 8/1: 03: Al prom: improving colt who should
be suited by further than today's 6f trip: acts on yldg grd and should find a maiden.   42
--   UNPAID MEMBER [16] (J Sutcliffe) 2-9-0 M Hills 33/1: 4: Kept on well inside final 2f
on racecourse debut and improvement seems certain: cost only 7200 gns as a yearling and
dam won over 12f: should be suited by 7f+: acts on yldg grd and is one to keep an eye on.   41
--   BAYOU BLUES [22] 2-8-11 S Dawson 33/1: 0: Led over 4f on debut: promising eff: first
foal whose dam was a sprint winner and is a speedily bred filly: acts on yldg ground.   35
--   DISTANT RULER [8] 2-9-0 J Reid 10/1: 0: Should improve for this first experience of
the racecourse: cost 12,000 gns as a yearling and acts on yldg ground: should stay 7f.   32
--   INFRA RED BOY [24] 2-9-0 N Howe 33/1: 0: Never nearer 7th on racecourse debut and
should do btr: can improve.   00
--   INSTINCTIVE [4] 2-9-0 B Thomson 7/1: 0: Chance over 1f out: should come on for run:
cost 170,000 gns as a yearling and is aa half brother to sev winners: will be suited by 7f:
acts on yldg ground.   00

NEWBURY   Thursday October 23rd   -Cont'd

2119 PALM REEF [26] 2-9-0 R Weaver 8/1: 40: Abs: fin 9th: see 2119 (gd).   00
-- **RIVA MARQUEE** [14] 2-9-0 S Whitworth 13/2: 0: Nearest fin on debut, showing future promise:
half brother to the very useful sprinter Roaring Riva and also the speedy Rio Riva: will improve   00
-- **PRAISEWORTHY** [3] 2-8-11 Pat Eddery 15/2: 0: Easy to back: prom much: can do btr.   00

2491 Wonderful William [19] 9-0		--	Encore Lamour [13] 8-11
2531 Coldwater Canyon [1] 8-11		2782	Fourth Protocol [21] 9-0
-- The Refrigerator [25] 9-0		--	Black Love [11] 8-11
2812 Saxon Mircel [23] 9-0	-- Crown And Horns [18] 9-0		
-- Matching Wood [27] 9-0		--	Melrow [17] 9-0
3037 Puppet Show [6] 9-0	2717 Swiss Connection [5] 9-0		
2514 Treble Top [15] 9-0	-- Vanitas [2] 9-0	--	Wazn [9] 9-0
-- Kopjes [7] 8-11			

27 ran   2½,1½,½,1,2,nk,½,1½,½   (Bob Lanigan)   R Hannon East Everleigh, Wilts.

3110 GREAT WESTERN HANDICAP (0-50) 3YO   £4363   1m 5f   Good/Soft 92 +19 Fast   [55]

2974 REFORM PRINCESS [6] (M Ryan) 3-7-10(bl) G Bardwell(7) 25/1: 1030001: 3 ch f Reform -
Bally's Princess (Salvo) Returns to form when a 25/1 winner of fast run and quite val 3yo
h'cap at Newbury: ran on under press to lead cl home: earlier successful in h'cap at Nottingham
very eff at 13/14f and prob stays 2m: acts on gd/firm and soft grd and on any track.   35
*2802 **REAL MOONSHINE** [2] (A Stewart) 3-7-12 M Roberts 9/2 FAV: 0400012: Led and drifted
left final 1f: just caught: fine effort and is running very well: acts on fast & yldg grd.   36
2955 **OSRIC** [10] (M Ryan) 3-8-11 P Robinson 11/1: 3204203: Led over 3f out: stays 13f: see 1578   44
*2923 **POKEYS PRIDE** [14] (R Sheather) 3-9-3(6ex) M Rimmer 8/1: 2203114: Ev ch over 1f out:
another gd effort on ground that was possibly too soft for him: in fine form: see 2923.   48
2850 **EBOLITO** [4] 3-8-7 J Reid 14/1: 0042100: Al there: lightly raced since 1393.   34
*2722 **VILLAGE HERO** [16] 3-7-11 Dale Gibson(7) 10/1: 00010: Made much: btr 2722 (firm).   20
1236 **WAVE DANCER** [7] 3-8-7 B Thomson 13/2: 4-130: Fin 7th after long abs: see 1236.   00
2834 **TEMPLE WALK** [12] 3-9-7 W Carson 6/1: 1301100: Has gone off the boil: btr 2665.   00
2201 **HUSNAH** [8] 3-9-0 R Cochrane 10/1: 3121200: Abs: btr 2028, 1848 (made running).   00
2720 **STEP IN TIME** [13] 3-7-10 G Carter 10/1: -000440: No threat: can do btr: see 2720.   00

2533 Willow Gorge [1] 7-7	1481 Crystal Moss [5] 7-7(9oh)	
2937 Royal Dynasty [15] 9-5		2848 Autumn Flutter [9] 8-9
1694 Blushing Spy [17] 7-13		2988 Dark Sirona [11] 7-9
2430 Jimbalou [3] 7-7(9oh)		

17 ran   hd,3,1½,2½,2½   (Bill Gerhauser)   M Ryan Newmarket

DONCASTER   Friday October 24th   Lefthanded, Galloping Track

Official Going Given As GOOD/SOFT ON STRAIGHT COURSE : GOOD ON ROUND COURSE

3111 E.B.F. WHEATLEY PARK STAKES 2YO   £1291   7f   Good 44 -34 Slow

-- **PRIME PRINCE** [13] (R Armstrong) 2-8-11 B Thomson 13/2: 1: 2 b c Prince Tenderfoot -
Primed (Primera) Made a successful debut, quickly into his stride and was never hdd when a
cheeky winner of a 2yo stks at Doncaster: 36,000 gns yearling who is closely related to a
handful of winners: clearly very eff over 7f with forcing tactics, certain to stay further
and will be suited by mid dist next season: acts on gd grd and on a gall trk: can only improve   52
-- **QANNAAS** [4] (H T Jones) 2-8-11 A Murray 2/1 JT FAV: 2: Well bckd debutant: al front rank:
cmftbly beat rem tho' flattered by proximity to winner: fetched 280,000 gns as yearling and
is a half brother to sev winners, including useful 7f colt Lidhame: likely to be suited by
1m+: acts on gd grd and on a gall trk: will improve and win a race.   46
2852 **GLASS CASTLE** [12] (A Hide) 2-8-11 R Guest 4/1: 03: Nicely bckd and clearly all the
btr for his recent debut: quite cheaply bought colt who is a half brother to winning sprinter
Simla Ridge: eff over 7f on gd grd: acts on a gall trk.   38
-- **RICHEMONT** [8] (W Jarvis) 2-8-11 J Hills(5) 16/1: 4: Kept on same pace, but should
be btr for this experience: should be suited by mid dist next season: acts on gd ground.   36
-- **BUNCHED** [7] 2-8-8 M Fry 25/1: 0: Al prom on debut: fair eff and should improve:
closely related to sev winners, including useful jumpers The Liquidator & Baron Blakeney:
will appreciate longer dist next term: acts on gd ground.   30
-- **STRIKE ACTION** [3] 2-8-11 W R Swinburn 2/1 JT FAV: 0: Quietly fancied on debut: prom
most and was given an easy time once his chance had gone: cost $135,000 as yearling and is
a half brother to the topclass sprinter Indian King: certain to improve on this rating.   29
-- **COCKATOO ISLAND** [2] 2-8-8 G Duffield 7/1: 0: Ran a fair race to fin 7th on her debut
and seems certain to improve next time: half sister to winning juv Beach Ball: acts on gd
grd and on a gall trk.   ++
-- **SANDMOOR DANCER** [5] 2-8-11 M Birch 10/1: 0: Never got into the race, and clearly was
expected to do btr than this: may need longer dist and more time.   00

-- Twice Bitten [9] 8-8	-- Oriental Plume [10] 8-11	
-- Brega [1] 8-11	-- Rumba Royale [11] 8-11	

12 ran   ½,4,½,1½,2½   (George Tong)   R Armstrong Newmarket

3112 CANTLEY PARK SELLING NURSERY H'CAP   £1324   1m   Good 44 -29 Slow   [34]

*2994 U BIX COPY [14] (J S Wilson) 2-8-11(bl) Pat Eddery 5/1: 3000011: 2 b c Goldhills
Pride - Jubilee Princess (Tribal Chief) In gd form and led below dist, cmftbly in a selling
nursery h'cap at Doncaster (bought in 4400 gns): attracted no bid when recently successful in
a seller at Ayr: eff over 6f, stays 1m well: acts on gd & hvy grd and seems best in blinkers:
could well complete his hat trick in this form.   28
2470 BABY COME HOME [13] (P Rohan) 2-8-4 J Quinn(5) 12/1: 00042: Ran on well: see 2470.   15
2936 RUWI VALLEY [6] (P Haslam) 2-8-12 T Williams 8/1: 00203: Never nearer after trouble
in running: gd eff and seems best over today's trip: see 2841 & 2254.   18
3016 DREAM TICKET [20] (W Haigh) 2-8-9(bl) A Clark 20/1: 000004: Led over 2f out: see 2757   14
2325 DUAL CAPACITY [17] 2-8-10 M Wigham 9/4 FAV: 0000: Gambled on after showing only a
modicum of ability in btr company: al prom, tho' could not quicken: cheaply bought colt
who had been running over sprint dist prev, but clearly does stay 1m: acts on gd/firm.   15
2584 DAMART [9] 2-9-7 A Culhane(7) 25/1: 003000: Fair eff under topweight: best 1812 (7f).   26
2470 WESTGALE [8] 2-8-9 M Wood 10/1: 0030020: Fdd into 7th: see 2470 & 1137.   00
2872 LEG GLIDE [16] 2-8-3(BL) R Lines(3) 10/1: 00000: Never nearer 9th: see 2872: wore blnks today 00
3016 MASCALLS DREAM [18] 2-8-5 T Quinn 5/1: 000220: Wknd: much btr over 7f in 3016:see 2801. 00

*3016 Lyn Rae [2] 8-13(7ex)	3016 Katie Says [5] 8-10	3069 Unos Pet [11] 8-4
3016 Thatch Avon [10] 8-11(bl)		3081 Lisasham [4] 8-3
2872 Corofin Lass [15] 8-9(bl)		2396 Chantilly Dawn [19] 8-11
3031 Penbreasy [7] 8-8	2976 Market Man [12] 8-5	2801 Miss Pisa [1] 8-4
3069 Fireiron [3] 8-7(BL)(1ow)		

20 ran   1½,2½,hd,shthd,hd,1½, ½,4   (J B Russell)   J S Wilson Ayr, Ayrshire.

3113 HALBERDIER HANDICAP (0-50) 3YO+   £3447   1m 2f   Good 44 +04 Fast   [48]

*2255 ROMAN BEACH [19] (W Musson) 6-8-13 M Wigham 10/1: 0000411: 6 b h Averof - Lovage
(Linacre) Made stdy h'way to lead near fin in quite a fast run and val h'cap at Doncaster:
recently found his form when winning a similar race at Newmarket: prev last successful in
'84 at Doncaster: eff over 1m, stays 10f well: acts on fast & yldg grd and on any trk:
in fine form.   45
2995 SWEET DOMAIN [20] (J Dunlop) 3-8-10 B Thomson 14/1: 0011042: Led below dist, hdd
cl home: back to her best and should be winning again soon: see 2161.   46
2720 NORTH OCEAN [16] (L Cumani) 3-8-11 R Cochrane 9/2 FAV: 0303323: In grand form:see 2720. 46
2684 SOLO STYLE [8] (G Lewis) 3-9-2 P Waldron 9/1: 1411424: Not btn far: consistent: see 2684 50
2477 MISTER POINT [17] 4-9-0 W Goodwin(7) 11/1: 1130100: Cl 5th and clear rem: gd eff.   40
2706 AL ZUMURRUD [7] 3-9-0(1ow) S Cauthen 10/1: 2124220: Made much, eased: consistent sort.   36
1931 MASTER LINE [13] 5-9-0 P Johnson(7) 10/1: 0010300: Fin 7th after a fair abs: see 1636.   00
--   ALEGREMAN [23] 4-9-8 G Starkey 9/1: 11040-0: Belated reappearance: just in need of
race and certain to strip fitter next time: won his mdn at Doncaster last season, then followed
up in h'cap company at Folkestone: very eff around 10f: seems to act on any grd and any trk.   ++
2924 SAMHAAN [18] 4-9-1(bl) R Hills 10/1: 1323020: No show: btr 2924: see 2331.   00
3029 KNIGHTS SECRET [4] 5-8-10 M Birch 10/1: 4042220: Btn over 2f out: much btr 3029 (1m)   00
2686 MASKED BALL [3] 6-8-12 M Fry 10/1: 2021400: Much btr over this trip in 1820.   00

2420 Samanpour [14] 9-6	3050 Quiet Riot [10] 9-10	3030 Pentland Hawk [9] 8-7
*2978 Wild Hope [21] 9-0(4ex)		2091 Avec Coeur [1] 8-8
2850 Saryan [22] 8-9(bl)	2666 Misaaff [6] 9-3(bl)	2867 Gorgeous Algernon [12] 8-12(bl)
2443 Romantic Uncle [15] 8-11		2934 Red Russell [11] 9-6
2956 Qualitair Flyer [5] 9-1		2891 Aristocrat Velvet [24] 8-6
2343 Barrack Street [2] 9-5(bl)		

24 ran   ½,½,½,½,6,hd,1½,hd   (R C Canham)   W Musson Newmarket

3114 DONCASTER STAKES (LISTED RACE) 2YO   £7921   5f   Good 44 +16 Fast

2460 LA PETITE NOBLESSE [9] (D Haydn Jones) 2-8-8 J Reid 9/1: 0101: 2 b f Thatching -
Karella (Jukebox) Very useful filly: back to the minimum trip and led after ½ way, gamely in
a fast run, competitive Listed race at Doncaster: disapp over an extra furlong last time,
but earlier was a cmftble winner of her mdn at Salisbury: speedily bred sort who is a half
sister to juv winners Ulpha & Lovely Chimes: suited by a little cut in the grd and likes a
gall trk: highly regarded by her trainer and looks a highclass sprinter in the making.   58
*3037 AGLASINI [10] (F Durr) 2-9-1 Pat Eddery 11/4 JT FAV: 012: Led over ½ way, rallied
well under press and lost nothing in defeat against this speedy filly: improving with ev race. 63
2871 ARAMOR [6] (G Huffer) 2-8-6 M Miller 10/1: 33: Again stayed on strongly and seems
certain to improve further when tackling another furlong: clearly well suited by a gall trk.   48
*2881 ABHAAJ [2] (H T Jones) 2-8-8 A Murray 11/4 JT FAV: 2114: Another gd eff: see 2881.   49
2950 PUSHOFF [11] 2-8-3 M Roberts 12/1: 02230: Kept on well: consistent sort: see 2589.   38
2661 THE DEVILS MUSIC [10] 2-8-6 L Charnock 8/1: 00000: Kept on under press: see 2661, 515   35
2843 VIVALDI [5] 2-8-11 S Cauthen 10/1: 01030: Lost touch quickly after ½ way: fin 9th.   00
2805 ALI SMITH [1] 2-8-6 R Cochrane 9/1: 234020: Never really went pace: see 1791.   00
*2950 GALLANT GALLOIS [7] 2-9-1 M Birch 10/1: 110: Easy to back: showed gd early speed,
wknd quickly after ½ way and was not given a hard time: can do much btr than this: see 2950.   00

| *2696 Imaginary Sky [2] 9-1 | 2950 Altobelli [5] 8-6 |

11 ran   ½,2,nk,2,2   (North Cheshire Trading & Storage Ltd)   D Haydn Jones Pontypridd, Mid Glam.

3115 APPRENTICES' HANDICAP (0-35)   £1479   1m 4f   Good 44 -36 Slow   [30]

2924 MAGIC TOWER [10] (C Brittain) 3-9-4 John Egan(ire) 10/3: 4023431: 3 ch f Tower Walk -
More Fun (Malicious) Gained a deserved first success when leading at the dist, ridden out in
an app h'cap at Doncaster: has only once fin out of the money this term, usually found wanting
for foot and was clearly well suited by today's longer trip: eff over 10/12f on gd & fast
ground: likes a gall trk.   35
2959 HIGHLAND BALL [2] (G Wragg) 3-9-0(BL) Jenny Moller(swe) 8/1: 0043002: Made most:
gd effort: see 2217: wore blinkers for the first time here.   28
3030 STORM HOUSE [11] (K Brassey) 4-9-5 Lester Mcgarrity(belg) 4/1: 30-3103: Ran on well.   25
2995 SHINY KAY [7] (C Elsey) 3-9-0 Luca Sorrentino(ity) 10/1: 0440404: Mkt drifter: ev ch.   24
2880 MAKE PEACE [5] 3-8-10 Jesper Johansen(den) 3/1 FAV: 0000020: Well bckd, but below
form shown in 2880 (11f).   14
2959 ELEGANT GUEST [4] 3-8-8 Frank Werning(ger) 11/2: 0431D00: Twice below form shown 2874   11
2278 Ancilla [3] 10-0   675 Hobournes [6] 8-8   2978 Snarry Hill [9] 8-7
--   Silver Prospect [8] 8-12
10 ran   1½,nk,1½,4,1   (Miss M Carrington Smith)   C Brittain Newmarket

3116 ARMTHORPE HANDICAP (0-35) 3YO+   £2388   1m   Good 44 -16 Slow   [35]

3029 WELSH MEDLEY [2] (D Haydn Jones) 4-8-8 D J Williams(7) 20/1: 4000001: 4 b c
Connaught - Blessed Beauty (Rustam) Mkt drifter but returned to form, led after ½ way and
just held on in a h'cap at Doncaster: little form since an easy winner of a similar race at
Chepstow in May: eff over 8/10f on gd/firm and yldg grd: seems to act on any trk: likes to
be up with the pace.   24
2905 CANADIAN GUEST [13] (H Candy) 3-8-13 W Newnes 10/3 FAV: -002022: Looked unlucky: denied
a clear run and only just failed to get up: certainly deserves a race: see 2905, 1198.   33
3029 BELLA BANUS [3] (W Stephenson) 4-8-13 M Hindley(3) 20/1: 0030003: Not btn far: see 606.   26
2934 SIGNORE ODONE [7] (M H Easterby) 4-9-12 M Birch 11/1: 1120004: Had ev ch: see 2104, 1624 35
2497 MASHHUR [15] 3-9-7 Paul Eddery 20/1: 1-00000: Btr eff: see 465.   34
3029 HELLO GYPSY [9] 5-9-13 W Goodwin(7) 6/1: 1301100: Ran on much too late: see 2797.   32
2797 WARPLANE [11] 6-9-4 J Bleasdale 8/1: 3400100: Fin 8th: best 2728.   00
2581 INTRINSIC [10] 3-8-8(2ow) G Starkey 10/1: -000000: Fin 9th: yet to trouble the judge.   00
2998 NATIVE HABITAT [4] 3-8-11 T Lucas 10/1: 3333000: Btn 2f out: see 2171, 169.   00
1924 DUNLORING [1] 3-9-8 G Duffield 10/1: 0-40000: Abs and never went pace: see 216.   00
2483 HARRY HULL [5] 3-8-13 D Nicholls 10/1: 0004140: Sn well behind and can do much btr.   00
2728 Tip Tap [12] 8-9(BL)   2842 Young Puggy [18] 9-2   1999 Unexplained [6] 8-10
2891 O I Oyston [19] 8-6   2532 Velvet Pearl [8] 8-5   3078 Cbm Girl [16] 8-11
17 ran   hd,¾,2,hd,2,½,½,2,2½   (North Cheshire Trading & Storage Ltd)   D H Jones, Pontypridd

3117 E.B.F. WHEATLEY PARK STAKES 2YO   £1280   7f   Good 44 -60 Slow

2788 GOOD SAILING [13] (R Sheather) 2-8-8 A Shoults(5) 7/4 FAV: 01: 2 b f Scorpio - Mother
Of The Wind (Tumble Wind) Impr filly: weaved her way thro' the field to lead cl home in a
slowly run 2yo stks at Doncaster: sister to middle dist winner Dark Heritage: certain to stay
further than today's 7f trip: acts on gd grd and on a gall trk: still inexperienced and is
certain to rate more highly.   48
--   SIR HARRY LEWIS [6] (B Hills) 2-8-11 B Thomson 4/1: 2: Made smooth prog to chall inside
dist, ran on well and seems sure to go one btr soon: dam a very smart sprinter, but on this
evidence he looks likely to make his mark over middle dist: acts on gd grd and a gall trk.   48
2847 STAFILIO [1] (L Cumani) 2-8-11 R Cochrane 5/2: 03: Well bckd: went on 2f out, no
extra inside dist: still rather backward and should improve further: see 2847.   42
2889 WILL RAINE [5] (D Barron) 2-8-11 D Nicholls 33/1: 04: Had traffic problems: ran on
well but all too late: clearly on the upgrade and may prove btr than this rating: sprint
bred gelding who acts on gd ground.   37
2761 LINDIS GOLD [12] 2-8-11 W Ryan 20/1: 00: Made much: unable to quicken below dist
but did show considerable improvement here: acts on gd grd and on a gall trk.   36
2919 LING GOLD [4] 2-8-8 K Hodgson 16/1: 00: Ran on same pace: half sister to winning juv
Airling but her dam showed her best form over middle dist.   31
--   EIGHT MILE ROCK [9] 2-8-11 M Hindley(0) 8/1: 0: Al mid-div on racecourse debut: 66,000 gns
yearling whose dam is a half sister to the smart Ksar: active in mkt today and should
do better than this.   ++
--   SOYBEAN [10] 2-8-11 P Tulk 8/1: 0: Fdd into 9th after showing gd speed over ½ way:
first foal and will be btr for this experience.   00
--   JEFF HARRIS [7] 2-8-11 G Duffield 8/1: 0: Gd speed over ½ way: btr for race.   00
--   Westminster Waltz [11] 8-8   -- Mephistopheles [3] 8-11
--   Yorkbay [2] 8-11
12 ran   hd,2½,2½,½,1,1   (D O McIntyre)   R Sheather Newmarket

Official Going Given As SOFT

3118 MECCA BOOKMAKERS HANDICAP STAKES 0-70   £6300   6f   Soft 121 +01 Fast   [58]

3015 POWDER BLUE [8] (P Makin) 4-8-13 W R Swinburn 9/1: 4010041: 4 b f He Loves Me - Ridalia (Ridan) Useful filly: fin well to get up cl home in a val h'cap at Newbury: earlier successful in a h'cap at Kempton: in '85 won at Redcar & Yarmouth: very eff over 6f on firm & soft grd: prob acts on any trk: carries weight well. 54

2242 MARGAM [4] (P Walwyn) 3-8-0 A Mackay 14/1: 3104102: Led over 2f out: ran on well and just btn: fine effort after an abs: suited by today's softer ground: see 1900. 42

2953 CREE BAY [3] (J Spearing) 7-8-11(bl) B Thomson 25/1: 1000003: Gd hdwy over 1f out: not btn far in a close fin: clearly acts on firm & soft grd: see 1777. 50

2862 STOCK HILL LASS [2] (L Cottrell) 4-8-1 N Adams 20/1: 0000004: Ev ch 1f out: fair effort: see 2655. 37

2749 HAY STREET [5] 5-8-6 J Lowe 33/1: -000000: Never nearer: btr eff: see 2645. 42

2731 NO BEATING HARTS [1] 3-8-1 R Street 33/1: 1300000: Chance 2f out: best 1654, 1505. 38

2953 YOUNG INCA [6] 8-9-1 R Guest 10/1: 0300300: Fin 7th: dislikes soft: see 1777. 00

2862 TYROLLIE [11] 4-8-13 P Cook 10/1: 0400100: Prom much: twice below 2731 (5f). 00

*3055 PERFECT TIMING [14] 4-9-13(7ex) P Mcentee(7) 11/2: 2102110: Unsuited by soft: see 3055. 00

2947 NUMISMATIST [9] 7-8-5 C Rutter(3) 9/1: -404000: Made no show: see 1933 (gd/firm). 00

3054 BUTSOVA [13] 3-8-3 W Carson 5/2 FAV: 3442230: Sn prom and ev ch: well below 3054 (5f) 00

2488 Dream Chaser [10] 9-3   2674 Precious Metal [12] 9-7

3055 John Patrick [7] 8-3

14 ran   ½,½,1½,shthd,nk   (R P Marchant)   P Makin Ogbourne Maisey, Wilts.

3119 THAMES VALLEY EGGS HANDICAP 0-70 3YO+   £7387   1m 3f   Soft 121 +10 Fast   [59]

2848 PRINCE ORAC [9] (C Brittain) 3-8-7 A Murray 20/1: 0210101: 3 ch c Good Times - Hannah Darling (Match III) Useful colt: made ev yard, staying on very gamely, when a shthd winner of fast run and val h'cap at Newbury: earlier made ev yard to win a 3yo h'cap at Sandown and a mdn at Epsom: half brother to a winner in France: eff at 1m, stays 11f well: acts on firm and soft grd and on any trk: best out in front. 58

2692 EXCEPTIONAL BEAUTY [1] (M Jarvis) 3-8-4 B Rouse 20/1: 4201302: Ran on well final 1f and btn a whisker: 10l clear rem and should win before season's end: acts well on soft: see 2068 55

2148 GALACTIC HERO [3] (M Stoute) 3-8-11 W R Swinburn 7/1: 2-323: No chance with front pair: fair effort after an abs and has been very lightly raced this term: acts on firm & soft. 47

2649 QUEEN OF BATTLE [2] (M Ryan) 3-8-0 A Clark 14/1: 2234104: No extra final 2f but is a consistent filly: stays 11f and prob acts on any trk. 35

2848 BASTINADO [13] 3-7-12 S O'gorman(7) 13/2 JT.FAV: 3010030: No real threat: btr 2848 (10f) 28

2848 BILLET [15] 3-7-7(5oh) T Williams 20/1: 0-00100: Never nearer: twice below 2706 (10f) 18

2156 SENOR TOMAS [17] 3-9-0 R Fox 13/2 JT.FAV: -100: Abs: fin 8th: best 619 (C/D). 00

2845 KHOZDAR [4] 4-9-10 W Carson 10/1: 0-30320: Well btn: much btr 2845 (firm). 00

*2958 BROWN THATCH [6] 3-9-7(7ex) W Ryan 8/1: -30110: Prom most: btr 2958 (firm). 00

2693 INDIAN HAL [12] 4-8-4(1ow) B Thomson 10/1: 4000040: Active in mkt: no show: btr 2693. 00

2149 Torwada [14] 8-2   2850 Thorny Rose [5] 8-0   2942 Mailman [10] 9-1

1038 Thats Your Lot [7] 8-3   2260 Running Flush [16] 8-2(vis)

2942 Pato [8] 8-1(BL)   3038 Lobkowiez [18] 7-10   2686 Kings Crusade [11] 7-7(1oh)

18 ran   shthd,10,½,3,4   (Dimitris M Lemos)   C Brittain Newmarket

3120 DICK DAWSON STAKES 2YO   £5664   1m   Soft 121 -25 Slow

+2894 DOLLAR SEEKER [24] (M Ryan) 2-9-3 J Lowe 8/1: 003211: 2 b c Buckfinder - Syrian Song (Damascus) Useful, impr colt: mkt drifter but led well over 1f out, under press in a val 2yo stks at Newbury: last time out was a ready winner of a mdn at Newcastle: stays 1m really well and should be suited by middle dist next term: acts on firm & soft grd and a gall trk: a genuine and progressive sort who should win more races. 58

+2723 ARDEN [16] (H Cecil) 2-9-3 W Ryan 10/3: 212: Led over 3f out: kept on well when hdd: in gd form and acts on firm & soft ground: see 2723. 55

-- SHANNON COTTAGE [1] (D Elsworth) 2-8-11 A Mcglone 25/1: 3: Stayed on well final 1f, showing a deal of future promise: U.S. bred colt who looks sure to be suited by further than 1m: acts on soft grd and should win races. 46

-- PECHE DOR [22] (I Balding) 2-8-11 R Curant 33/1: 4: Kept on well on debut and this was a promising effort: half brother to sev winners and is bred to stay well: acts on soft ground and looks sure to win a race. 41

2675 KIND OF GLITTER [21] 2-8-8 B Thomson 8/1: 00: Ev ch 2f out: fair effort: cost 18,000 gns as a yearling and is a half sister to a winning 2yo: acts on gd/firm and soft: should be suited by today's 1m trip. 33

-- OUTRAGEOUS FORTUNE [8] 2-8-11 W R Swinburn 33/1: 0: Kept on well on debut: cost 8800 gns as a yearling and is a half brother to sev winners: should be suited by middle dist next term: acts on soft. 35

1629 YOUNG GHILLIE [10] 2-8-11 Paul Eddery 33/1: 000: Abs: fin 7th: lightly raced: see 1241 00

-- ABADARE [6] 2-8-11 J Matthias 33/1: 0: Nearest fin on racecourse debut: U.S. bred colt who acts on soft. 00

*2869 DRY DOCK [2] 2-9-3 W Carson 5/2 FAV: 010: Heavily bckd disapp: well below 2869 (gd/frm) 00

-- Hotel Lotti [23] 8-8   2951 Honey Dancer [9] 8-11 -- Clifford Street [19] 8-11 00

--	Dorver [3] 8-11	2698	Farmers Gamble [18] 8-11
--	High Aloft [4] 8-11	--	Highly Pleased [13] 8-11
--	Kashkiss [11] 8-11	2711	Mansio [5] 8-11 1629 Va Lute [17] 8-11
--	Leap In Time [14] 8-8	2527	Regal Rhythm [20] 8-8 -- Rise And Fall [15] 8-8
1518	Seragsbee [7] 8-8		
23 ran	1½,2,3,3,nk (R P Ramsden)		M Ryan Newmarket

3121 GROUP 3 ST SIMON STAKES   £16905   1m 4f Soft 121 +10 Fast

-- JUPITER ISLAND [8] (C Brittain) 7-8-9 A Murray 6/1: 14001-31: 7 b h St Paddy - Mrs
Moss (Reform) Smart horse: despite an abs was brilliantly produced by his trainer to win fast
run Gr 3 St Simon Stks at Newbury: led over 1f out and ran on gamely: in April was a fine 3rd
to Dahar in a Gr 1 event at Santa Anita, despite running with an injury: in '85 won a Gr 2
event at Longchamp and also an easy winner of Gr 2 Hardwicke Stks at Royal Ascot: first time
out won Gr 3 John Porter at Newbury: in '84 won again at Newbury: very eff over 10f, stays
14f: acts on firm & soft ground and is suited by a gall trk: genuine and consistent sort who is
is a credit to his trainer.   80
*2845 VERD ANTIQUE [7] (H Cecil) 3-8-7 W Ryan 5/4 FAV: -1212: Led over 2f out: kept on well
when hdd: another fine effort and acts on firm & soft ground: see 2845.   83
2868 QUEEN HELEN [3] (W Hern) 3-7-13 R Fox 33/1: 21-0043: Behind, nearest fin: gd eff and
she has been very lightly raced this term: acts on firm & soft and stays 12f well: see 755.   71
2565 NISNAS [1] (P Cole) 3-8-12 T Quinn 11/2: 1031104: Mkt drifter: chance 2f out: fair
effort at these weights: see 2222.   80
3006 AMONGST THE STARS [5] 3-8-7 J Lowe 66/1: 1014400: Prom much, belying her 66/1 SP:
has been running well all season in smart company: see 2236.   68
2825 COCOTTE [6] 3-8-4 W Carson 20/1: 0142300: Never showed: see 1932 (10f)   53
3001 HIGHLAND CHIEFTAIN [3] 3-8-12 B Thomson 12/1: 1210220: Fdd str: unsuited by soft: see 3001 00
*2752 KAZAROUN [9] 4-9-3 W R Swinburn 4/1: 210-310: Led 10f: well below 2752 (gd/frm)   00
510 TISNT [2] 3-8-7 A Clark 12/1: -1230: Very long abs and no show: see 510.   00
9 ran 1½,2,2½,4,7   (Lord Tavistock)   C Brittain Newmarket

3122 OCTOBER NURSERY HANDICAP 2YO   £4584   6f   Soft 121 -15 Slow   [65]

-2935 SUPREME ROSE [16] (W Musson) 2-7-13 A Mcglone 4/1 FAV: 01021: 2 b f Frimley Park -
Ragtime Rose (Ragstone) Fin well under press to lead cl home in a val nursery h'cap at
Newbury: earlier a winner of a fillies mdn at Beverley: eff at 5f, stays 6f well: acts on
gd/firm and soft grd and a gall trk: carries weight well.   47
3019 ROCK MACHINE [4] (N Callaghan) 2-8-1 B Rouse 10/1: 44102: Led inside final 1f, just
caught: gd effort and handles soft grd well: should find a similar event: see 2717.   48
3041 BECHEMAL [1] (B Hills) 2-7-11 W Carson 14/1: 33003: Chance final 1f: ran on well
and just btn in a cl finish: well suited by a stiff 6f: acts on gd/firm and soft grd.   43
2252 FOUR LAFFS [7] (H Whiting) 2-7-7(3oh) L Riggio(7) 20/1: -023104: Came from behind:
not the best of runs and btn 1l: unlucky? : fine effort after an abs: lightly raced filly
who acts very well on soft ground: see 353.   37
2954 SHARP REMINDER [3] 2-9-7 B Thomson 10/1: 0031300: Led over 1f out: most consistent:
acts on firm & soft: see 2694, 2561.   61
+2812 CAPTAIN HOLLY [2] 2-8-4 T Quinn 8/1: 010: Chance inside final 2f: see 2812.   43
2118 MASHBUB [9] 2-7-8 T Williams 8/1: 3220: Dsptd lead: fdd: abs since btr 2118 (5f)   00
-3072 FOURWALK [17] 2-8-3 P Cook 8/1: 3200120: Dsptd lead: quick reappearance and much btr 3072 00
1255 TENDER TIFF [8] 2-8-4 W Newnes 7/1: 14300: Active in mkt after long abs: made no
show: best 655 (heavy).   00
2729 Young Lochinvar [6] 7-7(9oh)   1925 Munaasib [3] 9-1
2677 Combined Exercise [12] 7-13   *2875 Kept Waiting [15] 7-11
2753 Keen Note [13] 7-7(2oh)   2677 Unity Farm Boy [5] 7-7(4oh)
3058 Mr Mumbles [10] 7-7(12oh)   2421 Enchanted Times [11] 7-8
17 ran hd,nk,¾,2½,shthd,3   (E A Badger)   W Musson Newmarket

3123 LETCOMBE HANDICAP STAKES 3YO+ 0-50   £5325   1m   Soft 121 -07 Slow   [47]

3021 GOLD PROSPECT [22] (G Balding) 4-9-8 B Rouse 12/1: 2301241: 4 b c Wolverlife - Golden
Darling (Darling Boy) Useful colt: switched over 1f out and stayed on well to lead cl home
in a 27 runner h'cap at Newbury: has been tremendously consistent this term, earlier winning
the Autumn H'cap on this trk and also first time out at Folkestone: has run many fine
races in defeat: eff at 6f, clearly stays 1m well: acts on firm & soft grd and on any trk:
genuine and a credit to his trainer.   52
2566 STAR OF A GUNNER [24] (R Holder) 6-9-9 A Mackay 11/1: 0003202: Led 1f out: kept on:
gd effort: see 2390, 248.   51
3060 DUELLING [14] (P Mitchell) 5-8-6(vis)(3ow) S Raymont 20/1: 4102043: Not clear run
and fin well: acts well on soft: see 1619.   33
2123 GURTEEN BOY [2] (R Hannon) 4-8-11 A Murray 16/1: 0001034: Chance final 1f: gd run
after abs: see 1553.   36
3050 PARIS TRADER [23] 4-8-5 G Bardwell(7) 20/1: 3002000: Chance 1f out: not btn far: see 2867. 29
2144 MERLE [12] 4-9-3 J Lowe 25/1: 0000000: Led 1½f out: abs: yet to be placed this term.   34
2934 GRANNYS BANK [7] 4-9-1 Dale Gibson(7) 15/2: 1221020: Chance 2f out: see 2934 (gd/frm)   00
2934 OPEN HERO [21] 3-9-6 W R Swinburn 6/1 FAV: 11-0030: Well bckd: much btr 2934 (gd/frm)   00
2934 SPRING IN MY STEP [25] 4-9-3 C Nutter 9/1: 110-340: No threat: btr 2934 (gd/frm)   00

```
3042 GREAT LEIGHS [18] 3-9-1 B Thomson 10/1: 2000020: Fdd: well below 3042 (gd)                    00
*2784 Altch N Bee [4] 9-8          2956 De Rigueur [1] 10-0          *2956 Flyhome [17] 9-11(6ex)
2956 All Fair [10] 9-9(vis)       2946 Meritmoore [6] 9-0           2867 Paris Turf [13] 9-8
2477 Smokeys Secret [8] 9-7       2879 Floating Asset [20] 8-11     -719 Framlington Court [27] 9-6
2749 Super Trip [5] 9-6           1560 Arctic Ken [11] 8-1          2928 Bowl Over [26] 9-0(bl)
2477 Conmayjo [9] 8-13            2784 Pounelta [15] 8-7            3078 Sovereign Love [16] 8-7(2ow)
2946 Prince Merandi [3] 8-8       2896 Foot Patrol [19] 8-1
27 ran   1,hd,1,shthd,4           (Harvey Spack)               G Balding Fyfield, Hants.
```

Official Going Given As GOOD/SOFT ON STRAIGHT COURSE: GOOD ON ROUND COURSE

3124 EUROPEAN APPRENTICES' H'CAP (0-60)   £3388   7f   Yielding 87 -05 Slow   [60]

3021 SAILORS SONG [6] (N Vigors) 4-8-10 Luca Sorrentino(ity) 6/1: 0120331: 4 ch g Song -
Balgreggan (Hallez): Gained a deserved win, al prom & led at the dist, ridden out in an app.
h'cap at Doncaster: has been in gd form since just getting home in a h'cap at Lingfield in
Aug: most consistent last season, winning at Pontefract: eff over 6/7f on fast & yld grnd:
acts on any trk.   54
3015 SEW HIGH [11] (B Mcmahon) 3-8-5 Lester Mcgarrity(belg) 14/1: 1030002: Sn held a clear
lead, kept on under press: best effort for sometime and may go one btr if reverting to a
shorter trip : see 1704.   46
3050 REINDEER WALK [10] (G Huffer) 4-8-5 M Lynch(gb) 14/1: -000403: Never nearer: see 2945.   38
3055 DORKING LAD [4] (M Tompkins) 4-8-7 Jenny Moller(swe) 10/1: 0000004: Ran on too late.   39
2870 SIR ARNOLD [5] 3-9-1 Jesper Johansen(den) 7/1: 2313130: Stayed on late: btr in 2870.   44
2674 CORN STREET [7] 8-8-6(1ow) Dominique Regnard(fr) 11/2: 0000000: Chased ldrs over ¼way:
likes some cut: see 172.   31
2144 COINCIDENTAL [8] 4-8-10 John Egan(ire) 6/1: 1-02300: Fdd into 8th: see 2072 & 1804.   00
3021 HILTON BROWN [2] 5-9-5 S Dawson(uk) 11/4 FAV: 3031020: Disapp after fine run in 3021.   00
2773 Amigo Loco [3] 9-1   2685 Gouverno [9] 8-7   1387 Si Signor [1] 10-0
11 ran   2½,2½,¾,3,nk,3   (Introgroup Holdings Ltd)   N Vigors Lambourn, Berks

3125 YORKSHIRE TV NURSERY H'CAP 2YO   £4480   7f   Yielding 87 -10 Slow   [54]

2830 MELODY MAKER [20] (B Hills) 2-8-10 J Reid 14/1: 03141: 2 b c Song - Lovage (Linacre):
Useful colt: led over 2f out & ran on strongly to win a nursery h'cap at Doncaster: lightly
rcd since winning his mdn at Chester in mid-July: very eff over 7/8f & is likely to stay
further next season: acts on fast & yld grnd & on any trk.   50
2777 IBNALMAGHITH [18] (H T Jones) 2-8-10 A Riding(7) 20/1: 143002: Ran on well under press
& this was a much btr effort: acts on fast & yld grnd: see 1735 & 1149.   45
*2607 MISS SARAJANE [19] (R Hollinshead) 2-7-12 A Culhane(7) 20/1: 00213: Al front rank:
gd effort in this btr company & could win a nursery before the seasons end: acts on fast
& yld: see 2607.   32
*2625 LAST STAND [17] (J Hindley) 2-7-12 A Shoults(2) 16/1: 003314: Made much: acts on yld.   26
-2859 SAUNDERS LASS [7] 2-7-7(1oh) S Dawson 16/1: 2103420: Nearest fin: acts on yld: see 2859.   18
3041 SPEEDBIRD [6] 2-8-12 P Robinson 12/1: 0040140: Ran on strongly: in fine form: see 2756.   37
2926 FORESIGHT [12] 2-9-3 Pat Eddery 13/2: 03430: Nicely bckd: fin 7th: acts on yld: see 2626   00
2997 COMMONSIDR GIPSY [9] 2-8-0 B Crossley 7/1: 0003020: Front rank over ½way: btr in 2444.   00
2949 PEATSWOOD SHOOTER [4] 2-9-7 K Darley 13/2: 0340100: Fdd under top weight: best
over 6f in 2325.   00
3019 PETER MOON [3] 2-9-1 C Asmussen 6/1 FAV: 03140: Well bckd: fdd after ½way: much
better in 3019 (6f, good/firm).   00
2677 PLAGUE ORATS [1] 2-9-6 S Cauthen 8/1: 014320: Raced alone far side, eased below dist.   00
2968 Fountains Choice [16] 8-0   2922 Clown Streaker [13] 8-5   2179 Hanseatic [15] 9-1
2628 Irish Brigadier [11] 8-9   2811 Moore Brass [14] 8-10   2777 Antinous [2] 8-12
2865 Derwent Valley [8] 7-12   2669 Premier Lad [5] 9-0
-2971 Kaleidophone [10] 8-4   2082 Wichita Springs [21] 8-3
21 ran   1½,½,3,1½,shhd,½,1,1½,½   (Mrs P Shaw)   B Hills Lambourn, Berks

3126 GROUP 1 WILLIAM HILL FUTURITY STAKES   £44120   1m   Yielding 87 -05 Slow

+2721 REFERENCE POINT [6] (H Cecil) 2-9-0 Pat Eddery 4/1: 311: 2 b c Mill Reef - Home On
the Range (Habitat): Proved himself an outstanding prospect for next season, soon in front
and galloped his rivals into the ground when a highly impressive winner of Gr.1 William Hill
Futurity Stakes at Doncaster: needed the race on his debut, but was a similar wide margin
winner of a stakes race at Sandown last time, when breaking the juveniles course record: half
brother to 3yo winner Top Range: very eff over 1m & looks certain to prove a high class
performer over middle dists next term: acts on fast & yld grnd & on a gall trk: a resolute
galloper who seems best ridden from the front: held in very high regard by his powerful stable
and has been installed fav. for next year's Derby.   86
*2771 BENGAL FIRE [4] (C Brittain) 2-9-0 M Roberts 6/1: 23112: Kept on well under press,
though always in vain pursuit of this very smart winner: lost nothing in defeat and is sure
to win more gd races: acts on yld grnd: see 2771.   74
```
```

*2732 LOVE THE GROOM [9] (J Dunlop) 2-9-0 P Robinson 14/1: 213: Stepped up considerably in
class here but ran a fine race and is clearly a fast impr colt: stays 1m well and looks
certain to stay further: acts on fast & yld: see 2732.   72
2771 MR EATS [2] (P Kelleway) 2-9-0 G Baxter 50/1: 124044: Outsider: ran a blinder in
this high class company: will be suited by middle dists next season: acts on fast & yld.   72
2849 ARABIAN SHEIK [5] 2-9-0 C Asmussen 3/1: 120: Hvly bckd: slightly hmpd inside dist
but would not have finished any closer: stays 1m: likely to prove best on a sounder surface.   71
*2521 TOLUCA LAKE [7] 2-9-0 R Cochrane 8/1: 41110: End of his winning run but this was a
creditable effort in a much higher grade of race: acts on fast & yld grnd: continues to
improve: see 2521.   65
+2860 SUHAILIE [10] 2-9-0 S Cauthen 2/1 FAV: 1110: Btr-bckd stable mate of winner: wknd
quickly 2f out & clearly totally unsuited by this much easier ground: much btr in 2860 (firm).   58
2771 SANTELLA SAM [8] 2-9-0 N Day 50/1: 3201200: Outclassed, but not disgraced: see 2571.   54
2336 STILLMAN [1] 2-9-0 M Birch 50/1: 001320: Outsider & never dngr: see 2336 & 1812.   00
2751 SHINING WATER [11] 2-8-11 J Reid 12/1: 2110130: Lack-lustre   performance: probably
unsuited by this easier grnd though may have just had enough for this season: much btr in
2751 and 2384 on fast grnd.   00
10 ran   5,½,shhd,½,3,3,1½   (Louis Freedman)   H Cecil Newmarket

3127 SOLAGLAS ENERGY SAVERS H'CAP (0-70)   £6400   6f   Yielding 87 +28 Fast   [65]

2538 QUE SYMPATICA [10] (R Boss) 4-10-0 J Reid 16/1: 0002401: 4 b f Young Generation -
High Finale (High Line): Smart filly: returned to her best form over this shorter trip, led
dist when cmftbly defying top weight in a very fast run & valuable h'cap at Doncaster: first
time out winner at Kempton last season & in '84 won her sole start at Yarmouth: has run over
lngr dists though seems best over 6/8f: acts on fast and soft ground and seems to handle any track.
: clearly carries weight well.   76
3106 CHAPLINS CLUB [14] (D Chapman) 6-8-5(bl) K Darley 4/1 JT FAV: 0430022: Quick reapp. &
again ran a fine race: deserves a win: see 1222 and 1026.   45
3104 JARROVIAN [11] (T Fairhurst) 3-7-9(bl) G Carter 12/1: 0040133: In fine form: see 2977.   36
3055 BATON BOY [4] (M Brittain) 5-7-7(4oh) A Proud 9/1: 4044344: Another gd effort: see 2277   32
2668 JOKIST [12] 3-8-8 Pat Eddery 11/2: 0211100: Had ev ch: see 2668 & 2343.   44
3055 MATOU [2] 6-9-0 C Asmussen 10/1: D100000: Prom most: best in 1810.   48
2947 CATHERINES WELL [7] 3-9-5 S Cauthen 4/1 JT FAV: 1111040: Well bckd, wknd into 9th.   00
3106 BRIDGE STREET LADY [9] 5-8-9 G Baxter 8/1: 1200300: Front rank over ½way: btr in
2402 (5f): see 327.   00
3015 Quinta Reef [8] 8-6   3055 Dawns Delight [1] 9-0(vis)
2953 Meeson King [5] 7-10   2970 Kathred [6] 7-11   3055 All Is Forgiven [15] 8-13(VIS)
2842 Tufuh [13] 8-9
14 ran   3,nk,hd,2,nk,nk,3,½   (Mrs Andry Muinos)   R Boss Newmarket

3128 WHITE ROSE SELLING STAKES 3YO+   £3840   1m 4f   Yielding 87 -04 Slow

1048 ALARM CALL [14] (D Morley) 3-8-10 R Cochrane 4/1: 4101: 3 b c Alleged - Sunelianne
(Cyanne): Dropped to selling company after a long abs & proved an easy winner, not clear run
but led inside dist in an all-aged seller at Doncaster (bought in 5,600 gns): earlier won his
mdn at Haydock, when trained by G Harwood: effective over 12f on gd & soft grnd: seems well
suited by a gall trk: btr than a plater & should be noted in h'cap company.   35+
2576 STONEBROKER [19] (D Haydn Jones) 4-8-11 J Reid 8/1: 1002232: Ran well: see 1747.   20
2964 DICK KNIGHT [4] (K Ivory) 5-9-0(vis) A Shoults(5) 14/1: 0020323: Led over 2f out: see 2964. 22
2480 DONT RING ME [18] (W Hastings Bass) 4-8-11(bl) Pat Eddery 3/1 FAV: 0402304: Well bckd:
every chance: see 675.   16
2280 SIR BRETT [6] 3-8-6(bl)(1ow) C Asmussen 8/1: 0414000: Ran on same pace: best on hvy in 790 16
2896 COSMIC FLIGHT [17] 3-8-3(1ow) M Wigham 25/1: 0000000: Led over 3f out: best early
season: see 67.   11
3071 HARBOUR BAZAAR [1] 6-9-0(vis) S Whitworth 10/1: D312030: Fin 8th: see 2432 (13f).   00
2415 MOON JESTER [7] 6-9-5 D Mckay 10/1: 0000330: Btr in 2415 (gd/firm): see 349.   00
2959 KERRY MAY SING [3] 3-8-5(bl) P Robinson 6/1: 0004030: Much btr on fast grnd in 2959.   00
2807 Skyboot [5] 9-5   *522 Mill Tern [8] 9-0(bl)
--   Judys Dowry [12] 8-11   2964 Hot Betty [13] 8-11   2722 Way Above [2] 8-5
2722 Belvel [9] 8-5   2874 No Stopping [16] 8-5(bl)
530 Flaming Pearl [10] 9-2   609 Cavalieravantgarde [15] 9-0
2974 Coleman Hawkins [11] 8-5
19 ran   4,½,1½,½,1½,1½   (D Morley)   D Morley Newmarket

3129 ELMFIELD PARK STAKES 3YO+   £2070   2m 2f   Yielding 87 -07 Slow

-- TROY FAIR [5] (J Edwards) 4-9-0 S Cauthen 11/1: -0000-1: 4 b c Troy - Happy Kin
(Bold Hitter): Made a successful reapp, staying on well to lead inside dist in an all-aged
stakes race at Doncaster: off the trk since splitting a pastern over hdles in Mar: last ran
on the Flat when 6th in last years St Leger: sole success previously came at Newmarket in '84:
well suited by a dist of grnd: acts on hard & yld grnd & is suited by a gall trk: sure to
be all the btr for this run & should pay his way when returning to hdles.   40
*3035 SHAHS CHOICE [3] (J Dunlop) 3-8-6(1ow) C Asmussen 13/8 FAV: 2221212: Well bckd fav:
led well over 2f out, no extra close home: clear of rem & has been most consistent this season   38

DONCASTER   Saturday October 25th   -Cont'd

1016 LA ROSE GRISE [7] (J Fitzgerald) 4-8-2 M Roberts 16/1: 024-003: Recently placed over
hdles & is in gd form: clearly well suited by a test of stamina: likes some cut in the grnd.   14
2809 SUN STREET [9] (C Brittain) 4-9-2 G Baxter 7/1: 2013004: Seems to act on any trk.   26
582 HOLLISTON [2] 4-9-5 J Reid 9/1: 10-00: Long abs: well clear of rem: very lightly rcd
colt who made a winning debut in a large field of mdns at Newbury last term: stays well:
likes soft grnd.   26
2647 HIGH RENOWN [10] 6-9-0 Pat Eddery 16/1: 0-00-00: Lightly rcd & little form.   00
2996 PALMAHALM [8] 4-8-2 A Shoults(5) 7/2: -300: Nicely bckd: well btn 9th over this much
lngr trip: see 1636.   00
-- Inlander [6] 8-5   2075 Smack [4] 8-5   -- All Flash [11] 9-0(vis)
-- Allimore [12] 8-5
11 ran   1¼,6,¼,1½,15   (R J McAlpine)   J Edwards Sellack, Herefordshire

3130 VARIETY CLUB MAIDEN STAKES 2YO   £3614   6f   Yielding 87 -18 Slow

2983 GEORGE JAMES [18] (J Dunlop) 2-9-0 C Asmussen 7/1: 0421: 2 gr c Mummy's Pet -
Pariscene (Dragonara Palace): Impr cat: easy to back, but stayed on well to lead inside
dist in a 2yo mdn at Doncaster: cost 35,000 gns as a yearling: very eff over 6f & seems
certain to stay further: acts on fast & yld grnd & on any trk.   53
2987 KNOCKIN EXPRESS [16] (G Huffer) 2-9-0 M Miller 4/1: 022: Continues to impr: broke well
& only just failed to make all: well suited by this extra furlong & must win soon: see 2626.   48
2939 CANANGO [9] (M Stoute) 2-9-0 Pat Eddery 1/1 FAV: 43: Hvly bckd to fulfil the promise
of his debut: al front rank, though may need further to get off the mark: see 2939.   47
1928 HENRIETTA PLACE [19] (G Pritchard Gordon) 2-8-12(1ow) S Cauthen 11/1: 04: Al up there.   41
2950 MA PETITE LASSIE [10] 2-8-11 J Reid 10/1: 0220: Dsptd lead most: stays 6f: see 2950.   37
-- MUNADHIL [21] 2-9-0 R Cochrane 20/1: 0: Easy to back on debut: al prom & sure to
come on for this experience: 42,000 gns yearling who is a half brother to several winners,
most notably the very useful 6/7f filly Kittyhawk: should be suited by 1m plus next term:
acts on yld grnd & on a gall trk.   40
-- AS SHARP [7] 2-8-11 M Roberts 20/1: 0: Mkt drifter on debut: al there, fin a promising
7th: speedily bred filly who is closely related to several winners: acts on yld grnd & on
a gall trk: likely to impr.   35
2782 SERGEANT SMOKE [23] 2-9-0 K Darley 25/1: 000: Fdd into 8th: acts on yld: see 2782.   37
2082 PROSPECT PLACE [2] 2-9-0 T Lucas 25/1: 030: Never nearer 9th: cheaply bought gelding
who has shown some promise in his start to date & is likely to do btr next season: acts on
gd/firm & yld.   35
2696 ZEN WEST THREE [5] 2-9-0 R Still 50/1: 000: Prom most: best effort to date.   33
-- HYPNOLOGY [20] 2-9-0 R Lines(3) 12/1: 0: Never beyond mid-div on debut: breeding
suggests he will probably need middle dists & more time to show his best form, but this was
a fair initial effort.   29
-- SHAMAYIL [22] 2-8-11 R Hills 12/1:   Easy to back on debut & no real threat:
$885,000 yearling whose dam Kilijaro was a high class performer over 7/10f: sure to do btr
than this.   25
-- Bick Benedict [15] 9-0   -- Water City [17] 9-0
-- Jobys Jet [4] 9-0   -- Pit Talk [12] 8-11   2328 Shannon River [22] 9-0
3014 Heatseeker [14] 9-0   -- Upwell [6] 9-0   -- Verdon Canyon [8] 9-0
1172 High Chateau [13] 9-0   2645 Taylors Revenge [11] 9-0
22 ran   1½,¼,1½,1,hd,1,nk,¼,nk,1½,shhd   (R G Percival)   J Dunlop Arundel, Sussex

LINGFIELD   Monday October 27th   Lefthanded, Sharpish Undulating Track

Official Going Given As GOOD/SOFT FOR FIRST 3 RACES: HEAVY FOR REMAINDER

3131 EBF WILLOW MAIDEN STAKES 2YO DIV I   £2628   7f   Yielding 102 -22 Slow

-3075 IRISH SAILOR [6] (Pat Mitchell) 2-9-0 J Reid 7/2 FAV: 30421: 2 b c Runnett - Wilden
(Will Somers): Consistent colt: gained a deserved win, led over 2f out, readily in a 2yo mdn
at Lingfield: cost I.R. 10,000 as a yearling and is a half brother to several winners, incl
useful Irish hurdler Yankee's Princess: very eff over 6/7f & should stay further: acts on fast
& yld grnd & on any trk.   46
-- RULING DYNASTY [7] (G Harwood) 2-9-0 A Clark 4/1: 2: Quietly fancied on debut: no ch
with winner, but ran on promisingly and should go on from here: half brother to useful winners
Nuravia and War Hero: should stay 1m plus: acts on yld grnd & on a sharp trk: will improve.   36
1946 MAGNOLIA EXPRESS [5] (S Dow) 2-9-0 W Ryan 33/1: 03: Ran on same pace: clear of rem
& this was a gd effort after a long break: half brother to several winners: stays 7f: acts
on yielding.   35

914

2895 **GOODNIGHT MASTER** [12] (A Moore) 2-8-11 A Mcglone 33/1: 0004: Front rank over ½way:
first real signs of form from this speedily bred filly: acts on yld grnd.   22
--   **SEPTEMBER SNAP** [1] 2-8-11 W Newnes 16/1: 0: Active in mkt on debut: no real threat after
½way, though likely to improve for this experience: half sister to 6f winner Madraco: may
prefer a sounder surface.   18
2788 **SNOWSDOWN** [11] 2-8-11 P Cook 12/1: 000: Never reached ldrs: cheaply bought filly who
has shown little form to date and may need more time.   17
2542 **LINE OF SUCCESSION** [3] 2-9-0 R Hills 13/2: 000: Led over ½way: fin 7th: see 1552.   18
2368 **HIGH CLIMBER** [14] 2-8-11 Pat Eddery 4/1: 0230: Prom most: wknd quickly: btr in 2368.   00

3067 Sahood [4] 9-0		--	Brigadier Thwaites [9] 9-0		
3081 Netzer [2] 9-0		1728 Minobee [10] 8-11		2846 Lullaby Baby [15] 8-11	
2095 William Pere [13] 9-0		--	Crest Of Glory [8] 8-11		

15 ran   4,½,6,2,½,½,½   (M Heinimann)   Pat Mitchell Folkington, Sussex

3132 EBF WILLOW MAIDEN STAKES 2YO DIV I   £2628   7f   Yielding 102 -12 Slow

2852 **BRACORINA** [7] (J Dunlop) 2-8-11 W Carson 5/4 FAV: 31: 2 b f High Line - Premier
Danseuse (Saritamer): Well bckd after her promising debut and led after ½way for an easy win
in a 2yo mdn at Lingfield: narrowly btn behind Tweeter and Bashayer at Newmarket earlier this
month: very eff over 7f & sure to stay at least 1m: acts on fast & yld grnd & seems to handle
any trk: well regarded & certain to rate more highly.   55
3053 **PONDERED BID** [11] (G Pritchard Gordon) 2-9-0 W Ryan 11/2: 02: Led to ½way: no ch with
winner though cmftbly too good for the rem: acts on gd & yld: sure to win a race: see 3053.   48
--   **ENGLISH RIVER** [9] (M Stoute) 2-9-0 M A Giles(7) 14/1: 3: Friendless in mkt on debut,
but showed plenty of future promise: closely related to several winners, incl useful 7/10f colt
My Volga Boatman: acts on yld grnd: June foal who seems certain to impr in time.   42
2718 **CABALLINE** [4] (M Haynes) 2-9-0 P Cook 25/1: 0000204: Mkt drifter, but al prom and
showed much impr form here: last month was btn in a seller & had since been well exposed in a
nursery: seems to need plenty of give in the grnd to show his best form: see 2580 & 200.   38
3053 **BIRWAZ** [1] 2-9-0 J Reid 10/1: 000: Led/dsptd lead over ½way: acts on yld: see 2782.   36
2547 **KIKUYU** [6] 2-9-0 Pat Eddery 11/2: 00: Not unduly punished: btr on firm ground in 2547.   32

2920 Say You [2] 9-0		2869 Hubba [13] 9-0		544 Balquhidder Boy [14] 9-0	
2700 Segovian [5] 9-0		2961 Marcovich [3] 9-0		2571 Convincing [8] 9-0	
-- Kash Juwain [10] 9-0		1262 Flying Chapeau [15] 8-11			

14 ran   3,3,2½,1,2,2½   (A Stirling)   J Dunlop Arundel, Sussex

3133 EBF WILLOW MAIDEN STAKES 2YO DIV II   £2794   7f   Yielding 102 -09 Slow

-2926 **DUNENNY** [14] (R Akehurst) 2-9-0 A Clark 13/8 FAV: 21: 2 br c Dunphy - Drora (Busted):
Hvly bckd but only just got home, had to be strongly ridden to lead on the post in a 2yo mdn
at Lingfield: totally unfancied when narrowly btn by the useful War Brave on his recent debut over
6f here: half brother to winning juvenile Beechwood Cottage: very eff over 6/7f &
seems sure to get further: acts on fast & yld grnd & likes this sharpish trk.   46
2920 **FOURTH LAD** [9] (R Hannon) 2-9-0 B Rouse 10/1: 0040042: Led/dsptd lead thro'out,
caught final stride: much btr effort: acts on fast & yld grnd: see 985.   45
2976 **DYNAMIC STAR** [4] (M Usher) 2-9-0 A Mcglone 25/1: 0033: Ran on well & only just btn:
clear of rem & this represented much impr form: acts on fast & yld grnd: see 2976.   45
2901 **SUTOSKY** [16] (I Matthews) 2-8-11 Pat Eddery 6/1: 44: No extra below dist: probably found
this easy grnd & shorter trip against her: likely to do btr: see 2901.   34
2717 **FEASIBLE** [2] 2-9-0 J Reid 25/1: 000: Never nearer over this lngr trip: previously twice
outpcd over the minimum: acts on yld grnd & on a sharp trk.   33
2847 **RUNNING STEPS** [5] 2-9-0 P Waldron 11/2: 00: No threat, but was picking up grnd at
the fin: seems likely to impr when tackling lngr trips next season: acts on yld grnd.   32
2119 **CHARLIE ME DARLING** [6] 2-9-0 P Cook 10/1: 00: Made no show after fair abs: see 2119.   00
2664 **TAP ON BLUE** [11] 2-8-11 R Hills 10/1: 000: Fin in rear: much btr in 2664 (firm).   00

2147 Lady Silca Key [13] 8-11				2926 Rectory Girl [12] 8-11	
2982 Eagles Nest [8] 8-11		2651 Viens Vite [17] 8-11		1241 Al Ludher [15] 9-0	
-- Balholm Express [10] 9-0				-- Lord Kilgayle [7] 9-0	
2070 Claires Buck [1] 8-11		3018 Jane Marple [3] 8-11			

17 ran   shhd,hd,5,2,hd,shhd   (E Reitel)   R Akehurst Epsom, Surrey

3134 EBF WILLOW MAIDEN STAKES 2YO DIV II   £2794   7f   Yielding 102 -03 Slow

--   **LYPHENTO** [13] (G Harwood) 2-9-0 A Clark 10/3: 1: 2 b c Lyphard's Wish - Hasty Viento
(Gallant Man): Made an impressive winning debut, nicely bckd & led inside dist, cmftbly in a
2yo mdn at Lingfield: American bred colt who fetched $37,000 as a yearling & is a half brother
to several winners in the States: likely to be suited by middle dists next season: acts on yld
grnd & on a sharpish trk: promising sort who can only improve.   50
--   **EXCELLERS SPECIAL** [9] (O Douieb) 2-9-0 R Machado 10/1: 2: Led below dist: not pace of
winner but this was a promising debut: speedily bred colt who cost $47,000 as a yearling: acts
on yld grnd: seems certain to win a race on this evidence.   46
2926 **THORNFIELD** [11] (R Akehurst) 2-9-0 N Adams 25/1: 03: Led briefly 2f out: well clear
of rem & clearly benefitted considerably from his recent debut: should stay at least 1m:
acts on yld grnd & on a sharpish trk.   42
--   **FAR TOO RICH** [5] (R Smyly) 2-9-0 W Ryan 20/1: 4: Attracted little support on debut &
never reached ldrs: half brother to a couple of winners: acts on yld grnd: likely to improve
for this run.   30

2878 DURBO [7] 2-9-0 W Newnes 9/2: 0000: Made much, wknd: best in 2542 (firm).   24
2957 FOR THE CRACK [3] 2-9-0 R Wernham 16/1: 000: Btr on fast grnd in 2957 (1m).   18
2895 DEGENERALE [8] 2-9-0 Pat Eddery 5/1: 000: Fdd into 7th: see 2895 (6f, firm).   00
-- CROSS KRISS [4] 2-9-0 R Street 10/1: 0: Mkt drifter on debut: made some late progress
into 8th & likely to do btr: half brother to useful 6f colt Kirchner: likely to prefer a
sounder surface.   00
2675 MAINMAST [6] 2-8-11 W Carson 11/4 FAV: 00: Well bckd: eased after ½way: stoutly bred
filly who is unsuited by°this soft grnd & is certain to do btr than this.   00
-- Never Been Chaste [1] 8-11   2847 Arquati Redwood [14] 9-0
-- Borreto [2] 9-0   1238 Gods Lil Lisa [15] 8-11
2652 Meldon Hill [12] 8-11   -- Nautical Belle [16] 8-11
3017 Neirbo Lass [10] 8-11
16 ran   1½,2½,7,4,4,2,2½   (Cecil J Hedigan)   G Harwood Pulborough, Sussex

3135 EBF WILLOW MAIDEN STAKES 2YO DIV I   £2628   7f   Yielding 102 -19 Slow

2782 TILTING COURT [5] (Lady Herries) 2-9-0 B Rouse 9/1: 01: 2 ch g Castle Keep - Peteona
(Welsh Saint): Bckd from 33/1 when a comfortable winner of a 2yo mdn at Lingfield, led after
½way & was sn ridden clear: stays 7f really well & on breeding is certain to be suited by
middle dists next season: acts on gd/firm & yld grnd & seems to like a sharpish trk: on
the up grade.   50
2675 CASTLE IN THE AIR [6] (J Dunlop) 2-8-11 W Carson 9/4 FAV: 302: Well bckd: led over
½way, not pace of winner: handled this softer grnd well & is sure to win a race: see 2675 & 2418   42
2939 ROYAL ROB [2] (G Harwood) 2-9-0 A Clark 7/2: 03: Ran on well: eff over 6/7f on gd
& yld grnd: seems to act on any trk: see 2939.   44
-- MINSTREL SINGER [12] (O Douieb) 2-9-0 R Machado 10/1: 4: Mkt drifter on debut: prom
thro'out & this was quite a promising effort: cost $100,000 as a yearling & is a half
brother to a couple of winners in the States: acts on yld.   40
3085 SYLVAN ORIENT [14] 2-9-0 A Mcglone 16/1: 0030000: Kept on under press: acts on yld.   34
2531 DAWN ROMP [10] 2-8-11 W Ryan 16/1: 400: Never beyond mid-div: see 2287.   28
2716 FEARLESS MAN [13] 2-9-0 W R Swinburn 3/1: 00: Well bckd: fdd into 8th: btr in 2716 (firm).   20
2838 Spring Forward [3] 9-0   2990 Red Sky At Night [8] 8-11
2987 Al Laventa [4] 9-0   -- Festive Occasion [9] 9-0
2254 Technocrat [7] 9-0(BL)   2270 Pollan Bay [11] 8-11
-- Tulla Water [1] 8-11
14 ran   2½,½,2½,3,1½,hd,3   (Lady Mary Mumford)   Lady Herries Littlehampton, Sussex

3136 EBF WILLOW MAIDEN STAKES 2YO DIV II   £2794   7f   Yielding 102 -09 Slow

2159 KASTAMOUN [15] (R F Johnson Houghton) 2-9-0 J Reid 6/1: 401: 2 br c Ile De Bourbon -
Kastiliya (Kalamoun): Broke well & was never hdd when a comfortable winner of a 2yo mdn at
Lingfield: first foal of a 7f winner in France, who is related to top class performers Kozana
& Karkour: very eff over 7f & will be suited by middle dists next term: acts on gd/firm &
yld grnd & on any trk: likes to be out in front.   46
3067 SPLASH ON [10] (M Stoute) 2-9-0 W R Swinburn 2/1 FAV: 02: Ran on well from ½way,
though was never going to peg back winner: $100,000 yearling who is a half brother to several
winners: acts on gd/firm & yld grnd: on the up grade & will win a race: see 3067.   39
-- BEL BYOU [9] (P Cole) 2-9-0 P Waldron 4/1: 3: Al up there on debut: promising effort
from this 36,000 gns yearling: acts on yld grnd: seems sure to improve.   38
-- FIGINI [12] (J Tree) 2-8-11 Pat Eddery 9/2: 4: Chall dist, no extra: friendless in the
mkt, but fin well clear of rem here: half sister to useful winners Electric and Les Arcs: acts
on yld grnd: will be suited to a lngr trip.   34
2904 MISS PENGUIN [13] 2-8-11 R Lines(3) 20/1: 00: Mkt drifter: never dngr.   16
2846 TABELLINA [1] 2-8-11 P Cook 20/1: 00: Al mid-div: half sister to middle dist winner
Northern Amethyst: likely to impr himself over lngr trips next season.   15
2782 CASTLE TRYST [11] 2-9-0 B Rouse 10/1: 000: Active in mkt: fin 8th & has yet to show
any worthwhile form: bred to stay middle distances.   00
-- Ramberge [3] 8-11   -- Endless Gossip [16] 8-11
-- Al Torfanan [7] 9-0   -- Dont Yer Know [6] 9-0 -- Kellys Comet [5] 9-0
2983 Profit A Prendre [4] 9-0   -- String Concerto [2] 9-0
-- Lady Homily [14] 8-11   2407 Wind And Wave [8] 8-11(VIS)
16 ran   4,½,nk,12,1,½,4   (H H Aga Khan)   R F Johnson Houghton Blewbury, Oxon

3137 KEN BUTLER WINES STAKES 2YO   £3409   7f140y Yielding 102 -23 Slow

-2920 BOCATOWER [2] (G Harwood) 2-8-11 A Clark 6/4 FAV: 1D1: 2 b c Tyrnavos - Orange Silk
(Moulton): Useful colt: well bckd & led at the dist to justify fav. in a 2yo stakes at Lingfield: first past the post in a mdn auction stakes at York early this month, though subsq.
placed 2nd behind Silk Topper: quite cheaply bought colt who is very eff over 7/8f & is
likely to stay further: acts on fast & yld grnd & on any trk.   48
2628 NONSUCH PALACE [9] (I Balding) 2-8-11 P Cook 20/1: 03002: Broke well & made most:
best effort for sometime: acts on firm & yld: see 1019.   46
1801 SHIRBELLA [14] (P Walwyn) 2-8-8 Paul Eddery 25/1: 03: No extra dist, but ran a gd race
after a long break: 92,000 gns yearling who should continue to impr: acts on yld.   36
2574 CAMMARINO [13] (H Candy) 2-8-11 W Newnes 11/2: 04: On the up grade: see 2574.   38

2547 SERGEYEVICH [6] 2-8-11 W Carson 5/2: 20: No threat: much btr on firm in 2547.   26
2936 BRANDY BOTTLE [10] 2-8-11 R Lines(3) 33/1: 000: Never dngr: see 2723 (firm).   24
-- TRAPDOOR [1] 2-8-11 Pat Eddery 8/1: 0: Al mid-div on debut: fetched $75,000 as a yearling & should do btr than this.   00
2829 JONITE [3] 2-8-11 S Whitworth 8/1: 000030: Fin 9th: btr on firm in 2829 (seller).   00
1049 SECOOT [8] 2-8-11 P Waldron 10/1: 030: Abs: lngr trip & no threat: see 1049 (firm).   00
-- Barnhill [12] 8-11   2418 Bamar Lad [16] 8-11   -- Gerunty [5] 8-11
3067 Grunidad [7] 8-11   -- Little Realm [11] 8-11
2811 White Minstrel [4] 8-11   -- Madam Trilby [15] 8-8
16 ran 1,4,nk,8,1,2   (J B Austin)   G Harwood Pulborough, Sussex

3138 FRIARY MEUX HANDICAP 3YO+ 0-50   £3111   6f   Yielding 102 +08 Fast   [47]

3124 DORKING LAD [7] (M Tompkins) 4-9-6 Pat Eddery 11/2 JT FAV: 0000041: 4 b c Cawston's Clown - High Voltage (Electrify): Quick reapp. & led below dist, gamely in quite a fast run h'cap at Lingfield: very useful sprinter on his day, won valuable h'caps at York & Sandown last season: best form over 5/6f on fast & yld grnd: acts on any trk.   50
2992 MUSIC REVIEW [14] (M Tompkins) 3-7-11 R Fox 14/1: 2034102: Ran on well: clear of rem and is still racing off an attractive mark: see 2775.   28
3055 LOFT BOY [17] (N Vigors) 3-8-11 P Cook 12/1: 2300003: Likes this trk: see 496.   34
3106 STEEL CYGNET [2] (Pat Mitchell) 3-9-0 J Reid 11/2 JT FAV: 3404034: Ev ch: see 3106.   36
3055 FERRYMAN [10] 10-9-5 W R Swinburn 14/1: 4000000: Gd effort: best in 1461.   35
2526 EASY DAY [11] 4-8-4(bl) A Mackay 16/1: 0100000: Best over 1m in 956 (firm).   18
2981 APRIL FOOL [13] 4-7-13(vis) T Lang(7) 8/1: 0030020: Never nearer 7th: see 2981.   00
3015 SNAP DECISION [18] 3-8-2(bl) A Mcglone 8/1: 0203330: Fin 9th: see 2530 & 1033.   00
3118 CREE BAY [19] 7-9-8(VIS) W Carson 8/1: 0000030: Quick reapp: btr in 3118.   00
2573 AL AMEAD [4] 6-9-9 B Rouse 9/1: 0414040: Course specialist, but prefers firm: see 1347.   00
3118 JOHN PATRICK [1] 5-9-0(VIS) Paul Eddery 9/1: 0000000: Wore a visor: made much: see 192.   00
3021 Downsview [12] 9-2   2929 Lady Windmill [16] 7-11
2842 Crete Cargo [5] 9-4(vis)   1245 Heart Of Glass [6] 8-11
2619 Kimble Blue [15] 8-2(1ow)   3065 Wykehamist [20] 7-13
2256 Umbelata [9] 7-12   3055 Corncharm [8] 8-4(bl)
19 ran ½,4,¾,2,1,2½,3   (John Freedman)   M Tompkins Newmarket

3139 ELM HANDICAP STAKES 3YO+ 0-35   £2340   2m   Yielding 102 +07 Fast   [35]

-2882 TIGERWOOD [2] (R Akehurst) 5-9-1 N Adams 9/2 FAV: 2102221: 5 b h Lombard - Smokey Dawn (March Past): Most consistent stayer who was a comfortable all the way winner of a competitive & quite fast run h'cap at Lingfield: first time out winner at Warwick, later successful at Chester & has only once fin. out of the first two this term: also a fair top of-the-ground hurdler: well suited by a test of stamina: best with front running tactics on a sharpish trk: acts on fast & yld grnd.   35
+3110 REFORM PRINCESS [1] (M Ryan) 3-8-7(bl)(3ex) G Bardwell(7) 7/1: 0300012: In fine form.   33
2974 COLLISTO [13] (K Brassey) 5-8-3(vis)(1ow) Paul Eddery 16/1: 2220203: Gd effort: see 2075.   14
2938 BALLET CHAMP [19] (R Holder) 8-8-9 S Dawson 6/1: 4204224: Below 2938: see 349.   08
1633 MISS BLACKTHORN [10] 4-8-8 P Cook 14/1: 0320300: Abs: never nearer: see 541.   02
2662 BENS BIRDIE [16] 6-8-5 A Mackay 8/1: 13-2140: Best over 12f in 2415 (gd/firm).   00
2733 HIGH PLAINS [18] 4-8-11 W Newnes 6/1: 0000400: Continues to disapp: see 1837.   00
942 SHINY COPPER [5] 8-8-5 B Rouse 10/1: 0243300: No threat after long abs: see 204.   00
2733 Staghound [4] 8-9   2944 My Charade [15] 8-0(vis)
204 Spring Philtre [7] 8-0   -- Pleated [17] 10-0
-- Copse And Robbers [14] 9-4   341 Mishrif [12] 9-3
-- Southernair [11] 8-11   2464 Le Moulin [3] 8-11   2492 Maricama [20] 8-9
2022 Dust Conquerer [6] 8-4(bl)   2809 Italian Sunrise [8] 8-4(vis)
2873 Alacazam [9] 8-1
20 ran 2,6,12,5,1½   (Miss Anne Healy)   R Akehurst Epsom, Surrey

3140 CHESTNUT HANDICAP 3YO+ 0-35   £2760   1m 2f   Yielding 102 +07 Fast   [35]

2333 KING TEFKROS [2] (M Tompkins) 3-9-5 Pat Eddery 8/1: 0033231: 3 ch c Star Appeal - Salamina (Welsh Pageant): Was gaining an overdue first success when gamely leading close home in a fast run h'cap at Lingfield: consistent sort who is eff over 8/11f on fast & yld grnd: seems to have no trk preferences.   44
3063 HOMME DAFFAIRE [10] (G Lewis) 3-9-1 P Waldron 7/2 FAV: 0100042: Just failed to make all: clear of rem & this was a fine effort: likes some cut in the grnd: see 459.   38
2300 SWISS NEPHEW [9] (J Dunlop) 3-9-1 R Fox 14/1: 00-3003: Gd effort: see 2300.   31
3078 GOLDEN BEAU [6] (D Morley) 4-8-11 T Williams 14/1: 1230004: Stays 10f: see 2189 & 1942.   16
+3029 FORWARD RALLY [12] 4-10-0(5ex) C Nutter 9/2: 1120210: Had ev ch: btr in 3029 (gd).   32
*2856 AUCHINATE [15] 3-9-3 A Clark 13/2: -430310: Much btr on firm in 2856 (1m).   24
3050 TOM FORRESTER [3] 5-8-13 W R Swinburn 13/2: 4423000: Fdd into 9th: see 2807 & 453.   00
*2799 WHILE IT LASTS [8] 3-9-12 P Hamblett 8/1: 3231010: Dwelt, no threat: see 2799 (gd/firm).   00
2985 NOBLE FILLE [13] 3-9-4 W Carson 10/1: 0440100: Btn 2f out: twice below, 2853 (firm).   00
2876 EMRYS [4] 3-9-3 P Cook 10/1: 3314000: Has proved disapp since 919 (firm).   00
2925 Rapid Lad [14] 9-2   997 Saalib [7] 8-12   2995 Noholmina [5] 9-0 2985 Tarletons Oak [1] 9-0
14 ran ½,5,4,½,3,3,½   (Athos Christodoulou)   M Tompkins Newmarket

Official Going Given As GOOD

3141 WOODBOROUGH MAIDEN STAKES 2YO   £1028   1m 2f   Good/Yld 71 -13 Slow

2886 AMADEUS ROCK [21] (J Hindley) 2-9-0 A Shoults(5) 12/1: 0041: 2 b c Touching Wood-
Skyey (Skymaster): Impr colt: al prom and led over 2f out, staying this 10f well in a 2yo mdn
at Nottingham: half brother to 3 winners: acts on gd/firm & yld grnd: suited by 10f on
a gall trk.   45
2957 STAR NORTH [13] (L Piggott) 2-9-0 R Cochrane 7/2: 042: Well bckd & stayed on final 1f:
suited by 10f & acts on firm & gd/yld: can find a race: see 2957.   42
3014 DARING DESCENT [10] (R J Houghton) 2-9-0 S Cauthen 5/2 FAV: 0023: Al prom: rated 48
in 3014 (1m).   39
2901 RUSSIAN LULLABY [1] (I Balding) 2-8-11 J Matthias 6/1: 04: Ran on well final 2f &
should win races next term: see 2901: acts on gd/firm & yld.   35
2813 MANDALAY PRINCE [9] 2-9-0 R Guest 16/1: 000400: Late hdway: well suited by 10f:
acts on fast & gd/yld grnd: see 2700.   33
3023 HIGHLAND BOUNTY [8] 2-9-0 P Robinson 20/1: 00: Gd late hdway over this lngr trip:
cost 43,000 gns as a yearling & is a half brother to the speedy filly Tyrollie: acts on gd/yld   32
2904 ALJAW [6] 2-8-11 A Murray 12/1: 000: Led 7f: lightly rcd since 2287.   00
2997 Mamamere [3] 8-11   -- Corbadge [20] 9-0   3014 Gouldswood [19] 9-0
3069 Ripster [18] 9-0(bl)   3073 Tabareek [7] 8-11   2987 Biotin [11] 9-0
1653 Lightfall [16] 9-0   2961 Ulysses [4] 9-0   2484 Zanussi Line [2] 9-0
2990 Donnas Darling [5] 8-11   -- Little Elly [14] 8-11
2527 Main Rocket [17] 8-11   3068 Petalouda [15] 8-11
20 ran   1¾,1¼,nk,3,nk,3,¾,¾   (R Corson)   J Hindley Newmarket

3142 FLAWBOROUGH E.B.F. STAKES 3YO   £3099   1m 2f   Good/Yld 71 +09 Fast

3026 FIRST KISS [1] (J Dunlop) 3-9-6 B Thomson 7/1: 0303331: 3 b f Kris - Primatie
(Vaguely Noble): Fairly useful filly: mkt drifter but led inside final 2f, readily in quite
fast run 3yo stakes at Nottingham: first time out won a mdn at Leicester: half sister to the
smart Millers Mate: very eff at 10f, though does stay 12f: acts on firm & gd/yld grnd &
on any trk.   51
--   **DECIDED** [10] (H Cecil) 3-9-0 S Cauthen 3/1: -2: Wk in mkt on debut: led over 2f out:
fair effort: Canadian bred colt who may stay further than todays 10f: acts on gd/yld grnd
& a fair trk: should find a race.   40
2948 GREENHILLS JOY [4] (M Ryan) 3-8-11 P Robinson 7/1: -033: Nicely bckd: led inside
final ½m & continues to improve: stays 10f: see 2948, 2546.   33
3038 AMBASSADOR [6] (W O'gorman) 3-9-0(bl) A Murray 11/4 FAV: 2232234: Never nearer & this
10f trip seems inadequate for him: well below 3038 (stiff 12f).   31
3061 DIRECTLY [9] 3-9-0 J Williams 10/1: -030: Prom ev ch: see 2691.   30
3030 SHEHANA [5] 3-9-8 T Quinn 9/1: 431-030: Led over 6f: see 3030.   34
--   **JUST TOO BRAVE** [2] 3-9-0 R Cochrane 8/1: -0: Friendless in mkt on debut & was al behind:
half brother to the useful sprinter Melody Park & is probably capable of btr than this.   00
--   Mavela [7] 8-11   3028 Richards Folly [3] 8-11
2534 Lowara [11] 8-11   1309 Idle Song [8] 9-0   -- East Limerick [12] 9-0
12 ran   3,2,3,nk,2½   (Sheikh Mohammed)   J Dunlop Arundel, Sussex

3143 WOODBOROUGH MAIDEN STAKES (DIV 2) 2YO   £960   1m 2f   Good/Yld 71 -12 Slow

3023 OUR ELIASO [3] (L Piggott) 2-9-0 J Matthias 11/4 FAV: 01: 2 b c Niniski - Kalazero
(Kalamoun): Promising colt: fulfilled the promise of race 3023 when winning a mdn at Nottingham: well bckd & led 2f out, readily: cost 46,000 gns as a yearling & is a full brother to the
smart '84 2yo Kala Dancer: well suited by 10f & should get further: acts on gd/firm & gd/
yld grnd & a gall trk: on the up grade & will rate more highly.   49
2675 LIPREADER [5] (G P Gordon) 2-8-11 P Robinson 20/1: 02: Stayed on well final 1f & is
on the up grade: American bred filly who looks certain to find a race: should be suited by
12f next season: acts on gd/yld & a gall trk.   40
2961 ALA HOUNAK [12] (F Durr) 2-9-0 B Thomson 10/1: 0033: Chall. over 2f out: another gd
effort & stays 10f: acts on firm & gd/yld & can find a race: see 2961.   41
2894 BONAFORTUNE [6] (D Morley) 2-9-0 R Guest 6/1: 0444: Kept on under press: consistent but
lacks a turn of foot: should find a race over 12f next term: see 2761.   38
3023 COUP DE FOUDRE [19] 2-9-0 B Crossley 20/1: 00: Late hdway & is making impr: clearly
suited by 10f: acts on gd/yld.   29
3016 PARKERS JOY [1] 2-9-0 D J Williams(5) 33/1: 0044000: Al there: stays 10f: see 1253.   23
2527 AMANDA JANE [9] 2-8-11 T Fahey 25/1: 000: Never nearer 7th: probably stays 10f:
half sister to several winners abroad.   20
2748 NATURALLY AUTUMN [13] 2-8-11 M Roberts 10/1: 00030: Led 3f out: btr 2748 (1m, firm).   00
--   **PASTEL SHADE** [17] 2-8-11 W Woods(3) 6/1: 0: Wk in mkt on debut & was never in it:
sure to impr on this effort: cost $200,000 as a yearling & is a half sister to several winners:
should be suited by this trip.   00
3011 CRYSTAL HAWK [8] 2-9-0 R Cochrane 9/2: 40: Mkt drifter & wknd: btr 3011 (1m).   00

918

2239 JACK STRAW [10] 2-9-0(BL) S Cauthen 7/1: 00: Bl first time: prom much, fdd: little
form in 2 outings from this first foal.   00
3014 IJAZAH [11] 2-8-11 A Murray 7/1: 00: Led 7f: see 3014 (1m).   00
2904 Vestal Flame [15] 8-11   2723 Banks And Braes [2] 9-0
2514 Lantern Boy [18] 9-0   2657 Royal Astronaut [14] 9-0
2708 Skraggs Plus Two [21] 9-0   2407 Spanish Connection [7] 9-0
-- Maycrest [4] 8-11   -- Minabella [20] 8-11
20 ran   2,1,1½,5,3,shhd   (Elisha Holding)   L Piggott Newmarket

3144 RAINWORTH APP. SELL. H'CAP (0-25) 3YO   £954   6f   Good/Yld 71 -32 Slow   [18]

3057 LE MANS [6] (J H Wilson) 3-8-11(bl) Julie Bowker 10/1: 0000031: 3 br c Mansingh -
Dwindle (Major Portion): Impr of late & led over 1f out, narrowly in a slow run selling h'cap
at Nottingham (no bid): eff at 6f on gd/yld grnd & a gall trk.   09
2508 QUITE A QUEST [11] (B Mcmahon) 3-9-7 J Hillis 25/1: -000002: Sn prom: chall. final
1f & just btn: gd effort: eff at 6f & stays 7f: acts on fast & gd/yld & should find a seller. 18
2854 AUSTINA [12] (D H Jones) 3-8-10 D J Williams 10/1: 0000003: Chall final 1f: just btn:
gd effort: eff at 6f on gd/yld grnd.   07
2884 CLASS HOPPER [10] (W Elsey) 3-7-9(bl) G Carter 16/1: 0000004: Prom, ev ch: see 2884.   00
3024 EVER SO SHARP [7] 3-8-10 J Carroll 25/1: 0000300: Sn prom: eff at 5/6f: see 2884.   02
3024 HOBOURNES KATIE [2] 3-8-11 A Culhane 10/1: 0000300: Al prom: see 2268.   02
*3057 PADDINGTON BELLE [18] 3-9-3(vis)(7ex) S Whitelam(5) 7/1: 0030010: No show under penalty. 00
3024 TOLLYS ALE [19] 3-8-13 L Riggio 9/2 FAV: 0040430: Prom much: well below 3024.   00
3057 SAMBA LASS [9] 3-9-4 A Shoults 9/1: 3201000: Never showed: best 1334.   00
2960 MISS HICKS [13] 3-9-3(BL) S Hibble(5) 10/1: 0000400: Tried in bl: made some: btr 2898.   00
3057 Rich Bitch [3] 8-3(BL)   2715 Witham Girl [15] 9-7(bl)
2616 Findon Manor [8] 9-5   963 Bandyann [10] 9-2   2960 My Mutzie [14] 8-13
3033 Nomad Boxer [4] 8-10   2322 Sly Maid [1] 8-10   2793 Bella Carina [5] 8-10(bl)
18 ran   nk,shhd,1½,½,nk   (Times Of Wigan)   J H Wilson Tarleton, Lancs

3145 KEGWORTH H'CAP STAKES (0-35) 3YO+   £2477   6f   Good/Yld 72 +06 Fast   [34]

2668 SULLYS CHOICE [1] (D Chapman) 5-9-13 S Cauthen 20/1: 2100001: 5 b h King Pellinore -
Salute The Coates (Solar Salute): Returned to form, making ev yd on his own on far side under
top weight in a h'cap at Nottingham: earlier successful in h'caps at Haydock, Thirsk & Ripon:
below his best in '85: in '84 won again at Ripon: seems equally eff over 5/6f, though does stay
further: acts on gd/firm & soft grnd: eff with or without blinkers.   41
3015 GOLDEN ANCONA [18] (E Eldin) 3-9-4 E Guest(3) 8/1: 2430002: Stayed on well final 2f:
tried in bl last time: see 2399 (1m).   30
2992 GODSTRUTH [10] (H T Jones) 7-8-8(bl) A Riding(7) 10/1: 0043443: Ch 1f out: quite
consistent: see 1344.   17
3046 CAPTAINS BIDD [25] (H Whiting) 6-8-2 W Woods(3) 16/1: 4100034: Sn prom: btr 3046, 2256(5f) 09
3104 GODS SOLUTION [21] 5-8-11 A Shoults(5) 12/1: 0004000: Front rank most: see 42.   14
2702 DANCING SARAH [26] 3-9-3 D J Williams(5) 20/1: 0032000: Al up there: lightly raced
since 1750.   22
2765 SYBIL FAWLTY [24] 3-9-3(vis) M Roberts 10/1: 0442100: Sn prom: twice well below 2488.   00
3015 TAYLOR OF SOHAM [15] 3-8-13 J Williams 6/1 FAV: 3232320: Well bckd: early speed.   00
-3046 STANBO [12] 3-8-4 P Robinson 10/1: 0204020: Early speed: much btr 3046 (5f gd/firm).   00
+2033 Sharp Times [2] 8-11   2775 Gentileschi [14] 8-1   2659 Linavos [3] 8-10
3104 Mary Maguire [6] 9-6   3021 Lyric Way [11] 9-1   820 Riverside Writer [17] 8-12
3015 Fawleys Girl [23] 8-10   3078 No Credibility [8] 8-8
2312 Grisette [22] 8-7(bl)   3065 Sahara Shadow [7] 8-3 3065 Lucky Starkist [13] 8-3
2981 Jianna [9] 8-3   3104 Pentoff [5] 8-0   2715 Burning Arrow [10] 8-1(1ow)
3104 Miami Dolphin [4] 7-12   1543 Aphrodisiac [19] 7-8
25 ran   1½,½,½,1½,shhd   (William Chapman)   D Chapman Stillington, Yorks

3146 WESTBOROUGH FILLIES NURSERY H'CAP 2YO   £1644   6f   Good/Yld 71 -04 Slow   [44]

*2962 SKYBOLT [24] (W O'gorman) 2-9-0(bl)(10ex) S Cauthen 7/1: 040011: 2 gr f Absalom -
Hum (Crooner): Fast impr filly: in fine form, making ev yd on the stands side under a 10lbs
penalty in a fillies nursery h'cap at Nottingham: last time out won a nursery h'cap at Warwick:
speedily bred filly who seems equally eff over 5/6f: acts on gd/yld & firm grnd & a sharp/
easy trk: suited by front running.   41
2756 INSHIRAH [26] (H T Jones) 2-9-6(bl) A Murray 8/1: 1014332: Al chasing winner: most
consistent: see 2756, 1920.   44
3014 CALL FOR TAYLOR [13] (D Leslie) 2-8-1 N Howe 33/1: 0000003: Ch inside final 2f:
fair effort: has been running over 1m lately but seems suited by 6f on gd/yld.   21
3019 TINAS MELODY [19] (J Winter) 2-9-2 R Cochrane 7/1: 312104: Prom, ev ch: another gd
run: see 2010.   34
2284 INDIAN SET [21] 2-8-6 R Curant 14/1: 00400: Abs: al prom: eff at 5/6f on firm &
yld grnd: best form on an easy trk.   23
2989 KATE IS BEST [12] 2-8-9(bl) P Robinson 14/1: 004400: Mkt drifter: late hdway: can do btr 22
2700 RANKSTREET [4] 2-8-6 T Quinn 33/1: 00300: Fin close up 7th: best 2283 (7f).   00
3122 FOUR LAFFS [14] 2-8-11 J Williams 11/2 JT.FAV: 0231040: Well bckd: no show: btr 3122.   00
2485 MADAM BILLA [16] 2-8-3 W Woods(3) 11/2 JT.FAV: 00000: Bckd from 10/1: never looked
likely: lightly rcd & little form: see 1297.   00

919

2788 Bleu Celeste [3] 8-7
3017 Illustrate [17] 8-1
2689 Surely Great [5] 7-13(bl)
1427 Pollys Song [8] 9-7
2472 Home Device [20] 8-10
2664 Seulement [9] 8-1
1059 Imperial Friend [23] 7-11
2982 Little Lochette [6] 8-1
2843 Good Game [10] 9-7
3032 Quite So [7] 8-9
3027 Dohty Baby [15] 8-0
3079 Meath Princess [2] 7-7(vis)
3056 Ring Back [22] 7-7(5oh)
2792 Emmas Whisper [1] 8-7
2846 Watered Silk [11] 8-11
2595 Auntie Cyclone [25] 8-6
2664 Petroc Concert [18] 7-12
26 ran 1,1½,¾,½,1½,shhd (Mrs Linda Yong) W O'gorman Newmarket

EDINBURGH Monday October 27th Righthand, Sharp Track

Official Going Given As GOOD

3147 **ALMA STAKES 3YO+** **£1081 1m Good 45 +02 Fast**

2973 GREAT DILEMMA [6] (P Makin) 3-8-4 G Baxter 7/2: 0022041: 3 b f Vaigly Great - Solo Reign (Space King): Mkt drifter, but sustained challenge to lead near fin in a stakes event at Edinburgh: earlier showed gd form when 2nd to Smooch in a fillies race at Goodwood: eff over 7f, well suited by 1m on gd grnd: acts on any trk but seems suited by an easy one. 34
3070 RETRIEVE [10] (W Jarvis) 3-8-7 M Birch 10/11 FAV: -002: Led over 3f out: just btn: hvly bckd here & should find a small race: eff at 7f/1m on gd & yld grnd & a sharp trk. 35
2426 LUCKY BLAKE [7] (C Thornton) 3-8-7 J Bleasdale 11/1: -040403: Sn prom: kept on: remains a mdn: see 605. 29
3104 CASSANDRAS DREAM [4] (R Whitaker) 5-8-9 D Mckeown 12/1: 0000004: Ch inside final 2f: fair effort, but is probably more at home in selling company: see 1102 (12f). 16
-- CATCH A LIGHT [9] 3-8-4 M Giles 12/1: -0: Friendless in mkt on racecourse debut & was never a threat: half sister to middle dist winner Hunza Water: may do btr. 04
3086 VIRAJENDRA [2] 3-8-8(bl)(1ow) D Nicholls 12/1: 0034000: Never dngr: see 3086. 07
2998 Gloriant [1] 8-7(bl) **-- Pretty Fly** [8] 8-9 **3086 Its Heaven** [5] 8-9(bl)
-- Park Oaks [3] 8-12
10 ran nk,2½,1,4,hd (Mrs Kate Livingstone) P Makin Ogbourne Maisey, Wilts

3148 **FERRERO ROCHER MAIDEN STAKES 2YO** **£1405 1m Good 45 +05 Fast**

2723 GLORY LINE [13] (P Cole) 2-9-0 G Baxter 11/8 FAV: 021: 2 b c Run The Gantlet - Gallina (Raise A Native): Justified heavy support, led inside final 2f & despite hanging left was a 2L winner of quite fast run 2yo mdn at Edinburgh: last time out a gd 2nd to Arden at Beverley: eff at 1m, half brother to winning stayer Brave The Reef & should get further: acts on gd & firm grnd & on any trk. 46
-2886 OKOSAN [1] (S Norton) 2-8-11(vis) J Lowe 5/1: 00022: Ch over 1f out: in gd form: see 2886 37
3074 SPY GIFT [11] (M Stoute) 2-8-11(vis) K Bradshaw(5) 5/1: 0330443: Set very fast pace till inevitably tiring final 1f: 12f clear rem: rated 41 in 2989. 31
2976 CREOLE BAY [16] (T Fairhurst) 2-8-11 M Fry 25/1: 0003004: Prom most: see 2724 (seller). 06
2377 ARIZONA SUN [7] 2-9-0 D Nicholls 12/1: 0000: Never nearer: best 1869 (6f). 05
2007 HERR FLICK [8] 2-9-0 G Dickie 16/1: 0240: Abs: lightly rcd since 94 (soft). 01
2936 LISETA [2] 2-8-11 J Bleasdale 15/2: 02200: Has twice ran badly since 2664 (7f). 00
2888 Geobritony [9] 9-0 **3099 Muntag** [15] 9-0 **3058 Just A Decoy** [5] 9-0
3069 Tootsie Jay [10] 8-11(vis) **3074 Daffodil** [3] 8-11
2976 Only Joking [12] 8-11 **965 Maestroman** [4] 9-0 **2377 Major Oakey** [14] 9-0
15 ran 2,3,12,1½,1½ (Fahd Salman) P Cole Whatcombe, Oxon

3149 **FOODBROKERS TROPHY H'CAP (0-35) 3YO+** **£2038 7f Good 45 -03 Slow** **[32]**

2931 POINTED LADY [16] (R Armstrong) 3-8-10 G Baxter 3/1 JT FAV: 0420021: 3 ch f Sharpen Up-Real Babe (The Axe): Lost her mdn tag when staying on well to lead near fin in a h'cap at Edinburgh: half sister to a couple of winners in the States: stays 7f well: acts on gd & firm grnd & is well suited by a sharp/easy trk. 24
2340 LITTLE NEWINGTON [10] (N Bycroft) 5-8-2(bl) K Darley 14/1: 1240002: Led inside final 1f: just btn: best effort for a long time: acts on gd & hvy: see 820. 11
2797 BOLD ROWLEY [8] (J S Wilson) 6-7-8(1ow) M Fry 10/1: 0100003: Stayed on well final 1f: best 1839 (seller). 00
2970 TIT WILLOW [11] (S Norton) 4-8-8(bl) D Nicholls 3/1 JT FAV: 0343244: Lost many lengths at start & did well to fin this close: in gd form: see 2816, 828. 09
3084 JANES BRAVE BOY [1] 4-7-11 P Burke(7) 20/1: 0000000: Prom, ev ch: has shown virtually no form since a first time out winner in 46. 00
3077 MOLLY PARTRIDGE [6] 3-7-13 A Proud 14/1: 0410000: Led over 6f: best 2585 (seller). 00
866 FLOMEGAS DAY [7] 4-9-2(bl) M Wood 5/1: -000340: Long abs: bckd from 10/1: no real threat: see 636, 369. 00
2998 Career Madness [5] 8-1(bl) **2743 Tree Fella** [9] 7-8(1ow)(7oh)
3033 Foretop [4] 8-12 **2884 Star Crimson** [2] 7-7(7oh) **3060 James Pal** [12] 9-9(BL)
12 ran ½,1½,2,½,¾ (Kinderhill Corporation) R Armstrong Newmarket

3150 **CHEMIST BROKERS SELLING STAKES 3 & 4YO** **£772 1m 4f Good 45 -35 Slow**

783 COME POUR THE WINE [4] (H Wharton) 3-7-9 J Quinn(5) 5/1: 00-0001: 3 b f Crofter - Walariki (Condorcet): Despite a long abs, al there & cruised into lead 2f out to cmftbly win

a slowly run seller at Edinburgh (bought in 1,500 gns): quite lightly rcd, has shown btr form
since racing over 12f & promises to stay further: acts on firm & yld & does well on a shrp trk.   18
2996 MISS BECCA [8] (W Haigh) 3-7-9 M Fry 4/1: 0-02: Ran rather green under press final 2f:
seems to stay 12f though dam was a miler: may impr further.   14
8   ALPHABETICAL ORDER [6] (R Simpson) 4-8-7(BLHood) G Baxter 9/4 FAV: -02-03: Equipped
with a hood & bl for the first time when returning after a very long abs, refused to settle
& wknd final 2f: seems to have his share of temperament but showed definite ability last year,
notably when 2nd to the useful Esquire in a Newbury mdn.   12
3076 JALOME [7] (R Whitaker) 4-8-4 D Mckeown 7/2: 0004004: Waited with, no threat: see 2789.   03
2054 ONLY FLOWER [3] 3-7-10(bl)(1ow) L Charnock 25/1: -00300: Abs: held up, no threat.   00
2125 SUNLIT [5] 3-7-9 J Lowe 11/1: 0-00000: Made much after abs: moderate.   00
2984 OKAADH [1] 4-8-7 J Bleasdale 7/1: 00-0040: Prom, wknd: btr 2984.   00
2361 Jay Bee Windows [2] 7-9
8 ran   1¼,5,2,4,2,shhd   (R D Atkinson)   H Wharton Middleham, Yorks

3151 ARMOUR NURSERY H'CAP 2YO   £1246   5f   Good 44 -07 Slow   [38]

2935 KALAS IMAGE [3] (G Moore) 2-8-9(BL) S Webster 6/1: 1400441: 2 br f Kala Shikari -
Hi Friday (High Line): Bl first time & al prom, forged ahead inside final 1f to win a
nursery at Edinburgh: has proved most consistent earlier winning a mdn auction at Beverley:
probably stays 6f but very eff over 5f: acts on firm & yld: now seems best in blinkers.   31
2993 DENSBEN [1] (Denys Smith) 2-8-3 L Charnock 8/1: 0440342: Dsptd lead: see 1421.   19
*3031 GARDENIA LADY [2] (D Barron) 2-8-5(bl)(5ex) M Fry 12/1: 0000013: Mkt drifter, not btn
far: see 3031.   21
2883 LINPAC NORTH MOOR [4] (C Elsey) 2-8-10(bl) J Lowe 10/1: 0344234: Made much: see 2588.   22
3058 BRUTUS [5] 2-9-7 D Mckeown 11/1: 3040000: Ev ch, btr 2815 (6f).   23
2606 ROSIES GLORY [10] 2-7-13 M Wood 12/1: 0023000: Outpcd: see 2279 (6f).   00
*3032 OUR GINGER [7] 2-7-12(5ow)(5ex)(5oh) R P Elliott 7/4 FAV: 04010: Disapp after 3032 (seller) 00
2859 LINN ODEE [12] 2-8-13 M Birch 6/1: 4040140: Badly drawn: best 2744.   00
2993 FIVE SIXES [11] 2-8-7 K Darley 9/1: 1130000: Badly drawn: best 1298 (seller)   00
2689 Able Abbe [9] 8-3   3031 Joyces Pet [6] 8-3(BL)
2994 Pretty Soon [8] 8-2(bl)
12 ran   1¼,hd,1¼,4,¾,2   (I W Parry)   G Moore Middleham, Yorks

3152 HIGHLAND SPRING H'CAP (0-35) 3YO+   £932   5f   Good 45 +02 Fast   [35]

3015 RAMBLING RIVER [1] (W Stephenson) 9-9-12(vis) M Brennan(7) 5/1: 0002101: 9 br h
Forlorn River - Who-Done-It (Lucero): Grand old sprinter: winning for the 2nd time in his
last 3 races, made most on stands side for a comfortable 4L win in a h'cap at Edinburgh:
earlier won similar h'caps at Haydock & Newcastle: in '85 won at Edinburgh & Newmarket: equally
eff at 5/6f & acts on any going & on any trk: best form nowadays in visor or blinkers:
terrific stable servant.   46
3083 WARTHILL LADY [2] (M Brittain) 4-8-8 K Darley 15/2: 1002302: Prom thro'out: see 3083.   18
2295 ANGELS ARE BLUE [8] (M Ryan) 3-9-7 M Giles 16/1: 2301003: Prom, stayed: gd effort
after abs: needs 6f now: see 1836.   29
3083 SPACEMAKER BOY [5] (D Leslie) 6-9-7 D Nicholls 7/2 FAV: 0000024: Prom, ev ch: btr 3083.   26
3046 KARENS STAR [12] 9-8-0 S Webster 14/1: 2000000: Poorly drawn, ran creditably: see 3046.   05
3055 PUCCINI [10] 4-9-1 G Baxter 7/1: 0000000: Raced centre-track, ev ch: best effort
this term: last season won at Lingfield and Sandown: appears to handle any trk & is eff
at 5 & 6f, best form on gd or faster grnd.   20
2322 GOLD DUCHESS [13] 4-8-10(bl) M Birch 10/1: 0024030: Poor draw, fin 7th: see 2322.   12
2632 BAY BAZAAR [11] 4-8-2 D Mckeown 10/1: 0000400: Moderate draw, fin 8th: best 2513 (6f).   00
*3083 DEBACH REVENGE [6] 4-7-12(7ex) R Morse(5) 7/1: 4002010: Much btr 3083 (yld/soft).   00
3057 Ackas Boy [15] 7-8(1ow)(5oh)   3046 Mandrake Madam [9] 8-13
3083 Tradesman [14] 7-7(5oh)   3012 Maybe Jayne [16] 7-8(bl)(1ow)
3083 Biochairn Skolar [4] 7-7(bl)(10oh)   2621 Tiddlyeyetye [7] 7-7(5oh)
1247 Culminate [3] 7-9(2ow)(2oh)
16 ran   4,¾,1½,shhd,hd,1¼,1   (Miss G Richardson)   W Stephenson Bishop Auckland, Co Durham

REDCAR   Tuesday October28th   Lefthanded, Flat Galloping Track

Official Going Given As GOOD

3153 EAGLESCLIFFE MAIDEN STAKES 2YO   £1899   6f   Firm 04 -13 Slow

3109 ABU MUSLAB [2] (B Hanbury) 2-9-0 G Baxter 5/1: 0021: 2 bc Ile de Bourbon - Eastern
Shore (Sun Prince): Useful, impr colt: overcame his low draw when gamely making all on the
far-side in a 2yo mdn at Redcar: recently gambled on when chasing home Game Thatcher in a
similar race at Newbury: 80,000 gns yearling who seems sure to stay further than 6f: acts
on fast & yld grnd & on a gall trk: clearly does well with forcing tactics.   52
2967 AZYAA [20] (H T Jones) 2-8-11 A Murray 11/4 FAV: 332: Won her race on the stands side,
but just failed to reach the overall leader: another gd effort & certain to win a race,
probably over a slightly lngr trip: see 2967.   47
2846 ICE CHOCOLATE [26] (W Jarvis) 2-8-11 B Thomson 3/1: 43: Al prom, ran on well & not
btn far: on the up grade: sure to stay further: see 2846.   46

2589 BELAKA [12] (R Sheather) 2-8-11 W Ryan 14/1: 404: Made most stands side, no extra close
home: well clear of rem & this was a much btr effort: acts on any trk: see 2070.   40
3082 BILLY CONNOLLY [13] 2-9-0 K Darley 10/1: 0230: Front rank over ½way, wknd: see 3082.   22
3082 ENTIRE [14] 2-9-0 C Nutter 14/1: 300: Seems best on fast grnd: see 2410.   18
3082 LONG VIEW [11] 2-8-11 D Nicholls 16/1: 000: Prom most: fin 7th: half sister to a
couple of winners & was showing her first signs of form here: acts on firm grnd & on a gall trk   00

3103 Autobahn [16] 9-0	2476 Introvert [10] 9-0	3056 Trickle [25] 8-11		
2975 Royal Tower [22] 9-0	1843 Cowlam Boy [9] 9-0	2396 Sally Foxtrot [24] 8-11		
2994 Absolutely Free [8] 8-11		2468 Nicophana [3] 8-11		
3103 Edenthorpe [6] 9-0	-- Willowtree Girl [7] 8-11		
-- Dawn Sky [19] 8-11	2961 Charious Choice [21] 9-0		
-- All Mar Hel [15] 9-0	-- Brega [5] 9-0	-- Eight Mile Rock [18] 8-11	
2625 Taylor Cares [17] 8-11		2975 Danadn [4] 9-0	
2482 Atakashack [23] 9-0	3048 Carols Heights [1] 9-0		
26 ran ½,½,2,8,1½,½	(Muttar Salem)	B Hanbury Newmarket	

3154 BRASS CASTLE SELL. H'CAP (0-25) 3YO+   £1022   1m 2f Firm 04 -19 Slow   [18]

2877 POLYNOR [6] (M Ryan) 5-8-10 G Bardwell(7) 7/1: 40-0001: 5 b h Polyfoto - Sorea
(La Varende): Was gaining his first win in this country when staying on well to lead inside
dist in a selling h'cap at Redcar (no bid): placed over hdles at the weekend, but both his
previous wins had come in Belgium last year: eff over 10f on fast & yld grnd: seems well
suited by a gall trk.   04
2102 SMART MART [11] (F Yardley) 7-8-5 B Thomson 11/1: -300302: Had ev ch: see 1374.   00
2340 CHARMING VIEW [5] (H Jones) 4-9-1 W Ryan 10/1: 0200003: Best here in 1139 (1m).   06
3101 CHEVET LADY [1] (R Whitaker) 3-9-4 D Mckeown 4/1: 0004004: Not btn very far: see 2604.   14
2604 GLENDERRY [14] 4-8-1(bl) W Carson 8/1: 0000000: Led 3f out, wknd dist: see 872.   00
1820 HALF SHAFT [15] 5-8-10 M Birch 13/2: 000-440: Twice fin unplaced over hdles since
his last run on the Flat: al prom, not qckn: see 1546.   00
2746 MR MUSIC MAN [4] 12-8-12 N Day 6/1: 4001000: Fin 7th: disapp since 2528 (12f).   00
2613 PATRICKS STAR [12] 3-8-11 A Murray 8/1: 0000200: Fdd into 8th: btr in 2083 (9f): see 1960   00
2863 MISS APEX [13] 4-9-7(vis) J Williams 9/1: 3300100: No show: twice well below form in 2690.   00
2787 MY DERYA [10] 3-8-6(bl) K Darley 8/1: 0041040: Does not seem to get this trip: best in 2302.00
2780 Fill Abumper [8] 8-6   2704 Gem Mart [7] 9-3(BL)   3084 Res Non Verba [2] 8-2(BL)(1ow)
-- Remainder Girl [3] 8-11
14 ran ½,½,nk,1½,1½   (M J Ryan)   M Ryan Newmarket

3155 LINKS MAIDEN STAKES 3YO+   £684   1m 4f Firm 04 -21 Slow

3061 AIRCRAFTIE [5] (B Hills) 3-8-5 B Thomson 4/1 CO FAV: 0300221: 3 b f Northjet -
Ian Maid (Determine): Went on over 2f out & held on well to win an all aged mdn at Redcar:
placed several times in similar company this term & was not winning out of turn: cost
$100,000 as a yearling and is a half sister to several winners: eff over 10/12f & may well
stay further: acts on gd & fast grnd.   34
2996 RARE LEGEND [1] (M Ryan) 3-8-5 P Robinson 4/1 CO FAV: 0-00242: Just held: in gd form.   32
3101 SOMETHING SIMILAR [6] (J Fitzgerald) 3-8-8 M Birch 5/1: 0000233: Found little under press
see 3101 and 2885.   32
2853 SIT ELNAAS [7] (H T Jones) 3-8-5 P D'arcy 5/1: 0-04: Al there: stays 12f: see 2853.   26
3061 MEVAGISSEY [15] 3-8-8 G Baxter 4/1 CO FAV: -200: Set off in front, no extra when hdd:
twice well below form shown on his debut in 2996 (11f).   26
2148 GOOD NATURED [11] 3-8-5 K Darley 20/1: -0000: Abs: held up, no threat: see 1954.   17
1435 HURRICANE HENRY [2] 3-8-8 W R Swinburn 10/1: 2-00430: Mid-div: fin 7th: abs since 1435.   00
2853 INDIAN LOVE SONG [10] 3-8-5 W Carson 10/1: 4302300: Fdd into 9th: btr in 2129: see 464.   00
2996 Ickworth [13] 9-0   -- Chief Jester [4] 9-0   2478 Raffles Rogue [14] 8-8
2726 Fissure [8] 8-5   3087 Paravane [12] 8-11   2978 Craigs Venture [3] 9-0
3036 Minders Man [9] 9-0(bl)
15 ran ½,1½,2,1½,3,4,nk,1½   (Howard Kaskel)   B Hills Lambourn, Berks

3156 PROVIDEO STAKES 2YO   £1769   5f   Firm 04 +13 Fast

*2993 CHILIBANG [4] (J Dunlop) 2-9-5 W Carson 8/13 FAV: 1011211: 2 ro c Formidable -
Chili Girl (Skymaster): In grand form & again readily landed the odds, making all in a fast
run 2yo stakes at Redcar: earlier successful in nurseries at Ayr (2) and Windsor, & a mdn
at Nottingham: half brother to 6/7f winner Hot Case: very speedy colt who is equally eff
over 5/6f: acts on gd & firm grnd & on any trk: very consistent juvenile who is best out
in front.   56
3048 SKI CAPTAIN [5] (J Etherington) 2-8-11(bl) M Wood 9/2: 0022: Quickly into his stride,
but al in vain pursuit of winner: sure to win a race: see 3048 and 2781.   40
-3044 BALKAN LEADER [3] (J Fitzgerald) 2-8-11 A Murray 7/2: 023423: Running well: see 3044.   40
2232 ICHI BAN SON [1] (A Smith) 2-8-11 K Hodgson 25/1: 004: Sn outpcd: best in 1869 (6f).   22
3037 DOMINEERING [2] 2-8-8 W R Swinburn 4/1: 00: Dwelt, well btn: half sister to several
winners, incl useful juvenile Throne of Glory & should do much btr than this.   00
5 ran 2,hd,7,10   (Mrs H Heinz)   J Dunlop Arundel, Sussex

3157 GANTON HANDICAP (0-35) 3YO+   £2845   7f   Firm 04 +05 Fast   [35]

2998 BROADHURST [21] (J Etherington) 3-8-2(bl) S Webster 15/2: 3003141: 3 b f Workboy -
Simbirica (Simbir): Waited with, & qcknd into lead below dist to win quite a fast run h'cap
at Redcar: earlier a facile winner of his mdn over 1m on this same course: acts on yld though
seems best suited by a sound surface: likes this gall trk: in gd form & may win again.   24
3029 BELLA BANUS [12] (W Stephenson) 4-8-13 M Hindley(3) 6/1 FAV: 0030002: Gd effort: see 606. 26
2934 SIGNORE ODONE [14] (M H Easterby) 4-9-12 M Birch 12/1: 1120003: Led briefly 2f out.   35
2891 BAXTERGATE [17] (J Payne) 3-7-11(VIS) G Bardwell(7) 14/1: 0000204: Visored: led ½way.   04
3029 ZIO PEPPINO [20] 5-8-6 J Carroll(7) 12/1: 0113000: Nearest fin: best 2762.   08
3057 KING COLE [18] 4-7-9(2ow)(4oh) J Callaghan(1) 20/1: 00304D0: Ran on too late: see 3057, 1830.00
2977 AITCHANDOUBLEYOU [8] 3-8-3 W Ryan 14/1: 0004000: Never nearer 7th: see 1793.   00
3078 SHARP SHOT [2] 5-8-11 W Carson 8/1: 0000200: Again well bckd: so far best 2891 (1m).   00
3104 HOPEFULL KATIE [7] 4-8-13 J Williams 7/1: 1301020: Fdd 2 out: best here 3104 (6f).   00
2905 Festivity [5] 8-12   3033 Haywain [4] 8-3(vis)   3104 Clawson Thorns [23] 7-11
2977 Off Your Mark [13] 7-9   3104 Thatchered [19] 8-9
2602 Top Othlane [11] 7-13(4ow)   3033 Just The Ticket [9] 7-7
2213 Humble Beauty [16] 8-5   2399 Affaitati [10] 8-2(3ow)
1259 Apprila [1] 9-0   2945 Mels Choice [6] 8-9   3060 Christmas Cottage [22] 9-4(bl)
21 ran   2,2,3,2,hd,1,1½,shhd   (Les Baker)   J Etherington Norton, Yorks

3158 E.B.F. MUNICIPAL STAKES 2YO   £1802   1m   Firm 04 -10 Slow

3075 ANUBI [9] (L Cumani) 2-8-11 W Carson 7/4 FAV: 041: 2 brr c Sharpen Up - Evgenia
(Green Dancer): Impr colt: well bckd & led under press inside final 1f in a 2yo stakes at
Redcar: American bred colt who cost $25,000 as a yearling: clearly stays 1m well & will
do even btr when tackling middle dist next term: acts on fast grnd & on a gall trk.   42
+2888 MUBDI [2] (H T Jones) 2-9-4 A Murray 11/4: 23012: Game attempt to make all, but this
extra furlong just found him out: consistent colt who seems to act on any trk: see 2888.   44
--   BARN FIVE SOUTH [12] (O Douieb) 2-8-11 R Machado 10/1: 3: Active in mkt on debut:
ran on strongly & this was a promising effort: well bred colt who fetched $90,000 as a yearling
& looks sure to justify that outlay over middle dists next term: acts on fast grnd & on
a gall trk.   35
3080 BOLD AS BOLD [13] (M Usher) 2-8-11 M Wigham 10/1: 404: Vigourously ridden:
lightly raced since 577.   23
3059 PRIMETTA PRINCE [8] 2-8-11 D Nicholls 4/1: 030: Nicely bckd: btn 2f out: see 3059.   00
3059 ANOTHER NONSENSE [6] 2-8-11 C Nutter 14/1: 00: Gd speed over ½way: see 3059.   00
3059 IN A SPIN [11] 2-8-8 K Darley 9/1: 300020: Well btn in 7th: much btr in 3059 & 1529.   00
2975 Golden Game [3] 8-11   -- Hatshepsut [1] 8-8   -- Mabuhay [10] 8-8
10 ran   2,½,6,12,1   (Studcrown Ltd)   L Cumani Newmarket

3159 LINKS MAIDEN STAKES 3YO+   £684   1m 4f   Firm 04 +04 Fast

2605 SNOW WIZARD [3] (O Douieb) 3-8-8(bl) W Ryan 4/1: --00421: 3 b c Shirley Heights
Idiot's Delight (Bold Ruler): Led below dist & stayed on well to win quite a fast run mdn
at Redcar: progressive type who is well suited by 12/14f: acts on fast & yld grnd & is well
suited by a gall trk: wears bl.   42
2930 LAKE ERIE [1] (M Stoute) 3-8-8 W R Swinburn 10/11 FAV: -22: Hvly bckd to go one btr
after a promising debut: ev ch, no extra close home: fin clear of rem: see 2930.   40
3105 NO DOUBLET [2] (B Hills) 3-8-5 B Thomson 10/1: 2220403: Made much: see 1639.   28
2516 COOL GALES [5] (G Pritchard Gordon) 3-8-5 Abigail Richards(7) 3/1: -002004: No extra
dist: btr in 1690 (10f): see 732.   25
2747 SOLVENT [6] 3-8-8 A Murray 14/1: 2002330: Btn 2f out: disapp sort: see 2620 & 116.   14
2366 TOUKSHAD [7] 3-8-8 K Darley 10/1: -30: Failed to impr on his debut effort in 2366.   08
2853 NINOTCHKA [9] 3-8-5 W Carson 11/2: 4-240: Fin 7th: much btr over 9f in 2593.   00
3035 Sagax [4] 9-0   2605 Fiesta Dance [15] 8-8   -- Oleandrin [10] 9-0
2593 Save It Less [13] 8-5   2415 Racing Demon [12] 9-0 2948 Sweet Delilah [11] 8-5
2893 No Idea [14] 8-8   106 Pretty Amazing [8] 9-0
15 ran   ½,5,1½,8,3   (S S Niarchos)   O Douieb Newmarket

3160 REPTON CLAIMING STAKES 3YO   £2113   6f   Good 70 -19 Slow

3083 DEBBIE DO [9] (C Thornton) 3-9-7 J Lowe 16/1: 0004001:3 gr f Absalom - Miss Eliza
(Mountain Call): Cmftbly defied top weight in a 3yo claiming stakes at Nottingham, led dist
& ran on strongly: had run several good races this term without adding to her juvenile wins
at Hamilton & Carlisle: equally eff over 5/6f: acts on firm & soft grnd & likes a gall trk.   40
--   VILMAX [20] (B Mcmahon) 3-7-13 G Carter 20/1: -2: Ran on well from ½way & should be
all the btr for this initial effort: half sister to a winning plater & on this evidence should
not be hard pressed to win in that grade: eff over 6f on gd grnd.   15
3024 HOPEFULL DANCER [18] (R Hannon) 3-8-8(BL) A Mcglone 33/1: -000003: Fitted with bl: not
qkn near fin, but this was a much btr effort: see 928.   18
2977 KINGS TOUCH [4] (P Makin) 3-8-10 Pat Eddery 9/4 FAV: 0400024: Well bckd: btr in 2977.   20
2367 SUPERCOOMBE [14] 3-8-12 T Quinn 14/1: 022D000: Btr effort: little form since 516.   21

923

3024 SPANISH INFANTA [2] 3-8-2 A Mackay 20/1: 0000300: Ran on too late: see 2854.   11
+3046 JACQUI JOY [16] 3-8-11 A Shoults(5) 12/1: 2124010: Not btn that far in 7th: see 3046.   00
2619 OCEAN TRADER [23] 3-9-0(bl) P Waldron 8/1: 0000000: Prom most: fin 8th: see 2143.   00
3062 COURT TOWN [21] 3-8-9 B Rouse 7/1: 0402000: No show over this shorter trip: see 2601, 2027.00

1927 Global [17] 8-5		3033 Imperial Sunrise [11] 8-5(bl)	
2670 Lunar Shamal Gal [19] 9-2(BL)		2906 Kings Ring [5] 8-12	
2842 Young Puggy [22] 8-11	3104 Low Flyer [7] 8-7	2275 Progo [3] 8-7	
1171 Kelly Lindo [6] 8-5	3066 Whos That Girl [8] 8-4(BL)		
3144 Paddington Belle [12] 8-3(vis)		2594 The Stamp Dealer [1] 8-2	
1312 Herminda [13] 7-13	3024 Love At Last [10] 7-13		
22 ran 1,2,shhd,nk,shhd,nk	(Norman Robinson)		C Thornton Middleham, Yorks

3161 FULL CHOKE HANDICAP 3YO 0-35   £1459   2m 2f Good 70 -32 Slow   [38]

2587 PATRIOTIC [16] (M Prescott) 3-7-8 A Mackay 12/1: 0-04101: 3 b f Hotfoot - Poppy
Day (Soleil II): Went on over 2f out & just held on in a 3yo h'cap at Nottingham: bought in
after winning a seller at Catterick in Aug & seems to be making steady impr: related to several
winners: eff around 14f, clearly stays 2m plus well: well suited by fast grnd & a sharp/easy trk.   12
2974 CAROUSEL ROCKET [10] (R Whitaker) 3-9-2 K Bradshaw(5) 12/1: 1034042: Just denied:
stays well: see 968.   33
*2892 NIMBLE NATIVE [15] (S Norton) 3-8-13 J Lowe 9/2: 0304113: Btn a whisker: in fine form.   30
2722 MILTESCENS [3] (A Jarvis) 3-9-7(BL) Paat Eddery 7/1: 0204004: Wore bl for the first
time: seems to stay 2m plus, but has proved disepp during the latter half of this season: see 1177.   33
2892 DENALTO [9] 3-7-12 B Crossley 10/3 FAV: 3020220: In gd form: see 2892 & 2760.   08
3036 RIDESIDE [7] 3-8-4(BL) R Fox 6/1: -04000: Bl first time: stayed on late: see 2682.   13
2363 DENBERDAR [2] 3-8-7 S Perks 10/1: 2030340: Disapp sort: see 1961 & 48.   00
*3049 LOST OPPORTUNITY [14] 3-8-7(vis)(7ex) W Newnes7/1: 0000410: Btr on a tight trk in 3049 (2m). 00

2874 Bully Boy [13] 7-7(3oh)		2148 Gex [1] 8-1	
2306 Cupids Bower [11] 7-7(3oh)		2128 Marina Plata [8] 8-10	
2988 Mistral Magic [12] 8-1		1873 Kasu [4] 8-1	
2605 Garthman [5] 7-8(1ow)(2oh)		2902 Go Flamingo [6] 7-7(8oh)	
16 ran shhd,shhd,3,½,½	(Mrs C Philipson)		M Prescott Newmarket

3162 BITTER END SELLING HANDICAP 3YO 0-25   £911   1m 2f Good 70 -34 Slow   [27]

2597 BAYDON QUEEN [6] (D Hanley) 3-8-4(3ow) S Whitworth 20/1: -000001: 3 b f Blakeney -
Opera Star (Appiani II): Stayed on well to lead inside dist, cmftbly in a 3yo selling h'cap
at Nottingham (no bid): had been well btn in all her previous starts this term: well suited
by 10f & gd grnd.   12
2787 DRESS IN SPRING [9] (G Blum) 3-8-5 M Rimmer 11/2 JT FAV: 0001002: Stays 10f: see 2238.   06
2161 DENIECE [1] (J Norton) 3-9-2(bl) A Culhane(7) 20/1: -0003: Dropped in class: behind,
ran on too late: acs on gd & firm grnd: see 1639.   17
3076 NAME THE DAY [11] (J Douglas Home) 3-8-2(BL)(2ow) W Newnes 20/1: 0-4004: One paced.   02
3045 DAVALLIA [10] 3-9-7(BL) R Cochrane 6/1: 3-00040: Bl first time: fair effort under
top weight: see 430.   20
2679 GROSVENOR COURT [13] 3-7-7(vis)(1oh) N Carlisle 20/1:0-00000: Prom most of way: see 2679 00
3084 MISS VENEZUELA [2] 3-7-10 G French 7/1: 0000000: Never nearer 7th: see 1288.   00
3076 TYRANNISE [8] 3-7-13 A Mackay 8/1: 0-00200: Made most, wknd qckly into 8th: see 1340(1m). 00
3065 BEE KAY ESS [5] 3-8-2 S Dawson 9/1: 4002000: Fin 9th: btr over 1m in 2616: see 1210.   00
2335 FOLKSWOOD [14] 3-8-0 J Lowe 11/2 JT FAV: 0-00020: Fin in rear: abs since 2335 (1m yld). 00

2853 Worth Debating [15] 8-12		932 Gary And Larry [16] 8-10	
346 Delta Lima [7] 8-10(bl)		2932 Linton Springtime [3] 8-4	
2093 Mossaul [4] 8-3	2778 Andreas Pride [12] 7-9		
16 ran 4,hd,½,½,hd	(A J Richards)		D Hanley Marlborough, Berks

3163 WHATTON MANOR STUD STAKES 2YO   £3766   1m 50y Good 70 -02 Slow

-- LEGAL BID [13] (H Cecil) 2-8-11 S Cauthen 11/8: 1: 2 ch c Spectacular Bid - Bold
Bikini (Boldnesian): Very promising colt: could not have made a more impressive debut, sn in
front & spreadeagled his rivals when an easy winner of a 2yo stakes at Nottingham: American
bred colt who is closely related to numerous winners, incl Irish Derby victor Law Society:
clearly very eff over 1m on gd grnd: highly regarded by connections & has a lot of potential:
has already been made one of the fav. for next year's Derby & indeed looks a high class prospect.   76
2847 TIQUEGREAN [12] (J Dunlop) 2-8-8 R Fox 10/1: 22: Kept on well to take the minor honours,
though had no ch with this runaway winner: stays 1m well: see 2847.   53
-- BY THE FIRESIDE [4] (C Nelson) 2-8-11 J Reid 50/1: 3: Stayed on promisingly on debut:
half brother to useful 10/12f winner Get The Message: seems certain to stay further than 1m
himself: acts on gd grnd: one to keep an eye on.   56
3011 GOLD SCEPTRE [10] (P Cole) 2-8-11 T Quinn 25/1: 04: Mkt drifter: front rank over
½way & this represented considerable impr on his debut run: see 3011.   51
3080 TRANBY CROFT [19] 2-8-11 B Crossley 33/1: 00: Never nearer: clearly all the btr for
his recent debut: looks the type of make his mark over middle dists next season: see 3080.   50
*2852 TWEETER [16] 2-9-2 A Clark 11/10 FAV: 10: Pulled hard, back pedalling from dist
& is btr than this: see 2852.   55
-- PALACE SONG [14] 2-8-11 R Cochrane 50/1: 0: Ran on quite promisingly after a slow
start: quite a speedily bred gelding who is likely to impr next time: acts on gd grnd.   48

2499 Dalby Dancer [8] 8-8	2847 Bronze Buck [11] 8-11	3018 Burly Native [1] 8-11
-- Holtermann [6] 8-11	3059 Midbadge [15] 8-11	-- Palais De Danse [5] 8-11
2852 Rathdrum [9] 8-11	2957 Ribobambino [17] 8-11	2847 Trapper [3] 8-11
3074 Canary Wharf [7] 8-8	2651 Debutante Ball [18] 8-8	
200 Scallykath [2] 8-8		
19 ran 7,hd,2½,¼,nk,¼	(W S Farish III)	H Cecil Newmarket

3164 LESTER PIGGOTT FINAL HANDICAP 3YO+ 0-35 £1797   1m 50y Good 70 +07 Fast   [35]

-3060 ACTUALIZATIONS [12] (L Cumani) 3-8-9 R Cochrane 4/1 JT FAV: 0342421: 3 b f Green Dancer-
Tom's Lass (Tom Rolfe): Finally got off the mark, led over 1f out & held on well in an all aged
h'cap at Nottingham: cost $125,000 as a yearling & is a half sister to a minor winner: previously
had proved rather frustrating, being placed in most of her starts this term: suited by good or
faster grnd & seems to act on any trk.   32
2746 BLACK COMEDY [7] (M Ryan) 3-8-8 G Carter 12/1: 1404042: Fin well, just btn: see 843.   30
3078 XHAI [1] (M Tompkins) 4-9-9 M Rimmer 4/1 JT FAV: 2000023: In gd form: see 3078.   34
2728 TIP TAP [19] (A Hide) 4-8-9 P Bloomfield 14/1: 0010404: Never nearer: gd effort: see 1870. 20
2963 FARAG [14] 3-8-8 D Mead(6) 14/1: 3200020: Made much: in gd form: see 2963.   23
2929 VAIGLIAN [9] 3-8-9(bl) Paul Eddery 16/1: 0000030: Not clear run: see 2929 & 64.   21

3033 Ivory Gull [8] 9-2	3060 Run By Jove [20] 8-13(vis)	
2931 Makalu [11] 8-12	3078 Highland Image [16] 9-1	
520 Brampton Grace [10] 9-10		3070 Sparky Lad [15] 9-3
3078 Every Effort [2] 9-1	1022 Floral Charge [3] 8-11	
2314 Chart Climber [4] 8-10		2973 Green For Danger [18] 8-9
3060 Silly Boy [5] 8-9	1257 Azelly [17] 8-8	1689 Rio Deva [13] 8-8
19 ran nk,3,shhd,¼,1½	(Richard G Stokes)	L Cumani Newmarket

3165 EAST MIDLAND NURSERY HANDICAP 2YO   £1734   1m 50y Good 70 +05 Fast   [49]

2798 CHESTER TERRACE [17] (P Walwyn) 2-8-4 Paul Eddery 12/1: 000031: 2 ch c Crofter -
Persian Mourne (Mourne): Qcknd clear at the dist to win quite a fast run nursery h'cap at
Nottingham: half brother to winning juvenile Realert & looked unlucky not to get off the
mark when a close 3rd to Rivers Secret in a nursery at Hamilton last time: stays 1m well:
acts on gd & fast grnd & seems to handle any trk.   38
2723 WOODPECKER [13] (H T Jones) 2-9-1 R Hills 6/1: 2032: Fin well: see 2723 & 2051.   42
2607 CAMMAC LAD [6] (C Tinkler) 2-8-6 G Carter 14/1: 0003233: Consistent sort: see 2471.   30
2897 KIERON PRESS [15] (D Arbuthnot) 2-8-8 A Clark 8/1: 1400404: Nearest fin: see 1495.   30
-2744 SUPREME STATE [9] 2-8-11 S Perks 12/1: 003220: Ran on same pace: stays 1m: see 2270.   27
2989 PERSIAN TAPESTRY [12] 2-8-3(BL) W Newnes 8/1: 4000000: Ran on too late: stays 1m: see 707. 18
-2968 PHARAOH BLUE [7] 2-8-3 M Roberts 4/1 FAV: 1204020: Ev ch: wknd into 7th: btr 2968.   00
*2829 TYRIAN PRINCESS [16] 2-8-4 A Shoults(5) 13/2: 010: Much btr over 7f in 2829 (firm, seller) 00

2878 Absinthe [19] 9-7	2878 Gunner Stream [1] 8-10	
2029 Skolern [14] 8-9	2663 Punta Calahonda [2] 9-7(BL)	
3041 Battleaxe [10] 9-2(bl)		2761 Foreign Knight [4] 8-8
2989 King Richard [18] 8-6	-2976 Melgrove [8] 8-3(bl)	2379 City Final [20] 8-3
2485 Souleiadou [5] 8-3(bl)		*2466 Ribogirl [3] 7-12
19 ran 2,1½,¼,2½,nk,½	(Leonard Sainer)	P Walwyn Lambourn, Berks

---

LONGCHAMP   Thursday October 23rd   Righthand, Galloping Track

Official Going Given As VERY SOFT

3166 GROUP 3 PRIX DES RESERVOIRS 2YO FILLIES £36389   1m   Very Soft

-- BINT ALNASR (A Fabre) 2-8-9 C Asmussen : 101: 2 b f Al Nasr - Corolina Very useful
French filly: made almost all, very gamely, in a Gr 3 2yo fillies event at Longchamp: a
first time out winner again at Longchamp: stays 1m well and can clearly handle very soft grd. 68
3088 LIBERTINE (R Collet) 2-8-9 Y Saint Martin : 1320222: Led inside final 1f: narrowly
btn and deserves another win: stays 1m well and acts on gd/firm & soft.   67
-- SAVONNERIE (C Head) 2-8-9 G Mosse : 213: Not btn far: last time out was a 2l winner
at Evry: acts on soft.   65
-- HOT SILVER (F Boutin) 2-8-9 F Head : 314: Cl.up 4th in a very cl fin: in gd form:
last time out winning at St-Cloud: acts on soft.   64
8 ran   hd,½,nk   (M F Dabaghi)   A Fabre France

Official Going Given As GOOD/FIRM

3167 ARDENODE STUD LEOPARDSTOWN STAKES 2YO   £14455   7f   Good/Firm

-- ANTIC BOY (J Oxx) 2-8-10 D Hogan 20/1: 31: 2 br c Nebos - Alaria Fast impr colt: caused a 20/1 surprise, led final 1f, all out, in a Gr 3 event at Leopardstown: first time out fin 3rd in a mdn at the Curragh: eff at 7f, should be suited by 1m: acts on gd/firm grd.   **66**

2721 MULHOLLANDE (P Cole) 2-8-10 P Waldron 7/2: 022: Led briefly 1f out: kept on well and narrowly btn: a fine effort and should win races next term: said to prefer some give in the ground: see 2721.   **65**

-- BLUEBIRD (M O'brien) 2-9-0 D Gillespie 7/2: 13: Not btn far: another gd run: on only other outing won over 5f at Phoenix Park: acts on gd/firm.   **65**

2739 CECINA (L Browne) 2-8-7 C Roche 14/1: 22024: Most consistent: see 2739.   **58**

-- BIG SHUFFLE 2-8-10 M J Kinane 11/8 FAV: 10: Heavily bckd: not btn far in 5th: made a winning racecourse debut over 7f at the Curragh on fast grd and is obviously held in high regard.   **61**

13 ran   hd,1½,shthd,shthd,2   (N Schibbye)   J Oxx Ireland

Official Going Given As SOFT

3168 GROUP 1 PRIX DE LA FORET 2YO+   £36389   7f   Soft

-3020 SARAB [1] (P Cole) 5-9-12 T Quinn : 1104121: 5 b h Prince Tenderfoot - Carnival Dance (Welsh Pageant) Smart colt: ended his career on a winning note in Gr 1 Prix de la Foret at Longchamp: led 1f out and battled on in his usual game style for a narrow win: an absolute model of consistency, earlier winning a Listed race at Goodwood and also successful abroad at Phoenix Park, Chantilly and Baden-Baden: in '85 won at Newcastle and Haydock: very eff over 7f/1m: acts on any grd: a genuine sort who is a credit to his trainer.   **81**

2866 RISK ME [4] (P Kelleway) 2-8-5 R Cochrane : 114422: Fin very well and just btn: grand effort by a 2yo and continues to improve: loves this soft grd: stays 7f well: see 2866   **80**

2915 WHAKILYRIC [3] (F Boutin) 2-8-2 E Saint Martin 1: 1412303: Made much and ran very well indeed: clearly handles soft grd well: see 2915, 2737.   **73**

*2918 SECRET FORM [5] (P Bary) 3-9-8 C Asmussen : 1-22214: Fav: ran on well over a trip that was prob too short for her: acts on firm & soft: see 2918.   **74**

2507 NORTHERN ASPEN [8] 4-9-9 A Badel : 01-0200: Creditable 5th: see 2359.   **68**

2002 RIVER DANCER [8] 3-9-8 M Philipperon : 4304310: Gd eff: last time out won a Listed race at Deauville: see 467, 155.   **69**

2506 WISE COUNSELLOR [16] 3-9-11 Pat Eddery : -120100: Was prob unfavoured by his high draw: twice below 2192 (1m).   **00**

3092 BAISER VOLE [14] 3-9-8 F Head : 1432020: Poorly drawn and below her best: see 3092.   **00**

2440 STATELY LASS [11] 3-9-8 S Cauthen : 3-10020: Fin down the field: see 2440, 59.   **00**

16 ran   hd,2,½,2,nk   (F Salman)   P Cole Whatcombe, Oxon.

3169 GROUP 1 PRIX ROYAL OAK 3YO+   £35492   1m7.5f Soft

*2741 EL CUITE [3] (H Cecil) 3-8-11 S Cauthen 11/2: 1-111: 3 b c Vaguely Noble - Assez Cuite (Graustark) Very smart colt who remains unbtn after success in Gr 1 Prix Royal -Oak at Longchamp: stayed on well to get up cl home by a nk: earlier successful in Gr 1 event at San Siro and first time out a ready winner of a val and fast run h'cap at Newbury: on sole start in '85 won a 27 runner event at Newbury: very eff at 12f, clearly stays 15.5f: acts on firm & soft grd and a gall trk: will stay in training next season and will prove hard to beat in any company.   **85**

2738 ALESSO [4] (D Smaga) 3-8-11 A Lequeux : 14122: Fin in fine style and nearly gained the day: a tremendous effort in this Gr 1 event: clearly relishs soft grd and Longchamp: see 2738.   **84**

*2844 VALUABLE WITNESS [8] (J Tree) 6-9-3 Pat Eddery : 11-1113: Had to make his own running: hdd in the str but battled on gamely and just btn: most genuine and this was a fine effort.   **80**

3004 FABUROLA [9] (P Biancone) 5-9-0 G Mosse : 1-22024: Ev ch in str: another fine run.   **76**

*2005 AGENT DOUBLE [6] '5-9-3 F Head : -333100: Gd eff: likes it soft: see 2005.   **76**

2565 SWINK [1] 3-8-11 Y Saint Martin : 3231240: Btr on firm grd? See 2565.   **77**

*2525 REJUVENATE [10] 3-8-8 B Thomson : -310010: Fin 9th: well below 2525 (14f, firm).   **00**

3006 Robertos Fighter [5] 9-0   2453 Denel [2] 9-3

*693 Ore [7] 9-3

10 ran   nk,shtnk,hd,2,1½,1½   (Sheikh Mohammed)   H Cecil Newmarket

DUSSELDORF   Sunday October 26th

Official Going Given As SOFT

3170 GROUP 3 EVENT 3YO+   £9887   1m 4f   Soft

-- GANYMED (S Von Mitzlaff) 4-8-9 P Schade : -1: 4 b c Alpenkonig - Gaunerel Stayed on
well for a 1l win in a Gr 3 event at Dusseldorf: was the lesser fancied of the trainers
2 runners: clearly well suited by 12f and may get further: acts on soft.   75
2525 ALTIYNA (M Stoute) 3-7-12(2ow) P Robinson : 2204032: Tried to make all and stayed
on gamely: in fine form: acts on firm & soft: see 2525, 463.   70
2824 TIBERIUS (S Von Mitzlaff) 3-8-2 P Alafi : -203: Fav: ev ch: consistent.   70
2824 CASSIS (H Bollow) 4-9-4 P Remmert : 1-23404: --   69
3038 FIRST DIVISION 3-8-2 A Clark : -111000: Prom, wknd: lightly raced since 883.   53
7 ran   1,2,4,1½,1¾   (Stall Simone)   S Von Mitzlaff Germany

NEWMARKET   Friday October 31st   Righthand, Stiff, Galloping Track

Official Going Given As GOOD/SOFT

3171 SOHAM HOUSE STAKES 2YO   £4099   1m   Good 68 -13 Slow

2852 PILLAR OF WISDOM [8] (O Douieb) 2-8-9 Paul Eddery 2/1 FAV: 01: 2 b c Blushing Groom -
Sleeke Belle (Vaguely Noble) Very promising colt: heavily bckd to confirm his promising debut
in race 2852 and was an impressive winner of a val 2yo event at Newmarket: led well over 1f
out and was ridden clear: cost $325,000 and is a half brother to sev winners: well suited by
1m and will stay further: acts on gd & firm grd and a stiff trk: should win races next season   65
-- OUR ACCOUNT [1] (L Cumani) 2-8-9 P Hamblett 33/1: 2: Ridden along but stayed on in
fine style: American bred colt who is very stoutly bred and will be well suited by middle
dist next term: acts on gd grd and a stiff trk: should make a decent 3yo.   57
-- ROYAL PAGEANT [2] (J Dunlop) 2-8-9 B Rouse 33/1: 3: Led 2f out: promising racecourse
debut: dam a winner over 1m/10f: stays 1m on a stiff trk: acts on gd grd and seems sure to
find a race.   56
2939 ALWASMI [15] (H T Jones) 2-8-9 R Hills 3/1: 34: Well bckd: not clear run over 2f out:
ran on: another gd effort: stays 1m well: see 2939.   55
-- MCCUBBIN [5] 2-8-9 R Guest 33/1: 0: Mkt drifter: ran on well inside final 2f and
looks certain to rate more highly: American bred colt who cost $320,000: looks sure to be
suited by 10f+ next season: acts on gd grd and a stiff trk: one to keep an eye on.   54
-- LUMBERJACK [6] 2-8-9 A Clark 10/3: 0: Ev ch inside final 2f: promising first effort
from this U.S. bred colt: should stay middle dist next term: acts on gd grd and a gall trk.   53
-- NATSKI [11] 2-8-9 R Cochrane 12/1: 0: Never nearer 7th on racecourse debut: improvement
likely from this 52,000 gns purchase: bred to stay well and is a half brother to 3 winners
abroad: acts on gd ground.   52
*3023 NINTH SAGA [7] 2-9-6 C Rutter(3) 14/1: 010: Wk in mkt: made much: stiff task at
these weights and again ran with credit: see 3023.   59
*2957 UPTOTHEHILT [12] 2-8-11 J Reid 12/1: 0010: Dsptd lead 2f out, fdd: not disgraced in
9th: prob acts on any trk: see 2957.   48
-- Swalk [13] 8-9   -- Golden Dirham [4] 8-9 -- Alphasonic [9] 8-9
3053 Icarus [10] 8-9   2645 Taweel [14] 8-9   -- Pulaski [3] 8-9
15 ran 3,nk,½,½,½,½,1½,½   (Edward Seltzer)   O Douieb Newmarket

3172 NOVEMBER SELLING HANDICAP 0-25   £2040   6f   Good 68 -09 Slow   [25]

2632 FOOLISH TOUCH [6] (W Musson) 4-10-0(vis) M Wigham 4/1: 4402401: 4 b g Hot Spark -
Nushka (Tom Fool) Heavily bckd when gaining 2nd successive win in a 3 & 4yo selling h'cap at
Newmarket: led inside final 1f, readily: trained by K Stone much of this season and has
retained his form well after a h'cap win at Kempton in May: in '85 won this same race and
also first time out at Ayr: in '84 won Yarmouth: eff at 5-7f: acts on any going and any trk:
seldom disappoints when the money is down.   35
3083 ALNASHME [20] (D Thom) 4-9-4 A Murray 9/4 FAV: -401442: A big gamble: led after
2f till hdd by winner: chance before seasons end in a similar event: see 3083.   18
2315 POCO LOCO [18] (A Davison) 4-8-4 G Baxter 20/1: 0230033: Prom, ev ch: fair eff: see 889. 00
2898 HEAVENLY CAROL [1] (P Cundell) 3-8-1(BL) W Carson 20/1: 0000004: Raced alone far side.   00
2890 OPTIMISM FLAMED [3] 3-8-8 M Beecroft 20/1: 2000000: Late hdwy: best 183 (1m).   01
2996 GODOUNOV [23] 3-8-13(bl) S Whitworth 14/1: -0400: Prom most: btr 2688 (firm).   03
3057 Golden Disc [8] 7-10(bl)   3160 Global [15] 9-7
2614 Cresta Leap [9] 9-3   3071 Manabel [7] 8-7   3083 Wesbree Bay [2] 7-9(1ow)
2906 Northern Lad [4] 8-9(VIS)   2960 Ideoligia [22] 7-7(2oh)
3160 Kings Ring [19] 9-2(BL)   *3144 Le Mans [5] 8-2(bL)
3057 Winning Format [12] 8-4   2898 Golden Straw [13] 8-12(bl)
1186 Oeil De Tigre [14] 8-3   281 Repealed [21] 9-9
113 Passooner [16] 8-3   3024 Avalon [11] 9-2(BL) 2659 Commander Meaden [10] 8-4(bl)
2960 Mr Panache [17] 7-13(VIS)
23 ran 3,3,nk,½,1   (M Chandler)   W Musson Newmarket
                                                                                            00

3173 GEORGE STUBBS EBF STAKES LISTED 3YO+   £8975   2m 24y Good 68 -29 Slow

2627 PAEAN [4] (H Cecil) 3-8-7 W Ryan 10/11 FAV: 1211121: 3 b c Bustino - Mixed Applause
(Nijinsky) Smart colt: justified hvy support with a narrow, but decisive win in a Listed race
at Newmarket: made ev yard and held on well: a genuine colt who has not fin out of the first
2 this season, earlier successful at Beverley, Newcastle, Pontefract & Newbury (first time out):
eff at 12f, stays 2m really well: acts on firm but prefers some give in the ground: consistent
sort who could develop into a very smart stayer next season.   65
2908 ROSEDALE USA [3] (J Dunlop) 3-9-2 W Carson 9/2: 2210222: 2nd most: kept on well but
the winner was al holding him: most consistent: stays 2m: see 2908.   73
-403 HOLY SPARK [6] (D Elsworth) 6-9-1 A Mcglone 33/1: -01223: Very long abs: al prom and
ran very well: clearly stays 2m: likes some give in the grd: see 312, 189.   56
2938 INSULAR [2] (I Balding) 6-9-1 S Cauthen 8/1: -310034: Ev ch: best 778.   55
3169 ORE [1] 8-9-7 M Wigham 4/1: 24/0100: No real threat: lightly raced: see 693.   57
3142 AMBASSADOR [5] 3-8-7(bl) T Ives 12/1: 2322340: Distant last: expensive to follow: see 3038. 37
6 ran   ½,4,nk,3,15   (Lord Howard de Walden)   H Cecil Newmarket

3174 POTTER TROPHY NURSERY HANDICAP 2YO   £3464   5f   Good 68 +06 Fast   [58]

*2871 ANOTHER GUEST [17] (R Sheather) 2-7-13 A Shoults(3) 9/2 JT.FAV: 011: 2 ch f Anfield -
Sharpway (Good Bond) In fine form and made gd hdwy to lead inside final 1f, under press, in
quite val and fast run nursery h'cap at Newmarket: last time out won her mdn at Wolverhampton:
cheaply bought filly who is a half sister to winner juv Shaves You Close: very eff. at 5f,
prob stays 6f: acts on gd & firm grd and does well on a gall trk.   40
*3058 MILLFAN [8] (W Musson) 2-7-13(7ex) A Mackay 7/1: 232012: Bckd from 12/1: led 2f out
and just caught: in grand form: see 3058.   37
3130 MA PETITE LASSIE [15] (M Francis) 2-8-8 J Reid 20/1: 02203: Not much room over 1f
out: ran on: a consistent filly: eff at 5/6f: acts on gd/firm & yldg: see 2950.   45
2983 MON BALZAR [14] (A Bailey) 2-7-8 J Quinn(2) 25/1: 0000004: Ev ch final 1f: ran well:
seems best over the minimum trip: see 2514.   30
*3146 SKYBOLT [18] 2-7-10(bl)(7ex) W Carson 9/2 JT.FAV: 0400110: Led 3f: another gd run.   31
*2987 ANOTHER RHYTHM [3] 2-7-13 J Lowe 12/1: 310: Chance over 1f out: not btn far: acts
on gd & firm: see 2987 (sharp trk).   31
-2606 PARADISE COFFEE [16] 2-7-7 G Bardwell(7) 11/2: 23120: Slow start, no show: best 2281   00
2162 Nawwar [5] 7-11   2950 Golden Cajun [12] 7-13
*3027 Father Time [13] 8-7(bl)(7ex)   3114 The Devils Music [19] 8-2
-2986 Lingering [1] 9-7   2962 Out On A Flyer [7] 7-7(8oh)
*2983 Beaulieu Bay [9] 8-10   +3072 Riot Brigade [11] 9-5(7ex)
2926 Dallors Conquest [10] 7-8(1ow)(8oh)   3027 Days Like These [4] 8-8
2261 Viva Ronda [6] 7-7(4oh)
18 ran   1,½,hd,½,1   (D O McIntyre)   R Sheather Newmarket

3175 JAMES SEYMOUR STAKES LISTED RACE 3YO+   £9443   1m 2f Good 68 +15 Fast

2911 RIYDA [3] (R J Houghton) 3-8-6 J Reid 12/1: 2230221: 3 ch f Be My Guest - Rilasa
(St Paddy) Smart filly: has been in fine form this season and led over 2f out, ridden out in
fast run and val Listed race at Newmarket: first time out winner of a mdn at Warwick and
later fine 2nd to Gesedeh at Kempton and also 2nd to Cockney Lass in a gd event in Ireland:
very eff over 10f: acts on gd & fast grd and on any trk: a genuine filly.   70
*3028 NADEED [1] (M Stoute) 3-8-9 A Kimberley 5/1: -0212: Nicely bckd: ev ch over 1f out:
fine effort in this much btr company: should win more races: see 3028.   70
1886 MAGIC SLIPPER [6] (H Cecil) 3-8-6 W Ryan 12/1: -212103: Stable companion of fav:
could not quicken over 1f out but stayed on well closing stages: a gd eff after a fair abs
and over a trip prob short of her best: most consistent: see 1600.   65
2825 BONSHAMILE [8] (A Hide) 3-8-9 R Guest 14/1: -103004: Never nearer: btr eff: see 2236.   65
3001 CHAUMIERE [5] 5-9-3(vis) W Carson 12/1: 0330300: Held up, never nearer: see 1526.   61
*2991 WATER CAY [9] 3-8-12 S Cauthen 6/4 FAV: 4123-10: Heavily bckd but rather uneasy fav:
ev ch 2f out: not stay 10f? See 2991 (1m).   59
3121 TISNT [2] 3-8-12 P Waldron 5/1: -12300: A distant last: very lightly raced since
fine eff in 510 and seems to·have regressed.   00
*2948 Soemba [11] 8-6   1596 Farewell To Love [7] 8-6
2867 Atoka [4] 8-11   3119 Queen Of Battle [10] 8-6
11 ran   1½,¾,1½,3,1½,½   (Aga Khan)   R J Houghton Blewbury, Oxon.

3176 EBF RED LODGE MAIDEN STAKES 2YO   £4341   6f   Good 68 -26 Slow

2750 ROCKFELLA [20] (R J Houghton) 2-9-0 J Reid 5/4 FAV: 231: 2 ch c Ballad Rock - Salabella
(Sallust) Very promising colt: heavily bckd when winning a val 2yo mdn at Newmarket: led over
1f out and was sn clear despite hanging left: dam is a half sister to Irish St Leger winner
M-Lolshan: eff at 6f, should get 7f: acts on gd & firm grd & gall trk: sure to win more races.   62
2626 PRESCRIPTION [2] (R Armstrong) 2-9-0 P Tulk 33/1: 02: Led 3f out: no ch with winner
but is fast improving: half brother to winning 2yo Twist Home: should stay further than 6f:
acts on gd grd and a gall trk and should find a race.   50
-- HATINA [21] (L Cumani) 2-8-11 R Cochrane 12/1: 3: Wk in mkt: al there: improvement
likely from this ¾ sister to useful 6/7f winner Al Amead: should be suited by 7f herself:
acts on gd grd and a gall trk.   46

2983 SHUKO [3] (M Jarvis) 2-9-0 W Woods(3) 33/1: 04: Ev ch over 1f out: much btr eff:
cost 19,000 gns as a yearling and dam was a winner in Ireland: acts on gd grd and a stiff trk
and on this evidence should find a small race.   47
--   ROMANTIC PRINCE [19] 2-9-0 T Lucas 20/1: 0: Dsptd lead 2f out: wknd: promising first
run from this ½ brother to sev winners including the very smart 7/8f filly Capricorn Belle:
bred to stay further than 6f: should improve.   46
3053 PICK OF THE PACK [6] 2-9-0 M Hills 5/1: 000: Chance inside final 2f: gd eff: see 2847   45
2983 UNWISE [17] 2-9-0 S Cauthen 11/2: 30: Led 3f, fdd: btr 2983 (sharper trk).   00

3146 Surely Great [8] 8-11	-- Deep Water Bay [10] 9-0		
2561 Gameshow [7] 9-0	3130 Verdon Canyon [9] 9-0	3109 Saxon Mircel [12] 9-0	
3067 Moulas [16] 9-0	-- Bradman [18] 9-0	-- Los Gigantes [15] 8-11	
-- Tilford [11] 8-11	-- Mr Majinty [1] 9-0	-- Abathatc [5] 9-0	
-- Tilley Lamp [4] 8-11	-- Chamonis [13] 8-11	1082 Court Command [14] 9-0	
21 ran 5,hd,¾,½,½	(Mrs G T Johnson Houghton)	R J Houghton Blewbury, Oxon	

Official Going Given As SOFT

3177 BEN MARSHALL STAKES (LISTED) 3YO+   £9754   1m   Yielding 100 +17 Fast

2481 CRESTA AUCTION [9] (G Pritchard Gordon) 3-8-8 G Carter 25/1: 1230431: 3 b c Auction
Ring - Baby Clair (Gulf Pearl) Useful colt: was a surprise winner on this rain softened grd,
led over 2f out and was ridden clear in a fast run Listed Race at Newmarket: has only once
fin out of the frame since early season successes at Wolverhampton & Nottingham (first time
out) in '85 won a mdn at Brighton: very eff around 7/8f: acts on fast & soft grd and on any
trk: genuine & consistent sort who carries weight well.   73
3002 LAND OF IVORY [6] (I Balding) 3-8-8 T Ives 12/1: 3310102: Fine eff: see 2691.   70
3094 MUMMYS FAVOURITE [5] (J Dunlop) 3-8-5 B Rouse 15/2: 4143333: Most consistent: see 1487   65
3020 HOMO SAPIEN [4] (H Cecil) 4-9-3 S Cauthen 7/2 FAV: 2-13234: Fin best of all: see 3020.   72
*2740 MY GENERATION [3] 3-9-1 A Murray 10/1: 01-3110: In fine form: acts on soft: see 2740.   73
3093 KABIYLA [12] 3-8-5 M Stoute 4/1: 1201320: Not btn very far: acts on yldg: see 2765.   62
+3020 LUCKY RING [11] 4-9-10 W Carson 4/1: -000410: Led ½ way: wknd into 7th: btr 3020 (gd/frm)   00
+2943 ABSHEER [10] 3-8-8 J Lowe 9/2: -0110: Prom over ½ way: fin 8th: btr 2943.   00

3078 Fair Atlanta [7] 8-5	2785 Charge Along [8] 8-9	3042 Prince Pecadillo [1] 8-13	
2940 Hidden Brief [2] 8-5			
12 ran 1½,1,¾,nk,¾	(Mrs H F Gevers)	G Pritchard Gordon Newmarket	

3178 JENNINGS ZETLAND STAKES (LISTED) 2YO   £9536   1m 2f Yielding 100 -04 Slow

+2796 GRAND TOUR [10] (W Hastings Bass) 2-8-11 G Starkey 10/1: 011: 2 b c Troy - Peculiar
One (Quack) Very useful, fast impr colt: went on over 2f out and drew clear for an easy win
in val Zetland Stks at Newmarket: earlier a narrow winner of a mdn at Hamilton: well suited by
fast grd, and clearly handles a softer surf well: eff over 8/10f and certain to stay further:
likes a stiff, gall trk: should be an even btr horse next season.   65
2767 ARRASAS [8] (H T Jones) 2-8-11 A Murray 9/1: 132: Outpaced by winner inside dist,
comftbly beat rem: gd eff on this softer ground stays 10f well: see 2767 & 2646.   54
2936 MORNING FLOWER [2] (R Williams) 2-8-11 T Quinn 16/1: 2F20133: No extra below dist,
tho' ran another fine race in this gd class field: stays 10f: acts on fast & soft grd: see 2936   46
*2878 BATTALION USA [1] (J Dunlop) 2-8-11 W Carson 4/1: 0214: Ran on much too late: seems
certain to be suited by further next season: acts on fast & soft grd: see 2878.   44
2444 NORDAVANO [6] 2-8-11 J Reid 10/1: 2440: Prom most: see 2444 & 1452 (firm).   42
3018 SONG OF SIXPENCE [4] 2-8-11 J Matthias 7/2: 00: Well bckd: much btr on gd/firm in 3018   30
2941 TROJAN SONG [9] 2-8-12(1ow) S Cauthen 9/1: 2100: No threat in 8th: best over 7f in 2645.   00
3009 KALGOORLIE [12] 2-8-11 T Ives 11/4 FAV: 02330: Made much: wknd into 9th: much btr 3009   00

2989 Shaine [11] 8-11	1174 Scottish Fling [7] 8-11		
2718 Sunset Boulevard [3] 8-11(bl)		3085 Trompe Doeil [5] 8-8(bl)	
12 ran 3,5,2,½,7	(Lewis M Schott)	W Hastings Bass Newmarket	

3179 MAIL ON SUNDAY 3YO SERIES H'CAP FINAL   £15114   1m 2f Yielding 100 -09 Slow   [56]

2946 GEORDIES DELIGHT [8] (L Piggott) 3-9-7 T Ives 15/2: 2132031: 3 b c Northern Baby -
Shout For Joy (Court Martial) Very useful and most consistent colt: giving weight all round
but ran on strongly to lead inside dist, ridden out in a val 3yo h'cap at Newmarket: has been
a model of consistency this season: earlier won val race at Ostend , a h'cap at Pontefract and
his mdn at Epsom: very eff over 8/10f: acts on firm & hvy grd and on any trk: carries weight
well: most genuine and is a credit to his trainer.   65
3123 PRINCE MERANDI [7] (M Francis) 3-7-11 C Rutter(3) 16/1: 0001002: Led below dist,
hung right and sn hdd: clear rem and ran to his best: see 2431.   36
2867 SWIFT TROOPER [5] (R Williams) 3-9-1 R Cochrane 5/1 JT FAV: 1420003: Late prog: best 919   47
2911 SHEER LUCK [1] (I Balding) 3-7-9 R Fox 6/1: 0010204: Led over 3f out: btr 3676 (gd/frm)   22
+3101 THUNDERDOME [9] 3-8-3(5ex) W Ryan 5/1 JT FAV:0001110: Ran on late: much btr 3101 (gd/frm). 29
3105 NIHAD [13] 3-8-1(BL) G Baxter 10/1: 0323230: Bl first time: made much: see 3105.   26
2763 HARD AS IRON [3] 3-8-2 T Williams 6/1: 1221200: Al rear: fin 9th: best 2426 (gd/frm)   00
2942 CAPTAINS NIECE [6] 3-8-12 S Cauthen 15/2: -011120: Never going well: much btr 2755(gd/frm) 00

2890 Nap Majestica [2] 7-8(1ow)(6oh)   1084 Georges Quay [10] 8-0
2946 Veritable [12] 8-11
11 ran   2¼,6,4,1,¾   (H E Letchiman)   L Piggott Newmarket

3180 ROYSTON STAKES 2 AND 3YO   £3813   7f   Yielding 100 +03 Fast

2650 MYSTICAL MAN [9] (E Eldin) 3-9-7 T Lucas 7/1: 0201: 3 b c Baptism - Miss Aglojo (Aglojo)
Revelled in this soft grd, went on over 3f out and held on well in quite a fast run stks
race at Newmarket: ex Irish colt who gained his only win last season on a similar surf: seems
best around 7f on gd or softer grd: likes a stiff, gall trk.   46
3126 STILLMAN [10] (M H Easterby) 2-8-1(1ow) J Bleasdale 5/2 FAV: 0013202: Well bckd:
al front rank, just held: gd eff against older horses: see 2336 & 1812.   45
3116 CANADIAN GUEST [12] (H Candy) 3-9-1 W Newnes 3/1: 0020223: Narrowly btn: see 3116.   37
810 MISTER COLIN [14] (R Hannon) 2-8-0 A Mcglone 10/1: 124344: Not btn far despite a
lengthy abs: stays 7f: acts on fast & soft grd and on any trk: see 27.   42
3103 SUNORIUS [11] 2-7-11(BL) G Carter 6/1: 042200: Bl first time: best on gd/firm 2922.   32
2459 HOT MOMMA [8] 3-9-1 J Reid 14/1: 4330000: No extra dist: see 89.   28
--   HIGH STORM [7] 2-8-0(3ow) M Hills 6/1: 0: No threat in 8th on racecourse debut: 16,000 gns
yearling who is bred to stay middle dist.   00
2992 CORRALS JOY [2] 3-9-4 S Cauthen 8/1: -100000: Early speed, fin 9th: best over 5f in 205.   00
3104 Britwydd [13] 9-4   2575 Mrs Waddilove [3] 9-1 1482 Fauve [15] 9-1
1059 O La Le [1] 7-11
12 ran   ¼,hd,¾,4,¼   (Miss C J McCulloch)   E Eldin Newmarket

3181 E.B.F. BALATON LODGE MAIDEN STAKES 2YO   £4820   7f   Yielding 100 -02 Slow

--   CITY IN FLIGHT [19] (H Cecil) 2-8-11 S Cauthen 9/4 FAV: 1: 2 b f Irish River - Spanked
(Cornish Prince) Promising filly: heavily bckd and made a successful debut despite a poor draw,
showed a gd turn of foot to get up cl home in a 2yo fillies mdn at Newmarket: stays 7f well
and her breeding suggests she will get middle dist next term: acts on yldg grd and on a stiff,
gall trk: seems certain to rate more highly.   58+
2675 PETSARIA [4] (C Nelson) 2-8-11 J Reid 12/1: 02: Al front rank far-side, led below dist
till caught cl home: fine eff and seems certain to win races: acts on gd/frm & yldg:see 2675   54
--   GOLDEN PAMPAS [3] (H T Jones) 2-8-11 R Hills 20/1: 3: With leaders far-side·: promising
debut from this Golden Fleece filly who is a half sister to useful French 9/11f winner Samalex:
acts on yldg grd and on a gall trk: easy to back today and should improve on this rating.   48
--   MAGIC JOKER [10] (P Cole) 2-8-11 T Quinn 16/1: 4: Led far side most: no extra inside
dist but showed plenty of future promise here: acts on yldg grd and on a gall trk: seems
sure to improve and should do well next season.   46
--   RAINED OFF [17] 2-8-11 W Ryan 25/1: 0: Prom most far-side: gd debut from this ½ sister
to smart miler Ever Genial: acts on yldg grd and on a gall trk: considerably less fancied
than her victorious stablemate but looks pretty useful herself.   42
3074 DAHAB [8] 2-8-11(bl) G Baxter 33/1: 000: Fitted with bl and ran her best race to date
here: acts on gd & yldg grd and on a gall trk.   41
3111 COCKATOO ISLAND [25] 2-8-11 G Carter 25/1: 00: Gd eff from her poor draw: acts on gd &
yldg grd: certain to do btr than this next season: see 3111.   39
2675 HEAD OF VICTORY [29] 2-8-11 W Carson 5/1: 00: Poorly drawn: prom most: was far from
disgraced in 8th: acts on gd/firm and yldg grd: will do btr than this: see 2675.   39
--   EMERKALA [7] 2-8-11 P Robinson 33/1: 0: Mkt drifter on racecourse debut: prom most
on far side eventually fin 9th: cheaply bought filly who acts on yldg grd and on a gall trk:
should do btr.   39
--   NORTHERN MOON [20] 2-8-11 A Kimberley 33/1: 0: Ran on well from below dist: very easy
to back today and seems certain to improve on this rating: likely to be suited by middle dist
next term: acts on yldg grd and on a gall trk.   38
--   FLORENCE STREET [28] 2-8-11 R Cochrane 13/2: 0: Nicely bckd debutant: showed gd speed
most of way from her adverse draw: 34,000 gns yearling who is a half sister to 6f. winner
Bambolona: acts on yldg grd: certain to improve.   00
3068 STRELLILANE [26] 2-8-11 T Ives 33/1: 020: Poor draw: btr on gd/frm in 3068.   00
--   Inbisat [27] 8-11   --   Brarena [13] 8-11   2933 Turtur NI [23] 8-11
--   Cool Tempo [5] 8-11   --   Electric Storm [22] 8-11
--   Gold Paint [16] 8-11   --   Grundys Flame [14] 8-11
--   Heydir [6] 8-11   --   Hopespringsforever [2] 8-11
--   Humboldt Fair [18] 8-11   3073 Kumzar [12] 8-11
3120 Leap In Time [1] 8-11   2933 Miss Martinique [11] 8-11
1440 Peerglow [21] 8-11   2555 Sensitive Material [9] 8-11
--   Tango Star [30] 8-11
28 ran   ¾,3,1½,2,½,1,shthd,shthd,½   (S S Niarchos)   H Cecil Newmarket

3182 SUFFOLK NURSERY H'CAP CLAIMING STAKES   £3839   6f   Yielding 100 -07 Slow   [39]

3146 MADAM BILLA [12] (N Callaghan) 2-8-8 R Cochrane 7/1: 000001: 2 b c Auction Ring -
Hunter's Isle (Huntercombe) Quick reappearance and ran on strongly to lead inside dist in a
nursery h'cap at Newmarket: speedily bred filly who cost 10,000 gns as a yearling: eff over
5/6f on fast & yldg grd: seems to act on any trk.   30
2993 RAINBOW TROUT [21] (M Camacho) 2-8-8 W Carson 8/1: 040202: Led below dist, no extra
cl home: eff over 5/6f on fast & yldg grd: see 2281 & 1958.   26

3085 KNOCKSHARRY [20] (R Hollinshead) 2-8-3 P Hill(7) 14/1: 0003003: Al up there: acts
on yldg: see 1279.   17
3079 GOOD TIME GIRL [17] (R Hannon) 2-8-2 A Mcglone 8/1: 1202304: Al prom: see 1570, 1190.   15
2535 ROYAL RABBLE [8] 2-7-12 G Carter 25/1: 1000000: Fin strong: acts on yldg: see 1059.   10
2476 GYPSYS BARN RAT [18] 2-7-7(1oh) R Morse(5) 8/1: 0300: Prom most: acts yldg: best 2095   03
3017 CIREN JESTER [11] 2-7-13(BL) A Mackay 5/1 FAV: 002400: Well bckd and made much, fin 9th 00
2920 MACS MAESTRO [16] 2-9-7(bl) T Ives 7/1: 04400: Nicely bckd, no show: best 2229.   00
2927 KIBARA [10] 2-7-8(VIS) T Williams 10/1: 01000: Fitted with a visor: al behind: best 1803 00

3081 Sharphaven [14] 8-4	2588 Hugo Z Hackenbush [13] 8-3		
2895 Spitzabit [5] 8-4	2897 Say You Will [9] 8-12(BL)		
2994 Malacanang [2] 8-2	3079 Bloffa [6] 8-7(BL)	3058 Flair Park [3] 8-8	
3016 Its Been Rumoured [7] 8-11		3058 Rose Loubet [19] 8-9(VIS)	
3081 Daunting Prospect [24] 8-6		3016 Rylands Reef [1] 8-3	
2813 Peroy [23] 8-1	2990 Bangkok Boy [15] 8-0	2994 Rabenham [22] 7-13(bl)	
3017 Sappharino [4] 7-7(3oh)			

24 ran   1,1½,½,½,1,1,½,1   (M Tabor)   N Callaghan Newmarket

---

3183 WYSALL E.B.F. STAKES 3YO   £2700   1m 2f   Good 47 -05 Slow

3042 DOCKSIDER [9] (A Stewart) 3-8-6 Paul Eddery 7/2: -021201: 3 ch c Hotfoot - Tanara
(Romulus): Useful colt: led dist, cmftbly in a 3yo stakes at Leicester: earlier an easy
winner of his mdn at Chepstow: half brother to very useful juvenile Count Pahlen: very eff
over 8/10f & likely to stay further: acts on fast grnd & seems best on a gall trk.   52
2848 ASIAN CUP [8] (G Harwood) 3-8-9 G Starkey 4/6 FAV: -102422: Hvly bckd: led 2f out,
not pace of winner: clear of rem & has been in good form recently: see 2848 and 528.   50
3030 BANQUE PRIVEE [10] (B Hills) 3-8-3 R Hills 10/1: 3314023: Friendless in mkt: made
much: prob. unsuited by this shorter trip & btr over 12f in 3030: see 1908.   30
3142 JUST TOO BRAVE [1] (M Ryan) 3-8-5(2ow) R Cochrane 11/1: -04: Close up 1m: see 3142.   22
3077 MALIN FLEET [6] 3-8-0 M Hughes(7) 20/1: -000: Late prog: probably stays 10f: see 3077.   13
3077 DO RUN DO [3] 3-8-0 C Rutter(3) 50/1: 0-400: Mkt drifter: no threat: see 2991.   11

3142 Lowara [7] 8-0	2704 Bledsoe [11] 8-5(2ow)	2532 Out Yonder [4] 8-3
3077 Corn Noil [5] 8-3		

10 ran   1½,7,4,1½,½   (A Villar)   A Stewart Newmarket

3184 E.B.F. FLECKNEY MAIDEN FILLIES STAKES   £1706   6f   Good 47 +01 Fast

3073 BRONZEWING [18] (J Dunlop) 2-8-11 W Carson 6/4 FAV: 321: 2 b f Beldale Flutter -
Starlust (Sallust): Useful filly: took command 2f out when easily justifying fav. in a 2yo
fillies mdn at Leicester: eff over 6/7f on gd & fast grnd: seems well suited by a gall trk:
progressive type who should do even btr next season.   48
3034 KASHAPOUR [3] (L Cumani) 2-8-11 R Cochrane 8/1: 032: Al prom, ran on well without
troubling winner: eff over 6/7f on gd & firm grnd: likes a gall trk: see 2846.   38
2982 SPECULATE [5] (L Piggott) 2-8-11 T Ives 6/1: 023: Led over ½way: stays 6f: see 2982.   30
3153 BELAKA [15] (R Sheather) 2-8-11 W Ryan 10/3: 4044: Al prom: best in 3153 (firm).   28
3073 JUST SOMETHING [17] 2-8-11 W Newnes 50/1: 00: Ran on same pace: half sister to 7f
winner Something Casual & should continue to impr.   24
--   DARK MAJESTY [9] 2-8-11 J Carroll(7) 33/1: 0: Front rank over ½way on debut: cost
    $45,000 as a yearling & is bred to be suited by middle dists in time.   23
2788 MISS DAISY [4] 2-8-11 J Matthias 16/1: 300: Never nearer 7th: best in 1930.   20
2814 IRENIC [14] 2-8-11 T Lucas 16/1: 0000: Al mid-div: fin 8th: see 2499.   18
--   GREENS PICTURE [10] 2-8-11 P Robinson 20/1: 0: Never dngr on debut: should do btr.   16

2191 Spanish Melody [16] 8-11		-- Quick Riposte [7] 8-11
3103 Eranthe [19] 8-11	3103 Johns Last [2] 8-11	-- Lost Moment [11] 8-11
-- Madame Lumiere [8] 8-11		3044 Olive Leaf [13] 8-11
3025 Royal Meeting [6] 8-11		2875 The Cross [12] 8-11

18 ran   2,3,½,1,nk,1,½,½   (Sir Thomas Pilkington)   J Dunlop Arundel, Sussex

3185 SEAGRAVE APP. SELLING H'CAP (0-25) 3YO   £746   6f   Good 47 -17 Slow   [22]

3172 WINNING FORMAT [7] (P Makin) 3-8-9(bl) L Jones 11/1: 0020001: 3 b c Tanfirion -
Nous (Le Johnstan): Was gaining his first win when leading over 1f out in an app. selling
h'cap at Leicester (sold for 1,250 gns): speedily bred colt who has shown his best form over
6f on gd or softer grnd: seems to act on any trk.   10
3024 SHY MISTRESS [1] (A Jones) 3-8-3 Julie Bowker(5) 33/1: 0000002: Best effort since 729 (C/D). 00
3076 SIRTAKI DANCER [11] (C Wildman) 3-8-9 S Quane(5) 20/1: 0040003: Never nearer: mdn
who has yet to show any worthwhile form: probably stays 1m: acts on gd & firm.   02
2863 ALEXANJO [2] (A Jarvis) 3-9-0 A Flannigan(5) 10/1: 0002034: Running well: see 2174.   07

2929 ROYAL BERKS [6] 3-8-13 T Lang(5) 15/2: 4302000: Nearest fin: see 2313.   04
3144 BELLA CARINA [10] 3-8-6(bl) J Adams 33/1: 3000000: No worthwhile form: see 1350.   00
2614 FAMILLE ROSE [14] 3-9-7(BL) R Carter 11/1: 4-00000: Bl first time: never nearer 7th.   00
3144 QUITE A QUEST [13] 3-9-3 J Hills 6/1: 0000020: Fdd into 8th: btr in 3144.   00
3144 AUSTINA [8] 3-8-6 D J Williams 13/2: 0000030: Visored first time: fin 9th: btr in 3144.   00
2139 OUR CHILDREN [18] 3-8-11 J Carroll(5) 8/1: -030100: Abs: best in 1815.   00
3144 HOBOURNES KATJE [16] 3-8-7   A Culhane(5) 10/1: 0003000: No threat after slow
start: see 2268 and 246.   00
3144 CLASS HOPPER [5] 3-7-7(bl)(2oh) J Quinn 5/1 FAV: 0000040: No threat: btr in 3144: see 2884. 00
3144 Witham Girl [4] 9-3   3057 Pink N Perky [17] 9-7(VIS)
3144 Bandyann [3] 8-12   3144 Nomad Boxer [12] 8-6(VIS)
3144 Sly Maid [19] 8-6   3144 Rich Bitch [15] 7-13(bl)
18 ran 1,1½,shhd,¾,½,½,hd,1½   (James Fox)   P Makin Ogbourne Maisey, Wilts

3186 WYSALL E.B.F. STAKES 3YO   £2679   1m 2f Good 47 +10 Fast

3142 GREENHILLS JOY [10] (M Ryan) 3-8-0 P Robinson 7/1: -0331: 3 b f Radetzky - Soheir
(Track Spare): Impr filly: led below dist & was sn clear in a fast run 3yo stakes at Leicester:
eff over 9/10f & should stay further: acts on fast & yld grnd & seems well suited by a gall trk.   42
2610 GREY SALUTE [5] (R Simpson) 3-8-3 W Newnes 8/1: -330302: Made most: see 2428 & 1899.   35
*3142 FIRST KISS [4] (J Dunlop) 3-8-13 W Carson 1/1 FAV: 3033313: One-paced: btr in 3142.   45
*2929 KINGSFOLD FLAME [1] (M Haynes) 3-8-3 T Williams 10/1: -00014: Kept on late: stays 10f.   30
2760 QUEEN OF SWORDS [2] 3-8-0 A Culhane(7) 50/1: 0400000: Never nearer: best in 769 (14f).   13
3105 JUNGLE BEAT [8] 3-8-0 N Carlisle 9/2: 0-40240: Can do much btr: see 3105 & 2550.   09
3105 Concordes Demon [7] 8-0   739 Woodlands Crown [3] 8-3
3066 Everyinchalady [11] 8-0   1061 Lockwood Prince [6] 8-3
-- Torre De Belem [9] 8-0
11 ran 5,hd,1½,5,1½   (L Andus)   M Ryan Newmarket

3187 SQUIRREL HANDICAP STAKES (0-35) 3YO+   £3181   1m 4f Good 47 -14 Slow   [35]

2548 CORNELIAN [15] (G Harwood) 3-8-7 G Starkey 6/1: -03041: 3 b f Great Nephew - Jacinth
(Red God): Looked well h'capped & duly led dist, cmftbly in an all aged h'cap at Leicester:
well bred filly who is a sister to a 12f winner & seems best over that trip herself: acts on
gd & fast grnd & likes a gall trk.   32
778 NIKOOLA EVE [22] (J Glover) 4-9-1 M Birch 25/1: -03102: Early ldr: no ch with winner
but ran well after a lengthy abs: likes gd or soft grnd: see 282.   28
2747 FORMIDABLE DANCER [4] (J Dunlop) 3-8-7 W Carson 10/1: 0004023: Never nearer: see 2747.   25
2955 MALADHU [3] (J Fitzgerald) 7-9-3 A Murray 7/1: 0-13044: Ran on same pace: see 2324.   24
2880 MAKE IT SHARP [20] 3-8-10 Paul Eddery 12/1: -03040: Made much: see 1368.   20
2985 JABARABA [6] 5-9-1 T Lang(7) 12/1: 1134040: Ran on late: see 2330 & 2188.   15
2959 TRACKERS JEWEL [13] 4-8-11 P Robinson 11/2 FAV: 0-00120: Much btr in 2959 (sharp trk).   10
3087 MILLERS TALE [1] 4-9-4 F Arrowsmith(7) 10/1: 0400440: Best on a sharp trk in 761.   00
*2959 ISOM DART [2] 7-8-5 N Adams 10/1: 1000010: No show: much btr in 2959 (sharp trk).   00
2430 Tonquin [14] 8-8(bl)   2237 Vickstown [7] 8-7   2959 Toscana [11] 9-1
3161 Marina Plata [21] 8-7   2285 Record Wing [18] 9-1   2807 Foche [5] 8-13
-- Rockys Gal [10] 8-13   2958 Swaalef [9] 8-10   3128 Dick Knight [16] 8-8(vis)
3115 Silver Prospect [8] 8-7   3164 Azelly [12] 8-7(BL)
-- Dudleys Star [17] 8-4
21 ran 2½,1½,2,2½,1½,1½,2,½   (D Harris)   G Harwood Pulborough, Sussex

3188 JOHN O'GAUNT NURSERY H'CAP 2YO   £2396   7f   Good 47 +01 Fast   [45]

2556 KAMENSKY [4] (R Smyth) 2-9-3 W Carson 8/1: 032201: 2 b c Kampala - Benita (Roan
Rocket): Broke well & was never hdd when winning quite a fast run nursery h'cap at Leicester:
cost 16,000 gns as a yearling & is a half brother to several winners: eff over 5/7f on fast
& yld grnd: acts on any trk: best out in front.   44
2922 KINGS VICTORY [8] (M Usher) 2-8-10 M Wigham 16/1: 42002: Fin well: stays 7f: see 1629.   32
3041 LYRICAL LOVER [6] (C Benstead) 2-8-11 T Williams 20/1: 003003: Stays 7f: see 2118.   30
3146 RANKSTREET [19] (M Haynes) 2-8-5 Paul Eddery 16/1: 003004: Never nearer: see 2283.   20
3085 ORIENTAL DREAM [14] 2-7-13(vis) J Lowe 17/2: 010030: Btr in 3085 (1m): see 1119.   14
3125 SPEEDBIRD [16] 2-9-7 P Robinson 11/2 JT FAV: 0401400: Ran on too late: see 2756.   36
3125 SAUNDERS LASS [17] 2-8-1 S Dawson 8/1: 1034200: Ran on same pace: see 2859.   00
3125 IBNALMAGHITH [10] 2-9-5 R Hills 11/2 JT FAV: 1430020: Btr on yld in 3125: see 1149.   00
2919 HIGHLAND LODGE [2] 2-8-5(1ow) R Cochrane 10/1: 00020: Gd speed over ½way: btr in 2919(6f) 00
3080 Musical Bells [12] 8-12   3122 Mr Mumbles [20] 8-2(1ow)
2596 Always A Lady [11] 8-0   *3017 Good Point [7] 9-7(7ex)
2541 Dandy [15] 8-10   3112 Damart [9] 8-10   2708 Saboteur [13] 8-9
3011 Rolfeson [5] 8-6   2813 Mendip Star [18] 8-2   3075 Riverboat Party [1] 7-13
2694 Susan Henchard [3] 9-5
20 ran 1½,1,1½,shhd,shhd,hd   (S T Oon)   R Smyth Epsom, Surrey

3189 E.B.F. FLECKNEY MAIDEN STAKES (DIV 2)   £1711   6f   Good 47 +07 Fast

-- SANSIYA [6] (M Stoute) 2-8-11 A Kimberley 4/1: 1: 2 b f Dalsaan - Santalina (Relko):
Promising filly: made a winning debut, led after ½way, cmftbly in a fast run 2yo fillies mdn

at Leicester: well regarded filly who is a half sister to 9/10f winner Salilia: sure to stay
further than todays trip: acts on gd grnd & on a gall trk: looks a nice prospect for next season. 54
-- NOM DE PLUME [11] (H Cecil) 2-8-11 W Ryan 8/11 FAV: 2: Hvly bckd debutant: al front
rank & cmftbly beat rem: American bred filly who is held in quite high regard & should be
a btr horse next year: acts on gd grnd & on a gall trk. 50
2494 FREE SKIP [10] (P Felgate) 2-8-11 J Williams 50/1: 003: Showed much impr form here:
al prom, though lacked pace of front pair: should do even btr when tackling middle dists
next year: acts on gd grnd & on a gall trk. 38
2658 SHELDON MILLS [7] (I Balding) 2-8-11 T Ives 12/1: 0444: Led over ½way: see 2658. 35
2939 MORTAL SIN [8] 2-8-11 R Street 8/1: 00: No dngr: see 2939. 17
3146 CALL FOR TAYLOR [13] 2-8-11 N Howe 33/1: 0000030: Early speed: see 3146. 05

2969 Anaka [9] 8-11		2788 Yamrah [1] 8-11	--	Rag Queen [2] 8-11
2895 Salinas [14] 8-11		3153 Willowtree Girl [4] 8-11		
3017 Canebrake Lady [16] 8-11			--	Loveable Princess [15] 8-11
2796 Soothing Word [3] 8-11			2875	The Victor Girls [5] 8-11

15 ran ¾,3,1,6,4 (Aga Khan) M Stoute Newmarket

FOLKESTONE   Monday November 3rd   Righthand Undulating, Easy Track

Official Going Given As GOOD

3190 BURWASH CLAIMING STAKES 2YO DIV I   £959   6f   Good/Soft 92 -24 Slow

1308 RATHER HOMELY [1] (P Cole) 2-8-8 T Quinn 7/4 FAV: 331: 2 b f Homing - Rather Warm
(Tribal Chief): Despite a long abs & a very poor draw, led close home under press in quite
slow run 2yo claimer at Folkestone: first time out a fine 3rd to Mountain Memory at Ascot:
half sister to winning '85 juvenile Sparky Lad & is quite a speedily bred filly: acts on
firm, seems suited by some give: can win in btr company than this. 31
2986 RAINTREE COUNTY [15] (P Felgate) 2-8-3 A Mackay 33/1: 0040002: Made almost all on the
far side and was just caught: much impr form & clearly is best on the soft: has an official
rating of only 1: suited by forcing tactics over an easy 6f. 23
3081 CODED MESSAGE [13] (R Simpson) 2-8-11 S Whitworth 12/1: 03: Al prom: impr effort from
this speedily bred colt: eff over an easy 6f on yld grnd. 26
2531 OH MY JOY [11] (M Usher) 2-8-4 A Mcglone 33/1: 004: Never nearer: lightly rcd filly
who should stay further than 6f: acts on yld grnd. 12
2796 BOLD MOJACQUES [17] 2-8-11(BL) P Cook 11/1: 0000: Bl first time & was prom most: best 2711. 15
2926 WHATTA BUSINESS [10] 2-8-11 J Reid 33/1: 000: Prom, ev ch: little form in 3 outings
but is a half brother to several winners. 08
2935 FRANK THE BANK [6] 2-8-11 M Hills 9/2: 40000: Mkt drifter: led stands side: see 1665. 00
2987 SARASOTA [8] 2-8-5 B Rouse 4/1: 4000340: Nicely bckd: btr 2927. 00

2596 Lundy Isle [16] 8-3		3017 Madness Not To [9] 8-11		
3079 Highland Laird [5] 8-11(bl)			3044 Motor Broker [14] 8-11	
3134 Neirbo Lass [18] 8-8		3182 Rose Loubet [12] 8-8(vis)		
2829 Jealous Lover [3] 8-6		2652 Miss Lawsuit [2] 8-3	2829 Sohams Taylor [7] 8-3(vis)	

17 ran ½,2,3,1½,3 (Richard Barber) P Cole Whatcombe, Oxon

3191 HURSTMONCEUX HANDICAP 0-35 3YO+   £1463   6f   Good/Soft 92 +09 Fast   [35]

2906 MERRYMOLES [20] (M Mccourt) 3-8-11(bl) R Wernham 15/2: 0004131: 3 b c Tyrnavos -
Sovereign Help (Sovereign Lord): Made ev yd on fav. far side in a h'cap at Folkestone: in
gd form lately, earlier successful in a h'cap at Salisbury: in '85 won again at Salisbury &
likes that trk: very eff at 6f, probably stays 7f: best out in front on firm & yld grnd:
suited by bl as he often hangs. 28
3138 CORNCHARM [19] (H Collingridge) 5-8-13 M Rimmer 12/1: 0000002: Ran on final 1f: best
effort since 135: likes this track. 26
2992 FREMONT BOY [13] (C James) 4-8-2 B Rouse 16/1: 3040303: Prom, kept on: see 679. 13
2755 PEANDAY [17] (H Beasley) 5-8-0 D Mckay 12/1: 0000344: Ch over 1f out: see 2370. 06
2981 FIRST OPPORTUNITY [14] 3-8-8(5ow) R Guest 25/1: 0400000: No real threat: flattered 1947. 08
2992 GALLANT HOPE [12] 4-8-4 M Hills 9/1: 2233420: No threat: btr 2992 (5f firm). 00
3138 MUSIC REVIEW [2] 3-8-10 A Mackay 15/2: 0341020: Poorly drawn: btr 3138. 00
3145 GODSTRUTH [16] 7-8-5(bl) A Riding(7) 13/2 FAV: 0434430: Can do btr: see 3145. 00

3065 Thatchville [15] 8-13		3138 Downsview [10] 10-0	3024 Madam Muffin [18] 8-6	
3138 Loft Boy [7] 8-10		3160 Kings Touch [3] 9-9	3152 Angels Are Blue [6] 9-6	
3106 Platine [5] 9-2(BL)		3138 Kimble Blue [9] 9-0	3138 Wykehamist [1] 8-12	
3065 Zillebeke [8] 8-9		3172 Cresta Leap [4] 8-8	3104 Rosie Dickins [11] 8-4	

20 ran 1,1,2½,4,3 (A J Bingley) M Mccourt Letcombe Regis, Oxon

3192 BURWASH CLAIMING STAKES 2YO DIV 2   £959   6f   Good/Soft 92 -04 Slow

3182 SPITZABIT [7] (Pat Mitchell) 2-8-11 R Curant 33/1: 000001: 2 b c Pitskelly -
Marsabit (Martinmas): Showed impr form when a 33/1 winner of a 2yo claimer at Folkestone:

led over 2f out & ran on well: clearly suited by this easier grnd here: does well when up with
the pace on a sharp trk over 6f.   36
2782 IN FAT CITY [12] (J Sutcliffe) 2-8-11 M Hills 7/4 FAV: 042: Ran on well final 1f but
probably needs another furlong: acts on gd/firm & yld: see 2782, 2491.   35
2941 MUAD DIB [10] (R Akehurst) 2-8-11 J Reid 5/1: 3020003: Prom, ev ch: has been tried in
bl & yet to win: see 2205.   30
3081 FREDDIE ASHTON [11] (D Morley) 2-8-11(bl) R Guest 12/1: 0000404: Stayed on: btr 3047 (7f). 24
2320 PINEAPPLES PRIDE [19] 2-8-8 G Baxter 8/1: 040: Prom most after abs: see 2320.   15
3079 STARS IN MOTION [3] 2-8-7 A Clark 20/1: 3000200: No dngr: twice below 2899.   10
3017 BOLD INTENTION [5] 2-8-6 N Day 4/1: 000020: Well bckd: disapp after 3017 (stiff 6f).   00
3081 MAIN BRAND [14] 2-8-3(bl) P Cook 10/1: 0040140: Never showed: twice below 2990 (1m firm) 00

3079 Danse Arabe [1] 8-4	3112 Leg Glide [20] 8-0(bl)		
3079 Castillito [16] 8-3	3081 Bee Bee Cee [6] 8-11	2707 Coral Hall [2] 8-11	
2615 Prince Mac [9] 8-8	2838 Sauce Of The Sea [15] 8-3		
2596 Mayfair Doll [13] 8-2	3017 Survival Kit [18] 8-2	--	Miss Style [4] 8-0
3146 Ring Back [17] 8-0	3135 Tulla Water [8] 8-2(2ow)		
20 ran ½,2,2½,2½,1½	(Mrs Catherine Reed)	Pat Mitchell Polegate, Sussex	

3193 BIDDENDEN SELLING STAKES 3 & 4YO   £927   1m 4f Good/Soft 92 -07 Slow

3100 MISS LAURA LEE [16] (P Felgate) 3-8-3 A Mackay 2/1 FAV: 0040111: 3 ch f On Your Mark -
Strawberry Blond (Red God): Completed her hat trick in a seller at Folkestone: led over 1f
out, easily (bought in 3,500 gns): earlier a winner of similar events at Redcar (ddht) and
again at Folkestone: half sister to a couple of winners: stays 12f well: acts on gd/firm &
yld grnd & probably acts on any trk: a genuine filly.   25
3100 MITALA MARIA [6] (A Stewart) 3-8-3(BL) M Hills 13/2: 0230242: Tried in bl: led till
final 1f: acts on gd/firm & yld: see 2902.   17
2807 PRIMROSE WAY [1] (M Blanshard) 4-8-12 J Reid 10/1: 0030003: Ev ch in straight: little
form this season in non plating company: see 341.   11
3139 SPRING PHILTRE [5] (D Elsworth) 4-8-12 A Mcglone 14/1: 000-004: Some late hdway: very
lightly rcd on the Flat & little form.   01
*3162 BAYDON QUEEN [7] 3-8-3 G Carter 9/2: 0000010: No show: much btr 3162 (10f, good).   00
3076 VISTULE [13] 4-9-1 S Whitworth 9/2: -000020: No extra over 2f out: btr 3076 (10f firm).   00

2182 Kilmington Castle [14] 8-12		3150 Okaadh [3] 9-1(bl)
2925 Tana Mist [10] 8-12	2984 Gulphar [2] 9-1	-- Val Prive [8] 9-1
2515 Blairs Winnie [9] 8-12		-- Wirral [11] 8-12
3076 Toda Forca Avanti [4] 9-1		3045 Tiber Gate [15] 8-6
15 ran 2,5,6,1,8	(Mrs Anita Quinn)	P Felgate Melton Mowbray, Leics

3194 LEEDS AMATEUR RIDERS STAKES 3YO+   £913   1m 4f Good/Soft 92 -39 Slow

2923 GALESA [7] (P Kelleway) 3-10-6(BL) Sara Kelleway 2/1 JT.FAV: 00-0221: 3 b f Welsh Pageant
- Escape Me Never (Run The Gantlet): Tried in bl & made ev yd, ridden out in slow run amateur
riders stakes at Folkestone: has been rather lightly rcd: half sister to 2 winners: eff at
12f, stays 14f: acts on gd/firm & yld & on any trk: seems suited by forcing tactics.   35
--   PRECIOUS LINK [13] (W Turner) 3-10-9 Mr T Mitchell 50/1: -2: Rank outsider: kept on
well: cheaply acquired gelding who is a half brother to 3 winners incl the speedy Sylvan
Barbarosa: clearly stays 12f on yld grnd.   30
3101 GLOWING PROMISE [4] (B Hills) 3-10-10(BL) Princess Anne 8/1: 1240003: Ev ch inside
final 2f: bl first time today: lacks a turn of foot: stays 12f: see 452.   26
2733 BARAOORA [9] (D Oughton) 4-11-5 Mr G Webster 33/1: 0040/04: Held ev ch: may be seen
over hdles shortly: acts on yld grnd.   20
3128 HARBOUR BAZAAR [8] 6-11-9 Tracy Bailey 12/1: 3120300: Never nearer: see 2432.   14
2096 TOMS TREASURE [1] 4-11-2 Mr J Akehurst 4/1: -3330: Fdd final 3f: abs since 2096 (gd/firm) 00
--   ALL INTENT [3] 4-11-5 Amanda Harwood 2/1 JT.FAV: -0: Quite well bckd but fdd into 9th:
half brother to winners in the States but needs to impr to find a race himself.   00

-- Geryon [10] 11-9	2929 Barbershop Quartet [5] 10-9	
2964 Arnab [6] 11-12	184 Loch Laddie [12] 11-5	-- Road To Kells [11] 11-5
3071 Resha [15] 10-9	2683 Elvire [2] 10-6	3105 Sousaga [14] 10-6
15 ran 3,2,3,4,10,hd	(Roldvale Ltd)	P Kelleway Newmarket

3195 APPLEDORE HANDICAP STAKES 3YO+ 0-35   £1502   1m 2f Good/Soft 92 -14 Slow   [35]

3050 MOUNT TUMBLEDOWN [7] (R Hannon) 5-9-6 P Cook 7/1: -000101: 5 b h Tumble Wind -
Dowdy (Sea Hawk II): In gd form & led after 4f, cmftbly in a h'cap at Folkestone: recently
successful in an app. h'cap at Bath: in '84 won at Pontefract, Beverley & Ayr: eff at 1m,
well suited by 10f: acts on fast & soft & on any trk.   37
2896 ON TO GLORY [13] (J Dunlop) 3-8-9 B Rouse 7/2 FAV: 3002102: Stayed on final 1f:
acts on firm & yld: see 2516.   26
2807 ELECTROPET [12] (A Ingham) 4-8-9 A Shoults(3) 11/2: 0-00403: Stayed on: fair eff: see 2807. 17
2925 HEAD OF SCHOOL [6] (Pat Mitchell) 3-8-8 J Reid 12/1: 4244304: Ev ch in straight: btr 2720 21
3105 HOLLY BROWN [1] 3-8-8 S Whitworth 11/1: -00000: Al there: see 3105 (stiffer trk).   13
2408 MUSICAL YOUTH [9] 3-9-4 T Quinn 12/1: -202000: Never nearer: abs & has been lightly
rcd this term: btr 1588, 459.   22
3078 LADY COOMBE [5] 4-9-8 G Baxter 15/2: 0400-00: Prom, fdd 2f out: has been very lightly
rcd on the Flat: best form coming over 1m on gd/yld grnd on a sharp trk.   00

3063 PULSINGH [15] 4-8-7 P Waldron 9/1: 3000200: Never showed: twice below 2985 (gd/firm).   00
2956 Grumble [3] 9-10   2154 Safe Custody [14] 8-9   3038 Tivian [2] 9-4(vis)
3140 Saalib [10] 8-13   3140 Tom Forrester [1] 8-12
1237 Coastal Plain [8] 8-8
14 ran   3,1½,½,4,½   (Mrs John Collins)   R Hannon East Everleigh, Wilts

3196 LEEDS AMATEUR RIDERS STAKES 3YO+   £908   1m 4f   Good/Soft 92 -23 Slow

3110 OSRIC [1] (M Ryan) 3-11-2 Mr J Ryan 8/15 FAV: 2042031: 3 b g Radetzky - Jolimo
(Fortissimo): Hvly bckd, led early & again inside final 1f under strong press in an amateur
riders stakes at Folkestone: earlier successful in a similar event at Yarmouth & has also
been placed on several occasions: half brother to the fair middle dist winner Joli's Girl:
eff at 11/13f on gd & soft grnd & on any trk: may be seen hurdling shortly.   35
2980 BLACK DIAMOND [4] (A Jarvis) 3-10-9 Elaine Burke 7/1: 0022222: Led after 3f: hdd
final 1f but battled on well: 10L clear 3rd & deserves a change of luck: eff at 9f-12f on
fast & yld grnd.   27
 -- MOLOJEC [10] (A Bailey) 5-11-9 Sharon Murgatroyd 16/1: -3: Kept on but no ch with front
2: Polish bred gelding who may be running over hurdles shortly: stays 12f & acts on yld.   14
721 ORYX MINOR [2] (S Mellor) 6-11-9 Dana Mellor 7/1: 01-0304: Ev ch but probably needed
this race after a long abs: a very useful h'cap hurdler & may be seen out in that sphere shortly.   02
3161 BULLY BOY [11] 3-10-9 Kelly Marks 33/1: 0000000: Rank outsider: ev ch: little form
previously: probably stays 12f.   00
2877 SHALLAAL [3] 7-11-9 Cate Reynolds 4/1: 000120: Surprisingly well bckd: stiff task: see 2877.   00
3139 BENS BIRDIE [15] 6-11-12 Anna Tompkins 10/1: 3-21400: No threat: best in 2415 (gd/firm).   00
2617 The Wooden Hut [14] 10-13   -- Ribble Star [6] 11-2
 -- Just Martin [12] 11-12   -- Badingham Boy [9] 11-5
3066 Popsis Pom Pom [7] 10-6   3105 Roberts Flower [8] 10-6
13 ran shhd,10,6,10,10   (Richard Scott)   M Ryan Newmarket

3197 FOSSE WAY CLAIMING STAKES 3YO   £2674   1m 2f   Good 52 -01 Slow

2876 PRIME NUMBER [10] (P Cole) 3-9-5 T Quinn 10/1: 0000341: 3 ch c Young Generation -
Picture Book (Silent Screen): Was gaining his first win when leading over 2f out, cmftbly in
a 3yo claimer at Leicester: earlier placed in similar company: best form over 10f on gd grnd:
seems to act on any trk.   24
3087 COMMON FARM [9] (M Brittain) 3-9-5 P Robinson 7/1: 0000202: Ran on well: see 2995.   16
3036 TURMERIC [2] (D Morley) 3-9-5 R Cochrane 6/1: 0423133: Al prom: clear of rem: see 2874.   15
3062 EASTERN PLAYER [15] (D Laing) 3-9-5 J Reid 16/1: 0000004: Ran on same pace: eff over
8/10f: see 1472.   05
3154 CHEVET LADY [8] 3-8-12(vis) K Bradshaw(5) 10/1: 0040040: Ch below dist: btr on firm 3154   00
2995 CAPRICORN BLUE [6] 3-9-5(vis) D Nicholls 6/1: 4110100: Made much: well btn: best in 2890.   00
423 MISS TIMED [13] 3-9-2 A Murray 7/1: -000: Fdd into 7th after long abs: see 423.   00
3060 PHILOSOPHICAL [7] 3-8-12 M Wigham 5/1 FAV: 3013000: Disapp fav in 8th: best in 2060 (1m).   00
2807 CARVERY [12] 3-8-8(VIS) T Ives 8/1: 233D400: Visored first time: fin 9th: btr in 2395.   00
3110 WILLOW GORGE [14] 3-9-5(BL) P Waldron 8/1: 0004300: Wore bl: much btr on fast grnd in 2533.   00
2985 Lydia Eva [3] 9-2   3162 Dress In Spring [11] 8-10
 -- Gay Starlight [4] 8-2   3070 Cheerful Times [5] 9-1(VIS)
14 ran 4,nk,6,2½,8   (F Jenkins)   P Cole Whatcombe, Oxon

3198 HOBY MAIDEN STAKES 2YO   £964   1m   Good 52 -19 Slow

-3074 BETTY JANE [14] (J Dunlop), 2-8-11 W Carson 6/5 FAV: 421: 2 ch f Morston - Indulgence
(Prominer): Impr filly: cmftbly justified fav. led ½way & ran on well in a 2yo mdn at
Leicester: cheaply acquired filly whose dam was successful over 8/12f, & she seems certain
to be suited by middle dists herself next year: acts on gd & firm grnd & is well suited by
this galloping trk.   48
--- DRAGONS BLOOD [6] (H Cecil) 2-9-0 Paul Eddery 4/1: 2: Easy to back on debut: al front
rank & ran on promisingly: well bred colt by Nijinsky, who is a half brother to a winner in
France: sure to stay over todays trip: acts on gd grnd & on a gall trk.   48
3080 CLOPTON [11] (M Ryan) 2-9-0 P Robinson 12/1: 0033: Al up there, edged right inside
dist: improving with every race & should do even btr next year: see 3080.   46
3137 JONITE [16] (R Akehurst) 2-9-0 S Whitworth 12/1: 0000304: Not btn very far, & fin
clear of rem: has been btn in sellers & this was easily his best effort to date: stays 1m: see 2829. 45
3163 PALACE SONG [1] 2-9-0 R Cochrane 10/1: 00: Ran on too late: see 3163.   35
2901 NABRAS [4] 2-8-11 A Murray 16/1: 33000: Front rank most: quite consistent: see 1996.   31
2936 FORUMS FOLLY [2] 2-9-0 M Hills 15/2: 040: Nicely bckd: fin 8th: see 2936.   00

935

-- Avenio [7] 9-0	3011 Charlie Dickins [5] 9-0	
-- Kurdish Prince [13] 9-0		2990 Design Wise [17] 9-0
3069 Magnolia Dancer [8] 9-0		3132 Marcovich [12] 9-0(BL)
-- Model Lad [3] 9-0	2712 Pialuci [15] 9-0	-- Needwood Nymph [9] 8-11
3111 Twice Bitten [10] 8-11		
17 ran 1,½,nk,5,shhd	(E J Price)	J Dunlop Arundel, Sussex

3199 HOBY MAIDEN STAKES 2YO   £964   1m   Good 52 -12 Slow

3053 SHOOTING PARTY [16] (H Cecil) 2-9-0 W Ryan 6/5 FAV: 01: 2 b c Posse - Norfolk Gal
(Blakeney): Well bckd & led below dist, easily in a 2yo mdn at Leicester: showed promise behind
stable mate Scarlet Blade when unfancied on his debut at Newmarket recently: eff over 1m, &
seems sure to stay further: acts on gd grnd & on a gall trk.   44
3135 FEARLESS MAN [5] (L Piggott) 2-9-0 T Ives 3/1: 002: Not pace of winner, but ran his
best race to date here & was well suited by this extra furlong: see 2716.   34
3018 LILY MAB [10] (P Kelleway) 2-8-11 Gay Kelleway(3) 16/1: 03: Made most & is clearly on
the up grade: acts on gd grnd & on a gall trk.   28
3136 RAMBERGE [4] (R Sheather) 2-8-11 M Rimmer 12/1: 04: Made steady late progress &
promises to be well suited by middle dists next year: acts on gd & soft grnd & on a gall trk.   26
2886 ANORADA [14] 2-8-11 A Geran(5) 20/1: 000: Prom most: eff over 7/8f on gd & firm: see 1382.25
-- GIFTED NEPHEW [9] 2-9-0 M Birch 33/1: 0: Showed gd speed for most of way on debut:
will be btr for this experience.   25
-- DEVON LASS [13] 2-8-11 W Carson 15/2: 0: Active in mkt on debut: fin 7th & should do
btr than this: half sister to several winners, incl fair 9/10f colt Emperador.   00

3143 Parkers Joy [2] 9-0	3137 Gerunty [7] 9-0	-- Connaughts Joy [17] 8-11
3141 Main Rocket [3] 8-11	3136 Dont Yer Know [15] 9-0(BL)	
-- Glovers Kind [11] 9-0	3141 Ulysses [12] 9-0	3068 Dreemskerry [1] 8-11
3068 Tuneful Flutter [6] 8-11		
16 ran 4,1,1,nk,1	(Louis Freedman)	H Cecil Newmarket

3200 HOBY MAIDEN STAKES (DIV 2) 2YO   £964   1m   Good 52 +03 Fast

-- FRENCH GONDOLIER [2] (O Douieb) 2-9-0 Paul Eddery 3/1: 1: 2 b c Riverman - Miss Gallivant
(Gallant Man): Made a successful debut, improved to lead below dist, cmftbly, in quite a fast
run 2yo mdn at Leicester: well bred colt who cost $425,000 as a yearling: eff over 1m, seems
certain to stay further next season: acts on gd grnd & on a gall trk.   48
-- BROKEN HEARTED [13] (P Cole) 2-9-0 T Quinn 15/8 FAV: 2: Well bckd debutant: led briefly
2f out, not qckn but certain to improve for this experience: cost 66,000 gns as a yearling:
eff over 1m on gd grnd.   42
-- GRAND ECLIPSE [1] (P Kelleway) 2-8-11 Gey Kelleway(3) 25/1: 3: Ran on promisingly on
racecourse debut: closely related to several winners, notably very useful 7/10f filly
Go Leasing: should be suited by middle dists next term: acts on gd grnd & on a gall trk.   30
3165 SOULEIADOU [6] (R F Johnson Houghton) 2-9-0(bl) J Reid 33/1: 003004: Ran to his best:
stays 1m: see 1816.   26
2847 CI SIAMO [8] 2-8-11 P Robinson 16/1: 000: Ran on same pace: has shown a little promise
in her starts to date, though looks the type to do btr next year: acts on gd/firm grnd.   20
-- PIRACY [14] 2-9-0 A Murray 33/1: 0: Prom most on debut: unfancied today & should be
btr for this run: 10,000 yearling who is a half brother to useful 9/10f winner Foche.   20
2133 CAJUN DANCER [16] 2-9-0 C Rutter(3) 10/1: 400: Wknd into 7th over this extra furlong.   00
-- SHARP EGO [11] 2-8-11 A Kimberley 5/2: 0: Front rank over ½way & not given a hard race:
cost $275,000 as a yearling & is a half sister to Preakness Stakes 2nd Bold Ego: should
do better.   ++

3023 Barmera [4] 8-11	3163 Burly Native [3] 9-0	-- Augustus Caesar [5] 9-0
3014 Home To Tara [15] 9-0	-- Pps Little Secret [18] 9-0	
2652 Fair Moon [7] 8-11	1801 Final Rush [10] 8-11	3069 Magnolia Princess [17] 8-11
3163 Scallykath [9] 8-11	3117 Westminster Waltz [12] 8-11	
18 ran 2½,2,1,1½,½,nk	(Maktoum Al-Maktoum)	O Douieb Newmarket

3201 HOBY MAIDEN STAKES 2YO   £964   1m   Good 52 -02 Slow

-- SALAZIE [9] (W Hastings Bass) 2-8-11 W Carson 8/1: 1: 2 b f Ile De Bourbon - Top Call
(High Top): Promisingly filly: fin strongly & although just failing to get up in a 2yo mdn at
Leicester, was subsq. awarded the race in the stewards room: half sister to 7f winner Coping:
eff over 1m on gd grnd & certain to stay further: acts on a gall trk: should rate more highly.   46
-- IMPERIAL BRUSH [16] (D Elsworth) 2-9-0 A Mcglone 4/1: 1D: Led 2f out, held on well
under press but slightly hmpd Salazie ,placed 2nd: cost 10,500 gns as a yearling & is a half
brother to winning Irish miler Bristle: acts on gd grnd & on a gall trk.   48
3037 SALOPARD [10] (M Jarvis) 2-9-0 T Lucas 16/1: 03: Made most & this was a much btr effort:
$32,000 gns who should do btr when tackling lngr dists next term.   44
3137 CAMMARINO [1] (H Candy) 2-9-0 W Newnes 5/2 FAV: 044: Wknd below dist: see 3137 & 2574. 32
3141 STAR NORTH [11] 2-9-0 T Ives 15/2: 0420: Btr over 10f in 3141: see 2957.   30
2607 SLIPPERY MAX [4] 2-9-0 G Carter 14/1: 040: No real threat: see 2607.   28
3018 CARPET CAPERS [15] 2-9-0 S Whitworth 10/1: 000: Fdd into 7th: btr in 3018: see 2782.   00
-- STATUTORY [14] 2-9-0 Paul Eddery 9/2: 0: Quite well bckd on debut: fdd into 8th &
should do btr than this: $210,000 yearling whose dam is a half sister to Northern Dancer.   00

-- Khattaf [13] 9-0	-- The Gaelcharn [6] 9-0	3025 Via Veritas [8] 8-11
2493 Market Spirit [17] 9-0(BL)		3014 One To Note [12] 9-0
1762 Ra Raver [7] 9-0	2791 Swing Singer [3] 9-0	2987 Try Hills Supplies [2] 9-0(VIS)
2703 Oh Wiggy [5] 8-11		
17 ran shhd,1½,7,1,nk	(James Wigan)	W Hastings Bass Newmarket

3202 BARSBY SELLING H'CAP (0-25) 3YO   £704   1m 4f   Good 52 -35 Slow   [18]

2163 JULTOWN LAD [2] (H Beasley) 3-8-2 R Morse(5) 10/1: -204021: 3 b c Creetown - Julita
(Rockavon): Gained his first win, led inside dist & ran on well in a selling h'cap at
Leicester (bought in 2,000 gns): placed over 7f early-on, though seems btr suited by middle
dists now: acts on gd/firm & soft grnd & on any trk.   01
3076 SLEEPLINE DUCHESS [11] (G Huffer) 3-9-1 R Carter(2) 6/1: 0200302: Led 3f out: see 2238.   11
3076 JUBILEE JAMBOREE [4] (A Hide) 3-9-0(BL) P Robinson 6/1: 3003003: Had ev ch: see 1349.   08
2309 GOLDEN AZELIA [12] (R Brazington) 3-8-5 J Williams 20/1: -000004: One-paced: lightly
rcd filly who has yet to show any worthwhile form over middle dists.   00
3128 WAY ABOVE [1] 3-8-12(bl) A Clark 11/4 FAV: 0000000: Poor middle dist 'maiden.   00
3150 SUNLIT [9] 3-8-6 J Bleasdale 10/1: -000000: Some late progress.   00
2125 FIRE LORD [6] 3-9-0 B Rouse 5/1: 0034020: Fdd into 9th: btr in 2125 (sharp trk).   00
2293 SANDY BILL [3] 3-9-4 R Cochrane 6/1: -0000: Al behind: lightly rcd & no form.   00
3162 NAME THE DAY [7] 3-8-9(bl) W Newnes 10/1: 0-40040: No threat: poor middle dist maiden.   00
3162 Tyrannise [15] 8-8   3045 Expert Witness [13] 8-7
3162 Worth Debating [10] 9-7   3076 Montbergis [14] 8-12(BL)
1942 Haj [8] 9-0   1562 Platinum Star [5] 8-3
15 ran   1½,1,1½,4,1½,6,½   (S Birkett)   H Beasley Rockley, Wilts

3203 FOSSE WAY CLAIMING STAKES 3YO   £2658   1m 2f   Good 52 -22 Slow

8180 HOT MOMMA [13] (R Boss) 3-8-12 Paul Eddery 9/2: 3300001: 3 b f Free State - Mummy's
Darling (Mummy's Pet): Made a quick reapp. & finally lost her mdn tag when leading at the
dist in a 3yo claimer at Leicester: has proved most frustrating since 4th in the Cherry Hinton
at Newmarket last season: seems best over 8/10f: acts on any going & on any trk.   25
*2963 PLAIN TALK [1] (A Hide) 3-9-1 P Brette(7) 7/2 FAV: -040012: Just held: stays 10f: see 2963. 26
3100 RYMOS [9] (R Simpson) 3-8-7(bl) S Whitworth 10/1: 0-33203: Led 3f out, no extra: see 2705   15
2964 BAYTINO [2] (H Collingridge) 3-9-2 M Rimmer 12/1: -030034: Ran to her best: eff. over10/12f 22
3150 MISS BECCA [6] 3-8-6 J H Brown(5) 14/1: 0-020: Btr over 12f in 3150 (slr).   04
3138 LADY WINDMILL [5] 3-9-2 G Morgan 20/1: 0000000: Lngr trip: one-paced.   08
3063 PORO BOY [15] 3-9-5 G Baxter 8/1: 4002400: Best in 352 (1m).   00
3160 VILMAX [10] 3-8-6 G Carter 8/1: -20: Much btr over 6f in 3160.   00
2925 JAAZIEL [3] 3-9-5(bl) R Wernham 10/1: 000140P: Broke down & destroyed: see 2293.   00
2613 No Bolder [11] 9-5   949 Royal Effigy [14] 9-2   2593 Hillison [8] 8-11
-- Dora Frost [4] 8-10   3162 Delta Lima [7] 8-6(bl)(1ow)
-- Pointons Progress [12] 8-5(bl)
15 ran   nk,1½,1,4,3,1½,shhd   (K Bethel)   R Boss Newmarket

3204 TUGBY E.B.F. STAKES 3YO+   £3586   7f   Good 52 +16 Fast

2231 BARCLAY STREET [5] (I Matthews) 3-9-0 J Reid 10/1: -000001: 3 b c Nureyev - Avanie
(Avatar): Useful colt: nicely bckd & returned to form when leading 2f out, cmftbly in a fast
run stakes race at Leicester: first time out winner over this C/D last season & is clearly
well suited by this gall trk: acts on gd & firm grnd.   58
2946 NAVARZATO [7] (R Sheather) 3-9-7(BL) A Shoults(3) 5/2 FAV: 2000002: Wore bl: gd effort.   58
*3164 ACTUALIZATIONS [10] (L Cumani) 3-8-10 R Cochrane 11/2: 3424213: Fine effort: see 3164.   45
1788 MAWSUFF [2] (H T Jones) 3-9-4 R Hills 11/2: -021234: Abs: al prom: see 1788.   48
+3077 SKEAN [19] 3-9-1 G Starkey 11/2: 0222110: Eased inside dist: see 3077.   41
3123 PARIS TRADER [3] 4-9-3 G Bardwell(7) 16/1: 0020000: Bckd at long odds & ran well.   39
-3077 SOMETHING CASUAL [11] 3-8-8(vis) R Guest 8/1: 4444020: Made much: fin 8th: see 3077.   00
2728 Pershing [16] 8-12   *3157 Broadhurst [6] 9-0(bl)
851 Lady Eurolink [17] 8-10   3145 Sybil Fawlty [18] 8-10(vis)
611 Palmion [9] 9-2   2943 Mia Jubes [14] 9-1   2291 Mudisha [4] 9-1
3127 Quinta Reef [20] 9-0(bl)   -- Bugatti [12] 8-13
3145 Sahara Shadow [1] 8-13   3164 Sparky Lad [15] 8-12(BL)
3149 Tit Willow [8] 8-12(bl)   *3149 Pointed Lady [13] 8-10
20 ran   2,½,3,2½,shhd,1½   (Lord Matthews)   I Matthews Newmarket

3205 HOBY MAIDEN STAKES (DIV 2) 2YO   £964   1m   Good 52 +01 Fast

3043 HAATIF [5] (H T Jones) 2-9-0 R Hills 1/1 FAV: 31: 2 ch c Damascus - Mashteen (Majestic
Prince): Promising colt: easily justified fav, went on after ½way for a very cheeky win in a
2yo mdn at Leicester: strongly fancied to make a winning debut when placed behind Neshad at
Newmarket last time: half brother to the smart '84 juvenile Foulaad: eff over 7/8f & will
be suited by middle dists next season: acts on gd grnd & on a gall trk: well regarded &
should rate more highly.   52
3014 RUSHLUAN [16] (P Cole) 2-9-0(VIS) T Quinn 7/1: 002: Fitted with a visor: flattered by
proximity to winner, though beat rem decisively & is improving with every race: see 3014.   44

3099 GRANNY BIMPS [7] (R Sheather) 2-8-11 A Shoults(3) 7/2: 043: Btr in 3099: see 1802.   30
3122 COMBINED EXERCISE [11] (R Smyth) 2-9-0 S Whitworth 14/1: 0043004: Ran on too late: see 2383.   28
3120 MANSIO [17] 2-9-0 W Newnes 20/1: 000: Gd speed over ½way: btr effort.   22
3134 NAUTICAL BELLE [12] 2-8-11 N Day 33/1: 00: Again well btn: half sister to winning
plater Cooper Racing Nail, amongst others & should do btr than this.   00

2493 Dreaming River [4] 8-11		-- Rosy Cheeks [15] 9-0	
-- Al Fayes [9] 9-0	2589 Hail A Cab [1] 8-11	3135 Festive Occasion [8] 9-0	
3134 Meldon Hill [18] 8-11	3133 Balholm Express [2] 9-0		
3120 Farmers Gamble [3] 9-0		2976 Linco King [13] 9-0	
-- Regal Brass [6] 9-0	-- Double Gift [14] 8-11		
17 ran 1,5,3,2,8	(Hamdan Al-Maktoum)	H T Jones Newmarket	

3206 PYTCHLEY STAKES 2YO   £3013   7f   Good 52 -01 Slow

3103 LOUD APPEAL [13] (M Stoute) 2-8-11 A Kimberley 14/1: 021: 2 b c Star Appeal -
Yell Aloud (Laugh Aloud): Impr colt: easy to back but ran on strongly to get up close home in
a 2yo stakes at Leicester: half brother to several winners, incl useful juvenile Mums: eff over
6/7f & seems sure to stay further: acts on gd & firm grnd & on a gall trk.   46
-- MIN ALLAH [1] (H Cecil) 2-8-11 Paul Eddery 12/1: 2: Mkt drifter on debut: led dist,
caught final stride: cost $200,000 as a yearling & is bred to be suited by middle dists in
time: acts on gd grnd & on a gall trk.   46
3067 JUILLIARD [14] (M Dickinson) 2-8-11 J Reid 12/1: 23: Led briefly below dist, ran on
well & only narrowly btn: see 3067.   45
+3075 STUBBLE FIRE [2] (J Dunlop) 2-9-3 W Carson 10/1: 014: Made most: not btn far: see 3075.   50
+2975 AFTERNOON WINNER [7] 2-9-2 G Starkey 1/1 FAV: 10: Narrowly btn in a blanket finish.   49
3037 JADE HUNTER [9] 2-8-11 W Ryan 14/1: 000: Not btn very far: stays 7f: see 2554.   42
3136 BEL BYOU [15] 2-8-11 T Quinn 11/1: 30: AI prom: fin 7th: see 3136.   00
2939 HENRYK [12] 2-8-11 S Whitworth 5/1: 20: Bckd from 12/1: front rank most: see 2939 (6f).   00
-- HARUSI [5] 2-8-8 A Clark 33/1: 0: Unfancied debutant from the Harwood stable: stayed
on promisingly from ½way & is sure to benefit from this experience.   00

3099 Busted Harmony [10] 8-8		-- Timbuck [17] 8-11	
-- Grape [18] 8-11	3134 Arquati Redwood [3] 8-13		
-- Lyncombe Boy [16] 8-11		3117 Jeff Harris [8] 8-11	
3048 Ash Dee Royale [6] 8-11			
16 ran shhd,nk,nk,shhd,1,2,¾	(Mrs Denis Haynes)	M Stoute Newmarket	

SAINT-CLOUD   Thursday October 30th   Lefthanded, Galloping Track

Official Going Given As GOOD/SOFT

3207 GROUP 3 PRIX DE FLORE 3YO+ FILLIES   £18091   1m2.5f Good/Soft

2868 GESEDEH [3] (M Jarvis) 3-8-13 J Reid 5/2: 1000121: 3 ch f Ela-Mana-Mou - Le Melody
(Levmoss) Smart filly: gained her first win in Pattern company when an easy winner of a Gr 3
fillies event at St-Cloud: began the season with impressive wins in a Salisbury mdn and val
Pretty Polly Stks (Listed) at Newmarket: last month won a val fillies race at Kempton: very
well bred, being a ½ sister to sev winners including topclass middle dist performer Ardross:
very eff around 10f: acts on fast grd tho' is well suited by some cut underfoot: acts any trk.   78
-- ONLY A RUMOUR [2] (D Smaga) 3-8-9 J Velasquez 1: -0212: Made most, no pace of winner:
earlier this month won a fillies race at Longchamp: very eff over 10/12f on gd/soft.   70
298 STAR ROSE [11] (J Audon) 4-8-11 A Gibert 1: 21-3003: Fin strongly: fine effort.   64
-- DROITURE [9] (C Head) 3-8-13 G Guignard 1: -201014: In gd form: recent winner of a
fillies race at Longchamp, and earlier successful at St-Cloud: eff over 10/12f on fast & yldg.   70
3006 LIASTRA [6] 3-9-2 F Head 1: 1210440: Ran to her best: see 1215.   72
-- CHILDRENS CORNER [1] 4-8-11 D Regnard 1: 4221400: Now to be retired.   56
2278 SWEET MOVER [5] 3-8-9 W Carson 1: 22-1220: Slightly hmpd on the home turn and she looked
unlucky not to fin closer: btr judged on her prev efforts: see 2278, 1912.   00
12 ran   1½,¾,¾,nk,3   (Sheikh Ahmed Al Maktoum)   M Jarvis Newmarket

MAISONS-LAFFITTE   Friday October 31st   Lefthanded & Righthanded Sharpish Track

Official Going Given As HEAVY

3208 GR 2 CRITERIUM DE MAISONS LAFFITTE 2YO   £21868   7f   Heavy

3041 NOBLE MINSTREL [7] (O Douieb) 2-8-7 A Badel 7/2: 4121: 2 b c The Minstrel - Noble Natisha
(Noble Commander) Smart colt: made most of the running when a game winner of a val Gr 2 race
at Maisons-Laffitte: last month won an easy winner of his mdn at Leicester: cost $100,000 as a
yearling: very eff over 6/7f and will stay further: handles hvy grd well tho' prefers a
sounder surface: seems to act on any trk: fast improving and certain to win more races.   78
3005 GRECIAN URN [1] (D Smaga) 2-8-4 A Lequeux 1: 3212042: Fin well: acts on hvy: see 3005.   73
3005 FOTITIENG [4] (F Boutin) 2-8-13 F Head 1: 13133: Fin best of all: not btn far: see 3005.   80
-- TREMPOLINO [2] (A Fabre) 2-8-7 D Regnard 1: 144: Ran well: earlier successful at Deauville.   68
8 ran   1,¾,3   (A Paulson)   O Douieb Newmarket

3209 GRADE 1 BREEDERS CUP 2YO FILLIES(DIRT) £314685   1m110y Fast

-- BRAVE RAJ [2] (M Stute) 2-8-7 P Valenzuela 4/1: 0211111: 2 b f Rajab - Bravest Yet
(Bravo) Smart filly: extended her winning sequence when trotting up in a Grade 1 fillies event
at Santa Anita: has won her prev 4 starts: clearly very eff around 1m on fast ground. .   80
-- TAPPIANO [2] (F Schulhofer) 2-8-7 J Cruguet 5/2: 1112: Lost her unbtn record.   70
-- SAROS BRIG [3] (J Manzi) 2-8-7 W Shoemaker 231/10: 110043: No chance with front pair.   64
2915 POLONIA [9] (J Bolger) 2-8-7 Pat Eddery 239/10: 0131200: Disapp 9th: has gone off the
boil: see 2235.   39
12 ran   5½,3½   (Mrs D Green)   M Stute USA

3210 GRADE 1 BREEDERS CUP SPRINT 3YO+(DIRT)   £314685   6f   Fast

-- SMILE [1] (F Schulhofer) 4-9-0 J Vasquez 11/1: 4113101: 4 br c In Reality - Sunny Smile
(Boldnesian) Smart American colt: ran on strongly to win Grade 1 Breeders Cup Sprint at Santa
Anita: narrowly btn by Precisionist in this race last year: successful 4 times prev this season
at 6/9f: loves fast grd.   90
-- PINE TREE LANE [8] (W Lukas) 4-8-11 A Cordero Jr 135/10: 1411112: Stepped up in class
here and put up a fine effort: has won her last 4 starts in lesser company: very eff over
6/7f on fast ground.   83
-- BEDSIDE PROMISE [4] (R Martin) 4-9-0 L Pincay Jr 91/10: 1021243: Fine effort: very
consistent colt.   82
-- GROOVY [9] (J Martin) 3-8-12 J Santos 2/5 FAV: 4111414: Odds-on flop: very speedy colt
who is at his best over 6/7f on fast ground.   77
*2916 DOUBLE SCHWARTZ [2] 5-9-0 Pat Eddery 209/10: 1212410: Never got into the race: see 2916 UU
2916 GREEN DESERT [5] 3-8-12 W R Swinburn 32/1: 0213140: Last to fin: forget this run: see 2474. 00
9 ran   1½,1½,1½   (F A Genter)   F Schulhofer USA

3211 GRADE 1 BREEDERS CUP MILE 3YO+ (TURF)   £314685   1m   Firm

+2233 LAST TYCOON [7] (R Collet) 3-8-11 Y Saint Martin 359/10: 111411: 3 b c Try My Best -
Mill Princess (Mill Reef) Topclass sprinter: off the trk for sometime but put up a brilliant
performance to win Grade 1 Breeders Cup Mile at Santa Anita: most consistent this season,
winning Gr 1 Wm Hill Sprint Championship at York, Gr 1 at King's Stand Stks at Royal Ascot,
and earlier successful in Gr 3 races at Chantilly and Longchamp: very eff over 5/6f, tho'
clearly gets 1m well on a sharp trk: acts on yldg tho' is well suited by fast grd: most
genuine and consistent.   89
2456 PALACE MUSIC [1] (C Whittingham) 5-9-0 G Stevens 7/2(CPLD): 1204012: Fin strongly,
just held.   87
-- FRED ASTAIRE [6] (R Reinacher) 3-8-11 R Romero 40/1: 2111243: Fine eff in smart company. 83
2507 THRILL SHOW [14] (C Whittingham) 3-8-11 C Asmussen 7/2(CPLD): -11120: Another gd effort. 80
*2507 SONIC LADY [9] 3-8-8 W R Swinburn 23/10 FAV: 3111110: Went on turning for home: given
an easy time and came home a very respectable 7th: has been on the go all season and has
just lost her edge: see 2507.   76
14 ran   hd,2½,nose,¾,hd,nose   (R C Strauss)   R Collet France

3212 GRADE 1 BREEDERS CUP TURF 3YO+   £629371   1m 4f   Firm

*2735 MANILA [2] (L Jolley) 3-8-10 J Santos 88/10: 2111111: 3 b c Lyphard - Dona Ysidra
(Le Fabuleux) Topclass American colt: despite being hmpd inside final 2f, showed a fine turn
of foot after being switched to lead in the closing stages of Grade 1 Breeders Cup Turf at
Santa Anita: this was his 6th consecutive victory and he has won 8 times from only 13 outings:
stays 12f well, acts well on firm ground: genuine sort.   93
2456 THEATRICAL [1] (R Frankel) 4-9-0 G Stevens 27/10(CPLD): 0002022: Led 1f out, hdd
closing stages: remarkable effort and seems to have adapted well to American conditions.   90
*2456 ESTRAPADE [6] (C Whittingham) 6-8-11 F Toro 27/10(CPLD): 3210113: Set a modest pace,
hdd 1f out and was rated higher in 2456 (10f).   82
*2917 DANCING BRAVE [10] (G Harwood) 3-8-10 Pat Eddery 1/2 FAV: 1211114: Never going easily
on this tight trk and a combination of these turns and a long season resulted in him running
well below his Arc form here: see 2917.   82
*3098 IVORS IMAGE [8] 3-8-7 W R Swinburn 1355/10: -414310: Never btr than mid-div, fin 6th.   67
2917 DARARA [7] 3-8-7 Y Saint Martin 19/1: 1121100: Prom early, wknd into 8th: much btr 2917   59
9 ran   nk,3½,2½,3½,2½,2½,1½,6   (B M Shannon)   L Jolley USA

3213 GRADE 1 BREEDERS CUP CLASSIC 3YO+(DIRT)   £944056   1m 2f   Fast

-- SKYWALKER [3] (M Whittingham) 4-9-0 L Pincay Jr 101/10: 1331131: 4 b c Relaunch - Bold
Captive (Boldnesian) Topclass American colt: ran out a 1¼l winner of Grade 1 Breeders Cup
Classic at Santa Antia, recording his 7th success from 15 outings: all prev wins came over 1m/9f
but he obviously stays 10f really well: seems a specialist on dirt and has yet to win on grass:
well at home on fast grd, has also won on sloppy.   92
-- TURKOMAN USA [1] (G Jones) 4-9-0 P Day 16/10 FAV: 1142122: Trying for his 5th success
in 8 outings this season, btn only 1¾l and is evidently a topclass performer over 9/10f on dirt 89
-- PRECISIONIST [2] (R Fenstermaker) 5-9-0 G Stevens 17/10: 1321213: Creditable 3rd: has
won 5 of his prev 9 races this season, all of them on dirt at around 1m/9f.   86

+3051 TRIPTYCH [7] (P L Biancone) 4-8-11 A Cruz 10/1: 2323310: Ran well below her best
form here tho' can hardly be faulted considering it was her 10th Gr 1 race of the season!   72
2507 BOLD ARRANGEMENT [5] 3-8-10 Pat Eddery 33/1: 2004000: Fin 7th: see 1389, 469.   72
2917 IADES [8] 4-9-0 C Asmussen 1933/10: 2020000: See 2917.   00
11 ran   1½,1½,1¾,nk,4,2,1½,hd,7,2¾   (Oakcliff Stable)   M Whittingham USA

SANTA ANITA   Sunday November 2nd

3214 GRADE 1 YELLOW RIBBON STKS F & M (TURF)   £167832   1m 2f   Firm

-- BONNE ILE (J Gosden) 5-8-11 F Toro 44/10: -3232-1: 5 b m Ile de Bourbon - Good Lass
(Reform) Very smart ex English mare: gained a narrow success in a cl fin to Grade 1 Yellow
Ribbon Stks (fillies & mares) at Santa Anita: most consistent last year when trained in
France: stays 10f well and acts on firm.   82
-- TOP CORSAGE (J Fanning) 3-8-6 G Stevens 36/10 FAV: -2: Just btn in a cl fin: eff 9/10f   81
3098 CAROTENE (R Attfield) 3-8-6 R Platts 214/10: -23: Canadian challenger, just btn in
a tight fin: see 3098.   80
+2568 ASTEROID FIELD (B Hills) 3-8-6 B Thomson 1: 0303014: Not btn far and seems equally
eff at 1m/10f: see 2568.   78
2638 GALUNPE 3-8-6 A Lequeux 1: 0031100: Fin 7th: see 2452.   75
2918 RELOY 3-8-6 P Day 1: 1103200: Fin 8th: see 2918.   69
*2909 DUBIAN 4-8-11 M Roberts 1: -010410: Below her best: see 2909 (gd)   66
12 ran   ½,nose,1,hd,hd,¾,3   (A M Budgett)   J Gosden USA

SAN SIRO   Sunday November 2nd

Official Going Given As VERY SOFT

3215 GROUP 2 PREMIO CHIUSURA 2YO+   £18246   7f   Very Soft

-- ASSISI DEL SANTO (G Benetti) 3-9-6 A Di'nardo 1: 12-1: 2 b c Arctic Tern - Anna Ivanovna
(Bonconte di Montefeltro) Smart Italian filly: showed impr form when narrowly winning a Gr 2
event at San Siro: evidently well suited by testing going, stays 7f.   73
286 MISCROWN (A Botti) 3-9-6 G Dettori 1: 1320-32: Just btn in a cl fin: see 286.   73
3020 ARGON LASER (J Dunlop) 3-9-3 W Carson 1: -100343: Fin 2l back in 3rd: see 3020.   66
2832 BRAZZAKA (M Jarvis) 3-9-3 T Ives 1: 1233320: Fin in rear and much btr 2832 (firm)   00
15 ran   shthd,2   (A Boesso)   G Benetti Italy

3216 GROUP 3 PREMIO CARLO PORTA 3YO+   £13408   1m 2f   Very Soft

*3008 ESDALE (F Turner) 3-8-11 M Planard 1: 1301211: 3 b c Fabulous Dancer - Esdee (Hail
To Reason) Smart ex English colt: gaining 2nd successive Gr 3 race when making all at San
Siro: prev made all at Florence: earlier trained by J Tree to win 3 minor events at Windsor:
very eff over 10f, prob stays 12f: acts on firm & soft grd and does well forcing the pace.   78
3093 SPLENDID MOMENT (R Collet) 3-8-8 G Guignard 1: 0-43232: Took 2nd place, near fin.   72
3094 WHITE WATER (A De Royer Dupre) 5-8-6 J Heloury 1: -443: Caught cl home for 2nd place.   64
3007 CHARTINO (G Huffer) 3-8-8 G Starkey 1: -003234: Creditable eff: see 2449.   69
2942 SULTAN MOHAMED 3-8-8 W Carson 1: 1300140: Fair eff: see 2438.   65
3096 BIG REEF 4-9-1 M Jerome 1: -003100: Twice below 2640 & seems to have had enough.   60
9 ran   1½,shtnk,1,2½,4   (K Abdulla)   F Turner Italy

EDINBURGH   Wednesday November 5th   Righthanded, Sharp Track

3217 TENNENTS 80 SHILLING ALE STAKES 3YO   £938   1m 4f   Good 72 -10 Slow

3113 NORTH OCEAN [5] (L Cumani) 3-9-0 R Cochrane 15/8 JT FAV: 3033231: 3 b c North Jet -
Spring in Deepsea (Captain's Gig) Tried a longer trip and gained an overdue win, ran on well
to lead inside dist in a 3yo stks at Edinburgh: only twice fin out of the frame this season:
eff over 8/10f, & clearly stays 12f well: acts on gd & fast grd and on any trk.   46
3086 SPRINGWELL [1] (G Huffer) 3-8-11 G Carter 9/1: -003342: Led 3f out: stays 12f: see 2400.   38
3155 SIT ELNAAS [3] (H T Jones) 3-8-11 R Hills 9/1: 0-043: Clear rem: improving: see 2853.   32
*3187 CORNELIAN [7] (G Harwood) 3-9-4 G Starkey 15/8 JT FAV: -030414: Quick reappearance:
never going well and ran well below form shown in 3187 earlier this week.   26
3115 SHINY KAY [6] 3-8-11 J Lowe 16/1: 4404040: Best over this trip in 1160 (gall trk)   18
3155 RARE LEGEND [9] 3-8-11(BL) P Robinson 16/1: -002420: Bl first time: much btr 3155 (gall)   16
3155 SOMETHING SIMILAR [11] 3-9-0(BL) M Birch 10/1: 0002330: Wore bl: made much: btr 3101.   00
*3150 Come Pour The Wine [8] 9-1   3159 Save It Lass [4] 8-11
2864 Marble Moon [10] 8-11
10 ran   1½,2½,8,nk,1½,½   (J Fradkoff)   L Cumani Newmarket

3218 TENNENTS MAIDEN AUCTION 2YO STAKES   £829   5f   Good 72 -39 Slow

-3156 SKI CAPTAIN [2] (J Etherington) 2-9-0(VIS) M Wood 15/8 FAV: 00221: 2 b c Welsh Captain -
Miss Nelski (Most Secret) Fitted with a visor and landed some gd bets when making most, gamely,
in a mdn auction race at Edinburgh: cost 7400 gns as yearling: well suited by forcing tactics
over this minimum trip: acts on gd & fast grd and on any trk, tho' does seem best on sharp one   40
2969 SLEEPERS [3] (C Booth) 2-8-11 J Matthias 7/2: 22: Led inside dist, no extra cl home
and just btn: seems to act on any trk: should win a small race: see 2969.   36
3174 THE DEVILS MUSIC [6] (N Bycroft) 2-9-0(BL) L Charnock 4/1: 0000003: Front rank most
of way and seemed improved by the application of bl: acts any trk: see 2661 & 515.   34
3044 PATIENT DREAMER [1] (H Collingridge) 2-8-11 G Starkey 20/1: 0044: Again no threat.   10
2805 MONT ARTHUR [5] 2-9-0 C Dwyer 7/1: 00: No chance from ½ way.   08
3044 HITTITE RULER [7] 2-9-0 D Nicholls 20/1: 000: Early speed, sn ridden along: see 3044.   06
2986 TAP THE BATON [4] 2-9-0(bl) R Cochrane 15/2: 0003440: Replated before race: btr than this.   00
7 ran   hd,2,6,2,nk   (J Etherington)   J Etherington Malton, Yorks.

3219 TENNENTS NOVEMBER HANDICAP   0-35   £1923   1m 7f   Good 72 -08 Slow   [32]

3139 REFORM PRINCESS [9] (M Ryan) 3-9-1(bl)(7ex) R Cochrane 5/1 CO FAV: 3000121: 3 ch f
Reform - Bally's Princess (Salvo) In fine form & led below dist, driven out in an all-aged
h'cap at Edinburgh: won a minor h'cap at Nottingham in the Summer and recently returned to form
in quite a val h'cap at Newbury: very eff around 13/14f, stays 2m well: acts on gd/firm & soft
ground and on any track.   36
3139 MISS BLACKTHORN [16] (N Vigors) 4-8-11 S Dawson 16/1: 3203002: Led briefly below dist,
ran on same pace: best effort for sometime: stays well: see 419.   20
3161 NIMBLE NATIVE [5] (S Norton) 3-8-11 J Lowe 9/1: 3041133: Stayed on: see 2892.   26
2587 STONE JUG [11] (S Hall) 6-8-7 M Birch 5/1 CO FAV: 0411424: Well bckd: held up and
stayed on well: loves this sharp trk: see 1745.   14
3087 PATS JESTER [7] 3-8-10 C Dwyer 16/1: 1323000: Btr eff: see 958 & 356.   23
2800 PONTYATES [2] 4-8-11 S Perks 33/1: 0041000: Best on this trk in 1909 (11f)   10
3102 KRISWICK [17] 3-9-2 T Quinn 11/2: 0040220: Fdd into 7th: see 3102, 2974.   00
*3102 KAFARMO [1] 3-9-10(4ex) G Starkey 5/1 CO FAV: -03410: Fin 9th: btr 3102 (gall trk)   00
3087 KEEP HOPING [13] 3-8-3 G Carter 10/1: 0013320: Led ½ way till below dist: btr 3087 (12f)   00
998 Miami In Spring [4] 8-10   3049 Treasure Hunter [6] 9-8
2280 String Of Beads [10] 7-7(vis)(3oh)   2885 Strathconon [15] 7-7(2oh)
2974 Pauls Secret [8] 7-8(1ow)(5oh)   2478 Princess Andromeda [14] 8-6
2536 Killary Bay [3] 9-10
16 ran   3,nk,nk,½,5   (Bill Gerhauser)   M Ryan Newmarket

3220 TENNENTS SPECIAL SELLING STAKES   £919   1m   Good 72 +01 Fast

3154 HALF SHAFT [16] (W Stephenson) 5-8-9 M Birch 7/1: 00-4401: 5 b g Broadway Forli -
One Quest (One Eyed King) Was gaining his first win on the Flat when leading over 1f out,
driven out in an all-aged seller at Edinburgh (no bid): a winner over hurdles and will now
revert to the jumping game: eff around 1m on gd/firm & soft grd: likes this sharp trk.   10
3033 MISS BLAKE [12] (M Brittain) 3-8-2 A Munro(7) 25/1: 0000002: Btr eff and seemed well
suited by this longer trip: well btn in all her prev starts this term: acts on gd grd and
on a sharp track.   03
3116 O I OYSTON [7] (J Berry) 10-9-0 J Carroll(7) 5/1: 2202003: Never got in front: btr 2549.   07
2977 ALWAYS NATIVE [3] (D Chapman) 5-9-0 K Darley 25/1: 0000004: Led below ½ way: stays 1m.   06
2964 COMPOSER [15] 8-9-0(bl) D Nicholls 14/1: 2400040: Never nearer: in fair form: see 1546.   06
3046 VIA VITAE [5] 4-8-6 A Culhane(7) 10/1: 0000040: Seems btr over shorter trips: see 1765.   00
3157 KING COLE [14] 4-8-9 J Callaghan(7) 8/1: 0304D00: Fin 7th: maiden: see 1830.   00
3149 CAREER MADNESS [13] 3-8-5(VIS) P Robinson 7/1: 0000000: Visored first time: no form
since 1691.   00
3149 BOLD ROWLEY [10] 6-9-5 G Starkey 7/1: 1000030: Best on gall trk in 1839 (7f)   00
2905 NATIJA [1] 3-8-2 T Quinn 3/1 FAV: 0002400: Well bckd in this lower grade: slow start
and never got into race: would have been a "cert" on form shown in 2534: see 1228.   00
1547 Avraeas [6] 9-5   3149 Tree Fella [11] 9-0   2964 Teejay [9] 9-5
3157 Top Othlane [2] 9-0   2972 Musical Aid [4] 8-2(VIS)
-- Natina May [8] 8-11(bl)
16 ran   1½,1½,hd,hd,5   (W A Stephenson)   W Stephenson Bishop Auckland, Co Durham

3221 TENNENTS LAGER MAIDEN STAKES 2YO   £1303   1m   Good 72 +01 Fast

2678 MISTS OF AVALON [7] (H Cecil) 2-8-11 W Ryan 11/4 JT FAV: 42421: 2 b f Nureyev -
Untitled (Vaguely Noble) Well suited by this longer trip and qcknd well to lead below dist,
cmftbly, in a 2yo mdn at Edinburgh: half sister to a winning French miler: placed in her prev
starts over shorter trips: acts on gd & firm grd and seems best suited by a sharp/easy trk.   40
-3148 OKOSAN [2] (S Norton) 2-8-11(vis) R Cochrane 7/2: 000243: Another gd eff: see 2886.   34
2798 PIT PONY [14] (H Wharton) 2-9-0 D Nicholls 25/1: 00003: Made most: much btr eff and
seemed well suited by the different tactics: cheaply bought colt who is a half brother to
winning juv Magdolin Place.   32
3178 SCOTTISH FLING [3] (J S Wilson) 2-9-0(bl) T Quinn 8/1: 3330204: Ev ch: stays 1m: see 1174   32
2904 TRIBAL PAGEANT [1] 2-8-11 C Dwyer 10/1: 00: Ran on too late: on upgrade: 21,000 gns
yearling who is a half sister to 5/6f winning juv Brave Bambino.   28

2748 WILLOWBANK [5] 2-8-11(VIS) R Hills 14/1: 002000: Best over 7f in 2379 (yldg). 22
2723 TREGEAGLE [8] 2-9-0 G Starkey 11/4 JT FAV: 0400: Fdd into 9th: best 2541 (7f firm). 00
2218 Royal Illusion [13] 9-0
3082 Hopping Around [12] 9-0
3099 Cedar Creek [6] 9-0
3153 Dawn Sky [11] 8-11
2436 Talland Bay [4] 8-11
3148 Tootsie Jay [9] 8-11
2150 Buy Nordan [10] 8-11
14 ran 2,1½,nk,hd,3 (S S Niarchos) H Cecil Newmarket

3222 LAMOT PILS NURSERY HANDICAP 2YO £1320 7f Good 72 -05 Slow [39]

3165 SUPREME STATE [6] (P Makin) 2-9-7(bl) T Quinn 14/1: 0032201: 2 gr c Free State - Trytravelscene (Dragonara Palace) Cmftbly defied top weight when leading at dist in a nursery h'cap at Edinburgh: 9200 gns yearling who is a half brother to a winning sprinter: seems best over 6/7f, tho prob does stay 1m: acts on gd & fast grd and on any trk. 40
3058 AFRABELA [14] (M Brittain) 2-8-13 K Darley 10/1: 0200102: Ran on well: stays 7f: see 2792 28
3058 CROWN JUSTICE [15] (N Callaghan) 2-8-10 R Cochrane 11/10 FAV: 0123: Heavily bckd: ev ch: see 3058. 24
1433 BUNDUKEYA [3] (H T Jones) 2-8-13(bl) R Hills 7/1: 34044: Ran well after abs: see 1433 25
3058 SUPREME OPTIMIST [3] 2-8-1 A Proud 10/1: 0000400: In fair form: see 2392 & 460. 11
3148 GEOBRITONY [7] 2-8-6(BL) J Quinn(5) 20/1: 0200000: Bl first time: never nearer: best 1480 14
2986 TAMASSOS [1] 2-8-7(3ow) G Starkey 10/1: 000300: No threat in 9th: best 2678 (5f) 00
3047 OH DANNY BOY [12] 2-9-7 E Guest(3) 9/1: 00030: No show: much btr 3047: see 1984. 00
2919 Our Horizon [13] 7-13
3085 Miss Emily [9] 8-4
3148 Herr Flick [4] 8-11(BL)
2971 Craigendarroch [16] 8-4(VIS)
3112 Katie Says [11] 8-5(VIS)
3148 Just A Decoy [2] 7-8(1ow)(2oh)
3153 Sally Foxtrot [10] 7-7
3148 Creole Bay [5] 7-8
16 ran 1½,¾,1,1,hd (T W Wellard) P Makin Ogbourne Maisey, Wilts

3223 DUNKIRK MAIDEN STAKES (DIV 1) 2YO £1176 6f Good 58 -28 Slow

3130 KNOCKIN EXPRESS [8] (G Huffer) 2-9-0 M Miller 7/4 FAV: 0221: 2 b c Bay Express - Gilded Lily (Sparkler) Gained a well deserved win when gamely making all on stands side in a 2yo mdn at Doncaster: cheaply bought colt who is a half brother to a winning sprinter in the States: eff over 5/6f on gd & fast grnd: seems to act on any trk: genuine sort who seems best out in front. 48
-- **MUNAWAR** [22] (A Stewart) 2-9-0 B Thomson 11/1: 2: Made a very promising debut: ran on well and only just denied: Sharpo colt who fetched 80,000 as a yearling: acts on gd grnd and on a gall trk: should win races. 47
3130 WATER CITY [4] (R Armstrong) 2-9-0 P Tulk 10/1: 03: Led far side, kept on well and narrowly btn: much closer to winner than on his recent debut and seems likely to improve further: American bred colt who is likely to prove best around sprint dist: acts on gd grnd and gall trk. 46
2961 PAGITEK [10] (S Norton) 2-9-0 D Nicholls 12/1: 044: Gd eff over this shorter trip: see 2961. 44
3117 YORKBAY [23] 2-9-0 T Williams 20/1: 00: Nearest fin: clearly all the btr for his recent debut: sure to stay further: 200,000 gns yearling who is a half sister to middle dist winner,and useful hurdler, Quickstep. 43
2029 INDIAN SOVEREIGN [9] 2-9-0 S Perks 25/1: 00: Not btn that far and this was quite an improvement on his debut-run: half brother to the useful miler Aventino: should stay further next year. 41
3176 SURELY GREAT [21] 2-8-11(VIS) T Quinn 14/1: 2020000: Wore a visor: fin 7th: see 1632. 36
3133 FEASIBLE [14] 2-9-0 J Reid 7/1: 0000: Fin 8th: seems to act any trk: see 3133. 38
3048 QUASSIMI [16] 2-9-0 G Starkey 8/1: 00440: No ch from ½ way: see 2983. 00
-- **Cafe Society** [2] 8-11
-- **Straw Vale** [19] 9-0
3056 Spring Sunset [5] 8-11
2218 Broom Star [20] 9-0
3133 Charlie Me Darling [15] 9-0
2584 Frendly Fellow [11] 9-0
3080 Higham Broke [18] 9-0
3153 Introvert [13] 9-0
3037 Raise A Flyer [12] 9-0
2554 Benz Belle [7] 8-11
2328 Cloudy Light [17] 8-11
-- **Rebel Nun** [3] 8-11
-- **Trial Bid** [1] 8-11
3153 Trickle [6] 8-11
23 ran nk,½,½,½,¾,½,shthd,½ (W H Joyce) G Huffer Newmarket

3224 WESTERN DESERT SELLING H'CAP (0-55) £1509 1m Good 58 -26 Slow [24]

•**2621 HIGHLAND TALE** [18] (A Jarvis) 3-8-12 R Hills 10/1: 0004011: 3 ch f Crofter - Tell The Truth (Monseigneur) Gamely made all in a selling h'cap at Doncaster (bought in 2200 gns): last month struck form when a decisive winner of a similar race at Yarmouth: little worthwhile form prev: seems best around 7/8f on gd or fast grnd: acts on a gall trk and clearly does well with forcing tactics. 20
3128 COSMIC FLIGHT [4] (M Usher) 3-8-8 M Wigham 16/1: 0000002: Ran on strongly: btn a whisker: best effort for sometime: see 67. 15
2972 MAFTIR [12] (N Callaghan) 4-9-1(bl) D Nicholls 16/1: 1220033: Ran well: see 2412 & 1979. 15
2171 MABEL ALICE [16] (P Felgate) 3-8-10 A Mackay 16/1: 0000004: Stayed on: see 651. 12

3076 SWEET GEMMA [6] 4-8-5 D J Williams(5) 14/1: 2300400: Ran on too late: see 1081.   02
3154 CHARMING VIEW [15] 4-8-9 W Ryan 14/1: 2000030: Al prom: see 1139 & 673.   05
1774 GOLD LOFT [19] 4-8-9 G Carter 7/1: 1000020: Hmpd below dist: fin 8th: abs since 1774.   00
3060 PATCHBURG [7] 4-9-8 R Cochrane 5/1: 0000030: No show: btr 3060: see 611.   00
2083 JELDAIRE [11] 3-8-7 Pat Eddery 4/1 FAV: 0-01030: Abs: disapp fav: best 666.   00
2931 DELTA ROSE [2] 3-8-7 T Williams 10/1: 0040000: Fin in rear: btr 1695 (7f sharp trk).   00
3203 Rymos [17] 8-12(bl)   3078 Tarrakan [9] 9-0   3172 Repealed [13] 9-10
3220 Natija [3] 9-4   3154 Miss Apex [5] 9-1(vis)
3193 Tana Mist [8] 8-11   3185 Quite A Quest [1] 8-11
850 Lucksin [20] 8-6   3105 Polly Worth [14] 8-5
19 ran   shthd,1½,¾,nk,½,½   (Mrs M A Jarvis)   A Jarvis Royston, Herts.

3225 UNKNOWN SOLDIER HANDICAP (0-70)   £3464   2m 2f Good 58 +06 Fast   [44]

3052 ACCURACY [11] (G Balding) 5-9-6 J Williams 8/1: 0100041: 5 ch m Gunner B - Veracious
(Astec) Led below dist and ran on strongly to win quite a fast run stayers h'cap at Doncaster:
in fine form early-season, winning h'caps at Newbury & Goodwood: successful over hurdles last
season and will now revert to the jumping game: well suited by a test of stamina: best form
on gd & softer grnd: acts on any trk: well suited by forcing tactics.   46
3052 WITHY BANK [7] (M H Easterby) 4-9-5(VIS) M Birch 9/1: 3002002: Did not have the best
of runs: ran on well and is clearly back to his early-season best: likes this gall trk: see 50   43
3052 PATHS SISTER [18] (C Thornton) 5-8-6 M Tebbutt(7) 5/1 JT FAV: 0000103: In gd form: see 2974.   28
3052 ACTINIUM [5] (P Cole) 3-8-11 T Quinn 16/1: 2441404: Led over 2f out: gd eff: see 2809   41
3052 MISRULE [17] 4-9-1 W Carson 5/1 JT FAV: 20-1230: Another gd eff: see 3052 & 2467.   35
3139 BALLET CHAMP [14] 8-8-1 S Dawson 14/1: 2042240: Stayed on too late: see 349.   20
3013 TOM SHARP [3] 6-8-2 R Fox 7/1: 0-00020: Fin 9th: best out in front: see 3013.   00
2760 IGHTHAM [12] 3-8-12 G Starkey 10/1: 0103100: Twice below form shown in 2647 (firm)   00
*3129 TROY FAIR [13] 4-9-13(3ex) Pat Eddery 11/1: 0000-10: C/D winner last month, but al
behind and never looked likely to follow up under topweight: see 3129.   00
3161 Carousel Rocket [15] 8-0   3035 Standard Rose [10] 7-8
3052 Contester [9] 8-7(bl)   3129 Holliston [8] 9-6   3052 Sweet Alexandra [21] 7-12(bl)
3129 La Rose Grise [4] 7-8   2376 Leprechaun Lady [20] 8-5
2591 Jackdaw [19] 8-6   2692 Elpotino [1] 9-6   2647 Bedhead [6] 8-9
3161 Miltescens [16] 8-6(bl)   3026 The Lodge Prince [2] 7-10
21 ran   1,1½,1,½,½,½   (Miss B Swire)   G Balding Fyfield, Hants.

3226 NORMANDY BEACHES NURSERY H'CAP 2YO   £2918   5f   Good 58 +06 Fast   [65]

3027 SANDALL PARK [13] (M W Easterby) 2-7-9 L Charnock 9/4 FAV: 4140421: 2 br c Frimley
Park - Imacarboncopy (Imacornishprince) Again well bckd and ran on strongly to lead inside
dist in quite a fast run nursery h'cap at Doncaster: easily landed the odds in a small race at
Catterick earlier this season: speedily bred colt who cost 11,000 gns as a yearling: acts on
firm & yldg grnd and seems to have no trk preferences.   44
3156 BALKAN LEADER [8] (R Hollinshead) 2-7-8 J Lowe 7/1: 0234232: Led below dist, not
quicken: consistent sort, but has yet to get his hd in front: see 3044 & 583.   38
3122 SHARP REMINDER [5] (D Laing) 2-9-7 B Thomson 10/1: 0313003: Fin well: another fine
effort under topweight: eff over 5/6f on fast & soft grnd: see 2561.   63
3174 MON BALZAR [14] (A Bailey) 2-7-7(6oh) J Quinn(2) 8/1: 0000044: Al up there: see 3174.   32
3146 FOUR LAFFS [11] 2-7-7(3oh) L Riggio(5) 10/1: 2310400: Nearest fin: see 3122 & 353.   30
3122 MASHBUB [10] 2-7-8 T Williams 10/1: 32200: Prom most: see 2118 & 1442.   30
*3048 MAZILIER [4] 2-9-2 G Starkey 8/1: 201010: Fdd onto 8th: btr 3048 (sharp trk).   00
+3044 STELBY [7] 2-7-11 B Crossley 8/1: 2003310: Gd early speed, tho' much btr 3044 (sharp)   00
+2781 LUCEDEO [2] 2-7-7(3oh) A Culhane(7) 9/1: 0010: Lost touch quickly ½ way: much btr 2781.   00
3122 Enchanted Times [12] 7-8(bl)   *3151 Kalas Image [1] 7-9(bl)(2ow)(7ex)(8oh)
3146 Pollys Song [3] 8-0   3130 Shannon River [9] 7-8(BL)(1ow)(17oh)
3174 Viva Ronda [6] 7-8(1ow)(11oh)
14 ran   1½,½,¾,1,1,hd,1½,nk   (Hippodromo Racing)   M W Easterby Sherriff Hutton, Yorks.

3227 ROYAL BRITISH LEGION STAKES 3YO+   £3672   1m 6f Good 58 +04 Fast

3121 QUEEN HELEN [17] (W Hern) 3-8-12 W Carson 4/9 FAV: 1-00431: 3 b f Troy - Edinburgh
(Charlottown) Looked to have a simple task, but had to be vigorously ridden to regain lead cl
home in al all-aged stks race at Doncaster: lightly raced this season, on latest start was a
fine 3rd to Jupiter Island in Gr 3 St Simon Stks at Newbury: last season was a ready winner of
a Listed race at Ascot: eff over middle dist, clearly stays 14f+: acts on gd & fast grnd and
likes a gall trk.   52
3105 SEA POWER [14] (W Hern) 3-7-12(BL) R Fox 8/1: 3-03422: Wore bl for the first time:
led inside dist and almost surprised his much btr fancied stablemate: see 2701.   36
3052 SPECIAL VINTAGE [10] (J Fitzgerald) 6-9-5 A Murray 8/1: 3304203: Kept on same pace.   42
2923 CAESAR IMPERATOR [5] (R Akehurst) 3-8-2(1ow) A Clark 33/1: -034: Never nearer: see 2923   30
3052 AYRES ROCK [2] 5-9-0 J Reid 33/1: 000030: Best early-season: see 617 & 360.   30
3139 COLLISTO [11] 5-9-0(vis) S Whitworth 25/1: 2202030: Consistent, though was prob. flattered.   24
2338 Jolis Girl [15] 8-11   3110 Crystal Moss [4] 7-12   3155 Good Natured [7] 7-13(BL)(1ow)
3102 Pinzaureole [9] 7-12   595 Fleurcone [16] 8-5   3196 Bully Boy [3] 8-1

--	Baytown Coke [13] 8-5	--	Chart Finder [1] 8-5	3159 Oleandrin [12] 8-5
629	Descartes [6] 9-0			
16 ran	nk,4,1,3,3	(Sir Michael Sobell)		W Hern West Ilsley, Berks

3228 DUNKIRK MAIDEN STAKES (DIV 2) 2YO   £1191   6f   Good 58 -14 Slow

2812 GILBERTO [19] (J Dunlop) 2-9-0 W Carson 4/1: 43231: 2 b c Runnett - Natasha (Native
Prince) Useful colt: held up and qcknd well to lead at the dist, easily, in a 2yo mdn at
Doncaster: odds-on flop at Goodwood last time, but earlier showed plenty of promise behind some
smart juv, notably when a 3l 2nd to Dewhurst winner Ajdal over this C/D: half brother to sev
winners, incl very useful sprinter New Express: very eff over 6f, likely to stay further
next season: acts on gd & firm grnd and is well suited by a gall trk.   56
2967 ZUAETREH [20] (H T Jones) 2-8-11 A Murray 7/4 FAV: 22: Heavily bckd to go one btr: al
front rank but lacked pace of winner: may need further: see 2967.   45
3130 JOBYS JET [22] (J Spearing) 2-9-0 D Nicholls 50/1: 03: Ran on really well, showing
considerable improvement on his recent debut: cost 17,500 gns and seems sure to stay further:
acts on gd grnd and on a gall trk.   45
3109 FOURTH PROTOCOL [15] (L Cottrell) 2-9-0 N Carlisle 33/1: 004: Mkt drifter but led
the field for most of way: much btr effort from this 27,000 gns yearling, who is a half brother
to sev winners: likely to prove best over sprint distances.   43
3109 SWISS CONNECTION [11] 2-9-0 J Reid 33/1: 000: Front rank most of way, and this was
much improved form: cheaply bought colt who is quite speedily bred: acts on gd and gall trk   42
3053 DOWSING [8] 2-9-0 Pat Eddery 4/1: 00: Well bckd: not given a hard time when the race
was beyond him: looks the type to do btr next year: see 3053.   38
3176 VERDON CANYON [7] 2-9-0 W Ryan 20/1: 000: Never nearer 7th: btr effort.   00
2976 SWIFT CHALLENGER [23] 2-9-0 J H Brown(5) 50/1: 4000: Fin 8th: first signs of form.   00
2847 PITCHFORK [5] 2-9-0 Paul Eddery 7/1: 000: Fin 9th: can do btr: see 2522.   00

3112 Thatch Avon [3] 9-0	3153 Autobahn [10] 9-0	-- Another Lucas [21] 9-0
3018 Arrowknight [2] 9-0	3099 Danensian [12] 9-0	-- Russian Affair [6] 9-0
3130 Taylors Revenge [9] 9-0		3103 Tiger River [14] 9-0
3109 Vanitas [17] 9-0	3153 Eight Mile Rock [16] 8-11	
3117 Ling Gold [4] 8-11	3146 Seulement [18] 8-11	3017 Sparkling Judy [1] 8-11(bl)
22 ran 2½,1,½,½,2	(Mrs Manuelita Landi)	J Dunlop Arundel, Sussex

---

3229 E.B.F. ARMISTICE STAKES 2YO   £1578   1m 2f   Yielding 82 -16 Slow

2716 ASHWA [10] (P Cole) 2-8-11 T Quinn 9/2: 2001: 2 b c Golden Fleece - Baby Brew (Green
God) Clearly well suited by this longer trip, ran on strongly to lead inside dist, gamely, in
a 2yo stks at Doncaster: cost 200,000 gns as a yearling and is a half brother to 7f winner
Feydan: eff over 7f, stays 10f well: acts on yld & firm grnd and is suited by a gall trk.   43
*3141 AMADEUS ROCK [16] (J Hindley) 2-9-1 M Hills 13/8 FAV: 00412: Led over 3f out, just
caught in a driving fin: continues to improve: seems sure to stay further next year: see 3141. 46
3111 ORIENTAL PLUME [8] (R Hollinshead) 2-8-11 S Perks 20/1: 03: Ran on well & clearly all
the better for his recent debut: bred to be suited by middle dist: acts yldg grnd.   36
3014 TROJAN LEGEND [11] (S Norton) 2-8-11 T Ives 10/1: 004: Nearest fin: see 3014.   36
-- BRAVE DEFENDER [14] 2-8-11 M Kettle 10/1: 0: No extra dist: half brother to 7f winner
Silly Abdull: acts on yldg grnd: shd do better next year.   30
3125 COMMONSIDR GIPSY [9] 2-8-11 M Brennan 8/1: 0030200: Has proved rather disapp: see 2444.   26
3037 CALAPAEZ [12] 2-8-11 T Williams 16/1: 000: Never nearer 7th: seemed btr suited by
today's longer trip: half brother to 8/10f winner Allured: acts on yldg grnd.   22

-- Princess Lily [3] 8-11	2869 Gallions Point [15] 8-11	
3069 Hemmingford Grey [5] 8-8		3133 Lord Kilgayle [6] 8-11
3103 Young Snugfit [1] 8-11		3171 Pulaski [7] 8-11
3099 Nicholas Mark [2] 8-11		3163 Debutante Ball [4] 8-8
3117 Lindis Gold [13] 8-11		
16 ran hd,3,shthd,4,2½,1½	(Fahd Salman)	P Cole Whatcombe, Oxon

3230 E.B.F. NURSERY HANDICAP 2YO   £11187   7f   Yielding 82 -20 Slow   [48]

3174 PARADISE COFFEE [4] (O Douieb) 2-8-3 Paul Eddery 14/1: 231201: 2 ch f Sharpo -
St Isabel (St Crespin III) Went on over 2f out and held on well to win a val nursery h'cap at
Doncaster: earlier made most in a fast run mdn at Newcastle: cost 26,000 gns and is a half
sister to numerous nursery winners: eff over 5f, stays 7f well: acts on fast & yldg grnd and on any
trk: likes to be up with the pace.   35
*3082 EL REY [14] (W Hastings Bass) 2-8-13 Pat Eddery 11/8 FAV: 012: Heavily bckd to follow
up his recent mdn success: al prom, kept on well: stays 7f: see 3082.   42
3125 HANSEATIC [3] (P Makin) 2-9-7 T Quinn 20/1: 0021003: Not btn far: stays 7f: see 2029.   49
-3188 KINGS VICTORY [12] (M Usher) 2-8-7 M Wigham 10/1: 420024: Ran on well: see 3188.   32
3082 RUN BY [6] 2-8-8 J Williams 14/1: 0040: Al prom over this longer trip: see 3082.   32

944

-3165 **WOODPECKER** [19] 2-9-2 R Hills 10/1: 20320: Another gd eff: see 2723 & 2051. 37
+2976 **CHOISUN** [18] 2-8-4 T Williams 8/1: 0010: Prom most: fin 7th: acts on yldg: see 2976. 00
•3131 **IRISH SAILOR** [15] 2-9-7(7ex) J Reid 8/1: 304210: No show under his penalty: much btr 3131 00
3165 **Battleaxe** [13] 9-3(bl) 3025 **Bold Duchess** [16] 9-3
3180 **Mister Colin** [17] 9-7 3192 **Freddie Ashton** [9] 7-13(bl)
2829 **Street Legal** [10] 8-0 3188 **Oriental Dream** [7] 8-5(vis)
3058 **Hey Amadeus** [20] 7-12 •2364 **Ardiles** [11] 8-9 3165 **Kieron Press** [1] 8-9
•3112 **U Bix Copy** [5] 8-4(bl)(7ex) 3165 **City Final** [8] 8-4
2680 **Master Pokey** [2] 8-8
20 ran 1,shthd,1½,½,1½,nk,½ (Joe Arriola) O Douieb Newmarket

3231 A.T. CROSS JOCKEYS C'SHIP HCAP 0-70 £6609 1m Yielding 82 -15 Slow [55]

3123 **GRANNYS BANK** [17] (W Hastings Bass) 4-8-8 W Carson 15/2: 2210201: 4 b f Music Boy - Sweet Elaine (Birdbrook) Most consistent filly: gamely led inside dist in a val h'cap at Doncaster: earlier twice successful in h'caps at Newbury and hasn't run a bad race this term: in '85 won her final 2 starts, h'caps at Pontefract & Doncaster: very eff around 1m on fast & yldg grnd: acts on any trk, tho' does seem best on a gall one: genuine sort. 46
•3113 **ROMAN BEACH** [6] (W Musson) 6-8-11(5ex) M Wigham 15/2: 0004112: Didnot have the best of runs and did really well to go so close: in grand form and loves this trk: see 3113. 48
3123 **STAR OF A GUNNER** [20] (R Holder) 6-9-1 Pat Eddery 11/4 FAV: 0032023: Heavily bckd: smooth prog to lead below dist, no extra cl home: another fine effort: see 2390 & 248. 49
3113 **QUALITAIR FLYER** [13] (K Stone) 4-8-4 P Robinson 25/1: 0000004: Btr eff: see 330. 36
2851 **RESOURCEFUL FALCON** [15] 3-9-10 T Quinn 11/1: 2000030: Fin best of all: fine effort under topweight: see 586. 59
1189 **REALLY HONEST** [8] 5-9-3 M Hindley(3) 20/1: 0-00000: Never nearer: fine effort after a long break: lightly raced and little form prev this season, tho' in '85 won a val app h'cap at Ascot: best form over 1m: acts on fast & yldg grnd and is best when up with the pace. 45
3123 **GURTEEN BOY** [2] 4-8-3 A Mcglone 8/1: 0010340: Never reached leaders: best 1553 (gd/frm) 00
2244 **PICTOGRAPH** [18] 4-8-8 T Ives 10/1: -000020: Cl.up over ½ way: best 2244. 00
3123 **FLYHOME** [3] 5-9-4 N Adams 12/1: 0110100: Led to ½ way: best on fast grnd: see 2596. 00
-- **Romoss** [14] 8-1 453 **Kazarow** [16] 8-6 2891 **Moores Metal** [4] 8-0
3104 **Taranga** [7] 8-3 3118 **Hay Street** [12] 8-9 3123 **Smokeys Secret** [11] 8-13(vis)
3123 **Conmayjo** [5] 8-5 3000 **Cumute** [1] 9-7 3123 **Framlington Court** [19] 8-13
3123 **All Fair** [9] 9-1 3029 **Try Harder** [10] 8-3
20 ran nk,1½,¾,½,1½,2½ (John H James) W Hastings Bass Newmarket

3232 WILLIAM HILL NOVEMBER HANDICAP 0-75 £13597 1m 4f Yielding 82 +20 Fast [58]

•2988 **BEIJING** [9] (P Cole) 3-8-4 T Quinn 16/1: 1144311: 3 b f Northjet - Protectora (Prologo) Useful filly: stayed on strongly to lead inside dist in val and very fast run Wm Hill November h'cap at Doncaster: earlier successful in h'caps at Bath & York, and more recently defied top weight in a stayers event at Warwick: half sister to very useful stayers Protection Racket & Safe River: very eff over 12/14f, stays 2m well: acts on fast & yldg grnd and on any trk, tho' is well suited by a gall one: genuine and consistent sort who carries weight well. 52
2693 **FIVE FARTHINGS** [10] (M Stoute) 4-9-1 W R Swinburn 9/1: 0121002: Well bckd: led over 2f out, kept on gamely: fine effort: see 2058. 55
2445 **DUAL VENTURE** [14] (J Fitzgerald) 4-8-10 A Murray 20/1: 2031043: Grand eff: see 1663. 49
3022 **SPROWSTON BOY** [22] (P Kelleway) 3-7-12 A Mackay 33/1: 1133004: Not btn very far: lightly raced since early-season and is best with some cut in the grnd: stays 12f: see 132. 42
3022 **FLEETING AFFAIR** [19] 3-9-8 G Starkey 15/1: 0223030: Most consistent this term: see 2257. 62
2769 **PUBBY** [17] 5-7-11 G Carter 20/1: 0001000: Stayed on: gd eff: see 2273. 30
-- **LITTLE EGRET** [18] 5-8-6 P Robinson 33/1: /0 : Stayed on well final 2f: fin 7th: little worthwhile form prev in this country, but much improved when racing in Italy winning sev races: stays 12f, tho' is equally eff over shorter trips: acts on gd/firm and yldg grnd. 00
3113 **AVEC COEUR** [5] 4-7-12 C Rutter(3) 20/1: 0-00400: Never nearer 8th: stays 12f: see 2091. 00
3052 **MILTON BURN** [20] 5-7-11 G Bardwell(7) 33/1: 2000000: Fin 9th: btr effort: see 1099 & 312 00
-3038 **ISLAND SET** [23] 4-9-10 R Cochrane 11/1: 2102120: No extra 2f out: much btr 3038. 00
-3119 **EXCEPTIONAL BEAUTY** [3] 3-8-6 B Rouse 5/1 FAV: 2013020: Gambled on: no show: btr 3119. 00
•3063 **Folk Dance** [15] 8-4 3119 **Senor Tomas** [7] 9-2 3038 **Rana Pratap** [24] 9-4
3119 **Thorny Rose** [21] 8-2(1ow) 1779 **Western Dancer** [25] 9-9
+3026 **Saronicos** [11] 8-2 3038 **Verardi** [4] 8-8 1150 **Main Reason** [2] 8-10
•3128 **Alarm Call** [1] 7-12(4ex) 3113 **Mister Point** [16] 8-4
3022 **Benisa Ryder** [12] 7-13 3119 **Running Flush** [6] 8-3(vis)
2686 **Ballydurrow** [8] 8-3 3119 **Thats Your Lot** [13] 8-4
25 ran 1,¾,nk,2,nk,shthd,hd,¾ (Binfield Manor Farms Ltd) P Cole Whatcombe, Oxon

3233 GEORGE FARNDON ENGINEERING HCAP 0-70 £6628 5f Yielding 82 +04 Fast [49]

3104 **ROYAL FAN** [19] (M H Easterby) 3-8-3 J Lowe 16/1: 0002001: 3 br c Taufan - Miss Royal

(Kings Company) Led after ½ way and just held on in quite a fast run and val h'cap at Doncaster: earlier won his mdn at Carlisle: didnot race last season: best form over sprint dist on gd/firm & yldg grnd: likes a gall trk.   36
*3106 BONNY LIGHT [9] (R Sheather) 3-9-10(bl)(6ex) A Shoults(3) 11/2: 0012112: Fin strongly, just held but would have won in another stride: has made tremendous improvement since mid-season: see 3106.   57
3145 TAYLOR OF SOHAM [6] (D Leslie) 3-8-0 D Mckay 25/1: 2323203: Just btn: fine eff: see 2758. 32
2953 ALL AGREED [1] (J Winter) 5-9-8 B Thomson 25/1: 1130004: Fin well, as usual, see 1986.   50
3106 DURHAM PLACE [7] 4-9-7(bl) S Whitworth 25/1: 4024100: Not btn far: gd eff: see 3012.   48
3127 BATON BOY [2] 5-8-4 K Darley 16/1: 0443440: Most consistent this year: see 2277.   28
2250 VAGUE LASS [8] 3-9-5 W Ryan 50/1: 3100000: Led briefly ½ way, fin 7th: see 228.   00
2921 BOLLIN EMILY [13] 5-9-10(vis) M Birch 16/1: 2342030: Not btn very far in 8th: see 2921.   00
3106 LAURIE LORMAN [10] 4-9-4 R Wernham 16/1: 0020000: Never nearer 9th: see 2065 & 660.   00
3127 CHAPLINS CLUB [5] 6-9-7(bl) Pat Eddery 4/1 FAV: 4300220: Well bckd: not clear run:see 1026. 00
3106 BROADWATER MUSIC [15] 5-9-7 R Carter(5) 8/1: 0000400: Front rank to ½ way, wknd quickly. 00
+2970 Viltash [12] 9-6   3106 Davill [21] 8-7   3145 Golden Ancona [4] 8-5
3127 Meeson King [11] 8-12   3145 Riverside Writer [3] 7-11
2921 Iberian Start [22] 8-11(bl)   3138 Steel Cygnet [18] 8-9
*3152 Rambling River [20] 9-4(vis)(6ex)   2632 Jackie Blair [14] 7-12(bl)
3054 Glikiaa Mou [23] 8-7   3152 Spacemaker Boy [16] 8-7
2775 Capeability Pound [17] 7-12
23 ran   shthd,hd,1½,hd,1,hd,nk,hd   (I Armitage)   M H Easterby Great Habton, Yorks.

3234 E.B.F. ARMISTICE STAKES 2YO   £1565   1m 2f   Yielding 82 -29.Slow

3143 ALA HOUŇAK [10] (F Durr) 2-8-11 G Starkey 3/1 FAV: 00331: 2 gr c Sexton Blake - Negligence (Roan Rocket) Led well over 1f out and held on well to win a 2yo stks at Doncaster: cheaply bought colt who is a half brother to the smart Ala Mahlik, who fin 4th in the 1000 Guineas: eff over 8/10f on fast & yldg grnd: seems well suited by a gall trk.   44
3099 GENTLE DARIUS [12] (M Ryan) 2-8-11 R Cochrane 9/1: 43402: Narrowly btn: see 2001.   43
3141 DARING DESCENT [15] (R F Johnson Houghton) 2-8-11 J Reid 7/2: 00233: Made much: best 3014. 36
2869 BREAKOUT [2] (C Brittain) 2-8-11 Pat Eddery 10/3: 04: Ran on same pace: see 2869.   35
2723 CHICO VALDEZ [14] 2-8-11 W Woods(3) 20/1: 000: Prom most of way: improved effort and seems likely to do best over middle dist: acts on gd & yldg: see 2067.   34
2664 MISCHIEVOUS MISS [1] 2-8-8 M Birch 5/1: 300: Too much to do: see 2664, 2436.   26
--   FAUX PAVILLON [7] 2-8-11 R Guest 25/1: 0: Never nearer after slow start on debut: cost 10,500 gns and is a half brother to sev winners, including middle dist colt Owen's Pride: acts on yldg grnd: should do better.   26
3133 Jane Marple [16] 8-8   3135 Spring Forward [9] 8-11
3181 Grundys Flame [11] 8-8   2043 Lascivious Intent [5] 8-8
3099 Rebel Grey [8] 8-11   3111 Rumba Royale [13] 8-8
2466 Tubeson [6] 8-11   --   Sivaji [4] 8-11
15 ran   ½,4,½,½,3,½,1½   (Capt F Samdan)   F Durr Newmarket

3235 REMEMBRANCE DAY E.B.F. STAKES LISTED   £8194   6f   Yielding 82 -17 Slow

3118 BUTSOVA [3] (R Armstrong) 3-8-2 W Carson 9/2: 4422301: 3 gr f Formidable - Nicholas Grey (Track Spare) Finally opened her account, well bckd and led below dist, ridden out in a val Listed race at Doncaster: prev had proved very expensive to follow, tho' had run sev fine races including a close 3rd to Gwydion in a Listed race at Newmarket: half sister to 10f winner Young Nicholas: seems best over sprint dist herself, acts on fast & yldg grnd and any trk. 52
3092 FILLEOR [10] (G Pritchard Gordon) 3-8-11 W Ryan 8/1: 0044102: Ran on well: see 2672.   56
3118 STOCK HILL LASS [1] (L Cottrell) 4-8-3 N Adams 33/1: 0000043: Ran remarkably well in this gd class race: seems back to her best: see 2655.   46
+3127 QUE SYMPATICA [13] (R Boss) 4-9-1 J Reid 7/4 FAV: 0024014: Heavily bckd, but ran well below her form- shown over this C/D in 3127.   52
3191 CORNCHARM [6] 5-8-6 M Rimmer 100/1: 0000020: Fine effort at weights: see 3191.   28
3124 SI SIGNOR [8] 4-8-6(vis) T Quinn 6/1: 0-42000: Made much: lightly raced this term:see 245. 24
3118 YOUNG INCA [12] 8-8-6 N Carlisle 16/1: 3003000: Fin 7th: btr over fast grnd: see 1777.   00
3020 GREY DESIRE [11] 6-9-7 K Darley 13/2: 0000000: Led stand-side: fdd into 8th: see 1631.   00
2940 MOONLIGHT LADY [7] 3-8-6 R Cochrane 15/2: -020000: Has proved very disapp since her fine run here in 2538 (7f gd/firm)   00
2691 Farncombe [14] 8-5   2940 Kick The Habit [2] 8-7
3015 Pine Hawk [9] 8-11   3127 Bridge Street Lady [15] 8-8
3127 Kathred [5] 8-3
14 ran   1½,hd,2½,3,1½,½   (W J Gredley)   R Armstrong Newmarket

3236 CENOTAPH STAKES 3YO+   £4487   1m 2f   Yielding 82 -09 Slow

*2996 PICEA [8] (M Jarvis) 3-8-7 T Lucas 2/1 FAV: -422011: 3 b c Mummy's Pet - May Hill (Hill Clown) Useful colt: made smooth prog to lead inside dist and held on well in a stks race at Doncaster: recently broke his duck in an Ayr mdn, after earlier being placed sev times in btr company: dam a smart middle dist performer: eff around 1m, seems btr suited by 10/11f: acts on gd & yldg grnd and likes a gall trk.   52
3050 NICORIDGE [1] (G Wragg) 4-8-6(1ow) Pat Eddery 7/2: 0000022: Just btn: in gd form:see 3050. 45

*3115 MAGIC TOWER [10] (C Brittain) 3-8-4 T Williams 7/1: 0234313: Led below dist, not btn
far: gd effort in this btr company and clearly likes this trk: see 3115.   46
3042 CENTREPOINT [9] (J Etherington) 3-8-7(VIS) R Cochrane 10/1: -443044: Ev ch: see 2934. 44
2676 SATIN AND SILK [12] 3-8-4 G Carter 12/1: 3002140: No extra dist: best 2548 (firm).   36
2978 GOLDEN FANCY [7] 9-8-12 D Nicholls 20/1: 3302300: Prob flattered here: see 1964.   38
3123 MERLE [3] 4-9-0 J Lowe 14/1: 0000000: Fin 7th: been running in h'caps: see 1526.   00
3175 FAREWELL TO LOVE [2] 3-8-5(1ow) T Ives 5/1: 1022000: Well bckd: wknd into 8th: much btr 955. 00
3070 Sunny Match [14] 7-11   2799 Casual Pass [5] 8-7   3029 Supreme Kingdom [11] 8-9
3060 Silver Cannon [6] 8-12   --   Reform Line [4] 7-11
3066 Gardinia Lad [13] 8-0
14 ran   ½,½,3,3,hd,½   (T G Warner)   M Jarvis Newmarket

Key To The Index

Age	Total prize money win & place	Seasons Form Figures	All Race References

3 ABSENCE OF MALICE 38   £2499   -200232   213 464 1043 1520- 1974 2161

Superform Rating

```
2 A PRAYER FOR WINGS  62    £9660    11    2494* 2865*
3 AAH JIM BOY  6    £259    40-0204    1087 1350 1690 2293
2 ABADARE  32    £-    0    3120
3 ABADJERO  34    £838    -020000    576 702 1511 2053 2201 2996
2 ABATHATC  0    £-    0    3176
4 ABBEE VALLEY  9    £-    --000-00    366 960
8 ABBEY AVENUE  0    £-    -0    1166
2 ABERGWRLE  13    £-    00    818 905
2 ABHAAJ  55    £3896    2114    2292 2596* 2881* 3114
2 ABIDJAN  31    £-    0000    544 685 1307 2806
3 ABIGAILS GEM  0    £-    000-00    1244 1686
4 ABJAD  3    £947    10000-100000    788* 1136 1500 1720 1976 2704
2 ABLE ABBE  0    £-    00F00    1650 2043 2185 2689 3151
4 ABLE MAYBOB  17    £2546    20000-1200    594* 689 1013 1870
2 ABLE SAINT  57    £5609    21320    2056 2205* 2677 2811 3041
4 ABLOOM  29    £-    02000-00    112 429
2 ABOVE THE SALT  10    £-    00400    57 125 181 2050 2138
2 ABSALOUTE HEAVEN  8    £742    000102000    766 826 1012 1168* 1358 1537 1599 2045 2212
3 ABSCILLA  0    £-    -00    2174 2302
3 ABSCONDING  0    £-    0-0    991
3 ABSENCE OF MALICE  38    £2499    -200232    213 464 1043 1520- 1974 2161
3 ABSENT LADY  0    £-    -0    1399
5 ABSENT LOVER  36    £317    31240-040    225 964 1173
3 ABSHEER  70    £6266    -0110    371 527* 2943+ 3177
2 ABSINTHE  42    £1855    40100    2036 2658 2748* 2878 3165
3 ABSOLUTE MASTER  17    £259    000-2000    64 334 677 992
3 ABSOLUTELY BONKERS  2    £-    30040-000400    656 1065 1281 1827 2088 2417
2 ABSOLUTELY FREE  0    £-    000    892 2994 3153
2 ABSOLUTION  34    £2226    32122000    503 1057 1339* 1445 1693 1891 2261 2903
4 ABSONANT  13    £-    10000-0    7
4 ABSURD  12    £-    31434-00    129 333
5 ABU KADRA  55    £2308    00000-200    72 189 265
2 ABU MUSLAB  52    £3199    0021    2645 3037 3109 3153*
3 ABUTAMMAM  36    £1626    -001300    835 1036 1277* 1691 2155 3021
2 ABUZZ  68    £26281    11104124    252* 440* 924* 1108 1454 2158* 2447- 2564
3 ABYDOS  13    £-    -000    347 714 2000
4 ACATENANGO  89    £228184    111-111110    896* 1493* 1861* 2197* 2502* 2917
5 ACCLAIMATION  39    £547    40    1047 2219
2 ACCOMPANIST  55    £1703    42    1643 1926
5 ACCUMULATE  0    £-    40-00000    1256 1614 1677 1904 2335
5 ACCURACY  46    £17188    0200-3210100041    11 58A 235* 462 663* 801 1099 2809 3052 3225*
2 ACCUSTOMED  35    £177    000300    1067 1440 2105 2287 2680 2888
5 ACE OF SPIES  36    £1390    22/00-20    235 634
2 ACERTAINHIT  0    £-    00    2801 3069
2 ACHILL BAY  0    £-    00    2561 2957
3 ACHILLEAN  0    £-    -00    688 1256
3 ACHNAHUAIGH  45    £531    0204    1874 2368 2531 3073
4 ACKAS BOY  0    £840    -0000000100    106 259 628 1610 1718 2124 2397 2884* 3057 3152
3 ACLIA  20    £206    -0030000    431 593 835 1943 2120 2519 2702
5 ACONITUM  43    £3731    00120-030024030    433 573 698 1109 1525 1890 2144 2443 2566
2 ACQUISITIVE  39    £1122    320    230 323 404
2 ACT OF TREASON  48    £376    03020    1778 2308 2589 2812- 3073
3 ACTINIUM  41    £7792    043-212441404    347 811* 1040 1484 1879 2317* 2809 3052 3225
5 ACTION TIME  24    £1035    -0U001034    126 731 856 1035 1195* 1679 1952 2169
3 ACTUALIZATIONS  45    £3367    -03424213    1043 1327 1472 1904 2497 3060- 3164* 3204
3 ACUSHLA  78    £49823    03-012114    1491 1858* 2503* 2772
3 ADALIYAN  33    £-    00-000    916 1278 1437
3 ADAMSTOWN  41    £3439    -3141    528 829* 1256 1783+
3 ADBURY  3    £-    -0000400    619 1031 1645 2148 2317 2722 2955
3 ADEEM  30    £-    04203-0    193
3 ADHARI  13    £-    -000400    109 844 1244 1838 2109 2217
3 ADMIRALS ALL  38    £1679    00-034030421    402 765 1031 1372 1690 1998 2129 2430 2583*
3 ADORAMUS  66    £1880    -4404    2112 2192 2633 2911
5 ADVANCE  64    £3065    22101-00204    248 573 1793 2144 2566
2 ADVENTURINE  0    £-    0    2113
2 AEGEAN DANCE  28    £1250    10    2334* 2535
2 AERIAL BALLET  0    £-    0    2651
2 AESCULAPIUS  0    £-    -0    2861
3 AFFAITATI  9    £612    030-0200000    451 650 874 1184 1959 2399 3157
4 AFRABELA  28    £2740    32040200102    254 364 536 938 1305 1612 2081 2425 2792* 3058 3222
5 AFRICAN MAGIC  20    £-    -0    8
2 AFRICAN OPERA  22    £257    0300    694 1270 1534 1812
3 AFRICAN REX  32    £-    22011-0000    1391 1505 1896 2250
2 AFRICAN SAFARI  0    £-    000    596 1629 2032
2 AFRICAN SPIRIT  55    £4309    1201    1764* 1863 1948 2284+
2 AFRICAN SUNRISE  54    £2350    30    1591 2634
2 AFTERNOON WINNER  51    £2677    10    2975+ 3206
2 AGAINST ALL ODDS  21    £-    0000    1675 2723 2841 3099
3 AGATHIST  40    £4748    00-4110000    194 697* 949* 1111 2240 2480 3022
5 AGENT DOUBLE  76    £27125    -333100    2005* 3169
3 AGGIE  0    £-    -00    2653 2931
2 AGLASINI  63    £7661    012    2651 3037* 3114-
2 AGLOWING  39    £-    0    2531
4 AGRA KNIGHT  40    £-    12131-0    85
4 AGUARICO  65    £9887    -10    1216* 1715
2 AID AND ABET  32    £3234    421203    1205 1738- 2007* 2380 2694 2962
2 AILSA PEARL  0    £-    00000-00    131 378
2 AIM TO PLEASE  34    £350    3    3011
6 AIR COMMAND  35    £1795    4200-0000020200    649 815 1026 1157 1810 1868 2039 2437 2526 2668
4 AIR DE COUR  82    £56260    11241-211    153 390* 756*
3 AIR DISPLAY  70    £10006    31220-2230    151 267 395 559
2 AIR OF SPRING  38    £931    030202    450 515 627 766 995 1090-
```

```
3 AIRCRAFTIE  34    £1583   -030300221    338 980 1193 1301 2183 2306 2520 3061 3155*
4 AIRLANKA  0   £-   00000-0   721
3 AITCH N BEE  56    £6261    -04012410    371 1046 1511 1981* 2170 2458 2784* 3123
3 AITCHANDOUBLEYOU  13    £-    01-004000004000    447 1093 1247 1398 1701 1885 2038 2424 2614 2905
   2977 3157
2 AJANAC  54    £794    024    985 1313 2561
2 AJDAL  85    £56355    111    2554* 2767+ 3039+
2 AKII BUA  35    £481    202    206 1345 1458
2 AKROTIRI BAY  25    £2836    000011    531 1059 1803 2405 2712* 2806+
4 AL ALAM  0   £-   -0   8
6 AL AMEAD  46    £3216    004-00040414040    192 508 680 922 1086 1263 1347+ 1805 2207 2573 3138
3 AL BASHAAMA  56    £18641    -0131040    229 368+ 546 692* 2155 2526 2867
3 AL DIWAN  37    £111    20-4000    159 438 1934 2063
2 AL FAYES  0   £-   0   3205
3 AL KAAHIR  70    £18234    202-31214    688 1042* 1448 1642+ 2257
2 AL LAVENTA  0   £-   00    2987 3135
2 AL LUDHER  25   £-   00   1241 3133
2 AL MAHAMRY  35   £-   000   1097 1914 2584
4 AL MISK  0   £-   -0000   8 104 448 2517
5 AL MURTAJAZ  0   £-   30210-000   282 519 789
4 AL RAHIB  71    £3551    30    1356 1594
3 AL SALITE  77    £10065    412-1104    416* 597* 1009 1913
3 AL SHAMIKH  38    £3263    00-1300    699* 1080 1417 1998
2 AL TORFANAN  0   £-   0   3136
6 AL TRUI  44    £4544    000-01000200000    616 846* 952 1145 1235 1429- 1852 2144 2457 2668 3015
3 AL UQ HUWAAN  54    £1639    0314-13    888* 1170
4 AL YABIR  48    £6114    20020-22000    1038 1383- 1929 2558 2693
3 AL ZAHYIA  0   £-   0-000    844 1516 2248
3 AL ZUMURRUD  43    £8442    00400-122124220    637* 730 989 1185* 1517 1636 2226 2706 3113
2 ALA HOUNAK  44    £1829    00331    1928 2095 2961 3143 3234*
3 ALA MAHLIK  79    £24543    11-3420    214 373 551 926
4 ALACAZAM  8    £4336    00000-300011000    126 336 735 1035 1952* 2134* 2403 2873 3139
3 ALAGOS  68    £5085    3-32    2004 2500
2 ALAJIB  34    £368    03    2626 2975
6 ALAN FORD  74    £38367    13    398* 1005
3 ALARM CALL  45    £6353    41010    351 669* 1048 3128* 3232
2 ALASKAN  32   £-   0040    1452 2225 2407 2673
2 ALBANY PARK  0   £-   00    2232 2750
2 ALBASAR  50    £3548    1000    777* 1129 2146 2849
3 ALBERT HALL  55    £13421    0002-21D221114    322 699 880 1084 1412* 1498* 1601* 1931
2 ALBERT HENRY  18   £-   4   1075
3 ALBION PLACE  35    £3914    4000441    870 1049 1376 2105 2377 2521 2936*
3 ALBURUJ  0   £-   -00    764 2294
2 ALBYN LADY  48    £360    2    1067
2 ALCATRAZ  42    £702    0402    1573 2225 2341 2718
4 ALCAZABA  0   £-   -0000-0    28
3 ALCEBA  0   £-   -0000000    479 832 982 1437 2515 2597 2697
3 ALCHAASIBIYEH  42    £528    33-0020    966 1192 2653 2856
4 ALDER ROSE  59    £956    0010004    3002
3 ALDINO  60    £7926    00-00112414    357 648 751* 1085* 1402 1829 2247+ 2553
5 ALDO KING  28    £584    -1000-4040    312 462 663 2809
3 ALECS DREAM  57    £2350    -331    579 1628 1880*
4 ALEGREMAN  48   £-   11040-0   3113
3 ALESSO  84    £21113    14122    2738 3169
3 ALEX NUREYEV  62    £15182    -03004    286 897 2145 2359 2559
3 ALEXANJO  12    £895    444-40000002034    447 929 1164 1338 1603 1849 1917 2174 2268 2863 3185
3 ALFARAZDQ  38    £2262    -1    1921*
8 ALFIE DICKINS  0    £185    00130-04403000    590 1016 1183 1348 1564 1897 2111 2326
2 ALHAMIYA  0   £-   0   3073
2 ALHAYAT  15    £510    4433000    1370 1501 1738 2177 2368 2989 3085
2 ALI MAR HEL  0   £-   0   3153
2 ALI SMITH  46    £3093    234020    1791 2119 2232 2554 2805 3114
3 ALICE HILL  5   £-   10040-000U0000    30 340 760 977 1227 1443 1971 2416
3 ALICE HOLT  0   £-   -000    774 941 1220
3 ALICE PARRY  10   £-   -40000    539 868 2170 2304 2719
2 ALIMATHA  67    £7321    2    3095
2 ALJAW  23   £-   000   2287 2904 3141
3 ALKAASEH  64    £5747    210-42101    227 2214- 2619+ 2785 3064*
3 ALKAAYED  30    £1818    40-104030    241* 309 628 1065 1272 1398
2 ALKADI  55    £8688    3123201320    382 503* 610 810 1014 1143 1261* 1430 1760 2047
3 ALL A DREAM  7    £221    04000-0004020    120 318 1281 1824 2184 2302 2560
5 ALL AGREED  50    £9151    4-0040021130004    327 550 836 1037 1145 1385 1536* 1986* 2378 2731 2785
   2953 3233
5 ALL FAIR  49    £14085    000000210110300    72 248 521 775 1109 1383 1619 2132* 2219 2296+ 2629*
   2867  2956 3123 3231
4 ALL FLASH  0   £-   -0   3129
3 ALL HASTE  68    £7960    -20111    370- 574 2030+ 2422* 2553*
4 ALL INTENT  0   £-   -0   3194
6 ALL IS FORGIVEN  40   £-   02030/000000    2524 2668 2833 2921 3055 3127
4 ALL IS REVEALED  27    £4032    1310-0413000000    11 375 582+ 735 921 1150 1470 1633 2346 2591
3 ALLATUM  46    £6922    -2041010    351 463 1535 1799* 2201 2480* 2647
4 ALLEZ  0   £-   -0000-00    256 366
3 ALLEZ MILORD  82    £109385    1-1101001    370+ 654* 878 1853+ 2222 2565 2824*
4 ALLIMORE  0   £-   04000-0    3129
3 ALLISTERDRANSFIELD  9    £3123    00010-004213000    380 608 1063 1398 1664+ 1765 1959 2295 2660
2 ALLOUSH  35    £229    04030    1675 2105 2225 2377 2595
2 ALMAARAD  65    £11150    00-1031    849+ 1642 2069 2769+
3 ALMAROSE  37    £2809    0012-02030    886 2242 2463 2953 3055
3 ALMUTANABBI  0   £-   -00000    253 619 806 2408 3070
2 ALN WATER  0   £-   00    681 853
4 ALNASHME  20    £1536    0/004-401442    182 260 495* 679 3083 3172
3 ALONE SUCCESS  64    £1485    -034-20    150 753
2 ALPENHORN  50    £1112    030024    1573 1903 2105 2439 2796- 3043
                              > 949 <
```

```
3 ALPHA HELIX  28   £338   -033400   33 90 247 823 2599 2722
4 ALPHABETICAL ORDER  12   £97   -02-03   8 3150
2 ALPHASONIC  0   £-   0   3171
4 ALQIRM  34   £3307   02400-002100000   71 265 812 1240+ 1590 2255 2545 2749 2867
3 ALSACE  0   £-   0-0000   838 1444 1827 2371
3 ALSHINFARAH  51   £-   211-00   407 1971
4 ALSIBA  18   £2439   04-000014040044   189 312 582 801 1035* 1265 1348 1757 2134 2403 2733 2882
3 ALTAYAN  88   £133892   122411   554 1009 1493 1595* 3091*
5 ALTDORFER  74   £3542   3   901
3 ALTIYNA  70   £18289   1-2204032   463 661 1128 1513 2236 2525 3170
2 ALTOBELLI  33   £-   000   2281 2950 3114
2 ALTOUNTASH  57   £1564   2   2869
2 ALVECOTE MAGIC  45   £1187   001   1510 1681 2997*
2 ALWASMI  55   £1354   34   2939 3171
2 ALWAYS A LADY  28   £236   34040   73 2089 2249 2596 3188
5 ALWAYS NATIVE  6   £-   030-00040000004   700 830 1013 1222 1761 1906 2039 2295 2743 2977 3220
3 ALYDARS PROMISE  0   £-   -0   2948
2 ALYNZONA  0   £-   0   3075
2 AMADEUS ROCK  46   £1466   00412   2341 2796 2886 3141* 3229
2 AMANDA JANE  24   £-   000   1518 2527 3143
3 AMBASSADOR  53   £4752   -22322340   2061 2176 2441 2610 2834 3038 3142 3173
3 AMBER CLOWN  7   £698   03000-240000   6 38 246 545 2361 2592
2 AMBER COOKIE  52   £1244   1   3073+
2 AMBER ESPANA  18   £-   00   2707 3073
3 AMBROSINI  46   £6740   0231-1020430010   454* 588 886 1065 1487 1991 2250 2674 2928* 3021
6 AMEGHINO  32   £1607   0-0040330000000   192 401 616 748 846 1037 1235 1852 2079 2258 2702 2783
2862
7 AMERICAN GIRL  0   £-   -00   542 841
6 AMERICK  16   £-   000-0-00   137 504
2 AMIABLE AMY  19   £-   040   2584 2757 2976
4 AMIGO ESTIMADO  28   £2264   00000-0041   358 541 1035 1348*
5 AMIGO LOCO  48   £6905   -02220004000300   18 70 165- 245- 408 587 1146 1306 1508 1777 2258 2619
2773 3124
2 AMIGO SUCIO  71   £29960   1133010   457* 781* 1097 1887 2221 2501* 2954
3 AMIR ALBADEIA  25   £1746   04-220400   253 316 822 1705 2339 2797
3 AMJAAD  42   £-   -004   371 1031 2061
2 AMMEED  0   £-   -00-000000   651 1066 1344 1638 1839 2318
3 AMONGST THE STARS  68   £24140   41200-101014400   49* 372 604* 1002 1596* 2236 2643 3006 3121
3 AMONIQUE  37   £4218   20   2349- 2633
3 AMPLIFY  0   £465   20-030300002000   46 93 237 305 426 718 889 1562 1979- 2174 2335 3057
2 AMWAJ  0   £-   0   1239
2 ANAKA  20   £-   000   2423 2969 3189
6 ANATAS  79   £41408   1   1712*
3 ANAZID  85   £17672   10211   2738*
2 ANCIENT TIMES  ?   £-   10   3003
4 ANCILLA  28   £1377   -2-2000   682 1111 2278 3115
3 ANDARTIS  52   £1780   01002-033404000   15 553 807 946 1409 1702 2438 2536 2867
3 ANDERBY  0   £-   00400-000   93 426 963
3 ANDIKA  45   £2787   -00103   250 359 1228* 1753 2155
5 ANDREA DAWN  5   £-   -3000-0000   841 1004 2985 3071
3 ANDREAS PRIDE  6   £-   004-404000   35 139 2125 2679 2778 3162
2 ANGARA ABYSS  75   £8605   411210   1232 1458* 1587* 2044 2332+ 2468
4 ANGEL CITY  45   £1800   00421   2044 2263 2628 2894 3059*
3 ANGEL DRUMMER  13   £466   00010-002200   120 275 620 838 1158 1695
3 ANGEL DUST  0   £-   020300   3100
3 ANGEL TARGET  18   £170   000-00003   217 1142 1651 1989 2344
3 ANGELS ARE BLUE  29   £2033   -023010030   138 1142 1277 1399 1836* 1995 2295 3152 3191
3 ANGELS SHARE  56   £4000   -14   2634
4 ANGIES VIDEO  12   £1623   -00003203210   344 620 727 1195 1400 1567 1747 1784 1969 2077* 2208
4 ANITAS APPLE  8   £-   -0400-000   893 1017 1473
3 ANN AESTHETIC  50   £-   0014-00   567 776
3 ANNABELLINA  21   £1133   000-40004230030   162 315 538 1257 1571 1830 2076 2313 2601 2905 3077
2 ANNIE NOONAN  46   £2374   412   1025 1132* 1527
4 ANNIE RA  3   £-   00-00-0000   419 743 912 1243
3 ANNUAL EVENT  5   £-   03400-0000   414 1425 2690 2795
2 ANONA BELLE  16   £223   02   86 125
2 ANORADA  20   £-   000   1382 2886 3199
4 ANOTHER BING  0   £751   00400-100000   122* 327 418 495 679 1264
3 ANOTHER GLAMGRAM  6   £-   20000-0   207
2 ANOTHER GUEST  42   £4181   011   2651 2871* 3174+
2 ANOTHER LUCAS  0   £-   0   3228
2 ANOTHER NONSENSE  16   £-   00   3059 3158
3 ANOTHER PAGEANT  16   £-   -000000   315 512 1061 2653 2857 2948
2 ANOTHER RHYTHM  30   £780   310   2875 2987* 3174
2 ANOTHER SEASON  32   £-   0400   870 1090 1681 2265
3 ANOTHER SMOKEY  0   £-   -00   1645 1880
3 ANOTHER WESTERN  29   £-   004-00   431 835
2 ANSWERS PLEASE  32   £-   0   2527
4 ANTHEUS  84   £123297   0-1230311   1352 1595 2637 2820* 3096*
3 ANTHONY  45   £600   -3   1710
3 ANTHONY GERARD  0   £-   0-000   1607 1937 2238
2 ANTIC BOY  66   £14455   31   3167*
2 ANTINOUS  34   £3696   321000   1225 1376 1634* 2297 2777 3125
2 ANUBI  42   £1802   041   2574 3075 3158*
5 ANY BUSINESS  29   £691   00040-0000240   262 399 578 709 940 1176 1551
3 ANY SONG  65   £2390   1031113   3002
2 ANYOW  41   £2330   3310   1403 1445 1993* 2618
5 ANYTHING ELSE  30   £-   204-0-0   349
3 ANZERE  36   £-   304-00   807 1200
4 APELDOORN  79   £41034   023-13010   391* 1118 2195 2359* 2507
5 APHRODISIAC  0   £340   42010-00043000   211 418 626 820 971 1338 1543 3145
3 APHROSINA  21   £-   -00000   213 431 1244 1375 1836
2 APIARIST  34   £-   0R00   2484 2626 2761 2957
```
> 950 <

```
3 APPEALIANA  22  £953   00-002   25 648 738
4 APPEALING  23  £1587   000-41240   8 58* 184 202 591
2 APPEALING DANCER  35   £151   03   2522 2904
9 APPLE WINE  0   £1049   02000020244000000   23 256 308  493 591 1052 1124 1226 1302 1416 1548 1744
  1909 2337  2415 2727 2819
3 APPLY  54   £6451   -1100   1259* 1630* 2236 3022
3 APPRECIATIVE  6   £105   000-00003   505 955 2432 2800 3076
3 APPRILA  24   £441   -4000   59 1002 1259 3157
2 APPROACHING STAR  55   £362   004   2215 2703 2933
2 APRES SKI  24   £-   000   1282 1634 2287
4 APRIL ARABESQUE  0   £-   -0-40000   1208 1494 2072 2319 2581
3 APRIL FLUTTER  0   £-   -0   1688
4 APRIL FOOL  24   £813   3020-0400030020   481 1390 1640 1911 2123 2189 2390 2581 2981 3138
3 APRIL FOX  12   £-   0-00000F   1193 1451 1580 1835 1951 2704
6 AQABA PRINCE  6   £360   020-00000000030   10 399 453 812 1018 1229 1609 1755 2091 2274 2549
6 AQUALON  3   £-   -0000   651 943 1166 1565
3 AQUARULA  46   £-   31130-0   814
3 ARAB HERITAGE  0   £-   -00   708 1036
3 ARABIAN BLUES  15   £-   001-0000000   352 719 847 1245 2274 2414 3062
7 ARABIAN SEA  30   £-   00300-0   609
2 ARABIAN SHEIK  71   £6942   120   1903* 2849 3126
2 ARADU  32   £-   00   2574 3067
2 ARAMOR  48   £1229   33   2871 3114
11 ARANCIA DORO  0   £-   000-00   9 163
2 ARAPITI  55   £4384   2120   170 230* 440 614
5 ARBOR LANE  28   £1986   30440-104   1183* 1348 1533
3 ARC  70   £2542   -3   2454
3 ARCH PRINCESS  6   £-   000-004400   35 356 697 1078 1326 1898
3 ARCTIC BLAST  66   £3385   1-2030143   302 1009 2639
3 ARCTIC KEN  25   £4469   0040-011034000   141 424* 540* 703 747 1028 1436 1560 3123
2 ARDASHIR  41   £-   00   2852 3023
2 ARDAY WEDNESDAY  9   £-   00   1905 2323
2 ARDEN  55   £4892   212   2239 2723+ 3120
3 ARDENT PARTNER  15   £2676   40-000302100000   545 760 1171 1438 1476 1687 2024* 2106 2416 2592
  2702 2906
2 ARDILES  36   £879   04010   1019 1442 2159 2364* 3230
2 ARDNACROSS  10   £458   00242300   417 633 831 987 1168 1449 1537 1803
4 ARDOON PRINCE  7   £-   -0000   8 41 199 591
6 ARDROX LAD  60   £4822   00-000000210040   165 272 550 660 1235 2258 2378 2469* 2537 2764 2833
  2953
3 ARE YOU GUILTY  38   £4588   20003-3000102   63 1065 1199 1316 2390* 2508 2681
2 AREA CODE  20   £-   400   108 1812 1863
3 ARGENT MASSIF  70   £1564   4   1117
5 ARGES  36   £2644   22422-204142   9 984 1223 1417* 1652 1871
3 ARGON LASER  71   £14875   -100343   250* 551 803 1466 3020 3215
5 ARIBIAN  2   £-   04400-000   50 137 542
2 ARISHAN  0   £-   0000   488 627 2410 2584
4 ARISTOCRAT VELVET  25   £1073   00023-00200000   439 584 1335 1539 2296 2536 2891 3113
2 ARIZONA SUN  25   £-   0000   544 1869 2377 3148
3 ARMADA  80   £15742   -1110   218+ 342* 1378* 1913
4 ARMITAGE  22   £-   20--0-000   401 815 2762
4 ARMORAD  16   £241   30000-00402   333 578 1567 1666 1784
3 ARMOUR OF LIGHT  28   £-   -00000   209 379 2314 2520
6 ARNAB  0   £-   -000   2621 2964 3194
3 AROKAR  81   £50692   --101-12003   289* 643 878 2195 2820
2 ARQUATI REDWOOD  0   £-   000   2847 3134 3206
3 ARRANMORE GIRL  3   £-   40000-0000   26 1064 2335 2705
6 ARRAS LASS  0   £-   -00   861 1424
3 ARRAS STYLE  0   £-   -00   862 1418
2 ARRASAS  54   £4983   132   2646* 2767 3178
2 ARRIVISTE  0   £-   0   2675
5 ARROW BEAK  27   £-   02011-040   9 88 2346
2 ARROW EXPRESS  28   £1039   000-002030   141 386 514 816 1432 1923
3 ARROW OF LIGHT  24   £256   -043000   535 676 1087 1689 1830 2076
2 ARROWKNIGHT  0   £-   0000   2263 2484 3018 3228
3 ART FRANCAIS  81   £28353   -330   389 900 1009
4 ARTAIUS MEAD  42   £-   11314-0   50
3 ARTAIUS ROSE  0   £-   -0   822
4 ARTESIUM  19   £630   0434-0022000   1 19- 121 358 590 1035
3 ARTFUL DAY  46   £1094   04-1330   911* 1300 1571 1924
2 ARTFUL DODGER  49   £450   43   2263 2484
2 ARTFUL MAID  23   £1031   010000   20 40* 1910 2047 2265 2529
3 ARTHURS GIRL  54   £-   0   560
3 ARTISTIC CHAMPION  20   £1189   000-30010000   174 335 1245 1401* 2533 2880 2959 3063
2 AS SHARP  35   £-   0   3130
3 ASCENDIT  0   £-   -00   1540 2110
7 ASCENMOOR  0   £-   00   1016 1183
10 ASCOT AGAIN  0   £-   -0   2130
7 ASH CREEK  23   £285   200   1186 1514 1702
2 ASH DEE ROYALE  0   £-   00   3048 3206
3 ASHFORD LASS  0   £-   -00   357 479
3 ASHINGTON GROVE  34   £2146   00-2233230   328 535 702 1062 1473 2023 2959
5 ASHLEY ROCKET  38   £3545   -0000-30010   1579 2123 2431 2544* 3078
3 ASHRAF  0   £-   000-0000   93 718 963 2616
3 ASHSHAFAK  0   £-   -0000   765 980 1259 1835
2 ASHWA  44   £2120   2001   1518 2547 2716 3229*
3 ASIAN CUP  54   £5660   02-102422   528* 764 2545 2749 2848 3183
3 ASK MAMA  49   £2598   002-8012020   659 847 1368* 2049 2489 2576 2720
3 ASPARK  13   £-   00-0000   937 1375 2132 2594
3 ASPATIA  0   £-   0-0   2430
4 ASSAGLAWI  35   £1860   -0022-0012003   196 452 959* 1280 1388 1577 1757
5 ASSAIL  0   £-   0000   202 851 1186 1265
                              > 951 <
```

```
3 ASSEER  55  £1379   -0012   371 806 1178* 1361-
3 ASSEMBLY  26  £-   04-00   479 714
3 ASSISI DEL SANTO  73  £18246   12-1   3215*
2 ASSULTAN  48  £3001   13   2716* 3067
6 ASSWAN  54  £1057   30121-0200   410 1365 1460 1781
3 ASTARTE  22  £1171   23330-40003203   205 431 760 1399 2210 2245 2416 2575
3 ASTEROID FIELD  78  £52905   2114-20303014   232 467 754 926 1932 2200 2568+ 3214
4 ASTICOT  15  £1119   00000-03024002   530 984 1243 1348 1694 1945 2403 2789
3 ASTICOUR  45  £943   2124-00204   762 1169 1669- 2143 2291
2 ASTON LASS  38  £822   14   206* 440
3 ASTRAL  25  £822   0-01004   1645 2129* 2478 2722 2874
2 AT RISK  72  £15140   311   2345 2651+ 3040*
2 ATAKASHACK  0  £-  0000   1916 2281 2482 3153
3 ATALL ATALL  76  £1241   12030-030   18 854 1146
2 ATHALEA CYNTRA  17  £-  44   57 86
2 ATHENS GATE  45  £2067   01   1872 2761*
2 ATHENS LADY  10  £-  400   43 711 1100
3 ATHLETES WEEK  8  £-  00000-00000   424 540 637 1191 1398
3 ATIG  35  £459   41404-0000340   63 597 883 1130 1314 1402 1588
3 ATLANTIC DREAM  0  £-  -0   754
3 ATLANTIC PASSAGE  0  £-  -0   1375
4 ATOKA  52  £12601   -0001134301000   222 330 413 745* 976+ 1526 1657 1931 2219 2443* 2568 2867
  3175
2 ATRAYU  30  £542   0200300   1552 1946 2167 2375 2600 2698 3079
3 ATROMITOS  33  £255   041-400002   157 234 807 1303 1540 2041
2 ATTEMPTING  58  £5882   31122   1728 2185* 2434* 2687- 2781-
2 ATYAB  00  £-  0   1722
3 AU DESSUS  45  £240   33110-400   233 443 808
3 AU REVOIR SAILOR  0  £-  -0   1063
3 AUCHINATE  43  £2375   -430310   1628 2321 2532 2622 2856* 3140
4 AUCHINLEA  27  £460   41000-30000   629 778 964 2337 2551
3 AUCTION FEVER  55  £10917   00333-20232102   386 553 676 883 1278 1509* 1588 1957
2 AUCTION GROUPIE  0  £-  00   1844 2514
3 AUCTION MAN  31  £1184   00003-0324000   14 141 247 478 637 816 1091
3 AUCTION TIME  30  £329   -0333   229 258 368 1122
3 AUERSBERG  30  £-  30040-0   2269
5 AUGUST  26  £-  04000-000   399 578 1018
2 AUGUST HILL  16  £-  00   457 834
2 AUGUSTUS CAESAR  0  £-  0   3200
7 AULD LANG SYNE  12  £1513   33/30-42400   11 50 144 590 869
3 AUNT ETTY  7  £-  -0000000   338 458 723 1079 1401 1497 1969
2 AUNT FRANCES  20  £135   03   2596 2899
3 AUNT ISMAY  1  £-  32000-0   1447
2 AUNTIE CYCLONE  23  £-  0400000   834 1030 1440 1604 2485 2595 3146
2 AUNTIE SYBIL  38  £-  40   2788 3108
3 AUSSIE GIRL  06  £242   00-0000330004   89 422 1158 1201 1369 1459 1656 1898 2654 2795
2 AUSTHORPE SUNSET  0  £-  0000   858 1012 2757 2976
2 AUSTINA  7  £122   00-00000030   937 1446 2170 2286 2495 2854 3144 3185
3 AUTHAAL  84  £55700   11011   2222 3004*
2 AUTHENTIC  56  £7176   2210010   3 1681 1982* 2297 2479 2669* 3019
3 AUTO ELEGANCE  30  £-  00340-000   1499 2928 3066
2 AUTOBAHN  0  £-  000   3103 3153 3228
3 AUTUMN FLUTTER  38  £3158   00-301000   334 484 690* 850 2848 3110
2 AVADA  19  £261   4-0004002   1256 1444 1540 2085 2230 2497 2688
3 AVALON  15  £84   -0340000   600 844 1277 2186 2312 3024 3172
4 AVEBURY  24  £330   01433-3000   85 462 541 2733
4 AVEC COEUR  30  £-  00400-00400   1525 1901 2091 3113 3232
2 AVENIO  0  £-  0   3198
2 AVENMORE STAR  7  £-  00004000   965 1194 1440 1832 2180 2405 2580 2712
3 AVENTINO  63  £31776   0001-011111334   480 812* 954* 1041* 1384* 1486+ 1729 1793 2234
2 AVINASESH  25  £1567   023400240   446 1076 1294 1528 1717 2178 2512 2806 2968
7 AVRAEAS  5  £1013   00204-001000   91 163 630* 970 1054 1547 3220
4 AXE VALLEY  55  £6913   42010-010010   877 1037* 1385 2402 2530+ 2966
6 AYLESFIELD  30  £337   -3202-000030   225 432 743 1325 1601 1929
5 AYRES ROCK  36  £1063   03000-30400000   280 360 617 1111 1779 2311 3052 3227
3 AZELLY  13  £-  020-00000   545 891 1257 3164 3187
3 AZUSA  10  £-  0-000   720 839 1426
2 AZYAA  50  £2195   332   2774 2967 3153
2 BABA KARAM  70  £20000   -2012   2635
2 BABY ALEX  0  £-  00   1550 2020
2 BABY COME HOME  16  £364   00042   646 1088 2364 2470 3112
3 BABY RAVENNA  0  £-  -0000   501 941 1244 1446
4 BABY SIGH  31  £-  3-200-0   441
4 BABY TURK  83  £98324   1004323120   299* 468 645 1115 1352 1456 2194 2453* 2824 2917
2 BACCHANALIAN  20  £-  000   834 1019 1197
5 BACHAGHA  0  £-  00000   7 176 263 652 761
4 BACKCHAT  63  £24295   0-411-400110   215 462 1293 2523* 2733* 3038
3 BAD CONDUCT  79  £30543   13   302* 643
2 BAD PAYER  26  £3909   43121000   34 603 1100* 1221 1893+ 2265 2334 2606
3 BADARBAK  57  £9105   103-31230300   190 411* 654 1015 1354 1988 2220 3022
4 BADINGHAM BOY  0  £-  -0   3196
2 BADOGLIO  24  £-  040000   728 974 1197 2178 2336 2512
3 BAG LADY  35  £1314   04034-32000   162 762 1515 1902 2314
2 BAG ORHYTHM  54  £11261   2122343   979 1082* 1925 2223 2501 2661 2835
2 BAILEYS TOPLINE  0  £-  0   3081
4 BAILLAMONT  84  £103603   10030-311004   154 468* 1355* 2195 2506 3051
3 BAISER VOLE  81  £88490   11131-01432020   155 467* 754 2003 2742 2916 3092 3168
5 BAKERS DOUBLE  0  £-  00000-0000   495 1273 1951 2378
3 BAKERS DOUGH  14  £-  0011-0000000   74 567 1169 1471 1830 2282 2594
3 BAKHAROFF  82  £135629   11321-233123   510 1009 1330 2157+ 2461- 2752
2 BALAKIREV  73  £6081   23   2574 2771
3 BALANCED REALM  0  £-  -0   1880
2 BALBONELLA  76  £34904   14   1714* 2358
                                                  > 952 <
```

```
6 BALGOWNIE 13   £5164    0042-1100002040    7* 36* 105 126 208 243 333 429 609 721
2 BALHOLM EXPRESS 0   £-   00   3133 3205
2 BALI MAGIC 70   £6800   210   1915- 2232* 2552
3 BALIDAREEN 0   £-   0-00000000400   195 255 318 608 871 1053 1158 1424 1662 1824 2060
2 BALIDUCK 32   £751   3020    450 544 717 2334
2 BALINESE DANCER 12   £-   000   2788 2982 3081
7 BALITOU 82   £8000   11410-2   645
3 BALIVIEW 0   £-   000-0000000000   175 418 580 884 986 1316 1463 1849 2024 2275
6 BALKAN 0   £193   00010-300030   975 1077 1703 1839 2014 2213
2 BALKAN LEADER 40   £2403   0234232   583 780 2476 2875 3044- 3156 3226-
5 BALKAN PRINCE 48   £16563   -1   2116*
5 BALKASH 0   £-   -0000-00   85 366
3 BALLAD ROSE 48   £5824   323-432124   359 656 1043 1244* 1991 2570
2 BALLANTRAE 11   £472   002000   482 852 1190 1483 2095 2618
8 BALLET CHAMP 22   £5813   -30300242042240   349 504 942 1099 1260 1582 2031 2134 2376 2591 2809
2938 3139 3225
3 BALLY FRED 0   £-   0   1288
9 BALLYDURROW 42   £8174   13-010402143030   166 629+ 698 879 1409 1636 1744* 1909 2237 2536 2686
3232
5 BALLYOWEN KING 0   £-   -0000-00   1274 1689
5 BALMACARA 14   £-   32230-0   208
3 BALNACRAIG 13   £-   0010-0000   480 623 730 951
3 BALNERINO 14   £2629   33140-004010030   650 874 1362 1701 1813* 1976 2264 2426 2671
2 BALQUHIDDER BOY 21   £-   00   544 3132
3 BALTHUS 0   £-   -0   806
2 BALTIC SHORE 55   £1646   021040   1381 1550 1826* 2221 2447 2843
5 BALUCHI 0   £-   -0000   208 358 1183 1533
2 BAMAR LAD 0   £-   00   2418 3137
3 BAMBOLONA 57   £-   210-000   214 599 1408
7 BAMDORO 0   £-   01020-0000000   4 23 50 101 308 449 2683
3 BANANAS 54   £2570   -23412   194 739 916 2110* 2275
3 BANASIYA 38   £552   03-24   969 1301
2 BANDROLL 51   £2000   3   898
3 BANDYANN 3   £233   00-2000000   113 454 624 809 963 3144 3185
4 BANG BANG 0   £-   -00000   1554 1620 1833 2319 2429
2 BANGKOK BOY 11   £-   0000000   962 1313 1555 1665 2707 2990 3182
2 BANK EXPRESS 0   £-   0   1279
5 BANK PARADE 46   £1019   00424-44033   176 410 1109 1450 1667
2 BANKS AND BRAES 0   £-   000000   685 2325 2491 2607 2723 3143
3 BANNEROL 55   £6761   -0111   832 2054* 2492* 2631*
3 BANQUE PRIVEE 40   £1942   0-3314023   1061 1317 1908* 2324 2489 3030 3183
3 BANTEL BANZAI 19   £1316   0-0000040100200   109 255 377 630 822 828 889 932* 1134 1201 1334
1424 1547
3 BANTEL BEAU 0   £-   0-0000   99 145 258 368
2 BANTEL BLAZER 13   £316   303000   40 108 133 603 1050 1137
2 BANTEL BOUQUET 10   £216   00000200   376 488 602 819 892 1298 1421 2150
3 BANTEL BOWLER 20   £681   44400-10   107* 380
4 BANTEL BUCCANEER 1   £-   03--0-000   58 144 366
3 BANTEL BUSHY 25   £1927   000-22222233   106 130 307 381- 492 631 1544 1721
3 BAO 3   £149   -43000000040   346 426 506 608 666 1063 1101 1334 1549 1815 2088
4 BARAOORA 20   £-   -04   2733 3194
2 BARBARY COURT 33   £-   00   2147 2788
3 BARBERSHOP QUARTET 0   £-   -00   2929 3194
3 BARCLAY STREET 60   £3586   14-000001   249 808 1147 1854 2231 3204+
2 BAREFACED 31   £-   04   834 1826
3 BARGAIN PACK 22   £4326   03040-00023110   768 961 1051 1360 1742 1959* 2055* 2424
2 BARGER 80   £29830   31   755 300*
3 BARLEY BILL 72   £6987   022-11110   141* 310* 414* 538+ 698
2 BARLEY TWIST 29   £1293   221   421 589 1076*
3 BARLEYBREE 0   £-   -0000   581 739 832 1733 2722
2 BARMERA 0   £-   00   3023 3200
2 BARN FIVE SOUTH 35   £246   3   3158
2 BARNABY BENZ 28   £-   000   1984 2232 2476
3 BARNACLE BILL 0   £-   -0   875
5 BARNBROOK AGAIN 0   £-   -0   2403
2 BARNBY DON 22   £-   0000   1203 2016 2218 2493
4 BARNES STAR 15   £245   32000-0330400   101 145 260 378 830 1074 1906
2 BARNHILL 0   £-   0   3137
3 BAROOD 74   £16958   3203112   289 3091
3 BARRACK STREET 37   £-   13440-0040000   1514 1793 1971 2021 2258 2343 3113
3 BARRACUDA BAY 16   £-   00-40000   253 659 1645 2076 2414
5 BARRY SHEENE 0   £-   -0000   248 433 698 1254
3 BARSHAM 67   £1575   -0010   739 1408 1749* 2236
2 BASHAYER 59   £4244   22   2852 3053
2 BASIC BLISS 27   £823   303000   601 707 1341 2081 2435 2588
3 BASICALLY BETTER 40   £4235   20-4000110   501 764 1244 1885 2314* 2670* 2765
3 BASOOF 40   £1655   304-0404031   406 1032 1487 1586 2550 2755 2973*
4 BASSIM 42   £-   --431-0   349
2 BASTILLIA 36   £2423   0013000   73 533 746* 927 1527 1910 3027
3 BASTINADO 38   £2506   3010030   351 849 1062* 1642 2489 2848 3119
4 BATAVE 75   £13984   11-1220   563 2347 2916
3 BATH 28   £2266   0300-4004210   436 624 914 1399 2184 2399* 2458
2 BATON BOY 33   £3585   00-20000443440   55 606 668 775 1377 1900 2204 2277 2437 3055 3127 3233
6 BATON MATCH 0   £84   00000-0304   185 595 2023 2175
3 BATTALION USA 45   £3860   0214   2044 2711- 2878* 3178
2 BATTLE FLEET 0   £333   00-000340   162 351 714 1605 1748 3035
2 BATTLE HEIGHTS 25   £119   0300   834 1458 1914 2310
2 BATTLE QUEEN 0   £-   0   2191
2 BATTLE STING 22   £-   00000   1162 1936 2118 2895 2983
2 BATTLEAXE 37   £2922   334130000   531 834 1143 1305* 1504 2485 3041 3165 3230
2 BAUMANIERE 0   £-   00   664 1082
9 BAVAL 0   £-   -0   44
3 BAVARIAN PRINCESS 10   £-   -000   377 487 787
                              > 953 <
```

```
3 BAXTERGATE  8    £313    0000-00000204    39 91 277 498 1701 2780 2891 3157
4 BAY BAZAAR  15   £652    0240003400000400    12 42 110 306 369 649 786 1101 1682 1796 1896 2124
2322 2513  2632 3152
2 BAY BOULEVARD  61   £2408    43   2732 3040
4 BAY POND  15   £-   4000-0   532
4 BAY PRESTO  14   £668    0200-3000000000    172 401 566 616 836 922 1347 2469 2797 3078
2 BAY WINDOW  44   £108    3   985
2 BAY WONDER  33   £942    00022240   746 988 1161 1576 2127- 2308- 2600 2987
3 BAYDON QUEEN  12*  £911    00400-0000010   730 1078 2304 2432 2597 3162* 3193
2 BAYOU BLUES  35   £-   0   3109
3 BAYTINO  22   £213    -030034   430 592 2110 2395 2964 3203
6 BAYTOWN COKE  0   £-   -0   3227
3 BAYVIEW GAL  5   £-   0-00000   259 527 932 1201 1369
2 BE CHEERFUL  35   £2533    43021   988 1322 1561 2897 3085*
4 BE LYRICAL  38   £-   03000-000   2921 3012 3106
3 BE MY MASTER  70   £33548    -324   297 555 1005
2 BE MY PRINCE  26   £-   0   1573
2 BE MY PROSPECT  40   £256    030   741 1175 1660
5 BE MY WINGS  14   £-   00230-0   1829
3 BE POSITIVE  8   £-   40000-000   275 845 2422
3 BE SO BOLD  14   £-   -0000000   501 656 842 1316 1695 2184 2520
6 BEAKER  4   £971    40000-423   137 336 526
3 BEARS REVENGE  0   £-   -000000   579 733 941 1471 1999 2399
2 BEAT STREET  38   £869    403   1289 1643 2920
2 BEATTYS LAD  0   £-   000   1825 2325 3017
2 BEAU BENZ  30   £1693    0004000240   583 694 1050 1175 1534 1920 2472 2680 2922 3085
3 BEAU DIRE  18   £-   -001D00   334 527 684 1087 1396
3 BEAU MIRAGE  35   £4874    003-01020040   1 54 193 416 461 738
2 BEAU NASH  42   £1011    32   2791 3047
5 BEAU NAVET  0   £-   -040   542 1195 1564
3 BEAU SHER  49   £1338    -02040   218 402 806 1444 1924
4 BEAU VISTA  26   £994    20304-01   805 1243*
2 BEAUCHAMP BUZZ  67   £2404    20   1778 2235
3 BEAUCLERC  13   £608    00000-304000   427 615 1178 1290 1551 1917
3 BEAUJOLAISE  74   £4739    20142-2   288
2 BEAULIEU BAY  52   £1664    0010   2574 2711 2983* 3174
2 BECCADELLI  42   £119    430   2229 2499 2716
2 BECHEMAL  43   £1338    33003   223 311 2696 3041 3122
2 BECKINGHAM BEN  19   £392    020000   610 859 1984 2606 2744 2859
3 BEDHEAD  38   £1510    0-022100   978 1304 1688 2306* 2647 3225
3 BEDROCK  0   £-   -00   1062 1404
4 BEDSIDE PROMISE  77?   £75524    3   3210
6 BEDTIME  82   £32424    1112/1200   736* 1095 1389 2200
2 BEE BEE CEE  14   £-   000   2484 3081 3192
3 BEE KAY ESS  0   £240    -4002000   1210 1567 1937 2616 2836 3065 3162
3 BEECHWOOD COTTAGE  20   £4360    0010014402020300   147 198  1367* 1443 1543 1610* 1664 1742
2033 2120- 2143   2424 2614 2659 2816 3104
2 BEENA STAR  0   £-   0   2323
3 BEES NEST  71   £3695    4-1303   470 754 1332
2 BEESHI  71   £17713    32214   1242 1587 1780 2571* 3009
3 BEIJING  52   £23943    000-1144311   833* 1048* 1410 2201 2864 2988* 3232+
2 BEJANT SKITE  9   £-   00000   602 701 864 1069 1175
2 BEL BYOU  38   £382    30   3136 3206
4 BEL OSCAR  27   £-   01-0000   453 750 976 2290
2 BELAKA  40   £-   4044   2070 2589 3153 3184
3 BELDALE STAR  65   £11550    21120-100000   273* 442 1098 1913 2845 3089
3 BELHILL  0   £342    00000-430003000   100 132 451 648 697 1053 1158 1699 2335
4 BELICE  46   £1481    -1004   209* 599 1596 1899
3 BELIEVE ME NOT  14   £-   -00   1953 2599
3 BELL WETHER  25   £-   0-00   1361 2085
4 BELLA BANUS  26   £1438    0302-0000300032   606 956 1139 1800 2086 2264 2891 3029 3116 3157
3 BELLA CARINA  0   £119    0-03000000   1228 1350 1690 2314 2719 2793 3144 3185
2 BELLA GEORGINA  0   £-   0   818
2 BELLA SEVILLE  31   £429    33   1266 1333
4 BELLANOORA  15   £-   00013-00   312 2141
3 BELLE OF BUDAPEST  23   £96    -00300   1418 1541 1947 2186 2513
2 BELLE OF STARS  25   £274    020   353 446 2147
4 BELLE TOWER  29   £3916    00000-02100100   30 122 266+ 508 1213 1319* 1940 2046
3 BELLEPHERON  14   £-   0-044400   111 276 1316 1560 2033 2417
2 BELLOTTO  80   £12795    11   1629* 2199*
3 BELOVED INFIDEL  0   £-   -0   1494
3 BELOW ZERO  50   £14235    -12200010140244   74* 178 216 352 514 1147 1245*- 1924 2063* 2431 2562
2674 2773 2870
4 BELS ANGEL  1   £-   -0000   452 875 1415 1787
3 BELVEL  0   £-   000-000000   64 356 2152 2478 2722 3128
4 BEN ADHEM  46   £11100    03014-12001   410* 2330 2693 2850 3050*
2 BEN LEDI  58   £9195    03113140   515 892 1161* 1528* 1978 2276* 2439 2971
3 BENAROSA  37   £1521    -3400042200   130 372 509 1002 1259 1368 1670 1726 2054 2408
4 BENFIELD MORPETH  25   £2225    0021031   40 446 543 821* 1279 1795 2138*
2 BENFIELD NEWCASTLE  0   £-   000   376 544 1294 1480
2 BENGAL FIRE  78   £50138    23112   1914 2159 2444+ 2771* 3126
2 BENGUELA  43   £1102    340   1021 1752 3074
3 BENISA RYDER  37   £4517    03-2241000   14 188 484 1023* 2156 3022 3232
2 BENNETTHORPE  27   £-   000   523 780 2936
6 BENS BIRDIE  20   £2759    30413-21400   2240 2415* 2662 3139 3196
2 BENTHAM BAZAAR  0   £-   00   3014 3099
2 BENZ BELLE  0   £-   00   2554 3223
3 BERESQUE  30   £241    030-40000   15 178 234 427 928
3 BERING  97   £358232    -31-11112   301* 562* 1009* 2639* 2917
3 BERMUDA CLASSIC  69   £5654    02110-3204D0   2192 2351 2506 2633 2740
3 BERNIGRA BOY  0   £-   -0   486
3 BERNIGRA GIRL  6   £-   02331-000000000   15 496 580 929 1257 1312 1970 2463 3083
5 BERNISH LADY  24   £244    -040000   613 1015 1417 1923 2054 2363
```

```
3 BERRY STREET  0   £-   -00   1614 1921
2 BERTHELIER  16   £-   000   1625 1872 2410
3 BERTIE WOOSTER  40   £6647   0-0310002202400   217 284 496* 624 808 1263 1457- 1654- 1852 2207
  2343 2463 2650
2 BERTRADE  32   £1096   403243000   621 707 1057 1308 1632 1938 2556 2700 2792
2 BERYLS JOKE  36   £-   0000   985 1452 2159 2673
2 BEST O BUNCH  50   £575   023   2341 2645 2838
2 BEST SOLUTION  58   £-   -10   2635
2 BESTPLAN  70   £10920   01111   405 497* 614* 840+ 1442*
3 BET OLIVER  10   £-   -00000   250 539 765 1236 1401
2 BETTA WIN  0   £-   00000   73 311 596 1238 1728
3 BETTER BEWARE  23   £614   00-34300300   140 347 506 623 697 1204 1497 2152
2 BETTY BLUE  0   £-   00   1050 1867
2 BETTY JANE  48   £1228   421   2838 3074- 3198*
3 BEYBARS  40   £334   230-034   347 669 833
3 BIAFRAN NEVILLE  0   £-   0-0   978
3 BIBI KHATOUN  40   £262   00-002404   402 1228 1677 2248 2548 2931
2 BICK BENEDICT  0   £-   0   3130
3 BICKERMAN  28   £6893   04-0010123010   677 1051 1299+ 1560 1906* 2497 2594 2728 2876* 2980
7 BIDDABLE  3   £-   -0200-0   179
3 BIEN DORADO  45   £7508   -00434000111   218 371 576 1065 1299 2149 2497 2622 2857* 2998* 3060+
3 BIG COUNTRY  0   £-   00000-00   908 1072
7 BIG LAND  0   £-   00000-0   2014
3 BIG LEAGUE  0   £-   -000   16 702 916
11 BIG PAL  21   £-   12000-0000   578 1788 2260 2807
2 BIG RED  0   £-   0   2852
4 BIG REEF  75   £19307   2211-003100   221 325 1000 2640* 3096 3216
2 BIG SHUFFLE  61   £-   10   3167
2 BILL LAVENDER  32   £-   00   979 2957
3 BILLET  34   £3061   0-00100   484 619 2706* 2848 3119
4 BILLIDOR  14   £-   30040-00   308 769
3 BILLILLA  0   £-   0-000   231 347 849
3 BILLS AHEAD  32   £3049   12000-404441200   14 637 816 1091 1425 1626* 1922 2126 2473
3 BILLS BELLE  0   £-   0-000   941 1749 2534
3 BILLS DAUGHTER  8   £-   -0000   379 487 2496 3086
2 BILLS HENRY  53   £3974   01310   965 1197* 1373 1504* 2468
2 BILLY CONNOLLY  33   £734   0230   2494 2804 3082 3153
4 BILLY WHITESHOES  4   £358   32001-00030000   540 680 1213 1834 2072 2319 2619 2702
3 BILLYS DANCER  32   £3778   040-13014   279* 335 690 970* 1054
2 BILUP  0   £-   0   2883
2 BIN SHADDAD  47   £-   00   1903 2251
8 BINCLEAVES  27   £1423   -1010-01400   12 182+ 412 1227 1940
2 BINGDON BUILDERS  40   £-   000   2127 2292 2675
2 BINGO QUEEN  11   £1330   202213004   329 354 537 633 865* 1121 1358 2026 2107
4 BINNEYS LASS  0   £-   -0-0   2302
2 BINT ALNASR  68   £36389   101   3166*
2 BINT PASHA  66   £8498   222104   601 944 1382 1752* 2540 2751
6 BIONDONI  0   £-   00-00-000   1432 1769 2037
2 BIOTIN  10   £419   0000323000   483 622 1059 1241 1496 1692 1832 2045 2987 3141
4 BIRAS CREEK  12   £-   10000-00   2627 2885
2 BIRCHGROVE CENTRAL  31   £132   030   1522 2179 3067
5 BIRCHGROVE LAD  0   £-   -00400   1880 2085 2583 2780 2964
2 BIRD DANCER  0   £-   0   1097
2 BIRWAZ  43   £-   000   2782 3053 3132
2 BISCHERO  0   £-   0   1629
2 BISCUIT TRADER  0   £-   0   1731
3 BISHAH  58   £3370   2-124   744* 1002 2131
6 BIT OF A STATE  11   £-   00300-000000000   91 196 611 700 1013 1202 1673 2340 2414
2 BIT OMAY  32   £-   004   1874 2301 2433
2 BITOFAGIRL  0   £-   -000   218 744 978
3 BLACK BANK  31   £1969   30000-034100   874 1220 1678 1838* 1974 2300
3 BLACK COMEDY  30   £1883   001-00001404042   193 331 459 615 843* 997 1325 2516 2623 2746 3164
5 BLACK DANCER  68   £4600   -3   3089
3 BLACK DIAMOND  27   £2543   0000-030022222   451 657 992 1081 1396 1813 2890 2980 3196
2 BLACK LOVE  0   £-   0   3109
2 BLACK MANS BAY  30   £176   04300   1050 1504 1982 2512 3085
5 BLACK RIVER  0   £-   00040-004000   46 378 611 2037 2102 3060
3 BLACK SOPHIE  51   £8398   14303-0010414   762 1640 1991* 2155 2385 2676* 2763
5 BLACK SPOUT  0   £621   00000-32000003   31 114 266 855 1165 1804 1990 2094
3 BLAIRINGONE  36   £672   -032   1036 1472 1626
4 BLAIRS WINNIE  0   £242   000-40000000200   28 119 201 343 838 1166 1265 2094 2208 2515 3193
2 BLANDELL BEAUTY  16   £-   00000   1440 1802 2070 2600 2927
2 BLANTON RESERVE  42   £489   3   2243
3 BLAZE OF GOLD  22   £1285   02234000   1333 1770 2029 2153 2364 2465 2814 3103
5 BLAZE OF TARA  39   £-   00-42-0000   176 445 775 1189
4 BLAZING HIGH  40   £303   034U4D3   1495 2167 2514 2698 2903 3048
3 BLEDSOE  0   £-   -000   2622 2704 3183
3 BLENCATHRA BOY  0   £259   -002   492 822 1135
4 BLENDERS CHOICE  50   £12218   00300-030111311   358 731 856 1274* 1559* 1787* 1929 2260* 2955*
6 BLESSIT  37   £-   30-01-0   2586
2 BLEU CELESTE  23   £-   0000000   1550 1801 2292 2433 2531 2788 3146
2 BLICO  44   £-   00   1936 2667
8 BLOCHAIRN SKOLAR  0   £-   00022-000000000   418 626 971 1131 1610 1638 2124 3083 3152
3 BLOCKADE  55   £6407   02-131D1   239* 607 1078 1605*
2 BLOFFA  18   £1262   30024000   596 927 1440 1828 2071 2272 3079 3182
4 BLOODLESS COUP  42   £703   41000-0300   235 312 403 735
2 BLOOPERS  0   £-   0   446
2 BLOW FOR HOME  2   £549   0020240   612 717 853 987 2724 2872 3069
7 BLOW MY TOP  0   £-   00   46 262
3 BLOW THE WHISTLE  26   £298   4004-0300   545 1164 1418 1803
3 BLUE BELLS STAR  17   £-   0000-0400   53 130 613 1794
4 BLUE BELLY  70   £4379   3   2357
3 BLUE BRILLIANT  32   £2675   00-000212440   276 703 880 1316 1560* 1901 2189 2369 2544
```

```
3 BLUE EYED BOY   57   £-    221-0   222
3 BLUE FANTASY   11   £266   300-000002   749 845 1476 1549 1937 2271
2 BLUE GRASS FIELD   45   £308   04   2675 3023
3 BLUE GUITAR   51   £8681   0430-44213123   923 1073 1571 1830+ 2291 2481* 2719- 2832
3 BLUE HORIZON   32   £1853   41303-0100   274 768* 1164 1398
4 BLUE PIAZZA   0   £-   -00-0   41
2 BLUE PIPER   0   £-   0   1075
3 BLUE STEEL   10   £-   00000-00044400   274 620 749 963 1212 1364 1439 1574
2 BLUE SYMPHONY   0   £-   0   1958
2 BLUE TANGO   58   £11669   243321330   311 482 746 848 1021 1238+ 1454 1789 2460
4 BLUE TIP   77   £31530   1103-3240133   98 298 391 2918 3098
2 BLUEBIRD   65   £2955   13   3167
7 BLUEBIRDINO   0   £-   1D000-0040   69 126 1133 1884
2 BLUEMEDE   55   £5665   11222   3* 43+ 77 242 771
4 BLUFF COVE   24   £-   04000-4   185
2 BLUSHER   18   £-   00   1261 2218
3 BLUSHING SPY   26   £1415   -0041000   140 351 751 1204* 1326 1694 3110
2 BO BABBITY   40   £2762   301030   725 848 1501* 2158 2284 2465
2 BOB FOREST   0   £-   0   1903
2 BOBACH BOY   9   £-   00   1392 1598
2 BOBSBENT   65   £6780   43143   2821 3003
4 BOCA WEST   0   £-   -0000-0000   1686 1945 2169 2517
2 BOCATOWER   52   £4715   1D1   2920- 3137*
5 BOCODA LAD   30   £232   44004-040   582 735 801
2 BOIS DE BOULOGNE   40   £1334   20300320   662 1049 1289 1504 1653 2089 2167 2421
2 BOLD AD   12   £-   0000   646 818 1867 2365
3 BOLD ADMIRAL   35   £334   -300   733 2857 2929
4 BOLD AND BEAUTIFUL   66   £5675   01D10-0330030   433 759 1489 1890 2234 2568 3094
3 BOLD ANSWER   3   £1611   000-00001030000   380 527 867 932 1158* 1362 1838 1964 2360 2603 2980
3 BOLD ARCHER   26   £4650   400-0002010100   175 424 874 1104 1264 1565+ 1835 2102* 2267 2720
3 BOLD ARRANGEMENT   83   £83549   1322D-332004000   5 469 878 1389 1877 2200 2507 3213
2 BOLD AS BOLD   25   £-   404   577 3080 3158
3 BOLD BORDERER   14   £605   3300-000033000   234 402 674 1061 1471 1540 1830 2170 2293
3 BOLD CELT   36   £520   0-440   2473 2562 2870
6 BOLD CONNECTION   25   £-   00200-000   4 176 1186
2 BOLD CRUSADER   50   £722   422   1162 1555 1764
2 BOLD DIFFERENCE   23   £2082   00021200044   21 136 603 1088 1221* 1566 2198 2310 2512 2841 2976
2 BOLD DUCHESS   35   £295   3040   2029 2675 3025 3230
2 BOLD EVENT   0   £-   00   548 944
3 BOLD FURY   20   £1516   -202   1927 2268 2394
2 BOLD GARCON   51   £2944   014220   1019 1555* 1936 2181- 2284 2753
2 BOLD HIDEAWAY   17   £248   0402004   1576 2026 2150 2608 2815 2927 3079
8 BOLD ILLUSION   22   £2470   20104-1U40   23* 263 349 420
5 BOLD INDIAN   63   £7847   -023000   248 433 945 1109 1715 2808
2 BOLD INTENTION   31   £853   000020   804 1232 1345 2829 3017 3192
3 BOLD LOREN   38   £-   -00   39 431
2 BOLD MOJACQUES   24   £-   0000   497 2711 2796 3190
4 BOLD PILLAGER   49   £8393   020-032114040   453 775 1041 1229* 1377* 1525 2431 2655 2773
5 BOLD REALM   47   £6593   12100-00110   616 855 952+ 1086+ 1235
4 BOLD REX   59   £3862   12031-44100   263 403 584* 695 1020
6 BOLD ROWLEY   0   £1398   0000-0001000030   46 520 1610 1839* 1983 2411 2602 2797 3149 3220
8 BOLD SCUFFLE   12   £-   00000-00   1438 2397
3 BOLD SEA ROVER   38   £6314   0303013010024   16 82 368 891 1028 1200* 1398 1704 1840* 2027 2266
   2481 2685
2 BOLD SHARK   59   £3634   103   3090
2 BOLD TANGENT   46   £-   400   2574 2782 2920
2 BOLD WORLD   20   £-   0   1392
4 BOLDDEN   55   £-   41210-0000   248 652 885 1790
5 BOLDERA   0   £-   1030-0000000000   308 449 547 1017 1133 1866 2008 2217 2467 2683
3 BOLERO MAGIC   50   £2922   -2213   1184 2622- 2893* 3028
3 BOLIVIA   12   £-   11040-000   203 344 435
5 BOLLIN EMILY   50   £10928   2314-0242342030   306 428- 550 660- 877 2469 2537 2668 2921 3233
4 BOLLIN KNIGHT   78   £25313   -01110002   17 55* 330+ 413* 598 945 2145 2785
4 BOLLIN PALACE   32   £314   02000-300   308 474 3013
3 BOLLIN UNCLE   25   £-   000-0004   368 528 875 1637
2 BOLT UP   0   £-   0   415
3 BOMBALONG   0   £-   -0   2593
5 BOMBARD   0   £-   4--00-0   770
3 BON ACCUEIL   26   £1306   2-0000230000340   546 733 1821 1901 2018 2139 2155 2250 2446 2483 2725
   3012 3104
2 BONAFORTUNE   38   £-   0444   2484 2761 2894 3143
9 BOND DEALER   28   £2183   03200-01   566 636*
3 BONHOMIE   86   £144649   111-2122   324 1098* 1330 1853-
5 BONNE ILE   82   £167832   -3232-1   3214*
3 BONNET TOP   48   £-   -4F   966 1375
3 BONNY BRIGHT EYES   0   £-   04000-000004   195 545 1158 1334 1917 2302
3 BONNY LIGHT   57   £12412   204-30012112   217 1900 2343 2483* 2783 2906* 3106* 3233
3 BONSHAMILE   68   £6709   1-103004   682* 926 2236 2525 2825 3175
2 BONZO   0   £-   00400   981 1262 1318 1557 2045
3 BOOFY   33   £1412   0340-2240010000   83- 175- 334 677 1147 1947* 2120 2370 2562 2659
4 BOOM PATROL   42   £370   31000-30   9 72
3 BOON POINT   72   £20394   3-0300111330   619 1022 1469 1645 1941* 2092* 2354* 2630 2808 3008
4 BOOT POLISH   52   £19569   10104-10013031   306* 687 1145 1429+ 1810 2204 2668 2945*
2 BOOTHAM LAD   13   £978   00004000013000   20 186 425 696 821 865 1012 1181 1478 1949* 2307 2425
   2535 2689
4 BOOTLE JACK   5   £334   23200-020000   1264 1319 1447 1676 1995 2429
7 BOREHAM DOWN   0   £172   00400-000300000   69 137 256 824 1071 2111 2745 2819 2885
2 BORN A STAR   0   £-   0   2179
2 BORN FREE AGAIN   35   £1236   002034400   497 780 1225 1307 1920 2035 2272 2465 3058
2 BORN TO RACE   54   £5754   0121000   685 974* 1255- 1754* 2223 2949 3019
2 BOROTOWN   0   £-   000   2434 2577 2710
2 BORRETO   0   £-   0   3134
4 BOSCHENDAL   0   £-   00-00-0   2605
                                          > 956 <
```

```
7 BOSSANOVA BOY   25   £-   32230-00   129 208
2 BOTHY BALLAD   38   £1609   1020   701* 1527 1895 2465
4 BOURBON BOY   72   £1615   10123-400   585 704 1127
2 BOURBON GIRL   63   £8310   1   2768*
2 BOWERS FOLD   50   £552   03   1510 2667
3 BOWL OVER   39   £6821   04302-103241000   157* 352 514 954 1245 1804+ 2207 2928 3123
2 BOX THE COMPASS   35   £-   00   2159 2541
2 BOXERS CHOICE   0   £-   00   633 1083
3 BOXERS SHUKEE   10   £450   0000-300203000   89 205 424 726 835 1063 1272 1614 2430
2 BOY JAMIE   20   £-   000   2852 2957 3080
7 BOY SANDFORD   5   £783   0220-0304004420   611 789 970 1202 1335 1565 1720 1976 2800 2995
2 BOY SINGER   40   £5186   04300010   3 77 437 571 685 2479 2663* 2971
3 BOYNTON   16   £705   0004-02024003   143 1178 1335 1614 1773 2149 2267 2583
2 BRACORINA   55   £3379   31   2852 3132*
3 BRADBURY HALL   18   £2139   000000022100020   6 i38 81 427 650 874 997 1122 1267 1426* 1548 1671
   2154 2300 2426
2 BRADMAN   0   £-   0   3176
3 BRADMORES GIRL   0   £-   -0   2599
2 BRADMORES SONG   36   £-   0   513
2 BRAINWAVE   17   £-   0000   1162 1914 2541 2989
4 BRAMPTON GRACE   30   £-   30000-000000   12 76 172 321 520 3164
4 BRAMPTON IMPERIAL   3   £1130   00000-100000   41* 131 1771 2340 2681 2863
2 BRAMPTON LYN   0   £-   00-00   1334 1562
3 BRANCH OUT   0   £-   00-0   1818
4 BRANDON GREY   0   £-   0-000-000400   828 1201 1546 1736 2141 2413
2 BRANDY BOTTLE   24   £-   000   2723 2936 3137
3 BRANITSKA   0   £-   00-00   1327 1541
6 BRANKSOME TOWERS   0   £-   01000-0000000   163 540 727 967 1079 1579 1901
2 BRANSTOWN SUNSET   21   £-   000   404 531 938
2 BRARENA   0   £-   0   3181
3 BRAVE AND BOLD   24   £3051   2001-2020004010   100 335 451 491 843 1074 1346 1540 1964* 2226
2 BRAVE DANCER   69   £11435   31013   777 1019* 1097 2133* 2251
2 BRAVE DEFENDER   30   £-   0   3229
3 BRAVE OWEN   73   £13154   13-223   802 1107 1286
2 BRAVE RAJ   80?   £314685   1   3209*
3 BRAVO FOX   73   £18504   044-01014   2505* 3000
2 BRAZILIAN PRINCESS   33   £286   002   1126 1501 2895
3 BRAZZAKA   63   £21394   22221-11233320   271* 575* 803 1114 2165 2449 2832 3215
4 BREADCRUMB   63   £-   10010-000   945 1286 1631
3 BREAKFAST IN BED   30   £1671   0030-32230   438 814 911 1200 1524
2 BREAKOUT   35   £-   04   2869 3234
4 BRECKLAND LADY   14   £2651   21010-03120   976 1551 1951* 2154 2226
2 BREGA   0   £-   00   3111 3153
3 BREGUET   5   £384   00-20000000   487 822 1055 1432 1678 1918 2395 3061
3 BRENT RIVERSIDE   0   £-   0000-00000   74 234 480 1520 1835
2 BRENTANO   56   £7408   010   2239 2522* 2721
2 BREWIN TIME   38   £8778   00311   685 1869 2026 2391+ 2465+
2 BRIARQUEEN   11   £-   00000   367 543 672 858 1358
2 BRICKENAY   61   £6923   20   1351 1744
3 BRIDE   20   £684   00-1000   123* 463 833 1326
3 BRIDESMAID   73   £17395   1430-0012334000   220 373 691+ 854- 1125 1491 1631 2233 2474 2537
3 BRIDGE OF GOLD   16   £1040   120-10040000   529* 768 1027 1131 1704 2322 2758 2906
5 BRIDGE STREET LADY   48   £5989   4200-2012003000   76 192 327+ 477 660 2258 2402 3106 3127 3235
2 BRIDGET OBIRD   44   £164   03   2774 3073
5 BRIG CHOP   00   £819   00004-3000R   374 616 687 952 1285
8 BRIGADIER HAWK   0   £-   0-000-0   1459
5 BRIGADIER JACQUES   18   £1335   02210-140   121* 204 485
2 BRIGADIER THWAITES   0   £-   0   3131
4 BRIGADIER TROY   26   £-   30-00   381 613
2 BRIGGS BUILDERS   32   £259   00200   404 1483 1883 2140 3041
3 BRIGHT AS NIGHT   68   £4352   22240-3031001   24 286 1042 1395* 1486 1655 1831+
4 BRIGHT BIRD   29   £397   -030   693 1068 1644
4 BRIGHT PATH 1   £-   04000-000   1324 1901 2312
5 BRIGHTNER   61   £6287   01110/0311   2203 2510 2809* 2965*
3 BRIMSOL   1   £-   -00   2790 3105
2 BRIMUR   36   £222   240   2140 2804 2920
3 BRITTONS MILL   25   £1283   00-0241   1055 1426 1739 1985*
3 BRITWYDD   20   £-   00-00400   2473 2928 3024 3104 3180
3 BROAD BRUSH   80   £35000   2111113   469
3 BROADHURST   24   £4367   32000-030031410   1281 1626 1864 2027 2413 2780* 2998 3157* 3204
5 BROADLEAF   49   £-   -0020-,0   1004
4 BROADWATER MUSIC   48   £7724   41210-010000400   12 165+ 272 408 660 2953 3054 3106 3233
2 BROADWAY STOMP   24   £89   03   722 905
2 BROKEN HEARTED   42   £264   2   3200
7 BROKEN SEAL   0   £-   -0P   2087 2326
4 BROKEN TACKLE   0   £-   -0-00000   617 751 1348 1559 2134
3 BROKEN WAVE   68   £16396   -103101   486* 926 1538 2028* 2525 2692+
2 BROLGA   0   £-   000   2368 2675 3014
2 BRONZALIAS   0   £-   0   853
2 BRONZE BUCK   43   £-   00   2847 3163
3 BRONZE OPAL   55   £5186   03320-00010140   455 586 1245 1472* 1854 1934* 2099 2545
2 BRONZE RUNNER   12   £403   30   1531 3067
2 BRONZEWING   48   £2236   321   2788 3073 3184+
2 BROOKHEAD GIRL   13   £-   00000   415 537 2743 2987 3056
3 BROOKS DILEMMA   46   £1629   -01200   787 1516* 1691 2362 2488
2 BROOKSIDE   0   £-   00   1825 2011
2 BROOM STAR   25   £-   0000   425 612 2218 3223
2 BROONS ADDITION   22   £1568   434310000   102 186 254 376 603* 1527 1978 2137 2265
2 BROONS ANSWER   12   £861   0013000   102 181 537* 633 717 1358 1622
2 BROTHER PATRICK   62   £8283   301203   1172 1452 2105* 2407- 2648 3107
4 BROWN BEAR BOY   33   £4167   00400-023301000   374 508- 734 986 1037 1182+ 1222 2295 2934
3 BROWN THATCH   65   £5012   -30110   371 723 1278* 2958* 3119
3 BRUISER   55   £4370   112-1   886*
                    > 957 <
```

```
5 BRUNDEAN BREEZE 0  £-   -0   1361
4 BRUNICO 75  £27257  -10100  9* 265 475* 704 1148
2 BRUSHFORD 0  £-  000  170 350 503
2 BRUTUS 31  £1070  0103040000  627 826* 1527 1717 1893 1978 2265 2815 3058 3151
3 BRYANTHUS 0  £-  -00  39 127
2 BU SOFYAN 20  £-  0  1826
4 BUBS BOY 15  £207  -0011-00300  12 110 710 2513 2602
2 BUCHAN NESS 65  £2770  1  1232*
3 BUCKLEY 62  £6377  -31212  1923 2042+ 2428 2864* 3022-
9 BUCKLOW HILL 24  £556  30010-00003400  782 933 1159 1359 1865 2040 2141 2492
5 BUCKMINSTER BOY 17  £-  -0010-0  92
2 BUCKRA MELLISUGA 47  £656  300  2239 2484 2920
4 BUCKS BOLT 8  £283  000-00300044000  41 262 540 630 668 943 1231 1951 2374 2585 2863
2 BUCKSWILL 0  £-  0  780
2 BUDDY RICH 38  £199  4040  382 523 728 859
2 BUDSHEAD 0  £-  00  987 1323
8 BUGATTI 0  £-  0/000-0  3204
2 BUGBERRY 0  £-  0000  2185 2308 2514 2743
3 BUHAAZ 15  £-  00000-00  424 1901
7 BULANDSHAR 0  £-  -000  28 1035 1346
6 BULLOM 0  £-  -0  256
3 BULLY BOY 0  £-  0-0000000000  535 832 1346 1833 2430 2722 2874 3161 3196 3227
3 BUMI HEIGHTS 0  £-  -0  1386
2 BUMI HILLS 6  £-  4  13
2 BUMPTIOUS BOY 26  £-  0000  965 1572 2625 2707
2 BUNCHED 30  £-  0  3111
2 BUNCHES 0  £-  00  1345 1483
6 BUNDABURG 27  £-  131-00000000000  196 248 453 775 1109 1390 1640 1890 2091 2296 2431
4 BUNDLING BED 12  £1140  00000-020400100  609 673 993 1140 1280 1482 1719* 2173 2704
2 BUNDUKEYA 30  £350  34044  317 722 1132 1433 3222
5 BUNRANNOCH HOUSE 0  £-  00-0  1908
5 BURAAG 34  £472  40000-0044034  196 243 429 521 956 1106 1139
5 BURBRIDGE KING ST 0  £-  00  1736 1845
2 BURCROFT 28  £823  00300  1762 1984 2218 2393 3103
3 BURHAAIN 30  £3617  033-010000  455 703* 1032 2155 2390 2810
2 BURLY NATIVE 0  £-  000  3018 3163 3200
3 BURNING AMBITION 0  £-  0-000  619 1589 3105
4 BURNING ARROW 2  £-  000000  994 1438 2104 2312 2715 3145
3 BURNING BRIGHT 35  £1138  002-02441  371 1080 1494 1615 2 556*
3 BUSHIDO 26  £426  -2403  486 1494 2620 3035
12 BUSHY BAY 0  £-  00000-000  1845 1969 2101
3 BUSTAMENTE 0  £-  0-0  739
3 BUSTARA 59  £7115  010-04030  214 397 1002 1343 2058
5 BUSTED FLAVOUR 18  £561  30030300  875 1015 1394 1985 2109 2360 2604 2818
2 BUSTED HARMONY 0  £-  00  3099 3206
6 BUSTOFF 12  £1941  00--0-2300103  44 772 933 968 1897* 2040 2280
3 BUTHAYNA 29  £669  022-0003300  431 656 1153 1995 2343 2614 2977
3 BUTSOVA 52  £13704  -0334422301  431 776 966 1228 2672 2793 2947 3054 3118 3235*
2 BUTTERFIELD ROAD 49  £1118  100  1307* 1925 2297
3 BUTTERFLY KISS 44  £1576  -00331  250 581 935 1160 1706*
4 BUTTS BAY 13  £-  0-000-00  23 724
2 BL Y MUMS ACT 0  £-  00  2119 2926
2 BUY NORDAN 0  £-  000  1958 2150 3221
4 BWANA KALI 18  £1339  4010-4330020000  36 196 238 310 750 893 1139 1829 2173 2372
3 BY CHANCE 7  £-  10130-04000  1164 1406 1830 2027 2417
2 BY THE FIRESIDE 56  £512  3  3163
2 BY THE GLEN 0  £-  00  1434 2180
2 CABALLINE 38  £337  030000204  115 200 544 1232 2071 2310 2580 2718 3132
4 CABANAX 42  £365  0-220-30  525 1222
2 CABOT 42  £366  200  2001 2468 2847
5 CABRAL 30  £815  -0024  330 943 1166 1502
2 CACHONDINA 46  £487  4  1154
2 CADEAUX DAMIE 63  £3395  30  2644 2915
4 CADENETTE 0  £1175  0030-0042010000  163 238 522 993 1201 1699* 2102 2414 2885 3087
4 CADMIUM 33  £1541  13331-30343000  215 375 743 1667 1992 2290 2523 2955
2 CAERINETTE 22  £765  04340003000  1287 1440 1668 2013 2178 2310 2479 2648 2830 2968 3085
4 CAERNARVON BOY 15  £415  00000-3200  42 145 378 630
3 CAESAR IMPERATOR 30  £715  -034  2701 2923 3227
3 CAFE NOIR 26  £187  0431-30400  1316 1487 1830 2184 2516
2 CAFE SOCIETY 34  £-  0  3223
3 CAGLIOSTRO 36  £119  -300  66 334 928
2 CAJUN DANCER 30  £477  400  1780 2133 3200
2 CAJUN MOON 0  £-  00  2801 2990
3 CALAMETTA 63  £1987  -022-330  269 560 754
2 CALAPAEZ 22  £-  000  2869 3037 3229
2 CALIBOGUE 44  £5382  0011  404 2225 2707* 2968+
4 CALIFORNIAN LINK 7  £-  000-0  201
5 CALIPH 21  £-  0-000-000  1186 1429 1649
12 CALISOLON 0  £-  00--0-0  119
2 CALL FOR TAYLOR 21  £222  000000030  186 383 2147 2325 2468 2607 3014 3146 3189
4 CALL ME CLAIRE 5  £-  04000-0  41
3 CALL TO HONOR 49  £3634  -431  357 613 2441*
2 CALLACE 14  £-  004000  859 1373 1634 2153 2748 2935
3 CALS SYMPHONY 0  £-  -0  3024
3 CALVADOS 9  £-  -000  941 1087 1494
3 CALVINETTE 39  £-  -040  250 1062 2546
2 CALYPSO KID 0  £-  000  1550 1803 2829
3 CALYSTEGIA 37  £343  -003  1142 1586 2299
2 CAMALLINO ROSE 0  £-  0  2651
2 CAMBRIDGE REBEL 31  £-  0  664
2 CAMILLAS GIRL 20  £-  0  2527
2 CAMMAC LAD 32  £800  00003233  20 136 685 1675 1883 2471 2607 3165
2 CAMMARINO 38  £-  044  2574 3137 3201
                        > 958 <
```

```
2 CAMPEGGIO   0   £-   000    2007 2511 2886
5 CAMPUS BOY   0   £-   --032-000400000    243 358 542 824 1177 2305 2492 2727 2885
3 CANADIAN GUEST  37   £2271   -0020223    1198 1586 1751 2314 2905 3116 3180
2 CANADIAN MILL  73   £12096   13   1464+ 2831
3 CANADIAN STAR  44   £9454   0-0241122    357 980 1278 1637* 2091+ 2266 2730
2 CANANGO  47   £975   43   2939 3130
2 CANARY WHARF   0   £-   00    3074 3163
8 CANDAULES   9   £1033   -01    177 343*
2 CANDLE DANCER   0   £-   0    437
2 CANDLE IN THE WIND   62   £5561   0401000    1021 1287 1454 1874* 2246 2504 2753
4 CANE MILL  25   £-   2142-00000    282 519 1047 1176 1976
2 CANEBRAKE LADY   0   £-   ------00    3017 3189
3 CANESARA  46   £498   -30    1586 1934
5 CANIF  40   £8070   04000-0100100    192 1157* 1347 1849 2277+ 2573 2862
9 CANIO   0   £-   -0    11
3 CAP DEL MOND  60   £18189   -11111    2096* 2517* 2834* 2938* 3013*
6 CAPA   8   £982   004-220    1274 1569 2467
2 CAPE WILD  55   £5005   2120    1928 2229* 2563 2753
3 CAPEABILITY POUND  25   £3418   0-1000200000300    147+ 443 670 814 1027 1283 1524 1810 2055 2245
2632 2775 3233
3 CAPISTRANO CLIMAX   9   £-   300-00000    14 997 1917 2174 2361
2 CAPITAL FLOW  31   £202   043000    323 834 1555 2025 2205 2782
3 CAPITATION   0   £-   0-0P    592 1029
4 CAPO NORD  73   £3128   1343-2    287
3 CAPRICORN BEAU  35   £246   -04403    1046 1954 2170 2333 2857
3 CAPRICORN BLUE  26   £4626   00S-02424110100    650 960 1303 1719 1985 2083* 2344* 2549 2890* 2995
3197
3 CAPTAIN HAWAI  69   £15434   -1    297*
2 CAPTAIN HOLLY  52   £959   010    2696 2812+ 3122
6 CAPTAIN WEBSTER   4   £-   /0314-00    663 1260
6 CAPTAINS BIDD  15   £5940   002020414100034    355 679 1077 1438 1542 1649 1849 1950+ 2124 2256+
2402 2592 2775 3046 3145
3 CAPTAINS JADE   0   £-   0-0000    806 1554 2230 2490
3 CAPTAINS NIECE  50   £9843   -011120    941 1220* 1755* 2755* 2942 3179
3 CAPULET   4   £-   00-00000    980 1497 1733 2093 2787
3 CARANGE   0   £-   00-0    2161
2 CARAS QUEST   0   £-   00000    543 647 858 957 1012
3 CARD PLAYED  44   £982   -2330    941 1431 2550 2947
3 CARDAVE  18   £-   00    570 951 1204
3 CARE IN THE AIR   0   £-   00030-000    564 837 1549
5 CAREEN  22   £690   40030-22440    8 129 1079 1274 1519
4 CAREER BAY  18   £-   00300-00    2467 3028
3 CAREER MADNESS   0   £-   -00000000    1691 1836 1947 2099 2854 2998 3149 3220
3 CARELESS WHISPER  38   £2063   010-302U000    168 228 2204- 2446 2537 2674 2765
3 CARHUE LADY  65   £5586   22142-204    269 754 1110
4 CARILLON  43   £-   01200-00    2623 2766
2 CARINGMORE   0   £-   0    20
2 CARJUJEN  16   £-   000    503 1504 1625
4 CARLOPS  11   £-   -0004-000    522 651 960
2 CARLS PRIDE  10   £-   00000    1333 1634 2007 2756 2994
2 CARLTON GLORY   0   £-   F0    2185 2658
3 CARNATION  72   £3019   /0414-3040    288 755 904 1116
6 CARNEADES  20   £1587   1000-1300    44* 69 137 366
3 CARNET SOLAIRE  61   £1564   -04    288 1713
3 CARNIVAL ROSE  18   £-   0300-0000    436 615 961 1164
2 CAROLS HEIGHTS   0   £-   00    3048 3153
3 CAROLS LUCK  72   £6250   -1-0200    269 294 470 1331
5 CAROLS MUSIC  14   £-   01020-00    1081 1374
2 CAROLS TREASURE  73   £38193   211103134    614 715* 953+ 1143* 1467 1876 2223* 2564 2695
3 CARORIVER  48   £-   -0-0    150
5 CAROS GIFT  52   £3233   30003-130    52* 243 363
3 CAROTENE  81   £63725   -23    3098 3214
4 CAROUSEL NOUGAT   0   £-   00-00-000    2104 2335 2585
3 CAROUSEL ROCKET  33   £5448   3-3104210340420    100 130* 416 491 823 968* 1124 1661 1745 2627
2974 3161 3225
8 CARPENTERS BOY  13   £-   20000-0000040    742 1101 1638 1718 1765 1973 2322
2 CARPET CAPERS  38   £-   000    2782 3018 3201
3 CARR WOOD  12   £950   -00010    1184 1288 1562 2335* 2549
3 CARRIBEAN SOUND  32   £6186   000-24310042000    368 518 575 713* 925 1487 1821 2038 2250 2459
2719
3 CARRIBEAN TYME  45   £-   220-0000    1 49
2 CARSE KELLY   7   £618   0220000400    627 819 1050 1205 1681 2105 2310 2817 3016 3085
3 CARVERY  17   £1429   40-0233D400    1278 1657 1820 2217 2395 2807 3197
2 CAS EN BAS  44   £153   043    2487 2710 2901
3 CASA ROSADA   0   £-   0-000    1586 2186 2929
3 CASBAH GIRL  40   £9558   0002-011010    886 1257* 1398+ 1571 2842+ 3055
5 CASBAR KID   0   £-   00040-00    201 343
5 CASCABEL  34   £386   00012-04300    521 1240 1460 1581 2601
3 CASCADING   0   £-   -0000    1815 2186 2622 2793
3 CASH TO BURN   0   £-   -0    2306
10 CASHED IN   0   £-   -0    185
2 CASHEL VIEW  23   £247   030    548 665 2029
3 CASHEW KING  24   £2578   0010-0044021)0    411 857 1103 1685 1951 2102 2360* 2578 2727
2 CASHMERE N CAVIAR  47   £547   3    2036
5 CASSANDRAS DREAM  16   £-   -00000000    1102 1417 1620 1841 2264 2602 3104 3147
2 CASSE COU  37   £500   3    1708
4 CASSIS  72   £13659   41-23404    896 1328 2197 2824 3170
4 CASTIGLIONE   3   £-   -32-000004    199 449 582 731 942 1579
2 CASTILLITO   0   £-   000    2812 3079 3192
2 CASTLE CORNET  22   £406   000440030    187 350 1129 1993 2177 2435 2625 2813 2936
2 CASTLE CREEK  57   £1423   3    3108
2 CASTLE HEIGHTS  34   £599   03030    1197 1572 1735 2071 2209
2 CASTLE IN THE AIR  51   £855   302    2418 2675 3135
                              > 959 <
```

```
2 CASTLE MELODY  0   £-   0   2487
4 CASTLE POOL  20   £481   -04002   519 743 943 1349 1577
3 CASTLE ROCK  43   £925   0-020   2148 2441 2923
2 CASTLE TRYST  0   £-   000   1936 2782 3136
2 CASTLE WARD  44   £1399   32   2811 2961
3 CASUAL PASS  9   £-   -00   2799 3236
2 CATALONDA  52   £-   4   1591
3 CATCH A LIGHT  4   £-   -0   3147
5 CATCH THE THATCH  0   £-   -00   2109 2432
3 CATECHISM  14   £-   -0   87
2 CATHEDRAL PEAK  58   £1382   3   2951
3 CATHERINE MARY  62   £5300   -32   148 2450
2 CATHERINE SCHRATT  48   £-   00   1855 2147
3 CATHERINES WELL  65   £24380   11-030331111040   588 1027 1151 1524 1704 2084+ 2151+ 2242* 2362+
2668 2947 3127
5 CATMAN  9   £-   00-00-00000040   748 943 1243 1519 2123 2319 2490 2836
4 CATS LULLABY  0   £-   00020-000000   401 508 679 992 1211 1319
2 CAUSEWAY FOOT  15   £296   0000042030   602 694 948 1599 1955 2150 2212 2323 2608 2743
3 CAVALEUSE  37   £320   0-00020   1031 1941 2068 2546 3105
8 CAVALIER SERVENTE  0   £-   -000   2087 2326 2492
4 CAVALIERAVANTGARDE  13   £708   -0000-1000   22* 184 609 3128
2 CAVENDISH QUEEN  30   £-   00   2846 2926
5 CAWARRA BELLE  1   £-   4--00-00   126 485
2 CAWKELL TROOPER  0   £-   000   446 589 1137
2 CAWSTONS COMEDIAN  3   £106   0340   27 1318 1692 2927
2 CAWSTONS PREJUDICE  0   £-   00   2323 2472
5 CBM GIRL  16   £642   10000-320000   594 727 789 970 3078 3116
2 CECINA  58   £7080   22024   2739 3167
2 CEDAR CREEK  0   £-   0F0   2961 3099 3221
2 CEDRICO  66   £-   21100   2552 2907
2 CEE EN CEE  0   £-   00000   664 804 1019 1518 1643
2 CELCIUS  26   £-   00   1780 3075
4 CELEBRITY  59   £-   -2421-00   221 879
3 CELESTIAL DRIVE  22   £1266   23000-2001400   454 837 1001 1827* 2318 2702 2905
3 CELESTIAL STORM  91   £94320   0-132122   1469* 1912 2062 2257* 2565 3051-
2 CELLO SOLO  0   £-   00   848 1238
8 CELTIC BELL  0   £-   -0   1994
6 CELTIC BIRD  33   £6366   000-00023113000   742 784 877 1101- 1196 1638+ 1896+ 2362 2469 2858
2921
3 CELTIC BOW  0   £-   -0   1246
3 CELTIC DOVE  20   £-   -404000   169 209 338 506 730 949
3 CELTIC HEIR  74   £-   02010-000   60 249 920
4 CELTIC IMAGE  0   £-   00042-0040   967 1079 1459 1845
5 CELTIC QUEST  0   £-   -00-0000   8 381 541 912
6 CELTIC STORY  0   £-   0-0   1833
3 CELTIC SWORD  0   £-   -00   535 1062
4 CELTONA PEACH  0   £-   -0-0   844
2 CENTAURI  61   £6079   12244   1936+ 2179 2435 2907 3107
3 CENTRALSPIRES BEST  9   £279   0440-0000200000   540 637 966 1066 1401 1671 1951 2132 2360 2497
3 CENTREPOINT  44   £1324   001-443044   244 411 1768 2934 3042 3236
3 CEROC  18   £177   000-40003   74 141 335 637 1396
3 CERTAIN AWARD  31   £1594   014320   861 1425* 1864 2038 2602 2832
3 CHABLISSE  18   £2473   0-0P40310441323   64 424 700 857 1136 1369* 1773 2102 2360 2412* 2603
2778 3100
2 CHACONIA GIRL  18   £-   0   2070
3 CHAGUNOLA  0   £-   00000-0   346
4 CHAISE LONGUE  14   £-   00000-400   91 174 399
6 CHALET WALDEGG  0   £-   0/000-00   343 761
3 CHALFONT MO  29   £-   03000-00   37 1200
3 CHALICE OF SILVER  39   £1615   30-432323   315 978 1251 1535 2306 2974
3 CHALK STREAM  57   £2432   21124-20000   708 1110 1851 2145 2385
2 CHAMBER MASTER  46   £823   010   536 633* 927
2 CHAMONIS  0   £-   0   3176
2 CHAMPION JOKER  0   £-   00   2011 2325
4 CHANCE INA MILLION  52   £-   10000-0   706
3 CHANCE REMARK  26   £-   0-4040   247 1880 2706 2857
4 CHANGANOOR  16   £-   40432-000   208 282 860
2 CHANTILLY DAWN  17   £1769   00012000   813 905 1279 1635* 1795 2050 2396 3112
2 CHANTILLY LACE  26   £1008   1000   819* 1975 2498 2798
2 CHANTRY BOY  0   £-   0   2645
5 CHAPEL COTTAGE  80   £1564   00020-3   287
6 CHAPLINS CLUB  48   £5208   000000204300220   12 76 165 742 1026 1157 1222- 1385 1810 2469 2537
2668 3106 3127 3233
3 CHARCOAL  16   £-   00-0000   334 498 1316 1687
3 CHARDONNAY  13   £554   0-3000000400   431 658 764 966 1316 1835 2275 2394 2616 2697
4 CHARGE ALONG  55   £1841   34400-0400400   708 945 1514 1851 2241 2785 3177
3 CHARIOTS OF FIRE  0   £-   -0   2902
4 CHARISMA MUSIC  0   £-   03002-0000000   28 177 495 620 1186 1310 1574
2 CHARITY DAY  0   £-   U   2263
2 CHARLIE DICKINS  24   £-   000   1903 3011 3198
2 CHARLIE ME DARLING  25   £-   000   2119 3133 3223
2 CHARLIE MILORD  29   £-   04   2522 3059
11 CHARLOTTES CHOICE  0   £-   -0   1035
2 CHARLOUS CHOICE  0   £-   0000   2320 2791 2961 3153
3 CHARLTON KINGS  21   £390   030-04000034000   553 716 946 1130 1468 1685 2149 2230 2399 2497 2603
3 CHARMED PRINCE  35   £-   0400   1082 1241 1915 2118
2 CHARMING GRACIE  0   £-   0000   2167 2499 2698 2878
4 CHARMING VIEW  6   £1702   0400-0102000030   310 673* 1013 1139 1565 1870 2104 2340 3154 3224
3 CHART CLIMBER  23   £170   0-03000   732 1516 1953 2314 3164
4 CHART FINDER  0   £-   -0   3227
6 CHARTFIELD  2   £446   300033   121 204 582 841 1243 1694
3 CHARTINO  70   £11185   11112-003234   802 1912 2266 2449 3007 3216
2 CHASING MOONBEAMS  64   £10998   2214300   999 1238- 1453+ 1910 2158 2235 2954
```

```
3 CHATTERSPARK  24  £-  0030-00  1830 2049
2 CHAUDENNAY  55  £-  000  1914 2540 2768
5 CHAUMIERE  66  £34917  3-0000010330300  251 325 475 617 921 1526* 1712 2116 2354 2642 2845
  3001 3175
3 CHAUTAUQUA  24  £4165  0-42141240  51 377 670+ 760 910* 1283 1476 1687
3 CHAUVE SOURIS  69  £14723  0-020120  231 572 1098 1530* 2220 2523
2 CHAYOFA  14  £381  200000  515- 913 1105 2298 2757 3016
3 CHEAL  0  £-  00-0000  328 809 1472 1540
2 CHECKPOINT  42  £220  400  571 1129 1452
3 CHEERFUL TIMES  10  £763  000-02000000  535 716 843 1362 2807 2931 3070 3197
3 CHEETAK  0  £-  -000  95 219 1022
2 CHEFITALIA  0  £-  0  813
10 CHEKA  8  £3212  00000-201000  137 336 504* 712 1058 1183
3 CHEPSTOWED  07  £832  00000-12004  93* 279 335 845 2417
3 CHERCHEUR DOR  75  £22392  -310-4144  303 1214* 1597 3089
3 CHEREN HILL  0  £-  000-00  1472 2306
3 CHERNICHERVA  65  £2512  113-20  264 599
3 CHEROKEE  0  £-  -0  1954
2 CHEROKEE GOLD  0  £-  00  1311 1668
3 CHERRY GLORY  0  £-  00-00000000  458 1580 1749 2314 2532 2659 2929 3105
3 CHERRY LUSTRE  24  £403  -0003300  368 448 875 1303 1426 1799 2253
8 CHERRY PIT  0  £-  -0  1166
2 CHERRYWOOD SAM  12  £916  404013000  27 61 840 1082 1318* 1557 2047 2284 2712
2 CHERRYWOOD STAR  22  £-  0  345
2 CHESHAM SQUIRE  65  £12649  02  2711 3107
2 CHESTER TERRACE  38  £1930  000031  800 1629 1914 2663 2798 3165+
2 CHESWOLD  31  £936  4003030  610 915 1203 1625 2276 2663 2756
2 CHEVELEY CHOICE  0  £-  00  852 1194
3 CHEVET LADY  14  £3448  0-1242000040040  54* 132 331 461 648 883 1089 2128 2604 2727 3101 3154
  3197
2 CHEVREFEUILLE  51  £732  32  2710 3099
2 CHEVSKA  37  £128  30  353 536
2 CHIC ANTIQUE  27  £168  03  1683 2334
5 CHICAGO BID  27  £2975  00023-020010  374 700 855 1165 1324* 1727
4 CHICLET  46  £1911  12130-02040403  265 432- 698 1038 1526 1929 2121 2958
2 CHICO VALDEZ  34  £-  000  2067 2723 3234
7 CHIEF BLACKFOOT  0  £-  000-0-00  1833 1951
6 CHIEF JESTER  0  £-  -4-0  3155
3 CHIEF PAL  50  £6073  4-212340203  677- 941* 1080 1486 1655 1924 2612 2867 3070
4 CHIEF RUNNER  0  £-  -0000  2187 2271 2429 2981
4 CHILDRENS CORNER  56  £-  4221400  3207
2 CHILIBANG  56  £12698  41011211  1495 1816+ 2272 2421+ 2689* 2843- 2993* 3156+
2 CHIME TIME  72  £25305  11211343  741* 915* 1129 1506* 1697+ 2221 2552 2949
7 CHINA GOLD  33  £4756  030042020001000  550 784 877 1101 1268 1380 1649 1849 1896 2469 2537
  2586* 2858 2921 2966
3 CHINOISERIE  75  £33684  022-02112211  216 868 989* 1208* 1444 1554- 1912+ 2808*
4 CHIVWAIN  0  £-  0-00-0  1056
3 CHLOROPHYLL  7  £-  -0  1141
2 CHOCO  31  £-  00  61 186
2 CHOICE MATCH  0  £-  00040  627 696 821 1121 1297
2 CHOISUN  33  £1196  0010  2625 2829 2976+ 3230
3 CHORAL PARK  9  £-  0-0000000  546 937 1257 1398 1687 2106 2683
3 CHORISTERS DREAM  20  £-  01440-000000  339 507 1171 1272 1476 1827
2 CHORITZO  60  £4221  22211  2433 2596 2788 2895+ 2967*
3 CHRISTABELLE  0  £-  -0  560
4 CHRISTIAN SCHAD  49  £-  30040-000  17 265 349
8 CHRISTMAS COTTAGE  24  £-  -0000-000  2998 3060 3157
5 CHRISTMAS HOLLY  4  £1713  -000-31002000  23 105* 184 366 493 590 675 3087
4 CHRISTO  24  £818  -32300  19 185 199 360 526
3 CHUCKLESTONE  35  £1516  00-0000413400  806 1036 1315 1645 1833 2023* 2164 2311 2733 2955
2 CHUKATALK  0  £-  0  2577
3 CHUMMYS OWN  22  £3376  0-1020130  35* 416 908 951 1302* 1479 2034
3 CHUMMYS PET  55  £16977  -02133121124  217 255 377* 703 886 928* 1065 1312* 1457+ 1777 1900
2 CHUNKY SUPREME  0  £-  000  446 612 3032
2 CHURCH STAR  0  £-  0000  1528 2218 2364 2491
2 CHURCHILL LADY  0  £-  000  852 1067 1322
2 CI SIAMO  20  £-  000  1464 2847 3200
4 CIARAS LAD  5  £-  01000-00  1579 1784
3 CIGAR  30  £-  00-0000000  619 739 1469 1899 2173 2720 2848
8 CIMA  40  £670  304  235 312 634
2 CINDERELLA DEREK  19  £-  04  1282 3056
4 CINDIE GIRL  13  £-  01300-000  1243 1667 1939
4 CINDYS GOLD  0  £-  20000-000  540 1013 1482
2 CIREN JESTER  16  £259  002400  1570 1825 2095 2888 3017 3182
2 CITY FINAL  24  £414  40403000  473 612 1105 1253 1534 2379 3165 3230
3 CITY FORTRESS  73  £1840  4  2357
2 CITY IN FLIGHT  58  £4820  1  3181*
2 CLAIRES BUCK  0  £-  00  2070 3133
5 CLANTIME  58  £22645  0-0223412203300  165 272 408- 550 660 877* 1268- 1508- 1889 2065 2289
  2641 3054
3 CLAP YOUR HANDS  0  £-  0000-000  1784 1937 2174
5 CLARANCES HOPE  0  £-  -0  344
2 CLARENTIA  63  £16400  21403200213  180 400* 533 1641 1910 2047 2172 2284 2694 2843+ 2954
3 CLASS ACTION  23  £-  0-40  1516 1607
3 CLASS HOPPER  0  £-  20000-000000040  1917 2126 2174 2361 2585 2688 2884 3144 3185
4 CLASSIC CAPISTRANO  30  £118  -03  71 177
3 CLASSIC STYLE  66  £650  0-4  394
2 CLASSIC TALE  75  £8639  210  1488- 1780* 2199
3 CLASSY SCOUSE  0  £-  -000000  305 426 524 1142 1734 1824
3 CLAWSON THORNS  4  £-  0000-00000000  78 1142 1269 1425 1983 2980 3104 3157
2 CLEAR HER STAGE  51  £1263  310  1440 1802* 2252
2 CLEARWAY  11  £1111  0120440  170 502* 1163 1279 1832 2020 2580
3 CLEAVAGE  0  £-  -0000  1246 1953 2092 2787
                              >  961  <
```

```
3 CLEOFE  42   £9909   4-0033340010310   656 907 1228 1375 1487 1626 1902 2245 2367+ 2488 2650 2832*
2905
3 CLEONAIR  0   £-   0-00   1690 1831
3 CLEVELAND BOND  7   £-   -00000   1317 1472 1670 2309 2528
6 CLEVER ANGLE  0   £-   -0   177
2 CLIFFORD STREET  0   £-   0   3120
4 CLIPSALL  10   £-   14201-00000   547 727 992 1787 1901
3 CLIVEDEN  76   £23834   213-00310   224 384 920 1107* 2538
2 CLOPTON  46   £391   0033   2484 2645 3080 3198
4 CLOTILDA  3   £-   00000-0000   1017 1547 1800 2104
3 CLOUD CHASER  16   £-   000-40000   1317 1645 1833 2170 2576
4 CLOUD DANCER  3   £-   4-000-0   591
3 CLOUDLESS SKY  15   £1054   3400-0304021   857 1288 1701 2103 2361 2585 2887*
2 CLOUDY LIGHT  22   £-   00   2328 3223
4 CLOVEN DANCER  26   £844   4   2349
3 CLOVIO  75   £8963   -1-24   289 562
2 CLOWN STREAKER  32   £5297   210104200   47 364+ 515 1570* 1893 1962 2137- 2922 3125
5 CLUEDO  0   £-   10000-004000   131 419 889 1071 1195 1719
5 CLUGA GURM  0   £-   -000   8 176 751
2 COAST BOY  0   £-   00   715 913
4 COASTAL PLAIN  15   £-   4--00-000   582 1237 3195
3 COCCOLUTO  46   £1683   00-022200   402 863- 1539 1797 2327 2572
2 COCK SPARROW  0   £-   00   2159 2878
4 COCKALORUM  0   £-   -0   70
2 COCKATOO ISLAND  39   £-   00   3111 3181
4 COCKED HAT SUPREME  18   £1445   03040-442220   1092 1226 1477 1737 2152 2683
3 COCKNEY LASS  76   £10941   120-1111   2911*
3 COCOTTE  70   £13082   224-00142300   372 708 1580* 1932 2196 2462 2825 3121
4 CODED LOVE  0   £-   -0000   7 906 1101 3012
2 CODED MESSAGE  26   £119   03   3081 3190
3 CODICES  48   £4251   42340-001012000   217 1145 1607* 1934 2099* 2369 2463 2810 2945
11 COFFEE HOUSE  0   £-   00000-00   88 126
3 COINAGE  56   £6391   3-23101104   484 720 1102* 1314 1623* 1894* 2201 2834
4 COINCIDENTAL  45   £1219   00001-02300   1109 1804- 2072 2144 3124
2 COLD LASER  0   £-   000   21 612 1105
4 COLD LINE  34   £-   210-000   585 778 964
2 COLDWATER CANYON  38   £-   000   2147 2531 3109
3 COLE BAY  0   £-   -000   1142 1399 2077
3 COLEMAN HAWKINS  19   £358   -000403400   316 486 832 1258 2109 2386 2722 2974 3128
2 COLLEGE BOY  42   £-   0   149
2 COLLEGE WIZARD  21   £922   4214000   1323 1557 1692* 2298 2425 2625 2829
5 COLLISTO  16   £2807   10-00022202030   121 235 485 542 1757 1884 2075 2169 2346 2974 3139 3227
3 COLLYWESTON  27   £3544   -001211   656 2186 2394* 2427 2603* 2818*
2 COLNEY HEATH LAD  0   £-   00   1561 2105
3 COLONEL HALL  1   £170   000-00000030   67 237 451 491 673 1156 1267 1699
4 COLONEL JAMES  38   £1808   02200-140   199* 474 879
4 COLONEL POPSKI  0   £-   00-0   2495
3 COLONIAL KING  14   £-   0400-00000   650 874 2149 2508 2746
2 COLOR ARTIST  58   £2370   013000   1464 1801* 2057 2751 3040 3108
3 COLORSPIN  88   £114604   11-34140   551 926 1592* 2202 2506
3 COLOURFIELD  16   £-   00-40   1396 2128
3 COLWAY COMET  49   £-   21203-0000   228 387 1028 1532
3 COLWAY RADIAL  7   £-   00-044000   82 626 784 961 1200 1627
2 COLWAY RALLY  48   £5641   203240031   437 583 1798 1984 2198 2479 2680 2777 3103*
3 COMANCHERO  50   £522   3-33   916 1178
3 COMAZANT  18   £259   -00020   1469 1645 2464 2682 2892
2 COMBERMERE  20   £-   0000   685 870 1373 2535
3 COMBINED EXERCISE  36   £580   00043004   662 1458 1665 2044 2383 2677 3122 3205
2 COME ON CHASE ME  61   £5279   31130   602 780* 2162+ 2447 2564
2 COME ON OYSTON  34   £257   43300   1296 1770 1972 2423 2584
7 COME ON THE BLUES  52   £5968   0000-0000410030   441 706 1109 1389 1729 1890* 2234 2475 2749
3021
3 COME POUR THE WINE  18   £772   00-00010   194 379 783 3150* 3217
3 COME TO THE BALL  27   £1223   00000-0304100   1806 2017 2184 2659 2793* 2906 3065
3 COMEDY PRINCE  24   £820   000-0010   276 522 564* 1210
2 COMEDY SAIL  0   £-   000   457 577 3099
3 COMELY DANCER  46   £4696   4-3114340   452 631* 958* 1130 1663 1865 2551
5 COMHAMPTON  16   £833   02022-3200   940 1271 1569 2111
3 COMICAL LAD  0   £-   0-00   51 113
3 COMMANCHE BELLE  38   £841   2320   2048 2304 2726 3105
3 COMMANDER MEADEN  3   £106   000-03040000   339 726 929 986 1438 2592 2659 3172
4 COMMANDER ROBERT  40   £3138   04200-4011240   629 698 827* 1071* 1092 1988 2220
4 COMME LETOILE  74   £32615   121-31031   273 461* 1117 1484 2908*
4 COMMITMENT  12   £-   00000-00   2085 2413
3 COMMON ACCORD  22   £2989   000-000001   66 191 275 928 1281 1835*
3 COMMON FARM  18   £3100   000000100000000202   63 196 611 789 946 1017 1122* 1295 1374 1507
1678 1909 2173 2267 2415 2995 3087 3197
2 COMMONSIDR GIPSY  32   £1331   0200030200   523 685 1149 2108 2276 2444 2806 2997 3125 3229
2 COMMONTY  0   £-   -0   235
3 COMPLEAT  50   £1807   02331-0003200   314 580 1151 1391 1933 2343 2668
8 COMPOSER  9   £256   00-000002400040   163 378 1054 1274 1412 1546 1619 1990 2309 2836 2964 3220
3 COMPRIDA  72   £12429   130   1489* 2117 2454
4 COMRADE IN ARMS  81   £42636   0-21202330   901* 1356 2003 2347 2742 2916
7 CONCERT PITCH  25   £3605   44200-004100001   1447 1651 2123 2319+ 2431 2581 2715 3065*
3 CONCORDES DEMON  20   £283   -2000   2314 2442 3105 3186
3 CONDOVER SILK  0   £-   -000   1691 1937 2187
3 CONERSER  13   £-   00000-400   107 279 524
2 CONMAICHE  65   £17912   211   2914*
5 CONMAYJO  33   £6313   1020-0330100000   17 166 361 445 668* 1109 2123 2477 3123 3231
3 CONNAUGHT BROADS  0   £-   20000-000   828 1369 1815
2 CONNAUGHT FLYER  31   £1409   1000   544* 870 2198 2439
5 CONNAUGHT PRINCE  0   £-   0   2528
6 CONNAUGHT QUEEN  0   £-   -0   2996
> 962 <
```

```
2 CONNAUGHT ROSE  49   £1000   40   2739 2915
2 CONNAUGHTS JOY  0   £-   0   3199
2 CONNEMARA DAWN  23   £-   40000   1405 2019 2140 2498 2700
2 CONNUE  51   £447   3   1604
3 CONQUERING HERO  81   £18758   3113-11030   1000+ 1230+ 1597 2064 2222
6 CONTESTER  0   £-   -00000   360 462 2809 3052 3225
4 CONVINCED  62   £17744   1100-323103310   403 683 805 1112* 2237 2486 2769 2855+ 3038
2 CONVINCING  19   £-   000   2159 2571 3132
9 COOL DECISION  16   £-   --432-00   11 2944
5 COOL ENOUGH  1   £-   00000-400000000   12 65 306 520 649 1868 2295 2602 2977
3 COOL GALES  25   £259   33003-002004   732 1327 1690 2161 2516 3159
3 COOL MUSIC  35   £-   000-00   861 1184
3 COOL NUMBER  15   £1967   000-003312   843 1806 2187 2515 2679* 2965
3 COOL OPERATOR  34   £-   000-04040   39 183 451 487 857
2 COOL TEMPO  0   £-   0   3181
6 COOMBE SPIRIT  0   £-   -0   1837
3 COOPER RACING NAIL  22   £5070   2-3220023011140   39 237 276 464 666 932 1134 1334 1771* 1917*
2268* 2424 2854
4 COPLACE  0   £-   -04000   830 971 1120 1424 1908
3 COPLEYS WALK  29   £-   00-00   868 969
2 COPPER CREEK  44   £241   0034   1440 1604 1966 2529
2 COPPER RED  52   £6260   3231220   800 1039 1143 1728+ 2162 2482- 2804
3 COPPERMILL LAD  37   £5041   000-12000004001   38* 111 586 808 1235 1312 1669 1878 2143 2382 2573+
4 COPSE AND ROBBERS  35   £-   2431-0   3139
2 CORAL HALL  26   £-   40   2707 3192
4 CORAL HARBOUR  12   £119   40300-3000   8 984 1652 2188
2 CORBADGE  22   £-   0   3141
2 CORLEON  0   £-   000   2646 2707 2829
3 CORN NOIL  0   £-   -000   2406 3077 3183
8 CORN STREET  31   £5518   D4-010400000000   71 172+ 248 361 508 687 1145 1777 2390 2526 2674 3124
5 CORNCHARM  28   £1293   0-0203400000020   18 135 266 508 846 1263 2602 2715 2981 3055 3138 3191
3235
3 CORNELIAN  40   £3451   -030414   1645 2068 2304 2548 3187* 3217
3 CORNISH CASTLE  0   £-   -0   720
3 CORNISH PIXIE  0   £-   -P   506
3 CORNISH PRINCE  0   £-   -00000   90 430 613 2078 2305
2 COROFIN LASS  15   £1120   000004100   544 722 2080 2218 2396 2712 2801* 2872 3112
3 CORRALS JOY  20   £684   03200-100000   205* 431 2488 2614 2992 3180
3 CORRAN RIVER  40   £850   3402-1400   935* 1315 2420 2569
2 CORRIENDO LIBRE  49   £665   20   268 638
4 CORSTON SPRINGS  9   £-   00202-000   137 375 1582
2 CORVALENT  40   £-   0   2710
2 CORVIGLIA RUN  46   £275   400   2543 2675 2926
3 COSMIC FLIGHT  15   £2449   0-1033400000002   67* 193 356 480 659 762 1122 1540 1806 2807 2896
3128 3224
5 COSTOCK BUNNY  0   £-   00/00-0   2397
3 COUNT ALMAVIVA  15   £891   0-0002003000024   111 340 424 774 997 1063 1364 1567 1781 1990 2271
2429 2495
5 COUNT BERTRAND  12   £3139   0302-0000210000   36 281 420 689 1202- 1673* 2091 2189 2617 2755
4 COUNT COLOURS  31   £413   20204-002400   9 968 1417 1871 1963 2338
2 COUNT TREVISIO  45   £2421   1040   523* 781 1568 2025
2 COUNTER ATTACK  46   £2917   100   1872* 2383 2830
3 COUNTERMINE  39   £-   03-00   316 916
2 COUNTESS BREE  18   £301   00300002   621 1232 1363 1846 2310 2700 2829 2990
2 COUNTESS CARLOTTI  2   £349   00-0240003   1063 1134 1439 1699 2014 2495 2590
3 COUNTLESS COUNTESS  27   £1416   -201000   32 173 307* 949 1326 1582
3 COUNTRY CARNIVAL  11   £989   200-00300000001   183 451 907 1051 1257 1541 1701 2339 2603 2863
2972*
3 COUNTRY CRAFT  0   £-   00-0000   33 424 658 837
3 COUNTRY GENTLEMAN  48   £5478   040-00043011   328 1032 1245 1590 1835 2076 2274* 2497+
4 COUNTRY JIMMY  4   £-   00-400000   381 675 869 1102 1280 1769
2 COUP DE FOUDRE  29   £-   00   3023 3143
4 COURAGEOUS CHARGER  23   £-   30000-0   176
4 COURT APPEAL  0   £-   0-0-0   2704
2 COURT COMMAND  23   £-   0000   457 678 1082 3176
4 COURT JEWEL  0   £-   00000-00   28 963
3 COURT RULER  9   £-   0000-0000400   527 868 997 1424 1562 1671 1960
3 COURT TOWN  18   £733   04-00402000   1586 2027 2294 2459 2601 3029 3062 3160
2 COURTWOOD  0   £-   0   2846
3 COUTURE COLOR  28   £-   00400-000   247 328 528
3 COVA KESTREL  0   £-   -0   754
3 COVER INN  0   £-   00-000   528 874 2399
3 COWLAM BOY  0   £-   0000   612 780 1843 3153
3 COX GREEN  61   £8405   -142421   714+ 1642 1879 2058 2558 2786*
3 CRACON GIRL  0   £-   000C 00000000   480 966 1272 1447 2120 2417 2702 2854
6 CRADLE OF JAZZ  19   £-   32000-00   9 88
4 CRAGSIDE  76   £-   -0302-00   165 222
3 CRAIGENDARROCH  13   £3043   4001000000   1174 1561 1612 2050* 2276 2663 2724 2888 2971 3222
4 CRAIGS VENTURE  0   £-   00000-00   2978 3155
3 CRAMMING  38   £6371   000-123023010   318* 637 730 919 1179 1685 1939 2578* 2807
2 CRANCHETER  36   £375   004   1510 2067 2472
5 CRAVEN BOY  0   £-   -000   91 418 530
2 CREAM AND GREEN  20   £914   00020240   415 536 913 1379 1816 2310 2465 2711
7 CREE BAY  50   £16147   332004110000030   327 428 550 836 1037 1196 1385* 1777* 2204 2402 2446 2731
2953 3118 3138
4 CREEAGER  25   £5417   0040-0143000000   240 441* 573 815 1041 2390 2526 2730 2945 3078
2 CREES FIGURINE  33   £2794   310   415 882* 1108
3 CREETOWN SALLY  7   £98   00-03000   195 729 871 1344 1549
2 CREOLE BAY  8   £148   0000030040   40 367 1955 2050 2138 2724 2801 2976 3148 3222
2 CRESPIN  0   £-   000   2407 2571 3011
2 CREST OF GLORY  0   £-   0   3131
3 CRESTA AUCTION  73   £17212   0413-11230431   68* 210+ 344 676 1788 2165 2481 3177+
3 CRESTA LEAP  15   £1232   40-302400004000   205 339 431 657 929 2046 2210 2382 2416 2614 3172
3191
```

```
2 CRESTED 33  £-  4  2379
3 CRETE CARGO 40  £1924  -00000024200000  15 70 172 314 401 624 836- 994 1060 2242 2378 2731
2842 3138
2 CRETISE 7  £-  0  1421
11 CRI DE GRACE 0  £-  -0000  9 2338 2562 2627
4 CRICCEITH 27  £95  00-340  448 631 1074
3 CRICKET BALL 77  £24638  -33040410  156 291 644 1011 2003 2347* 2916
3 CRICKET HOUSE 0  £-  -00  487 2413
4 CRIMBOURNE 27  £-  02000-0  481
3 CRIMSON ROBES 18  £-  -04004  209 379 779 935 1250
8 CRISP AND KEEN 00  £-  -0000-00  1535 1787
2 CRISP HEART 36  £-  00  988 2651
3 CRISP METCALFE 0  £-  000-0000  309 516 666 1053
2 CROFT ORIGINAL 0  £-  0  818
3 CROFTERS CLINE 68  £22053  01111010  536 612* 870* 1174+ 1925* 2221 2447+ 2866
2 CROFTITO 65  £7345  2  2501
3 CROMWELL PARK 65  £4526  1-40041  190 1107 1286 1823 2262*
3 CRONKS QUALITY 40  £724  14000-000030300  76 233 443 884 1443 2258 2573 2842 3065
4 CROOK N HONEST 0  £-  )0040-00440000  208 341 542 841 1058 1260 1952 2111
2 CROSS BENCHER 0  £-  0  3037
2 CROSS KRISS 0  £-  0  3134
5 CROWFOOTS COUTURE 0  £206  00000-042000000  42 131 257 429 609 630 872 993 1271
3 CROWLEY 48  £5275  -0021331  1368 1580 2068 2299* 2569 2937 3030*
2 CROWN AND HORNS 0  £-  0  3109
3 CROWN COLONY 0  £-  000-00U  447 608 958
7 CROWN COUNSEL 12  £-  00300-0  112
4 CROWN ESTATE 24  £-  30220-00  9 310
2 CROWN JUSTICE 28  £2012  0123  1488 2396* 3058 3222
3 CROWN MINE 0  £-  -000  140 506 635
2 CROWN RIDGE 0  £-  0  2626
3 CROWNIT 1  £-  --000-000000  451 650 1885 2086 2973 3086
2 CRUSADE DANCER 49  £371  0200  2056 2229 2418 2677
2 CRY FOR THE CLOWN 56  £5623  111  1955* 2270+ 2435*
2 CRYPTIC 0  £-  0  3074
3 CRYSTAL DE ROCHE 75  £13993  -0302  302 644 900 2193
3 CRYSTAL GLASS 0  £-  0-00  371 579
2 CRYSTAL HAWK 32  £-  40  3011 3143
3 CRYSTAL MOSS 12  £-  -00000  250 1259 1481 3110 3227
3 CSILLAG 5  £-  00000-00000  480 1446 1989 2094 2271
2 CUBBY HOLE 31  £-  000  1464 2527 2901
3 CUCKOO IN THE NEST 16  £-  0000-00  1830 2148
4 CUDDLY 15  £-  0-400-0000  129 540 689 967
3 CUILLIN SOUND 38  £439  0-2000  607 978 2422 2665
2 CULINARY 0  £-  000  1561 1672 2801
3 CULLENS PET 0  £-  0-0  539
5 CULMINATE 0  £2674  -0031000  378 626 825 971+ 1131 1247 3152
3 CUMBRIAN DANCER 28  £3759  2-0430041200200  81 447 518 713 947 1051 1247+ 1338 1810 1959 2139-
2295 2411
3 CUMBRIAN NIJO 8  £-  01040-0000000  650 816 1091 1761 1864 2424 2688
6 CUMREW 11  £353  0--00-03  235 336
3 CUMUTE 45  £-  1110300  3000 3231
3 CUPIDS BOWER 0  £-  000-0400  1258 1786 2306 3161
3 CURIGA 29  £3686  000-041100  966 1671 1970* 2182* 2305 2709
2 CURRAGH DANCER 55  £-  0  2451
3 CURRENT WAVE 59  £1197  -2140-40  293 1593
3 CURVACEOUS 27  £606  -043303  581 862 1481 1939 2299 2610
2 CUSHINA 28  £-  0  2889
4 CUT A CAPER 5  £219  00002-02000  8 207 547 731 1201
2 CUTLER RIDGE 13  £-  0004  21 86 329 421
2 CUTTING BLADE 72  £26065  3110  685 962+ 1097* 1876
2 CUVEE CHARLIE 0  £-  0  2225
4 CYGNE 0  £128  00200-00034000  1264 1447 1609 1990 2282 2490 2836 2960
3 CYNOMIS 42  £4163  -30041  1639 2068 2299 2610 3105*
3 CYRANO DE BERGERAC 80  £7110  12111-200  1125- 1485 1631
3 DAARKOM 64  £15791  -2212320  625 875- 1290* 1538- 2220 2523 3022
3 DADS GUNNER 0  £-  000-000  331 718 889
3 DADS LINE 17  £-  02-00  593 910
2 DAFFODIL 24  £-  000  2894 3074 3148
2 DAHAB 41  £-  000  2080 3074 3181
3 DAHSALA 0  £-  -0  300
3 DAIS 0  £142  00-0003  1580 2300 2587 3045
3 DAISY STAR 2  £-  0000-000000  451 961 1257 1678 2409 2887
2 DALBY DANCER 0  £-  00  2499 3163
3 DALGADIYR 51  £6420  -3130022  316 625* 1130 1383 1526 1886 2247
3 DALLAS 81  £52934  -021131  218 527 764* 1147* 2559 2867*
5 DALLAS SMITH 4  £958  10000-000000410  91 975 992 1211 1374 1724 1845 1990* 2728
3 DALLONA 08  £210  00-00430  527 843 1204 1739 2709
2 DALLORS CONQUEST 15  £-  0000  2696 2782 2926 3174
2 DALROUMA 21  £-  0  2658
3 DALSAAN BAY 8  £-  00-040000000  31 111 175 496 1164 1947 2046 2416 2575
3 DALSAANITO 0  £-  -00  937 2129
3 DALVEEN PASS 0  £-  -0000  1954 2327 2603 2874
2 DAM INQUISITIVE 0  £-  0  1572
2 DAMART 26  £119  0030000  320 437 1812 1982 2584 3112 3188
3 DAMASCUS DEW 0  £-  -0  209
2 DAME CAROLINE 0  £-  00/00-0  1273
4 DAMISTER 82  £140069  13313-304320  221 468 641 2200 2735 3051
4 DAN MARINO 55  £1646  -11-04  462 1293
2 DANADN 29  £598  404033240040  278 544 627 781 1069 1421 1717- 1907 2482 2606 2975 3153
2 DANCE A JIG 0  £-  0  2531
2 DANCE UP 12  £-  400  1707 2334 2554
3 DANCER DO 6  £148  00-003  2216 2267 2780
2 DANCER TO FOLLOW 31  £-  000  1903 2239 2407
                              > 964 <
```

```
6 DANCING ADMIRAL  22   £-    04000-0   137
5 DANCING BARRON  14   £450   004-00003040403   349 532 750 851 1473 1559 1787 2190 2533 2807 2877
2 DANCING BELLE  38   £902   00001304   317 376 944 1253 1738+ 2100 2380 2606
3 DANCING BRAVE  101   £979971   11-11211114   226* 407* 878- 1389+ 1790+ 2557+ 2917* 3212
2 DANCING DIANA  44   £5581   214000133   417 531* 924 1552 1910 2090 2320* 2472 2753
3 DANCING EAGLE  48   £8257   01-3230023   386 556 899 1230 1486 1971 2262
3 DANCING FROG  0   £128   0-30   1842 2129
4 DANCING HABIT  0   £-   00-10-0   963
3 DANCING SARAH  23   £1394   2210-4000032000   443 580 671 1060 1447 1584 1750- 2120 2702 3145
3 DANCING TOM  24   £183   3101-4000004400   81 168 478 534 671 768 972 2139 2424 2660
3 DANCING ZETA  63   £3450   13013-20000   273 574 1098 1526 1793
2 DANDY  26   £-   0000   1442 2159 2541 3188
2 DANE DOLLY  0   £-   00   848 999
3 DANEAGLE GLORY  0   £-   -0   307
4 DANEDANCER  0   £196   30040-20000   22 343 399 845 1201
2 DANENSIAN  0   £-   000   2889 3099 3228
3 DANESMOOR  17   £-   -000000   776 1375 1511 1880 2508 2690
4 DANGERS HOUR  82   £59182   3   2735
3 DANISHGAR  70   £7775   22-041204   362 442 739* 1152 1853 2206
2 DANISHKADA  78   £57479   131   3005*
3 DANRIBO  0   £250   0-00002   486 733 1061 2135 2316
2 DANSE ARABE  0   £-   000000   1075 1598 2177 2889 3079 3192
3 DANSKI  55   £6398   22322-242   384 887 1046
2 DANUM DANCER  29   £-   0044040   571 685 973 1138 1978 2336 2756
2 DANUM LAD  8   £-   0000   1634 1984 2138 2976
3 DANZICA  69   £70491   1230   397* 642 2909 3093
2 DAPPING  0   £-   0   2852
3 DARARA  88   £89784   1121100   2196* 2638* 2917 3212
2 DARCYS THATCHER  73   £8130   1D2   2451 2821
3 DARE SAY  54?   £2148   -240   218 1045 1776
2 DARING DAMSEL  0   £-   0   2696
2 DARING DESCENT  39   £1076   00233   1510 2547 3014 3141 3234
3 DARING DOONE  66   £11629   -111   2248* 2653* 2940*
4 DARK CYGNET  0   £-   -000-0000   449 631 875 1092
3 DARK HERITAGE  34   £2666   00-004100   619 1130 1733 2381* 2516 2755
2 DARK MAJESTY  23   £-   0   3184
3 DARK PROMISE  56   £7575   21020-001323020   465 586 814* 947 1524- 1750 1900 2084 2242
4 DARK RAVEN  72   £-   0   641
2 DARK ROSAAN  20   £-   0   3025
3 DARK SIRONA  29   £4660   000-02210220   1022 1404 1706 2152* 2403 2745 2988 3110
2 DARK WINTER  0   £-   0   2814
2 DARLEY KNIGHT  68   £11470   12020   1049* 1242 1467 2460 2695
3 DARLING DADDY  6   £-   -04   1677 2413
4 DARNIT  43   £3455   43000-00021020   240 310 594 1176 1500* 1774 2126 2390
3 DARTIGNY  25   £-   01-0004000   514 747 1263 1648 2139 2370 2519
3 DASA QUEEN  34   £855   03223-02000   338 539 1472 1788 1953
3 DASHAKI GOLD  0   £-   00000-0000   729 1344 1836 2992
5 DASHING LIGHT  15   £1120   03202-404323343   432 591 709 1017 1321 1559 2098 2188 2516
5 DASSELLS  0   £-   -0   2517
5 DAUN  71   £24338   -1123-4034303   896 1712 2004 2354 2502 2824 3091
2 DAUNTING PROSPECT  17   £-   00000   1914 2159 2205 3081 3182
3 DAVALLIA  20   £-   3-00040   430 2734 2890 3045 3162
3 DAVEMMA  36   £334   0-40004030   128 372 509 926 1375 1788 2853 3105
4 DAVILL  28   £1429   12-000000300240   76 428 977 1268 1730 1900 1950 2256 2731 2966 3106 3233
3 DAWN COYOTE  48   £-   -0   151
3 DAWN LOCH  28   £-   0040   1469 2306 2464 2610
3 DAWN LOVE  29   £1692   0100-00014   671 1989 2171 2508* 2980
3 DAWN MIRAGE  0   £-   22000-0000   1971 2131 2429 2616
2 DAWN ROMP  30   £-   400   2287 2531 3135
2 DAWN SKY  0   £-   00   3153 3221
4 DAWN SPIRIT  0   £-   0000-0000   19 1871 2102 2374
8 DAWNS DELIGHT  53   £10534   00140-000100000   18 165 401 616+ 2537 2668 2956 3055 3127
2 DAYS LIKE THESE  49   £2068   41200   2301 2514* 2835 3027 3174
2 DAZY  58   £6821   230100   848 1108 1454 2368* 2540 2751
4 DE RIGUEUR  54   £19377   4324-1010100140   91+ 196 453* 578 680+ 930 1455 2773* 2956 3123
3 DEADBOLT  37   £-   11420-000   2562 2674 3021
8 DEADLY GOING  0   £-   -0   2030
3 DEAFENING  32   £154   0-00340   619 765 868 969 1556
5 DEALT  11   £-   -0000-000   775 1227 1901
2 DEAR DOLLY  0   £-   0000   376 905 1181 1635
2 DEAR GLENDA  22   £2672   200001   13 2270 2433 2580 3032 3081*
3 DEAR MARGIE  65   £-   0-110   373
3 DEARHAM BRIDGE  0   £-   000-04000   14 109 380 1160 1617
2 DEBACH DEITY  0   £-   000   197 746 1282
2 DEBACH DELIGHT  55   £873   0320   2185 2664 2901 3040
4 DEBACH REVENGE  8   £2439   -00004002010   452 613 960 1324 1727 1901 2033 2322- 2632 3083* 3152
3 DEBBIE DO  40   £2562   1322-4000004001   588 628 1027 2084 2204 2277 2670 2970 3083 3160*
3 DEBCO  36   £272   -023   1278 1556 1786
4 DEBRIS  18   £-   22014-0   889
2 DEBUTANTE BALL  0   £-   000   2651 3163 3229
2 DECCAN PRINCE  21   £-   00040   206 596 948 1083 1968
4 DECEMBRE  0   £-   0-000-00000   207 524 956 1336 3084
3 DECIDED  40   £864   -2   3142
4 DECOY BELLE  0   £-   000-00   1394 1567
4 DEEKAYS  22   £-   00430-0   185
2 DEEP RAPTURES  0   £-   004   852 2527 2899
2 DEEP TAW  17   £788   04301   337 502 939 1076 1449*
2 DEEP WATER BAY  40   £-   0   3176
4 DEERFIELD BEACH  0   £-   30021-000000000   129 202 530 838 2008 2173 2528 2789 2984
2 DEFTLY  0   £-   000   317 741 1253
2 DEGENERALE  28   £-   000   2229 2895 3134
2 DEINOPUS  8   £-   000   3 602 1944
2 DEJOTE  18   £-   0   3056
```

```
3 DEL BOY  15   £-    23200-00    1400 1827
4 DELAWARE RIVER  18   £814    04000-02400040    508 748- 1086 1213 1367 2370 2619 2715
2 DELICATE DESIGN  28   £-    -034-04    8 184
2 DELITE MUFFIN  5   £104    0030040    944 1253 1905 2050 2470 2724 2872
2 DELLA ROBBIA  0   £-    00    2577 2904
4 DELLWOOD RENOWN  0   £980    0-000-033003    399 709 860 1226 1884 2683
2 DELPHINIA  26   £-    044    2070 2185 2803
3 DELTA LIMA  10   £110    4200-00300    39 141 346 3162 3203
3 DELTA ROSE  4   £-    000-0000040000    340 624 886 1191 1560 1695 2184 2601 2931 3224
4 DELTA WIND  18   £-    00000-0    1202
2 DEMDERISE  56   £5323    113    242* 304+ 571
3 DEMISEMIQUAVER  0   £-    -0    498
3 DEMON FATE  28   £279    04-0000330    479 605 996 1304 1578 1688 1961
3 DENALTO  14   £2192    00-0033020220    744 959 1140 1700 1980 2280 2492 2760 2892 3161
3 DENBERDAR  20   £1296    0-2030040    48 411 1029 1304 1961 2363 3161
4 DENBOY  26   £6185    00400-0012010    262 532 731* 1035 1209 2330* 2467
7 DENEL  72   £24057    112000    153* 390 2453 3169
3 DENIECE  17   £116    -0003    1080 1639 2161 3162
2 DENSBEN  19   £725    0440342    1069 1421 1612 2410 2588 2993 3151
2 DEPUTY GOVERNOR  0   £-    -000    501 842 1036
2 DEPUTY GOVERNOR USA  77   £34480    31122    1780 2044* 2146* 2552- 2771
6 DEPUTY HEAD  38   £5997    00003133003002000    192 327 401 616 836 1060* 1263 1347 1608 1834
2160 2402 2537 2731 2764 2953 3106
3 DEPUTY MONARCH  22   £1077    040-02223    744 894 1072 1250 2759
3 DEPUTY TIM  31   £1570    0002-4000021    340 703 1065 1245 1521 2060 2174*
4 DERAMIN  26   £-    40030-00    333 410
5 DERBY DAY  14   £3647    00030-004203001    58A 618 750 856 1209 1321 1517 1788 2022*
2 DERRING DEE  47   £11529    0101001    404 533+ 927 1828* 2181 2485 2753+
3 DERRY  0   £-    -00    1337 1775
5 DERRY RIVER  39   £6086    22-000000104300    172 272 477 660 1730 1852 2160* 2402 2537 2764 2953
3106
4 DERRYRING  18   £805    0210-0000004020    92 349 432 1383 1590 1788 2121 2260 2578 2699
3 DERUTA  0   £-    0-00    351 1192
2 DERWENT VALLEY  24   £6934    1030    2218* 2563 2865 3125
3 DESAREM  11   £-    40000-00    451 517
4 DESCARTES  16   £571    0001/3300    80 144 629 3227
3 DESERT OF WIND  41   £1858    -02100    334 1055 1361+ 2053 2489
3 DESERTED  46   £1938    00-04210    699 1372 1799 2000* 2525
2 DESIGN WISE  16   £-    000040    1495 1728 2044 2561 2990 3198
7 DESTROY  0   £-    -04    1035 1243
5 DESTROYER  70   £459    41300-40    1779 2203
5 DETROIT SAM  38   £4646    00000-22104    179 341 569* 2809 2938
7 DEVIL TO PLAY  0   £-    -0    1183
3 DEVILS RUN  68   £1875    10010-3    151
2 DEVON LASS  0   £-    0    3199
5 DEW  2   £-    0/00-000    19 2111 2794
3 DHALEEM  46   £2709    -104    2085* 2458 3050
6 DHOFAR  35   £2565    -1000-1    179*
3 DHONI  43   £1356    0-40230    619 1022 1435 1879 2240
3 DIALECT  0   £-    -4000    1921 2327 2496 2948
2 DIAMOND FLIGHT  46   £4502    0144002    170 261* 456 804 1097 2677 2941
2 DIAMOND SEAL  56   £-    130    2910
2 DIANES BEST  0   £-    0    2846
6 DICK E BEAR  0   £-    -0    812
5 DICK KNIGHT  22   £2785    0000002000100203230    4 105 238 333 532 1056 1416 1559 1755 1952 2101*
2175 2395 2528 2727 2925 2964 3128 3187
3 DICKS BOY  0   £-    000-0000    545 809 1288 2014
7 DICKS FOLLY  16   £-    1224-0000    7 566 1689 1781
5 DIENAUS TROVE  18   £2496    -32140    959 1102 1226* 2861 3036
3 DIGGERS REST  73   £27728    303-130210    216* 605 1107 1911 2234* 2538
4 DIHISTAN  82   £89611    01112-11300103    653* 1144* 1593 1790 2200 2461+ 2917 3096
3 DIME AND A DOLLAR  0   £-    -0000    1437 1686 2030 2464
4 DIMENSION  9   £4514    00-014104000    8 399* 453 578* 709 812 1018 1211 2755
5 DINADAN  20   £121    00--0-03    940 1686
3 DIPPY  0   £-    0000-0    2992
4 DIPYN BACH  18   £1571    11000-044030200    166 782 912 1412 1509 1980 2337 2467 2955
3 DIRECTING  81   £12063    011340    1597 2195 2507
3 DIRECTLY  32   £94    -030    2691 3061 3142
3 DISCIPLE  41   £2388    -00004012    75 164 231 538 738 883 998* 1497
5 DISCOVER GOLD  11   £-    22223-00    1880 2549
4 DISPORT  5   £-    00000-0000    724 1018 1273 1945
2 DISTANT RULER  32   £-    0    3109
4 DISTING  0   £-    04000-00    845 1056
4 DIVA ENCORE  36   £5667    000-00011223030    623 738 978 1326* 1569+ 1694 1817 2015 2273 2873 3026
2 DIVINE CHARGER  25   £-    00040    230 876 1313 1458 1968
3 DIVINE DESTINY  49   £1920    0-410    1022 1304* 2201
3 DIVINE FLING  0   £-    0-0000    205 658 1191 2291
7 DIVINE TRUTH  0   £-    -00    121 179
4 DIVISSIMA  28   £1351    20031-0230    922 1196 1385 1649
4 DIVULGE  85   £169451    24    2456 2735
3 DIWAAN  34   £-    030-0040    486 833 1042 2430
3 DIX ETOILES  6   £1217    4-100034    305* 426 932 1201 1699 2041
6 DJANGO  28   £-    04-00-00    1438 1542
3 DO RUN DO  11   £-    0-400    2991 3077 3183
3 DOBEY THATCHER  65   £6770    22    295 472
2 DOCKIN HILL  18   £290    030300    304 864 965 1119 1528 1635
3 DOCKSIDER  52   £5187    -021201    1628 2085 2321* 2784 3042 3183*
3 DOGMATIC  50   £3980    2301-41000    178 478* 881 1189 2072
3 DOHTY BABY  16   £1599    030010000    818 1180 1253 1895 2323* 2625 2744 3027 3146
2 DOLITINO  0   £-    000    1764 2423 2814
3 DOLKA  68   £8353    1-1004    803* 1107 2385 2940
2 DOLLAR SEEKER  58   £9491    003211    2108 2225 2646 2761 2894+ 3120*
4 DOLLY  12   £438    0-004D003443000    112 344 481 762 950 1166 1349 1804 2132 2260 2490 2807
                                            > 966 <
```

```
3 DOM EDINO      0   £-      00-0     2931
3 DOM STAR      44   £-      -0       739
5 DOMINATE      32   £851    03002-00230    215 735 984 1348 1679
2 DOMINEERING    0   £-      00       3037 3156
5 DOMINION PRINCESS 16  £2296  2000-4433031200   310 606 745 960 1231 1558 1800* 2037 2182 2360
2 DOMINION ROYALE 74  £32077  413120   632 800+ 1126 1591+ 1876- 2113
2 DOMINO FIRE    43   £2441   1220403   985* 1275 1552- 1891 2577 2859 3072
2 DOMINO ROSE    28   £2465   23220230   236 473 826 1069 1501 1814 2172 2535
3 DON DIEGE       0   £-      10-10    2112
2 DON MARIO      70   £7176   -120     2636 3005
5 DON MARTINO    57   £-      3-000-00   1365 1911
4 DON ORAZIO     77   £10700   -1120-1   296*
4 DON PIPER       0   £-      02113-00   2572
4 DON RUNI       22   £2971   13000-0000210   23 50 137 308 731 860* 964
2 DONNA IMMOBILE  4   £-      00004    1832 2168 2471 2580 2927
2 DONNAS DARLING  0   £-      000      1083 2990 3141
3 DONNAS DREAM   62   £1436   40-310   173 338* 2765
2 DONNELLYS HOLLOW 0  £-      00       981 1449
4 DONOR          15   £264    -2000000   1602 1880 2030 2490 2622 2746 3071
6 DONT ANNOY ME   0   £-      -0000-000   827 1016 1133
2 DONT FORGET ME 78   £53554   4111    1242 1392* 1887* 2552+
2 DONT KNOCK IT   0   £-      000      2788 2926 3103
4 DONT RING ME   20   £1315   43100-0402304   675 1004 1633 1952 2326 2480 3128
3 DONT TELL VANESSA 6  £-     0000-0   718
2 DONT YER KNOW   0   £-      00       3136 3199
2 DOODLIN         0   £-      00       1225 3037
3 DOON VENTURE    5   £1209   03000-00003401   867 1089 1250 2478 2679 2778 2874 3045*
4 DOPPIO         13   £-      0-000-04   594 906
3 DORA FROST      0   £-      -0       3203
3 DORADE         12   £1518   00000-003010400   284 426 568 673 1824* 1917 2060 2238 2898
5 DORAME          3   £-      00000-004000   369 922 1066 1482 1727 2728
2 DORCET PLAN    10   £103    3        125
4 DORKING LAD    50   £3362   4210-0000000041   374 616 1026 1145 1306 1640 2947 3055 3124 3138*
2 DORMESTONE LAD 22   £1965   0041104   488 596 813 987+ 1163* 2472 2777
6 DORNEY          9   £-      20240-000000   508 679 734 890 1066 2370
3 DORS GEM       22   £1615   000-01100   67 139* 365* 648 949
4 DORSET COTTAGE 51   £8547   -021-032010000   17 344 573 1109 1525* 1793 2296 2566 3050
2 DORVER          0   £-      0        3120
3 DOUBLE BED     86   £112173   344D2120   302 900 2193* 2506 3051
4 DOUBLE BENZ    47   £3696   12200-0120   243 319* 695 917
3 DOUBLE CHAI    20   £-      04300-000040440   447 961 1398 1664 1701 1774 2086 2594 2977
2 DOUBLE GIFT     0   £-      0        3205
5 DOUBLE OPTION  19   £255    30-20-042   1056 1321 1459
5 DOUBLE SCHWARTZ 87  £126715   1D012-11212410   408+ 705* 1146- 1889+ 2233- 2474 2916* 3210
2 DOUBLE TALK    19   £277    042000   73 170 353 737 1261 1585
3 DOUBLE TANGO    0   £-      -00      1446 1580
3 DOUBLER         0   £-      -000     1288 1607 1831
2 DOUBLY GREAT    0   £-      00       1731 3075
2 DOWN AGAIN     68   £10842   1213D   2350* 2504
6 DOWN FLIGHT    34   £-      30000-400   85 121 235
4 DOWNSVIEW      33   £5526   0-0100004001000   748 855* 1213 1347 1608 1805 2046 2370 2519 2655* 3021 3138 3191
2 DOWNSVIEW LADY  0   £-      -0000    345 482 1187 1555
3 DOWNTOWN BROWN  0   £-      -00      576 2931
2 DOWSING        38   £-      00       3053 3228
2 DR BULASCO     64   £6234   213420   1357 1660* 2146 2199 2468- 2830
3 DRAGONARA BOY  18   £-      000-000   1901 2274 2681
3 DRAGONS BLOOD  48   £264    2        3198
2 DRAGUSA         0   £-      000      1801 2167 2596
2 DRAW LOTS      36   £142    3        2957
6 DREADNOUGHT    12   £-      004-00   1156 1223
3 DREAM CHASER   55   £4894   0024U-01000300   496 732+ 1631 1851 2021 2242 2488 3118
2 DREAM DOLLAR   32   £-      000      2531 2774 3082
2 DREAM LAUNCH   64   £9041   012140   773 1162+ 1261 1527* 2158 2223
2 DREAM TICKET   15   £-      000004   236 2476 2535 2757 3016 3112
5 DREAMCOAT       0   £-      -0       163
2 DREAMING RIVER  0   £-      00       2493 3205
2 DREEMSKERRY     0   £-      00       3068 3199
3 DRESS IN SPRING 8   £2247   0001-0000010020   183 733 1104 1316 1571 2238* 2549 2787 3162 3197
2 DRESS UP        8   £-      000      1843 2607 2920
3 DROITURE       70   £1564   -201014   3207
4 DRUMBARRA       0   £-      -000     '863 2085 2335
2 DRY DOCK       60   £5196   010      2673 2869* 3120
3 DRY GIN        16   £84     0000-0300   1078 1556 1952 3102
2 DRYGALSKI      37   £148    043      1634 1948 2584
2 DUAL CAPACITY  16   £-      0000     1550 1665 2325 3112
4 DUAL VENTURE   52   £7313   00-42-22031043   519 782 1112 1417 1663* 2220 2445 3232
5 DUBAVARNA      10   £251    0/034-000020   282 609 993 1102 2008 2101
4 DUBIAN         75   £56874   22331-010410   1144 1593* 2157 2506 2909* 3214
2 DUBLIN BELLE    8   £-      40000    1248 1370 1955 2757 3032
2 DUBLIN DANCER   0   £-      0        421
3 DUBLIN DAYGO    0   £-      -0       2339
3 DUBLIN LAD     74   £9358   3200-0000314400   408 550 660 903 1151 1268+ 1387 1508 1889 2065
3 DUBLINAIRE     77   £365    00303-03300000   1272 1447 1836 2024 2312 2530 2702 2992
3 DUCA DI BUSTED 67   £23286   1131143   1218 2741 2908
4 DUCK FLIGHT    35   £253    00030-000000   192 327 477 1805 2065 2151 2402
2 DUCKINGTON     44   £514    40       2522 3018
4 DUDLEYS STAR   16   £-      03002-0   3187
4 DUELLING       33   £3744   40000001410204 3   7 72 265 432 532 709 851 1231* 1517 1619* 1698 1720 2059 3060 3123
3 DUFF           35   £649    0423-340004   402 579 847 1520 1607 2321
4 DUFFERS DANCER 28   £6571   40004-0134110   1101 1765* 2012 2245 2513* 2816* 3104
7 DUKE OF DOLLIS  8   £1587   -0102-00000120   44 366 1071 1140 1422 1477* 1897 1980
```

```
3 DUKE OF MILLTIMBER  0   £-   000-040000    51 279 960 1439 1824 2268
4 DUKESWOOD  0   £-   0-000-00    399 568
3 DUNAN HILL  36   £520   -30   619 3061
3 DUNCAN IDAHO  48   £926   -0342   231 347 552 1276
2 DUNENNY  50   £3335   21   2926- 3133*
2 DUNGEHILL STAR  0   £-   000   353 1433 1816
2 DUNLIN  38   £5117   12310014   627* 785 1138 1740* 1920 2588 2815* 3058
3 DUNLORING  33   £334   20000-40000   216 455 692 1924 3116
2 DUNNINALD  51   £4724   12040   1604* 1919 2350 2694 2865
3 DUNOOF  42   £-   012-0004   459 642 2676 2786
3 DUNSTON  48   £2710   0-003034140   357 506 714 978 1646 2148 2305* 2665 3052
3 DUPLORI  70   £3812   -3   3010
4 DURASINGH  40   £3603   -2210   2312 2619 2758+ 3106
2 DURBO  30   £-   0000   2036 2542 2878 3134
4 DURHAM PLACE  50   £5534   0-0430004024100   877 1037 1268 1631 1852 2065 2289 2402 2758- 2953
   3012+ 3106 3233
3 DUSK APPROACHES  0   £-   -00   862 991
5 DUST CONQUERER  0   £-   -000   1755 2022 3139
3 DUSTY DIPLOMACY  22   £959   0-10B0   66* 331 716 1166
3 DUSTY DOLLAR  78   £38616   44-31221   253 923* 1466- 2568- 2868*
2 DUTCH AUCTION  38   £964   100   1573* 2081 2391
2 DUTCH COURAGE  48   £3260   44331440   405 565 728 918 1585* 1785 2081 2421
3 DUTCH QUEEN  0   £-   -040   863 1797 2339
3 DUWANTO  18   £-   -000   549 811 1072
3 DYNAMIC BABY  8   £-   00000-000   113 276 568
2 DYNAMIC STAR  45   £544   0033   1930 2179 2976 3133
3 EAGLE DESTINY  44   £4879   -0212001   334 822 1184* 1743- 2165 2684 3066*
2 EAGLES NEST  24   £718   00000230   2698 2982 3133
4 EAGLING  80   £9482   11310-200   251- 475 617
10 EARLS COURT  4   £124   00002-0400340   993 1432 1502 2008 2101 2374 2964
3 EARLY DOORS  0   £-   0000-0   1959
2 EASA  44   £959   10   345* 1113
3 EAST LIMERICK  0   £-   -0   3142
4 EAST STREET  2   £-   00-00-000   1056 1400 1567
6 EASTBROOK  18   £6804   00000-21324100   321- 369* 1222 1840 2033 2295* 2681 3104
6 EASTER LEE  24   £2926   -0122-00100   1633 1875 2432* 2733 2938
4 EASTER RAMBLER  11   £156   41100-000000300   403 530 620 851 1056 1310 1439 1666 1937
3 EASTERN COMMAND  11   £216   34-43000   1446 1751 2314 2534 2929
3 EASTERN HEIGHTS  0   £-   00-0000   516 891 2509 2972
3 EASTERN HOUSE  49   £8705   3022-021201   213 923 1725* 2155 2291 2570*
3 EASTERN LASS  0   £-   -0000   338 593 726 2174
4 EASTERN MYSTIC  81   £44039   21211-4132   360* 545* 704 1127
3 EASTERN OASIS  6   £907   44003-0040014D   961 1334 1734 1959 2055 2417* 2884
3 EASTERN PLAYER  10   £-   0000-0000000004   95 191 351 480 723 967 1303 1472 3062 3197
2 EASTERN PRINCESS  8   £-   00000   848 1194 1528 2927 3032
3 EASTERN SONG  57   £8653   20-01314   1107 1511* 1858 1995+ 2446
4 EASY DAY  20   £4030   0000-0410100000   10 281 499* 606 956+ 1202 1455 1727 2526 3138
4 EASY KIN  0   £1569   30400-0010000   164 381 519 1016* 1183 1419 1745 1952
3 EASY LINE  44   £9724   -100143112   64* 436 624 2143* 2213 2313 2424* 2614+ 2842-
3 EASY ROMANCE  0   £-   00-00   422 729
3 EATON SQUARE  36   £-   04-00   231 479
3 EAU COURANTE  0   £-   -00   806 1880
3 EBOLITO  38   £3354   -0042100   218 832 980 1265 1393* 2850 3110
2 EBONY PRIDE  38   £616   0403243   400 497 1844 1946 2089 2421 2596
4 EBOR GREY  0   £-   00000-0   673
2 ECHEVIN  44   £812   2   1872
2 ECHO VALLEY  52   £964   410   944 2215* 2540
2 ECHOING  51   £4471   1432100   766* 1527 1707 1893- 2172* 2661 2843
2 EDENTHORPE  8   £-   000   2919 3103 3153
3 EDGEWISE  35   £-   01200-00000000   216 455 624 929 1151 1312 2473 2655
4 EDNICA  73   £15758   00-11110   1857* 2503
2 EDRAIANTHUS  34   £519   040402   533 725 944 2136 2498 2792
4 EDWINS PRINCESS  6   £-   00400-0   30
4 EECEE TREE  27   £2936   11000-000000140   192 327 508 952 1077 1438* 1542 1849
3 EFFICIENT  3   £-   0-0000   1141 1481 2300 2978
4 EFFIGY  61   £2897   42221-00012   879 1112 1383 2406* 2861
4 EFISIO  84   £84035   02110-04120330   313 598 897* 1094- 1877 2195 2770 3020
2 EIGHT MILE ROCK  0   £-   000   3117 3153 3228
2 EILEEN A LEE  0   £-   00   400 852
2 EINSTEIN  48   £8119   01130   1155 1296* 2052* 2252 2563
4 EISTEDDFOD  17   £113   00000-3   828
3 EL ALAMEIN  17   £-   01004-000   38 103 529
2 EL BE DOUBLEYOU  39   £5580   0201420   460 596 717 1483* 1920 2035- 2178
3 EL CONQUISTADOR  53   £7731   -02022210   811 1029 1111 1633- 1875 2078 2882+ 3052
3 EL CUITE  85   £110247   1-111   2156+ 2741* 3169*
2 EL DELGADO  38   £119   300   1665 2301 2805
3 EL FABULOUS  73   £22350   -413   300 561* 1215
4 EL FAYEZ  40   £-   21100-0   629
4 EL HAR LE HAR  17   £-   0-020-4   524
2 EL REY  45   £4132   012   2926 3082* 3230
3 EL SALTO  77   £24982   -214   2197 2454* 2913
2 EL ZETA  42   £260   040   1242 1510 1780
3 ELA MAN HEE  20   £-   -0000   862 1953 2304 2726
3 ELAAFUUR  40   £4279   100-44410000   459 883 1236 1685* 2156 2558 2834 3022
7 ELARIM  13   £369   -00004400000003   310 609 745 956 1017 1106 1254 1374 1964 2037 2173 2604
   2746 2978
3 ELBANDARY  0   £-   -000   862 1220 1639
3 ELBURY PARK  47   £2373   -11   2534* 2879-
2 ELECTRIC STORM  0   £-   0   3181
5 ELECTRIFIED  6   £-   0-040-000   199 308 590
4 ELECTROPET  20   £202   00410-00-403   263 709 851 2807 3195
3 ELEGANT BILL  22   £2954   00000-010100   14 100* 322 380* 491 648
```

```
4 ELEGANT FASHION 18   £420    00200-0003200    420 578 992 2728 2887 2998 3086
3 ELEGANT GUEST  15   £747   -00431D00    494 1256 2613 2714 2874 2959 3115
2 ELEGANT ISLE  59   £5571   1242   2051* 2439 2663 2830
3 ELEMENTARY  53   £-   -0   3004
4 ELEPHANT BOY  0   £-   -0000   176 564 943 1447
2 ELEVEN LIGHTS  0   £-   0   2494
6 ELGENDON  0   £-   -00   968 1417
4 ELISHARP  71   £7291   2   901
3 ELLE SEULE  82   £39229   101341002    904 1215 2002* 2195 2507 2918
2 ELLIS BELL  0   £-   00   1345 1752
4 ELMCOTE LAD  0   £226   40000-0200   177 568 963 2960
6 ELMDON  10   £-   03300-0000   172 495 727 1447
3 ELNAWAAGI  58   £12106   31123-110040   588* 895* 1044 1486 2155 2446
3 ELOQUENCE  9   £-   -0000   2048 2248 2386 2546
4 ELPLOTINO  40   £4030   21100-30100   695 782 2403* 2692 3225
2 ELSENHAM STAR  0   £-   0   2796
3 ELSOCKO  34   £1393   0300-3033020   309 464 677 817 1043 2483 2660
3 ELVIRE  18   £-   -0040400   779 1259 1578 2300 2572 2683 3194
3 ELWADHNA  55   £705   21-2   157
3 EMANCIPATED LADY  0   £-   -0000   431 891 1375 2793
2 EMBARCADERO  0   £-   0   785
3 EMBLA  78   £19587   2111-40201   214 373 1110 1466 2851*
4 EMERALD EAGLE  33   £12275   010000300201000010   1  17  79 238 689 956 1176 1698 1774 1976*
1983 2231 2437 2629 2685* 2945
3 EMERALD POINT  54   £1207   3-010   273 1494* 2665
3 EMERALD WAVE  26   £3666   004-001000   806 982 1586* 1804 2250 2459
5 EMERGENCY PLUMBER  26   £1534   00400-42403   135 306 374 525 700
2 EMERKALA  39   £-   0   3181
2 EMILYS PRIDE  39   £-   40   2703 2901
3 EMMA HARTE  0   £-   00-0P   1472 2550
2 EMMAS WHISPER  25   £-   0003D0   985 1382 2191 2792 3146
2 EMMER GREEN  35   £2862   401001000   47 818 938* 1370 1893 1978* 2137 2465 2669
4 EMPAPAHERO  56   £-   22001-0   17
2 EMPEROR HOTFOOT  45   £823   2   1504
9 EMPEROR NAPOLEON  0   £-   -0   1519
3 EMPIRE BLUE  45   £5663   11240-010   455 880* 3066
4 EMPIRE SANDS  0   £-   00440-00   673 2509
2 EMPLOY FORCE  0   £-   00   2531 3011
3 EMRYS  28   £5884   002-103314000   33* 216 352 538 919* 2331 2404 2876 3140
2 EMSLEYS HEIGHTS  20   £-   0000   437 2043 2082 2664
3 ENBARR  73   £21291   0-21310121   357 535* 1284 1588+ 1912 2066* 2438 2567*
2 ENCHANTED COURT  1   £-   0000   1528 2050 2279 2608
2 ENCHANTED TIMES  31   £2335   13000000   187* 456 953 1828 2047 2421 3122 3226
2 ENCORE LAMOUR  0   £-   0   3109
2 ENDLESS GOSSIP  0   £-   0   3136
3 ENFOLD  13   £-   -0   90
3 ENGLE DALE  0   £-   -00   528 723
2 ENGLISH RIVER  42   £358   3   3132
4 ENGLISH SPRING  80   £43465   00112-4410100   221 325 651* 920 1095* 1331 1932
3 ENIGMA  32   £752   204-02020   835 1399- 1878 2367- 2483
3 ENSIGNE  43   £1482   -202410   720- 980 2183 2373 2759* 3026
2 ENTIRE  24   £85   300   2410 3082 3153
3 ENTOURAGE  30   £-   4-00   907 2216
3 ENTRANCING  59   £12049   12-0002120   264 708 1655 2262 2440* 2765 3021
3 ENZELIYA  42   £-   3-440   581 744 1192
4 EPHIALTES  72   £27301   443-0012444   2* 391 901 1118 2827
3 EPICURES GARDEN  65   £19799   ---13-4133   294 470* 1596 2450
2 EPPY MARNER  0   £-   000   1180 1561 1883
3 EQUATOR  70   £4750   -20   395 753
4 EQUIPPED FOR DUTY  7   £-   0-400-00   568 2271
3 ERA  21   £-   2000-0   1399
2 ERANTHE  0   £-   00   3103 3184
6 ERICS WISH  0   £-   -0   1686
2 ERINDALE  64   £6228   23210120   1591 2504 2910
4 ERNIES CHOICE  10   £-   00000-0   452
5 ERROL EMERALD  24   £3769   02300-0113   1254 1432* 1548* 1769
4 ERYDAN  0   £-   -0   1127
2 ESCUDERO  0   £-   000   2711 2796 3081
3 ESDALE  78   £40497   2-2011301211   190- 370 1087+ 1315* 1448 1912 2419 2640 3008* 3216*
3 ESFAHAN  48   £7516   -0201313   431 576 1043 1541* 1934 2291* 2570
2 ESKIMO MITE  47   £264   40   1903 2673
4 ESQUIRE  76   £38126   44010-2112422   265 445* 573* 652 920 1492 2004
3 ESS JAY ESS  0   £-   0000-000   2208 2315 2597
2 ESTA BONITA  40   £-   00   1287 2215
2 ESTATE CARLTON  56   £1254   2   292
6 ESTRAPADE  90   £570629   13   2456* 3212
4 ETAT MAJOR  74   £12519   22   98 1118
2 ETONNANTE  42   £-   0   2147
3 ETTAS PET  6   £128   00-40030000   1451 1586 1924 2161 2314 2548 2948 3101
4 EUCHARIS  12   £762   00000-00002403   399 540 992 1264 1727 1901 2033 2213
3 EUPHEMISM  0   £-   -0   231
2 EUROCON  18   £848   000002400000   364 931 1478 1635 1883 2050 2140 2439 2498 2680 2798 2936
7 EVEN BANKER  4   £-   00-00-00000   211 355 499 709 850
2 EVENING PRAYERS  19   £-   000   2308 2472 2535
4 EVER GENIAL 70?   £3106   21133-0400   920 1094 1466 1851
2 EVER SHARP  32   £272   40   1930 2118
2 EVER SO GENTLE  40   £-   4   752
3 EVER SO SHARP  6   £106   0000-000000300   910 1171 1399 2312 2394 2592 2884 3024 3144
2 EVERLOFT  0   £-   000   2472 2781 3011
4 EVERY EFFORT  23   £5094   0-401D341200040   112 481 930 1041 1189 1581* 1781 1890 2144 2545 3078
3164
2 EVERY WEDNESDAY  8   £100   430   1100 1298 1611
3 EVERYINCHALADY  0   £-   0-00000   2314 2534 2991 3066 3186
                              > 969 <
```

```
3 EVES ERROR  78  £37029  112-041131  226 476 1788* 2449* 2640 3007*
4 EVROS  22  £222  10004-00040000  166 225 403 652 750 1038 2173 2360
4 EXACTLY RIGHT  71  £3330  3  2828
3 EXAMINATION  40  £6621  00030-121040  168* 228 340* 478 1182 1222
7 EXCAVATOR LADY  10  £1820  0303-0043220220  519 629 772 968 1106 1223 1336 1621 1744 1808
3 EXCELBELLE  44  £662  -234  506 1259 1639
2 EXCELLERS SPECIAL  46  £784  2  3134
3 EXCEPTIONAL BEAUTY  55  £6255  02-42013020  599 862 1130 2068* 2278 2692 3119- 3232
3 EXCLUSIVE CAT  38  £347  4312-3000  760 884 1283 1704
3 EXCLUSIVE NORTH  45  £2310  2330-01040  229 1756* 2099 2183 2443
4 EXERT  6  £1645  00-344403000000  114 266 401 508 748 922 1086 1211 2021 2079 2258 2519
3 EXOTIC RIVER  60  £2500  -30  152 407
2 EXOTIC SOURCE  42  £363  2  2191
3 EXPERT WITNESS  0  £-  -040000  1396 1775 1985 2590 3045 3202
6 EXPLETIVE  18  £3353  00000-0430122  850 1081 1273 1394 1689* 1951 2173
2 EXPORT PRICE  70  £20134  14  1351* 1714
2 EXPRESS GROUPAGE  0  £-  000  1883 2511 2607
3 EYE SIGHT  31  £1232  -3432  723 2393 2546 2864
9 EYELIGHT  1  £-  00000-0  710
6 EYTON MILADY  0  £-  0-0  185
5 FAARIS  0  £-  -0  2516
3 FAATIK  18  £290  03400-004000  334 424 886 1065 1864 2333
3 FABLED MONARCH  0  £-  -00  941 1080
2 FABRINA  44  £1114  02  1982 2628
3 FABULOUS NOBLE  70  £18749  1  1713*
3 FABULOUS QUEEN  72  £4140  -4  755
5 FABUROLA  76 - £31799  421-22024  2453 3004 3169
2 FACEVIEW  0  £-  00  2869 3099
3 FACTOTUM  40  £1305  00-003200  941 1184 1841 2009 2536 2720
2 FAH SO LAH  0  £-  0  3073
2 FAHAD  51  £-  004  2056 2418 2542
5 FAIDROS  0  £-  -0  85
2 FAILIQ  49  £1086  041  1791 2547 2657*
3 FAIR ATLANTA  22  £3666  003-24010030300  141 209 335 505* 843 2274 2459 2719 2876 3078 3177
3 FAIR CADETTE  0  £-  -00  2299 2670
4 FAIR CHARTER  16  £-  00000-0  2697
4 FAIR COUNTRY  55  £28618  0300-0323110110  481 762 930 1240 1590* 1781* 1890 2566* 2749* 2867
2 FAIR MOON  0  £-  000  2434 2652 3200
4 FAIR OF THE FURZE  78  £65205  /2201-413010  470 641* 1095 1331 2868
5 FAIR TRADER  0  £-  -000  281 936 1016
3 FAIR ZINNIA  6  £-  000-000  1841 2103 3101
2 FAIRBURN  0  £-  000  197 2007 2334
8 FAIRDALE  0  £134  -0003000  84 174 418 495 679 727 2992
8 FAIRGREEN  9  £1170  00403-004004301  56 163 260 369 495 788 1131 1344 1424*
3 FAIRSEAT CLOSE  24  £-  0-00  1586 2622
2 FAIRTOWN  0  £-  000  979 1294 1570
2 FAIRWAY LADY  52  £1865  01024  292 638 752 876
2 FAIRY CHIMES  18  £128  34  1100 1496
2 FAIRY GOLD  38  £370  44  2133 2904
2 FALDWYN  20  £499  33020040  543 938 1090 1180 1305 2178 2284 2380
3 FALINE  33  £542  -300  16 109 2483
2 FALLING LEAF  45  £964  010  2105 2225* 2423
3 FALLONETTA  7  £-  304-00  1201 1340
3 FALLOWFIELD LAD  33  £1133  -31  1799 1961*
3 FAMILLE ROSE  12  £-  04-00000  1375 1541 1999 2614 3185
3 FAMILY FRIEND  69  £17852  41240-441000  348 597 902* 1354 2114 2565
3 FANAAN  54  £-  03-0  887
3 FANCY FINISH  17  £-  04-04000  911 1142 1541 2312 2793
3 FANCY PAGES  3  £-  11000-000000000  340 760 1191 1391 1499 1849 1943 2370 2417
3 FANCY PAN  38  £2750  -03041030  194 863 966 1868 1999* 2155 2837 3029
3 FANDANGO KISS  0  £-  00-00000  941 1288 1813 2060 2371
5 FANDANGO LIGHT  40  £2058  2020  1004 1150 1342- 1582
3 FANNY ROBIN  08  £2044  040-000400420  769 1123 1743 1904 1981 2424 2690 2795 2887
2 FANTINE  10  £1887  004421400340  57 446 543 711 821 939* 1181 1622 1795 1997 2609 2757
4 FAR TO GO  0  £-  0000-000000  199 358 590 990 1102 1419
3 FAR TOO BUSY  20  £2560  -000100  431 658 1036 1515* 1922 2072
2 FAR TOO RICH  30  £-  4  3134
3 FARAG  24  £2221  031-20020300020  74 386 919 1199 1581 1819 2171 2490 2581 2963 3164
3 FARAWAY DANCER  83  £42855  111-2140  226 476* 878 1230
3 FARAWAY LAD  10  £-  0000-0400  1315 1807 2169 2432
3 FARCEUSE  0  £-  000-000  2131 2546 2877
3 FAREWELL TO LOVE  45  £4685  20-21022000  162 315* 463 688 955 1596 3175 3236
2 FARFURR  52  £-  00  1488 1915
3 FARM CLUB  44  £3665  10-000300100  234 386 692 1084 1468 2226 2699* 2879 3050
7 FARM LANE  0  £-  -00  2381 2517
4 FARMER JOCK  14  £2548  -00030210000000  12 56 815 1066 1171 1438 1542* 1627 1730 1940 1950
   2160 2256 3012
2 FARMERS GAMBLE  0  £-  000  2698 3120 3205
2 FARNCOMBE  20  £-  00-00R000  70 159 407 1934 2691 3235
3 FASHADA  57  £714  01-03000  232 600 950 1655 2151
3 FASHIONABLY FORBES  38  £-  4000  2341 2484 2646 2852
3 FASSA  18  £-  1000-0000  955 1486 1989 2426
3 FAST AND FRIENDLY  24  £2347  0000-00431021  35 171 356 517 767* 949 1428 1759*
4 FAST DEALER - 13  £-  22200-0  2545
3 FAST REALM  30  £-  -000  218 765 1102
7 FAST SERVICE  18  £548  000-00002400000  578 706 930 1211 1346 1460 1942 2091 2288 2490 2755
3 FAST TAXI  0  £-  -00  1288 1540
3 FAST TOPAZE  90  £177006  -1113  152* 389* 643* 2736
3 FASTWAY FLYER  0  £-  000-00  275 1444
2 FATAL CHARM  46  £-  40  2531 2703
2 FATHER TIME  41  £2987  000200010  187 777 1019 1442 1550 2476 2717 3027* 3174
```

```
3 FAUVE   29   £-   42-0000   516 1200 1482 3180
2 FAUX PAVILLON   26   £-   0   3234
5 FAVOURITE NEPHEW   18   £-   -0000   9 104 185 381
4 FAWLEYS GIRL   23   £1522   00-002000400400   172 306 520- 687 1026 1536 2378 2526 2715 2862 3015
   3145
3 FAYRUZ   72   £10227   11022-000003122   600 705 854 1146 1387 2672 2833+ 3012 3054-
2 FE 0   £-   0   3023
2 FEARLESS ACTION   61   £2299   12   2001* 2732
2 FEARLESS MAN   34   £264   002   2716 3135 3199
2 FEASIBLE   38   £-   0000   2514 2717 3133 3223
3 FEATHER GIRL   0   £-   3000-000000   38 447 871 1701 1824 2508
3 FEBRINO   0   £-   -0   2923
3 FEDRA   42   £10845   000-12212423140   117* 331 648 908* 1048 1388 1605 1875 2311* 2647 3052
5 FEI LOONG   26   £5971   1400-0442143000   91 262 566 668 930* 1365 1553 2091 2655 2837
3 FELIPE TORO   60   £33409   00000-21111123   768 961* 1283* 1414+ 1524+ 2537* 2668- 2947
2 FELSTED BOY   0   £-   0   1082
3 FEMME ELITE   68   £-   110-0   300
4 FENCALINA   0   £-   00-0   258
5 FENCHURCH COLONY   14   £979   204000/3030000   429 591 1024 1159 1563 2727 2959
2 FENN TRAP   20   £-   000   715 948 1483
3 FERDINAND   85   £244755   3-21321   469*
2 FERRY MEADOWS   0   £-   000-0   1372
10 FERRYMAN   38   £7605   -00001214000000   401 660 846 952 1263* 1347 1461* 1730 1933 2537 2668
   2731 3055 3138
3 FESTIVAL CITY USA   52   £4319   3-030014330   224 887 1098 1469 1818* 2237 2536 2763 2946
2 FESTIVE OCCASION   0   £-   00   3135 3205
3 FESTIVITY   22   £352   000-00200000   431 1228 1451 1628 2027 2550 2905 3157
3 FETE CHAMPETRE   46   £-   4-0   599
5 FEYDAN   33   £4553   04000-0443123   1041 1273 1521 1890 2123+ 2268- 2544
3 FIC VIC   9   £757   0000-0100   120 207* 346 1303
2 FICKLE YOUNG MAN   38   £3822   13010403   1333* 1814 1907 2081+ 2198 2753 2843 3027
3 FIDAYTIK   0   £-   -0000   250 765 1259 2709
2 FIDGETTY FEET   10   £-   000   1221 1370 1843
6 FIEFDOM   30   £1388   40400-20140   968 1124 1223* 1963 2360
4 FIELD HAND   82   £37032   03121-2100   221 313* 468 1094
3 FIELDS DIAMOND   0   £-   00-0   41
3 FIESTA DANCE   10   £-   -000   2327 2605 3159
3 FIGHTING BELLE   0   £-   000   1522 2080 2577
3 FIGHTING HARD   0   £-   -0   1330
2 FIGINI   34   £-   4   3136
4 FILL ABUMPER   0   £-   -000000040   199 448 861 1139 1565 2264 2496 2780 3154
3 FILLE DU NORD   72   £7567   2   1215
3 FILLEOR   66   £8902   132-0044102   1286 2241 2457 2524 2672* 3092 3235
4 FILM CONSULTANT   8   £221   00-00300   592 940 1951 2109 2381
2 FINAGLE   35   £-   00   2522 2997
3 FINAL ALMA   20   £-   -000000   535 625 849 1258 1497 1806
3 FINAL AMBER   0   £-   -0   1431
3 FINAL CURTAIN   23   £-   00-00   183 2230
2 FINAL DELIGHT   0   £-   000   497 741 1948
2 FINAL MOMENT   57   £2157   23   2999
2 FINAL RUSH   20   £-   000   1238 1801 3200
3 FINAL SELECTION   35   £-   30-400   2275 2422 2720
3 FINAL TRY   66   £4231   01230-00012   384 1230 1912 2790+ 2958
3 FINDING   40   £548   0-032   806 941 1309
3 FINDON MANOR   11   £-   0340-0000000040   283 593 760 1319 1499 1927 2060 2417 2616 3144
2 FINGERS CROSSED   23   £-   00000   1067 2080 2185 2535 2792
2 FINLUX DESIGN   3   £303   03000000   870 1155 1294 2168 2470 2712 2872 3069
3 FINLUX FLAIR   0   £-   -00   1142 1420
3 FIORAVANTI   73   £4140   11-10000   466* 640 878 2200 2740
5 FIRE BAY   30   £-   32130-040   2121 2617 2896
8 FIRE CHIEFTAIN   0   £-   -00   343 1579
4 FIRE HAZARD   0   £-   0-000-0   2495
3 FIRE LORD   8   £375   00000-00034020   279 517 1304 1428 1767 1892 2125 3202
4 FIRE OF LIFE   75   £-   0   3096
3 FIRE ROCKET   27   £861   00-0042400   90 459 880 997 1401 2190 2594
3 FIREAL   26   £366   4-2400   338 2653 2734 2948
2 FIREIRON   12   £-   00000   2499 2678 2814 3069 3112
3 FIREPROOF   27   £3780   00-042014400   67 480 623 880 951* 1233 1386 1970 2386
3 FIRES OUT   0   £-   0000   1242 1445 1550 1844
2 FIRGROVE   30   £-   0   999
3 FIRM LANDING   81   £21993   310-01003   406 945+ 1107 2538 2772
2 FIRMLY ATTACHED   31   £5471   02000130   242 304 927 1825 2265 2535* 2859 3058
3 FIRST ALARM   7   £-   -00000   237 305 426 524 718
2 FIRST APPLAUSE   0   £-   0   3073
2 FIRST AVENUE   22   £-   0   1475
3 FIRST BILL   27   £1516   00000-204   2467 2709 3101
3 FIRST DIBS   50   £2965   2-31220   229 937* 1141- 1325 1912
3 FIRST DIVISION   55   £6763   000-111000   430* 648* 883* 1130 3038 3170
4 FIRST EXPERIENCE   10   £2586   12000-0010000   784 977 1196* 1438 1638 1950 2245 2592
3 FIRST KISS   51   £6287   -1003033313   723+ 1045 1233 1829 2131 2558 2799 3026 3142* 3186
3 FIRST OPPORTUNITY   14   £-   0-0400000   1836 1947 2319 2497 2594 2981 3191
3 FIRST ORBIT   2   £231   00000-0204000   111 346 620 749 845 1364 1439
3 FIRST RANK   14   £-   00-400400   832 1022 1520 2381 2876 3078
3 FIRST SUMMER   0   £-   -0000   937 1220 2017 2253
2 FIRWOOD   31   £-   00   1555 1722
2 FISHERGATE   35   £-   400   236 437 627
5 FISHPOND   20   £1093   23240-200030   419 663 1099 1243 2882 3052
2 FISSURE   22   £-   00-0040   194 1102 2726 3155
2 FIT THE SCRIPT   0   £-   00   1434 1684
4 FITNAH   80   £39388   12120-102010   100 1355 2200 2736* 2918
4 FIVE FARTHINGS   55   £23399   23100-0121002   584 1020+ 1509 2058+ 2220 2693 3232-
3 FIVE QUARTERS   0   £-   -00000   937 1246 1451 1751 1943
2 FIVE SIXES   17   £2627   01D421130000   186 337 647 813 957* 1298* 1785 1893 2815 2993 3151
```
> 971 <

```
2 FLAG BEARER 17  £853   00001000   497 834 938 2118 2180* 2320 2579 2903
2 FLAIR PARK  19  £2242  01243000000   773 1083* 1294 1483 1828 1965 2669 2865 3017 3058 3182
2 FLAKY LADY  0   £-   0   27
4 FLAME FLOWER  5   £-   30030-00   88 341
3 FLAMELIGHT  0   £-   0-000   1960 2515 2787
3 FLAMING DANCER  35   £503   0-2002   173 509 1368 1807
2 FLAMING EMBERS  40   £172   3   1067
5 FLAMING PEARL  20   £774   33/20-100   201* 530 3128
2 FLAPPER GIRL  11   £-   0000000   223 353 417 1287 1545 2180 2433
3 FLASH DONNA  30   £-   000-00   966 1246
3 FLASH OF STEEL  88   £110150   -0111-1100   395* 640* 878 1330
3 FLASHDANCE  52   £4143   -3100   806 1902* 2385 2719
2 FLAUNTING  36   £-   00440   2105 2283 2584 2748 2968
2 FLAWLESS IMAGE  58   £-   1000   2113 2635 2910
2 FLAXLEY  40   £4213   134300   460* 781 1014 1411 2025 2804
2 FLAXON WORRIOR  0   £-   00   2494 2761
6 FLEET BAY  13   £1163   0-000-0100   1450 1579* 1787 2132
2 FLEET FACT  36   £1279   2002   565 1464 1641 2025
3 FLEET FOOTED  25   £732   31004-0020300   49 461 843 1179 1590 1976 3050
3 FLEET FORM  71   £24295   01300-1221002   24* 210 406- 586* 1107 1286 1455
4 FLEET SPECIAL  38   £-   D2000-0   196
3 FLEETING AFFAIR  66   £10775   -1110223030   479* 570* 1209* 1408 1685 1992 2257 2525 3022 3232
6 FLEETING KNIGHT  0   £-   -0   2809
3 FLEETING SNOW  61   £2636   -1-3   1007
3 FLEUR DE THISTLE  09   £719   0000-00332023   28 177 749 838 975 1063 2094 2371
3 FLEUR ROYALE  80   £50900   -0120   754 1331* 1592 2202
4 FLEURCONE  10   £-   3000-0000   208 333 595 3227
2 FLIGHT WON O WON  0   £-   0   1914
2 FLIP THE BIRD  38   £150   400   2554 2774 3103
2 FLIRTING  34   £329   024400   848 988 1275 1966 2658 2989
3 FLITTER FLUTTER  6   £-   00000-0   1244
2 FLITTERISS PARK  13   £-   0   2589
3 FLOATER  26   £576   -0041   2478 2776 3028 3100*
3 FLOATING ASSET  43   £826   00124-4034440   386 615 847 1034 1520 2784 2879 3123
5 FLODABAY  1   £-   00000-000   812 967 1195
4 FLOMEGAS DAY  25   £294   10000-000340   110 369 525 636 866 3149
2 FLOOD MARK  58   £1296   3   3053
2 FLOOSE  65   £7732   1120   728+ 1003* 1411 1876
2 FLOPET  0   £-   0   2696
3 FLORAL CHARGE  23   £-   2-00000   486 625 832 1022 3164
2 FLORAL CHARMS  44   £-   0   28.
3 FLOREAMUS  0   £-   000-0   2963
4 FLOREAT FLOREAT  4   £-   03300-0000   36 341 851 1086
2 FLOREAT TINA  0   £-   00   2499 3082
2 FLORENCE STREET  0   £-   0   3181
2 FLORET  0   £-   0000   502 681 1083 1449
3 FLOWER BOWL  61   £5519   22-21   359 966+
4 FLOWER OF TINTERN  33   £-   34100-0   3078
6 FLOYD  47   £1134   04200-20   2403 3052
2 FLUTEAU  30   £378   0043   1869 2270 2657 2968
2 FLUTTER MONEY  37   £-   000   2159 2673 2852
3 FLUTTERY  45   £4743   -30224320   250 1327 1586 1902 2161 2440 2670 2842
3 FLY MY STAR  0   £-   -0   218
3 FLYAWAY BRIDE  51   £1284   0131-002000   59 294 732- 1151 1933 2214
5 FLYHOME  50   £18282   00-223030110100   399 578 706 930 2244 2490 2545+ 2730* 2867 2956* 3123 3231
3 FLYING BIDDY  31   £6261   000-3001320   997 1257 1701 2027* 2184 2459 2676
2 FLYING CHAPEAU  0   £-   00   1262 3132
3 FLYING FAIRY  44   £248   00-33   209 839
3 FLYING FLYNN  26   £826   321-2240   67 117 193 356
9 FLYING OFFICER  14   £-   40040-04000   11 336 504 634 1058
5 FLYING PIDGEON  82   £-   0   2456
2 FLYING SILENTLY  18   £432   0330200   337 421 537 939 2045 2535 3016
3 FLYING TRIO  72   £16912   21102-1044   224+ 442 574 1644
3 FLYING ZIAD  8   £-   000-40000000   1743 2104 2189 2413 2728 2876 2998 3060
5 FOCHE  18   £-   00000-00   2807 3187
4 FOGAR  33   £317   -10-300   92 532 683
4 FOLK DANCE  43   £5074   441-44202040210   189 485 1020 1209 1523 1935 2273 2558 2937 3063* 3232
3 FOLKSWOOD  2   £264   0000-00020   141 740 1428 2335 3162
2 FOLLIES BERGERES  50   £1001   320   1855 2215 2967
4 FOLLOW THE BAND  38   £7233   23200-004110   262 448 1156 2017* 2536* 2942
3 FOLLY AGAIN  0   £-   00000-0   2088
2 FOLLY GALE  20   £850   000001   252 350 2080 2287 2700 3069*
2 FONDOUK  77   £12006   2   756
4 FOOLISH TOUCH  35   £8678   1-0031004402401   10 65 306 401+ 687 922 1157 1285 1810 2256- 2411 2632 3172*
5 FOOT PATROL  25   £7566   -00001021043220   10 399 453 812 1139* 1579 1689 1967* 2059 2288 2617 2837 2896 3123
2 FOOTBRIDGE  0   £-   0   848
4 FOR A LARK  20   £358   01300-000300   312 462 735 1755 1935 2164
2 FOR THE CRACK  26   £-   000   2542 .457 3134
2 FOR YOU AND ME  0   £-   00   2191 2652
2 FORBIDDING  65   £2000   -2   393
2 FORCE MAJEURE  0   £-   00   571 741
3 FORCELLO  39   £5789   0342-1242430020   106* 444 553 604 807 888 1956 2149 2536 2995
2 FOREIGN KNIGHT  29   £147   3000   1234 1572 2761 3165
3 FOREMAST  25   £1668   0-13034040   822* 1073 1507 1637 1974 2267 2709 3087
3 FORESIGHT  48   £1171   03430   777 2626 2750 2926 3125
2 FOREST FLOWER  85   £135279   111211   601* 1108* 1454+ 2113- 2695* 2831+
3 FORETOP  16   £147   -0020000   891 1142 1300 1626 2481 3033 3149
4 FOREVER TINGO  0   £318   0000-0000003000   547 689 875 1079 1651 1870 2126 2401 2602 2728
3 FOREVER YOUNG  10   £1255   000-401420   195 783 993* 1267 1369 1699
5 FOREWARN  14   £-   10003-00   1349 1694
                              > 972 <
```

```
3 FORFLITE  36    £1231    -3100   937 1705* 2255 2837
4 FORGIVING  14   £962   04000-040300200   547 838 1079 1188 1321 2022 2182 2372 2807
4 FORLAWAY  66    £8198   02-30323   471 2192 3000
3 FORLIS FAIR  29   £-   -000   567 776 2518
4 FORMATUNE  20    £5958   -10233203000000   10* 71 481 668 812 1013 1640 1911 2258 2390 2773 2867
  2945 3078
3 FORMIDABLE DANCER  25   £890   000-00004023   982 1281 1520 1830 2182 2372 2747 3187
4 FORMIDABLE LADY  14   £195   40400-0030   727 812 1274 1450
4 FORT DUCHESNE  5   £-   33140-0000000   177 495 1066 1319 1937 2271 2519
3 FORT LINO  45    £2582   4-22221   832 1535 1721 2366 2620*
6 FORT NAYEF  16   £-   00--0-0   341
3 FORT PROSPECT  60   £-   -1-4   151
4 FORTUNE FINDER  16   £-   00100-0   860
2 FORTYNINER  7   £-   00000   1197 1528 1955 2320 2712
2 FORUMS FOLLY  25   £243   040   2716 2936 3198
3 FORWARD MOVE  0   £-   -00000   402 619 739 1085 1806
4 FORWARD RALLY  45   £19002   0021-1120210   609* 698+ 888 1038 2797 3029+ 3140
2 FOSSARD  0   £-   000   1955 2026 2325
2 FOTITIENG  80    £40147   13133   1714 2826* 3005 3208
3 FOUL SHOT  12    £1536   000-2202   29 171 331 949
3 FOUNDRY FLYER  12   £-   -040400   732 1418 1691 2106 2210 2409
4 FOUNTAIN BELLS  43    £4368   04000-2014240   161 233 507+ 884 986 1391 2382
3 FOUNTAIN OF YOUTH  20+   £-   -0   2622
2 FOUNTAINS CHOICE  30    £2808   33200201200   859 1050 1138 1675 2198 2364 2439 2595 2888 2968
  3125
2 FOUR CROWNS  0   £-   00   2609 2990
2 FOUR LAFFS  32    £2050   -02310400   34 136 252 353* 2252 3122 3146 3226
4 FOUR STAR THRUST  30    £8685   004020202321121 4 308 419 629 872 1024 1226 1416 1563 1809 2683
  2819* 2885* 2944 3036*
3 FOURNO TRUMPS  0   £-   000-00P   51 517 958
2 FOURTH LAD  45    £1355   0040042   985 1232 1731 2019 2198 2920 3133
2 FOURTH PROTOCOL  43   £-   004   2782 3109 3228
4 FOURTH TUDOR  23    £5537   -2000113   595 751 1918 2134 2800* 2995* 3087
2 FOURWALK  52    £5983   00241003200120   544 780 931 1305 1397* 1568 1814 1936 2081 2227 2588 2804*
  3072- 3122
3 FOUZ  46    £3027   13020-3400002   60 220 344 1084 1758 2879 3062
2 FOWL PLAY  14   £-   000   73 2698 2814
2 FOX PATH  0   £-   000   2223 2626 3037
2 FOX STEEP  0   £-   -0   2314
3 FOXCROFT  7   £-   10022-00000   356 620 993 1267 1759
4 FOXY DYKE  20   £-   2--00-00   620 1171
3 FOXY PRINCE  42    £1193   -010   231 1726* 2240
4 FRAGRANT CALAMITY  0   £-   -0   1251
3 FRAME OF POWER  11   £-   0-0000   868 1055 1724 1964
3 FRAMLINGTON COURT  47    £4825   0200-2D10200   234 352* 604 719- 3123 3231
3 FRANCHISE  46    £1421   -0123   1580 1786* 2096 2665
9 FRANCISCUS  0   £-   0-0   2111
3 FRANDIE MISS  3   £-   20-000000   14 237 426 626 1070 1771
3 FRANGNITO  41    £706   0-4002200   328 402 613 765 1061 1167 2477
2 FRANK THE BANK  24   £-   40000   1665 2089 2514 2935 3190
9 FRASASS  12    £762   00000-100400   257* 366 541 630 824 869
3 FRED ASTAIRE  83    £75524   3   3211
4 FRED THE TREAD  23   £-   000   751 943 1290
2 FREDDIE ASHTON  25   £-   000004040   1984 2229 2511 2756 2889 3047 3081 3192 3230
3 FREE CLARE  14   £-   0-000   658 2483 2816
3 FREE HAND  48   £-   3-4   625
4 FREE ON BOARD  29    £2340   30000-002022   189 432 709 1079 1729 2121
2 FREE SKIP  38    £230   003   2080 2494 3189
4 FREE TO GO  18    £219   0-3   164
2 FREEBYS PREACHER  47    £604   02   1903 2615
3 FREEDOM LINE  0   £-   00-0   1327
4 FREEDOMS CHOICE  62    £8570   21213-42D100   344 573 1047* 1216 2566
4 FREMONT BOY  15    £1478   03000-23040303   266- 679 1213 1367 1940 2256 2992 3191
3 FRENCH DESIGN  0   £-   -00   1961 2363
4 FRENCH EMPEROR  3   £-   0-000-00   2617 2896
3 FRENCH FLUTTER  40    £2523   30020-04130334   409 978 1160+ 1410 1732 2478 2623 2799
2 FRENCH GONDOLIER  48    £964   1   3200+
2 FRENCH KING  36    £519   02   985 1397
2 FRENCH PLAIT  0   £-   00   400 1382
4 FRENCH SCHOOL  72    £4416   10-0003   1493 2114
2 FRENCH SONNET  57    £488   020   2056 2377- 2635
2 FRENCH TUITION  48    £4123   233103   187 212 565 678* 876 1039
2 FRENCHGATE  32   £-   0000   1510 2082 2325 2607
2 FRENDLY FELLOW  26   £-   000   1812 2584 3223
2 FRENSHAM MANOR  7   £-   0   2881
4 FRESH THOUGHTS  45    £776   020   707 1341 1855
2 FREV OFF  17    £709   3000403430   672 913 1105 1294 1413 1480 1635 1862 1955 2279
6 FRIENDLY LASS  0   £-   -000   2370 2519 2656
4 FRIENDS FOR EVER  20   £-   02103-0   2207
2 FRIENDS FOR LIFE  0   £-   0000   1175 1253 2050 2138
2 FRIMLEY PARKSON  0   £-   00   2871 3072
2 FRIMLEY QUEEN  0   £-   000   1501 2308 2433
4 FRINGE OF HEAVEN  25   £-   111001-00000   1125 1286 1514 1702 2039
4 FRISCO  25   £-   30041-0   22
4 FRISKY HOPE  9   £-   0-110-0   2964
3 FRITHIOF  0   £-   -0   484
3 FRIVOLE  36    £4638   000-4011020   637 1446 1695* 1885* 2027 2291 2459
2 FRIVOLOUS FANCY  0   £-   00000   722 999 2019 2177 2514
2 FRIVOLOUS LADY  10   £-   44000000   1668 1946 2301 2579 2698 2987 3032 3056
3 FRUITY OROONEY  22   £-   0002-0000000   436 624 1036 1312 1608 1840 2183
2 FU LU SHOU  26    £1647   001200   1576 2150 2470* 2798 2897 3085
3 FUDGE  14    £1286   000-2000002   534 855 1032 1257 1927 2274 2991
3 FULL FLOW  0   £-   0-0   559
```

```
5 FULL OF DREAMS  0   £-    -00000    312 403 761 856 1559
3 FULL OF LIFE  35   £898   4321-0002200403   534 847 1169 1579 2132 2282 2581 2837 2879 3062
2 FULL OF PRIDE  60   £5946    120120   1266* 1707 1925 2265+ 2398- 2482
5 FULL OF SPEED  8   £-   0-100-00   2094 2274
3 FULL SPEED AHEAD  23   £535   0-0000200   484 739 980 1535 2093 2420 2709
2 FULTONS FLYER  0   £-   00   446 696
3 FUNNY LASS  0   £-   -0   2996
3 FUR BABY  0   £-   00000-0000   1420 1603 1734 2125
4 FUSILIER  42   £11131   003-30000001003   17 71 361 1383 1525 1793 1911 2165* 2255 2566 2773
3 G G MAGIC  19   £2886   -03042000421310   331 380 648 1309 1479 1739 1945 2128 2654 2679 2789*
2902 2964* 3100
2 GAELIC CROSS  30   £745   003   57 102 2352
3 GAELIC FLUTTER  36   £3096   4200-3010000   500 713 1436* 1934 2288 2473 3062
2 GAELIC LOVER  28   £1651   212   2466 2817* 3085
3 GAILY GAILY  68   £-   141-00100   560 754 2196 3002
5 GAINVILLE LAD  0   £-   -000   44 126 2794
2 GALA NIGHT  42   £-   4   2487
3 GALACTIC HERO  56   £2286   2-323   1554 2148 3119
3 GALAXY GALA  0   £-   0000-0040000000   237 309 426 871 1142 1334 1482 1662 2083 2778
3 GALAXY PATH  27   £84   0-004030   83 276 507 846 2312 2573
3 GALAXY PRINCESS  6   £120   -30   2008 3061
3 GALESA  42   £2444   00-0221   2419 2734 2923 3194*
4 GALLA PLACIDIA  83   £57071   11030-101020   298* 645 1115* 1493 2357 2453
2 GALLANT GALLOIS  52   £4305   110   2805* 2950* 3114
4 GALLANT HOPE  16   £3059   -00002022233420   679 846 1060 1273 1447 1581 1834- 2046 2318 2519
2702 2858 2992 3191
2 GALLANT RIBO  0   £-   000   2493 2657 2961
2 GALLIC TIMES  48   £3632   3113043   57 77+ 146+ 304 571 781 934
2 GALLIONS POINT  0   £-   000   2721 2869 3229
5 GALLOIS BOSQUET  6   £-   01300-0000   1173 1374 1651 2467
6 GALLOP DYNA  0   £-   -00   2195 2507
3 GALUNPE  80   £61656   114-0031100   300 755 1116 1353* 2452* 2638 3214
2 GALWAY EXPRESS  8   £-   00000   425 1105 1305 2470 2724
4 GAMBART  17   £93   40000-300   119 343 721
9 GAMBLERS DREAM  13   £-   00000-0000000   1390 1781 1901 2123 2381 2490 2549
2 GAME FEATHERS  26   £-   0000   20 818 2375 2482
2 GAME LIGHT  8   £-   00000   223 425 905 1844 2212
3 GAME SET MATCH  24   £-   0-00   452 790
2 GAME THATCHER  51   £4315   01   2939 3109*
2 GAMESHOW  38   £-   0000   513 834 2561 3176
3 GANOON  25   £426   2200-23000   751 1167 1315 1833 2489
4 GANYMED  75   £9887   -1   3170*
2 GARCON NOIR  32   £-   0004   1958 2100 2805 2871
3 GARDAS GOLD  8   £487   0033-0330004000   677 787 972 1104 1299 1742 1999 2126 2313 2399
2 GARDENIA LADY  25   £1513   3000000013   646 818 1025 1962 2425 2588 2792 2919 3031* 3151
3 GARDINIA LAD  22   £-   -040   2593 3066 3236
2 GARNET  53   £12508   014120   383 1297* 1754 1910+ 2297- 3040
6 GARRICK  64   £2740   43-3   1490
3 GARTHMAN  2   £-   -00000   595 959 1251 2605 3161
3 GARY AND LARRY  8   £-   00-00000   593 729 774 932 3162
5 GAUHAR  6   £224   00300-444000000   174 727 1018 1500 1609 1901 2123 2319 2755
3 GAVEA  0   £-   -00   213 774
3 GAY APPEAL  32   £4734   003-030011U0   615 822 1032 1503 2253* 2709* 2885 2985
4 GAY CAPTAIN  57   £12015   1-00-0002010   4 72 265 511 706 879* 2693
3 GAY CARUSO  21   £124   00-00030   351 486 625 1310 1666
5 GAY MINSTREL  72   £23606   13   1594* 2827
3 GAY STARLIGHT  0   £-   -0   3197
2 GAYANE  77   £15946   11   1778* 2460*
2 GAYS FLUTTER  25   £1646   403320   800 1108 1501 1683 2052 2198
3 GAYWOOD GIRL  0   £-   04240-00000   871 1288 1574 1827 2088
2 GEBLITZT  35   £-   004   1495 2345 2812
2 GELTSER  63   £2805   241   1019 1376 1552+
4 GEM MART  7   £-   03020-004000   967 2182 2422 2516 2704 3154
3 GEM OF GOLD  21   £-   0224-000   1472 1830 2120
2 GEMINI FIRE  67   £20358   0413131   531 780 931* 1082 1421* 1585 1850*
3 GEMMA KAYE  42   £-   00-00   661 1043
3 GEMMA LOUISE  0   £-   0000-00   279 673
6 GENERAL CONCORDE  0   £-   00   2480 2850
4 GENERAL KNOWLEDGE  60   £3802   2   1856
2 GENERAL MEILLAND  36   £811   03330   2341 2491 2716 2804 3075
4 GENERATION GAP  0   £-   -00-0000   258 1744 2211 2346
2 GENGHIZ  77   £21491   11033'   2036* 2243* 2737 2866 3039
2 GENNARO FR  44   £-   0   3018
2 GENOBRA  0   £-   0   2750
3 GENOTIN  10   £305   000-2   2743
4 GENTILESCHI  5   £681   -00-0000000000   18 70 412 742 922 1882 1950 2340 2513 2775 3145
2 GENTLE DARIUS  43   £609   43402   1816 2001 2723 3099 3234
5 GENTLE FAVOR  26   £588   01210-0403   519 693 1159 1582
2 GENTLE PERSUASION  62   £9608   144   1021* 1789 3040
4 GENTLE STREAM  21   £974   00000-20004034   282 519 617 942 1271 1473 1745 2098
4 GEOBRITONY  15   £-   0400200000   108 364 627 1050 1480 2379 2607 2888 3148 3222
3 GEOFFS FOLLY  0   £-   0-0000   33 195 237 356
3 GEORDIES DELIGHT  65   £33261   210414222132031   68 277* 344 719 1202+ 1325 1575 1753 1998- 2353*
2500 2567 2763 2946 3179*
2 GEORGE HARRY  12   £-   000000   94 544 834 1948 2829 3017
2 GEORGE JAMES  53   £4078   0421   2561 2791 2983 3130*
5 GEORGE WILLIAM  40   £6583   0000-2230100020   412 525- 687 836 2402* 2537 2731 2772 2921- 3106
3 GEORGES CHOICE  0   £-   000-0   454
3 GEORGES QUAY  32   £3683   000-4013400   229 386 480* 615 919 1084 3179
3 GEORGIA RIVER  63   £5257   3-12020   546* 950 1147 2691 2867
3 GEORGIAN ROSE  0   £-   0-04000000200   217 283 423 774 1334 1549 1898 2073 2208 2560 3076
3 GERAGHTY AGAIN  43   £873   00-04100   127 210 2339* 2594 2763
3 GERSHWIN  20   £5184   000-12001000214   729* 1367 1447 1990 2088* 2120 2463 2594 2702 2787* 2928
```

```
2 GERUNTY  0   £-  00   3137 3199
5 GERYON  0   £-  -0   3194
3 GESEDEH  78   £45437   -11000121   162* 372* 926 1128 2202 2462* 2868 3207*
2 GET ON GERAGHTY  53   £4540   2114   1510 1825* 2082* 2352
2 GET SET LISA  24   £3024   0040022210   364 515 905 1161 1305 1672 1881 1955 2298* 2756
3 GEX  0   £-  -0000   535 1087 2148 3161
2 GHANAYIM  65   £8806   022102   1154 1802 2043 2448* 2687 2999
2 GHAWWAS  48   £178   3   2229
3 GHOFAR  2   £-  -0   2386
3 GIANT REDWOOD  0   £-  00-0000   1337 1372 1544 1759
3 GIBBERISH  23   £5665   03000-20412132   674 823 960 1396* 1773 1974* 2226 2344
4 GIBBOUS MOON  14   £1019   20-002000   344 709 1018 1274 1689 2581
2 GIFT OF PEARL  15   £120   3   181
2 GIFTED NEPHEW  25   £-  0   3199
2 GILBERTO  56   £3049   43231   1488 1915 2554 2812 3228*
4 GILDERDALE  44   £-  04310-0000   433 706 879 1109
4 GILLANBONE  0   £140   30004-003   107 673 1201
2 GILLOT BAR  24   £1740   000021404   43 167 913 1105 1622 1795* 2050 2279 2471
2 GILLYS COMET  0   £-  00   2032 2180
3 GILSAN GREY  0   £-  0-00   45 130
4 GINAS MATCH  0   £-  00400-0   2960
3 GINGERLAND  23   £-  -4   2078
4 GIOVANNI  10   £119   43000-03   1939 2422
3 GIRDLE NESS  17   £3931   0-40011300   500 764 1193 1540* 1960* 2041 2426 2800
2 GIROTONDO  55   £4823   4123   2345 2493* 2865 3019
3 GIVING IT ALL AWAY  24   £4075   00-300002103240   74 436 615 1245 1432 1651 1819* 2230 2497 2594
2730 2928
3 GLACIER LASS  12   £532   00-000200   379 1198 1794 2230 2508 2797
3 GLADE  29   £-  -00000   1228 1586 2248 2676 2719
3 GLAMGRAM  0   £-  -0   422
2 GLAMGRAM FOR GRAMS  42   £2501   04143   1059 1475 2011+ 2479 2680
2 GLAMIS GIRL  23   £-  -0000   345 938 2434 2804
3 GLANGWILI  37   £353   0230-4200   1246 1446 1885 2313
2 GLASS CASTLE  38   £171   03   2852 3111
3 GLAZEPTA FINAL  0   £-  -000   941 1080 1193
3 GLEADHILL PARK  5   £358   004-0000002000   339 454 545 1277 1499 1584 2106 2312 2575 3065
3 GLEAM OUT  71   £6877   2   1117
5 GLEN KELLA MANX  33   £5472   40000-000100000   1235 1608 1852 2021+ 2160 2258 2402 2530 2862
2 GLEN WEAVING  0   £-  00   2044 2673
2 GLENCROFT  51   £2714   0010   320 515 602+ 1014
4 GLENDERRY  0   £331   100-00030000000   281 611 745 872 1024 1374 1985 2154 2395 2604 3154
4 GLENMORE CAPTAIN  13   £-  00000-0   282
4 GLIDE BY  58   £4184   24200-3200   950 1514 1851 2538
3 GLIFAHDA  73   £8314   400024   155 2742
3 GLIKIAA MOU  29   £2480   2F00-2420014000   26 228 516 884 1151 2210* 2488 2672 3054 3233
2 GLINT OF GLORY  35   £-  0   1382
2 GLINT OF VICTORY  63   £-  03D   2768 3040
3 GLITTER  42   £1154   -030400   250 359 599 1061 1630 3105
3 GLOBAL  7   £509   000-0020000   615 703 1051 1436 1927 3160 3172
2 GLOBAL LADY  40   £3415   21030   1668 1843* 2485 2611 2941
2 GLOIRE DE DIJON  8   £-  00   2651 3043
2 GLORIAD  13   £294   00002   354 446 543 603 2994
3 GLORIANT  0   £100   00040-034000000   39 109 284 368 2086 2424 2660 2998 3147
2 GLORIOUS DAN  0   £-  0000   1495 1555 2177 2535
2 GLORY BEE  23   £2576   01004100   1083 1262* 1522 1828 1938 2097* 2435 2529
2 GLORY FOREVER  71   £26371   44101   915 1097 1452* 2384 3088*
2 GLORY GOLD  11   £115   004003000   261 415 537 813 948 1680 2180 2588 3031
2 GLORY LINE  46   £1917   021   2239 2723 3148+
3 GLORY TIME  7   £-  00000-000   194 1415 1562
2 GLOVERS KIND  0   £-  0   3199
2 GLOW AGAIN  55   £12440   31112000   548 672* 995* 1255+ 1506 2198 2465 2687
3 GLOWING PROMISE  33   £1687   02-1240003   452* 690 875 2062 2286 3101 3194
3 GLYNCORRWG  0   £-  00-0   3102
5 GO BANANAS  51   £271   31000-000400   248 433 573 680 706 1047
3 GO FLAMINGO  0   £-  0-400440   1068 1416 1784 2590 2902 3161
2 GO HENRI  42   £561   30   1510 2547
8 GO LISSAVA  0   £-  -0   199
2 GO MY PET  25   £-  00000   383 533 2147 2287 2561
6 GO SPECTRUM  0   £-  00000-00000   42 131 257 1543 1719
2 GODFORD  0   £-  00   2596 2829
6 GODLORD  0   £-  0000-000000000000   369 540 943 1054 1689 1871 1987 2102 2173 3029
3 GODOUNOV  15   £-  -0400   2361 2688 2996 3172
4 GODS HOPE  18   £480   0--00-000402   36 129' 1829 2093 2175 3063
3 GODS ISLE  26   £1738   1010-0200033000   246 443 588 814 1638 1896 2055 2224 2378 2775
5 GODS LAW  5   £4446   000-01321302000   594 710* 830 956- 1074* 1156 1335 1547 1800 2414 2762
2 GODS LIL LISA  0   £-  000   1030 1238 3134
3 GODS PATH  20   £-  000-000000   512 739 980 1314 1589 1806
5 GODS SOLUTION  15   £1899   104020040004000   42+ 65 369 520 890- 1182 1338 1536 1882 2012 2537
2816 2970 3104 3145
7 GODSTRUTH  19   £466   44100-000434430   977 1344 1543 2322 2592 2775 2992 3145 3191
6 GOING BROKE  31   £1565   4/342-1300   204* 366 504 542
2 GOING EASY  29   £-  0400   1241 1522 1583 2729
7 GOING GOING  48   £3230   42114-013   349 532* 782
2 GOING GREEK  0   £-  000   2901 2990 3069
5 GOLD AND IVORY  76   £4491   101200-3000   251 475 885 1144
3 GOLD CARAT  70   £12975   -10   151* 293
3 GOLD CHIP  19   £1185   00013-4202000   431 936- 1247 1701 2104 2264 2508
4 GOLD DUCHESS  20   £4514   0-0424310024030   42 124 182- 240 355 412* 525 628 784 890 971 2322
3152
2 GOLD FEE  71   £8804   312   2675 2846* 3108
9 GOLD FLOOR  0   £-  40-0   201
6 GOLD HUNTER  0   £-  -0   343
2 GOLD JUSTICE  0   £-  000   1518 1660 1812
                                                > 975 <
```

```
4 GOLD LOFT  10   £1569   0--02-1000020   177+ 262 399 499 1662 1774 3224
2 GOLD MINORIES  21   £84   0030   2249 2812 2987 3082
3 GOLD MONOPOLY  0   £-   -00   1062 1315
2 GOLD PAINT  0   £-   0   3181
4 GOLD PROSPECT  52   £21182   0-1220402301241   31* 192- 374 616 952 1145 1521 1777 1852 2674*
  2773 3021 3123*
2 GOLD SCEPTRE  51   £-  04   3011 3163
3 GOLD SOVEREIGN  0   £-  -0   1961
2 GOLD STATE  16   £-   00000   544 728 1279 2323 3031
3 GOLD TOUCH  39   £-   0442-0   954
2 GOLDCHAN  2   £-  004   813 1221 2396
2 GOLDEN AIR  0   £-  0   1764
3 GOLDEN ANCONA  30   £2724   00-100024300020   284* 387 586 1091 1864 2266 2399 2475 2862 3015
  3145 3233
3 GOLDEN AZELIA  0   £-   -000004   937 1444 1670 2068 2309 3202
4 GOLDEN BEAU  16   £3034   40-033301230004   281 499 566 680 1013 1942* 2189 2369 2655 2762 3078
  3140
3 GOLDEN BOURNE  0   £-   0-00   774 1288
4 GOLDEN BOY  0   £-   00000   8 106 378 490 636
5 GOLDEN BOY(ITA)  66   £11178   -44------4   296 897 3093
2 GOLDEN BRAID  70   £11572   120   1382* 2246 2751
2 GOLDEN CAJUN  33   £216   0040   1207 2805 2950 3174
3 GOLDEN CROFT  15   £-   000-00400   193 331 623 850 2432
2 GOLDEN DIRHAM  0   £-  0   3171
4 GOLDEN DISC  0   £488   03333-430240000   710 1013 1136 1610 1765 2126 2863 3057 3172
9 GOLDEN FANCY  38   £3868   000223432D3302300   4  142  256  429 827 1024 1185 1412 1548 1866
  1964 2130 2267 2604   2776 2978 3236
2 GOLDEN GAME  0   £-   000   2725 2975 3158
3 GOLDEN GUILDER  30   £10291   02120313333U224   38 168 198* 447 545 670 947* 1414 1959 2277 2397
  2411 2660 2970 3104
3 GOLDEN HANDCUFF  0   £-   00000-0   2184
3 GOLDEN HEIGHTS  50   £7334   43-121423201   351* 435 635* 1152 1674 2142 2665 2776 2979*
3 GOLDEN ORIOLE  56   £540   30   466 754
2 GOLDEN PAMPAS  48   £709   3   3181
2 GOLDEN PLEASURE  50   £160   3   2487
4 GOLDEN SECRET  0   £-   0-000-0   2401
4 GOLDEN SLADE  33   £5349   0114-0013300300   112 499 762* 1018 1189 1365 2123 2207 2369 2544
3 GOLDEN STRAW  15   £246   -0000020   334 500 844 1324 1560 2898 3172
2 GOLDEN TOPAZ  0   £-   000   1665 2229 2423
2 GOLDEN TREE  47   £1160   000033   1049 1296 2468 2628 2894 2971
5 GOLDEN TRIANGLE  13   £-   00401-00000   940 1035 1523 1939 2134
3 GOLDENA  0   £-   -0   699
2 GOLDENDOUBLEYOU  22   £469   230   864 1088 1221
2 GOLDORINA  15   £578   100   86+ 2090 2421
3 GOLFLINES  0   £-   0000-00000   1160 1361 2327 2683 2857
2 GOMEZ  0   £-  0   2199
2 GONE FOR IT  0   £-   000000   1194 1305 1550 1803 1946 2045
3 GONE OVERBOARD  36   £474   -040020   779 991 1535 2015 2217 2520
2 GOOD BUY BAILEYS  40   £1326   140343   186* 515 1105 1568 1828 1962
2 GOOD CAUSE  0   £-  0   2750
2 GOOD GAME  37   £652   23000   905 1' ￠5 1683 2843 3146
5 GOOD N SHARP  1   £393   00000-200404   1766 2126 2264 2414 2797 2891
3 GOOD NATURED  17   £-   -00000   1530 1954 2148 3155 3227
2 GOOD POINT  40   £4115   020010   583 777 2225 2615 3017* 3188
2 GOOD SAILING  48   £1280   01   2788 3117*
3 GOOD TIME GIRL  15   £4776   011202304   533 763* 1190* 1570 1828 2026 2935 3079 3182
2 GOOD WOMAN  17   £-   400   2153 2365 2555
2 GOODNIGHT MASTER  22   £-   0004   2263 2788 2895 3131
3 GOODTIME HAL  25   £815   0-432300   430 769 996 1386 1700 2034
2 GOODWOOD PARK  0   £-   000   1289 1488 1555
2 GOODWYNS LAD  26   £-   00   2961 3067
3 GOOSE HILL  40   £3532   10-1040304   81* 216 575 716 1091 1292 2063
3 GORGEOUS ALGERNON  40   £6643   30-010202040000   74 178* 326 615- 692 1384 1486 2155 2624 2763
  2867 3113
4 GORGEOUS PRINCESS  12   £-   2000-00   129 341
3 GORGEOUS STRIKE  67   £11247   123-0203443402   191 348 411 946 1409 1538 2112 2454 2693 2912
3 GOSSIPER  51   £-   41400-0000   600 691 1044 1151
2 GOULDSWOOD  0   £-   0000   1504 1883 3014 3141
5 GOURTIONIST  15   £-   --000-00   420 1056
7 GOUVERNO  35   £-   00341/00   2685 3124
3 GOVERNOR GENERAL  68   £23874   001-011000   190 600+ 1044* 1631 2538 2785
2 GOVERNORSHIP  56   £980   2  583
5 GRACIOUS HOMES  13   £283   02004-40000   441 636 727 1500 1868
4 GRAND CELEBRATION  22   £2182   -0-040001110   41 106 786 890 1074 2094* 2208* 2315* 2467
2 GRAND CHELEM  70   £18031   -11   2636*
2 GRAND ECLIPSE  30   £124   3   3200
3 GRAND FLING  5   £168   00000-402   139 347 2315
6 GRAND HARBOUR  55   £-   12204-0000   598 1094 1389 1811
2 GRAND PAVOIS  78   £10534   2   1010
4 GRAND QUEEN  0   £-   -0-0000000   145 489 971 1423 1616 2124 2411
2 GRAND TOUR  65   £11489   011   2243 2796+ 3178*
3 GRANDANGUS  12   £4184   000-000103103   356 514 1309 1656* 1898 2060 2184* 2399 2508
4 GRANDCOURT  70   £6603   -333010   153 390 2114
2 GRANDE COUTURE  0   £-   -0   373
3 GRANGE FARM LADY  21   £1798   -0302001   1927 2186 2367 2409 2575 2793 3024*
2 GRANNY BIMPS  44   £124   043   1802 3099 3205
2 GRANNY TAKESA TRIP  0   £-   00   834 1440
4 GRANNYS BANK  46   £20326   33211-12210201   1018* 1189 1229 2144+ 2566 2934 3123 3231*
3 GRANNYS MONEY  60   £2394   3   293
2 GRAPE  0   £-   0   3206
3 GRATIFY  12   £512   00-00034034   484 832 1078 1260 1477 2492 2760 2892
5 GRAUER WICHT  75   £34192   -41   759 1715*
2 GREAT ACT  43   £501   30   1928 2476
                                      > 976 <
```

```
2 GREAT ASPECT   61   £9332   11   2067* 2439*
2 GREAT CAESAR   0   £-   00   2646 2957
3 GREAT DILEMMA   41   £2410   -0022041   402 656 982 1244 1487 2973 3147*
3 GREAT EXCEPTION   45   £3434   0232-31013   779 1481* 2324 2779* 2979
3 GREAT GANDER   30   £-   -044   1444 1799 2306
3 GREAT LEIGHS   50   £11236   02-012000020   213 359* 575 1153 1854 2165 2459 3042 3123
2 GREAT MEMORY   30   £-   0000   612 728 965 2140
4 GREAT OWING   0   £-   00--0-00   1574 1990
4 GREAT RELATIVE   5   £-   00-0000   8 58 260 355
2 GREAT STANDS BY   0   £-   0000   537 939 1076 2805
3 GREAT TOPIC   21   £381   0-004003   191 635 998 1303 1578 2034
9 GREATEST HITS   0   £-   04041/00   28 119
2 GRECIAN JOS   34   £433   0330   612 1895 2140 2512
2 GRECIAN URN   73   £13294   3212042   3005 3208
5 GREED   18   £3494   4-2443240424033   1185 1335 1565 1673 1820 1964 2154 2267 2415 2477 2683 2800
   2995
3 GREEK MUSIC   0   £-   -00   2085 2483
3 GREEK SWIFT   0   £-   00-0   849
5 GREEN   76   £5906   3   756
3 GREEN ARCHER   5   £116   -30000   524 651 960 1678 2305
3 GREEN DESERT   88   £168677   21214-120213140   220* 407 640 1096 1485* 2233 2474+ 2916 3210
3 GREEN DOLLAR   48   £982   10210-00300300   401 587 1805 1889 2155 2214 2655 2842
3 GREEN FOR DANGER   28   £672   -30030   213 464 862 2973 3164
2 GREEN GLORY   30   £735   2030   1075 1241 2007 2167
2 GREEN LALEEK   35   £-   000   2574 2878 2961
4 GREEN ROOM GAMBOLS   28   £-   40000-0   861
5 GREEN RUBY   62   £66828   03030-0331411   1235 1429 1608 1852* 2021 2204+ 2668+
4 GREEN STEPS   40   £234   -0430   452 863 1278 2706
2 GREEN VEIL   47   £1130   02   2056 2254
5 GREENACRES GIRL   1   £-   -0-00   282 743
2 GREENCASTLE HILL   53   £2697   012   1874 2555+ 2881
2 GREENHIL JAZZ TIME   46   £166   030   2147 2433 2658
3 GREENHILLS BOY   15   £944   -004201   1574 1815 1937 2342 2621 2795*
3 GREENHILLS GIRL   15   £637   001-0002403200   380 1394 1689 1909 2217 2300 2597 2705 2797 2932
3 GREENHILLS JOY   42   £3639   -0331   2546 2948 3142 3186+
3 GREENS GALLERY   24   £3135   01120000   353 589* 948* 1585 1693 2181 2485 2579
2 GREENS HERRING   28   £2300   0410   800 931 1155* 1397
2 GREENS OLD MASTER   40   £851   20303   1573 2001 2423 2716 3103
2 GREENS PICTURE   16   £-   0   3184
2 GREENS SEYMOUR   0   £-   00   813 1949
2 GREENSWARD   40   £959   100   2069* 2308 3019
2 GREENSWARD BOY   18   £453   0030003   1495 1599 1723 2212 2323 2588 2689
4 GREETLAND DANCER   5   £275   00000-40000   815 1377 1624 2154 2411
3 GREGORIAN CHANT   14   £-   00000400   217 576 835 1398 1806 2109 2190 2360
3 GRENDEL   0   £-   -000   328 546 1062
2 GRENVILLE LASS   12   £104   030   1803 2020 2405
3 GRETAS SONG   0   £-   -00   2793 3070
5 GREY CARD   0   £-   -000   366 449 611
4 GREY CREE   0   £-   -0000   594 1077 1765 2104
6 GREY DESIRE   65   £58690   1,124120230000000   18+   60*   222 413 587* 705 945 1485 1631 2003 2145
   2233 2259 2474 3020 3235
3 GREY DRAGON   12   £-   004-000   14 140 568
3 GREY GODDESS   75   £13106   03-10113   1107 2633* 2911
2 GREY ROD   8   £-   004   497 763 1599
3 GREY SALUTE   35   £1793   -330302   1674 1899 2148 2428 2610 3186
4 GREY STARLIGHT   16   £1392   00200-00130   182 355 906* 1104 1338
2 GREY TAN   38   £800   3240   931 1296 1397 2052
3 GREY WALLS   38   £-   013-00000   271 1487 2131 2649 2719
2 GREY WOLF TIGER   40   £5492   0224114002   404 483 927 1059 1405* 1522* 1891 2272 2485 2813
3 GRIMESGILL   21   £-   -004440   576 776 1540 2017 2216 2394
2 GRIMESGILL USA   55   £1539   31   2645 3067+
3 GRISETTE   22   £259   030-000240   837 1272 1516 2210 2312 3145
2 GROOM DANCER   75   £18928   1101   3090*
3 GROOVY 72?   £48951   4   3210
2 GROSSEN   0   £-   00   2889 3103
3 GROSVENOR COURT   0   £-   0-00000   751 1364 2495 2679 3162
3 GROVE TOWER   21   £-   003-400000   75 273 416 1884 1952 2306
3 GROVECOTE   4   £126   003-0000030   171 620 740 1310 1666 2125 2789
4 GRUMBLE   31   £-   11300-000   2545 2956 3195
4 GRUNDY LANE   58   £-   /0234-0   166
2 GRUNDYS FLAME   0   £-   00   3181 3234
3 GRUNDYS OWN   10   £-   0-000000   1372 1530 1688 2306 2605 2714
2 GRUNIDAD   0   £-   0000   2418 2869 3067 3137
2 GUARD ROOM   0   £-   0   3073
3 GUESSING   46   £1050   -00214   739 1833 2228 2363* 2745
4 GUEST IMAGE   7   £-   00003-00   1804 2109
2 GULF KING   72   £37500   0210101   405 571- 664* 1129 2198* 2737 3003*
2 GULF OF GOLD   11   £-   000   2491 2607 2936
5 GULFLAND   60   £17651   0-00-1321011214   129* 333 429 686* 1024 1502* 1963+ 2237 2389* 2912
3 GULL NOOK   81   £41551   -1100   549* 1128* 2202 2638
4 GULPHAR   6   £96   -0440-0000030   1103 1231 1784 1937 2515 2984 3193
4 GUNDREDA   44   £2399   01000-0040332   17 72 1498 1931 2062 2303 2443
3 GUNDULINA   0   £-   -0   371
3 GUNNER GO   6   £151   000-0300   14 41 195 237
3 GUNNER MAC   0   £-   0-000000   239 381 631 823 2042 2682
2 GUNNER STREAM   31   £227   03000   1275 1583 2159 2878 3165
2 GUNSHIP   0   £-   000   632 1181 1434
4 GURTEEN BOY   36   £3259   0001-000010340   453 566 668 881 1189 1553* 1890 2123 3123 3231
3 GUTSY   0   £-   24200-000   871 2743 2854
3 GUYMYSON   18   £264   -0030   328 1062 1404 1990
4 GWILLIM ENTERPRISE   2   £-   -0000-04   1195 1310
3 GWYDION   80   £56044   11-433124321   232 1146 1485 1631+ 1889- 2233 2538 2772- 3054+
4 GWYN HOWARD   11   £-   30000-04000   23 121 263 541 2432
                                    > 977 <
```

```
2 GWYNBROOK  13  £158  003400000  364 515 813 913 1566 2298 2466 2757 2919
2 GWYNRAS  25  £-  000  2542 2771 3067
4 GYPS GIFT  0  £-  -0  769
2 GYPSYS BARN RAT  10  £119  0300  715 2095 2476 3182
3 GYPSYS PROPHECY  42  £2616  0230-324100  507 624- 2370 2518* 2659 3015
2 HAATIF  52  £964  31  3043 3205+
2 HABCAN  43  £158  30  2541 2869
3 HABER  60  £8882  -2314303  229 465 667* 1007 1455 1655 2691
3 HABOOB BALADEE  50  £678  -20  1064 1469
4 HABS LAD  37  £-  11200-00000  481 616 706 815 1229
3 HACHIMITSU  8  £1077  00-000001034  111 338 480 907 1063 1937* 2594 2960 3065
5 HADDAK  0  £-  -0  164
3 HADDON LAD  23  £1172  0000-0004201  198 402 540 845 1212 1444 1666*
4 HADEER  83  £68984  0/044-204110100  920 1109 1286 1823* 2145+ 2259 2538* 2770 3020
2 HAIL A CAB  0  £-  000  2434 2589 3205
3 HAIL AND HEARTY  28  £633  400-0200  233 340 507 760
3 HAIL TO ROBERTO  76  £7590  20  302 407
2 HAILEYS RUN  34  £1975  430334032  323 632 927 1296 1475 1762 1946 2625 2829
3 HAITI MILL  28  £-  303-04404  309 768 907 1169 2399
3 HAJ  3  £283  02-240000  684 932 1063 1364 1942 3202
2 HAJJI BABA  0  £-  0  3080
5 HALF SHAFT  10  £919  3-000-4401  1546 1820 3154 3220*
3 HALINA  64  £4430  -3-2  470
3 HALLGATE  86  £65748  1111-3041031213  249 407 587 854+ 1146 2084 2241+ 2474- 2772+ 2916
4 HALLOWED  0  £-  000-0400  1473 1747 1952 2093
3 HALO HATCH  46  £3628  42203-030012003  234 570 1520 1783 1971* 2149 2481 2617 3066
3 HAMLOUL  38  £5052  00030-00220210  528 829 1281 1431 1864 2076 2288+ 2879
3 HAMPER  42  £10242  -43121  1880 2339 2401* 2807 2946*
5 HAMPTON WALK  0  £-  00000-000004  30 1165 1264 1346 1579 2014
4 HANDLEBAR  43  £8874  -0031-00112230  410 584 1017* 1636* 2066 2267 2566 2934
3 HANDSOME SAILOR  69  £13029  10412-0311  2258 2382 2725* 2947*
2 HANG LOOSE  15  £-  33042-0  2386
3 HANGLANDS  34  £-  0-040  923 1244 1580
3 HANKLEY DOWN  20  £-  -00040  714 978 1530 1726 2075
3 HANOOF  43  £1593  -431040  982 1291 1775* 2623 2855 3026
2 HANSEATIC  49  £4810  0021003  1019 1241 1512 2029+ 2179 3125 3230
3 HANSOM LAD  39  £1222  00303-02323  217 284 447 961 1142
3 HAPPY BREED  29  £648  31-0040400  224 1147 1509 2058 2569 2834 3022
2 HAPPY HARRIET  0  £-  000  2423 2667 2889
3 HARAABAH  54  £932  00200-010  478 1758* 2390
6 HARBOUR BAZAAR  14  £2882  4203003D3120300  8 199 967 1106 1186 1416 1578 1602 2190 2309* 2432 2591 3071 3128 3194
2 HARD ACT  58  £6656  011000100  457 632* 1057* 1129 1643 1925 2071* 2384 2598
3 HARD AS IRON  38  £15603  000-4111221200  620 1079* 1179* 1284* 1755 2404 2426* 2624 2763 3179
2 HARD LEAF  64  £7130  212  2914
6 HARD OAK  0  £-  -00  1274 1755
3 HARD ROUND  71  £29526  041-2443120  159 465 802 1107 1514* 1823 2145
3 HARDY CHANCE  14  £324  0-00303000  213 338 423 907 1299 1885 2313 2702
3 HARE HILL  13  £1041  00010-00100040  141 451 684* 997 1678 1838 2083 2427
2 HARLEM SHUFFLE  66  £9039  1023  2907 3088
4 HARLESTONE LAKE  38  £11701  320-00341401130  419 542 841 1058 1260* 1348 1875 2169* 2455* 2809 3052
3 HARLEYFORD LAD  8  £298  400-00003000  455 936 1299 1677 1921 2339 2497 2602
3 HARMONY BOWL  22  £-  000-00040  33 111 1191 2575 2816
3 HARMONY HEIGHTS  3  £-  300-00000  624 1246 1751 2546 2981
2 HARRY EM  0  £-  000  1550 1993 2615
3 HARRY HULL  30  £685  000-00004140  309 516 1091 1224 1627 2409* 2483 3116
2 HARRY HUNT  30  £5278  310001010  320 488* 785 1203 1379 1680* 2025 2279* 2798
2 HARRY QUINN  52  £7752  221320  149 752 1329 1591
2 HARRYAKER  0  £-  00  2919 3103
3 HARRYS COMING  19  £1853  02130020200  13 102 181* 711 813 1088 1680 1881 2150 2298 2588
3 HARSLEY SURPRISE  24  £2193  4040-3314104  608 740 889* 1201 1267* 1678 1800
2 HARTS LANE  17  £-  00000  1440 1604 2292 2527 2813
2 HARUSI  0  £-  0  3206
5 HATCHING  4  £414  00000-0200430  1165 1942 2123 2319 2519 2981 3065
3 HATINA  46  £634  3  3176
2 HATSHEPSUT  0  £-  0  3158
5 HAUTBOY LADY  13  £324  04032-03004  1804 1971 2189 2837 2981
2 HAUTBOYSLITTLEGIRL  0  £-  0  2698
3 HAUWMAL  68  £17221  020-1204122  501* 667 1147 1468 1886* 2156 2692-
7 HAVENS PRIDE  0  £-  -00  1412 1787
5 HAVERS ROAD  0  £-  -0  343
2 HAWAIAN CAT  55  £1421  23  1629 2118
3 HAWAIIAN PALM  61  £6072  13-001001  234 586 1084* 1468 2066 2617*
3 HAWARDEN  50  £3179  -4001320  218 384 1178 1797* 1956 2572 2924
4 HAWSER  18  £-  -0004-0  2900
5 HAY STREET  37  £-  34000-0000000  17 2437 2545 2668 2749 3118 3231
5 HAYASHI  0  £-  00000-0  137
2 HAYGATE PARK  26  £-  0440  2080 2494 2678 2814
2 HAYTAL  40  £-  00  685 1242
3 HAYWAIN  13  £2930  000-0300010440  874 1257 1579 1783 2184 2601* 2681 2905 3033 3157
3 HAZEL BEE  30  £102  03  2167 2589
2 HAZELS GIRL  13  £790  2304020000  20 118 254 404 1180 1635 1955 2100 2323 2609
3 HEAD OF SCHOOL  28  £1022  00020-004244304  619 839 1167 2017 2152 2599 2720 2925 3195
2 HEAD OF VICTORY  46  £-  00  2675 3181
6 HEADIN ON  8  £186  -3000  1102 1349 1535 2154
3 HEADIN WEST  38  £-  -0  148
3 HEART OF GLASS  33  £684  4-10000  83+ 111 255 1245 3138
4 HEART OF STONE  37  £9959  00000-00103110  432 652 851+ 1209 1441 2049* 2285* 2692
4 HEATHGRIFF  8  £1665  0102-3000023031  399 578 709 976 1188 2014 2342 2621 2836 2960*
2 HEATSEEKER  0  £-  000  1883 3014 3130
2 HEAVEN ONLY KNOWS  0  £-  00  2494 3074
```

```
3 HEAVENLY CAROL  0  £-  -0000004  835 928 1142 1695 2312 2898 3172
2 HEAVENLY HARMONY  0  £-  0  2487
3 HEAVENLY HOOFER  17  £5783  0-0101103100000  377 608* 1073 1103* 1547* 1678 1758 1864* 2039
  2264 2629 2891 3101
3 HEAVENLY STROLLER  0  £-  -0  1691
3 HEAVY BRIGADE  48  £6057  -11  247* 775*
2 HECKLEY LOCH  0  £-  0  2043
2 HEDERA HELIX  18  £460  0220  149 1496 2020 2180
3 HEIGHLAD  50  £5717  -133  409* 552 1152
2 HEIGHT OF ELEGANCE  56  £-  0  2675
5 HEIGHT OF SUMMER  10  £5082  100-04003001341  984 1209 1416 1559 1945 2098 2492 2727* 2900
  2959 3071*
3 HELAWE  41  £4834  22100-030140010  228 580 1033 1191* 1499 1991 2382 2659+ 3055
6 HELDIGVIS  0  £-  -0  9
3 HELEN BOY  0  £-  000-0  875
2 HELENS CONTACT  25  £684  1  13*
2 HELENS HERO  0  £-  0  2118
3 HELENS PLEASURE  39  £142  04404-30  29 120
3 HELIETTA  43  £4317  -04231210  1368 1481 1842 2248 2546* 2690 2980* 3101
3 HELLO BENZ  34  £3047  -400423322  322 699 916 1055 1220 1507 1671 1866 2053-
3 HELLO BLUE  0  £-  00-000  175 454 954
3 HELLO ERNANI  71  £31562  203-22321200  60 286 384 753 1045* 1343- 1715 2112
3 HELLO GEORGIE  0  £-  0-000  347 506 1281
5 HELLO GYPSY  36  £6810  00000-21301100  1500 1720* 2059 2264 2414+ 2797+ 3029 3116
3 HELLO SAM  0  £-  -00  2534 2991
7 HELLO SUNSHINE  26  £747  00144-000040004  192 481 680 1018 1640 1804 1911 2144 2674
2 HELLO TROUBLE  27  £-  0  2159
3 HELSANON  8  £1018  00-0004400  194 779 1078 1661 1721 1961 2280
3 HELVICK BAY  7  £-  0000-0000  454 671 954 1169
2 HEMMINGFORD GREY  5  £-  00  3069 3229
3 HENAADI  30  £738  -0002  2085 2314 2650 2998
2 HENDEKA  67  £9467  31120  1488 1915+ 2263* 2444- 2849
2 HENNERTON  0  £-  0  531
2 HENRIETTA PLACE  41  £-  04  1928 3130
6 HENRY GEARY STEELS  0  £-  -0  526
3 HENRY PADWICK  10  £-  24400-00  447 961
2 HENRYK  54  £2242  20  2939 3206
4 HENRYS PLACE  12  £2195  03300-002000100  10 114 378 499 689 745 866* 970 1104
4 HENRYS VENTURE  11  £4736  -00001130343000  42 182 266 1070 1120* 1338* 1423 2213 2295 2397
  2715 2816 2891 2970
4 HERALDISTE  80  £2369  23100-30  2 468
3 HERB ROBERT  0  £-  00040-0000000  1053 1134 1613 2139 2361 2508 2778
3 HERMINDA  8  £-  024-00000  507 884 1033 1312 3160
3 HERNE MISS MADAM  0  £-  -00  1446 2321
2 HERR FLICK  22  £267  02400  34 94 2007 3148 3222
5 HERRADURA  50  £6646  2-2302D32033144  743 921 1293 1349 1963 2211 2338 2627 2666 2776* 2873
  2979
2 HEXTHORPE DELL  0  £-  0  13
2 HEY AMADEUS  22  £581  0200300  1495 1803 2162 2485 2729 3058 3230
2 HEYDIR  0  £-  0  3181
2 HEYSHOTT  50  £1075  1  2961*
4 HI DIDDLE  0  £-  -00-0  448
4 HI TECH GIRL  52  £287  40340-400  1385 1508 1852
2 HIAAM  76  £11994  210  1464- 1789* 2235
2 HIDDEN ASSET  0  £-  00  2147 2434
3 HIDDEN BRIEF  65  £21510  00-120020123120  37* 59 406 1532 2021- 2241 2473* 2562 2765 2870*
  2940 3177
3 HIDDEN MOVE  14  £266  000-000340  357 452 631 969 1479 2152
2 HIERO FALCO  0  £-  00  1872 2105
2 HIGH ALOFT  0  £-  0  3120
3 HIGH BAZAAR  0  £-  00-0  2705
3 HIGH BORN BIDDER  14  £-  -00  1278 1726
2 HIGH CABLE  0  £-  00  1105 1413
2 HIGH CHATEAU  19  £-  000  685 1172 3130
2 HIGH CLIMBER  40  £514  0230  1345 2070 2368 3131
3 HIGH CONDUCT  24  £-  4-400  1756 2085 3062
3 HIGH CROWN  61  £1043  -42  370 1291
5 HIGH DEBATE  54  £-  00-40-00  617 964
6 HIGH EAGLE  0  £-  -000000  211 418 836 1447 1649 1940
4 HIGH FOREST  0  £-  0-000-00040  1923 2109 2306 2528 2714
3 HIGH HALO  37  £931  0-14  89+ 271
3 HIGH IMAGE  41  £1555  -01000  250 835* 1878 2362 2783
3 HIGH KNOWL  54  £8736  0-42311110  1206 1578 2042 2269* 2599+ 2701* 2937* 3038
5 HIGH MORALE  0  £-  -0  2134
5 HIGH PITCHED  23  £-  00404-0000  112 262 481 578
4 HIGH PLAINS  20  £-  21010-00000400  235 462 801 1099 1388 1837 2733 3139
7 HIGH PORT  8  £383  02100-000024440  101 594 830 943 1156 1338 1482 1698 1774
5 HIGH REEF  20  £-  02104-0  9
6 HIGH RENOWN  14  £-  0-00-00  2647 3129
2 HIGH STORM  0  £-  0  3180
4 HIGH TENSION  53  £18022  0044-2412210123  618 805 1177* 1409 1551- 1809* 2220 2551+ 2686 2855
2 HIGH TOWN  0  £-  000  86 181 446
3 HIGH VELOCITY  0  £-  -0  3070
2 HIGH WIND  63  £4318  143  268* 638 1006
2 HIGHAM BROKE  0  £-  000  2645 3080 3223
10 HIGHAM GREY  0  £-  10-000040044000  80 144 358 526 675 860 1745 1884 2087 2211 2280 2492
3 HIGHBLEST  0  £-  0-0  1934
4 HIGHDALE  10  £1471  00404-10000  163* 429 578 724 956
3 HIGHEST HONOR  82  £69964  -122  156* 389 900
3 HIGHEST NOTE  16  £1725  0400-3004324100  37 209 991 1369 1656 1898 2034 2163* 2217 2714
3 HIGHEST PEAK  34  £1835  000-2320200  140 357 512 2061 2401 2442 2622
3 HIGHEST PRAISE  45  £7126  403-01331030  455 677+ 914 1001 1640* 2155 2674 3021
2 HIGHFALUTIN LYMEY  5  £-  00000  483 596 2609 3017 3081
                                    > 979 <
```

```
4 HIGHFIELDS LAD  0   £-    0-0   1652
3 HIGHLAND BALL  28  £419   00-0043002   213 575 1755 2217 2623 2959 3115
2 HIGHLAND BELLE  34  £483   30   2067 2664
2 HIGHLAND BOUNTY  32  £-    00   3023 3141
2 HIGHLAND CAPTAIN  0  £-    00040000   865 1076 1413 1537 2298 2512 2724 2872
3 HIGHLAND CHIEFTAIN  79  £66499   12114-01210220   1098 1448* 1712 2004* 2461 2752 3001 3121
3 HIGHLAND DAISY  0   £-    -0   32
3 HIGHLAND GLEN  16  £-    04200-00040   516 1682 1973 2055 2139
4 HIGHLAND IMAGE  22  £798   00030-00200   1086 1804 2072- 3078 3164
2 HIGHLAND KATE  0   £-    00   1650 2396
2 HIGHLAND LAIRD  18  £-    0000000   777 2239 2444 2806 3031 3079 3190
2 HIGHLAND LODGE  25  £1256   00020   622 834 965 2919 3188
3 HIGHLAND TALE  20  £2516   00000-00004011   424 500 637 1257 1771 2238 2621* 3224*
4 HIGHLY PLACED  1   £-    -0000-0040   710 992 1104 1324
2 HIGHLY PLEASED  0   £-    0   3120
3 HIGHLY RECOMMENDED  40  £7914   -00031212   806 1036 1277 2120 2463* 2659- 2810* 2928
4 HILDALARIOUS  0   £-    0-00-000400   266 508 1319 1940 2046 2318
3 HILL RYDE  9   £247   34000-0020000   247 356 740 1158 1267 1540 1839
3 HILLGATE LADY  0   £-    -00   2314 2430
2 HILLIARD  1   £-    0000400   415 892 1105 1413 1672 2298 2724
3 HILLINGDON JIM  0   £-    0-00000   729 844 1340 2271 2515
2 HILLISON  0   £-    -000   2110 2593 3203
3 HILLS BID  64  £7565   00212-10032   615+ 692 1147 1383 1788
4 HILMAY  11  £1765   00-003040320100   211 355 418 636 842 977 1171 1940 2312 2592* 2858 3083
4 HILTON BROWN  61  £13216  313002243031020   12 76* 272 550 877 922 1285 1429 1640 1911 2021 2369* 2668 3021 3124
7 HIMORRE  0   £-    0-000-000   1969 2900 2985
4 HINCKLEY LANE  18  £-    -000-40   10 101
2 HINTON ROSE  25  £-    000   1238 2308 2788
2 HIS HIGHNESS  65  £5403   1322   1270* 1658 2133 2556
3 HISTON BRONZE  0   £-    -000   66 140 426
2 HIT LUCKY  25  £-    000   270 400 596
8 HIT THE BUTTON  0   £-    -000   1013 1542 1839
5 HIT THE HEIGHTS  17  £1606   00000-2232   177 530 2091 2274
3 HITCHENSTOWN  14  £-    0000-0000000   444 829 1055 1220 1503 1961 2128
2 HITTITE RULER  6   £-    000   2781 3044 3218
5 HIVE OFF  7   £-    043-2-000   532 1056 1459
3 HIYA BUD  0   £-    000-004000   379 650 1072 1954 2366 3045
4 HO MI CHINH  61  £10638   44000-110003   374* 687* 1145 1455 1777 1900
3 HOAD HILL  0   £-    00-00   381 631
4 HOBOURNES  8   £-    00400-00   675 3115
3 HOBOURNES KATIE  0   £408   -03000000003000   38 246 339 677 910 1360 1399 1687 2106 2268 2409 3024 3144 3185
2 HOBOURNES PERCY  0   £-    00   962 1197
2 HOCKLEY  39  £403   034   1019 1345 2329
9 HODAKA  12  £933   100   1546* 1951 2309
3 HOIST THE AXE  45  £1532   -21OO   53 82* 232 586
4 HOKUSAN  12  £411   01-034000000002   30 122 160 620 710 992 1338 1567 2094 2533 2697 3084
3 HOLBROOKE SUTTON  69  £5503   14-402400   1153 1466 1851 2231 2440 2568
2 HOLD DEAR  43  £124   3   3068
2 HOLD ON PLEASE  22  £-    4000   848 1205 1782 2365
3 HOLIDAY MILL  0   £-    30300-00400   29 880 1053 1288 1310
3 HOLLISTON  28  £-    10-000   582 3129 3225
3 HOLLOW HAND  64  £1269   22-1   688+
4 HOLLOW OAK  0   £-    -0   176
3 HOLLY BROWN  21  £-    -00000   498 733 1246 3105 3195
6 HOLLY BUOY  20  £-    13211-04   80 256
2 HOLLYWOOD MAN  0   £-    00   1234 2263
4 HOLME CODE  0   £-    040-0-0   207
3 HOLME ROOK  0   £-    -00   356 767
2 HOLST  68  £18808   2211   2907*
4 HOLT ROW  16  £-    00000-0000   65 428 525 836
2 HOLTERMANN  0   £-    0   3163
2 HOLTS WAY  22  £-    0000   1782 2167 2287 2494
6 HOLY SPARK  56  £6879   -01223   4 189* 312- 403- 3173
2 HOLY WILLIE  0   £-    0   2796
4 HOLYPORT VICTORY  36  £3836   32230-401133000   9 85 202* 341* 449 532 683 721 2692
2 HOLYROOD  10  £-    000   2396 2757 3034
4 HOME COUNTY  0   £-    -0   1290
2 HOME DEVICE  24  £-    0400   1874 2249 2472 3146
3 HOME FLEET  27  £-    000-0000   980 1481 2148 2430
2 HOME JESTA  0   £-    0000   1518 1869 2270 3069
3 HOME OR AWAY  0   £-    00-000   484 765 1835
4 HOME PLEASE  48  £1695   -3   895
4 HOME RULE  0   £-    0-00   868 1244
3 HOME RULE FR  59  £2944   01200-0100   62 227* 600 1107
4 HOME TO TARA  0   £-    000   2522 3014 3200
6 HOMEWARD  0   £-    0-030-0   2093
4 HOMING IN  42  £2018   0421400   136 1308 1427 1770* 1925 2035 2227
3 HOMME DAFFAIRE  38  £3180   000-0100042   217 459* 919 2404 2671 3063 3140
4 HOMO SAPIEN  78  £19084   11--2-13234   222* 330 945- 3020 3177
4 HONEST TOIL  35  £8035   000-340041D4110   14 48 451 553 956 1295 2053 2149* 2267* 2671
7 HONEST TOKEN  0   £-    40000-00000   257 630 788 1302 1619
4 HONEY DANCER  42  £-    00   2951 3120
2 HONEY PLUM  9   £-    44040000   115 261 1570 2032 2178 2471 2580 2757
5 HONEYDEW WONDER  40  £-    11103-00   4 349
2 HONEYWAY MIST  0   £-    00   2511 2584
4 HONG KONG VENTURE  0   £-    00000-0   1195
3 HOOKED BID  46  £2112   -00031323   1228 1375 1586 1953 2532* 2653 2973 3077
3 HOORAY HAMILTON  0   £-    00000-0000000   74 111 340 809 1349 1497 1656
2 HOORAY LADY  45  £273   04   2147 2436
4 HOPEFUL HEIGHTS  33  £-    04020-000   649 700 1157
4 HOPEFUL KATIE  27  £7358   430 402030301301020   65 240 355 481   710 992 1211 1324 1521 1727 1942 2213* 2340 2601 2715* 2945 3104 3157
```

```
3 HOPEFUL LINE   18   £-    0-0040    409 1645 1961 2363
3 HOPEFULL DANCER 18   £284   00001-000003    340 455 928 2463 3024 3160
2 HOPESPRINGSFOREVER 0  £-    0   3181
2 HOPPING AROUND  0   £-    000   2476 3082 3221
4 HOPTONS CHANCE  4   £916   22-000000243340    378 594 906 963 1338 1761 1839 2104 2414 2602 2797
2998
2 HORNBLOWER GIRL 35   £3980   11    446* 596*
3 HORNS LODGE  0   £-    0-0   3105
3 HOROWITZ  30   £1291   02-010    2216 2613* 2799
3 HORTON GLORY  0   £-    -00   2593 3077
6 HOT BETTY  10   £1095   -30000004001000    28 121 263 336 419 761 841 1260 1459 1694 2008* 2604
2964 3128
3 HOT GEM  15   £-    1-000000    216 326 880 1520 2458 3063
3 HOT LINING  22   £572   0000-00000240    863 997 1091 1362 1613 1989 2508 2594
3 HOT MOMMA  28   £3681   2022-2043000001    89- 264 464 1198 1415 1690 1953 2459 3180 3203*
3 HOT ORDER  20   £-    0000-000    1164 1443 1542
3 HOT RULER  11   £374   0202-300300    35 69 185 365 1016 2974
2 HOT SILVER  64   £2760   314   3166
3 HOT TWIST  13   £1096   0-00031    1446 1580 2188 2495 2705*
2 HOTEL LOTTI  30   £-    0   3120
3 HOTEL STREET  60   £2634   -120    2304* 2649 2952
3 HOTU  37   £-    -4P   486 765
5 HOUSE HUNTER  49   £4854   34000-02004124    265 363 801 1209 1441 1667* 1829 1992
3 HOW BLUE  3   £-    00-000   911 1257 1617
2 HOW VERY TOUCHING  50   £2451   222   2243 2418 2667
2 HUBBA  22   £-    00   2869 3132
3 HUBBARDS LODGE  46   £357   0032-33   25 75
3 HUDSONS MEWS  42   £5947   000-314012    451 650* 713 914 972* 1959
2 HUGO Z HACKENBUSH  14   £1034   40440042232000    415 536 612 785 913 1294 1680 1741 1949 2150
2307 2465 2588 3182
3 HUMBLE BEAUTY  0   £-    -00000    422 501 658 2213 3157
2 HUMBOLDT FAIR  0   £-    0   3181
3 HUNGRY GIANT  66   £592   --220-04    471 1332
3 HUNGRY GRIEBEL  41   £-    0   1632
2 HUNT BALL  44   £-    000   1464 2215 2368
4 HUNTERS FEN  24   £-    02340-04    23 69
2 HUNTERS LEAP  20   £1793   0020100400    197 236 544 870 973* 1529 1925 2276 2512 3085
2 HUNTING COUNTRY  24   £-    00   2499 2716
3 HUNTING GOLD  0   £-    -00   1141 1337
3 HUNTING IRISH  0   £-    -0   90
3 HUNTINGDALE  83   £25626   221-340    407 640 1096
4 HUNTS KATIE  17   £-    30030-00400    262 620 1319 1649 1804
2 HURRICANE DODO  33   £-    0   149
3 HURRICANE HENRY  30   £668   02-00430    452 738 1048 1435 3155
2 HURRICANE VALLEY  37   £-    00000    1632 1874 2057 2577 2788
2 HUSH KIT  0   £-    000   1067 2095 3068
3 HUSNAH  50   £5393   02-333121200    549 682 955 1192* 1620 1848* 2028 2201 3110
5 HUYTONS HOPE  0   £-    0-000-00000    636 940 1079 1394 2309
2 HYDRAULIC POWER  70   £3162   01   2345 2626+
2 HYGENA LEGEND  0   £-    00   1914 2997
3 HYMN OF HARLECH  53   £4659   21300-0032232    62 216 478 747 1028 1390 1532
4 HYOKIN  36   £5969   400032132002004   282 569 675 984 1226 1336 1359* 1563 1652 2211 2403 2727 2776
2985 3030
2 HYPNOLOGY  29   £-    0   3130
2 HYTAK PET  0   £-    000   2153 2710 2967
5 I BIN ZAIDOON  54   £-    04120-00    879 1111
2 I PROMISED  0   £-    00   2334 2491
2 I SWEPT IN  6   £262   4   1506
2 I TRY  57   £13688   311   2016 2615* 3041*
4 I WANT TO BE  77   £30626   41212-002313    704 1127 1513 2157 2450* 3004
4 IADES  82   £46468   2020000    645 1010* 1389 2194 2917 3213
3 IBERIAN START  37   £7221   0302-2103200300    628 1027* 1268 1796 1896 2224 2586 2858 2921 3233
2 IBN BEY  52   £3216   41   2251 3011*
4 IBN MAJED  18   £-    -0000-0000    11 2754 2937 3052
2 IBNALMAGHITH  45   £4026   1430020    694* 1149 1735 2272 2777 3125 3188
2 IBTIDAAR  60   £2026   10   2527* 2768
3 ICARO  28   £3476   2301-0220323320    29 380 609 883 989 1295 1613 1659 2426 2848
2 ICARUS  0   £-    00   3053 3171
2 ICE CHOCOLATE  47   £590   43   2846 3153
2 ICE HOUSE  48   £964   1   2710*
8 ICEN  10   £1081   04400/1000300    28* 179 1124 1909 2175 2415 3087
3 ICHI BAN SON  33   £-    004   1869 2232 3156
3 ICHNUSA  48   £3601   -412   733 2550* 2893
4 ICKWORTH  12   £-    40444-0040000    1280 1652 1873 2346 2496 2996 3155
4 IDEOLIGIA  0   £-    20-000440000040    160 812 992 1186 1324 1727 2033 2213 2370 2621 2960 3172
3 IDLE SONG  18   £-    -000000    140 414 635 790 1309 3142
4 IDLE TIMES  17   £4772   00-113000030000    110* 240+ 321 815 970 1429 1638 2039 2151 2390 2446
2970
2 IF YOU PLEASE  27   £-    0   2013
3 IGHTHAM  46   £3858   -00103100    347 1304 1688* 2075 2317 2647* 2760 3225
2 IJAZAH  26   £-    00   3014 3143
3 IKRAAM  0   £-    -0000000    402 535 849 1941 2184 2274 2709
4 IKTIYAR  36   £4568   03320-00100130    805 1041 1156* 1519 1788 2059* 2260 2581
7 IL PONTEVECCHIO  0   £-    -00   2093 2432
3 ILE DE ROI  51   £1162   -4-020    1469 1645 1899
2 ILIONA  55   £1861   0012   1996 2215 2658* 3025
7 ILLICIT  0   £-    -00000    260 378 1139 1338 1616
4 ILLINEY GIRL  27   £-    -0410-0    42
3 ILLUMINEUX  57   £1817   1-00002    226 586 1028 2842 2945
2 ILLUSTRATE  22   £-    000440    1867 2232 2436 2883 3017 3146
4 IM EXCEPTIONAL  9   £971   0-000-030032    1747 2173 2467 2604 2727 2819
2 IMAGINARY SKY  45   £3372   010   350 2696* 3114
3 IMPALA LASS  23   £5172   40301-11000000    339* 443* 670 884 1027 1344 1505 2906
```

```
4 IMPECUNIOSITY  32   £1109    30300-1    104*
2 IMPERIAL BRUSH  48   £264    1D    3201
3 IMPERIAL FALCON  80   £10695    -0-11    150* 396*
2 IMPERIAL FRIEND  20   £246    0300    350 913 1059 3146
2 IMPERIAL FRONTIER  71   £10980    210    2626 2849* 3107
4 IMPERIAL JADE  67   £13574    42030-302130    408 705 877 922* 1508 1631
3 IMPERIAL PALACE  29   £5414    -00021104    720 916 1055 2027 2171* 2313* 2399 2684
3 IMPERIAL SUNRISE  16   £2006    -40343002030100    309 447 768 961 1051 1418 1627 1917 2027 2268
2483 2688* 3033 3160
2 IMPERIAL WAY  36   £2589    0010    2118 2493 2708* 2989
9 IMPERIUM  0   £-    00000-0    526
3 IMPROVISE  19   £852    30010-2000000    81 373 518 2104 2340 2437 2681
2 IN A SPIN  34   £640    300020    1529 1812 1982 2920 3059 3158
3 IN CONTENTION  14   £586    -3003    2122 2776 2923 3102
3 IN DREAMS  43   £5598    40-2113    769 996* 1410* 1894
3 IN FACT  64   £5018    22-11    994+ 1463*
2 IN FAT CITY  48   £259    042    2491 2782 3192
2 INAAD  36   £-    0    2750
2 INANNA  61   £14535    11    2739*
2 INBISAT  0   £-    0    3181
9 INCHGOWER  12   £367    10000-0300    341 485 731 984
2 INCINDERATOR  52   £724    43    1653 2732
4 INDE PULSE  64   £6811    011100-01043440    215 280* 360 462 693 1099 1148 1470
2 INDEXS  57   £11120    2100    558 1006* 1108 2634
2 INDIAN FLARE  32   £-    00    2147 2555
2 INDIAN FOREST  68   £1100    101014    1714 2954
4 INDIAN HAL  39   £3540    24231-044000040    248 433 706 1109 1793 2144 2303 2693 3119
2 INDIAN JUBILEE  22   £-    004    1238 2292 2829
2 INDIAN LILY  64   £15182    14430    707* 1021 2235 2634 2831
3 INDIAN LOVE SONG  29   £1852    0400-2304302300    464 911 1055 1198 1337 2030 2129 2327 2853 3155
3 INDIAN ORATOR  35   £2037    22222-3134400    1023 1135* 1502 1732 2432 2683 2892
2 INDIAN SET  25   £-    00400    252 1550 1782 2284 3146
2 INDIAN SKIMMER  50   £350    4    2852
2 INDIAN SOVEREIGN  41   £-    00    2029 3223
3 INDIAN SUMMER  30   £724    0-200000    658 776 1487 2072 2143 2601
2 INDIRAJI  28   £-    00    548 2283
3 INDIVIDUALIST  42   £3301    01    2672 2713*
2 INFAMY  48   £598    4    3053
2 INFANTA DE CASTILE  0   £-    0    2239
2 INFANTA MARIA  39   £3602    0202210    621 882 1161 1938 2172 2307* 2694
4 INFANTRY OFFICER  39   £808    -20000    651 943 968 1450 1929
2 INFRA RED BOY  31   £-    0    3109
2 INGABELLE  30   £-    0    1591
2 INGLISTON  26   £291    033404    304 488 785 965 1568 2334
4 INHERIT  0   £-    00000-0    263
4 INIMEG  0   £-    -0    1400
3 ININSKY  71   £10660    210-400341102    950 1147 1588 1854 2144 2244* 2559* 2867 2956
3 INISHEER  70   £6350    33    559 2348
4 INISHPOUR  45   £5589    00-003034314400    17 374 1157 1222 1377 1673 1840 2039+ 2296 2475 2566
2945
5 INLANDER  19   £-    02220-0    3129
3 INNISHMORE ISLAND  55   £5313    0312-30322143    1237 1526 1792 1994 2353 2582* 2666 2861
2 INSHAD  44   £1323    031    2308 2555 2899*
2 INSHIRAH  44   £5968    1014332    646* 1174 1920* 2209 2479 2756 3146
2 INSTINCTIVE  30   £-    0    3109
6 INSULAR  58   £5379    00421-310034    618 778* 1111 2766 2938 3173
2 INTELLECT  0   £-    000    2678 2883 3031
2 INTEREST RATE  0   £-    0    2869
2 INTERVAL  74   £9377    12    999* 2235-
2 INTHAR  42   £413    003424    565 2229 2514 2717 2875 3027
3 INTO THE GAP  37   £-    410-00    2155 2488
3 INTRINSIC  0   £-    -000000    372 509 862 1202 2581 3116
2 INTROVERT  0   £-    000    2476 3153 3223
4 INTUITION  29   £1733    00000-100030    69* 235 358 485 541 663
2 INVITED GUEST  79   £52530    1111    852* 1926* 2246* 2751*
2 IOSIFA  73   £9496    313    1287 1855* 2246
2 IRENIC  18   £-    0000    1782 2499 2814 3184
2 IRISH BRIGADIER  40   £1007    4200    1872 2067 2628 3125
4 IRISH COOKIE  44   £14914    31320-01410200    112 508+ 687 1026* 1145 2258- 2668 2773
3 IRISH DILEMMA  12   £-    -00000400    140 430 535 635 1204 1558 1666 1845
5 IRISH FOLLY  56   £13969    1    2349+
4 IRISH HERO  16   £385    42-00402000003    452 812 943 1156 1558 2017 2406 2467 2623 2807 2887
2 IRISH LINK  0   £-    0    125
3 IRISH PASSAGE  43   £8855    1-02D001214    518 816 956 1224 1922* 2508 2684* 2946
2 IRISH SAILOR  46   £3994    304210    2205 2561 2847 3075- 3131* 3230
4 IROKO  79   £15045    20111-2430    325 736 1144 1712
2 IRON DANCE  0   £-    0    2710
3 IS BELLO  45?   £564    -0320300    370 535 723 1220 1372 1639 1908
4 ISHKHARA  1   £250    400-00300004    449 591 675 942 1159 1271 2415 2819
4 ISLAND EXILE  26   £205    10344-0404    542 712 1533 1772
2 ISLAND KING  40   £-    0    3023
2 ISLAND LOCKSMITH  31   £117    030    2026 2364 2472
2 ISLAND REEF  65   £11550    124120    2451* 3003
4 ISLAND SET  64   £15654    03411-022102120    410 1254 1412 1935* 2220 2486- 2850+ 3038- 3232
7 ISOM DART  16   £4139    -00-11000010    1056* 1473* 1837 2093 2533 2699 2959* 3187
3 ISTIKAL  74   £9824    22    757 2827
3 ISTORIATO  70   £10060    21142    2740 3000
5 ITALIAN SECRET  16   £-    30000-0    606
5 ITALIAN SPRING  0   £-    000-00    679 1165
6 ITALIAN SUNRISE  0   £-    -00000    2164 2403 2647 2809 3139
2 ITS BEEN RUMOURED  22   £1171    001440    1966 2180 2609* 2919 3016 3182
4 ITS GOOD ERE  11   £-    00010-00    1079 1226
```

```
6 ITS HEAVEN  0  £-  000-4-000000  490 628 2816 2996 3086 3147
4 ITS NOW OR NEVER  57  £680  -01-20  2074 2236
2 ITS VARADAN  23  £-  000  497 531 1172
3 ITTIHAAD  38  £1880  000-0302330  117 331 459 833 1085 2403 2432
2 IVE NO IDEA  0  £-  0000  2177 2625 2841 3069
5 IVOR ANTHONY  0  £-  -0  282
4 IVOROSKI  12  £4786  -00000332100441  80 519 629 1017 1106 1271 1359 1548 1769* 1918 2604 2885
   2978 3087*
3 IVORS IMAGE  85  £153411  21301-414310  463 642* 1116 2202 3098* 3212
2 IVORY FIELDS  48  £1396  031  2215 2527 2904*
3 IVORY FIRE  0  £-  -0  83
3 IVORY GULL  26  £-  041-0000000  514 713 1272 1447 2905 3033 3164
3 IVY MAY  0  £-  -0  1246
3 IYAMSKI  44  £5774  -202300411  16 127 423 1032 1515 2655 2810 2905* 3062*
3 IZZY GUNNER  16  £2392  0030-0022001400  14 194 240 491 611 857 2361* 2481 2684 3060
3 JAAZIEL  18  £2465  -000000140P  501 764 928 1316 1830 2190 2293* 2699 2925 3203
5 JABARABA  22  £4748  00-000411134040  481 680 1274 1473 1747* 1945* 2188* 2330 2558- 2766 2985
   3187
2 JABE MAC  26  £1242  000130  678 1082 1583 1832* 2272 2421
2 JACK STRAW  0  £-  00  2239 3143
6 JACKDAW  22  £7001  000300231204000  11 137  336 462 634 712 942 1140 1470 1633+ 1865 2031
   2240 2376 2591 3225
4 JACKIE BLAIR  23  £1628  0040-0300003200  30 211 272 784 1086 1171 2245 2402 2632 3233
5 JACKIES LASS  0  £-  -0  23
4 JACKS ISLAND  36  £-  11031-0  23
5 JACKS LUCK  31  £1624  -1230  8* 199 493 686
3 JACQUETTE  35  £-  -000  452 935 2419
3 JACQUI JOY  11  £3817  003000002124010  1164  1476 1734 1836 2088 2210 2416 2592 2621 2743* 2854
   2906 3024 3046+ 3160
3 JADE ESSENCE  8  £-  000-0  113
2 JADE HUNTER  38  £-  000  2554 3037 3206
2 JAH BLESS  39  £1148  220040  350 497 1162 1938 2261 2421
2 JAISALMER  52  £9260  10200222302  350* 655 773 1108 1287 1910- 2136 2261- 2485 2865 3019-
4 JALOME  3  £-  0000-0000004004  58 107 522 1703 2335 2549 2789 3030 3076 3150
5 JAMEENA  12  £-  0-000-0  2572
4 JAMES DE COOMBE  15  £1636  00230-00024234  114 355 566 679 855 1086- 1165 1264
2 JAMES OWL  20  £469  0243  515 701 2281 3058
4 JAMES PAL  24  £-  00211-000000  321 1120 2397 2513 3060 3149
2 JAMES STANLEY  0  £-  0  2239
5 JAMESMEAD  52  £1949  01012-0303  1099 1148 1633 2311
4 JANAAB  10  £-  03020-0000000  341 532 709 751 984 1694 1829
2 JANE MARPLE  20  £-  000  3018 3133 3234
4 JANES BRAVE BOY  0  £931  3-1000000000000  46* 101 310 594 710 2340 2414 2681 2728 2762 2863
   3084 3149
3 JANIE O  21  £139  -0300400  209 379 991 1198 1569 1964 2098
3 JANISKI  67  £9693  100-421  654 807 1150*
2 JANS CONTESSA  34  £910  23030  482 852 1282 2803 3074
2 JANS DECISION  0  £-  0004  115 421 681 981
8 JANUS  22  £1407  /0-40-02020  92 202 569 942 2591
3 JAREER  70  £-  210-00  878 1098
2 JARRETIERE  45  £-  0  3037
3 JARROVIAN  43  £5966  0421000400000040133  18  134 241 309 387  586 814 947 1028 1292 1524
   1648 2411 2715 2762 2870 2977* 3104 3127
3 JARYAN  0  £-  -000  218 806 1256
3 JAY BEE WINDOWS  0  £-  -00  2361 3150
2 JAY GEE ELL  50  £8645  314100  383 548* 646 927* 1021 1287
2 JAYS SPECIAL  38  £5160  40001233  197 1050 1225 1916 2025* 2198 2276 2669
4 JAZAIR  25  £167  10000-000000  403 582 761 856 2188 2850
3 JAZETAS  45  £5224  4-11404040200  14* 127* 226 407 605 706 1064 2562 2713 2851 3066
3 JAZZ DANCER  0  £-  000  1075 2894 2976
3 JAZZ MUSICIAN  68  £6971  24200-424  466 1007 1107
2 JEALOUS LOVER  14  £-  00000  1826 2308 2491 2829 3190
2 JEAN JEANIE  10  £-  00000000  364 646 934 1958 2127 2323 2781 2919
3 JEANNE JUGAN  0  £-  -00  346 1404
2 JEFF HARRIS  0  £-  00  3117 3206
3 JELDAIRE  15  £1611  00000-01030  447 666* 1701 2083 3224
4 JELDORA  0  £-  -0  31
3 JELLY JILL  2  £-  -00000  605 822 969 2129 2427
3 JELLYGOLD  50  £-  01100-0  244
3 JENIFER BROWNING  10  £302  00-200000  82 318 874 972 1626 1917
5 JENNY WYLLIE  9  £275  32300-0002  204 419 750 1056
3 JERSEY MAID  20  £330  3120-0000000420  451 650 814 1051 1885 2397 2513 2602 3057 3084
. 3 JESSIE ELLIS  16  £-  04000-0  529
3 JESSIE TIMMINS  0  £-  -0000  631 790 969 1053
2 JETMORE  11  £258  02000  1083 1262 1483 1803 2045
3 JEWEL MIST  0  £-  00-0  2931
3 JEWELLED REEF  59  £-  10-0P  384 902
4 JIANNA  14  £345  0040-002400  431 760 1476 1943 2981 3145
3 JIMBALOU  0  £-  -0000  849 1061 2430 3110
6 JIMJAMS  0  £-  -0  71
4 JIMMY TARPS  0  £-  -0  104
3 JIMMYS SECRET  9  £-  04030-0000  14 1418 1543 2361
6 JIMNASTICS  0  £-  -00  943 2028
3 JIPIJAPA  0  £172  00000-000030000  1226 1416 1700 1884 2141 2492 2666 2819 3049
2 JJ JIMMY  21  £-  00400  77 602 1270 1965 2894
6 JO ANDREW  0  £-  00000-00000  56 1394 1624 1774 1870
2 JOANIES STYLE  41  £-  0  3068
2 JOARA  0  £-  0  2901
2 JOBYS JET  45  £152  03  3130 3228
2 JOCKS BROTHER  19  £-  0000  1495 1629 1936 2547
2 JOE SUGDEN  45  £1269  030140  694 873 1510 1762* 1893 2223
2 JOEY BLACK  0  £-  0  1143
3 JOHN DOREY  38  £4558  40-1110  1072* 2683* 2760* 2802
```

```
4 JOHN GILPIN  25   £5065   04100-2121    46 101* 439 1081*
5 JOHN PATRICK  33   £-   10003-00000000    18 192 306 374 992 3055 3118 3138
3 JOHN RUSSELL  52   £3288   -2110    994- 1142* 1420* 1648
3 JOHN SAXON  51   £1848   033-002033    283 615 703 1147 1371 1677
3 JOHN TULLY  28   £-   0-4    68
2 JOHNKEINA  25   £-   40000    73 167 2596 2698 2903
5 JOHNNY FRENCHMAN  0   £-   02000-000000    8 594 863 993 1703 2008
2 JOHNNY ROSE  51   £377   20    1345 1883
2 JOHNNY SHARP  21   £2104   002001000    1155 1534 1675 1869 1984 2498* 2663 2798 2968
4 JOHNNYS SHAMBLES  19   £-   -0400-0    1686
2 JOHNS BABY  9   £-   000    1665 2320 2708
2 JOHNS LAST  12   £-   000    2982 3103 3184
2 JOHNSONS PRIDE  0   £-   0    2470
3 JOHNSTAN BOY  18   £-   0-00000440    194 328 650 857 997 1281 1471 2238
2 JOINT SERVICES  33   £316   3000    715 1653 2082 2465
4 JOIST  22   £3606   22010-002432103    541 634 933 1071 1183 1772 2040* 2647 2745
3 JOKER MAN  0   £-   -000    1607 2163 2253
3 JOKIST  49   £9505   44000-0211100    830 1272 1669+ 2079+ 2343+ 2668 3127
5 JOLI WASFI  17   £714   30300-0000002    410 618 879 1667 2558 2699 3071
3 JOLIE PELOUSE  30   £-   -400    1192 1639 2520
4 JOLIS GIRL  33   £1532   40420-0303000    7 72 189 225 363 2338 3227
2 JOLLIENNE  0   £-   0    1874
2 JONITE  45   £421   0000304    1019 1587 2044 2580 2829 3137 3198
5 JONIX  8   £-   -0000-000    23 121 801
2 JONLEAT  35   £2272   4122000    212 332* 523 664 927 1828 2310
4 JONNEY GEM  0   £-   --000-00    1201 1839
2 JOSIE SMITH  21   £1113   0100300    482 831* 965 1483 2178 2405 2700
3 JOUSTING BOY  28   £-   000-00    1868 2242
4 JOUVENCELLE  29   £1280   -0244-23    805 1004
3 JOVEWORTH  30   £812   00440-1400300    283* 355 914 1028 1610 1870 2086
2 JOVICK  30   £2418   310001    1320 1665* 2272 2435 2729 2986+
2 JOYCES PET  9   £-   000040    905 1680 2678 2969 3031 3151
6 JOYFUL DANCER  30   £4405   0400-0021030000    815 1109 1460 1729* 1890 1967 2288 2431 2674 2837
2 JOYFUL MISTRESS  0   £-   000    1782 2177 2990
5 JUBILANT LADY  0   £-   400-00000000000    9 44 419 827 1071 1302 1477 1737 1772 2101 2683
2 JUBILEE AGAIN  0   £-   0    2484
3 JUBILEE JAMBOREE  8   £523   -003003003    720 991 1349 1686 2015 2613 2714 3076 3202
3 JUDYS DESIRE  0   £-   0000-0    1267
5 JUDYS DOWRY  18   £-   1-100-0    3128
2 JUILLIARD  45   £806   23    3067 3206
2 JULIA SPRINGS  0   £-   00    848 1187
2 JULIOS LAD  10   £91   0300    446 821 1121 2471
2 JULTOWN LAD  1   £1096   40000-204021    93 346 718 1428 2163 3202*
2 JUMA MONTY  13   £-   000    1675 1984 2225
3 JUMBO HIRT  60   £4658   30-230    219 442 597
7 JUMP JAR  28   £216   00100-20    1070 1101
3 JUMP TO IT  13   £-   0030-00    910 1070
3 JUNGLE BEAT  36   £1601   0-40240    2550 2734 2948 3105 3186
7 JUPITER ISLAND  83   £16905   14001-31    3121+
8 JUPITERS GEM  0   £-   -0    770
3 JURISPRUDENCE  39   £5069   -000113    702 916 1278 1884* 2087* 2631
4 JUST A BIT  0   £-   03230-4000000    1013 1482 2335 2397 2602 2681 3057
2 JUST A DECOY  2   £-   0040000000    1298 1611 1741 1905 2298 2396 2994 3058 3148 3222
2 JUST A FLUTTER  68   £9106   1102    1488+ 1916+ 2221 2598
4 JUST A HALF  7   £-   00000-00    912 1223
2 JUST A PICNIC  0   £-   00    1903 2846
4 JUST CANDID  14   £837   -000-0033423240    1243 1558 1937 1969 2094 2187 2271 2509 2714 2964
3 JUST CHRISTENED  0   £-   000-00    1257 1747
2 JUST CLASS  36   £210   402    2589 2967 3082
3 JUST DAVID  56   £7559   -12102    506* 909 1879* 2220 2647
2 JUST ENCHANTING  2   £-   00000    502 717 831 2518 2658
2 JUST KALA  45   £832   4323    2147 2434 2658 2814
8 JUST MARTIN  0   £-   -0    3196
3 JUST MET  20   £-   000-000    1787 2497 2581
2 JUST MINE  0   £-   0    2846
2 JUST ON TIME  9   £88   0300    1440 1599 2177 2498
2 JUST ONE MORE  30   £496   4040020    678 780 1311 1475 2265 2425 3058
2 JUST SOMETHING  24   £-   00    3073 3184
3 JUST THE TICKET  4   £936   000-010000    1257 1562* 1824 2602 3033 3157
3 JUST TOO BRAVE  22   £-   -04    3142 3183
3 JUSTTHEWAYYOUARE  0   £-   0000-000    130 239 1417
2 JUVENILEDELINQUENT  26   £1207   1244000    1612* 1936 2047 2090 2307 2669 2815
5 K BATTERY  67   £28963   00000-100202000    17+ 221 325 1216 1526 1811- 2194 2461 2867
3 KAASIB  1   £-   -0000    500 1444 2183 2275
3 KABIYLA  73   £33077   1-1201320    386* 599 692 2765+ 2867 3093 3177
2 KACERE  31   £416   40000    602 780 1225 1893 1978
2 KADAN  42   £-   0    2673
5 KADESH  18   £-   00024-400    92 731 772
3 KADIAL  77   £15978   -2142102    371 572* 1098 1661- 2074* 2200 2496
3 KADROU  80   £7314   23413-02    301 644
3 KAFARMO  34   £2088   -03410    2306 2605 2923 3102* 3219
3 KAIYRAN  30   £2466   3-0001    1628 1981 2339 2594*
4 KALA NASHAN  33   £5580   -0020-0030120    176 420 652 750 1237+ 1659 2116
4 KALA PANI  0   £-   00000-0    1804
2 KALADIOLA  24   £-   019    1752 2531
3 KALANDARIYA  43   £1681   4-302200    422 1198 1511 1783- 1947 2155
2 KALAS IMAGE  31   £4001   03230314004410    364 536 892- 995 1161 1357 1561* 1919 2100 2472 2669
                                            2935 3151* 3226
2 KALEIDOPHONE  41   £2017   0034420    1266 1510 2379 2664 2796 2971- 3125
2 KALGOORLIE  71   £7917   02330    2225 2341 2522 3009 3178
4 KALIMPONG  0   £-   0-000    2517 2572 2900
3 KALISTAN  70   £8717   -203    152 389 1859
4 KALKOUR  55   £17937   10-0-010120400    71 432+ 805 1038* 1217 1383 1811 2354 2566
                                   > 984 <
```

```
2 KALORAMA  60   £1248   30   638 2634
4 KAMARESS  5   £2193   00002400431000000   10 91 745  893 1103 1394 1482 1610 1774 1901 2104* 2213
  2340 2549 2629 2797 2891
2 KAMENSKY  44   £3554   032201   614 678 1082 1993 2556 3188+
4 KAMPGLOW  20   £572   00004-030000300   17 71 238 374 481 1073 1906 1987 2340
3 KAMPHALL  6   £-   000-4000   822 969 1054 1769
2 KAMSTAR  0   £-   00000   13 181 988 1190 1723
2 KANDAWGYI  22   £-   0000   1253 1433 2191 2514
3 KANGAROO  20   £-   00033-000   1446 1953 2401
3 KANMARY  72   £7452   24130-0020   288 467 1713 2002
2 KARABAT  43   £-   0000   2179 2484 2869 3014
4 KARAKTER REFERENCE  0   £-   -0   2269
4 KARAMANAD  0   £-   00004-00   578 845
5 KARAMOUN  0   £-   20000-00000   88 547 721 856 1195
9 KARENS STAR  5   £265   -00000002000000   306 355 428 649 1093 1196 1638 2124- 2204 2322 2743
  2775 3046 3152
5 KARNATAK  11   £192   00--0-0300   420 943 1188 1558
2 KARONGA  0   £-   0   2901
2 KASH JUWAIN  0   £-   0   3132
2 KASHAPOUR  38   £710   032   2846 3034 3184-
2 KASHKISS  0   £-   0   3120
10 KASSAK  00   £-   -3020-00   943 1273
2 KASTAMOUN  46   £2794   401   1791 2159 3136*
3 KASU  7   £-   -0404^0   969 1123 1372 1544 1873 3161
2 KATE IS BEST  31   £-   004400   1287 1430 2511 2651 2989 3146
7 KATELL  72   £28367   22   392 897
4 KATES PRIDE  27   £345   -0244-00430   208 420 547 724 1038
8 KATHRED  34   £-   00000-000   2970 3127 3235
3 KATHY W  53   £3518   -1140   720+ 1206* 1630 2247
3 KATIE BRIDGE  0   £-   -00   1290 2034
2 KATIE CUDDLES  0   £-   000   1478 1795 2994
3 KATIE RHODES  0   £-   000-00000   183 284 451 874 1281
2 KATIE SAYS  14   £168   04003000   672 864 2043 2479 2757 3016 3112 3222
5 KATY QUICK  0   £-   -0   1417
4 KAVAKA  16   £2492   00-00012D020000   91 481 680 1567* 2037 2173 2303 2419 2496 2549 2706
5 KAYTU  74   £9001   -0000-310   511 617* 1115
4 KAZAROUN  82   £20296   11210-310   2557 2752* 3121
5 KAZAROW  34   £2548   02022-1000   71+ 265 453 3231
4 KEATS  32   £2653   232-001030   196 441 1077* 1429 1649 1840
3 KEDRON  54   £6901   012-11320   138+ 455* 588 914 1147
2 KEECAGEE  0   £-   0000   834 1039 1518 2407
2 KEEL  0   £-   00   985 2829
5 KEELEY LOUISE  0   £-   -00   121 204
2 KEEN CUT  60   £8236   10   638* 2451
2 KEEN EDGE  29   £2810   42200303024   531 577 678 927 1381 1612 1717 2166 2272 2529 2677
2 KEEN NOTE  35   £830   002200   1464 2153 2375 2600 2753 3122
3 KEEP COOL  10   £4274   3400100002004333143   '53 120 424 637 774* 1224 1362 1540 1739 1960 2060
  2282 2427 2509 2621 2778 2863* 2963 3084
3 KEEP HOPING  22   £2814   0--00013320   765 991 1569 1739* 1822 1980 3087 3219
3 KEEPCALM  45   £4354   -04041   231 444 739 2408 2671*
2 KEITHS WISH  0   £-   000   125 821 957
5 KELLY BAY  0   £-   -000   10 131 142
3 KELLY LINDO  15   £804   00000-000100   205 339 418 726* 1171 3160
2 KELLYS COMET  0   £-   0   3136
4 KELLYS ROYALE  43   £-   00000-0000000   192 327 550 748 1037 1227 1385
4 KELLYTALK  70   £7319   14330-02   1490 2641
2 KEMAGO  68   £12993   -1-10300   394* 764 2006 2192 2633
3 KEN SIDDALL  3   £-   -00440000000000   6 64 198 246 670 961 1101 1638 1704 2469 2592 2743 2854
  3024
3 KENANGA  70   £6898   -011120   402 991* 1437+ 1988+ 2236 2525
3 KENOOZ  34   £2930   0040-204001   657 972 1257 1695 2681 3033*
2 KENTONS LAD  26   £-   000   2029 2889 3082
2 KENTUCKY AIR  47   £264   02   2487 2710
4 KENTUCKY QUEST  35   £953   00000-002000   4 72 189 263 921 1020
5 KEPT ON ICE  0   £-   -0   104
2 KEPT WAITING  40   £1164   02010   2089 2514 2589 2875* 3122
2 KERALI  46   £-   0   2939
4 KEREDEM  0   £-   -0   8
3 KERRY MAY SING  16   £118   21031-000004030   807 989 1325 1685 1871 1945 2346 2959 3128
5 KEY ROYAL  10   £522   02400-000040204   363 449 1293 1737 1897 2141 2779 2885 3049
3 KEY TO THE KEEP  50   £212   20-3   1749
4 KEYANLOCH  3   £-   00040-000   2335 2884 2977
6 KEYNES  0   £270   141044/4   2943
2 KHADRUF  50   £4658   10310   437* 898 1255 1965* 2968
2 KHAKIS LOVE  50   £3832   30110   1238 1641 2191* 2292* 2543
3 KHAMSIN RED  20   £-   0000-00   217 495
3 KHARRANA  35   £2206   201-10000   1164* 1406 2143 2291 2858
2 KHARSHUF  52   £2928   200   1006 2451 2821
2 KHATTAF  0   £-   0   3201
3 KHETA KING  30   £4367   0-0311   625 951 1258* 1497*
3 KHLESTAKOV  23   £-   -000000   217 516 835 1164 1669 1836
4 KHOZDAR  62   £6635   10120-30320   653 2419 2693 2845 3119
2 KIBARA  5   £986   01000   1576 1803* 2298 2927 3182
3 KICK THE HABIT  46   £5177   0-00002100400   264 551 803 1628 1981 2131* 2404 2557 2752 2940 3235
2 KIERON PRESS  31   £1418   0314004040   404 1207 1495* 1968 2272 2677 2756 2897 3165 3230
3 KIKI GREEN  0   £-   000-000   38 198 237
4 KIKI STAR  10   £784   12021-0000001   341 504 569 943 2697 2984 3076*
2 KJKUYU  41   £-   00   2547 3132
2 KILAUEA  0   £-   00   2664 3099
4 KILIMANJARO BOB  20   £792   24230-0000200   176 1186 1325 1829 2034 2152 2372
4 KILLARY BAY  28   £-   31300-000   2443 2536 3219
4 KILMINGTON CASTLE  4   £-   400-00   2182 3193
2 KILVARNET  50   £3474   01314   21 167* 278 515+ 1255
                              > 985 <
```

```
3 KIMBLE BLUE  15   £-   11300-04000000    455 624 814 1312 2488 2619 3138 3191
2 KIMS TICKET  32   £-   00   1552 1844
2 KIND LADY  24   £1314    4231020    681 987- 1083 1358* 1795 1905 2138
2 KIND OF CLASS  16   £-   0000    999 1282 2283 2657
2 KIND OF GLITTER  39   £-   00   2675 3120
2 KING AMONG KINGS  0   £-   00   2494 3075
2 KING BALLADEER  57   £5746    03123320    777 979 1175* 1529 1926 1975 2611- 3041
7 KING CHARLEMAGNE  35   £871   11000-004340000    1268 1508 1796 1882 1986 2469 2537 2586 2632
4 KING COLE  0   £114   40-004000304D00    1104 1247 1839 1983 2086 2411 2585 2816 3057 3157 3220
3 KING JACK  44   £2312   -00214220    535 720 1062 1301* 1559 1837 2142 2665
2 KING KRIMSON  45   £3763    010   1903 2254* 2922
4 KING LUTHIER  78   £42710   -121201    299 1115 2114*
4 KING OF COMEDY  37   £-   00100-00000    735 1004 1388 1779 2220
3 KING OF GEMS  0   £-   00000-0000    809 1063 2017 2861
2 KING OF MERCIA  55   £757   3   2869
3 KING OF SPADES  42   £2380    3013-1000000    26* 228 588 1911 2250 2463 2674
7 KING OF SPEED  28   £5481    20300-1041030    112* 262 499 566* 750 1229 1804
3 KING RETAIN  0   £-   0   1330
2 KING RICHARD  35   £477    30030    1993 2179 2615 2989 3165
3 KING TEFKROS  45   £3746   -0033231    334 625 1206 1620 1775 2333 3140*
4 KINGS BADGE  21   £-   00000-000000    10 260 689 1976 2086 2629
3 KINGS CRUSADE  35   £3918   -4404233100    90 191 484 1284 1498 1806 1998 2300* 2686 3119
4 KINGS HEAD  65   £4169    120-3000    1109 1931 2234 2562
3 KINGS RING  0   £120   00-30000    2316 2702 2906 3160 3172
4 KINGS RIVER  72   £21256    1000    1007* 1094 1492 2192
4 KINGS ROCK  0   £-   -000    1554 1831 2183
3 KINGS TOUCH  35   £612   01-04000240    216 455 1032 1224 1520 2977 3160 3191
2 KINGS VICTORY  32   £2108    420024    1629 1816- 2108 2922 3188- 3230
3 KINGSCOTE  82   £-   13112-0    232
3 KINGSFOLD FLAME  30   £957   -00014    1516 2210 2367 2929* 3186
6 KINGSWICK  31   £-   20100-000    2240 2486 2692
2 KINGSWOOD RESOPAL  20   £-   000000    678 1057 1239 1518 2159 2841
2 KINSHAM DENE  16   £128   03400    1802 2045 2168 2334 2580
2 KIP KEINO  0   £290   40   1658 2957
2 KIREEN  0   £-   00   2133 2542
3 KIRINYAGGA  35   £-   -0   393
3 KIRKELLA  9   £-   0000-0000    674 960 1256 2361
5 KIRMANN  80   £-   1-103-0    1144
2 KIROWAN  42   £783   032   1928 2108 3080
2 KIRPAN  42   £630   03   2852 3109
3 KITTY CLARE  20   £735   0020-000010    765 1169 1835 2076 2187* 2807
3 KLAMMERING  17   £299   -02   666 1063
2 KLARARA  46   £643   42   1382 1982
3 KLOSTERBRAU  2   £-   00000-0000    940 1169 1309 1819
3 KNESSET  61   £-   00   2351 2503
3 KNIGHT HUNTER  0   £-   00-00    1080 1567
3 KNIGHTLY DIA  22   £84   -30000    87 423 806 1257 2656
5 KNIGHTS HEIR  8   £1874    30-020000020200    11 85- 137 712 1099 1569 1884 2015 2111 2326 2492
2745
3 KNIGHTS LEGEND  69   £10485   -21210    849 1040* 1111 1556* 2738
2 KNIGHTS NEVERGREEN  39   £359    0003    1289 1660 2019 3014
5 KNIGHTS SECRET  37   £12922   -21134034042220    441 606+ 815* 1176 1292 1455 1868 1987 2126 2390
2526 2629 3029 3113
2 KNOCKANDO  40   £-   00   2852 3023
2 KNOCKIN EXPRESS  48   £2364    0221    2626 2987 3130 3223*
2 KNOCKSHARRY  17   £3241    1100003003    1248* 1279* 1570 2081 2178 2708 2792 2968 3085 3182
2 KNOWLES BANK  0   £-   00   206 741
2 KNOWN LINE  50   £2951    421    2527 2703- 3014*
2 KNOWN POINT  10   £-   00   2651 2886
3 KNOYDART  18   £288   -02   14 608
3 KNYF  54   £6256   332-3201002    322 465 692 816* 1147 1486 1821
3 KO ISLAND  15   £405   32000-0000022    81 259 414 491 740 828 1053
4 KOFFI  29   £-   24000-0000    263 801 917 1342
3 KOLGONG HEIGHTS  66   £2264    1300-02003    273 597 654 2206 2553
4 KONIGSTRAUM  64   £5000   -2   1328
3 KOOKYS PET  21   £2938   -0000040130    357 512 720 1471 1830 2184 2414 2604* 2709 3087
2 KOPJES  0   £-   0   3109
7 KORYPHEOS  48   £3681    00000-00210    248 361 566 748+ 1145
3 KOUS  22   £1318   -103010    838* 951 1231 1310 1767* 2187
2 KRIBENSIS  49   £3733    01   2225 2628*
4 KRISLIN  0   £-   -00    12 84
2 KRISTAL ROCK  56   £772   03   1930 3037
3 KRISWICK  28   £1162   -0040220    479 1192 1646 2701 2974 3102 3219
3 KRUGUY  69   £10888    1132    2825 3006
4 KUBLAI  72   £-   12200-000    251 704 1127
3 KUDZ  70   £12220   22-21112013    239 592* 782* 1342+ 1484 2220 2510+ 2754
4 KUFUMA  70   £8528   23220-0001203    736 1000 1788 2496* 2740 2808 2943
2 KUMZAR  0   £-   000    2967 3073 3181
2 KURDISH PRINCE  0   £-   0   3198
4 KUWAIT MOON  18   £191   23202-000030    532 686 964 1441 1787 2093
4 KUWAIT MUTAR  29   £-   00-0-0    349
2 KYVERDALE  55   £6352   2011323300    1161 1407 1427* 1683+ 2261 2421- 2563 2687 2865 3019
3 L B LAUGHS  28   £431   430-00242    430 714 959 1304 1961
3 LA BELLE OF SANTO  1   £492   00330-002000000    447 1200 1299 1482 1761 1906 2126 2424 2972
2 LA BRETONNE  35   £1000   2   1708
2 LA CARABINE  0   £-   00   2418 2703
3 LA CAZADORA  15   £1010   -004031    770 991 1340 1759 2163 2597*
3 LA CHULA  0   £-   40000-00000    338 783 1056 1369 1898
3 LA DIVINA  5   £-   004-0400    496 726 2024 2417
4 LA DRAGONIERE  00   £-   000-00    1349 1558
3 LA DUSE  23   £102   -0300    1705 2129 2520 2610
3 LA GRANDE DAME  16   £-   -00000    581 1259 1646 2701 2802
3 LA JAMBALAYA  32   £3136   040-340210    424 867 1257 1835 2340* 2728
                              > 986 <
```

```
3 LA MALMAISON    22  £199    000-40000    314 418 580 760 1277
3 LA MANGA PRINCE  1  £-    30000-0000000   279 426 871 1200 1288 1360 1767
3 LA MUSCADE      24  £-    0-000000    1061 1554 1941 2148 2304 2520
3 LA NUREYEVA     36  £231   433-40   1902 2294
2 LA PETITE NOBLESSE 58 £9378  0101   1407 2118* 2460 3114+
4 LA ROSE GRISE   14  £270   -024-0030   590 1016 3129 3225
3 LA SERENATA     23  £-    0340-00000   271 1084 1694 2299 2520
3 LA SHAKA         0  £-    -000   2408 2653 2931
2 LA TROIENNE     22  £-    04   944 1650
2 LA VERTE GLEAM   0  £-    00000   197 741 1050 3011 3099
2 LA VIE EN ROSE  37  £-    00   2675 2901
3 LA ZINGARA      52  £-    0410-0   1284
3 LAABAS          58  £2885  04-330   231 654 1111
3 LABRAG          26  £-    0300-00   274 1081
3 LACED            0  £-    -0   2793
2 LACK A STYLE    62  £11520  002332100   405 1289 1373 1465 1660 1975 2251* 2384 2849
2 LACK OF PEARLS  35  £-    40404004   685 944 1132 1566 1975 2218 2468 2498
3 LACOVIA         86  £194209 ---01-2113   300 755* 1116* 2638
3 LADINA          67  £4780  0101002   2557 2911 3002
2 LADIZ            0  £-    P   2487
5 LADY ABINGER     0  £-    00-00-0000   164 1273 1546 1758
2 LADY ARTFUL      0  £-    000   1382 2283 2710
3 LADY ATTIVA     19  £960   00020-0000041   779 1085 1444 1841 2103 2603 2778*
2 LADY BEHAVE     20  £1677  302010000   746 924 1363* 1576 2421 2792 2919
2 LADY BENTLEY    59  £4643  1   3018*
3 LADY BISHOP     26  £326   0000-00300   338 436 637 955 1404
3 LADY BRIT       23  £-    00020-00000   132 379 674 907 1425
6 LADY CARA       29  £4968  014-00202411020   742 971 1131 1344 1682 1950 2124+ 2322+ 2469 2586 2858
4 LADY COOMBE     27  £-    -0400-00   3078 3195
4 LADY DAY        68  £-    011D4-0   298
4 LADY EUROLINK   27  £-    -1000-000   453 851 3204
4 LADY FIREPOWER   0  £-    -0002-000   8 36 2182-
3 LADY FOR TWO    46  £4087  -4041D213   708 1043 1327 1541 1841 2294* 2463
4 LADY GRIM        5  £-    10000-00   41 163
2 LADY HOMILY      0  £-    0   3136
4 LADY KILLANE    11  £-    04020-00   1473 1952
3 LADY LA PAZ     27  £5787  0-0402333031000   38 454 624 1032 1245 1515 1753 1830 2314 2459* 2676 2867 3062
3 LADY LAMB        1  £-    000-000000   1228 1830 2401 2576 2704 2972
2 LADY LAX         0  £-    0   3073
5 LADY LIZA        4  £166   10400-3000   202 420 532 841
3 LADY LOIRE      66  £4850  -011-24   394 560
2 LADY LUCINA     28  £582   040304   848 999 2185 2529 2792 2881
4 LADY NATIVELY   13  £545   00000-3002   160 495 845 906
3 LADY OF HAMPTON  8  £-    -400   684 767 1053
5 LADY OF LEISURE 16  £-    00000-00000   418 628 784 906 1070
2 LADY OF RIGA     0  £-    00   2334 2814
3 LADY OWEN        0  £-    2004-000000   356 730 928 1288 2060 2963
2 LADY PAT        51  £7035  241131240   27 818 905* 1025* 1275 1568* 1746- 2162 2472
3 LADY SIEMATIC    0  £-    -00   1927 2394
2 LADY SILCA KEY  31  £-    0000   1238 1440 2147 3133
4 LADY SONGE       0  £-    00-0-00   2992 3046
3 LADY SOPHIE     64  £10212  01-20120   214 373 1064* 2385- 2496
3 LADY ST CLAIR   26  £-    1404-0040   49 132 908 998
2 LADY SUNDAY SPORT 10 £1303  402300040   1190 1294 1528 1907 2071 2218 2465 2608 3031
6 LADY TUT         6  £-    0-010-0   137
2 LADY WESTGATE   10  £-    000000   601 1604 1801 2708 2792 2927
2 LADY WESTOWN     0  £-    0000   2434 2710 2788 2901
3 LADY WINDMILL    8  £374   000-400000000   158 232 955 1284 2534 2601 2929 3138 3203
4 LADY WOODPECKER 20  £-    00003-0   19
4 LADYS BRIDGE    45  £3086  214-10030   419* 921 1293 1633 2220
2 LADYS MANTLE    34  £1140  00000331   1604 1801 2069 2249 2433 2698 2881 3056*
2 LAENA           40  £263   300   1518 1914 2407
2 LAGTA           28  £-    000   1518 2527 2904
3 LAJNATA         29  £167   -0340   402 1055 1431 1806
3 LAKE CHAMPLAIN  71  £62979  2-21220231   560* 754 1331 1592 2633 2740 3002*
3 LAKE ERIE       42  £443   -22   2930 3159
3 LAKE ONEGA       0  £-    -000   250 581 1036
2 LAKE TANA        0  £-    0   2846
2 LAKEDGE         30  £-    4   1266
4 LAKINO          19  £2670  000-1-0000100   675 869 1226 1569 1866* 2267 2974
3 LAKISTE         11  £236   -0443040   714 894 1700 2040 2587 2760 2892
3 LALESTON        40  £2942  10400-210   418 760* 977
2 LALUCHE         72  £25730  111   1282* 2057* 2540*
2 LANCE           68  £5639  02200-2210   24 414 605* 802
3 LAND OF IVORY   70  £14579  1404-1D43310102   264 561 661 982 2135+ 2385 2691* 3002 3177-
3 LANDMARK        16  £-    -000   348 619 3102
3 LANDSKI         48  £5054  -40130313400   60 273 765* 1064 1147 1462 1768* 1994 2438 2642 2763
2 LANE PATROL      0  £-    0   2107
2 LANTERN BOY      0  £-    000   1803 2514 3143
3 LARCHES          0  £-    00-00000   25 67 740 809 963
5 LARCHMONT        0  £-    -0   1148
2 LARLOCH          0  £-    0   2522
3 LARNEM          10  £1396  4000-00021000   368 447 1055 1158 1662* 1824 1960 2083
2 LASCIVIOUS INTENT 0 £-    000   1119 2043 3234
2 LASHING         60  £1834  31   773 1322+
2 LAST CHORD      28  £272   03   2791 3044
3 LAST CRY         0  £-    -000   842 2186 2557
2 LAST DANCE      58  £8005  04231201   497 1207 1381 1512 1728- 2119 2252 2830*
3 LAST JEWEL      10  £-    00000-00040   608 1303 1815 2174 2585
3 LAST POLONAISE  09  £248   000-003000040   512 951 1078 1386 1497 1873 2152 2253 2528
2 LAST RECOVERY   38  £2247  303210   206 345 1059 1568 1693* 1814
                              > 987 <
```

```
5 LAST SECRET 0 £127 04000-00003000 626 1344 1543 1682 2124 2322 2775 3046
2 LAST STAND 35 £3317 003314 773 927 1105 2227 2625* 3125
3 LAST TYCOON 90 £450440 111411 563* 1011* 1146+ 1485 2233+ 3211*
3 LASTCOMER 60 £9209 1-00122 216 946 1468+ 1792 1929
3 LATCH STRING 52 £14494 40024-1100 516* 808+ 1151 1285
3 LATE PROGRESS 25 £2422 -000000332110 34 236 603 858 1012 1181 1434 1611 1684 1905* 2168*
2595
2 LATERAL 13 £663 200020000 43- 108 437 536 1333 1478 1920 2140 2466
3 LATRIGG LODGE 0 £- 00-0000 829 1426 2483 2893
3 LAUGH A LOT 22 £620 42223-3200 54 318 648 958
3 LAUGHTER 70 £4664 1-200 509 926 2236
5 LAURAS CHOICE 0 £- 30000-00 490 630
4 LAURIE LORMAN 41 £14440 00-010000020000 508 660+ 922 1145 1385 1730 1852 2065 2160 2537
3106 3233
3 LAURIES TROJAN 0 £- 00-0000 699 1272 2046 2106
2 LAURIES WARRIOR 66 £14616 402121124 3 404 974 1253* 1658 1731* 1968* 2251 2598
2 LAURISTON COTTAGE 0 £- 0 2069
2 LAVANDOU LEGEND 40 £- 040 2147 2555 2788
3 LAVENDER MIST 61 £9272 12-1400 1002* 1489 2462 2567
2 LAVROSKY 44 £- 0 2673
3 LAW COURT 38 £2479 0-00401 351 506 811 1022 1089*
2 LAWNSWOOD LAD 40 £921 410 34 136+ 3072
2 LAZIM 30 £119 043004 531 1082 1495 2329 2529 2895
2 LE FAVORI 53 £3776 1 1653*
3 LE MANS 12 £1109 0-00000310 1981 2394 2775 2854 3024 3057 3144* 3172
9 LE MARSH 0 £- -0 592
3 LE MOULIN 35 £566 0-0040020 357 619 1497 1806 2175 2464 3139
3 LE NID 0 £- 000-00 940 1316
3 LE ROC 60 £7514 -423 895 1490 1860
4 LE SOIR 18 £- 4-000-0 917
3 LEAD ON TIME 85 £35531 121-21 249 2003*
4 LEADING COUNSEL 79 £6014 01021-144 2348* 2637 3004
2 LEADING PLAYER 34 £119 0340 1161 1561 2100 2729
2 LEADING ROLE 16 £756 00010400 230 1234 1483 1684* 2032 2166 2466 2712
4 LEADING STAR 70 £8079 1-010-4302410 251 617 896 1644 2064 2206+ 2630
2 LEADING WREN 0 £- 00 1825 2100
4 LEAN STREAK 0 £- 03000-00000 30 177 495 838 1310
3 LEANDERS PEARL 0 £- -0000 539 723 1953 2174
2 LEAP IN TIME 0 £- 00 3120 3181
4 LEAP YEAR 2 £- /0000-0000 122 727 1165 1521
2 LEAVENWORTH 0 £- 0 2869
3 LEES DOMINION 0 £- -0 1628
3 LEFT RIGHT 11 £1477 00-030030441000 38 255 910 1191 1399 1476 1687 1847 2106* 2488 2906
2966
2 LEG GLIDE 9 £- 000000 1305 1598 2608 2872 3112 3192
2 LEGAL BID 76 £3766 1 3163*
3 LEI 24 £- -00 2853 3105
6 LEIPERS FORK 55 £782 30 1643 2146
2 LEMELASOR 23 £1783 30420-03232000 10 91 174 441 636 680 1553 1689
4 LEMHILL 75 £33539 1D232-134430 251+ 475 1144 1593 2203 2692
4 LEON 34 £2275 41104-22024330 80 126 582 675 778 2324 2395 2492 2944
8 LEONIDAS 22 £3345 00100-00410000 940 1188 1450 1539* 2022 2516 2617 2896
4 LEPRECHAUN LADY 24 £4505 0040-2000120220 69 144 319 419 590* 824 933 1533 2376 3225
4 LES ARCS 68 £- 0-144-00 706 1095
4 LESOTHO 70 £4913 3 2193
3 LETBY 0 £- 34000-00000 7 1310 1578 1884 2363
3 LETOILE DU PALAIS 3 £508 40-040004042434 177 568 845 975 1212 1666 1969 2077 2309 2597
2787 3076
2 LEVEN LASS 20 £441 003420 450 741 2323 2410 2609 2919
4 LEVIGATUS 14 £526 03240-002 618 976 1432
2 LEWISTA 0 £- 00 2127 2365
4 LHASA 30 £- 43200-000 319 2376 2523
3 LHIRONDELLE 19 £- -040 1444 1686 2520
3 LIAM 46 £3229 222-00101404140 60 226 1317* 1468 1690+ 1956 2404 2419 2576* 2612 2704
3 LIASTRA 72 £29559 21210440 904 1215* 2452 3006 3207
6 LIBERATED GIRL 00 £- -00000 1923 2182 2406 2572 2861
2 LIBERTINE 67 £45914 1320222 1351 1714 2826 3088 3166
3 LIBERTON BRAE 17 £- 40020-44400 161 339 545 837 1414
7 LIBERTY WALK 0 £- -0 119
2 LIBRAN STAR 62 £316 044 1629 1915 2270
5 LIBRATE 4 £- 00000-0000 85 126 2134 2432
4 LIDHAME 78 £12739 3-100'-100 267* 641 2145
3 LIDO DANCER 0 £- -0 835
3 LIE IN WAIT 54 £5843 0-144133 448* 688 1085 1435* 1642 2201
5 LIGHT ANGLE 13 £- 40000-000 1896 1986 2124
3 LIGHT BEE 48 £- 12103-04 264 1462
3 LIGHT HILLS 27 £- 10440-00000 534 747 886 952 1191
3 LIGHT THE WAY 12 £1395 0-021 2656 2972 3084*
2 LIGHTFALL 0 £- 00 1653 3141
2 LIGHTFOOT PRINCE 25 £- 000 1234 2036 2407
3 LIGHTNING BYTE 25 £226 -03000 175 277 402 512 764
4 LIGHTNING DEALER 72 £- 221-1-00 221 313
2 LIGHTNING DISC 55 £- 00 2540 2774
2 LIGHTNING LASER 32 £2000 003330100 544 800 1075 1483 1576 1722 1907* 2010 2177
2 LIGHTNING LEGEND 43 £1744 44041 513 655 927 1373 1598*
2 LIGHTNING WIND 11 £291 04300-40003000 514 615 1245 1471 1819 2076 2534 2810
3 LIHBAB 43 £- -40 1291 1469
3 LIKENESS 33 £1594 033-0300344 213 1043 1444 1645 2030 2532 2857
2 LILARDIA 11 £- 0 2493
4 LILIOM 62 £1271 4 2449
2 LILLYS DOUBLE 0 £- 000B 2080 2279 2757 2801
4 LILTING LAD 14 £872 000-00010 10 46 310 524* 967
2 LILY MAB 28 £124 03 3018 3199
```

```
2 LIME BROOK  10    £-   400    1949 2472 2987
3 LINASH  30    £692   -004433    862 1193 1818 2110 2393 2928
3 LINAVOS  23    £1413   000-0100440200    277 837* 961 1164 1398 1603 2171 2519 2659 3145
2 LINCO KING  0    £-   00   2976 3205
2 LINDAS MAGIC  70    £17142   2311310    1232 1464 1650* 1919+ 2235 2687+ 2910
2 LINDAS TREAT  37    £-   004   1440 1801 2069
2 LINDIS GOLD  32    £-   000   2761 3117 3229
3 LINDON  0    £-   0-0   2327
2 LINDRICK  20    £-   0000   1735 2468 2723 3014
2 LINDVARO  20    £-   0000   2056 2493 2717 2926
3 LINE OF CARDS  52    £2756   -41   849 1639*
4 LINE OF FIRE  62    £3348   1-021-0020    221 511 653 1112
2 LINE OF SUCCESSION  36    £-   000   1552 2542 3131
2 LINEBACKER  0    £-   00   2791 2926
3 LINEOUT LADY  0    £-   -0000   25 194 769 1419
2 LING GOLD  31    £-   000   2919 3117 3228
2 LINGERING  52    £1743   24120   1187- 1381 2167* 2986- 3174
4 LINGFIELD LADY  5    £-   00400-4000000    31 177 499 530 851 1056 2647
2 LINN ODEE  28    £4741   2314040140    317 425 665* 766 1527 2010 2380 2744+ 2859 3151
3 LINPAC MAPLELEAF  28    £-   000-0   1431
2 LINPAC NORTH MOOR  25    £1085   00240344234    353 602 665 1119 1427 1696 2265 2425 2588- 2883 3151
3 LINRIBO  0    £-   -P   2316
3 LINTON SPRINGTIME  0    £-   000-000000    553 782 1204 1651 2932 3162
5 LINTON STARCHY  0    £302   0-000-003000000    266 679 855 1367 1521 1940 2046 2619 2836
2 LIPREADER  40    £259   02   2675 3143
4 LIRUNG  85    £128893   232131    759 1355 1715 2195* 2507 2823*
2 LISA NICOLA  30+    £-   0   1604
6 LISAILY  0    £-   -000   1866 2008 2152
3 LISAKATY  10    £946   00-000000043010    162 277 500 940 1310 1471 1751 1898 2253 2560 2590* 2902
3 LISANA  53    £5296   0-2011   1160- 1535 2428* 2766*
2 LISASHAM  9    £200   00030000    848 1440 1801 1881 2608 2927 3081 3112
2 LISETA  40    £1465   02200   2043 2365 2664 2936 3148
2 LISIANTHUS  39    £767   03300   707 1382 1722 2383 2888
4 LISMORE  24    £187   20004-003   2093 2403 2819
3 LITTLE ARMIER  10    £306   00000-200   51 145 195
2 LITTLE BOLDER  48    £817   322   1782 2185 2434
4 LITTLE BORI  5    £-   02000-00   477 906
4 LITTLE DIMPLE  0    £100   -0300   540 718 993 3065
5 LITTLE EGRET  0    £-   -0   3232
2 LITTLE ELLY  0    £-   0   3141
3 LITTLE FIRE  28    £-   0-00   822 1073
5 LITTLE KATRINA  0    £-   -0   1556
2 LITTLE KEY  25    £-   40   345 602
2 LITTLE LAW  0    £-   000   2609 2817 3031
2 LITTLE LOCHETTE  19    £-   0000040   1826 1946 2600 2829 2927 2982 3146
5 LITTLE NEWINGTON  11    £6162   -04100121240002    58 101 131* 184 257 378* 594 820* 866 970 1054 2264 2340 3149
3 LITTLE PIPERS  36    £-   04000-000000   314 387 703 1032 1153 1783
2 LITTLE REALM  0    £-   0   3137
2 LITTLE SACY  32    £-   040   332 1313 1475
4 LITTLE SLOOP  33    £-   01200-0   9
8 LITTLE STARCHY  20    £-   00000-000   477 877 986
3 LITTLE TOKEN  0    £-   -00   2853 2991
2 LITTLE UPSTART  26    £-   044   383 1972 2375
2 LITTLEFIELD  59    £2927   21030   1440 1583* 2057 2543 2687
4 LIVE IN HOPE  0    £-   -0   1148
3 LIVING ROUGH  78    £1140   2-24D0   466 754 1107
2 LIZZY HARE  47    £964   01   2215 3068*
2 LJAAM  50    £2968   1040-4010   138 534 1091* 1335
3 LLANARMON  42    £4423   0-03102   253 444 702* 1130 1237
8 LO BROADWAY  18    £-   1000-0440   9 166 243 629
3 LOBBINO  36    £-   03-00   570 832
7 LOBKOWIEZ  27    £-   00210-000   208 3038 3119
3 LOCAL HERBERT  68    £20286   02-42012   231 411 555 899* 1218
3 LOCAL SILVER  51    £4338   0-0144   1046 1628* 1934 2244
3 LOCH AVICH  0    £-   -0   2583
4 LOCH BLUE  0    £-   00-0   2422
3 LOCH FORM  27    £1637   00-01200320400   64 255+ 339 529 814 1360 1543 1718 2224 2322 2586
4 LOCH LADDIE  5    £-   20300-00   184 3194
3 LOCH SEAFORTH  72    £17831   44-2111121   430 613* 909* 1441* 1994* 2406 2624*
4 LOCHABBEY  3    £-   0000-000   256 1574 2585
3 LOCHANIER  0    £-   -00   175 205
4 LOCHFAST  10    £-   00030-0   207
3 LOCHLAIREY  0    £-   -00   1337 3012
3 LOCHMAR  0    £-   -0000   1244 1451 1607 3057
3 LOCHONICA  52    £696   2140-0000030000   245 387 808 1044 1758 1821 2084 2204 2668 2862
7 LOCHTILLUM  41    £2931   100-00100040000   327 550 836+ 1037 1268 1385 2402 2537 2668 2764 2953
2 LOCKTON  78    £100314   2011312   810 1097 1529* 1658* 2384 2635* 3005
3 LOCKWOOD PRINCE  0    £-   000-000   625 1061 3186
3 LOFT BOY  34    £4291   030-1323000030   62+ 111 314 496 624 947 2842 3055 3138 3191
2 LOMA BREEZE  25    £365   -300003   345 497 746 1050 2848 2806
3 LONDON BUS  55    £8259   00-11220   259* 553* 946 1507 2475
3 LONDON CONTACT  30    £179   00133-00403   637 919 1173 1309 1747
2 LONDON CRIES  0    £-   00   2147 2920
3 LONDON TOWER  72    £27213   203312200   293 471 639 903 1491* 1858 2006 2351 2503
3 LONE GALAXIE  9    £-   03-000000   431 907 1927 1999 2103 2174
5 LONELY STREET  34    £5430   002-20203201430   855 1171 1263 1387 1521 1730- 1933 2046* 2160 2318. 2519
4 LONG BAY  17    £468   00001-0000043   399 611 1165 2602 2762 2836 3029
2 LONG VIEW  0    £-   000   2423 3082 3153
5 LONGBOAT  83    £105120   3-142-01111   617 704* 1127* 1888* 2539*
3 LONGGHURST  34    £1643   00-1000   75* 191 597 983
```

```
3 LONGRIVER LADY  0   £-   -0   173
4 LONGSTOP  26  £2456  1134-3003001024   179 349 569 750 1133 1450 2098* 2175 2372 2727
4 LONTANO  77  £-   1-0   1715
2 LORAS GUEST  43  £-   00   1464 3040
5 LORD BUTCH  0   £-   -000   121 201 343
3 LORD CAPILANO  0   £-   0-00   2148 2464
2 LORD COLLINS  46  £1235   4042044   979 1307 1675 2071 2178 2648 2997
3 LORD HONING  66  £2250   4-3   556
3 LORD IT OVER  26  £824   -00002000   765 1062 1160 1497 2022 2190 2516 2617
2 LORD JUSTICE  43  £532   03   2468 2628
2 LORD KILGAYLE  0   £-   00   3133 3229
2 LORD OF CANEWDON  0   £-   000   2270 2484 2812
2 LORD PATRICK  29  £-   00   1488 1681
4 LORD SUN  24  £-   20404-0   3086
2 LORD THATCH  34  £-   0   3099
2 LORD WESTGATE  48  £2083   0020210   664 1019 1253 1828 1962 2595* 3019
3 LOREEF  25  £761   -044000   739 1002 1530 1690 2546 2853
2 LORI GARBACZ  36  £-   000   2229 2658 3073
2 LOS GIGANTES  0   £-   0   3176
3 LOST IN FRANCE  23  £-   0-00000   372 599 2110 2373 2532
3 LOST ISLAND  20  £-   000-00   2534 2931
2 LOST MOMENT  0   £-   0   3184
3 LOST OPPORTUNITY  18  £1756   4-200040000410   99 229 997 1103 1300 2171 2445 2536 2727 2802
   3049* 3161
4 LOTTIE  0   £-   0-400-000   30 160 266
3 LOTTIE LIMEJUICE  0   £-   -0000   183 1073 1142 1960
2 LOTUS ISLAND  40  £-   0   3037
5 LOTUS PRINCESS  25  £2662   33203-01400   547 789* 967 1951 2102
2 LOUD APPEAL  46  £3891   021   2626 3103 3206*
3 LOUD APPLAUSE  62  £1425   20   560 754
3 LOUD LANDING  18  £1239   0-034002   1290 1652 2300 2467 2604 2932
3 LOUISALEX  0   £-   0-0   41
4 LOUKOUM  52  £11042   -2-1   1709*
3 LOUP DOR  65  £2300   4   301
2 LOUVANKAL  27  £-   00   1683 1919
3 LOUVECIENNES  42  £482   -3334   991 1818 2048 2400
3 LOVE AT LAST  21  £1572   -333320   501 928 1256 1927 3024 3160
5 LOVE LETTER  72  £13559   32-13   290* 896
2 LOVE THE GROOM  72  £13812   213   2522 2732* 3126
2 LOVE TRAIN  44  £-   4400   985 1307 2263 2782
5 LOVE WALKED IN  20  £3771   3-000-001310420   9 23 126* 204 358* 712 990 1183 1564
3 LOVE YOU ROSY  20  £693   -1   2902*
2 LOVEABLE PRINCESS  0   £-   0   3189
2 LOVELY BAND  59  £2496   2   638
5 LOVELY BUTTERFLY  4   £937   00000-32000   7 36 184 256 1271
2 LOVENKO  20  £-   00   2646 3080
3 LOW FLYER  2   £1161   04-030243000000   42 198 447 545 671 866 1051 2602 2854 2977 3104 3160
3 LOW KEY  28  £-   2-000   83 217 2213
2 LOW LINE  34  £-   40   1518 2044
4 LOW MOOR  23  £-   03304-0   783
3 LOW RATION  0   £-   000-0   1784
3 LOWARA  15  £-   -0000   2321 2534 3142 3183
3 LOYAL DOUBLE  74  £20005   1   757*
2 LUBRICAN  44  £399   400   1049 2232 2696
2 LUCAYAN KNIGHT  55  £5364   2110   2345 2491* 2667* 3041
3 LUCAYAN PRINCESS  73  £2244   110-3   463
2 LUCEDEO  34  £1463   0010   3 47 2781+ 3226
2 LUCIANAGA  41  £4691   220100040   834 1003 1143 1313* 1731 2090 2529 2815 3041
2 LUCK BE A LADY  12  £-   00   2433 2596
2 LUCKLEY  0   £-   0   2901
4 LUCKSIN  0   £-   00000-000   333 850 3224
3 LUCKY BLAKE  29  £143   -040403   605 868 1677 2339 2426 3147
3 LUCKY HUMBUG  16  £1006   00-22240   365 517 697 2415 3087
3 LUCKY LAD  17  £-   00-00040   739 980 1444 1556 1807
6 LUCKY LENA  0   £-   -0   1417
2 LUCKY PICK  30  £-   00   2436 2788
4 LUCKY RING  83  £24096   21114-000410   598 920 1823 2785 3020+ 3177
3 LUCKY SO SO  55  £7236   134-410304340   234 427* 692 925 1153 1507 1630 2278 2568
4 LUCKY SONG  50  £-   -0001-0   1292
2 LUCKY STARCH  0   £-   0   2180
4 LUCKY STARKIST  16  £2908   0-0031400040020   211 836 906 1213* 1447 1608 1834 2033 2207 2601
   2837 3065 3145
2 LUCKY STONE  60  £5073   2010   1604 1855 2436* 2751
3 LUCKY TAS  0   £-   -0   2129
3 LUCKY WEST  27  £1073   -001001D2   322 608 1053* 1361 1613 1800 1985
2 LUCRATIF  56  £8747   110414   1403* 1785* 2252 2435 2618+ 2949
3 LUCY AURA  0   £-   -0000   656 923 1061 1246
2 LUCYS MELODY  21  £-   000   1090 1770 1958
3 LUIGIS STAR  19  £-   0-000   64 175 424
2 LUKMARIE  22  £270   43000   1341 2013 2368 2700 2806
2 LULLABY BABY  0   £-   000   2436 2846 3131
3 LULLABY BLUES  21  £3620   -00121200000   237 377 489* 786 890+ 971 1927 1973 2322 2424 3083
2 LUMBERJACK  53  £-   0   3171
3 LUMIERE  27  £-   0-000   359 1628 2676
5 LUMINATE  21  £-   --000-0400   429 2337 2445 2727
3 LUNA BID  69  £2875   11130-02040   220 387 600 808 1457
3 LUNAR SHAMAL GAL  18  £-   01-000000   447 874 1515 1727 2670 3160
2 LUNDY ISLE  12  £-   00000000   725 1238 1433 1650 2308 2433 2596 3190
4 LUNDYLUX  65  £23167   01320-001020   617 1150 1856* 2220 2642 2850
3 LUQMAN  69  £2979   14114-040440   286 556 1096 2351 2505 2785
2 LUREX GIRL  27  £-   0   2531
4 LUSH PATH  0   £-   -000   19 164 1841
3 LUTH DOR  68  £5106   101043   2825 3006
```

```
2 LUZUM 60    £7963   232100    870 1129 1392 1914* 2146 2732
3 LYAPKIN TYAPKIN 45   £1842   04-412    861 1055* 1303
3 LYDIA EVA 16   £2683   000-00010400    1036 1401 1589 2386* 2599 2864 2985 3197
3 LYDIA LANGUISH 17   £800   42400-0020004    1001 1191 1540 1835 1991 2601 2854
2 LYN RAE 20   £2000   000403310    317 957 1622 1795 2050 2298 2470 3016* 3112
2 LYNCOMBE BOY 0   £-   0   3206
2 LYNDA BROAD 0   £-   00000    531 722 1803 1997 2283
3 LYNS GIRL 0   £-0-00    1451 1941
3 LYON COEUR 0   £-   -0   430
4 LYPHARITA 78   £13846   04-11420    1355 2002 2195
2 LYPHENTO 50   £2794   1   3134*
3 LYPHLAW 55   £6949   0-0033111    546 1184 2053 2275 2400* 2690* 2924*
2 LYREEN RIVER 48   £-   4   149
4 LYRIC WAY 19   £2072   2200-0000100000    192 321 727 1060 1211* 1324 1804 2207 3021 3145
2 LYRICAL LOVER 30   £870   003003    1936 2118 2254 2561 3041 3188
4 LYSANDER 35   £-   1-02-00    686 1173
2 LYSHAAN 56   £3953   23104    1329 2540
2 M KELLY 15   £-   0   2678
3 MA FEATHERS 0   £-   0-0000    486 723 1061 2709
2 MA PETITE LASSIE 45   £2044   02203    1826 2717 2950 3130 3174
5 MAAZI 40   £7518   01001-01000    361 881* 1390 1640 2369
3 MABEL ALICE 12   £-   0040-0000004    141 448 651 875 1226 2171 3224
2 MABUHAY 0   £-   0   3158
2 MACE BEARER 50   £646   002    1629 2547 2782
7 MACMILLION 22   £-   30-00-00    727 940
2 MACROBIAN 53   £3606   1000    2056* 2552 2865 3041
3 MACS MAESTRO 32   £-   04400    2229 2493 2646 2920 3182
4 MACS REEF 77   £11153   03202-1004    5* 1094 1230
2 MAD MAX 42   £1774   43202    1928 1984 2108- 2529 2708
2 MADAM BILLA 30   £3839   000001    1143 1297 1550 2485 3146 3182*
3 MADAM GERARD 14   £-   02000-444    45 164 517
3 MADAM MUFFIN 22   £966   2-2002002400    87 283 657 1066 1272 1571 2416 2702 3024 3191
2 MADAM TRILBY 0   £-   0   3137
2 MADAME FLORA 28   £-   04   497 1057
2 MADAME LAFFITTE 20   £1662   0210004    741 1413 1622* 2050 2471 2708 2994
2 MADAME LUMIERE 0   £-   0   3184
2 MADDYBENNY 12   £-   400000    20 47 186 415 1248 2396
4 MADE FOR LIFE 0   £-   0000-0    3087
3 MADEMOISELLE MAGNA 20   £-   30010-000400    1257 1436 1840 1959 2816 2905
3 MADISON GIRL 25   £4240   300-03411020000    130 770 959 1250* 1479* 1615 1739 1866 2237 2662
2864
2 MADNESS NOT TO 0   £-   00000    1019 1629 2011 3017 3190
3 MADRACO 22   £6169   0404-11020    447* 545* 947 1157 1638
3 MADRAMA 25   £-   -0   2734
3 MAELSTROM 16   £-   30-00    492 790
2 MAESTROMAN 26   £-   00000    236 544 685 965 3148
3 MAESTRUM 0   £-   -0   1686
4 MAFTIR 19   £1678   0-0000001220033    124 260 374 566 1066 1347 1979+ 2412 2495 2790 2863 2972
3224
4 MAGIC BID 35   £-   03212-000    238 700 1240
2 MAGIC FLUTTER 32   £-   0   2711
2 MAGIC JOKER 46   £334   4   3181
6 MAGIC MINK 20   £-   00200-0    9
3 MAGIC SLIPPER 65   £6825   -212103    315 862* 1170 1600* 1886 3175
3 MAGIC TOWER 46   £3402   0-40234313    1841 1953 2110 2286 2623 2924 3115* 3236
3 MAGIC VISION 50   £1976   -0001    581 849 1776 2734*
2 MAGICAL LACE 49   £759   30   2847 3023
3 MAGICAL WONDER 83   £111431   4-111041    393* 644* 900* 2195 2507 2827*
2 MAGISTROS 68   £-   340104    3088
5 MAGNIFICA 13   £-   -00-0    176
2 MAGNOLIA DANCER 0   £-   000000    1262 2019 2168 2990 3069 3198
2 MAGNOLIA EXPRESS 35   £358   03   1946 3131
2 MAGNOLIA PRINCESS 0   £-   000    2990 3069 3200
3 MAHABAD 0   £-   -0000    423 764 1303 2315
2 MAHAFEL 0   £-   0   1629
3 MAHOGANY RUN 48   £4511   11420-00010200    605 719 880 1224* 1532 1637 1924 2296
2 MAHRAJAN 35   £-   000    614 2159 2542
3 MAID OF HONFLEUR 22   £547   -10   1340* 2787
4 MAIDEN BIDDER 4   £2608   0000-0210310000    119 495 963* 1086 1319 1447* 1676 2519 2601 3065
7 MAILMAN 52   £24945   31000-40312200    511 879 1498 1931* 2260 2693 2942 3119
2 MAIN BRAND 20   £550   0040140    2499 2625 2708 2829 2990* 3081 3192
4 MAIN REASON 42   £3908   41002-1000    695* 1020 1150 3232
2 MAIN ROCKET 0   £-   000    2527 3141 3199
4 MAIN STAR 15   £-   00000-00    2381 2533
2 MAINMAST 34   £-   00   2675 3134
2 MAINTAIN 50   £2109   01   777 1225*
4 MAIRS GIRL 0   £-   00000-000000    445 724 1273 1447 1500 2581
3 MAIYAASAH 40   £766   -224    2532 2856 3077
3 MAJAAHED 58   £9978   -010300    806 1046* 2438 2567 2749 2946
2 MAJD 52   £2722   33210    1522 2232 2392 2499* 2695
2 MAJESTIC MISS 36   £-   000    2051 2936 3099
4 MAJESTIC RING 38   £240   -0012-040    58A 280 618
9 MAJESTIC STAR 0   £-   -000    1845 2101 2602
3 MAJESTIC VOICE 74   £9430   42   757 1594
3 MAJESTICIAN 62   £8241   -002122340    357 669 770 1029* 1326 2203 2376 2539 2913
6 MAJOR DON 38   £-   00000-0000    815 1249 1525 1758
3 MAJOR JACKO 41   £5536   000-0140000200    62 228* 274 387 616 886 1245 2143 2250 2437
2 MAJOR OAKEY 0   £-   00   2377 3148
4 MAJOR WALLER 15   £-   -0   2428
4 MAJORS REVIEW 24   £-   10300-000    177 495 748
5 MAJUBA HILL 0   £-   0   1582
3 MAKALU 24   £119   2340-030    2622 2931 3164
3 MAKE IT SHARP 26   £119   -03040    863 1368 2393 2880 3187
```

```
2 MAKE OR MAR  30    £3424    01000    1311 1632* 2047 2421 2694
3 MAKE PEACE  25    £1052    3-330000020    183 484 625 1023 1503 2275 2430 2880 3115
2 MAKIN MISCHIEF  13    £-    00000    187 577 664 1731 1948
2 MAKING HISTORY  36    £-    000    2491 2703 2920
2 MAKSAB  35    £-    0    2750
2 MAKSOUD  23    £-    0    3080
3 MAL Y PENSE  23    £-    32010-0000    2728 2879 2963 3033
2 MALACANANG  12    £142    00030    1625 2472 2535 2994 3182
2 MALACHI LAD  0    £134    30000    1163 1318 1496 1692 2899
3 MALADETOC  27    £-    -000    1327 1602 2110
7 MALADHU  26    £3644    03240-13044    2324* 2467 2861 2955 3187
3 MALAKIM  70    £8464    2-1422    302 2639
3 MALEIHA  18    £259    -02000    422 656 911 1669 2046
5 MALEVIC  71    £10324    -1    287*
2 MALIBU TOAST  52    £1369    011    2301 2589* 2883*
3 MALIN FLEET  17    £-    -000    2704 3077 3183
4 MALMO  0    £-    -000-0000    46 145 1139 1361
2 MAMADORA  19    £-    0000    1238 1632 2070 2485
2 MAMAMERE  21    £-    00    2997 3141
2 MAMOUNA  68    £2013    2    2675-
3 MAN IN THE MOON  13    £-    000-000040    328 1398 1917 2174 2238 2560
4 MANABEL  10    £782    0-0000000024400    129 196 441 1013 1104 1482 1565 2109 2340 2401 2549 3071
3172
3 MANASTA  0    £-    -00    608 684
7 MANCHESTERSKYTRAIN  44    £2401    00-300000200200    401 616 706 1109 1286 1640 2123 2431 2544 2655
2773 2867
2 MANDALAY PRINCE  35    £-    000400    1232 1587 2407 2700 2813 3141
5 MANDOWN LAD  5    £-    0-000-0    2591
3 MANDRAKE MADAM  20    £965    232-00003300300    518 814 929 1044 1380 1505 1796 2065 2688 3046 3152
2 MANDUB  56    £4492    131240    662* 1014 1746+ 2162 2460 2954
3 MANGAYAH  75    £2300    2210104    2918
4 MANGO EXPRESS  77    £2432    -1124-20    617 704
5 MANGO MAN  11    £162    00000-300    30 114 495
4 MANHATTAN BOY  13    £-    -1100-00    530 1666
3 MANIFIC  70    £-    0    644
3 MANILA  93    £925280    11    2735* 3212*
9 MANILOW  23    £-    00000-0    418
6 MANIMSTAR  56    £15502    430-00002110000    172 361 616 836 1145 1285* 1933* 2258 2446 2862 3055
5 MANIX  0    £-    4000    1766 2264 2413 2970
2 MANLY BOY  31    £693    02    2847 3081
3 MANNDESH  0    £-    -0    289
2 MANSIO  22    £-    000    2711 3120 3205
2 MANSOOJ  77    £42749    310124    405 810* 1097 1467* 2221- 2866
6 MANTELANO  71    £1498    23-3    290
5 MANTERO  74    £10862    -1    392*
3 MANTIQUE  20    £-    20000-F    716
3 MANTON DAN  65    £23499    012-20101100    227 387 1648* 1852 2224+ 2446* 2668 2953
3 MANTON MARK  26    £2494    1000-0001000000    814 1027 1524 1882* 1986 2224 2362 2858 3033 3104
3 MANVIL  18    £183    0-00030    322 702 969 1158 1267
4 MAORI WARRIOR  8    £-    0-0000-0    530
4 MARAVILLA  23    £2222    0300-0002420000    936 1104 1292 1627- 1761 2039 2340 2397 2513 2681
3 MARBLE MOON  18    £-    -000000    862 996 2464 2682 2864 3217
2 MARBLE ROCK  23    £-    000    2574 2869 3043
3 MARCEE  0    £-    -0    720
4 MARCELLINA  3    £-    0-00-0000    164 381 522 783
2 MARCHING MOTH  20    £3078    14000    236* 367 450 1576 1893
3 MARCOTTE  40    £1300    -2    1710
2 MARCOVICH  0    £-    000    2961 3132 3198
3 MARCREDEA  36    £1776    -002010    516 835 1246 1541 1943* 2189
2 MARDAS  43    £-    00    1465 1629
3 MARETH LINE  18    £2442    -041    2129 2366 2478*
3 MARGAM  42    £7825    0-3104102    593 787+ 1171 1312 1900+ 2242 3118
4 MARIA FUMATA  68    £-    -0    2917
3 MARICAMA  18    £119    -4003000    435 494 1022 1807 1879 2492 3139
2 MARIE BABY  0    £-    000    1802 2118 2434
3 MARIE DE BEAUJEU  78    £3300    -2    155
3 MARIE GALANTE  30    £1880    300-2323030    128 239 458 811 1048 2306 2745
2 MARIE ZEPHYR  13    £-    0    2975
2 MARIENBOURG  49    £461    43    2484 2796
3 MARIES VALENTINE  30    £-    04-0000000    431 835 1451 1947 2210 2653 2853
2 MARIKO GOLD  0    £-    000    383 2418 2710
2 MARIMBA  43    £2359    2331440    400 707 1030 2127+ 2292 2618 2865
3 MARINA PLATA  20    £2688    '0-01100000400    33 99* 322* 414 491 823 1223 1871 2128 3161 3187
4 MARINAVILLE  0    £-    -0    381
8 MARINE  0    £-    -0    1788
5 MARINERS DREAM  20    £5958    00000-100113    366* 933 1477 2141* 2745* 3049
4 MARINERS STAR  13    £-    22340-000    2428 2604 2800
2 MARK ANGELO  36    £450    2000    61 571 685 2852
9 MARK EDELSON  0    £-    -0    142
3 MARK EDEN  22    £146    -0003    438 546 1142 1420
3 MARK MY CARD  0    £-    000-000    1626 1864 2104
2 MARK OF GOLD  0    £-    0000    40 167 446 537
3 MARK SEAGULL  20    £-    0000    34 350 938 2320
3 MARKELIUS  15    £-    000-00000    75 659 919 2623 2930
2 MARKET MAN  11    £-    04000    612 892 2757 2976 3112
2 MARKET SPIRIT  0    £-    000    2177 2493 3201
2 MARLEY MONARCH  0    £-    00    2407 3067
4 MARLEY ROOFUS  16    £-    30200-0000    72 263 2164 3063
5 MARLION  32    £19940    0120-0032413312    144 366 917 1159 1280 1865* 2031 2169 2944* 3052
3 MAROUBLE  72    £4970    14023-0030    408 2233 2503 2672
2 MARQUEE CAFE  20    £-    000    513 2179 2472
2 MARQUETERIE  22    £-    0    2889
5 MARSH HARRIER  37    £6267    1-0002004130210    344 709 984 1188 1667 1788 1994 2190* 2406-2516
2617 2837* 2925
                              > 992 <
```

```
3 MARSHAL MACDONALD  38   £1624   40-00440300   60 387 1036 1384 1998 2404 2624 2848
3 MARSHALL DRILLS  0   £-   00000-0000000   626 910 1334 1505 1839 1917 2268
4 MARSILIANA  6   £2633   0000-0403401000   606 820 1013 1139 1624 1774 2086* 2340 2602 2762
4 MARSOOM  3   £711   32010-0002000   91 453 636 750 1188 1581 2226
4 MARTELLA  0   £83   00000-030000000   41 107 788 828 963 1201 1424 1662 1839
3 MARTESSANA DANCER  48   £196   -024   218 422 723
2 MARTHA STEVENS  0   £-   0   1464
2 MARTHAS PRIDE  0   £-   00   86 543
4 MARTIAN BABY  31   £-   00200-0   439
2 MARTIAN MELODY  0   £-   0000   1665 2433 2698 2878
8 MARTON BOY  6   £738   -0030-01   630 975*
4 MARY GUARD  66   £6148   1-020   392 1219 3094
9 MARY MAGUIRE  24   £1437   00-000032200000   110 306 355 490 820 1120 1182- 1338 1429 1610 3104
3145
3 MARY MILFORD  23   £-   0-00   423 2068
3 MARY SUNLEY  30   £151   -00430   1444 1690 2048 2548 2676
2 MASCALLS DREAM  24   £747   000220   1550 2070 2434 2801 3016 3112
2 MASHBUB  35   £955   32200   1442 1665 2118 3122 3226
3 MASHHUR  34   £-   02301-00000   465 807 1394 2497 3116
3 MASHKOUR  83   £138027   2211-31134230   226 362* 510* 878 1330 2222 2822 3091
6 MASKED BALL  39   £21040   11230-112021400   166* 439* 698- 1254 1526 1820* 2536 2686 3113
4 MASKEEN  11   £-   00000-0   1755
3 MASNOON  0   £-   -0   2148
7 MASTER BLOW  0 .  £-   /0000-0   9
7 MASTER CARL  12   £384   20230-000303   23 449 590 721 860 2587
2 MASTER COMEDY  0   £-   00   2541 2878
2 MASTER DRUMMER  0   £-   0   118
4 MASTER FRANCIS  9   £-   20300-000000   202 485 856 1035 1195 1784
2 MASTER KNOWALL  0   £-   000000   332 1197 1289 1452 1903 2645
3 MASTER LAMB  9   £-   000-404000   690 867 1089 1295 1637 1838
5 MASTER LINE  40   £3391   30110-0010300   265 445 709* 879 1636 1931 3113
3 MASTER MUSIC  5   £-   0-0004000000040   25 99 194 258 451 1904 2076 2264 2427 2602 2762 2887
3060
2 MASTER PIPPIN  0   £-   000   780 948 2396
2 MASTER POKEY  32   £13551   011100   136 1180* 2479* 2563* 2680 3230
3 MASTER THAMES  53   £84   2-430   546 861 1245
8 MASTER VINCE  25   £-   0/4   3035
3 MATBAR  10   £201   0400-04400   839 1029 1336 2129 2317
7 MATCH MASTER  00   £-   0--0-00   1166 1558
2 MATCHING WOOD  0   £-   0   3109
3 MATELOT ROYALE  17   £1252   0-01200   31 113* 356 738 1806
6 MATOU  53   £11266   011-4202D100000   192 1026 1145 1536 1810+ 2204 2668 2947 3055 3127
4 MATTSAWARD  7   £-   00-00-0   22
4 MATTYE LEE  0   £-   00000-00   1676 1870
4 MAUNDY GIFT  0   £-   00030-00   727 3076
2 MAUREENS CAVALIER  0   £-   000   1665 2609 3017
3 MAVELA  0   £-   -0   3142
4 MAVITTA DEE  0   £-   -U0   1223 1278
3 MAWDLYN GATE  18   £1796   -00400132200000   247 328 414 527 960 1134* 1547 1699 1808 1976 2427
2562 2776 3101
3 MAWSUFF  62   £6406   -021234   593 764 1036+ 1463 1788 3204
3 MAX CLOWN  8   £1019   000-00130   279 718 1428* 1898 2101
3 MAX DOR  70   £13064   -01   286 1114*
2 MAX IS CUTE  0   £-   0   1495
2 MAX STAR  0   £-   000   2107 2580 2801
5 MAY BE THIS TIME  18   £387   310-0-2P   1564 2492
2 MAY BELFORT  28   £-   00   2433 2555
3 MAYBE JAYNE  0   £-   0-4400000000000   377 489 825 972 1418 1505 1687 1973 2139 2409 2660 3012
3152
2 MAYBEMUSIC  16   £1111   00100030   612 931 1181* 1528 1717 2298 2712 3016
2 MAYCREST  0   £-   0   3143
2 MAYFAIR DOLL  0   £-   00   2596 3192
3 MAYOR  30   £605   43110-34000430   6 168 216 427 1257 1704 2018 2224
2 MAYRONI  0   £-   00   2675 2847
3 MAYSOON  84   £90305   130-12320   232* 373 926 1932 2456
2 MAYSPARK  19   £-   0400   612 948 1825 2100
2 MAZILIER  53   £2663   201010   985 1129 1550* 2843 3048* 3226
2 MAZURKANOVA  25   £1662   004204100   548 892 1069 1297 1527 1770 2026* 2391 2669
2 MCCALLUN  18   £-   40000   332 965 1675 2178 3085
2 MCCUBBIN  54   £-   0   3171
3 MEADOW MOOR  34   £-   01020-0000   15 62 234 496
2 MEADOWBANK  46   £931   00310   1282 2527 2652 2814* 3058
5 MEADOWBROOK  40   £3793   31423-230   11 58A 3052
3 MEASURING  56   £982   11320-300000   59 600 1235 1631 1852 2351
2 MEATH PRINCESS  9   £228   02000000   167 376 488 1155 2010 2178 3079 3146
2 MEBHIL  46   £1506   332   614 804 1175
2 MEDALLION MAN  17   £122   00300   186 2396 2580 2707 2994
3 MEDDY  3   £-   0403-000   426 608 1815
2 MEDRIAN  0   £-   00   2875 2982
2 MEESON JOSE  0   £-   0   1433
5 MEESON KING  34   £2168   01000-200000   2289- 2537 2783 2953 3127 3233
3 MEESON MORE  0   £-   -00   1437 1688
3 MEET THE GREEK  54   £22058   202-21120122301   352 514* 719+ 847 1147 1365* 1854 1967 2431 2867
3021*
3 MEGADYNE  2   £-   -0000007   205 733 907 1316 1943 2313 3046
4 MEGANOT  0   £-   40000-00000   22 207 963 1201 1482
3 MEGANS MOVE  24   £1861   004-01000   779 867* 1054 2128 2300
2 MEGS MONEY  0   £-   0   108
7 MEIKLEOUR  37   £-   12100-0   44
5 MELAURA BELLE  33   £-   04004-0000   649 1682 1840 1986
2 MELBURY LAD  72   £28700   2112   21- 170+ 898* 3009
2 MELDON HILL  0   £-   0000   2527 2652 3134 3205
3 MELENDEZ  42   £3758   -0021   751 951 1386 1732*
                        > 993 <
```

```
2 MELGROVE  30   £1584    0400120    523 1916 2105 2479 2757* 2976- 3165
2 MELODY LINER  0   £-  000   2325 2491 2607
2 MELODY MAKER  50   £6665    03141    405 1311 1534* 2830 3125*
4 MELODY PARK  62   £1475    33404-430    70 245 361
2 MELROW  0   £-  0   3109
8 MELS CHOICE  15   £-  00040-0000000    112 174 260 668 2685 2945 3157
8 MEND IT  12   £-  -1100-0   629
2 MENDELS LAW  0   £-  0   3017
5 MENDICK ADVENTURE  19   £1996   230000032000000  56 135 441 550 922 1026 1157 1338 1536 1810 1840
  2079 2151 2586 2632
2 MENDIP STAR  23   £2743    40410240    1445 1629 1746 2209* 2465 2700 2813 3188
5 MENINGI  30   £4781    00-00-31414330    185 308* 493 591* 721 869 1052 2955
2 MENZIES FLYER  0   £58   3   1474
2 MEPHISTOPHELES  0   £-  0   3117
3 MERANO  63   £4353    -321   1589 2148*
3 MERCADAH  70   £-  34340-0   288
2 MERCE CUNNINGHAM  66   £4123   323   1914 2199 2673
3 MERCIA GOLD  0   £228    03000-3000000    38 83 246 910 1334 1815 1960
3 MERDON MELODY  52   £15622    1034-1220041030    387* 496 808- 1044 1911 2242 2378* 2573 2842 3055
3 MERE MUSIC  28   £2618    000000100200    425 602 766 892 1075 1958 2150* 2334 2472 2535 2744 2903
3 MERHI  31   £3267    200-2343000300    143 244 604 698 946 1147 1503 1831 1923 2386
3 MERITMOORE  42   £1036    00-0200    1431 2442 2946 3123
4 MERLE  36   £-  0000-0000000000    433 573 706 879 1526 1792 1929 2144 3123 3236
3 MERLINS MAGIC  24   £-  001-00    1384 1558
4 MERRY MEASURE  20   £-  01000-000000    17 71 196 578 775 1013
3 MERRY RIDGE  0   £-  -0   67
3 MERRYMOLES  28   £3622    34130-000004131    480 545 1001 1669 1783 1991 2120+ 2906 3191*
4 MERSEY  84   £50284    23111-2104    468 2637* 2917 3097
3 MERSEYSPEED  0   £-  -400   2176 2400 2464
4 MESSALINE  25   £-  -040   959 1519 1831
3 METAL WOODS RULE  0   £-  0000-0000    339 545 1400 1567
5 METELSKI  18   £98    40100-000340    201 967 1569 1845 2101 2290
3 METEOR MISS  25   £-  20000-0   986
3 METEORIC  65   £5545    0120-01030    214 776+ 1107 2241 2772
2 METROMAN  0   £-  000000    1225 1741 2150 2323 2805 2987
3 MEVAGISSEY  32   £285    -200   2996 3061 3155
2 MEXICAN HONEY  40   £123   3   1802
4 MEXICAN MILL  10   £-  03000-00000    8 166 613 1964 2102
5 MEZIARA  10   £410    00420-224000    119 201 343 530 1058 2699
2 MI OH MY  31   £1288    302334020020    13 57 181 329 354 589 696 939 1221 1279 1363 1483
4 MIA JUBES  5   £-  00000-00000    1018 2046 2319 2943 3204
2 MIAMI BAY  28   £-  000   571 870 2511
3 MIAMI BLUES  20   £2050    000-00100100    26 431 749* 907 2189 2560* 2719 3101
4 MIAMI COUNT  66   £1581    24200-4400    267 639 945 2192
6 MIAMI DOLPHIN  2   £4139    00-001310300000    46 378 490+ 626 786* 890 1120 1247 2277 2411 3104
  3145
3 MIAMI IN SPRING  26   £2929    3000-1130    517* 823* 998 3219
2 MIAMI LASS  0   £-  000   1583 2044 2177
4 MICHELE MY BELLE  0   £-  00000-0000    137 526 731 1016
2 MICRO LOVE  34   £1930    3012000    187 804 1445* 1785 2485 2564 2986
2 MIDBADGE  0   £-  00   3059 3163
2 MIDDAY SANITO  22   £84    3000    27 118 1518 2097
2 MIDDLELANE LAD  0   £-  00   13 102
3 MIDWAY LADY  88   £221196    2111-11    373* 926+
2 MIDYAN  75   £15775    1421    979* 1467 1887 2949+
2 MIESQUE  83   £88666    1311    2358 2737* 2915*
2 MIGHT MOVE  39   £826    003-0020    32 95 274 436
3 MIGHTILY  19   £228    0-3000    276 351 512 738
2 MIGHTY BOLD  30   £-  004000    382 1512 1869 2485 2753 2935
3 MIGHTY FLASH  49   £8459    00-0001100010    581 849 1062 1236* 1523* 1886 2156 2525 2880* 3022
2 MIGHTY GLOW  44   £-  00   2852 2951
5 MIGHTY SUPREMO  9   £-  10000-00   1374 1432
3 MIGIYAS  55   £5712    1240-1000    158* 1002 2440 2568
5 MIJAS GOLF  22   £-  00043-P   341
2 MILAN FAIR  35   £-  0000   2418 2732 3037 3107
2 MILCREST  0   £-  0   1232
2 MILEAGE BANK  69   £5071    41014    614 1275* 1572 1760* 2384
3 MILEOMETER  35   £2673    0020-0201    461 816 1091 1394*
4 MILETRIANS LASS  0   £-  0-000-000    31 76 114
3 MILFORD QUAY  25   £-  -00   669 2366
2 MILITARY ATTACHE  0   £-  0   2243
3 MILL ON THE FLOSS  78   £49472    10-312202    372 509* 1128 1408- 2357 2952
7 MILL PLANTATION  52   £3343    -0110-00104    445 652 1325* 2686 2924
4 MILL TERN  22   £872    00200-10   522* 3128
2 MILL TRIP  30   £1338    030203    2051 2320 2626 2707 2829 3079
2 MILLENNIA  27   £-  000   2147 2434 2703
3 MILLERS DUST  50   £4285    -02323    384 1031 1469 1776 2061
4 MILLERS TALE  26   £2804    0002-2010400404    208 363 761* 1004 1366 1837 2766 2877 3087 3187
2 MILLFAN  37   £3448    232012    938 1844 2011- 2421 3058* 3174-
2 MILLFIELD BLUE  0   £-  000   446 589 1137
2 MILLFIELDS HOUSE  33   £-  00   2589 2933
2 MILLIE DUFFER  14   £-  004400    57 102 125 865 1012 2298
2 MILLIGRAM  80   £22341    12   2675+ 2915
2 MILLPOND BOY  25   £-  000   1234 2179 3075
3 MILLRACER  46   £2634    40-014    1184 1375* 1783
3 MILLS AMEND  0   £-  00-0   1953
3 MILTESCENS  33   £2992    033-10302040040    357* 552 635 883 1177 1679 1809 2478 2722 3161 3225
5 MILTON BURN  25   £14953    -01102232000000    11 58A* 312+ 475 735 801 1099 1150 1388 1779 2164
  2220 3052 3232
2 MIN ALLAH  46   £823   2   3206
4 MIN BALADI  28   £2609    3411-32002040    410 629 743 2066 2273 2551 2776 2855
2 MINABELLA  0   £-  0   3143
3 MINATZIN  68   £8180    -1431-4404    289 643 1009 2193
                              > 994 <
```

```
4 MIND THE TIME  0    £-   -00   344 2271
4 MINDERS MAN  0    £-   00000-0000000   1820 1981 2413 2583 2681 3036 3155
3 MINHAH  37   £236   -030   1580 1833 2430
2 MINI ROSE  0    £-   0   1955
8 MINIBANK  0    £-   -0   88
3 MINISTRAILIS  24    £-   00-0000   351 570 843 1199
2 MINIZEN LAD  0    £-   000   108 186 1883
2 MINIZEN LADY  16   £91   03   57 102
2 MINIZEN LASS  36   £5567   0422022420031   450 548 672 913 995 1266 1370 1545 1867- 2127 2261
2606 2678*
2 MINOBEE  0    £-   00000   118 565 848 1728 3131
2 MINSTREL SINGER  40    £-   4   3135
2 MINSTRELLA  83   £256713   4212112   383 548 1129+ 1454- 2113+ 2634+ 2831
8 MINUS MAN  11   £6110   0200-0003042311   281 547 710 1079 1188 1870 2190 2381 2807* 2896*
4 MIRACLE TOOL  0    £-   -0   568
4 MIRACLES TAKE TIME  35   £2678   13003-000422   70 192 508 734 952- 1235-
3 MIRAGE DANCER  40   £3733   0204-023424020   60 362 494 765 1315 1469 2408 2620 2930
3 MIRANDA JULIA  19   £2075   440-13000004000   276* 455 659 925 1032 2120 2291 2601 2702 2879 3063
3 MIRANOL VENTURE  7    £-   000-0000   162 347 1304 1807
3 MIRATAINE VENTURE  22   £713   022-30003000400   271 656 925 1153 1446 1571 2076 2333 2546 2676
2876
4 MIRPUR  0    £-   -04   1548 2587
3 MISAAFF  37   £2828   0213-411000   989 1336* 1808* 2247 2666 3113
2 MISCHIEVOUS MISS  40   £596   300   2436 2664 3234
3 MISCROWN  73   £12942   11320-32   286 3215
4 MISHRIF  24    £-   04010-00   341 3139
2 MISK  60   £3564   22013   974 1311- 1453 1984* 2392
2 MISK EL KHASHAB  35   £945   2000   1752 2215 2377 2577
3 MISNAAD  51   £5061   4220-120   15* 234 2463
4 MISRULE  36   £11866   0120-1230   2467* 2754 3052 3225
2 MISS ACACIA  10   £999   000303220200   819 944 1067 1221 1294 1647 1832 1997 2608 2927 2994 3031
4 MISS AGGRO  15    £-   20000-000   10 91 310
4 MISS APEX  8   £2113   2-0430233001000   91 420 673 963 1439 1689 1870 2154 2303 2697* 2863 3154
3224
3 MISS ARON  30    £-   00-0000   209 615 1395 2148
2 MISS ATWELL  0    £-   0000   2167 2308 2577 2707
3 MISS BECCA  14   £209   0-020   2996 3150 3203
2 MISS BESWICK  4    £-   40000-0000   426 608 871 1562
3 MISS BETEL  0    £-   00-04000000   209 767 978 1288 1369 1369 1567 1838
4 MISS BLACKTHORN  20   £1953   00001-03203002   69 419 541 801 1058 1633 3139 3219
3 MISS BLAKE  3   £251   00000-00000002   997 1257 1626 1761 1885 2268 3033 3220
3 MISS BLUEBELL  0    £-   -000   1751 2048 2430
2 MISS BOLERO  0    £-   000000   47 425 2396 2471 2712 3031
3 MISS BRADY  35    £-   0-4   33
3 MISS BRAHMS  0    £-   -00000   123 338 423 839 1210
3 MISS COMEDY  3    £-   00000-0000   845 1212 1364 1937
2 MISS DAISY  25   £595   300   1930 2788 3184
2 MISS DIAMANTE  0    £-   000   364 1180 1741
2 MISS DISPLAY  1    £-   0044000   236 627 826 1379 1611 2410 2689
2 MISS DRUMMOND  16   £2242   0002001313040   47 646 948 1323 1528 1680 1741* 1949 2107* 2425 2606
2744 2859
2 MISS EMILY  13   £786   000220000   701 1088 2100 2323 2396 2535 2669 3085 3222
3 MISS HARLEQUIN  1    £-   0200-0000   67 352 620 1210
3 MISS HICKS  7    £-   -0000400   213 1228 2186 2312 2898 2960 3144
3 MISS JADE  8    £-   0000-000400   581 843 1471 1970 2098 2386
2 MISS JASMINE  20    £-   004   1778 2320 2835
3 MISS KNOW ALL  30   £207   10-00030   624 884 1584 1940 2106
3 MISS KOLA  0    £-   -0000   656 1327 1541 2076
2 MISS LALIE  0    £-   0   2675
2 MISS LAMB  0    £-   0   317
3 MISS LAURA LEE  25   £2227   40-4000040111   368 676 779 1106 1688 1952 2478 2984* 3100 3193*
2 MISS LAWSUIT  0    £-   0000   999 1483 2652 3190
3 MISS MAGGIE  2    £-   40-00   498 837
4 MISS MAGNETISM  2    £-   00040-0   990
5 MISS MAINA  0    £-   -00   1290 1727
2 MISS MANAGEMENT  0    £-   0000   1090 1958 2127 2365
2 MISS MARIPOSA  24   £164   3   2471
2 MISS MARJORIE  6   £544   010000   200 337* 596 1785 1938 2927
2 MISS MARTINIQUE  34    £-   00   2933 3181
4 MISS METAL WOODS  9   £1713   00423-40400010   418 1171 1344 1542 1940 2274 2370* 3065
2 MISS MILVEAGH  42   £5055   32221300   1545 1826 1972 2272 2380* 2465 2588 2729
4 MISS MONROE  0    £-   03244-0000   812 1186 1240 1939
4 MISS MORLEY  2    £-   10100-0000004   7 80 129 333 782 1079 1124
3 MISS MOTH  0    £-   -000   431 732 835
2 MISS PENGUIN  16    £-   00   2904 3136
2 MISS PISA  10   £511   -03030430F0   34 167 254 647 957 1622 1862 2138 2801 3112
2 MISS PONTEVECCHIO  24    £-   000   2080 2375 2600
2 MISS PRECARIOUS  0    £-   0   2470
3 MISS PRIMULA  15   £495   000-03030004000   545 628 814 890 1247 1774 1959 2362 2632 2775 2966
2 MISS RUNAWAY  36   £648   04230   1308 1604 1966 2365 2600
2 MISS SARAJANE  32   £2237   00213   1883 2011 2325 2607* 3125
3 MISS SERLBY  15   £470   00000-000020   784 961 1399 1959 2055 2312
2 MISS SHEGAS  25   £4256   22100304   167 261 473* 873 1527 1760 2172 2588
2 MISS SHERBROOKE  0    £-   0000   317 450 1137 1413
3 MISS SHIRLEY  40   £3217   0-302241323   751 980 1700 2023 2304 2520+ 2599 2733 2988
3 MISS STANWAY  0    £-   -0000   829 1472 1953 2282
2 MISS STORM BIRD  61   £2494   20   2768 3040
2 MISS STYLE  0    £-   0   3192
2 MISS SUNDAY SPORT  52   £684   1   118*
3 MISS TAUFAN  0    £-   00000-040000   670 825 1070 1360 1734 2055
2 MISS TIMED  11    £-   -000   213 423 3197
3 MISS TONILEE  24   £4576   03-322431   67 426 666 809 1827 1927*
3 MISS VAIGLY BLUE  0    £-   00-0   966
                              > 995 <
```

```
3 MISS VENEZUELA 0  £-  0-0000040000000  455 615 703 954 1288 1549 1827 2088 2429 2898 2960
  3084 3162
2 MISS ZOLA 36  £1114  0010  1722 2043 2584* 2971
3 MISSELFORE 9  £313  00-000300  1031 1444 1941 2102 2709 3063
2 MISSION BIRD 0  £-  00  544 2365
5 MIST OVER PENDLE 0  £-  -0  2528
4 MISTA SPOOF 0  £-  24004-0000  174 540 727 845
3 MISTAKEMENOT 0  £-  0-0  581
3 MISTER BIG LOUIE 62  £3441  0-40003  643 2738
2 MISTER COLIN 46  £1601  1243440  27* 115 118 622 810 3180 3230
2 MISTER MAJESTIC 74  £49690  1211144014  212* 382 610* 804+ 859* 1129 2501 2695 2866* 3039
3 MISTER MARCH 24  £7051  000014112000302. 161 855 1171 1344 1406* 1584 1718* 1742* 2024 2033 2519
  2702 2810 2928 3033
4 MISTER POINT 36  £5903  200-00011301000  9 166 609 1054* 1133* 1254 2173 2374+ 2477 3113 3232
6 MISTER PRELUDE 15  £466  00020-002000  174 333 1081 1240 1519 1781
2 MISTER WIZARD 20  £-  0000000  1039 1522 1629 1915 2108 2514 2835
3 MISTER WONDERFUL 80  £21902  210-33331  216 406 692 1147 1286+
3 MISTRAL MAGIC 0  £-  0-00000000  500 982 1830 2109 2548 2743 2988 3161
3 MISTRESS CHARLEY 0  £-  00-0000  14 284 377 630
2 MISTS OF AVALON 45  £2537  42421  1322 2013 2215 2678 3221+
3 MISTS OF TIME 13  £640  000-03003  506 823 1258 1671 2109
2 MISTY RUNNER 0  £-  00000  701 1221 1480 1635 1955
3 MITALA MARIA 17  £755  -0230242  1080 1481 1908 2299 2902 3100 3193
6 MITILINI 0  £-  -0  336
3 MITNER 14  £-  00044-000000  534 775 1018 1303 1835 2060
2 MITRAL MAGIC 0  £-  00  2499 3031
3 MITSUBISHI VISION 68  £3340  012214  903 1858
2 MIXEDUP MHAIRI 0  £-  00  2584 2796
2 MODEL LAD 0  £-  0  3198
3 MODENA REEF 44  £3024  300-3010  157 352 730* 1236
6 MODERN MAN 0  £-  -0  28
5 MODEST 0  £-  -0  408
3 MOEL FAMMAU 17  £493  -0300400  371 527 699 1085 2009 2171 2508
3 MOGOAR 24  £-  030-0400  1451 1751 2963
3 MOHICAN 15  £151  3220-0300  45 492 697 1362
2 MOLASSES MAN 16  £-  0  2626
3 MOLLIKIN 0  £-  -0  1589
3 MOLLY PARTRIDGE 3  £1133  03-000300410000  89 674 857 1074 1471 2441 2509 2585* 2854 2973
  3077 3149
3 MOLOCH 9  £-  00000-000  1841 1960 2268
5 MOLOJEC 14  £121  -3  3196
3 MOLTO RAPIDO 0  £-  -0P  1206 1646
3 MOLUCELLA 12  £-  000-000  458 833 2306
5 MOLYBDENUM 0  £-  -000  1535 1686 2528
3 MOMA 0  £-  -0  2430
2 MOMENT IN THE SUN 0  £-  00  1464 2215
2 MOMENT OF TRUTH 0  £-  0  2869
2 MOMENTS OF SILVER 47  £124  340  2341 2645 3037
2 MON BALZAR 32  £229  00000044  1255 1552 2514 2667 2875 2983 3174 3226
2 MON COEUR 58  £2052  0423034  1232 1587 2105 2329 2498 2830 2971
3 MONA LISA 62  £8389  -0100  218 264* 463 3051
5 MONARTO 0  £-  -0  851
3 MONATATION 0  £-  000-000000  455 1273 1471 1581 2120 2659
7 MONCLARE TROPHY 13  £2737  010-00100030000  36 163 420* 547 731 1079 1173 1274 1829 2374 2549
2 MONETARY FUND 35  £584  020  1381 2328 2493
2 MONFEM 0  £-  0  2127
7 MONIAR 10  £1811  -001  912 1223 1621*
5 MONINSKY 9  £3338  -20030031040000  260 606 830 956 1077 1338 1624 1774* 1906 1983 2536 2629
  2728 2816
2 MONS FUTURE 17  £2335  0142221000  86 354* 672 696 1012 1358 1611* 2680 2798 2888
6 MONSANTO LAD 0  £-  -00  993 1703
3 MONSARAH 18  £-  01000-400  1272 1443 1584
3 MONSTROSA 5  £439  0300-0030003000  335 538 857 997 1560 1885 2104 2594 2715 3065
5 MONSWART 2  £-  00000-0000000  12 135 369 1093 1247 1638 1761
2 MONT ARTHUR 8  £-  00  2805 3218
3 MONTBERGIS 0  £-  00020-00000  1310 1437 1686 3076 3202
4 MONTEFIASO 0  £-  0000000  863 1068 1102 1415 2335 2621 2743
2 MONTERANA 62  £8005  1210  1996* 2436 2611+ 3040
2 MONTFORT 64  £7246  01230  1464 1722* 2057 2504 2751
6 MONTICELLI 0  £-  20404-002000  710 812 1231 1676 1976 2274
2 MONTYS GUNNER 0  £-  0000  1339 1665 2270 2468
2 MOODYBINT 12  £-  000-000  935 1589 2211
2 MOON INDIGO 41  £4201  01000000  187 1381* 1925 2136 2252 2694 2843 2993
6 MOON JESTER 12  £1412  040-00240000330  92 189 349 532 731 1112 1633 1939 2273 2415 3128
3 MOON MADNESS 89  £169916  4-11111313  484* 807+ 946+ 1130* 1661+ 2222 2565* 2824
5 MOON MELODY 16  £-  000-0-0  2401
5 MOONDAWN 22  £268  00040-02000  10 343 689 789 893
2 MOONEE POND 12  £482  2000003  57 317 446 589 1088 1137 1672
3 MOONLIGHT LADY 60  £8095  00320-020000  214 2538 2770 2868 2940 3235
3 MOONLIGHT MADNESS 0  £-  -00  2275 2653
6 MOONLIGHTING 10  £-  -04  1799 2130
2 MOONSHINE 0  £-  0  2147
3 MOONSTRUCK 42  £1527  0-2004233  127 370 1469 1601 1818 1954 2110
2 MOORE BRASS 36  £728  4040  2243 2522 2811 3125
3 MOORE STYLISH 24  £871  -00204  371 1220 1921 2300 2948
4 MOORES METAL 26  £2830  000 0004000032030000  17 441 573 815 1047 1109 1249 1525 1758 1870
  1987 2144- 2234 2390 2566 2730 2891 3231
3 MOORESTAR 2  £-  -0000  835 2575 2619 2981
2 MOORESTYLE GIRL 22  £119  30  2493 2774
4 MOORLAND LADY 20  £-  20130-0000  349 582 856 1260
4 MORESPEED 72  £-  130432-2200  468 1493
2 MOREWOODS 66  £13055  11434  1241* 1606* 2221 2460 2635
9 MORGANS CHOICE 18  £7238  -00000003010000  11 58A 336 462 504 942 1058 1150 1293 1388* 1533
  1779 1875 2591
```

```
3 MORGIANA  0   £-   -00000    422 806 1327 2381 2807
3 MORICA  37   £160   1-40404   1515 1854 2072 2676 3071
2 MORNING FLOWER  46   £6446   032F20133    728 965 1207 1363 2177 2405 2813* 2936 3178
7 MOROCCO BOUND  0   £-   -0   541
2 MORTAL SIN  17   £-   00   2939 3189
7 MORVERN  0   £-   -00   1837 1945
3 MOSSAUL  0   £-   000-000   1670 2093 3162
5 MOSSBERRY FAIR  5   £502   00000-000240   126 449 770 869 1052 1271
2 MOST WELCOME  77   £13792   110   1928* 2252* 2866
3 MOSTANGO  15   £865   0-000000410   498 733 1231 1396 1788 2060 2342 2616* 2697
2 MOTOR BROKER  24   £-   00040000   662 1583 1728 2118 2476 3027 3044 3190
3 MOTOR MASTER  0   £113   00-000300000   183 491 932 1617 2268 2409 2688 2743 2884
2 MOULAS  20   £-   0000   979 2983 3067 3176
4 MOULKINS  7   £2158   000-00013040400   592 772 917 1052* 1177 1422 1980 2324 2800 3028 3087
4 MOUNT ARGUS  0   £262   -00000030   70 199 344 1473 1551 1833 2305 2492
4 MOUNT EPHRAIM  0   £-   00000-0   2587
2 MOUNT HOLYOKE  31   £-   00   2675 3025
3 MOUNT OLYMPUS  43   £1121   04-0320   357 597 744 2996
6 MOUNT RULE  1   £-   32000-0   44
3 MOUNT SCHIEHALLION  14   £312   02030-33004   171 307 833 1078 1605
5 MOUNT TUMBLEDOWN  37   £3520   -0000-000101   2490 2578 2755 2877* 3050 3195*
2 MOUNT VENUS  30   £1099   0402   1632 1802 2177 2405
3 MOUNT WOOD  0   £-   -00   1404 1666
2 MOUNTAIN ISLE  59   £1732   33   2574 2768
2 MOUNTAIN MEMORY  73   £20628   122   1154* 1789 2751
3 MOURADABIA  25   £-   002-000   1830 2422 2810
3 MOVING PERFORMANCE  0   £-   0-00000   99 247 381 787 1334
3 MOWSOOM  0   £-   -00   1818 2228
3 MOZART  19   £-   -000440   576 787 1431 2120 2256 2416
3 MR ADVISER  21   £-   -00-400000   188 527 1602 1880 2216 2373
5 MR BENNINGTON  0   £-   -000   861 960 1102
2 MR BERKELEY  17   £-   000000   254 1333 2100 2410 2919 3058
2 MR CHRIS CAKEMAKER  0   £-   000   1634 2325 2920
3 MR COFFEY  18   £1537   0000-400022100   82 910 1200 1546 1703 1767 1892* 2861 3036
2 MR CORMAN  42   £1780   00100   1232 2239 2379* 2677 2813
2 MR CRICKET  20   £120   030   1625 1716 1984
2 MR EATS  72   £13808   124044   876* 1149 1887 2384 2771 3126
3 MR FIZYCAL  0   £-   000-0   2271
4 MR GARDINER  10   £1004   20401-20000040   92 179 1412 1551 1`29 2188 2467 2786
2 MR GRUMPY  38   £4352   02201110000   40 133 367 457 647+ 785* 934* 1697 1907 2425 2588
4 MR JAY ZEE  32   £9225   00-013130210200   42 936+ 992 1222+ 1292 1521 1640 1727* 1868 2059 2165 3021
3 MR JESTER  0   £-   000-400   93 305 729
3 MR JOHN  74   £67630   3100-4120042404   395 471* 640 878 1330 1492 2192 2200 2506 2822
3 MR KEWMILL  14   £2140   000-301400000   99 216 451* 747 874 1299 2226 2426 2594
4 MR LION  4   £4037   000-30122220004   105 142 493* 591 721 860 1052 1124 2154 2330 2683
2 MR MAJINTY  0   £-   0   3176
3 MR MATCHMAKER  0   £-   -000   501 733 849
4 MR MCGREGOR  18   £684   03440-00001000   31 71 174 344 842* 952 1263 1590
3 MR MOSS  15   £-   -000000   714 1031 1386 1700 2280 2464
2 MR MUMBLES  18   £-   0040000000   678 834 1550 1938 2090 2729 2903 3058 3122 3188
12 MR MUSIC MAN  2   £1354   00-000024001000   36 119 333 1056 1845 1969 2132 2282 2528* 2654 2746 3154
4 MR PANACHE  0   £-   00-00-00000000   540 784 977 992 1101 2104 2960 3172
3 MR PASTRY  34   £128   -0300   183 2532 2622 3101
7 MR QUICK  34   £959   -10   19+ 542
6 MR ROSE  23   £3475   000-00042010040   30 160 262 636 775 943 1901* 2123 2189 2544 2681
3 MR SAVVAS  21   £-   0000-000000   484 625 2061 2184 2422 2656
2 MR TINK  0   £-   0   627
3 MR WHATS HIS NAME  25   £308   4400-24400   25 95 790 1233 1410
4 MRS BARRIE  0   £-   00000-0   489
4 MRS CHRIS  21   £1720   34400-040001030   10 46 142 281 1226 1416* 1636 1737 2978
2 MRS DARLING  30   £185   2   3056
3 MRS MAINWARING  25   £-   03-04400000   379 1511 1677 1953 2314 2393 2853 3061
3 MRS NAUGHTY  14   £1188   2000-4000304323   650 816 1081 1288 1562 1917 2335 2549 2863 2963
2 MRS PISTOL  35   £438   3   3025
4 MRS SAUGA  16   £2120   04000-02104400   10 1171 1344* 1438 1882 2079 2702 2858
3 MRS SCATTERCASH  2   £114   -3   169
3 MRS WADDILOVE  32   £259   304-00200   214 387 500 2575 3180
3 MSHATTA PALACE  26   £302 .  -0043   1899 2422 2605 2892
3 MTOTO  74   £9152   3-210224   479 916* 1098 1600 2219 2770
2 MUAD DIB  30   £1422   23020003   1495 1629 1936 2205 2618 2753 2941 3192
3 MUBAARIS  63   £8861   3-111400   219* 381+ 552* 1111 1642 2257
3 MUBAASHIR  0   £-   -0   842
3 MUBAH  0   £-   -000   1880 2099 2216
7 MUBARAK OF KUWAIT  23   £2847   20-20-010   1829 2034* 2528
2 MUBDI  45   £2627   23012   741 1232 2423 2888+ 3158
2 MUBKIR  24   £1077   302002000   497 632 1339 1555 2136 2498 2700 2806 2989
3 MUDISHA  42   £3414   32130-004013000   496 747 1065 1457 1571* 1847 2038 2291 3204
3 MUDRIK  37   £5465   00041-412400000   62 234* 455 615 847 1147 1520 1924 2879
3 MUFARRIH  52   £-   00120-0   151
2 MUGATH  42   £259   02   2225 2494
2 MUGHTANIM  32   £249   0340   800 1397 1812 2680
4 MUHAJJAL  32   £-   -4   448
2 MUHIM  40   £-   000   2254 2541 2791
3 MUHTARIS  26   £3137   0-0222000000100   217 507 580 734 1001 1164 1391 1521 2242 2519 2575+ 2702 2906
2 MUKHABBR  50   £10925   0303111110   115 270 678 1693 1938+ 2047+ 2166* 2261* 2579* 2694
2 MULHOLLANDE  65   £6930   022   1914 2721 3167
2 MULTI SPIRAL  0   £-   000   864 1545 2678
3 MUMMYS FAVOURITE  67   £21264   24111-34143333   808 1044 1487* 1851 2505 2633 3094 3177
2 MUMMYS LUCK  52   £2610   210   1930 2249* 2611
                                 > 997 <
```

```
3 MUMMYS SECRET  51  £1075   20400-3030    227 733 1878 2224
3 MUMTAZ MAYFLY  16  £-    00-000    658 1246 2601
2 MUNAASIB  54  £5938   3101200    457 622* 1097 1430* 1643 1925 3122
2 MUNADHIL  41  £-   0  3130
2 MUNAWAR  47  £321   2  3223
2 MUNTAG  17  £-   00000000    3 197 781 1138 1296 2663 3099 3148
2 MURAJAH  24  £-   0400000    800 1039 1313 1828 2035 2383 2677
3 MURFAX  30  £1888   -04-14040    164* 239 416 983 2175
3 MURHAF  0  £-   -00    806 1396
10 MURILLO  8  £1209   2-0032040010300    46 131 257 630 788 993 1081 1703 1845* 2008 2309 2762
2964
2 MURPHY  40  £1307   04210    1253 1660 1812 2140* 2276
3 MURPHYS WHEELS  47  £8924   3-04112321    516 677 1131* 1360* 1443 1682 1810- 2018*
3 MURRYL CANNON  0  £-   000-0000000    447 529 857 1051 1334 1734 1917
2 MUSEVENI  34  £1429   400410    133 544 741 1357 1566* 2052
2 MUSIC DELIGHT  24  £300   0004000020    1057 1308 1576 1738 1955 2180 2396 2712 3031 3048
5 MUSIC MACHINE  31  £8522   0440410112000000    122 272 477 877 977 1171* 1268 1805+ 1849* 1986
2124 2245  2783 2921 2992 3054
3 MUSIC MINSTREL  19  £1858   0-00014400    231 506 841 1078* 1564 2111 2403 2492
3 MUSIC REVIEW  28  £4998   000-22220341020    910 1191 1418 1574 2106 2416 2715 2775+ 2992 3138
3191
2 MUSIC STAR  12  £-   000    818 905 1770
8 MUSIC STREAK  69  £-   23000-0   3092
3 MUSIC TEACHER  10  £1095   3300-0102000400    41 145* 198 489 608 768 972 1917 2139 2268
3 MUSICAL AID  10  £-   0000-0000000440    786 910 1070 1420 1617 1734 2409 2893 2972 3220
2 MUSICAL BELLS  30  £-   0040040    777 1488 1573 2172 2479 3080 3188
2 MUSICAL CHORUS  1  £308   0030244000    717 965 1262 1379 1599 1803 1944 2298 2625 2712
2 MUSICAL DANCER  0  £-   00    2791 3103
2 MUSICAL REVIEW  48  £880   4200    1778 2283 2527 3108
2 MUSICAL RHAPSODY  26  £280   00440    1308 1604 2279 2535 3081
4 MUSICAL SHADOW  0  £-   -0000    689 936 1104 1394
4 MUSICAL WILL  7  £398   /0210-004030200    105 530 783 993 1892 2008 2101 2412 2509
3 MUSICAL YOUTH  31  £1936   004-202000    459 1130 1588 1886 2408 3195
3 MUSKET WET  0  £-   -00    1317 2930
2 MUST BE MAGIC  0  £-   00    1238 1440
2 MUSTAKBIL  21  £512   3004    1606 1816 2615 2968
5 MUSWELL HILL  0  £-   -00-0    330
3 MY ANNADETSKY  0  £-   000-00000    124 991 1290 1577 2985
2 MY BEST LADY  0  £-   0  3053
2 MY BUDDY  50  £6204   0011100    460 577 1480* 1711* 2115* 2391 2648
8 MY CHALLENGE  0  £-   -0  11
5 MY CHARADE  15  £4130   0-0001402000040    23 204 358 485* 582 735 917 1035 1388 1633 2134 2944
3139
3 MY CUP OF TEA  9  £2377   0-03224201    51 113 809 867 1122 1824 2238 2371*
3 MY DARLING  0  £-   -00    656 1228
3 MY DERYA  8  £1125   0-0034030041040    6 38 103 147 335 564 1398 1815 1989 2302* 2361 2787 3154
2 MY ELANE  25  £-   00000    536 852 1059 1844 2283
3 MY GENERATION  75  £20951   301-3110    1702 2219* 2740* 3177
3 MY GREAT MONTI  50  £-   -0  150
4 MY HANDSOME BOY  10  £-   43330-000000    10 101 452 960 1074 1139
2 MY IMAGINATION  63  £6625   110004030    73* 320+ 440 1129 1454 2057 2246 2540 2751
2 MY ISABEL  45  £1604   120    482* 725 1442
3 MY KIND OF TOWN  46  £5231   -1104404    16* 335* 478 1199 2149 2255 2691
2 MY MABEL  0  £-   000000    13 57 446 1088 1795 2050
2 MY MATCH  0  £-   0  1692
3 MY MUTZIE  6  £-   04000-0000400    1164 1344 1584 1827 2024 2960 3144
4 MY MYRA  4  £-   00430-00040    1346 1439 1613 1719 2187
2 MY NOBLE LORD  53  £2214   210    1234 2019* 2521
2 MY PROMISED LAND  16  £-   00    2491 2875
2 MY SERENADE  15  £-   04400    450 819 1764 2391 3016
5 MY SON MY SON  29  £-   00000-00    420 547
3 MY TON TON  40  £-   00410-00000    224 510 1130 1507 2219
3 MY WILLOW  45  £2953   -42102    1337 1908 2142* 2665 2979
3 MYCENAE CHERRY  44  £1353   0-14200    173* 458 1848 2031 2647
3 MYRAS SPECIAL  51  £2934   01010-00100    1347 1457 1750+ 2258 2573
3 MYSTERIOUS DANCER  52  £250   010-30    128 1630
3 MYSTERY CLOCK  25  £259   0000-200    635 849 1559
3 MYSTICAL MAN  46  £4889   0201    295 2473 2650 3180*
3 MYTENS  62  £11323   3-110413    1031* 1350* 2219 2567 2848+ 2942
3 MYTH  54  £6970   2424-2113010    1259 1535* 1763* 1918 2236 2666+ 2850
5 MYTHICAL BOY  0  £-   -00 · 1757 2134
2 MYTYME  21  £-   000    2177 2607 2936
3 NAATELL  61  £3161   112    861+ 1141+ 1317
2 NABRAS  38  £470   33000    818 1996 2215 2901 3198
4 NACACYTE  75  £5000   42-2    557
3 NADAS  34  £1086   -423043    592 669 790 959 1102 1623
3 NADEED  70  £6650   -0212    370 2786 3028* 3175-
5 NADER  0  £-   -0  1035
4 NADRON  0  £-   -0000-0    2012
4 NAFTILOS  42  £1610   11120-020000    58A 215 375 582 2237 2445
2 NAFUAT  15  £-   00    1681 1863
3 NAGEM  20  £4556   0000-04234231    910 1438 1505 1687 2592 2906 2992 3104*
2 NAHEEZ  71  £41967   131    1791* 2849 3107*
2 NAIVE CHARM  55  £5850   120100    47* 2097 2252 2482+ 2634 2843
2 NAJABA  34  £-   00400    601 1604 1801 2531 2675
7 NAJAM  0  £-   -0  201
2 NAJIDIYA  51  £10895   3-02021144    937 1503 1818 2030 2275* 2763* 2848 3026
2 NAMARAI BAY  20  £-   0  2651
3 NAME THE DAY  2  £-   0-40040    2560 2597 3076 3162 3202
4 NAME THE GAME  0  £-   00000-000000    124 240 788 1077 1839 2397
2 NANCY NONESUCH  30  £-   000    988 1573 2167
3 NANOR  12  £1219   4-0030000001300    37 274 340 399 620 809 845 1191 1319 1574* 1603 1695 1943
3 NAOUSSA  20  £-   03-4200    423 861 1626 2856
```

```
3 NAP MAJESTICA   28   £1535    42300-001043230    713 861 1256* 1821 2038 2427 2603 2890 3179
2 NAPARIMA   37   £119    0300    999 2069 2433 2788
4 NARCISSUS   10   £1888    -0-30001    522 838 1208 1694 2075*
3 NASHAMAA   75   £38515    122-231    1332 1492 3001*
3 NASHIA   59   £-   21120-00000    587 705 1851 2457 2570
5 NASHOOD   0   £-   00004-0   2111
3 NASKRACKER   26   £946    0-00020303    579 839 1260 1559 1945 2896 2925 3063
3 NATCHAKAM   32   £2152    -420400100    39 90 328 703 880 1199 1346* 1540 2928
3 NATIJA   15   £380    0-00024000    1228 1446 2314 2534 2719 2905 3220 3224
5 NATINA MAY   2   £-   00440-0   3220
9 NATIONAL IMAGE   0   £-   01002/0   2958
2 NATIONS ROSE   13   £115    040403    1997 2212 2609 2801 2990 3069
2 NATIONS SONG   28   £6706    041022121400031    515 603 681* 785 948 1248 1323* 1403 1576* 1693 2307
   2421 2689 2781 2903+
2 NATIVE DRESS   51   £2501    310    2561 2782* 2926
3 NATIVE HABITAT   22   £1970    -413333000    89 169* 459 874 2171 2282 2414 2998 3116
3 NATIVE IMAGE   12   £713    -000010    535 625 790 1248 2014* 2171
3 NATIVE OAK   71   £9972    313-4211423    406 600 733* 950* 1486 2135- 2562
2 NATIVE PAWN   30   £-   00000    1253 1488 2029 2297 2472
5 NATIVE RULER   23   £3352    40000-012300313    211 1070* 1344 1543 2289 2632 2775 2992* 3064
4 NATIVE SKIER   41   £-   00000-00    508 877
3 NATIVE WIZARD   50   £-   3012-0000    220 1147 1655 3042
2 NATSKI   52   £-   0   3171
2 NATURALLY AUTUMN   36   £215    00030    944 1030 2527 2748 3143
2 NATURALLY FRESH   61   £8454    411400    223 383* 773+ 1108 1789 2954
3 NAUGHTY NIGHTY   5   £116    000-00000003400    338 992 1164 1603 2046 2189 2238 2417 2743 2884 3057
3 NAUTICA   23   £348    -00300    1444 2068 2176 2516 2709
2 NAUTICAL BELLE   0   £-   00   3134 3205
3 NAUTICAL STEP   0   £-   -000    347 458 669
3 NAVARZATO   59   £4522    11-2000002    1147- 1912 2219 2612 2867 2946 3204-
2 NAVOS   35   £267    003    685 1067 1282
3 NAWADDER   29   £1118    0-24010300    205 438 837 1073* 1436 1651 1989 2704
3 NAWOB   0   £-   -0   218
2 NAWWAR   27   £-   0000    985 1629 2162 3174
2 NEAR HEAVEN   27   £-   00    2341 2796
2 NEARLY GREAT   37   £253    040    1872 2254 2476
5 NEBRIS   77   £34827    10110-1110230    72* 265* 511* 736 1230- 1715 2064
3 NEDS EXPRESSA   36   £8667    00400-0003411    447 545 857 1028 1224 1371* 2038*
3 NEEDLE SHARP   25   £188    -3000    1880 2314 2532 2853
3 NEEDLEWOMAN   34   £1161    -0004302    217 402 546 739 1034 1998 2381
2 NEEDWOOD NUT   35   £515    0420    905 1194 2080 2472
2 NEEDWOOD NYMPH   0   £-   0   3198
2 NEIGHNAY   0   £-   0   3017
2 NEIRBO LASS   0   £-   0000    2045 3017 3134 3190
5 NELSONS LADY   5   £-   40310-0040000    1346 1515 1990 2309 2601 2836 2964
3 NELSONSUPERYANKEE   0   £-   0-000000    774 1303 1656 2034 2163 2789
4 NEMAIN   81   £45825    03414-20010    641 885 1144 2822* 2917
3 NENUCO   0   £-   004-00    346 726
5 NEOCENE   0   £-   -00    1186 1519
2 NERRAD   27   £-   040    621 717 882
3 NERVOUS RIDE   68   £1166    1-02    326 605
2 NESHAD   58   £-   1   3043*
6 NESTOR   43   £-   12000-00    92 189
2 NETTLE   68   £15191    141    2119+ 2246 3108*
2 NETZER   0   £-   00    3081 3131
2 NEVADA MIX   0   £-   00    2301 2494
3 NEVER BEE   0   £-   00-000000    32 188 506 739 1264 1560
2 NEVER BEEN CHASTE   0   £-   0   3134
2 NEW ATTITUDE   70   £4490    10    2159* 2384
4 NEW BARNET   1   £-   -0040-00000    547 745 1177 2891 2998
4 NEW BRUCE   75   £6900    00301044    1594 1715 2507 2736 2820
4 NEW CENTRAL   11   £726    21400-00002000    453 636 775 1273 1590 1870 2091 2730
3 NEW EDITION   27   £-   10000-000    168 1571 1695
3 NEW EVIDENCE   24   £2658    00400-000223203    447 545 961 1257 1515 1725 1885 2230 2601
2 NEW MEXICO   39   £554    40020    962 1143 1634 2007 2181
5 NEW MOON   62   £5367    34-34    1216 1715
5 NEW TARGET   74   £18211    -20-10    96* 299
5 NEW TIMES   0   £-   -0   19
3 NEW TROJAN   79   £20615    140-4024    510 654 1098 1853
5 NEW ZEALAND   22   £-   43120-0   532
5 NEWMARKET SAUSAGE   28   £ŗ   0/000-4   526
3 NEWQUAY   49   £2790    3-0221320    1259 1646 1786 2048* 2211 2569 3026
5 NEWSELLS PARK   53   £19797    312-P-2122244    778 1004* 1293- 1470 1779 2220 2523
3 NEXT DANCE   16   £128    -000030    625 887 1554 1951 2582 2876
5 NICANIC   0   £-   00000-400    177 343 566
3 NICCOLO POLO   60   £3368    10300-330244    26 387 600 884 1151 1380
3 NICE LADY   36   £288    -2   379
3 NICE PRESENT   0   £-   -0000    1198 1494 2017 2271
2 NICHOLAS GEORGE   20   £772    0100400    1279 1434* 1814 2172 2307 2535 2744
2 NICHOLAS MARK   15   £-   000    2997 3099 3229
3 NICKLE A KISS   42   £728    4-10000    422* 689 966 1312 1648
4 NICKY DAWN   0   £105    -0000003    259 448 770 888 1201 1424 1976 2302
5 NICKY NICK   10   £-   44000-00000    481 1590 1804 1901 2123 2549
3 NICOLA WYNN   48   £1654    -13000    458* 833 1128 1642 2257
3 NICOLINI   17   £1516    00-00332033    779 1250 1864 1989 2399 2508 2980 3086
2 NICOPHANA   16   £-   400    2051 2468 3153
4 NICORIDGE   46   £2726    22330-0000022    196 441 775 1018 1189 3050 3236
2 NIFTY GRIFF   37   £7252    0011010    696 913 1088* 1294* 1504 1962* 2669
2 NIGHT CLUB   0   £-   0   2791
4 NIGHT GUEST   1   £-   04000-000    631 827 2627
3 NIGHT LINE   72   £6440    300    2453 2643 2824
3 NIGHT OF THE COMET   0   £-   000-04    2088 2309
3 NIGHT OUT PERHAPS   63   £15693    0-114013303    229* 465* 1147 1486 1924* 2438 2624 2763 3042
                                                    > 999 <
```

```
2 NIGHT VISITOR  34   £-   000   1239 2541 2920
4 NIGHT WALLER  0   £-   00000-000   568 620 1166
4 NIGHT WARRIOR  25   £869   00-004030334200   10 184 238 310 609 745 970 1124 1918 2130 2995 3087
2 NIGHTDRESS  18   £768   0030100   1427 1782 1944 2138 2212* 2279 2609
3 NIHAD  38   £2827   0-400323230   213 315 776 1169 1337 2676 2799 3105 3179
4 NIKOOLA EVE  28   £3903   -03102   8 58 282* 778 3187
3 NILAMBAR  65   £4286   02-0231143   806 1087- 1395 1554+ 1670* 1912 2092
3 NILE LARK  27   £489   0-2000   1833 2299 2620 3063
2 NILOJEN  30   £-   40   2001 2225
3 NIMBLE NATIVE  30   £4829   00-104003041133   45* 331 416 519 648 949 1159 1435 2587* 2892* 3161 3219
3 NINO BIBBIA  69   £18133   2-110423000   371* 579* 920 1096 1286- 1514 1823 2567 2956
3 NINOTCHKA  30   £349   4-240   2593 2853 3159
2 NINTH SAGA  59   £4610   010   2159 3023* 3171
3 NIORO  45   £2108   40-132   498* 954 1987
2 NIPIKAN  0   £-   0   2159
5 NIPKNOWES  4   £-   40000-00000   490 606 2414 2818 2887
2 NIPPED OFF  0   £-   0   270
3 NIPPER SMITH  0   £-   00000-000   729 1734 1839
3 NIPPY CHIPPY  8   £679   0041-000000100   318 451 997 1295 1839 2126 2342* 2621 2762
3 NISNAS  83   £65769   143-131031104   190+ 362 494* 878 1098 1913* 2222* 2565 3121
3 NITIDA  14   £329   03-00000330   130 381 779 1700 1961 2128 2363 2478
3 NO BEATING HARTS  38   £8577   0-1304021300000   217* 534 649 817 1060 1414 1505* 1654 1878 2143 2469 2731 3118
3 NO BOLDER  19   £683   00-00200   1927 2092 2293 2613 3203
3 NO CAN TELL  28   £-   0-400   937 2408 2622
2 NO CONCERN  6   £146   00300   2542 2707 2801 2990 3069
4 NO CREDIBILITY  16   £412   42030-0000030   812 1041 2526 2728 2816 3078 3145
3 NO DOUBLET  30   £1509   33-32220403   862 1192 1368 1639 2023 2299 3105 3159
6 NO FLUKE  0   £-   -00   44 137
3 NO IDEA  0   £-   -000   1626 2893 3159
3 NO JAZZ  9   £480   0000-0002000   161 480 886 1165 1346 1471 2581
2 NO LIE  30   £1216   0323   1996 2191 2625 2708
3 NO MORE ROSIES  37   £2478   -01   1677 2327*
3 NO RESTRAINT  45   £3104   -0431130   33 911 1425 2216* 2704* 2879 3050
3 NO STOPPING  14   £1591   040-0003232200   480 534 1061 2073 2253 2560 2597 2787 2874 3128
8 NO U TURN  33   £1984   00200-004432   801 1004 1159 1342 2290 2955
2 NOALIMBA  20°   £-   000   136 913 2511
2 NOBLE BID  55   £2168   4012   1914 2159 2541* 2838
4 NOBLE FIGHTER  84   £27523   12310-333   299 645 1493
3 NOBLE FILLE  34   £2512   -00440100   1031 1278 1589 2054 2430 2853* 2985 3140
3 NOBLE HILL  20   £-   31-4004   171 1402 1733 2315
5 NOBLE JACK  0   £-   -0   743
2 NOBLE KALA  0   £-   000   515 957 1100
2 NOBLE MINSTREL  78   £28074   4121   2418 2711+ 3041 3208*
5 NOBLE MOUNT  14   £-   -4200-0   7
9 NOBLE PHILIP  0   £-   -0   343
3 NOBLE RISE  38   £-   3-440   1690 2042 2430
3 NOBLE SAXON  7   £-   40-40000   78 183 932 1134 1334
3 NOBLE VIKING  0   £-   000-000   357 535 2134
5 NOEL ARMS  0   £-   -00   1700 1808
2 NOFANDANCER  0   £-   0000   353 446 1137 1647
3 NOHOLMINA  30   £119   -03400   1953 2183 2327 2995 3140
2 NOM DE PLUME  50   £477   2   3189-
3 NOMAD BOXER  0   £-   -004000   2339 2441 2713 3033 3144 3185
3 NOMINATION  76   £5000   01104-0200   249 639- 1146 2772
3 NOMROOD  78   £58061   12-120023   442* 574 878 1597 2808 3001
2 NON FICTION  26   £352   3430   1194 1403 2375 2969
5 NONSENSE  24   £-   21230-00   1636 1808
2 NONSUCH PALACE  46   £1100   03002   1019 1239 1587 2628 3137
4 NOORA ABU  39   £2109   3   2349
2 NORAPA  45   £5708   31001   1869 2080* 2270 2687 2935+
3 NORAS BOY  0   £-   0000-0000   340 454 980 2184
3 NORCOOL  14   £124   0000-0000300   124 491 875 1068 1602 1880 2213
3 NORDAVANO  48   £1898   2440   1452 1926 2444 3178
6 NORDIC HAWK  0   £-   -0   36
3 NORDIC PLEASURE  48   £1482   -331   667 1503 1736*
4 NORDIC SECRET  10   £2241   -0000-001200   58 381 675* 772 888 2789
3 NORDICA  55   £8725   -00124110   581 849 1327+ 1724 1998 2458* 2719+ 3002
3 NORETTA  67   £16950   4222   1596 2117 2643 2913
3 NORFOLK SONATA  49   £648   0431-300003000   191 510 983 1130 1913 2206 2553 2845 2955
2 NORGABIE  52   £2632   1230   1867+ 2153 2482 2687
3 NORHAM CASTLE  19   £-   40-000   1184 2072 2422
3 NORMAN INVADER  51   £-   0   2869
3 NORMANBY LASS  55   £2296   00320-00200   271 575 925 1153 1487
3 NORPELLA  64   £8065   000-1414   2061+ 2462 2569* 3022
2 NORS GOD  42   £688   0020   1629 1826 2878 2961
3 NORTH LAKE  48   £-   -004   1046 1776 2030
3 NORTH OCEAN  46   £3882   -03033231   1036 1269 1395 2255 2442 2720 3113 3217*
2 NORTH PACIFIC  43   £5539   0301   1855 2531 2658 2971+
5 NORTH STAR SAM  0   £630   -0000402000   7 69 126 243 333 609 912 1133 2360 2549
2 NORTH TELSTAR  63   £664   2D   2350
3 NORTH VERDICT  70   £13466   210-0032410   555 1098 1378 1702 1886 2112* 2454
2 NORTHERN ALLIANCE  0   £-   0   3023
3 NORTHERN AMETHYST  48   £7474   022-32202321223   625 839 978- 1111 1642 2148 2408 2430* 2599 2701 2930
4 NORTHERN ASPEN  75   £7958   1001-0200   330 2359 2507 3168
4 NORTHERN CHIMES  49   £876   0-000-20000   817 1026 1455 1525 1729
3 NORTHERN DATE  73   £1300   -41-004   289 559 753
2 NORTHERN DECREE  24   £-   0000   583 780 1253 1883
3 NORTHERN ETERNITY  77   £-   112-0   232
3 NORTHERN EXPRESS  72   £11753   10   2351* 2916
3 NORTHERN FLING  0   £-   -00   99 258
                              > 1000 <
```

```
3 NORTHERN GUNNER 25   £1660  02000-0430321   31 424 809 928 2394 2413 2509*
4 NORTHERN HOPE 21   £-  03000-0  19
3 NORTHERN IMPULSE 14   £346  -03000000   500 567 842 994 1669 2294 2458 2783
3 NORTHERN LAD 8   £992  00-00002020U000   62 314 580 835 1277 1476 1584 1836 2416 2659 2906 3172
3 NORTHERN MEETING 45   £1034  000-1  379*
3 NORTHERN MELODY 33   £1222  -003100   14 67 138 195* 451 1169
2 NORTHERN MOON 38   £-  0  3181
3 NORTHERN PREMIER 80   £41435  1021  288* 467 1008 1356*
4 NORTHERN RIVER 0   £-  00000-000   2412 2686 2745
4 NORTHERN RULER 17   £2386  000-20000000100   280 358 462 590 778 1099 1280 1477 1737* 1865 2395
2 NORTHERN SECURITY 0   £-  000   1869 2482 2975
3 NORTHERN SOCIETY 37   £224  0-043   619 839 1304
3 NORTHERN TRUST 38   £1651  1020-3300020000   233 314 580 760 1033 1704- 1950 2160 2382 2530
3 NORTHERN VELVET 0   £-  00-0  969
3 NORTHINCH 11   £-  000-000   29 331 1236
2 NORTHSHIEL 50   £2504  4313  1238 1874 2287* 2577
2 NORTON MELODY 30   £1027  33300   1634 1958 2051 2479 2669
3 NORTON WARRIOR 8   £-  04000-0   2891
6 NORWHISTLE 8   £107  -00-000003   19 788 1073 1300 1546 1719
2 NORWICH CASTLE 11   £-  0   2975
6 NOSTER PUER 0   £-  31/00-0   485
3 NOT A PROBLEM 29   £1012  0000-3004320403   134 309 451 702 867 998 1295 1426 2300 2690
2 NOT ALONE 65   £1152  3   1778
2 NOT BY MYSELF 0   £-  0   1305
2 NOT READY YET 0   £-  00   938 1162
3 NOT SO SHARP 0   £-  -00   2034 2253
2 NOT SO SILLY 0   £-  000   2007 2281 2410
2 NOVA LAD 0   £-  0   2379
3 NOZET 12   £-  0031004   2890
2 NUAS 34   £2208  22   1711 2352
4 NUGOLA 0   £-  0-0000000040000   547 689 789 1054 1185 1374 1613 1820 2154 2360 2604 2800 2978
7 NUMISMATIST 36   £1909  31204-404000   1933 2573 2668 2862 2947 3118
2 NUNS ROYAL 0   £-  000   831 1083 1684
2 NURYANA 46   £-  0   2846
3 NUTSHAMBLES 19   £-  0-00   923 1259
2 NUTWOOD LIL 59   £9352  11203000   317* 450+ 924 1108 1850 2223 2843 2949
10 O I OYSTON 14   £2829  0030002022202003   260 441 606 710 936 1249 1424 1546 1758 1906 2264
   2390 2549 2891 3116 3220
2 O LA LE 28   £-  000   810 1059 3180
2 OAK FIELD 0   £-  0000   2127 2423 2814 3032
3 OAKDALE 0   £-  0000-00   2317 2528
2 OBIDOS 32   £2637  010   2341 2841* 2936
2 OCEAN HOUND 12   £-  00000   1440 2287 2657 2878 2989
3 OCEAN LAD 1   £-  000-0004   809 1288 1439 1656
4 OCEAN LIFE 0   £-  00-00   8 308
3 OCEAN TRADER 26   £-  30122-0000000   70 387 1457 1750 2143 2530 2619 3160
5 OCEANUS 1   £-  23000-00   44 144
2 OCONNELL STREET 21   £-  0004404   425 536 1207 1598 1846 2035 2227
3 OCTIGA 6   £692  .00300-00030200   54 740 1369 1662 1960 2238 2361 2795
4 OCTOBER 49   £224  10000-00400   433 573 775 1109 1455
3 ODEMIRA 0   £-  0-0  1063
3 ODERVY 0   £-  00000-000004   113 809 1212 1310 1666 2073
2 ODIAXERE 18   £-  00   2270 2527
4 OEIL DE TIGRE 0   £-  -0000   592 842 1186 3172
6 OFF YOUR MARK 0   £-  10000-04000000   42 1610 1676 2012 2411 2816 2977 3157
2 OFFICER KRUPKE 30   £-  4   2626
5 OG BOY 1   £-  4-000-00   28 177
3 OH BOYAR 46   £681  1300-30000   228 387 808 2160 2530
2 OH DANNY BOY 40   £380  00030   1984 2444 2667 3047 3222
2 OH MY JOY 12   £-  004   2292 2531 3190
2 OH WIGGY 0   £-  00   2703 3201
4 OKAADH 6   £-  20000-00400   2381 2490 2984 3150 3193
2 OKAY YAH 0   £-  00   1248 1862
2 OKOSAN 37   £933  000222   1132 1634 2377 2886- 3148- 3221-
3 OLD DOMESDAY BOOK 60   £7109  0-1330303   444+ 599 1002 1408 1886 2438 2786
2 OLD EROS 36   £1788  100   873* 2611 2888
2 OLD MAESTRO 48   £303  020   2407 2657 2894
4 OLD MALTON 12   £2562  0-4-0001330044   176 532 778 990* 1280 1577 1865 2031 2492 2794
3 OLE FLO 33   £382  24233-0330   6 161 339 507
4 OLEANDRIN 0   £-  00-00   3159 3227
2 OLIVE LEAF 0   £-  000   2982 3044 3184
2 OLORE MALLE 36   £5829  1423001   270* 664 1968 2136 2383 2648 2718*
2 OLYMPIC CHALLENGER 0   £-  00   2871 3103
3 OLYMPIC EAGLE 0   £-  -0   3062
2 OMANIA 15   £-  400-4400000   277 570 923 1586 2488 2719 2880
2 OMEN 38   £-  000   2829 2936 3018
3 ON IMPULSE 13   £1219  0000-0321000   620 684 845 1212* 1571 1885 3078
2 ON TAP 67   £9151  41112   1430 1675* 1863+ 2511* 2949
3 ON TENTERHOOKS 42   £3794  43-10403   980* 1484 2156 2766 2880
3 ON THE AGENDA 14   £-  0-00000   581 1192 2520 2682 2988
2 ON THE MARK 8   £-  0040000   858 1012 1611 1741 1905 2466 2757
2 ON THE STEEL 0   £-  40   268 292
3 ON TO GLORY 27   £2825  000-00B3002102   275 480 716 1199 1609 2184 2373 2516+ 2896 3195
3 ON WATER 20   £242  -0003   229 334 1705 2103
2 ON YOUR PRINCESS 37   £1814  00202030   405 1555 1958 2301 2476 2561 2717 2903
5 ONE FOR THE DITCH 0   £-  -00000   164 769 943 1424 1500
2 ONE LINER 48   £1282  22   212 460
3 ONE TO MARK 42   £726  00-210   1073 1300* 1486
2 ONE TO NOTE 17   £-  000   2377 3014 3201
4 ONESTO 64   £6045  23   1860 2823
2 ONGOING SITUATION 66   £13205  01312223   800 1090+ 1307 1707* 2010- 2252 2485 2907
3 ONISKY 52   £4607  410-112303   116* 519* 983 1276 2156 2338
3 ONLY A RUMOUR 70   £7199  0212   3207
                                    > 1001 <
```

```
3 ONLY FLOWER  0   £119    -00300   744 935 1135 2054 3150
2 ONLY JOKING  0   £-   00   2976 3148
3 ONLY STAR  73   £28078   132   1008* 1353 3094
3 OPAL FLOWER  9   £-   032-000000   500 1257 2314 2508 2931 3086
3 OPEN HERO  54   £679   04211-0030   2303 2624 2934 3123
2 OPERATIC SCORE  58   £461   23   1239 2657
3 OPTIMISM FLAMED  1   £222   033-2000000   183 553 604 1091 2818 2890 3172
2 OPTIONAL CHOICE  27   £-   000   2341 2484 2761
3 OR VISION  80   £10120   1300-1   155*
3 ORANGE DALE  37   £-   0-000   402 764 887
4 ORANGE HILL  33   £33634   0001-000422041   235 462 942 1633 2031 2169 2591 2754 3052*
2 ORANGEADE  0   £-   0   2703
3 ORBAN  60   £4181   -132   1080* 1468 1899
2 ORDINA  28   £-   400   1282 1782 2365
8 ORE  67   £3876   4224/0100   617 693* 3169 3173
2 OREMBO  54   £-   0   2821
3 ORFANO  73   £18899   334   1861 2197 2824
3 ORIENT  70   £19455   40-111300   593* 929+ 1151+ 1457 1889 2233
2 ORIENT LINE  44   £9411   02111   1059 1846 2095* 2677* 2922*
2 ORIENTAL DANCER  0   £-   0   2105
2 ORIENTAL DREAM  26   £1250   0100300   979 1119* 2310 2718 3085 3188 3230
3 ORIENTAL EXPRESS  10   £1698   000-01033000   247 487* 631 767 1258 2478 2760 3030
2 ORIENTAL JADE  28   £1386   041302   1207 1478 1599* 1846 2227 2298
2 ORIENTAL PLUME  36   £210   03   3111 3229
3 ORIENTAL SOLDIER  71   £11859   12210-02001   476 1114 1332 2234 2475*
2 ORIOLE DANCER  18   £1649   0002410000003   94 186 261 404 622 1069* 1527 2307 2435 2588 2729
   2843 2986
2 ORNE  65   £4897   12434   1239* 1465 2146 2598 2849
4 OROJOYA  75   £7393   31313-020020   222 413 587 901 1857 2003
3 ORTICA  22   £2281   -4023330430   667 829 1269 1794 1885 2063 2483 2660 2793 2977
5 ORVILLES SONG  0   £-   -00   1223 1689
6 ORYX MINOR  36   £190   20401-0304   9 519 721 3196
3 OSCAR DE SOUSA  0   £-   -004   16 67 113
3 OSRIC  45   £6598   -412D32042031   25 1578+ 1923 2066 2290 2517 2766 2855- 2955 3110 3196*
3 OSTENSIBLE  70   £13512   1-3000111   435 597 1009 1330 1757* 2201* 2627*
4 OSTENTATIOUS  00   £255   00400-0330400   399 620 845 1165 1649 1901 1990
4 OTABARI  50   £14298   -4414-003421   263 532 778 942 1099 1148*
2 OTHET  46   £2335   2233   1522 1869 2547 2941
2 OUR ACCOUNT  57   £1233   2   3171
3 OUR ANNIE  0   £-   000-0000040   183 279 517 1428 2008 2412 3100
9 OUR BARA BOY  0   £-   000/000   2647 2745 2944
3 OUR CHILDREN  8   £1024   20400-030100   1169 1476 1627 1815* 2139 3185
3 OUR CRAIG  0   £-   00-0   253
5 OUR DYNASTY  65   £3405   00000-03000   374 587 687 854 1125
2 OUR ELIASO  49   £960   01   3023 3143*
2 OUR FREDDIE  38   £222   444044   270 457 1728 1915 2696 2805
3 OUR GENERATION  0   £-   -0   1807
2 OUR GINGER  24   £1075   04010   1067 2365 2743 3032* 3151
3 OUR HERO  20   £457   -0020   1818 2110 2900 3061
2 OUR HORIZON  8   £248   20040000   612 701 1225 2025 2279 2744 2919 3222
3 OUR JAMIE  0   £-   00   2690 2799
4 OUR JOCK  62   £16691   2200-0004104202   70 361 616 1145 1306+ 1852 2258 2446 2668 3055
2 OUR LENA  0   £-   00   722 3068
2 OUR LUCKY NATIVE  20   £-   00   722 2652
3 OUR MABLE  18   £-   -0   1554
4 OUR MASTER MARK  0   £-   -0   1686
3 OUR MUMSIE  0   £458   00040-200400000   103 198 241 740 871 1200 2335 2884 3057
2 OUR NATHALIE  40   £259   42   1683 2069
3 OUR NOORA  8   £-   -000000   423 991 1372 1589 1954 2548
2 OUR PET  24   £2687   00001   73 223 852 2287 2700*
3 OUR REMEDY  0   £-   00000-0000   1316 1603 1999 2213
3 OUR TILLY  31   £-   2120-00000   26 326 1603 2715 2842
2 OUR TONY  25   £-   00   1345 1653
2 OUR ZOUZOU  47   £500   42   777 962
5 OUT AND ABOUT  0   £-   0   2112
7 OUT OF HAND  27   £3182   00000-401200   1077 1211 1521* 1649 1840 2295
3 OUT OF HARMONY  15   £-   010-0000000   454 534 1312 1695 1830 2184 2719
3 OUT OF KINDNESS  0   £-   -0000   1036 1315 1831 2620
3 OUT OF STOCK  12   £189   00000-004000044   140 316 1651 1835 2171 2327 2489 2932 3062
2 OUT ON A FLYER  20   £2630   0021324220   1604 1802 1944 2020* 2421 2579 2729 2903- 2962 3174
3 OUT YONDER  10   £450   000-003000   980 1208 2135 2313 2532 3183
2 OUTER COVER  0   £-   0   1982
2 OUTRAGEOUS FORTUNE  35   £-   0   3120
4 OVER THE OCEAN  81   £32218   /1003-23310   154 391 1010 2194* 2456
2 OVERDRIVE  47   £667   03   2768 3023
2 OVERNITE SENSATION  0   £-   00   2100 2150
2 OVERPOWER  15   £-   00000   1376 1634 1958 2281 2756
9 OVERULE  0   £-   -00   683 1165
4 OWENS PRIDE  25   £4760   03000-13000   263* 363 618 735 2873
3 OWL CASTLE  33   £1424   00000-32410000   32 95 117 171* 275 738 883 1130
3 OWLS WAY  3   £-   04000-00000000   451 677 857 1200 1482 1841 2339 3033
4 OWN UP  27   £1645   -000-10   2747* 2937
2 OXFORD PLACE  0   £-   0000   612 813 1561 1843
4 OXHEY BAY  37   £762   43112-00303   306 520 649 846 1077
2 OXSTALLS LADY  0   £-   0   2365
2 OXYMERON  0   £-   0   2847
2 OYSTER GRAY  28   £555   3200   197 425 612 2479
3 OZOPULMIN  69   £9366   -10-1232   1702* 2206 2419 2557
2 PACIFIC BASIN  47   £1617   023403   405 965 1313 1552 1925 2035
3 PACIFIC DRIFT  74   £4700   30   753 1330
4 PACIFIC PRINCESS  28   £-   21B40-00000   238 413 789 1249 1525
3 PACKAGE PERFECTION  18   £310   3320-00400200   593 677 891 994 1051 1420 1704 2106
3 PACT  0   £-   -000   217 283 438
                              > 1002 <
```

3 PACTOLUS 62 £15868 410-01231110 1166 1349* 1519 1935 2164* 2290* 2591+ 3052
3 PADDINGTON BELLE 8 £1312 000-00000300100 734 1077 1319 1827 1940 2088 2417 2981 3057* 3144 3160
2 PADDY MALONEY 0 £- 000 1862 2470 2976
2 PADDY WILL 7 £- 00 1680 2150
4 PADDYCOUP 29 £- 3100-00 582 663
4 PADDYSTOWN 17 £- 40000-000 355 594 976
5 PADRE PIO 46 £5522 01021-02002300 616 846 1145 1852 2151 2446 2668 2953
6 PADYKIN 11 £- 00/0 3035
3 PAEAN 70 £18244 2-1211121 231* 409 607* 1674* 2338* 2627 3173*
2 PAGAN RITE 55 £488 4 1453
5 PAGAN SUN 46 £4890 40040-201 4 410 474+
2 PAGITEK 44 £- 044 2232 2961 3223
2 PAGODA DANCER 0 £- 0 1680
7 PAJANJO 31 £- -00 519 651
2 PALACE FIELDS 0 £- 000 681 1083 1668
5 PALACE MUSIC 87 £157343 02 2456 3211
2 PALACE RULER 7 £- 400000 858 1100 1413 1881 2471 2724
2 PALACE SONG 40 £- 00 3163 3198
4 PALACE YARD 11 £- 0240-400 731 841 984
3 PALAESTRA 64 £7603 0212-002110 386 719 1249 1460* 1710* 2296
2 PALAIS DE DANSE 0 £- 0 3163
2 PALEFACE 53 £4526 33221230 544 1253 1572 1965 2178* 2383 2512 2813
3 PALEWELLS COMET 0 £- 000-0 193
2 PALLASS BLUE 62 £1000 42140 2910 2999
2 PALM REEF 43 £244 40 2119 3109
4 PALMAHALM 36 £84 -300 1736 2996 3129
4 PALMION 28 £980 02240-02000 10 196 521 611 3204
4 PAMELA HEANEY 3 £198 00030-0030400 119 578 727 850 2319 2581 2960
2 PANACHE 39 £7348 003121D30124 230 332 717 965* 1483 1570 1891 1925 2136* 2465- 2556
2 PANAMA JACK 0 £- 0 2493
2 PANBOY 18 £1926 312400000 3 108* 197 242 440 1962 2052 2398 2465
4 PANDI CLUB 0 £- 00000-00000000 112 176 262 578 856 984 1310 1459
2 PANIENKA 25 £- 00 2847 3025
3 PANNANICH WELLS 34 £4585 00430-02104300 520 588 671+ 1044 1283 1664 2224 2378
3 PANOVA 13 £- 23000-00 593 906
5 PANTO GIRL 0 £- -00 1251 1799
2 PAPARELLI 48 £3774 012 2301 2476* 2993
3 PAPER POLKA 0 £- -0 1540
3 PAPUN 4 £284 -0030 2653 2853 2991 3070
4 PARADE GIRL 2 £2043 003-01000404000 12 56+ 182 266 628 786 1543 1718 1896 2124 2322
2 PARADISE COFFEE 35 £13865 231201 1782 2127 2281+ 2606- 3174 3230*
5 PARANG 20 £709 01230-033 349 761 1342
4 PARAVANE 1 £- 000-00000 381 2683 3028 3087 3155
3 PARIJOUN 0 £- -000 2534 2793 3066
5 PARIOLI 84 £51213 10413-4121 2347 2742* 2916 3092*
2 PARIS GUEST 32 £2210 0100000 230 404* 513 1453 1585 1938 2136
4 PARIS MATCH 33 £- 21040-000000000 245 306 374 441 521 700 1173 1365 1450
6 PARIS NORTH 0 £- -0 984
4 PARIS TRADER 39 £615 -00000030020000 7 547 609 860 1156 1374 1565 1636 2490 2762 2867 3050 3123 3204
3 PARIS TURF 52 £5217 -00310300 218 328 576 1028* 1284 2458 2867 3123
3 PARK EXPRESS 88 £377741 02-13042D112123 148* 294 754 1128 1331 1408+ 1932* 2202- 2506* 2822 3051
2 PARK FROLICS 0 £- 000 2100 2325 2589
4 PARK MILL 0 £- 00000-0 3104
4 PARK OAKS 0 £- 0-00-0 3147
2 PARKERS JOY 20 £- 000440000 632 962 1105 1253 1480 2465 3016 3143 3199
3 PARKES SPECIAL 0 £- -00000 45 195 487 1824 1904
3 PARKIES BAR 19 £- 00100-00 120 356
2 PARKLANDS BELLE 32 £2942 0240201333 118 270 400 655 1083 1262 2045* 2405 2718 2897
3 PARSONS CHILD 30 £367 -0024300 581 1646 1873 2000 2228 2346 3036
3 PARTS IS PARTS 26 £- -000400 75 209 1244 1794 2059 2734
2 PARTY MATCH 0 £- 00 985 1262
3 PAS DE REGRETS 14 £- 04-4000 593 2382 2674 2929
2 PAS DENCHERE 58 £6779 0301220 1039 1261 1381 1891* 2332 2663 2941
2 PASHMINA 18 £3449 102103330000 57* 533 603 696* 873 1893 2137 2265 2425 2680 2792 3081
2 PASS THE CATCHUP 0 £- 00 2580 2841
3 PASSION PLAY 8 £244 003-0300 120 774 1656 2315
3 PASSO FINALE 0 £- 00-0 2488
3 PASSOONER 2 £- 0P-000 31 113 3172
7 PAST GLORIES 52 £12747 00-031042101200 572 699 969* 1206 1359 1809 1957* 2201 2337* 2662 2769 3022
3 PASTA JANE 0 £- -000 932 1053 1340
2 PASTEL SHADE 0 £- 0 3143
3 PASTICCIO 65 £13345 1-322211300 68 427 713 1199 1821* 2155* 2526 2867 3020
6 PAT ON THE BACK 2 £- 0-010-0 2190
4 PATCHBURG 22 £4746 02-213010000030 7 142* 281 429 611+ 893 1103 1335 2037 2360 3060 3224
3 PATCHOULIS PET 20 £101 00443-0003 1444 1637 1902 2077
2 PATELS GOLD 0 £- 00000 446 813 957 2396 2535
7 PATERNOSTER ROW 19 £- 02000-0 69
2 PATHERO 30 £- 00000 1373 1510 1812 2468 2723
2 PATHIAS 11 £166 003 2270 2405 2466
5 PATHS SISTER 28 £2900 13111-00000103 215 462 1099 1875 2445 2974* 3052 3225
2 PATIENT DREAMER 10 £- 0044 2487 2651 3044 3218
4 PATO 35 £1058 03210-000404000 511 921 1038 1792 1931 2219 2477 2942 3119
4 PATRALAN 7 £- 10000-00000 121 308 731 1052 1310
4 PATRIACH 71 £42928 03411-2011 248- 433 1109+ 1455*
5 PATRICK JOHN LYONS 9 £635 10030-30030 856 1035 1274 2578 2786
3 PATRICKS STAR 7 £350 -0000200 916 1160 1372 1960 2083 2613 3154
3 PATRIOTIC 12 £2411 00-04101 1386 1892 2125* 2587 3161*
3 PATS JESTER 24 £2444 00040-41263000 67 356* 648 958 1223 1871 3087 3219
3 PATSY KELLY 0 £- 00-0 2597

> 1003 <

```
6 PATTOMMY   0   £-   -0   2780
3 PAULS SECRET   0   £-   03000-000000000   54 322 650 829 1184 2399 2603 2974 3219
3 PAUSE FOR APPLAUSE   20   £1188   00-0000013   656 923 1246 1733 2190 2515* 2985
2 PAY DIRT   22   £698   030300   186 236 415 1843 1978 2781
3 PEACE KEEPER   25   £-   -040   1880 2314 2726
5 PEANDAY   14   £748   0000-0030000344   112 401 481 724 1240 1553 1870 2370 2755 3191
2 PEARL BAY   43   £124   3   2703
3 PEARL FISHER   25   £2850   -133040002   140* 416 623 719 1084 1581 2267 2594 2876
4 PEARL PET   12   £1526   00000-20022340   850 1079 1689 1787 2533 2746 2925 3086
5 PEARL RUN   54   £13938   -1320-1101222   85* 137* 235 336* 462- 634 693
2 PEARLITIC   0   £-   0000000   404 612 938 2177 2608 2829 3079
3 PEARLY KING   41   £1179   -400200   219 409 714 1236 2134 2403
2 PEATSWOOD SHOOTER   55   £8943   1110340100   21+ 197+ 278+ 571 1506 1697 1925 2325+ 2949 3125
2 PECHE DOR   41   £390   4   3120
2 PECKING ORDER   54   £632   4   2774
2 PEERGLOW   0   £-   000   1067 1440 3181
3 PEGASUS LADY   0   £-   0000-0000000   340 464 734 855 1444 1549 1827
4 PEGGY CAROLYN   38   £1716   31100-0033030   58A 778 964 1159 2850 2944 3052
3 PEGGY DRIVE   0   £-   -0   2929
2 PEGGYS TREASURE   8   £306   00344334   353 717 957 1076 1647 1741 2212 3032
3 PEGMARINE   31   £-   -000   218 479 699
4 PELEGRIN   14   £-   00000-400   1415 1590 1923
2 PELF   40   £1020   20200   1322 2185 2555- 2687 2871
6 PELHAM LINE   12   £1982   -31000   137 526* 634 712 942
4 PELLINCOURT   21   £4648   320-40020214000   179 265 432 532 750 1209 1366* 1523 1837 1992 2290
3 PELLINKO   50   £4883   00-412001300   127 334* 518 615 914 1199* 1436 1854 2536
3 PELLS CLOSE   2   £-   -0000000000   16 247 309 997 1418 1794 2027 2300 2360 2549
2 PEN BAL LADY   55   £8038   1211330   722* 1105 1341* 1895* 2198 2391 2687
4 PEN TAW   14   £94   -0200-30   22 207
2 PENANG BEAUTY   35   £3008   100000   1407* 1828 2057 2198 2648 2922
2 PENBREASY   16   £144   0400000030   1194 1333 1501 1764 1893 2137 2265 2465 3031 3112
2 PENCIL SHARPENER   42   £506   32   2080 2493
3 PENDOR DANCER   28   £6260   002300010102324   284 760 871 910 1164 1414 1476 1584* 1687 1940* 2322
2469 2586 2632 2783
2 PENELOPE STRAWBERY   46   £-   0   2846 3037
5 PENLLYNES PRIDE   10   £-   02204-0   2582
7 PENNILESS DANCER   0   £-   00000-00   875 993
4 PENNINE WALK   87   £175703   13140-11133   433* 920* 1094+ 1877 2456
2 PENNY FORUM   10   £-   000   2711 2841 3069
2 PENNY LOVER   0   £-   00000   332 544 717 965 2177
2 PENNY PRACTICE   0   £-   0   2847
3 PENRYN BOY   0   £-   00000-4000   257 365 517 522
2 PENSURCHIN   43   £5403   1312000   61* 115 434* 804 1126 1891 2435
5 PENTHOUSE C   16   £710   0-0-02   282 2175
5 PENTLAND BEAUTY   9   £-   -0   1556
3 PENTLAND HAWK   31   £4066   4-0000011D20000   33 386 692 1080 1486 1671* 1956 2109 2300 2536 3030
3113
4 PENTOFF   4   £-   01000-004400000   110 240 321 490 606 2715 2970 3104 3145
3 PENWARD   50   £-   0-0   229
4 PEPENON   22   £-   -000   1841 2085 2666
3 PERCIPIO   18   £1530   300-00003042100   6 161 809 906 1334 1549 1574 1603 1734* 1917 1959
2 PERCYS LASS   72   £10874   111   2070* 2529* 2941+
4 PERFECT APPROACH   32   £-   4030-4   541
5 PERFECT DOUBLE   3   £1359   -32-00403220002   185 493 770 1016 1071 1422 1745 1980 2666 2819 3036
2 PERFECT FOIL   37   £-   004   1778 2191 2652
2 PERFECT STRANGER   48   £11057   0310111   1305 1598 1846* 2336 2383* 2648+ 2989+
4 PERFECT TIMING   69   £38542   3-0433232102110   660 877 1145 1285 1608 1852 2160 2289+ 2524 2764
2953+ 3055* 3118
2 PERFUMERIE   25   £-   0000   1958 2191 2476 2777
8 PERGODA   29   £1749   0-0001010400400   56 182 626 825* 1423 1543* 1638 1896 2124 2322 2586 2775
2921
2 PERIGRIS   0   £-   00000   252 345 1668 2070 2283
4 PERION   47   £18254   000-10111040332   30+ 84 272+ 428+ 477* 877 1608 2160 2537 2783 2953-
4 PERISIAN KNIGHT   32   £1259   00000-0100   532 1124* 1441 2273
2 PEROY   12   £-   000000   621 2069 2292 2433 2813 3182
5 PERSHING   22   £2853   100-02032200220   310 611- 745 967 1017 1374- 1565 2102 2360 2728 3204
2 PERSIAN BALLET   12   £84   0-0340400   229 842 1164 1560 2367 2602 2876
3 PERSIAN BAZAAR   0   £-   10000-000000   1191 1443 1499 2024 2088 2416
2 PERSIAN DELIGHT   40   £5494   40-211   1705 1904* 2250*
2 PERSIAN DYNASTY   28   £-   000   985 1225 1518
2 PERSIAN STYLE   52   £924   00044   662 876 1097 1465 2767
2 PERSIAN TAPESTRY   24   £236   4000000   707 1030 1552 1752 2675 2989 3165
4 PERSONA   75   £22944   0030110   2357* 2637
2 PERTAIN   10   £538   0400220400000   94 136 425 612 1100 1181 1635 1881 2032 2298 2396 2805 3032
2 PETALOUDA   0   £-   00   3068 3141
2 PETANGO   0   £-   00000   1205 1333 1683 2127 3082
3 PETE MARSH   20   £-   -00   2856 3028
3 PETENCORE   0   £-   -00000000   16 109 241 1418 1420 1734 2322 2409
2 PETER MOON   46   £1563   03140   985 1203 1475* 3019 3125
2 PETERS BLUE   31   £2967   041110   589 1012 1478* 1723* 2588+ 2903
5 PETERS KIDDIE   0   £221   00000-00300003   490 611 909 1052 1424 1565 1703 1977
6 PETFORD CHIRU   0   £-   -0   1251
2 PETICOV SHADES   48   £259   020   2281 2499 2667
3 PETILLER   9   £472   0000-20   198 529
4 PETIT BOT   7   £1002   00000-000014   499 710 1074 1901 2282* 2581
4 PETOSKI   87   £13846   22011-330   885 1456 1790
3 PETRIFY   36   £1275   -0100   1246 1446* 1885 2905
5 PETRIZZO   60   £25604   4-00003040131D0   11 58A 360 474 585 704 1127 1293 1779* 1888 2539 2754
2 PETROC CONCERT   14   £-   40000   701 882 2436 2664 3146
4 PETROL BLUE   0   £-   0   2507
4 PETROVICH   66   £8268   11120-300033030   705 877 1146 1387 1857 2351 2641 2833 3042
2 PETRUS SEVENTY   22   £2088   00311   21 596 1413 2724*. 2872*
2 PETSARIA   54   £1458   02   2675 3181
> 1004 <
```

```
7 PETT VELERO   6    £2540    0/0-001010000    176 566 727* 1165 1264* 1346 1609 2319 2544
2 PETTING PARTY  37   £-    000    1311 2561 2717
2 PEWTER QUARTER  0   £-    00    1629 2159
2 PHAETONS GLORY  0   £-    0    2484
2 PHARAOH BLUE   29   £3195   001204220    1373 1731 1883* 2276 2391 2595 2756 2968- 3165
4 PHARDANTE   78   £65164   00230-010133402    221 385* 885 1217* 1513 1712 2157 2502 2844
5 PHAROAHS TREASURE  16   £-   10-00-00    1441 1551
3 PHEASANT HEIGHTS  16   £199   00000-440040    307 949 1304 1564 1688 2326
2 PHELIOFF  0   £-   000   2541 2782 3067
3 PHEOPOTSTOWN   47   £-   0   3002
3 PHILCLASS  0   £-   -0   2583
2 PHILEARN  18   £412   440002030    167 376 722 1480 1622 1362 2050 2138 2298
2 PHILGWYN  24   £743   0230000    848 1433 1752 2019 2577 2859 3025
4 PHILIP  60   £15433   03000-000311300    12 306 428 477 550+ 742+ 1026 1145 1508
3 PHILIPO  66   £-   0   2004
4 PHILLY ATHLETIC  10   £-   00-0   106
3 PHILOSOPHICAL  7   £2437   2041-0003013000    141 666 1224 1701 1774 2060* 2230 2497 3060 3197
2 PHILOTAS  38   £416   4020    1050 1376 1825 2669
2 PHILS PRIDE  0   £-   000   1012 1413 2976
5 PHILSTAR  11   £1132   000300303000040    355 428 628 1182 1438 1638 1676 1849 1986 2124 2469 2513
    2775 2966 3012
2 PHOEBE  4   £113   0030000    482 681 831 1083 2580 2927 2990
2 PIALUCI  8   £67   0000300    537 633 939 1012 1168 2712 3198
6 PICADILLY PRINCE  0   £-   -000    349 856 1099
3 PICATRIX  70   £356   00111-3   210
3 PICEA  56   £7460   42-422011    371 546 887 1469 2996* 3236*
2 PICK OF THE PACK  45   £-   000   2847 3053 3176
2 PICNICING  48   £724   3   2846
4 PICTOGRAPH  42   £950   13014-000020    265 1018 1590 1890 2244 3231
3 PIED DOR  0   £-   -0   720
2 PIFFLE  46   £-   02   2847 3043
3 PILFER  31   £-   3030-00    512 775
2 PILGRIM PRINCE  30   £1501   0000103    118 536 1119 2405 2608* 2804 2919
2 PILLAR OF WISDOM  65   £4099   01   2852 3171*
3 PILLOWING  25   £959   0400-0100    1171 1399+ 1687 1878
3 PILOT BIRD  60   £8506   3-100    599* 1128 2525
3 PILOT JET  69   £7010   41-3410    220 691 2214+ 3020
2 PIMMS PARTY  0   £-   0   2180
4 PINCTADA  0   £-   -000    519 743 1226
2 PINE AWAY  42   £2052   3012    944 1175 1618* 1740
5 PINE HAWK  13   £4317   43004-410100000    84 355* 418 679* 836 2046 2378 3015 3235
4 PINE TREE LANE  78?   £157343   2   3210
2 PINEAPPLES PRIDE  34   £-   040    621 2320 3192
4 PINETUM  16   £-   0--01-000    211 520 977
2 PINK FONDANT  22   £-   00   2070 2147
3 PINK N PERKY  10   £-   0400-000    2793 3057 3185
2 PINK PUMPKIN  7   £1095   0020140000    270 905 981 1318 1496* 1585 1938 2172 2284 2962
3 PINK PYJAMAS  0   £-   00-0   1375
3 PINK SENSATION  18   £270   00000-000420    867 958 1158 1428 1759 1892
2 PINK SWALLOW  24   £-   040    1440 2191 2368
3 PINSTRIPE  60   £19951   0330-011212230    747 1032* 1390* 1486 1575* 1655 2250 2655 2773
2 PINTAFORY  12   £-   00000    73 353 722 1088 1599
3 PINTURICCHIA  2   £-   00-0040000    379 688 958 1372 1615 2128 3036
4 PINWIDDIE  13   £4399   00003-042114000    9 126 366 449* 721* 1024 1223 1871 2403
3 PINZAUREOLE  10   £-   -00040    1372 1873 2682 3102 3227
6 PIP  15   £1035   -010    1265 1694* 2882
2 PIPERS ENTERPRISE  15   £106   030    200 763 2396
2 PIPIOLA  0   £-   0   2788
2 PIPSTED  37   £-   400    2016 2345 3018
4 PIQUE PAN  62   £4819   -2   296
2 PIRACY  20   £-   0   3200
2 PIT PONY  32   £175   00003    931 1090 2325 2798 3221
2 PIT TALK  0   £-   0   3130
2 PITCHFORK  45   £-   000    2522 2847 3228
4 PITKAITHLY  13   £934   04300-0100000    262 530* 689 851 2093 2190 2714
3 PITPROP  42   £-   30104-0   386
3 PLADDA PRINCESS  0   £-   -00000    422 980 1198 1396 1666
2 PLAGUE ORATS  46   £3112   014320    1241 1681* 2383 2521 2677 3125
2 PLAID  58   £8579   132-31304000    224 348* 476 1098 1448 1644 2749 3038
3 PLAIN TALK  26   £2321   04-040012    500 928 1281 2230 2963* 3203
2 PLANE  32   £208   400    1529 1948 3080
3 PLANET ASH  42   £3755   320-2414403    15 49 183* 326 427 604 1202
3 PLANNING ACT  0   £-   0000-0000    1158 1562 1824 2361
3 PLANTER  11   £1364   4033-0102400000    6 51* 145 195 237 305 426 1734 1771 1917
3 PLATINE  23   £2258   00-100020002000    111* 314 443 657 760 884 1001 1051 2488 2731 3106 3191
3 PLATINUM STAR  0   £-   00-0000    139 673 1562 3202
3 PLAXTOL  49   £-   -000    316 572 1046
6 PLAYTEX  20   £536   33400-4000    2151 2277 2526 2715
7 PLAZA TORO  0   £-   -0   1837
3 PLEASING PROSPECT  21   £240   300-03000    1511 1797 2327 2400 2684
3 PLEASURE ISLAND  18   £1700   0-001000    217 464 857* 1104 1830 2171
4 PLEATED  38   £-   2413-0   3139
6 PLIANT  14   £-   40000-00    10 129
3 PLUM BOSSY  0   £-   -04000    458 1404 1580 1786 1969
2 PLUM DROP  58   £2761   21300    383 621* 924 1108 2694
3 PLYMOUTH HOE  51   £3204   -1123    770* 894* 2122 2247
4 POCHARD  59   £9308   12323-3113230    189 403+ 805* 1038 1441 1957 2769
4 POCO LOCO  3   £776   0-0340230033    41 106 495 727 889 1056 1439 2271 2315 3172
3 PODEROSO  47   £1772   30-0040314    60 226 1184 1776 2009 2593* 2958
3 PODSNAP  0   £-   -000    832 2366 2620
3 POINT DARTOIS  68   £18971   /31-220000    301 562 1009 2639
2 POINT OF VIEW  0   £-   0   1855
3 POINTED LADY  24   £2871   -0004200210    217 567 861 1691 2213 2513 2601 2931 3149* 3204
                              > 1005 <
```

```
3 POINTONS PROGRESS  0   £-   -0   3203
4 POKA POKA  64   £-   40   2006 2192
3 POKEREE  12   £-   03000-00000   424 487 1538 1959 2174
7 POKERFAYES  0   £448   0301-0000204000   866 890 1066 1182 1447 1761 2012 2126 2213 2340 2602
4 POKEY  16   £-   03000-004   36 80 163
3 POKEYS PRIDE  50   £6114   0020-02203114   219 1206 1530 1899 2269 2605* 2923* 3110
3 POLECROFT  0   £-   00-0000   347 619 811 1260
7 POLEMISTIS  0   £1110   000-00000100000   445 676 1156 1273 1412 1703* 2014 2282 2374 2549 2964
2 POLEMOS  64   £10774   1200   685* 1097 1467 2501
2 POLLAN BAY  0   £-   000   1238 2270 3135
2 POLLENATE  60   £5208   01   2418 2847*
4 POLLY DANIELS  61   £2939   30231-100   817* 1125 1306
3 POLLY WORTH  10   £192   0000-003400   309 518 871 1134 3105 3224
2 POLLYS SONG  39   £272   02400   1030 1194 1427 3146 3226
2 POLONIA  78   £76657   110131200   558* 752* 1097 1329* 2113 2235+ 2634 2915 3209
4 POLYKRATIS  82   £39081   030-00031240312   222 854 1146 1306 1387+ 1631- 1889 2347 2474 2764*
  3010
5 POLYNOR  4   £1022   0-440-0001   2490 2533 2877 3154*
4 POMMES CHATEAU  10   £-   00000-00040004   679 1066 1211 2012 2126 2189 2513 2977
2 PONDERED BID  50   £736   02   3053 3132
4 PONTYATES  15   £1334   --24-3400041000   439 519 743 968 1074 1808 1909* 2604 2800 3219
4 POOELLA  7   £-   00300-0   341
3 POP THE CORK  50   £-   220-400   143 600 3042
2 POPS WILKINSON  0   £-   0   1421
11 POPSIS JOY  21   £-   00001-000   58A 215 375
3 POPSIS POM POM  0   £-   -00000   1670 2546 2931 3066 3196
3 POPTHORN  0   £-   -00   2248 2734
3 POPULARITY  62   £650   11044   1592 2450 3001
3 PORO BOY  20   £701   00-340004002400   127 352 444 615 723 847 2408 2534 2656 2818 3063 3203
3 PORT ETIENNE  69   £5308   30   301 643
2 PORT HELENE  59   £5150   2100   1855 2407+ 2540 2751
4 PORT MIST  0   £-   00000-000000   266 355 679 786 2342 2397
2 PORT OF TIME  0   £-   00   1812 1982
3 PORT PLEASE  24   £340   -4002P   651 863 1431 1800 2009
3 PORTE DAUPHINE  0   £-   -0000   500 764 937 1689
2 PORTENTOUS  29   £-   000   1928 2254 2645
7 PORTER  00   £-   --000-0000   199 366 493 1336
3 PORTHMEOR  39   £719   22044-424030   175 277 496 657 1463 1560
3 PORTLAND DANCER  25   £-   0204-0   1360
5 PORTLY  0   £-   -00   1799 2096
4 PORTO GREEN  0   £-   -00   448 522
6 PORTO IRENE  0   £-   000-0-0000   1056 1188 1565 1703
8 PORTOGON  32   £1130   000-00003000002   248 433 930 1189 1365 1460 1890 2091 2296 2431 2925
4 POSITIVE  54   £5782   21120-01D202   363 695 921- 1409 1963
3 POSSEDYNO  62   £8296   01-31100200   1312 1443* 1654+ 2347 2474 2672 2772 2842
4 POSTORAGE  62   £5888   10020-00010043   172 361 945 1292+ 1455 1793 2437 2685
3 POUNELTA  41   £2278   34133-420404030   63 271 459 925 1630 2247 2420 2784 3123
2 POUR LITALIE  0   £-   0   2846
3 POUSSEZ  28   £-   -40   528 1451
4 POWDER BLUE  54   £9218   33101-04010041   846 1060 1145 1608* 2537 2668 3015 3118*
4 POWDER KEG  81   £12171   11113-134   245+ 557 705
4 POWER BENDER  56   £43482   00222-430111123   452 651 1042 1929+ 2062* 2226* 2693* 2867 3050
2 POWER OF LOVE  0   £-   00   2708 2804
2 PPS LITTLE SECRET  0   £-   0   3200
2 PRADEL  0   £-   000   1488 2646 2716
3 PRADIER  81   £17480   1110   303* 554* 1009
3 PRAIRIE NEBA  68   £32203   211   1596 2643* 2913*
3 PRAIRIE OYSTER  32   £696   -0324   1431 2216 2339 2671
2 PRAISEWORTHY  0   £-   0   3109
4 PRAOS  0   £-   -0   176
3 PRASINA MATIA  35   £-   -0000   218 371 887 2321
3 PRECIOUS LINK  30   £254   -2   3194
3 PRECIOUS METAL  54   £15994   21200-103001000   657* 929 1235 1654 1933 2258+ 2382 2674 3118
5 PRECIPICE WILL  0   £-   -0   19
3 PRECISIONIST  88   £226573   3   3213
3 PREJUDICE  40   £1326   30030-3200   814 1091 2085 2481
3 PRELUDE  54   £7289   3-340101   581 1259 1589 2078* 2236 3022+
2 PREMIER LAD  46   £2892   030120   780 1161 2325 2423* 2669 3125
4 PREMIER ROLE  78   £35235   23443-413   299 645* 1115
2 PREMIER VIDEO  18   £1368   302020020   627 973 1155 1294 1545 2127 2883 3032 3056
4 PREMIERE CUVEE  74   £23007   --030-2103   1011 2457* 2916 3092
2 PREMIUM GOLD  22   £131   430000   21 483 533 938 1059 1180
2 PRESCRIPTION  50   £1308   02   2626 3176
4 PRESIDIUM  70   £11973   12-03-102410   344* 653 1000- 1514 2231* 3020
5 PRETTY AMAZING  0   £-   -00   106 3159
6 PRETTY FLY  0   £-   -0   3147
3 PRETTY GREAT  38   £634   -340020   33 217 593 891 2321 2784
2 PRETTY SOON  12   £-   40000000   1297 1370 2375 2535 2607 2678 2994 3151
4 PRICEOFLOVE  12   £1415   20040-0100   1156 1766* 2130 3060
2 PRIDE OF PARIS  0   £-   0   3073
3 PRIMARY  67   £47918   01-44114   324 494 1837* 2220+ 2692
3 PRIME NUMBER  24   £3000   0-0000341   247 334 615 1985 2293 2876 3197*
2 PRIME PRINCE  52   £1291   1   3111*
5 PRIME STONE  0   £-   -0   44
2 PRIMETTA PRINCE  30   £85   030   2607 3059 3158
2 PRIMITIVE RISING  48   £1969   1   3080*
4 PRIMO DOMINIE  77   £-   241220-00   587 705
4 PRIMROSE WAY  11   £900   0000-0020030003   341 731 1079 1274 1689 2154 2381 2490 2807 3193
2 PRINCE BOCA  55   £361   4   3037
3 PRINCE BOLD  16   £-   -0004   2030 2275 2464 2930
3 PRINCE DE LA TOUR  0   £-   -0   289
2 PRINCE MAC  0   £-   000000   27 345 1190 1495 2615 3192
3 PRINCE MERANDI  36   £9929   0-1330001002   25* 116 348 459 805 1034 2431* 2946 3123 3179
```

```
2 PRINCE NEWPORT  28   £-   000   2646 2852 3075
5 PRINCE OBERON  6   £609   00000-20   101 629
3 PRINCE ORAC  58   £14242   -30210101   1776 1934 2092 2333+ 2536 2720* 2848 3119+
3 PRINCE PECADILLO  60   £-   11000-00000   406 692 2870 3042 3177
4 PRINCE RELKO  0   £-   -00   8 452
6 PRINCE REYMO  74   £493   302D2-400   222 408 705
4 PRINCE SABO  76   £-   41020-00   408 1889
3 PRINCE SATIRE  38   £1498   -010403   140 492* 912 1939 2164 2324
4 PRINCE SKY  55   £10070   40114-4301402   172 616 1145 1235+ 1852 2151 2573-
2 PRINCE SWIFTFOOT  0   £-   0   2708
2 PRINCE ZAMARO  0   £-   000   2468 2628 2997
2 PRINCEGATE  26   £-   00400   236 1174 1625 1762 2218
3 PRINCELY ESTATE  36   £2073   000-222241   33 259 570 1301 1588 2373*
3 PRINCESS ANDROMEDA  17   £918   0-001000   402 774 2041* 2399 2478 3219
4 PRINCESS BELLA  0   £-   00-0000   492 888 1677 2413
3 PRINCESS EMMA  30   £816   -04230   1327 1953 2327 2520 3061
4 PRINCESS JENNY  22   £-   00002-0   841
2 PRINCESS LILY  0   £-   0   3229
2 PRINCESS MICHICO  6   £203   03030   533 1692 2625 2872 3079
3 PRINCESS NAWAAL  50   £13721   44-1100032   539* 925* 1153 1713 2404 2719 2946
3 PRINCESS PAMELA  18   £-   0010-000   240 451 637
2 PRINCESS PELHAM  5   £-   00400   1311 1528 1905 2168 2712
3 PRINCESS RYMER  0   £-   000-000   545 733 932
2 PRINCESS SEMELE  38   £-   000   1629 2577 2788
2 PRINCESS SINGH  14   £2166   0031044312000   186 354 696 858* 1088 1221 1279 1358 1537* 1907 2336
  2512 2756
4 PRINCESS WENDY  22   £-   044141/40000   30 877 977 2256 2469
2 PRINCESSE DU BOURG  75   £20134   114   2644* 2915
7 PRINGLE  6   £128   30   1424 1703
2 PRINT  65   £19833   2111   2301- 2410* 2694* 3019+
3 PRIOK  10   £481   00000-030003   117 275 1023 1236 1497 1748
2 PRIOR WELL  13   £522   002000   47 186 415 672 1528 1680
3 PRISSY MISS  22   £-   4320-00000   454 624 923 1245 1695
4 PRIVATE AUDITION  26   £575   -433   19 176 282
3 PRIVATE SUE  3   £-   0000-000000   359 835 1438 1687 2088 2210
3 PROBLEM CHILD  17   £395   00003-3000   274 480 843 1314
3 PRODIGAL DANCER  30   £-   -04   1589 2023
2 PRODIGIOUS LADY  0   £-   000   818 1187 2127
2 PROFIT A PRENDRE  0   £-   000   2547 2983 3136
3 PROGO  0   £-   -00   2275 3160
3 PROHIBITED  42   £3505   00-11000   90* 316* 538 1384 1783
4 PROHIBITION BOY  7   £-   0-000-00   524 783
3 PROMENADER  21   £-   00-0000   1036 1469 1628 2399
5 PROMISED ISLE  55   £19563   32002-32314040   432 706- 1047 1383+ 1793 1931 2557 2867
3 PROMISING TIMES  20   £-   -4   87
2 PROPENSITY  66   £11937   122   848* 1108 2543
2 PROSILIENT  37   £-   00   1239 1731
2 PROSPECT PLACE  35   £188   030   1872 2082 3130
4 PROTECTION  78   £5054   12110-300   313 598 736
4 PROUDEST HOUR  0   £-   -0   2916
2 PRYDWEN  0   £-   0   2768
3 PSALM  24   £1149   03100-03413   447 932 1334 1617* 1771
2 PSALMODY  51   £3757   002100   1376 1634 1948 2329+ 2598 3041
3 PSYLLA  54   £6333   -0111   1193 1953* 2170* 2286*
3 PUB ROYAL  80   £2760   1001340   2453 2738
5 PUBBY  29   £10255   3310-1120001000   225* 363* 584 698 1112 1409 2273* 2486 2769 3232
2 PUBLIC PRAISE  0   £-   00   415 741
4 PUCCINI  22   £-   00000-00000000   854 1037 1145 1900 2160 2256 3055 3152
2 PUGET  24   £-   0-320-0   2591
2 PULASKI  0   £-   00   3171 3229
3 PULHAM MILLS  38   £6219   4400-0000122010   54 247 427 747 1169+ 1471 1999 2343 2681* 2879
2 PULLANDESE  0   £-   00000   633 831 1083 1190 1449
5 PULSATE  35   £-   02002-0   432
4 PULSINGH  17   £2765   -00000103000200   31 70 176 499 709 850* 1035 1393 1551 2533 2699 2985-
  3063 3195
2 PUMPING IRON  49   £773   24   2999
3 PUNCLE CREAK  15   £1000   S00-40000023302   103 147 377 822 1334 1424 1617 1824 1917 2124 2268
2 PUNTA CALAHONDA  42   £2465   010000   1253 1975* 2251 2444 2663 3165
2 PUPPET SHOW  0   £-   00   3037 3109
3 PUPPYWALKER  0   £-   0000-0000   275 1349 1898 1969
4 PURCHASEPAPERCHASE  71   £17835   00000-010400100   433 708+ 1095 1466 1851 2194 2385+ 2568 2868
5 PURPLE  9   £918   -0010   530 1056 1459* 1952
2 PUSHOFF  38   £1708   02230   1874 2589 2696 2950 3114
3 PYJAMA PARTY  27   £2133   -4401   1941 2092 2430 2794*
2 QANNAAS  46   £358   2   3111
3 QUADRILLE  10   £-   0-0   388
7 QUADRILLION  11   £1286   -024333   917 1419 1582 1884 2111 2794
4 QUALITAIR FLYER  36   £443   000000000000004   17 330 433 573 706 1109 1455 1793 2234 2566 2693 2867
  2956 3113 3231
4 QUALITAIR KING  11   £3494   -03000312000000   14 78 284 447 677 961 1051* 1324 1664 1701 2513
  2602 2715 2998
7 QUALITAIR PRINCE  14   £-   04000-0   812
4 QUALITAIRESS  8   £8238   30003400302201212000   101 240 378 689 963 1074   1139 1338 1482 1761
  1870 1983 2173 2264* 2414- 2549*   2755 2832 2891 3029
5 QUALITY CHORISTER  18   £1850   00002-40100   142 281 893* 956 1335
5 QUALITY SQUARE  0   £-   -0   1908
3 QUARANTINO  17   £-   0000-000   307 381 595
3 QUARRYVILLE  38   £438   24413-00440000   172 228 387 567 808 1669 1852 2079
3 QUARTERFLASH  19   £-   00-000   75 1317 1497
2 QUASSIMI  28   £-   00440   2646 2782 2983 3048 3223
2 QUE PASA  26   £592   02400   2032 2334 2405 2625 2724
4 QUE SYMPATICA  76   £11245   404-33000024014   18 222 408 587 945 1125 2231 2440 2538 3127+ 3235
3 QUEEN HELEN  71   £8549   21-00431   755 2202 2868 3121 3227*
```

```
2 QUEEN MATILDA   0   £-   000    383 1427 1881
2 QUEEN MIDAS  44   £-   4   1722
3 QUEEN OF BATTLE   46   £3480   0-0022341040    213 372 1193 1327- 1575 1725 2393* 2649 3119 3175
3 QUEEN OF SWORDS   13   £-   40400-00400000    416 720 769 1089 1251 1435 2760 3186
2 QUEENS BRIDGE  60   £15632   41   2768 2999*
2 QUEENS CONNECTION   0   £-   000    602 2281 3103
2 QUEENS LAKE  0   £-   0   1778
3 QUEENS SOLDIER  74   £11894   131-11200    1015+ 1343+ 1913 2064 2845
3 QUEENS VISIT  36   £507   -404000    250 359 549 1062 1259 2304
2 QUEL ESPRIT  66   £21953   121113022420    20* 146- 382* 456* 571+ 915 1097 1591 1754 2223 2451
2695
2 QUELLE FILLE  52   £1693   32   1641 2527
2 QUESSARD  48   £1707   032   2721 2860 3011
3 QUEZAL  44   £3132   00-014   357 512* 730
3 QUICK DANCER  24   £-   00-00000    402 579 919 1041 1281
5 QUICK FLING  7   £197   3   163
3 QUICK REACTION  25   £2252   0-0002120    25 66 1577 2111 2211* 2305 2492
2 QUICK RIPOSTE  0   £-   0   3184
2 QUICK SNAP  58   £10599   43221011200    187 323 456 918 1039* 1143 1320* 1512* 1606 1876 2307
2 QUICK STICKS  0   £-   0000   21 108 415 1132
3 QUICKEN THE BID  12   £-   00400-0000    74 2103 2397 2581
3 QUICKSAND  42   £-   2202-0   575
2 QUIET BLUSH  0   £-   00   1855 2283
5 QUIET COUNTRY  21   £-   44040-0   724
2 QUIET HERO  44   £990   0323   2229 2494 2716 2886
4 QUIET RIOT  46   £4298   34304-0100000    71 429* 698 2419 2693 3050 3113
2 QUIETLY MINE  0   £-   000   852 2140 2710
4 QUINOA DE SAISY  51   £4969   -2   2116
3 QUINTA REEF  48   £5145   00-120024000    438* 671- 844 1044 1900- 2084 3015 3127 3204
3 QUITE A QUEST  14   £261   4-00000200    1193 1337 1751 1953 2508 3144 3185 3224
3 QUITE POKEY  0   £-   -000   1142 1415 1961
2 QUITE SO  25   £1781   -010000    34 565* 995 1785 3032 3146
3 QUIVERING  0   £-   00000-000    257 365 1759
3 QURRAT AL AIN  5   £-   000-00000    674 997 1142 1256 1562
5 R NANCY  18   £-   0--00-0   19
7 RA NOVA  26   £2599   10   683* 851
4 RA RA GIRL  31   £1005   11000-000002030    306 441 1026 1429 1508 1676 1852 2079 2322
2 RA RAVER  0 . £-   000   304 1762 3201
2 RAAHIA  65   £7492   1   2939*
3 RAAS  28   £1003   0-2340224    109 241 255 677 787- 891 1200
3 RAAWIYEH  25   £-   0020-000    1228 2063 2483
3 RABAB  0   £-   0-00   422 570
2 RABENHAM  10   £-   0040004000    236 515 741 965 1294 1528 1965 2298 2994 3182
5 RABIRIUS  31   £536   0-010-2000    745 956 1202 1525
3 RACEFORM RHAPSODY  0   £-   00000-000004    22 139 630 932 1481 1759
4 RACING DEMON  0   £145   03404-30000000    104 366 590 1016 1092 2054 2415 3159
3 RACKSTRAW  69   £1869   130-320   2231 2559 2808
5 RADWHAW  10   £-   00430-0   2338
3 RAF  21   £-   -000   806 1291 2408
3 RAFFIA RUN  30   £637   040-044023340    275 538 857 1065 1264 1394 2373 2656 2720
3 RAFFLES ROGUE  11   £-   0000-00   2478 3155
3 RAFFLES VIRGINIA  30   £757   02000-40200400    732 911 1200 1446 1885 2214 2313 2473
2 RAG QUEEN  0   £-   0   3189
6 RAGABURY  12   £-   0-000-04   164 1908
2 RAGOVN  0   £-   0   1684
2 RAGTIME PARTY  0   £-   00   2107 2323
2 RAGTIME SOLO  16   £279   00042   1307 1522 1948 2580 2712
2 RAHWAH  37   £335   030   1802 2878 3074
2 RAINBOW TROUT  26   £1648   040202   1634 1958 2127 2281- 2993 3182
2 RAINED OFF  42   £-   0   3181
2 RAINTREE COUNTY  23   £259   000040002    236 320 1305 1475 1723 2107 2743 2986 3190
4 RAISABILLION  1   £143   -40-0003   164 449 770 1897
2 RAISE A FLYER  0   £-   00   3037 3223
3 RAISINHELL  44   £1631   0200-3120   464 656* 907 2250
3 RAJ KUMARI  0   £-   -000   666 1053 1303
5 RAJA KHAN  0   £-   000/1-0   1582
3 RAJA MOULANA  30   £684   04-1000   907* 1228 2207 2650
2 RAJIVS DEBT  23   £132   003   1550 1665 1803
4 RAKAPOSHI KING  79   £40997   21120-311432    1020 1409+ 1513+ 2114 2461 2630-
2 RAMBERGE  26   £-   04   3136 3199
9 RAMBLING RIVER  46   £11384   0200021000021010    626 742- 784 1268 1380 1638- 1796* 2065 2204
2632 2668 2775- 2858* 3015 3152* 3233
4 RAMICH JOHN  56   £12908   320000   325 360 468 2450 2506 3004
4 RAMILIE  7   £207   00100-00340000    675 869 1416 1737 1892 2509 2745 3030
3 RAMPAGE  79   £16500   0-11414   469
6 RANA PRATAP  56   £22028   -04332042014100    17 71 248 445 879 1109 1383 1931 2219 2331* 2630
2686* 3038 3232
2 RANDOM ROVER  57   £894   23   2263 2542
3 RANELAGH  10   £175   00-0000030   194 572 989 1497 2260 2762 3101
4 RANGE ROVER  72   £1128   13041-020   617 1015- 1144
2 RANKSTREET  22   £169   003004   1930 2191 2283 2700 3146 3188
2 RANT ON  0   £-   00000   1345 1495 1692 1944 2168
5 RAPID ACTION  13   £821   03420-30330000    46 196 310 521 1018 1202 2104 2264
3 RAPID FLIGHT  0   £-   0000-0000    183 247 451 857
8 RAPID LAD  21   £1420   0-000-014000000    1017 1106* 1374 1563 1787 2102 2360 2925 3140
6 RAPID MISS  16   £271   20000-00000    784 1213 1367 1542 1649 1849
3 RAPID STAR  0   £144   00000-30000000    51 131 195 305 524 788 889 993
5 RAPIDAN  6   £1725   30-000000100   19 592 772 959 1140 1569 2395* 2467 3087
3 RARE LEGEND  32   £881   0-002420    1538 1600 2853 2996 3155 3217
2 RARE MEMORIES  50   £989   222   2287 2487 2652
3 RARE SOUND  21   £1031   1-23000    1725 1999 2385 2719 3078
3 RARE WIND  0   £-   -00   2931 3066
2 RARELY AT ODDS  0   £-   00   2159 2405
> 1008 <
```

```
2 RARELY IRISH  56  £1605  20   1287 1464
4 RASHAH  9   £-   0-300-000   184 860 1271
2 RATHDRUM  0   £-   00   2852 3163
2 RATHER HOMELY  50   £2121   331   1154 1308 3190*
3 RATTLE ALONG  46   £7732   0-010210   980 1193* 1444 2131 2404* 2676
2 RAUNCHY RITA  0   £-   000   2625 2919 2994
6 RAVARO  60   £-   0   1148
3 RAVELSTON  6   £-   00-000   82 426 718
4 RAVENS PEAK  11   £-   0-000-00   745 1017
4 RAVENSCRAIG  0   £-   0-000-00   1558 1945
2 RAW ENERGY  35   £-   0   3075
3 RAYHAAN  45   £8894   -0113000   111 431* 884* 1033 2160 2382 2764
2 RAYMONDS STAR  0   £-   00   2364 2511
4 RAZZAMATAZ GLORY  0   £-   -0   1073
4 RAZZLE DAZZLE BOY  0   £-   -0   1243
5 READY WIT  41   £18287   000-22100000202   71- 112 361+ 433 706 1109 2072 2144 2475 2629 2749
3 REAL MOONSHINE  36   £3318   -0400012   806 1220 1818 2230 2497 2802* 3110-
2 REAL RUSTLE  26   £1072   0003410   47 425 813 858 957 1012* 1635
3 REALITY  55   £5735   0-110300   1246* 1753* 1924 2385 2568 2956
5 REALLY HONEST  45   £-   4--10-00000   70 248 433 1189 3231
6 REAR ACTION  30   £389   02001-0030   262 499 748 855
3 REASON TO BE  64   £3030   3   1111
2 REATA PASS  23   £-   0000   1305 1561 2140 2607
4 REBECCAS PET  0   £-   -000   1300 1602 1841
2 REBEL GREY  0   £-   00   3099 3234
2 REBEL NUN  0   £-   0   3223
2 REBEL RAISER  59   £2664   03010   1653 2554 2695 2838* 3107
3 REBELLO IMP  0   £-   000-00000   111 340 424 666 1310
3 RECAPTURE  0   £-   0-00   500 842
4 RECHARGE  13   £-   204-0000   19 164 333 439
4 RECOLLECT  18   £-   0230-0000   2602 2685 2885 2995
2 RECORD BANGLER  0   £-   00   1105 2471
2 RECORD FLIGHT  17   £345   00023   206 350 1083 1647 2107
4 RECORD HAULIER  0   £87   4300   673 889 993 2401
5 RECORD RED  0   £-   -040   36 129 530
8 RECORD WING  22   £4339   14000-21330040   23 92* 208 263 474 1502 2285 3187
2 RECORDED TIME  0   £-   0   3079
2 RECREATION  40   £1526   3320   400 655 852 1108
2 RECTORY GIRL  20   £-   00   2926 3133
3 RED BILLY  0   £-   04000-4400000   29 54 1346 1671 2497 2746 2876
3 RED BREEZE  0   £-   -0   744
5 RED COUNTER  0   £-   00404-0P   2008 2152
6 RED DUSTER  6   £394   100-43000000000   44 50 319 366 462 933 1016 1071 1223 2480 2627
2 RED HERO  38   £412   003340   915 1914 2225 2595 2711 2997
3 RED IN THE MORNING  25   £-   000-00   1199 2076
2 RED RIDING HOOD  25   £-   0400   1030 1407 1966 2658
3 RED RIVER BOY  34   £533   -0023000   1061 1315 1472 1648 1804 2186 2532
5 RED RUSSELL  41   £-   40000-00000   361 521 1109 2934 3113
3 RED SHOES  32   £3480   0-3032232244   458 849 1031 1630 1941 2131 2304 2548 2734 3061
2 RED SKY AT NIGHT  15   £68   030   2580 2990 3135
2 RED TIMBER  44   £428   030   2239 2468 2869
2 RED TWILIGHT  30   £119   340   1681 1863 2423
5 RED VANITY  0   £-   0--0-0   46
3 RED ZULU  15   £884   22003-000040001   198 309 426 608 774 960 1201 1288 1364*
3 REDALLY  10   £201   -0024   194 2478 2590 2679
4 REDCROSS MISS  12   £-   03300-00   940 1106
8 REDDEN  18   £2565   14000-1404000   750* 1188 1441 2049 2617 2807 2925
4 REDEEM HERSELF  69   £5668   -111022   2505
2 REDWOOD EVE  0   £-   0   3073
2 REEF OF GOLD  32   £-   00000   2001 2263 2571 2894 3103
2 REFERENCE POINT  86   £47659   311   2407 2721+ 3126*
3 REFORM LINE  0   £-   -0   3236
3 REFORM PRINCESS  36   £9421   0-0034103000121   120 275 1326 1577 1817* 2015 2087 2403 2647 2974
3110+ 3139 3219*
4 REFORMED HABIT  0   £1444   0-000-3013300   630 963 1201* 1546 1703 1839 2412
2 REGAL BRASS  0   £-   0   3205
4 REGAL CAPISTRANO  19   £1522   32040-20134   104 184 783* 1302 1422
3 REGAL CASTLE  42   £1081   -21   1977 2366*
2 REGAL RAIDER  27   £-   000   2225 2491 2607
2 REGAL RHYTHM  18   £-   0000   2089 2418 2527 3120
3 REGAL SAM  2   £-   04000-00   2017 3076
3 REGAL STATE  82   £29059   31120-40420   288 467 2002 2195 2507
8 REGAL STEEL  23   £11380   0020322022214030020   43 52 243 308 474 686 964 1150 1359 1502 1769
1918* 2066 2290 2389 2551 2855 3026- 3087
2 REGALCROFT  0   £-   00   1869 2108
2 REGENCY FILLE  68   £23503   1222321220   223* 450- 655 876 1113 1453 1708* 1850 2158 2503
3 REGENCY SQUARE  16   £3930   000-3204414400   697 1089 1223 1326 1706 2109* 2226 2372 2604 2720
2 REGENT LAD  23   £-   4000000   320 571 685 915 1253 2310 2607
7 REGENT LEISURE  0   £-   -00   801 942
2 REGENT SQUARE  0   £-   0   1225
3 REHEARSING  53   £-   -4   150
3 REIGNBEAU  58   £11061   03-31120310   83 175+ 274* 501 1107 1384 1911* 2349
4 REINDEER WALK  38   £913   10003-000403   775 2562 2674 2945 3050 3124
4 REINE KA  67   £3864   44   298 1010
3 REJUVENATE  77   £65505   -310010   264 551* 926 2202 2525* 3169
4 REKADLO  0   £-   -000   1908 2054 2152
2 RELAMPEGO  2   £-   0000400   621 882 1253 1803 1997 2466 2712
3 RELATIVELY EASY  36   £4683   -001120   613 951 1404* 1822* 2128 2478
6 RELIABLE VYNZ  0   £-   0-0   2413
5 RELKISHA  10   £-   21000-000   204 336 419
2 RELKOORA  27   £-   00   1239 3080
3 RELOY  77   £50501   -31103200   904* 2196 2638 2918 3214
4 RELZA COCCINEA  4   £-   400-00   1195 1473
> 1009 <
```

```
2 REMAIN FREE   27   £3629    3304130    1305 1405 1883 2095 2272* 2380 2472
5 REMAINDER GIRL   0   £-    -0   3154
4 REMAINDER TIP   0   £-    0-00-000000    46 124 820 1077 1567 1703
5 REMEMBRANCE   3   £-    00000-040000000    378 540 636 943 1093 1156 1761 2104 2390
3 REMINISCING   12   £438    -2000    1749 2327 2726 3078
7 RENDSLEY GIRL   0   £-    -0   2517
3 RENO RALPH   40   £906    -00414    806 1469 1600 1721* 2096
4 REPEALED   17   £722    233000    1 10 112 281 3172 3224
3 REPETITIVE   0   £-    000-0   863
3 REPORT EM   10   £282    -0002000    806 1142 1399 1943 2186 2497 2726
3 RES NON VERBA   0   £67    0-300000    1340 1567 2335 2495 3084 3154
3 RESCUE PACKAGE   34   £204    4-04403000    579 1395 1554 1776 2294 2458 2685 2959
3 RESHA   9   £-    20-000    356 3071 3194
6 RESISTER   0   £-    -0   343
3 RESOURCEFUL FALCON   60   £9729    0111-022000030    226 586 692 1107 1486 2234 2674 2851 3231
3 RESPECT   57   £16884    43-213104124002    217 580* 660 1033* 1151 1654 1878+ 2224 2382 2764 3055
3064
4 RESPONDER   4   £67    -230-0030000000    8 142 259 441 490 830 936 1013 1439 2014
4 REST AND WELCOME   2   £-    40030-00000    31 174 499 2132 2274
3 RESTIVER   70   £11470    --411-30200    561 1116 1353 2002 2196
3 RESTLESS RHAPSODY   25   £1852    23134-240403100    246 529 760 1414 1476 2024 2416* 2659 3046
4 RESTORATION   20   £215    4-000-00300    1482 1627 1761 2102 2340
3 RESTORE   42   £5987    23-203214    593 1151 2224 2382 2660* 2764
3 RETHYMNO   35   £825    04000-002    49 344 928
3 RETRIEVE   35   £300    -002    334 3070 3147
3 RETURN TO TARA   14   £-    -040    1444 1670 2092
3 REVANORA   0   £-    -00   1751 2275
4 REVEILLE   40   £6015    000-22010030210    65 172- 374 1066* 1285 1429 2033 2277 2715 2981* 3065
2 REVELINA   15   £280    003000    73 223 261 483 882 2514
4 REVISIT   31   £3023    01-000343443000    58A 312 462 801 1150 1388 1679 2376 2445 2523 2692 2938
2 REVOLVER VIDEO   16   £-    000    77 819 1132
2 RHABDOMANCER   7   £316    333000    364 612 701 2396 2919 2994
3 RHAPSODY IN BLACK   14   £1021    -1000    39* 68 1122 2319
6 RHEIN COURT   0   £432    13000-0000020    547 940 1473 1787 1951 2374 2549
10 RHEINFORD   0   £-    0-340-000    9 137 519
3 RHODE ISLAND RED   24   £618    -40020    714 959 1372 1822 2128
2 RHONDALING   65   £8071    3113    2070 2283* 2577+ 2910
2 RHYTHM MAKER   0   £-    0   1311
3 RHYTHMIC BLUES   57   £3299    -110    978+ 1276* 2031
5 RIBBLE STAR   2   £-    00000-0   3196
6 RIBBONS OF BLUE   5   £-    -1320-00   44 80
2 RIBO BE GOOD   3   £-    004004    180 261 853 1262 1458 1557
3 RIBO MELODY   13   £129    00000-0003    779 862 1204 1759
2 RIBOBAMBINO   0   £-    00   2957 3163
8 RIBODEN   0   £-    -0   1689
2 RIBOGIRL   20   £1249    0000010    1067 1282 1570 1846 2364 2466* 3165
4 RIBOKEYES BOY   6   £-    -0000    1349 1494 1831 2017
3 RIBOVINO   20   £386    -03    1061 1732
4 RICCO STAR   0   £-    00440-00000    202 349 420 724 1243
3 RICH BITCH   0   £739    0-000002000000    51 145 195 545 871 972 1051 1742 2424 3057 3144 3185
2 RICH CHARLIE   75   £38546    0110    1097 1510+ 1876+ 2221
3 RICHARDS FOLLY   30   £829    0-0000020    1022 1259 1437 1787 2876 3028 3142
2 RICHEMONT   36   £-    4   3111
3 RICHMOND STREET   0   £-    -0   980
3 RICMAR   0   £-    00-00   720 1233
3 RIDESIDE   13   £-    -04000    2400 2682 2726 3036 3161
8 RIDGEFIELD   32   £502    00000-004    7 23 72
2 RIDGIDUCT   0   £-    00   1427 1683
6 RIG STEEL   16   £-    /0002-0   2809
4 RIGTON LAD   0   £-    -0   1415
2 RIJISTAN   26   £-    0   2646
7 RIKA MIA   0   £-    -0   121
6 RIKKI TAVI   42   £11157    01213-033010400    215 375 712 1099* 1293 1470 1875 2754 2938
5 RIMAH   42   £4587    20340-0113    547 912* 1166* 1519
3 RIMBEAU   32   £2179    4241000    230 345 460 717* 1313 1568 1938
2 RIMOVE   1   £-    000    865 1050 1221
2 RING BACK   4   £-    00400000    21 415 763 1075 1881 3056 3146 3192
2 RING OF PEARL   0   £-    000    383 800 2600
3 RIO DEVA   18   £-    10-2-0040    1079 1539 1689 3164
2 RIO PIEDRAS   45   £1780    10    2377+ 2543
2 RIOT BRIGADE   50   £6341    0033140410    382 694 1653 1754 2016+ 2485 2611 2941 3072+ 3174
2 RIOT SQUAD   0   £-    0   2847
2 RIPE CHRISTINA   45   £1507    0033424    621 1108 2185 2292 2563 2651- 2814
2 RIPSTER   14   £108    00400340    1762 1846 2045 2405 2724 2817 3069 3141
2 RISE AND FALL   0   £-    0   3120
4 RISING   66   £1929    404    475 1127 1856
3 RISK ANOTHER   0   £-    -0000    625 739 980 1497
2 RISK ME   80   £40441    114422    323* 737* 1126 2737 2866 3168
2 RITZS PEARL   0   £-    0   2434
2 RIVA MARQUEE   27   £-    0   3109
3 RIVA RENALD   19   £1150    -1400    868* 1141 1361 2360
3 RIVART   46   £682    -00324    806 1045 2085 2400 2622
3 RIVER BLUES   71   £2172    -04-34    150 471
3 RIVER DANCER   73   £16182    124-4304310    155 467 1008 1356 2002 3168
3 RIVER GAMBLER   21   £821    0000-002003    723 1087 1806 2173 2516 2802
3 RIVER HAWK   69   £6264    -2   3008
2 RIVER JIG   48   £1145    01    1464 2901*
3 RIVER LULLABY   0   £-    -0   560
2 RIVER MEMORIES   62   £7521    312    3090
3 RIVER MYSTERY   0   £-    0   470
2 RIVERBOAT PARTY   15   £-    0040000    1241 1522 1843 2019 2847 3075 3188
3 RIVERBRIDE   72   £17634    00042244    2196 2452 2638 2909
3 RIVERS NEPHEW   12   £305    -0003    430 595 751 1724
                          > 1010 <
```

```
2 RIVERS SECRET 20    £1459    0000414    627 818 1132 1622 2138 2798* 3085
4 RIVERSIDE WRITER 34    £1445    02000-103404000    84* 124 182 306 412 525 820 3145 3233
2 RIVERSTYLE 22    £85    003    2365 2781 3056
3 RIVIERA SCENE 33    £802    022-0020000    624 1001 1312 1524 2573 2842 3015
3 RIYDA 70    £18196    -12230221    423* 733 966 1153 1468 2462 2911 3175+
4 ROAD TO KELLS 8    £-    00000-0    3194
3 ROAMING WEIR 08    £-    000-0000    193 275 459 2984
2 ROAN REEF 8    £313    0343040000    711 987 1088 1190 1323 1576 1647 2608 2987 3081
3 ROARING RIVA 75    £2645    21000-440000    165 249 691 808 2474 2742
2 ROB ROY MACGREGOR 20    £-    4    953
3 ROBBAMA 60    £3796    110-432040    348 1214 1988 2257 2845 3038
3 ROBBIE GRANT 0    £-    000-00    517 1103
4 ROBERTOS FIGHTER 69    £6762    00403-0200    298 2828 3006 3169
3 ROBERTS FLOWER 0    £-    -00    3105 3196
6 ROBERTS GIRL 2    £-    -0000-00    177 343
3 ROBIS 26    £537    33000-4000200    24 368 545 733 1256 1998 2216
5 ROBROB 13    £-    14000-0000    84 172 495 836
5 ROCABAY BLUE 32    £-    10003-000    196 789 2296
2 ROCHES 0    £-    000    2716 2878 3080
2 ROCK A LITTLE 0    £-    00000    1650 1883 2095 2580 2990
2 ROCK CHANTEUR 68    £10000    0030    2232 2384 2635 2771
3 ROCK ISLET 66    £-    -0    389
2 ROCK MACHINE 48    £3346    44102    2167 2423 2717* 3019 3122
2 ROCK OF AGES 33    £-    00    2418 2703
4 ROCK SALT 0    £-    -00-0000    651 1136 2322 2891
3 ROCKALL 14    £511    34030-043000004    132 380 461 609 823 958 1089 2230 2344
2 ROCKETS OAK 0    £-    00    2026 3059
2 ROCKFAST 41    £-    0    752
2 ROCKFELLA 62    £6243    231    800 2750 3176*
3 ROCKHOLD PRINCESS 13    £-    000-00000    171 658 774 1540 2092
4 ROCKMARTIN 46    £1006    10020-000200    248 432 724 1581 1793 2431
3 ROCKVILLE SQUAW 0    £-    00440-0000    1244 1364 1827 1990
2 ROCKY HORROR 14    £-    0000    1075 1555 2646 2841
3 ROCKY ROYALE 0    £-    -0    2515
5 ROCKYS GAL 25    £-    41-11-0    3187
3 RODISTYLE 0    £-    -0000    732 966 1472 2533
2 RODOMONT 54    £650    043    571 2869 3099
2 ROEWOOD 0    £-    0    1675
3 ROHILA 39    £-    -040    941 1193 1580
3 ROI DE SOLEIL 1    £145    000-00030000    535 843 1309 1705 1989 2184 2497 2857
2 ROKER ROAR 15    £-    000    515 780 1296
3 ROLAMPAGO 0    £-    -0    1102
2 ROLFESON 28    £-    4400    2029 2499 3011 3188
6 ROMAN BEACH 48    £9438    04400-00004112    433 680 706 976 1551 2255* 3113* 3231
2 ROMAN BELLE 32    £493    0304    1322 1632 2043 2969
2 ROMAN GUNNER 60    £5390    0130    1903 2239* 2571 2830
7 ROMAN RULER 18    £-    00000-0040    1066 1367 1461 2021
4 ROMAN TRACK 0    £-    -000    1068 1186 1349
4 ROMANA 26    £-    00101-000    235 375 526
2 ROMANTIC PRINCE 46    £-    0    3176
3 ROMANTIC UNCLE 42    £1409    23021-0200040    196 478 586 914 2390 2443 3113
2 ROMANY LAD 24    £223    02    502 763
4 ROMIOSINI 39    £5202    32103-04110000    584 695 872* 1024* 1112 1409 1509 2220
8 ROMOSS 29    £-    23000-0    3231
2 ROOF GHOST 27    £337    2    2168
3 ROPER ROW 37    £6765    020-0113323    516 1418* 1627+ 1922 2204 2277- 2660
5 ROSANNA OF TEDFOLD 6    £-    00043-000000    176 432 709 984 1923 2034
2 ROSE DUET 18    £1458    00100320    181 446 711* 813 1100 1181 1478 1741
2 ROSE LOUBET 21    £269    00003000    417 1067 2364 2652 2815 3058 3182 3190
2 ROSE MEADOW 0    £-    000    450 1225 3103
3 ROSE OF THE SEA 71    £6542    43-00330    155 373 1011 1889 2916
2 ROSE OF TUDOR 4    £-    0000    1376 1881 2127 2872
3 ROSE PORT 0    £-    -00    684 1063
2 ROSE REEF 60    £5191    22    2750- 2951
4 ROSE ROCKET 6    £-    0400-0    1871
3 ROSE WINDOW 0    £-    0-0000    247 328 907 1104
4 ROSEDALE USA 74    £45334    ----2-212210222    231 347* 552 902 1218* 1679 2201 2908 3173
3 ROSI NOA 22    £1544    0-30000102    315 423 822 1031 1558 1969* 2103 2515
4 ROSIE DICKINS 13    £5781    1222403043140000300    124* 211 355 490 649 820 1093 1182 1347
    1542 1649* 1840 2033 2204 2397 2858 2977 3104 3191
2 ROSIES GLORY 9    £652    0023000    376 1881 2107 2279 2425 2606 3151
2 ROSIES IMAGE 0    £-    000000    197 523 610 2127 2323 2471
5 ROSIES MEMBER 0    £-    -0    3030
2 ROSINSKY 0    £-    00    1622 1795
7 ROSSETT 3    £2918    0000-0004002100    830 1074 1136 1547 1761 1839 1976 1983* 2086 2891
4 ROSTHERNE 31    £7673    0023-4210400020    4 52 215* 585 686 917 1293 2237 2445 2591
2 ROSY CHEEKS 0    £-    0    3205
4 ROTHERFIELD GREYS 68    £16295    00000-1101011    418* 626* 1145 1508+ 1796 2783* 2921+
3 ROUBAYD 49    £4369    -11000    1833* 2176* 2389 2553 2855
2 ROUGH DANCE 33    £1123    042430    1598 2067 2320 2625 2922 3079
3 ROUGH PASSAGE 38    £-    -000    90 1437 1833
2 ROUMELI 30    £5213    4423031220    353 544 722 1968 2178 2310 2512* 2648- 2806- 2989
2 ROUNDLET 71    £7970    4102    1452 1643* 1887 2146
2 ROUSHAYD 56    £1331    24    2484 2673
3 ROVE 38    £4316    0301-124300    6* 233 428 671 814 1001
2 ROWEKING 45    £2124    0201343    21 86- 242 367* 440 523 610
3 ROWIE 0    £-    -0    16
10 ROYABER 0    £-    34000-000    710 1074 1139
3 ROYAL ARIES 0    £-    000-00    2411 2660
2 ROYAL ASTRONAUT 15    £-    00    2657 3143
8 ROYAL BAIZE 0    £-    -0    1837
4 ROYAL BEAR 0    £1018    000-22043000000    30 84 124 211 266 418 734 1066 1344 1610 1616
```

```
3 ROYAL BERKS    4   £584   3000-0004302000    83 454 1472 1836 1942 2186 2313 2581 2929 3185
6 ROYAL CONDOR   0   £-    0   2317
5 ROYAL CRAFTSMAN 8  £785   .00-10-00303000    92 341 582 841 1035 1348 1388 2733
2 ROYAL CROFTER  44  £1256   32224   1090 1305 1561 2100 2380
3 ROYAL CRUSADER 0   £-    0-00   937 1340
8 ROYAL DUTY     5   £-    10000-000   1703 1839 2762
3 ROYAL DYNASTY  49  £1260   -0001240   371 720 1031 2042- 2666- 2937 3110
3 ROYAL EFFIGY   17  £259   000-01D400000    25 66 140 357 506 623 949 3203
6 ROYAL EXPORT   4   £135   -0000-030   163 993 1374
3 ROYAL FAN      36  £8111   -00100002001    438 593 891* 1371 1794 2038 2295 2397 3015 3104 3233*
5 ROYAL HALO     60  £12300   30234-2011102    176 265 1186* 1517* 1792* 2331 2477
2 ROYAL ILLUSION 10  £-    0000   43 1660 2218 3221
3 ROYAL INFATUATION 73  £-   0   901
3 ROYAL LOCH     0   £-    -0   402
3 ROYAL LOFT     69  £22783   1-22144   1153 1487 1851* 2145 2633
2 ROYAL MEETING  0   £-    00   3025 3184
3 ROYAL NATIVE   0   £-    -0   2929
3 ROYAL NUGGET   45  £780   322-0403   213 776 1220 1902
2 ROYAL PAGEANT  56  £596   3   3171
2 ROYAL RABBLE   10  £1901   0204231000000    73 118 261 417 681 882 1059* 1440 1522 2218 2405 2535
3182
2 ROYAL RESPECT  0   £-    0   2710
2 ROYAL ROB      44  £358   03   2939 3135
3 ROYAL ROCKS    58  £3390   -2   895
3 ROYAL ROUSER   20  £2467   00000-00001300    997 1371 1637 2027 2139+ 2424 2681 3033
2 ROYAL SPECIAL  7   £-    000   1370 1738 1949
2 ROYAL TOWER    21  £-    000   1869 2975 3153
3 ROYAL TREASURER 83  £38445   3   3097
2 ROYAL TREATY   28  £2064   000331100    47 186 425 865 1012 1137* 1413* 1566 2512
3 ROYAL TROUBADOR 44  £1477   0-0004302   229 600 2294 2534 2713 2784 3070
6 ROYAL VALEUR   3   £-    00   1985 2101
6 ROYSIA BOY     46  £12376   101-00003000110    374 952 1285 1608 1933 2079 2519 2715 2862+ 3015*
3055
3 RUE ST JACQUES 18  £1155   0-3330000    498 764 1036 1821 2155 2294 2594
5 RUFCHA         0   £-    10000-0   1348
5 RULE OF THE SEA 38  £602   13000/20   144 308
2 RULING DYNASTY 36  £736   2   3131
2 RUMBA ROYALE   0   £-    00   3111 3234
2 RUMBOOGIE      62  £7780   010300   2232 2392* 2460 2695 2907 3039
2 RUN BY         34  £-    0040   460 2717 3082 3230
3 RUN BY JOVE    22  £6533   0-0012002230000    194 357 674* 789 956 1091 1371 1613 1924 2508 2671
3060 3164
3 RUN CHARLIE    16  £219   000-0020   1256 1937 2077 2293
4 RUN FOR FRED   0   £-    20030-000000    41 963 1201 1567 1703 1839
3 RUN FOR YOUR WIFE 18  £1370   40004-302430230    1212 1439 1748 2075 2346 2492 2714 2874 2988
3 RUN HIGH       36  £959   -010   625 1700* 2240
2 RUN LITTLE LADY 40  £1598   421   1187 2814 2982*
2 RUN TO WORK    17  £740   422334040   633 865 957 1248 1478 1717 1955 2323 2588
3 RUNAWAY        35  £-    20004-000000000    6 165 443 914 1283 1505 2378 2469 2660
2 RUNLAD         0   £-    00   2696 3037
5 RUNNING BULL   8   £-    42000-000000   399 855 1870 2039 2602 2728
4 RUNNING FLUSH  38  £2990   040-00430010400    17 112 248 453 618 1109 1519* 1931 2260 3119 3232
2 RUNNING MONEY  23  £-    00000   2177 2379 2468 2798 2936
3 RUNNING RAINBOW 6  £-    30000-0000   6 241 784 910
2 RUNNING STEPS  32  £-    00   2847 3133
3 RUPERT BROOKE  10  £494   40000-0024200   335 538 963 1288 1562 1824 2083
3 RUPERTS DAUGHTER 0  £-   00000-000   1277 1451 1549
7 RURAL SCENE    0   £-    -00   105 308
2 RUSHLUAN       44  £264   002   2847 3014 3205-
8 RUSHMOOR       27  £3244   -0330-4003144    319 462 634 933 1159* 1417 2338
4 RUSSELL CREEK  24  £-    41100-000000   238 433 1047 1987 2219 2443
4 RUSSELL FLYER  5   £100   0-0000040300000    30 122 327 495 1086 1213 1367 1574 1849 1990 2370
2519 2621
2 RUSSIAN AFFAIR 0   £-    0   3228
3 RUSSIAN LADY   61  £22188   2   397
3 RUSSIAN LOGIC  51  £2518   -2221   191 1167- 1290 1807*
2 RUSSIAN LULLABY 35  £-    04   2901 3141
5 RUSSIAN NOBLE  50  £6025   03402-22300   976- 1112 1409 2220 2523
3 RUSSIAN RELATION 46  £883   -031   1818 2996 3061*
2 RUSSIAN ROVER  49  £240   4   2056
2 RUSSIAN STEPPE 54  £964   ,1   2341*
2 RUSSIAN WALTZ  39  £111   003   773 2270 2658
11 RUSSIAN WINTER 0  £2224   03000-00003100    412 890 1131 1196 1616 1682* 1718 2632
3 RUSSKI         28  £-    0-000   479 1607 2132
3 RUSTIC AMBER   74  £12866   02210-3100   472 639+ 903 1125
2 RUSTIC EYES    15  £641   23000   1625 1764 2050 2218 2608
6 RUSTIC TRACK   5   £2385   031-32000300100   131 281 609 827 1432 1744 1909 2037* 2360 2762 3060
4 RUSTLING       25  £741   00320-0032   8 2093 2401 2490
2 RUSTY LADY     50  £-    10200   2999
4 RUSTY LAW      30  £-    3-030-000000   1038 1237 1935 2303 2699 3050
2 RUWI VALLEY    20  £904   00203   2254 2748 2841 2936 3112
2 RUWIYDA        42  £-    4   3068
5 RYANS DOVE     0   £-    -00   164 2958
3 RYE HILL MARINER 30  £125   04-030   357 894 1022
2 RYESONG        0   £-    40   1298 2138
2 RYLANDS REEF   16  £-    404400   882 1161 1339 1635 3016 3182
3 RYMOS          15  £779   ---00-332030   2705 2795 2984 3100 3203 3224
3 S S SANTO      22  £3154   0-2200012300   35 169 356 774 1656 1898* 2386 2604 2727 3087
5 SAALIB         25  £184   40-20000   283 438 997 3140 3195
2 SABLE LAKE     48  £272   3   558
2 SABOTEUR       25  £-    0000   1253 2095 2708 3188
2 SAD CAFE       47  £518   04   1287 1641
3 SADEEM         75  £13467   -3112   849 1152* 1652* 2257
```

```
4 SAFE CUSTODY  15   £207    40100-0000400    453 566 775 1390 1781 2154 3195
4 SAFE RIVER  52   £7276    01221-4401302    225 363 519 801* 1293 2220 2510-
3 SAFEERA  52   £5145    41411-034100    387 929 1169 1532* 1854 2390
2 SAFETY PIN  50   £2820    14    1869* 2252
3 SAFFAN  44   £8822    03-321222122    188 1123 1362* 1615 1671 1763 2861* 2978 3101-
2 SAFFRON LIGHT  0   £-  0    3037
3 SAGAREME  23   £-    00400-400000    66 123 839 1688 2048 2304
4 SAGAX  31   £184    00/0020    448 613 3035 3159
2 SAGRES  0   £-  0    2707
4 SAHARA SHADOW  6   £3174    000-12100000000    845* 1211 1273* 1394 1500 1581 2132 2282 3065 3145
3204
2 SAHOOD  0   £-  000    2547 3067 3131
3 SAHRAAN  25   £556    -0200000    229 528 1469 1951 2226 2602 2931
5 SAILOR MISS  0   £-  -0    1519
4 SAILORS REWARD  39   £2763    03004-04100    126 504 634* 663 942
4 SAILORS SONG  54   £8797    4-0000000120331    374 616 687 1145 1429 1608 2072 2207* 2544 2773 2945
3021 3124*
4 SAINT ESTEPHE  86   £121852    32123-131220    154* 468 885+ 1493 2736 2917
3 SAINT SAMBA  75   £24435    -11    1219* 3094*
2 SAINTE JOIE  66   £10596    321    2215 2540 2933*
4 SAINTLY LAD  28   £-    0004-000    403 532 618
2 SAINTS ABOVE  0   £-  0    3047
3 SAIYYAAF  6   £-    -0004    183 258 334 2585
3 SAKER  59   £1660    -04010    371 572 714 2622+ 3021
2 SAKURA REIKO  79   £59222    11123    2358* 2737 2915
2 SALAZIE  46   £964    1    3201*
3 SALCHOW  75   £29232    1112-1023    463* 1128 2525 2952
3 SALES PROMOTER  16   £-    000-04000    275 342 420 832 1551
2 SALINAS  27   £137    0030    852 2600 2895 3189
4 SALLOOM  25   £302    02100-0300400    652 912 1166 1243 1744 2837 2896
3 SALLOW KITTEN  0   £-  -0    209
4 SALLUSTIO  3   £-    -0000-0    1543
2 SALLY FOXTROT  2   £-    00000    515 1972 2396 3153 3222
3 SALLY SAYS SO  45   £1104    10-40200    803 1107 1768 2196 2851
2 SALLYS WON  0   £-    00    2574 2708
2 SALOP ROUGE  0   £-    0000    2365 2757 2919 2994
2 SALOPARD  44   £124    03    3037 3201
3 SALTCOTE HOPEFUL  19   £-    13100-0    729
4 SALUS  56   £1802    3    1856
3 SALYF  64   £1250    -3134-3    303
3 SAMANPOUR  48   £8685    0001-1113020330    193* 275* 547* 683 1130 1462 2053 2331 2420 3113
3 SAMARID  76   £13246    3140-010104    945 1332* 1823 2419* 2740 2808
3 SAMBA LASS  6   £965    000-03201000    237 377 729 871 1334* 1627 3057 3144
2 SAMEEK  52   £5840    213002    405 583* 876 2460 2511 2725
4 SAMHAAN  43   £16307    2.410301121323020    310 578 689* 812 976 1112 1335+ 1450* 1553 2121* 2219
2331 2477 2693 2924 3113
2 SAMLEON  48   £4843    412340310    61 200* 278- 513 1003 1585 2047 2181+ 2694
3 SAMOSA  0   £-    -0000    688 862 1220 1337
2 SAMPREKI  0   £-    00    2471 2707
2 SAMS REFRAIN  15   £540    301D04402    86 354 502 633 831 1449 1949 2180
5 SAMS WOOD  39   £4666    00000-010000    976 1189* 1601 2755 2867 2934
4 SAN CARLOS  21   £-    04340-0    204
2 SAN JUAN SONG  0   £-    0000    2270 2518 2841 3080
3 SANA SONG  6   £357    040-20000030    134 258 605 891 1051 1617 2412 2679
2 SANAABELL  56   £3329    21    1996 2531+
2 SANAM  77   £65993    4101211    1019 1149* 1465 2035+ 2384- 2821* 3009*
3 SANCILIA  13   £-    00-00000000    1228 1516 1654 1730 2143 2256 2653 2948
4 SAND DOLLAR  24   £1806    00-133003    1614* 1904 2037 2149 2581 2891
3 SAND SHIP  68   £25732    241    1214 2642 2912*
4 SANDALL PARK  44   £5455    4140421    583 771* 859 2689 2843 3027 3226+
4 SANDBOURNE  14   £-    30-00-00000    481 636 830 1273 1394
7 SANDCRACKER  0   £-    -0    319
2 SANDHURST  40   £119    300    180 404 614
2 SANDIS GOLD  12   £-    4000    337 543 939 1083
3 SANDITTON PALACE  45   £4517    000-00404310120    516 670 910 977 1171 1344 1476* 1542 1687* 1878-
2055
2 SANDMOOR DANCER  0   £-  0    3111
3 SANDMOOR PRINCE  0   £-    000-00000    307 648 697 1042 1141
3 SANDRON  2   £367    00020-0303003    67 237 377 1549 1990 2174 2616
3 SANDS OF TIME  31   £2826    41032    1363 1672* 1936 2081 2218
3 SANDY BILL  0   £-    -0000    1690 2034 2293 3202
5 SANDYLA  22   £233    20--0-0240    19 1071 1251 1652
3 SANET  30   £1102    -440030    123 273 926 1589 2152 3061
2 SANNOX BAY  49   £964    01    2675 3074+
2 SANSIYA  54   £1711    1    3189+
4 SANTA DOMINGA  35   £1750    4-3    1709
2 SANTELLA GREY  60   £2266    0222    678 953 1241 1660
3 SANTELLA MAC  70   £5065    01-10002    847* 1147 1912 2475 2851
7 SANTELLA MAN  0   £-  0    2034
5 SANTELLA PAL  0   £877    00000-020430000    174 540 727 940 1211 1581 2046 2374 2617
2 SANTELLA SAM  63   £8055    23201200    1289 1452 1731 2384 2468+ 2571 2771 3126
3 SANTIKI  78   £53483    3-241331312    372 551 779* 1128 1408 1811+ 2452 2630+ 2909
3 SANTO BOY  17   £-    00-00    2400 2683
2 SANTO PRINCESS  0   £-    00400000    252 483 939 1693 1949 2298 2712 2872
4 SANTOPADRE  8   £247    -0003-30    893 2267
2 SAPPHARINO  1   £-    000000    1405 1738 2470 2994 3017 3182
2 SARA LANE  0   £-  0    2651
5 SARAB  81   £110415    10304-311104121    413 759* 1118* 1492* 2259 2538 2785* 3020- 3168*
2 SARASOTA  19   £344    0024000340    21 94 354 483 1828 2071 2272 2927 2987 3190
3 SARASOTA SPRING  70   £14002    -14    556* 1114
4 SARAVANTA  0   £-    -0000-000000    679 855 1400 1567 1937 2697
4 SAREMA  6   £-    -0424-00    41 710
3 SARFRAZ  70   £28012    42-01110111    430 841* 983* 1058+ 1388 1875* 2031* 2754*
                                                > 1013 <
```

```
2 SARIETTA  0   £-   0   2531
2 SARIHAH  42   £3554   012230   728 1075* 1531 1916 2097 2482
3 SARIZA  40   £1706   -42232   941 1228 1375 1541 1947
3 SARONICOS  46   £7217   00-32230304410   194 388 739 1645 1912 2170 2408 2551 2769 3026+ 3232
2 SAROS BRIG  64?   £75524   3   3209
2 SARSHARA  57   £1594   2   3037
3 SARYAN  40   £2602   00-041100300   402 1290 1372* 1620* 1923 2486 2704 2850 3113
5 SASEBO  63   £7247   42   1712 2354
3 SATCO  73   £18818   2-11440   1117* 1354 2738 3091
3 SATIAPOUR  52   £4852   043-20122220   438 593 844* 1001 1169- 1436 1648 2123
3 SATIN AND SILK  38   £2164   -3002140   1244 1902 2170 2393 2548* 2676 3236
3 SATISFACTION  58   £12005   00-2200102   619 1023 1130 1469 1776* 2219 2763
3 SATIVA  0   £-   00-0   1340
2 SAUCE DIABLE  60   £4557   210010   1030 1311+ 1850 2158 2729* 2865
2 SAUCE OF THE SEA  0   £-   000   2645 2838 3192
2 SAUCIER  9   £-   0004000   73 473 1083 1262 1537 1692 1949
3 SAUGHTREES  14   £1108   000-003001   637 874 1567 1990 2174 2429*
2 SAUNDERS LASS  20   £2815   021034200   725 1434 1647* 2137 2435 2792 2859- 3125 3188
3 SAVAGE LOVE  35   £-   30-40   506 839
2 SAVANNA KING  0   £-   000   1681 2029 2325
3 SAVE IT LASS  8   £-   -400   2593 3159 3217
2 SAVONNERIE  65   £6872   213   3166
2 SAWDUST JACK  13   £-   00000   364 515 603 2470 2607
3 SAXELBYE PARK  0   £-   00-000   546 733 868
3 SAXON BAZAAR  6   £-   004-000400000   83 157 328 837 1065 1231 1560 1835 2429
2 SAXON MIRCEL  24   £-   000   2812 3109 3176
2 SAXON STAR  53   £4943   144434   311* 601 737 995 1925 2181
3 SAY PARDON  32   £2786   23220-2200100   1033 1391 1505 1654 2312* 2416 2483
7 SAY PLEASE  0   £-   -00   381 607
2 SAY PRINCESS  58   £4140   10   292* 638
3 SAY SOMETHING  30   £368   000-22000   45 123 381 769 991
2 SAY YES  53   £627   3   292
2 SAY YOU  26   £-   00000   2205 2561 2812 2920 3132
2 SAY YOU WILL  22   £238   40040440   503 728 1363 1570 1785 2178 2897 3182
2 SCALLYKATH  20   £184   200   200 3163 3200
3 SCARBOROUGH  16   £-   000-04   247 492
2 SCARLET BLADE  60   £8974   1   3053*
2 SCARLET CREST  0   £-   0   3067
3 SCARLET DANCER  0   £-   -0000   862 1198 1469 2497
2 SCARNING SHADYLADY  0   £-   00000   1059 1308 1496 1723 1832
2 SCARNING SPARKLER  0   £-   0000   40 181 329 3031
2 SCATTERED SHOWERS  40   £315   02   2119 2904
2 SCAWSBY LEES  27   £752   03430   1161 1370 1561 2052 2140
3 SCENTED SILENCE  0   £-   0-0000   937 2314 2442 2876
2 SCHMUTZIG  42   £930   02   1928 2889
5 SCHOLAR  0   £-   -0000   19 164 420 530
6 SCHULA  22   £460   00400-0034   12 30 1060 1227
2 SCHUYGULLA  35   £870   342340   694 927 1475 1762 2615 2798
2 SCIERPAN  40   £2026   2200   533- 1874 2158 2871
2 SCIMITARRA  69   £4654   011   2436 2788+ 3025*
3 SCINTILLATOR  8   £503   000-000000033   1028 1281 1362 1788 1864 1989 2394 2818 2932
5 SCOOP THE KITTY  0   £-   00-00-0000   46 163 960 1156
2 SCOTCH IMP  31   £147   2   254
2 SCOTTISH FLING  38   £1259   3330204   108 146 242 571 1174 3178 3221
8 SCOTTISH GREEN  0   £-   00   1766 2374
4 SCOTTISH REEL  88   £98250   11240-2120   313- 598+ 1877 2259
4 SCOTTISH ROSE  19   £-   2000-00   50 185
7 SCOUTSMISTAKE  39   £1405   00020-000332   815 1018 1109 1335 1500 1673
5 SCREES  36   £3091   -0213   7 88 208* 256
3 SEA BARN  0   £-   -0   1444
2 SEA DARA  70   £28663   13101   1030* 1381 1641* 2235 2910*
3 SEA POWER  42   £2504   03-03422   806 2408 2701 3105 3227
3 SEA SHANTY  5   £-   0040-00   1943 2088
3 SEA TROUPER  0   £-   00-00000   500 839 1694 2271 2597
3 SEA VENOM  0   £-   000-000   1898 2060 2417
2 SEABURY  18   £-   00000   780 864 1069 1421 1681
2 SEAGO  8   £-   00000-0040   1171 1521 1819 2271
3 SEAMERE  8   £489   0-000200   1607 1841 2399 2746 2985 3086
6 SEAN BE FRIENDLY  0   £-   00-00-00   745 936
2 SEARCH THE WIND  0   £-   0   1097
7 SEASONS DELIGHT  9   £-   00/40-0   126
4 SEAT OF LEARNING  6   £-   -000   1494 1652 2096
2 SEATON GIRL  13   £1042   420014000   40 108 376 957 1121* 1358 1622 1881 2323
3 SEATYRN  26   £303   42430-340000   487 699 916 2441 2551 2682
2 SEBS MARK  0   £-   00   1311 1869
3 SECLUSIVE  25   £-   01400-040000   538 674 816 1956 2053 2604
2 SECOOT  45   £869   030   927 1049 3137
3 SECRET FACT  0   £-   -000   835 1516 1902
7 SECRET FINALE  3   £-   2-200-0   2141
3 SECRET FORM  81   £119429   11-22214   467 755 1116 2918* 3168
3 SECRET LIFE  67   £-   -00   300 1594
2 SECRET TELLER  0   £-   0   2080
3 SECRET WEDDING  47   £1241   30310-2324   209 505 779 2068
5 SECURITY CLEARANCE  36   £656   00000-0030020   375 542 590 712 841 1016 1159
3 SECURITY PACIFIC  20   £-   03040-000000   518 1840 2084 2816 3033 3104
3 SEE NO EVIL  16   £2052   40000-0000010   455 637 928 1245 1471 1989* 2508
4 SEEHASE  46   £3203   2   1148
2 SEEK THE TRUTH  52   £2886   214   1650 2043* 2368
2 SEGOVIAN  9   £978   200000000   230 497 565 678 1241 1693 2421 2700 3132
4 SEISMIC WAVE  80   £61880   00122-0322204   251 385 585 704 1005 1127 1456
2 SELECT COMPANY  29   £-   0   2225
3 SELL IT KILROY  32   £1855   -000130   546 806 941 1309* 2300 2551
3 SELORCELE  0   £-   -U0000   284 426 516 1562 1734
```

```
2 SEMIS  23   £-   000000   252 577 848 1162 2254 2524
2 SEND IT DOWN  0   £-   000000   488 785 1069 1843 2150 3048
3 SENDER  31   £1679   -01202000   357 595* 1204 1559 1964 2175 2604 2937
2 SENDIM ON SAM  31   £234   00003   1090 1266 1972 2127 2969
4 SENOR RAMOS  33   £4000   3200-0000000110   17 308 429 584 629 933 1254 1374+ 1613* 1909
3 SENOR TOMAS  54   £3820   -1000   619* 2156 3119 3232
2 SENSATIONAL LADY  17   £-   0   1996
2 SENSITIVE MATERIAL  0   £-   00   2555 3181
3 SEPARATE LIVES  0   £-   -0   2152
2 SEPARATE REALITIES  32   £-   400   2019 2615 2761
2 SEPTEMBER SNAP  18   £-   0   3131
3 SEQUESTRATION  0   £-   00-400000000   203 496 760 1066 1191 1364 1549 1827 2898
3 SEQUESTRATOR  21   £1696   3000-0001000403   424 886 1169 1316* 1664 1922 2313 2463 2681 3033
2 SERAGSBEE  0   £-   00   1518 3120
3 SERAPHINO  0   £-   -0   1586
2 SERGEANT MERYLL  22   £409   00300   685 1050 2050 2512 2798
2 SERGEANT SMOKE  37   £-   000   2554 2782 3130
2 SERGEYEVICH  52   £465   20   2547 3137
2 SERVE N VOLLEY  38   £-   4   2926
5 SESIN  72   £3031   -1-44   557 3010
2 SETTER COUNTRY  25   £1242   0143030   170 329* 596 948 1294 2181 2529
2 SEUL ETOILE  0   £-   0   1097
2 SEULEMENT  17   £533   30000   999 1187 2664 3146 3228
3 SEVEN HILLS  33   £6134   000-000311130   487 648 958 1615 2015* 2128* 2346* 2647 2834
5 SEVEN SWALLOWS  15   £1569   01230-10000000   184* 263 439 609 1787 2049 2260 2746
2 SEVENTH SONG  0   £-   0   2774
4 SEVERN BORE  76   £-   32203-00   325 413
3 SEVERS  60   £3954   -031   546 1046 1291*
3 SEW HIGH  46   £12994   1-0010411030002   6 65 246+ 447 814 1044 1704+ 1852 2151 2362 2870 3015
3124
2 SHABIB  47   £-   40   715 1129
4 SHAD RABUGK  3   £-   000-0-000000   36 129 333 547 731 850
2 SHADE OF PALE  34   £5166   12243   2032* 2391 2479 2611 2707
3 SHADES OF AUTUMN  16   £-   -000400   431 656 923 2186 2367 2601
5 SHADES OF BLUE  16   £446   03000-20040000   160 266 508 748 1066 1649 1852 2046
2 SHADES OF NIGHT  40   £5443   221414   73 252 376* 2172 2485* 2865
2 SHADIYAMA  26   £253   020   1440 1716 2191
2 SHADY BLADE  6   £477   0202000   672 858 1012 1121 1684 2743 2919
3 SHADY HEIGHTS  81   £28444   122   2418+ 2695 3039-
2 SHAFT OF SUNLIGHT  25   £-   00   2696 2846
3 SHAFY  64   £5834   32-4110   402 863+ 1507* 2784
3 SHAHAAB  65   £-   14-0   224
2 SHAHDJI  42   £-   0   3037
3 SHAHRASTANI  95   £688544   2-111144   324* 574* 878+ 1330+ 1790 2917
5 SHAHREEN  0   £217   00000-0003000   977 1319 1542 1849 2033 2213 2621
3 SHAHS CHOICE  38   £4821   -00-0432221212   579 1295 1517 1980 2188 2492 2682* 2802 3035* 3129
2 SHAIKIYA  69   £10937   124   1946* 2564- 2831
2 SHAINE  12   £-   00000   979 1289 2341 2989 3178
3 SHAJAR AD DURR  20   £119   -030   1554 1670 2048
3 SHAKANA  37   £-   2-000   1043 1469 3077
3 SHAKE THE KING  0   £-   00-000   164 307 697
3 SHAKEEB  22   £-   00-0000   688 849 1639 1726
4 SHALBEE  3   £-   00000-00000   734 1037 1235 1521 2046
7 SHALLAAL  8   £1394   000120   119 1056 1459 2654* 2877 3196
2 SHAMAYIL  25   £-   0   3130
3 SHAMIYDA  44   £909   0-03440   980 1444 1645 1776 2170
2 SHANAMA  0   £-   0   2768
4 SHANDON BELLS  2   £-   -0000   381 492 770 1416
2 SHANNON COTTAGE  46   £829   3   3120
2 SHANNON LADY  32   £-   00   1843 2082
2 SHANNON RIVER  13   £-   00000   1936 2089 2328 3130 3226
3 SHANNON VALE  35   £-   01-004   2458 2650 3070
6 SHANOUSKA  13   £2256   0/400-2100   110 135+ 369 412
2 SHANTAROUN  53   £1384   02   2484 3023
6 SHARAD  0   £1284   40440-000000100   734 986 1196 1344 1940 2245 2318* 2731 2783
3 SHARANIYA  79   £37019   2111   2825* 3006*
3 SHARASAR  8   £-   0400-0000   174 507 726 963
2 SHARBLASK  48   £803   22   2423 2791
4 SHARDARI  94   £286944   21D11-2412102   475 885 1456* 1790- 2200+ 2917 3097
3 SHAREEF  20   £-   -0040   371 576 2430 2701
3 SHARI LOUISE  27   £-   004P0-000   1033 1443 1584
3 SHARK FIGHTER  15   £-   01310-000000   414 465 830 1051 1500 1689
3 SHARKEN  76   £11960   4-3144   1009 1595
7 SHARLIES WIMPY  22   £2132   0400-0240000030   520 687 881 1182 1536 2295 2411 2715 2966 3104
3 SHARONS ROYALE  30   £7334   0-0003244144141   936 1081 1309 1614 1794 2076 2264 2413* 2426 2728
2891* 3029 3078*
2 SHARP EGO  0   £-   0   3200
3 SHARP GIRL  72   £7429   0143020   2825 3006
4 SHARP NOBLE  61   £3517   12001-0222400   17 166 263 445 618 1095 3008
3 SHARP REEF  0   £-   -000000   1244 2092 2422 2546 2988 3063
2 SHARP REMINDER  63   £3342   00313003   457 804 1241 2561* 2694 2954 3122 3226
4 SHARP ROMANCE  70   £5902   00-233000000004   18- 70 165 705 903 1146 1268 1823 2538 2772 2916
3092
5 SHARP SHOT  18   £743   -4000-0000200   499 1273 2189 2581 2891 3078 3157
5 SHARP SONG  18   £2444   030-3-13   1271* 1422
3 SHARP STABLE  0   £-   0-000   431 842 1499
3 SHARP TIMES  25   £4808   0-0210210   140 305 809* 1312 1742 2033+ 3145
2 SHARP VICTOR  68   £4096   012   2119 2547* 2767-
3 SHARPETTO  56   £8111   -00110400   218 402 576* 1001* 1145 1457 2343 2446
2 SHARPHAVEN  20   £4290   340302410020230   170 317 417 819 934 1119 1294 1379* 1528 1907 2279 2396
2777 3081 3182
3 SHARROOD  82   £57302   01111-04303220   226 407 640 878 1096 1597 2259 2506
3 SHAYI  15   £-   -0000   217 1399 1607 2659
                              > 1015 <
```

```
4 SHE KNOWS IT ALL  15   £-   11000-000000   1060 1344 1834 2245 2592 2702
7 SHEEPSCOTE  0   £-   -0   943
2 SHEER AUDACITY  22   £-   0   2652
3 SHEER CLASS  0   £-   -00000400   764 1063 1340 1827 2073 2208 2515 2597
3 SHEER LUCK  38   £5349   04-0010204   937 1193 1657* 2217 2676 2911 3179
3 SHEER NECTAR  30   £986   -0001   2131 2304 2548 3086*
2 SHEER ROYALTY  49   £5286   0410020   167 1996 2153* 2485 2611 2753- 2843
3 SHEHANA  38   £165   4431-030   372 3030 3142
2 SHELDON MILLS  37   £-   0444   2147 2434 2658 3189
4 SHELLEY MARIE  0   £-   00000-00   2271 2621
4 SHELLMAN  33   £1618   0300000000000030   17 248 410 584 698 872 1047 1698 1820 2066 2219 2296 2437 2475 2629
2 SHENLEY ROMP  0   £-   000   187 513 913
2 SHER SHAH  30   £-   0   3075
3 SHEREEKA  29   £819   2-3000   158 422 1055 1695
3 SHERGOR  42   £693   -2020   2269 2464 2759 2996
3 SHERKRAINE  64   £950   32-200   148 294 754
4 SHERPAMAN  0   £-   00000-0000   36 105 542 1124
3 SHERZAD  50   £306   -404   806 1046 1503
3 SHESINGH  0   £-   0-0000   546 774 1063 1340
3 SHIBIL  55   £13525   33-443222104   224 384 555 1022 1437- 1923 2183* 2438 2582
5 SHIELDAIG  6   £-   00000-0   1058
3 SHINING POPPY  49   £628   23244-20   37 982
3 SHINING SKIN  34   £1849   420-000130   982 1246 2294 2726* 2893 3030
2 SHINING WATER  75   £29063   42110130   852 1282 1440+ 1668* 1919 2384+ 2751 3126
8 SHINY COPPER  16   £1626   10000-00243300   58A 121 204 235 504 663 942 3139
4 SHINY KAY  24   £-   -004404040   549 702 935 1160 1530 1822 2995 3115 3217
3 SHIP OF STATE  60   £4420   23-4010   362 572 1645* 2156
3 SHIPBOURNE  47   £4789   -0003031130   430 619 669 1233 1569 1873 2111* 2280* 2591 3052
5 SHIPWRIGHT  0   £-   -0000   92 358 542 735
2 SHIRBELLA  36   £461   03   1801 3137
8 SHIRLEY GROVE  0   £-   -00   1952 2169
3 SHIRLSTAR TAXSAVER  20   £-   00-0400000   351 635 849 1085 1939 2148 2432
4 SHIRLY ANN  0   £449   00000/2000200   31 710 1077 1771 2960 3057 3084
3 SHIRZAD  21   £1015   0-004330   231 458 1023 1402 1733 2134
3 SHMAIREEKH  61   £5724   22000-2020000   330- 433 881 1109 1490 2359 2773
2 SHOOT THE MOON  0   £-   000   1555 1802 2185
2 SHOOTING PARTY  44   £964   01   3053 3199*
4 SHORT SLEEVES  45   £8350   -310-0100   310 521* 1047 1176
5 SHOSTAKOVITCH  0   £-   3-104-0000   72 189 265 453
4 SHOW HOME  29   £-   2-233-00000   742 977 1145 1380 1542
10 SHOW OF HANDS  11   £492   00000-0200   606 1074 1547 1906
3 SHOWDANCE  0   £127   0-0003000   444 1535 1639 2335 2412 2705 2795
3 SHTAIFEH  52   £260   1-024   1408 2338 2627
3 SHUJUN  25   £-   30200-0000   1327 1751 2161 2393
2 SHUKO  47   £297   04   2983 3176
2 SHUTTLE COCK  61   £10004   220   898 1113 1714
2 SHUTTLECOCK GIRL  30   £2763   4303310   311 722 1187 1528 2025 2137+ 2485
4 SHUTTLECOCK STAR  5   £-   03300-00040   312 504 663 856 1035
3 SHY MISTRESS  0   £207   -040000002   309 729 932 1134 1562 1824 2854 3024 3185
2 SHY PRINCESS  75   £13937   3120   2358 2915
4 SI SIGNOR  56   £7719   11040-42000   245 587 1387 3124 3235
3 SIANS PET  0   £-   -00   769 959
3 SICA SUE  2   £-   0000-000   1841 2184 2795
2 SICILIAN TONY  0   £-   0   2625
5 SIDELAND  0   £-   -0   842
3 SIDONS DAUGHTER  45   £2053   03040-002041   518 886 1224 1371 1541 1677*
4 SIGNORE ODONE  35   £7282   320-40011200043   594 698 912 1415* 1624* 2104 2234 2437 2934 3116 3157
5 SIGNORINA ODONE  0   £-   -00   92 349
3 SIGYM  73   £5000   30   1331 1592
4 SILBANDO  10   £427   00000-000300   734 1060 1344 1730 2124 2715
3 SILCA CHIAVI  34   £642   -00-02   535 1756
4 SILENT GAIN  8   £845   00000-0233000   481 842 1213 1627 2033 2312 2981
4 SILENT JOURNEY  30   £4064   -3030-1200232   256* 398 474 1112 1393 1621 2324
3 SILENT MAJORITY  53   £19822   44-030131141100   241 624 784 977* 1086 1227+ 1391* 1443 2245* 2382* 2731 2783
3 SILENT RUNNING  10   £185   000-00030000400   63 535 623 843 1023 1085 1231 1520 1614 1813 2599
2 SILHOUETTE DANCER  0   £-   0   2847
3 SILK THREAD  48   £-   2-00   370 739
2 SILK TOPPER  55   £4357   01   2159 2920+
4 SILLITOE  7   £-   10300-0000000   429 745 956 1202 1698 2414 2629 2998 3060
6 SILLY BOY  16   £357   000-04000000300   698 893 1249 1335 1525 1976 2296 2762 2998 3060 3164
2 SILVER ANCONA  32   £789   343343   332 437 741 1197 1566 1863
3 SILVER BAND  62   £4000   -1-030   303 562 1009
4 SILVER CANNON  24   £2253   21000-10000000   281* 441 521 724 1081 2998 3060 3236
3 SILVER DRAGON  40   £-   -0   501
5 SILVER EMPRESS  0   £-   -0   2132
3 SILVER FORM  9   £1097   00400-03402000   657 837 1001 1245 1499- 1695 2120 2519
2 SILVER GLANCE  0   £-   00   944 1534
5 SILVER GREEN  76   £16955   1   2828*
2 SILVER HAZE  52   £2134   222   781 973 1634
5 SILVER PROSPECT  14   £-   00304-00   3115 3187
3 SILVER WORD  71   £9328   -42030   1354 2114
2 SILVERCOAST  44   £339   033   2365 2651 3074
4 SILVERMERE GOLF  0   £-   0-00   1400 2422
2 SILVERS ERA  26   £3305   02040034103   383 473 627 873 1050 1828 2010 2137 2425* 2843 2903
2 SILVINO  73   £-   31032-0   226
4 SIMLA RIDGE  35   £3609   -00130020400   245 330 628* 977 1125 1268 1805 2160 2530 2833 3046
3 SIMON DAMIAN  0   £-   0-0   839
4 SIMON SACC  66   £24500   31   2457 2641*
3 SIMONS FANTASY  11   £2493   00-0443410000   127 843 1087 1309 1553 1724* 1838 2109 2381 2709
2 SIMPLE TASTE  62   £24862   2210   1154 1641 2504* 2751
                              > 1016 <
```

```
3 SIMPLON  64  £1650  4  559
3 SIMPLY DELICIOUS  36  £164  -03  1580 2593
2 SIMPLY SILK  0  £-  00  1874 2069
3 SIMSIM  69  £5409  41-2320  326 604 1068 1409
2 SINCLAIR LADY  58  £3868  000011200  47 197 317 818 1205* 1370* 1697- 2235 2511
3 SINDUR  8  £-  0-00  1167 2400
4 SINFEROPOLI  10  £-  33-00-00  58 259
2 SING FOR THE KING  0  £-  000  826 1069 1741
5 SING GALVO SING  0  £-  30044-000000000  418 495 636 906 1077 1438 1676 1839 2012
4 SING OUT LOUD  0  £-  -000000  58 448 651 2397 2513 2602
4 SINGERS TRYST  21  £-  11020-00000  584 1293 1533 2169 2480
5 SINGING BOY  28  £2582  34410-00000140  333 578 992 1394 1553 1987* 2132 2303
2 SINGING PARTNER  32  £2517  031  2308 2535 2698*
2 SINGING STEVEN  70  £34322  2211230311  332 457 536+ 834* 1143 1453 2113 2297 2661+ 2954+
4 SINGLE  39  £7326  00020-01141300  112 174+ 262* 399 481* 930 2544 2730
6 SINGLE HAND  4  £-  0-4000000000000  42 65 124 124 260 525 700 2012 2264 2397 2728 2762 2891
3 SINGLETTA  76  £25568  12-30113  509 1128 2117* 2278* 2868
2 SINJAAB  40  £341  34  962 2205
4 SINSA  57  £-  -4  392
3 SIOUX SWEET  0  £-  0-0  528
3 SIR ARNOLD  57  £5270  -2313130  844 1511 1691* 2099 2650+ 2870 3124
7 SIR BLESSED  24  £-  42410-00  1441 1551
3 SIR BRETT  20  £1339  -0414000  90 512 790* 951 1497 2280 3128
3 SIR CHESTER  26  £-  -04  613 996
2 SIR HARRY LEWIS  48  £355  2  3117
2 SIR JAMESTOWN  44  £-  00  2847 3023
3 SIR PERCY  47  £3736  -1003000  253* 442 654 1600 2201 2551 2850
3 SIR SPEEDY  0  £-  -000000  175 498 765 1210 1364 1969
4 SIR WILMORE  32  £3159  01000-000100030  936 1093 1482 1698* 1983 2126 2296 2629 3029
3 SIRDAR FLYER  2  £-  4300-0000000  338 505 1104 2109 2360 2876 3076
4 SIRDAR GIRL  1  £-  33--0-40000  2028 2363 2704 2985 3086
2 SIRIUS RIVER  0  £-  0  2846
4 SIRIUS SYMBOLI  80  £11224  003-04204  299 2194 2637 2917 3091
3 SIRK  81  £46377  423-1323032000  48* 324 442 574 878 1853 2157- 2453 2565 3097
3 SIRTAKI DANCER  2  £304  -0040003  1691 1836 2135 2463 2787 3076 3185
3 SISTER NANCY  5  £119  40000-43000000  41 195 305 608 666 871 1200 2268
3 SIT ELNAAS  32  £122  0-043  2853 3155 3217
3 SIT IN THE DARK  0  £-  -0  2599
3 SIT THIS ONE OUT  56  £4048  10-303000000040  159 362 802 920 1286 1514 2021 2241 2566 2674
2851 3042
4 SITAR THEME  16  £-  003-4000  683 856 1035 1260
8 SITEX  3  £1702  22000-004100  734 1077 1211 1616* 2319 2731
4 SITTING BULL  28  £705  10300-04200  429 1254 1601 1792 2226
3 SITZCARRALDO  23  £1114  03300-2002000  62 161 436 2319- 2394 2810 3066
2 SIVAJI  0  £-  0  3234
2 SIXTY MINUTES  0  £-  000  2472 2708 2829
4 SIYAH KALEM  75  £41789  00211-412003220  330 706+ 1109- 1332 1514 2259 2823 3007 3051
2 SIZZLING MELODY  78  £43800  1121301  34+ 115* 840- 1126+ 1467 2113 2564+
3 SKEAN  49  £6265  -00222110  1031 1368 2248 2550 2857 2931* 3077+ 3204
3 SKEEB  42  £617  3114-0300  228 732 2526 2730
3 SKELTON  20  £1259  20100-000300230  318 650 857 1103 1257 1959 2086 2670 2905
2 SKERNE ROCKET  12  £150  0304000  1137 1279 1413 1955 2396 2757 2976
4 SKERNE SPARK  0  £-  24000-0000  591 860 1159 1769
3 SKEVENA  32  £265  -030  2304 2734 3105
2 SKI CAPTAIN  44  £1729  00221  892 2781 3048 3156- 3218*
3 SKI DOWN  0  £-  0-00  849 2078
11 SKI RUN  10  £2340  03-00-4130  23 80* 184 308
2 SKI SLOPE  34  £-  00  2013 2418
2 SKINNHILL  0  £-  000  1050 1480 1622
3 SKINNY DIPPER  0  £-  000-00  2175 2282
2 SKIPAWAY  35  £-  04  2651 2967
2 SKOLERN  30  £-  4000  934 1958 2029 3165
2 SKRAGGS PLUS TWO  20  £190  00043000  206 834 965 1172 1566 1846 2708 3143
2 SKY CAT  34  £834  400220  694 864 1175 1421 1978 2307
5 SKY MARINER  0  £-  00030-0004000  594 1500 1651 1703 2401 2582 2836
2 SKY NINSKI  61  £7300  2  2910
2 SKY ROBBER  10  £128  002  596 831 1474
3 SKYBIRD  4  £131  0003-0000003000  677 768 830 1200 1701 1927 2361 2688 2863 2972
2 SKYBOLT  41  £3006  0400110  1665 1844 2089 2792 2962* 3146* 3174
7 SKYBOOT  8  £526  00440-03240000  7 88 142 308 474 1017 2807 3128
2 SKYDREAM  20  £821  1  125*
3 SKYLIN  9  £-  01000-000000  339 1584 2256 2513 2906 2992
4 SKYWALKER  92  £944056  1  3213*
3 SLANGI VAH  47  £7407  -330231  479 1589 2148 2489 2701 3038+
3 SLAP BANG  15  £177  40000-4300  505 908 1089 1706
2 SLEEPERS  36  £725  22  2969 3218
3 SLEEPLINE DUCHESS  11  £953  40000-00200302  418 1063 1656 1845 2060 2238 3076 3202
2 SLEEPLINE FOR BEDS  13  £257  42300  1168 1449 1684 2107 2580
2 SLEEPLINE FOR PINE  0  £-  00  350 596
2 SLIM HOPE  45  £170  030  2016 2249 2561
4 SLIP ANCHOR  88  £9753  11122-2  385
2 SLIP DANCER  39  £391  03000  1653 1872 2239 2556 2806
2 SLIPPERY MAX  28  £-  040  2036 2607 3201
3 SLY MAID  0  £-  -000000  1574 1815 1917 2322 3144 3185
3 SLY WHEELER  0  £-  -0  1193
4 SLYDONBYE  7  £-  0040-00  2490 2601
4 SMACK  0  £386  00020-0020000  185 542 841 1016 1897 2075 3129
7 SMART MART  5  £673  00000-300302  1374 1432 1565 1720 2102 3154
2 SMART SALUTE  36  £-  0  2436
3 SMASHNG MILLIE  48  £2761  0-144  581* 2286 2649
4 SMILE  85?  £314685  1  85? 3210*
3 SMILING BEAR  38  £613  00-030  1880 2250 2594
4 SMOKEYS SECRET  41  £298  03113-04000  1047 2303 2477 3123 3231
```

```
3 SMOOCH  54   £5054   103-0010040   232 575 982* 1219 1851 2496 2765
3 SMOOTH GLIDER  36   £-   -0   1291
2 SNAAN  37   £292   030   1869 2615 2894
4 SNAKE RIVER  26   £2248   24001-433102240   22 207 530 620* 745 943 1273 1581 2132
3 SNAP DECISION  26   £1928   31300-040203330   846 1033 1669 1943 2120 2530 2731 3015 3138
3 SNAPDRAGON  32   £-   0-0   183
2 SNAPPY DRESSER  54   £2111   33   149 2350
2 SNAPSHOT BABY  0   £115   003000   483 681 853 1318 2045 2927
3 SNARRY HILL  12   £-   04-00000   1511 1841 2027 2978 3115
6 SNEAK PREVIEW  52   £34353   01043-11000   375* 712+ 1293+ 2873* 3052
2 SNO SURPRISE  40   £5663   40020110   425 536 1305 1843 2137 2227* 2336* 2648
2 SNOW FINCH  63   £3672   011024   2113 2350 2451
3 SNOW WIZARD  42   £874   -00421   506 714 2441 2605 3159*
3 SNOWFIRE CHAP  30   £450   -0334   448 996 1251 1623
2 SNOWKIST  0   £-   0   3082
2 SNOWSDOWN  17   £-   000   1522 2788 3131
3 SNOWTOP  54   £-   00   472 754
3 SO DIRECTED  58   £-   40   295 691
2 SO KIND  51   £1786   3442   2043 2297 2687 2803
2 SO STYLISH  46   £489   32   1433 1722
2 SOARING EAGLES  0   £-   000   1862 2138 2535
9 SOCKS UP  14   £4210   04003-040301200   1 984 1223 2022 2093 2173* 2285 2467 2955
3 SOEMBA  38   £3804   4-00010   213 1043 2719 2948* 3175
3 SOFT SHOE SHUFFLE  24   £940   000-00001   765 1831 1941 2406 2495*
3 SOFTLY SPOKEN  26   £5686   0100-012022100   628 784* 1247- 1398 1765 2012 2519* 2785 2947
3 SOHAIL  39   £4308   03234-031220   1104 1361 1956* 2395 2709 2959
3 SOHAMS TAYLOR  7   £-   00004000000   382 596 728 1168 1684 2168 2298 2609 2712 2829 3190
3 SOHO SAM  12   £-   -00400   402 535 666 838 1898
3 SOHO SUE  22   £2519   00040-100001030   426* 809 1065 1201 1549 1784* 2305 2790 2958
3 SOKOLOVA  39   £-   30-0000   338 422 765 991
2 SOLANY  41   £800   4   1329
4 SOLAR CLOUD  37   £347   -002   251 519 2704
6 SOLAR LIGHT  3   £-   42403-00   2517 2654
3 SOLENT BREEZE  0   £-   0000-0400   45 365 1428 2430
3 SOLENT DAWN  0   £-   00000-000   1567 2094 2528
3 SOLENT EXPRESS  6   £297   00010-004042   1970 2073 2187 2581 2705 3045
2 SOLENT GOLD  0   £-   0000   633 853 1583 1803
2 SOLENT KNIGHT  0   £-   00   2547 2608
3 SOLENT LAD  0   £185   00000-200000   139 356 1310 2787 2984 3100
6 SOLITAIRE  0   £-   -00   841 1348
3 SOLO SINGER  15   £627   -0402000   250 431 776 1516 2143 2210 2601
3 SOLO STYLE  50   £14670   00-300101411424   454 624 886 1065* 1245 1651* 1854 2076* 2303* 2629
   2684 3113
3 SOLOMON LAD  21   £252   -2000F   1686 1833 2078 2432 2704
4 SOLSTICE BELL  5   £1212   00440-40010   564 709 845 1439* 1967
3 SOLVENT  22   £1072   4-2002330   116 219 690 2422 2620 2747 3159
2 SOMBRERO GOLD  27   £-   00   1175 2105
2 SOME DREAM  31   £-   400   2080 2494 3068
3 SOME GUEST  0   £-   0-0000000   835 941 1062 1401 1579 1947 1995
8 SOME JET  3   £-   00--0-0   9
2 SOMEONE ELSE  40   £2682   03000323   230 577 1097 1289 1914 2439 2521 2700
3 SOMEONE SPECIAL  70   £11357   -21330   250 658* 803 1110 1466
3 SOMETHING CASUAL  47   £3396   10-000034444020   386 575 1153 1507 1655 1924 2250 2459 2650 2765
   3077- 3204
2 SOMETHING EXTRA  48   £2008   021   962 1762 2108+
3 SOMETHING SIMILAR  32   £815   0204-00002330   613 714 2042 2400 2885 3101 3155 3217
3 SOMEWAY  0   £-   03-000000000   87 205 424 624 835 1549 1827 2088 2417
3 SON OF ABSALOM  11   £-   00-0000   605 868 1267 1428
3 SON OF SPARKLER  17   £467   00043-00000023   535 849 1540 1942 2171 2381 2560 2697
3 SONG AN DANCE MAN  14   £228   000-40000000200   116 191 210 1520 1581 1783 1937 2238 2371 2429
   2863
2 SONG N JEST  36   £1133   320004   583 715 2029 2221 2871 3103
2 SONG OF SIXPENCE  52   £-   00   3018 3178
3 SONIC LADY  90   £423885   1-13111110   214+ 373 754* 1110* 1466+ 1877* 2507* 3211
3 SONNENDEW  0   £-   0-000   688 1029 3057
3 SONNENELLE  8   £3931   22-120004001000   103* 147- 255 971 1131 1360 1524 1917 1973* 2424 2688
   3083
3 SONNING  0   £-   0-000   1064 1368 1516
5 SONNY ONE SHINE  8   £-   -0-0   104
2 SONOCO  30   £213   400   252 2675 2987
4 SOON TO BE  28   £-   21133-000000   441 616 881 1213 1521 1852
2 SOOTHING WORD  0   £-   000   2487 2796 3189
6 SOPHISTICATION  0   £-   -400   968 1417 1652
4 SOPHYS FOLLY  6   £119   -00-30000   143 258 630 673 828
2 SORROWFUL  0   £-   00   1100 1358
3 SOUGHAAN  62   £-   1-000   384 1823 2231
2 SOULEIADOU  26   £200   003000   1082 1522 1816 2485 3165 3200
2 SOUND AS A POUND  17   £86   000340   612 913 1181 1323 1434 1741
4 SOUND DIFFUSION  14   £4504   0-2210030000004   590 712 933+ 1099 1183 1419 1533 1772 2087 2745
   2794 2873 3013
3 SOUND REASONING  41   £-   22104-040   1443 1699 1834
4 SOUND WORK  0   £-   14000-000000   184 449 547 869 1185 1374
3 SOUSAGA  0   £-   -000   2958 3105 3194
6 SOUTH GALE  76   £4600   33020-44   390 756
3 SOUTH THATCH  73   £2193   -40   286 556
2 SOUTHERN COMFORT  56   £311   04   2645 3018
6 SOUTHERNAIR  0   £-   -0   3139
3 SOUTHJET  94   £209702   1   3097*
8 SOVEREIGN CELLAR  0   £-   0/000-0   1374
3 SOVEREIGN LOVE  27   £8839   2-0031323020000   1 15 49 178 1487 1924 2027 2381 3078 3123
3 SOXOPH  25   £1804   -4100000   16 53* 127 322 604 1885 2508
2 SOYBEAN  0   £-   0   3117
3 SPACE HUNTER  49   £-   -4   393
```

```
3 SPACE TROOPER  23    £5872    0400-4011320430    132 451 1295* 1678* 1773 1974 2300 2478 2671 3101
6 SPACEMAKER BOY  35   £4702    2410032F000000240    12 76 211* .272 418 742 1037 1196 1380 1730
  2469 2586 2783 2966 3083 3152 3233
2 SPANISH CALM  49     £5577    031    1936 2301 2472+
2 SPANISH CONNECTION  0   £-    0000    1232 1518 2407 3143
2 SPANISH GALLEON  0   £-    00    2056 2218
3 SPANISH INFANTA  11    £205    04000-0000300    447 961 2139 2602 2854 3024 3160
3 SPANISH INTENT  0   £-    -0000000    431 501 764 1272 1516 2060 2417
2 SPANISH MELODY  0   £-    0000    533 852 2191 3184
4 SPANISH REEL  30    £927    14040-2030    420 724 850 940
2 SPANISH SKY  35    £1207    010030004    350 1194* 1585 1910 2090 2435 2579 2792 2962
2 SPANISH SLIPPER  44    £8131    422412210    450 818 1205 1814 1972* 2265- 2472 2777* 2935
3 SPANSYKE  13   £-    000-000    322 744 2605
3 SPARE THE BLUSHES  0   £-    000-00    1369 1567
4 SPARKFORD LAD  4    £1358    400000000213000    122 266 399 495 679 845 1213 1319 1521 1937 2271* 2429
  2697 2836 2960
2 SPARKLER BOY  0   £-    00000    780 1296 2105 2494 2584
5 SPARKLER SPIRIT  9    £2777    4-000-024010    1188 1609 1942 2288 2581* 2837
3 SPARKLIN PERFORMER  25   £-    00-004440    1652 1923 2211 2517 2620 2988
2 SPARKLING BRITT  28    £119    0340    1440 1550 1867 2261
3 SPARKLING HOCK  0   £-    -0    2548
2 SPARKLING JUDY  4   £-    00000    337 543 987 3017 3228
4 SPARKLING WIT  12   £-    10-00-04    3057 3084
3 SPARKY LAD  20   £-    10-00000000    496 580 1044 2143 2650 3070 3164 3204
2 SPARSHOLT  50    £3170    3121    21 483+ 934 1105*
2 SPARSHOLT BREEZE  0   £-    0    2767
3 SPARTAN VALLEY  46    £5246    -0-2321433    448 744 1372 1646* 1894 2523 2834
2 SPATS COLUMBO  14   £-    0    2051
3 SPECIAL GUEST  16    £1371    01200-033240340    1034 1224 1560 1695 1885 2340 2490 2681 2876
5 SPECIAL SETTLEMENT  0   £-    04400-0    2141
6 SPECIAL VINTAGE  44    £3750    03304203    778 1533 1679 2220 2480 2631 3052 3227
4 SPECTAME  67    £1564    4    1594
2 SPECULATE  30    £612    023    2651 2982 3184
3 SPEED STICK  14    £309    -0030    1315 1607 1756 2294
2 SPEEDBIRD  38    £3134    000401400    353 1996 2215 2283 2611 2756* 3041 3125 3188
4 SPEND IT LASS  11   £-    00324-000    449 590 721
3 SPENDING CONTINUES  70    £4354    2-1122    2112 2348
3 SPERRY  80    £28472    03210-202100    220 406 691- 1125+ 2003 2772
5 SPICY STORY  68    £24662    04214-3032043    360 756 1127 1888 2157 2203 2844
3 SPINNAKER LADY  20    £1165    020-00000010020    352 538 637 730 1656 1951 2073* 2381 2462 2582
  2787
3 SPINNING TURN  35   £-    -034000    130 388 607 699 1511 1677
2 SPIRE  39   £-    0    3073
2 SPITTIN MICK  37    £5490    1213110040    421* 647 813* 1527 1717+ 1814* 2252 2606 2689 2935
2 SPITZABIT  36    £959    000001    2574 2717 2812 2895 3182 3192*
2 SPLASH ON  39    £784    02    3067 3136
2 SPLASHIN OUT  0   £-    00    1816 2976
3 SPLENDID MAGNOLIA  11   £-    00000-0004    749 1212 1316 1784
3 SPLENDID MOMENT  76    £28976    310-43232    389 2359 2820 3093 3216
2 SPOILED BRAT  38   £-    00    2711 2920
8 SPOILT FOR CHOICE  21    £365    40000-00020    42 163 281 369 525
2 SPORTIN HONORS  36   £-    0    2215
3 SPORTING SOVEREIGN  24    £3291    000-042201000    141 670 837 1164 1398 1701* 1774 1999 3029
2 SPOTTER  36    £1583    010200    999 1433* 2071 2178 2595 2806
2 SPRATS BRAT  0   £-    0    2791
3 SPRING FLIGHT  36    £10678    000-01323113124    356 740* 1179 1362 1678 1773* 2154* 2267 2490*
  2671 2807
2 SPRING FORWARD  25   £-    04000    1162 1320 2838 3135 3234
3 SPRING GARDEN  0   £-    00000-000000000    246 447 911 1051 1158 1543 1734 2268 2409
4 SPRING IN MY STEP  44    £818    -1110-340    2730 2934 3123
4 SPRING PHILTRE  6   £-    000-004    204 3139 3193
5 SPRING PURSUIT  7   £-    04020-000000    399 812 1136 2319 2621 2836
2 SPRING SUNSET  0   £-    00    3056 3223
2 SPRING TIDE  0   £-    0    2080
3 SPRINGWELL  40    £677    -003342    732 966 1981 2400 3086 3217
2 SPRINGWELL LADY  0   £-    0    2365
3 SPROWSTON BOY  42    £4873    04322-1133004    78* 132* 193 342 604 3022 3232
2 SPRUCE BABY  40    £602    033    2716 2889 2997
3 SPUN GOLD  62    £5683    14-041000    373 509 1170* 2202 2525 2952
2 SPY GIFT  41    £441    0330443    1604 1801 2105 2479 2989 3074 3148
2 SPY TOWER  38    £3179    -00410    678 1475 2328 2556* 2677
2 SQUIGGLE  21   £-    0000    425 612 2225 2841
2 ST CLAIR CHARGER  0   £-    0    3080
3 ST CROINS CASTLE  60   £-    00020-4    148
4 ST HILARION  76    £44059    33111-002024    653 885 1144 1493 2502 3096
3 ST JAMES RISK  14   £-    0100-000044    1384 1540 2103 2429 2515 2697
2 ST JOHNS BAY  0   £-    0000    913 1253 1483 2032
11 ST TERRAMAR  0    £604    02D20-0000000    30 977 1070 1213 1521 1730 2992
2 ST WENDRED  20    £84    0300    1322 1480 1883 3068
2 STAFILIO  42    £170    03    2847 3117
2 STAGE  38    £1044    00100    186 632 892+ 1105 2052
3 STAGE HAND  48   £-    010-00000    234 370 946 1538 1957
4 STAGHOUND  18   £-    -334-000    2572 2733 3139
2 STAINSBY GIRL  0   £-    0000    1555 1802 2119 2926
3 STALKER  70    £568    34121-400    854 1146 2833
5 STAMPY  1   £-    00--0-0    2656
4 STAN THE MAN  43   £-    01142-00    215 778
3 STANBO  20    £743    300-00040204020    62 233 1730 1995 2143 2575- 2715 2758 2906 3046- 3145
4 STANDARD BREAKFAST  22   £-    -1400-0000040    474 1150 1533 1935 2175 2346 2467
3 STANDARD ROSE  19   £-    0-40000    1580 2068 2734 3035 3225
3 STANDON MILL  12    £680    000-0004000420    14 132 416 648 823 998 2175 2305 2478 3087
5 STANELLY  0   £-    -0    452
3 STANFORD ROSE  1   £-    02003-0040000    960 1267 1960 2083 2427 2585 2795
```

```
3 STANFORD VALE  38   £6612   400-02231100    352 480 538 719 874* 997* 1231 3042
3 STANGRAVE  2    £193   33330-03000   356 666 928 1199 2060
9 STANS PRIDE  36   £-    -1124-00   208 419
4 STANWOOD BOY  23   £448   30100-30   319 541
3 STAR ADDIE  0    £-   -000   1705 2714 2874
2 STAR AFFAIR  0    £-   0  2628
8 STAR ALLIANCE  0    £-   -00/3-0   824
2 STAR CITY  0    £-   00   633 831
3 STAR COMMAND  0    £-   -00   35 767
3 STAR CRIMSON  0    £-   000-0000   2884 3149
3 STAR CUTTER  79   £27835   -2111   1036- 1269* 1854+ 3093*
3 STAR MAITE  74   £9660   -2   3089
2 STAR NORTH  42   £278   0420   2522 2957 3141 3201
6 STAR OF A GUNNER  51   £14758   100-01100032023   17 196* 248+ 433 573 1240 2144 2390 2566 3123 3231
6 STAR OF IRELAND  40   £4303   3--00-10104   88+ 333 349* 420 724
3 STAR OF POLY  0    £-   -0   1688
3 STAR OF TARA  10   £-   000-000   379 631 1904
2 STAR PLAY  3    £-   000000   523 741 864 2177 2466 2724
4 STAR ROSE  67   £6808   21-3003   298 3207
3 STAR SHINER  24   £208   -00-000030   229 1314 1569 1733 2078 2169
3 STARBOARD  4    £-   00-004000   328 822 1269 1571 2762 2973
2 STARCH BROOK  19   £-   400000   206 717 2127 2218 2320 2535
4 STARDYN  12   £387   00-03040   176 569 683 761 856
2 STARK REALITY  30   £-   00   2541 2878
3 STARLIGHT FREDDIE  0    £-   -00   1589 2110
3 STARMAST  34   £673   0-40300033   535 625 1830 1951 2173 2381 2534 2856
4 STARS DELIGHT  14   £3404   00030-23421   105 611 745 970 1136*
2 STARS IN MOTION  24   £474   0003000200   531 694 1232 1675 2026 2618 2744 2899 3079 3192
2 STARSIGN  0    £-   00   2514 2788
2 START COUNTING  0    £-   0   1955
2 START RITE  54   £2053   0201   1653 2016- 2179 2345*
3 STARTINO  75   £15955   2-11144   328* 1538+ 2236* 2525 2952
2 STARTLE  58   £4142   10   1930* 2199
4 STARWOOD  10   £295   000-20   1892 2714
2 STATE BALLET  49   £4579   01001   1232 1518* 2071 2529 2897*
5 STATE BUDGET  45   £7671   31230-13120   333* 547 618* 851 1020
3 STATE JESTER  16   £2944   00-00000001   744 916 1055 1503 1677 2085 2394 2932*
4 STATELY FORM  67   £23080   41140-021401   189 474- 921+ 1112 2220 2486+
3 STATELY LASS  67   £9273   23-10020   59+ 1110 1286 2440 3168
2 STATUTORY  0    £-   0   3201
3 STAVORDALE  70   £21070   0-44100   388 720 1111* 1513 1888
2 STAY LOW  59   £18856   211331403   223 425+ 513+ 621 840 1113* 1411 1454 2325
4 STEADY EDDIE  37   £3270   010-00003010000   952 1235 1455 1640 1804 1911 2072+ 2165 2207 2544 2674
2 STEAMSHIP  64   £5052   2134   2914 3090
8 STEEL COMMANDER  62   £526   02032-40   472 2503
3 STEEL CYGNET  36   £1267   1002-0034040340   62 233 443 580 2783 2921 3055 3106 3138 3233
8 STEEL PASS  0    £-   30010-000000   1609 1971 2189 2282 2370 2836
2 STEELOCK  38   £677   203   646 1025 1132
10 STEEPLE BELL  38   £648   11200-0340   1041 1781 1967 2244
3 STEINLEN  57   £1200   -3   393
2 STELBY  44   £4978   02242003310   544 632 873 1161 2082 2325 2447 2661 2805 3044+ 3226
4 STELLA GRANDE  76   £7498   10002-23   2 96
2 STEP BY STEP  0    £-   000   741 2364 2994
3 STEP IN TIME  30   £-   -000440   371 739 1469 2489 2720 3110
3 STEP ON  10   £180   00-3000   318 608 828 1053
3 STEPHENS SONG  27   £5374   24000-1100000   161* 233* 443 929 1654 2160 2469 2731 3106
5 STERLING VIRTUE  06   £-   0-004-4   591
2 STERN LASS  0    £-   0   1874
4 STERNE  42   £-   2--11-004   462 663 917
4 STEVEJAN  0    £411   00000-330400   65 124 355 378 3015 3057
3 STICKY GREENE  29   £2700   0-3342044   658 923 1043 1628 1953 2442 2856
3 STILL DREAMING  22   £765   030-204040   424 703 954 1256 2027 2238
3 STILL MARCHING  20   £-   000-000   1104 2400 2948
2 STILLMAN  56   £4096   0013202   571 741 1812* 2199 2336 3126 3180
3 STILLOU  22   £6102   104-34001001000   117 275 505 738 955* 1231 1657 1806* 2182 2404 2490
4 STOCK HILL LASS  46   £1596   03000-00000043   616 687 952 2530 2655 2862 3118 3235
3 STOCK PHRASE  21   £-   00400-00   624 703
2 STOLEN STAR  0    £-   00   1561 2011
6 STONE JUG  17   £3195   03401-0411424   319 590 1422* 1745* 2141 2587 3219
3 STONEBROKER  20   £2668   0-00-0441002232   8 207 530 718* 1274 1450 1747 2282 2576 3128
4 STONEYDALE  30   £3214   000-00100002000   412 550 734* 836 1037 1268 1608 2033- 2256 2411 2519
3 STOP THE CLOCK  0    £-   0-0000   723 1022 1111 1428
4 STORM CLOUD  40   £-   314-00   235 336
2 STORM HERO  45   £999   3224   870 1197 1534 1735
4 STORM HOUSE  28   £2283   32230-3103   2699 2900* 3030 3115
3 STORM LORD  0    £-   000-00000   648 769 949 1759 3045
4 STORM WARNING  75   £30289   -4310-03000221   408 563 903 1146 1889 2503 2833- 3010*
3 STORMGUARD  20   £1139   0-30042   1141 1578 1818 2313 2463
3 STORMY PROSPECT  36   £3157   -34010   409 669 1160 2175* 2467
3 STRAIGHT BAT  9    £234   -20   1815 2174
2 STRAIGHT EDGE  12   £-   0000   741 1225 2423 2712
3 STRAIGHT THROUGH  41   £6688   00024-21210043   63 120* 275 1034 1233* 1393 2049 2404 2489
3 STRAIGHTAWAY STAR  0    £-   -0000   656 941 1451 1943
2 STRANGE MUSIC  0    £-   0   3014
5 STRAPHANGER  0    £-   -000   1417 1556 2175
3 STRATCH  36   £-   000   1287 1874 2185 2555
2 STRATHBLANE  57   £2973   10130   1187+ 1522 2090+ 2556 2815
5 STRATHCONON  0    £-   00000-00   2885 3219
5 STRATHEARN  12   £-   000000   243 449 584 686 933 1159
3 STRAW BOATER  48   £3293   -001320   209 991 1337* 2649 2790- 3050
2 STRAW VALE  35   £-   0   3223
```

```
2 STRAW VOTE 0  £- 0  1522
3 STRAWBERRY SPLIT 0  £- 00-00000  247 328 593 871 963
2 STRAY NO MORE 0  £- 000  2423 2894 2976
2 STREET LEGAL 20  £- 00000  1082 1345 1816 2829 3230
2 STREET PARTY 57  £2285  323  2147 2531- 2933
2 STRELLILANE 44  £268  020  2574 3068 3181
4 STRICTLY BUSINESS 0  £- 0-000-400000  1185 1432 1820 2109 2414 2549
2 STRIKE ACTION 29  £- 0  3111
3 STRIKE HOME 53  £3125  -0231  739 991 1192 1829*
2 STRIKE RATE 48  £2469  12330  180* 434 2209 2332 2556
2 STRING CONCERTO 0  £- 0  3136
4 STRING OF BEADS 0  £360  40200-00000240  308 449 772 1226 1980 2141 2280 3219
2 STRING SECTION 40  £869  03300  1392 1731 2019 2628 2989
3 STRIVE 22  £776  23100-024000000  157 436 534 808 1245 1783 2810 2928 3078
3 STROMBERG 6  £- 0000-000  38 339 1471
2 STRONG SEA 0  £- 000  2628 2894 3099
3 STRONGARM 27  £- -4  32
2 STUBBLE FIRE 50  £2008  014  2878 3075+ 3206
2 STUMBLE 12  £- 000  962 2007 2218
2 STYLISH ENTRY 38  £1749  410  1681 2375* 2689
2 STYLISH GIRL 17  £202  03000  1322 1650 2127 2375 2792
3 SUBLIME MIME 0  £- -0  549
4 SUDDEN IMPACT 26  £2885  00040-100433000  65* 306 525 1235 1461 1536 1852 2021 2378
6 SUE CLARE 0  £- 00400-000  636 727 1273
2 SUE FOREVER 22  £974  0100  317 1862* 2336 2936
3 SUE GRUNDY 73  £4456  013-10040  128* 463 1128 1408 2236
3 SUEDE LADY 0  £- -0  2299
2 SUESANDY 7  £- 0000  1972 2153 2325 2994
3 SUEZ 0  £- -00  1645 1833
5 SUGAR PALM 28  £5732  10010-03042221  235 341 485 801 990 1260 1388 1582*
2 SUHAILIE 78  £19213  1110  1465* 2598* 2860+ 3126
2 SUIVEZ MOI 0  £- 00  2270 2847
4 SULAAFAH 77  £2170  01010-430  5 392 759
5 SULLYS CHOICE 41  £17190  -01310032100001  124 321+ 412 520+ 687 1026 1638 1796 2065* 2151
2446 2537 2668 3145*
3 SULTAN MOHAMED 65  £15131  0242-121300140  887* 1208 1462* 1644 1931 2219 2438* 2942 3216
5 SULTAN ZAMAN 11  £- /0004-40  105 144
3 SUMMER GARDEN 25  £192  -4030000  658 923 1246 1451 2719 2948 3105
3 SUMMER POSY 63  £2058  42  2675 2933
2 SUMMER SKY 55  £2683  1130  417* 725* 1746 1910
5 SUMMER STOP 6  £- -0  1659
2 SUMMER TRIP 0  £- 0  1241
3 SUMMERHILL ROCK 0  £- -00  90 351
3 SUMMERHILL SPRUCE 27  £1726  00000-001300  274 514 871* 1191 1360 1847
2 SUMMERHILL STREAK 55  £5506  2310  1049 1149 1376* 1512
4 SUMMERS DARLING 24  £- 30-00000  2617 2943
3 SUN 70  £2500  2  303
2 SUN FLEECE 0  £- 0  3018
4 SUN STREET 26  £3243  2240-4002013004  366 462 712 2040 2111 2326* 2480 2647 2809 3129
5 SUNAPAS OWLET 21  £555  00000-2  449
2 SUNAVA 0  £- 0  1634
2 SUNBRIDGE 35  £- 000  2147 2577 2838
3 SUNDAY CHIMES 25  £- -04000  1375 1981 2248 2550 3077
3 SUNDEED 59  £- 110-0000  1777 1889 2084 2672
4 SUNDOWN SKY 2  £- 00104-0000  893 1054 1567 1839
2 SUNERTA 46  £3882  010  2232 2664* 3040
3 SUNK ISLAND 10  £- 400-000404  656 1164 1580 2088 2174 2361
2 SUNLEY PARK STREET 0  £- 0  3108
2 SUNLEY PROJECTS 0  £- 0  2185
3 SUNLEY SAINT 28  £955  20-02240  423 1198 2299 2520 2925
2 SUNLEY SELHURST 24  £- 000  1440 2069 2703
3 SUNLEY SINNER 58  £- 23110-00  1630 1886
3 SUNLEY SPIRIT 0  £- 0000-0000  1081 1471 1951 2098
3 SUNLIT 0  £- 0-000000  702 1700 1892 2125 3150 3202
3 SUNMAIDEN 13  £- 00-0000  528 699 1204 1479
2 SUNNY GIBRALTAR 0  £- 0000  450 603 647 1379
3 SUNNY LIZ 35?  £259  2-200  498 658 2294
3 SUNNY MATCH 25  £1574  000-002002000  507 835 1836 2120 2313 2570 2810 3070 3236
2 SUNORIUS 44  £1377  042200  1869 2108 2491 2922 3103 3180
2 SUNSET BOULEVARD 46  £1820  040140  1345 1572 2001 2310* 2718 3178
3 SUNSET DANCER 0  £- 00-00  111 423
3 SUNSET SAM 0  £- 0  2707
4 SUNSTART 78  £- 11-21-0  267
3 SUNTAN 0  £- -0  1567
5 SUPER EXPRESS 14  £- -3P00-00  542 942
3 SUPER FRESCO 33  £147  0-0020  438 516 1425 1927
2 SUPER GAMBLER 9  £- 000  1137 1413 2466
7 SUPER GRASS 19  £3682  00--0-311  358 541* 772*
2 SUPER LUNAR 42  £1017  422  2243 2646 2975
4 SUPER MOVE 74  £11700  30  641 885
3 SUPER PUNK 47  £3954  031-3000410  436 703 1147 1436 1753 2879+ 3042
3 SUPER SIHLOUETTE 0  £- -0000  1062 1256 1941 2508
3 SUPER SMART 0  £- 0-000  356 535 951
2 SUPER SURPRISE 40  £- 00  2147 2596
5 SUPER TRIP 40  £13630  1400-0021421000  129 432 680- 1013* 1109 1292- 1793* 2234 2749 3123
3 SUPER TRUCKER 18  £- 00  2085 2339 2483
3 SUPERCOOMBE 21  £693  4-3022D000  516 677 835 1200 1607 2367 3160
2 SUPERCUBE 40  £199  04340  944 1225 1825 2043 2423
4 SUPERFROST 10  £1126  0430-0001004030  36 88 481 568* 845 1273 1609 1755 2121 2381
3 SUPREME COMMAND 4  £- -000000  140 328 426 684 1079 1201
3 SUPREME KINGDOM 24  £2926  032000430000000  15 49 244 461 538 954 1532 1783 2076 2266 2481 2594
2905 3029 3236
4 SUPREME LEADER 79  £55972  40030-11330040  221* 325* 598 736 1095 1790 2259 2506
```

```
2 SUPREME NEPHEW  12   £-   0   974
2 SUPREME OPTIMIST  12   £296   30000400   460 632 934 1050 1568 2392 3058 3222
2 SUPREME ROSE  49   £6745   01021   1996 2365* 2514 2935- 3122*
2 SUPREME STATE  40   £2154   0032201   1522 1826 2270 2410 2744- 3165 3222*
3 SURE BLADE  87   £73602   1113-10110   244* 407 1096* 2770+ 3051
3 SURE GROUND  43   £2317   -00-0301   506 832 2148 2464*
3 SURE LANDING  35   £1104   -0420340204   465 764 937 1046 1607 1750 1991 2216 2442 2704
2 SURELY GREAT  36   £2562   0202402020000   400 621 707 1025 1180 1454 1632 1789 1844 2689 3146
  3176 3223
2 SURF BOARD  38   £-   000   2239 2522 2723
3 SURFING  34   £1444   003-243   1245 1436 2027
5 SURPRISE ATTACK  0   £-   -0000-0000   1290 1951 2401 2704
3 SURPRISE CALL  45   £3045   310-0312   553 716 1303* 1565-
2 SURVIVAL KIT  14   £214   003300   596 848 981 2180 3017 3192
2 SUSAN HENCHARD  35   £919   1000   2308+ 2434 2694 3188
2 SUSSARANDO  0   £-   00   2308 2514
3 SUTIMARK  0   £-   -00   218 328
2 SUTOSKY  38   £-   44   2901 3133
2 SUTTERS MILL  3   £-   00   21 483
5 SUVADERA  0   £-   000-0   1280
3 SVELT  75   £28956   -1   286*
3 SWAALEF  26   £223   -0300   1431 2726 2958 3187
2 SWALK  0   £-   0   3171
2 SWALLOW BAY  22   £1687   00310   170 596 1379 1881* 2178
3 SWALLOW TIME  0   £-   000-0   95
4 SWAY  14   £-   21030-00   10 101
3 SWEDISH PRINCESS  25   £-   -00000   338 720 862 1829 2346
3 SWEEPY  23   £-   -0000   658 1368 2314 2440
3 SWEET ADELAIDE  65   £2875   130-20300   158 394 708 925 1107
3 SWEET ALEXANDRA  23   £3641   -43112000   829 1072 1686* 2093* 2420 2623 3052 3225
7 SWEET ANDY  0   £2089   -00043010000   578 679 992 1165 1188 1346 1609* 1727 2381 2490 2730
3 SWEET DELILAH  0   £-   -400   1602 2948 3159
3 SWEET DOMAIN  46   £4158   0320-0011042   277 747 1841* 2161* 2578 2995 3113
4 SWEET EIRE  2   £376   33400-00004032   310 906 1424 1771 1979 2585 2743 2884
4 SWEET EXPLANATION  7   £-   030-0   207
3 SWEET FOOL  0   £-   0-000   205 346 564
4 SWEET GEMMA  4   £407   00-40-02300400   22 107 1081 1273 2429 2863 3076 3224
2 SWEET MARY LOU  0   £-   00   2153 2423
3 SWEET MOVE  0   £-   -0   559
3 SWEET MOVER  66   £10678   22-1220   1503* 1912- 2278 3207
2 SWEET PICCOLO  9   £93   0030   728 1323 1537 1997
7 SWEET RASCAL  0   £-   -000   1208 1535 1686
2 SWEET RIBOT  0   £-   000   711 1881 2032
4 SWEET SALORA  5   £-   03000-0   1171
3 SWEET SNUGFIT  0   £-   000-00   1481 1623
3 SWEET SPICE  0   £-   -000   656 937 2321
4 SWEETWATER LASS  7   £-   00030-0   2958
2 SWEPT AWAY  24   £-   0   2846
4 SWIFT ASCENT  46   £-   42024-0   1519
2 SWIFT CHALLENGER  0   £-   4000   146 2323 2976 3228
9 SWIFT PALM  21   £-   24330-000   10 112 399 1018
2 SWIFT PURCHASE  35   £4907   3000104010   434 614 918 1082 1557* 1938 2097 2218 2405* 2708
4 SWIFT RIVER  10   £1147   0/0-20203033044   131 378 522 606 788 889 1054 1133 1613 1659 1699
3 SWIFT TROOPER  48   £19877   30410-121420003   63* 193 326* 692 919 1034 2693 2867 3179
3 SWIFTS PAL  48   £4605   1000-0030410002   216 326 881 1032 1343 1520+ 2475 2730 2879 3066
5 SWIFTSPENDER  0   £-   00234-000000000   9 745 956 1231 1624 1870 2309 2414 2887
4 SWIMMER  51   £14849   31013-1430021   964* 1166 1325 1509 2536 2766 2942*
2 SWING SINGER  13   £283   3300000   771 826 2398 2493 2680 2791 3201
4 SWINGING GOLD  24   £-   20000-00440   784 1101 1423 1543 1649
2 SWINGSIGN  0   £-   0   1232
3 SWINK  82   £69292   0-3231240   1117 1354* 2114 2565 3169
2 SWISS CONNECTION  42   £-   000   2717 3109 3228
3 SWISS NEPHEW  35   £798   00-3003   512 751 2300 3140
2 SWYNFORD LADY  0   £-   000   2032 2279 2994
3 SWYNFORD PRINCE  3   £3629   3-0012030000000   14 54 331* 416 648 738 949 1284 1685 2276 2337
  2467 2551
2 SWYNFORD PRINCESS  8   £1009   -0410300000   34 446 543* 647 1076 1294 2010 2606 2744 2919
3 SYBIL FAWLTY  30   £2290   020-04421000   338 656 1607 2186 2488* 2765 3145 3204
3 SYBILLY  0   £-   -0S0000   1184 1375 1626 1841 2110 2603
3 SYLVAN EXPRESS  65   £22891   00211-0100100   326 406+ 808 1147 1490* 1655 2006
4 SYLVAN JOKER  12   £-   -2010-000   58A 504 841
2 SYLVAN ORIENT  34   £306   00030000   270 513 1587 2044 2556 2718 3085 3135
2 SYLVAN WHISPER  0   £-   0   1232
6 SYMBOLIC  27   £153   10--2-00043   11 44 1577 1769 2528
3 SYNDROM  71   £7728   02   301 1859
3 SYNTHETIC  24   £-   4010-0000   352 575 1885 2184
3 SYRIENNE  57   £3606   3   1713
2 SYSTEMS GO  32   £119   03400   722 1187 1555 2276 2652
2 TA WARDLE  25   £-   000   1458 1936 2615
3 TABACOS  27   £-   0-40044   479 619 832 1040 1400
4 TABARDAR  40   £5069   03400-3010000   265 433 652* 879 2219 2692 3038
2 TABAREEK  0   £-   00000   1653 1928 2308 3073 3141
2 TABELLINA  15   £-   00   2846 3136
2 TABLE TURNING  18   £704   00-243304   258 874 1362 1813 2027 2171
3 TACHOMETER  19   £-   00-0000   283 624 1001 1120
4 TACHYON PARK  28   £3244   00000-002100   1086 2519 2592 2702* 2783 2992
2 TACITURN LADY  0   £-   00   2069 2147
2 TAFFY TEMPLAR  42   £124   300   1573 1928 2036
2 TAFFYS DELIGHT  20   £800   2   2115
4 TAFFYS PRIDE  0   £-   -0000000   943 1186 1208 1837 2190 2282 2533
4 TAGORE  6   £-   00000-000   1649 1942 2189
2 TAHARD  12   £143   000000030   694 1129 1504 1634 2026 2334 2781 3032 3079
2 TAHGREBA  34   £-   00   2147 2577
                              > 1022 <
```

2 TAHILLA 71 £9919 111 2147* 2433+ 2543*
2 TAIANA 0 £- 0 2270
3 TAIS TOI 24 £- 00-400400 422 843 1198 1749 2017 2429
4 TAJ SINGH 8 £189 00000-0000443 453 606 830 1133 1302 1613 1766
3 TAKE A BREAK 23 £1232 20020-010002003 209 346* 637 1064 1303 1400 1439 1567 1666
7 TAKE A CARD 15 £- 00404-04 7 80
2 TAKE A HINT 26 £1154 4414000 180 536 864* 1203 1570 2813 2941
2 TAKE EFFECT 17 £540 333000000000 20 47 136 332 1180 1333 1561 1717 2011 2535 2919 3081
3 TAKE THE BISCUIT 0 £306 -00000020003000 14 54 491 740 932 1063 1210 1400 1567 1759 1767 1845 1969 2014
3 TAKFA YAHMED 72 £19703 11140-2143 156 291* 644 757
2 TALE OF INTRIGUE 0 £- 00 2675 3011
4 TALE QUALE 64 £4514 11301-040044 585 704 1127 1513 1888 2844
2 TALIESIN 15 £103 0030000 632 864 1339 2284 2465 2757 3081
5 TALK OF GLORY 28 £3460 000-02002230020 174 453 706 1041 1240- 1450 2049 2121 2578 2699 2925
2 TALLAND BAY 0 £- 00 2436 3221
2 TALUS 44 £295 02 2847 2957
3 TAMALPAIS 12 £384 000-300000340 283 534 837 1198 1989 2424 2614 2793 2906
3 TAMANA DANCER 22 £1954 00-0001 328 593 837 1288*
2 TAMASSOS 24 £322 000300 1802 1966 2301 2678 2986 3222
3 TAMATOUR 47 £2743 -021234 1578 1954 2228* 2517 2733 3038
3 TAMBOUR BATTANT 62 £- 00 301 643
4 TAME DUCHESS 7 £- 00040-04000 28 119 343 495 564
3 TAMED SHREW 33 £- 4-0 832
5 TAMERTOWN LAD 12 £676 40000-20000 262 499 578 930 1829
2 TAMOURAD 0 £- 0 2 59
4 TANA MIST 4 £- 00000-0000 735 2925 3193 3224
3 TANAGON 0 £- -00 357 2275
3 TANAOS 77 £2964 314-10 1068* 1456
3 TANCRED SAND 0 £- 00-0 2464
7 TANCRED WALK 20 £885 02210/2 2873
5 TANFEN 27 £7473 0-0310210401000 18 369 525+ 687 820 1093+ 1157 1616 1810 2012* 2378 2537 2816
5 TANG DANCER 12 £- 144-0-00 1676 2213
2 TANGALOOMA 35 £139 340 417 746 1946
2 TANGDONTPAY 21 £736 01 13 102*
3 TANGLED LOVE 0 £- -0 1645
2 TANGO STAR 0 £- 0 3181
3 TANIAS DAD 34 £- 00400-0 15
3 TANOUMA 61 £4294 1-30003 232 467 754 2231 2940
3 TANYAS PRINCESS 08 £349 03-30020 829 1299 1482 1662 2083
3 TAP DUET 6 £276 000-0420000 234 318 767 1258 2366 2478 2679
3 TAP EM TWICE 43 £2619 04-2330431 164 430 983 2030 2269 2464 2610*
2 TAP ON BLUE 33 £- 000 852 2664 3133
2 TAP THE BATON 22 £1130 43230003440 186 404 622 1618 1717 2172 2421 2744 2781 2986 3218
2 TAPPIANO 70? £157343 2 3209
3 TARA DANCER 5 £- 00010-0000000 35 54 318 451 524 767 889
3 TARANGA 38 £4255 002-11020400200 109* 134+ 228 309 1900 2143 2343 2674 2870 3104 3231
5 TARAS CHARIOT 32 £372 02200-303 2075 2403 2517
3 TARGET SIGHTED 34 £819 2-0220 25 75 790 1130
3 TARIB 70 £32538 21112-2142120 203 758* 1125 1387- 1860* 2457 3054
6 TARISTEAC 0 £- 40000-0 1839
9 TARLETON 0 £259 00300-200000 788 993 1156 1500 2037 2309
6 TARLETON ELM 21 £- 00 930 1349
3 TARLETONS OAK 28 £- 000-4000 1806 2373 2985 3140
4 TARRAKAN 10 £634 04131-000200 1450 1651 2022 2581 3078 3224
5 TARS HILL 22 £1085 20012-0200034 499 724 942 1150 1450 1837 2134
2 TARSA 54 £1498 020 2651 2846 3103
5 TARTAN TAILOR 22 £158 -3 381
2 TARTUFFE 71 £20127 01113 1518 2542* 2811* 2951* 3041
4 TARVISIO 59 £3824 -3 398
4 TASHONYA 23 £- 00040-0 1831
3 TASHTIYA 78 £23020 0-211 581 2649* 2952*
2 TASJIL 42 £456 4003 434 1518 2119 3075
5 TASKFORCE VICTORY 19 £- 00001-000 306 649 890
3 TATE GALLERY 75 £1953 --011-30 267 407
2 TAUBER 50 £2422 032330 497 1162 1653 2056 2782 3037
3 TAUFAST 0 £- -00 448 2103
2 TAUSTAFF 38 £- 000 1778 2527 2788
3 TAVIRI 54 £4600 -2411 1934 2333 2572* 2930*
6 TAW CROSSING 0 £- -0 211
2 TAWEEL 28 £- 000 2341 2645 3171
2 TAWNY PIPIT 0 £- 00 21 186
3 TAX ROY 47 £4678 30121-001002200 671 947 1380* 1524 1654 1950- 2079 2224 2672
3 TAXI MAN 10 £1951 00-010000000000 702 960* 1303 1563 1838 2103 2300 2478 2603 2760 2890 3100
4 TAXIADS 27 £3554 20200-01100300 542 743* 984* 1035 1243 1871 1963 2211
4 TAXINETTE 0 £- 04000-00 28 105
2 TAYLOR CARES 0 £- 00 2625 3153
3 TAYLOR OF SOHAM 32 £7988 2340300413232323203 38 84 241 387 545 836 1066 1191 1603* 1695 1847 2143 2295 2473 2614 2758 3015 3145 3233
3 TAYLORMADE BOY 40 £10655 330-31230310100 48 258* 553 690 1179 1412 1794* 1974 2266* 2475 2684
2 TAYLORS REVENGE 0 £- 000 2645 3130 3228
3 TAYLORS TAYLORMADE 14 £333 40020-0302 339 489 910 1549
2 TEACHERS GAME 21 £173 434000 1583 1867 2127 2435 2595 2792
2 TEAM EFFORT 56 £5156 0301121300 3 43 197 254+ 1138* 1203 1373* 1697 2479 2552
8 TEARS OF GOLD 0 £- -0 2517
3 TEARS OF LAUGHTER 16 £375 000-0020 506 697 1258 1822
3 TEBITTO 38 £7587 000-01012024 402 738* 1085 1733* 1939 2247 2551 2850
2 TECANA 51 £1296 444 1464 1855 3108
2 TECHNOCRAT 20 £- 0000 622 1629 2254 3135

```
3 TEED BORE      21   £849    0-2043002      39 123 335 650 867 1773 3086
7 TEEJAY          4   £1284  -030000100     163 851 1079 1412 1985 2102 2836* 2964 3220
2 TELEGRAPH FOLLY 18   £1092   043310000     118 329 502 681 853* 1598 2097 2405 2625
6 TELEPROMPTER   89   £88862  12120-2333021   598- 1094 1389 1811 2456 2770- 3000*
2 TELESTO        30   £-     04400    1039 1234 1345 2097 2529
3 TELL EM NOWT    0   £-     -0   1807
2 TELL ME NOW    13   £-     00040    1550 1665 1843 3034 3073
4 TELWAAH        54   £2985  11010-20240     815 1109 1390 1911 3055
3 TEMPEST TOSSED 31   £3426   0003-040323010    637 955 1559 1726 1918 2182 2217 2372* 2489
3 TEMPLE HEIGHTS 40   £2714   -012400    458 1251* 1623 2164 2647 2882
3 TEMPLE WALK    54   £7513  0-1301100    1198* 1315 1886 2376* 2665* 2834 3110
3 TEMPTING SILVER 42  £-     -004   916 1031 1437
3 TENASSERIM     10   £-     -004000    891 1142 1420 1626 1959 2268
3 TENDER LOVING CARE 56  £-   120-0000    373 1128 1932 2650
2 TENDER TIFF    42   £2931   14300    655* 773 953 1255 3122
3 TENDER TYPE    42   £6880   -00012134030    357 570 1167 1615* 1678 1998+ 2156 2420 2692 2850 3038
2 TENTH DIMENSION 0   £-     0   2159
3 TERMIENNE      76   £21540  -41-13    97* 300
3 TERMINATOR     45   £2133   341-3030    326 615 1520 1854
5 TERN           24   £-     21000-00    336 526
3 TERN OF A CENTURY 14  £-   -000   1327 2299 2726
2 TERTIARY ZONE  61   £2817   322   1392 2542 2860
5 TEST OF TIME   46   £731    03300-20    1173 1335
3 TESTAROSSA      0   £-     0-0004    1210 1364 1666 2163
4 TESTIMONIAL    17   £-     2--00-0   801
2 TEZ SHIKARI    41   £3946   04222021    170 350 536- 728 1059 1405 1583 2328*
3 THAI SKY        0   £-     3440-0000000000    113 177 1210 1316 1499 1943 2210 2417 2597 2616
3 THALASSINO ASTERI 48  £-   014-000    216 386 946
4 THALESTRIA     30   £-     4-300-0000    325 618 1286 1755
2 THAMEEN        64   £7635   414   2159 2673* 3003
2 THANK HAVON    40   £5157   4040341    1067 1225 1984 2105 2336 2512 2680*
6 THARALEOS       0   £171    04200-0400300    80 827 1017 1280 1477 1737 2974
3 THARITA         0   £-     -000   162 702 862
2 THAT CERTAIN SMILE 37  £618  3230   1427 1696 1826 2181
3 THATCH AVON    17   £-     40000000    94 186 685 2535 2723 3016 3112 3228
5 THATCHERED     14   £1380   00000-0010000    1774 1839 2397* 2513 2816 3104 3157
3 THATCHINGLY    11   £1434   23300-104000000    176* 263 569 652 856 1166 1365 1558 1945
4 THATCHIT        4   £-     -0000-000    1195 1535 1784
4 THATCHVILLE    20   £2817   44040-044000100    30 114 520 668 762 1263 2966* 3065 3191
2 THATS MOTORING  0   £-     000   353 834 3072
4 THATS YOUR LOT 36   £-     1-140-0000000    72 248 445 706 1038 3119 3232
3 THE BATCHLOR    7   £-     041-0000    845 1213 1367 1549
3 THE BEAN SIDHE 74   £28585  03110-130100    294* 394 472 2006* 2145 2633
4 THE BERWICK     0   £-     -0   1923
4 THE BETSY      28   £3353   00000-0401314    121 595 751 856* 1265 1321+ 1393
3 THE BIGHT       0   £-     0100-00000    198 825 1664 1959 2055
2 THE BRAZILIAN  17   £366    0402   415 1155 1480 1618
3 THE CANNY MAN  30   £547    -000100    699 790 1055 1544* 2326 2627
4 THE CHALICEWELL 0   £-     00200-4040000    145 489 1070 1438 1543 1662 1950
2 THE CHIPPENHAM MAN 18 £1643  02213300    1190 1318 1723 1944* 2168 2609 3016 3081
5 THE CLOWN      30   £3940   22200-011    225 1140* 1419*
2 THE CROSS       0   £-     00000    1683 2080 2375 2875 3184
4 THE CRYING GAME 9   £3055   00000-400210    409 591 731 1133 1659* 1809
3 THE DABBER      0   £195    000-003300    22 41 139 279 673 2585
2 THE DEVILS MUSIC 34 £107    0000003    515 1916 2100 2661 3114 3174 3218
2 THE DOMINICAN  50   £5367   322132    350 503 694 918* 1003 1162
3 THE FINK SISTERS 19 £-     0440-000    2401 2520 2800
10 THE FOODBROKER  0  £-     -0   2572
4 THE FOOTMAN    29   £220    13010-00040040    263 1112 1325 1539 2121 2273 2406 2533
2 THE GAELCHARN   0   £-     0   3201
5 THE GAMES UP   40   £5792   30300-44101    265 445 940* 1109 1188*
3 THE GODFATHER   0   £-     0-000    688 1315 1646
4 THE GOLF SLIDE  0   £443    00000-020003000    889 1201 1338 1394 1574 1839 2104 2335 2697
2 THE GRANITTON  22   £1411   1000    133* 304 1174 2265
2 THE GREAT MATCH 32  £280    004400    583 715 918 2398 2606 2744
2 THE GRIFTER    25   £-     0000    2205 2542 2711 2926
4 THE HEIGHTS     0   £-     -0   176
3 THE HILCOTE CLUB 40 £205    00044-4004    06 62 507 1505
5 THE HOUGH      15   £-     -044000    770 888 1361 2152 2413 2604
4 THE HOWARD     26   £-     -0101-000400    71 238 652 976 1335 1523
6 THE JOKER      38   £1496   -040043    693 1000 1148 1523 1935 2285
3 THE LEGGETT    12   £-     R0024-000    307 430 684
3 THE LIDGATE STAR 9  £-     -000000    14 229 928 1603 1917 2614
2 THE LIONHEART  50   £1178   020   350 1903 2105
3 THE LITTLE JOKER 0  £-     00000-0000    39 246 309 438
4 THE LODGE PRINCE 10 £-     00000-0000    2861 2924 3026 3225
2 THE LONDONDERRY 0   £-     000   1555 2080 2584
2 THE MAGUE      22   £1350   0042210200    425 612 696 1137 1279 1474* 1955 2138 2919 3016
2 THE MAIN MAN   36   £-     0040    1345 2468 2889 3099
5 THE MANOR       0   £-     -0000    211 636 1101 1338
6 THE MAZALL     42   £14497  001202211001200    321 594 700* 830 1157 1377 1482 1761* 1868* 2039 2437
                                                 2526* 2685 2945 3021
3 THE MECHANIC   34   £9948   00000-0212311    64 977 1101+ 1227 1283 1730+ 1834+
5 THE MISSISSIPPIAN 25 £2683  00000-421D10    208 538 542- 869* 984
3 THE MOON AND BACK 0 £-     0-00000    334 498 963 1439 1784
7 THE NUB        29   £-     33/00-0    265
2 THE PRICE IS RIGHT 0 £-    0   2761
4 THE PRUDENT PRINCE 52 £14115 32-2111230    613 769* 1092* 1470* 1679 2539 3052
3 THE QUIETSTAN   0   £-     -000   253 402 928
2 THE REFRIGERATOR 0  £-     0   3109
3 THE ROMFORD ROAR 0  £-     -000   1073 2214 2339
5 THE RUSK        1   £-     -0000    1361 1769 2008 2101
                                    > 1024 <
```

3 THE SPORTSMAN 12 £- 040-00 335 564
3 THE STAMP DEALER 11 £142 -00003000 438 733 842 1288 2174 2473 2594 3160
3 THE STRAY BULLETT 6 £760 30-002000302000 51 377 529 768 910 1200 1418 1627 1734 1927 2322 2743
2 THE TAIN 0 £- 0 2499
3 THE TALETELLER 68 £1548 -12 1444* 1831-
3 THE TENDER MATADOR 5 £- 34010-000 93 346 749
4 THE UPSTART 15 £- 00000-00 2132 2699
3 THE UTE 23 £3555 -02023201204221 399 564 620 749 1210 1364 1459 1549* 1827 2132 2271 2370 2417 2898*
2 THE VICTOR GIRLS 0 £- 000 2678 2875 3189
2 THE WHITE LION 0 £- 000 543 813 2138
3 THE WOODEN HUT 6 £1420 00430-120000400 29* 120 331 623 738 1733 2190 2617 3196
4 THE YOMPER 12 £428 -0200-4203004 341 592 959 1808 2059 2395 2510
4 THEATRICAL 90 £328134 10200-0202 1144 1861 2456 3212
2 THEKKIAN 24 £2059 130000 415* 766 1138 2391 2563 2859
3 THEN AGAIN 84 £55870 -01-101212D 676* 878 1655* 2064- 2259* 3020
3 THEREAFTER 24 £168 000-000300 486 730 955 1451 2135 2659
4 THERESA 1 £- 00000-0 731
6 THETFORD CHASE 0 £- -0 419
4 THIRTEENTH FRIDAY 3 £631 -0000-400034300 259 745 893 1054 1774 1906 1983 2602 3060
3 THORCASTLE 40 £- -40 316 1677
2 THORNFIELD 42 £382 03 2926 3134
4 THORNY ROSE 33 £- 12110-000 2850 3119 3232
2 THORNYHILL 0 £- P0 1647 2308
4 THREE BELLS 14 £255 20-0-0004300000 950 1213 1521 1834 2046 2295 2519 2715 2861 3078
2 THREE GENERATIONS 74 £1564 140 2644 2915
2 THREE TAILS 70 £16709 011 2574 2703+ 3095*
3 THREE TIMES A LADY 30 £4324 -0002232200 224 372 551 1042 1410 1530 1732 2000 2202 2610
3 THRESH IT OUT 52? £3435 0223-23032 334 586 719 1184 1415
3 THRILL SHOW 88 £66293 -11120 1859* 2507 3211
5 THRONE OF GLORY 34 £1328 -00004400230430 182 260 355 606 742 1682 1852 2204 2411 2513 2537 2632 2816 2858
6 THROW ME OVER 12 £- 00-00-P 91
5 THUNDER ROCK 0 £- -0 44
3 THUNDERDOME 44 £6224 -00001110 806 1327 1953 2274 2746* 2925* 3101+ 3179
3 TIBER GATE 0 £- 000-0000000000 998 1258 1898 2125 2590 2679 2789 2902 3045 3193
2 TIBER RIVER 38 £583 3 1587
3 TIBERIUS 72 £7062 -203 2454 2824 3170
3 TICAROCK 70 £- 00 300 467
3 TICKFORD 44 £1673 1-431D00 1237 1523 1663 1939 2551
5 TIDDLYEYETYE 0 £- 21440-00000000 135 936 1182 1839 2086 2411 2621 3152
3 TIEATRE 15 £1002 00000-001000 379 894 1123* 1250 1615 2280
2 TIGER RIVER 0 £- 00 3103 3228
2 TIGER RUN 66 £1564 11D 2914
5 TIGERWOOD 35 £13791 0-000-12102221 942* 1058- 1533+ 1875 2311 2591- 2882- 3139*
2 TIKLAS 20 £1109 000434343 1067 1161 1650 1883 2011 2310 2498 2680 2841
2 TILFORD 0 £- 0 3176
2 TILLEY LAMP 0 £- 0 3176
2 TILLOUJO 0 £- 000 1059 1832 2107
2 TILTING COURT 50 £2628 01 2782 3135*
2 TILTING YARD 0 £- 000 73 717 1576
5 TIMBER MERCHANT 28 £- 00304-00 976 1188
3 TIMBERWOOD 48 £184 4040-120 388* 861- 1046
2 TIMBUCK 0 £- 0 3206
3 TIME BIRD 25 £- 333-000 335 1065 1245
2 TIME ODYSSEY 0 £- 0 2574
3 TIME WARP 0 £- 00-0 3070
2 TIMEFIGHTER 50 £1131 1 1234*
2 TIMELLA 0 £- 0 722
2 TIMES ARE HARD 34 £485 3 2696
2 TIMESWITCH 45 £4318 200220021 531 632 715 2090- 2227 2479 2648 2989- 3079+
4 TIMEWASTER 10 £- 00000-000000 10 160 208 1273 1400 1519
4 TIMMINION 14 £291 03330-3000034 44 69 308 449 2683 2789 3036
3 TIMSOLO 0 £- -00000 2085 2174 2509 2963 3100
4 TIMURS GIFT 4 £- -0000-000 36 860 1477
2 TIMURTASCH 0 £- 000 497 1598 1936
7 TIN BOY 10 £- 0 2072
3 TINA ROSA 0 £- 000-00000 1346 1943 2313 2416 2896
2 TINAS BEAUTY 26 £238 00300 1576 1844 2032 2352 2625
3 TINAS LAD 0 £- 00000-000000 1212 1600 1671 1898 2128 2613
2 TINAS MELODY 38 £4012 312104 1205 1545* 1683 2010+ 3019 3146
3 TINSEL ROSE 0 £- 40-000000 346 749 1264 1400 1666 2984
3 TINTEROSSE 75 £15388 11-11110 557* 2772
4 TIP TAP 20 £2656 02003-000104004 709 930 1558 1870* 2217 2545 2728 3116 3164
3 TIP TOP BOY 0 £- -0000 309 516 891 2339
2 TIPATINA 60 £959 010 2013 2652+ 2933
3 TIPPLE TIME 28 £- 03300-00 175 454
2 TIPTREE 18 £- 00000 1019 1289 1495 2405 2841
2 TIQUEGREAN 53 £2622 22 2847 3163
3 TISNT 75 £19185 -12300 60* 224- 510 3121 3175
2 TISSERANDS 0 £- 000 2069 2191 2596
2 TISZTA SHAROK 46 £959 1P 2089* 2421
4 TIT WILLOW 12 £3333 0-0221203432440 9 41 163 828* 1136 1547 1976 2340 2411 2816 2970 3149 3204
3 TITAN KING 11 £- 00001-00 1079 1281
2 TITANIAS STAR 0 £- 0 2969
6 TIVIAN 25 £3324 13010-1000000 4* 92 215 584 698 3038 3195
2 TO MONAKRIVO MOU 0 £- 0 2791
3 TOBAGO DANCER 54 £5987 02404-01223 234 464* 659 1085 1588
9 TOBERMORY BOY 35 £4639 -00020000040200 428 742 922 1306- 1429 1810 2079 2204 2586 2731 2764 2862 2921 3015
3 TOCA MADERA 80 £45005 ---11-101 293* 407 559*
                              > 1025 <

```
4 TODA FORCA AVANTI  0   £325   000-02D00000000    36 262 511 750 888 1264 2208 2342 3076 3193
3 TODAY EDDY  0   £-   -0   1639
3 TOGDALE  0   £-   000-00P   2085 2400 2682
2 TOKANDA  13   £212   0000030   1625 1764 1862 2323 2757 3016 3069
2 TOLL BAR  42   £1343   01000   1376 1735* 2198 2276 2680
7 TOLLYMORE  2   £-   03004-00   135 3104
3 TOLLYS ALE  18   £423   0304-4300040430    83 175 545 2106 2312 2409 2775 2884 3024 3144
4 TOLLYS BEST  06   £-   0-000-00000   211 626 1093 1482 1547
4 TOLLYS TONIC  4   £-   3000-00   2342 2414
2 TOLUCA LAKE  66   £9276   41110   1197 1948* 2352* 2521* 3126
5 TOM FORRESTER  19   £1597   003-03044230000    453 578 680 1041 1229 2516- 2807 2925 3050 3140
  3195
3 TOM RUM  14   £243   000-000034    193 331 535 1062 1609 1835
6 TOM SHARP  24   £1214   04000-00020    11 375 2591 3013 3225
3 TOMMY WAY  82   £193761   -021-311120    411 555* 1005* 1328* 2741 3096
5 TOMORROWS WORLD  0   £-   0-000-00   201 530
2 TOMS LITTLE BET  22   £-   0000   1057 1341 1518 2044
5 TOMS NAP HAND  0   £266   -000002400U    636 727 1344 1519 1834 1990 2518 2619 2655 2836
4 TOMS TREASURE  30   £523   -3330   1208 1494 2096 3194
3 TONDELA  29   £-   4-0   169
3 TONQUIN  24   £382   -0003430    484 832 1469 2000 2228 2430 3187
3 TONY BIN  79   £71968   3-14132    555 2741 3096
3 TOO PHAR  55   £5200   4   1592
2 TOOT TOOT  20   £67   340   1297 1696 2878
2 TOOTSIE JAY  0   £-   0   3221
2 TOOTSIE JAY  8   £647   30032400000000    77 223 278 589 711 1137 1483 1599 2465 2588 2724 2990
  3069 3148
3 TOOTSIE ROLL  6   £-   -400000    1463 1626 1971 2367 2659 2816
3 TOP AND LADY  74   £10410   ----1-22    97 561
2 TOP AND TAIL  38   £1818   01   223 2969*
3 TOP CORSAGE  81   £55944   -2   3214
2 TOP COVER  0   £-   00   1801 2069
3 TOP DEBUTANTE  35   £2036   -300210    218 359 1589 1953 2316* 2459
4 TOP FEATHER  0   £-   4004-00000000    262 499 578 1349 1686 2132 2271 2697
7 TOP GOLD  0   £-   -3-000    547 1056 1459
3 TOP GUEST  70   £38049   0222-122211    194* 476 1045 1378 1899+ 2642*
2 TOP OF MAI FIELD  0   £-   0   1583
9 TOP OTHLANE  0   £-   0100-0400000000    1377 1424 1624 1839 2039 2104 2340 2602 3157 3220
3 TOP RANGE  50   £4489   -030221    253 328 625 916 1284 2408*
2 TOP ROBE  0   £-   00   1622 1862
3 TOP ROW  10   £-   04300-00000    1503 1808 2028 2129 2360 2473
3 TOP RULER  46   £-   134-000000    220 574 802 1468 1655 2234
3 TOP SHOT  45   £1024   00-1   1842*
5 TOP THAT  26   £4236   000-00201400200    12 56 124- 428 649* 1093 1157 1222 1973 2295 2397
2 TOP WAK  0   £-   00   1382 1855
3 TOP WING  42   £2747   2-1030400    188* 370 713 1028 2255 2390 2674
2 TOPAS  40   £678   3   2448
3 TOPEKA EXPRESS  18   £1329   000-0000320244    228 340 719 1080 1281 1560 1761 2171 2274 2929
2 TOPICAL ISSUE  0   £-   0   1770
7 TOPORI  8   £807   130   119+ 201 341
3 TOPPESHAMME  46   £-   2311-000    478 1028 1922
2 TORRANCE  20   £-   000   2484 2717 2926
3 TORRE DE BELEM  0   £-   -0   3186
2 TORRES VEDRAS  44   £382   03   2036 2711
7 TORREY  28   £1137   00-10-2234    499 710 1264 1500
3 TORREYA  28   £738   -0423234    458 779 935 1123 1544 1970 2428
3 TORRIGGIA  0   £-   00-0000000    1080 1337 2152 2427 2508 2603 2818
3 TORWADA  46   £2592   204-100300    191* 1130 1642 1848 2149 3119
3 TORY BLUES  0   £-   -000   1198 1580 2068
4 TOSARA  52   £5066   0-24110    452 613 875+ 1254* 1526
5 TOSCANA  22   £2235   13200-221000    1243 1349 1871* 2861 2959 3187
3 TOUCH ME NOT  5   £119   40000-3000400    64 168 241 377 608 729 1051
3 TOUCH OF GREY  54   £27511   0-0011201400000    15 62 534+ 624+ 929 1027 1145* 1524 1669 1777 2668
  2772 2842
4 TOUCH OF LUCK  5   £256   00333-00000030    164 358 541 917 1042 1223 1817 1952
2 TOUCH OF SPEED  29   £-   00000400    20 437 728 1958 2167 2476 2805 2875
3 TOUCH THE SAIL  4   £262   0000-0420400    809 1617 1771 1927 2621 2898 3084
5 TOUCHEZ LE BOIS  16   £-   12-00-0000000    225 872 990 1470 2093 2627 2776
2 TOUCHING LOVE  63   £6923   2   2644
2 TOUGH N GENTLE  51   £6441   32123120234    664 915 1172* 1320 1552 1798* 2166 2252 2511 2618 3072
3 TOUKSHAD  18   £102   -30   2366 3159
3 TOUR VIEILLE  33   £-   000-00   816 1065
6 TOURNAMENT LEADER  6   £-   02130-000    709 943 984
3 TOWER BAY  0   £-   00   2607 2796
3 TOWER FAME  8   £-   04-000040000    14 90 650 874 1724 1998 2173 2426 2683
2 TOWN ABLAZE  48   £-   4   292
3 TOWN FAIR  0   £-   -0000   966 1244 1516 1827
3 TOWN JESTER  41   £-   310-0000    216 1854 2870 2946
3 TOWN OF ENNIS  0   £-   00-0000    379 651 1063 1158
2 TOWNSHIP  30   £-   -000   1628 2061 2430
2 TOY CUPBOARD  52   £1697   42   1874 2147
4 TRACING  53   £-   14321-00    921 1038
4 TRACK MARSHALL  16   £1013   00300-322320    343 718 783 1195 1666 1784
3 TRACK THE BEAR  9   £-   20000-000    201 620 729
4 TRACKERS JEWEL  20   £2157   0--00-00120    709 984 2714* 2959 3187
7 TRADE HIGH  16   £2639   -00300000401000    110 260 378 490 700 830 1074 1546 1676 1839 2126* 2264
  2411 2549
6 TRADESMAN  0   £1064   000,000103000000000    56 490 626 786 ,825 971 1423* 1616 1718 2124 2322
  2411 2586 2775 2816 3046 3083 3152
5 TRAFFITANZI  16   £2271   30--2-0001S    349 569 761 1265* 1667
2 TRAFFORD WAY  0   £-   0000   425 931 2325 2396
3 TRALTHEE  74   £11959   31-100    661* 926 1932
2 TRANBY CROFT  50   £-   00   3080 3163
                                              >  1026  <
```

```
2 TRANISKI  0   £-   0    2852
3 TRANSCENDENCE  47   £1074   -020   209 549 1192
7 TRANSFLASH  36   £1995   000-43003030000   55 192 361 508 952 1145 1525 1890 2437 2566 2773
3 TRANSFORM  0   £-   0-00   1626 2393
2 TRAPDOOR  0   £-   0    3137
5 TRAPEZE ARTIST  34   £13090   0400211002220000   11 58A 215 375 582 735+ 917* 1099 1293 1709
  2164 2389 2523 2733 2873 2944
2 TRAPEZE DANCER  41   £-   0    2852
2 TRAPPER  0   £-   00   2847 3163
6 TRAVEL HOME  0   £-   -00   1361 1736
3 TRAVEL MAGIC  50   £7640   -010221400   806 1451* 1821 2063 2255 2437* 2568 2719 2940
3 TRAVEL MYSTERY  45   £5279   0-1330210   1061* 1437 1657 1912 2286 2489* 2769
7 TREASURE HUNTER  26   £415   030-400020   869 1177 1293 1533 3049 3219
3 TREASURE KAY  72   £20551   010-142321   314* 600 1151- 1387 2241- 2524*
2 TREBLE TOP  0   £-   000   2249 2514 3109
9 TREE FELLA  0   £-   00000-00000000   1546 1703 1839 2126 2411 2743 3149 3220
3 TREGEAGLE  30   £-   0400   1780 2541 2723 3221
2 TREIZE QUATORZE  0   £-   00000   818 1770 2043 2472 2757
2 TREK  60   £4371   1043   2504 2739
3 TRELALES  0   £-   00-000   729 1574 1824
3 TRELAWNEY  32   £2505   000-0001120   117 277 841 1210* 1310* 1667 1806
5 TREMBLANT  73   £13892   30111-200033440   5 433 1109 1455 1823 2145 2461 2867 3051
3 TREMENDOUS JET  18   £1758   00-0001000223   351 535 625 1063* 1830 2132 2516 2697 2836 2898
2 TREMPOLINO  68   £1840   144   3208
3 TRENT END  0   £-   -0   498
5 TRENTULLO BLUE  0   £-   00000   863 1182 1546 1839 2014
4 TRESIDDER  28   £858   13410-04042400   11 52 1024 1663 2087 2326 2445 2662
2 TREVA  32   £-   0400   985 1239 1518 2209
4 TREYARNON  16   £1395   -43433000443223   58 142 449 631 827 912 1223 1336 2037 2173 2374 2583
  2818 2885
2 TRIAL BID  0   £-   0    3223
2 TRIBAL PAGEANT  28   £-   00   2904 3221
4 TRICENCO  09   £118   02000-00000300   369 788 889 1201 1424 1979 2124 2585
3 TRICK OR TREAT  42   £3466   1300-14440   518* 914 1371 1922 2481
2 TRICKLE  0   £-   000   3056 3153 3223
3 TRICKY  12   £-   030-000000   447 911 1200 1664 1742 2312
4 TRIKKALA STAR  0   £-   23000-00000   23 179 856 1310 1459
2 TRIKYMIA  44   £158   3   988
3 TRIPLE BLUFF  39   £3553   00-031P   253 674 1034* 1284
2 TRIPLE ENTENTE  38   £403   3200   662 1172 1948 3067
4 TRIPTYCH  91   £506224   0303-4212323310   468 885- 1352* 1389 1790 2200- 2506 2917 3051+ 3213
3 TRIPWIRE  67   £5650   32010-1   2500*
2 TRIVIA  0   £-   00   2531 2904
3 TRIXIE BELLE  0   £-   0-00   33 1375
4 TROJAN GOD  5   £226   -0000-303   2208 2429 2654
2 TROJAN LEGEND  36   £-   004   2628 3014 3229
2 TROJAN MISS  51   £2930   21   2249 2487*
4 TROJAN PRINCE  56   £-   00133-0   782
2 TROJAN SONG  50   £1228   2100   2225 2645* 2941 3178
3 TROJAN SPLASH  0   £-   -0004   1494 1690 1937 2371
2 TROJAN WAR  46   £410   43   1392 2721
4 TROJAN WAY  21   £1735   030-00001   519 675 1092 1280 1577*
5 TROMEROS  8   £346   10000-30   2337 3036
2 TROMPE DOEIL  32   £966   00024100   979 1155 2364 2584 2798 2886+ 3085 3178
2 TROPICAL BOY  25   £-   00000   985 1518 2019 2225 2615
2 TROPICAL FLOWER  0   £-   0   3068
3 TROPICO  23   £3692   02-004231021   318 637 992 1288 1401 1471* 2060 2103 2427*
4 TROY FAIR  45   £2070   -0000-10   3129* 3225
2 TROYES  45   £631   4   2951
2 TRUE GENT  56   £3983   1   2574*
3 TRUE NORA  52   £2532   1110-0030040203   443 550 994 1508 1878 2065 2204 2362- 2488 3012
4 TRUE WEIGHT  17   £1145   01000-00010   341 1188 1273 1558* 2896
3 TRUELY BILLY  43   £684   32-10   32* 3022
3 TRUELY NUREYEV  72   £8089   231-02000   1286 2145- 2538 2770 3020
4 TRULY RARE  61   £6901   -4141-00023   248 433 879 1109 1890 2234
6 TRUMPS  0   £-   23104-00000   36 343 750 1165 1188
2 TRY DANCER  32   £484   0002   1604 1782 2678 3034
3 TRY HARDER  31   £611   21400-00340000   816 1147 1532 1758 1922 2443 3029 3231
2 TRY HILLS SUPPLIES  0   £-   0000000   2379 2444 2626 2723 2950 2987 3201
2 TRY MY BRANDY  34   £-   000   1452 1872 2889
4 TRY SCORER  13   £1793   4-2100002004000   58 143* 260 310 611 700 1054 1139 1636 1866 2066 2414
  2797
3 TRY SIR  24   £-   -04000   438 787 891 1281 1540
2 TRY THE DUCHESS  57   £10148   10031   1067* 1287 1641 2133 2297+
5 TRY TO STOP ME  49   £9781   13000-0032104   79 698 879 1047 1249* 1383 1526
2 TRYNOVA  31   £5383   0202110   1322 1598 1846 2032 2177* 2471* 2798
2 TUBESON  0   £-   000   1373 2466 3234
8 TUDOR BOB  0   £-   -0   2706
3 TUDOR DOR  20   £-   -4000   173 351 458 1078
4 TUDOR JUSTICE  0   £-   -0-4   909
3 TUDORIO  0   £-   -0   1469
2 TUESDAY EVENING  0   £-   00000   589 1088 2377 2466 2724
2 TUFTY LADY  46   £2686   0022010   852 1752 2019 2329- 2652 2803* 2941
3 TUFUH  51   £1074   31140-020040   228 567 814 2526 2842 3127
7 TUGBOAT  26   £5199   34104-0212   11 663 1772* 2455
2 TULLA WATER  0   £-   00   3135 3192
2 TUMBA  10   £-   -00   635 996
3 TUMBLE FAIR  15   £-   4014-00000   340 837 1943 2370 2488
2 TUMBLE TIME  0   £-   00   2782 2926
2 TUNEFUL FLUTTER  0   £-   00   3068 3199
3 TUNEFUL LASS  29   £-   0000-00   111 431
5 TURCY BOY  2   £-   -000000   333 399 499 727 1186 1990
3 TURFAH  56   £14469   3400-0211122300   347 829 1431* 1743+ 2009* 2234 2458 2684 2867 3042
                                        >  1027  <
```

```
4 TURFFONTEIN  0   £-   00-00-00    22 257
7 TURI  5   £2443   003312   712 860 1016 1336 1564* 2317
3 TURINA  10   £119   0-00300040    1337 1614 1775 2042 2175 2630 2759 2923
4 TURKOMAN USA  89   £472028    2   3213
3 TURMERIC  24   £3298   2-0000020423133    409 570 723 1384 1637 1838 2190 2386 2613 2722 2874*
  3036 3197
3 TURN EM BACK JACK  20   £133   -0030000   134 247 1743 2085 2190 2426 2704
3 TURN FOR THBETTER  0   £-   000-00   570 751
3 TURNAWAY  33   £-   0220-0   205
2 TURTUR NI  0   £-   00   2933 3181
3 TUSSAC  76   £6421   112-1130   203* 567* 691 1387
4 TUTBURY  37   £2949   42102-44100   79 196 238* 429 521
2 TWEETER  60   £5156   10   2852* 3163
2 TWICE BITTEN  0   £-   00   3111 3198
3 TWICE BOLD  45   £10049   01-0342120432   386 880 1314 1468- 1551+ 2058- 2201 2389 2551 2776
3 TWICKNAM GARDEN  10   £126   00020-00003   438 1065 1199 1426 1960
4 TWO COUNTIES  0   £-   -00   8 258
2 TWYLA  70   £6389   110   944* 1287* 1454
3 TYMBAL  0   £-   0-0000   458 1080 1471 2653
3 TYRANNISE  0   £147   0-002000   356 524 1340 3076 3162 3202
2 TYRED NSNOOKERED  13   £-   00000   1050 1253 1635 2466 2607
2 TYRIAN PRINCESS  31   £3132   010   2707 2829* 3165
4 TYROLLIE  51   £11286   402-12200400100   192+ 401- 616 877 1145 1777 2258 2537 2731* 2862 3118
3 TZU WONG  30   £1810   424-00001300   527 624 1061 1273 1751* 2319 2459 2905
2 U BIX COPY  28   £3033   03230000110   108 446 488 973 1294 1681 2396 2817 2994* 3112* 3230
2 ULTRA NOVA  58   £5087   32011401   533 1501 1632 1782* 2100+ 2308 2694 2835*
3 ULTRESSA  9   £-   0400-000400000   259 779 935 1179 1337 1671 2264 2508 2726
2 ULYSSES  0   £-   000   2961 3141 3199
3 UMBELATA  18   £-   -00000   764 1036 1947 2256 3138
2 UN BEL DI  60   £1314   01004   773 1308* 1850 2158 2482
3 UN DESPERADO  84   £36136   12-031   302 554 1597*
2 UNCLE TOMS CASTLE  0   £-   0   1844
2 UNCLE WILKO  00   £-   0   1625
4 UNCORNERED  16   £-   00020-0   2582
4 UNDER THE STARS  12   £265   00300-0042   343 530 1056 1310
2 UNDERSHAFT  40   £604   20   1270 3099
2 UNEXPLAINED  21   £797   000-4202D20000   141 335 427 650 857 1065 1673 1999 3116
2 UNIFORMITY  50   £1370   0130   1936 2179* 2511 2677
8 UNIT TENT  0   £231   00314-04040002   119 201 343 975 1755 1990 2309 2654
2 UNITE  62   £2890   2   2774
3 UNITY FARM BOY  33   £383   000200   1059 1483 1629 2270 2677 3122
2 UNOS PET  17   £509   33000020   34 94 278 1279 1672 2806 3069 3112
2 UNPAID MEMBER  41   £295   4   3109
2 UNSELFISH  0   £-   000   2476 2696 3017
3 UNTOLD  86   £121254   0111-23130   926- 1592 2202+ 2565 3051
2 UNWISE  40   £224   30   2983 3176
2 UP THE LADDER  34   £-   000   1903 2036 2711
3 UP TO ME  43   £383   -020   572 714- 1022
3 UP TO UNCLE  39   £8490   -00022132233130   63 117 335 883 1233 1314* 1497 1733 1970 2093 2432
  2533* 2766 2942
4 UP TOWN BOY  0   £-   14443-04000   2271 2429 2515 2697 2836
2 UPDATE GAL  0   £-   0   2089
3 UPHORIA  32   £325   3020-4030   498 1246 1669 1943
5 UPLAND GOOSE  0   £214   2000   1195 1745 2040 2101
2 UPPER  51   £4437   1230   818* 995 1919 2057
2 UPSET  27   £2205   231003   1132 1407 1696* 2425 2687 2993
2 UPTOTHEHILT  48   £1057   0010   1928 2598 2957* 3171
6 UPTOWN GIRL  24   £500   00111-02   412 626
3 UPTOWN RANDBS  10   £406   21040-4300000   37 81 240 518 874 1299 1482
4 UPTOWN SWELL  84   £41958   4   2456
2 UPWELL  0   £-   0   3130
2 URRAY ON HARRY  42   £1896   140   913* 1895 2198.
3 URUGUAY  42   £1030   -0220   966 1880 2294 2440
3 USEFUL  42   £5219   31020-023010230   507 947 1406 1608 1847* 2143 2343 2488 2674
4 USEFUL ADDITION  0   £-   00-00   1417 1845
3 USFAN  61   £16333   -0221211   1395 1607 2099 2442* 2810 2934* 3042*
2 VA LUTE  0   £-   00   1629 3120
3 VAGADOR  55   £3087   -10100   839* 1538 1923* 2156 2776
3 VAGUE LASS  38   £5400   320-3100000   1 18 228 1950 2250 3233
4 VAGUE MELODY  41   £9417   4-2301134412300   91- 129 812 943* 1173* 1249 1788 2022 2355* 2623
  2706 2942 3050
3 VAGUE SHOT  62   £11272   40300-11100   436* 659* 914* 1486 2784
4 VAGUELY ARTISTIC  30   £-   03040-0   2517
3 VAIGLIAN  21   £119   42303-400000030   64 436 624 886 2120 2463 2715 2929 3164
2 VAIGLY BLAZED  24   £-   400000   662 804 1019 1891 2071 2383
6 VAIGLY REL  20   £205   04/0-2   28
3 VAIGLY TYRESOME  0   £-   000-0   22
2 VAIGLY YELLOW  0   £-   000000   931 1203 1376 2301 2511 3079
2 VAINGLORIOUS  76   £838   31102-0040   249 407 586 1107
4 VAL PRIVE  0   £-   -0   3193
3 VALDARNO  0   £-   04-0000000   145 195 451 545 1734 1824 2778
3 VALDOSTA  12   £64   00300   21 86 337 502 763
2 VALENTINE SONG  23   £-   00   2846 3056
6 VALLEY MILLS  39   £887   31000-030040000   306 520 616 815 1026 1292 1429 1810 3015
4 VALRACH  28   £462   00100-000200   594 1066 1198 1394 1651 2059
6 VALUABLE WITNESS  83   £57518   -1111-1113   360* 2203* 2844* 3169
3 VALVINORA  0   £162   00-0000   111 276 498 734
3 VAN DER PUP  3   £-   000-40000   99 130 380 491 2130
2 VANITAS  0   £-   00   3109 3228
3 VANTASTIC  0   £162   000-30000   120 331 506 951 1078
3 VARSITY  0   £-   -00   1160 1290
3 VAULA  16   £-   -04   1831 2790
8 VELESO  6   £473   3   2955
                                    >  1028  <
```

```
6 VELINDRE  0   £-   -0   185
6 VELOCIDAD  7   £270   00010-30000400   56 182 986 1171 1542 1638 1849 3046
5 VELOCITUS  7   £-   0300-00   1565 1870
3 VELVET PEARL  16   £-   -00000   338 501 1228 2532 3116
2 VELVET SLEW  0   £-   0   1914
3 VENDREDI TREIZE  34   £954   42100-1000   260* 518 2424 2602
3 VENEZ TRADER  22   £313   02214-40000   1027 1283 1380 2758 2966
2 VENHERM  25   £701   0003023   1825 2150 2323 2396 2689 2757 2888
4 VENTURE TO REFORM  0   £-   000-0-000000   91 540 620 783 1569 1845
3 VENUS SAGA  0   £-   00-000   1818 2253 2532
3 VERARDI  52   £6356   -30114200   370 572 1589* 1977* 2486 2850- 3038 3232
4 VERBADING  5   £389   -2000-02300040   256 524 783 993 1195 1374 2008 2964
6 VERBARIUM  9   £2213   41031-23200000U   10 79 238 281 930 1176 2303 2549 2762
2 VERBIER  0   £-   00   2600 2982
3 VERD ANTIQUE  83   £25834   -1212   384* 494 2845* 3121-
3 VERDANT BOY  74   £17094   03-31021132   414 747* 1455 2165 2562* 2612* 2785 2943-
2 VERDON CANYON  0   £-   000   3130 3176 3228
3 VERITABLE  46   £4891   43-0213400   409 1469 1954* 2496 2686 2946 3179
3 VERONICA ANN  32   £278   -00030   315 549 1031 1580 2676
4 VERTIGE  74   £23215   13420-2100000   96 98* 641 2195 2637
4 VERY SPECIAL  24   £3921   10143-03010303   591 686 1177 1563* 2058 2240 2733 3013
2 VERYAN BAY  38   £1415   000120   473 2127 2514 2600* 2883 2986
2 VESTAL FLAME  0   £-   000   2675 2904 3143
2 VESTRIS  48   £-   00   2869 3023
4 VESUVE  0   £-   -0   8
2 VEVILA  55   £3137   2210   707 1801 1966+ 3041
4 VIA SATELLITE  8   £214   23440-3000   110 266 369 499
2 VIA VERITAS  0   £-   0000   2472 2703 3025 3201
4 VIA VITAE  3   £-   00040-00000040   710 1104 1338 1765 2012 2797 3046 3220
3 VIANORA  64   £16804   3-01121304   213 402* 500* 579 1153* 1851 2385 2765
4 VICEROY BOY  8   £-   00000-00   530 1243
3 VICEROY MAJOR  27   £-   04040-00000   496 703 880 1384 1560
2 VICHY VAL  1   £-   000   13 57 102
4 VICKSTOWN  14   £-   13010-000000   235 360 584 964 2237 3187
3 VICTORIA FALLS  60   £13248   3   397
2 VICTORIA STAR  12   £236   004002   186 1413 2466 2607 2757 2872
2 VICTORY BALLARD  33   £6506   000104210   1241 1522 1728 1844* 2284 2579 2729 2859+ 3019
4 VIDEO  3   £-   03000-000   673 1195 1567
5 VIDEO LAD  0   £-   -0   530
2 VIENS VITE  0   £-   00   2651 3133
3 VIF ARGENT  71   £8051   43   2502 2913
2 VIGLIOTTO  40   £-   444   2721 2878 3014
3 VIKRIS  0   £-   -000   527 702 862
3 VILEE  10   £-   -0000   1691 2518 2697 2929
3 VILLAGE HERO  31   £1798   00010   1 2275 2599 2722* 3110
5 VILLAGE POSTMAN  0   £-   0   1546
3 VILMAX  15   £589   -20   3160 3203
3 VILTASH  46   £5691   00-003000000410   671 947 1044 1524 1922 2084 2378 2446 2668 2725 2970+
3233
4 VIN DE FRANCE  78   £1564   23140-0040   313 2195 2359 2507
4 VINTAGE LADY  0   £-   -0044-00   2509 3057
4 VINTAGE PORT  40   £5291   -000002214   617 653 854 1342 1559 1935 2098 2240* 2403
6 VINTAGE TOLL  46   £1700   20000-03003400   4 52 243 439 584 698 943 1047
3 VIRAJENDRA  10   £245   00200-0034000   198 283 491 1813 2414 3086 3147
5 VIRGIN ISLE  39   £2708   034-02000404003   17 79 248 361 652 930 1047 1455 1890 1987 2681
2 VISION OF WONDER  22   £909   0010   1653 1948 2580* 2897
4 VISTULE  6   £218   34424-000020   164 1554 1873 2317 3076 3193
4 VISUAL IDENTITY  23   £421   0020-0000004330   31 578 680 1086 1165 1558 1831 2572 2656 2733
2 VITAL CARGO  37   £-   4400   1534 1982 2140 3011
3 VITAL FORM  25   £-   -000   576 733 2442
3 VITAL STEP  3   £272   00-00042000   1425 1614 1841 2268 2361 2427 2495 2705
6 VITIGESON  19   £-   00000-0   262
3 VITRY  20   £302   00-000300   486 723 916 1089 1558 1871
2 VIVA RONDA  19   £1028   14000   981* 1261 2261 3174 3226
2 VIVALDI  47   £1645   01030   777 2301+ 2514 2843 3114
6 VIVRE POUR VIVRE  0   £-   -0   1833
7 VODKATINI  2   £-   -0   2572
2 VOL VITESSE  23   £-   0400   1561 1825 2100 2281
3 VOLIDA  57   £781   10400-40400   26 373 661 926 1110
7 VORACITY  53   £10871   0/004-2321410   569 1209 1366 1992* 2290 2558* 2769
2 VORTRACK  30   £-   0000   1844 2341 2494 3079
9 VORVADOS  38   £568   00004'-4000000   18 70 172 374 508 881 1461
4 VOUCHSAFE  40   £958   0100-041D000000   474 921 1112 1456 1790 2237 2551 2769 3038
3 W SEAFIELD  0   £-   0-00   875 1141
4 WAAFI  43   £-   -0000-0   2699
3 WAAJIB  62   £10202   02-2133201   1395 1602+ 1941 2296 2566 2867 3070*
2 WABARAH  50   £4151   311242   482 988* 1357* 1798 2052 2577-
6 WAGONER  73   £13394   3040-2220   1 398 756
4 WAHIBA  34   £1226   0302   1488 1948 2584 2936
2 WAIT TILL MONDAY  68   £15105   21332   2821 3003
3 WALCISIN  30   £5574   0-0002201040224   117 275 459 761 951 1236 1386* 1879 2015 2134 2722 2794
2988
4 WALENSEE  77   £-   00   1493 2357
6 WALHAN  1   £-   000-0-00   1104 1500
3 WALK ON AIR  57   £1346   -2   806
4 WALLER FIELD  12   £-   -00   628 817
4 WALTER THE GREAT  7   £254   12220-004000300   519 743 933 1016 1223 1419 1772 1897 2087
5 WALTERS WEDNESDAY  0   £-   -00   1077 1951
4 WANDERING WALTER  3   £-   00000-000000   126 358 541 772 2776 2984
2 WANTAGE PARK  36   £199   2   2871
3 WANTON  66   £-   33012-00   1151 1889
2 WAR BRAVE  58   £7055   24111   2561 2667 2791* 2926+ 3047*
2 WAR CHILD  16   £419   0030020   252 1105 1622 2310 2512 2817 2990
```

```
3 WAR HERO  71   £19932   013-0032   273 597 1048 1354
3 WAR PALACE  0   £-   -0   185
3 WAR WAGON  40   £4006   0000-0000101   514 703 886 1032 1499+ 2046 2189*
8 WARILY  0   £-   -00   2282 2490
3 WARM BREEZE  0   £-   ----0-00   1278 1953
3 WARM WELCOME  34   £4347   42-0030100   661 991 1290 1657 2053+ 2404 2934
6 WARPLANE  25   £2553   03100-003400100   1047 1335 1619 2059 2303 2414 2728* 2797 3116
2 WARRIOR BRAVE  0   £-   0   1629
4 WARTHILL LADY  20   £6159   04004000040101002302   12 56 182 306 1120 1247 1338 1676 1906 2295
2397 2411* 2513 2632* 2775 2816 2858 2970 3083 3152
4 WARWICK SUITE  22   £-   03000-0   52
3 WASMI  51   £-   00-2D4   253 527
5 WASSEM  8   £400   04/00-2   1945
3 WASSL REEF  67   £13553   22-2310101100   342 572 1167+ 1886 2122* 2206 2445* 2662* 2834 3022
3 WASSL TOUCH  83   £17337   1-01014   249 1644* 1913 2064+ 2222
3 WATENDLATH  13   £1949   0330-0300000100   309 529 593 911 1299 1773 1960 2103* 2335 2427
2 WATER BOATMAN  57   £672   3   3018
5 WATER CANNON  35   £-   0-040-00   801 1099
3 WATER CAY  74   £2124   14123-10   2991* 3175
2 WATER CITY  46   £149   03   3130 3223
3 WATER MUSICK  0   £-   00000-0   2988
2 WATER OF LOVE  0   £-   000   400 2703 3074
3 WATERDALE  29   £1418   000-003332   451 714 958 1250 1706 1894
2 WATERED SILK  33   £279   0300   2147 2328 2846 3146
3 WATERFORD WAY  10   £836   00-0401000   237 305 491* 648 823 1054
4 WATERLOW PARK  40   £2360   42422-22P   375 504 735
3 WATERSIDE LODGE  0   £-   -00   2593 2874
4 WATFORD GAP  24   £-   04040-0   363
3 WAVE DANCER  43   £2408   4-130   832* 1236 3110
3 WAVE GOODBYE  8   £184   300-0200   1281 1736 2152 3101
3 WAVEGUIDE  35   £-   424-00   340 844
3 WAVERLEY ROSE  0   £-   -00   733 844
3 WAY ABOVE  0   £-   0300-000000000   67 356 1087 1554 2152 2478 2722 3128 3202
2 WAYAK  43   £-   0   1914
2 WAZN  0   £-   0   3109
3 WEBSTERS FEAST  18   £2636   -00000204300010   507 836 947 1001 1182 1406 1704 1927 2106 2224
2416 2688 2854* 3083
3 WEIGHT IN GOLD  74   £16376   102   269* 373 471
5 WELL COVERED  34   £3012   00100-0001034   17 410 609 967* 1112 1539 1957
9 WELL MEET AGAIN  17   £324   34-20-3000000   36 72 333 547 652 850 1517
5 WELL RIGGED  43   £13837   31321-2120040   17- 79* 521 706 1525 2039 2475
4 WELL WISHER  17   £-   -00   1923 2517
2 WELSH ARROW  42   £1978   1340   1207* 1916 2391 2611
3 WELSH BARON  40   £437   00-30   219 430
3 WELSH CROWN  7   £84   -304   95 951 1620
3 WELSH FANTASY  72   £24620   -210-021000   269 396 753* 1331 1592 2633
2 WELSH FLITE  0   £-   0   1955
4 WELSH GUARD  0   £-   000000400   8 58 104 358 590 942 1419 1564 1772
4 WELSH MEDLEY  24   £5618   000-03214000001   281 420 547 724* 850 2121 2273 2578 2755 3029 3116*
3 WELSH NOTE  64   £8423   22214-4440200   408 903 1146 1889 2524 2672 3054
3 WELSH PAGEANTRY  21   £-   0-000000   941 1193 1503 2173 2339 2532
5 WELSH SPY  12   £-   40000-00   23 199
2 WENSLEYDALEWARRIOR  57   £5958   0320112220   304 523 627 864 1050* 1203* 1430 1735 1920 2221
4 WESBREE BAY  0   £1431   4-0022023000030   65 145 825 1423 1542 1718 1973 2124 2322 2397 2592
3083 3172
3 WESHAAM  58   £12494   30-201322012   78 406 716* 919 1130 1314 1642 2623* 2769-
4 WESSEX  35   £7429   33-412431340110   50 144* 319 358 542 824* 990 1177 1897 1980* 2130* 2445
3 WESSEX KINGDOM  48   £684   0-100   87* 134 241
3 WEST CARRACK  40   £1293   120-33003000040   62 203 314 514 884 1001 1391 1608 1890 2262 3106
2 WESTAJAMES  0   £-   00   2761 2975
4 WESTERHAM  25   £-   04000-00   112 2431
5 WESTERN DANCER  60   £20639   12124-013430   58A 462+ 1112 1470 1779 3232
2 WESTGALE  19   £467   0030020   544 685 1137 1279 1622 2470 3112
2 WESTMINSTER WALTZ  0   £-   00   3117 3200
2 WESTPARK PRINCESS  0   £-   00   2476 3025
4 WESTRAY  10   £343   130-00040403000   126 225 695 872 1052 1563 1871 2028 2175 2415 2623
2 WHAKILYRIC  73   £14664   121412303   2737 2915 3168
3 WHAT A GUY  33   £200   4004   1512 1653 1936 2332
4 WHAT A LINE  7   £-   -2430-4000   104 259 522 960
3 WHAT A PARTY  32   £-   22002-000   464 1256 1404
8 WHAT WILL I WEAR  0   £-   -00   199 282
2 WHATS A GUINEA  3   £-   0000   882 1305 2045 2990
2 WHATTA BUSINESS  8   £-   000   2717 2926 3190
2 WHICH DIRECTION  0   £-   0   2997
3 WHILE IT LASTS  50   £5239   -333231010   338 539 1193 1580 1909 2217* 2330 2799* 3140
3 WHIPCRACKAWAY  35   £306   -00320   1178 1700 2054 2363 2722
9 WHIPPER IN  69   £15710   1122   1958* 2398+ 2661- 2954-
2 WHIPPET  64   £7518   120003330   577* 737 1097 1467 1876 2223 2398 2524 2866
3 WHIRLING WORDS  32   £5715   004-002112   335 480 874 1104* 1281* 1624
2 WHISTLING WONDER  35   £3314   0104303000002032   40 94* 118 304 367 515 1174 1527 1895 1978
2137 2465 2815 2919 3017 3079-
3 WHITE CLOVER  68   £4582   -12   1022+ 2553
2 WHITE JAZZ  31   £-   0   1752
4 WHITE MILL  40   £11148   400-03110   850 1092 1280* 1679+ 2220
2 WHITE MINSTREL  19   £-   00   2811 3137
2 WHITE MISCHIEF  69   £14656   12   2774* 3040
2 WHITE OF MORN  27   £4172   00410   2320 2476 2698 2919* 3059
3 WHITE REEF  52   £1239   ----3-410   409 1873* 2201
5 WHITE WATER  65   £7304   -443   2640 3094 3216
2 WHITRIDGE  40   £-   000   1936 2133 3011
2 WHITSTABLE  60   £3972   314   2263 2484* 2571
3 WHITTINGHAM VALE  20   £84   -300   45 185 767
2 WHO KNOWS  74   £29334   312430   1019 1242* 1467 1876 2552 2771
                                    >  1030  <
```

```
3 WHOBERLEY WHEELS  0   £-   -000000000   593 891 1046 1436 1687 1959 2312 2728 3104
4 WHOKNOWSTHEBOWLER  12  £-   02000-0   9
3 WHOS THAT GIRL  0   £-   0-000   2929 3066 3160
2 WHOS ZOOMIN WHO  25  £1595   000102   1440 1632 1802 1997* 2529 2618
4 WHY TUMBLE  4   £-   04430-00   2496 2861
2 WICHITA SPRINGS  38  £349   3040   1376 1825 2082 3125
4 WIDE BOY  25   £2974   03230-11000   185* 542+ 1150 2754 2882
2 WIGANTHORPE  76  £61386   02201111410   242 320 602- 741 1014+ 1252* 1411* 1531* 2113 2221+ 2552
4 WILD GINGER  16  £2945   10030-020003341   341 485 683 856 1035 1366 2372 2900 2985+
5 WILD HOPE  38  £9054   33000-004210010   812 940 2062 2296- 2477* 2536 2850 2978* 3113
7 WILDRUSH  23  £2818   10002-10340   243* 493 591 860 1016
7 WILL GEORGE  48  £6153   22003-131100   12* 76 114* 160* 401 508
2 WILL RAINE  37  £-   04   2889 3117
3 WILLBE WILLBE  15  £2219   0000-0000001304   340 545 689 857 1391 1695 2230* 2581 2728 2896
2 WILLESDON  71  £3606   130   2826 3005
2 WILLIAM PERE  0   £-   000   1665 2095 3131
8 WILLIE GAN  15  £2685   00000-000320010   46 321 866 1093- 1247 1338 1500 1676* 2012
3 WILLIE THE MOON  35  £-   -0   1395
2 WILLIESWRIGHTONCUE  46  £310   204   1307 2239 2716
3 WILLOW GORGE  20  £373   -00004300   625 887 1290 1945 2330 2533 3110 3197
2 WILLOW THE KING  28  £-   040   1225 2325 3103
2 WILLOWBANK  28  £488   002000   1427 2029 2379 2664 2748 3221
2 WILLOWTREE GIRL  0   £-   00   3153 3189
3 WILLWOOD  0   £-   -000   229 357 1303
2 WILLY JUMP  0   £-   0   2405
2 WILLYS NIECE  0   £-   00000B   858 1181 2168 2470 2724 2801
2 WIND AND WAVE  0   £-   00000   621 1440 1801 2407 3136
2 WIND OF PEACE  34  £919   0100   741 1716* 2178 2498
3 WINDBOUND LASS  8   £-   00-000040   546 832 1439 1579 2576 2807
3 WINDING PATH  5   £109   33120-000400300   335 489 670 871 1398 1734 1815 1917 2238
2 WINDMEDE  24  £516   2300   34 61 2218 2922
8 WINDPIPE  44  £4395   -0040-04130   573 668 1176* 1698 2219
3 WINDS OF LIGHT  67  £2394   1-0100   224 435* 654 2206
4 WINDSOR KNOT  51  £2518   31000-400224   653 1095 1514 2091- 2431 2578
3 WINDY HOLLOW  0   £-   0-000000   832 1494 1833 2211 2581 2836
3 WINE FESTIVAL  0   £-   -00   356 517
3 WING BEE  0   £-   0000-0000   32 276 950 1560
2 WING PARK  0   £-   00   2847 3053
2 WINGED PHARAOH  0   £-   00   2584 2723
2 WINK GULLIVER  0   £-   00   2542 2721
2 WINNER ALRIGHT  0   £-   0   102
2 WINNIES LUCK  0   £-   0000   948 1221 1528 3031
3 WINNING FORMAT  10  £974   00-000020001   217 454 545 891 1521 1827 2088 2417 3057 3172 3185*
5 WINNING STAR  0   £-   -000   9 199 282
3 WINSONG MELODY  7   £-   -4400000   516 835 1516 2210 2312 2898 3065
3 WINTER HAVEN  19  £-   -00   2464 2605
4 WINTER PALACE  28  £-   13240-000000   618 850 1223 1829 2098 2406
7 WINTER WORDS  18  £3530   30000-001100   775 992+ 1165* 1500 2602
3 WINTERS BETA  0   £-   -000   205 346 838
4 WIRRAL  0   £-   00-0   3193
3 WISE COUNSELLOR  78  £23700   -120100   559 878 2192* 2506 3168
5 WISE CRACKER  6   £-   -00000   9 199 282 2415 2800
2 WISE TIMES  38  £2770   00223200   252 311 513 1891 1965 2209 2310 2687
3 WISHLON  62  £8411   -1010011   95* 370 623* 1130 1468 1939* 2420*
4 WITCHCRAFT  44  £7837   00020-244313   225 584 1020 2058 2237* 2662
5 WITH A LOT  0   £-   02000-0   1579
2 WITH GODS HELP  50  £3450   100   149* 752 1006
3 WITH HOPE  74  £2500   4-2   758
3 WITHAM GIRL  8   £-   120-000000   340 455 961 2715 3144 3185
2 WITHAM LAD  0   £-   0   965
4 WITHY BANK  43  £18289   40220-113002002   11+ 50* 462 712 1533 2480 2809 3052 3225
5 WIZZARD ART  22  £1725   43130-000010   850 1166 1667 2356* 2617
3 WIZZARD MAGIC  18  £1065   00-032020   844 1499 1616 2681 2929 3065
2 WOLF J FLYWHEEL  14  £451   020000200   47 186 332 1105 1480 1528 16¹1 1795 1905
3 WOLLOW BIRD  4   £-   40000-400   1158 1267 1369
2 WOLSEY  55  £2338   114   1345* 1572* 2468
4 WOLVERSTAR  69  £13538   1012034   639 903* 2503
7 WONDER WOOD  20  £268   -03   1952 2134
2 WONDERFUL WILLIAM  30  £-   440   2179 2491 3109
5 WONGALILLI  0   £-   30000-00   770 1432
2 WOOD CHANTER  48  £308   4   2239
2 WOOD CHISEL  45  £332   02´   2232 2541
2 WOOD LOUSE  42  £-   000   1914 2159 3099
2 WOODBERRY  18  £-   000   2433 2703 2841
5 WOODFOLD  42  £4078   02330-13000200   986* 1227 1387 1889 2402 2530- 2764 2953
3 WOODLANDS CROWN  0   £-   0-00   739 3186
3 WOODMAN  76  £2069   -1110-3   295
2 WOODMAN WEAVER  20  £1331   00043200   1552 1936 2108 2218 2579 2689 2744 2962
2 WOODPECKER  42  £1361   10320   2051 2225 2723 3165- 3230
6 WORDSWORTH  7   £-   04000-0   336
4 WORKADAY  38  £1852   00020-0003100   182 521 594 1101 1482* 2012 2126
2 WORKING MODEL  0   £-   0   3073
3 WORLD COURT  71  £720   30   396 1330
3 WORTH DEBATING  10  £-   -04000   2593 2747 2853 3162 3202
2 WORTHY PRINCE  30  £1782   100   1625* 2051 2744
2 WOW WOW WOW  22  £1778   10110-31002030   147 237* 447 545 670- 768 1070 1131
3 WRANGBROOK  7   £84   0-30000   123 770 1251 1686 2098
5 WRITE THE MUSIC  24  £494   12200-20   526 634
2 WUJUD  51  £-   000   2561 2782 3018
3 WUTHERING HEIGHTS  77  £4820   2   1593
2 WUZO  50  £3619   10   1289* 1465
3 WYKEHAMIST  16  £-   -000000   1947 2186 2294 3065 3138 3191
5 WYLFA  74  £15189   2243300   410 736 1095 1230 1913 2200 2461
                        >  1031  <
```

```
4 WYOMING  0   £-   00000-00   993 1103
4 XHAI  34   £7362  110-40202000023   17 72 361 525 649 748 1109 2629 2867 3078 3164
4 XYLOPHONE  6   £994   20003-1000   1400* 2059 2381 2863
4 Y I OYSTON  18   £-   00004-000   825 1101 1247
2 YAHEEB  55   £2449   31   2761 3099*
3 YAKA  75   £24379   -1   3089*
3 YAMMA  0   £-   -0   209
2 YAMRAH  0   £-   000   2418 2788 3189
4 YANI  0   £-   20000-0000   550 734 855 2731
2 YAQUT  40   £3020   221   1407 2748 3034*
2 YASIR  20   £-   0   1207
2 YAVARRO  24   £-   0000   482 834 1187 1341
4 YELLOW BEAR  7   £-   00001-000   46 110 594
3 YELLOW CANARY  0   £-   -0   1677
2 YLDIZLAR  50   £2010   10   2013* 2383
2 YODA  0   £400   3   1711
3 YOKO  0   £-   -0   288
2 YORKBAY  43   £-   00   3117 3223
4 YOUNG ANGEL  27   £-   11000-000   262 508 636
2 YOUNG BENZ  15   £-   00040   1253 1529 1883 2011 2512
3 YOUNG BLADE  75   £23350   01103-1104   295* 472* 639 1491
4 YOUNG BORIS  0   £-   -00-00000   31 499 975 1662 2884
4 YOUNG BRUSS  11   £1205   -0004-001300000   441 606 830* 936 1429 1536 2126 2390 2681
2 YOUNG CENTURION  15   £1033   000000001   728 1059 1305 1883 2177 2405 2580 2804 2927*
8 YOUNG DANIEL  0   £-   -0   750
3 YOUNG FLAME  28   £-   0000-0   455
2 YOUNG FOOL  0   £-   0000   421 543 858 3079
2 YOUNG GHILLIE  34   £-   000   1241 1629 3120
3 YOUNG HEROINE  0   £-   -0   338
8 YOUNG INCA  46   £2968   0-0000003003000   616 660 881 1145 1455 1777 2258 2475 2668 2862 2953
3118 3235
3 YOUNG JASON  39   £14541   40011-001223300   38 228 1272* 1461 1852 2288 2545 2773 3055
2 YOUNG JUDGE  52   £1605   200   2232 2522 3037
2 YOUNG LOCHINVAR  21   £-   00000   800 1241 2159 2729 3122
3 YOUNG LUCY  3   £-   41000-0   2417
2 YOUNG MORETON  0   £-   00   497 1019
3 YOUNG PUGGY  20   £681   400-02000000000   26 138 387 588 1151 1959 2143 2758 2842 3116 3160
4 YOUNG RUNAWAY  66   £2156   41010-4000   313 1094 1492 2449
2 YOUNG SNUGFIT  24   £-   000000   1958 2281 2476 2922 3103 3229
2 YOUNG WARRIOR  16   £-   4000   488 627 1119 1296
3 YOURS GRENVILLE  0   £-   -40   1350 3062
2 YSTRAD FLOWER  20   £-   000   1550 2118 2180
3 ZAAJER  40   £1525   -323   486 811 1040
3 ZAGAZIG  15   £-   -00   2321 2650
3 ZAHDAM  82   £38229   11-10220   159* 389 1595 2005 2454
2 ZAIBAQ  73   £13094   1324   405* 737 1126- 1850
2 ZAIZOOM  67   £2748   202   2159 2771 3018
2 ZAJAL  70   £7351   1   2750+
3 ZALATIA  59   £6413   22-1020043   213* 264 776- 1107 2440 2832 3055
2 ZAMPANO  54   £1356   2   2448
2 ZANUSSI LINE  29   £-   000   2205 2484 3141
2 ZARBYEV  52   £5391   3214   1791 2036 2889* 3067
2 ZAREEF  35   £-   0   2522
3 ZAUBARR  45   £9947   00-0011310   253 959 1402* 1484* 1569 1748* 1879
3 ZEELANDIA  6   £-   0000-400000   53 379 2401 2413 2704 2780
11 ZELDAS FANCY  0   £-   -0   344
2 ZEN WEST THREE  33   £-   000   2179 2696 3130
2 ZERO WATT  63   £1704   2   2673
2 ZEUS  51   £222   2   2607
3 ZIADS ALIBY  20   £303   -4300   2210 2483 2550 2793
2 ZILDA  40   £-   0000   601 2710 3040 3108
3 ZILLEBEKE  20   £697   -0033030   658 1246 2367 2518 2970 3065 3191
3 ZINDELINA  32   £1503   0440-2040200   505 623 762 1657 2333 2676 3105
5 ZIO PEPPINO  12   £5124   0320444030113000   260 490 606- 710 789 936 1136 2126 2264 2549 2602*
2762* 2797 2891 3029 3157
7 ZIRCONS SUN  0   £-   /0000-000   336 841 1058
2 ZITELLA  35   £-   000   1632 2118 3068
2 ZOLA ZOOM  25   £-   4   200
2 ZUAETREH  48   £907   22   2967 3228
3 ZULU KNIGHT  38   £2402   2240-0000212200   455 703 846 1312 1995- 2186* 2518 2650- 2842 3055
3 ZUMURRUDAH  57   £9256   -00140   213 549 1043* 1378 2236
```

USING THE RATINGS

The ratings in this book are expressed in pounds on a scale 0-100.
To assess any race where the horses are all the same age, simply subtract
the weight each horse is set to carry from 10-0 and add the result to the
rating:

E.G. Dunan 4-9-2 rated 61. 10-0 minus 9-2 = 12. 12 + 61 = 73.
Make these calculations for each horse in turn. The horse with the
highest adjusted rating is most favoured at the weights.

To assess a race in which there are horses of different ages, consult
the scale of age, weight and distance found on page 1056

On consulting the scale, according to the distances of the race, the
month in which it is taking place (and time within the month) and the
age of the horse, subtract the weight the horse is set to carry from the
weight now pinpointed in the table. Then add the result to the horse's
rating:

E.G.   7 furlong race on 11th April

Dunan 4-9-2 rated 61: Table wt.10-0 minus 9-2 = 12: 12 plus 61 = 73
Grady 3-8-1 rated 61: Table wt.8-12 minus 8-1 = 11: 11 plus 61 = 72
Budge 3-7-10 rated 60: Table wt.8-12 minus 7-10 = 16: 16 plus 60 = 76
            Budge has the best chance at the weights

Now that four year old horses receive no allowances from older
animals, nearly all your calculations will be done from 10-0 in the early
part of the season. It is usually a month or so before the 3 yo's start
to take on the older horses.

The following table is a fair guide to class.

90 plus	-	Top class: able to win Group 1 races.	50-60	- Useful handicapper
80-90	-	Very smart, able to win Group 2 races	40-50	- Fair handicapper
			30-40	- Moderate handicapper
70-80	-	Smart handicapper: also should be capable of winning Group 3 events.	30 and below	- Poor handicapper and selling class
60-70	-	Very useful handi-capper.		

Using The Ratings

A great time saving method of rating any meeting is to make calculations only for
those horses mentioned in the betting forecast. This will apply to the majority of bread
and butter races. Rich handicaps need more detailed treatment. Working through only
horses mentioned in the betting forecast should take about 20 minutes per meeting -
with practice. Another advantage of working this way is that you can then compare the
odds on offer with the ratings calculated. It should not take long before you become
adept at spotting value for money.

Value of Recent Form

Please remember that ratings are not magic figures. You must take into account
firstly whether the horse is racefit. Unless you have a direct stable link the only way
to be sure of fitness is to have printed evidence of a good recent run. By recent we mean
not more than four weeks old. Thus try to make sure that the rating which you are using
was achieved by the horse recently. Form more than four weeks old must be treated with
caution.

Look For The Pattern of Events

Don't become so tied up with figures that you miss the broad pattern of
events in racehorse performance. Most horses need a set of conditions before they
are able to produce their best. The distance must be right. Their going requirements
must be met and for many horses, particularly front runners, the course must be
suitable. Generally horses that win in stiff galloping tracks can win anywhere, but
those that win at sharp tracks like Chester, Epsom, Lingfield etc are often unable to
reproduce that form elsewhere.

TIME AND PACE FIGURES

Time And Going Figures

While making no attempt to produce 'time figures' we do take race times into consideration when calculating our handicap ratings.

Firstly we compare the race time with the standard time for the track. When this is calculated on a per furlong basis over 6 races, a pretty accurate picture of the prevailing going emerges.

For example a race over 5f produces a time of 63 seconds. The standard time for the track is 59 seconds. Thus the race was run in 4 seconds slower than standard time. Divide 4 (seconds) by 5 (furlongs) which equals .80. Do this for all 6 races which typically give figures of 80, 100, 65, 110, 115, 105. Add the figures - total 575 for 6 races. Divide 575 by 6 (races) and we have an average per furlong figure of 96 (95.83 rounded up).

This would indicate that the going was on the soft side of good since we use the following table as a guide :-

160 and upwards	HEAVY going
120 to 160	SOFT
80 to 120	YIELDING
40 to 80	GOOD
20 to 40	GOOD/FIRM
Below 20	FIRM

The average figure for each meeting is printed after the going in each race - thus - Good 60.

If the official going report differs from our figures, we state this at the start of each race meeting.

Pace Figures

We also find this going figure useful in determining the relative <u>pace</u> of each race.

In the above example the average per furlong figure for the meeting is 96. The third race produced a figure of only 65 and was therefore run at a relatively fast pace.

Conversely the fifth race with a figure of 115 was a fairly slow run affair

We indicate in the results whether the race was fast or slow run. This figure is calculated by comparing the figure for each race with the average for the meeting. Thus the first race would be 16 Fast - 96 minus 80. Race five would be 19 slow (96 - 115).

The general conclusions to be drawn from the pace figures are -

Slow pace -	form might be suspect particularly with regard to the placed horses. Easy winners might be flattered.
Fast pace -	form can be relied on and the form of the placed horses should work out well. Easy winners can be followed with confidence.

Compiling The Ratings

Compiling The Ratings

The race results in this annual cover the first six horses past the post plus all horses quoted up to and including 10/1 in the betting.

The ratings published here are expressions of opinion, based wherever possible on collateral form. Our ratings are presented on the 0-100 scale as used by the official Jockey Club Handicappers.

In studying form and assessing racehorse performance, we are trying to do a complex jigsaw puzzle. The whole picture is not complete until the end of the season and sometimes not even then! Many of the parts are definitely shaped and slot into obvious positions (the older handicappers), but so many of the pieces have no precise shape and we can only place them in tentative positions until more of the picture is revealed, and some of the shapes are changing as we study them! These non precise and changing shapes are mainly the 2yo's and those 3yo maidens that did not run or were lightly raced in their first season.

However, experience helps greatly in rating these animals. Collateral form is the basis for out ratings but of course none exists with the early 2yo's. Experience shows that the early two year old maiden races are won by the same standard of animal each year. Thus we start by giving the early winners 'average' figures that one expects for each particular maiden race, and pretty soon the winners or placed horses begin to race against one another and we have the beginnings of collateral form.

As results unfolded and our handicappers discovered that any race had been under-rated or overrated by 5lb or more, the ratings for the race in question were revised before printing.

OFFICIAL RATINGS

At the start of each handicap race, in the right hand margin, the figure in brackets represents the Official Rating of a horse set to carry 10-0 in that race. If the figure is 50, horse B carrying 10-0 is officially rated 50. Horse C, set to carry 8-8 is rated 30 since it carries 20lb less than 10-0 - and so on. In this way it is possible to work out the official mark of each horse in any handicap right through the season.

RACECOURSE GUIDE

ASCOT   A right handed triangular track: quite a stiff course with an uphill finish.
5,6,7 furlong tracks and the straight mile on which the Royal Hunt Cup is run are undulating
with a stiff uphill climb in the last two furlongs.
Round mile, 10, 12 furlongs and upwards: undulating: the run in is short, only 2½ furlongs,
and it is not a good track for coming with a late run: a particularly testing track when the
ground is soft: nowadays the draw seems of little consequence.
AYR   A left handed, flat galloping track: a very fair course which favours the big and strong
galloping types: 5, 6 furlong tracks are straight and easy and high numbers hold a slight
advantage: races run over 7 furlongs and upwards are on the turn, left handed; and low numbers
hold an advantage: there is a good run in of 4½ furlongs: drainage and turf are excellent and
rarely produce extremes of going.
BATH   A left handed, galloping, oval track with quite a steep uphill finish: 5 furlong and 5
furlong and 170 yds tracks bend to the left and are stiff: low numbers are favoured in races up
to 1 mile: the run in for races over 7 furlongs is a good half mile: the course stands on old and
lush downland turf, so that the going is rarely firm.
BEVERLEY   A right handed oval course with a stiff uphill finish: the 5 furlong course has a
slight bend to the right and high numbers have an advantage in races up to 1 mile: a particularly
tough test for two year olds: the run in is a short 2½ furlongs and this is not a track for coming
with a very late run.
BRIGHTON   A left handed, undulating track which is against the big long striding animal,
and favours the handy types, the front runners, and those who might have lost some of their zest
for the game: 5 and 6 furlong tracks are sharp and easy and on the turn, so that a low number,
speed from the gate give much advantage: run in is 3½ furlongs: course stands on chalk and the
going is rarely very soft: a course for specialists.
CARLISLE   A right handed, undulating, pear shaped course with a stiff uphill run in of 3½
furlongs: the undulations are pronounced and the track is a testing one: the subsoil is clay
and the going tends to extremes: 5, 6 furlong tracks are on the turn and high numbers are
definitely favoured in races up to 1 mile: another course for specialists.
CATTERICK   A very sharp, left handed, oval track: only 9 furlongs in circumference: front
runners are very much at home here but the course is hopeless for long striding animals: the
accent is on speed and there is little demand on stamina: the 5 furlong course bends to the
left and low numbers have the advantage in all races up to 7 furlongs: very much a course for
specialists.
CHEPSTOW   A left handed oval circuit of 2 miles: there are undulations but the course is
considered a galloping track: all races up to 1 mile are run on a straight track which provides
quite a stiff test and the accent is on stamina: high numbers have the advantage: the run in is
5 furlongs and this is not a front runner's track.
CHESTER   An extremely sharp, left handed track, only 1 mile round: this is a front runner's
track where all the racing is done on the turn: it suits those animals who need a bit of kidding
and is most definitely a course for specialists: unfortunately form shown here is so often not
repeated elsewhere: low numbers have a definite advantage in all races and early speed in the
sprints is essential.
DONCASTER   A left handed flat galloping track: ideal for the big, long striding horse, and
the powerful galloper: the run in is 5 furlongs: the accent is on stamina and courage: there is
a round mile track where there seems to be no advantage in the draw: there is also a straight
mile where in the past high numbers had an advantage but nowadays low numbers seem to be
favoured: this is not a track for the faint hearted.
EDINBURGH   A right handed, oval track, 10 furlongs in circumference: an easy course and
it is on the sharp side: front runners do quite well here: over the 5 furlongs straight and in
races up to 1 mile on the round course, high numbers have some advantage: the course drains
well and has a watering system so that the going is usually good and rarely extreme.
EPSOM   A left handed track with pronounced undulations and a fairly short run in of 3½
furlongs: it is totally against the tall, long striding horse: front runners have a good record
here and the many gradients seem to rekindle enthusiasm in those horses who may have lost
some zest for racing: the sprint tracks are very sharp and fast, being downhill nearly all the
way: speed from the gate is essential and low numbers are favoured in all races up to 1 mile:
not a track for the inexperienced 2 year old: the course stands on chalk, rarely rides very
soft, but despite the possession of a watering system, it can be very firm: very much a course
for specialists.

Dancing Brave quickens clear and holds on well from Shardari in the King George VI & Queen Elizabeth Diamond Stakes at Ascot.

Top class sprinter/miler **Last Tycoon** (nearside) holds off Double Schwartz in the five furlong Kings Stand Stakes at Royal Ascot.

FOLKESTONE   A right handed, undulating track with a fairly short run in, just over 2½ furlongs in length: it is not a stiff track and no great demand is made on stamina: low numbers have an advantage in sprints.

GOODWOOD   A right handed track with very severe undulations: it is totally unsuited to the big long striding animal: the small, handy types with good conformation who can keep good balance galloping downhill, have the advantage: the 5 furlong track is very fast and speed from the gate is essential: high numbers have a definite advantage, particularly in big fields, both on this and the 6 furlong track: in races over 1 mile and upwards, the track seems to suit front runners.

HAMILTON   A right handed, undulating course with a run in of 5 furlongs: the run in contains a dip 3 furlongs from the winning post and a fairly stiff uphill finish: the course stands on clay and in wet weather it rides very heavy: the 5 and 6 furlong tracks are quite straight and on the stiff side: there is no obvious advantage in the draw.

HAYDOCK   A left handed, flat galloping track, with a run in of some 4½ furlongs: the home stretch is on the rise and the accent is on stamina and courage: in races up to 1 mile, low numbers have the advantage: however when the going rides soft, the ground on the Stands rails drains better and high numbers have the advantage in sprints.

KEMPTON   A right handed triangular track with a 3½ furlong run in: the bends are quite sharp and in races over 7 furlongs, the nippy or handy type of horse has the advantage: quite a good track for front runners: the 5 and 6 furlong tracks are straight and easy and low numbers have a slight advantage: on the round course, in races of 7 - 10 furlongs, high numbers are favoured.

LEICESTER   A right handed, oval, galloping track with a run in of 5 furlongs: definitely a galloping course where the accent is on stamina and courage: all races up to and including 1 mile are run on a straight track: the straight mile is not for the faint hearted: a low draw has some advantage on the straight course, but it is slight: the track stands on clay and limestone and in wet weather it rides pretty heavy.

LINGFIELD   A left handed, very undulating track with a short run in of 3½ furlongs: the gradients and the steep downhill turn into the straight are very much like Epsom, the track is not for the big, long striding horse: races from 5 furlongs to 7 furlongs and 140 yards are run on a straight track which is mainly downhill and is therefore, fast and easy: fast starters and front runners do well here: on the straight track, high numbers are favoured when the going is good, but on heavy ground low numbers have the advantage: a course for specialists.

NEWBURY   A left handed, oval, galloping track with a long run in of 5 furlongs: the sprint course is quite straight and there are also straight 7 furlong and mile tracks: on this straight course the draw has little advantage, but in big fields, or on soft going, high numbers seem to do best: the course stands on gravel and drains well: the accent is on stamina and courage and it is not an easy track for front running types.

NEWCASTLE   A left handed, oval, galloping course with a good 4 furlong run in which rises steadily: the 5,6 and 7 furlong tracks are straight and quite stiff and a high number seems to have a very slight advantage: a very fair course where stamina and courage are needed.

NEWMARKET   Rowley Mile Course: All races from 5 - 10 furlongs are run on a straight track with an uphill finish: courage and stamina are needed and it is no place for the faint-hearted: races over 12 furlongs and upwards are run right handed and the course is a good stiff galloping test: all meetings, except the Summer meetings in June, July and August are held on this course.

July Course: All races up to, and including, one mile are run on a straight track, with the final furlong being uphill: races over 10 furlongs turn right into the straight: again a stiff galloping track: the meetings of June, July and August are held on this track.

Officially the draw has little advantage on either course, but in big fields in races up to 10 furlongs on the Rowley Mile course, high numbers seemed to have some advantage.

NOTTINGHAM   A left handed, flat, oval track with a long run in of 5 furlongs: a very fair course where the draw has little significance, possibly favouring high numbers over 5 and 6 furlongs and low numbers over 7 furlongs and 1 mile.

PONTEFRACT   A left handed, sharp and undulating track, with a short run in of 2 furlongs and a stiff uphill finish: the undulations and the sharp turns give the track similar character - istics to Brighton and Epsom and it is ideal for the smallish, speedy and front running types: the 5 and 6 furlong tracks turn left handed into the straight and low numbers have the advantage but a fast break is also very helpful: the course is a stiff one and stamina is all important: the going tends to extremes, getting very hard or very heavy: very much a course for specialists.

REDCAR   A left handed, flat, galloping track with a long run in of 5 furlongs: a very fair course and is ideal for the big, long striding horse: all races up to and including 9 furlongs, are run on a straight track and the 8 and 9 furlong events are not for those lacking in resolution: high numbers are best in sprints no matter where the stalls are placed since the field usually

Midway Lady holds on well under pressure from Maysoon (left), Sonic Lady· and Ala Mahlik in the General Accident 1,000 Guineas at Newmarket.

Showing a grand turn of speed, **Sonic Lady** defeats Scottish Reel and Pennine Walk in the Swettenham Stud Sussex Stakes at Goodwood.

comes across to the stands rail: the first three furlongs of the straight track drain much more quickly than the rest of the course so that quite a change of going can be encountered.

RIPON   A right handed, oval track with a long run in of 5 furlongs which is slightly on the ascent: the bends are just on the sharp side: the undulations in the straight are not nearly as severe as they appear to the eye and they are accentuated by the line of the running rail: the drainage is good and going is rarely extreme: when it is hard elsewhere it is on the firm side of good at Ripon: a good track to ride from behind.

SALISBURY   A right handed track, but little racing is done on the turn and there is a long run in of some 7 furlongs: the last 4 furlongs of the home straight are uphill: the course is a stiff galloping track where stamina is all important: all races up to and including 1 mile are straight and the uphill finish is a stiff test for a two year old: the ground seems slightly better on the stands side and most riders track over to that side which gives low numbers some advantage: it takes a genuine sort to win here and the form works out well elsewhere.

SANDOWN   A right handed, oval, galloping track with a stiff uphill run in of 4 furlongs stamina is all important: the 5 furlong track is quite separate and is uphill all the way so that it provides a real test of stamina for a two year old: high numbers have a decided advantage in big fields on soft ground over 5 furlongs.

THIRSK   A left handed, flat, oval track, some 10 furlongs round with fairly easy turns: not a stiff course and the emphasis is on speed: the 5 and 6 furlong track is straight with slight undulations and high numbers do have an advantage in big fields: over 7 and 8 furlongs, a high draw nowadays is preferred: the run in is 4 furlongs.

WARWICK   A left handed, circular track with a short run in of 3 furlongs: there are undulations on the back straight but all races up to 1 mile are run on flat ground: the 5 and 6 furlong tracks bend left into the short straight and low numbers are preferred: not a course to delay making a challenge and it seems to suit front runners.

WINDSOR   The track is in the form of a figure of eight: only in races over 12 furlongs and upwards do they gallop both right and left handed: only right handed turns are encountered in races up to 1 mile: the 5 and 6 furlong tracks are nearly straight, flat and quite easy: high numbers have the advantage: the run in of 5 furlongs makes this a very fair track despite the turns.

WOLVERHAMPTON   A left handed, pear shaped course, with a good 5 furlong run in: the 5 and 5 furlong 190 yards track is straight, flat and easy and high numbers have a slight advantage: a very fair track.

YARMOUTH   A left handed course with a good 5 furlong run in: races up to and including 1 mile are run on a straight track, and the mile is quite testing: the draw seems to have little advantage: suitable course for delivering a late challenge.

YORK   A left handed, flat, galloping course: ideal for the big, powerful galloper and stamina and courage are required to win here: the 5 and 6 furlong track is quite straight and low numbers have some advantage on soft ground: the going does tend to extremes and it gets heavy pretty quickly.

Sure Blade gamely accounts for Green Desert (rails) and Sharrood in the St. James Palace Stakes at Royal Ascot.

The immensely promising **Ajdal**, unbeaten in three starts, makes an impressive debut at Doncaster.

1,000 Gns

The French filly Mesque 15/8 FAV
slaughtered her rival, being hampered
1 out showed electric turn of
foot to beat Milligram + Interval
by 1½ length.

2,000

Don't forget me made all
to gallop his rivals into the
ground and win by ½ length,
Adjal 6/5 FAV got hampered
by would not have run.

Derby.

6/4 Fav Reference Point
makes virtually all to
grind the opposition into the
ground. Most Welcome
33/1 battles on to get
within 1½ lengths of Point

Oaks

Mich M States Unite 11/1
Impressivly beats her rivals
by 5 length. Bantoom Girl
stays on well to go seconc
Race marred by the break
down of the Cecil trained
½ Fav Simmitowrg when sh
looked sure to win

Champion 2yo filly, **Forest Flower**, cruises clear of Propensity and Dazy in the Queen Mary Stakes at Royal Ascot.

Minstrella sprints well clear of Chime Time and Luzum in the Chesham Stakes at Royal Ascot, setting a new 2yo course record.

SUPERFORM TOP PRIZE WINNERS

TOTAL PRIZE MONEY WIN & PLACE

2YO

£	
314685	BRAVE RAJ
256713	MINSTRELLA
157343	TAPPIANO
135279	FOREST FLOWER
100314	LOCKTON
88666	MIESQUE
76657	POLONIA
75524	SAROS BRIG
65993	SANAM
61386	WIGANTHORPE
59222	SAKURA REIKO
57479	DANISHKADA
56355	AJDAL
53554	DONT FORGET ME
52530	INVITED GUEST
50138	BENGAL FIRE
49690	MISTER MAJESTIC
47659	REFERENCE POINT
45943	LIBERTINE
43800	SIZZLING MELODY
42749	MANSOOJ
41967	NAHEEZ
40441	RISK ME
40147	FOTITIENG
38546	RICH CHARLIE
38193	CAROLS TREASURE
37500	GULF KING
36389	BINT ALNASR
34904	BALBONELLA
34480	DEPUTY GOVERNOR USA
34322	SINGING STEVEN
32077	DOMINION ROYALE
29960	AMIGO SUCIO
29334	WHO KNOWS
29063	SHINING WATER
28700	MELBURY LAD
28663	SEA DARA
28444	SHADY HEIGHTS
28074	NOBLE MINSTREL
26371	GLORY FOREVER
26281	ABUZZ
26065	CUTTING BLADE
25730	LALUCHE
25305	CHIME TIME
24862	SIMPLE TASTE
23503	REGENCY FILLE
22341	MILLIGRAM
22053	CROFTERS CLINE
21953	QUEL ESPRIT
21491	GENGHIZ
20628	MOUNTAIN MEMORY
20358	GEMINI FIRE
20134	PRINCESSE DU BOURG
20134	EXPORT PRICE
20127	TARTUFFE
20000	BABA KARAM
19833	PRINT
19213	SUHAILIE
18928	GROOM DANCER
18856	STAY LOW
18808	HOLST
18031	GRAND CHELEM
17912	CONMAICHE
17713	BEESHI
17142	LINDAS MAGIC
16709	THREE TAILS
16400	CLARENTIA
15946	GAYANE
15775	MIDYAN
15710	WHIPPER IN

3YO

£	
979971	DANCING BRAVE
925280	MANILA
688544	SHAHRASTANI
450440	LAST TYCOON
423885	SONIC LADY
377741	PARK EXPRESS
358232	BERING
244755	FERDINAND
221196	MIDWAY LADY
209702	SOUTHJET
194209	LACOVIA
193761	TOMMY WAY
177006	FAST TOPAZE
169916	MOON MADNESS
168677	GREEN DESERT
153411	IVORS IMAGE
144649	BONHOMIE
138027	MASHKOUR
135629	BAKHAROFF
133892	ALTAYAN
121254	UNTOLD
119429	SECRET FORM
114604	COLORSPIN
112173	DOUBLE BED
111431	MAGICAL WONDER
110247	EL CUITE
110150	FLASH OF STEEL
109385	ALLEZ MILORD
94320	CELESTIAL STORM
90305	MAYSOON
89784	DARARA
88490	BAISER VOLE
83549	BOLD ARRANGEMENT
75524	FRED ASTAIRE
73602	SURE BLADE
71968	TONY BIN
70491	DANZICA
69964	HIGHEST HONOR
69292	SWINK
67630	MR JOHN
66499	HIGHLAND CHIEFTAIN
66293	THRILL SHOW
65769	NISNAS
65748	HALLGATE
66505	REJUVENATE
63725	CAROTENE
62979	LAKE CHAMPLAIN
61656	GALUNPE
58061	NOMROOD
57302	SHARROOD
56044	GWYDION
55944	TOP CORSAGE
55870	THEN AGAIN
55700	AUTHAAL
53483	SANTIKI
52934	DALLAS
52905	ASTEROID FIELD
50900	FLEUR ROYALE
50692	AROKAR
50501	RELOY
49823	ACUSHLA
49472	MILL ON THE FLOSS
48951	GROOVY
47918	PRIMARY
46377	SIRK
45437	GESEDEH
45334	ROSEDALE USA
4005	TOCA MADERA
42855	FARAWAY DANCER
41551	GULL NOOK
41435	NORTHERN PREMIER

4YO+

£	
944056	SKYWALKER
570629	ESTRAPADE
506224	TRIPTYCH
472028	TURKOMAN USA
328134	THEATRICAL
314685	SMILE
286944	SHARDARI
228184	ACATENANGO
226573	PRECISIONIST
175703	PENNINE WALK
169451	DIVULGE
167832	BONNE ILE
157343	PINE TREE LANE
157343	PALACE MUSIC
140069	DAMISTER
128893	LIRUNG
126715	DOUBLE SCHWARTZ
123297	ANTHEUS
121852	SAINT ESTEPHE
110415	SARAB
105120	LONGBOAT
103603	BAILLAMONT
98324	BABY TURK
98250	SCOTTISH REEL
89611	DIHISTAN
88862	TELEPROMPTER
84035	EFISIO
75524	BEDSIDE PROMISE
68984	HADEER
66828	GREEN RUBY
65205	FAIR OF THE FURZE
65164	PHARDANTE
61880	SEISMIC WAVE
59182	DANGERS HOUR
58690	GREY DESIRE
57518	VALUABLE WITNESS
57071	GALLA PLACIDIA
56874	DUBIAN
56260	AIR DE COUR
55972	SUPREME LEADER
51213	PARIOLI
50284	MERSEY
46468	IADES
45825	NEMAIN
44059	ST HILARION
44039	EASTERN MYSTIC
43482	POWER BENDER
43465	ENGLISH SPRING
42928	PATRIACH
42710	KING LUTHIER
42636	COMRADE IN ARMS
41958	UPTOWN SWELL
41789	SIYAH KALEM
41408	ANATAS
41034	APELDOORN
40997	RAKAPOSHI KING
39388	FITNAH
39081	POLYKRATIS
38542	PERFECT TIMING
38367	ALAN FORD
38126	ESQUIRE
37032	FIELD HAND
35235	PREMIER ROLE
34917	CHAUMIERE
34827	NEBRIS
34353	SNEAK PREVIEW
34192	GRAUER WICHT
33634	ORANGE HILL
33539	LEMHILL
32424	BEDTIME
32218	OVER THE OCEAN

FREE OFFER !
Superform Computer Handicap

If you have never before subscribed to **Superform Computer Handicap** now is your chance to try it free of charge. Take up this free offer and discover how much time it will the Computer Handicap will save you.

Superform Computer Handicap is published five times each week at the 4 days stage and posted first class to you, at least two days before racing.

You can if you wish, subscribe only at weekends for Friday/Saturday racing.

Write now for your copy to

Dept. Comp. H'cap
Furlong Press
High Street
Shoreham By Sea   **FREE SAMPLE AVAILABLE**
West Sussex. BN4 5LH

Usual subscription rates are:

2 Weeks £11   4 Weeks £20

5 Fri/Sat only £10   12 Fri/Sat only   £20

VISA/ACCESS card holders phone 0273 455586 for immediate despatch.

Get Up To Date With Current Form

SUPERFORM WEEKLY

If you have enjoyed using this annual why not keep up to date with current form using our weekly publication, **SUPERFORM WEEKLY**.

To start with you receive a handsome vinyl filing book complete with all results from the start of the 1987 season.   It's the same size as this annual and the information is laid out in exactly the same way.

Superform covers every horse in each race in Britain.

Each week by first class post on Tuesdays, we mail you the latest set of results (inclusive of Saturday's) compiled in exactly the same way as in this annual. Also enclosed is a computerised index which contains the reference number of a horse's latest race and also the current handicap rating for fast easy reference.

Superform provides the fastest weekly form service in the country.   Why wait until Friday/Saturday for the latest form when with Superform you can have it by Wednesday!

3 Week Trial	£10
8 Weeks	£20

Complete season on application.

From Furlong Press, High Street, Shoreham, West Sussex.   BN4 5LH

VISA/ACCESS card holders phone 0273 455586 for immediate despatch.

Past Annuals

Have you missed earlier copies of the Superform/Haig Annuals?

Then bring your collection up-to-date with mint copies of the earlier editions.

Any single annual £5 but you can buy two or more copies at £4 per copy.
Tremendous value!

Remember each Annual covers the previous season's form so that 1983/84 covers the 1982/83 season, etc.

NATIONAL HUNT

1979/80	Not Available
1980/81	(Covers 79/80 Season)
1981/82	80/81
1982/83	81/82
1983/84	82/83
1984/85	83/84
1985/86	84/85

FLAT

1980	Not Available
1981	(Covers '80 Season)
1982	'81
1983	'82
1984	'83
1985	'84
1986	Not available

VISA/ACCESS card holders phone 0273 455586 for immediate despatch.

Only direct by post from
Furlong Press, High Street, Shoreham,
West Sussex. BN4 5LH

SCALE OF AGE WEIGHT AND DISTANCE

		March & April	APRIL	MAY		JUNE		JULY	
		1–15	16–30	1–15	16–31	1–15	16–30	1–15	16–31
5 Furlongs	2	6 11	6 13	7 2	7 5	7 7	7 9	7 10	7 13
	3	9 1	9 2	9 3	9 4	9 5	9 6	9 7	9 8
6 Furlongs	2	–	–	6 13	7 1	7 2	7 4	7 6	7 8
	3	8 13	9 0	9 1	9 2	9 3	9 4	9 5	9 6
7 Furlongs	2	–	–	–	–	–	–	–	–
	3	8 12	8 13	9 0	9 1	9 2	9 3	9 4	9 5
8–9 Furlongs	2	–	–	–	–	–	–	–	–
	3	8 10	8 11	8 12	8 13	9 0	9 1	9 2	9 3
10 Furlongs	3	8 9	8 10	8 11	8 12	8 13	9 0	9 1	9 2
11–12 Furlongs	3	8 8	8 9	8 10	8 11	8 12	8 13	9 0	9 1
13–14 Furlongs	3	8 7	8 8	8 9	8 10	8 11	8 12	8 13	9 0
15–16 Furlongs	3	8 6	8 7	8 8	8 9	8 10	8 11	8 12	8 13
2¼ Miles	3	8 5	8 6	8 7	8 8	8 9	8 10	8 11	8 12
2½ Miles	3	8 3	8 4	8 5	8 6	8 7	8 8	8 9	8 10

		AUGUST		SEPTEMBER		OCTOBER		NOV
		1–15	16–31	1–15	16–30	1–15	16–31	
5 Furlongs	2	8 2	8 4	8 6	8 8	8 10	8 12	8 13
	3	9 9	9 10	9 11	9 12	9 13	10 0	10 0
6 Furlongs	2	7 9	7 12	8 1	8 3	8 4	8 6	8 9
	3	9 7	9 8	9 9	9 10	9 11	9 12	9 13
7 Furlongs	2	–	–	7 12	8 0	8 1	8 3	8 5
	3	9 6	9 7	9 8	9 9	9 10	9 11	9 12
8–9 Furlongs	2	–	–	7 7	7 8	7 10	7 12	8 0
	3	9 4	9 5	9 6	9 7	9 8	9 9	9 10
10 Furlongs	3	9 3	9 4	9 5	9 6	9 7	9 8	9 9
11–12 Furlongs	3	9 2	9 3	9 4	9 5	9 6	9 7	9 8
13–14 Furlongs	3	9 1	9 2	9 3	9 4	9 5	9 6	9 7
15–16 Furlongs	3	9 0	9 1	9 2	9 3	9 4	9 5	9 6
2¼ Miles	3	8 13	9 0	9 1	9 2	9 3	9 4	9 5
2½ Miles	3	8 11	8 12	8 13	9 0	9 1	9 2	9 3

For Horses Aged 4 Years and Upwards, Use 10-0 In All Cases